KT-495-031

THE AUSTRALIAN NATIONAL DICTIONARY

EDITORIAL STAFF

THE AUSTRALIAN NATIONAL DICTIONARY

A DICTIONARY OF AUSTRALIANISMS
ON HISTORICAL PRINCIPLES

Edited by W. S. Ramson

MELBOURNE
OXFORD UNIVERSITY PRESS
OXFORD AUCKLAND NEW YORK

OXFORD UNIVERSITY PRESS

Oxford New York Toronto
Delhi Bombay Calcutta Madras Karachi
Petaling Jaya Singapore Hong Kong Tokyo
Nairobi Dar es Salaam Cape Town
Melbourne Auckland

and associated companies in
Beirut Berlin Ibadan Nicosia

First published 1988

National Library of Australia
Cataloguing in Publication Data

The Australian national dictionary : Australian
words and their origins.

Bibliography.
ISBN 0 19 554736 5.

1. English language — Australia —
Dictionaries. I. Ramson, W.S. (William
Stanley), 1933-

423

Typeset by Abb-typesetting Pty Ltd
Printed in Australia by The Book Printer

CONTENTS

INTRODUCTION

For the purposes of this dictionary an Australianism is one of those words and meanings of words which have originated in Australia, which have a greater currency here than elsewhere, or which have a special significance in Australia because of their connection with an aspect of the history of the country. The aim of the dictionary is to provide as full an historical record of these as possible.

In the simplest analysis Australian English, the English used by Australians, differs from that used elsewhere in the ways and to the extent that the circumstances of life in this country and the history of its people have been distinctive. Most obviously, there are words and meanings of words which have originated in Australia because of the need to give a name to a bird, a plant, an artefact, or a feature of the landscape encountered here for the first time: the application of a largely descriptive nomenclature to species of indigenous flora and fauna, and the borrowing from Aboriginal languages of terms for Aboriginal implements and weapons are illustrations of this.

But Australian English reflects also the composition of the immigrant population and an experience which while in part distinctive was in part common to other British colonies. Regional dialect and slang words which have remained non-standard in Britain became generally current in Australia. Occupational vocabularies, made up in part of traditional, often dialect, terms, in part of new terms required by new circumstances, acquired greater prominence: some mining terms, for instance, obtained general currency when gold-mining, in several parts of the new world, became a popular as distinct from a specialized pursuit. Words necessary to describe the opening up of an unfamiliar country, often originating in another colony or common to more than one, became part of an active vocabulary in Australia, of a largely passive one in Britain. Words formed from standard elements, as compounds formed on main elements like *bullock, canvas, cattle, sheep*, and *stock*, acquired a special significance because of the importance of the activity with which they were associated.

It is a reasonable presumption that a word recorded by the *Oxford English Dictionary* and its four-volume Supplement (OED(S) or the *English Dialect Dictionary* (EDD) as British regional dialect is rightly so described even if it can be antedated in Australian use. In many instances, also, a substantially earlier American history establishes an American origin for a word borrowed into Australian. But it would be hazardous to argue an Australian origin for *round up* or *puncher* (as in *bullock puncher*) simply on the ground that both are recorded earliest in Australia. And, in fields like gold-mining, sheep-raising, shearing, and Services speech, New Zealand and Australia have so many words in common that the location of the earliest written evidence may well be fortuitous. It has therefore seemed best to interpret 'Australianism' liberally, not making undue claims but including in the dictionary many words which are of undoubted significance in the Australian context but about the precise origin of which there remains uncertainty.

The first stage in the compilation of any dictionary on historical principles is the establishment of a bibliography of sources and the implementation of a reading programme. It was determined from the outset, in 1978, that the dictionary would be published in 1988. The bibliography was therefore necessarily selective and the reading programme contained. We were fortunate to obtain the services of Pauline Fanning, formerly Director of the Australian Humanities Collection in the National Library of Australia, to compile, from Ferguson's *Bibliography of Australia* (to 1900), the National Library catalogues and accession lists, and her own inspection of likely titles, a bibliography of some 9,500 items, including runs of newspapers and journals. Some idea of the range of these sources can be gained from the *Select Bibliography*. It became clear very early that any attempt to emulate the Oxford model by using voluntary readers would protract the reading programme interminably and so, as the acquisition of grant monies permitted, a team of trained readers was employed to read with and under the direction of the Editor and Associate Editor. Working mostly in the one library readers were able to compare findings and so improve their sensibility in the identifying of items and their selectivity in recording them. In five years some 250,000 citations were collected, of which about one in four appear in the dictionary. In the *Instructions* readers were asked to be alert to:

- words and phrases they believed were Australian
- words and phrases in occupational vocabularies, especially those used 'on the job'
- words and phrases in other specialized vocabularies
- names for animals, birds, fish, plants, and geographical features
- words and phrases apparently borrowed from Aboriginal languages
- colloquial expressions
- proverbial expressions and catch-phrases
- familiar words and phrases used in unusual ways
- family or local expressions
- words and phrases not in common use, especially those which appear obsolete
- words and phrases which others have found unfamiliar.

This was deliberately casting a wide net but we wanted readers to make inclusive rather than exclusive judgements. Our intention was to record as fully as possible that part of the vocabulary which could be regarded as readily accessible to most Australians. We have not sought to cover specialist or occupational vocabularies occurring only or mostly in specialist sources, though inevitably we have gone to many such sources in order to document more fully the history of words established as being in common use. One result of this policy is that the vocabularies of occupations such as gold-mining and shearing, which have a substantial popular literature, are more prominent than those of occupations such as cane-cutting and timber-getting, which have had their own importance in the social or economic history of the country. It should be noted also that common names in natural history checklists are included only if there is adequate evidence of sustained popular use.

Any dictionary draws to some extent on its predecessors and in this instance the literature of the subject was searched, at the conclusion of the reading programme or during the editing process. Our intention in so doing was to allow the reading programme to proceed without the participants forming preconceptions about what might, or might not, properly belong in the dictionary while at a later stage not denying ourselves the opportunity to supplement our own findings from those of previous studies, or to make good omissions, always provided of course that material from such studies could be verified. Of particular assistance were E.E. Morris's *Austral English*, the several works of Sidney J. Baker, the monographs published by the Australian Language Research Centre, University of Sydney, the two editions of G.A. Wilkes' *Dictionary of Australian Colloquialisms*, and R.W. Burchfield's four-volume Supplement to the *Oxford English Dictionary* (OEDS). Citations from OED(S have in the main been silently accepted, though for a small number which it would have been impossible to verify an attribution is given after the citation in parentheses.

The editing of the dictionary has taken three years, the method followed, like that of Mathews' *Dictionary of Americanisms*, being a modification of that established by the Oxford editors. The first task was to work through the data-base of citations, the raw material of the dictionary, identifying and grouping into parts of speech and senses those citations illustrating the use of words likely to be included in the dictionary. The file was then split, draft entries for all items in the general vocabulary being prepared by the Associate Editor, for all those items requiring scientific expertise by the Science Editor. The Science Editor built up a 'directory' of consultants in many specialist fields and drew on these on a regular basis. At this stage it was for both strands necessary to consult other historical dictionaries, in particular OED(S, EDD, Mathews' *Dictionary of Americanisms*, Craigie and Hulbert's *Dictionary of American English*, and Partridge's *Dictionary of Slang and Unconventional English*, and to decide, on the basis of the dictionary evidence available, whether or not a word warranted an entry in AND. Somewhat less than a third of the citations were rejected at this stage, as illustrating words, colloquial words particularly, common to British English, belonging to another branch of English, or insufficiently attested. Searches were made for further instances of words for which there was insufficient evidence, but many, particularly words from Aboriginal languages and names for plants and animals which never became established in English, languish in the file, perhaps to find a place in a later edition.

A selection was then made of those citations which most fully represented a word's life and most definitively and vividly illustrated its use and meaning. In the case of names of flora and fauna the selection was intended to include descriptive material and in many cases to substantiate the particular uses of names which have often been used loosely. Particular care was taken to select citations which established the Australianness of the word or its referent, not crudely in a quest for colour but in the recognition that, as the words added to a language by a people are an index of their history and culture, so the actual context of use provides evidence of their social and cultural attitudes and preoccupations. AND has used citations copiously, more with the interests of the historian in mind than because there are lexical features (variant forms, etc.), which require documentation. There nonetheless remains a surplus file of slightly larger size than the dictionary file itself. The cost of entering into a computer a data-base of which at best one in four items would ultimately be used was one factor in our decision to edit the dictionary in the traditional manner, on cards.

All draft entries, together with their surplus citations, then passed to the Editor for approval or revision. Entries in their 'final' form were checked by the copy editors, for consistency of style, and of the form and dating of bibliographical reference, and for the verification of detail where this appeared necessary. To this stage the text remained handwritten, but a word-processed version was now prepared for the use of outside consultants, and to facilitate cross-referencing and further revision. As sections of this were completed they were sent to Oxford, where John Simpson, a Senior Editor of the Supplement and, from 1985, Co-Editor of the *New Oxford English Dictionary*, not only gave extensive and valuable advice but had extracted from the unpublished files of OED(S citations which usefully supplemented our own holdings. The text was also read by three consultants, Stuart Macintyre as an historian, Barry Andrews as a sports historian, and H.W. Orsman as the editor of the forthcoming dictionary of New Zealand English on historical principles, all of whom gave information or advice which has improved the dictionary.

The dictionary consists of approximately 6,000 main entries. Many of these have subdivisions, especially those forming simple combinations and collocations (which do not require definition) and special combinations and collocations (which do require definition) so that the total number of entries is actually much larger. By far the most common method of expanding the Australian vocabulary has been by the formation of compounds and two-word combinations and collocations and it has seemed both helpful and economical to follow the Oxford practice of grouping combinations and collocations under main entries, except in such cases as the elements have coalesced to form a single, unhyphenated, word or where the combination or collocation requires fuller treatment.

The essence of an entry in an historical dictionary is its set of citations: these establish the chronology of a word's use, substantiate the definition or definitions, and illustrate the range of registers within which a word has been used. We have taken the view that, while it is sometimes a proper part of the descriptive process to use a subject label to indicate that a word is restricted to a particular field of activity, there is a danger that using labels to indicate register can be over-interpretative and over-restrictive. This seems particularly true of Australian English, which allows easy movement between formal and informal usage. It should be clear from the citations if a word belongs mainly in colloquial use or to the slang of a particular group, and equally clear if it is for some reason taboo in some contexts. Labels like *coarse, colloq., derog., slang*, and *vulgar*, which tend unnecessarily to categorize, have therefore been omitted. Inclusion of words that many will find offensive does not mean that the editors endorse the sentiments they frequently express: our responsibility has been to record the language as it has been used and to supply the evidence of this use in citations which enable users of the dictionary to form their own judgements about both the words and their users.

Our perception of the vocabulary of Australian English as an entity has made us wary also of using regional labels for many items in the colloquial vocabulary which are commonly supposed to be localized in their use. With the names of species of flora and fauna the evidence is sometimes unequivocal and attributions can be given with confidence. And in the case of a small number of items of peripheral interest – the names given to glasses of beer, for example – the written evidence is adequate. But for many more interesting items, words like *port* for instance, the evidence is unconvincing: we have frequently allowed popular opinion a voice in a citation but until there is a survey of regional usage which takes account of the spoken as well as the written word – and such a survey is a natural consequence of the completion of this dictionary – it must remain opinion.

The dictionary's concern is with the English used by or accessible to the majority of Australians. It thus necessarily takes account of what is referred to in AND as *Australian pidgin*, the language of contact between European settler and Aboriginal, used particularly in the earlier part of the nineteenth century and now largely obsolete, and what is referred to as *Aboriginal English*, that set of terms which is used mostly by Aborigines and which relates to their attitudes and concerns, made up partly of standard English words like *business* and *clever*, which have been given new meanings, partly of Australian pidgin words which have outlived the stigma attaching to a contact language, and partly of words originating in Aboriginal languages, especially words like *koori*, which manifest a pride in Aboriginality. In both cases, what is offered in AND is a preliminary account – in the case of pidgin because what is recorded is that which has at least in part been absorbed into Australian English, in the case of Aboriginal English because, while its spoken life is undoubtedly vigorous, its emergence into written English is mostly late.

Entries recording the popular nomenclature of flora and fauna are a significant component of the dictionary. Many names for plants and animals are descriptive, and have been similarly used elsewhere, many are new applications of words used in British and American English, and it has often been difficult to determine whether or not to include a word. In general we have erred on the side of inclusiveness: descriptive collocations in which for instance the distinguishing epithet denotes a colour (as *black-backed wren, black bream, black cormorant*, etc.) are included as probably independent of a similar use elsewhere; names used earlier elsewhere but applied in Australia to species of different genera are included; names used elsewhere for species within the same genus are included if the name has been applied in Australia to a new species, or if the degree of specificity in Australian use appears narrower or broader. Latin generic names like *Banksia* and *Zygomaturus* are included if there is adequate evidence of their use in an English context as the name of an individual and not that of a genus. (The use of the label *Obs.*, as in the entries for *Leipoa* and *Menura*, carries no implication that the word is no longer a valid scientific name for a genus.) Every effort has been made to comply with official changes in the Latin names of flora and fauna, the name most recently adopted being preferred, with a common alternative sometimes also supplied. The classification of plant families adopted in *Flora of Australia* (Bureau of Flora and Fauna, 1981—), has been followed. The distribution of a plant or animal has been given where possible. The formula 'all States' includes the Northern Territory and the Australian Capital Territory unless otherwise indicated.

The dictionary is intended to stand alone and to this end entries include all information likely to be useful to a reader enquiring into the Australian use of a word. But, as has been noted above, many of the words included are or have been in use elsewhere. And many standard English words given new meanings in Australia, like *run* and *station*, have long and interesting histories behind them. The *Oxford English Dictionary* and its Supplement is the only historical dictionary of international English and therefore the obvious next point of reference. Wherever it has seemed useful, a cross-reference to the corresponding entry in OED(S has been included in the etymology. Pursuit of such cross-references will help the reader to place an AND entry in a larger context: in some cases an earlier history will be revealed, in some an editorial judgement confirmed, in some an editorial doubt exposed. The symbiotic relationship between Australian English and New Zealand English has already been noted: it has seemed sensible to illuminate a word's earlier history by including in AND any citation from a New Zealand source which antedates the earliest Australian record, such citations being either supplied by H.W. Orsman or taken from OED(S.

The information provided in the etymologies is deliberately limited. No attempt has been made to provide more than a word's immediate derivation, and then only when it is not self-evident (as it most frequently is in descriptive compounds). As noted earlier cross-references to the corresponding entries in OED(S are provided in many instances. An important feature of AND is its inclusion of etymologies for words borrowed from Aboriginal languages: these are for the first time treated with a degree of comprehensiveness and, in the majority of instances, a specific source language is identified.

Etymologies for borrowings from Aboriginal languages have been provided by R.M.W. Dixon, Clare Allridge, Lysbeth Ford, Linda Macfarlane, and David Wilkins. A standardized orthography, using letters of the Roman alphabet with the addition of ŋ*, is employed in most instances, the orthography being that used by R.M.W. Dixon and described in his *Languages of Australia* (p. xxi):

The basic system . . is:

	apico-alveolar	apico-postalveolar (retroflex)	lamino-(inter)dental	lamino-palatal	dorsal	labial
stop	*d*	*rd*	*dh*	*j*	*g*	*b*
nasal	*n*	*rn*	*nh*	*ny*	*ŋ*	*m*
lateral	*l*	*rl*	*lh*	*ly*		
rhotic	*rr*	*r*				
semi-vowel				*y*		*w*

If there is a single apical series, the symbols, *d, n* and *l* are used; if there is a single laminal series *j, ny* and *ly* are used. For the few languages (e.g. Diyari . .) where there is a distinction between two series of stops, both voiced and voiceless symbols are used.

Systems of three vowels are shown as *i, a, u*; where there are five vowels *i, e, a, o, u* are used. Contrastive length is shown by doubling the letter, thus *ii, aa* etc.

For languages that have an accepted practical orthography, that is in daily use by speakers, we quote forms in this spelling. Western Desert [uses] *p, t, rt, k* and *ng* in place of our standard *b, d, rd, g* and ŋ. In addition, Western Desert uses *tj* for the laminal stop [etc.].

The writing system employed for languages of the Yolŋu subgroup – perhaps the best established practical orthography in Aboriginal Australia – uses underlining for postalveolar (retroflex) sounds i.e. $\underline{d}$, $\underline{t}$, $\underline{n}$, $\underline{l}$ corresponding to our standard *rd, rt, rn* and *rl*; it also employs *dj, tj* for lamino-(alveo) palatals and ' for the

* Where ŋ appears as the initial letter in the name of a language and is capitalized it is written as *Ng*.

glottal stop . . The Yolŋu orthography uses letters *e, o, ä* for long vowels, in place of *ii, uu, aa.*

For a description of the phonology of Aboriginal languages, the reader is referred to R.M.W. Dixon, *The Languages of Australia* (Cambridge 1980). In almost all instances a borrowing's first meaning in English is the same as that in the Aboriginal language: where there has been a change the original meaning is supplied. Some 400 borrowings are recorded. For most of these a source language has been identified, no small task given that there were over 200 languages at the time of European settlement, of which many are now dead and a good number of the remainder in decline. In cases where there are good grounds for believing a word is of Aboriginal origin but a source language cannot be identified a formula is used indicating the probability of the word being from an Aboriginal language in a given State (or Territory). For a list of the Aboriginal languages borrowed from, and for their location, see the table on p. xi and map on p. x.

Our policy on hyphenation has been conservative, largely because the citation evidence is so inconclusive. In general we have left two-word combinations and collocations unhyphenated unless grammatical function, sense, or stress dictate otherwise. If there is clear evidence that a combination or collocation has become a compound entity, it is treated as a main entry. Pronunciations are given only for those words which are new to standard English, as borrowings from Aboriginal languages, survivals from British regional dialects, or colloquial formations and, occasionally, in those instances where a word has more than one pronunciation elsewhere and the preferred Australian pronunciation needs to be indicated. Pronunciations are given in International Phonetic Alphabet notation, using the system established by A.G. Mitchell and A. Delbridge in *The Pronunciation of English in Australia*, revised edition (Sydney 1965). Where there have been variant spellings - and there was much early uncertainty about the representation of the sounds of Aboriginal words - the main variants are listed. These may sometimes indicate the existence of earlier or variant pronunciations but as a rule the evidence is too slight to permit of any systematic attempt at the identification and interpretation of these. For words which are now obsolete and which have not been heard in use the spelling evidence is often all that is available.

It is a pleasure to acknowledge both the institutional support which has made the undertaking and completion of the dictionary project possible, and the help and advice given freely by numerous colleagues. The Australian National University has made special provision for the project from August 1981, when my duties and those of Joan Hughes were varied to enable us to give our full time to the dictionary, and has given additional support, particularly in the provision of accommodation and through the agency of the Faculties Research Fund. The Faculty of Arts has given moral as well as financial support, and I am grateful also to the English Department and the Humanities Research Centre for their help, particularly in the early stages. The second major source of funding has been the Australian Research Grants Scheme which supported the project with annual grants from 1979 to 1986, and the third Oxford University Press Australia, which has advanced royalties over the four year period, 1984–87. Grants were received also from the Australian War Memorial Research Grants Scheme (1985–86), the University of the Northern Territory Planning Authority (1984), and the Australian Academy of the Humanities (1979). On an earlier Australian Research Grants Scheme grant (1970–72), Jean Fielding was employed in preliminary citation collecting.

I am glad to be able to make acknowledgement of the help given by R.W. Burchfield, Editor of the Supplement to the *Oxford English Dictionary*, and by A.J. Aitken and J.A.C. Stevenson, Editors of the *Dictionary of the Older Scottish Tongue*, in the several planning stages. And I particularly want to record our indebtedness to those who read and commented on the full text, John Simpson, H.W. Orsman, Stuart Macintyre, and Barry Andrews, and to R.M.W. Dixon for his help, particularly in establishing the etymologies of words borrowed from Aboriginal languages. Many others contributed, by responding to queries or by volunteering information, and I would like especially to thank the following, in the main from this University: D.W.A. Baker, S.C. Bennett, R.F. Brissenden, Clyde Cameron, G.W. Clarke, C. Cunneen, O.F. Dent, C.I.E. Donaldson, Tamsin Donaldson, E.C. Fry, J.A. Grieve, C.P. Groves, T.P. Grundy, J.P. Hardy, A.D. Hope, G.S. Hope, I.M. Hughes, K.S. Inglis, A.H. Johns, W.A. Krebs, Hans Kuhn, D.C. Laycock, F.W. Lewins, K.W. McDermott, C.C. Macknight, A.W. Martin, J.A. Merritt, J.N. Molony, Howard Morphy, D.J. Mulvaney, Nicolas Peterson, D.W. Rawson, J.D. Ritchie, F.W. Shawcross, F.B. Smith, P.N. Troy, and I.F.H. Wilson.

For the help they were able to give the Science Editor I would like to thank people from this and other universities, from the Bureau of Flora and Fauna, from various divisions of the Commonwealth Science and Industrial Research Organization, from botanic gardens, State museums, and Departments of Primary Industry and Agriculture, in particular J.A. Armstrong, S.A.F. Bain, A. Bragg, J.H. Calaby, M. Carver, A. Chapman, R.J. Chinnock, G.M. Chippendale, D.C. Christophel, I.A. Clark, H.T. Clifford, P. Coleman, A.B. Court, M.D. Crisp, W.M. Curtis, B.A. Fuhrer, A.S. George, C.J.M. Glover, M.R. Gray, G.P. Guymer, H.J. Hewson, R.J. Hnatiuk, W.L. Hoffman, M. Lazarides, B.Y. Main, H.R.C. Meischke, A.S. Mitchell, I.D. Naumann, E.S. Nielsen, R.W. Purdie, M.O. Rankin, B. Richardson, A.N. Rodd, R. Schodde, P.S. Short, M. Southwell-Walters, R.W. Taylor, I.R.H. Telford, M.J. Tyler, N.M. Wace, J.G. West, K.L. Wilson, P.G. Wilson, and J.C. Wombey.

A small number of people who have helped voluntarily deserve mention: John D'Arcy, Rosemary Balmford, D. Cox, L.J. Downer, B.L.C. Johnson, Delia Johnson, Michele Lang, M.C. Michell, F. Morris, and, in particular, R.G. Kimber. I would like to thank also staff in the Petherick Room and Newspaper Reading Room of the National Library of Australia, and in the Mitchell Library, for their assistance.

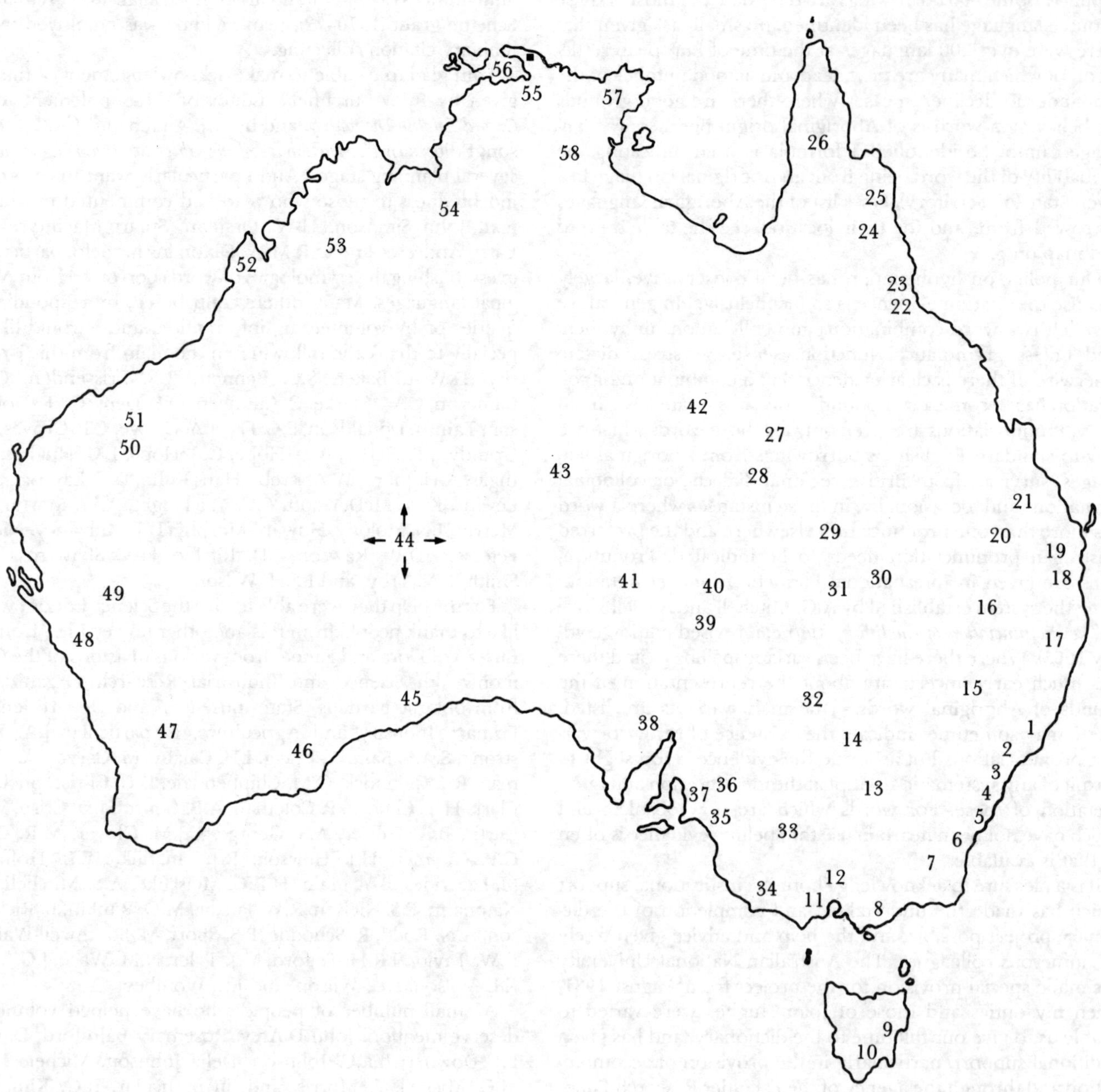
56
55
57
58
26
25
24
54
53
52
23
22
42
27
51
50
43
28
21
44
29
20
19
18
41
40
31
30
16
39
49
48
17
15
45
32
38
1
47
14
2
46
3
36
37
13
4
35
33
5
6
7
34
12
11
8
9
10

ABORIGINAL LANGUAGES

39 Adnyamadhanha – in the vicinity of Lake Torrens, S.A.
41 Arabana Waŋgaŋuru – west of Lake Eyre and in the Simpson Desert, S.A.
43 Aranda – in the vicinity of Alice Springs, N.T.
3 Awabakal – on the coast from north of Sydney to Newcastle, N.S.W.
32 Bagandji – along the Darling River, N.S.W.
17 Bandjalang – in the Clarence and Richmond Rivers district in n.e. N.S.W. and s.e. Qld.
38 Baŋgala – south of Lake Torrens to the Gawler Ranges, S.A.
52 Bardi – north of Broome and on Sunday Island, in n. W.A.
5 Dharawal – on the coast from Jervis Bay to Port Hacking, N.S.W.
4 Dharuk – in the vicinity of Port Jackson, Sydney, N.S.W.
6 Dhurga – on the coast from Bermagui to Jervis Bay, N.S.W.
40 Diyari – in the Cooper Creek district, east of Lake Eyre, S.A.
1 Djaŋadi – in the Macleay River district, N.S.W.
23 Dyirbal – in the Tully River district, n. Qld.
19 Gabi – in the Mary River district from Redcliffe to Fraser Island, s.e. Qld.
8 Ganay – in Gippsland, Vic.
34 Gangubanud – on the coast at Portland Bay, Vic.
21 Gangulu – in the Dawson River district, s.e. Qld.
28 Garuwali – in the Ferrar Creek district, n.e. of Birdsville, s.w. Qld.
37 Gaurna – in the vicinity of Adelaide, S.A.
20 Goreng Goreng – in the vicinity of Bundaberg, s.e. Qld.
55 Gunwinygu – from upper Cooper Creek to the Liverpool River, Arnhem Land, N.T.
30 Gunya – between Charleville and Cunnamulla in s.w. Qld.
25 Guugu Yimidhirr – in the vicinity of Cooktown, n. Qld.
18 Jagara – in the Moreton Bay district, s.e. Qld.
46 Kalaaku – at Israelite Bay and inland around the Fraser Range and Norseman, W.A.
15 Kamilaroi – in the Namoi River district, n. N.S.W. (closely related to Wiradhuri and Ngiyambaa).
2 Kattaŋ – on the coast from Port Stephens to Port Macquarie, N.S.W.
24 Kuku-Yalanji – in the Bloomfield River district, n. Qld.
27 Majuli – in the upper Diamantina River district, s.w. Qld.
16 Manandjali – in s.e. Qld.
31 Margany – in the upper Paroo and Warrego Rivers district, s.e. Qld.
56 Margu – on Croker Is. and mainland
45 Mirniŋy – along the coast of the Great Australian Bight, W.A. and S.A.
54 Ngaliwuru – in the upper Victoria River district, N.T.
7 Ngarigo – from Canberra across the Monaro tablelands to the Snowy Mountains and Omeo, N.S.W. (incl. A.C.T.) and Vic.
53 Ngarinjin – in the central Kimberley district, W.A.
36 Ngayawuŋ – in the lower Murray River district, S.A.
14 Ngiyambaa – in the Darling and Macquarie Rivers district, N.S.W. (very closely related to Wiradhuri, and closely related to Kamilaroi).
48 Nhanta-anmaŋu – on the coast from Dongara to the Murchison River, W.A.
47 Nyungar – over a wide area of s.w. W.A., including Perth and Albany.
9 Oyster Bay language of Tasmania – in the vicinity of Oyster Bay, east coast of Tasmania.
50 Panyjima – in the Pilbara region of n.w. W.A.
42 Pitta Pitta – in the Boulia district, n.w. central Qld.
29 Punthamara – in the Grey Range district, s.w. Qld.
10 South eastern language of Tasmania – from Hobart south to Prion Bay, including Bruny Island.
58 Warndarang – on the west coast of Arnhem Land, N.T. from Roper River to Rose River.
22 Warrgamay – in the Herbert River district, n. Qld.
11 Wathawurung – in the vicinity of Geelong, Vic. (closely related to Wuywurung and Wemba).
49 Watjari – in the Murchison River district, W.A.
33 Wemba – in the Glenelg and Loddon Rivers district, Vic. (closely related to Wuywurung and Wathawurung). Has several dialects including Djadjala, Wemba Wemba and Wergaia.
44 Western Desert language – spoken in the Desert areas of S. and W. Australia, and in s.w. N.T. (has many dialects including Luritja, Mantjiltjara, Yulbaritja, Pitjantjatjara and Yankunytjatjara).
26 Wik Munkan – in the Archer River district, n. Qld.
13 Wiradhuri – over a wide area in central N.S.W. in the region of the Murrumbidgee River and Lachlan River districts (very closely related to Ngiyambaa and closely related to Kamilaroi).
12 Wuywurung – in the vicinity of Melbourne, Vic. (closely related to Wathawurung and Wemba).
35 Yaralde – on the coast at Encounter Bay and at Lake Alexandrina, S.A.
51 Yinjibarndi – in the Fortescue River district, W.A.
57 Yolŋu Sub-group – a group of closely related languages spoken in n.e. Arnhem Land, N.T.
15 Yuwaalaraay – near Lightning Ridge, n. N.S.W. (a dialect of the same language as Kamilaroi).

EXPLANATION OF THE STYLE AND ARRANGEMENT OF ENTRIES

The entry. Each entry is designed to present the information it contains in the most illuminating, convenient, and economic form. Entries range from the simple, one word recorded as one part of speech and in one sense, to the complex, subdivided first according to part of speech and then according to sense. Combinations and collocations of which the headword is the main element are normally listed in a sub-section of the entry, with derivatives of minor importance at the end of the entry. In a sequence of combinations and collocations the main element is listed in the first instance but thereafter understood. Combinations which have coalesced into one, usually unhyphenated, compound, which require fuller treatment, or which are essentially independent of the bulk of the entry, are listed in their own alphabetical place. The elements of an entry (not all of which may be required) appear in the following order.

Headword. The headword, the word which is the subject of the entry, appears at its head in bold roman. Subordinate items – combinations, collocations, and phrases of which the headword is the main element, as well as derivatives, appear in their place in the entry in bold roman. Words which normally have an initial capital, as place-names used in a transferred sense and proprietary names, retain the capital, all other initial letters being in lower case. Superscript numerals are used to distinguish two or more headwords having the same spelling. If a word has separate entries according to its parts of speech these are arranged chronologically, the noun usually preceding the verb, unless the logic of the word's history demands otherwise.

Pronunciation. Where a pronunciation is given it follows the headword, marked off by slashes and in International Phonetic Alphabet notation (see table on p. xvi).

Part of speech. If a word is recorded only as a noun, and there is no other noun in the same form, no part of speech is given. Otherwise the part of speech is given in abbreviated form in italics.

Subject or restrictive labels. Subject labels (designating an occupation, sport, etc.) and restrictive labels, such as *Obs.* (obsolete), *Hist.* (now only in an historical context), and *N.S.W.* (used chiefly in New South Wales), are printed in italics and with an initial capital. In run-on entries, as sequences of special combinations and collocations, such labels (other than abbreviations of proper names) have a lower-case initial letter.

Variant spellings. The main variant spellings are given in bold roman after the headword (pronunciation, part of speech, label) and before the etymology. Spellings which are clearly aberrant or which do not help establish main directions are not listed. Some standard English spelling variants, as *color* for *colour, license* for *licence, parrakeet* for *parakeet, pigmy* for *pygmy* and *waggon* for *wagon*, are not remarked.

Etymology. The etymology is enclosed in square brackets. An etymology which informs all senses of a word precedes any numbered or lettered subdivision. An etymology which informs a specific sense follows that sense's number or (in the case of special combinations or collocations) the second element of the combination. The etymon, or primary word which is the basis of a derivative form or sense, is given in italics, unless it is a word for which there is a main entry in the dictionary, in which case it is in roman small capitals with initial full capital. The locations of Aboriginal languages are given in a table (p. xi) and on a map (p. x). In many instances a cross-reference to the corresponding entry in OED(S is supplied.

Ordering of senses. Senses within an entry are arranged chronologically, first according to part of speech and then according to sense. If an entry is divided according to parts of speech more than one part of speech label will follow the headword (as *n.* and *attrib.*, or *n., a.*, and *adv.*).

Definition. The definition is either discrete, if there is no division, or subdivided according to the division. The definition may include cross- references to words which have main entries or are subordinate items. These are readily identified as follows:

a word printed in small capitals with an initial full capital, as BOBUCK, has a main entry in the dictionary (part of speech is given only if necessary to distinguish the main entry being referred to; a numbered sense is specified when appropriate);

a word printed in italics is either a subordinate item in the main entry in which it appears (so **sheep tobacco** is defined as *sheep-wash tobacco* which is in the same entry), or a subordinate item in a main entry indicated in capitals (so, for **sheep-shed,** the definition given is *shearing shed*, see SHEARING B. 3). A reference to a subordinate item in a main entry may vary in form as required by its place in the text, as 'shortened form of *shearing shed* (see SHEARING B. 3)' or 'see also *shearing shed* SHEARING B. 3'.

Cross-references. There are two main forms of cross-reference:

if a word is defined by another in the dictionary, as **sorcerer** by KORADJI, or listed without qualification in the definition as, in the entry for **Major Mitchell cockatoo,** are LEADBEATER'S COCKATOO, *pink cockatoo*, see PINK *a.*, and WEE JUGGLER, the synonymy is exact;

if the cross-reference is introduced by 'see also' the synonymy is not exact but the information provided under the word referred to is complementary or in some other way useful.

Variant forms. Variant forms (as distinct from spellings) are listed at the end of the definition.

Citations. Sets of citations provide substantiation for the definition and illustrate the history of the word's use. Some words are more copiously exemplified than others, this being a reflection of their intrinsic interest. A citation is preceded by a date (of utterance, when this can be established, or publication) and a short bibliographical reference which is in most instances sufficient to enable the reader to identify the text or edition used. The name of the author of an article published in a periodical or of a story in a collection is not normally given. Volume numbers are given in upper case roman, numbers of issues or parts in lower case roman. (Fuller information on sources which have been used heavily or which may be difficult to identify is contained in the select bibliography.) Every effort has been made to record the earliest use of a word and to provide a reasonably spaced sequence of citations to the present day. Citations are given as they appear in the source except that, in the interests of elegance and economy, extraneous material has been omitted (medial ellipsis is indicated by . . and an ellipsis including a stop by . . .). Care has been taken not to distort the author's intent.

PROPRIETARY NAMES

This dictionary includes some words which are, or are asserted to be, proprietary names or trade marks. Their inclusion does not imply that they have acquired for legal purposes a non-proprietary or general significance, nor is any other judgement implied concerning their legal status. In cases where the editor has some evidence that a word is used as a proprietary name or trade mark this is indicated, but no judgement concerning the legal status of such words is made or implied thereby.

LIST OF ABBREVIATIONS

Abbreviations are listed in the form in which they most commonly occur: those printed in italics may in some contexts be in roman, and vice versa. Abbreviations may similarly be printed with or without an initial capital, as the context requires.

a.	adjective
a.	adaptation of, adoption of
a (before a date)	*ante*, before
A.A.O.	Australian Archives Office
abbrev.	abbreviated, abbreviation (of)
absol.	absolute, -ly
A.C.T.	Australian Capital Territory
adj. phr.	adjectival phrase
adj(s).	adjective(s)
adv. phr.	adverbial phrase
adv(s).	adverb(s)
Advt.	advertisement
AJCP	Australian Joint Copying Project
ALR	Australian Law Reports
Amer.	American
Ann. Rep.	annual report
app.	apparently
AR	Industrial Arbitration Reports
assoc.	association
attrib.	attributive, -ly
Aust.	Australia
Austral(s).	Australian(s)
Br.	British
Br. dial.	British dialect
Brit.	Britain, British
c (before a date)	*circa*, about
c. (as 19th c.)	century
CAR	Commonwealth Arbitration Reports
cf.	*confer*, compare
CLR	Commonwealth Law Reports
collect.	collective, -ly
colloq.	colloquial, -ly
Comb.	combination(s)
Comm.	commission
compar.	comparative
conj.	conjunction
const.	construed (with)
C.P.D.	Commonwealth of Australia Parliamentary debates
C.P.P.	Commonwealth of Australia Papers presented to Parliament
cv.	cultivar
Cwlth.	Commonwealth
DAE	*Dictionary of American English*
def.	definition
deriv.	derivative, -ation
dial.	dialect
Dict.	dictionary
dimin.	diminutive
DOST	*Dictionary of the Older Scottish Tongue*
Du.	Dutch
e.	east, eastern
ed.	edition, editor
EDD	*English Dialect Dictionary*
e.g.	*exempli gratia*, for example
ellipt.	elliptical, -ly
Eng.	English
esp.	especially
etc.	*et cetera*, and the rest
etym.	etymology
et al.	*et alii*, and others
euphem.	euphemism, euphemistically
exc.	except
excl.	exclusively
exclam.	exclamation
f.	formed on, from
fam.	family, families
Fed.	federal
fem.	feminine
fig.	figurative, -ly
fl.	*floruit*, flourished
Fr.	French
freq.	frequent, -ly
G.	German
G.B.P.P.	Great Britain Parliamentary papers
Gr.	Greek
Grose	F. Grose, *Dictionary of the Vulgar Tongue*
H.C.	House of Commons
Hist.	now only in an historical context
Hist.	historical, history
H. of R.	House of Representatives
Hotten	J.C. Hotten, *Dictionary of Modern Slang*
HRA	*Historical Records of Australia*
Ibid.	*ibidem*, in the same book or passage
i.e.	*id est*, that is
imit.	imitative
imp.	imperative
incl.	including
infl.	influenced (by)
Inst.	Institute
int.	interjection
intr.	intransitive
Ir.	Irish
irreg.	irregular, -ly
Is.	island
It.	Italian
joc.	jocular, -ly
L.	Latin
L.A.	Legislative Assembly
L.C.	Legislative Council
Let(t).	letter(s)
m.	metre(s)

masc.	masculine
Mathews	M.M. Mathews, *Dictionary of Americanisms*
ML	Mitchell Library
mod.	modern
Morris	E.E. Morris, *Austral English*
n.	noun
n.	north, northern
N. Amer.	North American
N.G.	New Guinea
NLA	National Library of Australia
no.	number
n.p.	no place of publication
N.S.W.	New South Wales
NSWPD	New South Wales Parliamentary debates
N.T.	Northern Territory
N.Z.	New Zealand
obj.	object
Obs.	obsolete
occas.	occasional, -ly
OED	*Oxford English Dictionary* 13 vols.
OEDS	Supplement to the *Oxford English Dictionary* 4 vols.
OED(S	(reference to) Dictionary and Supplement
orig.	originally
p.	page
pa. pple.	past participle
past pple.	past participle
Parl.	parliament, -ary
Partridge	E. Partridge, *Dictionary of Slang and Unconventional English*
pass.	passive, -ly
perh.	perhaps
Pg.	Portuguese
phr.	phrase(s)
pl.	plural
Pl.	plate
pop.	popular, -ly
poss.	possibly
ppl. a.	participial adjective
pple.	participle
pr.	present
prec.	preceding (word or entry)
predom.	predominantly
Pref.	preface
pref.	prefix
prep.	preposition
pres.	present
pres. pple.	present participle
prob.	probably
pron.	pronoun
pronunc.	pronunciation
Proc.	proceedings
pr. pple.	present participle
pseud.	pseudonym
Qld.	Queensland
QPD	Queensland Parliamentary debates
quot(s).	quotation(s)
q.v.	*quod vide*, which see
R.	Royal (in names of periodicals, etc.)
R. Comm.	Royal Commission
Rec.	records
redupl.	reduplicating
ref.	reference
refl., reflex.	reflexive
Rep.	report(s)
repr.	representation, representing
s.	south, southern
S.A.	South Australia
S. Afr.	South Africa, South African
SAPD	South Australian Parliamentary debates
S. Austral.	South Australian
sb.	substantive
sc.	*scilicet*, understand or supply
Sched.	schedule
Scot.	Scottish
Scot. dial.	Scottish dialect
Ser.	series
Sess.	session
sing.	singular
SND	*Scottish National Dictionary*
spec.	specific, -ally
sp(p).	species (singular, plural)
ssp.	subspecies
subfam.	subfamily
subj.	subject
subsp.	subspecies
suff.	suffix
superl.	superlative
Suppl.	supplement
syn.	synonym
t.	tense
Tas.	Tasmania
T.H.A.J.	Tasmania House of Assembly Journals
tr.	translation (of), translator
trans.	transitive
Trans.	transactions
transf.	transferred (sense)
ult.	ultimate, -ly
U.S.	United States
usu.	usually
v.	verb, verbal
V & P	Votes and Proceedings
var. (in scientific nomenclature)	variety
var(r).	variant(s) of
vbl. n.	verbal noun
vbl. phr.	verbal phrase
vbl. sb.	verbal substantive
Vic.	Victoria
vol(s).	volume(s)
v.p.	various places
VPD	Victorian Parliamentary debates
w.	west, western
W.A.	Western Australia
W. Austral.	Western Australian

PRONUNCIATION

List of symbols used

Vowels

i	heat
ɪ	hit
ɛ	bet
æ	bat
a	part
ɒ	hot
ɔ	sort
ʊ	put
u	hoot
ʌ	hut
ɜ	hurt
ə	another

Diphthongs

eɪ	hay
oʊ	hoe
aɪ	high
aʊ	how
ɔɪ	toy
ɪə	tier
ɛə	dare
ʊə	tour

Consonants

p	pat
b	bat
t	tap
d	dot
k	cat
g	goat
f	fat
v	vat
θ	thin
ð	that
s	sat
z	zap
ʃ	shot
ʒ	measure
tʃ	choke
dʒ	joke
m	mat
n	not
ŋ	song
l	long
r	ring
h	hang
j	young
w	way

A

Abbott's booby. [f. the name of W.L. *Abbott* (1860–1936), U.S. naturalist, who collected the type specimen on Assumption Island in 1892.] The gannet *Sula abbotti*, which now breeds only on Christmas Island in the Indian Ocean.

1964 A.L. Thomson *New Dict. Birds* 331 Abbott's Booby is a tree-nester. **1983** P. Harrison *Seabirds* 290 Abbott's Booby *Sula abbotti*. . . Confined to Christmas I., Indian Ocean, where 2,000–3,000 pairs breed. **1984** *Canberra Times* 13 Apr. 3/5 The Government knew Christmas Island was . . the only known breeding ground of the endangered Abbott's booby bird.

Abdul. *Hist.* [Transf. use of the proper name, common in Turkey.]

1. A nickname for a Turkish soldier, esp. during the war of 1914–18. Also collectively, the Turkish army. Also **Abdullah.**

1915 'Lance-Corporal Cobber' *Anzac Pilgrim's Progress* (1918) 71 Here my thoughts have lost that goodly colour, An' I delight in strafing poor Abdulla. **1916** 'Men Of Anzac' *Anzac Bk.* 59 So though your name be black as ink For murder and rapine, Carried out in happy concert With your Christians from the Rhine, *We* will judge you, Mr Abdul, By the test by which *we* can—That, with all your breath, in life, in death, You've played the gentleman. **1916** B. Baly *Patrolling Desert* 1 What's up, Abdul scooped the pot? **1918** *Kia Ora Coo-ee* Mar. 4/3 He stood there . . listening to Abdul's trench-diggers half-a-mile away. **1919** E. Dyson *Hello, Soldier* 18 Little Abdul's quite a fighter, 'n' he mixes it with skill; But the Anzacs have him snouted, 'n' oh ma, he's feelin' ill. **1949** G. Berrie *Morale* 92 I'd give a quid to be planted somewhere where I could watch some Abdul go in.

2. A nickname for an Afghan.

1919 R.J. Cassidy *Gipsy Road* 57 Abdul and his inelegant 'hunchies' are an essentiality of life on the lone, level lands that stretch away back o' sunset.

Abo /ˈæbou/, *n.* and *a.* Pl. **Abos.** [An abbreviated form, perh. brought into written currency by its use in a column entitled 'Aboriginalities', appearing in the Sydney *Bulletin* from 15 Oct. 1887: see quots. 1904 and 1906. See also Aboriginality.]

A. *n.*

1. Abbrev. of Aboriginal *n.* 1 a.

[**1904** *Bulletin* (Sydney) 8 Sept. 16/2 Have any 'Abo's' [*sc.* readers of 'Aboriginalities'] noticed that Willie is a one-man-one-job advocate? **1906** *Ibid.* 18 Oct. 17/3 Remarkable the number of 'Abo' writers who have been chased by snakes.] **1908** *Ibid.* 12 Mar. 14/3 At one time when a stranger approached a blacks' camp the juvenile King Billies . . would disappear into the gunyahs . . and the departing visitor was always well out of coo-ee before the little black nuts would bob out. . . The little abos. of the present day have not much trace of shyness. **1911** *Ibid.* 2 Nov. 14/1 The Protector of Abos. has resigned owing to the interference of clerks and office boys down south. **1912** *Truth* (Sydney) 29 Dec. 2/4 An idea of getting the nigs of the North to do the bulk of the necessary work. Well, it might be good work at which to put an Abo, better by far than having him bumming around the pubs. **1922** 'Te Whare' *Bush Cinema* 27 The guileful abos. put off in their tree-trunk canoes. **1926** A.A.B. Apsley *Amateur Settlers* 76 (*note*) In Australia 'native' means a born-and-bred Australian white man, while the black native Australian is referred to as an 'Aboriginal', or 'Abo' for short. **1929** K.S. Prichard *Coonardoo* (1961) 92 We sling off at the man who makes his abos 'sir' or 'boss' him. He's a new-chum, or a sleeping partner. **1944** S. Campion *Pommy Cow* 193 They're the only craftsmen left in Australia, them aboes. **1965** M. Patchett *Last Warrior* 30 I've seen what over-civilisation in our pattern has done to other Abos. **1965** G.H. Fearnside *Golden Ram* 10 When you're on the wallaby you get t'thinking like the Abos., the Old People. **1977** F.B. Vickers *Stranger no Longer* 148 The navy wouldn't have a bloody Abo. Why the ratings wouldn't sit with him on the mess deck! **1981** C. Wallace-Crabbe *Splinters* 51 Not much of a place, Canberra. Sometimes I reckon it should be given back to the Abos.

2. Abbrev. of Aboriginal *n.* 2.

1918 *Bulletin* (Sydney) 9 May 22/2 A booly (abo. for whirlwind) visited our little mission-school. **1952** C. Simpson *Come away, Pearler* 229 He speaks three or four languages, not counting abo.

B. *adj.* Abbrev. of Aboriginal *a.* (in some cases of Aboriginal *n.* 1 a. used *attrib.*).

1911 *Bulletin* (Sydney) 2 Nov. 14/1 All the Abo. Protector crowd are being run down by Chow white-men. **1915** *Ibid.* 29 Apr. 22/2 Up there it is known as the 'stone'-fish, and amongst some abo. tribes as the 'bullerow'. **1922** 'Te Whare' *Bush Cinema* 38 An 'abo' legend attaches to the great bluff between Bermagui and Tathra. **1932** W. Hatfield *Ginger Murdoch* 65 The futility of looking for those horses—unless they had with them a particularly good abo. tracker. **1940** *Bulletin* (Sydney) 6 Mar. 17/4 Jack . . managed to . . build a fire and cook his lizard abo. style. **1966** H. Gye *Father clears Out* 103 The abo family went walkabout. **1975** X. Herbert *Poor Fellow my Country* 322 He's a beautiful child, isn't he . . despite the Abo features. **1980** N. Watkins *Kangaroo Connection* 54 An abo woman, and I'm the last person to be interested in bedding down with one.

abolitionist. *Hist.* [f. the use of *abolition(ist)* with reference to slavery.] One who advocates the cessation of Transportation. See also Anti-transportation.

1847 (*title*) The abolitionists and transportationists. **1847** *Launceston Examiner* 1 May 277/3 Admitting that it could be shewn that all the evils which the anti-abolitionists predict should really follow, the abolition of transportation is nevertheless our most sacred duty. **1852** J. West *Hist. of Tas.* I. 282 To neglect the offer of social freedom would be infamy unexampled. To this feeling the abolitionists appealed. **1884** J. Fenton *Hist. of Tas.* 183 The abolitionists were in the majority. **1911** R.G.S. Williams *Austral. White Slaves* 72 The Fusionists were overthrown with great slaughter, and the leg-iron abolitionists reigned in their stead. **1945** S.J. Baker *Austral. Lang.* 245 *Abolitionists*, the section of the Australian public who, between 1820 and 1867, fought for the cessation of convict transportation to Australia—they were also known as *anti-transportationists*, and people in favour of continued importation of convicts were called *transportationists*.

Aboriginal, *a.*, *n.*, and *adv.* [Spec. use of *aboriginal* dwelling in a country before the arrival of (European) colonists: see OED *a.* 2 and *sb.*]

A. *adj.*

1. Of, pertaining to, or characteristic of the Aborigines; Aborigine *a.*

1829 *Colonial Times* (Hobart) 7 Mar., In furtherance of the Lieutenant Governor's anxious desire to ameliorate the condition of the Aboriginal inhabitants of this Territory, His Excellency will allow a Salary of Fifty Pounds per annum to a steady person of good character . . who will take an interest in effecting an intercourse with this unfortunate race. **1835** Backhouse & Tylor *Life & Labours G.W. Walker* (1862) 219 A Government School for half-caste and aboriginal children. **1842** *Colonial Observer* (Sydney) 24 Aug. 421/3 The reported removal of the blacks from their water-holes . . by certain stock holders, that their cattle might be saved at the expense of their aboriginal fellowmen. **1844** *Sydney Morning Herald* 1 Feb. 4/4 The title of the proposed 'Jury Bill' was altered. . . The 1st clause was adjusted to the following reading: 'Every man, being a subject of Her Majesty, and not an aboriginal native . . shall be qualified', etc. And the word 'aboriginal' before the word 'native', in the second paragraph, was introduced to make sense of it. **1850** *Australasian Sporting Mag.* 39 Artists . . can place before us the occupations and manners of the new denizens of the bush, as well as of the Aboriginal inhabitant in his more picturesque state of savage life. **1861** L.A. Meredith *Over Straits* 161 Three Sydney natives ('currency' not aboriginal). **1878** G. Walch *Australasia* 9 Unwilling to expose her to the chance of being captured for her plumpness by an aboriginal chief in Tasmania. **1909** W.G. Spence *Aust.'s Awakening* 11 When the white man came to Australia he found in possession the aboriginal squatter, whose runs were tribal and whose stock were kangaroos and opossums. **1910** *Bulletin* (Sydney) 22 Dec. 13/4 The bullock waggons were driven . . by aboriginal Billjims. **1914** *Ibid.* 2 Apr. 24/3 Decided by the legal advisers of the S.A. Government, that 'aboriginal' does not include half-caste, for the purposes of the Birds' Protection Act. **1930** 'Brent Of Bin Bin' *Ten Creeks Run* (1952) 125 One of the aboriginal old hands had requested a drink. **1951** C. Simpson *Adam in Ochre* 196 In 1949 . . two aboriginal boxers held four national titles. **1963** X. Herbert *Disturbing Element* 82 Half the crowd were 'murris', people of aboriginal stock. **1980** Ansell & Percy *To fight Wild* 134 The whole trip . . was as good an example as you could wish to see of Aboriginal bushcraft.

2. In collocations: **Aboriginal black, black man, black native, English, Establishment, Mission, native, police, reserve, school, settlement, station, trooper.**

1824 *Hobart Town Gaz.* 29 Oct., About twenty **Aboriginal blacks** approached the house and stock-yard. **1828** *Austral. Q. Jrnl. Theol., Lit. & Sci.* Jan. p. x, The population . . is entirely British, there having been no amalgamation with the Aboriginal Blacks. The noble hound hunts not with the cur. **1839** *Sydney Standard* 4 Feb. 3/3 *Henry Bartley*, man-slaughter of an aboriginal black, acquitted. **1846** *Tasmanian Jrnl. Nat. Sci.* II. 118 One of the Aboriginal blacks of Newcastle. **1899** *Progress* (Brisbane) 13 May 7/3 Walk-about Kanakas are a far greater disgrace to this colony than ever our aboriginal blacks were. **1963** X. Herbert *Disturbing Element* 1 Two or three cross streets . . ended in a sandy scrubby waste in which there was a fringe settlement of Afghan camel drivers and the dispossessed aboriginal blacks. **1839** *Port Phillip Patriot* 26 Dec. 3 The whole country only a few short months ago was uninhabited, save by the **aboriginal black man.** **1827** *Australasian Almanack* 95 An **aboriginal black native** admitted within the pale of the Church, by the rites of baptism. **1848** *Bell's Life in Sydney* 10 June 2/5 Timothy Duffy, holding a ticket-of-leave, was arraigned for shooting at aboriginal black natives at Moreton Bay. **1883** E.M. Curr *Recoll. Squatting Vic.* 117 This was the party which the blackfellow had described as consisting of 'Towsan', which all the country over, is the **aboriginal English** for any number over half-a-dozen. **1981** Ngabidj & Shaw *My Country of Pelican Dreaming* 4 The speech style called loosely 'Aboriginal English' . . is now a *lingua franca* . . across the north of Australia. **1841** *Geelong Advertiser* 7 Aug. 1/4 *Strayed . . two working bullocks*. . . Whoever will bring the same to the **Aboriginal Establishment** near Killembeet . . will receive the above reward. **1844** *Port Phillip Gaz.* 6 July 2 The vessel was chartered to convey 530 sheep to the Aboriginal Establishment on that Island. **1826** L.E. Threlkeld *Statement* (1828) 19, I was endeavouring to direct the conversation from other concerns to the concerns of the **Aboriginal Mission.** **1838** *Sydney Herald* 21 Sept. 2/4, I have this evening perused in the columns of the *Colonist*, an account of the *progress* of an Aboriginal Mission; and I certainly conceive it to be one of the most glaring and oppressive outrages on the public funds, that has met my observation. **1844** *Sydney Morning Herald* 30 Apr. 2/6 We have received a copy of the Third Annual

Report of the Apsley Aboriginal Mission to the Aborigines. **1846** *Moreton Bay Courier* 27 June 2/3 Aboriginal Missions. The missions for spiritually enlightening the Blacks, and ameliorating their wretched conditions, two of which were for some years existant in this area, are now both at an end. **1820** *N.S.W. Pocket Almanack* 74 Institution for the Children of the **aboriginal Natives** of this Colony, founded at Parramatta. **1827** *Tasmanian* (Hobart) 14 June 4 This native black was an aboriginal native. **1830** *Launceston Advertiser* 8 Mar. (Suppl.) 2 The Lieutenant Governor has directed that a reward of five pounds shall be given for every adult Aboriginal native, and two pounds for every child who shall be captured and delivered alive at any of the Police stations. **1841** *Port Phillip Patriot* 16 Sept. (Suppl.) 5/1 *Bonjon*, an aboriginal native, stood indicted for the wilful murder of Yammowing. **1853** J. SHERER *Gold Finder Aust.* 26 The emu is . . an object of sport to the aboriginal native as well as to the settler. **1855** H. CAPPER *Austral. Colonies* 29 The aboriginal natives are almost extinct, the few who remain living willingly in one place, protected and supported by the Government. **1862** *Bell's Life in Sydney* 15 Mar. 4/2 The aboriginal native, Kipper Billy. **1842** *Portland Mercury* 19 Oct. 3/1 Captain Dana with his party of **aboriginal police** . . went in pursuit of the robbers. . . The sable corps showed much anxiety to overtake and capture the 'myalls', i.e. wild blackfellows. **1842** *Colonial Observer* (Sydney) 5 Nov. 587/3 Native Police.—Eight of the aboriginal police . . started from Melbourne with the intention of forming a police station at Mount Rouse. **1868** J.K. TUCKER *Aborigines & Chinese Question* 26 Another mission was established . . on the **aboriginal reserve** at *Lake Condale*. **1886** E.M. CURR *Austral. Race* I. 104 The Colonial Governments have . . collected the remnants of some or all of the tribes, and located them on what in Victoria are called Aboriginal Reserves. **1895** A. MESTON *Qld. Aboriginals* 12 There are ninety-four aboriginal reserves, representing 23,900 acres. **1911** J.C. FOX *Social Workers' Guide* 13 There are large Aboriginal Reserves throughout the state, on which natives are allowed to camp unmolested. **1929** 'OLD STOCKMAN' *Sensational Cattle-Stealing Case* 81 Peter lived to a great old age, eventually passing out . . on an aboriginal reserve on the Queensland border. **1950** A. GROOM *I saw Strange Land* 42 Known as 'Native Pastoralists', they graze their small herds far out at little-known waters and in hidden grass-land valleys over the vast Aboriginal Reserve that is theirs to the exclusion of all white men other than missionaries and Native Affairs Patrol Officers. **1846** *Melbourne Argus* 23 Oct. 2/2 We regret extremely to learn that the fund for the support of the **Aboriginal School** at the Merrai Creek, has fallen so low. **1886** E.M. CURR *Austral. Race* I. 42 In our Aboriginal schools, it has been found that the pupil masters reading, writing, and arithmetic more quickly than the English child. **1978** *Nungalinya Occasional Bull.* (Darwin) iii. 13 We can develop 'modern Aboriginal' schools. **1897** *Bulletin* (Sydney) 24 July 11/1 One of Meston's niggers at the White Cliffs **Aboriginal Settlement**. **1955** *Ibid.* 12 Oct. 13/2 The lads of the Woorabinda Aboriginal Settlement . . managed to get that huge trunk out of the bush. **1964** P. ADAM SMITH *Hear Train Blow* 107 On the New South Wales side of the Murray was the aboriginal settlement of Cummeragunja where full-bloods and half-castes lived in humpies made of flattened-out kerosene tins. **1841** *Port Phillip Patriot* 31 May 2/4 No damage whatever was done to Mr Darlot's property by the temporary formation of the **aboriginal station** on the land claimed as his run. **1844** *Port Phillip Gaz.* 6 July 3 Fifty sheep belonging to the aboriginal station at Flinders. **1847** *Port Phillip Herald* 15 Apr. (Suppl.) The natives . . are a most orderly and obliging set, partly attributable no doubt to the good instructions they receive from Mr Parker, whose aboriginal station they all frequent. **1878** R.B. SMYTH *Aborigines of Vic.* I. 260 Medical men are in Victoria most zealous and painstaking at all the Aboriginal Stations. **1911** J.C. FOX *Social Workers' Guide* 13 There are nine Aboriginal stations under the management of officers appointed by the Board, which serve as a refuge for women and children, while the men are away in search of employment. **1913** *Bulletin* (Sydney) 21 Aug. 17/4 The Victorian aboriginal station of Lake Condah is being asked to show cause why it shouldn't maintain itself. **1843** *Port Phillip Patriot* 19 Jan. 2/3 Captain Dana started on Tuesday evening with five of his **aboriginal troopers**. **1890** R.S. BROWNE *Romances Gold Field & Bush* 32 The Native Police Officer . . is sent out into unsettled districts with a camp sergeant—the only other white man in the party—and, say, six aboriginal troopers.

B. *n.*

1. a. (For the pl.: see ABORIGINES.) One of the Aborigines; ABORIGINE *n.* 1.

1828 *Hobart Town Courier* 19 Apr. 1 Nothing herein contained shall authorize, or be taken to authorize, any Settler, or Settlers, Stockkeeper, or Stockkeepers, Sealer, or Sealers to make use of force (except for necessary self-defence) against any Aboriginal. **1828** H. DANGAR *Index & Directory River Hunter* 113 It is a custom amongst these aboriginals . . to make the women perform every drudgery. **1839** *Port Phillip Patriot* 6 Mar. 4 Sam, an aboriginal of Sydney, pray do sit four hours in the stocks—it will cure drunkenness. **1842** *Portland Mercury* 7 Sept. 2/5 The aboriginal Roger . . still denies that he committed the murder. **1849** C. STURT *Narr. Exped. Central Aust.* I. 116 There can be no doubt but that the Australian aboriginal is strongly susceptible of kindness. **1856** V. PEARCE *Life* 7 The aboriginals of this Island and of the neighbouring Continent of New Holland, are decidedly the most wretched, unintellectual, debased savages upon the surface of the globe. **1859** W. KELLY *Life in Vic.* I. 46 He felt as uncomfortable as an aboriginal in tight boots. **1863** J. MORRILL *Sketch of Residence* 17 The aboriginals . . are a fine race of people. **1873** A. TROLLOPE *Aust. & N.Z.* I. 60 It will be as well to call the race by the name officially given to it. The government styles them 'aboriginals'. **1881** W. ALLEN *Immigration & Co-operative Settlement* 1 Without population and settlement this territory remained uncivilized, and for ages was the home and hunting ground of the aboriginal. **1893** S. NEWLAND *Paving Way* 17 The dead and dying white men were alike hacked and speared in the blood-frenzy and love of slaughter common to all the aboriginals of Australia. **1902** L. BECKE *Breachley, Black Sheep* 67 In using the term 'nigger', instead of 'blackfellow' or 'black', I adopt the Queensland expression for aboriginal. **1914** R. KALESKI *Austral. Barkers & Biters* 30 The aboriginals were the first people to tame the dingo. **1929** K.S. PRICHARD *Coonardoo* (1956) 126 He was a pure-blooded young aboriginal to look at. **1932** E.R.B. GRIBBLE *Problem of Austral. Aboriginal* 68 A young aboriginal . . saved a large number of the white people. **1938** X. HERBERT *Capricornia* 163 He said he did not mind trying a nameless prisoner if he were an Aboriginal. **1949** I.L. IDRIESS *One Wet Season* 258 Call yourself an *aboriginal*! . . a true son of the forest! **1961** *Bulletin* (Sydney) 15 Feb. 32/1 The aborigines at the Settlement said that if you were an aboriginal you did not have to do anything. **1963** V.B. CRANLEY *27,000 Miles through Aust.* 40 They are relics of prehistoric years, unchanged to this day, like the Aboriginals. **1977** H. TOWSON *Black & White* 15 The Aboriginals went to their tribal grounds during their walk-about. **1985** *Canberra Times* 7 July 22/7 Many more Aboriginals are going into Years 11 and 12.

b. *Obs.* An early settler; an Australian-born colonist.

1837 *Perth Gaz.* 21 Jan. 838 As long as the noble and *graceful Swan* shall row her majestic 'state' to the ocean, so long will *the memorial* last of the attachment and gratitude of the first settlers to Sir James Stirling. I am, Sir, An Aboriginal. **1880** *Bulletin* (Sydney) 18 Sept. 1/1 The sensitive ears of our white aboriginals.

2. An (unspecified) Aboriginal language; ABORIGINE *n.* 2.

1845 J.O. BALFOUR *Sketch of N.S.W.* 8 You may see a *gin* (the aboriginal for a married woman). **1969** J. HIBBERD *Dimboola* (1974) 26 Speaks Italian, Spanish, Cretin, Greek and Aboriginal. **1974** A. BUZO *Coralie Lansdowne says No* 18 The address is 18 Jacka Avenue. Jacka. The Aboriginal for bourgeois.

C. *adv.* In a manner characteristic of the Aborigines; cf. ABORIGINALLY.

1959 L. ROSE *Country of Dead* 112 He's begun to think aboriginal. . . He's been out here too long.

Aboriginality. [Spec. use of *aboriginality* the quality of being aboriginal: see OED and also ABO.] The quality of being Aboriginal; the culture of the Aboriginal people.

1897 J.J. MURIF *From Ocean to Ocean* 72 Physically the natives to be seen about are very good samples of aboriginality. **1977** X. HERBERT *Dream Road* p. viii, One of the most important and pervasive elements of *Poor Fellow My Country*: its aboriginality. **1977** K. GILBERT *Living Black* 93 A few catch-phrases are mouthed . . 'we must get back our Aboriginality'—but there is no coherent drive to achieve any of these things. **1978** *Nungalinya Occasional Bull.* (Darwin) iii. 13 The current expressions of Aboriginality (whether they be the use of Aboriginal languages, kinship requirements or avoidance rules . .) are respected and assumed normal. **1982** *Canberra Times* 9 Nov. 1/3 The other five skeletons were people of mixed descent involving Aboriginality. **1984** *Austral.* (Sydney) 11 Sept. 1/7 By trading on his Aboriginality, Mr Dixon hopes to pressure, cajole and wheedle results from federal and State governments. **1985** *Canberra Times* 7 July 22/6 Consciously or unconsciously, the white population has suppressed Aboriginality.

Aboriginally, *adv.* In an Aboriginal language.

1863 J. MORRILL *Sketch of Residence* 19 The native small plum, aboriginally known as the Bolemo, botanically as the Ficus aspera. **1917** *Bulletin* (Sydney) 5 July 22/2 Leach's kingfisher is aboriginally known as kitticarrara.

Aborigine, *n.* and *a.* Formerly also **Aboriginee.** [A singular form derived analogically from ABORIGINES. ABORIGINAL is now preferred (see ABORIGINES quot. 1978).]

A. *n.*

1. ABORIGINAL *n.* 1 a.

1829 H. WIDOWSON *Present State Van Diemen's Land* 187 An aborigine has occasionally been seen in Hobart Town, but not of late years. **1845** T. MCCOMBIE *Adventures of Colonist* 185 About half-a-dozen men were very agreeably employed in making an aborigine tipsy. **1869** W.M. HOWELL *Reminisc. Aust.* 33 A black man, an aboriginee, walked in. **1906** J.W. GREGORY *Dead Heart Aust.* 60 In Australia the term 'native' is always used for white men born in Australia. The original inhabitants are called Black-fellows or Aborigines; from the last term is derived the singular Aboriginee. **1933** C.W. PECK *Austral. Legends* (ed. 2) 209 You should say 'aborigine' when you mean a person, but 'aboriginal' when you mean the kind of person. **1969** R.A. GOULD *Yiwara* 88 To the Aborigine a person's footprints are almost as distinctive as his physical appearance, his way of walking, or the sound of his voice. **1978** P. PORTER *Cost of Seriousness* 28 A man and a boy are eating with an aborigine In a boat.

2. ABORIGINAL *n.* 2.

1879 'AUSTRALIAN' *Adventures Qld.* 39 Bony . . spoke a curious jargon—a mixture of bad English and aborigine—freely intermixed with snatches of profanity. **1893** *Bulletin* (Sydney) 18 Feb. 15/2 The word 'warrigal' was current aboriginee ere the British Lion deposited 'our forefathers' here.

B. *adj.* ABORIGINAL *a.* 1.

1835 G.C. INGLETON *True Patriots All* (1952) 163 Captain Pigeon, and his company, are placed on the 'Aborigine Establishment', which forms an item in an expenditure, of *only* £1899 per annum. **1887** *Bulletin* (Sydney) 12 Feb. 13/4 The 'aboriginee' missionaries in S.A. are well nigh despairing. **1925** *Smith's Weekly* (Sydney) 7 Feb. 17/7 In the aborigine towns of the lower Murray, the members of the tribes that were chosen as ambassadors . . were generally of lower mentality than average. **1967** D. WHITINGTON *In Search of Austral.* 98 The Government should take over all Aborigine education. **1969** R.A. GOULD *Yiwara* 15 Aborigine children are indulged to an extreme degree, and sometimes continue to suckle until they are four or five years old.

Aborigines, *pl.* Formerly also **Aboriginees.** [Spec. use of *aborigines* those believed to have been the inhabitants of a country *ab origine*, i.e. from the beginning. At first, in Aust. as earlier elsewhere, used only in the pl.: see OED. Now the preferred pl. (but see quot. 1978 and, for examples of *Aboriginals*, ABORIGINAL *n.* 1 a.).] The indigenous inhabitants of Australia; their descendants.

1803 Banks Papers VIII. 221 Nature not having furnished it with food sufficient to maintain any other race of men than the Aborigines. **1804** *HRA* (1921) 3rd Ser. I. 281 The Aborigines of this Country are . . under the Protection of the Laws of Great Britain. **1811** D.D. MANN *Present Picture N.S.W.* 33 Some of the white men would frequently be more severe with the Aborigines . . but the circumstance of several settlers being capitally convicted of the murder of a native boy, in January, 1800, acts as a check. **1814** *HRA* (1916) 1st Ser. VIII. 313 It has long been in Serious Contemplation with me to Endeavour to Civilize the Aborigines of this Country. **1816** *Ibid.* (1917) 1st Ser. IX. 139 The hostile and Sanguinary disposition Manifested for a Considerable time past by the Aborigines of this Country. **1817** *Hobart Town Gaz.* 24 May, Several Settlers and others are in the habit of maliciously and wantonly firing at, and destroying, the defenceless *Natives* or *Aborigines* of this Island. **1819** W.C. Wentworth *Statistical, Hist., & Pol. Descr. N.S.W.* 4 The aborigines of this country occupy the lowest place in the gradatory scale of the human species. **1824** J. Lycett *Views in Aust.* 4 Every means which wisdom and humanity can suggest for the civilization of the aborigines, have been resorted to by succeeding Governors, a period of thirty years has passed away, without affording much hope of the attainment of that object. **1834** J.D. Lang *Hist. & Statistical Acct. N.S.W.* II. 112 Every habitable district in the colony has its tribe of aborigines or black natives. **1841** *England & her Colonies* 1 The Aborigines who may be termed British, amount at a low estimate, to one Million inhabiting Australia. **1847** A. Marjoribanks *Travels N.S.W.* 10 The words *aborigines* and *natives* are kept up with peculiar strictness in New South Wales; the former, a Latin word, signifying the original inhabitants of the country, who, of course, are the blacks; and the latter signifying those born in the country of white parents. **1849** C. Sturt *Narr. Exped. Central Aust.* I. 44 They were in truth two fine specimens of Australian aborigines, stern, impetuous, and determined, active, muscular, and energetic. **1859** H.M. Hull *Experience Forty Yrs. Tas.* 16 One of the black ladies, who married a few years ago a sawyer named *Smith*, has recently presented her husband with a little black 'pledge of affection' of which the other aborigines are very proud. **1867** 'Clergyman' *Aust. as it Is* 51 The aborigines have something very nearly approximating to an intuitive knowledge of eligible territory. **1872** Mrs E. Millett *Austral. Parsonage* 127 The 'aborigines', as they are now styled .. Captain Cook would in his older time have called 'Indians'. **1881** J.C.F. Johnson *To Mount Browne & Back* 7, I was introduced for the first time to the coloured carriageocracy. . . I had often been informed that the aborigines of the North were the *crême de la crême* of niggerdom. **1889** J.H.L. Zillmann *Past & Present Austral. Life* 113 My personal recollections .. serve the .. purpose of illustrating the character of the Aboriginees. **1919** *Smith's Weekly* (Sydney) 22 Mar. 15/1 Our aborigines are not over gifted with intellect. **1936** *Publicist* (Sydney) i. 3/1 The patriot in Australia may be a dwindling species, like the koala, the lyrebird, the platypus, and the Aborigines themselves. **1944** J. Devanny *By Tropic Sea & Jungle* 20 Left to themselves, the aborigines were the best self-governed and biggest-souled people you could meet. **1958** R. Ward *Austral. Legend* (1970) 201 No white man has ever been the equal of the Aborigines in essential bush skills. **1969** D. Cusack *Half-Burnt Tree* 14 We're Aborigines, see? Not blackfellers or *Boongs* or niggers. Aborigines .. with a capital A. **1978** *Style Manual* (ed. 3) 11 When referring to the first inhabitants of Australia, prefer the forms *Aboriginal* (singular noun), *Aboriginals* (plural noun) and *Aboriginal* (adjective). While the form *Aborigine* is not acceptable as an alternative to *Aboriginal* for the singular noun, *Aborigines* may be used as an alternative plural form. **1986** *Canberra Times* 3 Mar. 2/6 Health and education would do more, for urban Aborigines in particular, than land rights.

abscond, *v. Hist.* [Spec. use of *abscond* to depart (usu. to elude the law) secretly.]

a. *intr.* Of a convict: to escape from custody.

1788 D. Collins *Acct. Eng. Colony N.S.W.* (1798) I. 32 One of these [convicts] had absconded, and lived in the woods for nineteen days. **1808** *Sydney Gaz.* 18 Sept., The following Convict Servants have absconded from the employ of their respective masters. **1816** *Hobart Town Gaz.* 5 Oct., Richard Maynard .. has absconded and is now at large. **1820** H.G. Bennet *Let. to Earl Bathurst* 89 There are great herds containing some thousands of wild cattle. . . Their existence is considered to be a great evil .. as holding out an inducement to convicts to abscond. **1827** *Colonial Times* (Hobart) 13 Jan., Matthew Macavoy having in breach of his Engagement absconded from my Service, the Public are hereby cautioned from employing him. **1842** *Colonial Observer* (Sydney) 13 Dec. 718/2 Three men who absconded from the New England road party, have been apprehended. **1850** *Irish Exile* (Hobart) 16 Mar. 7 The woman stated that she had asked her mistress for a 'pass', and she had refused to give her one, when she immediately took French leave, and absconded. **1863** C. Gibson *Life among Convicts* II. 275 The condition of a convict, who takes to the backwoods, is a desperate one. It is thought that 75 of the 116 who absconded from Macquarie Harbour, perished in the woods.

b. In the phr. **to abscond into the woods, bush,** (of a convict) to escape into unsettled country.

1790 *Hist. Rec. N.S.W.* 391 If any person, male or female, shall desert or abscond into the woods, every such person or persons shall be deemed and held to be of the most dangerous and pernicious consequence to the community at large, and therefore be adjudged to suffer death. **1801** G. Barrington *Sequel to Voyage N.S.W.* 29 William Crozier Cook, having rendered himself obnoxious to the law, had absconded into the woods. **1818** *Hobart Town Gaz.* 28 Feb., My Wife .. absconded into the woods with Benjamin Gibbs, an absentee. **1824** J. Lycett *Views in Aust.* 13 Howe very soon absconded into the woods and joined a gang of bushrangers. **1827** *Colonial Times* (Hobart) 21 July, The Lieutenant Governor has much pleasure to announce the Capture of the three remaining Convicts, who after attempting to surprise the Emma Kemp cutter, absconded into the bush. **1832** J. Bischoff *Sketch Hist. Van Diemen's Land* 190 Desperate characters amongst the prisoner population .. absconded into the woods.

Hence **absconder** *n.*

1840 *Tasmanian Weekly Dispatch* 27 Mar. 7/4 An unusual number of absconders have been dealt with. **1852** J. Morgan *Life & Adventures W. Buckley* 118 An absconder from the operations of the sentence imposed upon me by the authorities. **1855** J. Bonwick *Geogr. Aust. & N.Z.* (ed. 3) 27 Two Irish absconders had there been killed and eaten by the blacks. **1865** 'Special Correspondent' *Transportation* 48 Difficulties arose from the sympathy and assistance absconders from the probation parties receive from the freed criminals.

absconding, *vbl. n. Hist.* The act of escaping from custody.

1804 *Sydney Gaz.* 15 July, *Wm. Cheshire*, for absconding from public labour at Castle Hill. **1805** J. Turnbull *Voyage round World* I. 113 One of the prisoners formed and executed the extravagant resolution of absconding into the glens. **1822** J.T. Bigge *Rep. State Colony N.S.W.* 99 At Windsor and in the adjoining districts, the offence termed bush-ranging, or absconding in the woods, and living upon plunder, and the robbing of orchards, are the most prevalent. **1834** J. Mudie *Vindication* p. xxiii, *Absconding*, is a term given to the first act of departure from an assignee. When the convicts have been absent a short time, they cease to be called *absentees*; they are then termed *bushrangers*. **1835** *Colonist* (Sydney) 30 July 243/2 Punishments of runaways have not been sufficiently felt to discourage a repetition of the crime of absconding. **1846** L.W. Miller *Notes of Exile Van Dieman's Land* 268 Nothing can be more wicked than to attempt avoiding your punishment by absconding. You take to the bush, you rob, you plunder, you even murder your victims, but you are soon taken, tried and hanged. **1852** J. Morgan *Life & Adventures W. Buckley* 15 Four of us agreed to take to the bush, as absconding is called.

absent, *v. Hist. trans.* (usu. *refl.*) Of a convict: to remove (oneself) from custody.

1806 *Sydney Gaz.* 23 Nov., *Ralph Summer* was ordered 50 lashes and the gaol gang for absenting himself from Government labour. **1810** *Ibid.* 28 Jan., The following Prisoners have absented themselves from Public Labour in the Town and other Gangs at Sydney.

absentee.

1. a. *Hist.* A convict who has escaped from custody and remains at large.

1805 *Sydney Gaz.* 29 Dec., Wm. Page, an absentee into the woods. **1809** *Ibid.* 9 Apr., The following Persons having lately absconded from Public Labour, all Persons are hereby cautioned against harbouring or employing either of the said Absentees. **1817** *Hobart Town Gaz.* 2 Aug., *Taylor*, the absentee alluded to in a Government and General Order in this page, was on Monday last sent back here from Port Dalrymple and lodged in prison. **1827** *Colonial Times* (Hobart) 29 Sept., John Williams who has been four years an absentee from Sydney, was taken in the streets of Hobart-town. **1833** *Trumpeter* (Hobart) 13 Aug. 130 *If Peter Bellamy* .. formerly an Assigned Servant .. does not present himself at this Office to take up his Ticket-of-Leave .. it will be cancelled, and he will be advertised as an Absentee. **1837** *Rep. Select Committee Transportation* 24 By the word 'absentee' which you have used just now, you mean a runaway convict?—I used it as it was used in the Committee-room; but my own term for such a person was an absconding person. 'Absentee' may be used as a word to express it.—Is it not a common word in the Colony?—It may be; it is a very proper word to use; I do not dispute that the word is very common in the colony. **1840** *Tasmanian Weekly Dispatch* 13 Mar. 6/3 George Jilks, an absentee, sentence of transportation extended 12 months. **1850** C.A. King *Life* 22, I became an absentee from the government gang .. when .. one of the government inspectors .. found fault with what he was pleased to term neglect of work. **1899** G.E. Boxall *Story Austral. Bushrangers* 4 Some of the issues of these *Gazettes* contain columns of the names and descriptions of persons variously styled 'absconders', 'absentees', 'bolters' or 'bushrangers'.

b. In the phr. **absentee from public labour**.

1805 *Sydney Gaz.* 3 Nov., *Lee*, one of the absentees from public labor. **1809** *Ibid.* 31 Dec., One *Hutchins*, an absentee from public labour.

2. [Spec. use of *absentee* a landlord who lives abroad: see OED 2.] A non-resident landholder, esp. one who lives in the British Isles. Also *attrib.*

1831 *Sydney Herald* 15 Aug. 2/3 Immense absentee grants will be less frequently met with. **1842** *Colonial Observer* (Sydney) 23 Nov. 630/2 A great number of our absentee colonists are returning by those ships. **1872** 'Resident' *Glimpses Life Vic.* 305 The owner has left his property in charge of an overseer, and has gone to swell the list of absentees who yearly return to the old country. **1892** *Bulletin* (Sydney) 6 Aug. 5/3 His back is growing rounder—slaving for an absentee—And his toiling wife is thinner than a country wife should be. **1911** V. Desmond *Awful Austral.* 72 A squatter's son is a chip off the old blockhead. When he's about twenty he's sent to England for a brush up, and he either becomes an absentee or returns to help make Australian cities more vicious. **1932** D.B. O'Connor *Belle of Barrine* 4 The harvests of our heritage are squandered by absentee bosses and their chromos in the casinos of Europe. **1955** J. Cleary *Justin Bayard* 90, I just hate the guts of the absentee landowners. . . The stations with the worst homesteads and with the least improvements on them are all those owned by men in Perth or Sydney or London. **1965** A.W. Upfield *Lure of Bush* 100 Can you open up the land as it should be opened when .. the absentee squatters have grabbed the lot?

absenteeism. *Hist.* The practice of being an Absentee (esp. sense 2).

1831 *Sydney Monitor* 7 May 3/4 A female assigned servant of Mr Whitaker was brought before the Police on a charge of *absenteeism*. **1844** *Sydney Morning Herald* 24 Jan 3/3 Absenteeism, like everything else, may be carried to excess, but for a colony a due proportion of absentees—of proprietors residing in the mother country—is a thing much to be desired. **1872** 'Resident' *Glimpses Life Vic.* 305 Absentees .. yearly return to the old country to spend the fortune amassed in the colonies. This absenteeism .. gives a very unsettled character to the society in town and country. **1892** 'E. Kinglake' *Austral. at Home* 85 All good Australians hope to go to England when they die. Not only does everybody, now-a-days, go 'home' when able to do so, but many stay there. Absenteeism is becoming common. **1917** *Truth* (Sydney) 28 Jan. 4/3 Absenteeism has been the curse of Australia in the past, and would be vastly increased under Imperial Federation.

absolute emancipation. *Hist.* Absolute pardon.

1799 D. Collins *Acct. Eng. Colony N.S.W.* (1802) II. 268 Absolute emancipation, with permission to quit the colony. **1802** *Gen. Orders issued by Governor King* 8 June 102 Those who have obtained Absolute Emancipations, and who leave the Colony, will do well to enquire if the counterpart of such Pardon has been sent to England; otherwise they may be taken up. **1805** *HRA* (1915) 1st Ser. V. 477 The enclosed are Twelve Counterparts of Absolute Emancipations, which I have granted to enable the objects thereof to enter on board His Majesty's Ship, Investigator.

absolute pardon. *Hist.* A complete remission of (a convict's) sentence, including restitution of the right of return to the British Isles; Free pardon.

1802 *N.S.W. Gen. Orders* 1 Oct. (1806) 1 To any convict, an Absolute Pardon, the Governor's Interest to get a Passage home. **1811** *Sydney Gaz.* 19 Jan., The whole of the Free Men on and off the Stores, including such as came free into the Colony, such as have become free from their Sentences of Transportation having expired, and such as are free by Absolute Pardon or Conditional Emancipation. **1820** H.G. BENNET *Let. to Earl Bathurst* 7 No one under sentence of transportation for life, shall ever apply for an absolute pardon until he or she shall have resided for the space of *Fifteen Years* in the colony. **1822** J.T. BIGGE *Rep. State Colony N.S.W.* 119 An absolute pardon of the governor of New South Wales contains a declaration under his hand, and the seal of the territory, that the unexpired term of transportation of the convict is absolutely remitted to him. **1838** *Tegg's N.S.W. Pocket Almanac* 130 *Principal Superintendent of Convict's Office*... Fee on absolute pardon, 5s. 6d. **1844** *Colonial Times* (Hobart) 6 Feb., The Lieutenant-Governor directs it to be notified to the under-mentioned persons, that it is his intention to recommend Her Majesty the Queen to grant them Absolute Pardons.

acacia. [Transf. use of *acacia* (fam. Mimosaceae), a genus of leguminous trees and shrubs (the most common sense in Aust.): see WATTLE.]

1. Any of several trees and shrubs of the genus *Cassia* (fam. Caesalpiniaceae) bearing some resemblance to species of *Acacia*.

1903 *Proc. Linnean Soc. N.S.W.* XXVIII. 764 *Cassia laevigata*... Known as 'Acacia'; a very bad weed. **1942** *Council Sci. & Industr. Research Bull.* no. 156 43 Acacia, African .. *Cassia laevigata*.

2. Any of several trees of the genus *Albizia* (fam. Mimosaceae), perh. confused with *Acacia* because members of both genera rapidly colonize burnt ground.

1938 C.T. WHITE *Princ. Bot. Qld. Farmers* 182 The tree colloquially known as 'Acacia' in the Queensland sugar-belt is a species of *Albizzia* (*A. procera*). Another species extensively planted in the central-west and familiarly known as 'Acacia' is *A. Lebbek*, a native of India.

3. Special Comb. **acacia cedar,** the tree *Albizia toona* (fam. Mimosaceae) of Qld.

1926 *Qld. Agric. Jrnl.* XXV. 435 Albizzia toona .. Mackay Cedar, Acacia Cedar (Cairns). **1930** V. KENNEDY *By Range & River* 73 A full list of Atherton timbers would include such building timbers as: .. acacia cedar. **1944** J. DEVANNY *By Tropic Sea & Jungle* 128 Acacia cedar is red striated with cream, with an open, wide grain.

acca /'ækə/. Also **acker.** Alteration of 'academic'.

1977 *Meanjin* 90 (*heading*) Accas and ockers: Australia's new dictionaries. **1982** *Sydney Morning Herald* 3 Sept. 12/7 N.S.W. University market day... Intended for the whole community, not just for accas (academic persons). **1984** *Age Weekender* (Melbourne) 2 Mar. 11/2 Ackers from the university.

accommodation house. [In Br. use freq. with reference to a house of ill repute: see OEDS.] A house providing board and lodging for travellers, and in which refreshments are served; HOUSE OF ACCOMMODATION.

1843 *Church in Aust.* (Soc. Propagation Gospel) (1845) ii. 39 We reached Mr Owen's accommodation-house. **1849** J.P. TOWNSEND *Rambles & Observations N.S.W.* 167 We at last reach 'an accommodation-house', a term applied to places that are to all intents and purposes grog-shops, although professing to sell nothing of the kind. **1858** R. ROWE *Peter 'Possum's Portfolio* 94 The acid anxiety of an old woman that keeps an 'accommodation house' .. on my eagerly inquiring whether she doesn't sell grog upon the sly. **1869** J. MARTINEAU *Lett. from Aust.* 125, I went to one 'accommodation-house' (an inferior kind of inn). **1872** G.S. BADEN-POWELL *New Homes for Old Country* 129 The squatter encourages the erection of an 'accommodation house'... This soon becomes an 'hotel'; and thus is formed the nucleus of a township. **1886** P. CLARKE *'New Chum' in Aust.* 124 In this accommodation house near the forest you will have culinary delicacies .. you never expected to see out in the bush. **1895** *Bulletin* (Sydney) 14 Dec. 7/1 An accommodation-house—a grog-shop and store combined. **1899** *Northern Tas.* (Northern Tasmanian Tourists' Assoc.) 57 An accommodation house, consisting of a living room and two sleeping apartments—one for the ladies and one for their escorts. **1907** *Bulletin* (Sydney) 7 Nov. 14/2 Half the cooks are yellow, the boarders at pubs and accommodation houses have never made a real effort to oust them. **1918** W. ROBERTSON *Sunshine & Shadow* 116 Near it is a place called the 'Galah', once an accommodation house. **1933** *Bulletin* (Sydney) 1 Nov. 21/3 An accommodation-house that has never received its due meed of notoriety is the Wingadee station mail-box on the Coonamble-Walgett (N.S.W.) road.

Hence **accommodation tent** *n.*

1861 T. M'COMBIE *Austral. Sketches* 90, I determined to endeavour to reach a station or accommodation-tent.

accommodation paddock. An enclosed area for the confinement and pasturing of travelling stock.

1843 *Colonial Observer* (Sydney) 22 Feb. 838/1 Four miles from town, near the accommodation paddocks. **1843** *Sydney Morning Herald* 22 Sept. 4/6, I sent the inspector to ascertain if any cattle in the town had been sold which were stolen... I saw them at Wright's accommodation paddock. **1860** 'LADY' *My Experiences in Aust.* 102 To pitch our tent in an accommodation paddock, some 2 or 3 miles out of town. **1874** R.P. FALLA *Knocking About* (1976) 8 There is a very fine accommodation paddock attached to the above hotel. **1910** *Bulletin* (Sydney) 6 Jan. 13/1 They had absolutely no feed and the usual accommodation paddocks were bare. **1920** B. CRONIN *Timber Wolves* 14 Half a dozen paling shanties built along the side of the accommodation paddock as they calls it.

accord. An agreement between the Australian Labor Party and the Australian Council of Trade Unions negotiated as part of a prices and income policy.

1983 *Sydney Morning Herald* 17 Feb. 12/4 As a result of the months of painstaking consultation, discussion and work, we, the representatives of the incoming Labor Government, have reached an historic accord with the trade union movement which will form the basis for a firm, genuine and workable prices and incomes policy for this nation. **1983** *Age* (Melbourne) 30 June 3/7 Pay accord may take years, unions tell the bench... The ACTU yesterday launched its claim for a national 2.2 per cent wage rise, and said it was prepared to wait years for the prices-and-incomes accord to be implemented. *Ibid.* 3 Mar. 19/1 As accord stands, so does Labor. **1985** *Canberra Times* 4 Aug. 1/5 Sweetheart deals break the accord. **1986** *Nat. Times* 18 Apr. 41/1 (*heading*) Accord begins to creak: major surgery advised.

ace. [Fig. use of *ace* a single dot or symbol on a die or playing-card.] In the phr. **on one's ace,** on one's own, using one's own resources; alone.

1904 *Truth* (Sydney) 2 Oct. 3/1 As a burglar bold, Kelly works strictly on his ace, believing that comradeship in crime is dangerous. **1908** E.G. MURPHY *Jarrahland Jingles* 58 And Brim.'s in London on his 'ace', Of Andrew Barr a trifle 'jack'. **1914** E. DYSON *Spats' Fact'ry* 34 It's one of them little things yeh can't do on your ace. **1934** A. RUSSELL *Tramp-Royal* 213 'They're capable of good work at times,' said a 'boss cattleman' to whom I had applied for his opinion of the merits and demerits of the aboriginal as a stockman, 'but you've got to be with them. Send 'em out "on their ace" and they'll probably "go camp" under the first shady tree they come to.' **1953** S.J. BAKER *Aust. Speaks* 131 *Ace, on one's*, on one's own [in a glossary of prison slang].

acher, var. ACRE.

acid. [f. *acid test* a test in which gold is distinguished from other metals by its resistance to nitric acid.] In the phr. **to put (ply, try) the acid (on),** to exert a pressure which is difficult to resist; to exert such pressure on (a person, etc.); to be successful in the exertion of such pressure. Hence **to take the acid off.**

1906 E. DYSON *Fact'ry 'Ands* 210 E's er hartist—got er touch like velvet. 'E put's ther acid on so't yeh think it's ther milk 'iv 'uman kindness. **1906** *Ibid.* 215 Evidently it was Mr Cato's intention to try the acid on Feathers again. **1910** L. ESSON *Three Short Plays* (1911) 9 Don' you worry. I'll come back orl rite... Take the acid orf. **1911** *Bulletin* (Sydney) 6 July 43/1 The Detective Office, where the experts could 'put the acid' on him nicely and quietly. **1915** A. WRIGHT *Sport from Hollowlog Flat* 21 He scented fair game, and determined to 'put the acid' on forthwith. **1919** P.S. CLEARY *One Big Union* 4 It seemed to be nobody's business to 'put the acid' on bogus social programmes. **1919** V. MARSHALL *World of Living Dead* 85 Since first I put the acid on a lifer fer a snout An' me traffickin' in contraband begun. **1927** A. WRIGHT *Squatter's Secret* 115 Go and put the acid on the old man, and get it over. **1938** J. MOSES *Nine Miles from Gundagai* 10 The barber's shop's a witness-box (They ply the acid there). **1939** G. DIGBY *Down Wind* 264 They tell me he's put the acid on the best-looking girl in the district. **1963** J. CANTWELL *No Stranger to Flame* 125 She was going to have my kid, but she dropped it when another bloke put the acid on. **1965** J. O'GRADY *Aussie Eng.* 9 'To put the acid on' a female does not mean that you dab a little sulphuric or hydrochloric behind her ears. It implies a question, and whichever way you phrase it, the answer will most likely be an astounded look, followed by a well-swung arm or handbag. **1968** *Swag* (Sydney) iii. 39/1 'A witty quip, very cleverly put,' he says, ducking off to cleverly put the acid on someone's spouse.

acker, var. ACCA.

ack-willie. *a.* Also **ack-willy.** [f. a superseded military signalling code in which *a* was represented as *ack* and *w* as *William*, A.W. being a shortening of A.W.L. or A.W.O.L.] In Services' speech: absent without leave.

1943 *Signals* (Melbourne) Christmas 39 Is it Stylish to go Ackwilly so consistently at night? **1944** S. KELLEN *Camp Happy* 95 Did anybody witness that haircut, or did you go ack willy to see your wife? **1946** A.J. MARSHALL *Nulli Secundus Log* 15 One HQ Company member was thought ack-willie, but he had merely returned to the convoy with personnel of a famous British battle-cruiser. **1948** H.W. CRITTENDEN *Rogues' Paradise* 86 Desertion in wartime is a serious and ugly sounding term for a military crime punishable by death. In Australia it is invariably called A.W.L. (absent without leave), or even more euphemistically 'Ack willy'. **1957** J.M. HOSKING *Aust. First & Last* 120 The officers are Duntroon men who did not volunteer. We go 'ack-willy' to the pub, and curse them over our beer. **1968** D. O'GRADY *Bottle of Sandwiches* 45 He was two weeks ack-willie from the job. **1977** R. BEILBY *Gunner* 22 While he wore it he was merely 'ack-willie', A.W.L., Absent Without Leave.

Hence **ack-willie** *n.*, one absent without leave.

1951 E. LAMBERT *Twenty Thousand Thieves* 31 Another couple of ack-willies.

acre. Also **acher.** [Fig. use of *acre* an expanse.] A euphemism for 'arse'.

1965 J. O'GRADY *Aussie Eng.* 9 'A kick in the acre' does not mean a kick in four thousand eight hundred and forty square yards of earth. Female 'acres' are generally referred to as 'rears'. **1971** F. HARDY *Outcasts of Foolgarah* 18 Wiping between his toes and falling on his acre. **1971** *Ibid.* 94 I'll give you a free kick up the acher if you're not careful.

addle, var. ATTLE.

Adelaidean. Also **Adelaidian.** [f. the name of the capital city of S.A.] A resident of Adelaide. Also **Adelaider, Adelaidonian,** and *attrib.*

1839 *Port Phillip Patriot* 20 Mar. 3/2 Australia Felix .. is as *free* from being a *penal* settlement as the most Antipenal Adelaidian can wish. **1845** R. HOWITT *Impressions Aust. Felix* 210 Little short of a million of money passed from the Adelaiders into the old colonies, for cattle, sheep, and farm produce. ***c* 1848** 'SICK MAN' *Voyage Sydney to S.A.* 10 The Adelaidonians would justly oppose the commentary. **1848** *Adelaide Miscellany* 9 Sept. 90 Adelaideans, who had apparently visited the port on business. **1852** S. SIDNEY *Three Colonies* 206 New arrivals from England fortunate enough to be admitted to the delightful evening parties given by a lady of the 'highest ton', the leader of the Adelaidean fashion, were astonished. **1873** A. TROLLOPE *Aust. & N.Z.* II. 182, I liked Adelaide much,—and I liked the Adelaideans. **1878** F.L. RAINS *By Land & Ocean* 17 The Adelaideans must be a pious people indeed. **1888** 'SPECIAL CORRESPONDENT' *Barrier Silver & Tin Fields* 8 To Adelaideans unaccustomed to any other scenes in the streets than the City of Churches presents on Sundays the sights furnished at Broken Hill have no common interest. **1924** A. GASK *Secret of Garden* 123 The Adelaidians were delighted. **1954** W.K. HANCOCK *Country & Calling* 116 Some ass of a publicist had called Adelaide the City of Culture. Too many Adelaidians recalled this tribute too often and too unctuously.

Adelaide pheasant. *Obs.* See quot.

1881 J.C.F. JOHNSON *To Mount Browne & Back* 13, I was met with the startling information that all Adelaide men were croweaters, and that the parson-coated birds were known on the border as 'Adelaide pheasants' because it was asserted that the early settlers of 'Farinaceous Village', when short of mutton, made a meal of the unwary crow.

Adelaide rosella. [f. *Adelaide* (see quot. 1900), first applied as the specific name *Adelaidae* by English zoologist J. Gould (*Proc. Zool. Soc. London* (1841) VIII. 161) + ROSELLA *n.*[1] 1.] The parrot *Platycercus elegans adelaidae*, a subspecies of the crimson rosella, restricted to wooded country in S.A. from the Flinders Ranges to the Fleurieu Peninsula; *pheasant parrot*, see PHEASANT 2.

1900 A.J. CAMPBELL *Nests & Eggs Austral. Birds* 631 The Adelaide Rosella or Pheasant Parrakeet is a beautiful species in radiant colouring... It was named *adelaidensis*, from the circumstance that Gould, in 1838, procured some of his first specimens in the very streets of Adelaide. **1952** A.C.C. LOCK *Travels across Aust.* 198 The tuneful notes of Adelaide rosellas. **1969** J.M. FORSHAW *Austral. Parrots* 189 The Adelaide Rosella is very variable and .. no change in plumage can be adequately correlated with distribution.

adjigo /ˈædʒɪgoʊ, ˈædʒɪkoʊ/. Also **adjiko, ijjecka.** [a. Nhanta-anmaŋu *ajuka*.] The native yam *Dioscorea hastifolia* (fam. Dioscoreaceae) of near-coastal s.w. W.A.; the edible underground part of this plant; WARRAN.

1863 *Jrnls. & Rep. Two Voyages Glenelg River* 1 Aug. (1864) 27/2 Edible roots .. identical with those of Champion Bay (warrein and adjiko). **1903** H. TAUNTON *Australind* 28 She it was that showed me the 'ajigo' plant, and taught me how to dig up its succulent root, which when cooked resembles a cooked yam in size, shape, and flavour. **1933** J.E. HAMMOND *Winjan's People* 28 The 'Warryn' or 'Adtjikoh' was a white root which grew best amongst the loose stones and rocks of the Darling Ranges. **1975** M.A. BAIN *Ancient Landmarks* 151 The people in the vicinity of the Bowes River lived mainly on the ijjecka root. **1979** E. SMITH *Saddle in Kitchen* 20 'Adjigo', a native creeper... Grandpa said the tuber .. was good to eat and tasted like sweet potato.

Adrian Quist, *a.* [The name of an Austral. tennis player, b. 1913.] Rhyming slang for 'pissed', inebriated. Also *ellipt.* as **Adrian.**

1978 *Austral.* (Sydney) 31 May 9/5 I'm on the turps again—got Adrian Quist somethin' terrible the other night. **1978** *Boozer's Diary* (1979) 80 Adrian (= drunk). **1982** *Sydney Morning Herald* 2 Nov. 9/4 They didn't look particularly decorous, .. collapsed, Adrian Quist, as the racing men say, under the hedge.

Advance Australia. A patriotic catch-phrase, used freq. in song and verse and, independently, as a slogan.

[**1828** L.E. THRELKELD *Austral. Reminisc. & Papers* (1974) II. 245 Joseph speaks fluently to the Blacks we having only six at present but are 'Advancing Australia'.] **1832** *Sydney Herald* 21 June 1/3 (Advt.), Advance Australia! **1841** *Ibid.* 12 Feb. 2/1 First a canopy of wreaths surmounted a gorgeous floral crown which overtopped a meadow coloured arch, on which the words *Advance Australia* appeared formed of the brilliant orange coloured flowers of the Xeranthemum. **1843** *Sydney Morning Herald* 25 May 4/4 Advance Australia is the poet's song! Advance Australia patriot hearts prolong! **1844** *Ibid.* 6 Aug. 2/7 Advance Australia Felix! now the cheapest country in the world, and destined .. to become probably the most populous, powerful, and opulent nation of either the southern or northern hemisphere. **1846** *Ibid.* 28 Jan. 3/4 The colonial motto—'Advance Australia'. **1851** *Empire* (Sydney) 5 Dec. 435/1 Slab huts succumb to weather-boarded tenements, and brick yards are already talked of. Gold abounds more profusely than ever and the universal watch-word seems to be 'Advance Australia'. **1855** W. HOWITT *Land, Labor & Gold* II. 426 Let us cordially cry, 'Advance, Australia!' and so treat her in her infancy that she shall remember us with grateful affection in the power and splendor of her maturity. **1888** *Morning Bull.* (Rockhampton) 11 Apr. 3/6 Advance Australia! Yes, my boys, And this seems something *like* advancing! **1899** *Tocsin* (Melbourne) 29 June 1/1 Advance Australia on a 30 bob a week 'living' wage! **1904** *Nineteenth Century* (London) July 105 'Advance Australia' is our national motto. **1917** *Huon Times* (Franklin) 19 Oct. 3/4 They have proved to the Hun that 'Advance Australia' is not a mere phrase, but a virile, palpitating reality. **1956** S. HOPE *Diggers' Paradise* 18 The old popular slogan 'Advance Australia' has gained special significance since the Second World War. **1965** G.H. FEARNSIDE *Golden Ram* 114 Be a visionary businessman, a public-minded citizen, a mother-of-five with a love of the wide open spaces. Advance Australia Fair! **1981** *Advance Aust.* iii. 3/1 Victoria's 1981 Moomba Festival carried a key theme of 'Advance Australia' with an Advance Australia float leading the parade. **1984** *Canberra Times* 8 Mar. 21/7 Legislation to prevent unauthorised use of the Advance Australia logo was introduced into the House of Representatives yesterday... Advance Australia was now a self-funding, private-sector project.

Adventure Bay pine. [f. the name of a bay and township in Tas.] CELERY-TOP PINE.

1821 *HRA* (1921) 3rd Ser. III. 507 Q. Did you observe any Turpentine in them? A. There may be in the Adventure Bay Pine. **1827** P.P. KING *Narr. Survey Intertropical & Western Coasts* I. 157 *Podocarpus asplenifolia* .. is known to the colonists by the name of 'Adventure Bay Pine', and grows on Bruny Island in Storm Bay. **1844** C. LYON *Narr. & Recoll. Van Dieman's Land* 36 The blackwood, the hoar pine, and Adventure Bay pine, are valuable trees. **1934** J.W. AUDAS *Native Trees Aust.* 102 *Phyllocladus rhomboidalis* .. the Adventure Bay Pine, is another fine tree of Tasmania, growing in dense forests and near rivers.

aerial ping-pong. [So called because the play is characterized by freq. exchanges of long and high kicks.] A jocular (freq. derisive) name for Australian National Football: see quots.

1964 *Footy Fan* (Melbourne) II. viii. 23 Sydney folk are generally curious about this religion or mania which they term 'aerial ping pong' or 'Aussie Rules'. **1965** F. HARDY *Yarns of Billy Borker* 43 That's not football, mate, it's aerial ping-pong. **1973** J. DUNN *How to play Football* 28 Sydneysiders like to call Australian Rules 'aerial ping-pong'. **1980** H. LUNN *Behind Banana Curtain* 187 I won't comment much on their football—called aerial pingpong in Queensland—because I don't understand it. **1985** *Bulletin* (Sydney) 24 Dec. 53/1 In Europe .. cycling is about the same mad preoccupation as aerial ping pong is to the Melbourne crowds.

Afghan. Formerly also **Affghan.** [Spec. use of *Afghan* an inhabitant of Afghanistan.] An Afghan immigrant to Australia, esp. one engaged in camel-driving or camel-breeding (but see quot. 1933); 'GHAN 1. Also *attrib.*

1869 *S. Austral. Register* (Adelaide) 2 Sept. 3/8 Sheep-dogs, the property of Lalloo, Eleme, and Pioo, three Affghan shepherds. **1873** P.E. WARBURTON *Journey across Western Interior* (1875) 154, I sent off the Afghan on my riding camel. **1892** *Truth* (Sydney) 1 May 1/7 Afghans are rather more objectionable than Kanakas; they come here, unaccompanied by their womenkind, and we know what that means. **1897** J.J. MURIF *From Ocean to Ocean* 62 From Hergott to Alice Springs the population is grouped under three generic headings—'Whites', 'Afghans', and 'Blackfellows'. **1905** *Bulletin* (Sydney) 21 Dec. 44/2 The Afghan may go on the 'bust' in his own country, but he certainly doesn't do it here. **1921** K.S. PRICHARD *Black Opal* 5 Riding together in the Afghan storekeeper's sulky. **1933** R.B. PLOWMAN *Camel Pads* 4 All Mohammedan camel-drivers in the Inland are classed as Afghans. **1936** L. KAYE *Black Wilderness* 11 The smaller houses and date palms of the Afghans, and camel yards and dumps of pack saddles. **1950** G.M. FARWELL *Land of Mirage* 23 The term Afghan, with its implication of contempt. **1959** D. STUART *Yandy* 52 His mother was blackfeller, his father some Afghan camelman of the old teamsting days, but Dugald was blackfeller. **1969** T.L. MCKNIGHT *Camel in Aust.* 126 Camel drivers brought from Baluchistan and Pakistan, but invariably referred to as 'Afghans'. **1981** *Bulletin* (Sydney) 3 Mar. 117/4 That little Afghan camel driver.—National Party minister Russ Hinze, referring to Liberal Aboriginal Senator Neville Bonner.

agate. *Obs.* [Fig. use of *agate* playing marble: see OEDS 1 b.] In the phr. **to toss in one's agate,** *to throw one's alley,* (etc.) *in,* see ALLEY 1.

1906 E. DYSON *Fact'ry 'Ands* 152 They put th' steam on her, 'n' she tossed in her agate.

agile wallaby. [f. *agile*, first applied as the specific name *agilis* by English zoologist J. Gould (*Proc. Zool. Soc. London* (1841) IX. 81) + WALLABY 1.] The large sandy-brown wallaby *Macropus agilis* of W.A., N.T., Qld., and New Guinea.

1857 J. GOULD *Mammals of Aust.* II. Pl. 25, The Agile Wallaby appears to be abundant on all the low swampy lands of the northern coast of Australia. **1926** A.S. LE SOUEF et al. *Wild Animals Australasia* 190 The agile wallaby is a tropical species. **1981** D. LEVITT *Plants & People* 20 The island's Agile Wallabies have very acute hearing.

agricultural, *a.* [Spec. use of *agricultural* pertaining to agriculture (including the rearing of animals): see OED.]

1. Of, pertaining to, or engaged in the cultivation of land for the production of crops, as distinct from the use of land for grazing. See PASTORAL.

1806 *HRA* (1915) 1st Ser. V. 711 Our principal Agricultural settlement at Hawkesbury. **1808** *Ibid.* (1916) 1st Ser. VI. 324 Bargains made at the Agricultural Settlements were for the produce of the Ground at the Store prices. **1828** *Tasmanian* (Hobart) 16 Sept. 2 When cattle can be purchased at 20s. to 30s. a head, it would be exceedingly advantageous for agricultural settlers, to purchase lots in proportion to their means, feed them with the crop of their farms, and get them salted. **1831** *Sydney Herald* 23 May 3/4 Superintendent and Overseer. Wants a Situation, in an Agricultural or Stock Establishment. **1834** *Perth Gaz.* 14 June 303 Agricultural settlers have selected and commenced cultivating their grants. **1843** J.F. BENNETT *Hist. & Descr. Acct. S.A.* 96 Agricultural farmers .. have generally a few head of cattle to supply their families with milk, butter and cheese. **1849** A. HARRIS *Emigrant Family* (1967) 82 You'll do no good .. here, unless you mean taking to the axe and plough, and having a regular agricultural farm. This is no sheep country, nor is it good for cattle. **1853** *Visit to Aust. & Gold Regions* (S.P.C.K.) 83 There is a wide difference between an agricultural and a pastoral farmer. The former is most frequently the proprietor of the land he cultivates, while the latter is no more than a 'licensed squatter', a tenant at will to the Crown. **1871** *Austral. Handbk.* 40 Country land .. is divided into (1) agricultural; (2) first-class pastoral; and (3) second-class pastoral. **1887** W. BANNOW *Emigrant's Hand-Bk.* 59 In an 'agricultural area' the maximum which may be selected by one person is 1,280 acres... In 'grazing areas' the maximum may vary from 20,000 to 2,500 acres. **1900** *Austral. Handbk.* 97 Agricultural Selections... Land open to selection as Agricultural Farms is not available for Agricultural Homesteads unless so proclaimed. **1910** *Bulletin* (Sydney) 20 Jan. 14/2 In the Territory .. a number of agricultural blocks were taken up for cotton and tobacco plantations. **1925** J.A. COLLUM *New Settlers' Handbk.* 111 By locking up the unlimited supplies of water .. in the larger rivers .. sufficient storage may be provided for stock and agricultural irrigation. **1946** A.J. HOLT *Wheat Farms Vic.* 18 There was a legal bar to the subdivision of his leased pastoral block into agricultural allotments. **1965** G.H. FEARNSIDE *Golden Ram* 160 Australia has the potential .. of being both a great agricultural-pastoral and industrial country.

2. In special collocations: **agricultural high school**, a secondary school offering a general education with special courses in agriculture; **reserve** *Qld., obs.*, land close to towns reserved for small farms.

1905 *Victorian Yr. Bk. of Agric.* 25 In a country centre where an attendance of 50 to 100 pupils could be guaranteed, the **Agricultural High School** should be worked in connexion with the local State school. **1910** *Acts* (Vic.) mmccci. Sect. 25, In agricultural localities the district high school may be styled the 'District Agricultural High School', and the course of study shall include a practical course in experimental agriculture at a school farm. **1913** *Official Yr. Bk. N.S.W.* 307 A special Agricultural High School (Hurlstone) is established at Ashfield, and forms part of the Technical Education system; the grounds . . are used for teaching practical operations and for experimental work. **1918** *Calendar Hawkesbury Agric. College* 34 Those proceeding from one of the Farm Schools . . or from the Agricultural High Schools will be admitted to the second year. **1935** P.R. COLE *Educ. of Adolescent in Aust.* 284 Fees for . . agricultural high schools are fixed by regulation. **1948** R. RAVEN-HART *Canoe in Aust.* 46 One of the finest homesteads . . had become a Government School, an 'Agricultural High School'. **1971** *Agric. Educ. in W.A.* 98 The agricultural high school wings are expected to provide vocational training at a relatively early age, for farmers' sons who intend to return to their family properties and eventually become farm owners. **1986** *Good Weekend* (Sydney) 1 Mar. 14/1 At Carlingford, in Sydney's north-western suburbs . . an agricultural high school is unexpected. **1855** W. CAMPBELL *Crown Lands Aust.* 9 The pastoral interest was the only interest beyond the settled district, and did not require either townships or **agricultural reserves**. **1861** F. ALGAR *Handbk. to Colony Qld.* 10 Tracts of land termed 'agricultural reserves' are to be proclaimed and set apart for cultivation on the shores of Moreton Bay, Wide Bay, Port Curtis and Keppel Bay, and an area of not less than 10,000 acres, within five miles of every town containing more than 500 inhabitants. **1866** 'J.W.T.' *Land Question in Qld.* 23 The several farms on the Agricultural Reserves in each district. **1871** *Austral. Handbk.* 40 In 'agricultural reserves' land may be selected, without having been put up to auction, under what are called 'conditional sales'.

agriculturist. One engaged primarily in the production of crops. Also **agriculturalist.**

1820 C. JEFFREYS *Van Dieman's Land* 149 The agriculturist in Van Dieman's Land, always reckons upon at least thirty-five bushels [*sc.* of wheat per acre.]. **1828** H. DANGAR *Index & Directory River Hunter* 98 The lands upon the Hastings are . . adapted to the agriculturist, and not for the extensive grazier. **1842** *Colonial Observer* (Sydney) 23 Feb. 162/4 Bush fires . . have been raging on all sides much to the detriment and danger of stockholders and agriculturists. **1845** *Observer* (Hobart) 4 Nov. 4/6 The present season will be more advantageous both to the squatter and the agriculturist. **1855** P. SAUNDERS *Two Yrs. Vic.* (1863) 12 The agriculturists in Victoria are so termed because they are *not* agriculturists. The squatters are classed in the census as agriculturists, but they have no permission to grow a potato or a cabbage beyond what they themselves can consume, and they are constantly reminded by Government of the *illegality* of cultivating their runs. **1866** 'J.W.T.' *Land Question in Qld.* 111 The agriculturist must take the place of the squatter if we expect to be successful. **1872** 'CAPRICORNUS' *Bush Essays* 41 Whatever the Australian selector may profess to be—whether called selector, farmer, or agriculturist—he is nearly always more a grazier than anything else. **1880** *Bulletin* (Sydney) 21 Aug. 3 (Advt.) *Preliminary Notice.* To capitalists, graziers, agriculturalists, and others. **1913** *Ibid.* 3 Apr. 15/1 It isn't always the cow farmer. Sometimes it is the agriculturist devoted to onions, and on occasion it is the squatter whose speciality is poultry.

agro-politician. One politically active on behalf of the rural sector; a lobbyist.

1978 *Cattleman* (Rockhampton) Sept. 20/1 Mr Barry Cassell, national director of the Cattlemen's Union, does not beat about the bush. . . Men such as Mr Cassell prefer to be styled 'agro-politician', a reflection of the importance the union places on its role as a political lobbyist.

Hence **agro-politics** *n.*

1986 *Canberra Times* 5 Mar. 2/3 What Mr Kerin rather neatly referred to as 'agropolitics'.

alarm bird.

1. *Obs.* SPUR-WINGED PLOVER.

1827 *HRA* (1923) 3rd Ser. VI. 271 The 'Alarm Bird' . . is in the Body not so large as a Partridge. . . Flying round without Gun shot, and disappointing a person of his Game by alarming it; hence 'Alarm Bird' by Sealers. **1896** F.G. AFLALO *Sketch Nat. Hist. Aust.* 103 The Wattled Plover (*Lobivanellus*), or 'Spur Wing', spoils many a day's kangaroo stalking by its provoking habit of rising just in front of one and putting every living thing on the alert by its piercing cries—for which peculiarity colonials have dubbed it the 'Alarm Bird'.

2. (App. recorded only in Dicts.) The kookaburra *Dacelo novaeguinea.*

1943 S.J. BAKER *Pop. Dict. Austral. Slang* (ed. 3) 5 *Alarm bird,* the Kookaburra. Cf. 'Bushman's Clock'.

Albany doctor: see DOCTOR *n.*[3]

Albany pitcher plant: see PITCHER PLANT.

Albert lyre-bird. [f. the name of Prince *Albert* (1819–61), Consort of Queen Victoria, first applied as the specific name *Alberti* by English zoologist J. Gould (*Proc. Linnean Soc. London* (1850) II. 67) + LYRE-BIRD 1.] The lyre-bird *Menura alberti,* restricted to a small area of rainforest in n. N.S.W. and s. Qld. Also **Albert's lyre-bird.**

1851 J. GOULD *Birds of Aust. Suppl.* (1869) Pl. 19, Albert Lyre Bird. . . I have great pleasure in naming this species *M. Alberti,* in honour of His Royal Highness Prince Albert, as a slight token of respect for his personal virtues. **1906** *Emu* VI. 39 Mr E. Ashby showed a specimen of the Albert Lyre-Bird (*Menura alberti*), from Queensland, and named after the late Prince Consort. **1951** L.H. SMITH *Lyrebirds of Sherbrooke* 11 The Albert lyrebird differs considerably in colouring and in plumage from the southern species. **1975** *Ecos* vi. 7/1 The paradise rifle-bird, rufous scrub-bird, and Albert's lyrebird live only in subtropical rainforests. **1985** *Parks & Wildlife News* Summer 19 Four endangered bird species have their home in this park—the Albert Lyrebird [etc.].

Alberts. *Obs.* Shortened form of PRINCE ALBERTS.

c **1892** STEWART & KEESING *Old Bush Songs* (1957) 203 Through his boots his toes were shining And his feet looked very sore, I knew his feet were blistered From the Alberts that he wore. **1904** L. LAWSON *Lonely Crossing* 5 Alberts you are wearing?

alcheringa /æltʃəˈrɪŋgə/. Also **alchuringa.** [a. Aranda *altyerre* dream + *nge, ablative suffix* from, meaning 'in the dreamtime'.] DREAMTIME 1. Also *attrib.*

[**1891** *Trans. & Proc. R. Soc. S.A.* XIV. 242 They pretend that these *tjurunga arknanoa* were *altjira*—that is, were not made—but I suspect . . that the old men and sorcerers make them themselves.] **1897** *Proc. R. Soc. Vic.* 23 All the ceremonies were concerned with mythical ancestors who lived in what the natives call the 'alcheringa' or dream times. **1912** T.E. SPENCER *Brindawalla* 86 Alcheringa . . is the name used by the natives when speaking of the far past time during which their mythic ancestors lived. **1933** C.W. PECK *Austral. Legends* (ed. 2) 37 The word 'Alcheringa' was never used except when at the time and from the happening an ancestor was brought into being. **1940** R. INGAMELLS *Memory of Hills* 22 Spirits shall haunt this land. O we shall roam a dim Alcheringa. **1944** A.W. UPFIELD *No Footprints in Bush* 196 Here were kept the tribe's churinga stones, the head of the sacred pole decorated with bird's down and hair alleged to have belonged to the tribe's Alchuringa ancestor, bull-roarers and other sacred objects. **1946** A.M. LAPTHORNE *Mildura Calling* 9 We feel the old contentment where the gums An age-old tryst with alcheringa keep. **1953** A.W. UPFIELD *Murder must Wait* 188 It happened a long, long time ago in the days of the Alchuringa, when the world was young and waiting for the aborigines to come and take possession of it. **1974** D. IRELAND *Burn* 51 Where did the white man find the iron for knives? There was none found in the beginning, in Alcheringa.

alec. Also **aleck.** [Shortened f. (orig.) U.S. *smart alec* a conceited person or show-off: see OEDS.] A fool or simpleton.

1919 C.L. DREW *Doings of Dave* 161 Yes, Blind Alec could see that. **1941** *Air Force News* (Melbourne) 4 Oct. 10 'You big Alecs . . ' came drifting . . across the green. **1944** J. HOLMES *Punter,* A man's a 'big Alec', it's a flaming mug's game. **1962** A. SEYMOUR *One Day of Yr.* 64 He looked such a big aleck, marching along as though he'd won both wars single-handed. **1965** K. SMITH *OGF* 89 Don't be an alec. **1968** S. GORE *Holy Smoke* 31 What sort of an Alec does he take *me* for. **1978** S. BALL *Muma's Boarding House* 109 That mug of a doctor wouldn't know dust if he saw it. I bet he's never been near a mine, the alec.

Alexandra palm. [f. the name of *Alexandra* (1844–1925), Princess of Wales and later Queen-Consort of King Edward VII, first applied as the specific name *Alexandrae* by the botanist F. von Mueller (*Fragmenta Phytographiae Australiae* (1865–6) 47).] The palm *Archontophoenix alexandrae,* restricted to the e. coast of Qld. from near Cape York to just south of the Tropic of Capricorn.

1881 F. VON MUELLER *Select Extra-Tropical Plants* (ed. 2) 273 The Alexandra-Palm. The tallest of Australian Palms, and one of the noblest forms in the whole empire of vegetation. **1908** E.J. BANFIELD *Confessions of Beachcomber* 252 The heart of the Alexandra palm . . would stand as vegetables. **1944** J. DEVANNY *By Tropic Sea & Jungle* 23 A glorious grove of Alexandra palms was cut down to make way for an aerodrome. **1982** A. BLOMBERY *Palms* 48 The Alexandra Palm has a number of different geographical forms.

Alexandra parakeet. [f. *Alexandra* (see prec.), first applied as the specific name *Alexandrae* by English zoologist J. Gould (*Proc. Zool. Soc. London* (1863) 232).] PRINCESS PARROT. Also **Alexandra parrot.**

1900 A.J. CAMPBELL *Nests & Eggs Austral. Birds* 624 Mr A. Zeitz, Assistant Curator of the Adelaide Museum, was successful in getting the Alexandra Parrakeets to breed in captivity. **1902** *Emu* I. 129 When the Alexandra Parrot sits on a bough, it generally does so lengthways. **1903** *Ibid.* III. 73 Mr Keartland's adoption of the vernacular 'Princess' Alexandra Parrakeet will not stand. Gould originally called the bird 'Princess of Wales' Parrakeet. But that gracious lady is now our 'Queen'. Why not simply call the beautiful bird the Alexandra Parrakeet? **1921** *Bulletin* (Sydney) 29 Sept. 20/2 For the four most beautiful of Australian parrots I plump for the green leek (superb parrot), the Mallee and Alexandra parrots, and the yellow parrot or 'Murray smoker'. **1935** H.H FINLAYSON *Red Centre* 144 Several men are now engaged in . . quest . . of the . . beautiful Alexandra parrakeet.

Alf. [Abbrev. of the proper name *Alfred.*] A derogatory term for the type of the uneducated and unthinkingly conservative Australian. See also ROY. Also *attrib.* and as *adj.*

1960 *Encounter* (London) May 28 The Australian worker, the 'Alf' as we call him. *Ibid.* 29 This, I thought, would give our own *Alfs* new heart, and liberate a tremendous . . dynamo of *Alf*-energy in Britain. **1964** *Oz* (Sydney) July 8/2 Every week day about 5 million Australian Alfs (or Alves) invade the capital cities to plot against *you* and *your* families. They work as Accountants, Executives, Bank Managers, Doctors, Lawyers, Salesmen, Wharfies, Bus Conductors. . . Nearly everyone is an Alf these days. . . Aims of the evil *Alf* movement. . . To convert *you* to a clean living, all Australian, anti-erotic, healthy, mentally retarded citizen. **1965** *Nation* (Sydney) 27 Nov. 21/3 Middle-class 'Roys' in sports cars and yachting jackets, and red-necked 'Alfs' who want to fight those who swear in front of ladies. (It was Sope [*sc.* Neil C. Hope] who invented the now-ubiquitous term.) **1966** J. SPENCER *Cross Section* 34 See man, the thing is that all the oldies and the alfs are in it together to stop the really creative people like you and me from making it. **1971** *Bulletin* (Sydney) 31 July 45/3 The division now is not only between the extremes of the alf drinker and the mystic head. The earnest cerebral Left see the head scene as 'privatist, anti-rational, and male chauvinist'. **1980** *Weekend Austral. Mag.* (Sydney) 18 Oct. 7/1 To be gay could very easily become very Alf in a few years time.

Alfred, Royal: see ROYAL ALFRED.

all about, *adv., attrib.,* and *pron.* Orig. *Austral. pidgin.*

1. *adv.* Everywhere.

1848 H.W. HAYGARTH *Recoll. Bush Life* 25 All travellers are universally welcome throughout the far districts, literally stopping, as the blacks call it, 'all about'. **1863** *Adelaide Observer* 12 Dec. 6/5 The blacks up there say, 'Very good country this one, all about flour, sugar, tea, clothes, and sheep.' **1951** E. HILL *Territory* 443 *All-about* (Pidgin) Everyone. Everywhere.

2. *pron.* Everyone, all those present; esp. of Aboriginal employees on a rural property.

1908 MRS A. GUNN *We of Never-Never* 302 Cheon was announcing dinner in his own peculiar way. 'Dinner!

Mis-sus! Boss! All-about!' he chanted. **1935** M. & E. DURACK *(title)* All-About: the story of a black community on Argyle Station, Kimberley. **1956** T. RONAN *Moleskin Midas* 235 'What this yarn allabout got where you going to send my boy to whitefeller school?' she demanded. **1976** C.D. MILLS *Hobble Chains & Greenhide* 9 'All about' employed as gate-openers, we took our first jaunt in the open.

3. *attrib.* In the phr. **all-about-gin,** a domestic servant. See GIN.

1962 C. GYE *Cockney & Crocodile* 75 And back to hot baths, the water heated over wood fires in kerosene tins and poured in by tousle-headed, cotton-frocked 'all-about-gins', the house-girls who arouse such envy in the servantless cities of the south.

all-Australian, *a.*

1. Exclusively or distinctively Australian in character or provenance.

1926 *Film Weekly* 4 Nov. 10 A new all-Australian movie. **1927** *R. Comm. on Wireless* 175 Is this local crystal?—Yes, it is all Australian. **1972** *Bulletin* (Sydney) 4 Mar. 13/2 Spacious all-Australian gardens. *Ibid.* 22 July 54/1 The traditional, standard all-Australian hotel whose primary function has been to serve beer. **1986** *Canberra Times* 13 June 8/6 It is possible to build the 'all-Australian house' in any price range.

2. Of, pertaining to, or representative of the whole, as distinguished from part, of Australia; ALL-STATE. Also **all-Australia.**

1927 *R. Comm. on Wireless* 2514 The cultivation of an All-Australian attitude that State consciousness shall gradually die out. **1963** X. HERBERT *Disturbing Element* 164 The wine saloon has been an all-Australian institution; but I don't think the attitude to wine drinking was ever in the other States what it was in W.A. **1965** L. WALKER *Other Girl* 157 Four . . hold State records and one is an all-Australia champion. **1973** P. MCKENNA *My World of Football* 94 My first All Australian Blazer.

all clear, *phr.*, also used as *n. Australian National Football.* See quot. 1968.

1925 *Laws of Football* (Australasian Football Council) 10 Field and goal umpires are not allowed to come to an understanding by signalling 'All Clear' by nodding of head, holding up fingers, etc. **1931** J.F. MCHALE et al. *Austral. Game of Football* 48 The 'All-Clear' signal . . given . . by the field umpire . . indicating that the goal umpire is at liberty to decide whether a goal or behind should be recorded. **1968** EAGLESON & MCKIE *Terminology Austral. Nat. Football* i. 9 *All-clear,* the signal given to the goal umpire by the field umpire to indicate that there was no breach of the rules just prior to an attempt at goal or behind and that the goal umpire is at liberty to give a decision on whether a goal or behind has been scored. (This is the standard term, used in all States.)

all day sucker. A large, long-lasting sweet, usually on a stick.

1935 K. TENNANT *Tiburon* 92 He's only fit for pickin' on Johns and takin' all-day suckers from kids. **1959** C. & E. CHAUVEL *Walkabout* 37 Children crowded in with pennies . . for ice-cream cones and 'all day suckers'.

alley. Also **ally.** [Fig. use of *alley* playing marble; cf. AGATE, MARBLE.]

1. In the phr. **to throw (chuck, pass, roll, sky, sling, toss) one's alley (in),** to die; to acknowledge defeat. See also AGATE, MARBLE 1.

1903 *Sporting News* (Launceston) 25 Apr. 2/8 Most of the cricketers have thrown in their 'ally' and the various clubs have stored away the paraphernalia until next spring. **1913** *Bulletin* (Sydney) 6 Nov. 22/2 Died, . . thrown in his alley. **1916** C.J. DENNIS *Moods Ginger Mick* 97 But if I dodge, an' keep out uv the rain, An' don't toss in me alley 'fore we wins. **1917** *Bulletin* (Sydney) 17 May 24/1 The lamented cannibal was not wasted after he had thrown his alley. First, choice cuts were devoured. **1918** C.J. DENNIS *Digger Smith* 60 Uv course, I threw me alley in right there. This Princess was a dinkum Aussie girl. **1919** E. DYSON *Hello Soldier* 33 When Ulrich stopped a Port bookay he rolled his alley in. **1924** C.J. DENNIS *Rose of Spadgers* 23 When my pal, Ginger Mick, Chucked in 'is alley in this war we won, 'E left things tangled; fer 'e went too quick Fer makin' last requests uv anyone. **1927** F.C. BIGGERS *Bat-Eye* 18 'Is alley's skied. An' then yer reads: *'Killed by a fall uv coal.'* **1933** N. LINDSAY *Saturdee* (1936) 25 'This book says a bloke kicked the bucket, . . so what's it mean?' 'Means a bloke passed his alley in.' **1960** *Khaki Bush & Bigotry* (1968) 228 Don't sling in yer alley, missus. There's a good time comin'.

2. In the phr. **to make one's alley good,** to exploit a situation; to improve one's position. See also MARBLE 2.

1924 C.J. DENNIS *Rose of Spadgers* 160 'E 'ad swore to git me one uv those Fine days, an' make 'is alley good with Rose. **1952** T.A.G. HUNGERFORD *Ridge & River* 209 It makes Wilder's alley good, but it doesn't win any popularity stakes for you. **1964** *Sydney Morning Herald* 10 Aug. 2/6 The dark, knowing whisper . . 'Hey Tom! Joe is making his alley good with Nellie Bli down be th' crik!' carries its own significance. **1975** *Bronze Swagman Bk. Bush Verse* 16 And did my very darndest To make my alley good.

alligator. [Transf. use of *alligator* a genus of the subfam. Alligatorinae, found chiefly in the Americas.] Either of the two species of crocodile *Crocodylus,* subfam. Crocodylinae, found in Aust.

1770 J. COOK *Jrnls.* 23 Aug. (1955) I. 395 In the Rivers and salt Creeks are some Aligators [*sic*]. **1829** R. MUDIE *Picture of Aust.* 302 Small rivers, which abounded in alligators. **1846** *Portland Gaz.* 28 Apr. 4/5 What is called alligator is no alligator, but a crocodile. **1876** 'EIGHT YRS.' RESIDENT' *Queen of Colonies* 278 The alligator is not found south of the Fitzroy River. **1880** *Bulletin* (Sydney) 1 May 2/1 A native policeman has had one of his arms mangled by a Herbert River alligator. **1884** G. WIGHT *Qld.* 83 In the northern rivers alligators, and in the southern rivers sharks, too frequently show themselves for the composure of bathers. **1931** 'L. KAYE' *Tybal Men* 187 We went to the museum and . . found they were crocodiles—that there wasn't any alligators *anywhere in Australia.* It's just blasted ignorance calling them alligators. **1978** TEECE & PIKE *Voice of Wilderness* 113 Crocodiles—'alligators' the bushmen called them, meaning the salt-water man-eating variety.

alligator pike. [Cf. U.S. *alligator-gar*: see OEDS.] Any of several marine and estuarine carnivorous fish of the fam. Belonidae, having long jaws; LONG TOM 2.

1908 E.J. BANFIELD *Confessions of Beachcomber* 154 The 'long tom' . . or alligator-pike, which shoots from the water and skips along. **1930** C.M. YONGE *Yr. on Great Barrier Reef* 95 The alligator pike or 'long tom' (*Tylosurus*). **1935** DAVISON & NICHOLLS *Blue Coast Caravan* 236 We saw the alligator pike . . about eighteen inches long and shaped like torpedoes.

allotment. *Hist.* [Spec. use of *allotment* allotted portion of land: see OED 4.]

1. A piece of Crown land granted to a particular person or (see quots. 1821 and 1828) for a specified purpose.

1788 *HRA* (1914) 1st Ser. I. 48 The land will be granted with a clause that will ever prevent more than one house being built on the allotment. **1793** J. HUNTER *Hist. Jrnl. Trans. Port Jackson* 537 In laying out the different allotments, an intermediate space . . was retained between every two allotments, for the benefit of the crown. **1793** W. TENCH *Compl. Acct. Settlement* 171 To every non-commissioned officer, an allotment of one hundred and thirty acres of land. **1796** *Instruct. for Constables Country Districts* 13 They have been promised Grants but have not had their Allotments measured or marked out for them. **1803** *HRA* (1915) 1st Ser. IV. 309 The People on the Banks of the Hawkesbury . . having others placed immediately behind them had no means of having their allotments enlarged for their increasing and acquired stock. **1804** *Ibid.* (1915) 1st Ser. V. 7 The allotments of land already granted, occupy nearly the whole of the disposable and profitable land. **1816** *Ibid.* (1917) 1st Ser. IX. 122 He had been allowed to select a certain Tract of Land in expectation of its forming a part of his allotment. **1821** *Austral. Mag.* 29 The site of this building is in Macquarie-street, being a choice allotment which was handsomely presented by His Excellency the Governor. **1826** *Colonial Times* (Hobart) 20 May, Several Allotments in Hobart Town, as well as in the different Towns and Townships of this Colony . . have been assigned to Parties for the Purpose of Building. **1828** J.D. LANG *Narr. Settlement Scots Church* 67 The contemplated buildings were immediately commenced, partly on the allotment of the Scots Church. **1834** *Perth Gaz.* 6 Sept. 350 When approved by the Governor, he receives permission to select an Allotment in any place suited to small Settlers. **1843** *Teetotal Advocate* (Launceston) 22 May 2/3 Many old soldiers . . had sold their allotments, and were now miserable. **1865** 'SPECIAL CORRESPONDENT' *Transportation* 7 Old colonists give lively descriptions of how ladies, blood horses, pianos, and carriages, were landed on a desolate coast . . and no one knew where his particular allotment lay.

2. A piece of land: in towns, a building block or section; in the country an area used for pasture or cultivation.

1811 *Sydney Gaz.* 12 Jan., Dwelling House . . with an extensive allotment of garden ground. **1819** *Ibid.* 13 Feb., Upwards of 300 Acres of this valuable Allotment are already cleared and enclosed in various Paddocks of different sizes. **1831** *Sydney Herald* 20 June 1/1 To Be Sold . . the old No. 4 Watch-House, together with the Allotment on which it stands. **1835** R. TORRENS *Colonization of S.A.* 81 Building allotments in Sydney Town . . could be readily purchased in 1825, for from £70 to £150. **1838** *Colonist* (Sydney) 3 Jan. 1/5 Some of the allotments have been richly manured and worked to a high state of cultivation. **1839** *Port Phillip Patriot* 6 Feb. 3 The Government . . caused to be laid out 24 Blocks, of 20 Allotments each Block, consisting of 76 Perches each allotment. **1841** 'AUSTRALIAN COLONIST' *Resources Aust.* 92 The waste lands of New South Wales have hitherto been sold in sections or allotments of a square mile or 640 acres each. **1853** W. WESTGARTH *Vic.* 71 The first sale of the public lands of the province . . was held at Melbourne, and consisted of a portion of the allotments or half-acre sections of that township. **1870** *Sydney Morning Herald* 2 July 3/6 *St. Leonard's* adjoining Post-office. Allotment for *sale*—cheap. **1880** R. ROSE *Vic. Guide* 7 He may obtain a lease of his allotment for seven years, at 2s. per acre. **1884** *Austral. Tit-Bits* (Melbourne) 19 June 1 Magnificent Block of Land, comprising 80 Acres, charmingly sub-divided into 309 Allotments. **1919** *Smith's Weekly* (Sydney) 10 May 5/2 Messrs Marshall and Dempsrell disposed of 11 allotments of the Fairholm Estate. **1930** V. PALMER *Passage* (1957) 26 He'll root out all the trees and slice it up into filthy little pocket-handkerchief allotments. **1933** N. LINDSAY *Saturdee* (1936) 12 They drifted across the road to a vacant allotment, where there was grass. **1939** A. BROOKSBANK *Air Raid Precautions* 50 Australian suburbs which have the minimum allotments of 50 x 150 feet have five houses per acre; those with a minimum of 40 x 120 feet have nine houses per acre. **1967** F.T. MACARTNEY *Proof against Failure* 8 The house . . still stands . . on its narrow allotment.

all right: see RIGHT *a.* 1.

all-State, *a.* ALL-AUSTRALIAN 2.

1943 H.W. MALLOCH *Fellows All* 99 Christesen is a University 'blue' and State and all-State champion athlete and footballer. **1973** P. MCKENNA *My World of Football* 144 Also a player worthy of leading an All State side such as this.

all-up, *a.* [Spec. use of *all-up* all-inclusive.] In the phr. **all-up bet,** a progressive bet, the stake and winnings from the first race being placed on the next, and so on, the sum accumulating for as long as the bet is successful; an accumulator. Also *absol.*

1933 R. SPARGO *Betting Systems Analysed* 24 All Up. The super optimist's method. . . For making sure of a losing day after picking a winner the all-up method is 'one hundred per cent. the goods'. **1949** L. GLASSOP *Lucky Palmer* 15 'Does this bookie pay full odds?' 'No limit on all-up bets.'

Hence as *v. intr.* and **all-upper** *n.*

1959 S.J. BAKER *Drum* 84 *All-upper,* a punter who bets 'all up' on a number of horse or greyhound races. **1978** D. STUART *Wedgetail View* 111 He . . practically all-upped all the way, so you can guess he'd made a killing.

alluvial, *a.* and *n.* [Spec. use of *alluvial* pertaining to alluvium.]

A. *adj.* Of or pertaining to gold-bearing alluvium, a sedimentary deposit of earth, sand, etc., found on flood-plains and in river-beds.

[**1851** *Empire* (Sydney) 7 Aug. 23/3 The licenses issued . . to dig, search for, and remove gold found in its natural place of deposit, will in future be limited in their operation to alluvial gold.] **1892** T. BRACKEN *Dear Old Bendigo* 14 In the alluvial days the gold passed through the hands of a large number of persons. **1898** D.W. CARNEGIE *Spinifex & Sand* 134 So far the alluvial men had been working on a false bottom. **1911** E.D. CLELAND *W. Austral. Mining Practice* p. xvi, During 1893 Hannan's alluvial find at Kalgoorlie employed 3000 men. **1921** W.H. PHIPPS *Bush Yarns* 20 Chance alone made men rich on the alluvial grounds.

B. *n.*

1. Gold-bearing alluvium; gold found in alluvium.

1871 *Austral. Town & Country Jrnl.* (Sydney) 18 Mar. 335/2 At the bottom of the ridge there is alluvial which has never been thoroughly tested for water. **1888** 'R. BOLDREWOOD' *Robbery under Arms* (1937) 273 We were digging up gold like potatoes... There never was a richer patch of alluvial, I believe, in any of the fields. **1936** J. KIRWAN *My Life's Adventure* 56 It looked country where there might be alluvial. We found colours of gold. **1940** E. HILL *Great Austral. Loneliness* (ed. 2) 319 Five hundred barrackin' a football match from this little hill, and betting in handfuls of alluvial! **1946** K.S. PRICHARD *Roaring Nineties* 348 The men . . understood by alluvial, any loose soil, earth, or rocky substance containing, or supposed to contain, gold not running in a lode or quartz vein. **1963** A. MOOREHEAD *Cooper's Creek* 5 Nearly all the surface alluvial was exhausted and now gold had to be mined . . in deep shafts.

2. *Obs.* Alluvial mining; an alluvial mine.

1871 *Austral. Town & Country Jrnl.* (Sydney) 7 June 15/4 In alluvial, things are quiet. **1877** *Free Trade Papers* xi. 1 The alluvial's pretty well done for, and quartz mining requires capital. **1891** *Braidwood Dispatch* 16 May 2/2 The chain of shafts that mapped the lead marked an alluvial of yore.

C. In Comb. and collocations: **alluvial claim, digger, digging, diggings, miner, mining, rush, working.**

1859 *Colonial Mining Jrnl.* June 79/1 Claims are divided into three sorts—**alluvial claims**, river claims, and quartz claims. **1865** *Rep. Mining Surveyors & Registrars* (Vic. Dept. Mines) Dec. 18 The general appearance of both quartz and alluvial claims in this division is . . good. **1931** W. BARAGWANATH et al. *Guide for Prospectors in Vic.* 72 Claims shall be divided into three classes, namely, quartz claims, alluvial claims, and mineral claims. **1944** M.J. O'REILLY *Bowyangs & Boomerangs* 17 We wanted quick returns, which could be got from the alluvial claims. **1893** A.F. CALVERT *W.A. & its Gold Fields* 32 The reefs are so rich at the surface that some of the **alluvial diggers** in slack times have earned fair wages by simply dollying the stone. **1941** D. O'CALLAGHAN *Long Life Reminisc.* 249 Alluvial diggers at Bulong were fined £10 . . for sticking up for what they considered their alluvial rights. **1946** K.S. PRICHARD *Roaring Nineties* 394 Tributors suspected of dummying for the company began to move ore from dumps claimed by the alluvial diggers. **1858** T. MCCOMBIE *Hist. Colony Vic.* 310 The gold had been obtained . . from **alluvial digging**, and by individual exertions. **1872** 'RESIDENT' *Glimpses Life Vic.* 144, I purchased a cradle and other necessary implements for alluvial digging. **1880** J. BONWICK *Resources Qld.* 108 Most of the alluvial digging is conducted by the Chinese. **1935** L. MANN *Human Drift* 101 The alluvial digging must peter out. It's shallower here than at Ballarat. **1853** A. MACKAY *Great Gold Field* 16 As a considerable space of ground . . is granted to holders of quartz claims, on each side of the veins, their claims . . include the adjacent **alluvial diggings**. **1865** *Illustr. Sydney News* 15 July 3/3 The alluvial diggings proved more extensive. **1871** *Austral. Town & Country Jrnl.* (Sydney) 11 Mar. 303/3 The alluvial diggings are doing pretty well. **1894** G.H. GIBSON *Ironbark Chips* 199 That land of rumour and vague reports, Alluvial diggings, and reefs of quartz. **1950** W.M. HUGHES *Policies & Potentates* 91 'Sully' . . challenged me to meet him in debate at the new alluvial diggings at Captain's Flat. **1858** *Colonial Mining Jrnl.* Oct. 28/3 The reef was taken up by **'alluvial' miners**—men who had . . exhausted their little means in the deep wet sinking. **1867** R.L.M. KITTO *Goldfields of Vic.* 63 *Quartz* mining is a much more profitable speculation than ***alluvial* mining**. **1895** *Colonial Mining Jrnl.* Feb. 84/2 Alluvial Mining, when the surface will be but comparatively disturbed. **1871** *Austral. Town & Country Jrnl.* (Sydney) 15 Apr. 454/1 The **alluvial rush** to Eurongilly, in the Wagga Wagga district, has not been turning out satisfactorily. **1898** D.W. CARNEGIE *Spinifex & Sand* 58 We . . arrived at the Red Flag, an alluvial rush that had 'set in' during our sojourn in the sand. **1901** H. LAWSON *Joe Wilson & his Mates* 47 Gulgong was about the last of the great alluvial 'rushes' of the 'roaring days'. **1865** *Rep. Mining Surveyors & Registrars* (Vic. Dept. Mines) Mar. 22 In the **alluvial workings** . . a strong leader has been cut. **1870** *Sydney Morning Herald* 4 July 2/4 The gullies, where our alluvial workings are situated, are in such a miry and swampy state that it is dangerous to work underground. **1889** *Braidwood Dispatch* 12 Oct. 2/2 A new mundic reef has been found in the alluvial workings... The company are doing too well in the alluvium to turn their attention to reefing.

Hence **alluvialist** *n.*

1956 J.E. WEBB *So much for Sydney* 24 Had the 'alluvialists' had their way Kalgoorlie might . . have become a deserted camp, the surface gold cut out and the English companies gone to other countries.

alpine ash. The tall tree *Eucalyptus delegatensis* (fam. Myrtaceae) of mountains in N.S.W., Vic., and Tas.; the wood of the tree.

1942 R.T. PATTON *Know your Own Trees* 31 Alpine Ash is found above an elevation of 3,000 feet. **1956** N.K. WALLIS *Austral. Timber Handbk.* 5 The mountain forests yielding the highest grades of timber such as mountain ash and alpine ash for sawmilling. **1967** E. HUXLEY *Their Shining Eldorado* 174 Another . . stringybark (*E. delegatensis*) sometimes called Tasmanian oak and sometimes called Alpine ash. **1983** *Ecos* xxxvii. 7/3 For more than 50 years, natural stands of alpine ash . . in northern Tasmania have been . . declining in vigour.

alunqua /əˈlʌŋkwə/. [a. Aranda *alangkwe.*] The twining plant *Leichhardtia australis* (fam. Asclepiadaceae) of drier Aust., the young fruit of which is edible; the fruit itself; *bush cucumber*, see BUSH C. 3. See also *native pear* NATIVE *a.* 6 a.

1935 H.H. FINLAYSON *Red Centre* 84 The alunqua; a green cucumber-like fruit borne by a plant which climbs upon the mallee in the sand-hills. **1974** M. TERRY *War of Warramullas* 151 The alunqua, or bush cucumber, is an important source of food... The fruit looks rather like a large banana passionfruit . . is deep green in colour and tastes like fresh green peas.

amalgamated claim. Two or more originally discrete gold-mining titles which have been combined into one (see also quot. 1869).

[**1857** *Vic. Govt. Gaz.* 9 Jan. 58 *Amalgamation.* Claims may be permitted to be amalgamated.] **1864** *Ibid.* 22 Jan. 144/1 An amalgamated claim shall mean any number of claims . . the owners whereof have combined to facilitate the working thereof. **1869** R.B. SMYTH *Gold Fields & Mineral Districts* 602 *Amalgamated claim*, claims adjoining one another which have been thrown temporarily or permanently into one claim for more economical working. **1874** *Jrnl. Legis. Council N.S.W.* (1875) 1015 'Amalgamated claims' shall mean two or more claims legally united and registered as one claim. **1931** C.B. SMITH *Austral. Gold Prospectors' Handbk.* 62 The following claims must be registered within twenty-eight days after possession is taken... Amalgamated claims.

amber, *a.* Used as a distinguishing epithet in collocations designating beer, esp. as **amber fluid.** Also *absol.* as *n.*

1906 *Truth* (Sydney) 22 July 1/3 The amber fluid is the cause why most men amble to the lock-up. **1918** *Ibid.* 3 Feb. 9/1 (*heading*) Rogue Reggie—runs amuck with a rug—but blames the amber beverage. ***c* 1929** 'F. BLAIR' *Digger Sea-Mates* 60 The amber beverage of the Golden West was thoroughly enjoyed that day. **1943** H.M. MURPHY *Strictly for Soldiers* 30 Just a quart of amber liquid with a bonzer sort of smell, Like an angel's breath from heaven, as the poets often tell. **1962** A. SEYMOUR *One Day of Yr.* 9 It's too cold for beer anyway. . . Never too cold for the old amber, love. **1968** G. DUTTON *Andy* 199, I was . . going to pour myself a glass of the old amber fluid. **1972** *Bulletin* (Sydney) 19 Aug. 6/2 Barry Crocker as Bazza is beautiful. He shows off remarkable cultural achievements, like being able to open a tube of the chilled article with one hand and give himself a swift amber transfusion. **1972** A. BUZO *Tom* (1975) 15 I'll stick with the old amber article. **1980** S. THORNE *I've met some Bloody Wags* 18, I was gifted with the capacity for copious quantities of amber fluid. **1985** *Canberra Times* 1 Oct. 15/2, I do trust you've got enough of the amber liquid over there.

ambit. *Industrial Relations.* [Spec. use of *ambit* extent or compass.] The definition of the limits of an industrial dispute: see quots. 1974 and 1980. See also LOG *n.*[2] Also *attrib.* and *transf.*

1972 SYKES & GLASBEEK *Labour Law in Aust.* 514 For practical purposes the log of claims sets out the ambit of the dispute. *Ibid.* 522 A line must be drawn somehow in deciding what is and what is not within ambit. **1974** *MOA* (Melbourne) Sept. 1/5 Many years ago MOA made a claim on these employers which was designed mainly to do two things: 1. Give the association an 'ambit', 'bounds', 'compass' in which to make claims for some time in the future. 2. Create a dispute—because without a dispute being found you cannot bring a log of claims before the Australian Conciliation and Arbitration Commission. **1974** J.J. MACKER *Austral. Industr. Laws* 48 He has no jurisdiction to make or vary any award other than within the confines of the ambit of the dispute created by the demand and refusal of the contestants. **1976** *10 A.L.R.* 467 Rather, the minima, in my opinion, are stated in the log in an endeavour to set a lower limit to the ambit of the dispute it is hoped to create whilst at the same time precluding the possibility of there being an upper limit to that ambit. **1979** G.H. SORRELL *Law in Labour Relations* 114 The practical effect of this in a period of rising prices and wages is that if a union wishes to get a *variation* of an award to take account of changes in wages it must 'have ambit' within which to operate. **1980** MCCALLUM & TRACEY *Cases & Materials Industr. Law* 174 An 'ambit' log of claims, that is, a log of claims designed to create a dispute with a very extensive coverage of both employers and matters and with extremely large claims for each of the individual items so as to provide an ambit of sufficient scope that the award, when made, would be capable of variation for a considerable time so reducing the need for further logs to be served. **1985** *Canberra Times* 20 Oct. 1/5 The hard-line ambit claim from Thatcher opponents was put by the Indian Prime Minister . . when he called . . for comprehensive mandatory sanctions.

American, *a.*

a. Applied to conveyances, constructions, etc., of American origin, or having characteristics believed to be American.

1828 *Hobart Town Courier* 12 July 4 Wanted, two or three Men . . to cut the timber, and put up 2 to 3000 rods of the American water fence. **1846** F. DUTTON *S.A. & its Mines* 203 There are the 'ditch and bank', 'American or log-fence' and the 'dog-leg-fence'. **1848** W. ARCHER Diary 25 Oct., Rode along the boundary line . . and found that our side wd furnish logs enough (I think) for an American-log fence. **1848** J. SYME *Nine Yrs. Van Diemen's Land* 132 Lands . . are protected . . either with a brush fence or with . . the American, consisting of trunks of trees piled upon each other. **1855** W. HOWITT *Land, Labor & Gold* II. 210 They have seen a sort of American waggon, and other carriages which have carried passengers to the races. **1857** *Illustr. Jrnl. Australasia* III. 207 Nobody knew of any carts to be had. 'Would he go in a 'Merican wagon?' **1861** *Austral. Settler's Handbk.* 13 The American slip-rails . . consist of three posts put outside the fence (not in the same line) and long saplings run through the whole of the posts; and these sapling rails are only pushed along when you wish to enter the field. **1864** *Bell's Life in Sydney* 12 Mar. 3/4 *The Australian Buggy.* An improvement on the American Buggy. **1872** G.S. BADEN-POWELL *New Homes for Old Country* 108 In Tasmania alone is found the regular 'stager' of the olden style; elsewhere the coach species is represented by that variety locally known as 'American'. **1893** 'OLD CHUM' *Chips* 17 New Brighton—a suburb of Melbourne some six or seven miles away—to which an American car ran. **1902** *Truth* (Sydney) 23 Feb. 7/3 They ought . . to give him an American jacket, that is, a warp of tar and a nap wove of feathers. **1903** *Sporting News* (Launceston) 27 June 2/1 Plumb's celebrated American Axes. Tasmanian Pattern with light square poles and broad blades.

b. In the collocation **American shout,** *Yankee shout*, see YANKEE.

1945 S.J. BAKER *Austral. Lang.* 170 We have versions of the shout, such as the *American shout.*

ampster. Also **amster.** [Perh. abbrev. of *Amsterdam* rhyming slang for RAM *n.* 2.] The accomplice of a sideshow operator or salesman, who dummies as the purchaser of a ticket or article with the intention of persuading others to do likewise.

1941 K. Tennant *Battlers* 144 The ampster rushes eagerly up to the ticket-window and says: 'Right-o, mister, I'll have a ticket.' His brother-ampsters form into an impatient queue . . at the head of the multitude who, like sheep, will follow the leader. **1945** S.J. Baker *Austral. Lang.* 138 An *amster* is a decoy who works with a sideshow operator to induce the public to spend its money. **1955** *Overland* iv. 10 Holdens rub hubs with old four-wheelers; So do the amsters and their shielas With bunnies walking country sorts. **1957** D. Niland *Call me when Cross turns Over* 101 Barbie, playing ampster, went up and bought a bottle. . . Others followed to buy. **1975** H. Porter *Extra* 244 A shady Soho club patronised by dips, amsters, off-duty prostitutes.

Hence **ampster** *v. intr.*

1941 K. Tennant *Battlers* 143 Mr Fosdick was agreeable, provided the busker would 'ampster' for him.

anabranch. [See quot. 1834.] An arm of a river which separates from and later re-joins the main stream. Also *attrib.* and *fig.*

[**1834** *Jrnl. R. Geogr. Soc. London* IV. 79 Such branches of a river as after separation re-unite, I would term anastomosing-branches; or, if a word might be coined, ana-branches.] **1839** T.L. Mitchell *Three Exped. Eastern Aust.* (rev. ed.) II. 40 We proceeded along the right bank of the Lachlan, crossing at five miles a small arm or ana-branch which had been seen higher up diverging from the river. *Ibid.* 90 Having experienced on this journey the inconvenient want of terms relative to rivers, I determined to use such of those recommended by Colonel Jackson in his able paper on the subject, in the Journal of the Royal Geographical Society for 1833, as I might find necessary. They are . . *Ana-branches*—Such as after separation unite [etc.] **1844** L. Leichhardt *Jrnl. Overland Exped. Aust.* 10 Nov. (1847) 35 The river itself divided into anabranches, which with the shallow watercourses of occasional floods from the hills, made the whole valley a maze of channels. **1853** B. Wannan *Treasury Austral. Frontier Tales* (1961) 49, I once found fourteen head of slaughtered cattle in one pond of water. They had been driven in by the natives, it being an ana-branch of the river. **1859** *Rambles at Antipodes* 30 The Edward river . . is little more than an ana-branch of the Murray. **1862** W. Landsborough *Jrnl. Exped. from Carpentaria* 103 The creek was too small to be the Barcoo River, and the ground on both sides of it too high to admit of it being an ana-branch. **1881** W. Feilding *Austral. Trans-Continental Railway* 21 The river is nothing but a series of disjointed water holes, and full of 'ana' branches. **1902** *Blackwood's Mag.* (Edinburgh) May 644/1 We set out again . . camping at night on an 'Ana' Branch or back-water of the famous Cooper. **1913** H. Lawson *Triangles of Life* 234 The station was not far away, but on a branch track of its own, an anabranch track, in fact. **1943** *Bulletin* (Sydney) 7 July 12/3 In an anabranch of the Copperfield (N.Q.) my mate and I stumbled on about a score of Johnston crocodiles. **1951** G. Farwell *Outside Track* 93 The yarn flowed as sluggishly as his river, with many anabranches, and deep waterholes of reminiscence, and irrelevant snags and sandspits to check its course. **1978** R.J. Britten *Around Cassowary Rock* 13 The water going through the scrub would have picked up the river again in the ana-branch down near the beach. This anabranch served as a sort of a back-water in an ordinary flood season; now it was a mad, boiling torrent.

Hence as *v. intr.*, to form an anabranch.

1956 T. Ronan *Moleskin Midas* 46 He swung away into the top of the bend and came to the end of a long, clear, claybanked billabong anabranching off the main creek channel.

Andersonian, *a.* and *n.* [f. the name of John *Anderson* (1893–1962), Challis Professor of Philosophy in the University of Sydney (1927–58).]

A. *adj.* Of, pertaining to, or characterized by the philosophy and attitudes of John Anderson and his followers.

1950 *Australasian Jrnl. Psych. & Philos.* XXVIII. 138, I am concerning myself not with the fate of inflationist doctrines which have been under fire for so long in both hemispheres, but with one position which is peculiarly Andersonian. **1958** *Austral. Highway* 72 For others, the interest is in all aspects of Andersonian doctrine, including the polemical criticism of orthodoxy and bourgeois values or of the unaesthetic in all its forms (sentimentalism, Puritanism and Bacchanalianism). **1962** *Bulletin* (Sydney) 20 Oct. 36/1 A lifetime interest in philosophy (*Andersonian* philosophy of course). **1976** *Quadrant* Jan. 8/3 Kamenka describes certain aspects of the earlier Marx, such as his hatred of censorship and of servility, and his advocacy of freedom of enquiry, and these are very Andersonian qualities.

B. *n.* A follower of the philosophical doctrines of John Anderson; one who founds on them a way of life and a set of moral, social, political, and anti-religious attitudes.

1958 *Austral. Highway* 72 It has always seemed to hostile critics that Andersonians have always followed a single line, opposing orthodoxy with an orthodoxy, repeating the master's arguments and even his phrases, in too narrow, sectarian and slavish a fashion. **1962** *Bulletin* (Sydney) 30 June 27/1 The Andersonians were supposed to be apostles of Free Thought. **1967** D. Horne *Educ. Young Donald* 212 To be an Andersonian was as self-sustaining as being a Marxist or a Freudian: it provided an answer to everything. **1977** *Nation Rev.* (Melbourne) 19 May 749 The split between left and right which had divided andersonians since the 1930s, was no less evident in 1977. **1983** *Quadrant* Jan. 43/2 Not, of course, that even the most simple-minded Andersonian believed in anything but the continuance of conflict.

Hence **Andersonianism** *n.*

1958 *Observer* (Sydney) 653 Philosophically, nothing has yet come from Andersonianism other than Andersonianism. **1967** D. Horne *Educ. Young Donald* 212 The first freethinkers I met in the Quad were mere outriders of Andersonianism. **1977** *Quadrant* June 50/3 'Realism . . proposes as the formal solution of any problem *the interaction of complex things*.' That, one might say is Andersonianism.

angel stone. See quot. 1961. See also Shin cracker.

1940 E. Hill *Great Austral. Loneliness* (ed. 2) 260 Holes in the ground . . fantastic with the gleam of potch and angel-stone and fragments of opal itself. **1961** F. Leechman *Opal Bk.* 132 Angel Stone has had two meanings; we now use it sometimes to describe a clay which has cracked in consequence of having been baked hard and dry; in these wavering and wandering cracks precious opal, often very brilliant, has formed making pretty pieces. . . The name was first used at White Cliffs . . to refer to the layer of intensely hard stone just above the opal level. **1973** C. Austin *I left my Hat in Andamooka* 189 So far they had found no 'nobbies' but only patches of 'angel stone' which is a very hard, white clay containing thin veins of potch.

Anglo-Australian, *a.* and *n.*

A. *adj.*

1. a. *Obs.* Of British descent, but born in Australia.

1827 *Monitor* (Sydney) 19 Nov. 774/3 By shutting up the Convict women in the Factory, lest they should turn prostitutes or concubines, we add to the temptations by which our free Anglo-Australian female youth, of the lower orders, are daily and hourly beset in a Colony, where the sexes are so unnaturally disproportioned. **1852** *Austral. Gold Digger's Monthly Mag.* iii. 78 The fertile and laughing isles of the South Seas shall be colonized by an Anglo-Australian race. **1863** J. Bonwick *Wild White Man* 36 We have known Anglo-Australian boys very fond of picking out grubs from old fallen timber. **1881** *Macmillan's Mag.* (London) Apr. 114/2 Will the Anglo-Australian race degenerate?

b. *Obs.* Of British birth, but resident in Australia.

1888 *Plea for Separation* 26 An Anglo-Australian Bishop of the Anglican Church refused to administer the church sacraments to those Australians who had availed themselves of the Deceased Wife's Sister Act. **1891** *Fortnightly Rev.* (London) 395 The old Anglo-Australian generation . . is quietly but swiftly passing away. **1899** *Austral. Tit-Bits* (Sydney) 6 May 199/3 William Caffyn, the old Anglo-Australian cricketer, is publishing his reminiscences.

c. *Obs.* Of Australian birth, but resident in Britain.

1894 *Bulletin* (Sydney) 17 Nov. 7/1 The Anglo-Australian officials in England. **1896** *Ibid.* 11 Jan. 16/1 In place of 'Anglo-Australian, absentee-parasite', etc., what's the complaint with 'Exhaustralian'?

d. Born (or resident) in Australia and of British, as distinct from European, Asian, etc., descent.

1984 *Canberra Times* 23 Feb. 1/2 It was asserted . . that Anglo-Australian students were rewarded for making their knowledge look natural.

2. Involving both British and Australian interests; of jointly British and Australian origin.

1848 J. Fowles *Sydney* 6 There are four Banks of Issue—the Bank of New South Wales, and the Commercial Bank, both *Colonial*; and the Union Bank of Australia, and the Bank of Australasia, *Anglo-Australian*. **1888** A.P. Martin *Oak-Bough & Wattle-Blossom* p. ix, Mrs Campbell Praed, so well known . . by her remarkable series of stories of Anglo-Australian life. **1927** *R. Comm. Moving Picture Industry* 145, I . . produced . . the Anglo-Australian semi-historical film. **1950** G.F. McCleary *Cricket with Kangaroo* 14 The third Anglo-Australian Test Match was played at Melbourne. **1962** I. Southall *Woomera* 48 Anglo-Australian rocketry . . has to solve its problems on tight budgets and ingenuity.

B. *n.*

a. *Obs.* A person born in Australia of British descent.

1836 J.F. O'Connell *Residence Eleven Yrs. New Holland* 100 Beside the transported population, there are growing generations of Anglo-Australians. **1843** R.D. Murray *Summer at Port Phillip* 194 She is a native of this new world—an Anglo-Australian. **1855** W. Howitt *Land, Labor & Gold* II. 420 There appears already an obvious tendency in the Anglo-Australian to run up into height. **1872** 'Resident' *Glimpses Life Vic.* 392 The fervent summers, while they blanch the cheek of English beauty . . impart at the same time a perceptible degree of languor to the constitution . . more observable in the young, and especially among the native-born Anglo-Australians. **1893** F.W.L. Adams *Australs.* 5 The Anglo-Australian of Melbourne rushes away with the English 'new chum' whom he has generously engaged to 'show round', and proudly points out to him the second-rate imitations of the second-rate results of English contemporary civilization.

b. *Obs.* A person born in Britain but resident in Australia.

1894 E.H. Canney *Land of Dawning* 132 Excessive drinking is for the most part confined to the Anglo-Australian . . with the native born it is very uncommon.

c. *Obs.* A person born in Australia but resident in Britain.

1902 *Bulletin* (Sydney) 25 Oct. 25/1 A well-known Anglo-Australian now in London.

d. A person of British (as distinct from European, Asian, etc.) descent born or resident in Australia.

1979 J.J. Smolicz *Culture & Educ.* 273 We have used the term Anglo-Australian for people bred in the Anglo-Saxon-based 'core' or 'dominant' culture. The label 'Anglo-Australian' is designed to distinguish them from arrivals from continental Europe and their descendants to whom we refer as 'ethnic-Australians'. **1983** *Canberra Times* 20 Oct. 3/3 The higher migrants come in the hierarchy, the more difficult it becomes for them to get promoted on merit. . . Very often when a migrant competes with other people, all things such as skills and experience being equal, chances are that the person who has an accent or who speaks with his hands will not get the promotion in favour of the Anglo-Australian. **1984** J. Jupp *Ethnic Politics in Aust.* 11 Are the methods and avenues used by ethnics the same as those used by comparable groups of Anglo-Australians?

Anglo-Celtic, *a.* Of or belonging to the British Isles, including Eire; of British descent or provenance (see quot. 1977). Also as **Anglo-Celt** *n.*

1888 E.W. O'Sullivan in *NSWPD* 1st Ser. XXXV. 597, I believe that the centre of power of the Anglo-Celtic race no longer lies in London. The majority are now to be found in the west, in America, and in the south, in Australasia. **1912** *CPD* LXV. 2695 If England were to go down, the result would be disastrous to the Anglo-Celtic-Saxon race all the world over, whether they were living under the Stars and Stripes, the Union Jack, or our Australian flag. **1965** B.E. Mansfield *Austral. Democrat* 263 From the beginning he held up as an ideal the racial union of the 'Anglo-Celtic' peoples.

1977 P. O'FARRELL *Catholic Church & Community in Aust.* 233 But fundamentally—Anglo-Celt—the self-description of the prominent layman E.W. O'Sullivan may also be applied to Moran; indeed he used the term himself. However elevated his estimate of the religion and culture of the Celt, he derived his political principles, his ideas of proper constitutional structure, his concepts of appropriate social behaviour, from Victorian England. **1985** *Austral. Hist. Assoc. Bull.* Sept. 13 If we view ethnicity in the same way, the process we observe is a gradual agglutination of the various groups and tribes of Britain into something recognisably 'Anglo-Celtic' by the time of the Kaiser's War. **1986** *Canberra Times* July 3/2 Dr McMichael said the intention was to balance non-British displays with Aboriginal and Anglo-Celtic material, so that the influence and history of migrant groups was recorded in the museum's overall display.

Anglo-colonial, *a. Obs.* Involving British and Australian interests; ANGLO-AUSTRALIAN *a.* 2. Also as *n.*

1843 *Colonial Observer* (Sydney) 1 Apr. 921/3 The selfishness and the griping and grasping policy of their Anglo-Colonial neighbours. **1844** *Sydney Morning Herald* 1 Aug. 2/2 As to the Anglo-Colonials, while in the Bank of Australasia, the deposits have *decreased* nearly 4 per cent, in the Union they have *increased* more than 5½ per cent.

Anglo-native. *Obs.* A person of British descent born in Australia; ANGLO-AUSTRALIAN *n.* a.

1827 *Monitor* (Sydney) 1 Nov. 736/2 The Captain, three mates, Carpenter, and boat-steerer, *are all native-born*. From the natural intrepidity of the Anglo-Natives, they seem peculiarly adapted for the adventurous calling of Mariners.

angophora /æŋ'gɒfərə/. Formerly also **angophera.** [f. Gr. ἄγγος jar + Φορός bearing, alluding to the vase-like fruits. The name was coined as the scientific name of the genus (see quot. 1797).] Any tree or shrub of the genus *Angophora* (fam. Myrtaceae) of e. mainland Aust. See also *apple tree* APPLE 3.

[**1797** A.J. CAVANILLES *Icon. et Descr. Plant.* IV. 21 *Angophora* . . quia fructus huius generis vasis formam referunt.] **1827** *HRA* (1923) 3rd Ser. VI. 580 Here is seen a magnificent specimen of Angophera. **1892** 'R. BOLDREWOOD' *Nevermore* III. 14 Beneath a wide-spreading angophora Estelle Chaloner seated herself. **1933** H.J. CARTER *Gulliver in Bush* 21 Jewel-beetles are special attendants on the angophora flowers. **1942** *Southerly* iii. 14 The angophora preaches on the hillsides With the gestures of Moses. **1974** D. IRELAND *Burn* 1 The tall ragged eucalypts and angophora cast little shade.

animated stick. *Obs.* The stick insect *Acrophylla titan* of e. coastal Aust., the female of which is one of the world's longest insects. Also **animated straw, twig.**

1805 J.H. TUCKEY *Acct. Voyage to establish Colony Port Philip* 164 The species of insects are almost innumerable: among them are . . several kinds of beetles, the animated straw, etc. **1833** G.R. GRAY *Ent. Aust.* 19 The *Titan tailed Spectre*, or Diura Titan . . is found on shrubs in the scrubby parts of the Colony . . and is locally termed 'Walking Straw', or 'Animated Stick'. **1839** J. STEPHENS *Land of Promise* 60 Mr Gouger mentions one very extraordinary insect, called the 'animated twig'. It somewhat resembles the mantis.

ankle-biter. A child.

1981 *Sun-Herald* (Sydney) 2 Aug. 167/4 The middle-aged Petula Clark does the Julie Andrews bit, skipping and trilling over the edelweiss with the Von Trapp ankle-biters. **1984** *Sydney Morning Herald* 26 Jan. 9/1 Travelling overseas with an ankle-biter has its advantages. It keeps you out of museums, cathedrals and temples and shows you the raw side of life: playgrounds, supermarkets, laundrettes and public toilets. **1984** *People Mag.* 7 May 28/2 When he was still just an anklebiter his father got a posting in Sydney. At North Sydney High, Ian was a top athlete.

Annie's room. Orig. in Services' speech: see quot. 1919.

1919 W.H. DOWNING *Digger Dialects* 8 'In Annie's room'—an answer to questions as to the whereabouts of someone who cannot be found. **1920** 'RETURNED SOLDIER' *Anzac Mem.*, Baldy Evans, the cook, went up in the shell burst. . . 'Where's Baldy? . . ' 'Up in Annie's room.' **1945** *Newsreel* (Launceston) May 7 The curtain falls once more on the general jottings in and around 'Annie's Room'. **1982** N. KEESING *Lily on Dustbin* 83 Had Christopher Robin been an Australian child the answer to his plaintive query, 'Has anybody seen my mouse?' might have been 'It's up in Annie's room behind the clock.'

Anniversary Day. A name given formerly, in some States, to the anniversary of the beginning of British settlement at Sydney Cove. See AUSTRALIA DAY a.

1846 *Sydney Morning Herald* 27 Jan. 2/1 *Celebration of the fifty-eighth anniversary of the foundation of the colony.* The 'Anniversary Day', as it is pretty generally called, is now a regularly established holiday in Sydney. **1880** *Argus* (Melbourne) 26 Jan. 5/6 *Sydney, Saturday.* To-morrow being anniversary day, will be observed as a general holiday. **1892** 'E. KINGLAKE' *Austral. at Home* 69 Besides the ordinary festivals . . each colony has one peculiar to itself, commemorating its own foundation. In New South Wales it is known as Anniversary Day. **1911** *Sydney Morning Herald* 26 Jan. 6/2 Our Anniversary Day has in mind the hour of our very birth; for before that January day of 1788 when Phillip's little craft made haven within these waters, we were not. **1932** *Ibid.* 27 Jan. 10/5 Anniversary Day, which was proclaimed a public holiday in 1838, will still be perpetuated by the Anniversay Regatta, which, since 1837, has held its annual function on that day and under the same name. **1971** *Bulletin* (Sydney) 30 Jan. 11/2 The eastern States could learn from them and try to make Anniversary Day not a national day but a State day and celebrate their own communities modestly. **1972** *Ibid.* 1 Apr. 43/1 *As an old* pro-Macarthur and anti-Bligh man, my sympathies go to anyone who signed the requisition calling for the overthrow of that absurdly romanticised bully Governor Bligh on Anniversary Day 1808.

anothery. Also **anotherie.** Another one.

1963 X. HERBERT *Disturbing Element* 24 The pity was the dog could not talk, because when I got home and excitedly related my adventure, the family laughed. Mother said: 'Garn . . give us anothery!' **1973** *Kings Cross Whisper* (Sydney) clix. 4/3 'One door closes, another door opens,' says Thimbles. . . 'I'll get into anothery tomorrer.' **1979** B. HUMPHRIES *Bazza comes into his Own*, 'Scuse I, gotta go and shake hands with the unemployed! Line us up anotherie! **1981** D. STUART *I think I'll Live* 178 We'd . . kill fast, put all the guts in the skin and shove the skin well under a big spinifex and off back to camp. . . We'd eat the lot in three meals, no trouble, an' get anothery next afternoon.

antarctic beech: see BEECH.

antbed.

1. a. An earth mound built by termites to house their nests.

1846 *Sydney Morning Herald* 22 June 2/5 They discovered five ant beds, which had been hollowed out to make ovens. **1935** F. BIRTLES *Battle Fronts Outback* 182 One [*sc.* young buffalo] was amusing himself by driving his powerful horns into a big ant-bed. . . Near him two birds . . were skipping about picking up the swarms of white ants rendered shelterless. **1975** X. HERBERT *Poor Fellow my Country* 12 Small spiked grey termites' nests, or Ant Beds, as called in these parts.

b. Earth from termite mounds, esp. used as a simple flooring material. Also *attrib.*, as **antbed floor.**

1913 *Bull. N.T.* vi. 6 The floors are of cement . . or are merely of rough earth or 'ant-bed'. **1930** J.S. LITCHFIELD *Far-North Memories* 20 The ant-bed floors needed only a daily damping and sweeping to be kept in perfect order. **1933** A.M. DUNCAN-KEMP *Our Sandhill Country* 20 The walls of the house . . are of pisé brick (ant-bed clay), built by the owners over thirty years ago. **1960** R.S. PORTEOUS *Cattleman* 25 It had the usual slab walls and bark roof, and a floor of antbed, puddled and stamped down until its surface was hard and smooth. **1973** C.E. GOODE *Stories Strange Places* 146 There was only a wooden hotel there, with the desert scrub right up to the doors and its ant-bed verandah was not particularly comfortable. **1977** A. THOMAS *Bulls & Boabs* (1980) 112 The stones were bonded together with a mortar made from antbed mixed with water.

2. The nest of any of various true ants (Formicidae), such as the *meat ant* (see MEAT).

1965 L. HAYLEN *Big Red* 164 Only for Johnny last night you'd have written your poetry on an ant bed with your arse bitten off by the bull joes.

3. Special Comb. **antbed parrot,** ANTHILL PARROT.

1964 M. SHARLAND *Territory of Birds* 206 The Golden-shouldered Parrot . . is sometimes called the 'ant-bed parrot'.

ant cap. A shield placed on top of a building support to discourage termites from entering the building from below.

[**1947** C.J. VIRGO *Australasian Building Knowledge* I. 46 As a precaution against the ravages of white ants . . the piers must be capped with galvanised iron caps. **1951** P. MAYES *Austral. Architects Price Bk. & Guide* p. vii, Anti-Ant Caps.] **1955** K. SHERROTT *Your House* 39 Fit termite-shields (ant-caps) to all foundation walls, piers and stumps. **1984** *N.S.W. Contract Reporter* 24 Jan., The presence of a correctly-designed and installed ant cap will not prevent a colony of termites from gaining access to a house. . . It will . . cause subterranean termites to form a visible bridge over the cap.

Hence **ant capping** *vbl. n.*

1973 *Sun-Herald* (Sydney) 26 Aug. 108/4 There should be no danger if effective ant-capping had been provided during construction of your house. **1984** *Rawlinson's Austral. Construction Handbk.* 211, 0.50 mm aluminium (standard grade) ant-capping.

anteater.

1. ECHIDNA.

1817 J. O'HARA *Hist. N.S.W.* 432 A species of ant-eater is found in addition to the luxuries of the table. **1833** W.H. BRETON *Excursions* 89 The only specimen we saw was one of those singular animals the Anteater (Echidna). **1846** N.L. KENTISH *Work in Bush* 28 The wombat, and porcupine or ant-eater (a species of hedge-hog) are almost the only animals found in the sombre Myrtle forest. **1911** E.M. CLOWES *On Wallaby through Vic.* 288 The ant-eater not being unlike the English hedgehog in appearance, and covered with similar prickles. **1928** B. SPENCER *Wanderings in Wild Aust.* 152 The latter [*sc.* Echidna] is very hardy, feeds on insects, principally ants—hence another of its fanciful popular names, 'the ant-eater'. **1975** D. STUART *Walk, trot, canter & Die* 39 Here in the flat creek bed they found tracks of an anteater, and . . he marvelled at the casual ease with which one of the men followed the track to where the echidna was hiding under a spinifex.

2. NUMBAT.

1853 S. SIDNEY *Three Colonies* (ed. 2) 293 (*caption*) Bonded [*sic*] Myrmicobius, or ant-eater. **1888** O. THOMAS *Catal. of Marsupialia & Monotremata* 313 *Myrmecobius fasciatus* . . Marsupial Anteater. **1952** J.F. HADDLETON *Katanning Pioneer* 101 The ant eater or numbat . . is a small animal, runs on four legs, part of the body light brown, back part dark brown with bands of white a quarter of an inch wide across his back.

ante-up, *n.* Also **anty-up.** [f. (orig.) U.S. *ante* the initial stake in the game of poker.] The game of poker.

1881 A.C. GRANT *Bush-Life Qld.* II. 169 Two or three men crawl out from underneath the tarpaulin of the nearest dray, where they have been playing 'Anty-up' (a favourite game with cards) for tobacco. **1883** *Illustr. Austral. News* (Melbourne) Nov. 194/3 Some have spent their money with the itinerant hawkers; others have lost it in 'ante-up'. **1893** S. NEWLAND *Paving Way* 282 To settle about the Star, I'll play you ante-up who shall take him. **1954** T. RONAN *Vision Splendid* 305 Sit in at a small game of nap or ante-up. **1955** STEWART & KEESING *Austral. Bush Ballads* 232 Some will be playing music, while some play ante-up.

ante-up, *v.* [Transf. use of *ante-up* to put up an *ante* (see prec.).] *trans.* To provide (money) in advance, often as a contribution to a collective expense. Also *absol.*

1878 'IRONBARK' *Southerly Busters* 181, I works a little 'on the cross', I never trusts to luck; I hates to have to 'ante-up', And likes to 'pass the buck'. **1890** *Quiz* (Adelaide) 11 Apr. 2/3 Subscription lists have been sent around. . . The Bank was going to ante-up £1,000. **1895** *Bulletin* (Sydney) 28 Sept. 26/4 The boss comes on the board and announces that he is thinking about raffling a couple of horses at £1 per member. . . If you don't ante-up your 'quid' you can bet an oil-rag against a grind-stone that you'll get the 'sack' the day after the raffle. **1904** *Advocate* (Burnie) 30 June 2/6 All outstanding milk accounts . . will be placed in a solicitor's hands. His clients should take the hint and 'ante-up'. **1912** S. LOCKE *Dawsons' Uncle George* 90 The push had anted-up to put one aboard the boat. **1926** 'S. WESTLAW' *Mystery of Lombardy Chambers* 176 Hasn't anteed up that cash yet, I suppose? **1936** E. SCOTT *Aust. during War* in *Official Hist. Aust. 1914–18* XI. 731 The children hand their pennies in, all dressed in colours gay, The townsmen 'ante up' their cheques—to help Australia Day. **1948** V. PALMER *Golconda* 33 Ante up for your union-ticket and the cut for the cook. **1984** *Canberra Times* 24 Mar. 12/3 Mr Phillips . . decided to make a donation to support the pickets. 'I hope to be a catalyst to other self-employed guys to ante up and do the same thing,' he said.

anthill parrot. See quot. 1964; *antbed parrot*, see ANTBED 3.

1929 A.H. CHISHOLM *Birds & Green Places* 104 Bushmen of old had gazed wide-eyed at the male bird, resplendent in green, blue, red, brown and black, and knew him . . as the . . ant-hill parrot (because of the habit of nesting in termites' mounds). **1964** M. SHARLAND *Territory of Birds* 205 Three species of parrots use termites' mounds for nesting—the Hooded Parrot of the Northern Territory, the Golden-shouldered Parrot of north Queensland, and the rare Paradise Parrot of southern areas in Queensland. They are known by the common name of 'ant-hill parrots'.

Anti-Billite. *Hist.* One who opposes the terms of the Bill to constitute the Commonwealth of Australia, while supporting federation. Also *attrib.*

1898 *Argus* (Melbourne) 10 May 7/4 It completely destroys the arguments of the anti-billites that in the settlement of a deadlock the wishes of the majority of the people in the Commonwealth cannot prevail. **1899** *North-Western Advocate* (Devonport) 22 July 2/3 The anti-Billites in Sydney have resolved to offer no further opposition to the Commonwealth Bill. **1901** G. COCKERILL *Scribblers & Statesmen* (1944) 109 It is not true that I do not distinguish between the Anti-Billite and the Anti-Federalist. **1931** H.L. HALL *Vic.'s Part in Austral. Federation Movt.* 141 There was a band of young men who went to the 'Anti-Billite' meetings and moved amendments to hostile motions against the Bill.

anti-convict, *a. Hist.* ANTI-TRANSPORTATION; esp. in the collocation **anti-convict league,** an organization opposed to the reintroduction of transportation.

1852 *Four Colonies Aust.* 16 Amongst other events which occurred between 1846 and 1850 were the attempt to re-introduce convicts into Australia, the consequent formation of the anti-convict league. **1853** W. WESTGARTH *Vic.* 161 The anti-convict league, although waging a triumphant war in the northern colonies, was here sadly depressed. **1855** W. HOWITT *Land, Labor & Gold* II. 404 The anti-convict league cut short his operations by depriving him of the labor he employed.

antipodal, *a. Obs.* ANTIPODEAN *a.*

1849 A. HARRIS *Guide to Port Stephens* 11 If anything suggests the antipodal locality of the spot it is the timber, with which it takes some time for the eye to become familiar in Australia. **1878** G. WALCH *Australasia* 8 It's a sort of Antipodal Isle of Wight, I should say, Polly. **1882** J. SCHLEMAN *Life in Melbourne* 3 A dull wet night in the month of June—antipodal winter. **1924** LAWRENCE & SKINNER *Boy in Bush* 96 You were grilling under a fierce sun and the rush of the intense antipodal summer.

antipodeal, *a. Obs.* [Br. *antipodeal*, 'rare and erroneous form of prec.' (OED 1881).] ANTIPODEAN *a.*

1854 W. SHAW *Land of Promise* 21 The river Paramatta—the antipodeal Thames below bridge.

antipodean, *a.* and *n.* [Spec. use of *antipodean* of the opposite side of the world: see OED(S.]

A. *adj.* Of or pertaining to the British antipodes; Australian.

1835 *Hist. Van Diemen's Land* 152 It remains to be decided whether the Colonists generally, or the Antipodean Princes, are of most consideration in the eyes of our Home Rulers. **1839** W.H. LEIGH *Reconnoitering Voyages* 203 Windsor, in Australia, is a little different from its name-sake in Britain—it is the Antipodean Windsor. **1847** *Moreton Bay Courier* 31 July 3/2 How many generations may pass away before the Antipodean flockmaster becomes assimilated to his neighbour—the wild native of the soil. **1859** F. FOWLER *Southern Lights & Shadows* 70 The great fault of all the antipodean orators is the rapidity of their utterance. **1883** BEESTON & MASSIE *St. Ivo & Ashes* 5 The Antipodean batsmen got the same favour from him in their second attempt. **1936** E. SCOTT *Aust. during War* in *Official Hist. Aust. 1914–18* XI. 534 Vast stocks of wheat, meat, tallow, and other products lay in the antipodean stores ready to be carried for the Allies' use. **1951** G. FARWELL *Outside Track* 125 They were driven to the milking by a very antipodean lad with sun-browned skin and pitched Australian drawl. **1971** A. BUZO *Macquarie* (1973) 27 All white brick and plaster with a wide verandah ranging all the way round. . . Completely Antipodean. **1984** *Canberra Times* 12 Feb. 2/4 For my part, as the owner of many eucalypts of many sizes and habits, I take the view that they were here before us and that they have a perfect right to behave in an antipodean way.

B. *n.* An Australian.

1843 *Sydney Morning Herald* 25 May 4/3 *Antipodeans* here—I see them sit Before me in the middle of the pit. **1869** S.T. DUNCAN *Jrnl. Voyage to Aust.* 91 We were glad to retire to rest, which was the first time to many of us amongst the *Antipodeans.* **1897** *Bulletin* (Sydney) 27 Feb. 10/4 An Australian K.C.M.G., lately in England, says that a similarly-titled Antipodean was threatened with prosecution. **1917** *Truth* (Sydney) 13 May 1/8 They strafe the men from down under for a day or two and decide that they are dead, when up pop the 'mad Antipodeans' and blow their Guard to blazes. **1939** H.W. DINNING *Austral. Scene* 160 Atmospheric effects in London make it . . a kind of fairyland to the antipodean. **1972** *Southerly* iv. 281 Brook always rose to dinner invitations for they represented to him that order and elegance and cultured society he felt should have been his, had he not been born an antipodean.

antipodes. [Restricted use of *antipodes* places on the earth's surface directly opposite each other: see OED 3.] Usu. with **the**: the British antipodes, spec. Australia, the calendar of the seasons and unusualness of the flora and fauna strengthening the sense of oppositeness (see quots., esp. 1857).

1833 *Sydney Herald* 12 Dec. 3/1 These are the Antipodes! 'The world is turned upside down!' **1842** H. PARKES *Stolen Moments* 98 I've wandered where the Southern Cross Glows o'er th'Antipodes. **1854** F. ELDERSHAW *Aust. as it really Is* 115 Native Dog-hunting is, in fact, neither more nor less than the Fox-hunting of the Antipodes. **1857** W. WESTGARTH *Vic. & Austral. Gold Mines* 33 The trees without leaves, of which the native cherry tree and several species of the 'she-oak' are the most common. The former gives the standing instance of everything going by contraries at the antipodes, by producing a cherry with the stone on the outside. **1862** G.T. LLOYD *Thirty-Three Yrs. Tas. & Vic.* 447 The colleges at the Antipodes are of equal rank with those of Oxford and Cambridge. **1867** 'CLERGYMAN' *Aust. as it Is* 222 It is very common at the Antipodes for persons to change their names when they wish to make a fresh start in life. **1872** 'RESIDENT' *Glimpses Life Vic.* 409 Girlhood is precocious at the Antipodes, and passes at an early age into young-ladyhood. **1881** *Bulletin* (Sydney) 18 June 4/2 At the antipodes we reverse things. **1898** A.P. MARTIN *Beginnings Austral. Lit.* 34 Such verses . . are now almost as familiar in London drawing-rooms and on suburban platforms, as in the remote sheep-stations or bush shanties of the Antipodes. **1910** *Huon Times* (Franklin) 17 Aug. 4/6 Hobart will become the greatest maritime port in the Antipodes. **1936** E. SCOTT *Aust. during War* in *Official Hist. Aust. 1914–18* XI. 190 He never ceased to take the liveliest interest in Australian affairs, maintained correspondence with friends at the Antipodes, and delighted to entertain them. **1978** B. OAKLEY *Ship's Whistle* (1979) 32 Lessons that the Mother Country has painfully learned over centuries must be learned yet again, apparently, in the Antipodes.

anti-sosh, *a. Hist.* [See SOSH.] Opposed to socialism; anti-socialist.

1906 *Gadfly* (Adelaide) 18 July 20/1 The anti-sosh crowd wanted us to breakfast with them. **1908** *Bulletin* (Sydney) 17 Sept. 14/4 A great Anti-Sosh cry was 'Give us back our eleven days. You stole our eleven days.' **1909** *Ibid.* 14 Oct. 14/2 If the virulent Anti-Sosh farmer or grazier can only cram another gramme of Sosh into his already Socialism-sodden system and use the virus supplied by the Government . . there is little to fear from bad virus.

anti-squatter. *Hist.* [See SQUATTER.] One politically active in opposing the squatting interest.

1847 *Atlas* (Sydney) III. 222/2 'Dermid' . . appears to be an 'anti-squatter'. **1847** *Melbourne Argus* 27 Aug. 4/3 No, I'm not an anti-squatter; I wish to become a squatter myself. **1865** 'W.R.L.' *Our Wool Staple* 28 No part of the anti-squatters' conduct seems more absurd than their consigning the Orders in Council to oblivion. **1867** J. BONWICK *J. Batman* 38 One of the so-called party of anti-squatters, Mr Evans, assured me that he went with the avowed intention to run sheep. **1867** *Pasquin* (London) 2 Feb. 9 The ancient and modern anti-squatters—dogs and duffers—have restored the waste land to its former peaceful simplicity—from Dan to Beersheba there isn't a bite for a bandicoot.

Also **anti-squatterish, anti-squatting** *adjs.*

1853 J.R. GODLEY *Extracts Jrnl. Visit N.S.W.* 11 The Legislative Council of Victoria is decidedly '**anti-squatterish**' in its tendencies. **1848** *Maitland Mercury* 20 May 2/1 In the spirit of Hannibal, the leader of the **anti-squatting** party has sworn eternal hatred to the Land Orders. **1865** 'W.R.L.' *Our Wool Staple* 19 It is accompanied with cries . . from the anti-squatting public of 'See what another big sop for the squattocracy!' **1873** A. TROLLOPE *Aust. & N.Z.* I. 455 The Order in Council . . was . . objectionable to the anti-squatting interests.

anti-transportation. *Hist.* Used *attrib.* to designate an association, proposal, etc., opposed to the continuance of the convict system. See also TRANSPORTATIONIST.

1847 *Atlas* (Sydney) III. 122/3 The mean system of 'burking', or the petty expedient of attempting to 'damn with small sneers', is pursued towards those gentlemen who . . have the manliness to brave the hootings of an anti-transportation meeting. **1848** *Maitland Mercury* 6 Sept. 2/5 Many . . after appending their names to anti-transportation petitions, did all in their power to neutralise the effect of such petitions. **1850** *Illustr. Austral. Mag.* (Melbourne) Aug. 154 An anti-transportation committee was also appointed, in order to watch over the interests of the settlement, and protect it from this commencement of a frightful inundation of crime. **1852** W. HUGHES *Austral. Colonies* 111 Strenuous efforts have recently been made to procure an exemption from the further influx of convicts, a great 'Anti-transportation League' . . having been formed for the purpose. **1855** W. HOWITT *Land, Labor & Gold* II. 411 Though the anti-transportation agitation was of old standing, and though Sydney had got rid of it in 1840, yet the great anti-transportation league here was formed almost contemporaneously with the discovery of the gold. **1864** *Illustr. Sydney News* Dec. 6/1 The Ballarat Ladies Anti-Transportation Society has forwarded a petition to the Queen, and an address to the women of England signed by 16,000 persons. **1865** 'SPECIAL CORRESPONDENT' *Transportation* 49 The anti-transportation party is insignificant in numbers and influence.

Hence **anti-transportationist** *n.*

1847 *Port Phillip Herald* 23 Sept. 2/7 Mr McCombie . . attempted to charge the anti transportationists with inconsistency, and endeavouring to prevent the importation of convicts and Pentonvilles, and employ them after. **1852** *Bell's Life in Sydney* 8 May 1/3 Crime was much less than what our more virulent anti-transportationists will admit. **1884** J. FENTON *Hist. of Tas.* 182 The anti-transportationists—the most numerous class—were the first to move. **1948** F. CLUNE *Wild Colonial Boys* 116 Then the anti-transportationists held a . . meeting . . on 22 October 1846. . . The 'Antis' then drew up a petition of protest.

anvil-bird. [See quot.] *Noisy pitta*, see NOISY.

1918 *Bulletin* (Sydney) 21 Nov. 24/2 The anvil-bird . . is a very rare and exceedingly shy creature. Its clear metallic notes ring out 'Kling, kling, kling, kling', several times in measured tones. **1976** *Reader's Digest Compl. Bk. Austral. Birds* 330 Noisy pitta... Other names Anvil-bird... The pitta holds a snail in its bill and repeatedly strikes the shell against an 'anvil'.

Anzac, *n.* and *attrib.* [Acronym f. the initial letters of *Australian and New Zealand Army Corps* orig. used as a telegraphic code name for the Corps.]

A. *n.*

1. The Australian and New Zealand Army Corps.

1915 C.E.W. BEAN Diary 25 Apr. 67 *Col. Knox to Anzac.* 'Ammunition required at once.' *Ibid.* 6 May 33 Anzac has become the sort of code word for the Army Corps. **1917** C.E.W. BEAN *Lett. from France* 231 They are proud of Anzac as the name of the corps, and as the name of that hill-side in Gallipoli where their graves lie side by side. **1920** *Aussie* (Sydney) May 13/1 The Army ceased to be officially known by the name Anzac some time after its arrival in France, and became the 'Australian Corps'. **1952** J. MAXWELL *Hell's Bells* 25 One of the many ditties I recollect (sung to the tune of *Greenland's Icy Mountains*) was:- We are a ragtime army The A.N.Z.A.C. We cannot shoot, we won't salute What—use are we.

2. Abbrev. of 'Anzac Cove': see quot. 1916.

1915 I. HAMILTON *Second Dispatch* 26 Aug., Lieut.-Gen. Sir W.R. Birdwood has been the soul of Anzac. Not for a single day has he ever quitted his post. Cheery and full of human sympathy, he has spent many hours of each twenty-four inspiring the defenders of the front trenches. **1915** J.D. BURNS *In Dawning of Day* 4 Sept. (1916) 10 The mine sweeper which is to take us across to Anzac on the peninsula, is alongside now. **1916** 'MEN OF ANZAC' *Anzac Bk.* p. ix, I was asked by General Headquarters to suggest a name for the beach where we had made good our precarious footing, and then asked that this might be recorded as 'Anzac Cove'—a name which the bravery of our men has now made historical, while it will remain a geographical landmark for all time. Our eight months at 'Anzac' cannot help stamping on the memory of every one of us days of trial and anxiety, hopes, and perhaps occasional fears, rejoicings at success, and sorrow—very deep and sincere—for many a good comrade whom we can never see again. **1917** *Huon Times* (Franklin) 13 July 3/1 The men who sleep at Anzac died with the word 'Australia' on their lips. **1925** *Bulletin* (Sydney) 1 Jan. 22/1 They'll not forget the men who saved Their land so fair, so fine, Though some lie dead at Anzac, And some in Palestine. **1952** J.R. TYRRELL *Old Bks.* 69 An old Gallipoli Digger.. recalls seeing him hunched down on his heels.. over a small fire in a trench at Anzac, cooking gruel. **1979** W.D. JOYNT *Breaking Road for Rest* 62 Their lack of hard training, for they had been living in the trenches at Anzac, made the effort too much for them. **1981** P. SEKULESS *Fred* 149 The Turks continue to recognize the sacred nature of Anzac, but they also make use of vantage points along the barren.. coastline to keep a watch on shipping.

3. The Gallipoli campaign.

1915 *Honk* x. 6/1 The whole Italian Press praises the valour of the Australasian troops in the Dardanelles at Anzac. **1918** R.H. KNYVETT *Over there with Australs.* 113 The whole nation brooded over these young men, guardians of Australia's honor, and waited anxiously for them to wipe out this slur. That explains Australia's pride in 'Anzac'. It meant for us not merely our baptism in blood—it was more even than a victory—for there, with the fierce search-light of every nation turned upon it, our representative manhood showed no faltering. **1918** L.J. VILLIERS *Changing Yr.* 38 *This* Anzac was the biggest flamin' show That ever I wuz in... There's none cud touch this fer a willin' go. **1927** K. BURKE *With Horse & Morse* Foreword, What mortal men could do these magnificent men from Anzac did. **1984** *Canberra Times* 25 Apr. 2/2 Sixteen military commanders, from Anzac to 1970.

4. A member of the Australian and New Zealand Army Corps who served in the Gallipoli campaign.

1916 *Truth* (Sydney) 9 Apr. 8/4 Lord Mayor Dick Meagher has decided to entertain returned Anzacs at luncheon at the Town Hall. **1916** C.E.W. BEAN Diary 25 Apr. 93 Bought two bottles of champagne.. and we drank the health of all Anzacs. **1916** *Truth* (Sydney) 15 Oct. 12/6 'Brave as an Anzac' has become a household word, and those of the Australian and New Zealand Army Corps are, many of them, descendants of the pioneers who made the picturesque history of Australia. **1916** *Bulletin* (Sydney) 28 Dec. (Red Page), On Christmas Eve, 1914, in Cairo, I and about 50 other Australians and M.L. boys ('Anzac' was not coined then).. got rather lively. **1916** 'MEN OF ANZAC' *Anzac Bk.* 95 The children unborn shall acclaim, The standard the Anzacs unfurled, When they made Australasia's fame The wonder and pride of the world. **1917** C.E.W. BEAN *Lett. from France* 231 The reason why they always avoid calling themselves 'the Anzacs' is that the term was at one time associated in the Press with so many highly coloured, imaginative, mock heroic stories of individual feats, which they were supposed to have performed, that its use from that time forth was, by a sort of tacit consent, irrevocably damned within the force. The picture which it called up was that of the 'Anzac' in London, with his shining gaiters and buttons and generally unauthorised cock's feathers in his hat, reaping the glory of the acrobatic performances which his battered countrymen, very unlovely with sweat and dust, were credited with achieving in No Man's Land. **1918** *Truth* (Sydney) 24 Feb. 5/5 You know that the accused is one of the original Anzacs, with three years and 10 days active service? **1918** *Kia Ora Coo-ee* Mar. 1/1 To all the sons of Australia and New Zealand whose blood has made sacred the scarred hillsides of Gallipoli, and enriched its barren soil, to all those sons whose cognomen, ANZAC, has become synonymous for bravery.. PEACE. **1918** R.H. KNYVETT *Over there with Australs.* 135 To-day the name Anzac is the envy of all other soldiers. **1919** W.J. DENNY *Diggers* 5 The offical recognition of the distinction between 'Anzacs' and 'Australians' is an order which prescribes that every Australian officer and soldier who took part in the Gallipoli campaign shall wear a brass letter 'A' over the regimental colours which every Australian soldier must wear on his sleeve. **1919** O. HOGUE *Cameliers* 47 On came the Turks, yelling, 'Allah finish Australia', 'Allah finish Australia'—a rather unique battle-cry, which tickled the Anzacs immensely. **1921** E. WELLS *Fragments* 12 The Anzacs!—their ranks are but scanty all told—Have a separate record illumined in gold. Their blood on Gallipoli's ridges they poured... These are the Anzacs! The other may claim Their zeal and their spirit—but never their name. **1956** B.J. RAYMENT *My Towri* 11 However, Charlie (an old Anzac) is still going strong. **1967** A. SEYMOUR *One Day of Yr.* 97 They put Australia on the map, they did, the Anzacs did. And bloody died, doin' it. **1975** X. HERBERT *Poor Fellow my Country* 1356 They say we were Blooded as a Nation at Anzac. With all due respect to you as an old Anzac, I say we were only *Bloodied* then. **1981** Q. WILD *Honey Wind* 72 Jeez some of the pubs in the middle of Sydney look old. You expect to find Anzacs drinking in them. **1984** *Canberra Times* 25 Apr. 2/2 The Gallipoli campaign should.. be kept in perspective and more emphasis placed on those Australians who were not Anzacs.

5. Used emblematically to reflect the traditional view of the virtues displayed by those who served in the Gallipoli campaign, esp. as these are seen as national characteristics.

1916 *Man. War Precautions* (Dept. of Defence) (1918) 158 No person shall, after the first day of July, One thousand nine hundred and sixteen, without the authority of the Governor-General or of a Minister of State.. assume or use in connexion with any trade, business, calling, or profession the word 'Anzac' or any word resembling the word 'Anzac', or any word notified by the Governor-General, by notice in the *Gazette*, to be for the purposes of this Regulation a prohibited word. **1916** *Truth* (Sydney) 28 May 8/2 There is every indication that the Federal City will be re-named Anzac. **1917** *Huon Times* (Franklin) 2 Mar. 4/4 The deathless name of 'Anzac' That thrills from pole to pole. **1918** *Poems by Austral. Soldiers* 1 There's an immortal name. The deathless name of 'Anzac'. **1918** N.P.H. NEAL *Back to Bush* 7 My thoughts go back to that chill morn When Anzac's soul first saw the dawn By lonely Samothrace. **1918** *Huon Times* (Franklin) 11 Oct. 3/1 The marvellous spirit and genius of the Australian and the immortal name of Anzac. **1919** O. HOGUE *Cameliers* 97 I'm sick to death of this discipline. That proves I'm an Anzac. **1919** 'SCOTTY'S BROTHER' *Desert Trail* 2 How much blood was spilt in helping to write the immortal letters ANZAC on the history of the world. **1920** J.N. MACINTYRE *White Aust.* 191 Hundreds and thousands of heroes of the Empire.. gladly come out to these smiling 'plains of promise'.. and multiply and prosper, and breed up a race of future Anzacs. **1927** T.S. GROSER *Lure of Golden West* 209 Suffice it to say that 'Anzac' is a household word for valour and endurance. **1929** H.J. TUCKER *Weather Prophet* 27 Anzac, immortal word. **1946** A.H. CHISHOLM *Making of Sentimental Bloke* 104, I think of Anzacs when the dusk comes down Upon the gums—of Anzacs tough and tall Guarding this gateway, Diggers strong and brown. **1952** T.A.G. HUNGERFORD *Ridge & River* 33 'You big Anzac!' scoffed White, in line behind him. 'You couldn't fight a sick moll!' **1962** A. SEYMOUR *One Day of Yr.* 98 That isn't all the story, there is something more in Anzac still, even now. **1965** K. SMITH *OGF* 164 The traditions of Anzac, forged in the harsh crucible of war, are forgotten while the brewers' profits mount. **1976** K. CLIFT *Soldier who never grew Up* 88 Before I went to school, he would proclaim if I were hurt, 'never cry, be an Anzac'. **1986** *Canberra Times* 25 Apr. 2/1 The spirit of Anzac has not been weakened by the passing years.

6. Generally, an Australian (or New Zealand) soldier or ex-soldier.

1917 T.E. RUTH *Mannixisms* 8 We are called, called by the Anzacs who have fallen, called by the Anzacs who are maimed. **1917** R.W. JONES *With 'Roos* 13 We heard a Cockney cook calling out: 'How much more of this Anzac stuff is coming ashore?' He thought the initial letters in Australian and New Zealand Army Corps—A.N.Z.A.C.—stencilled on a number of boxes.. indicated a new kind of tucker. And, from thence on, the fatigue that was unloading these stores, and those who were receiving them, were jocularly called the 'Anzacs'. **1918** A.C. STEPHEN *Austral. in R.F.A.* 84 Anzacs are pouring in—an endless stream of tattered bloody figures—night and day. **1919** W.A. CULL *At All Costs* 8 As a result of many disappointments both before and after enlistment, I missed the historic landing at Gallipoli, and to an Anzac that must ever be a matter of regret. **1919** E. DYSON *Hello, Soldier* 18 Little Abdul's quite a fighter, 'n' he mixes it with skill; But the Anzacs have him snouted, 'n' oh ma, he's feelin' ill. **1919** W.J. DENNY *Diggers* 6 'Anzac' is a word which is more frequently used by those who are not 'Anzacs' than by Australian soldiers. **1941** H. PERCY *Here's H. Percy* 4 The exploits of the Anzacs are known in every land. Hitler knows 'em, to his sorrow—he's tackled 'em before, So he's sent his side-kick 'Musso' to face 'em in this war. **1941** 'P. HARDY' *Torch of Remembrance* 30 When the War is done, after Peace they've won, We will remember the 'Anzacs'! **1950** H.C. WELLS *Earth cries Out* 99 They don't know that they are breaking all the traditions of Australian unions—the things our Anzacs are fighting for. **1959** E. LAMBERT *Glory thrown In* 114 Couldn't the big bronze Anzac wait, was he so passionate for his Sophie?

7. See quot. 1923; *Anzac biscuit*, see ANZAC B. 2.

1923 MRS H.W. SHAW *Six Hundred Tested Recipes* (ed. 9) 54 Anzacs: 2 breakfast cups John Bull oats, ½ breakfast cup sugar, 1 scant cup plain flour, ½ cup melted butter, 1 tablespoon golden syrup, 2 ditto. boiling water, 1 teaspoon carb. soda. Mix butter, golden syrup and soda together, pour boiling water on, then add dry ingredients. Put on oven sheet or scone tray with teaspoon. Slow oven till browned. **1929** L. DRAKE *Home Cookery* 160 *'Anzacs'—crisp brown biscuits.* Economical. **1975** D. MALOUF *Johno* 33 Pikelets or pumpkin scones for morning tea.. and in the afternoon, date slices, anzacs and cream puffs. **1980** MCKENZIE & ALLEN *Look at Yesteryear* 126 Cakes and biscuits, which became known as *Anzacs*, were sent to the soldiers to keep them in touch with home.

B. *attrib.* **1.**

1915 C.E.W. BEAN Diary 17 May 4 The beach was fairly clear but I could see men going about working careless of any fire, in the good old Anzac way. **1916** A. ST. J. ADCOCK *Australasia Triumphant* 87 'The Anzac Corps fought like lions,' says Mr Ashmead Bartlett. **1916** *Astra* (Melbourne) Oct. 5/1 Anzac men of the first contingent. **1918** *Truth* (Sydney) 5 May 15/8 There are still a few who haven't heard of the English war bride who remarked modestly that her Anzac hubby was not very well off; all he had was a little place called Tasmania. **1919** *Smith's Weekly* (Sydney) 29 Mar. 11/6 A certain Anzac bride lately arrived in Perth. **1937** C.D. MITCHELL *Backs to Wall* 20 In the cold winter winds we were debarred from the Anzac national sport of 'reading our shirts', sometimes also called 'chatting by the wayside'. **1942** *Aust. Week-End Bk.* 12 The Anzac perkiness has stemmed out of the English conception of courage. The Anzac is frankly cockier, but not disagreeably so. **1966** G. MCINNES *Humping my Bluey* 80 The wearing of the Digger hat—the Anzac hat—made me feel one with the heroic tradition. **1967** D. HORNE *Educ. Young Donald* 59 The Anzac spirit—endurance, commitment, the expression of will. **1968** K. DENTON *Walk around my Cluttered Mind* 117 I've looked in vain for the Aussie of My Youth, the big, bronzed Anzac hero. **1970** *Coast to Coast 1967–68* 77, I . . do remember feeling Anzac-tall and commando-masculine. **1971** *Sydney Morning Herald* 20 Apr. 18/7 The Anzac campaign is regarded as having created the spirit and identity of Australia as a nation. **1979** D. MAITLAND *Breaking Out* 113 The abortive baptism of fire at Gallipoli, which gave birth to the myth of the Anzac nation. **1981** B. GREEN *Small Town Rising* 143 An Anzac soldier on top of the town's tall clock forever saluted a marbled honour roll.

2. Comb. **Anzac biscuit, button, march, overcoat, parade, wafer.**

1943 *Austral. Home Cookery* 257 **Anzac biscuits**. . . These biscuits should be stored in an airtight tin, immediately they are cold. **1977** B. HUMPHRIES *Dame Edna's Coffee Table Bk.* 35 Many young lasses couldn't run up a batch of Anzac Biscuits or a decent Pavlova these days and couldn't care less furthermore. **1983** M. FOX *Possum Magic*, They ate Anzac biscuits in Adelaide, mornay and Minties in Melbourne, steak and salad in Sydney and pumpkin scones in Brisbane. **1986** *Sydney Morning Herald* 21 Apr 3/1 It is illegal to sell Anzac biscuits in Tasmania. **1919** W.H. DOWNING *Digger Dialects* 8 **Anzac button**, a nail used in place of a trouser button. **1978** P. ADAM SMITH *Anzacs* 106 Stretcher bearer Jim McPhee of the 3rd Division Field Ambulance told me '. . We had some silly sayings. An Anzac Button was a nail in place of a trouser button.' **1945** I.L. IDRIESS *Horrie Wog-Dog* 32 We're going home so you can lead the **Anzac march** through Melbourne. **1957** D. NILAND *Call me when Cross turns Over* 157 He wore a dyed blue **Anzac overcoat** with the collar up. **1980** J. SEAGER *Kangaroo Island Doctor* 44, I farewelled my host, who insisted upon my keeping warm in his Anzac overcoat. **1966** J. ALDRIDGE *My Brother Tom* 164 As usual on the twenty-fifth of April the Australian activity nearest to God, the **Anzac parade**, was held in the town. **1971** *Bulletin* (Sydney) 1 May 10/3 Some things move us deeply here in Melbourne—football, dawn Anzac parades and air pageants. **1975** *Age* (Melbourne) 25 Apr. 5/3 The RSL expects about 12,000 men and women to march in the Anzac Parade today. **1918** C.L. HARTT *Diggerettes* 15 We were out for a spell, and from our billets could see the light railway crawling along laden with whizz-bangs and **Anzac wafers**. **1918** *Aussie* (Sydney) Oct. 13/2 He felt that winding up the war would literally be taking the Anzac wafers and margarine out of his mouth. **1919** *Ibid.* Jan. 7/2 Rus. and I often spoke of the bonzer feed we would have on Anzac wafers and bully beef when we got back to our own lines. **1929** *Ibid.* Apr. 33/1 Wafers—Anzac Wafers. . . Makes me smile to think about 'em; They were made of bricks and mortar, and a little dash of flour. . . And they exercised our molars, bitin' at 'em by the hour.

Anzac Day. April 25, the anniversary of the landing at Gallipoli: a national public holiday commemorating all Australia's war dead. Also *attrib.*

1916 *Truth* (Sydney) 9 Apr. 1/8 What? We're going to have an Anzac Day, A night of Fireworks and Illumination, For which ratepayers they will have to pay To hold high revelry and jubilation, Strange conduct this is, truly be it said, To hold a picnic o'er Australia's dead. **1916** Tas. Non-State Rec. 103/11 28 Apr., So after lunch we proceeded to carry out the programme arranged for Anzac Day. **1916** *Desert Dust Bin: Official Organ 3rd L.H.F.A.* 3 May 8/1 Tuesday, 25th . . Anzac Day today. The 'Dinkums' put on blue ribbons. **1918** *Kia Ora Coo-ee* Apr. 16/2 It will have been noticed in recent cables, that the Returned Soldiers' Imperial League holding its annual meeting for Australia, decided that Anzac Day should be kept as a Public Holiday. **1920** H. HANSELL *Everlastin' Ballads* 91 As he who passed for ever from Her life on Anzac Day. **1924** *Bulletin* (Sydney) 22 May 24/1 Some went to pray and others to play on Anzac Day. **1942** *Welcome to Aust.* 23 Anzac Day (April 25, the anniversary of the Gallipoli landing) is in peace-time one of the most closely-kept holidays of the year. **1957** J.M. HOSKING *Aust. First & Last* 32 The men of the original A.I.F. were far away the best, The chockoes throw their chests out on Anzac Day parades, But all those daffodils were fit for was putting on charades. **1964** *Bulletin* (Sydney) 25 Jan. 10/2 For more than 40 years, under an Act of Parliament, Anzac Day in Queensland has been a total day of mourning. **1967** A. SEYMOUR *One Day of Yr.* 32 England? Bugger England. I'm a bloody Australian, mate, and it's because I'm a bloody Australian that I'm gettin' on the grog. It's Anzac Day next week, that's my day, that's the old digger's day. **1971** *Bulletin* (Sydney) 8 May 41/2 'The reason why the old soldiers get so pissed and vomitous on Anzac Day is nothing to do with a Militaristic Plot,' explicates Boddy. **1976** *Age* (Melbourne) 24 Apr. 15/1 Isn't Anzac Day just a bit passé? **1981** *Daily Mirror* (Sydney) 24 Apr. 7/1 Arneil will be marching tomorrow, just as he has every year since the war ended. 'Anzac Day, to me, is the spirit of this country. It *is* Australia,' he says. **1982** *Sunday Tel.* (Sydney) 14 Mar. 20/2 The threat of violence during next month's Anzac Day ceremonies is looming again. **1982** *Canberra Times* 15 Apr. 1/2 The Police Commissioner . . has given three groups permission to join the Anzac Day march.

apostle. [See quot. 1928.] **a.** The predom. grey bird *Struthidea cinerea*, which builds its nest of mud and lives in family groups of about nine (twelve, according to tradition) in wooded parts of e. Aust.; LOUSY JACK. **b.** HAPPY JACK. **c.** Rarely, CHOUGH. See also HAPPY FAMILY, TWELVE APOSTLES. Also **apostle bird.**

1894 G. BOOTHBY *On Wallaby* 291 The Apostle Bird's peculiarity is always to move about with eleven of his fellows. **1903** *Emu* II. 164 Apostle-Bird (*Struthidea cinerea*). **1911** *Bulletin* (Sydney) 26 Jan. 15/2 The babbler or chatterer. In the bush . . these birds are variously known as 'the happy family', 'twelve apostles' or plain 'apostles' (sharing the appellation with the grey jumper). **1928** G.H. WILKINS *Undiscovered Aust.* 31 The Apostle-birds have gained their local name because of their habit of congregating together . . in groups of twelve. **1941** I.L. IDRIESS *Great Boomerang* 77 The antics of the scolding apostle-birds. **1962** B.W. LEAKE *Eastern Wheatbelt Wildlife* 87 White-browed babblers or apostle birds travel around in groups from seven to twelve. **1973** V. SERVENTY *Desert Walkabout* 62 Apostle-birds scolded us heartily, in between building their communal mud nests. **1975** D. STUART *Walk, trot, canter & Die* 52 A group of apostle birds . . flew off in a squawking tantrum from trees that shaded the meathouse.

appearance money. A payment made to employees presenting themselves for work irrespective of its availability: see quot. 1979. Also **attendance money.**

1947 *58 CAR* 20 App., Any waterside worker who refuses to accept work which he is capable of performing . . shall not be paid such attendance money in respect of any day or days upon which he so refuses. **1947** *59 CAR* 154 To provide for a fortnight's annual leave and the payment of appearance money in cases where draggers report for work and no work is available. **1965** F. HARDY *Yarns of Billy Borker* 22 But there's no money to be made on the waterfront these days—except appearance money. **1979** S. MORAN *Reminisc. of Rebel* 29 During the struggle for the payment of appearance money, i.e. payment for the days on which the employers were not able to offer employment but on which the wharfies had to report for work, the Sydney Branch organised a march to the Sydney Domain. **1981** *Canberra Times* 30 Oct. 2/7 Appearance money is another claim which we think will succeed. We reckon the presence of a highly qualified academic in a tutorial is worth something in its own right, regardless of whether he or she actually says anything, or conducts a tutorial. Just showing up is worth big bickies.

apple.

1. Any of several fruits which in some way resembles the apple.

1770 J. COOK *Jrnls.* 23 Aug. (1955) I. 394 There are indeed found growing wild in the woods a few sorts of fruits . . which when ripe do not eat a miss, one sort especially which we call'd Apples. **1829** R. MUDIE *Picture of Aust.* 150 The apple on the tropical coast belongs to the same genus as the Malay apple (*Eugenia*); but it is so exceedingly sour that it cannot be eaten. **1928** M.E. FULLERTON *Austral. Bush* 130 The sheoak 'apple', as it is called, is armed with semi-pricks, placed like the covering of the pine-cones.

2. Abbrev. of *apple tree*.

1825 B. FIELD *Geogr. Mem. N.S.W.* 463 Excepting . . the wild apple (achras australis) . . the wood-cutters had no names for the many trees of gigantic growth which cover this mountain. **1861** W. LANDSBOROUGH *Jrnl. Exped. from Carpentaria* (1862) 9 The higher parts are more thickly grassed, and are slightly wooded with stunted timber, consisting of box, apple, white gum. **1880** J. BONWICK *Resources Qld.* 37 The White Box and Apple take the lower, but still fertile districts. **1902** *Proc. Linnean Soc. N.S.W.* XXVIII. 579 *E. conica* is fairly plentiful. It is locally known under the names of Box, Apple, and Woolly-butt. **1965** *Austral. Encycl.* I. 218 Several eucalypts are called 'apples', particularly *E. bridgesiana* (the but-but) and *E. cinerea* (Argyle apple). **1984** D.J. BOLAND et al. *Forest Trees Aust.* (rev. ed.) 186 'Apple' is believed to have originated from the apple-tree appearance of the first observed species, *A[ngophora] hispida*.

3. Special Comb. **apple berry,** any of several climbing plants of the Austral. genus *Billardiera* (fam. Pittosporaceae), some of which have edible fruits; **box,** any of several myrtaceous trees having a soft, fibrous bark and dull green leaves, as *Eucalyptus bridgesiana*; also *attrib.*; **bush,** a shrub with features reminiscent of the apple tree, as *Pterocaulon sphacelatum* (fam. Asteraceae) which emits a fruity aroma when crushed; **gum,** *apple box*; **isle (island, land),** Tasmania, so called because of its popular identification as an apple-growing region; also **islander** (or **lander**), a Tasmanian; **tree,** any of several trees thought to resemble the apple (*Malus*), esp. of the genera *Eucalyptus* and *Angophora* (fam. Myrtaceae); **tree flat,** see FLAT *n.*[1] b.

1793 J.E. SMITH *Specimen Bot. New Holland* 1 *Billardiera* scandens. Climbing **Apple-berry**. **1842** J. BACKHOUSE *Narr. Visit Austral. Colonies* (1843) p. xxxii, Apple Berry. B[illardiera] murabilis has a green cylindrical fruit becoming lighter green or amber colour, when ripe, possessing a pleasant, sub-acid taste but the seeds are numerous and hard. **1888** *Proc. Linnean Soc. N.S.W.* III. 491 'Apple Berry.' The berries are acid and pleasant when fully ripe. From their shape children call them 'dumplings'. **1942** C. BARRETT *Austral. Wild Flower Bk.* 43 The climbing apple-berry ranges from Queensland to South Australia and is also a Tasmanian species. **1890** *Argus* (Melbourne) 9 Aug. 4/6 An ironstone hill . . with **apple-box** and ironbark dotted about. **1902** *Proc. Linnean Soc. N.S.W.* XXVII. 525 *Eucalyptus bicolor* . . 'Apple Box' or 'Red Box' of Lachlan River. **1946** *Bulletin* (Sydney) 10 July 28/1 When the couch gives way t'kangaroo an' red grass, cut over the spur where there's a stray applebox or two. **1953** E. MITCHELL *Flow River, blow Wind* 89 They . . walked into the shade of the great spreading applebox-trees. **1979** DOUGLAS & HEATHCOTE *Far Cry* 85 It was utterly wild, fairly open bush of stringy barks and grey apple-box trees. **1983** *Warwick Daily News* 14 June 3/1 In the valley's 10 square kilometres, important wildlife habitats are represented: . . stands of apple box, brush box and Casuarinas. **1900** *Proc. Linnean Soc. N.S.W.* XXV. 710 *Heterodendron oleaefolium* (locally called **Apple Bush**, though in most places it is known as Rosewood). **1903** G. SUTHERLAND *Australasian Live Stock Man.* (ed. 2) 384 The following are likewise very good feed for stock, namely . . Apple Bush and Orange Bush. **1936** I.L. IDRIESS *Cattle King* 252 The rabbits had killed all the white wood, apple-bush, and butter-bush. **1968** K. WEATHERLY *Roo Shooter* 38 There was the willie wagtail that lived in the apple bush behind their tent. **1982** D. HARRIS *Drovers of Outback* 50 We cut apple bush, . . and any other edible scrub that we could find. **1845** L. LEICHHARDT *Jrnl. Overland Exped. Aust.* 22 May (1847) 264 The rocky ridges were occupied by . . another Eucalyptus, with a scaly butt like the Moreton Bay ash, but with smooth upper trunk and cordate ovate leaves. . . We called it the **Apple-gum**. **1846** *Sydney Morning Herald* 26 Mar. 2/6 They are timbered with box, apple-gum, (a new species of gum with the foliage of the apple-tree of the Darling Downs, and with the black butt of the Moreton Bay ash). **1867** F.J. BYERLEY *Narr. Overland Exped. Northern Qld.* 9 The timber of the ridges was cheifly [*sic*] . . the apple-gum. **1888** *Centennial Mag.* (Sydney) 132 The apple gum is well named, for the leaves are dusted with a pea-green bloom much like that of a growing apple, while when its spring vigor is greatest the tree gives off a soft aroma suggestive of stone pippins mellowing in the straw. **1940** H. ELLIS *My Life* 122 There was the clump of apple-gums with the delicious soft grey trunks so subtly in harmony with my mood as I passed them. **1952** D. STEWART *Sun Orchids* 69 Day's clear blue and sunlight dappling Apple-gum. **1979** DUSTY & LAPSLEY *Walk Country Mile* 12 The cows had gathered under the apple-gums, waiting to be taken down for milking. **1901** [**apple isle**] *Advocate* (Burnie) 3 Oct. 2/5 The term 'apple-land' and Tasmania grew to be synonymous. **1906** *Gadfly* (Adelaide) 7 Mar. 19/1 The apple isle still continues to *fête* Senator Keating and his bride. *Ibid.* 21 Mar. 17/3 The apple island still continues to attract a few stragglers from our city. **1914** H.M. VAUGHAN *Aus-*

tralasian Wander-Yr. 130 For Tasmania is essentially a land of the temperate zone, and the summer visitor to the 'Apple Isle' can revel in a profusion of the most luscious fruits. **1926** *Film Weekly* (Sydney) 14 Oct. 32 His return from the Apple Island. **1926** A. EDEN *Places in Sun* 74 To us in England Tasmania is, in the main, pictured as appleland. **1927** 'VIATOR' *From up along Down Under* 273 'The apple-land of Australia' as Tasmania claims to be. **1945** *Bulletin* (Sydney) 25 July 12/1 Following on the successful acclimatisation of the koala in Tasmania, the Apple Island received a consignment of lyre-birds. **1945** A. THURIAN *Bunyips & Bushland* 9 My apple isle, dearest Tassy. **1948** *Bulletin* (Sydney) 24 Mar. 28/2 Tasmania's oldest apple-tree .. is no more. Fierce gales and storms in the Apple Isle early this year were too strong for the veteran. **1965** R.H. CONQUEST *Horses in Kitchen* 141 Another bloke, Tassie, hailed from the Apple Isle. **1981** *Yates Garden Guide* (rev. ed.) 247 Wherever you live in Australia—sunny Queensland, the Apple Isle or any place in between—you can grow garden-fresh fruit. **1986** *Austral.* (Sydney) 23 Jan. 11/1 (*heading*) Clash of opposites in Apple Isle. **1914** [**apple islander**] *Truth* (Sydney) 15 Feb. 8/6 Three Applelanders arrived in Sydney this week. **1928** *Aussie* (Sydney) Apr. 15/3 The newly-arrived Apple Islander blinked his eyes nervously. 'Well, you're a disgrace to Tasmania!' he roared. **1982** J.A. SHARWOOD *Vocab. Austral. Dried Vine Fruits Industry* 3 Names for people from different states .. sandgropers, apple islanders [etc.]. **1801** *HRA* (1915) 1st Ser. III. 415 The timber on the low ground is principally blue-gum and **apple-tree**. **1805** J.H. TUCKEY *Acct. Voyage to establish Colony Port Phillip* 228 The apple-tree takes its name from the leaf, the limbs are large and crooked. **1820** J. OXLEY *Jrnls. Two Exped. N.S.W.* 187 That species of eucalyptus, which is vulgarly called the apple tree .. again made its appearance on the flats. **1829** R. MUDIE *Picture of Aust.* 150 The apple-tree of the colonists (*angophora lanceolata*) is of no value whatever as a fruit tree. **1830** R. DAWSON *Present State Aust.* 195 The resemblance of what are called apple-trees in Australia, to those of the same name at home, is so striking at a distance in these situations, that the comparison could not be avoided, although the former bear no fruit, and do not even belong to the same species. **1844** L. LEICHHARDT *Jrnl. Overland Exped. Aust.* 7 Oct. (1847) 9 The well-known tracks of the Blackfellows are everywhere visible; such as trees recently stripped of their bark, the swellings of the apple-tree cut off to make vessels for carrying water. **1852** G.C. MUNDY *Our Antipodes* II. 25 Pomona would indignantly disown the apple-tree, for there is not the semblance of a pippin on its tufted branches. **1869** H. KENDALL *Leaves from Austral. Forests* 34 The evening-coloured apple-trees Are faint with July's frosty breath. **1876** 'EIGHT YRS.' RESIDENT' *Queen of Colonies* 218 Rafters of small saplings are placed for the roof, and the whole is covered in with large sheets of bark of the stringy bark, turpentine, black-bull, or apple-tree. **1890** G.J. BROINOWSKI *Birds of Aust.* IV. Pl. 27, The wattled honey-eater .. builds, either on a branch of an Angophora (apple-tree), or in a bush. **1897** *Worker* (Sydney) 16 Oct. 6/1, I smoked some gum-leaves (an old lag camped and christened them apple-tree). **1938** C.T. WHITE *Princ. Bot. Qld. Farmers* 190 *Angophora* is closely allied to Eucalyptus... The two commonest and most widely spread are those trees known as Apple Trees (*A. subvelutina* and *A. intermedia*). **1967** A.M. BLOMBERY *Guide Native Austral. Plants* 252 The common name Apple Tree is chiefly confined to *Angophora*, but some species of *Eucalyptus* are also given this name.

4. *pl.* Rhyming slang for 'apples and spice' (or 'rice'), nice. Used *ellipt.* (esp. as **she's apples**), to indicate general approbation; all right, in good order.

1943 J. BINNING *Target Area* 140 If everything is running smoothly 'she's apples'. **1958** F.B. VICKERS *Mirage* 113 He pulled up his singlet and showed Freddie a blue mark and an indentation where his ribs had been crushed in. 'She's apples now, mate. But she wouldn't have been apples with me if that coon hadn't come along.' **1961** *Realist* (Sydney) vii. 5 Whenever Harry had taxed Barney about taking a serious stand, Barney had always repeated stubbornly, 'She's sweet for me', or 'I'm apples'. **1963** S. MUSSEN *Beating about Bush* 36 When I asked a conductor whether his bus went to Glebe and he replied, 'She's apples!', I knew it went in the right direction. **1965** K. TENNANT *Summer's Tales* 227 Stuck m'head under the tap. She's apples now. I'm sober. **1968** S. GORE *Holy Smoke* 35 God was just making sure the Jews'd all be apples when the whistle blew. **1970** R. BEILBY *No Medals for Aphrodite* 52 Suddenly the engine leapt alive... 'She's apples, George.' **1978** *Overland* lxxii. 16 'Is the fire safe .. ?' 'Yeah, she's apples.' **1979** B. HUMPHRIES *Bazza comes into his Own*, She's apples your Grace!

Arbitration. [Spec. use of *arbitration* settlement, with reference to industrial contexts.] Used *attrib.* in Special Comb. **arbitration award,** an award made by a court of industrial arbitration (see AWARD); **system,** the organization and method of the settling of industrial disputes, determining of awards, etc., federally and in the States.

1897 *Argus* (Melbourne) 7 Apr. 6/1 An unusual application was made to-day to the Chief Justice, sitting in Equity, that execution should issue against the Crown in respect to an unsettled **arbitration award. 1904** *Sydney Morning Herald* 30 Dec. 8/4 The class of work now being done at his colliery was not in evidence when the arbitration award was made. **1979** *Courier-Mail* (Brisbane) 5 Mar. 5/5 While arbitration awards were legally binding upon employers, labor was always entitled to strike for as much more as it thought it could get. **1920** E.G. THEODORE *Some Industr. Problems* 5 The criticism I speak of was mostly directed against the Commonwealth Government **arbitration system. 1971** *Canberra Times* 24 June 2/7, I believe that the institution of the arbitration system will endure in Australia. **1979** *Austral.* (Sydney) 16 Oct. 7/1 Australia's unique arbitration system grew out of the volatile industrial climate of the 1890s. **1980** *Canberra Times* 23 Dec. 7/5 The power of the whole arbitration system in Australia is now under attack from both the Government and the Public Service Board.

area school. A school formed by the amalgamation of several small rural schools, offering both primary and secondary education: see quot. 1974. Also *attrib.*

1940 *Educ. Studies & Investigations* (Austral. Council Educ. Research) 226 He paid two visits to Tasmania during 1939 in order to examine the working of the newly established Area Schools. **1942** *Tasmanian Area School* (Tas. Educ. Dept.) 28 The pupil who has satisfactorily completed the work of Grades VII and VIII is entitled to an Area School Certificate. **1950** C.E.W. BEAN *Here, my Son* 155 The most interesting experiment carried out by Australian schools is probably that of the Tasmanian (State) area schools. **1966** R.N. FARQUHAR *Agric. Educ. in Aust.* 49 In 1963 there were two main types of government secondary schools in Tasmania—high schools, and area schools. **1970** R.T. FITZGERALD *Secondary School at Sixes & Sevens* 97 Tasmania's area schools present a striking illustration of changing social aspiration. Founded a generation ago complete with their own farm lands, the area schools have enjoyed a great deal of autonomy in developing their own curricula. **1974** J. MCLAREN *Dict. Austral. Educ.* 27 Area School. The name used in Tasmania and South Australia for schools formed by the consolidation of a number of small rural schools, and offering both primary and secondary courses... The first area schools were established in Tasmania in 1936. **1980** A. BARCAN *Hist. Austral. Educ.* 298 From the beginning of 1957 first-year high school classes, organised on comprehensive lines, were introduced at three Area schools.

Argyle apple. [f. the name of *Argyle* County in the Goulburn district of N.S.W.] The small tree *Eucalyptus cinerea* (fam. Myrtaceae), native to a small area of N.S.W. and Vic., and cultivated as an ornamental; (formerly) the similar *E. pulverulenta.*

1867 W. WOOLLS *Contribution to Flora Aust.* 236 *E. pulverulenta*, and .. *E. cinerea* seem to be two varieties of the small tree usually called 'Argyle Apple'. It is similar in appearance to *Angophora subvelutina* or the 'Apple' of the colonists, as the leaves are opposite, and the bark furrowed and wrinkled. **1885**—*Plants of N.S.W.* 55 E. *pulverulenta* (including *E. cinerea*) is a small tree, very like the apple (Angophora) in its bark, and hence sometimes called 'Argyle Apple'. **1932** R.H. ANDERSON *Trees of N.S.W.* 65 Argyle Apple .. is distinguished by the rather striking bluish-grey or silvery appearance of the leaves. **1956** T.Y. HARRIS *Naturecraft in Aust.* 142 Argyle Apple .. often picturesque in habit, occurring on poor sandy and shaley soil in the southern parts of New South Wales and in Victoria. **1979** *Ecos* xix. 15/2 The other strongest performers are Argyle apple (*E. cinerea*) and the swamp gum (*E. ovata*).

aristotle. Rhyming slang for 'bottle'. Also **Arrystottle.**

1897 *Bulletin* (Sydney) 7 Aug. (Red Page), Bottle (of anything)—'Aristotle' .. rarely used, and only of late. **1936** K.L. SMITH *Sky Pilot's Last Flight* 29 He went on to explain that 'stripes and silk' mean milk, 'Aristotle'—bottle, 'Johnny Horner'—corner, and on through a lengthy list. **1965** *Kings Cross Whisper* (Sydney) Mar. 5/2 A free dozen aristotles on offer and no one to claim them. **1967** J. HIBBERD *White with Wire Wheels* (1970) 203 More beer, chaps... Must go and get another Aristotle. **1968** D. O'GRADY *Bottle of Sandwiches* 93 How about stickin' around till I knock off at seven, an' then we'll take a few Arrystottles out to your joint. **1985** H. GARNER *Postcards from Surfers* 68 They fought in the pub, and bloody McLaughlin had a fuckin' aristotle behind his back while poor Chappo had his fists up honourable like this.

arm. *Obs.* A narrow tract of open land projecting into forested and mountainous country, as a tributary valley.

1834 J.D. LANG *Hist. & Statistical Acct. N.S.W.* II. 108 The valley of the Wollombi .. is bounded on either side by mountain-ranges .. and throws off numerous *arms*, as the settlers call them, to the right and left, some of them extending for a distance of twenty or thirty miles among the mountains. These arms, as well as the principal valley, abound in excellent pasture. **1838** *Lit. News* (Sydney) 6 Jan. 225 The valley of Wollombi .. is bounded on either side by mountain ranges, covered with timber to their summits. Numerous valleys, or, as the settlers call them, *arms*, branch off on either side. **1874** R.W. MAYNE *Two Visions* 8 Inland in Australia 'arm' is used conversely to denote a continuation, or inlet as it were, of open land from a plain.

arse.

1. Dismissal (from employment). Also *fig.*

1955 *Overland* v. 4 We cleaned up that concreting before 9 a.m. only to get the arse just as Plugger had intended... He told us that if we cared to come back next week, there might be another couple of hours' work going. **1969** W. DICK *Naked Prodigal* 19 'What's up?' I asked. 'They give me the arse,' he answered loudly... 'They let me work right up till finishin' time without even tellin' me.' **1974** J. POWERS *Last of Knucklemen* 50 I'm not worth a day's pay a week. I'm lucky Tarzan doesn't give me the arse out of the place. **1978** J. DINGWALL *Sunday too far Away* 15 He wrote to me just when I'd decided to give the fish market the arse. **1983** L. CLANCY *Perfect Love* 238 She's been playing around with half the town. So I went home and gave her the arse.

2. Insolence, effrontery, 'cheek'.

1958 F. HARDY *Four-Legged Lottery* 188 See all the snooker balls going into the pockets—he had more arse than a married cow playing snooker, I can tell yer. **1960** 'N. CULOTTA' *Cop This Lot* 8 He laughs... A man would need plenty of arse to pinch another bloke's book. **1963** J. CANTWELL *No Stranger to Flame* 76 The johns'd never have the arse to frisk every house in a dump like this—people'd feel their word was being doubted. **1979** *Bulletin* (Sydney) 11 Sept. 86/3 Since the place was set up 25 years ago there have been less than 200 visitors in total and I only got there through sheer arse and lots of it.

arsehole, *v. trans.* To dismiss or get rid of (a person).

1965 W. DICK *Bunch of Ratbags* 153 It's orright when yuh young, but when yuh get a bit old and yuh can't keep up with the younger stickers .. they'll arsehole yuh. **1974** D. IRELAND *Burn* 125 They want to clear us right out. Arsehole us completely.

arsey, *a.* Also **arsie, arsy.** [Alteration of *tin arse* TIN *n.*[2] 2.] Lucky.

1953 S.J. BAKER *Aust. Speaks* 104 *Arsey*, lucky. **1960** J. WALKER *No Sunlight Singing* 23, I was real arsy to pick up a job here. **1968** S. GORE *Holy Smoke* 95 *Arsey*, lucky. **1977** R. BEILBY *Gunner* 87 She's apples. Now you just lie back an' take it easy. Ya got a homer, mate, you arsey bastard. **1978** T. DAVIES *More Austral. Nicknames* 25 *Arsie*, is very lucky at cards and raffles.

artesian. *a.* and *n.* [Spec. use of *artesian* of the type of well found in Artois.]

A. *adj.* In the collocation **artesian bore,** an artesian well; a well formed by drilling through impervious strata to tap water held under sufficient pressure to cause it to rise spontaneously to the surface. See BORE.

1897 R. NEWTON *Work & Wealth Qld.* 14 Artesian bores have been put down in numbers to tap these stores. **1910** *Huon Times* (Franklin) 27 July 4/2 The holdings comprise an area of 120,000 acres, well subdivided, and watered by two flowing artesian bores. **1914** E.F. PITTMAN *Great Austral. Artesian Basin* 5 An Artesian bore is one in which water is subject to a pressure sufficient to force it above the surface of the ground. **1942** H.H. PECK *Mem. of Stockman* 75 More artesian bores than on any other run in Australia, and some of them of great depth, with bore drains running out, and watering otherwise waterless country. **1955** F. LANE *Patrol to Kimberleys* 105 He snouted straight into an artesian bore. **1965** R.H. CONQUEST *Horses in Kitchen* 134 It was the artesian bore . . that made Queensland the rich pastoral State it is today. **1977** W.A. WINTER-IRVING *Bush Stories* 7 We passed a couple of artesian bores belching up hot water that came from hundreds of metres underground.

B. *n. transf.* A name for beer: see quot. 1892.

1892 K. LENTZNER *Dict. Slang-Eng. Aust.* 1 *Artesian*, colonial beer. People in Gippsland, Victoria, use *artesian* just as Tasmanians use *cascade*, in the sense of 'beer', because the one is manufactured from the celebrated *artesian* well at Sale, Gippsland, and the other from the *cascade* water. **1941** S.J. BAKER *Pop. Dict. Austral. Slang* 6 *Artesian*, beer, originally that made with artesian water at Sale, Gippsland. **1948** R. RAVEN-HART *Canoe in Aust.* 166 Another . . tried to entrap me into tasting the sulphuretted-hydrogen-loaded water—it gave Australia one of the slang names for beer, 'artesian', apparently because the beer made with this water was . . good.

artist. [Orig. U.S.: see OEDS 10.] A person practised or habitually engaged in an activity which requires little skill or is reprehensible; now esp. as final element in Comb., as **booze, bullshit artist**, etc. See also *grog artist* GROG *n.* 3, *fang artist* FANG *n.*[1] b., *stoush artist* STOUSH *n.* 3.

1889 J.L. HUNT *Bk. of Bonanzas* 9 The twenty-seven artists on the roof spat on their hands . . and pulled away at the rope. **1892** *Truth* (Sydney) 1 May 1/3 Imperialist and Jingoist and Chartist, Each in his pettifogging way an 'artist'. **1915** A. WRIGHT *Sport from Hollowlog Flat* 111 Dinan, highly pleased, turned his attention to his gang of pick and shovel artists. **1918** G.A. TAYLOR *Those were Days* 10 It merited the smart saying of a Bohemian that the Club was still a club of 'Writers' and 'Artists', from the fact that most of its members could easily write their names at the end of a cheque, but it was the work of an artist to get it cashed. **1927** J.M. WALSH *Man behind Curtain* 165 'I've never killed a man in my life,' he declared. 'I'm an artist, I am, not a thug.' **1929** F. MANNING *Middle Parts of Fortune* I. 54 Every bugger was trying to get the bayonet away from the other artist. **1938** X. HERBERT *Capricornia* 23 These men . . were what are called Booze Artists, fellows who can drink continuously without getting drunk. **1940** H. DRAKE-BROCKMAN *Men without Wives* (1955) 132 Scared I'll turn into a booze-artist if I'm left alone? **1951** CUSACK & JAMES *Come in Spinner* 308 And are they booze-artists! Boy, we thought we could put it away, but they beat us hollow. **1951** D. STIVENS *Jimmy Brockett* 20 'I was getting fitted for my ten suits.' 'You said six last time. . . You bull artist.' **1953** T.A.G. HUNGERFORD *Riverslake* 3 Urgers, touts, bludgers, bash-artists and straight-out crooks. **1966** D. NILAND *Pairs & Loners* 13 Pig's bum to your reputation! Get your hands up now, you big bull artist. **1969** F. MOORHOUSE *Futility & Other Animals* 97, I was a bullshit artist and I wrote bullshit letters. **1969** A. BUZO *Rooted* (1973) 78 What a lot of bull-artists. Bloody scientists. What were they doing in an art gallery, anyway? **1979** C. STONE *Running Brumbies* 55 The stationhands on Lyndhurst and surrounding properties were a good bunch but I'd never met such a mob of booze-artists. **1981** F. HARDY *Who shot George Kirkland?* 141 The greatest bullshit artist who ever poked his head through a bridle.

art union. [Spec. use of *art union* a union of persons for the purpose of promoting art, orig. by subscription to the purchase of works of art, which were then distributed among the subscribers by lottery: see OED(S *art* V, and also quots. 1841 and 1846.] A lottery organized to raise funds for a charity or public cause, with prizes in cash or kind. Also *attrib.*

[**1841** *Sydney Herald* 15 Dec. 3/3 The Subscribers to *Mr Felton's Art Union*, who have not paid their subscriptions, are respectfully requested to do so without delay, as the distribution of the Paintings will take place as soon as the above is complied with. **1846** *Sydney Morning Herald* 9 Jan. 2/5 *Art Union*—The first distribution of pictures in the colony by this, now in England, very popular medium, came off at the Court House on Monday. The Art Union had its origin in Mr Howard Bower, the artist, being desirous to proceed to England as early as possible, and finding it impossible to find eight-and-twenty purchasers for as many pictures at any thing like remunerating prices, hit on the present idea. . . Sixty subscribed at £1 1s. each, entered for the chances of the eight-and-twenty prizes.] **1849** *Ibid.* 27 Nov. 1/4 The undersigned guarantees the respective sums of £50 and £40 to the drawers of the 1st and 2nd Prizes, in his Art Union. **1872** *Argus* (Melbourne) 8 Feb. 6/1 The latest novelty in 'art unions' has been discovered by the Glendaruel Society, which proposes to distribute amongst the members several pigs and fowls, besides watches and agricultural implements. **1893** *Ibid.* 17 Mar. 6/3 Senior-Constable Gleeson . . has completed his enquiries concerning the art union held by the Australian Natives' Association at the Exhibition-Building on Foundation Day. **1897** *Bulletin* (Sydney) 7 Aug. 24/2 The one just past probably absorbed £7000 of public money, of which £1700 went to the charities, £1500 went in art-union prizes, the balance being swallowed up in bicycle prizes and expenses—chiefly expenses. **1902** *Truth* (Sydney) 2 Feb. 5/6 Then there is the art union man, a *smart-spoken spieler*, who talks half-crowns out of silly women's kicks as easily as a penny-pinching parson talks the 'trays' into the plate. **1903** *Ibid.* 7 June 2/5 Why a wretched lottery that does not, in the slightest degree, encourage or assist Art should be called an 'art union', we are at a loss to understand. **1919** T.G. RABBETS *Whimplin Whimsies* 45 Now that it is all over, and I have not been gazetted as having won the first or any subsequent prize in the Golden Casket Art Union, I desire to add my voice to those who are kicking against this art union. **1960** S. WOODFIELD *A for Artemis* 53 The ambulance art union was in full swing. Carnival held sway. **1966** *Courier-Mail* (Brisbane) 5 May 3/11 A Scottish couple . . yesterday won first prize in a Queensland consultation, the Scarborough art union. **1977** *National Times* (Sydney) 17 Jan. 36/6, $60,000 . . is expected to come from the proceeds of an art union for which Volvo has donated a top-of-the-range saloon, a boat and five outboard motors.

arvo /'avoʊ/. [Modified pronunc. of *af(ternoon* + -O.]

1. Afternoon. Esp. in the phr. **this arvo**. Also *attrib.* See SARVO.

1927 *Sunday Sun* (Sydney) 9 Oct. (Sunbeams Suppl.) 1, I told young 'Ocker' Stevens to come up and say that so I could go shooting with him with his new pea rifle this arvo. **1933** *Bulletin* (Sydney) 6 Dec. 42/1 The flicker in his chest heaved once up into tumult and was still, the shell of Grandfer being alone on the beach this Sunday arvo. **1945** M. RAYMOND *Smiley* 30 Please, sir, I'll 'elp you with the bees this arvo. **1957** 'N. CULOTTA' *They're Weird Mob* 41 Pat said, 'You comin' back this arvo?' 'Yeah. See yer about four.' **1960** J. WYNNUM *Sailor Blushed* (1962) 81 I've really got a prize-winning thirst this arvo. **1963** D. ATTENBOROUGH *Quest under Capricorn* 130 We had already relished the local taste for amputating words, whereby an afternoon became an 'arvo' and an oiling and greasing, a 'lube'. **1965** G. MCINNES *Road to Gundagai* 123 You the lads making a nuisance of yourselves up at the High Street corner this arvo? **1977** A. MACKAY *Life Pieces* II. 81 He cruises the school on sports arvos in his kinky car. **1978** B. ST. A. SMITH *Spirit beyond Psyche* 20 You an' me, like, when we retire, we can go down t' the RSL of an arvo an' grog on regardless. **1980** E. METCALFE *Garden Party* 98 You remember the time you popped out for *two* minutes—to get me cakes for 'arvo tea'—or whatever? **1981** K. MCARTHUR *Bread & Dripping Days* 19 Saturday was children-cleaning day in the morning and children visiting day in the afternoon (never 'arvo' for that was unpermissable slang), when other children came to play.

2. Afternoon tea (but see quot. 1972).

1950 A.W. UPFIELD *Widows of Broome* 42 He hoped the 'arvo' would soon be served. **1972** *Bulletin* (Sydney) 17 June 62/3 The watercress salad and cheeses came with a masked bottle, which was voted the top wine of the 'baked arvo'.

ash. [See quot. 1957.] Any of many trees, usu. of the genus *Eucalyptus* (fam. Myrtaceae), yielding a valuable timber; the timber, which is typically pale, strong, and straight-grained. Also *attrib.*, and with distinguishing epithet, as **alpine, mountain, red, white** (see under first element).

1801 *HRA* (1915) 1st Ser. III. 170 Here [*sc.* Ash Island] we found plenty of different sorts of wood, and the ash trees of considerable magnitude. **1803** J. GRANT *Narr. Voyage N.S.W.* 159 The ash cut on Ash Island is not . . so light as English Ash. **1841** *Geelong Advertiser* 5 June 4/3 Various kinds of native oak, pine, ash. **1888** *Sydney Morning Herald* 24 Jan. (Centennial Suppl.) 1/6 The finest trees in the Northern districts are the Flindersia, commonly called the ash, and the . . bean tree. **1895** *Proc. Linnean Soc. N.S.W.* X. 585 *Albizzia (Pithecolobium) muelleriana* . . locally known as 'Ash'. **1896** A. MACKAY *Austral. Agriculturist* (rev. ed.) 297 The Australian ash tree is different from the ash of Great Britain; ours is a gum. **1926** A. EDEN *Places in Sun* 72 The ash or swamp-gum towers to 300 feet and more, a glorious, gracious tree. **1957** *Forest Trees Aust.* (Cwlth. Forestry & Timber Bureau) 132 The ash group of eucalypts . . includes some of the most important timber trees of Australia . . . The name 'ash' was applied in the early days of settlement because of a superficial resemblance of the timber to that of the European ash (*Fraxinus* spp.) Botanically, however, there is no close relationship between the two groups of trees.

Ashes. *Cricket.* [See quot. 1882. Recorded earliest in Aust.] The symbolic trophy awarded to the winner of a series of test matches played periodically between Australia and England; the actual wooden urn containing the ashes of a cricket stump and remaining permanently at Lord's Cricket Ground, headquarters of the Marylebone Cricket Club. Chiefly in the phr. **the Ashes.** Also *transf.* (see quot. 1948).

[**1882** *Sporting Times* (London) 2 Sept., In Affectionate Remembrance of English Cricket Which died at the Oval on 29th August, 1882. Deeply lamented by a large circle of sorrowing friends and acquaintances. R.I.P. N.B.—The body will be cremated and the ashes taken to Australia.] **1883** BEESTON & MASSIE *St. Ivo & Ashes* 3 Mr Bligh humorously declared that he and his eleven had come to 'beard the kangaroo in his den, and try to recover *those* ashes.' *Ibid.* 8 So the battle for the 'ashes' was over, and once more the Englishmen had regained their lost supremacy in the cricket field. **1903** *Sporting News* (Launceston) 19 Sept. 2/3 The ashes of English cricket remain in Australia. **1912** *Truth* (Sydney) 18 Feb. 1/7 We're just at present in a sorry plight, Our sun at noonday plunged in sudden night, Our cricket's dead, and we've a lesson learned, And only ashes now Australia's 'urned'. **1934** *Austral. Ring* IX. iii. 8 The term 'Ashes' had not been thought of at that early period in its application to cricket. **1947** *Sydney Morning Herald* 6 Mar. 8/4 Compton and Hutton found their best form too late to have any great influence upon the destination of the 'ashes'. **1948** *Australs.' Tour Official Souvenir* (Rugby Football League) 4, I am told that the Australian Rugby League side, the 'Kangaroos', hope to win back the 'Ashes' from England this year. **1961** S.C. CAPLE *Ashes at Stake* 211 Even Australian supporters were glad that for the ultimate good of the game the 'Ashes' had at last returned to England. **1981** *Sydney Morning Herald* 16 July 36/4 The Australians are confident that they can repeat their Trent Bridge win and take a firm grip on the Ashes.

assign, *v. Hist. trans.* To make over the services (of a convict) to a private individual. Occas. with services as obj.

1789 *Hist. Rec. N.S.W.* I. ii. 258 It is Our Will and Pleasure, that in case there should be a prospect of their employing any of the said convicts to advantage, that you assign to each grantee the service of any number of them. **1791** P.G. KING Jrnl. Norfolk Island 12 Nov. 2 The service of convicts to be assigned them on its appearing that such Settlers can Maintain, Feed, Cloath, and Employ them to advantage. **1800** *Gen. Orders* 31 Oct., Officers and others, to whom the Labour of Prisoners is assigned, are to conform to the following conditions. **1801** *HRA* (1915) 1st Ser. III. 253 Every person, civil and military, to whom the labour of prisoners victualled from public stores is assigned. **1804**

Ibid. 1st Ser. V. 89 The best behaved convicts will continue . . being assigned to such settlers as may prefer continuing on Norfolk Island. **1812** *Ibid.* (1916) 1st Ser. VII. 614, I always Assign as Many of them to Married Settlers, as Servants, as Can be disposed of in that Way. **1817** *Hobart Town Gaz.* 27 Sept., Settlers who are desirous of having Crown Servants assigned off the Store, are requested to send in Applications. **1822** J.T. BIGGE *Rep. State Colony N.S.W.* 16 Those who are not so allotted, are distributed amongst the public works at or near Hobart Town, and are afterwards assigned, as they are applied for, by the settlers, the application being invariably made to the lieutenant-governor. **1826** *HRA* (1919) 1st Ser. XII. 252 No Convict will be assigned to any non-resident Settler. **1828** *Blossom* (Sydney) i. 62 It was in the power of the Superintendent . . to assign women from the Factory as servants. **1831** H. SAVERY *Quintus Servinton* III. 186 When married men were joined by their wives . . the latter, in capacity of free settlers, claimed their husbands to be assigned to them, thus virtually removing many of the pains of transportation. **1833** *HRA* (1923) 1st Ser. XVII. 202 To assign a shipload of 200 Convicts occupies from 5 to 6 hours of constant and assiduous attention. **1837** *Rep. Select Committee Transportation* 294 When you say the mechanical convicts have not been assigned lately, you mean they have not been permanently assigned?—Yes; they are assigned on loan. **1837** J. MUDIE *Felonry of N.S.W.* 54 General Darling had reclaimed a convict servant who had been *lent*, not assigned, to a free emigrant in Sydney. **1840** A. RUSSELL *Tour through Austral. Colonies* 108 Farmers usually get convict labourers assigned to them by government, which is of much consequence, where free labour is yet scarce. **1840** *HRA* (1924) 1st Ser. XXI. 16 With respect to the discontinuance of the system of Assigning Convicts. **1843** *Ibid.* (1925) 1st Ser. XXIII. 92 Heretofore it had been the custom to assign Convicts, whose ultimate destination was Norfolk Island, to the Lt. Governor of Van Diemen's Land. **1847** R. WELCH *Convict & Free Labour* 19 Until convicts were assigned in New South Wales, they were employed on Government and Colonial works. **1858** C. ROWCROFT *Tales of Colonies* 216 Shortly after my landing, I was assigned to a very good master. **1863** C. GIBSON *Life among Convicts* II. 216 The Act 5 Geo. IV. c. 84, gave the governor of a penal colony a *property* in the services of a transported convict, and authorized him to assign the prisoner to any other person. **1865** *Glenorchy Murders* 7 He was sentenced to seven years' transportation. Under this sentence he arrived in Tasmania . . on the 31st July, 1852. . . Soon after his arrival he was assigned to Mr Turnley. . . While in his assigned service he frequently manifested habits of intemperance. **1871** M. CLARKE *Old Tales of Young Country* 89 The convicts in their prison clothes were landed and marched up to the prisoners' barracks . . and in due course 'assigned'.

assignable, *a. Hist.* Of a convict: eligible to be assigned to a private individual.

1829 Tas. Colonial Secretary's Office Rec. 1/32 198 It has to supply not only the Washerwomen belonging to the Assignable Class, but also those in the Crime Class with hot water. **1834** *Austral. Almanack* 140 Convicts . . returned by their respective masters with complaints touching their conduct, are to be considered as 'probationary', and not assignable . . for six months. **1839** *Tasmanian Weekly Dispatch* (Hobart) 4 Oct. 7/4 State of the Female House of Correction at Hobart Town. . . Number assignable for Hobart Town, 19. **1842** *Colonial Observer* (Sydney) 16 Feb. 159/2 There are at present a number of female servants in the factory assignable. **1850** *Britannia* (Hobart) 4 July 4/4 The introduction of convicts under the new name of assignable passholders. ***c* 1860** 'PRISON CHAPLAIN' *Life T. Jones* 37 The six months passed away without any report against me, and I was once more 'assignable'.

assigned, *ppl. a. Hist.*

1. Of a convict: made over into the service of a private individual. Also applied to convict service and with **out.**

1806 *Sydney Gaz.* 16 Mar., Any *assigned Prisoner* off the Stores with Individuals, who do not appear as above will . . be sentenced. **1814** L. MACQUARIE *Let.* 10 Sept. (1821) 88 Ticket of Leave Men are to muster on the right of Assigned Government Men. **1825** *Tasmanian* (Hobart) 12 Jan. 2/2 Mr Rose, having occasion to require the services of Samuel Davies, an assigned Crown servant, called out. **1834** J. BACKHOUSE *Extracts from Lett.* (1838) ii. 40 Men, whom from their appearance, we judged to be soldiers and assigned prisoner-servants. **1842** *Colonial Observer* (Sydney) 7 Dec. 662/4 Within the last few days, three assigned men have taken the bush from one farm alone. **1845** *Southern Queen* (Sydney) 66/1 That the assigned labour of the convict in town and country has been most beneficial to the colony we have never heard disputed. **1854** *Illustr. Sydney News* 11 Nov. 356/3 The master is bound to keep his assigned woman clothed and in return has a full right to all the services which he can exact from her. **1879** C.P. WILLIAMS *Southern Sunbeams* 13 Do you wish to stay here, like this, and to die, nothing but an assigned-out lag? **1928** 'BRENT OF BIN BIN' *Up Country* (1966) 20 Mazere . . with the aid of several assigned men as bullock-drivers, made the pilgrimage.

2. In collocations: **assigned convict, convict servant, servant, service.**

1827 *HRA* (1920) 1st Ser. XIII. 137 The **Assigned Convicts** are on all occasions forwarded by the Government to the Persons, to whom they are assigned. **1831** *Ibid.* (1923) 1st Ser. XVI. 34 The tax, proposed by them, is only ten shillings a year for each assigned convict. **1839** *Port Phillip Gaz.* 4 Dec. 3 The Governor said there were now 25,000 assigned convicts. **1854** MRS C. CLACY *Lights & Shadows* II. 192 They had with them two men and one woman as servants, all assigned convicts. **1862** BACKHOUSE & TYLOR *Life & Labours G.W. Walker* 54 The term of servitude for the assigned convict varied according to his sentence of transportation. **1824** E. CURR *Acct. Colony Van Diemen's Land* 160 Colonial regulations touching the summary jurisdiction of magistrates over the relation of master and **assigned convict servants.** **1834** 'EMIGRANT' *Party Politics Exposed* 31 The open turbulence and desperate demeanour of certain assigned convict servants. **1840** *HRA* (1924) 1st Ser. XXI. 88 The Government has a claim on you for One hundred and forty Nine Bushels of Maize for the Services of assigned Convict Servants. **1847** J.D. LANG *Phillipsland* 68 The masters of assigned convict-servants in New South Wales were allowed to carry these servants along with them if they removed. **1817** *Regulations respecting Assigned Convict Servants* 28 Mar. (1821) 5 **Assigned Servants** will clearly understand, that the Settler or Inhabitant to whom they are appropriated by Government has a Right to their extra Time for the Wages above specified. **1819** *Hobart Town Gaz.* 1 May, The Settlers are apprized that they are prohibited from allowing their assigned Servants to go on their own Hands. **1827** *Monitor* (Sydney) 27 Aug. 611 Seventy five convict labourers, were forwarded to Parramatta on Saturday for distribution among the numerous applicants for assigned servants. **1835** 'IMPARTIAL OBSERVER' *Illustr. Present State N.S.W.* 52 There are masters, who give their assigned servants (prisoners) regular wages. **1839** *Port Phillip Patriot* 20 May 7 The wives of emigrant farm labourers, are not proof against the seductive arts of assigned and emancipist servants, when living on the same establishments. **1848** C. COZENS *Adventures of Guardsman* 156 The extent to which tyranny was formerly carried on with regard to the assigned servants throughout the Colony, is almost incredible. **1866** *Austral. Monthly Mag.* (Melbourne) III. 205 Dreadful deeds of crime done by 'the assigned servants'. **1891** W.B. DEAN *Notorious Bushrangers* 31 And from persons whom he robbed he distributed tobacco amongst their assigned servants. **1931** *Century of Journalism* 14 The 'assigned servant'—otherwise the convict handed over for a term to work in legalised slavery for some free settler or public official—laboured everywhere against odds for his ticket-of-leave. **1970** *Sunday Mail Mag.* (Brisbane) 1 Mar. 12/6 Assigned servants (convicts) in the area had become quite undisciplined through lack of supervision. **1818** *Hobart Town Gaz.* 28 Mar., The Lieutenant Governor makes known his intention of sending up to Port Jackson, to be placed in the Factory there, such Female Prisoners as . . cannot be continued in **Assigned Service.** **1837** *HRA* (1923) 1st Ser. XIX. 96 Some intermediate step is required between a Chain Gang and assigned service. **1839** *Sydney Standard* 7 Jan. 2/2 Gross and Glaring partiality . . has been exercised in the Assigned Service system. **1840** *Tasmanian Weekly Dispatch* 24 Jan. 4/3 The assigned service plan we never could see the least reasonable excuse for continuing. **1865** *Glenorchy Murders* 7 While in his assigned service he frequently manifested habits of intemperance. **1900** *Bulletin* (Sydney) 13 Jan. 14/2 Old hands still point out the spot where a famous 'bolter' from his assigned service made his home in the bush.

assignee. *Hist.* A person to whom the services of a convict are made over. Also *attrib.*

1825 *HRA* (1917) 1st Ser. XI. 496 His labor belongs to the Crown and the Crown's Assignees. **1830** *Ibid.* (1922) 1st Ser. XV. 352 The Convict, being no longer the property of the original Assignee, is of necessity once more at the disposal of the Governor. **1834** *Austral. Almanack* 142 Assignees of convict servants will be allowed to lend them to free and respectable individuals. **1835** *Tegg's N.S.W. Pocket Almanac* (1838) 85 The Sessions, or Magistrate, as the case may be, shall not recommend as assignee for Convict servants of any description, any person who is not free, of good character, capable of maintaining the servants applied for, and to whose care and management they may not in their, or his opinion, be safely entrusted. **1843** *Sydney Morning Herald* 23 Aug. 3/5 No convict assigned under these regulations . . shall be permitted to remain within the limits of the town of Sydney for more than one week at any one time . . upon pain of such servants being withdrawn, and the assignee considered incapable of receiving convict servants in future.

assignment. *Hist.*

1. The making over to a private individual of the services of a convict; the state of being so placed.

1822 T. REID *Two Voyages N.S.W. & Van Diemen's Land* 252 The Superintendent of convicts is . . perfectly apprized of everything requisite for directing a just and satisfactory assignment of the prisoners. **1826** *HRA* (1922) 3rd Ser. V. 231 The number of Convicts in Van Diemen's Land is so limited that their Assignment to Settlers is a matter of favor. **1829** *Ibid.* 1st Ser. XIV. 767 The Governor may revoke the assignment of a Convict Servant made to A and reassign him to B. **1835** T.B. WILSON *Narr. Voyage round World* 295 It is to be distinctly understood that whenever the word 'Assignment' is used by the Government, with reference to convict servants, it is intended to imply merely a temporary appropriation of their services. **1840** *Tasmanian Weekly Dispatch* 7 Feb. 7/1 An assigned servant, was returned to the Crown for assignment in the interior. **1843** *Sydney Morning Herald* 15 Sept. 2/3 Assignment, whether for good or for evil, exists no longer. **1845** *HRA* (1845) 1st Ser. XXIV. 250 Of these Convicts, one half at least have been placed in what is called 'Assignment' (a species of domestic Slavery) as Servants to the Settlers. **1856** J. BONWICK *Bushrangers* 37 He also required a place as an intermediate penitentiary, where those who had been in gangs of punishment could be drafted for a time, previous to their transmission to Hobart Town for assignment.

2. Comb. **assignment system.**

1838 *Colonist* (Sydney) 10 Jan. 2/2 In regard to the Assignment System, *Dr Lang* gave it as his opinion that it ought to be discontinued forthwith. **1844** *Colonial Times* (Hobart) 27 Feb., While transportation was limited to the arrival of as many convicts in the year as that best of all means of providing for them, the assignment system could dispose of, the settlers were happy to receive them. **1845** *Sentinel* (Sydney) 15 Jan. 2/5 The merciful assignment system wrought well both for master and 'government man' in every important respect. **1854** W. SHAW *Land of Promise* 46 The leading principles of the old 'assignment system' were that those banished for offences against the laws of the mother country, should be made serviceable to Infant Settlements. **1871** M. CLARKE *Old Tales of Young Country* 124 There is no need to expatiate upon the 'assignment system'.

assimilation.

1. The acceptance, by non-British immigrant minorities, of Australian cultural values; the integration of such minorities into Australian society.

1927 J. LYNG *Non-Britishers in Aust.* 105 The question of 'assimilation' has of late been raised in Australia, more frequently in connection with Italian immigrants than with any other foreign nationals. **1942** W.D. FORSYTH *Myth of Open Spaces* 190 Northern Europeans have a long tradition of assimilation into Australian life. **1953** H.E. HOLT *Aust. & Migrant* 156 Assimilation is a two way process as we now realize and naturally we are interested in what migrants are going to do to us. **1956** A. LODEWYCKX *People for Aust.* 172 The experience of assimilation in the last 10 years is most encouraging. **1965** R. TAFT *From Stranger to Citizen* 34 The degree of assimilation of the children was . . greater than that of their parents. **1977** *Ethnic Studies* I. iii. 3 In the post-war period, the assimilation model has become increasingly difficult to sustain.

2. The integration of Aborigines into white Australian society: see quots. Also *attrib.*

1951 *CPD* (H. of R.) CCXIV. 875 Assimilation means, in practical terms, that, in the course of time, it is expected that all persons of Aboriginal blood or mixed blood in Australia will live as do white Australians. **1963** *Aboriginal Welfare* (Conference Cwlth. & State Ministers) 3 The policy of assimilation means that all Aborigines and part-Aborigines will attain the same manner of living as other Australians and live as members of a single Australian community enjoying the same rights and privileges, accepting the same responsibilities, observing the same customs and influenced by the same beliefs, hopes and loyalties as other Australians. **1978** C.H. & R.M. BERNDT *Pioneers & Settlers* 125 The word 'assimilation' was interpreted in various ways, but in practice it was always intended to mean absorption. **1980** L.R. SMITH *Aboriginal Pop. Aust.* 3 The new official policy of preservation and protection as a prelude to assimilation gained acceptance. **1984** P. READ *Down there with me on Cowra Mission* 129 What did you make of the Assimilation policy? I think its a load of crap.

assisted, *ppl. a.* Of or pertaining to Government-subsidized immigration to Australia.

1848 *HRA* (1925) 1st Ser. XXVI. 578 We propose sending out Assisted Emigrants as they are passed, in the Ships we charter for the conveyance of the Free Emigrants. **1855** R. CALDWELL *Gold Era Vic.* 87 In 1853, out of 14,578 assisted emigrants, no fewer than 6737 . . could not write. **1861** W. WESTGARTH *Aust.* 249 The plan for the present is one of 'assisted emigration', by which, on payment in the colony of a sum equal to about from one-half to one-fourth of the usual fare, on the part of friends or employers of intending emigrants, the colonial government pays the remainder. **1863** *Lett. from Emigrants* 18 The new system of *assisted passages*, as given by the Queensland Government, is now in full working . . the class of persons eligible for Assisted Passages, are Farm Laborers, Mechanics, and Female Domestic Servants. **1871** *Austral. Handbk.* 44 Assisted emigration to Tasmania is effected by means of 'Bounty Tickets', which are procurable in the colony, or from . . the emigration agent . . in London. **1881** W. ALLEN *Immigration & Co-op. Settlement* 23 The idlers, the loafers, and ne'er-do-wells of the United Kingdom are shipped off, by the help of public subscription, as *assisted* emigrants, and the best of the joke is that these *assisted* emigrants are persons who pay £1 for their kit, the free emigrants getting their kit free. **1890** W.F. BUCHANAN *Aust. to Rescue* 23 Assisted emigration was liberally encouraged by our governments until lately. **1896** J.M. PRICE *Land of Gold* 180 The Government grant assisted passages to Western Australia to nominated immigrants, upon the payment of £7 10s. per adult by sailing vessel. **1912** *Cwlth. of Aust. for Farmers* (Dept. External Affairs) 94 *Assisted immigrants*—Approved immigrants can obtain a passage from London to any port in Queensland for £5, provided they deposit with the Agent-General the sum of £50 as a guarantee that they have some means of support. This sum is refunded to the immigrant upon arrival in Queensland. **1932** *Brit. Migrants' Case for Repatriation* (Brit. Migrant Movt. S.A.) 4 This *country is not ready for assisted migrants* of any kind, having regard to the enormous number of Australians who are unemployed. **1963** *Bulletin* (Sydney) 3 Aug. 5/3 A young Englishman . . hears of the £10 Assisted Passage scheme, and his problem is solved. **1972** ANDERSON & BLAKE *J.S. Neilson* 7 After his compulsory two years shepherding as an assisted migrant. **1984** *Yr. Bk. Aust.* 112 From May 1981 the grant of assisted passage was restricted to refugees.

attendance money: see APPEARANCE MONEY.

attle. *S.A. Obs.* Also **addle**. [Cornish mining *attle* mine refuse: see EDD *attle* and *addle*.] Earth or rock which contains no ore; refuse from a mine; MULLOCK *n.* 1.

1850 *S. Austral. Register* (Adelaide) 2 July 2/5 And have spoiled to (many eyes) the appearance of these places, by putting in the addle, but they have nevertheless left ore in sight. **c 1860** 'AURIFERA' *Victorian Miners' Man.* 101 *Attle*, deads. Unproductive stone. **1865** *Wallaroo Times* (Kadina) 23 Sept. 5/2 The 48 stopemen are putting in stull and loading the same with addle. **1914** *Wallaroo & Moonta Mines* 12 Crushed waste rock, locally known as 'attle'. **1962** O. PRYOR *Aust.'s Little Cornwall* 35 When the ore was brought up to the surface, it was sorted by 'pickey boys' under the supervision of a 'grass captain', or surface boss. They graded it into 'prill' (rich ore), 'alvins' (low grade), and 'attle' (waste).

aunty. *Aboriginal English.* Used as a mode of address: see quot. 1963.

1963 D.E. BARWICK *Little more than Kin* 287 'Aunty' . . and 'coz' are here significant terms of address. . . Aunty is used as a courtesy title of address and reference for older women belonging to the same regional population, regardless of their genealogical connection to the speaker. **1980** *N.S.W. Parl. Papers* (1980–81) 3rd Sess. IV. 1794 The teachers are not just their teachers; they are their aunties. They are part of the extended family process that Aborigines have always kept. All the teachers are called auntie. It was a bit awkward for the European teachers when they first came. *Ibid.* 2007, I consider myself an elder when these people around the area call me auntie. This is an indication of my eldership. They expect me to give them my thoughts and pass on information to them.

Aurora Australis. [mod. L. 'the southern lights' (OED 1741) by analogy with *aurora borealis* the northern lights.] An illumination of the night sky occurring in a belt about the southern magnetic pole and irregularly visible, esp. in southern parts of Australia.

1788 J. WHITE *Jrnl. Voyage N.S.W.* (1790) 214 About half after six in the evening, we saw an aurora australis, a phenomenon uncommon in the southern hemisphere. **1841** *Sydney Herald* 19 Apr. 2/3 *Aurora Australis.* On the evening of the 10th instant, between the hours of eight and eleven, we had a very beautiful display of the 'polar lights'. **1843** *Colonial Observer* (Sydney) 4 Mar. 859/2 On Thursday night, a faint Aurora Australis, was visible in Sydney. **1846** J.L. STOKES *Discoveries in Aust.* I. 233 On our first arrival at Swan River in November last, we saw the Aurora Australis very bright. **1854** F. ELDERSHAW *Aust. as it really Is* 59 Aurora Australis . . rose in the shape of a low and long-extended arch of pale yellow light. **1870** *Illustr. Sydney News* 26 Oct. 66/1 A most beautiful Aurora Australis was visible at Sydney. The whole of the Heavens to the S.S.E. of the city was of a bright crimson—throughout which all the stars remained distinctly visible. **1917** *Huon Times* (Franklin) 14 Aug. 3/5 The Aurora Australis reported to have been observed throughout the island on Thursday last was also witnessed here by many residents shortly before seven o'clock. **1937** D. GLASS *Austral. Fantasy* 109 Stars bright as Aurora Australis dust the black velvet of the sky. **1953** D. STIVENS *Gambling Ghost* 10 It is like looking at a giant maypole or about a dozen Auroras-Australis. **1983** B. CORBETT *Fistful of Buttercups* 118 'It could be the aurora australis,' said my father. . . Sure enough, there was a faint flickering in the southern sky.

Aus, var. Oz.

Aussie /ˈɒzi/, *n.* and *attrib.* Also **Aussey, Ossie, Ozzie.** [f. AUS(TRALIA or AUS(TRALIAN + -Y.]

A. *n.*

1. Australia.

1915 G.F. MOBERLY *Experiences 'Dinki Di' R.R.C. Nurse* (1933) 30 A farewell dance for the boys going home to 'Aussie' tomorrow. **1917** P. AUSTEN *Bill-Jim* 5 Well, I'm back again in Aussie. **1918** *Kia Ora Coo-ee* June 4/3 Say, Sir, this leave pass is for Cairo, can't you alter it to Aussie? **1920** T.E. TAYLOR *Peregrinations* 7 To men mostly used to the open-air life and the wide spaces of 'dear old Aussie' it was a terrible time. **1924** 'TWINKLER' *Happy Days* 136 Ginger was very sentimental. He was always talking the dear old 'Aussie' stunt; and the wattle-blossom was heavy on his mind. **1941** M.L. SKINNER *WX* 3 The young girls are more forward here than they are in old Aussie. **1953** G.H. FEARNSIDE *Bayonets Abroad* 163 The Wagga men now prepared to travel, as their own sheep had travelled back in dear old Aussie in the almost forgotten days of peace. **1954** J. CLEARY *Climate of Courage* 126 Me, I believe in Aussie for the Aussies! **1965** G. MCINNES *Road to Gundagai* 35 People with complaints were so glad to be back in dear old Aussie that they forgot their troubles. **1969** G. JOHNSTON *Clean Straw for Nothing* (1971) 165 'But how do you get on living with these bloody Wogs?' the spokesman wanted to know. . . 'You ought to get back to good old Aussie, you know.' **1973** J. POWERS *Last of Knucklemen* (1974) 55 We're the first bit of Aussie they see comin' in. An' the last goin' out. Sometimes you can see the planes as clear as you like. Miles up.

2. An Australian; orig. an Australian soldier serving in the war of 1914–18. Also *fig.*

1918 *Truth* (Sydney) 28 July 6/5 We consider the term Aussie or Ossie as evolved is a properly picturesque and delightfully descriptive designation of the boys who have gone forth from Australia. **1918** N.P.H. NEAL *Back to Bush* 20 Seven little Aussies came to France with Nix, Started a two-up school, Then there were six. **1918** *Kia Ora Coo-ee* Dec. 5/1 The Maorilanders applied the term to members of the A.I.F. soon after arrival in France implying that the Aussies were real dinkum mates. **1919** C.H. THORP *Handful of Ausseys* p. xiii, I have endeavoured to picture the Aussey as he really is—a lovable, humorous, if somewhat crude product of the great Commonwealth. **1919** C.A. SMITH *New Words Self-Defined* 15 The fondness between the soldiers was mutual. There was nothing an Ozzie liked so much as fighting with a Yankee company. **1925** E. MCDONNELL *My Homeland* 68, I have often noticed Jacky in the Sydney parks, where the little Aussie has to battle with the pommy pest—the English house sparrow. **1932** R.W. THOMPSON *Down Under* 21 A 'dinkie die Aussie'; she looked as if she was capable of anything. **1946** 'A. SPENCE' *Mystery of Red Gum* 210 'It's not so bad in the summer, but the winter's a fair cow.' 'She's getting quite an Aussie, is Mrs Turner.' **1951** R.H. WHITECROSS *Slaves* 235 The game was tough and rugged, but we were Aussies, and we didn't moan. **1955** F. LANE *Patrol to Kimberleys* 48 'And how do you like Australia?' Constable Norton asked politely. 'I think you Aussies ought to give it back to the abos,' Glen said with a grin. **1956** 'A.B.C.' *What is A?* 4 An Aussie is truth with a sunburned face—reassurance with a grin a mile wide and the hope of the future—heading for a game of Swy! **1963** V.B. CRANLEY *27,000 Miles through Aust.* 147 A thin, spare, rather angular body with a stiff-gaited walk. . . Upright, with shoulders well back, a longish angular face deeply lined, a prominent nose, all in a sort of reddish coppery hue with little blue veins. Blue eyes staring straight at you . . that's him, that's the Aussie. **1971** *Bulletin* (Sydney) 16 Apr. 40/1 Damned Aussies. No sense of style. **1976** D.B. HUTLEY *Clement* 43 You wouldn't be an Aussie. You wouldn't be true blue. If Arnott's biscuits didn't mean something to you. **1978** J. ANDERSON *Tirra Lirra* 84 If you stay more than five years you become a pommified Aussie, than which there is no more pitiful creature on God's earth. Unless it's an aussiefied Pom. **1981** A.B. FACEY *Fortunate Life* 275 We had arranged the guard down to Headquarters so that we had an Australian soldier in the lead . . then a Turk, another Aussie, then another Turk, and so on.

3. Australian English.

1945 'MASTER-SARG' *Yank discovers Aust.* 64 This one was dinkum (which is Aussie for O.K.) **1952** 'N. SHUTE' *Far Country* 2, I don't speak Lithuanian. . . Aussie's good enough for me—Aussie or English. **1968** K. DENTON *Walk around my Cluttered Mind* 96 He hadn't spoken pidgin, he'd said it in straightforward Aussie. **1972** B. REED *Mr Siggie Morrison* 93 Oh, crayfish is Aussie for lobster. I think.

B. *attrib.* passing into *adj.* Australian.

[N.Z. **c 1910** A.E. WOODHOUSE *N.Z. Farm & Station Verse* (1950) 49 We'd a bunch of Aussie shearers, and they come from New South Wales.] **1916** G.F. MOBERLY *Experiences 'Dinki Di' R.R.C. Nurse* (1933) 51 One of our Aussie officers. **1927** K. BURKE *With Horse & Morse* 161 Our much-prized Aussie hats. **1929** C.E.W. BEAN *Official Hist. Aust. 1914–18* III. 601 Usually wearing an old 'Aussie' tunic (as worn by a private). **1944** A.S. SMITH *Boys write Home* 9 That's the spirit of the Aussie boys. **1946** A.H. CHISHOLM *Making of Sentimental Bloke* 124 For they talked the Aussie lingo all their days. But the Man from Snowy River strives to change his 'Oi' to 'I', And Clancy of the Overflow now wears an old school tie. **1948** J. FAIRFAX *Run o' Waters* 38 Sleeping buttresses, a necessary adjunct to Aussie architecture, hold up the posts along the streets. **1965** C. KOCH *Across Sea Wall* 54 'Now don't make fun of the Aussie accent,' Michael says. **1969** *Bulletin* (Sydney) 4 Jan. 14/1 The first clear picture of the new Prime Minister which Australians got just on a year ago was John Gorton, in good old Aussie rig of sports shirt and strides. **1972** *Ibid.* 8 Apr. 4/3 The good old Aussie principle of 'when in doubt, knock.' **1980** A.S. VEITCH *Run from Morning* 129 One of your original Aussie battlers. Started with a horse and dray at Bullabakanka. **1986** *Sydney Morning Herald* 8 Mar. 28/1 At the Adelaide Festival lurked that perennial ghost at every literary banquet, the starving Aussie writer.

Hence **Aussieism** *n.*, AUSTRALIANISM 1.

1966 *Sunday Truth* (Brisbane) 23 Dec. 22/7 We of the 'weird mob' are noted for the wealth of our idiomatic language and the sooner Aussieisms are coined for our new currency the better will people understand the decimal units of exchange.

Aussieland. Australia.

1920 *Aussie* (Sydney) Aug. 34/2 The girl he left in Aussieland Went nearly out her mind. **1969** *Kings Cross Whisper* (Sydney) lxxviii. 5/2 We want to make him into Knuckler Grogon, Aussieland's forthright, thrusting leader—the punchiest PM since Mauler Ming. **1976** *Evening Times* (Glasgow) 30 Nov. (Advt.), *The Emigrants.* Last episode of ponderous and badly acted series about life for British family in Aussie-land.

Hence **Aussielander** *n.*

1941 S.J. BAKER *Pop. Dict. Austral. Slang* 6 *Aussie* .. whence, 'Aussieland', 'Aussielander'.

Aussie rules. Shortened form of AUSTRALIAN RULES.

1941 S.J. BAKER *Pop. Dict. Austral. Slang* 6 *Aussie Rules*, Australian Rules football. **1953** *Bulletin* (Sydney) 15 July 13/1 Mat's Aussie Rules player .. couldn't play but made things awkward for those who thought they could. **1960** *N.T. News* (Darwin) 26 Jan. 5/2 Dunbah was at the Gardens Oval watching the Aussie Rules. **1965** *Bulletin* (Sydney) 15 May 35/1 Results .. are closer than in Rugby Football or Aussie Rules. **1967** F. HARDY *Billy Borker yarns Again* 81 They tell me Aussie rules is a religion in Melbourne. **1972** E. SPENCE *Nothing-Place* 5 'We came here from Melbourne.' 'Did you have to play Aussie Rules?' Shane asked sympathetically. 'No. I was born in New South Wales.' **1978** D. STUART *Wedgetail View* 92 Played Aussie rules, under eighteen, he said. **1983** *Nat. Times* (Sydney) 13 May 50/3 A lot of people will bag Aussie Rules, calling it a sheila's game, but the guys that are playing it are top class sportsmen, there's incredible skill involved.

Austral. *a.* and *n.* [Spec. use of *austral* belonging to the south, southern.]

A. *adj.*

1. Australian. Freq. poetic.

1823 W.C. WENTWORTH *Australasia* 21 Grant that yet an Austral Milton's song .. flow deep and rich along;—An Austral Shakspeare rise. **1833** *N.S.W. Mag.* (Sydney) 39 No common talent grac'd the Austral Bard. **1839** *Port Phillip Gaz.* 6 Nov. 4 It was singular to hear the blending of our highland music with the deep monotonous chaunt and beat of the Austral aborigine. **1843** 'POLICEMAN' *Headlong Rhymes*, Thus too the Exile views the seasons four Rule with inverted course the Austral year. **1849** *Bell's Life in Sydney* 29 Dec. 1/3 Will our loved Gov'nor be as great As now, on Austral grounds. **1866** *Bronze Trumpet* 6 Her Austral sister turned With lips that faltered, but with heart That burned. **1874** *Illustr. Sydney News* 28 Mar. 10/1 History proves their success in discovering and touching at certain points of the Austral continent. **1881** ANDERSON & BLAKE *J.S. Neilson* (1972) 10 Gordon and Kendall, men who rung On Austral desert bells the chimes Full of the wildest, sweetest notes. **1885** J. HOOD *Land of Fern* 15 Ah, fair, Austral land, are thy yellow-haired daughters. **1891** *Bohemia* (Melbourne) 9 July 19 And just at present, are we not all waiting to be astonished by the Austral Minuet which is to be danced at the forthcoming ball? **1898** *Bulletin* (Sydney) 2 Apr. 6/2 Real Australian Federation may be postponed for a few centuries till after the great Austral-Chow civil war is fought out. **1911** *Ibid.* 9 Nov. 13/4 The only way the Austral boy deals with a letter or a paper is to tear it up and strew it in the streets. **1922** J. LEWIS *Fought & Won* 144 Yes, we remember Anzac .. that dazzling and glorious concentration of Austral love and Austral courage. **1937** *Publicist* (Sydney) viii. 15/2 We shall continue with Austral-English. Basic English is another absurdity born of the British World-Dream. **1948** F. CLUNE *Wild Colonial Boys* 29 The chorus to this Austral ballad was sung with fervour as a kind of national anthem. **1972** *Bulletin* (Sydney) 9 Dec. 41/2 Mr Rushton's other funny song captured some of that Austral naivety.

2. Used as the first element in the names of some plants. See also AUSTRALIAN *a.* 2.

1833 J. BACKHOUSE *Narr. Visit Austral. Colonies* (1843) 166 This [*sc.* Bruny] island is nearly covered with wood like that of the main land, and has a few Austral Grass-trees interspersed among them. **1956** B. BEATTY *Beyond Aust.'s Cities* 198 A remarkable feature of the North-West landscape is the Austral baobab, Australia's most grotesque tree.

B. *n. Obs.*

1. Australia.

1868 *Colonial Soc.* (Sydney) 31 Dec. 3 That we're sons of old England we ne'er shall forget, And must think of our own native home with regret—But, aye let us remember in Austral's bright strand We live in a free,—perhaps a happier, land. **1891** H. NISBET *Colonial Tramp* I. 64 Fair daughters of sunny Austral.

2. A non-Aboriginal Australian.

1884 D.B.W. SLADEN *Summer Christmas* 231 She was slim, As Australs are, of waist and limb at wrist and ankle.

Australasia. *Obs.* [a. Fr. *Australasie* the Australian continent and neighbouring islands; ult. f. L. *australis* southern + *Asia.*] The Australian mainland; Australia.

[**1756** C. DE BROSSES *Histoire des Navigations* I. 80 L'une dans l'océan des Indes au sud de l'Asie que j'appellerai par cette raison *australasie.* **1766** J. CALLANDER *Terra Australis Cognita* I. 49 The first [division] in the *Indian Ocean* to the south of *Asia*, which, for this reason we shall call *Australasia.*] **1794** G. SHAW *Zool. New Holland* 2 The vast Island or rather Continent of Australia, Australasia, or New Holland, which has so lately attracted .. particular attention. **1802** —— *Gen. Zool.* III. i. 62 Smooth ovate Tortoise, with extremely long neck.. . This species is a native of Australasia or New Holland. **1810** *Sydney Gaz.* 9 June, And *Australasia* hail her *George's* Natal Day. **1823** *Hobart Town Gaz.* 8 Mar., It is headstrong, unwise, and untrue too, to say that Australasia is excelled by Van Diemen's Land. **1823** *First Fruits Austral. Poetry* (ed. 2) 16 This must be the place Where our Columbus of the South did land; He saw the Indian village on that sand, And on this rock first met the simple race of Australasia. **1829** E.G. WAKEFIELD *Let. from Sydney* 1 By Australasia, I mean Australia and all the smaller islands in its neighbourhood, including Van Diemen's Land. **1829** R. BURFORD *Descr. View Sydney* 4 Australasia, or New Holland, the largest island in the world. **1832** *Emigrant's Guide N.S.W.* p. v, The latest intelligence from Australasia has produced abundant proof of the intense anxiety which prevails .. in that distant land. **1842** *Tasmanian Jrnl. Nat. Sci.* I. 4 We consider Tasmania to have the *first* claim upon our attention, we shall not fail .. to furnish information .. of scientific interest in the other countries of Australasia. **1846** J.L. STOKES *Discoveries in Aust.* I. 255 It is a prevalent theory that the whole of the vast plains of Australasia have but recently emerged from the sea. **1880** *Bulletin* (Sydney) 31 Jan. 4/1 [Darlinghurst Gaol] .. the most populous prison of Australasia. **1890** H.A. WHITE *Crime & Criminals* 68 No country in the world could offer such numerous facilities as Australasia.

Australasian, *a.* and *n. Obs.*

A. *adj.* Of, pertaining to, or characteristic of Australia.

1802 G. SHAW *Gen. Zool.* III. iii. 506 An extremely good general representation of this species .. as well as of some other Australasian snakes. **1826** *Monitor* (Sydney) 2 June 19/2 What opinions of Colonial policy does this old Colonist and the Father of Australasian-merino wool *really* entertain at the present moment? **1832** *Hill's Life N.S.W.* (Sydney) 7 Dec. 1 Climates similar to those of the favoured Australasian colonies. **1841** *Colonial Observer* (Sydney) 18 Nov. 54/2 The kangaroo and emu, the characteristic animals of our Australasian continent. **1843** W. PRIDDEN *Aust.* 281 Western Australia, (which is, perhaps, all things considered, the most desirable of our Australasian colonies for a respectable Englishman to fix himself in). **1851** H. MELVILLE *Present State Aust.* 59 There is at present more unemployed capital in Adelaide than in any of the other Australasian settlements. **1891** *Bohemia* (Melbourne) 3 Dec. 20 As a matter of fact we deliver either by post or messenger a copy of our annual pamphlet to every house to be found in these Australasian Colonies and New Zealand. **1898** M. DAVITT *Life & Progress* 251 Any 'M.L.C.' can resign when he pleases and seek the more popular letters, 'M.L.A.' at the hands of the electors. Upper House members .. travel free over all the Australasian railway lines. **1903** *Truth* (Sydney) 19 Apr. 3/1 The annual session of the Australasian Natives' Association was opened .. on Tuesday. **1916** *Ibid.* 5 Mar. 11/6 Zam-Buk has such a wide range of usefulness that it should be kept handy in every Australasian home, workshop, farm-stead, sheep-run, and cattle-station. **1972** *Bulletin* (Sydney) 18 Nov. 58/1, I came upon a tattered copy of Philip Mennell's 'The Dictionary of Australasian Biography, 1855–1892, Comprising Notices of Eminent Colonists from the Inauguration of Responsible Government Down to the Present Time.'

B. *n.*

1. A non-Aboriginal Australian.

1819 *Edinburgh Rev.* XXXII. 40 The Australasians grow corn; and it is necessarily their staple. **1823** W.C. WENTWORTH *Australasia* p. ix, An Australasian myself, I am anxious .. to testify my gratitude for the services which you have rendered to that country. **1832** J. HENDERSON *Observations Colonies N.S.W. & Van Diemen's Land* 89 The young Australasians, are .. an idle and degraded race. **1917** *Huon Times* (Franklin) 1 May 4/1 In remembrance of the Australasians who had counted their lives not their own as they went forth to suffer and to die.

2. An Aboriginal.

1845 P.E. DE STRZELECKI *Physical Descr. N.S.W.* 349 Since the time that the fate of the Australasian awoke the sympathies of the public, neither the efforts of the missionary, nor the enactments of the Government, and still less the protectorate of the 'Protectors', have effected any good.

Australasiatic, *n.* and *a. Obs.*

A. *n.*

1. A non-Aboriginal Australian.

1824 *Hobart Town Gaz.* 30 Apr., The mind of an Australasiatic is not formed to be bounded by the Blue Mountains, and a bullock's hide.

2. Australian English.

1890 *Cornhill Mag.* (London) July 98 It was neither Cockney nor Yankee, but a nasal blend of both.. . In a word, it was Australasiatic of the worst description.

B. *adj.* Australian.

1819 *Blackwood's Mag.* (Edinburgh) V. 96 Craf-callee, which is a kind of Australasiatic Delos. **1827** *Hobart Town Courier* 10 Nov. 3 The Sydney Gazette, and the Australian, to say nothing of the Colonial Times of this place, are highly worthy of our gratitude in thus adding to the *copia verborum*, of Australasiatic literature. **1827** *Monitor* (Sydney) 3 Dec. 803 On the 1st January, 1828, will be Published, *Murray's Austral-Asiatic Review.* No. 1. **1828** *Tasmanian* (Hobart) 25 Apr. 2 The magnificent assemblage of Ladies and Gentlemen at Government House, in the evening, displayed a collection of beauty and fashion, never before equalled in either of the Austral-Asiatic Colonies. **1833** H. MELVILLE *Van Diemen's Land* p. ix, Erroneous conceptions obtain in the Mother Country, with regard to the two Austral-Asiatic Colonies of New South Wales and Van Diemen's Land. **1835** *Van Diemen's Land Monthly Mag.* Sept. 11 The females of all indigenous Austral-asiatic animals have a marsupium or pouch. **1838** *Bent's News* (Hobart) 21 Dec. 1 *The* Austral-asiatic Public are respectfully informed, that *Bent's News* .. will, as a Hobart Town journal, cease at the end of the present year, with a view to its re-appearance at Sydney. **1842** *S. Austral. Mag.* (Adelaide) June 313 (*heading*) Union of the Australasiatic colonies under a General-Governorship. **1859** D. BUNCE *Travels with Dr Leichhardt* 92 Sydney .. one of the most important cities in the Austral-Asiatic colonies.

Austral Felician. *Hist.* A resident of AUSTRALIA FELIX. Also as *adj.*

1839 *Port Phillip Patriot* 21 Oct. 3/1 The .. paragraph .. caused feelings of surprise to arise in our mind, and in the minds of the Austral-Felicians generally. **1840** *Sydney Herald* 5 Oct. 2/5 Nothing has been spoken of in Melbourne since the arrival of the overland mail, but Sir George Gipps' denunciations of the Austral-Felicians. **1841** *Port Phillip Patriot* 18 Jan. 2/1 The *Southern Australian*, avails itself of the opportunity .. to proffer the right hand of fellowship to the Austral-Felicians. **1843** *Colonial Observer* (Sydney) 25 Jan. 770/2 This is the first trial of Austral-felician beef in the English market. **1845** R. HOWITT *Impressions Aust. Felix* 89 Pleasant instances of the good feeling and gentlemanliness of the Austral Felicians.

Australia. [An anglicization of (*Terra*) *Australis* the southern land, a name used to designate the islands and supposed continent s. of Asia from the early sixteenth century. With spec. reference to the known continent it was preferred by Matthew Flinders (1774–1814), and popularized by Lachlan

Macquarie (1762–1824): see quots. 1805, 1814, and 1817.]

1. The continent in the Southern Hemisphere bounded by the Indian, Southern, and Pacific Oceans (in early use often restricted to the mainland or to N.S.W. as the known part of the mainland); the federated States and Territories which together make up the Commonwealth of Australia.

[**1770** J. COOK *Jrnls.* 14 Aug. (1955) I. 376 The Islands discover'd by *Quiros* call'd by him Astralia [*sic*] del Espiritu Santo lays in this parallel. **1773** J. HAWKESWORTH *Acct. of Voyages Southern Hemisphere* III. 602 The islands which were discovered by Quiros and called Australia del Espiritu Santa, lie in this parallel.] **1794** G. SHAW *Zool. New Holland* 2 The vast Island or rather Continent of Australia, Australasia, or New Holland, which has so lately attracted .. particular attention. [**1803** W. FADEN *Chart of Indian Ocean (caption)*, *Australis Incognita* and *Terra Australis* of the Ancient Cosmographers named afterwards New Holland.] **1805** M. FLINDERS Memo. 14 May Adm. 55O76 *AJCP* 1587/77, It is necessary, however, to geographical propriety, that the whole body of land should be designated under one general name; on this account, and under the circumstances of the discovery of the different parts, it seems best to refer back to the original Terra Australis, or Australia; which being descriptive of its situation, having antiquity to recommend it, and no reference to either of the two claiming nations, is perhaps the least objectionable that could have been chosen; for it is little to be apprehended, that any considerable body of land, in a more southern situation, will be hereafter discovered. **1814** —— *Voyages to Terra Australis* I. p. iii Introd., I have ventured upon the re-adoption of the *original* Terra Australis... Had I permitted myself any innovation upon the original term, it would have been to convert it into Australia; as being more agreeable to the ear, and an assimilation to the names of the other great portions of the earth. **1816** L. MACQUARIE Diary 30 Sept., I talked to Secretary Campbell this day, *for the first time*, on the important subject of his collecting the necessary materials and information for writing a correct and impartial '*History of New South Wales*'—alias 'Australia';—and he has promised me to take this subject into his serious consideration. **1817** L. MACQUARIE in *HRA* (1917) 1st Ser. IX. 356, I beg leave to acknowledge the Receipt of Captn. Flinders' Chart of *Australia*. *Ibid.* 747 Lieut. King expects to be absent from Port Jackson between Eight and Nine Months, and I trust in that time will be able to make very important additions to the Geographical knowledge already acquired of the Coasts of the Continent of *Australia*, which I hope will be the Name given to this country in future, instead of the very erroneous and misapplied name, hitherto given it, of 'New Holland', which properly speaking only applies to a part of this immense Continent. **1820** C. JEFFREYS *Van Dieman's Land* 19 There does not appear throughout the whole of Australia, as New Holland is now denominated, a more convenient place for docks and ship building, than the river Tamar. **1821** T. GODWIN *Descr. Acct. Van Diemen's Island* 3 Van Diemen's Land Or Tasmania .. is divided from New Holland, or Australia, by a strait, about 90 miles wide, called Bass's Strait. **1821** *Hobart Town Gaz.* 1 Sept., The Industry and Spirit of Enterprize, exhibited generally by the Inhabitants of Hobart Town .. bids fair to render it one of the handsomest and most flourishing in Australia. **1826** G.C. INGLETON *True Patriots All* (1952) 110 The parties hied to a certain delectable spot two miles short of Parramatta where the intrinsic merit of *sterling* and *currency* blood was about to be decided.—For the *honour* of Old England on the one hand, and the *fame* of Australia's Sons on the other. **1826** C. TOMPSON *Wild Notes* 21 Hope, 'neath the veil of future years, Sees proud Australia to an empire rise. **1827** *Tasmanian* (Hobart) 22 Mar. 2 We have shown to the Mother Country, and to our Fellow-Colonists of Australia, that .. in public spirit, we are prepared to go hand in hand with them. **1827** P. CUNNINGHAM *Two Years in N.S.W.* I. 9 The climate of Tasmania is generally cooler than that of New South Wales (or *Australia* as we colonials say). **1828** *Tasmanian* (Hobart) 18 Jan. 2 Australia received the most fostering protection which could be afforded by the Mother Country, for, at least, thirty years. Tasmania has a right to a similar protection. **1829** E.G. WAKEFIELD *Let. from Sydney* 1 As the Australasian settlements are known indifferently by several names, I must introduce the following account .. by requesting you to understand that, by Australia, I mean the large island of which one half is called New Holland, and the other New South Wales. **1830** 'RETIRED OFFICER' *Friend of Aust.* p. x, The island of Van Diemen's Land is called the 'Island of Tasmania', or simply Tasmania. The continent is called 'Australia'. **1838** *Counsel for Emigrants* (ed. 3) 204 Australia. Under this general name are included the large island of New Holland and the smaller one of Van Dieman's Land. **1841** H.S. CHAPMAN *New Settlement Australind* 26 Australia is the name given by modern geographers to .. what was formerly known as New South Wales and New Holland. **1853** S. SIDNEY *Three Colonies* (ed. 2) 13 The name 'Australia', now universally adopted to designate the whole island-continent. **1887** *NSWPD* 1st Ser. XXIX. 1476 Sir Henry Parkes rose to move: That leave be given to bring in a bill to confer on the colony the name of Australia, and to make constitutional and legal provision for and in respect of all changes in designation or title consequent thereon. **1899** *Tocsin* (Melbourne) 30 Mar. 5/1 A letter was received from Tasmania warning Victorians against the alluring but lying advts. appearing in Australia relative to the amount of work available at Mt. Lyell, Queenstown, and Gormanston... Yet shiploads of Australians continue to arrive. **1917** *Huon Times* (Franklin) 14 Dec. 2/6 The cry in Australia was 'Australia for the Australians', and a 'White Australia'. **1944** K.M. GORDON *Youth Centres* 29 Church youth organizations have interstate and Australia-wide machinery. **1956** *Sydney Morning Herald* 1 Dec. 1/1 Within three hours at the Olympic Games today Australia won six medals. **1976** R. ROBINSON *Shift of Sands* 117 My Australia. She is like a beautiful, mysterious woman.

2. *Obs.* In the collocation **the Australias**: the several Australian colonies considered collectively; regions of Australia so considered.

1846 *Sydney Morning Herald* 20 Apr. 2/2 It is a coincidence somewhat out of the ordinary course of events, that all the Australias, Eastern, Western, and Southern, should have experienced a change in the person of their respective rulers within a few months of each other... There are at least two great interests in which the Australias have a common stake. **1852** *Austral. Gold Digger's Monthly Mag.* i. 1 We write for the whole of the Australias. **1854** *Guardian* (Hobart) 7 Jan. 3/3 Has never been equalled in the Australias. **1872** G.S. BADEN-POWELL *New Homes for Old Country* 57 Of all the Australias Tasmania reminds one most of home. **1876** 'EIGHT YRS.' RESIDENT' *Queen of Colonies* 78 In 1861 and 1862 many were in the habit of regarding the Darling Downs as the most valuable section of country in the whole Australias. **1884** *Austral. Tit-Bits* (Melbourne) 3 July 2/1 We make it the journal *par excellence* of the Australias. **1893** *Bulletin* (Sydney) 9 Sept. 4/1 The electorate of Smith's Curse and its member may be found all over the Australias. They are both the embodiment of the spirit of parochialism, and represent the 'road and bridge interest' pure and simple. **1910** *Huon Times* (Franklin) 3 Dec. 2/7 A panorama of mountain and valley opens out before the eye, the grandeur of which is not excelled anywhere in the Australias.

Australia Day. a. A name given to the day, 26 January, on which the anniversary of the beginning of British settlement, at Sydney Cove in 1788, is celebrated. Formerly (in some States) ANNIVERSARY DAY. **b.** *Hist.* A name given in the Roman Catholic community to the day, 24 May, formerly celebrated as Empire Day, in protest at its allegedly Protestant character (see quots. 1911). **c.** *Hist.* The name given to a day, 30 July, so proclaimed in connection with an Australian Red Cross Society fund-raising campaign (see quots. 1915). Also *attrib.*

1911 *Sydney Morning Herald* 19 Jan. 5/7 And that, as a help to the cultivation of the patriotic spirit, May 24 should be formally set apart as 'Australia Day', under the auspices of Our Lady, Help of Christians. *Ibid.* 23 May 6/3 But in arrogantly setting up an Australia Day of its own, with no historical or other reference to our universal Australia Day, January 26, that Church assumes a prerogative it has no right, human or divine, to exercise. The proper authority to proclaim an Austalia Day, if one is wanted, is the Parliament of the Australian Commonwealth. *Ibid.* 25 May 5/2, I look upon Anniversary Day as Australia Day .. and upon Empire Day as the day for celebration of our broader citizenship. **1911** *Argus* (Melbourne) 25 May 8/2 Australia Day was celebrated by the Roman Catholic section of the community for the first time today. The Irish flag and the Australian ensign were flown from the central tower of St. Mary's Cathedral. **1915** *Sydney Morning Herald* 30 July 7/7 The object of Australia Day is to raise a fund of sufficient proportions to provide comforts and nursing assistance for our men who have fought so valiantly, and suffered so grievously. **1915** *Bulletin* (Sydney) 16 Sept. 18/1 Australia Day committee purred over the cream-puff at Government House. **1916** V.G. DWYER *Conquering Hal* 296 The papers are just full of praise for the Australians at Gallipoli, and Australia Day, last Friday, the 30th of July, proved how full of appreciation the people's hearts are too. **1931** *Century of Journalism* 447 This 'Australia Day' was held on the 30th of July, 1915, and the *Herald* devoted the space to it in its issue of the following day that its unique interest demanded. We quote from the general columns of the paper a description of the scenes in the city during the height of the excitement... There was never anything like it before. 'Australia Day' will assuredly never be forgotten. **1932** *Sydney Morning Herald* 27 Jan. 10/5 Anniversary Day was celebrated under a new name yesterday. For more than 100 years the day has been commemorated as Anniversary Day, but the State Cabinet decided that it should be observed in future as Australia Day. **1971** *Bulletin* (Sydney) 30 Jan. 11/2 For the rest there is a lesson to be learnt from South Australia and Western Australia, which have never really recognised Australia Day. They have Anzac Day as the national day, and, beyond that, Commemoration Day and Foundation Day as State days. **1981** A.J. BURKE *Pommies & Patriots* 38 The name Australia Day is a tribute to Joe Lyons who died in office of Prime Minister in 1939 and he largely sponsored the change of name from Foundation Day to Australia Day in 1932. **1981** *Sydney Morning Herald* 25 Apr. 37/8 Australia Day, no matter how much we may try to hide it, is now seen as celebrating the beginning of the British occupation of Australia. Anzac Day celebrates not only comradeship and sacrifice, but also remembers Australian fealty to Britain. Both days celebrate not independence, but dependence. **1986** *Canberra Times* 19 Feb. 16/1 Canberra's recent Australia Day celebrations were an insult to the intellect, and lacked 'class'.

Australia Felix. *Hist.* [f. L. *felix*, *felicis* happy, fertile, productive.] The name given by Thomas Mitchell in 1836 to the region south of the Murray River which, in 1851, was separated from New South Wales and named Victoria.

1836 *HRA* (1923) 1st Ser. XVIII. 590 He has also gone over .. rich and well watered Country deserving as he thinks the name of Australia Felix. **1839** T.H. MITCHELL *Three Exped. Eastern Aust.* (rev. ed.) II. 333, I named this region Australia Felix, the better to distinguish it from the parched deserts of the interior country. **1839** *Port Phillip Patriot* 19 Aug. 5/2 Australia Felix, a country larger than England .. is thus thrown open. **1845** T. MCCOMBIE *Adventures of Colonist* 18 We do not include the rich soil of Australia Felix, where droughts are almost unknown. **1852** *Murray's Guide to Gold Diggings* 28 The district not ill-named by Sir Thomas Mitchell, Australia Felix .. Phillipsland of Dr. Lang, Port Phillip of the masses and common parlance, and Victoria .. are all the same country. **1865** MRS A. CAMPBELL *Rough & Smooth* 48 The fertility of the soil surrounding the chief city of Australia Felix. **1888** R. THOMSON *Austral. Nationalism* 6 Till all our land, Australia Felix called, Become one Continent-Isle of Emerald. **1930** BILLIS & KENYON *Pastures New* 19 Latrobe minuted that despatch when sent him from Sydney for comment: 'They shall not get one acre of Australia Felix.' **1965** G. MCINNES *Road to Gundagai* 143 This was Australia Felix, the scene that inspired Streeton and the Heidelberg Group of painters.

Hence **Australia Felician, Australia Felixian** *n.*, AUSTRAL FELICIAN.

1839 *Port Phillip Patriot* 24 Apr. 4/1 Would not a standing committee be useful in our rising Capital? Could we not meet in such a committee, not as Vandemonians, or Sydneyites, but as Australia Felixians? *Ibid.* 17 June 4/2 The people of Adelaide .. are terribly hurt too, like many of the silly Australia Felicians, because, forsooth, the Protector cannot do impossibilities. **1840** A. RUSSELL *Tour through Austral. Colonies* 176 The day is not far distant when the Australia Felicians, will have the privilege of sending representative members to the legislative council at Sydney.

Australian, *n.* and *a.* [Spec. use of *Australian* inhabitant of *Terra Australis*, a. Fr. *australien* southern: see OED.]

A. *n.*

1. An Aboriginal.

1814 M. FLINDERS *Voyage Terra Australis* II. 205 Several natives were seen on the shore abreast of the ship and lieutenant Fowler was sent to communicate with them . . . They staid to receive him, without showing that timidity so usual with the Australians. **1825** B. FIELD *Geogr. Mem. N.S.W.* 197, I do not think the difference between the New Hollander and the Islander of Van Diemen by any means sufficient to class the Australians into two varieties, like those of the Birmanese and the Great Andamaners. **1829** R. MUDIE *Picture of Aust.* 246 The Australians are cunning and treacherous where they dread hostility. **1835** C.J. NAPIER *Colonization* 147 So it is with the poor Australians. Their country . . contains many nations, or, as we call them, tribes. **1840** *S. Austral. Rec.* (London) 6 June 310 The Australians were comparatively new, and were not a people *de facto*; the New Zealanders were more advanced, divided into distinct tribes, and not absolute savages. **1847** E.W. LANDOR *Bushman* 198 Did the fathers of science live on bark and roots, like the wretched Australian? **1863** J. BONWICK *Wild White Man* 63 All these institutions failed in doing any lasting good for the heathen Australians. **1878** R.B. SMYTH *Aborigines of Vic.* I. p. xviii, As may be expected, there were no insane persons and no idiots among the Australians, and suicide was unknown when they were living in their wild state. **1886** E.M. CURR *Austral. Race* I. 61 The second relation of the Australian is with his tribe. **1935** DAVISON & NICHOLLS *Blue Coast Caravan* 188 In speaking to them, of themselves, the expression 'coloured people' was used. The term, apparently, was acceptable to them, but when they spoke of themselves they used the term 'Australian'. **1960** D. MCLEAN *Roaring Days* 93 No other native people but Australians ever discovered the secret of the bent hardwood throwing-stick called the boomerang.

2. A non-Aboriginal person native to or resident in Australia.

1822 M. EDGEWORTH *Let.* 5 Jan. (1971) 307 Mr Rolfe has lately seen and questioned one of the men from new South-Wales—I should say an *Australian*—So they chuse to be called. **1825** *Australasian Pocket Almanack* 116 John Frazier, the second eldest Australian, a settler at Kissing-point, lost his life while venturing to bathe, in a state of perspiration. **1826** *HRA* (1919) 1st Ser. XII. 656 Presuming myself (altho' an Australian) capable from experience of undertaking such an expedition. **1828** *Blossom* (Sydney) i. 38 Oh! Australians and British Colonists, divest yourselves of this degrading feature,—lest too late you find your country in a state of abject vassalage. **1836** *Bent's News* (Hobart) 11 June 3 *Three Thousand* a year for the salary of the Lord Bishop alone—two thirds to be paid by the Australians, and one third by the poor impoverished Tasmanians. **1841** *Port Phillip Patriot* 22 Mar. 3/1 On Saturday last, she became the wife of Mr Russell, an Australian by birth. **1847** T. MCCOMBIE *Austral. Sketches* 21 The Australian carries, in his tall, light, elegant person, and wild sparkling eye, the noble and independent air of one who cares not a straw for any one on earth. **1859** F. FOWLER *Southern Lights & Shadows* 23 Your London gamin pales into utter respectability before the young Australian. **1863** *Bell's Life in Sydney* 15 Aug. 4/1 We may cite the many instances around us of Australians whose intellectual attainments reflect honor on themselves. **1886** H. DE CASTELLA *John Bull's Vineyard* 1 Early in 1859, being already a naturalised Australian, but at that time a visitor in Rome, I stood often watching with keen interest a bright young Englishman. **1886** D.M. GANE *N.S.W. & Vic.* 39 True Australians; not merely English recently domiciled, but a peculiar type of humanity which has sprung from the varied effects of climate, food, and mode of life, and frequent intermarriages of the English with the French, Germans, and Americans, and we regret to say, to some extent, with the Chinese. **1900** *Advocate* (Burnie) 8 Mar. 4/2 Taking up a safer position, the Australians covered the Tasmanians' retirement. **1906** *Truth* (Sydney) 4 Nov. 7/2 Quey Noz, the slant-eyed Australian. **1917** *Ibid.* 15 July 12/2 As long as imported people come out here *to be good Australians* I have no fault to find with them. **1919** *Huon Times* (Franklin) 17 Oct. 4/2 He is an Australian and the pioneering blood courses freely through his veins. **1932** D.B. O'CONNOR *Belle of Barrine* 4 You will know Australians by their free athletic gait, their suntanned handsome features, and their unrestrained laughter radiating something of their native sunshine in defiance of the brooding fogs of the Thames Valley. **1949** E. HILL *Lady Gowrie Centres* 13 An 'Australian' is usually considered to be one who is born in Australia of Australian-born parents. **1960** D. MCLEAN *Roaring Days* 127 That pommy turned out to be one of the best Australians I ever met. He became a rich station-owner and married a squatter's daughter. **1979** D. MCCARTHY *Fate of O'Loughlin* 10 You can tell an Australian anywhere. You just look out for a big man who wears a felt hat, calls his best friend a bastard, spells Jesus with a small 'j', and farts at the breakfast table.

3. Australian English, esp. as it is popularly characterized.

1902 *Bulletin* (Sydney) 14 June (Red Page), The schoolboy reciting . . to the inspector in 'perfect English' and then calling for the inspector's horse in pure Australian. **1915** *Honk* xi. 2/1 Then he began to speak some pure Australian, and the language that came out of the hole in that driver's face heated the air for yards around. He had spoken about 232 violent adjectives without repeating the same one twice, when his second driver laid a restraining hand on his shoulder. 'Can't you see he's a Belgian,' he said. 'He can't understand you, and, it's a pity to waste all that good bad language.' **1916** O. HOGUE *Trooper Bluegum at Dardanelles* 36 Nor shall we ever forget the laborious days and nights which that shopkeeper who put out the sign must have spent in mastering our language—'English and French spoken; Australian understood.' **1920** *Huon Times* (Franklin) 30 Apr. 3/2 He cursed them first of all in good round Australian, which really does not give a man much scope for variety. **1929** D.J. HOPKINS *Hop of 'Bulletin'* 17 On her arrival in Sydney, my mother had some difficulty in making herself undertood by the tradespeople. She did not know 'Australian', and called a spade a spade, and a 'cracker' just a 'cracker'. **1969** L. HADOW *Full Cycle* 101 The other women of her age still spoke the tongue of their native Jugoslavia . . but . . except in moments of excitement, of strain, of great joy, Australian was the currency.

B. *adj.*

1. Of, characteristic of, or belonging to Australia.

1814 R. BROWN *Gen. Remarks Bot. Terra Australis* 7 The existence of certain natural classes is already acknowledged, and I have, in treating of the Australian natural families, ventured to propose a few that are perhaps less obvious. **1821** *Austral. Mag.* I. 157 With the advancement of civilization in these numerous Isles, the improvement of Australian commerce must always keep pace. **1827** *Tasmanian* (Hobart) 3 Mar. 2 The great benefits for which our Australian brethren are now struggling. **1829** *HRA* (1922) 1st Ser. XV. 58, I myself glory, and shall die glorying, in the name of *Englishman*, yet my children glory in *another* name. To be *Australian* is their signal-word. **1832** *Currency Lad* (Sydney) 1 Sept. 2 More than three thousand bushels of Australian wheat have been sold in Sydney this week. **1840** A. RUSSELL *Tour through Austral. Colonies* 238, I arrived . . when the country was just recovering . . from one of those visitations these colonies are sometimes subjected to, known as Australian droughts. **1845** *Colonial Lit. Jrnl.* 27 Feb. 131/1, I wish you would abolish the use of the word 'Colonial' at any rate with regard to literature, and call it either 'Australian' or 'National'. Depend upon it that Australia will never be more than a cipher among the nations, until her sons assume to themselves national characteristics. **1850** J.B. CLUTTERBUCK *Port Phillip* 9 Two Australian lads now educating at Rome were, not more than two years ago, wild in the bush. One belonged to a cannibal tribe, and had himself eaten human flesh. **1859** F. FOWLER *Southern Lights & Shadows* 22 The Australian boy is a slim, dark-eyed, olive-complexioned young rascal, fond of Cavendish, cricket, and chuckpenny, and systematically insolent to all servant girls, policemen, and new-chums. **1861** L.A. MEREDITH *Over Straits* 64 There were Australian squatters and Tasmanian settlers. **1870** C.H. ALLEN *Visit to Qld.* 190 Australian dialects abound in these double words, of which Yarra Yarra is a well-known example. **1878** R.B. SMYTH *Aborigines of Vic.* I. 51 That there are instances, occasionally, of culpable negligence should not warrant us in stating that the affection of the Australian parents for their children is less than that of the best educated amongst Europeans. **1886** E.M. CURR *Austral. Race* I. p. xiv, Something positive might be learnt from language in connection with the past history of the Australian race. **1892** 'R. BOLDREWOOD' *Nevermore* III. 204 Then she raised her voice, in the high-pitched Australian call—originally borrowed from the blacks, but since heard (unless modern novelists lie) in the streets of London—ay, even in the 'Eternal City' itself. **1894** *Bulletin* (Sydney) 20 Jan. 14/2 The newly-branded Australian ennoblees are nearly all native born. **1899** *North-Western Advocate* (Devonport) 23 Jan. 2/7 The union of the Australian colonies and Tasmania. **1907** *Bulletin* (Sydney) 11 Apr. 15/3 For 20 years I've punched cattle with the roughest of 'em, but my chips go on that old sundowner for the most fluent command of Australian vernacular. **1908** *Ibid.* 23 Jan. 14/4 In Elmhurst (Vic.) lives an old Australian she-native of 75. . . This old bush girl was always dressed in ancient, but clean, skirt and blouse. **1909** *Ibid.* 21 Oct. (Red Page), It has been urged locally that the adjective 'Australian' should be reserved for that literature in English which has been produced by the white natives of Australia. **1936** *Publicist* (Sydney) i. 16/1 Above me the Australian blue sky, and about me the hard bright light of the Australian sun. **1940** A. HASKELL *Waltzing Matilda* 35 The Australian twang is by no means universal, though it is growing in the younger generation. **1948** R. RAVEN-HART *Canoe in Aust.* 187 'Australian flag' is a shirt-tail sticking out, their own slang. **1951** G. FARWELL *Outside Track* 21 It is out there that the mode of life we have come to call the Australian Tradition still persists. **1956** S. HOPE *Diggers' Paradise* 122 Mostly all the talk about 'the Australian way of life' refers to being matey, taking an interest in sport and enjoying a drink and a flutter. **1964** K. TENNANT *Summer's Tales* 13 How Australian-looking you are, my dear! . . It's a look. I would know it anywhere. **1965** E. LAMBERT *Long White Night* 85 A still wind blowing straight out of the west . . whipped up the wide brim of my Australian hat. **1971** *Bulletin* (Sydney) 9 Oct. 65/1 *Once upon* a time building a weekender for holidays—and eventual retirement—was an integral part of the Australian dream, like owning a Holden, a Victa lawnmower, and one's own home.

2. Used as the first element in the names of flora and fauna, esp. when the second element is a common English name: see quots. and cf. NATIVE *a.* 6.

1819 *First Fruits Austral. Poetry* 3 When first I landed on Australia's Shore . . A Flower gladden'd me above the rest . . The Australian 'fringed Violet' Shall henceforward be my pet! **1827** P. CUNNINGHAM *Two Yrs. in N.S.W.* I. 317 Our *porcupine*, or Australian hedgehog, serves for another native dish. **1836** J. BACKHOUSE *Extracts from Lett.* (1839) iv. 13 We heard the voice of the Australian pheasant, so celebrated for its splendid tail, on account of which it is sometimes called the New Holland Bird of Paradise. **1839** W.H. LEIGH *Reconnoitering Voyages* 198, I recollect seeing . . two tame Australian magpies. **1842** J. GOULD *Birds of Aust.* (1848) VI. Pl. 4, Australian Bustard . . Turkey, Colonists of New South Wales. **1842** *Tasmanian Jrnl. Nat. Sci.* I. 70 The adventurers . . being by this time entirely out of provisions, were reduced to live upon the Australian bear or monkey. **1843** J. GOULD *Birds of Aust.* (1848) VI. Pl. 15, Many years must probably elapse before anything is known of the habits and economy of the Australian Dottrel. **1845** R. HOWITT *Impressions Aust. Felix* 101 The laughing jackass, the Australian jay, or settler's clock as it is called, making merry with the first glimpse of daylight. **1853** J. SHERER *Gold Finder Aust.* 28 The dingo, or Australian dog, is extremely fierce. **1906** D.G. STEAD *Fishes of Aust.* 262 Australian Salmon. *Arripis Trutta.* **1948** F.D. MARSHALL *Let's go Fishing* 98 The perch (also known as Australian bass and grunter) is found in all the streams flowing east from the Great Divide. **1953** A. RUSSELL *Murray Walkabout* 25 It was an Australian bittern, or boomer. **1964** M. SHARLAND *Territory of Birds* 163 Beside the track a sprightly little Australian Dotterel, an inhabitant of inland places, dodged out of our way.

3. In collocations designating an Aboriginal: **Australian Aboriginal, Aborigine, black, savage.**

1861 W. WESTGARTH *Aust.* 17 Pickering has remarked the noble bust of a well-conditioned **Australian aboriginal**. **1911** *Huon Times* (Franklin) 22 July 6/1 At a little before 3 o'clock on Saturday afternoon, there strolled onto the ground an Australian aboriginal. **1948** E.H. COLLIS *Lost Yrs.* 98 In the shearing-shed, the boss-of-the-board was an Australian aboriginal. **1965** M. PATCHETT *Last Warrior* 9 Then the irises would lose their brilliance and would give no indication of the incredibly keen sight of the Australian Aboriginal unblinded by trachoma. **1843** *Arden's Sydney Mag.* Oct. 66 To arrive at any definite end in legislating for the existing races of the **Australian aborigine**, it is necessary to take a plain and truthful view of his character and state by nature. **1851** *Empire* (Sydney) 22 Oct. 284/3 The habits and customs of the Australian Aborigines. **1870** *Illustr. Austral. News* (Melbourne) Feb. 52/3 Times have changed since the Australian aborigines were troublesome to the white settlers. **1927** M. DORNEY *Adventurous Honeymoon* 51 The Australian aborigines are not beyond the stone age. **1963** W.E. HARNEY *To*

Ayers Rock & Beyond 192 To me he epitomized the Australian aborigine. People who helped us freely in the past, yet because of their colour and nomadic way of life, were on the scrapheap in our social structure. **1975** R.J. MERRITT *Cake Man* (1978) 12 The Australian Aborigine, that's who I am and what I am. **1845** J.O. BALFOUR *Sketch of N.S.W.* 9 The **Australian blacks**, both male and female, are most expert swimmers. **1854** W. HOWITT *Boy's Adventures* 297 Travellers and writers agree in considering the Australian blacks as very low in the scale of humanity. **1862** G. BOURNE *Jrnl. Landsborough's Exped. from Carpentaria* 5 The persons composing the land party were . . two Native Police Troopers; and two Australian Blacks. **1883** E.M. CURR *Recoll. Squatting Vic.* 291 The Australian Black generally performs well at cricket. **1911** A. MARSHALL *Sunny Aust.* 46 The Australian blacks are not high in the anthropological scale. **1944** M.J. O'REILLY *Bowyangs & Boomerangs* 30 As our natives are not of the negroid type they should be called Australian blacks. **1948** A. MARSHALL *Ourselves writ Strange* 73, I had heard so often that the Australian black could only be given a rudimentary education, his brain being incapable of retaining what a white child of twelve absorbs without difficulty. **1965** *Tracks we Travel* 169 With the Australian blacks the hunt for food was so continuous and necessary because they used no store houses. **1833** *Jrnls. Several Exped. W.A.* 197 To the **Australian savage** it is of little use. **1845** *Sentinel* (Sydney) 29 Jan. 2/6 The Australian Savages have their customs and ceremonies, as well as the civilised nations. **1847** *Moreton Bay Courier* 25 Sept. 2/4 The 'poor blacks', as certain philanthropic gentlemen, who know little or nothing of the peculiarities of the Australian savage, designate a race of beings, possessing all the worst passions of man, with scarcely any of his redeeming qualities. **1879** *Native Tribes S.A.* p. viii, The Australian savages . . are wandering savages. **1883** W.A. BRODRIBB *Recoll. Austral. Squatter* 19 From old experience, we knew it was necessary to keep the Australian savages at a distance.

4. In special collocations: **Australian adjective,** the epithet 'bloody'; also **great Australian adjective; ballot,** a form of secret ballot; also *attrib.*; **blue** *obs.*, light blue; **crawl,** CRAWL; **feathers,** gum leaves; **football, game,** AUSTRALIAN NATIONAL FOOTBALL; **language, (a)** an Aboriginal language; **(b)** Australian English; **(c)** blasphemous language (see SLANGUAGE); **metropolis** *obs.*, Sydney; **salute,** see quots; **slanguage,** see SLANGUAGE; **terrier,** a small, sturdy breed of dog; *Sydney silky*, see SYDNEY 2; **ugliness,** see quot. 1960.

1894 *Bulletin* (Sydney) 18 Aug. 22 The 'Bulletin' calls it the **Australian adjective** simply because it is more used and used more exclusively by Australians than by any other allegedly civilised nation. **1897** A. HAYWARD *Along Road to Cue*, But round the push and in the bush They're not so strangely sensitive: Unmasked and bare it riots there, The Great Australian Adjective. **1898** *Tocsin* (Melbourne) 3 Feb. 5/1 A good instance of the usefulness as a logical argument of the Great Australian Adjective is supplied in the story of the young man who during the elections asked a voter and a brother 'What is this here One Man One Vote they're all gabbering about?' 'Don't you see, Bill; it's this way—one ··· man, one ··· vote! Don't you see?' 'Yes, of course! I wondered what all the jaw was about.' **1913** *Truth* (Sydney) 2 Mar. 7/4 Tongues are too prone to utter with constant iteration the Australian adjective. **1944** *Aust. Week-End Bk.* 121 Compared with the poetic profanity of the Latin Europeans, with the colourful cuss-words of the East, our Great Australian adjective looks dull and anaemic. **1956** V. COURTNEY *All I may Tell* 56 Although he was no wowser, he kept his conversation on a high level and in all the years I knew him, I never heard Curtin tell a risque story or indulge in anything stronger than the great Australian adjective. **1964** P. ADAM SMITH *Hear Train Blow* 138 He spoke simply, with no heroics, and used the great Australian adjective whenever he became distressed. **1888** *Nation* (N.Y.) 2 Aug. 91/2 By introducing the secret '**Australian ballot**' in Congressional elections . . the use of bribery in the choice of Congressmen might be discouraged to some extent. **1889** J.H. WIGMORE *Austral. Ballot System* 2 It is proposed in the following introductory pages to sketch the history of the measure known as the Australian ballot system, as it passed from state to state in Australasia, on to the mother country in Europe, thence westward to Canada and eastward to continental countries, and finally westward again to these United States. **1917** E.C. EVANS *Hist. Austral. Ballot System* 17, 1. The origin of the Australian ballot. As the name implies, this system originated in Australia. . . The secret ballot was first proposed by Francis S. Dutton in the Legislative Council of South Australia in 1851 . . became a law in 1857–58. **1955** N. PULLIAM *I traveled Lonely Land* 282 The system of voting which we in the United States know as the Australian Ballot originated in South Australia. **1968** L.E. FREDMAN *Austral. Ballot* p. xii, Three pieces of Australian social engineering . . have been considered for borrowing by Americans. . . The third instance is the Australian ballot which has been well and truly borrowed as it has been adopted by name in every state. **1972** C. PEARL *Brilliant Dan Deniehy* 73 The 'Australian ballot', as it was called, was not introduced into Britain until 1872. **1843** *Sydney Morning Herald* 26 June 4/1 The flag borne at the head of this procession, was **Australian blue**, fringed with true blue. **1893** D. HEALEY *Cornstalk* 53 The generally accepted typical Cornstalk is an artistically drawn creature of some six feet, two inches, or thereabouts, in height, picturesquely habilitated in a red shirt, wide blue sash, a blue necktie (Australian blue, of course), a cabbage-tree hat, high boots, and a stock-whip wound in graceful loops on his arm. **1906** TAYLOR & GIBSON *Extra Dry* 32 Arthur Haddock . . swam out with a rope in his teeth, using the **Australian crawl**. **1914** R. STOCK *Pyjama Man* 28 Headed for the raft with what he fondly imagined to be the Australian 'crawl stroke'. **1930** D. HELLMRICH *How to swim Correctly* 14 It was that great sportsman, the late Cecil Healy . . who . . developed the Australian 'Crawl' as a distance stroke. **1963** F. CARLILE *On Swimming* 140 Cecil Healy of Australia was the disciple of the heavy 2-beat leg-kick which became known as the *Australian Crawl* and was used by Healy himself. **1969** G. JOHNSTON *Clean Straw for Nothing* (1971) 162 She taught him diving and the Australian crawl. **1975** O. MASS *Dangerous Waters* 70 Tina was soon away, doing an exaggerated Australian crawl—splashing a lot. **1980** M. BAIL *Homesickness* (1981) 14 The Australian Crawl . . requires the mouth to regularly turn sideways for breathing giving the swimmer the appearance of a sergeant shouting to men behind him. **1853** *Austral. Gold Digger's Monthly Mag.* iv. 123 '**Australian feathers**! What are they?' cried I. 'Gum leaves to be sure', said he. **1905** *Shearer* (Sydney) 4 Mar. 8/1 Luxuries, like 'bacca', fire-water, peanuts, theatres, race-books, 'nobs' and 'greys', &c, the writer has had to do without. Wood, water, gum leaves (Australian feathers) and camps cost him nothing. **1968** L. BRADEN *Bullockies* 106 He camped in a tent, sleeping on 'Australian feathers' (Mallee leaves) and his food bill averaged 8s. per week. **1910** *Argus* (Melbourne) 11 Nov. 7/1 The **Australian Football** Council further discussed the proposal to co-operate in an oversea tour. **1927** T.S. GROSER *Lure of Golden West* 143 Australian football is a hybrid type of game—a sort of cross betwixt 'Soccer' and Rugby, with a few quite original features thrown in. **1943** *Bulletin* (Sydney) 23 June 12/4 The big fellow's chief sport was Australian football; for all others he entertained indifference or contempt. **1963** *Footy Fan* (Melbourne) I. v. 18 Australian football has come to be accepted by Victorians almost as a way of life. **1903** *Sporting News* (Launceston) 30 May 3/7 Hon. treasurer of the Rugby union; on being asked his opinion of the **Australian game** said [etc.]. **1906** *Truth* (Sydney) 5 Aug. 1/5 The St. Kilda team of kickballers arrived in Sydney . . their mission being to popularise what is termed the Australian game of football. **1912** *Ibid.* 11 Feb. 1/4 At the present time our (in their own opinion) Big cricketers are really playing, football, the Australian game, all bounce. **1935** A. FRANCIS *Then & Now* 57 The football we played was known as the Australian Game. **1872** G.S. BADEN-POWELL *New Homes for Old Country* 402 **Australian language** is chiefly noticeable for the general absence of all dialect. . . Of course a certain number of peculiar words have crept in, among which may be noticed, *plant* for hide, *plum* for perfection, *bogie* for bath. **1886** E.M. CURR *Austral. Race* I. p. xv, The Australian languages have not unfrequently two words in the same sense. **1888** J. FRASER *Aborigines of Aust.* 35 In no Australian language is there any word for 'five'. **1891** M. ROBERTS *Land-Travel & Sea-Faring* 69, I tried to back the bullocks, but they scorned me utterly, in spite of the Australian language I used. **1915** *Honk* ix. 4/2 All barracking to be screamed, yelled, or bellowed in French. Australian language barred. **1945** *Oceania* XVI. 146 However widely Australian languages differ among themselves, they are in their general phonetic structure the same all over Australia. **1848** C. COZENS *Adventures of Guardsman* 130 The country immediately adjacent to Sidney . . the **Australian Metropolis**. **1853** *Visit to Aust. & Gold Regions* (S.P.C.K.) 70 The shops and warehouses are not inferior to any in the Australian metropolis. **1858** T. MCCOMBIE *Hist. Colony Vic.* 45 If the land were offered at Sydney . . the Australian metropolis. **1972** I. MOFFITT *U-Jack Soc.* 65, I flopped a hand at the flies (the **Australian salute**). **1980** B. HORNADGE *Austral. Slanguage* 14 Since all things and all actions in Australia have to be assigned a nickname, the fly-swatting action quickly became known as *the Australian salute*. **1986** *Canberra Times* 13 Nov. 1/5 The Australian salute: Prince Joachim brushes flies away yesterday. **1906** *R. Agric. Soc. N.S.W. Ann.* 122 There were 17 rough-haired terriers, some of them possibly progenitors of our **Australian terriers**. **1945** E. GEORGE *Two at Daly Waters* 83, I already had Flossie, my little Australian terrier, for company. **1960** *Bulletin* (Sydney) 6 July 18/2 A few weeks ago the American Kennel Club swallowed its long-held objections to the Australian Terrier and admitted it to its book of registry as a separate breed. **1976** *New Yorker* 26 Jan. 37/1 Most people had never heard of an Australian terrier. . . 'A small, sturdy, rough-coated terrier of spirited action and self-assured manner', according to the American Kennel Club. **1960** R. BOYD (*title*) The **Australian ugliness**. *Ibid.* (1968) 251 The Australian Ugliness begins with fear of reality, denial of the need for the everyday environment to reflect the heart of the human problem, satisfaction with veneer and cosmetic effects. It ends in betrayal of the element of love and a chill near the root of national self-respect. **1967** E. HUXLEY *Their Shining Eldorado* 12 What the architect Robin Boyd has called 'The Australian Ugliness' is rampant. Poles and pylons, cables and T.V. masts, roads and hoardings, shops and signs. **1972** *Bulletin* (Sydney) 18 Nov. 56/3 Perhaps it is churlish, but I think Betjeman, instead of contrasting the rural calm of 19th century houses with a Boydish Australian Ugliness of power lines and fluorescent lights, could have contrasted the past with the present by showing us the houses that the Alcorso family had built in Hobart. **1981** SANDERCOCK & TURNER *Up where, Cazaly?* 130 In the 1950s the spread of car ownership reinforced . . preference for low density living, otherwise known as suburban sprawl or, by some, as the Great Australian Ugliness.

Australiana. [f. AUSTRALI(A 1 + *-ana*, L. suffix attaching to names to denote memorabilia relating to the subject.] Items relating to or characteristic of Australia.

1845 (*title*) The Australiana. A weekly paper. **1855** *Putnam's Monthly* (N.Y.) V. 598 (*title*) Australiana. The Campbell Town election. **1886** R. HENTY (*title*) Australiana or my early life. **1907** *Native Companion* Aug. 55 Collectors of 'Australiana'. **1926** W.A. CAWTHORNE *Kangaroo Islanders* p. iii, Much sought after by Australiana collectors. **1935** MUNN & PITT *Austral. Libraries* 43 This library, bequeathed by Mr David Scott Mitchell, is a magnificent collection of Australiana. **1943** H.W. MALLOCH *Fellows All* 69 The Club has exhibited Australiana at the Public Libraries. **1952** J.R. TYRRELL *Old Bks.* 38 George Robertson . . was the driving force in launching the firm's own invaluable contribution to Australiana, the publishing of books by Australian authors. **1957** 'D.L. SANDERS' *Ribbons in her Hair* 150 They sat and talked Australia, Australiana and Australian people for another hour. **1970** G. DE FRAGA *Murder by Wash of Light* 3 A weekly round up of South Pacific politics along with whatever other Australiana he thought the chain's fifteen million readers might enjoy. **1972** *Daily Mirror* (Sydney) 12 Oct. 4/5 The rest of the audience kept its guffaws for genuine Australiana: the Big Spit, the Technicolor Yawn, Laughing at the Ground. **1974** *Gayzette* (Sydney) 17 Oct. 3/4 We seem to have a reputation for Australiana and outbackery. **1982** *Austral. Financial Rev.* (Sydney) 5 Feb. 40/4 But there may not be much Australiana left in the cupboard. Then prices could soar.

Australian-born, *a.* Born in Australia (but not of Aboriginal descent). Also *absol.* as *n.*

1829 *HRA* (1922) 1st Ser. XIV. 594 Refused me pasture for my cattle, and the cattle of eight Australian born children. *Ibid.* XV. 55 Particularly of the Australian-born population, who are of course rapidly rising to the *leading* population. **1842** *Colonial Observer* (Sydney) 6 Apr. 212/3 For I am an Australian born, And want no praise of thine; Go herd, I say, with your *own* friends, And let me keep to mine. **1850** *Britannia* (Hobart) 10 Jan. 2/5 To show that, independent of his being an Australian born, he has other especial claims. **1888** T.V. FOOTE *My Weird Wooing* 146, I as an Australian-born endorse the sentiment. **1916** *Truth* (Sydney) 8 Oct. 3/6, I have two Australia-born sons away fighting. **1926** A. EDEN *Places in Sun* 106 The Governors of those States should be Australian-born. **1927** J. LYNG *Non-Britishers in Aust.* 107 The Italian children in our State schools are Australian born. **1947** F. CLUNE *Roaming around Aust.* 3 Hamilton Hume, an Australian-born battler, who was a keen bushman, and the first of the real Australian-born explorers. **1965** N. LINDSAY *Bohemians of Bulletin* 5 The *Bulletin* was . . Australia in concrete form. Up to its appearance, the Australian-born were wandering in a limbo. **1972** *Bulletin* (Sydney) 17 June 51/1 The traditional Australian company's management team . . will usually be Australian born, little travelled, and generally have an outlook which is decidedly uncosmopolitan.

Australianese. *Obs.* Australian English.

1902 *Truth* (Sydney) 19 Oct. 2/6 Several toadies, lickspittles, cringelings, crawlers and sneaks, or, in Australianese, 'smoodgers'. *Ibid.* 30 Nov. 1/2 All sorts of dirty tools, including sharpers (called in Australianese, Sir, 'spielers') and even fraudulent bankrupts, have here been made magistrates. **1918** R.H. KNYVETT *Over there with Australs.* 83 The Australianese that the 'Gyppos' picked up is not commonly used in polite society. **1953** *Advertiser* (Adelaide) 2 Oct. 2/2 *Australianese.* 'The first scientific study of the Australian accent' has been embarked upon by Dr Franklin Hunt, a Fulbright scholar from the United States. **1965** *Listener* (London) 2 Sept. 340/1 It seems that Australianese is developing.

Australianism.

1. A distinctively Australian word or phrase.

1883 R.E.N. TWOPENY *Town Life Aust.* 245 There is room for a very interesting dictionary of Australianisms. **1894** A.F. CALVERT *Coolgardie Goldfield* 19 Some are lucky and strike 'pay dirt', (to use an Americanism), others fail to make 'tucker' (to use an Australianism). **1902** *Truth* (Sydney) 20 Apr. 5/1 The class of female under notice has, to use an Australianism, a chiv as tough as the rear end of a native bear. **1929** 'F. BLAIR' *Digger Sea-Mates* 193 Cobbers, how strange, these Australianisms, they sparkle among your speech like fireflies in the summer night. **1970** J.S. GUNN in W.S. Ramson *Eng. Transported* 50 Another warning should be issued against the habit of regarding as Australianisms occasional short-lived, local expressions. **1981** *Macquarie Dict.* 12 Our dictionary is not merely a dictionary of Australianisms.

2. Pride in, or loyalty to, Australian nationalism; a character distinctively Australian.

1909 *Bulletin* (Sydney) 11 Nov. 14/2 Wherever Australian products go outside of Australia they make many converts to Australianism. **1916** *Truth* (Sydney) 6 Aug. 6/6 (*heading*) Awaking Australianism. Will national spirit of Australia revive? **1920** *Aussie* (Sydney) Apr. 12/2 *Aussie* stands for Australianism. Australianism means to give all your physical and moral strength to the advancement of your country, to support its industries, enhance its reputation, build up its future, obey its laws, defend its rights, to put its interests before all others, to give it all your affection and loyalty, and to know only one patriotism, Australian. **1937** *Publicist* (Sydney) viii. 8/1 Her book fascinates me by its healthy Australianism. **1938** *Point* (Melbourne) I. i. 12 What sort of language is this? Is it the language of 'Australianism' or of 'democracy'? **1956** J.T. LANG *I Remember* 6 Aggressive Australianism has been the keystone of Labor's real appeal to the people of this country. **1965** G. MCINNES *Road to Gundagai* 281 Yet paradoxically they would prove their Australianism by rallying to England's defence. **1973** *Bulletin* (Sydney) 6 Jan. 28/1 Evatt struck me, first and foremost, as an Australian nationalist, as an Australian patriot. . . I do not believe his Australianism can be challenged. **1985** *Canberra Times* 26 Jan. 23/8 Sir Arthur called for more organised demonstrations of 'Australianism'.

Australianity. A character distinctively Australian.

1936 *Publicist* (Sydney) i. 3/1 Bunyip is the presiding god of Australianity, a religion scarcely yet born and therefore certainly not yet extinct. **1967** *Southerly* iv. 265 We take pleasure in the Australianity of our literature.

Australianize, *v. trans.* To render (a person, institution, etc.) Australian in character. Chiefly as *pa. pple.*

1883 *St. James's Gaz.* (London) 10 May 7/1 Are the latter wronged, then, in having to become, for instance, 'Australianized'? **1888** D.B.W. SLADEN *Austral. Ballads & Rhymes* p. xxiv, Swinburne Australianised à la Gordon. **1889** *Bulletin* (Sydney) 13 July 5/4 The reading books used in the state schools of New South Wales and Victoria are, it is said, about to be Australianised. **1904** *Truth* (Sydney) 15 May 5/3 The longer a man has been in Australia, if it be sufficiently long for him to have become 'colonized', or, as we prefer to say, Australianised, the more remote become his chances of employment. **1913** H. LAWSON *Triangles of Life* 100 He was not an Englishman, as far as I could see, and not an Australian—not yet what is next best to it, an Englishman Australianized. **1919** *Aussie: Austral. Soldiers' Mag.* Feb. 10/1 Mr Standatease was the 'one pip' in charge of our platoon. He had not lived in Aussie long enough to become Australianised. **1928** *Bulletin* (Sydney) 9 May 23/1 Joe, who was thoroughly Australianised, got even. **1960** *Encounter* (London) May 27/1 A good many years' obedience could be expected before they became Australianised and the unions got them. **1972** *Bulletin* (Sydney) 7 Oct. 33/1 (*heading*) Australianising soccer. **1983** *Age* (Melbourne) 1 Oct. (Saturday Extra) 3/1 Werner Herzog has employed Bob Ellis to Australianise his script, but it is not peppered with jokes.

Australian National Football. The formal name of a game of football originating in the mid-nineteenth century in Victoria and played according to rules now determined by the Australian National Football Council. See also AUSTRALIAN RULES.

1927 *Argus* (Melbourne) 9 Aug. 10/6 The name of the council was altered to that of the Australian National Football Council, and all of the States will place before the word 'football' in the title of their organisations the words 'Australian National'. **1931** J.F. MCHALE et al. *Austral. Game of Football* 10 At the present time the N.S.W. Australian National Football League comprises seven clubs in the metropolitan area. **1952** *New Settler in W.A.* (Perth) July 7 Most of you have not seen Australia's biggest football game played before. It is called Australian National Football and is played in all States. **1971** B. ANDREW *Austral. Football Handbk.* 12 The necessity of having a national controlling body was often expounded by State administrators until, in 1906, the Australian National Football Council was formed.

Australian native.

1. An Aboriginal. Also *attrib.*

1839 T.L. MITCHELL *Three Exped. Eastern Aust.* (rev. ed.) I. 34 The white man is known as yet only by name—or as the manufacturer of this most important of all implements to the Australian native. **1845** J. DREDGE *Brief Notices* 12 As to their moral and spiritual condition . . the Australian Natives, with no deficiency of ordinary mental capabilities, are extremely wicked and degraded. **1845** E.J. EYRE *Jrnls. Exped. Central Aust.* II. 153 The character of the Australian native has been so constantly misrepresented and traduced, that by the world at large he is looked upon as the lowest and most degraded of the human species, and is generally considered as ranking but little above the members of the brute creation. **1852** J. SHAW *Tramp to Diggings* 16 It has been customary among some writers to dignify the Australian natives by the appellation of 'human monkeys', and to describe them as not being possessed of the common intellect and almost common feelings of humanity. **1854** MRS C. CLACY *Lights & Shadows* II. 15 The Australian natives are cannibals, and have been known to eat their own children. **1859** *Rambles at Antipodes* 26 If the Australian native is to perish irretrievably before us, let us take steps to enable him, like Caesar, to gather his robes about him, and to fall with decency. **1872** J.L.A. HOPE *In Quest of Coolies* 2 You have but to ask an Australian native to chop a little wood, to send him stalking off. **1879** *Native Tribes S.A.* p. xi, All who have written upon the subject of the Australian native tribes acknowledge that they vanish before the white settler. **1927** M.H. ELLIS *Long Lead* 238 The Australian native question still exists. **1936** M.E.P. SHARP et al. *Early Days St. Peter's College* 53 Even the Australian natives from the Poonindie station came over to play cricket with the St Peter's boys.

2. A non-Aboriginal Australian. Also *attrib.*

1872 *Argus* (Melbourne) 2 July 6/4 An entertainment was given by the Australian Natives' Association . . last night, in celebration of the first anniversary of that body. **1876** *Ibid.* 28 Apr. 5/3 The members of the Australian Natives' Association celebrated their fifth anniversary last night. **1882** A.J. BOYD *Old Colonials* 60 The peculiar type of the Australian native (I do not mean the aboriginal blackfellow, but the Australian white), which has received the significent *sobriquet* of 'The Nut', may be met with in all parts of Australia. **1888** *Bulletin* (Sydney) 11 Feb. 9/2 No Australian native spoke at the Sydney Centennial banquet. **1889** *Illustr. Austral. News* (Melbourne) July 2/3 A large percentage of the new House consists of young men returned on the Australian Native ticket. **1892** H.C.J. LINGHAM *Juvenal in Melbourne* 39 Australian Natives are too much inclined To honor muscle at the expense of mind. **1893** D. HEALEY *Cornstalk* 97 The native Australian, i.e. aboriginal, bursts into spontaneous expressions of loyalty, or joyousness—'Good man, de Queen; plenty blankets and bacca'—at the periodic distribution of those bounties. The Australian native, i.e. the white lord of the soil, gives utterance to his expression of loyalty, or custom, 'God Save the Queen', when custom renders the repetition of that platitude necessary. **1900** *Tocsin* (Melbourne) 18 Oct. 2/3 We Women are pleased to note that it is at last dawning on the intelligence of the A.N.A. that there are Australian native women as well as men.

Australianness. A quality or character distinctive of Australia or of Australians.

1954 *Landfall* (Christchurch) 27 An essential Australianness which is apt to recede when too deliberately pursued. **1960** *Encounter* (London) May 28/1 The migrant . . must not, of course, attack the country itself or its Australianness. **1967** D. HORNE *Educ. Young Donald* 66 On Anzac Day we attempted a formal synthesis of Australianness and Christianity as two examples of brotherhood. **1971** *Bulletin* (Sydney) 23 Oct. 62/3 Few of them . . seem able to live unself-consciously with the fact of their Australian-ness. **1981** P. SEKULESS *Fred* 5 More importantly, he acquired qualities of individualism and mateship, a distinctive Australianness.

Australian rules. The rules under which Australian National Football is played; the game itself. Also *attrib.*, esp. as **Australian rules football.**

1903 *Truth* (Sydney) 19 Apr. 3/1 They had accorded their patronage to the Australian Football League and the game as played under Australian rules. **1904** *Ibid.* 4 Sept. 1/4 Another good man killed playing 'Australian rules' football. **1928** H.C. PERRY *Son of Aust.* 68 Young Harrison became a champion athlete, a cricketer and footballer of note and was instrumental in establishing the Australian Rules of football. **1931** J.F. MCHALE et al. *Austral. Game of Football* 2 There's nothing quite so Australian in all our sport as football under Australian rules. **1948** R. RAVEN-HART *Canoe in Aust.* 144 A game of 'Australian Rules' football, at its best in Melbourne. **1956** E. LAMBERT *Watermen* 173 In the fishing-ports of Western Victoria football meant Australian Rules, and soccer and rugby were distant aberrations. **1962** O. PRYOR *Aust.'s Little Cornwall* 165 Before Australian rules football was played at Moonta, there was a rough-and-tumble form of the game there without rules or scores, in which spectators often joined. **1968** K. DENTON *Walk around my Cluttered Mind* 153 Fanatic about Australian Rules football, that bastard child of Rugby, played on an oval pitch with four goal-posts at each end and with the power to rouse a missionary fervour in all its adherents. **1973** K. DUNSTAN *Sports* 217 The famous battle of 1858 between Melbourne Grammar and Scotch College gets the credit for being the first Australian Rules match. **1976** N.V. WALLACE *Bush Lawyer* 96 To live in Melbourne, one must accept the alternative local religion of Australian Rules football.

Australienne. [f. AUSTRAL(IAN *n.* 2 + *-ienne*, Fr. feminine suffix.] A non-Aboriginal Australian woman.

1895 *Bulletin* (Sydney) 16 Feb. 14/3 The Australienne, having got her medical diploma, thought she would like to settle into a practice at Darstadt. *Ibid.* 17 Aug. 12/4 An Australienne in England. **1903** J. FURPHY *Such is Life* 144 Vivian was a type Englishman, of his particular sub-species; his wife was a type Australienne, of the station-bullock-driver species. **1904** *Truth* (Sydney) 3 Jan. 6/3 As a free born Australienne, I protest. **1909** H.H. BOOTH *Opalodes* 52 *'Fair Australiennes.'* Fair maids and matrons! **1916** *Truth* (Sydney) 8 Oct. 3/7 We have a number of letters from Australiennes proving conclusively that the Currency Lass can wield a pen as well as the Currency Lad can shoulder a rifle, but space precludes publication. **1934** *Bulletin* (Sydney) 18 Apr. 11/4, I have just been reading the complaint of an Australienne, now resident in India.

Australioid, var. AUSTRALOID.

australite. An Austral. tektite, a small glassy body considered to be of extra-terrestrial origin; *black-fellow's button*, see BLACKFELLOW *n.* 2, *button stone*, see BUTTON *n.*; OBSIDIANITE.

1909 *Geol. Mag.* (London) VI. 411 Occurrences of the related 'obsidianites' (referred to by Professor Weinschenck as Billitonite and Australite) in the Malay Peninsula. **1912** *Bull. Geol. Survey Vic. No. 27* 13 Original forms of australites are remarkable for their symmetry, and are quite unlike other mineral bodies. **1916** *Geol. Survey Bull. No. 67* (W.A.) 135 Neglecting as of unknown origin the many thousands of 'Australites' or 'Obsidianites' which have been discovered on the surface of the central plateau of the State, only twelve undoubted meteorites have been found. **1918** W. HOWCHIN *Geol. of S.A.* 10 The peculiar, black, glassy, and button-like objects found throughout Australia, known as *Australites*, and formerly thought to be of volcanic origin ('obsidian bombs'), are now generally considered to be a peculiar form of meteorite. **1928** B. SPENCER *Wanderings in Wild Aust.* 42 Scattered over these open table-lands and on the Gibber fields, agates and obsidian bombs are met with lying on the surface of the ground. The latter, often called Australites, consist of a brownish or dark green coloured vitreous material. **1933** C. FENNER *Bunyips & Billabongs* 39 Most of us have seen an Australite, either in our own or in a friend's collection, or in a museum. **1937** R.H. CROLL *Wide Horizons* 85, I noticed an Australite near his polishing wheel. He called it a 'plainer' and mentioned that he cut that class of stone for mourning jewellery—the blackest stuff he knew. **1946** C. FENNER *Gathered Moss* 101 The blacks are still the best collectors of australites, and with the grim humour of the outback they are called 'black-fellows' buttons'. **1968** *Victorian Naturalist* LXXXV. 344 Tektites from America are called 'Amerikanites' . . Island of Billiton, 'Billitonites'; and Australia, 'Australites'. **1973** V. SERVENTY *Desert Walkabout* 28 The stone was a tektite or Australite as they are often called. **1985** *West Austral.* (Perth) 25 June 30/5 Till about 20 years ago tectites—or australites—were thought to be glassy meteorites from the moon. But more recent studies showed that their composition was like clayey sandstone.

Australoid, *a.* Of, allied to, or resembling the ethnological type of the Aborigines. Also as *n.*, and formerly **Australioid.**

1869 J. LUBBOCK *Pre-Hist. Times* 378 Prof. Huxley . . divides mankind into four groups, the Australoid, Negroid, Mongoloid, and Xanthochroid. . . The Australoid type contains all the inhabitants of Australia, and the native races of the Deccan, with whom he also associates the Ancient Egyptians. **1870** T.H. HUXLEY in *Jrnl. Ethnol. Soc. London* New Ser. II. 405 The chief representive [*sic*] of the Australioid type is the Australian of Australia. **1913** H. JOHNSTON *Pioneers in Australasia* 49 When races of superior intellect and bodily strength were developed in Europe and northern Asia, the ancestors of the Tasmanians and the Australoids were driven forth into the forests of Africa and southern Asia. **1925** H. BASEDOW *Austral. Aboriginal* 59 There are considerable racial differences between the other races and the Australoids, the most highly specialized and cultural division of which is now represented by the modern Caucasian. **1938** A.P. ELKIN *Austral. Aborigines* 3 In view of the differences which exist between the Aborigine and other great divisions of mankind . . the Australian Aborigine is now classified in a special group, the Australoid. **1967** B. YAMAGUCHI *Comparative Osteol. Study* 7 It may be called, therefore, Australoid type and is characterized by the narrow cranial vault, flat and inclined frontal squama, protruding superciliary arches, nearly triangular orbital margins, deep canine fossae and marked alveolar prognathism. **1976** KIRK & THORNE *Origin Australs.* 91 It is very interesting to note here that many skulls of early *Homo sapiens* exhibit some Australoid features, or more precisely, are described as Australoid.

Australorp. [f. AUSTRAL(IAN *a.* 1 + *Orp(ington)*, the name of a town in Kent, England.] An Australian fowl belonging to or descended from the Orpington breed; the name of the Australian breed developed from the Orpington and given distinct status in 1930. Also *attrib.*

1922 *Daily Mail* (London) 9 Dec. 14 (Advt.), Australorps imported. Australian Black Orpingtons. World's Record Layers—1,750 eggs 6 birds, 12 months. **1930** *Australasian Poultry World* 1 Nov. 174/1 Now that the Australorp has come to be recognised as such in the land of its birth, the time is opportune to have the type and character of the breed clearly defined and preserved. **1933** *Bulletin* (Sydney) 8 Feb. 21/1 A sinister and suspicious happening at Townsville . . has set the town by the ears. . . An Australorp hen entered for the N.Q. egg-laying competition . . was a comparative unknown on starting, . . rapidly forged to the front . . then . . was discovered in the pen at the Show Ground with the head missing and the body badly battered. **1939** *Victorian Poultry Jrnl.* 1 July 27/1 The Australorp cockerel secured grand champion fowl of the show. **1944** *Bulletin* (Sydney) 2 Aug. 14/1 A Vic. Mallee contractor, put a dozen Australorp eggs in a Lowan nesting mound last spring. **1948** R.A. PEPPERALL *Emigrant to Aust.* 66 White Leghorns were his fancy in the poultry world while I took up the Black Orpington breed renamed 'Australorp'. **1961** A.A. MCARDLE *Poultry Managem.* 64 Great credit is due to Australian breeders for evolving the Australorp—the Australian Utility Black Orpington. **1978** W.J. NOWLAND *Modern Poultry Managem.* 49 In 1930 the breed was called Australorp, with a standard designed to embody a first-class utility fowl of the true Orpington type. As a result, Australorp has become standardised. **1981** D. READING *Guide to keeping Poultry* 32 The Australorp is a large, handsome bird, with glossy black feathers having a greenish sheen. It is so well feathered and so large that the Australorp assumes almost a square shape.

awake up, var. WAKE UP.

award, *n.* and *attrib.*

A. *n.* A determination made by a State or Federal industrial court or commission regulating conditions of employment.

1886 *Arbitrations between Proprietors & Miners* 115 The award given on that occasion reads—'that an advance of 3d. per ton be given on the coal worked on No. 1 Heading'. **1910** *Bulletin* (Sydney) 19 May 14/1 He is paid a princely 30s. a week, and . . engaged under an award which sets a working week of 48 hours. **1913** W.F. HAMILTON *Compulsory Arbitration* 1 The award can fix not only the minimum rates of wages to be paid to the workers, the hours of labour, and all other conditions of labour, but may also settle questions as to dismissal of or refusal to employ any worker or workers and claims of preference for unionists. **1936** P. STAAL *Foreigner looks at Aust.* 145 As early as 1891 a Council of Conciliation and an Arbitration Court were created. Neither of these institutions however had authority to summon the parties to appear before them, nor were they granted the power to enforce their decisions ('awards' as they were called). **1957** V. PALMER *Seedtime* 165, I was one of the first wages-men on the field and I don't forget the way you worked to get us a little bit more than the current award. **1966** *Realist* (Sydney) xxi. 20/2 Y'gotter stick by the award, y'gotter fight for better conditions and y'never scab on a mate. **1973** J. O'GRADY *Survival in Doghouse* 33 Your union gets you a new award, and your wages go up. **1984** *People Mag.* (Sydney) 7 May 40/3 All were unionists who denied working outside the award.

B. *attrib.* **award conditions, rates, wage, work.**

1983 *Bulletin* (Sydney) 4 Jan. 24/3 Wide combs will break down their **award conditions** and create unfair competition between shearers. **1919** *Smith's Weekly* (Sydney) 19 Apr. 10/6 Workers belonging to the Railway Workers' Branch of the A.W.U. are . . denouncing the Commissioners, who refuse to pay **award rates.** **1936** E. SCOTT *Aust. during War* in *Official Hist. Aust. 1914–18* XI. 669 The ship owners maintained that the existing award rates were adequate. **1948** *Austral. Cwlth. invites U.S. Veteran to New Life in Aust.* 10 Only in some rural areas, where no award rates apply, are workers not guaranteed this minimum. **1967** ISAAC & FORD *Austral. Labour Econ. Readings* 220 If the rise of overaward pay could be checked, it would reduce the pressure on the commission for 'excessive' increases in award rates. **1941** *Bulletin* (Sydney) 3 Sept. 15/1 He knew all about **award wages**, keep and economics in general. **1957** A. O'CONNOR *Worker's Legal Man.* 7 Employees who are not unionists but whom a Federal award requires to be paid award wages have no personal right to enforce the award. **1967** J.E. ISAAC *Austral. Labour Econ. Readings* 220 Overaward pay does not rise faster than award wages. **1941** O. DE R. FOENANDER *Solving Labour Problems Aust.* 119 A respondent may in certain circumstances engage these persons to do **award work** outside the workshop or factory.

away back, var. WAYBACK.

axe-handle.

1. Used *attrib.* in Special Comb. **axe-handle wood,** any of several tree species producing wood suitable for axe handles, such as the native elm *Aphananthe philippinensis* (fam. Ulmaceae) of rainforests in N.S.W., Qld., and n. to the Philippine Islands, and *Planchonella myrsinoides* (fam. Sapotaceae) of n. N.S.W., s. Qld., and Lord Howe Island.

1898 *Proc. Linnean Soc. N.S.W.* XXIII. 130 'Axe-handle Wood' . . An ornamental small tree with foliage reminding one of that of a Camellia [Lord Howe Island] **1926** *Qld. Agric. Jrnl.* XXV. 438 *Aphananthe Philippinensis* . . Axehandlewood.

2. A rough unit of measurement. Esp. in the fig. phr. (so many) **axe-handles across the arse.**

1958 R.G. HOWARTH et al. *Penguin Bk. Austral. Verse* 268 My arms are aching and I'm dripping sweat But the sun is three axe-handles in the sky And I must toss sheaves till dark. **1965** E. LAMBERT *Long White Night* 65 She's as heavy as you. About six axe handles across the arse. **1968** S. GORE *Holy Smoke* 95 *Axe-handle*, old bush unit of measurement. **1977** *Austral.* (Sydney) 11 Apr. 6/8 A big woman, but not a big man, would be described as being 'two axe handles across the arse'. **1982** *Sun-Herald* (Sydney) 19 Dec. 127/2 There was this giant Yugoslav bodyguard there, about four axe-handles across the chest and he had to wrestle with them to keep them away.

azure kingfisher. The kingfisher *Alcedo azurea* of n. and e. Aust., New Guinea, and adjacent regions, having deep blue plumage on the head, back, and wings. Formerly also **azure kingsfisher.**

1801 J. LATHAM *Gen. Synopsis Birds* Suppl. II. 372 Azure K[ingsfisher]. . . Inhabits *Norfolk Island.* **1808** J.W. LEWIN *Birds of New Holland* 5 (*caption*) Azure Kingsfisher . . visits dead trees from whose branches it darts on its prey in the water beneath, and is sometimes completely immersed by the velocity of its descent. **1845** J. GOULD *Birds of Aust.* (1848) II. Pl. 25, With the exception of Swan River, every colony of Australia, from Port Essington on the north-west to Van Diemen's Land in the extreme south, is inhabited by Azure Kingsfishers. **1945** C. BARRETT *Austral. Bird Life* 143 The azure kingfisher . . darts past like 'a living flash of blue'. **1980** M. GRANT *Barrier Reef* 12 The Azure kingfisher, so called because of the full azure blue of his head and body, an intense blue . . and, despite his size, well able to deal with small fish, frogs and crabs.

B

baal /'bal/, *adv. Austral. pidgin. Obs.* Also **bael, bail, bale.** [a. Dharuk *bial.*] Used to express negation: cf. BORAK *adv.* Also as *adj.*

1790 D. SOUTHWELL Corresp. & Papers 149 *Bei-yăl* or *bey-ăl*, no. **1803** J. GRANT *Narr. Voyage N.S.W.* 108 They began a conversation . . using many words which seemed to resemble the Sydney dialect, such as *Bail*, signifying *No*, and *Maun* to *take away* or *carry off.* **1818** J. HOLT *Mem.* (1838) 154 He said 'Bail bail', that is, never fear. **1827** *Monitor* (Sydney) 13 Jan. 276/3 Mr J. desired Oleinthebrook to place his hands behind him, that he might tie them together. '*Baal tie me!*' said the savage, and sprang from them like an arrow from a bow. **1828** *Sydney Gaz.* 2 Jan., Casting his eyes wistfully around him, and giving a melancholy glance at the apparatus of death, he said, in a tone of deep feeling, which it was impossible to hear without strong emotion, 'Bail more walk about', meaning that his wanderings were over now. **1830** R. DAWSON *Present State Aust.* 65 The word *bael* means no, not, or any negative. **1843** *Arden's Sydney Mag.* Oct. 130 His Honor then, in a most impressive manner, passed sentence of death upon the prisoner. When the sentence was explained to him, he shook his head and said 'bail me' (it was not I). **1844** *Bee of Aust.* (Sydney) 2 Nov. 4/1 The learned member for Sydney: Who in baal gammon style of eloquence will no doubt, Let my Lord Stanley's mother know 'that he is out'. **1848** *Atlas* (Sydney) IV. 121/2 Nay the aboriginal jabber is pressed into the service, as if the forty or fifty thousand words of the standard dictionaries in our language were inadequate to express or dissemble all our ideas '. . payala, patter, bel' etc. are all reckoned elegances of a particular kind among certain classes of society. **1859** W. BURROWS *Adventures Mounted Trooper* 102 The answer he got, in his own lingo, was, 'suppose you no cut waddy (wood) you bale get tucker'. **1870** C.H. ALLEN *Visit to Qld.* 183 There are certain native terms used by the whites also as a kind of colonial slang, such as 'yabber', to talk; 'budgeree', good; 'bale', no. **1876** J.A. EDWARDS *Gilbert Gogger* 115 Baail that fellor—something fool; yarraman plenty cooler; Misses Gilber baail jarrand; . . budgeree rideum their fellor. **1897** *Bulletin* (Sydney) 3 July (Red Page), 'Bale' was the pure negative. 'Bo-rák' carried the idea of good-humored repudiation or denial—something equivalent to our 'gammon!' or 'no dash fear!' **1914** T.C. WOLLASTON *Spirit of Child* 109 'Baal spying,' I answered swiftly in the old lingo. **1923** T. HALL *Short Hist. Downs Blacks* 34 'Baal you cry', 'Baal you tell 'em Master' was all they could say.

bab. Abbrev. of BABBLING BROOK.

1936 *Bulletin* (Sydney) 22 July 21/1 Old 'Forty-Mile Tom' is the 'bab' on our station, But, though he is famed all along the Paroo, He sets little store by his great reputation For making a duff or concocting a stew. **1943** S.W. KEOUGH *Around Army* 19 It is axiomatic that a bab. should either have had absolutely no experience of cooking or experience confined to hash-houses where, instead of customers getting serviettes, they wipe their greasy hands on the establishment's large woolly dog, which is washed every Wednesday, and mulligatawny soup is on the menu every Thursday. **1959** *Bulletin* (Sydney) 1 July 18/2 The bab's present rate for cooking for more than seven is £14 4s. 11d., *plus* keep and overtime for Sundays and holidays, *plus* (in the north-west) 14s. 8d. parity-rate. **1965** R. FAIR *Treasury Anzac Humour* 34 We have a tame Babbling Brook, who in civvy life was a parson. . . Fritz put up another salvo. . . The Bab. ducked.

babbler. BABBLING BROOK.

1904 *Worker* (Sydney) 6 Aug. 7/1 Ninety per cent of the cooks do their full share of work. The offsider gets a third and emerges for next season as a full-fledged Babbler—that is if he takes to the game. **1915** *Bulletin* (Sydney) 28 Oct. 22/3 The cook is 'the babbler' or 'dough-puncher', the former an allusion to 'the babbling brook'. **1918** *Kia Ora Coo-ee* Sept. 14/3 Cooks range from the grease-besmudged 'babbler', who dishes up a monotonous succession of 'teas straight', bad language and an occasional stew, to the natty, smart-looking chef. **1926** *Bulletin* (Sydney) 11 Feb. 24/1 The shearers have their 'babbler' set—he's feeding them now on hash. **1942** *Ibid.* 22 Apr. 13/3 The babbler . . remarked: 'I see youse blokes don't seem to care much about my slapdab. If y'll wait a mo, I'll change it into a queen puddin'.' **1943** S.W. KEOUGH *Around Army* 19 In base camps, barracks, and other pleasant places where military life, in terms of scran, approximates civvy spheres, it amounts almost to a sacrilege to refer to the lordly being who presides over the kitchen as a greasy or a babbler. **1946** *Bulletin* (Sydney) 3 July 29/1 That woman, I'll give in, was a wizard of a babbler—she could pretty well disguise anything. **1962** *Ibid.* 3 Feb. 43/2 The . . babbler had a feed of cold cuts all prepared—from ham to colonial goose. **1977** F.A. REEDER *Diary of Rat* 63 We came back to camp with the ute loaded down to the Plimsoll with jams, milk, beans, bully and tinned fruit. If that did not give the babblers encouragement nothing would.

babbling brook. Rhyming slang for 'cook', esp. one catering for a party of shearers or stockmen; an army cook.

1913 *Bulletin* (Sydney) 25 Sept. 24/1 I'll touch the babblin' brook here for . . scran today . . and work the other sheds down to Yanco. **1916** *Ibid.* 3 Feb. 24/4 Noticed . . a shearers' 'babbling brook' (cook) saying he was sick and tired of the smell of barbers. **1918** *Kia Ora Coo-ee* Oct. 4/3 They knew the cook-house call as well as we did, if not better. I reckon they used to watch the 'babbling brooks'. **1920** *Aussie* (Sydney) Apr. 20/3 Indignant Digger to Babbling Brook: 'Tea! Tea! D'yer call this tea? It's nothing but innocent water scalded to death!' **1933** H.B. RAINE *Whip-Hand* 35 'And who is Porky?' inquired Jean. 'The Babbling Brook. That is to say, our sergeant cook in France,' answered Bluey. **1940** I.L. IDRIESS *Lightning Ridge* 59 The white-whiskered old Babbling Brook used to make scrumptious brownies. **1955** M. DURACK *Keep him my Country* (1966) 138 'Seen our illustrious Babbling Brook?' he asked. 'He's in the kitchen as far as I know.' **1967** G. JENKIN *Two Yrs. Bardunyah Station* 2 There was a colossal racket coming from the Hut as the 'babbling brook' belted away at . . iron pipes suspended under the verandah and told the bush that dinner was ready. **1975** B. FOLEY *Shearers' Poems* 11 They had no Christmas pudding Because the 'Babbling Brook' was dead. He'd not been much of a 'bait layer' But not a bad sort of a bloke. **1977** F.A. REEDER *Diary of Rat* 60 Next day a couple of our babbling brooks were feeling a bit off colour.

Hence **babble** *v. trans.*, to cook. Also as *vbl. n.*

1938 *Bulletin* (Sydney) 19 Jan. 20/1 I've bin babblin' for fifty-four years, Cookin' all sorts o' scran—yairs, from wombats to steers. **1962** *Sydney Morning Herald* 24 Nov. 12/1 Gaily aproned women do the 'babbling' (cooking).

bach, var. BATCH *n.* and *v.*

bachelor's buttons. Also **bachelors' buttons** and as sing. [Spec. use of *bachelor's buttons* any of various plants with button-like flowers: see OED *bachelor* 6.] BILLY BUTTONS.

1852 W. HOWITT *Land, Labor & Gold* 7 Nov. (1855) I. 109 In the grassy places, the Murnong of the natives, like a yellow hawkweed, and a yellow bachelor's button (*Craspedia Ridua*), are very gay. **1855** *Ibid.* II. 92 A sort of bachelor's buttons, or golden balls, different to the ordinary ones of this colony. These balls were round and firm as if of solid gold, and covered with little points. **1908** E.J. BANFIELD *Confessions of Beachcomber* 221 The little yellow diurnal moth commonly known as 'the wanderer' has a partiality for the nectar of the 'bachelor's button' as yellow as itself. **1921** K.S. PRICHARD *Black Opal* 65 Bachelor's buttons paint the earth raw gold. **1944** G. COCKERILL *Scribblers & Statesmen* 71 Joe walked over the hills . . gaily whisking off the grass beads [*sic*] and bachelors' buttons with his myall stick. **1981** E. POTTER *Scone I Remember* 23 The silver-stemmed, silver-leaved yellow balls of a flower we used to call 'bachelors' buttons'.

bachelor's hall. *Obs.* Also **bachelors' hall.** [Transf. use of *bachelor's hall* a bachelor's establishment.] BACHELORS' QUARTERS.

[**1846** *Bell's Life in Sydney* 27 June 1/5 The dwelling-houses of the principals are mostly very neatly built, and for bush houses have many little comforts scarcely expected in the bachelor's hall of a bushman.] **1875** *Austral. Town & Country Jrnl.* (Sydney) 180/2 The five buildings shown in the engraving is the general manager's residence, then there are to the right and left, the bachelor's hall, overseer's, storekeepers, and accountant's cottages, the mens' quarters, &c. **1881** A.C. GRANT *Bush-Life Qld.* I. 56 The building John had dined and slept in . . was called 'The Bachelors' Hall.' **1891** *Truth* (Sydney) 15 Mar. 7/3 Take for instance, Billy Bangsall, whose mother is a friend of King William's. You can't well send him to the hut, so he goes to the barracks, or bachelors' hall. **1906** W.A. HORN *Notes by Nomad* 82 The traveller simply turns his horse into the station paddock, and, according to his social grade, goes either to the 'Government House' (owner's dwelling), 'Bachelor's Hall' (overseer's), or to the men's kitchen, and the next morning pursues his journey. **1913** W.K. HARRIS *Outback in Aust.* 46 The 'Batchelors' Hall' was a better structure than is usually found so far outback, and consisted of eight separate rooms, with two entrances.

bachelors' quarters. *Obs.* Accommodation provided on a station for single men, esp. jackeroos and overseers; BARRACKS *n.*[1] 2.

1878 G. WALCH *Australasia* 19 The unconscious object of his threats was seated on the verandah of the bachelors' quarters. **1881** MRS C. PRAED *Policy & Passion* I. 135 'Not even the Bachelors' Quarters would be sacred to Mrs. Maddox,' answered Cathcart, shortly. **1890** 'R. BOLDREWOOD' *Squatter's Dream* 123 The bachelors' quarters made ready for occupation. **1891** D.E. FALK *Rick* 295 The pretty cottage, with its detached kitchen and outhouses, the fine orchard, the roomy stables, the store and wool-store, the bachelors' quarters, termed familiarly the 'barracks', the men's huts at the rear—all were pointed out to him. **1964** J.S. MANIFOLD *Who wrote Ballads?* 86 Next below the homestead socially comes the 'narangy barracks', 'bachelors' quarters' or 'jackaroos' quarters'. . . It would be rare indeed to find a piano in the bachelors' quarters, but in the '80s and '90s you might bet on finding the highly fashionable banjo.

back, *a.*, *n.*[1], and *adv.* [Spec. use of *back* distant, outlying.]

A. *adj.*

1. Inland of settled districts.

1800 *HRA* (1914) 1st Ser. II. 411 Those of the back Farms and above the Creek in remote situations are exposed to great Danger from the Natives. **1849** *Britannia* (Hobart) 12 Apr. 3/2 There is every reason to believe the robbers are lurking about some of the back stations. **1864** 'E.S.H.' *Narr. Trip Sydney to Peak Downs* 23 A high range behind the township shuts it out from the back grazing country. **1886** *Argus* (Melbourne) 13 Mar. 4/2 There is nothing so beautiful as these swans which breed in the Back Lakes. **1900** *Bulletin* (Sydney) 19 May 14/3 One of the speakers complimented said tradesman upon having worked so hard to get a road opened to some back place. **1904** M. WHITE *Shanty Entertainment* 39 And it was good to hear the old back-hut hatter's laugh.

2. Distant from a permanent watercourse.

1837 *Perth Gaz.* 14 Oct. 988 A party relinquishes 3,000 acres of his original back grant on the Swan, for which he receives a choice of selection elsewhere for 1000 in fee simple. **1843** *Sydney Morning Herald* 8 May 3/5 The station is first-rate, being situated on the banks of the never-failing stream, Murrumbidgee, where all the natural conveniences for sheep-washing it is well known cannot be surpassed, with back pasture to an almost unlimited extent. **1851** *Empire* (Sydney) 10 June 3/4 It was a first-rate flood, and within three feet of the great flood, overflowing the banks and filling all the back creeks and lagoons. **1855** *Illustr. Sydney News* 20 Jan. 20/3 Large numbers of diggers coming in from the back gullies where water is not to be had and settling down on the banks of the Bendigo. **1886** R. Henty *Australiana* 17, I was on the back plains of the Murrumbidgee [*sic*]. **1890** 'R. Boldrewood' *Squatter's Dream* 36 There's always plenty of back-water on this run. **1899** *Bulletin* (Sydney) 7 Jan. 14/1 During '88 drought was fixing flood-gates in a back creek anticipating a fresh. **1956** T. Ronan *Moleskin Midas* 193 If ever we strike one of them droughts there'll be a big smash on this river. There ain't enough back water on any of these joints barring my place.

3. In the sparsely populated interior, remote from towns and settled districts. See also Outback *a.*

1848 J.A. Jackson *National Emigration* 7 The illimitable and easily accessible back-pastures of the Australian continent. **1849** *Belfast Gaz.* (Port Phillip) 21 Sept. 3/1 The inhabitants of the back districts should not be content with yielding a tacit consent. **1872** 'Demonax' *Mysteries & Miseries* 30/2 The head reporter of that important back-district journal was a thin meagre individual. **1880** J. Bonwick *Resources Qld.* 32 In the back plains of Queensland there are still some dangers. **1885** *Bulletin* (Sydney) 28 Feb. 5/4 Squatter from the back Barcoo and a couple of friends are actively engaged in 'painting the city red' when waiter enters and the shepherd king calls out. **1887** A. Nicols *Wild Life & Adventure* p. vii, Life in the back Bush of Queensland may prove interesting. **1896** D. Stewart *Thousand Miles & More* 55 In these back districts you frequently obtain the finest and best of commodities although the price is very high. **1902** *Bulletin* (Sydney) 30 Oct. 16/2 Mail . . in Queensland back towns . . has been known to finish the journey in a wheelbarrow. **1902** *Blackwood's Mag.* (Edinburgh) May 642/1 Only the niggers knows what it is, an' no white man barrin' us back boys has iver got any. **1906** *Bulletin* (Sydney) 24 May 15/2 The frequency with which the country joskin loses himself in the city is even worse than the persistency with which the city cove gets bushed in the back regions. **1917** *Ibid.* 5 July 24/1 Near the boundary fence of a back run on the north-west coast of Tasmania I came across a horrible example of the cruelty of the casual white trapper. **1920** C.H. Sayce *Golden Buckles* 21 His mother was one of those stock mares for which the back stations are famous. **1930** 'Brent Of Bin Bin' *Ten Creeks Run* (1952) 24 Racially he was a born conversationalist or monologist: the solitary conditions of the boundaries of the back runs and the taciturnity of the colonials restricted his life. **1975** G. Page *Smalltown Memorials* 1 Out on back-roads the churches are dying.

B. *n.*[1] Chiefly in the phr. **at (out,** etc.) **the back of.**

1. The part of a station most distant from the homestead or from permanent water.

1878 'R. Boldrewood' *Ups & Downs* 22 But the herd had spread by degrees over the wide plains of 'the back', as well as over the broad river flats and green reed-beds of 'the frontage'. **1884** —— *Old Melbourne Memories* 62 An expedition had been made to a . . desolate tract of country which lay at 'the back' of the run. **1888** —— *Robbery under Arms* 78 One day we were out at the back making some lambing yards. **1930** V. Palmer *Passage* (1957) 172 Living out at the back of runs, too, on wells and potholes.

2. A part of the interior which is remote from towns and settled districts. See also Outback *n.*

1897 *Bulletin* (Sydney) 4 Sept. 32/1 On a little old bush-racecourse at the back of No Man's Land. **1905** *Truth* (Sydney) 26 Mar. 1/8 A couple living together in a settlement at-the-back-of-out-back . . were often attacked by the visiting parson. **1910** *Bulletin* (Sydney) 9 June 15/1 Struck a quaint old card . . out at the back of the Barcoo. **1911** *Ibid.* 26 Oct. 13/2 Away out on the myall country at the back of the Hodgkinson. **1929** A.H. Chisholm *Birds & Green Places* 99 North into the 'back' of New South Wales. **1938** C.P. Conigrave *Walk-About* 34 A fair number of stockmen had come in with the 'mob' that was being held out on the grassy plains at the back of the Bastion Ranges. **1953** D. Stivens *Gambling Ghost* 1, I was in the back of the outback, two hundred miles from anywhere, with a broken leg. **1959** J. Cleary *Strike me Lucky* 185, I could be out the back of Alice Springs, out on me own in the mulga, and there'd allus be some nosey parker shoving his nose in to complain.

C. *adv.* At or to the back of: see quots.

1878 'R. Boldrewood' *Ups & Downs* 232 The well-marked but unfrequented track which led 'back'—that is, to the indifferently-watered, sparsely-stocked, and thinly-populated region which stretched endless at the rear of the great leading streams. **1890** —— *Colonial Reformer* III. 115 Every hoof of stock was off the frontage now and away back, where there was good shelter and a trifle of feed. **1894** G.H. Gibson *Ironbark Chips* 15 There are still adventures to be met with if you go far enough 'back' to seek them. **1911** *Huon Times* (Franklin) 4 Feb. 2/5 Do you know the Upper Huon very well?—I have been back about 20 miles, and know the country pretty well. **1936** I.L. Idriess *Cattle King* 63 He rode back bush, nearing Wilcannia.

D. In phr.

a. back of (or **o'**) (a town or place): behind; beyond. Freq. **back o' sunset.** See also Sunset 1.

1891 J. Fenton *Bush Life Tas.* (1964) 127 This summer I have grown in pots and boxes . . the native indigo, the thorny acacia from the mountains back of Melbourne, and the glory pea from seeds out of your garden. **1898** *Bulletin* (Sydney) 13 Aug. 14/3 Nothing warms the heart of a backblocker in town more than to meet a man who knew 'that big fence back of McBride's'. And, of course, the spieler does. **1900** *Ibid.* 31 Mar. 15/2 Swagging it recently back of the Darling, I called at a boundary-rider's hut. **1903** *Ibid.* 30 July 17/2 Lamb-marking is now general in the Milparinka-Tibooburra district. . . This part of Back-o'-Out-Back does get rain occasionally. **1911** *Ibid.* 30 Nov. 14/3, I know an old corn and pumpkin cocky on the Mulgrave River, back o' Cairns. **1912** L. Esson *Red Gums* 30 Beyond the world—the track is never ended—Back o' the sunset, there the region splendid The Unknown, lures men ever. **1918** B. Reynolds *Dawn Asper* 5 She waited by the open slip-rails back of her selection home. **1919** R.J. Cassidy *Gipsy Road* 57 Yet Abdul and his inelegant 'hunchies' [*sc.* camels] are an essentiality of life on the lone, level lands that stretch away back o' sunset. **1944** 'S. Campion' *Pommy Cow* 203 Back of Kylie is the desert. **1963** I.L. Idriess *Our Living Stone Age* p. ix Prospecting in that marvellous tableland back o' Cairns.

b. back of beyond: see Beyond.

c. back of Bourke: see Bourke.

back, *n.*[2] *Timber-getting.* [Spec. use of *back* the opposite to the front.] The side of a tree trunk opposite the Belly. See quot. 1909. Also *attrib.* as **back-cut.**

1901 *Advocate* (Burnie) 28 Nov. 2/6 Bryan put in excellent work and was the first to turn to the back cut despite his handicap. **1909** R. Kaleski *Austral. Settler's Compl. Guide* 55 Standing timber is *chopped* through by cutting two scarfs or notches in it, which run out in the centre; the first one on the side the tree is to fall (the 'belly' scarf), the second on the reverse side or 'back'. The 'belly' scarf is cut first so that the tree won't fall on the cutter; if he wants to commit suicide he cuts the 'belly' last. **1916** *Bulletin* (Sydney) 8 June 24/3 When referring to the cut made by axe or saw, they spoke of it as the 'belly-cut' or the 'back-cut'. **1959** *Overland* xv. 14 In no time I was climbing up onto the springboard up the trunk and putting in the belly cut while one of them put in the back cut.

back, *n.*[3] [Spec. use of *back* situated to the rear.] That part of a gaol in which prisoners are kept in solitary confinement. Also *attrib.*

1896 M. Hornsby *Old Time Echoes Tas.* 173 'Fourteen days in the back cells,' said Boyd. **1962** J. Brown *Harpoon* 50 McLeod lost two stone in weight while he was in solitary confinement. When he was released, and appeared in the exercise yard, prisoners . . came up and asked him how he was. It was obvious that anyone who had done a stretch out 'the back' was treated with respect.

back, *v.*[1] [Poss. transf. use of *back* to mount (see OED(S *v.* 10), but prob. of independent development.] *intr.* Of a sheep dog: to run across the backs of yarded sheep and, by barking, cause the sheep to move in the required direction.

[N.Z. **1934** J.E. Lilico *Sheep-Dog Mem.* 26 Finest backing dogs . . any keen dog constantly forcing in yards can be trained to back . . but stockmen in Addington have evolved a race which take naturally to backing.] **1942** R.B. Kelley *Animal Breeding* 142 In sheep yards the dog that will 'back' probably is the most specialized.

Hence **backing dog** *n.*

1934 [see Back *v.*[1]]. **1941** S.J. Baker *Pop. Dict. Austral. Slang* 6 *Backing dog*, a sheepdog that will run across the backs of sheep to aid mustering or droving. **1942** R.B. Kelley *Animal Breeding* 142 At the big sale yards . . 'backing' dogs . . go forward up the races and down the lanes, over the tightly packed sheep's backs and, by barking vigorously, cause the leading sheep to keep moving. **1955** N. Pulliam *I traveled Lonely Land* 370 *Backing dog*, a sheepman's dog which runs across the backs of the sheep to help round them up.

back, *v.*[2] *Timber-getting.* [Spec. use of *back, v.* to set back.] *trans.* With **off**: to trim (a post, sleeper, etc.) with a broad-axe.

1855 'Rusticus' *How to settle in Vic.* 10 If good sound timber be employed, and the posts split in the way the splitters term *backing off*, they will probably last for twenty years. **1908** *Bulletin* (Sydney) 27 Feb. 15/1 The sawn sleeper is inferior because it is cut across the grain, while the sleeper-chopper 'backs' his off with the grain.

back block, *n.* and *attrib.*

A. *n.*

1. A tract of land in the remote interior; in *pl.*, sparsely populated country beyond the closely settled districts.

1870 *Argus* (Melbourne) 22 Mar. 7/2 Fancy the change, the transition from a cis-Darling back block to Melbourne and the Theatre Royal! ***c* 1872** J.C.F. Johnson *Over Island* 2 You'll have to go many miles out of your course, and perhaps get bushed altogether out in the back blocks. **1876** 'Capricornus' *Colonisation* 21 The talk is . . of new country, back blocks, waterless plains, spinifex, and mulga scrub. **1882** A.S. Armstrong *Austral. Sheep Husbandry* 3 Winters seldom pass without a rich water supply being received in the back blocks. **1884** *Austral. Tit-Bits* (Melbourne) 17 July 2/1 A new arrival in Melbourne from one of the back blocks . . had never been in a big town in his life before. **1891** *Quiz* (Adelaide) 3 July 7/2 The lending of books in the back blocks is a great institution . . country folk are generous. **1892** *Braidwood Dispatch* 7 Dec. 4/2 These timber-getters are very good citizens. They are men who have gone into the back blocks of the country and have been real pioneers. **1897** E. Soldene *My Theatr. & Mus. Recoll.* 210 It seemed terrible when people one knew said they had been 'up country' in the 'back blocks', in 'the bush' for six months at a time. **1902** *Blackwood's Mag.* (Edinburgh) May 638/1 The back-blocks, generally, are the western divisions of Queensland and New South Wales. **1908** Mrs A. Gunn *We of Never-Never* 181 'Back blocks!' he said in scorn. 'There ain't no back blocks left. Can't travel a hundred miles nowadays without running into somebody!' **1923** *Bailey, M.L.A. Exonerated* (Austral. Workers Union) 24 Do you consider Wagga out in the backblocks? **1932** H. Priest *Call of Bush* 56 It is difficult to keep up-to-date with one's reading in the 'back blocks'—and very expensive. **1950** E.M. England *Where Turtles Dance* 88 He's attaining his majority—a big event, even for a William Mumble of the backblocks. **1977** J. Wallace *Memories Country Childhood* 46 As I reached across the table to help myself to jam, an aunt said: 'If you do that, people will think you come from the back blocks.' **1981** A. Wilkinson *Up Country* 109 'It's way out in the back blocks,' my informant continued, ' . . the first hut built in the district.'

2. Land behind that with a water frontage; land on which there is no permanent watercourse. Also *attrib.*

1871 *Austral. Town & Country Jrnl.* (Sydney) 29 Apr. 518/4 The feed on both frontage and back blocks looks splendid. **1872** 'Resident' *Glimpses Life Vic.* 31 We were doomed to see the whole of our river-frontage purchased. The back blocks which were left to us were insufficient for the support of our flocks, and deficient in permanent water-supply. **1879** *Austral.: Monthly Mag.* (Sydney) II. 527 We allude to our policy in dealing with dry country or 'back blocks'. **1885** P.R. Meggy

From Sydney to Silverton 27 The state of things on this back block has been so bad for five years or more. **1887** W.H. SUTTOR *Austral. Stories Retold* 99 Down to the year 1857 . . squatting was almost entirely confined to the lands permanently watered. No one thought of settling on the back blocks. **1890** 'R. BOLDREWOOD' *Squatter's Dream* 24 He had been permanently located upon a back block, where economy in the use of water was a virtue of necessity. **1949** *Bulletin* (Sydney) 5 Jan. 29/4 He bought a back block on Dingo Creek and built himself a hut. **1974** J. HORNER *Vote Ferguson* 2 Newchum squatters were forced to buy the dry, waterless 'backblocks', unfenced and useless for keeping stock. **1980** P. FREEMAN *Woolshed* 132 Wargam was a 'back block' run—there were no permanent watercourses, and only the sinking of wells or the ownership of other riverside property could make such properties useful in the last century.

3. *transf.* and *fig.*

1944 F. BRUNO *Sa-eeda Wog!* 32 The fortunes of war . . deposited us thirstily in this back-block of the Balkans. **1968** *Swag* (Sydney) ii. 6 A scruffy house on the back-blocks of St Kilda. **1972** *Bulletin* (Sydney) 26 Feb. 41/1 Ringside tables are all labelled 'reserved'. . . But the back blocks are full of wide open spaces and you can settle down to wait for curtains up at nine.

B. *attrib.* Located in a remote and sparsely populated inland district; characteristic of those who live in such a district. Also **backblocks.**

1868 *Adelaide Punch* 19 Dec. 11/1 And this is the daily city life of the hardy back-block pioneer. **1887** *Boomerang* (Brisbane) 31 Dec. 11/2 Without a forwarding agent at Rockhampton a backblocks purchaser is dependent on influences altogether independent of him. **1900** *Western Champion* (Barcaldine) 10 Apr. 9/1 This is typical of the average back-block colonial. His sole ambition is to become proficient in profanity. **1906** J. BARBOUR *Pencillings on Wallaby* 31 They yearned for beer with a backblock thirst. **1910** *Huon Times* (Franklin) 30 Nov. 3/4 With a fine accuracy which would delight the soul of a back block teacher of the past generation, the Treasurer announced that the expenditure for 1911 would be £16,841,629. **1920** *Smith's Weekly* (Sydney) 11 Sept. 17/4 The Australian hopbush, a great standby for stock in drought time, is also useful in the backblocks home. Many old bushwhackers declare that the flowers . . are superior to the common hops. **1930** N.F. SPIELVOGEL *Old Eko's Note-bk.* 177 The great civilizing good it was doing by sending these cultured, handsome lassies to the back-block schools. **1956** R.G. EDWARDS *Overlander Songbk.* 102 I'm only a backblocks shearer, as easily can be seen, I've shore in almost every shed in the plains of the Riverine. **1965** E. LAMBERT *Long White Night* 79 Bocker in his backblocks innocence had absorbed it all, and become sick with suspicion. **1975** L.H. CLARK *Rouseabout Reflections* 12 For I'd heard by 'back-block wireless' That old Danny 'tanked' and tireless, Had been tramping round the shanty pubs, and having quite a spree. **1978** B. ST. A. SMITH *Spirit beyond Psyche* 97 No matter where the tiny backblocks pub in which they were drinking might be, people always seemed to know him, to recognise him.

backblocker. One who lives in the back blocks: see BACK BLOCK *n.* 1.

1870 *Argus* (Melbourne) 22 Mar. 7/2, I am a bushman, a back blocker, to whom it happens about once in two years to visit Melbourne. **1881** W.E. ABBOTT *Notes Journey on Darling* 60 The back-blocker must get leave from the owner of the nearest tank where water can be got to draw it out in waggons to where the work is to be done. **1889** J.S. MANIFOLD *Who wrote Ballads?* (1964) 104 Gordon is the favourite—I may say the only—poet of the backblocker. **1898** *Bulletin* (Sydney) 13 Aug. 14/3 Nothing warms the heart of a backblocker in town more than to meet a man who knew 'that big fence back of McBride's'. And, of course, the spieler does. **1902** *Blackwood's Mag.* (Edinburgh) May 638/1 On the streets of Sydney or Melbourne the appearance of a copper-skinned back-blocker excites as much comment as might a being from another planet. **1905** *Steele Rudd's Mag.* (Brisbane) May 449 No one knows the art of 'making the best of things' better than the back-blocker. **1906** J. PARSONS *Thirty-Six Yrs. amongst Criminals* 37 As a rule, when the 'backblockers' first came in they purchased a new suit of clothes and made a great show for a few days. **1908** W.H. OGILVIE *My Life in Open* p. x, The feeling, of boundary-riders and back-blockers, of men unspoiled by culture. **1923** J. BOWES *Jackaroos* 18 Coaches even stopped far short of the 'back blockers', and the only mode of travel was by bullock- or horse-team. **1929** 'OLD STOCKMAN' *Sensational Cattle-Stealing Case* 7 The backblockers were a hard-riding, hard-swearing lot, but they opened up the country. **1948** M. UREN *Glint of Gold* 155 Like most back-blockers he was prematurely grey, but possessed the keen eyes of the bushman, the easy walk of a man used to long trails.

back country, *n.* and *attrib.* [U.S. *back country* country at the rear of a settled district: see OEDS.]

A. *n.*

1. Country lying inland of settled districts.

1798 *Hist. Rec. N.S.W.* (1895) III. 820 A report which some artful villain in the colony had propagated amongst the Irish convicts lately arrived, 'That there was a colony of white people at no very great distance in the back country—150 or 200 miles—where there was abundance of every sort of provision without the necessity of so much labour.' **1802** M. FLINDERS *Voyage to Terra Australis* (1814) I. 111 No hill, nor any thing behind the shore could be perceived, but it does not certainly follow that there are no hills in the back country, for the haze was too thick to admit of the sight extending beyond four or five leagues. **1825** B. FIELD *Geogr. Mem. N.S.W.* 467 The cedar grounds end before Shoal Haven . . and Mr Berry need not be alarmed lest any occupation of the immediate back country should shut in his cattle-run. **1840** *S. Austral. Rec.* (London) 1 Aug. 70 Every day is increasing our knowledge of the back country, and adding to our flocks and herds. **1845** C. HODGKINSON *Aust.* 18 The back country being very hilly, densely wooded, and intersected by narrow ravines, and brushy hollows . . rises to an altitude of 3000 feet. **1846** G.H. HAYDON *Five Yrs. Experience* 15 The whole of the back country of Australia is denominated the bush. **1848** T.L. MITCHELL *Jrnl. Exped. Tropical Aust.* 428 On the occupation of that back-country must . . depend the establishment of a direct line of communication between Sydney and the Gulf of Carpentaria. **1864** *Port Denison Times* 26 Mar. 3/2 Another party consisting of Messrs. Scott, Tully, Dallachy and myself went to explore the back country, and ascended the range to survey the back valley of the ranges. **1873** A. TROLLOPE *Aust. & N.Z.* I. 31 Great difficulty of immigration . . prevents . . speedy filling up of the back country. **1882** G. RANDALL *Aust. for Industrious* 17 If this back country was taken up and fully stocked, it is capable of carrying not seven but fifty millions of sheep! **1891** J. FENTON *Bush Life Tas.* (1964) 168 Mr Smith was the first to thoroughly explore the back country of West Devon. **1897** L. LINDLEY-COWEN *W. Austral. Settler's Guide* 58 A sheep owner will lay baits of meat or fat poisoned with strychnine, or occasionally set a trap if he finds that a dingo has been harrying his stock, but the dogs are allowed to breed in their fastnesses in the back country almost undisturbed. **1905** E.C. BULEY *Austral. Life* 5 The Australian of the cities speaks of the rest of his continent as 'the bush'. The dwellers in the agricultural country speak of the district further inland as the 'back country'. Those themselves in the back country have behind them a land, partly unknown, and therefore attractive to the adventurous, which they call the 'Never-Never Land'. **1921** J. MATTHAMS *Rabbit Pest in Aust.* 203 Have been attracted by the female dingo into the back country, where many of them have remained. **1938** *Bulletin* (Sydney) 12 Oct. 21/1 The tallyman at the timber-mill that I haul logs to knows the back-country well. **1953** T.G. TUCKER *Aust. as Home* 38 Settlement has now crept out far into the interior and 'back' country. **1968** K. WEATHERLY *Roo Shooter* 25 Ben . . had been a miner and knocked about all parts of the back country with his mate.

2. Land removed from a permanent watercourse; BACK GROUND 2; BACK LAND 1. See also BACK BLOCK *n.* 2.

1839 T.L. MITCHELL *Three Exped. Eastern Aust.* (rev. ed.) I. 302 Grass is only to be found on the banks of the river. . . None may appear in the back country. **1845** L. LEICHHARDT *Jrnl. Overland Exped. Aust.* 23 Oct. (1847) 450 These hills separated the valley of the river from an open well grassed, but extremely stony back country; from which creeks carried the water down to the river, through gaps and openings between the hills. **1848** *Sydney Morning Herald* 27 May 2/7 All the creeks in the back country are dry, and the stock are forced into the Murrumbidgee to obtain a supply of water. **1865** *Austral. Monthly Mag.* (Melbourne) I. 17 We experienced considerable difficulty in crossing the back country from Balronald [*sic*] to the Darling, owing to a total absence of feed. **1868** C.W. BROWNE *Overlanding in Aust.* 6 It is this want of water that makes it so hazardous a speculation to take up back country (by back country I mean country away from any of the principal rivers, and only just taken up; all the inner boundaries of the colonies are called back country). **1883** F. BONNEY *On Some Customs Aborigines* 2 On that occasion their only water supply was at the few springs in the back country and at the rivers. **1889** *Illustr. Austral. News* (Melbourne) 1 Oct. 3/1 Along the course of the Murray the river in many places overflowed its banks and covered large stretches of back country with its waters. **1890** 'R. BOLDREWOOD' *Colonial Reformer* III. 117 By degrees it began to be asserted that 'back country', *i.e.* the lands remote from all visible means of subsistence for flocks and herds, as far as water was concerned, paid the speculative pastoral occupier better than the 'frontage', or land in the neighbourhood of permanent creeks, and of the few well-known rivers. **1892** *Trans. & Proc. R. Soc. S.A.* 195 Next came the wool-grower, who stocked the back country (*i.e.* back from the rivers). **1927** A. CROMBIE *After Sixty Yrs.* 96 Development of the Lachlan back country. **1944** C. FENNER *Mostly Austral.* 114 Gnamma-holes . . are well-known features to those who know the back country. **1954** H.G. LAMOND *Manx Star* 64 Bores had been started out from the river in the back-country.

3. The hinterland of a port; BACK LAND 2.

1849 *Belfast Gaz.* (Port Phillip) 14 Sept. 3/1 Melbourne boasts of itself as the capital, Geelong as the 'commercial emporium', Warrnambool as possessing a fine back-country, and snug little harbour. **1861** J.D. LANG *Qld., Aust.* 126 Gladstone . . will be the outlet of a very large back country. **1876** 'EIGHT YRS.' RESIDENT' *Queen of Colonies* 167 There is no back country to the port.

4. Land immediately beyond settled districts, or adjacent to stations, used as supplementary grazing land.

1876 'CAPRICORNUS' *Colonisation* 8 The unsold back country was left open in an easy way, so that the settlers might get the use of the grass. **1878** R.B. SMYTH *Aborigines of Vic.* I. 33 The tract [*sc.* north-western Vic.] is hot in summer and cold in winter, and much of it cannot be regarded but as 'back-country' for the tribes bordering on it, to be used only at certain times during each season, when the productions which it affords might tempt the Aboriginals to penetrate several parts of it. **1881** W. FEILDING *Austral. Trans-Continental Railway* 27 Malvern Hills Station. . . There are now about 120,000 sheep and 5,000 cattle on this station, but it would carry more if the back country could be given water. **1887** W.H. SUTTOR *Austral. Stories Retold* 105 The back country was used as a common by the frontage proprietors. **1889** H. EGBERT *Pretty Cockey* 44 The Wallaby Station had an extensive run adjoining it, besides a good deal of back country. **1890** 'R. BOLDREWOOD' *Colonial Reformer* III. 109 The sheep also you may as well keep: they'll pay their own wages if you put 'em on a bit of spare back country, and there's plenty your cattle never go near. **1897** H. HUSSEY *Colonial Life & Christian Experience* 303 Notice of the meeting was sent to those on and about the station, and I undertook to go out in the afternoon to one or two families residing in the back country, two or three miles from the station. **1899** *North-Western Advocate* (Devonport) 16 Jan. 3/4 Access to its splendid area of back country. **1911** *Huon Times* (Franklin) 18 Feb. 4/4 The back country is first-class grazing land. **1927** A. CROMBIE *After Sixty Yrs.* 74 Tarrawong Station . . had been the headquarters for Tyson's back country.

5. Land in the sparsely populated interior, remote from towns and closely settled districts.

1887 'OVERLANDER' *Austral. Sketches* 1 You want to know how I first took to the roads and the back country. **1889** E.E. MORRIS *Cassell's Picturesque Australasia* IV. 143 Then in September the teams would come in from the back country, groaning under the weight of tons of wool neatly packed in bales. **1889** *Braidwood Dispatch* 2 Oct. 2/3 A sun-downer on the run, seeking honest employment in the back country. **1891** 'SMILER' *Wanderings Simple Child* (ed. 3) 95 He had let out to one of the women that he had been nine years in the back country dealing in stock, and had made a big pile. **1892** 'J. MILLER' *Workingman's Paradise* 145 There are 20,000 men in the back country altogether and I don't believe 5000 of them have votes and they're mostly squatters and their managers. **1897** A.F. PATERSON *'Mid Saltbush & Mallee* 2 One of the ladies said to her, 'You will find the back-country dull after this nice holiday, Mrs. Gage.' **1918** B. REYNOLDS *Dawn Asper* 176 It was nearing noon . . and the family were gathering round the long table for that substantial meal called dinner in the back country. **1921** C.E.W. BEAN *Official Hist. Aust. 1914–18* I. 47 The long journeys in droving bullocks down the great stock routes across the 'back country' offer many conditions similar to those of a military expedition. **1929** K.S. PRICHARD *Coonardoo* (1961) 9 As a young man he spent all the money he had made on sprees in the coastal towns, and went off into the back-country again when his cheque gave out. **1948** G. FARWELL *Down Argent Street* 1 They drifted in from the back country . . drovers and boundary riders. **1951** —— *Outside Track* 21 For an earlier generation there seemed something queer in men who preferred to exist in the back country, rather than try their luck in closer-settled lands Inside. **1954** T. RONAN *Vision Splendid* 236 Grog is the ruination of the back country. **1956** B.J. RAYMENT *My Towri* 61 When I was living there, it was not served by that one modern blessing to the back country, the Flying Doctor. **1962** MARSHALL & DRYSDALE *Journey among Men* 52 But in the back country, the far north, the land of the Never-Never, in a way of life that offers little comfort and few luxuries, it is cold beer that has the special place. **1976** MULLALLY & SEXTON *Stir Possum* 13, I had just returned from the back country from a droving trip which had taken me south to Mullewa. **1979** D. LOCKWOOD *My Old Mates & I* 82 The beef roads had reached into the back country, bitumen to Wave Hill and beyond.

B. *attrib.*

1888 'R. BOLDREWOOD' *Robbery under Arms* 234 Dad was dressed up to look like a back-country squatter. **1894** *Bulletin* (Sydney) 6 Jan. 7/3 All back-country men will remember Bogan. **1899** *Ibid.* 25 Feb. 3/2, I struck a back-country selector, named Patrick McDonald O'Day. **1910** *Emu* X. 16 A large express waggon, built for the back country roads. **1926** L.C.E. GEE *Bush Tracks & Gold Fields* 23 Bother and blunder in getting a back country expedition started. **1937** W. HATFIELD *I find Aust.* 91 A strange back-country code seems to place cattle-stealing outside mere low-down thieving. **1944** *Bulletin* (Sydney) 26 Jan. 13/4 Back-country milkers never forget their birthplace, and no river-fence will stop them making back there to calve. **1962** T. RONAN *Deep of Sky* 79 The McKays were, in back-country idiom, 'smart men', and there was never a version of the English tongue so prone to understatement as back-country idiom. **1962** *Bulletin* (Sydney) 20 Jan. 11/3 Some young, back-country shearers 'inside' for the first time reckon wide-open Yass the Paris of the south, with grog on all the time. **1968** E.M. NOBLET *Winds that Blew* 60 Her face was very thin and had what I called the 'uncooked look' of many of the back-country women.

back ground. *Obs.* [f. BACK *a.* + GROUND *n.*[2] 1.]

1. Land immediately behind an allotment or settlement, used as grazing land; BACK LAND 3.

1804 *Sydney Gaz.* 11 Nov. A number of labourers had been employed in clearing and burning off a back ground contiguous to the cultivated lands. **1829** *Extracts Lett. Swan River* 13 Nov. (1830) III. 3 We sailed beyond the Upper Government Farm, twenty miles above Perth, and finer land I never beheld; you could not show me finer tares within ten miles of your farm than I saw there.—I am now speaking of the alluvial soil on the *banks* of the river; the *back* grounds are not to be depended on for a quarter of a mile together. **1832** G.F. MOORE *Diary Ten Yrs. W.A.* 9 Aug. (1884) 127 The brook traverses my grant twice, and makes the back ground valuable.

2. *pl.* BACK COUNTRY *n.* 2.

1842 *Colonial Observer* (Sydney) 6 July 318/3 The Commissioner observes that an extended portion of water frontage is occupied, and the back grounds kept in a state of idleness. **1854** W. HOWITT *Land, Labor & Gold* 12 Mar. (1855) II. 183 In the unsettled district, where agricultural land is required, it may be accommodated with large back-grounds of mere barren ranges fit for the wandering over of flocks and cattle.

back land. *Obs.* Also in *pl.*

1. BACK COUNTRY *n.* 2.

1814 M. FLINDERS *Voyage Terra Australis* I. 127, I do not think that any stream, more considerable than perhaps a small rill from the back land, falls into it. **1820** J. OXLEY *Jrnls. Two Exped. N.S.W.* 82 The back lands (with the exception of the ranges) were always lower than the immediate banks of the river itself. **1831** W. BLAND *Journey of Discovery Port Phillip* 43 The back land is excellent, superior perhaps to that on the northern or right bank. **1835** *Cornwall Chron.* (Launceston) 28 Mar. 3 *To let . . a farm*. . . Part of the back land is fit for agricultural purposes. **1842** *Colonial Observer* (Sydney) 6 July 318 In order to make the back land, as well as the land with water frontage, available for occupation. **1881** W.E. ABBOTT *Notes Journey on Darling* 61 These back lands had little or no value in their natural state.

2. BACK COUNTRY *n.* 3.

1824 *HRA* (1921) 3rd Ser. IV. 148 The Back lands at Swan Port to the northward communicate through Tiers of Hills with an extensive Country.

3. BACK GROUND 1.

1846 *Sydney Morning Herald* 17 Feb. 3/1 He is *at least* entitled *freely* to the use of the detached pond in his back land, for which he is indebted to a casual and providential fall of rain, and which is for half the year as likely to be a mere 'water *hole*' as a hole of water.

4. Land in the sparsely populated interior. See BACK COUNTRY *n.* 5.

1850 J.W. MELVIN *Emigrant's Guide to Colonies* 22 As to marriage, however in the back lands or bush. **1891** J. FENTON *Bush Life Tas.* (1964) 172 Mr W.R. Bell knows perhaps more of the backlands of the western districts than any other man.

Hence **backlander** *n.*

1928 B. CRONIN *Dragonfly* 66 Too many canary-grass backlanders in these parts. They live on the land, not for it.

back-loading, *vbl. n.* Freight carried on a return journey, after delivery of the principal load. See LOADING *vbl. n.*[1]

1925 M. TERRY *Across Unknown Aust.* 85 These long treks without back-loading (i.e. both ways). **1936** I.L. IDRIESS *Cattle King* 120 The Wilcannia teams don't like going out. There's not enough diggers out there yet, and there's no back loading. **1956** *Bulletin* (Sydney) 15 Feb. 13/4 You had to 'run the rabbit'; pulling a handcart loaded with rivets and coke to the lines of butty gangs, and returning with clinker and scrap as backloading. **1975** L.R. SMITH *Memories of Hall* 40 A resident . . would bring loads of goods from the Queanbeyan railways goods shed, with his waggon and team of horses, as 'backloading', after despatching a load of wool or other farm products, rather than return to Hall with an empty waggon. **1984** *N.T. News* (Darwin) 30 Oct. 25/5 Furniture pantec unloading Darwin . . require backloading Brisbane.

backman. *Australian National Football.* One who plays in a defensive back position.

1928 G. MORIARTY *Teaching Game of Football* xi. 2 A Backman's motto should be:- that '*no kicks to the Forwards mean no goals to their side*'. **1930** W.S. SHARLAND *Sporting Globe Football Bk.* 29 The forward player is trying to work into position all the time, and to lose his back man. It is the corresponding duty of the back man never to let the forward wander off on his own. **1931** J.F. MCHALE et al. *Austral. Game of Football* 66 The back man was worthy of mention, as he kept his forward in check. **1959** PARNELL & ANDREW *Austral. Football* 37 Every ruckman is a 'forward' when his own side has the ball, and is a 'backman' when the opposing side has the ball. **1963** L. RICHARDS *Boots & All!* 66 Coleman knew as well as anyone that the last thing a forward wants to do is 'mix it' with a backman—that he must put as much distance between himself and a defender as quickly as possible. **1973** J. DUNN *How to play Football* 82 A backman, and especially a back pocket, should always remember that his job is to restrict scoring.

back paddock. A paddock distant from the main source of water on a station, or from the station homestead.

1898 A.S. MURRAY *Twelve Hundred Miles* 28 The most effectual plan, in the back paddocks, away from the river (the Murrumbidgee), was poisoned water in troughs. **1911** C.E.W. BEAN *'Dreadnought' of Darling* 70 Some of their back paddocks run out over the horizon on to the Cobar-Wilcannia coach road, sixty miles away. **1929** *Bulletin* (Sydney) 9 Jan. 25/3 We were mustering the back paddocks when seven eagles appeared. **1947** N. LINDSAY *Halfway to Anywhere* 75 Bill having planted his half-bottle of sherry in the back paddock, came lounging innocuously back. **1965** A.W. UPFIELD *Lure of Bush* 57 He with the squatter and Dugdale went off on a tour of the back paddocks. **1974** J. JOST *This is Harry Flynn* 17 One of his clearest recollections was the day she dropped dead in the back paddock and he had found her, an object of curiosity for a couple of poddy calves.

back pocket: see POCKET.

back run. *Obs.*

1. An area of Crown land immediately behind a holding and available to the landholder as supplementary grazing land: see quot. 1833.

1824 *Hobart Town Gaz.* 30 July, A Farm of 400 acres . . with a large back run. **1827** P. CUNNINGHAM *Two Yrs. in N.S.W.* II. 161 You must secure, if possible, a good grazing *back-run* behind your location. **1828** *Tasmanian* (Hobart) 29 Feb. 3 *A valuable dairy farm* . . commands an unbounded back Run of unlocated Land. **1832** *Sydney Herald* 27 Feb. 1/3 *A small farm* . . an extensive back run of Forest and Swamp, affording abundance of grass and water in every extreme of seasons. **1833** *HRA* (1923) 1st Ser. XVII. 112 On three fourths of the Grants on the Hunter River . . the Proprietors enjoy the advantages of what is called a 'back run' for their Cattle, etc., namely, Land not appropriated, nor ever likely to be appropriated, as separate Farms, *being only useful in connection with the Neighbouring Estates*, which latter must in a multitude of instances be passed through to arrive at the unappropriated land. **1843** J.F. BENNETT *Hist. & Descr. Acct. S.A.* 96 When a person purchases land with the intention of keeping stock, he, if possible, makes a selection which commands good water and a 'back run'—that is a track of hill country, which is not surveyed, or likely to be purchased for agricultural purposes, but yet affords good pasture. **1843** A. CASWALL *Hints from Jrnl.* 45 Mares can be kept on a farm with a good back run (unbought land belonging to the Government), which is rented at a trifle a section. **1845** *Port Phillip Gaz.* 23 July 2 No sooner is he [*sc.* the squatter] circumscribed in his natural resources than he will improve his back run at least by artificial reservoirs of water, if not by fencing. **1846** *Sydney Morning Herald* 17 Feb. 3/1 It is a positive injustice to charge the grazier ten pounds for the occupancy of a water hole on his 'back run' which no living soul beside himself could make any use of. **1858** C. ROWCROFT *Tales of Colonies* 43 A spot, which pleased me at once, from the back run for sheep and cattle which it afforded.

2. A run distant from a water frontage, or from a station homestead.

1876 'CAPRICORNUS' *Colonisation* 8 Of those inland pastures one acre was worth three of the poorer country to the eastward; and if water was scarce on the back runs, there were miles and miles of frontage to running rivers. **1891** W.B. DEAN *Notorious Bushrangers* 72 The unfortunate woman . . was discovered in one of the ravines on Barnes' back run.

back settlement. *Obs.* [U.S. *back settlement* a remote settlement: see Mathews *back, a.* 1.] An isolated settlement, inland from settled districts; in *pl.*, the sparsely populated interior.

1791 G.C. INGLETON *True Patriots All* (1952) 10 We have four different settlements—viz. Sydney Cove—Rose-Hill—and two back settlements which are not yet named. **1817** *Hobart Town Gaz.* 9 Aug., Ticket of Leave Men, in the District of New Norfolk, the Back Settlement, & District of Melville. **1831** *Sydney Herald* 15 Aug. 4/1 Having a water communication with the back settlement of our Colony. **1841** *Colonial Mag.* (London) IV. 63 The small rustic capitalist locates himself as squatter or proprietor in the back settlements of New Holland. **1862** G.T. LLOYD *Thirty-Three Yrs. Tas. & Vic.* 134 Heated and over-driven stock from the back settlements. **1866** *Adventures ashore & Afloat* (1887) 154 In the winter of 1851 I was making a long journey on horseback along the back settlements of Australia. **1896** M. HORNSBY *Old Time Echoes Tas.* 21 On the following day some young children brought word . . that the bushrangers had stuck up a family called Worsley near the back settlement.

back settler. *Obs.* [U.S. *back settler*: see Mathews *back, a.* 2.] One who lives in a remote settlement, or in the interior.

1829 E.G. WAKEFIELD *Let. from Sydney* 103 Bushranging is a dreadful evil, being a kind of land piracy. None but back settlers, it is true, are exposed to its burnings, rapes, and massacres. **1840** *S. Austral. Rec.* (London) 25 July 54 The 'roughing it out' system . . is necessarily encountered by country settlers in a *new* colony, and by back-settlers in an older one. **1853**

J. Capper *Emigrant's Guide to Aust.* (ed. 2) 41 Mrs Chisholm 'went about doing good' amongst the back-settlers of Australia. **1891** J. Fenton *Bush Life Tas.* (1964) 136 The back settlers . . were the victims of indescribable torment, no provision having been made for roads. **1901** *Advocate* (Burnie) 24 Aug. 4/3 They would . . turn to the back settlers and say, 'You only pay a sixpenny rate.' **1911** *Huon Times* (Franklin) 10 June 6/4 No saw-mill would be allowed to remain on any public road, as in the case of Toby's Hill Road, to the injustice of back settlers.

back station. Out-station 2 a.

c **1887** R.G. Gallop In Never Never Land, Life on these back stations is necessarily rather rough. **1891** 'R. Boldrewood' *Sydney-Side Saxon* (1925) 60 When I got up to the 'back station' at Yugildah, as it was called, I was struck all of a heap with the look of the place. **1906** J.W. Gregory *Dead Heart Aust.* 35 The usual food allowance on the back stations consists of 10 lb. of meat, 10 lb. of flour, 2 lb. of sugar, and ¼ lb. of tea per man per week. **1910** C.E.W. Bean *On Wool Track* 59 There had been an old back station at the tank. **1949** J. Morrison *Creeping City* 42, I was dragged up on a back-station in a tin and hessian hut—fly-blown meat, sour water, bung eyes, bare feet, and Bathurst burrs. **1953** *Bulletin* (Sydney) 30 Sept. 12/2 When I was a nipper Top Hut was always known as an out-camp of Arumpo, which was itself a back-station of Tarcoola. . . Now Top Hut is a station in its own right. **1979** W.D. Joynt *Breaking Road for Rest* 44, I had two fights on the station—the first while doing some boundary riding on a back station.

back to, *adv., n. phr.,* and *attrib.* [f. *back, adv.,* in the reverse direction + *to.*] Used with reference to a reunion of former residents or associates, with appropriate festivities.

1925 *S. Eastern Star* (Mount Gambier) 31 Dec. 3/2 The activities of the publicity committee of the 'Back-to-Mount Gambier' movement have brought many advantages other than the 'boosting' of the March celebrations. **1927** B. O'Dowd (*title*), Souvenir of 'back to Beaufort'. **1944** A.J. & J.J. McIntyre *Country Towns Vic.* 237 '*Back to's*' are . . infrequent . . usually occurring only every ten, or even fifteen to twenty years. Their chief aim is to give the town a financial boost. **1948** *Bulletin* (Sydney) 10 Nov. 22/4 The back to Bunglebobba celebrations are in full swing and a large crowd of former pupils in their schoolday costumes, are playing hop-scotch. **1958** *Ibid.* 24 Sept. 16/2, 1400 people were swapping yarns at the back-to-Kanowa (W.A.) celebrations. **1960** *N.T. News* (Darwin) 2 Feb. 8/1 By the time 'Back to Katherine' week comes up the race club committee is confident the track will be as good as any in the north. **1971** B. Lester *Verses* 15 The clay bird shoot attracted many shooters Saturday night And the 'Back to' Ball was crowded, the music sweet and light. **1985** *Mid-Coast Observer* (Kempsey) 16 Oct. 2/6 Back to Bowra celebrations.

back track. A little-frequented and often indirect road or track, away from the main route. Also *attrib.*

1867 G. Walch *Fireflash* 10 So if you'll please say good-bye to the worthy owner of this delightful property, we'll start to-morrow morning on the back track. **1878** 'R. Boldrewood' *Ups & Downs* 48 He had nosed out an unfrequented back track, where the feed was unspoiled by those marauding bands of 'condottieri', travelling sheep. **1895** *Worker* (Sydney) 4 May 3/1 The back-track boys will engage the Walgett band, and go out and meet them with all honour and conduct them to Dungalear. **1896** *Bulletin* (Sydney) 8 Feb. 28/1 Mac. and I were driving a two-horse sulky down one of the back tracks to the Culgoa. **1907** *Lone Hand* Nov. 19 If he knew of a place where there was a chance of a job, on the back track, he'd fix up a swag, water-bag and tucker. **1928** 'Brent Of Bin Bin' *Up Country* 72 There was a mountainous back track by which horsemen could avoid the big stream. **1938** F. Blakeley *Hard Liberty* 120 Leaving Anna Creek, we made by back track for an out-station. **1948** B. Cronin *How runs Road* 42 On the back tracks, the little tracks, the mud-and-slush-and-corduroy tracks, the bullock-driver was . . king of the roads. **1977** V. Priddle *Larry & Jack* 22 'Which way are you going home, Pop?' 'I really wanted to go by the back track.' . . 'I think you'd be a wise man to go home the shortest route on the best roads.'

back up. A second helping of food. Also as *v. trans.* and *intr.*

1929 'F. Blair' *Digger Sea-Mates* 19 'Our first meal aboard.' . . 'Any 'buckshee', Boy?' he enquired. 'Yes, back up yer cart.' Tom's plate received another slice of beef. **1946** R.D. Rivett *Behind Bamboo* 93 An exclusive monopoly of all 'back-ups' or 'gash', as the Perth boys called second helpings. **1953** T.A.G. Hungerford *Riverslake* 199 'Bloody burned widows for breakfast—who'll be in a back-up?' 'I don't know about a back-up, but you'll be in a blue if Verity cops you,' Randolph advised him. **1959** *Bulletin* (Sydney) 30 Dec. 16/1 That stew was a beaut, with plenty for 'back-ups'. **1966** S.J. Baker *Austral. Lang.* (ed. 2) 217 *Back up*, to seek another helping or share.

back verandah: see Verandah.

back yard. Also *attrib.* (usu. as **backyard**).

1. An enclosure, usually including a garden in which fruit and vegetables are grown, at the back of a house.

1793 W. Tench *Compl. Acct. Settlement* 44 Baneelon no sooner found himself in a back-yard, than he nimbly leaped over a slight paling. **1831** *Sydney Herald* 11 July 3/3 Going into the back yard, he secured the male prisoner. **1843** *Teetotal Advocate* (Launceston) 26 June 1/2 Cottage to be Let or Sold . . a well in the back yard. **1884** 'R. Boldrewood' *Old Melbourne Memories* 12 For years after it stood in the back yard with cracked panels. **1896** N. Gould *Town & Bush* 58 It occasionally arises that a man may find his neighbour's back-yard opposite his front gate. **1903** *Bulletin* (Sydney) 10 Sept. 35/2 All slops are emptied on the sandy soil of the back yard. **1930** K.S. Prichard *Haxby's Circus* 144 She rarely went beyond the garden in Bergen's back-yard. **1933** *Melbourne University Mag.* 39 If the Harbour is the emblem of Sydney, it might with equal truth be claimed that, beneath the Melbourne motto—'*Vires acquirit eundo*'—there should be a back-yard rampant, gules, on a field crêpe-noir. **1936** J. Devanny *Sugar Heaven* 16 The Lees' shack, being new, had its frontage cheek by jowl with giant ti-trees and stringy bark and its back yard still waited to be stumped. **1941** *Southerly* iii. 25 A little bottle of jam 'from our own tree in the back yard'. **1954** *Bulletin* (Sydney) 16 June 13/1, I had a bumper backyard tomato-crop. **1963** X. Herbert *Disturbing Element* 164 Everybody who had a backyard in W.A. grew grapes, and . . would brew a drop of what was called Pinky. **1965** G. McInnes *Road to Gundagai* 76 It was one of the delights of life in Melbourne that, despite brief raw winters, you really could go out into your own back yard and pick oranges and lemons right off the tree. **1978** L. White *Memories of Childhood* 41 Backyard lawns now lap aridly around backyard barbecues. **1983** *Canberra Chron.* 19 Jan. 8/3 Death by drowning in backyard pools occurs mainly in the five-year-and-under age group.

2. *fig.* Used of a business conducted in domestic premises and often implying small-scale work that may be inferior or illegal. Usu. *attrib.*

1927 *R. Comm. Moving Picture Industry* 151 'The Sentimental Bloke' was also made in the back yard for something like £2,000. **1939** J. Campbell *Babe is Wise* 214 'Backyard' factories, Mrs McDougall called them, denouncing them with all the righteous indignation of one whose own man's employers were beyond reproach. **1964** *Austral.* (Sydney) 31 Dec. 6/7 In Britain, where fees are much higher and wages lower, there is a significant preponderance of backyard abortionists. **1976** *Sun* (Sydney) 11 Aug. 94/3 If a woman decides, however, that she does want her pregnancy terminated, it is no longer a nightmare of backyard operators for those who couldn't afford three hundred guineas for a highly qualified surgeon. **1984** *Canberra Chron.* 15 Aug. 4/3 The P.A. People . . began in Canberra eight years ago as a small backyard business.

backyarder. One who conducts a backyard business: see Back yard 2.

1948 C.B. Maxwell *Cold Nose of Law* 19 Unfortunately the less admirable type of 'backyarder' got hold of the breed about 1930, after which it embarked on a period of major decline. **1971** *Bulletin* (Sydney) 7 Aug. 13/2, 250 legal abortions a day, price range from $60 to $200 . . still leaving plenty of scope for cheaper backyarders. **1972** Berman & Childs *Why isn't she Dead!* 45 Doctor finally had to pay . . $300 to the backyarder, who in turn passed it on to the detective who was standing over him. **1984** *National German Shepherd Dog Mag.* Jan. 5/3 A cynic might construe this combination of circumstances as one way of easing the 'hobbyists', 'backyarders', 'small timers', call us what you will, out of business. **1984** *Open Road* Apr. 9/1 Be careful of the backyarder! The man who repairs cars from a shed behind his house . . the man who buys cars at auction and 'does them up' for resale from his home.

bacon-and-egg(s): see Eggs-and-bacon.

bad, *a. Obs.*

1. [Ironic use of *bad* wicked.] Applied to a convict who dissociates himself from his fellows and co-operates with the prison officers.

1835 J. Backhouse *Narr. Visit Austral. Colonies* (1843) 278 He [*sc.* a convict] could no longer join in many of the evil practices in which they indulged and he became in their estimation and language, 'a bad fellow'. Before when he ran with them into the depths of iniquity, he passed among them as a 'good fellow'; for thus, among this depraved portion of our race is good too generally called evil and evil good. **1838** W. Molesworth *Rep. Select Committee Transportation* 17 Dr Ullathorne likewise said: 'I was very much struck with the peculiar language used by the convicts at Norfolk Island. . . A prisoner . . said, that it was the habitual language of the place . . that a bad man was called a good man; and that a man who was ready to perform his duty was generally called a bad man.'

2. [U.S. *bad* hostile, dangerous: see Mathews.] Of an Aboriginal: hostile, opposed to white settlement.

1910 *Bulletin* (Sydney) 20 Oct. 14/1 Although he had travelled through country infested with 'bad' niggers, he was never troubled by them. **1932** I.L. Idriess *Flynn of Inland* (1965) 152 Numbers wore cartridge belts, for men generally go armed in the north if travelling through 'bad-nigger' country. **1933** R.B. Plowman *Man from Oodnadatta* 195 On the fringe of bad black-fellow country, controlled with a firm hand a large number of bush blacks. **1948** M. Uren *Glint of Gold* 246 All this country in the North-West was 'bad native' country. The natives resented the penetration of the white men . . and . . tried to hold off the invaders.

badger. a. *Obs.* Any of several indigenous marsupial mammals. **b.** Chiefly *Tas.* Wombat *n.* 1.

1803 *Sydney Gaz.* 23 Oct. The Margaret's sealing party at King's Island, who have brought round a number of very fine Kangaroos and *badgers.* **1829** R. Mudie *Picture of Aust.* 173 The *Parameles*, to which the colonists sometimes give the name of badgers. **1831** *Van Diemen's Land Anniversary & Hobart-Town Almanack* 265 That delicious animal, the wombat, (commonly known at that place [*sc.* Macquarie Harbour] by the name of badger). **1834** C.O. Booth *Jrnl.* 8 Mar. (1981) 172 Pair of very fine Badgers (very improperly so named) called wambats [*sic*] by the natives. **1850** J.B. Clutterbuck *Port Phillip* 37 The rock Wallaby, or Badger. **1852** F. Lancelott *Aust. as it Is* I. 35 The bandicoot, or pouched badger. **1897** *Papers & Proc. R. Soc. Tas.* (1898) 177 In places, wallaby and kangaroo are to be found, but, as a general rule, the 'badger' (*i.e.* wombat) is the only game. **1920** B. Cronin *Timber Wolves* 163 Here in Tassie we . . got names of our own for things this side the straits. . . For instance they ain't no wombats here; we call them badgers. **1951** D. Collins *Vic.'s my Home Ground* 31 When I was first prospecting round these parts, back in the nineties, we often had wombat. Used to smoke it in the chimney just like ham. Called it badger ham, we did, and it went down bonzer.

badger box. *Tas. Obs.* [f. Badger + *box* shelter.] A makeshift hut or shelter.

1864 *Papers & Proc. R. Soc. Tas.* (1876) 100 Took rations to the Badger box. **1875** *Ibid.* 99 The dwellings occupied by the piners when up the river are of the style known as 'Badger-boxes', in distinction from huts, which have perpendicular walls, while the Badger-box is like an inverted V in section. **1896** M. Hornsby *Old Time Echoes Tas.* 27 There must exist a breakwind, a mi-mi, or badger-box up the gully, as bolters would hardly trouble to erect a hut. **1911** *Huon Times* (Franklin) 1 Mar. 2/7 It is interesting to watch the gradual development in houses here. First comes the bush hut or 'badger box', with the fire often outside.

bael, var. Baal.

bag, *n.*[1] [Abbrev. of *bagging* sacking.]

1. Used *attrib.* in Comb. to distinguish a contrivance, structure, etc. made of (used) hessian sacks.

1903 *Bulletin* (Sydney) 6 June 17/1 He places a bag-swag and jam-tin billy outside his front gate so that travellers . . will pass . . on their way, thinking that *that* beat is occupied. **1906** *Ibid.* 12 July 17/1 When the nomad is utterly stiff and swagless, he obtains three or four discarded corn sacks and sews them together. That is a 'Wagga rug', and, when it is rolled up, behold the bag-swag. **1911** 'S. RUDD' *Bk. of Dan* 101 Uncle . . fell ill one day and took to his old bagbed. **1913** W.K. HARRIS *Outback in Aust.* 136 Kerosene-tin huts, bark huts, and bag huts are the common dwelling-houses. **1916** *Bulletin* (Sydney) 7 Sept. 24/2 *Re* 'flies' on bag humpies . . a young architect had put in a good while camping in tents. **1921** K.S. PRICHARD *Black Opal* 67 A score or so of bark and bag huts were ranged on either side. **1924** H.E. RIEMANN *Nor'-West o' West* 96 He fished out a tin matchbox from the head of his bag-bunk. **1926** J. POLLARD *Bushland Man* 157 Tess also was tethered away from trees, the men rigging a bag-manger on the lee side of a line of scrub. **1930** K.S. PRICHARD *Haxby's Circus* 91 The child, asleep in a bag hammock she had rigged up for him. **1932** J. TRURAN *Green Mallee* 80 He fed the horses, pouring plenty of chaff into the bag-feeders. **1934** C. MACKNESS *Young Beachcombers* 95 They're bag bunks—two fold-up wooden crosses for legs, and bagging stretched tightly across. **1935** R.B. PLOWMAN *Boundary Rider* 121 The padre already knew several pensioners . . half starving in tin sheds or bag humpies. **1935** K. TENNANT *Tiburon* 42 Okker Slade's bag shelter had joined those of Dutch and Old Grey in the little circle round the fire. **1948** M. UREN *Glint of Gold* 26 Women . . followed their men to the goldfields and gladly shared the discomforts of a bag humpy. **1950** C.E. GOODE *Yarns of Yilgarn* 11 He . . rolled over on the bag stretcher. Harry threw a wagga over him. **1961** D. STUART *Driven* 42 Some in sandshoes, some in sandals . . others with bag boots, all, to the last man, sore-footed. **1972** C. DUGUID *Doctor & Aborigines* 140 The houses are no more than 'bag huts', with walls of hessian surrounding floors of earth or cement. **1979** C. STONE *Running Brumbies* 110 We had two blankets and a bag wagga apiece. A bag wagga is a kind of quilt made from a sack stuffed with anything that will keep you warm. **1981** A.B. FACEY *Fortunate Life* 25 The old lady used to put the milk into flat tin trays, each one holding about two gallons. She would then put these into a large bag cooler and let them stand like that for about twelve hours.

2. In the phr. **rough as bags,** lacking in refinement.

1919 *Ça ne fait Rien: 6th Battalion A.I.F.* 10 Jan. 1 As we've said before [Belgian girls]'re as rough as bags. **1927** K.S. PRICHARD *Brumby Innes* (1974) 96 He's rough as bags; but he'll treat Mrs Innes proper. **1938** F. CLUNE *Free & Easy Land* 51 Hill-billies of Australia; distillers of moonshine, rough as bags. **1944** *Bulletin* (Sydney) 18 Oct. 13/3, I will advertise for 50 silky-haired bitches to foster-mother lambs from my rough-as-bags crossbreds. **1957** D. NILAND *Call me when Cross turns Over* 174 Don't think of the Apostles as silvertails, all mokkered up in the best, and a cheque-book for every pocket. They were nobodies. Rough as bags. **1977** C. KLEIN *Pomegranate Tree* 55 She talked rough as bags, but she acted pure as the Virgin Mary, she was a doer, that one. **1984** M. ELDRIDGE *Walking Dog* 89 'Rough as bags', people said of Raelene, and in the same breath, 'heart of gold'.

bag, *n.*[2]

1. *Horse-racing.* [Fig. use of (bookmaker's) *bag.*] In the phr. **in the bag,** applied to a horse being run to lose. See also quot. 1982.

[N.Z. **1900** J. SCOTT *Tales of Colonial Turf* 3 The neddy was in the bag in the Cup; he was no trier.] **1903** *Sporting News* (Launceston) 6 June 3/3 Had I not known for certain she was a fair trier, would have thought she was 'in the bag'. **1911** A. WRIGHT *Gambler's Gold* (1923) 98 Getting Alf Price, the bookmaker, to put Red Flag in the bag. **1945** S.J. BAKER *Austral. Lang.* 174 A horse set to lose a race is said to be *in the bag.* **1955** N. PULLIAM *I traveled Lonely Land* 369 It's interesting to note there are various slangisms which both the Australian and the American use often, but with almost opposite meaning, e.g. . . 'in the bag'. **1982** J. ANDERSON *Winners can Laugh* 148 Sam rejected many offers from the smart bookmakers to put him in the bag, meaning that, in return for preventing a horse from winning, a rider received a percentage of the money the bookmaker won on the race as a result of the arrangement.

2. *pl.* [Abbrev. of *sand-bag.*] In the phr. **over the bags,** over the sand-bags protecting a trench, 'over the top'; also *fig.*

1918 *Aussie* (Sydney) Jan. 10/2 *Over the bags*, the intensive form of danger; denoting a test of fitness and experience for Billzac and his brethren. **1919** W.A. CULL *At All Costs* 36 On the Somme we were twice over the bags in something more imposing than trench fighting.

3. [Orig. U.S.] In the phr. **bag of fruit,** rhyming slang for 'suit'.

1924 *Truth* (Sydney) 27 Apr. 6, *Bag of fruit*, a suit. **1950** *Austral. Police Jrnl.* Apr. 110 *Bag of fruit*, suit of clothing. **1962** D. MCLEAN *World turned Upside Down* 45 His little grey-haired mother pulled the lapels. . . 'Strike me roan!' cried Skinny. 'What sort of a bag of fruit is that?' **1966** G. WYATT *Strip Jack Naked* 72 The big boot-licking bludger made me drag off the top half of me bag of fruit. **1981** P. BARTON *Bastards I have Known* 92 She dressed me up fit to kill in my best 'bag of fruit'.

4. [Prob. abbrev. of *bag of tricks* stock of resources: see OEDS *bag, sb.* 17 and cf. BOX *n.*[6].] In the phr. **out of the bag,** unexpected, surprising.

1954 T.A.G. HUNGERFORD *Sowers of Wind* 44 The only difference is, it was all done with one bloody bomb—that's what makes it one out of the bag. One place that's been skittled is like any other, otherwise. **1961** T. RONAN *Only Short Walk* 135 She was something out of the bag, was Hetty. **1980** ANSELL & PERCY *To fight Wild* 9 Anyway, that was out of the bag. Writing poetry.

bag, *v.*

1. [f. BAG *n.*[2] 1.] *trans.* See quot. 1958. Also as *vbl. n.*

1958 F. HARDY *Four-Legged Lottery* 174 'Don't back that horse, Paul. It's been bagged.' 'Bagged?' This can be done by the owner or the jockey, but more often it is done by the trainer. . . A trainer gets a horse 'in the market'. He approaches a bookmaker or a group of bookmakers through an intermediary. The horse will not win if they pay up; he is prepared to 'bag it', to run it for the bookmakers. **1983** HIBBERD & HUTCHINSON *Barracker's Bible* 19 'Bagging' may be arranged by owner, trainer, or jockey. The bookmaker will then guarantee a kickback.

2. [Fig. use of *bag* to sack, dismiss.] *trans.* To denigrate. Freq. as *vbl. n.*

1969 *Daily Tel.* (Sydney) 20 Mar. 6/6 In the last couple of decades the poor old Poms have taken such a bagging from the rest of the world . . that they'd relish any chance to get back to a bit of good, old-fashioned British sneering. **1975** *Daily Mirror* (Sydney) 15 May 11/1 The only publicity I ever got in the first 12 months was a baggin'. **1975** *Austral.* (Sydney) 11 Nov. 10/2 Sigley is also 'bagged by the blokes'. He says the world is full of big-noters who reckon if a little fat guy can stand up there and talk for an hour then they can too. **1983** *Canberra Times* 9 June 14/2 In private to him Mr Lewer had engaged in 'bagging' Mr Farquhar. . . He was saying things quite uncomplimentary about Mr Farquhar. **1986** *Bulletin* (Sydney) 22 Apr. 73/2 Telecom is a pretty suspect outfit, deserving of the consistent bagging it gets from exasperated subscribers.

bagman, *n.*[1] [Prob. orig. a facetious application of *bagman* commercial traveller.]

1. A swagman. Also *attrib.*

1866 H. SIMCOX *Rustic Rambles* 21 See the dummies and the mediums, Bagmen, swagmen, hastening down. **1896** H. LAWSON *While Billy Boils* 51 'So you're a native of Australia?' said the bagman to the grey-beard. **1897** *Bulletin* (Sydney) 10 July 3/2 The horsemen can dally with bagmen, For they're wanted no more on the camp. **1904** *Ibid.* 1 Sept. 36/2 Their name is legion—the bright, capable young men who get the 'bagman' brain-twist and go out and waste their splendid forces carrying preposterous swags about the bush. **1914** *Ibid.* 17 Sept. 24/2 Struck a burning-off camp . . which is bossed by a Chow. . . He keeps an excellent Chow cook, who never turns a bagman down. **1923** *Ibid.* 25 Oct. 22/2 Niggers are not the only Aussies who are 'good on the hoof'. . . A bewhiskered old bagman . . landed a job from my dad, and after getting a 'bit on the hip' trundled Matilda out on the road again. **1930** *Ibid.* 16 July 20/2 The time seems not far distant when the Queensland swaggie and the bagman will deign to accept a lift from the motorist. For years past the motorist's proffered lift has met with a nasty 'Open the ··· gates yerself.' **1937** *Ibid.* 4 Aug. 21/2 Why do swagmen shy clear of fettling gangs?. . . The dinky-di bagman will invariably give fettlers a miss, and even when 'sleeper-walking' he will detour to avoid them. **1954** T. RONAN *Vision Splendid* 291 God bless de Boss and all his rich relations, And don't let the bagmen camp around the stations. **1962** J. MACKENZIE *Austral. Paradox* 108 And there in that lonely place an ancient swagman, Traveller, bagman, sundowner, what you will—His rolled up blankets slung aslant his shoulders. **1977** J. DOUGHTY *Gold in Blood* 23 The swagman—or bagman, as he was always called in Queensland—scorning the trains and striding the roads like a free man. **1981** K. GARVEY *Rhymes of Ratbag* 56 Took the trousers off a bagman who had died from drinking booze.

2. *spec.* A mounted swagman.

1902 *Bulletin* (Sydney) 8 Feb. 32/3 Of 'bagmen', the slang W. Queensland word for mounted travellers, there are . . several grades. **1905** E.C. BULEY *Austral. Life* 53 From the tucker-bag, a sort of pillow slip with the mouth in the middle, which is slung across the front of the saddle so that a bulging end hangs down on either side, he gets his bush name of 'bag-man'. The bag-man . . is generally a shearer first and a handy-man when shearing is over. **1911** E.S. SORENSON *Life in Austral. Backblocks* 72 Two terms that are often confounded one with the other are swagman and bagman. The first is a footman, the other a mounted man who may have anything from one to half a dozen horses. **1926** *Bulletin* (Sydney) 11 Feb. 24/1 The shabby pack-horse bagmen sneer, who pass on their shoddy crocks, And the 'gun' who 'rung' till the wet set in has auctioned his flashest socks. **1947** E. HILL *Flying Doctor Calling* 17 The only others that you meet in the heart of the bush are pilgrims—drovers, . . wild-dog hunters, an occasional trooper on patrol, an occasional bagman wandering for no apparent reason with a packhorse and a couple of spares. **1967** M. SELLARS *Carramar* 44 Itinerant bagmen, 'jes ridin' round'; and most colourful of all, the swaggie.

3. In the Depression of the 1930s: one of the itinerant unemployed, in search of work or sustenance. See TRAVELLER 1.

1935 K. TENNANT *Tiburon* 8 The shelter-shed on the travellers' reserve, unlike most of the structures erected by charitable town councils, actually did shelter . . and . . during the long rainy spells had saved many a bagman from lying stiff with rheumatism under a bridge. **1941** —— *Battlers* 24 No one welcomes the bagman. The local unemployed watch jealously lest he get a job, the police lest he show signs of lingering, the charitable lest he impose on their charity, and the shopkeeper lest he steal. **1963** HARNEY & LOCKWOOD *Shady Tree* 89 The swaggies I knew were complex and often quite well-educated men. Many were travelling recluses who detested the swarms of 'bagmen', as distinct from 'swagmen', who took to the roads during the Depression. **1979** G. STEWART *Leveller* 20 A bagman was an unemployed person whose only possessions were bags: a water bag, a tucker bag, flour bags washed and sewn together called a Wogga; all carried in yet another bag.

4. In special collocations: **bagman's gazette, leg, Bagmen's Union,** see quots.

1936 K.L. SMITH *Sky Pilot's Last Flight* 210 Ned has been arrested. The aeroplane travels quicker than the **'bagman's gazette'**, so of course you have not heard of it. **1955** H.G. LAMOND *Towser* 185 'Th' good old *Mulga Wire's* still functioning,' Watson explained. 'There'll be a leading article about it in th' next *Bagman's Gazette.*' **1959** —— *Sheep Station* 46 The men had heard by *The Mulga Wire* and *The Bagman's Gazette* of Jack's exploits with Mat Branigan. **1968** B. HUMPHRIES *Bk. Innocent Austral Verse* 130 There is a paper outback which all bushmen quote; From Derby right out to Brunette, 'Tis a paper to which subscriptions are free And 'tis known as The Bagman's Gazette. **1970** W. FEARN-WANNAN *Austral. Folklore* 27 The *Bagman's Gazette* was an imaginary swagmen's newspaper; a mythical source of bush rumours, i.e. 'According to the Bagman's Gazette.' **1977** STIRLING & RICHARDSON *Memories of Aberfeldy* 27 There had been several accidents caused by 'taking her on the fly' (jumping on when the train was moving at speed). This resulted in a new addition to the language, **'bagman's leg'** (loss of limb by falling under the train). **1954** *Coast to Coast 1953–54* 77 'How'd you come to do a thing like that—it's against the **Bagmen's Union** rules.' 'Ah, the Bagmen's Union is a thing of the past,' says the sundowner, rattling the corks to chase the flies off his face. **1965** F. HARDY *Yarns of Billy Borker* 48 'What? Sundowners never pay fares. It's against the rules of the Bagmen's Union.' 'Bagmen's Union? Never heard of it.' 'Easy to see you weren't on the track during the Depression.'

bagman, *n.*[2] [f. BAG *n.*[2]]

1. A bookmaker's clerk.

[**1972** J.S. GUNN in G.W. Turner *Good Austral. Eng.* iii. 53 We find that the bookmaker is also a *bagman* or *bag boy.*] **1973** F. PARSONS *Man called Mo* 140 Having a brother who was a bookmaker, he knew the best bagmen to bet with—those who gave him the best odds. **1980** S. ORR *Roll On* 62 In the main betting ring, bookies and their bagmen sweated away. **1984** *Nat. Times* (Sydney) 21 Dec. 8/6 According to the transcripts of the illegal N.S.W. police tapes, Coombs had been 'a bagman for a major SP bookmaker'.

2. *transf.*

1972 *Sunday Sun* (Brisbane) 2 July 14/2 Now he [*sc.* the drug supplier] is called the connection, the bagman, the wingman, the dealer. **1973** *Nat. Times* (Sydney) 25 June 18/3 The money is always paid in cash. . . The police 'bag man' will call once a month to collect. **1976** *Courier-Mail* (Brisbane) 15 Dec. 9/3 He had never acted as a 'bagman' for a former commissioner when he was a constable, and . . had not accepted the one bribe offered to him. **1980** S. ORR *Roll On* 59 The rent bagman with his little leather satchel still calls on Saturday mornings. **1981** *Canberra Times* 6 Nov. 3/7 The Leader of the NSW National Country Party, Mr Punch, told State Parliament yesterday that the Deputy Police Commissioner, Mr Bill Allen, was the 'bag man' for the Premier, Mr Wran.

bagpipes, *pl.* [f. the tubular appearance of sugar cane.] See quot. 1938.

1938 F. CLUNE *Free & Easy Land* 285 *Bagpipes*, an armful of cane picked up and carried on the shoulders. **1976** S. WELLER *Bastards I have Met* 7 One day I picked up the bundle wrong and was slipping and sliding on the tops. . . Keith burst out laughing and said, 'Give us a tune on your bagpipes Sam.'

bail, var. BAAL.

bail, *n.* [Spec. use of *bail* a bar used to confine an animal (see OED *sb.*[3] 4). Prob. Br. dial. but recorded earliest in Aust. and N.Z. (see OED(S *sb.*[3] 5 and EDD *sb.*[2]).] Orig. a frame to secure a cow's head during milking (see quot. 1876); now usu. a stall, or one of a number of stalls in a milking shed, in which a cow is confined during milking, the head being held steady in a frame. Also *attrib.*

1841 [see BAIL *v.* 1 a.]. **1843** J.F. BENNETT *Hist. & Descr. Acct. S.A.* 101 In the yard 'bails' are erected, in which the cow is held while she is being milked. **1849** S. & J. SIDNEY *Emigrant's Jrnl.* 67 The other man takes hold of the end of the rope and runs to the post fixed by the side of the bail for pulling up the cows. **1852** MRS C. MEREDITH *My Home in Tas.* II. 19 It is necessary to have a kind of pillory, called a 'milking bail', in which . . their heads are held fast . . making them quiet. **1872** G.S. BADEN-POWELL *New Homes for Old Country* 51 Some six or eight head would be draughted from a large yard into a small one; then one of these would be urged into a small stall or 'bail'. **1876** 'EIGHT YRS.' RESIDENT' *Queen of Colonies* 221 In one corner of the yard the 'milking bail' is put up, which consists of two strong posts with a cross-piece on the top, and a thin rail, fastened to a bottom cross-piece, and working on a pin. . . The cow puts her head inside this moveable piece against the post, and it is then pushed forth close to her neck behind the ears and secured by a peg running through it and the cross-piece. The cow is thus prevented from moving her head while being milked. She is in fact 'bailed up'. **1892** *Bulletin* (Sydney) 28 May 21/1 The boy drives a dusty, discouraged-looking cow into the 'bail'. **1899** G.E. BOXALL *Story Austral. Bushrangers* 45 It is always unsafe to milk one of these cows unless her head is fastened in 'a bail' and her leg tied. **1911** I.A. ROSENBLUM *Stella Sothern* 32 I'll just see if she is down the bail-yard. **1912** *Bulletin* (Sydney) 2 May 15/1 For you might all the gods of greatness woo With that bail-bursting, leg-roped, milky moo! **1942** E. LANGLEY *Pea Pickers* 81 Past the first farm I strode, where the crumpled wet manure flowed in the bails. **1979** DOUGLAS & HEATHCOTE *Far Cry* 54 Like all my cows; it hardly ever messed in the bail.

bail, *v.* Also **bale.** [f. prec.] Usu. with **up.**

1. a. *trans.* To confine (a cow) in a bail for the purpose of milking. Also *intr.*, to accept such confinement (see quot. 1881). In quot. 1843 the part of speech is uncertain.

[N.Z. **1841** N.M. TAYLOR *Jrnl. Ensign Best* 6 Apr. (1966) 285, I saw a small herd of Cows driven into a little stockyard bailed up and milked all by a *mauri* lad.] **1843** *Port Phillip Patriot* 23 Feb. 3/5 Thirty cows, broken-in to bail. **1874** C. DE BOOS *Congewoi Correspondence* 154 When we wanted to bail up a cow, the fust thing we had to do was to let out the carf. **1881** H.W. NESFIELD *Chequered Career* 251 When it came to the vicious cow's turn to be milked, I determined to try a soothing and gentle mode of proceeding. I was told that she objected to the 'leg-rope'. She baled up quietly enough. **1886** *Once a Month* (Melbourne) June 512 'Bailed up' (a dairyman's expression, as when milch cows are secured with their neck in a 'bail' whilst they are milked). **1892** *Bulletin* (Sydney) 28 May 21/2 The boy will lamb the cow down with a jagged yard-shovel, let her out, and bail up another. **1898** *Ibid.* 14 Nov. 27/3 Bailing up cows is nice, too. . . When you have got them bailed, it's ten to one that the first you go to leg-rope plants her foot in your stomach. **1911** *Ibid.* 12 Oct. 14/1 If I'm at home, I bail up for them, or I might even milk a few. **1946** F. CLUNE *Try Nothing Twice* 112 'Bail up a cow and get started!' yelled Ma Roberts, as she powerfully squirted two sizzling streams of lactic fluid into her bucket.

b. *intr. imp.* A call with which a cow is encouraged into a bail. Also in fig. contexts.

1847 T. MCCOMBIE *Austral. Sketches* 2 The women and children now get long branches of trees, and lay on with a will, crying 'bail up, Coffee', or whatever name she is known by, 'bail up'. **1876** 'EIGHT YRS.' RESIDENT' *Queen of Colonies* 222 An unbroken heifer will need to be hauled up to the bail a few times . . after which on hearing the cry 'bail up' she will walk up to the bail of her own accord. **1876** J.A. EDWARDS *Gilbert Gogger* 154 It is customary to say of a man who cannot understand English, 'He cannot say bail up to a cow.' **1899** G.E. BOXALL *Story Austral. Bushrangers* 45 When driving the cows into the bail it was the custom to order them to 'bail up'. **1905** L. BECKE *Tom Gerrard* 98 Now, bail up, Maggie, and if you try to kick over the bucket you'll feel sorry. **1974** P. ADAM SMITH *Desert Railway* 17 'Hoosh! Hoosh! Hooshta!' The call was as well known on the construction of the Transcontinental line as the cry of 'Whoa!' to horses in city streets, and of 'Bail up!' on the bush farms of the cow-cockies. **1981** A.B. FACEY *Fortunate Life* 25 The old lady called out, 'Bail up, bail up', and the cows seemed to understand.

2. a. *trans.* Orig. of bushrangers: to confront (a person or persons) usu. with intent to commit robbery, preventing resistance by threat, force, or some means of confinement. Also *intr.*, to submit to such treatment without offering resistance (see quots. 1845 and 1892). See also STICK *v.* 1 b.

1838 *Colonist* (Sydney) 20 Oct. 3/2 They '*bail up*' the inmates, and commence plundering. **1838** *Cornwall Chron.* (Launceston) 17 Nov. 1 They then *baled up* all the servants by the hands, but treated Mrs ··· very respectfully. **1839** *Sydney Standard* 6 May 3/2 Made all the persons who were in the house come out and what is called 'bail up'; that is, they were all placed together and made to lie with their faces on the ground. **1844** MRS C. MEREDITH *Notes & Sketches N.S.W.* 132 Bushrangers . . 'bail up', *i.e.* bind with cords, or otherwise secure, the male portion, leaving an armed guard over them, whilst the rest of the gang ransack the house. **1845** *Standard* (Melbourne) 19 Feb. 3/2 He said I have settled him. . . I said what for? 'Because he would not bail up,' was his reply. **1847** A. MARJORIBANKS *Travels N.S.W.* 72 Being baled up is the colonial phrase for those who are attacked, who are afterwards all put together, and guarded by one of the party of the bushrangers when the others are plundering. **1849** J.P. TOWNSEND *Rambles & Observations N.S.W.* 75 From this group of Aborigines, one came running to us, saying that he had 'bailed up', or secured, a white fellow in a neighbouring hut, having caught him without a pass. **1854** W. SHAW *Land of Promise* 95 This system of bailing-up can scarcely be credited. . . The gang generally consists of three men, two of whom seize the arms of the victim, pulling them behind him, while the third pins or 'bails' him against a wall. **1866** *Australasian* (Melbourne) 7 Apr. 23/3 A party of four men . . bailed up the inmates, and took away what money they found on them. **1875** CAMPBELL & WILKS *Early Settlement Qld.* 39, I and two more will go bail up a dray. **1888** H.S. RUSSELL *Genesis Qld.* 351 A large mob of blacks had 'baled up' seven men. **1892** *Western Champion* (Barcaldine) 19 Apr. 1/2 Suddenly as he gained the 'drop' on them, he thundered out—'Bail up, you donkeys; throw up your arms. I'm Power!' They 'bailed'. **1900** *Ibid.* 16 Jan. 10/2 Me and the young master was going to 'bail you up' an' if you made any resistance we was goin' to shoot you in your tracks. **1920** C. CROWE *One Big Crime* 10 Two months later, they bailed up Younghusband's Faithful Creek Station, about four miles from Euroa. **1935** J.P. MCKINNEY *Crucible* 72 'The jacks were tailing me up.' 'What was the matter,' John asked. 'Just a bit of stoush,' said Roberts. 'Two of them bailed me up for my pass. I dropped them and beat it for the bush.' **1947** *Bulletin* (Sydney) 11 June 28/1 When he was camped by Naracan Creek a couple of louts bailed him up. . . The amateur Kellies rushed. **1980** *Sydney Morning Herald* 16 May 1/7 Two of the men, all barefooted and wearing only short pants, were armed with Armalite rifles. A third man carried a pistol. They bailed up Mr Dyason in his cabin and demanded the ship's money.

b. *Hist. intr. imp.* A bushranger's challenge, requiring those challenged to submit without resistance to being robbed.

1842 *Geelong Advertiser* 4 Apr. 3/2 *Bushranging at Sydney*. On Thursday evening, about ten o'clock, while Mr Grey of Balmain was sitting in his room, three bushrangers, heavily armed, rushed in, presenting their muskets and calling on him and his family to 'bail up'. **1852** G.C. MUNDY *Our Antipodes* I. 179 The passengers were ordered severally to get out and to 'bail up'—like cows prepared for milking—at the fence side. **1854** MRS C. CLACY *Lights & Shadows* I. 155 'Bail up' in a rough voice, and the click of a pistol, made him think it advisable to pause. **1864** *Sydney Punch* 9 July 50/2 And the noodles sang out, With a mock savage shout, 'Bail up, or I'll blow out your brains.' **1870** *Sydney Morning Herald* 1 July 4/6 McNab said, 'Bail up, and down with your hands; turn your heads to the fire all of you.' **1872** 'RESIDENT' *Glimpses Life Vic.* 323 The robbers . . ordered all the men to 'bail up!' This order signified that they should place their arms behind them. **1887** A. NICOLS *Wild Life & Adventure* 317 Many a richer man had perforce answered to his imperative summons, 'bail up'. **1888** 'R. BOLDREWOOD' *Robbery under Arms* (1937) 452 The same talk for cows and Christians. That's how things get stuck into the talk in a new country. Some old hand like father, as had . . spent all his mornings in the cowyard, had taken to the bush and tried his hand at sticking up people. When they came near enough . . he'd pop out from behind a tree . . , and when he wanted 'em to stop 'Bail up, d-- you', would come a deal quicker and more natural-like to his tongue than 'Stand'. So 'bail up' it was from that day to this. **1893** S. NEWLAND *Paving Way* 273 Scarcely was this accomplished, when a quick step sounded on the verandah, and he found himself confronted by a revolver at full-cock pointed straight at his head, while a rough voice said in imperative tones—'Bail up, or I'll blow the b--y roof off your head!' **1929** J.J. KENNEALLY *Compl. Inner Hist. Kelly Gang* 58 Suddenly Ned Kelly cried out, 'Bail up! Throw up your arms.'

3. a. *trans.* To bring (an animal) to bay.

1870 E.B. KENNEDY *Four Yrs. in Qld.* 93 Two Kangaroo hounds (they sometimes resemble coarse deer hounds) one day 'bailed up' a Kangaroo in a water-hole. **1887** A. NICOLS *Wild Life & Adventure* 275 The kangaroo . . planted his back against a large gum-tree fairly 'bailed up' at last. **1891** M. ROBERTS *Land-Travel & Sea-Faring* 127 To stand on the fallen trunk and cut out the comb while a thousand bees are flying round one's head in a thick cloud, gives a sensation of daring adventure not often afforded by 'bailing up' a wretched kangaroo. **1899** *Bulletin* (Sydney) 14 Oct. 14/4 Once saw two magpies with a mud-turtle bailed-up near a waterhole. **1916** *Ibid.* 31 Aug. 22/1 The dog's part was to bail up the pig; then it was lassoed. **1937** D. GUNN *Links with Past* 208 The shepherd's dog had baled up an old man kangaroo in a shallow waterhole. **1973** R. ROBINSON *Drift of Things* 112 The greyhounds would overtake and 'bail up' a kangaroo.

b. *intr.* Of an animal: to stand at bay.

[N.Z. **1894** J.K. ARTHUR *Kangaroo & Kauri* II. 98 The pigs will oftentimes 'bale up', or stop, and with their backs to a rock, tree, or other obstacle, keep two or more dogs at bay.] **1934** 'S. RUDD' *Green Grey Homestead*

125 He stuck to a black sow, in and out, and over everything, till he ran her to a standstill. And when she bailed up she had a snout on her as long as the nose of the smithy's bellows. **1956** B.J. RAYMENT *My Towri* 109 They managed to get half-way when the sheep bailed up. **1976** S. WELLER *Bastards I have Met* 116 They'd just yarded up at the Broughton and one big brahman bullock had bailed up. He was real stirry—would blow snot and throw dirt even if you looked his way. **1980** ANSELL & PERCY *To fight Wild* 102 Cows gallop too hard and fast, bulls get hot and bail up under trees.

4. *trans., transf.* and *fig.* Also (rarely) *intr.*

1841 *Geelong Advertiser* 14 Aug. 2/3 A 'barker' is a barefaced fellow who lays hold of you by the collar, drags you into a dark den .. bails you up in a corner, and holds you fast until you purchase some of his goods 'all as better as new'. **1845** *Parramatta Chron.* 28 June 3/1 The Bench, considering it clearly a case of *wool gathering, baled up* the accused until the Quarter Sessions settled the quality of the *fleece.* **1853** N. BARTLEY *Opals & Agates* (1892) 67 Bailed up by rain. **1855** W. HOWITT *Land, Labor & Gold* II. 303 The land question is the grand cardinal point. Set that right, and all will soon right itself. So long as that is wrong, the whole community will be wrong,—in colonial phrase, 'bailed up' at the mercy of its own tenants. **1877** *Vagabond Papers* iii. 153 It soon became known around the Stockade that he had bailed up the Super. in his office. **1879** 'AUSTRALIAN' *Adventures Qld.* 46 During floods, when people were bailed up, large numbers would stay for days successively. **1895** *Bulletin* (Sydney) 31 Aug. 27/1 A voice bailed me up: 'Say, mate; is this Friday or Saturday?' ***c* 1907** C.W. CHANDLER *Darkest Adelaide* 45, I knew a man that once sold a machine and he's been a blithering idiot ever since, going about and bailing up everybody he met and telling of his great feat. **1916** *Truth* (Sydney) 26 Nov. 5/1 The wages board has stepped in with a heavy and ignorant hand, *bailing up* the pork trade. **1931** *Bulletin* (Sydney) 4 Feb. 20/2 A seedy-looking individual bailed me up with a novel tale. **1944** C. WILMOT *Tobruk* 40 Italians driving to surrender .. were 'bailed up' by Major Gordon Hayman. **1967** J. WYNNUM *I'm Jack, all Right* 96, I wouldn't care to be bailed up in a tree with one. **1977** T. RONAN *Mighty Men on Horseback* 32, I reckoned it was about time I bailed up. **1986** *Canberra Chron.* 12 Mar. 5/1 Secondary-school students will 'bail up' Canberrans on Friday for donations for the .. Royal Blind Society.

Hence **bailed-up** *ppl. a.*, **bailing (up)** *vbl. n.*.

1963 X. HERBERT *Disturbing Element* 22, I grew up on tales of what a fearsome thing a **bailed-up** old man 'roo could be. **1841** *Sydney Herald* 17 Apr. 2/4 On the road from Goulburn upwards a single bushranger .. has been levying contributions, the most serious of which is the robbery of her Majesty's mail .. and the '**bailing up**' of the coachman. **1853** H.B. JONES *Adventures in Aust.* 296 'Bailing up' is stopping a man for the purpose of robbing. Either waylaying him, or going into his hut or store in gangs of three or four, and obliging him to reveal his wealth, and deliver it up. **1863** R. THERRY *Reminisc. Thirty Yrs. N.S.W. & Vic.* 126 '*Bailing up*' .. consisted in our being grouped together on the roadside, whilst one of the three bushrangers was placed as a sentinel over us, with instructions from the captain to shoot the first man that stirred without permission. **1872** A. MCFARLAND *Illawarra & Manaro* 48 The driving of cows from the paddocks into the yards, the 'bailing', the milking. **1888** G. ROCK *Colonists* 98 The process of 'bailing up' consisted generally in tying up the victim to a tree, robbing him of all his valuables, and leaving him to take his chance of being rescued. **1916** *Ross's Monthly* June 14/2 Webster said he would not discuss such matters (the 'bailing-up' in the post-office of 'Ross's Magazine' and the 'International Socialist') on a public platform, but in the proper place.

bailer shell. Also **baler shell.** Any of several volutid molluscs of the genus *Melo*, used by Aborigines in n. Aust. for bailing out canoes, for digging, and as a cooking utensil; the shell of such a mollusc.

1908 E.J. BANFIELD *Confessions of Beachcomber* 148 The bailer shell (*Cymbium aethiopicum*) [is] the 'Ping-ah' of the blacks... The bailer shell alive is like an egg, in the fact that it is full of meat. **1926** K. DAHL *In Savage Aust.* 290 These knives were made from bits of the large 'bailer shell'.., a gigantic snail, whose shell is almost the size of a wash-hand basin. **1936** T.C. ROUGHLEY *Wonders Great Barrier Reef* 111 One of the largest and most interesting of the univalves .. inhabiting the waters of the Great Barrier Reef is the bailer- or melon-shell, which is very common on the reef flats... It has received the former name because of its extensive use by the blacks as a bailer for their canoes .. and the latter from its resemblance both in shape and pattern to a water-melon. **1949** *Bulletin* (Sydney) 19 Jan. 29/1, I recently observed something rare: a bailer shell .. laying its eggs. **1978** N. COLEMAN *Look at Wildlife Great Barrier Reef* 69 Entirely carnivorous, baler shells feed almost exclusively on other molluscs.

baked, *ppl. a. Obs.* [Br. dial.: see EDD *bake, v.*[1] 4.] Exhausted.

1861 *Burke & Wills Exploring Exped.* 22 The horse, Billy, being completely baked, next morning we started at day-break, leaving the horse short hobbled. **1861** 'OLD BUSHMAN' *Bush Wanderings* 213 Often have I turned in fairly 'baked' and put my supper off till morning. **1866** *Australasian* (Melbourne) 22 Dec. 1188/5 Poor Harry was .. rather 'baked' the last mile or two. **1871** *Austral. Jrnl.* Aug. 663/2 'Moke seems rather baked?' says he at length. 'Yes,' returned Dick. 'Had a hard day's work?' 'Yes.' **1888** 'R. BOLDREWOOD' *Robbery under Arms* (1937) 86 Pulled up before if I knowed your horses were getting baked.

baker. FLOURY BAKER.

1860 G. BENNETT *Gatherings of Naturalist* 271 Many of the species of this insect have various parts of the body covered with a whitish secretion; hence they are named *Millers* and *Bakers* by the colonial youth. **1903** *Agric. Gaz. N.S.W.* XIV. 418 A well-known 'locust', to the Sydney boys is popularly known as the 'Floury Miller', or the 'Baker', on account of the rich, silvery pubescence, which makes it look as if it had been dusted with flour.

bal /bæl/. [Cornish *bal* a mine or cluster of mines: see OED.] In Cornish mining settlements in S.A.: see quot. 1971. Freq. *attrib.*

1867 *Wallaroo Times* (Kadina) 28 Aug. 2/3 We have had several of the 'bal bills' from the Moonta Mines left at our office to show the actual earnings of a number of the tributers. **1869** *Ibid.* 31 July 3/2 The mine is improving in value and exhibits all the signs of a permanent 'bal'. **1900** *Yorke's Peninsula Advertiser* (Moonta) 26 Jan. 3/1 Mr Leslie Davey is doing well in Broken Hill.—Bal friends send hearty congratulations. **1962** O. PRYOR *Aust.'s Little Cornwall* 15 The working people of Cornwall lived hard, and the women shared the work. In mining communities they were the *bal-maidens*, skilled in the dressing of ore for the smelters. **1971** *AUMLA* xxxvi. 167 *Wheal* and *bal* .. seem to have been widely used in South Australia... *Bal* seems to have been the word regularly used to describe a mine or group of mines together with the associated buildings, plant, and machinery, as .. in .. *scatterin' the bal* .. the closing down of a mine and disposal of the plant, .. *bal bill* 'statement of a miner's earnings', *bal friend*, and *bal-maiden* .. a woman working on the surface, especially in the dressing of ore.

balander /bəˈlændə/. *Aboriginal English.* Also **balanda, ballanda.** [a. Maccasarese *balanda*, a. Malay *bĕlanda* (corruption of *Hollander*), a Dutchman, a white man.] A white man. Also as *adj.*

1845 L. LEICHHARDT *Jrnl. Overland Exped.* 2 Dec. (1847) 503 They knew the white people of Victoria, and called them Bálanda, which is nothing more than 'Hollanders'; a name used by the Malays, from whom they received it. **1915** E.R. MASSON *Untamed Territory* 112 The blacks rushed up to the house calling 'Ballanda, Ballanda'—white man—and the Boss and Missus ran out. **1927** *Trans. R. Soc. S.A.* LI. 192 White man, balanda. **1943** W.E. HARNEY *Taboo* 203 On the natives' side are .. fear of the Ballander-whiteman and the thought of losing their country. **1976** C.C. MACKNIGHT *Voyage to Marege'* p. ix, Friends in the Northern Territory, both Aboriginal and Balanda .. trusted me to tell the story. **1978** J. MIRRITJI *My People's Life* 48 Then I understood that this 'balanda' means people with skins like the white clay. **1978** *Nungalinya Occasional Bull.* (Darwin) iii. 7 The balanda fishing supervisor, himself a keen sailor, considered B-- an expert sailor. **1978** *Austral.* (Sydney) 6 Oct. 7/2 Balander .. is an Aboriginal name for a white man—corruption of the word Hollander. The tribes of Arnhem Land knew the tough, phlegmatic Dutchmen of the East Indies before Cook was born. Now a balander means any white man. **1982** A. POWELL *Far Country* 36 The word 'balanda', originally referring to the 'Hollanders', was adopted widely in Arnhem Land to designate all white men.

baldcoot. [Transf. use of *baldcoot* the coot *Fulica atra.*] *Swamp hen* see SWAMP *n.*

1829 H. WIDOWSON *Present State Van Diemen's Land* 182 The baldcoot, and a large bird, called the native hen .. frequent the lakes and lagunes. **1912** *Emu* XII. 119 *Porphyrio melanonotus.* Bald-Coot... This bird is terribly destructive to the eggs of the Black Swan. **1939** *Bulletin* (Sydney) 3 May 21/1 Two bad pests in the cane-fields in N.Q. are the bald coot, known occasionally as the 'waggy', and the scrub turkey. **1953** A. RUSSELL *Murray Walkabout* 50 The bald-coot is .. among the loveliest of all the Australian swamp-dwellers; its red legs and bill, blue vest, and upright form give it a singular beauty.

baldy, *n.* and *a.* Also **bally.** [f. Br. dial. *bald* marked with white: see EDD *adj.* 1.]

A. *n.* A Hereford, so called from the white face of the breed; a white-faced beast (see quot. 1946).

1887 *Bungendore Mirror* 19 Oct. 3, 50 18-months old Heifers—nearly all ballies. **1918** C. FETHERSTONHAUGH *After Many Days* 99 'Ballys' (Herefords) were introduced. **1924** C. BLOXSOME *How Wonder won Cup* 46 We came to a herd of cattle. Most of them seemed to be Herefords. 'By jove,' said Jim, 'I own all those ballys.' **1925** *Bulletin* (Sydney) 21 May 24/4 He's for ever skiting of ancient times when there were always Shorthorns and no Baldies. **1927** *Smith's Weekly* (Sydney) 15 Jan. 14/2, I helped a 'baldy' out of a wombat hole. He showed his gratitude by chasing me up the nearest sapling. **1939** J.G. PATTISON *'Battler's' Tales Early Rockhampton* 113 He drafted off the best of the herd to take with him, and left all of what 'Banjo' calls the Goulburn roans and polled ballys. **1946** *Bulletin* (Sydney) 24 July 28/3 The bullock team, a strung-out procession of baldies, brindles and blacks, plods slowly along. **1947** *Ibid.* 5 Nov. 28/3 The Carters .. brought the Herefords down from the slopes above Tigercat Creek. The baldies quietly plodded the well-worn track. **1949** *Ibid.* 19 Oct. 12/1 With the baldies bedded down, we mooched into the little township. **1961** D. STUART *Driven* 138 One beast, a light red baldy, dodged back almost under Khaki's nose, and the mare pivoted with it. **1976** C.D. MILLS *Hobble Chains & Greenhide* 145 If I say Hereford, the Shorthorn blokes'll gang up to prove that I'm wrong, and if I defend the 'baldies' against 'em, the Polled Angus champions will show me pictures provin' they've won the export body of beef.

B. *adj.* **a.** Hereford (cattle). **b.** Of other animals: white-faced or with a white marking on the face. Also applied to the face itself.

1890 *Braidwood Dispatch* 30 Apr. 4/1 Now Jack you take the bally mare And ride right round Gum Swamp today. **1914** C.H.S. MATTHEWS *Bill* 137 A nice-looking chestnut called Pink 'un, with four white legs and a 'baldy' face. **1924** C. BLOXSOME *How Wonder won Cup* 72 Oh! I'd take £8 for her; I wouldn't sell her at all, only I can't stand a horse with a bally face. **1938** F. RATCLIFFE *Flying Fox & Drifting Sand* 76 She .. knew .. every beast on the place—not as 'that bally cow with a crooked horn', but as an individual being. **1944** *Bulletin* (Sydney) 26 July 13/1 Every spring a mob of long-horned bally-faced Herefords come down from their winter habitat. **1981** A. WILKINSON *Up Country* 149 Good baldy (Hereford) cattle in the paddocks.

bale, var. BAAL, BAIL *v.*

baler shell, var. BAILER SHELL.

ball. *Obs.* [Prob. metaphoric use of *ball* as fired by a musket (cf. *slug*). The slang use of *ball* glass of spirits, is attested by *ball of fire* glass of brandy (OEDS *ball, sb.*[1] 6 b. 1821), U.S. *highball* (OEDS 1898), and the chiefly Irish *ball (of malt)* glass of malt whisky (OEDS *sb.*[4] 1925).] A glass of spirits.

1832 *Hill's Life N.S.W.* 3 Aug. 2 The party then adjourned to a *max*-house, and drowned their sorrows in a few *balls.* **1833** *Sydney Herald* 11 Mar. 3/1 The inhabitants not much relishing their visitor, and knowing that he was attached to a ball, gave him as much rum as he thought fit to imbibe. **1841** *Port Phillip Patriot* 29 Nov. 3/1 Several bloated looking creatures, who were awaiting the dreaded question, 'Were you drunk, Sir?' hobbled away to drink 'long life to Sir George' in another *ball.* **1843** *Satirist & Sporting Chron.*

(Sydney) 1 Apr. 2/4 The waiter being called, each gent. ordered his ball or pot of swipes which ever suited his palate. **1843** *Melbourne Times* 29 Aug. 3/1 Mr Baker stated that the man had been on the spree for the last week, and being refused liquor within doors, was constantly going out for 'balls'. 'Balls', said the Major, what, is he such an inveterate waltzer? No, your Worship. Then, what do you mean by 'balls'? A 'ball' is a 'drain', your Worship. And pray what is a 'drain'? A 'drain' is a 'nobbler', your Worship. And what is a 'nobbler'? A small glass of spirits, your Worship. **1848** *Maitland Mercury* 10 May 2/5 *Newington Races* . . A large room is being prepared for a Ball in the evening, though we have no doubt the sporting gents will be taking a *ball* during the day. **1849** J.P. TOWNSEND *Rambles & Observations N.S.W.* 209 A few ants in his tea give it an additional flavour, and the summit of his bliss is a 'brandy ball'. **1850** T. MCCOMBIE *Colonist in Aust.* 182 When shall we have a ball of rum? **1854** C.A. CORBYN *Sydney Revels* 7 Lizzy received two shillings from him; procured the alcohol and poured him out a 'ball'. **1855** W. HOWITT *Land, Labor & Gold* I. 144 A glass, denominated a nobbler—if half a glass, a nip or a ball. **1867** J.R. HOULDING *Austral. Capers* 246 Bill, come to the 'Badger', and let's have a ball. **1879** 'AUSTRALIAN' *Adventures Qld.* 9 A fellow could always coax a stiff ball of the right sort of stuff out of him. **1888** A. MCLEAN *Harry Bloomfield* 13 'Sure ye know what a *ball* is?' 'For a gun?' . . 'Ye'd vex St. Patrick himself; sure ye ken undherstand a good glass of whiskey?'

Hence as *v. trans.*

1845 *Parramatta Chron.* 1 Feb. 3/3 At a public-house, near the police office . . they were apparently accidentally joined by a man named Adams—who also 'balled it' off—which done, they separated.

ballander, var. BALANDER.

Ballarat (seedling): see STEWART'S BALLARAT SEEDLING.

ballart /'bælat/. [a. Wergaia and Djadjala dial. of Wemba *balaad.*] **a.** Any of several shrubs or small trees of the partly-parasitic genus *Exocarpos* (fam. Santalaceae) having a swollen and often edible cherry-like pedicel. **b.** With distinguishing epithet, as **cherry ballart,** *native cherry* (a), see NATIVE *a.* 6 a. See also CHERRY 1.

1889 J.H. MAIDEN *Useful Native Plants Aust.* 30 'Oringorin' of the Queensland aboriginals; and 'Ballat' of those of Gippsland. The fruit is edible. **1930** A.J. EWART *Flora Vic.* 418 *E[xocarpus] cupressiformis* . . Cherry Ballart. A small tree . . with a graceful habit and dense, dark-green branches. **1952** E. WALLING *Austral. Roadside* 79 The Ballart is cypress-like in appearance. **1967** V.G.C. NORWOOD *Long Haul* 79 A troop of green-wings quit the light-green foliage of a drooping cherry ballart. **1980** G.R. COCHRANE et al. *Flowers & Plants Vic. & Tas.* (rev. ed.) 111 The common name 'Ballart' is not used in Tasmania.

ball of muscle. [Cf. *ball of fire.*] A person of dynamic energy; one who is physically very fit.

1914 A.B. PATERSON in C. Semmler *World of Banjo Paterson* (1967) 321 The handicap king, Moonlighter, bounds along, a ball of muscle, in last place. **1939** K. TENNANT *Foveaux* 160 Rolfe was again 'a ball of muscle', as he termed it, working on the Slum Abolition Committee. **1945** C. MANN *River* 137 All of them shake except Spider Hayes, who's a ball of muscle, one of the fittest of the whole bunch. **1951** CUSACK & JAMES *Come in Spinner* 251 'Hullo,' he said pleasantly. 'You look a ball of muscle tonight.' **1963** D. ATTENBOROUGH *Quest under Capricorn* 26 'G'day,' we said, slipping into the vernacular. 'Yer right?' 'Ball o' muscle,' he replied with gusto. . . 'If I felt any better I couldn't stand it.'

ball-tearer. [Fig. use of *ball* testicle.] Something outstanding of its kind; a source of exasperation or dismay.

1971 J. MCNEIL *Chocolate Frog* (1973) 25, I mean you bein' pinched for street fightin' . . yer must be a real little ball-tearer. **1978** J. DINGWALL *Sunday too far Away* 30 Phew, she's a ball-tearer of a day. **1978** *Nat. Times* (Sydney) 27 May 29/3 Ron Blair's play about the Christian Brothers stood out as a 'ball-tearer'. **1984** *Sydney Morning Herald* 26 Mar. 2/6 He thought the Opposition might have done better in the country and not quite as well in the city. 'The result in the city shows that corruption is a ball-tearer in the city.'

ball-up. *Australian National Football.* The bouncing of the ball by the field umpire to start or restart play, at the beginning of a quarter or after certain interruptions of play. See BOUNCE.

1890 J. SADLER *Lyrics & Rhymes* 143 'Jump on him!' 'Kick it!' 'Ball up!' **1928** G. MORIARTY *Teaching Game of Football* ii. 3 If there is a scrimmage in front of goals, and the Umpire blows his whistle for 'Ball up', your tall ruckman should get in position. **1931** J.F. MCHALE et al. *Austral. Game of Football* 57 If the ball strikes a player above the knee after being kicked, and it goes out of bounds—ball up. **1964** *Footy Fan* (Melbourne) II. xvi. 19 No matter what decision I made, I could not win, so, like any courageous umpire, I could not make up my mind, and I called for a 'ball-up' and settled for a draw. **1973** B. HOGAN *Follow Game* (rev. ed.) 63 The field umpire may throw the ball in the air if the ground surface is unsuitable to bounce the ball. . . (Umpires must not resort to a 'ball up' in preference to awarding a free kick against the first infringement observed). **1983** G. ATKINSON *Bk. Austral. Rules Finals* 202 Umpire Schwab blew his whistle for a puzzling 'ball-up' decision.

bally, var. BALDY.

Balmain bug. [f. *Balmain* the name of a Sydney suburb + *bug*: see quot. 1974.] The edible marine crustacean *Ibacus peronii* of s. Aust., having a dorsoventrally flattened body. See also SHOVEL-NOSED LOBSTER.

1952 W.J. DAKIN *Austral. Seashores* 184 The flapjack, also known to trawlermen as the Balmain bug. **1974** J.M. THOMSON *Fish Ocean & Shore* 77 The Balmain bug owes its name to the trawlermen who pioneered the trawling industry in New South Wales. . . The trawlers were based at Balmain. . . Any jointed crawly thing was a bug to the locals. **1979** L. MORRISSY *Austral. Crustacean Cookery* 9 The 'northern shovel-nosed lobster' or 'Moreton Bay bug', *Thenus orientalis* . . is considered to have more flavour than the 'southern shovel-nosed lobster' or 'Balmain bug', *Ibacus peronii.* **1983** J. JONES *Macquarie Dict. Cookery* 200 Balmain bugs are usually orange-brown to orange-red in colour. . . They are caught from Moreton Bay round New South Wales and the southern states to Western Australia.

Balt /bɔlt/. [Transf. use of *Balt* native or inhabitant of one of the Baltic states.] An immigrant to Australia from one of the Baltic countries in the period following the 1939–45 war; loosely, any non-British immigrant from Europe. Freq. in *pl.*

1945 *Queanbeyan Age* 28 Sept. 1/7 Officials believe it will be impossible to repatriate at least 300,000; while 25,000 refuse to be sent home. Of this number 170,000 Balts refuse to be returned to Russian controlled areas. **1948** *Bulletin* (Sydney) 3 Mar. 23/4 Those Balts who are starting in the big timber in W.A. . . will make a good job of their work. **1957** J.M. HOSKING *Aust. First & Last* 123 We call them New Australians now; once we called some Dagoes, Others Balts and Squareheads, Pongoes, Brills and Rice and Sagoes. **1957** 'N. CULOTTA' *They're Weird Mob* 53 You gunna let 'em talk that stuff out here? Dagoes an' Jerries an' Balts an' Poles an Lithu-bloody-wanians? **1959** D. HEWETT *Bobbin Up* 150 Only the four New Australians went on working doggedly. . . 'Look at them bloody Balts, all with their heads down and their arses up.' **1963** B. BEAVER *Hot Summer* 85 Balts you call us. Well, I am central European. **1973** R. ROBINSON *Drift of Things* 410, I had heard that the fettlers' gangs were filled with 'Balts', which was what the war migrants from Europe were called. **1976** N.V. WALLACE *Bush Lawyer* 161 The name Baltic was easy to say, so not only in Naracoorte but throughout the country, European immigrants came to be called Balts, even though they may have hailed from lands overlooking the Adriatic or Aegean seas. **1979** B. SCOTT *Tough in Old Days* 77 There was a New Australian in the compartment, though they were called 'Balts' in those days.

ban: see *black ban* BLACK *a.*[4] 2, GREEN BAN.

banana.

1. Used *attrib.* in Special Comb., chiefly with reference to Queensland.

a. Banana land, State, a name for the State of Queensland.

1880 *Bulletin* (Sydney) 26 June 3/1 (*heading*) Notes from **Banana Land** (From our Brisbane Correspondent). **1887** *Lantern* (Adelaide) 12 Mar. 22 A Queensland Exchange tells . . how Sunday closing works in Banana Land. **1899** *Worker* (Sydney) 14 Jan. 1/3 The Premier of Bananaland seems to be indulging in an unnecessary degree of hauteur towards us poor Southern worms. **1900** *Bulletin* (Sydney) 3 Mar. 15/1 Even the Bananaland Chow is patriotic just now—when it pays. **1906** *Truth* (Sydney) 20 May 6/2 How many residents of Bananaland ever saw a respectable married Kanaka with a loving white wife and fragrant piebald family? **1916** *Bulletin* (Sydney) 24 Feb. 24/1 His blood relation . . *does* imitate the call of the wonga, just as he would that of the whampoo if he lived in the Bananaland scrubs. **1938** *Ibid.* 6 July 20/3 The queerest fence I've seen was a bandicoot-blocker enclosing a vegetable garden in the elbow-bend of a small Bananaland creek. **1950** E.M. ENGLAND *Where Turtles Dance* 35, I give Pen a month in that Bananaland backwater. **1960** *N.T. News* (Darwin) 5 Feb. 15/5 Andrew Walsh will go to Queensland soon. . . I'm tipping it will mean a gain to some Bananaland organisation. **1974** D. IRELAND *Burn* 32 Had my eighteenth birthday in camp. Up in bananaland. Canungra. **1977** C. MCCULLOUGH *Thorn Birds* 247 It's your first bit of genuine Bananaland food. I tell you, there's no place like Queensland. **1916** *Truth* (Sydney) 17 Dec. 10/4 He *was going to Roma*, in the **Banana State**. **1979** H. POST *Maintain your Rage* 55 Pouring rice over the heads of the young marrieds when they leave for their honeymoon to the banana-state.

b. Banana-bender, -lander, -skin, a nickname for a Queenslander.

1964 D. LOCKWOOD *Up Track* 110 We are so close to Queensland that I think we should hop over the border. What do you say to a quick look at the **banana-benders**? **1967** G. JENKIN *Two Yrs. Bardunyah Station* 2 The boss was a native of Queensland . . still very conscious of being a Bananabender and pretended to despise the 'Damned Crow-eating custom' of drinking wine. **1979** H. POST *Maintain your Rage* 87 He's not a Victorian any more, the state where he lived for a long time; he's a straight-out banana-bender now. **1980** M. GRANT *Barrier Reef* 33 To the rest of the country Queensland was the home of the 'Banana Benders'. This, to Queenslanders . . was not a term of endearment. **1983** *Weekend Austral. Mag.* (Sydney) 30 July 18/3 Don't these ignorant banana-benders know that Italian cooking is *based* on tomatoes? **1887** *Bulletin* (Sydney) 26 Feb. 6/4 He made all arrangements for being married on that day, and his friends rallied up to congratulate him, and see him through, after the custom of the simple **Bananalanders**. **1890** *Quiz* (Adelaide) 18 July 3/3 The Premier of Queensland . . has given up the idea. . . It is a saying with the Bananalanders that he has more head than brains. **1892** *Truth* (Sydney) 19 June 4/7 A Queenslander accepts as a compliment the title Bananalander. **1899** *Progress* (Brisbane) 4 Mar. 10/2 It seems to me that the only step which will effectively rouse the Bananalanders will be the appointment of Chinese and Kanaka policeman. **1918** *Kia Ora Coo-ee* May 4/3 The Bananalander made a rush for the nearest Turk. **1928** *Bulletin* (Sydney) 25 July 25/2 Victorian settlers refer to these as 'Queensland gates', while the Bananalanders blame the Victorians for introducing them. **1949** D. WALKER *We went to Aust.* 72 The people of Queensland are known in Australia as the Bananalanders. **1953** *Bulletin* (Sydney) 22 July 13/4 'It's rosella jam—it's made out of rosellas,' insisted Stan. 'Gaw starve the crows,' breathed his best mate. . . 'Now I suppose you'll tell me them Bananalanders make pickles out of peewees and tomato-sauce out of galahs?' **1968** K. DENTON *Walk around my Cluttered Mind* 3 Ya can't fool me sport. I c'n tella banana-lander any time. I c'n pickem. You come from Queensland 'n' I *know it!* **1921** F. GROSE *Rough Y.M. Bloke* 148 Combat the pestilential attacks of 'Cornstalks', 'Croweaters' and '**Bananaskins**'.

c. Banana city, Brisbane; **curtain,** the Queensland border; **-man** *obs.*, **(a)** a Queenslander; **(b)** a (Queensland) drink.

1893 J.A. BARRY *Steve Brown's Bunyip* 181 He had, he flattered himself . . been making rapid progress with the damsels of the **Banana city**. **1955** N. PULLIAM *I traveled Lonely Land* 370 *Banana City*, Brisbane. **1979** *Austral.* (Sydney) 28 Dec. 1/1 We know the Fleet Street system, Henry. Even up here behind the **banana curtain.** **1980** H. LUNN *Behind Banana Curtain* 202 Someone at Parliament House had twigged that I was a northerner and asked me how things were 'behind the Banana Curtain'. **1868** *Wallaroo Times* (Kadina) 9 Sept. 6/2 The '**Bananah Men**' have struck some really splendid patches of gold. **1876** 'EIGHT YRS.' RESIDENT' *Queen of Colonies* 151 With all this increase of population very little new ground was opened, and great was the ire of the Southerners against the 'Banana men', as they choose to call the Queenslanders, for their luck in holding all the payable ground. **1880** *Bulletin* (Sydney) 14 Feb. 4/3 When a Cooktown man arises he goes to the bar and takes what is variously known as a 'Queenslander' or a 'Bananaman'. To make this delectable beverage . . you mix in a lemonade tumbler, a big nobbler of gin, ditto of whiskey, some limejuice, curacoa, cloves, absinthe, and Hostetter's bitters together with a teaspoonful of cayenne, and a little of the grounds of a bottle of Worcestershire sauce. **1886** P. CLARKE *'New Chum' in Aust.* 66 A Queenslander is . . distinguished by the title of 'banana-man'. **1930** *Bulletin* (Sydney) 8 Jan. 20/2 A favorite drink of the old days in N. Queensland . . was a 'bananaman'. You paid the publican 5s. and then went behind the bar with a long glass and poured into it something out of every bottle that chanced to catch your eye. **1971** D.G. WILSON *New Ships* (1975) 46, I said, 'By God and this big right hand You must recognise a banana man.'

2. In the names of animals: **banana bird,** any of several birds, esp. the blue-faced honeyeater *Entomyzon cyanotis*, *Lewin honeyeater* (see LEWIN), and FIGBIRD; **prawn,** the crustacean *Penaeus merguiensis* of warm waters from India to New Caledonia, including n. Aust., fished commercially in the Gulf of Carpentaria.

1931 N.W. CAYLEY *What Bird is That?* 9 Lewin Honey-eater *Meliphaga lewini*. . . Also called Yellow-eared Honey-eater and **Banana-bird**. **1948** *Bulletin* (Sydney) 3 Nov. 28/2 The banana-birds shrill their alarms like official awakeners. **1967** V.G.C. NORWOOD *Long Haul* 80 A yellow-eared Lewin honey-eater or banana bird swooped across the shallow flow. **1976** *Reader's Digest Compl. Bk. Austral. Birds* 468 Like other large honeyeaters, the blue-faced species has a varied diet. . . It will damage cultivated fruits such as pears and especially bananas—in coastal Queensland it is called the banana bird. **1953** *Fisheries Newsletter* XII. ii. 23/1 The King and Banana are 'summer' prawns. **Banana prawns** are not particularly common in Moreton Bay, but large catches of them are made in the Mary and neighbouring rivers. **1965** M. PATCHETT *Last Warrior* 21 He saw the banana prawns which barramundi love. **1965** *Austral. Encycl.* VII. 256 The banana prawn has a pale cream body and the tail-fan is coloured in a combination of yellow, green and brownish shades, giving the appearance of ripening bananas. **1977** *Commercial Fish of Aust.* (Dept. Primary Industry) 84 Banana prawns . . form large schools and adults are rarely found in water deeper than 40 metres. **1984** *N.T. News* (Darwin) 12 Sept. 40/1 (Advt.), A steal. Whole green banana prawns. Only $6.80 per kg. . . Special while stocks last.

band. *Opal-mining.* A layer of sandstone containing some opal, above and below which larger deposits are likely to occur.

1902 *Geol. Survey Rep.* (Qld. Dept. Mines) clxxvii. 10 The opal-bearing stratum 'band' in which the sandstone opal is found, occurs in the falsely-bedded series of sandstones and clays at the base of the sandstone, and at its junction with the underlying clay. **1910** *Lone Hand* Mar. 494 Through this rock the gem seams also run in a generally flat direction above and below a harder formation, called the 'band', averaging about two feet in thickness. This 'band' is your principal guide. **1932** I.L. IDRIESS *Prospecting for Gold* 249 'Matrix opal' is opal in many veins running through 'the band'. **1940** —— *Lightning Ridge* 86 'We're right on the band!' the gouger would call up to his mate. 'Better knock off,' would come the reply; 'we'll bottom in the morning.' . . Next morning they'd break through the band and expose the first of the bottom. **1960** D. McLEAN *Roaring Days* 62 We gouged them from a white clay below the band, and the country round the ugly bush town was like a rabbit warren of shafts and white dumps left by the opal gougers.

banded stilt. The wading bird *Cladorhynchus leucocephalus* of s. Aust., which feeds and breeds in salt lakes: see quot. 1968.

1841 J. GOULD *Birds of Aust.* (1848) VI. Pl. 26, The Banded Stilt is an inhabitant of the southern and western coast of Australia. **1890** G.J. BROINOWSKI *Birds of Aust.* II. Pl. 35, The Banded Stilt is found to inhabit Eastern, Southern and Western Australia. **1968** R. HILL *Bush Quest* 4 Even more shy were the banded stilts, handsome white birds with dark brown backs and a chestnut band on their breast.

bandicoot, *n.* Also **bandycoot.** [Transf. use of *bandicoot* (lit. 'pig-rat'), the Indian eutherian mammal *Bandicota indica*, to which the Austral. animals bear some resemblance.]

1. Any of several marsupial mammals of the fam. Peramelidae and Thylacomyidae of Aust., New Guinea, and nearby islands, having long, pointed heads, esp. *Isoodon macrourus* of n. and e. Aust., which frequents suburban gardens. Also with distinguishing epithet, as **pig-footed, rabbit, short-nosed:** see under first element. Rarely **bandicoot rat.**

1799 D. COLLINS *Acct. Eng. Colony N.S.W.* (1802) II. 188 The bones of small animals, such as opossums . . and bandicoots. **1803** J. GRANT *Narr. Voyage N.S.W.* 137 He supposed it to be the Bandicoot rat, an animal that seldom appears by day-light. **1804** *Sydney Gaz.* 21 Oct., A large tree in which three apertures had been cut for the purpose of searching after the *bandycoot*. **1818** J. HOLT *Mem.* 14 Jan. (1838) II. 69 An animal somewhat like a rabbit, called a bandy-coot, on which we afterwards dined, and found it of good flavour. **1825** *London Mag.* May II. 58 The bandy coot is a small animal, not so big as a rabbit, but very fat, and very fine eating. **1827** 'PINDAR JUVENAL' *Van Diemen's Land Warriors* 21 His gun would not go off and shoot, That noble animal—the *bandicoot*! **1832** J. BISCHOFF *Sketch Hist. Van Diemen's Land* 177 The only creatures inhabiting these large forests, appeared to be opossums and bandicoot rats [etc.]. **1841** *Sydney Herald* 27 Oct. 3/1 The maize is particularly exposed, immediately after planting, to the ravages of Bandicoots; who root up and eat the seed. **1865** G.F. ANGAS *Aust.* 73 The *Perameles*, or bandicoot, of which there are several species peculiar to Australia, is a pretty little creature about the size of a guinea-pig. **1870** E.B. KENNEDY *Four Yrs. in Qld.* 99 The animal I liked best cooked on a bush fire was a bandicoot. **1887** A. NICOLS *Wild Life & Adventure* 94 Put a close fence round it, to keep out the pademelons and bandicoots. **1897** MRS L. RAWSON *Austral. Cook & Laundry Bk.* 42 A bandicoot is a very disagreeable animal to clean, therefore it should be done as soon after killing as possible. **1924** A.B. PEIRCE *Knocking About* 68 And the delicious meaty bandicoot, or native rat, the flesh of which reminds one of a sucking pig. **1928** *Bulletin* (Sydney) 29 Feb. 19/2 How many different sorts of bandicoot does Australia possess? I have met the pig-footed 'coot, the striped 'coot, the long-nosed, the short-nosed, the golden, the spiny-furred and the grizzled-yellow. **1935** F. BIRTLES *Battle Fronts Outback* 104 There was one old dame with a necklace of dead bandicoots hung around her skinny neck. **1952** B. BEATTY *Unique to Aust.* 37 The Bandicoot is . . omnivorous and insectivorous and of burrowing habits. . . They . . are usually small . . in appearance like a rat, with a long tail and hind legs like those of a kangaroo. **1962** MARSHALL & DRYSDALE *Journey among Men* 65 At night, bandicoots, sharp-nosed little insect-hunters, foraged around our camp and were held in the rays of our flashlights. **1983** J. HEPWORTH *Birds & Beasties Aust.* The Bandicoot is rather beaut. Neat and clean, No way a fool: Like a rat that's been To finishing school. **1983** R. STRAHAN *Compl. Bk. Austral. Mammals* 93 Of the seven genera of bandicoots, three are restricted to Melanesia.

2. *transf.* and *fig.* Used in various phrases as an emblem of deprivation or desolation.

1837 H. WATSON *Lecture on S.A.* 20 The land here is generally good; there is a small proportion that is actually good for nothing; to use a colonial phrase, 'a bandicoot (an animal between a rat and a rabbit) would starve upon it'. **1845** J.O. BALFOUR *Sketch of N.S.W.* 26 When hungry, cold, or unhappy, the Australian black says that he is as miserable as the bandicoot. **1857** J. ASKEW *Voyage Aust. & N.Z.* 98 The bandecoots, and kangaroo rats, are little lean animals, that burrow in the earth. 'As poor as a bandecoot', is a very common expression in the Australian colonies. **1867** *Pasquin* (London) 2 Feb. 9 The ancient and modern anti-squatters—dogs and duffers—have restored the waste land to its former peaceful simplicity—from Dan to Beersheba there isn't a bite for a bandicoot. **1871** *Williams's Illustr. Austral. Ann.* 63 Why, I declare, the man looks as sad as a misanthropical bandicoot! **1873** M. CLARKE *Holiday Peak* 37 When you're bald as a bandicoot, *then*, Jack, 'Twill be time to be solemn and slow! **1890** *Quiz* (Adelaide) 12 Dec. 7/2 He looked . . as miserable as a widowed bandicoot. **1901** *Truth* (Sydney) 17 Nov. 5/4 Looking as *hungry and lugubrious* as 'a bandicoot on a burnt ridge'. **1904** *Bulletin* (Sydney) 24 Mar. 16/3 'Miserable as an orphan bandicoot on a burnt ridge' was a favorite expression of Henry Parkes, but don't know if he originated it. **1909** C. SHELDON *Chewin' Rag* 16 Some . . wos [*sic*] always as hard up as a bandycoot. **1911** V. DESMOND *Awful Austral.* 69 There is an expression in Australia, 'Blind as a bandicoot'. It's at variance with natural history. **1920** C.L. HARTT *More Diggerettes* 9 That's the worst of them French tabs. They look oright, but they're as ignorant as blanky bandycoots. **1927** J. POLLARD *Rose of Bushlands* 74 'Oh, goody!' the girl exclaimed. 'I'm as hungry as a bandicoot.' **1940** 'K. BRUCE' *Digger Tourists* 112 I'm as lousy as a bandicoot and I'm getting dog poor carrying the damn chats round with me. **1953** D. STIVENS *Gambling Ghost* 12 We were sitting on the veranda, as mournful as a trio of blistered bandicoots on a burnt-out ridge because the old man's plough was at the bottom of the estuary and the corn paddock was not turned. **1965** R.H. CONQUEST *Horses in Kitchen* 50 He had a mate, a dour Western Australian who was as bald as a bandicoot. **1972** *Ten Award Winning Stories* 41 Second class land with a reputation that it wouldn't even run a bandicoot. **1980** ANSELL & PERCY *To fight Wild* 110, I remember the way they had of putting things, like if a bit of country was hard country, they'd say: 'Aw, she's bad, that end of the place. Saw a bandicoot with a cut lunch round his neck out there.'

bandicoot, *v.* [f. prec.]

1. *Obs. intr.* To hunt the bandicoot.

1825 *London Mag.* May II. 59 You can always tell . . where the blacks have been bandy cooting.

2. *trans.* To remove (potatoes) surreptitiously from the ground, leaving the tops undisturbed.

1896 *Bulletin* (Sydney) 12 Dec. 26/4, I must 'bandicoot' spuds from the cockies—Or go on the track! **1899** *Ibid.* 2 Dec. 14/1 'Bandicooting' . . is a well-known term all over Western Vic. potato-land. The bandicooter goes at night to a field of ripe potatoes and carefully extracts the tubers from the roots without disturbing the tops. **1914** *Ibid.* 13 Aug. 26/1 The Tasmanian bandicoot is a friendly little chap . . but his burrowings have given him an undeserved reputation for bandycooting potatoes. **1918** *Two Blues: Mag. 13th Battalion A.I.F.* 24 Dec. 5 Bandicooting Spuds . . is a triumph in the art of camouflage. **1926** *Illustr. Tasmanian Mail* (Hobart) 7 Apr. 6/2 By digging amongst potatoes and rooting out the tubers, they have given to the language a new verb, 'to bandicoot'. **1930** E.R. GRIBBLE *Forty Yrs. with Aborigines* 63 We discovered that the blacks at night 'bandicooted' the potato patch, carefully removing the young tubers and covering up the roots again with the soil. **1942** E. LANGLEY *Pea Pickers* 273 All the pumpkins and maize we can pinch, every potato we can bandicoot. **1978** W. LOWENSTEIN *Weevils in Flour* 326 We learnt to bandicoot spuds. We'd feel the drill where the potatoes were and take a good sized one. We'd fill the earth back so it wouldn't interfere with the rest of his crop. **1980** P. PEPPER *You are what you make Yourself* 12 Men at the station had threatened to shoot them because they had bandicooted the potatoes. [*Note*] Removed the potatoes and replaced the plant.

3. *Mining. intr.* To fossick, esp. in previously worked ground.

1907 *Bulletin* (Sydney) 29 Aug. 15/3 Chows are the very worst botchers of mining work in the world. I've seen thousands of them bandicooting in Australia . . and not a miner in the whole yellow horde. **1940** *Ibid.* 29 May 17/4 Me an' cobber Bill 'ad bin doin' a bit o' bandicootin' on some old workin's on the Macquarie, but we slings it in after on'y gittin' about 18 'weights after three munce yakka.

Hence **bandicooted** *ppl. a.*, **bandicooter** *n.*

1916 J. FURPHY *Poems* 15 And trade away your pin and studs, To live on **bandicooted** spuds. **1899** *Bulletin* (Sydney) 2 Dec. 14/1 The **bandicooter** goes at night to a field of ripe potatoes. **1937** *Ibid.* 28 Apr. 21/1 To discourage 'bandicooters' an old cocky I knew tried entombing rabbit traps in the rows of spuds . . but the murphies went just the same.

bandicoot gunyah. *Obs.* A makeshift shelter. Cf. BADGER BOX.

1849 S. & J. SIDNEY *Emigrant's Jrnl.* 34 They will make a bandicoot gunya, that is to say, a house in the shape of a large dog kennel. **1867** F.J. BYERLEY *Narr. Overland Exped. Northern Qld.* 56 At night, on camping, a 'bandicoot gunyah' was erected, and covered with the broad pliable paper bark of melaleuca, which made a snug shelter for the night from the still pouring rain.

banditti. *Obs.* [Spec. use of *banditti* (It. *banditi*) pl. of *bandit*, also as a collect. sing. (see OED *bandit*).]

A. *pl.* Bushrangers.

1796 *HRA* (1914) 1st Ser. I. 554 We have now, my Lord, a band or two of banditti, who have armed themselves and infest the country all round, committing robberies upon defenceless people, and frequently joining the natives for that purpose. **1800** *Ibid.* II. 583 The whole of the above named Banditti be securely Imprisoned. **1804** *Sydney Gaz.* 11 Mar., If any of the prompt measures that were adopted on the exigence of the moment had been omitted, the Banditti would have increased their numbers. **1814** *HRA* (1916) 1st Ser. VIII. 307 Settlers are now Subjected to the plunder of these Banditti, Commonly Called '*Bush Rangers*'. **1824** J. LYCETT *Views in Aust.* 13 The daring outrages of these lawless banditti . . spread universal terror through the colony. **1827** 'PINDAR JUVENAL' *Van Diemen's Land Warriors* 14 The Parson's Clerk then rose with speech most witty, Hoping they'd kill the rascally banditti. **1831** *Sydney Monitor* 8 Jan. 2/1 Your Lordships . . may probably have heard of the innumerable robberies committed in this Colony during the last four years, by a species of banditti called bushrangers. These men are run-a-way convicts from the Government barracks, road-gangs, and iron-gangs. **1838** *Cornwall Chron.* (Launceston) 27 Oct. 2 The Bushrangers. . . The career of these banditti—seems to be unchecked by the Government. **1845** J.O. BALFOUR *Sketch of N.S.W.* 112 The mounted police corps is composed of 100 soldiers, the élite of the regiments quartered in the colony. Their duty is to apprehend bushrangers (a sub-genus banditti). **1853** H.B. JONES *Adventures in Aust.* 297 There was a most formidable band, composed of liberated and run-away convicts at Victoria, headed by a lag who has been celebrated in the colony as an excellent race-jockey. Happily for society these desperate banditti have been taken up. **1855** G.H. WATHEN *Golden Colony* 203 Their country is ruined, their houses pillaged, their roads infested by banditti.

B. *collect. sing.* Pl. **bandittles.** A gang of bushrangers.

1803 *Sydney Gaz.* 5 Mar., We should here observe that this banditti is entirely composed of Irish prisoners. **1816** *Hobart Town Gaz.* 3 Aug., The Robbery committed upon Mr John Beamont by one of the Bandittíes of Bush Rangers . . was . . at his house near Jericho. **1818** T.E. WELLS *M. Howe* (1945) 18 This Banditti, now consisting of Twenty-nine persons . . availed themselves of the proffered clemency and surrendered to Government. **1826** *Austral.* (Sydney) 5 Jan. 2/1 The banditti of bushrangers . . made two sea excursions. **1836** *Bent's News* (Hobart) 17 Sept. 2 The lawless bandittíes of Bushrangers. **1843** C. ROWCROFT *Tales of Colonies* I. 178, I have your house completely surrounded by a banditti. **1847** *Port Phillip Herald* 18 Feb. (Suppl.), There is a regular banditti in town, well armed with skeleton keys, pick-locks, and other ingenious devices. **1852** G.C. MUNDY *Our Antipodes* I. 168 Many a formidable banditti broken up, or hunted down until they yielded in despair.

bandy. Abbrev. of BANDICOOT *n.*

1895 *Proc. Linnean Soc. N.S.W.* X. (*note*) 400 Mr Barry on one occasion noticed two bandicoots near a native grave and told some blacks of it. . . The natives were hard pressed for food, but they would not touch the 'bandies' because they believed them to be the dogs of the dead. **1902** *Bulletin* (Sydney) 25 Oct. 16/3 What is the difference between bandy and small kangaroo rat? **1911** *Ibid.* 30 Mar. 13/3 The march of Mrs Chow is driving 'bandy' from his haunts. **1928** E. FOREMAN *Hist. & Adventures Qld. Pioneer* 44 The bandicoots dug up every grain we planted before it got a chance to sprout. Somebody then advised us to tar the seed. So we did, and the bandies were euchred. **1945** *Bulletin* (Sydney) 5 Sept. 12/1 In my early days many of the windows cut in the prostrate trunks of trees by the abos. were intended to provide a draught for the very purpose of smoking out a bandy or kanga-rat.

bandy-bandy /ˈbændi-bændi/. [a. Kattaŋ *bandi bandi.*] Either of two small elapid snakes patterned with black and white bands around the body, *Vermicella annulata* of e. and central Aust. and *V. multifasciata* of n. W.A. and N.T. See also RING SNAKE. Also **bunda-bunda.**

1911 *Bulletin* (Sydney) 22 June 14/4 The small and slender coral snake of South America . . is no larger than our 'bandy-bandy'. **1918** *Ibid.* 22 Aug. 24/4, I have struck a great number of bunda-bunda snakes (commonly known as 'bandy-bandy'). **1962** B.W. LEAKE *Eastern Wheatbelt Wildlife* 99 The bandy bandy . . seems to be holding its own in sandy bush country. About fourteen inches long full grown it is pretty but venomous and shows fight when disturbed. **1978** B.P. MOORE *Life on Forty Acres* 110 The Bandy Bandy (*Vermicella annulata*), dramatically patterned with alternate black and white rings.

bandycoot, var. BANDICOOT.

bang, *v. trans.* To cut (the tail of an animal), usually square across (but see quot. 1911).

1900 *Advocate* (Burnie) 15 Aug. 1/6 They are like yearlings or weedy two-year-olds of the hack breed, and have their tails 'banged' and manes 'hogged', which gives them the look of big foals. **1905** *Bulletin* (Sydney) 19 Jan. 17/1 The squatter had maliciously adopted the low-down practice of banging his horses' tails before they were broken. **1911** E.J. BRADY *King's Caravan* 241 Station hands were busy 'banging' the mob; which operation consists chiefly in cutting the hair of the animal's tail in different ways for different paddocks. **1926** *Bulletin* (Sydney) 21 Oct. 22/3 Some cranks still inflict cruelty on their horses by 'banging' their tails. **1933** R.B. PLOWMAN *Camel Pads* 290 They are then counted and their tails are banged, or, in other words, about three inches of hair is cut off the end of its tail, after the manner of a 'long bob'. A bang-tailed beast is as conspicuous among other cattle as a girl with a shingled head. **1942** W. GLASSON *Our Shepherds* 24 A bullock's tail . . could be 'banged' or shortened to the desired length. **1967** E. KETTLE *Gone Bush* 65 The tails were then 'banged'. . . The hairy end of the tail was chopped off. . . Stray cattle . . were readily detected by their long tails.

Hence **banged** *ppl. a.*

1905 *Bulletin* (Sydney) 19 Jan. 17/1 The 'broken' horses were commandeered by night, being known by their banged tails.

bangalay /ˈbæŋgəleɪ, bæŋˈgæli/. [Prob. f. a N.S.W. Aboriginal language.] The tree *Eucalyptus botryoides* (fam. Myrtaceae) of N.S.W. and Vic., commonly found on saline coastal soils; *bastard mahogany*, see BASTARD *a.*

[*c* **1810** *Agric. Gaz. N.S.W.* (1903) XIV. 990 Bengaly robusta, Swamp Mahogany.] **1861** *Catal. Natural & Industr. Products N.S.W.* 28 Bang alay . . a crooked growing tree, the timber much valued for knees and crooked timbers of coasting vessels. **1880** *Proc. Linnean Soc. N.S.W.* V. 464 *E. botryoides* . . , the 'Bastard Mahogany' or 'Bangalay' of workmen, occurring for the most part in moist sandy places near the coast. **1884** A. NILSON *Timber Trees N.S.W.* 59 '*Bangalay*' (of carpenters). A tree of crooked growth and gnarled appearance, never attaining any considerable height, with a rough furrowed persistent bark. **1934** J.W. AUDAS *Native Trees Aust.* 66 Known as Swamp Mahogany, Blue Gum, 'Bangalay' and Mahogany Gum, it is indigenous to Victoria, New South Wales and Queensland—a handsome tree. **1962** N.C.W. BEADLE et. al. *Handbk. Vascular Plants Sydney & Blue Mountains* 278 Near the sea. Deep, usually wet and often saline soils . . *Bangalay.*

bangalow /ˈbæŋgəloʊ/. Formerly also **bangally, bungalow.** [Poss. a. Manandjali *baŋgalu.*] The tall palm *Archontophoenix cunninghamiana* (fam. Arecaceae) of N.S.W. and Qld., having arching, feather-like fronds; (occas.) a similar palm. See also PICCABEEN.

1826 J. ATKINSON *Acct. Agric. & Grazing N.S.W.* 4 To their other productions are then generally added the bangally, much resembling the cabbage tree in appearance, but having long and wide leaves of a thick and tenacious texture. **1836** J. BACKHOUSE *Extracts from Lett.* (1839) iv. 12 Seaforthia elegans, known here by the native name of bangalee, is also plentiful in shady places. **1851** J. HENDERSON *Excursions & Adventures N.S.W.* II. 229 The Bangalo, which is a palm, and a native of the brushes. . . The germ, or roll of young leaves in the centre, and near the top, is eaten by the natives . . either raw or boiled. **1887** H. GULLET *Tropical N.S.W.* 9 The tall slender stems of the graceful bungalow palms struggle upwards for air and light. **1933** H.J. CARTER *Gulliver in Bush* 75 Both Bangalow and cabbage-tree, and a few patches of tea-tree gave some little harvest to the bottle. **1943** *Bulletin* (Sydney) 7 July 12/1 Bangalow palms arise Above them all towards the lilac skies. **1980** C. KELEN *Punks Travels* 51 In the filtered sun of the rainforest floor . . bangalow palm at my shoulder.

bange /ˈbændʒi/, *v.* Also **bandge, banje.** [Of unknown origin; prob. f. Br. dial. *benge* to lounge lazily: see EDD.] *intr.* To rest; to sleep. Also with **off** and **to bange it.**

1845 D.G. BROCK *To Desert with Sturt* (1975) 142 Sullivan never has cared about getting birds—he prefers what is called here 'Banging it'—that is, ever lying under the dray. **1849** A. HARRIS *Emigrant Family* (1967) 123 I'm thinking there'll be enough for us all to do directly. We'll all have to leave off bandging it for a bit. **1873** J.C.F. JOHNSON *Christmas on Carringa* 16 'Banjing' is bush slang for sleeping or lying full length under a tree. **1877** W. ARCHER in R. Stanley *Tourist to Antipodes* (1977) 65 Around the fire the men were 'banjing' (i.e., resting) in all sorts of different positions. **1976** C.D. MILLS *Hobble Chains & Greenhide* 7 'We'll 'bange off' for a few days, and let the big bloke settle down,' remarked the Boss, well pleased.

bange /ˈbændʒi/, *n. Obs.* [See prec.] A rest; a sleep.

1844 *Parramatta Chron.* 15 June 2/1 *Michael Cahill* . . was doomed to experience the fallacy of his conceptions by a four days' 'bange' in the cells. **1849** S. & J. SIDNEY *Emigrant's Jrnl.* 20 The shepherd . . then lights his pipe, and when it is out very often takes a bange (*Anglice*, a sleep). **1850** B.C. PECK *Recoll. Sydney* 98 We may enjoy a quiet 'bange' on the greensward, and contemplate the little ferry steamers and sailing ships, *en route* across the placid bay, from the metropolis to . . Balmain. **1867** *Sydney Punch* 23 Feb. 104/1 He saw once more the dark-eyed gin Taking a bange at noon. **1873** J.C.F. JOHNSON *Christmas on Carringa* 16 So Sunday, Monday, Tuesday I Jogs upon my way With a little banje or whaling To just fill up the day. **1880** J.B. STEVENSON *Seven Yrs. Austral. Bush* 42 We were having a 'bange' in the bush, in the heat of the day, and had dozed off. **1902** E.B. KENNEDY *Black Police Qld.* 184, I should follow their example . . and . . turn on to my bunk for a 'bange', *i.e.*, sleep, and in such manner get my one day of rest.

banger. [Of unknown origin. Cf. *bang-up* stylish: see OED(S but see also FLOGGER.] A morning-coat. Formerly also **fantail banger.**

1882 *Sydney Slang Dict.* 10 The Parson is on the highfly in a fantail banger. **1886** *Bulletin* (Sydney) 13 Feb. 7/3 Behold the smart blue tie The 'two-ten' fantail-banger, and The health-glow in his eye! **1921** F. GROSE *Rough Y.M. Bloke* 26 All bar one bloke with a long-tailed banger and a shiny hat. **1978** D. VAWR *Ratbag Mind* 17 He left three of his old morning-coats ('bangers' in the slang of the day) hanging in a bedroom.

bangtail, *n.* Abbrev. of BANGTAIL MUSTER. Usu. *attrib.*

1931 *Bulletin* (Sydney) 29 July 20/4 On the big cattle stations of western Queensland . . a general muster on such occasions as the sale of the run is necessary. . . There is nothing for it but the tedious 'bangtail' count through the races. **1939** J.G. PATTISON *'Battler's' Tales Early Rockhampton* 125, I have often heard controversy re the merits of buying a property on a walk-in, walk-out, or bookmuster delivery, and the bang-tail system. **1951** E. HILL *Territory* 391 We're sellin' Merryfield, an' now the buyers have asked for a bang-tail. **1974** D. STUART *Prince of my Country* 212 'Reckon we oughta have a muster, along our boundary with you? . . ' 'No, I can't see we need a bangtail.'

bangtail, *v. trans.* To bang the tails of (horses or cattle), esp. as a means of counting or identifying.

1908 MRS A. GUNN *We of Never-Never* 252 'Well I'm blest!' he said. 'If we didn't forget all about bangtailing that mob for her mattress.' **1949** H.E. THONEMANN *Tell White Man* 46 All the cattle had to be 'bangtailed'. That meant that they had to be mustered, and the hair of their tails cut off as they were counted so that they should not be counted twice. **1959** H.G. LAMOND *Sheep Station* 143 They bang-tailed over twenty-five thousand cattle that year! **1976** C.D. MILLS *Hobble Chains & Greenhide* 164 We rode to the rail yards to 'bang-tail' our mob.

Hence **bang-tailed** *ppl. a.*, **bangtailing** *vbl. n.*

1933 R.B. PLOWMAN *Camel Pads* 291 A **bang-tailed** beast is as conspicuous among other cattle as a girl with a shingled head. **1943** H. LAMOND *From Tariaro to Ross Roy* 76 Pise is easily erected: it is just mud mixed with straw, with grass, or . . with hair from bang tailed cattle. **1922** *Bulletin* (Sydney) 26 Oct. 20/4 He had an outsize pocket-knife (as used for '**bangtailing**'), keen as the average barber's razor. **1938** *Ibid.* 26 May 20/4 Pisé is mud of a clayey consistency mixed with cow-, bullock- or bull-hair, and a bangtailing would supply plenty on those old cattle stations. **1976** C.D. MILLS *Hobble Chains & Greenhide* 164 Bang-tailing is simply cutting a square bang on a bullock's brush by removing the tip, and is a method used to identify a beast more readily when drafting.

bangtail muster. A muster of the stock on a station during which the tail of each beast is banged, to distinguish it from those still to be counted.

1886 *S.A. Parl. Papers* III. no. 54 1 The manager of the station, Mr Lindsay Crawford, was instructed to make a bang-tail muster and classify the stock on the run. **1887** W.S.S. TYRWHITT *New Chum in Qld. Bush* 61 Every third or fourth year on a cattle station, they have what is called a 'bang tail muster'; that is to say, all the cattle are brought into the yards, and have the long hairs at the end of the tail cut off square, with knives or sheep shears. **1911** *Bulletin* (Sydney) 31 Aug. 43/1 After completing a 'bang-tail muster', all hands on Avoca station were drafting and branding. **1923** *Ibid.* 7 June 24/3 During a bang-tail muster . . in '88 we had about 300 yarded. **1933** R.B. PLOWMAN *Camel Pads* 290 A bang-tail muster is of rare occurrence, and takes place only when a station is being sold—and not always then. **1951** E. HILL *Territory* 328 A glass of beer and a counter lunch at a 'billabong' near by, and they are off . . to watch the 'big mobs' galloping past like a bang-tail muster. **1960** R.S. PORTEOUS *Cattleman* 165 The only way to tell how many head he owns would be to put a good team of men on and do a bang-tail muster. **1971** W.A. WINTER-IRVING *Beyond Bitumen* 47 A bang-tail muster turned up Father's estimated number of livestock.

banjo. [Fig. use of *banjo* musical instrument, as applied to objects similar in shape.]

1. A shoulder (of mutton).

1897 *Bulletin* (Sydney) 7 Aug. (Red Page), Shoulder of Mutton—'Banjo'. **1899** *Ibid.* 30 Dec. 14/3 Free meat is a certainty on any station, because it pays the squatter better to *give* a 'banjo' than to risk having sheep killed on the run for the sake of a 'piece'. **1905** *Shearer* (Sydney) 17 June 6/2 The squatter gives him . . a 'banjo' of mutton. **1930** *Bulletin* (Sydney) 5 Feb. 25/1 Some who merited it fully Would get a 'banjo' from a woollie. **1974** B. KIDMAN *On Wallaby* 32 What a 'hand-out' I received! A banjo (shoulder) of mutton . . a big piece of brownie.

2. A shovel.

1915 *Bulletin* (Sydney) 9 Dec. 22/1, I was wielding the pick and banjo in a gang on a big channel job once. **1918** *Aussie* (Sydney) Sept. 4/2 We have a bloke I'd back as a banjo-swinger against any cove in the A.I.F. . . He shovels so fast that he can work in the shade of the muck he shifts. **1928** L.A. SIGSWORTH *Verse* 7 A ploughman roots up tons of 'muck' for the banjo men to shift. **1946** F. CLUNE *Try Nothing Twice* 117 'You're a big enough lad', he said, 'to swing a banjo with the best of them.' 'What's a banjo?' I queried. 'A shovel!' was his explanation. **1956** *Bulletin* (Sydney) 4 Jan. 13/1 On the loco.-run, Bricky . . swung on the Banjo for more steam. **1972** D. SHEAHAN *Songs from Canefields* 62 They expect him to go hell for leather The minute the whistle says when As if the banjo were a feather And the pick were the point of a pen. **1983** *Sun-Herald* (Sydney) 9 Oct. 71/4 My dad and I laid our 80 to 90 yards of gravel a day, working with a banjo (shovel) and a two-horse dray.

3. *Mining.* A device for washing tin: see quot. 1932.

1932 I.L. IDRIESS *Prospecting for Gold* 17 A banjo is simply an open box, about four feet long. The 'head' of the box may be two feet high, with the sides sloping to six inches. The width is two feet at the head, tapering to eighteen inches at the end. . . The bottom is covered with bagging. **1969** B. GARLAND *Pitt Street Prospector* 30 There was more to setting up a banjo than had been described in the books which Chow had read. **1985** M. KENNEDY *Born Half-Caste* 33 The men would get the banjo (sluice-box) ready for washing the tin.

4. FIDDLER. Also *attrib.* as **banjo ray.**

1969 J. POLLARD *Austral. & N.Z. Fishing* 573 The brown fiddler or banjo ray occurs along the Australian east coast from south Queensland to Tasmania and is common down the coast of New South Wales. **1986** *Canberra Chron.* 29 Jan. 19/1 There are a few cockies and a lot of banjos mixed in with them but they provide good fishing.

bank, *n.*[1] *Gold-mining.* [Cf. U.S. *bank-diggings*: see Mathews.] Used *attrib.* to designate a place being mined in the bank as opposed to the bed of a creek or river.

1851 *Empire* (Sydney) 7 Oct. 231/7 The bank or dry diggings are being worked in situations that excite astonishment in the visitor. **1852** *Moreton Bay Free Press* 24 June 3/5 Not only are the bed claims on the creeks yielding well, where workable (for water is abundant there now) but . . the bank diggings are also now yielding largely. **1931** W. BARAGWANATH et al. *Guide for Prospectors in Vic.* 75 Possession may be taken of a bank sluicing claim—that is an alluvial claim which does not include the bed of a river or creek—not exceeding 75 feet in width by 390 feet in length for each holder of miner's right. **1944** M.W. PEACOCK *Dead Puppets Dance* 22 I've only got a creek claim. If I had a bank claim—including the bank as well as the bed of the creek—I'd sink a shaft.

bank, *n.*[2] [Prob. generalized use of *bank* as in gambling.] A sum of money; spec. one reserved for a particular purpose, i.e. for drinking, gambling, etc.

1919 C. DREW *Doings of Dave* 28 Did you have any bank to kick off with? **1967** *Kings Cross Whisper* (Sydney) xxxii. 6/3 *Bank,* the amount of ready money for a purpose. A drinking bank, races bank, etc. **1978** D. STUART *Wedgetail View* 47 A few quiet bottles, just once a week. . . This way, a feller'll get a bank together in no time.

banker.

1. A creek or river swollen to the top of, or overflowing, its banks. Freq. in the phr. **to run** (or **come down**) **a banker.**

1848 H.W. HAYGARTH *Recoll. Bush Life* 129 Now that I take a second glance at the river, its waters look very muddy, which is a sure sign of its being high, not to say a 'banker'. **1867** 'S. MCTAVISH' *Chowla* 4 Great, then, was the joy, when a telegram was received from Fort Bourke, announcing that the sluggish Darling was at length coming down 'a banker'. **1871** *Austral. Town & Country Jrnl.* (Sydney) 20 May 615/4 We had a nice day's rain (yesterday). The Macquarie River commenced to rise on Saturday, and is now a banker. **1894** W. CROMPTON *Convict Jim* 28 An' the river is a banker, an' its current's running strong, An' I don't think I'll be waiting for Death's cooee very long. **1905** *Shearer* (Sydney) 4 Feb. 4/1 The rain fell in torrents, until every creek and billabong was a banker and the river itself miles wide. **1911** C.E.W. BEAN *'Dreadnought' of Darling* 20 When the river comes down a banker, or even half a banker, small steamers can get up to a point 1696 miles from the sea. **1919** V. PALMER *Prisoner* (1924) 39 The river's running a banker—rising every minute, too—and there's five hundred cattle in the home paddock. **1935** K.L. SMITH *Sky Pilot Arnhem Land* 267 The thirsty ground was unable to absorb it all. . . Every creek and depression ran a banker. **1944** J.J. HARDIE *Cattle Camp* (ed. 3) 85 As easy to try to block the Barker coming down a banker as to stop horsemen talking. **1959** D. STUART *Yandy* 36 They came to . . a stretch of silted floodland, thick with tangled scrub and the rubbish of past bankers. **1977** D. WHITINGTON *Strive to be Fair* 40 The creek came down a banker, I tied the car to a tree, but it was submerged in the raging waters.

2. *fig.*

1898 *Examiner* (Launceston) 11 Oct. 6/3 Feeling is running a banker at Devonport in reference to the coming election. **1910** *Truth* (Sydney) 30 Oct. 1/8 For their lingual rivers often run a banker, Run a banker, And the oaths they uses sometimes weighs a ton, Weighs a ton. **1966** P. MATHERS *Trap* 95 Colin's arse-cleft ran a banker with sweat.

bank high, *a. Obs.* [Used elsewhere but recorded earliest in Aust.] Of a river in flood: swollen to the top of its banks.

1847 *Atlas* (Sydney) III. 3/1 Two creeks, now bank high, although probably dry in ordinary seasons. **1848** *Moreton Bay Courier* 19 Feb. 2/3 Several of the creeks are bank high, and a great number of drays are detained in consequence. **1852** *Moreton Bay Free Press* 1 Jan. 3/2 There has been a most unusual amount of rain in this district, the rivers all being flooded, and the Burnett half-bank high. **1875** CAMPBELL & WILKS *Early Settlement Qld.* 4 Upon arriving at the Condamine found it running bank high.

banksia. [f. the name of Joseph *Banks* (1743–1820), English botanist, given by J.R. and G. Forster in 1776 to a N.Z. plant genus now classified as *Pimelea.* The name was applied to the Australian plant genus by the younger Linnaeus (*Suppl. Plantarum* (1782) 15, 126).]

1. Any tree or shrub of the genus *Banksia* (fam. Proteaceae), usu. with leathery leaves and dense flower spikes forming thick woody cones as the fruits mature. Also *attrib.*

1788 J. WHITE *Jrnl. Voyage N.S.W.* (1790) 221 (*heading*) The different species of Banksia. **1794** T. WATLING *Lett. from Exile Botany Bay* 16 The various Banksias do not more appear to belong to one common family, than the Kangaroo, Opossum, and Kangaroo-rat, to that of the Kangaroo. **1801** *HRA* (1915) 1st Ser. III. 175 The hills are covered with excellent verdure without trees, except in the valleys, and they are chiefly Banksia new, or what is commonly called the white honeysuckle. **1820** J. OXLEY *Jrnls. Two Exped. N.S.W.* 267 A species of banksia was seen to-day under the same meridian as on the Macquarie. **1833** *Jrnls. Several Exped. W.A.* 25 In the barren land the banksia and stunted swamp oak, and grass tree, held undisputed sway. **1840** T.J. BUCKTON *W.A.* 67 The *Banksia,* called the honeysuckle tree, from a sweet tasting substance contained in its flowering cone. **1847** E.W. LANDOR *Bushman* 40 The banksia is a paltry tree, about the size of an apple-tree in an English or French orchard, perfectly useless as timber, but affording an inexhaustible supply of firewood. **1857** W. HOWITT *Tallangetta* II. 143 But Dinah Slaughter sits alone Under the Banksia tree. **1886** P. CLARKE *'New Chum' in Aust.* 94 Down in the hollows, growing best near the marshy 'pockets', the orange, green, scarlet, and brown blooms of the banksia scent the air and beautify the scene. **1911** A. MACK *Bush Days* 29 The sad-hued banksias, with their dry dead cones, which do their best to turn the landscape into that dreary wilderness it is so often accused of being. **1916** E. & M.S. GREW *Rambles in Aust.* 17 The banksia . . looked as if a fir-cone had suddenly burst into bristling pink flowers. **1935** DAVISON & NICHOLLS *Blue Coast Caravan* 9 There were spreading banksias with cones of honey-coloured bloom mingling with last year's withered flowers, dark, like little bearded men roosting among the branches. **1955** P. WHITE *Tree of Man* 240 It was a big old banksia, full of dead heads, the trunk and branches of the tree tortured into abominable shapes, full of dust and ugliness. **1965** *Coast to Coast 1963–64* 82 Marilyn's suburb was one of those new . . suburbs . . where pink boronia, red grevillea, hairy banksias leant in discarded profusion against the tiny houses on land lit by the rich purple of Paterson's Curse. **1979** E. SMITH *Saddle in Kitchen* 26 Grandpa had strange names for some things too—native names many of them. Banksias he called what sounded like 'mungites', though I've never heard the term used by anyone else.

2. Special Comb. **banksia man,** a name for the large woody cone of any of several *Banksia* species; orig. applied to a type of character in a children's story (see quot. 1918).

1918 M. GIBBS *Snugglepot & Cuddlepie* 74 She could see the glistening, wicked eyes of Mrs. Snake and the bushy heads of the bad Banksia men. **1927** K.S. PRICHARD *Bid me to Love* (1974) 36 *Louise*: . . See what I've got in my pocket for you. . . *Bill*: (diving into a pocket of her coat and pulling out a banksia cone) A banksia man. Oh Mum! **1937** N. MASS *Austral. Wild-Flower Fairies* 128 Banksia men used to do dreadful things once upon a time, carrying off poor little fairies and gumnuts and making them captive. **1974** M. PAICE *Dolan's Roost* 83 A fire-blackened banksia tree leaning over the top of the rock, its hairy little banksia-men lined up along a branch. **1979** E. SMITH *Saddle in Kitchen* 64 Hell was under the well near the cow paddock, deep and murky and peopled by gnarled and knobby banksia men who lurked there waiting for the unguarded to fall in.

Banksian cockatoo. [See prec. and quot. 1822.] A black cockatoo, esp. the *red-tailed black cockatoo* (see RED *a.* 1 b.).

1787 J. LATHAM *Gen. Synopsis Birds* Suppl. 63 Bankian [*sic*] Cockatoo. . . The tail is pretty long. . . The two middle feathers are black; the others the same at the base and ends; the middle of them, for about one third, of a fine deep crimson. . . Inhabits *New Holland*. **1788** J. WHITE *Jrnl. of Voyage N.S.W.* (1790) 139 We this day discovered the Banksian Cockatoo. **1822** J. LATHAM *Gen Hist. Birds* II. 199 Banksian Cockatoo. . . Sir Jos. Banks first brought this with him into England, on his return from his Voyage round the World. **1945** C. BARRETT *Austral. Bird Life* 71 The Banksian or red-tailed black cockatoo . . ranges throughout the continent. **1956** A.C.C. LOCK *Tropical Tapestry* 148 A Banksian black cockatoo added a splash of avian beauty to the landscape.

banyan. Formerly **banian.** [Transf. use of *banian* the Indian fig tree *Ficus benghalensis*. The name Banian (or Banians') Tree was orig. given by Europeans to an individual tree near the Persian Gulf under which the Banians (Hindu traders) had built a pagoda: see OED *banian* 5.] Freq. *attrib.*, esp. as **banyan tree.**

1. Any of several trees of the genus *Ficus* (fam. Moraceae), the adventitious roots of which form buttresses around the trunk, as *F. virens* of n. Aust. and Asia.

1845 J.O. BALFOUR *Sketch of N.S.W.* 40 The tree which has excited most interest in the colony is the banian tree lately discovered to the northward of Moreton Bay. **1886** F. COWAN *Aust.* 16 The Banyan-tree: the grandest of the Figs: in its expansion and extension, self-supporting its long arms with outward-leaning, life-renewing, supplemental props. **1886** F.A. HAGENAUER *Rep. Aboriginal Mission Ramahyuck, Vic.* 46 On the road to Cooktown . . where the stately cedar and the venerable Banian tree (*ficus religiosa*) are laced and festooned together. **1896** J.W. FAWCETT *Narr. Terrible Cyclone Townsville* 9 Mr Clayton had his kitchen verandah and out-buildings, as well as several trees in the garden, including a mango tree 18 years old, torn up by the roots, and a banyan three feet in circumference broken off short. **1934** WARBURTON & ROBERTSON *Buffaloes* 170 Between us and the lagoon, we could see a huge banyan-tree, the space covered by the aerial roots appearing to have a diameter of about fifty feet. **1963** X. HERBERT *Larger than Life* 235 From his left [shoulder] hung a long bag of banyan-cord containing his big painted didgeridoo and music-sticks. **1985** *Vogue Aust.* Oct. 178 We head towards . . Valley of the Shadows, a mysterious and aptly named forest of banyan trees.

2. Special Comb. **banyan rum**, a spirituous drink: see quots. 1944 and 1977.

1938 F. CLUNE *Free & Easy Land* 252 Two bottles of banyan-rum. **1944** J. DEVANNY *By Tropic Sea & Jungle* 26 When they ran out of the real stuff, the grog-sellers would manufacture Banyan Rum while you waited—a mixture of boot black, Condy's crystals and methylated spirits. **1977** LOWENSTEIN & LOH *Immigrants* 26 The traditional recipe for Banyan Rum was very simple. 'Two gallons of overproof rum, a pound of salt to keep you drinking, two tablespoons of water, an armful of leaves off a stinging tree and a pound plug of tobacco nailed to the bottom of the keg. Allow to mature for five minutes. If you're a fussy bastard you can strain it through a greasy horse blanket.'

baobab. [Transf. use of *baobab* the African tree *Adansonia digitata*.] **a.** The swollen-trunked tree *Adansonia gregorii* (fam. Bombacaceae) of n.w. Aust. **b.** BOTTLE TREE. Also **baob, boab, boabab,** and *attrib.*

1863 *Jrnls. & Rep. Two Voyages Glenelg River* (1864) 17 Noticed some poor sandalwood, also acacia, baobab, and palms, and a rose-like vine. **1864** *Ibid.* 59 We fell in with an enormous Baobab tree (Adansonia) with the drupe containing ripe seed. **1880** A. FORREST *N.-W. Exploration* 12 We saw a boab tree today, about ten feet in diameter. **1886** F. COWAN *Aust.* 17 The Boabab: the Gouty Stem, the Monkey-bread, Sour Gourd, or Cream-of-Tartar-tree: . . a huge, aerial, aborescent [*sic*] yam! a bulb become a tree without a bole! . . its gourd-like fruit filled with a mealy melting acid mass: a desert substitute for lemonade! **1905** A. SEARCY *In Northern Seas* 18 Remnants of a half-consumed meal of roasted baobab-nuts were lying about. **1909** *Bulletin* (Sydney) 7 Jan. 14/2 The fruit of the baobab is . . evidently the true Australian bread-fruit, or bread-nut. **1930** E.R. GRIBBLE *Forty Yrs. with Aborigines* 169 The names of the party are still to be seen on a large baobab-tree. **1933** C.H. HOLMES *We find Aust.* 62 In the Kimberleys we were introduced to that amazing tree, the baobab, a bald, defiant-looking tree, which grows like a bottle. . . Dampier described the baobab as the 'dragon tree'. **1934** T. WOOD *Cobbers* 45 Underneath a baobab tree whose nuts looked like kidneys dressed in green velvet. **1937** D. GLASS *Austral. Fantasy* 28 The plump and dimpled Baobab, offspring of the bottle-tree and able to provide sweet water for the thirsty traveller out of its capacious trunk. **1946** *Bulletin* (Sydney) 21 Aug. 28/1, I suppose Binghi's pictorial efforts with the baob nut as a canvas should really be classed as engraving. **1947** F. CLUNE *Roaming around Aust.* 170 Baobab trees—usually called 'Boab' for short—look something like a bottle with a tuft on top—a big bottle, up to 30 or 40 feet around at the base. **1953** L. & C. REES *Spinifex Walkabout* 106 The baobabs, or boabs, were . . unbelievably like stone-ginger bottles that had unaccountably taken root. **1955** F. LANE *Patrol to Kimberleys* 28 'That's a baobab tree,' his uncle said. 'This northwest section of Australia has a copyright on them. It's also called the 'boab' or 'bottle-tree'—and it's mighty important to the natives.' **1970** J.V. MARSHALL *Walk to Hills of Dreamtime* 106 The myalls tried tapping the baobab for water. But the tree was dry . . even its gum had solidified to a desiccated paste. **1977** A. THOMAS *Bulls & Boabs* (1980) 20 It was, she said, a historic tree. It was a sad tree and, of all the boabs I was to meet, easily the most forlorn. Boabs tend to be merry rather than sombre. **1981** *Bulletin* (Sydney) 6 Oct. 18/3 The baobab tree . . is prolific in the adjoining Kimberley area of Western Australia and called the boab, and bottle tree in the Northern Territory.

bar, *n.*[1] [Transf. use of *bar* bank of sand at the mouth of a river, applied to banks formed by currents upstream. Used elsewhere but recorded earliest in Aust.: see OED *sb.*[1] 15 b.] A bank of sand or silt formed by river currents, either mid-stream or on river bends. Also *attrib.*

1843 R.D. MURRAY *Summer at Port Phillip* 55 One of those bars, from which no river in Australia is wholly free. **1847** *Atlas* (Sydney) III. 8/1 The largest sized vessels can lay there without encountering 'bars and flats' in the progress up the river. **1851** *Empire* (Sydney) 5 Aug. 15/1 The most successful were those who were working steadily on 'bars', or banks of sand and gravel formed on the many points along the winding river. *Ibid.* 7 Oct. 231/7 The water having subsided, bar diggings are again being worked, but the water still interferes to a great extent. **1851** S. RUTTER *Hints to Gold Hunters* 9 What in California they call a *bar*, which we should call a sand bank, is formed in the middle of the river, or on its sides. **1852** F. LANCELOTT *Aust. as it Is* II. 22 A long sloping bend (called a bar by the Australian diggers) . . would be found a good locality. **1857** F. DE B. COOPER *Wild Adventures* 153 We made for the river, and prospected different 'bars', or points of ground deposited by the stream in its windings. **1860** W.B. CLARKE *Researches Southern Gold Fields N.S.W.* 87 Points of obstruction, or in gold-digger's phraseology, where 'bars' occur. **1967** G. HUME *River Murray Guide* 5 Grounding was deliberate to find how far out into the River these submerged bars stretch.

bar, *n.*[2] *Opal-mining.* [Spec. use of *bar* a stripe.] Banding within a layer of opal.

1932 I.L. IDRIESS *Prospecting for Gold* 241 Some opals are sand-pitted, others are milky, cloudy, smoky, broken barred, etc. Judge by the 'bar' and the brilliance of the colour. **1962** WHITING & RELPH *Occurrence of Opal* 9 The seams are thick in comparison with the rest of the field and some large pieces of potch were found. Some bars of opal were up to one-half inch in thickness.

bar, *n.*[3] [Of unknown origin.] In the phr. **not to like (have, be able to stand) a bar of,** to be unable to tolerate (someone, etc.), to dislike intensely; to reject utterly (a course of action).

1933 J. MCCARTER *Love's Lunatic* 238, I didn't like a bar of him when he was alive—an' I'm not shook on lookin' at his dead chivvy. **1945** G. CASEY *Downhill is Easier* 25 Reg wanted to have another drink . . but I wouldn't have a bar of it. **1964** J. POLLARD *High Mark* 28, I thought hard at one stage about tossing it in and coming over to play with Richmond . . but East Perth wouldn't have a bar of it. **1972** A. CHIPPER *Aussie Swearers Guide* 75, I don't care if his mother's won *Tatts*. I can't stand a bar of him. **1978** D. STUART *Wedgetail View* 11 No use sayin' I'll do his nightwatch for him. He wouldn't have a bar of that. He's a proud stubborn old bastard. **1985** *Canberra Times* 26 Feb. 1/5 Australia should not have a 'bar' of the insane notion of a winnable limited nuclear war.

bar, *v.* [f. *to bar the dice* to declare the throw void.] *trans.* In the game of two-up: to disallow (a throw of the coins).

1897 *Worker* (Sydney) 18 Dec. 3/4 Hey, bar that toss! Heads it is! **1911** A. WRIGHT *Gamblers' Gold* (1923) 57 The coins fell 'heads', but they had been barred, and curses fell thickly on the head of the youth who had 'barred the toss'. **1949** G. BERRIE *Morale* 251 Anyone not satisfied with the fairness of the spin has the right to call 'bar 'em'. **1977** R. BEILBY *Gunner* 299 Slight shock put Gunner off his toss so that the coins drifted up sedately, not turning. 'Floater,' several voices shouted. 'Barred,' shouted the ringie.

barb. [Prob. from the name of an individual dog: see quots. 1911 and 1914.] A black strain of KELPIE. Also *attrib.*

1898 *Sydney Morning Herald* 4 July 3/1 To sheepmen the dogs are known as kelpies, barbs, or Clydes, and the origin of the breed is said to be the smooth-haired 'coolie' [*sic*] and the English fox. **1908** W.H. OGILVIE *My Life in Open* 162 The barb dogs are all prick-eared and have a peculiar crouching and watchful carriage. . . They fight like Japs and resent a thrashing from their masters with tooth and nail. **1911** *Australasian* (Melbourne) 29 Apr. 1043/1 Mr King called his dog 'Barb', after the horse of that name that won the Melbourne Cup in the old days. **1914** R. KALESKI *Austral. Barkers & Biters* 47 There have been some awful fights and arguments as to where the barb originated; this is the truth about it. Kelpie was a bitch owned by C. King, of Woollongough. One of her pups . . had been called Barb. Barb turned out a great worker. . . Mr Edols bought him . . and kept him on Burrawang, where he got many fine pups. These all took after him, so they were called Barb's pups, and then, as the name spread, just barb. **1917** 'PEGASUS' *So Drover Said* 3 His mother was Kelpie, pure and clean, His father a Barb, the best I've seen. **1923** *Austral.* (Sydney) June 7 It is said that a top-notch barb can yard chickens into a hat. **1943** *Bulletin* (Sydney) 20 Oct. 12/1 A Forbes (N.S.W.) farmer has only to appear at his back door, rubbing up a knife on a steel, and his black barb will depart for whatever paddock they happen to be in and bring the killers up. **1975** L.A. POCKLEY *Handbk. for Jackeroos* 56 *The Kelpie*: Is of Australian development and uncertain origin. The Black variety are usually called 'Barbs' and others 'Kelpie'.

barber, *n. Obs.* A nickname for a shearer; *jumbuck barber*, see JUMBUCK 2; *sheep barber*, see SHEEP 2.

1898 *Bulletin* (Sydney) 19 Nov. 14/1 When I took to dabbing tar, And 'picking up' on Blaringar, The cook when 'barbers' came at morn To get a snack, would say, with scorn: 'Tea on the left.' **1910** *Ibid.* 5 May 15/1 Every sheep station . . has had its 'shearers' paddock', so named because in shearing time it was reserved for the barbers' horses. **1914** *Ibid.* 22 Oct. 13/4 Shearing cut out at Glengarrie . . yesterday. A barber . . who comes from Sydneyside, I think, put up, on the last day, the respectable total of 304. **1936** A.B. PATERSON *Shearer's Colt* 17 Wears a barber's delight (silk shirt) and jemimas (elastic-sided boots), but the dressier they are the hotter they are.

barber, *v. Obs. trans.* To shear (a sheep). Also *absol.*

1910 *Bulletin* (Sydney) 22 Dec. 13/2, I took a hand in the formation of the Shearers' Union in 1885, previous to which shearers had to barber the jumbucks at the sweet will of the shed bosses, whether wet or dry. **1915** *Ibid.* 14 Oct. 24/2 The old-timer who only barbers with the shears is 'queer' or 'cranky'. **1929** C.H. WINTER *Story of 'Bidgee Queen* 94 But still they 'barbered' cheerfully—though roughly.

Hence **barbered** *ppl. a.*, **barbering** *vbl. n.*

1922 *Bulletin* (Sydney) 16 Mar. 22/1 The cocky gazed gloomily upon the **barbered** jumbucks in the ringer's pen. **1912** *Ibid.* 28 Nov. 16/4 The next most meagre **barbering** was that of the aforesaid Nugget, and my friend had wagered him a bottle of whisky he would disrobe more jumbucks than Nugget on the following day.

barbie /'babi/. [f. *barb(ecue* + -Y.] A barbecue; a meal cooked on a barbecue. Also *attrib.*, and *fig.*

1976 *Austral.* (Sydney) 14 Aug. 20/4 He propounded the natural and national virtues of the Aussie beach barbie with beer and prawns, and the big chunder. **1977** K. McArthur *Bread & Dripping Days* 14 Before the barbecue ceremony you have to work out what steaks to buy, what fuel to buy, where to build the barbie if it's buildable, where to port it if it's portable. **1977** E. Mackie *Oh to be Aussie* 15 The trainee Aussie must make sure a barbie is the genuine article—beef, booze and shielas. **1981** *Weekend Austral. Mag.* (Sydney) 11 July 6/8 A few tinnies and an impromptu barbie. **1984** *Overlander* June 52 Refuse to give some cove who's . . y' know . . a few snags short of a barbie—refuse to give him a job as a brain surgeon and . . you're up in front of the bloody Discrimation Board. **1986** *Austral. Geographic* Jan. 19/1 It . . like most barbie guests, enjoys a drink.

Barcoo /ba'ku/, *attrib.* and *n.* [The name of a river in w. Qld.; applied also to the surrounding country.]

A. 1. *attrib.* Of or pertaining to the district traversed by the Barcoo River; in some way characterizing the people or living conditions of that part of the country or of the remote inland generally.

1882 *Bulletin* (Sydney) 6 May 9/4 There were two young squatters and a Barcoo banker on the box seat. **1895** K. Mackay *Yellow Wave* 205 Billy, giving the 'Barcoo back cut', drove his horse down the face of the hill. **1904** L.M.P. Archer *Bush Honeymoon* 58 The long lash is deftly flicked on to the leaders and wheelers. '*Gave them a Barcoo start*, that time!' he remarks, as they rear up. **1912** J. Bradshaw *Highway Robbery under Arms* (ed. 3) 24 Three more blows, and down they chopped on to the thigh; with the Barcoo snap, over the tail they go, up the backbone and on to the cobbora, down the whipping side. **1919** *Bulletin* (Sydney) 24 Apr. 20/2 I've heard the half-crown piece called the 'Barcoo shell'. **1927** J. Mathieu *Backblock Ballads* 44, I boiled me bloomin' billy and knocked up a 'Barcoo Bun'. [*Note*] Barcoo Bun—Small Damper. **1933** J. Hamilton *Nights Ashore* 100 The parrot's language would have shamed the choicest repartee of a Blue-nosed bosun or a Barcoo bullocky. **1936** *Bulletin* (Sydney) 8 Apr. 21/4 How many of the present generation would know how to load a Barcoo pistol? **1937** D. Gunn *Links with Past* 245 I'm from the Murrumbidgee For Western tracks I make, None of your small and ridgey, A Barcoo blow I take, When I was in the West afar I shore two hundred without tar. **1967** F. Hardy *Billy Borker yarns Again* 3 Anyway, there was this battler in Sydney, see. Shabby as a Barcoo tramp. **1972** J. Byrne *Horse Riding Austral. Way* 20 Australia has its own peculiar types of *Station Bridles*, with such names as: Barcoo Bridle, Drover's Bridle, and Station Bridle. **1973** P. Adam Smith *Barcoo Salute*, 'I see you've learnt the Barcoo Salute,' said a Buln Buln Shire Councillor to the Duke of Edinburgh. 'What's that?' said His Royal Highness, waving his hand again to brush the flies off his face. 'That's it,' said the man from the bush. **1973** R. Edwards *Austral. Bawdy Ballads* 26 He grabbed the black bitch, Made her fast to the tree with a Barcoo half-hitch.

2. Special Comb. **Barcoo dog,** see quots.; **grass,** Flinders grass; **rot,** scurvy (see quot. 1894); also **rotted** *a.*; **sandwich,** see quots.; **shout,** see quot. 1919; **sickness,** a condition characterized by attacks of vomiting; Belyando spew; **sore,** an ulcer on the skin symptomatic of Barcoo rot; **spew, vomit,** *Barcoo sickness.*

1936 *Bulletin* (Sydney) 9 Sept. 20/2 A winner among discordant bush noises is the **Barcoo dog**—an elaboration of a baby's rattle that some genius long ago invented for scaring sheep up into the forcing pens and down the drafting race. **1952** A.M. Duncan-Kemp *Where Strange Paths go Down* 96 Sally's wooden staff was topped by a battered jam tin which she rattled vigorously—a contraption known as the 'Barcoo dog' and exceedingly useful for driving sheep or goats without a dog to work them. **1977** B. Scott *My Uncle Arch* 55 Now, a Barcoo Dog isn't a dog. . . It's a six inch circle of eight gauge fencing wire with seventeen tin lids on it that rattle like hell when you shake it. **1979** R. Edwards *Skills of Austral. Bushman* 158 And I thought, well, that just shows you the stupidity of grown-ups, all these years they've been rattling Barcoo dogs and screeching their throats out all for nothing. **1880** J. Bonwick *Resources Qld.* 45 The *A[nthistiria] membranacaea* is the brittle, dry **Barcoo grass**. **1903** E. Palmer *Early Days N. Qld.* 237 The Flinders or Barcoo grass, is an annual of a reddish colour, found all over the western plains. **1956** A.C.C. Lock *Tropical Tapestry* 96 Barcoo grass . . is a favourite with graziers. **1870** E.B. Kennedy *Four Yrs. in Qld.* 46 Land Scurvy . . is better known in Queensland by local names, which do not sound very pleasant, such as **'Barcoo rot'** . . according to the district it appears in. **1871** *Great Northern Run Case* 31 An almost intolerable existence, made up of toil and privation, fever and ague, sand flies and sandy blight, mosquitoes, colonial fevers, and Barcoo-rot. **1894** *Intercolonial Q. Jrnl. Med. & Surg.* I. 218 'Barcoo rot', in which the slightest scratches or abrasions of the skin pass speedily into rapidly spreading, freely suppurating, yet superficial and painless, circular ulcers, often of extraordinary persistence. **1911** 'Rose Boldrewood' *Complications at Collaroi* 102, I don't know how the station would get on without his vegetables! We should suffer 'Barcoo rot' only for Ah See's efforts. **1927** *Bulletin* (Sydney) 24 Nov. 27/1 His hands were barcoo-rotted and his shoulders labor-bowed. **1933** M. Terry *Untold Miles* 28 Apart from the delight of fresh vegetable, the beauty of munuyeroo is that it banishes that curse of hard living inseparable from prospecting far afield. With the juices of this plant coursing through your veins, the misery of barcoo rot is banished. **1937** F. Clune *Dig* 95 McDonagh . . began to feel alarming symptoms of the scurvy (now called Barcoo Rot). **1946** K.S. Prichard *Roaring Nineties* 51 They were nothing to the torture he endured when barcoo rot attacked him. The great sores festered on his back, hands and legs: his lips split and were raw and bleeding. **1963** X. Herbert *Larger than Life* 4 The venture . . lasted long enough to lay up half the males of the family with swamp fever, leech rash, and Barcoo rot. **1982** P. Adam-Smith *Shearers* 230 The old bushman's disease they called 'Barcoo Rot', a form of scurvy caused from lack of fresh food and vegetables. **1968** W.N. Scott *Some People* 120 Before he went he taught the little bloke . . how to make a **Barcoo Sandwich**, which is a curlew between two sheets of bark. **1976** B. Scott *Compl. Bk. Austral. Folk Lore* 380 A Barcoo sandwich is a goanna between two sheets of bark, or a double rum between two beers. **1919** *Bulletin* (Sydney) 20 Mar. 22/1 West of Winton (Q.) a gargle costs a bob. A pound-note buys 20 drinks; but if three thirsts breast the bar and place thereon a half-crown, it buys the three drinks. This is the **'Barcoo shout'**. **1936** *Ibid.* 8 Apr. 21/4 Remember the 'Barcoo shout' when, though drinks were a bob a time, a man could claim three for half-a-crown? **1896** B. Spencer *Horn Sci. Exped. Central Aust.* IV. 132 There is a complaint, from which those long resident in the distant bush frequently suffer severely, which has received the name of the '**Barcoo Sickness**' or simply 'Barcoo'. . . To Queenslanders it is known as the 'Belyando Spew'. **1909** F.E. Birtles *Lonely Lands* 105 Barcoo sickness, so common about here, is caused by the flies getting into the system and causing severe retching. **1918** C. Fetherstonhaugh *After Many Days* 272 What I called the Belyando Spue was a most trying ailment. . . The Western fellows called it the 'Barcoo sickness', the Northern men termed it the 'Burdekin vomit'. **1898** D.W. Carnegie *Spinifex & Sand* 420 Sudden changes in temperature made any **'Barcoo' sores** most painful. **1951** E. Hill *Territory* 79 His legs is black . . and his arm in a sling and he's full of Barcoo sores. **1967** E. Huxley *Their Shining Eldorado* 234 Drought held them up. . . The water . . was poisonously alkaline. They suffered from scurvy and 'Barcoo sores'. **1901** P.D. Lorimer *Songs & Verses* 20 **Barcoo spew**, rot, and sandy blight, Dingoes howling all the night. **1911** E.J. Brady *King's Caravan* 134 Already we were both suffering a nausea known as 'The Barcoo Spews', through drinking bad water. **1922** J. Lewis *Fought & Won* 65 The flies were horrid, and people were suffering from nausea—'Barcoo spew'. **1932** K.S. Prichard *Kiss on Lips* 261 Because a woman has the barcoo spew and is a bit done up with it, you'd dig a hole in the ground and leave her to rot. **1938** C.P. Conigrave *Walk-About* 78 Wilson was suddenly taken most violently sick with what the northerner calls the 'Barcoo spew'. . . It is generally believed that a species of small fly, with a vicious bite, brings about the trouble. The disorder begins suddenly with extreme dizziness, this being immediately followed by sharp vomiting. **1957** D. Niland *Call me when Cross turns Over* 52 Don't try the Barcoo spews. A cow of a thing. Get a feed into you, and then you want to chuck it up again. You chuck it up and you're right as pie till you eat again. And so it goes on. **1977** G.W. Lilley *Lengthening Shadows* 6 'Barcoo Spews' was another complaint characterised by violent vomiting at the taste or even the thought of food. **1881** J.C.F. Johnson *To Mount Browne & Back* 23 The '**Barcoo vomit**', which here usually accompanies dysentery, is a very distressing complaint. **1890** E.T. Towner *Selectors' Guide to Barcoo* 20 From what I can learn from the people on and near the coast, they imagine that the Barcoo is out of the world; that it is hot, that everyone has fever and Barcoo vomit, and that the flies are unbearable. **1899** *Bulletin* (Sydney) 10 June 14/4 Barcoo vomit is caused, in my opinion, by the scent (or pollen) of some herb or plant. **1912** J.B. Cleland *Some Diseases Aust.* 43 '*The Barcoo*', '*Barcoo vomit*', or '*Belyando Spue*' . . is . . a peculiar and often distressing condition characterized by vomiting at meal times, and found in Central Australia, extending as far westward as the coast of West Australia, and eastwards to the Dividing Ranges.

B. *n.*

1. *Barcoo rot.*

1885 *Once a Month* (Melbourne) Jan. 55 In Queensland and all the pioneer stations . . every one is liable to have festering sores on his hands, and it is briefly designated as Barcoo. **1898** D.W. Carnegie *Spinifex & Sand* 148 Nothing but an entire change of diet and way of living can cure the 'Barcoo'; constant washing, an impossibility 'out-back', being essential. **1935** J.K. Ewers *Story of Pipe-Line* 51 The absence of fresh food caused many of the prospectors to break out in sores, known as Barcoo, which took a long time to heal. **1977** F.B. Vickers *Stranger no Longer* 25 Onions and dried apricots. Best things in the world for keeping the barcoo away. **1979** D.R. Stuart *Crank back on Roller* 30 The corporal, a red headed long gangling young fellow, with pink barcoo scars on the back of his hands, was nonplussed.

2. *Barcoo sickness.*

1891 *Adelaide Observer* 16 May 37/1 We were warned against 'barcoo'—an epidemic which is very prevalent when the Cooper is in flood. The popular antidote for the unpleasant sensation of vomiting immediately after a meal is Lea and Perrins' sauce. **1898** *Bulletin* (Sydney) 8 Jan. 14/1 Gidgea tea . . gives you the 'barcoo' for a week after. **1915** *Ibid.* 15 Aug. 22/4 'Barcoo', the summer sickness of the western cattle camps, collars a man at the hour when he's busy with his food. **1932** M.R. White *No Roads go By* 191 Barcoo was rife among the kiddies and station-hands; vomiting attacks lasting for days laid each low in turn.

3. *fig.*

1920 *Bulletin* (Sydney) 24 June 20/2 The bloke who rode 100 'whistlers' in one day gives me the barcoo.

4. See quot.

1934 *Bulletin* (Sydney) 21 Nov. 21/2 So far as I know there are no sandstone ridges at Longreach (Q.), but the electrical storms . . there—called Barcoos—are terrific and take toll of both human and stock life.

5. Language characterized by profanity.

1875 R. Thatcher *Something to his Advantage* 18 Old Daddy objurgates and blesses their eyes and limbs in choicest Barcoo.

bardie /'badi/. Chiefly *W.A.* Also **barde, bardee, bardi.** [a. Nyungar *bardi.*] **a.** The edible larva or pupa of the cerambycid beetle *Bardistus cibarius*, found in the stems of grass-trees, eucalypts, and acacias. **b.** The edible larva or pupa of any of several species of hepialid moth, esp. *Trictena argentata*, found underground, feeding on roots of eucalypts and acacias. See also Witchetty. Also **bardie grub.**

1840 T.J. Buckton *W.A.* 97 The *Bar-de* (the native name for the white grub alluded to), has a fragrant, aromatic flavour; and is eaten either raw or roasted. **1841** G. Grey *Jrnls. Two Exped. N.-W. & W.A.* II. 289 If the top of the tree is observed to be dead, the native gives it a few sharp kicks with his foot, when, if it contains any *barde* or grubs, it begins to give. **1845** J. Brady *Descr. Vocab. Native Lang. W.A.* 14 *Bardi*, the edible grub in the grass tree. **1890** *Trans. & Proc. R. Geogr. Soc. Australasia Vic.* 93 When hungry they simply go forth with a strong stick . . and dig for 'bardies' or large white grubs that attack the jam trees. **1917** *Bulletin* (Sydney) 30 Aug. 24/2 Don't fancy the tree-grub? Try it this way. A dozen bardies, a similar quantity of mushrooms, butter, pepper and salt cooked together on a shovel over a camp-fire. **1922** *Ibid.* 29 June 22/1, I have by me a piece of wood with one old man bardie's blazed trail running clean through a half-inch railway dog-spike which had been driven into the tree. **1926** R.J. TILLYARD *Insects Aust. & N.Z.* 233 The 'bardee' of Western Australia, *Bardistus cibarius* . . , ranges right across to New South Wales; its larvae are found in the stems of grass-trees and 'black-boys' (*Xanthorrhoea*) and are eaten both by aborigines and white people. **1938** D. BATES *Passing of Aborigines* 217 For constipation a cooked iguana liver . . and a few bardie grubs. **1944** K.S. PRICHARD *Potch & Colour* 75 'You bankrupt?' Gus jeered. 'You'd do in an abo for his bardies.' **1959** A. UPFIELD *Bony & Black Virgin* 150 The bardee grubs came from tree-trunks and up from tree-roots to split their skins and emerge as great winged moths the size of a man's hand. **1971** J. GOODE *Guide to Austral. Insects* 112 The Murray River ghost moth (*Trictena argentata*) is large and grey. . . Its grubs breed in red gums along the rivers and are known as 'barti' or 'bardee' grubs, often used by fishermen as bait. **1977** J. O'GRADY *There was Kid* 52 Sandgropers are not like us 'from the East'. They called . . witchetty grubs 'bardies'.

bare-belly. See quot. 1965.

[N.Z. **c 1875** G.L. MEREDITH in A.J. Harrop *Adventuring in Maoriland* (1935) 143 Naturally, the easiest-shorn sheep—'bare-bellies' and 'bare-points'—are selected first.] **1897** *Worker* (Sydney) 11 Sept. 1/2 At a 'clean point' 'bare belly' he'd hardly ever scoff. **1899** *Bulletin* (Sydney) 28 Jan. 14/4 Generally the first sheep to go are the bare-bellies, or rosellas; then the animals with much whisker; but the worst in the pen is the last. **1905** *Steele Rudd's Mag.* (Brisbane) July 661 Wool away, you young beggars! . . A bare-belly, Bill—there's a cobbler for you! **1965** J.S. GUNN *Terminol. Shearing Industry* i. 6 *Barebelly*, a sheep with defective wool growth caused by a break in the fibre structure. This causes the wool to fall off the belly and legs. **1982** P. ADAM SMITH *Shearers* 278 A gate-opener is barrowing a bare-belly at smoke-O. . . Translation: . . the wool-roller kid is learning to shear by finishing off an old sheep for a shearer after the bell has gone.

Hence **bare-bellied** *a.*

1912 J. BRADSHAW *Highway Robbery under Arms* (ed. 3) 23 In came the bare-bellied ewes. Then the pickers-up were bogged in wool, the penner-up was up to his rump in trouble, and the tarboys were almost blind from perspiration. **1918** *Huon Times* (Franklin) 29 Nov. 3/5 The famous ringers established their records on light-woolled and bare-bellied ewes. **1982** P. ADAM SMITH *Shearers* 403 *Bare-bellied Joe*, or *yoe*, said to be Irish for ewe. A sheep that has lost its belly wool.

barilla. *Hist.* [Transf. use of *barilla* a maritime plant *Salsola soda* (fam. Chenopodiaceae); the alkali obtained by burning the plant.] Any of several coastal plants, esp. of the fam. Rhizophoraceae and Chenopodiaceae; the alkaline ashes, formerly used in soap-making, obtained by burning the plants.

1826 Tas. Colonial Secretary's Office Rec. 1/36 201 The most important production however, is the Vegetable from which Barilla is made:- and which is, itself, commonly called British Barilla;—from which that important article *soap* is principally manufactured. **1828** *HRA* (1922) 1st Ser. XIV. 134 The *Barilla*, obtained from the Mangroves which line parts of the Coast and Creeks . . is found to be of so superior a quality for Making *Soap*. **1834** *Hobart Town Almanack* 134 The Barilla shrubs (*Atriplex Halimus, Rhagodia Billardieri*, and *Salicornia arbuscula*) . . with some others, and under the promiscuous name of Botany Bay greens, were boiled and eaten . . by the earliest settlers. **1835** *Ibid.* 69 Barilla . . is the plant so common on the shores of Cape Barren and other islands of the Straits, from which the alkaline salt is obtained and brought up in boats to the soap manufactory at Hobart-town. It has been set down as the same plant that grows on the coast of Spain and other parts of Europe. **1841** *Kerr's Melbourne Almanac* 114 Barilla . . per ton 2s. 6d. **1847** E.W. LANDOR *Bushman* 358 It would be worth inquiry at what price we could afford barilla as an export. **1850** *S. Austral. Register* (Adelaide) 2 Nov., The body of Richard Curtis, the barilla-burner, who was drowned on Tuesday, was found on Thursday. **1891** *Papers & Proc. R. Soc. Tas.* (1892) 1 These petrels choose islands where the soil is composed of a loose sand, covered in places by a bush with a blue flower called 'barilla'.

bark. [Used *attrib.* in Comb. not always excl. Austral. but of local importance.]

1. Applied to items made of bark by Aborigines: **bark canoe, shield.**

1830 R. DAWSON *Present State Aust.* 246 A fleet of small **bark-canoes**, belonging to the natives, was lying moored to some mangrove-trees. **1833** C. STURT *Two Exped. Interior S. Aust.* II. 201 The natives launched their bark canoes . . formed of an oblong piece of bark, the ends of which are stuffed with clay, so as to render them impervious to the water. **1844** *Sydney Morning Herald* 29 Oct. 4/5 Mrs Guise was with two infants on the roof-tree of her hut for several days, until rescued by the blacks in a bark canoe. **1870** E.B. KENNEDY *Four Yrs. in Qld.* 76 The coast Blacks . . can always obtain an abundant supply of fish, and therefore frequently have permanent camps on the sea shore, consisting of well-built 'gunyahs', or huts of bark: they also have bark canoes. **1878** R.B. SMYTH *Aborigines of Vic.* I. p. lix, The bark canoe, it may be safely assumed, is Australian—as much as the boomerang. **1892** MRS F. HUGHES *My Childhood in Aust.* 48 You should see them on a rough day skimming along in their little bark canoes, with nothing but a spear for a paddle. **1798** D. COLLINS *Acct. Eng. Colony N.S.W.* (1798) I. 328 One native of the tribe of Cammerray . . was suffered indeed to cover himself with a **bark shield**, and behaved with the greatest courage. **1801** G. BARRINGTON *Sequel to Voyage N.S.W.* 25 He was indulged with a bark shield, and defended himself with great skill and resolution. **1845** D. MACKENZIE *Emigrant's Guide* 223 Their weapons are the following:- spears, boomerang, nulla-nullah, bark shield. **1856** *Moreton Bay Free Press* 2 June 4/6 Boomerangs and spears flew in marvellous confusion, and heavy waddies thumped on bark shields.

2. Used with reference to the gathering and processing of bark as a source of tannin: **bark chopper, cutter, -cutting, gatherer, getter, licence, mill, peeler, stripper, -stripping.**

1835 *True Colonist* (Hobart) 7 Feb. 3/2 They told us they were going to a **bark-chopper's** hut. **1843** *Arden's Sydney Mag.* Oct. 107 Many of the harbours which abound along the southern coast of the colony were frequented by sealers, whalers, and **bark cutters.** **1854** T.F. BRIDE *Lett. Victorian Pioneers* 24 Apr. (1898) 54 The fame of the place was spread far and wide by the returned bark cutters. **1853** *Austral. Gold Digger's Monthly Mag.* v. 187 By begging or **bark cutting** they obtain money. **1908** E.J. BANFIELD *Confessions of Beachcomber* 13 If you have had no actual experience in bark-cutting . . you will put your elation to a shockingly severe test. **1848** *Adelaide Miscellany* 21 Oct. 183/1 The ruthless stripping knife of the **bark gatherer**, and the eager search of the gum collectors. **1931** *Bulletin* (Sydney) 26 Aug. 21/4 A party of bark-gatherers crossed from Launceston to Westernport in November, 1834. **1849** A. HARRIS *Guide Port Stephens* 43 He had better, if possible, secure the services of a few blacks: they are capital **bark-getters**, but usually strip off merely the butt sheet from the tree as it stands. **1944** E.M. ANDERSON *Typist Tales* 77 He . . decided to look for him first at the bark-getter's camp. **1844** *Portland Mercury* 1 May 2/2 Monthly list of persons who have taken out **bark** and timber **licenses** for the District of Portland Bay. **1885** *N.T. Times Almanac* (1886) 75 A timber or bark licence will not authorise the holder to fell, cut, or remove timber, strip bark, on or from any lands surveyed. **1833** *Trumpeter* (Hobart) 15 Oct. 203 For Sale. A **Bark Mill**, complete, on the most improved principle. **1835** *Cornwall Chron.* (Launceston) 30 May 3 One of the latest bark mills, complete, by Lambert. **1845** R. HOWITT *Impressions Aust. Felix* 148 These loiterers were the **bark-peelers**, their wives and children . . enjoying the sea-breeziness of a fine cheery Australian Sabbath. **1829** *Sydney Monitor* 23 May 1613/2 'The **bark-strippers**' may be numerous as a class in the Colony; but one thing we know, they do not strip enough bark to tan all the shoes that are consumed in the Colony. **1847** A. HARRIS *Settlers & Convicts* (1953) 133, I was told of a poor bark-stripper getting mimosa bark. **1891** W.B. DEAN *Notorious Bushrangers* 81 Attract the attention of the bark-strippers and lime-burners. **1928** M.E. FULLERTON *Austral. Bush* 36 Not a landowner himself . . a rail-splitter, a bark-stripper, a 'possum-trapper maybe. **1944** E.M. ANDERSON *Typist Tales* 77 Hearing the sound of an axe he diverged towards it, and soon saw the bark-stripper at work. **1881** A.C. GRANT *Bush-Life Qld.* II. 156 Owing to the long dry season, the boys found **bark-stripping** exceedingly arduous work.

3. Applied to dwellings or buildings made of bark: **bark gunyah, humpy, school.**

1847 *Portland Guardian* 1 Mar. 4/4 Having erected a **bark gunnee** as token of possession, the squatter's next measure is to hasten away unto the Commissioner of Crown Lands, and put in his application for the run. **1847** *Moreton Bay Courier* 23 Oct. 4/1 It enlarged into a chain of large deep water-holes, which seemed to be the constant resort of numerous natives, who had constructed their bark gunyas at most of them. **1848** S. & J. SIDNEY *Emigrant's Jrnl.* 5 We were living, rather sleeping, in a bark gunnyer, that is to say, we slept in a place made of bark, like a large dog kennel in England. **1851** *Empire* (Sydney) 3 May 2/4 The increased desire for squatters to make themselves contented, and the rumours of nice brick cottages which are superseding the 'bark gunyahs'. **1853** J. SHERER *Gold Finder Aust.* 38 Tents, from the bark gunya and the comfortable marquee down to the 'rustic bower'. **1878** *Squatters' Plum* 39 A bachelor station-hand gets 10s. to £1 per week, lives in a bark gunyah, draughty and damp. **1884** 'R. BOLDREWOOD' *Old Melbourne Memories* 43 Joe must have felt pretty lonely at night, camped in a bark gunyah, with the black pillars of the stringy-bark trees around him, and not a soul within reach or ken. **1887** A. NICOLS *Wild Life & Adventure* 117 Pompey, the old black fellow, who had long been a hanger-on at the station, living in his own bark gunyah near the wash-pool. **1872** C.H. EDEN *My Wife & I in Qld.* 281 Every man has an innate desire to own some place . . even though that home may be only a **bark humpie.** **1881** W. FEILDING *Austral. Trans-Continental Railway* 44 A bark humpy . . does duty for a station on Mr Sutherland's run. **1890** A.J. VOGAN *Black Police* 36 The . . town . . is now emerging from the 'bark-humpy' to the 'iron' age. **1898** *Worker* (Sydney) 22 Jan. 7/1 If you and I go mates on a selection it will often be desirable that you should go on clearing or ploughing for both, while I mend the roof of the bark humpy for both. **1935** F. CLUNE *Rolling down Lachlan* 96 Gradually the bark humpies, . . the tents and the calico huts have all gone away. **1949** B. O'REILLY *Green Mountains* 97 In earlier generations a bark humpy formed the nucleus of the homes of thousands of Australian selectors. **1895** *Worker* (Sydney) 20 July 4/1 Bill and Jim and Joe went to the old **bark school** through Long Gully and over the Gap. **1903** *Bulletin* (Sydney) 9 Jan. 17/1, I was once head-master of a bark school.

4. Special Comb. **bark hut.**

a. *Obs.* A name given by colonists to a temporary shelter constructed by an Aboriginal.

1793 J. HUNTER *Hist. Jrnl. Trans. Port Jackson* 60 We sometimes met with a piece of the bark of a tree, bent in the middle, and set upon the ends, with a piece set up against that end on which the wind blows. . . These bark huts (if they deserve even the name of huts) are intended . . for those employed in hunting. **1814** M. FLINDERS *Voyage Terra Australis* I. 145 Many straggling bark huts, similar to those on other parts of the coast, were seen upon the shores of Port Lincoln. **1820** J. OXLEY *Jrnls. Two Exped. N.S.W.* 253 Natives appear to be very numerous; their guniahs (or bark-huts) are in every direction. **1827** P.P. KING *Narr. Survey Intertropical & Western Coasts* I. 213 Near the watering-place were some natives' bark-huts and gourds. **1834** J.D. LANG *Hist. & Statistical Acct. N.S.W.* I. 38 It seems . . to be a general appointment of Divine Providence that . . the miserable bark-hut of the aborigines of New Holland, should be utterly swept away by the flood-tide of European colonization. **1846** *Tasmanian Jrnl. Nat. Sci.* II. 418 One tribe was discovered living in a village, if it may be so termed, of bark huts or break-winds. **1860** 'LADY' *My Experiences in Aust.* 203 Even while they remained in our paddock they would change the site of their little bark huts or *guneyahs* every eight or ten days.

b. A dwelling of which the walls and roof are made of bark.

1810 E. BENT Let. 30 July II. 192, I mean to . . make the Stockmen build themselves a Bark Hut. **1815** *HRA* (1921) 3rd Ser. II. 461 There must also be a Strong Temporary Bark Hut, for the accommodation of the Guard. **1825** *Austral.* (Sydney) 28 Apr. 3 Five of the desperadoes . . had constructed a bark hut . . where a black girl . . was kept for their convenience. **1834** G. BENNETT *Wanderings N.S.W.* I. 101 A neat little inn (which now supplied the place of a rude bark hut). **1837** W.B. ULLATHORNE *Catholic Mission Australasia* 111, I have celebrated the mysterious rites of our religion in the bark hut, beneath the gum tree in the valley. **1844** *Bee of Aust.* (Sydney) 9 Nov. 4/2 It was a new bark hut, but on entering it I was much struck by the many symbols of refinement it contained. A handsome collection of books, a pianaforte [*sic*], and a guitar, gave evidence that its owner was one of cultivated taste. **1847** *Port Phillip Herald* 4 Mar. (Suppl.), But as time passes by, And beauty will fly, I'm determin'd no longer to tarry; So now I declare, I am willing to share A bark hut in the bush with dear Harry. **1862** 'W.T.G.' *Quite Colonial* (*c* 1948) 7 He built himself a bark hut; that is, he erected a wooden frame, splitting the necessary timber himself from the trunk of a large peppermint tree he had felled for the purpose, and then covered the roof and sides with sheets of bark. **1879** 'AUSTRALIAN' *Adventures Qld.* 105 Two bark huts were built... The upper hut was for the two principals, the lower one for the men. A bark hut is easily built, and keeps out the weather effectually. **1905** A.B. PATERSON *Old Bush Songs* 12 In an old bark hut. In an old bark hut. I'm forced to go on rations in an old bark hut. **1913** W.K. HARRIS *Outback in Aust.* 136 Kerosene-tin huts, bark huts, and bag huts are the common dwelling-houses. **1937** D. GUNN *Links with Past* 11 On arrival at Wyaga we found the head station house was a bark hut with an earth floor, but there was a good woolshed. **1962** D. LOCKWOOD *I, Aboriginal* 46 Our permanent 'camp'—and I doubt if it deserved any more pretentious title—was a bark hut, twelve feet square, consisting of but a single room. **1981** *Austral. Women's Weekly* (Sydney) 15 Apr. 62/1 Bark huts, when well constructed, were comfortable and durable. In the one recently restored at Aireys Inlet, Vic., a bark dividing wall, protected from the weather, was still in perfect condition after more than 100 years, as was the framework.

barking, *ppl. a.* Used in the names of various animals to describe the sounds they produce or are supposed to produce, esp. **barking bird** *obs.*, *barking owl*; **gecko, lizard,** any of several lizards, esp. the thick-tailed gecko *Underwoodisaurus milii* of s. Aust.; **owl,** the owl *Ninox connivens* of all exc. the arid parts of Aust.; SCREAMING-WOMAN BIRD; WINKING OWL; **spider,** see quot. 1976.

1844 L. LEICHHARDT *Jrnl. Overland Exped. Aust.* 25 Oct. (1847) 23 The stillness of the moonlight night is not interrupted by.. the monotonous note of the **barking-bird** and little owlet. **1855** J. BONWICK *Geogr. Aust. & N.Z.* 198 Barking birds.. are in North Australia. **1962** B.W. LEAKE *Eastern Wheatbelt Wildlife* 105 The **barking gecko**, about four inches long, differs from other lizards and goannas by its habit of barking softly when disturbed. **1916** *Bulletin* (Sydney) 31 Aug. 24/3 Binghi will have nothing whatever to do with.. the 'weelitcha' or **barking lizard**. **1952** A.M. DUNCAN-KEMP *Where Strange Paths go Down* 21 Here beneath a shrub they had unearthed a barking lizard, a grotesque frog-like creature with reddish brown upper part and tough creamy looking skin on its lower regions. **1984** W.W. AMMON et al. *Working Lives* 140 The barking lizard.. when disturbed.. will raise itself on its hind legs.. and bark several times at you. **1844** L. LEICHHARDT *Jrnl. Overland Exped. Aust.* 20 Nov. (1847) 47 The glucking-bird and the **barking-owl** were heard throughout the moonlight nights. **1968** D. FLEAY *Nightwatchmen* 25 Both Barking Owls and Boobooks brood from the moment of laying. **1986** *Canberra Times* 19 May 20/2 The first animal to move into camp was a barking owl. Its call, a cross between a cough and a soft bark, came from a branch overhead. **1896** B. SPENCER *Rep. Horn Sci. Exped. Central Aust.* I. 130, I was also especially anxious.. to watch the so-called '**barking spider**' in its natural state. **1976** B.Y. MAIN *Spiders* 78 *Selenocosmia* [*stirlingi*] is the legendary barking spider or whistling spider of inland Australia... Although the spider does apparently produce a whistling sound its 'bark' was more likely attributable to.. quails which frequent the same localities.

bark painting. A picture painted on bark, traditionally that of the stringybark *Eucalyptus tetrodonta*, as part of the ceremonial of Arnhem Land Aborigines; now a widely practised Aboriginal art form. Also *attrib.*

1897 T. WORSNOP *Prehistoric Arts Aborigines* 37 A copy of a bark painting from Port Essington natives is figured in one of the volumes of the Linnean Society of New South Wales. **1939** *Trans. R. Soc. S.A.* LXIII. 370 The bark paintings described in this paper are.. the work of the Mau tribe, who live on the mainland opposite Goulburn Island. **1951** R.M. BERNDT *Kunapipi* 10 There are also bark paintings, with sacred totemic clan designs, used on the ceremonial ground, or with copies of chest drawings. **1964** C.P. MOUNTFORD *Aboriginal Paintings* 11 The most beautiful examples of aboriginal graphic art are, without doubt, the cave and bark paintings. **1964** R.M. & C.H. BERNDT *World First Australs.* 219 If a rite or myth or song, or bark or cave painting, is secret to the men of a community, and women or children are conventionally prohibited from seeing it or approaching it, the tendency is to label it 'sacred'. **1965** K. KUPKA *Dawn of Art* 61 Bark painting is beyond doubt the most characteristic of the different art-forms practised by the Aborigines. As its name indicates, the painting is executed on panels of bark; they are taken from the eucalyptus, the most widespread tree in Australia. **1969** H. PORTER *Eden House* 42 Oh, the shop was all tizzed up with saris and bullfight posters and things dangling from the ceiling, and bark paintings supposed to be done by boongs. **1983** *Canberra Chron.* 31 Aug. 5/1 Students demonstrated Aboriginal bark-painting techniques.

bark ringer. *Obs.* RING BARKER.

1894 J.K. ARTHUR *Kangaroo & Kauri* 24 A station of 100,000 acres may have for two or three months in the year 15 to 20 bark-ringers at work.

bark-ringing, *vbl. n. Obs.* See RING-BARK *v.*

1926 *Illustr. Tasmanian Mail* (Hobart) 6 Jan. 59/4 Early spring is the best season for wholesale bark-ringing.

barley grass. [Transf. use of U.S. *barley grass* meadow barley: see DAE.] Any of several annual grasses bearing seeds in awned spikelets, esp. naturalized species of *Hordeum.*

1846 *Sydney Morning Herald* 8 Dec. 2/6 Along the banks of the Narran, the grass is of the very best description, *Panicum laevinode*.. (barley-grass.. of the colonists) growing on plains or in open forests... The seeds of the *Panicum laevinode* constitute the chief food of the natives, who bruise these seeds between stones, and bake the dough into cakes. **1849** J.P. TOWNSEND *Rambles & Observations N.S.W.* 181 The feed.. on some stations.. is composed of barley grass, wild carrots, and wild melons. **1861** *Austral. Settler's Handbk.* 25 *Barley Grass* is a flourishing native grass, growing wild in the Kurrajong and adjoining neighbourhoods... I have called it *barley grass* because it much resembles barley in appearance. **1880** G.A. BROWN *Sheep Breeding in Aust.* 321 Black salt flats, growing barley-grass, clover-burr. **1890** A. MACKAY *Austral. Agriculturist* (ed. 2) 140 Andropogon refractus and pertusus, both powerful growers and rich grasses,.. are commonly called barley grasses. **1903** G. SUTHERLAND *Australasian Live Stock Man.* (ed. 2) 384 Among the grasses of Riverina he mentions as meriting special attention—Umbrella Grass, Silver Grass, Barley Grass,.. and wild carrot. **1955** STEWART & KEESING *Austral. Bush Ballads* 204 There spear-grass grows, and barley-grass, And crow-foot green and high.

barmaid's blush. See quot. 1970.

1912 *Huon Times* (Franklin) 3 Apr. 6/2 The plaintiff urged that he could not have been drunk because he had swallowed nothing beyond 'barmaid's blush'. **1943** *Bulletin* (Sydney) 5 Jan. 12/1 Whatever you think of a Lady's Waist Or a Barmaid's Blush or a Horse's Neck, A Bull-whale's Crush or a Slippery Deck, There's nothing solid in what ghosts drink. **1970** W. FEARN-WANNAN *Austral. Folklore* 32 Usually in old-time bushmen's meaning, a drink of rum and raspberry is a Barmaid's Blush.

barney, *n.* [Br. dial.: see OED(S and EDD.] A dispute or altercation; a fight.

1858 *Bell's Life in Sydney* 30 Jan. 2/4 After the usual bit of *barney* that follows a mistake. **1858** C.R. THATCHER *Colonial Songster* (rev. ed.) 68 A barney first commences With a little bit of 'skiting', But calling names is not enough, And so it ends in fighting. **1869** *Adelaide Punch* 4 Mar. 64/2 Then *Jones* and me made it up amicable, after which the game proceeded without no more barney. **1888** *Centennial Mag.* (Sydney) 222 Roper's a rum chap when his monkey's up. I don't go there now; we had a barney about some calves. **1908** 'FIFTY-THREE YRS.' MINER' *So Long* 44 After a lot of 'barney' and angry words between them. **1918** *Kia Ora Coo-ee* Apr. 20/2 You chaps ride up to the driver, and get up a barney with him and his mate. **1938** X. HERBERT *Capricornia* 379 The musician was playing *The Red Flag.* Andy chuckled and said, 'Muster been trouble in the camp... Joe always plays tunes like that when there's been a barney with the men.' **1968** S. GORE *Holy Smoke* 10 One or two of the other jokers.. heard all this barney goin' on. **1981** *Business Review* (Sydney) 11 Jan. 2/3 Andrew Peacock is planning to pull-on a barney with the unions. If he wins the face of industrial relations may never be the same again.

barney, *v.* [f. prec.] *intr.* To dispute or argue. Freq. as *vbl. n.*

1861 *Bell's Life in Sydney* 9 Nov. 2/4 After considerable 'barneying' the dusky darling was induced to retire. **1871** *Austral. Town & Country Jrnl.* (Sydney) 11 Mar. 316/2 There was more disagreement over it, and what is usually called barneying, than ever I had seen over a similar match. **1887** G. WALCH *Victorian Jubilee Bk.* 32, I don't know what you're barneyin' about. ***c* 1894** 'I. SC-TT' *How I stole over 10,000 Sheep* 32 At last after no end of barneying he agreed to pay three-quarters of the money down. **1914** E. DYSON *Loves of Lancelot* 59 He was barneying with the policeman. **1922** J. LEWIS *Fought & Won* 169 After a great deal of 'barneying' the blacksmith sold it to him for £60. **1947** V. PALMER *Hail Tomorrow* 63 No more barneying with pannikin bosses about the length of a smoko or whether the sheep's wet or dry.

barra /ˈbærə/. Abbrev. of BARRAMUNDI.

1900 *Bulletin* (Sydney) 1 Sept. 15/1 When a 'barra' is hooked he strives hard to entangle the line. **1913** *Ibid.* 6 Feb. 15/4 *Re* the barramundi of the Wide Bay (Q.) streams. Was recently holidaying on the upper reaches of the Mary River, where the 'barra' were like shoals of mullet. **1959** *Never kill Dolphin* (Writers' Guild Qld.) 91 He was sore at the hole in the net, and the fact that they had not netted either a barra or a king. **1978** R.J. BRITTEN *Around Cassowary Rock* 71 He wanted to.. help him set a few 'barra' nets. **1981** P. RICE-CHAPMAN *Food at Top End* 10 Probably the fish most associated with the Top End is barramundi, known colloquially as Barra. **1983** *Ecos* xxxv. 7/3 Customs officials confiscated many tonnes of 'bogus barra'.

barrack, *n.*[1] Freq. *pl.* [Spec. use of *barrack* a building for the accommodation of troops.] Also *attrib.*

1. *Hist.*

a. A building or set of buildings for the temporary accommodation of convicts; *convict barrack*, see CONVICT B. 3.

1826 *Colonial Times* (Hobart) 6 May, Malcolm Laing Smith, Esquire, to act as Barrack Master. **1826** *Monitor* (Sydney) 1 Sept. 126/3 The perambulator will have noticed in his peregrinations through Sydney Streets on a Saturday, every corner occupied by numerous groups of barrack-men. **1828** *Tasmanian* (Hobart) 12 Sept. 2 There are now upwards of 600 prisoners in Barracks.. waiting until their masters in the interior arrive to take them away. **1834** *HRA* (1924) 1st Ser. XXII. 461, I would also propose that the Office of Barrack Overseer be abolished as the number of Prisoners now in the Barracks are daily diminishing. **1836** J.F. O'CONNELL *Residence Eleven Yrs. New Holland* 65 Neither bushrangers or barrack prisoners, however, often betray runaways. **1837** G. LOVELESS *Victims of Whiggery* 13, I now began to feel the effects of transportation. I worked on the roads with the chain-gang in the day, and slept in the barracks at night, without a bed, or covering. **1838** *S. Austral. Rec.* (London) 14 Nov. 116 There are no huge barracks in Adelaide, full of wicked and condemned men—no female factories or penitentiaries. **1842** *Austral. & N.Z. Monthly Mag.* 48 His rations and his lodgings are the same.. in the great barrack his bed either of wood or iron, a straw pallet under, and a common rug over him. **1865** J.F. MORTLOCK *Experiences of Convict* 88 Necessity.. obliged me to become once more a denizen of the 'Barracks', where the officers having become acquainted with me, a little favour was shown. **1905** *Bulletin* (Sydney) 6 July 16/2 In 1848 Governor Gipps ordered the demolition of all prisoners' stockades or barracks in the locality, and wiped away.. the traditions of lagdom.

b. A building or set of buildings for the temporary accommodation of immigrants.

1841 *Hunter River Gaz.* 11 Dec. 3/4 Shortly before we left Sydney we happened to pass the Immigration Barrack yard, and overheard, in spite of ourselves, the conversation of a knot of these immigrants. **1847** J. SIDNEY *Voice from Far Interior* 18 Ship-loads of emigrants were idling in the government barracks. **1852** S. SIDNEY *Three Colonies Aust.* 244 We were received in the Immigration Barracks.

2. BACHELORS' QUARTERS.

1876 *Austral. Town & Country Jrnl.* (Sydney) 9 Sept. 422/3 To the barracks also were relegated those just too exalted for the men's hut, while not eligible for the possibly distinguished company occasionally entertained at 'the cottage'. Such were cattle-dealers, sheep buyers, overseers of neighbouring stations, and generally unaccredited travellers whose manners or appearance rendered classification hazardous. **1891** *Truth* (Sydney) 15 Mar. 7/3 But the most difficult step of all is from hut to barracks. I know some young and some old station hands who would lose ten years of their life to *tucker in the barracks.* **1899** *Bulletin* (Sydney) 19 Aug. 32/2 The overseer was seen walking across from the 'barracks' to the woolshed. **1903** J. FURPHY *Such is Life* 292 Go on to the barracks; I'll be after you in two minutes. **1942** J. DEVANNY *Killing Jacqueline Love* 3 A hundred yards from the house the low wooden barracks, the home of the overseer and jackeroo and occasional workmen. **1964** J.S. MANIFOLD *Who wrote Ballads?* 86 Next below the homestead socially comes the 'narangy barracks', 'bachelors' quarters' or 'jackeroos' quarters'.

barrack, *n.*[2] [f. BARRACK *v.*] Banter; provocative or derisive language.

1892 *Bulletin* (Sydney) 5 Nov. 17/2 While in her guileless presence he ceased to chew or swear, He knew the kind of barrack that can fetch a square affair. **1900** *Advocate* (Burnie) 22 Oct. 4/1 Mr Midgely stated that when he was present there seemed to be a certain amount of 'barrack' between Mr Simmons and Mr M'Mahon. **1914** N.F. SPIELVOGEL *Gumsucker at Home* 76 There is laughter, banter, 'barrack', till the street hums, but there is no stay. **1924** F.J. MILLS *Happy Days* 43 The 'barrack' from the onlookers .. was vociferous. The score stood at deuce. **1932** M. TERRY *Out Back* 2 Good honest work, hard tucker—with plenty of it—long nights and regular beneath the stars, a joke and some barrack. **1948** V. PALMER *Golconda* 60 His flood of good-humoured barrack made the newcomers feel at home. **1959** —— *Big Fellow* 44 'Surely to God you can take a bit of barrack!' 'Not that kind of barrack,' said Donovan.

barrack, *v.* [Prob. Br. dial. (N. Irel.) *barrack* to brag, to be boastful of one's fighting powers: see EDD and OEDS. It is unlikely that there is any connection with BORAK.]

1. *trans.* To ridicule, jeer at, verbally abuse (a person, etc.). Also *absol.*

1878 [see *barracking, vbl. n.*]. **1887** G. WALCH *Victorian Jubilee Bk.* 32 That's what I meant by actin' fair, not fightin' and barrackin' one another. **1892** A.B. PATERSON in C. Semmler *World of Banjo Paterson* (1967) 130 And if you want to get your two eyes knocked straight into one, go and 'barrack' against the land of Erin. **1898** *Western Champion* (Barcaldine) 26 Apr. 3/2 He barracked persistently all the time we were in the field and his language was simply lurid blasphemy. ***c* 1907** C.W. CHANDLER *Darkest Adelaide* 59 They were always barracking me with being a frightened baby and not going out with boys like they did, and nearly all said they got a lot of money by meeting men after work. **1911** E. DYSON *Tommy Hawker* 19 Life wouldn't be liveable here if those beggars knew. They'd barrack the soul out of a man. **1915** C.J. DENNIS *Songs of Sentimental Bloke* 22 Me! that 'as barracked tarts, an' torked an' larft, An' chucked orf at 'em like a phonergraft! **1924** F.J. MILLS *Happy Days* 112 Those trousers .. were what was known as half-masters. There was a space of three inches between the bottom of each leg and the top of each boot... Other boys 'barracked' him. **1943** *Coast to Coast 1942* 165 Dingo kept his pipe in his mouth all evening, not saying a word till even Ward barracked him. **1951** D. STIVENS *Jimmy Brockett* 54 'Not Jimmy Brockett... I'm still a working man, even if I sport a white collar.' 'Yes .. I was only barracking you, pal.' **1962** V.C. HALL *Dreamtime Justice* 43 Out there on the islands there'll be nobody to barrack a man about looking like a monk. **1972** J. MCNEIL *Familiar Juice* (1973) 82 Like in Cairo they had this monkey and a bloody stupid donkey... We used to barrack the monkey every time it went off.

2. *intr.*

a. With **for**: to give support or encouragement to (a person, team, etc.), usu. by shouting names, slogans or exhortations. Also *trans.* (see quot. 1892).

1890 *Bull-Ant* (Melbourne) 8 May 14/1, I alwus barrack fer the club I put my stuff on, an' .. I'd backed the South for a tanner. **1891** *Bulletin* (Sydney) (1892) 7 May 17/1 Old dad was in his glory there—it gave the old man joy To fight a passage thro' the crowd and barrack for his boy. **1892** A.B. PATERSON in C. Semmler *World of Banjo Paterson* (1967) 129 The Australians impartially barracked both sides. **1894** *Bulletin* (Sydney) 17 Mar. 11/1 The 'fashionable' element of the N.S.W. Female Suffragists openly 'barracks' for the so-called 'Free-trade' cause. **1895** *Ibid.* 28 Sept. 8/2 That god near the ceiling Was proudly revealing His Love for poor Gentleman Joe, Ho! ho! He barracked for Gentleman Joe. **1908** P. TREVOR *With M.C.C. in Aust.* 230 An obviously well-conducted young man or an unimpeachable young woman will say frankly: 'I'm going to 'barrack' for the Englishmen today; my brother is 'barracking' for the Australians.' That barracking consists simply and solely in cheery partisan applause. **1910** *Huon Times* (Franklin) 28 May 4/1 Accused, on oath, stated that he had merely been 'barracking' for Fitzroy, and took no part in the stone-throwing. **1914** T.C. WOLLASTON *Spirit of Child* 31 You love the dear old gums, of course, and 'barrack' for them in a general way. **1923** *Bulletin* (Sydney) 12 July 23/2 The crows were barracking for him when he went out 'roo shooting. **1941** D. O'CALLAGHAN *Long Life Reminisc.* 11, I often had a bit of a scrap after school. Some of the girls .. would barrack for me. **1950** G.S. CASEY *City of Men* 278 Trucks! .. I always barracked for 'em, and I always will. They're more essential here than they are anywhere. **1960** D. MCLEAN *Roaring Days* 195 You gave me a hiding once, because I barracked for a different team than yours. **1971** D. WILLIAMSON *Don's Party* (1973) 24, I take it you'll be barracking for Labor tonight?

b. *transf.* To argue or agitate for (a cause, etc.).

1897 A. HAYWARD *Along Road to Cue*, For the lawyer chaps to speak, The coves in wigs that barrack for the drunks. **1903** *Truth* (Sydney) 8 Mar. 1/6 North Shore is barracking for the establishment of a technical college. **1904** L. LAWSON *Lonely Crossing* 31 And take the tightest pinch of all From dire misfortune's screw; And humbly barrack for a job The hated cockatoo. **1909** *Truth* (Sydney) 10 Jan. 1/5 Those barracking for a bridge across the harbor will have a walk-over when they get it. **1912** *Ibid.* 7 July 1/6 Paddington women are barracking .. for a gallery. **1916** *Ibid.* 12 Nov. 1/6 It is only natural that a Bathgate should be death on sly grog and barrack loudly for cold water. **1948** V. PALMER *Golconda* 32 We oughtn't to barrack for the spending of public money.

Hence **barracking** *vbl. n.* and *ppl. a.*

1878 *Pilgrim* (Sydney) 2nd Ser. iv. 39 Douglass mumbled over a 'petition' .. for the edification of assembled roughs and larrikins; but was received with noisy insult and cries of 'cheese your barrickin' and 'shut up'. **1884** *Austral. Tit-Bits* (Melbourne) 26 June 14/2 The umpire .. was grossly insulted by some of the 'barracking' rowdies. **1889** J.L. HUNT *Bk. of Bonanzas* 66 The 'barracking' of the bystanders is distasteful to young men who seek to meet their antagonists and contend with them in all good humour and friendliness as befits English gentlemen. **1899** *Austral. Tit-Bits* (Sydney) 25 Nov. 14/1 'Barracking' is the jeering and hooting of the roughs, which forms such an objectionable feature at cricket and football matches in the big Australian towns. **1907** G.R. WITTON *Scapegoats of Empire* 3 A man could judge fairly his chance of success by the applause or 'barracking' as he passed the crowd. **1915** *Honk* ix. 4/2 All barracking to be screamed, yelled, or bellowed in French. Australian language barred. **1930** V. PALMER *Passage* (1957) 76 She laughed lightly as she flung back jest for jest; it would take more than a little barracking to disturb that cool poise of hers! **1939** J. CAMPBELL *Babe is Wise* 252 Me an' me girl-friends going on the scoot, Mac .. Mrs Mac. would inform her husband in her usual barracking way. **1960** *Bulletin* (Sydney) 10 Aug. 16/3 Tiger, who's only too willing to back-up his footy barracking with his dooks, was warned by the police-sergeant. **1973** J. MURRAY *Larrikins* 52 But the barracking was by no means confined to football matches. The 'gods' in the theatres, sixpence a seat, were a wonderful place for a push to be.

barracker. [f. BARRACK *v.*] One who barracks.

1889 *Bulletin* (Sydney) 6 July 8/2 (*caption*) Become a barracker in a Melbourne football club. **1890** *Bull-Ant* (Melbourne) 8 May 14/1 A barracker can't get a show when th' club he's talkin' for is walkin' all over the other push, and can lick em on their heads. **1891** *Bohemia* (Melbourne) 18 June 20, I know I'm an awful barracker .. but I do so hope the South Melbourne Club will be premiers this year. **1900** *Tocsin* (Melbourne) 4 Jan. 6/1 The Barracker is the Critic in embryo; the primeval reviewer of other men's deeds. **1908** *Austral. Mag.* (Sydney) Nov. 1251/1 In the old days a barracker was a person who poked borak at the opponents of the side he favoured, and it was not until comparatively recent years that he became identified with the person who yelled encouragement to his own and discouragement to the other side indiscriminately. **1913** E.W. HOWE *Travel Lett.* 180 A man who attends all cricket games, and knows all the fine points, is called a 'barracker'. But he does not abuse the players, as do our baseball fans; a 'barracker' seems to be more of a gentleman than a 'fan'. **1916** *Truth* (Sydney) 19 Mar. 4/2 De Foe .. was a great 'barracker' for that dirty Dutch he-goat, Billy the Beast, in whose defence he wrote his well-known poem. **1922** A. WRIGHT *Colt from Country* 13 He must take an active part in the game, for he did not love sport from a distance. Doug was no barracker; he butted right in, and got there. **1942** H.H. PECK *Mem. of Stockman* 26 John Murray Peck, always wearing the red and black Sturt's Desert Pea in his coat, was for years vice-president and chief barracker. **1960** R.S. PORTEOUS *Cattleman* 161 He heard the shrill-voiced barracker yell, "It 'im in the guts, McReady! Ya can't 'urt them bloody boongs' 'eads.' **1979** K. DUNSTAN *Ratbags* 14 The barracker of the nineteen-seventies tended to be a bore.

barracouta. Also **barracoota.** [Transf. use of *barracuda, barracouta* a West Indian fish: see quot. 1843.] The sea fish *Leionura atun* of the fam. Gempylidae, widespread in southern waters, including those of s. Aust. and N.Z.; COOTA.

1835 J. BATMAN *Settlement in Port Phillip* 28 May (1856) 10 Two fine, long, bright, and well-tasted barracoutas, fish peculiar to the coast of Australia, were caught. **1837** J. BACKHOUSE *Extracts from Lett.* (1839) v. 3 Many barracootas were taken from the stern by large hooks baited with pieces of red rag. **1843** J.F. BENNETT *Hist. & Descr. Acct. S.A.* 47 Barracouta .. [*Note*] In Colonial parlance so called, from a supposed resemblance to that fish. **1900** *Advocate* (Burnie) 6 Dec. 4/4 M'Guire is sitting down like a dried barracouta. **1934** W.A. OSBORNE *Visitor to Aust.* 84 Some are coarse in flesh but nutritious and cheap, such as .. barracouta. **1966** *Courier-Mail* (Brisbane) 17 Sept. 3/8 Fish processors and distributors have for some time been disturbed at the frequent mistaken association between the barracouta netted for commercial purposes in Australia and the ferocious tropical barracuda... They advocated a change of name and the Australian Fisheries Newsletter for September says the barracouta will henceforth be known as the snoek, the name by which it is known in South Africa. **1976** *Ecos* ix. 3/3 Just before and after World War II, the research vessel *Wareen* .. explored the possibilities of fishing for .. snoek (barracouta). **1984** *Canberra Chron.* 3 Oct. 19/5 The barracouta appear to be giving it away for the season, which should cause a sigh of relief among anglers who are getting short of sinkers and hooks.

barramundi /bærəˈmʌndi/. Also **barramunda.** [Prob. f. a Qld. Aboriginal language.] **a.** Any of several n. Austral. fish found in rivers, now chiefly *Lates calcarifer* of warm rivers and coastal waters from Japan to the Persian gulf and s. to W.A., N.T., and Qld., valued as food. **b.** LUNGFISH. **c.** Either of the osteoglossids *Scleropages leichhardti*, of n. N.T. and Qld., and *S. jardini.* Also abbrev. as BARRA.

1864 'E.S.H.' *Narr. Trip Sydney to Peak Downs* 28 There is also a fine large fish in the river, called by the aborigines 'Barramundi', which attains a weight of more than 20 lbs. **1872** C.H. EDEN *My Wife & I in Qld.* 192 The *Barri mundi*, or Australian salmon .. much resembling the English salmon, for running water and access to the sea are indispensable to it. **1880** A.C.L.G. GÜNTHER *Introd. Study Fishes* 357 The Barramunda is said to be in the habit of going on land, or at least on mud-flats; and this assertion appears to be borne out by the fact that it is provided with a lung. **1881** *Proc. Linnean Soc. N.S.W.* VI. 256 *Osteoglossum Leichardti* .. 'Burramundi' of the Aborigines of the Dawson River. **1896** F.G. AFLALO *Sketch Nat. Hist. Aust.* 211 The Fitzroy perch .. known locally as the 'barramunda', a name that more properly belongs to the *Ceratodus*, or Lung Fish.

1905 A.B. PATERSON *Old Bush Songs* 6 For we'll bob for barramundies Round the banks of a lagoon. **1935** A. FRANCIS *Then & Now* 49 The very rare Barramundi, sometimes called lung fish. **1962** C. GYE *Cockney & Crocodile* 114 We were after crocs and barramundi, that delicate Kimberley fish which yields large steaks of creamy white flesh that melts in your mouth. **1983** *Ecos* xxxv. 5/1 Until a few years ago, only three commercially important Australian fish were known to change sex: barramundi, coral trout, and threadfin salmon.

barrel, *v.* [Perh. f. (rifle-)*barrel* orig. in Austral. Services' speech.] *trans.* To kill, esp. by shooting; to knock down; to manhandle. Also *intr.*, and *fig.*

1966 S.J. BAKER *Austral. Lang.* (ed. 2) 169 *Barrel*, to shoot and kill. **1972** J. DE HOOG *Skid Row Dossier* 106 I'll barrel her... The only thing that stopped me shovin' her through the window was a charge of assault and breakin' and enterin'. **1977** *Cattleman* (Rockhampton) Mar. 2/3 Keep barrelling away at Government and get into every field of endeavour.

barrow, *v.* [Of unknown origin: perh. a Gaelic *bearradh* shearing, clipping.] *intr.* Of one learning to shear: to shear, or shear partially, a sheep (see quot. 1930). Freq. as *vbl. n.*

1887 *Gen. Rules* (Amalgam. Shearers' Union) 13 No 'barrowing' shall be permitted in any shed. [*Note*] 'Barrowing' means shearing done by persons other than those engaged to shear in the shed. **1891** *Conference Amalgam. Shearers' Union & Pastoralists' Fed. Council* 29 A learner . . will go barrowing, will pick out three or four of the best sheep in the pen to practise upon. They are shorn, and they are counted to the fast man without his mate getting any advantage. **1905** *Shearer* (Sydney) 23 Dec. 7/5 They strut and skite round the woolroom and the galley-fire like 'first-battle' grenadiers to the great amusement of the 'barrowing' boys. **1915** *Bulletin* (Sydney) 28 Oct. 22/4 Barrowing has been stopped by the last Arbitration award. **1930** *Aussie* (Sydney) May 27/3 In those blade days 'barrowing' was a most important institution. When the shearer knocked off for smoke-oh, a picker-up or other lad about the shed would take his shears over and learn to shear by taking the belly wool off the sheep in the pen, and perhaps trimming woolly legs. The shearer watched with good advice, and by the system of barrowing most youngsters turned into fine shearers. **1964** H.P. TRITTON *Time means Tucker* (rev. ed.) 40 Shearing started at two o'clock and there was a race to shear the first sheep in the shed... I spent most of the afternoon watching and 'barrowing', i.e. finishing off. **1965** *Tracks we Travel* 96 The picker-up who had been barrowing . . was ready to be a shearer. **1979** B. HARDY *World owes me Nothing* 78 But then he began to do a bit of 'barrowing'. At the end of a run Jack Healy, Billy Bath, or another experienced shearer would let him finish off a sheep and stand over him, telling him what to do.

Hence **barrower** *n.*

1911 *5 CAR* 107 None of the respondents shall permit 'barrowing' during 'smoke-ohs' or meal hours if it interfere in any way with the 'smoke-oh' or meal hour of any member of the claimant organization (other than the 'barrower'). **1915** *Bulletin* (Sydney) 28 Oct. 22/4 A 'barrower' is one who tries his 'prentice hand at shearing during the smoke-o's. **1917** *11 CAR* 430 None of the respondents shall permit 'barrowing' during smoke-ohs or meal hours if it interfere in any way with the smoke-oh or meal hour of any member of the claimant organization other than the 'barrower'.

bar-shouldered dove. The ground-feeding pigeon *Geopelia humeralis*, of n. and e. Aust. and New Guinea, having a brown back barred with black. Formerly **barred-shouldered dove.**

1844 J. GOULD *Birds of Aust.* (1848) V. Pl. 72, *Geopelia humeralis.* Barred-shouldered Ground-Dove . . Mangrove Pigeon. **1903** *Emu* II. 154 *Geopelia humeralis* (Barred-shouldered Dove)... These birds have a wide range over Northern Australia. **1935** D. THOMSON *In Arnhem Land* 17 June (1983) 39 Shot a Bar-shouldered Dove—our only fresh meat for the day—a few mouthfuls each. **1964** M. SHARLAND *Territory of Birds* 186 Double cuckoo-calls of 'River Pigeons' (Bar-shouldered Doves). **1978** N. COLEMAN *Look at Wildlife Great Barrier Reef* 33 Frequently seen in small groups, the bar-shouldered dove is a seed and vegetation feeder which spends most of its time foraging on the ground.

bart. *Obs.* Rhyming slang for TART.

1879 *Truth* (Sydney) 23 Dec. 5/4 Adores the fair sex... Lately spirited away Sol's 'bart'. **1882** *Sydney Slang Dict.* 1 *Bart*, a girl, generally applied to those of loose character. **1898** *Bulletin* (Sydney) 4 June (Red Page), And his lady love's his 'donah', Or his 'clinah' or his 'tart', Or his 'little bit o' muslin', As it used to be his 'bart'. **1900** *Western Champion* (Barcaldine) 26 June 16/1 He makes a dart ter see his 'bart', Goes on th' randy dan.

basement. *Obs.* [f. *basement* lowest storey, from the position of solitary confinement cells.] In prison speech: solitary confinement.

1919 V. MARSHALL *World of Living Dead* 33 He'd done lots o' basement, lots o' bread an' water, an' it hadn't killed him.

bash, *v.* [Transf. (often joc.) use of *bash* to strike.] *trans.* In various informal phrases, **to bash the spine (scrub**, etc.): see EAR-BASH, SCRUB-BASH, SPINE-BASH *v.*

1945 I.L. IDRIESS *Horrie Wog-Dog* 6 At our tent all the Rebels were 'bashing the spine', sprawled out in various attitudes of 'I don't care'. **1965** F. HARDY *Yarns of Billy Borker* 56 Always bashing their ear about how much money he was making, about having shares in the B.H.P., a barbecue in the backyard and a didee in the house. **1968** *Swag* (Sydney) i. 40/3 In temperatures around the 100 mark, the police shore the sheep, and bashed scrub to keep them alive. **1977** T. RONAN *Mighty Men on Horseback* 30 Here I have been bashing your ears.

Hence **bashing** *vbl. n.*

1920 *Land of Lyre Bird* (S. Gippsland Pioneers' Assoc.) 74 In the heavy blackbutt spar country a style of scrub-cutting, known as 'bashing' or 'wild-dog flash', was adopted after a few years.

basic wage. A standard minimum wage for an adult unskilled worker as determined by arbitration, orig. based on an assessment of living costs. Also *attrib.*

1911 *5 CAR* 14 There seems to be no doubt that the cost of living is increasing; but the evidence does not justify me in saying how much, or in altering the amount of what I may now call the basic wage by any definite sum. **1916** *10 CAR* 477 It is also reassuring to see a consensus of opinion as to the need for finding a basic wage, based on the cost of living. **1919** *Age* (Melbourne) 29 Nov. 16/3 The Prime Minister stated . . that the commission would be fully clothed with power to ascertain what was a fair basic wage. **1929** G. ANDERSON *Fixation of Wages* 187 The term 'basic wage' was first used by Mr Justice Higgins, and is the term commonly used in Australia. **1937** W. HATFIELD *I find Aust.* 205, I got a job painting, and was . . overjoyed to get on to something *supposed* to have a margin of skill in it and lift it above basic-wage labouring. **1947** E. GEORGE *January & August* 164 I'm sure I don't know what he expects me to do, with him on the basic wage, and eight of us to put our feet under the table at every meal. **1953** H.P. BROWN *Basic Wage Case* 74 In the March Quarter 1951 . . the basic wage was up 73% but average earnings were up 81%. **1961** *Bulletin* (Sydney) 8 Feb. 11/1 Men who are not found employment will be entitled to receive the State basic wage of £14 5s. weekly for six months. **1965** *Austral. Encycl.* I. 445 To most Australians the idea of a 'basic wage' is so familiar that few realize that it is almost unique to the Commonwealth. **1978** R.H. CONQUEST *Dusty Distances* 18 That's ten bob a week more than Queensland's basic wage.

basket, *attrib.* and *n.*

A. Used *attrib.* in Special Comb. **basket fence**: see quot. 1890.

1872 G.S. BADEN-POWELL *New Homes for Old Country* 208 For sheep . . is made the 'basket fence'. Stakes are driven in, and then pliant 'stuff' interwoven, as in a stake hedge in England. **1890** A. MACKAY *Austral. Agriculturist* (ed. 2) 32 'Basket' Fence . . is made by driving five feet six inch stakes in the ground with mauls, to a depth of 9 to 12 inches, and four feet six inches apart; saplings from about two inches in diameter are then closely entwined with the stakes to a height of four feet six inches. [**1913** M.A. MCMANUS *Reminisc. Maranoa District* 27, I knew three men to put up a large 'basket' sheep yard in three days, made of saplings woven basket fashion between upright stakes.] **1979** J. BIRMINGHAM et al. *Austral. Pioneer Technol.* 33 In the brigalow country of Queensland a 'basket fence' was made, interweaving saplings around posts sunk into the ground. This was cheap and quick to erect.

B. *n.* [Cf. U.S. *basket lunch, meeting, picnic*: see OEDS *sb.* B. 2.] PLATE. Also *attrib.*

1900 *Advocate* (Burnie) 3 Dec. 3/5 A Monster Picnic... Heads of families are requested to *provide 'baskets'*; the committee will find hot water and crockery. **1946** *Coast to Coast 1945* 178 Eight tonight sharp. Supper following. Ladies bring a basket. **1965** R.H. CONQUEST *Horses in Kitchen* 35 Bush dances were usually basket affairs. Married ladies brought baskets, in which were cakes and sandwiches.

bastard, *a.* and *n.* [Transf. use of *bastard* illegitimate child. The adjectival use is common elsewhere but produces some distinctively Austral. collocations. The weakened and generalized use of the noun is also widespread though often remarked on as characteristically Austral.]

A. *adj.* Incorporated in the names of some plants and animals which closely resemble their namesakes, as **bastard box,** any of several rough-barked *Eucalyptus* trees; **dory,** any of several fish of Australian coastal waters (see quots.); **mahogany,** BANGALAY.

1814 *HRA* (1916) 1st Ser. VIII. 222 The **Bastard Box** Bark No. 4 . . is very thick and hard. **1824** *Austral.* (Sydney) 11 Nov. 3 A described, but unpublished species of eucalyptus, very generally known and distinguished throughout the Colony (perhaps from its want of legitimate worth, as a timber), by the name of bastard-box. **1834** G. BENNETT *Wanderings N.S.W.* I. 253 Different species of *Eucalypti* . . among them . . 'Bastard box tree', (Bargan of the aborigines). **1845** C. GRIFFITH *Present State & Prospects Port Phillip* 120 The principal trees are the six kinds of Eucalyptus, namely, the white gum, the red gum, the bastard box or peppermint, the box, the stringy bark, and the iron bark. **1880** J. BONWICK *Resources Qld.* 37 Peppermints are often content with inferior ground, like the Bastard box, Yellow Iron-bark. **1902** *Proc. R. Soc. Qld.* XVII. 92 No ringbarked country, but white-stemmed gum trees, rough barked bastard box, and silver-leafed peppermints. **1904** J.H. MAIDEN *Notes on Commercial Timbers N.S.W.* 14 A Yellow or Bastard Box . . will be found, in some districts, to display a great affinity to the true yellow box. **1957** F. CLUNE *Fortune Hunters* 13 Level sheep country, sparsely treed with wilga, mulga, saltbush and bastard box (which polite people call 'shiny-leaf box'). **1896** F.G. AFLALO *Sketch Nat. Hist. Aust.* 225 The Old Wife of Port Jackson and elsewhere is a remarkable little member of the perch family. The names by which it is known in the Melbourne Market, 'Zebra-fish' or '**Bastard Dory**', are considerably more appropriate. **1906** D.G. STEAD *Fishes of Aust.* 176 The Silver Dory (*Cyttus australis*) . . in Tasmania . . is known as 'Bastard Dory'. **1924** C.E. LORD *Synopsis Vertebrate Animals Tas.* 66 Zebra fish (*Enoplosus armatus*) known in NSW as 'Old Wife'. It is also called the Bastard Dory. **1827** *HRA* (1923) 3rd Ser. VI. 503 The Banks on both sides are covered with very large timber . . such as **Bastard Mahogany**. **1880** *Proc. Linnean Soc. N.S.W.* V. 464 *E. botryoides* . . the 'Bastard Mahogany' or 'Bangalay' of workmen, occurring for the most part in moist sandy places near the coast. **1915** *Bulletin* (Sydney) 2 Sept. 26/2 The bastard mahogany is a galloping grower.

B. *n.*

1. Used variously of a person; sometimes derogatory (but without any suggestion of illegitimacy), freq. good-humoured if sometimes edged. See quots.

1892 *Bulletin* (Sydney) 26 Mar. 19/2 Here's the bleedin' push, me covey—here's a bastard from the bush! **1899** *Ibid.* 7 Oct. 31/4 Anyone trespassing in this paddock will be . . prosecuted by the --- bastard who owns this run. **1902** *Truth* (Sydney) 11 May 7/4 They called me all sorts of names, from *an Irish washerwoman* to *a bastard.* **1918** C.E.W. BEAN *Official Hist. Aust. 1914–18* (1942) VI. 16 'Would yer, yer bastard!'—and you look out of the window and find that it is all spoken with a grin. **1929** F. MANNING *Middle Parts of Fortune* I. 39 'Has anyone seen anything of Redmain?' 'Yes, sir,' cried Pike, with sullen anger in his voice. 'The poor bastard's dead, sir.' **1932** R.W. THOMPSON *Down Under* 26 We were gradually being initiated into Australian slang... 'Listen, brother. If a man calls you a bastard, don't get sore—it don't mean nothing.' **1939** G. DIGBY

Down Wind 275, I know the boss of that pub, and he's a vindictive little bastard. **1944** J. DEVANNY *By Tropic Sea & Jungle* 164 As regards humans, if they like a man he's all right; if they don't like him he's just a bastard. No venom; just plain facts. **1961** L. GLASSOP *We were Rats* (ed. 3) 149 'G'day, ya old bastard,' said Jim, and I was amused again by the thought that the Tommies could never get used to our main term of endearment. **1968** *Sydney Morning Herald* 4 July 4/2 The Premier, Mr Askin, was clapped and cheered yesterday when he told a luncheon meeting that he had advised a policeman to run over demonstrators trying to block President Johnson's motorcade in Sydney in 1966... He had turned to the policeman and had said 'Run over the bastards.' **1972** *Bulletin* (Sydney) 1 Apr. 62/3 If they drank a bit more wine they wouldn't be such miserable bastards. **1978** R.H. CONQUEST *Dusty Distances* 128 There are times when I even think the good bastards outnumber the bad bastards.

2. Anything considered disagreeable or unpleasant.

1919 V. MARSHALL *World of Living Dead* 12 Bastard, ain't it! Fer the love o' Gawd, give us a taste o' snout. **1942** A.L. HASKELL *Waltzing Matilda* 36 Too right; it's a fair cow of a day, the bastard's boiling over. **1954** T. RONAN *Vision Splendid* 157 It's a bastard to be old. **1963** J. O'GRADY *Things they do to You* 158 It was a bit of a bastard being stuck in hospital. **1965** D. MARTIN *Hero of Too* 324 Life's a bastard, and we're all bastards together. **1972** *Bulletin* (Sydney) 2 Sept. 50/1 A bastard of a Budget—for the next Treasurer. **1979** D. LOCKWOOD *My Old Mates & I* 147 Biggest bloody dunny in the world. Thirty thousand square miles of the bastard.

bastardization. [f. *bastardize* to debase.] In some educational institutions: a college ritual of physical and psychological harassment, in which newly-enrolled students are required to perform certain (usu. humiliating) tasks.

1964 *Bulletin* (Sydney) 6 June 22/2 Fourth Class cadets suffer what is known as 'bastardisation'. They have to listen to the 6.45 a.m. news and they may have to repeat this back at breakfast, item by item. **1969** *Canberra Times* 19 Sept. 2/1 'Bastardisation' is the unofficial term for what is officially known at RMC as 'the assimilation and regimental training of the fourth class'. Initiation was outlawed more than 10 years ago: the continuing process of 'bastardisation' seems to be taking its place. **1969** *Kings Cross Whisper* (Sydney) lxxix. 5/3 The certificates are designed to prove to the public that bastardisation has ended at the college. **1970** *Bulletin* (Sydney) 11 July 19/2 Bastardisation recurs in cycles, a bit like long hair and short skirts. **1974** *Telegraph* (Brisbane) 9 Oct. 48/1 Tasmania's police training college is to have a new superintendent following an inquiry into bastardisation. **1983** *Sydney Morning Herald* 13 Apr. 1/3 Bastardisation, or the systematic hazing of junior cadets, has been back at Duntroon for 10 years.

bastardry. Unpleasant treatment or activity: see quot. 1945.

1945 S.J. BAKER *Austral. Lang.* 156 *Bastardry*, ill treatment, injustice, anything unpleasant, especially when done at the whim of a superior officer. **1948** *Khaki Bush & Bigotry* (1968) 98 Strikes me old Wimp will be slower on the bastardry than he used to be... Old swine he is. **1965** E. LAMBERT *Long White Night* 127 If it were anyone else but Tony stuck up there with those two, I'd think up some real bastardry. **1978** H.C. BAKER *I was Listening* 161 What sort of new bastardry they were cooking up now. **1983** *Age* (Melbourne) 27 Oct. 13/3 People in the Kremlin.. will undoubtedly store up the Grenada episode as a good excuse for their future bastardry.

batch, *v.* Also **bach.** [f. U.S. *bach* to live as a bachelor: see OEDS *sb.* and *v.*] *intr.* To live on one's own, or provide for oneself, simply and without the usual domestic conveniences. Also **to batch it.**

1882 W. SOWDEN *N.T. as it Is* 154 Supposing he lives in a hut and 'batches', this is the kind of bill he is confronted with. **1890** *Bull-Ant* (Melbourne) 28 Aug. 17/1, I have not seen the little white-headed.. girl that batches lately. I wonder if something has gone wrong with the works. **1892** G.L. JAMES *Shall I try Aust.?* 116 Boarding-houses soon spring up, where he can be very well fed at about 2s. daily; but, if he elects to 'batch' himself, I have heard many declare that they can live well for 7s. weekly. **1900** *Bulletin* (Sydney) 2 June 31/1 She 'batched' for economy's sake. **1907** *Native Companion* Sept. 20 He had no liking for company, and 'batched' in an old, tin-roofed, paling skillion. **1911** E.M. CLOWES *On Wallaby through Vic.* 128 Various men.. 'batch' in places such as these, getting their meals out at some handy tea-room or restaurant. **1914** C. MACKNESS *Gem of Flat* 11 Grandfather and child 'batched it' in the old house. **1920** W. MCGUFFIN *Austral. Tales of Border* 156 He could also cook fairly well, so he batched for himself. **1926** A.A.B. APSLEY *Amateur Settlers* 52 The farmer is 'baching'—that is to say, has no wife and is living, or rather camping on his block. **1940** G.W. LOVEJOY *In Journeyings Often* 18 At Brewarrina we only 'batch' once a day (for tea) at the Rectory and go out to the Far West Boarding House for breakfast and dinner. **1960** *Overland* xix. 7 He who'd batched in content since his old mother died. **1977** *Nat. Times* (Sydney) 17 Jan. 6/2 Evidently well enough for the two men to 'batch' at the Lodge for a few nights last week while their wives and families enjoyed holidays. **1985** P. CAREY *Illywhacker* 69 Goog stood on the veranda with the leg of mutton still grasped in his bony hand. 'Go on,' the father bellowed, 'get on with it before I come and give you a clout across the ear-hole.'.. 'They're good boys,' Stu said, 'but they never batched before.'

Hence **batcher** *n.*, **batching** *vbl. n.* and *ppl. a.*

1895 *Bulletin* (Sydney) 28 Sept. 27/1 The two Macks were the best '**batchers**' in the district; they were as neat and as careful of things as two old women. **1896** *Worker* (Sydney) 11 July 4/2 The luxury of being alone with his sorrow was denied him, however, for anon neighbouring 'batchers' kept dropping in. **1901** *Illawarra Mercury* (Wollongong) 7 Feb. 2/5 He would like to call under the notice of the assessors the unfair way in which 'batchers' 'huts were rated in his ward. **1931** *Bulletin* (Sydney) 1 Apr. 20/1, I think I'll sling this **batchin'** game, an' get meself a bride. **1936** M. FRANKLIN *All that Swagger* (1980) 126 There was no such feast as at Wong's, but the baching was improved by rice and potatoes boiled in the one billy-can with the salt junk.

batch, *n.* Also **bach.** [f. prec. but prob. infl. by N.Z. *bach* a makeshift dwelling: see OEDS *sb.* 2 and quot. 1911.] A holiday house or WEEKENDER, often simple and freq. at the beach.

[N.Z. **1911** *N.Z. Truth* (Wellington) 28 Jan. 6/1 A room in the 'batch' formerly occupied by Munn, whose belongings were still stored there.] **1929** C.H. WINTER *Story of 'Bidgee Queen* 98 In seaside 'bach' or far-back pub. **1957** D. NILAND *Call me when Cross turns Over* 122 She stood in the yard close to the bach, but in the shadows. **1973** *Overland* lvi. 19 They have what they call 'batches' (derived from bachelor and batching) which, in the main, are badly built weekenders. **1981** *Sydney Morning Herald* 3 Oct. 44/4 It [*sc. The Macquarie Dictionary*] lists over 1,000 distinctive items of vocabulary from New Zealand.. such as hoot (money), bach or batch (in the sense of a weekend cottage) [etc.].

bathers, *pl.* A swimming costume.

1930 K.S. PRICHARD *Haxby's Circus* 230 If they went down the lakes to the coast perhaps they would find Mart and his mother there on the beach in bathers. **1940** G.B. PHILIP *Sixty Yrs. Recoll. Eastern Suburbs* 62 Grandma and grandpa went out.. in their 'skirted' costumes and 'baggy bathers' to dare the waves. **1946** A. GREEN *We were (Riff) R.A.A.F.* 22 Soldiers clad in bathers, sun-glasses and a service brand of sun-helmet.. read books. **1951** R. DORIEN *Venturing to Aust.* 182 After the picnic, we lazed, then put on bathing suits, called 'bathers'. **1965** L. ROWLANDS *Bird in Hand* 105 'Doesn't Syd look a treat in his bathers,' Violet said. Clem hadn't heard anyone say bathers since he couldn't recall when. It reminded him of country river banks and people cavorting round in old motor tyres in the water, avoiding snags. **1968** E. PAGRAM *Never had it so Good* 67 On to the clothing department to buy myself a swimming costume, and some panties. I came away with 'bathers' and a pair of 'gussies'. **1981** A.B. FACEY *Fortunate Life* 114 We lay on the sand on the beach, then hired some bathers and went for a swim. **1985** *Good Weekend* (Sydney) 7 Dec. 58/2 We fled through the gravelly schoolyard down the back streets to snatch our bathers from home before mum knew what we were up to.

bathing togs: see TOGS.

Bathurst burr. [f. the name of a town in central N.S.W.] The S. American plant *Xanthium spinosum* (fam. Asteraceae), the spiny stems of which bear fruits covered with numerous slender hooked spines; the fruit of the plant.

1853 *Moreton Bay Free Press* 1 Feb. 3/4 The Bathurst Burr is spreading widely in some stations on the Downs. **1865** *Sydney Punch* 6 May 395/2 Trimmed with a curtain of the fragrant Bathurst Burr; which from its crochet-hook nature is admirably adapted to hold on the hair arranged beneath it. **1880** J. BONWICK *Resources Qld.* 47 The Bathurst Burr is a great annoyance to the animal's skin, and an injury to wool. **1894** *Bulletin* (Sydney) 23 June 24/4 The men who introduced the first Kanakas to Australia will go down to posterity arm in arm with the calamitous persons who introduced the Bathurst burr. **1898** *Western Champion* (Barcaldine) 10 May 3/3 And what is the matter with sending a pair of dingoes (the Royal Family are fond of dogs), and also a few bunches of bathurst burr for placing in vases about the royal drawing rooms. **1903** *Truth* (Sydney) 4 Jan. 8/2 Mr Crick smiled like a Bathurst burr in full bloom. **1913** W.K. HARRIS *Outback in Aust.* 149 Like many of the noxious things in Australia, the Bathurst burr is an imported article. **1924** 'S. RUDD' *Me an' Son* 139 All the time I clung to his mane like a Batherst [*sic*] burr. **1937** D. GUNN *Links with Past* 219 When gold was discovered horses were in great demand, and some enterprising person imported a ship load.. from Valparaiso... These horses were.. driven to Bathurst... The horse-breakers.. combed lots of burr out of their tails; this seed came up after the first rain and the plants got the name of 'Bathurst burr'. **1949** J. MORRISON *Creeping City* 42, I was dragged up on a back-station in a tin and hessian hut—fly-blown meat, sour water, bung eyes, bare feet, and Bathurst burrs. **1967** E. HUXLEY *Their Shining Eldorado* 191 Bathurst burr. It gets into the fleece and ruins the quality. **1977** K. GILBERT *Living Black* 242 When we caught the little bastards on their own we sat them down on top of Bathurst burr bushes by way of apology.

battery. *Mining.* A set of stamps used for crushing quartz. Also *attrib.*

1858 *Colonial Mining Jrnl.* Sept. 11/3 The machinery used in crushing quartz consists of 3 batteries of 12 stamps each, and one of 8 stamps and a Chilian mill. **1888** 'R. BOLDREWOOD' *Robbery under Arms* (1937) 247 We heard the row of the cradles and the clang and bang of the stampers in the quartz-crushing batteries. **1895** A.C. BICKNELL *Travel & Adventure Northern Qld.* 117, I hear the ring of the battery stamp, I guess I'm coming to a mining camp. **1895** *Worker* (Sydney) 21 Dec. 2/1 Within a radius of two miles there were some 15 or 16 batteries working, and the din to the unpractised ear was terrible, though old stagers could not sleep without the dread accompaniment. **1951** G. FARWELL *Outside Track* 33 He and his first partner had bought up an old government four-stamp battery for £300. **1966** H. GYE *Father clears Out* 16 An offshoot from our old reef provided the quartz that Chester was to cart down to our little home battery.

battery gang. *Hist.* [f. *battery* fortified gun emplacement + GANG.] A party of convicts assigned to labour in the construction of a (gun) battery.

1801 *HRA* (1915) 1st Ser. III. 257 If a prisoner either makes the purchase or sells the article, he will be severely punished and work six months in the battery gang. **1803** *Sydney Gaz.* 10 July, The Prisoner Dobson is to receive 100 Lashes, and to labour in the Battery-gang at George's Head.

battle, *v.*

1. *intr.* Usu. of one with few natural advantages: to work doggedly and with little reward, to struggle for a livelihood, to display courage in so doing.

1895 [see *battling*, *vbl. n.*]. **1896** H. LAWSON *In Days when World was Young* 40 But the men who never 'battle' always seem to travel aft. **1897** *Antipodean* (Melbourne) 92 He went in and 'battled', when better players were failing hopelessly. **1903** *Truth* (Sydney) 19 Apr. 1/2 You, no more than any other Premier, can maintain your position without 'battling'. **1925** A. WRIGHT *Boy from Bullarah* 22 When a man's battling, it's no good bein' particular as to how he makes a rise, as long as he don't take anyone down. **1932** J. TRURAN *Green Mallee* 84 He's a returned soldier, battlin' for a livin' like a whole lot more of 'em. **1937** D. GUNN *Links with Past* 11 After battling for two years, father sold Wyaga. **1939** K. TENNANT *Foveaux* 178 All her life Mrs Thompson had been what she called 'battling for a crust', and although in this epic battle she had never been quite knocked out, many a time she had only been saved by the gong. **1955** M. DURACK *Keep him my Country* (1956) 158 Well, I'm battling now to send Penny away to school—down to the Alice maybe. **1970** *Bulletin* (Sydney) 21 Mar. 23/1 Frank Husey, the wharfie, . . became a national figure in the 1950s when he battled for his right to refuse payment of a political levy to the Waterside Workers' Federation. **1978** D. STUART *Wedgetail View* 234 She battled on, poor, trapped, with a crook heart, and a mob of hungry kids to be fed and clothed and sheltered. **1981** A.B. FACEY *Fortunate Life* 137 She thinks it's a shame that a boy your age has to battle along on his own.

2. Of an unemployed itinerant.

a. *intr.* To seek to subsist, esp. while seeking employment.

1897 *Worker* (Sydney) 11 Sept. 1/1 And while in search of shearing work he rides from hut to hut, He says he's merely 'battling' round and looking for a 'cut'. **1899** *Bulletin* (Sydney) 19 Aug. 32/1 Mick Sheedy and Jack Devine had battled from the Diamantina to the 'North West Corner' without having so much as got their hands into wool during the whole dreary ten weeks. **1903** *Ibid.* 10 Sept. 36/2 Jenkyn Jessop (*aetat* 70) . . battled about in the Bakblox until he could battle no more. **1944** *Ibid.* 8 Nov. 12/3 I've seen coves like you on the track, game little battlers who get a bit o' tucker in a fair-dinkum way an' then have it taken from 'em by loafin' bullies too lazy t' battle for themselves. **1965** R.H. CONQUEST *Horses in Kitchen* 113 We regarded giving assistance to battlers as a sort of insurance, as there was always the chance we'd be battling ourselves some day.

b. *trans.* To obtain (sustenance or a means of subsistence) by the use of one's wits; to employ one's wits against (a person, etc.) to obtain sustenance. Also *intr.*

1902 H. LAWSON *Children of Bush* 88 They were tramping along the track towards Bourke; they were very hard-up and had to 'battle' for tucker and tobacco along the track. **1947** *Bulletin* (Sydney) 1 Oct. 28/3 A cove from the Marthaguy battled a hunk of corned beef from a Narromine butcher. **1948** *Ibid.* 19 May 23/1 We had inspected an emu-bobbing contract, battled the owner to a price and were set to start. **1950** *Ibid.* 13 Sept. 12/2 We'd battled Wagga for a bit of tucker and were chewing it under the bridge when Mat said, 'I got a job this afternoon cleanin' windows. Worth half a nicker.'

3. *intr.* To attempt to earn one's living at racecourses, esp. by punting (in a small way).

1895 [implied at BATTLER 3]. **1898** T. HAYDON *Sporting Reminisc.* 118, I don't believe there is another man living who can present such a healthy and youthful appearance after so many years of 'battling', and its attendant excitement. **1915** A. WRIGHT *Sport from Hollowlog Flat* 20 Battling on the pony courses for a living, soon began to pall.

4. *intr.* To work as a prostitute.

1898 [implied at BATTLER 4]. **1901** *Truth* (Sydney) 18 Aug. 5/3 After a few years of 'battling' in the Chow's baneful brothel, they were cast adrift to swell the ranks of the toe-rag crowd. **c 1907** C.W. Chandler *Darkest Adelaide* 35 Prostitution though most terrible and degrading in any shape or form reaches its most forbidding form when married women are found out battling for cash. **1912** L. ESSON *Red Gums* 37 All the tarts is waitin', Linin' Little Lon, In ther [*sic*] flashest clobber, Battlin' ter git on.

Hence **battling** *vbl. n.* and *ppl. a.*

1895 *Bulletin* (Sydney) 13 Nov. 27/2 Six long years' battling in the bush is not so very gay, And so I chucked the job and took once more the Sydney way. **1897** *Ibid.* 7 Aug. (Red Page), *Battling—i.e.*, struggling—On the Johnnie Russel. A city term, quite new in the bush. Used in Q. and N.S.W. towns—mainly by public-house loafers. **1900** H. LAWSON *Verses Pop. & Humorous* 58 For 'battling' is a trade to learn, and I've served seven years. **1918** *Bulletin* (Sydney) 6 June 22/2 In the battling days I was operating a slaughter-yard for 'stags' and other game at an out-station on a Riverina squattage. **1919** A. WRIGHT *Game of Chance* 43 Some of his sharp acquaintances of the 'battling' fraternity. **1960** *N.T. News* (Darwin) 8 Jan. 11/6 One highlight of the game was the battling of young . . Muir for Saints. **1977** V. PRIDDLE *Larry & Jack* 172 They were so dirty . . that the girls actually laughed at them. Jack said: 'This is the penalty you pay when you are just a battling cow cocky'. **1982** PAGE & INGPEN *Aussie Battlers* 5 Only the acid test of 'battling' can prove the true metal of Australians.

battle, *n.* [Back-formation from BATTLER 4.] In the phr. **to be on the battle,** to work as a prostitute.

1944 L. GLASSOP *We were Rats* 146 She tells me how she useter be on the battle. . . To think she'd been a chromo all the time! **1969** F.B. VICKERS *No Man is Himself* 17 She's charged with being on the battle.

battleaxe. *Obs.* [Fig. use of *battle-axe* weapon.] Rum.

1871 *Austral. Town & Country Jrnl.* (Sydney) 18 Mar. 335/2 To brace up his nerves with a drop of 'battle-axe', as the christening was conducted on strict temperance principles. **1888** G.O. PRESHAW *Banking under Difficulties* 66 Carmichael put a bottle of the best 'battle-axe' into my valise. **1899** P.W. MCNALLY *Life & Adventures* 30 Several good stockmen . . were made special constables. . . These 'specials' had a 'rare old time of it' in Roma, billiards and battleaxe being the game and the tipple.

battler. [f. BATTLE *v.*]

1. One who battles: see BATTLE *v.* 1. Also *attrib.*

1896 H. LAWSON *While Billy Boils* 26, I sat on him pretty hard for his pretensions, and paid him out for all the patronage he'd worked off on me . . and told him never to pretend to me again that he was a battler. **1897** *Antipodean* (Melbourne) 91 In the latest Colonial slang . . a man who plays a determined game is called a 'battler'. **1911** *Huon Times* (Franklin) 29 Apr. 6/4 At any rate, battlers for 'Yes' say they are scoring heavily off the sympathies of those who think both sides should be reported. **1919** C.A. BERNAYS *Qld. Politics during Sixty Yrs.* 128 He was a battler for the grievances of the manual worker. **1926** L.C.E. GEE *Bush Tracks & Gold Fields* 65 And so he rambles on, this cheerful, hardy old battler, and in the unsteady glance of his honest, old eyes and his disconnected speech, I read the mark of the Australian solitudes—'white ants' they call it up north. **1939** I.L. IDRIESS *Cyaniding for Gold* 9 A surprising amount of gold has been . . won . . by battlers who have rigged up a rough plant and treated the material just by 'chucking in a bit of cyanide and a lump of lime'. **1941** K. TENNANT *Battlers* 182 She was a battler, Snow admitted; impudent, hardy, cool, and she could take a 'knock-back' as though it didn't matter, and come up to meet the next blow. **1946** *Austral. New Writing* 27, I once saw Old Madge, a metho-stewed old battler, weeping. **1954** T. RONAN *Vision Splendid* 222 Most of the travelling stock was also the property of the battlers. These were hard-bitten men who had spent years building up herds on country which, for the most part, was theirs only because it was so poor the big holding companies didn't want it. **1959** D. LOCKWOOD *Crocodiles & Other People* 76 He is still what the Territory knows as a Battler. That means that he is building up a station from scratch, battling against lack of capital, isolation and distance from markets. **1965** F. HARDY *Yarns of Billy Borker* 102 Tom and Ron would go around Footscray collecting bets off old sheilas and battlers. **1965** K. SMITH *OGF* 58 Everybody in Australia has his position. Roughly speaking, there are three kinds of people in this country: the rich, the middle class and the battlers. **1970** *Bulletin* (Sydney) 14 Mar. 28/2 Battler pastoralists in the Northern Territory . . cannot see any cause to resist the Americans with bulging wallets. **1974** BLAZEY & CAMPBELL *Political Dice Men* 37 Sneddon . . is the essence of the Australian 'battler'. His life has been a long struggle to rise above his depressed background. **1986** *Nat. Times* (Sydney) 10 Jan. 18/1 'You bloody trendies,' he shouted, 'you move . . and the housing prices go bloody berserk. And what happens to your poor Aussie battler. . . One day this whole place'll be just like Balmain—a refuge for the terminally smug.'

Also *fig.*

1919 *Smith's Weekly* (Sydney) 15 Mar. 2/1 That remarkable battler, the sparrow, is to be met with in every part of the civilized world nowadays. **1968** D. O'GRADY *Bottle of Sandwiches* 128 But the chooks were really up against it. . . Real battlers.

2. Of an unemployed, or irregularly employed person.

a. In the country: a swagman or itinerant worker. See BATTLE *v.* 2 a.

1898 *Bulletin* (Sydney) 2 Apr. 14/3, I found patch after patch destroyed. Almost everyone I met blamed the unfortunate 'battler', and I put it down to some of the Sydney 'talent' until . . I caught two Chows vigorously destroying melon-vines. **1906** *Ibid.* 19 Apr. 39/1 They were old, white-bearded, travel-stained battlers of the track. **1910** *Ibid.* 15 Dec. 30/4 The first to arrive was the Lost Cat, one of the most noted of the Battlers in the West. **1919** R.J. CASSIDY *Gipsy Road* 89 For three days the Old Union Battler had trudged across the plains. **1932** D.B. O'CONNOR *Belle of Barrine* 3 Then laugh, ye sturdy station hands, Ye drovers, gougers, battlers, Ye farmers of the tablelands, Ye men who man the rattlers. **1938** *Bulletin* (Sydney) 5 Jan. 21/1 Putting rum in one's boots . . is by no means restricted to old battlers on the track. **1952** *Ibid.* 9 Jan. 17/4 In the days when an outback battler could live well enough on a few bob a day 'Tarcutta' Ted used to do odd jobs. **1960** *N.T. News* (Darwin) 22 Jan. 6/3 Bella was a first-class bush cook and very generous in her handouts to many a battler travelling this district in the depression days. **1965** R.H. CONQUEST *Horses in Kitchen* 173 Tourist? Me? No. A b-- old battler, that's me. A hobo. **1976** B. SCOTT *Compl. Bk. Austral. Folk Lore* 302 Oh, yes, I am a battler of the old-time shearin' push, We humped Matilda often o'er the plain land and the bush. **1982** PAGE & INGPEN *Aussie Battlers* 6 The average Australian's image of a battler does seem to be that of a kind of Henry Lawson character: a bushie of the colonial era, complete with quart pot and swag, down on his luck but still resourceful and cheerful.

b. In an urban context: an unemployed person who lives by opportunism. See BATTLE *v.* 2 b.

1946 F. CLUNE *Try Nothing Twice* 7 George was a great battler. His technique was to get us into a crowded tram, and wait until 'Mrs Fares-please' came. Then . . look pathetic, and tell the truth—'We haven't any money.' **1965** F. HARDY *Yarns of Billy Borker* 104 Any Footscray battler could get a few quid off Murphy, just for the asking. **1976** S. WELLER *Bastards I have Met* 100 He was a battler, into all the lurks about the place and just one jump ahead of the coppers all the time.

3. One who frequents racecourses in search of a living, esp. from punting. See BATTLE *v.* 3.

1895 C. CROWE *Austral. Slang Dict.* 7 Battlers, broken-down backers of horses still sticking to the game. **1914** A.B. PATERSON in C. Semmler *Banjo of Bush* (1966) 310 A battler is a turf hanger-on who has not capital enough to be a backer, not personal magnetism enough to be a successful whisperer, and not sense enough to get work. **1925** A. WRIGHT *Boy from Bullarah* 23 He betook himself with his few remaining shillings to the home of the battler—Randwick. **1936** A.B. PATERSON *Shearer's Colt* 8 The speaker was Dear Boy Dickson, turf urger, battler and general hanger-on at race-meetings. **1966** S.J. BAKER *Austral. Lang.* (ed. 2) 236 *Battler*, a small-time bettor who attempts to live on what he can earn by following horses.

4. A prostitute. See BATTLE *v.* 4.

1898 *Bulletin* (Sydney) 17 Dec. (Red Page), A *bludger* is about the lowest grade of human thing, and is a brothel bully. . . A *battler* is the feminine. **c 1907** C.W. CHANDLER *Darkest Adelaide* 8/2 He evidently wished to impress me that he was no mug so far as bludging was concerned. I told him I would not mind taking on a tart myself—an extra good battler preferred. **1956** PARK & NILAND *Drums go Bang* 142 A battler is Sydneyese for prostitute. **1978** R.J. RODDEWIG *Green Bans* 7 A battler was also the name given a woman who earned a few extra quid for her old man by sleeping around.

bauera /'baʊərə/. [The plant genus *Bauera* was named by Joseph Banks (in Henry C. Andrews *Botanist's repository for new and rare plants* (1801) Pl. 198) after Austrian botanical artists Franz (1758–1840) and Ferdinand (1760–1826) *Bauer*.] Any shrub of the Austral. genus *Bauera* (fam. Saxifragaceae), of spreading habit and with wiry branches. Freq. *attrib.*

1801 H.C. ANDREWS *Botanist's Repository* III. Pl. 198, *Bauera rubioides*. Three-leaved Bauera. **1835** *Hobart Town Almanack* 70 Madder leaved Bauera. **1888** R.M. JOHNSTON *Systematic Acct. Geol. Tas.* 6 The Bauera scrub is met with in the wet flats along the stream courses. On open hill sides it is a tiny, beautiful shrub with soft verticillate leaf whorls and lovely pink and white blossoms. **1891** J. FENTON *Bush Life Tas.* (1964) 38 We got entangled in a wiry maze of bauera scrub. **1968** P. ADAM SMITH *Tiger Country* 15, I gathered . . great garlands of a gay woodland type of wild rose, pale pink and pretty. The bushmen howled when they saw it. 'Bauera!' they shouted . . and told me . . that this is the most dreaded growth . . crawling and tangling itself around growing things. **1980** B. ROBERTS *Penalty of Adam* 14 He introduced him to the bush, to bull-ants, jack-jumpers, leeches, snakes, cutty-rushes, bauera.

bauple nut, var. BOPPLE NUT.

Bay. Usu. with **the.**

1. *Obs.*

a. BOTANY BAY 1.

1841 J. WARD Diary of Convict 113 The roll was called—and the gangs gone ashore; when we for Bay, as it is called were mustered into the Chapel, to wash. . . All the washing or wetting bustle is over; all the Bay men on Deck for inspection. **1842** *Legends of Aust.* Feb. 2 Mr Howard found himself on board the 'Pandora', bound for that place which the mate, who had been on two previous occasions to New South Wales, was pleased to designate, '*the* Bay'. **1843** *Sydney Morning Herald* 8 June 2/7 Would you rather be sent to the Hulks or the Bay? **1852** J. WEST *Hist. of Tas.* II. 150 They departed from the prison with huzzas . . exclaiming, 'what a glorious kangaroo hunt we will have at the Bay.' **1857** *V & P* (Vic. L.A.) III. 86, I have scarcely more than one or two men to try at weekly visits out of my 1000 men; whereas in the Bay you see no end of it.

b. Special Comb. **bay ship,** a ship carrying convicts from England to Botany Bay.

1825 *London Mag.* May II. 49 When they first leave the hulks, every man pulls of [*sic*] his hulk dress, and has given him a fresh dress . . then goes on board the Bay ship. **1834** H.W. BUNBURY *Early Days W.A.* (1930) 2 Here I am at last embarked in a 'Bay Ship', as the convicts call those bound to Botany Bay. **1836** 'W. R--s' *Fell Tyrant* 46 When a bay ship is ready you are sent on board with a written character. **1865** J.F. MORTLOCK *Experiences of Convict* 54 We learned that a 'bay ship' (vessels for New South Wales being so called) had anchored at Spithead.

2. Locally: an abbrev. of a place-name; a place by the sea.

a. Glenelg, S.A.

1883 *Adelaide Punch* 5 Jan. 422/1 At the Bay on the 28th. . . We went to commemorate the plantin' of the flagstaff by Capting Indmarsh. **1891** *Quiz* (Adelaide) 6 Mar. 7/2 The Bay, as we are apt to call Glenelg. **1933** *South Australiana* (1963) Sept. 69 Recent shells were collected on the shores of St. Vincent Gulf at 'the Bay' as Glenelg was mostly called then, and at the Semaphore.

b. Port Phillip Bay, Vic.

1915 C.J. DENNIS *Songs of Sentimental Bloke* 81 We're honey-moonin' down beside the Bay. **1934** V. PALMER *Swayne Family* 4 From the heavy seas outside they had slipped before the daylight into the quiet of the Bay. **1965** G. MCINNES *Road to Gundagai* 115 In Melbourne . . a ship was . . just going 'down the Bay' to Queenscliff, Portarlington or Geelong.

c. Long Bay Gaol, Sydney.

1918 V. MARSHALL *Jail from Within* 16 'If yer lucky yer might get a bite at the Bay tonight,' said the officer with brutal unconcern. **1939** K. TENNANT *Foveaux* 350 They can't send you out to the Bay on a Sunday, so you spend Sunday yarning with the chaps at Central and then Monday morning at six you get out to the Bay and put in your week. **1966** G.F. TROST *Call me Cabbie* 39 'I have just done ten years hard labour at Long Bay. For murder!' . . After ten years at the Bay, I had a pretty good idea what his next destination was. **1974** ADAMSON & HANFORD *Zimmer's Essay* 29 Long Bay Penitentiary is the largest prison in New South Wales. . . There are three reasons for the high turnover in The Bay.

Bay of Biscay, *attrib.* and *n.* [f. the popular association of stormy seas with the *Bay of Biscay.*]

A. *attrib.* Terrain of heavy clay soils forming mounds and depressions, often linear in form; lattice GILGAI. Freq. as **Bay of Biscay country, ground.**

1854 C.H. SPENCE *Clara Morison* II. 231 The occasional interruptions caused by a bad gully or an awkward piece of 'Bay of Biscay ground'. **1855** G.H. WATHEN *Golden Colony* 133 The soil is much richer than it is in those volcanic plains which, from their wavy surface, are known as 'Bay of Biscay Land'. **1872** 'RESIDENT' *Glimpses Life Vic.* 93 This dead level is occasionally varied by a tract of country known as Bay of Biscay ground, where the soil rises in countless small mounds, called 'dead men's graves', which resemble tiny solid waves. **1893** D. LINDSAY *Jrnl. Elder Sci. Exploring Exped.* 33 Travelled up a densely scrubby flat of hard yellowish clay, in which were some Bay of Biscay holes containing, in one or two instances, a little water. **1897** J.J. MURIF *From Ocean to Ocean* 152 Then came three miles of dangerous 'Bay of Biscay' ground; . . five miles of still treacherous track, on which were many patches of 'Biscay holes' and lengths of fallen timber; and then again the jungle. **1901** F.J. GILLEN *Diary* 24 Oct. (1968) 305 Our stage consisted of 22 miles of undulating country mostly forest with bay of biscay soil seamed in all directions with great cracks and very heavy travelling. **1944** M.J. O'REILLY *Bowyangs & Boomerangs* 124 There were a number of mud springs in very dangerous country. This is known as 'Bay of Biscay country'. It is a soft springy tract of swelling soil . . soft and silky smooth to touch, resembling Fuller's earth in quality and consistency. It bears a rough appearance; to walk on it is soft and silent, leaving a clear imprint as in snow. The soil does not drift, wind has no influence on it. **1951** E. HILL *Territory* 294 The mob goes drifting down through the pindan, light scrub in red sand, 'Bay o' Biscay' country, raggedy gullies and hills like tumbled waves in a big sea, 'drummy' country, a crust over limestone. **1968** LINKLATER & TAPP *Gather no Moss* 55 Mustering was dangerous work on Lawn Hill, because there was much Bay of Biscay country.

B. Rarely, as *n.*

1901 O. OSBORNE *Golden Jubilee* 8 And in the Bay of Biscay bogged Some teamsters were delayed for weeks. **1933** *Bulletin* (Sydney) 20 Dec. 34/1 The alternation of wet seasons or floodings on the one hand and of droughts on the other induces characteristic alternations of depressions and rises in heavy soils. These have received various local names, of which melonhole, gilgai, Bay of Biscay, devil-devil and crab-hole are the most frequently met. **1953** *Ibid.* 23 Dec. 12/2 In S.A., and probably in other parts of Australia, are tracts of soil called 'Bay of Biscay'. It's soil excellent for growing things, but very treacherous to build on.

bay whale. *Hist.* The southern right whale *Eubalaena australis.*

1820 *HRA* (1921) 3rd Ser. III. 458 In June, July and August the Bay or Black Whale Fishery is best carried on. That is the season when the whales come into the Bays to Calve.

bay whaler. *Hist.* **a.** One engaged in bay whaling. **b.** A boat used for bay whaling.

1867 *Australasian* (Melbourne) 12 Jan. 37/3 My first acquaintance with the bay-whaler was made at St. Paul's Island, or Amsterdam Island. *Ibid.* 2 Feb. 132/3 The coasts of New Zealand presented great attractions to the bay whalers. **1913** R. MCNAB *Old Whaling Days* 6 The *Waterloo* returned on the twenty-third with 14 tons of flax. During the following month—November—the remaining bay whalers returned to Sydney. **1934** W.J. DAKIN *Whalemen Adventurers* 28 The capture of Right whales could just as easily be undertaken from a shore station with row-boats of the usual whaling type, and this method became the common practice of the Bay whalers.

bay whaling, *vbl. n.* and *ppl. a. Hist.* Whaling from shore stations; engaging in this.

1837 W.B. RHODES *Whaling Jrnl.* 6 May (1954) 102 The season . . would be far advanced for Bay Whaling. **1838** T.H. JAMES *Six Months S.A.* 45 Men who have been discharged from the bay-whaling gangs, on the coast, and have come up to Adelaide to spend their wages. **1841** E.J. EYRE *Jrnls. Exped. Central Aust.* 14 June (1845) II. 77 He had some intention of calling at King George's Sound, when the Bay whaling was over. **1865** J.F. MORTLOCK *Experiences of Convict* 83 Formerly, bay-whaling returned large profits; now a whale or a seal is only seen at intervals few and far between. **1867** *Australasian* (Melbourne) 12 Jan. 37/3 There is no likelihood whatever of bay-whaling ever reassuming its ancient importance as a native industry. **1880** L.A MEREDITH *Tasmanian Friends & Foes* 235 It was bay-whaling we were, for black whales. . . There was no ship only boats employed. The station ashore was made in the neighbourhood of good whaling-ground, and the boats started out of a morning mostly before daylight. **1924** LORD & SCOTT *Synopsis Vertebrate Animals Tas.* 294 In the year 1806 the first 'Bay whaling' station was established at Ralph's Bay, River Derwent. **1954** W.B. RHODES *Whaling Jrnl.* p. xvi Introd., The pursuit in coastal waters of black whales was known as 'bay whaling'.

beachcomber. *Pearling.* [Spec. use of *beachcomber* one who seeks a subsistence living on a beach: see OED(S.] See quot. 1907.

1907 A. MACDONALD *In Land of Pearl & Gold* 289 The poorer class of pearlers are termed 'beachcombers' by their more fortunate fellows. ***c* 1920** E. WOOD *Under Southern Cross* 113 Even 'beachcombers' had to pay four pounds for a licence to allow them to search for pearls. **1940** E. HILL *Great Austral. Loneliness* (ed. 2) 242 Taking out a beach-comber's licence and a permit to employ native labour, you hire an old lugger at Broome for £1 a month . . and set out for where you fancy 'up east'.

beacher. *Surfing.* A wave which a body-surfer rides to the beach.

1930 *Surf: All about It* 10 The gentle art of scraping your nose . . on the sand of the beach itself, is in both senses of the word, the high-water mark of surfing. But don't, for this reason, imagine that the glory of the Beacher is reserved for a chosen race of experts alone. **1949** C.B. MAXWELL *Surf* 9 Striving always to see who could 'crack a beacher' and ride it the farthest. **1956** S. HOPE *Diggers' Paradise* 166 The beacher . . takes you from deep water right to the shallows.

beakie. [Cf. *half-beak* any of various garfish (see OED).] Any of several GARFISH, esp. *Hyporhamphus australis* of coastal waters in Qld. and N.S.W., *H. ardelio* of Qld., N.S.W., Vic., S.A., and W.A., and *H. melanochir* of s. Aust.

1924 LORD & SCOTT *Synopsis Vertebrate Animals Tas.* 42 The Sea Garfish . . is often referred to as the 'Beakie' in New South Wales. **1935** *Bulletin* (Sydney) 4 Dec. 20/1 Best bait for barramundi . . is a 4 in. to 8 in. sprat or 'beakie' on live-bait tackle. **1983** *Canberra Chron.* 14 Dec. 18/4 Best bet is that it was a . . yellowfin, but a beakie could not be ruled out at this time of the year.

beal, var. BULL *n.*[1]

bean tree. Any of several trees bearing podded seeds, esp. *black bean* (a) (see BLACK *a.*[2] 1 a.) and some species of *Erythrina* (fam. Fabaceae) incl. STUART'S BEAN TREE; the wood of these trees. Freq. *attrib.*

1861 J.M. STUART *Explorations in Aust.* 4 Apr. (1865) 265 After crossing the range, we found the bean-tree in blossom; it was magnificent. I have obtained a specimen of it; also some beans, a number of which were of a cream colour; we have roasted a few of them, and find that they make very good coffee. **1861** *Burke & Wills Exploring Exped.* 8 The tree grows to fifteen or twenty feet, and bears numbers of flat brown pods, each containing from four to six hard light brown beans, known by us as the bean tree. **1864** E.A. OPPEN *Descr. N.T.* 30 Near here I saw some bean-trees in bloom (*Erithrina*) [*sic*]. The blossom of these trees is rich and handsome, of a reddish colour. **1889** W.H. TIETKENS *Jrnl. Central Austral. Exploring Exped.* 29 Mar. (1891) 7 Obtained specimens of the bean tree, from which natives make their shields and procure fire. **1895** W.H. WILLSHIRE *Thrilling Tale Real Life* 18 Chillberta . . was making a necklace out of the red beans that fall from the bean-tree. **1908** E.J. BANFIELD *Confessions of Beachcomber* 252 One pudding might certainly be included, *vermicelli* (shredded bean-tree nuts—'tinda-burra') with honey. **1916** *Bulletin* (Sydney) 20 Apr. 22/4 When placed partly in the ground beantree rots 'between wind and water' in four or five years. **1928** B. SPENCER *Wanderings in Wild Aust.* 196 Their most picturesque ornament is made from the bright red seeds of the Bean tree (*Erythrina vespertilio*). **1941** I.L. IDRIESS *Great Boomerang* 125 Then scrub-covered hills, creeks with mulga and gidgee on the flats, wattle and beantree. **1958** O. RUHEN *Naked under Capricorn* 39 Never gallop—bean-tree country. Always holes. ***c* 1960** C. MACKNESS *Clump Point & District* 5 Most roots and seeds were macerated in running water to free them of poisonous elements. The big beans from the bean-tree pod were treated thus, after a preliminary roasting.

bear. *Obs.* [Transf. use of *bear* any of several large mammals of the genus *Ursus*, to which the Austral. animal displays a fancied resemblance.] KOALA 1.

1827 *Monitor* (Sydney) 30 Mar. 363/1 A small paddock is enclosed . . for a menagerie, and we have in it . . the Bear found in the mountains. **1849** J.P. TOWNSEND *Rambles & Observations N.S.W.* 57 The curious little creature called 'a bear' . . , but which is much more like a monkey covered with fur. **1911** I.A. ROSENBLUM *Stella Sothern* 49 She heard the mopoke and the bear complaining against fate.

bearded dragon. The lizard *Amphibolurus barbatus* of e. Aust., having large spiny scales on the throat pouch and other parts of the body; JEW LIZARD 1. Also **bearded lizard.**

1861 *Catal. Natural & Industr. Products N.S.W.* 136 Lizards . . the Bearded ditto. **1886** F. MCCOY *Prodromus of Zool. Vic.* (1890) II. xiii. Pl. 121, Bearded Lizard. . . This is commonly called the Jew Lizard by colonists, and is easily distinguished by the beard-like growth of long, slender spines round the throat and parotoids. **1909** LUCAS & LE SOUEF *Animals of Aust.* 228 The Bearded Dragon is usually found on the ground or fallen trees, or on fences. **1956** *Bulletin* (Sydney) 18 Apr. 13/1 Does anyone know whether the bearded-dragon, or jew-lizard, hibernates? There are lots of them about our Queensland gardens and lawns in summer. **1973** V. SERVENTY *Desert Walkabout* 102 In the days that followed we found many old nests of wedgetail eagles, most of which had a rim of bearded dragon skeletons on the ground below.

beardie. *Hist.* Also **Beardy.** A nickname for a follower of John Wroe (1782–1863), founder of a sect called the Christian Israelites, who visited Australia several times between 1843 and his death in Melbourne in 1863. Chiefly in *pl.* Also *attrib.*

1851 *Empire* (Sydney) 9 Sept. 135/5 A party of Israelites, Beardies, Southcotarians or by whatever signification they may be known . . have just left for Sydney with 75 oz of clean gold. **1856** W.W. DOBIE *Recoll. Visit Port-Phillip* 50 Here were to be seen small flocks gathered around their particular pastors, who were generally of that class of preachers called, in the colony, Beardies, from the patriarchal length of that facial adornment. **1857** N. PIDGEON *Life, Experience, & Jrnl.* 83 At three went to the Market to hold an open air service; the Beardies had taken up our stand. **1875** *Spectator & Methodist Chron.* (Melbourne) xvi. 190/1 The Beardies or Christian Israelites of Ballarat—as the followers of that ignorant old Yorkshireman, John Wroe, are called—are quarrelling among themselves. **1967** F.T. MACARTNEY *Proof against Failure* 13 Music was provided by a brass band, consisting of the male members of a sect who, as their religion prohibited them from cutting any of their hair, each had a coil of it on his head, surmounted by a large belltopper hat peculiar to themselves. They were known as the Israelites, but we boys called them the Beardy-bucks.

beaut, *n.* and *a.* [Abbrev. of BEAUTY. Recorded earliest in U.S.: see OEDS.]

A. *n.* Abbrev. of BEAUTY *n.*

1898 M. CANNON *That Damned Democrat* (1981) 13 He is known as a 'Beaut' by his scavenging, slabbering [*sic*], suckless face. **1904** *Truth* (Sydney) 18 Dec. 4/3 Bird, you're a 'beaut' after the bunce. **1906** *Ibid.* 21 Oct. 2/7 Twig his boko. It's a beaut. **1909** *Ibid.* 21 Mar. 1/3 (*heading*) Block beauts and their blokes *tear, swear, trouble and tussle* in lower George-street. **1915** DREW & EVANS *Grafter* 106 What a 'beaut' he is, always figuring out schemes for getting money. **1921** F. GROSE *Rough Y.M. Bloke* 26 Strike me! Yer should er seen the feed they slapped up that night! It was a beaut. **1928** B. CRONIN *Dragonfly* 110 'You old beaut!' Birkett enthused. He smacked uncle Marmie on the back. **1930** *Bulletin* (Sydney) 9 Apr. 19/1 That was a beaut I missed, said Alf, as he threw back his hook. **1945** A.W. UPFIELD *Death of Swagman* 202 The sergeant's gruff voice repeated and repeated: 'You beaut! You little beaut!' **1946** A. MARSHALL *Tell us about Turkey, Jo* 61, I leaves this piece—she isn't much and gets in with 'em. They are on the pirate. . . We drives along the beach and, near Hampton, sees four beauts. **1952** T.A.G. HUNGERFORD *Ridge & River* 148 A big blonde . . sitting in a bath. . . She had two big beauts. **1972** *Bulletin* (Sydney) 18 Nov. 63/3 Therefore, one gets the distinct impression that the deal which is currently being negotiated could be a 'beaut'. **1978** SAW & MILBANK *Back to back Tango* 1 I'd be crazy to pretend that what I had going with National was anything but a marvellous job. It was a beaut.

B. *adj.* Exciting admiration; pleasing, satisfying. Also as *exclam.* (cf. BEAUTY *a.*).

1918 L.J. VILLIERS *Changing Yr.* 8 Twould be beaut Ter 'ave the cow w'ere he mus' foller suit. **1945** L. JILLET *Moresby's Few* 31 Gee, that's a beaut mo. How long did it take you to grow it, mate? **1948** *Bulletin* (Sydney) 12 May 29/4 Heaps of dough and a beaut. daughter. **1952** *Ibid.* 20 Feb. 12/3, I got a couple o' beaut nibbles . . last season. **1965** *Ibid.* 16 Jan. 17/2, I had a beaut time. Parties went on and on. **1973** *Ibid.* 24 Feb. 15/2 *The Lodge, Wednesday*. Fabulous. Only way to describe beaut culture night. **1979** S.W. DUTHIE *Fidlers Creek* 29 Oh, darling, look at them beaut crays, only 3 dollars a serve. **1981** C. WALLACE-CRABBE *Splinters* 22 'And could somebody type these three letters for me?' . . 'OK, Mr Bessier. I'm not particularly busy.' . . 'Beaut. Thanks.' **1983** *Weekend Austral. Mag.* (Sydney) 29 Oct. 12/5 The rugged 'you beaut' oddities expected from this strange southern continent.

beauty, *n.* and *a.* Also **beaudy, bewdy.** [Generalized use of *beauty*: see OED(S (esp. 5 and 7).]

A. *n.* Anything outstanding of its kind.

1852 J. BONWICK *Notes of Gold Digger* 34 A bullock driver spied a nugget at the foot of a tree; he scratched up a handful of beauties. **1895** *Worker* (Sydney) 14 Sept. 4/2 Yes, they are beauties on that station. **1903** *Sporting News* (Launceston) 5 Dec. 3/6 Inskip . . bowled him with a 'beauty'. **1919** C.J. DENNIS *Jim of Hills* 31 So I fetches him a beauty with a lovely left-arm swing. **1936** N. CALDWELL *Fangs of Sea* 175 The net was full of the beauties. **1953** D. STIVENS *Gambling Ghost* 99 And afterwards he heard the owner and the trainer telling each other what a beauty, a pearler and a trimmer the other racehorse was. **1964** K. TENNANT *Summer's Tales* 69 You little beauty, you bottler! I knew you could do it. **1969** C. BRAY *Blossom* 193 You drove like a beauty. **1978** SAW & MILBANK *Back to Back Tango* 56 'Turn on the booze,' I said. 'And don't forget it's on the house.' . . 'You little bloody bewdy,' said the biggest bikie. 'Free piss.' **1982** R. HALL *Just Relations* 113 The publican . . gives young Annie Lang a pat on the bottom as a compliment but she dongs him a beauty.

B. *adj.* Good, pleasing, esp. as an exclamation of approval or satisfaction.

[N.Z. **1960** N. HILLIARD *Maori Girl* 80 Beauty, boy! room to myself.] **1968** F.J. THWAITES *Sky full of Thunder* 100 'How's our tucker going?' 'Will be ready soon.' 'Beauty—.' **1969** A. BUZO *Front Room Boys* (1970) 43 Righto, lunchtime. . . Beauty. Coming down the rubbity, Gibbo? **1969** B. BREYDOR *You oughta seen Us!* 153 'Aussies, eh? Fair dinkum? Beauty, mate!' And laughing loudly he went through a whole string of Aussie slang. **1971** *Nation* (Sydney) 20 Feb. 22/1 *What* can a thinking man say to *The Wonderful World of Barry McKenzie* except hosannah and beauty bottler? **1972** *Bulletin* (Sydney) 3 June 17/2 That used car ad with Ron Frazer saying 'Beaudy'. **1977** *Southerly* ii. 160 'How are you, Raelene?' 'Beau-dy,' she said. 'It's great being back home.'

beaver rat. *Water rat*, see WATER.

1861 'OLD BUSHMAN' *Bush Wanderings* 51 We used to kill a large species of water rat, which we called the *Beaver Rat*. **1865** G.F. ANGAS *Savage Life & Scenes* 77 The Hydromys or 'beaver rat' inhabits the banks of the Murray and other rivers, and is also met with on some parts of the sea-coast. **1896** F.G. AFLALO *Sketch Nat. Hist. Aust.* 11 The true Water Rats or Beaver Rats as they are called. **1949** B. O'REILLY *Green Mountains* 106 The culprit proved to be a brush tail water rat. . . This rat is sometimes called the Beaver rat because of his aquatic habits. **1981** WATTS & ASLIN *Rodents of Aust.* 67 Water-rats from south-western Australia are dark . . and are commonly known as the 'sooty beaver rat'.

bed. *Tas. Obs.* A stand of trees.

1871 *Mercury* (Hobart) 5 Apr. 2 The piners have to go some 15 or 20 miles up the Davey River to the timber beds. **1903** *Advocate* (Burnie) 18 Sept. 3/4 There were some good beds of timber in the district. **1904** *Ibid.* 28 May 4/2 Fair beds of pine were met with in the early days of the settlement. **1911** *Huon Times* (Franklin) 14 Jan. 3/2 How much blue-gum is there? There are some fine beds back in the hills, and you can always get it down hill.

bed claim. *Mining. Hist.* [f. *bed* river bottom + CLAIM.] A claim, part or all of which is situated in the bed of a river or creek. Also *attrib.*

1851 *Empire* (Sydney) 8 Dec. 443/2 Heavy and continuous showers, with thunder, have again sunk the hopes of the bed-claim diggers, who are now flocking either to the mountains or the metropolis. **1852** *Moreton Bay Free Press* 18 Mar. 3/2 Sheep Station Point still continues a brisk place, the bed claims, in many instances, turning out very rich. **1853** J.R. GODLEY *Extracts Jrnl. Visit N.S.W.* 17 'Bed claims' . . can only be worked in very dry weather . . being fitted with a machinery of pumps and pipes, to remove the water which is constantly flowing in. **1855** *Ovens & Murray Advertiser* (Beechworth) 27 Jan. 4/3 The water holes in the river have paid and are paying very handsomely; the dry season, otherwise so unfavourable to pastoral purposes has been a great benefit to the diggers in aiding them in working their bed claims. **1867** *Illustr. Sydney News* 16 Feb. 123/3 Down among the bed claims and working ground fringing the river, diggers began to cluster like bees.

Hence **bed claimant** *n.*, one who works a bed claim.

1851 *Bell's Life in Sydney* 20 Dec. 2/3 The hopes of the bed-claimants. **1852** S. SMITH *Whether to Go* 115 The yield of gold . . is daily increasing, and the bed claimants are hard at work.

Bedourie /bə'duri/. [The name of a town in s.w. Qld.]

1. A dust storm: see quot. 1954.

1931 D.B. O'CONNOR *Black Velvet* 29 And the warm Bedouries blowing Stir the dust eternally? **1945** A. THURIAN *Bidgeroo & Jumbucks* 34 Brown dust down here and across the sky A Bedourie like a red fog. **1954** H.G. LAMOND *Manx Star* 257 *Bedourie*, a storm from the west which brings dust and sand, no rain. **1959** —— *Sheep Station* 32 'There's a Bedourie comin'.' He was right! The dust-storm, named after the township in the area where such abominations originated, came with a rush. **1978** TEECE & PIKE *Voice of Wilderness* 22, I had only gone about thirty miles when a big Bedourie dust storm hit me late that afternoon. It was my first experience with the dreaded Bedourie. I couldn't see my hand in front of me.

2. A type of camp oven: see quot. 1960. Also *attrib.*, esp. as **Bedourie dish, (camp) oven.**

1936 C.T. MADIGAN *Central Aust.* 94 It is usual to carry a small, pressed steel, camp oven, the 'Bidourie'. **1946** —— *Crossing Dead Heart* 19 Another item of camp equipment peculiar to Australia . . is the Bedourie camp oven, a flat round pressed-steel oven. **1960** B. HARNEY *Cook Bk.* Camp ovens . . have been largely supplanted by Bedourie ovens, which were first made in West Queensland. Bedourie ovens are made of steel, so that you could put a Bedourie on a packhorse and, if the horse bucked and threw its pack, the steel oven would not break as the old brittle cast-iron pots did. **1964** *Meanjin* 60 Syd had taught him the simple skills of making damper, and of cooking a brownie in a Bedourie oven. **1974** W. ROEDIGER *We Survived* 90 The horses . . grew sleek and fat . . , while the old cows carried udders like a bedourie oven. **1975** D. STUART *Walk, trot, canter & Die* 44 Joe brought out sugar and a yeast loaf that showed the shape of the Bedourie dish. **1982** J. & R. ABSALOM *Outback Cooking in Camp Oven* 11 The Bedourie camp oven made of pressed steel with the lid that fits over the top was made for Bedourie Station.

beech. [Transf. use of *beech* a forest tree of the genus *Fagus*, incl. *F. sylvatica*.] Any of several trees, esp. of the genus *Nothofagus* (fam. Fagaceae); the wood of these trees. Often with distinguishing epithet, as **antarctic beech,** *N. cunninghamii* and *N. moorei*; **deciduous beech,** *N. gunnii* (see TANGLEFOOT); **myrtle beech,** MYRTLE 1; **negrohead** (or **niggerhead**) **beech,** *N. moorei* of n.e. N.S.W. and s.e. Qld.; **white beech,** any of several trees of the genus *Gmelina* (fam. Verbenaceae), esp. *G. leichhardtii*.

1790 J. HUNTER *Hist. Jrnl. Trans. Port Jackson* (1793) 390 The live-oak, yellow-wood, black-wood, and beech, are all of a close grain. **1810** *HRA* (1921) 3rd Ser. I. 571 The Oak Trees or Beech Wood generally speaking are very diminutive and unfit for any useful purpose. **1845** *Sydney Morning Herald* 29 Nov. 2/5 There was some discussion whether a description of timber which grows at Brisbane Water, and is known as colonial beech, is adapted for making casks. **1855** J. BONWICK *Geogr. Aust. & N.Z.* (ed. 3) 203 The Beech of Cunningham reaches 100 feet. **1882** *Austral. Handbk.* 391 One of the most useful of Queensland timbers is the 'Beech' (*Gmelina Leichhardtii*). **1884** A. NILSON *Timber Trees N.S.W.* 78 *Negrohead Beech.*—A beautiful tree, attaining a height of 150 feet and a diameter of 4 feet. **1892** W.H. WARREN *Austral. Timbers* 11 *Gmelina Leichhardtii* .. Beech, or White Beech, of New South Wales (found also in Queensland). ***c* 1910** W.R. GUILFOYLE *Austral. Plants* 177 *Fagus* Gunnii .. 'Deciduous Beech' (shrub, 5 to 8 ft.)—Tas. **1917** *Advocate* (Burnie) 11 Aug. 4/2 The red myrtle or beech, encumbered by the botanists with the name of Fagus Cunninghami .. resembles the hardest and heaviest English beech. **1920** B. CRONIN *Timber Wolves* 162 Here in Tassie we call them myrtles, though they're beech right enough on the mainland. **1922** J.H. MAIDEN *Forest Flora N.S.W.* VII. 365 *Nothofagus Moorei* .. 'True or Negro-head Beech' of New South Wales, the latter name being given owing to the rich dark colour of the foliage. **1933** H.J. CARTER *Gulliver in Bush* 88 The many rotten logs of the nigger-head beech (*Nothofagus*). **1938** C.T. WHITE *Princ. Bot. Qld. Farmers* 152 Nothofagus, the so-called Antarctic or southern beeches. They are of interest botanically, as representative of the so-called Antarctic element in the Australian flora. **1944** J. DEVANNY *By Tropic Sea & Jungle* 128 White beech used for flooring. **1949** B. O'REILLY *Green Mountains* 28 On either side, and meeting overhead, were the ancient Antarctic beeches, covered with moss. **1975** *Ecos* vi. 4/3 The scattered Antarctic beech forests of Victoria, and the much more extensive ones in western Tasmania, are the temperate rainforests. **1981** H. HANNAH *Together in Jungle Scrub* 75 Rainforest trees are now rare, especially the Negrohead Beech, which was once on Comboyne. **1981** M. SHARLAND *Tracks of Morning* 70 Deciduous beech strikes an odd note in its winter bareness amongst surrounding trees and scrub. It is Tasmania's only deciduous native tree, and belongs to this island entirely.

beef. [Archaic in Br. Eng. but common in U.S.: see OED(S *sb.* 3 b.]

1. A bull, cow, or steer, esp. one reared for human consumption. Freq. *attrib.*

1873 *Illustr. Sydney News* 16 Apr. 4/1 The style of house .. is a common one at an out-station. To the left is the yard and that necessary appendage the beef gallows. **1902** *Bulletin* (Sydney) 7 June 16/4 When meat-hungry they shoot the handiest beef. **1911** *Ibid.* 30 Nov. 13/2 Is there any man who leads a more leisurely life than the small beef-fattener? **1920** *Ibid.* 2 Sept. 24/3 The station's beef rations had been yarded, and my father was preparing to finish the business with a .44 Winchester. **1938** *Ibid.* 24 Aug. 20/2, I was took orf boundary-ridin' last week to muster the beefs. **1942** *Ibid.* 9 Sept. 13/2 It's a long time since I padded behind the cow's tail, and for all I know modern beef conductors may have evolved a newer technique. **1977** *Caravan World* Jan. 63/2 On the beeves that were dried out, no good horns. Where there were good horns there was still too much meat attached to them.

2. Special Comb. **beef road**, an all-weather road built for trucking cattle from remote areas.

1962 *N.T. News* (Darwin) 1 Sept. 5/1 The Government's big road construction program since 1956–57 had included a special beef roads project to improve roads serving the higher-carrying country and so boost beef exports. **1963** *Bulletin* (Sydney) 16 Nov. 81/2 The meeting expressed its determination to persevere with .. a beef road from Bourke to Wyndham. **1964** D. LOCKWOOD *Up Track* 33 Now huge motor trains carry cattle along wide beef roads bisecting the Territory. **1972** J. GOODE *Austral. Cars & Motoring* 32 The improvement of roads in Northern Australia had been partly due to the development of 'Beef Roads' .. roads with good level surfaces which now extend for hundreds of miles through the outback north .. to enable huge diesel prime movers to tow trailers which transport cattle from the isolated stations to the slaughter houses. **1979** D. LOCKWOOD *My Old Mates & I* 82 The beef roads had reached into the back country, bitumen to Wave Hill and beyond.

beefer. BEEF 1.

1945 *Bulletin* (Sydney) 27 June 14/1 We pass a paddock in which a few Angus beefers graze. **1964** B. WANNAN *Fair Go, Spinner* 67 Twenty 'beefers' were slaughtered for each meal.

beef tree. BEEFWOOD.

1845 J.O. BALFOUR *Sketch of N.S.W.* 40 To these may be added .. the tree named by the colonists, from a peculiarity in the grain, beef tree, Australian maple, and black wood. **1876** *Observer Miscellany* 9 Dec. 830/2 The 'beeftree', so termed, I was told, because of the likeness of the grain of the wood to beef. **1931** MRS E.P. HALFORD *Pioneers of Yesterday* 16 Good beeftree, saltbush, grass, and native geranium grow well in this jumble of hills.

beefwood. [See quot. 1885.] **a.** The tree *Grevillea striata* (fam. Proteaceae) of drier Australia; its timber. **b.** Any of several other trees having similar wood, esp. *Stenocarpus salignus* (fam. Proteaceae) and some species of the fam. Casuarinaceae. Also *attrib.*

1803 Banks Papers 9 May VII. 192, I have also sent a quantity of our Beefwood, or She-Oak to Sir E. Nepean. **1805** *Ibid.* 7 Jan. XX. 129 A species of Casurina [*sic*] different to that of Port Jackson (called the Beefwood) and I think equally beautiful. **1826** J. ATKINSON *Acct. Agric. & Grazing N.S.W.* 16 *Forest Oak* .. the wood is well known in England by the names of Botany Bay wood, or beef wood. **1829** R. MUDIE *Picture of Aust.* 137 There are three principal species [of *Casuarinae*] to which the colonists have given names, and the timber of which is indiscriminately called oak or beef-wood. **1852** G.C. MUNDY *Our Antipodes* II. 25 A shingle of the beef-wood looks precisely like a raw beef-steak. **1885** *Once a Month* (Melbourne) June 455 A tree, known as beefwood, is widely distributed. The wood is dark red, with a purple tinge, coarse-grained, and soft. **1893** D. LINDSAY *Jrnl. Elder Sci. Exploring Exped.* 163 There are several beefwood or 'yarra' trees growing around the well. **1904** J.H. MAIDEN *Notes on Commercial Timbers N.S.W.* 26 *Red Silky Oak* or *Beefwood* .. has been long used by Illawarra dairy farmers for such purposes as butter kegs. **1936** F. CLUNE *Roaming round Darling* 161 Beefwood grows forty feet high, and, besides being a fodder-tree, is the best fencing timber. **1947** J.W. GORDON *Under Wide Skies* 36, I drop my swag in a beefwood shade. **1963** X. HERBERT *Larger than Life* 120 Stunted beefwood trees and mean clumps of sun-scorched grass. **1973** A. BURNETT *Wilful Murder in Outback* 26 Five miles further on they came across his saddle and an empty water bottle in the fork of a beefwood tree. **1976** C.D. MILLS *Hobble Chains & Greenhide* 40 Mick carried his swag over to a great, fallen beef-wood log this night.

beer-chewer. A heavy drinker of beer. Also **beer-eater (-guzzler, -sparrer, -sucker).** Also **beer-chewing** *vbl. n.* and *ppl. a.*

1891 'SMILER' *Wanderings Simple Child* (ed. 3) 81, I called him a 'beer-eater', and thought him a mean-spirited cur. **1895** *Worker* (Sydney) 20 Apr. 1/3 Real good beer chewers, I admit, they could drink anything from clay-pan water to Port Mackay rum. **1903** *Truth* (Sydney) 4 Jan. 1/8 There is a beer-eater in Sydney who seems to swallow pints of beer one after another without the liquor touching his throat. **1907** *Bulletin* (Sydney) 28 Feb. 15/3 Seventeen beer-chewers went into a Winton (Q.) bar the other day, and came out an hour later, having .. surrounded 28 drinks each. *Ibid.* 19 Sept. 39/1 There was not a solitary beer-sparrer to help him dissipate the cheque. **1910** *Ibid.* 2 June 14/2 'Buzz' is the pastime which has the greatest vogue among beer-sparrers. **1912** *Truth* (Sydney) 28 Jan. 12/2 That foul, beer-chewing skunk I was speaking of. **1925** *Smith's Weekly* (Sydney) 24 Jan. 23/5 Two hairy beer-chewers .. made themselves a nuisance at Blind Creek races. **1929** *Bulletin* (Sydney) 26 June 23/4 Here's my entry for the beer-chewing championship... Three swipers for a wager consumed respectively 45, 44 and 42 ordinary glasses of beer. **1965** *Kings Cross Whisper* (Sydney) Jan. 5/3 He has entered for Sydney's Best Beer-Guzzler title and is flat out to clinch a place in the finals. **1971** D. IRELAND *Unknown Industr. Prisoner* 231 Have you mob ever thought of the inhabitants of this pretty little earth before we started brewing beer on it? .. Just picture them, you beer-suckers. **1975** K. WILLEY *Ghosts of Big Country* 52, I don't drink much .. but when I do tackle the stuff, I *drink* it! I'm not a beer-chewer.

beer-up. A beer-drinking party or session; a 'booze-up'.

1919 W.H. DOWNING *Digger Dialects* 10 *Beer-up*, a drunken orgy. **1921** *Aussie* (Sydney) July 40/2 They reckoned that they'd had a cheap beer-up at the price. **1941** K. TENNANT *Battlers* 146 A gang of assorted showmen broke into the temporary bar .. and the camp indulged in a general 'beer-up'. **1944** A. MARSHALL *These are my People* 168 Every six months or so life got them down and they had a 'beer-up' together. **1968** G. DUTTON *Andy* 175 'An excuse for a'—Andy paused—'bloody good beer-up at the mess.' **1978** K. GARVEY *Tales of my Uncle Harry* 62 We had a good beer-up at the pub that night.

before, *prep. Obs.* In the phr. **before the gold** (or **diggings**), prior to the discovery of gold in Australia.

1855 G.H. WATHEN *Golden Colony* 22 The discovery of gold in Victoria forms the great epoch in its history, to which all events are referred, as having happened 'before' or 'after the gold'. **1884** 'R. BOLDREWOOD' *Old Melbourne Memories* 119 It was in a year 'before the gold' that I had occasion to ride to Kalangadoo. **1891** J. FENTON *Bush Life Tas.* (1964) 77 The circumference of a sovereign 'before the diggings' had a very much wider gauge than it has now.

beggar. [Prob. familiar or playful use of *beggar*: see OED *sb.* 6 b.] In the phr. **beggar on (the) coal(s)**, a small damper (see DAMPER 1). Formerly also **beggar-in-the-pan.**

1847 G.F. ANGAS *Savage Life & Scenes* I. 161 Our cook had not been idle: there were 'dampers', 'dough-boys', 'leather-jackets', 'johnny-cakes', and 'beggars-in-the-pan', awaiting our arrival, for in the Australian bush, flour and water are transformed into a variety of shapes, designated by as many colonial appellations. **1848** C. COZENS *Adventures of Guardsman* 141 There is another sort of bread made when in a hurry, called 'beggars on the coal', which is made very thin like our girdle-bread, and merely placed on the hot ashes, and afterwards turned. **1902** R.C. PRAED *My Austral. Girlhood* 45 If the ashes be not properly prepared, the Johnny-cake will be heavy and no longer a Johnny-cake; it is then a 'Leather-jacket', or it is a 'Beggar on coals', when little bits of the sticks are turned into charcoal and make black marks on the dough. **1909** E. WALTHAM *Life & Labour in Aust.* 132 The usual bush hospitality of tea and damper, varied sometimes by an occasional 'dough-boy' or 'beggars on the coals'. **1918** C. FETHERSTONHAUGH *After Many Days* 277 The troopers cooked good food for us and most delicious 'beggars on the coals', sort of Johnny cakes. **1951** E. HILL *Territory* 108 We watered the horses and made some johnnie-cakes... We called them beggars-on-the-coals. Mr Knuckey was so delighted that he was moved to poetry—'The greatest enjoyment under the sun Is to sit by the fire till the beggars are done.' **1980** P. TAYLOR *End to Silence* 70 They made johnnie cakes out of flour, salt and water, which they called beggers-on-coals [*sic*].

beg-pardon. [f. the phr. *to beg pardon* to excuse (oneself): see OED *v.* 3.] An expression of apology; esp. in the phr. **no beg-pardons,** without concern for the niceties.

1906 E. DYSON *Fact'ry 'Ands* 137 'Twas quick business down below here, 'n' no beg-pardons with Bunyip. **1916** J.B. COOPER *Coo-oo-ee!* 11 Then without a 'beg pardon', off she goes again. **1922** 'J. NORTH' *Black Opal* 54 Finishing with a fast fighting round, in which there were no beg-pardons. **1967** *Sunday Mail Mag.* (Brisbane) 8 Jan. 6/2 There were no beg-pardons about Mrs Hodges (or Debbie, as she insisted I call her). **1974** D. STUART *Prince of my Country* 122, I just want him to accept the fact that he's half blackfeller, half white feller and be a strong enough character to make everyone else accept it without any beg pardons.

behind. *Australian National Football.*

1. a. *Hist.* The kicking of the ball over the *behind line*, a 'near miss' (see quot. 1876). **b.** A scoring kick that earns one point (see quot. 1925); the score itself.

1866 *Australasian* (Melbourne) 28 July 523/2 The umpires be instructed to count the number of times the ball is driven behind goal; and in the event of no goal, or one goal by each being obtained, the side obtaining the greater number of 'behinds' should be declared the winners. **1876** T.P. POWER *Footballer* 9 A struggle for it results in it being seized by a nimble player, who kicks it forward, where a friend awaiting, if he can, kicks it towards the goal-posts, outside which it goes, and within the 20 yard posts, and the goal umpire calls 'Behind!' This is looked upon as an honor for the attacking team, though nothing counts in the game but goals. **1880** *Melbourne Punch* 29 Apr. 173/2 'Forward Carlton' is now the cry, And we rush it like the wind, A roar from ten thousand throats goes up, For we've kicked another behind. **1882** *Ibid.* 26 Oct. 168/2 The scrimmage brought in dear papa, Who's conduct was unkind, And with unerring shot he kicked—He kicked—well a 'behind'. **1888** *Australasian* (Melbourne) 23 June 1373/4 M'Inerney . . added a behind just before the first bell sounded. The visitors had up to this scored only one behind to Carlton's 2 goals 5 behinds. **1904** *Truth* (Sydney) 4 Sept. 2/6 Queensland, 4 goals 15 behinds (39 points). **1925** *Laws of Football* (Australasian Football Council) 4 A behind shall be won when the ball passes over the line drawn between the goal posts after being touched by any player or touches either of the goal posts, or is kicked or forced over the line drawn between the goal posts and behind posts. **1927** *Melbourne Univ. Mag.* Nov. 154 Attacking with the wind, Adelaide took several behinds. **1964** B. WANNAN *Fair Go Spinner* 135 We're not doing too well. We've only kicked twenty-five behinds. **1971** B. ANDREW *Austral. Football Handbk.* 12 The first series of matches by the Victorian Football League was played in 1879, when the 'little mark' was abolished, and the system of scoring by points was introduced. For the first time, Behinds or 'near misses' were included in the score. **1978** J. POWERS *Coach* 150 North gained the vital 'jump'—a goal and a behind, to lead by 7 points to nil.

2. Special Comb. **behind line,** the line between the goal post and the behind post; **post,** either of a pair of posts, in line with and flanking the goal-posts.

1930 W.S. SHARLAND *Sporting Globe Football Bk.* 24 The space occupied by the goal-line and the **behind lines** in all makes twenty-one yards. **1963** *Laws of Football* (Austral. Nat. Football Council) 6 The lines between the goal and behind posts shall be called the behind lines. **1983** B. HOGAN *Follow Game* (rev. ed.) 57 It is necessary for him to go back over the goal or behind lines to take his kick. **1925** *Laws of Football* (Australasian Football Council) 4 Should the ball touch a **behind post** it shall be out of bounds. **1950** *Austral. Nat. Game Football* (Austral. Nat. Football Council) 7 When near the behind posts do not 'throw in' too far. **1963** *Laws of Football* (Austral. Nat. Football Council) 11 A behind shall be scored in any other case when the ball passes over the goal line, or touches or passes over a goal post or passes over a behind line without touching a behind post. **1965** A. SCOTT *Man. Austral. Football* 67 Because he has over twenty yards to cover from one behind post to the other, the goal umpire has to be active. **1979** *Murray's Austral. Football* 105 There are two goal and two behind posts at each end of the ground. The distance between each post should be 6.4 metres.

belah /bəˈla/. Also **belar, billar.** [a. Dharuk *bilar.*] Any of several trees or large shrubs of the fam. Casuarinaceae with slender jointed branchlets and woody cones, esp. *Casuarina cristata* of drier regions of Aust. Also *attrib.*

[**1798** D. COLLINS *Acct. Eng. Colony N.S.W.* I. 612 *Billarr*, a spear with one barb, cut from the wood. **1834** J.S.C. DUMONT D'URVILLE *Voyage de Découvertes: Philologie* 11 Casuarina. *Bela.*] **1862** H. KENDALL *Poems & Songs* 18 A voice in the beela grows wild in its wail. **1887** W.H. SUTTOR *Austral. Stories Retold* 117 On the low-lying, black, flooded land, the belar, a species of native oak or casuarina, is found, casting so dense a shade as to prevent all other vegetation from showing. **1897** *Bulletin* (Sydney) 19 June 28/1 They're fetching in 'stores' to the station Through tangles of broken belar. **1899** *North-Western Advocate* (Devonport) 8 Mar. 4/1 The scrub now being felled for feed is chiefly billar. **1911** E.J. BRADY *King's Caravan* 105 He looked tired, as tired as a man with eight children and 2,500 acres of belah scrub might be. **1918** *Emu* XVIII. 65 Found a Brown Hawk's nest, which was high up in a tall, straight belar tree (casuarina). **1935** F. CLUNE *Rolling down Lachlan* 196 Here, ibis, ducks, and swans swam in the shade of box-trees, mixed with belahs and yarran. **1944** A.E. MINNIS *And All Trees are Green* 126 A prone belar log lit at one end will burn steadily along its length like a fuse. **1953** *Bulletin* (Sydney) 27 May 13/4 Lopping belah for drought-stricken sheep is no job for those whose nerves are frayed. **1976** J.H. TRAVERS *Bull Dust on Brigalow* 16 In no time millions of grubs were scattered in the belah scrub. **1986** *Trees & Natural Resources* Mar. 7 (*caption*) Belah woodland in sound condition.

bell, *n.* Used *attrib.* in the names of animals and birds having calls which resemble the sound of a bell: **bell frog,** a frog of the genus *Litoria*, esp. *L. aurea*, a green species with patches of brown or gold, found in or near water in coastal N.S.W.; **magpie,** any of the three species of CURRAWONG; **miner,** BELLBIRD 1.

1834 G. BENNETT *Wanderings N.S.W.* I. 138 The peculiar sound uttered by that species known by the name of the '**bell frog**' is . . very similar to a sheep-bell. **1881** F. MCCOY *Prodromus of Zool. Vic.* (1885) I. vi. Pl. 53, So completely alike was the sound of these Bell-Frogs in an adjoining pond at night to the noise of the men by day. **1930** H.H. RICHARDSON *Fortunes Richard Mahony* (1931) 92 Hundreds of bell-frogs, which were like hundreds of hissing tea-kettles just about to boil. **1916** S.A. WHITE *In Far Northwest* 45 The liquid call of the **bell magpie** . . was heard far on ahead of us. **1929** A.H. CHISHOLM *Birds & Green Places* 18 Those mountain roysterers which bird-men term bell-magpies, and which bush-dwellers know as currawongs. **1950** *Bulletin* (Sydney) 27 Dec. 12/3 People talk of black magpies, currawongs, bell magpies and jackdaws—four names for one bird. **1967** E. HUXLEY *Their Shining Eldorado* 61 At sun-up . . the bell-magpie . . utters his well-named bell-like call. **1900** A.J. CAMPBELL *Nests & Eggs Austral. Birds* 417 The **Bell Miner** is . . gregarious to an extent, living in companies in certain restricted areas. **1903** *Emu* II. 176 The Bell Miner (*Manorhina melanophrys*) was identified. The clear, bell-like notes of the male are frequently answered by a chuckling call from the female. **1932** *Bulletin* (Sydney) 11 May 21/3 The tinkling note of the bell-birds, whether the bell-miner of the coastal regions or the crested bellbird of the interior, are always a sure indication of water being close at hand. **1942** C. BARRETT *From Bush Hut* 46 Wattle Creek folk will follow the bell miners' example: they've migrated three miles downstream, because timber cutters disturbed the old colony. **1968** R. HILL *Bush Quest* 11 The bell-miners, which had made such a dreadful fuss when I arrived, were settling down. Their alarm call is similar to a finger squeaking over a balloon.

bell, *v.* [See OED *v.*[5] 1.] *trans.* To furnish (a grazing animal) with a bell, so that its whereabouts remain known.

1882 A.J. BOYD *Old Colonials* 68 As soon as the animals were attended to, hobbled and belled, the billies were slung on the fire. **1921** W.H. PHIPPS *Bush Yarns & Town Sketches* 73 He unyoked the bullocks, belled them, and turned them into a paddock. **1942** W. GLASSON *Our Shepherds* 8 Six big wethers, all having shown some signs of independent leadership when the mob was let out to graze, would be 'belled'.

Hence **belled** *ppl. a.*

1959 C. & E. CHAUVEL *Walkabout* 12 The ringing of the bells is only intermittent and quite like the sound which 'belled' horses make when feeding.

bellbird. [Cf. BELL *n.*]

1. The bird *Manorina melanophrys* (fam. Meliphagidae) of woodlands in s.e. Aust., typically living in colonies and maintaining contact by frequent calls; *bell miner*, see BELL *n.*

[**1770** J. BANKS *Endeavour Jrnl.* 17 Jan. (1962) 455 This morn I was awakd [*sic*] by the singing of the birds ashore from whence we are distant not a quarter of a mile, the number of them were certainly very great who seemd [*sic*] to strain their throats with emulation perhaps; their voices were certainly the most melodious wild music I have ever heard, almost imitating small bells but with the most tuneable silver sound imaginable to which maybe the distance was no small addition.] **1799** D. COLLINS *Acct. Eng. Colony N.S.W.* (1802) II. 91 The melancholy cry of the bell-bird (dil boong, after which Bennilong named his infant child). **1803** J. GRANT *Narr. Voyage N.S.W.* 134 The *Bell Bird* . . has no remarkable plumage, but a note not unlike the tinkling of a bell. **1827** P. CUNNINGHAM *Two Yrs. in N.S.W.* II. 157 The note of the bell-bird, tinkling like a dull sheep bell, announces . . the welcome presence of water. **1846** G.H. HAYDON *Five Yrs.' Experience Aust. Felix* 72 The bell bird . . is a small brown creature with yellow legs and bill. **1867** *Sydney Morning Herald* 25 Nov. 5/6 And, softer than slumber and sweeter than singing, The notes of the bell-birds are running and ringing. **1890** G.J. BROINOWSKI *Birds of Aust.* IV. Pl. 13, The Bell-bird . . is met with in companies, varying in number from ten to forty. **1912** B. O'DOWD *Bush* 24 Acolyte bell-birds the Angelus are pealing, And boobooks moan lone vespers in the dusk. **1950** H.C. WELLS *Earth cries Out* 25 The bellbirds, small and quick, chattered amongst the blossom, pealing out their bell-like notes. **1980** F. MOORHOUSE *Everlasting Secret Family* 43 Bellbirds could send you demented, too, the incessant single note.

2. *Crested bellbird*, see CRESTED.

1843 J. GOULD *Birds of Aust.* (1848) II. Pl. 81, *Oreoica gutturalis* . . Bell-bird, Colonists of Swan River. **1903** *Emu* III. 91 *Oreoica cristata* (Bell-bird, Pan-pan-pannella) . . Their songs were a distinct nuisance when one wanted to locate the horse bells. **1960** *Bulletin* (Sydney) 6 July 16/3 Next to cuckoos, the chief patron of hairy-caterpillars is the crested bellbird. . . Every self-respecting bellbird actually stocks its nest with 'stingarees' and other such larvae.

bellowser. *Obs.* [Br. dial. *bellowser* a violent blow or hard task which takes one's breath away: see EDD.] A sentence or term of transportation for life; one who serves this.

1812 J.H. VAUX *Mem.* (1819) II. 225 *Wind*, a man transported for his natural life, is said to be *lag'd for his wind*, or to have *knap'd a winder*, or *a bellowser*, according to the humour of the speaker. **1837** *Cornwall Chron.* (Launceston) 27 May (Suppl.) 5 He says that we're all damned drunken bellowsers. **1844** *Parramatta Chron.* 29 June 2/1 What is termed in colonial phraseology a 'Bellowser' vulgo, a transport for life.

bell sheep. A sheep secured by a shearer just before the bell rings to signal the end of a period of work.

1897 *Bulletin* (Sydney) 20 Feb. 3/2 And rip 'em through and yell for 'tar' and get the bell-sheep out. **1900** *Ibid.* 13 Jan. 32/3 He times himself to get so many sheep out of the pen *before* the bell goes, and *one more*—the 'bell-sheep'—as it is ringing. **1911** E.S. SORENSON *Life Austral. Backblocks* 245 There is also hard cutting among greedy persons for a bell sheep (the one caught just as the bell is about to ring off). **1918** *Truth* (Sydney) 1 Dec. 10/2, I, together with thousands more of roussies, would like to see this whistle or bell sheep business knocked on the head. **1965** J.S. GUNN *Terminol. Shearing Industry* i. 7 The 'bell sheep', or 'the catch' as it is often called, may be an easy one.

belltopper. [f. *bell*, from the shape of the crown + *topper* top hat.] Any of various types of tall hat. Also **belltopper hat.**

1858 C.R. THATCHER *Colonial Songster* (rev. ed.) 64 Who can cut it jolly fat, Without a mag, on Ballarat, Wear a bad belltopper hat? **1863** B.A. HEYWOOD *Vacation Tour Antipodes* 59 My chief offence in his eyes was my wearing a black hat, known by many as a bell-topper. **1866** *Austral. Monthly Mag.* (Melbourne) III. 47 Hat emporiums, whereat the number of 'cabbage-trees' is marvellously in excess of the quantity of 'bell-toppers'. **1872** MRS E. MILLETT *Austral. Parsonage* 87, I was the only woman whom Isaac had ever seen in a black beaver riding-hat, of the shape commonly called in the colony a 'bell topper'. **1886** D.M. GANE *N.S.W. & Vic.* 42 Bell-toppers, the colonial nick-name for tall hats, are nearly as much worn by the well-to-do inhabitants as at home. **1899** *Progress* (Brisbane) 10 June 5/2 Great reform questions are never settled by kid-gloved politicians who were born in bell-toppers. **1924** F.J. MILLS *Happy Days* 153 First there was his shiny 'belltopper' which was placed on me when he returned from his wedding. **1934** 'S. RUDD' *Green Grey Homestead* 152 A galaxy of horsemen, buggy-pairs, fours-in-hand, horse-women (these all in belltoppers). **1942** H.H. PECK *Mem. of Stockman* 42 He knocked his hat, a beautiful new silk bell-topper, into the pen among the bullocks. **1967** F.T. MACARTNEY *Proof against Failure* 13 As their religion prohibited them from cutting any of their hair, each had a coil of it on his head, surmounted by a large belltopper hat. **1980** P. FREEMAN *Woolshed* 128 Jacky Dow was of the old breed of strict squatter-managers; he was among the last of the wearers of the white bell-topper hat once fashionable among squatters.

Hence **bell-toppered** *a.*, wearing a belltopper.

1874 *Adelaide Observer* 26 Dec. (Christmas Suppl.) 40/1 The now buttoned and bell-toppered page. **1903** *Truth* (Sydney) 4 Jan. 7/2 Occasionally a bell-toppered swell—mashers they were called in those days, and 'toffs'—came along.

belly. *Timber-getting.* [Spec. use of *belly* the front, inner, or lower surface as opposed to the *back.*] A scarf or notch cut in that side of the trunk facing the direction in which the tree is intended to fall. Also *attrib.*, esp. as **belly cut, scarf.**

1848 *Maitland Mercury* 26 July 1/6 Making a 'belly' in the timber .. means cutting that side of the tree to which it leans and on which side it is calculated it will most likely fall. **1909** R. KALESKI *Austral. Settler's Compl. Guide* 55 The 'belly' scarf is cut first so that the tree won't fall on the cutter; if he wants to commit suicide he cuts the 'belly' last. **1916** *Bulletin* (Sydney) 8 June 24/3 When referring to the cut made by axe or saw, they spoke of it as the 'belly-cut' or the 'back-cut'. **1940** *Ibid.* 9 Oct. 17/3 He puts in the belly cut on the side to which it is to fall. **1959** *Overland* xiv. 14 In no time I was climbing up onto the springboard up the trunk and putting in the belly cut while one of them put in the back cut.

belly board.

1. See quot.

1960 K. SMITH *Word from Children* 156 The soapbox has gone; in its place is a flat piece of something for lying on going down hills; this is called a 'belly board'.

2. *Surfing.* [Used elsewhere but recorded earliest in Aust.] A short surf-board, ridden in a prone or kneeling position. Also *attrib.*

1964 *Surfabout* (Sydney) I. vi. 17 Lee has been riding a belly board for many years. **1967** *Ibid.* IV. iii. 13 Though belly-board riding has reached a degree of sophistication, it is just entering a new phase of development in what the board and its rider are able to do.

belly-buster. A dive in which the front of the body strikes flatly on the water, a 'belly-flop'. Also **belly-thumper** and *fig.*

1941 S.J. BAKER *Pop. Dict. Austral. Slang* 9 *Belly-buster*, a bad fall, an ungainly dive into water. Also 'belly-flopper'. **1968** S. GORE *Holy Smoke* 51 You'll come a big belly-thumper if you don't watch out! **1971** D. IRELAND *Unknown Industr. Prisoner* 281 From an upright position the body fell forward into a flat position, like a diver entering the water with a belly-buster.

belly wool, *n.* Wool shorn from the belly of the sheep. Also *ellipt.* **belly** (chiefly in *pl.*).

[N.Z. **1851** F.A. WELD *Hints intending Sheep-Farmers* 10 Their mothers do not lose the belly-wool as they would do by lambing in spring.] **1871** *Austral. Town & Country Jrnl.* (Sydney) 18 Mar. 331/2 Sheep that strip at the points, and lose the belly-wool, having a clean head without topknot. **1891** *Conference Amalgam. Shearers' Union & Pastoralists' Fed. Council* 8 The belly wool to be taken off first and laid aside. **1899** G. JEFFREY *Princ. Australasian Woolclassing* 51 The locks are picked up from the floor by the boys and taken to the 'Belly and Lock Picker', who sees that all the large 'dags' are kept out before placing the locks in a heap ready for pressing. **1908** W.H. OGILVIE *My Life in Open* 39 The belly-wool and the 'locks' or sweepings which fall through the bars of the wool-tables. **1928** C.E. COWLEY *Classing Clip* 45 The wool that has good length, is bulky and comparatively light in condition, will constitute the leading line. The balance will make up the bellies. **1948** R. RAVEN-HART *Canoe in Aust.* 54 'Bellies', losing in value because they have picked up burrs from the pastures, shorn separately. **1980** P. FREEMAN *Woolshed* 20 There are three main types of shorn wool; the 'locks', from the sheep's legs, .. the 'bellies' from the sheep's underside, .. and the 'fleece' itself.

belly-wool, *v.* [f. prec.] *trans.* To shear the underside of (a sheep). Also *ellipt.* as **belly** (in quot. as *vbl. n.*).

1902 *Bulletin* (Sydney) 1 Feb. 16/2 The shearers had men belly-woolling their sheep. **1930** D. COTTRELL *Earth Battle* 123 Fifty rams and wethers .. had been flyblown, and needed shearing round the belly and horns—'wigging and bellying' as it was called.

belt. *Surf life-saving.* The wide canvas belt with line attached worn by the member of a surf life-saving team who swims to the rescue. Usu. in Comb., as **belt man, belt (and line) race.**

1914 *Newcastle Morning Herald* 14 Nov. 6/2 Another bather, whose name was not ascertained, and N. Mason, went to his assistance, the former putting on the belt. **1918** *Ibid.* 19 Jan. 8/4 By the time the beltman reached him, he was safe in 3 or 4 feet of water. **1929** *Sydney Morning Herald* 11 Feb. 12/7 A lifeline was sent out after the man, but the heavy sea prevented the beltman getting through the surf. **1942** M.L. MACPHERSON *I heard Anzacs Singing* 21 First comes the belt-man whose task it is to swim out, carrying the line to the drowning person. *Ibid.* 23 There are boat races, belt-and-line races, 'chariot' races. **1963** J. POLLARD *Austral. Surfrider* 52 It is a wise idea for board riders to know the accepted signals .. : *Beltman needed.* One arm raised vertically above the head. **1964** *Austral. Surf Life Saving Competition Handbk.* (Surf Life Saving Assoc. Aust.) (ed. 4) 14 For dead-heats in belt races, the beltmen concerned shall be required to no-contest the event on the same day.

Belyando spew /bɛljændoʊ 'spju/. [f. the name of a river in central Qld.] *Barcoo sickness*, see BARCOO A. 2. Also *ellipt.*

1889 R.B. ANDERSON tr. Lumholtz's *Among Cannibals* 58 *Beliander* is also a common disease in Queensland; without the slightest apparent cause, a person is suddenly seized with vomiting, but is relieved just as suddenly. **1896** B. SPENCER *Rep. Horn Sci. Exped. Central Aust.* IV. 132 There is a complaint .. which has received the name of the 'Barcoo Sickness'... To Queenslanders it is known as the 'Belyando Spew' from the Belyando district where it is .. a common complaint. **1912** J.B. CLELAND *Some Diseases Aust.* 43 *'Belyando Spue'* .. is .. a peculiar and often distressing condition characterized by vomiting at meal times, and found in central Australia. **1918** C. FETHERSTONHAUGH *After Many Days* 272 What I called the Belyando Spue was a most trying ailment... The Western fellows called it the 'Barcoo sickness', the Northern men termed it the 'Burdekin vomit'. **1976** B. SCOTT *Compl. Bk. Austral. Folk Lore* 375 The worst of the lot Is the Bellyando Spew.

bencher. BENCHMAN.

1904 *Bulletin* (Sydney) 2 June 16/1 But the bencher jams the billets 'gainst the saw with all his might.

benchman. In a saw-mill: the employee responsible for feeding the log or length of timber being cut through the saw.

1895 *Bulletin* (Sydney) 3 Aug. 3/2 Few know the song—for the tailer-out, And the benchman swart and his underlings, and the truckerman, and the trammer stout, Have their souls in the flitch and in wooden things. **1937** *N.S.W. Parl. Papers* (1938–40) 2nd Sess. VI. 667 The Aborigine Protection Board is running this sawmill... The same benchman has been there for the last five years. **1984** *Canberra Times* 16 Jan. 9/1 Working as a top-line benchman at several mills. **1985** *Ibid.* 30 Aug. 8/4 He .. was employed as a benchman by Grant Timbers.

bend, *n.* [U.S. *bend* a tract of land within a bend of a river: see DAE *n.* 1 b.] The land bordered by a curve in a river.

1860 *Trans. & Proc. R. Soc. Vic.* (1861) 142 Points of land or 'bends' of the river. **1878** 'IRONBARK' *Southerly Busters* 25 He'd known the time, not long ago, When half the year he'd spend In idleness, and comfort too, A-camping in a 'bend'. **1890** 'R. BOLDREWOOD' *Squatter's Dream* 95 His horses had not done so badly in the long grass of the 'bend'. **1905** H. LAWSON *When I was King* 85 She loved me! And why? Ask the she-oaks that sighed in the bends. **1913** —— *Far Aust.* 182 River banks were grassy—grassy in the bends.

bend, *v.* [Spec. use of *bend* to turn from a straight line.] *trans.* To head off and turn back (a mob of stampeding cattle). Also as *n.* (see quot. 1923).

1923 *Six Austral. One-Act Plays* (1944) 9 By gum, tho', look at the old bloke putting a bend on them. He's got them... Wheeled 'em a treat... You should have seen him bending that mob. **1951** E. HILL *Territory* 293 Sometimes they ring in midstream, or scatter when they reach the bank, which makes adventurous riding, gallop and smash through the scrub to 'bend' them.

bendee /ben'di/. Also **bendi.** [Prob. f. a Qld. Aboriginal language.] The tree of Qld. and N.T. *Acacia catenulata* (fam. Mimosaceae), found on shallow stony soils and (usu.) having a deeply-fluted trunk; the wood of the tree.

1881 W. FEILDING *Austral. Trans-Continental Railway* 18 The road enters a scrub .. of 'bendee'. **1898** C.L. MORGAN *Rabbit Question in Qld.* 98 Posts to be of .. bendee or yapunyah. **1911** ST. C. GRONDONA *Collar & Cuffs* 69 Bendi, as a very thick scrub is called, is almost impenetrable... It is most awkward if the stock you are after take it into their heads to investigate the interior of a patch of bendi. **1978** H.J. LAVERY *Exploration North* 78 Lancewood and bendee occur on shallow rocky soils on slopes and ridges.

benjamin. *Obs.* [Prob. transf. use of the name of the patriarch Jacob's youngest son, hence a favourite son: see OEDS.] See quot. 1870.

1870 C.H. ALLEN *Visit to Qld.* 183 With the black people a husband is now called a 'benjamin'... All white men are called 'Willy', all white women 'Mary'. **1897** W.E. ROTH *Ethnological Studies* 2 He can pronounce *shirt* quite correctly, but when he comes to *fish* he calls it *bish* or *pish*, and speaks of a woman's husband or *Fancy-man* as her *Benjamin.* **1909** E. WALTHAM *Life & Labour in Aust.* 66 While these gins are occupied in searching for their daily food, the 'Warriors' and the 'Benjamins' are out hunting in the Bush.

Bennett's wallaby. [Applied as the specific epithet *Bennetti* by English naturalist G.R. Waterhouse (*Proc. Zool. Soc. London* (1837) 103) after E.T. Bennett (1797–1836), secretary of the Zool. Soc. London.] The brownish-grey wallaby *Macropus rufogriseus rufogriseus* of Tas. and Bass Strait islands. Formerly also **Bennett's kangaroo.**

1838 *Proc. Zool. Soc. London* 137 In Bennett's Kangaroo there are twenty-four caudal vertebrae. **1894** R. LYDEKKER *Hand-Bk. Marsupialia & Monotremata* 27 Bennett's Wallaby (var. *M. bennetti*), from Tasmania, has longer and thicker fur and a more sombre tone of coloration than the typical form [of Red-necked Wallaby]. **1941** E. TROUGHTON *Furred Animals Aust.* 203 The Tasmanian race has hitherto been known as Bennett's Wallaby in natural history books owing to its earlier description as a full species (*bennetti*) named in honour of a distinguished Secretary of the Zoological Society of London. **1973** S. & K. BREEDON *Wildlife Eastern Aust.* 114 A small group of Bennett's Wallabies rise lazily to their feet and hop from the cover of a patch of wattle trees. **1986** *Austral.* (Sydney) 18 Feb. 3/2, 18 animals—eastern grey and red kangaroos and bennett's wallabies—at the Barringo Wildlife Reserve near Gisborne, 85 km. north-west of Melbourne.

berdan. [Of unknown origin.] '*Berdan*, a circular revolving iron inclined pan in which concentrates are ground with mercury and water by an iron ball' (H.A. Gordon *Mining & Engineering* (1906), 576.). Also *attrib.*

1901 O. OSBORNE *Golden Jubilee* 5 Cornish buddles and berdan That saved sludge gold so fine. **1939** I.L. IDRIESS *Cyaniding for Gold* 200 The job can also be done in a Berdan pan.

berg. *Obs.* [a. G. *berg* mountain.] See quot. 1839.

[**1834** *Jrnl. R. Geogr. Soc. London* 82 *Berge* (a German word) .. means those heights now at some distance (greater or less) from the river, but which seem to have been at one time its immediate banks.] **1839** T.L. MITCHELL *Three Exped. Eastern Aust.* (rev. ed.) II. 90 Having experienced on this journey the inconvenient want of terms relative to rivers, I determined to use such of those recommended by Colonel Jackson in his able paper on the subject, in the Journal of the Royal Geographical Society for 1833, as I might find necessary. They are .. *Berg—bergs* heights now at some distance, once the immediate banks of a river or lake. **1845** L. LEICHHARDT *Jrnl. Overland Exped. Aust.* 15 Mar. (1847) 180 The general course of the river was about southwest... Its bed is broad and shallow, with numerous channels, separated by bergues. **1848** T.L. MITCHELL *Jrnl. Exped. Tropical Aust.* 134 Grass was excellent and abundant on the bergs and near the river, but thick scrub crowned these bergs on our side. **1867** F.J. BYERLEY *Narr. Overland Exped. Northern Qld.* 14 Leichhardt describes the stream .. as stony, and with conical hills .. near the river banks, 'Bergues' running into it on each side.

berley, *n.* Also **burley.** [Of unknown origin.]

1. Ground-bait.

1874 *N.S.W. Rep. R. Comm. Fisheries* (1880) 1292 The bait should be crabs. It is usual to wrench legs and shell off the back, and cast them out for berley. **1890** *Jrnl. & Proc. R. Soc. N.S.W.* (1891) 115 They would go with their torches and throw in handfuls of the blue crabs as 'berley'. **1895** C. THACKERAY *Amateur Fisherman's Guide* 10 The black breamer can .. throw berley away without stint and allow his bait to be chewed and worried by .. yellowtail. **1909** F.E. BIRTLES *Lonely Lands* 61 His mode of fishing was to camp near a homestead and at an opportune moment approach the fowl run, scatter a handful of breadcrumbs over the fence and drop his well-baited line among the 'burley'. **1933** C.W. PECK *Austral. Legends* (ed. 2) 25 A little chewed burley from the seed of the burrawang. **1936** *Bulletin* (Sydney) 19 Feb. 20/4 A kerosene-tinful of rabbit carcases boiled to a pulp makes the best 'burley' for Murray cod. **1944** *Ibid.* 23 Feb. 12/3 Hung over the stern of the moored flattie such a bag, given an occasional shake, discharged a stream of tasty meat particles... The modern angler would probably call it 'burley'. **1983** *Canberra Chron.* 16 Mar. 18/2 The best bait is what he calls a 'Montague mullet'... Once the tuna are biting, other trash fish make useful berley.

2. *fig.*

1903 *Truth* (Sydney) 30 Aug. 1/4 The public have already had more than a bellyful of this Bartonian bunkum; they're not taking any more Bartonian burley, thank you. **1972** J. FINGLETON *On Cricket* 24 Hall gave Favell a loose one outside the off-stump for 'burley' and to take his attention away from his leg trap.

berley, *v.* Also **burley.** [See prec.] *trans.* To scatter ground-bait on (the water), in order to attract fish. Also *absol.*, esp. as **berley-up.**

1852 G.C. MUNDY *Our Antipodes* I. 388 The first operation was the baiting of the spot—locally termed 'burley-ing'—with burnt fish. **1895** C. THACKERAY *Amateur Fisherman's Guide* 13 Black bream fishermen frequently spend a lot of time in berleying their spots, and the *modus operandi* is as follows—a bucket or two of bones and crushed oyster shells is quietly tipped over in some sequestered nook close inshore, and about a day or two after is prospected generally with excellent results. **1975** *Meanjin* 186 I'm not tempted, said Kit, By dry-fly or wet. And one never berleys a flood. **1978** J. ROWE *Warlords* 206 Let's burley-up on the reef here and see what comes sniffing about.

Berry blight. *Hist.* [f. the name of Graham *Berry* (1822–1904), Victorian politician.] A name given to a period of economic depression in the Colony of Victoria: see quot. 1886, and also *Black Wednesday* BLACK *a.*[3]

1879 *Australasian* (Melbourne) 4 Jan. 16/4 The year that is gone .. will be painfully memorable hereafter as the sinister epoch of Black Wednesday and the 'Berry blight', and it has acquired an evil pre-eminence for acts of political turpitude in which we hope it will stand alone. **1883** R.E.N. TWOPENY *Town Life Aust.* 92 The 'Berry blight', as it is called, which has fallen over Victoria, is .. a reaction against the selfish and inconsiderate policy of the squatters when they were in power. **1886** R.C. SEATON *Six Lett. from Colonies* 36 Mr Berry is a well-known Radical politician. It is about six years ago since, in one day, he dismissed the greater number of Civil servants in consequence of a disagreement between the two Houses. Most of them had to be quickly restored to their places, but public confidence was so much shaken by this arbitrary act that a large amount of capital was transferred to New South Wales... This period is known as the Berry-blight. **1892** H.C.J. LINGHAM *Juvenal in Melbourne* 14 Time was, the 'Berry Blight' fell on the land. And then no property was in demand.

Also **Berryism** *n.*, **Berryite** *n.* and *a.*

1878 *Australasian* (Melbourne) 9 Feb. 178/4 The Queensland papers had been unanimous in opposing **Berryism.** **1879** *Victorian Rev.* Nov. 25, I have used the word 'Berryism' to denote the latest development of so-called Liberalism in the Colony of Victoria. **1880** *Bulletin* (Sydney) 31 July 1 He likes Mr Berry and believes in Berryism. **1879** *Victorian Rev.* Nov. 45 The ruling principle of the **Berryite** system. **1880** *Bulletin* (Sydney) 3 Apr. 1 The wind which drove the Berryite ship to destruction. **1905** J. FURPHY *Rigby's Romance* (1946) 70 I'm Berryite to the bone; and Binney's tarred with the same stick as yourself—with this difference, that he's a sound Conservative, and you're a rotten one.

best, to give (someone, something): see GIVE 2.

betcherrygah, var. BUDGERIGAR. Also **betshiregah.**

bettong /ˈbɛtɒŋ/. [a. Dharuk *badaŋ*.] A rat-kangaroo, esp. either of two small species of the genus *Bettongia*, *B. penicillata* of drier regions of s. Aust., and *B. gaimardi* of s. and e. Aust.; SQUEAKER 3. See also WOYLIE.

1802 Banks Papers 1 June VIII. 103 Betong. I think this is the one with the slender tail. **1831** *Proc. Zool. Soc. London* I. 149 That to which I have given the name of *Hyps. setosus* is known in the colony of New South Wales by the native name of *Bettong Kangaroo.* **1925** *Bulletin* (Sydney) 3 Sept. 22/2 One of the prettiest little animals of the Tassie bush is the bettong, known to bushmen as the rat-kangaroo. **1972** *Sunday Mail Mag.* (Brisbane) 3 Sept. 4 Bettongs, which occur in many parts of Australia but are nowhere common except in some parts of Tasmania, are the 'nest-making rat-kangaroos' and use their long flexible tails for the transport of nesting materials. **1986** *New Scientist* (London) 6 Feb. 27 Lesser-known species such as the .. burrowing bettong are truly endangered, but are ignored.

betty. *Obs.* [Transf. use of *betty* bar used to force a door or window.] An instrument for picking locks; a skeleton key.

1812 J.H. VAUX *Mem.* (1819) 156 *Betty*, a picklock; to *unbetty*, or *betty* a lock, is to open or relock it, by means of the *betty*, so as to avoid subsequent detection. **1848** *Port Phillip Herald* 3 Feb. (Suppl.), He might have searched him, and found either a 'Jemmy' or a 'Betty' (a master-key) in his possession. **1854** *Illustr. Sydney News* 20 May 63/1 John Flynn alias Henry Fagan was charged with having in his possession three skeleton keys and a 'betty'. **1882** *Sydney Slang Dict.* 1 Betty, skeleton key, or picklock.

bewdy, var. BEAUTY.

beyond. [Spec. use of *the back of beyond* humorous phr. for a distant place: see OED *beyond* quasi-*sb.* b.] In the phr. **back of** (or **o'**) **beyond,** (country) far inland, remote from large towns or closely settled districts. Also used adverbially. See BACK COUNTRY *n.* 5.

1888 'R. BOLDREWOOD' *Robbery under Arms* (1937) 149 You'll mostly find that these far-out-back-of-beyond places have got men and women to match 'em. **1904** *Bulletin* (Sydney) 15 Sept. 18/2 The back-o'-beyond Jay Pee is often a tricky bit of mulga. **1911** A.L. HAYDON *Trooper Police Aust.* 51 A little-known country which the bushman speaks of as the 'back of beyond', the 'Never-Never land'. **1926** L.C.E. GEE *Bush Tracks & Gold Fields* Pref., The 'Back of Beyond' is to most of us a land of fascination. **1935** DAVISON & NICHOLLS *Blue Coast Caravan* 149 Knew a chap who reckoned there was nothing to touch the country out west—the red sand-hill country, back-of-beyond. **1948** G. FARWELL *Down Argent Street* 1 Every man comes up to town to yarn .. or to mingle with newcomers and station people in from a hundred or two miles back o' beyond. **1963** D. ATTENBOROUGH *Quest under Capricorn* 24 This isn't the back of beyond any more—though people down south still seem to think we're a rough mob here. **1974** P. ADAM SMITH *Desert Railway* 21 Port Augusta is Beyond. Anywhere beyond this is truly Back o' Beyond.

beyond the black stump: see BLACK STUMP.

beyond the boundaries: see BOUNDARY *n.*

beyond the limits: see LIMITS.

beyond the limits of location: see LOCATION 4.

bib. [Fig. use of *bib* upper garment.] In the phr. **to push (put, stick) one's bib in,** to interfere; **to keep one's bib out,** to refrain from interfering.

1952 T.A.G. HUNGERFORD *Ridge & River* 57 Here was Wilder .. sticking in his bib. **1959** S.J. BAKER *Drum* 89 *Bib in*, any interference, any action of a busybody, esp. in the phrases stick one's bib in, put (or push) one's bib in. **1966** J. WATEN *Season of Youth* 80, I don't know what possessed me to push my bib in but I asked a question in a rather nervous, unusually high voice. **1974** BLAZEY & CAMPBELL *Political Dice Men* 201 Askin 'thanked the pussy-footing Victorians to keep their bib out of New South Wales politics'. **1984** *Canberra Times* 1 Sept. 3/4 The doctors should not 'stick their bibs' into negotiations on building workers' wages and conditions.

Bible-basher. [Cf. *Bible-pounder*: see OEDS. Used elsewhere but recorded earliest in Aust.] A clergyman; a religious zealot. Also **Bible-banger.**

1904 *Bulletin* (Sydney) 21 Jan. 16/3 The clerical calling gathered a rich store of opprobrious appellations from irreverent Australians. Some that I have heard: Sky-pilot, devil-dodger, gospel-puncher, snuffler, amen-snorter, bible-banger. **1904** *Truth* (Sydney) 18 Sept. (Suppl.) 1/6 The tray-trapping Bible-banger .. fears that his churchwardens and prominent patrons may *sink their thrumbos* in long sleevers, instead of planking them into the empty plate. **1958** R. STOW *To Islands* 74 They were Bible-bashers and humourless clods. **1962** D. MCLEAN *World turned upside Down* 42 Old man Fenton was a bloody old Bible-banger. **1975** X. HERBERT *Poor Fellow my Country* 254 The bigger the case, the more the publicity. That's what the Anthrops and the bible-bashers want. **1978** T. DAVIES *More Austral. Nicknames* 30 *The Bible Basher* sprouts about religion.

Hence **Bible bash** *v. intr.*, **Bible-bashing** *ppl. a.*

1944 L. GLASSOP *We were Rats* 124, I doan want any bible-bashing bastard who's never seen me before mumblin' any bull-- over me. **1967** H. SAINT-THOMAS *Night of Long Shadows* 117 The cow, always Bible bashing. **1976** A. REID *Whitlam Venture* 58 The National Country Party Premier of Queensland, Joh Bjelke-Petersen, whom Whitlam in a fit of petulance described publicly as that 'Bible-bashing bastard'.

biccies, bickies, varr. BIKKIES.

bidgee-widgee. [Altered form of N.Z. *biddy-biddy* burr of the piripiri, a. Maori *piripiri*: see OEDS *biddy-biddy*.] Any of several creeping perennial herbs of the genus *Acaena* (fam. Rosaceae) having a burr-like fruit, esp. the widespread *A. novae-zelandiae* and related species; BUZZY.

***c* 1910** W.R. GUILFOYLE *Austral. Plants* 390 Bidgee-widgee *Acaena Sanguisorbae.* **1975** A.B. & J.W. CRIBB *Wild Food in Aust.* 177 Bidgee-widgee .. was used as a tea substitute. **1980** J. WOLFE *End of Pricklystick* 30 The bidgee-widgee plants threw their deep-green creepers over the land and a million little stems shot up from the creepers. Each stem carried a green, spiked ball that looked something like a sea-urchin.

big, *a.*

1. a. *Austral. pidgin.* Great in size, quantity, duration, importance, or intensity, esp. in the collocations **big fellow, mob, one.**

1840 J.P. JOHNSON *Plain Truths* 17 The natives appeared equally afraid of the horses and bullocks, which they called big dogs. **1845** L. LEICHHARDT *Jrnl. Overland Exped. Aust.* 17 Mar. (1847) 185 Charley cried out, 'Look there, Sir! what big water!' **1847** G.F. ANGAS *Savage Life & Scenes* I. 129 The natives ran back to their fires, saying, 'no care if big sheepy [*sc.* horse] die'. **1867** W. MILTON *Victim Nineteenth Century* 23, I heard the blacks talking very much about '*big one emu*', meaning the camels, from which I inferred that Burke had crossed the Murray, and very likely the Darling by this time. **1870** C.H. ALLEN *Visit to Qld.* 182 'Big fellow waddy', a large quantity of wood. **1872** MRS E. MILLETT *Austral. Parsonage* 83 A large quantity of anything is expressed by the words 'big-fellow', as 'big-fellow-rain', 'big-fellow fond of'. **1887** 'OVERLANDER' *Austral. Sketches* 37 He told me that Jim had a big-fellow growl at him. **1890** 'R. BOLDREWOOD' *Colonial Reformer* I. 201 I've never seen our main city or the big waterhole, as the blacks call it. **1895** J. KIRBY *Old Times in Bush* 110 One of their habits is to hold 'big yabbers', and they begin talking quietly at first about the tribe they are at variance with, and by degrees talk louder and faster, until they work themselves up into a state of great anger and excitement. **1925** *Bulletin* (Sydney) 24 Dec. 22/2 A big-fellow shark is to be seen near Murray Island. **1930** A.E. YARRA *Vanishing Horsemen* 17 The boss was a big feller medicine man, able to smell out the sleeping-places of lazy scrub choppers. **1949** I.L. IDRIESS *One Wet Season* 267 The 'Big Sick'—the actively virulent form of leprosy. **1954** *Bulletin* (Sydney) 18 Aug. 12/1 There was bigfella trouble among the plantation kanakas. **1955** F. LANE *Patrol to Kimberleys* 13 Additionally, there were cases of the 'big sick'—leprosy—to investigate. **1968** S. GORE *Holy Smoke* 16 God's make 'im all this one country longa you. Make 'im land, make 'im sea—big mob water.

b. *Obs.* **big one** (used advb. with (*ppl.*) *a.*), very, extremely.

1856 W.W. Dobie *Recoll. Visit Port-Phillip* 91 The ground was *big one* hard, and his back was *big one* tired. **1872** 'Resident' *Glimpses Life Vic.* 191 'Me big one frightened.' [*Note*] 'Big one' signifies in the black's English 'very' or 'very much'.

2. [Orig. *pidgin.*] **big smoke,** a town or city.

1848 H.W. Haygarth *Recoll. Bush Life* 6 He gradually leaves behind him the 'big smoke' (as the aborigines picturesquely call the town). **1857** F. de B. Cooper *Wild Adventures* 41 If you send him to the 'Toom-virran' (literally, 'Big-smoke', *i.e.*, Brisbane), they will hang him! **1894** A.B. Bell *Austral. Camp Fire Tales* 103, I heard Jack had gone to Melbourne, so I made for the big smoke, as that city was called by the diggers. **1903** *Truth* (Sydney) 18 Jan. 1/6 'I believe you had a pretty tough time in Sydney,' said the pumpkin squatter to his friend who had just returned from a trip to the big smoke. **1908** *Ibid.* 26 July 1/6 The latest cricket news from the Big Smoke says that Middlesex won the match against the Philadelphians at Lords. ***c* 1937** J.M. Harcourt *It never Fails* 71 The big smokes—Brisbane and Sydney and Melbourne. **1965** R.H. Conquest *Horses in Kitchen* 119 Toowoomba . . had a population of about 22,000 . . but to Hoppy's amazed eyes it was the biggest Big Smoke in creation. **1975** T. Schurmann *Shop!* 129 There were men from the city and the world outside, who returned to the big smoke every weekend and actually went to see the big games of football.

3. [Prob. strongly influenced by sense 1.]

a. In collocations implying (a person's) superiority: **big bloke, boss, cog, fellow, man, squatter,** a powerful or successful person.

1916 *Bulletin* (Sydney) 6 July 24/1 Here are a few of the pet names given by the wielder of the pick and banjo to the ganger: 'The red light', 'the **big bloke**', [etc.]. **1978** W. Lowenstein *Weevils in Flour* 97 Yes! The Big Bloke was definitely a product of the 1890s. **1964** P. Adam Smith *Hear Train Blow* 151 He . . said his father was no longer the '**big boss** cocky'. **1925** *Bulletin* (Sydney) 12 Mar. 22/3 In south-west Queensland many station managers are known as 'the **big cog**'. This title was originally earned by Clement Ladbury, of Milo, who explained to a station-hand that everyone working on the place was a 'cog in the machine'. 'And I,' he added, 'am the big cog.' **1907** *Ibid.* 14 Nov. 15/2 The managers of tin sluicing and dredging concerns . . are all called, irrespective of size, 'the **Big Feller**'. **1938** F. Blakeley *Hard Liberty* 90 The big fellow was Mr McTaggart, who owned the station. **1940** *Bulletin* (Sydney) 28 Feb. 16/4 The big fellow was stiff in a Victorian dairy town, so he took a job with a cow-cocky at 25s. a week and keep. **1983** *Austral. Dict. Biogr.* IX. 664 The end of the industrialists' drive for power since 1916 was the ascendancy of a maverick parliamentarian, 'the Big Fella' [*sc.* J.T. Lang]. **1911** R.G.S. Williams *Austral. White Slaves* 99 But when those five million acres were abandoned by '**big men**' in the Western division of New South Wales how many small men took their places? **1951** S. Hickey *Travelled Roads* 10 It [*sc.* dummying] was a good thing for the Big Man until he began to be double-crossed. **1845** *Port Phillip Gaz.* 4 June 2 We cannot see that the **'big' Squatters**—as the phrase goes—have any right to claim any more than is just sufficient for their stock. **1888** 'R. Boldrewood' *Robbery under Arms* (1937) 61 The 'big squatter', as he was called on our side of the country, was Mr Falkland.

b. In collocations describing a tract of land or type of vegetation distinguished by extent or dimension: **big bush, country, paddock, sand, scrub, timber**.

1909 *Bulletin* (Sydney) 8 Apr. 43/1 We was special settlers, an' we had a hundred acres of **big bush**. **1959** H.G. Lamond *Sheep Station* 64 He was imbued with the creed of the big bush: he would never let a mate down! **1968** *TV Times* (Sydney) 28 Aug. 8/1 A new half-hour programme dealing with the big issues that confront people living outside the cities. Titled A **Big Country**. **1970** R. Beilby *No Medals for Aphrodite* 39 A couple of ecstatically free-booting seasons with shearing teams in the Nor'-west, the 'Big Country'. **1974** *Austral. Folksongs* (Folk Lore Council Aust.) 2 Our land Australia—a big country. **1937** M. Terry *Sand & Sun* 26 We would wander in the **Big Paddock** where Jackey, the black-fellow, is still King. **1899** *Bulletin* (Sydney) 9 Dec. 19/2 On the further edge of the **Big Sand** is a hut. **1881** R. Crawford *Echoes from Bushland* 102 There's a **big scrub** right a-head! **1893** D.J. Frost *Crown Lands N.S.W.* 7 In this Richmond district is an area of country some 60 miles long by 30 miles broad, known as the big scrub, which is of wonderful richness. **1898** *Bulletin* (Sydney) 26 Nov. 14/3 For solid cheek the Murrumbidgee Whaler 'ain't in it' with the Big Scrub Swaggie. **1948** P.J. Hurley *Red Cedar* p. ix, Red Cedar was the 'red gold' of the 'big scrubs'. **1959** *Never kill Dolphin* (Writers' Guild Qld.) 165 Unbidden, his mind returned to the timber camps of the big scrubs, with their broken melody of running water, their fragrance that was the fragrance of a thousand earth scents. **1976** *Ecos* ix. 31/3 Large areas of northern New South Wales for example—the 'Big Scrub'—were once covered with rainforest. Now they support run-down dairy farms. **1904** *Bulletin* (Sydney) 13 Oct. 18/2 Smith was a settler far out in mountainous **big-timber** country. **1914** *Ibid.* 3 Dec. 13/2 When the bushman goes off to yakker in the big timber he does not, as a usual thing, carry a medical outfit. **1925** *Smith's Weekly* (Sydney) 20 June 15/7 In the big timber country of the North Coast of N.S.W. timber-getters had to produce a licence when visited by a forest ranger.

c. In collocations denoting the duration or severity of seasonal phenomena: **big blow, dry, rain, wet.**

1944 J. Devanny *By Tropic Sea & Jungle* 3 That's the **big blow** season. **1947** H. Drake-Brockman *On N.-W. Skyline* 15 Even from the air we could see the tarpaulin cover over part of the hospital roof, reminder of the last 'big blow'. **1942** L. & K. Harris *Lost Hole Bingoola* 51 The long rainless season which the natives called the '**big dry**' had begun. **1965** L. Haylen *Big Red* Pref., The struggle of the poor farmer to break his bonds to the boss, the banker and the 'big dry' in the years prior to World War II. **1903** *Bulletin* (Sydney) 3 Jan. 16/2 A **big rain** is magnified under glaring head-lines in the daily press. ***c* 1960** C. Mackness *Clump Point & District* 85 The big-rains country, with its tall, fast-growing grasses, does not suit sheep. **1927** M. Dorney *Adventurous Honeymoon* 95 We would never have got through before the '**big wet**'. **1981** Q. Wild *Honey Wind* 33 Less than a thousand years ago streams on the plains between the high ground and the coast spilled into enormous lagoons and paperbark swamps. Only in the Big Wet did they now link up with the tidal reaches where they once routinely flowed.

d. In miscellaneous collocations denoting greatness of extent, dimension, or number: **big fence,** see quot.; **house** [orig. U.S.: see OEDS *big house* 1], the homestead on a sheep or cattle station; **mob,** a large number (of animals or people); a large quantity; **ring,** a game played with marbles; **spit,** the act of vomiting; esp. in the phr. **to go for the big spit,** to vomit; **stoush,** see Stoush *n.* 2.

1940 E. Hill *Great Austral. Loneliness* (ed. 2) 57 He is a rider of the **Big Fence**, the only fence in the world that cuts a continent into two mighty paddocks—the Number One Rabbit Proof. **1881** A.C. Grant *Bush-Life Qld.* I. 57 'There,' said Stone, pointing to the **big house**, 'nobody has lived in the *cawbawn humpy*—that is what the blacks call it—since Mr Cosgrove went away.' **1927** 'S. Rudd' *Romance of Runnibede* 7 The 'big house', as it was called, with father's office at the end of a wide, high verandah, was walled and floored with dressed slabs. **1943** H.G. Lamond *From Tariaro to Ross Roy* 21 Candles . . were the illuminants of the homestead—the 'big' house, or 'gov'ment' house as it was known in the bush vernacular. **1959** K.S. Prichard *N'Goola* 16 When you were away on the bullock muster . . I went to the big house for stores. **1977** C. McCulloch *Thorn Birds* 190 All the other men . . turned their mounts into the stockyard and headed for either the big house or the jackaroo barracks. **1951** E. Hill *Territory* 328 A glass of beer and a counter-lunch at a 'billabong' nearby, and they are off . . to watch the '**big mobs**' galloping past like a bang-tail muster. **1964** K. Willey *Eaters of Lotus* 28 More than a hundred people—what they call a 'big mob' in this country—have gathered for the fun. **1983** *Yulngu* July 25 The Community have . . built a new basketball court. It has taken biggest mobs of sweat, time and concrete. **1984** *N.T. News* (Darwin) 27 Oct. 36/4 Big mobs of finches including Stars, Longtails, Double Bars. **1947** M. Raymond *Smiley gets Gun* 44 Blue joined them and suggested a game of marbles. They chalked a rough circle on the wooden floor of the shed and started to play **big-ring.** **1966** A.R. Chisholm *Familiar Presence* 78 Marbles . . gave rise to a large number of special expressions. 'Big ring' and 'little ring' may still exist. **1977** R. McKie *Crushing* (1978) 107 'I just have time for one game of Big Ring. . .' They marked a Big Ring. One sweep with a stick without a join. **1983** J. Hepworth *Extraordinary Austral. Landmarks*, And with marbles like these there's another thing: The game you play must be *Big Ring!* **1959** *R.A.N. News* (Sydney) 20 Mar. 4 Down in the Strait The wave rolled high The waves rolled wide And the '**Big Spit**' starters lined the side. **1960** J. Wynnum *Sailor Blushed* (1962) 85 He retired to the stern-sheet, and without any ceremony, 'went for the big spit' into the darkness in the lee of the launch. **1964** B. Humphries *Nice Night's Entertainment* (1981) 78 The bastard barely swallowed it When he went for the big spit And he chundered in the old Pacific sea. **1967** F. Hardy *Billy Borker yarns Again* 63, I did want to be a grog guzzler and live on side bets, but they'll bar me here in Darwin just because I go for the big spit occasionally. **1969** A. Buzo *Rooted* (1973) 43 Remember the time he got sick at Davo's twenty-first and went for the big spit?

e. *Australian National Football.* In collocations denoting height: **big man,** a tall player, esp. a Follower; **ones, sticks** *pl.*, the goal posts (see Stick *n.* 1).

1920 *Australasian* (Melbourne) 8 May 911/2 Hiskens, a **big man** and strong, a younger brother of a famous football family, hailed from Rutherglen. **1928** G. Moriarty *Teaching Game of Football* iv. 2 If you put a big man to watch him he will be all the time giving the little fellow free kicks. **1931** J.F. McHale et al. *Austral. Game of Football* 78 In addition to being the fastest big man in the game, he was very accurate with long drop kicks for goal. **1955** *Herald* (Melbourne) 1 Apr. 23/1 At that time Richmond had a formidable line-up of big men. **1969** A. Hopgood *And Big Men Fly* 44 And there's the bounce. And the big men fly! **1984** *Canberra Times* 3 Feb. 16/1 These two players will add to our big-man strength and allow us more scope to switch players around. **1979** *Herald* (Melbourne) 7 Sept. 2 *It's through*: A score worth six points. . . *Bisects the* **big ones**—Right through the centre: Likewise. *Bangs it through the* **big sticks**: Ditto. **1981** L. Money *Footy Fan's Handbk.* 37 *Terms for a goal*: . . Bangs it through the big sticks!

Big Brother. [Fig. use of *big brother* elder brother.] A member of a voluntary organization founded in 1925 to provide foster-care for British youths emigrating to Australia. Also **Big Brother Movement** (or **Scheme**).

1925 *Youth* (Big Brother Movt.) 2 The Big Brother Movement is founded upon the belief that the outstanding need of Australia is more population. **1926** F.M. Sky *Our most Important Problem* 4 Mr Henry E. Budden . . gave . . an address on the Big Brother movement, and in response to his appeal . . readily signified, in writing, their willingness to become a 'Big Brother'. **1929** W.A. Carrothers *Emigration from Brit. Isles* 284 Through what is known as the 'Big Brother Movement', selected boys going to Victoria, South Australia and New South Wales are placed under the care of responsible men who act as 'Big Brothers' to them until they reach the age of 21. **1939** J.T. McMahon *Bushies' Scheme in W.A.* 37 The 'Big Brother' assumes a paternal interest in some immigrant boy, promising to care for him when out of employment, and to guard him while in it. **1959** E. Webb *Mark of Sun* 101 Big Brothers are Australian men who promise to keep an eye on us, and help any way they can. **1986** *Bulletin* (Sydney) 18 Feb. 58/3 The Hawke government's first Immigration and Ethnic Affairs Minister . . put a stop to the Big Brother scheme under which British youngsters were brought out to Australia as settlers.

big-note, *v. refl.* In the phr. **to big-note** (oneself), to display or boast of one's wealth; to exaggerate one's own importance.

[**1950** *Austral. Police Jrnl.* Apr. 111 *Big-note man*, wealthy.] **1953** K. Tennant *Joyful Condemned* 23 'Morton the bustman!' Rene sneered. 'Listen to him big-note himself. He's going to do a bust.' **1960** K. Smith *Word from Children* 157 Any father who wants to big-note himself with his boy has only to look back into the past to get a clue or two. **1970** R. Beilby *No Medals for Aphrodite* 252 Helping her! Taking the guilt from her! Just big-noting himself, that's what it was. **1972** J. O'Grady *It's your Shout, Mate!* 16 You can't big note yourself by shoutin' for us an' then pissin' off. You got two more pots to come yet. **1977** A. Mackay *Life Pieces* II. 134 He'd tell lies just to big-note himself. **1983** *Age* (Melbourne) 2 June 1/2 He agreed that Mr Farquhar was egotistical, a name-dropper and frequently big-noted himself.

Hence **big-noter** *n.*, one who tries to impress others.

1967 *Kings Cross Whisper* (Sydney) xxxii. 6/3 *Big noter*, a braggart who uses money to impress birds. **1972** A. CHIPPER *Aussie Swearers Guide* 26 The big note the *Big Noter* sounds is in his own glorification. He is easy to spot because he invariably suffers from chronic Verbal My-itis. . . In basic Australian, he's *got tickets on himself*. **1975** *Austral.* (Sydney) 11 Nov. 10/2 He says the world is full of big-noters who reckon if a little fat guy can stand up there and talk for an hour then they can too.

bike. [Fig. use of *bike*, abbrev. of *bicycle*.]

1. See quot. 1945.

1945 S.J. BAKER *Austral. Lang.* 123 A willing girl is sometimes described as *an office bike, a town bike*, etc. **1951** D. STIVENS *Jimmy Brockett* 178 The little bitch got up with a squeal and tried to cover herself with a cushion. Young Herb looked scared. . . 'I might have known you were the bloody town bike.' **1965** L. HAYLEN *Big Red* 186 The Socialist . . whose wife now had openly become the 'village bike'. **1972** L. IRISH *Time of Dolphins* 121 Piss off. Keep your twitchy hands and shanks to yourself. . . I'm not, I repeat *not*, the neighbourhood bike. **1977** W. MOORE *Just to Myself* 99 Elsie Patterson was the town bike. . . 'Give her a guzzle of cherry cocktail', Merv would say, 'and she's a moral.' **1981** *Nat. Times* (Sydney) 5 Apr. 38/3 Girls at school were called 'slut', 'dog', and 'bike' for sleeping with anyone.

2. In the phr. **to get off** (or occas. **on**) **one's bike,** to become angry.

1938 X. HERBERT *Capricornia* 565 Don't get off your bike, son. I know you're tellin' lies. **1943** J. BINNING *Target Area* 34 Don't get off your bike, old man. **1968** S. GORE *Holy Smoke* 46 And at that, o' course, as the Bible says, he gets properly off his bike. **1973** F. MOORHOUSE *Austral. Stories* 33 Come on, Hel, don't get off your bike. **1986** *Sydney Morning Herald* 12 Apr. 45/1 Magistrate Blisset is a fair magistrate and a 'good bloke'. 'I've never heard anyone get on a bike about him.'

bikie. [Abbrev. of *motor-)bike (rider* + -Y.] See quot. 1967.

1967 *Kings Cross Whisper* xxxii. 6/3 *Bikie*, a member of a gang or a club of people interested in motor bikes. **1968** *Everybody's* (Sydney) 20 Mar. 4/2 'Before the bikies came to the Wayside Chapel, they spent most of their spare time drinking in hotels and other places,' Mr Noffs said. **1973** F. MOORHOUSE *Austral. Stories* 107 I'd rush to friend's houses in gumboots and sou'wester shouting, that's the last affair I have with a Chinese, a Greek, a bikie. **1976** J. JOHNSON *Low Breed* 228 'You were raped by a dozen bikies,' suggested David. 'No such luck,' Winnie replied agreeably, 'I spent last week at an Encounter Group.' **1978** SAW & MILBANK *Back to Back Tango* 55 The bikies arrived. There must have been twenty of them on as many bikes, roaring and rattling: in obscene fibreglass helmets, tight leather jackets, and boots and goggles. **1984** *Canberra Times* 6 Sept. 2/2 'Bikies' are the outlaw types, while 'bikers' are ordinary motorcyclists. **1984** *Open Road* Oct. 10/5 All he asked was that the motorist remember he had been 'helped by a bikie'.

bikkies, *pl.* Also **biccies, bickies.** [Facetious use of *bicky* biscuit.] Money.

1966 *Kings Cross Whisper* (Sydney) xx. 8/1 Here in Kings Cross cabbage means money, and so does . . lolly, bikkies and fat. **1972** *Ibid.* cxxiii. 2/1 As for their other bikkies, like stolen money, everyone knows Australian currency is worthless. **1975** B. DAWE *Just Dugong at Twilight* 7, I reckon now I've got it made: My Earth Dynamics thesis in, There'll be more biccies in the tin! **1981** *Canberra Times* 30 Oct. 2/7 We reckon the presence of a highly qualified academic in a tutorial is worth something in its own right, regardless of whether he or she actually says anything. . . Just showing up is worth big bickies.

bilby /'bɪlbi bɪlbi/. [a. Yuwaalaraay *bilbi*.] **a.** The rabbit-eared bandicoot *Macrotis lagotis*, a small, burrowing marsupial of woodlands and plains of drier parts of mainland Aust.; DALGITE. **b.** (Occas.) the smaller *M. leucura*, now rare and poss. extinct. See also *rabbit bandicoot, rat* RABBIT A. 1. Also *attrib.*

1885 *Once a Month* (Melbourne) May 376 There are several kinds of burrowing animals . . everywhere. . . The most remarkable is the Bailby—some call it Billby—about the size of a rabbit. **1896** T. HENEY *Girl at Birrell's* 14 'Possum and bilby-skin rugs. **1900** *Bulletin* (Sydney) 24 Mar. 14/2 The 'bilby' is the smallest variety of plains wallaby, lives underground, and never comes out till after dark. **1921** *Ibid.* 14 Apr. 26/4 A rare animal nowadays is the bilby . . which was one time very plentiful in Central Australia. **1954** C. BARRETT *Wild Life Aust. & New Guinea* 32 'Bilbies', or 'bielbies', as these beautiful little marsupials are commonly termed, have long tails as well as rabbit-like ears. **1972** V. SERVENTY *Singing Land* 85 Another flesheater is the dalgite, or bilby. . . Once widespread, its stronghold today is the desert lands. **1984** *Austral.* (Sydney) 12 July 3/1 It might sound like something from Tolkien, but the bilby is real.

Biljim, var. BILLJIM.

billabong /'bɪləbɒŋ/. Also formerly **billibong, billybong.** [a. Wiradhuri *bila* river + *-baŋ*, signifying a watercourse which runs only after rain; orig. as a place-name, with reference to the Bell River in s.e. N.S.W.]

1. An arm of a river, made by water flowing from the main stream, usu. only in time of flood, to form a backwater, blind creek, anabranch, or, when the water level falls, a pool or lagoon (often of considerable extent); the dry bed of such a formation. Also *attrib.*

[**1836** T.L. MITCHELL *Three Exped. Eastern Aust.* (1838) II. 21 The name this stream receives from the natives here, is Billibang. **1848** *Port Phillip Herald* 15 Feb. 3/1 The cattle station of W. O'Sullivan, Esq., at Billy Bong forest. **1851** *Britannia* (Hobart) 13 Feb. 4/5 In the Billebong country, water is an unknown treasure.] **1853** J. ALLEN *Jrnl. River Murray* 31 This station is situated about half-a-mile inland, over a 'billy-bong' (the native name for a small creek or backwater). **1861** *Burke & Wills Exploring Exped.* 27 At the end of a very long waterhole, it breaks into billibongs, which continue splitting into sandy channels until they are all lost in the earthy soil. **1863** W.J. WILLS *Successful Exploration Interior Aust.* 227 We struck the first of several small creeks or billibongs, which must be portions of the creek with the deep channel that we crossed on going up. **1872** *Eclectic* (Adelaide) I. x. 40/1 Tingling of the horse bells, which ring out sweetly and musically as the animals graze about in the green bed of a neighbouring 'billabong'. **1878** R.B. SMYTH *Aborigines of Vic.* II. 314 The Billybongs . . run inland for miles, and served as reservoirs to hold the waters which were brought down by the floods. **1887** 'COMMERCIAL TRAVELLER' *Diary Three Months Trip Qld.* 54 The road to Winton winds along the Western River. When we arrived at any of the inlets or billybongs, caused by its overflow, the mailman would gallop ahead to take soundings. **1887** 'OVERLANDER' *Austral. Sketches* 32 We camped in a sort of billabong running out of the creek. **1893** S. NEWLAND *Paving Way* 238 Another line of timber . . denoting to the practised eye that there was a long billabong, receiving its waters in flood-time from the great stream, and restoring them to it many miles lower down, probably after filling several lakes and pools. **1896** *Bulletin* (Sydney) 7 Mar. 19/2 'Billabong' . . is the aboriginal equivalent of 'anabranch'—a natural by-wash or secondary channel, running, as a rule only in flood-time. The Billabong Creek is a billabong of the Murray; so are the Edwards, the Gulpa, the Wakool, and a host of minor intermittent streams. A billabong may form the flood-connection of two separate rivers; the Willandra Billabong is an example. **1906** J.W. GREGORY *Dead Heart Aust.* 112 We passed several billabongs—some of them curved, others horse-shoe shaped—and we searched their beds for fossils. **1914** 'B. CABLE' *By Blow & Kiss* 234 If the river would rise another three foot, we might have it running up the billabongs. **1925** M. TERRY *Across Unknown Aust.* 150 Where one finds a disused channel of a river, holding water and filled during flood, the term 'billabong' is used. A billabong may be a backwash, blocked by debris at its mouth, or an old detour, abandoned after a new course has been found by the stream. **1927** R.S. BROWNE *Journalist's Memories* 76 In the shearers' huts in the West, on mustering camps and at these little meetings of 'billabong whalers' where two or three were gathered together the name of 'Billy' Lane was reverenced. **1930** HIVES & LUMLEY *Jrnl. of Jackaroo* 65 Just before reaching the river itself I had to cross a 'billibong', or extra channel, generally dry except for a pool in the centre of its course. **1933** D. MACDONALD *Brooks of Morning* 67 Bayou in Florida, billabong in Riverina—the same thing everywhere, with different geographical names. **1951** *Bulletin* (Sydney) 15 Aug. 13/1 The river . . gradually rose and rose and presently flowed out over its banks and backed up the creeks and swelled the billabongs ('Lake Forbes' is a billabong) until the water overflowed their banks. **1956** T. RONAN *Moleskin Midas* 250 The rain which occurred almost every day created bogholes in every gilgai and billabong. **1965** G. McINNES *Road to Gundagai* 179 Our camp at Warrandyte was on a peat-and-sand isthmus between the Yarra and its billabong. **1973** R. ROBINSON *Drift of Things* 108 It sloped down to a creek which ran into billabongs and swamps filled with reeds and bulrushes. **1986** *Sydney Morning Herald* 26 Apr. 6/3 Wetlands in the upper Lachlan were usually linked to the river with billabongs, the remnants of earlier river channels, which formed lagoons with moderate to high river flows.

2. *transf.* and *fig.*

1895 *Bulletin* (Sydney) 23 Nov. 3/2 And down the beds of dried-up creeks They wandered all day long Till life seemed, in a trooper's view, one endless billabong. **1899** W.T. GOODGE *Hits! Skits! & Jingles* 170 Jack McCamley, Lank and long. Ox-persuader, Billabong. **1930** J.S. LITCHFIELD *Far-North Memories* 6 Their amazement at the harbour, which they described as a 'whopping big billabong', was very funny. **1935** H. MCCRAE *My Father* 57 My billabong of intellectual solitude is the London Library. **1936** *Publicist* (Sydney) ii. 6/2 Australia's intellectual, political, social, and financial life has been in a billabong for twenty years past. **1950** G. FARWELL *Surf Music* 23 His life was a billabong, closed in upon itself, joining up with the outer world at rare floodtimes. **1951** E. HILL *Territory* 328 A glass of beer and a counter-lunch at a 'billabong' near by. **1959** J. CLEARY *Strike me Lucky* 188 Out in the paddocks, above the pale green billabong of young lucerne, a few crows flapped in sluggish flight. **1962** T. RONAN *Deep of Sky* 58 He told them about Crooked Mick—the one great hero of billabong mythology. In a matter of thieving a drink or a feed for bullocks or horses he was not only a willing accomplice but a joyous one. **1969** G. JOHNSTON *Clean Straw for Nothing* (1971) 168 The consciousness of being in a mainstream of human conflict and aspiration, not in a backwater or stranded on some remote dry billabong.

Hence as *v. intr.*, to follow a circuitous route in leisurely fashion, to meander; **billabonger** *n.*, a swagman.

1886 *Illustr. Sydney News* Dec. 33/3 The shearers grinned, and Sam the Billabonger, Whose noted points were ribaldry and beer, Exclaimed, when, after a protracted laugh he Could speak, 'The super, to an ephigraphy!' **1908** MRS A. GUNN *We of Never-Never* 1 It [*sc.* the train] was out of town just then, up-country somewhere, billabonging in true bushwhacker style, but was expected to return in a day or two. **1908** *Ibid.* p. xi, A strange medley of Whites, Blacks, and Chinese; of travellers, overlanders, and billabongers, who passed in and out of our lives. **1954** T. RONAN *Vision Splendid* 217 They dispensed tactfully casual invitations for lunch or tea to billabongers who hadn't eaten a really square meal for months.

billar, var. BELAH.

billet. [Transf. use of *billet* soldier's lodging place: see OEDS *sb.*[1] 4 b.]

1. A job, employment; a particular task (see quot. 1911); a sinecure (see quot. 1909). Also *fig.*

1843 *Adelaide Observer* 9 Dec. 4/1 If men have to walk ten or twelve miles to their labour . . it is not to be wondered at that they should fly off at a tangent, or look out for what they not inaptly term *a better billet*. **1846** L.W. MILLER *Notes of Exile Van Dieman's Land* 280 Grant, Gemmell and Beemer continued to be 'good coveys', and our overseer made a fine billet of it. **1849** T. ROGERS *Corresp. relating to Dismissal* 141 Before a month both these men were in billets: one as hut-keeper to the police, and the other as a policeman. **1855** *Illustr. Sydney News* 20 Jan. 3/1 A Happy New Year (For Government Officers.)—The utmost excitement is prevailing on the camp in consequence of the uncertain tenure of their respective 'billets'. **1872** W.M. HUGO *Hist. First Bushman's Club* 30 A swagsman, and not ashamed to own it. I have done the 'wallaby' for years past in search of a billet. **1884** *Austral. Tit-Bits* (Melbourne) 26 June 8/3 Will take a saleman's billet at the Fish Market. **1887** *Bulletin* (Sydney) 26 Feb. 6/4

Already Sir Henry Parkes has found that the Premiership is not the very rosiest of billets. **1896** *Ibid.* 14 Mar. 27/2 One Barrier speculator-squatter has £50,000 looking for a billet. **1903** *Ibid.* 15 Oct. 35/1 A dashing young softgoodsman came from Sydney to take a billet in the leading store in Quantook. **1909** W.G. Spence *Aust.'s Awakening* 267 One Premier after another retired to a good fat billet. **1911** St. C. Grondona *Collar & Cuffs* 112 My billet for that day was to boundary ride the seven-mile spring paddock. **1930** V. Palmer *Passage* (1957) 65 Fred was talking of finding a billet on one of the sugar-boats going up the coast. **1945** M. Hodges *Veil of Time* 157 My next billet was as 'procurer' in the country order department of a well-known city drapery emporium. **1980** Brennan & White *Keep Billy Boiling* 82 Times being bad I had to take a billet of boundary rider.

2. Comb. **billet-hunter, -seeker.**

1894 *Bulletin* (Sydney) 16 June 8/3 He was constantly worried by **billet-hunters**. **1899** *Ibid.* 4 Mar. 15/2 A billet-hunter lately applied to a N.S. Wales M.P. for a reference. **1876** 'Capricornus' *Colonisation* 4 The youth of the colony crowding into the towns to become stock-jobbers and **billet-seekers**.

billeted, *ppl. a.* Orig. of convicts: quartered (see quot. 1850); having certain privileges in return for service.

1848 R. Marsh *Seven Yrs. of My Life* 88 There were five or six old hands, billited men, about the station, that would steal our cloths, and often we were punished for loosing them. **1850** W. Gates *Recoll. Van Dieman's Land* 130 There are usually at every station what are termed billeted men, who are prisoners that can work at such trades as blacksmithing, carpentry, masonry, &c. It is the law that they can work only for government. **1870** M. Cash *Adventures* 45, I . . spent the . . afternoon in watching the billetted hands, thinking that they might be doing the same for me. **1883** 'One Who Was There' *Prison Sketches* 8 Independent of this some are allowed tea in the morning—these are what are termed 'billeted men'. **1895** *Bulletin* (Sydney) 24 Aug. 7/3 The food sent in is overhauled by a 'searcher'—not a warder, but a 'billeted' prisoner—and—well good care is taken by him that I shall not grow fat from overfeeding.

Hence **billeter** *n.*

1847 *Hobart Town Herald* 6 Mar. 2/2 With 112 prisoners, billiters, to clean the rooms.

billibong, var. Billabong.

Billite. *Hist.* A supporter of the Constitution Bill, enacted as the Commonwealth of Australia Constitution Act by the Parliament of the United Kingdom on 9 July 1900.

1898 *Riverine Grazier* (Hay) 7 June 2/6 A band of billites, wearing badges, marched up Lachlan-street, singing. **1899** *Austral. Star* (Sydney) 3 May 5/3 There are many who opposed the old bill who are supporting the present one, but few, if any, have changed from Billites to Anti-Billites. **1900** 'Uloola' *Fable* 46 But he was a Billite firm and true. **1969** A.W. Martin *Essays in Austral. Federation* 179 The change in the coastal voting block from opposition to the Bill in 1898 to its support in 1899 is more easily seen in terms of the Australia-wide trend towards a rise in Billite support than in terms of any particular local interest. **1975** R. Norris *Emergent Commonwealth* 22 As the Billites defeated their opponents one must assume that the majority were readier to believe in them than in the anti-billites.

Billjim. *Obs.* Also **Biljim.** [Blend of the proper names *Bill* and *Jim*, a coinage of popular journalism.]

1. The typical Australian, the 'man in the street'.

[**1893** *Bulletin* (Sydney) 18 Nov. 20/4 Half the bushmen are *not* called 'Bill', nor the other half 'Jim'. We knew a shearer whose name was Reginald! *Ibid.* 31 Oct. (Red Page), The harrowing tale of the lost Bill or Jim in the Australian desert whose eyes are picked out by the crow almost before his death-struggle ceases.] **1898** *Ibid.* 12 Mar. 14/3 Billjim saddled his favourite cuddy about tea-time, pushed on, and struck the Bushman's Rest at dawn next day. **1902** *Truth* (Sydney) 16 Nov. 6/4 Uncle Sam has his George Washington. Why not Biljim Cornstalk have his ditto? **1903** *Bulletin* (Sydney) 6 Aug. 25/1, I really think these ballads are the songs of truthful men, Who do not wrap their Billjim in a cloak. **1904** *Truth* (Sydney) 6 Nov. 1/5 The name of the Czar's new baby is Kuroindiksiiskiczropikizits Scnikizikinstzitzi. In plain English that means Bill Jim. **1907** *Lone Hand* Nov. 17 A certain man from anywhere, call him Biljim, . . leaves a sick mate at the Half-way Pub.

2. The typical Australian soldier of the 1914–18 war. Cf. the British 'Tommy (Atkins)'.

1915 *Truth* (Sydney) 28 Feb. 3/6 These exemplary young gentlemen are still doing the 'Block', either too proud to consort with Billjim, or too cowardly to risk their precious skins in defence of the country. **1917** 'Patrius' *Hoisting our Flag* 5 These 'dare devil billjims' that all of us love. **1918** R.H. Knyvett *Over there with Australs.* 125 'Bill-Jim', which is Australia's name for her soldier-boy, always makes the best of things. **1918** *Aussie: Austral. Soldiers' Mag.* Oct. 2/2 I'm worried about this name Billjim that some of the Aussie papers have tacked on to us. I don't like it. Has anybody ever heard a Digger address another as Billjim? I haven't. **1918** *Bulletin* (Sydney) 3 Oct. 45/2 The pupils have erected two cottages for returned Billjims. **1919** *Souvenir 'Demosthenes' on Voyage Mother Country to Aust.* 6 The word 'Billjim' has become attached to the Australian Light Horseman as an expression for his type, and usage has forced the acceptance of it. **1920** *Bulletin* (Sydney) 6 May 22/3 The returned Digger was perspiring on a job for the local Road Board in front of the pub, and Bung was standing on the verandah gazing on the exertions of Billjim. **1939** H.W. Dinning *Austral. Scene* 172 The Armistice found the 'Bill-Jims' of Palestine in the heart of a barren country-side. **1961** C. McKay *This is Life* 132 When the parties took to the hustings Thomas Joseph Ryan jumped on to the Digger band-wagon. He acclaimed 'Billjim', so he called the Digger, as the saviour of his country.

billy, *n.*[1] [f. Scot. dial. *billy-pot* cooking utensil, cf. *bally, bally-cog* milk pail: see SND.]

1. A vessel for the boiling of water, making of tea, etc., over an open fire; a cylindrical container, usu. of tin, enamel ware, or aluminium, fitted with a lid and a wire handle.

[N.Z. **1839** J. Heberley Autobiogr. 87 [We] boiled the Billy and made some Tea out of tawa bark.] **1849** G.B. Wilkinson *Working Man's Handbk. S.A.* 79 Singing, near the wooden fire, is what is called the *billy*, or tea kettle. **1853** J. Rochfort *Adventures Surveyor* 63 We must needs purchase a 'billy' (a tin pot for boiling tea, coffee, meat, or anything you may have the luck to get), to make our tea in. **1859** W. Burrows *Adventures Mounted Trooper* 14 A 'billy' is a tin vessel, something between a saucepan and a kettle, always black outside from being constantly on the fire, and looking brown inside from the quantity of tea that is generally to be seen in it. **1866** *Sydney Punch* 4 Aug. 83/1, 7 ozs. 9 dwts. of gold from one 'Billy'-full of dirt. **1870** C.H. Allen *Visit to Qld.* 172 The Australian bushman . . carries . . his tin 'Billy', or large mug, slung at his horse's side. **1874** *Illustr. Sydney News* 25 July 18/2 In the fire is a large tin 'billy' containing a delicious stew of wallaby. **1881** A.C. Grant *Bush-Life Qld.* I. 41 A billy (that is, a round tin pitcher with a lid) in his hand. **1889** R. Etheridge et al. *Lord Howe Island* 20 The beautiful striped eel . . afforded equally good sport, whilst endeavouring to secure it in a 'billy'. **1892** *Missing Friends: Adventures Danish Emigrant Qld.* 97 The billy serves all purposes: in it the meat is cooked, the tea is boiled, and on extra occasions the plumduff too. **1909** *Bulletin* (Sydney) 25 Feb. 14/1 There are many phases and manifestations of mulga madness; but only three distinct stages—(1) wearing corks on the rim of the hat; (2) carving quondongs; (3) carrying puppies in the billy. **1912** *Huon Times* (Franklin) 17 Jan. 4/1 He saw defendant's daughter, nine years of age, carrying a billy of beer from the Preston Arms Hotel. **1930** 'Brent Of Bin Bin' *Ten Creeks Run* (1952) 162 Our only hope of distinguishing ourselves is with the raspberries. If you'll hold the billy, I'll pick. **1937** D. Glass *Austral. Fantasy* 89 The name 'billy' originated on the goldfields, where the miners drank tinned soup from France, and used the 'bouilli-cans' for tea-making afterwards. **1945** *Aust. Week-End Bk.* 96 The well-blackened billy—the traditional hall mark of the true Australian picnic. **1947** E. Hill *Flying Doctor Calling* 19 There are billies, pint, quart, gallon, and sets of flat-side billies for the pack. **1955** M. Corben *Not to mention Kangaroos* 80 A billy—a small pail with a lid, Australia's universal container. The name comes from the aboriginal word for water, *billa*, but it is used for anything liquid. **1965** *Bulletin* (Sydney) 9 Jan. 30/2 You earned an honest penny on the way from school . . by 'running the cutter' for the miners who lined the gutter outside the Shamrock Hotel and were glad to pay a penny for the services of an agile boy who would keep the three-quart billies, that passed down the line from mouth to mouth, rolling from bar to gullet without pause till the shillings paid for them ran out. **1972** *Meanjin* 327 What could be more natural than that a *royal George* [*sc.* a large iron pot] should have become a *royal William*, hence a *William* and hence a *billy*, after Prinny's death and the accession of King William IV in 1830, and that *billy* should have become fixed in popular usage as fitting the object it describes by the time of his death in 1837? **1980** Brennan & White *Keep Billy Boiling* 86 The 'billy', of course was synonymous with the Swagman and lost opportunities or maybe of opportunities that were never really there.

2. Abbrev. of *billy tea.*

1900 *Albury Banner* 5 Jan. 16/3 Farmers, selectors, and halves-men seem to care very little about comfort in their small shantys, as long as they get plenty of black billy, tough burnt chops, and half-baked bread.

3. Comb. **billy boy, -can, -full, tea.**

1944 *Bulletin* (Sydney) 19 July 13/3 By noon 300-a-day sheep-barbers were only pickers-up, while brickies who couldn't put away their thousand in eight and three-quarters were only **billy-boys.** **1949** *Ibid.* 13 July 11/4, I was billy-boy on that job, and lunch-times were wonderful occasions for me. **1955** *Overland* v. 3 No billy boy can ever brew his tea exactly right, so he prefers to make it himself. **1973** D. Wolfe *Brass Kangaroo* 144 That girl can be billy boy. . . What about making us some tea? *c* **1870** H. Baylis *Reminisc. Bush-Ranging Days N.S.W.* 9 A small fire was burning, on which was a **billy-can** half-full of tea. **1883** G.E. Loyau *Personal Adventures* 8 Tom and I passed Penrith, and made our first acquaintance with damper, johnny-cake, and billy-can tea at a bullock-driver's camp. **1896** *Bulletin* (Sydney) 11 Jan. 11/2 'Billycan' . . is obviously a corruption of 'boiling-can'. **1908** C.H.S. Matthews *Parson in Austral. Bush* 155 In addition to his swag, the swagman carries a couple of 'billy-cans', one inside the other. **1914** 'B. Cable' *By Blow & Kiss* 27 'Er 'air's black as the bottom o' an old billy-can, an' shiny as a sweatin' nigger. **1927** M. Dorney *Adventurous Honeymoon* 22, I cooked the turkey in a billy-can. **1930** Hives & Lumley *Jrnl. of Jackaroo* 27 At the end of each hour 'smoko' would be called . . when every man would light up his pipe and take long swigs of cold tea from his 'billy can'. **1938** D. Bates *Passing of Aborigines* 83 My first billy-can of gruel, the billy being a two-gallon one. **1945** *Bulletin* (Sydney) 25 Apr. 14/2 Billycans, a necessity to all bricklayers, were hard to get. **1955** *Ibid.* 4 May 12/2 When a new billycan is issued to a stock-camp in Centralia the first ceremony of its initiation is the discarding of its lid. **1970** *Kings Cross Whisper* (Sydney) xcv. 1/3 Australia entered the space race today when it became the first country in the world to successfully land a billy can on the moon. **1980** N. Watkins *Kangaroo Connection* 7 The toothless little bandy-legged station cook handed around steaming enamel mugs of strong black billy-can tea. **1861** *Bell's Life in Sydney* 16 Nov. 2/5 Fifty-four ounces . . out of only just a **billy-full**. **1889** E. Giles *Aust. twice Traversed* II. 115 We agreed to sacrifice a small billyful of our remaining stock of water for this unfortunate last victim to our enterprise. **1902** *Bulletin* (Sydney) 22 Mar. 32/2, I . . made a billyful of coffee. **1915** *Ibid.* 16 Sept. 24/2 Pippies are collected when the tide is *out*. And these people collected a billyful. **1938** F. Blakeley *Hard Liberty* 14 A continuous line of water-carts was passing. . . We would ask for a drink, but only the older men would give us a billyful. **1981** A.B. Facey *Fortunate Life* 210 Jock made a big billy-full of tea. **1890** Mrs R.D. Douglas *Romance at Antipodes* 83 We had a small fire on which to boil our oddly-shaped tin tea-kettles, or billy cans, in order to make '**billy tea**'. **1895** *Bulletin* (Sydney) 13 Aug. 27/1 For 12 months straight-off I take nothing stronger than billy-tea, and then I get full-up. **1898** C. Bond *Goldfields & Chrysanthemums* 35 No billy tea, which seems a part of bush life, but we have to put up with billy cocoa. **1903** *Bulletin* (Sydney) 10 Jan. 17/2 But *is* it necessary to boil the tea brew to make 'billy tea'? **1916** 'T.O. Lingo' *Austral. Comic Dict.* 57 *Billy Tea*, a milkless beverage flavoured with Eucalyptus and ants; takes some ability to make and some agility to drink. **1924** F.J. Mills *Happy Days* 65 Finally Melba's health was drunk in billy tea. **1937** D. Glass *Austral. Fantasy* 88 Billy-tea has its own distinctive flavour, due to the habit of sprinkling tea-leaves into creek water, hot and dancing, stirring the mixture with a twig and allowing a gum-leaf or two to share in the infusion. **1939** *Bulletin* (Sydney) 25 Jan. 21/1 Bush billy-tea doesn't get its flavor from twigs dropped into it. That tang is bred into the billy through years of coating with tannin and caffeine. **1943** *Jest: Digestion Good Humor* 37 The Pearly Gates he'll open wide and, sure enough, I'll see An angel Aussie making up a fire for billy-tea. **1977** P. ADAMS *Unspeakable Adams* 24 How many restaurants are willing to serve billy tea? How many head waiters know how to swing one over their head? **1986** *Sydney Morning Herald* 8 Mar. 1/8 More than billy tea and damper may be taken away on Sunday when environmentalists . . hold a protest campfire.

4. In collocations with a qualifying term: **black billy,** a fire-blackened billy; **Christmas billy,** a billy containing donated Christmas gifts, as distributed to Australian service personnel during the war of 1914–18; **rugged billy** *obs.*, an insulated billy.

1862 C. MUNRO *Fern Vale* II. 24 **Black Billy** . . a name applied by the diggers to the tin pot in which they boil their water. **1943** *Bulletin* (Sydney) 8 Sept. 13/2 Long Jack left the old black billy and a white enamelled mug standing on a rock. **1940** E. HARRINGTON *My Old Black Billy* 2 My old black billy, my old black billy, whether the wind is warm or chilly I always find when the shadows fall My old black billy, the best mate of all. **1964** P. ADAM SMITH *Hear Train Blow* 10 The driver and guard climbed down carrying a black billy of beer each. **1916** I.L. IDRIESS Diary 22 Dec. vi. 15 We are back with the regiment again. . . The **Xmas billies** have arrived, one each to a man. **1919** J. ANDREWS *Garrison Ginger* 15 'Twas a case of your Christmas billies. How we danced and we cheered when the billies appeared, and each man was duly presented. **1902** *Bulletin* (Sydney) 1 Feb. 16/2 The process of swathing billies in bagging is called 'rugging' (horsey term). Hence '**rugged billy**'. **1911** E.S. SORENSON *Life in Austral. Backblocks* 277 Some swagmen have a special water-billy, carried in the hand, with a tightly-fitting bag drawn over it to keep it cool. . . This is called a rugged billy.

5. a. In the phr. **to boil the billy,** to brew tea.

1839 [see BILLY *n.*[1] 1]. **1867** G. WALCH *Fireflash* 13 Our noble selves are grouped 'waiting for the billy to boil'. **1883** 'KEIGHLEY' *Who are You* 31 In a calm content by the fire we lie And watch while the billy boils. **1895** *Worker* (Sydney) 11 May 4/1 And while my mate . . boiled the billy I pitched the fly. **1899** *Western Champion* (Barcaldine) 23 May 10/1 They last had foregathered and 'boiled the billy' by some distant creek or tank in the far distant Never Never country. **1928** E. FOREMAN *Hist. & Adventures Qld. Pioneer* 31 What about lighting a fire in the camp oven and boiling the billy? **1938** D. BATES *Passing of Aborigines* 25 Boiling the billy by an old tank out on the plain. **1955** F. LANE *Patrol to Kimberleys* 27 Boiling the billy, Glen found out, meant brewing tea in a metal container which bushmen called a billy-can. **1979** D. LOCKWOOD *My Old Mates & I* 154 We stopped beside a crystal-clear creek to boil the billy.

b. billy-boiled *ppl. a.*, **billy-boiler** *n.*, **billy-boiling** *vbl. n.*

1898 G. GARNET *Barrier Bride* 77 He took his cup of **billy-boiled** tea, too, from her hands, and deemed it nectar. **1954** T. RONAN *Vision Splendid* 37 There was a tang about the billy-boiled tea unlike anything he had ever drunk. **1957** F. CLUNE *Fortune Hunters* 44, I acted as **billy-boiler** and steak-griller. **1934** C. MACKNESS *Young Beachcombers* 82 It's up to us to go and help with the **billy-boiling** and the lunch. **1961** D. STUART *Driven* 143 As he watched the dexterous unharnessing and hobbling, the fire-lighting, the billy-boiling, he smiled.

6. In the phr. **to sling** (or **swing**) **the billy (kettle, pot),** to prepare to make tea, esp. as an act of hospitality.

1848 *Bell's Life in Sydney* 4 Mar. 1/2 Jack Jones and his good wife made much of us, slung the pot in double quick time. **1862** G.T. LLOYD *Thirty-Three Yrs. Tas. & Vic.* 125 Four or five times in one day . . was the over-welcome command, 'Spell O, and sling kettles', responded to. **1879** W.J. BARRY *Up & Down* 9 The proprietor immediately 'slung the billy' and you were made welcome to 'Damper, mutton and tea'. **1893** J. DEMARR *Adventures in Aust.* 106 That was a signal for the people at the station to 'sling the pot' for the coming guest. **1896** M. HORNSBY *Old Time Echoes Tas.* 25 Bush folks always slung the billy when they saw a stranger approaching. **1920** W. MCGUFFIN *Austral. Tales of Border* 132 There we lighted a fire, slung the billy, and soon were replenishing the inner man. **1928** M.E. FULLERTON *Austral. Bush* 119 The cracking of stock-whips among the tree-ferns near may cause the lonely hut dweller to 'swing the billy' on hospitable thoughts intent, for the approaching stranger who, however, fails to materialise. **1944** F. BRUNO *Sa-eeda Wog* 22 We had just crawled out of our scrub bedrooms to have a cup of tea. All good machine-gunners, in particular, 'swing the billy' at this time. **1957** D. NILAND *Call me when Cross turns Over* 13 Like me to swing the billy, and get you a drink of tea? **1976** B. BENNETT *New Country* 37 Come on. Let's swing the billy! **1981** *Sydney Morning Herald* 2 May 42/2 One of them, Ken Esgate, has been a bushie round these parts all his life, as was his father. Esgate gave James Mason a lesson in how to swing the billy.

billy, *n.*[2] *Obs.* [Abbrev. of BILLYCOCK.] A low-crowned hard felt hat.

1862 C. MUNRO *Fern Vale* II. 40 On his head stood erect a black cylindrical deformity, designated in the vulgar parlance of the colony, a 'Billy' . . but which he . . called a hat. **1864** *Bell's Life in Sydney* 13 Feb. 3/1 His hat . . fell into the street and immediately fell a victim to the unbridled fury of the mob, who crashed, dashed, gashed, and smashed the unhappy 'billy' in a most frightful manner. **1867** J.R. HOULDING *Austral. Capers* 227 Some of the 'cabbage-tree boys' were there too, indulging in their favourite holiday rollick of knocking all the 'black billies' from the heads of the wearers.

billy, *n.*[3] Shortened form of GREY BILLY.

1967 R.O. CHALMERS *Austral. Rocks* 313 The sapphire occurs principally in a wash consisting of fragments of basalt, 'Billy', sand, and clay.

billybong, var. BILLABONG.

billy buttons. Also as sing. [f. *billy*, dim. of *William*, popular name of some plants + *button* button-like flower.] Any of several herbaceous plants of the fam. Asteraceae, esp. of the genus *Craspedia*, having button-shaped or globular flower-heads; BACHELOR'S BUTTONS. Also *attrib.*

1909 *Bulletin* (Sydney) 4 Nov. 13/2 A Mulga mate of mine writes to say that there are wonderful expanses made yellow with everlastings and 'billy-buttons'. **1916** S.A. WHITE *In Far Northwest* 37 A short growth of Billy Buttons . . had sprung up. **1940** E. HILL *Great Austral. Loneliness* 304 Across vast plains of buck-bush, through a Mohammedan paradise of Billy Button daisies, yellow and white. **1946** A.M. LAPTHORNE *Mildura Calling* 9 Billy-buttons shedding dusty gold On sun-seared grass. **1961** *Meanjin* 6 Billy-buttons were already waving their little pompoms. **1978** B.P. MOORE *Life on Forty Acres* 43 We have the bright yellow globular heads of Billy Buttons (*Craspedia glauca*) for much of November. **1981** J. BURT *Shutterbug in Bush* 74 The ribbon of water flanked by sandy plains carpeted with poached egg daisies and yellow billy buttons.

billycart. [Perh. f. *billy(goat* male goat + *cart.*] A small handcart, sometimes drawn by a goat; a go-cart.

1923 *Anthony Hordern Catal.* 304 Very Strong 2-wheel Billy Cart, Iron Axle and Wheels, long handle . . 17s. **1936** N. CALDWELL *Fangs of Sea* 76 He [*sc.* a goat] was a big white chap who had won many billy-cart races. **1952** J.R. TYRRELL *Old Bks.* 2 As boys, Fred & I delivered books round Sydney in a billycart. **1957** M. PAICE *Valley in North* 9 The goat moved restlessly as the weight of water increased in the drum, tilting the billy-cart back on the shafts. **1960** K. SMITH *Word from Children* 156 When I was a boy, a billy-cart was called 'a truck', and those strong, castiron wheels and the soapbox behind were the last word in speedy leg-breakers for old ladies using the footpath. **1981** E. POTTER *Scone I Remember* 78 Most boys had billycarts, homemade from fruit boxes held together with nails, strips of metal from kerosene tins or even pieces of leather such as old belts or scraps of harness. **1984** *Canberra Times* 11 Nov. 6/4 He graphically described the screech of billy-carts sweeping down Sunbeam Avenue and scything to the ground every one of Mrs Branthwaite's poppies.

billycock. *Obs.* [Br. *billycock* low-crowned felt hat; app. rare: see OED.] Any of several styles of round, low-crowned hat worn by men. Also **billycock hat.** See BILLY *n.*[2]

[N.Z. **1865** B.L. FARJEON *Shadows on Snow* 61 All are alike attired in rough jackets, moleskin trousers, and billy-cock hats.] **1867** J.S. BORLASE *Night Fossickers* 54 Billy-cock or cabbage-tree hats, blue or red serge suits. **1884** *Austral. Tit-Bits* (Melbourne) 25 Dec. 22/2 An elderly man dressed in moleskin trousers, drab coat, and billy-cock hat, and carrying an extremely clean swag. **1892** *Braidwood Dispatch* 17 Dec. 6/1 'Two hundred fiddlesticks!' shouted the wretched digger . . throwing down his battered billycock. **1902** *Truth* (Sydney) 16 Nov. 1/6 Burke only wears a 'billycock' on off occasions. His professional cady is a silk cylinder. **1906** E. DYSON *Roaring Fifties* 65 Cabbage-tree hats or billycocks were on every head, and for the rest a gray or blue jumper tucked into clay-stained trousers and Wellington boots satisfied the majority. **1908** A.M.W. STIRLING *Coke of Norfolk* 167 Another matter in which he gained temporary and amusing notoriety was as wearer of a billycock (Billy Coke) hat.

Billzac. *Obs.* [Blend of BILL(JIM + AN)ZAC.] BILLJIM 2.

1918 *Aussie: Austral. Soldiers' Mag.* Jan. 10/2 *Home*, the place or places where Billzac would fain be when the job is done. **1918** *Kia Ora Coo-ee* Sept. 3/2 This term Digger . . has supplanted 'Billjim' and 'Billzac'. *Ibid.* Dec. 5/1 'Billzac' has no place except in print, and then only used by persons who have no more than a nodding acquaintance with us. **1926** 'DRYBLOWER' *Verses* 22 When Billzac and his mates Belted the Huns.

bim: see BIMBO.

bimble box. [a. Wiradhuri *bimbil.*] The tree *Eucalyptus populnea* (fam. Myrtaceae) of N.S.W. and Qld., having a fibrous, brownish-grey bark and glossy green leaves. Also **bimble,** and *attrib.*

1839 T.L. MITCHELL *Three Exped. Eastern Aust.* (ed. 2) II. 55 The 'bimbel' (or spear-wood) which grows on dry forest land. **1900** *Proc. Linnean Soc. N.S.W.* XXV. 718 *Eucalyptus populifolia* (Bimble Box, sometimes spelt Bimbil; I understand that Bimble is the aboriginal name for this tree). **1901** K.L. PARKER in M. Muir *My Bush Bk.* (1982) 102 A few bibbil, wide-leaved box trees . . whose leaves after rain or in sunlight look as if they had been dipped in liquefied silver. **1904** J.H. MAIDEN *Notes on Commercial Timbers N.S.W.* 15 Bimble Box . . is an exclusively western box, with shiny leaves and a poplar-like habit. **1953** *Bulletin* (Sydney) 28 Jan. 13/4 The bimble-boxes seemed hung with leaves of glass. **1961** *Ibid.* 29 Mar. 42/1 A flock of Happy Jacks ran merrily and noisily up and down the bimble-box trees. **1962** *N. Austral. Monthly* Mar. 21 Another inland tree, a eucalypt, is known by the pretty name 'bimble', but some still prefer to call it 'shiny-leaved poplar box' which is quite a mouthful. **1976** *Ecos* viii. 10/2 A large region of woodland—dominated mainly by bimble box (a eucalypt), mulga, and white pine . . stretches north into southern Queensland.

bimbo. [U.S. *bimbo* fellow, chap: see OEDS.] A male companion, esp. a homosexual. Also abbrev. **bim.**

1961 X. HERBERT *Soldiers' Women* 208 Got a Yank in tow too. . . Well, are you going anywhere particular with your bimbo? **1962** R. TULLIPAN *March into Morning* 46 Get out of here and take your bimbo with you. **1966** E.J. WALLACE *Sydney & Bush* 144 That 'mate' as you call him is a queer. . . You know, a queen. I think they're called 'Bimbos' on the track. **1973** F. HUELIN *Keep Moving* 140 The older man claimed the younger as his nephew and that may have been so, but we concluded there was also a more intimate sexual relationship—that the younger was the older man's 'bimbo'. **1978** D. STUART *Wedgetail View* 243 He's just what's needed in a bimbo. Fresh and neat, dapper, a real well-dressed little bastard; he'll polish Piggy's boots, make his bed, do his washing; just a regular little handmaiden. *Ibid.* 242 You're a clown, even for a bimbo. Anyone knows a bim has to be stupid, but you're the world's expert at stupidity.

bin. *Wool bin*, see WOOL 2.

[N.Z. **1865** M.A. BARKER *Let.* 1 Dec. in *Station Life N.Z.* (1870) 32 Armfulls of rolled-up fleeces [were] laid on the tables before the wool-sorters who . . pronounced . . to which bin they belonged.] **1867** J.C. JORDON *Managem. Sheep & Stations* 92 When a fleece is folded and tied, the classer will place it in the proper bin or compartment, according to its class. **1883** *Illustr. Austral. News* (Melbourne) 28 Nov. 194/3 Having the various fleeces placed one after the other into the 'bins' or partitions set apart for their reception. **1900** A. HAWKESWORTH *Austral. Sheep & Wool* 242 Under the table there are three or four small bins, into which are put the smaller sorts. **1928** C.E. COWLEY *Classing Clip* 155 Another very necessary item in the equipment of a modern woolshed is 'bin space'... Wool cannot be properly handled unless the various sorts made can be carefully stacked away in bins and so kept distinct and clean. **1941** *Sheep Industry* (Vic. Dept. Agric.) (ed. 6) 61 The position of the bins, press, and rolling and skirting table in the plan are only suggestions. **1970** HARMSWORTH & PAGE-SHARP *Sheep & Wool Classing* 60 The rolled fleece must be classed so that all fleeces in one bin are as similar as possible.

bindi-eye /'bɪndi-aɪ/. Also **bindy-eye** and formerly with much variety, as **bindei, bindiyi.** [a. Kamilaroi and Yuwaalaraay *bindayaa*.] Any of several plants bearing barbed fruits, esp. herbs of the widespread genus *Calotis* (fam. Asteraceae); the fruit of these plants. Also **blindy-eye.**

1896 K.L. PARKER *Austral. Legendary Tales* 7 In the country of the Galah are lizards coloured reddish brown, and covered with spikes like bindeah prickles. *Ibid.* 129 Bindeah, a prickle or small thorn. **1905** *Steele Rudd's Mag.* (Brisbane) Feb. 142 Tyres are now .. puncture proof against the Bindei, that little ball of spikes so plentiful on the ground in many parts of Australia. **1911** E.J. BRADY *King's Caravan* 115 That night I lay awake .. on my blankets, prickly with bindiyi burrs. **1920** J.H. MAIDEN *Weeds N.S.W.* 12 Everybody in the country knows the pest called Bindi-eye or Bogan flea. **1930** K.G. TAYLOR *Pick & Duffers* 254 If you'd've been pelted off in the bindey-eyes and got your pants full o' them you wouldn't think it so extremely amusing. **1948** R. RAVEN-HART *Canoe in Aust.* 73 The prickly 'bindi-eye', the flowers looking like lavender daisies that had elegantly curling-tong'ed their petals; but sheep thrive on this feed. **1959** H. LAMOND *Sheep Station* 35 He scraped the blindy-eye burrs from the soles of his bare feet. **1977** J. O'GRADY *There was Kid* 52 Sandgropers .. call .. bindi-eyes 'doublegees'. **1981** *Overland* lxxxvi. 58 'Bendei' (spelled variously, e.g. 'bindy-eye') .. was standardly used to describe various species of both *Bassia* and *Emex*, which are not related to one another.

Hence **bindi-eyed** *a.*

1984 K. LETTE *Hit & Ms* 95 Though you violently disagree with your host's economic, emotional and political persuasions, it's a long, bindi-eyed walk back to town.

bingey, var. BINGY.

Binghi /'bɪŋgi/. [a. Awabakal (and neighbouring languages) *biŋay* (elder) brother.]

1. An Aboriginal; the typical Aboriginal. Also *attrib.*

1830 R. DAWSON *Present State Aust.* 224 We were all bingeyes (brothers). **1849** A. HARRIS *Emigrant Family* 225 Binghi (brother) you, belonging to black fellow. **1867** J.R. HOULDING *Austral. Capers* 294 Lost his gun, which he had given to a black fellow to hold... On his return to the coach he found that Bingi had run away with the gun. **1894** G. BOOTHBY *On Wallaby* 130 A collection of Binghis (aboriginals). **1910** *Bulletin* (Sydney) 29 Dec. 14/3 When Binghi, jun., is dragged to a mission station, the.. authorities.. feed him on 'white pfellers'' tucker. **1920** *Smith's Weekly* (Sydney) 20 Mar. 9/1 Binghi doesn't believe in citronella or these new-fangled mosquito chasers. **1925** *Bulletin* (Sydney) 23 Apr. 23/3 So long as the witch-doctor leaves him alone, Binghi in his wild state is a hardy customer. **1930** *Aussie* (Sydney) Sept. 38/1 Binghi has a keen ear... Many of the names he has given to birds are simply imitations of the birds' own notes. **1936** *Bulletin* (Sydney) 23 Sept. 21/4 When speaking of a Binghi in earlier days they generally referred to the natives who had come from far inland. When these arrived at the coast their eyes were flybitten, and they .. were at first referred to as 'bungeyes', which gradually became Binghi. **1937** J.M. HARCOURT *It never Fails* 79 We know that the only good *binghi's* a dead binghi, but you'd think a black was a human being the fuss that's made if one or two of them get shot. **1940** E. HILL *Great Austral. Loneliness* (ed. 2) 63, I followed the flat simian footprints of the 'Binghi-pads' to the turtle-feasts and sing-abouts of the good Australian blackfellow. **1946** *Bulletin* (Sydney) 21 Aug. 28/1, I suppose Binghi's pictorial efforts with the baob nut as a canvas should really be classed as engraving. **1960** *Ibid.* 13 Apr. 19/1 That binghi hospital-patient .. drew roses and the most delicate flowers. **1964** M. SHARLAND *Territory of Birds* 48 Are we .. to accept purely as fantasy all we've heard .. about 'Binghi' transmitting .. over hill and plain for the enlightenment of distant tribes? **1985** J. MILLER *Koori* 156 The popular Press of Australia makes a joke of us by presenting silly and out-of-date drawings and jokes of 'Jacky' or 'Binghi', which have educated city-dwellers and young Australians to look upon us as sub-human.

2. *transf.* See quot.

1918 R.H. KNYVETT *Over there with Australs.* 25 The 'Binghies' (natives of New Guinea).

bingie, var. BINGY.

bingle. [Prob. f. Br. dial. *bing* thump, blow: see EDD and OEDS *bing, sb.*[3]] A fight or skirmish; a collision. Also **bingle-bingle.**

1945 'MASTER-SARG' *Yank discovers Aust.* 17 A 'bingle' is a fight, a 'do' is a battle. **1945** *Mud & Blood* 51 After a lapse, the old 'bingle-bingle' was going this morning with a vengeance. After watching those Stukas diving .. one was left with the impression that tremendous damage must have been caused. **1966** R. CARR *Surfie* 122 There was this clang of metal on metal and both cars lurched over to the shoulder and we nearly went for a bingle. **c 1975** 'BLUEY' *Bush Contractors* 117 The bingle hadn't knocked the conceit out of him. He told Con he was going to be on crutches. **1976** A. BUZO *Martello Towers* 14 There could be a bingle on here in a minute. **1984** J. HIBBERD *Country Quinella* 80 Who stacked the car? .. Fangio here... I claim full responsibility for the second bingle.

bingy /'bɪndʒi/. Also **bingey, bingie, binjie, binjy.** [a. Dharuk *bindi*.] The stomach; the belly. Also *fig.*

1791 W. TENCH *Compl. Acct. Settlement* (1793) 122 Belly .. Bin'-dee [name at the Hawkesbury]. **1798** D. COLLINS *Acct. Eng. Colony N.S.W.* I. 615 Ben-de (inland), belly. **1845** D. MACKENZIE *Emigrant's Guide* 215 They lay .. with their hands rubbing their bellies, exclaiming, 'Cabonn buggel along bingee' (that is, I am very sick in the stomach). **1859** H. KINGSLEY *Recoll. Geoffry Hamlyn* II. 94 Don't you fret your bingy, boss. **1875** CAMPBELL & WILKS *Early Settlement Qld.* 39 With savory 'possum their 'binjies' to fill; And the sweet flying-fox and the delicate grub. **1892** *Truth* (Sydney) 19 June 5/7 And each small boy went home and told his parents that he warn't going to be a butcher or a baker, but to be a member of Parliament, have a big binjie, wear a gold chain, and cut about among the toffs! **1902** *Ibid.* 23 Mar. 3/5 If I could be a Pre-me-eer It's very likely I must say, I'd fill my bingie up with beer Some five and forty times a day. **1912** *Ibid.* 24 Nov. 4/3 Scant of thatch and protuberant of bingy. **1927** *Bulletin* (Sydney) 3 Nov. 27/1 Of boiling-down and burning-up we've had our bingie full. **1936** N. CALDWELL *Fangs of Sea* 218 It made me fair sick to watch it; even now me bingy is feelin' real bad thinkin' of it. **1948** I.L. IDRIESS *Opium Smugglers* 149 My bingey was demanding whether my throat was cut. **1952** H.P. DOWN *Out Fishing* 110 A four-gallon petrol tin, half filled with crawfish, taken from the 'bingy' of a 90 lbs Murray cod—ugh! **1969** E. O'CONNER *Second Helping* 194 Probably got a pain in her bingie from eating too much goanna. **1979** J. WILLIAMS *White River* 82 The pregnant Aboriginal girl .. sat up suddenly and spoke. 'Got pain in bingy.'

Hence **bingied** *a.*, **bingyful** *n.*

1913 H. LAWSON *For Aust.* 159 They're patting their binjies with pride, old man, and I want you to understand, That a **binjied** bard is a bard indeed. **1917** *Truth* (Sydney) 16 Sept. 1/7 The big-bingied blokes have been forced to walk. **1907** *Ibid.* 7 Apr. 1/7 Daddy Hayseed, staggering homewards .. under a heavy **bingeyful** of purge, reckons that the 'Frisco and Valparaiso earthquakes were trivial affairs.

bird. Abbrev. of *dead bird* (see DEAD 2).

1941 S.J. BAKER *Pop. Dict. Austral. Slang* 10 *Bird*, a certainty. **1980** A. HOPGOOD *And here comes Bucknuckle* 20 Let me give you a tip. Next race .. Bolivia. It's a bird. Look .. twenty five to one. **1980** [see BIRDCAGE].

birdcage. [Transf. use of *birdcage* the paddock at the Newmarket racecourse, England, in which horses are saddled.] An enclosure at a racecourse, freq. surrounded by a high wire mesh fence, in which jockeys mount and dismount.

1893 *Antipodean* (Melbourne) 48 The betting ring is at the far end of the grandstand, and then comes the 'bird cage', where an extra charge of five shillings is made to keep the crowd away from the horses. **1903** *Sporting News* (Launceston) 14 Mar. 3/6 Will find many improvements, including a birdcage in the saddling paddock. **1907** *Clipper* (Hobart) 28 Dec. 4/2 I'm in one of the outorfices in the bird-cage. **1923** C.E. SAYERS *Jumping Double* 114 In a rage he left the ambulance room and hurried into the birdcage. **1933** H.B. RAINE *Whip-Hand* 272 He wandered about the saddling paddock examining the horses for the first race with an expert eye, he gloated over the parade in the bird cage. **1949** L. GLASSOP *Lucky Palmer* 244 Before each race, the jockeys mounted their horses in the birdcage and then rode out on to the track. **1980** *Age* (Melbourne) 16 Sept. 3/1 You have a big serve on a bird and you are relaxing over a glass by the birdcage waiting for it to trot in... This means that you have a big bet on a certain winner and you are in a bar at the races waiting for the event which your chosen animal will win with ease.

birder.

1. Abbrev. of BLACKBIRDER 1.

1898 *Bulletin* (Sydney) 2 Apr. 29/2 'Harry Monck' .. I take to be an ex 'birder desirous of showing that his craft isn't quite as black as painted.

2. Abbrev. of *mutton-birder* (see MUTTON-BIRD *v.*).

1986 *Weekend Austral.* (Sydney) 29 Mar. 5/4 The cruel and insensitive killing methods used by many amateur birders often results [*sic*] in chicks not even being stunned when their head and entrails are wrenched from their bodies.

birding, *vbl. n.* See MUTTON-BIRD *v.*

1896 *Papers & Proc. R. Soc. Tas.* (1897) p. vi, Mutton-birding, a unique industry, and only carried on in the Furneaux Islands as a regular one... The 'birding' begins on March 20. **1943** *Bulletin* (Sydney) 15 Dec. 13/3 The majority of the mutton-birders are taken to the islands of the Furneaux Group .. at the close of 'birdin''. **1969** J. WOODBERRY *Garland of Gannets* 26 'Do you go birdin', Ben?' .. 'Me!' Ben was insulted. 'Me! Birdin'? I'm a respectable bloke. Work for the guvermint. Can't stand the things. Taste nothing like mutton, nor bird, neither.'

bird of paradise. [A name applied to birds of the fam. Paradisaeidae: see OED(S *bird, sb.* 7.] In sense 1 the name has been applied to an unrelated bird also having a long and beautiful tail.]

1. *Obs.* LYRE-BIRD.

1800 D. COLLINS *Acct. Eng. Colony N.S.W.* (1802) II. 300 The first bird of paradise ever seen in this country had been shot. **1837** J. BACKHOUSE *Narr. Visit Austral. Colonies* (1843) 506 The Blacks often bring in the splendid tails of the Lyre-bird, *Menura superba*, which is called in Australia, the Pheasant, or the Bird of Paradise.

2. Any of several Austral. bird species in the fam. Paradisaeidae, esp. *Ptiloris victoriae* (see VICTORIA RIFLE-BIRD).

1853 J. SHERER *Gold Finder Aust.* 26 The lyre-bird and the bird of Paradise, two of the most beautiful of the feathered species. **1889** R.B. ANDERSON tr. Lumholtz's *Among Cannibals* 171 It was an Australian bird of paradise, the celebrated Rifle-bird (Ptiloris victoriae), which, according to Gould, has the most brilliant plumage of all Australian birds.

bird of providence. *Obs.* MOUNT PITT BIRD.

1790 J. HUNTER *Hist. Jrnl. Trans. Port Jackson* (1793) 182 This *bird of Providence*, which I may with great propriety call it, appeared to me to resemble that sea bird in England, called the puffin... We were highly indebted to Providence for this vast resource.

Birdsville. [The name of a town in s.w. Qld.] A condition of horses caused by eating the central Austral. plant *Indigofera linnaei* (fam. Fabaceae) and characterized by staggering and toe-dragging. Also **Birdsville disease.**

1915 *Bulletin* (Sydney) 28 Jan. 22/2 The Birdsville horse disease is peculiar to the lower Diamantina country... A horse may .. be fit and well in the morning, and by midday may suddenly collapse, struggle in agony for perhaps half an hour, and then pass out. The victims may go through several fits before finally throwing a seven. . . It is easy to kill a horse that has had a touch of 'Birdsville'. **1974** S.L. EVERIST *Poisonous Plants Aust.* 316 A known 'Birdsville disease paddock' was made safe for horses by grazing with sheep. **1976** C.D. MILLS *Hobble Chains & Greenhide* 1 'Walkabout' and Birdsville had taken heavy toll of our horses. **1981** G.M. CUNNINGHAM et al. *Plants Western N.S.W.* 398 It [*sc. Indigofera dominii*] is toxic to horses and causes 'birdsville disease', resulting in dullness, muscular incoordination and loss of condition.

birdwing. [From the butterfly's appearance in flight; cf. *bird-winged butterfly* an Indonesian species of the genus *Ornithoptera*: see OEDS *bird, sb.* 8 c.] Any of several large colourful butterflies of the tropical genus *Ornithoptera*, occurring in n.e. coastal Aust. and elsewhere. Also **bird's wing butterfly.**

[**1882** J. ALLEN *Hist. Aust.* 195 The golden-green bird-winged butterfly is found all through Queensland.] **1933** H.J. CARTER *Gulliver in Bush* 100 The splendid green butterfly that floats so serenely among the vines, commonly called the 'Bird's Wing' butterfly. **1972** COMMON & WATERHOUSE *Butterflies of Aust.* 189 *Ornithoptera priamus pronomus* . . Cape York birdwing.

birthstain. *Hist.* [See quots. 1892 and 1899; the lines written by Kipling with reference to Sydney were adapted and used by William Lygon, 7th Earl Beauchamp, on his arrival as Governor of N.S.W. in 1899.] The stigma attached to the convict period or to convict ancestry. See also STAIN.

1892 R. KIPLING in *Eng. Illustr. Mag.* (1893) X. 537 Greeting! My birth-stain have I turned to good; Forcing strong wills perverse to steadfastness; The first flush of the tropics in my blood, And at my feet Success! **1899** *Sydney Morning Herald* 11 May 5/6 Greeting,—Your birthstain have you turned to good, Forcing strong wills perverse to steadfastness, The first flush of the tropics in your blood, And at your feet success.—Beauchamp. **1901** *Truth* (Sydney) 17 Nov. 1/1 The Snob hangs upon the words of a cheeky young Earl who has the patronising assurance to express a hope, loudly, that Australians will live to wash out their so-called 'birthstains'. **1909** *Ibid.* 20 June 1/8 John Bull's tainted legacy has somehow come to stay, The 'birthstains' on the blanket they will *never* wash away. **1910** *Bulletin* (Sydney) 17 Mar. 14/1 The district was spotted with 'birth stain'. The 'old hands' formed almost a community of themselves. **1918** C.H. NORTHCOTT *Austral. Social Dev.* 40 The sociological significance of this experiment in colonization is great. It is customary in Australia to dismiss the whole subject with a deprecatory reference to 'a birth-stain'. **1936** *Publicist* (Sydney) iii. 8/1 'Birth stains'—i.e., the origin of settlement in Australia through transportation of convicts from England. **1945** J.A. ALLAN *Men & Manners in Aust.* 19 Viewed soberly, convictism was neither a shameful 'birth-stain'—as Lord Beauchamp called it—nor a sentimental romance. **1956** J.T. LANG *I Remember* 195 Beauchamp had started off badly by trying to add a literary flourish to one of his statements, when he declaimed, Your *birth stains, you have turned to good.* It didn't make him very popular in squatter society.

Hence **birthstained** *a.*

1904 *Truth* (Sydney) 29 May 7/3 An invitation to Government House, in the first quarter of the nineteenth century, was in the nature of a command, or was it that the 'exclusives' were toadies enough to go to Government House, knowing well Macquarie's partiality for the 'birthstained'?

Biscay. Abbrev. of BAY OF BISCAY.

1897 J.J. MURIF *From Ocean to Ocean* 163 'Devil-devil' . . is applied to clay . . similar to 'Biscay', but . . in contracting after rains, in the quick-drying rays of fierce tropical sun it cracks, while the 'Biscay' becomes distressingly bumpy.

biscuit bomber. An aircraft which used to drop supplies to troops in remote parts of New Guinea during the war of 1939–45.

1943 A. DAWES *Soldier Superb* 58 The biscuit bombers—the transport planes—had gone over. **1944** G. HAMLYN-HARRIS *Through Mud & Blood* 48 We saw the biscuit-bombers dropping food far below. **1948** W. HATFIELD *Barrier Reef Days* 24 Keith said it was one of the 'biscuit bombers' that parked on the inlet just across from the wharves. **1974** D. WAUGH *Master White Grass* 35 Food will be dropped where necessary by the biscuit-bombers, or carried by boong-train—by native carriers. **1978** R. MACKLIN *Newsfront* 99 Above they could see old 'Biscuit Bombers', resurrected from war service, dropping supplies.

Bishop Barker. *Obs.* [f. the name of Frederic *Barker* (1808–1882), Anglican Bishop of Sydney: see quot. 1892.] A large glass of beer.

1886 F. COWAN *Aust.* 32 *Long-sleever, Bishop Barker,* and *Deep-sinker*, synonyms of Yankee Schooner. **1892** *Bulletin* (Sydney) 9 Jan. 14/1 Dr Barker . . was so abnormally tall that (incited thereto also by the fact that he was a teetotaller) the tavernites called the 'longest' drink of beer procurable at a public-house 'a Bishop Barker'. **1902** *Ibid.* 18 Oct. 14/4 A 'long beer' used to be called in Sydney a 'Bishop Barker'—the bishop was a very tall man.

bit. [Cf. *bit of muslin* woman: see OED *muslin, sb.* 2.] In the phr. **a bit of** (or **o'**) **skirt,** a woman, esp. a young woman (regarded sexually).

1898 *Truth* (Sydney) 17 Apr. 3/1 Demanded free admission for himself and his 'bit o' skirt'. **1899** *Ibid.* 19 Nov. 6/6 Certain dance rooms in Balmain, where the 'rorty' talent congregate . . and with preternatural gravity slowly gyrate with their 'bits o' skirt'. ***c* 1907** C.W. CHANDLER *Darkest Adelaide* 42 He encountered a rather chic bit o' skirt, whom he accosted with the remark—'How are you darling?' **1913** C.J. DENNIS *Backblock Ballads* 60 But she 'ad brains this bit o' skirt. **1919** O. HOGUE *Cameliers* 13 What about that letter you promised to write to my bit of skirt, Sister? **1965** J. WYNNUM *Jiggin' in Riggin'* 35 I'll lay even money she can line up a bit of skirt for me, too.

bite, *n.* [f. *bite* swindler (OED *sb.* 9 b.), prob. influenced by BITE *v.*]

1. A cadger.

1944 *Bulletin* (Sydney) 2 Aug. 14/1 Bush lawyers, cockies who insist they can help you make out your tax return, . . the tobacco 'bite', the chap who wants to borrow everything. **1982** J. MORRISON *North Wind* 54 Your old mates have had a win in Tatts . . and all the bots and bites in Victoria are on to them.

2. That which is cadged; the act of cadging.

1919 W.H. DOWNING *Digger Dialects* 10 *Bite* (n. or vb.), (1) a borrowing, to borrow; (2) an attempt to borrow. **1941** K. TENNANT *Battlers* 33 The unwanted, crouched in little groups on the edge of the gutter, talking and smoking and comparing 'handouts' and 'bites' and good towns and 'hungry tracks'. **1967** *Kings Cross Whisper* (Sydney) xxxiv. 4/5 Whereas a snip is only a small loan a fang is a large 'bite'.

3. In the collocation **good bite,** one who responds favourably to a cadger, a 'soft touch'.

1965 R.H. CONQUEST *Horses in Kitchen* 192 He was . . considered a good 'bite' by down-and-outs. **1966** D. NILAND *Pairs & Loners* 38 He was a good bite, and the men soon realised that.

4. In the phr. **to put the bite on** (someone), to cadge from; also **on the bite,** cadging, 'on the scrounge'.

1941 H. PERCY *Here's Hal Percy* 23 He used to dine on meat pies at Mother Bourke's Cafe, And was always on the bite for a few bob till next pay day. **1955** R. LAWLER *Summer of Seventeenth Doll* (1965) 98 Your money's runnin' out, you know you can't put the bite on me any more, and so here's the new champion, all loaded and ready. **1967** F. HARDY *Billy Borker yarns Again* 3 Puts the bite on a Yankee tourist for a quid. **1967** D. HEWETT *This Old Man* (1976) 92 Yeah, Mumma put the big bite on 'im. Georgie moved out faster'n a Bondi tram. **1976** S. WELLER *Bastards I have Met* 5, I said, 'How about a few scraps for a stew, butch?' and he roared 'God strike me pink—I've had ten customers this morning—four on the bite and six on the nod.'

bite, *v.* [Abbrev. of *to bite the ear* to borrow money from (someone): see OEDS *bite, v.* 16.] *trans.* To solicit money, etc., from; to 'touch' for; to scrounge (food). Also *intr.*

[**1895** *Worker* (Sydney) 5 Jan. 1/5 Mitchell bit the cook's ear for a bit of meat, and tea, and sugar. **1898** *Bulletin* (Sydney) 4 June (Red Page), If he borrows money off you He will say he 'bit your lug'.] **1912** *Truth* (Sydney) 8 Dec. 7/4 They 'bit' him not merely for 'tens' or 'twenties', but for hundreds and even thousands. **1919** V. MARSHALL *World of Living Dead* 70 The 'hum', the unskilled derelict or derelict-to-be who stands upon the 'pub' corner kerb, 'bites' all and sundry. **1922** C. DREW *Rogues & Ruses* 67 He'd been a member of the leadin' sportin' clubs, but he'd bitten his way out of all of them. **1935** K. TENNANT *Tiburon* 24 An' would y' go bitin' people for coppers if y' weren't forced to it? **1941** ——*Battlers* 172 I'm here to cook for you men, and not for any lousy bagmen that come biting tucker. **1942** *Plane Speaking from R.A.A.F. Amberley* 3 Sept. 7 Sgt. Ron Minett, who went around the alcoves 'biting' the occupants for five bobs. **1957** *Overland* ix. 4 We'll go up and bite Rene for a cuppa. **1968** *Meanjin* 18 Look I'm not going to bite you for a couple of bob or the price of a drink. I just want to say 'hullo', that's all. **1980** *Westerly* i. 7 Could I bite you for a few bucks? Pay day tomorrow.

biter. BITE *n.* 1.

1955 *Bulletin* (Sydney) 26 Oct. 13/3 Ned looked the supplicant quizzically up and down and said, 'Hmnn, have you ever bit me before?' 'No,' beamed the biter confidently. 'Well,' replied the big bloke . . 'I ain't puttin' on no new customers!' **1967** *Kings Cross Whisper* (Sydney) xxxvi. 7/2 Outraged, biter leaps to his feet saying he couldn't possibly take her money—how much has she got by the way.

bitser, var. BITZER.

bitter bark. Any of several trees having a bitter bark, esp. *Alstonia constricta* (fam. Apocynaceae) of N.S.W. and Qld. See also QUININE TREE.

1881 *Proc. Linnean Soc. N.S.W.* VI. 742 The beautiful flowering shrub *Clerodendron floribundum*, which is here mistaken for the 'Bitter-bark' (*Alstonia constricta*). **1890** A. MACKAY *Austral. Agriculturist* (ed. 2) 151 'The bitter bark' . . , a fine upright tree reaching forty-five feet in height in the rich scrub of Northern Queensland, is believed to contain quinine. **1926** *Bulletin* (Sydney) 14 Jan. 22/3 The 'fever'-tree . . is the native quinine, *Alstonia constricta*, commmonly known on the North Coast of Bananaland as 'bitter bark'. **1965** *Austral. Encycl.* II. 17 Bitter-bark . . is also called fever-bark or quinine bush. Its thick fissured bark is intensely bitter and contains a febrifugal tonic principle.

bitumen.

1. A road with a tarred surface; a sealed road.

1948 G. MEREDITH *Lawsons* 1 Wongalee is . . an impressive little one-horse town whose few hundred yards of bitumen, straggling at each end into dusty dirt roads, rouse no excess of enthusiasm. **1962** C. GYE *Cockney & Crocodile* 61 By some miracle found myself in the starlight on 'the bitumen', i.e. a macadam road. **1965** *N. Austral. Monthly* Oct. 17 We decided to take the new cattle road to the bitumen and on to Katherine. **1980** C. KELEN *Punks Travels* 58 Driving down the long loose edged bitumen thru endless miles of scrub. **1983** *Open Road* Feb. 17/3 Because of the difficult terrain and weather conditions in the shire that means about a kilometre and a half of new bitumen a year.

2. *spec.* The Stuart Highway between Darwin and Alice Springs.

1949 H.E. THONEMANN *Tell White Man* 149 There were the workmen who made a beautiful road now called the 'Bitumen'. **1950** *New Settler in W.A.* (Perth) Feb. 50 Once you leave the 'Bitumen' you return to the timeless atmosphere of the Never Never. **1951** G. FARWELL *Outside Track* 147 Even along the 'Bitumen'—as the modern Alice Springs-Darwin highway is always known—you are aware of history, the hardships that went to the making of the back country. **1953** A. MOOREHEAD *Rum Jungle* 66 Engineers moved into the Northern Territory and built the Stuart Highway. . . The local people always call it 'The Bitumen' . . saying they are 'East (or West) of the bitumen', or simply 'Up (or down) the bitumen'. **1959** D. LOCKWOOD *Crocodiles & Other People* 209 They called The Bitumen the Stuart Highway after explorer John McDouall Stuart. **1960** *N.T. News* (Darwin) 5 Feb. 15/5 Fishing downstream from the bitumen at the Elizabeth. **1977** T. RONAN *Mighty Men on Horseback* 74 If you are in Darwin you go 'up the bitumen' to get down to Alice Springs. If you are in the Alice you go 'down the bitumen' to get up to Darwin.

bitumenize, *v. trans.* To surface (a road, etc.), with bitumen.

1959 H. DRAKE-BROCKMAN *West Coast Stories* 194 The company told him they were going to bitumenize the pearl-shell road. **1964** *Mount Isa Mail* 30 Jan. 1/3 The car bays have not been bitumenised.

bitzer. Also **bitser, bitza.** [f. abbrev. of *bits (and pieces.*]

1. A contraption made from previously unrelated parts.

1924 *Smith's Weekly* (Sydney) 6 Dec. 24/5 Toombes built the body himself, and made a fair job of it. Thence emerged the super Bitza . . and those who do not know that its ragged bonnet hides a Vauxhall engine ponder over the origin of its cheek. **1951** S. HICKEY *Travelled Roads* 27 George had a big 'bitza' clock with a powerful knock at each hour, but it struck one every time.

2. A mongrel dog. Also *attrib.*

1936 *Bulletin* (Sydney) 4 Mar. 21/4 The 'bitzer'-bred dog belonging to a resident of the Hawkesbury River. **1940** *Ibid.* 6 Nov. 17/4 Joe the rouseabout . . not only refused to acknowledge the canine as a blue-blooded poodle, but also made a few tactless references to 'bitzers'. **1960** J.E. MACDONNELL *Subsmash!* 78 'Strike me, this plurry cat's a prize Persian or somethin'?' 'No, she's a bitzer—bits of everything.' **1969** P. ADAM SMITH *Folklore Austral. Railwaymen* 154 This young navvy began to sool their 'bitza' on with a stick. **1978** B. ST. A. SMITH *Spirit beyond Psyche* 10 Jim bent and scratched the dog's ears. Poor old Seidlitz, a bitzer if ever there was one!

bizzo. [Abbrev. of *bus(iness* + -O.] Something to which the speaker does not wish to refer precisely; cf. 'thingummy'.

1969 A. BUZO *Front Room Boys* (1970) 27 Do the overall tallies in the squares provided on the bizzo. **1972** G. MORLEY *Jockey rides Honest Race* 62 Sheilas sitting down against the wall, legs up in the air, showing their bizzos. **1984** *Canberra Times* 6 May 6/6, I hear Jim was on to Parramatta the other day after fixing up the Michelle bizzo.

black, *n.*, *a.*[1], and *attrib.* [Spec. use of *black* dark-skinned (person).]

A. *n.*

1. An Aboriginal.

1795 D. COLLINS *Acct. Eng. Colony N.S.W.* (1798) I. 434 Samuel Chinnery (a black) servant to Mr Arndell. **1809** *Sydney Gaz.* 3 Sept., A man . . was attacked near Parramatta by three blacks. **1826** *Monitor* (Sydney) 25 Aug. 117/3 We have read the account in the Gazette, of the accidental killing of the black. **1832** J. HANSON *Let.* 8 He had been out all morning, and had had but one shot at a Black!! **1833** C. STURT *Two Exped. Interior* I. 20 The men went to bathe, and blacks and whites were mingled promiscuously in the stream. **1837** *Perth Gaz.* 21 Oct. 992 His Britannic Majesty's *blacks* are really a very singular race! **1843** *Sydney Morning Herald* 22 Nov. 3/2 He is a strong muscular man, about the middle size, is very intelligent for a black, and possesses a remarkably fine set of teeth. **1855** W.H. HOVELL *Reply to Hamilton Hume* 20 At the time we were encamped on the coast the blacks became somewhat troublesome. **1865** *London Soc.* Dec. 446/1 Nearly all the members of the corps of rangers are men of classical education and good birth, who can quote Homer or Virgil as well as they can shoot a kangaroo, or kick a black. **1886** E.M. CURR *Austral. Race* I. p. xviii, Our Blacks do not mark the boundaries of tribal territories. **1899** R. SEMON *In Austral. Bush* 45, I had caught a considerable quantity of Platypus. . . My blacks were hardly able to furnish me with any information as to the customs of this animal. **1911** ST. C. GRONDONA *Collar & Cuffs* 60 The blacks have all been transported to Frazer, the dingoes are nearly all poisoned. **1928** B. SPENCER *Wanderings in Wild Aust.* 195 They are commonly spoken of as 'niggers' or 'blacks', but in reality are neither 'nigger' in race nor black in colour, but are long-headed Caucasians, belonging to the same great race as ourselves, only to a dark variety of it. **1937** J.M. HARCOURT *It never Fails* 79 You'd think a black was a human being the fuss that's made if one or two of them get shot. **1955** D. CLARK *Boomer* 30 The blacks, the Australian tribesmen, wandered still as they had wandered for countless ages. **1963** 'E. LINDALL' *Springs of Violence* 55 'What about the blacks?' 'Soon as we start the round-up they'll scamper outa this territory mighty fast.' **1971** A. BUZO *Macquarie* (1973) 32 We shall hope to see the birth not only of integration and assimilation, but of participation by blacks in the building of our society. **1984** *Age* (Melbourne) 24 Aug. 4 (*heading*) Blacks may have arrived 130,000 years ago.

2. In the collocation **black's bread,** *native bread* NATIVE *a.* 6 a.

1904 *Bulletin* (Sydney) 13 Oct. 18/3 A 7lb. lump of 'black's bread' has been unearthed in the neighbourhood of Bathurst (N.S.W.). . . According to the oldest and least reliable inhabitant, this bread was once plentiful in the Oberon district. . . It has a tough crust, but the inside is soft, resembling sago, and is not unpalatable. There is no visible root or germ about it, and its origin is a mystery.

B. *adj.* and *attrib.*

1. Aboriginal. See also BLACKBOY 1, BLACKFELLOW.

1788 [see *black man*]. **1820** *HRA* (1921) 3rd Ser. III. 363 Are the native Black Children, who have been Baptized, brought in by their Parents? **1835** *Cornwall Chron.* (Launceston) 15 Aug. 1 Does Mr Batman mean to convey, that in purchasing 500,000 acres of land from a black chief, he has also . . bought the sovereignty, of the soil? **1840** F.J. MEYRICK *Life in Bush* 16 June (1939) 115 Our black guides were excellent hands at stalking kangaroo. **1843** C. ROWCROFT *Tales of Colonies* (1858) 309 Those black chaps have a knack of tracking in the bush. **1856** W.W. DOBIE *Recoll. Visit Port-Phillip* 93 A black doctor, according to Syntax, is like a white poet, *nascitur, non fit.* **1867** 'CLERGYMAN' *Aust. as it Is* 51 Those who . . are accustomed to the work of pioneering and 'taking up country', are always careful to avail themselves of the services of one or two trusty black attendants. **1872** 'RESIDENT' *Glimpses Life Vic.* 310 The black cricketers who lately visited England belonged to western district tribes. **1882** *Bulletin* (Sydney) 11 Feb. 10/3 A young black larrikin, . . arrested the other day for pelting the 'peelers' with rocks. **1910** *Ibid.* 22 Dec. 13/4 The board comprised 24 black shearers; picking up was done by gins and sweeping by piccaninnies. **1921** K.S. PRICHARD *Black Opal* 105 He had worked half a million . . acres . . in the days before runs were fenced, with only a few black shepherds and one white man. **1944** *Aust. Week-End Bk.* 10 The blunder of our dealings with the black Australians whose land we stole. **1960** V. CARELL *Naked we are Born* 68, I didn't do no shooting and ya must have seen somebody else with the black sheila. **1970** *Bulletin* (Sydney) 24 Oct. 28/1 The NTC wants the affairs of black Australians controlled by black Australians. **1974** M. GILLESPIE *Into Hollow Mountains* 53 The Builder's Arms is supposedly Melbourne's 'black-pub', although . . a black activist from Sydney says it doesn't deserve the title. 'A black pub is full of black people talking about black topics.'

2. In Comb. and collocations: **black camp, girl, -hunting, man, people, police, population, trooper, woman.**

1826 R. DAWSON *Private & Confidential* 15 He . . carried it a considerable way to the **black camp**, as they call it. **1842** *Portland Mercury* 7 Sept. 3/5 Within a mile of one of the out-stations the party found the dead bodies of thirty-five of the animals, and continuing on their tracks came to a black camp. **1865** G.S. LANG *Aborigines of Aust.* 31 They reached the black camp before dawn. **1815** *HRA* (1921) 3rd Ser. II. 95 The **Black Girl** . . is a Native of the Island. **1825** *Tasmanian* (Hobart) 12 Jan. 3/2 Recollects of a black girl being at his hut, and of seeing spears and waddies there. **1827** *Ibid.* 18 Oct. 3 We have been informed that a black girl, a native of this Colony, commonly known by the name of *Black Kate*, is now in an advanced state of pregnancy by a Lascar named *Boxhall*. **1879** 'AUSTRALIAN' *Adventures Qld.* 25 They dared not call out loudly—that was against all rules on **black-hunting** expeditions—for the natives' ears are sharp as well as their eyes. **1926** W.A. CAWTHORNE *Kangaroo Islanders* 65 A little wrecking, stabbing, and black-hunting. **1788** R. CLARK *Jrnl.* 29 Feb. 129 Two **black men** . . received sentence of death. **1827** *HRA* (1920) 1st Ser. XIII. 404 Thomas Farnham . . delivered the Blackman over to the Mounted Police. **1839** *Sydney Standard* 19 Aug. 3/6 It is an offence punishable by death for a white man to kill a blackman. **1844** *HRA* (1925) 1st Ser. XXIII. 486 They believe White Men to be Black Men returned to life again. **1856** *Plea on Behalf of Aboriginal Inhabitants Vic.* 4 The worst vices of the black man are those we have taught him. **1873** A. TROLLOPE *Aust. & N.Z.* II. 84, I do not say that the black men were ill-treated. **1956** S. GORE *Overlanding with Annabel* 47 The coast was looked upon as a 'black man's country'. **1965** G. MCINNES *Road to Gundagai* 40 Troopers fired on aborigines and despatched maimed and writhing black men with a shot from a carbine. **1974** F. STEVENS *Aborigines in N.T. Cattle Industry* 113 Borroloola, on the Gulf, also seemed to be taking the role of the 'Blackman's Brighton'. Stations . . often drove their workers to Borroloola . . loaded down with food, camping gear and happy children. **1826** *HRA* (1919) 1st Ser. XII. 672 The advice you are supposed to have given in the cases of the **Black People** and Bushrangers. **1838** *S. Austral. Rec.* (London) 14 Nov. 110 The black people here would make you smile; they are quite naked, men, women, and children; they have no shame, and are very gentle. **1843** C. ROWCROFT *Tales of Colonies* I. 231 The black people had set fire to the thatch of native grass. **1825** B. FIELD *Geogr. Mem. N.S.W.* 33 Should the runaways even escape the **black police**, they are almost sure to perish by hunger or the hostility of the other Indians. **1844** *Colonial Observer* (Sydney) 7 Nov. 2/4 The advanced guard of Captain Dana's black police, arrived in town. **1847** *Atlas* (Sydney) III. 69/2 Slaughter of the aboriginies [*sic*] by the black police. **1863** J. BONWICK *Wild White Man* 74 Our Black police were horrible instruments of colonial law. **1893** S. NEWLAND *Paving Way* 242 The 'black police' were men selected principally from the remnants of coastal tribes, which were hostile to those of the interior. They were trained to arms, and, loving slaughter for slaughter's sake, were absolutely unaffected by any feelings of humanity towards their fellow-countrymen. **1902** L. BECKE *Breachley* 97 You ought to be an officer in the Black Police, and go in for nigger-shooting as a regular business. **1969** A.A. ABBIE *Original Australs.* 233 The whites . . enlisted (legally) 'Black Police' (or 'Troopers') and 'Black Trackers' from distant tribes. **1828** *Blossom* (Sydney) i. 43 Much . . has been said, as to the impracticability of ever civilizing the **black population** of Australia. **1839** *S. Austral. Miscellany* Dec. 53 In accounting for the very great decrease in the black population. **1847** *Colonial Intelligencer* (London) I. 70 The nearest hospital is in Goulburn, which does not contemplate the reception or relief of the Black population. **1862** BACKHOUSE & TYLOR *Life & Labours G.W. Walker* 278 The embryo town of Adelaide . . was . . much frequented by the black population. **1843** *Portland Mercury* 25 Oct. 3/4 The serjeant with five of the **black troopers** . . returned back at full speed. **1865** G.S. LANG *Aborigines of Aust.* 46 When the black troopers are let loose they are completely beyond the control of their officers. **1882** A.J. BOYD *Old Colonials* 184 There is a native police station opposite the ford, and the help of the black troopers is often very acceptable to the escort. **1899** *Bulletin* (Sydney) 18 Nov. 31/2 The sub-inspector told him that he would come out himself with a black trooper. **1911** A.L. HAYDON *Trooper Police Aust.* 81 The duties of the black troopers, or 'Joes', as they were commonly called. **1845** L. LEICHHARDT *Jrnl. Overland Exped. Aust.* 12 Feb. (1847) 149 We soon came in sight of three **black women.** **1862** E. STRICKLAND *Austral. Pastor* 60 They were welcomed . . by two black women and a coloured girl. **1888** G. ROCK *Colonists* 76 A 'lady of color' is a black woman. **1915** N. DUNCAN *Austral. Byways* 86 He had fallen in with a roving band of gins (blackwomen).

3. Used tautologously to qualify nouns which themselves denote Aboriginality: **black Aboriginal, Aborigine, gin, lubra, native, piccaninny, tribe.**

1870 C.H. ALLEN *Visit to Qld.* 98 The **black aboriginals** lying in ambush. **1926** A.A.B. APSLEY *Amateur Settlers* 91 Certain amount of black Aboriginals. **1842** *Colonial Observer* (Sydney) 24 Aug. 421/2 His own views of the relation between the whites and the **black aborigines.** **1837** *Rep. Select Committee Transportation* 18 Apr. (1838) 27 What are the native women called by the assigned convicts?—**Black gins.** **1843** C. ROWCROFT *Tales of Colonies* I. 76 I've seen a black gin get up a stringy-bark tree after a 'possum as well as any one of the men could. **1848** C. COZENS *Adventures of Guardsman* 128 The 'black *gins*', as the women are styled, are not remarkable either for beauty or stature. **1882** A.J. BOYD *Old Colonials* 195, I enjoyed a hearty meal, although the damper was kneaded by an old black gin and the beef salted by native troopers. **1899** *Bulletin* (Sydney) 2 Sept. 14/2 In far-out Westralia . . two white men are the owners of a couple of black-gins. **1922** *Smith's Weekly* (Sydney) 29 July 17/6 There lived in a township near the Queensland border a black-gin. **1938** X. HERBERT *Capricornia* 73 She was a full-blooded blackgin. **1959** E. WEBB *Mark of Sun* 10 You stubborn pommy bastard. . . Take your bloody blackgin and get out of it! **1984** P. READ *Down there with me on Cowra Mission* 108 Well the woman that's got him, she was a blackgin—she couldn't have no kids. **1841** *Geelong*

Advertiser 7 Aug. 2/3 Tender-hearted creatures would no doubt be wonderfully edified at the sight of a **black leubra** suckling a pup at her breast, while her own emaciated offspring was squalling at her back!! **1845** T. McCombie *Adventures of Colonist* 74 'And make love to the black *lubras*,' interrupted the settler. **1860** R.B. Smyth *Aborigines of Vic.* (1878) I. 264, I knew one instance of this disease becoming most distressing to a white man, in a respectable position, who was continually cohabiting with black lubras. **1939** T.E. Jones *These Twenty Yrs.* 66 'Mary' was only a black lubra. **1816** *Hobart Town Gaz.* 31 Aug., A few days ago a party of about twenty **Black Natives** pursued three of the Government Stock-keepers. **1818** T.E. Wells *M. Howe* (1945) 18 Howe, accompanied by a black Native Girl named Mary. **1821** *Sydney Gaz.* 17 Mar., A Member of each of the . . Committees of the Male Orphan Institution, Female Orphan Institution, and Black Native Institution. **1827** *Monitor* (Sydney) 3 Feb. 299/2 The black natives are completely tranquil. **1828** *Tasmanian* (Hobart) 18 Apr. 3 Capt. Dalrymple with his whole company, is about to proceed to the interior to scour the country of black natives and all other human pests of society. **1839** *S. Austral. Rev.* 14 The character and condition of the black natives is another repulsive feature of the older colonies. **1848** J. Syme *Nine Yrs. Van Diemen's Land* 255 The quickness and sagacity peculiar to the black natives in tracing footsteps. **1852** D. Mackenzie *Gold Digger* 73 In Australia you have nothing to fear, either from quadrupeds or from the black native bipeds. **1873** A. Trollope *Aust. & N.Z.* II. 229 At the Wallaroo mines I found a set of black natives employed on surface work. **1923** T. Hall *Short Hist. Downs Blacks* 5 A lot of **black picaninnies** (children) clapping their hands. **1808** *Sydney Gaz.* 6 Nov., Your sage Correspondent affects to describe The Habits that grace Australia's **Black Tribe**. **1848** C. Cozens *Adventures of Guardsman* 128 The men were for the most part tall, muscular and well formed, particularly above the knee; but below that they greatly fell off, having little or no calves . . as is the case with most black tribes.

4. Used in collocations to evoke, (often) ironically, the image of the 'noble savage', as **black gentleman, gentry, ladies, lords (of the soil), proprietors (of the soil).** Cf. Child.

1839 W.H. Leigh *Reconnoitering Voyages* 85, I . . saw . . two black gentlemen from whom the 'coo-ēē' proceeded. **1840** J.P. Johnson *Plain Truths* 55 The black gentlemen begin thrashing the black ladies. **1848** *Observer* (Melbourne) 25 May 75/4 The very loose and incorrect notions which these black gentry have of the rights of *meum* and *tuam* [*sic*]. **1851** H. Melville *Present State Aust.* 52 The white population . . have always acted kindly towards these black proprietors of the soil. **1854** Mrs C. Clacy *Lights & Shadows* II. 23 Their wives or lubras . . do all the disagreeable work, whilst their black lords recline lazily upon the grass. **1859** H.M. Hull *Experience Forty Yrs. Tas.* 16 One of the black ladies, who married a few years ago a sawyer named *Smith*, has recently presented her husband with a little black 'pledge of affection'. **1867** 'Clergyman' *Aust. as it Is* 54 The territory . . they proposed taking possession of from the black proprietors. **1875** G.M. Newman *N.T. & its Gold-Fields* 16 The black lords of the soil . . on all occasions show the utmost contempt for civilization and labor.

5. Used pejoratively in collocations, as **black animal, bastard, brother, crow, cur, game, savage, sister.**

1838 *Sydney Herald* 5 Oct. 3/1 The whole gang of black animals are not worth the money which the Colonists will have to pay for printing the silly documents. **1847** *Moreton Bay Courier* 6 Feb. 2/4 The circumstances attending the deaths of several of the white population who have been slaughtered by the black savages. **1857** F. Gerstaecker *Two Convicts* 13 If I were certain . . I would make the black curs pay for it dearly enough. **1882** W. Sowden *N.T. as it Is* 20 Even now it is considered a joke all along the coast beyond Cooktown . . to shoot down black-fellows . . and some men pride themselves on the 'row of stiff 'uns' they have made in their time, and others talk pleasantly of 'black-crow shooting'. **1895** A.C. Bicknell *Travel & Adventure Northern Qld.* 66, I might get a brace or two of black game before the morning. **1909** *Bulletin* (Sydney) 25 Nov. 14/4 Our black brother is soaking in education. . . The other day he was awarded two years for forging and uttering a cheque for £6. **1943** *Ibid.* 25 Aug. 12/2 Black sister of the Murchison and the Nullagine (W.A.) could do one quite remarkable thing with her coolamon or yandi. **1946** *Ibid.* 30 Oct. 29/4, I remain sceptical as to the possibility of endowing Black Brother with commercial acumen. **1975** R.J. Merritt *Cake Man* (1978) 27 Come back with my property! Black bastard! Mission Rat!

6. In special collocations: **black tracker,** Tracker; **velvet,** Aboriginal women as the focus of a white man's sexual interest; sexual intercourse with an Aboriginal woman.

1862 *Leader* (Melbourne) 5 July, The **black trackers** could only discover the tracks of six horsemen. **1865** 'Special Correspondent' *Transportation* 33 The prisoners know . . that if they attempted an escape . . with . . the sureness of the black trackers employed to follow them up, their chance would be poor. **1878** R.B. Smyth *Aborigines of Vic.* 7 When any one is lost in the bush the whites rely . . on the sagacity and skill of the 'black-tracker'. **1889** W.H. Tietkens *Jrnl. Central Austral. Exploring Exped.* 14 Mar. (1891) 2 A black-tracker (Billy, from the ranks of the native police at Alice Springs). **1912** S.A. Payne *Orig. Austral. Verses* 28 For a terror to ride and Australia's pride Is this keen-eyed and wily black tracker. **1919** *Smith's Weekly* (Sydney) 5 July 11/5 Blacktrackers have not always been a success in Victoria. Once one got bushed in the police-paddock at Dandenong. **1948** C.B. Maxwell *Cold Nose of Law* 54 Queensland still depends on black-trackers alone—is still without trained dogs. **1960** *N.T. News* (Darwin) 5 Feb. 5/3 He got two black trackers from Bagot and searched the whole area. **1975** D. Stuart *Walk, trot, canter & Die* 7 It's the black police, not the whites, that's the danger. Never a sight of a wanted man would they get if it weren't for the blacktrackers. **1900** H. Lawson *Verses Pop. & Humorous* 57, I know the track from Spencer's Gulf and north of Cooper's Creek—Where falls the half-caste to the strong, **'black velvet'** to the weak. **1906** *Truth* (Sydney) 8 Apr. 4/6 The acquired taste of 'black velvet', like that of alcohol, is never entirely eradicated. **1929** K.S. Prichard *Coonardoo* (1961) 46 You're one of those god-dammed young heroes. No 'black velvet' for you I suppose? **1934** S. Howard *You're telling Me!* 131 You preacher fellers can talk all you like, but . . you'll never get rid of black velvet. **1938** *Publicist* (Sydney) xix. 13/2 As each new outback district is pioneered, the white pioneers cannot resist the lure of Black Velvet. **1940** W. Hatfield *Into (Great?) Unfenced* 80 Then go an' cool off with a Jin. That's our cut. The black velvet, son. **1958** G. Casey *Snowball* 17 Did you see the girls, when you were out there? . . The sort of black velvet that makes me sometimes wish I wasn't a policeman. **1976** T. Shepherd *Children of Blindness* 139 Don't you fancy a bit of black velvet, eh?

7. *Hist.* In Special Comb. and collocations: **black line,** a dragnet operation in 1830 in which the military and police, aided by settlers and their convict servants, moved systematically across eastern Tasmania in an attempt to round up the Aboriginal population; **protector, protectorate,** Protector, Protectorate; **string, war,** *black line.*

1835 H. Melville *Hist. Van Diemen's Land* 99 In September, of 1830, the **black line** was projected, and proved a very innocent amusement for the various Government officers, as also for a very large portion of the settlers, and their convict servants. **1851** —— *Present State Aust.* 365 The parties forming the 'black line', composed as they were, of a curious melange of masters and servants, took their respective stations. **1862** G.T. Lloyd *Thirty-Three Yrs. Tas. & Vic.* 234 Many country residents dated their success in life from circumstances connected with the memorable 'Black Line'. **1898** G.W. Walker *Notes on Aborigines Tas.* 4 The deadly feud between the natives and the settlers which raged between 1825 and 1830, led to Governor Arthur's military operation known as the 'Black Line'. **1986** *Bulletin* (Sydney) 11 Mar. 98/3 Boyes was in Van Diemen's Land when . . the Black line, the decision to restrict Aborigines to an area, effectively leading to their extermination, was set. **1842** *Melbourne Times* 16 July 2/6 We have not for some weeks seen a **Black Protector** in town, which is indeed something new, as they may be generally seen sauntering about our streets as unconcernedly as if there was not a single black in the colony. **1843** *Portland Mercury* 23 Aug. 2/3 A Black protector, aye, *black* indeed, was the voluntary ally in this dreadful prosecution. **1865** G.S. Lang *Aborigines of Aust.* 45 Any complaint would bring a black protector or his deputy. **1870** E.B. Kennedy *Four Yrs. in Qld.* 67 The 'Black question' gives rise to more argument than almost any other . . the settlers on one side and certain individuals styled 'Black protectors' on the other. **1893** E. Favenc *Last of Six Tales* 50 The new super. was a black-protector. **1844** *Portland Mercury* 31 Jan. 3/5 Such a rotten, dangerous system known as the **Black Protectorate**? **1859** R.H. Horne *Austral. Facts & Prospects* 40 It was adjoining the station of the 'Black Protectorate' (meaning a place where blankets, tobacco, bread, and other articles were periodically given to the aboriginal tribes of that locality). **1870** J. Bonwick *Last Tasmanians* 163 Some good stories of theLine, or **'Black String'**. **1830** P.L. Brown *Clyde Co. Papers* (1941) I. 110 The **Black War** ended here after 2 months' campaign of 3,000 men. **1833** *Launceston Advertiser* 31 Oct. 3 A Proclamation in last Gazette puts an end to the Black War. **1834** *Colonist* (Hobart) 25 Mar. 3/1 The Sydney Natives, who were employed here during our Black War, . . have come back to the Colony. **1855** J. Bonwick *Geogr. Aust. & N.Z.* (ed. 3) 157 Through the narrow East Bay Neck, into Forrestier's Peninsula, the settlers sought to drive the natives in the Black War. **1869** J. Martineau *Lett. from Aust.* 72 The crowning event, the great joke of the time . . was the 'black war', as it is ironically called. **1890** A.J. Vogan *Black Police* 42 What's wanted here is a Black war like they had in Tasmania.

8. a. Of or pertaining to a Kanaka. Also used instrumentally.

1876 [see Black 8 b.] **1896** N. Gould *Town & Bush* 69 Black labour must be employed on the Queensland sugar plantations. **1901** *Brisbane Courier* 1 July 9/1 There was . . trouble over the black labour question in Queensland. **1904** *Advocate* (Burnie) 14 Nov. 2/4 Black-grown sugar enjoys a protection of £3 per ton, and white-grown sugar of £5 per ton. **1964** R. Connolly *John Drysdale & Burdekin* 111 Black-grown cane, 947,105 tons . . White-grown cane, 379,884 tons.

b. Special Comb. **black-labour man, party,** a person or faction favouring the use of Kanaka labour in Queensland.

1876 'Eight Yrs.' Resident' *Queen of Colonies* 300 A very strong public opinion developed itself, yet the **black-labour men**, as they are called, had influence enough with Government to cause the matter to be hushed up. **1901** *Bulletin* (Sydney) 30 Mar. 20/1 Brisbane Courier issues its 'ticket' of six for Q. Senate. All are black-labor men. **1876** 'Eight Yrs.' Resident' *Queen of Colonies* 301 So strong is the **black-labour party** in the colony—the premier himself being a large employer of Polynesians on his station. **1895** *Worker* (Sydney) 2 Mar. 1/1 This Convention . . protests against the 'black labor party' in Queensland imperilling the future welfare of white Australia by the maintenance of the Kanaka Act. **1899** *Progress* (Brisbane) 29 Apr. 9/1 The revolt against the rule of the black-labour party will come from the white men who have the misfortune to live in those parts of the colony where the Curse most abounds.

black, *a.*[2] [Spec. use of *black* characterized by the colour.]

1. a. Used as a distinguishing epithet in the names of plants: **black apple,** any of several trees bearing a dark fruit, esp. *Planchonella australis* (fam. Sapotaceae) of N.S.W. and Qld., which also yields a fine-grained timber; *bush apple*, see Bush C. 3; **bean, (a)** the large tree *Castanospermum australe* (fam. Fabaceae) of e. Qld. and n.e. N.S.W., having dark green leaves and a hard, heavy pod containing poisonous chestnut-like seeds; the dark brown, attractively figured wood of the tree; Chestnut *n.*; *Moreton Bay chestnut*, see Moreton Bay; see also Bean tree; **(b)** the tree *Erythrophleum chlorostachys* (see Camel poison); **oak,** any of several trees of the genera *Allocasuarina* and *Casuarina* (fam. Casuarinaceae), incl. *C. cristata* (see Belah); **sallee** (or **sally**), the small tree of s.e. Aust. *Eucalyptus stellulata* (fam. Myrtaceae), having a rough black lower trunk and smooth olive green to grey upper trunk; Muzzlewood; **wattle, (a)** any of several dark-barked trees of the genus *Acacia* (fam. Mimosaceae), esp. *A. mearnsii*; **(b)** the shrub or small tree *Callicoma serratifolia* (fam. Cunoniaceae), which bears wattle-like heads of flowers.

1888 *Proc. Linnean Soc. N.S.W.* III. 485 *Achras australis* . . **'Black Apple'**, 'Brush Apple', 'Wild' or 'Native Plum' of colonists. **1938** C.T. White *Princ. Bot. Qld. Farmers* 192 *Family Sapotaceae*. . . About twenty species are natives of Queensland. These include the Black Apple. **1968** J. Carter *Stout Hearts* 96 Joe made boomerangs. . . At first he went to the Gloucester and Kempsey districts, in search of . . black apple. **1981** A.B. & J.W. Cribb *Useful Wild Plants Aust.* 143 The most distinctive feature of the black apple is its purple-black, plum-like fruits containing a few large, shiny brown seeds. **1895** *Agric. Gaz. N.S.W.* V. 1 The **black bean** or Moreton Bay Chestnut... Because of the seeds, which are very large beans, this tree goes under the name of bean-tree; and because of the dark colour of the wood.. it is usually known by timber merchants as black bean. **1930** V. KENNEDY *By Range & River* 73 A full list of Atherton timbers would include such building timbers as.. black bean. **1948** A. MARSHALL *Ourselves writ Strange* 92 Many had bundles of the large beans from the black bean tree suspended from their waists. **1967** V.G.C. NORWOOD *Long Haul* 72 Enormously spreading black bean or Moreton Bay chestnut trees whose elongated seed pods harboured swarms of droning bees. **1974** S.L. EVERIST *Poisonous Plants Aust.* 296 *Erythrophleum chlorostachys*... In Western Australia it is also known as *camel poison* and *black bean*. **1980** B. SCOTT *Darkness under Hills* 45 Downstream was a tall stand of black bean trees. **1860** J.M. STUART *Exploration of Interior* 5/1 Alternate sandhills and grassy plains, consisting of mulga, malay, and **black oak.** **1868** *Colonial Monthly* Sept. 68 Here and there, I saw a few thickets of black-oak; or, as some call it, he-oak. **1893** D. LINDSAY *Jrnl. Elder Sci. Exploring Exped.* 31 Some good patches of black oak (*Casuarina glauca*). **1900** R. BRUCE *Benbonuna* (1904) 86 The foliage of the black oak is not fodder for cattle, and its wood is only useful for firewood. **1923** J. ARMOUR *Spell of Inland* 32 They met at a clump of black oaks. **1936** I.L. IDRIESS *Cattle King* 326 Where had all the mulga gone.. the black oak and nelia, and bullocky bush..? **1972** R. ERICKSEN *West of Centre* 50 The black oak.. grows to thirty feet or more and occasionally has exclusive possession of the ground in heavy stands two and three miles wide. **1889** J.H. MAIDEN *Useful Native Plants Aust.* 522 In Gippsland it [*sc. Eucalyptus stellulata*] is known by the names of '**Black Sallee**' and 'Muzzle-wood'. **1942** R.T. PATTON *Know your Own Trees* 42 Black Sallee.. is to be seen chiefly in the alpine area. **1963** C. BURGESS *Blue Mountain Gums* 48 '*Black Sally*' was named *Eucalyptus stellulata* by Sieber. **1980** J. WRIGHT *Big Hearts & Gold Dust* 84 It was pleasant.. listening to the jingle of hobble-chains and camp gear as he rode beneath the black-sallys and blue-gums. **1797** D. COLLINS *Acct. Eng. Colony N.S.W.* (1802) II. 63 A similar timber was called the **Black Wattle.** **1805** *HRA* (1921) 3rd Ser. I. 344 The Bark of the Trees, called the Blue Gum and Black Wattle of this country, can be used successfully in tanning. **1822** J.T. BIGGE *Rep. State Colony N.S.W.* 160 The mimosa decurrens, that has received in New South Wales the name of the black wattle. **1829** R. MUDIE *Picture of Aust.* 138 The *acacia melanoxylon* is called the black wattle. **1841** *Colonial Mag.* (London) IV. 452 The *Acacia decurrens*, or *black wattle*, an elegant tree, a native of Van Diemen's Land. **1853** *Illustr. Sydney News* 15 Oct. 10/3 In the forests or bush we meet the golden blossoms of the black wattle or mimosa. **1881** *Proc. Linnean Soc. N.S.W.* VI. 771 In the early days of the colony.. *Callicoma serratifolia* was the Black Wattle.. but now the terms Black and Green Wattle are applied almost universally to the two varieties of *Acacia decurrens*. **1921** A.J. CAMPBELL *Golden Wattle* 44 The Black Wattle (*Acacia mollis*) of commerce—a tree highly prized by 'unrighteous mammon', because of the maximum percentage of tannic acid its bark produces. **1935** E. COLEMAN *Come back in Wattle Time* 19 A few, like the Black Wattle (*A[cacia] mollissima*), are ravished by certain wood-moths. **1955** P. WHITE *Tree of Man* 206 Sometimes in stormy weather gulls came.. and glided and dipped above the black wattles. **1978** K. GARVEY *Tales of my Uncle Harry* 9 Gum and pine and black wattle so thick a dingo couldn't hear himself bark in it.

b. In the names of animals: **black and white fantail,** WILLY WAGTAIL; **and white swallow,** *white-backed swallow*, see WHITE *a.*[2] 1 b.; **-backed wren,** the small bird *Malurus splendens*, a species of *fairy wren* (see FAIRY *n.*[1] 1) of inland s.e. Aust.; the breeding male is largely blue above, but the lower back and rump are black; **bream,** any of several dark-coloured fish, esp. the estuarine *Acanthopagrus australis*, ranging from Qld. to Vic., and *A. butcheri* of s. Aust.; **-breasted buzzard** (or **kite**), the large bird of prey *Hamirostra melanosternon* of central, n. and w. Aust., characterized in flight by its short, square-ended tail; **cap,** any of several honeyeaters with black crowns in the genus *Melithreptus*; **-capped sittella,** a common bird of woodlands in s. but not s.e. Aust., being one form of the SITTELLA, and having a black top and sides to the head; **-cheeked falcon,** the peregrine falcon *Falco peregrinus*, which swoops on prey at high speed and occurs throughout Aust. and in all exc. the polar continents; **cockatoo,** any of the five species of large crested parrot with predom. black plumage of the Austral. genus *Calyptorhynchus*; also with distinguishing epithet, as **red-tailed, white-tailed, yellow-tailed** (see under first element); **cormorant,** *black shag*; **currawong,** the predom. black bird *Strepera fuliginosa* of Tas.; see also *black magpie*; **duck,** the common water fowl and game bird *Anas superciliosa*, predom. brown and distinguished by a dark line from the bill to behind the eye, bordered by pale lines; **-eared cuckoo,** the pale brownish cuckoo *Chrysococcyx osculans*, typically occurring in drier parts of Aust., and on islands to the north, named for a dark line extending from the bill to the ear-covert feathers; **-faced cuckoo-shrike,** the mainly grey bird of woodland *Coracina novaehollandiae*, the adult having a black patch extending from the forehead to the throat and behind the eyes; *blue jay*, see BLUE *a.*; see also *summer bird* SUMMER; **-faced wood swallow,** the grey bird *Artamus cinereus*, with a black patch between the bill and eyes, occurring widely in relatively dry parts of Aust., and in Timor and New Guinea; **falcon,** the dark brown, fast-flying, Austral. bird of prey *Falco subniger*; **-fronted dotterel,** the wading bird *Elseyornis melanops*, having a black V-shaped mark on its white breast, of Aust. and N.Z.; **-gloved wallaby,** the wallaby *Macropus irma* of s.w. Aust., having black forefeet; **-headed honeyeater,** the brownish honeyeater *Melithreptus affinis* of Tas., having a black head; **jay,** CHOUGH; CURRAWONG; **magpie, (a)** CHOUGH; **(b)** *pied currawong*, see PIED; **(c)** *black currawong*; **prince,** the predom. black cicada *Psaltoda plaga* of e. Qld. and N.S.W.; **rock cod,** the fish *Epinephelus damelii* of rocky coasts and estuaries in the s.w. Pacific, including Qld. and N.S.W., the adult being almost uniformly black or dark grey; **shag,** a widely distributed water bird, the predom. black cormorant *Phalacrocorax carbo*; **-shouldered kite,** the widespread bird of prey *Elanus axillaris*, having a black area at the 'shoulder' or bend of the wing's leading edge; **snake,** either of two species of elapid snake, the red-bellied *Pseudechis porphyriacus* of s.e. Aust. and coastal e. Qld., and the spotted *P. guttatus* of s.e. Qld. and n.e. N.S.W.; **swan,** the large water bird *Cygnus atratus* of s. Aust., with plumage mainly black in adults, the faunal emblem of W.A.; SWAN; **trevally,** any of several marine fish, usu. of the fam. Siganidae, esp. *Siganus spinus*.

1900 A.J. CAMPBELL *Nests & Eggs Austral. Birds* 118 The **Black-and-white Fantail** is exceedingly persevering in nest-building. **1917** *Bulletin* (Sydney) 17 May 22/2 The vocabulary of willy wagtail, or black and white fantail.. is about the best known of any bird in the bush. **1962** B.W. LEAKE *Eastern Wheatbelt Wildlife* 90 The black and white fantail or Willie Wagtail. **1842** J. GOULD *Birds of Aust.* (1848) II. Pl. 12, *Atticora leucosternon*.. White-breasted Swallow.. **Black and White Swallow** of the Colonists. **1901** *Emu* I. 127 In some hard sandy cliffs on the beach several Black and White Swallows (*Cheramoeca leucosternum*) had their nests. **1922** A.H. CHISHOLM *Mateship with Birds* 159 The more retiring of the bi-colored species, such as.. the Black and White Swallow. **1841** J. GOULD *Birds of Aust.* (1848) III. Pl. 20, *Malurus melanotus*.. **Black-backed Wren.** [**1912** SPENCER & GILLEN *Across Aust.* 173 Three different species inhabit the Ranges, of which the one called the black-backed warbler.. is perhaps the most beautiful.] **1982** *Wrens & Warblers of Aust.* 12 Because it lives far from towns and cities the black-backed blue wren is not often seen. **1857** J. ASKEW *Voyage Aust. & N.Z.* 228 The harbour abounds with fish, of which the.. **black** and red **bream**.. are used for food. **1882** J.E. TENISON-WOODS *Fish & Fisheries N.S.W.* 43 The 'black bream' (*Chrysophrys australis*) and the 'tarwhine'.. are both excellent fishes... In Port Jackson line-fishing for 'black bream' is a very favourite sport. **1906** D.G. STEAD *Fishes of Aust.* 99 Macquarie's Perch.. is another of the fishes of Western New South Wales... It is often known to western folk as 'Black Bream'. **1948** F.D. MARSHALL *Let's go Fishing* 65 The blackfish is also known as.. black bream. The 'darkie' or 'nigger', as this fish is called, is a most worthy opponent. **1949** *Bulletin* (Sydney) 2 Feb. 14/2 It was dark, and right at the top of a 'king' tide, so the visitor to the little seaside holiday resort decided to give the black bream a go. **1977** *Commercial Fish Aust.* (Dept. Primary Industry) 34 Black bream.. have white, tender flesh and are rated one of Australia's best table fish. **1842** J. GOULD *Birds of Aust.* (1848) I. Pl. 20, The **Black-breasted Buzzard** generally flies high in the air, through which it soars in large circles. **1896** B. SPENCER *Rep. Horn Sci. Exped. Central Aust.* II. 107 Black-breasted.. Kites were seen, but no specimens secured. **1956** A.H. CHISHOLM *Bird Wonders of Aust.* 205 The Black-breasted Buzzard, a fine large Hawk of the inland areas. **1976** *Reader's Digest Compl. Bk. Austral. Birds* 120 Six or more black-breasted kites will gather to feed at ravaged emu nests. **1855** J. BONWICK *Geogr. Aust. & N.Z.* (ed. 3) 198 In the island [*sc.* Tas.].. are **Black Caps.** **1903** *Bulletin* (Sydney) 31 Jan. 36/1 We had no knowledge of scientific terms. To us they were.. gillies,.. coachies, black-caps. **1908** *Emu* VIII. 41 The Black-throated Honey-eater (*Melithreptus gularis*), often called the 'Black-cap'. **1928** R.H. CROLL *Open Road Vic.* 103 Blackcaps,.. those charming honey-eaters. **1844** J. GOULD *Birds of Aust.* (1848) IV. Pl. 104, *Sittella pileata*.. **Black-capped Sittella.** **1849** C. STURT *Narr. Exped. Central Aust.* II. 35 App. *Black-capped Sittella.* A creeper, with a black head, and grey brown plumage. **1896** B. SPENCER *Rep. Horn Sci. Exped. Central Aust.* II. 98 Black-capped Sittella... The Orange-winged Sittella loves to work head downwards, or hopping along under the limbs of trees inspecting the crevices in the bark in search of spiders or small insects. So in Central Australia we found the little black-headed species behaving in exactly the same manner. **1976** L.R.M. HUNTER *Woodline* 41 Black-capped sitellas with their funny upturned beaks especially adapted for probing under the bark. **1841** J. GOULD *Birds of Aust.* (1848) I. Pl. 8, **Black-cheeked Falcon**.. *Blue Hawk*, Colonists of Western Australia. **1902** *Emu* II. 10 The Black-cheeked Falcon.. will audaciously come into trees alongside a dwelling. **1945** C. BARRETT *Austral. Bird Life* 36 Australia's boldest and swiftest bird of prey, the black-cheeked falcon.. or 'duck-hawk'. **1949** D. WALKER *We went to Aust.* 107 A black-cheeked falcon, the dive bomber of Victoria that will swoop and kill a cockatoo with one wicked sweep of talon. **1770** S. PARKINSON *Jrnl. Voyage to South Seas* (1773) 144 We found.. large **black cocatoes**, with scarlet and orange-coloured feathers on their tails. **1799** D. COLLINS *Acct. Eng. Colony N.S.W.* (1802) II. 241 The black and the white cockatoo.. were seen here. **1806** *Sydney Gaz.* 4 May, A beautiful black cockatoo.. so remarkably tame as to be already capable of *conversing*. **1834** G. BENNETT *Wanderings N.S.W.* I. 183, I have seen, more than once, small trees lying prostrate, occasioned by the powerful bills of the large black cockatoos. **1852** W. HUGHES *Austral. Colonies* 82 There are both black and white cockatoos—two species of the former. **1911** *Bulletin* (Sydney) 17 Aug. 13/2 The black cockatoo.. is the best meteorologist in the bush... Wherever I see the blackies flying inland I can safely bet on wet and squally weather. **1964** M. SHARLAND *Territory of Birds* 102 The cries of Black Cockatoos, whose red tail patches in flight seem a mobile part of the sunset. **1982** R. HALL *Just Relations* 156 A flock of black cockatoos swept past. **1864** *Papers & Proc. R. Soc. Tas.* 63 The **black cormorant** (*Phalacrocorax carboides*) will, I apprehend, prove a worse poacher than any other bird. **1903** *Emu* II. 167 Black Cormorant.. Common in suitable places. **1976** *Reader's Digest Compl. Bk. Austral. Birds* 71 The black cormorant swims underwater for periods of up to half a minute or more. **1945** C. BARRETT *Austral. Bird Life* 215 Of currawongs or bell-magpies (*Strepera*) there are six species, two—the **black currawong** (*S. fuliginosa*) and the hill strepera (*S. arguta*)—being restricted to Tasmania. **1984** SIMPSON & DAY *Birds of Aust.* 340 The Black Currawong, considered a race of the Pied by some, now has full species status based on differing plumage and call. **1820** C. JEFFREYS *Van Dieman's Land* 35 This lake abounds with black swans, **black ducks**, widgeons. **1852** J. MACGILLIVRAY *Narr. Voyage H.M.S. Rattlesnake* I. 55 *Anas superciliosa*, the 'black duck' of the colonists, the richest and best flavoured of the Australian water-fowl. **1886** R. HENTY *Australiana* 60 The sportsman was creeping warily for a shot at black duck or teal. **1945** C. BARRETT *Austral. Bird Life* 48 Australia's premier sporting bird, the black duck,.. occurs in New Guinea and the Dutch East Indies. **1977** *Ecos* xi. 21/2 A black duck banded at Lake George near Canberra was shot next day at Dowd's Morass—400 km to the south-sou'-west in Victoria! **1847** J. GOULD *Birds of Aust.* (1848) IV. Pl. 88, *Chalcites osculans*.. **Black-eared Cuckoo**, Colonists of Swan River. **1902** *Emu* I. 138 Black-eared Cuckoo.. one or two noted on the Diamantina. **1976** *Reader's Digest Compl. Bk. Austral. Birds* 297 Black-eared cuckoos are migratory or nomadic. **1900** A.J. CAMPBELL *Nests & Eggs Austral. Birds* 96 Under various trivial vernacular names, such as Blue Dove, Summer Bird, etc., the **Black-faced Cuckoo Shrike** is found through the length and breadth of Australia. **1926** *Official Checklist Birds Aust.* (R. Australasian Ornith. Union) p. v, A few long names such as White-throated Grass-Wren and Black-faced Cuckoo-Shrike have so far defied efforts for improvement. **1937** *Bulletin* (Sydney) 6 Oct. 21/4 Why is the bird commonly known as the blue-jay called in our bird books the black-faced cuckoo-shrike? **1964** M. SHARLAND *Territory of Birds* 37 Some black-faced Cuckoo-shrikes are black right down to the abdomen. **1896** B. SPENCER *Rep. Horn Sci. Exped. Central Aust.* II. 68 **Black-faced Wood Swallow** . . great variation in the size of this species. **1973** V. SERVENTY *Desert Walkabout* 74 Soon a pair of black-faced wood-swallows joined in. **1848** J. GOULD *Birds of Aust.* (1848) I. Pl. 9, *Falco subniger* . . **Black Falcon**. **1954** H.G. LAMOND *Manx Star* 44 They recognized a master-slayer in action, a black falcon. **1976** *Reader's Digest Compl. Bk. Austral. Birds* 133 Small birds cower and scatter when they hear the harsh scream of an attacking black falcon. **1845** J. GOULD *Birds of Aust.* (1848) VI. Pl. 20, *Hiaticula nigrifons*. **Black-fronted Dottrel**. **1849** C. STURT *Narr. Exped. Central Aust.* II. 49 App. *Black-fronted Dotrell*. . . A pretty little bird with a plaintive note. **1967** N.A. WAKEFIELD *Naturalist's Diary* 31 Black-fronted Dotterels . . beautiful little wading birds, sparrow-sized, black about the face and breast, white on throat and belly, and with red about the eyes. **1886** F. COWAN *Aust.* 36 Wallaby being a generic term of native origin for a number of kangaroo-like animals specifically distinguished as the rock-wallaby, **black-gloved-wallaby**, . . and the like. **1954** C. BARRETT *Wild Life Aust. & New Guinea* 6 The black-gloved wallaby of south-western Australia, whose fingers and toes are black or 'gloved'. [**1801 black-headed honeyeater:** J. LATHAM *Gen. Synopsis Birds* Suppl. II. 167 Black-headed Cr[eeper] . . Inhabits *New South Wales*.] **1822** —— *Gen. Hist. Birds* IV. 175 Black-headed Honey-eater. **1898** E.E. MORRIS *Austral Eng.* 198 Black-headed H[oneyeater]—*M[elithreptus] melanocephalus*. **1945** C. BARRETT *Austral. Bird Life* 153 The black-headed honeyeater . . and the strong-billed honeyeater . . are restricted to Tasmania and the Bass Strait islands. **1976** *Reader's Digest Compl. Bk. Austral. Birds* 493 It is not uncommon to see black-headed honeyeaters working furiously to feed a young cuckoo. **1900** *Tocsin* (Melbourne) 9 Aug. 6/1 For some days lived on an abundance of magpies and **black jays**. **1912** *Emu* XII. 114 White-winged Chough (Black Jay) . . A very mournful note. **1981** M. SHARLAND *Tracks of Morning* 75 Black jays (currawongs) haven't got much love for eagles either. **1832** J. BISCHOFF *Sketch Hist. Van Diemen's Land* 177 We also occasionally heard the trumpeter, or **black-magpie**. **1836** J. BACKHOUSE *Narr. Visit Austral. Colonies* (1843) 438 Some of the birds of V.D. Land abound; such as . . the Jay or Black Magpie, *Coronica fuliginosa*. **1855** *Trans. Philos. Soc. Vic.* I. 63 The white-winged chough, or black magpie. **1889** *Proc. Linnean Soc. N.S.W.* IV. 403 *Strepera graculina* . . Known locally as 'Black Magpies'. **1911** *Bulletin* (Sydney) 26 Jan. 15/2 The name 'black magpie' is given to both the white-winged chough and the pied crow-shrike, while the latter is called by various onomatopoeic renderings of its cry, such as charawack or corowong. **1928** G.H. WILKINS *Undiscovered Aust.* 104 The 'white-winged chough', or black magpie as it is generally called . . builds a big, rough nest of mud and rubbish. **1950** *Bulletin* (Sydney) 27 Dec. 12/3 People talk of black magpies, currawongs, bell magpies and jackdaws—four names for one bird. **1951** CUSACK & JAMES *Come in Spinner* 106 'Mine's a Floury Baker . . and mine's a **Black Prince**!' Young Jack and Andrew held up their fists for her to peep at frosted fawn body and tan-and-black. **1959** A. VON BERTOUCH *February Dark* 124 Through the shimmer of heat and the drilling song Helen saw the beautiful cicadas of childhood, the Black Prince [etc.]. **1974** R. MCKIE *Mango Tree* 18 He had talked to her about his first puppy, the Black Prince and the Double-drummer he had caught in the garden. **1982** N. KEESING *Lily on Dustbin* 95 His tally for today (which he keeps in a shoe box . .) has been two 'green-grocers', a 'black prince' and one 'yellow Monday'. . . It is a bumper year for cicadas. **1880** *Proc. Linnean Soc. N.S.W.* V. 317 *Serranus Damelii* . . '**Black Rock Cod**' of the Sydney Fishermen. **1936** T.C. ROUGHLEY *Wonders Great Barrier Reef* 246 A near relative of the Queensland groper . . is the black rock cod which grows to . . about a hundred pounds. It is common and widespread, and when young is a delicious table fish. **1834** J. BACKHOUSE *Narr. Visit Austral. Colonies* (1843) 189 The pools of Jordan, in which, as well as in the other rivers of Tasmania, and on the sea-coast, **Black Shaggs** are often seen fishing. **1847** G.F. ANGAS *Savage Life & Scenes* I. 57 A few scattered gum-trees grow along the water's edge; and these are the resort of multitudes of black shags. **1981** K. GARVEY *Rhymes of Ratbag* 168 On a log sits preening The cormorant . . And bushmen call him The old black shag. **1821** J. LATHAM *Gen. Hist. Birds* I. 231 **Black-shouldered Kite**. This is full two feet in length. **1945** C. BARRETT *Austral. Bird Life* 35 The black-shouldered Kite . . ranges over the greater part of the mainland. **1981** B.J. BROCK *Catharsis* 25 And black-shouldered kites 'ave goed 'coz their weed patch woz all 'oed for a car-park. **1795** D. COLLINS *Acct. Eng. Colony N.S.W.* (1798) I. 404 A convict, on entering the door of his hut, was bit in the foot by a **black snake**; the effect was, an immediate swelling of the foot, leg, and thigh, and a large tumour in the groin. **1804** *Sydney Gaz.* 9 Dec., The *black snake* . . is generally known to be from about *fourteen* to *eighteen* inches in length, the back of a dusky disagreeable colour. **1827** P. CUNNINGHAM *Two Yrs. in N.S.W.* I. 332 Our two most venomous snakes, the brown and black, appear to me to be male and female, as I have twice met them lying very suspiciously coiled up together. **1845** *Sydney Morning Herald* 19 Feb. 4/5 The black snake I have seen eaten, and I have eaten of it myself; when cooked it is as white as an eel, and tender as a chicken. **1865** G.F. ANGAS *Aust.* 104 The black snake is from five to eight feet in length, of a glossy black above, and crimson beneath. **1885** MRS C. PRAED *Austral. Life* 34 That especial delicacy, the eggs of the black snake. **1910** *Huon Times* (Franklin) 5 Mar. 2/7 A large black snake was found under the bed of a lad who was sleeping out on the verandah. **1951** G. FARWELL *Outside Track* 17 One trip to the city was enough for me. . . I stood on a street corner, watching the people pass. . . If ever I nodded or said 'Good-day', they looked as though a black snake had bitten them. **1982** R. HALL *Just Relations* 499 The black snake that has been curled beside him in the warmth glides out to enquire into the disturbance. **1698** *Philos. Trans. R. Soc. London* (1699) XX. 361 Here is returned a Ship, which by our *East India* Company, was sent to the South Land, called *Hollandia Nova*. . . **Black Swans**, Parrots, and many Sea-Cows were found there. **1788** *HRA* (1914) 1st Ser. I. 29 We saw a large black swan; it was larger than the common swan and when it rose, . . the wings appeared to be edged with white. **1789** A. PHILLIP *Voyage to Botany Bay* 98 A black swan, which species, though proverbially rare in other parts of the world, is here by no means uncommon. **1826** *Monitor* (Sydney) 19 May 3 This land of Kangaroos and black Swans. **1845** C. HODGKINSON *Aust., Port Macquarie to Moreton Bay* 208 Black Swans frequent the mouths of rivers, and salt lagoons, and are easily shot. **1857** *Illustr. Jrnl. Australasia* II. 51 A flock of black swans go off in single file, uttering their peculiar harsh note. **1870** *Illustr. Austral. News* (Melbourne) 21 May 98/2 The skins of the black swan are much sought after for the down, which, notwithstanding the feathers are black, is of pure whiteness and great in quantity. **1895** A.B. PATERSON *Man from Snowy River* 113 Oh! ye wild black swans, 'twere a world of wonder For a while to join in your westward flight. **1926** W.A. CAWTHORNE *Kangaroo Islanders* 6 They were black swans making a bee-line across the straits. **1956** S. HOPE *Diggers' Paradise* 57 The black swan is Western Australia's emblem. **1967** R. DONALDSON et al. *Cane!* 114 'It's a black swan from western Aussie,' he said without much interest. **1874** *N.S.W. Rep. R. Comm. Fisheries* (1880) 1294 The **black trevally** is a very good eating fish when used at once. **1906** D.G. STEAD *Fishes of Aust.* 139 The fish known in New South Wales as the Black Trevally (*Siganus nebulosus*). **1973** *Kings Cross Whisper* (Sydney) cxlvii. 4/4 Black trevally are known by smarties as happy moments, because anybody who gets stung by them has happy moments remembering all the times it wasn't hurting.

2. In special collocations: **black billy**, see BILLY *n.*[1] 4; **book** *hist.*, a book in which the offences of a convict were recorded; also as *v. trans.*; **hat** *obs.* [from the unsuitability of dress], NEW CHUM *n.* 2; **money** *Austral. pidgin, obs.*, a copper coin; **peter,** a solitary confinement cell; see PETER 1.

1816 *N.S.W. Pocket Almanack* 43 Gaoler's Fees. . . From every person receiving a certificate of his or her term of transportation being expired (reference being always had to the **black book** in his possession). **1828** *Hobart Town Courier* 26 July 2 It is important to make the 'Black Books', or Registers of Offences, as complete as possible. **1835** *True Colonist* (Hobart) 29 Jan. 2/4 Would have been tried for the offence, and, if not punished at least 'black-booked'. **1837** *Cornwall Chron.* (Launceston) 18 Nov. 2 Being already in the 'black books', he was ordered three months to a road party. **1852** J. WEST *Hist. of Tas.* II. 229 Black and white books were kept, in which meritorious actions and the reverse were recorded. **1876** *Austral. Town & Country Jrnl.* (Sydney) 15 July 102/2 It is more a bush expression than a town one, and rather slangy. A '**black hat**', in Australia [*sic*] parlance, means a new arrival. **1881** MRS C. PRAED *Policy & Passion* II. 265 You remember that 'ere long chap from England as wur a-stopping here! Lord! if I were Mr Dyson Maddox I'd never let it be said that a *black hat* had cut me out sweetheartin'. **1839** W. MANN *Six Yrs.' Residence* 285 'De be no good—no money but **black money**'; by which they mean pence. **1845** *Melbourne Standard* 1 Mar. 2/6, I think he can be made to understand the difference between right and wrong, as he knows the difference between black and white money, and also the comparative value of a bob and a tanner. **1848** *Adelaide Miscellany* 9 Sept. 90/1 Some natives coming up, asked me for black money. **1886** R. HENTY *Australiana* 19 They were very expert in picking off 'blackmoney' (a penny or halfpenny) from the top of a short upright stick. **1953** K. TENNANT *Joyful Condemned* 259 The prison doctor was walking down from the gate. He had once got a girl two days in the **black peter** for saying good-day to him. **1968** J. ALARD *He who shoots Last* 261 [*Note*] *Black Peter*, name given the feared severe solitary confinement cell. **1974** ADAMSON & HANFORD *Zimmer's Essay* 63 When he wasn't tanked in the black peter, the administration tried to get him a segregated cell. **1980** M. WILLIAMS *Dingo!* 93 It was time to exercise for two hours in a tiny yard outside the black-peter. **1984** P. READ *Down there with me on Cowra Mission* 109 They put you in the Black Peter. They take your shoes off. . . Take your belt off you. You're put in this 'ere cell, you can't even see your hand in front of you.

black, *a.*[3] [Spec. use of *black* malignant, disastrous.] In special collocations qualifying the name of a day of the week: **Black Thursday,** 6 Feb. 1851, a day on which devastating bushfires occurred in Victoria; **Wednesday,** 9 Jan. 1878, the day on which the Victorian Government, having failed to pass its Appropriation Bill, dismissed a large number of public servants; also *v. trans.*, to dismiss (a public servant); see BERRY BLIGHT.

1851 *Illustr. Austral. Mag.* (Melbourne) July 26 The 6th of February last, which received around Port Phillip the ominous designation of '**Black Thursday**', will be long remembered in Victoria for its intense heat and burning winds, and the extensive conflagrations that occurred over all the country. **1859** *Fifth Ann. Rep. Melbourne C. of E. Mission* 10 We have had scorching north winds for a week. . . Such north wind as is talked of in Melbourne for a long time as 'equal to black Thursday'. **1870** W.H. KNIGHT *W.A.* 14 There are no 'brickfielders' to choke you with their clouds of dust, as in Sydney; no 'Black Thursdays' to smother you, as in Victoria. **1889** J.H.L. ZILLMANN *Past & Present Austral. Life* 39 The old colonists still repeat the most terrible stories of 'Black Thursday'. **1898** *Bulletin* (Sydney) 8 Jan. 11/2 On the Victorian Black Thursday—1851—cinders and burning twigs from the blazing Gippsland forests were blown right across the Straits on to the beach of Northern Tasmania. **1914** *Ibid.* 26 Mar. 22/1 The Vic. bushfires on the anniversary of Black Thursday swept away a few homesteads. **1926** *Illustr. Tasmanian Mail* (Hobart) 24 Feb. 6/1 The fires of Black Thursday . . swept a much wider area. **1878** 'Y.O.-B.A.' *Proclamation!* 3 The Government announced . . on the celebrated **Black Wednesday**, that they had dispensed with the services of . . many of the civil servants. **1880** *Bulletin* (Sydney) 17 Apr. 4/3 As a result of Black Wednesday, Victorian civil servants are becoming practical. **1880** *Argus* (Melbourne) 7 Feb. 6/6 Mr Symonds is an official liable to be 'Black Wednesdayed' at any moment.

black, *a.*[4] [Spec. use of *black* incurring censure, as in *black list*: see OED(S *black, a.* 11 and *black list, sb.* 1 c. Sense 1 is used elsewhere but recorded earliest in Aust.]

1. Used to designate a category or place of work, person, piece of machinery, etc., declared subject to a boycott by a trade union during a dispute.

1911 ST. C. GRONDONA *Collar & Cuffs* 100 None of these gentlemen here is blacklegs. . . Anyone wantin' to prove who's black let him step out here, and I'll d--n quick settle the dispute by blackenin' his eyes for him. **1914** *Pastoral Rev.* Feb. 105 Action . . may be taken by . .

the wharf workers when . . what is labelled 'black' wheat is handled. **1917** *Huon Times* (Franklin) 16 Jan. 4/1 The regular cleaners . . declined to clean the catch because an industrial dispute existed, and consequently the fish were 'black'. **1923** *Argus* (Melbourne) 13 Dec. 14/2 The Building Trades' Federation declared the job 'black' on Monday, in consequence of its failure to convince the foreman . . that the claim for 'grinding time' should be paid. **1927** *Ibid.* 6 Sept. 14/4 A whole State may be menaced with chaos by the comparatively simple expedient of declaring somebody or something 'black'. **1949** *Daily Tel.* (Sydney) 29 July 2/6 Union leaders declared the Haligonian Duke 'black' without even bothering to find out if the Communist claim that it was concerned in the Canadian Seamen's strike was true or not. **1955** J. Morrison *Black Cargo* 215 Don't you know this ship's black? **1971** *Austral.* (Sydney) 19 Jan. 2/7 Any employer who calls in police against federation officials will be declared black and 'driven out of the industry'.

2. In the special collocation **black ban,** a prohibition (esp. as imposed by a trade union) which prevents work from proceeding: see quot. 1981. Also as *v. trans.* See also Green ban.

1972 *Sydney Morning Herald* 11 Aug. 3/7 The Builders Labourers' Federation of N.S.W. lifted its eight-months-old black ban on restoration work in the $500-million East Rocks redevelopment scheme yesterday. **1978** B. Kennedy *Silver, Sin, & Sixpenny Ale* 146 (*note*) The unions could declare a shop or business out of bounds to unionists and their families or under a 'blackban'. **1976** *Bulletin* (Sydney) 7 Aug. 9/1 The Plumbers' Union has black-banned a number of private citizens who want to build homes in Pascoe Vale Road, Broadmeadows. The union's attitude is that the homesites are too close to Tullamarine. The land-owners, who bought the land three years ago, naturally agree that it's none of the union's business. **1981** Sheehan & Worland *Gloss. Industr. Relations Terms* (ed. 2) 9 *Ban*, an organised refusal by employees to undertake certain work, to use certain equipment or to work with certain people. They are generally known as 'black bans'. **1983** *Mercury* (Hobart) 20 Aug. 11/4 'We will be summing up the situation and deciding what industrial action is needed,' Mr Bacon said. The action may include black-banning of some sites.

blackbird, *n.*

1. *Obs.* An Aboriginal. Esp. in the phr. **blackbird shooting.**

1865 *London Soc.* Dec. 448/1 Men travelling up country used to provide themselves with . . a kind of 'licence to shoot blacks'. . . The sport-loving traveller would frequently indulge in what we should call a decidedly sensational pastime, which he called 'black-bird shooting'. But this sort of thing is all of the past now. **1893** S. Newland *Paving Way* 131 Squatting won't pay . . nor is it an agreeable occupation, when attended with frequent black-bird shooting on a large scale. **1909** E. Waltham *Life & Labour in Aust.* 71 A day's 'Blackbird' shooting.

2. *Hist.* A Pacific islander brought to Australia as a labourer, a Kanaka. Also *attrib.*

1869 P.A. Taylor *Colony of Qld. & Alleged Slave Trade* 11 Polynesian labourers were employed, who had been taken from their homes by fraud. Ships went to the New Hebrides to 'catch blackbirds', and they caught them by utter deceit for three years' engagements. **1872** S. Walch *True-Blue Beard* 15 Out 'blackbird catching' some are gone, 'Mongst the islands near the Golden Horn. **1875** G.S. Searle *Mount & Morris Exonerated* 7 They were going to take a cruise round the islands 'blackbird' catching. **1895** *Western Champion* (Barcaldine) 26 Feb. 16/2 The local 'blackbirds' escorted the visitors to a couple of carriages. **1900** *Bulletin* (Sydney) 13 Jan. 10/3 A Queensland black-bird captain tells of a curious form of funeral rite current at Santo, New Hebrides. **1919** C.A. Bernays *Qld. Politics during Sixty Yrs.* 67 Voyages across the Pacific with cargoes of 'black-birds' for the Queensland coast.

blackbird, *v. Hist.* [Back-formation from Blackbirding.]

a. *intr.* To engage in blackbirding. Also *fig.*

1894 J. MacDonald *Thunderbolt* 304 I've been down to the islands, sir, with a schooner 'blackbirding', and the skipper felt it his business to get useful labour for the Queensland tropics, where a white man can't work all day in the sun. **1952** C. Simpson *Come away, Pearler* 7 They say his mother was a Rotuma woman Bully got hold of when he was blackbirding down Fiji way.

b. *trans.* To kidnap (a Pacific islander).

1901 *Tocsin* (Melbourne) 5 Sept. 4/4 Savages . . who can be blackbirded and whipped into working for nothing more than the cost of keeping them alive. **1929** K.S. Prichard *Coonardoo* (1961) 105 One crew of Swan Point boys, a pearler I knew black-birded, was so dangerous he had to drive 'em overboard when he got to sea. He and his mate, with loaded guns behind the nigs. **1946** K. Tennant *Lost Haven* 4 Although he claimed to have made his money pearling, he had really made it blackbirding natives. **1969** J. Dingwell *One String* 5 There were twelve fully certificated nurses whom Mr Felix had persuaded . . or had it been 'black-birded', Charlotte sometimes wondered. **1979** A.J. Burke *Bite Pineapple* 86 Kanakas were blackbirded as slaves for the Queensland sugar plantations, the cost to some cane farmers being as low as six shillings per head.

blackbirder. *Hist.*

1. One engaged in blackbirding.

1880 *Bulletin* (Sydney) 17 Apr. 4/3 Three well-known 'blackbirders', alias Government labour agents . . are known as 'The world, the flesh and the angel'. **1898** *Ibid.* 19 Mar. 20/3 The men are all used up on the islands, and the black-birders have to fall back on children. **1924** *Smith's Weekly* (Sydney) 19 Apr. 17/6 In the middle of last century . . the famous blackbirder, Bully Hayes, . . arrived at Port Adelaide with a number of gold-miners and a large stock of grog. **1949** I.L. Idriess *One Wet Season* 52 A blackbirder smoked lazily while on watch with a rifle, for lubras used to crawl in from the bush at night and feed the prisoners. **1954** N. Bartlett *Pearl Seekers* 128 When a blackbirder had collected some forty or fifty natives, by fair means or foul, he steered for the Torres Straits and handed over his captives at so much a head. **1978** M. Paice *Shadow of Wings* 74, I had read about the blackbirders, . . how they brought men—and women too—from the islands of the New Hebrides and New Guinea to work the plantations of Queensland.

2. A ship used for blackbirding.

1903 *Bulletin* (Sydney) 4 Apr. 17/1 Things happened pretty suddenly those days on board a black-birder.

blackbirding, *vbl. n. Hist.* The act or practice of kidnapping, or otherwise obtaining, Pacific islanders and trafficking in them as labour, mainly for the Queensland cotton and sugar plantations; Recruiting. Also *fig.*

1871 G. Palmer *Kidnapping in South Seas* 120 Of late English traders find '*black-birding*' far more lucrative than bêche-de-mering. **1875** G.S. Searle *Mount & Morris Exonerated* 8 All the three methods, however, of obtaining labour in the South Seas—that which was just and useful, that which was of suspicious character, and that which was nothing, more or less than robbery and murder—were in use at the same time; and all three went by the same general slang term of 'blackbirding', or 'blackbird catching'. **1886** F.A. Hagenauer *Rep. Aboriginal Mission Ramahyuck, Vic.* 36 The most serious and grievous part of the whole labour business is certainly the South Sea labour traffic—the 'blackbirding' of the poor Kanakas. **1892** *Truth* (Sydney) 5 June 4/4 *Truth* has had some experience of the way in which the niggers are trapped and treated and unhesitatingly affirms that 'black-birding' and slave-trading are so very much alike. **1903** *Ibid.* 6 Dec. 1/7 Ever since black-birding was made legal . . time expired islanders have been returned in boat loads. **1920** *Smith's Weekly* (Sydney) 18 Sept. 17/4 In the old blackbirding days . . they played mean tricks on the ignorant islanders. **1955** N. Pulliam *I traveled Lonely Land* 45 The Kanakas moved onto the Australian stage in a hideous scene called 'blackbirding', familiar reading once again to the American recalling the cotton-and-cane days. **1971** *Bulletin* (Sydney) 6 Nov. 43/1 Her Majesty's ships were still trying . . to suppress blackbirding, which killed 10,000 out of 50,000 imported islanders in 40 years of the Australian sugar business. **1981** Sandercock & Turner *Up Where, Cazaly?* 58 There was acrimonious argument . . about Victoria's 'black-birding'. In 1911, a Tasmanian delegate . . urged that an interstate player should be required to establish two years' residence before he was permitted to transfer to a Melbourne club.

blackboy.

1. *Hist.* An adult Aboriginal male, esp. one accompanying explorers or employed on a station. See also Boy.

1810 *Sydney Gaz.* 1 Dec., My servant, Nussee, a black boy, has absconded from my Employ. **1838** T.H. James *Six Months S.A.* 232 We heard a low 'cooe' from the opposite side of the river; I wished the black boy to answer it. **1855** H. Hume *Brief Statement* 3 A black boy, a native of Appin, started on an exploring journey. **1867** F.J. Byerley *Narr. Overland Exped. Northern Qld.* p. xi, Native blacks, or as they are commonly called in the colonies, Black-boys. **1896** W.H. Willshire *Land of Dawning* 65 Neither the wild nigger up the tree nor my blackboys understood one word of that eloquent address. **1913** W.K. Harris *Outback in Aust.* 26 We pulled up for a chat with a couple of 'blackboys'. [*Note*] Aboriginal stockmen. **1930** *Bulletin* (Sydney) 1 Jan. 20/2 One of the black-boys . . had a very small opinion of the explorer. **1950** 'N. Shute' *Town like Alice* 82 Black boys—black stockmen.

2. Chiefly *W.A.* **a.** Grass-tree 1. **b.** The resin of the grass-tree; also **blackboy gum.**

1834 J. Roberts *Two Yrs. at Sea* 97 Near our encampment . . was a tree of a singular though not very ornamental form: it was called 'grass tree', from its grassy head, and 'black boy', from the dark colour of its stem. **1847** *Atlas* (Sydney) III. 111/2 Blackboy Gum. . . This very powerful gum is now in constant use by our boat and shipbuilders as a substitute for pitch. **1853** I. Chamberlayne *Austral. Captive* 107 Blackboy is the colonial name of a large growing herbaceous plant, as well as of the gutta percha-like substance which it furnishes. **1860** G. Bennett *Gatherings of Naturalist* 365 'Black-boy gum', which the aborigines use as a cement for fastening stone heads on their tomahawks. **1865** 'Special Correspondent' *Transportation* 17 The grass tree of the eastern colonies, known in the west as the 'black boy'. **1872** Mrs E. Millett *Austral. Parsonage* 45 The 'blackboys' . . when seen for the first time, and from a distance, might easily be mistaken for savages dressed up in the traditional wavy head-dress of a South Sea Islander. **1897** L. Lindley-Cowen *W. Austral. Settler's Guide* 7 If you want to grow corn or fruit trees, find a place in which redgums and blackboys cluster thickly. **1928** M.E. Fullerton *Austral. Bush* 107 The 'black boy', a resinous West Australian grass-tree . . has one of the toughest and best fibres for brooms known. **1949** D. Walker *We went to Aust.* 178 Black boy, an indescribably peculiar tree holding one stump straight into the air. **1978** Mullally & Sexton *Libra & Leprechaun* 98 Past clumps of blackboy, long hair-like leaves and spear-like flowers pointing at the sky.

blackbutt. Any of several trees of the genus *Eucalyptus* (fam. Myrtaceae) with a characteristic fire-charred fibrous bark on the lower trunk; esp. *Eucalyptus pilularis* an important source of hardwood timber in the coastal ranges of N.S.W. and s. Qld. Formerly also **black-butted gum.**

1801 *HRA* (1915) 1st Ser. III. 414 The finest stringy-bark and black-butted blue-gum trees I ever saw. **1803** *Ibid.* IV. 106 Box and black butted Gum abound. **1820** J. Oxley *Jrnls. Two Exped. N.S.W.* 331 The timber was chiefly black butted gum. **1836** J. Backhouse *Narr. Visit Austral. Colonies* (1843) 445 One called here, the Woolly-butted Gum, seems identical with the Black-butted Gum of Tasmania. **1847** A. Harris *Settlers & Convicts* (1953) 29 Fine tall black butts, even as a gun-barrel, and as straight in the grain as a skein of thread. **1880** J. Bonwick *Resources Qld.* 79 The colonial *Blackbutt* is *Eucalyptus pilularis*, growing near Moreton Bay to 100 feet and more. **1904** J.H. Maiden *Notes on Commercial Timbers N.S.W.* 12 *Blackbutt* . . is a strong, durable, thoroughly safe and well-tried timber. **1935** Davison & Nicholls *Blue Coast Caravan* 14 Cargoes of blackbutt, bluegum, and tallow-wood logs. **1955** N. Pulliam *I traveled Lonely Land* 168 Many of those called blackbutt because they look as though they'd been dipped in tar to about six or eight feet above the ground. **1960** D. Ireland *Image in Clay* (1964) 100 It takes a blackbutt wedge to split the blackbutt. **1977** *Ecos* xii. 30/2 Carbon resulting from charring of the bark during bush-fires is a particularly troublesome material when making printing or writing papers. It is this blackening that gives the blackbutt its name. **1983** *Open Road* Aug. 24/3 The Bird Tree and Benaroon, the two largest blackbutt trees known in the State—69 metres tall and 64 metres tall respectively.

blackee, blackey, varr. Blackie.

blackfellow, *n., a.,* and *attrib.* Also **black fella, blackfeller.** [f. BLACK *a.*[1] + *fellow* familiar synonym for *man*, widespread in pidgin.]

A. *n.*

1. An Aboriginal.

1798 D. COLLINS *Acct. Eng. Colony N.S.W.* I. 590 Car-ru-ey strenuously urged him . . to shoot the Botany Bay black fellows. **1800** *HRA* (1914) 1st Ser. II. 405 What Sentence shall we pass upon these black Fellows. **1825** L.E. THRELKELD *Aboriginal Mission, N.S.W.* 13 Massa, you know black fellow no tell lies! **1827** *Tasmanian* (Hobart) 21 Dec. 3, I have heard some say, that they would never give a black fellow the chance to approach them, but level him to the ground without hesitation. **1836** J.F. O'CONNELL *Residence Eleven Yrs. New Holland* 87 They appear to have recognised their title 'black fellows', and in return dub the English 'white fellows', seemingly perfectly content with the distinction, and considering white the worse hue, decidedly. **1841** G. GREY *Jrnls. Two Exped. N.-W. & W.A.* I. 159 I shouldn't think nothing at all of having shot that there black fellow; why, Sir, they're very thick and plentiful up the country. **1859** J.D. MEREWEATHER *Diary Working Clergyman* 180 These stupid blacks mistook this poor American black for one of themselves. . . A black expressed . . great indignation at their stupidity, saying, that they ought to have known the difference between 'black fellow' and 'white man's black fellow'. **1879** *Natives Tribes S.A.* p. xiii, It was suggested that the blackfellow should be dipped like the sheep. ***c* 1891** J. GARDINER *Twenty-Five Yrs. on Stage* 21 He was a splendid actor, a most versatile one, but about as much fit to be a manager as a blackfellow. **1913** *Truth* (Sydney) 30 Nov. 6/6 The British bucolics are not the only ones to imagine that Australians are a race of blackfellows. **1927** M. DORNEY *Adventurous Honeymoon* 52 A shield that must have taken a blackfellow weeks of patient work. **1938** A. UPFIELD *Bone is Pointed* (1966) 52 I've known lots of fine blackfellers and more 'n one extra good half-caste. **1952** *Bulletin* (Sydney) 16 Apr. 16/2 An aborigine sees nothing offensive in the term 'blackfellow', but 'nigger' is an insult. **1958** F.B. VICKERS *Mirage* 194 No matter how he dressed her up, she was a gin—a black fella. **1961** *Bulletin* (Sydney) 1 Feb. 32/3 His approach to the aboriginal is one of intuitive sympathy. . . His sole interest is in what kind of blokes blackfellows are. **1969** D. CUSACK *Half-Burnt Tree* 13 Dad got mad when he said 'blackfeller'. 'Don't use that word, Kem,' he said. 'We've got a name like every other race.' **1979** D. LOCKWOOD *My Old Mates & I* 35 'Not on your life,' he said. 'I'd hold my own with any blackfeller.' I looked at his black skin again and realised that by 'blackfeller' he was simply distinguishing between full-blood and mixed-blood. **1984** P. READ *Down there with me on Cowra Mission* 29 That's the poor blackfeller standing there all the time, didn't know nothing about that.

2. In special collocations: **blackfellow's bread,** *native bread*, see NATIVE *a.* 6 a.; **blackfellow's button,** AUSTRALITE; **blackfellow's oven,** *native oven*, see NATIVE *a.* 5; **blackfellow's wash,** see quot. 1915; **blackfellow's well,** *native well*, see NATIVE *a.* 5.

1902 *Proc. Linnean Soc. N.S.W.* XXVII. 542 *Polyporus mylittae*. . . The sclerotium of this species is of common occurrence in the eastern States of Australia as well as in Tasmania under the name of **'Black Fellows' Bread'**. **1914** N.F. SPIELVOGEL *Gumsucker at Home* 122 He even uses the fungus known as 'Blackfellow's Bread' for the crooks of sticks. **1943** *Bulletin* (Sydney) 7 July 12/2 'Blackfellow's bread' . . looks like a potato, and, cut in sections, it closely resembles sago boiled to the consistency of cheese; but as it has no seed, bud, root, branch or anything else to indicate its age or stage of development, it is difficult to understand how it is propagated, or how long it takes to reach maturity. **1977** LESLIE & COWIE *Wind still Blows* 107, I picked up what was called 'blackfellows' bread' or manna. It was in small white bunches like the beaten white of an egg, and sweet and pleasant to taste. **1933** C. FENNER *Bunyips & Billabongs* 40 Most of us have seen an Australite. . . They are also known as **'blackfellows' buttons'**, obsidianites, emu-stones, and 'trans-line' meteorites. **1952** B. BEATTY *Unique to Aust.* 93 Blackfellows' buttons, the nickname for Australites, are small meteorites . . no bigger than buttons. **1883** *Jrnl. & Proc. R. Soc. N.S.W.* (1884) 37 **Blackfellows' ovens** or cooking-places have been a fertile source of argument for many years, some holding that they are not cooking places at all, but tumuli . . left by some race long since passed away. **1911** C.E.W. BEAN *'Dreadnought' of Darling* 190 Somebody explained that they were called 'blackfellows' ovens', and that they were the remains of the heaps of fuel which the blackfellows had piled over their meat when they wanted to cook it. **1918** A.M. MOORE *Autumn Grey* 104 Blackfellows' ovens . . are large mounds of earth resembling huge ant-beds, their soil being jet-black. . . The blacks before journeying from one place to another, made a fire, cooked their meal and before leaving covered the ashes with earth; then on each return to the old spot the earth was scraped away and glowing ashes were revealed. To these sticks were added, and the fire blazed into life once again, this process being repeated until the mound was formed. **1932** M.R. WHITE *No Roads go By* 235 The little hummocks of hard-baked sand and stones which we call blackfellows' ovens in which the black cooked his food. **1979** B. MARTYN *First Footers S. Gippsland* 55 There's a blackfellow's oven out on the rise where we're working. **1915** N. DUNCAN *Austral. Byways* 68 In outward aspect he was not by so much as a **black fellow's wash** (which is no wash at all) improved above his wretched neighbor. **1945** K.D. YOUNG *Born to Adventure* 64 My mother . . accused me of having had a 'blackfellow's wash'. **1944** M.J. O'REILLY *Bowyangs & Boomerangs* 107 Such waterholes are known as 'enama holes' or **blackfellows' wells.** **1954** *Bulletin* (Sydney) 20 Jan. 13/4 I've seen proof positive that the natives of Queensland's sou'-west . . knew how to cut . . rock to provide water-storage. . . A gourd-shaped hole capable of holding several gallons . . was carved at the lowest point of a large rock-table. . . Narrow channels cut in the flat rock led to the opening, which was only a few inches wide and was covered by a flat stone to reduce evaporation or use of the water by animals. . . There were similar 'blackfellows' wells' at many other places. **1960** D. MCLEAN *Roaring Days* 166 Anna knew where there was a blackfellows' well four-five miles away.

B. 1. *adj.* and *attrib.* Aboriginal.

1829 D. BURN *Bushrangers* (1971) 30 Well, matta, how you like black fello corobbora? **1886** R. HENTY *Australiana* 244 There were very few red kangaroos of the old man species (old man, blackfellow for 'big'). **1900** *Bulletin* (Sydney) 25 Aug. 16/1 There is a big revival of blackfellow lingo in the Australian Parliaments. Native names spurious or real, are in great demand for the Federal constituencies. **1920** C.H. SAYCE *Golden Buckles* 63 A girl about 16 years old, with blackfellow features. **1936** K.L. SMITH *Sky Pilot's Last Flight* 14 We augmented our food-supply with water-lily roots, stems, and seeds; also goannas, flying foxes (bats), mussels, and other 'blackfellow tucker'. **1944** M.J. O'REILLY *Bowyangs & Boomerangs* 48 Yandying, in blackfellow language, means shake-about. **1959** D. STUART *Yandy* 52 His mother was blackfeller. **1968** S. GORE *Holy Smoke* 16 You have to do it all in blackfeller yabber. **1974** N. PHILLIPSON *As Other Men* 174 She had shown him then how the man should position himself blackfeller style, kneeling between her legs. **1981** NGABIDJ & SHAW *My Country of Pelican Dreaming* 9, I had to distinguish between the 'white man way' . . and 'blackfeller Law'.

2. In Comb. and collocations: **blackfellow country, doctor, fashion.**

1863 J. BONWICK *Wild White Man* 86 The white man . . 'take him everything **blackfellow country**'. **1962** T. RONAN *Deep of Sky* 105 He observed normal 'blackfellow country' precautions. **1965** R.H. CONQUEST *Horses in Kitchen* 66 They persisted in referring to Queensland, Victoria, and States other than New South Wales as 'blackfellow country'. **1884** A.W. HOWITT *On Some Austral. Ceremonies Initiation* 5 His father . . was a renowned '**blackfellow doctor**' of the Wirajuri tribe. **1886** —— *On Austral. Medicine Men* 24 The term 'Doctor' or 'Blackfellow Doctor' is always used . . for those men in a native tribe who profess to have supernatural powers. **1910** *Bulletin* (Sydney) 1 Sept. 44/2 A thooligal . . can only be driven away by incantations, which none but a bangal (a blackfellow doctor) knows how to say. **1862** A. POLEHAMPTON *Kangaroo Land* 106 Our meat we . . threw . . on the ashes to cook itself—**black-fellow fashion.** **1887** A. NICOLS *Wild Life & Adventure* 128 Bill, after stirring one of the fires into a blaze, laid a wallaby upon it in its skin, and left it there to cook, remarking 'We'll have *that* black-fellow fashion.' **1889** E. GILES *Aust. twice Traversed* II. 319 Another way of getting some of these wallabies was by knocking them over, blackfellow fashion, with a short stick. **1956** T. RONAN *Moleskin Midas* 67 Goanna or any wild life . . could be stalked, blackfellow fashion, with a stick. **1963** X. HERBERT *Larger than Life* 89 He swam, dived for cockles, caught yabbies, and had a meal cooked blackfellow-fashion in the coals.

blackfish. Any of several dark-coloured marine and fresh-water fish, esp. the LUDERICK and *Gadopsis marmoratus*, of fresh water in s.e. Aust.

1790 R. CLARK *Jrnl.* 15 June 176 Four fish of which number there was a large black fish. **1831** *Acct. Colony Van Diemen's Land* 54 Some fine fish are caught in this river, called black fish, occasionally from 2 to 3 feet in length. **1848** *Port Phillip Herald* 27 Apr. 3/2 A black-fish, weighing 7 lbs. was taken in the Yarra. **1873** F. DE CASTELNAU *Edible Fishes Vic.* 14 The Blackfish (*Gadopsis marmoratus*) . . inhabits nearly all the rivers and streams of the southern part of the colony. . . It is considered a good edible fish. **1880** *Proc. Linnean Soc. N.S.W.* V. 407 *Girella tricuspidata* . . 'Black Fish' of the Sydney Fishermen. **1908** *Bulletin* (Sydney) 23 Jan. 15/1 A peculiar feature along the Murray billabongs this season has been the absence of the ubiquitous blackfish. **1941** *Ibid.* 26 Mar. 16/4 My blackfish was the southern freshwater kind (*Gadopsis marmoratus*). **1948** F.D. MARSHALL *Let's go Fishing* 65 The blackfish is also known as luderick or black perch. **1963** B. CROPP *Handbk. for Skindivers* 120 Luderick (*Girella tricuspidata*). This fish is often referred to as a nigger, or blackfish, in New South Wales and black bream in Queensland. **1974** L. WEDLICK *Sporting Fish* 30 As the ancestral home of the blackfish is the dark, overgrown pools in Tasmania . . blackfish only reach their potential size in icy cold waters. **1985** *Canberra Times* 26 Jan. 23/3 When Dad caught a blackfish the little boys got very excited.

blackie. Formerly also **blackee, blackey, blacky.** [Transf. use of *blacky* a Black: see OED *sb.* 1.] An Aboriginal. Freq. used facetiously, and now uncommon.

1827 P. CUNNINGHAM *Two Yrs. in N.S.W.* II. 21 The instant *blacky* perceives *whity* beating a retreat, he vociferates after him—'Go along, you dam rascal.' **1834** G. BENNETT *Wanderings N.S.W.* I. 277 He took a piece of charcoal and sketched some figures upon a sheet of bark . . ; blackee called them 'white fellers'. **1844** *Sydney Morning Herald* 12 Apr. 2/7 To . . the wonderment of 'blackee', and the envy of passing bullock-drivers. **1856** *Full & True Acct. Murder of P. Brown*, There's nothing looming in the distance, To cheer the heart or glad the eye; There's nothing certain for old blackey, But the doom that, he must die. **1868** *Illustr. Sydney News* 3 Oct. 53/2 The flesh of the opossum is highly relished by the blackee, who is not nice in his eating. **1967** M. BARRETT *Gold of Lubra Rock* 110 Them blackies don't jest prance around playin' stupid games. **1977** T.A.G. HUNGERFORD *Wong Chu* 2 Scarecrow 'blackies' and their stick-insect children, whose tangled black hair and blazing black eyes I can still see.

black soil. [Not exclusively Austral. but of local importance.]

1. A black, cracking, clay soil characterizing natural grasslands, valued for its fertility but soft and hazardous to travel across in wet weather. Also *attrib.*

1874 J.J. HALCOMBE *Emigrant & Heathen* 57 In some places the road is deep with sand, in others it is a dry hard gravel; while the decomposed '*trap*' makes a rich black soil, which in wet weather is most tenacious. **1876** 'EIGHT YRS.' RESIDENT' *Queen of Colonies* 81 The Darling Downs squatters, often spoken of in colonial parlance as the Black Soil men, had no intention of foregoing the privileges they enjoyed as occupiers of this fruitful district. **1894** G.H. GIBSON *Ironbark Chips* 12 The genuine black soil 'bull-puncher' with his team well bogged in a bad crossing can hold his own with the mate of a Yankee whaler and curse a Thames bargee into—despondency and an early grave. **1913** W.H. OGILVIE *Overlander* 57 Loiterers in the lignum where the blacksoil traps the weak! **1932** W. HATFIELD *Ginger Murdoch* 1 Scores of miles of black-soil bog where the Diamantina and Georgina rivers meet. **1939** M.B. ELDERSHAW *My Aust.* 15 The black soil is unique. In time of rain it is a veritable glue pot making travel impossible. In times of drought the soil dries hard and great cracks make their appearance, some large enough to take a modern car. **1947** J.W. GORDON *Under Wide Skies* 26 There are gaping cracks in the black-soil tracks That lead to the Queensland creeks. **1955** D. NILAND *Shiralee* 78 Nobody but a bunny . . would venture a black-soil road with a sky ready to leak at any tick of the clock. **1962** MARSHALL & DRYSDALE *Journey among Men* 20 In the hot dry weather this covering of blacksoil compacts into a solid, cement-like surface over which one can travel fast. Yet a mere thirty points of rain will turn it to glutinous bog in which vehicles get hopelessly stuck.

2. Comb. **black soil country, flat, plain, plainsman.**

1882 G. RANDALL *Aust. for Industrious* 11 The Darling Downs—magnificent **black soil country. 1918** R.H. KNYVETT *Over there with Australs.* 216, I have been bogged in a sulky in the 'black soil' country. **1934** T. WOOD *Cobbers* 192 The rains overtook us when we were on the black-soil country. **1953** *Bulletin* (Sydney) 11 Nov. 12/2 The young matron of the 'blacksoil country' whom the artist depicted in the nuddie killing a snake . . did a good job. **1976** B. NORMAN *Bush Pilot* 242 Walter Lawrence would never let anyone burn his blacksoil country. You could look across these plains—or prairies as they call them in Canada and the United States—for miles. It was beautiful rich Flinders grass country. **1894** *Bulletin* (Sydney) 10 Mar. 20/1 They may be at Mundooran now, or past the Overflow—Or tramping down the **black-soil flats** across by Waddiwong. **1938** W. HATFIELD *Buffalo Jim* 169 Soft green clothed the black-soil flats as far as the eye could reach. **1976** B. NORMAN *Bush Pilot* 211 From there on there would be blacksoil flats, boggy and rough perhaps, but a landing was possible. **1867** A.J. RICHARDSON *Private Jrnl. Surveyor Exped. Cape York* 4/1 We encamped near some waterholes, on the western side of a small **black-soil plain. 1880** *Argus* (Melbourne) 7 Jan. 5/7 Hundreds of acres of our best black soil plains, from whence our largest yields have in former years come, are almost a total failure this season. **1897** *Bulletin* (Sydney) 8 May 27/2 The tableland is merging in the big and black-soil plains. **1914** C.H.S. MATTHEWS *Bill* 197 The merry-go-round got bogged in the middle of a black-soil plain, and there we left it. **1939** M.B. ELDERSHAW *My Aust.* 15 The townships are situated on the New South Wales-Queensland border and are surrounded by the famous 'blacksoil' plains. **1959** *Never kill Dolphin* (Writers' Guild Qld.) 73 It went on and on, endlessly repeating itself—a great sweep of black soil plain, surrounding the gravel ridge. **1977** C.T. CASSIDY *Random Thoughts* 14 The water's creeping slowly, Across the black soil plain, As the last mob from Argyle, Move out ahead of rain. **1986** *Sydney Morning Herald* 15 Jan. 13/1 The rich blacksoil plains of western N.S.W. were dotted with cavernous holes, entrances to 30-metre burrows which were homes for hairy-nosed wombats until rabbits appeared. **1977** C. MCCULLOUGH *Thorn Birds* 188 Let Sydney and Melbourne brides petition him for forecasts; the **black-soil plainsmen** would stick with that old sensation in their bones.

black stump. [Spec. use of *black* fire-blackened. From the use of the ubiquitous black stump as a marker when giving directions to travellers (see quot. 1900).]

1. An imaginary marker at the limits of settled and, by implication, civilized country. Also *attrib.*

[**1900** *Bulletin* (Sydney) 31 Mar. 31/1 A rigmarole of details concerning the turns and hollows, the big tree, the dog-leg fence, and the black stump.] **1957** J.M. HOSKING *Aust. First & Last* 16 There must be some of that Black Stump left, It's out near the Queensland border. **1964** D. LOCKWOOD *Up Track* 94 Tennant Creek is no longer black stump country. I don't think of it as being 'Way Out, or even Outback. **1968** R. MAGOFFIN *We Bushies* 33 No this is not The Bush my friend, The Bush is nowhere near, The Black Stump was just around the Bend, But it's no longer here. **1972** *Bulletin* (Sydney) 30 Dec. 28/3 The new government is looking into the possibility of establishing a separate system of Australian awards and if it decides to do so, what's funny about that? There won't be an Order of the Boiling Billy or an Award of the Black Stump Third Class. **1974** *Austral. Gem & Minerals Fossicker* I. 98/1 Reach the turn-off onto the Mudgee Road, which leads seventy-one miles on to Mudgee, first main town en route to the Black Stump. **1978** R.H. CONQUEST *Dusty Distances* 142 Haven't you heard of the black stump court?

2. a. In the phr. **this side of the black stump,** in the world known to the speaker.

1954 T. RONAN *Vision Splendid* 264 You're looking . . at the best bloody station bookkeeper this side of the black stump. **1956** 'N. SHUTE' *Beyond Black Stump* 74 'The kindest people this side of the black stump.' 'The black stump?' 'It's what they say round here. It just means—anywhere.' **1958** J.R. SPICER *Cry of Storm-Bird* 241 The biggest bloody rat this side of the black stump. **1960** M. HENRY *Unlucky Dip* 10 Best-looking governess this side of the black stump. **1968** C. SINCLAIR *Tall Bronzed & Handsome* 29 Why, Australians are the couthest people this side of the Black Stump. **1981** P. BARTON *Bastards I have Known* 63 Wolfy . . was a German and turned out to be one of the best bastards this side of the black stump.

b. In the phr. **beyond the black stump,** in the remote outback.

1965 G.H. FEARNSIDE *Golden Ram* 78 Fair go, mate, we're out beyond the black stump here. **1967** J. WYNNUM *I'm Jack, all Right* 18 It's way back o' Bourke. Beyond the Black Stump. Not shown on the petrol station maps, even. **1972** *Bulletin* (Sydney) 7 Oct. 38/1 He was born not in the capital cities, A.D. Hope's 'five teeming sores', but somewhere beyond the Black Stump, the edge of the world. **1974** *Bronze Swagman Bk. Bush Verse* 55 'Beyond the black stump' is a saying That is well-known to everyone, It used to refer to the country North-West of the Black Stump Run. **1979** D. MAITLAND *Breaking Out* 83 Beyond the mythical Black Stump, where, as Hunt often joked, the crows flew backwards to keep the sun and the flies out of their eyes.

3. A local name for the State Office Block in Sydney. Also *attrib.*

1970 J. CLEARY *Helga's Web* 263 His office was in the State Government block, a beautiful dark grey tower that the citizens, with the local talent for belittling anything that embarrassed them with its pretensions, had dubbed the Black Stump. **1975** *Bulletin* (Sydney) 24 May 29/1 Legal & General Assurance fairly recently built a 17-storey 'black stump' type office on the North Shore. **1981** *Sun-Herald* (Sydney) 28 June 135/1, I gather that Nifty himself went around turning off a few lights in the Black Stump, setting an example to the troops.

blackwood. The tree *Acacia melanoxylon* (fam. Mimosaceae) of Qld., N.S.W., Vic., Tas., and S.A.; the reddish-brown wood of the tree; *Tasmanian blackwood*, see TASMANIAN *a.* 2. Also *attrib.*

1790 J. HUNTER *Hist. Jrnl. Trans. Port Jackson* (1793) 390 The live-oak, yellow-wood, black-wood, and beech, are all of a close grain, and durable. **1810** *HRA* (1921) 3rd Ser. I. 762 The only Tree of a Species not known in New Holland is the Black Wood. **1822** G.W. EVANS *Geogr., Hist., & Topogr. Descr. Van Diemen's Land* 52 Van Diemen's Land . . wants the cedar, mahogany, and rose-wood; but has very good substitutes for them in the species of oak called black wood and in the Huon pine. **1835** *Hobart Town Almanack* 62 *Acacia melanoxylon.* Lightwood. Blackwood. This tree obtains its first name from the gravity of its wood, the second from its colour. **1847** G.F. ANGAS *Savage Life & Scenes* I. 50 The presence of the blackwood tree denotes a rich and good country. **1873** 'LADY IN AUST.' *Memories of Past* 68 We were staying to have luncheon under a beautiful tree called 'blackwood'. **1910** *Huon Times* (Franklin) 30 Mar. 4/3 Bush fires have devastated the thickly-timbered Bridgetown blackwood districts in the south-east. **1964** P. WHITE *Four Plays* (1965) 306 You'll pick up the track just down there . . behind that big blackwood standing on its own.

blacky, var. BLACKIE.

bladder saltbush. [f. *bladder*, referring to the appearance of the fruits + SALTBUSH 1.] Any of several small shrubs of the genus *Atriplex* (fam. Chenopodiaceae), the fruits of which have large inflated appendages, esp. *A. vesicaria* and *A. hymenotheca.*

1897 L. LINDLEY-COWEN *W. Austral. Settler's Guide* 426 *(caption) Atriplex vesicaria* . . 'Bladder salt-bush.' **1903** G. SUTHERLAND *Australasian Live Stock Man.* (ed. 2) 379 Vast areas of the salty interior of Australia . . are covered with three varieties of the *Atriplex* saltbush, namely, *A. vesicaria, A. holocarpa*, and *A. halimoides.* Popular names for the two former are the 'Bladder saltbush' and the 'Whole-fruited saltbush'. **1982** *Ecos* xxxiii. 19/1 One widespread type of pasture land, the bladder saltbush . . community.

blade. *Shearing. Hist.*

1. *pl.* Hand shears. Also (in *sing.*) *attrib.*, and **blade shears.**

1897 *Worker* (Sydney) 11 Sept. 1/1 That's what he calls his shears at work; he calls them 'blades' in songs. **1905** A.B. PATERSON *Old Bush Songs* 26 All among the wool, boys, keep your wide blades full, boys. **1915** *Bulletin* (Sydney) 14 Oct. 24/2 The old-timer who only barbers with the shears is 'queer' or 'cranky', and his implements of destruction are 'the blades'. **1937** *Ibid.* 14 July 20/1 Anyone who shore In blade-sheds of a bygone day Will tell you what men labor for. **1946** F. CLUNE *Try Nothing Twice* 89 Those were the old days when shearing machines were new, replacing the old-fashioned 'blades'. **1958** F.B. VICKERS *Mirage* 110 'Is he still shearin' with the blades?' 'Still pokin' it off, Fred.' **1965** R.H. CONQUEST *Horses in Kitchen* 193 His father had shorn at Isisford in the old blade days, as had Jacky Howe. **1980** P. FREEMAN *Woolshed* 20 Until the introduction of the mechanical handpiece in 1888, 'blade' shears were exclusively used.

2. Comb. **blade-man, -shearer, -shearing** *vbl. n.*

1918 *Huon Times* (Franklin) 29 Nov. 3/5 They got through upwards of 400,000 sheep per year there, and some of the champion **blade-men** gathered. **1937** *Bulletin* (Sydney) 14 July 20/1 No blademen sought For artificial aids to pace. **1924** *Ibid.* 10 Jan. 24/4 Howe proved himself to be absolutely the world's champion **blade-shearer. 1935** R.B. PLOWMAN *Boundary Rider* 159 The blade-shearer finds it hard to cut through the gritty mass of wool and sticks and sand, and the machine-shearer finds the edge worn off his comb in a few minutes. **1965** R.H. CONQUEST *Horses in Kitchen* 191 His father was a contemporary of Jacky Howe, reckoned the greatest Australian blade shearer of all time. **1977** D. WHITINGTON *Strive to be Fair* 27, I worked at the shearing . . picking up for three blade shearers. **1945** *Bulletin* (Sydney) 14 Mar. 15/1 Sam was doing casual **blade-shearing. 1949** *Ibid.* 23 Feb. 14/4 In an old ballad of the blade-shearing days . . the shearers are skiting in a hotel bar in Hay. **1978** D. STUART *Wedgetail View* 18 Davey roamed the land making a few quid here and there at horse-breaking or blade-shearing. **1980** P. FREEMAN *Woolshed* 36 Blade shearing was difficult. The good blade shearer made three cuts at each blade position.

3. In the phr. **to go out with the blades,** to become obsolete.

1958 J.R. SPICER *Cry of Storm-Bird* 2 Others . . were still on the pedal-wireless system, but most wirelesses were up-to-date and pedalling had 'gone out with the blades'. **1965** J.S. GUNN *Terminol. Shearing Industry* i. 29 *Gone out with the blades*, old-fashioned, no longer wanted.

blady grass. Also **bladey grass.** [f. *blady* blade-like.] Any of several grasses (fam. Poaceae), esp. the perennial *Imperata cylindrica* var. *major*, the mature blades of which are stiff and fibrous, with sharp edges. Formerly also **blade of grass.**

1827 P. CUNNINGHAM *Two Yrs. in N.S.W.* I. 209 The blady grass grows often to the height of two or three feet, and from its broad strong leaf makes excellent thatch. **1844** L. LEICHHARDT *Jrnl. Overland Exped. Aust.* 1 Dec. (1847) 59 A bush-fire . . had left very little food for our cattle: the blady-grass, however, had begun to show its young shoots. **1847** A. HARRIS *Settlers & Convicts* (1953) 132 Here and there a little meadow-like spot covered with the coarse grass called 'blade of grass'. **1908** S.W. JACKSON *Field Trip Notebk.* 169 Small houses covered on the roof & sides with the blady grass (*Imperata arundinacea*) which grows so abundantly & so very long in this part of Queensland. **1955** F. LANE *Patrol to Kimberleys* 152 Glen and Dave rode on one of the rear flanks of the herd as it moved southward through the dry, hip-high blady-grass. **1963** *Meanjin* 42 The small mattress he'd stuffed with bladey-grass. **1972** D. SHEAHAN *Songs from Canefields* 80 The horses' reign is ended—the ridge now holds their bones If bush fires haven't got them—'mong blady grass and stones. **1981** T. SHAPCOTT *Stump & Grape & Bopple-nut* 13 When they tugged at the bladeygrass they cut their fingers.

blank. Of a waterside worker: one who holds an unendorsed licence for casual work (see PREFERENCE 2).

1947 J. MORRISON *Sailors belong Ships* 32 Work on these ships sometimes trickles out to the Blanks, but to-day the Seconds rush it. **1955** —— *Black Cargo* 28 First Preference men (Federation and Jacks) possess, in addition to their licences, little oblong cardboard dockets inscribed with their name and Bureau numbers. Blanks have nothing but their Licences. **1982** LOWENSTEIN & HILLS *Under Hook* 78 About 1933 I went in for a licence. The First Preference was P and C and Federation men. The Second Preference was men that used to follow the wharf as much as they could and the Third Preference was the blanks. And when you first paid you were a blank.

blanket.

1. *Hist. Government blanket*, see GOVERNMENT B. 4. Also *attrib.*, as **blanket day** (see quot. 1857).

1857 *Moreton Bay Free Press* 29 Apr. 3/1 *Blanket Day.*—The blankets and articles of clothing usually distributed to the aborigines on the Queen's birth-day, were given out last Thursday (St. George's Day). **1880** *Bulletin* (Sydney) 19 June 21/9 Queen's Birthday (the annual 'blanket-day' of the Wide Bay blacks). **1881** *Ibid.* 18 June 4/2 The Queensland officials now distribute blacks' blankets by hanging them on the boughs of trees. The blankets are invariably red and blue, and are usually cut into stripes to ornament the head-dress of gins and braves. **1897** *Western Champion* (Barcaldine) 10 Aug. 3/2 As blanket-day comes around every year complaints about the niggardliness of the Government . . are regularly made. **1930** J.S. LITCHFIELD *Far-North Memories* 51 Blanket day dawned bright and clear. **1940** E. HILL *Great Austral. Loneliness* (ed. 2) 273, I get the blacks' rations, a little tea, sugar and flour from the Government every week, with a gin's frock of blue galatea and a blackfella's blanket once a year.

2. *Gold-mining. Obs.* A device for trapping particles of water-borne gold; a blanket-sluice (see quot. 1871). Also **blanket-table.**

1862 J.A. PATTERSON *Gold Fields Vic.* 260 If blanket-tables, or revolving blankets, are added only impalpable gold can escape. **1871** J. BALLANTYNE *Homes & Homesteads* 42 A table, or platform of wood, so laid as to have a gentle incline, and covered with what diggers call 'a blanket'—in other words, a cloth made of green baize or some other coarse material—is prepared as the bed over which the water with its precious freight is to flow. **1881** H.W. NEWMAN *Extracts & Rep. on Lucknow* (1888) 42 The rest of the stone is put through an eight-stamper battery and over quicksilver and blanket tables, by means of which most of the free gold is obtained and the pyrites collected. **1891** H. NISBET *Colonial Tramp* II. 88 The gold . . is so fine that much of it escapes the 'ripples' and 'blankets'.

3. Used *attrib.* in Special Comb. **blanket cheque,** a large cheque; **muster,** see MUSTER *n.* 5.

1905 *Bulletin* (Sydney) 16 Mar. 3/2 My cheque was not the size of shearing-cheques of long ago (The good old days of '**blanket' cheques** were dead).

blanketing, *vbl. n. Obs.* See quot. 1825.

1825 *Colonial Times* (Hobart) 19 Nov., The common practice in the gaol called *blanketing.* When a prisoner receives a loaf or other provisions, before he has time to commence his repast, a blanket is thrown over him, he is wrested of his food, and held in durance until the whole is devoured out of sight. **1826** *Ibid.* 2 Sept., Disgraceful attempts to rob a fellow-prisoner by *blanketing.*

bleeders, *pl. Obs.* [Survival of Br. slang *bleeder* a spur: see F. Grose *Dict. Vulgar Tongue* (1811).] Spurs.

1812 J.H. VAUX *Mem.* (1819) II. 156 *Bleeders,* spurs. **1849** *Bell's Life in Sydney* 29 Dec. 2/3 Cutts tried the whalebone and bleeders, but all to no purpose, as Higgerson landed his horse a winner by a length. **1915** T. SKEYHILL *Soldier-Songs from Anzac* 14, I urged and forced him to his best, and plied the whip and bleeders, And truly well he stood the test, and rattled past the leaders.

blew, var. BLUE *v.*[1]

blight. SANDY BLIGHT.

1807 *Sydney Gaz.* 8 Feb., The blights which affect the eye perhaps in a much greater degree here than elsewhere are more severely felt this season than ever before remembered. **1827** P. CUNNINGHAM *Two Yrs. in N.S.W.* I. 184 An inflammation of the eyes, called 'the blight', often follows. . . The lower palpebrae are the chief seat of the disease, becoming red and swollen, and discharging a glutinous sort of matter, which seals the eyelids together. **1834** G. BENNETT *Wanderings N.S.W.* I. 303 There is an affection of the eye, which much prevails at this season of the year in the interior of the colony, attacking both European settlers and natives, and is called by the colonists the 'blight': it occurs only during the summer season: the attack is sudden, no doubt proceeding from the bite of a gnat, or some other insect. I had an opportunity of witnessing a case of this malady, which occurred in a native. The integuments surrounding the orbit were puffed up so much, as totally to close the eye, which was found much inflamed, as in acute opthalmia, and attended with symptoms, in some degree similar, with severe itching and pricking pain, as if sand had been lodged in it, with a profuse flow of tears. **1852** J. SHAW *Tramp to Diggings* 260 Ophthalmia . . arising from the bite of a fly, and commonly termed *blight,* and not at all a serious complaint. **1859** W. BURROWS *Adventures Mounted Trooper* 149 The dust frequently causes them to be affected by what is called 'blight'. **1869** 'E. HOWE' *Boy in Bush* 80 A good many people in Jerry's Town had got 'the blight'. Their eyes were bunged up just as if they had been fighting. **1917** *Bulletin* (Sydney) 8 Mar. 22/2 Our timber-getters' bullocks are suffering from what is termed blight. It mostly affects only one eye, but some animals go totally blind in both eyes. **1929** K.S. PRICHARD *Coonardoo* (1961) 173 Phyllis went down to an attack of blight, which kept her to her room for days.

blind, *a.*

1. [Spec. use of *blind,* of a geographical feature that terminates abruptly: see OEDS *a.* 11 c.] In collocations: **blind creek, gully** (see CREEK, GULLY).

1834 *Sydney Herald* 1 Sept. 2/4 All those lagoons have, what they term here, '**blind creeks**', (or a hollow made by floods). **1838** T. WALKER *Month in Bush Aust.* 27 There were many blind creeks and ridges between the ranges to get over. **1852** S. SMITH *Whether to Go* 108 On the Wollondilly river, nearly the whole of the country presents a similar appearance to Braidwood, having innumerable rich blind creeks, swamps, and flanked by granite hills. **1853** J. CAPPER *Emigrant's Guide to Aust.* (ed. 2) 160 These diggings are situated on a 'blind creek'. **1853** A. MACKAY *Great Gold Field* 38 Some men are working in a gully or a blind creek near Golden Point. **1868** J. BAIRD *Emigrant's Guide Australasia* 221 Deep indentations suggested to the unpractised beholder the openings of creeks, or the estuaries of rivers. These blind creeks, as they are called, lead to nowhere, but terminate in . . bays of black mud, fringed, even below high water mark, with the never failing mangrove. **1889** F.C. CLIFFORD *Richmond River District* 13 This is a matter that could easily be affected by damming one of the blind creeks or gullies running from the Moonumbar division of the Richmond Range. **1902** *Bulletin* (Sydney) 4 Oct. 36/2 They were approaching one of the brief, blind creeks of Centralia, which, after a course of a mile or two, exhaust themselves in sand, or merge into a tiny swamp. **1905** *Emu* V. 59 One nest was situated in the side of one of the short, deep channels ('blind creeks') that drained the swampy portion of the river flat. [N.Z. **1848** C.J. PHARAZYN *Jrnl.* 15 Jan. 97 Teddy and W. to lambs to drive them to pen, smother'd 10 in a **blind gully.**] **1852** D. MACKENZIE *Ten Yrs. Aust.* 22 The best places to look for gold are . . along the sides of gullies (especially 'blind' gullies, as they are called, that lose themselves in the hills). **1852** G.C. MUNDY *Our Antipodes* III. 387 It was the first attempt Mr Hardy had seen of working in the 'blind gulleys' as they are called here—'gulches' as they are styled in California. **1853** A. MACKAY *Great Gold Field* 38 After having seen the manner in which all the creeks, blind gullies, and hills in the vicinity of the Turon have been worked or tried, I am astonished to find that the ground adjacent to the Summerhill Creek has been almost wholly untouched. **1891** E.H. HALLACK *W.A. & Yilgarn Goldfields* 18 The battery-house . . is situated near the head of a blind gully. **1892** *Western Champion* (Barcaldine) 26 Apr. 12/1 Please, sir, I have been over by the blind gully, about two miles back, and I notice it is filling and spreading over the lignum swamp. **1896** J. HOLT *Virgin Gold* 21 If he should, perchance, get bushed at night at any time, he need not be at all alarmed, as he can procure a drink in the blind gullies. **1899** *Western Champion* (Barcaldine) 25 July 3/2 He spun up a blind gully, then over a gum flat, and up a boree spur, on to a spinifex tableland.

2. In the collocation **Blind Freddie** [poss. the nickname of a Sydney hawker], a most unperceptive person (as a type).

1946 D. STIVENS *Courtship of Uncle Henry* 188 He doesn't want to go on with tonight. Blind Freddy could see that. **1952** T.A.G. HUNGERFORD *Ridge & River* 136 We might've come two miles . . and leaving a trail old Blind Freddie could follow. **1953** —— *Riverslake* 200 'You are poofter, Slim. One day I fix it you. *Kaput.*' 'You couldn't fix old Blind Freddie.' **1972** *Bulletin* (Sydney) 12 Aug. 7/2 'Do you find that expressions containing proper names are liable to fall into neglect?' I asked. 'With a few exceptions, yes,' she said. 'Blind Freddy is still around and seeing things, I'm glad to say.' **1975** G.A.W. SMITH *Once Green Jackaroo* 52 Blind Freddie himself could have picked the ace. **1985** *Bulletin* (Sydney) 4 June 12/2 It was obvious to blind Freddie there was no real impediment to air safety.

blind, *n.* In the phr. **on the blind,** on chance, without prior information.

1917 *All abaht It* (London) (1919) Feb. 62 What about getting it—'one on the blind'? **1929** J.L. MOORE *Canine King* 30 The dog is 'cast off' 'on the blind' to use the expression by which a sheep-man admits his own impotence. **1936** I.L. IDRIESS *Cattle King* 63 He had taken up country on the 'blind', without ever having seen it. **1960** D. MCLEAN *Roaring Days* 62 When you're on opal country . . you have to sink 'on the blind'.

blind grass. [See quot. 1926.] Either of the perennial plants *Stypandra grandiflora* and *S. imbricata* (fam. Liliaceae) of s.w. W.A.

1897 L. LINDLEY-COWEN *W. Austral. Settler's Guide* 589 The Candyup poison, or blind grass, has been identified with *Stypandra glauca,* a liliaceous plant met with from King George's Sound to the Swan and Murchison. **1915** *Bulletin* (Sydney) 2 Sept. 26/4 A vegetable much abused in parts of Westralia is commonly known as 'blind grass'. . . The woolly-coats, as a rule, won't tackle it. **1926** *Poison Plants W.A.* (W.A. Dept. Agric.) 62 The Blind Grasses . . are reputed to cause blindness in stock. **1977** *Jrnl. R. Soc. W.A.* LIX. 72 A number of cyanogenetic plants, particularly the blind grasses.

blindy-eye, var. BINDI-EYE.

blind-your-eye. Also **blind-your-eyes.** Either of the trees *Excoecaria agallocha* (see *milky mangrove* MANGROVE) and *E. dallachyana* (fam. Euphorbiaceae), the milky sap of which can cause temporary blindness.

1888 *Proc. Linnean Soc. N.S.W.* III. 380 *Excaecaria agallocha* . . 'Blind-your-eyes'. **1908** E.J. BANFIELD *Confessions of Beachcomber* 202 Another denizen of the partially reclaimed area of the mangrove swamp is the 'milky mangrove', or river poison tree, *alias* 'blind-your-eyes'. **1928** B. SPENCER *Wanderings in Wild Aust.* 533 For the first time we met with . . gutta-percha or india-rubber tree. . . When the bark is cut it exudes a thick whitish fluid that soon sets like gutta-percha. . . If it comes in contact with the soft membrane of the eye, it sets up severe inflammation that often results in temporary blindness, indeed one of the bushman's names for it is 'blind-your-eye'. **1934** *Bulletin* (Sydney) 5 Sept. 20/2 The milky or 'blind-your-eyes' variety of mangrove . . is a remedy for the sting of the stone-fish. **1974** S.L. EVERIST *Poisonous Plants Aust.* 199 Blind-your-eye . . is reputed to be capable of causing blistering and blindness in man.

blister, *n.*[1] [Abbrev. of *blister pearl* irregularly shaped pearly excrescence.]

1. See quot. 1919.

1913 *Cwlth. Parl. Papers* III. 640 Do the Japanese divers break up the shells to get the pearl blisters? **1919** *Smith's Weekly* (Sydney) 10 May 11/2 Seed pearl and 'blisters' (pearls of irregular shape attached to the oyster's inner shell) are fairly common. **1937** I.L. IDRIESS *Forty Fathoms Deep* 85 The pearl was a blister, a bubble of nacre filled with caked mud. A shellfish had bored into the oyster which had formed a coating of nacre over the wound. This gradually grew into a blister.

2. An oyster shell having a protuberance which contains a pearl; the protuberance as distinct from the shell.

1937 J.M. HARCOURT *It never Fails* 130 The pearl-cleaner sat at a table working on a blister with a file. **1940** E. HILL *Great Austral. Loneliness* (ed. 2) 66 Hawkes is an artist in shell carving. He has covered the dash-light of his car with a 'blister'. **1941** K.S. PRICHARD *Moon of Desire* 72 T.B. chuckled about the pearl, sold for one hundred pounds, he had found in a blister on some old shells used for a doorstep. **1944** *Bulletin* (Sydney) 12 July 15/4 Men . . treasured blisters, finally cracking them, to find therein a pearl fit for a queen's necklace. . . Most blister-crackers merely went round the junction of the bulge with the shell, punching a circle of small holes with a sharp-pointed tool.

blister, *n.*[2] [f. *blister* summons: see OEDS *sb.* 6.] A debt.

1934 T. WOOD *Cobbers* 134 Men talked about their blister . . which means a mortgage, with complacency. **1951** E. HILL *Territory* 431 Never carry a 'blister', a bill or an account.

blithered, *ppl. a.* [f. *blither* to talk nonsense: see OEDS *v.*] Drunk.

1911 *Bulletin* (Sydney) 12 Oct. 14/2 Who ever hears . . of a man being 'drunk'? . . The staid and dignified citizen will say he is 'intoxicated' . . , the average boy that he is 'shickered', 'blithered' or 'tonicked'. **1921** K.S. PRICHARD *Black Opal* 37 Old Ted! . . He's blithered! **1940** *Bulletin* (Sydney) 27 Mar. 16/4 Well blithered, and with the remnants of his cheque from a clearing job, Big Tom struck the town. **1944** *Ibid.* 2 Aug. 15/2 A Mildura settler was making home in the dusk one night slightly blithered. **1946** *Southerly* ii. 78 'Blithered.' 'Stonkered.' 'Full as a tick.'

blitz. [Transf. use of *blitz* attack.] **a.** An army sobriquet for an open truck, esp. a personnel carrier. **b.** Any modified heavy-duty ex-army vehicle. In full **blitz buggy (truck, wagon).**

1943 *Troppo Tribune* (Mataranka) 8 Feb. 3 The blitz-buggy in the vanguard of the returning Concert Troupe. **1950** G.M. FARWELL *Land of Mirage* 110 It turned out to be Ron Michell, whose Ford 'blitz' wagon had passed us. **1950** A. GROOM *I saw Strange Land* 82 A blitz-wagon called for me at sunrise and bundled me off to the large landing field. **1955** A.W. UPFIELD *Cake in Hat Box* 56 I wouldn't take a blitz-buggy across them ranges. **1956** A.C.C. LOCK *Tropical Tapestry* 124 When a youngster he never imagined he would one day travel in a blitz buggy through country where Burke and Wills had tramped wearily and desperately along. **1968** G. MILL *Nobody dies but Me* 29 They turned up, piling out of the back of the Blitzwagon and clowning around the place. **1970** D. BAIRD *Incredible Gulf* 18 Just after dawn the rumble of the 'blitz' truck engine awakens me. . . Baker is backing the blitz up to the drums of fuel scattered in one corner. **1981** P. BARTON *Bastards I have Known* 55 A youth . . was on hand to . . assist with the transfer of supplies on to an old army 'blitz'. . . We were sitting on the back of the 'blitz' heading for the homestead . . up a winding, sandy track.

block, *n.*[1] [U.S. *block* each of the parcels of land in which a town is laid out for subdivision, orig. with reference to a mass of contiguous buildings wholly or mainly occupying an area bounded by four streets: see Mathews 1 b.]

1. One of the parcels into which a town site or other land made available for settlement and development is divided.

1833 *Sydney Herald* 4 Mar. 2/5 A large site of ground is occupied by the new arrangement. . . This is divided into sections, or what are professionally designated 'blocks', . . each block containing ten acres. **1838** *Southern Austral.* (Adelaide) 30 June 2/2 *To let*, together or separately, for a term of years, at a moderate Rent, a block of four Town Acres, in North Adelaide. *Ibid.* 3 Nov. 4/3 J.E.W. Bull, *Land & Stock Agent*, &c. begs to announce that he has for sale, or to be let in Farms of various sizes, several Country Sections in District A. . . Parties may be suited in blocks of from six to eight, or in single sections. **1839** *Port Phillip Patriot* 6 Feb. 3 The Government . . caused to be laid out 24 Blocks, of 20 Allotments each Block, consisting of 76 Perches each allotment. **1841** *Geelong Advertiser* 11 Sept. 2/2 The sale of Town Allotments in North Corio, which is to take place in December next, will consist of one entire block of ten acres, divided into twenty allotments. **1870** C.H. ALLEN *Visit to Qld.* 110 Broad, straight streets, running in parallel lines, cut the square town into numerous smaller squares, which form what are called 'blocks'. Each block consists of about ten divisions, containing some two roods of land. These are put up and sold by the Government. **1884** *Austral. Tit-Bits* (Melbourne) 19 June 1 The . . magnificent Block of Land, comprising 80 Acres, charmingly sub-divided into 309 Allotments. **1885** F.A. BOYD (*title*) The farmer and settler's guide to the Gosford five acre model farm blocks. **1896** W. BANNOW *Colony of Vic.* 9 Melbourne glorying in possessing these rectangular streets occupies only thirty-two 10 acre blocks. **1911** *Huon Times* (Franklin) 28 Jan. 6/5 The council's idea was blocks not larger than 200 acres. **1943** H.G. LAMOND *From Tariaro to Ross Roy* 108 The land was cut up into 20,000-acre blocks. **1952** J.F. HADDLETON *Katanning Pioneer* 9 The first block selected was 100 acres, Kojonup Location 66.

2. A parcel of land which is entire and of a piece, esp. one taken up for settlement.

1835 J. BATMAN *Settlement in Port Phillip* 6 June (1856) 20, I purchased two large blocks or tracts of land, about 600,000 acres, more or less, and, in consideration there for, I gave them blankets, knives, looking glasses, tomahawks, beads, scissors, flour, &c., and I also further agreed to pay them a tribute or rent yearly. **1839** W. MANN *Six Yr.'s Residence* 42 Permission has been obtained of His Majesty's Government to select one block of 20,000 acres at Circular Head. **1845** *Port Phillip Gaz.* 23 July 1 The present holders of large blocks of land, will be allowed to retain out of each block as many runs as they choose to pay for at the rate of £10 per annum for each run. **1870** *Sydney Morning Herald* 2 July 3/6 Block of unstocked country, securely fenced; capabilities, 15,000 sheep. **1886** P. FLETCHER 'Hints to Immigrants' in P. Fletcher *Qld.* 8 All Queensland is not open for anyone to go and pick out a piece of land, but from time to time large districts are proclaimed open, and you can take up your block anywhere in those districts. **1899** *Progress* (Brisbane) 17 June 1/1 You can hear it in the mulga on the million-acre block. **1911** *Huon Times* (Franklin) 17 June 6/4 About 80 miles east of Tanami there is a block with an area of 500 square miles of good Country, carrying Mitchell grass and saltbush. **1929** 'OLD STOCKMAN' *Sensational Cattle-Stealing Case* 74/1 They are taking up the country in large blocks, and excavating big tanks for the water supply. **1972** ANDERSON & BLAKE *J.S. Neilson* 11 Victoria's Land Act of 1869 permitted anyone over the age of eighteen to select up to 320 acres of first class land, peg each corner of the block chosen, and then lodge an application with the nearest land board. **1979** W.D. JOYNT *Breaking Road for Rest* 45 When the time came to leave the station, I took on a contract with another fellow to clear and burn the mallee scrub on a six hundred acre block at a place in a newly developed district north of Ouyen.

3. A variously defined unit of measurement used to limit the size of a piece of land taken up for settlement or to determine the rent payable on it.

1843 *Adelaide Observer* 18 Nov. 7/1 *Waste Lands Bill.* On laying this Bill on the table, his Excellency stated that its object was chiefly, to lease runs in the neighbourhood of purchased land; the runs would be divided into blocks of a square mile, and be let at one pound for that quantity of land. **1847** *Port Phillip Herald* 5 Jan. 2/2 Blocks of twenty-five square miles, or four thousand sheep, are to be rented at £10 per annum. **1863** *Cassell's Qld.* 6 The quantity of country held in one block is limited to 200 square miles. **1865** R. HENNING *Lett.* (1952) 87 A block of land is supposed to contain twenty-five square miles. . . In general, there is about half as much again in a block, as, of course, the squatters go to the utmost limit in taking up country, and the Government allow so much for 'unavailable land'; that is, scrubs and dense forest where sheep cannot feed. **1867** 'CLERGYMAN' *Aust. as it Is* 50 The land in the country to be discovered must be taken up in 'blocks', each block being estimated to sustain four thousand sheep, and six hundred and fifty head of cattle; and for each block there is to be paid ten pounds annually at the Government treasury, besides a small assessment on the stock. **1882** *Austral. Handbk.* 367 Water frontages are leased in blocks of not less than 50,000 acres, non-frontage land can be had in blocks of 20,000 acres. **1897** L. LINDLEY-COWEN *W. Austral. Settler's Guide* 133 Formerly the settlers would only put the plough in where the York, red gum, and manna trees stood, but now that an enlargement of work has to be provided for owing to the growing requirements of the colony, the white gum blocks are no longer passed over. **1937** *Bulletin* (Sydney) 30 June 21/4 For 25 years I've lived on the edge of a large block of tropical jungle.

4. A building allotment.

1874 J.J. HALCOMBE *Emigrant & Heathen* 16 The school . . was built by the Bishop in 1849, on a block of land. **1899** *Progress* (Brisbane) 11 Feb. 1/3 Working men's blocks as a means of settling families of the artisan class in the suburbs, will have to get a fair trial in the near future. **1900** *Advocate* (Burnie) 2 May 2/6 The block on the corner . . is also said to have changed hands. **1960** *N.T. News* (Darwin) 2 Feb. 1/3 One block owner who paid £104 above 'upset' for a block at Nightcliff was this week offered £300. **1972** ANDERSON & BLAKE *J.S. Neilson* 4 His son . . had the private township of Penola or Penoola surveyed and sold town blocks. **1976** *Meanjin* 380 Trip overseas, holiday block, washing-machine, dishwasher, colour TV upstairs.

5. *Mining.* See quots. 1869 and 1870. Also *attrib.*

1858 *Colonial Mining Jrnl.* Oct. 28/3 The amount of litigation in connection with this lead is great, some of the claims being under the frontage, and others the block system. **1862** 'W.T.G.' *Quite Colonial* (*c* 1948) 7 With right good will he went about stripping the worthless soil off his 'block'; and before dinner time he had laid bare some couple of square yards of auriferous stratum. **1869** R.B. SMYTH *Gold Fields & Mineral Districts* 604 *Block-claim*, a claim bounded by right lines (except where in very rare cases a creek or river forms a boundary) which are fixed and defined by pegs, posts, or trenches at each angle of the claim; either at the time of taking possession, or within a prescribed time thereafter by survey, prior to registration. **1870** W.B. WITHERS *Hist. Ballarat* 126 The block claim is a fixed area, with bounds ascertained from the first. **1890** 'R. BOLDREWOOD' *Miner's Right* 131 All shallow sinking and block claims; none of your confounded frontages. **1910** *Huon Times* (Franklin) 22 Oct. 6/3 No fewer than nine syndicates have been formed, and representations sent to the west to secure options over blocks. **1941** D. O'CALLAGHAN *Long Life Reminisc.* 143/2 They had an option on the pioneer lease first and without a deposit. They tried hard to get mine without a deposit, but they had no chance. . . My block was only a position block and no payable ore to break. **1950** G.S. CASEY *City of Men* 57 Three blocks from the Irish Luck and right on the line of the reef. **1972** N. KING *Nickel Country* 25 Soon she found what she called 'some interesting stone', pegged the ground, and sold several blocks to companies.

6. A small holding; esp. an irrigated orchard or vineyard near Mildura, Vic.

1888 *Illustr. Austral. News* (Melbourne) 3 Mar. 35/1 The property . . will be cut up into small farms, orchard blocks and vineyards. **1913** W.K. HARRIS *Outback in Aust.* 71 We received a hearty invitation to spend the week-end with one of the packers on his 'block' at Merbein. **1920** T.E. TAYLOR *Pioneer Irrigationists' Man.* xxxvi. 1 The cost of planting a block of trees or vines. **1938** F. BLAKELEY *Hard Liberty* 30 One could find in Mildura . . dozens of men who bought their blocks from a rise made on White Cliffs. **1944** A.J. & J.J. MCINTYRE *Country Towns Vic.* 185 The irrigation districts, and particularly the Mildura district, present a contrast . . because the blocks are comparatively closely set around the town. **1946** A.M. LAPTHORNE *Mildura Calling* 43 Already life is astir on neighbouring vineyards (locally called 'blocks'). **1960** N. CATO *Green grows Vine* 24 He was the champion grape-picker on the block, a Yugoslav who had once had a vineyard of his own in Europe. **1968** J. BEGLEY *Block with One Holer* 18 They admired the miles of orange groves as they sped by. 'I was twenty-five years too late for one of those blocks,' mused Bluey.

block, *n.*[2] [Spec. use of BLOCK *n.*[1]] Also *attrib.*

1. A street or block in which it is fashionable to promenade.

a. In Melbourne: Collins Street between Swanston and Elizabeth Streets.

1868 [see sense 2]. **1872** 'RESIDENT' *Glimpses Life Vic.* 349 A certain portion of Collins Street, lined by the best drapers' and jewellers' shops . . is known as 'The Block', and is the daily resort of the belles and beaux. **1880** *Bulletin* (Sydney) 6 Nov. 9/4 Female block-walkers are a feature of Melbourne. . . They are simply 'fetching', and have 'sugar'—for they are allied to that fraternity which revels in interest. **1887** *Illustr. Austral. News* (Melbourne) 25 June (Suppl.) 15/2 There is now a dress promenade every afternoon at 4 o'clock down Collins-street, in which Melbourne ladies display their taste for millinery in lavish profusion on what is termed locally 'the block'. **1894** *Antipodean* (Melbourne) 32 I'm a giddy little tart, And I'm up to every dart; You should see me when I go upon the knock-O! And the chappies all declare, That the girl with golden hair Is the rortiest little titter on the block-O! **1905** W. MOORE *City Sketches* 12 The Block is still the hub of our little universe. It is here that you observe the free swinging stride of the Melbourne girl. **1912** O. WOOD *Cup Week* 12 Ladies airing dresses Every tint and shade, Make the Block a sort of Butterfly parade. **1912** *Huon Times* (Franklin) 31 Jan. 4/2 The Swanston-street end of 'The Block' is another place much frequented by persons who apparently have no other purpose than to force their attentions upon women. **1928** *Melbourne Univ. Mag.* Oct. 14 We sell more buttons on the Block on Saturday morning than at any other time. **1947** *Ibid.* 31 The annual 'block parade' in Commencement Week. **1973** K. DUNSTAN *Sports* 36 The young man took his lady to . . the old basement café on the Block. There he gave her a 'schoolgirl's dream' which was a sickly affair with a milk and ice-cream base.

b. In Sydney: see quot. 1872.

1872 BUNSTER & THATCHER *It runs in Blood* 60 '*The Block*' is supposed to extend down George-street, from King-street to Hunter-street, round Pitt-street, and up King-street into George-street again. But George-street is the 'subs'-walk' *par excellence.* **1890** *Truth* (Sydney) 7 Dec. 2/6 A rough grey suit with the broad arrow for the dainty ones in which I had . . mashed many a belle on the block. **1900** *Ibid.* 15 Apr. 5/6 King-street has taken fright, the block is deserted, fashion has fled, and the obstruction by 'fashionable ladies' so often complained of has ceased. **1904** *Ibid.* 8 May 8/3 The Block has always been woman's Rialto, where beauty is knocked down to the highest bidder. **1914** *Ibid.* 19 July 1/5 London has its Piccadilly, but in Sydney we can pick a dilly daily on the Block. **1945** H.M. MORAN *Beyond Hill lies China* 131 Challis's mind slipped back to the days when, as a student, he 'did the block' on Saturday mornings. Down George Street and around the Post Office, up Pitt Street, past King Street, and through the Arcade, then back to George Street again.

c. In Brisbane: the rectangle formed by Queen, Edward, Elizabeth, and Albert Streets.

1878 E. BRADDON *Lett. to India from Tas.* (1980) 15 We have done the block thoroughly; 'doing the block' being the local expression for wearing out one's shoe-leather on the Brisbane-street pavement. **1899** *Truth* (Sydney) 2 Apr. 2/6 Any quantity of Northerners have come and are coming to swell the gang who consider it *the* thing to do the wretched little block.

2. In the phr. **to do the block,** to promenade along 'the block'.

1868 *Australasian* (Melbourne) 6 June 721/4, I was slinking down the sunny side of Collins-street to avoid a bailiff . . and I was surprised to see so many people 'doing the block'. **1872** BUNSTER & THATCHER *It runs in Blood* 60 A Sydney swell could not sleep comfortably if he had not 'done the block' during the day. **1878** F.L. RAINS *By Land & Ocean* 30 In Collins Street . . the 'world and his wife' turn out in best bib and tucker to see and to be seen; which, in colonial slang is called 'doing the block'. **1888** *Bulletin* (Sydney) 25 Feb. 8/3 Girls are doing the Block who did it ten years ago, and who have each worn out a hundred pairs of boots in vainly trotting about after the husband who has never come. **1896** W. BANNOW *Colony of Vic.* 19 From 3 to 5 p.m. it is fashionable to 'do' the 'Block', that is, parade the northern footpath of Collins-street. **1910** *Truth* (Sydney) 13 Feb. 9/5 Of types of beauty, Sydney's a rare stock, You'll daily see them gaily do the block. **1920** *Land of Lyrebird* (S. Gippsland Pioneers' Assoc.) 360 And one sturdy scrubcutter was seen doing the 'block' in a top hat and claw-hammer coat surmounting a pair of old moleskins with 'bowyang' trimmings. **1930** H. REDCLIFFE *Yellow Cygnet* 110 Here the fashionable lounger, lately of Collins Street, Melbourne, redolent in attar of roses and the scent of opoponax, 'doing the block' in spatted boots.

block, *n.*[3] In the phr. **to do** (or **lose**) **one's block, (a)** to lose one's temper; **(b)** to lose one's heart (to someone).

1907 C. MACALISTER *Old Pioneering Days* 19 At this Mr Donovan 'lost his block' completely. **1915** C.J. DENNIS *Songs of Sentimental Bloke* 34 She knoo. I've done me block in on 'er, straight. A cove 'as got to think some time in life An' get some decent tart, ere it's too late, To be 'is wife. **1918** *Aussie: Austral. Soldiers' Mag.* Sept. 7/2 A bloke must be barmy to do his block on a froggie bint, when there's tarts like these in Aussie. **1919** C. DREW *Doings of Dave* 41 Did you lose your block last night or what? **1927** A. WRIGHT *Squatter's Secret* 130 He lost his block and settled her. **1952** C. SIMPSON *Come away, Pearler* 108 What's her game, Ty? Is she doing this to get a ride to Darwin—or has she done her block on you? **1967** J. WYNNUM *I'm Jack, all Right* 60 I'd do my block a lot less if I was treated differently. **1974** J. JOST *This is Harry Flynn* 47 Look cobber . . I didn't mean to do me block the other night. . . You know. When I pushed you in the face. **1980** ANSELL & PERCY *To fight Wild* 112 Of course I did my block: 'Get off that fuckin' horse and come over here, you old bastard.'

block, *n.*[4] *Obs.* A block of wood used in road-making: see quot. 1954. Freq. *attrib.*

1894 W.A. SMITH *On Austral. Hard Woods* 10 In Sydney, there are blocks which have been laid thirteen years in one of the busiest streets of the city, which are today in a perfect state of preservation. **1934** J.S. NEILSON *Autobiogr.* (1978) 53 We . . got a contract for making a road and a culvert on a black flat near Swanhill. It was a wet autumn and we got badly caught on the block ground. **1954** *Bulletin* (Sydney) 3 Nov. 12/2 Section of an old 'block' road, last of its kind in W.A., is to be preserved as a memorial to the pioneers who built it. . . The road was built by felling trees up to 3 ft. in diameter, sawing off rounds about 9 in. thick, and laying them side by side on a formed sand foundation.

block, *v.*[1] *Mining. Obs.* [Spec. use of *block* to cut out: see OED *v.* 10.] *trans.* In the phr. **to block out,** to excavate (gold-bearing wash-dirt) in sections. Also *intr.*

1862 J.A. PATTERSON *Gold Fields Vic.* 128 When the tunnel is driven . . and the drives are made, and the roof propped . . 'blocking out' the wash-dirt begins, and the stuff is . . piled at the bottom till the supply of water permits 'washing-up' to take place. **1871** *Austral. Town & Country Jrnl.* (Sydney) 15 Apr. 463/3 A shaft 52 feet deep has been sunk, and the shareholders are engaged night and day blocking out. **1877** G. WALCH *Hash* 61 We were *blocking out* near our western boundary, in a fair way to work out the claim in four days.

block, *v.*[2] *Obs.* [Spec. use of *block* to mark out: see OED *v.* 9.] *trans.* In the phr. **to block off** (or **out**), to place markers at the angles of (a mining claim), as required by law. Also *intr.*

1871 *Austral. Town & Country Jrnl.* (Sydney) 4 Feb. 143/3 This claim is not yet lawfully blocked off. *Ibid.* 11 Feb. 166/4 No. 7 has blocked off, having defeated the 'jumpers'. ***c* 1882** T.F. DE C. BROWNE *Miners' Handy Bk.* (ed. 2) 11 On a frontage lead the block claim is exactly the same size that a frontage claim for the same number of miners is, when 'blocked off'—see Regulation 20.

block, *v.*[3] *Obs.* [Spec. use of *block* to make with blocks of wood: see OED *v.* 11 and BLOCK *n.*[4]] *trans.* To surface (a road) with blocks.

1891 *Argus* (Melbourne) 25 Nov. 7/8 Only those streets in which the most traffic takes place will be blocked.

block and tackle. [Fig. use of *block and tackle* rope and pulley-block (also U.S.).] A watch and chain.

1899 *Western Champion* (Barcaldine) 25 Apr. 12/5 One of our own crowd had his 'block and tackle' (watch and chain) taken from him not so long ago. **1962** D. MCLEAN *World turned upside Down* 105 Somewhere Arnot had a gold watch and chain, known in the 'Loo as a 'block and tackle'.

block boy. A street-cleaner.

1918 *Shire & Municipal Rec.* X. Feb. 275/2 *Log of the Federated Municipal and Shire Council Employees' Union of Australia.* Wages and Working Conditions. . . Block Boys . . £1 16 0. **1919** *Bulletin* (Sydney) 1 Mar. 19/3, I live at 639 Harris Street, Ultimo, and am in the employ of the City Council as a block boy. **1942** *Guinea Gold* 27 Nov. 4 Several boys employed as 'block boys' by the Melbourne City Council left their street-cleaning jobs. **1945** E.W. CAMPBELL *Hist. Austral. Labour Movt.* 99 The block boys, employed by the City Council, objected to pursuing their usual calling while horses driven by free laborers remained on the streets, and . . struck work.

blocker. [f. BLOCK *n.*[1] 2.]

1. *Obs.* One who occupies a small block of rural or semi-rural land.

1890 *Quiz* (Adelaide) 9 May 2/1 *Quiz* has never lost his mental balance in gushing on the subject of homestead blocks, but at the same time he heartily congratulates the blockers on the success of their show. **1892** E.H. HALLACK *Our Townships, Farms, & Homesteads* 128 The homesteads of four blockers are seen in the gully to the left, and I was thankful to note that there is a good deal of unalienated Government land. **1897** L. LINDLEY-COWEN *W. Austral. Settler's Guide* 189 The Midland district is not the place for 'blockers' *i.e.,* 10 and 20 acre men. **1899** *Progress* (Brisbane) 11 Feb. 1/3 Workmen's trains at suitable times and cheap fares are run to take the blockers to their work and bring them back. **1901** *Bulletin* (Sydney) 23 Mar. (Red Page), The Adelaide gutter-snipe and the sand-hopping son of the 'blocker' are much alike in their speed, and supply 'types' of 'Australese'. **1910** *Huon Times* (Franklin) 16 Mar. 4/3 As the result of the rain-storms, the properties of many blockers near Murray-bridge were inundated.

2. *spec.* The proprietor of a small holding: see BLOCK *n.*[1] 6.

1934 J.S. NEILSON *Autobiogr.* (1978) 131 I reported the matter to the blocker's wife. **1943** *Bulletin* (Sydney) 1 Sept. 12/4 There's more outback color around the Mid-Murray's oldest town Euston . . than in any place I know. . . The population includes whalers . . grape blockers and even wheat cockies over the river. **1946** A.M. LAPTHORNE *Mildura Calling* 45 The word 'blocker', or 'blockie' as it is often called, originally referred to the owner of a block of land comprising ten or more acres, but is now used for smaller land-holders of fruit properties. **1948** *Bulletin* (Sydney) 10 Mar. 22/3 We took a job with a blocker in Mildura. **1963** R. MCGREGOR-HASTIE *Compleat Migrant* 62 Every year the Murray rises more than ever before, which is very good business for the blockers who see new faces during the raising of levees to keep the river off their oranges. **1968** J. BEGLEY *Block with One Holer* 14 During late February and early March Bluey and Flo picked grapes for other blockers.

3. *Mining.* An occupant of a category of claim (see BLOCK *n.*[1] 5).

1890 'R. BOLDREWOOD' *Miner's Right* 76 Some of the impatient holders of claims on 'the line' frontages and others who were merely 'blockers' or occupants of ordinary chance claims anywhere in the vicinity, were more impatient.

blockie. Also **blocky.** [f. BLOCK *n.*[1] 6 + -Y.] BLOCKER 2.

1944 A.J. & J.J. MCINTYRE *Country Towns of Vic.* 185 The irrigation districts, and particularly the Mildura district, present a contrast. . . Here the blockies' wives are in everything, and it is the town women who are in the minority. **1950** G. FARWELL *Surf Music* 22 Don't bring him up to be a blockie, girl. . . Growing grapes, that's no life for a man. Send him out in the bush. **1967** E. HUXLEY *Their Shining Eldorado* 112 Round Mildura the irrigated land is squared off into rectangular blocks and many of the blockies, as the owners are called, are Greeks or Italians. **1979** C. STONE *Running Brumbies* 120 There we found a 'blocky', who owned one of the irrigation blocks, who gave us work but drove a pretty hard bargain. **1983** *Austral.* (Sydney) 11 Feb. 7/1 You must remember that bushies, from graziers through to the fruit and vegetable blockies, are getting a rough deal. **1986** *Sydney Morning Herald* 15 Feb. 7/1 The opening of a coal mine . . and a gradual influx of 'blockies'—small subdivision farmers—has picked up most of the slack from the rural downturn.

bloke. A person in authority or of superior status.

1841 B. WAIT *Lett. from Van Dieman's Land* (1843) 265 These removes are always made 'under the rose', (in secret) principally when the 'bloke' (proprietor) is out. **1913** W.O. LILLEY *Reminisc. of Life in Brisbane* 9, I had heard the term 'bloke' applied to a clergyman, but I was told that the word was not intended to be uncomplimentary, and that it was a common term used by young colonials, for dignitaries, both of Church and State. **1915** *Bulletin* (Sydney) 28 Oct. 22/3 The part of the woolshed where the barbering is done is 'the board', and the party who supervises the work is the 'boss of the board', 'the boss', 'pitch-en-toss', 'the bloke'. **1966** T. RONAN *Once there was Bagman* 2 See if you can work me in for a yarn with the Bloke. I'll bite him if you won't.

blood. [Spec. use of *blood* red.] In the names of birds: **blood-bird,** either of two birds, the *scarlet honeyeater* (see SCARLET), and the *red-headed honeyeater* (see RED *a.* 1 b.); **-finch,** *crimson finch*, see CRIMSON.

1843 J. GOULD *Birds of Aust.* (1848) IV. Pl. 63, *Sanguineous Honey-eater*. . . **Blood-bird** of the Colonists of New

South Wales. **1917** *Bulletin* (Sydney) 5 July 24/1 The gorgeous black and yellow regent-bird takes some beating, but I think the rare blood-bird . . runs it very close in the beauty competition. **1964** M. SHARLAND *Territory of Birds* 136 Resembling [a humming bird] in the manner in which it hovers in front of flowers, in the shape of its bill, the flickering movements, the brilliant hood and back, is the Red-headed Honeyeater, the 'blood-bird', as it is usually known. **1928** G.H. WILKINS *Undiscovered Aust.* 143 **Blood-finches** passed through each year in migration. **1944** K.S. PRICHARD *Potch & Colour* 115, I got a blood-finch this morning . . and he's rare. See, the brown bird, all red on his back and breast. **1964** M. SHARLAND *Territory of Birds* 137 The Crimson (Blood) Finch . . is restricted to pandanus palms on the banks of permanent water.

blood house. [f. *blood* bloodshed + *(public) house*.] A disorderly public house; one with a reputation for violence.

[N.Z. **1951** *Evening Post* (Wellington) 13 Jan. 12 For many years its customers earned it the reputation of a 'blood house' and the licensee's job of keeping the peace was a hard one.] **1952** A.C.C. LOCK *Travels across Aust.* 140 In Queensland it would have been called a 'blood house'; a hotel whose management was interested only in getting the maximum number of people drunk in the minimum time. **1965** K. MCKENNEY *Hide-Away Man* 25 'This place is a real blood house of a Saturday.' . . 'Think I'll need a bodyguard?' **1970** *Kings Cross Whisper* (Sydney) lxxxi. 8/5 *Drinkers* must not call pubs blood houses. **1977** R. BEILBY *Gunner* 128 You bloody booze hound! . . I've hauled you out of every boozer and blood house from here to Perth.

blood tree. *Obs.* BLOODWOOD.

[**1805** J. GRANT Jrnl. 40 Un arbre cède, sur une incision fait avec mon Canif—une liqueur rouge comme le Sang—Une Vigne aussi donne la même—appellé de leur Nature—l'arbre de Sang, Vigne de Sang.] **1827** *Trans. Linnean Soc. London* XV. 271 *Mun'ning-trees*, or *Blood-trees* of the colonists (a species of *Eucalyptus*). **1859** *Bell's Life in Sydney* 18 June 1/1 Split posts of iron bark, blood-tree, or other durable timber are substituted for saplings. **1892** *Proc. Linnean Soc. N.S.W.* VI. 412 That (kino) from a species called 'Blood-tree' is heated . . by the blacks of Lake Macquarie . . and applied to external wounds. **1903** *Ibid.* XXVII. 539 *E. Squamosa* . . is now found to extend as far north as Putty, 50 miles south of Singleton, where it is known as 'Blood-tree'.

bloodwood.

1. Any of many trees of the genus *Eucalyptus* (fam. Myrtaceae), typically having a rough, tesselated, persistent bark and exuding a viscous reddish kino when damaged; the wood of these trees, usu. having abundant veins and pockets of kino; BLOOD TREE. Also *attrib.*

1827 *HRA* (1923) 3rd Ser. VI. 503 The Banks on both sides are covered with very large Timber . . such as . . Blood Wood. **1846** *Portland Gaz.* 14 Apr. 4/5 The bloodwood and ironbark are generally of a good size for building huts. **1851** J. HENDERSON *Excursions & Adventures N.S.W.* II. 214 The Bloodwood is a rather handsome tree, crowned in its season with a pretty white blossom. It gets its name from the red colour of its wood. A good deal of blood-coloured gum exudes from it. **1882** W. SOWDEN *N.T. as it Is* 45 The initials of the distinguished journeyers had been deeply graven in the impervious bloodwood. **1904** J.H. MAIDEN *Notes on Commercial Timbers N.S.W.* 19 *Bloodwood* . . one of the most durable of all Australian timbers. **1938** R. INGAMELLS *Sun-Freedom* 38 Bleached bones tied to a bloodwood tree! **1963** C. BURGESS *Blue Mountain Gums* 18 The kino, blood red when fresh, trickles slowly down the bark, hence the name 'Bloodwood'. **1977** R. MCKIE *Crushing* (1978) 151 A bloodwood whose sap cured dysentery.

2. Special Comb. **bloodwood apple,** a rounded gall formed on the smaller branches of the tree in response to insect damage.

1903 H. BASEDOW *Jrnl. Govt. N.-W. Exped.* (1914) 108 Our natives have collected a bagful of what they call 'bloodwood apples'. **1927** M. TERRY *Through Land of Promise* 203 Among its leaves are bloodwood apples. **1969** A.A. ABBIE *Original Australs.* 69 Among the less likely items of vegetable food are grubs found in the galls ('mulga apple', 'bloodwood apple') formed on trees by insect parasites. **1975** A.B. & J.W. CRIBB *Wild Food in Aust.* 215 'Bloodwood apples' have nothing to do with the fruit of the rough-barked eucalypts known as bloodwoods.

bloody, *a.* and *adv.* Also in tmesis. [Used as in general English but from its frequency and ubiquity often thought of as characteristically Austral.: see *Australian adjective* AUSTRALIAN *a.* 4.]

A. *adj.*

1. An intensive, ranging in force from 'mildly irritating' to 'execrable'.

1814 *HRA* (1916) 1st Ser. VIII. 363 He said Bloody Main at the Toll bar; he said that Main informed against some Bushrangers. **1817** *Ibid.* (1917) 1st Ser. IX. 596 They heard some of the Guard on the Quarter Deck call out, Shoot the bloody Doctor. **1847** A. MARJORIBANKS *Travels N.S.W.* 57 The word bloody is the favourite oath in that country. One man will tell you that he married a bloody young wife, another, a bloody old one; and a bushranger will call out, 'Stop, or I'll blow your bloody brains out.' I had once the curiosity to count the number of times that a bullock driver used this word in the course of a quarter of an hour, and found that he did so twenty-five times. I gave him eight hours in the day to sleep, and six to be silent, thus leaving ten hours for conversation. I supposed that he had commenced at twenty and continued till seventy years of age . . and found that in the course of that time he must have pronounced this disgusting word no less than 18,200,000 times. **1849** C. STURT *Narr. Exped. Central Aust.* I. 111 Nadbuck . . whispered to us, 'Bloody rogue that fellow, you look after jimbuck.' **1894** M. ROBERTS *Red Earth* 101 Devil a man will you get to sharpen his shears to put into your bloody wool. **1927** A. CROMBIE *After Sixty Yrs.* 142 Although the word 'bloody' may have been more frequently in use 50 years ago than it is to-day, the man of the West used it in the same sense as the Johnnie used the words, jolly, or consummate. The bush adjective was neither obscene nor profane. **1929** F. MANNING *Middle Parts of Fortune* 170 'Beer here's bloody,' said Marlow. **1940** A. HASKELL *Waltzing Matilda* 35 'Bloody' is the great Australian adjective. **1944** M.J. O'REILLY *Bowyangs & Boomerangs* 80 You must think yourself a damned clever bushman, talking about tracking a bloody dingo over bloody ground where a bloody regiment of newly-shod horses would scarcely leave a bloody track. **1955** 'M. HILL' *Land nearest Stars* 108 We came to the first ramp and gate—on which was printed in letters a foot high *shut the bloody gate*. **1967** A. SEYMOUR *One Day of Yr.* 28 I'm a bloody Australian and I'll always stand up for bloody Australia. **1976** B. SCOTT *Compl. Bk. Austral. Folk Lore* 303 Shootin' kanga-bloody-roos At Tumba-bloody-rumba. **1980** ANSELL & PERCY *To fight Wild* 16 He might decide he doesn't want to go to bloody Hall's Creek after all and go home.

2. In the collocation **(my) blood(y) oath,** an intensive form of *my oath* (see OATH).

1848 R. MARSH *Seven Yrs. of my Life* 70 Come along you bloody crawlers, you'll have to walk faster than this tomorrow, with a cart load of stone—my bloody oath you will. **1932** R.W. THOMPSON *Down Under* 56 My bloody oath—drunk all the time—every bloody minute. **1967** M. & M. LEYLAND *Where Dead Men Lie* 20 Bloody oath. . . Most important part of any fishing trip is the ice box. **1968** K. DENTON *Walk around my Cluttered Mind* 5 One of the blokes said to me, 'Y' gonna havanutha cuppa, digger?' And I said, 'Blood oath, mate!' **1971** D. WILLIAMSON *Don's Party* (1973) 27 'Did he say that?' . . 'Bloody oath he said it.'

B. *adv.* An intensive: extremely, very.

1823 *HRA* (1917) 1st Ser. XI. 45, I know bloody well who the Captain meant to shoot. **1846** L.W. MILLER *Notes of Exile Van Dieman's Land* 280, I caught our worthy overseer *putting away* (eating) what he called 'a bloody good feed', which he had obtained from the wardsman whose dirty work we were performing. **1859** W. KELLY *Life in Vic.* I. 76 He declared 'we were a bloody rubbishy gang of lime-juicers'. **1872** J.M. CONROY *False* 42 He did not say 'bloody'; thus he had no kin with those sanguine wits who, whether they wear moleskins or frock-coats, unconsciously, by the use of the word, indicate the natural family they belong to. **1914** *Bulletin* (Sydney) 30 July 22/2, I see how a bloke in the old dart named Shaw has wrote a play and makes a tart say 'bloody'. **1934** T. WOOD *Cobbers* 175 'It's bloody high, Bill,' said an admirer from the backblocks, gazing up at the tower of Brisbane's City Hall. 'Aw,' said Bill, 'not so bloody.' **1944** C. WILMOT *Tobruk* 53 Here we bloody-well are; and here we bloody-well stay. **1958** *Coast to Coast 1957–58* 51 Good day, missus. Bloody hot, ain't it? **1975** R.J. MERRITT *Cake Man* (1978) 16 Know what happens when y' cross a black crow with a white rooster? Y' get a magpie. That's why we got so bloody many magpies in Australia and parts elsewhere.

blot. [Transf. use of *blot* dark patch.] The anus.

1945 S.J. BAKER *Austral. Lang.* 156 [World War II slang.] *Blot*, the posterior or anus. **1965** W. DICK *Bunch of Ratbags* 262 He pushed me away and he gave me a kick up the blot. **1967** *Kings Cross Whisper* (Sydney) xxxix. 8/4 *Too Many Bums on Buses* . . 'They have travelled to many capitals of the world, calculating the size of the average Anglo-Saxon khyber. . . There are not enough people with average-sized blots,' Mr Horror said. **1971** F. HARDY *Outcasts of Foolgarah* 57 'Well, we just thought we'd ask your advice,' Tich said, disappointed but still respectful. 'Get out of his blot,' Chilla said. **1974** D. IRELAND *Burn* 146 Maybe he'll grab this last chance for some action after sitting on his blot all these years.

blotch, *v. Obs.* [Spec. use of *blotch* to mark, disfigure.] *trans.* To obscure (a brand on an animal).

1899 G.E. BOXALL *Story Austral. Bushrangers* 355 The manner in which brands might be 'faked' was endless, and when it was impossible to 'fake' a brand it was 'blotched' or burned over, so that the original design could not be recognised.

Hence **blotch-brand** *n. Obs.*

1880 'ERRO' *Squattermania* 111 Dan appeared with the well-heated blotch-brand, and clapping it over the letters I.R., previously stamped on the near side of the bullocks, soon rendered them . . illegible.

blow, *n.*[1] *Obs.* [Chiefly Br. dial. and U.S. *blow* boast: see OED *sb.*[2] 2 and EDD *sb.*[1] 6.] A boast; boasting.

1867 *Sydney Punch* 19 Oct. 169/2 Australia's hope and 'blow'. [*Note*] 'Blow', *Anglice*, Boast. 'Quite Colonial!'—Ed. **1871** *Austral. Town & Country Jrnl.* (Sydney) 25 Mar. 359/2 They are undoubtedly a very good lot of bullocks, but certainly do not deserve all the blow that has been bestowed upon them. **1885** *Australasian Printers' Keepsake* 162 A European typo, working in Sydney, was grievously galled by the 'blow' of the cornstalks. **1892** F.A. HARE *Last of Bushrangers* 127 Kelly often said . . that it was no use resisting, . . as he had eight armed men outside . . but this was only 'blow'. **1895** *Bulletin* (Sydney) 19 Oct. 7/4 The beginning and end and the whole was blow—Australian blow, Our own blow, Not the Brummagem foreign kind—Oh no! But good old, genuine, 'possum—and platypus, bright Australian blow. **1918** *Huon Times* (Franklin) 29 Oct. 3/2 He was inclined at first to regard the reports of their prowess as, to use his own words, mere 'blow' because, being an Australian he knows how some of them can 'blow'.

blow, *n.*[2] *Shearing.* [Spec. use of *blow* firm stroke, recorded in EDD Suppl. as meaning 'the mark left by the shears'.] A stroke of the shears.

1870 *Austral. Town & Country Jrnl.* (Sydney) 5 Nov. 11/2 Every 'blow' of the shears is acutely painful. **1878** 'IRONBARK' *Southerly Busters* 180 My tally's eighty-five a day—A hundred I could go, If coves would let me 'open out' and take a bigger 'blow'. **1895** *Worker* (Sydney) 27 July 1/3 Small blows first, then open wider as the stiffness leaves your wrist. **1912** J. BRADSHAW *Highway Robbery under Arms* (ed. 3) 23 Then came the woolly hoggets, which took a bit of doing with a big blow. **1936** E.W. COX *Evol. Austral. Merino* 149 The crutching should be a thorough one—well over the tail—say, two 'blows' of the machine. **1956** R.G. EDWARDS *Overlander Songbk.* 101 *Click go the Shears* . . *Chorus:* Click go the shears, boys, Click! Click! Click! Wide is his blow, and his hands move quick. **1975** L.A. POCKLEY *Handbk. for Jackeroos* 103 A 'belly blow' may be made to clean the wool from around the udder to make it easier for the lamb to find the teat and not start sucking a lock of wool in error. **1979** HARMSWORTH & DAY *Wool & Mohair* 153 Sufficient wool must be removed over the tail . . so that the sheep will not have to be lifted for the last few blows.

blow, *n.*[3] [f. *blow* to erupt: see OED *v.*[1] 26.] A body, usu. outcropping, of quartz or other mineral substance.

1871 *Austral. Town & Country Jrnl.* (Sydney) 25 Mar. 367/4 And when 7 feet had been driven, the reef, or a kind of a 'blow' was met with. The holders then started to drive on this 'blow', but when 4 feet had been driven it changed into a well-defined reef of blue-looking quartz. **1881** A.C. GRANT *Bush-Life Qld.* II. 263 They came upon a large 'blow' or outcrop of quartz, sticking out of the earth, over the surface of which were scattered detached blocks of the same substance. **1887** *N.T. Times Almanac* 108 The term generally used by the miners for the outcrops of the heads of a vein is a 'blow', and the idea of their origin is connected with the action of fire. **1898** D.W. CARNEGIE *Spinifex & Sand* 107 Strange inner urgings . . make him examine a certain quartz reef or blow that others have passed. **1909** *Bulletin* (Sydney) 18 Mar. 13/1 Some diggers near Gundagai used the floaters from a neighbouring 'blow' for a fireplace wherein to boil their billies. **1918** J.A. PHILP *Jingles that Jangle* 46 Dives owns the hoards of gold, Every reef and 'blow'. **1946** K.S. PRICHARD *Roaring Nineties* 40, I prospected the big blow and got gold at both the north and the south ends. **1976** *Tracks we Travel* 121 A lifetime of deserts and dried watercourses, of outcrops of reef beneath rotten granite and 'blows' of quartz among shale.

blow, *n.*[4] [f. *blow* to smoke (tobacco): see OED *v.*[1] 9 b.] A rest (from the association between smoking and relaxing).

[**1855** R. CARBONI *Eureka Stockade* 10 He must have a 'blow', but the d--d things—his matches—had got damp, and so in a rage he must hasten to his tent to light the pipe.] **1910** *Huon Times* (Franklin) 26 Feb. 2/3 We didn't even get time to have a blow before we were called on to get on with the job again. **1915** J.P. BOURKE *Off Bluebush* 66 Hello, on top! Hello! Ease off, and have a blow! We've a crushin' in the paddock, and there's more below! **1952** T.A.G. HUNGERFORD *Ridge & River* 129 'Have a blow,' said Shearwood. 'Five minutes—and don't smoke.' **1959** *Overland* xvi. 18 Time we had a cup of brew. One more and we'll take a blow. **1978** H.C. BAKER *I was Listening* 139 Panting, he added, 'What about a blow? That's . . nearly . . four rounds!' **1984** W.W. AMMON et al. *Working Lives* 24 Look, they've been in the scrub belting their guts out. . . Don't you think they're entitled to a bit of a blow.

blow, *n.*[5] A cyclone; a very strong wind.

1935 *Frontier News* July 6/1 The week before our arrival they had had a blow which lasted three days and three nights. Afterwards she took forty-two kerosene buckets of sand out of her two front rooms. **1941** K.S. PRICHARD *Moon of Desire* 85 The divers were becoming disgruntled when a blow threatened. They reported that queer agitation along the floor of the sea which presaged a storm. **1949** C. BENHAM *Diver's Luck* 101 That cyclone was not an isolated calamity. The nor'-west coast has had more than a fair share of cockeyed-bobs, and willy-willies. Those blows . . have blasted the fortunes, lives, and property of so many men. **1950** *Coast to Coast 1949–50* 58 We're in for a bad blow. . . There's a cyclone not far off. **1961** *Bulletin* (Sydney) 8 Feb. 26/3 During the blow, huge waves swirled over the sea-wall. **1979** T. ASTLEY *Hunting Wild Pineapple* 163 She was given to those underplay phrases so dear to our myth: 'After the blow,' she'd say, referring to our worst cyclone in years. **1981** Q. WILD *Honey Wind* 149 Then quite suddenly the wind came in heavily from the North-East, hot and dry. . . 'There's a big blow coming,' Galiali told Harry.

blow, *v.*[1] [Chiefly Br. dial. *blow* to deposit eggs: see OED *v.*[1] 28 c. and EDD *v.*[1] 10.] *trans.* Of a fly, to deposit eggs on (meat, etc.).

1827 P. CUNNINGHAM *Two Yrs. in N.S.W.* I. 270 Meat is blown here, as soon as killed, by our bottle-flies; nay, even the very meat roasting on the spit, or smoking on the table, not always escapes. **1855** W. HOWITT *Land, Labor & Gold* I. 192 The blow-flies we are quite contented with if they don't fly-blow ourselves. They blow your blankets or anything that has a particle of woollen in it. **1861** 'OLD BUSHMAN' *Bush Wanderings* 105 The flies blow so quickly, that I have often taken a bird out of my bag, killed but a few hours, a living mass of maggots. **1899** G.E. BOXALL *Story Austral. Bushrangers* 10 Great care has always to be taken to prevent sores on man or beast from being 'blown'. **1930** HIVES & LUMLEY *Jrnl. of Jackaroo* 55 Keep away the flies that would have 'blown' them. **1941** *Bulletin* (Sydney) 8 Jan. 17/4, I have seen flannel shirts, blankets and even the tail of a foal 'blown'. Going out in the paddock the other morning to gather mushrooms I found that every one was 'blown'. **1975** A. MARSHALL *Hammers over Anvil* 32 I've never seen a woman take meat out of a safe without smelling it all over. If it had just been blown there was a little pile of maggots.

Hence **blown** *ppl. a.*, fly-blown.

1910 *Bulletin* (Sydney) 7 July 7/4 The blowfly pest means big trouble. . . The sheep are continually 'blown', which means great suffering to the animals. **1954** *Ibid.* 13 Jan. 12/2 One spring we had an abnormal rush of blown sheep and the boss put on a couple of extra hands to help.

blow, *v.*[2] [Chiefly Br. dial. and U.S. *blow* to boast: see OED *v.*[1] 6 a.] *intr.* To boast; to exaggerate.

1858 C.R. THATCHER *Colonial Songster* (rev. ed.) 35 About your talents *blow*, Mind, that's the regular caper. **1865** *Sydney Punch* 16 Dec. 649/2 'Tis money makes the mare to go—That makes the Mayor 'shout', For tho' without it he may blow, He never can 'blow out'. **1879** 'NEW CHUM' *Ramble in Launceston* 53 The Victorian 'swell' . . is slightly intoxicated, and 'blows' greatly. **1887** A. NICOLS *Wild Life & Adventure* 87 Why, many a squatter goes flashing round and blowing about 'his run'. **1899** *Progress* (Brisbane) 3/2 Some people blow about the Chow being a law-abiding individual. **1907** C. MACALISTER *Old Pioneering Days* 129 Two teamsters, one from Cooma, and the other from Queanbeyan, got 'blowing' over the merits of their horses. **1917** *Life & Experiences of Successful W. Austral.* 45 The great feature of the young Australian was his tendency to 'blow'. **1930** 'BRENT OF BIN BIN' *Ten Creeks Run* (1952) 20 Aw, you're allers blowing about the old days. **1952** J. CLEARY *Sundowners* 88 'It was no worse than a landslide I was in in the Himalayas.' 'Always blowing. . . '

Hence **blowing** *vbl. n.* and *ppl. a.*

1858 A. PENDRAGON *Queen of South* 55 Wilson, from his constant habit of romancing, peculiar to colonists, and colonially termed 'blowing'. **1878** 'J.W.A.' *Mike Healy's Tip* 3 If we do go in, at times for great 'blowing', Our cricket and rowing show that we well may. **1882** *Sydney Mail* 23 Dec. 1123/3 Jonathan was a blowing, blatherskiting fool. **1895** G. RANKEN *Windabyne* 94 A lie, a blowing advertisement, the wind and gas of trickery, formed the staple of his speech. **1910** *Huon Times* (Franklin) 27 Apr. 3/6 You will have been warned, as I was, against the 'blowing', bragging propensities of the people. **1917** *Life & Experiences of Successful W. Austral.* 45 After all it is better to be guilty of 'blowing' than hiding your light under a bushel.

blow, *v.*[3] *Horse-racing. trans.* To lengthen the odds on (a horse, etc.) Also with 'odds' as obj., and *absol.* Freq. with **out**.

1911 A. WRIGHT *Gamblers' Gold* (1923) 93 'They'll have us up!' whined Nelson. 'I wish y'd never started th' bally horse. A nice thing to be blown out just as—.' 'We won't get blown out,' growled Ralph. 'Alan's book will show that I backed Rikai.' **1922** —— *Boss o' Yedden* 129 'Ain't Lobitout fav'rit?' he gasped. 'Lobitout? No!' snapped the stranger. 'Got blown right out.' **1949** L. GLASSOP *Lucky Palmer* 63 I've got the commission for it this end of the ring, and I'm trying to blow the price out. **1968** J. ALARD *He who shoots Last* 86 'She's blown in the bettin',' said a suspicious Ragged.

blow, *v.*[4] [Phrasal use of *blow* to leave hurriedly: see OEDS *v.*[1] 12 e.] *intr.* With **through**: to leave, esp. in a hurry.

1950 *Austral. Police Jrnl.* Apr. 110 Blow through . . Go away, leave. **1968** J. HIBBERD *Who?* (1970) 141 Why don't you take a hint? Why don't you blow through, clear off, right now? **1970** R. BEILBY *No Medals for Aphrodite* 14 'I didn't land her. She just came along.' . . 'Then tell her to blow through.' **1978** L. HORSPHOL *Turn down Empty Glass* 41 I can't see any future in us hanging around here. I reckon we ought to blow through! **1981** A. MARSHALL *Aust.* 37 'When he is down, don't hang round, blow through,' a king-hit expert once told me. 'When he gets up you might find he can scrap.'

blow, *v.*[5] *Obs.* In the phr. **to blow the froth (off),** to drink beer. Also *fig.*

1910 L. ESSON *Three Short Plays* (1911) 17, I don' forget 'ow you stuck to me. . . Ah, blow ther froth orf. **1912** —— *Red Gums* 36 Give the push the office, Pass the 'at erlong, . . Won't we blow the froth orf! Jugger's owt ter-d'y. **1931** D.B. O'CONNOR *Black Velvet* 30 There's a pub around the corner You must blow the froth with me.

blower. *Obs.* [Br. dial. and U.S. *blower* boaster: see OED *sb.*[1] 5.] A boaster.

1864 J. SNODGRASS *N.S.W. as Is* 8 He was not only communicative, but talkative. . . He was, what is usually termed in colonial parlance, a 'blower' i.e., one who never ceases talking of himself in particular, and everything in general. **1876** 'EIGHT YRS.' RESIDENT' *Queen of Colonies* 141 Day after day you see men sitting on their ground from eleven to twelve, chaffing each other, or listening to a 'blower' spinning a yarn. **1890** 'R. BOLDREWOOD' *Colonial Reformer* III. 149 A regular Sydney man thinks all Victorians are blowers and speculators. **1899** J. BRADSHAW *Quirindi Bank Robbery* 24 He was the ringer at Hammond's, and not a blower.

blowey, *n.*[1] Also **blowie.** [f. *blow(fly* + -Y.] A blowfly, esp. *Lucilia cuprina* , introduced to Australia in the twentieth century.

1916 J.B. COOPER *Coo-oo-ee!* 84 A dead jumbuck is buzzing with blowies. **1952** H.P. DOWN *Out Fishing* 69 'We catch our fish on flies.' . . 'What sort of flies? March flies or Blowies?' **1972** K. DUNSTAN *Knockers* 14 Finally there was the blowfly, better known as the Blowey, which was unquestionably a native of this country. **1972** P. MATHERS *Wort Papers* 36 Resplendent in navy singlet, white jodhpurs, sandshoes and digger hat with dangling corks black with blowies. **1981** B. HUMPHRIES *Nice Night's Entertainment* 83 Beryl had given the home a good going over with the Flytox so we wouldn't have to race the blowies to our dinner.

blowey, *n.*[2] Chiefly *W.A.* Also **blowy.** [f. *blow(fish* + -Y.] A blowfish, esp. *Torquigener pleurogramma*, a marine fish with potentially poisonous flesh.

1916 *Bulletin* (Sydney) 24 Feb. 22/2 It has been stated that the toad fish is rarely found outside of Japanese waters. In the Swan River and in the waters surrounding Fremantle 'blowy', as he is named, abounds. **1945** *Ibid.* 24 Jan. 13/4 Fish were plentiful, and none more so than the 'blowey'. **1960** *Ibid.* 9 Mar. 16/1 Many tailer lately caught north and south of Fremantle have had blowfish in them, so it looks as though they've developed a taste for the blowies and a resistance to their poisonous properties. **1974** *Ibid.* 16 Nov. 10/1 Japanese gourmets relish a variety of blowfish. . . The big nor'-west blowies seem to be just what the cook ordered.

blowfly. [Fig. use of *blow-fly.*] One who acts officiously.

1899 *Bulletin* (Sydney) 26 Aug. 16/2 Police are sometimes called 'blowflies'. On the Condamine (Q.) I heard—'Going to kill the brindle steer today father?' 'No, Sonny; the blowflies are too bad. I asked Sonny what his father meant, and he explained that 'the old cove must have heard that the police are about'. **1918** *Truth* (Sydney) 15 Dec. 6/6 Under the rule of the Blowflies, the A.W.U., if all unionists belonged to it, would really be . . an 'industrial blowfly', a most serious parasitical pest to the people and a menace to democracy. **1977** J. O'GRADY *There was Kid* 68 The 'blow flies' [Army hygiene personnel] insisted that we construct a urinal.

Hence **blowflyism** *n.*

1918 *Truth* (Sydney) 28 July 7/1 The spurious form of One-Big-Unionism favoured by some of the A.W.U. officials (which has been aptly named 'Blowflyism'). *Ibid.* 4 Aug. 6/7 Its unionism is not industrialism, but 'Blowflyism'. It has destroyed the individual existence and identity of the unions that have amalgamated with it, and has simply swallowed them.

blow-hole. [Transf. use of *blow-hole* hole through which a whale 'blows'.] **a.** In coastal rock, a hole through which air or water rushes in response to the action of waves. **b.** Inland, a vent through which air passes, often with some force, to or from an underground air reservoir in response to temperature variation.

1849 J. TOWNSEND *Rambles & Observations N.S.W.* 141 At Kiama is a cavern running horizontally into the cliffs on the sea-side, and open to the sea. . . A gigantic fountain spouts through the opening, or 'blow-hole', to the height of sixty feet. **1855** *Illustr. Sydney News* 28 Apr. 204/3 It is a blow-hole particularly grand when in full blast. The entrance to the subterranean passage is in the form of a vast arch opening into a cavern from the sea. . . The advancing sea enters and swells onwards with only a gentle murmuring for a distance of about

200 feet—then a wall of black basalt stands before it against which it throws itself with a deafening roar and then dashes up through an opening forty feet deep, rising in a column in the air. **1894** A.F. CALVERT *Coolgardie Goldfield* 51 Our route was . . through salt bush and cotton bush country. . . The formation is of a limestone character full of blow holes. **1923** H. LEAF *Under Southern Cross* 71 A peculiar feature of some parts of the plain are 'blowholes', openings in the surface connected with the underworld. **1936** J. KIRWAN *My Life's Adventure* 263 The ground beneath the surface is honeycombed with caves—. . . They are approached by 'blow-holes' through which wind comes. **1938** D. BATES *Passing of Aborigines* 132 Scattered over the surface are numerous blow-holes through which the ocean winds sweep violently and hot gusts of summer are sucked down with a loud roaring. **1966** N. SIDNEY *Beyond Bay* 43 'Then for the blowhole,' Sandra called, and rushed to squash down the wet swimsuits in her haversack. **1980** G.R. COCHRANE et al. *Flowers & Plants Vic. & Tas.* (rev. ed.) 162 The spectacular cliffs, blowhole and tessellated pavement at Eaglehawk Neck are formed in Permian mudstone.

blowie, var. BLOWEY *n.*[1]

blow-in. [f. (orig. U.S.) *blow in* to turn up unexpectedly: see OEDS *blow v.*[1] 12 d.] A newcomer or recent arrival; an intruder.

1937 E. HILL *Great Austral. Loneliness* 32 They had been painted by a 'blow-in', an Englishman named Malcolmsen, said to have been a crack steeplechase rider in his day. **1950** G.S. CASEY *City of Men* 252 They were known as 'blow-ins' and worthy citizens who had remained on the goldfields during the lean years . . found virtue in the fact that they had stood by the town, resented the newcomers and shouted their dislike to the skies. **1952** C. SIMPSON *Come away, Pearler* 223 You get the blow-ins—coves who're wanted in other States. **1957** D. WHITINGTON *Treasure upon Earth* 97 'I felt like an interloper. This fight isn't our fight. We're—we're—.' 'Blow-ins.' **1968** J. O'GRADY *Gone Troppo* 94 'Every Australian kid ought to know something about the history of his country.' 'I agree. But all they taught was about you blow-ins.' 'Blow-ins?' 'Yes. White men.' **1973** L. OAKES *Whitlam PM* 51 There were also people in the local ALP who simply resented a man they regarded as an academic blow-in who was in the habit of lecturing them like a schoolteacher. **1979** D. LOCKWOOD *My Old Mates & I* 61 They came just as the Indonesian blow-ins do every year. **1986** *Sydney Morning Herald* 14 June 44/6 Some blow-ins to Canberra . . said recently that the 'board under Wilenski' had lost its once powerful position.

blow my (or **me**) **skull (off),** *n. phr.* An alcoholic drink: see quots. Also **blow-your-hat-off.**

1853 C.R. READ *What I heard, saw, & Did* 172 '*Blow my skull off*'. . . Some of the ingredients . . were as follows:- 'Cocculus indicus, spirits of wine, Turkey opium, Cayenne pepper and rum'; to this was added about five times the quantity of water, and sold at 2s. 6d. per wine glass. **1864** *Colonial Cook Bk.* (1970) 152 Blow my skull. This was a colonial beverage in use in the earlier days of Tasmania, and was named and drank by an eccentric governor. . . It was made in the following proportions:- Two pints of boiling water, with 'quantum sufficit' of loaf sugar, and lime or lemon-juice, one pint of ale or porter, one pint of rum, and half a pint of brandy. **1888** G. ROCK *Colonists* 28 'Blow me skull off'. This expression . . is the popular name by which the most common decoctions sold at the diggings are known—a name too, which is well deserved. **1949** D. WALKER *We went to Aust.* 189 The great drink of the miner was 'Blow me Skull off', a mixture of wine, opium, cayenne pepper and rum that sold at 2s. 6d. a glass. **1956** *Bulletin* (Sydney) 28 Nov. 13/3 Wine purveyed there graded from 'dynamite' and 'blow-your-hat-off' to 'belltopper' brand and was pretty potent.

blow-up. [f. BLOW *n.*[4] + *-up.*] The signal that a rest period is over, and work about to begin. Also as *exclam.*

1873 THOMSON & GREGG *Desperate Character* I. 63 As his watch marked six, he shouted, in stentorian tones, 'Blow up'; and all the men fell to. **1889** H. EGBERT *Pretty Cockey* 80 When the highest scorer thought it time to set to work again, he would stand up and call out either—'Roll up!' or 'Blow up!' as he thought fit. **1951** *Bulletin* (Sydney) 21 Feb. 12/2 When, at blow-up, the 'pannikin' succeeded in bringing him back to life he crawled back to work like a blue-tongued lizard. **1968** D. IRELAND *Chantic Bird* 3 The rest of the workers liked having me around. Their day had more kick when I was there. Until each blow-up and heave-ho. **1978** H.C. BAKER *I was Listening* 130 At the call of 'Blow up!' each day, he carefully marked his place with his pencil.

blowy, var. BLOWEY *n.*[2]

blucher. [Br. *blucher* a type of boot, having local significance as part of the dress of the bushman: see quot. 1881.] A strong leather half-boot. Also *attrib.*

1839 *Southern Austral.* (Adelaide) 17 July 1/3 Just received . . Blucher boots and gents. half dress ditto. **1843** *Adelaide Observer* 16 Dec. 5/1 Tenders will be received . . for the supply of the Police Force . . with blue cloth jackets, . . blue cloth caps, and blucher boots. **1850** *Monthly Almanac* (Adelaide) 9 And in their place appear the sober Guernsey—the humble moleskin—the strong fossil shaped colonial Blucher. **1881** R. CRAWFORD *Echoes from Bushland* 77 Put him into the squatting costume of the period, namely, a twill shirt open at the neck, and a pair of moleskin trousers, a size too big, tucked over a pair of *blootcher* boots. **1911** L. STONE *Jonah* 108 The watertight bluchers with soles an inch thick that a woolwasher from Botany had ordered and left on his hands. **1930** H. REDCLIFFE *Yellow Cygnet* 110 The fashionable lounger . . was now clad in loose cotton shirt, guiltless of collar, much-worn pants tied at the shins with coarse twine, earning for him admission into the ranks of the 'boyangs', and feet encased in heavy bluchers. **1966** T. RONAN *Once there was Bagman* 14 This character wore blucher boots, slack on his feet, with the laces trailing through the scanty vegetation. **1981** G. MITCHELL *Bush Horseman* 37 If he was a timber cutter or a person who did little riding in his work, the boots could be quite heavy with hob-nailed soles. These were the Blucher boots so often mentioned in the writings of Henry Lawson.

bludge /blʌdʒ/, *v.* [Back formation from BLUDGER.] Usu. with **on.**

1. *intr.* To evade one's own responsibilities and impose on, or prey upon, others; to live off the efforts of others.

1899 *Truth* (Sydney) 12 Mar. 1/7 What else could they expect from the gang who bludge on cricket in Sydney? **1910** *Ibid.* 27 Mar. 5/1 The scallywags and scoundrels, skunks and scabs, who batten and bludge on the Bushworkers' broadsheet in Bathurst-street. **1916** *Ibid.* 25 June 11/6 This subscription-cadging practice is a standing inducement to every loafing parasite, two-up spieler, and shypoo joint-runner to bludge on the bona-fide toiler by cringing and smoodging for monetary help. **1933** J. TRURAN *Where Plain Begins* 40 'E must needs come 'ome to bludge on us, becos 'e knows 'e can allus get 'is three meals an' a bed without 'avin' to do any work for 'em. **1937** L. MANN *Murder in Sydney* 212 Britannia may be, as they say yonder she is, an immoral woman, but there's no need for Australia to bludge on her. **1957** D. WHITINGTON *Treasure upon Earth* 53 Trade union secretaries were actually bludging on the 'workers'. **1965** L. HAYLEN *Big Red* 119 He's no good. Bludging on the shed. **1967** *Kings Cross Whisper* (Sydney) xlii. 1/4 They had decided to work for a living because they were 'sick of bludging on the public'. **1976** J. JOHNSON *Low Breed* 231 A very good living was to be had bludging off radicals, drop-outs and students. **1978** R.H. CONQUEST *Dusty Distances* 128 A man has to eat. Bludge on the bastards, right and left.

2. *intr. Obs.* To live on the earnings of a prostitute.

1903 *Truth* (Sydney) 20 Dec. 5/3 The increasing number of these fellows . . togged up in fine linen and fashionable clothes, procured with sin-money wrung from the unfortunate females upon whom they bludge, is a disgrace. ***c* 1907** W.C. CHANDLER *Darkest Adelaide* 16 Until recently Connolly was bludging at Broken Hill on a frail creature named Bessie Connors. **1910** *Truth* (Sydney) 20 Feb. 7/4 *The brother 'bludges' on his sister*. . . A vile fellow who lives on the prostitution of *his own sister.*

3. *intr.* To idle, usually (by implication) at someone else's expense.

1942 *Ack Ack News* (Melbourne) Aug. 2 Three men knocked out, rest of instrument crew bludged. **1953** T.A.G. HUNGERFORD *Riverslake* 226 Poor bastards—I don't know whether I hate them or pity them or despise them, with their right to strike and rest and bludge, time-and-a-half for this and double-time for that, their danger money and their stop-work meetings. **1958** J.R. SPICER *Cry of Storm-bird* 70 He always appeared to be in the act of lighting a cigarette or sharpening his axe. This gave Rob a feeling of angry satisfaction: 'Bludging over there while I'm working like hell,' he thought. **1967** J. WYNNUM *I'm Jack, all Right* 107, I convince George he's crook and fix it so he's got at least a day bludging. **1973** J. POWERS *Last of Knucklemen* (1974) 24, I like to just mosey about—do what I wantta do—work when I gotta work, and bludge as much as I can. **1979** *Bludgers* (Petersham Techn. College) 25 After a while I did all my work in my own time and at my own speed. But I wasn't bludging. **1980** *Sunday Tel.* (Sydney) 20 Apr. 43/4 Ask him, for instance what he does to relax and he replies, 'Bludge.'

4. *trans.* To cadge or scrounge (food, etc.).

1954 T. RONAN *Vision Splendid* 98 It makes me a man in work again, not just a bloke bludging a lift. **1963** J. O'GRADY *Things they do to You* 129, I might be able to bludge a bit of raw potato from him to put in my tobacco tin. **1969** F. MOORHOUSE *Futility & Other Animals* 87 The old man was fair dinkum and had to bludge a living. **1979** CAREY & LETTE *Puberty Blues* 37 The girls smiled, bludged smokes and looked attractively bored.

Hence **bludging** *vbl. n.* and *ppl. a.*

1903 *Truth* (Sydney) 11 Oct. 3/3 She had called him a 'bludging bastard', to which he replied, 'Like your mother, who keeps a brothel.' ***c* 1907** W.C. CHANDLER *Darkest Adelaide* 2/1 That bludging has been reduced to a fine art here in Adelaide cannot be gainsaid. Here the bludger is an institution. **1914** *Truth* (Sydney) 26 Apr. 7/8 *Bludging 'Beauty'.* Sends his paramour on the streets. **1942** *Ack Ack News* (Melbourne) July 3 He knows that this may cover anything from three years' undiluted bludging at the worst. **1965** L. HAYLEN *Big Red* 94 That would fix the greedy squatter, the stupid banker, the bludging city merchant. **1979** DUSTY & LAPSLEY *Walk Country Mile* 58 Look at yers lying there, you bludging pack of no-hopers. **1983** *Woman's Day* (Sydney) 27 June 19/1 He has often been quoted as saying he won't do more because he is lazy or simply that he likes bludging.

bludge /blʌdʒ/, *n.* [f. prec.]

1. An undemanding job; a period of idleness, usually at someone else's expense.

1943 J. BINNING *Target Area* 24 They realised you had not come down there just for a joke or a 'bludge'. **1943** D. FRIEND *Gunner's Diary* 18 'I've been three weeks in hospital with measles.' 'Ah—that's not a bad bludge.' **1949** L. GLASSOP *Lucky Palmer* 152 A man's got to earn a living and this is a good bludge. **1959** D. HEWETT *Bobbin Up* 71 'I dunno what they do on that night shift,' Julie grizzled. 'Must be the biggest bludge on earth.' **1960** J. WALKER *No Sunlight Singing* 159 This job of yours with Native Affairs would be a fair old bludge, wouldn't it? You chaps can do just about what you like, can't you? **1978** D. STUART *Wedgetail View* 50 Sandy was a bit away, havin' a little bludge, I s'pose. **1979** CAREY & LETTE *Puberty Blues* 48 Phew. The class sat back for a bludge.

2. An imposition or exaction.

1947 V.C. HALL *Bad Medicine* 160 The history of the Northern Territory is the story of one long bludge on the aboriginal. **1957** D. NILAND *Call me when Cross turns Over* 75 What's the big idea, coming the bludge on us? Haven't you got anywhere to go? **1979** CAREY & LETTE *Puberty Blues* 89 We bought our ten cents worth of lollies. That was our daily bludge from Mr Knight.

bludger /ˈblʌdʒə/. [Survival of Br. slang *bludger*, shortened form of *bludgeoner*: see OED(S.]

1. One who lives on the earnings of a prostitute.

[**1856** H. MAYHEW *Great World of London* 46 'Bludgers' or 'stick slingers', who rob in company with low women.] **1882** *Sydney Slang Dict.* 1 *Bludgers*, or *Stick Slingers*, plunderers in company with prostitutes. **1897** *Bulletin* (Sydney) 16 Oct. 7/1 The Church as a 'Bludger'. **1900** *Truth* (Sydney) 13 May 5/3 This 'shop' is not occupied by girls, but by 'bludgers',—the men who own the girls and live on their prostitution. **1901** *Ibid.* 23 June 3/1 Girls of no more than 13 years of age smoked their cigarettes and *mopped up booze* as freely as their bludgers. **1905** *Ibid.* 5 Feb. 1/1 In Australia . . bludger means what in London and other large English cities is known as a 'ponce'. . . In other words, it seems that the Australian bludger lives on the earnings of a prostitute, with whom he cohabits. **1915** *Ibid.* 19 Sept. 7/3 To enter Australian politics, to abide there, and to succeed therein, a man must have the instincts of a loafer, the aptitudes of a pickpocket, the conscience of a whore, and the honor of a bludger. **1933** H.B. RAINE *Lash End* 67 You've ruined this kid's life—made a prostitute out of her. You're only a rotten bludger! **1945** R.S. CLOSE *Love me Sailor* 70 'I got a young island girl fer yer, and she don't look more'n sixteen.' . . 'Wot you got is a couple of fat bludgers who will knock me on the 'ead an' take me money.' **1950** K.S. PRICHARD *Winged Seeds* 290 The bludger who owns the place picks up drunken soldiers and sailors and tells them Lili's a high-class French piece. **1959** D. HEWETT *Bobbin Up* 115 'But what about libel?' 'There's a name for a man who lives off women!' 'Can't you get pinched for callin' a man a bludger?' **1963** X. HERBERT *Disturbing Element* 96 Two other famous protectors of molls, Bludgers as they were called, were an Irishman . . and a negro. **1973** R. EDWARDS *Austral. Bawdy Ballads* 32 O, a strapping young harlot lay dying, A pisspot supporting her head. And all the young bludgers were 'round her.

2. a. A generalized term of abuse, esp. as applied to a person who appears to live off the efforts of others.

1900 *Truth* (Sydney) 28 Jan. 5/4 Lyttleton's battalion of Bludgers. **1906** *Ibid.* 5 Aug. 1/3 Dancing, according to a Salvarmy bludger in Melbourne, is sinful and wicked. It is no sin for sour Salvarmy sallies to . . hug the officers, though. **1948** H.W. CRITTENDON *Rogues' Paradise* 239 Let us shout Rafferty! Sinn Fein! Traitor! in a volume that will drown Pommy, Wowser, Bludger, Rat and Scab, which our conquerors have used as their vicious pass-words into power. **1953** D. CUSACK *Southern Steel* 140 Great birds! I reckon any bludger who'd shoot one of 'em deserves the bad luck of the Ancient Mariner. **1956** J.E. MACDONNELL *Commander Brady* 58 If we're to get back to the beach, we've got to leave enough dead Japs behind us to make the bludgers think we're a much bigger force. **1957** *Westerly* i. 4 Some bludger's pinched my clothes. **1958** J.R. SPICER *Cry of Storm-bird* 136 He . . turned to look proudly at the box-like shape of the Geiger counter on the table beside his bed. 'You'll bring me luck, you little bludger,' he told it, and spat. **1967** W. WATKINS *Shadow of Whip* 47 'C'mon in y'u bludgers,' and her guests trampled inside. **1977** *Bronze Swagman Bk. Bush Verse* 58, I charged him like a scrubber that's got murder in its mind, And with a roarin' shout, I donged the bludger from behind.

b. *spec.* A derogatory term for a person engaged in non-manual employment, a white-collar worker.

1910 *Truth* (Sydney) 27 Mar. 5/3 Blackguard band of blatant, bumptious bummers and bludgers, who bum and bludge on Labor. **1957** D. WHITINGTON *Treasure upon Earth* 53 'Bludgers' he dubbed them early, because in his language anyone who did not work with his hands at a laboring job was a bludger. **1961** *Realist* (Sydney) vi. 10 Workers' precious blood has flowed like wine To stroke the lust of bludgers in the line. **1967** D. HEWETT *This Old Man* 36 The working class can kiss me arse I've found a bludger's job at last. **1969** A. BUZO *Front Room Boys* (1970) 36, I don't like those la-di-da hoity-toity upper-crust bludgers with their fancy accents, so I chucked Lord Muck out the window. **1978** K. GARVEY *Tales of my Uncle Harry* 42 Like all bureaucrats, he's a bludger. **1979** *Canberra Times* 19 Sept. 2/2 It was when you came to analyse the reasons for the uncomplimentary stereotype of public servants as a pack of tea-swilling bludgers.

3. An idler, one who makes little effort.

1942 *Ack Ack News* (Melbourne) Apr. 3 By the way, who said our sappers are bludgers? **1949** L. GLASSOP *Lucky Palmer* 9 Lot of bludgers. . . That's all they are, them coppers. **1950** J. CLEARY *Just let me Be* 135 Everything I backed ran like a no-hoper. Four certs I had, and the bludgers were so far back the ambulance nearly had to bring 'em home. **1956** E. LAMBERT *Watermen* 39 'Boats?' Finnigan nodded. 'Durrant's, the bludger. Last out and first in, as usual.' **1965** K. SMITH *OGF* 188 Don't be a bludger, Bert—get stuck into it. **1976** T. SHEPHERD *Children of Blindness* 55, I said, look mate, the blackfellows we've got up here are bludgers who sit around. **1978** D. STUART *Wedgetail View* 30 Good poor old bastard, Bill. Toiler. State Battery, bush work, Road Board, anything. Not a bludger, old Bill. **1980** *Sydney Morning Herald* 4 Jan. 7/8, I suspect there are far more bludgers in jobs than there are on the dole.

4. One who does not make a fair contribution (to a cost, enterprise, etc.); a cadger.

1955 D. NILAND *Shiralee* 46 Put the nips into me for tea and sugar and tobacco in his usual style. The biggest bludger in the country. **1961** X. HERBERT *Soldier's Women* 370 You'd only piss it down the sink or let some bludger take it off of you. **1971** J. O'GRADY *Aussie Etiket* 66 When it comes to your turn, return the 'shout'. Otherwise the word will spread that you are a 'bludger', and there is no worse thing to be. **1972** A. CHIPPER *Aussie Swearers Guide* 30 The great Australian cadger, the *Bludger* is out for anything he can get—and never return. **1978** J. ANDERSON *Tirra Lirra* 46 But you always say Les is a bludger. I'll do the swearing round here! He's a bludger all right, but naturally, he had to kick in *some*thing. **1982** R. HALL *Just Relations* 137 Just look at the bludger, Billy roared. Can't get his thieving hands on the cash fast enough.

Hence **bludgerdom** *n.*, **bludgeress** *n.*

1903 *Truth* (Sydney) 19 July 3/5 Another case, savoring somewhat of **bludgerdom**, was heard at the same court. ***c* 1907** C.W. CHANDLER *Darkest Adelaide* 12/1 In the face of this thriving state of affairs in Bludgerdom, the police don't seem over-anxious to swoop down on the carrion with a big swoop. **1908** *Truth* (Sydney) 27 Dec. 1/5 Latterly, bludgers, so the police say, are marrying **bludgeresses.**

blue, *n.*[1] [Back formation f. BLUEY.]

1. *Obs.* BLUEY 1 a. Also as *adj.* in the collocation **blue one.**

1896 *Bulletin* (Sydney) 30 July 32/2 'Neddy' the tucker-bag is of more importance than the 'blue one', and by way of precedence dangles in front, mostly hanging to Matilda's apron-strings. **1905** A.B. PATERSON *Old Bush Songs* 24 We'd whips and whips of Rhino as we meant to push about, So we humped our blues serenely. **1916** *Truth* (Sydney) 11 June 3/7 I've humped my 'Blue' from the back Paroo To the fringe of the distant north. **1918** 'LANCE-CORPORAL COBBER' *Anzac Pilgrim's Progress* 14 Coo-ee! Coo-ee-ee! Hump yer blue an' away.

2. BLUEY 4.

1939 K. TENNANT *Foveaux* 348 Before we get any more blues for obstructin' the traffic, there's something I want to tell you. **1965** *Tracks we Travel* 13 They put a blue on you if you pick up a hitch-hiker. **1980** B. HORNADGE *Austral. Slanguage* 267 A legal summons is a *blue* (or *bluey*) and the origins of this is not hard to fathom since summonses are printed on blue paper.

3. BLUEY 6.

1932 L. MANN *Flesh in Armour* 56 Blue McIntosh, No. 1, red in the head. **1946** E.A. FELDT *Coast Watchers* 37 Being red-haired, he was, following the Australian custom, called 'Blue'. **1957** R. OLLIS *101 Nights* 207 Joe and his red-headed companion whom he called 'Blue' would collapse in spasms of laughter. **1966** A.R. CHISHOLM *Familiar Presence* 79 A boy with red hair was automatically called 'Blue'. **1978** H.C. BAKER *I was Listening* 141 In American a red-headed man is 'Red', in England 'Carrots' or 'Ginger'; only an Aussie could make him 'Blue'.

blue, *n.*[2] [Poss. from *blue* characterized by swearing, as in *to make the air blue*: see OEDS *blue, a.* 9 b.]

1. A fight; an altercation; a disagreement.

1943 A. DAWES *Soldier Superb* 29, I heard the 'blue' (battle) was still on. **1953** T.A.G. HUNGERFORD *Riverslake* 67 One of the cooks there had a blue with a Balt in the mess. **1964** B. BEAVER *Hot Men* 12 Bunch of Eyeties and Germans had a blue over the local beauty contest winner. **1969** A. BUZO *Front Room Boys* (1970) 77, I was in the pub having a quiet beer with a few Werris Creek identities, when this bloke came up and started picking a blue with Simms. **1978** D. STUART *Wedgetail View* 51 If a feller gets in a blue, he can talk his way out, or he can grab a pick handle and break a leg on the bastard that's tryin' to force a fight on him. **1981** —— *I think I'll Live* 84 'Yes, there was a bit of a blue. What did you hear about it?' 'Nothing much, except three of you had told one of your sergeants what he could do.'

2. In the phr. **to smack a blue,** to run into trouble.

1939 K. TENNANT *Foveaux* 290 You can always get a bet 'cause there's sure to be some bloke wiv a life sentence an' a wireless. As long as you don't smack a bad blue, you ought to 'ave a 'appy time. **1967** *Kings Cross Whisper* (Sydney) xl. 4/4 *Smack a blue*, to strike trouble along life's way. **1968** J. ALARD *He who shoots Last* 24, I know the kid never had a chance. . . I did my best to stop him smacking a blue; but it wasn't enough.

3. A mistake, a faux pas.

1941 *Action Front: Jrnl. 2/2 Field Regiment* Sept. 8 Decided he'd made a 'blue'. **1941** S.J. BAKER *Pop. Dict. Austral. Slang* 11 *Blue*, an error or mistake; a loss. **1957** R. STOW *Bystander* 187, I reckon you ought to tell your missus she made a bit of a blue. **1960** S. WOODFIELD *A for Artemis* 159 'I'm sorry about the blue,' said Bill. . . 'It will be hard to explain. If there is anything I can do, I'll fix it.' **1965** L. HAYLEN *Big Red* 47 It was the only way he could wipe out the 'blue' he made at the dance. **1972** *Bulletin* (Sydney) 12 Aug. 34/1 I've made a lot of blues in my personal life. **1983** *Sun-Herald* (Sydney) 4 Dec. 168/6 Labor Party chappies were quick to jump in last week and score off Nick Greiner's tactical blue in saying the Opposition wasn't ready to govern yet.

4. In the phr. **to bung (put, stack) on a blue,** to make a fuss, to create a disturbance.

1950 *Austral. Police Jrnl.* Apr. 118 If it is said that a particular mug 'sings' well, then it means that he pays well without 'bunging on a blue'. **1953** D. CUSACK *Southern Steel* 137 'Luke-bloody-warm. It's time we put on a bloody blue for a ziggin' refrigerator.' 'Unions's got it in hand, Slap.' **1965** *Tracks we Travel* 76 When the publican refused to serve him a drink on the grounds that he was an Aborigine under the Act, the town-workers really stacked on a blue. **1967** *Kings Cross Whisper* (Sydney) xlii. 8/5 The guard has been mounted to prevent the dirty yellow bastards getting out and bunging on a blue. **1974** D. IRELAND *Burn* 28 You tryin' to bung on a blue? I'll give you a smack in the chops in a minute. **1978** H.C. BAKER *I was Listening* 19 Your mate straightaway bungs on a blue.

blue, *v.*[1] Also **blew.** [Br. slang *blue* to spend lavishly (see OEDS *v.*[2] 1). Not excl. Austral.] *trans.* To squander (money to hand, earnings for a period, etc.). Esp. in the phr. **to blue a cheque.**

1881 G.C. EVANS *Stories* 300 When the old fool found a piece of gold, instead of blueing it in a proper manner [etc.]. **1890** 'R. BOLDREWOOD' *Miner's Right* 59 Then we can 'blue the lot' and your tucker account can go with many another good pound, as we've seen the last of. **1891** M. ROBERTS *Land-Travel & Sea-Faring* 75 Like many bush workers, he had made quite enough money for a spree, and was ready for it. Yet Jack only went down to town to 'blue his cheque' at reasonable intervals. **1894** *Antipodean* (Melbourne) 8 As long as the creeks don't rise and block us goin' to the big smoke to blue our cheques. **1906** G.M. SMITH *Days of Cobb & Co.* 58 But she wasn't having any When I'd blued my final pound. **1909** *Bulletin* (Sydney) 23 Sept. 14/3 The woman with the swag . . having blued her cheque . . was turned out of the hotel. **1924** *Ibid.* 30 Oct. 24/4 The customer who has blewed his cheque . . is no ornament to a pub verandah. **1930** HIVES & LUMLEY *Jrnl. of Jackaroo* 140 All their lives they had been accustomed to 'blueing' their wages in an annual spree, and old habits stick. **1948** V. PALMER *Golconda* 148 We blued all we had. **1962** MARSHALL & DRYSDALE *Journey among Men* 56 Then they would enter the bar and hand over their cheque to the publican. Thus they would 'blue' their cheques. **1969** D. NILAND *Dead Men Running* 62 Hen money. Egg money. A few bob from me. Then blues it all on that bloody commercial traveller. **1985** H. GARNER *Postcards from Surfers* 68, I got the bottle off McLaughlin. At least if you blue you should do it proper.

blue, *v.*[2] [Cf. BLUE *n.*[2]] *intr.* To argue, fight.

1969 W. DICK *Naked Prodigal* 27 'I thought youse were still goin' together, Kenny, even though youse bin bluein' a bit,' Raincoat said. **1976** D. IRELAND *Glass Canoe* 26 While the others were blueing, I thought of all that energy exploding during the few minutes the fight lasted. **1977** R. EDWARDS *Austral. Yarn* 82 We'd been blueing in Camooweal at the bottom pub.

blue, *a.* Used as a distinguishing epithet in the names of flora and fauna: **blue-billed duck,** the diving duck *Oxyura australis* of s.e. and s.w. Aust., so called because the bill of the male turns blue in summer; **bonnet, (a)** the parrot *Northiella haematogaster*, having a blue face and occurring in relatively dry areas of s. Aust.; **(b)** *red-collared lorikeet*, see RED *a.* 1 a.; **bush,** any of several shrubs of inland plains and arid shrublands esp. of the genus *Maireana* (formerly *Kochia*), fam. Chenopodiaceae, the hairy leaves of which give the low bushes a blue-green to grey-green appearance; **caladenia,** the slender orchid *Caladenia caerulea* (fam. Orchidaceae) which bears a blue flower on a stem less than 20 cm. high; **cap,** any of several fairy wrens, the males having blue crowns; **cattle dog,** *blue heeler*; **couch,** any of several grasses (fam. Poaceae) with couch-like creeping root-stocks and blue-green leaves, esp. the African *Cynodon incompletus*, widespread in N.S.W., and *Digitaria didactyla* of Qld. and n.e. N.S.W.; **crane,** *white-faced heron*, see WHITE *a.*[2] 1 b.; **dog,** *blue heeler*; **eye,** the fish *Pseudomugil signifer* of N.S.W. and s. Qld., occurring mainly in brackish but also in fresh and salt water; **fig,** QUANDONG 1 c.; the wood or fruit of the tree; **fish,** the marine fish *Girella cyanea* of N.S.W., New Zealand, and nearby islands, having a blue back and sides with small golden spots; **flyer,** an adult female *red kangaroo* (a) (see RED *a.* 1 b.); **grass,** any of several perennial grasses (fam. Poaceae) having flower-head spikes of a blue or purple colour, esp. of the genera *Bothriochloa* and *Dichanthium*; **groper,** the blue or brown parrot fish *Achoerodus gouldii* (fam. Labridae) of rocky coasts of s. Aust.; **gum,** any of several trees of the genus *Eucalyptus* (fam. Myrtaceae) having a smooth bluish-grey bark or bluish-grey juvenile foliage; the wood of these trees; also with distinguishing epithet, as **southern, Sydney, Tasmanian** (see under first element); **heeler,** the blue, or Australian cattle dog, a breed having a blue or red flecked coat, developed in Australia in the nineteenth century by crossing dingo with merle collie from Scotland and subsequently with Dalmatian and black-and-tan kelpie; **jay,** *black-faced cuckoo-shrike*, see BLACK *a.*[2] 1 b.; **mallee,** the bluish-leaved mallee tree *Eucalyptus polybractea* (fam. Myrtaceae) of central Vic. and N.S.W.; also **blue-leafed mallee; martin, (a)** *fairy martin*, see FAIRY *n.*[1] 1; **(b)** a wood swallow, esp. the *masked wood swallow* (see MASKED); **mountain parrot (lorikeet, parakeet),** *rainbow lorikeet*, see RAINBOW 2; also **mountaineer; -ringed octopus,** the small venomous octopus *Hapalochlaena maculosa* of Austral. coasts; **swimmer (crab),** the edible blue crab *Portunus pelagicus*, widely distributed in sheltered estuaries and inlets; also **swimming crab; -tongue(d) lizard,** any of several lizards with a blue tongue, prominent when the animal is threatened, esp. BOBTAIL or certain species of the closely-related genus *Tiliqua* (see also SLEEPING LIZARD); **-winged kookaburra,** the large kingfisher *Dacelo leachii* of woodlands in n. Aust. and New Guinea, having conspicuous blue areas on the wing; LEACH'S KINGFISHER; **wren,** any of several Austral. wrens of the fam. Maluridae, the adult male having blue on the crown and other parts of the body, esp. the *superb blue wren* (see SUPERB).

1844 J. GOULD *Birds of Aust.* (1848) VII. Pl. 17, *Erismatura australis*... **Blue-billed Duck** of the Colonists. **1901** *Emu* I. 137 Blue-billed Duck .. owing to their quickness in diving, were hard to shoot. **1974** *Ecos* ii. 28/3 The sedentary musk duck, blue-billed duck, and hardhead tended to breed most regularly each year in winter or spring. **1865** J. GOULD *Handbk. Birds Aust.* II. 62 Red-vented Parrakeet... **Blue bonnet** of the Colonists of New South Wales. **1888** W.H. WILLSHIRE *Aborigines of Central Aust.* 6 Parrots of many kinds—ring-necks, blue bonnets, and goolahs, furnish the natives with many a meal. **1933** *Bulletin* (Sydney) 8 Feb. 20/4 A blue bonnet, in the absence of a lady of his own kind, mated with a pale-headed rosella hen. **1948** R. RAVEN-HART *Canoe in Aust.* 82 Bluebonnets were feeding on the road-side grass, almost as tame as sparrows: they are little parrots, in general effect brownish especially when on the ground, but with brilliant blue daubs on their cheeks and eyes. **1964** M. SHARLAND *Territory of Birds* 36 The gaudy Red-collared Parrots, usually referred to around Darwin as 'blue bonnets', have .. heads of rich blue, fringed with a scarlet collar, and with vermilion beneath the wings. **1985** P. CAREY *Illywhacker* 428 When he at last succeeds in trapping a one-guinea blue bonnet he can sit happily for hours marvelling at the beauty of its feathers, the rich blue around its parrot's beak, the yellow of its lower breast in which lovely sea you find a soft-edged island of rich blood red. **1862** W.R.H. JESSOP *Flindersland and Sturtland* II. 37 Before we reached this, however, we passed through a couple of miles of **blue bush**, a sign of good feed... This curious bush, so plentiful in Sturtland, is about the size of a gooseberry or currant bush, of the colour of sage, and of a very saltish taste. **1881** J.C.F. JOHNSON *To Mount Browne & Back* 11 Bush nags.. will eat anything... Mulga leaves .. and blue bush they will tackle with a will. **1895** *Bulletin* (Sydney) 13 July 23/2 And you'll travel to the shearing, up across the open plain, Through the salt and blue-bush country, and you'll camp one night again. **1903** J. FURPHY *Such is Life* 216 There's boun' to be a bit o' blue-bush, if not crows-foot, on them sand-hills. **1929** W.J. RESIDE *Golden Days* 21 We left Percy with blue-bush round his hat, brushing the flies away. **1937** E. HILL *Water into Gold* 113 Humorous tales are told of those 'speak-easies' of the blue-bush in the bad old times when Mildura was prohibition. **1974** P. ADAM SMITH *Desert Railway* 34 The bluebush is particularly conspicuous with its leaves bluish-white, a shade which no other plant can quite rival. **1835** *Hobart Town Almanack* 74 *Caladenia caerulea*. **Blue Caladenia.** Smells like honey or meadow-sweet. It derives its name from *kalos*, beautiful. **1978** B.P. MOORE *Life on Forty Acres* 41 The dainty Blue Caladenia (*Caladenia caerulea*) with its solitary azure flower on a short stem. **1981** A. MARSHALL *Aust.* 143 Blue Caladenias grow from the mossy ground. [*c* **1872 blue cap**: J.C.F. JOHNSON *Over Island* 11 A tiny 'blue-capped wren'.] **1903** *Emu* III. 27 Long-tailed Blue Wren... Under various names, such as .. 'Blue-cap' .. is this beautiful little species known to us. **1911** E.J. BRADY *Bells & Hobbles* 78 High-poised upon his bending rush, a bluecap warbles clear. **1928** *Bulletin* (Sydney) 25 Apr. 23/1 Mrs Daisy Bates .. records that the fairy or blue-cap wren and his mate .. are known to many tribes of natives by the euphonious names of *Miril Yiril Yiri* and *Minning Minning*. [**1909 blue cattle dog:** R. KALESKI *Austral. Settler's Compl. Guide* 24 Cattle-Dog—The best to get is a pure-bred blue one.] **1935** DAVISON & NICHOLLS *Blue Coast Caravan* 148 With them came two blue-cattle dogs. **1951** W. HATFIELD *Wild Dog Frontier* 121 Working like a trained team of blue cattle-dogs, silent heelers. **1979** D. STIVENS *Demon Bowler* 49, I had gone for a short walk with Bluey, our blue cattle dog—no other dog was worth owning except a kelpie, declared my father, a country man to the end. **1923** *Bulletin* (Sydney) 27 Dec. 23/4 To .. **blue couch** .. and .. sweet potato vines .. I can add another common bush plant with generally unsuspected poisonous properties. **1941** *Qld. Agric. Jrnl.* LV. 7 Blue couch is one of the commonest lawn grasses in the southern coastal districts of Queensland, where it does quite well. **1976** *Ecos* vii. 25/2 Buffalo grass .. survives best in the parks where there is little pedestrian pressure, but it's no good for playing fields... To date, blue couch .. and green couch .. have given the best service for these purposes. **1814** M. FLINDERS *Voyage Terra Australis* II. 226 The aquatic birds were **blue** and white **cranes.** **1847** J. GOULD *Birds of Aust.* (1848) VI. Pl. 53, *Ardea Novae-Hollandiae*... White-fronted Heron... Blue Crane of the Colonists. **1884** 'R. BOLDREWOOD' *Old Melbourne Memories* 11 There did I shoot, and bear home with schoolboy pride, a blue crane—the Australian heron. **1955** P. WHITE *Tree of Man* 108 The paddocks undulated with a greater joyfulness, in which the blue crane stalked. **1968** R. HILL *Bush Quest* 21 The brolga .. is one of Australia's largest birds and our only crane—despite the popular use of the name 'blue crane' for the white-faced heron. **1979** C. THIELE *River Murray Mary* 53 The blue cranes stood like carved birds of stone in the backwaters. **1949** *Bulletin* (Sydney) 26 Jan. 15/1 The visiting salesman was gingerly patting the **blue dog.** **1981** A. WILKINSON *Up Country* 30 The old blue dog .. that with age and years of competent work earned its place on the verandah. **1906** D.G. STEAD *Fishes of Aust.* 71 The tiny, but beautiful, **Blue-eye** (*Pseudomugil signifer*). **1938** *Bulletin* (Sydney) 26 May 20/4 The world's best and most effective larvae-destroying fish, the 'blue-eye' .. is abundant in every N.S.W. and S.Q. coastal stream and deep lagoon. **1980** R.M. MCDOWALL *Freshwater Fishes S.-E. Aust.* 137 Southern blue-eye... Eye surrounded by an iridescent blue ring. **1884** A. NILSON *Timber Trees N.S.W.* 55 **Blue Fig.**—A tall slender tree... *Timber* close-grained and soft, but little used. **1932** R.H. ANDERSON *Trees of N.S.W.* 150 *Elaeocarpus grandis* .. is generally known as Blue Fig or Brush Quandong, and is a fairly large tree with grey bark and greenish-white flowers. **1965** *Austral. Encycl.* III. 365 *E*[*laeocarpus*] *grandis* .. has large blue drupes known to children as blue figs, and sometimes, but incorrectly, as quandongs. **1985** P. CAREY *Illywhacker* 117 Blue fig for struts. **1790** R. CLARK Jrnl. 19 Apr. 159, 16 fishes consisting of Snappers **Blue Fish** and one Rock Cod. **1889** *Lord Howe Island* 56 *Girella cyanea* .. the 'Blue-fish' is abundant at all seasons. **1956** B. BEATTY *Beyond Aust.'s Cities* 158 To the accompaniment of screams from the hundreds of terns circling your launch you can land fish after fish after fish, .. blue-fish, zebra-fish, and maybe a shark or two. **1851** J. HENDERSON *Excursions & Adventures N.S.W.* II. 170 The **blue-flyer** is the swiftest, and tries the speed of the best kangaroo-dogs. **1872** G.S. BADEN-POWELL *New Homes for Old Country* 329 The kangaroo of the flats is the most numerous, .. the best-looking being the 'red soldier', with his fleet wife the 'blue flier'. **1953** H.M. EASTMAN *Mem. of Sheepman* 79 'Going to skin the 'roo?' 'No, she's a Blue Flyer, not worth skinning. I only skin the Foresters.' **1973** V. SERVENTY *Desert Walkabout* 60 The 'red' is the kangaroo of the inland plains... The females are bluish grey, the 'blue flyer' of the bushman—a tribute to her speed and beauty. **1862** J.M. STUART *Explorations in Aust.* 5 June (1865) 359 At four o'clock arrived at the **blue-grass** swamp. **1881** A.C. GRANT *Bush-Life Qld.* II. 145 At times they feed on the luscious herbage and luxuriant blue-grasses of a limestone country. **1890** A. MACKAY *Austral. Agriculturist* (ed. 2) 140 Chloris barbata, commonly termed blue grass, is naturally very rich, and suffers greatly from over-stocking. **1895** *Bulletin* (Sydney) 14 Dec. 7/4 Store cattle from Nelanjie! Their breath is on the breeze; You hear them tread, a thousand head, in blue grass to the knees. **1907** *Ibid.* 4 Apr. 14/1 On the great plains the blue and Mitchell grasses at full growth stand as even as a wheat field. **1923** J. BOWES *Jackaroos* 16 'Blue grass', one of the best of the Australian natural grasses, the saccharine qualities of which made it a great fat producer. **1943** L. MCLENNAN *Spirit of West* 46 We met on the blacksoil plain, Where the furlongs rolled like ribbon and the blue grass waved like grain. **1985** *Austral. Financial Rev.* (Sydney) 18 Dec. 25/3 When the settlers arrived the country had a parklike appearance, with unending stretches of perennial native grasses such as kangaroo grass and blue grass. **1874** *N.S.W. Rep. R. Comm. Fisheries* (1880) 1294 The gruper .. popularly called in this country **blue** or black **groper**—no doubt from the fact of these fishes groping in and out of the caverns and crevices of rocks in search of crustaceae. **1913** *Bulletin* (Sydney) 27 Nov. 22/4 Recently caught a large fish known as 'blue groper' near Kirribilli Point, Sydney. **1963** B. CROPP *Handbk. for Skindivers* 115 Blue Groper (*Achoerodus gouldii*). This species is the most popular of the large fish taken by spearmen. **1799** D. COLLINS *Acct. Eng. Colony N.S.W.* (1802) II. 145 A sort of gum tree .. its leaf, that of the **blue gum** tree. **1803** *Sydney Gaz.* 15 May, 20 casks of Blue Gum Bark which has been so successfully used in the colony for *Tanning leather*. **1810** *Ibid.* 21 July, Stolen... Nine large Pieces of well-seasoned Honey-suckle, together with several Planks of Blue Gum, which are all fit for ship-building. **1827** P. CUNNINGHAM *Two Yrs. in N.S.W.* I. 200 Blue, spotted, black-butted, and woolly, gums are so nominated from the corresponding appearance of their respective barks. **1836** J. MORPHETT *S.A.* 8 Blue-gum .. is a most elegant tree of great magnitude. **1852** G.C. MUNDY *Our Antipodes* III. 206 The largest trees being the blue-gum for which the island is famous—so called I suppose, because the leaf has much of the colour of the bloom on the Orleans-plum. **1870** *Illustr. Austral. News* (Melbourne) 13 Aug. 150/1 Cantelevers covered with blue gum planking. **1880** J. BONWICK *Resources Qld.* 79 The *Euc. saligna* is known as Blue Gum, White, Gray, or Flooded, according to locality. **1906** *Emu* V. 138 Lorikeets were screaming and feeding on the flowering 'blue gum' trees (Eucalyptus leucoxylon). **1920** J.J. GLADSTONE *Tragedy of Gallipoli* 39 The blue-gum tree, Australian! we Should very loyally love it. **1928** M.E. FULLERTON *Austral. Bush* 117 Just to hear the magpies warble in the bluegum on the hill. **1934** W.A. OSBORNE *Visitor to Aust.* 66 Fine groves of Australian Blue Gum may be found in all Mediterranean lands, in California, where it is called the Californian Gum (!), in Mexico, South America, and India. **1949** W. LAWSON *Blue Gum Clippers* 114 A feature of the *Tasman* was that her masts and spars were of blue-gum; she was the only blue-gum clipper to have spars of this timber. **1965** G. MCINNES *Road to Gundagai* 173 The landscape was one of open paddocks dotted with bluegum, sheoak, and cootamundra. **1981** *Woman's Day* (Sydney) 16 Sept. 6/1 Pink and grey galahs wheeled over the shining tin roof of the infants' school and fluttered through the pepper trees and the blue gums. **1908** W.H. OGILVIE *My Life in Open* 52 The **blue 'heelers'** or cattle dogs. **1943** *Bulletin* (Sydney) 14 July 12/3 He rode up to a cattle station in Queensland .. with a blue heeler in tow and asked for a job. **1968** J. O'GRADY *Gone Troppo* 4 He said, 'There're only two kinds of dogs worth feeding. Sheep dogs and cattle dogs. Kelpies and blue-heelers.' **1980** Holth & Barnaby *Cattlemen of High Country* 102 The Blue Heeler dog . . was bred to drive cattle by snapping at their fetlocks. **1986** *Sydney Morning Herald* 12 Apr. 1/4 Bill Morley, his faithful blue healer [*sic*] Gove, and an equally weary old red truck have travelled back and forth. **1861** 'Old Bushman' *Bush Wanderings* 131 The bird that we called the **Blue Jay** resembled its British namesake in no one particular. **1886** W.J. Woods *Visit to Vic.* 23 The shrill whistle of the Blue-jay. **1913** *Emu* XIII. 95 Black-faced Cuckoo-Shrike . . commonly known as 'Blue Jay'. **1954** *Coast to Coast 1953–54* 1 He heard the chattering of blue jays and wattle-birds over his head as he passed through the first group of manna gums. **1901** *Proc. Linnean Soc. N.S.W.* XXV. 692 *Eucalyptus Polybractea*, sp. nov. '**Blue Mallee**'. . . A glaucous Mallee, with quadrangular branchlets. **1948** H.A. Lindsay *Bushman's Handbk.* 7 The blue mallee, whose leaves are as large as the palm of the hand and of the same grey-blue colour (glaucous) as the familiar blue-gum. **1983** *Bogong* IV. v. 4 Blue mallee is economically important, being the basis of the eucalyptus oil industry in the West Wyalong area. **1984** *Sun News-Pictorial* (Melbourne) 2 Aug. 3/4 The contraption, run on 'only the best of blue-leafed Mallee gums', brews 87-per-cent pure 'euky oil'. **1924** *Bulletin* (Sydney) 10 Jan. 22/2 The **blue martin**, or bottle-swallow, seems to stop his flight by gripping the landing-place with his claws. **1934** H.G. Lamond *Aviary on Plains* 112 It is the blue martin (masked wood-swallow). **1961** *Bulletin* (Sydney) 31 May 35/3 We call them blue martins, and they're common from the eastern coast to the western border in Queensland. Ornithologists refer to them as some species of wood swallow. **1804** G. Caley in A.E.J. Andrews *Devil's Wilderness* (1984) 39 A deal of **Blue Mountain Parrots** (Psittacus haematotus novae Hollandia) on the road. **1822** Mrs E. Hawkins in G. Mackaness *Fourteen Journeys Blue Mountains* (1950) ii. 26 There are but few birds on the mountains, but their plumage is more beautiful than I ever beheld before. They are called 'Blue Mountaineers.' **1827** P. Cunningham *Two Yrs. in N.S.W.* I. 323 Our parrot tribes are of infinite variety, . . the *blue-mountain* decked out in all the colours of the rainbow. **1842** R.G. Jameson *N.Z., S.A., & N.S.W.* 71 The Blue Mountain paroquet, the rosella, and the lory, are the most beautiful. **1845** L. Leichhardt *Jrnl. Overland Exped. Aust.* 31 Aug. (1847) 382 A strange mess was made of cockatoo, Blue Mountaineers, an eagle hawk, and dried emu. **1888** *Centennial Mag.* (Sydney) 131 It is in the taxidermist's window that we see most of the Blue Mountain parrot and its kind. **1948** P.J. Hurley *Red Cedar* 179 Loquat trees were loaded with Blue Mountain parakeets. **1952** B. Beatty *Unique to Aust.* 52 The gaudily plumaged Blue Mountain parrots may be seen in large numbers along the whole eastern coast. **1956** A.C.C. Lock *Tropical Tapestry* 177 The silence was disturbed by the screeches of blue mountain lorikeets flashing past us with a brilliant display of colours. **1933** *Victorian Naturalist* XLIX. 238, I have seen the small, **blue-ringed octopus** (*Octopus maculosus*), common in Sydney Harbour, sitting on about fifty small, white, pea-shaped eggs. **1968** *Sun-Herald* (Sydney) 24 Mar. 2/1 Officials at the Commonwealth Serum Laboratories . . say the venom of the blue-ringed octopus is more deadly than the poison of a tiger snake. **1970** Deas & Lawler *Beneath Austral. Seas* 48 It is a yellowish colour with iridescent blue-purple markings on its tentacles and body which show up particularly well when it is disturbed. It is commonly called the 'blue-ringed octopus'. **1986** *Canberra Times* 14 Jan. 9/4 A man and a teenage boy bitten by deadly blue-ringed octopuses at Nelson's Bay, north of Newcastle . . have both recovered. [**1897 blue swimmer:** W. Saville-Kent *Naturalist in Aust.* 238 The so-called Blue Crab, *Neptunus pelagicus*. It belongs to the group known as swimming crabs.] **1905** D.G. Stead *Crustaceans* 28 Some crabs swim about freely in the waters, their legs being flattened, and the last pair turned into oars to enable them to propel themselves readily through the water. To this pelagic kind belongs our common Blue Swimming Crab. **1952** W.J. Dakin *Austral. Seashores* 196 The well-known and widely distributed blue swimming crabs, *Portunus pelagicus*, and they are caught for eating. **1953** *Bulletin* (Sydney) 25 Mar. 12/2, I have a boyhood memory of catching 'blue-swimmer' crabs on a tuppenny fishing-line. **1984** *Canberra Chron.* 15 Aug. 23/3 Freshly boiled blue swimmers and mussels and pipis grilled alive in the shells. **1848** W. Carron *Narr. Exped. Rockingham Bay & Cape York* (1849) 74 The natives . . gave us a **blue-tongued lizard**, which I opened and took out eleven young ones, which we roasted and ate. **1882** F. McCoy *Prodromus of Zool. Vic.* (1885) I. viii. 15 These Lizards are very sluggish, so that the popular name 'Sleepy Lizard' as well as 'Blue-tongue' comes to be applied to both. **1923** *Bulletin* (Sydney) 3 May 24/4 What's the proper tucker for blue-tongue or shingle-back lizards? **1951** *Ibid.* 28 Feb. 13/4 A blue-tongued lizard is a master of profanity. His hiss, when a dog has him bailed-up, is a gem of threatening invective. **1962** Marshall & Drysdale *Journey among Men* 10 Blue-tongued stumpy-tailed lizards—'bobtails'—were plentiful. **1968** R. Hill *Bush Quest* 30, I . . flicked away a few lumps of earth only to reveal a blue-tongue lizard. . . Its Prussian-blue tongue flowed out of the gaping mouth with a life of its own. **1945** C. Barrett *Austral. Bird Life* 143 The **blue-winged kookaburra** (*Dacelo leachi*) is more brightly coloured than its cousin of Eastern and South Australia. **1955** F. Lane *Patrol to Kimberleys* 121 Near a creek lined with tea-trees and gums, Glen saw kingfishers and their larger cousins, the blue-winged kookaburra. **1962** Marshall & Drysdale *Journey among Men* 90 We saw a blue-winged kookaburra, the tropical one that does not laugh. **1841** J. Gould *Birds of Aust.* (1848) III. Pl. 18, *Malurus Cyaneus* . . Superb Warbler, **Blue Wren**, etc., of the colonists. **1847** G.F. Angas *Savage Life & Scenes* I. 58 The brilliant blue wrens are constantly fluttering like blossoms. **1892** 'Mrs A. Macleod' *Silent Sea* I. 97 Here she loved to watch the little blue wrens taking their feeble flight from one tussock of grass to another. **1926** L.C.E. Gee *Bush Tracks & Gold Fields* 95 At a friend's house up the gully the blue wrens come hopping. **1948** P.J. Hurley *Red Cedar* 32 Birds of all kinds found this sanctuary . . piping spine-bills, pretty trilling blue-wrens. **1983** *Advertiser* (Adelaide) 12 Dec. 17/1 In the mythology of the Adnjamathanha people, Chambers Gorge in the Flinders Ranges was created by a boomerang throw of the Blue Wren.

bluebell. Any of several small herbs of the genus *Wahlenbergia* (fam. Campanulaceae) bearing blue flowers reminiscent of the related Scottish bluebell; *native bluebell*, see Native *a.* 6 a.

1839 *Southern Austral.* (Adelaide) 16 Oct. 4/1 May. . . The blue bell is almost the only flower in bloom this month. **1903** *Proc. Linnean Soc. N.S.W.* XXVIII. 412 Under *Campanulaceae* . . the Australian 'blue bell', *Wahlenbergia gracilis*. **1932** *Victorian Naturalist* XLIX. 190 The ubiquitous Bluebell (*Wahlenbergia*) makes 'lakes of blue' in the distance. **1975** A.B. & J.W. Cribb *Wild Food in Aust.* 164 Flavour of the bluebells is very mild, but the attractive appearance makes them worth using in salads.

blue-blind, *a. Obs.* [U.S. *blue* intoxicated (see OEDS *a.* 3 b.) + *blind (drunk).*] (Extremely) drunk. Also **blue-blind paralytic**.

1911 *Bulletin* (Sydney) 12 Oct. 14/2 Who ever hears . . of a man being 'drunk'? . . The staid and dignified citizen will say he is 'intoxicated', . . the dustman that he is 'blue-blind paralytic'. **1913** *Ibid.* 25 Sept. 22/2 'Inebriated'. . . In the number, aptness and variety of its colloquial equivalents I consider it commandeers the pastry. For instance:- loaded, primed, beered, . . blind, blue-blind. **1918** H. Dinning *Byways on Service* 107 'If I could get drunk,' said a man wearing his equipment, 'I would—blue-blind paralytic. I never felt so like it in my life.'

Also **blue-blinded** *ppl. a.*

1914 E. Dyson *Spats' Fact'ry* 65 'Well, I'm blue-blinded,' murmured Nippo O'Kieffe.

bluebottle. The Portuguese man o' war, the blue marine siphonophore *Physalia physalis*, having a floating jelly-like body bearing a crest and trailing tentacles that sting on contact and may be several metres in length.

1911 *Bulletin* (Sydney) 27 Apr. 13/4 The famous 'blue-bottle', which at times infests the ocean beaches, and whose greeting resembles that of a much-magnified stinging nettle. **1931** *Surf: All about It* 43 To every rose its thorn, and to the surf its bluebottles. **1949** C.B. Maxwell *Surf* 111 The Bluebottle (*Physalia*), the major hazard in the surf. . . Small, bright-blue bladders . . trail long threadlike tentacles which tend to wrap about the limbs of the surfers, inflicting stinging weals that set up a dull rheumaticky ache. **1968** V. Serventy *Southern Walkabout* 19, I was able to explain to the children the build of these 'balloons', really marine creatures called the Portuguese-men-of-war and locally known as a bluebottle. The bluebottle of the west is a different jellyfish. **1986** *Canberra Times* 17 Jan. 9/1 A Batemans Bay doctor said he knew of one death recently in N.S.W. when a man had accidentally swallowed a bluebottle while swimming at Bondi Beach.

blue duck. [Of unknown origin, but cf. (orig. U.S.) *dead duck.*] A lost cause, a failure.

1895 C. Crowe *Austral. Slang Dict.* 10 *Blue duck*, no good; no money in it. **1902** R.C. Praed *My Austral. Girlhood* 21 One evening as he sits smoking outside the hut, without a moment's warning, he finds a spear in his chest! Darn'd, but he would have been a blue duck if I hadn't ridden up that very moment and scared the natives off. **1916** *Truth* (Sydney) 16 Jan. 1/7 Hopes of Lord Mayoralty are a blue duck. **1939** I.L. Idriess *Cyaniding for Gold* 138 But now his growling rhythm was 'She's a blue duck—she's a blue duck. She's a blue duck.' **1942** F. Clune *Last of Austral. Explorers* 101 Not a trace of gold! It was a Blue Duck. **1962** J. Naish *Cruel Field* 50 'She's no gude,' sighed Pedro unhelpfully. 'She's a blue duck.' **1978** R. McKie *Bitter Bread* 142 He had rung round the usual contacts. But this Saturday had, early, an unmistakable feeling of being a blue duck for news.

blue metal, *n.* [f. *blue metal* bluish stone used in road-making: see OEDS *blue, a.* 12 c.] Pieces of stone used as missiles, esp. in street fights. Also *attrib.* and *fig.*

1891 *Truth* (Sydney) 8 Mar. 4/6 Federalists, at the next polling-day, will get more 'blue metal' than Union votes. **1904** *Ibid.* 5 June 5/1 Strategically retreated from *these bombarding bandits* with their blue metal. **1906** *Ibid.* 5 Aug. 1/4 When the Collingwood tigers fail to win a football match, they get even with the opposition players by pelting them with blue metal. **1917** A.B. Paterson *Saltbush Bill* 34 There's some what likes blue-metal for to throw. **1935** F. Clune *Rolling down Lachlan* 59 A large heap of blue metal being used by an imp and an urchin for duelling purposes. **1946** —— *Try Nothing Twice* 5 The streets of Woolloomooloo were paved with blue-metal stones, which came in quite handy for the larrikin 'pushes' in their frequent fights. **1949** *Coast to Coast 1948* 34 But Butch could fight. He could also hurl goolies, gibbers, and plain bluemetal with devastating accuracy.

blue-metal, *v.* [f. prec.] *trans.* To attack (someone) by throwing stones; to pelt with stones.

1891 *Truth* (Sydney) 18 Jan. 1/4 A gentleman named Charles Durkin was painting the atmosphere of Cowper-Street blue when a constable remonstrated, whereupon Durkin blue-metalled *him*. **1901** *Ibid.* 10 Feb. 7/3 If he should be unwise enough to resent this outspoken pleasantry, he will be very lucky if he does not get kicked or bluemetalled. **1946** F. Clune *Try Nothing Twice* 71 In Woolloomooloo . . larrikin pushes blue-metalled one another.

blue orchid. [From the colour of the uniform and with reference to its supposed smartness.] During the war of 1939–45: a member of the R.A.A.F. Chiefly in *pl.*

1940 *Ack Ack: Jrnl. 2nd Anti Aircraft Regiment* 17 Oct. 9 Gordon Orchard has joined the 'Blue Orchids'. **1941** *Action Front: Jrnl. 2/2 Field Regiment* Sept. 3 Flower show . . to aid R.A.A.F. trainees. Display of blue orchids, probably. **1943** G.H. Johnston *New Guinea Diary* 76 In the hearing of a Port Moresby digger never call a R.A.A.F. pilot 'Blue Orchid'! **1955** N. Bartlett *Island Victory* 62 Airfield construction units and radar personnel on the L.S.T . . stubbornly remained what they were, skilled artisans rather than soldiers, hardened up 'blue orchids'. **1968** G. Mill *Nobody dies but Me* 61 There's about as much love between the Army and the Air Force as there is between a pork chop and a Jew. They call us Blue Orchids, amongst other things. Menzies' Blue Orchids, in fact. **1972** K. Clift *Saga of Sig* 57 Some A.I.F. bitterness toward the Air Force, generally referring to them as 'Blue Orchids' and indicating that the initials R.A.F. stood for 'rare as f--k.'

bluestone. [Spec. use of *bluestone* a building stone of a bluish grey colour.] In e. Aust., a basalt used for building, road making, etc.; in S.A., an argillite or quartzite. Also *attrib.*

1850 *Illustr. Austral. Mag.* (Melbourne) Dec. 389 It is constructed of blue-stone, with granite in the arch and parapet. **1851** *Britannia* (Hobart) 9 June 3/1 A six-story steam mill, built entirely of blue stone. **1855** G.H. WATHEN *Golden Colony* 15 The basalt of the plains has become familiar under the name of 'blue-stone'. **1871** J. BALLANTYNE *Homes & Homesteads* 143 On the banks of the river they have now erected a comely structure of bluestone, 104 feet square. **1889** *Illustr. Austral. News* (Melbourne) 1 July 23/3 A number of masons were working on the hard, sonorous basalt (called bluestone by the colonists) a hundred yards from my house. **1903** *Truth* (Sydney) 4 Jan. 8/3 The outer walls of Pentridge are . . constructed of rough bluestone. **1926** 'S. WESTLAW' *White Peril* 227 Dick sat down on the low blue-stone wall that fronted the sand and pondered. **1961** M. KIDDLE *Men of Yesterday* 283 The homes of the squatters, made of the volcanic bluestone which littered the District, merged into the landscape. **1969** MORGAN & GILBERT *Early Adelaide Arch.* p. viii, A greyish-blue young slate which in Adelaide is called bluestone; this is neither as black nor is it as hard as the basalt which was so individual to early Melbourne and which is also called, or miscalled, bluestone. **1975** L.H. CLARK *Rouseabout Reflections* 5 'Neath the ancient shade of the elms and birches Stands the last of the Outback's bluestone churches. **1979** *Westerly* ii. 27, I moved out the same day. Into a renovated cottage in North Adelaide. Bluestone on the outside, white walls and Picasso prints inside. **1983** *Heritage Aust.* II. ii. 26 The bluestone of Adelaide . . is a dark-coloured (brown, grey, black and orange but never blue) argillite related to siltstone, slate or quartzite . . and is visible everywhere in nineteenth century buildings of all kinds.

blue-tongue.

1. Shortened form of *blue-tongue lizard* (see BLUE *a.*).

1882 F. MCCOY *Prodromus of Zool. Vic.* (1885) I. viii. 15 These Lizards are very sluggish, so that the popular name 'Sleepy Lizard' as well as 'Blue-tongue' comes to be applied to both. **1911** *Bulletin* (Sydney) 28 Sept. 13/2 The only weapon of defence of the blue-tongue ('bogi', 'bob-tailed gohanna', or 'sleepy lizard') is a jaw that closes like a rat-trap. **1949** *Ibid.* 11 May 10/3 First cousin to the blue-tongue, the prickly-tailed lizard of W.A.'s central tablelands is also blue-tongued and sleepy. **1979** C. KLEIN *Women of Certain Age* 60 A blue-tongue opened a sudden mouth at her feet, almost catapulting her down the stairs.

2. *transf.* (Esp. in allusion to the supposed sleepiness of lizards.)

1900 *Bulletin* (Sydney) 18 Aug. 14/3 The shearer terms the rouseabout variously a 'loppy', 'bluetongue', 'wop-wop', 'leather-neck', 'crocodile', etc. **1913** C.J. DENNIS *Backblock Ballads* 20 Pass that whip, you blasted blue-tongue! **1925** *Bulletin* (Sydney) 12 Feb. 22/2 A blue-tongue is a station manager, from the usual color of his remarks when addressing common lizards [*sc.* boundary riders]. **1936** *Ibid.* 29 Jan. 20/4, I have heard boundary-riders referred to by many names. Blue-tongues, lizards . . and paddock parasites are just a few of those which will pass the censor. **1956** C.D. MILLS *Stockwhip & Spur* 48 But the blue-tongues were different and chancing no loss, For wet days like dry days were paid by the boss. **1968** L. BRADEN *Bullockies* 119 Dad used to take his bullocks and dray as far as Whittlesea. . . They used to call off-siders Fridays or blue-tongues. **1975** L. RYAN *Shearers* 124 'Righto, you blue-tongues!' he bellowed out. 'Get stuck into it!'

bluey. [f. *blue* + -Y.]

1. a. A swag (so called because the outer covering was traditionally a blue blanket); BLUE *n.*[1] 1.

1878 *Squatter's Plum* 42 If a Minister wishes to gain information on anything connected with station-work, he need not go to a kangaroo-drive. . . Rather let him arm himself with a billy, and 'hump bluey' *incognito* in search of work. **1888** 'SPECIAL CORRESPONDENT' *Barrier Silver & Tin Fields* 23 Teams full of diggers' swags pushed on for the great silver-fields. Crowds of men placed their 'blueys' upon their backs and tramped off. **1892** 'E. KINGLAKE' *Austral. at Home* 132 He carries a swag containing all his personal property wrapped in a blue blanket which is folded like a horse collar. The swag is called in the vernacular a 'bluey'. **1899** W.T. GOODGE *Hits! Skits! & Jingles* 143 There's the everlasting swaggie with his bluey on his back Who is striking out for sunset on the Never-never track. **1930** *Aussie* (Sydney) 15 July 27 After 'Matilda', 'Bluey' is probably the favourite 'pet' name for the Australian swag. 'Bluey' originated from the blue blanket that is generally found in a swag, and is given preference, as blue shows the dirt less than any other colour. **1942** *Bulletin* (Sydney) 29 Apr. 13/4 The knight of the road mournfully thudded his bluey down and peered wistfully over the fence. **1955** D. NILAND *Shiralee* They'll tell you he took that child from the city . . and carried it . . in a sugar-bag that swung as a balance to his bluey. **1981** G. CROSS *George & Widda-Woman* 10 A swaggie suddenly appearing out of the bush, unshaven, with wild, haunted eyes, his bluey and billycan on his back.

b. *transf.* Luggage.

1959 *Overland* xv. 13 To get there I had to swim the Russell River with my bluey, a tin trunk. I had been carrying the trunk on my shoulder. **1963** J. DUFFY *Outsville Pub* 22 Where's yer bluey? No luggage?

2. A swagman's (usu. blue) blanket.

1888 J. POTTS *One Yr. Anti-Chinese Work in Qld.* 10 Then fancy hears a snake hissing as it glides along the ground—perhaps to curl with you in 'bluey'. **1891** *Truth* (Sydney) 15 Mar. 7/3 This kit consisted of a tin can, a tin mug, a blanket, and a good deal of assurance. These, in bush parlance, are *billy, pannikin, bluey,* and *knocker.* **1894** W. CROMPTON *Convict Jim* 39 With his bluey wrapped around him peacefully asleep he lay. **1920** *Character Glimpses: Australs. on Somme* 19 With my old bluey curled tightly on top of my pack. **1924** LAWRENCE & SKINNER *Boy in Bush* 92 'Now, roll up y'r bluey'—meaning the new rug, which was yellow. **1956** R.G. EDWARDS *Overlander Songbk.* 87 Wrap me up with my stock whip and bluey, And bury me deep down below. **1965** B. JAMES *Collecting Austral. Gemstones* 83 Humping his water-bags and a few simple tools wrapped in his dusty bluey.

3. Orig. and in early use chiefly *Tas.* A heavy grey-blue woollen outer garment or coat, protective against cold and wet (see quots. 1899); *Tasmanian bluey*, see TASMANIAN *a.* 3. Also *attrib.*

1890 A.M. ANDREWS *Card Only* (1891) 6 The ordinary camp costume of a miner, moleskins and light 'bluey', with broad, slouched hat. **1899** *Bulletin* (Sydney) 11 Feb. 17/1 Term 'bluey' never applied to swag in Tasmania. The Tas. 'bluey' is a rough overcoat of blue-grey woollen, and never seen by writer in any other part of Australasia. **1899** *North-Western Advocate* (Devonport) 1 Sept. 4/1 The winter costume . . is incomplete without . . a 'bluey'. A bluey is a sort of smock such as is worn by carters in Great Britain, made of rough blue or grey serge, and will keep the water out for a whole long day's journey. **1903** *Advocate* (Burnie) 27 June 3/3 His father . . told him to put on his bluey as the morning was cold. **1918** *Bulletin* (Sydney) 2 May 22/1 They hitched their long-sleeved boots up to their waistbelts, shed their 'blueys' and . . started. **1929** *Ibid.* 12 June 23/4, I bought a 'bluey' nine years ago, and have worn it every winter since. **1953** K. GRAVES *Tasmanian Pastoral* 59 From the little farms high on the mountain walls above the men had gathered, wearing 'bluey' coats, oil-skin slickers, or even chaff-bags slung over their shoulders, since sudden squalls sweep across the highlands. **1964** P. ADAM SMITH *Hear Train Blow* 118, I found most of my 'clobber' in the wash-house—an old pair of dungaree trousers and an old 'bluey', a bushman's coat. **1984** *Canberra Times* 6 July 6/1 Bluey Jackets, boots and overalls without the normal 10 days' qualifying period.

4. A summons; BLUE *n.*[1] 2.

[**1895** C. CROWE *Austral. Slang Dict.* 58 *Piece of blue paper*, a summons.] **1909** 'H. THOMPSON' *Ballads about Business* 13 I'll show you valls papered mit blueys. **1958** V. KELLY *Greedy Ones* 134 'What's the warrant for?' . . 'It's for wife-desertion, and a wife-starver's bluey can keep a man out of circulation for quite a while.' **1965** G. MCINNES *Road to Gundagai* 242 A uniformed John Hop with a tall patent leather helmet rang the bell and handed me the dreaded 'bluey', the summons for riding a bike without lights. **1973** *Kings Cross Whisper* (Sydney) cl. 16/4, I was down at Central today on a small matter of a traffic bluey. **1979** J. LINDEMAN *Red Rumps & White Faces* 104 She showed me a 'Bluey' from the Taxation Department, wanting to know why she had not sent in a tax return for the war years. **1986** *Choice* Apr. 2/1 Imagine my shock upon returning to a bluey at the end of the day.

5. A familiar hypocoristic form of any of a number of popular names for birds, animals, etc., usu. beginning with 'blue'; a bird, animal, etc., predom. blue in colour.

1903 *Bulletin* (Sydney) 31 Jan. 36/1 We had no knowledge of scientific terms. To us they were . . bluies, diamonds, big and little silver-eyes. **1912** *Ibid.* 22 Aug. 13/1 Have no fear of the lick of the blue-tongued lizard. Have seen a terrier's ear torn in three strips by a bite from 'bluey' with no ill-effects. **1923** *Ibid.* 14 June 24/4 The wonga's love-call can bring dozens of the blueys cooing on the branches overhead. **1961** *Ibid.* 31 May 35/3 We call them blue martins. . . Ornithologists refer to them as some species of wood swallow. . . They're all 'blueys' to us. **1979** S.W. DUTHIE *Fidlers Creek* 32 We get . . red mullet, a bluey, a couple of flounder.

6. A nickname given to a red-haired person; BLUE *n.*[1] 3.

1906 *Truth* (Sydney) 28 Oct. 9/4 The Perilous Adventure of Red-headed 'Bluey', a Dealer in Greens. **1936** A.B. PATERSON *Shearer's Colt* 123 'Bluey', as the crowd called him, had found another winner. (All red-haired men are called 'Bluey' in Australia for some reason or other.) **1950** J. MCLAREN *New Love for Old* 8 Many Australians called him Bluey, their odd nickname for people with reddish hair. **1962** P. WHITE *Season at Sarsparilla* (1974) 173 'Ugh, I don't like the red, freckly men! . .' 'Don't go much on the blueys meself.' **1978** R.H. CONQUEST *Dusty Distances* 32, I found out later that he was a native of New South Wales, called 'Bluey' because of his red hair—typical Australian logic.

7. In *pl.* Denim working trousers or overalls.

1917 *Stretcher* (Melbourne) Mar. 15 Yes, combination blueys are still fashionable in France. **1921** K.S. PRICHARD *Black Opal* 282 Their working clothes, faded blueys, or worn moleskins. **1946** —— *Roaring Nineties* 219 When he's had a shower, washed his blueys and put on a clean shirt, it makes me happy just to see him. **1950** J. MORRISON *Port of Call* 243 You'll be back in time to catch her, Jim, only you won't get home to change. How would it be if you turned up in the blueys? You could get a wash and brush-up at the station.

boab, boabab: see BAOBAB.

boang, var. BUNG.

board.

1. The part of the floor of a shearing shed upon which the sheep are shorn (see quot. 1893); *shearing board*, see SHEARING B. 3. Also *attrib.*

[N.Z. **1857** R.B. PAUL *Lett. from Canterbury* 90 One of these huts must serve for your first year's wool-shed, with the help of a few hurdles in front, and a tarpaulin or a few boards to shear on. **1867** J.C. JORDAN *Managem. Sheep & Stations* 90 The shearing boards should be kept constantly swept and clean from pieces and locks.] **1870** *Austral. Town & Country Jrnl.* (Sydney) 5 Nov. 11/3 So unreasonable are they, that an act of simple justice is often the signal for a strike, which includes a third or a half of the men 'on the board', as the shearing floor is by them termed. **1873** A. TROLLOPE *Aust. & N.Z.* (1967) I. 126 The floor, on which the shearers absolutely work, is called 'the board'. **1883** *Illustr. Austral. News* (Melbourne) 23 Nov. 194/2 The centre of the woolshed is given up to pens, the long shearers' floor, or 'board' as it is called, running on either side. **1893** 'OLD CHUM' *Chips* 42 Down each side . . is a clear space about ten feet wide called the 'board'. Here the shearing is done by a long row of men on each side. In the middle is a large enclosure, or 'pen', into which the sheep are driven from outside, and there are smaller pens, called 'catching pens', on each side, which are fed from this large one. **1904** L.M.P. ARCHER *Bush Honeymoon* 61 There are two boards, *i.e.*, narrow passages which run the length of the shed; here the shearers stand about two yards apart. **1917** C.L. DREW *Reminisc. Dick Gilbert* 17 Be cleaning your machine whenever he happens to be coming along the board, and he won't have a chance of seeing what a rough shearer you are. **1933** R.B. PLOWMAN *Camel Pads* 194 Yet the rough bough-shed, the rudely constructed yards, and the dried bullock-hide which was the 'board', were emblems of amazing courage and heroic endeavour in subduing the wilderness. **1946** *Bulletin* (Sydney) 11 Dec. 21/1 'I'm walkin' orf the board,' he yelled. 'I won't work with scabs who shear for shed-hand's wages.' **1954** *Ibid.* 24 Feb. 13/3 He was able to stride bowyanged and 'Jackie Howe'd' to his place on the board and snarl at the tarboy, 'Outer me way! I hate the smell of a rouseabout!' **1979** HARMSWORTH & DAY *Wool & Mohair* 150 The *board boy* picks up the fleece, carries it to the skirting table, throws it so that it spreads evenly over the table.

2. Used with reference to the employment of shearers at a shed, esp. in the phr. **on the board;** also **full board,** a full complement of shearers.

1879 S.W. SILVER *Austral. Grazier's Guide* 51 There are fifty or seventy of the smartest shearers in the land 'on the board'. **1891** 'ROUSEABOUT' *Jackeroo* 63 Mr Jowle was known to the shearers as an old skinflint... Every man on the 'board' knew that Jowle would levy blackmail in some shape or other. **1904** *Shearer* (Sydney) 3 Sept. 5/4 Cobran started on the 16th ult. with a full board. Everything going splendidly. Shearers booked for sheds to follow. **1912** T.E. SPENCER *Bindawalla* 65 There were men enough at the camp now to make a full board, and next week shearing would be in full swing. **1926** *Bulletin* (Sydney) 14 Jan. 24/3 With a board of 16 shearers a jumbuck-barbering firm this season cut out 105,000 sheep. **1956** F.B. VICKERS *First Place to Stranger* 233 So there were five of the old team and three new men come up from Perth to fill the board at Brentwood Station. **1965** *Tracks we Travel* 95 The only cleanskin on the board.

3. In the phr. **over the board,** used to designate the overseer of a shearing gang, the contractor; esp. in the collocation **boss over** (or **of**) **the board**: see quots. 1908 and 1979. Also **man over the board.**

1893 H. LAWSON *Collected Prose* (1972) I. 105 The 'boss over the board' comes along to tell the men not to swear, 'there's ladies coming.' **1895** *Worker* (Sydney) 4 May 3/1 After finishing Abbott's shed he.. was made boss over the board. **1896** *Ibid.* 11 Jan. 3/4 Mr Stokes, the person over the board. **1896** T. HENEY *Girl at Birrell's* 109 The shed overseer, the 'man over the board', was present to see that the shearing was properly done. **1896** H. LAWSON *While Billy Boils* 89 Lies about getting the best of squatters and bosses-over-the-board. **1899** *Western Champion* (Barcaldine) 13 June 7/4, I know another pastoralist who, when over the board, never 'chipped'. **1908** W.H. OGILVIE *My Life in Open* 39 The shearing-board is supervised by an overseer, commonly known as the Boss of the Board, whose duties are to keep the shearers in check, to see that the sheep are properly shorn, and to act generally as a middle man between shearers and owner. **1912** J. BRADSHAW *Highway Robbery under Arms* (ed. 3) 37 You could not leave the shed without the permission of the man over the board, or you would be fined the ensuing pen of sheep. **1925** *Bulletin* (Sydney) 9 Apr. 24/1 The shed overseer or boss of the board is the 'red light'. **1937** D. GUNN *Links with Past* 139 George Jenkins was over the board. At Callandoon the sheep.. were shorn in the grease. **1943** H.G. LAMOND *From Tariaro to Ross Roy* 27 The boss of the board would appeal for sheep washers from among the shearers. **1956** C.D. MILLS *Stockwhip & Spur* 49 'We'll meet at the crutching,' said the boss of the board, 'So send her down Hughie,' the rouseabouts roared. **1965** L. HAYLEN *Big Red* 97 Next came the 'boss of the board', the shearing contractor. **1979** HARMSWORTH & DAY *Wool & Mohair* 151 The *boss of the board* is generally in charge of the team. He supervises the shearers, seeing that they shear the sheep correctly, counts the sheep from the counting out pens, enters the number shorn to the credit of each individual shearer in a tally book and writes up the daily tally board.

Hence **boss of the boarding** *vbl. n.*

1944 A.E. MINNIS *And All Trees are Green* 97, I suppose he does the boss of the boarding himself?

bob-in. *Shilling-in*, see SHILLING 2.

[N.Z. **1889** W. DAVIDSON *Stories N.Z. Life* 5 From tricks at cards, the fun changed to 'a bob in' the winner shouting.] **1919** *Smith's Weekly* (Sydney) 15 Mar. 14/3 Forty of them gathered him up and made for the bar. 'A bob in' was suggested... After paying for the shout he salvaged a whole quid. **1922** *Ibid.* 21 Jan. 17/4 Blinks rang me up to apologise for his non-attendance at the Bob-in school. **1933** *Bulletin* (Sydney) 28 June 36/3 What say we rig a few bob-ins for the poor cow? **1949** *Coast to Coast 1948* 104 'Have this with me.' Buzzer and Tiger had it with Blue; then there was a bob-in; then they had one with Chrissie who'd been pulling beer at the Exchange since they were kids. **1961** *Bulletin* (Sydney) 15 Feb. 7/1 A 'bob-in' testimonial opened by the 'Courier-Mail'.. raised a total of over £500.

bobtail. [Transf. use of *bob-tail* animal with tail cut short.] The slow-moving lizard *Trachydosaurus rugosus* of s. mainland Aust., having large ridged scales on the back and a short rounded tail; SHINGLEBACK; STUMP LIZARD; STUMPY TAIL. See also *blue-tongue lizard* BLUE *a.*, SLEEPING LIZARD. Also **bob-tail(ed) goanna** (or **lizard**).

1872 MRS E. MILLETT *Austral. Parsonage* 180 The lizard which the colonists call the 'bob-tailed' guana, or in colonial pronunciation 'gew-anna'. *Ibid.* 181 A lizard of exactly the same shape as that of the 'bob-tails'. **1911** *Bulletin* (Sydney) 28 Sept. 13/2 The only weapon of defence of the blue-tongue ('bogi', 'bob-tailed gohanna', or 'sleepy lizard') is a jaw that closes like a rat-trap. **1937** R. FAIRBRIDGE *Pinjarra* 197 It was difficult to avoid running over bob-tailed lizards sleeping in the hot dust. **1943** *Bulletin* (Sydney) 6 Jan. 12/4 Always regarded the bobtail goanna as being in the snail class. **1978** L. WHITE *Memories of Childhood* 1 Father showed us the bobtail was harmless. He picked one up and put his finger crossways in the blue-tongued mouth.

bobuck /ˈboʊbʌk/. [Prob. f. a N.S.W. Aboriginal language.] The possum *Trichosurus caninus* of mountain forests in s.e. mainland Aust.

1953 E. MITCHELL *Flow River, blow Wind* 75 'A young bobuck!' said Charlie... Joseph let the possum sit on his shoulder. **1970** W.D.L. RIDE *Guide Native Mammals Aust.* 70 In Victoria it and the Bobuck are destructive in plantations of introduced pine trees.

boco, var. BOKO.

bodger. *Obs.* [Prob. f. Br. dial. *bodge* to work clumsily: see OED *v.* and EDD *v.*[1], and cf. *botch.*] Something (occas. someone) which is fake, false, or worthless. Also *attrib.*

1945 *Biscuit Bomber Weekly: Mag. 1st Austral. Air Maintenance Co.* 18 Feb. 3 This when the Bodgers, or sly guys place themselves in the most concealed.. places in the line. **1950** F.J. HARDY *Power without Glory* 383 This entailed the addition of as many more 'bodger' votes as possible. **1954** *Coast to Coast 1953–54* 76 Well, we stuck together all through the war—we was in under bodger names. **1966** S.J. BAKER *Austral. Lang.* (ed. 2) 292 An earlier underworld and Army use of *bodger* for something faked, worthless or shoddy. For example, a faked receipt or false name.. is a *bodger*; so is a shoddy piece of material sold by a door-to-door hawker.

bodgie, *n.*[1] [f. BODG(ER + -Y: see quot. 1983.] A male youth, esp. of the 1950s, distinguished by his conformity to certain fashions of dress and larrikin behaviour; analogous to the Br. 'teddy boy'. Also *attrib.*

1950 *Sunday Tel.* (Sydney) 7 May 47/3 The bizarre uniform of the 'bodgey'—belted velvet cord jacket, bright blue sports shirt without a tie, brown trousers narrowed at the ankle, shaggy Cornel Wilde haircut. **1951** *Sydney Morning Herald* 1 Feb. 1/9 What with 'bodgies' growing their hair long and getting round in satin shirts, and 'weegies' cutting their hair short and wearing jeans, confusion seems to be arising about the sex of some Australian adolescents. **1951** *Bulletin* (Sydney) 18 Apr. 14/1 The bloke with the bodgie haircut. **1956** *Truth* (Sydney) 1 Jan. 38/1 The current outbreak of vicious crimes by teenage louts who glory in the tag 'Teddy Boy' or 'Bodgie' is causing widespread concern. **1963** D. LOCKWOOD *We Aborigines* 155 The birth of black bodgies and the advent of juvenile delinquency among our tribespeople dates from the very time of these edicts. **1979** K.R. MACKENZIE *Cosmic Fun* 14 There was a bonzer bodgie, He was a lovely male, He whipped his widgie so humanely, She didn't even quail. **1983** *Age* (Melbourne) 12 Aug. 2/7 Mr Hewett says his research indicates that the term 'bodgie' arose around the Darlinghurst area in Sydney. It was just after the end of World War II and rationing had caused a flourishing black market in American-made cloth. 'People used to try and pass off inferior cloth as American-made when in fact it was not: so it was called 'bodgie',' he says. 'When some of the young guys started talking with American accents to big-note themselves they were called 'bodgies'.' **1986** *Canberra Times* 23 Feb. 8/7 Set in Brisbane in the bodgie and widgie era, the novel is the beautifully honed story of Lola and Brownie.

bodgie, *n.*[2] Altered form of BODGER, infl. by BODGIE *n.*[1]: see quot. 1952. Freq. as *adj.*

1952 *Sun* (Sydney) 6 Mar. 1/7 An office in town has a mail file marked *bodgies*. It's for letters that don't seem to come under any of the regular classifications. The misfits, in other words. **1964** J. IGGULDEN *Clouded Sky* 10 'I've had that bloody altimeter!' shouted Ern. 'It's a bodgie. I'll throw it in the bloody river.' **1967** G. JENKIN *Two Yrs. Bardunyah Station* 27 The Boss reckoned he could throw a boomerang... The Boss argued that he was getting all the bodgie ones, and that Jacky was using the only 'come-back' ones. **1975** LATCH & HITCHINGS *Mr X* 200 To avoid any suspicions in case they were picked up by the Transport Regulation Board, it was decided.. to take a 'bodgy' receipt for the tyres with them. **1978** O. WHITE *Silent Reach* 173 This heap is hot—else why did they give it a one-coat spray job over the original white duco and fix it with bodgie number plates? **1984** *Canberra Times* 27 Aug. 1/2 Allegations.. of branch-stacking and the use of hundreds of 'bodgie' members in the electorate.

Hence **bodgied up** *a.*

1972 A. CHIPPER *Aussie Swearers Guide* 31 'In he *lobs, bodgied up* and smelling like *dead horse gully*.' ('He arrived wearing a new suit and after shave lotion.')

body bullock. [Spec. use of *body* main part of a collection.] See quots. 1872 and 1959. Also *ellipt.* as **body.**

1872 C.H. EDEN *My Wife & I in Qld.* 36 Twelve bullocks is the usual number in a team, the two polers and the leaders being steady old stagers; the pair next to the pole are called the 'pointers'.. the remainder being called the 'body bullocks'. **1904** *Bulletin* (Sydney) 15 Dec. 40/1 Eighteen to twenty constitute a team, which includes polers—those nearest the waggon—clampers, body bullocks and leaders. **1959** H.P. TRITTON *Time means Tucker* 36 A bullock-team is made up in four parts: polers, pin, body and leaders... The body is the bulk of the team, sometimes 20 of [*sic*] more, the labourers of the team, mainly noted for their strength. **1968** L. BRADEN *Bullockies* 34 A bullock team is comprised of leaders .. clampers .. polers .. and body bullocks.

body-line, *a. Cricket. Hist.* Usu. in the collocation **body-line bowling.** Fast, leg-theory (bowling), intimidatory in effect: see quots. 1933.

1932 *Australasian* (Melbourne) 10 Dec. 27/4 It has many names, such as bowling at the leg stump, the author's definition, a clever one, leg theory, or bodyline offensive. *Ibid.* 17 Dec. 49/5, I have been repeatedly asked in reference to the umpires' powers respecting the rules of fair and unfair play in this body-line attack. **1933** *Age* (Melbourne) 19 Jan. 11/1 The Australian Board of Control has forwarded the following cablegram to the Marylebone club:- Body-line bowling assumed such proportions as to menace best interests of game, making protection of the body by batsmen the main consideration... Unless stopped at once is likely to upset friendly relations existing between Australia and England. **1933** BLUNDELL & BRANSON *Bodywhine* 36 In a sincere effort to stamp out body-line bowling the Australian Board of Control suggested a new rule, enabling the umpire to call a no-ball if he thought the bowler intended to injure the batsman. **1937** F. AUSTAL *City & Country Life* 43 The danger to the life and health of the batsman has been removed by the prohibition of body-line bowling. **1956** 'W. GODFREY' *Malleson at Melbourne* 99 The only means by which this placing could be rendered dangerous was.. by the discredited body-line bowling. **1966** E.W. SWANTON *World of Cricket* 126 *Body-line.* A term coined by the Australian journalists to describe the fast leg-theory bowling adopted extensively by H. Larwood, and to a lesser degree by W. Voce and W.E. Bowes, on the tour of D.R. Jardine's MCC team of 1932–33. **1979** K. BONYTHON *Ladies' Legs & Lemonade* 21, I was there on that memorable day in 1933 when the English Captain, Douglas Jardine, directed his fast bowler Harold Larwood to bowl the infamous 'bodyline' at the Australian team under Bill Woodfull.

Hence **body-liner** *n.*

1933 BLUNDELL & BRANSON *Bodywhine* 27 (*caption*) A former body-liner plays bowls.

body surf, *v. trans.* To ride (a breaking wave) towards the beach, streamlining the body and holding it rigid like a board: see SURF *n.* and *v.* Also *absol.*, and **body shoot.**

1956 T.I. THOMPSON *Pop. Handbk. Swimming* Pref., It is surprising how little has been written on the technique of body surfing which is so popular on the ocean beaches. **1956** S. HOPE *Diggers' Paradise* 166, I can't remember seeing anyone 'body-shoot' a wave in the way the lads do it now. **1963** J. POLLARD *Austral. Surfrider* 35 The broken water will help carry you to the beach or you can body shoot a wave in. *Ibid.* 41 Those who wish to enjoy the delights of body surfing should be strong swimmers experienced in the surf. **1981** *Nat.*

Times (Sydney) 20 Dec. 26/2 To body surf a big wave is to feel briefly like Superman or Superwoman.

Hence **body surfer** *n.*

1963 *Bulletin* (Sydney) 30 Mar. 10/3 The Surfies had only one real complaint. That was that while they were banned from swimming in the be-flagged area on beaches .. body-surfers were not prevented from swimming in the board area. **1963** J. Pollard *Austral. Surfrider* 14 Most beaches have special areas marked out for board riders, so keep clear of the sections reserved for body surfers.

bog, *v.* [Prob. fig. use of *bog* to sink, 'to get stuck into'.]

1. In the phr. **bog in(to),** to engage (in a task or activity) with vigour or enthusiasm; esp. to begin eating.

1907 *Bulletin* (Sydney) 24 Oct. 14/3 As for 'Bog into it!' that expression is a good deal older than I am. I heard, a few days since, a little girl request her brother to 'bog his frame down here'. **1910** *Huon Times* (Franklin) 23 July 6/1 For the defence, Mr Secomb said Jones heard someone call out, 'You can't win the match—bog into them.' **1916** 'Men Of Anzac' *Anzac Bk.* 164 Vaulting the parapet and bogging into a dinkum bayonet charge. **1917** C.T. O'Neill *Soldiers' Poems*, An' like a lot of cannibals we bog into the stew. **1927** F.C. Biggers *Bat-Eye* 14 Nights fer bucks, 'Oo bog in straight, an' try their 'and at stoushin's arts. **1932** I.L. Idriess *Flynn of Inland* (1965) 212 'Bog in!' called the cook; and all hands 'bogged in'. **1948** K.S. Prichard *Golden Miles* 83 If he saw a trucker in difficulty, he would just bog in and give a hand: not wait to be asked. **1968** W.N. Scott *Some People* 120 He made it up that the two of them should each cook a feed and the contract men could bog into it. **1978** G.A. Wilkes *Dict. Austral. Colloquialisms* 41 'Two, four, six, eight; bog in, don't wait' is a mock 'grace'.

2. *intr.* Chiefly *W.A. Mining.* To work underground, in a coal or gold mine, shovelling ore or mining refuse away from the workface, usu. into trucks for transport to the surface. Also *trans.*

1935 *Bulletin* (Sydney) 8 May 20/1 Back in the early days of the Golden Mile the writer, then a 'shoveller', was frequently urged to 'bog' his frame into a big heap of mullock or ore. Now, 35 years later, from the verb 'to bog' has descended the noun 'bogger'. **1946** K.S. Prichard *Roaring Nineties* 302 He was bogging on the Boulder, and the first day shovelling ore took the stiffening out of a man. **1947** G. Casey *Wits are Out* 175, I put in six months bogging underground on the goldfields once. **1959** *Bulletin* (Sydney) 6 May 16/2 Main feature of this year's Kalgoorlie-Boulder (W.A.) Community Fair was a shovelling competition. By bogging 35 shovelfuls each minute, 32 lb. at a throw, a Kalgoorlie miner .. shifted a ton of ore in under two minutes. **1968** K. Denton *Walk around my Cluttered Mind* 19 'Bogging' meant shovelling up mullock. **1982** M. Wattone *Winning Gold in W.A.* 64, I then went back to Kalgoorlie... I got a job for the Croesus Proprietory [*sic*] Ltd, bogging (shovelling) down the mine.

Hence **bogging-out** *vbl. n.*, **bog-in** *n.*

1943 *Jest: Digestion Good Humor* 43 **Bogging out** is the use of a shovel, commonly known as a *banjo* to shovel ore or mullock (usually off flat sheets) into trucks. **1954** J. Cleary *Climate of Courage* 58 Two suburban ladies .. sat toying with their food and wishing they had gone to Sargent's where they could have had a real **bog-in** for less than half the price.

Bogan /'boʊgən/. [The name of a river in w. N.S.W.] Used *attrib.* in Special Comb. **Bogan flea,** any of several prostrate annual plants of the genus *Calotis* (fam. Asteraceae) esp. *C. hispidula*, the seeds of which have small rigid spines; see also Bindi-eye; **gate,** see quot. 1980; **shower,** a dust storm.

1905 *Proc. Linnean Soc. N.S.W.* XXX. 44 The 'burr'-like fruiting heads of several species of *Calotis* are regarded with disfavour by sheep-owners... The pappus surmounting each achene is composed of barbed bristles or sharp spines, and sometimes causes great irritation to those who camp out. Hence stockmen call these fruits '**Bogan Fleas**'. **1920** J.H. Maiden *Weeds N.S.W.* 12 Everybody in the country knows the pest called Bindi-eye or Bogan flea. The principal weed (a native) which goes under this name is *Calotis cuneifolia*. **1981** G.M. Cunningham et al. *Plants Western N.S.W.* 653 In its early stages of growth bogan flea is relatively acceptable to stock but the plants are shunned once the seeds have matured. **1980** J. Wright *Big Hearts & Gold Dust* 45 Don stopped at a **bogan gate**... Though I'd seen many of these intricate contraptions of barbed wire and sticks, I'd never had the pleasure of trying to open one. Usually bogan gates were erected as a temporary block but almost invariably remained to become a jigsaw puzzle of flesh devouring spikes. **1904** A.B. Paterson *Rio Grande's Last Race* 29 We don't respect the clouds up there, they fill us with disgust, They mostly bring a **Bogan shower**—three rain-drops and some dust. **1945** *Queanbeyan Age* 2 Jan. 1/2 People are getting very tired of hearing 'a few showers are expected in a day or so', as a change is approaching from the west, but most of them are just Bogan showers. **1953** *Bulletin* (Sydney) 20 May 13/1 The main street in Trundle (N.S.W.) is so wide that in a Bogan shower its pretty hard to see the other pub.

bogey /'boʊgi/, *n.* Also **bogie.** [f. Bogey *v.*] Also *attrib.*

1. A swim or bathe; a bath.

1847 A. Harris *Settlers & Convicts* (1953) 132 In the cool of the evening had a 'bogie' (bathe) in the river. **1869** Mrs W.M. Howell *Diggings & Bush* 247 Florence was much amused the other evening by her enquiring if she (Flory) was going down to the water to have a 'bogey'. Flory was much puzzled till she found out that a 'bogey', in colonial phraseology, meant a bath. **1876** J.A. Edwards *Gilbert Gogger* 149 Gilbert and his two companions decided to have a bogie; they accordingly began to swim about in a large water-hole. **1894** G. Boothby *On Wallaby* 246 An hour's sharp tennis (for these Queenslanders are never tired) prepares the body for the evening bath, or *bogie* as it is usually called. **1912** *Truth* (Sydney) 11 Aug. 3/6 He may risk taking a bogie once a year or be induced to change his sox once a quarter. **1924** *Bulletin* (Sydney) 22 May 24/1 A boar was discovered by two of us having a bogey in a 16,000-yard tank about five miles from the river. **1955** H.G. Lamond *Towser* 136 We'll go down to the water-hole and have a bogey. **1974** D. Stuart *Prince of my Country* 110 Take a bogey .. there; keep an eye on your soap, the gins are always pinching mine. **1981** G. Mackenzie *Aurukun Diary* 36 A bogey is the Queensland outback word for a bath or bathe.

2. Comb. **bogey hole.**

1913 *Newcastle Morning Herald* 31 Dec. 5/3 They .. went to Blackwood's Beach, a treacherous bogey-hole. **1926** M. Forrest *Hibiscus Heart* 134 Leant thankfully against the bole of a piccabeen that came to the edge of the bogie hole. **1949** B. O'Reilly *Green Mountains* 274 The 'bogie hole' was .. a large basin three feet deep sculptured from the living granite. **1983** *Newcastle Herald* 10 Jan. 11/6 More than 200 people attended the Greek Orthodox Church's Blessing of the Waters service at Newcastle's Bogey Hole yesterday morning. The highlight of the service was when 30 men tried to retrieve the holy cross from the bottom of the old convict-built pool.

bogey /'boʊgi/, *v.* [a. Dharuk *bu-gi.*] *intr.* To swim; to bathe.

1788 *Hist. Rec. N.S.W.* (1893) II. 700, I have bathed, or have been bathing .. Bogie d'oway. These were Colby's words on coming out of the water. **1790** D. Southwell Corresp. & Papers, *Bō-gie*, to dive. **1830** R. Dawson *Present State Aust.* 166 'Top bit, massa, bogy,' (bathe) and he threw himself into the water. **1841** *HRA* (1924) 1st Ser. XXI. 472, I suppose you want your Boat, Sir; Yes, said Mr Dixon; well, said Crabb I suppose we must bogey for it. Yes, said Mr Dixon, any two of ye that can swim. **1876** 'Eight Yrs.' Resident' *Queen of Colonies* 43 Bathing, or bogying, for that is the colonial phrase borrowed from the blacks. **1904** *Bulletin* (Sydney) 3 Mar. 35/2 They 'bogey' at all hours of the day; the dwellers along the river are almost amphibious. **1923** T. Hall *Short Hist. Downs Blacks* 12 The males were allowed to bogey in the forenoons and the females in the afternoons. **1949** B. O'Reilly *Green Mountains* 274 We kiddies 'bogied' with never a bathing costume. **1960** V. Carell *Naked we are Born* 47 One blackfella, him take lubra go bogey-bogey... They wash wash, they play about. **1974** *Smoke Signal* (Palm Island) June 7 'Bogey' with plenty of soap and water *every day.*

bog-eye, var. Boggi.

boggabri /'bɒgəbraɪ/. [Prob. f. a N.S.W. Aboriginal language. Also the name of a town in n.e. N.S.W.] Any of several low herbs, esp. *Amaranthus mitchellii* (fam. Amaranthaceae), *Chenopodium pumilio* and *C. carinatum* (fam. Chenopodiaceae), and *Commelina cyanea* (see Scurvy grass).

1893 *Antipodean* (Melbourne) 95, I cud do a bit of doughboy, an' that theer boggabria'll eat like marrer, along of the salt junk. **1959** H.G. Lamond *Sheep Station* 72 'This is th' best vegetable there is, Boss,' Harry stated, lifting a steaming mass of green stuff from a boiling tin of water. 'This 'ere's that there scurvy-grass. Some fellows call it *Boggybri*.' **1964** P. White *Burnt Ones* 284 A smell of sink strayed out of grey, unpainted weatherboard, to oppose the stench of crushed boggabri and cotton pear.

bogger. Chiefly *W.A. Mining.* [f. Bog 2.] One who works underground shovelling mullock or ore. Also **bogger-out.**

1935 *Red Star* (Perth) 29 Nov. 3/4 The Ivanhoe uses a cunning method of making boggers stay on the shaft more than eight hours. **1938** H. Drake-Brockman *Men without Wives* (1955) 146 What's a bogger? Sounds awful... Man who shifts the ore down the stope. **1943** *Jest: Digestion of Good Humor* 43 It was *necessity*—the italics emphasise the truth—which first sent me underground to earn my living as a *bogger-out*. **1950** *Coast to Coast 1949–50* 149 As soon as he could say in English to a pannikin boss, 'Here is ten pound; I want-a da job on-a your mine,' he started work as a bogger, underground, at sixteen and ten a shift. **1959** K.S. Prichard *N'Goola* 45 Undersized and runty, a bogger on the South Kalgurli, he had been told too often that he 'wasn't a miner's bootlace' to have any opinion of himself. **1968** K. Denton *Walk around my Cluttered Mind* 19 When a skip is filled, the bogger trucks it, which means he busts a gut to get it started. **1983** *Advertiser* (Darwin) 15 Dec. 1/1 They buried Joe 'Bogger' Young at Pine Creek last Saturday... He was a wielder of the shovel at the mine and that's where his nickname came from .. shovellers are 'boggers'.

boggi /'bɒgaɪ/. Also **bog-eye, bogi,** etc. [Prob. f. a N.S.W. Aboriginal language.]

1. Sleeping lizard.

1911 *Bulletin* (Sydney) 28 Sept. 13/2 The blue-tongue ('bogi', 'bob-tailed gohanna', or 'sleepy lizard'). **1965** R. Ottley *By Sandhills* 29 A bog-eye ain't much. They seldom bite you.

2. The handpiece of a shearing machine: see quot. 1915.

1915 *Bulletin* (Sydney) 14 Oct. 24/2 The jumbuck barber has a vocabulary of his own... In a shed where the barbering is done by machinery he always alludes to his handpiece as 'a bog-eye'. This from the likeness to the lizard of that name. **1918** *Truth* (Sydney) 7 July 5/5 Swinging the humming boggi, Shaving the jumbucks clean. **1946** *Bulletin* (Sydney) 11 Dec. 21/1 Those of us station-hands who could handle the bogai were set to barbering the woolled stragglers which had eluded the shearing-time musterings. **1962** *Ibid.* 3 Feb. 43/2 A tough wether shed too—thousands of them—weeks of unrelenting head down, backsides up for the bogghi boys. **1970** *Matilda* (Winton Tourist Promotion Assoc.) 7 The 'bogis' freed from nerveless hands went clattering o'er the board. **1977** C. McCullough *Thorn Birds* 232 He graduated from tar boy to shed hand, running down the board catching the great heavy fleeces as they flew off the boggis in one piece. **1982** *Sydney Morning Herald* 23 Oct. 29/3 'I grabbed my boggi and I ran her down the whipping side.' .. Which, translated, means that the shearer took up his handpiece—named after the boggi lizard of inland Australia which it is said to resemble—and ran the clippers down the last side to be shorn while the sheep is on its back.

boggins, *pl.* [Of unknown origin.] An abundance.

1849 A. Harris *Emigrant Family* (1967) 97 There must be very nigh a hundredweight of meat there: boggins for a whole week. **1906** *Bulletin* (Sydney) 22 Nov. 16/4 The rain came—boggins of it—within three days. **1916** H.L. Roth *Sketches & Reminisc. Qld.* 4 Francis Henry eventually got round the old man, pretending he wanted to buy 'boggins' of things and showing his money. **1927** 'S. Rudd' *Romance of Runnibede* 34 There was always boggins of rains and grass that he used to lose his horses in.

bogi, var. Boggi.

bogie, var. Bogey.

bogong /ˈboʊgɒŋ/. Formerly **bugong.** [a. Ngayawuŋ *buguŋ*.] The brown noctuid moth *Agrotis infusa*, which breeds on plains in s. Aust. The adults, which migrate to hills where they aestivate in rock crevices, were formerly eaten by Aborigines. Now usu. **bogong moth.**

1834 G. BENNETT *Wanderings N.S.W.* I. 265 It is named the 'Bugong Mountain', from the circumstance of multitudes of small moths, called Bugong by the aborigines, congregating at certain months of the year about masses of granite on this and other parts of the range. **1845** E.J. EYRE *Jrnls. Exped. Central Aust.* II. 253 A species of moth which the natives procure from the cavities and hollows of the mountains in certain localities . . is called in the dialect of the district, where I met with it, Bōōguōn. **1878** R.B. SMYTH *Aborigines of Vic.* I. 207 The Bugong moths . . are greedily devoured by the natives. **1901** *Bulletin* (Sydney) 5 Oct. 16/3 When camped on the tops of the highest mountains in Victoria, I have seen at sundown, countless numbers of the huge 'bogong' moths arise from the rocks. **1926** *Ibid.* 25 Nov. 24/2 Bogong moths . . have been invading Sydney suburbs in millions. **1948** F. CLUNE *Wild Colonial Boys* 92 He gave the wild children black sugar and johnny-cakes made of cracked corn. . . They gave him quandongs and wild honey . . and choice bogong grubs, roasted. **1953** *Meanjin* 239 The audible fluttering of thousands of Bogong moths feeding on the white tea-tree blossom that clothed the heatherlands. **1962** J. HEDGE *Trout Fishing N.S.W.* 42 Some were using 'Bogong' moths, others worms; spinners were also being thrown. **1981** *Austral. Women's Weekly* (Sydney) 23 Sept. 5/3 We were driven crazy by the Bogong moths last year and nearly had to leave home.

boil, *n. S.A. Mining. Obs.* [f. *boil* to seethe, upheave.] A mineral outcrop, esp. one giving surface indications of the presence of a lode.

1850 *S. Austral. Register* (Adelaide) 11 July 3/1 There is apparently a great boil of copper ore—the whole surface, for many yards round, being covered with specimens of copper ore. **1865** *Wallaroo Times* (Kadina) 5 Aug. 2/2 The new discovery at the Yeeba bar proved to be nothing more than a 'boil' of copper ore. It has . . been completely worked out. **1882** *Yorke's Peninsula Advertiser* (Moonta) 13 Jan. 3/5 A valuable lode was reported. . . By some miners it was described as a 'big boil'.

boil, *v.*[1] [Spec. use of *boil down* to lessen the bulk of (anything) by boiling: see OED *v.* 8.]

1. *trans. Hist.* With **down.** In the preparation of tallow: to reduce (animal carcasses) by boiling. Also *absol.*

[**1843** *Sydney Morning Herald* 24 June 2/4 A sheep shorn may live to be shorn again; but a sheep boiled is gone for ever.] **1843** M. HINDMARSH *Lett.* (1945) 43 Sheep are now being boiled down by thousands for to extract the tallow from their carcases. **1847** J.D. LANG *Phillipsland* 155 They had recently realized, from the hides and tallow only, of a lot of cattle which they had *boiled down*, as it is called in the colony, £3 12s. per head in London. **1852** G.B. EARP *Gold Colonies Aust.* 115 In 1849, there were boiled down in New South Wales, 165,701 sheep, and 33,097 head of cattle, producing 60,841 cwt. of tallow. **1863** J. DAVIS *Tracks of McKinlay* 383 Spelled here to boil down old horse. **1888** 'R. BOLDREWOOD' *Robbery under Arms* (1937) 83 There's a mob in most towns, though, I think, that wants boilin' down bad. Some day they'll do it, maybe; they'll have to when all the good country's stocked up. **1899** *Austral. Tit-Bits* (Sydney) 25 Feb. 34/2 In January, 1843, sheep were first boiled down in Australia. **1937** D. GUNN *Links with Past* 211 W.H. Walker of Tenterfield, had a boiling down place, where in 1892 I had some old ewes boiled down. . . My father seems to have been among the very first to boil down; he started in 1843.

2. *fig.* [So used elsewhere but seeming in Aust. to draw its connotations from the prec.]

1872 'CAPRICORNUS' *Bush Essays* 19 Bankers and merchants had stations on hand which they wanted to sell. One customer had got the length of his tether and it was time to 'boil him down' and get a new one into the concern. **1898** *Worker* (Sydney) 14 May 1/4 Barton's Bill boiled down. **1903** *Truth* (Sydney) 27 Dec. 1/8 The British Empire, boiled down, is a handful of fat-jowled loafers, and another handful of hook-nosed Jews. **1904** *Bulletin* (Sydney) 24 Nov. 40/1 We just useter let things slide till our cheques b'iled down, an' there weren't any bones left either. **1910** *Huon Times* (Franklin) 2 Mar. 4/2 Sam Cooney spreads himself over a lot of paper while denying Mick Dooley's report of the Logue-Cooney fight. Boiled down, Sam says Logue undertook to knock him out in 15 rounds. **1932** J.J. HARDIE *Cattle Camp* (1944) 26 Boiled down, the reason seems to me that people here do more thinking than talking.

boil, *v.*[2] [Spec. use of *boil* to bring to boiling point.] *intr.* With **up**: to make tea (see also BILLY *n.*[1] 5 and QUART POT 1).

1923 J. ARMOUR *Spell of Inland* 30 Alex., accompanied by George and Robertson, rode in the direction of the Mulga Well, where they proposed to 'boil up'. **1960** R.S. PORTEOUS *Cattleman* 41, I boil up and 'ave a bit of tucker down along the creek.

Hence **boil-up** *n.* Also *fig.*

[N.Z. **1934** *Canterbury Mountaineer* Aug. 52 We had a welcome boil up.] **1936** C.T. MADIGAN *Central Aust.* 210 We emptied our cans of the Glauber's-salt solution from Glen Helen, and filled up with this beautiful liquid, and had a boil-up and good tea for the first time in the last few days. **1975** M.B. ROBERTS *King of Con Men* 68 The main method of gold stealing was to palm rich 'tailings' and when enough had been stolen there would be a 'boil-up' in the scrub.

boiler. [f. BOIL *v.*[1]]

1. *Hist.* A vessel in which animal carcasses are boiled down.

1843 *Sydney Morning Herald* 18 July 3/2 They have clearly shown that they will not be driven like sheep either to the shambles or to the boiler. **1844** *Ibid.* 11 Nov. 2/7 The 'boilers' will doubtless be in requisition to an immense extent after the clip is taken off.

2. a. *Hist.* An animal relegated to be boiled down.

1884 'R. BOLDREWOOD' *Old Melbourne Memories* 109 Two hundred and seventy 'boilers' are safe in the small yard, the which will be started for their last drive on the following morning.

b. *fig.* [Prob. influenced latterly by *boiler* boiling fowl.]

1862 *Bell's Life in Sydney* 14 June 4/3 On asking a night guardian where a night's lodging is to be obtained, he tells you 'all the old boilers are full, the verandah at the post-office is overcrowded; and, mate, if you mean to sleep under a door-way why you will have to turn out somebody else'. **1965** *Kings Cross Whisper* (Sydney) Mar. 6/3 Bad landladies are known as dragons or boilers. **1967** *Ibid.* xxxii. 7/1 *Boiler*, an old female with still a little life. **1967** A. SEYMOUR *One Day of Yr.* 51 He . . patronized the old boilers. **1980** B. HORNADGE *Austral. Slanguage* 197 By extension an older, tougher hen (or woman) is known as a *boiler*.

3. *Hist.* With **down**: one who operates a boiling down establishment.

1848 *Maitland Mercury* 13 May 3/1 *Tallow Casks*. . . A loss of fifteen per cent. has lately been sustained by a settler, which has arisen solely from bad casks which were supplied by his 'boiler-down'.

boiling, *vbl. n. Hist.* [f. BOIL *v.*[1] 1.] Usu. with **down.**

1. The process of separating fat from animal carcasses in the preparation of tallow: see quot. 1848. Also *attrib.*

1843 *Adelaide Observer* 15 July 5/3 When our Sydney friends trumpeted forth the boiling down of sheep as a discovery of their own, they found a mare's nest. . . Sheep boiling has been quietly going on in Adelaide from the commencement of the present year. **1843** *Sydney Morning Herald* 26 Dec. 2/3 They are each calculated to contain about 400 carcases at a single boiling. **1848** H.W. HAYGARTH *Recoll. Bush Life* 71 'Boiling down' is a very simple and rapid process. The whole carcase, having been cut up into pieces, and thrown into large cast-iron pans . . is boiled to rags, during which operation the fat is skimmed off, until no more rises to the surface. The boiled meat is then taken out of the pans, and, after having been squeezed in a wooden press, which forces out the remaining particles of tallow, it is either thrown away, or used as food for pigs, vast numbers of which are sometimes kept in this manner, in the neighbourhood of a boiling establishment. **1852** G.B. EARP *Gold Colonies Aust.* 116 Boiling-down has become a safe speculation. **1873** A. TROLLOPE *Aust. & N.Z.* I. 55 The boiling down is an old trade in Australia. **1882** W. COOTE *Hist. Colony Qld.* 51 Another, and still more beneficial consequence, was the introduction of the 'boiling down' process, by which unsaleable sheep and cattle were converted into saleable tallow. **1916** J.M. CREED *Recoll. Aust.* 46 The village had about 250 inhabitants, a considerable number of whom were employed at the principal industry of 'boiling down' for the production of tallow from the many fat cattle, which, otherwise, would have had no market. **1927** *Bulletin* (Sydney) 3 Nov. 27/1 Of boiling-down and burning-up we've had our bingie full. **1942** H.H. PECK *Mem. of Stockman* 40 The first contractor for all injured stock at the railway siding . . combined a fairly large boiling-down business with his shop trade.

2. An establishment for boiling down; the site of a boiling-down operation.

1857 F. DE B. COOPER *Wild Adventures* 66 Fletcher, the proprietor of the boiling-down. **1898** G. DUNDERDALE *Bk. of Bush* 236 On every station in New South Wales the paddocks still called 'the boiling down' were devoted to the destruction of sheep and cattle and to the production of tallow. **1905** *Truth* (Sydney) 26 Feb. 1/8 If Heaven were situated directly over the high-smelling 'boiling downs' that are located in that suburb, Peter or one of the boss angels would drop a rock . . on the heads of some of the proprietors. **1910** *Bulletin* (Sydney) 27 Oct. 14/3 Cadwallader's 'boiling down' . . worked pretty well all the year round. **1939** J.G. PATTISON *'Battler's' Tales Early Rockhampton* 149, I was meeting and taking delivery of mobs of cattle for the boiling-downs.

3. Comb. **boiling (-down) establishment, house, pot, season, system, works.**

1843 *Duncan's Weekly Register* (Sydney) 29 July 2/1 **Boiling establishments** are being erected on the Parramatta-road. **1844** *Guardian* (Sydney) 65/4 The great nuisance which was springing up in the city, in the shape of the boiling-down establishments. **1854** W. SHAW *Land of Promise* 69 Two boiling down establishments in full play . . emit villanous odours. **1857** J. ASKEW *Voyage Aust. & N.Z.* 265 Beyond this is a large boiling down establishment, the immediate vicinity of which was a complete Golgotha. **1870** E.B. KENNEDY *Four Yrs. in Qld.* 54 Boiling down establishments offer a market to holders of stock, and a relief to those who wish to realize and have no market for their fat or aged stock. **1891** 'SMILER' *Wanderings Simple Child* (ed. 3) 2 My carcase wouldn't fetch seven farthings a pound at the boiling-down establishment. **1910** *Huon Times* (Franklin) 27 July 4/2 With regard to boiling down establishments stringent requirements had been insisted on to prevent them being a public nuisance. **1846** *Cumberland Times* (Parramatta) 28 Feb. 1/2 The Mayor of Sydney has commenced a crusade against those detestable nuisances, the small **boiling houses**, some of which are in the heart of the city, and in the chief thoroughfares—the stench arising from these receptacles of corrupt filth is beyond endurance, and most offensive to passengers. **1852** G.B. EARP *Gold Colonies Aust.* 115 Boiling-houses are necessarily placed at some distance from the towns. **1870** C.H. ALLEN *Visit to Qld.* 139 The killing-yards and boiling down houses are on a very extensive scale. **1844** *Bee of Aust.* (Sydney) 9 Nov. 2/6 To the **boiling pot** daily, I wend my sad way, And gaze on my flocks as they wither away. **1849** J. PATTISON *N.S.W.* 91 In 1840, £80,000 was spent in Irish beef and pork, while the colony had no markets for its own beef and mutton except the boiling-pot. **1853** MOSSMAN & BANISTER *Aust. Visited & Revisited* 71 Sending their surplus stock to the boiling-down pots. **1920** *Bulletin* (Sydney) 22 Apr. 20/3 For catarrh the only remedy was the boiling-down pot. **1943** H.G. LAMOND *From Tariaro to Ross Roy* 105 They just about cleared their costs at the boiling-down pots. **1848** *Maitland Mercury* 8 Mar. 3/3 The squatters are making extensive preparations for the **boiling-down season** just beginning. **1853** *Moreton Bay Free Press* 1 Feb. 3/4 A quantity of tallow from the last boiling season—now five months over—is not shipped yet. **1857** J. ASKEW *Voyage Aust. & N.Z.* 265 During the boiling down season several hundreds of cattle and sheep were slaughtered there every week. **1843** *Sydney Morning Herald* 22 June 2/8 Stock-owners may with certainty avail themselves of the convenience held out by the **boiling system** to realize at all seasons from their herds and flocks. **1844** *Parramatta Chron.* 24 Feb. 2/3 *Effect of the late rains*. . . Feed and water are proportionably abundant, and fat cattle are likely to increase in consequence, despite the boiling-down system. **1847**

J. SIDNEY *Voice from Far Interior* 49 The boiling system is only useful to get rid of scabby sheep. **1901** *Bulletin* (Sydney) 7 Dec. 31/3 He smelt like a **boilin'-down works** an' had ernuff grog in him to cure all the toothache in the Commonwealth. **1905** *Truth* (Sydney) 19 Feb. 1/8 A ranter . . runs a Sunday night meeting for sinners out near the boiling-down works at Botany. **1943** H.G. LAMOND *From Tariaro to Ross Roy* 105 The ewes went to the boiling-down works.

boilover. Orig. *Horse-racing.* [Fig. use of *boil over* to overflow: see HOT POT.] **a.** A surprise result; the unexpected defeat of the favourite.

1871 *Austral. Town & Country Jrnl.* (Sydney) 18 Feb. 217/3 The sensation has this week been the Launceston Champion Race, with its boil over; and the knowing fraternity now begin to wonder if there be a possibility, no matter how remote, of a favourite pulling off this great event. **1878** *Ibid.* 30 Mar. 602/1 How often is the favourite amiss, or 'nobbled', the rider 'off his head', the certainty a 'boil over'! **1882** *Sydney Slang Dict.* 1 *Boilover*, favorites not winning. Bookmakers and sporting men out in their calculations. **1898** *Western Champion* (Barcaldine) 11 Jan. 9/2 The two principal events both resulted in a 'boil over'. **1922** C. DREW *Rogues & Ruses* 42 Punters who had backed Mohawk and had separated themselves from their tickets raced around with their lamps skinned in the hopes of findin' them again. . . Takin' it altogether, it was a fine boil-over. **1964** *Footy Fan* (Melbourne) II. viii. 23 In recent years, with a general summing up of standard, a feature of Australian Rules Football has been the number of surprise results, or 'boil-overs' to use the colloquial expression. **1973** J. POWERS *Last of Knucklemen* (1974) 21 I've seen too many boil-overs to get sucked into mug bets any more. **1986** *Canberra Times* 31 Mar. 19/3 St. Kilda provided a boil-over to win at Moorabbin when the two teams met last year.

b. *transf.*

1974 J. GABY *Restless Waterfront* 222 We got caught up in one senseless dispute, a demarcation issue, a most frustrating and hopeless affair. . . There was a boil-over for you.

boko /ˈboʊkoʊ/. Also **boco.** [Prob. f. a Qld. Aboriginal language.] An animal or person blind in one eye. Also as *adj.*

1847 C. DE BOOS *Congewoi Correspondence* 119 They useter call him Boco because he'd only got one eye, and I suppose boco is French for bein blinder one eye, for that's what they callser one eye man up the country. **1880** 'ERRO' *Squattermania* 37 'Your boco' (a term for a one-eyed horse) 'is rather rough for yer.' **1886** *Adelaide Observer* 17 July 42/2 A camp with four or five lubras and one old boko blackfellow. **1890** *Quiz* (Adelaide) 29 Aug. 3/1 He returned, leading a darkey who was 'boko', that is blind in one eye. **1906** A.B. PATERSON *Outback Marriage* 243 The boco's one eye's worth any horse's two. Me an' the boco will be near the lead when the whips are crackin'. **1953** H.G. LAMOND *Big Red* 154 As horses, men and other animals, were liable to infection, it can be assumed 'roos also ran the risk. If they did, the curse never got beyond the initial stages—boko, scummy-eyed kangaroos were unknown.

bollocky /ˈbɒləki/, *a.* Also **bollicky.** [f. *bollock* naked (see OEDS 3) + -Y.] Of a person: naked. Also as *n.*

1952 T.A.G. HUNGERFORD *Ridge & River* 161 Remember that time . . we're all stark bollocky and that jeep-load of Yank nurses comes down. **1967** *Kings Cross Whisper* (Sydney) xxxii. 7/1 *Bollicky*, to be in the bollicky is to be completely nude. **1968** *Ibid.* lxi. 9/2 Australian housewives may soon be serving breakfasts in the bollocky if a current American craze catches on in this country. **1971** F. HARDY *Outcasts of Foolgarah* 18 Chilla heard because he had turned the shower off and come out bollicky. **1985** *People Mag.* (Sydney) 22 July 43/3 Completely bollicky except for a pair of woollen socks.

bolly gum /ˈbɒli gʌm/. [f. *bolly* (prob. f. a N.S.W. Aboriginal language) + GUM *n.* 1.] Any of several trees esp. of the genera *Beilschmiedia*, *Litsea* and *Neolitsea* (fam. Lauraceae), and *Blepharocarya* (fam. Anacardiaceae); the wood of these trees. Also **bolly wood.**

1904 J.H. MAIDEN *Notes on Commercial Timbers N.S.W.* 29 *Bolly gum* . . yields a soft whitish timber valuable for boxes, meat casks, and for many other purposes. **1926** *Qld. Agric. Jrnl.* XXV. 433 There is a Bolly Gum which is not a gum at all, but a timber resembling Queensland Maple, which is not a Maple either. **1931** J. DEVANEY *Earth Kindred* 31 Two by two in a toiling line, Lumbering bolly-gum, box, and pine. **1956** N.K. WALLIS *Austral. Timber Handbk.* 4 Other timbers have special uses, such as . . bollywood (aircraft construction).

bolt, *v.* [Spec. use of *bolt* to take flight.]

1. *intr. Obs.* To abscond, either abandoning one's debts or in possession of illicit gains.

1829 *Sydney Monitor* 24 Oct. 2/2 *The family* . . are now departed or departing, save *the scion.* Mr Giulding *has bolted.* **1838** *Colonist* (Sydney) 21 Mar. 2/3 Any individual who might suspect any of his debtors of *bolting* by the said vessel, might see whether the *bolter* was on board. **1838** *Cornwall Chron.* (Launceston) 27 Oct. 2 This week the town has again suffered the loss of about £3,000, by the *Bolting* of two persons, who contrived to gull the credulous to that amount. These cases are now of so frequent occurrence, that the enquiry, *'Anybody bolted?'* is as common as *'Good morning to you.'* **1843** R.D. MURRAY *Summer at Port Phillip* 47 Let him be defrauded by a debtor who has absconded,—or, as it is called, 'bolted',—without paying. . . We find half a column of eloquence devoted to its refutation by the parties aggrieved. **1846** *Argus* (Melbourne) 4 Dec. 2/4 John Anderson . . is stated to have *bolted* from Adelaide by the *Will Watch*, schooner, having (colonially speaking) *done* the people there, at no small allowance. **1849** *Belfast Gaz.* (Port Phillip) 4 May 4/3 John Kent (. . 'Doctor Kent' during his 'practice' in Melbourne and subsequently a publican at the Grange) . . in company with a Mrs Morrice, bolted from Portland, having 'let in' the good folks there to the amount of some £150. **1852** D. MACKENZIE *Gold Digger* 45 The partner intrusted with the keeping of the gold *bolted*, that is, walked off with the earnings of the whole party. **1871** *Austral. Town & Country Jrnl.* (Sydney) 4 Mar. 259/4 Samson, clerk of the National Marine Insurance Company, has bolted; his accounts are deficient.

2. *Hist.* Of a convict: to escape from custody.

1832 *Currency Lad* (Sydney) 13 Oct. 3 He hoped the Magistrate would excuse him, because it was *only* the second time of his bolting, and he went the three days he was absent to see the races. **1837** *Cornwall Chron.* (Launceston) 27 May 2 He bolted from the Perth chain-gang about 18 months ago. **1842** *Tasmanian Jrnl. Nat. Sci.* I. 28 His comrade . . declared he had 'bolted'. . . Boardman was accordingly reported as an absconder. **1846** S. SNOW *Exile's Return* 16 If a convict, sent out from England, or any of her colonies, is retaken after bolting, he is sure to have an addition made to his sentence and be flogged, and obliged to work in irons. **1851** J.F.L. FOSTER *New Colony Vic.* 17 A shepherd may abscond, or, in the colonial language, 'bolt'. **1857** J. BONWICK *Early Days Melbourne* 62 It was customary, in order to give notice to the military of any attempt at bolting, to maintain near each out-working station some smouldering fires. **1865** J.F. MORTLOCK *Experiences of Convict* 58 He 'bolted', as it is termed, from Van Diemen's Land, in 1849. **1874** *Illustr. Sydney News* 19 Sept. 153 Taking advantage of the absence of his keepers, he quietly scaled the stockade and bolted.

Hence **bolt** *n.*, **bolting** *vbl. n.* and *ppl. a.*

1838 *Colonist* (Sydney) 21 Mar. 2/2 The facilities afforded for escape, or, in other words, for making a successful **bolt.** **1848** J. SYME *Nine Yrs. Van Diemen's Land* 195 The sentenced man . . is . . possibly forming the plan of his next 'bolt', and ascertaining who will accompany him to obtain the ineffable pleasure of a *whiff of the weed*, and *doing* a settler. **1897** H. HUSSEY *Colonial Life & Christian Experience* 59 Others, who had determined to defraud their creditors if possible, made a 'bolt' in any vessel that would take them away. **1833** *Trumpeter General* (Hobart) 29 July 3 We are happy to find that some check is put to the **bolting** system, it has long been wanting (and highly commendable it is) that persons about leaving this colony must produce certificates from their employers before they can obtain the signature of our Assistant Police Magistrate. **1843** *Portland Mercury* 13 Sept. 3/5 If the Bolting system receive negative encouragement through the silence of the Press, the industrious tradesman and honest dealer will soon be victimized by a parcel of scoundrels. **1867** J. BONWICK *J. Batman* 11 These rough fellows were either runaway sailors or bolting convicts.

bolter. [f. BOLT *v.*]

1. *Hist.* A runaway convict.

1832 *Hill's Life N.S.W.* 17 Aug. 2 *Margaret Champion*, assigned to Mr Wood of George street, was brought in by a constable, who said, he had just *grabbed* her, and knowing her to be a *bolter*, took her under his *protection.* **1833** *Sydney Herald* 19 Sept. 2/3 John Jones, was charged as a bolter from his master's house. **1844** MRS C. MEREDITH *Notes & Sketches N.S.W.* 132 A party of the mounted police went in search of a very daring gang of bush-rangers, or, as they are sometimes called, 'bolters'. **1849** *Portland Gaz.* 9 Feb. 2/1 *Abraham Bramford. A bolter. All* persons are hereby warned against receiving or employing Abraham Bramford, who absconded from my service on the morning of the 13th instant. **1854** F.J. COCKBURN *Lett.* (1856) 65 Admirers of liberty (elegantly called 'bolters' here). **1865** J.F. MORTLOCK *Experiences of Convict* 109 A damsel at the gold fields often received a 'nugget' for washing a shirt, so that feminine 'bolters' to the 'diggings' became pretty numerous. **1874** *Illustr. Adelaide Post* 6 Aug. 19/1 Sulky Joe was an old hand and a bolter besides, that is, having obtained a ticket-of-leave from the Sydney authorities, he had taken French leave by crossing the Murray into Victoria, and was thereby liable to be arrested at any time. **1900** *Bulletin* (Sydney) 13 Jan. 14/2 Near New Norfolk, Tas., old hands still point out the spot where a famous 'bolter' from his assigned service made his home in the bush.

2. *Hist.* An absconder.

1838 *Sydney Herald* 10 May 2/3 *'Bolters'.* This class of animals adds one or more to its number by every vessel that leaves the port. . . Several fellows (Jews and Gentiles) are making arrangements to defraud their creditors by leaving the Colony in a few days. **1843** *Port Phillip Patriot* 15 May 2/3 *Another bolter. Report* says a well-known character in the commercial circles of Melbourne has given leg-bait to his constituents by the *Bolina*, which sailed yesterday for New Zealand. **1843** *Sydney Morning Herald* 14 Aug. 2/4 Another Bolter—Within the last three weeks an accountant, named Rollason, has contrived to leave the colony, and to carry with him about £700. **1869** *Wallaroo Times* (Kadina) 21 Apr. 5/1 In the vicinity of Mt. Gambier traders are victimised annually to a considerable amount by bolters who when they get into debt slip across the Border. **1897** H. HUSSEY *Colonial Life & Christian Experience* 59 Others, who had determined to defraud their creditors if possible, made a 'bolt' in any vessel that would take them away. . . One of the vessels that took away several . . had conferred upon her the . . designation of 'the bolters' clipper'.

3. One with only a remote chance of succeeding, an outsider; freq. in the phr. **a bolter's (chance)** (cf. BUCKLEY'S).

1941 S.J. BAKER *Pop. Dict. Austral. Slang* 35 *Haven't (hasn't) the bolter's*, used of a person or racehorse that has no chance at all in a contest or situation. **1964** H.P. TRITTON *Time means Tucker* (rev. ed.) 33 At the race game 'The Bolter' always won when the favourite 'Esmeralda' was well backed. **1970** *Matilda* (Winton Tourist Promotion Assoc.) 7 They never had a bolter's chance when Brumby went to war. **1973** *Sydney Morning Herald* 17 Sept. 1/7 A South Coast publican who continually spurns the big money of Sydney Rugby League was the 'bolter' in the Australian team announced last night to tour France and England. **1975** *Sun-Herald* (Sydney) 14 Sept. 42/5 Books cheer as 'bolter' gets home. **1984** *Canberra Times* 23 July 20/6 The English bookmakers give Baker-Finch only a bolter's chance. He is quoted at 14–1 to win the title, with Watson a 7–4 on favourite.

bomaring, var. BOOMERANG *n.* 1.

bomb. [Fig. use of *bomb* explosive projectile.] An old or unreliable motor vehicle; (by extension) anything in a dilapidated condition.

1950 *Austral. Police Jrnl.* Apr. 110 *Bomb*, . . a dud—usually refers to second-hand motor vehicles in poor mechanical shape. **1956** *Bulletin* (Sydney) 30 May 13/1 No longer is 'It's a bomb' restricted to senile cars; the word has become synonymous with worn-out or up-to-putty anything. **1963** M. BRITT *Pardon my Boots* 25 The next morning, George departed in his ancient and unreliable 'bomb' with a gleam of anticipation for the bright lights of Mt. Isa in his eye. **1968** *Southerly* i. 3 The decent old-style sedans, the mini-cars, the bombs, the Holdens. **1978** H.C. Baker *I was Listening* 121 Merv and me were travellin' out west in Merv's old bomb.

bombo /ˈbɒmboʊ/. [Prob. as prec. + -O, and independent of *bombo* or *bumbo* a spiced alcoholic drink (see OED *bumbo*).]

1. Cheap (often fortified) wine of inferior quality. Also *attrib.*

1942 *Sun* (Sydney) 26 Aug. 4/8 Bombo has replaced plonk as a term for cheap wine. **1943** H.E. Beros *Fuzzy Wuzzy Angels* 37, I wasn't full of bombo. **1952** P. Gladwin *Desert in Heart* 34 He built a tumble-down shanty . . and when it was finished he went on a bombo-jag which lasted a week. **1959** H. Drake-Brockman *West Coast Stories* 139 Last time I saw Wheelbarrow he had been drinking heavy – the bombo again. 'Just to nudge me liver,' he says. **1972** *Bulletin* (Sydney) 12 Aug. 7/3 Lots of young Australians have never heard of burgoo or cocky's joy. They hardly know what it means to get shickered on bombo. **1976** B. Bennett *New Country* 44 Sitting around in parks sucking bombo. **1980** Hepworth & Hindle *Boozing out in Melbourne Pubs* 17 The men who ran the bombo bars seemed, by and large, to be chaps who had suffered, but who had become finer chaps because of it.

2. An habitual drinker of such wine.

1966 P. Pinney *Restless Men* 69 Saves winos and bombos from drinkin' their selves mad.

bombora /bɒmˈbɔrə/. Formerly also **bumbora.** [Prob. f. a N.S.W. Aboriginal language.]

1. A wave which forms over a submerged off-shore reef or rock, sometimes (in very calm weather or at high tide) merely swelling but in other conditions breaking heavily and producing a dangerous stretch of broken water; the reef or rock itself.

1871 *Industr. Progress N.S.W.* 789 Some [fishing grounds] are on sunken rocks in about 8 fathoms water, 'Bumborers', as they are generally termed, from 1 to 3 miles distant from the shore others on rocky patches in deeper water. **1871** *Ibid.* 791 A cable-length or so distant from 'Jibben Head', the southern point of the entrance to Port Hacking, lies Jibben 'bumborer', a fishing-mark of great repute. **1880** *V & P* (N.S.W. L.A.) III. 1132 A few 'Bumboras' are found in this bight, and they (like all 'Bumboras' on the coast) have been and still are the favourite resort of the schnapper-men during particular conditions of the currents. **1895** C. Thackeray *Amateur Fisherman's Guide* 21 At the mouth of Lake Macquarie and within coo-ee of Reid's Mistake, a bumbora, will be found, and alongside it tremendous black and red rock-cod. *Ibid.* 25 At Botany Head alongside the Botany bumbora is a favourite place during calm weather. **1910** *Truth* (Sydney) 14 Aug. 5/7 Bold bucks at bonny Bondi, where the big bomborahs bom. **1927** A. Wright *Squatter's Secret* 15 'It's the Bomborah,' he almost screamed. **1933** *Bulletin* (Sydney) 24 May 27/1 'Bombora' is an aboriginal word applied to the high-crested wave which breaks, even on windless days, over submerged rocks near the coastline and in some cases at entrances to coastal harbors and inlets. **1963** J. Pollard *Austral. Surfrider* 24 Dave Jackman used a 'gun' when he rode the famed Queenscliff bombora which is very treacherous with waves standing up to 30 ft. **1967** *Surfabout* (Sydney) III. vii. 42 A fast breaking bombora is found at the north end of the beach, with a very hollow left and a slow but full right-hander. **1972** K. Willey *Tales Big Country* 75 Bristow and Owen told the lads to hang on and began breaststroking, grimly plugging away to the north while the bombora crashed and surged close behind them.

2. *transf.* and *fig.*

1969 W. Moxham *Apprentice* 44 The trouble with Lenny was like a bombora. There was a commotion followed by an uneasy calm, a feeling it was likely to blow up again any old time, cause harm to someone. **1979** D. Maitland *Breaking Out* 73 He married Shirley and inherited her bitch of a mother at Coogee, the Eastern Suburbs beach community . . and got sucked into a deadly *bombora* of domesticity.

bomerang, bommerang, varr. Boomerang *n.* 1.

bommie. Also **bommy.** [f. Bom(bora + -Y.] Bombora.

1949 C.B. Maxwell *Surf* 112 Surfmen, swimmers and the 'surfboat happy' . . wondered what it might be like to 'crack the bommy' out there. **1960** R.D. Murphy *Speak to Strangers* 15 The westerly comin', flattenin' the combers like grass, No time to make the beach, I pulled between The big and little bommy. **1963** J. Pollard *Austral. Surfrider* 100, I had to break through a heavy sea before reaching the swell outside and then to where the 'bommie' was breaking a long way above normal sea level. **1968** J. O'Grady *Gone Troppo* 153 So, with the glasses, he looks for 'bommies' . . coral boulders on top of the Reef. **1970** G. Bahnemann *Calling Reef* 31 Bandy, wearing the helmet and corselet, had gone down deep on Lark Reef and had found the line entangled on a coral-bommy. **1978** N. Coleman *Austral. Fisherman's Fish Guide* 42 Large specimens will often patrol areas around coral 'bommies'. **1981** G. Ellis *Hey Doc, let's go Fishing!* 53 The echo-sounder produced evidence of some isolated 'bommies' (big coral upgrowths) in a sandy surround.

bomring, var. Boomerang *n.* 1.

bond, *a. Hist.* [Spec. use of *bond* not free.]

1. Of convict status.

1800 *Gen. Orders issued by Governor King* 26 Nov. (1802) 26 He strictly forbids all officers, and every person, bond or free, from striking or ill using any other person in this colony. **1817** *Hobart Town Gaz.* 4 Oct., All Persons, Free as well as Bond. **1829** *Launceston Advertiser* 16 Nov. 3 Government likes to see every man, free or bond, do well. **1838** A. Maconochie *Thoughts on Convict Managem.* 124, I believe the convict constabulary to be most vexatiously officious, both as regards the free and the bond. **1844** *Colonial Times* (Hobart) 7 Oct., First, the community is composed of three classes, the *free*, the *freed*, and the *bond*. **1856** W.H.G. Kingston *Emigrant's Home* 6 Western Australians . . arranged to receive a certain proportion of free emigrants with the bond. **1865** 'Special Correspondent' *Transportation* 9 Every other man he sees is a 'ticketer' – as the criminal class, whether bond or free, are termed. **1898** *Western Champion* (Barcaldine) 20 Dec. 1/3 What business is it of yours whether I'm free or bond? **1902** *Bulletin* (Sydney) 31 May 31/2 The Spider, Rajah Riley, Pincher Wilson, and three other greycoats comprised the representatives of the bond, and compared very favorably with the six freemen, amongst whom was the gaol wood-carter.

2. In collocations indicating convict status, as **bond labour, list, man, servant, stockman, population, woman.** Also **bondsman.**

1827 *Monitor* (Sydney) 30 Mar. 363/1 My bond-woman is offered as a prize to the best deserver or truest lover, and 30 acres in fee. **1830** *Ibid.* 12 May 2/2 The labour of this country, agricultural as well as commercial, is chiefly performed by bond-men. **1835** *Colonist* (Sydney) 30 July 243/3 Five of the persons convicted of cattle stealing were originally bond or freed stockmen. **1839** *Sydney Standard* 7 Jan. 2/4 The hard work and menial labour of the colony, is only performed by bondsmen. **1845** A. Maconochie *On Managem. Transported Convicts* 3 The last Census of Bond Population that I took on Norfolk Island in September 1843. **1845** D. Mackenzie *Emigrant's Guide* 77 The bond-man frequently saves his few shillings, received as indulgences for good conduct, in order that when he becomes free he may buy a horse to carry him. **1845** *Sydney Morning Herald* 30 Dec. 2/6 Not a single free case of drunkenness, and only three charges for such on the bond list, all ticket holders. **1847** J. Lackland *Common Sense* 16 Bond labour requires an extra oversight. **1848** C. Cozens *Adventures of Guardsman* 160 His master . . could not obtain another bond servant, and . . if he retained his services after he obtained his ticket, he would be compelled to pay him a free man's wages. **1850** *Irish Exile* (Hobart) 19 Oct. 2/1 The man of wealth and influence, the employer and the employed, the bondsman and the free, can once for all cooperate for the common good. **1857** D. Puseley *Rise & Progress Aust., Tas., & N.Z.* 153 In 1840 New South Wales ceased to be a place to which convicts might be transported from the United Kingdom, since which period the number of 'bondmen' have gradually decreased. **1865** 'Special Correspondent' *Transportation* 38, I was kindly furnished with a return of the bond population in confinement in the colony. **1919** *Smith's Weekly* (Sydney) 1 Mar. 8/2 Flogging died hard; in the good old days of Australian bond labour it was dealt out in the most casual and even humorous fashion.

bondage. *Hist.* [Spec. use of *bondage* servitude.] The state or condition of being a convict; penal servitude.

1831 Tyerman & Bennet *Jrnl. Voyages & Travels* II. 174 Those who were never in bondage are naturally jealous of those who bear the barbarous name of *emancipists.* **1837** W.B. Ullathorne *Catholic Mission Australasia* 14 The entire number in actual bondage, is, in New South Wales, nearly 30,000. **1849** J.P. Townsend *Rambles & Observations N.S.W.* 220 When, as he terms it, his 'bondage' is over, he generally comes from the hands of his master an useful man. **1851** 'Female Transport' *Let.*, Here am I in bondage, in a foreign land.

bondi /ˈbʊndi, ˈbʌndi, ˈbɒndaɪ/, *n.*[1] Also **boondie, bundi, bundy.** [Prob. a. Wiradhuri and Kamilaroi *bundi.*]

1. A heavy Aboriginal club.

1844 C. Wilkes *Narr. U.S. Exploring Exped.* II. 202 Their weapons are the spear, club, or nulla nulla, boomerang, dundumel and the bundi. **1846** *Cumberland Times* (Parramatta) 4 Apr. 4/1 Fishhook held his bundy over his head, saying, *'bail you saucy, or pie cobra belonging you'*, meaning he would strike me on the head. **1851** *Empire* (Sydney) 30 Dec. 519/6 Jackey was found lying dead. . . A bondi, or club, was seen near him, with marks of blood on it. **1892** J. Fraser *Aborigines N.S.W.* 74 The 'bundai'—also a war club—which has knob end nicely tapered off. **1896** *Bulletin* (Sydney) 18 Apr. 27/1 In the Sydney dialect 'coojee' was an oyster, and 'Bondi' the heavy nulla. **1900** *Advocate* (Burnie) 24 July 3/4 Jimmy Governor pursued and overtook them, and felled Miss Kerz with his 'boondie'. **1918** K.L. Parker *Walkabouts of Wur-Run-Nah* 24 Making weapons such as he had never seen before: boomerangs, boondees, and shields such as were unknown to his tribe then. **1949** *Oceania* XX. 92 Formerly, children used play *bundis* (cropped sticks). . . In place of the whittled sticks, the term is used today for rough sticks selected for their length and rounded head, or for tubes of iron surmounted by ornamental knobs taken from old bedsteads. **1976** C.D. Mills *Hobble Chains & Greenhide* 98 If it comes to a stoush, get in first. . . A coon doesn't like fighting with his hands, 'finger-fight' he calls it, and doesn't give *you* any points if *you* do. He is brought up with a bundy in his hand as soon as he can toddle. **1978** E. Simon *Through my Eyes* 115 There were no more bundis used after he had gone. The last law man to use the stick with the big knob had gone. **1978** *Nat. Times* (Sydney) 2 Jan. 6/3 They had a boondi (a club the shape of a baseball bat but carved usually from heavy myall or yarran).

2. [Poss. of independent development and apparently infl. by the form and pronunc. of the place-name (see Bondi *n.*[2]).] In the phr. **to give** (someone) **bondi,** to attack savagely.

1890 *Truth* (Sydney) 19 Oct. 3/6 A live policeman is on the ground while the gay and festive members of a 'push' are 'giving him Bondi'. **1891** *Ibid.* 3 May 1/6 A cabman named Butler, who amused himself by knocking Emily Dallas down and then dancing on her and yanking her round by the hair and otherwise 'givin' her Bondi', . . was . . sentenced to three months' gaol. **1894** *Bird o' Freedom* (Sydney) 1 Dec. 5/3 Such a biffing push of biffers ne'er before were on that beach, Such 'chawing' and such 'jobbing', and such 'give 'em Bondi' tricks. **1910** *Truth* (Sydney) 26 June 11/3 *Give 'em Bondi.* Furious Fishermen's Funny Fight. **1951** D. Stivens *Jimmy Brockett* 67 Then Snowy got Maxie in a corner and began to give him Bondi. **1973** J. Murray *Larrikins* 84 Many a push battle was called in the dark, to the cry of 'Give 'em Bondi!', a memorial echo of defiance . . . 'To bondi' someone, especially a policeman, became a very transitive verb, with boots, bottles and all, as the push were 'dealing out stoush'.

Hence as *v. trans.*

1907 C. MacAlister *Old Pioneering Days* 124 They were mercilessly speared and 'boondied' (beaten to death with nullas) by the blacks.

Bondi /ˈbɒndaɪ/, *n.*[2] [The name of a suburb in Sydney.] Used allusively to designate a hasty departure, esp. in the phr. **to shoot through like a Bondi tram.** See also *shoot through* Shoot *v.* 3.

1945 D. Robinson *Pop's Blonde* 62 The Choco went through like a Bondi tram. **1947** D. Goodhart *We of Turning Tide* 60 The runners had their hands up. They, too, were going through like a Bondi tram for the P.O.W. cage in Alex! **1951** 'S. Mackenzie' *Dead Men Rising* 53 'Shot through like a Bondi tram.' 'Not 'ere today, Sar' Major.' **1952** T.A.G. HUNGERFORD *Ridge & River* 46, I got a shock, too, the first time I was jumped—I damn' near filled me strides, but by hell, I never diced me gun and took off like a bloody Bondi tram. **1956** K. TENNANT *Honey Flow* 151 We collected Mike from where he and Hertz was mixing it, and we went through like a Bondi tram. **1965** K. SMITH *OGF* 171 After a moment's stunned silence the value of the idea hit the others as it hit me and the motion went through like a Bondi bus. **1972** *Bulletin* (Sydney) 12 Aug. 7/2 'Are many of our native idioms threatened with extinction?' I asked. 'More than you could poke a stick at,' Dr Bottler replied. 'For example, we are concerned about the future of 'shooting through like a Bondi tram'.' **1976** B. SUTTON *Comrade George* 53 When she got her copy she shot through like a Bondi tram. **1979** A.J. BURKE *Bite Pineapple* 36 The War Cabinet did not agree to this in Sydney on 18 March, 1942 and told the Chiefs to 'take a Bondi tram' which is a fate not to be envied.

bone, *n.*

1. In Aboriginal ritual practice: a bone pointed at a person whose death is willed; DEATH BONE; *pointing bone*, see POINTING. Chiefly in the phr. **to point the bone.**

1884 A.W. STIRLING *Never Never Land* 89 The blacks in the neighbourhood of the Peake, a well-known region of South Australia, believe that if one of a tribe at a feast with evil intent 'points a bone' at a fellow black, the latter is doomed. **1895** *Proc. Linnean Soc. N.S.W.* X. 399 (*note*) This superstition is evidently the same as the 'pointing of a bone', believed in by most of the Australian indigenes. **1899** *Ibid.* XXIV. 331 Probably at one time the 'pointing of the bone' was a common form of sorcery in eastern N. S. Wales. **1907** *Bulletin* (Sydney) 17 Jan. 40/1 Others merely say 'Rats', or its aboriginal equivalent, when any half-tame myall points a bone at them. **1927** M. DORNEY *Adventurous Honeymoon* 56 They believe they can do great harm to an enemy by magic and have a practice that is called 'Pointing the bone' or 'Singing to death'. **1944** A.W. UPFIELD *No Footprints in Bush* 59 He had become proficient in the black art of pointing the bone. **1952** B. BEATTY *Unique to Aust.* 12 To point the bone the native adopts the correct ritual attitude, squatting on his haunches. He chants the prescribed song then suddenly points or jerks the bone in the direction of his victim. **1958** V. KELLY *Greedy Ones* 98 Now, when an abo points the bone at an enemy you know what happens? The enemy just packs up and dies. **1963** I.L. IDRIESS *Our Living Stone Age* 89 Only one kind of fear could be shown without shame—fear of the supernatural. This might take the form of fear of the Bone from a malicious witch-doctor. **1978** 'B. WONGAR' *Track to Bralgu* 4 Some of your Riratjingu mob had pointed bones at you or finished you off with a spear.

2. *transf.* and *fig.*

1943 D. FRIEND *Gunner's Diary* 21 The bone is pointed at myself and a few others. We are to be transferred to a draft battery. **1945** L. JILLET *Moresby's Few* 101 These instances are not cited to 'point the bone' but to emphasise the debt Australia owes to the men who did so much with such scanty material in days so full of peril to this country. **1951** CUSACK & JAMES *Come in Spinner* 367 'I just thought you been off the last coupla mornin's, you mightn't be too good like.' Guinea poked her in the ribs. 'Pointing the bone at me, are you, you old witch?' **1966** M. BROWN *Jimberi Track* 11 'Shove it into him, Jacky! Point the bone at him, matey!' the white blokes called. **1972** A. CHIPPER *Aussie Swearers Guide* 33 The greatest sin against the Australian spirit of mateship is to *point the bone* at a cobber, i.e. sneak on a friend or leave him in the lurch. **1975** D.J. TOWNSHEND *Gland Time* 22 With the racing season comin' up, I don't want a bone pointed at me. **1982** *Overlander* Sept. 5 Just so I don't get labelled as a cranky old bugger who does nothing but complain and point the bone at people.

Hence **bone-pointer** *n.*, **bone-pointing** *vbl. n.*

1956 A. UPFIELD *Battling Prophet* 11 The quack's a **bone-pointer**, like. He wouldn't know. **1960** D. IRELAND *Image in Clay* (1964) 98 We won't have that old skinny bone-pointer nagging at us, where we're goin'. **1963** W.E. HARNEY *To Ayers Rock & Beyond* 95 She was the first of the 'bone-pointers', her breath was the lethal song-chant which could destroy. **1928** W. ROBERTSON *Coo-ee Talks* 80 The method of **bone-pointing** differed among the tribes. **1959** D. LOCKWOOD *Crocodiles & Other People* 16 Then followed two nights of terror during which he was subjected to bone-pointing: he was 'sung' by the blacks. **1959** L. ROSE *Country of Dead* 58 'You don't believe in the efficacy of bone-pointing, Hern?' 'Oh, no, I didn't say that. But before the pointing is effective you've got to believe that the bone *can* kill.' **1977** J. CARTER *All Things Wild* 58 They had heard nothing of 'bone pointing', although they acknowledged this form of tribal justice is still practised.

bone, *v.* [f. prec.] *trans.* In Aboriginal ritual practice: to influence (a person at whom a bone is pointed), with the intention of causing the person's death.

1901 F.J. GILLEN *Diary* 21 Aug. (1968) 235 The Puntudia crept up and 'boned' him with their pointing sticks... He became very ill and finally died. **1915** *Bulletin* (Sydney) 4 Nov. 26/1 A walkabout Binghi of the same colony of abos. told him he had been 'boned'... He took to his humpy, and in 10 days' time was dead meat. **1928** W. ROBERTSON *Coo-ee Talks* 78 When it was found that he refused to believe that he was being 'boned', they arranged that he should behold the tribal doctor pointing the death-bones in the direction of his mia-mia. **1936** 'L. KAYE' *Black Wilderness* 158 An old man sitting in the dust with a long bleached bone pointing before him toward someone he could not see—that was all. But death went out from him. Someone would die... 'Who's the old devil 'boning'?' Lex wondered. **1938** F.J. HAYTER *Deadly Magic* 14 Our own people in the back blocks of Australia .. might perhaps say that the black fellow when 'boned' dies of funk. **1941** K.S. PRICHARD *Moon of Desire* 175 Gabriel asserted he had been 'boned' by an old man of the tribe he had fallen in with; Mission boy though he was, and 'a good Christian', he had been powerless to avert the death willed on him. **1959** L. ROSE *Country of Dead* 80 Old Unda had once 'boned' a man for selling his tjuringa to a white man. **1963** I.L. IDRIESS *Our Living Stone Age* 90 Stricken ones have gazed up at me, a white man, as if asking for help, after their witch-doctor has shaken his head and walked away, making it plain that a stronger doctor than he has 'boned' their tribesman. **1985** B. ROSSER *Dreamtime Nightmares* 47 They think the other tribes are out to kill them or bone them.

Hence **boning** *vbl. n.*

1925 M. TERRY *Across Unknown Aust.* 147 There is a custom, common to all Australian natives, whereby an enemy can be killed without violence. It is called 'boning', or 'singing'. **1933** C.W. PECK *Austral. Legends* (ed. 2) 154 In the same category, it is considered, is 'Boning'. Provided a person knew what marks to make in clay on the face, and what incantations to indulge in, he could kill by pointing a bone. **1929** K.S. PRICHARD *Coonardoo* (1961) 139 Hugh knew, of course, that a black ordinarily would succumb to a 'boning'. **1938** A. UPFIELD *Bone is Pointed* (1966) 140 Well, they could get on with their boning. He would fight it with all the strength of his mind, and again he would triumph over his aboriginal ancestry.

boneseed. [See quot. 1973.] The introduced South African shrub *Chrysanthemoides monilifera* (fam. Asteraceae), naturalized and regarded as a troublesome weed in s. Aust. incl. Tas.

1962 N.C.W. BEADLE et al. *Handbk. Vascular Plants Sydney & Blue Mountains* 387 *Osteospermum*... Ray flowers .. long, yellow... Sand dunes; roadsides. Fl. chiefly spring. Introd. from Africa. Boneseed. *O. moniliferum* L. **1973** W.T. PARSONS *Noxious Weeds Vic.* 100 'Boneseed' refers to the colour and hardness of the seed... Boneseed was first introduced to Victoria in 1858. **1981** D.G. & S.G.M. CARR *Plants & Man Aust.* 186 Boneseed (*Chrysanthemoides monilifera*) ..) was introduced in 1858 and is now widespread in southern States... It is of special interest because it is not a weed of agriculture but a strong competitor with native plants in our bushlands. **1986** *Your Garden* Jan. 20 In the Adelaide Hills (S.A.) and the Mornington Peninsular, Dandenong Ranges and You Yang Ranges (Vic.), Boneseed has created havoc because it can compete so vigorously with the natural vegetation.

bong, var. BUNG A.

bong tong. *Obs.* [Altered form of *bon-ton* good style, breeding: see OED.] A term applied ironically to a supposed social elite. Also *attrib.*

1892 *Truth* (Sydney) 5 June 3/6 This is the latest in 'bong tong' circles. **1892** *Ibid.* 7 Aug. 5/5 Some of the 'bong-tong' ladies of our geebung aristocracy. **1899** *Worker* (Sydney) 18 Feb. 1/3 Municipal Labor candidates are not appreciated by the 'bong-tong' up Gunnedah way. ***c* 1907** C.W. CHANDLER *Darkest Adelaide* 63 A sycophantic licensee would receive her in the most obsequious fashion, bowing as he escorted her into the parlor kept specially for the bong tong of harlotry.

bontosher /bɒn'tɒʃə/. [See quot. 1904 (2) and cf. BONZER.] BONZER *n.* Also as *adj.*

1904 *Bulletin* (Sydney) 14 Apr. 29/1 A bontosher is a real slasher, a fair hummer, virtually a past master .. but no female has yet achieved the dignity of a bontosherina. *Ibid.* 5 May 17/3 'Bonster' is a corruption of Bontojer, pronounced Bontodger; and Bontojer is a corruption of the two French words *bon* and *toujours*—'always good'. **1906** *Ibid.* 22 Nov. 17/2 Occasionally one hears of a dabster (a variety of boshter) and a bontoshter, which denotes something abnormal in the boshter line. **1907** *Truth* (Sydney) 30 June 9/5 Bill's a 'daisy' and a 'boshter' When he does a bullock rush, But he's 'jest a real bontosher' When he crashes through the crush. **1908** *Austral. Mag.* (Sydney) Nov. 1250/2 Bonanza was another Californian term brought over, but the Australian soon turned it into bonzer, and he has been varying it ever since till we have bosker, boshter and bontoger. **1951** D. STIVENS *Jimmy Brockett* 141 It was a bontosher of a flat though. **1953** —— *Gambling Ghost* 100 And they called him a beauty, a trimmer, a bobby-dazzler, a sizzler, a pearler, a dazzler, a ripsnorter, a honey, a bon-tosher and everything they could think of.

bony bream. The fresh-water fish *Nematalosa erebi* (fam. Clupeidae), widespread in mainland Aust.

1882 J.E. TENISON-WOODS *Fish & Fisheries N.S.W.* 106 A fish of the herring tribe is also found in these rivers... By the white settlers it is sometimes known as the 'bony bream'. **1951** T.C. ROUGHLEY *Fish & Fisheries Aust.* 219 The bony bream is usually avoided by anglers because it contains an excessive number of troublesome bones that render it unpopular as a food-fish. **1980** R.M. MCDOWALL *Freshwater Fishes S.-E. Aust.* 48 Bony bream *Nematalosa erebi*... Not a bream, but a herring.

bonz, *a. Obs.* Also **bonze.** Abbrev. of BONZER *a.*

1920 *Bulletin* (Sydney) 4 Nov. 20/1 'Struth! its bonz to be the skipper of a full-rigged racin' stripper. **1935** A. CROCKER *Aust. hops In* (1941) 54 'Wasn't that bonze, Alick?' he wanted to know, when he could speak; and Alick agreed between his own chuckles that it was bonze.

bonzarina /bɒnzə'rinə/. *Obs.* [f. BONZER + *-ina* L. fem. suffix.] A beautiful woman. Also *attrib.*

1906 *Bulletin* (Sydney) 22 Nov. 17/2 Bonzarina, feminine of bonza. **1934** T. WOOD *Cobbers* 212 She was a little bonzarina. **1950** F.J. HARDY *Power without Glory* 45 She's a bonzarina shiela, like a colleen from old Ireland. **1951** D. STIVENS *Jimmy Brockett* 141, I got her undressed. She was a bonzerina, as we used to say when I used to knock around with the Livers.

bonzer /'bɒnzə/, *n.*, *a.*, and *adv.* Also **bonza.** [Perh. formed in word-play on F. *bon* good, infl. by U.S. *bonanza*: see early quots. and BONTOSHER. See also BOSHTER and BOSKER which may have a similar origin.]

A. *n.* Something (or someone) which excites admiration by being surpassingly good of its kind.

1904 *Bulletin* (Sydney) 14 Apr. 29/1 *Re* that bulwark of Austral Slanguage—'Bonster'... A bonser or bonster is comparatively superior to a bons. **1904** *Truth* (Sydney) 28 Aug. 1/7 King Ned is a 'bonser'. **1906** *Bulletin* (Sydney) 22 Nov. 17/2 There is a bónza, a sort of improvement on the boshter. **1908** 'DRY-BLOWER' *Jarrahland Jingles* 164 The banquet was a bonza, a rare recherche feed. **1914** A. WRIGHT *In Last Stride* 14 Blime, th' car's a bonser; travel! why, she bloomin' well flies. **1915** G. SARGANT *Sweet Heart of Bush* 45 The parson's as good as 'e looks if 'e ain't better; 'e's a bonzer. **1918** A. WRIGHT *Over Odds* 11 Cherry—in the language of the boys of the village.. was a 'bonser'. **1918** *Aussie: Austral. Soldiers' Mag.* Apr. 2/1 And I tell yer it's a bonzor w'en we're feeling cold and stunned And we trudges for our issue ter the little 'Comforts Fund'. **1927** *Canberra Community News* 11 Apr. 5 The returned 'Diggers'' social last month was a 'bonzer'. **1934** T. WOOD *Cobbers* 87 'She's a bonza,' said Mr Dean jerking his head towards the door through which the flower-girl had withdrawn. **1960** S. WOODFIELD *A for Artemis* 21 'I've put a bit on the side for yer Maggie,' he used to say... 'A coupla nice kidneys, Maggie, real bonzers.' **1972** B. FULLER *West of*

Bight 18 A suitable caravan turned up at last. . . 'She's a bonzer. I guess you'll be lucky.'

B. *adj.* Surpassingly good. Formerly also **bonz.**

1906 *Bulletin* (Sydney) 5 July 17/1 There's allers bits o' jobs about ther Farm; Doin' Polly, breakin' metal, keeps a bloke in bonza fettle. **1908** *Clipper* (Hobart) 19 Sept. 2/2 Molross took a bonza mark on the wing, and from a pass Rait scored a sixer amidst great applause. **1910** L. Esson *Three Short Plays* (1911) 19 Look, we'll 'ave real bonzer times goin' out tergether. **1913** C.J. Dennis *Backblock Ballads* 85 The bonzer smell o' flow'rs is on the breeze. **1916**—— *Moods Ginger Mick* 32 'E's 'ad 'is visions uv the Bonzer Tart; An' stoushed some coot to ease 'is swellin' 'eart. **1918** 'Lance-Corporal Cobber' *Anzac Pilgrim's Progress* 54 Oh, the Turk is a bonzer man to fight, He'll stick to his enemy hard an' tight. **1919** C.H. Thorp *Handful of Ausseys* 144 You know, I like ter see all these bonzer tabbies blowin' the smoke from their classy little mouths. Blimey, I wish we knew some uv them—bonzer tarts! ***c* 1923** L.A. Warren *Speaking Silence* 64 ''E's got a bonzer face,' she said. **1924** F.J. Mills *Happy Days* 118, I was on with a taxi-driver named Phyllis. Now, she was the neatest tart outside of a baker's shop. . . She 'ad the bonzerest ankles I ever seen. **1932** J.J. Hardie *Cattle Camp* (1944) 270 Bonzer! Best pair of legs I've ever seen! Great idea, these short skirts. No more buying a pig in a poke! **1938** X. Herbert *Capricornia* 204 You'll make the bonzerest couple ever seen this side the Tropic. **1950** E.M. England *Where Turtles Dance* 5 Cool as a cucumber; in a new frock—oh, looking bonsa, I'll admit. **1959** H. Drake-Brockman *West Coast Stories* 2 Hail, beauteous land! hail, bonzer West Australia; Compared with you, all others are a failure. **1964** M. Hilliard *Running through Rain* 169 They're a bit rough, this class, but they're bonzer kids when you get to know them. **1974** *Gayzette* (Sydney) 19 Sept. 19/2 Since Big Gough Whitlam and Bonzer Bob Hawke, the maleness of Australian society is becoming more, rather than less, emphatic. **1984** *Canberra Times* 12 Feb. 2/1 The gallery has nothing of the ocker oeuvre of Rolf Harris . . that bonzer Bronzino. **1986** *Nat. Times* (Sydney) 10 Jan. 14/1 Should there be a national breast-beating . . over our lost reputation as a bonzer little nation of sportsmen?

C. *adv.* Beautifully, splendidly.

1914 'B. Cable' *By Blow & Kiss* 246 Came back grinning widely, with the assurance that it [*sc.* the rain] was coming down 'Bonzer'. **1916** 'Men Of Anzac' *Anzac Bk.* 22 An' 'ere's some er the dinkum coc'nut-ice the tart uster make. . . 'Ow er yer orf fer socks, cobber? . . Take these—bonzer 'and-knitted. **1918** *Aussie: Austral. Soldiers' Mag.* Dec. 5/1 We sat down . . to try and forget about squad drill, and managed bonzer. **1936** F. Clune *Roaming round Darling* 67 Quite a score of people . . passed pleasant remarks about the weather. 'Bonza sunny day.' **1944** A.S. Smith *Boys write Home* 215 It's a bonzer clear day, perhaps the Zeros think so, too. **1951** D. Collins *Vic.'s my Home Ground* 31 When I was first prospecting round these parts, back in the nineties, we often had wombat. Used to smoke it in the chimney just like ham. Called it badger ham, we did, and it went down bonzer.

boobialla /bubiˈælə/. Also **boobyalla.** [a. Oyster Bay and s.e. Tas. *bubiala.*] **a.** The shrub or small tree of coastal sand dunes *Acacia longifolia* var. *sophorae* (fam. Mimosaceae). **b.** Any of several shrubs or small trees of the genus *Myoporum* (fam. Myoporaceae) with pale flowers and globular, often purplish, fruits. Also *attrib.*

1832 J. Backhouse *Narr. Visit Austral. Colonies* (1843) 59 The sand-banks at the mouth of Macquarie Harbour are covered with Boobialla, a species of *Acacia*, the roots of which run far in the sand. **1835** *Hobart Town Almanack* 63 *Acacia sophora.* Sophora podded Acacia or Booby-aloe . . a large shrub on the sand hills of the coast. . . [The seeds are] roasted in pods among the ashes by the Aborigines. **1861** L.A. Meredith *Over Straits* 62 Boobyalla bushes lay within the dash of the ceaseless spray. **1880** *Argus* (Melbourne) 2 Feb. 6/7 Now in bloom:- . . a variety of myoporum serratum, called by the aborigines of the Western district the 'boobiala'. **1912** *Emu* XII. 68 Under the shade of a boobialla tree. **1948** H.A. Lindsay *Bushman's Handbk.* 8 South of the Murray mouth . . through a stretch of coastal sand-dunes more than a hundred miles in length, we find the boobialla, a small-leafed wattle-like tree, whose long roots are often exposed. **1976** C. Eagle *Four Faces* 168 He came out, straight into the barley sown right up to the boobyalla hedge on the western side of the house.

boobook /ˈbubʊk/. [a. Dharuk *bug bug.*] The owl *Ninox novaeseelandiae* of Aust. and elsewhere, having a characteristic two-note call; Mopoke *n.* 1 a. Also **boobook owl.**

***c* 1790** W. Dawes Grammatical Forms Lang. N.S.W., *Bōk bōk*, an owl. **1801** J. Latham *Gen. Synopsis Birds* Suppl. II. 64 Boobook O. Description. Size of the Brown Owl. . . Place. This inhabits *New Holland*, where it is known by the name of *Boobook.* **1827** *Trans. Linnean Soc. London* XV. 188 Boobook Owl. . . 'The native name of this bird', as Mr Caley informs us, 'is *Buck'buck.* It may be heard nearly every night during winter uttering a cry corresponding with that word. . . The note of the bird is somewhat similar to that of the European *cuckoo*, and the colonists have hence given it that name.' **1846** *Portland Gaz.* 18 Sept. 4/5 The boobook or barking bird, and the curlew called during the night. **1849** C. Sturt *Narr. Exped. Central Aust.* II. 17 App. *Boobook Owl.* . . This bird has a dark brown plumage, spotted white. **1881** E. Davies *Story Earnest Life* 380 A species of owl, the boobook of Australia, that has the cuckoo's note. **1898** W. Redmond *Shooting Trip* 64 This bird . . keeps on crying out 'Mo-poke, mo-poke' and from this it derives its name although some people call it the 'Boobook owl' and others . . do call it the 'night-cuckoo'. **1912** B. O'Dowd *Bush* 24 Boobooks moan lone vespers in the dusk. **1917** *Bulletin* (Sydney) 23 Aug. 22/2 In the lingo of some Victorian abos. wook-ook stands for the boobook owl. **1925** *Ibid.* 23 Apr. 23/2 The blacks usually named a bird from its call, and good examples are currawong and boobook (though the latter cry was 'mopoke' to the white-man). **1945** T. Ronan *Strangers on Ophir* 144 You get up in the night and sing out like a boobook owl so you won't forget what talkin' sounds like. **1968** D. Fleay *Nightwatchmen* 87 An injustice of the bird world involving the Boobook Owl persists even today in many parts of Australia. It is the insistent misnomer of 'morepork' for the Tawny Frogmouth because this open-perching master of camouflage, which is not an owl at all, is occasionally found sitting by day in trees from which the Boobook Owl has 'mopoked' the prior night. **1976** *Reader's Digest Compl. Bk. Austral. Birds* 303 The boobook owl . . is the smallest and most abundant of the Australian owls.

boodgery, var. Budgeree.

boodie /ˈbudi/. Also **boody.** [a. Nyungar *burdi.*] A burrowing rat-kangaroo *Bettongia lesueur*, formerly widespread on mainland Aust. but now rare or extinct exc. on islands off the W.A. coast; Lesueur's rat-kangaroo. Also **boodie rat.**

1857 W.S. Bradshaw *Voyages* 114 Many of the animals of the forest . . are very good for food, namely, the opossums, bandicoots, boodies. **1872** Mrs E. Millett *Austral. Parsonage* 201 Binnahan . . on finding a picture in 'Punch' of rats dressed in coats and trousers, exclaimed, 'Look at the *boodies*, missis! They have all got on comfortable clothes.' **1897** L. Lindley-Cowen *W. Austral. Settler's Guide* 33 Boodie rats . . do some damage among the fruit trees and cereal crops. **1946** K.S. Prichard *Roaring Nineties* 49 The way the white men burrowed in the earth like boudie rats. **1952** J.F. Haddleton *Katanning Pioneer* 98 The boodie . . is very much like the kangaroo rat . . but lighter grey and . . with about ½ inch of white on the tail. The boodie makes a burrow like a rabbit . . and gets his food at night. **1975** R. Beilby *Brown Land Crying* 271 The orange-tinted, calcined earth was stamped with the prints of wallabies and boodie rats.

boofhead. [Prob. from *bufflehead* (lit. bullock head), fool: see quot. 1945.]

1. A fool or simpleton.

[**1941** *Daily Mirror* (Sydney) 12 May 15/1 (*caption*) Boofhead looks fishy.] **1945** S.J. Baker *Austral. Lang.* 130 *Boofhead*, from the English *bufflehead*, a stupid person, or dialectal *boof*, stupid. *Boofhead* is the name of a cartoon strip character in the Sydney 'Mirror', since 1941. [**1953** *Daily Mirror* (Sydney) 21 Jan. 29/1 'Did my medicine do any good, Boofhead?' 'It was a wonderful remedy, Doctor. I took three spoonfuls and my cough went, I rubbed four spoonfuls into my knee and it cured my rheumatism and I just left my mother at home using the rest of it to clean the silver.'] **1968** G. Dutton *Andy* 42 Now look, boofhead, your job is guarding me. **1976** J. Johnson *Low Breed* 57 At first I thought you were a bit of a boofhead to become a primary teacher. **1983** *Weekend Austral. Mag.* (Sydney) 27 Aug. 20/7 *Boofhead* is a word you don't hear often these days. Which is a pity. It has a certain charm, along with undeniable clarity of meaning. According to published evidence this week, Mr Bill Hayden used the word to the Hope Royal Commission, defining it as a person who is 'brash, barging and a bit bumptious'. **1986** *Canberra Times* 15 Feb. 2/5 You bunch of boofheads.—The Special Minister of State, Mr Young, on the Opposition.

2. A person or animal having a big head.

1946 R.D. Rivett *Behind Bamboo* 395 *Boof head*, one with a big head. **1981** A. Marshall *Aust.* 132 'What a boofhead of a foal,' he had thought—and so it was named. The foal did indeed have a large head, a hairy head, whiskered like a draught horse.

Hence **boofheaded** *a.*, **boofheadedness** *n.*

1965 J. Beede *They hosed them Out* 171 Tubby . . asked, 'Who's that **boofheaded** old bastard, anyway?' It was an apt description and from then on . . he was known as 'boofhead'. **1984** *Sydney Morning Herald* 19 Apr. 31/2 He is a big, clumsy, boofheaded type of a horse. **1983** *Sun-Herald* (Sydney) 18 Sept. 143/4 It is a scandal that they have been allowed to get away with this **boofheadedness** for so long.

boojeree, var. Budgeree.

book. Abbrev. of 'bookmaker'.

1891 *Truth* (Sydney) 11 Jan. 5/7 It must be evident to those who are not blind that bona fide bookmakers must soon cease to attend pony meetings; and experience shows that when the 'books' begin to leave, the game is up. **1896** *Bulletin* (Sydney) 11 Apr. 17/4 Of the small 'books' who bet outside the Sydney race-courses one is a Chinaman. **1904** *Shearer* (Sydney) 5 Nov. 8/2 His party . . have him coupled with every horse in the Melbourne Cup, and most of the 'books' are now considering how they are going to get out. **1915** Drew & Evans *Grafter* 63 The books kept the horse well under the odds for a time. **1933** S. Griffiths *Rolling Stone on Turf* 35 The news that several amateur bookmakers were to bet on a practically unlimited scale—'strike-breakers', the recalcitrant 'books' called them—proved a splendid attraction. **1955** P. White *Tree of Man* 271 At that time Ray was still associated with Bernie Abrahams, the book, whom nobody had met yet, because Bourkes did not go for bookies. **1984** *Sun-Herald* (Sydney) 25 Nov. 152/6 A local rails book was abused by a professional punter.

book muster. An inventory based upon the evidence of the stockbook, rather than an inspection of the actual stock. Also *attrib.*

[**1849** A. Harris *Emigrant Family* (1967) 128 Every beast being examined, as described by his or her marks in the stockbook; if female and possessed of this-year's calf, that calf is minutely described, and booked to her.] **1880** J.B. Stevenson *Seven Yrs. Austral. Bush* 108 A book muster, particularly upon an outside scrubby station is never to be depended upon. **1939** J.G. Pattison *'Battler's' Tales Early Rockhampton* 125, I would not have liked to buy any properties the late Government bought on book muster. *Ibid.*, I have often heard controversy re the merits of buying a property on a walk-in, walk-out, or bookmuster delivery, and the bang-tail system.

bool, var. Bull *n.*[1]

Booligal /ˈbuligəl/. [The name of a town in w. N.S.W.] Used *fig.* to designate a place of the greatest imaginable discomfort, 'the last place on earth', esp. in the sequence **Hay, (and) Hell, and Booligal.**

1888 *Illustr. Austral. News* (Melbourne) 12 Jan. 10/1 The grass everywhere is gone, and, to use the expression of a landholder there, 'there was not enough to whip a mosquito with'. Added to this, both flies and mosquitos are more plentiful than anything else, so that, when the climate is taken into consideration, Booligal seems to fully earn its place in the comparison instituted by residents and visitors, who place it thus—Hay, Hell and Booligal. **1896** *Bulletin* (Sydney) 25 Apr. 7/4 And people have an awful down upon the district and the town—Which worse than hell itself they call; In fact, the saying far and wide Along the Riverina side Is 'Hay and Hell and Booligal'. **1898** *Ibid.* 2 July 32/1 Hot? Great Scot! [*sic*] It was Hell, with some improvements, worse than Booligal, a lot! **1916** O. Hogue

Trooper Bluegum at Dardanelles 58 It was generally thought that he had spent some time in hell, or Booligal, so familiarly did he speak of the infernal regions. **1917** C.E.W. BEAN *Lett. from France* 214 Tradition in New South Wales puts the climate of Hay, Hell, and Booligal in that order. **1955** J. MORRISON *Black Cargo* 11 We've cursed the Federation from Hell to Booligal for all the muck they've tossed out at us. **1966** M. BROWN *Jimberi Track* 158 You're mad! Hay, hell and Booligal! **1972** *Sydney Morning Herald* 10 Apr. 17/1 'Hay, hell and Booligal', they say—but out there at Hay in the early morning it was still cardigan-cool.

boomalli, /bu'mæli/, *v.* [Prob. f. an Aboriginal language.] *trans.* To beat (an animal); see also quot. 1876.

1876 *Austral. Town & Country Jrnl.* (Sydney) 2 Dec. 902/4 To-night yan longa camp; boomalli (shoot, slay) Hutkeeper. **1945** T. RONAN *Strangers on Ophir* 99 A thousand head of bullocks, hungry and mostly thirsty, boomallied and knocked about as these had been, are hard to hold. **1981** K. GARVEY *Slowly sweats Gun* 177 I'll tell yer what yer spoilt, pampered little Guardsman needs! A bloke with a good heavy whip to boom-alley him into a corner of the yard and flog the legs off him until he faces up and takes the bridle.

boomareng, var. BOOMERANG *n.* 1.

boomer, *n.*[1] Also **boomah.** [Br. dial. *boomer* anything very large of its kind: see EDD.] Also *attrib.*

1. Orig. *Tas.* A large kangaroo, esp. an adult male *Macropus giganteus* (see *grey kangaroo* (a), GREY *a.*) or *M. rufus* (see *red kangaroo* (a), RED *a.* 1 b.). Also *fig.*

1830 *Hobart Town Almanack* 111 The fore-legs of a kangaroo are scarce one-third so long as the hind ones. For this reason, if a boomah attempts to run down a hill on all fours he is very apt to tumble head over heels. **1831** *Ibid.* 265 The forest or boomah kangaroo, which delights in rich and open pastures. **1835** J. BATMAN *Settlement Port Phillip* 5 June (1856) 19 In this forest, which was well grassed, we caught one of the largest kangaroos I have ever seen, measuring nine feet. This *was a boomer.* **1841** G. GREY *Jrnls. Two Exped. N.-W. & W.A.* I. 320 We killed a large Boomer, or old male kangaroo. **1843** C. ROWCROFT *Tales of Colonies* III. 191 We saw five kangaroos—foresters—in the middle, and one prodigious fellow, whom the natives greeted with the title of boomah! boomah!. . . The boomah! stood in the midst looking with a sort of defiance on his enemies. **1845** *Atlas* (Sydney) I. 258/1 The large full-grown male is termed Buck or Boomer, and attains a great size. **1854** W. HOWITT *Boy's Adventures* 197 The great red kangaroo, called a boomah, or old man . . is often six feet high or more. **1872** MRS E. MILLETT *Austral. Parsonage* 195 A kangaroo's feet are, in fact, his weapons of defence with which, when he is brought to bay, he tears his antagonists the dogs most dreadfully. . . This peculiar method of disposing of his enemies has earned for him the name of *Booma,* which in the native languages signifies to strike. **1893** R. BRUCE *Echoes from Coondambo* 162 There's a red old man and flying doe; *Ware doe* and *after* the boomer! **1917** T.J. BRIGGS *Life & Experiences Successful W. Austral.* 126 The average weight of 'boomer' skins was about two and a half pounds when dry. **1936** *Bulletin* (Sydney) 15 Apr. 20/2, I have seen many an old-man 'roo so helpless and frantic with the 'roo-flies that any one could approach to within a few feet without the boomer taking the slightest notice. **1951** I.L. IDRIESS *Across Nullarbor* 140 'He was a boomer right enough,' agreed Bill. 'The biggest 'roo I've ever seen.' **1981** A. WELLER *Day of Dog* 109 The old man . . has the look of an old warrior boomer, with the mongrel dogs of wasted time and circumstance cornering him and dragging him bloodily to the ground.

2. A large or otherwise remarkable specimen of its kind.

1843 C. ROWCROFT *Tales of Colonies* III. 96 'Wool! No Boomahs [*sc.* fleas]! I hope—Eh! Dick?,' beginning to scratch himself instinctively at the sight of the wool. **1849** *Bell's Life in Sydney* 21 Apr. 2/5 'There's a boomer of a gum tree,' said he, pointing to an enormous trunk. **1856** W.W. DOBIE *Recoll. Visit Port-Phillip* 77 She would sometimes relate . . how successful she had been in flea-hunting, and what a *boomer* she had caught that morning. **1885** *Australasian Printers' Keepsake* 76 When the shades of evening come, I choose a boomer of a gum. **1887** A. NICOLS *Wild Life & Adventure* 128 They generally run about three to six pounds; but there's some boomers out there in the middle, in the deep water. **1892** 'MRS A. MACLEOD' *Silent Sea* II. 272 'A boomer nugget! a boomer nugget!' The cry flew like wildfire, and strange excitement ensued. **1909** R. KALESKI *Austral. Settler's Compl. Guide* 92 If rain comes the crop will be a boomer. **1924** *Aussie* (Sydney) 15 Mar. 48 The simultaneous jolting and stopping of the boat, suggested that we had hooked a boomer. **1936** 'L. KAYE' *Black Wilderness* 52 And the southern haze was a good sign: the *booma* duststorms came from there. **1949** C.B. MAXWELL *Surf* 2 Great 'boomers' of waves had been crashing farther out. **1968** G. DUTTON *Andy* 262 Some bloody boomers, boy, be in it. But some hairy-nosed dumpers as well. **1977** F.B. VICKERS *Stranger no Longer* 77 It's sure a boomer of a morning. **1979** D. BURKE *Darknight* 7 'There has to be a story in this,' he said to himself. 'It could be a real boomer.' . . 'I could get a byline.'

boomer, *n.*[2] [f. *boom* to call resonantly.] The Austral. bittern *Botaurus poiciloptilus,* a swamp bird with a booming call, occurring in s. Aust. and New Zealand; *brown bittern,* see BROWN *a.* 1; *bull bird,* see BULL *n.*[3]; BUNYIP 4.

[**1857** *Australasian* (Melbourne) ii. 11 The boom-boom . . the bittern]. **1951** *Argus* (Melbourne) 14 Dec. (Suppl.) 2/5 The hollow boom so often heard on the margins of reedy swamps . . is the mythical bunyip. . . Our brown bittern is the culprit. He it is who cries at night from the depths of lonely swamps. Bushmen call him the 'Boomer'. **1953** A. RUSSELL *Murray Walkabout* 25 It was an Australian bittern, or boomer.

boomerang /'buməræŋ/, *n.* Formerly also with much variety, as **bomerang, bommerang, bomring, boomareng, boomering, bumerang.** [a. Dharuk *bumarin*ʸ.]

1. An Aboriginal weapon: a crescent-shaped wooden implement used as a missile or club, in hunting or warfare, and for recreational purposes. The best-known type of boomerang can be made to circle in flight and return to the thrower. See also SWORD, THROWING STICK b., THROW-STICK 1, WADDY *n.* 1 a., WOMERA. Also *attrib.*

c **1790** W. DAWES Grammatical Forms Lang. N.S.W., *Boo-mer-rit,* the Scimiter. **1825** B. FIELD *Geogr. Mem. N.S.W.* 292 The spear is universal, as is also the throwing-stick; the *boomerang* or *woodah,*—a short crested weapon which the natives of Port Jackson project with accurate aim into a rotary motion, which gives a precalculated bias to its forcible fall,—was also seen at Port Bowen on the east coast, and at Goulburn Island on the north. **1827** P.P. KING *Narr. Survey Intertropical & Western Coasts* I. 391 A boomerang whizzed past his head, and struck a tree close by with great force. **1828** *New Monthly Mag.* (London) Sept. 218 We were amused after dinner by the throwing of the Bomaring, or crooked stick . . making it come back to where they stand. **1832** *Hill's Life N.S.W.* (Sydney) 21 Sept. 4 Unerring his aim when his barbed spear flew, Nor less so, when wamrah, or bomring, he threw. **1833** *Currency Lad* (Sydney) 9 Mar. 3 Quarrels . . arose among the tribes assembled, and an engagement took place with boomarings, in which several natives were severely wounded. **1834** G. BENNETT *Wanderings N.S.W.* I. 116 'Bomerang' . . is a peculiar weapon thrown by the hand, and possesses the apparent anomalous property of striking an object in the opposite direction from that in which it is at first propelled. **1839** T.L. MITCHELL *Three Exped. Eastern Aust.* (rev. ed.) II. 348 The bommereng, a thin curved missile, can be thrown by a skilful hand, so as to rise upon the air, and thus to deviate from the ordinary path of projectiles, its crooked course being, nevertheless, equally under control. **1846** *Portland Guardian* 22 Sept. 4/2 At the Macarthur we still saw the bommerang, which is unknown at the Alligator River or Port Essington, where the throwing stick and the goose spears are the means of obtaining game. **1848** *Bell's Life in Sydney* 12 Feb. 2/1 Those Bills . . like Boomerangs, came back to you. **1851** J. HENDERSON *Excursions & Adventures N.S.W.* II. 145 The weapon next in importance is the boomerang, or, as the natives pronounce it, bumering. **1861** T. M'COMBIE *Austral. Sketches* 158 They are equally expert in killing birds with the bumerang. **1863** J. BONWICK *Wild White Man* 51 It was difficult at our safe boomerang distance always to distinguish the part of these Amazons. **1871** 'IOTA' *Kooroona* 119 Harry awoke the next morning just in time to see most of the men, armed with spears and waddies, go off for the day's hunting. Two or three carried boomoorangs; the dogs followed them. **1885** *Australasian Printers' Keepsake* 26 The verdant plain! The happy time is past! The white-folk wallaby, in numbers vast, Fill all the valleys where my fathers sprang When Jacky Jacky hurled his boomerang. **1893** S. NEWLAND *Paving Way* 58 Rolls had a spear through his shirt, Jem got a clip from a waddy on the shoulder, and a boomerang took my hat off; thank heaven it wasn't my head! **1916** *Truth* (Sydney) 23 Jan. 2/7 When this writer read the outburst he thought it may possibly, boomerang-like, return to the Department. **1923** T. HALL *Short Hist. Downs Blacks* 15 It will be noticed that I have always used the word 'Boomering', not 'Boomerang', because the latter word was a white man's 'Cockneyism'. **1929** W.J. RESIDE *Golden Days* 160 Another weapon which is in prevalent use is the boomerang, Kailla or Kylie. Crescent-shaped, or angular, it is flat on one side and occasionally ingeniously ornamented. **1942** E. LANGLEY *Pea Pickers* 112 He . . sent the decorated boomerang wheeling and winging out across the paddock on a slanting angle. **1963** D. ATTENBOROUGH *Quest under Capricorn* 148 Charlie referred to these objects as 'boomerangs' and 'wommaras', for our benefit. The names were not Walbiri ones and Charlie had learned them from the white men. **1981** P. CORRIS *White Meat* 31 He lifted the arm and threw in a short, chopping motion that launched the boomerang off in a skipping, dancing spin; it arced out and came back humming like a model plane.

2. *transf.* and *fig.*, esp. with reference to something which returns to or recoils upon its author. Also *attrib.*

1846 *Boston Daily Advertiser* 5 May, Like the strange missile which the Australian throws, Your verbal *boomerang* slaps you on the nose. **1894** *Bulletin* (Sydney) 7 July 11/4 The argument that there should be no profitable industrial prison-labour is a boomerang with a wicked recoil. **1911** *Pastoralists' Rev.* 15 Mar. 59 Labour-Socialist legislation is boomerang legislation, and it generally comes back and hits those it was not intended for. **1921** J.P. OSBORNE *Nine Crowded Yrs.* 14 The principle was sound enough, but in practice it proved cumbersome and expensive, and strange to relate, became a veritable 'boomerang' to the Party responsible for its introduction. **1932** *Austral. Ring* II. xx. 4 The 'bird' given the Editor of this paper by certain leading (or shall we say misleading) sport writers for boosting a country 'White Hope' proved a boomerang when the country clouter lived up to his publicity and came through a winner. **1944** J. DEVANNY *By Tropic Sea & Jungle* 4 Trevally with red flesh are considered uneatable and are thrown back into the sea. Boomerangs, the men call them. **1945** T. RONAN *Strangers on Ophir* 19 The cheque was a boomerang. McGarry knew it and Bugworthy knew that he knew it. **1949** P.A. JACOBS *Lawyer Tells* 102 The circular did not disclose the name of the person who composed or authorised it. . . It probably acted as a boomerang and may have done me more harm than good. **1969** D. NILAND *Dead Men Running* 77 The wind was the sweeper there judging by the boomerang bend on the banksia trees that grew here and there. **1980** B. SCOTT *Darkness under Hills* 62 No cloud marred the brilliant stars and the moon was a thin boomerang of palest light on the western horizon. **1981** Q. WILD *Honey Wind* 109 'I believe there is a kind of boomerang law,' Galiali said to Harry. 'And that the way you treat the world around you . . will rebound and reflect like a mirror.'

3. Comb. **boomerang thrower, throwing;** also *fig.*, as **boomerang bill, cheque.**

1884 *Bulletin* (Sydney) 12 July 20/4 One of Barnum's troop of Australian **boomerang throwers** died recently. **1901** *Ibid.* (Sydney) 2 Mar. 15/1, I am a pretty fair boomerang-thrower, except with the 'returner'. **1956** S. HOPE *Diggers' Paradise* 32 The expert boomerang throwers . . still make their own by hand for competitive displays. **1981** *Woman's Day* (Sydney) 16 Sept. 45/2 Away from his clerical duties . . [he] is one of Australia's top boomerang throwers. **1910** W.C. WALL *Sydney Stage Employee's Pictorial Ann.* 74 The blacks gave an exhibition of **boomerang throwing** and so on. **1915** *Honk* xi. 3 A very interesting exhibition of boomerang throwing and stockwhip cracking. **1971** *Bulletin* (Sydney) 30 Oct. 24/2 The whole colonial lot—boomerang throwing and a touch of farm hospitality. **1981** *Woman's Day* (Sydney) 16 Sept. 45/2 The Boomerang Association of Australia wants boomerang throwing to be accepted as a serious sport. **1961** *Bulletin* (Sydney) 21 Oct. 8/1 The delegates had decided to go far beyond the issue of the **'boomerang' bills** and press for: a fully elected Legislative Council. **1951** E. HILL *Territory* 237 He had a notice put in the Northern Territory Times:

Old hands still welcome at the Depot but . . **boomerang cheque** artists take another track. **1956** T. RONAN *Moleskin Midas* 286 Bob was good with the pen in his day, mainly for signing boomerang cheques. **1962** —— *Deep of Sky* 48 Having acquired the science of writing his signature, Alby soon devoted his knowledge to the signing of cheques. His life then became one boomerang cheque after another.

4. Special Comb. **boomerang leg, (a)** a disease characterized by flattening and forward bowing of the shinbone; **(b)** a leg affected by the disease; also as **boomerang-legged,** *a.*

1894 *Intercolonial Q. Jrnl. Med. & Surg.* I. 223 The condition is well recognised by the residents who, not inaptly, describe the natives so affected as 'boomerang-legged'. **1899** SPENCER & GILLEN *Native Tribes Central Aust.* 44 Not infrequently platycnemia, or flattening of the tibial bones, is met with, and at times the curious condition to which Dr Stirling has given the name of Camptocnemia. The latter consists in an anterior curvature of the tibial bone and gives rise to what the white settlers have, for long, described by the very apt term 'boomerang-leg'. **1913** CASTELLANI & CHALMERS *Man. Tropical Med.* (ed. 2) 1447 Boomerang leg. This disease . . occurs among the aboriginal natives of the north of Western Australia, and exists in the northern territory of the Commonwealth and the Torres Straits Islands. . . The first symptom is tenderness and pain in the tibia and fibula, which become soft, and bend gradually till they assume the 'boomerang' curve. **1915** *Jrnl. Tropical Med. & Hygiene* XVIII. 218 The disease has for some time been known as 'boomerang leg', on account of the similarity of the shape of the legs to that of a boomerang. **1936** C. CHEWINGS *Back in Stone Age* 34 The legs of the natives thus affected are referred to by the whites as 'boomerang legs'. **1969** A.A. ABBIE *Original Australs.* 87 Usually the worst permanent sequela of yaws is a bony thickening that produces a forward curving of the long bones of the legs and especially of the shin bone where the condition is popularly called 'sabre tibia' or 'boomerang leg'. **1973** P.M. MOODIE *Aboriginal Health* 236 It seems very likely that 'boomerang leg' is a disease of complex aetiology.

boomerang /ˈbuməræŋ/, *v.* [f. BOOMERANG *n.* 2.] *intr.* To return in the manner of a boomerang; to recoil (upon the author); to ricochet.

1891 *Worker* (Brisbane) 16 May 8 Australia's a big country An' Freedom's humping bluey And Freedom's on the wallaby Oh don't you hear her Cooee, She's just begun to boomerang She'll knock the tyrants silly. **1919** C. DREW *Doings of Dave* 11 [The billiard ball] boomeranged off the jaw, and . . rolled into the left-hand middle pocket. **1934** *Austral. Ring* IX. cxi. 13 Now and again a joke will 'boomerang', and then it's a case of the biter being bitten. **1967** R. DONALDSON et al. *Cane!* 166 Christ, the whole thing had boomeranged on him. **1979** T. ASTLEY *Hunting Wild Pineapple* 141 She . . cried his name over and over against the hurlings of the wind. Nothing. His name boomeranged back into her mouth, was tasted and flung out again. **1979** *Canberra Times* 13 Nov. 28/6 Greg Chappell's decision to send England in appeared to have boomeranged.

boomeranging, *vbl. n.* The throwing of a boomerang.

1880 J.B. STEPHENS *Misc. Poems* 26 No faint forhearing of the waddies banging, Of clubs and heelaman together clanging, War shouts, and universal boomeranging? **1899** *Longman's Mag.* (London) XXXIII. 475 Boomeranging is dangerous for on-lookers, till the thrower is a perfect master of his weapon.

boomerang propeller. *Hist.* A steamship propeller the design of which was inspired by the Aboriginal weapon; invented by the explorer Thomas Mitchell (1792–1855), but never developed commercially.

1849 T.L. MITCHELL *Let.* 22 Oct. in *Mechanic's Mag.* (London) (1850) LII. 448/2 A boomerang propeller, whose diameter was 22 inches. **1851** *Sydney Morning Herald* 11 Jan. 2/2, I . . had a boat built at Sydney, and attached a small bomareng propeller to the bow. **1852** *Austral. Gold Digger's Monthly Mag.* i. 36 Who is to say that Australia in twenty years may not boast of a mighty fleet of Boomerang Propellers? **1878** R.B. SMYTH *Aborigines of Vic.* I. 319 By attaching a thin slip of wood to the inner part of a boomerang, and using the point of a needle for a support, the weapon may be balanced and made to rotate freely. . . This discovery . . was made many years ago by the late Sir Thos. L. Mitchell, and in his 'Lecture on the Bomareng-Propeller' . . this and many other interesting facts . . are mentioned. **1913** J.C.L. FITZPATRICK *Good Old Days of Molong* 38 He was a man of most versatile type—for instance, he published a trigonometrical survey of Port Jackson, patented a boomerang-propeller for steamers, and translated 'The Lusiad' of Camoens. **1928** W. ROBERTSON *Coo-ee Talks* 112 It is said that Sir Thomas Livingstone Mitchell, the great explorer, had made a special study of the peculiar gyrations of the returning boomerang, and when he revisited England in 1853 he patented the boomerang-propeller for steamers. **1937** *Publicist* (Sydney) viii. 11/1 Mitchell was interested in a project for the formation of a company . . to exploit the 'Boomerang propeller', an invention of his own based on the aboriginal weapon.

boonaree /ˈbunəri/. Also **boonery.** [a. Kamilaroi *bunari.*] The plant *Heterodendrum oleifolium* (see ROSEWOOD).

1932 R.H. ANDERSON *Trees of N.S.W.* 7 Rosewood or boonery (*Heterodendron oleaefolium*). A small to medium-sized tree, but sometimes little more than a shrub. **1935** B.E. PHELPS *Austral. tells England* 193 Those wonderful little trees . . myall, wilga, boonerie. **1944** *Bulletin* (Sydney) 23 Feb. 13/3 Rosewood or Boonery (*Heterodendron oleaefolium*) is also called whitewood. **1966** J.F. MACADAM *Some Poisonous Plants N.-W.* 77 Boonery, or rosewood grows into a medium sized tree and is commonly found on the slopes and plains. **1974** S.L. EVERIST *Poisonous Plants Aust.* 438 Boonaree is one of the most useful fodder trees in inland Australia and sheep and cattle often live on it during drought periods.

boondie, var. BONDI *n.*[1]

boondie /ˈbundi/. [Prob. f. a W.A. Aboriginal language.] A stone.

1952 T.A.G. HUNGERFORD *Ridge & River* 94 See that bastard, practising grenade-throwing with bits of boondies? **1957** R. STOW *Bystander* 132 The stone hit the middle of the roof. . . 'He's chucking boondies on the roof.' **1963** —— *Tourmaline* 116 And he stooped to pick up a small stone . . and tossed it . . to lob on Byrne's stomach. . . 'I didn't mean chuck boondies at him,' Deborah objected. **1977** D. STUART *Drought Foal* 7 It doesn't matter if she sees them pissing and throwing boondies. **1986** A. WELLER *Going Home* 40 He could fight, chuck boondies . . and run better than anyone.

boonery, var. BOONAREE.

boong /bʊŋ/. [a. Wemba Wemba dial. of Wemba *beŋ* man, human being.]

1. A name for an Aboriginal (see also quot. 1933).

1924 *Smith's Weekly* (Sydney) 2 Aug. 16/2 The abos. or boongs around Cairns cure headaches by placing a grass plaited band, about two and a half inches wide, across the forehead. **1933** F.E. BAUME *Tragedy Track* 51 'So then our job is to catch 'em,' Simon says. He and George usually speak 'bung', or blackfellow 'pidgin'. It is the custom of the country. **1937** M. TERRY *Sand & Sun* 269 My word, we've got plenty of names for 'em too. Let's see. There's nigger, boong, coon, blackfellow, myall. **1940** *Bulletin* (Sydney) 28 Feb. 17/4 Binghi soon coiled up in the shade and went to sleep . . and by the time the boong had rubbed the sleep out of his eyes the bullocks were off in a mad rush across the desert. **1947** O. GRIFFITHS *Darwin Drama* 34 Women were scarce in Darwin and it was said that, to the lonely sailor, soldier and airman, the 'boongs' and 'creamies' got whiter every day. **1950** 'N. SHUTE' *Town like Alice* 82 'Nine boongs we had'. . . 'Nine what?' 'Black boys—black stockmen. Abos.' **1960** R.S. PORTEOUS *Cattleman* 161 He heard the shrill-voiced barracker yell, "It 'im in the guts, McReady! Ya can't 'urt them bloody boongs' 'eads.' **1969** D. CUSACK *Half-Burnt Tree* 14 We're Aborigines, see? Not blackfellers or *Boongs* or niggers. Aborigines. . . With a capital A. **1972** *Kings Cross Whisper* (Sydney) cxxii. 2/4 Queensland Premier, Mr Jolly Prattleon, said that giving things to Aboriginals was standard practice in his state. 'We're always giving boongs things,' he said. **1974** *Bulletin* (Sydney) 13 July 20/3 To them the Aborigines and Islanders who make up some 10 percent of the town are . . 'darkies' or 'boongs' (both neutral expressions). **1982** P. GOLDSWORTHY *Archipelagoes* 55 Frank remembered . . when they'd ambushed the abo on his morning rounds. . . The three of them might still have been at school, but were old enough to know how to treat a boong. **1986** *Nat. Times* (Sydney) 10 Jan. 25/4, I get called 'wog' by the ethnics because I'm not an Aborigine. . . The girls who are Aborigines get called boongs or chocos. There's heaps of name-calling but it is mostly just fun.

2. *transf.* An indigenous inhabitant of New Guinea, Malaysia, etc. Also *attrib.*

1943 *Survey Sentinel: 2/1 Austral. Army Topogr. Survey Co.* 2 May, If near a native village, just follow the 'boongs'. **1944** A.S. SMITH *Boys write Home* 117 *Believe* me, when this war is over, and its history written, there is one chap that should get a large share of the praise. He is the lowly 'boong'. **1944** *Bulletin* (Sydney) 26 July 12/4 That boong who had the possum's tail fast in a split stick . . was probably acting according to Papuan lore. **1945** *Aust. Week-End Bk.* 170, I am now an old hand at dealing with the 'boongs', angelic or otherwise. **1946** *Southerly* iv. 208 In Malaya . . the chooks we had got from a boong's place.

3. Special Comb. **boong line,** a team of native bearers, as employed in New Guinea during the war of 1939–45.

1943 A. DAWES *Soldier Superb* 58 Suddenly there was a shout and a cheer, and in at the double burst the carriers—the 'boong line', as the Australian soldiers (much against the grain of Angau, for 'boong' is an Australian Aboriginal word) call them. **1946** A.J. MARSHALL *Nulli Secundus Log* 83 We had a 'boong-line' of 40 native carriers to carry . . other essential gear.

Hence **boongess** *n.*

1945 *Aust. Week-End Bk.* 153 Isn't there a fancy boongess somewhere around this joint? Classy bit of colour?

boongarry /ˈbʊŋgəri/. [a. Warrgamay *bulŋgari.*] The tree-kangaroo *Dendrolagus lumholtzi* of forests in n.e. Qld.; MAPI.

1889 R.B. ANDERSON tr. Lumholtz's *Among Cannibals* 102 According to the statement of the blacks, it was a tree-kangaroo. . . It had a very long tail . . and was called *boongary.* **1890** A.J. VOGAN *Black Police* 197 Boongaries (tree-kangeroos) squeak and bark to their mates. **1913** *Bulletin* (Sydney) 5 June 15/4 The boongarry was long thought an aboriginal myth, like the bunyip; but it isn't and the Melbourne Zoo has a couple to prove it. **1944** J. DEVANNY *By Tropic Sea & Jungle* 19 There are a lot of tree-kangaroos in the Cardwell Ranges. Boongarrie, the natives call them.

boorah, var. BORA.

boorie /ˈbʊri/. Also **burry.** [a. Wiradhuri (and neighbouring languages) *buray* boy, child.] A name for an Aboriginal.

1955 N. PULLIAM *I traveled Lonely Land* 369 The abo is sometimes called a blackfellow or binghi, burry or blackman, etc. **1972** K. WILLEY *Tales Big Country* 170 Some Queenslanders still disparage Aborigines as 'abos' and 'boories'. **1974** N. PHILLIPSON *As Other Men* 137 The deliberately provocative references to 'gins' and 'boories' . . would have earned him a swift smack . . policeman or no policeman. **1977** M. TUCKER *If everyone Cared* 50 Children are either *pang pang gooks*, or *boories*; their mothers are *lerrooks*; women, *kring-krings*.

boot, *n.*[1]

1. [Now used elsewhere.] In the phr. **to put** (or **sink**) **the boot in, to put in the boot.**

a. To attack savagely, esp. when the opponent is disadvantaged, or in a manner which is otherwise conventionally unacceptable.

1915 C.J. DENNIS *Songs of Sentimental Bloke* 42 'It's me or you!' 'e 'owls, an' wiv a yell, Plunks Tyball through the gizzard wiv 'is sword, 'Ow I ongcored! 'Put in the boot!' I sez. 'Put in the boot!' **1918** J.A. PHILP *Jingles that Jangle* 28 In the game Ginger Mick was a tricky galoot, He might 'trip', he might 'rabbit'—or 'put in the boot'. **1932** J. TRURAN *Green Mallee* 18 Get on wi' the job, or I'll put the boot inter yer. **1962** E. LANE *Mad as Rabbits* 81 Father had a dreadful job stopping him from rushing after the offender, and without a word, 'sinking the boots in' as punishment.

b. *fig.*

1916 *West Austral.* (Perth) 11 Nov. 7/7 Don't scab on the unemployed. Slow work means more jobs, more jobs less competition, higher wages. Fast workers die young. Someone has to be slowest—let it be you. Get wise to the I.W.W. tactics. Organise on the job. Put in the boot. Sabotage. Kick like hell. **1917** *Railway Strike* (Labor Council N.S.W.) 4 The employers, backed up by the Government, are taking full advantage of the surplus labor and hungry unemployed, and are 'putting the boot in' with a vengeance, regardless of the misery and suffering of the innocent women and children. **1919** *Smith's Weekly* (Sydney) 19 Apr. 10/6 Unless the Commissioners study the men a bit and leave off 'putting the boot' into them, then it is useless to talk of remedying industrial discontent. **1935** K. TENNANT *Tiburon* 33 If they're puttin' the boot in, they'll get you sooner or later. **1946** D. STIVENS *Courtship of Uncle Henry* 75 He was mad as a cut snake about everything and wanting to put the boot in. **1968** S. GORE *Holy Smoke* 36 As per usual when things go crook, the first bloke they put the boots into is their own leader, Moses. **1973** J. MURRAY *Larrikins* 197 'Putting in the boot' has continued to be a fairly common practice, only reprehensible when someone with a criminal background is doing it literally.

2. In the phr. **boots and all,** without reservation, with no holds barred.

[N.Z. **1947** O.M. DAVIN *Rest of our Lives* 96 The next thing he'll do is counter-attack, boots and all.] **1950** *Arna* (Sydney) 27 Their [*sc.* Marxists] historical science informs them that ruling classes in the period of their decline resort increasingly to violence and repression—'boots and all', to use the phrase of a Democratic Prime Minister, as he threw police and troops against striking mine-workers. **1953** D. CUSACK *Southern Steel* 260 When you do a thing you go into it boots and all. **1964** P. ADAM SMITH *Hear Train Blow* 185 Settling down in the 'Big Smoke', Melbourne, was an adventure of a different kind and Kevin and I went into it 'boots and all', as his grandfather said. **1973** J. POWERS *Last of Knucklemen* (1974) 72 You lift your arse off that floor, mate, an' I'm gonna come wadin' into you—boots an' all! **1985** *Weekend Austral.* (Sydney) 28 Sept. 4/4 Canberra's cabbies go in boots and all for a fair deal.

boot, *n.*[2] [Br. *boot* that which is given to make up a deficiency of value (*obs.* exc. Scot. dial.): see OED *sb.*[1] 2.] Something added in from one side to ensure the equality of an exchange.

1863 *Frank Gardiner, or Bushranging in 1863* 10 If I had known that the boot was only fifteen notes and a ticker, I wouldn't have started on such a wet night. **1871** M. CLARKE *Old Tales of Young Country* 38 Rum was taken morning, noon and night, was paid as 'boot' in exchanges and received as payment for purchases. **1903** J. FURPHY *Such is Life* 10 'And how much boot are you going to give me?' I asked, with a feeling of shame which did honour to my heart.

booyong /ˈbujɒŋ/. [a. Bandjalang *buyaŋ.*] Any of several ornamental and timber trees of the genus *Argyrodendron* (fam. Sterculiaceae) of N.S.W. and Qld.; *crowsfoot elm*, see CROWSFOOT; TULIP OAK.

1908 *Emu* VII. 203, I arrived at the Booyong scrubs from Sydney on the 4th of October, 1899. **1923** T. HALL *Short Hist. Downs Blacks* 25 The boomerings were made from the booyong (or Black Jack) tree, which was considered the finest timber to be had for that purpose. **1926** *Qld. Agric. Jrnl.* XXV. 433 There is a Crow's Foot Elm which is also called Booyong. **1933** H.J. CARTER *Gulliver in Bush* 102 Almost immediately we plunged into a gorgeous forest of eucalypts, tristania, booyong (*Tarrietia*). **1949** B. O'REILLY *Green Mountains* 102 The tree, a long straight Booyong, fell squarely into the fork of the next tree. **1981** A.B. & J.W. CRIBB *Useful Wild Plants Aust.* 110 Buttressing of the trunk base . . is particularly noticeable in booyong, where the upper edge of the buttress is typically concave in outline.

booze bus. A police vehicle carrying equipment for the random breath-testing of motorists.

1982 *Sydney Morning Herald* 16 Dec. 2/1 (*heading*) Police 'booze buses' gear up for start of random breath tests. **1984** *Bulletin* (Sydney) 29 May 54/2 There were buses everywhere to take guests to and from their motels and thereby avoid any cruising booze bus. **1984** *Open Road* Dec. 3 (*caption*) Booze buses operating through the night.

bo-peep. A peep, a look.

1941 *Coast to Coast* 67 'I'll 'ave a bo-peep,' he said. 'You gotter watch 'er. We don't want no dead pups.' **1954** I.L. IDRIESS *Nor'-Westers* 125 One morning the butcher drove past. Tommy Ryan . . glanced up quizzically. 'Why the bo-peep at the butcher?' inquired a friend. **1968** D. O'GRADY *Bottle of Sandwiches* 165 We'll have a bo-peep at the damage. **1983** *Sydney Morning Herald* 21 May 35/4 Sister prowled in regularly for a bo-peep at my progress.

Hence *v. intr.*

1949 I.L. IDRIESS *One Wet Season* 24 'Bo-Peep at that bunch of pretty girls,' shouted Bunch.

bopple nut. Chiefly *Qld.* Also **bauple nut.** [See quot. 1975.] MACADAMIA. Also *ellipt.* as **bopple.**

1927 H.J. RUMSEY *Austral. Nuts* 5 The Australian Nut . . has been variously known as 'Queensland Nut', 'Bush Nut', 'Mullumbimby Bush Nut', 'Bauple Nut', 'Popple Nut'. . . The term 'Poplar Nut' is absurd, and should be dropped, as the word is only a demoralised form of 'Bauple', from Mount Bauple, in Queensland. **1948** H.A. LINDSAY *Bushman's Handbk.* 64 Queensland has two food plants not mentioned in the books; one of which is the Queensland nut or 'bopple' (*Macadamia ternifolia*). It grows in gullies and has leaves with serrated edges, quite like those of a banksia. The nut is an inch in diameter and has a remarkably hard shell. **1975** A.B. & J.W. CRIBB *Wild Food in Aust.* 88 This species was once well known in the rainforests of the Mt Bauple [*sc.* s.e. Qld.] area, and for this reason was commonly called Bauple nut, a name sometimes corrupted to bopple or popple nut. **1981** T. SHAPCOTT *Stump & Grape & Bopple-Nut* 12 Never forget, in the bopple-nut season; never forget under the house, under the verandah: cracking 'em with a hammer.

bora /ˈbɔrə/. Also **boorah, borah, boree, borer.** [a. Kamilaroi *buuru.*]

1. An initiation ceremony: a ceremony at which an Aboriginal youth is admitted to the privileges of manhood. Also *attrib.*

1851 *Colonial Intelligencer* (London) III. 316 They have to observe the difficult and unpleasant custom of 'borra', in order to make them *men.* **1860** 'LADY' *My Experiences in Aust.* 222 There are other meetings they hold, known in our part of the country as 'Boroes', which they acknowledge are for the purpose of celebrating some superstitious rites practised when their youth arrive at years of manhood. . . The call to 'boro' is . . urgent and imperative. **1864** J. MORRILL *Sketch of Residence* 215 They went through the rites and ceremonies of the Boree, or making young lads men. **1870** E.B. KENNEDY *Four Yrs. in Qld.* 79 A 'Boorah' . . consists of the surrounding tribes congregating to perform a mysterious ceremony. **1872** G.S. BADEN-POWELL *New Homes for Old Country* 398 Black boys . . are made men of by passing through the mysteries of the 'Borer'. **1874** *Illustr. Sydney News* 2 May 6/3 As in the Borah (another important native rite), females are carefully excluded. **1885** MRS C. PRAED *Austral. Life* 24 The great mystery of the Blacks is the Bora—a ceremony at which the young men found worthy receive the rank of warriors and are henceforth called *kippers.* **1895** R.H. MATHEWS *Bora* 413 The Aborigines' Protection Board, on being informed that the Bora was to be held, authorised the issue of rations to the aged blacks and children. **1925** *Smith's Weekly* (Sydney) 4 July 15/7 Attendance of whites at a native Borah dance was forbidden. **1942** L. & K. HARRIS *Lost Hole of Bingoola* 21 Many times Binda had heard the blackfellows talk about the Bora, the sacred dance or ceremony by which young boys were initiated into manhood and became warriors of the tribe. **1966** K. WALKER *Dawn at Hand* 21 Today at the Bora Terrified but eager Boy becomes man.

2. The site at which a bora is held.

1937 D. GUNN *Links with Past* 17 All the boras I know consist of two round patches of ground cleared of grass and sticks. The larger ring is where the men of the tribe meet and pass laws, which are confirmed by the old men who meet at the smaller ring. **1969** A.A. ABBIE *Original Australs.* 134 Special ceremonies are sometimes held on a particularly sacred piece of ground called a *bora*; this title may also be applied to the ceremony itself. The *bora* ground is usually defined by a circular earthen bank or by a ring of large stones, hence the common name of '*bora ring*'. **1970** J.V. MARSHALL *Walk to Hills of Dreamtime* 89 They . . were approaching the 'boree', the meeting ground of the tribes. **1971** K. GILBERT *End of Dreamtime* 24 Once again the tribe is gathered—on the bora—by the sea!

3. Comb. **bora ceremony, circle, ground, ring.**

1896 *Bulletin* (Sydney) 18 Apr. 27/2 The white quartz crystal used at the **bora ceremony**. **1904** *Ibid.* 4 Aug. 17/1 The blacks are very reticent concerning the 'bora' ceremonies, most of which were trials of endurance. **1923** T. HALL *Short Hist. Downs Blacks* 8 Knowing the object of the Bora ceremonies, and seeing the symbols on the trees at the Bora ring. **1928** W. ROBERTSON *Coo-ee Talks* 87 The *Bora*-ceremony required not only water but fire. **1896** *Bulletin* (Sydney) 18 Apr. 27/3 The small pathway from the large to the small **bora circles**. **1928** W. ROBERTSON *Coo-ee Talks* 4 To-day cotton grows over the sites of both these camps; the *Bora*-circles and the people are no more. **1885** MRS C. PRAED *Austral. Life* 24 The **Bora ground** is usually in a retired spot, on a slight elevation, level at the top. **1923** T. HALL *Short Hist. Downs Blacks* 5, I at once came to the conclusion that this must be the sacred place they called the Bora ground, and having heard old hands say that no white man or black gin had ever seen the Bora ground when the ceremonies were to take place, made me very inquisitive. **1931** 'L. KAYE' *Tybal Men* 185 Mac saw . . the markings of a native *bora* ground in the scrub. **1965** M. PATCHETT *Last Warrior* 102 When they reached the bora ground, the other tribesmen were dancing and singing. **1976** C.D. MILLS *Hobble Chains & Greenhide* 22 We . . pulled up in a thick patch of ant-beds close to a clear space about forty yards across. It looked like a 'bora' ground or something. **1923** T. HALL *Short Hist. Downs Blacks* 8 Knowing the object of the Bora ceremonies, and seeing the symbols on the trees at the **Bora ring**. **1926** *Smith's Weekly* (Sydney) 9 Oct. 18/2 Two well-defined bora rings have been discovered. **1935** DAVISON & NICHOLLS *Blue Coast Caravan* 192 The Bora-rings. There was a low mound of earth in the shape of a circle about a road's width across, with an opening at one side through which the young men had entered for the several days' period of their trial by ordeal. **1981** T. SHAPCOTT *Stump & Grape & Bobble-Nut* 7 Tribes preparing for this initiation rite at the sacred bora ring.

borak /ˈbɔræk/, *adv.* and *n.* Also **borack, borax.** [a. Wathawurung *burag.*]

A. *adv. Austral. pidgin. Obs.* Used to express negation: cf. BAAL.

1839 *Port Phillip Gaz.* 13 Nov. 3 Constable—Plenty white man I got here—borack me give 'em anything to eat. **1842** *Geelong Advertiser* 25 July 3/2 The prisoner at the bar was the chief of the tribe and I saw him strike the blow; I swear positively to his identity, and that I saw him do it. (This part of the evidence was interpreted to the prisoner, who cried out, 'no, no, borack'.) **1843** *Port Phillip Patriot* 11 Sept. 3/1 Policeman no good—too much wet—borak come all along from Melbourne. **1845** *Standard* (Melbourne) 2 Aug. 2/5 In his defence, the prisoner merely denied the charge by using the word 'borac'. **1847** T. MCCOMBIE *Austral. Sketches* 110 At the very name of work their countenance falls. 'Borack work!' they exclaim. **1856** W.W. DOBIE *Recoll. Visit Port-Phillip* 92 Borak, you quamby dead, me suck 'im blood and water and all pull away. **1903** J. FURPHY *Such is Life* 176 'Borak this you paddock, John?' 'My plully paddock, all li.'

B. *n.*

1. Nonsense, rubbish; GAMMON *n.* 2. Also *attrib.*

1845 T. MCCOMBIE *Adventures of Colonist* 273 *Borack*, gammon, nonsense. **1876** J.A. EDWARDS *Gilbert Gogger* 185 'O! Hume; that is all borack. . . ' Borack: humbug. Thus it is a common saying amongst bushmen, when any person is attempting to make them believe something improbable. 'O! don't poke borack at me!' **1885** *Australasian Printers' Keepsake* 124 Oh, we were bad—no borack, mind, boys. **1895** *Worker* (Sydney) 9 Mar. 4/1 And in this matter, one wants to know who has the biggest 'kink', the jury who whimper because they are not fed on an aldermanic scale, or the judge who sympathetically pats them on the back (with a lot of borak which they are too dense to see) and promises to improve the menu? **1899** *Bulletin* (Sydney) 30 Dec. 32/2 Witticisms fly—Borak, slang, and guyver—What a wag am I! **1950** *Southerly* iii. 142 The borak-pokers, with grouch Against all lordship. **1978** *Warrumbungle Bk. of Verse* 36 We had a Chinese cook on Quandong Vale, Slant-eyed and silent, with a poker face, Who took our borak with a guileless smile And let us pull his leg with Eastern grace.

2. In the phr. **to poke borak** (at a person), to deride. See also POKE *v.*

1873 J.C.F. JOHNSON *Christmas at Carringa* 4 Oh! he's a [*sic*] awful cove for to poke borack at a feller, that old O'Niel. **1885** *Australasian Printers' Keepsake* 75 Bob in my misery had 'poked borack' at me. **1890** *Truth* (Sydney) 26 Oct. 2/2 It is not possible to drive across any of our Western plains without thousands of bunnies bobbing up and poking 'borak' at the traveller. **1895** *Worker* (Sydney) 6 Apr. 4/1 Mike eyed his visitor dubiously, as if he were poking borak at him. **1901** *Truth* (Sydney) 12 Jan. 1/6 Bloodyard Drippling's preposterous 'pome', which virtually pokes borak at England's helplessness. **1902** *Ibid.* 16 Mar. 4/3 This is the sort of 'light and airy persiflage' in which Elijah, the Prophet of the Lord, 'poked borax' at the poor prophets of Baal. **1908** *Austral. Mag.* (Sydney) Nov. 1251/1 Borak . . is alleged to be the origin of the term 'barracker'. In the old days a barracker was a person who poked borak at the opponents of the side he favoured. **1919** C.H. THORP *Handful of Ausseys* 203 When the train pulls out, they leans out uv the carriage and 'pokes it' at the Jacks. 'Struth! they seem ter like jeerin' an' pokin' borax at those blokes. **1948** H. DRAKE-BROCKMAN *Sydney or Bush* 204 Why should Dick have to trap rabbits if he didn't want to? 'They cry, Mum,' he'd whispered to her when he was a kid and the others poked borak. **1960** E. NORTH *Nobody stops Me* 149, I sort of subscribed to his ravings about women, while everybody else about the place poked borak at him. **1968** S. GORE *Holy Smoke* 48 And when he slings in a rider that in future anyone who tried poking borak at their God'd be cut to pieces . . everyone starts barrackin' for the Lord.

Hence **borak** *v. trans.*

1885 *Bulletin* (Sydney) 25 Apr. 10/1 And what had this young gentleman been doing to be so deprived of sweetness and light and the songs of birds and the innocent delights of expectorating on street corners and gaily 'borracking' the passers-by?

border. [Spec. use of (also U.S.) *border* frontier: see OED *sb.* 3 c.]

1. The outer limit of land surveyed and available for tenure; land at or beyond that boundary. See also BOUNDARY *n.* and LOCATION 4. Also *attrib.*

1827 *Tasmanian* (Hobart) 21 Dec. 3 [Signature to a letter.] A Border Settler. **1840** *Colonist* (Sydney) 20 Oct. 3/2 They . . were supposed by the inhabitants to have been either mounted or Border troopers. **1844** D.G. BROCK *Jrnl.* 5 Sept. 10 We this day crossed the Eastern boundary line of S. Australia—the land we are now in may be called Borderland as it belongs neither to Adelaide or Sydney. **1846** *Portland Gaz.* 2 June 3/5 We beg to caution newcomers into the district against a practice which has lately become very prevalent, especially about 'the borders' and in the 'new country', of men going to them and offering to point out runs for a certain fee. **1847** *Port Phillip Herald* 9 Dec. 2/3 Many horses supposed to be stolen from the Melbourne side have come up to the borders lately. **1849** S. & J. SIDNEY *Emigrant's Jrnl.* 139 Montefiores . . is about 250 miles from Sydney, situate upon the borders of the colony, I might say upon the borders of location. **1859** F. SINNETT *Acct. 'Rush' Port Curtis* 71, I believe the border warfare about the Fitzroy, the Dawson, and the adjacent districts, to be as savage to this day as any war with the aborigines. **1872** H. PARKES *Speeches* 19 June (1876) 340 The Government said—not that they desired in any way to favour the remote border settlers. **1879** 'AUSTRALIAN' *Adventures Qld.* 2 In the year 184-, Maryborough was a border town in the northern portion of the colony of New South Wales—but now part of Queensland. By 'border' town is meant an outside settlement, composed of a few scattered wooden houses or huts.

2. The boundary between two Colonies; after Federation, between two States. Also *attrib.*

1847 *Port Phillip Herald* 29 July 2/3 The South Australian and Port Phillip boundary line offers no terrors to the 'border' thief. **1848** *Ibid.* 23 May 2/3 A crime described on the calendar as 'an attempt at murder', has been committed on the Port Phillip and South Australian 'Borders'. **1859** W. FAIRFAX *Handbk. to Australasia* 172 Albury, a border-town of New South Wales and Victoria. **1871** J. BAIRD *Emigrant's Guide to Australasia* 10 Disputes, and agitation for 'Riverine [*sic*] Independence' . . have now been ended by the arrangement respecting 'border custom', agreed to by Victoria and New South Wales. **1880** G. WALCH *Vic. in 1880* 123 Echuca was at one time more thriving than it is today. . . The border duties . . at present severely militate against its progress. **1891** M. ROBERTS *Land-Travel & Sea-Faring* 42, I settled on Albury in New South Wales as . . the Border City must after all be a very important place. **1896** *Bulletin* (Sydney) 18 Apr. 13/4 When Federation arrives, and there are no border tariffs . . Port Augusta should start on a career that will ultimately make it almost . . the greatest seaport in Australia. **1901** *Ibid.* 27 Apr. 15/1 Two New England (N.S.W.) border-farmers, weary of the drought . . hired waggons. **1906** *Ibid.* 11 Oct. 17/1 A gatekeeper on the tick fence (Queensland border) is a State official. **1926** *Ibid.* 15 Apr. 24/1 One of the greatest farces out back is the rabbit-proof fence on the N.S.W.-Queensland border. **1940** *Ibid.* 4 Dec. 17/3 'Waddy wood' . . grows about 12 miles north of Birdsville, in Western Queensland, near the S.A. border. **1945** F. CORK *Tales from Cattle Country* 25 At the border the mob is met by the police and stock inspector who rides through the herd. **1960** *Bulletin* (Sydney) 5 Oct. 16/3 They were waiting their turn at the border-gate. **1969** E.C. ROLLS *They all ran Wild* 49 Australian rivers change names disconcertingly, sometimes on a State border, sometimes mid-State. **1972** ANDERSON & BLAKE *J.S. Nielson* 13 John Neilson, who had planned in August 1879 to become a Victorian selector, can scarcely be accused of being a moonlighter or border-flitter. However, more than one South Australian had 'done a moonlight flit' across the border and left debts. **1976** *Austral.* (Sydney) 29 Mar. 7/1 Another fruit fly . . infests large parts of the east coast from North Queensland to the Victorian border.

3. Special Comb. **border fence,** a vermin-proof fence at the outer limit of a settled district or on a Colonial (later State) boundary; **police** *obs.*, a police force established to maintain law and order at or beyond the border (sense 1).

1895 *Bulletin* (Sydney) 5 Jan. 23/4 No grass this side the **Border-fence**! and all the mulga's dead. **1912** *Ibid.* 12 Dec. 48/2 Anyone who does not know the Border Fence has no conception of the magnitude of the work. **1927** *Ibid.* 26 May 24/2, I can bear witness to the uselessness of Queensland's expensive vermin-proof border fence. **1944** M.J. O'REILLY *Bowyangs & Boomerangs* 137 Dingoes, one of the reasons for the border fence, are fairly numerous on the South Australian side. **1954** T. RONAN *Vision Splendid* 148 It's a long hard lead to the Border Fence, But the money rolls in as the miles roll by. **1980** S. THORNE *I've met some Bloody Wags* 9 At the ripe old age of nineteen I decided that I was sick of Australia, and would go back to Queensland—back to where the scrubs are deep and dense, to God's own land where the pikers roam, across the border fence. **1839** *Sydney Standard* 11 Mar. 4/2, I object to settlers being obliged to supply the **Border police** with tea and sugar. **1840** *Port Phillip Gaz.* 25 Jan. 4 The Brickmakers . . are always close upon the town, and cannot therefore be said to live beyond the bounds of location, a position which can alone demand the protection of a Border Police. **1843** R.D. MURRAY *Summer at Port Phillip* 106 A third force, termed the Border Police, as its name implies, affords protection to the settlers on the furthest verges of location. **1847** *Port Phillip Herald* 23 Nov. 2/7 Yesterday, Dr Thomas, assisted by Dr Campbell, amputated the leg of the black sergeant, of the Border Police, at the thigh. **1850** *V & P* (N.S.W. L.A.) II. 396 In order to preserve the continuity of the history of the Police, which has been observed in the Reports of the Committees of 1835 and 1839, it may be proper to record here that the Border Police established in the latter year, for the protection of the then Squatting districts, and which was originally composed of military convicts, was wholly disbanded in 1846, upon the expiry of the local enactment 2 Vict., No. 27, in pursuance of which it had been raised.

bore, *n.*

1. An artesian well. See also *government bore* GOVERNMENT B. 4. Also *attrib.*

1897 *Western Champion* (Barcaldine) 31 Aug. 3/3 It used to be a dry country out there in years gone by, but bores have changed all of it to a white man's land, carrying many sheep. **1899** *Progress* (Brisbane) 26 Aug. 5/2 Longreach is a bore town without enjoying the enormous privilege of being able to use the bore water without stint. **1901** *Brisbane Courier* 4 July 7/5 There was a natural fall in the country, so that one bore could be made to serve four or five farms. **1912** *Bulletin* (Sydney) 25 Jan. 14/2 When Trivett counted up the Ma State's bores . . he found 487 left, after eliminating all that walked on legs—211 of them public bores and 276 private. **1923** F.A.C. BISHOP *Rep. on Inspection Pastoral Holdings Barkly Tablelands* 5 The stock route comes out at this bore and continues on to the Crow's Nest bore, 16 miles on. **1934** T. WOOD *Cobbers* 198 Bores have been sunk, and water gushes to the surface. **1950** G.M. FARWELL *Land of Mirage* 30 It is the possession of three good bores that gives this property its first-rate grazing for sheep and cattle. **1960** *N.T. News* (Darwin) 5 Jan. 3/6 The new bore at the 10-mile has gone salty and is unfit for human consumption. **1965** M. PATCHETT *Last Warrior* 172 We'll ride out to the bore paddock then come back for you after breakfast. **1977** T. RONAN *Mighty Men on Horseback* 32 Shifting cattle onto the back bores. **1986** *Canberra Times* 19 Feb. 14/3 Police were trying . . to determine the events that preceded the death of a group of six people . . on a lonely bore road on a Northern Territory pastoral station.

2. Special Comb. **bore drain,** a channel which carries water from a bore; **head,** the point at which the underground water surfaces; **stream,** *bore drain*; **water,** water from a bore.

1914 *Bulletin* (Sydney) 18 June 16/4 The sheep were still alive, and even had sufficient strength to make a frenzied dash for the **boredrain.** **1917** A.L. BREWER *'Gators' Euchre* 29 He tackled a bore-drain and followed it through the Gidgee for hours. **1942** H.H. PECK *Mem. of Stockman* 75 More artesian bores than on any other run in Australia, and some of them of great depth, with bore drains running out, and watering otherwise waterless country. **1959** H.G. LAMOND *Sheep Station* 62 It was on Mulga Creek, on the bore drain which ran down the gully of that name. **1968** R. MAGOFFIN *We Bushies* 69 So we'll skim it Or we'll swim it Where the boredrain overflows. **1980** *Sydney Morning Herald* 14 Oct. 3/7 Gordon Murray's dam water is almost dry and he'll now have to depend entirely on a metre-wide bore drain coming from another property. **1932** M.R. WHITE *No Roads go By* 157, I called loudly for a tub, mustard, and hot water from the **bore-head.** **1947** M. RAYMOND *Smiley gets Gun* 179 Around the borehead the crowd continued to grow. **1902** *Bulletin* (Sydney) 19 June 16/2 Dozens of **bore-streams** in W.Q. well adapted for irrigation. **1922** V. PALMER *Boss of Killara* 117 If he had only a bore-stream running through these undulating ridges, they would carry another thousand head of cattle. **1935** R.B. PLOWMAN *Boundary Rider* 216 The coach . . got bogged in a bore-stream which crossed the track. **1899** *Bulletin* (Sydney) 9 Sept. 17/1 *Re* quality of **bore-water**. . . The Richmond . . Govt. bore gives splendid water. **1917** A.L. BREWER *'Gators' Euchre* 45 The Nebine in this part was now a constantly running stream, rising principally from a bore lately put down. . . There are many similar places in West Queensland to-day, where the traveller drinks bore-water at the river. **1937** J.M. HARCOURT *It never Fails* 124 He felt that to bathe even in the sticky, evil-smelling bore-water that ran from the bathroom taps . . was a luxury. **1942** F. CLUNE *Last of Austral. Explorers* 98 His gloomy narrative flowed on like his bore-water. **1960** *N.T. News* (Darwin) 5 Jan. 3/3 Bore water there is salty and fit only for stock. **1979** *Ecos* xx. 25/3 The need to reserve . . large volumes of water, to carry us over periods of low flow, costs no considerable amounts of capital to build the required reservoirs. The use of bore water is one way around this problem.

bore, *v.* [Fig. use of *bore* to push or thrust (esp. in sporting context).] *trans.* In the phr. **to bore it up** (or **into**) (someone), to attack with vigour, 'to let (someone) have it'.

1947 *Coast to Coast 1946* 76 He bored into Wally and chopped his face about—cut his eyes and ears and smashed his mouth. **1951** E. LAMBERT *Twenty Thousand Thieves* 178 A provost I got into a blue with in Tel Aviv was barkin' the orders. Christ! Did that bastard bore it up me? **1959** 'D. FORREST' *Last Blue Sea* 84 'Into it!' he yelled at Three Platoon. 'Bore it into them!' **1972** N. MILES *Opal Fever* 4 Hey, that's good. O.K., bore it up 'er, Chilla. **1972** K. CLIFT *Saga of Sig* 58 Hitler, presumably after a bit of carpet chewing, decided to 'bore it up us' and sent his crack troops. **1984** *West Austral.* (Perth) 21 Feb. 79/1, I handed out a lot of rockets as a captain but I also handed out a lot more praise than most captains. If players did badly I would bore it right up them and if they did well I would heap praise on them.

boree, borer, varr. BORA.

boree /'bɔri, bɔ'ri/, *n.* [a. Wiradhuri and Kamilaroi *buri.*]

1. a. Any of several *Acacia* species (fam. Mimosaceae), esp. *A. tephrina*, the phyllodes of which are covered with short white hairs. **b.** *N.S.W. spec.* *A. pendula* (see MYALL *n.*[2]). Also *attrib.*

1845 D. MACKENZIE *Emigrant's Guide* 212 In the heart

of the main root of a small sapling, called the *Myall* or *Boree*. **1875** *Austral. Town & Country Jrnl.* (Sydney) 13 Feb. 263/4 Myall and boree belts of timber, never known to grow upon 'poor' or 'sour' land . . betokened that Elysium of the Squatter, 'sound fattening country'. **1878** 'IRONBARK' *Southerly Busters* 144 Where the tangled 'boree' blossoms, Where the 'gidya' thickets wave, And the tall yapunyah's shadow Rests upon the stockman's grave. **1886** R. HENTY *Australiana* 167 Half of this water was mud. Our plan of cleansing it was to throw in salts and Boree ashes. **1898** D.W. CARNEGIE *Spinifex & Sand* 362 Funereal is the aspect of the dead scrub and dark tops of the 'boree' (a kind of mulga). **1915** *Bull. N.T.* xiv. 10 Boree (camel bush or bullock bush). **1921** 'J. O'BRIEN' *Around Boree Log* 11 Yet spend another night with me around the boree log. **1955** H.G. LAMOND *Towser* 82 Stately borees dotted the open downs. **1977** G.W. LILLEY *Lengthening Shadows* 171 Boree . . is confined to the western districts of Queensland north of Tambo. Myall (acacia pendula) is also called 'boree' in western N.S. Wales, but although the trees are closely related botanically acacia canae is the genuine boree. **1979** J. WILLIAMS *White River* 80 Stunted boree spreads its stiff green fans.

2. Comb. **boree scrub**.

1864 J.G. MACDONALD *Jrnl. Exped. Port Denison to Gulf of Carpentaria* (1865) 17 Next through belts of boree scrub, one and a half mile. **1905** *Emu* V. 15 More or less covered with boree scrub. **1959** M. RAYMOND *Smiley roams Road* 48 Out west they had swum only in the muddy pools of the drought-stricken Warrego River and the even muddier waterholes in the boree scrub. **1976** L.R.M. HUNTER *Woodline* 69 A definitely Australian vista of boree scrub.

boring, *vbl. n.* used *attrib.*

1. Of or relating to an artesian well, or the drilling thereof.

1901 *Bulletin* (Sydney) 28 Dec. 14/1 *Re* reported recent discovery of fish in 'boring'-water. **1912** *Emu* XII. 30 We . . moved . . to a Government boring camp near the little-known Sunset country. **1935** R.B. PLOWMAN *Boundary Rider* 200 His next destination was the camp of some boring engineers near Clayton Dam. **1948** G. FARWELL *Down Argent Street* 105 His mate, a boring contractor, had been sixty feet below the paddock's surface, shovelling sand and earth to release the jammed bore casing, when the walls caved in. **1954** T. RONAN *Vision Splendid* 112 He saw two of the lubras who had sought protection, coming back from the boring camp.

2. Special Comb. **boring plant,** equipment used to sink a bore.

1911 'S. RUDD' *Bk. of Dan* 1 Dan turned up one morning in possession of a boring plant and asked for a job. **1956** B.J. RAYMENT *My Towri* 60 We had a paddock nine miles long with water in only one end, and I had no boring plant. **1973** *Dusts of Time: Lake Cargelligo & District* 62 Later on a boring plant entered the district and many bores were sunk.

boronia /bəˈroʊniə/. [The plant genus *Boronia* was named by English botanist J.E. Smith in honour of his former assistant, the Milanese botanist Francesco *Borone* (1769–1794).] Any shrub of the genus *Boronia* (fam. Rutaceae), the flowers of some species being highly aromatic.

[**1798** J.E. SMITH *Tracts Nat. Hist.* 288 The country of New Holland, so rich in botanical novelties, has made us acquainted with several new genera of M. de Jussieu's natural order of *Rutaceae*. . . No genus among the whole tribe is more worthy of notice than that to which I have given the name of *Boronia*. **1814** R. BROWN *Gen. Remarks Bot. Terra Australis* 13 *Boronia* is both the most extensive and the most widely diffused, existing within the tropic, and extending to the South end of Van Diemen's Island.] **1848** *Maitland Mercury* 6 Dec. 4/3 Boronia, the latter plant of such exceeding beauty that the aborigines, unpoetical as they are supposed to be in their composition, name their gins or women after it, in the same manner as we (their more cultivated brethren) do our wives and daughters from the rose and other favourite plants. **1856** *Jrnl. Australasia* I. 38 Variable boronia . . is, perhaps, one of the most handsome among our indigenous herbaceous flora. **1910** L. ESSON *Woman Tamer* (1976) 78 What's up? Blime, you've cleaned the knives. Cake? 'Struth, we are hotties. Boronia? Are you expecting the gawd Mayor for tea? **1914** T.C. WOLLASTON *Spirit of Child* 27 While there are Acacias in many corners of the earth, the shy Boronia is exclusively our own. **1939** J. CAMPBELL *Babe is Wise* 364 Sprays of the marvellously sweet, delicate brown bells yellow lined which she had come to know were 'boronia'. **1963** O. RUHEN *Flockmaster* 7 The heavy, heady scent of boronia from the golden-flowered bushes on the bank. **1985** *New Idea* (Melbourne) 7 Sept. 141 If you enjoy the perfume of boronias, most varieties are small growing but seem to prefer a moist soil and need to be trimmed when flowering is finished.

bosca, boscar, varr. BOSKER.

bosey, var. BOSIE.

boshter /ˈbɒʃtə/, *n.* and *a. Obs.* [Of unknown origin: see BONZER.] BONZER.

A. *n.*

1903 *Sporting News* (Launceston) 2 June 1/4 George, although within 10 yards of the last-named, escaped a penalty. With what result. This, a 'boshter' in the mile and a half at a great disadvantage, and an absolute 'nong' in this, under more favorable circumstances. **1904** *Advocate* (Burnie) 3 Sept. 4/3 Arthur Hanigan's leap was a boshter. **1904** *Bulletin* (Sydney) 8 Dec. 16/1 'She's a little boshter!' he said vehemently. **1906** *Ibid.* 22 Nov. 17/2 What is known here [*sc.* Victoria] as boshter is called bosker in Sydney. We never hear of a bosker here. **1906** *Ibid.* 20 Dec. 15/3 Boshter is as common as bosker—perhaps even more so—in Sydney. **1906** *Steele Rudd's Mag.* (Brisbane) Mar. 110 That car is a boshter, right enough. **1908** *Bulletin* (Sydney) 19 Mar. 14/2 This south Groperland climate is a boshter. **1910** B. DUBOIS *High Light* 36 A thunderstorm came on. It was a boshter! **1911** E. DYSON *Tommy Hawker* 75 He remembered that the punch was a boshter. **1911** ST. C. GRONDONA *Collar & Cuffs* 9, I got quite near enough to an old boar to kick him. . . He was a 'boshter', and had tusks about three inches long. **1916** *All abaht It* (London) Nov. 13 He's proved himself a boshter.

B. *adj.*

1908 *Bulletin* (Sydney) 10 Dec. 17/1 It was Sam's eye-drop taw! . . 'Me only boshter taw!' he roared. **1910** L. ESSON *Three Short Plays* (1911) 7 Ye're boshter with ther tarts, ain't yer. **1911** W.H. ELSUM *Aust.* 42 We're th' boshter comin' nation o' th' earth. **1913** C.J. DENNIS *Backblock Ballads* 96 'Er eyes! Soft in the moon; such boshter eyes! **1915** —— *Songs of Sentimental Bloke* 29 The champeen backs an' fills, becos 'E doesn't feel the Boshter Bloke 'e was. **1919** C.H. THORP *Handful of Ausseys* 131 P'r'aps the owner uv the station 'll drive over with some boshter girls who been stayin' at the homestead. **1929** W.J. RESIDE *Golden Days* 377, I didn't mind our luck—'Twas bad, but then, I'd struck A boshter mate.

bosie /ˈboʊzi/. *Cricket.* Also **bosey.** [f. the name of the English cricketer, B.J.T. *Bos(anquet* (1877–1936) + -Y.] A googly, a ball which breaks in the direction opposite from that suggested by the action of its delivery. Also *attrib.*

[N.Z. **1909** *N.Z. Truth* (Wellington) 23 Oct. 3/2 Geo. Schmoll fell a victim to a 'bosie' delivery from Senior, the ball coming back from the opposite way in which the hand delivery indicated.] **1912** *Australasian* (Melbourne) 2 Mar. 481/2 Then he lifted the 'Bosie' bowler high to the on, the ball bouncing just inside the fence. **1920** P.F. WARNER *Cricket Reminisc.* 12 Mr Bosanquet, as all the world knows, was the inventor of the googlie, and in Australia this particular type of ball is invariably called 'the Bosie ball', in honour of its author. **1930** C.V. GRIMMETT *Getting Wickets* 22 It was at this time that I learned to bowl the 'bosie' or 'googly'—an off-break with a leg-break action. **1932** H.V. HORDEN *Googlies* 48 It was during this season of 1905–6 that I worked out the method of bowling the googly or 'Bosie', after its inventor, Bosanquet. **1954** A.G. MOYES *Austral. Batsmen* 190 One thing the 'bosey' did—it introduced a new touch of science into bowling, and nothing more beautiful has been seen on Australian cricket fields.

bosker /ˈbɒskə/, *n., a.,* and *adv. Obs.* Also **bosca, boscar.** [Of unknown origin: see BONZER.] BONZER.

A. *n.*

1904 *Truth* (Sydney) 3 Apr. 6/1 The show is described as a 'bosker', the horses, cows, and pigs are in great condition. **1907** *Bulletin* (Sydney) 20 June 14/1 The 'skirt' somehow got her foot caught in the pocket of the bloke in front, and came down a 'bosker'. **1908** *Austral. Mag.* (Sydney) Nov. 1249/1 You will hear a young Australian, perhaps, all in the one conversation, say that a certain girl is a bosker, a football hero is a bosker, a murderer is a bosker, a storm is a bosker, and a calm placid evening is a bosker. **1950** F.J. HARDY *Power without Glory* 221 'Ain't he a bosker?' said the leader of the deputation. **1968** F.J. THWAITES *Sky Full of Thunder* 23 After a lot of coaxing, we got Gerald off to the Yass Picnic Races; came back a different person—a girl, of course! Real little bosker. **1973** H. LEWIS *Crow on Barbed Wire Fence* 49 'If they'd been some beer in the town,' he muttered, 'it would have been a bosker.'

B. *adj.*

1905 *Steele Rudd's Mag.* (Brisbane) Oct. 835 Oh, she's a real bosker gal is Matildee. **1908** *Bulletin* (Sydney) 9 July 15/2 *Re* wombat as a cursed nuisance to ground-sluicers. . . He is a bosker curse, and I live among dozens of old sluicers who can verify my statement. **1910** L. ESSON *Three Short Plays* (1911) 17 W'ere did yer pinch ther lovely cray? Ain't 'e bosker? **1913** C.J. DENNIS *Backblock Ballads* 97 An' when she looked at me I sorter felt that bosker feelin' that comes o'er a bloke, And makes 'im melt. **1918** R.H. KNYVETT *Over there with Australs.* p. v, There is a thrill in war, as all must own, The tramplin' onward rush, The shriek o' shrapnel and the followin' hush, The bosker crunch o' bayonet on bone. **1920** H.J. RUMSEY *Pommies* 66 My word, mum, this is a bosca place. I should like you to see it. **1922** 'TE WHARE' *Bush Cinema* 49 They spoilt a bosker funeral. **1934** J.C. LEE *Boshstralians* 141 Wasn't that bosker? Staunton caught him a beauty on the jaw. **1942** *Plane Speaking from R.A.A.F. Amberley* 29 Oct. 7 Jerry and I find ourselves sitting in a very bosker-looking lounge in one of the Nicer Suburbs. **1958** T. QUILTY *Drover's Cook* 47 Now, I'm not an imposter, you pile on the oscar, the win will be bosker. **1968** F.J. THWAITES *Sky Full of Thunder* 86 'Fine clubhouse.' 'Bosker—cost a mint.' **1972** F.R. POWER *My Fight* p. v, The bosker boy from Bamganie, Sir Henry Bolte, has turned over the bullock waggon of State to one who might not hold so tight or authoritarian a rein.

C. *adv.*

1923 J. MOSES *Beyond City Gates* 32 It's a bosker big river, the Clarence. **1943** G. MCIVER *Bunyip & Other Verses* 31 But if I liked to buy some stores, My half was there for sure—And boscar rich whenever struck, In weighty nuggets pure. **1953** D. STIVENS *Gambling Ghost* 43 Things went along bosker for a couple of years.

boskerina. *Obs.* Var. of BONZARINA.

1905 *Steele Rudd's Mag.* (Brisbane) July 701 Joe . . murmured in a tone of mingled admiration and endearment—'You're a—boskerina.'

boss cocky. [See COCKY *n.*[2]]

1. A small farmer who has achieved a degree of prosperity (esp. one able to employ labour to supplement his own).

1879 'DOCTOR DORIC' *Unsophisticated Rhymes* 3 The iron heel you know; 'Tis Boss-Cokie Law Fit for an Indian squaw. **1883** *Bulletin* (Sydney) 1 Dec. 5 (*caption*) The Boss Cockie Deputation (To The Land Minister):- 'Now you mustn't pass this Land Bill.' **1897** *Tocsin* (Melbourne) 11 Nov. 6/3 'Boss cockies', or prosperous farmers, with unencumbered freeholds, grab the holdings of the small fry, and deprive them of a living. **1906** *Bulletin* (Sydney) 14 June 14/3 *Re* women farm-hands . . nearly all the present boss cockies around Maroona (Vic.) built their farms with the labor of their daughters. **1911** E. DYSON *Tommy Hawker* 189 Wheelan was something between a boss-cockie and a small squatter, and was doing well. **1914** *Truth* (Sydney) 22 Mar. 3/6, I was working for a boss cockie, getting £1 a week and keep. **1958** G. CASEY *Snowball* 12 The chief stock-and-station agent, and the head officials of the local Road Board were often linked up with some of the boss-cockies from round about to form a clique.

2. One who assumes or who is accorded, often grudgingly, authority or superior status.

1902 *Truth* (Sydney) 19 Oct. 4/8 He might be the grand high boss cocky in Australia's political world, but he was no friend of Queensland's. **1918** *Kia Ora Coo-ee* Nov. 18/1 I'll easy be able to hold down a job as boss cocky of a restaurant. **1938** H. HODGE *Death in Morning* 38 Who paid you to do it? Who's the boss cocky? **1945** W. NOONAN *Surprising Battalion* 111 He was the big military man of the district, and was 'boss cocky' of our particular show. **1950** A. GROOM *I saw Strange Land* 50 Abel is a sort of boss cocky, leader of the native evangelists, bell-ringer in chief, organizer and community foreman. **1965** R.H. CONQUEST *Horses in Kitchen* 195 It is worth remembering that even in the early days of radio in Australia, the A.B.C. was boss cocky. **1979** D. MAITLAND *Breaking Out* 327 'Who're we going to negotiate with?'. . . 'The Governor, I guess . . whoever's the boss cocky in New South Wales.' **1981** D. STUART *I think I'll Live* 168 Yes, mate, an' some clever bastard said he knew the Boss Cocky of that far off land, eh?

boss over (or **of**) **the board**: see BOARD 3.

bot, *n.* [Fig. use of *bot* parasitic worm or maggot, as in 'Had a situation . . near Cobargo (N.S.W.) what time the bot-fly was botting there with much vigor.' (1907 *Bulletin* (Sydney) 10 Jan. 14/2).]

1. *Obs.* A scheme for illicit gain, a 'lurk'.

1888 'R. BOLDREWOOD' *Robbery under Arms* (1937) 42 'You think you can't be tracked,' says I, 'but you must bear in mind you haven't got to do with the old-fashioned mounted police as was potterin' about when this 'bot' was first hit on.'

2. A cadger.

1916 *All abaht It* (London) Nov. 24 Lit in time for the 'Bot's fatigue'. **1943** *Bulletin* (Sydney) 6 Oct. 12/3 The young John Hop sent to take charge of the country station showed too much zeal. Deadbeats and pub bots he made a dead-set at. **1963** B. BEAVER *Hot Summer* 51 As they passed the pub the usual babble, . . the tinny wheeze of a concertina could be heard. . . Some old bot playing for beers, thought Danny. **1964** P. ADAM SMITH *Hear Train Blow* 118 None of those who came to our house were 'bots'. While Mum was boiling the water for their billy they would go over to the wood-heap, unasked, and cut a pile of wood, or stack what Dad had cut. **1965** J. O'GRADY *Aussie Eng.* 24 'Bots' are allergic to work, and impervious to insult, and although they have no visible means of support, are nearly always drunk. **1982** J. MORRISON *North Wind* 54 Your old mates have had a win in Tatts. . . They're a bit scared of all the commotion it's stirred up. The track down from the township is worn bare, and all the bots and bites in Victoria are on to them.

bot, *v.* Also **bott.** [f. prec.]

a. *trans.* To cadge.

1921 F. GROSE *Rough Y.M. Bloke* 73 However, I had firmly made up my mind that the boys were not going to be disappointed, and I eventually 'botted' (the diggers' word for begged, borrowed or stolen) a lorry. **1940** *Sentry Go* (Keswick) Dec. 20/1 Mind if I bott a cigarette? **1966** *Overland* xxxv. 39 I'll bot a cuppa tea meself if you don't mind. **1974** *Austral. Folksongs* (Folk Lore Council Aust.) 30 He'd botted handouts by the score. **1986** *Nat. Times* (Sydney) 3 Jan. 11/1 Johnson botted a smoke and tried to let the conversation die.

b. *intr.* Usu. with **on**: to borrow from, to impose upon.

1934 *Bulletin* (Sydney) 7 Nov. 46/2 Settle up when I sell me next picture. . . Never did like botting on a bloke. **1941** S.J. BAKER *Pop. Dict. Austral. Slang* 12 *Bot, to,* to borrow money, to 'sponge'. **1965** K. TENNANT *Summer's Tales* 82 They'll bot on property owners or missions. That's where they're going.

Botany. *Obs.* Abbrev. of BOTANY BAY. Also *attrib.*

1787 R. CLARK Jrnl. 27 Dec. 106, I wish to God that we had got to Botany that I might be able to get some greens. **1822** *Giovanni in Botany* 9 Now he's courting, So transporting, Nothing his mind can fix,—Not even *Bot-a-ny*! **1827** P. CUNNINGHAM *Two Yrs. in N.S.W.* I. 15 If you chance to . . burst forth perhaps in praise of the beauties of *Botany* . . he measures you over and over with a most suspicious eye.

Botany Bay. [The name given by James Cook to a bay south of Sydney, the site of his first landing in Australia.]

1. *Obs.* A name used variously to refer to Port Jackson, to New South Wales, and to other Australian Colonies, individually and collectively. Also *attrib.*

1787 J. WHITE *Jrnl. of Voyage N.S.W.* (1790) 1, I this day left London, charged with dispatches . . relative to the embarkation of that part of the marines and convicts intended for Botany Bay. **1789** 'OFFICER' *Authentic & Interesting Narr. Exped. Botany Bay* 7 Even some folks apparently well settled in their circumstances . . became candidates for their passage to Botany Bay. **1805** J. TURNBULL *Voyage round World* III. 182 The circumstances under which the colony was settled . . has had a very visible effect upon the general manners, or what may be called the national character, of Botany Bay. **1820** C. JEFFREYS *Van Dieman's Land* 143 The term Botany Bay, has a very extensive signification, including, in the general acceptance of the word, all our Australian territories. **1825** M. HINDMARSH *Lett.* (1945) 23 You may tell R. Dunn he may think his old master a gentleman if he chooses. But he is only a Botany Bay one. **1835** *Colonist* (Sydney) 16 July 225/4 All we want is permission *to oil the wheels* of our own little Botany Bay state-carriage ourselves. **1838** 'A.L.F.' *Hist. S. Terry* 12 The treatment of convicts generally, and the manner in which they are employed in Botany Bay (the Australian Penal Colonies). **1839** *Sydney Herald* 7 Jan. 2/2 The American Government, too, unlike our Botany Bay Government, will not allow the whites to be butchered by the blacks with impunity. **1845** D. MACKENZIE *Emigrant's Guide* 31 The town of Melbourne is represented by one member, and the Port Phillip district generally by five members, in our Botany Bay Parliament. **1846** *Cumberland Times* (Parramatta) 3 Jan. 4/4 It is now five and thirty years, since I landed in Botany Bay, as it was then called, but some of the swells, having got rich, and finding when they got home, and talked of Botany Bay, people looked queer, and buttoned up their breeches pockets, managed to get it called New South Wales, and then getting hold of some chap, who made up fine words out of the old languages christened it, over a bottle, Australia. **1852** S. SIDNEY *Three Colonies* 20 Colloquially, until very recently, Botany Bay, the first landing-place of Captain Cook, was vulgarly and popularly the designation given to Australia. **1870** J. BONWICK *Curious Facts* 115 The 'Botany Bay' residents could not, generally speaking, have received much scholastic advantage. **1880** *Bulletin* (Sydney) 28 Feb. 4/4 To consider himself 'the coming man'—the Berry of Botany Bay—is a monstrous day-mare or delusion. **1896** *Ibid.* 18 Jan. 9/3 Many things are upside-down in Australia. In England, Howard is the name of a philanthropist; in Botany Bay he is the hangman.

2. *transf.* Penal servitude; a penal colony. Also *attrib.*

1789 *Times* (London) 20 Nov. 3/3 Men of profligate principles empowered with empanelling of juries, may give away the lives of every honest Englishman, and send people to the New-drop, or Botany Bay, who ought to go to some better place. **1794** G. THOMPSON *Slavery & Famine* ii. 9 If guilty, he is taken to a cart wheel to receive a Botany Bay dozen, which is twenty-five lashes. **1796** D. COLLINS *Acct. Eng. Colony N.S.W.* (1798) I. 502 The word 'Botany Bay' became a term of reproach that was indiscriminately cast on every one who resided in New South Wales. **1828** *Austral. Q. Jrnl. Theol., Lit. & Sci.* Jan. p. iv, It [*sc.* the colony of N.S.W.] is still considered a mere Botany Bay, an immense hulk as it were, or common sewer, into which the refuse of the Jails in England periodically drains. **1832** *Emigrant's Guide N.S.W.* 7 She was an obscure penal settlement . . scarcely thought of by the mother country but as *Botany Bay*—the emporium of felons. **1837** J. MUDIE *Felonry of N.S.W.* 173 He was . . sent to Wellington Valley, a sort of Botany Bay elysium for the reception of *gentlemen* convicts. **1848** *Atlas* (Sydney) IV. 377/1 *Botany Bay* must no longer be the synonyme for a receptacle for banished vice. **1852** J. WEST *Hist. of Tas.* I. 29 Thus, Van Diemen's Land was colonised; first as a place of exile for the more felonious of felons—the Botany Bay of Botany Bay. **1854** W. SHAW *Land of Promise* 29 Men and women with broken noses and black eyes, which are the 'Botany Bay coat of arms'. **1890** J.E. RITCHIE *Austral. Ramble* 135 To talk of the taint of Botany Bay is the silliest of bunkum in the world. There is no trace of it now. Young Australia knows nothing of transportation. **1903** *Truth* (Sydney) 5 Apr. 5/3 Botany Bay law, while hampering an outraged husband 'under the ban', aided and abetted the adulterous wife. The old lag law is still law. **1955** H. ANDERSON *Colonial Ballads* 18 To the ballad-monger, Australia was Botany Bay, a place of blood, sweat and tears.

3. Special Comb. **Botany Bay aristocracy,** see quots.; **greens,** see quot. 1834.

1832 *Colonial Times* (Hobart) 9 May, **Botany Bay Aristocracy**; or, Shop-boys and Groggy Dunderheads converted into Justices and Esquires, performing Works of Antiquity. **1838** 'A.L.F.' *Hist. S. Terry* 16 Some . . of the Botany Bay aristocracy possess fifty, seventy, one hundred, and three hundred convicts (gratuitously given away white slaves). **1872** BUNSTER & THATCHER *It runs in Blood* 61 When we find 'The Block' thronged with this Botany Bay aristocracy, whose insufferable pretensions would be unbearable in the bluest blood to be found in 'Debrett', one cannot help reminding these gaudy tulips that they spring from very dirty roots. **1900** *Bulletin* (Sydney) 29 Dec. 15/2 Darlinghurst . . is the pet prison of Old Lagdom, which some of the 'Botany Bay Aristocracy', or their convict pregenitors [*sic*], helped to build. **1802** M. FLINDERS *Voyage Terra Australis* (1814) I. 114 The soil . . was overspread with shrubs, mostly of one kind, a whitish velvety plant—(*artriplex* [*sic*] *reniformis* of Brown), nearly similar to what is called at Port Jackson, **Botany-Bay greens.** **1827** *Tasmanian Almanack* 72 In the years 1806 and 1807 . . the people were without a morsel of bread, flour, or biscuit! During this period, they lived for the most part on kangaroo and Botany Bay greens. **1834** *Hobart Town Almanack* 134 The Barilla shrubs (*Atriplex Halimus, Rhagodia Billardieri*, and *Salicornia arbuscula*) . . with some others, and under the promiscuous name of Botany Bay greens, were boiled and eaten along with some species of sea-weed, by the earliest settlers, when in a state of starvation. **1873** J. BONWICK *Tasmanian Lily* 123 'What are the Botany Bay greens?' 'These were eaten in a terrible famine at Port Jackson in the days of the first settlement. We have the same plant here [*sc.* Tas.] It belongs to the goosefoot family.'

bott, var. BOT *v.*

bottle, *n.*[1] *Obs.* [Abbrev. of *bottle jaw.*]

1. A fluke infestation of sheep characterized by a swelling under the throat: see quot. 1871. Also *attrib.*

1827 *Monitor* (Sydney) 3 Sept. 631 During a period of extreme drought . . all the finest sheep were dying of the bottle, and other diseases, for want of grass and water. **1871** *Austral. Town & Country Jrnl.* (Sydney) 27 May 647/4 This remedy, among his own lambs, caused the 'bottle' to disappear. The 'bottle'—a swelling under the throat from the point of the jaw to the throat—is a sure sign of worms in lambs. **1888** *Bungendore Mirror* 3 Mar. 2 We hear that the disease known as 'bottle' has broken out amongst them [*sc.* the sheep] and as a remedial measure Mr Rutledge is sending them to pastures new.

2. Special Comb. **bottle plant** (or **weed**) *obs.*, the plant *Drosera peltata* (fam. Droseraceae), the consumption of which was mistakenly believed to cause the disease in sheep.

1876 *Jrnl. & Proc. R. Soc. N.S.W.* (1878) 24 With reference to the 'bottle' disease—a selector about two years ago pointed out to me a small plant which he called the bottle weed, and he assured me that sheep contracted the disease by eating it. The plant grows to a height of from four to six inches, bearing a small pink flower. . . It is botanically known as *Drosera peltata.* **1880** J. BONWICK *Resources Qld.* 47 The Bottle plant, three inches high, having a small pink flower, is carnivorous, and the cause of the Bottle disease in sheep; it is a Drosera, delighting in swamps of granite regions.

Hence **bottled, bottley** *adjs.*

1871 *Austral. Town & Country Jrnl.* (Sydney) 21 Jan. 74/4 Flukey ewes especially get 'bottled' in the neck, and die off rapidly at six years of age. **1908** *Bulletin* (Sydney) 4 June 14/3 Death . . claims many an old ewe an hour or so before it is due, when the cocky has decided it is not possible to save her. She may be 'bottley'.

bottle, *n.*[2] [Perh. by analogy with the phr. *no bottle* no good.] In the phr. **the** (or **a**) **full bottle,** (an) expert.

1968 S. GORE *Holy Smoke* 39 It wouldn't have entered their nuts that God . . just happened to be the real full-bottle on Natural Forces as well. **1976** *Bulletin* (Sydney) 28 Feb. 25/3 A consciousness that he is intellectually superior to most of his colleagues, 'a full bottle'. **1984** P. CORRIS *Winning Side* 107 Colin had had a year at a teacher's college on an Aboriginal scholarship and he was full bottle on the Aboriginal struggle.

bottle, *v. trans.* To attack, using a bottle as a weapon.

[**1917** A.B. PATERSON *Saltbush Bill* 34 There's some what likes blue-metal for to throw: But as for me, I always says for layin' out a 'trap' There's nothin' like an Empty Bottle-O!] **1917** *Advocate* (Burnie) 11 July 3/9 And moved down the street, because he had heard that some person was going to 'bottle' him. **1977** K. GILBERT *Living Black* 304 If you stand over . . the goomees you get bottled or kicked.

bottlebrush. a. Any shrub or small tree of the Australian genus *Callistemon* (fam. Myrtaceae), the flower spikes of which are shaped like a bottle brush. **b.** Any of several other plants with similar flowers esp. of the genera *Melaleuca* (fam. Myrtaceae) and *Banksia* (fam. Proteaceae).

[**1823** G. BLAXLAND *Jrnl. Tour Blue Mountains* 31 May (1913) 36 The flowers of the honeysuckle tree . . which are shaped like a bottle-brush, are very full of honey.] **1841** *Kerr's Melbourne Almanac* 134 Kalistemon, lopanthes and crestata (bottle brush). **1851** J. HENDERSON *Excursions & Adventures N.S.W.* I. 134 The immediate verge of the stream is fringed with the bottle-brush, a tree which produces a brilliant red flower, of the size and shape of the domestic instrument from which it derives its name. **1869** J. MARTINEAU *Lett. from Aust.* 109 To the south you may ride in an hour and a half over glorious open country, amongst scarlet bottle-brush. **1885** MRS C. PRAED *Austral. Life* 112 We composed jointly . . while we sat on a log that bridged the river, with the bottle-brush flowers of the ti-trees touching our shoulders. **1926** M. FORREST *Hibiscus Heart* 105 Bottle-brush, scarlet and bee-filled. **1934** M. GILMORE *Old Days* 25 The bottle-brush soaked in soft water yielded syrup for sore throats and colds. **1935** T. RAYMENT *Cluster of Bees* 89 At Gunbower . . the dairy-farmers have allowed to remain in their paddocks clumps of bottle brush trees to afford shade for the cows. [*Note*] *Callistemon paludosus*. **1948** R. RAVEN-HART *Canoe in Aust.* 69 The quite unmistakeable 'Bottle Brush', great heads of it, magenta or red, exactly like its name, the cylindrical brushes on wire handles. **1974** D. IRELAND *Burn* 1 A single seedpod, brown and dry, left from another year on a thin twig of bottlebrush.

bottle-oh. Also **bottle-o.** [f. *bottle* + -O.]

1. A dealer in used bottles. Also *attrib.*

1898 *Truth* (Sydney) 3 Apr. 5/2 The 'bottle-oh men' (*i.e.*, the dealers in bottles), a Sydney class corresponding in some degree to the London costers. **1901** *Ibid.* 6 Jan. 8/5 The crowd in this street was largely of the 'bottle-oh' variety, and mercilessly chaffed the procession. **1902** *Bulletin* (Sydney) 11 Oct. 36/1 The driver showed himself to be very different from what one would expect from his . . occupation of 'bottle-oh'. **1904** *Ibid.* 14 Jan. 15/1 An East Sydney man has named his bottle-oh cart after George Reid. **1915** A. WRIGHT *Sport from Hollowlog Flat* 49 Jacko Parker, late bottle-oh, of Surry Hills. **1921** *Smith's Weekly* (Sydney) 1 Jan. 9/4, I know a lady Bottle-O. **1933** *Bulletin* (Sydney) 31 May 20/3 Times is that bad, Mrs Stidgers. My pore husband was ashamed to face the bottle-o this mornin', we 'ad so few to offer him. **1947** O. GRIFFITHS *Darwin Drama* 32 Darwin became renowned for its 'empties', broken or whole. It did not pay to collect them; there were no 'bottle-oh' men, so the bottles were just left everywhere. **1954** J. WATEN *Unbending* 82 The bottle-oh jumped off his cart holding a chaff bag in hand and made towards the grounds strewn with empty bottles and the papers of sweets. **1967** D. HORNE *Educ. Young Donald* 57 The Bottle-oh (calling, 'Bottles! Bottles!' with a glottal stop instead of a double 't'). **1978** S. BALL *Muma's Boarding House* 38 Each Monday morning I waited for the Bottle-oh. **1983** L. CLANCY *Perfect Love* 103 'Did you get rid of those bottles?' she asked him. 'I got the bottle-oh out. He gave me six bob for them.'

2. A name for a marble: see quot. 1981. Also **bottley.**

1956 *Bulletin* (Sydney) 22 Aug. 13/1 Heard a couple of our old-timers reminiscing about marbles: 'Remember when we used to exchange chows for stonkers, knock over a commons or a bottley and trade conks for smokies?' said one old chap. **1959** *Ibid.* 22 July 18/3 I'm old enough to remember the small bottles of soft-drink that were corked with a built-in glass marble—known to us kids as a 'bottle-oh'. **1972** *Ibid.* 6 May 63/3 He managed to win a few 'birdcages', bottle-os, connie agates and other middle-class marbles. **1981** A. MARSHALL *Aust.* 74 Marble games seemed to vary in each State. Even the terms used were different. . . The glass marble obtained from the top of a soft drink bottle was called a 'bottley'.

bottler. [Of unknown origin.] Something (or someone) which excites admiration. Also *attrib.*

1855 *Bell's Life in Sydney* 19 May 2/4 He has proved himself, as the saying is, 'a bottler'. **1876** *Austral. Town & Country Jrnl.* (Sydney) 9 Sept. 422/1 He's more than three-parts bred. . . He's a bottler, that's what he is. **1881** J.C.F. JOHNSON *To Mount Browne & Back* 12 Carona Copper Mine is what they term in the neighborhood a 'regular bottler', meaning thereby that it is AA1 at Lloyd's. **1952** T.A.G. HUNGERFORD *Ridge & River* 122 The old bastard! The old hooer! What a bloody bottler! **1957** D. WHITINGTON *Treasure upon Earth* 98 'You bottler,' Mick breathed. 'You bloody beaut.' **1964** *Qld. Guardian* 8 Apr. 5/4 This bottler little booklet. **1971** *Bulletin* (Sydney) 11 Dec. 50/3 Back to Australia. It now appears that things are on the improve, you little bottler! **1975** R. HALL *Place among People* 109 'I might get drowned in this weather.' 'Yes, it's brewing up for a real bottler.' **1978** B. ST. A. SMITH *Spirit beyond Psyche* 208, I seen some terrific acts in me time, but the old Jim's must a bin a bottler to make 'em take 'im out' the looney-bin in a 'nambulance. **1981** D. STUART *I think I'll Live* 223 Saw a feller once on a Road Board job. . . He was a bottler.

bottle-swallow. [See quot. 1898.] *Fairy martin*, see FAIRY *n.*[1] 1.

1898 E.E. MORRIS *Austral Eng.* 47 Bottle-Swallow, . . a popular name for the bird *Lagenoplastis ariel*, otherwise called the *Fairy Martin*. . . The name refers to the bird's peculiar retort-shaped nest. **1924** *Bulletin* (Sydney) 10 Jan. 22/2 The blue martin, or bottle-swallow, seems to stop his flight by gripping the landing-place with his claws. **1949** *Ibid.* 19 Oct. 12/1 The bottle-swallows . . came in a flock.

bottle tick. [f. *bottle*, prob. alluding to the animal's shape when engorged + *tick* parasite.] *Scrub tick*, see SCRUB *n.* 5.

1876 'EIGHT YRS.' RESIDENT' *Queen of Colonies* 44 There are two kinds of these in the scrub, the black and the bottle tick. **1917** *Bulletin* (Sydney) 1 Nov. 24/3 After a few hours in a Queensland scrub . . a battler often finds himself the host of the bottle-tick and the cudgera. **1936** K.C. MCKEOWN *Spider Wonders Aust.* 250 The common tick, the attacker of picnic parties, is known under a number of popular names, the Bush Tick, Dog Tick, or Bottle Tick. **1965** *Austral. Encycl.* VIII. 498 *I*[*xodes*] *holocyclus*, the dog, bush or bottle tick (this last name is merited only by the female in its fully engorged state).

bottle tree. Any of several trees having a swollen trunk, esp. of the genus *Brachychiton* (fam. Sterculiaceae); BAOBAB b. Also *attrib.*

1844 L. LEICHHARDT *Jrnl. Overland Exped. Aust.* 11 Oct. (1847) 13 The Bottle-tree (Sterculia, remarkable for an enlargement of the stem, about three feet above the ground) was observed within the scrub. **1844** *Sydney Morning Herald* 12 Dec. 4/4 The serculia [*sic*] or bottle-tree is a very singular curiosity. It generally varies in shape between a soda water and port wine bottle, narrow at the basis, gradually widening at the middle, and tapering towards the neck. Its girth in the middle may vary from twelve to thirty feet; its height from fifteen to thirty feet. **1855** J. BONWICK *Geogr. Aust. & N.Z.* (ed. 3) 205 The Bottle tree . . so bulging out as to be called the Gouty tree. **1874** *Illustr. Sydney News* 28 Feb. 3/2 For water he was rarely at a loss, as in dry country he could always obtain a sufficiency for his wants from the mulga root, the bottle tree and currajong. **1881** *Echoes from Bushland* 44 A patch of dwarf myall with one of those absurd-looking bottle-trees growing in the middle of it, with a bunch of leaves like a small carrot growing out of the top. **1902** *Bulletin* (Sydney) 8 Nov. 16/1 He was feeding his horse on a mixture of boiled prickly-pear and bottle-tree chaff in a trough. **1908** *Ibid.* 3 Dec. 15/2 In some parts of the Territory the tree has a symmetrical shape, looking like a huge beer bottle with a plant stuck in the neck. This is called locally the bottle-tree, and is clearly a distinct species from the common gouty stem. **1923** *Ibid.* 16 Aug. 24/3 Hunting for the luscious roots of young kurries and young bottle-trees was a favorite pastime of mine. **1936** *Austral. Writers' Ann.* 21 They came to bottle tree scrub—grey monolythic boles, stillness and a sense of solitude. **1946** *Bulletin* (Sydney) 20 Nov. 29/4 Trunks of bottle-trees in the Dawson Valley (Q.) are bringing the drought price of £2 each. The pith makes passable fodder. **1955** N. PULLIAM *I traveled Lonely Land* 316 There's a story in these parts—this is one of the few places the bottle tree grows—that one was used for a jail years back. **1972** *Bulletin* (Sydney) 26 Aug. 16/2 With the council's plans for change, will go most shrubs, palms and bottle trees. **1975** X. HERBERT *Poor Fellow my Country* 456 The 'Bamgulut', the bottle-trees, said George, were people in the Beginning, the ancestors of the yam called 'Miyakka'. **1986** *Herald* (Melbourne) 28 Jan. 9/2 Bottle trees and Kurrajongs have a long life. Some of the trees on my property were quite large when I was a kid.

bottley: see BOTTLE-OH 2.

bottling, *ppl. a.* [Prob. f. BOTTLER.] Excellent.

1894 A.B. BELL *Austral. Camp Fire Tales* 87 Full of gold nuggets—thick as plums in a bottlin' Christmas puddin'. **1955** R. LAWLER *Summer Seventeenth Doll* (1965) 35, I had to put me foot in it . . by tellin' him how they made Dowdie ganger in his place, and what a bottling job he done. **1976** C.D. MILLS *Hobble Chains & Greenhide* 180 Tumble-up found some bottlin' sugar-bags too.

bottom, *n.*[1] *Mining.* [See BOTTOM *v.*] A mineral-bearing stratum, esp. an auriferous stratum. Also *attrib.*

1853 *Austral. Gold Digger's Monthly Mag.* v. 192 Many a hole has now yielded two, three, and even four bottoms of treasure. **1855** G.H. WATHEN *Golden Colony* 70 It is customary to sink a square or round shaft . . down to the gold-bearing deposit or 'bottom', and then to *drive*, or excavate horizontally, in search of the precious metal. **1864** J. ARMOUR *Diggings, Bush & Melbourne* 5 We have learnt how the diggers wash their bottom stuff, and hurry up for some of our tin dishes. **1887** 'OLD GOLD DIGGER' *Gold Digger's Guide* 8 Where the bottom is only up to 5 or 6 feet in depth . . one man can throw back as much headings as two men could do by pulling it up. **1901** O. OSBORNE *Golden Jubilee* 14 In depth John paddocked thirty feet, And picked two feet of bottom up, And thus the work, done so complete, Left not a colour in the stuff. **1928** R.M. MACDONALD *Opals & Gold* 82 Some new chum . . not knowing that opal was found only on a well defined 'bottom', and not underneath it. **1932** I.L. IDRIESS *Prospecting for Gold* 12 Next day take up the bottom and dish it. **1941** D. O'CALLAGHAN *Long Life Reminisc.* 46/2 They should have done down another 3 or 4 inches to get real bottom, where the gold did not go any deeper.

bottom, *n.*[2] In the phr. **bottom of the harbour,** the depths of a harbour (orig. Sydney Harbour), the fig. destination of a company stripped of its assets and sold off as a means of evading a taxation liability: see quot. 1984. Also *attrib.*

1980 *Austral. Financial Rev.* (Sydney) 11 Jan. 1/1 The tax schemes are jokingly referred to as 'Bottom of the Harbour Pty Ltd', by members of the Sydney tax avoidance fraternity, as many of the documents have gone to a watery grave. **1982** *Canberra Times* 23 Sept. 1/3 The progress of government action against 'straw companies' or bottom-of-the-harbour tax avoidance schemes. **1983** *Sydney Morning Herald* 13 Aug. 4/4 The Federal Government's introduction of the Taxation (Unpaid Company Tax) Act last year is expected to recoup about $250 million in unpaid tax from the bottom-of-the-harbour participants. **1984** *Canberra Times* 11 Apr. 3/1 An example of a simple bottom-of-the-harbour scheme would begin with a 'target' company with large assets, say $1 million, and a large tax liability, say $400,000. Net value of shares would be $600,000. The shareholders sell the company to a promoter for that $600,000 (plus a commission). The promoter and his clients then convert the $1 million to cash and keep it (thus getting $1 million for about $600,000). The shares in the company are 'sold' to fictitious people and the company's office is transferred to a fictitious address, and the company can never meet its $400,000 tax liability—it has been sent to the bottom of the harbour.

bottom, *v.* [Spec. use of *bottom* to reach the bottom of: see OED *v.* 4.]

1. *Mining.* **a.** *trans.* To excavate (a hole, etc.) to the level of a mineral-bearing stratum. **b.** *absol.* To reach this stratum. Also with **on:** to strike (gold, etc.).

1852 F. TRELOAR Extracts from Diary 5 Apr., Went to our claim, Bottomed hole—a blank—about 24 feet deep. **1853** MRS C. CLACY *Lady's Visit to Gold Diggings* 206 Often when a man has—to use a digger's phrase—'bottomed his hole', (that is, cut through the rocky strata, and arrived at the gold layer). **1855** R. CARBONI

Eureka Stockade 6, I had marked my claim in accordance with the run of the ranges, and safe as the Bank of England I bottomed on gold. **1862** J.A. PATTERSON *Gold Fields Vic.* 182 They bottomed on the 29th of June, 1861, having been five years in getting through the bluestone. **1872** 'RESIDENT' *Glimpses Life Vic.* 145 To look at the hole where he was at work, and which, to use the technical phrase, he had just 'bottomed', having reached the layer of pipe-clay among which the gold is usually found. **1886** W.J. WOODS *Visit to Vic.* 32 On Thursday morning the miners 'bottomed on wash', that is, they found gold. **1896** *Bulletin* (Sydney) 12 Dec. 26/4 Just a weight! And she bottomed at forty—A miner will know what it means. **1902** E.B. KENNEDY *Black Police Qld.* 44 These were waiting for the owners to 'bottom' *i.e.*, reach the description of earth which contains the gold. **1921** K.S. PRICHARD *Black Opal* 168 Roy O'Mara's bottomed on opal there... Got some pretty good colours, and we're goin' to peg out. **1932** I.L. IDRIESS *Prospecting for Gold* 242 If you are one of those new chums who go to an opal-field and 'bottom on it' first go, give your opals to a professional cutter. **1968** *Swag* (Sydney) i. 12/2 Scores of abandoned claims have never been properly 'bottomed', according to old prospectors. Clean them out and a couple of shovels full may put you onto paydirt. **1977** J. DOUGHTY *Gold in Blood* 82, I bottomed at six-and-a-half feet, the last nine inches being composed of a red puggy wash tightly packed with pebbles of quartz, ironstone, and ochre.

2. *fig.*

1861 L.A. MEREDITH *Over Straits* 250 Not unfrequently in danger of 'bottoming a shycer' by slipping into it. **1886** *Bulletin* (Sydney) 2 June 10/1 And in big boots stump after the heavenly 'push' Who are hastening to 'bottom' on souls at the rush. **1891** *Truth* (Sydney) 19 Apr. 1/3 We hope they'll treat 'our Nellie' well, and not in pocket let her suffer, Her 'prospects' good and soon she'll tell We hope, she's 'bottomed' on no 'duffer'. **1903** J. FURPHY *Such is Life* 209 Bottoming on gold this time, she buried the old man within eighteen months, and paid probate duty on £25,000. **1969** *Southerly* i. 61 Towards the end of his life he must have had the feeling that he had 'bottomed on mullock'.

Hence **bottoming** *vbl. n.*

1856 S.C. BREES *How to Farm & Settle in Aust.* 56 Deep-sinking was connected with the later practice of 'bottoming', in which the mass of the 'drift', that was previously wont to be washed in its entirety, was passed over, excepting a small quantity immediately adjacent to the rock or bottom on which it rested. **1868** J. BAIRD *Emigrant's Guide Australasia* 172 Parties were sometimes obliged to blast through three successive layers of hard blue stone at different depths ere they succeeded in 'bottoming', that is, in reaching the ancient rivulet's bed, where amid a bluish mud and smooth-worn quartz pebbles the gold lay embedded.

bottom end. In local use: the lower part of the Murray River and its surrounding country. See also TOP END 2. Also *attrib.*

1947 W. LAWSON *Paddle-Wheels Away* 16 'Bottom-end?' Dan Dalley asked. 'Where's that?' 'Down near the mouth—Goolwa, Murray Bridge, Mannum, Blanchetown, Morgan—they're all 'bottom-end' ports. This is the only 'top-end' one, and we're busy, I tell you.' 'What divides the two classes—'bottom-end' and 'top-end'?' Dan asked. 'The Darling. She comes in 500 miles down.' **1956** B. BEATTY *Beyond Aust.'s Cities* 172 Eventually the river transport split into two factions—'top end' and 'bottom end' boats—the former based at Echuca, and the latter using Morgan and Goolwa as their chief ports. **1981** B.J. BROCK *Catharsis* 54 You came through clear tonight, mate, On the tape from Stenhouse Bay, Talking of shells and Bottom End lore Over a black and tan.

Hence **bottom-ender** *n.*, a member of the crew of a Murray River boat: see quot. 1953. See also TOP-ENDER 2.

1947 W. LAWSON *Paddle-Wheels Away* 103 There were about a dozen 'bottom-enders' in the brawl. **1953** A. MORRIS *Rich River* 53 The crew .. made merry in the Wilcannia hotels where top-enders (Echuca men) vied with bottom-enders, their rivals from South Australia. **1982** LOWENSTEIN & HILLS *Under Hook* 7 Work on the mail ships was handled by the Port Phillip Stevedores, the 'bottom-enders'.

bough. Used *attrib.* in Comb. to denote a type of structure: made in a rough and ready way from branches.

1848 *Maitland Mercury* 6 Dec. 4/4 The careful manner in which they appeared to manage their sheep—making very neat and substantial bough yards. **1849** A. HARRIS *Emigrant Family* (1967) 89 Bough-yards are formed by merely felling the trees that surround an area of sufficient size for the folding of the flock .. and then, after lopping off all the limbs, running the barrels into a line of circumference, and piling them on the lopped limbs, till a fence of four or five feet is made good; an entrance way being left, which is stopped by a rough frame of any sort that can be quickly knocked together. **1851** *Empire* (Sydney) 14 Nov. 362/4 For the most part, Sofala presents to the spectator a strange jumble of tents of every possible variety of shape—canvas, osnaburgh or calicos, slab and bark huts, bough gunyahs, and nondescripts, presenting several varieties in one. **1875** P.E. WARBURTON *Journey across Western Interior* 301 The Colonel and his son were lying down near their bough-hut. **1896** W.H. WILLSHIRE *Land of Dawning* 44 One lubra gave birth to a child on this occasion just as easily as if it was an every-day occurrence. No-one seemed to take any notice of her but me. When I saw her situation I had a bough wurley made, and had her removed into it. **1902** *Bulletin* (Sydney) 1 Feb. 16/2 At one N.S.W. wool-scour, where the scouring lasts from two to four months every year, there is nothing but a rough bough shed .. under which the men eat their meals. **1927** A. CROMBIE *After Sixty Yrs.* 75 The first year 4,500 sheep were shorn under a bough-shed. **1931** LAWSON & BRERETON *H. Lawson* 161 A township of calico tents and bough humpies. **1937** C. WARBURTON *White Poppies* 253 He noted the killing-pen—a bough shelter had been erected above it. **1953** *Bulletin* (Sydney) 30 Dec. 12/1 In the cutter's-camp out from Lakewood (W.A.), thirsts were once quenched with a potent brew of hop-beer, dispensed in bough-shed shanties. **1959** *Overland* xv. 25 We put up the tent, and also, because it was the height of summer, a bough shed—that great mound of green leaves which completely blocks out the sun and gives a blessed cool shade. **1968** LINKLATER & TAPP *Gather no Moss* 86 Of course there was a bar close to the bough shed grandstand, and horses, carts, and even a few buggies, and the general excitement helped to make it a gala scene. **1983** *Yulngu* Dec. 9 Most of the kids will have seen the improvement in the bough shelter area.

boulder opal. See quot. 1974.

1928 R.M. MACDONALD *Opals & Gold* 35 The opal was a specimen of 'boulder opal' cut from a boulder. **1932** I.L. IDRIESS *Prospecting for Gold* 248 In most Queensland fields, the values occur as 'boulder opal'. **1962** D. MCLEAN *World turned upside Down* 144 It'll probably bring fifty quid an ounce and I estimate there's six ounces in it. It's what's known as boulder opal. **1974** B. MYATT *Dict. Austral. Gemstones* 134 The term boulder opal or Queensland opal is commonly used by miners for some stones found in Queensland. These consist usually of brownish coloured iron stained sandstone containing scattered veins or coatings of opal or of opal coated concretions.

bounce, *v. Australian National Football. trans.* To bounce (the ball) in a BALL-UP, esp. with reference to the beginning of the game.

1900 B. KERR *Silliad* 35 The ball is bounced, the glorious game renewed. **1908** *Clipper* (Hobart) 19 Sept. 2/2 The ball was bounced in a thunderstorm. **1936** E.C.H. TAYLOR *Our Austral. Game Football* 43 The field umpire shall bounce the ball .. at the start of each quarter, and after each goal has been kicked.

Hence **bounce** *n.*

1910 *Huon Times* (Franklin) 18 May 4/3 Immediately on the bounce they swooped down on the leather. **1958** B. HUMPHRIES *Nice Night's Entertainment* (1981) 18 Had the usual trouble parking the vehicle... However, found a possie in the long run just when I was thinking I'd be late for the bounce. **1960** *N.T. News* (Darwin) 5 Jan. 8/6 They attacked from the bounce through McClindon and Sparks for a single. **1963** *Footy Fan* (Melbourne) I. ii. 24 Ray Gabelich took some clever knock-outs from the bounce. **1969** A. HOPGOOD *And Big Men Fly* 44 And there's the bounce. And the big men fly! **1982** *Sun-Herald* (Sydney) 4 Apr. 87/2 Finally they got around to the bounce and the Sydney Swans were off and running. **1985** H. GARNER *Postcards from Surfers* 11 He turns on the TV in time for the bounce.

bound. In the phr. **bounds of location:** see LOCATION 4.

boundary, *n.* and *attrib.* [Shortening of 'boundary of location': see LOCATION 4.]

A. *n. Hist.* The boundary defining that part of a Colony in which land is surveyed and available for legal tenure: see quot. 1845. See also BORDER 1. Freq. in the phr. **beyond** (or **within**) **the boundaries.**

1803 *Sydney Gaz.* 27 Nov., A Settler at the Northern Boundary .. on Monday last employed a thresher. **1822** *Australasian Pocket Almanack* 49 An account of the Government cattle, which had strayed, was received by the Governor by a young man who frequented the bush, and was so far incorrigible as not to be kept within boundary by any limit of the law. **1835** *Sydney Times* 6 Jan. 2/5 We have the particulars of another dreadful outrage by bushrangers, at the remotest part of the county of Argyle, we believe beyond the boundaries. **1840** *HRA* (1924) 1st Ser. XXI. 127 Beyond the Boundaries, that is to say, upon the unalienated lands of the Crown. **1842** *Colonial Observer* (Sydney) 28 Sept. 498/3 Government should .. encourage the licensed occupation of land within the boundaries by small settlers. **1845** J.O. BALFOUR *Sketch of N.S.W.* 87 The settlers, properly speaking, are those who, either by purchases or grants, are possessed of landed property within the boundary; and the squatters those who live and depasture their sheep and cattle outside the boundary. By the boundary is meant a line that separates the land already surveyed .. from the lands in the interior, called in the colony 'bush', which are not surveyed. **1849** J.P. TOWNSEND *Rambles & Observations N.S.W.* 69 The father, although his headquarters were within the boundaries, was a squatter, and annually sent overland many fat cattle. **1857** F. DE B. COOPER *Wild Adventures* 66 The overlanders are the pioneers of civilization in Australia and their employment consists in taking large herds of cattle beyond the boundaries far into the bush, and finding a 'run' or tract of land. **1893** J. DEMARR *Adventures in Aust.* 56 All this part of the country was 'beyond the boundaries' and occupied only by 'squatters'.

B. *attrib.*

1. Of or pertaining to the perimeter of a rural property.

1808 *Sydney Gaz.* 5 June, Three allotments of 30 acres each: the boundary line continuing further as far as Burk's Farm. **1816** *Hobart Town Gaz.* 10 Aug., The Public are hereby cautioned against grazing any Stock on my Farm at New-Town (the Boundary trees being marked with white paint, and known to Stock-keepers). **1843** R.D. MURRAY *Summer at Port Phillip* 124 With regard to boundary fences the colonial laws enforce several equitable provisions. **1871** *Great Northern Run Case* 2 The names of certain defined boundary creeks. **1888** *Bulletin* (Sydney) 7 July 8/4 And our reason almost totters Through our squabbles with the squatters, And their watchful bound'ry-trotters who were always on our track. **1891** M. ROBERTS *Land-Travel & Sea-Faring* 64 With a little odd boundary work, I began to ride fairly well even before the winter or rainy season was over. **1894** J.K. ARTHUR *Kangaroo & Kauri* 21 Boundaries are usually indicated by wire fences... Sometimes the boundary-line is merely a clearing cut through woodland. **1917** *Bulletin* (Sydney) 5 July 24/1 Near the boundary fence of a back run on the north-west coast of Tasmania I came across a horrible example of the cruelty of the casual white trapper. **1929** 'OLD STOCKMAN' *Sensational Cattle-Stealing Case* 7/1, I have ridden the boundary wires with you. **1949** H.G. LAMOND *White Ears* 73 White Ears and his companions stayed several days in the boundary paddock of Tooloopa Station. **1965** R.H. CONQUEST *Horses in Kitchen* 161 And there the fiction writers leave the squatter's daughter—up to her neck in happiness in a remote boundary hut, cooking, washing nappies and hanging up curtains.

2. Special Comb. **boundary rider,** an employee responsible for maintaining the (outer) fences on a station, or a publicly owned vermin-proof fence. Also *fig.* (see quot. 1919).

1864 H. JONES *New Valuations* 13 Fencing does not decrease the expenses of working a station... Instead of shepherds we have to get boundary riders. **1869** *Colonial Soc.* 18 Feb. 10 The humble position of a boundary-rider, a man whose life is passed in performing tedious journeys about miles of post and rail, log, dog-leg, and brush fences. **1885** *Illustr. Austral. News* (Melbourne) 30 Sept. 162/3 The duties of a boundary rider for the most part consist in riding round the fences every day, seeing that they are all in good order, blocking up any panels that may be broken, putting out strangers (that is stock that have strayed on to the run), and, in fact, doing all that may pertain to keeping his master's stock on his own land, and everybody's else out of it. **1897** A.F. Paterson *'Mid Saltbush & Mallee* 18 Combaowie was very isolated, the next-door neighbour being twenty miles away, and the nearest habitation of any kind being a boundary-rider's hut, six miles off. **1899** *Western Champion* (Barcaldine) 2 May 13/1 Some weeks ago the Darling Downs Rabbit Board called for applications for the position of boundary-riders of the rabbit fence. **1906** *Bulletin* (Sydney) 13 Sept. 16/1 Boundary-riders .. are now supplied with strychnine, to destroy dingoes in their spare time. **1919** H.B. Fletcher *Boundary Riders Egypt* 24 The supports are brought up and a very lively scrap takes place, almost inevitably in Billjim's favour, as the Turk has a holy fear of the 'Boundary Riders'. **1936** *Bulletin* (Sydney) 29 Jan. 20/4, I have heard boundary-riders referred to by many names. Blue-tongues, lizards, hatters, boundary-jerkers, wire-inspectors and paddock parasites are just a few of those which will pass the censor. **1950** G.M. Farwell *Land of Mirage* 24 Today the only men working camels are Australian; two boundary riders on the dog-fence north of Marree .. some brumby-shooter in the Diamantina sandhills. **1965** A.W. Upfield *Lure of Bush* 25, I would rather be a boundary-rider than an army general, or a bullock-driver than an Under-Secretary. **1981** *Austral. Women's Weekly* (Sydney) 26 Aug. 5/2 (*caption*) Boundary rider Neville Beauchamp calls his neighbours by radio.

boundary-ride, *v. trans.* and *intr.* To ride (round) the boundaries of a station: see prec. (sense 2). Also *transf. and fig.*

1889 W.R. Thomas *In Early Days* 21 He used to boundary-ride the pegs [on a mining claim] once a day. **1894** *Bulletin* (Sydney) 6 Jan. 23/3 Whether boundary-riding, burr-cutting or droving he did not like being called Doctor. **1899** *Ibid.* 19 Aug. 15/1 Station-hand to injured mate in bed, as the priest leaves the room: 'What sorter cove's that? Looks like a cross atween a doc, an' a parson.' Mate: 'No, them ain't his lines; he's boundary-ridin' for the Pope.' **1911** St. C. Grondona *Collar & Cuffs* 112 My billet for that day was to boundary ride the seven-mile spring paddock, and as it was not more than twenty-five miles round .. I would be back in good time. **1935** I.L. Idriess *Man Tracks* 306 Their flour became ropey and they had to boundary-ride the dampers, toasting the crust. **1956** T. Ronan *Moleskin Midas* 201 'You boundary ride that mob', said the foreman, 'and let me know if they're heading this way.' **1980** R. Bropho *Fringedweller* 77 His reply was not direct. He boundary-rided most of the important questions.

Hence **boundary-riding** *vbl. n.*

1878 *Squatters' Plum* 39 The wife is expected to cook, wash, make beds, and bake bread; and the husband to do boundary-riding, cut and cart wood, kill and dress sheep, and be always doing something. **1923** *Bulletin* (Sydney) 22 Feb. 24/4 It is boundary-riding of the real old-fashioned kind, too, for there are no fences up there. **1965** A.W. Upfield *Lure of Bush* 9 He spent twenty years in the bush, working at many kinds of jobs: boundary riding, cattle droving, opal gouging, rabbit trapping, as cook, swagman and general station worker from one end of Australia to the other.

boung, var. Bung *a.*

bounty. *Hist.*

1. A sum of money paid by the government to an immigrant, or to an individual or company who sponsors certain categories of immigrant; an immigrant so sponsored.

1832 *Emigrant's Guide N.S.W.* 23 Females desirous to emigrate to New South Wales .. will be admitted as candidates for the bounty of £8. **1833** *N.S.W. Mag.* (Sydney) 125 The 'assistance' of Government consisted of *advances*, or loans, to be repaid by the emigrants after their arrival in the Colony; and *bounties*, or gifts not to be repaid at all. **1836** *HRA* (1923) 1st Ser. XVIII. 556 A Bounty of £30 will be allowed for every married couple. **1837** J. Macarthur *N.S.W.; its Present State & Future Prospects* 149 The offer of a bounty by the local government of the colony, for the introduction of agricultural families from the continent of Europe, having excited remark in this country, it may be proper to explain the enlightened principles upon which His Excellency Sir Richard Bourke was led partially to adopt this provision. **1844** *Port Phillip Gaz.* 30 Nov. 3 Twenty probationers from the new model prison of Pentonville .. are the very best we could have, inasmuch as they cost us nothing, and are like a free supply of labour, while the 'bounties' were brought here at a cost of £8 to £12 to the Colony. **1847** *Ibid.* 8 May 1 Bounties will not be allowed .. for persons above the labouring class, such as Overseers. **1848** *HRA* (1925) 1st Ser. XXVI. 663 They had been informed that they would receive in the Colony a Bounty apparently of £2 10s. a head. **1873** A. Trollope *Aust. & N.Z.* I. 33 Queensland had found it necessary to offer higher bounties than have sufficed with the other colonies,—or .. re-emigrating immigrants would not trouble themselves to come to Queensland.

2. Comb. **bounty agent, emigrant, emigration, immigrant, immigration, order, ship, system, ticket.**

1841 *Port Phillip Patriot* 16 Aug. 2/6 He (Mr Arden) would attract the attention of his listeners to the manner in which the work of the **Bounty agents** had been performed. **1843** *HRA* (1925) 1st Ser. XXIII. 19 None of the Bounty Agents engaged in Emigration, were permitted to send out People without a previous approval of their ships. **1852** S. Sidney *Three Colonies* 135 The bounty agents were pouring in a crowd of most unsatiable [*sic*] persons. **1840** *S. Austral. Rec.* (London) 4 July 4 The *Arkwright*, from Liverpool, arrived at Sydney on the same day, having on board 172 **bounty emigrants.** **1843** *N.S.W. Monthly Mag.* Sept. 470 That amount paid for bounty emigrants amounting to £957,000 is one of the principal causes of the present distress. **1844** C. Lyon *Narr. & Recoll. Van Dieman's Land* 40, I have been acquainted with a number of these bounty emigrant women. **1846** C.P. Hodgson *Reminisc. Aust.* 124 Coming out as Bounty Emigrants, you must remain three years in the Colony. **1840** *S. Austral. Rec.* (London) 21 Mar. 129 The materials of **bounty emigration,** from the very nature of the case, must ever be superior to those of government emigration. Bounty emigrants are selected, with few exceptions, on behalf of capitalists in the colony, and good engagements are made with them. **1846** *Melbourne Argus* 5 June 2/3 Under the system of Bounty Emigration which continued in operation until the end of the year 1841, many married couples are represented to have emigrated to this colony without their children. **1842** *Sydney Herald* 3 Feb. 2/3 (*heading*) **Bounty immigrants.** **1847** J.D. Lang *Phillipsland* 57 A large portion of the Bounty Immigrants imported into Port Phillip. **1851** *Bell's Life in Sydney* 19 Apr. 3/1 Free passages to the colony .. for such of their children who were left at home by married bounty immigrants who left Great Britain on or before 7th January, 1842, have been cancelled. **1841** *Port Phillip Patriot* 5 Aug. 2/1 The danger which threatens this Province from the stoppage of **Bounty Immigration.** **1845** *Sentinel* (Sydney) 15 Jan. 2/2 Nearly one million of money was sent out of the Colony to pay for Bounty Immigration, of which about one-fourth part was withdrawn from the Banks in the single year 1841. **1855** 'One Who Has Handled Spade' *Bounty Immigration* 45 It does not follow—in fact, it is impertinence to assume—that Bounty Immigration, or the Direct Remission Scheme, should be adopted. **1842** *Colonial Observer* (Sydney) 9 Feb. 145/3 His Excellency's **Bounty Orders** have been selling publicly, under the name of 'Botany Bay Emigration Scrip', we presume, in the Stock Exchanges of London, Liverpool and Glasgow. **1844** *HRA* (1925) 1st Ser. XXIV. 3 Settlers, to whom Bounty orders were first issued, never executed them. **1840** *S. Austral. Rec.* (London) 26 Dec. 409 Letters have been received from many .. emigrants .. urging all poor families who desire to emigrate to Australia to come out in the government ships, and not in the **bounty ships.** **1843** *Duncan's Weekly Register* (Sydney) 30 Sept. 137/1 The means taken in the mother country to fill the bounty ships, was well described by the Attorney General. **1848** J.C. Byrne *Twelve Yrs.' Wanderings Brit. Colonies* I. 281 The emigrant barracks, where new arrivals in bounty ships, who have come out at the Government expense, are housed for a few days. **1839** *HRA* (1924) 1st Ser. XX. 43 The comparative state of health which has existed on board the Government Ships and those sent out on the **Bounty System.** **1840** *Ibid.* XXI. 18 The extraordinary cheapness of the Bounty System is so greatly extolled. **1842** *Geelong Advertiser* 7 Mar. 2/3 An abuse in the Bounty System has existed unperceived for a considerable time, namely, a traffic in bounty orders, from one party to another. **1854** S. Sidney *Gallops & Gossips* 129 It was the emigrant ship 'Cassandra', bound for Australia during the period of the 'bounty' system, when emigration recruiters, stimulated by patriotism and a handsome percentage, rushed frantically up and down the country, earnestly entreating 'healthy married couples' and single souls of either sex, to accept a free passage to 'a land of plenty'. **1854** Backhouse & Tylor *Life & Labours G.W. Walker* (1862) 536 The Government furnishes **Bounty Tickets** for each adult emigrant. **1863** F. Algar *Handbk. to Colony Tas.* 15 Satisfactory arrangements are made for the reception of immigrants coming to this colony by means of the bounty tickets issued by the Colonial Government. **1871** *Austral. Handbk.* 44 Assisted emigration to Tasmania is effected by means of 'Bounty Tickets', which are procurable in the colony, or from .. the emigration agent .. in London.

Bourke /bɜk/. [The name of a town in n.w. N.S.W.] In the phr. **back of** (or **o'**) **Bourke,** the remote and sparsely populated inland. Also used adverbially.

1896 *Bulletin* (Sydney) 15 Feb. 3/2 Where the mulga paddocks are wild and wide, That's where the pick of the stockmen ride, At the Back o' Bourke. **1904** *Ibid.* 4 Aug. 17/3 You wonder that my nose is red! I got that done out back o' Bourke! **1919** R.J. Cassidy *Gipsy Road* 88, I could dump you into the desert at the Back o' Bourke, and you'd only be a speck. **1927** *Bulletin* (Sydney) 29 Dec. 31/4 We were takin' a mob of ewes across a dry stage back o' Bourke. **1937** W.R. Glasson *Musings in my Saddle* 42 The story of the child, born at the back of Bourke, who, on coming to Sydney, encountered rain for the first time and complained to his mother that some naughty person was throwing water on him, is a true one. **1947** M. Maclean *Drummond of Far West* 115 'I'll have to live out Back o' Bourke and become a he-man,' he said. **1963** *Bulletin* (Sydney) 6 Apr. 27/1 Newly returned from the lush 'back o' Bourke' (over a foot of rain in some places since Christmas). **1972** *Ibid.* 11 Mar. 65/1 In one day .. you can see superb tropical beaches, rolling prairie country, Hawaiian gauchos, lush Englishy farmland, and back-of-Bourke bushland. **1975** L.H. Clark *Rouseabout Reflections* 98 Should our Queen pen a letter, her armies and navy may bear it, it's true; But the back-o'-Bourke postie, the government rover, must still get it through. **1983** *Daily Tel.* (Sydney) 10 Oct. 11/1 He can make TV viewers in Nagasaki laugh as heartily as those in Barcelona, Brighton or the back of Bourke.

Bourke parrot. [f. the name of Richard *Bourke*, Governor of N.S.W. (1831- 1837).] The parrot *Neophema bourkii* of inland Australia, having pink on the underside of the body and blue areas on the wings. Formerly **Bourke parakeet.**

[**1841** J. Gould *Birds of Aust.* (1848) V. Pl. 43, *Euphema Bourkii.* Bourke's Grass Parrakeet.] **1934** *Bulletin* (Sydney) 18 Apr. 20/3 One of our most elusive birds is the Bourke parrakeet. **1937** R.H. Croll *Wide Horizons* 51 An observant station owner .. pointed out the large eyes of the Bourke Parrots and said that these parrots assuredly fly by night. **1950** *Bulletin* (Sydney) 26 July 12/2 The Bourke parrot .. appears to have survived both foxes and trappers. **1973** V. Serventy *Desert Walkabout* 40 Next morning I was delighted to see Bourke parrots drinking at the watering trough.

Bourke-street, *attrib.* [The name of a street in Melbourne.] Citified; cf. Pitt Street.

1944 *Bulletin* (Sydney) 10 May 12/2 We've all heard Bourke-street pioneers giving tongue to the alleged Aussie call as they battled through the trackless wilds of the Sherbrooke Forest. **1946** *Ibid.* 4 Dec. 29/4 Bourke-street bushmen .. marvel at the tolerance of the wedge-tail eagle.

bower. A structure, made by the male of certain species of bower-bird to attract a mate, consisting of an avenue of sticks or other vegetation and decorated with numerous natural or man-made objects collected by the bird.

1841 *Proc. Zool. Soc. London* VIII. 94 These constructions, Mr Gould states, are perfectly anomalous in the architecture of birds, and consist in a collection of pieces of stick and grass, formed into a bower. . . They are used by the birds as a playing-house, or 'run', as it is termed, and are used by the males to attract the females. **1846** J.L. STOKES *Discoveries in Aust.* II. 97, I found matter for conjecture in noticing a number of twigs with their ends stuck into the ground, which was strewed over with shells, and their tops brought together so as to form a small bower. **1886** P. CLARKE *'New Chum' in Aust.* 223 We pass the bower of a bower-bird, that curious little alley built by this bird-architect. **1926** K. DAHL *In Savage Aust.* 198, I found a very beautiful nest or playing bower of the 'bower-bird'. **1959** L. ROSE *Country of Dead* 63 He saw a bower-bird suddenly rise from the dried grass, in its beak the prize of a bleached rabbit-bone for its bower. **1976** *Reader's Digest Compl. Bk. Austral. Birds* 552 The smallest of the bower birds builds the biggest bower.

bower-bird.

1. Any of several species of bird in the fam. Paradisaeidae, occurring in Australia and New Guinea. (Most Austral. species build a bower.)

1841 J. GOULD *Birds of Aust.* (1848) IV. Pl. 9, *Chlamydera nuchalis.* Great Bower-bird. **1865** G.F. ANGAS *Aust.* 93 The 'bower-birds' possess the singular habit of constructing bower-like structures of twigs upon the ground, which they decorate with gaily-coloured feathers, bones and shells. **1882** W. SOWDEN *N.T. as it Is* 33 The bower-bird, the cockatoo, a sort of magpie, and others—piped out cheerily. **1916** L. FERRIS *John Heathlyn of Otway* 97 The blue-hued bower bird with his mottled mate. **1948** J. FAIRFAX *Run o' Waters* 30 In the spring the bower birds come down into Frederick's garden, and steal blue flowers to take back into their bowers in the mountains to dance around. **1980** ANSELL & PERCY *To fight Wild* 75 Up in the fig trees there were bower-birds, looking for ripe figs.

2. *fig.* A person who collects objects, ideas, etc.; a hoarder; a thief. Also *attrib.*

1926 H.W. FOWLER *Dict. Mod. Eng. Usage* 193 Use of French words... Only fools will think it commends them to the English reader to decorate incongruously with such bower-birds' treasures as *au pied de la lettre. Ibid.* 194 Every writer .. who suspects himself of the bower-bird instinct should .. remember that acquisitiveness & indiscriminate display are pleasing to contemplate only in birds & savages & children. **1941** K. TENNANT *Battlers* 301 George the Bower-bird .. was up to his old tricks, prowling around deserted camps, swooping on rubbish. **1943** S.J. BAKER *Pop. Dict. Austral. Slang* (ed. 3) 13 *Bower bird,* a petty thief. **1944** M.J. O'REILLY *Bowyangs & Boomerangs* 58/9 A young fellow known as the 'Bower Bird', on account of his natural tendency to pick up anything bright... One night .. he lifted a case of cheap watches. **1953** *Sydney Morning Herald* 3 Jan. 6/1 Those eccentric bower birds, the students of Australiana. **1969** P. ADAM SMITH *Folklore of Austral. Railwaymen* 27 All fettlers are bower birds, the most notorious in railways... They're never given a stock of anything so if they didn't pinch every bit of railway gear they can get hold of and salt it away they'd have nothing to draw on in a hurry. **1973** *Southerly* ii. 139 All my novels are an accumulation of detail. I'm a bit of a bower-bird. **1981** *Sunday Mail* (Brisbane) 14 June 13/1 Brisbane State High School principal Mr Ray Fitzgerald admits to being a bit of a bower bird. Indicating his executive-size office he says: 'I don't know how I'm going to get this cleaned out by June 26.'

Hence as *v. trans.* and *absol.*

1941 K. TENNANT *Battlers* 301, I don't want him bower-birding round this camp. **1948** W. HATFIELD *Barrier Reef Days* 66 What a mess-up things would be if we couldn't put a thing down and turn our backs without somebody bower-birding it. **1980** E.R. HALL *Can you hear Me?* 16 A .. warrant officer who .. 'bower-birded' radio spares in his garage.

Bowser /ˈbaʊzə/. Also **bowser.** [Proprietary name.]

1. A petrol pump; a petrol tanker used for refuelling aircraft, tanks, etc. Also *attrib.*

1918 *Austral. Official Jrnl. Patents* (Canberra) 31 *Bowser* 22,099... Pumps. *S.F. Bowser and Company, Incorporated,* Fort Wayne, Indiana, United States of America, oil storage engineers. **1930** *Bulletin* (Sydney) 7 May 20/2 Wallerbrith .. keeps the general store, the garage and the bowser palace in our village. **1930** V. PALMER *Passage* (1957) 124 Cars from the hills were pouring past to Lavinia, or pulling up at the bowser for petrol. *c* **1933** V.C. BUCKLEY *With Passport & Two Eyes* 152 At the first garage .. I asked the man which pump had 'Shell' in it. He looked at me blankly and then said: 'Oh you mean which Bowser is the 'Shell' in,' from which I gathered petrol pumps were called Bowsers. **1942** W. SIMPSON *One of our Pilots is Safe* 18 All this was changed by the arrival of the hundred odd vehicles of our M.T. columns—petrol bowsers, tractors, office trailers. **1947** G. CASEY *Wits are Out* 163 He first branched out for himself in the motor business years ago, with just an agency for petrol pourers, before there were any bowsers. **1957** D. WHITINGTON *Treasure upon Earth* 43 In the winter he took a job as a bowser attendant at a service station. **1963** D. IRVING *Destruction of Dresden* 139 The bowsers were waiting to top up the tanks once again. **1968** J. ALARD *He who shoots Last* 34 The big, black Buick came to a stop in front of a bowser. **1978** C. RUHEN *Crocodile* 34 The Kombi-van stood beside the petrol bowsers, connected to one of them by the hose that pumped the vital fluid into the depleted tank. **1985** *Town & Country Mag.* (Goulburn) 15 July 4/2 (*caption*) A bowser showing 61.5 cents per litre at Cobargo.

2. *transf.* and *fig.*

1937 *Bulletin* (Sydney) 20 Oct. 20/2 Nature played a shabby trick on the dormouse-opossum... The first four to arrive are set, each having a teat to fasten to. The late arrivals find that there are no more bowsers available and quickly die. **1976** S. WELLER *Bastards I have Met* 25 In the days before bowsers, when beer was a zac and spirits a deener, it was customary to give the bloke the bottle and let him pour his own.

bowyang /ˈboʊjæŋ/. Also **boyang.** Usu. in *pl.* [f. Br. dial. *booyangs* straps buckled over trousers below the knees: see SND and also EDD *bowy-yanks* leather leggings.]

1. A string or narrow strap tied round the trouser-leg below the knee: see quot. 1893.

1893 *Warracknabeal Herald* 22 Sept., To those not in the cult of 'boyang worship', it may be necessary to explain that the two straps used to hitch the lower part of labourers' trousers are 'boyangs'. **1897** *Antipodean* (Melbourne) 35 Moleskin trousers, which were tied under the knees with the customary 'bowyangs'. **1902** *Bulletin* (Sydney) 12 Apr. 14/2 Boyangs are merely used to keep trousers from dragging over the knee in stooping-work. **1913** H. LAWSON *For Aust.* 9 The spirits of our fathers have belts and bowyangs on (Oh, Father! do you live again and know?). **1915** A. WRIGHT *Sport from Hollowlog Flat* 52 Moleskin pants of various hues and shapes, held below the knees with the article of navvy apparel known as the bowyang. **1931** *Aussie* (Sydney) May 36/2 The navvies' union used to regard bowyangs as their trade-mark. **1944** M.J. O'REILLY *Bowyangs & Boomerangs* 45 Another thing that helped when carrying the swag was 'Bowyangs'—that is, straps or strings around the trousers just below the knee cap. These helped keep the full weight of the trousers off the waist-belt or braces. **1964** E. LANE *Our Uncle Charlie* 27 'Dungaree is such a cuss to shrink,' he used to say as he tied his binder-twine bowyangs beneath his knees. **1978** J. ANDERSON *Tirra Lirra* 18 How all the girls went on about the nightman .. a thin man, with bowyangs round his trouser legs. **1981** P. RADLEY *Jack Rivers & Me* 90 We're wearin' bowyangs... That's like when you tie a rope round the legs of your pants to stop snakes from crawling up. The boys call them shit-catchers.

2. *transf.* and *fig.* Used *attrib.* as a symbol of engagement in manual labour: limited in education and outlook.

[**1905** *Bulletin* (Sydney) 23 Mar. 16/1 Bill Bowyangs faced the local J.P. (and shopkeeper) on the usual charge of drunkenness. **1916** 'T.O. LINGO' *Austral. Comic Dict.* 57 *Bowyang,* the Garter of Labor.] **1951** S. HICKEY *Travelled Roads* 48 His artistry and polish made him the foremost propagandist in Labour's early days, and helped counter the cry that it was a bowyang party. **1969** L. HAYLEN *Twenty Yrs.' Hard Labor* 53, I have heard Chifley referred to by latter day Laborites as one of the 'bowyang boys'. **1972** A.A. CALWELL *Be Just & fear Not* 257 Anti-Labor parties have their troubles, too, but being composed of well-bred, middle-class, properly-educated people who are concerned with the preservation of the status quo, they are better able to reconcile their personal and other differences than those possessing what conservatives have called 'bowyang' mentalities. **1983** *Austral.* (Sydney) 18 Feb. 11/2, I think it has to do with the increasing conservatism of the electorate and the disappearance of the true-blue, boots and bowyangs Labor man.

Hence **bowyanged** *a.*

1915 J.P. BOURKE *Off Bluebush* 92 For the world wags fine with the bow-yanged blokes While they work for a miner's pay! **1915** A. WRIGHT *Sport from Hollowlog Flat* 52 The last of the bowyanged travellers fell inside. **1946** A. MARSHALL *Tell us about Turkey, Jo* 118 The windlass that had once creaked to the slow winding of bowyanged miners now slept.

box, *n.*[1] [Transf. use of *box* the tree.]

1. Any of several trees of the fam. Myrtaceae, esp. of the genus *Eucalyptus,* having close-grained timber resembling that of the European *Buxus* and (usu.) a fibrous bark; the wood of these trees. Also *attrib.*, and with distinguishing epithet, as **apple, brush, red, white, yellow** (see under first element).

1801 *HRA* (1915) 1st Ser. III. 177 The banks of the river covered with cedar, ash and what is called box. **1805** J.H. TUCKEY *Acct. Voyage to establish Colony Port Philip* 227 Box (so called from its leaves) is a sound and very tough wood; its size about two feet and a half, and would answer for any purpose of ship-building. **1829** R. MUDIE *Picture of Aust.* 131 To another eucalyptus, which is very hard, close, hardy, and weighty, though like most of the genus, liable to splinter, the colonists give the name of box. **1848** T.L. MITCHELL *Jrnl. Exped. Tropical Aust.* 392 Marks of former inundations on the trunks of box trees ('*Coborra*'). **1872** G.S. BADEN-POWELL *New Homes for Old Country* 152 The bark of the box gum-tree is .. very good, for roofing purposes. **1878** 'R. BOLDREWOOD' *Ups & Downs* 1 Many a ton of .. box had burned away in the great stone chimney. **1912** R.S. TAIT *Scotty Mac* 27 His dog, tied up under a box tree. **1927** *Bulletin* (Sydney) 21 July 27/3 Near Balmoral (Vic.) .. one of our bush-walks was to 'the manna trees', locally known as box-gums. **1948** R. RAVEN-HART *Canoe in Aust.* 34 The ones with pale, smooth, peeling bark are gums; those with rougher, darker bark are box (the 'Coolabah tree' in Waltzing Matilda is a box). **1965** *Austral. Encycl.* III. 406 Box eucalypts also range from Victoria to the Northern Territory and are so named from their hard tough timbers (like European boxwood); the barks consist of finely matted fibrils .. tending to flake away in small pieces.

2. Comb. **box bark, creek, flats, forest.**

1827 P. CUNNINGHAM *Two Yrs. in N.S.W.* I. 206 The bark of the .. box and the stringy-bark makes good roofs for cattle, as also cart-sheds, and workmen's huts, the **box-bark** possessing considerable incombustible properties. **1894** H. LAWSON *Short Stories* 72 The strong pine rafters creaked and strained, 'Til we thought the roof would go; And we felt the box-bark walls bend in And bulge like calico. **1972** *Bulletin* (Sydney) 2 Dec. 39/1, I put my Bible down on a sheet of box bark and as far as the eye could see there was nothing but empty Australia and I do believe I heard God's authentic call. **1847** *Moreton Bay Courier* 23 Oct. 4/1, I am inclined to believe that the open box country of the four last mentioned creeks extends in an easterly direction round the scrub we had crossed to the first **box creek.** **1861** *Burke & Wills Exploring Exped.* 7 Then crossed an open plain with claypans, the drainage of which, running westward, forms numerous small box creeks. **1902** S.C. GUBBIN *Journey Wilgena to Everard Ranges* 10 There is a box creek coming in on the south-east side which fills the Woorung after heavy rains. **1844** L. LEICHHARDT *Jrnl. Overland Exped. Aust.* 23 Dec. (1847) 83 The country begins to open, with large **Box-flats** extending on both sides. **1896** B. SPENCER *Rep. Horn Sci. Exped. Central Aust.* III. 24 The 'box flats', which are met with on the sides of the Finke Channel, are flood plains, on which *Eucalyptus microtheca* flourishes in large numbers. **1935** *Bulletin* (Sydney) 30 Oct. 21/3 Chinese ringbarkers .. rang most of the box flats along the Murray (N.S.W.). **1946** A.M. LAPTHORNE *Mildura Calling* 46 The firewood is cut many miles from Mildura, up-stream, down-stream, on the box flats adjoining the Murray River. **1847** E.B. KENNEDY *Extracts Jrnl. Exped. Central Aust.* 232 Continued our journey .. through a flooded **box-forest.** **1863** W.J. WILLS *Successful Exploration Interior Aust.* 162 We then came to a box forest, where the soil was loose and earthy, similar to polygonum ground. **1880** J. BONWICK *Resources Qld.* 36 Such phrases as 'Box forest', 'Iron-bark ranges', 'Apple-tree flats' .. have all had their own respective associations in the minds of those interested in the pastoral or agricultural capabilities of land.

3. Special Comb. **box poison,** the shrub poisonous to stock *Oxylobium parviflorum* (fam. Fabaceae) of s.w. W.A.

[**1865** 'SPECIAL CORRESPONDENT' *Transportation* 14 There are no less than fourteen known varieties of these plants, but only four are commonly pointed out. These are the York-road, the heart-leaf, the rock, and the box-scrub .. gastrolobium anylobiaides.] **1872** MRS E. MILLETT *Austral. Parsonage* 50 The 'box' poison (one of the *Gastralobrum* [*sic*] tribe, I believe) takes its name from a fancied resemblance between the pernicious shrub and the well-known box-tree. **1891** E.H. HALLACK *W.A. & Yilgarn Goldfields* 8 York-road and box poison plants, as they are called, abound here, principally on the ironstone ridges. **1903** *Emu* III. 105 The gullies .. have a scrub of their own .. consisting mostly of box poison. **1926** *Poison Plants W.A.* (W.A. Dept. Agric.) 23 Box Poison (*Oxylobium parviflorum* ..). An erect shrub of 3–6 ft. occasionally 8 feet high, the branches erect or rather spreading, leafy .. is widely distributed through the Wheat Belt. **1962** B.W. LEAKE *Eastern Wheatbelt Wildlife* 12 Most of the aboriginal shepherds were careless and there was a constant leakage of sheep through some eating box poison. **1974** S.L. EVERIST *Poisonous Plants Aust.* 338 *Box poison* .. is regarded as one of the most toxic plants of Western Australia.

box, *n.*[2] *Hist.*

1. A moveable box-like shelter in which convicts were confined at night; CARAVAN.

1836 J. BACKHOUSE *Extracts from Lett.* (1839) iv. 5 At the quarries the men are lodged in 'boxes' or caravans, a little more than seven feet wide; four tiers of men, of five each, occupy one box. **1838** W. MOLESWORTH *Rep. Select Committee Transportation* 16 They are locked up from sunset to sunrise in the caravans or boxes used for this description of persons, which hold from 20 to 28 men, but in which the whole number can neither stand upright nor sit down at the same time (except with their legs at right angles to their bodies), and which, in some instances, do not allow more than 18 inches in width for each individual to lie down upon the bare boards. **1843** J. BACKHOUSE *Narr. Visit Austral. Colonies* 457 The prisoners on Goat Island .. are lodged in twelve wooden 'boxes', which are whitewashed inside and out, and are very clean. Each of these boxes is furnished with a few Bibles, Testaments and Prayer Books. **1863** C. GIBSON *Life among Convicts* II. 228 They were locked up from sunrise to sunset, in caravans or boxes, which held from twenty to twenty-eight men each; but which were not high enough to allow of the men standing.

2. A moveable shelter in which a shepherd could sleep while remaining close by his flock.

1843 J.F. BENNETT *Hist. & Descr. Acct. S.A.* 97 The shepherd or hut-keeper, with his dog, sleeps in a moveable box placed close to the fold. **1847** T. MCCOMBIE *Austral. Sketches* 99 The duty of a hut-keeper is to keep the hut, cook the victuals of his fellow servants, and sleep in a box close by the hurdles during the night. **1909** H. BUTTON *Flotsam & Jetsam* 103 He followed his sheep over immense plains, sleeping in a portable 'box' fixed on wheels.

box, *n.*[3] [Prob. f. the phr. *to be in a (the same, wrong) box* to be in a fix: see OED *sb.*[2] 21.] A mixing of two flocks or herds. Also **box-up.**

1868 C.W. BROWNE *Overlanding in Aust.* 2 A. and B. represent two shepherds on a run. They live not far apart, and in consequence occasionally meet, each man having his flock with him. On such an occasion A. comes over to B. to have a chat and a smoke with him. The flocks meanwhile are left to take care of themselves, and in process of time come feeding closer and closer to each other. Suddenly the leading sheep in A.'s mob lifts up his head, gives a preparatory 'Bah!' and charges straight at B.'s followed by all his companions. The two thus become amalgamated. This is a box, and it has occurred through the negligence of both parties. **1872** C.H. EDEN *My Wife & I in Qld.* 67 A 'box' .. causes an infinity of trouble, which is the reason that the stations are so far apart. **1917** A.L. BREWER *'Gators' Euchre* 97 'Have to go some to prevent a box-up,' he mutters. Now his whip flies round; his horse props and wheels in all directions; and the station cattle are turned after a determined resistance.

box, *n.*[4] *Mining.* Abbrev. of 'sluice box'; a compartment of a sluice box.

1870 *Sydney Morning Herald* 5 July 2/4 The Big Engine claim is the only fresh one that has started washing... They have, I am informed, come on to some payable dirt... The boxes are going, which will soon test its quality. **1889** *Braidwood Dispatch* 18 Sept. 2/1 During the week I have had a good supply of water, and in consequence have got a fair quality of wash through the boxes, the prospects being fully up to the average. **1931** W. BARAGWANATH et al. *Guide for Prospectors in Vic.* 12 A box sluice consists of a long wooden trough or series of troughs .. each length being called a 'box'.

Hence **box** *v. intr.*

1932 I.L. IDRIESS *Prospecting for Gold* 26 Now for a much faster method of gold working, 'boxing'. *Ibid.* 51 You can box in a running stream under conditions where it would not be advantageous to hand sluice your whole claim in a face.

box, *n.*[5] [Fig. use of *box* dice-box.] In the collocation **the whole box and dice:** everything, the whole lot.

1888 'R. BOLDREWOOD' *Robbery under Arms* (1937) 74, I could see him turn his head and keep watching me when I put on the whole box and dice of the telegraph business. **1938** X. HERBERT *Capricornia* 374 'When the bust-up comes the job will close down for good.' 'What—the construction?' 'The whole box and dice.' **1978** D. STUART *Wedgetail View* 257 There'd've been con men, slick bloody jewel thieves, international spies, the whole bloody box an' dice. **1985** J. CLANCHY *Lie of Land* 80 Everything's changed. The whole box and dice.

box, *n.*[6] [Var. of U.S. *to look as if one came out of a bandbox* to look very smart: see OEDS *bandbox* c.] In the phr. **out of the box:** unusually good.

1926 *Sun* (Sydney) 1 July 1/4 Two out of the box. These Siamese cats are just looking at the world from the box in which they travelled. **1931** F.D. DAVISON *Man-Shy* 50 'She's one out of the box, alright,' he said. **1941** *Coast to Coast* 63 You talk about it as if 'avin' kids is somethin' out of the box. **1953** D. STIVENS *Gambling Ghost* 100 You trimmer! Won by streets, didn't you? Out of the box! **1968** J. ALARD *He who shoots Last* 73 It was nothing out-of-the-box, even as bush pubs go. **1975** *Sun-Herald* (Sydney) 9 Nov. 111/2 To be frank, the novel is nothing out of the box, and neither is the movie.

box, *v.*[1] [f. BOX *n.*[3]]

1. *trans.* To allow, either by accident or design, (discrete flocks or herds) to become mixed. Also with **up.**

[N.Z. **1864** Puketoi Diary 19 Apr., Lambs boxed.] **1870** J.C. WHITE *Qld. Progressive* 27 But if the sheep do get mixed, or 'boxed' as the saying is, you must yard them. **1872** G.S. BADEN-POWELL *New Homes for Old Country* 124 Station shepherds, who feed along the road, may be forewarned, and thus save their own flocks getting 'boxed' with the travelling 'lots'. **1884** 'R. BOLDREWOOD' *Old Melbourne Memories* 10 As his cattle were drawing into camp, I cheerfully 'boxed' mine therewith and relieved myself by the act of further anxiety. **1890** 'MRS A. MACLEOD' *Austral. Girl* (1894) 181 Some sheep got boxed up at the seven-mile hut, and we had a high old time of it drafting them. **1913** M.A. MCMANUS *Reminisc. Maranoa District* 20 The reason all these sheep were 'boxed' in one large flock was in consequence of all their men leaving through being frightened at some hostile natives. **1925** M. TERRY *Across Unknown Aust.* 84 When far enough distant to avoid getting 'boxed' (mixed), the unrequired beasts were allowed to disperse. **1932** I.L. IDRIESS *Flynn of Inland* (1965) 61 They were discussing a coming muster, an important event out on the unfenced frontiers where the cattle herds sometimes become 'boxed'. **1942** W. GLASSON *Our Shepherds* 15 When mobs belonging to different owners became 'boxed' they have been known to completely separate themselves and each lot return to its own fold. **1949** H.G. LAMOND *White Ears* 136 Three more men with another mob of ewes and lambs joined the first lot. They boxed the two flocks and drove them down Brandy Creek. **1959** H.P. TRITTON *Time means Tucker* 16 In the event of two mobs getting 'boxed' they would have to be taken to the nearest yard and drafted out.

2. *transf.* and *fig.*

c 1884 *Punchialities from Punch* 50 *Squatter's daughter*— We had such a jolly lark to day. In going out for a walk we got boxed with another school; we had to be mustered, and then drafted out. **1893** *Bulletin* (Sydney) 28 Oct. 3/1 If the Heavenly hosts got 'boxed' now, as mobs most always will, Why who'd cut 'em out like William, or draft on the camp like Bill? **1909** J.C.L. FITZPATRICK *When we were Boys Together* 25 Followers and opponents alike could get their liquor free at one pub, and then go on to another, and another, and so on, until they had completely 'boxed the compass'—and boxed themselves, for that matter. **1911** E.J. BRADY *King's Caravan* 251 Once and only once have I experienced that beastly sensation which bushmen term 'getting boxed'. I was certainly 'boxed'. My sense of direction had gone. **1960** *Sydney Morning Herald* 19 July 1/10 Thurber's moral is: Those who live in grass houses shouldn't stow thrones. Emile boxed it.

Hence **boxing** *vbl. n.*

1868 C.W. BROWNE *Overlanding in Aust.* 62 He must be, moreover, constantly on the move, and on the alert to prevent boxing with other flocks, or those of the run he may be passing through. **1879** 'AUSTRALIAN' *Adventures Qld.* 107 To prevent the possibility of their boxing with any other flocks on the run, they were sent to an out-station. **1893** 'PIONEER' *Reminisc. Austral. Early Life* 31, I had settled myself down between the two flocks, to keep them from 'boxing' (a term well known to shepherds). **1924** L. ST. C. GRONDONA *Kangaroo keeps on Talking* 54 Care must be taken to prevent their 'boxing'—or mingling—with the sheep belonging to the stations through which we are passing. **1944** *Bulletin* (Sydney) 30 Aug. 13/3 Jack .. kept the mass of mutton moving; the trouble was to prevent their boxing with station sheep. **1964** H.P. TRITTON *Time means Tucker* (rev. ed.) 26 He would have time to shift his stock off the route and avoid getting them mixed up with the travelling mob. This was known as 'boxing up'.

box, *v.*[2] *intr.* With **on:** to fight, to persevere.

1919 W.H. DOWNING *Digger Dialects* 13 *Box on*, (1) continue; (2) fight. **1937** C.E.W. BEAN *Official Hist. Aust. 1914–18* V. 516 'You dig in where you are .. and 'box on' with us,' said the Australians. **1962** V.C. HALL *Dreamtime Justice* 109 The party had crossed the first nightmare salt-arm with surprising ease and then had boxed on with varying fortunes. **1968** S. GORE *Holy Smoke* 26 He boxes on with a yarn about this old joker who had two sons. **1980** M. WILLIAMS *Dingo!* 76, I got five years' hard labour. Five years! .. The big shots said I was lucky. Box on with it, they said.

boxer, *n.*[1] [Prob. Br. dial. *boxer* tall (hard) hat: see OEDS 4.] A bowler hat. Also *attrib.*

1895 *Bulletin* (Sydney) 29 June 3/2 You might chance to meet a spectre on some God-forgotten track Wearing spectacles and boxer with a lib'ry on his back. **1910** *Huon Times* (Franklin) 7 Dec. 4/1 He wore a dark sack coat and blue dungaree trousers and a boxer. **1981** A. MARSHALL *Aust.* 25 It was the days of boxer hats, ankle-choker pants, handlebar moustaches and Charlie Chaplin gallantry.

boxer, *n.*[2] *Two-up.* [Prob. fig. use of *boxer* one who boxes in the ring.] The person in charge of the game; a payment to this person, either as a percentage of some winnings or by contribution. See also *ring-keeper* RING *n.*[2] 2.

1911 L. STONE *Jonah* 216 The spinner threw down the kip, and took his winnings from the boxer. **1935** H.R. WILLIAMS *Comrades of Great Adventure* 184 So large were his wagers on each spin that it necessitated the help of two boxers, who saw that every bet was covered. **1949** L. GLASSOP *Lucker Palmer* 169 'What about a boxer?' The man running a two-up game takes a percentage of the winnings of the spinner when there is a run of heads, but when tails are falling he depends on contributions from the tail backers. In response to the fat man's appeal for a 'boxer', a few florins and shillings were tossed into the ring. **1950** F.J. HARDY *Power without Glory* 323 Gambling was the favourite pastime. 'Two-up' was the most popular form... Big Bill was 'Boxer'. He held the money for which the spinner threw the pennies. **1955** N. PULLIAM *I traveled Lonely Land* 76 The players usually take up a collection, a sort of tipping idea, for the cockie, and they call this emolument a 'boxa' or sometimes a 'boxer'. **1965** *Kings Cross Whisper* (Sydney) Nov. 1/2 He must learn that phrases like 'Flip again' are only for the boxer and not for the common player. **1972** K. CLIFT *Saga of Sig* 21 He disclosed that he was quite well cashed up having been the 'boxer' at the swy game. **1977** R.E. GREGORY *Orig. Austral. Inventions & Ideas* 116 The man in charge of a game of two-up is called the boxer. He chooses a 'spinner' who bets that he will 'head 'em'.

box jellyfish. [See quot. 1976.] Any of the jelly-like

sea animals of the class Cubozoa of the phylum Cnidaria, having stinging tentacles; STINGER 3.

[**1958** *S. Austral. Naturalist* XXXII. iv. 58 One group of jellyfish of special interest to Australians are the Cubomedusae, which are often referred to as 'sea wasps' in the tropics. The writer believes however that the term 'box-jelly' or 'jelly-box' is a more suitable popular name.] **1971** *Bulletin* (Sydney) 25 Sept. 26/1 The sea-wasp, or box-jelly fish, is said to have killed some 70 swimmers this century. **1976** E. WORRELL *Things that Sting* 56 Also called the Box Jellyfish, the Sea Wasp can be recognised from other less dangerous jellyfish by its box-shaped body, with long venomous tentacles suspended from the four corners. **1984** *People Mag.* (Sydney) 7 May 8/1 (*caption*) Lifesavers don pantyhose to thwart the box jellyfish's poison stingers.

box-on. [f. BOX *v.*[2]] See quot. 1919.

1919 W.H. DOWNING *Digger Dialects* 13 *Box-on*, a fight; a battle; a tussle. **1956** J.T. LANG *I Remember* 202 The meeting was high lighted by a box-on between Frank Burke and Molesworth. **1968** S. GORE *Holy Smoke* 8 Yair, here we are—around the time of the Israel-Philistine box-on, in the Holy Land.

boy. [Spec. use of *boy* coloured servant or slave: see OED(S *sb.*[1] 3 c. and 3 e.] A non-white male employee (of any age). See also BLACKBOY 1. Also *attrib.*

1864 R. HENNING *Lett.* (1952) 68 He takes with him Alick, one of the blackboys—they are always called 'boys' though the said Alick must be thirty-five at least. **1876** 'EIGHT YRS.' RESIDENT' *Queen of Colonies* 58 The blacks who work on a station or farm are always, like the blacks in the Southern States, called boys. **1886** E.M. CURR *Austral. Race* I. 102 The massacre concluded, the English officer gives over the women . . to satisfy the lust of his 'boys', as he calls the troopers. **1893** 'OLD CHUM' *Chips* 27 The quiet waiting of the Chinese 'boys' appeared to me perfect. **1898** D.W. CARNEGIE *Spinifex & Sand* 154 It is marvellous how soon a tame boy comes to despise his own people, when he far outstrips any white man in his contemptuous manner of speaking about a '-- black-fella.' **1907** *Truth* (Sydney) 7 Apr. 10/6 The Chow boy is everywhere to be seen nursing and washing the baby . . making beds, and doing all domestic work. The boy institution is ruining the rising generation and Northern Territorians generally. **1916** S.A. WHITE *In Far Northwest* 36 During the afternoon the boys became very excited, and, pointing to footprints in soft sand, repeated 'Wild Blackfeller' several times. **1922** 'J. BUSHMAN' *In Musgrave Ranges* 102 Yarloo was a good boy. . . He had not had many masters. **1934** *Red Star* (Perth) 15 June 3/2 Squatters were in the habit of referring to aborigines in their employ as 'my boy' and 'that boy of mine'. **1944** M.J. O'REILLY *Bowyangs & Boomerangs* 153 One may have a boy in his employment (male natives of all ages are called boys) whom he looks on as a stupid, dopy, ignorant native, yet that boy may be possessed of more real, practical knowledge about the ways and means of life and the secrets of nature than his egotistical boss. **1960** *N.T. News* (Darwin) 5 Feb. 5/5 Aborigine Wally . . described himself as 'number one boy' at the station. **1981** A. GRANT *Camel Train & Aeroplane* 103 One white man who is to drove the horses to Oodna and his seven 'boys' form a semi-circle round the mouth of the yard and into this the mob rushes.

boylya /ˈbɔɪljə/. Also **bullya.** [a. Nyungar *bolya.*] KORADJI. Also *attrib.*

1841 G. GREY *Jrnls. Two Exped. N.-W. & W.A.* II. 84 The 'Boyl-yas' would acquire some mysterious influence over him, which would end in his death. . . The Boyl-ya is the native sorcerer. **1843** W. PRIDDEN *Aust.* 129 Yes, unconsciously he rested In a slumber too profound; While vile Boyl-yas sat and feasted On the victim they had bound. **1846** J.L. STOKES *Discoveries in Aust.* I. 81 'Boyl-yas'. . . The natives in the neighbourhood of Swan River give this name to their Sorcerers. **1863** J. BONWICK *Wild White Man* 59 Venus . . that Boyl-ya dame now raised on high. **1929** W.J. RESIDE *Golden Days* 158 They also place faith in the powers of the 'bullya', or the sorcerer of the tribe.

bracken. [Transf. use of *bracken* a fern.] The perennial fern *Pteridium esculentum* (fam. Dennstaedtiaceae), sometimes divided into *P. esculentum*, *P. semi-hastatum*, and *P. revolutum*, and abundant in forests which are subject to frequent burning. Also **bracken fern.**

1844 N.L. KENTISH *Work in Bush Van Diemen's Land* (1846) 12 Thicket of fern or braken, growing to the height frequently of 8 or 9 feet. **1859** H. KINGSLEY *Recoll. Geoffry Hamlyn* II. 192 Then they sauntered away . . among the knolls of braken. **1888** *Proc. Linnean Soc. N.S.W.* III. 540 *Pteris aquilina, Linn.* . . 'Brake-fern' or 'Bracken'. Formerly called 'Tara' by the aboriginals of Tasmania. **1897** L. LINDLEY-COWEN *W. Austral. Settler's Guide* 217 In fern (bracken) country ring-barking appears to be of doubtful benefit. **1931** B. CRONIN *Bracken* 53 Full of weeds, Martin. Full of bracken-fern. Get the fern-hook to work, man. **1956** T.Y. HARRIS *Naturecraft in Aust.* 114 Those, like the common Bracken Fern, that are able to grow in fairly dry places make new plants by putting out runners.

Braddon Blot. *Hist.* [f. the name of Edward *Braddon* (1829–1904), Premier of Tasmania and member of the first Federal Parliament.] See quot. 1936.

1899 *North-Western Advocate* (Devonport) 6 Feb. 3/3 The so-called 'Braddon Blot' had been retained, but in a modified form. **1899** *Ibid.* 19 Apr. 2/4 The amendment which Sir Edward Braddon managed to carry through the Melbourne session of the Convention, and which has since been known as the Braddon Blot. **1936** J. KIRWAN *My Life's Adventure* 179 He . . succeeded in embodying in the Constitution what is known as the Braddon Clause, by which for the first ten years after Federation the Commonwealth Government had one-fourth of the Customs and Excise revenue and the balance went to the States. Many called it 'The Braddon Blot'.

brain-fever bird. [Transf. use of *brain-fever bird* an Indian cuckoo which calls repeatedly.] PALLID CUCKOO.

1924 *Bulletin* (Sydney) 14 Aug. 22/3 Several of our cuckoos—including . . the pallid cuckoo (brain-fever-bird)—are migratory. **1970** J.V. MARSHALL *Walk to Hills of Dreamtime* 41 The cry of the brain-fever bird, a fluted longdrawn coo-ee, haunting as an invocation to the moon.

bramble. Any of several introduced or native prickly shrubs of the genus *Rubus* (fam. Rosaceae), incl. the naturalized blackberries *R. discolor* and *R. ulmifolius.*

1827 *Hobart Town Courier* 29 Dec. 3 It may be acceptable to those who are disposed to attempt the culture of the silk worm to know, that the mulberry tree thrives here with astonishing luxuriance . . and that the leaves of the common wild bramble of Van Diemen's Land, form a very good substitute. **1842** *Tasmanian Jrnl. Nat. Sci.* I. 37 The common bramble of the Colony has a well-flavoured fruit. **1867** 'CLERGYMAN' *Aust. as it Is* 39 The only really valuable wild fruit is the raspberry—more properly, the bramble—found in cold districts. **1912** *Huon Times* (Franklin) 27 Apr. 6/2 The tints of autumn amongst the orchards, the red and gold leaves of the bramble etc. make a pleasing sight to lovers of nature.

brand, *v. trans.* With **up:** to brand (an animal or animals) with an identifying mark. Also *absol.*

1879 S.W. SILVER *Austral. Grazier's Guide* 21 It is usual for the stockmen and proprietors of the neighbouring runs to assemble at one another's homesteads . . for the purpose of aiding the owner to 'brand up'. **1890** 'R. BOLDREWOOD' *Colonial Reformer* III. 108 I'm glad these crawlers of cattle are branded up. **1921** G.A. BELL *Under Brigalows* 111, I have to muster the horses and brand up the foals. **1929** 'OLD STOCKMAN' *Sensational Cattle-Stealing Case* 18, I stopped there some days spelling my horses. While I was loafing on him, I gave him a hand to muster and brand up his horses.

Hence **branding-up** *vbl. n.*

1919 *Bulletin* (Sydney) 25 Sept. 22/3 Owing to the rise in price of cattle and the difficulty stations have in branding-up, 'poddy-dodging' has become an established trade.

brand-fake, brand faker: see FAKE *v.*

branding, *vbl. n.* Used *attrib.* in various Comb.: of or pertaining to the branding of stock.

1848 H.W. HAYGARTH *Recoll. Bush Life* 70 The fence of the branding-yard is more closely constructed than that of the other divisions, and is provided with what is called a 'branding panel', which is, in fact, a sort of screen, behind which the men take refuge, if suddenly charged by an infuriated animal. **1849** A. HARRIS *Emigrant Family* (1967) 67 We shall have to speak of a branding-day. **1854** S. SIDNEY *Gallops & Gossips* 71 The Branding Feast was over. A week's hard work, hard riding, hard swearing, with interludes of blood and dust, stockmen tossed, and horses gored, rails jumped—in fact, a sort of Spanish bull feast without the costume or the idle audience—was ended. **1856** J. BONWICK *Bushrangers* 43 It was the usage of a settler to proclaim a branding season. **1857** F. DE B. COOPER *Wild Adventures* 58 It was at branding-time, and the greater part of the beasts had been mustered. **1880** J. BONWICK *Resources Qld.* 48 Branding directories are regularly published. **1881** A.C. GRANT *Bush-Life Qld.* I. 227 The branding-pen is getting particularly lively now. **1934** W. HATFIELD *River Crossing* 152 Men were injured . . in their man-handling of grown beasts on the branding-camps. **1943** *Bulletin* (Sydney) 22 Sept. 12/1 The twisted ropes, three-, four-, and five-stranders were always made in the manner indicated for use on the branding camps. **1954** H.G. LAMOND *Manx Star* 118 The stock-camp was completing the final branding muster of the year.

brass razoo: see RAZOO.

breadcarter. An itinerant vendor of bread, etc.

1908 *Truth* (Sydney) 12 Apr. 7/3 (*heading*) Breadcarter's battle against buns. **1914** *Ibid.* 12 July 11/3 A bread carter named George Buckworth . . had been charged with aiding the nurse. **1933** R.D. TATE *Doughman* 34 He may ooze horsey gold, and me but a common breadcarter, but I've got all youse dames taped. **1956** *Bulletin* (Sydney) 14 Mar. 13/1 Our local breadcarter and his horse always struck me as a happy combination.

breadfruit. [Transf. use of *breadfruit* the farinaceous fruit of a tree, esp. that furnished by *Artocarpus altilis*, which is cultivated in Aust.] Any of several native plants bearing an edible fruit, esp. SCREW PINE; the fruits of these plants. Also *attrib.*

1830 W.J. HOOKER *Bot. Miscellany* I. 250 On the beach were thickets of *Hibiscus tiliaceus*, and *Pandanus pedunculata*: the latter is called *Bread-fruit*, and eagerly eaten by the natives. **1842** *Colonial Observer* (Sydney) 7 Dec. 662/2 The scrubs are also rich in a fruit, 'Buerwi', (bread fruit) of which the natives are very fond. **1864** J. MORRILL *Sketch of Residence* 228 The bread fruit grows on the mountains. **1888** *Proc. Linnean Soc. N.S.W.* III. 536 'Screw Pine', 'Bread fruit'. The 'Wynnum' of Queensland aboriginals. **1909** *Bulletin* (Sydney) 7 Jan. 14/2, I don't think there are any baobabs in the Northern Territory *east* of the Victoria River. . . The fruit of the baobab is . . evidently the true Australian bread-fruit, or bread-nut. **1926** *Ibid.* 27 May 22/2 There is another Queensland coastal nut frequently misnamed 'breadfruit'. This fruit has something of a shape of a pineapple, is yellow and red, and shines as if varnished. **1930** M.M.J. COSTELLO *Life J. Costello* 229 Here the beautiful Breadfruit Palm, now in full bearing and utilised by the blacks in making a food which when pulverised, moulded into dough and baked in the ashes results in a product resembling a sodden damper in which no baking powder had been used. **1938** C.T. WHITE *Princ. Bot. Qld. Farmers* 157 The true Bread Fruit is not to be confused with the Pandanus tree—common along the coast and often called 'Bread fruit' by Queenslanders.

break, *n.* [Spec. use of *break* an interruption of continuity.]

1. A temporary barrier: see quot. 1876.

1876 J.A. EDWARDS *Gilbert Gogger* 143 Breaks: Temporary brush fences, built by parties travelling with sheep, to count their sheep through, upon the road. **1888** 'R. BOLDREWOOD' *Robbery under Arms* (1937) 32 It's a 'break' he said, almost in a whisper. There's a 'duffing-yard' somewhere handy. **1913** M.A. MCMANUS *Reminisc. Maranoa District* 20 At night he put them in a large 'break', or half-yard on one side of which was a large waterhole in the Maranoa River. **1918** *Bulletin* (Sydney) 30 May 48/1 Even with four dogs and an improvised break, it was too dangerous. . . The flock would put forward every endeavour to return to their habitual watering-place. **1934** A. RUSSELL *Tramp-*

Royal 54 Rolled in our 'nap' with the break at our heads and the camp fire at our feet.

2. A fire-break.

1925 M. TERRY *Across Unknown Aust.* 244 To burn a break around it . . i.e. burn off the grass so as to leave the yards surrounded by cleared ground, over which the flames could not leap. **1927** T.S. GROSER *Lure of Golden West* 191 The law demands that 'breaks' be ploughed around the areas to be burned off. **1935** N. HUNT *House of David* 156 She's euchred, boss! She's hemmed in on all sides! She can't pass them there breaks, nohow. **1956** F.B. VICKERS *First Place to Stranger* 26 The greedy tongues of flame licked the stubble faster than we could dig a break. **1965** G. MCINNES *Road to Gundagai* 248 To see him burning a break, dipping sheep or leaning over a wire fence talking to a stock-rider, was to recognize a grazier's hierarchy in which everyone was equal because everyone had his place.

3. The point at which the swell of a wave 'breaks'. Also with qualifying word, as **beach, reef, shore break.**

1963 J. POLLARD *Austral. Surfrider* 20 The next one you might take right to the 'shore break', the waves breaking on the very edge of the beach. *Ibid.* 27 The highlight of the Duke's performance came when he picked up a wave in the northern corner, stood erect and ran the board across the bay, continually beating the break. **1965** *Surfabout* (Sydney) II. ix. 25 There is a reef break which occasionally produces good right slides. **1967** *Ibid.* III. vii. 8 The other popular surf, the left beachbreak, works best at 3–4 feet on high tide.

break, *v.* [Spec. use of *break, v.* to escape from restraint; with *out* to burst out (as of fire); with *down* to demolish.]

1. *intr.* Of stock: to stampede. Also *transf.*

1888 'R. BOLDREWOOD' *Robbery under Arms* (1937) 35 Stop 'em from breaking or running clear away from the others. **1891** —— *Sydney-Side Saxon* (1925) 104 It'll take some galloping to wheel that poley brindle's mob, and if they once break there's no headin' 'em. **1909** J.S. RYAN *Splinters on Wall* 61 But the night watch gallops with them When the cattle break at night. **1914** C.H.S. MATTHEWS *Bill* 99 Sometimes they 'break' in the night, and it is then that the drovers have their toughest job and run their greatest risks. **1927** K.S. PRICHARD *Brumby Innes* (1974) 73 If the bullocks start breakin' like that, they make a habit of it. **1938** F. RATCLIFFE *Flying Fox & Drifting Sand* 124 The camp [of flying foxes] 'broke' at precisely 6 P.M . . first forming a packed wheeling mass above the trees. **1981** A.B. FACEY *Fortunate Life* 155 The rain was tumbling down. It hadn't let up since the cattle broke.

2. *intr.* With **out.**

a. Of a goldfield: to become the centre of a rush; to burst into life. Also as *vbl. n.*

1855 G.H. WATHEN *Golden Colony* 43 When first the gold 'broke out' (to use the diggers' phrase), the general excitement . . almost put an end to private convivial meetings. **1857** W. WESTGARTH *Vic. & Austral. Gold Mines* 200 Ballan, a poor-looking little township, but now likely to get larger and richer from some gold fields that have since 'broken out' in its vicinity. **1867** *Sydney Punch* 5 Jan. 51/2 We've got a tremendous new diggings *broke out* here at the Weddin Mountains. **1879** *Kelly Gang* 13 Here . . the young couple resided until the breaking out of the diggings, the husband pursuing his adopted calling of splitter and fencer. **1881** A.C. GRANT *Bush-Life Qld.* II. 227 A year or two had been spent in station work, but a gold-field having broken out, the lad had forsaken steady employment to become 'a wandering digger'. **1892** 'R. BOLDREWOOD' *Nevermore* II. 138 Some of these new goldfields . . were 'breaking out' every day. **1919** *Smith's Weekly* (Sydney) 12 Apr. 18/5 When Peak Hill diggings first broke out Jim Small . . successfully tendered for the carriage of mails. **1938** F. BLAKELEY *Hard Liberty* 30 Of all the mining fields that ever broke out in Australia . . White Cliffs was by far the best. **1951** E. HILL *Territory* 266 In fever and fatality Umbrawarra broke out—'broke out', that apt Australian phrase.

b. To go on a drinking bout: see BREAK OUT *n.*

[N.Z. **1899** J. BELL *In Shadow of Bush* 161 He had though it best on the occasion in which Dan had 'broken out', to give him a wide berth.] **1965** F. HARDY *Yarns of Billy Borker* 126 The old Ragged was a good bloke, a good worker and a good unionist, but he was fond of the gargle, see. He'd break out now and then and when he did, you couldn't get him out of the cart to turn to. Cart? Bed.

3. In the imp. phr. **break it down,** 'desist!'

1941 *Coast to Coast* 127 Ah, break it down, feller. Everybody knew you had her on the town. **1950** F.J. HARDY *Power without Glory* 358 'I'll start the fund off with five thousand, and I want you to give a thousand, if you've got it.' 'Break it down, Jack. I'll come to the meetin'.' **1953** T.A.G. HUNGERFORD *Riverslake* 186 'You underrate your charm.' 'Ar—break it down!' **1963** D.H. CRICK *Martin Place* 154 'Oh, hang the expense. I'll shout.' 'Break it down, Paula.' She slapped him playfully. 'Stop arguing.' **1968** S. GORE *Holy Smoke* 12 'Break it down,' says the King. 'He's been a bash artist ever since he was a tin lid—.' **1972** D. MARTIN *Frank & Francesca* 16 Jeez, you talk exactly like my mum now. Break it down!

breakaway.

1. An animal that rushes free from a flock or herd. Also *attrib.*

1881 A.C. GRANT *Bush-Life Qld.* I. 223 After a good deal of shouting, cracking of whips, and galloping after odd breakaways, the cattle were yarded amid clouds of dust. **1947** E. HILL *Flying Doctor Calling* 15 To see him . . roping a big 'mickey' on the stockyard, or breaking in, or bringing back a breakaway on the big buff Mitchell grass plains is a classic for an Australian 'Wild-wester'. **1955** H.G. LAMOND *Towser* 167 As soon as the sheep started to run odd ones gave the usual 'break-away' call.

2. Chiefly *W.A.* A low escarpment. Also *attrib.*

1896 D. STEWART *Thousand Miles & More* 54 The appearance and contour of this district is very picturesque—abrupt ironstone 'breakaways' and quartz hills and blows are passed through. **1911** E.D. CLELAND *W. Austral. Mining Practice* 2 Good natural sections of these sediments can be seen along the small 'breakaways' forming the western edge of the lake country. **1916** *Jrnl. R. Soc. W.A.* (1917) 72 Cliffs, often 50 to 100 feet high, usually cut from weathered granite . . are known on the fields as 'Breakaways', probably from some idea that the ground has broken and fallen along them. They show no sign, however, of being fault scarps. **1933** M. TERRY *Untold Miles* 187 They are wholly associated with the sedimentary breakaways—the Westralian bushman's term for escarpment or, as others say elsewhere, 'jump up'. **1937** —— *Sand & Sun* 141 High sandstone cliffs lay close ahead, beyond them a scrub-covered 'breakaway'. **1959** A. UPFIELD *Bony & Mouse* 1 The breakaway was the granite lip of a vast and shallow saucer, on which grew a mulga forest the like of which is exceedingly rare in modern Australia. **1973** *Meanjin* 253 My father's mine was about a quarter of a mile south. Rich, too, until they lost the lode. It's tricky here. Breakaway country. **1980** R. DAVIDSON *Tracks* 220 A twisted freakish wasteland of sandstone break-aways, silent, and seemingly aloof from the rest of the earth's evolution.

3. A rush of floodwater bursting from its usual course; the channel thus eroded.

1926 A.A.B. APSLEY *Amateur Settlers* 98 'Washouts' and 'breakaways' as the run-offs made by the terrific rainfall in 'the wet' are called. **1935** I.L. IDRIESS *Man Tracks* 25 Then the desert face broke into chasm-like wrinkles that were 'breakaways', rocky cracks, enormous channels one after the other down into which and across the labouring camels had to be coaxed and driven. **1956** T. RONAN *Moleskin Midas* 151 The Yates's Place caravan swung around the breakaways below the police station. **1963** M. BRITT *Pardon my Boots* 67 And finally thundered back over red iron-hard ground gashed by deep break-aways, with the bullock now glad to return to the mob.

break o' day bird. *Obs.* [See quot. 1872.] MAGPIE *n.* 1 a. Also **break o' day boy.**

1872 MRS E. MILLETT *Austral. Parsonage* 42 The business of the lark as harbinger of morning devolves in Australia upon the magpies, which on this account are commonly called 'break-of-day birds'. **1878** R.B. SMYTH *Aborigines of Vic.* II. 213 Kooree. . . The large magpie, break o' day bird, *gymnorhina tibicen.* **1916** E. & M.S. GREW *Rambles in Aust.* 28 The magpies . . are called 'break o' day boys' in the country, because, like our cocks, they call the neighbourhood.

break out. *Obs.* A drinking bout.

1847 A. HARRIS *Settlers & Convicts* (1953) 142 The notion of a 'spree' gets into their head, they are never easy till they have their 'break out' over. **1888** 'R. BOLDREWOOD' *Robbery under Arms* (1937) 81 He saw him once in one of his break-outs.

breakweather. *Obs.* BREAKWIND 1.

1839 *Royal S. Austral. Almanack* 110 It being now sunset we formed a native 'breakweather' of boughs, and passed the night in this place. **1843** J.F. BENNETT *Hist. & Descr. Acct. S.A.* 63 Their dwellings or encampments consist of slight temporary erections, forming nothing more than a kind of break-weather. **1845** C. GRIFFITH *Present State & Prospects Port Phillip* 2 The mi-mi is a kind of break-weather, formed of branches of trees and bark, which the natives use instead of buildings of any kind. **1852** G.C. MUNDY *Our Antipodes* I. 331 The natives . . squatted before a fire and behind a sloping sheet of bark turned from the wind—in bush lingo, a break-weather.

breakwind.

1. An Aboriginal shelter.

1832 J. BACKHOUSE *Extracts from Lett.* (1838) i. 55 We went into their breakwinds (as their huts are called) and took leave of them. **1842** *Tasmanian Jrnl. Nat. Sci.* I. 369 A few boughs of the tea-tree shaped into a break-wind formed their only protection. **1847** W.H. LEIGH *Emigrant* 189 Busied himself in the erection of a 'bower' (in polite discourse) for the habitation of their domestics, but which in rude Colonial phraseology is yclept a 'break wind'; but we prefer calling it a bower, rather than use the other flatulent appellation. **1861** *Burke & Wills Exploring Exped.* 5 They made me a breakwind in the centre of their camp. **1873** J. BONWICK *M. Howe* 186 Temporary huts, or *breakwinds*, had been reared. These were of sticks, boughs, and leaves, with a stray rug of opossum or kangaroo skin thrown upon the top. **1898** G.W. WALKER *Notes on Aborigines Tas.* 6 These 'breakwinds' were thatched roofs sloping to the ground, with an opening at the top to let out the smoke. **1938** D. BATES *Passing of Aborigines* 52 Old breakwinds on the slopes surrounding the valley of Nambeet Well showed that the place was once a favourite camping-ground. **1943** *Bulletin* (Sydney) 17 Nov. 12/2 Most times a breakwind of bark and boughs suffices the Kimberley abo. for a roof.

2. Any temporary shelter; a wind-break.

1840 *S. Austral. Rec.* (London) 17 Oct. 251 Arrived upon his estate, his [*sc.* the settler's] primary object is to erect a brush-hut or break-wind, which is formed of the boughs of trees, and sometimes thatched in a rude manner with long grass. This serves for a shelter until a log-hut can be constructed. **1875** P.E. WARBURTON *Journey across Western Interior* 34 The whole party proceeded to make break-winds of boughs before lying down for the night. **1891** J. FENTON *Bush Life Tas.* (1964) 31 Our men had made a breakwind of tea-tree poles and boughs. **1900** H. LAWSON *On Track* 128 Close at hand, 'butcher's shop'—a bush and bag breakwind in the dust, under a couple of sheets of iron, with offal, grease and clotted blood blackening the surface of the ground about it. **1938** D. BATES *Passing of Aborigines* 190, I built an enclosing breakwind of mulga bushes, and set up the little household that was to be my domain for 16 years.

bream /brım/. Also **brim.** [Transf. use of *bream* as applied to certain fish, either fresh-water (fam. Cyprinidae), or marine (various fam).] Any of several fresh-water and marine fish, esp. *black bream* (see BLACK *a.*[2] 1 b.); see quot. 1963. Also with distinguishing epithet, as **bony, red, silver** (see under first element).

1699 W. DAMPIER *New Voyage round World* (1703) III. 140 In the night while Calm we fish'd with Hook and line, and caught good store of Fish, *viz* Snappers, Breams, Old Wives, and Dog-Fish. **1770** J. COOK *Jrnls.* 23 Aug. (1955) I. 394 The sea is indifferently well stock'd with Fish of various sorts, such as . . Breames. **1789** 'OFFICER' *Authentic & Interesting Narr. Exped. Botany Bay* 38 Bream and mackerel are the most plenty of any fish, but none are so delicate as those caught in the European seas. **1825** B. FIELD *Geogr. Mem. N.S.W.* 149 The large cod and bream (as they are called) of the waters falling westerly . . have not been observed in this river. **1839** W. MANN *Six Yrs.' Residence* 237 Bream are quite a drug at Melbourne, which the natives take in great quantities. **1842** *Port Phillip Gaz.* 17 Dec. 1 (Advt.), *Melbourne Retail Market . . Fish*—Bream and Schnapper, average per lb., 3d. **1856** G. WILLMER *Draper in Aust.*

225 The bream and mullet are similar to those caught in England. **1861** 'OLD BUSHMAN' *Bush Wanderings* 245 The Australian bream, or brim, was certainly the best of all our fresh-water species. **1906** D.G. STEAD *Fishes of Aust.* 125 The bream family (. . *Sparidae*) . . includes two, at least, of our most important food-fishes. **1951** T.C. ROUGHLEY *Fish & Fisheries Aust.* 82 There are six species of bream in Australian waters. **1963** B. CROPP *Handbk. for Skindivers* 116 There are two common species—black and southern bream. Bream are mainly found in New South Wales and Queensland. . . Southern bream (*Mylie butcheri*) are confined to the southern section of Australia. **1969** L. HADOW *Full Cycle* 120 The brim are on the bite. **1984** B. DIXON *Searching for Aboriginal Lang.* 34 Joe's sons were diving into the stream and spearing fish—barramundi and bream—which the women wrapped in ginger leaves to cook in the coals of fire they had made on the sand.

breast, *v.* [Fig. use of *breast* to face.] Esp. in the phr. **to breast the bar,** to approach (a bar) purposefully. Also *transf.* and *fig.*

1909 E. WALTHAM *Life & Labour in Aust.* 31 No sooner do we 'breast the bar' than a huge rough-and-ready miner accosts us thusly 'Well mate, what's your poison?' **1909** F.E. BIRTLES *Lonely Lands* 75 Plucky little Burketown came up smiling every time to 'breast the bar' and 'face the music', as the local language so pithily expressed it. **1968** S. GORE *Holy Smoke* 26 Yair, he didn't even have the price of the fare home; let alone feeling too much of a crumb to breast the old man again and give him the score. **1979** DUSTY & LAPSLEY *Walk Country Mile* 118 Then the stockman rides up with his dry dusty throat, He breasts up to the bar and pulls a wad from his coat, But the smile on his face quickly turns to a sneer, As the barman says sadly, the pub's got no beer.

breezer. *Shearing.* In the phr. **from the breezer** (or **sneezer**) **to the sneezer** (or **breezer**), from nose to tail. Also *transf.*

***c* 1895** CLARK & WHITELAW *Golden Summers* (1986) 133 So I . . catches my bird, gives him two blows, from his sneezer to his breezer. **1899** J. BRADSHAW *Highway Robbery under Arms* (1912) 36 Cut the sheep from the breezer to the sneezer. **1929** *Aussie* (Sydney) 15 Apr. 17 'I went from the sneezer to the breezer in three chops up the neck and down the whipping side in a couple more.' That is to say, he did one side of a sheep in three blows of the shears, then shore the neck and the last side in a couple more. **1978** J. DINGWALL *Sunday too far Away* 88, I hope you've got clean hands doctor—you've cut him from the sneezer to the breezer.

brewer. In special collocations: **brewers' asthma,** see quots. 1953 and 1967; **droop** [used elsewhere but recorded earliest in Aust.], alcohol-induced flaccidity of the penis; **goitre,** see quot. 1953.

1953 S.J. BAKER *Aust. Speaks* 137 **Brewer's asthma,** shortness of breath, allegedly due to habitual drinking of strong waters. **1967** *Kings Cross Whisper* (Sydney) xxxii. 7/1 *Brewers' asthma,* a very severe hangover. **1971** B. HUMPHRIES *Bazza pulls it Off,* I know you've had a few but don't tell me you've copped the **brewer's droop**! **1976** M. POWELL *Down Under* 31 All this beer-drinking had given some of the men such enormous stomachs that they looked pregnant. . . The condition is known as 'brewers goitre', and it eventually leads to 'brewers droop'. **1984** B. DRISCOLL *Great Aussie Beer Bk.* 128 *Droop, brewer's,* sad condition, caused by too much beer, preventing a man from rising to the occasion. **1953** S.J. BAKER *Aust. Speaks* 137 **Brewer's goitre,** a paunch allegedly acquired by consuming beer in large quantities. **1980** N. WATKINS *Kangaroo Connection* 37 Danny Andrews . . now supported a definite 'brewer's goitre' beneath a wide leather belt.

brick, *n.*[1] Chiefly *Tas. Obs.* [Prob. ironic use of *brick* good fellow: see OED *sb.*[1] 6.] A member of a street gang; a hooligan.

1840 *Tasmanian Weekly Dispatch* (Hobart) 31 July 7/1 Some of the vagabonds of the Town, who call themselves 'Bricks', had much annoyed Clark. **1843** *Port Phillip Patriot* 27 Mar. 5/6 All Van Diemen's Land rung with the exploits of a number of idiots, who, calling themselves 'Bricks', used to sally forth at night, when the streets were deserted, and amuse themselves by breaking honest men's windows. **1845** *Standard* (Melbourne) 30 Aug. 2/6 On the night of Tuesday last, some youths of that genus who in the sister colony have earned, by their exploits, the distinguishing title of 'bricks', took a fancy to a model of a key which hung over the shop of Mr Wharton, Ironmonger, Collins street. **1848** J. SYME *Nine Yrs. Van Diemen's Land* 285 They pride themselves in being termed 'bricks', that is, because they do not flinch at the lash. **1853** C.R. READ *What I heard, saw, & Did* 132 He is only fined one pound, which the chap pulls out, gambling like fun, and abuses all the Commissioners like bricks. **1866** *Sydney Punch* 13 Jan. 687/1 How very hard headed both Scotch and Colonial 'bricks' are.

Hence **brickism** *n.*

1841 *Geelong Advertiser* 14 Aug. 2/4 *Midnight Marauders.*—We had hopes that this gang of mischievous youths had been broken up. . . If the police would only keep a sharp eye upon them for a few nights, and lay a few of them fast by heels, the spirit of 'brickism' would soon be broken.

brick, *n.*[2] *Obs.* [From the colour of the note.]

1. In gambling: a ten-pound note; ten pounds.

1914 A.B. PATERSON in C. Semmler *World of Banjo Paterson* (1967) 324 Pop it down, gents, if you don't put down a brick you can't pick up a castle! **1949** L. GLASSOP *Lucky Palmer* 103 'Lucky's' eyes lit up as he stared at the note in his hand. . . 'I don't feel lucky tonight. . . You give this brick a fly. Back the tail.' **1954** *Coast to Coast 1953–54* 175 You'll win a brick, matey. I can see y' know this game. **1967** A.E. DEBENHAM *All Manner of People* 89 The husband sold his new suit for £10 and put the 'brick' on the dead cert. **1976** S. WELLER *Bastards I have Met* 103 In gambling parlance, money-wise, 10's a 'brick', 100's a 'spot', 500's a 'monkey', etc.

2. In the phr. **London to a brick,** see quot. 1972.

1965 F. HARDY *Yarns of Billy Borker* 108 'Close: but Magger by a head,' the course announcer Ken Howard says, 'London to a brick on Magger.' **1972** *Bulletin* (Sydney) 8 Apr. 53/1 *A well-known* Sydney race caller has been heard to utter the phrase 'London to a brick', to describe the seemingly indisputable chances of certain horses at Royal Randwick. **1985** *Sydney Morning Herald* 10 Sept. 2/5 Mr Hayden invited the rebels to consider the fact that 'the moment they set foot in South Africa, it is London to a brick that Brisbane will have to kiss the Olympic Games goodbye'.

brick, *n.*[3]

1. *attrib.* In the collocation **brick area,** a residential area in which the houses are of brick or brick veneer, and which therefore has a certain social cachet.

1935 *Austral. Home Beautiful* July 28 The 'better class' suburbs have their brick areas in which no weather-board may show its face. **1958** F.B. VICKERS *Though Poppies Grow* 97, I blocked him turning One Tree into a brick area. He had a brick house so he thought everybody else ought to have one. **1981** B. HUMPHRIES *Nice Night's Entertainment* 4 It's a brick area, of course, and our neighbours are all a very nice type of person.

2. In the collocation **brick veneer.** Usu. hyphenated as *adj.*

a. *adj.* Of a house (or other small building): having external walls which consist of a timber frame faced with a single, non-structural skin of bricks (see quot. 1937).

1935 *Austral. Home Beautiful* July 22 The construction is brick veneer on timber frame with the rear portion in timber. **1937** *Building* (Sydney) 24 Apr. 35/1 A brick veneer job consists wholly of timber frame walls with an outer 4½ in. brick veneer external wall which is tied to the studs at intervals either with 8 in. lengths of 20 gauge 1¼ galvanised hoop iron bent strapping or by special No. 8 gauge galvanised wire ties with ends bent to form eyes and double nailed to the stud. **1951** D. COLLINS *Vic.'s my Home Ground* 103 Five generations have lived there, and the original house of pine logs had been encased in hundred-year-old homemade bricks. Surely our earliest example of brick veneer? **1980** I. WARDEN *Worst Of* 89 The Marquis de Sade would have languished unnoticed and uninspired in a brick-veneer bungalow in analgesic Rivett. **1983** *Canberra Chron.* 7 Sept. 1/2 Some of the fibro houses .. have been replaced with attractive brick-veneer government houses and some have been bought by tenants.

b. *n.* A house built with brick-veneer walls: see quot. 1977.

1968 *Swag* (Sydney) iii. 22/1 Our new ranch-style brick veneer in a little court in outer suburban Melbourne. **1977** P. ADAMS *Unspeakable Adams* 1 It's 1944 and I'm five years old, living with my grandparents in an old weatherboard in what has become a middle-class suburb of brick veneers with flouncy curtains. **1978** B. ST A. SMITH *Spirit beyond Psyche* 14 I'd be a Professional Man and would bring home lots of money and move into a brick-veneer. **1981** B. HUMPHRIES *Nice Night's Entertainment* 30 Where the cream brick veneers stay hygienic for years In Highett, the place of my dreams.

brickfielder. [f. the name of *Brickfield* Hill, a hill in what is now central Sydney where, until *c* 1850, there was a brickworks.]

1. *Hist.* In Sydney, a sudden squally wind from the south, bringing relief at the end of a hot day but sometimes characterized also by an accompanying dust-storm: see quot. 1835.

1829 *Sydney Monitor* 10 Oct. 2/6 On Monday last His Excellency and family were placed in considerable danger whilst sailing in consequence of a *brickfielder* coming on, which nearly capsized the boat. *Ibid.* 14 Nov. 2/6 During the *Brickfielder* (as these South-east hurricanes are vulgarly called). **1835** J. BACKHOUSE *Narr. Visit Austral. Colonies* (1843) 236 The thermometer rose to 100° in the shade. About two o'clock the wind rose, with violence, from the south east, and the temperature fell to 70°. It rained in the evening. This kind of wind has occurred a few times before, since our arrival: it is frequent in the summer, and coming upon the town from the direction of some old brickfields, has obtained the name of a Brick-fielder. It brings small pebbles pelting like rain, and clouds of red dust, formed, not however entirely from the brickfields, but also from the reddish sand and soil in the neighbourhood. This dust penetrates the houses, in spite of closed doors and windows, till it is seen upon everything, and may be felt grating between the teeth. **1837** *Colonist* (Sydney) 5 Jan. 3/1 The weather during the last week has been exceedingly sultry, on Tuesday the hot wind was most oppressive, and the day not having terminated with that usual and useful clearer of the atmosphere, a Brickfielder, the agreeable relief of a cool night was not experienced. **1845** D. MACKENZIE *Emigrant's Guide* 7 In Sydney and its neighbourhood there occasionally blows a hot wind, which continues for a few hours, and raises the thermometer sometimes to 120° Fahrenheit; but is almost invariably succeeded by what is here called 'a brickfielder', which is a strong southerly wind, which soon cools the air, and greatly reduces the temperature. **1846** *Citizen* (Sydney) 26 Dec. 139/1 Those you trusted have deceived you, Never more in them place trust—But drive them from their seats in Council As Brickfielders drive the dust. **1857** J. ASKEW *Voyage Aust. & N.Z.* 234 During summer, the southerly wind, or Brickfielder, as the Sydney people used to term it, is . . most annoying. It is now commonly styled the Southerly Burster. **1865** *Sydney Mail* 15 Apr. 9/1 So comes the Southern gale at evenfall (the swift 'Brickfielder' of the local folk). **1891** *Truth* (Sydney) 17 May 3/6 In upper Balmain dust storms rage which, if put in competition with 'a real old Brickfielder', would knock it out in one 'blow'. **1915** N. DUNCAN *Austral. Byways* 130 A southerly buster would blow—a Sydney brickfielder.

2. Elsewhere (but see quot. 1851) a hot wind, usu. from the north and accompanied by a dust-storm. Also *attrib.*

1840 A. RUSSELL *Tour through Austral. Colonies* 206 The hot winds are oppressive, particularly in the neighbourhood of the sandy districts so common here, and at Adelaide. These winds are generally termed *brickfielders.* **1847** *Maitland Mercury* 2 Oct. 2/6 The early part of the day was oppressively warm, and accompanied with hot winds, but towards five or six o'clock a storm set in from the north-west, which stirred up a regular brickfielder, and for a time eclipsed the town in dust. **1851** H. MELVILLE *Present State Aust.* 27 At Sydney, the . . soil in the immediate neighbourhood, westward of the city, is of a red colour, and when the wind blows from the interior it is, in consequence, called a 'brick-fielder'. **1861** 'OLD BUSHMAN' *Bush Wanderings* 231 In Melbourne a hot-windy day is called a 'brick-fielder', on account of the dust which darkens the sky. **1885** *Illustr. Austral. News* (Melbourne) 19 Dec. 218/2 *Riverina.* The feed has wholly disappeared; the soil, parched and browned by the almost vertical rays of the sun, becomes impalpable dust, which, when a brickfielder rages, rises in enormous volumes in the air not unlike a waterspout when seen from a distance, and is driven with the violence of a tornado before the wind. **1899** H. FURNISS *Austral. Sketches* 66 Melbourne is proud of its fine streets and its trams, Sydney of its harbour, but Adelaide 'blows' about nothing. Still Adelaide has its 'brick-fielder', which blows like all creation. **1909** LINDSAY & HOLTZE *Territoria* 7 Although during the wet season the atmosphere is humid and moist, inducing profuse perspiration, we do not consider it as unpleasant as the dry heat and 'brickfielders' experienced in South Australia during the same period. **1924** J. NISBET *Scraps* 4 'Let us get on,' said John; 'there's a brickfielder coming.' I was ignorant as to what he meant, but ere many minutes we were enveloped in thick red dust which darkened the air and filled one's eyes and nostrils. **1935** H.H. FINLAYSON *Red Centre* 21 'Brickfielder' dust-storms .. occasionally cloud the towns. **1950** J. MORRISON *Port of Call* 163 Nothing had cooled the heat from yesterday, and the deceptive little breeze stirring the curtains at the window had in it all the incipient menace of a Melbourne brickfielder. **1965** G. MCINNES *Road to Gundagai* 61 We started off with our first Melbourne summer. It was like living at the open door of an oven, and its instrument was the hot north wind or 'brickfielder'. **1975** X. HERBERT *Poor Fellow my Country* 1164 A battering nor'wester was blowing, a wind known locally as a Brickfielder, a name betraying how tenuous was the grasp of these people on the Continent they had presumed to have won.

brickie. [f. *brick(layer* + -Y. Used elsewhere but recorded earliest in Aust.] A bricklayer.

1900 *Tocsin* (Melbourne) 6 Sept. 5/2 On Monday I went along, accompanied only by the 'brickie'. **1912** *Truth* (Sydney) 1 Sept. 4/8 A deputation of brickies waited on our very own Preemeer Jim. **1933** 'TRAMWAY WORKERS' *Shock Brigader* 8 Being mid-winter, you can well imagine how the 'brickies' were 'kidded' on to nobler efforts by our chaps. **1942** *Bulletin* (Sydney) 18 Feb. 12/2 The boys on the job were arguing about a brickie who was supposed to be able to pick up four bricks with one hand. **1956** V. COURTNEY *All I may Tell* 106 For several years both of us were earning less than bricklayers' wages, although we worked much longer hours than any brickie. **1972** *Bulletin* (Sydney) 1 Jan. 39/2 Michael, probably in his early twenties, is a brickie's laborer who came to Sydney from Manchester four years ago. **1981** G. CROSS *George & Widda-Woman* 68 Up would go the barrow, as slow as a funeral train, until it reached the brickies, where it was unloaded. **1986** *Good Weekend* (Sydney) 1 Mar. 36/2, I worked for two days recently as a brickie's labourer but it was too hard.

bricklow, var. BRIGALOW.

bridled nail-tailed wallaby: see NAIL-TAILED WALLABY.

brigalow /ˈbrɪgəloʊ/. Formerly also **bricklow.** [Poss. a. Kamilaroi *burigal*.] Any of several trees of the genus *Acacia* (fam. Mimosaceae), esp. the N.S.W. and Qld. tree *A. harpophylla*, having a dark furrowed bark and silver foliage. Also *attrib.*

1844 L. LEICHHARDT *Jrnl. Overland Exped. Aust.* 8 Oct. (1847) 9 The Bricklow scrub compelled us frequently to travel upon the flood-bed of the river. **1848** T.L. MITCHELL *Jrnl. Exped. Tropical Aust.* 192, I found myself gradually entangled in a bad scrub of brigalow and rosewood. **1860** W.L. MORTON *Notes of Visit Northern District Qld.* 194 The peculiar shade of the brigalow scrub was but too plainly visible. **1880** J. BONWICK *Resources Qld.* 82 The Brigalow of good scrub soil is an acacia, and its timber is much used in building and fencing. **1884** *Once a Month* (Melbourne) Sept. 206 Briglow scrub (always called *bricklow* scrub by Dr Leichhardt, but spelt here according to what is believed to be the native pronunciation) is an acacia which differs from other varieties, as it produces no seeds. **1908** *Emu* VII. 188, I found a Jumper's nest in a small brigalow. **1918** C.E. BOSWORTH *Shoe & Leather Trade* 37 There is a large supply of *Acacia harpophylia* [*sic*], or Brigalow, which has a tannin content of 16–14 per cent. **1935** A. FRANCIS *Then & Now* 45 The brigalow .. grows in such profusion as completely to cover the land and render it useless for grazing... In times of great drought .. sheep and cattle will eat the leaves, which are cut down to keep the stock alive. **1944** C. FENNER *Mostly Austral.* 81 The brigalow wood has a violet-like perfume when fresh. **1952** *Bulletin* (Sydney) 21 Jan. 13/3, I was out in the brigalow country between the Ward and Langlo Rivers when the rain came. **1967** E. HUXLEY *Their Shining Eldorado* 342 Brigalow is only to be found in eastern Queensland, save for a little in the north of New South Wales... The brigalow is like the Hydra; no sooner do you fell one trunk than half a dozen .. spring up in its place. **1975** R. MACKLIN *Queenslander* 110 The branches of the brigalow were stiff and the black trunks as hard as iron.

brim, var. BREAM.

brindabella /brɪndəˈbɛlə/. [The name of a range of mountains, and (formerly) a sheep station, near Canberra.] See quot. 1959.

1959 *Bulletin* (Sydney) 23 Dec. 16/1 Most sheep-barbers either drink one or two bottles of beer between knocking-off and going in to tea or slap a brace of rums down. The last 'run' of the day is traditionally called 'The Rum Run'. Some go for the 'brindabella'—rum with a beer-chaser. **1962** *Ibid.* 3 Feb. 43/3 We oldies .. hit ourselves first up with a Brindabella—OP rum with a beer chaser.

brindle. [f. *brindle(d* of two colours.] A person of part-Aboriginal, part-white descent. Also *attrib.*

[**1905** *Truth* (Sydney) 16 July 5/5 The law of New South Wales deals with a white man found in an aborigines' camp, and while we have this colored cove business to deal with we should extend its provisions to all copper coons. We do not want a brindled Australia; we want it white.] **1934** C. SAYCE *Comboman* 20 There must have been fifty niggers all told at Kendal Station, counting the brindles. **1937** W. HATFIELD *I find Aust.* 286 We'll all turn out, every man-Jack of us, black, white and brindle. **1941** *Bulletin* (Sydney) 5 Nov. 14/1 At a church service at Alice Springs .. recently the white, black and brindle congregation didn't know at one stage of the service whether they should kneel or not. **1959** D. NILAND *Big Smoke* 30 The white women .. never drew the colour-line when the black or brindle had money to throw about. **1985** *Canberra Times* 5 Mar. 3/6 They cannot march alone... This is the same whether they're black, white or brindle. The rules are the rules.

bring, *v.* In the phr. **bring your own** (beer, wine, etc.), an intimation to patrons of an unlicensed restaurant that they may bring into the restaurant liquor purchased elsewhere. Also used adjectivally. See also B.Y.O.

1967 *This Week in Melbourne* 28 Jan. 13/3 The only French seafood restaurant in Melbourne La Bouillabaisse 1455 Malvern Road Glen Iris—20 3685 (Closed Mondays) Bring your own liquor. **1976** *Advertiser* (Adelaide) 19 July 4/8 Bring-your-own wine restaurants are the best thing that could happen to Adelaide with its fine wine areas so near. **1976** *Melbourne BYO's* (Consumers' Assoc. Vic.) 2 Victoria is fortunate and somewhat unique in having a large number of restaurants which have a 'bring-your-own' liquor permit.

brinny. [Prob. f. an Aboriginal language.] A stone, esp. one used by children for throwing as a missile.

1943 S.J. BAKER *Pop. Dict. Austral. Slang* (ed. 3) 14 *Brinny*, a stone. **1977** P. MOTHERWELL *Mr Bastard* 43 A devilish scheme clicks in my delighted brain and I slowly crouch to pick up two brinnies from the ground. **1979** *Age* (Melbourne) 2 July 9 You should have included 'brinny' and 'yonny' as synonyms for 'stone'. **1981** B. GREEN *Small Town Rising* 104 The copper's dog hadn't even been friendly though. 'How'd we kill him?' 'Toss a few brinnies at him, and when he comes out lay into him.'

Brisbane line. [f. the name of the capital city of Queensland.] See quot. 1943 (1).

[**1943** *West Austral.* (Perth) 3 May 2/4 The defence plan of Australia provided for all of Australia north of a line north of Brisbane and following a diagonal course to a point north of Adelaide to be abandoned to the enemy.] **1943** *Ibid.* 4 May 2/7 A military plan to defend Australia south of the 'Brisbane line'. **1946** *'Brisbane Line' Lie Exposed* (Austral. Country Party) 2 It was proposed, according to the Brisbane line plan, to abandon Western Australia without providing any adequate method of evacuation. **1971** *Bulletin* (Sydney) 2 Jan. 38/1 Anyone who tried to get a schoolboy excited about what the Brisbane Line controversy was all about would be no more successful than a schoolteacher who was trying to persuade his pupils that Hitler was not a wicked man. **1979** A.J. BURKE *Bite Pineapple* 36 Australian Army Chiefs were prepared to allow the Nips to occupy all of Queensland and also West Australia and Tasmania. The Australian Chiefs of Staff were undoubtedly in agreement that the cattle country north of Brisbane was to be surrendered. This was known as the Brisbane line. **1985** *Canberra Times* 5 Dec. 1/4 A new 'Brisbane Line' concept .. has been put up by the Australian Army.

bristlebird. Any of the three species of *Dasyornis*, brown ground birds having prominent bristles on the face, and restricted to certain coastal areas of mainland Aust. Also with distinguishing epithet, as **rufous, western** (see under first element).

1827 *Trans. Linnean Soc. London* XV. 232 [Dasyornis] Australis... This bird Mr Caley procured in a scrubby place on the north side of Paramatta [*sic*]... He calls it in his notes '*Bristle Bird*'. **1921** S.A. WHITE *Bunya* 79 On that bright morning the musical notes of the bristle bird .. could be heard. **1976** *Reader's Digest Compl. Bk. Austral. Birds* 422 The eastern bristlebird builds a dome-shaped nest close to the ground.

brittle gum. Any of several trees of the genus *Eucalyptus* (fam. Myrtaceae), having brittle timber, esp. *Eucalyptus mannifera* subsp. *maculosa* and *E. haemastoma* (see SNAPPY GUM).

1896 *Proc. Linnean Soc. N.S.W.* XXI. 451 *E. viminalis* .. known under several vernacular names such as .. 'Brittle Gum'. **1897** *Ibid.* XXII. (1898) 706 *E. haemastoma* var. *micrantha* .. usually goes under some name referring to the softness or brittleness of its timber, *e.g.* .. 'Brittle Gum'. **1932** R.H. ANDERSON *Trees of N.S.W.* 103 *Snappy Gum* .. also known as Scribbly Gum, Brittle Gum, and White Gum. **1967** N.A. WAKEFIELD *Naturalist's Diary* 26 The scattered trees were Long-leaf Box .. and Brittle Gum. **1983** *Canberra Chron.* 14 Sept. 18/1 The three species which form the canopy layer are .. brittle gum (*E. mannifera* ssp. *maculosa*) [etc.].

broad-leaved ironbark. The tree *Eucalyptus fibrosa* subsp. *fibrosa* (fam. Myrtaceae) of N.S.W. and Qld., bearing broad juvenile leaves. Also **broad-leaf ironbark, broad-leafed ironbark,** and *attrib.*

1861 J.D. LANG *Qld., Aust.* 277 It is generally covered with the broad or silver-leaved iron-bark tree. **1870** E.B. KENNEDY *Four Yrs. in Qld.* 32 Small *broad*-leaved ironbark .. denotes poor country; while silver-leaved ironbark .. shows good country. **1899** *Proc. Linnean Soc. N.S.W.* XXIV. *E[ucalyptus] siderophloia* .. var. *glauca* var. nov. This is the glaucous interior form of the species, which goes under the names of 'Blue-leaf Ironbark' .. and 'Broad-leaf Ironbark', in allusion to its broad sucker-leaves. **1963** C. BURGESS *Blue Mountain Gums* 56 *Broad-leaved ironbark* was described by Mueller in 1859.

broken, *ppl. a.* Of wool: see quot. 1950.

1880 J. BONWICK *Resources Qld.* 43 The proportion of broken wool, pieces, and locks. **1928** C.E. COWLEY *Classing Clip* 44 *Broken*, the largest and most bulky wool of good length, colour, and light condition. These portions will be the first trimmed to remove skirty ends, etc. **1950** H.G. BELSCHNER *Sheep Managem.* 692 *Broken*, a trade term applied to the best wool of the skirtings, having the characteristics of fleece wool.

broker. *Obs.* A bankrupt; one who is 'broke'.

1882 *Sydney Slang Dict.* 9 Dick's a broker, and has gone out snow-dropping. **1889** H. EGBERT *Pretty Cockey!* 134 When the drunkard becomes 'fly-blown', 'lambed down', 'a broker', or bankrupt, he is usually 'chucked out' to look for another job. **1890** *Truth* (Sydney) 28 Sept. 2/4 He soon learned that his claim had proved to be one of the greatest duffers that ever disgraced a diggings, and had landed him a broker. **1898** *Western Champion* (Barcaldine) 20 Dec. 13/2 He did well, but getting into fast company squandered his earnings and realised one morning that he was a 'broker'. **1915** 'ALPHA' *Reminisc. Goldfields* i. 73 Most of the boarders, who knew nothing about cards, would be found playing with others more skilful than themselves, and in due course became 'brokers'—their week's earnings gone and unable to pay their board and drink bill.

brolga /'brɒlgə/. [a. Kamilaroi *buralga.*] A large bird, the crane *Grus rubicundus,* living near water in e. and n. Aust. and in New Guinea; *native companion,* see NATIVE *a.* 6 b. Also *attrib.*

1896 *Westminster Gaz.* (London) 6 Oct. 2/1 The native companion crane, otherwise known as the brolga. **1897** K.L. PARKER *Austral. Legendary Tales* (ed. 2) 27 Paddymelons came in haste... After them .. came the Bralgahs. **1902** *Bulletin* (Sydney) 10 May 17/2 Brolgas are sold in numbers at the best poulterers' shops in Melbourne in the season. **1922** *Smith's Weekly* (Sydney) 5 Aug. 19/4 The Brolga dance was Binghi's conception of the frolicksome movements of the native companion. **1947** J.W. GORDON *Under Wide Skies* 40 The brolgas dance in stately grace, The jackass laughs a greeting. **1963** F. FLYNN *Northern Gateway* 214 The one-legged 'Four-o'clock stance' or 'Brolga pose' is typical of native men when standing at ease. **1979** D. LOCKWOOD *My Old Mates & I* 133 Galah, kangaroo and brolga figured prominently in their diet. One of them said of brolga, 'You could re-sole your boots with the breast meat.' **1986** *Courier-Mail* (Brisbane) 15 Jan. 1 The brolga .. was adopted by State Cabinet yesterday as the official bird emblem of Queensland.

brombie, var. BRUMBY.

brome. *Obs.* [Transf. use of *brome* a grass of the genus *Bromus.*] *Kangaroo grass* (a), see KANGAROO *n.* 5.

1827 *HRA* (1923) 3rd Ser. VI. 580 The brome or Kangaroo grass was here seen in great abundance. **1830** W.J. HOOKER *Bot. Miscellany* I. 229 Here I first observed the *Brome* or *Kangaroo grass* of New South Wales in great luxuriance. **1848** T.L. MITCHELL *Jrnl. Exped. Tropical Aust.* 61 There I also observed a brome grass, probably not distinct from the Bromus australis of Brown; it called to mind the squarrose brome grass of Europe.

broncho /'brɒŋkoʊ/, *n.* used *attrib.* [See *v.*]

1. Of or pertaining to the practice of roping cattle for branding, etc., while on horseback.

1932 J.J. HARDIE *Cattle Camp* (1944) 47 That's old Belle—she used to be a great broncho-mare. **1946** W.E. HARNEY *North of 23°* 39 On Coorabulka, the bronco system was in vogue.

2. Special Comb. **broncho bail, panel,** see quot. 1964; **yard,** a yard or set of yards in which a mob is held, esp. while calves are branded.

1964 *N. Austral. Monthly* Nov. 11/2 A **broncho bail** .. is a panel of stout fence... The focal point is the actual bail itself .. two posts, about a foot apart, stoutly built and firm in the ground. When the calf is roped it is dragged .. to the bail. The lassoo rope slides over the panel and runs along on top of that to slot between the two main posts. **1968** D. O'GRADY *Bottle of Sandwiches* 26 'Hear yer want some yards built... How much, an' what size?' 'Seventy quid each, hundred yards square, with a **bronco panel** in the guts.' **1976** C.D. MILLS *Hobble Chains & Greenhide* 104 You've got your yard, and your wing and your gate and your bronco-panel. What more do you want? **1977** W.A. WINTER-IRVING *Bush Stories* 13 There were cattle yards nearby and a bronco panel. **1923** F.A.C. BISHOP *Rep. on Inspection Barkly Tableland* 3 The improvements on Newcastle are few, and consist of—Two paddocks containing 8 miles of fencing, with the addition of a check fence extending through the gap over the Ashburton Range, and continuing on into the Downs country. There are two cattle yards, and two **broncho yards.** **1935** M. & E. DURACK *All-About* (1940) 64 The first event is the lubras' obstacle race. The course set through the broncho-yard over the killing-pen and out into the open. **1977** T. RONAN *Mighty Men on Horseback* 168 Not this new fashion rubbish broncho yard but properly post and rail drafting yards.

broncho /'brɒŋkoʊ/, *v.* Also **bronco.** [f. *bronco* unbroken horse.] *trans.* To rope (a calf, etc.), usu. for branding, while on horseback. Chiefly as *vbl. n.* Also *absol.*

1914 Austral. Archives CRS A3 Item 14/2576, All our boarding and herding is done in wire yards, making a small yard to broncho in. **1927** M. TERRY *Through Land of Promise* 230 The man who does the 'bronco-ing' (the local term for this roping of cattle, only found in the most bushy out-Bush stations) rides amongst the mob. **1932** J.J. HARDIE *Cattle Camp* (1944) 47 Sometimes it's too far to drive the calves to a yard to brand them, so they hold the mob on a level piece of ground, and a couple of the boys on steady horses ride through them, rope the unbranded calves and drag them to the fire, where they're thrown and branded. They call that 'bronchoing'. **1937** C. WARBURTON *White Poppies* 152 For years they had endeavoured to quieten their herd by constant handling and yarding. 'Broncoing', as this method of roping and branding a calf was termed, frightened the beasts and made them unmanageable. **1945** F. CORK *Tales from Cattle Country* 28 It takes two men to broncho a calf, and so rapidly and deftly is it done that to the onlooker it appears easy. **1964** *N. Austral. Monthly* Nov. 11 'Bronchoing' .. is the job of lassoing calves from horseback, pulling them to a branding place, throwing them there, doing the necessary jobs, letting them go while the rider returns to the mob to rope another calf.

bronze. The anus; the backside. Also **bronza, bronzo.**

1953 S.J. BAKER *Aust. Speaks* 105 *Bronzo,* anus (a variation of *bronze,* used similarly). **1957** D. NILAND *Call me when Cross turns Over* 139, I know the one with the ugly face like a handful of bronzas. Who's the other? **1959** —— *Big Smoke* 164 He roared laughing and gave her a slap on the seat. 'The biggest bronza in the world—and just think, you're all mine.' **1975** L. RYAN *Shearers* 104 Go and sit on your bronze while we give scabs your jobs. **1982** *Austral.* (Sydney) 25 Nov. 10/2 In the age of innocence (1953), we fell about at the lines: 'There's rust on me bust and me bronze is all tarnished.'

bronze cuckoo. Any of several species of cuckoo in the genus *Chrysococcyx,* having more or less bronze-coloured feathers on various parts of the body and occurring in Aust. and nearby regions.

1841 J. GOULD *Birds of Aust.* (1848) III. Pl. 18, The female [Blue Wren] .. is also the foster-parent of the Bronze Cuckoo (*Chalcites lucidus*), a single egg of which species is frequently found deposited in her nest. **1847** *Ibid.* IV. Pl. 89, *Chrysococcyx lucidus.* Shining Cuckoo... Golden or Bronze Cuckoo of the Colonists. **1860** G. BENNETT *Gatherings of Naturalist* 209 The note of the Shining or Bronze Cuckoo is an exceedingly melancholy whistle. **1949** B. O'REILLY *Green Mountains* 50 The bronze cuckoos commenced their pre-dawn wailing. **1970** K.E.C. GRAVES *Third Chance* 109 When it flew across the river he saw the shining green back and the checked brown and white breast of a bronze cuckoo. **1976** *Reader's Digest Compl. Bk. Austral. Birds* 299 The little bronze cuckoo and the rufous-breasted bronze cuckoo are separated from other Australian bronze cuckoos by their small size and red around the male's eye.

bronze-wing. a. Any of several pigeons having bronze-coloured markings on the wings, esp. the common bronze-wing, *Phaps chalcoptera,* widespread in Aust., and the *brush bronze-wing* (see BRUSH *n.*[1] B. 2); also **bronze-wing(ed) pigeon. b.** *fig.* A person of part-Aboriginal, part-white descent (see quot. 1956).

1789 A. PHILLIP *Voyage to Botany Bay* 162 Bronze-winged Pigeon... The greater [*sc.* coverts] .. have each of them a large oval spot of bronze. **1801** J. LATHAM *Gen. Synopsis Birds* Suppl. II. 266 Bronze-winged P[igeon]... The name it is known by, in *New Holland,* is *Goad-gang,* and by the *English, Ground Pigeon,* being unable to take long flights, and seen chiefly on the ground or low trees; called by some also *Brush Pigeon.* **1827** P. CUNNINGHAM *Two Yrs. in N.S.W.* I. 321 We have .. two varieties of our beautiful *bronze winged pigeons,* the *crested pigeon* of Illawarra, and the *large green pigeon* of Port Macquarie. **1834** G. BENNETT *Wanderings N.S.W.* I. 164 The more gentle 'Bronze-winged pigeons' (*Columba chalcoptera*) were also very numerous .. unmindful of the near approach of the horses. **1843** J. GOULD *Birds of Aust.* (1848) V. Pl. 64, Although .. the Bronze-wing is an excellent article of food, it must yield the palm in this respect to .. the Partridge Bronze-wing (*Geophaps scripta*), whose flesh is white and more delicate in flavour. **1857** *Illustr. Jrnl. Australasia* III. 196 The mournful cooing of the bronze-winged pigeon is heard, as he woos his mate with every antic and gesture of love. **1881** C.F. CHUBB *Fugitive Pieces* 18 Back to their forest homes, erst the abode of the bronzewing and the bunyip. **1905** A.B. PATERSON *Old Bush Songs* 66 Oh! had I the flight of the bronzewing, Far o'er the plains would I fly. **1935** DAVISON & NICHOLLS *Blue Coast Caravan* 271 A pair of bronzewing pigeons—cinnamon brown with wings of iridescent green. **1956** T. RONAN *Moleskin Midas* 161 If there is a few bronzewings being born about my place there's nearly as much chance of your being their daddy as me. The blacks reckon that since your hoppy leg keeps you from riding colts you seem to make up for it with the fillies. **1962** H.J. FRITH *Mallee-Fowl* 53 A bronzewing pigeon will explode from a shrub. **1981** A.B. FACEY *Fortunate Life* 90 The bronze-winged pigeon lived on seeds and such like and was good to eat—it was half the size of a chicken.

bronzo, var. BRONZE.

brook. Used as elsewhere of a stream. Now, exc. in W.A., generally superseded by CREEK. Also *attrib.*

1770 G.W. ANDERSON *New Collection Voyages* 22 Aug. (1784) 70 There are several salt creeks, running in many directions through the country, where there are also brooks of fresh water, but there are no rivers of any considerable extent. **1790** J. HUNTER *Hist. Jrnl. Trans. Port Jackson* (1793) 403 On the opposite side of the brook there is a farm-house. **1820** J. OXLEY *Jrnls. Two Exped. N.S.W.* 291 This valley was watered by a fine brook. **1839** W.H. LEIGH *Reconnoitering Voyages* 140 The River Torrens is an unnavigable country brook. **1851** *Australasian* (Melbourne) 469 The brook .. runs over a rocky bed through a pretty wooded dell. **1874** J.J. HALCOMBE *Emigrant & Heathen* 33 On the opposite side of the brook was an unfinished stone church. **1882** ARMSTRONG & CAMPBELL *Austral. Sheep Husbandry* 164 The rule that all wools shall be washed, or subjected to a deduction of one-third, to put them on a par with brook-washed wools, operates very unequally. **1897** *Bulletin* (Sydney) 24 July 11/1 In Westralia .. they call their employer 'the master', a creek a 'brook', an overseer a 'foreman'. **1902** *Emu* II. 73 The dense thickets on the coastal brooks. **1928** J. POLLARD *Bushland Vagabonds* 238 The fruit-shed of jarrah slabs among the apple-trees had historic interest in that it was formerly a flour-mill worked by the brook. **1940** *Bulletin* (Sydney) 17 July 17/2 In Eastern Australia a 'creek' is any stream too small to be called a river. In the West such streams are properly called brooks, and dozens of examples could be quoted.

broom. [Transf. use of *broom,* as applied to shrubs of the genera *Cytisus* and *Genista.*]

1. The name is used in Aust. both for several naturalized European species of broom and for any of several native broom-like shrubs, esp. *Viminaria juncea* (fam. Fabaceae), which has long, wiry, apparently leafless branchlets and yellow flowers.

1841 *S. Austral. Mag.* Oct. 123 The strata of the banks, through which it [*sc.* the Torrens] directs its course, are usually composed of a clayey or marlish substance, in many places ornamented with the native broom, and myrtle, or honeysuckle. **1882** G.F. MOORE *Diary Ten Yrs. W.A.* 14 Sept. (1884) 133 Mahogany is indicative of sandy land .. and the broom and dwarf grass tree, of what we term *shrubby herbage.* **1888** *Proc. Linnean Soc. N.S.W.* III. 385 *Melaleuca uncinata...* One of the common 'Tea-trees'. (Called 'Broom' in South Australia, according to Mr Tepper). **1929** I.A. SCOULER *Dowerin Story* 6 The heavy land is thickly timbered .. interspersed with .. broom. **1955** 'M. HILL' *Land nearest Stars* 173 In addition to wattle there was the soft yellow broom in profusion.

2. Special Comb. **broom-bush,** any of several shrubs, esp. *Templetonia egena* (fam. Fabaceae) and *Melaleuca uncinata* (fam. Myrtaceae); also *attrib.*

1883 F. BONNEY *On Some Customs Aborigines* 5 The root of broom-bushes (*poontee*). **1911** *Emu* XI. 111 Patches of broom-bush country relieved the monotony. **1962** H.J. FRITH *Mallee-Fowl* 24 In some types of vegetation, including broom-bush, the bushes grow closely and shed large numbers of very small leaves, so that the ground is covered by a fairly deep layer. **1977** J. DOUGHTY *Gold in Blood* 80 Thatched it with broom-bush, making it rain proof except in the heaviest of downpours. **1981** L. COSTERMANS *Native Trees & Shrubs S.-E. Aust.* 196 *Templetonia egena* Round Templetonia, Broombush (NSW).

broomie. *Shearing.* [f. *broom* + -Y.] One employed to sweep in a shearing shed: see quot. 1915.

1895 *Bulletin* (Sydney) 13 July 23/3 There's the flying hurry-scurry up and down the greasy floors Of the pickers and the broomies; there's the banging of the doors. **1915** *Ibid.* 28 Oct. 22/3 The 'broomie' is the 'blue-tongue' who sweeps the board free of locks, etc. **1948** R. Raven-Hart *Canoe in Aust.* 56 The sweepers, the 'broomies' (who deal with the floor-locks and the bellies). **1975** L. Ryan *Shearers* 142 That stupid broomie . . oh, Gawd! . . what a scream. **1982** P. Adam Smith *Shearers* 151 As old Ray Watley, a shearer of the 1920s, says, 'By the time a Broomie reaches town with a few bob in his pocket he's a gun shearer!'

brother colonist. *Hist.* A resident of an Australian Colony other than that in which the speaker resides. Cf. Sister.

1834 *Hobart Town Mag.* May 115 Why should not we be allowed the privilege of a ten years' purchase, like our brother-Colonists of New South Wales? **1838** *Colonist* (Sydney) 7 Apr. 2/4 Our brother colonists of South Australia have got this important requisite already. **1840** *S. Austral. Rec.* (London) 25 July 54 In the year 1831 Tasmanian wool-growers were enabled to export 20,000 lbs. more wool than their brother colonists in the senior settlement of New South Wales. **1845** *Atlas* (Sydney) I. 323/1 It seems a strange accusation to bring against our brother colonists of Port Phillip.

brown, *a.* and *n.* [Spec. use of *brown* the colour.]

A. *adj.*

1. Used as a distinguishing epithet in the names of flora and fauna: **brown barrel,** the timber tree of e. N.S.W. and n.e. Vic. *Eucalyptus fastigata* (fam. Myrtaceae) which has a brown fibrous bark on the trunk; see also Cut tail 1; **bittern,** Boomer *n.*[2]; **flycatcher,** *Jacky Winter*, see Jacky *n.*[2]; **gannet,** the large seabird *Sula leucogaster* of n. Aust. and other tropical regions; **goshawk,** the hawk *Accipiter fasciatus*, found throughout Aust. and in neighbouring areas, having predominantly brown plumage; **hawk,** the falcon *Falco berigora*, having pale or dark brown upperparts, and found throughout Aust. and in New Guinea and nearby islands; *orange-speckled hawk*, see Orange; **-headed honeyeater,** the honeyeater *Melithreptus brevirostris* of s. Aust., having a grey-brown head and pale line across the nape; **honeyeater,** the honeyeater *Lichmera indistincta* of tropical woodland, a summer visitor to s.w. and s.e. Aust., having brown upperparts; **pigeon,** the pigeon *Macropygia amboinensis* of rainforests in coastal Aust., and n. to the Philippines, having brown upperparts; *pheasant-tailed pigeon*, see Pheasant 2; **quail,** the plump bird *Coturnix ypsilophora* of grassland and swamps in Aust., New Guinea, and nearby islands; *swamp quail*, see Swamp *n.*; see also Partridge; **snake,** any of several more or less brown snakes, esp. the venomous *Pseudonaja textilis* of e. Aust. and New Guinea and *P. nuchalis* of central and w. Aust.; see also *western brown snake* Western; **song-lark,** the widespread brown bird *Cincloramphus cruralis*; **thornbill** (or **tit**), the small bird *Acanthiza pusilla* of s.e. Aust., having a pale brown body with red-brown feathers on the head and tail; **treecreeper,** the grey-brown tree-climbing bird *Climacteris picumnus* of e. Aust.; **warbler,** the small brown-backed bird *Gerygone mouki* of forests in coastal e. Aust.

1896 *Proc. Linnean Soc. N.S.W.* XXI. 810 '**Brown-barrel**' at Queanbeyan. **1956** R.H. Anderson *Trees of N.S.W.* (ed. 3) 121 *Brown barrel* . . (Also known as . . Blackbutt, and Cut Tail.) **1970** N. Hall et al. *Forest Trees Aust.* 180 Brown barrel is a moderately large tree. **1986** *Sydney Morning Herald* 22 Feb. 11/5 The Coolangubra forest with its brown barrel . . and swamp gum trees spearing straight to the skies compares with many of the North Coast rainforests. **1945** C. Barrett *Austral. Bird Life* 55 'Bunyip-bird' and 'bull bird' are nicknames for the large **brown bittern.** **1976** *Reader's Digest Compl. Bk. Austral. Birds* 85 In size, voice, habits and habitat the Australian brown bittern is virtually identical to the bittern *Botaurus stellaris* of Eurasia and South Africa. **1845** J. Gould *Birds of Aust.* (1848) II. Pl. 94, *Microeca flavigaster*. . . **Brown Flycatcher,** Residents at Port Essington. **1917** *Bulletin* (Sydney) 23 Aug. 22/2 Some appropriate names bestowed by the white pfella are . . Peter Peter (the brown fly-catcher) [etc.]. **1929** A.H. Chisholm *Birds & Green Places* 203 The chanting Jacky Winter, or brown flycatcher. **1846** J. Gould *Birds of Aust.* (1848) III. Pl. 78, *Sula fusca*. . . **Brown Gannet** . . Brown Booby . . *Booby*, of the Colonists. **1890** G.J. Broinowski *Birds of Aust.* I. Pl. 6, Travellers have often seen the Brown Gannet kept as a pet, and allowed perfect freedom, in the native villages on the islands and coasts which it inhabits. **1955** V. Serventy *Aust.'s Great Barrier Reef* 56 Gannets or Boobies are also common in the area. The best known is the Brown Gannet. **1968** R. Hill *Bush Quest* 81 Gos was a young **Brown goshawk.** **1977** *Ecos* xi. 21/2 A brown goshawk travelled 900 km in 7 months. **1777** G.W. Anderson *New Collection Voyages* (1784) 426 The principal sorts of birds are **brown hawks** or eagles. **1844** J. Gould *Birds of Aust.* (1848) I. Pl. 11, *Ieracidea berigora*. . . Berigora, Aborigines of New South Wales. . . Brown Hawk, Colonists of Van Diemen's Land. **1935** H. Basedow *Knights of Boomerang* 68 They lost many of the fish . . owing to the daring of a swarm of brown hawks, which swooped upon them almost as fast as they were thrown on to the land. **1968** R. Hill *Bush Quest* 28 Brown hawks were common, sitting on the fence posts and hunting over the paddocks. **1900** A.J. Campbell *Nests & Eggs Austral. Birds* 365 *Melithreptus brevirostris*. . . We found **Brown-headed Honeyeaters** somewhat numerous. **1932** A.H. Chisholm *Nature Fantasy in Aust.* 185 Walking recently in a patch of casuarinas I saw a pair of brown-headed honeyeaters and a pair of yellow-faced honeyeaters dancing attendance on a pallid cuckoo. **1976** *Reader's Digest Compl. Bk. Austral. Birds* 491 (*caption*) The brown-headed honeyeater builds its small cup-shaped nest of bark, grass and spiderweb in the outer foliage. **1846** J. Gould *Birds of Aust.* (1848) IV. Pl. 31, *Glyciphila ocularis*. . . **Brown Honey-eater**. . . Brown Honeysucker of the Colonists. **1896** B. Spencer *Rep. Horn Sci. Exped. Central Aust.* II. 93 Brown honey-eater[s] . . are very plentiful in the stunted mallee and acacias at Davenport Creek. **1964** M. Sharland *Territory of Birds* 185 First came the notes of a Brown Honeyeater, hesitant and tentative, as though it were not fully awake. **1917** *Bulletin* (Sydney) 9 Aug. 24/4 Guess he hasn't tasted the green-pigeon, which . . excels the wonga as the latter excels the **brown-pigeon.** **1976** *Reader's Digest Compl. Bk. Austral. Birds* 234 Widespread clearing of rainforest and illegal hunting have resulted in a decline of the brown pigeon. **1843** J. Gould *Birds of Aust.* (1848) V. Pl. 89, *Synoicus australis*. Australian Partridge. . . New Holland Quail. . . **Brown Quail**, Colonists of Swan River and Van Diemen's Land. **1903** *Emu* II. 155 (Brown Quail). . . These birds are plentiful in the Northern Territory. **1980** C. Allison *Hunter's Man. Aust. & N.Z.* 130 Brown quail populations have decreased somewhat alarmingly. **1805** *Sydney Gaz.* 13 Jan., A **brown snake** was killed a few days ago on the Blackwattle Swamp. **1827** P. Cunningham *Two Yrs. in N.S.W.* I. 332 Our two most venomous snakes, the brown and black, appear to me to be male and female, as I have twice met them lying very suspiciously coiled up together. **1841** *Geelong Advertiser* 3 Apr. 3/1 He was bit by a snake of the most dangerous kind (the brown snake). **1867** J.R. Houlding *Austral. Capers* 228, I hate them worse than brown snakes or deaf adders. **1880** *Bulletin* (Sydney) 21 Feb. 4/2 Near Gayndah, Queensland, recently, a brown snake crawled up the arm of a coach passenger. **1976** E. Worrell *Things that Sting* 13 There are several Brown Snake species in Australia. . . The largest variety, the Common Brown Snake, grows to just over two metres. **1898** E.E. Morris *Austral Eng.* 259 **Brown Song Lark**—*Cincloramphus cruralis*. **1900** A.J. Campbell *Nests & Eggs Austral. Birds* 277 The Black-breasted or Brown Song Lark appears partial to grassy plains. **1976** *Reader's Digest Compl. Bk. Austral. Birds* 407 (*caption*) The brown song lark lives on vast open plains. **1984** E. Rolls *Celebration of Senses* 17 The male Brown Songlark with his harem of six or seven half-sized females ignores everything but himself. [**1844 brown thornbill:** J. Gould *Birds of Aust.* (1848) III. Pl. 54, *Acanthiza diemenensis*. . . Brown-tail, Colonists of Van Diemen's Land.] **1900** A.J. Campbell *Nests & Eggs Austral. Birds* 230 *Brown tit* . . is an active little bird. . . Some recent authors use the term Thornbill—a name already applied to a number of Humming Birds—as a vernacular name for the Acanthizas. **1945** C. Barrett *Austral. Bird Life* 186 The brown thornbill . . and the striated thornbill . . are common birds of the bush. **1976** *Reader's Digest Compl. Bk. Austral. Birds* 435 Cuckoos often use the brown thornbill as a host. **1841** J. Gould *Birds of Aust.* (1848) IV. Pl. 93, *Climacteris scandens*. . . **Brown Tree-Creeper.** **1912** *Emu* XII. 116 Brown Tree-creeper. . . Note similar to the English Chaffinch. **1976** *Reader's Digest Compl. Bk. Austral. Birds* 456 The loud ringing cries of the brown treecreeper are commonly heard in eucalypt woodland over much of eastern Australia. **1929** A.H. Chisholm *Birds & Green Places* 32 When thinking of jungle choristers generally I think chiefly of scrub-wrens, shrike-thrushes, flycatchers and robins, golden-breasted whistlers and **brown warblers.** **1956** A.C.C. Lock *Tropical Tapestry* 279 The exquisite notes of a brown warbler.

2. In the collocation **brown bomber** *N.S.W.*, an officer employed to police parking regulations; also *attrib.*

1953 *Sydney Morning Herald* 3 Jan. 6/2 The year produced many slang words. Some of them were inherited from previous years but acquired wide usage in the past 12 months. . . 'Brown bombers', Sydney parking police, probably derived from the colour of their uniforms and influenced by the use of 'bomb' for an old car. **1954** *Sun* (Sydney) 8 June 1/7 New name for the Brown Bomber boys is Walkie-Chalkies. **1964** *Oz* (Sydney) June 4/1 In Melbourne, they are known as Traffic Officers; in Sydney, as Brown Bombers, and the world over as those little bastards who materialise out of thin air to book your car the moment your back is turned. **1971** *Kings Cross Whisper* (Sydney) civ. 11/2 One of Sydney's most hated Brown Bombers is a well-known female impersonator. When he's not happily booking motorists, he's on stage in drag. **1985** *Bulletin* (Sydney) 24 Dec. 10/2 In a poll of what vexed motorists most, the hat-wearing male driver was listed third, behind only radar cops and brown bombers.

B. *n. Obs.* A penny.

[**1812** J.H. Vaux *Flash Dict.* (1819) II. 159 Browns and whistlers, bad halfpence and farthings.] **1845** *Parramatta Chron.* 15 Mar. 2/1 The charged was not only descanting most learnedly on the evolution and revolutions of 'three up' and with upturned eyes and outstretched body intently watching the fall of some 'Browns', but had just given tongue to an expressive predilection for *heads*, when Fox laid him by the *heels*. **1853** J. Sherer *Gold Finder Aust.* 22, I never saw anything in the shape o' money but whites and browns (silver and copper). **1869** *Colonial Soc.* (Sydney) 14 Jan. 5 My temp'rance pledge, alas! I broke—In beer I spend each brown. **1885** *Australasian Printers' Keepsake* 24 *We found no change in him*—no, not a brown. **1891** 'Smiler' *Wanderings Simple Child* 10 Upon this were placed a couple of 'browns', as the pennies were called by the aesthetic circle. **1919** *Smith's Weekly* (Sydney) 15 Mar. 15/2 The humble brown is a token that signifies a wide divergence between the city boy and the bush boy. The city boy is always on the lookout for a penny. **1946** F. Clune *Try Nothing Twice* 67 'Without a single brown' was the truth as far as I was concerned, as I had spent Mum's twopence on an apple.

brownie, *n.*[1] Also **browny.** [f. *brown* + -Y.]

1. A sweetened currant bread.

1883 J.E. Partington *Random Rot* 312 It was an amusing sight to see the three of us, each with a huge hunch of 'browny' (bread sweetened with brown sugar and currants) in one hand. **1889** H. Egbert *Pretty Cockey* 80 Some would munch a bit of 'browny' with their beverage. This was a species of cake or sweetened loaf, by no means nasty. **1899** R. Semon *In Austral. Bush* 66 We even baked a sort of cake on particularly festive occasions, the 'Browny' or 'Johnny cake' of the Australians. Its production is based on the same principle as that of the damper, but the dough is made rich by adding some sugar, suet, and, if possible, some currants and raisins. **1911** E.S. Sorenson *Life Austral. Backblocks* 86 The brownie (which is simply a damper with currants and sugar added) is placed in the naked ashes. **1925** M. Terry *Across Unknown Aust.* 52 To partake of 'smoko' (morning tea), about 9.30—just a mug of tea and some 'brownie'. The latter is a kind of currant and raisin loaf. **1937** D. Gunn *Links with Past* 138 On Sundays . . they got doughboys with black sugar, and vinegar spread over them; and they had no brownies for smoke-ohs. **1954** T. Ronan *Vision Splendid* 42 On the alternate nights when one of the ovens contained an eggless, but still very appetizing cake mixture called 'brownie', which required longer and more careful cooking, Jack would always ask, 'Is she a puddin', Marty, or is she a cake?' **1963** M. Britt *Pardon my Boots* 112 Most of the male cooks made brownies (utility cakes) in huge meat roasting tins to last the week. 'It's me busy day today. I'm making me brownies.' **1978** M. Walker *Pioneer Crafts Early Aust.* 151 Cooking for shearers was testing work for the self-opinionated connoisseurs of damper, meat, 'dough boys', Johnnie cakes, brownies (simply damper with sugar and currants) were harsh critics.

2. Special Comb. **brownie gorger,** see quot. 1982.

1939 *Bulletin* (Sydney) 26 Apr. 20/4 We were shearing out Hungerford way. Joe was one of the 'brownie gorgers'. **1982** P. ADAM SMITH *Shearers* 403 *Brownie gorger*, hungry shed-hands (usually young boys with big appetites).

brownie, *n.*[2] [f. BROWN *n.* + -Y.] A penny.

1899 *Western Champion* (Barcaldine) 13 June 7/4 To shoot at my 'headpiece' with ordinary, common, low-down 'brownies' (coppers) is a bit too stiff. **1903** *Truth* (Sydney) 18 Jan. 4/7 Bad Bill's boy bought a brownie's worth of ice cream from a monkey-faced Dago. **1938** F. BLAKELEY *Hard Liberty* 29 He took me to a big two-up school, and . . there was Scram, spinning the pennies. . . He smiled at me. 'Hard luck, Fatty! The brownies went against me.' **1951** CUSACK & JAMES *Come in Spinner* 7 'Two-up.' . . 'It's the great Australian pastime . . just a matter of spinning a couple of brownies.'

bruce auction. [Prob. f. the name of John Vans Agnew *Bruce* (1822–1863), construction contractor and philanthropist.] An auction of donated goods, the proceeds which are dedicated to a charitable cause; used esp. in church fund-raising. Also *transf.* (see quot. 1959).

1868 *Yass Courier* 1 Dec. 2/4 Blessed be the name of Bruce—the Bruce of Victoria (now in his grave) who invented the description of auction to which his name is irrevocably linked. How many struggling communities have been relieved from embarrassment by his means that might otherwise have languished under a load of debt. How else could the Wagga Wagga Presbyterians have raised the magnificent sum of £700 to build a church, but by means of a Bruce auction. Honour to the memory of Bruce who discovered the secret of combining business with pleasure. **1868** *Christian Herald* Dec. 146/2 Monday, the 30th November, was the day appointed for holding a bazaar and Bruce auction for the purpose of extinguishing the debt still due on St. Andrew's Church, in this town [*sc.* Yass]. **1878** *Austral. Churchman* (Sydney) 23 May 561/2 On Thursday May 2nd a very successful Bruce auction and tea-meeting was held to raise funds for fencing in the Church ground . . nearly fifty persons having given donations to the Bruce auction. **1880** *Express* (Sydney) 8 May 6/6 The bazaar, luncheon, bruce auction, and athletic sports, lately held, have realised this sum and a few odd pounds besides. **1899** *North-Western Advocate* (Devonport) 12 Apr. 2/6 The evening's proceedings concluded with a Bruce auction, at which the fruit and vegetables used for decoration purposes . . were disposed of. **1903** *Bulletin* (Sydney) 28 Feb. 15/1 A Bruce Auction is proposed in aid of N.S.W. drought victims. **1911** *Huon Times* (Franklin) 7 Jan. 3/6 Councillor Harris—I think, Mr Warden, this matter is being carried too far. It is practically being put up by bruce auction. **1959** *Southern Mail* (Bowral) 14 May, A famous annual event was the 'Bruce Auction' . . held by the late George Lake at his barber and tobacconist shop every New Year's Eve. . . This auction did not require a licensed auctioneer. George himself offered the goods at a certain price which came down if there were no takers, until a price was reached satisfactory to both seller and buyer. He would offer a job lot comprising a cherrywood pipe, plug of tobacco and a box of matches, or such like bundle, and cleared off a lot of stock.

brum. Abbrev. of BRUMBY.

1936 J.C. DOWNIE *Galloping Hoofs* 102 This is goin' to be a 'dinkum nark' of a 'brum', and I reckon I'll take it out of 'im, and ride 'im till he quits. **1951** *Bulletin* (Sydney) 16 May 12/3 Some well-meaning railway official had unloaded the brums into the cattle-yard for a drink. **1955** STEWART & KEESING *Austral. Bush Ballads* 195 They stared to see him stick aloft—The brum. bucked fierce and free.

brumby /ˈbrʌmbi/. Also **brombie, brumbie, brummy.** [Of unknown origin.]

1. A wild horse.

1880 *Australasian* (Melbourne) 4 Dec. 712/3 Passing through a belt of mulga, we saw, on reaching its edge, a mob of horses grazing on the plains beyond. These our guide pronounced to be 'brumbies', the bush name here [*sc.* Qld.] for wild horses. **1885** *Once a Month* (Melbourne) Jan. 53, I came to the conclusion that he was a 'Brummy'—the New South Wales name for wild horses. **1889** *Illustr. Austral. News* (Melbourne) 9 Nov. 18/4 When 'brumbies' become a nuisance they are usually run into a yard and the stallions shot, any of the rest that are of any use being sent to market and sold. **1896** *Bulletin* (Sydney) 21 Mar. 27/4 'Brumby' . . is derived, writes a Bulletin correspondent, from Baramba, the name of a creek and station in the Burnett district of Queensland. In the early 40's this . . station was formed, and a choice lot of mares with three or four stallions were sent to stock the place. . . The total abandonment of the station and most of the stock . . occurred within two or three years. It was from the remnants of this stud that the wild horses on the Lower Burnett and the head of the Brisbane descended from being the 'Baramba horses', got by easy stages to be called 'Barambas', and finally 'Brumbies'. **1913** *Ibid.* 24 Apr. 13/2 The brumbies were yarded by stratagem and hard riding. **1920** *Ibid.* 24 June 20/2 A brumby (no unbranded cove under seven years old merits the term) is a grown horse and hits the ground much harder than a 'green' thing. **1935** M. GILMORE *More Recoll.* 13 Australia first called the wild horses warrigals from the black tribes of Warri, and then brumbies, the latter name said to have been derived from a Mr Brumby (or was it Bromby?) who lived in Tasmania. **1947** *Bulletin* (Sydney) 13 Aug. 28/3 The word 'brumby' . . comes from Captain (or Major) Brumby, who had a reputation as a horsebreeder in the early part of last century. . . The other—and less-likely—origin is the abo. word booramby. **1968** LINKLATER & TAPP *Gather No Moss* 87 Today, we hear that the brumbies are bad in the north, and there is a suggestion that a bonus should be paid for every pair of ears brought in. **1977** *Ecos* xiii. 13/3 Brumbies usually exist in scattered mobs consisting of a stallion and 6–15 mares. **1986** *Star Weekly* (Canberra) 10 Apr. 6/2 Authorities are monitoring the brumbies and are concerned with the damage they are inflicting on the native habitat.

2. A (partially) tamed wild horse (see quot. 1948); a worn-out or ill-bred horse.

1891 T. BATEMAN *Valley Council* 4 Five of my station hands, a motley crew, horsed on brumbies, as we call our unbroken half-wild horses. **1898** D.W. CARNEGIE *Spinifex & Sand* 15, I would ride into Coolgardie . . our faithful little chestnut 'brumby', *i.e.*, half-wild pony, of which there are large herds running in the bush near the settled parts of the coast. **1915** *Bulletin* (Sydney) 22 July 24/3 He climbed up on the brumby again and leathered old Daisy home in No. 1 Australian style. **1943** *Coast to Coast 1942* 106 The bottle-o winked to himself and urged his lean brown horse on with a 'Git up, can't yer, yer brumby.' **1948** M. UREN *Glint of Gold* 105 They purchased a spring cart and two hardy brumbies. . . A bush horse of questionable breeding and ownership which, because of its hard life spent in the bush, was much in demand by prospecting parties. **1969** B. GARLAND *Pitt Street Prospector* 115 The old blokes used to go out and round up the cattle bare-back, on a brumby.

3. *transf.* and *fig.* Also *attrib.*, passing into *adj.*

1890 *Truth* (Sydney) 16 Nov. 4/5 It is wonderful to witness the number of sky-pilots, devil-dodgers and brumby parsons who visit the House. **1903** *Ibid.* 8 Mar. 4/2 A few flat-chested, flat-footed female brumbies can't supply the place of the splendid breed sprung from Eden's stock. **1911** ST. C. GRONDONA *Collar & Cuffs* 98 They were a brumbie lot of rotters, all swagmen, and to all appearance at least, considerably down on their uppers. **1921** *Aussie* (Sydney) Nov. 21/1 I've just started in to fence my new selection in the scrub, All unbroken, brumby mallee, limestone ridge, an' loam an' sand. **1925** M. TERRY *Across Unknown Aust.* 121 Taken part in a brumbie (wild) bull hunt. **1926** *Bulletin* (Sydney) 2 Dec. 22/4, I nominate the Galong (N.S.W.) 'brumbies' as the ugliest and worst pigs in Australia. **1930** 'BRENT OF BIN BIN' *Ten Creeks Run* (1952) 3 Mrs Saunders had an ex-sailor in the kitchen and in the house proper a couple of brumby girls. **1954** H.G. LAMOND *Manx Star* 74 'He came to Queensland, a remittance man.' 'What's that in a white man's language?' 'A black sheep or a brumby bull,' Wilson explained. **1979** A.J. BURKE *Bite Pineapple* 22 She was a steam, twin screw of 909 tons, much faster than the Tinana but a rough old brumby. **1980** H. LUNN *Behind Banana Curtain* 108 The red-beaked finches that live around the bores don't bother to fly away; man doesn't harm them here. And because they fly so dangerously close, Chris Hermann calls them 'brumby birds'.

4. Special Comb. **brumby hunter,** one who rounds up wild horses; also **-hunting** *vbl. n.* and *pr. pple*; **runner, (a)** *brumby hunter*; **(b)** a horse used for brumby hunting; also **running** *vbl. n.*

1891 H.W. HARRIS *Shearers or Shorn* 26 One young Queenslander who has lived the greater portion of his life in the bush, has worked as a shearer, drover, **brumby hunter,** and scalp collector. **1911** A.L. HAYDON *Trooper Police Aust.* 269 Brumby hunters, men who rounded up the wild horses of the ranges. **1892** *Western Champion* (Barcaldine) 26 Jan. 5/3 **Brumbie hunting** at Jericho. . . About half-a-dozen really smart horsemen left here . . with the object of running in wild horses. **1908** *Bulletin* (Sydney) 9 Jan. 39/1 They were brumby hunting on Taromeo. **1937** C. WARBURTON *White Poppies* 153 Mounted on one of the **brumby-runners,** Big Head thundered away in a swirl of dust. **1968** LINKLATER & TAPP *Gather No Moss* 97 It was during 1894 that men known as the brumby runners of the McDonnell [*sic*] Ranges began passing through Newcastle Waters. **1897** *Western Champion* (Barcaldine) 23 Nov. 10/3 In **'brumby' running** of the immediate future the . . 'Lord of the Hills' will at last be yarded by the station Platt-Betts astride his steel-rubber 'moke'. **1913** *Bulletin* (Sydney) 20 Mar. 15/1 It is the fast, rough work, such as cattle drafting, brumby-running, polo, etc. that begets horsemen. **1945** F. CORK *Tales from Cattle Country* 36 Brumby running, besides providing an exciting form of sport often proves highly remunerative for the riders. The best animals are kept for hacks and pack horses, the mongrels are shot and the remaining 'sellers' are shipped to the markets, where they often bring fair prices.

brummy, var. BRUMBY.

brummy, *n.* and *a.* [f. *Brumm(agem* counterfeit coin + -Y.]

A. *n.* A counterfeit coin; a dud.

1921 *Bulletin* (Sydney) 11 Aug. 24/2 The decent cove rang true, in the same way as a dinkum coin rang true when thrown down, whereas the brummy fell with a thud. **1962** J. WYNNUM *Tar Dust* 38 'But you pay through the nose for it and I'm not clewed up enough to know whether or not I'm getting the genuine article.' '*We* might slip you a brummy for that matter.' **1966** G. WYATT *Strip Jack Naked* 17 If I go around telling everyone they can buy a watch for seven pounds ten, they'll suspect it is a brummy.

B. *adj.* Counterfeit; sham and often showy; cheaply made.

1900 *Truth* (Sydney) 24 June 4/4 It is down on the 'brummy' parsons and shark lawyers. **1964** K. TENNANT *Summer's Tales* 54 Ah, youth! With its brummy outsize ideals, its outsize ebony heart, its outsize dreams. **1965** I. HAMILTON *Persecutor* 37, I wouldn't take your word for a brummy two bob. **1967** F. HARDY *Billy Borker yarns Again* 125 Lose their wages every week. Borrow money, cash brummy cheques. **1979** T. SCHURMANN *Showie* 36 Jack threw down the pen. 'You—you broke the nib.' 'It was a brummy pen.' **1980** J. WRIGHT *Big Hearts & Gold Dust* 155 A claw-like hand . . glittered with jewelled rings—brummy jewels, I thought.

brush, *n.*[1] and *attrib.*

A. *n.* A tract of dense natural vegetation: orig. applied chiefly to the understorey, later to forest, esp. rainforest (see esp. quots. 1793, 1834, and 1843).

1789 D. COLLINS *Acct. Eng. Colony N.S.W.* (1798) I. 56 Lost their way in some of the thick and almost impenetrable brushes which were in the vicinity of Rose Hill. **1793** J. HUNTER *Hist. Jrnl. Trans. Port Jackson* 61 Those fires were intended to clear that part of the country through which they have frequent occasion to travel, of the brush or underwood, from which they, being naked, suffer very great inconvenience. **1805** *HRA* (1915) 1st Ser. V. 586 Brush—is a dark impenetrable Thicket consisting of plants and herbacious Shrubs. This kind of Land is oftentimes found of a good quality owing to its being a vegetable mould. **1820** J. OXLEY *Jrnls. Two Exped. N.S.W.* 40 We . . were obliged to stop in the middle of an acacia brush. **1829** R. MUDIE *Picture of Aust.* 168 The tangled woody surface in the latitude of Sydney being generally composed of small and stunted trees, and being called bush, or brush, and not forest. **1834** G. BENNETT *Wanderings N.S.W.* I. 201 A rugged road led through 'Bargo Brush', which is a dense forest, small portions only being occasionally seen cleared. **1843** J.D. LANG *Cooksland* (1847) 84 After much pains I got into this brush, and here all lower vegetation ceases at once. Every thing strives to get to the light. The climbers ascend to the tops of the trees, and display there their rich foliage and blossoms. The trees themselves rarely form branches under forty to fifty feet high. **1852** J. MACGILLIVRAY *Narr. Voyage H.M.S.*

Rattlesnake I. 88 Penetrating this shrubby border, one finds himself in what in New South Wales would be called a *brush* or *scrub*, and in India a jungle. **1871** *Austral. Town & Country Jrnl.* (Sydney) 1 Apr. 394/3 Every farm is backed or surrounded by the apparently impenetrable brush. **1882** *Proc. Linnean Soc. N.S.W.* VII. 569 The climbing fern . . clasps the stems of the tallest trees in succulent snake-like smooth vines about two inches in diameter, sending forth at every few inches enormous pinnate leaves a couple of feet in length. In New South Wales, such forests are called 'Brushes'. **1890** G.J. Broinowski *Birds of Aust.* III. Pl. 1, The brushes . . extend along the coast from the Cardwell district in Northern Queensland to the extreme south-east of New South Wales. **1911** A. Mack *Bush Days* 39 Not at all an uncommon tree in the South Coast brush, where it chiefly flourishes. **1923** *Bulletin* (Sydney) 1 Mar. 24/3 A species known as the native cork-tree (*Duboisia myoporoides*) grows in the Richmond and Tweed River (N.S.W.) brushes. **1941** C. Barrett *Aust.* 87 Pythons up to twenty feet in length inhabit Queensland brushes. **1968** A. D'Ombrain *Fish Tales* 70 The term brush in Australia refers to a type of tropical country where dense undergrowth and palms, fig trees, lawyer vines, and all the flora that makes up such a spot is to be found. **1977** J. Carter *All Things Wild* 1 The 'brush' covered some hundred square kilometres with an almost continuous leaf canopy, through which the sun rarely penetrated.

B. 1. *attrib.*

1821 T. Godwin *Descr. Acct. Van Diemen's Island* 18 The ploughing will not stand him in more than 10s. the acre; which, added to the clearing makes £1 18s. per acre for preparing forest land for seed-corn, while the brush-land is £3 2s. **1837** *Colonist* (Sydney) 19 Jan. 19/4 There are about fifty acres of rich brush land. **1845** C. Hodgkinson *Aust., Port Macquarie to Moreton Bay* 68, I . . ordered them to cut some branches of . . brush-trees, (for all forest trees are of greater specific gravity than water). **1849** *Sydney Guardian* 155/3 The explorers had forced their way . . through a very difficult brush country. **1849** A. Harris *Guide Port Stephens* 14, I consider one acre of brush land, all things taken into consideration, fully worth three of ordinary forest land. **1852** J.D. Lang *Austral. Emigrant's Man.* 48 It could not, however, be considered as a disadvantage, having a portion of brush-land attached to each farm. . . It would not only afford timber for building, but would yield a ready . . supply of food. **1867** J.R. Houlding *Austral. Capers* 269 He had let off portions of his brush land to industrious, steady families, on clearing leases. **1903** *Bulletin* (Sydney) 26 Nov. 17/1 The brush-timber district, which takes in the middle reaches of the northern rivers, contains by far the greatest number of timber trees. **1915** *Forestry Question in N.S.W.* (Austral. Forest League) 4 The Rosewood, which still exists in large quantities in our northern brush forests, rivals the West Indian Mahogany. **1956** N.K. Wallis *Austral. Timber Handbk.* 2 In addition to the hardwood forests and the cypress pine belt, the coastal strip in Queensland and northern New South Wales provides 'rain' or 'brush' (scrubwood) forests.

2. In the names of flora and fauna: **brush apple,** *black apple*, see Black *a.*[2] 1 a.; **box,** any of several trees, esp. *Lophostemon confertus* (fam. Myrtaceae) of e. Qld. and n.e. N.S.W., with pinkish-grey scaly bark; the wood of these trees; **bronze-wing,** the pigeon *Phaps elegans* of dense vegetation in s. Aust.; **cherry,** any of several trees esp. *Syzygium australe* (fam. Myrtaceae) which bears succulent fruits; the wood of these trees; **kangaroo,** *brush wallaby*; **turkey,** the large, mound-building bird *Alectura lathami* of e. Aust., having a bare red head and neck, yellow wattles at the base of the neck, and otherwise mainly black plumage; *bush turkey*, see Bush C. 3; *New Holland vulture*, see New Holland 2; *scrub turkey* (a), see Scrub *n.* 5; **wallaby,** any of several macropodids, usu. larger wallabies, of coastal scrubs and more open inland forest, as the *red-necked wallaby* (see Red *a.* 1 b.); *brush kangaroo*; **wattle bird,** the large honeyeater *Anthochaera chrysoptera* of s.e. Aust. incl. Tas.; see also *little wattle bird* Little 2.

1888 *Proc. Linnean Soc. N.S.W.* III. 485 'Black Apple', '**Brush Apple**'. **1889** J.H. Maiden *Useful Native Plants Aust.* 367 The 'Black Apple', 'Brush Apple', 'Wild', or 'Native Plum', of the colonists, as it has a fruit very like a plum, though of coarse, insipid flavour. ***c* 1910** W.R. Guilfoyle *Austral. Plants* 333 Australian Brush or Bush Apple. **1933** C.W. Peck *Austral. Legends* (ed. 2) 39 Here he found the Achras australe or Brush Apple. **1889** J.H. Maiden *Useful Native Plants Aust.* 608 '**Brush Box**' . . timber is much prized for its strength and durable qualities. It is used in ship-building. **1904** —— *Forest Flora N.S.W.* I. 108 'Brush Box' . . 'Brush', because it is essentially a brush (an Australian word for luxuriant vegetation—jungle in fact) timber. **1909** R. Kaleski *Austral. Settler's Compl. Guide* 43 *Brush box*, like smooth-barked red box; mostly found growing in scrubs, hence its name; timber pink. **1948** P.J. Hurley *Red Cedar* 96 Trees for commerce . . brush box and tallow-woods. **1968** D. Fleay *Nightwatchmen* Pl. foll. 36 Giant flooded gum flanked by brush box trees at McLennan's Creek (south-eastern Queensland). **1979** *Sydney Morning Herald* 5 Sept. 6/5 These mighty veteran brushbox may be 70 metres tall and their crowns 70 metres across. [**1801 brush bronze-wing:** J. Latham *Gen. Synopsis Birds* Suppl. II. 267 Bronze-winged P[igeon] . . called by some also *Brush Pigeon*. **1843** J. Gould *Birds of Aust.*(1848) V. Pl. 65, *Peristera elegans*. . . Brush Bronze-winged Pigeon. . . Little Bronze Pigeon, Colonists of Swan River.] **1902** *Emu* II. 75 Phaps elegans (Brush Bronze-wing)—I flushed many of these birds in the sage scrubs. **1962** Marshall & Drysdale *Journey among Men* 73 In 1792 Labillardiere 'killed the charming yellow turtle dove, remarkable for six or eight golden feathers towards the base of its wings'. This was the brush bronzewing. **1976** *Reader's Digest Compl. Bk. Austral. Birds* 241 Half of the brush bronzewings' food was wheat and the other half acacia seeds. **1888** *Proc. Linnean Soc. N.S.W.* III. 512 *Eugenia myrtifolia* . . '**Brush cherry**' or 'Native myrtle'. The fruit is acid, and makes a good preserve. **1893** D.J. Frost *Crown Lands N.S.W.* 19 Brush cherry . . proved suitable for engraving. **1932** R.H. Anderson *Trees of N.S.W.* 153 Brush Cherry (*Eugenia myrtifolia*) . . is found fairly commonly in brush lands from the Illawarra northwards. **1956** T.Y. Harris *Naturecraft in Aust.* 150 Lillipillies and Brush Cherries, which belong to the rain-forest, have shining green leaves, smooth bark, small fluffy, rather inconspicuous flowers, and succulent pink, white or red fruits. **1980** L. Fuller *Wollongong's Native Trees* 51 Brush cherry (*Syzygium [sic] paniculatum*). **1802** Banks Papers 1 June VIII. 103 A **Brush Kangoroo** (Walaby) which is of a blackish colour. **1802** D. Collins *Acct. Eng. Colony N.S.W.* II. 153 It is singular, that a place wherein food seemed to be so scarce should yet be so thickly inhabited by the small brush kangooroo. **1833** H.W. Parker *Rise, Progress, & Present State Van Dieman's Land* 179 The brush kangaroo . . is found among thick scrubs. **1847** G.F. Angas *Savage Life & Scenes* I. 70 Numbers of the brush-kangaroo (*Halmaturus Greyii*) were put up constantly. . . This new and beautiful species . . is . . confined to the desert-scrub bordering on Lake Albert and the north-west end of the Coorong. **1864** *Illustr. Sydney News* 16 July 9/1 The dingo (wild dog) and wallaby (brush Kangaroo) are also hunted extensively in some districts. **1888** *Centennial Mag.* (Sydney) 14 The so-called brush kangaroo of Tasmania . . is, of course, really a wallaby. **1926** A.A.B. Apsley *Amateur Settlers* 219 Hunt either fox, dingo or 'brush' kangaroos. **1962** B.W. Leake *Eastern Wheatbelt Wildlife* 42 Previous to 1908 the Brush Kangaroo was found only in the areas, south and slightly north and east of the country between Dangin and Mt. Stirling. **1840** J. Gould *Birds of Aust.* (1848) V. Pl. 77, *Talegalla lathami*. . . **Brush Turkey** of the Colonists. **1845** C. Hodgkinson *Aust., Port Macquarie to Moreton Bay* 205 The brush-turkey is a foolish bird, very easily shot. **1851** J. Henderson *Excursions & Adventures N.S.W.* II. 177 The Brush Turkey, . . as indicated by its name, inhabits the brushes, or jungles. It is as large as the domestic turkey, though more beautiful, and is most excellent eating. **1865** G.F. Angas *Aust.* 87 That singular mound-building bird, the brush turkey, has also bred in confinement. **1890** G.J. Broinowski *Birds of Aust.* II. Pl. 58, The Brush Turkey is found principally in the scrubs on the eastern slopes of the Main Range. . . In the matted jungle . . of North Queensland, this bird (called there the 'Scrub Turkey') is hunted by the aborigines for food. **1935** G. McIver *Drover's Odyssey* 26 The brush turkey—that marvellous creation of nature which has deputed to mother earth the responsibilities of hatching its eggs and rearing its young. **1972** *Bulletin* (Sydney) 25 Nov. 75/2 To descend into a rainforest like the one at Dorrigo and see brush turkeys scurrying about like domestic fowls is an enriching experience for anyone. **1846** *Portland Guardian* 22 Sept. 4/1 At the Mitchell we met a **brush wallabi** of a brownish colour and very coarse hair, (halmaturus agilis gld.) which was common all round the Gulf of Carpentaria. **1872** G.S. Baden-Powell *New Homes for Old Country* 268 One is almost prevented from keeping still . . to obtain shots at a brush wallaby. **1890** *Braidwood Dispatch* 1 Jan. 3/4 *Price for scalps.* Brush wallaby 3d. **1925** H. Hannah *Together in Jungle Scrub* (1981) 73 The Brush Wallaby with dark reddish fur, a medium sized animal. **1941** E. Troughton *Furred Animals Aust.* 198 In accordance with their greater size the typical wallabies haunt the taller, usually less dense, brushwood. This has earned for them the generally appropriate term of Brush Wallabies. **1958** *Coast to Coast 1957–58* 209 He went as easily as a brush wallaby, hardly disturbing the leaf-pressing bush. **1841** J. Gould *Birds of Aust.* (1848) IV. Pl. 56, The **Brush Wattle-bird** . . constantly resorts to the Banksias. **1849** C. Sturt *Narr. Exped. Central Aust.* II. 34 App. Anthochaera Mellivora.—Brush Wattle Bird. This Honey-eater is of very limited range, and was so seldom seen during the progress of the Expedition up the Darling, that it may almost be said to be confined to the located district of South Australia. **1890** G.J. Broinowski *Birds of Aust.* IV. Pl. 28, The Brush Wattle-bird is comparatively rare in the interior of the continent. **1917** *Bulletin* (Sydney) 23 Aug. 22/2 Binghi's nearest approach to the brush wattle-bird's call . . was goo-gwar-ruc.

3. Special Comb. **brush hook,** a long-handled arcuate tool, used for cutting light scrub.

1904 *Bulletin* (Sydney) 15 Sept. 40/3 We have laid in a supply of brushhooks and axes . . for neither last long in chopping scrub. **1925** *Smith's Weekly* (Sydney) 23 May 19/6 He was a new Caesar, with a rusty brush-hook as his sword. **1948** P.J. Hurley *Red Cedar* 216 Only a razor-edged brush-hook could sever and rend the flesh-tearing lawyer vines. **1960** M. Vizzers *She'll do Me!* 140 Four months later we cleared the last acre. It was a solemn occasion when Bert and I swung our brush-hooks for the last time. **1979** L.C. Brien *Byron Connection* 7/1 Frank could recall cutting into the dense undergrowth with a brushhook.

brush, *n.*[2] [Abbrev. of *brushwood.*]

1. Brushwood, applied (chiefly *attrib.*) to dead or felled vegetation used for building purposes.

1840 *S. Austral. Rec.* (London) 17 Oct. 251 Arrived upon his estate, his [*sc.* the settler's] primary object is to erect a brush-hut or break-wind, which is formed of the boughs of trees, and sometimes thatched in a rude manner with long grass. **1847** A. Harris *Settlers & Convicts* (1953) 31 It is considered that no more is done by the brush-sawyer than just to break the logs down into planks. **1850** T. Woolley *Reminisc. Life Bushman* 31 With the aid of brush carpenters and sawyers . . you won't be much out of pocket. **1863** J. Davis *Tracks of McKinlay & Party across Aust.* 177 A native dog came into camp last night, and tried to get at a sheep in the fold (for at every camp we have to build a brush fold) but was shot by our native. **1871** *Austral. Town & Country Jrnl.* (Sydney) 25 Feb. 251/4 The yards, which were partly brush and partly chock-and-log, and were 100 yards distant from the nearest fence. ***c* 1891** J. Gardiner *Twenty-Five Yrs. on Stage* 45 There was the improvised brush-made stable for his horse, and beside it a mia-mia for himself. **1896** H. Lawson *While Billy Boils* (1975) 51 Further up along this water is a brush shearing shed, a rough framework of poles with a brush roof. This kind of shed has the advantage of being cooler than iron. **1897** L. Lindley-Cowen *W. Austral. Settler's Guide* 274 When grass or other small seeds are sown a brush harrow is quite sufficient to cover them with. **1926** L.C.E. Gee *Bush Tracks & Gold Fields* 26 The big brush gunyah . . was our office. **1948** E.H. Collis *Lost Yrs.* 83 Soon Coolgardie in the desert had a population of thousands, living in brush, hessian and galvanized-iron shanties. **1960** M. Henry *Unlucky Dip* 87 The row of lairy-shirted ringers sweating with their backs to the masculine end of the brush wall. **1961** *N. Austral. Monthly* Dec. 11 Gentlewomen . . braved the wilderness and lived under a brush shed that Australia should march with the older nations.

2. Comb. **brush fence, yard.**

1824 E. Curr *Acct. Colony Van Diemen's Land* 119 Those lands that are protected from depredations upon stock are generally surrounded . . with a **brush fence.** **1837** *Cornwall Chron.* (Launceston) 14 Oct. 1, I found this box in a brush-fence. . . It was laying with the lid uppermost and some brush over it. **1845** Mrs Thomson *Life in Bush* 17 Fifty sheep were enclosed within a brush fence. **1862** G.T. Lloyd *Thirty-Three Yrs. Tas. & Vic.* 276 Encircling himself with a light brush fence, constructed of the most brittle bushes to be found. **1898** D.W. Carnegie *Spinifex & Sand* 36 We noticed a large number of old brush fences . . which the natives had set up for catching wallabies. **1924** J.A. Reid *Pioneer Grazier Aust.*

4 Later on the country was fenced with brush fences made by falling the green timber, of which there was plenty, cutting the limbs off the trees and putting them together in a straight line with the butts of the limbs the way the fence was being built and the tops always back. **1962** E. LANE *Mad as Rabbits* 122 Mrs Paynter . . had cut and carted enough tea-tree from the scrub to build a high brush fence right round the garden. **1980** HOLTH & BARNABY *Cattlemen of High Country* 37 We'd cut the snow-gums off so high up and built what they call a brush fence. **1835** J. BATMAN *Settlement in Port Phillip* 1 June (1856) 16 We have not yet met with timber fit for the saw or splitting. **Brush yards** might be made for sheep or cattle. **1848** J.C. BYRNE *Twelve Yrs.' Wanderings Brit. Colonies* II. 252 There were a few stunted trees which might be made into a stockade and a brush-yard for the cattle. **1856** W.W. DOBIE *Recoll. Visit Port-Phillip* 57 The solitary shepherd . . gathering his flock at sundown in the adjoining brush-yard. **1892** *Western Champion* (Barcaldine) 26 Jan. 11/2 The monkeys are safe tonight in the brush yards which, with a little topping up, the boys have made perfectly secure. **1911** *Bulletin* (Sydney) 2 Feb. 13/2 Two dingoes got into a brush yard containing a flock of sheep. **1943** H.G. LAMOND *From Tariaro to Ross Roy* 33 The sheep were shepherded and enclosed in brush yards at night. If a wing of a flock was lost . . that lost flock would be torn by dingoes. **1980** P. FREEMAN *Woolshed* 18 Henry King had washed his sheep in the creek to the north of the shed, then herded them into brush yards until they were dry enough to shear.

brush, *n.*[3] Abbrev. of *brush kangaroo, wallaby* (see BRUSH *n.*[1] B. 2). Also *attrib.*

1834 *Colonist* (Hobart) 15 Apr. 3/5 The Kangaroos in the neighbourhood are mostly of the brush kind, which, not being gregarious like the forest or boomah species, are not numerous. **1839** J. STEPHENS *Land of Promise* 57 Kangaroos are of five distinct kinds; namely, the forester, the brush, the wallaby, the kangaroo rat, and the kangaroo mouse. They are all in great abundance. **1851** H. MELVILLE *Present State Aust.* 309 Each brush-skin is now worth, upon an average, fifteen pence. **1852** F. LANCELOTT *Aust. as it Is* I. 35 The forester is the largest, standing six feet high. . . The brush is about the size of a sheep, and the wallabi is rather larger than a cat. **1927** T.S. GROSER *Lure of Golden West* 213 The kangaroo is a fleet-limbed animal. . . The 'wallaby' and the 'brush' species. **1934** T. WOOD *Cobbers* 92 Lay a poor little brush dead in the road. He was a tiny kind of kangaroo. **1970** V. SERVENTY *Dryandra* 46 In the thicker sections of the forest are the haunts of the 'brush'.

brush, *n.*[4] [Prob. spec. use of *brush* animal's tail; cf. slang uses of *arse (ass), tail*, etc., for a woman as a sexual object.] A woman, esp. one regarded sexually.

1941 S.J. BAKER *Pop. Dict. Austral. Slang* 14 *Brush*, a girl or young woman. **1965** W. DICK *Bunch of Ratbags* 226 We were all hanging out the windows, whistling up some of the bits of 'brush' (sheilas) that were walking along. **1966** R. CARR *Surfie* 32 'How did you make out last night?' 'Forget last night. . . How about you picking up some brush for yourself, and coming round with us tonight.' **1968** S. GORE *Holy Smoke* 79 A young brush called Rahab cribs 'em away out of sight in her house. **1975** E. RILEY *All that False Instruction* 229 'Have another beer, mate.' 'Wouldn't mind another piece of tail.' 'Beer first. Brush later.' **1984** *Sun-Herald* (Sydney) 24 June 82/3 He carefully rehearsed some of the smart talk at the track; intrigued by the younger men's comments about the beautiful 'brush' (women) eager to be entertained by visiting trainers.

brush, *v.*[1] [f. BRUSH *n.*[1]] *trans.* To clear (land) of scrub. Also with **up.**

1914 *Bulletin* (Sydney) 10 Dec. 22/2 The old lady . . gazed at the fire-tortured timber. . . 'There's a bit of picking-up to be done over there this summer, and there's the gully to be 'brushed' again. It takes a lot of keeping down. **1929** *Ibid.* 25 Sept. 23/1 The wool-king . . was taking his rouseabout . . to show him some fencing that he wanted done. . . They came to a washaway that had to be brushed. **1981** *Bega District News* 27 Nov. 5/6 A track was brushed up with a tractor and the fire was allowed to burn itself out.

Hence **brushing** *vbl. n.*

1909 *Bulletin* (Sydney) 26 Aug. 15/2 You cut all the small undergrowth, vines, etc., with a slasher (or scrub-hook); this is 'vining' in N.S.W., 'brushing' in Queensland. **1920** C.W. BRYDE *Chart House to Bush Hut* 95, I got a small brushing job from a mean person who gave me ten shillings an acre to cut four acres thickly grown. **1924** E.J. BRADY *Land of Sun* 80 Timber tracks are first cut through the scrubs. The 'brushing' follows. This means a cutting down of all the higher vegetation, with vines and undergrowth, and felling such timber as remains after the more valuable logs have been removed.

brush, *v.*[2] [f. BRUSH *n.*[2]] *trans.* To build (a fence, etc.) with dead or felled vegetation. Also *intr.* and with **up.**

1913 *Bulletin* (Sydney) 16 Jan. 14/2 'Sydney' was sent ahead and told to 'brush up' the wire at the back of the canvas. . . When we arrived Sydney was still hard at work 'brushing up' the fence. But not with timber and small boughs. He had a tin of polish. **1934** W. HATFIELD *River Crossing* 45 They set off into the scrub close by for loads of boughs, with which to brush in from the veranda to the hut. **1958** F.B. VICKERS *Mirage* 277 'How's things?' he asked. 'Not so bad.' 'Brushing Ritchie's dam, aren't you?' 'Yes. Just made a start on it.' **1976** DRAGE & PAGE *Riverboats & Rivermen* 163 At Portree . . the Murray Waters Commission had built a 'spur'. This was a cunning contrivance consisting of a double row of red gum piles, stretching out at an angle from the bank, and then 'brushed' . . the process of forcing logs, tree tops, and similar material down between the rows of piles. . . Its effect was to divert the river current into midstream.

brusher, *n.*[1] *Obs.* [Perh. f. *brush, v.* to decamp.] In the phr. **to give** (someone) **brusher,** to defraud (someone); to abscond, avoid.

1878 *Pilgrim* (Sydney) 2nd Ser. x. 5 He subsequently victimised Mr Weber, Post Office Hotel; . . indeed anywhere this penniless Hebrew obtained admission he never failed to give 'brusher' to the confiding boniface. **1882** *Sydney Slang Dict.* 2 *Brusher (to give anyone)*, to obtain or borrow something and not pay for or return it. **1884** *Austral. Tit-Bits* (Melbourne) 26 June 14/1 A Mr Jones, of Adelaide, has been giving backers brusher. After laying the most liberal odds against Councillor and receiving the money, he was missed after the above-named animal had won. **1914** E. DYSON *Spats' Fact'ry* 77 The whole bloomin' fact'ry . . was thinkin' iv givin' the grip brusher, 'n' goin' into co. with the unemployed. **1918** *Bulletin* (Sydney) 30 May 24/3 The animal with the bristly-haired tail . . was probably the 'brusher' or scrub-wallaby, whose celerity in leaving a vacancy when he felt his presence was superfluous gave rise to the expression of the bookie with an empty bag when he sees the wrong number go up—'Give 'em brusher!' **1934** *Ibid.* 21 Nov. 20/3 It wasn't long before the fraternity kept to the Tambo-Blackall road on the other side of the Barcoo and, unless it was a case of starvation, gave the station 'brusher'.

brusher, *n.*[2] *Obs.* [Transf. use of Br. dial. *brusher* 'a boy who is quick and active': see EDD *brush, v.*[2] and *sb.*[2]] See quot. 1916.

1882 *Freeman's Jrnl.* (Sydney) 30 Sept. 17/1, I have often thought how admirably that decidedly vulgar phrase 'fussy little brusher' defines you. **1894** A.B. BELL *Austral. Camp Fire Tales* 105 Jack, old brusher, I bears no malice now, if you stands another drink, we'll cry quits. **1916** *Bulletin* (Sydney) 21 Sept. 22/3 *'Brusher'* (rare), any nondescript old chap, like the English 'geezer'. Said to be in reference to an old station cook who always commenced brushing boots when he was annoyed. Or possibly from a likeness to a horse or bullock run wild in the 'brush' (scrub).

brush-tailed, *ppl. a.* Used as a distinguishing epithet in the names of flora and fauna: **brush-tailed phascogale,** the arboreal marsupial *Phascogale tapoatafa*, widespread in wooded country of mainland Aust., having a bushy, 'bottle-brush' tail; see also TUAN; **possum,** the common possum, the widespread arboreal marsupial *Trichosurus vulpecula*, cat-sized with a long prehensile tail; VULPINE OPOSSUM; also abbrev. as **brush-tail; rock wallaby,** the wallaby *Petrogale penicillata*, widespread in rocky places of mainland Aust. and having a bushy dark tail; also **brush-tailed wallaby.**

[**1852 brush-tailed phascogale:** *Austral. Gold Digger's Monthly Mag.* i. 21 In South Australia there is a brush-tailed Kangaroo Rat.] **1926** A.S. LE SOUEF et al. *Wild Animals Australasia* 335 The brush-tailed phascogale is widely spread over the continent. **1979** DOUGLAS & HEATHCOTE *Far Cry* 121 The Tuan, or brush-tailed phascogale . . is a bandicoot sized marsupial carnivore, with a tail which is smooth at first, then like a stiff bottle-brush, which he holds up like a squirrel as he bounces about. **1887** [**brush-tailed possum**] *Illustr. Austral. News* 21 (Melbourne) Dec. 218/1 Two varieties of opossum are found, the ring-tail and brush-tail. **1970** W.D.L. RIDE *Guide Native Mammals Aust.* 70 Most Australians dwell in suburbs and, under these conditions, they have more contact with the common Brush-tailed Possum . . than they have with any other native mammal. **1977** J. CARTER *All Things Wild* 21 Trundling along a shelf was Thumper, the brush-tailed possum, happily nosing wineglasses and decanters down on to the floor. [**1887 brush-tailed rock-wallaby:** A. NICOLS *Wild Life & Adventure* 58 The agile brush-tailed rock kangaroos were springing over the broken surface with astonishing bounds.] **1926** A.S. LE SOUEF et al. *Wild Animals Australasia* 201 The eastern species (the brush-tailed rock-wallaby). **1978** M. DOUGLAS *Follow Sun* 115 Brush-tailed wallabies, startled by our presence, jumped up the almost perpendicular cliffs. **1983** *Sun* (Sydney) 17 Aug. 17 At similar peril are the regent and helmeted honeyeaters, the brush-tailed rock wallaby.

brushy, *a. Obs.* [f. BRUSH *n.*[1]] Covered with dense natural vegetation.

1805 *HRA* (1915) 1st Ser. V. 583 For the Brushy and Rocky Land that prevails from the first M to the River Side. **1813** J.W. LEWIN *Birds N.S.W.* 2 Variegated Warbler. Inhabits thick brushy woods. **1820** *Sydney Gaz.* 16 Dec., They had for the most part quitted the thinly wooded and more open tracts of the interior, and betaken themselves to the sea-coast, and brushy and broken country. **1828** *Tasmanian* (Hobart) 31 Oct. 3 The place being brushy, he succeeded in making his escape. **1843** J. GOULD *Birds of Aust.* (1848) V. Pl. 62, The Little Green Pigeon is sparingly dispersed in all the brushes of New South Wales, both those clothing the mountain ranges as well as those near the coast. . . The brushy districts are the localities peculiarly adapted to it. **1847** A. HARRIS *Settlers & Convicts* (1953) 134 Lost himself in the deep brushy Budawong gullies.

bubba. Also **bubby.** [Var. of *baby.*] A young child. Also **bub.**

1906 *Steele Rudd's Mag.* (Brisbane) Mar. 159 Why, in Australia, is every baby a 'bubba'? The word will be found in use from one end of the continent to the other. **1960** *Overland* xvii. 7 'All right. How's Bubby?' 'Fit as a Mallee bull! Got another tooth.' **1967** *Southerly* iii. 149 Nice fire in the waiting room. . . Nice and warm for the bubba. **1977** P. ADAMS *Unspeakable Adams* 75, I discovered that all the other kids from the bubs' grade were similarly attired. **1983** *Canberra Chron.* 5 Oct. 19/1 Wife and bub are well.

Bubble. *Obs.* [Spec. use of *bubble* something unsubstantial, delusive; often with reference to allegedly fraudulent commercial undertakings and so used of the South Australian Company's plan to finance immigration from land sales.] Used *attrib.* with reference to the South Australian Company or Colony. Used *attrib.*

1838 *Sydney Herald* 28 Nov. 2/1 *South Australia.* What a *rot* among the bubble Province officials! **1839** *Ibid.* 18 Jan. 2/1 (*heading*) The Bubble Company. *Ibid.* The scheming South Australian Company were straining every nerve to advance their own interests at the expense of the Colony of New South Wales . . in order to turn the tide of population to their own 'Bubble Province'. *Ibid.* 2/2 To raise the minimum price of land in the Colony for the benefit of the 'Bubble' gentry, is, in effect, a mild rebuke of their grasping propensities. **1840** *S. Austral. Rec.* (London) 15 Jan. 10 We are glad to perceive a more kindly spirit existing in our Sydney contemporaries with reference to the 'Bubble Company's Colony', as South Australia has generally been termed.

bubble-bubble. *Austral. pidgin. Obs.* See quot. 1888.

1888 E. FINN *Chron. Early Melbourne* I. 371 The 'wallaby trackers' would, on a certain evening, treat all the blacks that might cross the river to a big feast of 'bubble-bubble'—a mess of flour and water to which the Port Phillipian Aborigines were even more partial than to the squatters' rum or beef. **1923** H.C.A. Harrison *Story of Athlete* 21 The lubras . . were also very fond of boiled flour, which they used to call 'bubble bubble'.

bubbler. A drinking fountain.

1970 J.S. Gunn in W.S. Ramson *Eng. Transported* 57 Over a long period we have picked up odd terms like bubbler. **1983** *Canberra Times* 4 Mar. 1/4 She said the smell of the Gunning water had made her ill. Children were unable to drink from the school bubbler, and some parents were having difficulty affording prepared drinks for them. **1985** *Good Weekend* (Sydney) 24 Aug. 20/2 One wonders . . why the dedicatee's heirs weren't approached to discuss the alternative of a well-designed bubbler.

bubby, var. Bubba.

buck, *n.*[1] [Spec. use of *buck* male animal; used also of humans and derog. of the U.S. Indian or Black.]

1. A large male kangaroo. Also *attrib.*

1845 *Atlas* (Sydney) I. 258/1 The large full-grown male is termed a Buck or Boomer, and attains a great size. **1850** *Bell's Life in Sydney* 22 June 3/2 And with our waddy, after a really desperate conflict, for these fighting bucks are not to be trifled with. **1926** A.S. Le Souef et al. *Wild Animals Australasia* 177 The bucks grow fairly large, in rare cases almost equal to the Grey.

2. a. An Aboriginal male.

1870, 1879 [see *buck nigger*]. **1896** W.H. Willshire *Land of Dawning* 57 We discovered about fifteen blacks, who upon hearing our approach made most desperate attempts to get away. One old buck met with a geographical accident by falling flop into a dry gully and breaking his crupper-bone. **1898** D.W. Carnegie *Spinifex & Sand* 189 The strange procession started, the 'buck' (the general term for a male aboriginal) leading the way. **1919** *Bulletin* (Sydney) 18 Dec. 22/2 It caught sight of . . a big buck Binghi asleep under a gumtree. **1925** G. Wirth *Round World with Circus* 11 The bucks just carried their spears and boomerangs and nulla nullas (waddies), and a lighted fire-stick. **1931** *N.T. Times* (Darwin) 9 Jan. 3/1 A number of the married men wanted to buy the woomeras that the bucks used for beating their wives. **1952** *Bulletin* (Sydney) 2 Apr. 17/1 Several of the young bucks . . by collusion with a gin . . were able to squeeze nightly down the chimney of the ration-hut and take toll of the stores. **1965** M. Patchett *Last Warrior* 42 Burramurra stood with the other bucks. **1976** C.D. Mills *Hobble Chains & Greenhide* 22 She had been betrothed from birth to a young buck. He had picked up another, and was crooked on the world because the old fellas made him take this one.

b. Comb. **buck nigger.**

1870 E.B. Kennedy *Four Yrs. in Qld.* 29 We . . waited . . for the big 'Buck nigger' (or niggers), whom we were certain were within a few yards of us. **1879** 'Australian' *Adventures Qld.* 38 Take my advice and be more careful with those big buck niggers in future. **1909** F. Birtles *Lonely Lands* 84 When supper is ready the 'buck niggers' have first 'whack', the gins and piccaninnies second, while the dogs come in at the tail end. **1925** J.E. Liddle *Selected Poems* 120 In 'mia-mias' we could see Buck-niggers squatting like the Turk.

3. A foreman.

1906 *Bulletin* (Sydney) 5 July 17/1 Accept 'is invitation to ther Farm, Fur away from biffs an' rossers, bucks an' bats an' 'ooks an' dossers. **1937** *Ibid.* 4 Aug. 21/2 Why do swagmen shy clear of fettling gangs? The wherefore of it has always been a puzzle to me, especially as most 'bucks' would be good nips for . . a handout from their always loaded tucker-boxes. **1944** *Austral. New Writing* 34 'Does the buck know you've left?' 'I'm not worried. I wouldn't work to-night, not for King George.'

4. *attrib.* Exclusively male, esp. as **buck set.**

1898 D.W. Carnegie *Spinifex & Sand* 24 We . . had frequent sing-songs and 'buck dances'—that is dances in which there were no ladies to take part. **1900** *Western Champion* (Barcaldine) 12 June 13/2 Inside the dining room adjoining a 'buck set' had been formed waltzing indiscriminately to any tune. **1907** A. Searcy *In Austral. Tropics* 367 What grand 'buck sprees' we used to have there, to be sure; a lot of men together, pure fun and frolic. **1920** *Aussie* (Sydney) July 20/2 It was during a 'buck set' on the promenade deck. A rather 'naive'-looking little Corporal was dancing with a 'hard-doer'-looking Private. **1932** J. McCarter *Pan's Clan* 175 She left the drover and coaxed the men who were not dancing 'buck pairs' into the bar. **1934** J.C. Lee *Boshstralians* 121 The shearers held their fortnightly dances. These dances it might be explained were, save for the presence of Mag and Poppy, unavoidably 'buck' hops. **1937** *Bulletin* (Sydney) 27 Oct. 21/2 It was a buck station in W.Q., and there wasn't one poultry expert among them. **1942** F. Clune *Last of Austral. Explorers* 123 A 'buck dance' was put on in their honour—no ladies present. Booze was the chief attraction, with much singing of sentimental songs. **1960** I.L. Idriess *Wild North* 179 Revelry rang from the pub. . . Boards were creaking to heavy feet as men rollicked and sang to 'buck sets'. **1976** B. Scott *Compl. Bk. Austral. Folk Lore* 394 One outback dance—the Bullock-drivers' Schottische—was done by two men. Lack of women didn't stop the early shearers from holding a dance. They did all the traditional square dances and a few of the dances for couples in what they called buck sets.

5. In the collocation **buck(s') party** (or **night**), a party given for a bridegroom on the eve of his wedding by male friends.

1918 *Home Trail: Souvenir Issue Voyage H.M.T. 'A 30'* Dec. 5 It was a buck party. **1935** *Bulletin* (Sydney) 20 Nov. 20/3 It was a bucks' party, and Bert was the last to arrive. **1972** G. Morley *Jockey rides Honest Race* 261 Kon organized my bucks night, because he was going to be my best man. **1977** H.O. Tesher *Eleven Days* 31 Maria thought that more than buck-parties were keeping him away. **1980** S. Thorne *I've met some Bloody Wags* 94 We had a buck's party for him at Toby's woolshed, and during the night old Mick was skiting that he was as fit as any of us. **1984** *Sun-Herald* (Sydney) 15 July 125/1 The Prince and Princess of Wales had the RD '73 served at their wedding and Charles chose the '75 for his bucks' night.

buck, *n.*[2] [f. Buck *v.* 1.]

1. Buckjump *n.* 1.

1898 D.W. Carnegie *Spinifex & Sand* 98 Wait till you make your evening feed off mulga scrub and bark—that'll take the buck out of you! **1908** W.H. Ogilvie *My Life in Open* 7 Your own horse bites on the bit, and then, rearing straight up, makes a plunging buck forward. **1929** K.S. Prichard *Coonardoo* (1961) 49 He'd begin with a flying root and a couple of high bucks . . and go on buckin' and rootin' in a circle.

2. Buckjumper.

1944 *Bulletin* (Sydney) 20 Dec. 12/3 That phrase 'sit a buck' . . always brands its user, in my mind, as a cocky-country horseman. **1951** E. Hill *Territory* 318 They dragged a buck up from the yards and challenged him out. **1978** D. Stuart *Wedgetail View* 26 Davey's mount, a flashy chestnut . . was a willing buck but Davey made nothing of the hurried, flurried attempt at dislodging him.

Hence **buckrunner** *n.*, see quot. 1970.

1970 J.S. Gunn in W.S. Ramson *Eng. Transported* 59 *Buckrunner*, one who rounds up wild horses. **1980** Holth & Barnaby *Cattlemen of High Country* 172 They may avoid that yard for some time and many buckrunners of old would rotate the trapping procedure through two or three yards.

buck, *a. Mining.* [Of unknown origin.] Barren; not containing the mineral sought.

1875 G.M. Newman *N.T. & its Gold-Fields* 15 In this locality numerous barren or buck reefs are seen cropping above the surface. **1886** J.W. Anderson *Prospector's Handbk.* 116 *Buckstone*, rock not producing gold. **1894** *Bulletin* (Sydney) 11 Aug. 20/3 The *exception* is to find rich patches in 'buck' quartz. **1895** H.P. Woodward *Mining Handbk. W.A.* 177 *Buck*, a name given to large quartz reefs in which there is no gold. **1897** *Bulletin* (Sydney) 6 Mar. 28/4 Granite Creek, a country of buck-reefs and barren quartz. **1914** *Ibid.* 29 Oct. 14/4 You'd . . hurry off Londonward to float some 'buck' reef for £1,000,000 or so. **1922** R.L. Jack *Northmost Aust.* II. 726 The reefs were all very 'buck'- looking on the surface. **1929** W.J. Reside *Golden Days* 151 The discoverer . . had often previously used this big 'buck' quartz out-crop as a shield for shooting rabbits. **1932** I.L. Idriess *Prospecting for Gold* 177 With a little experience, you will begin to distinguish between 'likely stone' and 'buck' reefs, quartzite, etc. **1946** K.S. Prichard *Roaring Nineties* 455 He had left Jack beside a big outcrop of buck quartz. . . There was nothing more unpopular among the early prospectors than the cold, unkindly white stone which had betrayed their hopes so often in a likely looking outcrop.

buck, *v.* [Abbrev. of Buckjump *v.*]

1. *intr.* Buckjump *v.* Also *trans.*

1848 H.W. Haygarth *Recoll. Bush Life* 78 'Buckjumping', or as it is more familiarly called, 'bucking'. **1870** E.B. Kennedy *Four Yrs. in Qld.* 194, I have seen a man (a Sydney native) so much at his ease, that while the horse has been 'bucking a hurricane', to use a colonial expression, the rider has been cutting up his tobacco. **1876** J.A. Edwards *Gilbert Gogger* 146 No sooner did Stockman Bill let her head go, than up went her heels in the air, and buck! buck! she went, amongst pots and pans, tents, buckets, drays, and camp fires. **1896** M. Clarke *Austral. Tales* 10 How the bay filly had bucked off Black Harry. **1900** R. Bruce *Benbonuna* (1904) 108 Him too much buck all about. **1908** W.H. Ogilvie *My Life in Open* 82 Countess, in the parlance of the Bush, can 'buck a town down'. **1920** *Bulletin* (Sydney) 24 June 20/2 In far-western Queensland, where you *do* get brumbies and rough horses, they are considered soft snaps unless they can 'spin' and 'buck back'. **1928** 'S. Rudd' *Romance of Runnibede* 131 Tom called to the merry blacks on the yard-top, as he hitched his pants and approached the outstretched quivering outlaw, 'if he bucks me off some of you fellows will have to get on him'. **1936** I.L. Idriess *Cattle King* 315 It was Albert who rode the notorious outlaw until it 'bucked its brands off'. **1944** M.J. O'Reilly *Bowyangs & Boomerangs* 139 Have you ever seen a camel buck? Your brumby outlaws, circus horses, or wild west broncs are not in it. **1981** *Sun-Herald* (Sydney) 10 May 87/1 It's like keeping a horse stabled up over the weekend. You watch them at the track on Monday morning and they're all bucking their brands off.

2. *transf.* and *fig.* With **in.**

1900 J. Bufton *Tasmanians in Transvaal War* 3 Mar. (1905) 140 After tea had a grand game of football, our captain and doctor 'bucking in' well. **1903** *Sporting News* (Launceston) 2 May 3/6 The pluvial visitation did not stop the teams from 'bucking' in, as the barracker would say.

Hence **bucking** *vbl. n.*

1865 *London Soc.* Dec. 446/2 The horses of the bush are a native breed, and have a curious vice which the troopers call 'bucking'. **1884** 'R. Boldrewood' *Old Melbourne Memories* 145 That animal, being young and what the stockmen call 'touchy', immediately exhibited a fair imitation of that well-known Australian gambade known as 'bucking'. **1944** *Bulletin* (Sydney) 20 Dec. 12/3, I was brought up among old-timers, who spoke of 'sitting a couple' or 'ridin' a few roots', and who reserved 'bucking' for the activities of that one horse in thousands which can be ridden only by one man in many thousands.

buckbush. Any of several shrubs, esp. *Salsola kali* (see Roly-poly).

1898 D.W. Carnegie *Spinifex & Sand* 191 The scrub in the trough of the ridges became more open with an undergrowth of coarse grass, buck-bush or 'Roly-Poly' (*Salsola Kali*) and low acacia. **1916** S.A. White *In Far Northwest* 162 'Buckbush' . . grows in great spherical masses on this light, sandy soil. **1932** W. Hatfield *Ginger Murdoch* 156 Not a vestige of dry feed in the last fifteen miles. What about the buck-bush and bindy-eyes? **1946** C.T. Madigan *Crossing Dead Heart* 87 Andy made himself a beautiful bed of dead buckbush with two bags on it. **1951** W. Hatfield *Wild Dog Frontier* 153 Like tufts of crackly buck-bush before a light dawn breeze.

bucker.

1. Buckjumper.

1853 H.B. Jones *Adventures in Aust.* 143 A 'bucker' is a vicious horse, to be found only in Australia. His peculiarity consists in curling his back upwards, till he wriggles saddle, girth, and rider over his head. **1856** G. Willmer *Draper in Aust.* 122 No sooner had we put the tackling on, than he unfortunately escaped from us . . being a first-rate 'bucker', as they term them in this country. **1916** J.B. Cooper *Coo-oo-ee!* 17 He'll sit a bucker with the best. **1918** *Bulletin* (Sydney) 6 June 22/1 P'raps I can't sit buckers, but b'gosh, I'm game to try.

2. One capable of riding a bucking horse.

1979 Carey & Lette *Puberty Blues* 22 'Ah, Kim's a

good bucker!' cried Steve Strachan as Kim rode Conchise into the scene.

bucket, *n.* [Fig. use of *bucket* container.]

1. An ice-cream carton, now usu. small (see quot. 1972). See also DANDY, DIXIE.

1945 S.J. BAKER *Austral. Lang.* 195 An ice-cream carton is called a *dixie* in Melbourne . . and a *bucket* in Sydney. **1952** *Australasian Confectioner* Apr. 12 Where buckets are sold retail in a theatre, public hall or at a racecourse or showground, 1d. may be added to the above retail prices. *Ibid.* 10 Buckets, small, van[illa] 3s. 7d. [per dozen] do. large 6s. 3d. **1972** G.W. TURNER *Eng. Lang. in Aust. & N.Z.* (rev. ed.) 124 Why should . . a pot or tub of icecream be a dandy in Adelaide, a dixie in Melbourne and elsewhere a *bucket?*

2. *fig.*

a. In the phr. **to drop (tip, turn) the bucket (on),** to make damaging revelations (about someone, often a political opponent).

1950 *Austral. Police Jrnl.* Apr. 112 Drop the bucket. . . Drop the responsibility suddenly on to someone else. **1971** A. REID *Gorton Experiment* 219 But the position as regards Gorton could not go on indefinitely. Labor or 'somebody else' sooner or later would 'turn a bucket'. **1972** *Things I Hear* (Sydney) 11 Apr. 4 If the selection stands, Premier Askin has enough inside information to drop the bucket. **1972** *Bulletin* (Sydney) 13 May 17/3 In the golden days of bucket-tipping it was the DLP who were expected to do most of the dirty work. But an immigration scare is one of the several new buckets the DLP will not tip. **1983** *Austral. Weekend Mag.* (Sydney) 29 Oct. 12/3 Delivering the message to an English audience: 'I didn't come over here to tip the bucket on yas.'

b. A damaging revelation.

1986 *Nat. Times* (Sydney) 28 Feb. 7/4 In the Parliament under privilege . . where all skilled exponents of the bucket operate.

Hence **bucket-dropper** *n.*

1976 *Bulletin* (Sydney) 13 Nov. 25/1 In parliamentary parlance, 'bucket-droppers' are those who, under parliamentary privilege and hence free from any fear of legal action, raise subjects only marginally in the political arena which their more respectable and conventional parliamentary colleagues would not touch with a 40 ft bargepole.

bucket, *v.* [f. prec.] *trans.* To denigrate (a person, etc.).

1974 *Austral.* (Sydney) 1 Apr. 6/7 While it might be valid to find Brisbane lacking in Adelaide's grace or Sydney's vigor or Melbourne's dignity, it is not valid to bucket it in total. **1981** *Potato Grower* (Perth) July 11/1 Former NFF leader 'buckets' senators. Former National Farmers' Federation president . . unleashed an attack that is likely to earn him a stiff invitation from the Senate Standing Committee. **1984** *Canberra Times* 20 June 16/6 Here is a Minister for *Education*, a graduate of this university, ready enough to 'bucket' (her word) the academic staff who are part of her responsibility.

buckjump, *v.* [f. *buck* male animal + *jump*, from the resemblance to the leap of a (startled) male animal, perh. esp. the kangaroo (see BUCK *n.*[1] 1).]

1. *intr.* Of a horse: to leap with head down, legs drawn together, and back arched in an attempt to throw the rider. Freq. as *vbl. n.*

1838 S. HACK Let. 17 June, I bought a colt that had only been mounted a week to help him on the remaining journey to Portland Bay, I was vain enough to think I could ride him but in a week he convinced me of the fallacy of this idea by sending me up in the air like a skyrocket by buckjumping. **1848** H.W. HAYGARTH *Recoll. Bush Life* 78 Australian horses have a vicious habit known as 'buck-jumping', or as it is more familiarly called, 'bucking'. This trick . . is peculiar to colts bred in the colony and in Van Diemen's Land, and is decidedly the most expeditious way that could be devised for emptying a saddle. **1852** G.C. MUNDY *Our Antipodes* I. 364 The 'Agitator' colt will buck-jump a bit at starting. **1857** J. D'EWES *China, Aust. & Pacific Islands* 30 A complicated performance of a species of gymnastics called 'buck jumping', to which, from early habits in their almost wild state, and subsequent very imperfect breaking, Australian horses are particularly addicted. **1867** J.R. HOULDING *Austral. Capers* 277 He is the steadiest brute in the district, and was never known to bolt or buckjump. **1872** MRS E. MILLETT *Austral. Parsonage* 166 The universal trick of buck-jumping that prevails amongst Australian horses might be traced to the no less general practice of hobbling them. **1890** A.A. BOSWELL *Recoll. Some Austral. Blacks* 13 Suddenly the brute plunged and buck-jumped madly. **1909** E. ASH *Austral. Oracle* 13 Three glasses would make you buck-jump like a Sydney two-year-old. **1914** R. KALESKI *Austral. Barkers & Biters* 159 Buck-jumping is so called because the horse jumps like a buck—all four feet off the ground at once. **1924** C. BLOXSOME *How Wonder won Cup* 74 It was a bosker saddle, a buck-jumping one, with big knee pads. **1969** *Bulletin* (Sydney) 11 Jan. 5/4 Some horses have been buckjumping for 20 years. They like to buckjump. **1980** HOLTH & BARNABY *Cattlemen of High Country* 173 In the buckjumping events the brumbies enjoy a reputation of having 'more points than a porcupine'.

2. *fig.*

1876 'EIGHT YRS.' RESIDENT' *Queen of Colonies* 343 One of the blacks . . on seeing him approaching, cried out, 'Here Missa ---, you see 'em me Cabona (very much) me directly buck-jump!' referring to the convulsions directly caused by the poison, and which he called buck-jumping.

buckjump, *n.* [f. prec.]

1. The act of buckjumping. Also *attrib.*

[N.Z. **1873** M.A. BARKER *Station Amusements N.Z.* 233 The series of buck-jumps, of bites and kicks, with which [the mare] received the slightest attempt to touch her.] **1882** A.J. BOYD *Old Colonials* 200 It . . succeeded in making a succession of the most tremendous screwing buck-jumps I ever witnessed. **1917** 'D. DELANEY' *White Champion* 31 Kate Kildare, champion lady buckjump rider of Australia. **1919** *Bulletin* (Sydney) 16 Oct. 20/1 'The Cattle King', was the best buckjump rider I ever saw.

2. Abbrev. of *buckjumping event* (etc.).

1977 V. PRIDDLE *Larry & Jack* 157 He's won a novice buckjump and I'm sure he's not nominated for the Open. **1981** A. MARSHALL *Aust.* 24 A vivid, alert man . . stood in the ring of a buckjump show in a Queensland town telling tall stories to the crowd.

buckjumper. A horse which buckjumps (habitually).

1838 S. HACK Let. 1 Sept., I have bought the horse today for 65 guineas his name is Bucksfoot and he is rightly named for its my belief he is the worst buckjumper in South Australia. **1848** H.W. HAYGARTH *Recoll. Bush Life* 78 An expert 'buck-jumper' usually begins when his rider is in some degree off his guard and has not got him tight in hand. . . He flings down his head between his forelegs, sets up or 'arches' his back, and concentrating all his muscular force, gives a succession of short, quick plunges, all his legs being at times off the ground together. **1850** J.B. CLUTTERBUCK *Port Phillip* 87 Horses are here broken in and used at two years old, and the majority are buck-jumpers. **1852** G.C. MUNDY *Our Antipodes* I. 262 The poor brute is broken by force in a few days—broken in spirit if he be naturally gentle, made a 'buckjumper' for life if bad tempered. **1859** W. BURROWS *Adventures Mounted Trooper* 144 There are not many men who can sit a 'buck-jumper', although the chief qualification of a good horsebreaker is to be able to stand this test. **1886** D.M. GANE *N.S.W. & Vic.* 145 A youth, probably a clerk in a London merchant's office, leaves England in the hope of turning squatter, and riding about all day on a buckjumper, cracking his stockwhip. **1903** H. TAUNTON *Australind* 51 Shortly after my arrival here I made my first acquaintance with an Australian buck-jumper. **1911** A. SEARCY *By Flood & Field* 250 Better to be killed off a buckjumper than be branded as a coward. **1936** J.C. DOWNIE *Galloping Hoofs* 36 A lot of people in town call a pig-rooter a buck-jumper, which is wrong. A true broncho leaves the ground with all four feet at once, while a pig-rooter only lifts his hind legs. **1976** C.D. MILLS *Hobble Chains & Greenhide* 150 A peculiar thing with buck-jumpers is that they are often 'bread-eaters'—poddy-reared round a drover's cart. **1981** A. MARSHALL *Aust.* 24 The telling of these tales probably began as an impromptu, between-acts stunt to hold the audience while some refractory buckjumper was being brought in for riding.

buckle. [f. *buckle* to apply oneself vigorously (orig. from being buckled into armour).] In the phr. **in (good, great,** etc.) **buckle,** in good fettle.

1871 *Austral. Town & Country Jrnl.* (Sydney) 4 Feb. 153/4 We know little of how the New South Wales horses are getting on in Melbourne, but we hear from pretty good authority that Tim Whiffler is in good buckle. **1888** 'R. BOLDREWOOD' *Robbery under Arms* (1937) 216 The horses were in great buckle. **1891** *Truth* (Sydney) 26 Apr. 6/3 Joe . . was in town last Monday, and looked in superb buckle. **1898** *Worker* (Sydney) 15 Jan. 8/2 He was in good buckle, and went from the bell, and they never caught him. **1961** D. STUART *Driven* 103 They went on slowly, on the best feed they had seen yet, and the sunshine dried them out, and Tom, by midday, was in good buckle again.

bucklee /'bʌkli/. [Prob. a. Yinjibarndi *bagali.*] An Aboriginal initiation rite. Also *attrib.*

[**1929** K.S. PRICHARD *Coonardoo* (1961) 17 The older men took the boys off into the mulga thickets . . for the bucklegarroo ceremonies which no woman was allowed to see.] **1959** D. STUART *Yandy* 4 All the blackfellers had come together for a bucklee meeting, for the circumcision of two boys.

Also **bucklee** *v. trans.*

1969 F.B. VICKERS *No Man is Himself* 56 He went to give young Tommy . . the law before he's circumcised—*bucklee'd.*

Buckley's. [Poss. f. the name of William *Buckley* (1780–1856), an escaped convict who lived for 32 years with Aborigines in s. Vic.; but see also quot. 1953.] In full **Buckley's chance (choice, hope, show).** A forlorn hope; no prospect whatever.

1895 *Bulletin* (Sydney) 9 Nov. 13/1 'Buckley's chance'; the Maoriland Supreme Court vacant Judgeship. **1896** *Ibid.* 25 Jan. 25/2 Freemasonry and R.C.-ism . . are worked for all they are worth in Q'sland. . . Unless you are a 'child' of either party your chances of promotion are 'Buckley's'. *Ibid.* 22 Feb. 13/4 Old man Parkes hasn't 'Buckley's chance' for the Waverley seat. **1897** *Worker* (Sydney) 30 Oct. 2/4 He has 'Buckley's show' of working the mine with them. **1902** *Truth* (Sydney) 30 Mar. 1/8 It is wise to be contented With an humble lot, you know, Especially when it's obvious You haven't Buckley's show! **1903** *Ibid.* 22 Mar. 1/5 About the only chance Sir Teaman Lipton has of winning the American Cup is Buckley's. **1908** E.G. MURPHY *Jarrahland Jingles* 16 You've 'done the rattler in to-day', you ain't got Buckley's 'ope, But there's one goes down at night-time when the stoney-brokers slope. **1913** *Truth* (Sydney) 6 July 1/5, 'I suppose you think I have Buckley's chance of winning this case?' . . 'No, I think you have about the same chance as a celluloid dog would have of chasing an asbestos cat through hell.' **1927** *Bulletin* (Sydney) 28 July 24/4 Th' ole man got th' axe an' tried 'is dam'dest ter cut th' vine an' settle it; but 'e didn't 'ave Buckley's. **1940** *Sentry Go* (Keswick) Oct. 9/1 *Buckley's choice.* A new tunic was being issued to a recruit. 'We have two kinds, those too large and those too small. Which will you have?' **1953** H.M. EASTMAN *Mem. of Sheepman* 109 You may not have heard how this phrase, taken from the old firm 'Buckley and Nunn', came into the language some seventy years ago in dealing with one's chances. 'You have two chances, 'Buckley's and Nunn'' only one really, or 50–50 (as it sounds). **1972** M. CASSIDY *Dispossessed* 24 'Twenty-eight years among the abos and not a white man nearer than Sydney or Tasmania.' . . 'Buckley's chance, you might say.' . . 'Yes, that's how the expression Buckley's Chance came into the Australian vocabulary.' **1978** H.C. BAKER *I was Listening* 171 What chance have we got if the Nips land? Bloody Buckley's! **1981** P. BARTON *Bastards I have Known* 78 Faced with the extra load in the cage the brake had Buckley's chance of stopping the mangle roller from turning.

buck scraper. See quot. 1890.

1890 W.H. BUNDEY *Winter Cruise* 14 After the land is cleared and ploughed . . comes the 'grading for irrigation'. For this three instruments are used, viz. the 'buck scraper', an ordinary 'earth scoop', and the 'smoother'. **1925** A.N. SHEPHERD *Irrigation Farming N.S.W.* 11 If there are many 'bumps' to take off or holes to fill, the buck-scraper may be employed to produce an even surface.

Hence as *v. trans.*

1920 H.S. TAYLOR *Pioneer Irrigationists' Man.* xxxvi. 1 When the whole of the land is contoured, run a plough round each row of pegs, then start buckscraping the banks, terracing the land.

buck-shot. [Transf. use of *buck-shot* coarse shot: see OED 2.] A stratum of ironstone concretions: see quot. 1855.

1855 G.H. WATHEN *Golden Colony* 14 While describing these plains, I ought to allude to what the settlers have named 'buck-shot'. This is a kind of black gravel, mingled with the soil to a depth of a few inches, and consisting of small, irregular-shaped stones, about the size of a pea or of a small bean. This, though not universally diffused, is found over large areas. It may perhaps be a volcanic ash. **1948** G.W. LEEPER *Introd. Soil Science* (rev. ed.) 19 The ironstone gravel, which is known in Victoria as 'buckshot', often appears on the surface after erosion.

buck spinifex. Any of several plants, esp. the grass *Triodia longiceps* (fam. Poaceae) which has rigid pointed blades; *old man spinifex* see OLD MAN B. 3.

1883 W.J. O'DONNELL *Diary Exploring Exped.* 8 Aug. (1884) 15 Following the valley of a small creek, which joined the Margaret near here, we steered easterly, and soon reached the foot of some rough sandstone ridges, covered with buck spinifex. **1898** D.W. CARNEGIE *Spinifex & Sand* 177 There are two varieties of spinifex known to bushmen—'spinifex' and 'buck' (or 'old man') spinifex. The latter is stronger in the prickle and practically impossible to get through. **1909** *Emu* VIII. 175, I had the good luck to flush a female Emblema pictata from her nest in a huge clump of 'buck' spinifex. **1931** M. TERRY *Hidden Wealth* 36 The top feed (edible bushes), associated with buck spinifex . . is raising some of the highest priced wool in Australia. **1958** F.B. VICKERS *Mirage* 156 There was only buck spinifex for the cattle to nibble at now—coarse, hard spikes that had no nourishment in them. **1977** J. DOUGHTY *Gold in Blood* 174 This was not stock country: this was a land of small buck-spinifex, needle sharp, growing porcupine-like on the hard red earth.

budda /'bʌdə/. Also **buddha, budtha.** [a. Wiradhuri and Yuwaalaraay *budaa.*] Any of several shrubs or small trees of inland Aust. esp. *Eremophila mitchellii* (fam. Myoporaceae), the leaves and timber of which have a strong aroma resembling that of sandalwood; the wood of the plant. See also SANDALWOOD *n.*[2] Also *attrib.*

1890 *Sydney Mail* 14 June 1300/1, I would state that the tree known as sandalwood on the Darling and in the West generally, one of the 'Eremophylla', called 'Butha' by the natives, is not eaten by sheep, and is only attacked by rabbits when nothing better is to be had. **1895** *Worker* (Sydney) 26 June 4/1 The sun was just rising, and the dewdrops, still clinging to the drooping branches of the buddha scrub, were glittering like so many diamonds. **1899** *Truth* (Sydney) 31 Dec. 2/6 A Sahara tempered to the eye with clumps of budda-bush and ti-tree. **1901** K.L. PARKER in M. Muir *My Bush Bk.* (1982) 101 The bright shiny green budtha, with its nutty-scented white or pale heliotrope flowers, which every shower brings out so lavishly as almost to hide the leaves, should be near the homestead. **1921** K.S. PRICHARD *Black Opal* 5 Bunches of paper daisies and budda blossoms. **1930** *Bulletin* (Sydney) 17 Dec. 21/2 Up till quite recently N.S. Wales farmers (and bushmen generally) have remained blind to the many virtues of the budda-tree. . . Budda is now beginning to come into its own. . . The proper spelling . . is 'budtha', an aboriginal word meaning strong-smelling. **1956** T.Y. HARRIS *Naturecraft in Aust.* 193 Among the most persistent shrubs . . are Wilga, Budda. **1978** B. ST. A. SMITH *Spirit beyond Psyche* 93 The beating heart of the Black Opal Country was a painter's paradise with its characteristic lunar landscape of pearly-white mullock heaps backed by olive-dun, straggling low buddha scrub. **1985** *Age* (Melbourne) 23 Dec. 12/2 Even dry country is adversely affected by shrubby invaders like . . budda.

buddawong, var. BURRAWANG.

buddha, var. BUDDA.

budgeree /'bʌdʒəri, 'bʊdʒəri/, *a. Austral. pidgin.* Also with much variety, as **boodgery, boojeree, budgeri.** [a. Dharuk *bujari.*] Good.

1790 D. SOUTHWELL Corresp. & Papers *Boó-gē-reē* (boo-jē-ree), good, handsome, comely, pretty. **1793** W. TENCH *Compl. Acct. Settlement* 116 We were Englishmen, and Bud-yee-rée (good). **1793** J. HUNTER *Hist. Jrnl. Trans. Port Jackson* 213 They very frequently . . would apply to us for . . marks of our approbation of their performance; which we never failed to give by often repeating the word *boojery*, which signifies good. *c* **1795** G. BARRINGTON *Voyage to Botany Bay* 107 They . . appear highly delighted if you say '*boojerie cariberie*', a very good dance. **1803** J. GRANT *Narr. Voyage N.S.W.* 150 A native . . on seeing the boat had run down to it, crying out several times, *Whale Boat!* and *Budgerie Dick!* or *Good Dick.* **1830** R. DAWSON *Present State Aust.* 12 'Budgeree,' (very good,) he replied. **1849** W. CARRON *Narr. Exped. Rockingham Bay & Cape York* 89 Depositions were taken, before which he became faint; and a glass of wine revived him, which he told us afterwards, made him 'budgeree' (that is well again). **1852** *Empire* (Sydney) 6 Jan. 543/2 The niggers were at first frightened at the treacle, thinking it to be black paint, but after tasting, they pronounced it 'budgery sugar bag', and to work they went. **1870** C.H. ALLEN *Visit to Qld.* 183 There are certain native terms used by the whites also as a kind of colonial slang, such as 'yabber', to talk; 'budgeree', good. **1892** *Bulletin* (Sydney) 14 May 7/4 She tempted him with promises Of 'budgeree tuck out'—That's 'pigeon-talk' for pigeon pie, Roast goose and bottled stout. **1903** J. FURPHY *Such is Life* 200 'My word!' I exclaimed admiringly, 'you take-um budgeree rise out-a whitepeller, John!' **1912** J. BRADSHAW *Highway Robbery under Arms* (ed. 2) 20 To the tune of 'Budgery, you my boy, and more like it,' [*sic*] played by several young gins on the jel-pe jel-pe. **1944** C. FENNER *Mostly Austral.* 8 The approved spelling for this substance is 'pitjeri', but it is also commonly spelt 'pituri', a word that is said to be related to budgeri, which means 'good'. **1959** M. RAYMOND *Smiley roams Road* 169 Good, bonzer or budgeree—as the blackfellows say. **1981** A. WELLER *Day of Dog* 88 Valerie's budjarrie for me ya know. If she 'as a miscarriage from tonight's rip, I'll kill you, Doug, true's God.

budgerigar /'bʌdʒərigа/. Also **betcherrygah, betshiregah, budgerygar.** [a. Yuwaalaraay (and related languages) *gijirrigaa.*] The small green and yellow parrot *Melopsittacus undulatus*, occurring in drier mainland areas, often in large flocks, and a popular cage bird; LOVE-BIRD; SHELL PARROT; WARBLING GRASS PARAKEET; *zebra parrot*, see ZEBRA.

1840 J. GOULD *Birds of Aust.*(1848) V. Pl. 44, *Melopsittacus undulatus.* Warbling Grass-Parrakeet. . . Undulated Parrot. . . Canary Parrot, Colonists. Betcherrygah, Natives of Liverpool Plains. **1845** L. LEICHHARDT *Jrnl. Overland Exped. Aust.* 20 June (1847) 297 The rose-breasted Cockatoo and the Betshiregah (Melopsittacus undulatus . .) were very numerous. **1848** H.W. HAYGARTH *Recoll. Bush Life* 139 A most brilliant little parrot. . . It is about the size of a bullfinch, and is called budgery garr (budgery, in the black's language, meaning good or handsome). It is easily tamed. **1851** J. HENDERSON *Excursions & Adventures N.S.W.* II. 181 The *budgeryga*, a very small paroquet, whose plumage cannot be surpassed. **1854** *Southern Cross & Antarctic Gaz.* 15 Mar. 3/2 Ah, no! 'tis but a little bird, The gentle Budgery Gar! **1860** A. MACPHERSON *My Experiences in Aust.* 31 The well-known boodjerigah, or shell parrot, or love bird, as it is more commonly called. **1868** J.R. HOULDING *Austral. Tales* 116 She is as tender-hearted as a little 'budgery ghar', bless her! **1877** C.W. GEDNEY *Foreign Cage Birds* 19 The budgerigars are Australian birds, congregating in large flocks upon the inland pastures. **1878** R.B. SMYTH *Aborigines of Vic.* II. 303 A blackfellow with his girdle full of unfledged *Budgerygars* (shell parrakeets), which he had stuffed under by the heads. **1884** W.T. GREENE *Parrots in Captivity* I. 112 Budgerigars, we prefer this name to the long appellation of Undulated Grass Parakeet. **1890** G.J. BROINOWSKI *Birds of Aust.* III. Pl. xxxviii, The best known name is the native one, Budgerigar, signifying 'pretty bird'. **1902** *Emu* II. 17 Visitors of the parrot tribe are . . the little 'Betcherrygah' (Melopsittacus undulatus). **1933** D. MACDONALD *Brooks of Morning* 68 Budgerygah is the Australian word that has spread farthest over the world. **1949** H.C. JAMES *Gold is where you find It* 27, I knew then the water was permanent because there was thousands and thousands of budgerigars and blood-finches there. **1970** R. ROBINSON *Altjeringa* 64 Zig-zag lightnings of budgerigars. **1977** J. CARTER *All Things Wild* 51 Budgerigars are listed at $100 each. **1980** A.S. VEITCH *Run from Morning* 129, I married a good woman and a budgerigar and reformed.

budgie /'bʌdʒi/. [f. BUDG(ERIGAR + -Y. Used elsewhere but recorded earliest in Aust.] BUDGERIGAR.

1935 W. WATMOUGH *Cult of Budgerigar* 207 Although Budgies are so hardy . . reasonable care should at all times be exercised to protect them from chills. **1946** D. BARR *Warrigal Joe* 30 Wave after wave of budgies swept over the water. **1970** *Matilda* (Winton Tourist Promotion Assoc.) 58 A cloud of budgies settling, like a quilt of ruffled green. **1973** M. STEEL *Red Rover* 127 Budgerigars in the wild are quite different from budgies in cages. **1985** *Canberra Times* 11 Dec. 10/5 How do you degrease a budgie that has fallen into a pot of fat?

budtha, var. BUDDA.

buffalo grass. [U.S. *buffalo grass*, referring orig. to the low-growing perennial grass *Buchloë dactyloides* common on former buffalo ranges.] The introduced *Stenotaphrum secundatum* (fam. Poaceae), cultivated as a coarse lawn grass.

1875 *Illustr. Sydney News* 19 Jan. 18/2 It can be propagated either from seed or roots, the same as couch or buffalo grass. **1879** *Illustr. Austral. News* (Melbourne) 7 June 94/3 In the hot summer months the fresh springy buffalo grass will form a most welcome pathway. **1886** J.A. FROUDE *Oceana* 101 The coarse buffalo-grass eats, like a destroying monster, into its delicate English rival and kills it out of the way. **1903** *Proc. Linnean Soc. N.S.W.* XXVIII. 752 *Stenotaphrum americanum* . . the common Buffalo Grass of Australia, but not of America. **1917** EWART & DAVIES *Flora N.T.* 40 Buffalo grass. Useful as a coarse lawn grass in hot climates, but browned by frost, and a low-grade pasture plant. **1926** A.S. LE SOUEF et al. *Wild Animals Australasia* 330 The long buffalo-grass skirting a swamp. **1955** P. WHITE *Tree of Man* 261 So he went away in his sandshoes, over the spongy buffalo grass. **1968** G. DUTTON *Andy* 229 Andy and Feline lay on a rug on the bumpy buffalo grass of Merv's ill-kept lawn.

buffel grass. [S. Afr. *buffel grass*, f. Du. *buffel* buffalo.] The tussocky perennial African grass *Cenchrus ciliaris* (fam. Poaceae), valued as a forage plant and soil stabilizer.

1931 M. TERRY *Hidden Wealth* 324 A marsh on Wallal sown with buffle grass gives a great body of feed. **1958** O. RUHEN *Naked under Capricorn* 214 At the old camel camps a new kind of grass, a buffel grass, was growing among the spinifex. . . It came from the Middle East, and had been brought accidentally in the padding of the camel saddles. **1962** C. GYE *Cockney & Crocodile* 133 The road was white clay edged with buffel grass and wild yellow hibiscus. **1978** O. WHITE *Silent Reach* 122 A pair of hunting eagle hawks, soaring, dipping and wheeling above the expanse of bleached buffel grass.

bugeen /'bʌgin/. Also **buggeen.** [a. Wiradhuri *bagiin*ʸ, but cf. Br. dial. *bugan* evil spirit (see EDD).] A devil or evil spirit. See also quot. 1980.

1834 G. BENNETT *Wanderings N.S.W.* I. 126 They were afraid, if they buried them, the *Buckee*, or evil devil would take them away. **1948** F. CLUNE *Wild Colonial Boys* 102 By night they . . protected their hut with a 'buggeen' or devil-on-a-stump. This was a pumpkin, scooped hollow, with three holes to represent eyes and mouth, and a lighted candle inside, placed on a tree-stump outside the hut. **1958** R. ROBINSON *Black-Feller White-Feller* 111 Someone, a *bugeen* perhaps, is sneaking up on me to kill me with his *guneena*, his devils' stones. **1977** M. TUCKER *If everyone Cared* 79 She became frightened of *bugenge*, the same bogeyman as at Moonahculla or *becca* at Cummeragunga. **1980** P. PEPPER *You are what you make Yourself* 33 Their parents went to the *bugheen*, that's the clever bloke of the tribe and got him to sing the one who took the girls away.

bugle.

1. The nose.

1891 *Truth* (Sydney) 3 May 6/3 He got a good left flush home on George's mouth, and George met him full on the bugle, and drew first blood. **1901** *Ibid.* 14 July 8/3 Mr Dorward's 'bugle' had evidently received a business-like bash, which . . splintered the nasal bone. **1904** M. WHITE *Shanty Entertainment* 15 It was never known as a nose. It was sheer insult to call it anything less than a bugle.

2. In the phr. **on the bugle,** smelly; hence 'a bit off', crooked.

1943 J. DEVINE *Rats of Tobruk* 111 Everything was 'on the bugle' to him. By this he meant that he disliked it. Bugle stood for nose, and saying a thing was on the nose meant that it smelt. **1945** I.L. IDRIESS *Horrie*

Wog-Dog 9 'Perhaps the meat is too much on the bugle (smelly),' suggested Fitz doubtfully. **1962** J. WYNNUM *Tar Dust* 104 They dished up some greasy pork chops . . for breakfast—can you imagine that! Makes me feel crook just to talk about it. And into the bargain, they were on the bugle. **1967** *Kings Cross Whisper* (Sydney) xxxviii. 10/1 *On the bugle*, something fishy. A term used about a dud rort. **1968** G. DUTTON *Andy* 307 Yer know, matey, my name rhymes with perv but I'm not like that. I'm just a simple crook, you know that. There are some things that are on the bugle. I'm not interested. **1973** J. O'GRADY *Survival in Doghouse* 80, I . . tell Ray things are all right, and ask him how they are with him. He says 'They're a bit on the bugle, mate.' I say, 'What seems to be the trouble?'

bugong, var. BOGONG.

build-up. *N.T.* [Spec. use of *build-up* gradual accumulation.] The period of gradually increasing heat and humidity which precedes the wet season.

1977 K. COLE *Winds of Fury* 12 The transition from the Dry to the Wet, known as the 'build-up', takes place from October to December. **1985** *Centralian Advocate* (Alice Springs) 18 Dec. 2/4 The Wet Season arrived dubiously, not bringing many of its promised merciful downpours . . and the build-up keeps building.

bulk, *a.* [Prob. by analogy with *bulk-buying.*] Many.

1977 *Surf Wacks* 2 Bulk people camped at Cactus, and Witzig was raking in bulk money. **1984** *Advertiser* (Adelaide) 26 Jan. 17/3 They may be too busy writing bulk new scripts for the second series of the mega-trendy comedy, *Australia, You're Standing In It*. **1984** *Canberra Times* 14 Feb. 17/4 Bulk kisses and hugs, Marcus.

bull, *n.*^{1} *Hist.* Also **beal, bool.** [Spec. use of *bull* a drink made from spirit or sugar residue: see OED *sb.*^{6} and *v.*^{4}] A crudely sweetened or alcoholic drink formerly favoured by Aborigines: see quots. 1839 and 1840.

1821 Methodist Missionary Soc. Rec. 5 Oct., If they cut wood, or do any other trifling work, they are rewarded with what they call *bull*; sometimes this is composed of a mixture of spirituous liquors, and at others is the washing of liquor puncheons. **1826** R. DAWSON *Private & Confidential* 9 One of their great treats is to get 'Bull'—that is, an old sugar bag, cut into shreds and boiled in an Iron pot filled with water, which they place over a blazing fire and stir with the ends of their spears. **1834** G. BENNETT *Wanderings N.S.W.* I. 326 The camp was now one scene of tumult and confusion: the huts, of a weak and temporary construction, were thrown down; the men, inebriated with '*bull*', were chasing the women and children with sticks. **1838** T.L. MITCHELL *Three Exped. Eastern Aust.* II. 286 Piper explained the purpose for which these flowers had been gathered, by informing me that by steeping them a night in water the natives make a sweet beverage named 'bool'. **1839** W. MANN *Six Yrs.' Residence* 152 He asked for a vessel to mix the honey with some water, which mixture they call *bull*; the same term is applied if sugar be the substitute for honey. This they drank with great glee, which excited them almost as much as the same quantity of wine would affect Europeans. **1840** J.P. JOHNSON *Plain Truths* 55 Their grog, or bull, as it is termed, is a small quantity of boiling water put into a cask, out of which all the spirits have been drawn, or at any rate only leaving the dirt at the bottom. **1846** T.H. BRAIM *Hist. N.S.W.* 248 The natives . . are very fond . . of the refuse [honey]comb, with which they make their favourite beverage called Bull, and of this they drink till they become quite intoxicated. **1848** *Maitland Mercury* 18 Mar. 2/4 On Thursday night a party of aboriginals, who had got plentifully supplied with 'bool', or intoxicating liquor, had a corroborree in Maitland, followed by a quarrel, which eventually included nearly all of them, and led to an interference by some of the whites. **1878** R.B. SMYTH *Aborigines of Vic.* I. 210 In the flowers of a dwarf species of *Banksia* (*B. ornata*) there is a good deal of honey, and this was got out of the flowers by immersing them in water. The water thus sweetened was greedily swallowed by the natives. The drink was named *Beal* by the natives of the west of Victoria. **1975** A.B. & J.W. CRIBB *Wild Food in Aust.* 182 Sir Thomas Mitchell found that Aborigines in Victoria made a sweet drink called 'bool' by steeping the flowers of an ironbark in water. **1984** *Canberra Times* 21 Sept. 17/2 Aboriginals soaked the large flower spikes of *B. serrata* in water to obtain a dilute sugary drink known as 'beal'.

bull, *n.*^{2} *Obs.* [Transf. use of *bull*, former Br. slang for a five shilling coin.] Seventy-five strokes of the lash.

1859 J. LANG *Botany Bay* (1885) 30 There were slang terms applied to these doses of the lash: twenty five was called a 'tester', fifty, a 'bob',—seventy five, a 'bull' and a hundred a 'canary'.

bull, *n.*^{3} Used *attrib.* in the names of flora and fauna: **bull bird,** BOOMER *n.*^{2}; **head,** any of several unrelated plants bearing spiny fruits, esp. DOUBLE-GEE; also **bull (head) burr; mallee, (a)** a form of growth of mallee eucalypts (see quots. 1956, 1962, and 1982); **(b)** any of several mallee eucalypts, esp. *Eucalyptus behriana* (fam. Myrtaceae) of N.S.W., Vic., and S.A.; **Mitchell,** see MITCHELL GRASS 2; **oak,** any of several trees, esp. of the genera *Casuarina* and *Allocasuarina* (fam. Casuarinaceae) and usu. *A. luehmanii* of inland Qld., N.S.W., Vic., and S.A.; the wood of these trees; also **buloke; rout,** any of several fish, esp. *Notesthes robusta*, a scorpion fish (fam. Scorpaenidae) of e. Aust. and Irian Jaya coastal waters, estuaries and fresh-water streams, having venomous spines on the head which can inflict painful wounds.

1857 *Moreton Bay Free Press* 15 Apr. 3/7 The **bull-bird** has only been seen three or four times in Australia. **1970** J.V. MARSHALL *Walk to Hills of Dreamtime* 148 *Bittern*. . . Widely known as the Boomer or Bull-bird because of its call—'three or four deep booms, like the bellowing of a bull'. **1938** [**bull head**] *Qld. Agric. Jrnl.* L. 790 Cape spinach or prickly jack . . also called bull head burr, a name applied, however, to other burrs in Queensland. **1967** *Southerly* iii. 199 Weeds flourished, wait-a-whiles, bull-burrs, wild blackberries, Bathurst burrs. **1977** KLEINSCHMIDT & JOHNSON *Weeds Qld.* 178 In Queensland, spiny emex is also known as . . bullhead and goathead. It occurs in disturbed sites such as cultivated paddocks. **1890** W.H. BUNDEY *Winter Cruise* 13 **Bull mallee** is a problem to the ordinary grubbing contractor. **1934** J.S. NEILSON *Autobiogr.* (1978) 47 When I tackled cutting the bell bottomed mallee (or bull mallee) as we used to call it, my thumb gave way. **1946** *Bulletin* (Sydney) 24 July 29/2 The victim was said to have been found hanging from a shell-parrot's hole . . in a bull mallee hollow out on the Hopetoun-road. **1956** R.H. ANDERSON *Trees of N.S.W.* (ed. 3) 37 The larger Mallees which often become single-stemmed are called Bull Mallees. **1962** H.J. FRITH *Mallee-Fowl* 54 On heavy soils the eucalypts have only a few stems, perhaps six to eight inches thick, and are known as bull mallee. **1982** BARKER & GREENSLADE *Evol. Flora & Fauna* 153 In western New South Wales, most of the common mallee species . . can occur either as 1–3 stemmed trees known as 'bull' mallee up to 10 m in height or as multi-stemmed 'whipstick' mallee 1–3 m high. **1874** 'REV. F.T.P.' *Thirty-Shilling Horse* 40 'That wasn't she-oak you gave your horse, but **bull-oak**.' I had never heard of bull-oak before, so I asked the difference. He informed me that she-oak was sour, bull-oak was bitter. **1880** C. PROUD *S.-E. District S.A.* 10 'Bull oak'—a fine straight tree which looks like a pine in the distance. **1905** *Bulletin* (Sydney) 14 Dec. 23/1 And my heart is fain for the bush again—Far out, far out, where the bull-oaks grow! **1908** *Ibid.* 16 July 14/2 First-class country carrying salmon gum, gimlet and morrell equal to the Buloke and box country of the Wimmera. **1915** J.P. BOURKE *Off Bluebush* 108 And the shaft is there near the ridge's crown, By the foot of an old bull-oak. **1931** *Bulletin* (Sydney) 4 Feb. 20/3 'Sheoke' and 'buloke' are the names that have been adopted for two kinds of casuarinas. It was considered that 'she-oak' and 'bull-oak', the previous names, would suggest a relationship with the oak of Europe which the casuarinas cannot claim. **1944** J. DEVANNY *By Tropic Sea & Jungle* 130 The bull oak by itself is a harsh and formidable tree, with its heavy, dark green leaves and grey acorns. **1956** *Bulletin* (Sydney) 23 May 12/1 Spotted a bulloak backlog for my fireplace. **1960** *Ibid.* 16 Mar. 19/3 The paling-splitter . . may be flushed in an odd gully or two . . catering for a Macquarie Street farmer with some fancy bull-oak shingles. **1972** ANDERSON & BLAKE *J.S. Neilson* 19 Subsequently they built one and two-room huts of bull-oak spars driven into the ground and fastened at a height of seven to eight feet to a wall plate. **1983** *Age* (Melbourne) 31 Aug. 12/1 The native pine-buloke woodlands cannot regenerate as all seedlings are immediately eaten by kangaroos. **1986** *Trees & Natural Resources* Mar. 8 In the Wimmera, the Bulloak (*Casuarina luehmanni*) . . and Black box . . were found on the best wheat land and only vestiges on road and rail reserves now remain. **1851** J. HENDERSON *Excursions & Adventures N.S.W.* II. 207 There is a small fish, called the **Bull-rout**, which inhabits the rivers, and is capable of biting or stinging in a desperate manner. **1882** J.E. TENISON-WOODS *Fish & Fisheries N.S.W.* 48 It emits a loud and harsh grunting noise when it is caught. . . When out of the water the noise of the Bull-rout is loudest. . . The name of bull-rout may possibly be a corruption of some native word. **1916** *Bulletin* (Sydney) 3 Feb. 22/2 There are several remedies for bull-rout 'stings'. **1948** H.A. LINDSAY *Bushman's Handbk.* 85 In some of the coastal creeks up north the poisonous spines of the bullrout lie in wait for bare or lightly-shod feet. **1984** *Overlander* July 81 Bullrouts are a fair match for a stone-fish, and fishermen are a touch apprehensive about standing on them in the weedbeds.

bull, *n.*^{4} [Prob. fig. use of *bull* the animal, as chosen by a buyer in a sale-yard: see quot. 1975.]

1. A wharf labourer who is given preferential treatment when work is allocated by the foreman. See also PINK-EYE *n.*^{3}

1957 T. NELSON *Hungry Mile* 80 The employers were often responsible for the undermining of the union's attempt to prevent wrongful movement of men from job to job by indulging in illegal trafficking of 'bulls' to suit their own ends, or meet the request of other companies for early release of 'bulls' for new jobs starting. **1975** V. WILLIAMS *Yrs. of Big Jim* 71 The compound, now known as the Waterside Labour Bureau, resembled the Newmarket cattle yards. Members of the Federation were herded into one pen. **1978** W. LOWENSTEIN *Weevils in Flour* 244 Anyone who could get into a foreman's No. 1 or No. 2 gang was assured of a reasonable living. These were the bulls. The rest of you had to take the leavings. **1979** S. MORAN *Reminisc. of Rebel* 24, I earned about $3.50 per week. . . 'Bulls' (workers favoured by the foreman) earned 5, 6, or 7 times that. **1984** S. MACINTYRE *Militant* 71 In the cattle yard, down on the wharf Where only the 'bulls' can get a go, There isn't a chance to get picked up, Unless you're in the know.

2. Comb. **bull system.**

1957 T. NELSON *Hungry Mile* 77 The battle to end the bull system is unsurpassed in the history of Australian unionism. **1968** F. ROSE *Aust. Revisited* 92 Up to the nineteen-thirties the 'bull' system of recruiting labour was used. The men seeking work congregated at the wharf gates and the foreman . . selected what labour he wanted. **1979** S. MORAN *Reminisc. of Rebel* 24 In my first years on the Waterfront we worked according to the 'Bull System'. **1982** LOWENSTEIN & HILLS *Under Hook* 66 The bull system became entrenched on the Melbourne waterfront.

bull, *v.*^{1} *Mining.* [f. *bull* iron rod used in blasting: see OED *sb.*^{1} 5.] *trans.* See quot. 1958.

1889 *Braidwood Dispatch* 30 Oct. 2/4 He was engaged in 'bulling' three drills, and was very unwisely carrying all lighted fuses with plugs of dynamite attached in his hand. **1899** *North-Western Advocate* (Devonport) 15 Mar. 2/8 About half-past 4 deceased started to 'bull' a hole to put a charge in. **1902** *Bulletin* (Sydney) 27 Oct. 35/2 A drill bore will often be seen to terminate in a round cavity. That cavity is the result of 'bulling'. **1958** *Prospector's Guide* (N.S.W. Mines Dept.) 191 *Bull*, to enlarge the bottom of a drilled hole to increase the explosive charge.

bull, *v.*^{2} [Survival of Br. *bull* to adulterate: see OED *v.*^{4} and BULL *n.*^{1}.] *trans.* To adulterate. Also as *ppl. a.*

1891 *Truth* (Sydney) 8 Mar. 7/3 Then the whisky comes. That is watered and 'bulled'. You may say that there is no profit in that. Don't you know that a 'tanner' saved is a sixpence gained? **1929** W.J. RESIDE *Golden Days* 277 'Bulled' water is the condensed brackish fluid to which a proportion of uncondensed has been added to make the measurement when the sale is by the gallon. The term is obsolete. There are no condensers, and *few prospectors* in W.A. now. **1932** K.S. PRICHARD *Kiss on Lips* 232 It was decided to give the camels and horses 'bulled' water, brackish and pure water mixed. **1959** *Bulletin* (Sydney) 23 Dec. 16/1 The most heinous crime in the shearing-shed—next to 'scabbing'—is to 'bull' your room-mate's rum after surreptitiously swiping some.

Bullamakanka /bʊləmə'kæŋkə/. Also **Bullabakanka.** [Perh. based on pidgin *bulla macow* bully beef: see OEDS.] An imaginary place, remote and supposedly backward. See also WOOP WOOP 1.

1953 T.A.G. HUNGERFORD *Riverslake* 230 Hitch out to Bullamakanka and live with the blacks. **1977** *Southerly* i. 48 Because for a lazy man . . literary editorship of the Bullamakanka *Clarion's* Saturday Book page is a very sweet cop indeed. **1980** A.S. VEITCH *Run from Morning* 129 One of your original Aussie battlers. Started with a horse and dray at Bullabakanka.

bullan bullan /'bʊlən bʊlən/. *Obs.* Also **bullen bullen, buln buln.** [a. Wuywurung *bulin bulin.*] *Superb lyre-bird*, see SUPERB.

1843 *Port Phillip Mag.* Feb. (Advt.), Beautiful specimens of the 'Lyre Bird', 'Menura Superba', or 'Bullen Bullen'. **1845** *Atlas* (Sydney) I. 280/3 The lyre-bird, (bullen bullen, or native pheasant) was in great variety and number but very timid. **1858** *Illustr. Jrnl. Australasia* IV. 120 The native name of the bird is Bullan Bullan, and is said to be derived from a sort of gurgling noise which it makes when alarmed. **1865** J. GOULD *Handbk. Birds Aust.* 303 Bullan-Bullan is the name which the aborigines of the Yarra tribe give to this bird. **1896** F.G. AFLALO *Sketch Nat. Hist. Aust.* 132 Besides a mellow note of its own, from which the aboriginals know it as the Bullan-Bullan, the bird is a capital mimic. **1948** J. FURPHY *Buln-Buln & Brolga* 85 The Buln-buln and Brolga returned to their seat. **1965** *Austral. Encycl.* V. 393 Very few aboriginal names for the lyrebird have been recorded. The best-known one is *bullen-bullen*, or *buln-buln*.

bull-ant. Shortened form of BULLDOG ANT. Also *attrib.*

1880 J. BALLANTYNE *Our Colony* 93 Ants are numerous, . . the bull-ant being of large size. **1908** *Emu* VIII. 155 The stomach contained scores of the large brown bull-ant, well known to those who have accidentally rested upon one of their mounds. **1936** *Austral. Writers' Ann.* 31 Nothing takes the conceit out of a bumptious human quicker than a bull-ant; nothing in the bush impresses the new chum more than the electric shock of Bully's sting. **1941** *Bulletin* (Sydney) 9 Apr. 16/2 The true bull-ant (*Myrmecia genus*) invariably exhibits a wholesome aversion to fire. Bushmen working in bull-ant country always light a few gumleaves and twigs on any nearby nests so that they can work undisturbed. **1942** C. BARRETT *From Bush Hut* 15 Goanna oil's best for a cold, and splendid for bullant stings. **1953** D. CUSACK *Southern Steel* 25 You can't fool me. You'd be as mad as a bull-ant if they listened to you. **1972** K. WILLEY *Tales Big Country* 151 That red bull-ant is the biggest ant in the world. He'd swallow your finger. **1985** *Austral. Short Stories* 38 Old Pearson had died out in the bush. . . The bullants stripped him clean.

bullbar. A strong metal bar or frame mounted at the front of a vehicle to reduce damage to the vehicle in the event of a collision with a stray beast, kangaroo, etc; *kangaroo bar*, see KANGAROO *n.* 6; *roo bar*, see ROO *n.*[2] c.

1967 J. YEOMANS *Scarce Australs.* 97 Most beasts had been killed by one blow from the bull bars (the heavy horizontal steel tubing mounted as cattle guards) on the front of a road train. **1975** *Wheels* July 82 A bull bar is also handy in scrub country, where you may nudge the occasional tree. **1978** *Truckin' Life* II. vii. 32 Did you ever plod along behind a Road-Train, When you couldn't see your bull-bar for the dust. **1984** *N.T. News* (Darwin) 15 Sept. 42/3 Nissan MQ 4 x 4 S/wagon Diesel Air-con tow/bar Air shocks, Bullbar, Driving lights, F.W.H. long rego. **1985** *Canberra Times* 8 Feb. 2/7 'The roos are a bit of a risk aren't they?' . . 'Not since I got the bullbars fitted!'

bulldog ant. A large ant of any of several species of the genus *Myrmecia*, capable of inflicting a painful sting; BULL-ANT; BULLJOE. Also *ellipt.* as **bulldog.**

1851 W.B. CLARKE *Researches Southern Gold Fields N.S.W.* (1860) 120 It was difficult to find a spot on which to lay our blankets, on account of the 'Bull Dog Ants'. **1853** MRS C. CLACY *Lady's Visit to Gold Diggings* 134 The largest [ants] are called by the old colonists, 'bull-dogs', and formidable creatures they are . . about an inch and a half long, black, or rusty black, with a red tail. They bite like a little crab. **1855** W. HOWITT *Land, Labor & Gold* II. 113 One half of a bull-dog ant fights the other if cut in two. **1875** R. THATCHER *Something to his Advantage* 124 How can one happy be With 'bull-dog' ants inside your hat. And black ants in your tea? **1890** A. WOODHOUSE *Man with Apples* 99 It was a narrow shave with you—the bull-dog ants were already on you when I came along. **1903** 'BOONDI' *Boondi's Bk.* 37 When it comes to a matter of hanging on to a soft thing not even an Australian politician can come within cooee of the 'bull-dog' ant. **1932** *Bulletin* (Sydney) 27 Jan. 21/3 Puff cigarette smoke at a common black and tan ant or a bulldog ant, and he'll spring *at* you. **1941** *Ibid.* 9 Apr. 16/2 The true bull-ant (*Myrmecia genus*) invariably exhibits a wholesome aversion to fire. . . Nor does the bulldog display any liking for natural heat. **1975** DONALDSON & JOSEPH *Wilderness* 44 An army of inch-long ants spilled out bristling for war. 'Bulldogs,' commented Amy. **1981** *Woman's Day* (Sydney) 9 Sept. 75/1 She suggested a documentary on bulldog ants which are, like the funnel web, native to Australia. They are also the most primitive ant in the world.

bulldust, *n.*

1. [Prob. with ref. to powdered dirt in e.g. a stock yard, etc., but see also quot. 1962.] A kind of fine powdery dirt or dust. Also *attrib.*

1932 I.L. IDRIESS *Flynn of Inland* (1965) 170 Crossing the Arthur River . . they came down on to the flat country and the 'bull dust' (finer than sand yet not quite dust), a greasy sort of dust in which, in wet or dry, beast and car can bog very easily if they break through the crust. **1939** M.B. ELDERSHAW *My Aust.* 181 In places the crust is desiccated into 'bull dust', a crumbly dusty soil such as bulls like to roll in. **1947** O. GRIFFITHS *Darwin Drama* 205 The bush roads were covered with a thick carpet of fine 'bull' dust and . . everyone was impregnated from head to foot with, and had taken on the light pink colour of, the dust. **1955** A. GROOM *Wealth in Wilderness* 73 Bulldust rose in a choking, penetrating cloud with its suffocating thick smell. **1960** *N.T. News* (Darwin) 26 Jan. 5/4 He then complained my tail light was pink instead of red. I said its got bulldust on it. I've been out in the bush. **1962** C. GYE *Cockney & Crocodile* 74 The track was full of deep holes, filled up flat with fine dust as yielding as water and apt to break axles or bog you down. It was called bull dust, not from any connection with bulls but from its ferocity. **1968** D. O'GRADY *Bottle of Sandwiches* 16 The bull-dust gave us some strife for a while. That stuff's like talcum powder, and there was enough of it to cover the bottoms of all the babies in the world. **1979** DUSTY & LAPSLEY *Walk Country Mile* 153 Glarmkahn, a Pakistani country singer . . refused to believe it when he saw the Nullarbor signs warning: 'Bulldust—beware.' **1984** *4 × 4* July 30 A bulldust hole . . can just as easily trip up a 4WD.

2. [Orig. U.S.] Euphemistic var. of 'bullshit', *n.*

1951 'S. MACKENZIE' *Dead Men Rising* 70 He, while a soldier on active service—what bulldust . . did absent himself. **1952** P. GLADWIN *Desert in Heart* 132 He was a snide young bastard, chockablock with boarding-school bulldust. **1954** J. CLEARY *Climate of Courage* 264 'I'm seventy-five per cent Irish,' said Mick. 'You're seventy-five per cent bulldust, too,' said Joe. **1965** J. WYNNUM *Jiggin' in Riggin'* 114 'If Bulldust was music, that bloke would have his own private brass band,' he observed. **1967** B. BREYDOR *Flying is for Birds* 23 This administrative building was fondly known to the troops of Laverton as 'Bull-dust Castle'. **1970** E. & D. CAMPBELL *Demonstrator* 67 Fred had spent a lifetime in Universities filling his students with the golden bulldust of the ages. **1978** B. ST. A. SMITH *Spirit beyond Psyche* 213 Nerves? *Nerves is all bull-dust.*

3. Comb. **bulldust artist.**

1965 I. HAMILTON *Persecutor* 189, I know you'll pass for an honest man, even if you are a bull-dust artist. **1972** A. CHIPPER *Aussie Swearers Guide* 24 *Bulldust artist*, public relations or Con man.

bulldust, *v.* [f. BULLDUST *n.* 2.] *intr.* Euphemistic var. of 'bullshit', *v.* Also *trans.*

1967 F. HARDY *Billy Borker yarns Again* 58 He bull-dusted and yak-yaked while the ex-warder paid for the beer. **1975** C. PERKINS *Bastard like Me* 166, I was sick and tired of . . getting bull-dusted by all the Yanks and the people from the Australian Embassies. **1979** B. HUMPHRIES *Bazza comes into his Own*, Listen Kev, I reckon you've been overworkin'. Just quit bull-dustin' and drop me off at Mum's hospital.

Hence **bullduster** *n.*

1963 R. STOW *Tourmaline* 93 'I say he's a bloody good prospector,' said Kestrel; 'and the best bullduster I'm likely to meet.' **1975** 'N. CULOTTA' *Gone Gougin'* 104 Les an' Allan are not bulldusters, like some people I know.

bulldusted, *a.* [f. BULLDUST *n.* 1.] Of a (road) surface: covered in fine dust.

1975 *Bulletin* (Sydney) 20 Sept. 34/3 Until you get to Georgetown . . you are on corrugated, bull-dusted dirt. **1976** MULLALLY & SEXTON *Stir Possum* 11 I've travelled many a road in the outback And some which are no road at all, Pot-holed and stony, bull-dusted track.

bulldusty, *a.* Of or pertaining to BULLDUST *n.* 1.

1936 C.T. MADIGAN *Central Aust.* 172 At one cape we were forced close in to the shore, and tried a run on the land surface, but it was altogether too 'bull-dusty', and heavier than the lake surface. **1959** D. LOCKWOOD *Crocodiles & Other People* 43 We drove out along the bull-dusty track. **1968** D. O'GRADY *Bottle of Sandwiches* 28 We had to travel about 140 miles on a rocky, rutty, bull-dusty cattle-pad to get to it. **1979** D. LOCKWOOD *My Old Mates & I* 5 Thousands of hooves had assisted wheels in grinding the ground to bulldusty talc.

bullen bullen, var. BULLAN BULLAN.

Bulli soil /bʊlaɪ'sɔɪl/. [f. the name of a coastal town s. of Sydney, N.S.W.] A clay-rich soil taken from coastal headlands at Bulli and formerly used extensively for cricket pitches and lawn tennis courts.

1912 P.F. WARNER *England v. Aust.* 53 The almost impervious Bulli soil. **1965** *Austral. Encycl.* II. 180 Bulli soil is valued for turf cricket pitches.

bulljoe /'bʊl dʒoʊ/. [f. BULL(DOG ANT + the proper name *Joe*.] BULLDOG ANT. Also **bulljoe ant.**

1952 C. SIMPSON *Come away, Pearler* 222 When Bulljoe got on a trail he hung on to it, never let go—'just like those inch-ants with the big nippers, the ones we call bulljoes.' **1958** *Bulletin* (Sydney) 16 July 18/1, I threw a lighted cigarette-butt on the ground and it landed near a bulljoe-ant. Game as Ned Kelly, Bulljoe charged. **1976** E. WORRELL *Things that Sting* 40 The Red and the Black Bull Ants or 'Bulljoes' live in colonies.

bullo. [f. *bull* nonsense + -O.] Rubbish, nonsense.

1942 *Cheeriodical* (Rathmines) 5 Mar. 2 Believe me, that's no Bullo. **1944** L. GLASSOP *We were Rats* 174 'Mick—this time—they got—me.' 'Bullo,' I said. 'You'll be O.K.' **1974** M. PAICE *Dolan's Roost* 126 'Ah, bullo!' Dobbo decided at last. 'Who'd be mad enough to stick a bag of money in there?'

bullock, *n.*

1. Used *attrib.* in Comb. not necessarily excl. to Austral. but of local importance: **bullock cart, conductor, dray, driver, driving, paddock, persuader, team, track, train, wagon, watchman, whip.** See also OX.

1805 *Sydney Gaz.* 3 Mar., Two stout able men, as labouring servants, whose work will mainly consist in attending a **bullock cart**. **1843** C. ROWCROFT *Tales of Colonies* I. 91 A settler's bullock-cart fortunately was proceeding to Norfolk Plains. **1971** *Bulletin* (Sydney) 13 Nov. 27/1 There's a Cobb & Co. coach, a bullock cart with a white banner proclaiming 'Australia's living history'. **1915** *Ibid.* 1 Apr. 14/4 Don't let us miss the chance of securing a good, technical education to the coming generations of **bullock conductors**. . . The engineering of bullocks is a dying industry. **1847** L. LEICHHARDT *Jrnl. Overland Exped. Aust.* p. xvi, My friends had lent me a **bullock dray**. **1852** F. LANCELOTT *Aust. as it Is* II. 92 A bullock dray is a rude, ponderous affair: compared with the trim built British waggon, it may be likened to a brewer's dray, with the addition of rough unplaned wood sides, about 12 inches high. **1939** *Bulletin* (Sydney) 25 Jan. 20/4 The old German wagon can be included with the bullock-dray on the list of Australia's vanishing vehicles. **1948** J. FAIRFAX *Run o' Waters* 23 The time is past when the journey from Jamberoo to Gerringong and back in bumping bullock drays over vague cedar tracks took three whole days. **1836** *Cornwall Chron.* (Launceston) 24 Dec. 1, I am, Sir, your obedient servant, a poor **bullock driver**. **1858** C.R. THATCHER *Colonial Songster* (rev.

ed.) 17 If nice expressions you would learn, Colonial and new, Some bullock driver who is bogged, Is just the man for you. **1894** G.H. GIBSON *Ironbark Chips* 9 The bullock-driver, another typical Australian, popularly supposed to consist principally of boots, beard and blasphemy. **1901** *Truth* (Sydney) 9 June 3/3 But you have no estimation Of the great Australian nation, Till you listen to a bullock-driver swear. **1948** B. CRONIN *How runs Road* 42 On the back tracks, the little tracks, the mud-and-slush-and-corduroy tracks, the bullock-driver was .. king of the roads. **1847** J. SIDNEY *Voice from Far Interior* 48 **Bullock-driving** in the bush being almost a science, we say, 'any man can knock bullocks about, but very few can drive them.' **1867** 'COLONIST' *Life's Work* 31 Bullock-driving is an Australian accomplishment. **1933** R.S. SAMPSON *Through Central Aust.* 19 The old bullock-driving days. **1923** F.A.C. BISHOP *Rep. on Inspection Barkly Tableland* 5 The country traversed was through the **bullock paddock.** **1980** ANSELL & PERCY *To fight Wild* 102 The mickeys are cut and branded and put in a bullock paddock. **1916** *Bulletin* (Sydney) 6 Jan. 24/3 **Bullock-persuaders** vary in their methods, like other artists. **1829** J. ATKINSON *Distilling & Brewing N.S.W.* 5 It occupies a **bullock team** 12 days, and very often more, to perform a journey from this place to Sydney and back. **1947** J.W. GORDON *Under Wide Skies* 37, I can see the spires of a whirlwind curling In the dusty wake of a bullock team. **1848** *Maitland Mercury* 21 Oct. 2/4 An acquaintance of his was travelling on the Lower Murray, and passing along a **bullock track** .. within about five miles of a certain public-house. **1982** R. HALL *Just Relations* 73 A shelf which had once been a bullock track hewn out of the mountainside by hand. **1855** W. HOWITT *Land, Labor & Gold* I. 72 The colonials plough their way with their ponderous **bullock trains.** **1935** T. RAYMENT *Cluster of Bees* 212 The farm fences may disappear under a drift of sand, and the roads become almost too loose to carry the long bullock-trains. **1909** *Bulletin* (Sydney) 26 Aug. 15/2 Two men on the Victoria 'sat down' on a billabong with a **bullock-waggon**. In two years they had 600 cattle. **1982** R. HALL *Just Relations* 21 Men are still getting drunk here who drove bullock wagons up the range into the backcountry. **1849** S. & J. SIDNEY *Emigrant's Jrnl.* 25 Bullock-driving is more of an art .. but any one can make a **bullock watchman.** **1846** G.H. HAYDON *Five Yrs. Experience Aust. Felix* 138 A large emu .. in consequence of the noise made by the **bullock-whip**, was off. **1870** J. BONWICK *Last Tasmanians* 60 We hear of another who, having caught an unhappy girl, sought to relieve her tears, or subdue her sulks, as it was termed, by first giving her a morning's flogging with a bullock-whip.

2. Special Comb. **bullock bell,** a bell worn by a bullock to indicate its whereabouts; **bush,** the plant *Heterodendrum oleifolium* (see ROSEWOOD).

1845 *Bell's Life in Sydney* 20 Dec. 1/3 The Undersigned has on sale .. **Bullock Bells.** **1862** C. STRETTON *Mem.* II. 215 We could not even hear the cheering sounds of distant bullock-bells. **1895** *Bulletin* (Sydney) 21 Sept. 25/2 Brummy rings the bell, a crack'd old bullock-bell, Which every station cook has got. **1930** D. COTTRELL *Earth Battle* 227 The fading jingle of Luther's bullock-bells drifted to them under the starlight. **1951** G. FARWELL *Outside Track* 38 Only the rare sound of a bullock bell disturbed it or the chiming of the bellbirds, or the far cawing of a crow. **1981** A. MARSHALL *Aust.* 114 Years ago when a bullocky was about to buy a new bullock bell he always tested the ones available by ringing them over his felt hat. **1915** *Bull. N.T.* xiv. 10 Boree (camel bush or **bullock bush**). **1923** J. ARMOUR *Spell of Inland* 100 A black boy and Mr Dunn's eldest son watched the proceedings from behind a clump of bullock bushes. **1935** I.L. IDRIESS *Man Tracks* 35 He hurried away up the creek-bank .. and tied his camel to a bullock bush.

3. *Austral. pidgin. Obs.* BULLOCKY *n.* 1.

1847 A. HARRIS *Settlers & Convicts* (1953) 207 They soon began to ask for bread and 'bullock' (beef). **1849** —— *Emigrant Family* (1967) 254, I never give King Bondi .. bullock (beef). **1879** 'AUSTRALIAN' *Adventures Qld.* 50 Salamanca [*sc.* a thieving pet emu] plagued the poor blacks terribly. . . They often went up to the store with whining requests for 'more flour and bullock—that fellow S'manker been *patter* altogether'.

4. *Obs.* See quot. 1881.

1881 H.W. NESFIELD *Chequered Career* 346 He calls them his *bullocks*, a term used up country for men who work hard for the benefit of the publican. **1895** *Worker* (Sydney) 30 Mar. 4/2 On settling day the publican gives each of his 'bullocks' any small sum he thinks fit.

5. *transf.* A working camel.

1893 D. LINDSAY *Jrnl. Elder Sci. Exploring Exped.* 18 Hadji was breaking in one of the young bullocks, which he says will make a very good riding camel. **1978** D. STUART *Wedgetail View* 65 He never used a ridin' camel, just led the two bullock camels on foot.

6. Brute force, brawn.

1936 E.C.H. TAYLOR *Our Austral. Game Football* 91 Football is not all 'bullock' and 'sheer stupidity'.

bullock, *v.* [f. prec.]

1. *intr.* To work tirelessly (like a bullock). Freq. as *pr. pple.* Also *trans.*

1875 *Austral. Town & Country Jrnl.* (Sydney) 28 Aug. 343/4, I don't believe in running after new country; let other fellows, if they're fools enough, do all that bullocking. Wise men buy their work afterwards—and cheap enough, too. **1891** *Truth* (Sydney) 17 May 3/4, I was engaged as a laborer in the wood-blocking of Harris-street, and getting my nine bob a day, when one cove comes along and says to me, 'What the --- are you bullocking away there and spoiling of your figure for, Jim?' **1892** 'J. MILLER' *Workingman's Paradise* 105 Well, when a man's anxious to keep a job and afraid he won't get another he'll often nearly break his back bullocking at it. When he feels independent he'll do the fair thing, and sling the job up if the boss tries to bullock him. **1899** *Bulletin* (Sydney) 21 Jan. (Red Page), We two bullocked in a rough, wet gully for a fortnight—felling trees, making a track for the bullocks, and 'jacking' logs to it over stumps and boulders. **1903** J. MARSHALL *Battling for Gold* 192 What would the shareholders think of the party being out so long and never getting a colour? It was hard luck, indeed, after 'bullocking' as they had done. **1950** G.M. FARWELL *Surf Music* 44 They bullocked all afternoon with shovels and picks. **1957** 'N. CULLOTTA' *They're Weird Mob* 82 I'm trimmin' the back face an' chuckin' the clay up the top, an' 'e's bullockin' in under the foundations. **1965** H. ATKINSON *Reckoning* 88 Big fat Teresa .. possessed by her faith to the point of martyrdom or madness, bullocking over the tubs and coppers in a storm of soap suds and steam. **1980** R. BROPHO *Fringedweller* 23 Aboriginal people have dropped dead .. by standing in the heat of the sun and bullocking their guts out.

2. *fig.*

1930 V. PALMER *Passage* (1957) 5 Fred was tough as tarred canvas, able to bullock his way anywhere. **1950** *Coast to Coast 1949–50* 141 It was a good thing the other kids ate like rabbits and bullocked and banged through life. **1957** V. PALMER *Rainbow-Bird* 92 The only way to bullock through these air-journeys is to get a good feed inside you before you take off.

Hence **bullocking** *vbl. n.*

1888 'R. BOLDREWOOD' *Robbery under Arms* (1937) 57 It would have paid us better if we'd read a little more and put the bullocking on one side. **1895** *Worker* (Sydney) 7 Sept. 4/1 We felt almost sorry that our 'bullocking' was over or, rather, that we should have to change our free-and-easy Bohemian ways. **1904** *Rep. R. Comm. Non-British Labour* (W.A.) 92 Some people used to think that the Italians were better at the 'bullocking', *i.e.*, the unskilled work. **1923** *Truth* (Melbourne) 6 Oct. 8/1 The systematic game gave way largely to individual play of the 'bullocking' style. **1948** G. FARWELL *Down Argent Street* 72 The foreman disembarks. A thick-set powerful man in his late fifties, he has come up the hard way, with twenty-five bullocking years in stopes. **1977** J. DOUGHTY *Gold in Blood* 73 It was I who had done all the bullocking. **1986** *Good Weekend* (Sydney) 5 Apr. 36/1 It's bullocking labour. . . Each of those panels over there weighs about 82 kilograms.

bullocker. *Obs.* A bullock driver.

1889 BARRÈRE & LELAND *Dict. Slang* I. 197 *Bullockirs* in Australia are as proverbial as bargees or Billingsgate fishwives in England for the forcibleness of their language. **1892** N. BARTLEY *Opals & Agates* 209 Lucky 'bullockers' in the old Port Phillip cattle shipping trade, used to gladden the heart of Gipsy Poll in her noisy little hostelry. **1894** J.K. ARTHUR *Kangaroo & Kauri* 31 Men are employed to cut down shrubs and small trees for the sake of feeding the stock with the leaves. Roadmen, especially hawkers and bullockers have to do the same.

bullock puncher. [f. BULLOCK *n.* + PUNCH *v.* 1 + *-er.*] A bullock driver.

[N.Z. **1856** H. BEATTIE *Early Runholding Otago* (1947) 42 In the hands of an experienced 'bullock-puncher'.] **1859** W. KELLY *Life in Vic.* I. 172 The demon yells of the savage bullock puncher .. another sobriquet for the teamster, whose whip-shaft is always armed with a spike to punch an over-obdurate animal. **1870** *Illustr. Sydney News* 11 May 395/1 Bullock drivers, or as they are poetically called by gentlemen residing inland, 'bullock-punchers'. **1885** *Australasian Printers' Keepsake* 96 'Yes,' said that young bullock-puncher, promptly. 'I'm that scallawag—what about him?' **1897** *Bulletin* (Sydney) 2 Oct. 14/1 Peter was a common kind of man, with the vocabulary of a Yankee skipper, a 'Geordie' gaffer and a Vandemonian bullock-puncher, in one volume. **1910** *Ibid.* 24 Feb. 15/2 Consider the bullock-puncher's couch. . . Formerly it was slung under the waggon. Nowadays it depends from the rear of the vehicle. *c* **1919** E.S. EMERSON *Shanty Entertainment* 51 He was known as the only bullock-puncher on the road who could shift his team. **1928** E. FOREMAN *Hist. & Adventures Qld. Pioneer* 176 The picturesque language of the Queensland bullock punchers. **1956** R.G. EDWARDS *Overlander Songbk.* 121 And the hardy bullock-punchers throw Aside their occupation.

bullock punching, *vbl. n.* [See prec.] The activity of driving cattle. Also *attrib.*

[N.Z. **1868** H. PHILLIPS Jrnl. Rockwood & Point 10 Nov. (typescript), Heavy bullock punching—stone carting &c.] **1886** F. COWAN *Aust.* 29 Bullock-punching on the Cambridge downs of Kimberly. **1895** *Bulletin* (Sydney) 3 Aug. 6/3 The interests of the drought-stricken West were sacrificed to the teamster and bullock-punching vote of one constituency. **1903** *Truth* (Sydney) 2 Aug. 7/3 Narrow-minded, ignorant, bigoted brutes .. would be better employed at bullock-punching than in shepherding Christ's sheep. **1918** C.J. DENNIS *Backblock Ballads* 12 Daddy was, I pause to mention, livin' on an old-age pension Since he gave up bullock-punchin' at the age of eighty-three. **1926** *Bulletin* (Sydney) 28 Oct. 24/1 During my career of 15 years' bullock-punching .. I never came across a good driver who used the jingler. **1934** J.C. LEE *Boshstralians* 204 The possession of a fluent flow of lurid language is absolutely necessary if one wishes to be successful in the business of bullock-punching.

bullocky, *n.* [f. BULLOCK *n.* + -Y.]

1. Orig. *Austral. pidgin.* Beef; BULLOCK *n.* 3.

1839 *S. Austral. Rec.* (London) (1840) 1 Feb. 22 There was a public dinner given to the Adelaide tribe of Aborigines of roast beef and plum pudding, but they call it *bullocky.* **1846** 'SQUATTER' *Visit to Antipodes* 123 The black fellows have no bullocky, or sheepy; but in their stead they have plenty kangaroo. **1923** *Western Star* (Roma) 3 Jan. 2/1 One day one of these warrigals was up at the Glenormiston stockyard, with others, to get a supply of 'bullocky', otherwise beef. **1952** A.M. DUNCAN-KEMP *Where Strange Paths go Down* 16 No pastoralist can afford to pay a pensioned stockman or his dependents, but he is ever willing to give them a home and 'bullocky' (fresh meat), blankets and tobacco in return for odd jobs done.

2. A bullock driver.

1869 *Australasian* (Melbourne) 17 July 72/5 *Cornstalk* and *gumsucker* are both of colonial growth, and so, I think, is .. *bullocky* (a teamster). **1872** 'RESIDENT' *Glimpses Life Vic.* 311 Their [*sc.* Aboriginal cricketers'] familiar colonial appellatives, such as 'sun-down', 'bullocky', etc., did not please their fancy when among Englishmen, where they were prompt to detect the smile evoked by the nicknames whose absurdity had not previously occurred to their minds. **1886** P. CLARKE *'New Chum' in Aust.* 137, I knew a 'bullockie' (as these men are dubbed) who had a team of twelve beasts under his command which obeyed his every word and never received a word, which a 'high-born ladie' might not have listened to. **1894** G. BOOTHBY *On Wallaby* 219 Talking of bullock drivers, the driver himself is called the bullocky, while his mate or assistant is denominated the bullocky's offsider. **1900** *Truth* (Sydney) 28 Jan. 28/4 A gift for blasphemy that would be a godsend to any earnest bullocky. **1908** *Bulletin* (Sydney) 23 Jan. 15/2 He didn't care a bullocky's prayer for the bites. **1919** V. PALMER *Prisoner* (1924) 39 The Boss is nearly off his nut, racing round and swearing like a bullocky with his team bogged. **1934** T. WOOD *Cobbers* 82 He was a bullocky, one of a race which speaks straight and spares none, like the bargees. **1940** —— *Cobbers Campaigning* 152 They'd make rings round a bullocky—swearing—in five languages. **1955** *Bulletin* (Sydney) 4 May 13/1 There aren't any bullockies left in our district. **1964** H.M. BARKER *Camels & Outback* 67 One of the best bullockies in Queensland would swear at his son but not his bullocks. **1979** A.J. BURKE *Bite Pineapple* 94, I have never heard a Pope vituperate like a bullocky. **1986** *Bulletin* (Sydney) 11 Mar. 78/1 The garden is worked by Murray senior, a lithe man after years as a bullocky, dairyman and timber cutter.

3. An idiom or use of language supposedly characterizing bullock drivers. Also *attrib.* and quasi-*adv.*

1879 *Kelly Gang* 122 The perpetrators of the robbery were not known throughout to make use of a single 'bullocky' or colonially-emphasized expression. **1894** A.B. BELL *Oscar* 55 That made dad mad, he bounced out the house swearin' bullocky. **1916** 'MEN OF ANZAC' *Anzac Bk.* 103 Bang! bang! went a couple of bombs, followed by cries and shouts from Abdul, and above it all we were certain we heard fragments of language, or the category known in Australia as 'bullocky'. **1918** G.A. TAYLOR *Those were Days* 57 'Give her some bullocky language,' suggested someone who knew something. **1938** BRIGGS & HARRIS *Joysticks & Fiddlesticks* 58, I let that chap know what I thought of him in pure bullocky Australian.

4. In the collocation **bullocky's joy** (or **delight**), treacle or golden syrup.

1901 *Bulletin* (Sydney) 9 Mar. 31/3, I bitterly thought of . . the tin of 'bullocky's joy' reposing in a saucer of water to keep the ants out. **1902** *Ibid.* 5 Apr. 32/2 'Cockie's Delight', better known, perhaps, as 'Bullocky's Joy', occupies a prominent position on the table, and may be called the cockie's 'staff of life'. **1911** *Ibid.* 13 July 14/4 How many aliases does treacle travel on through the bush? Here are some of them: 'Cockies'-joy', 'Bullocky's-delight', 'Oh-be-joyful', 'Wild honey', 'Mallee honey', 'Bush honey', 'Cosmetique', and 'Varnish'. **1918** R.H. KNYVETT *Over there with Australs.* 158 And even relieve the monotony of marmalade jam with 'bullocky's joy'. This last is merely molasses or 'golden syrup' called 'bullocky's joy', sometimes 'cocky's delight' because it is the chief covering for slices of bread with the bullock-driver or cocky-farmer. **1926** S.F. CASHMORE *N. Coast Verses* 43 Yes, corned beef and dripping and bullockies' joy, With a damper just done to a turn. . . 'Tis feed that the gods wouldn't spurn. **1937** *Bulletin* (Sydney) 11 Aug. 21/3 Why waste 'bullocky's joy' to poison foxes? **1951** E. HILL *Territory* 136 She brought fresh flour, bully and bullocky's joy.

5. Comb. **bullocky bush,** *bullock bush,* see BULLOCK *n.* 2.

1963 A.E. FARRELL *Vengeance* 22 Their fringe was dotted with innumerable Callitris pines, quondongs and hardy bastard mulgas and bullocky bush.

bullocky, *a.* Of or pertaining to bullock driving or rural life generally. Also in the collocation **Bullocky Bill,** a nickname for a bullock driver.

1876 *Austral. Town & Country Jrnl.* (Sydney) 1 Apr. 544/4 Poor bullocky Bill! In the circles select Of the scholars he hasn't a place; But he walks like a *man*, with his forehead erect, And looks at God's day in the face. **1885** *Australasian Printers' Keepsake* 16 'When you *make* Mokepilly,' quoth one of the sunburnt bullocky men, 'keep on by the brush fence.' **1890** 'R. BOLDREWOOD' *Colonial Reformer* I. 196 'By George, Jack, you're a regular bullocky boy,' said old Mr Hasbene; 'you'd better get Mr Neuchamp here to put you on as stockman when he buys a cattle station.' **1897** *Bulletin* (Sydney) 10 July 7/3 He selected the bullocky-minded Brunker to be Acting-Premier. **1903** *Truth* (Sydney) 11 Jan. 1/6 There are 2720 languages in use all over the world, but the most expressive is that used by the Australian Bullocky Bills. **1962** *Daily Mercury Centenary Story Mackay* 30 Grinding through the romantic bullocky life of dust, heat and flies, the rugged settlers drove their straining teams. **1982** P. RADLEY *My Blue-Checker Corker* 75 The road to Bora Bora, still referred to as Gutshaker Road, its old bullocky name. **1985** *Canberra Times* 23 Mar. 2/5 Every word of it is true . . except a few bullocky yarns.

bull puncher. Abbrev. of BULLOCK PUNCHER.

1871 *Illustr. Sydney News* 23 Dec. 211/2, I, a new chum—the imported new material, used to nothing save quill-driving, striving to compete with bull-punchers, who had taken their colonial experience degree in Macquarie's or Darling's time. **1883** G.E. LOYAU *Personal Adventures* 8 The heavy pulling through black soil after incessant rains, together with a thousand other incidents which make up the life of a 'bull-puncher'. **1893** *Western Champion* (Barcaldine) 21 Feb. 3/4 Now the ancient Queensland bull punchers, if not the most aristocratic class in the country, had the merit of possessing all the high-bred vices. **1911** E. DYSON *Tommy Hawker* 28 'I don't care a tinker's damn . . ,' snorted one bull puncher. **1924** J. NISBET *Scraps* 14 The fluent 'bull puncher'.

Also **bull punching** *vbl. n.*

1879 'AUSTRALIAN' *Adventures Qld.* 111 Old Ben used to let him take the whip, and instructed him in the noble art of 'bull-punching'. **1883** G.E. LOYAU *Personal Adventures* 8 An insight was given us into the 'bull-punching' business.

bull-ring, *v. Obs. trans.* See quot. 1880. Also as *vbl. n.*

1880 *V & P* (N.S.W. L.A.) III. 1134 Inside the huge ring made by a mile or so of net, a boat from time to time throws off a small seine, which is 'bull-ringed', or drawn to the shore where practicable round as many fish as are required for the next trip of the steamer. **1897** *Worker* (Sydney) 25 Sept. 4/2 A fisherman doing that class of work which is professionally termed bull-ringing—that is, running a net around a shoal of mullett, and hauling into a boat. **1906** D.G. STEAD *Fishes of Aust.* 66 When fish are in large schools at the surface of the water . . the process followed is what is termed 'Bull-ringing'; the net being thrown in a circle right round the school.

bullroarer. [So called because of a fancied resemblance to the child's toy.] A sacred object of Aboriginal ceremony and ritual: see quot. 1898.

1848 *Adelaide Miscellany* 2 Sept. 77 The assembled 'bull-roarers', as those rude and mysterious instruments are popularly called, were swung round more vehemently than ever. **1884** A. LANG *Custom & Myth* 29 An Englishman, country-bred . . says to himself, 'Why, that is the bull-roarer.' If he knows the colony and the ways of the natives, he knows that the blacks are celebrating their tribal mysteries. The roaring noise is made to warn all women to keep out of the way. **1898** D.W. CARNEGIE *Spinifex & Sand* 333 They use flat carved sticks, some eight inches long, and of a pointed oval shape. Through a hole in one point they thread a string, with which the stick is rapidly swung round, making a booming noise—'Bull-roarers' is the general white-fellows' name for them. **1901** F.J. GILLEN *Diary* 5 July (1968) 157 A group of men at a place called Irril-lilya who were attending an initiatory ceremony . . had neglected to swing the bull-roarer. **1913** *Bull. N.T.* vii. 10 In the southern parts of the Territory this will take the form of a sacred stick called a churinga, or popularly a bull roarer. **1928** B. SPENCER *Wanderings in Wild Aust.* 273 The Central ceremony of Initiation is concerned with showing the youth the sacred bull-roarer or Churinga. **1942** L. & K. HARRIS *Lost Hole Bingoola* 21 Many times Binda had heard the blackfellows talk about the Bora, the sacred dance or ceremony by which young boys were initiated into manhood and became warriors of the tribe. But of the magic bull-roarer he knew no more than the lubras. **1956** *Bulletin* (Sydney) 5 Sept. 13/2 The bull-roarer, or churinga, still used in aboriginal ceremonies, is held to be the voice of the god Daramulum. **1966** K. WALKER *Dawn at Hand* 44 The weird whirring drone of the dread bullroarer. **1981** NGABIDJ & SHAW *My Country of Pelican Dreaming* 58 One thing we used to make a girl love us was the *djarada*, love magic of the *manabago* or *barang*, what the white men call a bullroarer.

bull run. Esp. in a country house, a wide passage dividing one part of the house from another and allowing free movement of air.

1935 DAVISON & NICHOLLS *Blue Coast Caravan* 112 The houses are mostly bungalows, that is a more or less four-square structure, with a 'bull run' passage through the centre. **1946** F. CLUNE *Try Nothing Twice* 78 He careered into the 'bull-run', an open corridor between the kitchen annexe and the house.

bullsh. Also **bulsh.** [Abbrev. of *bullshit*: see OEDS.] Rubbish, nonsense: see quot. 1919. Also *attrib.* as **bullsh artist.**

1919 W.H. DOWNING *Digger Dialects* 14 Bullsh . . (1) Insincerity; (2) an incorrect or insincere thing; (3) flattery; (4) praise. **1932** J. MAXWELL *Hell's Bells* 46 'Bullsh,' exploded Clarke. 'We're winning the war.' **1938** X. HERBERT *Capricornia* 377 This talk of invasion by the Japs is all plain bulsh. **1947** V.C. HALL *Bad Medicine* 299 Never mind Billy Hughes. He's a politician, and 'bulsh' is their stock-in-trade. **1949** G. BERRIE *Morale* 125 When he told them what gallant fellows they were, they promptly put him down as one more 'bulsh' artist. **1959** D. HEWETT *Bobbin Up* 38 A job for life, me bum. Who's been filling you up with all that bulsh. Dick I s'pose? **1970** R. BEILBY *No Medals for Aphrodite* 158 'The real Aphrodite was supposed to be born in Cyprus.' 'I wouldn't know about all that bullsh.' **1980** E. BARCS *Backyard of Mars* 53 He said, with a straight face, that if one wanted to say politely, 'nonsense' one used the word 'bulsh' or 'bullshit'.

bullswool. Also **bull's wool.** [So called from the resemblance to coarse hair.]

1. Fibrous bark, esp. that of some stringybark trees; any kindling material.

1881 G. WALCH *Vic.* 73 A few matches and some frayed fibres of stringy-bark—called by experts 'bull's wool'. **1911** E.M. CLOWES *On Wallaby through Vic.* 247 There is a little plateau . . on which to build one's fire, kindling it surely and quickly with what is called 'bull's-wool', the thick, dry fibre, like fine cocoa-nut matting, which forms the hair shirt of the gum-tree. **1944** M.J. O'REILLY *Bowyangs & Boomerangs* 151 A handful of finely shredded bark, known as bullswool which must always be kept dry, is carried. To make the fire, the block of soft-wood is placed on the ground; the pointed stick is inserted into the hole; around which the bullswool is placed. **1981** M. SHARLAND *Tracks of Morning* 65 Australian bark, easy to gather and quick to burn presents few problems, whether in strips or a handful of 'bull's wool' from a hoary stem.

2. A euphemism for 'bullshit'. Also *attrib.*

[**1904** C.W. JOHNSTON *Out-Back Homestead* 56 Say, Bullswool, you were a fool to ever work.] **1933** R.D. TATE *Doughman* 20 The way you harp on Honesty, and you the bull's-wool artist from the Devil's Sunday School! **1948** I.L. IDRIESS *Opium Smugglers* 88 'Fiddle-sticks!' I yawned. 'Bullswool!' **1962** MARSHALL & DRYSDALE *Journey among Men* 52 Ten million Australians drink about the same total quantity of wine as fifty million Britons. There is in Australia, of course, less *bullswool* associated with wine-drinking than in England. **1968** *Kings Cross Whisper* (Sydney) liv. 4/3 The ACT has long held prior right to the title of Bulland due to the vast amount of bull's wool issuing from it since the firs sod was turned.

bullwaddy, var. BULWADDY.

bull wire. [So called because of its strength.] A heavy gauge fencing wire.

1945 *Coast to Coast 1944* 56 Sand, gibbers; and crazy bull-wire fences staggering into infinity. **1968** A. D'OMBRAIN *Fish Tales* 11 For our fishing expedition he cut off two ten-foot lengths of what he termed 'Bull Wire', or heavy gauge fencing wire.

Bully. [f. *Bull(etin* + -Y.] *The Bulletin*, the name of an influential weekly journal published in Sydney from 1880; *bushman's bible*, see BUSHMAN 8.

1913 *Truth* (Sydney) 16 Nov. 5/8 The 'Bully' should be the last paper in the world to sneer at the advertisements other journals publish. **1916** *Ibid.* 30 July 7/7 The 'Bully' is great on literature: it kids itself *it is literature*. **1923** *Bulletin* (Sydney) 2 Aug. 22/4 Some chap in the *Bully* has been saying that green paw paw is poisonous. **1976** *Southerly* iii. 294 That's how the Bully got its pink page, I bet: saw red. **1981** L. MCLEAN *Pumpkin Pie* 43 My father kept a rolled up copy of the 'Bulletin' at the back of his seat. . . Some of Dad's early articles were published in the 'Bully', as we affectionately called this magazine.

bullya, var. BOYLYA.

buln buln, var. BULLAN BULLAN.

buloke, var. *bull oak*, see BULL $n.^3$

bulrush. [Transf. use of *bulrush* a tall rush of wet places, esp. *Typha latifolia*.] Any of several tall reed-like plants growing in or near water, esp. the native

Typha domingensis and *T. orientalis* (fam. Typhaceae) of all States, Asia, and N.Z.; CUMBUNGI; WONGA.

1798 J. HUNTER *Hist. Jrnl. Trans. Port Jackson* 339 The huts were very soon built .. and thatched with bull-rushes and flaggs. **1839** *S. Austral. Miscellany* Nov. 29, I understood that the 'Bolyan' or bulrush-root .. is the chief food of the natives. **1844** *Swan River News* June 1/2 The bull rush of Scripture is found in the colony, and used by the coopers to staunch their work. **1856** J. BONWICK *W. Buckley* 52 The net is an important feature of hunting. Those to entrap kangaroos .. are made out of bullrush root. **1888** *Proc. Linnean Soc. N.S.W.* III. 550 *Typha angustifolia*... Called 'Bullrush', and also 'Cat's tail' and 'Reed Mace'. It is the 'Wonga' of the Lower Murray aboriginals. The young shoots are edible, and resemble asparagus. **1916** *Bulletin* (Sydney) 21 Sept. 22/2 Southern coastal tribes used the bulrush or 'yacca' stick. **1965** K. TENNANT *Summer's Tales* p. vi, As different from the native narrative as a beautiful hot-house tuberose is from a bulrush.

bulwaddy /bʊl'wɒdi/. Also **bullwaddi, bull-waddie, bullwaddy.** [Prob. f. an Aboriginal language.] The tree of n. Aust. *Macropteranthes kekwickii* (fam. Combretaceae) which forms dense thickets.

1925 M. TERRY *Across Unknown Aust.* 194 Bull-waddi grows in .. thickets... It gives off greater heat than any other Australian wood... Gidgee is supposed to be one of the hottest, but it is cool compared with bull-waddi. **1936** 'L. KAYE' *Black Wilderness* 36 In a little patch of bulwaddy near the herd, Lex stopped and tethered his horse. **1945** T. RONAN *Strangers of Ophir* 111 He was in a tangle of lancewood and bullwaddy. **1951** E. HILL *Territory* 299 Hedgewood, *allumbo*, the 'bulwaddi'... These gnarled dark woods are the hardest timber on earth—when very old it will break and burn, but it never bends. **1959** D. LOCKWOOD *Crocodiles & Other People* 71 A few patches of the dreaded, low-slung bulwaddie, where wild cattle shelter from stockmen who dare not follow. **1964** K. WILLEY *Eaters of Lotus* 21 Grey, gnarled and knotted like an old bulwaddy tree and twice as tough, Jim does not worry much about anything. **1979** D. LOCKWOOD *My Old Mates & I* 60 I'm sure he'd prefer poetry to botany if he knew the banyans, the pandanus and the bulwaddie.

bum.

A. Used *attrib.* in Special Comb. **bum brusher,** a batman; **chum,** an intimate; **puncher,** a homosexual.

1941 S.J. BAKER *Pop. Dict. Austral. Slang* 15 **Bum-brusher,** an officer's servant. **1978** P. ADAM SMITH *Anzacs* 23 They did feel that being a 'foot-slogger' was only one rung up from being a 'bum-brusher' (officer's servant). **1972** G. MORLEY *Jockey rides Honest Race* 254, I can go round saying I'm Kon Malouf's **bum chum.** Know him? I've shared a flat with the bastard. **1977** D. WHITINGTON *Strive to be Fair* 31 There was no easy acceptance of homosexuals. They were still referred to scathingly as 'queans' [*sic*] and '**bum punchers**'.

B. *n.* In the phr. **bum to mum**: see quot. 1972.

1972 *Bulletin* (Sydney) 30 Sept. 45/1 Australian rules footballers in Melbourne, when forbidden sexual relations before an important match, are told: 'Bum to Mum'. The phrase is appealing, both for its conciseness and for its Melburnian assumption that the amorous activity of footballers is exclusively conjugal. **1980** B. HORNADGE *Austral. Slanguage* 241 Australian Rules has also given an amusing new phrase to the world in the form of *bum to mum*—this being another way of saying 'no sex with the wife'. **1983** HIBBERD & HUTCHINSON *Barracker's Bible* 40 *Bums to mum*... A phrase used by coaches, exhorting players to sexual abstinence on the evening before a game.

bumble tree. [a. Kamilaroi and Yuwaalaraay *bambul* + (Eng.) *tree.*] *Wild orange*, see WILD 1. Also **bumble.**

1846 C.P. HODGSON *Reminisc. Aust.* 150 The bumble (or *Capparis Mitchelii*) has three varieties. **1897** K.L. PARKER *Austral. Legendary Tales* (ed. 2) 15 Many and ripe are the bumbles hanging now on the bumble trees. **1901** K.L. PARKER in M. Muir *My Bush Bk.* (1982) 101 The dark green thick foliage of the bumbles (*Capparis mitchelli*) of which the blossom is like a gigantic myrtle flower. **1912** *Emu* XII. 72, I visited a large bumble or wild orange tree. **1932** *Victorian Naturalist* XLIX. 189 *C[apparis] Mitchellii* is the Bumble, which develops from an untidy straggling shrub into a shapely little tree... The fruit .. is edible... The taste suggested an over-mellow papaw with turpentine sauce. **1938** C.T. WHITE *Princ. Bot. Qld. Farmers* 31 The Bumbil Tree or Native Pomegranate.

bumboat. [Transf. use of *bumboat* a boat carrying provisions for sale to ships.] A travelling sly grog shop; the proprietor or stock of such a shop. Also *attrib.*

1851 *Bell's Life in Sydney* 25 Oct. 1/1 Scarcely a station in the interior but has been visited by the 'bum-boat' .. of the Bathurst sly grog-sellers. **1869** *Bushmen, Publicans, & Politics* 12 It is notorious that the principal 'bum boats' are small unlicensed hawkers travelling under colour of selling a few potatoes or some fruit. **1891** *Truth* (Sydney) 19 Apr. 7/3 Do you know what a bum-boat is? There are not many now—travelling sly-grog shops. **1905** D. REID *Reminisc.* 58 He was what was called a bum-boat man and had his cart and an immense puncheon of rum which he was selling at a good figure and intending to proceed to the diggings. **1913** J. BEUKERS *Humour & Pathos Austral. Desert* 77 What's that over there with the white cover on, a hawker or a bum-boat? **1933** R.B. PLOWMAN *Man from Oodnadatta* 132 Originally a stockman, he had been .. a 'bum-boat runner' (travelled with a buggy-load of illicit beer and spirits which he sold to the station-hands). **1946** I.L. IDRIESS *Crocodile Land* 219 The bumboats were teams of horses (sometimes camels) packed with alleged rum and various brands of firewater. **1954** T. RONAN *Vision Splendid* 84 The crowd of racing men, station hands, bagmen and surveyors gathered around the bumboats. **1974** P. ADAM SMITH *Desert Railway* 45 The talk of 'rough seas prevailing' causing 'Customs Department' to interfere with cargo of 'Bumboat' is a reminder that although it was illegal to bring booze into camp, it certainly got there.

bumbora, var. BOMBORA.

bumerang, var. BOOMERANG *n.* 1.

bump, *v.*

1. *trans.* To encounter (a person, etc.).

1907 *Truth* (Sydney) 5 May 1/5 Bumped a tramguard the other day .. who did not know where Grosvenor-street was. **1917** C. THACKERAY *Goliath Joe, Fisherman* 87 Wen 'e tried to scale on the tram for a section he bumped a rough guard who knew 'im by name an' repitation an' 'ad 'im prosecuted. **1922** A. WRIGHT *Colt from Country* 33 'Where did you see Helyer?' 'Bumped him in the train.' **1925** —— *Boy from Bullarah* 18 'I thought you was broke.' 'I bumped a better friend than you, Mosh,' said Hughie quietly. **1957** D. WHITINGTON *Treasure upon Earth* 115, I was pickin' up when I first bumped him. 'Tar, boy,' he'd yell and I'd rush up with the tar stick.

2. *trans.* To get the better of (someone).

1911 A. WRIGHT *Gamblers' Gold* (1923) 87 I'll bump you every time. You expect to win the Sydney Cup with the horse I have been robbed of, but let me tell you I'll down you if it costs me a thousand. **1956** T. RONAN *Moleskin Midas* 253 Ophir Downs always made sure it carried at least one man big enough and clever enough 'to bump Blake the half-caste' if he and his boss were caught with O.D.I. cattle.

bumper, *n.* [Of unknown origin.]

1. A cigarette butt. Also *attrib.*

1899 *Austral. Tit-Bits* (Sydney) 6 May 194/3 Bumper hunters .. are men and boys who, unable to buy tobacco, or in order to save money, make a practice of picking up and smoking all the 'butts' .. of cigars and cigarettes which they can find lying in the streets. **1899** *Truth* (Sydney) 25 June 2/8 The side-walks of the provincial city thoroughfare are black with great splodges of spittle, and littered with cigar and cigarette 'bumpers'. **1916** 'MEN OF ANZAC' *Anzac Bk.* 47 Along comes the bloomin' officer, so 'Enessy sticks 'is lighted bumper down south into 'is overcoat pocket. **1928** *Bulletin* (Sydney) 29 Feb. 21/2 We were out of matches except for a chip from the head of a waxie found in my 'bumper' pocket. **1933** H.B. RAINE *Whip-Hand* 46 You see this bumper I'm smokin'? Well, Lofty could stand over there and nick off the ash without touchin' the rest of the fag. Dinky di. **1944** *Bulletin* (Sydney) 2 Aug. 15/1 My matchbox bears the legend 'Stamp out that butt', and the lowly bumper is nominated as the cause of many a grassfire. **1959** D. NILAND *Gold in Streets* 63 'Hey, who's smoking cowdung?' 'Oh, good day, Mr Soaper,' Danno greeted. 'It's me,' he grinned. 'I'm on the bumpers again.' **1968** D. IRELAND *Chantic Bird* 56 You've picked up bumpers and spilled them out into cigarette papers or a twist of tissue paper. **1977** STIRLING & RICHARDSON *Memories of Aberfeldy* 24 Shabby figures in the shameful dull black shuffling along Collins Street... 'Bumper shooting' (picking up discarded cigarette butts). **1981** D. STUART *I think I'll Live* 149 Well, there's no chance o' getting a bit of weed for them, is there? Three of 'em smoke an' they haven't got a bumper between 'em.

2. In the phr. **not worth a bumper,** worthless.

1947 M. TRIST *Daddy* 164 My old man's not going to be worth a bumper that day. **1949** L. GLASSOP *Lucky Palmer* 28 Shielas don't interest me. They're not worth a bumper. **1968** S. GORE *Holy Smoke* 77 Sand, flies, wait-a-bit thorn, Joe Blakes—the lot, that place; not worth a bumper. **1974** D. IRELAND *Burn* 44 'Billy, you're not worth a bumper,' Joy says. 'You couldn't fight your way out of a paper bag.'

bumper, *v.* [f. prec.] *trans.* To make (a cigarette) from butts; to extinguish (a cigarette) and save the butt.

1968 D. O'GRADY *Bottle of Sandwiches* 30 Hope he brings the makin's we asked him to. Smokin' bumpers is all right when there's nothin' else, but by tomorrow we'll be bumperin' the bumpers. **1978** T. DAVIES *More Austral. Nicknames* 34 As soon as he came into the danger area they would have to bumper their cigarettes.

bumpy ash. [See quot. 1932.] The tree *Flindersia schottiana* (see CUDGERIE).

1925 *Bulletin* (Sydney) 15 Jan. 22/2 Another member of the family (*F[lindersia] schottiana*), bumpy ash or cudgery, might be put to better use. **1932** R.H. ANDERSON *Trees of N.S.W.* 138 Cudgerie (*Flindersia Schottiana*) is also known as Bumpy Ash owing to the presence of fairly large protuberances along the stem. **1981** A.B. & J.W. CRIBB *Useful Wild Plants Aust.* 135 Bumpy ash... The irregular swellings or bumps which commonly occur here and there on the trunk .. provide a good reason for one of its common names.

bunchy top. [See quot. 1921.] A viral disease afflicting banana trees and other crops, transmitted by the banana aphid *Pentalonia nigronervosa*.

1919 *Agric. Gaz. N.S.W.* XXX. 814 That Bunchy Top should occur in plants so widely separated botanically as the sugar cane and the banana, indicates that the disease is of physiological origin. **1921** *Bulletin* (Sydney) 10 Mar. 20/3 'Bunchy-top' in banana growth .. is caused by a white fungus that attacks the roots and eats away the covering thereof, leaving only a dried and dead fibre, which, of course fails to transmit the necessary food to the bulb of the plant—hence the dwarfed and unhealthy leaves, which 'bunch' together instead of spreading out, and so prevent the bananas from growing to fruition. **1929** VEITCH & SIMMONDS *Pests & Diseases Qld.* 117 Bunchy top is by far the most serious disease affecting the prosperity of the banana-grower in Queensland. **1981** P. BAXTER *Growing Fruit in Aust.* 167 Bunchy Top virus is potentially the most serious disease of bananas.

bunda-bunda, var. BANDY-BANDY.

bundi, var. BONDI *n.*[1]

bundle.

1. *Obs.* SWAG *n.* 1.

1853 [see BUNDLEMAN]. **1907** *Bulletin* (Sydney) 6 June 14/4 A swag is known .. as 'bundle', 'parcel', 'nap', 'matilda', 'drum'. **1920** *Smith's Weekly* (Sydney) 28 Aug. 9/4 No traveller likes to be on the road without a bluey of ordinary dimensions. A man might 'swamp his cheque' but he won't part with his bundle.

2. In the phr. **to drop one's bundle,** to go to pieces.

1897 *Antipodean* (Melbourne) 91 In the latest Colonial slang, a man who loses his nerve at a critical part of a game is said to 'drop his bundle', while a man who plays a determined game is called a 'battler'. **1906** *Gadfly* (Adelaide) 21 Mar. 14/2 Bowen put up a very spiritless game against the champion. In the language of the sporting pushite, he appeared to 'drop his bundle'. **1908** *Lone Hand* Dec. 170 Thieves rarely 'drop their bundle', that is, give information to the police; such information must be sought among the women. **1913** C.J. DENNIS *Backblock Ballads* 21, I nearly dropped me bundle as I looked at Dad McGee. **1927** K.S. PRICHARD *Bid me to Love* (1974) 18 Of course Kath Brown plays a rattling good game: there's no two ways about it. But Dick drops his bundle if he doesn't win at once. **1931** O. WALTERS *Shrapnel Green* 24 But I make allowances fer a man Wot's dropped 'is bundle an' lost 'is grip. **1944** L. GLASSOP *We were Rats* 191 There'll always be an England whether you bastards drop your bundles or not. **1957** D. WHITINGTON *Treasure upon Earth* 177 'The party's falling to pieces,' he reported. 'Half the boys have dropped their bundle. They're looking for a way out. So am I.' **1968** S. GORE *Holy Smoke* 54 It started to rain, too. And at this, he really drops his bundle. **1980** S. HAZZARD *Transit of Venus* 40 'We could all give in,' she said, when told that Miss Garside the librarian had completely dropped her bundle.

bundleman. *Obs.* [a. G. *bündelmann*, tr. of SWAGMAN.] SWAGMAN. Also **bundler.**

1853 F. GERSTAECKER *Narr. Journey round World* III. 64, I did not look like a common bundleman with my gun and knife, and the way I carried my blanket. ***c* 1856** —— *Life in Bush* 15 Not far off, beneath a tree, sate a foot passenger, one of the men known as bundlers, eating his breakfast very tranquilly in the open air. **1857** —— *Two Convicts* 10 The 'fine speaking' is left to the 'swells', that is, to those who have a decent coat upon their backs, and do not belong to the class of 'old hands' or 'bundlemen'.

bundy, var. BONDI *n.*[1]

bundy /'bʌndi/, *n.*[1] [a. Dharuk *boondah.*] Any of several trees of the genus *Eucalyptus* (fam. Myrtaceae), esp. the rough-barked *E. goniocalyx* of s.e. Aust.

1899 *Proc. Linnean Soc. N.S.W.* XXIV. 462 *E. goniocalyx, F.v.M.* . . In this colony this species is sometimes known as 'Yellow Gum'. . . It is known as 'Bundy' at Burraga and Rockley. **1904** J.H. MAIDEN *Notes on Commercial Timbers N.S.W.* 15 Bundy (*Eucalyptus Cambagei*, Deane and Maiden) . . is often termed 'Mountain Apple'. **1981** A.B. & J.W. CRIBB *Useful Wild Plants Aust.* 28 The bundy or long-leaved box, *E. goniocalyx*, of the Dividing Range areas of New South Wales and Victoria, extending into some of the South Australian Ranges.

Bundy /'bʌndi/, *n.*[2] Also **bundy.** [The proprietary name of a make of time clock.] A machine which records the times at which employees start and finish work; a clock used to regulate the punctuality of public transport services; *transf.*, a signal for the beginning or end of work. Also **bundy clock.**

1912 *Truth* (Sydney) 29 Dec. 5/6 The Sydney car conductor . . reckons it the joy of his life to beat bundy, and he will whiz the old car along . . so that he can have a couple of minutes' spell while waiting to get his correct time at every bundy along the route. **1922** *Smith's Weekly* (Sydney) 1 Apr. 19/4 Out of 365 days this year, the average Australian workman will ring the Bundy clock on 251 days—the remaining 114 being swallowed up by Saturdays, Sundays, and holidays. **1930** *Aussie* (Sydney) Mar. 47/1 It starts when the knock-off bundy sounds. **1933** 'TRAMWAY WORKERS' *Shock Brigader* 7 'Ting!' went the bundy. 'Let her go, Bill!' the tram started on the 8.30 am trip to Town. **1949** G. FARWELL *Traveller's Tracks* 16 There are no bitumen roads . . no rush hours or bundies to turn life into a milling ant-heap. **1965** *Realist* (Sydney) xx. 15 Passing the bundy clock there was a chorus: 'Punch mine, Betty.'—'And mine.'—'Mine too.' **1972** *Bulletin* (Sydney) 8 Apr. 48/1 Each worker has his own key. As he clocks in and out the bundy shows a record of how many hours he has worked that week and how many he still has to work in order to reach his minimum quota. **1979** D. LOCKWOOD *My Old Mates & I* 18 Look at Darwin—all those people, queues of 'em in cars, driving to work every morning, punching the Bundy at eight o'clock, punching it again at four-twenty-one. **1981** P. RADLEY *Jack Rivers & Me* 101 'They reckon they're puttin' in one of them bundy clocks.' 'You mean they're gonna time men the way they clock greyhounds and horses?'

Hence **bundy-puncher** *n.*

1943 A. DAWES *Soldier Superb* 99 The rotten minority—the schemer, the job stealer, the non-co-Operating boss and the non-co-operating bundy-puncher.

Bundy /'bʌndi/, *n.*[3] [f. *Bundaberg* the name of a town in Qld. and proprietary name of a brand of rum + -Y.] Bundaberg rum. Also **Bundy rum.**

1972 D. SHEAHAN *Songs from Canefields* 85 And some to drown their sorrow tore into Bundy Rum. Old Bundy is the dinkum stuff that serves a fellow well—Whether heading for Paradise or going to 'Inverell'. **1975** M. THORNTON *It's Jackaroo's Life* 66 We collected all our winnings, and a bottle of Bundy rum. **1980** S. THORNE *I've met some Bloody Wags* 83 We hadn't had any scran all day, and the 'Bundy' had made us reckless. **1984** *Nat. Times* (Sydney) 9 Mar. (Color Mag.) 6/1 The 'spirit of the game' was overproof Bundy rum and all the players entered freely into it.

bung /bʌŋ/, (formerly) bʊŋ, bɒŋ/, *a.* Orig. *Austral. pidgin.* Also **boang, boung** and formerly **bong.** [a. Jagara *baŋ.*]

1. *Obs.* Dead. Also in the (orig. pidgin) phr. **to go bung,** to die.

1841 *Colonial Observer* (Sydney) 14 Oct. 10/3 To the right the path to Umpie Boang or Old Settlement. **1847** J.D. LANG *Cooksland* 65 The black natives, whose nomenclature is always distinctive and appropriate—not like that of the Colonial Office—call it Umpie Bong, the 'Dead Houses', or 'Deserted Village'. **1857** F. DE B. COOPER *Wild Adventures* 58 'Boung!' said he, making use of the Cameleroi term for dead. **1879** 'AUSTRALIAN' *Adventures Qld.* 134 How you get out, Micky? Suppose mine open him door, spear come up, plenty—then you *bong* (dead). **1881** A.C. GRANT *Bush-Life Qld.* II. 175 'Yohi,' said the boy, still sitting on his horse, 'altogether bong' (dead), 'one fellow bail bong' (one not dead). **1882** A.J. BOYD *Old Colonials* 72 Sometimes you've got a horse . . an' you sells him, but just afore you hands 'im over and gets the money he goes bong on you. That's just what happened to C-- there. He sold a whippin' horse to a cove, and just as he was goin' to deliver him, the brute goes an' dies. **1886** A.M. HUGHES *Idylls of Bush* 13 'Good Lord! he's a stiff un!' 'Gone right bung?' sez Tim. So I feel his heart; it warn't beatin'. **1887** A. NICOLS *Wild Life & Adventure* 151 A few teeth or little bones belonging to some black fellow that had gone 'bong', as they call it.

2. *fig.* **a.** Bankrupt, in financial ruin. **b.** Incapacitated, exhausted, broken. Esp. in the phr. **to go bung,** to fail, to collapse.

1885 *Australasian Printers' Keepsake* 40 He was importuned to desist, as his musical talent had 'gone bung' probably from over-indulgence in confectionery. **1891** *Bohemia* (Melbourne) 3 Dec. 4 If we ever start a building society, and there is a possibility of it going bung, we will secure the services of Alfred Deakin as chairman. **1893** *Braidwood Dispatch* 26 Apr. 2/5 A man was fined £3 at the Sydney Water Police Court on Monday for having injured a notice posted at the Savings Bank of New South Wales. He wrote the words 'Gone Bung' on the notice, and advised the crowd to look after their money. **1897** *Worker* (Sydney) 25 Sept. 4/1 As soon as the Union was 'bung' the squatters would have nothing to fear. **1898** *Truth* (Sydney) 11 Dec. 2/3 It is more than a marvel that public indignation has not long since sent you morally and monetarily 'bung'. **1901** *Advocate* (Burnie) 11 Jan. 2/3 This was when 'boom' and 'bung' times were alike unknown. **1901** *Tocsin* (Melbourne) 19 Sept. 5/3 When their train was halted on the line in consequence of the mishap to its predecessor, they remarked confidently, 'It is that carriage gone bung.' **1916** 'T.O. LINGO' *Austral. Comic Dict.* 45 'Going Bung'—The Fat Man becoming insolvent; liquidating. **1926** *V & P* (W.A.) (1927) I. no. 3 51 Through the ravages of the blacks the station has practically gone bung. **1929** G. MEUDELL *Pleasant Career Spendthrift* 207 They . . saved enough money to buy deposit receipts in bung banks and make competencies. **1945** *Aust. Week-End Bk.* 178 A broken nose and two bung ears. **1951** J. DEVANNY *Travels N. Qld.* 186 'The stations would go bung without the Abos,' one of the missionaries told me frankly. **1954** J. CLEARY *Climate of Courage* 41 Even with that bung hand of his, he'd have knocked me arse-over-Bluey. **1965** R.H. CONQUEST *Horses in Kitchen* 64 The show went bung; everybody was left without a cracker. **1976** N.V. WALLACE *Bush Lawyer* 32 When the typewriter went bung, as it frequently did in its latter years, the local bicycle man fixed it up, and sometimes even made parts for it. **1980** HOLTH & BARNABY *Cattlemen of High Country* 122 He had been one of the mountain cattlemen who were severely hit by the weather in 1923 and he 'went bung'. **1983** I. WYNER *With Banner Unfurled* 154 We had a sort of society before that, but it went bung. . . That was how the union came to be formed.

bung /bʌŋ/, *v.* [f. *bung* to throw, put forcibly.] *trans.* With **on:** to stage (an event); to assume (a style of speech or behaviour, usu. pretentious or ostentatious), esp. in the phr. **to bung it on.** See also **to bung on a blue,** BLUE *n.*[2] 4.

1942 A.J. MCINTYRE *Putting over Burst* 4 So we say 'Go to it, Sergeant, Bung it on real thick.' **1950** *Austral. Police Jrnl.* Apr. 118 To commence an illegal game of chance. In N.S.W. it is 'bung a game on'. **1960** R.S. PORTEOUS *Cattleman* 11 'At least, I don't go bungin' on that la-di-dah accent you cultivate, me girl.' 'No, you 'bung on', as you term it, the crude vernacular of one of your own stockmen.' **1961** X. HERBERT *Soldiers' Women* 107 The hostess conducted her guests with such ceremony that one of them who had the right by long acquaintance to be rude, said, 'Don't bung it on, Sel. We're only going to stay an hour.' **1965** K. SMITH *OGF* 170 Lance Hogarty . . suggested that we should bung on a compulsory church parade next Sunday evening. **1969** A. BUZO *Rooted* (1973) 78 You don't bung on the bull like a lot of these blokes you see around the place these days. **1977** W. MOORE *Just to Myself* 71 Mum said she was bunging on side and thought she was a bit good for us. **1978** H.C. BAKER *I was Listening* 94 Every year she bungs on a Christmas party. **1980** B. HORNADGE *Austral. Slanguage* 92 Australians dislike anyone who they feel is a phoney or who acts in a way they consider as *putting on side*. When this happens the person concerned is said to be *bunging it on.*

bungalow, var. BANGALOW.

bungarra /'bʌŋærə/. *W.A.* Also **bung-arrer, bung-arrow.** [a. Nhanta-anmaŋu *baŋarra.*] The wide-spread monitor lizard, *Varanus gouldii*, usu. having a dark horizontal stripe through the eye, bordered by pale lines; *sand goanna*, see SAND. Also *transf.*

1897 A. HAYWARD *Along Road to Cue*, Ah, me! It grieves me sore To hear the batteries roar Where only roamed of yore The mild bungarra. **1908** E.G. MURPHY *Jarrahland Jingles* 25 He who dines on caviare, Or on boiled bungarra. **1927** M. TERRY *Through Land of Promise* 120 A larger breed known as the 'bung-arrer' is found up to 12 feet long. **1948** B. WANNAN *Treasury Austral. Frontier Tales* (1961) 105 The reproduction of St. George and the Dragon . . is Sir John Forrest . . on horseback spearing a bungarra. **1962** MARSHALL & DRYSDALE *Journey among Men* 170 Even the goannas, or bung-arrows, as the Western Australians call them, can be made into reasonable food. **1972** N. KING *Nickel Country* 91 One bough shed . . was often visited by a four-foot long bungarra. . . With its tongue flicking in and out, it always headed for the Coolgardie cooler where it knew eggs were kept. **1977** J. O'GRADY *There was Kid* 52 Sandgropers are not like us 'from the East'. They called goannas 'bungarras'. **1978** T. DAVIES *More Austral. Nicknames* 35 *Bungarra* (That's an Aboriginal word for Lazy Sun Lizard, I'm told.) He's not noted for overexertion.

bunged, *ppl. a.* Afflicted with BUNG EYE 1.

1912 SPENCER & GILLEN *Across Aust.* 50 If both eyes become 'bunged' at the same time, you are quite blind for so long as the 'bung' lasts. **1918** L.J. VILLIERS *Changing Yr.* 28 The flies 'a' got me bunged blind as a pup. **1928** B. SPENCER *Wanderings in Wild Aust.* 355 Fortunately, you do not often get both 'bunged' completely at the same time.

bunger. [Var. of *banger.*] A kind of firework which explodes with a loud report.

1929 D.J. HOPKINS *Hop of 'Bulletin'* 17 A parcel of gay fireworks, consisting of big bungers, little bungers, and strings of smaller ammunition. **1946** F. CLUNE *Try Nothing Twice* 21 The bunger burst with a deafening roar and John Chinaman . . jumped like Spring-heel Jack. **1960** K. SMITH *Word from Children* 142 On Guy Fawkes night, a bodgie threw a threepenny bunger in the window while Dad was watching TV. **1973** R.D. JONES *Mad Vibe* 21 Down the road there was a bang The familiar bang of a bunger in a letterbox. **1979** DOUGLAS & HEATHCOTE *Far Cry* 56 There followed the most colourful explosion and Catherine wheels and Big

Bungers and Flower Pots and Volcanoes exploded together.

bung eye.

1. An infection of the eye caused by the bite of the sandfly *Leptoconops stygius*, or transmitted by bush flies; an eye so affected; SWELLING BLIGHT. Also **bungey eye.**

1892 G.L. JAMES *Shall I try Aust.?* 242 [Sandy Blight] is also known as 'bung-eye', because, as an Irishman would say, when you open your eyes in the morning, the lids are tightly closed, and require no small amount of fomentation to get them open. **1895** A.C. BICKNELL *Travel & Adventure Northern Qld.* 79 He had got what is commonly called 'bung-eye'. This is brought on by allowing flies which have probably been feeding on carrion to settle on the face. **1901** K.L. PARKER in M. Muir *My Bush Bk.* (1982) 116 Sometimes they would only have swelling blight—'bungey eye' colloquially called—from a fly sting which the blacks used to cure by pressing on hot budtha twigs, and the whites with the blue-bag. **1910** *Truth* (Sydney) 16 Jan. 3/4 In the day time I have been *smothered in flies* and mosquitoes. Horses get 'hard eye' from these horrible insects, becoming totally blind. Men get 'bung eye', i.e., the eye swells and becomes closed from the poison. **1928** B. SPENCER *Wanderings in Wild Aust.* 355 A 'bung eye' is most uncomfortable. All of a sudden you feel a sharp prick and then your eyelids, both of them, begin to swell out and your cheek gets puffy. This goes on until you cannot open your eye. **1937** L.R. MENZIES *Gold Seeker's Odyssey* 87 We wore veils all day long to protect our eyes from the sting of the little devils, for if one was bitten the eyes were swollen shut several days. We called it 'bung-eye'. **1949** J. MORRISON *Creeping City* 42, I was dragged up on a back-station in a tin and hessian hut—fly-blown meat, sour water, bung eyes, bare feet, and Bathurst burrs. **1958** *Med. Jrnl. of Aust.* May 743/1 If the bite is on the face the area surrounding the eye is usually attacked and the sequelae may take the alarming form of bung eye. Both the upper and lower eyelids become oedematous, and the swelling completely closes the eye. **1967** E. KETTLE *Gone Bush* 59 A day out hunting in the bush meant 'bung' eyes; 'bung' being the popular expression used to describe an eye bitten by a fly.

2. Comb. **bung-eye fly.**

1932 H. PRIEST *Call of Bush* 147, I was stung in the eye by a small fly that inhabits the river country. I have heard it spoken of as the 'bung eye' fly—and very appropriately too. **1970** N. HALL et al. *Forest Trees Aust.* (ed. 3) 84 We camped at the Eight Mile. . . In the middle of lunch we were attacked by an immense swarm of 'bung-eye flies'.

bunging, *vbl. n. Obs.* [Of unknown origin.] In the collocation **bunging the mill**: see quots.

1895 J.T. RYAN *Reminisc. Aust.* 258 'Bunging the mill' was a term used for grinding flour with a steel mill . . among the first settlers. **1907** C. MACALISTER *Old Pioneering Days* 122 'Bunging the Mill', as it was called, was largely practised on the stations. This was simply the grinding of wheat in a little steel grinding machine (or mill).

bungwall /'bʌŋwɔl/. [a. Jagara *bangwal.*] The fern of swampy land *Blechnum indicum* (fam. Blechnaceae), occurring in Qld., N.S.W., N.T., and elsewhere; the rhizome of the plant, an important traditional foodstuff.

1824 *Austral.* (Sydney) 21 Oct. 2 The natives . . shewed them where to find and how to use the bungwa, as they call it—a very nutritious root, something like *ferne*, but larger; it is found in swamps. **1830** R. DAWSON *Present State Aust.* 92 Bungwall is fern-root. **1894** *Proc. Linnean Soc. N.S.W.* IX. 26 Almost every native tribe has a distinct name for this plant; the majority of the blacks now in Brisbane call it 'Tong-wun'; the word Bungwall is regarded by them as the white man's name. **1978** K. MCARTHUR *Pumicestone Passage* 43 Their principal vegetable food was 'bungwall', the root of a fern (*Blechnum indicum*), which is still very common in the swamps along the coast.

bunji-man. /'bʌndʒə-mən/. Also **bunjamun.** [f. Goreng Goreng (and other s.e. Qld. languages) *banji* friend + (Eng.) *-man.*] A white man with a predilection for Aboriginal women.

1975 R. BEILBY *Brown Land Crying* 4 'When you see one really crawling along you know it's a bunji-man.' A bunji-man, an adventurer in sex seeking something exotic. 'Black-velvet, that's what they call us Ab'rig'nes.' **1981** A. WELLER *Day of Dog* 54 Ya the cunning one, Val. But ya better not be givin' that ole bunji man a bit on the side. **1985** *Nat. Times* (Sydney) 12 Apr. 20/2 They were Bunji men. The origins of the term are unclear, but could be related to Bun-gyte, meaning an unbetrothed girl. Today the term, widely used by Aboriginal people around Perth, refers to lonely alcoholic old white men who wander the parks and back streets seeking 'black velvet'—sexual solace from Aboriginal women. . . The best free translation of Bunji is 'dirty old man'.

bunny. A simpleton or innocent; a scapegoat. Freq. in *pl.*

[**1914** E. DYSON *Spats' Fact'ry* 37 Garn, yiv got bunnies! . . You 'n' yer twitter about cats!] **1943** S.J. BAKER *Pop. Dict. Austral. Slang* (ed. 3) 16 *Bunny*, a simpleton or fool, an easy victim for exploitation. **1950** J. CLEARY *Just let me Be* 14 But you wait and see. I'm not gunna be like all them bunnies over there for the rest of my life. **1960** J. WYNNUM *Pinch Salt* (1963) 11 You can bet your socks they won't be putting a team of bunnies into the ring. **1962** *N.T. News* (Darwin) 4 Jan. 10/6 Agreed with Cr. Brandon but 'only provided the council is not eventually made the bunny and has to pay out for the work'. **1967** J. WYNNUM *I'm Jack, all Right* 10 In my opinion there should be a law to protect the dumb bunnies from spivs like Thumper. **1972** *Bulletin* (Sydney) 12 Aug. 16/3 Employers became increasingly fed up with being 'the bunnies' of the government.

bunya /'bʌnjə/. [a. Wiradhuri *bunya.*] The Queensland tree *Araucaria bidwillii* (fam. Araucariaceae), the cones of which contain seeds which are eaten raw, roasted, or pounded to a flour; the seeds of the tree. Also **bunya bunya,** and *attrib.*

1842 *Colonial Observer* (Sydney) 7 Dec. 662/2 The fruit is at present as large as a pear, and resembles a pine-apple: it grows, however, about five or six times larger, and is then covered with nuts, which contain the proper bunya fruit. **1855** J. BONWICK *Geogr. Aust. & N.Z.* (ed. 3) 205 The Bunya, a pine 150 feet high, bears a scented nut which is pounded and roasted. **1865** G.S. LANG *Aborigines of Aust.* 6 The Bunna-Bunna pine produces a very large cone, once in every two or three years, and all the tribes, from a great distance around, flock to it in the proper season. **1870** *Illustr. Sydney News* 6 July 3/1 The Government have proclaimed that the cutting and removal of certain timber named the 'Bunya Bunya' and the 'Queensland nut' is now absolutely prohibited. **1881** C.F. CHUBB *Fugitive Pieces* 18 Delighting the gins in their gunyahs, Grinning like wild cats, with pearly teeth chewing the bunya, Washing it down with a choogarbag. **1892** J. FRASER *Aborigines N.S.W.* 50 But there is proof that the blacks do gather from great distances and in great numbers and remain together while the temporary supply of food lasts. I refer to the annual feasting in the Bunya-bunya country . . about 50 miles to the north of the town of Dalby in Queensland. **1904** C.C. PETRIE *T. Petrie's Reminisc. Early Qld.* 11, I will pass now to their native customs, and tell you of the 'Bon-yi season'. 'Bon-yi', the native name for the pine, Araucaria Bidwilli, has been wrongly accepted and pronounced bunya. **1914** J. MATHEW *Ballads Bush Life* 24 Where elders squatted, children played And women roasted bunyas. **1931** M.M. BANKS *Memories Pioneer Days Qld.* 78 The bunya bears large cones with nuts, which are good eating when roasted. **1957** *Bulletin* (Sydney) 24 Apr. 19/1 The laden cones were dropping from our bunya-tree, but the nuts were always ratted before we got a look-in. **1964** R.M. & C.H. BERNDT *World First Australs.* 99 In the Bunya Mountains in Queensland, when bunya nuts were in season they were not all eaten at once. **1974** N. CATO *Brown Sugar* 181 The bunya's botanical name was *Araucaria Bidwilli*, in honour of John Bidwell who had sent the first specimens of this strange 'pine' back to England. **1982** K. MCARTHUR *Bush in Bloom* 12 In my mind January is strongly associated with Bunya Nuts. It is the time of their fall and although they are seldom marketed one can be lucky enough to be given a cone.

bunyip /'bʌnjəp/. [a. Wergaia dial. of Wemba *banib.*]

1. A fabulous amphibious monster supposed to inhabit inland waterways. Also *attrib.*

1845 *Sydney Morning Herald* 12 July 2/5 On the bone being shown to an intelligent black, he at once recognised it as belonging to the 'Bunyip', which he declared he had seen. **1845** *Observer* (Hobart) 18 July 4/5 The Bunyip . . is represented as uniting the characteristics of a bird and of an alligator. **1847** *Port Phillip Herald* 11 Feb. (Suppl.), Naturalists of every grade have, since the plantation of the Australian colonies, been racking their brains with fruitless researches as to the existence or non-existence of the supposed amphibious monster y'clept, amongst many other designations, the Bunyip. **1847** *Bell's Life in Sydney* 19 June 3/2 That apocryphal animal of many names, commonly designated 'The Bunyip' has, according to a correspondent of the *Sydney Morning Herald*, been seen on the Murrumbidgee. It is described as being about as big as a six months old calf, of a dark brown colour, a long neck, a long pointed head, large ears, a thick mane of hair from the head down the neck, and two large tusks. It is said to be an amphibious animal, as it has been observed floundering in the rivers, as well as grazing on their banks. **1848** *Austral. Sportsman* (Sydney) 2 Dec. 4/5 A picture of the Bunyip to my sporting friends I give sirs. An animal so very scarce, 'twas never caught alive sirs. **1857** *Moreton Bay Free Press* 15 Apr. 3/7 Mr Stocqueler informs us that the bunyip is a large freshwater seal, having two small paddles or fins attached to the shoulders, a long swan-like neck, a head like a dog, and a curious bag hanging under the jaw, resembling the pouch of the pelican. **1867** 'S. MCTAVISH' *Chowla* 47 'Rather,' said the noble girl, 'rather would I take the baleful bunyip to my bosom . . than give my hand to a man I loathe.' **1878** J.H. NICHOLSON *Opal Fever* 129 So all our studies we will sink; The Bunyip is the Missing Link Between the monkey and the man; We'll find that Bunyip if we can. **1888** *Illustr. Austral. News* (Melbourne) 1 Aug. (Suppl.) 2/2 The Bunyip is the evil spirit or devil of the blacks. **1901** 'A. FERRES' *Free Selector* 97 And the echo fierce of the bunyip's roar I heard from out the skies. **1907** A. MACDONALD *In Land of Pearl & Gold* 83 The presence of some natives fantastically adorned with snake, kangaroo, and emu skins—bunyip-men, as they are called—was a sign that developments might take place later. **1924** *Aust.* (Sydney) Mar. 64 The Paterson River is like all the others, in that it possesses a bunyip hole. **1932** J. TRURAN *Green Mallee* 67 Dad reckoned the bunyips must 'a' got yer; yer was so long comin' over to see us. **1947** W. LAWSON *Paddle-Wheels Away* 154 The gins at the homestead reckoned a new bunyip was livin' down here. **1965** R.H. CONQUEST *Horses in Kitchen* 92 There is hardly a river or creek that doesn't possess one 'bunyip hole' at least. **1975** *Bulletin* (Sydney) 9 Aug. 44/1 Literary gentlemen have tended to call the great Australian novel the bunyip, the monster that has never been revealed. **1979** D. MAITLAND *Breaking Out* 261 A terrible primeval lust rose up out of the deepest sludge of his mind like an ugly bunyip from the depths of a dark, misty, outback billabong.

2. *fig.* See quot. 1852. Also *attrib.*, esp. as **bunyip aristocracy.**

1852 G.C. MUNDY *Our Antipodes* II. 19 A new and strong word was adopted into the Australian vocabulary: Bunyip became, and remains, a Sydney synonym for *imposter, pretender, humbug*, and the like. **1853** *Sydney Morning Herald* 16 Aug. 5/3 Here they all knew the common water mole was transferred into the duck-billed platypus, and in some distant emulation of this degeneration, he supposed they were to be favoured with a bunyip aristocracy. **1867** J.R. HOULDING *Austral. Capers* 170 Another he described as a regular old Bunyip, who would be sure to want to sell him a station stocked with scabby sheep, a rotten ship, or a tumble-down house. **1956** R.G. EDWARDS *Overlander Songbk.* 103 The very large stations . . fostered the class feeling that was summed up with the title of 'Bunyip Aristocracy'. **1960** *Sydney Morning Herald* 8 Aug. 3/6 Bit by bit the A.L.P. in New South Wales is building up a bunyip peerage of its own even if the bunyips aren't titled, and sit in Lower, not Upper, Houses. **1972** *Bulletin* (Sydney) 21 Oct. 35/3 Even many members of Australia's bunyip aristocracy seem to be able to grasp the reasoning behind the need to eliminate God Save The Queen as the national anthem and to remove the Union Jack from the flag. **1975** X. HERBERT *Poor Fellow my Country* 661 'Bunyip Lord, dear boy?' 'A term applied to Australian holders of Imperial titles.' **1984** *Sydney Morning Herald* 31 Mar. 34/4 Now the quest for national identity (our century-long pursuit of the bunyip) is on again.

3. *transf.* See quot. 1952.

1875 R. BRUCE *Dingoes* 123 Six horsemen urge with voice and whip The cattle in the rear, And teach each surly bunyip A little wholesome fear. **1952** A.C.C. LOCK *Travels across Aust.* 271 'Now and again we have a combined muster... Sometimes we strike a few bunyips.' A bunyip.. was a beast that had grown to full size without being branded.

4. *transf.* BOOMER *n.*[2] Also **bunyip bird.**

1909 E. ASH *Austral. Oracle* 31 The bittern is certainly what our early colonists called the 'swamp bull' or 'bunyip'. **1954** C. BARRETT *Wild Life Aust. & New Guinea* 112 Bitterns are sometimes called 'Bunyip-birds'... When a booming call breaks the silence of a lonely swamp, it is the voice of the 'Bunyip-bird', largest of the five kinds of bitterns found in Australia. **1955** *Bulletin* (Sydney) 13 July 12/1 The brown bittern—the bunyip of our mythology—is loath to leave old haunts. **1955** D. CLARK *Boomer* 38 A great brown bittern—the 'bunyip bird', whose solemn booming brings fear to the myth-haunted blackfellows—posed motionless.

Hence **bunyipian** *a.*, fantastic.

1899 *Bulletin* (Sydney) 4 Feb. 14/4 His unique treasure utters small plaintive cries.. and was captured under bunyipian circumstances.

Burdekin /'bədəkən/. [The name of a river in n.e. Qld.] Used *attrib.* in Special Comb. **Burdekin duck, (a)** the shelduck *Tadorna radjah* of n. Aust., having a white head, neck, and underparts exc. for a chestnut band across the breast; RAJAH SHIELDRAKE; **(b)** a slice of meat, battered and fried; **plum,** the tree of Qld. and New Guinea *Pleiogynium timorense* (fam. Anacardiaceae) which yields both timber and a dark plum-like fruit, palatable when ripe; the fruit itself; *sweet plum*, see SWEET *a.*[1]; **vine** *obs.*, the vine of Qld. and N.S.W. *Cissus opaca* (fam. Vitaceae), the tubers of which are a traditional foodstuff; **vomit,** an attack of vomiting (see also *Barcoo sickness* BARCOO A. 2, BELYANDO SPEW).

1867 F.J. BYERLEY *Narr. Overland Exped. Northern Qld.* 6 The beautiful **Burdekin duck** (*Tadorna Radjah*). **1870** E.B. KENNEDY *Four Yrs. in Qld.* 116 The Burdekin duck is .. large, and bronze and white in colour. They are found in large numbers on the River Burdekin, from which they derive their name. **1896** W.H. WILLSHIRE *Land of Dawning* 48 My trackers shot Burdekin ducks. **1945** T. RONAN *Strangers on Ophir* 39 A meat fritter known in the Kimberleys as a 'Burdekin Duck', and on the Burdekin as a 'Kimberley Oyster'. **1960** B. HARNEY *Cook Bk.* 24 Burdekin Ducks (or Kimberley Oysters). Use either cold or corned beef... Beat the batter well, dip each slice into it and fry in hot fat. **1964** M. SHARLAND *Territory of Birds* 86 The handsome white heads of Burdekin Ducks were prominent among the green rushes. **1972** *Austral. Lapidary Mag.* Sept. 9/2 'The Burdekin Duck', so named from the bushman's name for salt beef rolled in flour and fried, was found by Jimmy Escreet and Jack Atherton. **1977** W.A. WINTER-IRVING *Bush Stories* 120 Burdekin duck .. is a thin slice of beef or mutton... Cover meat with batter as thickly as possible. Fry in fat. **1979** D. LOCKWOOD *My Old Mates & I* 51 The Burdekin ducks lay their eggs in hollow tree trunks, sometimes fifty feet up. **1889** J.H. MAIDEN *Useful Native Plants Aust.* 599 *Spondias pleiogyna* .. 'Sweet Plum', or '**Burdekin Plum**'. Wood hard, dark brown, with red markings, resembling American walnut. **1903** *Austral. Handbk.* 280 Some of the trees which furnish woods particularly suited for cabinet work:-.. 'Burdekin Plum' (*Pleiogynium Solandri*). **1946** A. THURIAN *Bush Tea & Overlanders* 23 He swore by the lignum and mulga, Not forgetting the saltbush too, That nothing seemed to be so vulgar, As Burdekin plums in a stew. **1951** *Bulletin* (Sydney) 7 Nov. 12/2 The Burdekin plum.. grew as far up as Exmoor, not far from the headquarters of the Bowen River. **1963** *N. Austral. Monthly* Dec. 11 Burdekin plum trees .. are fairly plentiful, and are often grown near stockyard for shade. It is a fair-sized tree, with large dark green pinnate leaves up to seven inches long. **1888** *Proc. Linnean Soc. N.S.W.* III. 553 *Vitis opaca*... '**Burdekin vine**'... The tubers .. are eaten after immersion in hot water. **c 1910** W.R. GUILFOYLE *Austral. Plants* 365 'Burdekin Vine' or 'Pepper Vine' of Fraser's Island (evergreen climber). **1918** C. FETHERSTONHAUGH *After Many Days* 272 What I called the Belyando Spue was a most trying ailment... The Western fellows called it the 'Barcoo sickness', the Northern men termed it the '**Burdekin vomit**'.

burka /'bəkə/. *Obs.* [a. Gaurna *burka.*] See quot. 1858.

1841 C.G. TEICHELMANN *Aborigines S.A.* 6 The male sex is divided into several ages, the last of which is called *burka*, an old, full adult. **1845** M. COLLISSON *S.A.* 44 The fifth stage is *burka* (a full man), when gray-headed. **1857** F. GERSTAECKER *Two Convicts* 31 Title of honour, Burka, the old man (aboriginal). **1858** W.A. CAWTHORNE *Legend of Kupirri* 30 'Burka.'—An aged man, the last stage through which men pass, and in whom the knowledge of all charms, ceremonies, &c., is deposited.

Burketown mosquito net. [f. the name of a town in Qld.] See quots. 1960 and 1976.

1960 B. HARNEY *Cook Bk.* 89 A Burketown Mosquito Net. Drink a bottle of O.P. rum with swamp-water. **1976** B. SCOTT *Compl. Bk. Austral. Folk Lore* 380 A Burketown mosquito net is a bottle of rum and a cowdung fire. **1980** N. WATKINS *Kangaroo Connection* 102 'Hope you've brought your Burke-town mosquito net?' .. Charles laughed, as the reference to a Burke-town mosquito net, meant a bottle of O.P. rum and swamp water!

burl. [Br. dial. (esp. Scot.) *birl, v.* to spin, twirl.] A try or attempt; esp. in the phr. **to give it a burl,** to venture an attempt.

[N.Z. **1917** *Chrons. N.Z. Exped. Force* 16 May 137/2 So up they [*sc.* pennies] went and spinning well And betters cried 'Fair 'burl'!' **1924** *Truth* (Sydney) 27 Apr. 6/3 *Burl*, to try anything.] **1927** F.C. BIGGERS *Bat-Eye* 10 These dancin' stunts was jakeloo—a bloke Jist prats 'is frame in, an' selects a girl: A sorter joint wear blokes can sit an' smoke, W'ile waitin' round ter give the 'op a burl. **1935** K. TENNANT *Tiburon* 95 'Come on,' Kahn murmured to Johnny as the crowd increased, 'give it a burl!' **1943** S.W. KEOUGH *Around Army* 57 The trouble is you're getting too flash after your burl in the bright lights. **1953** T.A.G. HUNGERFORD *Riverslake* 124 Well, you want to give it a burl—you want to come? **1965** R.H. CONQUEST *Horses in Kitchen* 169 The optimistic westerners who gave it a burl .. rushed and jumped all over the place. **1969** J. HIBBERD *Dimboola* (1974) 25 Shirl's very religious. Thinks of nothing else. We know all about you Shirl. Who's for a burl with Shirl! **1978** MULLALLY & SEXTON *Libra & Leprechaun* 12 Should be some fish out there I say. We'll give it a burl, eh? **1981** C. JAMES *Charles Charming's Challenges* 37 We're real thrilled You're giving *Timbertop* a burl, Your Grace.

burley, var. BERLEY *n.* and *v.*

burn, *v.*

1. *trans.* With **off:** to clear (land) for agricultural purposes by burning the vegetation; to burn (timber, stubble, etc.); to burn (sugar cane prior to its being cut). Also *intr.*

1793 D. COLLINS *Acct. Eng. Colony N.S.W.* (1798) I. 334 For cutting down the timber of an acre of ground, burning it off, and afterwards hoeing it for corn, the price was four Pounds. **1806** *Sydney Gaz.* 1 Sept., Wanted, a Gang of Men to burn off 20 or 30 acres of fallen timber on Clench's Farm at George's River. **1832** *Colonial Times* (Hobart) 21 Mar., About thirty labourers were employed to grub up the stumps and to burn off the timber. **1837** J. MACARTHUR *N.S.W.* 186 By degrees, however, the felled timber and the stumps are burnt off. **1839** *Southern Austral.* (Adelaide) 16 Oct. 4/1 May.—In the beginning of this month the feed was very scarce and the ground hard, especially where it had been burnt off. **1849** S. & J. SIDNEY *Emigrant's Jrnl.* 162 Other settlers do not burn off at all, but saw the logs into pieces and spare chain them off the land. **1870** W.B. WITHERS *Hist. Ballarat* 2 The ground afforded excellent pasture after the ranker growth had been burnt off. **1885** *Illustr. Austral. News* (Melbourne) 25 Nov. 202/2 To remove the undergrowth he generally begins by starting a fire through his land, or 'burning off' as it is called, after which he sets to work 'grubbing' and 'falling' the trees. **1891** E. HULME *Settler's 35 Yrs. Experience Vic.* 22, I often took my blankets and slept outside by the large fires, where the large logs were being burned off. **1913** W.K. HARRIS *Outback in Aust.* 186 Mr Gmeiner was out 'burning off' some scrub with his men. **1931** B. CRONIN *Bracken* 61 When first scrubbed and burned off it was remarkably free from fern or fireweed. **1977** F.B. VICKERS *Stranger no Longer* 30 We'll burn off the hundred acres today. If the easterly holds all morning we'll get a clean burn. **1979** D. MAITLAND *Breaking Out* 5 May I suggest you consider its merits next time you want to burn off a paddock for ploughing. **1981** A.B. FACEY *Fortunate Life* 69 We would set it alight all around the outside of the eighty acres, and let it burn quietly inwards. That was the correct way to burn off in the wheat-belt in those days.

Hence **burning off** *vbl. n.*

1804 *Sydney Gaz.* 11 Nov., Labourers had been employed in clearing and burning off. **1827** *Monitor* (Sydney) 30 Aug. 619/3 When '*the burning off*' commenced, the spare time would vary from two or three days, to nine or ten, out of a month. **1834** J.D. LANG *Hist. & Statistical Acct. N.S.W.* I. 89 The operation of *burning off* must precede the plough. **1849** A. HARRIS *Emigrant Family* (1967) 85 I'll look after the felling and burning off. **1879** 'RECENT SETTLER' *Emigration Tas.* 74 If he intends to clear only a few acres each year, he should arrange that the trees are rung three years before the burning off takes place. **1891** J. FENTON *Bush Life Tas.* (1964) 175 Happy homesteads and verdant meadows rise from the wreck of the 'burning off'. **1911** 'ROSE BOLDREWOOD' *Complications at Collaroi* 17 Joe Blundell was duly put on the strength of the 'burning-off' contingent next day. **1963** D. ROBERT *Look at me Now* 113 Before cutting, the cane fields are set alight... It is a strange and terrible sight to see a 'burning-off'. **1981** A.B. FACEY *Fortunate Life* 88 Burning-off season opened and several neighbours came to help put the fire through the chopped and burnt down timber.

2. To drive a motor vehicle at high speed. Also as *n.*

1963 G. BAHNEMANN *Hoodlum* 155 He parked his bike at the kerb and waited. Soon the others burned around the corner as if hunted by the devil in person. **1965** C. JOHNSON *Wild Cat Falling* 109 'What was the plan?' he asks. 'Pick up a car,' I say. 'Bust a store in this one horse town, then burn off out of the State.' **1967** J. HIBBERD *White with Wire Wheels* (1970) 164 He .. wants to know how the Valiant performs. I've promised to take him for a burn when I've driven it in.

burn, *n.* [U.S. *burn* burning of vegetation, in order to clear land.] In clearing land: the controlled burning of standing or felled vegetation; the area so burned; also, the burning of sugar cane prior to its being cut. Also **burn-off.**

1849 W. ARCHER Diary 14 Apr., Found that the threshers had finished .. and that the burn of rushes in Bull Pad[dock] was also at an end. **1897** L. LINDLEY-COWEN *W. Austral. Settler's Guide* 112 The poison plant.. is most deadly when it is making a new growth after a 'burn', or when it is in the flowering stage. **1910** *Emu* X. 127 Throwing together the branches and debris after the burn-off. **1911** A. MARSHALL *Sunny Aust.* 234 With a 'good burn' nothing is left but wood ash, which fertilizes the ground. **1916** L. FERRIS *John Heathlyn of Otway* 161 Anyone who has viewed the result of a good burn-off must know what a great advantage this element is to the settler who faced a dense primeval forest. **1920** *Land of Lyre Bird* (S. Gippsland Pioneers' Assoc.) 79 Perhaps the most anxious time of the year for the early pioneer lay between the finish of the scrub-cutting, usually about Christmas time, and the time for 'the burn'. **1940** G. MORPHETT *Simple Story Rural Dev.* 2/2 We had a beautiful burn of the second 100 acres, and so we had 200 acres in the second year. **1948** J.K. EWERS *For Heroes to live In* 5 Ross was over at the block, bashing suckers in preparation for a summer burn. **1952** J.R. SKEMP *Memories Myrtle Bank* 24 Then, on the fresh ashes after the 'burn', grass and clover seed was broadcast. **1953** H.G. LAMOND *Big Red* 197 The wallaroos understood that signal: they were on the burn almost before the smoke had cleared away. **1972** *Ten Award Winning Stories* 41 He brushed through a patch of dolly-bush and fire-weed that had taken over after a burn the year before. **1981** *Woman's Day* (Sydney) 16 Sept. 27/3 An announcement that a big daytime burn of cane would be used in the film had farmers clamouring for their burn to be seen around the world.

Burnett salmon. Chiefly *Qld.* [f. the name of the *Burnett* River in s.e. Qld., from which the type specimens came.] LUNGFISH. See also *mud fish* MUD 1.

1886 F. COWAN *Aust.* 18 The Burnett Salmon of the Queensland streams: Ceratodus: nor fish, nor flesh, nor good red herring. **1899** R. SEMON *In Austral. Bush* 87 The settlers call the Ceratodus the 'Burnett Salmon' on account of its reddish flesh. **1928** M.E. FULLERTON *Austral. Bush* 222 Among the best table-fish native to the fresh-water rivers is the Burnet [*sic*] River salmon. **1951** T.C. ROUGHLEY *Fish & Fisheries Aust.* 159 This lungfish [*Ceratodus forsteri*], now referred to always as the

'Queensland lungfish' . . was often called by the local settlers 'Burnett salmon'.

burnt, *ppl. a.*

1. With **up**: burned dry, scorched.

1828 Tas. Colonial Secretary's Office Rec. 1/12 98, The Grass is so completely burnt up that the Oxen are dyeing [*sic*]—Two of them have died this week. **1862** A. POLEHAMPTON *Kangaroo Land* 235, I travelled for some time over a burnt-up plain. **1882** A.J. BOYD *Old Colonials* 67 The blacks is about these water-holes, now the country is so burnt up. So it isn't very safe for a cove to camp alone. ***c* 1960** C. MACKNESS *Clump Point & District* 74 The memory of the bitter struggle on 'the bit of eaten-out, burnt-up bush that killed poor old Dad and his spuds and weedy cows' refused to die.

2. With **out**: destroyed by fire, esp. bushfire: (of people) afflicted by the loss of property so caused.

1851 *Empire* (Sydney) 13 Feb. 3/3 The flock masters . . are compelled to move their flocks, and such of them as have not runs in watered districts . . as are the unfortunate owners of the runs that are 'burnt out'. **1880** *Argus* (Melbourne) 13 Jan. 6/2 Extensive bush-fires are raging close to the town, and the heat has been excessive. Early in the afternoon it became rumoured that two people had been burnt out, but this proved subsequently to be incorrect. Only the fencing of the places was destroyed. **1910** H. LAWSON *Rising of Court* 15 Leader of subscription lists for burnt-out, flooded-out, sick, hurt, dead. **1920** *Huon Times* (Franklin) 7 Dec. 2/7 He had been burnt out twice and was likely to be so again if the scrub was not felled. **1980** ANSELL & PERCY *To fight Wild* 143 Once Luke McCall and the others began their ride home, they had to move as fast as possible because there was little feed for their horses on the burnt-out country.

3. In the collocation **burnt feed,** new and succulent growth following a fire.

[**1826** J. ATKINSON *Acct. Agric. & Grazing N.S.W.* 21 The grass in winter becomes withered by the frosts . . and as it impedes the growth of young grass, the common practice is to set fire to it. . . The young herbage that springs up . . is sure to attract the kangaroos and other game; and the horned cattle are also very fond of feeding upon this *burnt ground*, as it is termed in the Colony.] **1837** *Colonist* (Sydney) 27 Apr. 134/3 The young grass was shooting up with the usual vivid green peculiar to 'burnt feed'. **1842** *Colonial Observer* (Sydney) 23 Feb. 162/4 The rain . . is in good time to freshen the grass, and ensure young grass where it has been burnt (familiarly called *burnt feed*) before the Autumn frosts. **1859** W. BURROWS *Adventures Mounted Trooper* 141 They can get a patch of 'burnt feed', as the young shoots are called, which spring up on a piece of land that has been on fire. **1870** E.B. KENNEDY *Four Yrs. in Qld.* 31 The grass here had been burnt some weeks ago, and the young shoots were springing up. This is known in the bush as 'burnt feed'. **1886** H. FINCH-HATTON *Advance Aust.* (rev. ed.) 87 Directly the first shower falls these parts are immediately covered with beautiful young grass, 'burnt feed' as it is called.

4. *Mining. Obs.* In the collocation **burnt stuff**: see quot. 1852.

1852 J. BONWICK *Notes of Gold Digger* 38 The burnt stuff, or burnt quartz of the miners, is a ferruginous cement binding quartz pebbles. . . In the Ballarat holes the 'Burnt quartz' has been found ten feet thick. **1853** MRS C. CLACY *Lady's Visit to Gold Diggings* (1963) 65 This was succeeded by a strata almost as hard as iron—technically called 'burnt-stuff'.

'burra. Also **burra.** Shortened form of KOOKABURRA.

1901 'A. FERRES' *Free Selector* 97 The burra laughs the rosy dawn Into the sweet spring day. **1904** E.S. EMERSON *Shanty Entertainment* (1910) 10 While 'burras, magpies and galahs jeered at them. **1908** *Bulletin* (Sydney) 29 Oct. 14/3 The 'roos and the 'burra viewed the proceedings from afar. **1912** *Ibid.* 1 Feb. 13/1 The women laughed like 'burras at the townies' sudden spill.

burrawang /'bʌrəwæŋ/. Also **buddawong, burrawong.** [a. Dharuk *barawaŋ*.] Any of several plants of the genera *Macrozamia* (fam. Zamiaceae) and *Cycas* (fam. Cycadaceae), esp. *M. communis*, having palm-like fronds and pineapple-like cones yielding nuts edible after treatment (see quot. 1901). Also *attrib.*

***c* 1790** W. DAWES Grammatical Forms Lang. N.S.W., Names of fruit in N.S.W. . . buruwang [etc.]. **1825** B. FIELD *Geogr. Mem. N.S.W.* 244 A kind of dwarf palm, called *burrawang* by the natives (zamia spiralis). **1826** J. ATKINSON *Acct. Agric. & Grazing N.S.W.* 19 The burwan is a plant with leaves very much like the cocoa nut, growing out from a stem about a foot high; at certain seasons it produces a flower, which is succeeded by a cluster of nuts, enclosed in a hard woody shell. **1851** J. HENDERSON *Excursions & Adventures N.S.W.* II. 238 The Burrowan, which grows in a sandy soil, and produces an inedible fruit, resembling the pine-apple in appearance, has already been noticed. **1888** *Proc. Linnean Soc. N.S.W.* III. 525 'Burrawang Nut', so called because they used to be, and are to some extent now, very common about Burrawang, N.S.W. The nuts are relished by the aboriginals. **1901** *Bulletin* (Sydney) 21 Dec. 16/2 The buddawong nuts, when crushed and soaked in running water for about 10 hours, may with safety be boiled and eaten. They are very plentiful along N.S.W. South Coast. **1912** A. BERRY *Reminisc.* 192 An Australian plant . . which contains a nutritious fecula and a poison. . . The natives call this plant Burrawang; botanists call it *Macrozamia spiralis*. **1938** C.T. WHITE *Princ. Bot. Qld. Farmers* 134 Burrawang or Wild Pineapple is a name frequently given to species of Macrozamia, particularly to *M. spiralis*. All the Australian members have a bad reputation as plants poisonous to stock. **1943** *Bulletin* (Sydney) 7 July 12/1 Tree-fern tops and squatty burrawongs. **1968** F. ROSE *Aust. Revisited* 165 On Groote Eylandt it was the harvest of the fruit of the cycad or burrawang (*Cycas media*). **1981** Q. WILD *Honey Wind* 169 The grey spotted gums reflecting light above the deep green of the ancient burrawangs.

burr-cutter. One employed (in the country) to cut burr-bearing plants.

1890 *Braidwood Dispatch* 30 Apr. 4/1, I know . . the edge of Little Plain . . by the burr-cutter's old camp. **1896** T. HENEY *Girl at Birrell's* 207 In the country townships each clique, . . the 'gold-tops', the 'silver-tails', the 'burr-cutters'. **1949** *Bulletin* (Sydney) 26 Oct. 12/3 The trouble with Sandy's burrcutters started with the arrival of a young chap with very Leftist ideas of work. **1955** D. NILAND *Shiralee* 47 During the trip he had been thinking of the job at the burr-cutter's camp. **1964** H.P. TRITTON *Time means Tucker* (rev. ed.) 15 We met a chap who wanted burr cutters for Pine Ridge . . and thought we would have a go at it. . . Wool infested with burr was almost worthless. . . The only method of control used then was to dig them out, rake them . . and burn them.

Hence **burr-cutting** *vbl. n.*

1894 *Bulletin* (Sydney) 6 Jan. 23/3 Whether boundary-riding, burr-cutting or droving he did not like being called Doctor. **1902** *Ibid.* 18 Oct. 14/1 There will be no station work except burr-cutting. **1911** ST C. GRONDONA *Collar & Cuffs* 25 Our principal employment lately has been burr cutting. **1955** D. NILAND *Shiralee* 31 They would take a job burr-cutting, walking about with a long-handled hoe, and not minding it, so long as the burrs were not too plentiful. **1959** H.P. TRITTON *Time means Tucker* 10 All were looking for burr cutting, which was a seasonal occupation on the Liverpool Plains.

burry, var. BOORIE.

bursaria /bə'sɛəriə/. [The plant genus *Bursaria* was named by Spanish botanist A.J. Cavanilles (*Icon. et Descr. Plant.* (1797) IV. 30) f. L. *bursa* bag or satchel, referring to the pouch-like fruit capsules.] **a.** Any species of the Austral. genus of prickly shrubs and small trees *Bursaria* (fam. Pittosporaceae) which is cultivated in Aust. and w. Europe. **b.** With distinguishing epithet, as (*Vic.*) **sweet bursaria,** *B. spinosa*, bearing sweet-smelling flowers; *native box*, see NATIVE *a.* 6 a.; *prickly box*, see PRICKLY.

1814 R. BROWN *Gen. Remarks Bot. Terra Australis* 10 Both Pittosporum and Bursaria are found within the tropic. **1827** A. CUNNINGHAM *Gen. Remarks Vegetation* 22 Bursaria . . has been traced within the tropic to latitude 19° South on those eastern shores. **1914** E.E. PESCOTT *Native Flowers Vic.* 33 'Sweet Bursaria' . . is called in many localities the 'Christmas Bush'. **1928** R.H. CROLL *Open Road Vic.* 20 A solitary Bursaria of good stature. **1967** N.A. WAKEFIELD *Naturalist's Diary* 32 Sweet Bursaria (*Bursaria spinosa*) was in full bloom with its dense pyramids of small white flowers. **1984** *Gold Coast Bull.* 28 Apr. 56/4 Nectar is no longer available from . . Bursaria.

burst, *n.*[1] [Br. dial. *burst* an outburst of drinking: see EDD.]

1. A drinking bout, esp. in the phr. **on the burst.** See also BUST *n.*

1852 *V & P* (N.S.W. L.A.) II. 769, I should say perhaps one-third of the miners are incorrigible drunkards, who are eternally at these houses; many of these are very lucky; they frequently fall into good claims, and make large hauls in the course of the week; they then go 'upon the burst', as they call it, and drink until all their earnings are 'knocked down', and they then go to work again. **1875** *Austral. Town & Country Jrnl.* (Sydney) 21 Aug. 303/3 Well, there is a chap, but he's on the burst just now, as one might say. **1876** *Ibid.* 5 Aug. 222/4 'There would be a slight probability of some of the party going 'on the bust', after three or four months' teetotalism.' 'On the burst? I do not quite follow.' 'On the burst,' explained the colonist, 'vernacular signifying a protracted and utterly reckless debauch. It's an Australian malady.' **1880** 'ERRO' *Squattermania* 225 He paid for his board and lodging, and departed without making any effort to get 'on the burst', much to the landlady's disgust. **1888** *Bulletin* (Sydney) 10 Mar. 14/2 An appreciative and sympathetic audience of drovers, washers, shearers and 'knockabouts' on the 'burst' at a wayside hotel. **1896** T. HENEY *Girl at Birrell's* 32 For a week the Oonoondoo Creek Hotel was the scene of one of those indescribable debauches of drunkenness called an 'all-hands-burst'. **1904** A.B. PATERSON *Rio Grande's Last Race* 30 We all chucked-up our daily work and went upon the burst. **1912** S. LOCKE *Dawsons' Uncle George* 79 They all have the idea that Sydney's a fair petunia of a place. . . So when they want a burst, they hails a steamer, an' over here they comes an' lets themselves go. Blows themselves right out. **1916** A. WILSON *Lays & Tales of Mines* 24 Sam had had his share of the precious metal, and the 'bursts' he had after his lucky finds were talked about in the camp for years afterwards. **1924** *Smith's Weekly* (Sydney) 26 Apr. 25/6 Into the bush barber's walked a sleeper-cutter, just off a long burst, who demanded that his throat be cut. **1942** C. CASEY *It's Harder for Girls* 98 He was a real damn nuisance, allus in arguments an' stayin' on th' burst for as much as a fortnight at a time.

2. *fig.*

1912 E. FISHER *Kiss of Dolly Day* 57 Pure thoughts are borne to realms above. My soul is on the burst.

burst, *n.*[2] *Obs.* [Abbrev. of BURSTER *n.*[2]] SOUTHERLY BUSTER.

[N.Z. **1851** C.O. TORLESSE *Canterbury Settlement* 9 The north-west wind . . somewhat resembling the 'hot winds' of Australia . . is almost invariably succeeded by one from the south-west, which in the summer time is a cool and pleasant guest, but in the winter season what is aptly denominated 'a burst', and sometimes lasts for two or three days, being generally accompanied by rain, if not snow and sleet.] **1894** *Jrnl. & Proc. R. Soc. N.S.W.* XXVIII. 140 In the early morning on the day of a 'burst' the sky is white and hazy of aspect.

burster, *n.*[1] *Obs.* [f. *burst* to break (in various contexts).] A heavy fall from a horse; BUSTER *n.*[3]

1845 *Bell's Life in Sydney* 18 Jan. 2/2 In the first heat the rider of Rob Roy got a terrific burster, shortly after turning the sharper angle we have already complained of or rather on his way down the hill. **1850** *Ibid.* 25 May 2/3 Steeltrap crossed his legs or touched the rail, and threw Meharty a burster. **1864** *Illustr. Sydney News* 16 Dec. 12/1 Station life is not without its excitements—often in the saddle from daylight till dark over ranges and gullies heedless of 'crabholes' and 'bursters'. **1871** *Austral. Town & Country Jrnl.* (Sydney) 28 June 122/3 He got an awful burster from a notorious buckjumper. **1886** R. HENTY *Australiana* 245 A gallop after wild horses over the plains, with the prospect of a 'burster' when crossing the crab-hole country, was exciting.

burster, *n.*[2] *Obs.* [Shortened form of SOUTHERLY BURSTER.] A strong sudden wind, esp. from the south.

1854 M.B. MOWLE Diary 16 May, The Cosmopolite sailed today for Hobarton. . . All the vessels left the Bay with a N.E. wind, they have been detained here three weeks in consequence of the late constant southerly gales, occasionally being lured out for a few hours, or a day by the promise of a north-easter & then sent flying back by a '*burster*' from the southward. **1868** J.R. HOULDING *Austral. Tales* 222, I thought we might get to Sydney before the 'burster'. **1903** W. CRAIG *My*

Adventures 233 The intense heat and the clouds of dust raised by northerly 'bursters' during the summer season were hard to bear.

bursting, *vbl. n. Timber-getting.* The splitting of a log into four or more billets, out of each of which a sleeper is cut.

1882 A.J. BOYD *Old Colonials* 25 You want to be very particular in a tree for staves. They ain't split like palings or shingles. We run them off the 'bursting way', as it is called, across the grain. It isn't exactly across the grain, but that's the best way I can explain it. **1903** *Bulletin* (Sydney) 24 Dec. 36/3 Sleepers are split, 'on the flat', the 'boarding' way of the tree—*i.e.* if you can see in imagination, the sleepers in the log before they are cut out, they lie side by side round the bole. And herein is the reason why sleepers are split and not sawn. If sawn the most would be made of the block and the sleepers sawn 'on the flat' the 'bursting' way of the tree and be no use.

bush, *n., a.,* and *attrib.* [a. Du. *bosch* woodland. Used earliest in S. Afr. and U.S.: see OED(S *sb.*[1] 9 and Mathews.]

A. *n.* Freq. with **the.**

1. Natural vegetation of any kind; a tract of land covered in such vegetation.

1790 R. CLARK Jrnl. 15 Feb. 133 They had run into the bush, on there [*sic*] seeing the Boat pulling towards them. **1800** *HRA* (1914) 1st Ser. II. 419 Thirty Natives thereupon immediately came out of the Bush and saluted the witness. **1804** *Sydney Gaz.* 22 July, Being given to understand the infant had not been seen by any one, she rushed into the bush attended by several friends and neighbours. **1814** *HRA* (1916) 1st Ser. VIII. 176 The Bush is exceedingly thick, and bad travelling on account of the sharp Rocks. **1825** *Austral.* (Sydney) 28 Apr. 3 The great bush . . extends from Clegg's to within a short distance of [Liverpool]. **1827** *Monitor* (Sydney) 4 May 401/2 The perusal of your Weekly Paper costs me a long walk, through a wild bush. **1834** *Colonist* (Hobart) 10 June 4/1, I went to Maria Island when it was a bush, and I left it, after erecting thereon buildings to the amount of thousands. **1836** *Tegg's Monthly Mag.* (Sydney) I. 63 On the banks of rivers the bush changes its character very materially, for in these situations, instead of the open forest in which you can trot along briskly among the lofty trees, it becomes a sort of impenetrable jungle, or as the colonists term it, a *thick brush.* **1838** *S. Austral. Rec.* (London) 11 July 75 Go into the bush, as it is called (although that bush is here one of the most picturesque countries possible, with fine open plains and undulating uplands well watered and timbered). **1840** *Ibid.* 1 Aug. 69 What 'the bush' really is, may, we think, be most truly described as the very reverse of the 'more thickly wooded part of the country'. **1851** *Empire* (Sydney) 25 Jan. 4/1 Its banks are thickly covered with 'bush', the colonial name for all kinds of wild vegetation. **1857** *Illustr. Jrnl. Australasia* II. 133 A close bush of tea-tree scrub. **1865** *Glenorchy Murders* 26 He turned his horse out on Murray's run; thats the next bush ground to us. **1871** *Illustr. Sydney News* 23 Dec. 206/2 It was here, on the southern extremity, that the 73rd regiment encamped on its arrival in the colony in 1810. At that time Hyde Park was a forest, or to use a colonial term 'the bush'. **1873** A. TROLLOPE *Aust. & N.Z.* I. 78 Woods which are open, and passable,—passable at any rate for men on horseback—are called bush. When the undergrowth becomes thick and matted so as to be impregnable without an axe, it is scrub. **1893** 'OLD CHUM' *Chips* 50 Sheep . . had to be 'yarded' nightly in yards fenced with logs and bush, and made 'dog-proof' as far as possible. **1913** H. LAWSON *Triangles of Life* 212 It was a lonely place, which stood in a dark stringy-bark bush. **1948** A. MARSHALL *Ourselves writ Strange* 68 He guided me through thick bush, past tinipra trees laden with red fruit, through clumps of pandanus palms, by wattle trees, vine-covered figs. **1960** *Encounter* (London) May 31 Anything smaller than a river is a creek, anything not flat is a gully, any piece of land is a paddock, any vegetation is bush. **1965** G. MCINNES *Road to Gundagai* 40 The mysterious 'bush' clinging like hair to the shoulders of Mount Wellington. **1978** 'B. WONGAR' *Track to Bralgu* 25 The settlers cleared the bush long ago and the country hereabouts looks like a skinned beast.

2. Country which remains in its natural state; country which has not been settled or which has resisted settlement.

1803 *Sydney Gaz.* 17 Apr., Upon perusing a paragraph in one of your Papers, which suggested the propriety of converting the Rocks into an Academy for *tumblers*, I rather conceived that you might, with an equal promise of success, recommend some parts of the *bush* for an improvement in the talent of *dancing*, as there much instruction might be expected from the assistance of the accomplished *kangaroo.* **1824** E. CURR *Acct. Colony Van Diemen's Land* 12 Van Diemen's Land is half bush and barrenness. **1834** J.D. LANG *Hist. & Statistical Acct. N.S.W.* II. 35 The word *bush*, which sometimes signifies the country in general, but more properly the uncleared part of it, is merely the Dutch word *bosch*, signifying wood or forest. **1836** *Tegg's Monthly Mag.* (Sydney) I. 62 Our road lay through the *bush.* In India, I should have said the *jungle*, and in Europe, the *forest.* The bush is a generic term in the colony, and signifies a district of the country in a state of nature. **1841** *Sydney Herald* 6 Mar. 2/5 From the time you leave Yass, until you reach Melbourne, a distance of four hundred miles, you are fairly in what is called the *bush.* In short, you are beyond the region of civilization. **1842** *HRA* (1924) 1st Ser. XXII. 449 They live perpetually in the wilderness, or, as it is called in the Colony, 'The Bush'. **1843** W. PRIDDEN *Aust.* 8 All that country, which remains in a state of nature uncultivated and unenclosed, is known among the inhabitants of the Australian colonies by the expressive name of *the Bush.* **1849** R.J. MANN *Emigrant's Guide Aust.* 16 Beyond these districts, lies *the bush*, or wild and unreclaimed country, in which the sheep and cattle farmers are mere squatters on the soil. **1853** S. SIDNEY *Three Colonies* (ed. 2) 85 The vast territories beyond the surveyed limits of the colony (colonially, the Bush). **1865** J.F. MORTLOCK *Experiences of Convict* 83 Kangaroo . . are found in the 'bush', a generic term synonymous with 'forest' or 'jungle', applied to all land in its primeval condition, whether occupied by herds or not. **1896** W.H. WILLSHIRE *Land of Dawning* 62 'Bush' is the name given in Australia to thickly-wooded lands. They are composed largely of underbrush, clusters of vines clinging from tree to tree, and not only hiding the pathway but almost shutting out the light of heaven. **1908** W.H. OGILVIE *My Life in Open* 3 The great reach of hill and plain that men call the Bush. **1913** H. LAWSON *Triangles of Life* 18 London has more sameness and monotony, for its size, than the Bush. **1914** H.M. VAUGHAN *Australasian Wander-Yr.* 18 'Bush' is everywhere used in Australia to denote the uncleared primeval forest lands. To get 'bushed' is to become lost in the gum-forests. **1935** W. GRAY *Days & Nights in Bush* 15 The 'bush' is the country in its natural state—as it was before men cut down the trees and disturbed its flora and ousted the kangaroo, wallaby, and emu and annihilated the birds that keep our trees healthy. **1955** 'M. HILL' *Land nearest Stars* 113 Many people find the Australian bush terrifying at night, not only because of its immense loneliness but because of influences that remain of a period older far than either knowledge or experience can record. **1972** *Bulletin* (Sydney) 8 Apr. 39/1 We caught a glimpse of it when Arthur Boyd's Nebuchadnezzar cavorted through the Australian bush with flaming red testicles. **1978** R.A.F. WEBB *Brothers in Sun* 9 Huge areas of grasslands, dense jungles of rainforest, Texas-size deserts and great tracts of arid semi-desert, lush wheat lands set amid lonely splendour—all have one thing in common. They are called 'the bush'.

3. The country as opposed to the town; rural as opposed to urban life; those who dwell in the country collectively (see quot. 1983).

1825 *Howe's Weekly Commercial Express* 23 May 3 There is at this moment many a poor settler living up the country, buried in the bush. **1828** *Tasmanian* (Hobart) 12 Dec. 4 Blythly the lambkins skip and play As through the bush they roam. **1833** W.H. BRETON *Excursions* 46 'Bush' is the term commonly used for, country *per se*: 'he resides in the Bush' implies that the person does not reside in, or very near, a town. **1839** J.G. JOHNSTON *Truth* 13 Some . . fix their residence in the towns and villages, committing the management of their country affairs to an overseer, and ride out betimes to see how they are going on; others take themselves at once to the *bush*, and reside on the spot. **1843** *Port Phillip Patriot* 27 Feb. 1/2 Mrs Harvie will be happy to accommodate gentlemen from the bush during their brief occasional visits to Melbourne. **1847** *Melbourne Argus* 16 Feb. 4/1 The Bush, or what folks at home would call The Country, has charm for young and old. **1852** W. HUGHES *Austral. Colonies* 181 Hospitality is . . one of the virtues of 'the bush'. **1870** *Illustr. Austral. News* (Melbourne) 3 Jan. 7/3 A dweller in the bush, whether in proximity to a gold-field or on a lonely station, is more representative of Australian life than a denizen of the city. **1872** 'RESIDENT' *Glimpses Life Vic.* 37 There were a few ladies among the scanty society of the Bush. **1874** J.J. HALCOMBE *Emigrant & Heathen* 45 The sad but expressive saying, '*There's no Sunday in the bush.*' **1885** MRS C. PRAED *Austral. Life* 2 In the Bush, life is made pleasant to him. Wild horse-hunts, kangaroo *battues*, and camping out expeditions are organised for his amusement. **1893** *Antipodean* (Melbourne) 102 The grand Australian bush—the nurse and tutor of eccentric minds. **1895** *Bulletin* (Sydney) 14 Sept. 22/1 The land into two is divided, And everything's 'bush' but 'the town'. And they speak with a hush Of this terrible bush Where Nature does nothing but 'frown'. **1910** *Huon Times* (Franklin) 6 Apr. 4/3 As to the Federal Capital, he would never favor building a new city in the bush for that purpose. **1918** W. ROBERTSON *Sunshine & Shadow* 44 A great part of a minister's duty in the bush is to be a quickener of social life. **1940** G.W. LOVEJOY *In Journeyings Often* 3 To the warm-hearted people of the Bush and Sydney. **1953** T.G. TUCKER *Aust. as Home* 38 Long before that date he has learned to feel that he would not exchange the 'bush'—which is the Australian word for the newly-settled country even when there is not a bush upon it—for any home which he was even likely to acquire in the congested land from which he migrated years before. **1965** J. IGGULDEN *Dark Stranger* 6 They're city kids, and you're a kid from the bush, see? So naturally they hate you. **1972** *Bulletin* (Sydney) 2 Sept. 39/1 There is a strong counter-tradition that asserts that Lawson hated the bush and revelled in the city. **1983** *Ibid.* 22 Mar. 24/2 Labor found out in 1975 that it had alienated the entire rural electorate mainly because it had removed the petrol subsidy to the bush—a move of irrefutable economic responsibility. The coalition offered to restore the differential on petrol prices. It did not fully honor that promise, but it did win the bush.

4. In phr. with various verbs of motion, esp. **to take (to) the bush.**

a. Orig. of convicts: to escape from custody or justice; to run away; (of animals) to run wild. See also ABSCOND b.

1804 *Sydney Gaz.* 10 June, One of the ringleaders was apprehended, and two others escaped into the bush before they were accused. **1813** *HRA* (1921) 3rd Ser. II. 20 Betaken themselves to the Woods, *or Bush.* **1821** *Ibid.* IV. 22 To prevent Prisoners of the Crown from absconding from the former Town and running into the Bush. **1826** *Ibid.* (1922) 3rd Ser. V. 290 Prosecuting four other men, who had absconded from the Public Works and taken to the Bush. **1833** *Currency Lad* (Sydney) 23 Mar. 3 Mr B. . . gave the fellow sixteen shillings, who said, 'we would not take this only we are starving,' and jumping from the chaise, 'now you may hang us as soon as you please.' Then they took the bush. **1835** *Colonist* (Sydney) 30 July 243/2 Punishments of runaways have not been sufficiently felt to discourage a repetition of the crime of absconding. 'Taking to the bush', or roads, as usually termed, must in general be considered as taking to robbery. **1842** *Colonial Observer* (Sydney) 7 Dec. 662/4 Within the last few days, three assigned men have taken the bush from one farm alone. **1846** *Citizen* (Sydney) 26 Dec. 138/2 Others . . from an aversion to labour, would also 'take the bush'. What . . would be the consequence of all this dispersion of reckless characters through the wild bush? **1847** *Maitland Mercury* 10 July 2/4 The cart came in contact with a stump, and an overturn was the consequence, throwing out both men, and breaking off the shafts of the cart, with which the two horses immediately started, taking the bush. **1850** W. GATES *Recoll. Van Dieman's Land* 98 About this time, four of our number 'took the bush', as fleeing into the woods is called. **1888** 'R. BOLDREWOOD' *Robbery under Arms* (1937) 3 How do you think a chap that's taken to the bush—regularly turned out, I mean, with a price on his head . . can stand his life if he don't drink? **1894** J.K. ARTHUR *Kangaroo & Kauri* 55 Brumbies are . . the offspring of imported mares that at some time strayed from the herd and took to the bush. **1899** G.E. BOXALL *Story of Austral. Bushrangers* 1 The first bushrangers were simply men who took to the bush to escape work and enjoy freedom of action. **1911** *Huon Times* (Franklin) 29 July 6/5 The police are searching for his alleged assailant, who, after supplying himself with rations, took to the bush. **1918** C. FETHERSTONHAUGH *After Many Days* 366 Four young desperadoes . . were wanted by the police before they 'took to the bush'. **1936** N. LINDSAY *Saturdee* (1936) 61 They . . like other malefactors of their country's ill-fame, took to the bush. **1978** H.C. BAKER *I was Listening* 170 To disperse—take to the bush while the bombing was on.

b. To leave the town for the country. See *to go bush* BUSH *n.* 5c.

1829 E.G. WAKEFIELD *Let. from Sydney* 10, I bore my disappointment as well as could be expected; and, to use a colonial phrase, 'took boldly to the bush'. **1843** *Duncan's Weekly Register* (Sydney) 28 Oct. 202/3 This indisposition to take to the bush is constantly lamented by employers as a grievance of the utmost magnitude. **1886** *Few Lett. from Qld. Farmers* 5, I . . got along very well at digging, but I saw I could do better at other work—such as rough carpenter work—and after doing this for a time, I thought I could do better by taking to the bush and splitting slabs, palings, shingles, and doing anything else that came my way. **1904** *Bulletin* (Sydney) 1 Sept. 36/2, I met an old schoolmate recently . . who had 'taken to the bush' sixteen years before. . . And their name is legion—the bright, capable young men who get the 'bagman' brain-twist and go out and waste their splendid forces carrying preposterous swags about the bush and running down the Government.

c. Of Aborigines: to return to traditional life.

1841 G. GREY *Jrnls. Two Exped. N.-W. & W.A.* II. 371 You see the taste for a savage life was strong in him, and he took to the bush again directly. **1847** E.W. LANDOR *Bushman* 187 Most . . betake themselves to the bush, and resume their hereditary pursuits.

5. Freq. passing into *adj.*. In the phr. **to go bush.** Also with other verbs of motion.

a. To escape, to disappear from one's usual haunts.

1908 MRS A. GUNN *We of Never-Never* 90 Considering ourselves homeless, the Maluka decided that we should 'go bush' for awhile. **1926** A.A.B. APSLEY *Amateur Settlers* 94 The horses 'went Bush'. **1927** M. DORNEY *Adventurous Honeymoon* 51 Black figures darting through the trees and going bush as quickly as they could. **1935** K.L. SMITH *Sky Pilot Arnhem Land* 115 As soon as the engine turned, the native leapt in the air . . and dropping the plugs 'went bush'. **1940** E. HILL *Great Austral. Loneliness* (ed. 2) 60 Joe won £2,000 in a sweepstake, . . put it in the bank . . and went bush. **1960** *N.T. News* (Darwin) 11 Mar. 5/7 He went bush after absconding bail. **1962** C. GYE *Cockney & Crocodile* 50 We finished our job by lunch time the next day, having examined 111 of the 119 inhabitants of Kalumburu, the other eight having 'gone bush' or 'shot through' in local idiom. **1976** C.D. MILLS *Hobble Chains & Greenhide* 2 We . . cursed with a 'bluency' inspired by thoughts of the long and bitter riding ahead, and more horses 'gone bush'. **1977** *Bronze Swagman Bk. Bush Verse* 66 Then came the day he saved my life We'd both gone bush for we'd been in strife. **1984** *Sydney Morning Herald* 24 Mar. 6/3 A farmer 'went bush' for nine days after shooting a neighbour in a dispute over water supplies and boundary gates. . . After the shooting Elford ran off and lived for nine days in the bush, surviving on bird's eggs and sour lemons.

b. Of Aborigines: to return to traditional life. See also quots. 1922 and 1956.

1908 MRS A. GUNN *We of Never-Never* 170 Maudie, discovering that the house was infested with debbil-debbils, had resigned and 'gone bush'. **1910** *Bulletin* (Sydney) 31 Mar. 15/1 When notice has to be taken of nigger lepers—and there are a few in the Territory—they are put on the island, and . . provided they 'go bush' and stop there, no serious attempt is made to recapture them. **1914** *Ibid.* 11 June 24/2 Charlie . . and his two lubras and their piccaninnies had to . . 'go back bush', as they could get no jobs in Port Darwin. **1922** 'J. BUSHMAN' *In Musgrove Ranges* 247 It was a strange position for a white man to be in, and if Stobart had not had a stout heart he would have given way to despair, and either 'gone bush' entirely as some white men have done, and become a full member of the warragul tribe, or he would have committed suicide. **1929** *Bulletin* (Sydney) 3 July 23/2 The tribe went bush for their usual 'walk-about'. **1938** X. HERBERT *Capricornia* 291 When the necessary discipline was brought to bear, most of the converts went bush, and warned their ignorant brethren against the Mission. **1956** A.C.C. LOCK *Tropical Tapestry* 120 That's where you see the 'white' black fellows—white men who have gone bush with the natives, like. **1976** T. SHEPHERD *Children of Blindness* 134 They work through the dry and go bush in the wet. The whitefellows they work for can't afford to be paternalistic to them.

c. To leave the beaten track and travel cross-country.

1913 W.K. HARRIS *Outback in Aust.* 131 A little distance out we 'went Bush' (that is, left the track). **1925** *Bulletin* (Sydney) 15 Jan. 24/2 While travelling bush through Cape York Peninsula just after the wet season, the thick mat of tall grasses cuts the horses knees to pieces. **1957** R.S. PORTEOUS *Brigalow* 20 These were the occasions when Carson left the road and went bush. We were in thick box country when he did it the first time. 'To dodge a bit of rough stuff,' he explained. **1960** I.L. IDRIESS *Wild North* 184 My mate Harry and I, travelling 'bush' in the middle of a hard-luck prospecting trip, had located the isolated camp that afternoon. **1976** E. BAIN *Ways of Life* 37 They left the road and started bush.

d. To leave urban life for that of the country; to visit the country.

1916 *Bulletin* (Sydney) 17 Aug. 6/4 It was good to 'go bush', even a paltry 250 miles from Sydney. **1925** M. TERRY *Across Unknown Aust.* 49 After finishing all work in town, we 'went bush'. **1935** L.J. GOMM *Blazing Western Trails* 123 He could 'go bush' and earn big money, but it would melt when he reached the first public house. **1947** V.C. HALL *Bad Medicine* 251 Well, Doctor, in this country of Australia we are dealing with a people that won't go bush even down in the settled areas where they have roads, services, markets, and so forth. **1957** D. WHITINGTON *Treasure upon Earth* 87 What about coming bush with me? . . We'll go for a pickled pork into Queensland, pick up some work harvesting or cane cutting maybe. **1960** E. NORTH *Nobody stops Me* 6 Then I went bush again. I told myself I was through with the pavement jungles. **1963** B. HESLING *Dinkumization & Depommification* 227 Although many of my friends during the years have 'gone bush'—which usually means they have bought a chook farm some place—going bush never appealed to me, for I would as soon work with ad. men as with chooks. **1968** *Swag* (Sydney) iii. 6/3 That's when he'd head bush, to what he described later as the only place he knew. **1972** *Bulletin* (Sydney) 3 June 67/3 She'd be quite happy for him to throw it all up and go bush. **1977** D. WHITINGTON *Strive to be Fair* 32 The scion of a wealthy family from Melbourne who had 'gone bush' to prove something to himself or his family. **1986** *Nat. Times* (Sydney) 14 Feb. 3/4 Prime Minister Bob Hawke, who a few days earlier had been bush to talk with farmers in trouble . . reacted with considerable concern to the news.

e. Of flora and fauna: to become wild.

1921 *Bulletin* (Sydney) 13 Jan. 20/2 My dog put up a domestic cat 'gone bush' and chased it to twin saplings. **1930** *Ibid.* 9 July 21/2 Most native creatures kept as pets have a tendency to go bush. **1946** *Ibid.* 7 Aug. 29/4 The track crossed a bridge near our gunyah and Darley . . made a special point of bringing our rations. Then one day the horses went bush. **1953** *Ibid.* 28 Oct. 12/4 Domestic flowers are beginning to 'go bush'. **1965** R.H. CONQUEST *Horses in Kitchen* 148 The horses . . were mostly little short of the brumby class, descendants of horses that had gone bush earlier.

B. *adj.* and *attrib.*

1. a. Of or pertaining to natural vegetation or to a tract of land covered therein: cf. BUSH *n.* 1.

1828 *Tasmanian* (Hobart) 12 Dec. 4 Then give me still the bush-clad hill Where sweet the daisies blow. **1843** *Satirist & Sporting Chron.* (Sydney) 25 Feb. 4/1 Doctor I am a free man, and these constables have brought me here without a summons, nor yet a warrant—and I only came off the road, on your bush ground, when you sung out for a trap. **1854** *Hobarton Guardian* 7 Jan. 3/3 A fearful bush conflagration has taken place in this province, and which, we presume, has never been equalled in the Australias. **1857** 'RETURNED DIGGER' *Six Yrs. in Aust.* 15 Masses of wattle and tea tree scrub, with immense gum and stringy bark trees, shooting up from the bushwood. **1870** C.H. ALLEN *Visit to Qld.* 113 An unbroken expanse of bush country, without any scrub or low bushes. **1886** J. NORTON *Austral. Labour Market* 13 Forced to accept work at pauper wages at roadmaking, bush-clearing, stone-breaking on Government Relief Works. **1906** *Bulletin* (Sydney) 2 Aug. 3/2 In Hyde Park I hear you singing as your kind sang long ago On the bush-hills near the city. **1907** *Truth* (Sydney) 24 Feb. 3/1 They formed a lengthy chain, with a break at each crossing street or road. And there are not many breaks in a mile out in that bush suburb. **1924** *Smith's Weekly* (Sydney) 10 May 25/6 Charing Cross, in 1884, was a lonely bush scrub. **1945** G. CASEY *Downhill is Easier* 19 One of the firemen . . shoved the hard bush wood we were unloading under the boilers. **1948** P.J. HURLEY *Red Cedar* 13 It was wild and rugged; hills and deep gullies, bush-covered, alternating with fertile valleys. **1960** *Bulletin* (Sydney) 14 Sept. 16/2 A resident whipbird . . lurks in the bush-covered sand-dunes.

b. Of artefacts: made with branches, saplings, etc., as materials.

1839 D. MACKELLAR *Austral. Emigrant's Guide* 8 Great care ought to be taken that they are not folded in any of the bush folds that may be found by the road side, for fear of getting infected, *scab* and *catarrh* being very prevalent throughout the Colony. **1849** A. HARRIS *Emigrant Family* (1967) 39 He had a sufficient quantity of slabs split, and other bush-stuff ready, for the construction of two common huts. **1865** A.R. RICHARDSON *Early Memories Great Nor-West* 2 Sept. (1914) 31 Very busy getting a bush and bough shed ready for shearing. **1870** E.B. KENNEDY *Four Yrs. in Qld.* 123 A good rod is quite thrown away; you can always cut a bush rod. **1888** J.F. MANN *Eight Months with Dr Leichhardt* 30 Mr Hely . . constructed a 'bush bail' with the intention of milking the cow, who was inclined to be rather wild. **1900** 'CAS-HAMBA' *Sketchy Characters* 27 Can the reader picture mentally a canvas township, varied in architecture and building material, in the form of bush break-wind and calico roofs, scattered over an area of land as extensive as an estate of an English noble? **1911** ST. C. GRONDONA *Collar & Cuffs* 90 Davies . . began to build a V-shaped bush break, leading up to where the bridge would be. **1949** I.L. IDRIESS *One Wet Season* 244 Bert shouted 'Bush!' and as the bush gate swung open the frantic animal charged out and went limping back to the bush. **1979** J.J. MCROACH *Dozen Dopey Yarns* 80 Fritz . . pinions the snake in the middle of its length with an ordinary bushstick. **1981** A.B. FACEY *Fortunate Life* 10 Aunt's place, which was only a hut, was built near a big hill. It consisted of bush poles for uprights with hessian pulled tight around the poles.

2. a. Of Aborigines: living outside white society. **b.** Of flora and fauna: indigenous; also used of these as a source of food. Cf. BUSH *n.* 2.

1827 P. CUNNINGHAM *Two Yrs. in N.S.W.* II. 30, I have now taken out upwards of six hundred convicts . . versed in every species of cunning, address, and plausibility, yet none of that number ever exceeded in these particulars a bush acquaintance of mine on Hunter's River. **1830** T.J. MASLEN *Friend of Aust.* 129 It is the inland or bush tribes who are eaters of human flesh. **1841** G. GREY *Jrnls. Two Expd. N.-W. & W.A.* II. 90 They had the 'mondak kurrang kombar', or great bush fury, on them, or rather, were subject to wild untutored rage. **1870** E.B. KENNEDY *Four Yrs. in Qld.* 99 Bush game is poor eating when cooked on a camp fire. **1887** 'COMMERCIAL TRAVELLER' *Diary Three Months Trip Qld.* 44 Pituri is a bush which the natives chop up into small pieces and then chew. . . The effect of indulgence in this bush delicacy is simply to render its votaries half stupefied. **1911** *Bulletin* (Sydney) 13 July 14/4 What about the friendliest bush animal? I place them: (1) The W.A. boodie rat, (2) native cat, (3) carpet snake. **1926** J. MCLAREN *My Crowded Solitude* 128 The bush-tribe, in the course of its wanderings. **1948** M. UREN *Glint of Gold* 87 If they are still alive. The blacks might have got them. I didn't like the look of some of those bush bucks I saw near Mt Quin. **1955** *Bulletin* (Sydney) 21 Dec. 13/4 A mob of bush abos appeared and got a bit fractious. **1961** *Ibid.* 22 Feb. 45/3 These men would not remain at the mission. They were 'bush blackfellers'. **1978** PALMER & MCKENNA *Somewhere between Black & White* 50 'He's bush.' 'How far bush? What do you mean, gone walkabout?' **1986** *Centralian Advocate* (Alice Springs) 15 Jan. 5/2 There are numerous bush foods all over Australia.

3. a. Of or pertaining to rural, as opposed to urban, life: cf. BUSH *n.* 3.

1845 T. MCCOMBIE *Adventures of Colonist* 185 The landlord . . was not by any means a good specimen of Bush publicans. **1849** *Bell's Life in Sydney* 3 Feb. 3/1 Those gents in their annual visits are in the habit of introducing bush manners which do not exactly assimilate with the milder ones of the metropolitans. **1854** MRS C. CLACY *Lights & Shadows* I. 168 Butter-making, mutton-pickling, and innumerable other bush amusements. **1856** W.W. DOBIE *Recoll. Visit Port-Phillip* 44 The house was frequented mostly by the fraternity of squatters, or the bush aristocracy. **1859** W. BURROWS *Adventures Mounted Trooper* 168 The whole of the police in the town and bush districts . . at length came up with them. **1872** MRS E. MILLETT *Austral. Parsonage* 251 The wealth of a bush lady consisting principally in her poultry. **1873** A. TROLLOPE *Aust. & N.Z.* I. 251 Instead of a town mouse and a country mouse in Australia, there would be a town mouse and a bush mouse,—but mice living in small country towns would still be bush mice. **1877** *Illustr. Austral. News* (Melbourne) 14 May 74/3 Amid the joyous uproar of the house dogs we made our way to a bush-breakfast. The ham and eggs, the beefsteak pie, the clotted cream, the fruit and tea. **1886** P. CLARKE *'New Chum' in Aust.* 181 After such essentially bush chat we arrive at the paddock. **1897** *Bulletin* (Sydney) 2 Oct. 32/2 When young Wilkins, the Sydney jackaroo, began his course of 'experience' on Serano, he naturally thought the knowledge of how to crack a stockwhip was the very first requisite of a bush education. **1900** *Ibid.* 19 May 14/3 A bush-hawker . . was amusing some children with a music-box. **1905** *Steele Rudd's Mag.* (Brisbane) Jan. 68 She was a bush-bird. She followed the seasons at Bloomfield, the shearing, mustering, branding, and hay-making. **1918** C. FETHERSTONHAUGH *After Many Days* 121 Go and kill a sheep. This was what I heard a bush lady friend call 'baa-ing mutton'. **1935** G. MCIVER *Drover's Odyssey* 174 Billy lost his temper, and opened out on his hecklers with a flow of bush Billingsgate that staggered even the veterans of camp-life. **1950** J. MCLAREN *New Love for Old* 17 In a pronounced bush-Australian accent, said he must apologize for his wife's reception of him. **1959** D. LOCKWOOD *Crocodiles & Other People* 96 Roger's letter, being the word of a bush gentleman, was accepted as proof that the work had been faithfully done. **1964** *Bulletin* (Sydney) 14 Nov. 25/3, I feel half-way bush, half-way city. **1978** MULLALLY & SEXTON *Libra & Leprechaun* 142 What after all is a bush race meeting without a fight or two.

b. By extension, and with connotations depending on whether the perception is urban or rural: of artefacts, constructions, etc., simple, (crudely, ingeniously, etc.) improvised; of people, lacking an urban sophistication; of domestic animals, useless, unmarketable, fit to be put 'out to grass'.

1835 J. LHOTSKY *Journey from Sydney to Austral. Alps* 36 There is . . no *artificial road* whatever, nothing than better or worse bush-ways, tracked and kept in order as far as they are so, by the working of the iron wheels. **1840** A. RUSSELL *Tour through Austral. Colonies* 158 The glimmering and smoky light of the bush-made candle. **1848** *Adelaide Miscellany* 9 Dec. 301/1 Some bush-like stools, and a very primitive table, were less ornamental than useful. **1849** T. ROGERS *Corresp. relating to Dismissal* 62 They were in the habit of making what is called '*bush coffee*', with a little burnt maize corn, and small thin cakes of maize meal. **1849** S. & J. SIDNEY *Emigrant's Jrnl.* 53 If you have seen navvies in a beershop after twenty-four hours' drinking, you will know what Bush-drinking is like. **1852** S. MOSSMAN *Voice from Aust.* 10 Crop after crop is reaped . . until the land is impoverished; and then the bush-farmer seeks a new patch of ground. **1860** 'LADY' *My Experiences in Aust.* 197 Neither Dr Kitchener nor M. Soyer contemplated the very limited cooking apparatus of a bush-kitchen, or the very limited resources of a bush-larder. **1865** J.F. MORTLOCK *Experiences of Convict* 156 He was going to pluck a simple bush ignoramus, colonially termed a 'flat', with pockets full of nuggets. **1873** J.C.F. JOHNSON *Christmas on Carringa* 1 Luscious bush jam tarts in tin plates, the jam ingeniously concocted of brown ration sugar and water. **1878** E. BRADDON *Lett. to India from Tas.* (1980) 49 Heron promptly made for us a 'bush lantern': he put a little water into a bottle, placed the end of the bottle in the fire and in a minute or two withdrew the upper part, leaving the lower in the burning logs; then he held the bottle's neck downwards and dropped into it a lighted candle. **1890** 'R. BOLDREWOOD' *Colonial Reformer* II. 114 Whenever this 'pound' holds cattle of *only one class* you hear the deciding shouts of the cockatoo stockmen, who are doing the 'reviewing' safely on the fence, of 'Fat', 'Bush', 'Stranger', or 'Calf-yard', as the case may be. **1891** H. NISBET *Colonial Tramp* I. 208 We passed . . a little bush-chapel belonging to the Roman Catholic religion—a little corrugated-iron building, with a pointed spire. **1893** *Bulletin* (Sydney) 25 Mar. 13/1 The bush bride is a familiar study in Melbourne and Sydney. . . The clothes are fearfully and wonderfully made, the fashions of 30 years ago, raked out of Fosselman's mercery, at Wantabadgery. **1902** *Ibid.* 4 Jan. 14/2 The bush teacher is no more intellectual than the up-to-date shop assistant. **1905** *Truth* (Sydney) 9 Apr. 1/5 Bush rum fires the imagination. **1908** *Bulletin* (Sydney) 24 Dec. 39/2 There are dozens of bush post offices along the road. These are simply candle boxes, lolly tins, or kerosene tins, nailed to trees and gate posts. **1910** J. FLYNN *Bushman's Companion* 36 Usual bush bunk of two bags on poles is excellent. **1926** A.A.B. APSLEY *Amateur Settlers* 111 'Camp!' 'Pack!' and 'Bush!'—'camp', being for the best light-weight, riding horses; 'pack' for heavier horses to carry the pack-saddles, and 'bush' meaning those that are not wanted. **1928** *Bulletin* (Sydney) 25 Aug. 22/4 Bit of a bush-doctor are you George? **1942** F. CLUNE *Last of Austral. Explorers* 97 By nightfall the bush weld was completed, and looked a very strong and satisfactory job. **1948** H.A. LINDSAY *Bushman's Handbk.* 107 Do not rely upon bush 'barometers' such as ants, flies and spiders to forecast rain or storms. **1957** M. PAICE *Valley in North* 104 His favourite chair, a bush-made affair of poles and plaited rawhide, relic of pioneer days. **1959** J. WYNNUM *Down Hatch* 41 It was only the arrival of the Naval Police that averted bush justice. **1969** E. O'CONNER *Second Helping* 191 A bush line stretched from Silver Ridge to Green Glades. . . Fashioned from No. 8 wire, and looped from tree to tree for thirty miles, it was a tenuous and uncertain thread of communication. **1975** K. WILLEY *Ghosts of Big Country* 4 His beverages were rum and 'bush champagne', an invention of his own which consisted of a pannikin of methylated spirits mixed with riverwater and a spoonful of sal volatile. **1976** K. BROWN *Knock Ten* 59 She had the 'bush' nose for gossipy news, and keen-eyed curiosity for human motives. **1977** R. EDWARDS *Austral. Yarn* 153 He was such a nice looking horse, but when he turned him round he said, 'Bush, that horse got big eye'. When you are working in the crush they call 'Bush' and you open the gate and let the horse free. He's finished. **1978** D. BALL *Great Austral. Snake Exchange* 2 It's a piece of panty hose. A bush fan belt. **1982** *Open Road* (Sydney) v. 12/3 A bush retread—a tyre with good casing and tread which has blown at the beading, and which was fitted over the top of a worn tyre. They were often used as spares in the depression days.

C. 1. Comb. **bush ballad, balladist, bed, biscuit, black, blanket, boy, -bred** *a.*, **camp, carpenter, carpentering, constable, cook, costume, dress, duty, experience, eye, fare, fashion, feed, fence, girl, hand, horse, hospitality, hotel, hut, inn, knife, labour, labourer, land, life, lore, mad, madness, mile, missionary, native, nurse, paddock, parson, picnic, poet, pub, races, rider, riding, road, school, servant, shanty, shower, song, sport, style, tea, timber, town, township, track, traveller, travelling, tucker, work, worker, yard.**

[**1888 bush ballad:** D.B.W. SLADEN *Austral. Ballads & Rhymes* p. xxiv, Consequently the commonest types of Australian Poems are Bushman's Ballads à la Gordon, often very spirited, but often also very rugged.] **1895** A.B. PATERSON *Man from Snowy River* p. iii, In my opinion this collection comprises the best bush ballads written since the death of Lindsay Gordon. **1905** —— *Old Bush Songs* p. v, There will be no more bush ballads composed and sung, as these were composed and sung, as records of the early days of the nation. **1928** H.M. GREEN *Austral. Lit.* 8 He steeple-chased, farmed, rode after bushrangers, and dashed off rough, swinging, bush ballads on which was afterwards founded a school which has hardly yet died. **1955** STEWART & KEESING *Austral. Bush Ballads* p. vii, The purpose of this anthology is to preserve and present in the compact array of a single volume the Australian bush ballad of the nineties. **1965** L. WALKER *Other Girl* 247 One of the shearers produced his classical guitar and all the old bush ballads were sung. **1979** DUSTY & LAPSLEY *Walk Country Mile* 181 To this day I still only use a bass and ballad guitar for backing on bush ballads, but bush ballads are not the only songs about life in Australia. **1898** *Bulletin* (Sydney) 11 June (Red Page), One does not depreciate our prized **bush-balladists.** **1962** MARSHALL & DRYSDALE *Journey among Men* 41 The Australia of Banjo Patterson, Henry Lawson and the bush balladists of the 'nineties. **1986** *Bulletin* (Sydney) 11 Mar. 79/1 Goodge is . . more or less regarded as a bush balladist but he's . . a sophisticated verse experimenter. **1846** C. ROWCROFT *Bushranger Van Diemen's Land* III. 199 He left his **bush-bed** and came out into the clear space. **1866** *Australasian* (Melbourne) 22 Dec. 1188/3 The art of making a comfortable bush bed, viz., with bundles of light branches of trees and long grass, the blankets and 'possum rug above all. **1894** M. ROBERTS *Red Earth* 38 In the right-hand corner, near the fireplace, was an ordinary bush-bed, made of forked stakes driven into the ground, and poles with stretched sacks upon them. **1975** R. EDWARDS *Austral. Traditional Bush Crafts* 39 A common bush bed is constructed by simply burying four forked sticks into the ground. Poles go to these sticks, and bags are threaded through the poles to complete the bed. **1845** C. HODGKINSON *Aust., Port Macquarie to Moreton Bay* 28 Breakfasted on toasted bacon, and **bush biscuit,** (thin cakes of flour and water baked on hot embers). **1973** C. AUSTIN *I left my Hat in Andamooka* 58, I had 'bush biscuits' and honey for a light lunch. **1830** R. DAWSON *Present State Aust.* 123 Been see mandoehah (foot or footsteps) belonging to **bush black.** **1842** *Melbourne Times* 10 Sept. 4/5 The necessity of cautioning the men on Mr Jones's establishment against going out unarmed, as the bush blacks were looking out in the neighbourhood for the purpose of murdering them and taking away their sheep. **1876** 'EIGHT YRS.' RESIDENT' *Queen of Colonies* 343 Station blacks, as designating those who reside on station premises, in contradistinction from bush blacks. **1929** J.W BLEAKLEY *Aboriginals & Half-Castes* 32 Bush blacks with unlicensed guns. **1935** I.L. IDRIESS *Man Tracks* 74 At nearly every station a beast is killed regularly for these 'bush blacks', so that they may have no excuse for interfering with the cattle. **1950** J. MCLAREN *New Love for Old* 20 They were . . bush blacks, that is, nomads who ordinarily knew nothing about work as other people knew it, or regular hours or even time itself. **1954** T. RONAN *Vision Splendid* 164 A cringing, cadging, half-starved hanger-on in a bush-blacks' camp down at the Goldfield. **1845** *S. Austral. Odd Fellows Mag.* Apr. 67 With the assistance of an old **bush blanket** we sluiced. **1924** H.E. RIEMANN *Nor'-West o' West* 98 He unrolled his swag in the smoothest rut, crept into his bush blanket, and soon was snoring. **1958** G. CASEY *Snowball* 174 He was climbing sleepily between the great grey bush blankets. **1978** D. STUART *Wedgetail View* 7 Carefully he wrapped himself in the bush blankets. **1856** J. BONWICK *Bushrangers* 48 All naughty **bush boys** who surrendered themselves before a certain day were to be forgiven. **1889** J.H.L. ZILLMAN *Past & Present Austral. Life* 122, I was riding through the bush . . wearing a red shirt, such as bush-men and 'bush-boys' then affected. **1907** *Truth* (Sydney) 5 May 1/5 There are some noble intellects on Sydney trams since the bush-boys began to rush the job. **1909** *Bulletin* (Sydney) 11 Nov. 14/3 The more I see the toughness of the Australian bushboy the more hope I have for the future of our own white country. **1925** *Smith's Weekly* (Sydney) 23 May 19/4 The white bushboy takes naturally to tracking. **1951** E. LAMBERT *Sleeping House Party* 104 He's no more a successful entrepreneur than I am. He's a bush boy and he can't cope. **1964** P. ADAM SMITH *Hear Train Blow* 55 Young Pete . . could get the little grey yabbies out by hand; he was an excellent bush boy. **1849** A. HARRIS *Guide Port Stephens* 115 In three cases out of four, the **bush-bred** youth possesses at least the virtues of innocence. **1888** 'R. BOLDREWOOD' *Robbery under Arms* (1937) 246 Pleased enough with the nonsense of a couple of good-looking girls like these—regular bush-bred fillies as they were. **1946** A.H. CHISHOLM *Making of Sentimental Bloke* 103 The spirit of the bush-bred boy. **1964** P. ADAM SMITH *Hear Train Blow* 221 Australia had sent away armies . . famous for the bush-bred initiative that makes formal discipline unnecessary. **1969** T.M.A. GRAHAM *Paper Men* 96 They try to pass their poets off as sort of bush-bred Shakespeares. **1846** N.L. KENTISH *Work in Bush Van Diemen's Land* 83 **Bush Camp** at the junction of the 'Wilmot' with the 'Forth'. **1901** *Advocate* (Burnie) 8 June 4/2 Several stock riders and others who formed a typical bush camp, opposite which the train pulled up, and the Royal party alighted. **1913** *Bulletin* (Sydney) 6 Nov. 24/2 The most common subject of conversation in any bush camp, whether it's sheep, cattle, scrub cutters', fencing or any other . . is horse. **1934** *Red Star* (Perth) 28 Sept. 1/3 As far as the Government's attitude to fettlers living in bush camps is concerned trade union principles are brushed aside. **1948** A. MARSHALL *Ourselves writ Strange* 155 The bush camp, consisting of mia mias and galvanised iron huts. **1954** T. RONAN *Vision Splendid* Two adolescent trollops, recently promoted from the bush camp to 'learning for house lubra'. **1980** E. & J. TRANTMAN *Jinkers & Jarrah Jerkers* 19 As logging operations moved farther afield. . . A forward base—a bush camp—was necessary. **1841** G. ARDEN *Recent Information Port Phillip* 108 **Bush carpenters,** sawyers, splitters. **1848** *Maitland Mercury* 12 Apr. 4/5 *A bushman's funeral.*—What, or where is a more melancholy spectacle than this? Splints of green wood for his coffin, a bush-carpenter his undertaker. **1854** G.E. SARGENT *Frank Layton* 139 Its furniture . . was evidently the work of no rough bush carpenter. **1890** 'R. BOLDREWOOD' *Squatter's Dream* 49 These sawyers and bush-carpenters can't be depended upon. **1919**

O. Hogue *Cameliers* 155 A special letter of thanks came from the Flight Commander to the bush carpenter who had effected the repairs. **1978** H.C. Baker *I was Listening* 70 A 'sugar bag carpenter' suggested a bush-carpenter or tommyhawk carpenter, which were the most disparaging appellations to be flung at a tradesman. **1980** Holth & Barnaby *Cattlemen of High Country* 84 Brackets carved from snow-gums by a skilful bush carpenter embellish the mantelpiece. **1859** F. Sinnet *Acct. 'Rush' Port Curtis* 43 A powerful Scotchman .. has developed .. a genius for **bush-carpentering.** **1901** H. Lawson *Joe Wilson & his Mates* 48 Bush-carpentering, tank-sinking,—anything, just to keep the billy boiling. **1923** *Austral.* (Sydney) Mar. 41 I'm not a tradesman, but I've done a bit of bush carpentering. **1826** Tas. Colonial Secretary's Office Rec. 1/34 113, Three persons in the shape of **Bush Constables** .. called here. **1830** *Launceston Advertiser* 15 Feb. 3 It would of course Sir, be highly reprehensible in me .. to treat with levity a subject which has won so many Tickets of Leave for Bush Constables. **1836** J.F. O'Connell *Residence Eleven Yrs. New Holland* 65 Trusty natives are created 'bush constables'. These are about the only blacks who have guns and ammunition. **1870** J. Bonwick *Last Tasmanians* 196 At the end of the first year, he recommended that Pigeon and Crook should be made Bush constables. [N.Z. **1873** St. John *Pakeha Rambles* in N.M. Taylor *Early Travellers* (1959) 554 The untutored paws of a **bush cook.**] **1887** *Bulletin* (Sydney) 19 Feb. 8/4, I, once a Guardsman, now a bush-cook, was comparatively virtuous. **1905** *Shearer* (Sydney) 14 Jan. 8/3 How can the A.W.U. claim bush cooks as being eight hours' men when, by the very nature of their occupation, they have to work all hours to keep things going? **1946** *Bulletin* (Sydney) 8 May 29/1 Too many bush cooks I've met have to wait till the damper is cut to find out what it's goin' to turn out like. **1960** *N.T. News* (Darwin) 22 Jan. 6/3 Bella was a first-class bush cook and very generous in her handouts to many a battler travelling this district in the depression days. **1979** D. Lockwood *My Old Mates & I* 156 He said that no man could be considered a good bush cook before he could make tasty soup from a pair of dirty socks. **1847** G.F. Angas *Savage Life & Scenes* I. 118 All in **'bush' costume**, with tether-ropes and pannikins slung to our saddles, jogged on through the winding paths. **1853** Mossman & Banister *Aust. Visited & Revisited* 248 A neighbouring settler .. came in dressed in complete bush-costume, blue shirt, belt, and cabbage-tree hat. **1889** H. Egbert *Pretty Cockey* 38 In full bush costume, with his swag, billy and pannikin about him. **1891** D.E. Falk *Rick* 248 The conventional bush costume of moleskin trousers and Crimea shirt. **1836** *Hobart Town Almanack* 165 Bushrangers were committing outrages in different parts of the country, and a tall athletic man in a **bush dress**, and armed, had been seen three or four times. **1845** C. Hodgkinson *Aust., Port Macquarie to Moreton Bay* 50, I then put on the bush dress I usually wore in such excursions, which consisted of a scarlet woollen shirt, and light kerseymere trowsers, doubled in kangaroo leather down the legs, secured by a leather belt round my waist. **1852** S. Mossman *Gold Regions Aust.* 128 A good stock of lace-up boots, duck and moleskin trowsers, common shirts, and blue woollen frocks .. is the ordinary bush dress of the colonists. **1884** J.T. Hinkins *Life amongst Native Race* 48, I felt ashamed at the appearance of my child in her bush-dress and opossum-skin bonnet. **1833** *Hill's Life N.S.W.* (Sydney) 28 Dec. 2 The Police, who were on **bush-duty**, had taken up their quarters at a hut belonging to Mr O'Loughlin. **1841** *Port Phillip Patriot* 31 May 2/7 With the new year the number of ordinary constables is to be twenty-four, and two horses are to be kept for bush-duty. **1853** G.S. Morris *Convicts & Colonies* 16 For bush duties .. the native police is infinitely more effective than the English police. **1879** *Kelly Gang* 68 The local sub-inspector .. had .. recently arrived in the district from Melbourne, where his many years' residence .. had precluded the possibility of gaining any experience in bush duty. **1869** *Illustr. Sydney News* 29 Sept. 262/1 They even require advice in the laying out and clearing of their grants of land for building their houses or huts, and other matters learnt only by actual **bush experience.** **1888** *Bulletin* (Sydney) 10 Mar. 14/2 Never go to a Northern squatter bush experience to see. **1929** H. Macquarrie *We & Baby* 123 Here our New Zealand experience helped us. Innocent of what is called 'bush experience' in Australia, we are both experts with sand. **1878** *Austral.: Monthly Mag.* (Sydney) I. 491 'And I could not tell .. what were there—cows, or calves, or bullocks. I question if I could see them at all if I were not told where they were.' I had not got my **bush eyes.** **1927** M.H. Ellis *Long Lead* 42 With good Bush eyes, we might see. **1951** S.H. Edwards *Shooting & Bushcraft* 32 Game are sometimes hard to see, so use your 'bush eye'... The man with a 'bush eye' can see a rabbit or hare in a squat .. and point it out to the new-chum. **1827** P. Cunningham *Two Yrs. in N.S.W.* II. 158 Your muskets will furnish you with birds of various kinds; and with a brace of good grayhounds you will never lack kangaroos and emus; so that your **bush-fare** is a true sportsman's feast. **1844** *Colonial Times* (Hobart) 19 Oct., As the pulp of the grass tree is a purgative, people who live on this 'bush fare' of the island always get very lean. **1845** C. Hodgkinson *Aust., Port Macquarie to Moreton Bay* 52 The usual bush fare, quart pots full of tea, damper cake, and salt bacon, constituted our breakfast. **1852** S. Mossman *Voice from Aust.* 27 Live in a tent or under a bark 'Gunya' or a gum tree, partaking of good bush fare—tea, damper and mutton. **1843** R.D. Murray *Summer at Port Phillip* 257 Cooked .. after the **bush fashion**—that is to say, in a very indifferent style. **1852** J. Macgillivray *Narr. Voyage H.M.S. Rattlesnake* I. 55 We had them [*sc.* duck] cooked 'bush fashion' for supper. **1854** W. Shaw *Land of Promise* 156 It being the height of summer, I dressed Bush-fashion, in a blue woollen shirt and cabbage-tree hat. **1872** W.M. Hugo *Hist. First Bushmen's Club* 56 In the morning .. I arose (bush fashion) early. **1899** *Nineteenth Century* (London) June 969 Every one had, bush fashion, pannikins of hot tea to drink. **1913** H. Lawson *Triangles of Life* 205 It was Bush fashion to drop into Sunday dinner anywhere. **1972** *Bulletin* (Sydney) 25 Nov. 75/1 Squatting bush fashion, scratching modestly on the ground with a twig. **1975** X. Herbert *Poor Fellow my Country* 577 With knees crossed, one leg in the air, in true bush fashion. **1841** *Colonial Observer* (Sydney) 25 Nov. 59/1 **Bush feed** is abundant: we do not recollect since we knew the district having seen the Plains so truly verdant. **1845** *Standard* (Melbourne) 2 Apr. 3/3 *Bush feed*—We are informed that the whole of the pasture of the Pentland Hills, is as bare as parchment, the result of the late bush fires. **1848** *Maitland Mercury* 23 Feb. 4/5 The long and continued drought, which commenced in October, has parched bush feed for cattle quite as much as the drought in the year 1844. **1875** R. Thatcher *Something to his Advantage* 139, I was regaled with a regular 'bush feed' of damper and fried chops. **1897** L. Lindley-Cowen *W. Austral. Settler's Guide* 144 There is silver grass and bush feed at Mount Barker. **1828** Tas. Colonial Secretary's Office Rec. 1/47 33, About a quarter of a mile of Post and Railing fence has been put up, and there are now four to five acres of wheat growing within a **Bush fence.** **1845** E.J. Eyre *Jrnls. Exped. Central Aust.* II. 283 In making runs for taking the wallabie, the natives break the branches from the bushes, and laying them one upon another, form, through the scrubs, two lines of bush fence, diverging from an apex sometimes to the extent of several miles. **1876** 'Eight Yrs.' Resident' *Queen of Colonies* 115 The neighbouring ground .. is cleared of its timber, which serves to make a pig-proof bush fence. **1913** H. Lawson *Triangles of Life* 150 They were spelling in the shade of a bush fence, or pile of cut scrub, or something. **1936** J.E. Hammond *Western Pioneers* 123 The 'bush fence' .. was constructed by driving pairs of yam timber posts about 15 inches into the ground, with a space of about 12 inches between .. and about six feet between each pair. The spaces between the posts were then filled with sticks and brush, and the pairs of posts were tied at the top to keep the material in place. **1849** A. Harris *Emigrant Family* (1967) 221 The self-helpfulness of the **bush girl.** **1885** Mrs C. Praed *Austral. Life* 212, I went down a raw Bush girl to .. go to some Government House balls. **1895** A.B. Paterson *Man from Snowy River* 24 Quiet and shy as the bush girls are, But ready-witted and plucky, too. **1900** *Bulletin* (Sydney) 8 Dec. 21/2 This dowdily-dressed and freckle-faced little bush-girl .. wasn't by any means his ideal wife. **1916** V.G. Dwyer *Conquering Hal* 135 You'd make such a boska little bushgirl .. because you're a real genuine little Australian—not just an ordinary, towney one. **1932** C.M. Gray *Western Vic. in Forties* 19 My daughter Annie .. became, like most bush girls, fond of riding at an early age. **1944** 'S. Campion' *Pommy Cow* 278 She let the slip-rail down for him .. reaching up for a last kiss as any bush girl would do .. farewelling her lover. **1955** J. Cleary *Justin Bayard* 189 She's not a bush girl. City girls aren't exposed to nature as much as you are. **1850** S. Sidney *Female Emigration* 35, I should also require two or three good **bush hands** (*prisoners*) from Hyde-Park Barracks. **1869** *Bushmen, Publicans, & Politics* 7 The best of our bush hands leave us after a comparatively short stay. **1879** S.W. Silver *Austral. Grazier's Guide* 13 The Australian bush hand is, indeed, rather aristocratic than democratic. **1891** *Trans. & Proc. R. Soc. S.A.* XIV. 155 He is an old bush hand, with all the watchful alertness and powers of observation usually acquired by those who live lives of difficulty and danger. **1902** J.H.M. Abbott *Tommy Cornstalk* 239 An excursion train-load of shearers, or 'cockies', or ordinary 'bush hands' going down *en masse*, with their coats off, to 'blue their cheques'. **1842** R.G. Jameson *N.Z., S.A., & N.S.W.* 69 We should have been unable to continue our journey, but for the skilful piloting of an old **bush-horse** from Van Dieman's Land, whose rider gave him a loose rein. **1855** W. Howitt *Land, Labor & Gold* I. 45 Most of the horses which I have seen are bush horses, which have been brought down to Melbourne, and never had a bridle on or been in shafts before. **1863** B.A. Heywood *Vacation Tour Antipodes* 65 The general pace of a bush horse is a canter. **1873** A. Trollope *Aust. & N.Z.* I. 261 The bush horses are, generally, not shod... They are expected,—to use a bush phrase,—to cut their own bread and butter, or, in other words, to feed themselves by foraging. **1889** *Illustr. Austral. News* (Melbourne) 6 Apr. 58/1 For the purposes of mounted infantry a blood horse is unsuitable, and the strong little Australian Bush horses, which can keep going all day, and climb over rough country like dogs are pre-eminently adapted for the work. **1911** *Huon Times* (Franklin) 9 Aug. 3/3 The bush horses had passed down the line ahead of the trolley. **1975** Hardy & Mulley *Needy & Greedy* 46 These two battlers had a good bush horse and they took it from town to town winning cups. **1855** W. Howitt *Land, Labor & Gold* I. 173 Is this, thought I, **bush hospitality?** **1862** A. Polehampton *Kangaroo Land* 213 A man and his wife .. with true Bush hospitality, pressed me to join them at their dinner. **1909** E. Waltham *Life & Labour in Aust.* 132 The usual bush hospitality of tea and damper, varied sometimes by an occasional 'dough-boy' or 'beggars on the coals'. **1927** M. Dorney *Adventurous Honeymoon* 31 No exception to the rule of bush hospitality. **1956** A.C.C. Lock *Tropical Tapestry* 111 We went into the settler's frugal home where we enjoyed the inevitable bush hospitality. **1963** Harney & Lockwood *Shady Tree* 87 Another cause of vanishing bush-hospitality is probably that so few of the hotels are privately owned. In the past, a pub's name advertised its owner. **1865** *Illustr. Sydney News* 15 July 3/3 The **bush hotel** is .. little better than a sort of aristocratic extensive gunyah: walls of slab and roof of bark. **1885** P.R. Meggy *From Sydney to Silverton* 52 Some mutton, fed on the run, which I tasted by chance at the fine little bush hotel at Pooncarie was far superior to anything to be obtained in Sydney. **1886** D.M. Gane *N.S.W. & Vic.* 161 She kept her house very clean for a bush hotel, and in saying that, we would have it understood we are paying her a great compliment. **1897** *Western Champion* (Barcaldine) 9 Feb. 12/2, I struck a bush hotel or grog shanty about sundown, and feeling tired I thought I'd stick out the night there. **1928** B. Spencer *Wanderings in Wild Aust.* 105 A store, one or two houses and the inevitable bush hotel. **1830** *Sydney Monitor* 2 June 2/2 Three hundred decent families .. will be blown and washed out of their **bush huts** (for of *timber* there is none). **1834** *True Colonist* (Hobart) 30 Sept. 4/3 There was a bush hut near the place made of boughs. **1839** T.P. Besnard *Voice from Bush* 15, I wish you had a peep at my bush hut. It measures 24 feet by 13, and is built of slabs, (literally '*wooden walls*') covered with bark, having unglazed apertures in lieu of windows. **1845** C. Griffith *Present State & Prospects Port Phillip* 131, I have known many an evening pass agreeably in a bush-hut with the aid of a pianoforte and some singing. **1886** *N.T. Times Almanac* 95 Services in connection with the Church of England in North Australia, were first held in 1871 in a bush hut. **1891** D. Ferguson *Vicissitudes Bush Life* 30, I next entered the men's hut to see what arrangements were there provided for the comfort of the station hands. This, as a bush hut .. I found on the whole to be fairly satisfactory. **1913** *Bulletin* (Sydney) 21 Aug. 18/1 There was an outcamp hut, which, like a lot more bush huts, had the reputation of being haunted. **1979** W.D. Joynt *Breaking Road for Rest* 42, I found a small bark roofed bush hut with slab walls, and inside was a rough bunk made by two bush poles stretched through a couple of chaff bags. **1847** J.D. Lang *Phillipsland* 157 We halted at a respectable **Bush Inn.** **1851** J. Henderson *Excursions & Adventures N.S.W.* 162 We early retired to our 'stretchers', after a supper of the usual bush-inn fare. **1862** A. Polehampton *Kangaroo Land* 102 We .. breakfasted at a roughly built Bush inn. **1868** C.W. Browne *Overlanding in Aust.* 58 A shepherd will now and again .. leave his flock for half an hour, and stray away for a 'nobbler' into a bush inn.

1910 F.B. Boyce *Church on River Darling* 7 Widgery, a bush inn, seemed placed in one of the wettest and muddiest parts. **1843** C. Rowcroft *Tales of Colonies* III. 195, I took out my **bush-knife** and presented it to Musqueeto. **1853** *Austral. Gold Digger's Monthly Mag.* iv. 123 A passable substitute for the genuine bakery was soon . . enduring the incisions of a bush-knife. **1965** M. Patchett *Last Warrior* 78 A sparkling new bush-knife in a leather sheath with 'Boy' embossed on it. **1979** T. Shearston *Something in Blood* 94 The boys fetched green coconuts from the hut and opened them with a bush knife. **1846** *Port Phillip Gaz.* 11 Nov. 2 Very extensive employers of **bush labour** say that they find old convicts preferable to free or bound emigrants. **1848** *Sydney Daily Advertiser* 1 July 2/5 There is at present not any very urgent demand for bush labour; the lambing season is over. **1869** *Bushmen, Publicans, & Politics* 3 The different classes . . contribute to bush labour. **1872** W.M. Hugo *Hist. First Bushmen's Club* 194 There is very little bush labor [*sic*] engaged at this time of the year in the city. **1832** *Colonist* (Hobart) 23 Nov. 2/3 Depriving . . every settler, stock-keeper and **bush-labourer** of the only means of warning. **1856** W.W. Dobie *Recoll. Visit Port-Phillip* 72 Very few of this class of bush labourer are what can be called sober men. **1891** *Great Qld. Strike* (United Pastoralists Assoc. Qld.) 3 No man outside the various shearers' and bush labourers' unions shall be allowed to work in any shed. **1901** *Brisbane Courier* 23 July 7/6 Peter English, the plaintiff, said he was a bush labourer. **1929** J.W. Bleakley *Aboriginals & Half-Castes* 6 A few bush labourers, such as sleeper cutters' assistants . . receive 10s. per week. **1827** *Tasmanian* (Hobart) 3 Mar. 4 The report represents . . the maize as promising where it has been sown in rich alluvial soil—but a failure on **bush land.** **1835** *True Colonist* (Hobart) 11 Feb. 3/3 The fire ran along the grass . . but when it got into bush land the tops of the tallest trees were soon on fire. **1865** *Glenorchy Murders* 22/1 Work was being done on our bush land. We were falling a tree. **1871** J. Baird *Emigrant's Guide Australasia* 229 The bush lands—that is, the open forest lands. **1910** *Huon Times* (Franklin) 17 Dec. 5/2 It is nearly all bush land. **1939** M.B. Eldershaw *My Aust.* 222 In open bushland the Mock Sarsaparilla, the small purple flower of a little twining plant, can in its masses colour the whole ground. **1955** D. Clark *Boomer* 16 The rock face . . reared from the surrounding bushland like a gray fortress. **1971** *Bulletin* (Sydney) 13 Mar. 18/1 Where once the real-estate agents wrote up their lots of land as 'cleared', today they are more likely to advertise a 'bushland setting'. **1983** *Open Road* (Sydney) Aug. 24/4 Passengers go ashore for lunch in a bushland setting. **1831** *HRA* (1923) 1st Ser. XVI. 285 A **bush life** being attended with much less expense. **1839** *Port Phillip Patriot* 20 Mar. 3/2 As for the bush life, which many of our respected fellow colonists are obliged to lead, we would remind the Record that a pastoral life, is not necessarily a savage life. **1846** *Port Phillip Gaz.* 11 Nov. 4 They have learned bush life, shearing and splitting, and so forth. **1851** H. Melville *Present State Aust.* 63 He frequently expressed a desire to resume the bush life of the Aborigines. **1851** *Bell's Life in Sydney* 21 June 1/1 The hardship of a bush-life. **1874** A. Trollope *Harry Heathcote* 18 They who live away from the towns live a 'bush life'. **1886** R. Henty *Australiana* 9 He was one of my instructors in the mysteries of Australian bush life, such as throwing the boomerang, the kangaroo spear, the waddy. **1898** C. Bond *Goldfields & Chrysanthemums* 35 No billy tea, which seems a part of bush life, but we have to put up with billy cocoa. **1910** *Huon Times* (Franklin) 27 Apr. 3/7 Among the native-born Australians there is a marked growing dislike towards bush life. **1927** A. Crombie *After Sixty Yrs.* 32 A habit of observation which I found of great value during the long years of my bush life. **1862** G.T. Lloyd *Thirty-Three Yrs. Tas. & Vic.* 121 Accompanied by two companions learned in **Bush lore.** **1875** C.H. Eden *Aust.'s Heroes* (ed. 3) 290 Are their eyes deceiving them, or is their bush lore at fault, and have they missed the camp? **1893** S. Newland *Paving Way* 225 Proud of his bush-lore, and justly so, he mistook signs that a novice might have understood and acted upon. **1929** A.H. Chisholm *Birds & Green Places* 51 He had small opinion of the bush-lore of city men. **1968** *Swag* (Sydney) iii. 7/1 He'd . . go roaming along creek beds . . learning bushlore through observation, trial and error. **1977** J. Carter *All Things Wild* 13 It's all very impressive to city visitors, but there's really nothing mysterious or extraordinary about what is known as 'bushlore'. **1924** Lawrence & Skinner *Boy in Bush* 221 'The man's potty!' '**Bush mad,**' supplemented Rackett. **1974** *Gayzette* (Sydney) 19 Sept. 19/4 **Bush madness** was a common phenomenon. Therefore men were employed to work in pairs. One male was the actual worker, the other was his 'mate'. **1862** A. Polehampton *Kangaroo Land* 252 **Bush miles** are long, and evening closed in ere I reached the desired goal. **1976** B. Norman *Bush Pilot* 252, I think the bush mile will always hold its own in the minds of the Outback folk and will remain a form of measurement. Just what that measurement is, is the mystery. **1864** N. Shreeve *Short Hist. S.A.* 37 There are **bush missionaries**, who travel up the country for the purpose of preaching to the different shepherds. **1872** W.M. Hugo *Hist. First Bushmen's Club* 9 In the month of June, 1866, the Bush Missionary 'William' wrote a note to a friend of his . . representing to him the desirability of establishing an institution of a social nature as a home for bushmen. **1874** J.J. Halcombe *Emigrant & Heathen* 147 Once or twice lately a 'bush missionary', a kind of ranter, has been round. **1892** *Truth* (Sydney) 12 June 2/3 Sometimes the bush missionary selects a nigger for special training and then the fate of that unfortunate darkey is sealed. **1931** J.R. Fiddian *R. Mitchell of Inland* 117 The life of a Bush Missionary is many-sided. **1801** *Hist. Rec. N.S.W.* (1896) IV. 514, I mean to keep a **bush native** constant soon, as they can trace anything so well in the woods. **1803** J. Grant *Narr. Voyage N.S.W.* 158, I should be at a loss where to place my Bush Native, whether as the next link above the monkey, or that below it. **1840** *S. Austral. Rec.* (London) 12 Sept. 166/3 A very warlike tribe:—they are bush natives, and all heathens. **1871** *Austral. Town & Country Jrnl.* (Sydney) 14 Jan. 56/1 Brown and his wife were both 'bush natives', an appellation bestowed upon those descendants of Europeans who have been brought up in the backwoods of Australia. **1892** *Bulletin* (Sydney) 19 Mar. 18/2 Off-hand as most bush natives are, and freckled, tall and slim, A careless native of the land was 'Tambaroora Jim'. **1895** *Worker* (Sydney) 29 June 4/1 He was a 'typical bushman' or 'bush native'. **1903** J.T. Reilly *Reminisc. Fifty Yrs. W.A.* 686 He visits the sheep in charge of natives about once a week, but if bush natives are about he visits them oftener. **1928** G.H. Wilkins *Undiscovered Aust.* 72 My guide confessed that the 'bush' natives would not hunt for me. **1949** I.L. Idriess *One Wet Season* 209 Rolls of blankets . . yearly are issued to town natives, and where possible to bush natives. **1962** C. Gye *Cockney & Crocodile* 50 There a bush native, tall and thin and proud and black in a tiny red naga-naga (loincloth). **1909** *Truth* (Sydney) 17 Oct. 1/3 The ladies in the backblocks are to receive the doubtful benefit of '**bush nurses**'. **1920** G. Sargant *Winding Track* 15 A bush nurse had been installed. **1939** M. Morris *Dark Tumult* 151 His damaged ankle . . would, under his own ministrations and those of the capable Bush nurse, probably allow him to be about in a few days. **1946** *Bulletin* (Sydney) 18 Sept. 28/2 The nearest doctor's at Parkes, but I got an idea there's a Bush Nurse about here. **1962** V.C. Hall *Dreamtime Justice* 30 We were greeted by Mounted Constable Sheridan and his wife, a former Bush Nurse, one of two bush nurses who were married by policemen within a year of coming to the Territory. **1986** *Canberra Times* 22 Apr. 3/ (*heading*) Being a bush nurse is no fun. **1847** *Moreton Bay Courier* 17 July 3/2 What was once a **bush paddock** is now a well-appointed race-course. **1849** J.P. Townsend *Rambles & Observations N.S.W.* 14 When housed, the next object is to split up posts and rails, and fence in a part of the bush, which is then called 'the Bush Paddock', and is devoted to the use of the horses and working bullocks. **1852** S. Mossman *Voice from Aust.* 10 The slopes of Mount Lofty range . . yield heavier and more regular crops than the bush-paddock. **1890** 'Lyth' *Golden South* 166 Driving over very indifferent roads through bush paddocks. **1927** A. Crombie *After Sixty Yrs.* 6 Little more than a bush paddock. **1956** *Bulletin* (Sydney) 23 May 12/4 The bush-paddock was still enclosed by the original 'rough-and-tumble'; just saplings and heavier branches piled in line to resist big stock. **1873** M. Clarke *Holiday Peak* 19 It was considered a point of honour for all travelling clergymen ('**bush parsons**', the Bullocktowners called them) to give an evening at the 'brick edifice'. **1882** A.J. Boyd *Old Colonials* 224 A bush parson had a black fellow in his service. **1896** H. Lawson *While Billy Boils* 18 This Stiffner was a hard customer. He'd been a spieler, fighting man, bush parson, temperance preacher, and a policeman, and a commercial traveller, and everything else that was damnable. **1918** C. Fetherstonhaugh *After Many Days* 162 He was a model 'bush parson', and welcomed by high and low. **1977** S. Locke Elliott *Water under Bridge* 120 The bush parson had absentmindedly begun with the marriage service. **1901** *Advocate* (Burnie) 8 June 4/2 The **bush picnic** arranged on the Darling Downs, Queensland, for the Duke and Duchess. **1931** *Bulletin* (Sydney) 7 Oct. 20/2 At a bush picnic on the South Coast of N.S. Wales I was persuaded to act as a judge of the foot-racing. **1967** D. Horne *Educ. Young Donald* 10 Go for a bush picnic, the men in their cream trousers and blazers and ties and motoring caps, the women in tailored 'suits'. **1972** A. Chipper *Aussie Swearers Guide* 48 Her teas are like Bush picnics. *Rough as guts.* **1975** L. Walker *Runaway Girl* 94 We have bush picnics down south, too. Guess it's an old Australian custom. **1846** N.L. Kentish *Work in Bush Van Diemen's Land* 55 The **Bush-poet** blushes at the thought of . . great merit having been attributed to him. **1945** *Bulletin* (Sydney) 1 Aug. 12/1 'Yer strike all kinds of loons in the bush,' Ben said, 'an' the worst is bush poets.' **1963** W.E. Harney *To Ayers Rock & Beyond* 45, I am pretty sure that this bush school of oral teaching was the starting point with many a bush-poet and magsman, such as I, who kept up the yarning into later days. **1984** *People Mag.* (Sydney) 7 May 55/2 In Macksville, a bush poet immortalised the pair in a poem which was later put to music. **1880** J.B. Stevenson *Seven Yrs. Austral. Bush* 137 Dan . . kept a **bush pub** out on the River road. **1895** J. Kirby *Old Times in Bush* 150 A bush pub at the time I am writing about (the forties) served as a kind of 'labor depôt' as well as 'lambing down shop'. **1914** C.H.S. Matthews *Bill* 53 He gave the contract to a man called Maloney, who kept a little bush pub, on the track, some miles from our place. **1936** *Bulletin* (Sydney) 30 Dec. 20/2 Many a one of them was given an old saddle, a pack-saddle and a pair of pensioned horses just to get rid of him. That he jumped 'em over the bar at the first bush pub didn't matter. **1962** C. Gye *Cockney & Crocodile* 41 In the bush pub she had been too terrified to go to bed. **1978** D. Stuart *Wedgetail View* 110 She was a great one to run a bush pub. **1880** J.B. Stevenson *Seven Yrs. Austral. Bush* 133, I think it would be a good idea for **bush races,** to give a prize for the best man and horse at camp work. **1900** *Truth* (Sydney) 13 May 6/3 Usually the bush races are held at some lonely hotel or wine shop. **1947** E. Hill *Flying Doctor Calling* 35 The bush people met once a year—or once in five years—at the bush races, to which some of them still travel five hundred miles. **1850** *Bell's Life in Sydney* 22 June 3/2 Certainly the best **bush-rider** in this country. **1872** G.S. Baden-Powell *New Homes for Old Country* 397 Black boys . . frequently . . become invaluable as bush-riders. **1882** A.J. Boyd *Old Colonials* 178 A sore-backed horse is the terror of every sensible bush rider. **1893** E.D. Cleland *White Kangaroo* 55 To any one unaccustomed to bush-horses and bush-riders, it would have appeared impossible to gallop over such rough country. **1848** H.W. Haygarth *Recoll. Bush Life* 62 The native youths particularly excel in **bush-riding.** **1857** F. de B. Cooper *Wild Adventures* 58 Very different to the juvenile I broke into bush-work and bush-riding at M'Connel's. **1882** A. Tolmer *Reminisc.* I. 134 Bush-riding was only required to ensure effectiveness in the mounted police. **1935** B.E. Phelps *Austral. tells England* 209 Those Nolan girls beat all ever I heard of for bush-riding. **1827** P. Cunningham *Two Yrs. in N.S.W.* I. 123 A *made* **bush-road** is one where the brushes have been cleared, banks of rivers and gullies levelled, and trees notched, on the route, and cuts made on the faces or tops of hills when necessary, the remainder being all left in a natural state; while a *natural* bush-road signifies one to which nothing has been done except notching the trees, the carts simply following each other's tracks. **1834** J.D. Lang *Hist. & Statistical Acct. N.S.W.* II. 110 Bush-roads, as they are called in New South Wales, are formed by the person who first traverses the forest, notching the trees with an axe in the direction of his route. **1847** *Maitland Mercury* 27 Oct. 2/4 A 'bush road', on which the traveller has to encounter several abrupt, or rather precipitous elevations, impassable to any sort of wheeled vehicle. **1857** W. Westgarth *Vic. & Austral. Gold Mines* 197 We had now the unmade or bush road to put up with. **1886** W.J. Woods *Visit to Vic.* 21 Colonists distinguish between roads which have been 'made' and such as are mere tracks among the trees cleared of fallen timber. The latter are the bush-roads proper. **1942** E. Langley *Pea Pickers* 37 The slow sweet divulging of a bush road, being covered by two human feet. **c 1960** C. Mackness *Clump Point & District* 81 Mr Dunlop would drive a dray in there for supplies, using the old bridle-track, which, thanks to the timber-men, had grown into a bush road of sorts. **1963** D. Niland *Dadda Jumped* 97 Terrible. Just a bush road. Nobody uses it. Only farmers and some tourist cars. A five-ton limit on that road. **1852** G.C. Mundy *Our Antipodes* III. 61 There was a humble hedge-school—or rather **bush-school**, for there is hardly a mile of hedge in Australia. **1899** *Austral. Tit-Bits* (Sydney) 25 Nov. 4/1 Inexperienced girls . . are sent out to take sole charge of lonely bush schools. **1911** E.S. SORENSON *Life in Austral. Backblocks* 51 The bush school is often a small, isolated building standing among the trees. **1927** T.S. GROSER *Lure of Golden West* 73 Often the Bush school area is large. **1948** P.J. HURLEY *Red Cedar* 205 The felling of that scrub affected the bush-school youngster. **1965** *Coast to Coast 1963–64* 87 She had been teaching for seven years in this little bush school and she still experienced the greatest difficulty in distinguishing between insolence and laconicism. **1975** *Bronze Swagman Bk. Bush Verse* 34 Hear the phantom songs of children, Where the bush school used to be. **1842** *Geelong Advertiser* 10 Jan. 3/2 The **bush servants** being in the interior for some time, come to town to spend their money. **1847** T. MCCOMBIE *Austral. Sketches* 101 The bush servants form a most important class in our social scale. **1849** S. & J. SIDNEY *Emigrant's Jrnl.* 10 All Bush servants are allowed to cultivate as much garden ground as they like round their huts. **1852** S. SIDNEY *Three Colonies* 157 What, Mrs Chisholm! is it my business to find wives for bush servants? **1856** W.W. DOBIE *Recoll. Visit Port-Phillip* 75 A better specimen of an efficient bush-servant there could not be. **1885** *Illustr. Austral. News* (Melbourne) 2 Jan. 10/3 The true haven of the sundowner is the **bush shanty.** **1891** 'SMILER' *Wanderings Simple Child* (ed. 3) 159, I had pulled bridle in front of what I guessed was a bush shanty—half eating-house, half drinking-drum, and the rest a gambling-hell, and perhaps worse. **1923** *Bulletin* (Sydney) 11 Jan. 22/3 Among a crowd of us busy knocking down our cheques at a bush shanty was one who had just bought a new pair of boots. **1965** N. LINDSAY *Bohemians of Bulletin* 62 Only to be quenched by a billy of lukewarm beer from a bush shanty. **1981** *Austral. Women's Weekly* (Sydney) 18 Nov. 21/2 Good outback style: **bush shower** dangling from a gum tree, hessian-screened dunny (with reading material, of course) and even, a bath. **1846** N.L. KENTISH *Work in Bush Van Diemen's Land* 35 My **Bush song**, is much too long To need a peroration. ***c* 1892** J. CAMERON *Fire Stick* 35 Some were singing snatches of popular bush songs. **1964** P. ADAM SMITH *Hear Train Blow* 186 We all felt for a moment the nostalgia that had set her to singing that old bush song. **1967** MEREDITH & ANDERSON *Folk Songs Aust.* 19, I have always found that 'old bush songs' is a definition understood by most old folk. **1858** T. MCCOMBIE *Hist. Colony Vic.* 22 Like most young men born in Australia, he was much addicted to **bush sports.** **1902** *Axeman's Jrnl.* (Ulverstone) 30 Aug. 2/4 An association to organise the holding of bush sports, so that the settlers might be able to prove to their fellow men their wonderful skill with the axe, saw etc. **1903** *Sporting News* (Launceston) 20 June 2/4 A conference of enthusiasts on chopping, sawing and other bush sports. **1838** *Colonist* (Sydney) 9 May 4/1, I proposed to Mr Hill . . to make an excursion in our **bush style** to the banks of the Murray. **1845** T. MCCOMBIE *Adventures of Colonist* 149 Dinner was got up in the very best Bush style. **1852** *Austral. Gold Digger's Monthly Mag.* iii. 93 In bush style, the necks were broken, and the liquor passed around. **1855** W. HOWITT *Land, Labor & Gold* I. 129 Alfred and I mounted our horses, in bush style. **1859** W. BURROWS *Adventures Mounted Trooper* 29 The police thought it advisable to dress in plain clothes, and with blankets rolled up, and strapped in front of their saddle in true bush style. **1861** H. EARLE *Ups & Downs* 220 Your father furnished it in proper bush style . . a few boxes full of carpenters' and other kinds of tools, and a lot of logs for seats. **1918** *Kia Ora Coo-ee* Oct. 8/3 He counts his deferred pay in poddies and has a supreme contempt for 'townies' and their inability to do anything in proper Australian bush style. **1955** F. LANE *Patrol to Kimberleys* 134 He's a bush-style Sherlock Holmes when it comes to deduction. **1986** *Sydney Morning Herald* 1 May 1/8 An advertisement in the *Herald* for the sale of a North Brisbane property sang the praises of its 'bush-style landscape of flowering native fauna'. **1848** *Adelaide Miscellany* 2 Dec. 303 ***Bush* tea** . . is generally made excessively strong . . is seldom softened by milk, and always sweetened with very coarse, dark sugar. **1849** A. HARRIS *Emigrant Family* (1967) 80 There was true bush tea, with cream and new eggs. **1862** H. BROWN *Vic. as I found It* 116, I . . tasted . . bush tea, softened with brandy instead of milk. **1883** E. PALMER *Plants N. Qld.* 16 *Ocimum sanctum* . . White people make tea of the leaves dried, called bush tea. **1926** M. FORREST *Hibiscus Heart* 97 It's the genuine bush tea, of course, and *don't* dare to speak of milk. **1846** *Port Phillip Gaz.* 16 Sept. 3 (Advt.), Port Phillip **bush timber.** **1875** J. FORREST *Explorations in Aust.* 259 The telegraph line is most substantially put up; . . large poles of bush timber, often rather crooked. **1936** J.E. HAMMOND *Western Pioneers* 107 In the very early days the little homes were built of sun-dried bricks and very rough bush timber. **1946** K.S. PRICHARD *Roaring Nineties* 115 Here and there a windlass of bush timber stuck out against the clear sky. **1965** R.H. CONQUEST *Horses in Kitchen* 197 He and the station blacksmith fashioned out of bush timber two high aerial posts. **1974** D. STUART *Prince of my Country* 63 They put a bush-timber collar-set on the well. **1981** A.B. FACEY *Fortunate Life* 10 The roof was bush timber and galvanised iron. **1874** A. TROLLOPE *Harry Heathcote* 18 Small towns, as they grow up, are called **bush towns**—as we talk of country towns. **1893** *Bulletin* (Sydney) 19 Aug. 20/4 There are no 'villages' in Australia—there are townships, and bush towns, and country towns, but the term 'villages' is merely an atavistic paroxysm. **1922** A. WRIGHT *Boss o' Yedden* 24 Cooya, sleepiest of bush towns, was awake this afternoon. **1955** F. LANE *Patrol to Kimberleys* 62 From here on, to Blue Gum Downs, we're avoiding stations and bush towns—even drovers. **1880** J.B. STEVENSON *Seven Yrs. Austral. Bush* 117 A good specimen of a **bush township.** One long straggling street upon the bank of a river, the backs of all the houses on the river side turned upon the splendid sheet of water, fringed with giant gums, which lay below them. **1976** B. SCOTT *Compl. Bk. Austral. Folk Lore* 311 Small towns . . are usually called, 'bush townships'. **1837** *Tegg's N.S.W. Pocket Almanac* 46 **Bush track** leading across Kenyon's bush track into the great southern road. **1852** J.E. ERSKINE *Short Acct. Late Discoveries Gold* 71 We found a good bush track, and rejoined the Bathurst road at 'Meadow Flat'. **1872** 'RESIDENT' *Glimpses Life Vic.* 116 Travelling painfully along the rough boggy bush-tracks. **1891** J. FENTON *Bush Life Tas.* (1964) 138 Messrs Bell and Bertinck . . further improved the bush track. **1908** W.H. OGILVIE *My Life in Open* 34 Heavy drinking and riotous living in the hells of the Bush-track and township. **1920** W. MCGUFFIN *Austral. Tales of Border* 148 There were no roads, only bush tracks, and these very rough and dangerous. **1948** M. UREN *Glint of Gold* 22 From York bush tracks to the eastward would have to be followed. These tracks led from waterhole to waterhole. **1979** D. LOCKWOOD *My Old Mates & I* 85 The next two or three hundred miles of bush track was completely flood-bound during the wet season. **1834** G. BENNETT *Wanderings N.S.W.* I. 113 Tea, sugar, a tin-pot, and a blanket, are the requisites for a **bush-traveller.** **1845** T. MCCOMBIE *Adventures of Colonist* 185 The tap-room was filled with bullock-drivers, and the usual classes of Bush travellers. **1855** H. HUME *Brief Statement* 5 Mr Hume's character as a skilful bush traveller was . . fully recognized. **1844** *Sydney Morning Herald* 25 July 2/2 His supplies will be carried on pack-horses, it being evident that in **bush travelling** any sort of vehicle must cause great delay. **1847** A. HARRIS *Settlers & Convicts* (1953) 126 Practice in bush travelling gives great address in tracing such natural land-marks. **1855** H. HUME *Brief Statement* 29, I set out trusting to my . . knowledge of bush travelling. **1888** A. MCLEAN *Harry Bloomfield* 70 The bustle of camping, preparing food, packing and unpacking, with the other occupations connected with bush-travelling. **1895** W.H. WILLSHIRE *Thrilling Tale Real Life* 41 It is well known that after rain the natives want to wander about in search of **bush-tucker.** **1927** A. CROMBIE *After Sixty Yrs.* 45 Abundance of bush tucker. **1936** C.P. CONIGRAVE *N. Aust.* 226 Living entirely on bush tucker, he made no contact with the outside world. **1948** A. MARSHALL *Ourselves writ Strange* 166 The searching for food is a woman's daily task. . . The food she collects is called 'bush tucker', but the men often refer to it with some contempt as 'woman tucker'. **1952** N. GOREY *Alice* 22, I should mention 'bush tucker' . . a wide range of edible bush or native foods which have been the sweet-meats and luxury lines of the native tribes. **1954** *Coast to Coast 1953–54* 90 The blacks said that he had gone walkabout, that he was hungry for 'bush-tucker' and the life of his own people again. **1962** MARSHALL & DRYSDALE *Journey among Men* 169 In the pioneering days bush tucker of necessity formed the main diet in many places. **1972** C. DUGUID *Doctor & Aborigines* 135 All that the Aborigines could find in the way of 'bush tucker' were wild cucumbers and yelka—the roots of grass which grew in the banks of dry creeks. **1977** J. CARTER *All Things Wild* 12 From past experience he knows what type of bush tucker the various forms of wildlife prefer. So if he is asked to locate anything from cockatoos to kangaroos, he usually knows where to look. **1986** *Centralian Advocate* (Alice Springs) 15 Jan. 5/1 (*heading*) Bush tucker may find its way to the kitchen table. **1846** *Port Phillip Gaz.* 11 Nov. 4 They have been accustomed to sheep, and **bush work** generally. **1854** G.H. HAYDON *Austral. Emigrant* 145, I can do all sorts of bush work, splitting and fencing, carpentering, clearing, grubbing, ploughing. **1882** A.J. BOYD *Old Colonials* 142, I then started bush work, and in five weeks managed to earn two horses and a rig-out. **1897** R. NEWTON *Work & Wealth Qld.* 18 For the rest of the time there is a variety of bush work, fencing, yard-making, dam-making. **1920** *Bulletin* (Sydney) 6 May 20/2 About the toughest of all bushwork, not excepting wattle-barking or log-fencing, is burning. **1933** F.E. BAUME *Tragedy Track* 179 Trick them in their own game in bushwork. **1973** R. ROBINSON *Drift of Things* 79 Tom would take on any job of bush work—fencing, clearing, digging out rabbits, ring-barking or 'sucker-bashing'. **1891** M. ROBERTS *Land-Travel & Sea-Faring* 75 Like many **bush workers,** he had made quite enough money for a spree. **1900** *Tocsin* (Melbourne) 6 Sept. 5/1 In these wildernesses, fertile in sheep but sterile of the human race, the bushworker toils from dawn till dark. **1922** A. WRIGHT *Boss o' Yedden* 22 He wandered back to his home town, became a shearer and general bush worker. **1933** C.E.W. BEAN *Official Hist. Aust. 1914–18* IV. 663 (*footnote*) Capt. Beresford E. Bardwell, 51st Bn. Bush worker; of Geraldton and Broome. W. Aust. **1958** R. ROBINSON *Black-Feller White-Feller* 87 This was Jim, a good bush-worker and an axeman. **1980** J. WOLFE *End of Pricklystick* 23 Men from the mill-houses often sat on the verandah discussing the strike and the rates of pay for the bush-workers. **1846** C.P. HODGSON *Reminisc. Aust.* 41 The **bush-yard** . . received the herd from the run. **1851** J. HENDERSON *Excursions & Adventures N.S.W.* II. 6 Bush-yards, made by the tribe of stakes and boughs of trees. **1890** 'R. BOLDREWOOD' *Squatter's Dream* 41 A rough upper-shepherd sort of individual who counted sheep and helped to make bush-yards. **1902** F. RENAR *Bushman & Buccaneer* 57 They've built bush yards on Wild Horse Creek. **1922** E.C. SOMMERLAD *Land of Beardies* 23 We were all engaged in making a bush-yard for my sheep to sleep in. **1930** E.R. GRIBBLE *Forty Yrs. with Aborigines* 27 It was my duty to get each into its own yard—the branded cows into the bush-yard, and the 'clean skins' or unbranded cattle into the branding-yard.

2. Special Comb. **bush bass,** an improvised musical instrument (see quot. 1979); **bellows,** see quot. 1856 (2); **bread,** DAMPER 1; **(-bred) cattle,** wild cattle; **Contingent,** *Bushmen's Contingent*, see BUSHMAN 8; **craft,** see quots. 1883 and 1963; **fever,** a sickness associated with bush living; a longing to return to the bush; **happy** *a.*, mentally disturbed; **-head,** BUSHY *n.* 1; **honey,** honey from the nests of wild bees; **house, (a)** a roughly-built dwelling in the country; **(b)** a garden shelter in which plants needing protection are cultivated (see quot. 1890, 1); **(c)** a dwelling occupied by a rural commune (see quot. 1981); **liar,** one who tells tall stories; **oysters,** see quot. 1971; **pickles,** see quot. 1962; **walk, (a)** of an Aboriginal, WALKABOUT *n.* 2; **(b)** a hike; also **-walker, -walking** (see quot. 1945); **week, (a)** a time in which people from the country come to, and are reputed to go 'on' the town; **(b)** a period of licence, esp. in the phr. **what do you think this is—bush week?**; **(c)** at some universities, a period of student festivity.

1966 R. MORLEY *Cool Change* 81 She gets a brumby and goes miles off looking for someone with a **bush-bass** who can raise some sort of a band. **1967** MEREDITH & ANDERSON *Folk Songs Aust.* 17 The bush bass, a one-stringed, tea-chest affair. **1979** R. EDWARDS *Skills Austral. Bushman* 150 The standard bush bass is made by turning a tea chest upside down, boring a hole in the centre of the base, and passing a string from this hole to the top of the stick. . . The butt of the stick rests on the outer edge of the box, and varying tensions are applied to this to produce the changes in tone. **1856** J. BONWICK *Bushrangers* 52 While Michael stooped down to apply the **bush bellows,** his mate leaped upon him. **1856** G. WILLMER *Draper in Aust.* 155 But for our perseverance in puffing away with the bush bellows (our hats). **1840** *S. Austral. Rec.* (London) 7 Nov. 292 The mode of conversion to *damper*—the true **bush-bread**—is as unartificial as any other part of our unartificial repast. **1849** A. HARRIS *Guide Port Stephens* 78 The Australian bush bread is called damper. **1945** E. GEORGE *Two at Daly Waters* 10 Bush bread and rain water taste sweet after years of soft and pleasant living. **1955** F. LANE *Patrol to Kimberleys* 79 He filled the billy can with water from a canvas bag and, unlashing the tucker box, took out some bush bread and salt beef. **1975** DONALDSON & JOSEPH *Wilderness* 16 Garrett carved a handful of thick bacon slices and tossed them on the pan, using a hunk of bush bread to clean up the fat. **1833** J. KING *Information Van Diemen's Land* 10 Dairy cows bred up by the hand, sell at about £15 each... **Bush bred cattle** .. varying from £3 to £6 each. **1842** *Tasmanian Jrnl. Nat. Sci.* I. 319 A stock-yard, made and used for collecting bush cattle. **1847** A. HARRIS *Settlers & Convicts* (1953) 132 A flock of kangaroo, or a scarcely less wild flock of bush-cattle galloping down upon you at a charge pace. **1865** *Austral. Monthly Mag.* (Melbourne) I. 234 Some bush cattle came out of the forest. **1883** E.M. CURR *Recoll. Squatting Vic.* 297 Bush-bred cattle are, I believe, unerring; so that a herd driven from its run .. will, at pleasure, return step by step the way it went. **1897** J.D. HENNESSEY *New-Chum Farmer* 6 They were an average lot of bush cattle, of no particular breed or brand, and a bit wildish. **1934** C. SAYCE *Comboman* 127 To face a mob of bush cattle on foot would be courting death. **1963** M. BRITT *Pardon my Boots* 58 The track was steep and irregular, crossed at intervals by the pads made by bush cattle. **1900** *Advocate* (Burnie) 2 Jan. 2/8 The fund for the **Bush contingent** now amounts to £12,000. **1900** *Bulletin* (Sydney) 10 Feb. 7/3 I'm going to the war, and I don't know what its for But the other chaps are going with the Bush Contingent men. **1851** C.P. FORD *Emigrant Family* 54 The early age at which he had begun, had given him an opportunity of acquiring **bush-craft.** **1870** J. BONWICK *Last Tasmanians* 189 Of powerful frame, goodly stature, great activity, untiring energy, quick intelligence, and superior Bush-craft, he was fitted for leadership in the Black War. **1883** E.M. CURR *Recoll. Squatting Vic.* 428 By the term *a good man in the bush* .. is meant a man well versed in bush craft; one who can find his way fairly; track, shoot, and swim well; who can bear hunger, thirst and fatigue; is able to look after his horses under circumstances of every sort; understands the Blacks and their ways; has a good idea of where to look for water, and so on. **1932** H. PRIEST *Call of Bush* 12, I was either lacking in bushcraft, or more dependent upon the things that civilisation provides than I cared to believe. **1943** *Bulletin* (Sydney) 8 Dec. 13/2 The men .. were superb riders whose bushcraft was learnt within 100 miles of Sydney. **1963** I.L. IDRIESS *Our Living Stone Age* 16 Soon she will be following in mother's footsteps, using all her inborn and taught bushcraft to find her quota of the small game and particularly the plant foods for the tribe. **1980** ANSELL & PERCY *To fight Wild* 134 The whole trip .. was as good an example as you could wish to see of Aboriginal bushcraft. A lot of it was over very tough bad country with a general scarcity of water holes. **1854** W. HOWITT *Boy's Adventures* 135 He was attacked by a fever which the men called the **bush-fever.** **1892** *Bulletin* (Sydney) 20 Aug. 21/2 He 'rolled-up', very gladly, for he had bush-fever badly When he left the smoke 'to wander where the wattle-blossoms wave'. **1893** J.A. BARRY *Steve Brown's Bunyip* 184 The reverend gentleman had provided himself with two bottles of port, a wine which he had been told was a first-class specific in cases of bush-fever and dysentery. **1915** E.R. MASSON *Untamed Territory* 47 George has bush fever, and if the whole police force of Darwin were called out it could not keep him back. **1944** *Aust. Week-End Bk.* 104 '*Troppo*' is a new disease—or rather an old disease with a new name—sometimes known as '**bush happy**', 'mulga mania', 'Darwin dementia', 'Moresby Madness' .. or just plain 'nuttiness'. **1944** F. JOHNSON *F. Johnson's Laugh* 49 I'm camp happy, and *bush happy*, and you know it. **1950** J. MORRISON *Port of Call* 27 Looks to me she's got the ding-bats. Bush-happy. **1956** H. FRAUCA *In New Country* 35 Often, prospecting is only a wild goose chase and most prospectors become a bit funny in the long run. They go sort of bush-happy. **1950** J. MORRISON *Port of Call* 66 That ain't no reason for 'er to go pokin' mullick at the **bush-'eads.** These city sheilas are all the same. **1966** *Meanjin* 281 'See them lyrebirds.' Jack agreed. The two bush-heads were manifestly revelling in their rôle as hosts. **1973** J. MORRISON *Austral. by Choice* 123 They've all gone, the old employment agencies for bush-heads, the shabby but busy little shops where jobs were bought and sold .. teamsters, harvesters, fruit-pickers, fencers, shearers, boundary-riders. **1907** *Bulletin* (Sydney) 15 Aug. 44/2 Going for **bush honey** is sometimes called bee-hunting. **1912** A. GALE *Austral. Bee Lore* 103 True it was bush honey, that is, a mixture of rotten wood and whatever else the hollow spout contained. **1928** *Bulletin* (Sydney) 12 Sept. 23/2 Quartpot and Biddy were commissioned to get a bucket of bush honey. **1959** D. STUART *Yandy* 55 Worrai made honeycomb in hollow trees and filled it with the hotly-sweet bush honey. **1981** —— *I think I'll Live* 62 I've tried most of the bush tucker, y' know, .. bungarra, snake, all the birds, and o' course I was always a bit gone on bush honey, the ole sugar-bag. **1837** *Perth Gaz.* 21 Oct. 994 All he had to provide for in the first instance, was the erection of a **bush-house**, and the clearing and cultivating of a few acres of land. **1847** J.D. LANG *Phillipsland* 120 The hand of a woman can give even 'a bush house' an air of *domesticity*. **1870** C.H. ALLEN *Visit to Qld.* 163 A Queensland bungalow .. may be taken as a type of the best of the bush houses. **1890** A. MACKAY *Austral. Agriculturist* (ed. 2) 228 The Bush-House .. is becoming, and deservedly so, a special feature of the Australian garden... The principle is .. to get shade, and shelter, without shutting out the air... The roof should be as high as convenient, say eight feet at least. Then the sides and roof are covered with bush material, laid as evenly and neatly as possible. The brushwood of young tee tree answers admirably; laths are also used; also Chinese matting, and close-mesh wire netting .. and at no great outlay, the bush house may be ornamental as well as useful. *Ibid.* 229 Nurserymen and gardeners are taking more advantage of the opportunities the bush-house offers for raising seedlings of all kinds. **1914** C.H.S. MATTHEWS *Bill* 46 Our home was just an ordinary bush house built of slabs, with a bark roof, and it stood on the banks of a deep creek. **1925** *Bulletin* (Sydney) 21 May 22/2 Some desert pea seed [*sic*] .. were planted in a fresh-water river-sand bed in a corner of the bush-house and struck, giving a beautiful show of blooms. **1941** C. BARRETT *Aust.* 84 Australia's biggest land snail lives .. on Tamborine Mountain... I kept two of the giants, as pets, in my bushhouse, down in Melbourne. **1949** J. MORRISON *Creeping City* 56 Her gesture took in the entire gully, dim and cool and moist as a latticed bush-house. **1960** M. HENRY *Unlucky Dip* 86 It was four o'clock and the bush-house had filled up. 'What can I pass you, Mrs Garland? Another scone, or one of those marvellous lamingtons.' **1979** V. CRITTENDEN *Front Garden* 30 The Bush House .. provided the shade and cool situation for exotic plants and ferns. **1981** *Nimbin Newsletter* 19 Nov. 1 'Bush houses', those communal dwellings which have aroused much controversy on the North Coast, are now sanctioned—if they meet minimum standards—and multiple occupancy is recognised as an acceptable lifestyle. **1892** *Bulletin* (Sydney) 5 Nov. 20/2 We met the **bush liar** in all his glory. He was dressed like—like a bush larrikin... He had been to a ball where some blank had 'touched' his blanky overcoat. **1896** H. LAWSON *While Billy Boils* 89 Every true Australian bushman must try his best to tell a bigger outback lie than the last bush-liar. **1936** A. RUSSELL *Gone Nomad* 46 Probably the most dramatic Bush Liar I met with on the tablelands .. was 'Longbow' B--. **1957** R.S. PORTEOUS *Brigalow* 83 As a yarn spinner and bush liar Wonga had no equal. He could tell the most outrageous lies without a flicker of a smile. **1971** *Bulletin* (Sydney) 27 Nov. 48/3 Mick Hunter attributes his 'morbid, unbalanced lust for the opposite sex to over-indulgence in **bush oysters**'. He describes the taste this way: 'Testicles are to meat as monstera deliciosa are to fruit.' **1962** MARSHALL & DRYSDALE *Journey among Men* 170 **Bush pickles**, according to the old recipe, are made by stirring a bottle of Worcester sauce into a large tin of plum jam. This can be varied to suit individual tastes. **1846** J.L. STOKES *Discoveries in Aust.* II. 184 Malay boy, work, have house; Swan River boy, no work, **bush walk.** **1892** MRS F. HUGHES *My Childhood in Aust.* 83 Now let me tell you of some of our bush walks. **1911** A. MARSHALL *Sunny Aust.* 113 Every now and then some of them would desert for a 'bush-walk'. **1927** *Bulletin* (Sydney) 21 July 27/3 Near Balmoral (Vic.) .. one of our bush-walks was to 'the manna trees', locally known as box-gums. **1940** *Ibid.* 6 Mar. 17/4 Jack's oft-expressed desire for a feed of 'overland trout' induced a couple of us to take a bush walk. **1985** *Canberra Times* 20 Feb. 22/6 It would be a test of endurance and the ability to ignore pain rather than an enjoyable bushwalk. **1948** H.A. LINDSAY *Bushman's Handbk.* 137 For **bushwalkers**, who carry all their gear on their backs and are on the move most of the time, we have not yet worked out a method for killing the flies. **1965** *Tracks we Travel* 107 Only the dingo crouched behind a rock, and a party of bushwalkers camped in the western valley. **1980** H. STEPHENSON *Cattlemen & Huts High Plains* 67 The homestead was burnt, it is thought by walkers who lit a big fire in the fireplace... Years later, Arthur spoke to me about it. 'Two bushwalkers,' he said. Then .. he corrected himself. 'It was two tourists on foot,' he said. **1930** *Bulletin* (Sydney) 15 Jan. 23/2 Dave was busy scuffling corn when one of those **bush walking** enthusiasts shouted out to him. **1945** A. RUSSELL *Bush Ways* 57 Bush-walking is something more than tramping along a well-worn road by day, and sleeping at inns and lodging houses. It is something more than making a mountain traverse under the comfortable guidance of a compass. These things are .. only correlated parts of a transcending purpose—the search for the spiritual meaning of the hills. **1968** *Coast to Coast 1967–68* 125 His bush-walking days had given him a stamina which now kept him on his feet. **1979** P. COCK *Alternative Aust.* 159 His other interests were classical music, good wines, bush-walking and ecology. **1985** *Canberra Times* 20 Feb. 22/5, I have .. lectured on many occasions to Scout and school groups planning bushwalking trips. **1919** *Lone Hand* Feb. 10 **Bush week**... An excellent movement was started some time ago in a quiet way to organise a Bush festival in the City of Sydney. It is proposed that it should last a week, and thoroughly represent every phase of primary and secondary production. **1923** J. MOSES *Beyond City Gates* 57 We go to Sydney, too, with all our produce, and put it in the windows in George Street every year. They call it Bush Week, mister. **1945** S.J. BAKER *Austral. Lang.* 76 The time-honoured chant of derision *What's this, bush week?* **1948** *Bulletin* (Sydney) 11 Aug. 22/2 It was bush week or something in Murrayville, and when we blew off the train into the pub there was nothing between us and several long cool beers except most of the local cockies, townsmen, shophands, their friends, relatives and acquaintances. **1949** L. GLASSOP *Lucky Palmer* 37, I get smart alecks like you trying to put one over on me every minute of the day. What do you think this is? Bush Week? **1952** H.E. BOOTE *Sidelights Two Referendums* 37 *February:* Bush week and procession in town. Cobb & Co.'s coaches looked the real thing with lady passengers in crinolines. **1952** T.A.G. HUNGERFORD *Ridge & River* 95 'Grab your bloody brains!' he muttered tensely. 'What d'you think it is, bush-week?' **1960** J. WYNNUM *Pinch Salt* (1963) 66 As if it's not enough being adrift during working hours, you've got to further flout authority by turning up to training smellin' like a brewery. What d'you think this is—Bush Week? **1965** K. SMITH *OGF* 188 Don't be a bludger, Bert—get stuck into it. Not that one! Oh, you—finger out, Harry, it ain't Bush Week! **1972** *Bulletin* (Sydney) 12 Aug. 17 (*caption*) In Canberra, forestry students provided their commentary on the strike in the Bush Week procession. **1980** C. LEE *Bush Week* 67 The yellow form said Bush Week was to raise money for a Worthwhile Charity, to remind us of our debt to the Bush People who pioneered this country and to provide an occasion for Student Frivolity. **1986** *Canberra Times* 30 Mar. 3/1 Memo ANU Bush Week organisers: forget about the Australian Defence Force Academy and any planned hijinks.

3. In the names of flora and fauna: **bush apple,** *black apple*, see BLACK *a.*[2] 1 a.; **canary,** *white-throated warbler*, see WHITE *a.*[2] 1 b.; **cat,** a wild cat; **cucumber,** ALUNQUA; **devil,** *Tasmanian devil*, see TASMANIAN *a.* 2; **fly,** the fly *Musca vetustissima* (fam. Muscidae), which settles persistently on the eyes, mouth, and other moist parts of the body; **grass,** any of several native grasses used as fodder on uncultivated land; **hay,** hay made from native grasses; **kangaroo,** a medium-sized kangaroo; **lark,** the small bird *Mirafra javanica* (fam. Alaudidae) of n. and e. Aust., resembling the introduced skylark in plumage and song; **mouse,** any of many small native mammals, esp. the marsupial hopping mouse, *Notomys*, and the *marsupial mouse* (see MARSUPIAL 1); perh. also native rodents of the genus *Pseudomys*; **rat,** any of several rat-sized native marsupials and rodents, esp. native species of *Rattus*; **tick,** *scrub tick*, see SCRUB *n.* 5; **turkey,** *brush turkey*, see BRUSH *n.*[1] B. 2.

1935 DAVISON & NICHOLLS *Blue Coast Caravan* 40 Valleys dotted with dark clumps of **bush apple** and turpentine. **1918** *Bulletin* (Sydney) 14 Feb. (Red Page), *White-throated Flyeater* (**Bush Canary**) and other members of the genus *Gerygone*. **1924** *Ibid.* 9 Oct. 24/1, I have some feathered cobbers—a thrush, a bellbird and a bush canary. **1967** E. HUXLEY *Their Shining Eldorado* 288 The lemon-breasted flycatcher trills delightfully, and has been called the bush-canary. **1933** J. McCARTER *Love's Lunatic* 124 He had seen the same crazy look in **bush cats** inadvertently caught in rabbit traps. **1964** K. TENNANT *Summer's Tales* 25 Seeing how long it would take a bush cat to eat out of your hand. **1937** M. TERRY *Sand & Sun* 213 Another common bush delicacy was the alunqua, some call it the **bush cucum-**

ber. **1955** DEAN & CARELL *Dust for Dancers* 52 Bush cucumbers are the size of small gherkins, with a delicate cucumber flavour. **1974** M. TERRY *War of Warramullas* 151 The alunqua, or bush cucumber, is an important source of food... The fruit looks rather like a large banana passionfruit... The fruit is deep green in colour and tastes like fresh green peas. **1833** J. BACKHOUSE *Narr. Visit Austral. Colonies* (1843) 123 Another animal, .. black, with a few irregular white spots, .. is commonly known by the name of the Devil, or the **Bush-Devil.** **1841** *Launceston Courier* 4 Oct. 2/4 *Richmond hounds.*—The huntsmen had a capital run, and on the morning after the ball were again out to some fine sport after a bush devil. **1838** T.H. JAMES *Six Months S.A.* 71 The large **bush flies** had settled on him by thousands. **1903** A.G. CHARLETON *Gold Mining & Milling W.A.* 10 The dust-storms, which rage for days at a time, are certainly a nuisance, but a secondary source of annoyance compared with the bushflies which give rise to the common complaint of 'bungeye', a painful swelling of the eyelids. **1946** G.E.L. WATSON *But to what Purpose* 115 In the inland bush flies blackened all one's clothes. **1953** H.G. LAMOND *Big Red* 125 The flies came in their uncounted and uncountable millions of millions. They were the bush-fly, a cousin perhaps to the ordinary black-fly of the house, needing an entomologist to tell them apart. **1968** V. SERVENTY *Southern Walkabout* 85 The bushfly is very similar to the housefly but, unlike the housefly, only bothers humans in sunshine, dropping away when you move into deep shade or into a house. **1973** D. STUART *Morning Star, Evening Star* 49 And always .. the bush flies in clouds. **1827** *Monitor* (Sydney) 24 July 534/3 The discord of *3d. an acre rent* for the use of His Majesty's **bush-grass**, soon put an end to the *country* portion of this national chorus. **1841** *Geelong Advertiser* 14 Aug. 3/1 Bush grass begins to get short; and fodder for working bullocks and horses is every day becoming more scarce. **1851** J. HENDERSON *Excursions & Adventures N.S.W.* I. 162 Our nags eat their miserable allowance of maize and withered bush-grass. **1888** F. HUME *Madame Midas* 29 A particularly tempting tuft of bush grass growing in the moist ditches. **1896** N. GOULD *Town & Bush* 284 The ground is hard-baked, and the long rank Bush grass is shrivelled and dry. **1964** P. WHITE *Burnt Ones* 297 Over the paspalum clumps, before the thinner, bush grass. **1827** *Monitor* (Sydney) 1 Nov. 781/3 **Bush Hay** from £6 to £9 per ton. **1845** R. HOWITT *Impressions Aust. Felix* 314 A man mowing near us on the unoccupied land .. getting bush-hay. **1852** S. MOSSMAN *Gold Regions Aust.* 62 The grass throughout such land is mainly composed of the kangaroo grass (*Authistiria* [*sic*] *Australis*), attaining the height of five feet in favourable localities, when it is frequently cut for 'bush' hay. **1894** G. BOOTHBY *On Wallaby* 276 We took the precaution to obtain a fresh supply of bush hay to carry along with us. **1916** *Bulletin* (Sydney) 14 Dec. 22/2 Where Mitchell grass flourishes a good deal of bush-haymaking is done. **1927** 'S. RUDD' *Romance of Runnibede* 20 At intervals during the day when we had asked the governess if we could 'please go out', it was to stuff bush hay and more bush hay into those ponies. **1959** H. MYERS *Regions of Courage* 183 How they can get along on mulga, bush hay, water, the bit of nutriment in the grass, and other edibles such as dead-finish has me beat. **1978** M. NIXON *Rivers of Home* 16 Making a type of 'bush hay' out of natural grasses in the Pindan country just out of Derby. **1832** BACKHOUSE & TYLOR *Life & Labours G.W. Walker* (1862) 45 The Forest and the **Bush Kangaroo**, and the Wallaby. **1845** R. HOWITT *Impressions Aust. Felix* 330 The bush kangaroo is about the size of a sheep. **1865** J. GOULD *Handbk. Birds Aust.* I. 404 Horsefield's **Bush-Lark.** **1931** J. DEVANEY *Earth Kindred* 14 The little bushlark's spurt of glee. **1872** G.S. BADEN-POWELL *New Homes for Old Country* 321 The '**bush-mouse**', a perfect kangaroo of .. diminutive proportions. **1875** R. BRUCE *Dingoes* 38 The spotted native cats, Bush mice, or active leaping rats. **1902** *Bulletin* (Sydney) 21 June 16/4 Recently found, in a hollow stump, a bush-mouse's nest containing 33 young. **1936** K.L. SMITH *Sky Pilot's Last Flight* 121 In a big glass and fly-wire cage lived my little bush mice. Pretty brush-tailed marsupial honey-eating mice, with gentle eyes and movements. **1981** A.B. FACEY *Fortunate Life* 90 The owl .. lived on bush mice and rats. **1855** *Trans. Philos. Soc. Vic.* I. 70 The **bush rat** (*P*[*erameles*] *Gunnii*). **1893** S. NEWLAND *Paving Way* 200 The small bush-rats swept over the country like a wave and honeycombed the hills. **1899** R. SEMON *In Austral. Bush* 37 *Phascologale penicillata*, called a 'bush rat' by the Australians. **1929** *Bulletin* (Sydney) 23 Jan. 25/4 In the Far North there is an agile bush rat that can climb tall trees at the run. **1954** C. BARRETT *Wild Life Aust. & New Guinea* 41 The brush-tailed marsupial rats, particularly the species known as the 'bush-rat', are savage little creatures. **1972** K. WILLEY *Tales Big Country* 28 Great bush rats, the size of rabbits, scuttled away in hundreds. **1872** A. MCFARLAND *Illawarra & Manaro* 43 A former proprietor stocked it with hogs... The **bush-tick** .. settled upon, and killed every one of them. **1890** A.J. VOGAN *Black Police* 210 The two travellers .. pick the bush-ticks and scrub-itch insects from their flesh with the point of the long scrub-knife the old digger carries. **1917** *Bulletin* (Sydney) 1 Nov. 24/2 Blue-bottle tick and .. bush tick .. are one and the same insect. **1956** S. HOPE *Diggers' Paradise* 201 The bush tick *ixodes holocyclus* is a poisonous menace and the wise camper makes sure daily that he has not become a host to one. **1836** J. BACKHOUSE *Narr. Visit Austral. Colonies* (1843) 425 The **Bush Turkey**, *Allectura Lathami*, inhabits these forests. **1841** *Port Phillip Patriot* 9 Aug. 4/2 The wattled talegalla, or bush turkey of the colonists. **1898** W. REDMOND *Shooting Trip* 51 There is nothing to beat a good young Bush turkey, which is considered quite a delicacy. **1965** L. WALKER *Other Girl* 153 The bush turkeys came back—having had their feed of grasshoppers.

bush, *v.*[1] [f. prec.]

1. *intr. Obs.* Freq. with **it**: to camp, often involuntarily, in the bush. Also as *vbl. n.*

1825 *Austral.* (Sydney) 5 May 2 One of those fathers of the Colony .. recollects when it was a common thing for people to lose themselves in the bush at Wooloomooloo—and after walking about in the woods a whole day, lay themselves down in despair and 'bush it' within 10 minutes walk of the camp! **1838** T.H. JAMES *Six Months S.A.* 289 We bushed for the night under a low scrubby tree with nothing for the horses to eat, and *no water.* **1842** E. IRBY *Mem.* (1908) 60 A smart shower or two came on in the night, but on the whole we passed our first night's regular bushing pretty well. **1845** C. GRIFFITH *Present State & Prospects Port Phillip* 63 Some people never succeed in becoming good bushmen; and there have been instances of persons being *bushed* (that is, having to spend the night *al fresco*), within a mile of their own doors. **1845** *Standard* (Melbourne) 15 Mar. 3/1 His Excellency intended to bush it last night, and arrive at Wollongong this morning. **1851** *Australasian* (Melbourne) 470 Reached Geelong, jaded, footsore, and travel-torn, after having 'bushed it' eight nights. **1854** S. SIDNEY *Gallops & Gossips* 37 It was while bushing at night by a wood fire that we got in the way of telling yarns. **1870** B.L. FARJEON *In Austral. Wilds* 34 'We shall have to bush it, Trot,' I said. 'Yes, mate,' he said unconcernedly, but looking about him sharply .. for a suitable spot to camp in. **1891** 'E.H.' *Advance Aust.* 11 My first night's 'bushing' was a strange experience. **1894** R. CALDWELL *In our Great N.-W.* p. v, On reaching Anna Creek Station, after having been 'bushing it' for six or seven days.

2. *intr. Obs.* With **it**: to go into the bush; to make an expedition into unknown country.

1828 *Tasmanian* (Hobart) 15 Aug. 4 The bullocks bolted, and I had to *bush it* after them. **1846** *Bell's Life in Sydney* 27 June 1/4 Since the successful termination of Leichardt's expedition from this place to Port Essington, I, in common with many others, have felt an inkling to bush it in search of something wonderful and new.

3. *intr. Obs.* With **it**: to live, usu. under conditions of hardship, in the bush.

1839 *Port Phillip Patriot* 26 Aug. 3 For a young man, not afraid of bushing it, and determined to look after his shop himself, I am inclined to think that he would make more of £1000 at Port Phillip in five years, than he could at South Australia. **1841** *Sydney Herald* 13 Dec. 2/5 A continuousness of action would be too much to expect from those whose long habits of 'bushing it', with all its barbarisms, have so worn out all recollection of the stir and enterprise of more civilized life and more enlightened men. **1843** S. DAVENPORT *Lett.* 5 June in *S. Australiana* (1967) Mar. 35 For my part I enjoy bush life very much—if bush ours may be called. For certainly in our case there is no 'bushing it', in the former and, even now, general sense of the term, since we have here now all the comforts of home. **1854** G.H. HAYDON *Austral. Emigrant* 144 Many men have been bushing it for years and have not seen such adventures. **1874** R.P. FALLA *Knocking About* (1976) 20 Can you feast upon mutton, drink gallons of tea? Then come o'er the waves and bush it with me.

4. *trans.* To turn (cattle) out into open country. Also *fig.*

1959 *Bulletin* (Sydney) 16 Sept. 18/3 The cream-carter .. took one look at the cow and said positively: 'She ain't got brucellosis!' whereupon Daisy's owner said, 'Well, if the carter says she hasn't got the disease, we won't waste time testing her!' and he promptly bushed the cow. **1976** C.D. MILLS *Hobble Chains & Greenhide* 175 One old mare was very fizzy, and too old to try and break so, after branding her, we bushed her in the open country. She might breed on out there. **1980** ANSELL & PERCY *To fight Wild* 118 I'd smelt the rib bones hanging up the night before, and reckoned I'd get one more feed off them before I had to bush the rest—throw them out.

Hence **bushing (it)** *vbl. n.*

1839 W.H. LEIGH *Reconnoitering Voyages* 105 'Bushing it', was the only thing to be done; and, for this purpose, we struck into the woods. **1846** S. DAVENPORT *Lett.* 18 Feb. in *S. Australiana* (1971) Sept. 69 Bushing is the best life .. a man sleeps with the sun and rises with it too. **1850** *Australasian Sporting Mag.* 43 Share the dangers and delights of some of those extensive pic-nic trips, which are here more commonly recognised under the expressive appellation of '*bushing it*'. **1853** MRS C. CLACY *Lady's Visit to Gold Diggings* 269 The farther we went, the more uncivilized it became—hills here, forests there, as wild and savage as any one could desire. It was 'bushing it' with a vengeance. **1861** E.P. RAMSAY-LAYE *Social Life & Manners* 55 We were very fortunate in finding an agreeable party .. experienced in 'bushing it'. **1895** J. KIRBY *Old Times in Bush* 63, I had had a good deal of experience in 'bushing it'.

bush, *v.*[2] [Back-formation from BUSHED.] *trans.* To disorient (a person), to cause 'to lose one's bearings'.

1916 *Bulletin* (Sydney) 27 Apr. 22/3 A man I knew could find his way anywhere. You couldn't 'bush' *him.* **1928** *Ibid.* 23 May 23/1 If you should chance to go out back And 'bush' yourself on Gilgai Plain. **1937** W. HATFIELD *I find Aust.* 180, I rode with him down in the Georgina sandhill country, and you couldn't bush him anywhere, day or night. **1950** G. FARWELL *Surf Music* 216 'Takes more'n that to bush me, son'... 'If you'd not shown up by dark, I was sending Quartpot after you.'

bush-bash, *v.* [f. BUSH *n.* 1 + *bash* to strike.] *intr.* SCRUB-BASH 2. Also *trans.*

1967 L. BEADELL *Blast Bush* p. ix, Short cuts through mulga scrub (known as 'bush-bashing') can be an interesting experience but is attended with real dangers. **1970** D. STIVENS *Horse of Air* 215, I kept heading northwest, bush-bashing through the mulga scrub. **1972** R. ERICKSEN *West of Centre* 41 He had spent .. a large part of the preceding fifteen years bush-bashing new tracks and patrolling old ones. **1976** L. BEADELL *Beating about Bush* 179, I would bush-bash to the area, fix my own position from the stars. **1977** J. CARTER *All Things Wild* 73 Two Land Rovers eventually reached the grounded plane, after bush-bashing at snail's pace northward from the atom bomb testing area. **1979** D. LOCKWOOD *My Old Mates & I* 9 He was Tom Vegar, a qualified Territorian, which means twenty or more years of bush-bashing. **1986** *Canberra Times* 16 Mar. 6/2 (*heading*), 4WD models do more than 'bush-bash'.

Hence **bush basher** *n.*

1971 L. BEADELL *Bush Bashers* 1 Several hundred miles north was the road my little camp of six bush bashers had made, extending for nearly a thousand miles east to west. **1978** *Sydney Morning Herald* 22 Sept. 25/1 The 'bush-bashers' are alive and well, with various four-wheel-drive organisations campaigning heavily against the establishment of national parks which they see as a threat to their activities.

Bush Brother. A member of the BUSH BROTHERHOOD.

1908 C.H.S. MATTHEWS *Parson in Austral. Bush* 213 Bush christenings are a constant source of delight to the Bush brother. **1914** J.W.S. TOMLIN *Aust.'s Greatest Need* 129 The bush brother with his bridles in his hand enters the horse-yard. **1927** T.S. GROSER *Lure of Golden West* 110 Vocation to the life of a Bush Brother. **1940** G.W. LOVEJOY *In Journeyings Often* 36 A celebration at Brewarrina is usually followed, in the case of the Bush Brothers, by the saying of Mattins privately. **1947** M. RAYMOND *Smiley gets Gun* 169 The obvious man to be entrusted with the sealed confession was the Bush Brother. **1952** *Bulletin* (Sydney) 8 Oct. 13/1 Word came down from the homestead that a Bush Brother was coming on the Sunday, and the boss expected us to be shaven and clean and attend a service in the woolshed at 11 a.m. **1957** N. ELLISON *Flying Matilda* 75 The Bush Brothers were a small body of young Anglican ministers from Britain, specially picked to cope with the temporal and spiritual complexities of the Australian outback; in 1928 the stipend was £40 a year. **1963** J.F. HARLEY *Mantle of Safety* 178, I had heard of these Bush Brothers. They were travelling clergymen who covered an area of thousands of square miles of deep inland country. They held a service whenever they came across a settlement of people, however small, who wanted one; they baptised children, visited the isolated families and ministered as far as possible to all the people they met, regardless of race or creed. **1978** R.A.F. WEBB *Brothers in Sun* 9 Their title is expressive of their relationship with the people of the bush over the last three-quarters of a century—that of Bush Brothers.

Bush Brotherhood. [f. BUSH *n.* 3 + *brotherhood* a fraternity.] An Anglican missionary organization founded to provide a peripatetic ministry in remote areas.

1897 *Theology* (London) (1947) May 165 Bishop Dawes himself spoke. Half-humorously he called the venture a 'Bush Brotherhood'. **1908** C.H.S. MATTHEWS *Parson in Austral. Bush* 34 Largely through the efforts of the present Bishop of London . . the first of the Bush Brotherhoods was formed. **1915** *Bulletin* (Sydney) 7 Jan. 14/3 Anglican Parson Matthews . . used to be prominent in the Bush Brotherhood in the back-blocks of N.S. Wales. **1927** T.S. GROSER *Lure of Golden West* p. xi, The inauguration of the Bush Brotherhood system (as a substitute for the iniquitous 'Bush Parochialism' of former days). **1940** G.W. LOVEJOY *In Journeyings Often* 84 Their home was always 'open-house' to the Bush Brotherhood. **1953** H.M. EASTMAN *Mem. of Sheepman* 112, I learnt he was a member of the 'Bush Brotherhood', which stood for parson in those areas. **1962** *N.T. News* (Darwin) 9 Jan. 5/6 Changes in the administration of the Darwin Church of England parish will follow a reunion of the Bush Brotherhood.

bush capital. [f. BUSH *n.* 3 + *capital*.] A (derisive) name for Canberra, the capital city of the Commonwealth of Australia. (See also quot. 1911.)

1906 *Truth* (Sydney) 19 Aug. 1/3 The search for a Bush Capital has already cost Australia £14,406. **1911** A. MARSHALL *Sunny Aust.* 68 It is all very well to laugh at the 'Bush Capital'; but Washington was laughed at in just the same way before it grew to be the fine city it is. **1922** *Daily Mail* (Sydney) 19 Jan. 5/8 A party is to go down to the Bush Capital at Canberra. **1926** *Canberra Community News* 11 Oct. 19 Canberra had a glorious setting, but they should not look upon it as the 'bush' capital, but as the national city of Australia. **1928** M.E. FULLERTON *Austral. Bush* 20 Since it was to be a *bush* capital, Canberra was a good choice. **1978** *Truckin' Life* II. iv. 77 Some of my best friends are public servants but they often raise a giggle in the bush capital. **1986** *Canberra Times* 5 Mar. 18/2 Big flocks of galahs feeding on the parched nature strips around the Bush Capital.

bushed, *ppl. a.* [f. BUSH *v.*[1]]

1. Lost in the bush.

1844 H. MCCRAE *Georgiana's Jrnl.* 6 Feb. (1934) 107 Even with the aid of his compass, Captain Reid thinks we run the risk of being bushed for the night. **1847** *Moreton Bay Courier* 17 July 4/1 It is well known that scarcely a week passes that some traveller is not bushed for more or less longer periods. **1854** W. HOWITT *Boy's Adventures* 123 He was afraid of being bushed, as it is called, that is, lost in the bush. **1859** W. KELLY *Life in Vic.* I. 170 We kept a little wide of the track, but not out of sight, as there was timber in the distance, and we had our fears about getting bushed. **1880** J.B. STEVENSON *Seven Yrs. Austral. Bush* 28 A man gets bushed, that is, he suddenly realizes the fact that he does not know which way to go. **1883** *Bulletin* (Sydney) 13 Oct. 7/3 Reader, have you ever been 'bushed'? I mean . . hopelessly, inextricably lost in the unsainted wilderness of an Australian desert? **1898** D.W. CARNEGIE *Spinifex & Sand* 219 The poor fellow failed to follow back the outgoing tracks, got lost in the night, became hopelessly 'bushed', and perished, alone in the desert. **1912** *Huon Times* (Franklin) 17 Jan. 2/4 A 'bushed' horseman made the discovery, and he states that it would be impossible for him to find the place again. **1922** R.L. JACK *Northmost Aust.* I. 328 It is not for a moment suggested that the Leader of the expedition was 'bushed' during his wanderings. **1927** A. WRIGHT *Squatter's Secret* 92 All the harm I wish you is that you get bushed out in those gullies yonder, and never turn up again. **1935** G. MCIVER *Drover's Odyssey* 24 The experienced men knew . . the tendency of lost men to travel in curves. Hence the bushed men, even if they walked throughout the night . . could not be far distant. **1944** *Bulletin* (Sydney) 17 May 12/3 I've been bushed myself and also in searches for bushed mates, and I'm blowed if I ever heard the bush 'ring with cooees'. **1964** T. RONAN *Packhorse & Pearling Boat* 156, I was staggered. I'd never heard of an aboriginal being bushed, that is, lost. **1981** A. WILKINSON *Up Country* 49 After all . . we didn't find our cliff, and it was only John's sharp eyes which prevented us from being 'bushed' for the night.

2. *transf.* and *fig.*

1885 MRS C. PRAED *Austral. Life* 29 He added with true Australian simplicity, 'I get quite bushed in these streets. London is an awful place.' **1904** *Shearer* (Sydney) 10 Sept. 4/4 'Dauntless, dashing Jack', the elect of the Darling, got bushed in the House the other night. **1923** J. ARMOUR *Spell of Inland* 109 Ned persisted that he had a very good ear for music. 'Yes, that is right,' said Hughie. 'You have got one good ear, but the other is so d-- bad it gets you completely bushed.' **1943** S.W. KEOUGH *Around Army* 60 The lance-jack is the biggest mug of a map-reader in the A.I.F., and . . he'd get bushed in Hyde Park. **1956** *Bulletin* (Sydney) 26 Sept. 13/1 The beginner in ornithology is liable to get bushed in the jungle of avian nomenclature. **1963** E. LINDALL *Springs of Violence* 102 But we ain't talkers, are we, Lew? We'd get bushed among all them big words the Yank spits out. **1965** *N. Austral. Monthly* Oct. 7 Whilst flying down from the North they had difficulty in distinguishing towns from homesteads, and had thus become 'bushed'. **1978** M.J. BURTON *Bush Pub* 126 'That's got 'im completely bushed,' the Fanatic whispered to me. 'It would be all bloody Eskimo talk to 'im.'

bushfire.

1. A fire which burns through (freq. extensive) areas of natural vegetation, often causing loss of life and property. Also *attrib.*

1832 *Sydney Monitor* 1 Dec. 2/6 Another large bush fire has been very destructive in the neighbourhood of Windsor. **1833** *Perth Gaz.* 21 Dec. 203 On Saturday last, a valuable building . . recently the residence of Captain Irwin, our late Lieut. Governor, was destroyed by a *bush*-fire. **1841** *Launceston Courier* 11 Jan. 2/1 A bushfire broke out in Mr Lawrence's paddock, adjoining the suburbs of the town on Friday. **1843** R.D. MURRAY *Summer at Port Phillip* 144 The sole danger to be apprehended by the agriculturist from the 'bush fires', arises from their likelihood to communicate with his crops. **1846** C.P. HODGSON *Reminisc. Aust.* 179, I have seen a tremendous bush-fire which has burnt its way for some 300 yards. **1848** *Port Phillip Herald* 9 Mar. 2/4 Certainly of all the magnificent sights on earth none equals an extensive bush fire for grandeur and sublimity when seen by night. **1855** G.H. WATHEN *Golden Colony* 89 'Bush fires' are very common during summer. They originate from the spread of a camp fire, from a lighted match carelessly thrown on the dry grass, or some other accident. **1870** *Williams's Austral. Ann.* 18 Over on the ranges there hangs a black cloud of smoke. It is the Bush Fire—the Yule-log of Australia. **1872** MRS E. MILLETT *Austral. Parsonage* 96 Bush-fires are variously accounted for by different people, some inclining to the idea that the sun, striking upon the thick glass at the bottom of some of the many broken bottles which lie about the bush, acts upon them as if they were burning-glasses and sets the grass alight. **1876** 'RESIDENT' *Girl Life in Aust.* 137 Papa says I shall see a bush fire. . . I'd like to see a real jolly one, with a native scorching in the middle, and the half-roasted snakes and animals running about; it must be awfully horrid. **1887** A. NICOLS *Wild Life & Adventure* 102 The grass was kept carefully burnt down, in order to protect the hut and sheep-enclosures from Bush-fires. **1891** W. TILLEY *Wild West of Tas.* 84 The news spread like a bush fire. **1898** *Bulletin* (Sydney) 8 Jan. 11/2 The Tas. bush-fire recalls the fact that on the Victorian Black Thursday—1851—cinders and burning twigs from the blazing Gippsland forests were blown right across the Straits on to the beach of Northern Tasmania. **1910** *Huon Times* (Franklin) 26 Oct. 2/7 The only danger is that the extraordinarily luxuriant growth of grass and crops may lead to bush fires. **1929** A. YOFFA *Real Thing* 73 A single, terrified word burst from my palsied lips 'Bush-fire'. **1934** E. STOREY *Eve's Affairs* 21 Trains during the summer are the very devil for causing bush-fires. **1952** J. CLEARY *Sundowners* 81 'You ever seen a bush fire?' 'Not a real one . . just grass fires in a paddock.' **1956** A. MARSHALL *How's Andy Going?* 160 February—the bush-fire month. **1961** *Bulletin* (Sydney) 30 May 35/2 The smoke from a bushfire rings a tucker bell for many birds. **1974** BUCKLEY & HAMILTON *Festival* 10 The bush-fire jumped the firebreak and was crackling and bursting in the tree tops. **1985** *Bombala Times* 18 July 4/3 No funds are available . . for landholders affected by the bushfire.

2. *Obs.* A camp-fire; occas., a fire indoors (in the bush).

1832 *Currency Lad* (Sydney) 1 Sept. 3 She was sitting about an hour before daylight near a bush fire contiguous to the house. **1834** G. BENNETT *Wanderings N.S.W.* I. 136 We stopped to make a bush fire, prepared tea, turning out our horses to graze. **1843** C. ROWCROFT *Tales of Colonies* I. 215 We placed the afflicted lady on a log of wood before our bush-fire. **1852** F. LANCELOTT *Aust. as it Is* I. 24 These corrobories are generally held on moonlight nights, and during the performance large bush fires are kept burning. **1862** H. BROWN *Vic. as I found It* 74 Around the bush fire men will often, without the slightest reserve, tell the history of their lives. **1871** 'OLD BOOMER' *Story of Mathinna* 4 We shot them down over their bush fires, while the men slept and women suckled their babes. **1886** R. HENTY *Australiana* 20, I don't enjoy my tea now half as well as when made on the bush fire in a 'tin-billy' in the old time long ago! **1903** M. MOORE-BENTLEY *Sketched from Life* 43 The fire blazed and crackled as only Australian bush fires can, the blue smoke, escaping the chimney, filling the room with incense of eucalyptus fragrance.

3. *Obs.* A controlled burning of natural vegetation for a particular purpose: see quots. 1845 and 1865.

1844 L. LEICHHARDT *Jrnl. Overland Exped. Aust.* 29 Nov. (1847) 54 Recent bush fires and still smoking trees betokened the presence of natives. **1845** R. HOWITT *Impressions Aust. Felix* 70 The convicts, busily employed at their bush-fires, burning off and clearing the land. **1862** G. BOURNE *Jrnl. Landsborough's Exped. from Carpentaria* 10 Bush-fires, but no blacks visible. **1865** G.F. ANGAS *Aust.* 41 Many of these bush fires are caused by the blacks burning the scrub to drive out game.

4. *fig.*

1888 H.S. RUSSELL *Genesis Qld.* 163 Active, energetic, prince of 'bushmen' and good fellows, full of 'bush-fire', he was a man not likely to sit down satisfied with the first thing he happened to meet with. **1898** W. DOLLMAN *Bush Fancies* 59 A drop of whisky, or 'bush fire', used to get into the hut.

5. Special Comb. **bushfire blonde,** see quot. 1943; **brigade,** a volunteer fire-fighting organization; **fighter,** a member of a bushfire brigade.

1943 S.J. BAKER *Pop. Dict. Austral. Slang* (ed. 3) 17 **Bushfire blonde,** a red-haired girl. **1955** N. PULLIAM *I traveled Lonely Land* 111 That bushfire blonde didn't give you the first looko. **1968** J. HIBBERD *Squibs* (1984) 130, I love bushfire blondes. **1904** *Truth* (Sydney) 3 Jan. 2/6 A **bush fire brigade** has been formed at Brown's Creek. **1974** L. GRIERSON *Down by Riverside* 46 The bush fire brigade have been called but they said they couldn't contain it. **1981** *Bega District News* 27 Nov. 1/6 A number of bush fire brigade members. **1980** *Sydney Morning Herald* 4 Nov. 1/1 **Bushfire fighters** at Waterfall took advantage early today of a drop in wind to start back-burning operations. **1981** *Bega District News* 27 Nov. 1/5 Divided loyalties among bush firefighters.

bushie, var. BUSHY.

bush lawyer.

1. One who parades an only fancied knowledge of the law; one who 'lays down the law'.

1835 *True Colonist* (Hobart) 4 Sept. 7/4 The able oratory of the bush lawyer, whose time of servitude, in one of the worst of Mr O'Connor's gangs, expired last week. **1840** *Tasmanian Weekly Dispatch* (Hobart) 11 Sept. 6/3 Another forgery was produced . . bearing the indorsement of John Hodsol, the celebrated bush lawyer. **1853** *Guardian* (Hobart) 19 Feb. 3/3 The witness was sharply examined by the prisoner, who is somewhat of a 'Bush Lawyer'. **1862** G.T. LLOYD *Thirty-Three Yrs. Tas. & Vic.* 120 'Arrah, boys!' shouted the last sentry, the loquacious Bush-lawyer. **1869** *Argus* (Melbourne) 11 Sept. (Suppl.) 2/2 He established a sod-hut house of accommodation near the market reserve, hired out horses to inspecting visitors, practised as a bush lawyer. **1881** J.C.F. JOHNSON *To Mount Browne & Back* 13 An 'Adelaide man', who happened to be a bit of a bush lawyer, was getting the best of an argument. **1898** T. HAYDON *Sporting Reminisc.* 117 'Bush lawyers' . . would argue for hours over any conceivable subject, if they could only get an audience patient enough to listen to them. **1906** *Bulletin* (Sydney) 7 June 40/2 When Dan was released he talked big about illegal arrest (he's a bit of a bush-lawyer). **1928** G.H. WILKINS *Undiscovered Aust.* 88 The sundowner was a 'bush lawyer'; legally he was in the right and he got his cheque. **1940** W. HATFIELD *Into (Great?) Unfenced* 248 Klaas was careful that day how he handled this 'bush lawyer' as he was wont to describe any citizen citing his rights under the law. **1955** D. NILAND *Shiralee* 234 I've had all the bush lawyers and all the bush Solomons talking to me and they've had the world's problems carved up and solved. **1967** F. HARDY *Billy Borker yarns Again* 135 Well, in the old days in the bush, there were no registered lawyers, so some half-shrewd mug, usually a barber, would set himself up to advise all and sundry. So now anyone who throws around a lot of free advice is called a bush lawyer. **1976** B. SUTTON *Comrade George* 47 Prof. Edwards . . would have been a bush lawyer except that he lived in the city. **1985** *Daily Mirror* (Sydney) 25 July 41/2 (*heading*) Bush lawyer fires off telling shots.

2. A member of the legal profession who has a rural practice.

1976 N.V. WALLACE *Bush Lawyer* 181 A bush lawyer is perhaps in an even better position to study humanity in all its aspects than parson, priest, or doctor.

3. LAWYER VINE.

[N.Z. **1853** C.W. ADAMS *Spring in Canterbury Settlement* 44 Hour after hour we toiled on, sometimes making our way through masses of thorn, and the long and clinging bramble, called by colonists the 'bush-lawyer', sometimes scrambling down steep banks.] **1878** *Austral.: Monthly Mag.* I. 36 The 'bush lawyer' twists and twines, half strangling the eucalypti. **1905** A. SEARCY *In Northern Seas* 15 There is another pet plant, known as the 'waitawhile' or 'bush lawyer', both very appropriate names.

bushman.

1. One skilled and experienced in travelling through bush country and able to do so without getting lost or into difficulty.

1825 B. FIELD *Geogr. Mem. N.S.W.* 369 Set out . . from Bong Bong . . taking with us Joseph Wild (a constable of the district of Argyle, well known as a bushman on similar excursions to the one we were about to take). **1838** *S. Austral. Rec.* (London) 8 Aug. 86, I have just returned from an excursion into the interior, in which I was . . escorted by my trusty bushman, Tom Davis. **1841** G. ARDEN *Recent Information Port Phillip* 33 The bell-bird . . is always indicative of the proximity of water, a circumstance which the inexperienced bushman should bear in mind. **1845** *Cumberland Times* (Parramatta) 1 Nov. 4/1 Port Macquarie—to which the only road is one that requires a bushman's skill to make out, and no dray could possibly travel on. **1846** *Sydney Morning Herald* 20 Oct. 2/5, I have been a great bushman of late; I have had two excursions, occupying between them thirty-one days, and have ridden during that period about eight hundred miles, and am happy to say I stood the journey well. **1848** *Adelaide Miscellany* 5 Aug. 7 The Torrens flows through the plains to the Reed Beds near the sea-coast, where, like a bad bushman, it loses itself. **1865** J.M. STUART *Explorations in Aust.* p. xii, Mr Stuart's qualities as a practised Bushman are unrivalled, and he has always succeeded in bringing his party back without loss of life. **1870** J. BONWICK *Last Tasmanians* 186 The guides of the parties were either white Bushmen, or Natives. **1875** CAMPBELL & WILKS *Early Settlement Qld.* 34 They declared that he was no bushman but merely a good navigator. **1889** J.H.L. ZILLMAN *Past & Present Austral. Life* 117 No true bushman ever allows a black to follow him. **1909** *Emu* VIII. 243 Any person wishing to explore these scrubs needs to be a good bushman, possessed of a good bump of locality. **1924** C.E.W. BEAN *Official Hist. Aust. 1914–18* II. 812 In bush scouting at least the Turk was equally daring. Thus . . an Australian scout, a good bushman, who was lying out only twenty yards in advance of the trenches . . was found stabbed through the heart, with his skull broken in. **1931** M.M. BANKS *Memories Pioneer Days Qld.* 43 My father, as a good bushman, wished to ride to Brisbane by an untried route, 'blazing' a track through the scrub trees. **1942** H.H. PECK *Mem. of Stockman* 106 A wonderful bushman, able to strike across new country without tracks for hundreds of miles and never out in his reckoning. **1955** F. LANE *Patrol to Kimberleys* 80 Seasoned bushmen have come into the Kimberleys an' have got themselves lost so good they've never been seen again. **1965** H. ATKINSON *Reckoning* 98 Requiring only to obey instructions, the bushman's sense of direction and distance had been unalerted in them. **1979** DOUGLAS & HEATHCOTE *Far Cry* 107 My infallible bushman's experience at finding my way through trackless bush was no help to me here.

2. *Obs.* BUSHRANGER *n.* 1.

1827 'OFFICER OF LINE' *Military Sketch-Bk.* II. 322 She pointed to a man lying in the long grass, and bleeding profusely—it was a desperate Bushman of the name of Collyer. **1830** *Austral.* (Sydney) 5 Mar. 3/2 Here we met another curiosity of the morning. It was no less than the ruins of a hut, belonging to the notorious bushman, Michael Howe. **1847** A. MARJORIBANKS *Travels N.S.W.* 170 Many of the assigned convicts . . who were approaching the termination of the period of their probation, have, by the harshness of their task-masters, been driven into the woods to lead the lives of savages, and to become the terror of the surrounding neighbourhood. Such . . are the bushmen of New South Wales. **1863** J. BONWICK *Wild White Man* 17 The poor creature, alarmed for his safety from the dreaded bushmen, tried in vain to thwart his intention. **1897** M. CLARKE *Stories Aust.* 104 The bushranger, in high glee, filled a 'goblet'. . . 'There!' cried Howe; 'these fires have cost a pretty penny. Here's success to the bushman's tinder-box, and a blazing fire to his enemies!'

3. One who lives in the country as opposed to the town; one who displays the manners, practical skills, etc., of a country-dweller, with connotations often depending on whether the perception of the user is urban or rural; cf. BUSH B. 3 b.

1832 *Colonial Times* (Hobart) 21 Mar., What! go to Swan River and be sea-sick all the passage, and die before you get there; and, perhaps, not get a husband after all, or only get a bushman? **1836** *Tegg's Monthly Mag.* (Sydney) I. 134 Sydney, disagreeable as it is to the bushman on all occasions, was absolutely intolerable, even to the citizens. **1842** *Melbourne Times* 18 June 4/1 His flocks encrease, and the wool pays all, While his generous board's at the traveller's call; By the clear river side he improves his time—Oh, the Bushman's the stay of Australia's clime. **1852** S. MOSSMAN *Gold Regions Aust.* (ed. 2) 78 The stockholder, who is simply the country settler, like a farmer in England, would fain individualize his class, under the cognomen of 'Australian Bushmen'. Consequently, he dresses *outré*, wears a beard, affects Bobadilism, and looks with contempt upon the towns'-folk. **1862** A. POLEHAMPTON *Kangaroo Land* 234, I put up at an inn where were congregated a number of Bush men, who were drinking and fighting when I arrived, and had been . . all day. **1867** A.K. COLLINS *Waddy Mundoee* p. iii, Being a bushman, and loving the face of nature better than that of art, I would not live in those days to come. **1880** J.B. STEVENSON *Seven Yrs. Austral. Bush* 33 He was a genuine bushman, and I don't believe he had been in a town half a dozen times in his life. **1883** R.E.N. TWOPENY *Town Life Aust.* 243 Everyone who lives in the country, whether on a station or in a farm, but not in a township, is called a 'bushman', although properly speaking, this designation only applies to a person who lives in the 'bush' or unsettled country. **1892** H. LAWSON *Lett.* (1970) 50, I have already found out that Bushmen are the biggest liars that ever the Lord created. **1893** F.W.L. ADAMS *Australs.* 13 In another hundred years the man of the interior—the veritable 'bushman'—will be as far removed from the man of the sea-slope as the Northern Frenchman from the Southern. **1906** W.A. HORN *Notes by Nomad* 81 The term Bushman is applied to all who live on the outer fringe of civilisation. **1911** A. SEARCY *By Flood & Field* 228 She was a fine woman, and as good a 'bushman' as anyone around. **1916** V.G. DWYER *Conquering Hal* 133 In the country—on the farms clinging round the edge of the towns, on the 'cocky's' places within a few miles coo-ee of the sea . . you may meet the sawny country bumpkin. You've got to go out beyond—far out—to meet the bushmen. **1926** *Smith's Weekly* (Sydney) 22 May 19/7 An assorted crowd of bushmen and townspeople. **1934** WARBURTON & ROBERTSON *Buffaloes* 25 A bushman's not a bushman without a stockwhip. **1942** *Welcome to Aust.* 18 Aborigines or blacks (not bushmen; bushmen are white men who are at home in the outback) number from 50,000 to 60,000. **1944** M.J. O'REILLY *Bowyangs & Boomerangs* 62 The troopers up there were as different from the city police as a bushman's word is from a politician's promise. **1951** G. FARWELL *Outside Track* 19 The qualities of the bushman are those we have come to regard as specifically Australian. **1954** H.G. LAMOND *Manx Star* 75 The men pulled up, in the manner of bushmen, to have a yarn. **1965** M. PATCHETT *Last Warrior* 239 The thought of the coming of a handsome, moneyed bushman into her life. **1972** ANDERSON & BLAKE *J.S. Neilson* 5 He had the attributes of a skilful bushman: sturdy, self-reliant, a strong axeman and fencer, a shepherd and drover with practical knowledge of animal husbandry, a teamster and stationhand. **1982** R. HALL *Just Relations* 336 Course I'm only an old bushman sittin up on my little mountain like Jacky; and you've travelled the world.

4. A rural employee, esp. an (unskilled) labourer able to work in a range of capacities.

1843 J.F. BENNETT *Hist. & Descr. Acct. S.A.* 101 Stockmen . . searching for stray cattle . . are often in the 'Bush' for days. . . When night comes, the horse is unsaddled and . . the bushman . . covers himself with his blanket. **1849** R.J. MANN *Emigrant's Guide Aust.* 17 These Bushmen are altogether engaged in tending and managing the extensive cattle droves of the interior, in the neighbourhood of their masters' stations. **1850** J.W. MELVIN *Emigrant's Guide to Colonies* 21 It is much to be regretted that many labourers, or bushmen as they are called. **1855** G.H. WATHEN *Golden Colony* 34 The servants of the settlers, including shepherds, stock-keepers, and others, formed a fourth class, known as *Bushmen*. **1879** 'AUSTRALIAN' *Adventures Qld.* 2 They were bullock-drivers, shepherds, shearers, sawyers, and bushmen of all sorts—men who were accustomed to rough it; who had the constitutions of horses, and could work in earnest when they did work. **1891** D. FERGUSON *Vicissitudes Bush Life* 30 On the station several men were employed throughout the year—a bullock driver, two bushmen, and the home-station shepherd. **1895** J. KIRBY *Old Times in Bush* 156 It was usual to hire a couple of rough carpenters (bushmen they were called) to erect buildings. **1901** F. WILKINSON *Aust. at Front* 67 Then came the 'Bushmen', a corps of boundary-riders, station-hands, fencers, shearers and general 'rouse-abouts'—all those occupations, in fact, which go to make up life in the 'back-blocks' of Australia. **1918** B. REYNOLDS *Dawn Asper* 176 Tom Dalton, the young splitter . . arrived . . riding as bushmen only ride. **1933** C.E.W. BEAN *Official Hist. Aust. 1914–18* IV. 214 (*note*) Sgt. W.J. James (No 1364; 50th Bn.) Bushman, of Broken Hill, N.S.W. **1943** H.G. LAMOND *From Tariaro to Ross Roy* 27 Shearers then were bushmen, all round men, who did all classes of station work.

5. *Timber-getter*, see TIMBER.

1847 A. HARRIS *Settlers & Convicts* (1953) 86 If I wanted employment as a bushman I could not miss it here; as there were sawyers, splitters, squarers, firewood getters scattered through the bush hereabouts in all directions. **1896** M. HORNSBY *Old Time Echoes Tas.* 62 He requested to be allowed to change his clothes; this was no uncommon request with Bushmen, i.e. sawyers and splitters, in those days. **1900** *Bulletin* (Sydney) 9 June 32/2 How did I become a bushman? Well I believe I started up Parramatta way chopping down Geebung trees and 'Hellfires'. **1910** *Huon Times* (Franklin) 7 May 2/4 Owing to the heavy rain the bushmen have not been able to work, and so the mills have been closed for a couple of days. **1916** T. WARLOW *Mirage & Mulga* 85 Many men make a living by felling the high trees . . and splitting them into shingles for roofing houses, posts and rails for fencing land, and sawing others into boards and posts. . . The men that do this sort of work are called bushmen or timber-getters. **1920** *Huon Times* (Franklin) 14 Dec. 2/6 There was a big tree across the Arve road and he could not get a man to cut it out and do practically bushman's work for 11s. a day when other men in the bush were getting £1 a day. **1980** *Sydney Morning Herald* 30 May 7/2 A bushman out looking for timber to cut reported that he almost tripped over a tiger sleeping on a rock.

6. SWAGMAN.

1872 G.S. BADEN-POWELL *New Homes for Old Country* 428 The multitudes of 'swagmen', or 'bushmen', wandering about the country will do as little as possible for a living. **1889** H. EGBERT *Pretty Cockey* 46 The swag is almost as much a part of the bushman, as the shell is of the snail or cockle. **1896** H. LAWSON *In Days when World was Wide* 95, I suppose he's tramping somewhere

where the bushmen carry swags, Cadging round the wretched stations with his empty tucker-bags. **1909** *Bulletin* (Sydney) 30 Sept. 13/2 The white flour of the bushman's life does not often bloom into damper nowadays. **1915** N. DUNCAN *Austral. Byways* 112 The bushmen travel amazingly light. A billy-can and a blanket—the 'swag' of the bush—are equipment enough for any frugal man in places within reach. **1954** *Bulletin* (Sydney) 16 June 12/4 All this talk about 'blueys' and 'Matildas' may be O.K. for you blokes in the 'inside' country, but bushmen in the Territory and Kimberleys always refer to 'swags'.

7. *pl.* Abbrev. of *Bushman's Contingent*; in *sing.*, a member of this.

1900 *Truth* (Sydney) 4 Feb. 5/1 Another man failed in horsemanship for both the previous contingents, but managed to pass for the Bushmen. **1901** *Bulletin* (Sydney) 4 May 32/2 The derider of work was now one of a 'mob' . . upon their way to South Africa. He was a full-blown 'Bushman'—a 'Soldier of the Queen'. **1901** *Western Champion* (Barcaldine) 16 July 8/3 Our only idea of 'bushmen' are the big, strapping fellows who have been, and are still, doing Australia so much honor in South Africa. **1931** *Century of Journalism* 349 Of the New South Welshmen, about half were regular troops, while the remainder constituted a special force known as the 'Bushmen'.

8. In special collocations: **Bushman's Bible,** a name for *The Bulletin* (see BULLY); **bushman's clock,** *settler's clock*, see SETTLER 3 b.; **Bushman's Contingent,** a body of volunteer troops equipped through public subscription for service in the Boer War; **Bushman's Home** *obs.*, a guest house catering chiefly for country-dwellers (see quot. 1868).

1888 *Bulletin* (Sydney) 15 Dec. 5/4 (*heading*) *The Bulletin* is the **Bushman's Bible.** **1903** P.F. ROWLAND *New Nation* 204 A backblocks' shearer once told him that 'if he had only sixpence left he would buy the *Bulletin* with it'. Whatever may be thought of the anti-religious and separatist principles of this 'Bushman's Bible', it must be conceded to have done a very real service to Australia in the encouragement of literature. **1915** *Bulletin* (Sydney) 7 Jan. 14/3 Australia's unique illustrated paper, so popular in the Bush as to be nicknamed the Bushman's Bible—the Sydney Bulletin. **1948** R. RAVEN-HART *Canoe in Aust.* 187 'Bulletin' . . still influential out-back, 'Bushman's Bible'. **1973** R. EDWARDS *Austral. Bawdy Ballads* 4 The Sydney *Bulletin*, known as the 'Bushman's Bible' because of its keen appreciation of outback life. **1846** C.P. HODGSON *Reminisc. Aust.* 165 The Laughing Jackass is a comical creature . . well and truly stiled the **Bushman's clock.** **1862** C. ASPINALL *Three Yrs. Melbourne* 204, I heard the laughing jackass, which is . . from its regular habits, called the Bushman's clock. **1880** R. ROWE *Roughing It* 45 It is sometimes called the 'bushman's clock', because it laughs before sunrise, at noon, and at sundown. **1917** *Emu* XVI. 236 Now . . they [*sc.* kookaburras] have become plentiful again, and the 'bushman's clock' chimes regularly every morning. **1962** MARSHALL & DRYSDALE *Journey among Men* 90 To a south-eastern Australian a kookaburra that doesn't laugh is a bit of a fraud, for, from the earliest colonial days, the so-called bushman's clock has held a strong place in the affections of our people. **1970** D.C. BUTTS *Down Under* 58 In some areas, the kookaburra is found in such numbers that his morning call is known as the 'bushman's clock'. **1900** *Pastoral Times* (Deniliquin) 17 Feb. 2/3 When it was first decided to form a **bushmen's contingent** to go to South Africa Mr Frank V. Weir . . was one of the first to volunteer for service. **1978** G. HALL *River still Flows* 15 Those early British setbacks had heightened the fever of excitement in our country, and soon the recruitment of a 'Bushmen's Contingent' began. **1868** W.M. HUGO *Hist. First Bushmen's Club* (1872) 14 Some few months ago we called public attention to the importance of establishing a **Bushmen's Home**, in order to keep poor fellows who come down from the country out of the hands of harpies who prey upon them on their occasional visits to Adelaide. **1872** *Illustr. Sydney News* 13 Apr. 55/2 Some such considerations have led to the establishment of 'Bushmens Homes' in Adelaide and Melbourne. Already these have worked wonders in favour of the bushmen who periodically visit the chief towns of these colonies. **1872** W.M. HUGO *Hist. First Bushmen's Club* 10 It has been suggested that the establishmen of a Bushman's Home at Burra . . (on the same principles as a first-class Sailors' Home) . . would be of great benefit. **1875** *Illustr. Adelaide News* xiii. 2/4 *The Bushmen's Club*—It is proposed to raise funds to complete the Bushmen's Home so as to provide accommodation for the numerous applicants. **1921** *Bulletin* (Sydney) 19 May 20/4 Thanks to the people who run the 'Bushmen's Homes' in many outback towns. . . You just blow in, unroll your own nap on a decent bed, boil the 'knock me silly' and grill a chop.

Hence **bushmanlike** *a.*

1862 H. BROWN *Vic. as I found It* 89, I had crept up to the horses in . . a very scientific, bushman-like manner. **1894** *Bulletin* (Sydney) 10 Nov. 15/3 The other day a man of bushmanlike appearance brought to Melb. Hospital a boy whose face and hands were black as a veteran billy. **1951** G. FARWELL *Outside Track* 23 Bushmanlike, he never showed surprise, and never asked a question.

bushmanship. The ability to travel through, or live in, inhospitable country, esp. that which is unfamiliar and unsettled, without getting into difficulty.

1848 H.W. HAYGARTH *Recoll. Bush Life* 134 Notwithstanding all that has been said of the great sagacity of savages in tracking, and of their quickness in catching a distant sound, I strongly suspect that the white man, when he has been accustomed to this kind of 'bushmanship' at an early age, generally proves his superior. **1849** A. HARRIS *Emigrant Family* (1967) 142 Through the ignorance of their hut-mate of everything connected with bushmanship, they both hurried off . . with an agreement that whichever of them met with him should koo-eh. **1854** S. SIDNEY *Gallops & Gossips* 46 Robert's consummate bushmanship led him the true course, even when we were going fastest; every cattle-track was familiar to him; and bits of stone and grass and broken twigs, which I should have passed unregarded, were to him plain proofs of where the black stallion or his pursuers had passed. **1893** S. NEWLAND *Paving Way* 108 Out in that scrub, to lose the points of the compass is to lose your life, unless your luck be greater than your bushmanship. **1928** B. SPENCER *Wanderings in Wild Aust.* 14 No amount of bushmanship will suffice to take horses and human beings across more than a certain extent of absolutely dry country. **1933** W.L. OWEN *Cossack Gold* 73 Bushmanship was of the essence of the contract with nature. **1957** F. CLUNE *Fortune Hunters* 70 The wonderful endurance and skill in bushmanship of the quarry and the hunters. **1967** M. SELLARS *Carramar* 46 In recognition of their bushmanship these two young men were made Fellows of the Royal Geographical Society and were given grants of money.

bushrange, *v.* [Back-formation f. BUSHRANGER *n.* 1.] *trans.* To hold up and rob (travellers, dwellings, etc.); to steal. Also *absol.*, and *fig.*

1841 *Omnibus & Sydney Spectator* 4 Dec. 75/1, I, in company with two other men bushranging, was going along the road. **1850** *Bell's Life in Sydney* 15 June 3/1 Then black mugs an' white mugs can run a cleer race, Tal they bushrange the counthry right out uv a face. **1920** H.F. MOLLARD *Humour of Road* 65 Me mate had escaped and was shot while bushranging a farm. **1976** C.D. MILLS *Hobble Chains & Greenhide* 123 They were anathema to station managers in the matter of 'bushranging' feed for their bullocks. As well to stand between a lioness and her cubs as a bullocky on a bare route with feed through the bordering fence.

bushranger. [f. BUSH *n.* + *ranger* one who ranges over a tract of country. Prob. of U.S. origin: cf. BUSH *n.* and see Mathews *bossloper* and *bushranger.*] Also *attrib.*

1. One who engages in armed robbery, escaping into, or living in, the bush in the manner of an outlaw; orig. an escaped convict subsisting in the bush, often by resort to robbery (see quot. 1822).

1801 J. ELDER et al. *Jrnl. Rio to Port Jackson* 5 Mar. 25 It is said also, which we are very sorry to observe, that of these Bushrangers, that Williams . . is one. **1805** *Sydney Gaz.* 17 Feb., Three men whose appearance sanctioned the suspicion of their being bush-rangers. **1805** *Ibid.* 10 Nov., John Winch, a Bush Ranger and notorious character now in custody. **1809** *HRA* (1916) 1st Ser. VII. 161 It is a momentous concern that a Set of Free Booters (Bush Rangers as they are called) should be increasing in their numbers throughout the Country. **1810** *Sydney Gaz.* 8 Dec., *James Hutchinson*, the notorious bush-ranger, has again taken to the woods. **1816** *Hobart Town Gaz.* 3 Aug., The Robbery committed upon Mr John Beamont by one of Banditties of Bush Rangers . . was . . at his house near Jericho. **1822** J.T. BIGGE *Rep. State Colony N.S.W.* 108 The convicts assigned to military officers, according to the custom and necessities of that day, were obliged to furnish to their masters, and to procure for themselves, a certain quantity of kangaroo flesh; and having first gone into the woods for these temporary supplies of food, they gradually acquired a knowledge of the country, and of the means of supporting themselves in it. To this at length they were driven; and the predatory habits of these men, who have since received the common appellation of bush-rangers, have continued from the year 1805, with more or less of violence and rapacity, until the month of October in the year 1818. **1828** *Austral. Almanack* 87 *A Man holding a Ticket of Leave*, who shall apprehend Two Runaways, or one Bushranger . . shall have his Ticket of Leave extended to two or more Districts. **1836** *Tegg's Monthly Mag.* (Sydney) I. 242 The colonial term bush-ranger is applied equally to the outlaw, who attempts to gain a livelihood by levying contributions from the passing traveller, and to the simple runaway, who absconds from his master's employment with the hope of passing himself off as a free man. **1842** *Colonial Observer* (Sydney) 2 Mar. 172/1 Mr Wiseman's dray was stopped on the Wollombi Road . . by three or four armed bushrangers, and robbed of its contents. **1853** J. SHERER *Gold Finder Aust.* 16 Gangs of mounted bush-rangers, masked, and with pistols, are infesting all the roads, stopping the travellers, and even the gold transports. **1862** G.T. LLOYD *Thirty-Three Yrs. Tas. & Vic.* 158 No-one can tell Bush-rangers from Bush-gentlemen in such wilds as these. **1882** J.A. REID *Austral. Reader* 93 In October, 1878, the bushrangers known as the 'Kelly Gang' began their career of crime by murdering three policemen near the town of Mansfield. **1908** *Truth* (Sydney) 11 Oct. 1/5 The police might do worse than keep an eye on some of Sydney's picnicking rendezvous at holiday time for female bush-rangers. A few days ago a man reported that he had been assaulted and robbed in the bush at one of such resorts by two well-dressed young women. **1918** *Huon Times* (Franklin) 7 June 6/1 A mysterious bushranger is stated to be at large in the Rockvale district. **1938** F. CLUNE *Free & Easy Land* 106 Bashed on the boko by binghies or bushrangers, or both. **1955** F. LANE *Patrol to Kimberleys* 46 The King Leopold Range had to be crossed before they would be within striking distance of the two white bush-rangers. **1971** *Bulletin* (Sydney) 9 Oct. 23/3 W.A. has its own home-grown bushranger. . . He took his family to the bush about 100 miles north of Perth and supplemented his income by raiding farmhouses. **1978** R.H. CONQUEST *Dusty Distances* 53 It was our first, and last, meeting with bushrangers. There were many armed robberies during the Depression years, but there were no recorded instances of real bushranging—armed men, mounted on blood horses, holding up mail coaches and robbing banks. **1981** D. STUART *I think I'll Live* 141 Y'know, a Pommy bushranger, they called 'em highwaymen 'cause there's not enough bush in England for 'em to be called bushrangers.

2. *Obs.* One skilled in travelling through the bush; BUSHMAN 1.

1805 Banks Papers 19 July XX., If the Bush rangers will always bring plants from the remote parts of their tours, I can form a good idea of what distance they have been. **1825** *Austral.* (Sydney) 17 Feb. 1 We regret much that ever Mr Hume allowed such a person as Mr Hovell, who knows so little of the interior of the country, and possessed of such poor abilities as a bushranger, to be of his party. **1827** P. CUNNINGHAM *Two Yrs. in N.S.W.* II. 157 If pushing into a country at a distance from settlers, a pack-horse with provisions ought to accompany you. A steady white man who is a good bush-ranger, and a black native, complete your train. **1832** E.O.G. SHANN *Cattle Chosen* (1926) 147, I suffer little inconvenience for I am now an old bushranger. **1832** *Sydney Herald* 9 Jan. 3/3 A party of the Mounted Police were about starting for the purpose of bringing to the settlement the runaways from Sir John Jamison who were reported by Barker the Bushranger to have settled some little distance in the interior. **1835** *Colonist* (Sydney) 2 Apr. 108/2 An experienced bush-ranger told us there were certain wild cattle belonging to the Colonial Press, running at large around Sydney. **1843** J. HOOD *Aust. & East* 176, I confess I was again induced to wish that my boys had remained at home in Britain instead of becoming bushrangers in New Holland.

3. *transf.* and *fig.*

1855 F.H. WILSON Overland Expedition No. 2 19 Mar., He abused them terribly and said that we were a regular lot of bushrangers—going from one man's run to another and eating off all the grass—and did not care for anybody. **1861** 'OLD BUSHMAN' *Bush Wanderings* 49 The *Domestic Cat* sometimes wanders away from a station and turns bushranger. **1862** *Western Post* (Mudgee) 2 Aug. 3/2 Apart from the evil of a large quantity of grass—which is now very scarce—being consumed by these intruders [*sc.* travelling sheep], there is the risk of the sheep on the river being deteriorated, by accidentally mixing with these low-bred and ill-favoured bushrangers. **1900** *Western Champion* (Barcaldine) 27 Nov. 9/1 The Imperial men don't understand our fellows in the least. They refer to us as bushrangers, and all sorts of things complimentary. **1907** *Truth* (Sydney) 1 Sept. 1/4 The political bushrangers who have collared the £600. **1923** *Aussie* (Sydney) Dec. 7/1 This swine of a publican's a bushranger orright. **1932** D.B. O'CONNOR *Belle of Barrine* 4 The bushrangers from abroad have already sent out their agent to divide us and spy out the land. **1954** T. RONAN *Vision Splendid* 113 Member of all the big racing clubs down south. He don't like having to meet bushrangers like me and Mick on level terms. **1965** G.H. FEARNSIDE *Golden Ram* 109, 'I think I'm on to something you can really sink your teeth into'... 'Yeah? The bushranger's back in business?' **1977** R. MACKLIN *Paper Castle* 138 Basically, I suppose, everyone has the public interest at heart. But by Christ some of those bushrangers on the other side go the long way round.

bushranging, *vbl. n.*

1. The practice of the bushranger (sense 1); the committing of armed robbery by one who escapes into the bush; orig. living as a fugitive in the bush. Also *attrib.*

1813 *HRA* (1921) 3rd Ser. II. 441 There are no means which can be devised that will so effectually destroy the System of Bush-ranging, as a rigid observance of this order. **1818** T.E. WELLS *M. Howe* (1945) 36 The system of Bushranging .. might now be considered annihilated. **1820** C. JEFFREYS *Van Dieman's Land* 136 Nothing therefore can prevent a recurrence to the system of Bush ranging, but a total removal of every means of indulgence in the immoderate use of ardent spirits. **1825** *Howe's Weekly Commercial Express* (Sydney) 25 July 2 Bushranging is not infrequent in the vicinity of Bathurst. **1829** *Sydney Monitor* 24 Oct. 4/1 The only way and the cheapest way to prevent bushranging, is to give the iron-gangs better food and more of it, and to cover their nakedness, and to treat them with humanity. **1841** *Launceston Courier* 25 Oct. 2/4 This morning the last sentence of the law was carried into effect upon the person of Joseph Broomfield, convicted at the last session of the court upon the capital offence of bushranging. **1847** A. HARRIS *Settlers & Convicts* (1953) 10 He got twenty-five lashes for drunkenness, twenty-five for insolence, fifty for bushranging. **1857** *Illustr. Jrnl. Australasia* III. 91 Every provincial paper contains fresh reports of bushranging, a crime which appears to be very prevalent. **1864** *Port Denison Times* 2 Apr. 3/1 For the last two years bushranging has been carried on successfully in New South Wales, and is now showing itself here. **1874** J.J. HALCOMBE *Emigrant & Heathen* 86 The same immunity from robbery and violence prevailed throughout the greater part of the colony in respect of '*bushranging*', as it is called, or, in English language, highway robbery. **1886** R. HENTY *Australiana* 177 He commenced his bushranging tactics under the *rôle* of being the 'swagman's' friend. **1890** MRS H.P. MARTIN *Under Gum Tree* 197 Australian bushranging may now be ranked among the lost arts. **1904** *Bulletin* (Sydney) 4 Aug. 16/3 After a month's bushranging .. a blackfellow who escaped from Albany lock-up, has been recaptured. **1928** R.M. MACDONALD *Opals & Gold* 183 A well organized bush-ranging business. **1946** F. CLUNE *Try Nothing Twice* 18 In the streets and alleys we played 'Bobbies and Bushies', which was a memory of the bushranging period of Australia's wild west. **1955** N. PULLIAM *I traveled Lonely Land* 44 Kelly was hanged in 1880 and bushranging dwindled and finally died away.

2. *Obs.* Travelling cross-country, esp. in an unfamiliar or unsettled region.

1821 Macarthur Papers XII. 57, I reached Home in good time, and in much better health than when I set out bushranging. This sort of Life is to me an efficacious, and at the same time agreeable restorative. Roaming in lonely independence thro' almost trackless wilds, and contemplating without interruption the vast Sublimity of nature, we lose the recollection of those unpleasant circumstances which within the influence of Sydney's Pollutions continually to [*sic*] occur to harrass the Mind. **1839** W.H. LEIGH *Reconnoitering Voyages* 129 Night came on, and we again sought the bush, like all bush ranging, 'The mixture as before'.

3. *fig.* Also as *ppl. a.*

1939 K. TENNANT *Foveaux* 425 The once notorious Bud Pellager .. had taken to a mild and lucrative form of bushranging as owner of a garage on the Main Western Highway. **1951** D. CUSACK *Say no to Death* (1959) 258 You're a bush-ranging, cowardly old bitch! You've black-marketed here all the war, and you're black-marketing still. **1965** L. HAYLEN *Big Red* 36 What in thunder do you mean by pre-empting my lodge gates? It's sheer bushranging.

bush telegram. BUSH TELEGRAPH *n.* 2.

1894 J.M. MACDONALD *Thunderbolt* 143 These bush telegrams were a source of wonder to the police from the old country. A lighted fire, a burning tree, a slip-rail tied up, a tree allowed to fall across the road, blazed trees, the smoke of a leaf fire rising high in the air—these all had different meanings, cyphers to the bushrangers who could read them. **1913** J.B. CASTIEAU *Reminisc. Detective-Inspector Christie* 123 If any of the settlers, 'cockatoos', or wood splitters had noticed them, a bush telegram would have been sent through the forest immediately to warn the gang. **1927** A. CROMBIE *After Sixty Yrs.* 150 By some occult means, known far out as a mulga wire, or bush telegram, the approach of the visitors was conveyed to the people of Boulia from Winton, a distance of 225 miles. **1937** W.R. GLASSON *Musings in my Saddle* 117 As a system of 'bush telegrams' prevailed, information of the approach of the Inspector of Selections usually came in ample time. **1980** *Sporting Globe* (Melbourne) 1 July 2/7 Evidently the 'bush telegram' is .. fast as Carlton knew of South's plans to play Teasdale almost as quickly as the Swans.

bush telegraph, *n.*

1. *Hist.* One who alerts a bushranger to the movements of police or to a potential victim. Also *fig.*

1864 *Bell's Life in Sydney* 23 Apr. 2/5 Two or three noted 'bush-telegraphs' were among the crowd who had come in from the country to obtain one more look at the robbers. **1865** J.J. WESTWOOD *Jrnl.* 369 A number of men I saw about the verandah of the hotel, wearing cabbage tree hats, with their horses secured to the posts, were 'bush telegraphs', or men employed by bushrangers as spies, to inform them of the movements of the police. **1880** *Bulletin* (Sydney) 3 July 1/4 There were plenty of deeply-dyed villains, treacherous 'bush telegraphs', splendid horses, and a plucky priest. **1888** G.O. PRESHAW *Banking under Difficulties* 90, I have seen the bushrangers and they have been on the look out for me. Still I am glad to say I never got into their clutches. Oftentimes when at meals at the hotel I have been asked, 'When are you going home?' Noticing the bush telegraph close to or opposite me, I would reply, 'Tomorrow morning early.' As soon as the meal was over I would saddle up and away. **1894** *Western Champion* (Barcaldine) 5 June 2/2 That bloke was one of the Murray crowd, or one of their bush telegraphs. **1907** C. MACALISTER *Old Pioneering Days* 256 Gardiner's mates that day were Johnny O'Malley, and Dick T--r, a Fish River native, the smartest 'bush telegraph' of Gardiner's gang. **1916** *Truth* (Sydney) 18 June 12/7 Morgan's 'bush telegraphs' assembled at Mrs Negro's public-house in the 'Federal City', of course without the knowledge of the landlady, who was a highly reputable woman. **1920** B. CRONIN *Timber Wolves* 210 Them [*sc.* white cockies] and the red-bills seem to hold the job of bush telegraph for the rest of the wild things. **1926** M. FORREST *Hibiscus Heart* 199 Yet they felt secure enough, for they had had word by their special bush telegraph how MacPherson and his stockman had ridden over the ranges. **1955** STEWART & KEESING *Austral. Bush Ballads* 32 They studied all the time To guard against 'bush telegraphs' who sympathize with crime. **1967** S. SHUMACK *Autobiogr.* 29 Archibald, the proprietor of an hotel, was also arrested, together with a man named Taylor, one of their 'bush telegraphs'. **1976** B. SCOTT *Compl. Bk. Austral. Folk Lore* 343 Hall was betrayed by one of his 'bush telegraphs'.

2. An informal network by means of which information is conveyed in remote areas; the information or message so conveyed; a rumour; MULGA WIRE 1. Also *attrib.*

1864 *Sydney Punch* 13 Aug. 91/1 The following correspondence has been forwarded to us for publication. It was carried on through the medium of 'Bush Telegraphs'. **1900** H. LAWSON *Over Sliprails* 107 The nearest squatter's wife .. arranged (by bush telegraph) to drive over next morning. **1916** J.L. BEESTON *Five Months at Anzac* 35 Bush Telegraph .. is a tortoise in its movements compared with a Beachogram. **1933** S. GRIFFITHS *Rolling Stone on Turf* 200 In 'bush telegraph' fashion the news had spread far and wide. **1939** J.W. COLLINSON *Early Days Cairns* 56 The visits of revenue men were generally well-advertised along the line by bush telegraph. **1944** J. HETHERINGTON *Austral. Soldier* 15 Soldiers have a bush telegraph system of their own. The wildest furphies travel over it, but sometimes it carries the truth. **1947** M. MACLEAN *Drummond of Far West* 40 The report still goes that the shearers sent word by 'bush telegraph'. **1965** D. MARTIN *Hero of Too* 246 The bush telegraph had it that her lover had struck up a friendship with a rich landholder's son from Balranald. **1972** K. WILLEY *Tales Big Country* 159 Word filtered back on the 'bush telegraph' that he had been paid more than 2,000 dollars. **1981** *Sydney Morning Herald* 7 Aug. 16/3 Those seeking snapper off Broken Bay found them on the south marks. Those who were not linked to the bush telegraph went north and bombed out.

3. A means of long-distance communication used by Aborigines, usu. employing smoke signals; the message so conveyed; MULGA WIRE 2.

1930 A.E. YARRA *Vanishing Horsemen* 42 It was a signal that could be seen for miles—the smoke signal of the aboriginals: the bush telegraph. **1934** WARBURTON & ROBERTSON *Buffaloes* 112 The bush telegraph is the blacks' counterpart to our Morse code. They build a fire and place on it large quantities of green leaves or grass, and when a column of smoke has arisen, they break it at various intervals by putting on and removing a blanket or green bough. **1946** L. RHYS *My Ship* 110 It had been picked up from natives who had received it by 'bush telegraph', a quicker and more reliable method of communication than most. **1952** A.M. DUNCAN-KEMP *Where Strange Paths go Down* 11 Smoke signals, the bush telegraph which relays in some intricate secret code, tribal news to the outside world. **1967** M. SELLARS *Carramar* 49 The blacks had a different kind of radio—bush telegraph. Thin spirals of smoke curl into the still morning air as they signal to one another in scattered camps.

Hence **bush telegraphist** *n.*, **bush telegraphy** *n.*

1965 D. MARTIN *Hero of Too* 172 Peter was the greatest **bush telegraphist** of his time. Nothing went on but Quinn knew of it. **1900** *Truth* (Sydney) 17 June 6/3 The nature of the country and the system of **bush telegraphy** prevented arrests. **1922** 'J. BUSHMAN' *In Musgrave Ranges* 81 The columns of smoke... Natives .. near them .. sending messages... The simplicity of this bush telegraphy was fascinating. **1977** B. FULLER *Nullarbor Lifelines* 52 These tramps have a system of bush telegraphy very nearly as effective as that employed by the Aborigines.

bush telegraph, *v.* [f. prec.] *trans.* To communicate (information) by means of bush telegraph. Also *intr.* and with a person as obj.

1926 A.A.B. APSLEY *Amateur Settlers* 98 A set of blacks could 'bush telegraph'. **1953** *Bulletin* (Sydney) 11 Mar. 13/1 The ranger doing his annual round is bush-telegraphed long before he arrives, and it must be a continual surprise to him to note the rapid decline in the dog population. **1966** 'E. LINDALL' *Northward Coast* 160 They were now heading directly into tribal country. Every move they made would be bush-telegraphed ahead.

bushwhack, *v.* [Back-formation f. BUSHWHACKER.] *intr.* To work, esp. as an unskilled labourer, clearing ground in the country; to fell timber. Freq. as *vbl. n.* and *ppl. a.*

[N.Z. **1907** W.H. KOEBEL *Return of Joe* 287 Cutting good [plug] terbaccer as if you was bushwacking.] **1927** M.H. ELLIS *Long Lead* 187 The resulting regime was, to quote Mrs Aeneas Gunn, a 'friendly, bushwhacking old Government'. **1929** P.R. STEPHENSEN *Bushwhackers* 68 Only a few lived on after the white men came to whack the bush; lived as adjuncts, almost as spectators of the bushwhacking. **1935** H.H. FINLAYSON *Red Centre* 24 After weeks of bush-whacking in the mulga. **1946** *Bulletin* (Sydney) 4 Dec. 28/4, I bushwhacked with an old-timer who brought an unerring instinct to the locating of bee-hives. **1950** G. FARWELL *Surf Music* 180 The yarns he told them of his old bush-whacking days. **1959** *Overland* xv. 14 It was then that I started to bushwhack. Between cooking I would go out and brush for the men and from that I got to helping them fell the timber. **1973** H. LEWIS *Crow on Barbed Wire Fence* 210 Feeling flush, I broke all the rules of bushwhacking finally and forever by paying my fare down to Townsville. **1977** J. CARTER *All Things Wild* 12 He did most of his bush-whacking with a glass in one hand and his foot on the bar rail.

bushwhacker. [U.S. *bushwhacker* backwoodsman.]

1. One who lives in the country (as opposed to the town): cf. BUSHY *n.* 1.

1896 M. HORNSBY *Old Time Echoes Tas.* 60 Berresford was an old hermit, or bush-whacker. **1898** *Bulletin* (Sydney) 12 Mar. 14/3 A bushwhacker out my way recently had a harrowing experience. **1903** *Truth* (Sydney) 1 Mar. 3/3 Battalions of bush whackers . . chucked hard yakker for the less arduous and more congenial sport of Boer splitting. **1909** *Bulletin* (Sydney) 4 Feb. 13/1 Existence to a rough bush-whacker, With money tight and times grown slacker, Yields little more than long hard yakker. **1936** 'SWEENEY, EX-CROOK' *I Confess* 54 The easily-caught 'bush-whacker' is no longer a reality. **1948** C.B. MAXWELL *Cold Nose of Law* 39 I'd not bothered to put on a coat. . . I was still pretty much of a bushwhacker, in those days. **1953** 'CADDIE' *Caddie* 36, I must have looked a regular bushwhacker the day I stepped out of the train on to Central Station. . . Home-made skirt and blouse, mended cotton gloves. **1968** J. BEGLEY *Block with One Holer* 49 Any people living the other side of the Woods's place were considered to be bushwackers [*sic*], the term applying to settlers around the river towns who were too far away from the river to derive any benefit from it. **1973** H. LEWIS *Crow on Barbed Wire Fence* 161 You bushwhackers never see a newspaper and don't know what goes on the other side of the creek. **1981** P. BARTON *Bastards I have Known* 19 He hated city-slickers (we had many years to go before Jack accepted us as fellow bushwhackers).

2. *Hist.* A member of the *Bushman's Contingent* (see BUSHMAN 8).

1900 *Tocsin* (Melbourne) 22 Mar. 1/3 Bushwhacker Davey's case disclosed wretched bungling on the part of the Defence authorities. **1901** *Ibid.* 22 Aug. 4/4 You know 'Ginger' wot went away with the 'bushwhackers' to the war?

Hence **bushwhackery** *n.*

1961 *Bulletin* (Sydney) 1 Feb. 32/4 He is nowadays capitalising on his outback years and imposing a self-conscious bushwhackery on his gullible urban admirers.

bushy, *a.* and *n.* Also **bushie.** [f. BUSH *n.*3 + -Y.]

A. *adj.* Countrified; lacking the (supposed) refinements of urban life.

1843 *Satirist & Sporting Chron.* (Sydney) 18 Mar. 1/2 We have heard quite enough of *Flash Bill B.*, the horse-dealer. . . Bill has quite enough to do to look after Mary, and keep her from getting *bushy*. **1901** *Truth* (Sydney) 17 Nov. 1/2 Every wretched little larrikin . . jumps at the opportunity to take his blowzy, frowzy 'donah', 'clinah', or 'little bit of all-right' to some bushy seaside resort. **1906** G.M. SMITH *Days of Cobb & Co.* 71 He got a call girl up from town Who was good at cracking jokes, A thing quite indispensible To lamb down bushy blokes. **1922** C. DREW *Rogues & Ruses* 17 He was a bushie lookin' chap. **1927** M. TERRY *Through Land of Promise* 230 'Bronco-ing' (the local term for this roping of cattle, only found in the most bushy out-Bush stations). **1962** C. GYE *Cockney & Crocodile* 139 How 'bushy' we had become not to recognize our capital city on an ordinary everyday evening! **1972** DOUGLAS & OLDMEADOW *Across Top* 46 The Aborigines, far more reserved and 'bushy' than the mission people, accepted us readily. **1975** X. HERBERT *Poor Fellow my Country* 1029 'Someone'd sell you the Harbour Bridge within an hour.' 'D'you think I'm that bushy?'

B. *n.*

1. One who lives in the country as opposed to the town; one whose manner or appearance betrays this.

1887 *Tibbs' Pop. Song Bk.* 4 And they poke fun at our clothes. Their own are made to measure, Fitting neatly round the leg, And Bushy's got a tenner Where they've only got a peg. **1889** *Bulletin* (Sydney) 13 July 20/1 For the shanties are aw'fly alluring To the bushy that's hot from the track. **1892** *Ibid.* 26 Mar. 19/2 Said the stranger: 'I am nothing, save a bushy and a dunce.' **1897** *Western Champion* (Barcaldine) 22 June 3/3 He was a 'bushee' named Barney who had been enjoying himself for some days in the good old way among the various pubs in town. **1900** *Truth* (Sydney) 11 Feb. 8/2 The adaptability so eminently a characteristic of the true bushie. **1913** *Bulletin* (Sydney) 21 Aug. 18/4 The bushy doesn't 'chuck off' at the Englishman for his habit of doing without a bathroom. **1926** G. BLACK *Hist. N.S.W. Political Labor Party* v. 33 It was easily discernible that the 'bushies' were hopelessly divided on the question, and that the 'townies' were determined. **1939** J.T. MCMAHON *Bushies' Scheme in W.A.* 37 Catholic schools may organise a Bushies' Day, so that the children may see the problem of the isolated child, and learn to know how they may help the Scheme. **1948** I.L. IDRIESS *Opium Smugglers* 185 Like some other 'bushies' Billy looks nothing in particular on the ground but he is a picture on a horse. **1950** E.M. ENGLAND *Where Turtles Dance* 63 It's a wonder you didn't see me. We're true bushies—went round the back way. **1959** D. NILAND *Gold in Streets* 142 Ed's a bushy. . . First time in the Smoke. **1965** R.H. CONQUEST *Horses in Kitchen* 116 The lady bushies . . concentrate on buying new dresses, hats and shoes. **1983** *Austral.* (Sydney) 11 Feb. 7/1 You must remember that bushies, from graziers through to the fruit and vegetable blockies, are getting a rough deal. **1986** *Sydney Morning Herald* 15 Feb. 6/3 Tony Adams, an AWU member and lifelong Labor voter, takes his first break. . . 'Ever since they started treating bushies like dirt, I've stopped being keen on the bastards.'

2. *Hist.* A member of the *Bushman's Contingent* (see BUSHMAN 8).

1900 *Truth* (Sydney) 4 Mar. 5/1 One very drunk Bushie reeled all over the shop, and for a time disorganised the whole outfit. **1901** F. WILKINSON *Aust. at Front* 281 Austenberg, July 9th, 1900. Our 'Bushies' have had a fight with the Boers, and acquitted themselves well and bravely. **1903** J. GREEN *Story Austral. Bushmen* 188 Here a Bushie tipped me a knowing and unbelieving wink.

business. *Aboriginal English.*

1. Traditional lore and ritual; the exercise of this. Also *attrib.*

1943 W.E. HARNEY *Taboo* 170 'That not proper wind, but blackfellow business.' Blackfellow business! Some native in another tribe had cast some magic and sent this wind to destroy the tribe. **1961** F. DE GRYS *Cobba Cobba* 113 Whitefella Aspros were not likely to be much good for a headache caused by too much Blackfella Business. **1974** J. BERN Blackfella Business 26 Blackfella business is the expression of Aboriginal consciousness in general. **1977** J. & P. READ View of Past 12 Aug. (1978) 308 (typescript), A lot of these girls here are all, all educated when there are business ceremonies, ceremonial things, our custom way. . . They still join in. **1978** *Alywarra Land Claim: Transcript of Proc.* 9 Oct. 416 Do they also own the business and the story to that place? **1983** NATHAN & JAPANANGKA *Settle down Country* 114 Because of 'sorry business' [*sc.* mourning ceremonies] the people had moved from their normal site. **1985** I. WHITE et al. *Fighters & Singers* 13 They might make him a man . . this year at business time up here.

2. In the collocation **Sunday business,** an exclusive ritual (see quots. 1949 and 1962). Also **Sunday business ritual**.

1949 HARNEY & ELKIN *Songs of Songman* 143 The women . . go off to 'dance', that is perform their secret corroboree, their 'Sunday Business'. **1962** D. LOCKWOOD *I, Aboriginal* 32 Henceforth the ceremony was strictly men's Sunday-business . . in which [the women] could not take part. **1964** —— *Up Track* 124, I have seen dozens of corroborees and a few big Sunday Business rituals among today's aborigines. **1978** J. & P. READ View of Past 227 They going to be shown all that Sunday business . . do you reckon?

bust, *n.* [Br. dial. *bust* var. of BURST *n.*[1]: see OEDS *sb.*[3] a.] A drinking bout. Freq. in the phr. **on the bust.**

1865 *Sydney Punch* 23 Sept. 554/2, I may here explain that the term 'on the bust' is an expression having reference to a curious religious practice of the inhabitants of these parts, who . . enter into a solemn vow to spend a certain, or uncertain, sum of money, usually all they are possessed of, in the purchase of spirituous liquors. **1868** *Argus* (Melbourne) 28 Feb. 6/3 They have just put up their horses preparatory to 'goin' on the bust'. **1873** J.C.F. JOHNSON *Christmas on Carringa* 2 Watty served out old man Modder, the shanty-keeper, the last time he was on the bust at Tambo. **1891** J. FENTON *Bush Life Tas.* (1965) 164 A man's nothing without a 'bust' now and then. **1895** *Worker* (Sydney) 21 Dec. 6/4 He was evidently on the 'bust', and looked somewhat wild about the eyes. **1911** E.M. CLOWES *On Wallaby through Vic.* 106 Of course, men still go 'on the bust', cheques are planked down, and 'shouting' . . indulged in till all the money is finished. **1929** C.H. WINTER *Story of 'Bidgee Queen* 74 He'll never join the old hands in a flaring, crimson 'bust'. **1935** W. GRAY *Days & Nights in Bush* 29 They are reliable hands, but go in for a 'bust' from time to time. **1948** P.J. HURLEY *Red Cedar* 57 He lives frugally on the job, making the most of his periodic visits to town, when life takes on a red and rainbow hue during the sweet days of a real bust. **1963** X. HERBERT *Larger than Life* 18 Ben, if I win Tatts, you and I are going on the bust together.

bust, *v.* [f. prec.] *trans.* To squander (money), usu. on liquor. Formerly also with **up.**

1878 'IRONBARK' *Southerly Busters* 24 In Bathurst's busy streets He got upon the spree. . . He said he'd 'busted up his cheque'. **1884** *Austral. Tit-Bits* (Melbourne) 3 July 7/2 We are afraid he footed the journey and busted the money in a cook shop. **1898** *Critic* (Adelaide) 12 Feb. 5/3 Fur I've busted ev'ry penny that I 'ad. **1908** *Bulletin* (Sydney) 9 Jan. 14/1 If you've cheques, well, quickly bust 'em In the old, time-honoured way. **1960** L.H. EVERS *Make Way for Tomorrow* 45 One of our own blokes busted his pension money getting full in Hattersville. **1968** D. O'GRADY *Bottle of Sandwiches* 170 Been here three bloody days bustin' his shearin' cheque. **1980** J. WRIGHT *Big Hearts & Gold Dust* 153 Come on mate, we've got a fiver to bust.

buster, *n.*[1] *Obs.* [Prob. Br. dial. form of *burster* 'exhausting piece of exercise': see OED 1 b.] A cracking pace, something which 'takes the wind out of one'.

1865 *Austral. Monthly Mag.* (Melbourne) I. 234 He went it a buster for fifteen miles, and then gave in. **1868** *Sydney Punch* 15 Feb. 88/1 We're nowheres—so when there's a rush, Mind you go in a buster. **1887** A. NICOLS *Wild Life & Adventure* 223 The overseer, after bringing them round, gave the mob a 'buster' at a severe pace during the next half-hour, to take the wind out of them.

buster, *n.*[2] [Abbrev. of SOUTHERLY BUSTER.] A strong squally wind, esp. from the south.

1873 W. THOMSON-GREGG *Desperate Character* II. 179 We'll have a regular buster in no time; it was just such weather as this last year. **1880** *Argus* (Melbourne) 21 Jan. 6/6 This has been, perhaps, the hottest day we have had during the present summer. A northerly buster has been blowing throughout the day. **1888** W.T. PYKE *Bush Tales* 26 The revolutionary 'buster' from the south rose in opposition to the north winds. **1906** *Truth* (Sydney) 4 Nov. 6/1 Tuesday was the hottest day of the season, and its 'buster', which reduced the temperature 30 degrees in the twinkling of an eye, was a caution. **1913** H. WILSON *Log H.M.S. 'Encounter'* 133 We have had several busters accompanied by heavy rain during the day. ('Busters' is the local name for strong, squally winds; generally they are from the s.w.). **1928** E.M. ROBB *Lyrics* 7 There's nothing doing on a yacht when the naughty buster blows. **1956** S. HOPE *Diggers' Paradise* 71 Sometimes the south wind or a 'south-westerly buster' puts a chill on the city, but when this wind occurs in summer it is generally welcome. **1985** B. ROSSER *Dreamtime Nightmares* 120 We used to get a buster out in the bush, too.

buster, *n.*[3] [Prob. Br. dial. form of racing slang *burster* (see BURSTER *n.*[1]) a fall, a 'cropper' (cf. BUST *n.*).]

1. A heavy fall from a horse.

1878 G. WALCH *Australasia* 28 He wouldn't tell a lie to save his life, but he would put the parson in the way of a 'buster' without compunction. **1887** A. NICOLS *Wild Life & Adventure* 288 Joe's got such a 'buster' he won't be fit for a week, if he hasn't broken his arm. **1890** A. MACKAY *Austral. Agriculturist* (ed. 2) 283 The colonial 'buster', or a fall from horseback, very often results in a broken head, or in dislocation of an arm or leg, or both. **1902** R.C. PRAED *My Austral. Girlhood* 186 Had a buster into the bargain! No bones broke though. **1918** *Kia Ora Coo-ee* May 13/2 Seen some bad busters in my time.

1927 A. CROMBIE *After Sixty Yrs.* 61 A 'buster' from a horse. **1949** B. O'REILLY *Green Mountains* 136 Perhaps you are out riding, your horse falls and you get a 'buster'. As you pick yourself up out of the dust and finger a skinned nose, a loud laugh breaks out overhead. **1962** D. STUART *Yaralie* 153 So he'd had a buster off a rough horse, eh? **1980** ANSELL & PERCY *To fight Wild* 103 Go and hop on a rough horse and maybe take a buster.

2. *fig.*

1968 *Sunday Truth* (Brisbane) 30 June 20 The Australian Government has come an incredible double buster on the design for its Vietnam campaign medal.

but, *adv.* [Not in standard use.] At the end of a phrase or sentence: though, however; 'no doubt about it'.

1853 *Austral. Gold Digger's Monthly Mag.* iv. 125 The hero of (not a hundred fights, but) famed Whitechapel, doubtless considered such a feat of valour would greatly exalt him in the eyes of Cockneyism. **1938** E. LOWE *Salute to Freedom* 157 She had so few words to express her feelings. 'I love you—won't you kiss me, but!' **1952** C. SIMPSON *Come away, Pearler* 87 What a pity the young lady's afternoon's got to be spoiled but. She seemed to be enjoying herself. **1959** D. LOCKWOOD *Crocodiles & Other People* 72 'Slow,' Jack agreed, 'but faster than the old buggy, but.' **1965** H. PORTER *Cats of Venice* 186 He'd *do* him, but, the little tonk. **1971** J. O'GRADY *Aussie Etiket* 14, I was off on compo then, see with me crook foot. She was good enough to hobble around on, but, long as I took me time. **1972** —— *It's your Shout, Mate!* 89 'There's only bread and butter and bacon and eggs for breakfast,' I said, still mentally in Queensland, 'Shit, eh? No coffee, but?' **1977** *Southerly* ii. 160 'Your friend Hans . . was arrested for trafficking prostitutes.' 'Oh!—yes, I heard about that. He was a nice bloke but.' **1979** CAREY & LETTE *Puberty Blues* 67 She asked for it but! **1982** P. RADLEY *My Blue-Checker Corker* 3 'Wish we had ashfelt in the school playground, but.' 'Asphalt,' Grandad said. 'I thought Miss Cruikshank had you out of the habit of ending your sentences with 'but'.'

butcher, *n.*[1] *S.A.* [Prob. a. G. *becher* convivial drinking vessel, but see quot. 1956.] A glass or measure of beer; for size, see quots. 1908 and 1984.

1889 W.R. THOMAS *In Early Days* 14/2 Over a good fat 'butcher' of beer, he told me how he was getting on. **1891** *Quiz* (Adelaide) 16 Jan. 7/2 A butcher of beer, if you please, miss. **1895** *Worker* (Sydney) 12 Oct. 4/1 The landlady took her best 'butcher' and rubbed it clean and bright. Filling it to the brim with sparkling ale, she handed it to Dick. **1906** *Gadfly* (Adelaide) 4 Apr. 9/2 A Butchers' Conference was to be held in Adelaide. . . Butchers, butchers, everywhere, but not a drop to drink. **1908** M. VIVIENNE *Sunny S.A.* 255 He gives away a good few of what they call 'butchers of beer', which is a long, wide glass, holding more than a pint. **1916** *Bulletin* (Sydney) 21 Sept. 22/4 'Butcher.' A long beer. Local to S. Aust., I think. Said to refer to the habit of journeymen butchers always wanting a long one. **1929** H.M. NEEDHAM *Morepork* 11 The cool and grateful 'butcher', drawn by barmaid arch and pretty, Quickly fled from out the goblet. **1956** S. HOPE *Digger's Paradise* 232 And what is called a 'lady's waist' in some parts of the country is generally known as a 'butcher'. This originated in bygone days when workers from the abattoirs came unwashed to the pubs after their day's toil. A proportion of drinking mugs was kept separate for them, and a mob of slaughtermen would announce themselves as 'butchers' and be given those mugs. **1972** J. O'GRADY *It's your Shout, Mate!* 30 There was at one time a pub near the abattoirs. Employees were accustomed to visit it in their lunch hour, and because of the Australian custom of 'shouting', and the limited time available, they preferred to drink small beers. Six-ounce glasses were the smallest the publican had, and so a six-ounce glass became known as a butcher. **1984** B. DRISCOLL *Great Aussie Beer Bk.* 99 The South Australian six ounce (170 ml.) has Australia's oddest glass name, a 'butcher'.

butcher, *n.*[2]

1. As **butcher's (hook),** rhyming slang for 'crook'.

a. Ill; CROOK 1 c. **b.** In the phr. **to go butcher's (hook),** to complain vehemently; to speak angrily; *to go crook*, see CROOK 2 b.

1918 *Kia Ora Coo-ee* Aug. 5/1 A certain New Zealand Regiment, camped on the Jordan flats, recently came under the eagle eye of brother 'Jacko', who immediately went 'butcher's hook' or 'ram's horn' and launched forth much frightfulness. **1951** D. STIVENS *Jimmy Brockett* 126 As soon as Sadie came in I went butcher's hook. **1957** D. WHITINGTON *Treasure upon Earth* 78 'These galahs are going butchers.' Mick had no great sympathy with the wharf laborers at this stage. **1967** *Kings Cross Whisper* (Sydney) xxxii. 7/1 *Butchers in the comics*, sick in the guts from the rhyming butchers hook and the comic cuts. **1981** B. HUMPHRIES *Nice Night's Entertainment* 186 Still feeling butchers after your op, are you Mau?

2. In the collocation **butcher's picnic,** an occasion characterized by its lack of decorum; a motley assemblage.

1965 K. SMITH *OGF* 140 Behave yourself, Gadley, and shut your trap—this isn't a butchers' picnic. **1972** J. GOODE *Austral. Cars & Motoring* 38 In Australia, sedan or saloon car racing was always popular. The 'butchers' picnic' of two dozen sedans of every shape, size and colour setting-off in two rows at Fisherman's Bend . . was something which brought everyone to the rails. **1984** S. MACINTYRE *Militant* 137 Terms used to be bandied around like curses at a butchers' picnic.

butcherbird. [Transf. use of *butcher-bird* shrike (fam. Laniidae), referring to the bird's habit of impaling its prey on thorns.] Any of the four birds of the genus *Cracticus* (fam. Cracticidae) having black and white plumage and hooked bills, noted for their predatory habits, and (esp. the *pied butcherbird*, see PIED) as songbirds.

1827 *Trans. Linnean Soc. London* XV. 213 Mr Caley thus observes . . *'Butcher-bird.*—This bird used frequently to come into some *green wattle-trees* near my house, and in wet weather was very noisy; from which circumstance it obtained the name of *Rain-bird.*' **1866** *Australasian* (Melbourne) 14 July 476/1 Of the notes of the true butcher-bird, or 'old soldier', I have heard it admitted . . that in richness and volume they compete with those of the nightingale. **1886** H. FINCH-HATTON *Advance Aust.* 42 Close to the station, one or two butcher-birds were piping their morning song. **1896** *Bulletin* (Sydney) 12 Dec. 26/4 And I brood by the camp-fire alone, With the butcher-birds melody flowing. **1899** *Ibid.* 15 July 15/1 *Re* origin of term 'butcher' bird . . the British b.b. (Lanius excubitor) . . 'hangs up' portions of its prey till wanted. **1934** T. WOOD *Cobbers* 191 Butcher-birds greet daybreak with their beautiful call of a rising sixth. **1956** A.C.C. LOCK *Tropical Tapestry* 239 From a big mango tree . . came the peerless flute-like notes of a black and white butcher bird. **1974** N. CATO *Brown Sugar* 96 As purely as the butcher-birds singing in the dew of a Queensland morning.

butt. [Survival of Br. *butt* bale, pack: see OED *sb.* 10. 1.] A pack, esp. a bale of wool below standard weight.

1913 W.K. HARRIS *Outback in Aust.* 184 Mr Saxons . . 'hitched on' a well-filled 'butt' to the back of the sulky. **1921** L.G. JONES *Flockmaster's Companion* 81 *Butt*, an incomplete bale of wool weighing less than the standard weight (200 lbs. greasy, or 100 lbs. scoured). **1923** J. ARMOUR *Spell of Inland* 111 Ned lifted his young wife up on the waggon, and she seated herself on a butt of chaff. **1928** C.E. COWLEY *Classing Clip* 166 Those sections of the catalogue set apart for oddments, known as *butts* and *bags*. The former consist of packages of wool contained in the recognized woolpack, but under the acknowledged weight. **1973** V. SERVENTY *Desert Walkabout* 25 Two butts of euros were carried back to the camp to feed the rest of the group. **1976** DRAGE & PAGE *Riverboats & Rivermen* 75 To plug such holes we carried 'butts' (bags) of flour.

butterbush. [From a fancied resemblance to butter, prob. in the colour of the wood.] Any of several shrubs or trees esp. *Pittosporum phylliraeoides* (fam. Pittosporaceae), which yields seeds used for flour, an edible gum and a hard pale timber; *native apricot* NATIVE *a.* 6 a. See also *native willow* NATIVE *a.* 6 a.

1888 *Proc. Linnean Soc. N.S.W.* III. 538 *Pittosporum Phillyraeoides*. . . Called variously 'Butter-bush', 'Native Willow', and 'Poison-berry' tree. **1903** G. SUTHERLAND *Australasian Live Stock Man.* (ed. 2) 385 Another tree of considerable value, especially during droughts, is the . . 'Butter-bush'. **1936** I.L. IDRIESS *Cattle King* 252 The rabbits had killed all the . . butter-bush. **1944** *Bulletin* (Sydney) 23 Feb. 13/3 Little whitewood . . or butter-bush—they call it Berrigan on the Lachlan—not only provides good fodder but splendid wind-breaks.

butterfish. [From a fancied resemblance to butter, prob. in the flavour of the flesh.] Any of several unrelated fish, esp. (*S.A.*) MULLOWAY.

1849 *Adelaide Miscellany* 28 July 407 A really excellent fish for the table has fallen in my way, as large as a small salmon, and something like it in form; they call it 'butter fish': the flesh is white, but it is much richer than any other I have tasted. **1861** E.P. RAMSAY-LAYE *Social Life & Manners* 95 Butter-fish, a small kind of whiting. **1873** F. DE CASTLENAU *Edible Fishes Vic.* 10 [*Cheilodactylus*] *nigricans* is the *butter fish*, which is one of the commonest of all sorts on the Melbourne market. **1906** D.G. STEAD *Fishes of Aust.* 114 The Jewfish [*Sciaena antarctica*]. . . At the mouth of the Murray the fishermen call it 'Mulloway', or 'Butterfish'. **1933** D. MACDONALD *Brooks of Morning* 181 Any strange fish is to the fisherman a kind of butterfish. **1963** B. CROPP *Handbk. for Skindivers* 116 Butterfish (*Dactylopagrus morwong*) . . is the Victorian name for the dusky morwong.

butterfly, *v. Two-up. trans.* See quot. 1967. Freq. as *vbl. n.*

1949 G. BERRIE *Morale* 251 *Butterflying*—throwing the coins so that they turn once in the air and then come to the ground without spinning. The coins are always tails upwards and the spinner always backs heads; hence the idea. **1953** T.A.G. HUNGERFORD *Riverslake* 129 'I'll take thirty of it,' he announced sneeringly, looking at Novikowsky as though the Pole were butterflying the pennies. **1967** F. HARDY *Billy Borker yarns Again* 2 He was butterflying the pennies.—Butterflying?—Butterflying is to throw the pennies sliding off the kip so they flutter like a butterfly but don't really spin.

Also **butterfly** *n.* (*attrib.* in quot.), **butterflied** *ppl. a.*

1946 K.S. PRICHARD *Roaring Nineties* 152 The ring-keeper might object to a spin. . . A **'butterfly'** fall was in order over a sandy patch, but not if there were any stones about on which she might bounce and start an argument. **1967** F. HARDY *Billy Borker yarns Again* 2 Any experienced swy player can pick a **butterflied** penny from the genuine spinning article.

butterfly cod. *Fire fish*, see FIRE *n.*

1936 N. CALDWELL *Fangs of Sea* 116 Butterfly cod, their long streamers of colour extended, streak about in panic. **1976** E. WORRELL *Things that Sting* 51 Butterfly cod are so beautifully coloured and spectacularly finned that they are easy to see in the water.

button, *n.* [Fig. use of *button*.] Used *attrib.* in Special Comb. **button grass, (a)** the large, tufted sedge, *Gymnoschoenus sphaerocephalus* (fam. Cyperaceae) which forms distinctive plains, esp. in w. Tas. (see quot. 1898); **(b)** the short-lived annual grass *Dactyloctenium radulans* of mainland Aust.; **stone,** AUSTRALITE.

1881 *Tas. H. of A. Jrnls.* XLI. lv. 14 A narrow strip of barren **button-grass** land. **1898** E.E. MORRIS *Austral Eng.* 74 Button-grass. . . So called from the round shaped flower (capitate inflorescence), on a thin stalk four or five feet long, like a button on the end of a foil. **1921** B. CRONIN *Timber Wolves* 41, I touches my horse with the hooks and away we goes, helter-skelter across the button-grass. **1923** M.B. PETERSEN *Jewelled Nights* 10 The wagonette lumbered out on . . tremendous plains of button grass. **1960** *N.T. News* (Darwin) 11 Mar. 7/3 Without March rains hot weather might burn off . . annual grasses such as button grass. **1968** P. ADAM-SMITH *Tiger Country* 77 Button-grass is peculiar to Western Tasmania. It resembles tussock and gets its name from the button-like flowers on the end of long stalks. **1980** *Southerly* iv. 430 He looked at the swampy button grass, and thought of Christmas bells and snowberries. **1983** MORLEY & TOELKEN *Flowering Plants Aust.* 391 Among native grasses recorded as being used by Aborigines for food are . . *Dactyloctenium radulans*, button grass, which has its seeds adhering to large husks which were methodically removed [etc.]. **1855** *Q. Jrnl. Geol. Soc. London* XI. 403 The smaller very much resembles a button without the shank; and, from this appearance, the diggers call them **'button stones'**. **1934** C. FENNER *Australites* i. 65 Even as far back as 1855, and possibly earlier, australites were well known to the gold diggers, who called them 'button stones'.

button, *v. Obs.* [Back-formation f. BUTTONER.] *intr.* To act as a buttoner. Also as *vbl. n.*

1917 C. DREW *Reminisc. D. Gilbert* 131 His job was to do the 'buttoning'. To be seen in company with the other rogues would have been fatal. **1919** A. WRIGHT *Game of Chance* 116 'It was a slanter,' cried Mason. 'The dice were loaded; I saw that man next the thrower helping to ring the changes. He was buttoning for the other.'

buttoner. *Obs.* [Survival of Br. slang *buttoner* accomplice, decoy: see OED *button sb.* 9 and *buttoner* 3.] The accomplice of a confidence man.

1882 *Sydney Slang Dict.* 2 *Buttoners*, assistants of stage tricksters who mingle with the audience. **1885** G. DARRELL *Sunny South* 32 Here's a lark. The three card monte man and his buttoner. **1895** *Worker* (Sydney) 9 Nov. 1/4 Buttoners are common all through society, they are decoys and may be male or female, according to the class of person to be taken in. **1903** *Truth* (Sydney) 31 May 3/5 When out for a big haul three men are usually associated. One carries the stock of base money, and is apart from the other two; of the latter one goes into a public-house and calls for a drink, this he pays for with a genuine coin; his mate comes in and also calls for a drink, but tenders a base coin in payment. . . If the bartender doubts the coin the 'buttoner' asks to see it, and in the examination manages adroitly to exchange the bad coin for a good one. **1913** *Ibid.* 20 July 8/8 Asher was employed *as a buttoner* at Woolf's, and could be seen moving amongst the crowd suggesting prices to be bid for the articles put up. After running up the bidding to a big figure, he would bid and purchase the article himself; and shortly afterwards the very same, or an exactly similar, article would be again put up. **1918** J.H.C. SLEEMAN *Queer Qld.* 51 It is the same honorable tactics as the buttoner practises when assisting his friend, the card-sharper, to defraud the public.

buy, *v.* [Transf. use of the gambling expression *to buy into (a game).*] In the phr. **to buy in(to),** to involve oneself in (an activity).

1929 C.E.W. BEAN *Official Hist. Aust. 1914–18* III. 613 While part of the 5th Brigade, ostensibly fresh, had thus subjected itself to considerable strain by 'buying in' (to use an Australianism) to a struggle on its flank. **1943** *Coast to Coast 1942* 188, I haven't got to buy into every fight you pick! **1962** A. SEYMOUR *One Day of Yr.* 56 You fight your own battles. I'm not buyin' into any arguments. **1977** K. COOK *Man Underground* 122 As soon as we open the campaign we have Charlie on the air every day, buying in on everything that's going on.

buzzy. *Tas.* [Of unknown origin.] BIDGEE-WIDGEE.

1952 J.R. SKEMP *Memories Myrtle Bank* 94 Buzzy is the common Tasmanian name for a creeping native herb which has a very adhesive burr for a seed-head. It is sometimes called 'bidgee-widgee'. **1968** J. WOODBERRY *Come back Peter* (1974) 87 Treading on buzzies and prickles.

B.Y.O. /bi waɪ 'oʊ/. Acronym for the phr. *bring your own* (see BRING). Also **B.Y.O.G(rog).**

1968 *Catering* May 12/2 One important alteration in the new Liquor Control Bill is that B.Y.O. permits for unlicensed restaurants have been abolished. **1973** *Nation Rev.* (Melbourne) 31 Aug. 1460/6 Most people can only eat out on any regular basis if they dine at a BYO and avoid the licensed houses. **1976** *Advertiser* (Adelaide) 19 July 4/6 He was aware of objections by licensed-restaurant owners that BYO restaurants should be fully licensed, but he felt there was a need for both licensed and BYO restaurants. **1981** J. WALKER *Eating Out in Aust.* Cover, Concise information on hundreds and hundreds of leading restaurants from the famous and expensive to the very best BYOs. **1983** *Canberra Times* 11 July 9/7 The B.Y.O.G. restaurant is something of a rarity in Canberra. **1986** P. GOLDSWORTHY *Zooing* 13 Parties: monthly BYO affairs for a couple of hundred closest friends.

by-yu /'baɪ-ju/. [a. Nyungar *bayu.*] The seed of the cycad of s.w. W.A. *Macrozamia riedlei* (fam. Zamiaceae), formerly an Aboriginal plant food. Also **by-yu nut.**

1841 G. GREY *Jrnls. Two Exped. N.-W. & W.A.* II. 64 The natives had, according to their custom, buried a store of By-yu nuts. **1843** W. PRIDDEN *Aust.* 115 The pulp of the nut of a species of palm is called *by-yu* . . an agreeable and nourishing article of food. **1855** J. BONWICK *Geogr. Aust. & N.Z.* (ed. 3) 62 They were feasted with roast frogs and by-yu nuts. **1894** A.F. CALVERT *Aborigines W.A.* 29 The By-yu nut is also collected and eaten with relish. **1907** FOUNTAIN & WARD *Rambles Austral. Naturalist* 211 There is one palm (*Zamia media*—native, gherge), the nut of which, called bay-i-o by the blacks, is much sought after by them, as they are very fond of it.

C

cab. [Fig. use of *(taxi) cab.*] In the phr. **first cab off (on) the rank,** the first to seize an opportunity. Also as **next cab off the rank.**

1966 S.J. BAKER *Austral. Lang.* (ed. 2) 421 It must have been in the time of horse-drawn cabs that *the first cab on the rank* came to mean early in the day. **1967** *Kings Cross Whisper* (Sydney) xxxiv. 4/5 *First cab off the rank,* to do anything to anyone first. Next in line. **1977** *Austral.* (Sydney) 19 July 10/5 It is unlikely the Ranger partners will agree to new terms without concessions, such as being first cab off the rank if, as expected, the Government agrees to limited mining. **1982** *Sun-Herald* (Sydney) 15 Aug. 122/2 First cab off the rank this week was a luncheon fashion parade in Sydney Uni's Great Hall.

cabbage garden. A nickname for Victoria. Also **cabbage patch, cabbage State.**

1882 *Bulletin* (Sydney) 8 Apr. 8/1 There is a town in the 'Cabbage Garden', where, after a lot of exertion, two or three were gathered together to petition for rain. **1889** J.H.L. ZILLMANN *Past & Present Austral. Life* 30 'The cabbage garden', old cynical Sir John Robertson of New South Wales, once called Victoria. **1898** M. DAVITT *Life & Progress* 112 Victoria . . is referred to colloquially by people in sister colonies as 'the cabbage garden', owing to its relative smallness of area. **1905** *Bulletin* (Sydney) 7 Dec. 14/1 In Perth . . vegetables . . are cheaper than and equal to those I've met in Victoria the cabbage State. **1923** *Nat. Rev.* (London) Apr. 296 Only nine of the 48 United States equal Victoria for vastness, but in Australia, the land of bloated, weed-grown, unmanageable political estates, it has been nicknamed in derision 'the Cabbage Garden'. **1941** *Bulletin* (Sydney) 30 Apr. 16/2 In that same Cabbage Garden, in a spot infested with boxthorn hedges. **1951** *Ibid.* 14 Feb. 12/3 There's nothing new in maggies building among phone-wires in the Cabbage Garden. **1960** *Ibid.* 27 July 16/2 Two travellers from the Cabbage State on a six-week holiday trip to the Pacific Islands are taking their motor-scooter. **1967** G. JENKIN *Two Yrs. Bardunyah Station* 71 And I tell you what—I'll never go back to the Cabbage Patch again! **1970** *Austral.* (Sydney) 31 Oct. 3/3 'Cabbage patch history' was the way a leading Australian historian yesterday described the Victorian Government's Captain Cook bicentenary awards—now the centre of a growing literary career.

Hence **cabbage gardener, patcher, Stater** *n.*

1903 *Sporting News* (Launceston) 14 Feb. 3/6 Subsequently shipped to the other side, he opened the eyes of the '**cabbage gardeners**' by winning an important event. **1940** *Bulletin* (Sydney) 3 Jan. 16/2 Down on the Hopkins . . a shoal of what we Cabbage Gardeners call salmon trout had come in. **1955** N. PULLIAM *I traveled Lonely Land* 373 ***Cabbage patcher***, a person from Victoria. **1960** *Bulletin* (Sydney) 3 Aug. 19/1 **Cabbage-Staters** and Croweaters reading 'Curio's' dismissal of red-gum for fencing-posts . . must have been undecided whether he was having them on.

cabbage gum. [f. *cabbage* + GUM *n.* 1: see quots. 1889 and 1897, though the diversity of species to which the name applies makes it susceptible of other explanations (see quot. 1956).] Any of several trees of the genera *Eucalyptus* and *Angophora* (fam. Myrtaceae), esp. (*Tas.*) *E. pauciflora.*

1887 *Proc. Linnean Soc. N.S.W.* II. 279 'White', or 'Cabbage-gum'; useless for timber. **1889** J.H. MAIDEN *Useful Native Plants Aust.* 520 This timber is considered, in the Braidwood and Monaro districts, N.S.W., so soft and perishable for ordinary purposes that it is called 'Cabbage Gum', but it is nevertheless very durable underground. **1897** *Proc. Linnean Soc. N.S.W.* XXII. 706 'White Gum' . . usually goes under some name referring to the softness or brittleness of its timber, *e.g.* 'Cabbage Gum', 'Snappy Gum'. **1920** *Bulletin* (Sydney) 15 Jan. 22/1 Perfect gents. call this a cabbage-gum, while vulgar persons refer to it as a stinkin'-gum. **1938** C.P. CONIGRAVE *Walk-About* 67 Nothing is finer than cabbage-gum wood for 'live' coals. **1956** A.C.C. LOCK *Tropical Tapestry* 171 At last we reached some black soil plains, out of which rose some cabbage gums, so called because the smell they exude resembles that of boiled cabbage. **1975** D. STUART *Walk, trot, canter & Die* 43 Back at the shade of the solitary cabbage gum, the youngfeller had the billy on. **1981** M. SHARLAND *Tracks of Morning* 71 Specimens of the cabbage gum or weeping gum, always picturesque and lovers of high moist places.

cabbage palm: see CABBAGE TREE 1 a.

cabbageite, cabbager: see CABBAGITE.

cabbage saltbush. [f. *cabbage* + SALTBUSH: see quots. 1885 and 1887.] *Old man saltbush*, see OLD MAN *n.* 3 a.

1885 *Trans. & Proc. R. Soc. S.A.* VIII. 25 *Atriplex nummularium.* Often called the 'Cabbage' Saltbush, from the comparatively large size of its leaves. **1887** S. NEWLAND *Far North Country* 15 Cabbage saltbush is extolled as a table vegetable of surpassing excellence. **1902** *Bulletin* (Sydney) 21 June 16/1 *Re* the use of saltbush as a vegetable. On the Barwon and Darling, 40 years ago, what we called the 'cabbage saltbush' was pretty generally so used. ***c* 1910** W.R. GUILFOYLE *Austral. Plants* 65 'Old Man Salt Bush' or 'Cabbage Salt Bush'.

cabbage tree. [Spec. use of *cabbage tree* a name variously applied in other parts of the world.]

1. a. Any of several trees, usu. palms (fam. Arecaceae) of the genera *Corypha* and esp. *Livistona*, of n., e., and central Aust. and elsewhere, the young growing shoot of which is edible. See also FAN PALM. Also **cabbage palm, cabbage tree palm.**

1770 J. COOK *Jrnls.* 8 June (1955) I. 339 The trees we saw were a small kind of Cabbage Palms. **1788** J. HUNTER *Hist. Jrnl. Trans. Port Jackson* (1793) 306 We found a vast number of cabbage-trees. . . They are a very good substitute for other vegetables, but one tree produces only a single cabbage. **1826** J. ATKINSON *Acct. Agric. & Grazing N.S.W.* 3 The cabbage tree, with its slender stem, rising to 60 or 70 feet high, and circular head, is a conspicuous object in these shades. **1844** L. LEICHHARDT *Jrnl. Overland Exped. Aust.* 10 Dec. (1847) 72 Several of my companions suffered by eating too much of the cabbage-palm. The Blackfellows will doubtless wonder why so many noble trees had been felled here. **1852** W. HUGHES *Austral. Colonies* 72 In the Illawara district are still left a few specimens of the cabbage-tree palm, the leaves of which are used for making the kind of hat almost universally worn by colonists of all classes. **1855** J. BONWICK *Geogr. Aust. & N.Z.* (ed. 3) 23 The first huts were constructed of the cabbage palm. **1862** W. LANDSBOROUGH *Jrnl. Exped. from Carpentaria* 23 We got a fine potful of cabbagetree sprouts, which eat like asparagus. **1874** J.J. HALCOMBE *Emigrant & Heathen* 27 The cabbage-tree palms, with occasionally a tall ant-hill, three or four feet high, give a semi-tropical character. **1914** H.M. VAUGHAN *Australasian Wander-Yr.* 214 Here the tall straggling gum-trees are thickly interspersed with the 'cabbage-tree' and the bangalow palms. **1938** A. UPFIELD *Bone is Pointed* (1966) 89 He neck-roped the mare to a shady cabbage-tree. **1957** J. HAWKE *Follow my Dust* 79 It was eaten in the shade of the best shade-tree in the bush, the cabbage tree. **1979** D. LOCKWOOD *My Old Mates & I* 12 Spectacular cabbage palms grew in groves, straight trunks uniformly surmounted by fronded wigs. **1986** *Your Garden* Jan. 11 A small 'rainforest' of Staghorn . . and Cabbage Tree palms shelters in filtered sunlight.

b. The plant *Nuytsia floribunda* (see *Christmas bush* (b) CHRISTMAS).

1832 G.F. MOORE *Diary Ten Yrs. W.A.* 14 Sept. (1884) 136 The cabbage or beef-wood tree, with a splendid orange blossom. **1838** J. BACKHOUSE *Narr. Visit Austral. Colonies* (1843) 533 *Nuytsia floribunda* . . is called in the Colony, Cabbage-tree, because of a faint resemblance, in the texture of its branches, to cabbage-stalks. **1936** J.E. HAMMOND *Western Pioneers* 126 The bush around contained an interesting variety of timber, including . . cabbage (or Christmas) tree.

2. Ellipt. for CABBAGE-TREE HAT 1.

1844 *Dispatch* (Sydney) 20 Apr. 1/2 The very 'cabbage trees' of the squatters seemed to assume a something of defiance in their knowing cock, as their wearers laughed and joked. **1845** *Cumberland Times* (Parramatta) 15 Nov. 4/1 On Sunday evening a young man passing through Hyde Park, was met by a man dressed in white, and tiled with the omnipotent Cabbage-tree. **1858** R. ROWE *Peter 'Possum's Portfolio* 93 Chinamen, with silken nets hanging veil-wise from their cabbage-trees. **1873** W. THOMSON-GREGG *Desperate Character* I. 52 He of the beard and dilapidated cabbage-tree. **1883** R.E.N. TWOPENY *Town Life Aust.* 244 A 'cabbage-tree' is an immense sun-protecting hat, rather like the top of a cabbage-tree in shape. It is much affected by bushmen. **1906** *Bulletin* (Sydney) 4 Jan. 15/1, I reached for my boots and cabbage-tree, and rushed to the door. **1927** A. CROMBIE *After Sixty Yrs.* 110 A cabbage-tree hat was then *de rigueur* amongst stockmen, and . . when riding fast after cattle, the boot-lace hat fastener was generally gripped by the horseman's teeth, thus assuring the safety of his 'cabbage-tree', which might have cost anything up to £5. **1974** *Austral. Folksongs* (Folk Lore Council Aust.) 26 The squatter loves his cabbage-tree With streamers hanging down—He wears it always in the bush, And even when in town!

3. *Hist.* CABBAGE-TREE MOB (sense 1). Also *attrib.*

[**1833** *Currency Lad* (Sydney) 18 May 4 Mr J. McArthur . . displayed more manliness than the other cabbage gents, in expressing his sentiments at the Meeting.] **1848** *Austral. Sportsman* (Sydney) 14 Oct. 2/4 The visitors had to run the gauntlet of the 'cabbage-trees', who subjected each carriage to a critical inspection. **1849** *Bell's Life in Sydney* 26 May 2/6 The lads of the village, alias the young cabbage tree gents. **1867** J.R. HOULDING *Austral. Capers* 227 Some of the 'cabbage-tree boys' were there too, indulging in their favourite holiday rollick of knocking all the 'black billies' from the heads of the wearers.

4. *Hist.* See CABBAGE-TREE MOB 2.

1857 *Bell's Life in Sydney* 17 Oct. 2/1 Our young men, particularly the class familiarly termed the 'cabbage-tree' lads [*sc.* stockmen], are peculiarly fitted for this honorable duty.

Hence **cabbage-treed** *ppl. a.*

1857 *Illustr. Jrnl. Australasia* II. 6 A burly-looking carter, blue-shirted and cabbage-treed, according to custom.

cabbage-tree hat. [f. CABBAGE TREE 1 a.]

1. A wide-brimmed hat woven from cabbage tree leaves. Also **cabbage-palm hat.**

[**1802** G. BARRINGTON *Hist. N.S.W.* 335 This hat, made of white filament of the cabbage-tree, seemed to excite the attention of the whole party.] **1841** *Hunter River Gaz.* 11 Dec. 3/3 At present our principal manufactures are cabbage-tree hats and tomb stones. **1853** F. GERSTAECKER *Life in Bush* 13 A squatter from the Adelaide district, with a huge beard, a cabbage-palm hat, . . bush shoes, and a red silk neck handkerchief. **1869** 'E. HOWE' *Boy in Bush* 151 Long Steve's wife had plaited him a cabbage-tree hat. **1887** A. NICOLS *Wild Life & Adventure* 63 A cabbage-tree hat on his head . . and his trusty stock-whip looped in his hand. **1916** H.L. ROTH *Sketches & Reminisc. Qld.* 10 He was joined by a man, Bottle-Green, an eccentric shepherd up north noted for his cabbage tree (palm tree) hats. **1935** C.H. SOUTER *Lonely Rose* 54 An' on 'er shiny curls she wore My cabbage-tree hat! **1948** J. FAIRFAX *Run o' Waters* 44 The heart of the palm they cooked and ate. . . The leaves were used for thatching, for brooms, and the making of that famous cabbage-tree hat which led to the old cockney jibe 'That's an Orsetrillian, 'e's got on a cabbage-tree 'at.' **1968** LINKLATER & TAPP *Gather no Moss* 18 A cabbage-tree hat . . cost two pounds ten, but it was worth it to look like a stockman. **1981** G. CROSS *George & Widda-Woman* 84 Dan's horse always wore a cabbage-tree hat, with holes cut in the sides for her ears.

2. cabbage-tree hat mob: see next.

Hence **cabbage-tree-hatted** *ppl. a.*

1876 *Austral. Town & Country Jrnl.* (Sydney) 16 Dec. 982/2 The sabre stroke of a sixteen foot stockwhip dropped fair between the eyes, by a cabbage-tree-hatted black velvet-banded native. *c* **1914** A.B. PATERSON in C. Semmler *World of Banjo Paterson* (1967) 318 He saw a genuine bushman, bearded, cabbage-tree-hatted, sunburnt, and silent.

cabbage-tree mob. *Hist.* [f. CABBAGE-TREE 2 + MOB 3.]

1. A collective term for a class of young urban roughs distinguished by their wearing of cabbage-tree hats; a gang of these. Also **cabbage-tree hat mob.**

1848 *Atlas* (Sydney) IV. 390/2 The disturbances . . were not begun by the Irish party who were in favour of Captain O'Connell, but originated with a parcel of young blackguards, known by the name of the *Cabbage-tree mob.* **1852** G.C. MUNDY *Our Antipodes* I. 53 There are to be found round the doors of the Sydney theatre a sort of 'loafers', known as the Cabbage-tree mob, . . an unruly set of young fellows, native born generally, who . . amuse themselves by molesting those who can afford that luxury. **1861** *Bell's Life in Sydney* 5 Jan. 3/1 'Twas Thursday in old Sydney town. . . The 'cabbage-tree mobs' that you'd meet Were off to the Parliament Houses. **1907** C. MACALISTER *Old Pioneering Days* 54 George Hough . . was a bit inclined to act the bully, perhaps to show his credentials as a leading member of the lower strata of the 'cabbage-tree Hat' mob, which corresponded to some extent to the hooligans and larrikins of to-day. **1973** J. MURRAY *Larrikins* 30 There are suggestions of pushes much earlier than the larrikins themselves. The Cabbage Tree Mob was distinctive, its flamboyant use of the cabbage-tree hat marking it out.

2. *transf.* and *fig.* Used of other traditional wearers of the cabbage-tree hat, e.g. bushmen, squatters.

1891 *Truth* (Sydney) 5 Apr. 7/3 The fence and the sheep have sent the stockman to Queensland, and the cabbage-tree hat mob to the devil. **1898** *Bulletin* (Sydney) 19 Feb. 6/3 The remnant of the Cabbage-tree Mob has risen to announce that it will do all it knows to prevent any Federation unless N.S. Wales receives a special bribe by the establishment of the Federal capital in its territory.

cabbage tree palm: see CABBAGE TREE 1 a.

cabbagite. *Hist.* Also **cabbageite.** [f. CABBAGE-TREE 2.] A member of the CABBAGE-TREE MOB (sense 1). Also **cabbager.**

1838 *Colonist* (Sydney) 21 July 3/4 The Bench sentenced the young *cabbagers* to a month's industry at the treadmill. **1852** G.C. MUNDY *Our Antipodes* III. 131 Scurrilous and insolent abuse of the constituted authorities had been found to be a dainty dish to set before the Cabbageites. **1976** B. SCOTT *Compl. Bk. Austral. Folk Lore* 52 Unaware of the propensities of the Cabbagites, he was by them furiously assailed—for no better reason apparently than because, like 'noble Percy', 'he wore his *beaver* up'.

cable gum. *Obs.* [f. *cable* (see quots.) + GUM *n.* 1.] GIMLET a.

1833 *Perth Gaz.* 21 Sept. 151 An apparently different species of the Eucalyptus. . . From its peculiar appearance, some of our party named it the cable gum. **1846** J.L. STOKES *Discoveries in Aust.* II. 132 *Cable gum* . . Several stems twisted together, abundant in the interior. **1855** R. AUSTIN *Jrnl. Interior W.A.* 9 Interspersed with patches of gnaleruk, (fluted or cable-gum of Roe) a singular species of eucalyptus, with smooth, glossy bark, and three spiral channels along the trunk, which make it resemble a twisted clustered column growing on the loamy soil.

cabon /ˈkɒbɒn/, *a.* (and *adv.*) *Austral. pidgin. Obs.* [a. Dharuk *gaban.*] Also **cawbawn, cobborn,** etc.

A. *adj.* Big, great.

1827 P. CUNNINGHAM *Two Yrs. in N.S.W.* II. 28 They could not contain their astonishment . . that '*cobawn* (big) gobernor, had not mout *so* (screwing theirs in the appropriate shape), like the *narang* (little) gobernor'. **1838** 'ONE OF PARTY' *Month in Bush Aust.* 6 The blacks say, however, that there are two deep holes in it a 'cabonn' (large and deep) and a 'narang' (small). **1845** C. HODGKINSON *Aust., Port Macquarie to Moreton Bay* 216 The blacks . . seemed to recognise it, and said that it belonged to 'cobbaun water', (the ocean). **1849** S. & J. SIDNEY *Emigrant's Jrnl.* 311 He required a rig out, as a necessary preliminary that he might appear 'a cabon swell'. **1870** C.H. ALLEN *Visit to Qld.* 183 Certain native terms . . are used by the whites also as a kind of colonial slang, such as . . 'yan', to go; 'cabon', much; and so on. **1881** A.C. GRANT *Bush-Life Qld.* I. 57 'There,' said Stone, pointing to the big house, 'nobody has lived in the *cawbawn humpy*—that is what the blacks call it—since Mr Cosgrove.' **1923** J. BOWES *Jackaroos* 137 He elicited the information that three days ago a cobborn (big) mob of white pfeller rode in from the north.

B. *adv.* Extremely.

1881 A.C. GRANT *Bush-Life Aust.* II. 175 'Missis bail bong, only cawbawn prighten' (Missis not dead, only dreadfully frightened).

cacker, var. KAKKA.

cackle tub. [f. *cackle* loquacity + *tub* pulpit.] A pulpit. Also *fig.*

1882 *Sydney Slang Dict.* 2 *Cackle-Tub*, a pulpit. **1905** *Shearer* (Sydney) 26 Aug. 5/2 Miss Locke, like many of her sex, is terribly assertive when mounted on the political 'cackle tub'. **1973** J. MURRAY *Larrikins* 202 *Cackle tub*, a pulpit.

cactus, *n.* and *a.*

A. *n.*

1. In the phr. **in the cactus,** in difficulty.

1943 S.J. BAKER *Pop. Dict. Austral. Slang* (ed. 3) 18 *Cactus, in the*, in trouble. (R.A.A.F. slang.) **1984** A. DELBRIDGE *Aussie Talk* 56 *In the cactus*, in difficulties, in trouble.

2. *fig.* The backblocks.

1945 *Coast to Coast 1944* 174 He got in the car and started the engine. 'Well, it's back to the cactus,' he said. **1945** 'R. RENE' *Mo's Mem.* 120 Mo is very nostalgic. . . 'Oh to get back to the cactus. Just dying to get a saw in me hand.' **1980** *Sydney Morning Herald* 31 Dec. 7/9 We are today back to the cactus as our Antipodean friends would say.

B. *adj.* Ruined; finished.

1945 *Atebrin Advocate: Mag. 2/4 Austral. Armoured Regiment* Jan. 1 My Jeep's broken down. . . The starter's cactus. **1980** ANSELL & PERCY *To fight Wild* 29, I couldn't make up my mind about that dirty-water creek. . . If I was lucky I might find fresh water in a few hours. If not, if it ran back into salt pans, I'd be cactus. I'd never make up the lost time.

cadet. *Obs.* [N.Z. *cadet* young man learning sheep-farming: see OEDS 4.] JACKEROO *n.* 2.

1879 S.W. SILVER *Austral. Grazier's Guide* 13 The 'colonial experiencer', the 'jackàroo' or 'cadet', as he is variously designated in different colonies, always lodges with the proprietor or the resident manager. **1918** C. FETHERSTONHAUGH *After Many Days* 40, I had the opportunity of going to Woodlands as a 'cadet', as jackeroos were more euphoniously styled in those days. **1923** J. BOWES *Jackaroos* 17 They were cadets newly appointed to a cattle station, and from henceforth would be known as 'jackaroos'.

cakker, var. KAKKA.

calabash. *Obs.* [Transf. use of *calabash* vessel made from the shell of a gourd or fruit.]

1. COOLAMON 1.

1835 J. BACKHOUSE *Narr. Visit Austral. Colonies* (1843) 325 They [*sc.* the natives] likewise carry with them . . vessels for water, made of the large, tubercular excrescences of the gum-tree, hollowed out, which are here called Calabashes. **1845** L. LEICHHARDT *Jrnl. Overland Exped. Aust.* 15 Feb. (1847) 159 The natives . . made him several presents, among which were two fine calabashes which they had cleaned and used for carrying water. **1922** J. LEWIS *Fought & Won* 85 We spied a lubra. The moment she saw us she hid in a bunch of grass, and as we rode up seemed very frightened and ran away, leaving her wooden calabash.

2. *fig. Obs.* A promissory note: see quot. 1882.

1861 *Brisbane Courier* 23 Oct. 2/2 *Calabashes.* Agents or other parties resident in the country are requested to refrain from the practice of forwarding '*calabashes*' to this office by way of payment, since they are not looked upon as cash, and will invariably be returned to the person who transmitted them. **1882** W. COOTE *Hist. Colony Qld.* 82 The absence of a bank and the want of silver, led to the adoption of a system of what were called 'calabashes'—orders drawn upon some agent of the drawer, payable at various dates after presentation, and often for very small amounts. **1913** M.A. MCMANUS *Reminisc. Maranoa District* 53 Just fancy there being no silver or notes in the district . . and cheques, orders, and I.O.U.'s were sometimes valueless, and were known as 'calabashes'. **1916** J.M. CREED *Recoll. Aust.* 53 All other transactions were carried out by cheques or I.O.U.'s, which passed current everywhere. The latter were known as 'calabashes' and were of varying amounts, the smallest being sixpence, given by someone for a box of matches. **1938** *Smith's Weekly* (Sydney) 12 Nov. 6/3 Mention of 'shin-plasters' recently in 'Smith's Weekly' suggests a mention of 'calabash'. This was a form of currency in the early days.

calico, *attrib.* and *n.* [Spec. use of *calico* cotton cloth.]

A. *attrib.*

1. Applied to temporary or portable structures made of strong cotton or canvas.

1856 G. WILLMER *Draper in Aust.* 140, I was agreeably surprised to receive an invitation to dine with him in his calico-roofed house. **1871** J. BAIRD *Emigrant's Guide Australasia* 34 Lined on each side with shabby wooden and calico huts, on the brink of the Turon. **1896** M. HORNSBY *Old Time Echoes Tas.* 117 Wattle and dab, with a bark roof, the hut soon got slapped together; a slab floor and a calico window completed. **1907** *Bulletin* (Sydney) 10 Oct. 14/1 They were for years most valuable to drovers, saving night watches, dogs, calico fences, etc. **1911** ST. C. GRONDONA *Collar & Cuffs* 75 After inspecting the calico break in which the sheep had to be put for the night. **1917** *Bulletin* (Sydney) 18 Jan. 22/2 He . . set out for Maytown to deliver a billiard table at that calico township. **1935** F. CLUNE *Rolling down Lachlan* 96 The bark humpies . . the tents and the calico huts have all gone away. **1939** J.W. COLLINSON *Early Days Cairns* 130 Cooktown in 1873, Cairns in 1876, and Port Douglas in 1877, were each in turn calico towns. **1946** W.E. HARNEY *North of 23°* 16 Camped the sheep at night by erecting a calico yard. **1949** H.E. THONEMANN *Tell White Man* 38 With the party was also the hangman, cooks, and those to care for the large plant of horses. . . It was the largest calico town most of us had ever seen.

2. Special Comb. **calico muster:** see MUSTER *n.* 5.

B. *n.* A shirt.

1858 *S. Austral. Advertiser* (Adelaide) 13 July 3/2 He . . was fined for the assault . . and damage done to the constable's 'calico'. **1935** P.H. RITCHIE *North of Never Never* 154 Some don't even wear a 'calico'.

calico jimmy. *Obs.* [f. *calico* (see prec.) + the proper name *Jimmy.*] A member of a free-trade lobby advocating the importation of duty-free textiles; a textile merchant. Also *attrib.*

1889 *Braidwood Dispatch* 14 Sept. 2/4 It had been the habit three years ago when the Parkes Government came into power, for such men as Melville and O'Sullivan to rail at the Government as calico jemmies, but what did they find in Melbourne—why that calico was admitted free. **1895** *Bulletin* (Sydney) 10 Aug. 7/2 Every sinful calico-jimmy roaming at large is an insult to the doctrine of 'fair dinkum' which all men, rogues or otherwise, hold in respect. **1902** *Truth* (Sydney) 14 Sept. 4/4 The clique of calico jemmies who employ the cur. **1907** *Ibid.* 25 Aug. 4/7 Because Reid won't . . play the Freetrade farce in the Federal Parliament for these corrupt Calico Jemmies, they 'sool' their plutish prints on to proclaim him a cocktail, a renegade, a coward. **1917** *Advocate* (Burnie) 3 July 1/5 Why, farmers, you are placing your business in the hands of lawyers and calico jimmies.

Californian, *a. Hist.* In the gold-rush period: applied in collocations to machinery and wearing apparel similar to those used on the Californian goldfields, esp. as **Californian pump** (see quot. 1931). Also **California.**

[**1850** *Bell's Life in Sydney* 22 June 3/2 Being equipped a *la* Californy rig.] **1851** *Britannia* (Hobart) 26 June 4/5 Others add to it a blue serge shirt and a California hat. **1853** A. MACKAY *Great Gold Field* 30 At the waterhole, they cut a channel for the water of the creek to run off, and then soon emptied the waterhole with a Californian pump. **1854** C.A. CORBYN *Sydney Revels* 64 Addison William Blakely then put a California kiver on his cabbage head, and ambled out of court. **1862** H. BROWN *Vic. as I found It* 291 Besides similar machinery to ours of stampers and Californian tables, there were various others used to crush and wash the quartz rock. **1869** R.B. SMYTH *Gold Fields & Mineral Districts* 607 Californian pumps are used only in shallow alluvial ground. **1931** W. BARAGWANATH et al. *Guide for Prospectors in Vic.* 15 The California pump is an endless belt passing over rollers, and having buckets at intervals attached to it. When the belt is in motion the buckets, as they pass down into the water, fill themselves, and then travel with the belt to the top, where they discharge the water as they turn over into a shoot, by which it passes away.

Hence **Californiate** *v. trans.*

1854 W. SHAW *Land of Promise* 87 The efforts made by the tradespeople to Californiate their city, are rather amusing.

call, *v.* [Spec. use of *call* to announce.] *trans.* To commentate upon (a sporting event).

1906 *Gadfly* (Adelaide) 20 June 14/1 When the sporting writer whose task it is to 'call' an important hockey match focuses his spectacles on the frenzied girls, he talks like a lunatic. *Ibid., The Register* printed a paragraph about the glorious way in which 'Mostyn' 'called' an important race. **1959** D. LOCKWOOD *Crocodiles & Other People* 70, I haven't got time to drive this bastard and call the card, too. **1966** G. BARRY *Bed & Bored* 17 You're calling the wrong race if you think that. **1977** *Sun-Herald* (Sydney) 9 Jan. 67/5 He's calling the dogs for 2UE on Fridays from Richmond and on Saturdays from Wentworth Park.

Hence **caller** *n.*

1949 L. GLASSOP *Lucky Palmer* 247 There's no better race caller in Australia than 'Lucky' Palmer. When he was only fourteen he used to call the races from the verandah of a house. **1980** M. WILLIAMS *Dingo!* 14 The sound of a race caller droned monotonously.

callistemon /kəˈlɪstəmən/. [The plant genus *Callistemon* was named by British botanist Robert Brown in 1814 (see quot. 1814), f. Gr. καλλι-, comb. stem of κάλλος beauty + στήμων thread, referring to the conspicuous stamens of the individual flowers comprising the 'bottlebrush'.] Any plant of the chiefly Austral. genus *Callistemon* (see BOTTLEBRUSH a.).

1814 R. BROWN *Gen. Remarks Bot. Terra Australis* 15 Callistemon, a genus formed of those species of Metrosideros that have inflorescence similar to that of Melaleuca, and distinct elongated filaments. **1901** *Proc. Congress Engineers, Architects, Surveyors* (Melbourne) 44 Our heritage must be kept in sight,—our Gippsland stream and valley, our Blue Mountain escarpment .. for waratah, rock lily, calistemon, [etc.]. **1948** C.B. MAXWELL *Cold Nose of Law* 101 The prickly coastal shrub of the locality, casuarina and callistemon. **1985** *Age* (Melbourne) 3 Dec. 27/1 Prune callistemons after flowering.

callitris /kəˈlitrəs/. [The plant genus *Callitris* was named by French botanist E.P. Ventenat (*Decas generum nov.* (1808) 10), f. Gr. καλλι-, comb. stem of Gr. κάλλος beauty and τρεῖς three, referring to the arrangement of the leaves in whorls of three.] Any plant of the chiefly Austral. coniferous genus *Callitris* (fam. Cupressaceae). See also CYPRESS PINE.

[**1814** R. BROWN *Gen. Remarks Bot. Terra Australis* 42 *Callitris* of Ventenat is peculiar to Terra Australis, where it exists very generally. **1827** A. CUNNINGHAM *Gen. Remarks Vegetation* 10 Callitris, of which seven species are known, and principally found in the parallel of Port Jackson, has also been discovered upon the North-west Coast, in about latitude 15° South. **1834** G. BENNETT *Wanderings N.S.W.* I. 263 Were growing large quantities of a species of Callitrys, called the 'Murrumbidgee pine' by the colonists, from having been seen first on the hills in the vicinity of that river.] **1849** C. STURT *Narr. Exped. Central Aust.* II. 291, I saw no Callitris (Pine of the colonists) in all that country. **1855** W. HOWITT *Land, Labor & Gold* II. 106 One new tree, a calitris, I suppose the Murray pine, but large and lofty, and much handsomer than the calitris of the granite rocks in the Ovens country. **1963** A.E. FARRELL *Vengeance* 18 A great belt of Callitris pines. The sturdy, dark blue-green boles, capped with clumps of dark green, needle-like foliage stood out as exquisite etchings against the undulating pink coloured sandhills.

callop /ˈkæləp/. *S.A.* [Prob. f. a S.A. Aboriginal language.] *Golden perch*, see GOLDEN 3.

1921 *Rec. S. Austral. Museum* II. i. 88 *Plectroplites ambiguus* .. (Callop, Tarki). **1935** *S.A. Parl. Papers* II. no. 20 23 Larger quantities of Callop are marketed than of any other river fish. **1951** T.C. ROUGHLEY *Fish & Fisheries Aust.* 147 The name 'callop' has been customarily used for this fish in South Australia over a long period. **1974** L. WEDLICK *Sporting Fish* 11 This perch was officially called 'callop' but this name .. was ousted and today the fish is both officially and colloquially known as a golden perch or yellowbelly. **1986** *Daily Tel.* (Sydney) 24 Apr. 15/4 Callop and Murray Cod, two of Australia's most prized native fish.

camel bush. Any of several shrubs, esp. *Trichodesma zeylanicum* (fam. Boraginaceae), reputedly favoured by camels.

1900 A.A. DAVIDSON *Jrnl. of Explorations Central Aust.* 6 May (1905) 18 From the ridge we passed into a small flat, with a splendid run of camel bush. **1915** *Bull. N.T.* xiv. 10 Boree (camel bush or bullock bush). **1932** I.L. IDRIESS *Flynn of Inland* (1965) 1 Here and there grew camel-bush near stunted mulga whose dwarf shapes seemed dancing in the hazy plain. **1973** C.E. GOODE *Stories Strange Places* 141 That patch of land towards Mount Burgess is rich enough for anything. . . Plenty . . of camel bush.

camel-neck. [See quot. 1935.] A drought-emaciated rabbit. Also **camel-back.**

1935 D.G. STEAD *Rabbit in Aust.* 87 Rabbits had died out or were dying, and the remnant were all poor, miserable 'camel-necks'—just skin and bone, moving about feebly. **1969** E.C. ROLLS *They All ran Wild* 59 These superior rabbits do not drink. . . 'Camel backs' and 'camel-necks', they are called when the feed and water dry up.

camel poison. Any of several (poisonous) trees or shrubs, esp. the shrub *Gyrostemon australasicus* (fam. Gyrostemonaceae) and the extremely poisonous tree *Erythrophleum chlorostachys* (fam. Caesalpiniaceae) of n. Aust. See also *black bean* (b) BLACK *a.*[2] 1 a., IRONWOOD.

1926 *Poison Plants W.A.* (W.A. Dept. Agric.) 57 Camel Poison (*Erythrophloeum Labourcherii*) .. is more commonly known as 'Black Bean Tree', 'Ironwood', or 'Steelwood'. **1935** H.H. FINLAYSON *Red Centre* 45 Another poisonous plant, *Duboisia hopwoodi* [*sic*]—a camel poison of the whites—with which the blacks poison the smaller rock-holes, so that .. water-greedy emus become stupefied .. easy victims to the spear. **1976** L. BEADELL *Beating about Bush* 145 There could be no doubt that this specimen, with its 'goanna skin' patterned bark and light green foliage, was one of the dreaded camel poison bushes.

camp, *n.* [Spec. use of *camp* temporary quarters.]

1. *Obs.* A name given to Sydney and to any of several other towns which grew out of temporary settlements (see quot. 1792). Usu. with **the.**

1790 *Hist. Rec. N.S.W.* (1893) II. 724 He treats us with more affability, and is all at once so polite as to beg of my only companion, Mr Harris, and self, whenever we come to camp, to let him have our co. **1792** R. ATKINS Jrnl. 4 Apr., I walked by myself to the Brick fields, about a mile from the Camp, for so Sydney is call'd, from its having been on the Spot they pitch'd their tents on their first landing. **1827** P. CUNNINGHAM *Two Yrs. in N.S.W.* II. 70 The old resident . . still calls Sydney with its population of twelve thousand bustling inhabitants *the camp.* **1843** *South Briton* (Hobart) May 139 A bark hut, under a great gum tree, in the very middle of *Camp* as they then called the charming port of Hobart Town. **1852** J. WEST *Hist. of Tas.* II. 124 They gave, and long preserved to the site of the city, the name of *Camp.* **1887** MRS D.D. DALY *Digging, Squatting, & Pioneering Life* 44 The 'camp', to use the name so familiar to every one, and which to this day it [*sc.* Darwin] has retained, consisted of a number of log and iron houses on either side of the gully. **1929** I.A. SCOULER *Dowerin Story* 17 The more scattered mining towns (or 'camps', as they were generally called—Coolgardie is still spoken of by its old timers as the 'Old Camp').

2. An Aboriginal settlement, either temporary or permanent. Also *attrib.*

1840 *S. Austral. Rec.* (London) 18 Apr. 191 We have the chief or king (Wagamy), and his two black queens, or *jins*, always with us, who have their camp just beside us. **1850** J. PLATT *Horrors of Transportation* 13 When the sun goes down at night they begin to form their camp; if it is dry weather, they take the bark off the trees and form a kind of roof to a house. **1861** *Burke & Wills Exploring Exped.* 3 Mr Burke and Mr Wills went in search of the natives, to endeavour to find out how the nardoo grew. Having found their camp, they obtained as much nardoo cake and fish as they could eat. **1878** R.B. SMYTH *Aborigines of Vic.* I. 85 After a little fencing between the pair, the woman, if she has no serious objections to the man, quietly submits, and allows herself to be taken away to the camp of her future husband. *c* **1891** J. GARDINER *Twenty-Five Yrs. on Stage* 109 One . . was going to marry a halfcaste out of the camp of blacks on his run. **1910** *Huon Times* (Franklin) 9 Nov. 4/3 The two natives went to Kellerberrin on Saturday, and obtained liquor, which they took back to camp. **1922** 'J. BUSHMAN' *In Musgrave Ranges* 82 These niggers are wild. . . They're different from the camp blacks who hang round stations. **1936** C. CHEWINGS *Back in Stone Age* 13 Natives never make a bed, but scratch out a shallow hole or hollow which they call a camp-hole—*tmara junta.* **1977** X. HERBERT *Dream Road* 75 The collection of hovels on the river bank below the tanks—the blacks' camp?

3. A place where stock choose regularly to congregate; a resting-place for travelling stock; the place where a mustered herd is assembled; travelling stock (see quots. 1868 and 1944). Freq. in the phr. **on camp.** Also **cattle camp, sheep camp.**

1845 *Sydney Morning Herald* 23 Sept. 3/3 Any one who has been upon a cattle camp knows that cattle invariably face about, and stare at the intruder. **1855** W. RIDLEY *Rep. Journey Condamine, Barwon & Namoi Rivers* 5 While troops of aborigines roam about the runs, and especially if they go to the cattle camps and watering places, it is impossible to keep a herd together. **1861** H. EARLE *Ups & Downs* 10 Cattle . . become peculiarly attached to a particular camp or locality. **1868** C.W. BROWNE *Overlanding in Aust.* 38 When two sheep-camps meet on the road, there very soon springs up a friendly feeling between them. **1872** 'RESIDENT' *Glimpses Life Vic.* 61 They were driven first on to a large camp, when they were all rounded up together. **1881** A.C. GRANT *Bush-Life Qld.* II. 157 As the rains extended their period of duration .. the cattle were, perforce, obliged to remain about the sound, sandy country on which their instinct led them to select their camps. **1890** 'R. BOLDREWOOD' *Colonial Reformer* II. 133 A cattle 'camp' is a rendezvous, used by a subdivision of a herd of cattle for purposes apparently of friendly gathering, converse, and social recreation—a Bovine Club. **1915** *Bulletin* (Sydney) 23 Sept. 22/4 A mob of travelling cows was put on camp. **1923** *Ibid.* 29 Mar. 24/2 Are Australian-bred sheep changing their camping habits? Forty or fifty years ago a big leafy tree was selected for a camp and used year after year. The 'camping-tree' was a landmark in each station paddock. **1938** F. RATCLIFFE *Flying Fox & Drifting Sand* 80 In Queensland a 'camp' merely means a place where beasts (or men) can rest. **1943** *Bulletin* (Sydney) 7 Mar. 13/3 The bullock-muster was on. About a thousand head were being held on 'camp' while the best of them were being cut out to go on the road. **1944** J.J. HARDIE *Cattle Camp* (ed. 3) 82 Ken led his camp down the Barker on his first muster as head stockman. **1957** R.S. PORTEOUS *Brigalow* 21 Odd patches of green timber had been left to form shady camps for the cattle. **1976** E.H. MCFARLANE *Land of Contrasts* 20, I could ride out . . and spend the day helping to muster, and hold the cattle on camp while branding was done.

4. See quot. 1938 and FLYING FOX CAMP.

1881 A.C. GRANT *Bush-Life Qld.* II. 20 A little distance further on they come to a camp of flying-foxes. **1938** F. RATCLIFFE *Flying Fox & Drifting Sand* 12 A camp of flying foxes was to be found. (The daytime congregations of these beasts are known as 'camps'. A camp is not just a casual meeting place. Many have been inhabited year after year for half a century at least.)

5. A rest.

1899 'S. Rudd' *On our Selection* 127 Sometimes Dan used to forget to talk at all—he would be asleep—and Dad would wonder if he was unwell. Once he advised him to go up to the house and have a *good* camp. **1943** *Bulletin* (Sydney) 22 Dec. 12/3 Horses have a love for an early-morning camp, but old bushmen hold it as infallible the rule that a prad which lies down at sunset is ailing. **1960** R.S. Porteous *Cattleman* 95 'Run me in the best horse you've got and I'll get started.' 'You better have a bit of a camp first, after the ride you put up last night.' **1979** B. Scott *Tough in Old Days* 39 He stretched luxuriously on the grass as the sun warmed his bones. 'Think I'll have a camp,' he said.

6. Special Comb. **camp gang,** a convict working party; **horse,** see quot. 1886; **kettle,** a cooking vessel; variously applied to (iron) vessels used over a camp fire; **muster,** see quot. 1933; **oven, (a)** a heavy, iron, three-legged cooking vessel which stands in a fire and has a flat, usu. recessed, lid on top of which hot coals can be placed; **(b)** an Aboriginal cooking place (see quot. 1851); **pie,** a kind of cooked, usu. tinned, meat mixture; **work,** work associated with a camp muster.

1808 *HRA* (1916) 1st Ser. VI. 356 As employed in the **Camp Gang**, which Gang are supposed to be working for the sole advantage of the Crown. **1822** J.T. Bigge *Rep. State Colony N.S.W.* 47 Those whose services are not useful in the buildings are employed in what is called the camp gang, in clearing stumps of trees, and preparing the ground for building. **1886** H. Finch-Hatton *Advance Aust.* 63 A '**camp-horse**' is one used for cutting out cattle on a camp. **1897** *Western Champion* (Barcaldine) 23 Nov. 10/3 Next I expect to chronicle that the 'camp' horse has served his period of usefulness . . and retires in favour of the bike. **1907** *Bulletin* (Sydney) 30 May 15/2 The best camp horses in the world are found on the Belyando River (Q.) stations. They have the grit and stamina with which to gallop and twist and shoulder a beast out of any mob. Just let your camp horse see the beast you want cut out and he does the rest. **1922** 'J. Bushman' *In Musgrave Ranges* 183 For a camp-horse can turn right round at full gallop in its own length. . . A camp-horse is a horse which has been especially trained for cutting out cattle on a cattle-camp. **1940** W. Hatfield *Into (Great?) Unfenced* 116 He had *discovered* Miss Koongi as a camp-drafting mount, a *camp-horse*, to give her her trade designation. **1963** M. Britt *Pardon my Boots* 67 This little brown horse was a magnificent old camp-horse, who could always anticipate what a bullock's next move would be. **1976** C.D. Mills *Hobble Chains & Greenhide* 141 He is going to be a camp-horse. The most highly prized and hardest horse to replace on any cattle station. **1805** J. Turnbull *Voyage round World* I. 74 Some fish belonging to the sailors . . boiling in a **camp kettle** over the fire on shore. **1838** *Hobart Town Almanack* 71 It was cooked in a small camp-kettle. **1851** *Illustr. Austral. Mag.* (Melbourne) Nov. 257 The waterman standing at the head of the cradle, with camp kettle, tin-dish, or ladle of any sort fastened to a handle, bales the water continuously into it. **1892** 'R. Boldrewood' *Nevermore* II. 163 When you've finished your first beaker of tea, there's more in the camp-kettle, Australice 'billy'. **1912** R.S. Tait *Scotty Mac* 16 Brownie, damper, and scones baked in a camp-kettle. **1933** *Bulletin* (Sydney) 9 Aug. 21/3 The **camp muster** was an annual event in the old days before general fencing, when every station had a general muster on the main cattle camps, and men from all the stations came along to identify and cut out their own cattle. **1832** *Hill's Life N.S.W.* (Sydney) 28 Dec. 1 Iron **camp ovens**, all sizes. **1851** *Australasian* (Melbourne) 303 The 'camp ovens' where in happier times they roasted the kangaroo whole. **1852** J. Bonwick *Notes of Gold Digger* 20 The same camp oven has, perhaps, to turn out two loaves, a baked joint for dinner, and, mystery of mysteries, a boiled plum pudding. **1872** Mrs E. Millett *Austral. Parsonage* 91 Our pies and bread were baked upon the bars of the grate in camp-ovens, which are round flat-bottomed pots standing on three short legs, and with lids so contrived as to retain the hot embers with which they are heaped. **1910** *Bulletin* (Sydney) 22 Sept. 13/4 Cooked any old how wallaby is good . . braized [*sic*] in a camp oven with a few onions, bosker. **1916** J.M. Creed *Recoll. Aust.* 112 What is known as a camp-oven is used. This is a cast-iron, flat-bottomed vessel, from eighteen to twenty-four inches in diameter and nine deep, with perpendicular walls, two loops for a movable handle on opposite sides, and three legs about six inches high. It has a lid to fit it somewhat loosely, with a loop on the top for lifting with a hook. It is used for baking bread and cakes, for roasting joints, for frying, for boiling, or any of the ordinary purposes of a pot. For baking, it is placed over glowing wood embers and covered with others piled around and over it; when it cooks admirably. **1944** K.S. Prichard *Potch & Colour* 6 The camp-oven, a large black pot on short legs, squatted in the embers. **1955** *Bulletin* (Sydney) 18 May 13/1 Gidgee-wood gives off terrific heat and produces fierce red coals, which should be used sparingly when cooking in a camp-oven. **1982** R. Hall *Just Relations* 150 An iron camp-oven stood at the back. He removed the lid with a flourish. **1909** *Anthony Hordern Catal.* 1153 Preserved Meat . . **Camp pies**, Maconochie's . . 1s. tin 11s. 6d. doz. **1938** Mrs F.V. McKenzie *Electrical Assoc. for Women Cookery Bk.* 85 Camp Pie. Mince 1 lb. of lean beef with ¼ lb. of lean fat. Season well . . and bind with an egg. Steam in a covered basin for 2 hours, with the hotplate element on low. Serve cold and sliced. **1964** K. Tennant *Summer's Tales* 41, I boyishly punted a camp pie tin. **1984** P. Read *Down there with me on Cowra Mission* 97 We'd get our sandwiches, our bread and our devon, or camp-pie. **1876** *Austral. Town & Country Jrnl.* (Sydney) 23 Dec. 1022/4 In **camp-work**, there is little or no chance of oppression or hurt. After an hour's 'beating up', and ringing of whips, streams of cattle are seen pouring in from every point of the compass towards, let us say, the main camp. Generally situated at no great distance from the stockyard, this is supposed to be the central and principal trysting place. **1880** J.B. Stevenson *Seven Yrs. Austral. Bush* 126 There are usually a very small number of quiet cattle, generally only what is known as the milking mob, and therefore there is none of the work common upon ordinary stations. No camp work, or boundary riding.

camp, *v.* [See prec.]

1. *intr.* Of stock: to settle down to rest, usu. in some number (but see quot. 1872); to use an habitual resting place (see quot. 1849).

1843 A. Caswell *Hints from Jrnl.* 37 He then lets the cattle camp, or lie down. **1849** S. & J. Sidney *Emigrant's Jrnl.* 20 The sheep, for nearly nine months in the year after drinking, *camp*; that is, lie still under the shade, with all their heads turned towards one another. **1872** A. McFarland *Illawarra & Manaro* 121 Teams of bullocks—from 6 to 12 in number . . are to be met with 'camped' by creek and stream. **1882** A.J. Boyd *Old Colonials* 7, I follow the sheep, and camp when they camp. **1896** M. Clarke *Austral. Tales* 13 There was a herd of cattle camped at this place. **1904** *Bulletin* (Sydney) 8 Dec. 19/3 Cattle seldom 'rush' during the morning hours; they have by the time the last watch is called, generally settled down, although you must not rely too surely on their 'camping' even then. **1923** *Ibid.* 4 Jan. 22/2 If you want cattle to camp you must feed and water them well and not overdrive them. **1932** J. McCarter *Pan's Clan* 230 He rode slowly around the fringe of cattle, some of which were moving among their fellows sitting or 'camping' on the ground. **1942** W. Glasson *Our Shepherds* 9 Travelling sheep are often camped in a lane near this homestead. **1980** *Weekend Austral. Mag.* (Sydney) 23 Aug. 1/1 Close to the road a small herd of prize-winning short-horns are 'camping' in the early morning sun under a tree.

2. *intr.* To take a short rest, usu. for refreshment and not necessarily out of doors (see quots. 1870, 1892 and 1917). Also *fig.*

1848 *Maitland Mercury* 12 July 2/5 Having camped, to breathe the dogs, and partaken of refreshments and 'nobblers' round, the hounds started on a fresh scent. **1863** J.B. Austin *Mines S.A.* 29 We 'camped' in the middle of the day, to refresh man and beast . . amongst beautiful native flowers including sweet peas. **1870** 'Jackaroo' *Immigration Question* 8 An old gentleman from Bathurst . . camped at our hut in the middle of a broiling day recently. **1881** W. Feilding *Austral. Trans-Continental Railway* 50 Camped for dinner and to rest the horses, as the day was hot and oppressive. **1892** *Bulletin* (Sydney) 7 May 24/1 We'd camp in some old shanty-bar, And sit a-tellin' lies. **1912** *Ibid.* 10 Oct. 15/2, I have often met a party of shearers, camped for tucker-time, with their bikes all set up in a mulga garage. **1917** *Ibid.* 29 Mar. 22/2 Six teamsters with their waggons and 30 horses were camped for dinner at 'The Weatherboard'. **1944** A. Marshall *These are my People* 30, I camp about two hours for lunch. **1949** *Bulletin* (Sydney) 30 Mar. 15/4 The shearers as they go in for a sheep will naturally select the one they consider the easiest shearing, leaving the culls . . to last. Last one of all is called the 'cobbler'. A shearer just missing that 'choice' would have first pick of the new pen, and the vast difference between the two often leads shearers to 'camp' on their last sheep so that the other fellow would get the rough 'un.

3. *intr.* Of wild animals: to rest; to establish a resting place. Also with **up.**

1861 'Old Bushman' *Bush Wanderings* 9 It is a pretty sight to watch a mob [of kangaroos] camped up. **1895** *Bulletin* (Sydney) 2 Feb. 3/2 A kangaroo always wears his tail straight out behind. The scrub-wallaby, however, gets his between his legs when camped. **1926** *Smith's Weekly* (Sydney) 22 May 19/5 The large water-holes in Koopa Creek (Q.) . . are known as cockatoo holes, the birds flocking there at sundown to drink, and camp in the trees near by. **1941** C. Barrett *Aust.* 47 'Come and see our old Teddy. . . He's been here since last year: and nearly always camps in the same tree—that twisty-branched old manna gum. . . ' Close to the little schoolhouse an elderly koala had selected a home-tree. **1942** —— *From Bush Hut* 15 There's mobs of 'em [*sc.* snakes] around Wattle Creek. A big tiger used to camp in this hut.

4. *trans.* To keep (stock) together at a particular place, esp. for their rest and refreshment. Also with **out,** and *absol.*

1847 *Maitland Mercury* 28 Aug. 4/4 At stations where I cannot form paddocks, I make the shepherds camp the sheep out. **1847** *Moreton Bay Courier* 16 Oct. 4/1 Mr Wills of Port Phillip, recommends those persons who may be desirous of 'camping out' their flocks, to place rock salt on or about the spot on which they wish their stock to remain. **1848** *Maitland Mercury* 26 Aug. 2/4 Another mode of treatment [*sc.* of catarrh in sheep] which has been generally adopted, but in too many cases imperfectly carried out, is to travel with the flock upon high ranges, and camp them out every night. **1897** *Bulletin* (Sydney) 28 Aug. 29/2 Men from outback are camping for grass or water. **1916** *Ibid.* 24 Aug. 22/4 Has any . . orchardist tried camping sheep among his trees to eradicate codlin moth? **1936** L. Kaye *Black Wilderness* 86 Ben'd tell his offsider to camp the camels then, and he and Tobe would ride back.

camp draft, *n.* [f. Camp *n.* 3 + *draft* a selection.] A competitive equestrian event in which a rider isolates a steer from its fellows and drives it, against the clock, round a set course. Also *attrib.*

1951 *Bulletin* (Sydney) 23 May 15/2 He now has a horse to handle. It's not really a camp-draft champion. **1963** R.H. Conquest *Spurs are Rusty Now* 14 The girls who rode in the rodeos and camp-drafts in those days were hard-boiled customers. **1965** —— *Horses in Kitchen* 43 Hobo, an Americanism, crept into our language about the same time rodeo did—say, in 1929. Until then rodeos were known as camp-drafts, and hoboes were known as swaggies. **1977** V. Priddle *Larry & Jack* 188 The menfolk were talking Rodeo. George was of the opinion the Galway Downs horses were outstanding in the campdrafts.

Also **camp-drafter** *n.*, a horse used for camp-drafting.

1942 *Bulletin* (Sydney) 27 May 13/4 A sheep on the wheel will leave the best camp-drafter standing. **1973** R. Robinson *Drift of Things* 100 His name was Ovens, and he was a camp-drafter. He had won the camp-draft at the Warren Show. A camp-drafter is a specially trained horse for cattle. **1976** C.D. Mills *Hobble Chains & Greenhide* 138 When a new run of colts are brought into the yard for breaking, the first thought is—'Any suitable for camp-drafters?'

camp-draft, *v. trans.* Usu. as *vbl. n.*

1. To take part in a camp draft.

1921 *Bulletin* (Sydney) 14 Apr. 24/2 Cracks . . compete annually at one of the best camp-drafting and bull-tossing shows in Australasia. **1972** J. Byrne *Horse Riding Austral. Way* 103 Campdrafting is a true Australian bushman's sport and it started in this country using horses that worked with cattle. **1977** W.A. Winter-Irving *Bush Stories* 27 It was to be years before the imported breed of camp-drafting horses reached the north. **1981** *Weekend Austral. Mag.* (Sydney) 3 Oct. 9/2 Good shots of the Australian-invented sports of polocrosse (polo-cum-lacrosse) and campdrafting (cattle mustering in a showground).

2. To ride among yarded cattle, with the intention of isolating those required for branding, butchering, etc.

1945 E. MITCHELL *Speak to Earth* 56 Mitchell . . had as great a name for riding after cattle in rough country as he had a bad one for camp-drafting. **1951** E. HILL *Territory* 293 Stockmen, white and black, have been out for weeks 'riding tracks', mustering, branding, camp-drafting. **1956** T. RONAN *Moleskin Midas* 22 Until mid-night they worked erecting a rough but serviceable fork-and-sapling yard. In the morning they mustered their cattle into this, and . . Amos Sides started camp-drafting out the heifers.

camping, *vbl. n.* [f. CAMP *n.* 3, infl. by CAMP *v.* 1.] Used *attrib.* in Special Comb. **camping ground, place, reserve**: see CAMP *n.* 3.

1841 *Omnibus & Sydney Spectator* 27 Nov. 68/4 The whole course of the Mackie is full of dead bullocks, and I have heard that the skeletons of two hundred bullocks are bleaching on one **camping ground**. **1848** *Maitland Mercury* 26 Aug. 2/4 The sheep will camp quietly around the cart and watch-fire, after they become a little accustomed to it. . . A dray or cart will of course have to go round daily to take up any that may have died on the run, or camping ground. **1853** W. WESTGARTH *Vic.* 110 Shifts the hurdles for the camping-ground of the sheep during the night. **1872** 'RESIDENT' *Glimpses Life Vic.* 62 One by one the various parties met on the camping-ground, bringing in the herds each had collected. **1882** *Bulletin* (Sydney) 29 Apr. 10/1 A dummy selector took up an area comprising the squatter's camping ground. **1843** *Sydney Morning Herald* 11 May 3/5 Strayed from a **camping place**, about 25 miles north-east of Gloucester. A bay mare. **1845** D. MACKENZIE *Emigrant's Guide* 128 The cattle no sooner hear the loud crack of the stock-whip, than they scamper away towards their usual camping-place. **1849** A. HARRIS *Emigrant Family* (1967) 37 Willoughby left them to pursue their way on to the best camping-place within reach. **1934** 'S. RUDD' *Green Grey Homestead* 131 'There!' someone cried as the wild mob rose from their camping place, and off! **1903** *Bulletin* (Sydney) 21 Mar. 16/2 **Camping reserves** for travelling stock, which are reserved from sale and lease, are placed at suitable distances along almost every T.S.R. for the convenience of drovers. **1977** T.L. MCKNIGHT *Long Paddock* 60 In Eastern and Central Divisions of the state there are some long stretches of stock routes. . . These reserves are . . holding or resting paddocks . . called by three different names, Travelling Stock Reserve . . , Camping Reserve . . or Camping and Watering Reserve . . , but there are no precise distinctions between these.

canagong /'kænədʒɒŋ/. *Obs.* Also **canajong.** [a. e. Tas. *ganajaŋ* .] PIGFACE.

1834 *Hobart Town Almanack* 133 *Mesembryanthemum equilaterale*, pigfaces, called by the aborigines by the more elegant name of canagong. **1842** *Tasmanian Jrnl. Nat. Sci.* I. 38 The canagong of the Aborigines . . is the most widely diffused plant in Australia. **1889** J.H. MAIDEN *Useful Native Plants Aust.* 44 The 'canajong', of the Tasmanian aboriginal. The fleshy fruit is eaten raw by the aborigines. The leaves are eaten baked.

canary.

1. a. [See quot. 1829; prob. infl. by Br. slang *canary bird* jailbird (see OED 2).] A convict (from the colour of the clothing); *pl.* the clothing. Also **canary bird.**

1827 P. CUNNINGHAM *Two Yrs. in N.S.W.* II. 117 Convicts of but recent migration are facetiously known by the name of *canaries*, by reason of the yellow plumage in which they are fledged at the period of landing. **1829** R. BURFORD *Descr. View Sydney* 11 Convicts . . when first landed . . are termed Canaries, from their yellow clothing; they afterwards attain the more honourable distinction of Government Men. **1839** W.H. LEIGH *Reconnoitering Voyages* 201 These were the convicts dubbed canaries, from their yellow-and-brown dress. **1849** *Britannia* (Hobart) 26 July 2/6 Pray, are not some men in this colony called canary-birds, from the colour of their clothing? **1852** W. HUGHES *Austral. Colonies* 248 The prisoners at Port Arthur . . are dressed in a livery of green and yellow—whence the appellation of 'canary birds', by which they are familiarly known. **1857** W. HOWITT *Tallangetta* I. 206 He bolted to the woods in nothing but the bright yellow suit which the so-called canary-birds, the convicts, wear. **1871** *Austral. Jrnl.* (Melbourne) June 542/2 We can't bring him off . . in his canaries. He puts on these duds, d'ye see. **1876** *Austral. Town & Country Jrnl.* (Sydney) 5 Aug. 222/1, I goes up to the corporal, 'I say, mate,' says I, 'can't you get your canaries off the track here for about a quarter of an hour, and let my mob of cattle pass?'

b. A punishment of one hundred lashes.

1859 J. LANG *Botany Bay* (1885) 30 There were slang terms applied to these doses of the lash—a hundred was called a 'canary'. **1892** 'P. WARUNG' *Tales Convict System* 9 As he has to go through another little ceremony this morning I'll let him off with a 'canary'—(a hundred lashes).

2. Abbrev. of 'canary bird', a gold coin.

1853 MRS C. CLACY *Lady's Visit to Gold Diggings* 163 In digger's slang, a 'canary' and half-a-sovereign are synonymous. **1888** G. ROCK *Colonists* 40 Cheese yer clappers, old boy, I can look after the canaries. **1895** *Western Champion* (Barcaldine) 31 Dec. 9/5 A profitable profession it seemed, too, judging from the cool way they talked of 'John Dunns' (£1), 'thick 'uns' (sovs.), 'canarys' (half-sovs.), 'finn' (£5), &c. **1928** 'BRENT OF BIN BIN' *Up Country* 203 The 'Sweep Stakes', for which every entrant had to pay a 'canary'.

3. [From the skin colour.] A Chinese immigrant. Also *attrib.*

1898 *Bulletin* (Sydney) 1 Oct. 14/3 A few more W. Q. slang words. . . Tobacco is 'snout', opium 'twang', a Chinaman a 'canary', and a blackfellow is a 'swatser'. **1912** R.S. TAIT *Scotty Mac* 42 What's the matter, canary face? **1971** *Bulletin* (Sydney) 18 Sept. 47 Australian attitudes towards the almond-eyed celestials, the chinks, chows, pongs, canaries and dinks which have so resolutely clung to the fringes of the national consciousness.

candlebark. Any of several trees of the genus *Eucalyptus* (fam. Myrtaceae), esp. *E. rubida* of s.e. Aust. incl. Tas., having a smooth white bark which freq. develops reddish patches in summer and autumn before the bark is shed.

1899 *Proc. Linnean Soc. N.S.W.* XXIV. 456 The name 'Candle-bark' in use in the Queanbeyan district is in reference to its smooth and glaucous trunk. . . It has usually reddish or plum-coloured patches on the bark. **1912** S. LOCKE *Dawsons' Uncle George* 24 You won't know the place when I gets a floor down an' candle bark up the sides. **1946** *Bulletin* (Sydney) 6 Sept. 29/4 The candlebark (*E. rubida*) . . usually bears in clusters of threes shaped like a Maltese cross. **1952** E. WALLING *Austral. Roadside* 77 The chalk white trunks of the Candlebarks (assuming brilliant red and orange streaks and patches in autumn, before shedding their deciduous bark). **1967** N.A. WAKEFIELD *Naturalist's Diary* 32 Some of the Candlebark Gums were very picturesque indeed, with half the trunk coloured bright red . . on the weather side. **1974** BUCKLEY & HAMILTON *Festival* 71 'Aren't those pretty trees? Nice white trunks.' 'They're called candlebarks, Delcia.'

cane. [Shortening of *sugar cane*.]

1. Used *attrib.* in various Comb. with reference to the growing or harvesting of sugar cane.

1880 J. BONWICK *Resources Qld.* 73 The cane-growing prospects of Queensland are good. **1895** *Bulletin* (Sydney) 5 Jan. 3/2 Men do *not* fight in Australia so much as 'at 'ome'. But they talk fight. By 'they' I mean . . the shearing, harvesting, racing or cane-cutting lot. **1908** *Truth* (Sydney) 12 Jan. 7/7 The coal-lumpers who went cane cutting in Northern Queensland are back again with cheques of half a century upwards in their belts. **1909** *Bulletin* (Sydney) 7 Jan. 14/4 In the Mackay (Q.) district . . is a long, low shed that . . is used as a garage for cane-drays. **1927** *Ibid.* 7 July 27/4 A Queensland cane-planter always objected strongly to anyone throwing stones near a dry canefield. **1946** J.G. EASTWOOD *More about Cairns* 24 Dan got a place in one of the cane-cutting gangs. **1957** *Bulletin* (Sydney) 26 June 19/1 The old lady had managed canefarms and canecutters for decades, but this year she had a larrikin gang. **1965** J. BECKETT *New-Chum looks at Qld.* 53 Working for a cane farmer often meant batching which is very unpopular whilst cane cutting. **1971** *Bulletin* (Sydney) 30 Oct. 58/1 Such a trend would normally be welcomed by cane-growers. **1977** C. MCCULLOUGH *Thorn Birds* 260 'This is a cane knife. . .' It widened into a large triangle instead of tapering to a point, and had a wicked hook like a rooster's spur at one of the two blade ends. **1978** M. PAICE *Shadow of Wings* 5 The cane loco emerged from the field.

2. Special Comb. **cane barracks,** accommodation provided at a cane farm for itinerant workers; **beetle,** a beetle the larva of which attacks cane roots; any of several Austral. species of *Lepidiota* or *Dermolepida*; **cocky,** the proprietor of a cane farm; *sugar cocky*, see SUGAR 2; **-cutter,** an itinerant worker employed in the harvesting of sugar cane; also *transf.* (see quot. 1909); **inspector,** one responsible for regulating the supply of sugar cane to a mill, and for settling industrial disputes; **paddock,** cane field; **season,** the harvesting period (from June to December); **toad,** the large toad *Bufo marinus*, native to Central and S. America and introd. to n.e. Aust.

1967 *Meanjin* 30 His wife had left him in the **cane barracks** fifteen years ago. **1977** B. SCOTT *My Uncle Arch* 95 A bunk, obviously borrowed from somebody's cane barracks. **1902** *Agric. Gaz. N.S.W.* XXIII. 64 This destructive **cane beetle** . . is . . in general form somewhat like the typical cockchafer. **1975** J. DINGWELL *Cane Music* 87 'Are the toads peculiar to this state?' . . 'Yes, but they're not natives, they were brought here to eat the cane beetle.' **1899** *Bulletin* (Sydney) 18 Feb. 15/2 Not satisfied with cheap Jap. and kanaka-labor brought to their doors by a piebald Govt. many **cane-cockies** rope in the blacks and make them sink holes and plant and trash cane. **1938** F. CLUNE *Free & Easy Land* 137 Relations between cane-cockies and mills are harmonious. **1944** *Bulletin* (Sydney) 6 Dec. 12/2 A cane cocky out from Mackay (Q.) had a 20-acre block, mostly lantana and turkey-bush. **1967** D. HEWETT *This Old Man* (1976) 13 Only way I could win 'er orf all them good lookin', loaded young cane cockies was to give 'er a bun in the oven. **1881** *Bulletin* (Sydney) 30 July 13/4 **Cane-cutters** are scarce on the Clarence. **1909** *Ibid.* 17 Feb. 13/2, I have discovered the longest long beer in the Commonwealth . . is found on some of the Queensland sugar fields and is known as the 'cane cutter'. **1925** *Ibid.* 15 Jan. 24/3 What about a 'gun' cutter? . . The phrase is in common use on the canefields, a 'gun' among canecutters being the equivalent of a 'ringer' in the shearing-shed. **1938** F. CLUNE *Free & Easy Land* 234 Cane-cutters are considered to be amongst the finest physical types of Australian manhood. **1956** A.C.C. LOCK *Tropical Tapestry* 217 Two or three cane cutters, their faces and bodies covered in soot from burnt cane, pushed their bicycles homewards. **1972** *Bulletin* (Sydney) 29 July 7/2 Remember the cane-cutters, the brawny characters in their shorts, Jackie Howe singlets, the itinerants who travelled 1500 miles of sugar coast, wielding their cane knives? **1911** *Austral. Sugar Jrnl.* 6 Apr. 45/1 From the official synopsis of **cane inspectors'** reports . . we make the following extracts as to the condition of the cane crops. **1921** *Ibid.* 8 Apr. 35/1 However competent the Industrial Magistrate might be in the settlement of ordinary disputes, the questions involved in deciding the price for cutting cane were so intricate, and so bound up with other questions of which the Cane Inspector was the best judge, that it should be left for his decision as final. **1936** J. DEVANNY *Sugar Heaven* 134 The cane inspectors visited every Goondi gang, threatening them with victimisation and eviction from the barracks if they did not resume the knife. **1956** *S. Pacific Enterprise* (Colonial Sugar Refining Co.) 135 The cane inspectors in Australia and the field superintendents and the traffic officers in Fiji are responsible for the supply of cane to the mills. **1957** *Bulletin* (Sydney) 13 Nov. 19/1 The cutting-rate fixed by the cane-inspector and the Cairns (Q.) farmer not being acceptable to the gang, the industrial magistrate was called in to arbitrate. **1945** *Ibid.* 11 Apr. 13/2 The grasshopper swarm in the hopping stage arrived in the **cane paddocks.** **1978** R.J. BRITTEN *Around Cassowary Rock* 133 We took off along the headland of the cane paddock. **1955** R. LAWLER *Summer of Seventeenth Doll* (1965) 18 Seven months they spend up there killin' themselves in the **cane season**, and then they come down here to live a little. **1961** *Bulletin* (Sydney) 17 May 32/1 Towards the end of a cane season, getting on to Christmas, it was so hot that you used to wish you could work at night instead of in the day. **1963** HARNEY & LOCKWOOD *Shady Tree* 117 A . . **cane toad**, one of a species that had been introduced to Queensland to destroy beetles that were causing havoc to the crops of sugarcane. **1980** S. THORNE *I've met some Bloody Wags* 55 One of the last remaining waterholes . . was literally chock-a-block with canetoads.

canegrass. Any of several grasses (fam. Poaceae)

having cane-like stems, esp. *Eragrostis australasicus* of all mainland States. Also *attrib.*

1861 *Burke & Wills Exploring Exped.* 6 Cane-grass growing in great quantities. **1881** W.E. ABBOTT *Notes Journey on Darling* 55 A kind of coarse grass about 4 feet high, resembling small canes, called in some places cane grass. **1898** D.W. CARNEGIE *Spinifex & Sand* 90 Clay-pans . . containing drinkable water are often distinguishable by the growth of cane grass which covers the bed, a coarse, rush-like grass of no value as food for stock. **1906** J.W. GREGORY *Dead Heart Aust.* 101 A needle-bush to every two or three square miles, and a tuft of dead cane-grass and a dead 'wild carrot' to every five square yards. **1938** A. UPFIELD *Bone is Pointed* (1966) 50 Trees . . surrounded by what appeared to be a canegrass fence. **1950** A. GROOM *I saw Strange Land* 101 There were four blacks crouching and squatting about their fire by the canegrass hut. **1966** A. MORRIS *Plant-life W. Darling* 7 Near the river on the black soil plains clumps of . . Cane Grass, are met with.

Caneite. [Proprietary name.] A soft building board made from the fibres of sugar cane.

1938 *Austral. Official Jrnl. Patents* (Canberra) 1969 *Cane-ite* 72,201. Structural materials, including fibre board, fibre laths, fibre tiles. . . The Colonial Sugar Refining Company Limited. **1953** T.A.G. HUNGERFORD *Riverslake* 1 It was pinned on the Caneite at the foot of the bed. **1955** K. SHERROTT *Your House* 25 Caneite may be oil-painted, kalsomined, stained, dyed, or colored with casein-vehicle finishes. **1979** R. DUFFIELD *Rogue Bull* 91 It had developed from sugar-cane a fibre hardboard called Caneite.

cannibal. *Hist.* A term applied undiscriminatingly by the colonists to an Aboriginal. Also *attrib.*

1838 *Sydney Herald* 14 Nov. 21/1 We say, protect the whites as well as the blacks. Protect the white settler, his wife, and children, in remote places, from the filthy, brutal cannibals of New Holland. **1847** E.B. KENNEDY *Extracts Jrnl. Exped. Central Aust.* 269 We met some cannibals returning with bark. **1850** *Britannia* (Hobart) 9 May 4/5 The policy of telling a number of cannibal savages that a party of white men is supposed to be approaching. **1855** W. CAMPBELL *Crown Lands Aust.* 45 Were it not for the squatters, Melbourne would yet have been a small straggling village, and the gold fields still an unproductive hunting-ground, under a few barbarous, cannibal savages. **1864** *Illustr. Sydney News* 16 Nov. 3/2 The natives—who are said to be cannibals—have given much annoyance to the settlers.

canoe. *Hist.* A name given by the colonists to any Aboriginal boat. Also *attrib.*

1784 G.W. ANDERSON *New Collection Voyages* 71 The canoes are formed by hollowing the trunk of a tree, and it was conjectured, that this operation must have been performed by fire, as the natives did not appear to have any instruments for the purpose. The canoes are in length about fourteen feet, and so narrow, that they would be frequently overset, but that they are provided with an out-rigger. . . The canoes in the southern parts are formed only of a piece of bark four yards long, fastened together at each end, and the middle kept open by pieces of wood, passing from side to side. **1789** 'OFFICER' *Authentic & Interesting Narr. Exped. Botany Bay* 28 The canoes in which they fish are as despicable as their huts, being nothing more than a large piece of bark tied up at both ends with vine sticks. **1814** M. FLINDERS *Voyage Terra Australis* II. 198 The canoe was of bark, but not of one piece, as at Port Jackson; it consisted of two pieces, sewed together lengthwise, with the seam on one side; the two ends were also sewed up, and made tight with gum. **1820** C. JEFFREYS *Van Dieman's Land* 127 They make canoes from the adjoining woods. These when formed are not unlike a catamaran, and are sufficiently large to support from ten to six persons in crossing the largest rivers. **1835** BACKHOUSE & TYLOR *Life & Labours G.W. Walker* (1862) 212 A canoe was near, made fast to the shore. It was composed of a single sheet of bark. **1847** G.F. ANGAS *Savage Life & Scenes* I. 102 The canoe dance of the Rufus is one of the most graceful of these savage amusements. **1861** J.D. LANG *Qld., Aust.* 327 They make little canoes of the stringy-bark tree, which they call Dibil palam.

Canterbury cake. A kind of butter cake containing dried fruit or seeds: see quot. 1909.

1909 MRS H.W. SHAW *Six Hundred Tested Recipes* 65 Canterbury Cake. . . 1 cup of butter, 2 cups sugar, 1 cup milk, 4 eggs, 3 cups flour, 1 cup fruit or seeds, 2 teaspoons baking powder. Beat butter and sugar to a cream, add milk (a little at a time), well-beaten eggs, then flour with baking powder. Flavour with essence to taste. **1924** H.E. RIEMANN *Nor'-West o' West* 102 The tins of Canterbury cake and Queensland pineapples . . were certainly very tasty. **1929** W.J. RESIDE *Golden Days* 345, I have had a roaring feed, dinkum. I've had half a Canterbury cake and a tin of parsnips! **1973** A. BURNETT *Wilful Murder in Outback* 42 'Canterbury cake, jubilee Mick and lady drawers.' Meaning tinned cake, jubilee sweets mixture and women's underclothing.

canvas.

1. Used *attrib.* of dwellings, etc., made of canvas.

1855 'RUSTICUS' *How to settle in Vic.* 22 The *canvas-framed house* is merely a tent, brought into the form of a house by means of a timber framing, on which the canvas is stretched. **1862** H. BROWN *Vic. as I found It* 134 A few well-like holes had been sunk here and there, and a few canvass stores were standing. **1865** J.F. MORTLOCK *Experiences of Convict* 119 Quaffing Champagne, in the canvass hut of an hospitable Irish storekeeper. **1898** C. BOND *Goldfields & Chrysanthemums* 33 We pay a visit to a lady, who lives in a nice little canvas hut. **1902** *Bulletin* (Sydney) 22 Mar. 3/2 The canvas houses rose in scores, The camp-fires blazed away. **1938** F. BLAKELEY *Hard Liberty* 13 We lived in a new canvas house, and it was no protection from the storm. **1945** *Bulletin* (Sydney) 26 Dec. 13/2 Corny had a canvas-and-bark humpy by the lagoon.

2. Special Comb. **canvas muster,** see MUSTER *n.* 5; **town,** a settlement, initially of gold-miners, consisting largely of tents; also **canvas township.**

1851 [**canvas town**] *Empire* (Sydney) 14 Nov. 364/2 About the centre of this canvas village, stand the stores of Mssrs. Fentum and Edmiston and Mr Tucker. **1853** F.J. COCKBURN *Lett.* (1856) 5 'Canvass town', a town or village of tents, made since gold was found. **1853** W. WESTGARTH *Vic.* 212 The famous 'Canvass Town' . . with its airy mansions and its 4000 or 5000 inhabitants, lay in an opposite direction about a mile to the south-east, beyond the intervening stream of the Yarra. **1862** J.A. PATTERSON *Gold Fields Vic.* 195 Though long a 'canvas town', Maryborough has made considerable strides. **1891** H. NISBET *Colonial Tramp* II. 87 Passing through a little canvas town with its store. **1900** 'CASHAMBA' *Sketchy Characters* 27 Can the reader picture mentally a canvas township, varied in architecture and building material, in the form of bush breakwind and calico roofs, scattered over an area of land as extensive as an estate of an English noble? **1930** J.S. LITCHFIELD *Far-North Memories* 6 She had landed at Darwin in the early days, when it was little better than Canvas-town. **1955** STEWART & KEESING *Austral. Bush Ballads* 64 But there, quite unconscious of any mishap, I'll fix him up neatly in gay Canvas Town!

cap. [Spec. use of *cap* a part laid horizontally along the top of a structure.] See quot. 1849. Also **cap rail.**

1849 S. & J. SIDNEY *Emigrant's Jrnl.* 43 The stockyard ought to be made very strong; four rails with a cap; that is to say, a long, round rail on the top of all the posts, running from one to the other. . . The top rail is the cap. **1890** 'R. BOLDREWOOD' *Colonial Reformer* II. 111 If the 'ring' crowds too near the fence, the men on that side would walk along the middle rail holding on the while by the 'cap', or uppermost horizontal, always of rounded and not of split timber like the lower bars. **1897** *Bulletin* (Sydney) 11 Dec. 30/1 We heard them lift the post and wire and fling the cap-rails down. **1898** *Daily Tel.* (Sydney) 4 Oct. 3/8 All round the high 'caps' of the cattle-pens are perched long-limbed youths in clean 'moles'. **1911** *Bulletin* (Sydney) 31 Aug. 43/1 A jackeroo would fall flop over the cap-rail in an agitated attempt to escape the horns of an aggrieved cow. **1921** G.A. BELL *Under Brigalows* 110 With a quick spring he reached the rails again and sprang up on to the 'cap'. **1935** A. FRANCIS *Then & Now* 66 The boss takes up his position on the cap-rail of the drafting pen.

Cape. Used *attrib.* in Special Comb. designating species of flora brought from the Cape of Good Hope: **Cape barley** *obs.*, see quot. 1833; **spinach,** DOUBLE-GEE a.; **weed,** the widespread S. African herb *Arctotheca calendula* (fam. Asteraceae), naturalized in W.A. by 1833 and, although used as fodder, generally regarded as a weed.

1825 *Australasian Pocket Almanack* 84 [January is] the proper season for sowing winter (here commonly called **Cape**) **barley.** **1833** *Launceston Advertiser* 7 Mar. 2 *On sale* . . *Cape Barley*, (the produce of Seed imported last year from the Cape of Good Hope). **1841** *Port Phillip Patriot* 18 Mar. 2/6 For green crops this is the best sowing month, and Cape barley the very best crop to ensure heavy returns. **1852** F. LANCELOTT *Aust. as it Is* I. 177 The kinds cultivated are the English two-rowed, the Cape or four-rowed, and the skinless barley. **1897** L. LINDLEY-COWEN *W. Austral. Settler's Guide* 541 Mr Wansborough . . sowed a bed with the seed of this '**Cape Spinach**'. . . The seed was obtained from Mr Tanner. . . However, the plant did not prove a very palatable spinach. **1938** *Qld. Agric. Jrnl.* L. 790 Cape spinach or prickly jack. . . The name spinach is applied to it because the leaves have sometimes been used as a substitute for ordinary spinach. **1977** KLEINSCHMIDT & JOHNSON *Weeds Qld.* 178 In Queensland, spiny emex is also known as . . cape spinach. **1878** W.R. GUILFOYLE *Austral. Bot.* 60 **Cape weed** . . which has proved such a pest in many parts of Victoria, was, a few years ago, introduced from the Cape of Good Hope, as a fodder plant. **1897** L. LINDLEY-COWEN *W. Austral. Settler's Guide* 85 The dandelion, or Cape weed plant, so thickly covers the ground that [it] is a great assistance to the stock-owner in fattening his sheep in spring and early summer. **1911** A. MACK *Bush Days* 35 From Albury to Melbourne the green fields were changed to golden carpets by the bright, round faces of the Cape weed. **1928** R.H. CROLL *Open Road Vic.* 20 The capeweed, making ready for its early spring change from green to gold. **1978** L. WHITE *Memories of Childhood* 20 Again the frosted capeweed crackles under my bare feet. **1986** *Trees & Natural Resources* Mar. 9 Weed problems (including . . capeweed) . . increase the difficulties of establishment of trees.

Cape Barren. [f. the name of *Cape Barren* Island in Bass Strait.] Used *attrib.* in Special Comb. **Cape Barren goose,** the grey waterfowl *Cereopsis novaehollandiae* of s. Aust., breeding mainly on islands off the mainland s. coast; **tea** *obs.*, the shrub of Tas. and s.e. mainland Aust. *Correa alba* (fam. Rutaceae) commonly found on coastal dunes and cliffs; also *attrib.*

1832 J. BACKHOUSE *Narr. Visit Austral. Colonies* (1843) 87 We returned to the Lagoons with . . a man carrying two young **Cape Barren Geese**, one of which died on the way, from the effect of cold and rain. **1844** *Port Phillip Gaz.* 6 July 3 The Cape Barren or wild goose, is about the same in size as the tame bird, but when dressed is of a far superior flavour. **1861** 'OLD BUSHMAN' *Bush Wanderings* 71 The *Cape Barron* [*sic*] *Goose* . . looks like a cross between a goose and a turkey. **1945** C. BARRETT *Austral. Bird Life* 47 The Cape Barren Goose . . is related to an extinct giant goose of New Zealand, but has no living allies. **1968** R. HILL *Bush Quest* 94, I heard a honking, a wild wind-torn cry; I turned to see two Cape Barren geese. **1827** *HRA* (1923) 3rd Ser. VI. 267 '**Cape Barren Tea** Shrub' . . makes an acrid stimulating drink. **1833** J. BACKHOUSE *Narr. Visit Austral. Colonies* (1843) 179 *Corraea alba*, the Cape Barren tea, becomes a large bush, and covers the sand hills of the western head of the Tamar. **1873** J. BONWICK *Tasmanian Lily* 125 There is a correa called the Cape Barren tea. **1888** *Proc. Linnean Soc. N.S.W.* III. 502 *Correa alba.* . . Called 'Cape Barren tea' in Tasmania, on account of its use near that headland.

cap rail: see CAP.

captain. A person with money to spend, esp. one who buys drinks for an assembled company.

1961 W.E. HARNEY *Grief, Gaiety & Aborigines* 20 Doleites were calling to other doleite friends. . . Everywhere I heard the term 'captain' or 'a whale in the bay' and came to realise it meant someone was in town who had money to spend. **1967** *Kings Cross Whisper* (Sydney) xxxiii. 4/3 *Captain*, a person buying all the drinks. **1973** J. POWERS *Last of Knucklemen* (1974) 63 I'll be the captain for a round of beers. **1977** J. RAMSAY *Cop it Sweet* 20 *Captain*, person buying all the drinks. **1977** K. GILBERT *Living Black* 302 Have you seen 'em bludging up to a captain who's just come onto the mission with money in his pocket? [*Note*] The reserve people's name for a white man who visits them to trade money or grog for sex.

Captain Cook, *n.* and *a.* [The name of James *Cook* (1728–79), navigator and explorer.]

A. *n.* Rhyming slang for 'look'. See also COOK.

1932 L. MANN *Flesh in Armour* 179 Take a captain cook at love's young dream. **1946** D. STIVENS *Courtship of Uncle Henry* 70, I took a Captain Cook at him then and seen he had on a white coat like a dentist. **1957** D. WHITINGTON *Treasure upon Earth* 80 'Coppers,' he breathed. 'Take a Captain Cook at that.' **1974** D. O'GRADY *Deschooling Kevin Carew* 140 Got a Captain Cook at your dossier—it's thicker than your frickin' head.

B. *adj.* Rhyming slang for CROOK *a.* 1 c.; ill.

1959 E. LAMBERT *Glory thrown In* 46, I never saw anyone who was feeling Captain Cook get any sympathy from Doc.

Captain-General and Governor-in-Chief: see GOVERNOR-IN-CHIEF.

caravan. *Obs.* BOX *n.*[2] 1.

1835 BACKHOUSE & TYLOR *Life & Labours G.W. Walker* (1862) 219 The prisoners lodge in small caravans, capable of containing sixteen at a time, which are moved from one place to another upon small wooden wheels. **1839** *Corresp. on Secondary Punishment* (Great Brit. Parl.) 15 Feb. (1841) 77 The mode of incarceration in boxes or caravans, alluded to by the Committee . . as in existence in New South Wales, was never, so far as I am aware, even thought of in Van Diemen's Land.

carbeen /'kabin/. Also **carbean, karbeen.** [a. Kamilaroi and Yuwaalaraay *gaabiin.*] *Moreton Bay ash*, see MORETON BAY.

1888 *Centennial Mag.* (Sydney) 293 Tall and imposing carbeens and river-gums lined the bank of the Namoi. **1889** J.H. MAIDEN *Useful Native Plants Aust.* 527 Commonly called 'Moreton Bay Ash'. . . Another aboriginal name is 'Carbeen'. **1928** B. SPENCER *Wanderings in Wild Aust.* 525 One special gum tree was especially interesting (*Eucalyptus platypoda*). . . The tree is popularly called 'Karbeen'. **1935** DAVISON & NICHOLLS *Blue Coast Caravan* 156 The Moreton Bay ash—called by some the Carbeen—distinguished among the eucalypts. **1956** T. RONAN *Moleskin Midas* 114 The use of knives in this district is restricted to butchering and stockwork, and if you want to carve your name look for a carbean tree. **1970** *Matilda* (Winton Tourist Promotion Assoc.) 61 The grey galahs rise up from the carbean trees. **1984** D.J. BOLAND et al. *Forest Trees Aust.* (rev. ed.) 206 Carbeen occurs from far northern New South Wales through most of the eastern half of Queensland.

carby. Also **carbie.** [f. *carb(urettor* + -Y.] A carburettor.

1957 'N. CULOTTA' *They're Weird Mob* 47 'Carburettor, matey,' said Joe. 'We'll start on the carby.' **1963** D. ATTENBOROUGH *Quest under Capricorn* 130 Finally, he looked up, as mystified as we were. 'Well, I dunno,' he said, 'Yer maggie's right and there's mobs of 'ole in the carbie.' **1965** *Austral. Hot Rodding Rev.* i. 18 You had to use both the hard throttle and the accelerator to keep going because we had fouled up the linkages or something when we cleared the carbie. **1968** J. O'GRADY *Gone Troppo* 69 Ned said he'd fixed the carby. **1977** A. MACKAY *Life Pieces* II. 89 Randy had a double-overhead-camshaft Maserati with four webers. We were always pulling down the carbies to get more out of them. **1978** R.J. BRITTEN *Around Cassowary Rock* 52 It might take nearly all day of fooling around with the mixture on the 'carby' advancing and retarding the spark to get even one or two little promising, backfiring boots. **1983** *Overlander* Oct. 21 Slotting in . . 'proper' carbies was all very well but . . the only way to go was to make the beasties rev high and fit them with big bearings, so they didn't get hot.

carf. *Timber-getting. Obs.* Also **carve.** [Br. dial. *carf* an incision or notch: see OED 1 and EDD *sb.*[1]] The part of the trunk cut out as a tree is felled: see quot. 1885. Also as *v. trans.* (see quot. 1916).

1885 *Illustr. Austral. News* (Melbourne) 25 Nov. 202/2 Having put in the front 'carve', on the side the tree is to fall, the back one, which is usually a little higher than the front, is commenced and the tree is cut across. **1916** *Bulletin* (Sydney) 4 May 22/3 Tassy bushmen of 30 years ago always spoke of 'carfing' a tree, the cut being called front or back carf. The majority of bushmen . . on the mainland . . used the word 'scarf', which I took to be correct and smiled at the Speck splitters' corruption of the term. *Ibid.* 8 June 24/3 Tassy bushmen . . never spoke of 'carfing' a tree when they meant chopping or sawing it down. When referring to the cut made by axe or saw, they spoke of it as the 'belly-cut' or the 'back-cut'. The opening or angle taken out by the axe was the carf. . . If an axeman marked this angle on his tree before chopping . . he would be said to be carfing his tree.

cark, var. KARK.

cark, *v.* [Imitative.] *intr.* **a.** Of a crow: to caw. **b.** Of a person: to laugh or speak raucously. Also *trans.*, and redupl. as **cark-cark.** See also KARK.

1936 F. CLUNE *Roaming round Darling* 120 Big mob of crows carking. **1946** F.D. DAVISON *Dusty* 52 A lone crow flew closely overhead, carking loudly. . . The crow carked its way into the distance. **1971** F. HARDY *Outcasts of Foolgarah* 6 'Leave my bottles alone,' the Black Crow, who looked after the dump for the Council, cark-carked, poking his head out from under the front-end loader. **1981** —— *Who shot George Kirkland?* 6 Hall carked a laugh.

carn, *v.* Also **c'arn.** [Altered form of *come on.*] Esp. in supportive barracking at sporting fixtures, 'come on!'; an injunction to greater effort.

1968 B. DAWE *Eye for Tooth* 42 When children are born in Victoria they are wrapped in the club-colours, laid in beribboned cots, having already begun a life-time's barracking. Carn, they cry, Carn . . feebly at first. **1969** A. HOPGOOD *And Big Men Fly* 11 'C'arn the Crows' is the battle-cry of the greatest football machine in league history. **1979** *Overland* lxxvi. 41 That greatest of all Australian tribal chants: *'Carn the Tigers! Eat 'em alive!'* **1981** SANDERCOCK & TURNER *Up where, Cazaly?* 5 A deep-throated roar comes from the crowd: 'Carn the Tigers. . . Carn the Blues.' The umpire blows his whistle, bounces the ball, and the game is on. At this moment, Melbourne comes to life. **1985** *Canberra Times* 6 Nov. 18/4 Frenzied cries of 'Carn What a Nuisance'.

carney /'kani/. Also **carni, carnie.** [a. Wemba *gaani.*] Any of several lizards in the traditional diet of Aborigines, esp. BEARDED DRAGON.

1881 J.C.F. JOHNSON *To Mount Browne & Back* 13 The carnie or Jew Lizard is esteemed a luxury by many of the Central Australian men. **1902** *Bulletin* (Sydney) 8 Nov. 3/2 He cooks Some wood-grubs in a pan, Or carnies roasts in lonely nooks. **1916** *Ibid.* 31 Aug. 24/3 Next in favor is the 'carni' or frill-necked lizard. **1932** M.R. WHITE *No Roads go By* 233 Dick Willow, a full-blooded black, was licking his shiny chops after polishing off a large-sized carney, i.e., a lace lizard. **1961** F. LEECHMAN *Opal Bk.* 75 One of the old-timers lived on carneys—a kind of big lizard that forages round the camps by night.

carpet. [Spec. use of *carpet*, with reference to skin markings.] Used *attrib.* in Special Comb. **carpet shark,** WOBBEGONG; **snake,** the python *Morelia spilotes variegata*, widespread in Aust. and New Guinea.

1896 F.G. AFLALO *Sketch Nat. Hist. Aust.* 221 The Wobbegong or **Carpet-Shark** of Sydney. **1936** N. CALDWELL *Fangs of Sea* 36, I saw an unusual sight—a large carpet shark with a small shark of the black-tip species in its mouth. **1955** V. SERVENTY *Aust.'s Great Barrier Reef* 44 The wanderer on the reef itself is unlikely to meet anything more dangerous than the rather attractive Carpet Shark. **1833** *Perth Gaz.* 16 Feb. 27 A young man last week, imprudently laid hold of a **Carpet Snake.** **1836** J. BACKHOUSE *Extracts from Lett.* (1838) iii. 57 The largest species, called the carpet-snake, is harmless; its skin is sometimes prepared for making into slippers, &c. **1844** *Duncan's Weekly Register* (Sydney) 16 Nov. 245/3 The Carpet or Diamond Snake grows to a large size. **1849** *Adelaide Miscellany* 20 Sept. 26 The hideous countenance of a carpet-snake issued forth. . . I believe it to be the boa-constrictor of Australia. **1861** 'OLD BUSHMAN' *Bush Wanderings* 129 A pair of jackasses had disabled a carpet-snake under an old gum-tree. **1888** *Sydney Morning Herald* 24 Jan. (Centennial Suppl.) 1/6 The carpet snake . . is prettily marked, and lives on birds and small animals, but its bite is not poisonous. **1917** *Bulletin* (Sydney) 25 Jan. 22/2 Any of you ever tried carpet-snake for lining your belt? **1935** H. BASEDOW *Knights of Boomerang* 75 In Central Australia the recognised delicacy . . is a large brown variety of the carpet-snake. **1962** B.W. LEAKE *Eastern Wheatbelt Wildlife* 99 Carpet snakes are harmless and some farmers would like to protect them, because they do a lot of good keeping mice in check. **1972** J. HIBBERD *Stretch of Imagination* (1973) 14, I was merely the first of a string the length of a carpet snake. . . She had more love affairs than Lady Lucifer.

carrying gang. Chiefly *Tas. Hist.* A party of convicts assigned to hard labour at carrying, esp. the carrying of timber from where it is felled to where it is to be used: see quot. 1842. See also GANG.

1835 *Sydney Herald* 31 Aug. 3/2 He is immediately sent into the 'carrying gang', the severest of all, where he remains for some months. **1842** *Tasmanian Jrnl. Nat. Sci.* I. 287 The carrying gang is deemed the most severe. This body . . transport on their shoulders immense spars (the masts and yards of a 300-ton ship for example) from the forest to the dockyards. **1846** L.W. MILLER *Notes of Exile Van Dieman's Land* 329, I could not long endure the horrors of the 'carrying gang', as it was called. **1848** R. MARSH *Seven Yrs. of my Life* 120 He then put me in the carrying gang. Said he, 'You can carry light timber.' **1851** *Empire* (Sydney) 10 Feb. 3/1 The wood-carrying gang, the hardest and vilest at Port Arthur. **1856** J. FROST *Horrors Convict Life* (1973) 41 Myself and my fellow constables were in the bush, watching the carrying gang. **1896** M. HORNSBY *Old Time Echoes Tas.* 89 M'Intyre and M'Reynalds were a pair of beauties, and were over two carrying gangs or wood humpers.

cartwheel. A round damper marked with a cross (resembling the spokes of a wheel). Also **cartwheel damper.** See DAMPER.

1900 *Tocsin* (Melbourne) 13 Sept. 6/1 The march of years and of intellect has flattened the damper into a 'cart-wheel', in which form even the unskilled traveller fresh from the city can very easily produce a tolerably good baking. **1902** R. BRUCE *Reminisc. Old Squatter* 194 On my return to the hut I would put on some more salt junk to boil, or make a cartwheel damper, in order to meet the requirements of our mixed population. **1916** H.L. ROTH *Sketches & Reminisc. Qld.* 11 While thus rainbound they made a 'cart wheel' (a large 'damper'), which they cooked under great difficulties inside the tent. **1946** J.G. EASTWOOD *More about Cairns* 24 The food provided for us was . . salt beef and heavy 'cartwheel' damper. **1948** I.L. IDRIESS *Opium Smugglers* 174 He smacked it top and bottom—a bonzer damper, a dinkum 'cartwheel'.

carve, var. CARF.

case moth. Any of several moths of the fam. Psychidae, whose larvae make and inhabit cases: see quot. 1926.

1886 F. COWAN *Aust.* 18 The Case- or Lictor-moths . . marvelous among the marvels of the insect world. **1926** R.J. TILLYARD *Insects Aust. & N.Z.* 435 Psychidae (Case Moths, Bag Moths). . . The larvae construct bags or cases of strong silk into which they weave short twigs or dried leaves. **1956** S. HOPE *Digger's Paradise* 202 This basket affair was the home-made retreat of the Case Moth grub.

caser. [Br. slang *caser* a crown, five shillings, orig. f. Yiddish (cf. Heb. *kesef* silver). Recorded earliest in Aust.] (A coin worth) five shillings, a crown; formerly a dollar.

1825 *Austral.* (Sydney) 29 Sept. 3/4 A swell drew out his thimble and handed it to the time keeper, together with a few casers. **1832** *Hill's Life N.S.W.* (Sydney) 10 Aug. 3 'Why, here's a *caser* for you,' throwing down at the same time, what had the semblance of a dollar, but which turned out to be a piece of base metal. **1849** A. HARRIS *Emigrant Family* (1967) 104 A caser (dollar) if you give him a night of it. **1882** *Sydney Slang Dict.* 10 A bludger . . 'ticed a cully into the 'Deadhouse', and while he was parting for the booze buzzed him for three caser and a deaner. **1906** H. LAWSON *Lett.* (1970) 153, I want that quid—pound (otherwise four casers) tonight. **1943** H.M. MURPHY *Strictly for Soldiers* 17 And you throw the caser yonder to the boxer's waiting hand. **1957** D. WHITINGTON *Treasure upon Earth* 78 I'll lay you a caser to nothing there'll be a blue here this morning. **1969** D. NILAND *Dead Men Running* 312 'Be worth a caser to you,' Needle said. Five shillings was half my wages for the whole week.

casey. [f. the name of *Casey* Jones, hero of an American ballad.] A small mechanical conveyance used by railway workers. In full **Casey Jones.**

1939 T.E. JONES *These Twenty Yrs.* 66 It costs many pounds to use railway engines and . . 'Mary' was only a black lubra. 'Mary' must be taken in a 'casey', a small open trolley. **1955** *Overland* iii. 11 The fettlers, riding mechanical 'caseys', patrolled the line. **1964** P. ADAM SMITH *Hear Train Blow* 128 Because of the amount of traffic the fettlers did not use the Caseys or other motorized transport here. . . Instead, they pulled one-man and sometimes four-man hand trolleys. **1969——** *Folklore Austral. Railwaymen* p. x, The most common form of transport is a four-wheeled motor vehicle known to the old-timers as a Casey Jones but nowadays more often referred to as a section car. **1972** W. WATKINS *Suddenly of Age* 12 They milled around the casey, running pannikins of water and eating the food that had been left over from dinner.

cashed up, *ppl. a.* Well supplied with money, 'flush'. See also CHEQUED UP.

1930 L.W. LOWER *Here's Luck* (1955) 115 Straight from the Never-Never by the look of him. Is he cashed up? **1945** *Bulletin* (Sydney) 2 May 12/3 Well cashed up, we hit the town. . . There was nothing much to do in the place except absorb a few beers. **1951** *Ibid.* 18 Apr. 15/2 On board was Billy Mac, cashed-up and travelling down to Wentworth for a bender. **1972** K. CLIFT *Saga of Sig* 21 He disclosed that he was quite well cashed up having been the 'boxer' at the swy game. **1980** S. THORNE *I've met some Bloody Wags* 88 They had just sold a big 'parcel' and were cashed up and ready for some fun among the bright lights.

cask. A plastic or foil-lined container for table wine, fruit juice, etc., enclosed within a cardboard pack, and having a spigot so that wine not drawn off remains under a vacuum. Also *attrib.*, and **wine cask.**

[**1971** *Ann. Rep.* (Wynn Winegrowers Ltd.) 7/1 Based on this principle the Company has developed the *Wynn Winegrowers 'Winecask'* which has a capacity of six bottles or one gallon.] **1974** *Wine Buyer* Aug. 429 An agreeable, light cask wine. **1977** *Weekend Austral. Mag.* (Sydney) 22 Oct. 15/4 Already the cardboard cask has found an acceptable place on the table in most homes. **1981** *Canberra Times* 23 July 18/5 Britain has discovered the wine cask. With the curious name of 'bag-in-a-box', the wine container, which for many years was the exclusive domain of Australians, has been launched in London with a big bang. **1982** N. KEESING *Lily on Dustbin* 96 The 'rest of the mob' pours itself another glass all round from the 'cask', which is a plastic skin holding wine and fitted with a plastic tap. **1983** *Wine List* (A.N.U. Staff Centre), Our cask is launched with flags unfurled: Australia's blessing to the world.

Casket. Shortened form of *Golden Casket*: see GOLDEN 2. Also *attrib.*

1924 L.M.D. O'NEIL *Dinkum Aussie* 37, I worked an' belonged to me union, an' drew down a sizeable screw; Took tickets in Tatt's an' the Casket; was fairly contented with life. **1934** T. WOOD *Cobbers* 135 The alphabet of topics was A for Australia, B for Bradman, C for Casket. **1948** V. PALMER *Golconda* 24 A few loungers stood yarning at McClintock's hessian store, where the trade was mostly in tobacco and tickets for the Casket. **1958** G. COTTERELL *Tea at Shadow Creek* 156 When I was working up in Queensland there was a girl won five hundred, she had a half share in the casket, that's the lottery up there. **1972** D. SHEAHAN *Songs from Canefields* 133 If ever I hit the Casket Or hold a good ticket in Tatts I'll put it away in a basket I won't go for farms or flats. **1977** *Southerly* iii. 303, I found the present she had for me—it was really a whole lot of presents, a shirt, a tie, a pair of socks she'd knitted herself, a couple of paperbacks and a Casket ticket.

cassowary. [Spec. use of *cassowary* flightless bird related to the ostrich; in mod. usage restricted to members of the fam. Casuariidae, as in sense 2.]

1. *Obs.* EMU *n.*[1]

1788 J. WHITE *Jrnl. Voyage N.S.W.* (1790) 129 A New Holland Cassowary was brought into camp. This bird stands seven feet high, . . and, in every respect, is much larger than the *common Cassowary.* **1789** A. PHILLIP *Voyage to Botany Bay* 271 *New-Holland Cassowary.* . . The flesh is said to be in taste not unlike beef. **1801** M. FLINDERS *Observations Coasts Van Diemen's Land* 20 Marks of the emu, or cassuary, were met with. **1840** *S. Austral. Rec.* (London) 21 Mar. 125 The cassowary, or emu, is found in nearly all parts of Australia. **1857** *Illustr. Jrnl. Australasia* II. 263 Cassowaries, cranes, swans . . the Botany Bay menagerie.

2. A flightless bird of n.e. Qld., the Austral. cassowary *Casuarius casuarius*, having black plumage, a bare blue neck with red wattles, and standing up to 2 m. in height.

1848 W. CARRON *Narr. Exped. Rockingham Bay & Cape York* 4 Nov. (1849) 64 This morning Jackey . . shot a fine cassowary; it was very dark and heavy, not so long on the leg as the common emu, and had a larger body, shorter neck, with a large red, stiff, horny comb on its head. **1869** J. GOULD *Birds of Aust.* Suppl. v. Pl. 70, Australian Cassowary. . . In the neighbourhood of the latter locality [*sc.* Rockingham Bay] the bird was well known under the name of the Black Emu. **1872** *Illustr. Sydney News* 8 July 4/1 The cassowary stands, when erect between four and five feet high; its head is without feathers but covered with a blue skin. **1949** D. WALKER *We went to Aust.* 59 The fierce old cassowary . . which wears a kind of fireman's helmet. **1978** R.J. BRITTEN *Around Cassowary Rock* 96 The most dangerous of the lot—the cassowary. That big flightless bird of the Queensland jungle . . can kick with the leg power of any horse, taking a dog or man apart at will with those big toes and hissing, slashing beak.

cast, *n.* [Spec. use of *cast* the spreading out of hounds in search of a lost scent: see OED *sb.* 41.] The sweep that a trained dog makes in mustering sheep: see quot. 1966.

1929 J.L. MOORE *Canine King* 45 Of these, five points are awarded for the 'run out', or as we call it in Australia, the 'cast'. **1946** F.D. DAVISON *Dusty* 117 The trial had four phases; the cast, when the owner sent the dog forward by himself to find the sheep [etc.]. **1966** C. ODELL *Working Dogs* 18 Most dogs are taught to run towards the sheep in a wide arc, so that the sheep are not frightened, and any stragglers near the boundary fence will be rounded up. This is called a 'cast' and many sheep-dogs do it by instinct. **1978** N. EVERS *Tas. Paradise & Beyond* 46 His dog was a bit slow in bringing a mob back from a blind cast.

cast, *v.* [See prec. and OED *v.* 60.] *trans.* In mustering, to direct (a sheep-dog) to make a wide sweep; also *intr.*, to make such a sweep. Also with **off.**

[N.Z. **1911** W.H. KOEBEL *In Maoriland Bush* 77 He must acquire the art of 'casting' a sheep-dog.] **1920** J.B. CRAMSIE *Managem. & Diseases Sheep* 28 Have the dog behind you, and by a wave of the hand cast him out wide to the right. **1929** J.L. MOORE *Canine King* 30 The dog is 'cast off' 'on the blind' to use the expression by which a sheep-man admits his own impotence. **1942** R.B. KELLEY *Animal Breeding* 126 The easiest way to start a pup casting is to let some sheep move off down the paddock and urge the pup to head them. **1967** M. HAMILTON-WILKES *Kelpie & Cattle Dog* 45 To pick up the sheep the dog is 'cast' out in a curving run so that he comes round behind the sheep and drives them back to the stockman. **1970** R.B. KELLEY *Sheep Dogs* (ed. 4) 156 When the young dog casts proficiently on sheep which have been put together, he can be run on those which are scattered.

cast, *ppl. a.* [Spec. use of *cast* thrown aside, discarded.]

1. Rejected as of inferior quality; esp. in the Comb. **cast fleece.**

1921 L.G. JONES *Flockmaster's Companion* 77 *Cast* relates to wools that are rough or badly bred, found in a clip. **1948** R. RAVEN-HART *Canoe in Aust.* 54 'Cast fleeces', thrown out by the remorseless classer for lack of quality. **1980** P. FREEMAN *Woolshed* 20 This man determines the destination of the wool, for fine, clean and even fleeces will be used for 'combing', shorter fleeces for 'clothing', and poor fleeces are baled separately as 'cast fleeces'.

2. In the collocation **cast-for-age** *a.*, (of sheep) culled, as too old for good breeding stock.

1930 D. COTTRELL *Earth Battle* 140 He pulled out the particulars of the fifteen thousand 'cast-for-age ewes in lamb by Derford rams'. **1942** H.H. PECK *Mem. of Stockman* 87 The wethers and cast-for-age ewes of English Leicester-Merino crosses. **1946** *Bulletin* (Sydney) 11 Sept. 28/2 Evora paddock was the dead-end for scrags—cripples, cast-for-age ewes, double culls and other rubbish. **1959** H. LAMOND *Sheep Station* 194, I can get about four thousand cast-for-age ewes from Barcaldine Downs. **1977** A.G. BLACKBURN *Managem. Booms & Busts* 58 Cast-for-age ewes are sold off-shears and 1½ year old wethers are sold at the autumn break.

castor, *a.* [Poss. shortened form of *castor sugar* as (something) sweet.] All right; *apples*, see APPLE 4. Also as *n.* in the phr. **on the castor.**

1945 'MASTER-SARG' *Yank discovers Aust.* 75 'Castor' or 'sweet'—all right. **1950** *Austral. Police Jrnl.* Apr. 111 *Caster* [*sic*], . . O.K. **1953** K. TENNANT *Joyful Condemned* 294 These chaps . . why am I on the castor with them? **1963** J. CANTWELL *No Stranger to Flame* 103 'How is he today!' 'Castor, now you've arrived,' Max said easily. 'Just what the doctor ordered.' **1980** *Sydney Morning Herald* 3 Jan. 6/7 In the action where 'Simmo' won his Victoria Cross, when the situation appeared hopeless, Ray crawled over to me amid the intense enemy fire, and said: 'Don't worry, skipper, she will be castor,' and it was!

casuarina /kæʒjəˈrinə/. [The plant genus *Casuarina* was named by Swedish botanist Carl von Linne (Linnaeus) (*Amoenitates Acad.* IV. (1759) 143), from the fancied resemblance of the tree's drooping branches to the cassowary's plumage.] **a.** Any of many trees or shrubs of the fam. Casuarinaceae, of Aust., s.e. Asia, and the Pacific, the genus *Casuarina* formerly including all species of the fam. The plants have distinctive foliage consisting of whorls of tiny teeth-like leaves on jointed branchlets. **b.** The wood of these trees. See also HE-OAK, OAK 1, SHE-OAK 1.

1799 Banks Papers 28 Nov. XIX. 95 The wood which was so admired just before I left London is what I supposed it to be a Casuarina. **1814** R. BROWN *Gen. Remarks Bot. Terra Australis* 39 The maximum of Casuarina appears to exist in Terra Australis, where it forms one of the characteristic features of the vegetation. **1833** *Perth Gaz.* 27 July 119 The Shea Oak, or Casuarina of this Colony, admitted to be of a superior description to that of either our Eastern or Southern neighbours, is likely to become an article of more extensive export to the Cape than our Mahoganies. **1861** L.A. MEREDITH *Over Straits* 15 On the chief of them sits, snugly perched amidst . . dusky olive-coloured Casuarinas, the white cottage. **1878** 'R. BOLDREWOOD' *Ups & Downs* 66 The river, fringed by the graceful though dark-hued casuarinas. **1886** P. CLARKE *'New Chum' in Aust.* 232 The colonial oak, or casuarina, with its pine-like sombre foliage, speaks rather for use than for ornament. **1912** SPENCER & GILLEN *Across Aust.* 79 The 'desert oak' (casuarina) has completely lost its leaves and its apparent, dull-green, drooping foliage is made of little stiff, green twigs. **1935** DAVISON & NICHOLLS *Blue Coast Caravan* 27 Casuarinas, with their long leaves like emu-feathers, were powdered with bloom. **1948** C.B. MAXWELL *Cold Nose of Law* 57 He had built a little mia-mia with leaves and sticks and scrubby casuarina bush. **1982** *Austral. Financial Rev.* (Sydney) 5 Feb. 40/3 Due to the limited size of the tree, casuarina was used largely as a veneer. No fine piece of early colonial veneered furniture should now be without it. **1985** *Ecos* xlv. 23 In . . glasshouse experiments, casuarinas belonging to one of the genera, *Allocasuarina*, nodulated less frequently than those remaining in the *Casuarina* genus.

cat, *attrib.* and *n.* [From a fancied resemblance to the animal.]

A. Used *attrib.* in Special Comb. **cat bird, (a)** the green cat bird *Ailuroedus melanotis* of rainforests in e. Aust.; **(b)** any of the three Austral. species of *Ailuroedus* (fam. Ptilonorhynchidae); **(c)** any of several other birds (see quots. 1896, 1911, and 1928); **head,** any of several plants having spiny fruits, esp. the annual of all mainland States *Tribulus terrestris* (fam. Zygophyllaceae), often abundant on disturbed ground; also **cat's head; head fern,** any of several ferns, esp. (*Tas.*) *Blechnum nudum* (fam. Blechnaceae), widespread in e. Aust.; also **cat's head fern.**

1827 P.P. KING *Narr. Survey Intertropical & Western Coasts* I. 171 The discordant screams of a bird which had roosted over our fires, and which the people called the **cat-bird.** **1851** J. HENDERSON *Excursions & Adventures N.S.W.* II. 186 The Cat-bird is a pretty green bird . . and at night . . screams like a cat . . but still more, I think, like a child in distress. **1855** J. BONWICK *Geogr. Aust. & N.Z.* (ed. 3) 198 No two Cat-birds can meet without fighting. **1896** B. SPENCER *Rep. Horn Sci. Exped. Central Aust.* I. 120 The 'cat-bird' (*Pomatostomus rubeculus*) attracted attention to itself. **1911** *Bulletin* (Sydney) 26 Jan. 15/2 In the bush . . [babblers] are variously known as . . 'dog birds' or 'cat birds' in tribute to their vocal peculiarities. **1928** B. SPENCER *Wanderings in Wild Aust.* 540 Troops of cat-birds (*Struthidea cinerea*). **1976** *Reader's Digest Compl. Bk. Austral. Birds* 560 The green catbird is retiring in its behaviour. **1985** *Age* (Melbourne) 31 Oct. 11/6 In the distance behind us a cat bird cried out its piteous call. ***c* 1910** W.R. GUILFOYLE *Austral. Plants* 357 'Land Caltrops', 'Indian Caltrops', or **'Cat's-head'**. **1920** J.H. MAIDEN *Weeds N.S.W.* 12 The solid-angled fruits of the Cat's Head (*Emex australis*) and the Double Gee (*Tribulus terrestris*) present a sharp penetrating point to the feet of animals from all aspects. **1938** F. BLAKELEY *Hard Liberty* 160 Catheads . . of a giant kind . . burned within the flesh like red-hot needles. **1974** S.L. EVERIST *Poisonous Plants Aust.* 537 It [*sc. Tribulus terrestris*] is known in many districts as *bull-head* or *cathead* but these common names are applied also to unrelated plants with thick spiny fruits. **1981** G.M. CUNNINGHAM et al. *Plants Western N.S.W.* 438 Cat-head is not attractive to stock, although it may be eaten by hungry animals. **1880** L.A. MEREDITH *Tasmanian Friends & Foes* 220 The **cat's head fern** . . is full of beauty. **1900** *Bulletin* (Sydney) 30 June 14/3 The fern-tick . . does not patronise the cat-head fern. **1920** *Land of Lyre Bird* (S. Gippsland Pioneers' Assoc.) 41 You would enter perhaps a piece of more open scrub . . where cathead ferns covered the ground. **1935** T. RAYMENT *Cluster of Bees* 256 On the forest floor the maiden-hair and the cat-head ferns trembled in amongst the long hooked vines of the wild-raspberry.

B. *n.*

1. See *native cat* NATIVE *a.* 6 b.

2. *Mining.* See quot. 1977.

1950 K.S. PRICHARD *Winged Seeds* 23 Then a couple a little beauts turned up in the ripples and I got a thirty ouncer with a nest of small slugs in the 'cat'. **1977** J. DOUGHTY *Gold in Blood* 72 This was east of where the bar fell away like a small cliff, and was somewhat deeper than usual, being composed of four to five feet of yellow-striped crumbly clay known as 'cat'.

3. In the phr. **to whip the cat:** see WHIP *v.*

4. [Cf. *cat* 'regular guy' (OEDS *sb.*[1] 2 d.).] A passive homosexual.

1958 F. HARDY *Four-Legged Lottery* 117 The hospital was 'full of cats', as the crims say; a large percentage of its staff were flaunting homosexuals. **1967** B.K. BURTON *Teach them no More* 120 'Now that bloke's a cat,' the homosexual continues. 'Me—I'm no woman—I'm what we call a hock—I sort of take to cats like that one over there.' **1974** *Gayzette* (Sydney) 14 Nov. 13/3 The big losers in the prison sexual politic are the 'cats', who will not accept feminine status, but who are weak and so are raped. **1979** L. NEWCOMBE *Inside Out* 38, I would turn off completely at the sight of a cat going through 'her' paces and this revulsion stayed with me during my entire sixteen years of prison living. **1980** B. JEWSON *Stir* 109 'Are you fucken normal or what?' 'Normal?' asked Andrew returning to his bunk. 'Well, t' put it bluntly, are you a cat?' . . 'I don't know what gives you the idea that I might be, er, . . camp.'

catamaran. *Tas. Obs.* A name given by the colonists to an Aboriginal craft.

1804 M. HOOKEY *B. Knopwood & his Times* 21 June (1929) 25 Three of their cattemirans or small boats made of bark that will hold about 6. **1831** G.A. ROBINSON in N.J.B. Plomley *Friendly Mission* 27 June (1966) 366 *Worrady* manufactured several rush catamarans. **1832** J. BACKHOUSE *Narr. Visit Austral. Colonies* (1843) 103 She said, that when the rest were all dead, she made a 'catamoran', a sort of raft, and crossed D'Entrecasteaux Channel to Bruny Island, and joined a tribe there. **1851** H. MELVILLE *Present State Aust.* 361, I tell you dat, him own Wallaby ground—he make 't catamaran, come back so soon as yourself.

catarrh. *Hist.* [Spec. use of *catarrh* inflammation of a mucous membrane.] An infectious and often fatal disease of sheep: see quot. 1848.

1837 *Colonist* (Sydney) 13 June 3/2 The sheep are . . afflicted with the 'Catarrh'. **1838** *Cornwall Chron.* (Launceston) 10 Nov. 1 An Act for preventing the extension of the disease, commonly called the Influenza or Catarrh in Sheep and Lambs, in the Colony of New South Wales. **1840** *S. Austral. Rec.* (London) 19 Sept. 179 We are sorry to hear that severe losses have already taken place amongst the sheep in various parts of the colony. Catarrh and red water, it is said, are the most prevalent diseases. **1848** H.W. HAYGARTH *Recoll. Bush Life* 50 The scourge of the sheepowner is the catarrh; a disease peculiar to Australia. . . The principal symptoms are a discharge from the nostrils of a dark slimy matter, a drooping of the head, feeble gait, and loss of appetite; the infected animal . . dies, apparently in great pain, often within twenty-four hours from the time of its first seizure. **1851** *Empire* (Sydney) 3 Nov. 324/2 The disease commonly called catarrh, in New South Wales, is most improperly named, as it bears little or no affinity to that known by the same appellation in England. **1877** G. MITCHELL *Cumberland Disease* 2 We have now come to the opinion that catarrh originated in Australia, and through mismanagement of sheep. **1883** W.A. BRODRIBB *Recoll. Austral. Squatter* 37 During the winter, spring, and summer, of 1846 . . we lost, by catarrah, over 2,000 sheep. **1942** H.H. PECK *Mem. of Stockman* 133 An epidemic then called 'catarrh' later carried off a lot of the sheep.

Also **catarrhed** *a.*

1846 *Portland Guardian* 22 Sept. 3/2 The bill admitted of the boiling down of catarrhed sheep. **1848** *Maitland Mercury* 26 Aug. 2/4 In the present state of the colony, few sheep runs are so situated as to enable the proprietor to go off his own with catarrhed sheep, without subjecting himself to a penalty. **1890** 'R. BOLDREWOOD' *Colonial Reformer* III. 5 It was a blind trick of yours to go and bring those chaps here, like a lot of catarrhed sheep, all among your own stock.

catch. *Shearing.* BELL SHEEP.

[N.Z. **1933** *Press* (Christchurch) 23 Sept. 13/7 Just before stopping time in a wool shed, a shearer tries to finish the sheep he is on and catch another which he can finish at ease after knock-off. This is called *getting a catch.*] **1965** J.S. GUNN *Terminol. Shearing Industry* i. 7 The 'bell sheep', or 'the catch' as it is often called, may be an easy one. **1982** P. ADAM SMITH *Shearers* 404 *Catch*, last sheep in pen.

catching pen. [Also used elsewhere.] A pen in a shearing shed from which the shearer takes the sheep to be shorn.

[N.Z. **1857** R.B. PAUL *Lett. from Canterbury* 88 A post and rail catching pen.] **1867** A.K. COLLINS *Waddy Mundoee* 9 Catching pens front the shed. **1893** 'OLD CHUM' *Chips* 42 The shearing is done by a long row of men on each side. In the middle is a large enclosure, or 'pen', into which the sheep are driven from outside, and there are smaller pens, called 'catching pens', on each side, which are fed from this large one. **1914** H.B. SMITH *Sheep & Wool Industry* 34 Two shearers generally have one pen to catch their sheep from. They are called catching pens. **1928** C.E. COWLEY *Classing Clip* 148 The catching pens should be comparatively small. **1947** *Bulletin* (Sydney) 26 Nov. 29/3 She made for the catching-pen. **1980** P. FREEMAN *Woolshed* 18 Before shearing starts, the 'rouseabout', or general hand, drives some sheep into each of the 'catching' pens. The shearer 'catches' the sheep from these pens.

catfish. Any of several marine and fresh-water fish of the fam. Ariidae and Plotisidae, having long barbels near the mouth somewhat resembling a cat's whiskers, and harmful spines. See also *Murray catfish* MURRAY.

1827 P.P. KING *Narr. Survey Intertropical & Western Coasts* I. 31 The river appeared to abound in fish, but the only sort that was caught was what the sailors called cat-fish. **1834** G. BENNETT *Wanderings N.S.W.* I. 343 The '*Cat-fish*' (*Silurus*), said to have the power of stinging with the tentaculae or feelers. **1856** G. WILLMER *Draper in Aust.* 225 The cat-fish is singular in its appearance, having a large head and whiskers similar to the animal from which it derives its name. **1881** *Proc. Linnean Soc. N.S.W.* VI. 205 *Copidoglanis tandanus*. . . '*The Cat Fish*' of the Murrumbidgee. **1916** T.C. ROUGHLEY *Fishes of Aust.* 19 *Freshwater catfish*. . . As an edible fish this species is really valuable. It is far and away superior to its relative the Estuary Catfish. **1963** M. BRITT *Pardon my Boots* 61 Deadly poison, these cat-fish. . . I knew a bloke got spiked with one once. In agony 'e was. **1981** Q. WILD *Honey Wind* 33 The barramundi, the saltwater crocodile and the large catfish were seen on the walls of the rock caves.

Catholic frog. [See quot. 1923.] The yellowish frog *Notaden bennettii* of inland s.e. Aust.; HOLY CROSS TOAD. Also **Catholic toad.**

1891 *Proc. Linnean Soc. N.S.W.* VI. 265 *Notaden bennettii*, the 'Catholic frog' or, as I have heard it called, the Holy Cross toad. **1901** F.J. GILLEN *Diary* 11 June (1968) 113 He also brought us some specimens of frogs one of which Spencer thinks is Notaden Bennetti commonly called Catholic Toad. **1923** *Bulletin* (Sydney) 12 Apr. 24/3 Aestivation . . is practised by . . the 'catholic' frog, which gets its ecclesiastical moniker from the pale cross decorating its back. **1928** B. SPENCER *Wanderings in Wild Aust.* 142 All of these three species store water in their bodies, as also does the Catholic Frog.

cat-shag, *v. intr.* To 'fool around'.

1971 D. IRELAND *Unknown Industr. Prisoner* 143 These men are trained for years, they know more than us, they're bent over books and calculus and things we've never heard of while we're out cat-shagging around and learning to get on the piss. **1977** R. BEILBY *Gunner* 248 Now, lets stop cat-shagging about and get started.

cat's paw. a. PUSSY TAIL. **b.** Any of the smaller perennial herbs of the W.A. genus *Anigozanthos* (fam. Haemodoraceae) having a claw-like flower with a furry appearance (cf. *kangaroo paw* KANGAROO *n.* 5), esp. *A. humilis.*

1901 *Twentieth Century Impressions W.A.* 186 In the order Amarantaceoe [*sic*], Ptilotus leads with 36 species. . . In the eastern colonies it is known as the cat's paw. ***c* 1910** W.R. GUILFOYLE *Austral. Plants* 357 *Trichinium spathulatum* . . 'Australian Foxtail', or 'Catspaw' (herbaceous perennial). **1949** D. WALKER *We went to Aust.* 184 The catspaw is more straightforward, usually orange and resembling an orchid. **1959** C. & E. CHAUVEL *Walkabout* 33 Patches of 'Cats' paw', which is an edible little bush, enjoyed by the kangaroos. **1977** D. STUART *Drought Foal* 6 Miles of the brown and gold flowers of bacon-and-egg bushes, cat's paws and kangaroo paws.

cattle. Used *attrib.* in Comb. not always excl. Austral. but of local importance.

1. Comb. **cattle bitch, country, dip, draft, -drafting, holder, -holding, property, road, spear, -spearing, walk, work.**

1936 I.L. IDRIESS *Cattle King* 58 The best **cattle-bitch** on the Darling! **1944** E.M. ANDERSON *Typist Tales* 114 Charlie Smith's cattle-bitch took a bait. **1978** R.J. BRITTEN *Around Cassowary Rock* 11 Now these pups were a pretty solid sort of breed—a cross between a blue cattle bitch and a staghound dog. **1840** *S. Austral. Rec.* (London) 20 June 335, I think the lands nearest the settled districts which are desirable for purchase are . . the **cattle-country**, commencing, say, twelve miles north of Perth. **1847** G.F. ANGAS *Savage Life & Scenes* I. 149 We found a good cattle country, consisting of grassy flats scattered over with banksia or honeysuckle-trees. **1881** W. FEILDING *Austral. Trans-Continental Railway* 17 The route passed through fair cattle country, open box-forest flats. **1901** *Bulletin* (Sydney) 7 Dec. 30/1 At periodical intervals a boom in cattle-country arises in the cities. **1922** V. PALMER *Boss of Killara* 9 He had spent most of his time away from this belt of cattle-country that had bred him. **1932** M.R. WHITE *No Roads go By* 43 A big area of cattle-country cannot be worked from the head station with a night out now and again. **1953** A. UPFIELD *Venom House* 40 If you want to know why I left the cattle country to work on a place no bigger than a cattle station's backyard, I won't be telling you. **1981** A.B. FACEY *Fortunate Life* 167 We were crossing through cattle country so the Boss had put two extra men on the scouting team to help clear any station stock. **1909** *Bulletin* (Sydney) 14 Oct. 14/2 A **cattle-dip** stirred up is about the color, consistency and odor of Melbourne's Yarra. **1910** *Ibid.* 6 Jan. 14/3 The cattle dip for Territory cattle going into Queensland, is about 200 miles south of Borooloola. **1925** M. TERRY *Across Unknown Aust.* 84 Dipping is achieved by means of a race . . leading to a pit containing the cattle-dip solution. **1901** *Advocate* (Burnie) 8 June 4/2 The Duke expressed a desire to see a **cattle draft**, and in 'cutting out' certain animals and clearing them off, very fine stockriding was shown. **1952** *Bulletin* (Sydney) 16 Jan. 16/2, I got up then, picked up the cattle-draft from the saleyards and left the other mob. **1859** H. KINGSLEY *Recoll. Geoffrey*

Hamlyn II. 244 Sam, sir, has won a wife by **cattle-drafting.** **1886** R. HENTY *Australiana* 158 Next morning the cattle-drafting takes place. The 'strangers' are handed to their owners, the fat cattle are set apart. **1913** *Bulletin* (Sydney) 20 Mar. 15/1 It is the fast, rough work, such as cattle drafting, brumby-running, polo, etc. that begets horsemen. **1925** M. TERRY *Across Unknown Aust.* 78 Cattle drafting and dipping. **1843** *N.S.W. Monthly Mag.* June 270 The **cattle holders** and drivers of New South Wales. **1845** J.O. BALFOUR *Sketch of N.S.W.* 100 The boiling down of live stock for their tallow came, in 1843, very opportunely to the relief of the cattle-holder. **1876** *Austral. Town & Country Jrnl.* (Sydney) 16 Dec. 982/1 Banks pointed out the types which all cattleholders agree in desiring to 'get shut of'. **1893** 'PIONEER' *Reminisc. Austral. Early Life* 59 Cattle-holders of runs. **1854** W. SHAW *Land of Promise* 250 **Cattle-holding** differs totally from sheep-farming. **1950** A. GROOM *I saw Strange Land* 209 Henbury is one of the oldest and largest **cattle properties** along the mighty old Finke. **1969** G. JOHNSTON *Clean Straw for Nothing* (1971) 8 Steve . . was trying to get rid of a cattle property he had up north in the brigalow scrub. **1977** V. PRIDDLE *Larry & Jack* 5 He . . always seemed to be able to get a job on a big cattle property as a station hand. **1965** *N. Austral. Monthly* Oct. 17/2 We decided to take the new **cattle road** to the bitumen and on to Katherine. **1879** 'AUSTRALIAN' *Adventures Qld.* 12 Some blacks had got up the trees with their heavy **cattle-spears,** while another party had watched their opportunity till the cattle fed that way, when they rushed from their hiding-places, and hunted them pell-mell down the gully, for the fellows up the trees to spear as they passed under. **1894** *Bulletin* (Sydney) 23 June 24/1 We found the cattle, like hunted devils, cattle-spears—roughly scraped and fire-pointed saplings—all over the country. **1882** A.J. BOYD *Old Colonials* 193 If they are punished, it deters them for a certain time from committing any more overt acts of murder or **cattle-spearing.** **1898** D.W. CARNEGIE *Spinifex & Sand* 123 A band of marauding black-fellows, most of whom had 'done time' at Rotnest Jail for cattle-spearing, probably, on the coast stations. **1955** F. LANE *Patrol to Kimberleys* 13 Sometimes, there were areas to police against cattle-spearing by the natives, or cattle-duffing—rustling—by the whites. **1831** *Acct. Colony Van Diemen's Land* 117 Great part of this fine grazing country has now been located and converted into profitable sheep and **cattle-walks.** **1840** A. RUSSELL *Tour through Austral. Colonies* 164 The land in this neighbourhood is more taken up for sheep runs than cattle walks. **1926** A.A.B. APSLEY *Amateur Settlers* 112 Our '**cattle-work**' was . . amusing. **1936** W. HATFIELD *Aust. through Windscreen* 291, I have known men pull out of a droving-camp when we reached the country of fences. 'This isn't cattle work!' they said '— getting orf your horse every five minutes opening blasted gates. I'm a cattle man, and I'm orf back to cattle country.' **1937** —— *I find Aust.* 81, I got a little tired of sheep-work. Moore was always saying how much faster and harder cattle-work was, so I was itching to get amongst it.

2. Special Comb. **cattle camp,** see CAMP *n.* 3; **dog,** a dog bred and trained to work with cattle, such as the *blue heeler* (see BLUE *a.*); **driver,** *cattle drover*; **-driving** *vbl. n., obs.*, DROVING; **drover,** DROVER; **grazier,** see GRAZIER, so **-grazing** *vbl. n.*; **hunt** *obs., cattle muster*; **-hunting** *vbl. n., obs.*, MUSTERING; **king** [orig. U.S.] a large-scale cattle farmer; **muster,** see MUSTER *n.* 2; **pad,** a track made by cattle (see PAD 1); **run,** see RUN *n.*[2] 1 a. and 2; **slut,** a female *cattle dog*; **station,** see STATION 2 a. and 3; **track,** a route followed by cattle drovers (see TRACK *n.* 2 a.).

1868 *Illustr. Sydney News* 7 Aug. 27/4, I remember . . Robardi killed a **cattle dog** belonging to me. **1888** 'R. BOLDREWOOD' *Robbery under Arms* (1937) 70 He had as much chance of coming up with her as a cattle dog of catching a 'brush flyer'. **1900** *Truth* (Sydney) 4 Mar. 5/2 A cattle dog must bite and have no tongue. **1914** R. KALESKI *Austral. Barkers & Biters* 85 Nothing in the bush makes so good a mate as the cattle-dog. **1933** C.H. HOLMES *We find Aust.* 155 The cattle dog is larger and more thick-set than the kelpie, and its colourings are red-speckle, blue-speckle, and red. **1957** J.M. HOSKING *Aust. first & Last* 30 With the cattle dog under the tucker cart and the flankers swinging wide. **1981** P. RADLEY *Jack Rivers & Me* 59 Throw your butts in the spittoons not down there or you'll singe the cattle-dogs restin' underneath in the shade. **1843** *N.S.W. Monthly Mag.* June 270 **Cattle** holders and **drivers.** **1857** J. ASKEW *Voyage Aust. & N.Z.* 63 Cattle-drivers, and shepherds, with sheep and cattle destined for slaughter. **1843** R.D. MURRAY *Summer at Port Phillip* 232 You are now equipped for a steeple-chase of a desperate kind though it be under the modest name of **cattle-driving.** **1852** W. HOWITT *Land, Labor & Gold* 8 Dec. (1855) I. 140 We hear a deal of the adventures of such life [on squatting stations]—of cattle-driving amongst the hills, swimming rivers, sleeping out in tempests, and so on. **1844** *Sydney Morning Herald* 15 May 2/7 (*heading*) Caution to **cattle drovers.** **1857** *Queen v. Beaton* 14 A cattle drover brought a mob of cows and calves and put them on my grass. **1909** E. WALTHAM *Life & Labour in Aust.* 5 A splendid opening in the career of a cattle drover, whose work is usually spoken of as overlanding. **1963** V.B. CRANLEY *27,000 Miles through Aust.* 128 The cattle drovers of today up in the north and the distant west are after all no different from those who took their flocks and herds from stream to stream here in the eighties. **1845** D. MACKENZIE *Emigrant's Guide* 110 To the emigrant who intends to commence as a **cattle-grazier,** I would recommend to buy a *mixed* herd. **1852** *Four Colonies Aust.* 26 The occupation of a cattle-grazier is far more onerous than that of a sheep-farmer. **1884** *Qld. Handbk. Information* (Burns, Philp & Co.) 31 The cattle-graziers . . occupied the country. **1937** D. GUNN *Links with Past* 98 The Lows commenced their operations as cattle graziers. **1965** R.H. CONQUEST *Horses in Kitchen* 95 In Queensland's early years the Dawson region and the Burnett country were probably the best **cattle-grazing** areas in the State. **1968** D. O'GRADY *Bottle of Sandwiches* 29 We took off to improve the cattle-grazing situation by eliminating some of the roos. **1854** H.B. STONEY *Yr. in Tas.* 91 The settlers in the counties, when in the interior collecting cattle, which they allow to graze at large over the wilds, enjoy above all things a good **cattle-hunt.** **1829** H. WIDOWSON *Present State Van Diemen's Land* 159 From what I have seen of **cattle-hunting,** I must confess there is more fuss and noise made than are necessary. **1841** *Colonial Observer* (Sydney) 30 Dec. 100/2 A few of our Colonial Absentees will be obliged to exchange the pleasures of fox-hunting and pleasure-hunting in England . . for the good old realities of cattle and kangaroo-hunting in New South Wales. **1852** G.B. EARP *Gold Colonies Aust.* 118 None but riders thoroughly accustomed to their work should engage in cattle-hunting or collecting. **1885** D.E. MCCONNELL *Austral. Etiquette* 470 Cattle-hunting, or to apply the more correct Australian term, 'cattle-mustering', may be fairly classed as an Australian sport. **1901** *Truth* (Sydney) 16 June 5/7 Some of these **cattle kings** rig out their dark inamoratas in all the glory of a loud pink dress. **1903** *Bulletin* (Sydney) 6 Aug. 17/1 The budding 'cattle king' of Australia . . lately got back to Adelaide. **1919** *Smith's Weekly* (Sydney) 1 Mar. 6/3 The late James Tyson, and the present Cattle King, Kidman, both began moneyless. **1956** T. RONAN *Moleskin Midas* 12 The Ophir was a fit background for this, the last of the genuine cattle kings. **1972** G.C. BOLTON *Fine Country to starve In* 101 Shrewder entrepreneurs . . such as the 'cattle kings' Sam Copley and Isadore Emanuel, went off to live in London. **1845** D. MACKENZIE *Emigrant's Guide* 131 Divers extraordinary and incorrect accounts of Australian **cattle-muster** have been written. **1847** A. HARRIS *Settlers & Convicts* (1953) 14 The season for important farm operations, such as sheep washing, sheep shearing, wool pressing for exportation, reaping, cattle muster, etc. **1872** 'RESIDENT' *Glimpses Life Vic.* 61 Among the various operations that were customary on stations the cattle muster used to be one of the most exciting. **1955** A. UPFIELD *Cake in Hat Box* 62 Sometimes a cattle muster will net wild cattle, and the bulls are dangerous, and often of no use as beef. **1910** *Emu* X. 22 We . . got through to the west side on a **cattle pad.** **1919** *Bulletin* (Sydney) 7 Aug. 22/1 Was ridin' along on a cattle-pad when I finds a heap of human bones. **1929** H. MACQUARRIE *We & Baby* 103 Some difficulty in finding the cattle-pad near the Cooktown crossing; drovers usually allow their beasts to 'spread' some miles before reaching water. **1953** E. MITCHELL *Flow River, blow Wind* 13 The red-and-white beasts . . would move slowly along the drifting cattlepads. **1980** ANSELL & PERCY *To fight Wild* 46 Following cattle-pads is not a sure method, often they just lead to a dried-out swamp. **1823** *Hobart Town Gaz.* 4 Oct., Two small Farms, one 100 and the other 50 acres . . affording a good **cattle run.** **1834** J.D. LANG *Hist. & Statistical Acct. N.S.W.* II. 165 Proprietors will naturally suffer their land to remain in its present wild and uncultivated state as mere *cattle-runs*, till the increase of the population of the colony . . shall have rendered every acre ten times more valuable than it is at present. **1839** T.L. MITCHELL *Three Exped. Eastern Aust.* I. 11 The pasturage afforded by the numerous vallies on this side of the mountains, here called 'cattle runs', is more profitable to the owners of farms, than the farms they actually possess. **1840** *HRA* (1924) 1st Ser. XXI. 127 There is scarcely a man of any property who has not a Cattle Run or a Sheep station beyond the Boundaries. **1873** A. TROLLOPE *Aust. & N.Z.* I. 34 Small farmers do deal in beef, but they steal the cattle from the large cattle-runs. **1910** *Huon Times* (Franklin) 28 Sept. 2/5 Large areas that could be satisfactorily utilised for growing rootcrops are now used as cattle runs. **1934** *Red Star* (Perth) 7 Sept. 3/1 The old battler . . has pioneered the country for capitalism . . has thirsted and starved in gold rushes and on out back cattle runs. **1965** R.H. CONQUEST *Horses in Kitchen* 187 Thylungra . . is only a pup of a station compared with some of the huge cattle runs further north, but is nevertheless about 1,600,000 acres. **1974** B. ROLAND *No Ordinary Man* 80 He owns Tarcoola, one of the biggest cattle-runs in the west. **1915** *Pastoral Rev.* Mar. 239 A valuable **cattle slut** . . developed mange. **1933** J. MCCARTER *Love's Lunatic* 40 'Never brought th' cattle slut t'day,' he explained. . . 'Would your dog have made that much difference?' **1956** B.J. RAYMENT *My Towri* 87 Two of these were cattle sluts gone bush. **1832** *N.S.W. Govt. Gaz.* 14 Mar. 9/1, I arrived . . at Walamoul . . (a **cattle station** of Mr Brown). **1838** T.L. MITCHELL *Three Exped. Eastern Aust.* II. 136 One or two spots seemed very favourable for farms or cattle stations. **1843** J.F. BENNETT *Hist. & Descr. Acct. S.A.* 100 A 'cattle station' is sometimes formed on Government land, sometimes on the Settler's own property, but commanding a run. **1851** MRS R. LEE *Adventures in Aust.* 283 The Murray . . has its banks lined with cattle-stations. **1873** *Illustr. Sydney News* 5 July 11/1 The stock-keeper . . is usually found located at a cattle station far out. **1888** 'R. BOLDREWOOD' *Robbery under Arms* (1937) 369 He'd bought cattle-stations on the Lachlan just when the gold broke out first. **1911** *Bulletin* (Sydney) 10 Aug. 14/4 Among the cattle stations of the North-West Territory . . it is customary to have periodical poisonings-off of black-fellows' dogs. **1925** M. TERRY *Across Unknown Aust.* 24, I went sheep-droving and he went south, far away to a distant cattle station. **1955** F. LANE *Patrol to Kimberleys* 177 Far below, on the flats, sprawled a cattle station, its homestead, barns, and sheds looking like toy buildings. **1965** R. OTTLEY *By Sandhills* 173 Each cattle-station—then as now—has a boss, who is either the owner or a manager. Then there is an overseer, and also numerous stockmen, odd-job men, and general rouse-abouts. **1986** *Centralian Advocate* (Alice Springs) 15 Jan. 12/2 Benstead had worked as a cattle station manager for several years. **1849** *Belfast Gaz.* 14 Sept. 3/3 By following along a well-marked **cattle track** you will arrive at the mouth of the Shaw river. **1870** *Illustr. Sydney News* 17 Feb. 343/3 Sydney . . could have been truthfully represented by a drawing of a rough cattle-track, adorned with tree stumps, and intersected by water-courses. **1935** F. BIRTLES *Battle Fronts Outback* 25, I was following up the overlanding cattle-track that leads the drovers down from the far north-west. ***c* 1960** C. MACKNESS *Clump Point & District* 66 By that time, there was a cattle-track at least right through to Innisfail.

3. In the names of flora: **cattle bush,** any of several plants, esp. the perennial herb *Trichodesma zeylanicum* (fam. Boraginaceae); **pumpkin,** see quot. 1977.

1886 D. LINDSAY *Exped. across Aust.* 18 Good **cattle bushes** and blue-bush are plentiful. **1910** *Emu* X. 100 A nest in broken-down cattle-bush. **1931** M. TERRY *Hidden Wealth* 325 Cattle bush—which with its blue-hooded flowers is said to be valuable cattle fodder. **1944** *Bulletin* (Sydney) 23 Feb. 13/3 Cattlebush is indigenous to the western part of the State. **1925** *Ibid.* 5 Feb. 22/4 He has a mandolin fashioned out of a **cattle-pumpkin** shell. **1977** G.A.W. SMITH *Riding High* 181 Enough grass to fill the beast, using the artificial feed merely as a supplement: this was cattle pumpkin. The pumpkins were huge, twice the size of the table variety.

cattle duff, *v. intr.* To steal cattle; see also DUFF *v.* 1. Freq. as *vbl. n.*

1865 *Tumut & Adelong Times* 23 Mar. 3/1 A very lucrative business in the cattle-duffing at Kiandra. **1881** H.W. NESFIELD *Chequered Career* 305 On such stations 'cattle duffing' and similar abominations are regarded as things of the past. **1886** *Melbourne Punch* 15 July, Cattle duffers on a jury may be honest men enough, But they're bound to visit lightly sins in those who cattle duff. **1888** T.V. Foote *My Weird Wooing* 94 My father wouldn't cattle duff, not because he didn't understand it, but because he thought it dishonest—I've heard him say it was *stealing*. **1891** *Hist. Bushranging* 26 Followed the pursuit of stock-breeding, or rather 'cattle duffing' as the appropriation of animals from the herds of one's neighbour is designated. **1910** *Bulletin* (Sydney) 17 Mar. 14/1 Horse and cattle-duffing was not looked upon as a crime. **1935** F. Clune *Rolling down Lachlan* 123 Vane and Mick Burke, both of whom were eventually to join Ben Hall's gang, camped here with two others on the night before their first big job of cattle duffing. **1955** F. Lane *Patrol to Kimberleys* 119 They were after him for cattle duffing. **1978** O. White *Silent Reach* 159 'A couple of years back, I'd've said there was money in cattle duffin'.' 'Cattle stealing?' 'That's what I said.'

cattle duffer. A cattle thief; Duffer *n.* 1.

c **1872** J.C.F. Johnson *Over Island* 1 The wild Barrier Rangers, the haunt of the 'cattle duffer'. **1888** 'Special Correspondent' *Barrier Silver & Tin Fields* 22/2 It was generally looked upon as the haunt of the 'cattle-duffers', as the notorious cattle thieves were called. **1897** *Western Champion* (Barcaldine) 26 Jan. 3/3 It is supposed the body of the father was burnt after being shot, that being a favourite mode of 'cattle-duffers' in the country of disposing of the remains of sheep and cows. **1911** V. Desmond *Awful Austral.* 70 Many of the squatters to-day in Australia are the decendants of cattle 'duffers', as their nondescript herds amply testify. **1927** R.S. Browne *Journalist's Memories* 170 The cattle 'duffer' . . is just a plain thief. **1955** J. Cleary *Justin Bayard* 28 Old Man Crispin, who was so moral otherwise and hated cattle duffers, had reckoned that anyone who risked his neck going into those hills was entitled to keep what he found. **1978** R.H. Conquest *Dusty Distances* 46 Kangaroo beef . . which we said was cheap beef, bought from the cattle duffers.

caucus. [U.S. *caucus* a private meeting of the leaders or representatives of a political party: see OED 1.] A meeting of the parliamentary members of a political party; collectively, those eligible to attend such a meeting. Also *attrib.*

1887 *Tasmanian News* (Hobart) 25 Feb. 2/3 After the caucus broke up yesterday afternoon, Ministers entertained their supporters at lunch. **1893** *Mercury* (Hobart) 23 Dec. 2/8 The Opposition in caucus. **1906** *Truth* (Sydney) 20 May 4/6 The only difference between a Cabinet and a Caucus is that there are two C's in 'Caucus' and only one in 'Cabinet'. **1911** H.G. Turner *First Decade Austral. Cwlth.* 178 Some of his party had been injudicious in vaunting the powers of the Caucus. **1917** *Huon Times* (Franklin) 30 Mar. 5/4 We wanted to represent us in Parliament men who would not be bound by the dark and underhand ways of Caucus, but who would be in a position to express their thoughts and ideas of good citizenship. **1936** E. Scott *Aust. during War* in *Official Hist. Aust. 1914–18* XI. 47 Mr Hughes . . favoured the compelling of members of the party to subscribe to a pledge which bound them, 'on questions affecting the fate of a government, to vote as a majority of the Labour party may decide at a duly constituted caucus meeting'. **1943** R. Dixon *Story J.T. Lang* 6 He was not yet strong enough to dispense with Caucus meetings. **1956** J.T. Lang *I Remember* 7 There was trouble over the solidarity pledge and the rights of Caucus. **1976** K. Amos *New Guard Movt.* 5 Bitterly disappointed with the result, Hughes stormed from a Labor caucus meeting. **1986** *Canberra Times* 3 Mar. 2/3 About 35 members out of a total caucus of 82 put their stomachs ahead of dealing with the other matters on the agenda.

Hence **caucuser** *n.*, **caucusite** *n.*

1898 *Truth* (Sydney) 6 Nov. 4/3 These cursed, cowardly **Caucussers.** **1905** *Shearer* (Sydney) 14 Jan. 8/5 Merely a little Pedlington gang of blinding and bluffing clacquers, 'barrackers', and caucusers. **1904** *Ibid.* 27 Aug. 4/2 Albert is a well-known foot-baller, an earnest speaker, and a **Caucusite**.

caustic, *a.* Used in the names of plants from the irritant action of their sap: **caustic bush (plant, vine),** any of several plants, esp. the scrambler or bush *Sarcostemma australe* (fam. Asclepiadaceae) of all mainland States exc. Vic., which is variously regarded as good fodder (*W.A., S.A.*) or as poisonous to stock (*Qld., N.S.W.*); see also *milk-bush* Milk 1; **creeper** (or **weed**), any of several plants usu. of the genus *Euphorbia* (fam. Euphorbiaceae), esp. *E. drummondii* of Aust. and New Guinea which has a milky sap, and is reputed to have either healing or poisonous properties (see quots. 1917 and 1981).

1887 [caustic bush] Bailey & Gordon *Plants reputed Poisonous* 43 *Sarcostemma australe*. . . Known as 'Caustic plant' or 'Caustic vine' in Queensland. **1897** L. Lindley-Cowen *W. Austral. Settler's Guide* 591 'Caustic bush' or 'vine'. . . Reported poisonous in Queensland but sometimes found harmless. **1917** Ewart & Davies *Flora N.T.* 224 Caustic vine, a noxious weed, poisonous to stock. **1922** *Jrnl. & Proc. R. Soc. N.S.W.* LVI. 183 This plant, which occurs in all the Australian States except Victoria and Tasmania, is known as 'Caustic Vine', or 'Caustic Plant'. **1966** A. Morris *Plantlife W. Darling* 75 'Snake Plant' or 'Caustic Plant', leafless shrub, common on hills near Umberumberka. **1980** Ansell & Percy *To fight Wild* 96 One bush to avoid is an ordinary grey looking shrub, caustic bush, which brings you out in blisters if you brush against it. **1887** Bailey & Gordon *Plants reputed Poisonous* 79 *Euphorbia drummondii* . . **Caustic creeper**. . . This weed is unquestionably poisonous to sheep. **1917** Ewart & Davies *Flora N.T.* 170 Caustic Creeper . . is used by the Queensland natives in cases of snake-bite. The fresh milky sap possesses great healing properties, and is in constant use by bushmen. **1981** G.M. Cunningham et al. *Plants Western N.S.W.* 456 Caustic weed . . when eaten as part of a mixed diet . . has little effect on grazing animals. It has however been blamed for poisoning sheep, and on occasions, horses and cattle.

cawbawn, var. Cabon.

Cazaly /kəˈzeɪli/. [The name of Roy *Cazaly* (1893–1963), an Australian National Football player who played for South Melbourne (1921–1926).] In the phr. **up there Cazaly,** orig. a supporter's cry (see quot. 1943); now *transf.* as a cry of encouragement or approbation.

1943 S.J. Baker *Pop. Dict. Austral. Slang* (ed. 3) 86 *Up there Cazaly!* Used as a cry of encouragement. **1950** J. Morrison *Port of Call* 245 'Give it to him, Jack!' 'Up there, Cazally!' 'Throw the silly bastards over the side!' **1962** —— *Twenty-Three* 91 'Good on you Bo!' 'Up there, Cazally!' 'Rock it in, Bo!' **1963** *Sun-Herald* (Sydney) 13 Jan. 72/4 'Up there, Cazaly' became the battle cry of Australian soldiers of the Ninth Division in North Africa. **1970** C. Nolan *Bride for St. Thomas* 142 'Up there, Cazaley!' I said. . . Then had to explain that this was a phrase Australian crowds roared when a football hero made a spectacular leap for the ball. **1972** *Bulletin* (Sydney) 26 Feb. 11/1 While coolly robbing a jeweller's or sticking up a bank, one or other of them is usually heard to utter some give-away locution like 'Stone the crows' or 'Up there, Cazaly'. **1978** *Daily Mirror* (Sydney) 9 June 44/1 To many Australians the words 'Up there Cazaly' have a special meaning as a form of greeting and a sign of recognition between fellow countrymen. **1979** *Bulletin* (Sydney) 21 Aug. 31/1 Up there Cazaly, don't let 'em in Fly like an angel You're out there to win. **1981** B. Oakley *Marsupials & Politics* 71 I'm telling you the facts about your damn fool, insignificant, down-under, she'll-be-right, fill-'em-up-again, see-yer-later, 'ow-ya-goin', waltzing-matilda, up-there-Cazaly little country. **1983** G. Hutchinson *Great Austral. Bk. Football Stories* 140 One of the greatest players Australian Rules has ever known, the lean and wiry Roy Cazaly, specialised in spectacular leaps enabling him to mark over taller opponents. Rover Skeeter Fleiter first yelled 'Up there Cazaly' in a 1921 game when spurring his teammate on during a tense battle for possession of the ball.

cedar.

1. Any of several trees resembling the coniferous *Cedrus* in foliage or in the colour, grain, or smell of its timber, esp. the tall rainforest tree *Toona australis* (fam. Meliaceae) of e. N.S.W., e. Qld., and elsewhere, the wood of which is often attractively figured and usu. a deep red colour; the timber of these trees. Also with distinguishing epithet, as **native, pencil, red, Sydney, white** (see under first element). Also **cedar-tree.**

1795 *HRA* (1914) 1st Ser. I. 491, I have permitted the master of the Experiment to take with him a cargo of mahogany and cedar of this country. **1805** J.H. Tuckey *Acct. Voyage to establish Colony Port Phillip* 227 Cedar nearly resembles the mahogany of Honduras. **1820** H.G. Bennet *Let. to Earl Bathurst* 100 No light wood except cedar, which is dear and scarce, grows in the settlement. **1825** B. Field *Geogr. Mem. N.S.W.* 461 The humblest house is fitted up with cedar. **1834** Tas. Colonial Secretary's Office Rec. 1/11 276 He does not consider it [*sc.* furniture] suitable for a Government House, being generally of an inferior quality and principally composed of cedar. **1845** *Sydney Morning Herald* 22 Aug. 3/7, I had a quantity of slop clothing damaged by salt water, and they were permanently stained of a bright red colour wherever they had been in contact with the cedar. **1852** G.C. Mundy *Our Antipodes* II. 25 Here I saw for the first time the cedar—the most valuable timber in the country for upholstery—the mahogany, in short, of New Holland, a wood which it much resembles in colour and grain, although inferior in solidity. It has no affinity whatever with the cedar of other climes—the foliage nearly resembling the European ash; it is not even a coniferous tree. **1874** *Illustr. Sydney News* 2 May 18/2 A number of vessels sail pretty regularly to this point from Sydney for cargoes of cedar, which is to be obtained in abundant quantities on the mountain slopes inland. **1880** *Argus* (Melbourne) 26 Jan. 6/4 The large pinnate leaves during the spring and summer rival in beauty those of the well-known cedar tree of New South Wales and Queensland—cedrela toona. **1895** A.C. Bicknell *Travel & Adventure Northern Qld.* 42 We got into thick scrub, with cedar trees of enormous size. **1921** *Bulletin* (Sydney) 3 Nov. 22/3 The cedar-tree borer threatens to spoil what fire and axes have left in Queensland. **1960** E. O'Conner *Irish Man* 169 He heard the lonely call of a black cockatoo, and knew that this was what he had heard as he stood by the cedar-tree.

2. Comb. (chiefly with reference to *Toona australis*) **cedar brush, cutters, cutting, getter, grounds, party, sawyers, tracks.**

1836 J. Backhouse *Narr. Visit Austral. Colonies* (1843) 397 We took a walk into one of the luxuriant woods, on the side of the Hunter, such as are termed **Cedar Brushes**, on account of the colonial White Cedar . . being one of the trees that compose them. **1858** A. Harris *Secrets* (1961) 145 The cedar brushes are the most distinguishing feature. **1872** G.S. Baden-Powell *New Homes for Old Country* 351 This cedar-brush was very like a good thick wood at home, excepting for the huge trees projecting above it. **1827** *Monitor* (Sydney) 10 Feb. 308/1 Before the present **cedar-cutters** could wind up and get out of the trade, their loss of earnings will compel them to live on their capital. **1855** J. Bonwick *Geogr. Aust. & N.Z.* (ed. 3) 27 Two shipwrecked cedar cutters gave him information of a fine river. **1885** Mrs C. Praed *Austral. Life* 140 The men—small farmers and cedar-cutters—were a rude, independent set. **1946** J.G. Eastwood *More about Cairns* 23 A deserted cedar-cutter's hut (built entirely of red cedar). **1845** *Star* (Parramatta) 27 Sept. 3/2 *Moreton Bay*. . . **Cedar cutting** had been commenced on an extensive scale. **1857** *Vic. Parl. Papers* (1856–57) III. no. 48 77 Farming work and cedar cutting. **1876** 'Eight Yrs.' Resident' *Queen of Colonies* 133 A wandering miner . . presented himself at the camp of a **cedar-getter** on the upper waters of the Mary. **1946** J.G. Eastwood *More about Cairns* 24 All hands having gone on 'the drunk' as was usual with cedar-getters in those days. **1977** J. Carter *All Things Wild* 2 As the cedar-getters chopped down the forests, farmers took up the cleared land. **1833** *Monitor* (Sydney) 9 Mar. 3/1 The **cedar-grounds** within 100 miles of Sydney, are now bared of this wood. **1849** A. Harris *Emigrant Family* (1967) 68 He had been employed in the cedar grounds. **1832** *HRA* (1923) 1st Ser. XVI. 713, I collected the prisoner Settlers and these men, as well as many of the **Cedar party.** **1871** *Austral. Town & Country Jrnl.* (Sydney) 25 Mar. 363/1 Coglan's cedar party consists of three pairs of sawyers in the winter season, and two pairs in the summer. **1901** *Bulletin* (Sydney) 7 Dec. 22/2 The boys ast me to make a third in a cedar-party. **1845** C. Hodgkinson *Aust., Port Macquarie to Moreton Bay* 10 Ague . . was particularly prevalent among the **cedar sawyers.** **1865** *Illustr. Sydney News* 15 July 10/2 They were cedar sawyers guiding the logs down to the river mouth. **1871** *Ibid.* 23 Dec. 211/1 There are few rougher occupations one could name than that of a cedar sawyer in them days. **1851** J. Henderson *Excursions & Adventures N.S.W.* 125 Lost amid the various and endless mazes of **cedar tracks.** **1903** *Bulletin* (Sydney) 2 May 17/1 You have to trust to cedar-tracks and luck. **1948** J. Fairfax *Run o' Waters* 23 The time is past when the journey from Jamberoo to Gerringong and back in bumping bullock drays over vague cedar tracks took three whole days. **1948** P.J. HURLEY *Red Cedar* 211 Everywhere the bush and scrub was criss-crossed by cedar-tracks, and to get into this maze and out again tested the bushmanship of any venturesome traveller.

3. Special Comb. **cedar wattle,** the N.S.W. tree *Acacia elata* (fam. Mimosaceae) having large dark-green glossy bipinnate leaves, and freq. planted as an ornamental.

c **1910** W.R. GUILFOYLE *Austral. Plants* 33 *Acacia elata* . . 'Tall Acacia', or 'Cedar Wattle'. **1932** R.H. ANDERSON *Trees in N.S.W.* 73 *Cedar wattle* . . is one of the most ornamental of the wattles, the foliage being particularly attractive. **1942** *Junior Tree Warden* iv. 70 The Cedar Wattle, so called on account of a resemblance of its foliage to that of the White Cedar (*Melia azedarach*). **1956** T.Y. HARRIS *Naturecraft in Aust.* 159 Cedar Wattle . . belongs to the dense coastal rain-forests, particularly in the Blue Mountains of New South Wales. **1964** K. TENNANT *Summer's Tales* 210 Cedar-wattles in bloom, at each bend yellowly massed.

celery-top pine. The rainforest tree *Phyllocladus aspleniifolius* (fam. Phyllocladaceae) which is restricted to (mainly w.) Tas.; the timber of the tree, valued for its durability and resistance to chemicals; ADVENTURE BAY PINE. Also **celery-leafed pine, celery-topped pine,** and *ellipt.* as **celery-top.**

[**1820** *HRA* (1921) 3rd Ser. III. 466 There is another sort of Tree, which grows among the Huon Pine; it is called here the Celery Pine.] **1827** *Ibid.* (1923) 3rd Ser. VI. 265 The 'Celery-leafed Pine' of Van Diemen's Land . . is rather inclined to be knotty in the trunk in small trees. **1832** J. BACKHOUSE *Narr. Visit Austral. Colonies* (1843) 48 Celery-topped Pine—*Thalamia asplenifolia*—so called from the resemblance of a branch clothed with its dilated leaves, to the leaf of Celery, is well calculated for masts. **1842** D. BURN *Narr. Journey Hobart Town to Macquarie Harbour* 11 Apr. (1955) 25 A very fine resinous pine, called the Celery Top, from its resemblance to that production, is a native of these woods. **1849** *Tasmanian Jrnl. Nat. Sci.* III. 279 Next to the *Huon Pine*, the species called the *Celery-topped* or *Adventure Bay Pine*, is the best known to the colonists. **1891** W. TILLEY *Wild West of Tas.* 43 Celery-top is the only pine growing in any quantity in the Zeehan district. **1905** *Timber Products & Sawmilling* (Tas. Lands & Surveys Dept.) 11 *Celery-top Pine* . . is another valuable tree, which is generally distributed throughout Tasmania, but in limited quantities. **1956** N.K. WALLIS *Austral. Timber Handbk.* 8 Celery-top pine (boat-building and joinery). **1983** *Ecos* xxxvii. 5/1 A dead stag of celery-top pine amid button grass plain.

celestial. *Hist.* [Spec. use of *celestial* a Chinese: see OED(S *sb.* 2.] An immigrant from China; an Australian resident of Chinese descent. Chiefly *pl.*

1841 *Port Phillip Patriot* 11 Mar. 2/5, I am glad to find that our disagreements with the *celestials* promise soon to receive a pacific and satisfactory settlement. **1853** *Austral. Gold Digger's Monthly Mag.* iv. 116 The celestials of China and the Anglo-Africans . . these all seek in their ardent feelings of devotion to enter the chosen temple of this world's deity—Gold. **1856** *Plea on Behalf Aboriginal Inhabitants Vic.* 4 The Colonial was considered in no small danger of being overrun with Celestials. **1858** *Colonial Mining Jrnl.* Sept. 11/2 Every available piece of ground was pounced upon by the celestial diggers. **1871** *Austral. Town & Country Jrnl.* (Sydney) 10 June 711/4 Kiandra, were it not for a few Celestials, would be a deserted village. **1879** 'AUSTRALIAN' *Adventures Qld.* 116 Wing Lee was indeed a good shepherd . . and though a good deal chaffed and teased by his European mates—as all Celestials are sure to be—he was nevertheless well liked by them for his many good qualities. **1917** *Truth* (Sydney) 12 Aug. 5/4 (*heading*) *The Yellow Peril. Clinahs consorting with Chows.* Smelly celestials' strange fascination over frail flappers. **1939** J.W. COLLINSON *Early Days Cairns* 67 The 'Blackbird' arrived with 40 passengers and 10 or 12 Celestials. **1956** A.C.C. LOCK *Tropical Tapestry* 70 The mating of celestial and lubra had produced a woman with unusual features, which were reflected in her children. **1971** *Bulletin* (Sydney) 18 Sept. 47 Australian attitudes toward the almond-eyed celestials.

cement. *Mining*, esp. *gold-mining.* [Transf. use of U.S. *cement* 'gravel held firmly in a siliceous matrix or the matrix itself': see Mathews.] Any conglomerate. Also *attrib.*

1858 *Colonial Mining Jrnl.* Nov. 46/3 The singular auriferous conglomerate called 'cement', continues abundant and good. **1859** *Ibid.* May 145/1 Sandstone bottom, with two or three feet of cement, which . . can be got through with the pick. **1860** W.B. CLARKE *Researches Southern Gold Fields N.S.W.* 43 The ferruginous 'cement', overlying the auriferous lower Silurian slates of Bendigo. **1869** R.B. SMYTH *Gold Fields & Mineral Districts* 607 Cement—Conglomerate: quartzite; quartz gravel, with an argillaceous, silicious, or ferruginous cement; auriferous pudding stone. **1891** *Hist. Wedderburn Gold Fields* 8 Between the gullies, and surrounding the flats, are innumerable cement hills. These cement hills are mere remnants of ancient river beds. **1898** D.W. CARNEGIE *Spinifex & Sand* 133 Cement is composed of angular quartz-fragments, broken from the reefs or veins, and fragments of diorite and hornblend schists, cemented together by lime; it is very hard and solid, and, in places, continues to a depth of over twenty feet. **1921** K.S. PRICHARD *Black Opal* 23 Tracked every trace of black potch through a reef of cement stone in the mine. **1970** J.A. TALENT *Minerals, Rocks & Gems* 243 *Cement*, in gold mining, a gold-bearing consolidated clastic rock.

Centralia. [Blend of *centr(al* and AUSTR)ALIA 1.] A name orig. proposed for the Colony of South Australia (see quots. 1888 and 1896); now applied to the region surrounding Alice Springs. Cf. CENTRE 1. Also *attrib.*

1888 W. BADGER *'Land Transfer' Laws* p. vii, South Australia, geographically speaking, the 'Centralia' of 'The Australias'. **1896** J.S. LAURIE *Story of Australasia* 299 The name 'South' Australia, embracing as it does both the central and the northern territory, is anomalous . . why not *Centralia*; for West Australia, *Westralia*; for New South Wales, *Eastralia*. **1900** *Bulletin* (Sydney) 7 Apr. 11/2 Patriotic fervor was running high in Swilltown, Centralia. **1915** *Ibid.* 22 July 24/4 In the dry parts of Centralia there are journeys to be negotiated on which the abo. has to provide himself with water. **1932** I.L. IDRIESS *Flynn of Inland* (1965) 128 The doctor was voted the 'biggest-feller' medicine man in Centralia when he came to Alice Springs. **1944** M.J. O'REILLY *Bowyangs & Boomerangs* 115 She married a Centralia claypan squatter. **1955** *Bulletin* (Sydney) 4 May 12/2 When a new billycan is issued to a stock-camp in Centralia the first ceremony of its initiation is the discarding of its lid. **1980** C. ALLISON *Hunter's Man. Aust. & N.Z.* 13 The camel is found mostly in Centralia.

Hence **Centralian** *a.* and *n.*

1896 *Bulletin* (Sydney) 24 Oct. 19/3 Your sneer at Percy Hodgkinson's Centralian frogs is unjust. **1897** *Tocsin* (Melbourne) 4 Nov. 9/2 There are men from Northern Croydon, and a crowd of Maorilanders, Westralians and Centralians, round to Murrumbidgee whalers. **1912** *Bulletin* (Sydney) 21 Nov. 16/4 Perched among the elaborate trappings with which the Centralian fits his riding camel . . you might imagine yourself an Asiatic potentate. **1927** M.H. ELLIS *Long Lead* 208 Views of the Centralian future. **1953** J.K. EWERS *With Sun on my Back* 159 You would not find many like Mona Minnehan, who is as Centralian as her Centralian Stores. **1964** D. LOCKWOOD *Up Track* 47 Not that the Centralians worry much about dust. **1977** J. CARTER *All Things Wild* 12 He certainly spent quite a few years knocking about the Centralian back-blocks with a string of camels and his inevitable Aboriginal 'guides'. **1986** *Centralian Advocate* (Alice Springs) 15 Jan. 19/1 Take the opportunity now to nominate the person you think most deserves the title Centralian of the Year.

central school. A school providing post-primary courses for pupils from primary schools in the surrounding districts: see quots.

1905 *N.S.W. Parl. Papers* 2nd Sess. IV. 1140 The scheme for conveying children to central schools was brought into operation this year under rules specially framed, and the results have been satisfactory. **1924** *New Settlers' Handbk. Vic.* 24 There are also nineteen 'central' schools. **1927** G.S. BROWNE *Educ. in Aust.* 36 That the bush children should fare as well as town children [*sc.* in N.S.W.], Central Schools were established in 1903 to which children were conveyed free of charge. **1935** P.R. COLE *Educ. of Adolescent in Aust.* 9 Central Schools for pupils who remain at school for indefinite periods beyond the primary courses and for reasons of economy are collected into centres to continue their education while awaiting employment. **1974** J. MCLAREN *Dict. Austral. Educ.* 54 Central School. In New South Wales a country school classified as primary but providing both primary and secondary education. . . In Victoria, a metropolitan primary school with secondary classes for grades 7 to 8. **1980** A. BARCAN *Hist. Austral. Educ.* 219 In 1909 [in W.A.] eight of the largest elementary schools, six in the metropolitan area and two in the eastern goldfields, became Central schools taking advanced pupils from neighbouring primary schools.

centre.

1. With **the** and initial capital. Central Australia (see quot. 1965); *red centre*, see RED *a.* 2.

[**1840** C. STURT Let. 3 July, Eyre is gone expressly to penetrate to the centre if he can do so.] **1899** SPENCER & GILLEN *Native Tribes Central Aust.* 54 In common with all other Australian tribes, those of the Centre have been shut off from contact with other peoples. **1910** *Huon Times* (Franklin) 20 Aug. 5/3 He estimates that a great subterranean river flowing through the Centre is as much as 200 miles wide. **1932** I.L. IDRIESS *Flynn of Inland* (1965) 184 The spirit of Flynn of the Inland broods away up there over the Centre. **1940** W. HATFIELD *Into (Great?) Unfenced* 27 The Centre. The great alluring, mysterious Centre, the heart of a continent. **1951** G. FARWELL *Outside Track* 134 This was the style of country which had worn down Charles Sturt in his desperate attempts to reach the Centre, where bushmen had lost their tracks and cattle had perished. **1960** *N.T. News* (Darwin) 22 Jan. 1/6 Although some parts of the Centre are still in a bad way it is clear that cattlemen have the hardest part behind them. **1965** *Austral. Encycl.* II. 323 In popular present-day Australian usage 'The Centre' is an area roughly within a radius of 400 to 500 miles from Alice Springs. **1979** D. LOCKWOOD *My Old Mates & I* 77 And so I told him about the eight-year drought that hit the Centre in the late 1950s and early '60s.

2. *Australian National Football.* **a.** *Centre circle* (see sense 4). **b.** The player occupying the position in the centre circle.

1931 J.F. MCHALE et al. *Austral. Game of Football* 60 The centre and the half-forward centre are absolutely unguarded. **1936** E.C.H. TAYLOR *Our Austral. Game Football* 34 *Centre*, . . able to kick with either foot, and should be an expert stab kick or a long drop kick, and . . a good mark. **1973** P. MCKENNA *My World of Football* 107 *Centre*: This is where all the action is and it needs a very skilled player to handle the pressure involved with the position. **1982** G. ATKINSON *Everything about Austral. Rules Football* 203 Centres and half-forwards—keep your places and kick at once. Never run unless the coast be very clear.

3. *Two-up.* The central part of the ring, where the spinner stands and bets with the spinner are taken. Also *attrib.*

[N.Z. **1917** *Chrons. N.Z. Exped. Force* 16 May 137 The 'ringies' they were bending low And yelled for 'centre hoot!'] **1931** O. WALTERS *Shrapnel Green* 26 The centre was set, the side-bets on, and Mick was ready to toss. **1955** *Overland* iii. 16 Come on you tail punters, twenty quid in the centre! **1971** G. MORGAN *We are borne On* 87 In my first two spins I bet three pounds so I decided to give another pound a fly and went into the centre for my last gamble.

4. *Australian National Football.* Special Comb. **centre back,** the player occupying the central back position; **circle,** a circle in the middle of the field in which the ball is bounced by the field umpire to commence play at the start of each quarter and after a goal is scored; **half-back,** the player occupying the centre half back position, between the centre and back positions; **half-forward,** the player occupying the centre half forward position, between the centre and forward positions; **line man,** a player occupying one of the three centre positions; **man,** the player occupying the central position in the centre line; **wing,** a player occupying either of the wing positions in the centre line.

1931 J.F. MCHALE et al. *Austral. Game of Football* 59 The **centre back** must kick off to the windward side of the ground. **1936** E.C.H. TAYLOR *Our Austral. Game Football* 34 *Centre back*, . . a good kick and safe mark, cool and intelligent, with the ability to move quickly. **1964** J. POLLARD *High Mark* 16 The playing surface . . is oval-shaped and apart from the boundary line itself, a **centre circle** and the goal 'square' at each end there are no other markings anywhere on the field. **1942** H.H. PECK *Mem. of Stockman* 103 **Centre half-back** for

Essendon. **1963** L. RICHARDS *Boots & All!* 90 By far the greater part of his success has been at centre half-back. **1973** J. DUNN *How to play Football* 24 The centre-half-back's job is to stop the centre-half-forward bobbing up. **1963** L. RICHARDS *Boots & All!* 158 Big **centre-half-forward** Ray 'Joe' Poulter was another character. **1973** J. DUNN *How to play Football* 16 The rover, rucks or centreline players unload the goods from downfield and the centre-half-forward then distributes the chances. **1964** J. POLLARD *High Mark* 14 The 18 men comprise six defenders or backmen, six forwards or attacking players, three **centre line men,** and three followers who may move to any part of the ground. **1963** L. RICHARDS *Boots & All!* 46 A well-built six-footer, he was tall for a **centreman. 1973** J. DUNN *How to play Football* 18 Centremen usually are among the best players in the team and many times they are the stars. **1931** J.F. MCHALE et al. *Austral. Game of Football* 60 The half-backs—or . . the **centre wings.**

centre-board shed. [See BOARD 1.] A shearing shed in which shearing takes place in the middle rather than along each side.

1908 W.H. OGILVIE *My Life in Open* 36 In a 'centre-board' shed the pens containing the sheep are around the outside of this board. **1979** HARMSWORTH & DAY *Wool & Mohair* 141 Sheds may be classified as *side board* or *centre board* sheds.

century. *Shearing.* [Transf. use of *century* (in cricket) a hundred or more runs.] A tally of one hundred sheep.

1905 A.B. PATERSON *Old Bush Songs* 28 For some had got the century who'd ne'er got it before. **1957** STEWART & KEESING *Old Bush Songs* 258 Tomorrow I go with a sardine blow For a century or the sack. **1959** H.P. TRITTON *Time means Tucker* 62 Dutchy broke the 'century', and . . the rep. . . made a speech praising Dutchy, and welcoming him to the ranks of the big-gun shearers.

certificate. *Hist.* A document issued on the expiry of a convict's term of penal servitude, certifying the recipient's status as a freed person: see quot. 1822. Also **certificate of freedom.**

1796 *N.S.W. Instruct. to Watchmen* 11 If they call themselves Free People and off the Store, they are to produce their Certificates. **1802** *N.S.W. Gen. Orders* 28 Oct. (1806) 14 Any Settler or other Person employing any Prisoner without seeing his Certificate, will incur the Penalty pointed out by Former Orders. **1810** *Sydney Gaz.* 14 Jan., All Persons whose Term of Transportation to this Colony has expired, and who have not obtained a legal Certificate of Freedom. **1822** J.T. BIGGE *Rep. State Colony N.S.W.* 120 The certificates issued by the secretary attest, that after an examination of the indents, so many years have expired since sentence of that term was passed on the party entitled to it, describing the year and ship in which he arrived, and ending with a declaration, that by reason of the expired service, the said party is restored to all the rights of a free subject. **1826** *Austral.* (Sydney) 26 Jan. 1/1 Notice is hereby given, that no duplicate certificate of freedom or ticket of leave, will be granted in the future. **1834** 'EMIGRANT' *Party Politics Exposed* 20 A Certificate of Freedom is granted to all persons who have duly worked out the periods of their sentenced exile, and it expresses that the individual . . is restored to all the rights of a free British subject. **1843** *Sydney Morning Herald* 7 Aug. 3/5 Having lost my Certificate of Freedom, I do hereby caution all constables and others not to molest me in my lawful occupation. **1847** A. HARRIS *Settlers & Convicts* (1953) 67 Some stalwart young Briton transported at fifteen weathers his seven years, and at two and twenty gets his certificate of freedom and goes off to seek his fortune.

chain, *n.*[1]

1. *Hist.* Used *attrib.* in Special Comb. **chain gang,** a party of convicts assigned to hard labour in chains, such chains usu. being ankle fetters joined by a chain which, to allow reasonable freedom of movement, was tied up to the belt (convicts wearing irons were also chained together when moving from one place to another); IRONED GANG; see also GANG; hence **chain gangsman** *n.*

1822 J.T. BIGGE *Rep. State Colony N.S.W.* 35 The punishment of the chain gang is rightly described . . to be the least efficient, and most prejudicial. **1829** H. WIDOWSON *Present State Van Diemen's Land* 24 The chain gang . . are employed all day in mending the roads and streets. **1832** J. BACKHOUSE *Extracts from Lett.* (1838) I. 18 He was ordered by the Governor into a chain-gang, where, if he continue to improve, he will be assigned to private service. **1835** *Cornwall Chron.* (Launceston) 4 July 1 The punishment of death will no longer . . be the legal consequence of escape from a chain gang or penal settlement. **1840** T.P. MACQUEEN *Aust. as she Is* 10 Of all conditions in which convicts can be placed, that of *private assignment* is the most desirable; and that of a *chain gang*, or a penal settlement, the most degraded and miserable. **1846** H. EASY *Horrors of Transportation* 11, I now begin to believe what I have often heard old chain gangsmen say. **1849** J.P. TOWNSEND *Rambles & Observations N.S.W.* 233 Very many convicts in New South Wales were employed in 'chain-gangs'. . . At dusk you might observe, guarded by soldiers, a body of convicts (all heavily ironed, and in grey serge dresses) marched along the road, some dragging hand-carts . . their fetters ringing as they moved. **1856** J. BONWICK *Bushrangers* 38 The members of the Chain gang had the word 'Felon' stamped in several places upon their yellow dresses. **1872** MRS E. MILLETT *Austral. Parsonage* 242 Confirmed runaways . . were punished by being placed in the chain-gang at the 'Establishment'. **1900** W. DELAFORCE *Life & Experiences Ex-Convict Port Macquarie* 35 When a man had finished his sentence in the chain gang, he was sentenced to a road party, and it was Heaven to the chain gang. **1935** F. CLUNE *Rolling down Lachlan* 154 The Fitzroy Dock . . had been built of solid rock by chain-gangs from Cockatoo.

2. In the phr. **(up)on the chain.**

a. *Hist.* Of a convict: (so as to be) secured with a chain.

1835 J. BACKHOUSE *Extracts from Lett.* (1838) ii. 74 He was committed to jail in irons, with the rest of his fellows, and they were put upon the chain (i.e.) had a chain passed over their irons, and fixed outside of their prison to render them more secure. **1846** *Citizen* (Sydney) 26 Dec. 138/2 He would be put on 'the chain' and sent down to Sydney. **1881** W. FEILDING *Austral. Trans-Continental Railway* 51 The native constable and our Kanaka lad (Walter) . . got drunk. The former was sent to the police and placed 'on the chain' there. **1888** A. MCLEAN *Harry Bloomfield* 42 You must cut for your life, for here comes the troopers to put you on the chain. **1899** G.E. BOXALL *Story Austral. Bushrangers* 136 Later some boxes, made of corrugated iron, were put up as cells and those were known as 'the Dutch ovens' or 'the sardine boxes' and prisoners confined to them on hot summer nights suffered tortures and begged to be put 'on the chain' as a relief.

b. *fig.* See sense 3.

1980 *Nat. Times* (Sydney) 2 Nov. 36/2 Shearers are a competitive lot, and watch each other's tallies jealously. There's great prestige in being the ringer; no one wants to shear 'on the chain'.

3. *fig.* In the phr. **to drag the chain,** to lag behind one's fellow workers (orig. in shearing) or companions in an activity.

1912 *Bulletin* (Sydney) 28 Nov. 16/4 One of the fraternity confided to me on the board . . that he 'had peeled 88, and was dragging the chain behind Nugget Smith'. **1915** *Ibid.* 18 Nov. 24/4 The shearer at the tail-end of the list is 'the drummer' or 'the snagger', and is sometimes 'dragging the chain'. **1954** T. RONAN *Vision Splendid* 124 Pass the bottle, Top, you're dragging the chain. **1961** M. CALTHORPE *Dyehouse* 156 Maybe they could take it easy. Drag the chain just a little. **1968** G. DUTTON *Andy* 146 Rooster here's way behind; dragging the bloody chain. He's due to set 'em up.

4. *fig.* In the phr. **off the chain,** free from restraint.

1947 C. FENTON *Flying Doctor* 53 For what followed, little excuse can be offered, except that we were 'off the chain'; we had come from the bush, and our spirits were high with prospect of holiday in the gay town of Darwin.

chain, *n.*[2] [Spec. use of *chain* linear series (of objects).] In the collocation **chain of billabongs (lagoons, lakes, ponds, pools, waterholes),** a series of depressions in the bed of an intermittently flowing watercourse which continue to hold water after the connecting stream has dried up.

1799 D. COLLINS *Acct. Eng. Colony N.S.W.* (1802) II. 185 The creek runs winding between two steep hills, and ends in a chain of ponds that extends into a valley of great beauty. **1815** H.C. ANTILL *Early Hist. N.S.W.* 2 May (1914) 33 Our encampment this day was picturesque and beautiful, situated in a valley with a chain of ponds running through it. **1832** J. BACKHOUSE *Narr. Visit Austral. Colonies* (1843) 27 He has about a mile of frontage on the Clyde, which at this season of the year is little more than a chain of ponds—called here lagoons. **1835** BACKHOUSE & TYLOR *Life & Labours G.W. Walker* (1862) 219 The South Creek here forms a chain of ponds, or lagoons, that are never dry. **1840** A. RUSSELL *Tour through Austral. Colonies* 59 Adelaide stands on two hills of limestone, between which lies a chain of ponds, called the Torrens. **1845** L. LEICHHARDT *Jrnl. Overland Exped. Aust.* 10 Jan. (1847) 104 The creek . . joined a river. . . It was not, however, running but formed a chain of small lakes, from two to three and even eight miles in length, and frequently from fifty to one hundred yards broad. **1852** G.C. MUNDY *Our Antipodes* II. 40 A fine chain of water-holes, which, after heavy rains, puts on the guise of a continuous stream. **1863** J. DAVIS *Tracks of McKinlay* 230 'The running of the creek' is quite an event in many parts of colonized Australia, where the creek is, perhaps, for nearly all the year, or for several years together, merely a chain of ponds or natural cisterns. **1882** W. SOWDEN *N.T. as it Is* 39 The village is situated near a chain of billabongs. **1887** A. NICOLS *Wild Life & Adventure* 62 Chains of lagoons—some of extraordinary depth—marked the former course of the Maranoa. **1900** *Pastoral Times* (Deniliquin) 6 Jan. 2/1 Water is becoming very scarce and there is very little feed left, in fact another month like the past one will convert the river into a chain of waterholes. **1932** C.M. GRAY *Western Vic. in Forties* 8 During the night . . I camped at a chain of ponds called the 'Wardeyallock'. **1945** *Bulletin* (Sydney) 11 Apr. 12/3 Barramundi and other fish contrive to survive when the river is reduced to a mere chain of pools. **1951** *Ibid.* 6 June 15/3 Many of the North Westralian 'rivers' become chains of pools during the rainless season.

chain *v.*

1. *intr.* Of pools: to form a chain.

1926 *Bulletin* (Sydney) 8 Apr. 22/2 Dawdling down the Diamantina, squandering days where the deep pools chain.

2. *trans.* To clear (land), using a chain stretched between two bulldozers to flatten scrub, etc.

1968 R.M. FADDEN Land Clearing Team Daily Diary 4 Mar. 1 The two operators had no experience on chaining. **1985** *Newsletter* (Soc. for Growing Austral. Plants, Canberra Region) Sept. 10 His wildflower farm is at Coorow, where he purchased 3500 acres of sand-plain in 1978. The land had previously been chained and unsuccessfully cropped.

chain-lightning. [U.S. *chain-lightning* inferior whisky: see Mathews.] Any crudely-made spirituous liquor. Also *attrib.*

1876 J.A. EDWARDS *Gilbert Gogger* 96 At three o'clock in the morning, they lighted up, and began to retail 'stone fences', 'shandy gaff', 'chain lightning', 'all my own', etcetera, etcetera, to the assembled diggers. . . Australian fancy drinks. **1892** *Braidwood Dispatch* 31 Dec. 2/3 The sole stock-in-trade consists of an empty beer barrel and some chain-lightning rum, warranted to bite all the way down and scratch all the way back, and to be particularly soothing to the bush-man. **1898** *Worker* (Sydney) 26 Nov. 7/2 Drinking Cody's hand-made chain-lightning whisky. **1900** *Pastoral Times* (Deniliquin) 16 June 2/7 Had a rough night, and most of the men are getting the niggers to bring them grog and Portuguese wine at a shilling a bottle—regular chain lightning. **1901** *Bulletin* (Sydney) 13 Apr. 14/1 When the traveller asked for 'brandy and curacoa', he planked down a bottle of chain-lightning. **1925** A. WRIGHT *Boy from Bullarah* 118 I've heard about th' chain-lightin' whisky they dope a man with in the bush.

chalkie. Also **chalky.** [f. *chalk* + -Y.] A school-teacher.

[**1941** S.J. BAKER *Pop. Dict. Austral. Slang* 17 *Chalk-and-Talker*, a school-teacher.] **1945** *Bulletin* (Sydney) 2 May 12/1 A country chalkie of my acquaintance. **1953** T.A.G. HUNGERFORD *Riverslake* 29 'I was a chalky before the war—just couldn't settle down to it again, after.' 'Chalky?' 'School-teacher.' **1957** *Overland* x. 10 'E never 'it it orf with the lady chalkies. **1978** 'E. LINDALL' *Season of Discovery* 16 'You remind me of someone. . . A bloody chalkie up near Beetoota. . . A bossy bitch like you.' He peered at her. 'You're not a chalkie?' Ann looked at him coldly. 'If you mean schoolteacher, yes, I am.' **1979** L. CLANCY *Wife Specialist* 40 After I was taken on as a staff member I used to drink with a group of 'chalkies', as they like to call themselves. **1984** *N.T. News* (Darwin) 22 Dec. 13/5 'It's the fault of those chalkies,' he said 'they're supposed to be teachers.'

chaney. *Obs.* Also **chanie.** [Of unknown origin.] In the phr. **to play chaneys,** to exert influence; **to play chaneys with,** to bribe (someone).

1892 *Bohemia* (Melbourne) 4 Feb. 3 He hasn't any constitution or manifesto in his breeches-pocket, and only vents a growl at his successor, who really does not appear to have 'played all chanies' in the little game which ends with Berry out and Munro in. **1899** *Truth* (Sydney) 19 Mar. 3/3 She stows whatever morals she has in the south-western corner of her heel, plays chaneys with the police. **1900** *Ibid.* 29 Apr. 4/4 It is often better, being safer, to be a brazen 'bludger' or protected prostitute, an oft-convicted criminal, or a professed spieler, than an honest citizen or taxpayer—provided one 'plays chaneys' with or pays tribute to the blackmailing abettors of crime who swarm among the plain-clothes police.

change. *Hist.* [Scot. dial. *change* inn: see OED *change, sb.* 11 and *change-house.*] A staging-post at which coach horses were changed. See also *mail change* MAIL *n.*[1] Also **change** (or **changing**) **station,** and *attrib.*

1913 W.K. HARRIS *Outback in Aust.* 110 The pub-keeper drove the coach on to the next 'change'. **1926** C.B. FLETCHER *Murray Valley* p. ii, A small two- or three-house changing-station on the Murray. **1943** H.G. LAMOND *From Tariaro to Ross Roy* 90 Cobb & Co.'s change grooms were always versatile. **1947** W. LAWSON *Paddle-Wheels Away* 145 Might find shanty or a change-station and find out about the coach. **1975** G.A.W. SMITH *Once Green Jackaroo* 97 Essarate was a 'change' station en route and he had free agistment for two horses all the year round.

Hence **change** *v. trans.*

1911 *Bulletin* (Sydney) 19 Jan. 14/4 That crib was one of the busiest between Melbourne and Beechworth. Cobb's changed there, while the passengers got their tucker at three bob a time.

chanie, var. CHANEY.

channel-billed cuckoo. [From the channel or groove on each side of the beak.] The large-billed, predom. grey cuckoo *Scythrops novaehollandiae* of n. and e. Aust., a summer visitor from Indonesia and New Guinea, having a loud, harsh call traditionally presaging rain. See also STORM BIRD. Also **channel-bill (cuckoo).**

1801 J. LATHAM *Gen. Synopsis Birds* Suppl. II. 96 N. Holland Channel-Bill . . is not very common, and first appears about *Port Jackson* in *October.* **1837** *Colonist* (Sydney) 350/4 The *Toucans* find their representative in the Australian *channel bill.* **1890** G.J. BROINOWSKI *Birds of Aust.* III. Pl. 47, The Channel-Bill . . is insectivorous like the other Cuckoos. **1914** *Bulletin* (Sydney) 15 Jan. 24/2 The so-called storm-bird—who can't predict storms worth a cuss—is a cuckoo, the channel-bill cuckoo. **1964** M. SHARLAND *Territory of Birds* 130 The giant Channel-billed Cuckoo . . whose vocal talents are by no means melodious. **1983** *Open Road* Feb. 24/1 Most Australians wouldn't know a channel-billed cuckoo if one pecked them on the ear.

channel country. See quot. 1968.

1947 *Proc. R. Soc. Qld.* LIX. 158 Panicum Whitei . . is . . sometimes . . a prominent part of the pasture of the 'channel country'. **1950** G.M. FARWELL *Land of Mirage* 209 The 'Channel Country' comprises the area watered by the three great rivers of the Inland—the Cooper, Diamantina and Georgina. **1955** *Bulletin* (Sydney) 16 Feb. 13/4 Big inland rivers then flood out in a vast brown sea, flowing s.-w. away to Lake Eyre in S.A. They inundate hundreds of square miles of lush cattle-fattening Queensland 'channel country', making it independent of its sparse local rainfall, annual average of which is mostly well below 10 inches. **1963** I.L. IDRIESS *Our Living Stone Age* 13 That was in the Channel Country of south-west Queensland; there were still plenty of the Old Folk along the Cooper and Diamantina and Georgina then. **1968** A.M. DUNCAN-KEMP *Where Strange Gods Call* p. ix, The term 'channel country' is not necessarily the proper name of a geographical area, but a common expression used by outback residents to designate a definite order of geographical features. These are the wide, twisting rivers and creeks, and the great flood plains that form the inland river system, the natural irrigation channels of the far south-west of Queensland and the north of South Australia. **1981** *Austral. Women's Weekly* (Sydney) 2 Dec. 33/3 At Glengyle, another Kidman property, we meet one of the channel country's characters.

charcoal tart. A piece of dough baked on embers: see JOHNNY-CAKE.

1909 *Bulletin* (Sydney) 30 Sept. 13/2 The 'Johnny cake' . . is variously known as the 'charcoal tart' or the 'blanker on the coals'. **1923** *Ibid.* 22 Nov. 22/3 Most dry scrub timbers . . are . . excellent for cooking 'charcoal tarts'. **1927** J. MATHIEU *Backblock Ballads* 1, I don't succumb to swagging, July fogs, or charcoal tarts. **1976** C.D. MILLS *Hobble Chains & Greenhide* 73, I could hear the plant bells moving in as I flicked the 'charcoal tarts' out of the ashes next morning.

charge, *v. Australian National Football. trans.* To attack and push (a player) illegally. Also as *vbl. n.*

1929 W.S. SHARLAND *Sporting Globe Football Bk.* (1930) 86 The field umpire shall . . report to the controlling body every player who . . charges an opponent when such opponent is standing still or when he is in the air for a mark. **1931** J.F. MCHALE et al. *Austral. Game of Football* 30 In charging or meeting a player under the circumstances described above, you must be careful not to charge from behind, otherwise a free-kick will be given for 'a push in the back'. **1959** PARNELL & ANDREW *Austral. Football* 46 Charging takes place when a player bumps or pushes a player when the ball is *more than five yards away, on the ground or in the air.* **1982** J. WARREN *Austral. Football Fundamentals* 13 *Charging,* violently meeting or contacting a player in a manner not authorised by the game's laws, when he is in the air or not in possession of the ball or not being legitimately shepherded.

charge, *n.*[1] *Australian National Football.* [f. prec.] The act of pushing or bumping illegally.

1931 J.F. MCHALE et al. *Austral. Game of Football* 31 Every charge cannot be effective in upsetting an opponent, and so every player must expect to be charged as well as to charge. **1964** J. POLLARD *High Mark* 75 There is a vast difference between a deliberate charge and a shirtfront. **1965** J. DYER *Captain Blood* 190 If you see a charge coming, get out of the way if you can. If you can't, improvise. . . There is no set answer for a charge other than raising as dangerous a front to him as possible.

charge, *n.*[2] [Spec. use of U.S. *charge* a thrill, 'kick'.] A glass of an alcoholic beverage, esp. spirits. Also **charge-on.**

1963 D. ATTENBOROUGH *Quest under Capricorn* 19 Doug took the hint. 'It's my shout,' he said. 'You blokes can ease in another charge I reckon.' **1965** K. MCKENNEY *Hide-Away Man* 47 Early in the afternoon Ben . . walked into the long bar. . . 'Yer late,' Cholly said. 'Yer a coupla charges behind.' **1976** C.D. MILLS *Hobble Chains & Greenhide* 109 The few good 'charges' they had imbibed to 'steady their nerves', had them about half sprung. **1978** M.J. BURTON *Bush Pub* 73 Archie had been in town for about four days when he and the Fanatic came in for their morning charge. Bruce Burns, the local bread carter, always came in about nine o'clock, which was after the pair had downed a few pots with dashes of rum. **1984** P. READ *Down there with me on Cowra Mission* 115, I went over to where the Aborigine camp is alongside of that, and there's two old fellers having a charge-on.

charity moll. A prostitute who charges less than the usual rate.

[**1953** S.J. BAKER *Aust. Speaks* 125 An amateur harlot or one who undercuts regular professional prices . . is called a charity dame.] **1962** 'C. ROHAN' *Delinquents* 104 If the cops spring you here, I know nothing and no charity moll capers with my men. **1967** *Kings Cross Whisper* (Sydney) xxxiii. 4/3 *Charity moll,* a female frowned upon by the professionals. **1982** N. KEESING *Lily on Dustbin* 41 A 'charity moll' is the equivalent of a World War II 'EA' or 'enthusiastic amateur': a promiscuous woman whose sexual favours are theoretically not available for sale . . instead, for presents, dinners, theatre and show tickets.

charlie. Also **charley,** and in full **Charlie Wheeler.** [f. the name of *Charles* Wheeler (1881–1977), a painter of the nude.] Rhyming slang for 'sheila'.

1942 *Cheeriodical* (Rathmines) 5 Mar. 12 The Manager knew what they meant by 'Charlie Wheelers'. **1949** L. GLASSOP *Lucky Palmer* 41 'What do you mean by 'Charlie'?' 'Your 'Charlie',' repeated Max. 'Your canary.' 'Canary?' 'Ay, don't you speak English? Your sheila.' **1960** D. MCLEAN *Roaring Days* 1 A female may be my sheila, my bird, my charley, [etc.]. **1966** G. BARRY *Bed & Bored* 27 'Hey, here are the charlies.' I turned around to see a group of women emerge from the kitchen. **1968** D. O'GRADY *Bottle of Sandwiches* 123 Bloody bedlam. The joint jumps every night, the pubs make a fortune, the charlie-wheelers come in in droves, and the Docs work overtime tryin' to keep the VD rate down. **1973** *Kings Cross Whisper* (Sydney) cxlvii. 3/1 A little charlie from the match factory and her mother.

chase, *v.* In the phr. **to chase the dragon,** see quot. 1979; **the (penny) weight,** to prospect for gold; **the sun(set),** to tramp the country.

1979 B. DELANEY *Narc* 43 Charlie chased this elusive liquid and inhaled the fumes through the drinking straw! Hence the expression **'chasing the dragon'**. As the heroin burned off, Charlie expertly dropped more granules and sucked the gas into his lungs. **1936** J. KIRWAN *My Life's Adventure* 76 Prospectin' is a rotten life . . . I expect I'll be all my life **chasin' the weight.** **1949** I.L. IDRIESS *One Wet Season* 72 And the talk inevitably turned to gold. 'Ah!' sighed Womba. 'I too chased the pennyweight in the days when I had my Ena.' **1977** J. DOUGHTY *Gold in Blood* 175 They were all prospectors who had spent their lives 'chasing the pennyweight' and lesser minerals in places where few if any white men had ever been before. **1915** *Bulletin* (Sydney) 14 Oct. 24/4 Tell me a profession with more *aliases* than the swagman's? Here are a few: 'Waltzin' Matilda', . . 'humpin' the bluey', . . **'chasin' the sunset'**.

chat, *n.* [Br. slang *chat* louse: see OED *sb.*[7]]

1. A louse. Also *attrib.*

1812 J.H. VAUX *Mem.* (1819) 162 *Chats,* lice. **1916** *Battery Herald: Jrnl. 14th Field Artillery* 25 Sept. 2 *For sale.* Specially selected stud chats. **1918** C.L. HARTT *Diggerettes* 63 Just after we had left the lines a Digger was industriously holding the usual 'chat hunt', when a pal passing by remarked: 'Hello, Bill, picking 'em out?' Bill: 'No, just taking 'em as they come.' **1919** W.A. CULL *At all Costs* 10 There was the perennial problem of the little nuisances of life, the unbidden guests which come and abide with you—not as single spies, but in battalions. Had 'chats' been sheep, many of us were squatters. **1940** *Sentry Go* (Keswick) Aug. 9/11 A chat doesn't mind whose it crawls on. **1966** A.R. CHISHOLM *Familiar Presence* 55 Our most disagreeable guests were 'chats', from which we could never be freed until we got back . . and obtained a change of underclothes, handing in the soiled ones for fumigation. **1967** *Kings Cross Whisper* (Sydney) xxxiii. 4/3 *Chat,* a prison bed-bug. A term used to describe an obnoxious person. *Chats' yard,* the section of a prison where grubby people are segregated. **1974** ADAMSON & HANFORD *Zimmer's Essay* 99 George Orwell gives 'chat' as a term for 'louse' . . in usage among Kentish hop-pickers. . . In New South Wales prison argot, it means both 'louse' and a certain type of prisoner. A 'chat' is a social incompetent, though not necessarily a drunk. They are usually gaoled for nuisance offences, such as vagrancy.

2. *Transf.* and *fig.* A debased person. See quots. 1967 and 1974 above.

1967 B.K. BURTON *Teach them no More* 119 He had always felt for the alcoholics in the chat's yard. **1972** J. MCNEIL *Old Familiar Juice* (1973) 111 Yer a warb . . a chat . . a wino. . . Yer a *vagrant!* **1974** *Gayzette* (Sydney) 14 Nov. 13/4 Six chats were taken off for the chat-yard. **1980** M. WILLIAMS *Dingo!* 160 'He's a warb! A chat!' I exclaimed. 'A dirty drunk!'

Hence **chatty** *a.*, afflicted with lice.

1972 W. WATKINS *Don't wait for Me* 45 'I'm so chatty I can bloody near smell myself.' He scratched irritably at his crutch with his free hand as he spoke. **1978** H.C. BAKER *I was Listening* 112 We have to keep at him all the time to make him wash. And this morning I found he was chatty.

chat, *v.* [f. prec.] *trans.* To remove lice from (one's clothing or person). Also *absol.*

1919 *Waiting Times: Jrnl. 17 Battalion A.I.F.* 1 Mar. 4 A certain officer was one day chatting himself. **1928** 'C. DENISON' *Glimpses* 94 He always kept his distaste for the necessary process of 'chatting'. **1932** CUNNINGHAM & HARDY *Anzac* 10 Fletcher . . is seated near the table 'chatting' his shirt. **1933** E.J. RULE *Jacka's Mob* 16 Like the poor, the 'chats' were with us always, and most of us chatted twice daily. **1937** G.D. MITCHELL *Backs to Wall* 20 In the cold winter winds we were debarred from the Anzac national sport of 'reading our shirts', sometimes also called 'chatting by the wayside'.

cheerio. [N.Z., prob. from association with *cheerio* 'cheers'.] A small sausage of the frankfurter type. Also *attrib.*

1965 K. SMITH *OGF* 136 Vi looked towards the kitchen where eight pounds of cheerios were bubbling merrily on the stove; they would be splitting their sides already. **1972** *Sunday Mail Mag.* (Brisbane) 27 Feb. 2/3 Her hostess at the first Queensland party she attended after moving here from Victoria recently said she was going to put the 'cheerios' on. **1980** S. THORNE *I've met some Bloody Wags* 18 Keith . . tossed cheerio sausages into the fans, played the didgeridoo, and wrestled a stuffed crocodile. **1982** *N.T. News* (Darwin) 15 June 19/2 (Advt.), *Cheerios* $2.49 kg.

cheer-up. *S.A.* [f. the name of the *Cheer-Up* Our Boys Society, a patriotic organization founded in Adelaide in 1914.] Used *attrib.* in Comb. with reference to the activities of the Cheer-Up Our Boys Society (or of a similar organization). Also *absol.*, a member of the Society.

[**1914** *Register* (Adelaide) 3 Nov. 4/4 Our boys must not be allowed to believe for even one solitary hour that they are forgotten or neglected by the people for whom they have shown their willingness to make the supreme sacrifice or to fancy that nobody cares for them. . . Who will form the first Cheer Up Our Boys Society? *Ibid.* 5 Nov. 4/6 We are pleased to announce that The Register's suggestion of a 'Cheer Up Our Boys Society' has resulted in the formation of such a body.] *Ibid.* 10 Nov. 5/7 Yet, but for this 'Cheer Up' organisation, it is probable that little would have been done to adequately farewell this band. *Ibid.* 2 Dec. 6/4 Friends simply send the cash; the Cheer-ups do the rest! **1915** *Ibid.* 6 Mar. 9/5 The men in blue had a graceful and felicitous welcome at the Cheer-up tent. *Ibid.* 5 Nov. 6/4 The men were to regard themselves as the protectors of the Cheer-up girls. *Ibid.* 6/5 After the opening ceremony at the new Cheer-up Hut, there was a quiet little presentation. **1920** F.J. MILLS *Cheer Up* 25 The Cheer-Ups—150 strong—arrived with baskets of good things, including oranges and early peaches. **1924** —— *Happy Days* 136 In 1919 a bronzed returned wounded soldier entered the Cheer-up Hut, Adelaide. **1941** *Air Force News* (Melbourne) 12 Apr. 5 (*caption*) Air ace's portrait for S.A. Cheer-up Hut. **1942** *Whizz* (Perth) Aug. 3 Foote . . is thinking about starting a cheer-up society. **1954** N. BARTLETT *With Australs. in Korea* 236 He gave me a frosty smile. . . Another one of the Cheer Up boys!

cheque.

1. The total sum received, esp. by a rural worker at the end of a seasonal contract, or from the sale of a crop.

1857 F. DE B. COOPER *Wild Adventures* 66 Drawing my 'cheque' from Wilder, I felt my exchequer sufficiently strong to allow of my embarking in another career, namely, that of an overlander. **1868** *Colonial Soc.* (Sydney) 3 Dec. 2 There are . . cheques to be knocked down by a course of brutal debauchery in half as many days as it has taken weeks to earn them. **1875** *Austral. Town & Country Jrnl.* (Sydney) 10 Apr. 584/4 The shepherd hands his cheque across the bar—and, till every shilling, purchased by a year's work, abstinence, and solitude, disappears, drinks—madly drinks. **1880** 'ERRO' *Squattermania* 47 Are you going to shout, Billy? . . I thought you'd drunk your cheque out long ago. **1902** R.C. PRAED *My Austral. Girlhood* 236 And when the barkeeper sees he's had about enough, and is close on D.T., he comes up and says, 'Look here, my boy, your cheque is out and you must shift.' **1908** W.H. OGILVIE *My Life in Open* 29 Every sheep put down the shoot represents a few pence more towards the building of the coveted 'cheque'. **1919** E.S. SORENSON *Chips & Splinters* 67 He was down from Texas Station with a cheque for recreation, And he seemed to own creation by the way he put on side. **1929** K.S. PRICHARD *Coonardoo* (1961) 9 As a young man he spent all the money he had made on sprees in the coastal towns, and went off into the back-country again when his cheque gave out. **1932** J. MCCARTER *Pan's Clan* 164 Goody was on very intimate terms with Peter, having 'belted up a cheque' at the road-house on several occasions. **1940** E. HILL *Great Austral. Loneliness* (ed. 2) 134 Some epic cheques dissolve . . in the beer glasses of these outback pubs. **1950** *Bulletin* (Sydney) 30 Aug. 12/4 Old Smithers from Wiregrass blew down to the city with a record wool-cheque. **1962** T. RONAN *Deep of Sky* 6 Early on his first Sunday morning Calico Hat went for his private horses; at breakfast he asked for his cheque. **1976** B. SCOTT *Complete Bk. Austral. Folk Lore* 167 In a week the spree was over and the cheque was all knocked down, So we shouldered our Matildas and we turned our backs on town.

2. Special Comb. **cheque bu(r)sting** *ppl. a.*, spending freely, engaged in a spree; so **buster; man,** one who has received a cheque and is ready to spend it; **-proud** *a.*, 'flush', elated at being so.

1910 *Bulletin* (Sydney) 5 May 15/1 Shearers were then just about on a par with their present-day confrères in gambling and **cheque-bursting** habits. **1943** *Ibid.* 8 Dec. 12/2 More than once I saw a cheque-busting shearer, just on the verge of the d.ts. **1945** *Ibid.* 22 Aug. 12/1 Adelaide was the acme of cities, the vision of all vacationists, the **cheque-busters'** dream. **1962** MARSHALL & DRYSDALE *Journey among Men* 56 But the old cheque busters . . were mostly men who led unbelievably lonely lives maintaining a remote bore pump far out on some station run, or an equally solitary existence such as dogging. **1881** *Bulletin* (Sydney) 10 Sept. 12/1 Shearing . . is the season when the honest publican gets the 'shearer's bottle' ready under the counter and when he sees a little cloud of dust drawing nearer along the winding track, calls out to the 'stringer'—just brought up from town for the season—'Come into the verandah and smile, Mary Ann; here's another **cheque-man** coming.' **1896** T. HENEY *Girl at Birrell's* 67 These shearers are the most famous of cheque-men. These are they who earn money by working like machines and throw it away with an incredible prodigality. **1907** *Bulletin* (Sydney) 30 May 39/4, I know some towns . . that would be real glad to see a cheque-man. **1931** A.W. UPFIELD *Sands of Windee* 61 When a man from Windee or one of the smaller neighbouring stations went into Mount Lion to spend there a week or a fortnight, during which he was nearly always drunk, for there was no other form of amusement, he was known as a 'cheque-man'. **1937** —— *Winds of Evil* 184 'Will you have goat or galah,' she'd say. 'Course every one would say, 'Goat please, Mrs Nelson.' When a bankrupt chequeman said that, she'd say, 'Indeed, you won't. You'll have galah.' **1953** *Bulletin* (Sydney) 19 Aug. 12/1 Jimmy Beggs had spent most of the afternoon . . at the Gol Gol pub with two cheque men from up the river. **1966** T. RONAN *Strangers on Ophir* (rev. ed.) 76 Chequemen rolling in from three watersheds. **1904** L.M.P. ARCHER *Bush Honeymoon* 276 Any other fellow would have been **cheque-proud** long ago. **1911** E.J. BRADY *King's Caravan* 276 The 'cheque-proud' shearer who made the shanty-keeper's prey in past days is nowhere so frequent. **1913** *Bulletin* (Sydney) 25 Sept. 24/1 Narrandera . . is the first hurdle the shearer has to negotiate when, cheque-proud, he takes the train for Sydney or Melbourne. **1926** *Ibid.* 8 Apr. 22/1 Oh, come with a cheque-proud, carefree bagman. **1936** A.B. PATERSON *Shearer's Colt* 6 Some of the big sheds had just cut out and 'cheque-proud' shearers were there in scores.

chequed-up, *a.* In possession of a CHEQUE (sense 1), and ready to spend it. See also CASHED UP.

1905 *Bulletin* (Sydney) 16 Mar. 3/2, I was chequed-up for a wonder. . . Course my cheque was not the size of shearing-cheques of long ago. **1918** J.H.C. SLEEMAN *Queer Qld.* 45 So great is their prosperity, that many strikes are engineered because the men want to spend what they have—and for no other cause. In the language of the district, they are 'chequed-up'. **1926** *Aussie* (Sydney) Apr. 49/1 Chequed up and in town for a good time . . the miner was out for a spree. **1941** *Bulletin* (Sydney) 15 Oct. 15/1 The big fellow, chequed-up, had put his gear in the pub and was taking a stroll round the town. **1959** H.G. LAMOND *Sheep Station* 122 The men had about six weeks' work behind them: they should be well chequed-up. They should be financial. **1968** LINKLATER & TAPP *Gather no Moss* 17 In droving language, he was 'chequed up'; that is he had been paid for work done over a long period and had money galore. **1977** F.B. VICKERS *Stranger no Longer* 85, I was the lucky bastard who was chequed-up at the end of a run of shearing.

cherry.

1. *Obs.* Any of several plants, esp. those of the genus *Exocarpos* (see BALLART); the wood or 'fruit' of these plants; *wild cherry* WILD 1. See also *native cherry* NATIVE *a.* 6 a. Freq. *attrib.*, as **cherry-tree.**

1793 J. HUNTER *Hist. Jrnl. Trans. Port Jackson* 478 The fruit Captain Cook calls a cherry. **1799** D. COLLINS *Acct. Eng. Colony N.S.W.* (1802) II. 235 The blue gum, she-oak, and cherry tree of Port Jackson were common here. **1824** *Hobart Town Gaz.* 1 Oct., Colonial Timber may at any time be purchased of an inhabitant of this town. . . Cherry Tree and Pink Wood, for furniture and gun stocks. **1833** C. STURT *Two Exped. Interior S.A.* I. p. xxxviii, I noticed the wild fig and the cherry-tree, growing to a much larger size than I had seen them in any other part of the colony. **1843** C. ROWCROFT *Tales of Colonies* I. 147 The cherry-tree, as they call it, is a funny thing, indeed! a sour, squashy thing, with the stone forgotten in the middle, and so it was stuck outside, for the look's sake, I suppose. **1854** W. HOWITT *Boy's Adventures* 25 They call a tree, very much resembling the arborvitae, a cherry-tree, and its berries, not half so good as our English yew-berries, cherries! **1884** A. NILSON *Timber Trees N.S.W.* 98 M[emecylon] *cerasiformis*—Cherry. . . A singularly handsome tree, tall and straight. **1928** E.H.F. SWAIN *Timbers & Forest Products Qld.* 131 Cherry Alder . . is known also as Cherry in allusion to the small, globular, fleshy, subacid fruits which it bears.

2. Special Comb. **cherry bob,** a cherry-stone, esp. as used in a game played by children; the name of a game; **pick** *v. trans.* **(a)** to sort or remove (stones, etc.) manually; **(b)** to manipulate (monies in a superannuation fund) for the purpose of tax avoidance; also as *vbl. n.*; so **picker.**

1959 A.D. MICKLE *After Ball* 73, I played '**Cherry-bobs**', 'Kick the Tin', 'Charlie Over', and collected stamps. **1960** K. SMITH *Word from Children* 155 These days cherry stones are cherry stones. When I was a child they were 'cherry-bobs', eagerly sought after as currency in a schoolboy's game of skill called 'Bunny-holes'. **1976** B. LEWIS *Sunday at Kooyong Road* 112 It is cherry-bob time. Cherry stones take the place of pissies as currency and the aim is to transfer others' cherry pips to your own possession. **1975** L. BEADELL *Still in Bush* 22 Eric drove the workshop Rover, doing a dual job of helping everyone do everything as well as '**cherry picking**' the finished road for odd roots and stones left behind after the last pass of the grader. **1984** *Canberra Times* 5 Apr. 13/8 Legislation to combat the operation of 'cherrypicking' tax-avoidance schemes involving employee superannuation funds was introduced into Parliament yesterday. **1984** *CPD* (Senate) CII. 486 A way in which the employees . . for whose benefit ostensibly the fund was established, are deprived of their entitlements in that fund and the contributions on which exemption from taxable income has already been claimed and on which income earned within the fund has been tax exempt, are ultimately directed or harvested, if you like. I understand that the colloquial term is 'cherry picked'. **1970** B. FULLER *Nullarbor Story* 43 'When everything was set, we cut a track thirty-four feet wide to take a twenty-eight foot surface. And after us came the **cherry pickers.**' 'Cherry pickers?' 'Yeh. The name we had for the old blokes who did smoothing-off work, cleaning up the large stones that we had missed.' **1980** W.H. O'ROURKE *My Way* 180 Teams of men known as 'cherry-pickers' separated the barren stones from the ones containing [asbestos] fibre as the conveyor belt passed by. **1984** *CPD* (Senate) CII. 497 The cherry picker scheme is a most outrageous and reprehensible tax avoidance mechanism.

chestnut, *n. Obs. Black bean* (a), see BLACK *a.*[2] 1 a.

1833 W.J. HOOKER *Bot. Miscellany* I. 259 Close to our encampment we observed a number of fires, kindled by the natives, with quantities of *Chestnuts* (*Castanospermum*). **1854** F. ELDERSHAW *Aust. as it really Is* 43 The native Plum, Tamarind, Chestnut . . are . . well-recognised delicacies among the rising Anglo-Australian generation. **1880** J. BONWICK *Resources Qld.* 82 The Chestnut of the south-east is a *Castanospermum* of magnificent growth and luxuriance of foliage, with dark walnut-like wood.

chestnut, *a.* [Spec. use of *chestnut* the colour.] In the names of birds: **chestnut-breasted shelduck,** *mountain duck*, see MOUNTAIN; **-eared finch,** *zebra finch*, see ZEBRA; **teal,** the small duck *Anas castanea* of s. Aust., the adult male having chestnut underparts.

[**1844 chestnut-breasted shelduck:** J. GOULD *Birds of Aust.* (1848) VII. Pl. 7, *Casarca tadorïnodes*... Chestnut-coloured Shieldrake... Mountain Duck, Colonists of Swan River.] **1931** N.W. CAYLEY *What Bird is That?* 246 Chestnut-breasted Shelduck .. is generally shy and wary. **1945** C. BARRETT *Austral. Bird Life* 48 The chestnut-breasted shelduck .. also is handsome, but fortunately has no reputation as a table bird. **1948** R. RAVEN-HART *Canoe in Aust.* 71 A .. duck .. with warm chestnut breast and a silver ring separating this from the darker neck and head .. Jack called .. 'Mountain Duck', the usual name ('Chestnut-breasted Shelduck' is more official). **1848** J. GOULD *Birds of Aust.* (1848) III. Pl. 87, The **Chestnut-eared Finch** is one of the smallest of the genus yet discovered in Australia. **1896** B. SPENCER *Rep. Horn Sci. Exped. Central Aust.* I. 13 The approach to a water-hole can always be told .. by the twittering of innumerable chestnut-eared finches. **1948** *Austral. Bushcraft* (Austral. Army Educ. Service) 18 The chestnut-eared finch is another guide... Bushmen call it the 'headache bird' on account of its monotonous cry. [**1845 chestnut teal:** J. GOULD *Birds of Aust.* (1848) VII. Pl. 11, *Anas punctata*... Chestnut-breasted Duck... Teal, Colonists of Swan River.] **1945** C. BARRETT *Austral. Bird Life* 50 The chestnut teal .. is absent from northern parts of the mainland and the south-west. **1976** *Reader's Digest Compl. Bk. Austral. Birds* 105 The chestnut teal is an important game bird.

chew, *v. Obs.*

1. In the phr. **to chew** (someone's) **lug** (or **ear**), to cadge. See also BITE *v.*

1896 H. LAWSON *While Billy Boils* 14 Bill said: 'We'll have to sharpen our teeth, that's all, and chew somebody's lug... You know one or two of these mugs. Bite one of their ears.' So I took aside a chap that I knowed and bit his ear for ten bob, and gave it to Bill to mind. **1900** —— *Over Sliprails* 15, I know the barman here, and I think he knows me. I'll chew his lug for a bob or may be a quid. **1901** *Truth* (Sydney) 9 June 3/4 The bandsmen, who complained about being half-starved on the Royal yacht, had been indulging freely in the unromantic occupation of what, in polite circles, is called 'chewing a man's ear', or 'biting his lug'. In other words .. the Royal bandsmen .. were *obliged to cadge.*

2. *trans.* To drink (esp. beer). See also BEER CHEWER.

1904 *Shearer* (Sydney) 15 Oct. 8/1 They are well dressed and well behaved, and instead of chewing beer, they were reading good books. **1910** *Bulletin* (Sydney) 14 Apr. 14/3 Twenty years ago the average shearer was a derelict sort of person, whose main ambition in life was to earn a cheque and then chew it up at the nearest shanty. The old-time beer-chewer has been driven out to join the sundowners. **1911** *Ibid.* 20 Apr. 14/3 The Mount Morgan system of 'chewing' or 'running the cutter' is, as far as I can ascertain, unique in Australia. A party .. of miners on their way home .. take turn about to provide the nimble sprat; a billy-can is .. in return for the sixpence .. filled by R. Public House.

Hence **chewer** *n.*

1922 *Ibid.* 13 July 22/4 A chewer on the promise of a pint of beer swallowed a mixture of tar and kerosene.

chewbac. *Austral. pidgin.* [f. *chew (ing + to)bac(co.*] Tobacco.

1925 M. TERRY *Across Unknown Aust.* 286 There was much chew-bac to be handed to them. **1944** F. BERKERY *East goes West* 26 The black inhabitants .. found the men were not such bad fellows, and inclined to be liberal with the good old 'chewbac'.

chewy. Also **chewie.** [f. *chew(ing gum)* + -Y.]

1. (A piece of) chewing gum. Also *attrib.*

1924 F.J. MILLS *Happy Days* 115 The boys .. looked round for the chocolate and 'chewy' sellers. **1969** W. DICK *Naked Prodigal* 239 'Have a chewie, Kenny,' he said, passing me one. **1976** MCDONALD & HARDING *Norman Gunston's Finest Moments* 17 The easiest to prepare, cheap as mud to buy, and the slowest to eat, is a couple of pieces of chewy.

2. In the phr. **chewy on your boot,** a barracker's call intended to discourage a player from performing well (at kicking, running, etc.), or to deride one who is performing poorly.

1966 S.J. BAKER *Austral. Lang.* (ed. 2) 370 *Hope you have chewie on your boot!* used to express a wish that a football player kicking for goal misses because there is chewing gum on his boot. **1975** *Sydney Morning Herald* 8 Nov. 4/3 Mr Hawke puzzled the crowd when he described their reaction to the Khemlani disclosure as, 'You were wrong, chewy on your boot'. He did not seem to realise he had used an Australian Rules cat-call. **1980** A. HOPGOOD *And here comes Bucknuckle* 56 Bucknuckle says, see you later .. chewie on your boot .. and draws away to score another effortless win. **1981** L. MONEY *Footy Fan's Handbk.* 8 Chewy on Ya Boot!!!—Battle cry of *Spectatorus Mad-keenus.*

chiack /'tʃaɪæk/, *v.* Also **chyack.** [a. Br. slang *chi-hike*, apparently orig. a costermonger's cry of praise or commendation: see OED(S.) *trans.* To taunt, barrack, or tease (someone). Also *absol.*

1853 [see *chiacking, vbl. n.*]. **1874** G. WALCH *Adamanta* 27 I've learnt to chi-ike peelers. **1879** *Austral. Monthly Mag.* (Sydney) I. 742 The circle of frivolous youths who were yelping at and *chy-acking* him. **1885** *Australasian Printers' Keepsake* 139 My mates chyacked me all night. **1900** *Pastoral Times* (Deniliquin) 23 June 2/7 The police magistrate and others were 'chiaking' him about not paying the Chinamen. **1919** O. HOGUE *Cameliers* 166 The pilots and observers 'chiack' each other when they make a dud landing. **1919** *Aussie* (Sydney) Apr. 3/2 Diggers of the Yarra tribe .. like to chiack the Cornstalk variety about 'our 'arbour'. **1937** V. PALMER *Legend for Sanderson* 29 The other men did not chiack him about his eccentricities. **1944** 'S. CAMPION' *Pommy Cow* 112 They whooped, they made ribald noises, they chyacked one another. **1948** K.S. PRICHARD *Golden Miles* 180 The groomsmen all red in the face and looking as if they would choke in their stiff white collars, rocked the whole congregation with a desire to chuckle and chiack. **1968** S. GORE *Holy Smoke* 27 So half the time he's chyacking the pigs outa the way to have a go at their tucker. **1977** R. MCKIE *Crushing* (1978) 117 They chyacked their sissy mates and their sisters who were forced to attend late afternoon dancing classes. **1979** DOUGLAS & HEATHCOTE *Far Cry* 36 No-one chiacked me about snakes again.

Hence **chiacking** *vbl. n.* and *ppl. a.*

1853 C.R. READ *What I heard, saw, & Did* 148 The 'skyhacking', to which the police were subject .. was brought on principally by their own individual overbearing conduct. [*Note*] Blackguarding. **1887** W.H. SUTTOR *Austral. Stories Retold* 145, I was always civil to the chaps, for all the chyacking they gave me. **1906** *Gadfly* (Adelaide) 25 Apr. 19/3 Tommy Bent .. was a victim of most of the 'chyacking'. **1918** R.H. KNYVETT *Over there with Australs.* 79 They served out hot tea and in a few moments grumbling gave place to 'chiacking'; criticism that a few moments ago had been edged was now good-humored. **1944** 'S. CAMPION' *Pommy Cow* 69 Thus ended the relief of Rustenburg, in cheers and laughter and chyacking and sleep. **1955** D. STIVENS *Ironbark Bill* 54 Ironbark's face was red by this time with all the chyacking he got from the blokes. **1963** B. HESLING *Dinkumization & Depommification* 84 Next day at lunch-time I got the same chyacking treatment from Gordon's brother Frank. **1964** 'E. LINDALL' *Kind of Justice* 30 They were a vociferous crowd, ruggedly vocal in a loud, chiacking anticipation of the heady joys to come. **1967** D. HORNE *Educ. Young Donald* 81 Other types of humour—chyacking and leg-pulling, sardonic anecdotes, jolliness and exuberance. **1976** C.D. MILLS *Hobble Chains & Greenhide* 1 The Boss was strangely quiet during the meal, and did not join in the usual 'chiacking' as was his custom. **1984** M. ELDRIDGE *Walking Dog* 170 When their chiaking got too much I would go out and talk to the turkeys.

chiack /'tʃaɪæk/, *n.* Also **chyack.** [f. prec.] Banter, barracking.

1869 *Australasian* (Melbourne) 17 July 72/4 The hissing of gallery, or the gods, is called *chy-ike.* **1898** *Bulletin* (Sydney) 17 Dec. (Red Page), *Chyack* is more properly *chyike*, the cockney pronunciation of 'cheek'—impudent badinage. **1913** C.J. DENNIS *Backblock Ballads* 89, I felt as if I couldn't go that fur, An' start to sling off chiack like I used. **1940** *Action Front: Jrnl. 2/2 Field Regiment* 13 Jan. 2 Pleasant chi-ack in the billets. **1943** A. DAWES *Soldier Superb* 82 Australian soldiers with a passion for handing out 'chiak' in the form of nicknames can take it, too. **1971** F. HARDY *Outcasts of Foolgarah* 2 'Hullo, hullo,' Chilla said, always a bit too keen on the old chiack, especially when it came to Tich's unsuccessful carryings on with the female of the species.

chief. *Hist.* KING *n.*[1] 1 a.

1794 G. THOMPSON *Slavery & Famine* II. 11 There are three or four of the Chiefs who attend the Governor's house every day for their dinner and a glass of wine. **1817** *Sydney Gaz.* 4 Jan., His *Excellency* then assembled the chiefs by themselves, and confirmed them in the ranks of chieftains to which their own tribes had exalted them. **1835** J. BATMAN *Settlement in Port Phillip* 6 June (1856) 20 We sat down in the midst of these sooty and sable aboriginal children of Australia; amongst whom, we ascertained, were eight chiefs belonging to the country near Port Phillip. **1838** T.L. MITCHELL *Three Exped. Eastern Aust.* I. 198 The greater part of the tribe decamped... The chief, or *king* (as our people called him), continued with us. **1849** C. STURT *Narr. Exped. Central Aust.* II. 72 We observed a body of natives... The party consisted of two chiefs and fourteen young men and boys. **1863** J. BONWICK *Wild White Man* 80 Nominally, the old men are chiefs. **1874** J. RAE *Gleanings from Scrapbk.* 73 An *Australian Chief*, with his blanket, vaults, With hop, step, and jump, to the midst of the waltz. **1886** R. HENTY *Australiana* 21, I have seen two chiefs fight with shield and leeangle. **1912** A. BERRY *Reminisc.* 178 Two native gentlemen—Lager, the chief of Jervis Bay, and Wagin, the chief of Numba—who were induced to accompany me by the promise of a suit of clothes and an engraved brass plate each, as a badge of their dignity as chiefs or kings!!

child. *Obs.* Usu. in *pl.* In the phr. **child of the bush** and varr., applied to an Aboriginal. Cf. BLACK *a.*[1] 4.

1819 *Sydney Gaz.* 2 Jan., *His Excellency* the *Governor*, accompanied by the *Lieutenant Governor*, the Members of the Native Institution, and several other Gentlemen entered the circle where these Children of Nature were seated. Chairs were provided for the Chiefs of tribes. **1843** *Sydney Morning Herald* 30 Aug. 2/2 How far these children of the woods have been improved by their intercourse with the civilized colonists. **1859** R.H. HORNE *Austral. Facts & Prospects* 169 The children of the Southern climes, and tribes which partake of some of their characteristics, appear destined to succumb before those of the North. **1874** J.J. HALCOMBE *Emigrant & Heathen* 38 Those houseless, homeless children of the bush, the black natives.

child endowment. An untaxed allowance paid by a government (from 1941 by the federal government) to the parents or guardians of a child. Also *attrib.*

1926 *Sydney Morning Herald* 24 Dec. 1/1 The State Cabinet has approved of a child endowment scheme, the rate to be 6s. per child per week. **1933** J. TRURAN *Where Plain Begins* 159 He was drawing unemployment relief for his wife and children, and 'child-endowment' money in respect of five of the latter. **1935** K. TENNANT *Tiburon* 8 Twelve-year-old Jim could trap rabbits as cleverly as a man; and between rabbits and child endowment they managed well enough. **1943** R. DIXON *Story J.T. Lang* 6 Mr Lang has made great capital out of the fact that his Government introduced .. Child Endowment. **1950** V.E. TURNER *Ooldea* 152 The Child Endowment scheme made it possible for such amenities as milk and fruit and biscuits to be given to the camp children. **1961** *Bulletin* (Sydney) 1 Feb. 10/3 An increase in Southern European 'bride' migrants, greater child-endowment payments and propaganda for private-school grants would head the list. **1978** R.H. CONQUEST *Dusty Distances* 18 Child endowment, for what it's worth, was something for the distant future.

Children's python. [The specific epithet *Childreni* was given by English naturalist J.E. Grey (*Zool. Miscellany* (1842) 44), after J.G. *Children* (1777–1852), a colleague at the British Museum.] The nocturnal python *Liasis childreni* of n. Aust. Also **Children's snake.**

1869 G. KREFFT *Snakes of Aust.* 34 Children's rock snake. **1899** *Bulletin* (Sydney) 12 Aug. 14/2 The 'children's' or 'Rock' snake (*Liasis childreni*) is probably the reptile that my critics refer to as a carpet snake. **1970** P. SLATER *Eagle for Pidgin* 59 'It's a Children's python, isn't it, Dad?' 'That's right—not called after kids . . but after a Dr Children.'

Chinaman.

1. *Obs.* In the collocation **Chinaman's trot,** a slow but steady jogging pace; a shuffling gait. Cf. CHINKIE (quot. 1930).

1897 J.J. MURIF *From Ocean to Ocean* 22, I frequently caught myself going at a 'Chinaman's trot' where I could not do any riding. **1903** J. FURPHY *Such is Life* 108, I followed the buggy at a Chinaman's trot. **1904** *Sporting News* (Launceston) 10 Sept. 1/3 Why the stewards did not take action is certainly not understandable. It was a Chinaman's trot, in the fullest sense of the term, and should not be countenanced.

2. Used *attrib.* in Special Comb. **Chinaman fish,** any of several fish, esp. the sea perch *Symphorus nematophorus* of n. Qld. Also **Chinaman.**

1906 D.G. STEAD *Fishes of Aust.* 265 Yellow Leather-jacket or 'Chinaman'. *Monacanthus ayraudi*. N.S.W. **1944** J. DEVANNY *By Tropic Sea & Jungle* 81 The Chinaman fish is supposed to be poisonous at certain times of the year. **1978** N. COLEMAN *Austral. Fisherman's Fish Guide* 138 The chinaman fish inhabits coral reef and often hangs in water over deep gutters.

Chinese. In various collocations: **Chinese burr,** any of several burred plants, esp. *Centaurea melitensis* (see COCKSPUR); the burr itself; **pump** *mining*, a pump consisting of buckets on a continuous belt; **scrub** (or **shrub**), the aromatic shrub *Cassinia arcuata* (fam. Asteraceae) which, from its vigorous growth and seeding, is often regarded as a weed.

1900 *Bulletin* (Sydney) 15 Dec. 15/2 The **Chinese burr** in Cairns district (N.Q.) is densely thick. . . The Chow always leaves this legacy behind him when he quits leased land. It is supposed to have been brought from China in packing. **1920** J.H. MAIDEN *Weeds N.S.W.* 114 'Chinese Burr' . . does not come from China, nor am I aware that the Chinese have had anything to do with its introduction or dissemination. **1946** 'B. JAMES' *Cookabundy Bridge* 20 He wildly explored his feet for Chinese burrs. **1852** A. MACKAY *Great Gold Field* 9 Nov. (1853) 46 The claim . . is situated near the centre of the Bar, and what is called a Californian, but more properly a **Chinese pump,** which lifts a great deal of water, is employed to work it. **1869** R.B. SMYTH *Gold Fields & Mineral Districts* 607 *Chinese Pump*, . . a pump differing from the Californian only in its being made entirely of wood. **1931** W. BARAGWANATH et al. *Guide for Propectors in Vic.* 15 The water is . . pumped out of the wing dam by means of a 'Chinese pump', thus enabling the miner to reach the gravel over which the river formerly flowed. **1909** A.J. EWART *Weeds Vic.* 1 The following native plants are included under the head of proclaimed weeds: . . the **Chinese Scrub** (*Cassinia arcuata*) [etc.]. **1921** J. MATTHAMS *Rabbit Pest in Aust.* 248 Chinese Scrub . . A useless perennial native plant which occasionally grows to several feet in height. **1981** J.A. BAINES *Austral. Plant Genera* 83 Chinese Scrub was apparently so called because Chinese gold-miners brewed a kind of tea from the leaves; it certainly is not native to China. **1981** G.M. CUNNINGHAM et al. *Plants Western N.S.W.* 688 As chinese-shrub readily colonizes disturbed and bare soils it has some use in the reclamation of gravel pits or mine dumps. Its name originates from its frequent occurrence around gold diggings and the fact that the Chinese miners used it to thatch roofs of their dwellings.

Chingah, Chingi, varr. JINGY.

Chink. [Altered form of *Chinese*, poss. infl. by *chink* narrow aperture, slit, with reference to the eyes; not excl. Austral. but, like CHINKIE, recorded earliest in Aust.] A Chinese; usu. an immigrant or a descendant of an immigrant.

1887 'WANDERER' *Down on their Luck* 28 The white man must go, because the Chinks can live on the smell of an oil rag. **1911** A.L. HAYDON *Trooper Police Aust.* 46 The 'Chinks' were not to be tolerated so close. **1929** P.R. STEPHENSEN *Bushwhackers* 36 The peanuts of Willy Ah Foo were not only remarkably tasty in themselves, but they were grown by a Chinaman, a Chink, a Chow, a Pong, and they were most legitimate plunder for little white boys. **1946** D. BARR *Warrigal Joe* 80 Chinatown at Palmerston, as they called it in those days, was swarmin' with Chinks. **1965** *Coast to Coast 1963–64* 118, I take a little Chink with the slanty eyes, or a little Black Feller nobody wants. **1982** R. HALL *Just Relations* 465, I remember some pretty crook things went on there, did some of them meself. . . Ears? yes, cut off of Abos and Chinks and the like: we was young larrikins.

Chinkie. Also **Chinkee, Chinkey, Chinky.** [See prec.] CHINK. Also *attrib.*

1876 *Queenslander* (Brisbane) 18 Mar. 13/2 Our colonialised 'Chinkie', as he is vulgarly termed (with the single variation 'Chow'). **1879** W.J. BARRY *Up & Down* 51 The first Chinese war with Britain had broken out, and there was every appearance of plenty of fun to be shortly had with the Chinkies. **1889** F. CRAWFORD *Native Companion Songster* 23 As far as the Chinkies are concerned, I'd make them shut up shop, divide their property amongst yer, cut off their pig-tails, and make 'em clear. **1907** *Truth* (Sydney) 24 Feb. 12/5 The scallywags who would rob a chinkie's pie melon patch deserve nothing better than a seat on an ounce of shot. **1916** *Ibid.* 22 Oct. 12/1 Gesticulating chinkies were gathered about the door. **1930** *Bulletin* (Sydney) 6 Aug. 20/1 An' many a mile across the plains We done the 'chinkie-jog'. **1969** W. DICK *Naked Prodigal* 5 He didn't seem a bad bloke for a chinky-chink.

Hence **Chinkieland** *n.*, China.

1911 *Truth* (Sydney) 29 Oct. 1/5 He sees the Pong start off for dear old Chinkieland.

chip, *v. trans.* To hoe or break up (the surface soil); with **in(to),** to sow (seed) by hoeing it into the ground.

1797 D. COLLINS *Acct. Eng. Colony N.S.W.* (1802) II. 18 Some . . too idle and dissipated to hoe and properly prepare the ground for seed, have carelessly thrown the grain over the old stubble, and afterwards chipped it in, as they termed it, going lightly over the ground with a hoe, and barely covering the seed. **1810** *Sydney Gaz.* 12 May, Chipping in the seed . . 6s. 8d. per acre. **1817** *Hobart Town Gaz.* 18 Jan., Chipping in wheat. ***c* 1852** A. MANN *Goldfields Aust.* 107 A man with a hoe, and the labour of a few days, may 'chip' into the earth sufficient maize or Indian corn to sustain him for the entire year. **1879** 'RECENT SETTLER' *Emigration to Tas.* 73 Leave the land ready for chipping in the first grain crop. **1918** *Bulletin* (Sydney) 18 July 22/3, I have gone to fight the Germans, and I don't know when I'm coming back, somebody chip round my humpy against grass fire. **1945** J. DEVANNY *Bird of Paradise* 43 Their compatriots, chip and clear for them, for no money. **1965** J. BECKETT *New-Chum looks at Qld.* 22 If you don't get a job cutting, there's always chipping (hoeing) to be done.

Hence **chipper** *n.*

1978 D. BALL *Great Austral. Snake Exchange* 97 A work force of 2000 Aboriginal 'chippers', so called because they chip out weeds with five-foot long hoes.

chip heater. A domestic water heater which uses small pieces of wood as fuel.

1946 K. TENNANT *Lost Haven* 101 Grandpa led the way to the bathroom and expected the guest to admire the bath and the chip-heater! **1948** R. RAVEN-HART *Canoe in Aust.* 30 The 'chip heater', in essence a cylindrical fire-holder with a pipe chimney and a lidded hole in the top through which fuel is dropped, surrounded by an outer cylinder into which cold water is fed, and hot, piping water is taken. To light them, you drop in paper and small sticks and a match. **1962** C. GYE *Cockney & Crocodile* 98 Here was pure delight, a real hot bath. It is true that it was heated by that thoroughly Australian contraption, a chip heater. **1967** D. HORNE *Educ. Young Donald* 32 In the bathroom we had a 'chip heater' that worked on little bits of wood and pulsated like a ship's engine. **1975** R. THROSSELL *Wild Weeds & Wind Flowers* 221 She had loved wandering through the home paddocks . . gathering bundles of dry twigs, gum-leaves and pine-cones for the chip heater that snuffled and snorted to produce a trickle of tepid bath water. **1979** P. ADAMS *More Unspeakable Adams* 152 One's weekly shower was kindled by the Little Hero chip heater. **1984** P. READ *Down there with me on Cowra Mission* 26 They didn't have a chip heater, like we got here now.

chiv /tʃɪv/. [Abbrev. of *chiv(v)y* shortened form of *Chevy Chase*, rhyming slang for 'face'.] The face.

1902 *Truth* (Sydney) 20 Apr. 5/1 The class of female under notice has, to use an Australianism, a chiv as tough as the rear end of a native bear, and *a hide like a dugong*. **1903** *Ibid.* 19 Apr. 1/4 Seedy warts on a fellow's chiv are a sign of piety. **1905** *Steele Rudd's Mag.* (Brisbane) Nov. 961 I'm leaving here to-morrow, lads, and you may never see My chiv behind the bar again. **1916** C.J. DENNIS *Moods of Ginger Mick* 117 'Ow many times 'ave I sat in this chair An' seen is 'ard chiv grinnin' over there.

choc: see CHOCKO.

chock-a-block. See quots. Also abbrev. as **chocka.**

1971 F. HARDY *Outcasts of Foolgarah* 80 They caught me at it once on the sofa in the living room, caught me right in the bloody act with a woman who came to do the cleaning; chocker-block up her, I was, going for me life. **1979** R. DREWE *Cry in Jungle Bar* 146 It was as if he and Gigi had been the couple caught red-handed. On the job. Chocka—as the old schoolboy expression succinctly put it—chockablock. **1983** D. FOSTER *Plumbum* 305 Some cunt'll steal your mags while you're chock-a-block up your charlie.

chock-and-log. A kind of fence or wall built of logs resting on short, transversely-placed blocks of wood. Freq. *attrib.* as **chock-and-log fence.**

1869 E.C. BOOTH *Another England* 132 Tom . . put a 'chock and log' fence round his little property. **1872** G.S. BADEN-POWELL *New Homes for Old Country* 207 Another fence, known as 'chock and log', is composed of long logs resting on piles of chocks, or short blocks of wood. **1879** 'RECENT SETTLER' *Emigration to Tas.* 85, I think the 'choc and log' a better fence. . . The chocs are cut from three to four feet long, and are placed transversely about five yards apart. Resting on these the logs are laid longitudinally, and so on, in alternate layers until the required height is attained. **1892** A. CAMERON *Aust. Felix* 16 A hard half day's wrastlin' wi' a chock-an'-log fence. **1907** C. MACALISTER *Old Pioneering Days* 297 'Chock and log' fences erected around each small holding. **1917** *Bulletin* (Sydney) 19 Apr. 24/4, I . . found old Pat seated on the 'chock an' log'. **1929** C.H. WINTER *Story of 'Bidgee Queen* 24 It is partly a dog-leg, and part chock-and-log. **1956** T. RONAN *Moleskin Midas* 99 They mustered into the chock-and-log paddock. **1980** HOLTH & BARNABY *Cattlemen of High Country* 24 The construction of this hut was known to the cattlemen as 'chock 'n log'. **1984** *Australasian Post* 27 Dec. 54/5 Over the years the chock and log fences became victims of decay and bushfires and are hard to find today.

chocko /ˈtʃɒkoʊ/. Also **choco.** Shortened form of CHOCOLATE SOLDIER. Also **choc.**

1918 R.H. KNYVETT *Over there with Australs.* 154 We carried off the 'championship cup', beating the 'Chocolates' by two or three points. We might not have been so elated had not the 'Chocs.' been such 'nuts' on themselves. **1919** W.H. DOWNING *Digger Dialects* 16 *Chocs*, the 8th Brigade ('Twey's Chocolate Soldiers.' Originally an abusive name; now an honourable appellation). **1942** T. KELAHER *Digger Hat* 51 I've a letter here to hand, Saying Chockos, Yanks and Refugees Have overrun the land. **1943** D. FRIEND *Gunner's Diary* 39 Chocos (militia) shouldn't be allowed into the canteen, the conscript rats. **1945** D. ROBINSON *Pop's Blonde* 60 He had flinched when they had disparagingly referred to him audibly as 'Choco'. **1951** CUSACK & JAMES *Come in Spinner* 19 Hero be blowed. He's a choco. Caught in the draft. **1957** J.M. HOSKING *Aust. first & Last* 32 The sarge was only a chocko; I was a volunteer. **1968** G. MILL *Nobody dies but Me* 61 We call the soldiers Chockos—that's short for Chocolate Soldiers—because most of the army is conscripted like any other army. **1977** S. LOCKE ELLIOTT *Water under Bridge* 230 Joined up. Not one of those 'chockos' who had to be drafted.

chocolate frog. Rhyming slang for 'dog', an informer (see DOG *n.*[2]). Also *ellipt.* as **chocolate.**

1971 *Bulletin* (Sydney) 28 Aug. 17/2 He said he preferred any other prisoner to a 'chocolate frog' or an informer. **1973** J. MCNEIL *Chocolate Frog* 18 Trouble is, but, yer never know these days just who is a bloody chocolate, and who ain't! *Ibid.* 18 Yeah. I can remember when you'd never even bother to *spit* at a uniform or a dog. Look at it now, but: nobody worries about chocolate frogs any more.

chocolate lily. Any of the several perennial herbs

of the genus *Arthropodium* (fam. Liliaceae), the purplish flowers of which have a sweet scent reminiscent of chocolate or vanilla. Also *ellipt.* as **chocolate.**

1944 A. Marshall *These are my People* 201 Say diggers, do you remember picking the ham and eggs, the chocolates, the everlastings, the early nancy? **1965** *Coast to Coast 1963–64* 155 The mullock heaps in their pelts of paspalum and chocolate lilies. **1977** J. Galbraith *Wild Flowers S.-E. Aust.* 32 Chocolate lily . . with a scattering of bluish-mauve vanilla-scented ¾" flowers.

chocolate soldier. [Spec. use of *chocolate (cream) soldier* a soldier who will not fight (see G.B. Shaw *Arms and the Man* (1898) I. 17).]

a. *Hist.* In the war of 1914–18, a soldier in the 8th Infantry Brigade of the Australian Imperial Force, so called because the Brigade arrived in Egypt after the Gallipoli campaign.

1915 T. Skeyhill *Soldier-Songs from Anzac* 22 But 'e called me a chocolate soldier, A six bob a day tourist, too. 'E says, 'You'll not reach the trenches; Nor even get a view.' **1916** E.F. Hanman *Twelve Months with Anzacs* 74 We'll never get away from this hole—just think we are chocolate soldiers, they do! **1917** C.E.W. Bean *Lett. from France* 226 The 'Chocolate Soldiers' became veterans in one terrible struggle. **1918** R.H. Knyvett *Over there with Australs.* 153 There was a good deal of rivalry between us and another brigade known as 'The Chocolate Soldiers'. They received this nickname because they were the most completely equipped unit that ever left Australia.

b. Orig. in the war of 1939–45, a militiaman or conscript, called up for home service and unable, before 1943, to serve outside Australia and its territories.

1943 A. Dawes *Soldier Superb* 83 'Chocko' abbreviates 'chocolate soldier', formerly a term of opprobrium rather than affection applied by men of the A.I.F. to 'Saturday soldiers'—militiamen called up for home defence. **1944** G. Mant *You'll be Sorry* 54 'Chocolate Soldier' to us was merely a term of good-natured banter. **1979** *Southerly* iv. 368 He's in the University Regiment. He's a chocolate soldier.

chokey /'tʃoʊki/. [Anglo-Indian *choky* police station lock-up, used also in Br. slang from 1873: see OED 2.] A police station; a gaol. Freq. without article.

1840 A. Russell *Tour through Austral. Colonies* 190 He was politely handed up to the *chokey*, (colonially called) . . more generally known as the police office. **1845** *Star* (Sydney) 6 Dec. 1/1 A man named Fleming, was confined on Saturday night in the watch-house, for drunkenness, and . . paid 11s. on Sunday morning, to get out of the chokey. **1855** R. Carboni *Eureka Stockade* 55 Three of the ringleaders of the mob had been pounced upon, and were safe in chokey. **1869** *Colonial Soc.* (Sydney) 7 Jan. 11, I'll drag you to Sydney, and put you in chokey. **1897** *Bulletin* (Sydney) 2 Jan. 11/1 A stable is used as a lock-up at Queenstown. . . One night recently the improvised 'chokey' was occupied by a drunk, a horse, a pig, and a corpse. **1909** *Ibid.* 23 Dec. 43/1 Now this is the song of a prison—a song of a gaol or jug—A ballad of quod or of chokey, the ultimate home of the mug. **1923** J. Armour *Spell of Inland* 142 You are fined a quid, and if you don't part up you'll go into 'chokey' for a month—see? **1954** N. Bartlett *Pearl Seekers* 207 I've been in chokey, see . . for killing a nigger. **1962** D. McLean *World turned upside Down* 205 I'll put you in the chokey with the rest.

choko /'tʃoʊkoʊ/. [a. Brazilian Indian *chuchu.*] The cultivated vine of tropical America *Sechium edule* (fam. Cucurbitaceae), bearing an edible pear-shaped fruit; the fruit itself.

1909 Lindsay & Holtze *Territoria* 58 The choko, to give its Queensland name, likes a loose sandy or loamy substratum. **1914** *Bulletin* (Sydney) 18 June (Red Page), The chokos on the vine are turning white. **1945** C. Mann *River* 1 Pumpkin vines, the occasional pie-melons and chokos. **1956** S. Hope *Diggers' Paradise* 226 One vegetable which will probably be a novelty to British settlers is the choko. **1965** K. Smith *OGF* 57 Already, a long hungry-looking choko vine had crept up the side. **1979** Douglas & Heathcote *Far Cry* 46, I ate chokos steamed, fried, stewed, in salads, and every other way I could think of.

choof, *v.* Also **chuff.** [Fig use of *chuff* to puff (as a steam engine).] *intr.* To go or move.

1947 *Contact: Jrnl. Air Force Assoc. Victorian Division* Mar. 16 We hope you shall be able to choof along to the next function. **1963** J. Cantwell *No Stranger to Flame* 29 They only stayed the one night and I'd choofed into Cairns with Nugget. **1965** F. Hardy *Yarns of Billy Borker* 82 Up he choofs to the uniformed flunkey at the club door. **1971** D. Ireland *Unknown Industr. Prisoner* 83 We were choofing along Highway One about forty-five or fifty when all of a sudden we see the wheel going past. **1976** N. Sidney *Return* 28 Lou'll be choofin' up be'ind us. **1977** R. Beilby *Gunner* 139 It's just that the old bloke's sick so it might be better if you chuffed off. **1979** B. Hardy *World owes me Nothing* 156 'If my presence is going to cause trouble', I said, 'I'd rather not be here, so I think I'll choof off.'

choogar bag, var. Sugar bag 1.

chook /tʃʊk/. Also **chookie, chooky, chuckie, chucky.** [Br. dial. *chuck(y)* chicken, fowl: see OED *sb.*[2]]

1. A domestic fowl; a chicken. Also *attrib.*

1855 W. Howitt *Land, Labor & Gold* II. 148 They overtook a huge and very fat hen. . . They tied chuckey up in a handkerchief, and rode on. **1875** R. Thatcher *Something to his Advantage* 149 Gone! gone! are my chuckies, But where are the foes? **1880** *Bulletin* (Sydney) 17 July 4/2 A man was found in the cow-shed of Government House. . . Was he looking after the housemaid or the 100 little chookies? **1900** *Truth* (Sydney) 13 May 5/5 Lord Augustus Loftus . . spent . . his time coaxing 'choocks' to lay, and inducing venturesome chicks to emerge into light. **1903** *Bulletin* (Sydney) 19 Nov. 36/1 Chuck!—*Chook!*—Cho-ok! Why, there's that white 'un lost another chick today! **1905** *Ibid.* 27 Apr. 16/4 The mallee-hen is not . . any brainier than the barndoor chooky. **1916** *Truth* (Sydney) 4 June 8/6 The lady farmers should train their chooks on the American plan. **1927** *Bulletin* (Sydney) 3 Feb. 24/2 A Digger poultry-farmer . . received a letter from his wife . . announcing a chook hunger-strike. **1936** *Ibid.* 12 Feb. 21/4 Returning, with a blackboy, he found not a skerrick of tucker at the . . homestead, but the chooks had presented him with two eggs. **1945** R.S. Close *Love me Sailor* 160 Well, what do you expect aboard a bloody windjammer . . roast chook? **1957** V.H. Lloyd *Hidden Enemy* 142 He doesn't realise how much depends on his staying on his feet in this expedition. Without him we're like a headless chook. **1968** E. Pagram *Never had it so Good* 67, I went to the meat counter and asked for a chicken and some liver. I came away with a 'chook' and some 'lambs'-fry'. **1972** *Daily Mirror* (Sydney) 12 Oct. 4/5, I hope all yer chooks turn into emus and kick yer dunny down. **1985** *Nat. Times* (Sydney) 8 Nov. 49/3 A terrific dryish botrytis riesling which is now as rare as chook-fangs.

2. *transf.* and *fig.*

1914 *Bulletin* (Sydney) 22 Oct. 43/2 Over the gaol there is the inscription 'Erected 1836'. There is a rat (or kangaroo) and a common chook (or emu) flanking the inscription. **1915** C.J. Dennis *Songs of Sentimental Bloke* 80 'She's young—too young to leave 'er muvver's nest!' 'Orright, ole chook,' I nearly sez. **1918** *Bulletin* (Sydney) 13 Oct. 24/2, I plump for the diamond-sparrow . . and the barley-bird as the two smallest Australian chooks. **1955** D. Niland *Shiralee* 207 Some half-witted chook's got off with Mac's kid. **1964** C. Kunrathy *Impudent Foreigner* 133 The girls were teaching me many useful new words. They called . . an old woman a 'chook'. **1969** D. Niland *Dead Men Running* 63 What would he be making up to an old married chook like you for? **1984** *Nat. Times* (Sydney) 20 July 2/2 Clancy noted last week that Premier Joh had told his 'chooks' (press gallery members) to cease their practice of gathering outside the Cabinet room for interviews with ministers as they emerged from meetings.

3. Comb. **chook farm, house, raffle, -raiser, run, yard.**

1939 *Bulletin* (Sydney) 17 May 20/4, I called at a **chook-farm** recently when a batch of some thousands of eggs was about to hatch. **1946** *Ibid.* 23 Jan. 13/3, I . . invested in a chook farm. **1963** B. Hesling *Dinkumization & Depommification* 227 They have bought a chook farm some place. **1938** *Bulletin* (Sydney) 26 May 20/3 Went into the **chook-house** the other day and found a porcupine. **1946** *Ibid.* 10 Apr. 14/2 A native cat devastated our chookhouse. **1956** K. Tennant *Honey Flow* 348, I looked up from my papers to see Matt sitting with his feet up on the old cane lounge he had rescued from the chook-house and scrubbed down. **1981** P. Barton *Bastards I have Known* 30 The time we burned ten bales of hay, half a chookhouse, and frightened 250 fowls so badly that they never laid another egg. **1979** *Herald* (Melbourne) 18 Aug. 2 The Government is proudly announcing a casino venture . . while the local church footy club secretary can go to jail for running an unregistered **chook raffle.** **1981** Q. Wild *Honey Wind* 24 A young nurse came in, selling tickets in a 'Chook' raffle for the local hospital, run by the Uniting Church. **1985** *Bulletin* (Sydney) 18 June 72/3 Kevin Parry . . does not have to worry about chook raffles. Parry has personally guaranteed the $10 million budget drawn up. **1931** *Ibid.* 30 Dec. 20/2 A suburban **chook-raiser** added a wallaby to the population of a pen of Leghorn cockerels. **1934** C. Mackness *Young Beachcombers* 161 Cows and chooks are early risers, and cow-cockies and chook-raisers have to be. **1979** D. Maitland *Breaking Out* 23 'I'll admit I'm more of a hayshed man,' Henry confessed—a skinny fox ogling the surrounding **chook-run.** 'I get nervous in open country.' **1981** K. McArthur *Bread & Dripping Days* 8 There might have been a dunny in the backyard and probably a chook-run too, into which were thrown the kitchen scraps. **1942** G. Casey *It's Harder for Girls* 127, I seen one [*sc.* willy-willy] take the roof off my front veranda an' land it in th' **chookyard** at the back. **1945** *Bulletin* (Sydney) 16 May 14/3 There'd been an outsize goanna raiding Jud's chookyard. **1965** *Overland* xxxii. 6 Mr Treloar's place with chook-yards built right along the road. **1982** *Age* (Melbourne) 6 Feb. 11/5 This policy of trying to get a public opinion consensus before you do anything is the sort of thing you do in the chookyard.

choom /tʃʊm/. [Repr. Br. dial. pronunc. of *chum.*] **a.** In the war of 1914–18: an English soldier. **b.** An English person.

1916 Tas. Non-State Rec. 103/11 11 June, The 'Chooms', as our men call the men of Kitchener's new army, pulled the wire rope. **1918** *Kia Ora Coo-ee* Oct. 14/3 'Jock', 'Choom', 'Dinkum' and 'Cobber' are standardised monikers that do yeoman service. **1921** C.E.W. Bean *Official Hist. Aust. 1914–18* I. 126 'Ahv ye got a fahg, choom?' (which was Lancashire for 'Have you a cigarette, mate?') was almost the extent of their intercourse. The 'chooms' were the first British troops whom the Australian soldiers met. **1923** *Aussie* (Sydney) Nov. 7/2 A rouseabout was Freckled Jim, Tarts, chooms, and swagmen worshipped him. **1939** *Bulletin* (Sydney) 8 Feb. 21/4 Dad and Choom . . unearthed a bottle that the tractor-driver had planted. **1952** J. Cleary *Sundowners* 157 She's a Choom, like you, Rupe. I married her when I was over in the Old Dart during the war. **1971** F. Hardy *Outcasts of Foolgarah* 1 They'd know that good things come in a glass, wouldn't they choom? **1983** B. Dawe *Over here, Harv!* 18 'Yeah—mad with the work,' said Mick Bailey. 'These bloody Chooms, they're all alike.'

chop, *n.*[1] and *a.* [Generalized use of *chop* quality, class, a. Hindi *chhap* seal, mark of quality: see OED(S *sb.*[5] 4.]

A. *n. Obs.* Something to be valued or prized.

1827 *Monitor* (Sydney) 9 Aug. 575/2 Many native girls, after living in a very decent sort of a way (as they conceive at least) as concubines with several gentlemen, at length will do a Hawkesbury Settler *the honour perhaps to marry* him. And if she be a brisk good-looking active wench, the Settler blesses his stars at his rare luck in getting such *a chop.* **1849** A. Harris *Guide Port Stephens* (1967) 49 It is not 'a chop' at all times to have a good steel mill; your neighbours keep grinding sometimes till twelve o'clock at night. **1888** 'R. Boldrewood' *Robbery under Arms* (1937) 461 Life ain't no great chop to a man like me, not when he gets the wrong side o' sixty, anyhow.

B. *adj.* Of quality; good. Freq. in the collocations **no chop, not much chop,** no good, not up to much.

1847 *Moreton Bay Courier* 28 Aug. 3/1 You never hear of masters who, to use a colonial phrase, are no chop, who take very mean advantages of their men. **1865** J.F. Mortlock *Experiences of Convict* 21, I was in Australasia, dragging a hand-cart (reckoned 'no chop') when informed of it. **1882** *Sydney Mail* 8 July 45/2 There's good and bad of every sort, and I've met plenty that were no chop of all churches. **1895** *Bulletin* (Sydney) 31 Aug. 27/1 Thank you, mate; it's not much chop in the way of liquor, but I feel better for it. **1901**

Western Champion (Barcaldine) 14 May 18/2 Though we never knew Brigalo Jim, and we're not such a fop, To discredit bush yarns and say they're no chop. **1922** C. DREW *Rogues & Ruses* 17, I ain't much chop at poker. **1950** J. MORRISON *Port of Call* 225 Anyway, that verandah's not much chop in bad weather; the south wind blows right in. **1955** —— *Black Cargo* 174 'I've heard he's no chop, Rory.' 'No chop?—he's a bastard.' **1968** S. GORE *Holy Smoke* 10 Only o' course their language wasn't much chop. **1981** P. BARTON *Bastards I have Known* 121 Trying to get yourself into gear at 4 a.m. . . and riding 10 kilometres in pitch darkness before dawn . . wasn't much chop. **1982** J. MORRISON *North Wind* 113 To tell the truth . . he's not much chop. Too fond of bending the elbow.

chop, *n.*[2] An event or series of events in which axemen compete under certain rules in a contest of speed.

1899 *North-Western Advocate* (Devonport) 5 Apr. 4/1 'Mugs'' chop, 1 ft. blocks. **1903** *Sporting News* (Launceston) 11 July 2/4 Get the blocks for the champion chop. *Ibid.* 28 Nov. 2/3 Intending competition will note that the chop is registered with the Australasian Axemen's Association. **1910** *Huon Times* (Franklin) 24 Dec. 5/2 On Monday two chops will be contested at the Geeveston sports. **1926** K.S. PRICHARD *Working Bullocks* 48 He hewed his way through tough logs as though he were out to beat the champion in a chop. *Ibid.* 84 One of the best axe-men in the sou'-west, Duck was champion in his day, and . . he still entered the chops. **1934** G. PORTER *Wanderings in Tas.* 267 A nation which can abbreviate trotting-matches into 'trots', and chopping-matches into 'chops'. **1945** *Coast to Coast 1944* 42 And the chops . . I'd like to see Whaka Green make the chips fly. **1983** *Daily Mirror* (Sydney) 19 Jan. 48/3 During the chop the coach stood near the log advising the chopper where to direct his blows.

Also **chopping match** *n. Tas. Obs.*

1896 J.B. WALKER Corresp., Chopping match. A favourite contest for bush men in Tasmania. **1899** *North-Western Advocate* (Devonport) 15 Feb. 2/7 A chopping match took place. **1910** *Huon Times* (Franklin) 26 Feb. 2/3 The conclusion of the chopping matches held in connection with the Hobart Carnival.

chop, *n.*[3] [Fig. use of *chop* a slice or cut of something.] A share (usu. of winnings); a gain or advantage.

1919 W.H. DOWNING *Digger Dialects* 16 *Chop*, share. 'To hop in for one's chop'—to enter in, in order to secure a privilege or benefit. **1949** L. GLASSOP *Lucky Palmer* 21 'Here's a fiver for you,' said Fred, handing Max five crumpled one pound notes. 'That's your chop.' **1952** T.A.G. HUNGERFORD *Ridge & River* 212 There's got to be leaders, so hop in for your chop. Think of the dough and the privileges. **1968** S. GORE *Holy Smoke* 60 That's them sorta blokes all over, when they see someone else might be gettin' a few bob for a change—can't hop in for their chop fast enough. **1977** R. BEILBY *Gunner* 296 The ring-keeper was desperate, prowling around the ring at intervals, beseeching: 'What about a litta chop from you tailies? Come on, ya've had a good run.' **1986** *Good Weekend* (Sydney) 19 Apr. 11/1 A stutter and some early illness made Norm's schooling . . an ordeal with the nuns using the strap liberally. 'They all had their chop,' he says.

chopper.

1. *Obs.* One taking part in a wood-chopping contest.

1901 *Axeman's Jrnl.* (Ulverstone) Sept. 44/2 If the West Coast champion can down the 'Duke's Own' chopper, he will be a strong favourite. **1904** *Sporting News* (Launceston) 3 Sept. 2/3 There are not wanting those who scoff at the idea of nobleness or any manly virtue being connected with work or play among the choppers. **1910** *Huon Times* (Franklin) 26 Feb. 2/3 The choppers had no opportunity, after finishing one event, of getting a 'rub down'.

2. [From the chopping movement of the fish's jaws, most noticeable when a school is feeding in an estuary.] A small TAILOR.

1969 J. POLLARD *Austral. & N.Z. Fishing* 793 Tailor are silvery white on the belly and pale green to greyish or bluish above. . . The half-grown fish generally are spoken of by anglers as 'choppers'. **1981** *Sunday Mail* (Brisbane) 6 Dec. 91/7 Tailor fishermen on the North Coast beaches have been pleasantly surprised by the run of 'choppers' which has shown up on most of the surf areas. **1984** *West Austral.* (Perth) 10 Feb. 40/6 Chopper tailor have been taken from Mosmans downstream and several reports have come in of bigger tailor to 1.5 kg. being caught at Blackwall Reach.

chop picnic. An outdoor meal at which (lamb) chops are cooked and served.

1948 G. FARWELL *Down Argent Street* 5 When the stores close, soon after midday, the crowd rapidly ebbs, shifting to sports grounds and dog-races . . chop picnics or an afternoon's drive in the bush. **1962** *Texas Q.* 173 We're all going for a chop picnic in the scrub. **1980** M. DUGAN *Early Dreaming* 42 My mother took me and my friends for chop picnics by a waterfall.

chough. [Transf. use of *chough* a large black bird in fam. Corvidae. The Austral. bird looks similar but is unrelated.] The predom. black bird *Corcorax melanorhamphus* (fam. Corcoracidae) of s.e. Aust., living in groups and building nests of mud. Also **white-winged chough.**

1846 J. GOULD *Birds of Aust.* (1848) IV. Pl. 16, The White-winged Chough is a very early breeder. **1855** *Trans. Philos. Soc. Vic.* I. 63 The white-winged chough, or black magpie . . throughout the whole year associates in groups of ten or fifteen. **1929** A.H. CHISHOLM *Birds & Green Places* 130 She [*sc.* a lyre-bird] . . laughed like a kookaburra . . and wailed like a chough. **1962** MARSHALL & DRYSDALE *Journey among Men* 178 The chough is a conspicuous black bird . . with an unmistakable white 'window pane' in each wing. **1979** DOUGLAS & HEATHCOTE *Far Cry* 116 Choughs can't nest in saplings, they need big trees.

Chow /tʃaʊ/.

1. [Abbrev. of CHOW CHOW.] A Chinese, esp. an immigrant or a descendant of an immigrant.

[N.Z. **1872** G.L. MEREDITH *Adv. in Maoriland* (1935) 22 The solitary Chinaman to take up his abode amongst the hardy Scots at Dunedin. . . This 'Chow' wanted to study economy.] **1876** *Queenslander* (Brisbane) 18 Mar. 13/2 Our colonialised 'Chinkie', as he is vulgarly termed (with the single variation 'Chow'). **1880** *Bulletin* (Sydney) 28 Aug. 13/4 Ah Noon shot a brother Chow at Bathurst. **1892** *Ibid.* 10 Sept. 19/2, I like a native, and I'll liquor with a nigger, But I hate the skin and colour of these sanguinary chows! **1903** *Truth* (Sydney) 18 Jan. 1/6 An irate Flossie hit a Chow on the head with a large lump of road metal, and drew the 'claret'. **1911** *Bulletin* (Sydney) 20 July 14/3 Chows did invade the place some years ago, when the silver city was booming . . but . . they were . . escorted to the boat again. **1921** *Smith's Weekly* (Sydney) 29 Jan. 9/5 Chows are law-abiding citizens. **1933** H.B. RAINE *Lash End* 50 The Chows even get white girls to go to their dens about Sydney. **1948** F. CLUNE *Wild Colonial Boys* 205 The white miners . . formed an Anti-Chinese League and invited the co-operation of mining communities everywhere in expelling the 'Chows' from Australia. **1962** T. RONAN *Deep of Sky* 38 You start brooding about that poor old Chow having fat horses while you've got poor ones. **1977** T.A.G. HUNGERFORD *Wong Chu* 25 'The Chows.' She emphasised the word, long discarded I imagine, except among Australians, in a way which whisked me straight to my boyhood in South Perth, and my mother saying: 'Go down the Chows and get me. . .'

2. The name of a type of playing marble.

1909 J.C.L. FITZPATRICK *When we were Boys Together*, His 'Alley tors' were the choicest, and his 'Chows' the best. **1945** M. RAYMOND *Smiley* 14 Two stonks were equivalent to a chalky marble called a chow. **1956** *Bulletin* (Sydney) 22 Aug. 13/1 Heard a couple of our old-timers reminiscing about marbles: 'Remember when we used to exchange chows for stonkers . . and trade conks for smokies?' said one old chap. **1977** R. MCKIE *Crushing* (1978) 107 'Glassies or Chows allowed, Doc?' 'Certainly not. I've only got alleys.'

chowchilla /tʃaʊ'tʃɪlə/. [Imitative of the call of *Orthonyx spaldingii.*] LOG-RUNNER 1, esp. *Orthonyx spaldingii.*

1909 *Emu* VIII. 251 Other names given to different birds by the local aborigines are as follow . . Black-headed Log-runner ('Chow-chilla') [etc.]. **1934** A.H. CHISHOLM *Bird Wonders Aust.* 206 Settlers in northern Queensland know the Black-headed Logrunner . . as the 'Chow-chilla', since they say, a company of the birds freely shouts, 'Chow-chilla-chow-chow, Chowy-chook-chook, Chowy-chook-chook!' **1945** C. BARRETT *Austral. Bird Life* 135 The old name, 'spinetail', has been replaced by 'chowchilla', suggested by the curious notes uttered by the log-runners. **1973** S. & K. BREEDEN *Wildlife Eastern Aust.* 55 Chowchillas are dark brown birds, round in shape but also with very strong feet and legs. The male Chowchilla has a white throat, that of the female is orange.

Chow Chow /'tʃaʊtʃaʊ/. *Obs.* [Transf. use of *chow chow* a mixture or medley of any sort, e.g. mixed pickles: see OED *sb.*] A Chinese.

1864 C.R. THATCHER *Invercargill Minstrel* 72 Chow Chow his hands with glee did rub, 'Cause he'd washed out a halfpennyweight to the tub. **1869** 'E. HOWE' *Boy in Bush* 215 The Jerry's Town youngsters were pelting the Chinaman . . meanwhile shouting 'Chow-chow!' **1879** 'AUSTRALIAN' *Adventures Qld.* 38 Then I tell him, 'what for you *momkoll* Chow Chow?'

Chrissy. Also **Chrissie.** [f. *Chris(tmas* + -Y.] Christmas. Also *attrib.*

1966 S.J. BAKER *Austral. Lang.* (ed. 2) 372 *Chrissie*, Christmas. Whence *Chrissie prezzie*, Christmas present. **1971** *Kings Cross Whisper* (Sydney) cxvii. 5/2 The missing bag contains . . a beautifully gift-wrapped Chrissy present. **1974** *Bulletin* (Sydney) 30 Apr. 6/1 Was this article a prezzie for Chrissie to your readers in Australia? **1977** E. MACKIE *Oh to be Aussie* 42 If the trainee Aussie didn't get a chance to go broke over Chrissie, he can do it now—taking the wife and kids on holidays (they don't say holi*day* here), camping or caravanning.

Christmas. Used *attrib.* in Special Comb. designating flora and fauna, etc. associated with Christmas time: **Christmas beetle,** any of several scarab beetles of the genus *Anoplognathus*, so-called because the adults emerge in summer; **bells,** any of several species of the grass-like plant *Blandfordia* (fam. Liliaceae) of N.S.W., s.e. Qld., and Tas., so called from the abundance of their brightly-coloured red and yellow flowers (see quot. 1896); **billy,** see BILLY *n.*[1] 4; **bush** (or **tree**), **(a)** any of several unrelated trees or shrubs known for their decorative qualities, esp. (*N.S.W.*) *Ceratopetalum gummiferum* (fam. Cunoniaceae), the calyx lobes of which enlarge and turn deep pink in summer and (*Tas.* and *Vic.*) the aromatic summer-flowering *Prostanthera lasianthos* (fam. Lamiaceae); **(b)** *W.A.* the semi-parasitic arborescent mistletoe *Nuytsia floribunda* (fam. Loranthaceae) of s.w. W.A., bearing bright orange flowers (see quot. 1937); **eye,** see quot.; **hold** (or **grip**), see quot. 1953.

1932 *Bulletin* (Sydney) 27 Jan. 21/4 The various heavy-bodied flying beetles—the coleopt known in Australia as the '**Christmas beetle**' is notorious for it— . . deliberately butt their heads into every obstruction. **1966** R. MORLEY *Cool Change* 37 The drumming of the cicadas pulsated through the night air; and the busy Christmas-beetles zoomed into the window panes. **1980** S. ORR *Roll On* 59 You could still find Christmas beetles in the heart of the city. **1896** J.H. MAIDEN *Flowering Plants & Ferns N.S.W.* 51 Large **Christmas bells** . . Vernacular name.—Originally given, of course, because these beautiful flowers were to be seen during the Christmas season. **1911** A. MACK *Bush Days* 20 Christmas bells and Christmas bush are to the Australian what holly and mistletoe are to the Englishman . . emblems of the season of happiness. **1933** H.J. CARTER *Gulliver in Bush* 38 The lovely Christmas bells (*Blandfordia*) that occur sparsely throughout our sandstone areas. **1947** MRS A.H. GARNSEY *Romance Huon River* 30, I think Tasmania claims this beauty as her own—also the specially large and brilliant red and orange blandfordia or Christmas bells. **1962** R. ROBINSON *Deep Well* 48 The little fires of the Christmas-bells. **1980** M. DUGAN *Early Dreaming* 43 It was a story about a park ranger's children attempting to protect the Christmas bells in their sanctuary from flower thieves. **(a) 1817** A. CUNNINGHAM in I. Marriott *Early Explorers Aust.* 8 Mar. (1925) 171 Ceratopetalum gummiferum (**Christmas Bush**). **1838** J. MARTIN *Austral. Sketch Bk.* 264 'Christmas bushes' are plucked from a beautiful tree which is now becoming scarce in the vicinity of our towns. **1865** G.F. ANGAS *Aust.* 123 The 'Christmas bush', a pretty evergreen shrub, with masses of pink blossom, is used in New South Wales instead of holly, as a decoration at Christmas. **1881** E. DAVIES *Story Earnest*

Life 379 The Christmas tree, so called because of its use in decorations at their season, is laden with small crimson flowers. **1914** E.E. PESCOTT *Native Flowers Vic.* 33 'Sweet Bursaria' . . is called in many localities the 'Christmas Bush'. **1933** *Bulletin* (Sydney) 15 Nov. 20/3 The Christmas-bush got its name in Governor Macquarie's time. The regiment stationed in Sydney took great pride in the decoration of their mess on December 25, and a species of brilliant red flower was set aside for their especial use. This flower was known first as 'officers' bush' and later as 'officers' Christmas-bush'. **1953** *New Settler in W.A.* (Perth) Dec. 3 In the Eastern States there is the brilliant Australian Christmas bush in all its crimson loveliness. **1980** J. WOLFE *End of Pricklystick* 30 The flowering of the delicate Christmas Bush with its trumpet flowers and fine, fresh scent of peppermint told the people . . that the warm weather had at last arrived. **(b) 1901** M. VIVIENNE *Travels in W.A.* 65 A handsome painting of the Nutsyia [*sic*] fire-tree, or **Christmas-bush.** **1937** R. FAIRBRIDGE *Pinjarra* 196 The Christmas Tree, a queer parasite of the Mistletoe tribe, growing on roots, but reaching a height of 20 feet or so, which in December bursts forth into a startling blaze of bright orange blossom. **1946** 'A. SPENCE' *Mystery of Red Gum* 31 The first thing to meet her eye was the orange Christmas tree. **1968** V. SERVENTY *Southern Walkabout* 120 There are mistletoes, most of which grow on trees but one stands on its own trunk and flowers in early summer. This is called the Christmas tree, and its blackened trunk often disappears under a great golden blaze of blossom. **1972** B. FULLER *West of Bight* 3 He jerked a thumb at a Christmas Tree, . . just then a bonfire of orange-gold colour. **1984** *Canberra Times* 22 Sept. 11/2 The unpleasant habits of larvae of the steel-blue sawfly, or 'spitfires'. . . A sticky secretion from their mouths . . was high in eucalyptus oil and caused severe pain if it got into the eyes. . . The secretions made the eyeball bloodshot—a condition called **Christmas Eye.** **1953** S.J. BAKER *Aust. Speaks* 132 **Christmas hold,** a hold applied by grabbing an opponent's testicles (a 'handful of nuts'). **1956** T. RONAN *Moleskin Midas* 115 I'll do my time willin' if I can get a Christmas hold on him for half a minute first. **1964** —— *Packhorse & Pearling Boat* 126 Joe came in low, looking for that grip which the west-coast blackfellow learned from that other clean fighter, the Jap: The Christmas hold (the handful of nuts). **1981** *Weekend Austral. Mag.* (Sydney) 2 May 7/1 A woman in a dental surgery lying on the dentist's couch, put the Christmas grip on the dentist. When the dentist winced with pain, as anyone would wince if a Christmas grip were put upon him, she said, 'We are not going to hurt each other are we, Mr Dentist?'

chromo /'kroʊmoʊ/. [Fig. use of *chromo*, abbrev. of *chromolithograph* a picture lithographed in colours, with reference to the painted face of the prostitute.] A prostitute. Also **chrome.**

1883 *Bulletin* (Sydney) 19 May 11/4 'That fellow is so highly colored that he reminds me of a chromo,' remarked a man of a schnapper-nosed, dissipated-looking creature in a marine suburb. **1932** D.B. O'CONNOR *Belle of Barrine* 4 The harvests of our heritage are squandered by absentee bosses and their chromos in the casinos of Europe. **1951** D. STIVENS *Jimmy Brockett* 125 If you get stuck, I've got a good address for you. She's a chromo, but the goods. Dark and plump. **1960** J. IGGULDEN *Storms of Summer* 297 Some rotten poxy bitch of a chromo dobbed them in. **1977** T. RONAN *Mighty Men on Horseback* 65 He'd butted into some big bloke who had a chromo in tow.

chuck, *v.* [Colloq. substitution for *throw.*]

1. In the phr. **to chuck off,** see *throw off* THROW *v.* 2.

1901 *Bulletin Story Bk.* 147 Aggie 'chucked off' in a particularly nasty way at the porter at Cheltenham. **1913** *Bulletin* (Sydney) 21 Aug. 18/4 The bushy doesn't 'chuck off' at the Englishman for his habit of doing without a bathroom. **1915** C.J. DENNIS *Songs of Sentimental Bloke* 22 Me! that 'as barracked tarts . . An' chucked orf at 'em like a phonergraft! **1916** 'MEN OF ANZAC' *Anzac Bk.* 31 Sometimes one of 'em gets 'is back up and calls us sons of convicts in return for chuckin' off at 'im. **1922** A. WRIGHT *Boss o' Yedden* 140 'What y' chuckin' off about?' he growled. **1958** A.E. MANNING *Bodgie* 76 Virtue *may* be its own reward, but it's a poor reward if your friends 'chuck off' at you for being a 'goodie-goodie'. **1959** D. HEWETT *Bobbin Up* 150 She waddled away . . grinning at the good-humoured chucking off from the spinners and the reelers.

2. *trans.* To bring (something) up, to vomit. Also *absol.*

1957 D. NILAND *Call me when Cross turns Over* 53 Get a feed into you, and then you want to chuck it up again. You chuck it up and your right as pie till you eat again. And so it goes on. **1968** *Swag* (Sydney) i. 18 The Pommy bird woke up and chucked all over the multicoloured woollen blanket. **1970** *Kings Cross Whisper* (Sydney) lxxxviii. 2/3, I say drunkenness . . is the ideal solution to drug-taking. No one will want to experiment with dangerous drugs when they've got their heads down a toilet bowl chucking their guts up. **1972** G. MORLEY *Jockey rides Honest Race* 73 It's enough to make a bloke want to chuck. **1977** W. MOORE *Just to Myself* 53 He nearly chucked everywhere.

chuck, *n.* [See prec.] Vomit; an act of vomiting. Also *attrib.*

1966 *Kings Cross Whisper* (Sydney) Apr. 2/5 He sat down in the gutter to have a bit of a chuck and flaked out. **1972** *Bulletin* (Sydney) 5 Feb. 31/1 The chunder/ chuck/technicolor yawn sequences are in the planning stages. **1976** McDONALD & HARDING *Norman Gunston's Finest Moments* 12 Were there chuck stains around the toilet?

chuckie, var. CHOOK 1.

chuck in. [See CHUCK *v.* and cf. *to throw in* to put in as a supplement or makeweight.] A bit of luck; a bonus.

[N.Z. **1912** *N.Z. Truth* (Wellington) 11 May 4 Fancy landing thousands of the starving humans from Bull's country. . . What a chuck-in for the local squatters!] **1916** Tas. Non-State Rec. 103/11 Apr., Bound for the Soudan . . and if so their job would be no chuck in. **1920** *Land of Lyre Bird* (S. Gippsland Pioneers' Assoc.) 26 It was a 'chuck in' to strike a big fallen tree lying in the right direction, as you would get easy walking on top of it. **1961** D. STUART *Driven* 101 This was a real chuck-in for old Charlie.

chucky, var. CHOOK 1.

chuff, var. CHOOF.

chum. [Shortened form of NEW CHUM *n.* 2.] A recently arrived immigrant. Also **chummy.**

1846 *Britannia* (Hobart) 28 May 3/2 I'm the flashest, fliest chum upon the Derwent River. **1846** C.P. HODGSON *Reminisc. Aust.* 366 'Hand', synonymous with 'Chum'; not elegant appellations, but very significant. **1887** A. NICOLS *Wild Life & Adventure* 191 Hi, chummy, didn't quite know where you was jist now, did yer? **1889** *Bulletin* (Sydney) 15 June 13/4 Chummy scorns that ancient maxim, 'Do as Romans when in Rome', Oft avers—tho' no one ax him—'That's not how its done at home.' **1911** A. SEARCY *By Flood & Field* 299 This . . was not the only 'Colonial experience' the 'chum' had secured since starting. **1923** *Austral.* (Sydney) Mar. 24 Even if I did get thrown off like a 'chummy', I rode like a dinkum Australian. **1934** 'S. RUDD' *Green Grey Homestead* 65 You've . . heard the chums in the migrant colony over on the plain murmuring like a remnant of Philistines despairing. **1953** G. PIKE *Campfire Tales* (1981) 44 After we arrived at Atherton, all the money my father had left was enough to buy a ton of iron for our home to be, and being 'chums', we brought nothing with us.

chunder /'tʃʌndə/, *v.* [Prob. f. rhyming slang *Chunder Loo* for 'spew', after a cartoon figure *Chunder Loo of Akim Foo* orig. drawn by Norman Lindsay (1879–1969), and appearing in advertisements for Cobra boot polish in the Sydney *Bulletin* between 1909 and 1920.] *intr.* To vomit.

[**1914** *Geelong Racer: Paper of Troopship 'Geelong'* 29 Oct. 2 At the sign of the three onions Uncle Chunder the well known financier is prepared to do business. **1917** *Rabaul Rec.* 1 Aug. 5 They envy the cut o' me, and all make a butt o' me And sing out 'Hullo, Chunder-Loo.' **1918** *Kia Ora Coo-ee* June 15/1 My guide ('Chunder') halted before a low, squalid-looking mud hut.] **1950** 'N. SHUTE' *Town like Alice* 76 The way these bloody Nips go on. Makes you chunda. **1964** B. HUMPHRIES *Nice Night's Entertainment* (1981) 77 When I'd swallowed the last prawn I had a Technicolor yawn And I chundered in the old Pacific sea. **1965** *Times Lit. Suppl.* (London) 16 Sept. 812/2 His favourite word to describe the act of involuntary regurgitation is the verb to chunder. This word is not in popular currency in Australia, but the writer recalls that ten years ago it was common in Victoria's more expensive public schools. It is now used by the Surfies. . . I understand, by the way, that the word derives from a nautical expression 'watch under', an ominous courtesy shouted from the upper decks for the protection of those below. **1967** J. HIBBERD *White with Wire Wheels* (1970) 154 The man who can count the number of times he's chundered on one hand. **1976** *Bulletin* (Sydney) 28 Feb. 24/3 Newly-elected Federal MPs should celebrate their triumph by 'chundering' over the stern bronze statue of George V which graces the hall of Parliament House. **1978** R. MACKLIN *Newsfront* 100 On the eighth loop-the-loop the poor bugger couldn't take it any more and he chundered—urrh—right in me ear, and all down me collar. **1985** *Austral. Short Stories* xi. 42 And lamb chops and fluffy kenebecs drooling melted butter have been known to make me chunder!

2. *transf.* and *fig.* Also *trans.*

1968 B. HUMPHRIES *Wonderful World Barry McKenzie*, Hey Bazza? You chundering off [*sc.* departing] already! **1971** *Bulletin* (Sydney) 17 Apr. 40/1 Ellis with gum-ache, . . Boddy bilious, his candy-striped jeep chundering petrol all over Waverley. **1979** CAREY & LETTE *Puberty Blues* 117, I paddled out first. Sue couldn't stop laughing at me slipping off and getting chundered [*sc.* thrown into the sea].

Hence **chunderer** *n.*

1967 F. HARDY *Billy Borker yarns Again* 61, I know a better yarn called 'The Champion Chunderer from Cooper's Creek'. **1968** B. HUMPHRIES *Wonderful World Barry McKenzie*, We've been after the Brompton *chunderer* for a long time. We knew he'd go too far with the sweet corn one of these days.

chunder /'tʃʌndə/, *n.* [f. prec.] Vomit; an act of vomiting. Also *attrib.*

1960 G. TAYLOR *Crop Dusters* 111 Chunder-yellow. You couldn't miss it unless you were colour-blind. **1967** F. HARDY *Billy Borker yarns Again* 37 One of the boys asked him about the chunder and the Gargler says modestly: 'I never chundered in my life; I put it down and keep it down.' **1969** A. BUZO *Front Room Boys* (1970) 64 I'm a . . a white collar office employee. . . Oh God, bring me the chunder-bucket. **1970** *Private Eye* (London) 10 Apr. 16 Youse can bet your life Pom dogs have rolled around in stuff a lot worse than a nice fresh chunder! **1980** C. KELEN *Punks Travels* 40 Wiping the chunder from his mouth.

Hence **chunderous, chundersome** *adjs.*, sickening; revolting.

1967 F. HARDY *Billy Borker yarns Again* 66 'Yodeller, me old chunderous mate,' he says. **1971** *Kings Cross Whisper* (Sydney) cii. 3/2 Chunderous new telly series. Anglo-Australian film interests are planning their biggest venture yet—Coronation Street Meets Bellbird. **1971** *Bulletin* (Sydney) 4 Dec. 11/2 The Poms are rapacious, mean, cunning. Bazza is beery, chundersome, anal.

churinga /tʃə'rɪŋgə/. Also **tjuringa.** [a. Aranda *tywerrenge.*]

1. A sacred object of Aboriginal ceremonial (but see also quots. 1886 and 1917). Also *attrib.*

1886 *Proc. R. Geogr. Soc. Australasia: S.A.* (1890) 34 Every festival is called 'tjurunga'. They speak, for instance, of an 'emu tjurunga', a 'kangaroo tjurunga'. **1896** B. SPENCER *Rep. Horn Sci. Exped. Central Aust.* IV. 76 Ceremonial sticks and stones. Under this head I deal with a class of objects of some symbolic import which are common to a large group of natives in the interior. Concerning them a good deal of secrecy and mystery exists among the blacks, and very little has been said, or seems to be known of their true significance. Collectively, the term 'Churiña' is applied to them in the Arunta (Gillen). **1897** *Proc. R. Soc. Vic.* 24 Every alcheringa man and woman carried about a large number of the sacred churinga. **1912** SPENCER & GILLEN *Across Aust.* 22 Churinga is the name given to certain special objects possessed by the old mythic ancestors and hence regarded as sacred. **1917** M.W. JAMES *'Coo-ee' Call* 21 *'Churinga'* is an Aboriginal expression meaning 'Good Luck'. **1928** B. SPENCER *Wanderings in Wild Aust.* 274 The word *Churinga* is used both as a substantive and as a qualifying term. Anything associated with the totemic ancestors, a shield, a boomerang or a stone knife, anything, in fact, that they used or possessed is spoken of as being Churinga. **1935** H. BASEDOW

Knights of Boomerang 33 Then Romeo retires a short distance . . and softly swings a tjuringa, which at the final ceremony of his initiation, was dipped in the blood he lost during the operation. **1944** M.J. O'Reilly *Bowyangs & Boomerangs* 144 He is given his Tjuringa, which has been dipped in the blood of his circumcision. This is the most precious thing a black fellow possesses—he never parts with it. It is an oval-shaped piece of flat wood, only about six inches long with totem marks on it. **1950** G. Farwell *Surf Music* 13 If someone spoke of the river, his thin lips tightened. . . It was his churinga, the touchstone of his faith, not to be profaned by the currency of everyday speech. **1963** I.L. Idriess *Our Living Stone Age* 192 Churinga sticks . . are the sacred records of the tribe and the individuals within it, the symbols of their spiritual life, and are looked upon with great reverence. **1974** D. Ireland *Burn* 53 They have no tjuringa, no sacred stone to hold the spirits of their ancestors. **1981** Q. Wild *Honey Wind* 168 Mysterious, even 'holy' patterns, whorls and circles of the kind identified with the sacred Aboriginal Tjuringa.

2. Comb. **churinga stone.**

1933 W. Hatfield *Desert Saga* 26 He went then to the *ertnalunga* on Gallinanna Creek, the cave wherein lay the *churinga* stones, personal talismans of all the men in the tribe. **1936** L. Kaye *Black Wilderness* 114 Lex . . saw the *churinga* stones and the cutting stones and the witch doctor's stock in trade, and he knew that he trespassed on sacred ground. **1944** A.W. Upfield *No Footprints in Bush* 196 Here were kept the tribe's churinga stones, the head of the sacred pole decorated with bird's down and hair alleged to have belonged to the tribe's Alchuringa ancestor, bull-roarers and other sacred objects. **1959** —— *Bony & Black Virgin* 222 Now you go outside and rub your churinga stones against your forehead, and think up a yarn I can send down to the Aborigines Department.

chute, var. Shoot *n.*

chyack, var. Chiack *n.* and *v.*

cider gum. Any of several trees of the genus *Eucalyptus* (fam. Myrtaceae), esp. the Tas. tree *E. gunnii*, yielding a sweet potable sap. Also **cider tree.**

1826 *Colonial Times* (Hobart) 15 Apr., The tree called the cider tree by the stock keepers . . exudes a rich saccharine juice, capable of making wine or spirits. **1846** *Tasmanian Jrnl. Nat. Sci.* II. 140 On the Western Range there is a species of the *Eucalyptus* called the cider tree. . . The cider, or sap of the tree, has an agreeable subacid taste. **1857** D. Bunce *Australasiatic Reminisc.* 47 The *Eucalyptus resinifera*, or cider tree . . yields a quantity of slightly saccharine liquor, resembling treacle, which the stock keepers were in the habit of extracting, and using as a kind of drink. . . When allowed to remain any length of time, it ferments and settles into a coarse sort of wine or cider, rather intoxicating if drank to excess. **1903** *Tasmanian Timbers* (Tas. Lands & Survey Dept.) 20 *Cider gum* . . named from its sweet sap . . is rather a branching tree. **1920** *Bulletin* (Sydney) 16 Dec. 20/2 In districts only a few miles apart the cider-gum . . is identified as the swamp-gum, river-gum and white-gum. **1975** G. Blainey *Triumph of Nomads* 174 George Robinson had been travelling with Tasmanian aboriginals for almost two years before he saw them tap a cider tree in the early summer of 1831.

cigarette swag. A small swag, so called because of its size and shape (see Swag *n.* 1). Also **cigarette-paper swag.**

1938 J.F.W. Schulz *Destined to Perish* 33 Jack had brought a somewhat diminutive swag, a cigarette swag, as I was told later. **1946** *Bulletin* (Sydney) 2 Jan. 12/2 A kid of about 16 drifted to their fire. He had a cigarette swag and was pretty shy. **1953** L. & C. Rees *Spinifex Walkabout* 36 Ours was only what was known in these parts as a 'cigarette-paper swag', a light American ground-sheet and a blanket apiece, with an extra blanket and a tiny pillow for the lady. **1959** D. Stuart *Yandy* 16 He had been camped in the river with a cigarette swag and almost no tucker. **1975** X. Herbert *Poor Fellow my Country* 1016 He opened swag and suitcase and rolled bare necessities in the former, to make what was called a Cigarette Swag, fixing a towel through the straps for easy carrying. **1977** T. Ronan *Mighty Men on Horseback* 15, I noticed a bloke drifting along from the homestead way leading a cigarette swag.

cigger /'sɪgə/. [Shortened form.] A cigarette.

1922 A. Wright *Colt from Country* 78 'Wait till I get you a cigger,' said Bucks; 'I knew y'c'd do a smoke.' **1925** —— *Boy from Bullarah* 24 A fellow 'broke' approached, and reclining nearby requested a 'cigger'. Terry threw him his almost empty box of cheap smokes. **1967** *Kings Cross Whisper* (Sydney) xxxiii. 4/3 *Cigger*, a cigarette. **1973** R. Hall *Poems from Prison* 40 Last night as we enjoyed a quiet cigger, The stars reflecting open life outback, The knack we had of mateship was much bigger.

citizen. A civilian trained for military service in the event of a national emergency. Chiefly *attrib.*

1903 *Act* (Cwlth. of Aust.) no. 20 Sect. 30, The Defence Force shall consist of the Naval and Military Forces of the Commonwealth, and shall be divided into two branches called the Permanent Forces and the Citizen Forces. **1909** *Ibid.* no. 15 Sect. 6, The Citizen Military Forces shall consist of Active Forces and Reserve Forces. **1919** Fletcher & Hills *Conscription under Camouflage* 32 The citizen soldier is liable to be tried and punished by court-martial. *Ibid.* 48 Senator Dobson . . had been advocating for years—conscription, under the pretty title of Citizen Army. **1937** *Citizen Soldier Aust.* Oct. 31/1 There are few members of society, who have had in recent years, so many slurs and insults to contend with as the Citizen Soldier. **1944** C. Wilmot *Tobruk* 109 Morshead is a citizen-soldier in the Monash tradition. **1958** *Austral. Encycl.* VI. 81 On 31st May 1930, as the result of a vigorous recruiting campaign, the militia (as the citizen forces were renamed) numbered 29,334 in all ranks. **1964** *Act* (Cwlth. of Aust.) no. 92 Sect. 15, The Military Forces of the Commonwealth consist of two parts, namely, the Permanent Military Forces and the Citizen Military Forces. **1968** K. Denton *Walk around my Cluttered Mind* 183 About a year after I arrived in Australia I joined the part-timers, the Citizen Military Forces.

city of churches. Adelaide, the capital city of South Australia.

1873 A. Trollope *Aust. & N.Z.* II. 184, I have said that Adelaide has been called a city of churches. **1892** *Quiz* (Adelaide) 25 Mar. 7/2, 30 miles . . from the city of churches. **1909** *Truth* (Sydney) 1 Aug. 9/2 Not for nothing has Adelaide been called 'The City of Churches'. **1916** *Astra* (Melbourne) May 6/1 Adelaide . . the 'City of Churches'. **1937** D. Glass *Austral. Fantasy* 96 Adelaide should need no subtitle, but it is sometimes christened 'City of Churches'. **1956** S. Hope *Diggers' Paradise* 66 Adelaide is sometimes referred to as the 'city of churches'. **1983** J. Hepworth *Great Austral. Cities, Adelaide.* Supposed to be the 'City of Churches', but actually a city as sinful as they come.

civilize, *v. Hist. trans.* To impose upon (an Aboriginal people) a way of life alien to them. Also *absol.*

1827 P. Cunningham *Two Yrs. in N.S.W.* I. 134 We trust a strong injunction will be laid on every settler to abstain from all aggression or insult of the natives, who are described as a stately healthy race, easy to be civilized. **1893** S. Newland *Paving Way* 64 We found them a happy, healthy people; and wherever we have come in contact with them, in less than fifty years we have civilised them off the face of the land. **1901** C. Moynihan *Feast of Bunya* 17 As a set-off to the method of 'civilizing' practised by a bumptious, self-assertive class of pioneer-squatters. **1913** C.J. Dennis *Backblock Ballads* 154 They landed with some rum and Bibles and a gun or two, And started out to 'civilize', as whites are apt to do. **1916** 'T.O. Lingo' *Austral. Comic Dict.* 54 *Civilizing the Blacks*, presenting them with appendicitis, laryngitis, meningitis, and every other cultivated 'itis', and then wondering why they try to fight us, and to bite us.

civilized, *ppl. a. Hist.* Of an Aboriginal: having adapted to (some aspects of) the European way of life. See also Domesticated, Tame.

1843 C. Rowcroft *Tales of Colonies* III. 143 The civilized natives soon catching the colonial predilection for cloth of a superior quality. ***c* 1849** *Aust., Van Diemen's Land, & N.Z.* 25 They despatched an agent with a number of articles to give in exchange to the natives, together with seven civilized aborigines as interpreters. **1849** A. Harris *Emigrant Family* (1967) 39 A wandering tribe of natives pitched their camp. They were what are called 'civilized blacks'—one of the tribes who had been for several years in connection with the Europeans. **1857** J. Bonwick *Early Days Melbourne* 8 John Batman, and his seven civilized Sydney blacks. **1872** *Illustr. Sydney News* 28 Sept. 15/1 Not even a 'civilised Jacky' who, with a great deal of persistent loquacity, endeavours to make known that he is 'budgeree fellow'. **1886** F.A. Hagenauer *Rep. Aboriginal Mission Ramahyuck, Vic.* 14 At the Ravenswood and Charters Towers junction we met some so-called civilized blacks. **1900** T. Major *Leaves from Squatter's Note Bk.* 29 A civilized New South Wales black fellow named Jerry. **1920** *Smith's Weekly* (Sydney) 28 Aug. 9/4 When Sub-inspector Kaye was killed by warrigals near Woolgar diggings 40 odd years ago, civilised blacks on stations 100 miles away knew of it in less than 12 hours. **1935** R.B. Plowman *Boundary Rider* 224 His assistants were only partly civilized black boys.

claim. [Spec. use of (orig. U.S.) *claim.*]

1. A piece of land formally claimed and taken up for mining purposes. Also with distinguishing epithet, as **amalgamated, bed, creek, extended, reward** (see under first element).

1851 J.H. Burton *Emigrant's Man.* 121 Numerous claims have already been marked out, and the indications of the plentiful presence of the coveted metal are said to be unmistakable. **1852** J.E. Erskine *Short Acct. Late Discoveries Gold* 93 One or two *prospectors* were . . washing the soil, previous to fixing upon a *claim*, which is the name given to each man's or party's allotted portion of ground. **1856** S.C. Brees *How to farm & settle in Aust.* 57 The official regulations had . . been altered, as to allowance of surface, from eight feet square to twelve per man, four such 'claims' being permitted together to any one party consisting of at least four licensed individuals. **1862** H. Brown *Vic. as I found It* 151 Their claim (as the piece of ground they mine on is called) may be jumped. **1881** G.C. Evans *Stories* 11 Handsome George obtained a large amount of gold from the claim. ***c* 1882** T.F. de C. Browne *Miners' Handy Bk.* (ed. 2) 2 'Claim'—The portion of Crown land which any person or number of persons shall lawfully have taken possession of, and be entitled to occupy, by virtue of his miner's right or their miners' rights, for the purpose of mining therein for gold, or any number of such portions lawfully amalgamated by the holders. **1895** A.C. Bicknell *Travel & Adventure Northern Qld.* 50 He was lucky and struck a good claim, and having made his small pile, he determined to leave gold mining alone. **1916** A. Wilson *Lays & Tales of Mines* 65 Bill Scott and his son Bob . . had a 'claim' up Gum Creek way, in West Australia. **1944** M.J. O'Reilly *Bowyangs & Boomerangs* 11 A Reward Claim is granted to a prospector for finding new ground carrying payable gold, outside a specified distance from an existent goldfield. **1978** B. Oakley *Ship's Whistle* (1979) 37 Any more of that, and you'll get a whiff of grapeshot. Back to your claims! Do some work for a change!

2. *transf.* and *fig.*

1918 *Bulletin* (Sydney) 30 May 24/1 One night a red-backed spider pegged out a claim in the corner of my stable.

3. Special Comb. **claim holder,** the holder of a mining claim; **jumper,** Jumper *n.*[3]; also **jumping** *vbl. n.*

1853 A. Mackay *Great Gold Field* 49 **Claim holders** who wish to be employed on the work are to have preference over strangers. **1862** J.A. Patterson *Gold Fields Vic.* 49 One claimholder on the reef . . is strongly impressed. **1884** *Goldfield's Reminisc.* 120 The claim-holders . . were extremely shy of giving information. **1944** M.J. O'Reilly *Bowyangs & Boomerangs* 28 Not a colour could we find. All the other claim-holders seemed to be in the same boat. **1891** 'Smiler' *Wanderings Simple Child* (ed. 3) 167 A band of **claim 'jumpers'** had been at work and had secured all the best shows in that part of the field. **1913** W.K. Harris *Outback in Aust.* 165 The Parsonage household decided that 'The Long 'Un' and I were 'claim-jumpers'. **1863** *Bell's Life in Sydney* 3 Oct. 3/1 **Claim jumping** extraordinary. On Thursday afternoon a very extraordinary case of jumping a claim. **1892** T. Bracken *Dear Old Bendigo* 17 In 1857, a shindy over some claim-jumping business occurred at Long Gully. **1923** M.B. Petersen *Jewelled Nights* 66 There never has been any claim-jumping down here.

clamper. Pin-bullock.

1904 *Bulletin* (Sydney) 15 Dec. 40/1 Eighteen to twenty constitute a team, which includes polers—those nearest the waggon—clampers, body bullocks and leaders. **1968** L. Braden *Bullockies* 34 A bullock team is comprised of . . clampers, which are hooked onto a clamp at the end of the pole [etc.]. **1980** O. RUHEN *Bullock Teams* 172 On a crest of a road the pull of the bullocks ahead could put an increasing strain on each pair of body-bullocks as they topped it, culminating in that borne by the pin-bullocks; and many animals suffered death or a lesser permanent injury from this factor. Because of this pin-bullocks were often referred to as 'the clampers'.

clan. a. *Hist.* A name applied by the colonists to an Aboriginal community. **b.** A group of Aboriginal people of common descent. Also *attrib.*

1837 E. FRASER *Narr. of Capture* 14 We reached a cluster of inhabited tents of huts of another and more numerous clan of savages. **1865** G.S. LANG *Aborigines of Aust.* 10 The Moreton Bay blacks led me to understand that they were divided into four clans. **1868** J.K. TUCKER *Aborigines & Chinese Question* 10 Beside the shores of the Coorong, a few years ago, there were separate clans or tribes of the aborigines who were often engaged in war. **1885** A.W. HOWITT *Jeraeil* 301 The gathering of four clans of the Kurnai tribe who participated in these ceremonies was preceded by long consultations between the elders of the clan in which the initiative was taken. **1904** —— *Native Tribes S.-E. Aust.* 43 In order to prevent confusion between the lesser division of each of these different organisations of the tribe, the term 'clan' is used for the subdivision of a tribe which has descent in the male line, and 'horde' for that in which there is female descent. **1930** *Official Yearbk. Cwlth.* 692 The clans were again divided into lesser groups of people and each had its own definite tract of good country and food grounds. **1950** A.P. ELKIN *Art in Arnhem Land* 27 Living on cycad-nut bread; sitting there with white-stained fingers. Sitting there resting, those people of the sandfly clan. **1961** *Oceania* XXXII. 86 When at last they came near his clan-country two or three men went ahead, carrying a ceremonial spear. **1985** I. WHITE et al. *Fighters & Singers* 140 She painstakingly participated in painting clan designs with ochre on the young men—a very unusual and probably new role for a woman.

clap stick. An Aboriginal percussion instrument; MUSIC STICK: see quot. 1952. Usu. in *pl.* Also **clapping sticks.**

1952 R.M. BERNDT *Djanggawul* 310 Clapping sticks, sometimes called *bilma*: two sticks of resonant wood clapped together by a singing man, while another man blows on the drone pipe. **1979** A. WELLS *Forests are their Temples* 45 The old man, seated on the ground, began to clap his music-sticks for quietness. Then verse by verse he told the story while the clap-sticks marked each quiet pause between. **1980** L.G. FOGARTY *Kargun* 7 Dancing till sun alights the clap-sticks. **1984** *N.T. News* (Darwin) 22 Sept. 3/4 For those of you who aren't versed in Aboriginal instruments, the didjerido is a rhythmical instrument used in accompaniment with clap sticks during ceremonies and rituals.

claret ash. The ornamental ash tree *Fraxinus oxycarpa* cv. Raywood (fam. Oleaceae), orig. cultivated in S.A., and having purplish-red autumn leaves.

1934 H. SARGEANT *Flowering Trees & Shrubs* 77 Raywoodii is the purple or claret Ash. **1948** E.E. LORD *Shrubs & Trees* 84 One of the finest of all Australian-raised ornamental trees, the Claret Ash is a product of a South Australian nursery and was sent to London and named at Kew Gardens. **1962** L.D. PRYOR *Trees in Canberra* 97 *Fraxinus oxycarpa* 'Raywoodii' . . is apparently a horticultural selection from seedlings on *F. oxycarpa*, and is commonly called Claret Ash. **1980** R.F. BRISSENDEN *Whale in Darkness* 45 The dripping pinoaks and the claret ash Burn with the first fires of autumn.

class, *n. Hist.* A division of the convict population of a penal colony, graded according to the severity of the punishment to be undergone. Chiefly with distinguishing first element, as **crime, first, second, third,** etc.

1824 Tas. Colonial Secretary's Office Rec. 1/40 164, I was placed in the first Class in the Penitentiary on the Establishment of Classes by His Honor the late Lieut. Governor. **1829** *Ibid.* 1/32 198, It has to supply not only the Washerwomen belonging to the Assignable Class, but also those in the Crime Class with hot water. **1830** *Sydney Monitor* 6 Feb. 2/2 She having lately been condemned to third class . . her auburn locks were shorn or shaven off her fair head. **1831** *Sydney Herald* 9 May 3/2 Kate Pitt . . was sentenced to learn manners in the third class of the factory for six weeks. **1833** H.W. PARKER *Rise, Progress, & Present State Van Dieman's Land* 40 The first class, which is to consist of the most hardened offenders, is to be sent to the penal settlement at Norfolk Island. . . The second class, consisting of persons convicted of less heavy offences, and of whom there are some hopes of reformation entertained, is to be . . kept to labour in chains upon . . public works; and the third class, consisting of prisoners convicted of minor offences, is . . for distribution among the settlers. **1833** J. BACKHOUSE *Narr. Visit Austral. Colonies* (1843) 167 Prisoners are divided into a chain-gang, and a first and second class, distinguished by the kind of labour allotted them, by their clothing, and by the second class having an allowance of tea and sugar. **1837** *Colonist* (Sydney) 9 Mar. 78/3 Convicts of the second class sent here to labour for a certain period on the public works, before assignment to settlers. **1847** A. MARJORIBANKS *Travels N.S.W.* 229 Women sent to the factory for pregnancy, when not living with their husbands, may be sentenced to the second class. **1848** J. SYME *Nine Yrs. in Van Diemen's Land* 276 The third class is composed of the very worst men.

class, *v.*

1. *trans.* To grade (fleeces), esp. in a shearing shed. Also *absol.*, and with 'shed' as obj. Freq. as *vbl. n.*

1845 *Sydney Morning Herald* 8 Aug. 4/3 Large and really substantial Wool Shed . . with every convenience for classing and packing. **1885** Tas. Non-State Rec. 103/5 18 July, Going to Sydney . . to try a season's classing. **1889** H. EGBERT *Pretty Cockey* 44 Mr Thompson classed the wool into Long Clothing, Short Clothing [etc.]. **1899** G. JEFFREY *Princ. Australasian Woolclassing* 38 If the sheep are properly drafted . . the work of the Wool Classer is very much simplified, because he will be able to class each lot on its own merits. **1910** *Bulletin* (Sydney) 22 Dec. 13/4 A black did most of the classing. **1917** *Ibid.* 28 June 22/1 He'd 'class' at Gunneguldrie, muster sheep on Burrawang. **1934** T. WOOD *Cobbers* 196 Men would class the fleeces, and clean them. **1953** A. UPFIELD *Venom House* 78 Robin Foster's brother done the wool pressing. Bloke from over Manton way came to do the classing. **1961** *Bulletin* (Sydney) 21 Oct. 30/1 Woolclassers . . want to see that wool they've classed . . goes from wool-bin to wool-press unspoilt by floor sweepings. **1965** L. WALKER *Other Girl* 54 All this classing had been done in a technical school and on the wool floor of the brokers. **1977** D. WHITINGTON *Strive to be Fair* 28, I was paid £5 a week and my keep to class a small shed on Tasmania's east coast. **1981** A.B. FACEY *Fortunate Life* 185 Mr Kent showed me how to class wool and throw it so it would fall spread out over a special wool-table.

2. *Hist. trans.* To grade (a convict) according to severity of punishment; see CLASS *n.*

1851 *Irish Exile* (Hobart) 18 Jan. 3/1 Mr P. O'Donohoe arrived here on Wednesday evening last, and was 'classed' on Thursday morning, for a hard labour party.

classer. One who grades fleeces, esp. in a shearing shed; *wool-classer*, see WOOL 2.

1874 *Australasian Sketcher* 31 Oct. 119/3 Some hands then 'skirt' the wool . . and the 'classer' decides on the classification. **1894** *Bulletin* (Sydney) 10 Feb. 20/3 They throw the classer up the fleece, he throws it to the bin. **1915** *Ibid.* 28 Oct. 22/4 A 'pony' is a rouseabout who carries the fleeces from the classer to the wool-bins. **1926** A. EDEN *Places in Sun* 49 The classers . . class the wool with amazing speed and dexterity. **1941** *Bulletin* (Sydney) 10 Dec. 15/3 In a S.A. shed a classer came across a well-grown fleece with stripes in it. **1961** *Ibid.* 15 Mar. 40/2 A squatter came up to the classer's table and asked: 'How're they coming off? Not bad sheep, are they?' **1978** J. DINGWALL *Sunday too far Away* 48 The *classers, piece pickers, rousies* and *pressers* standing at one end of the shed, looking, waiting.

clay-hole. CLAYPAN 1.

1843 *Sydney Morning Herald* 31 Oct. 4/1 The rain has fallen generally on the interior plains and water may be found in the clay-holes for some months at least to come. **1861** A.C. & F.T. GREGORY *Jrnls. Austral. Explorations* 15 July (1884) 72 We only procured a little water at night in a clay-hole. **1889** E. GILES *Aust. twice Traversed* I. 145 We next saw a large clay-hole in the main creek—it was, however, dry. **1898** D.W. CARNEGIE *Spinifex & Sand* 425 It is a stony cotton-bush flat, and on it numerous white clay-holes of water. **1928** M. FORREST *Reaping Roses* 231 His horse stumbled in a dry clay-hole and pitched the rider right over his head.

claypan. [f. *clay* + *pan* a hollow or depression in the ground, esp. one in which water lies (cf. *saltpan*).]

1. A shallow depression with an impermeable clay base which holds water after rain: see quot. 1889. Also *attrib.*

1858 J.M. STUART *Explorations in Aust.* 23 June (1865) 9 At fourteen and a half miles we found a clay-pan of water, with beautiful green feed for the horses. **1861** J. MCKINLAY *Jrnl. Exploration Interior* 6 Oct. (1862) 4 The bottoms of the clay-pans are nearly as hard as bricks. **1867** W. MILTON *Victim Nineteenth Century* 24 July is the proper month to find water in the 'clay-pans'. **1889** E. GILES *Aust. twice Traversed* I. 39 A clay pan is a small area of ground, whose top soil has been washed or blown away, leaving this hard clay exposed; and upon this surface, one, two, three, or (scarcely) more inches of rain water may remain for some days after rain: the longer it remains the thicker it gets, until at last it dries in cakes which shine like tiles; these at length crumble away, and the clay pan is swept by winds clean and ready for the next shower. **1905** *Emu* V. 19, I did see one after a Native-Hen . . on a claypan flat where there was no shelter. **1929** 'OLD STOCKMAN' *Sensational Cattle-Stealing Case* 22 We startled a camp of wild blacks . . camped on a large water hole, a sort of clay pan, very deep. **1940** E. HILL *Great Austral. Loneliness* (ed. 2) 61 We left Hedland . . taking off from the clay-pan racecourse. **1954** *Bulletin* (Sydney) 27 Oct. 12/1 Speedways when dry, the wide claypans that make up much of the 'motor roads' through nor'-west W.A.'s outback stations are still firm and easily traversed after heavy rain. **1962** MARSHALL & DRYSDALE *Journey among Men* 12 After the rains come, suddenly in the claypans there are full-grown toads, and soon, their young. **1985** *Woman's Day* (Sydney) 1 July 21/3 Huge red clay-pans which pockmark the semi-arid country of the West Darling.

2. Special Comb. **claypan squatter,** one who occupies land without holding title to it, and grazes illegally acquired stock.

1905 *Observer* (Adelaide) 2 Sept. 47/1 The depredations of what are known as claypan, or waterhole, squatters are a serious menace to pastoralists in the unfenced country of the interior. Taking up a ridiculously small area of pasture, these men raid the outskirts of a run and gather in young unbranded cattle and horses. **1911** A. SEARCY *By Flood & Field* 290 The 'gentlemen' who stocked their stations by such purchases were known as 'Lagoon' or 'Clay-pan' squatters. **1936** I.L. IDRIESS *Cattle King* 34 He was a nomad, a 'claypan squatter'. **1944** M.J. O'REILLY *Bowyangs & Boomerangs* 110 As pretty a little mob of 'clean-skins' as would delight the eyes of any 'clay-pan' squatter. **1959** W.E. HARNEY *Tales from Aborigines* p. xvi, In the early days the native girls travelled around with their white companions, and being excellent cattle-and-horse-women they became the ones who helped the . . 'claypan squatters'.

Clayton's. [The proprietary name of a soft drink: see quot. 1980.] Something which is largely illusory or exists in name only.

[**1980** *Herald* (Melbourne) 6 Dec. 22/4 Actor Jack Thompson was commissioned for that Clayton's ad by D'Arcy-MacManus & Masius whose national creative director Noel Delbridge wrote the line that, with variations, is now part of the language. . . 'It's the drink I have when I'm not having a drink.'] **1984** *Canberra Times* 20 June 16/7 Academic staff of Commonwealth tertiary-education institutions will now have to pay back their 'Clayton's' pay rise. **1984** *Advertiser* (Adelaide) 31 July 2/5 There were plans to change the name of Mick Young's electorate to Claytons because he's the Minister you have when you haven't got a Minister. **1985** *Canberra Times* 13 July B1/1 Australian English is not a Clayton's sort of English, a sort of colonial doggerel you speak when you cannot manage Standard Southern. **1986** *Ibid.* 16 Feb. 6/5 I'm not sure if the advertisements boosted sales of Claytons Tonic, but they certainly made 'Claytons' a household word and one that will make 'The Macquarie Dictionary' before too long.

clean, *a.* and *adv.*

A. *adj.*

1. a. Of stock: uncontaminated by disease.

1839 *Port Phillip Patriot* 4 July 3/2 An opportunity of at once finding clean flocks. **1840** *Port Phillip Gaz.* 21 Mar. 4 These sheep are warranted perfectly clean, and never to have had the scab or any other disease. **1842** *Ibid.* 31 Oct. 1 To be disposed of, a gentleman's one-third interest in about three thousand perfectly clean sheep. **1844** *Ibid.* 1 Apr. 3, 2523 Clean Sheep, with Station capable of carrying from eight to ten thousand, given in, without reserve. **1960** *N.T. News* (Darwin) 28 Oct. 2/2 Mixing 'clean' cattle with a mob from a pleuro area cost a former transport driver 18 guineas.

b. Of pastoral land: uncontaminated by diseased stock; free from pests.

1840 *Port Phillip Gaz.* 29 Jan. 4 The above Run is . . quite clean. **1843** *Sydney Morning Herald* 4 Oct. 4/2 Price drove his sheep to a clean station, and none of them died. **1845** *Portland Gaz.* 9 Sept. 4/4 The land was clean upon which we put the two dressed flocks; it had been vacated for cleaning. **1849** A. HARRIS *Emigrant Family* (1967) 140 Shepherds . . when placed on a clean run must be made to keep upon it. **1898** C.L. MORGAN *Rabbit Question in Qld.* 62 Every mile of fencing is a protection to the clean country outside the rabbit districts. **1935** D.G. STEAD *Rabbit in Aust.* 50 The most important use of the Dog is in the final clearing up of a holding, and the keeping of it 'clean'. **1943** H.G. LAMOND *From Tariaro to Ross Roy* 121 Though the country is clean, the cattle are tied up on account of a fanciful tick line drawn between that station and the markets. **1975** L.A. POCKLEY *Handbk. for Jackeroos* 118 Treated sheep are put directly into 'clean' paddocks (i.e. have had no sheep in them for 21 days).

2. In collocations indicating a degree of completeness: **clean burn,** (in clearing land) a controlled fire which leaves little debris; **muster,** (of stock) a complete round-up.

1886 P. CLARKE *'New Chum' in Aust.* 268 He has cut them down so that they all lie in the fittest way for a '**clean burn**' when the opportunity comes. **1977** F.B. VICKERS *Stranger no Longer* 30 We'll burn off the hundred acres today. If the easterly holds all morning we'll get a clean burn. **1891** M. ROBERTS *Land-Travel & Sea-Faring* 72 The sheep hunting began. In this mountainous land they grow very wild; . . so good dogs are essential to anything like a **clean muster.** **1942** *Bulletin* (Sydney) 8 July 13/2 We had made what appeared to be a clean muster of ewes and summer lambs in a river paddock where careful mustering was always required. **1953** *Ibid.* 7 Oct. 13/2 It would take all morning to get a *clean* muster. **1975** L.A. POCKLEY *Handbk. for Jackeroos* 29 If the paddock is mustered 'up-wind' then once the sheep are started they will tend to continue to move up wind and not only is a clean muster more likely, it is done with much less effort and time.

B. *adv.* Of mustering: completely.

1925 M. TERRY *Across Unknown Aust.* 121 No country can be mustered 'clean', i.e. entirely. **1928** L.A. SIGSWORTH *Various Verse* 1 But the boys turn out, for the overseer harps loud and long on the early start, To muster clean in a circling sweep, with men well spread, half-a-mile apart. **1956** B.J. RAYMENT *My Towri* 79 Rough timbered country, but fairly well watered, the nature of the land being such that the station musterers rarely mustered clean.

clean, *v.*

1. *trans. Obs.* To decontaminate (pasture affected by diseased stock).

1845 *Portland Gaz.* 9 Sept. 4/4, I . . have to request your kind permission to vacate my head sheep station, where I have been both dressing and shearing for four months, in order that the run may be cleaned and the grass renewed.

2. *trans.* To clear (a paddock) of stock, to muster (stock from a paddock).

1886 P. CLARKE *'New Chum' in Aust.* 168 This is the paddock we have, in bush phraseology, to 'clean' or 'muster'. **1903** *Bulletin* (Sydney) 17 Jan. 16/2 The men could not have sighted and 'cleaned ' every part of the paddock—the true definition of mustering—in time to count 80,000 sheep.

cleanskin.

1. An unbranded animal; CLEARSKIN. Also *attrib.*

1881 A.C. GRANT *Bush-Life Qld.* I. 209 All hands are anxious to try their luck with the clean-skins. **1886** H. FINCH-HATTON *Advance Aust.* 98 We would . . hunt up some of the 'clean-skins' as the wild cattle are called, an allusion to their never having been branded. **1902** F. RENAR *Bushman & Buccaneer* 9, I have done a bit of brumby running in mountain country, although most of the cleanskin experience has been in mulgoa or brigalow. **1916** *Bulletin* (Sydney) 27 Jan. 22/3 He reckoned the Barkly being unfenced country was anyone's land, and he lived upon it, going from hole to hole, camping for months . . with his gin. . . His game was running in clean-skins. **1927** M. TERRY *Through Land of Promise* 230 When all the clean skins (those that have escaped branding) have been sorted out, they are driven to the branding-yard. **1935** M. & E. DURACK *All-About* (1940) 29 A three year old clean skin bull breaks suddenly from the edge of the mob. **1950** G.M. FARWELL *Land of Mirage* 47 If there's a mob of cleanskins out there, and you don't put your brand on 'em, you'll just as likely find the next joker will. **1960** R.S. PORTEOUS *Cattleman* 16 When it came to duffing he had few equals. A faint or blotched brand he regarded as a challenge to his artistry, a cleanskin a direct invitation. **1968** LINKLATER & TAPP *Gather no Moss* 100 Honesty is the best policy, but never pass an Ord River cleanskin. **1981** A.B. FACEY *Fortunate Life* 172 We have a surplus of thirty-eight head, and two of them are clean skins (unbranded).

2. *transf.* An Aboriginal who has not passed through an initiation rite.

1903 H. BASEDOW *Jrnl. Govt. N.-W. Exped.* 21 May (1914) 111 He is a so-called 'clean-skin', that is, he has not yet been the victim of any personal mutilation ceremonies. **1963** I.L. IDRIESS *Our Living Stone Age* 155 The 'cleanskins' the stockmen referred to were unbranded beasts; as the white man called an unbranded bullock a cleanskin, so he called a blackboy who had not been 'branded' with the initiation knife.

3. *fig.* One who has no criminal record; one new to (a situation or activity) and lacking experience.

1907 A. SEARCY *In Austral. Tropics* 112 The men I met with were good, honest, and hard working, although perhaps it might have been as well for a clean skin to fight shy of some of them. **1941** S.J. BAKER *Pop. Dict. Austral. Slang* 18 *Cleanskin*, a person of integrity, esp. in a political sense. **1945** —— *Austral. Lang.* 141 A man who has had no convictions recorded against him is a *cleanskin*. **1950** *Austral. Police Jrnl.* Apr. 111 *Clean-skin*, a person without convictions. **1965** R.H. CONQUEST *Horses in Kitchen* 71 The other seven were veteran trainjumpers. I was the only cleanskin. **1968** *Swag* (Sydney) ii. 6/2 He . . was, according to all reports, an industrious, intelligent kid, and in criminal parlance, a 'cleanskin'. **1973** L. OAKES *Whitlam PM* 84 He was a 'cleanskin' who could not be smeared as a dangerous radical or fellow traveller. **1978** D. HUTLEY *Swan* 60 'You're not a cleanskin?' 'What does that mean?' 'A joker who's never done it before at all. It was a joke we had. That's what the cops call you if they got nothing on you. No 'previous' you see, so you're a cleanskin.' **1979** W.D. JOYNT *Breaking Road for Rest* 80 How would we behave when under fire and in front of tough Anzacs, and what would be their reactions to us cleanskins?

clearing, *ppl. a. Hist.* In collocations referring to the clearing of land: **clearing gang,** orig. a detachment of convicts detailed to clear trees, undergrowth, etc., from a settler's land in order to fit it for cultivation or pasturage; any party so employed; **lease,** an arrangement under which a settler has the use of a tract of land, for little or no rent, in return for clearing it; also *attrib.*; **party,** *clearing gang.*

1824 *HRA* (1921) 3rd Ser. IV. 560 Respecting the appropriation of the **Clearing Gangs**. **1826** *Austral.* (Sydney) 5 Jan. 2/4 The Clearing Gangs, we observe by a Public Order, are about to be dissolved and the men distributed among the Settlers. **1834** J.D. LANG *Hist. & Statistical Acct. N.S.W.* II. 5 *Clearing-gangs*, or parties of convicts in the service of Government—each under the charge of an overseer—who were stationed for certain periods on the lands of private individuals to fell and to burn off the standing timber. **1853** S. SIDNEY *Three Colonies* (ed. 2) 86 In Macquarie's time the settler usually obtained, in addition to a supply of farm labourers, the use of a 'clearing-gang', which cut down, burned, rolled, and cleared the huge trees. **1924** LAWRENCE & SKINNER *Boy in Bush* 88 He can take the clearing gang over to his A'nt Greenlow's for the shearing. **1934** J.S. NEILSON *Autobiogr.* 122, I got a job in the clearing gang. **1808** *Sydney Gaz.* 4 Sept., Together with several allotments of land on **clearing leases** for 5 to 7 years. **1811** *Ibid.* 30 Nov., On Clearing Leases for Seven Years, in small lots of 100 Acres, the Farm of Copenhagen. **1819** *Ibid.* 17 July, To be *sold*, or *let* on a *clearing lease*, 60 *Acres* of *land.* **1834** J.D. LANG *Hist. & Statistical Acct. N.S.W.* II. 426 The ticket-of-leave man or emancipist . . takes a small farm on a clearing lease. **1843** *Sydney Rec.* 9 Dec. 76/4 We observe with satisfaction that twenty-three families left Sydney on Thursday, by the steamer, for Wollongong, accompanied by Mrs Chisholm, who has procured for them land in that neighbourhood, on clearing leases. **1849** J.P. TOWNSEND *Rambles & Observations N.S.W.* 136 In this district is to be found a numerous class of small settlers called 'clearing-lease men'. They take a small piece of uncleared land (each about thirty acres), on condition of having it rent-free for six years, and form on it a kind of shanty. . . By the time their original tenancy expires, they have generally got on pretty well in the world, and can afford to pay about ten pounds a-year for their now reclaimed land. **1867** J.R. HOULDING *Austral. Capers* 269 He had let off portions of his brush land to industrious, steady families, on clearing leases. ***c* 1886** *Few Lett. from Qld. Farmers* 11, I have two selections—a homestead taken up in 1873 . . and a conditional purchase of 100 acres. . . A portion of the last-named I have just leased (in the same state that I got it) on a seven years' *clearing* lease for £1 10s. per acre per annum. **1903** *Bulletin* (Sydney) 3 Sept. 17/2 All the old clearing leases in the Illawarra district were fenced in with what we now call dog-leg fences. **1980** L. FULLER *Wollongong's Native Trees* 11 Grants were divided and sold as smaller farms or the land-holders leased the land under 'Clearing Leases'. **1824** *Hobart Town Gaz.* 16 Apr., In New South Wales . . the settler may have his farm . . entirely cleared, and ploughed fit for the seed. . . This work is all done by **Clearing Parties**, consisting of several hundred Crown prisoners, employed in that manner by Government. **1827** *Monitor* (Sydney) 5 July 495/2 A detachment of defaulters . . had been previously selected . . for the purpose of forming *a clearing party*. **1846** N.L. KENTISH *Work in Bush Van Diemen's Land* 17 The placing of clearing-parties of probation pass-holders, on the rich tracts which may be selected for cultivation. **1879** 'AUSTRALIAN' *Adventures Qld.* 108 Mr Brown, George Martin, and the Malcolms, lent him two hands each, who, with his off-sider and himself, made a good strong clearing party.

clearing sale. A sale, esp. of surplus stock, farm machinery, and household goods at a rural property; a retailer's sale of superseded merchandise, usu. at reduced prices.

1884 *Austral. Tit-Bits* (Melbourne) 19 June 2/3 We have also . . clearing sales, land rackets, and bogus auctions. **1898** L. LINDLEY-COWEN *W. Austral. Settler's Guide* 775 It may be that a fair herd can be purchased at a *bona-fide* clearing sale, but that is only a chance in a lifetime. **1905** *Bulletin* (Sydney) 7 Sept. 35/1 Roney and Son's clearing sale was in full swing. **1941** *Ibid.* 12 Feb. 17/1 Old Job Haystack made a good job of the 'clearing sale' he had conducted on his Upthecreek farm. **1942** H.H. PECK *Mem. of Stockman* 33 In those days free grog was the understood thing at big clearing sales and . . the Heyfield sale must have been a record for the number of 'dead beats' who attended and spent the night sleeping it off. **1959** C.V. LAWLOR *All This Humbug* 148 At a clearing sale he had bought some good furniture for the lounge room. **1979** B. MARTYN *First Footers S. Gippsland* 89 There's a clearing sale up at Peter's in about a month. . . She's got some good dairy stuff if you want to stock up a bit. **1983** M. HAYES *Prickle Farm* 47 Clearing sales are big news in the bush. . . Many country people seem to gain satisfaction out of watching someone's property . . go under the hammer.

clearskin. CLEANSKIN 1.

1884 'R. BOLDREWOOD' *Old Melbourne Memories* 109 Calves and clear-skins, are separated at the same time. **1888** —— *Robbery under Arms* (1937) 10 I've seen them ride to chapel and attend mass, and look as if they'd never seen a 'clearskin' in their lives. **1893** *Bulletin* (Sydney) 4 Mar. 19/2 We rode up in the 'Bidgee where the clearskins mustered thick. **1917** *Emu* XVI. 149 He informed me that cattle—'clear-skins'—were fairly plentiful near the mouth of the river. **1920** *Land of Lyre Bird* (S. Gippsland Pioneers' Assoc.) 383 The lure of 'clear skins' failed to tempt 'Jimmy' from the paths of virtue; although in those days it was said that a rough bush yard and a branding iron . . were all that was required to lay the foundations of a handsome fortune. **1967** E. HUXLEY *Their Shining Eldorado* 247 The rest are 'clearskins' whose males grow up to be scrub bulls.

cleftie, clefty, varr. CLIFTY.

Cleopatra. [Transf. use of *Cleopatra* the name of a queen of Egypt renowned for her beauty.] A (chiefly Tas.) variety of eating apple. Also **Cleo.**

1936 *Austral. Writers' Ann.* 77 Cleopatras, sweet as Egypt's golden queen. **1947** MRS A.H. GARNSEY *Romance Huon River* 171 Next came Gravensteins, Cox's, Cleopatras. **1961** R. PARKER *Fiddlers' Place* 19 He . . fetched the apple out of his pocket. 'What'd you take a Cleo for?' demanded his brother. . . 'There were still some red ones.' **1973** J.C. FIDLER et al. *Biol. Apple & Pear Storage* 106 The season when the Cleopatra apples were abnormally large.

clever, *a. Aboriginal English.*

1. Wise; learned in traditional lore. Esp. in the collocation **clever man.** See KORADJI.

1909 *Folklore* (London) XIV. iv. 487 A 'doctor' or clever blackfellow can sometimes go and see a Wahwee. **1935** *Oceania* VI. 33 Several men had the reputation of being 'clever' men. **1944** A.P. ELKIN *Aboriginal Men High Degree* (1946) 85 Amongst these people there was a class of 'clever' men who specialized in meditation, hypnotism, thought-transference and 'seeing' what was occurring at a distance. **1947** *Oceania* XVII. 330 The two women, who were 'clever', and possessed a certain amount of magical 'power', had used . . a decoy. **1965** R. ROBINSON *Man who sold Dreaming* 12 The clever-feller is a witch-doctor, a rain-maker, one who can cast spells . . an old man who has specialised in magic. **1977** J. BARKER *Two Worlds* 71 They were just ordinary Aborigines and not reputed to be witch doctors or clever men. **1985** T. WISE *Self-Made Anthropologist* 246 At times, he seemed to think that many clever men used the knowledge that there was a certain element of faith on their viewers' part.

2. *Transf.* and *fig.*

1972 *Bulletin* (Sydney) 24 June 59/1 As widely reported, the clever-feller-money-magicians (who are *usually* right) are predicting a further 0.2 percent cut in the long term bond rate. **1986** HERCUS & SUTTON *This is what Happened* 229 There was a white cleverman at Port Augusta—white people call him 'doctor'.

clifty, *v.* Also **cleftie, clefty, cliftie.** [f. Gr. κλέφτης a thief; used in Services' speech and prob. not excl. Austral.] *trans.* To steal (something).

1918 *Kia Ora Coo-ee* June 8/1 You discover that the iron rations for your horse have been 'cleftied'. *Ibid.* Oct. 18/3 There stood the Great Pyramid, which had been 'cleftied' somehow, and shifted bodily to this spot. **1942** T. KELAHER *Digger Hat* 16 We 'clifteyed' a three-tonner from the Tommy A.S.C. **1956** *Harry Peck's Post* (Sydney) July 18, I cliftie a truck off the lines. **1961** L. GLASSOP *We were Rats* (ed. 3) 98 Too many bloody Wogs for my likin'. They'll *cliftie* the bloody shirt off yer back. **1977** F.A. REEDER *Diary of Rat* 51 We decided to make some cocoa on a little stove he had 'clifteed' from someone.

Hence **clifty** *a.*, thieving.

1943 H.E. BEROS *Fuzzy-Wuzzy Angels* 66 We'll remember how we had to watch those sneaking clifty wogs.

climbing, *ppl. a.* Used in the names of fauna: **climbing fish,** MUDSKIPPER; **kangaroo** *obs.*, *tree-kangaroo*, see TREE.

1880 *Proc. Linnean Soc. N.S.W.* V. 614 *Periophthalmus Australis* 'The **Climbing Fish**' of the Northern Queensland Settlers. **1952** B. BEATTY *Unique to Aust.* 75 Another amphibious fish of Queensland is the Mudskipper or Climbing fish. At low tide these small fish— . . about five inches—come ashore . . in hundreds hopping, skipping. **1890** *Braidwood Dispatch* 29 Jan. 2/5 Three **climbing kangaroos** . . are said to have been captured safe and sound. **1918** *Bulletin* (Sydney) 15 Aug. 24/2 One of the prettiest of the scrub residents in North Queensland, the 'climbing kangaroo' . . is about the size of an ordinary wallaby.

cliner /'klaɪnə/. *Obs.* Also formerly **clinah, kleiner.** [a. G. *kleine*: see quot. 1898.] A girl or girl-friend.

1895 *Bulletin* (Sydney) 9 Feb. 15/4 I'm ryebuck and the girl's O.K. Oh, she's good iron, is my little clinah. **1898** *Ibid.* 20 Aug. (Red Page), The 'clinah' of Goodge's 'Australian Slanguage' is simply the German *kleine* (fem. of *klein*, small, little, and meaning 'little', i.e., woman) Australised. I heard the term first in S.A. (where Germans abound) some years ago. **1899** *Truth* (Sydney) 10 Sept. 1/8 He'd wing his kliner with a sock, The toe of which contained some rock. **1902** *Ibid.* 29 June 6/2 He'd a little kleiner stoppin' With him. She went out awl day Workin'. **1915** C.J. DENNIS *Songs of Sentimental Bloke* 22, I carn't describe that cliner's winnin' ways. The way she torks! 'Er lips! 'Er eyes! 'Er hair! **1928** E.M. ROBB *Lyrics* 6 Oh, they're bonzer, are these cliners, with their dainty little frills. **1931** *Bulletin* (Sydney) 21 Jan. 20/1 No other cliner ever 'ad such 'air. **1942** M.L. MACPHERSON *I heard Anzacs Singing* 33 In Australia . . a girl is a cliner . . or (not quite so polite) a shiela, or (most impolite) a tart.

clock. [From the number of hours on a clock-face.] With **the:** a prison sentence of twelve months.

1950 *Austral. Police Jrnl.* Apr. 112 *Clock, The*, 12 months imprisonment. **1968** J. ALARD *He who shoots Last* 2 Anyhow I'd better stall; if I get picked up I'll at least get the clock.

clocker. [Used elsewhere but recorded earliest in Aust.: see Mathews.] One who (surreptitiously) times a racehorse, esp. during a training run.

1895 N. GOULD *On & Off Turf in Aust.* 117 Ruses are resorted to at times to deceive or out-general the 'clocker' on the look-out for a good gallop. **1978** *Sun-Herald* (Sydney) 1 Oct. 62/5 His time of 2 m. 32 ½ s. clipped five seconds from the previous Randwick record and three and three-quarter seconds from the Flemington record. The 'clockers' couldn't believe their eyes. **1980** *Daily Mirror* (Sydney) 1 Apr. 111/1 She's an absolute flying machine and today made clockers look twice when she recorded 35 sec. for her 600 m. task.

Cloncurry ringneck. [f. the name of a town in n.e. Qld. + RINGNECK.] The parrot *Barnardius barnardi macgillivrayi* of n.w. Qld. Also **Cloncurry parrot** (or **parakeet**).

1913 G.M. MATHEWS *List Birds Aust.* 134 Cloncurry Parrot . . Range: Interior of Mid-Queensland. **1967** E. HUXLEY *Their Shining Eldorado* 135 Here are colonies of Cloncurry ringnecks. **1977** J. CARTER *All Things Wild* 51 Cloncurry parakeets have a tag of $2500 a pair.

close out, *v. Surfing. intr.* Of a wave: to break simultaneously over its whole length, thus preventing a surfer from riding along the breaking crest.

1964 *Surfabout* (Sydney) I. vi. 9 The waves are always right-handers, with the bigger waves 4 ft.–5 ft. closing out. **1967** *Ibid.* III. vii. 8 The other popular surf, the left beachbreak, works best at 3–4 feet on high tide. Any bigger and it will close out.

closer settlement. *Hist.* A policy of closely settling land suitable for agricultural purposes, with a view to increasing land utilization and productivity; settlement in this manner. Also *attrib.*

1897 *Act* (S.A.) 60 & 61 Vict. no. 687 Sect. 1, An act relating to the Repurchase of Land. . . 1. This Act may be cited as 'The Closer Settlement Act, 1897'. **1902** *Bulletin* (Sydney) 12 Apr. 14/2 S.A. Govt. is at present very hot on Closer Settlement. **1910** *Huon Times* (Franklin) 1 Oct. 5/4 The powers that be are busy preparing for the Closer Settlement people who are to come out as the result of the tour of Europe and America by the Minister of Lands. **1912** *Cwlth. of Aust. for Farmers* (Dept. External Affairs) 99 *Closer settlement Purchase*, the terms under which closer settlement farms are made available are very liberal. **1934** 'S. RUDD' *Green Grey Homestead* 151 'The Mount' consisted of waste country reserved by a Government of squatters for 'closer settlement', and bordering this reserved area were mighty stations . . lying there within their cheap, pointed sheep fences, like living land sharks. **1958** E.O. SCHLUNKE *Village Hampden* 113 Is that all you can think of, when dozens of men in this district are going to be put off their farms any day? Two out of three of the Closer Settlement men, because the Government has decided that a thousand acres isn't an 'economic unit' in this area.

Hence **closer settler** *n.*

1913 *Bulletin* (Sydney) 9 Oct. 22/3 Victoria's closer settlers are not all craven shirkers of the conditions of their agreements. **1937** E. HILL *Water into Gold* 234 Soldier settlers and 'closer' settlers were not to be merely orphans in the storm.

close up, *adv. Austral. pidgin.* Near; nearly.

1853 H.B. JONES *Adventures in Aust.* 128 It was with some difficulty we could get them to be bearers of the skin, &c. of the bullock to the 'humpy', i.e. station, which was 'close up' (near), for they will not work at all if they are full. **1883** E.M. CURR *Recoll. Squatting Vic.* 349 Six or eight of them, knocking down their cheques . . were, as I heard, close up fly-blown (*i.e.*, nearly penniless) the day before yesterday. **1908** MRS A. GUNN *We of Never-Never* 305 He chuckled: 'Close up smash him Cognac all right.' **1929** K.S. PRICHARD *Coonardoo* 316 She was 'close up finish 'm,' she knew, as the trooper had said. **1935** M. & E. DURACK *All-About* 97, I bin go mad and kill that Masha. Might 'im close up dead now. **1946** W.E. HARNEY *North of 23°* 257 She is panting hard when she arrives, and complains about how she is 'close up been lose 'em wind'. **1951** E. HILL *Territory* 320 Rose was 'close up finish'.

clothes hoist. A rotary clothes-drier consisting of a square frame, between the arms of which run lengths of clothes-line, turning about a central pole and adjustable in height.

[**1923** *Austral. Home Beautiful* Aug. 66/1 An ingenious circular clothes-line . . revolves on the principle of the merry-go-round on windy days, and helps to dry the clothes quickly.] **1926** *Ibid.* Jan. 9 (Advt.), *Toyne's rotary clothes hoist. The perfect clothes line—props done away with—an ornament to your back yard.* . . Raises as desired up to 7 ft. 6 in. from ground to lines. **1964** F.M. CULLEN *Man. Home Econ.* 168 The best drying equipment is the rotary clothes hoist which rotates as the breeze catches the clothes thus shortening the drying time. **1972** *Southerly* iv. 291 The clothes hoist was blown gently round above them, its four aluminium arms spreading thin shadows across them.

clover. Used *attrib.* in the names of plants having a clover-like leaf: **clover burr,** any of several naturalized herbs of the genus *Medicago* (fam. Fabaceae) having a spiny fruit; **fern,** NARDOO.

1878 'R. BOLDREWOOD' *Ups & Downs* 49 We *must* have shearing over by October, or all this **clover-burr** that I see about will be in the wool. **1880** G.A. BROWN *Sheep Breeding in Aust.* 321 Black salt flats, growing barley-grass, clover-burr. **1956** *Singabout* Apr. 6 Shearing on the western plains where the fleece is full of sand, And the clover burr and corkscrew grass is the place to try your hand. **1878** R.B. SMYTH *Aborigines of Vic.* I. 209 The use, as a food, of the **clover-fern**, *Nardoo*. **1970** J.V. MARSHALL *Walk to Hills of Dreamtime* 155 *Nardoo cake*, cakes made by grinding up into paste and then baking the hard pea-like fruit of the nardoo or clover-fern.

clucky, *a.* [From the noise made by a broody hen.] Of a woman: pregnant; broody.

1941 S.J. BAKER *Pop. Dict. Austral. Slang* 18 *Clucky*, pregnant. **1977** H.O. TESHER *Eleven Days* 22, I told you I have been very clucky lately, and I wanted your child.

cluey, *a.* [f. *clue* prob. by analogy with *clueless*.] Knowledgeable; alert (to the possibilities of a situation); 'clued-up'.

1967 *Kings Cross Whisper* (Sydney) xxxiii. 4/3 *Cluey*, a cluey person is one who has many ideas of ways and means of getting money. **1969** A. BUZO *Four Austral. Plays* (1974) 59 He's in the know, mate. He's a cluey bloke, is Hendo. **1975** D.G. JENNER *Darlings* 21 Dad wasn't cluey enough to take up the offer.

clumper. A work-horse (see quot. 1980). Also *attrib.*

1916 L. FERRIS *John Heathlyn of Otway* 138 Heathlyn's first equine companion was a brown, hardy clumper. **1936** I.L. IDRIESS *Cattle King* 64 There were a lot of horses there with some good-looking clumpers amongst them. **1963** M. BRITT *Pardon my Boots* 50 At the first light, the men caught the big 'clumper' pack-horses, and I watched eagerly as they were packed. **1980** HOLTH & BARNABY *Cattlemen of High Country* 126 A 'clumper' or heavy type of mare crossed with a blood horse produced a strong horse suitable for a 'remount' or regimental mount.

coach, *v.* [Spec. use of *coach* to teach, train.] *intr.* To use tame cattle as a lure for wild cattle. Also *trans.*, to lure (wild cattle), and as *vbl. n.* and *ppl. a.*

1872 G.S. BADEN-POWELL *New Homes for Old Country* 183 In mountainous and rough districts the cattle are often very wild, and the method usually entered upon is that termed 'coaching'. **1880** J.B. STEVENSON *Seven Yrs. Austral. Bush* 128 We often worked all through a long winter's night, coaching round scrub after scrub, without coming across a single mob. **1905** *Bulletin* (Sydney) 13 Apr. 18/1 'Scrub-running' for clean-skins, a lot of which can only be got by tying, and then coaching them with quiet cattle. **1951** E. HILL *Territory* 308 Coaching was rougher riding. . . You take a couple of hundred cattle on to wild cattle tracks, circle the outlaws and work them into the coaches (N.B. the tame cattle). **1978** PALMER & MCKENNA *Somewhere between Black & White* 36 He used 'coaching cattle', tame cows that would do exactly as directed and the rougher . . animals tended to follow their lead.

coach, *n.*[1] Abbrev. of COACHER.

1872 G.S. BADEN-POWELL *New Homes for Old Country* 183 The 'coaches' are a mob of quiet cattle. **1929** K.S. PRICHARD *Coonardoo* (1961) 71 Got the rest of the mob next evening. . . But we had to turn in some coaches. **1962** D. LOCKWOOD *I, Aboriginal* 172 On clear nights we drove quiet decoy cattle we called 'coaches' on to the plains to attract others.

coach, *n.*[2] In the phr. **to rob this** (or **the**) **coach,** to be in charge of an operation.

1945 S.J. BAKER *Austral. Lang.* 251 Disapproval or disagreement is indicated by . . *who's robbing this coach?* [*Note*] Reputed to be associated with bushranging days, this expression is equivalent to 'mind your own business!' **1951** E. LAMBERT *Twenty Thousand Thieves* 206 Chip's boom shattered the . . feeling among them: 'Who's robbing this coach? Do you want to hear the news or not?' **1963** H. PORTER *Watcher on Cast-Iron Balcony* 108 'Shut up, you great lazy beasts,' the aunts cry back to the uncles. 'Who's robbing this coach, anyway? Just be patient, you hulking buggers.' **1971** F. HARDY *Outcasts of Foolgarah* 17 He carried on a dialogue with himself, his voice muffly-mimicky deep in the helmet. 'I'm going to rob all the men and fuck all the women': 'You can't do that, you dreadful man': 'Who's robbing this coach, you or Mister Kelly?' **1977** *Austral.* (Sydney) 1 Dec. 8/2 Apart from raising the question as to which of Labor's four Treasurers-elect is robbing the coach, where does this leave Labor policy—except in tatters?

coacher. [f. COACH *v.*] A tame beast used as a lure for others, esp. wild cattle; a tame horse used to attract brumbies.

1876 J.A. EDWARDS *Gilbert Gogger* 137 Now our coachers they start on the track they well know. **1880** J.B. STEVENSON *Seven Yrs. Austral. Bush* 109 A small mob of quiet cattle . . are termed 'coachers', and are indispensable in working for scrub cattle. **1889** *Illustr. Austral. News* (Melbourne) 1 May 76 (*caption*) There's some scrubbers over there—let the coachers go. **1916** J.M. CREED *Recoll. Aust.* 90 When the wild horses and cattle were not absolutely beyond control, attempts would be made to drive them into a tame herd, technically known as 'coachers', and with such guidance, which they are loath to leave, they could be driven to a stockyard. **1934** *Bulletin* (Sydney) 28 Mar. 20/1 Old Roany, a tough and ancient beast used as a coacher at the slaughter-yards . . was missing. **1945** F. CORK *Tales from Cattle Country* 34 Well-trained 'coachers' lure the brumbies into a winged yard. The 'coachers' are broken station horses which have been at the game for years. **1967** E. HUXLEY *Their Shining Eldorado* 247 Coachers are steady-going and reliable cattle, as it were the prefects, who exert a calming influence on the wild scrubs. **1980** ANSELL & PERCY *To fight Wild* 49 With, say, forty coachers you can handle about twenty-five bulls.

coachman. *Obs.* [Fig. use of *coachman*.] COACH-WHIP. Also **coachman bird, coachman's whipbird.**

1822 B. FIELD *Geogr. Mem. N.S.W.* 10 Oct. (1825) 440 Some [notes] are harsh and vulgar, like those of the parrot-kind, the cockatoo, the coachman's whip-bird. **1827** P. CUNNINGHAM *Two Yrs. in N.S.W.* II. 158 If you should hear a coach-whip crack behind, you may instinctively start aside to let *the mail* pass; but quickly find it is only our native *coachman* with his spread-out fan-tail and perked-up crest, whistling and cracking out his whiplike notes as he hops sprucely from branch to branch. **1836** *Tegg's Monthly Mag.* (Sydney) I. 64 The coachman-bird would almost persuade you that you were listening to the cracking of stage-coach whips on the London City Road. **1847** A. HARRIS *Settlers & Convicts* (1953) 109 You heard nothing but . . the startling note of the coachman bird. **1878** MRS MEREDITH *Grandmamma's Verse-Bk.* 35 He's known as 'the coachman', because his song Is just like a whistle shrill, And the last note mimics the crack of a thong, In a hand of practised skill. **1892** P.D. LORIMER *Songs & Verses* (1901) 202 And the *whacking* of the Coachman, From the thicket's leafy den.

coach-whip. [Fig. use of *coach-whip*: see quot. 1793.] The bird *Psophodes olivaceus* (see WHIPBIRD). Also **coach-whip bird.**

1793 W. TENCH *Compl. Acct. Settlement* 175 To one of them, not bigger than a tom-tit, we have given the name of coach-whip, from its note exactly resembling the smack of a whip. **1801** J. LATHAM *Gen. Synopsis Birds* Suppl. II. 222 It has a long single note, not unlike the crack of a coachman's whip, hence called the *Coach-whip Bird.* **1833** W.H. BRETON *Excursions N.S.W.* 273 The coachman, or coachwhip, is a small bird, with a note which terminates with a jerk. **1865** G.F. ANGAS *Aust.* 92 The 'coach-whip' . . is a handsome greenish bird. **1881** A.C. GRANT *Bush-Life Qld.* I. 213 That is the coach-whip bird. There again. Whew-ew-ew-ew-*whit*! How sharply the last note comes! **1903** *Victorian Naturalist* XX. 99 Nest and eggs of Coachwhip-bird, *Psophodes crepitans.* **1928** C.G. LANE *Adventures Big Bush* 113 Coach-whip birds cracked their vocal 'whips'. **1944** C. BARRETT *From Bush Hut* 19 The coachwhip birds had built their cup-shaped nest of rootlets in the midst of the tangle.

coachwood. [From the use of the timber in coach-building.] Any of several trees, esp. the N.S.W. and Qld. *Ceratopetalum apetalum* (fam. Cunoniaceae), having a fragrant bark and serrated leaves, and yielding a versatile light brown to pinkish brown timber; the wood of these trees. Also *attrib.*

1860 G. BENNETT *Gatherings of Naturalist* 325 Another species is named Coach-wood, Leather-jacket, and also Light-wood by the colonists (*Ceratopetalum apetalum*). **1880** J. BONWICK *Resources Qld.* 83 The Coachwood, a *Ceratopetalum*, rising 100 feet, has fragrant soft, light, but tough wood, suitable for furniture and coach-building. **1891** *Proc. Linnean Soc. N.S.W.* VI. 138 *Callicoma serratifolia*. . . Sometimes called 'Coachwood' in the Braidwood district. **1893** D.J. FROST *Crown Lands N.S.W.* 19 Among the timbers which these northern river forests contain are . . coach-wood, [etc.]. **1936** E. MCDONNELL *Land of Budgeriga* 48 Oh spot beloved, long lost to view, Where sassafras and coachwood grew. **1956** N.K. WALLIS *Austral. Timber Handbk.* 4 Coachwood is used for rifle furniture, motor body work, shoe heels, turnery, joinery, furniture and aircraft plywood manufacture. **1979** *Sydney Morning Herald* 5 Sept. 6/5 It is impossible to drop trees on these steep slopes without them crashing into the coachwood rainforest below.

coalie. Also **coaley.** [Prob. survival of Br. dial. *coaly* (see quot. 1846).] A wharf labourer who loads coal into ships, a coal-lumper.

[**1846** 'HON. F.L.G.' *Swell's Night Guide* 78 A most motly [*sic*] group of shicksters, flash-lads, loggers, coalies, watermen, and lightermen.] **1882** *Sydney Slang Dict.* 4 Two quarts of brimming porter, With several goes of gin beside, Drained Bet the Coaley's Daughter. **1907** *Truth* (Sydney) 26 May 1/4 The coalies will be down in the dumps when these machines arrive. **1909** *Bulletin* (Sydney) 9 Dec. 34/2 Shortly after twelve a mob of 'coalies' swarm into the dining-room like a plague of black beetles. **1911** *Truth* (Sydney) 5 Feb. 1/7 It is an ironical fact that houses built for wharf-lumpers and coalies should have a rent which only a middle-class semi-genteel city coin-counter . . could look at. **1955** J. MORRISON *Black Cargo* 214 The coalies congregated. **1982** *Access* Mar. 21 On the coal wharves, which were called *Siberia* because the work was so hard, the 'coalies' even had to provide their own shovels!

coalopolis. A name given to Newcastle, N.S.W., because of its traditional association with coal-mining.

1891 *Truth* (Sydney) 8 Feb. 1/3 The honest miners of Coalopolis. **1956** G. MACKANESS *Art of Bk.-Collecting Aust.* 10 Newcastle, the coalopolis and second city of New South Wales.

coast, *n.* Used *attrib.* in Special Comb. **coast disease,** a disease of sheep, formerly prevalent in parts of coastal s. Aust., caused by a deficiency of cobalt and copper; **myall,** the tree *Acacia binervia* (fam. Mimosaceae) of the e. coast, which has silvery foliage and often occurs in rocky soil near creek gullies and rivers; also **coastal myall; she-oak,** any of several coastal trees of the genera *Allocasuarina* and *Casuarina* (fam. Casuarinaceae); see also SHE-OAK 1; **wattle,** BOOBIALLA a.

1863 W. MILNE Notes on Journey S. Eastern District 9 Jan. 28 The frightful **Coast disease** which has always made such havoc all along this part of the Coast of So. Australia amongst Sheep & Cattle. **1871** *Austral. Town & Country Jrnl.* (Sydney) 21 Jan. 75/1 They call it the 'coast-disease'; but in many places it extends from the coast 100 miles inland. **1950** *Bulletin* (Sydney) 8 Feb. 12/3 Never knew kangaroos suffered from 'coast' disease. **1978** *Cobalt Deficiency in Sheep* (S.A. Dept. Agric. & Fisheries) p. xciv, Treatment for Coast Disease is ineffective unless both cobalt and copper are provided. **1980** J. SEAGER *Kangaroo Island Doctor* 86 Very little was known about coast Disease. . . Sheep became emaciated, their bones were fragile and broke easily. **1895** J.H. MAIDEN *Flowering Plants & Ferns N.S.W.* 13 The wood strongly resembles that of Myall, and as it is purely a coast and coast-range species we propose to designate it '**Coast Myall**'. **1935** E. COLEMAN *Come back in Wattle Time* 25 Only one of our Australian wattles is known to be poisonous. This is the Coastal Myall (*A. glaucescens*), an Eastern species, ranging from South Australia to Queensland. **1956** T.Y. HARRIS *Naturecraft in Aust.* 165 Found on the east coast, Coastal Myall has a pale grey-green appearance, fairly broad sickle-shaped phyllodes, and rod-shaped flowers of a delicate yellow in spring. **1981** L. COSTERMANS *Native Trees & Shrubs S.-E. Aust.* 306 *Acacia binervia* (syn. *A. glaucescens*) Coast Myall . . Scattered mostly on rocky sites near rivers and creek gullies. **1880** *Argus* (Melbourne) 2 Feb. 6/7 Casuarina quadrivalvis, the '**coast sheoak**'. **1903** G. SUTHERLAND *Australasian Live Stock Man.* (ed. 2) 384 One vegetable specific sometimes recommended is the foliage . . of the casuarina or 'Coast She-Oak'. **1984** *Canberra Chron.* 22 Feb. 15/2 C[*asuarina*] *equisetifolia* (coast she-oak). **1880** *Argus* (Melbourne) 2 Feb. 6/7 Acacia sophorae . . the '**coast wattle**'. **1921** A.J. CAMPBELL *Golden Wattle* 36 In tea-tree groves by the seashore, in sunny glade, and in shadowy scrub alike, the splendid Coastal Wattle (*Acacia longifolia*) runs riot. **1935** T. RAYMENT *Cluster of Bees* 171 Ten or twelve feet above me, in amongst a clump of coast-wattle, I discerned a face. **1948** H.A. LINDSAY *Bushman's Handbk.* 7 Though found inland as well as on the coast, it is usually called coast wattle and is the main vegetation of the coastal dunes as far down as Fremantle. **1985** *Age* (Melbourne) 13 Sept. (Suppl.) 6/4 Keep to the sandy shore, around a deep bay bordered by dense coast wattle.

coast, *v. Obs.* [U.S. *coast* to wander about aimlessly; orig. to travel downhill without exerting effort.] *intr.* With **about:** to travel as a tramp.

1878 'R. BOLDREWOOD' *Ups & Downs* 295, I ain't like you, Towney, able to coast about without a job of work from shearin' to shearin'. **1945** S.J. BAKER *Austral. Lang.* 104 Expressions to describe being on the tramp . . *to swag it, chase the sun, coast about.*

Hence **coaster** *n.*

1875 *Austral. Town & Country Jrnl.* (Sydney) 27 Mar. 503/3 A voluble, good-for-nothing loafing imposter, a regular 'coaster'. **1895** *Worker* (Sydney) 26 Oct. 4/1 The tramp, whaler, coaster, swaggy, traveller, sundowner and gipsy. **1955** N. PULLIAM *I traveled Lonely Land* 374 *Coaster*, a tramp.

coasty, *a.* Also **coastie.** Affected by *coast disease* (see COAST *n.*); associated with the disease.

1886 J.F. CONIGRAVE *S.A.* 108 Disease is almost unknown . . except occasionally on the swampy land of the coast, where the sheep sometimes become 'coastey'. **1887** *Adelaide Observer* 3 Dec. 27 Some of the coast is coasty in winter. **1911** *Bulletin* (Sydney) 30 Mar. 14/4 'Coastie' stock, when removed to an inland pasture, rapidly recover. **1976** *West of Peesey* (Warooka Hist. Committee) 68 Cattle from 'The Dairy' were pastured there to spell them from the 'coasty' areas.

coat. [Of unknown origin; but see quot. 1983.] In the phr. **to be on the coat,** to be ostracized, in disfavour, 'beyond the pale'.

1940 P. KERRY *Cobbers A.I.F.* 21 Once yer on the coat yeh stay there, an' yer pleadin's go fer nought. **1945**

J. HOLMES *Is it Dinkum?* 11 On election day, when law says 'tis compulsory to vote, Many show hostility, and say 'it's on the coat'. **1953** K. TENNANT *Joyful Condemned* 92, I happened to say something about that old hag Jess who runs it, and she's had me on the coat ever since. **1967** *Kings Cross Whisper* (Sydney) xxxviii. 10/1 *On the coat*, a person who is unpopular. **1973** F. PARSONS *Man called Mo* 47 It was the 'He's on the coat' sign, a gesture of supreme contempt. **1983** STURGESS & BIRNBAUER *Journalist who Laughed* 28 *On the coat*... To ostracize someone, particularly a strike-breaker. From the days when seamen or dock-workers would signal by jerking on the right lapel.. that a particular individual was a blackleg.. or that a specific job or ship was blacklisted.

coathanger. [Fig. use of *coathanger*: see quot. 1940.] A name for the Sydney Harbour Bridge.

[**1940** D. AUCHTERLONIE *Kaleidoscope* 7 Twinkle, twinkle little stars On a million motor-cars, Along the Harbour bridge so high, Like a coat-hanger in the sky.] **1943** *Troppo Tribune* (Mataranka) 12 Apr. 1 A number of New South Welshmen.. anxious for a glimpse of the famous 'coat-hanger' that means home. **1953** *New Settler in W.A.* (Perth) III. x. 1 Overshadowing the city is the Sydney-sider's proudest possession—the Harbour Bridge—fondly called by local residents 'The Coat Hanger'. **1955** 'S. RUDD' *Far & Near* 11 We reached the famous Sydney Harbour Bridge, or as Melbournites call it, the Coathanger. **1967** A. SEYMOUR *One Day of Yr.* 116 They'd come to look at the Bridge in the full moon.. .. The huge arch ('the bloody Coat-hanger' Ginge called it) had been part of the scene for ages now. **1979** A.J. BURKE *Bite Pineapple* 21 This coathanger was thought by seamen to be an ugly monumental blunder—especially to those who were familiar with the Golden Gate bridge. **1983** *Sydney Morning Herald* 18 June 31/5, I like it here [*sc.* Melbourne] but I'd give anything for a glimpse of the old coathanger.

Cobar /ˈkoʊbɑ/. [The name of a copper-mining town in w. N.S.W.]

1. *Obs.* A penny.

1898 *Bulletin* (Sydney) 1 Oct. 14/3 A few more W.Q. slang words. A penny is a 'Cobar', 3d. a 'traybit', 6d. a 'zack'. **1900** *Pastoral Times* (Deniliquin) 6 Jan. 2/5, I had accoomerlated a thrummer, and Bill 'ad a Cobar, but Tom, Jack and 'Arry 'adn't a bean. **1911** E.S. SORENSON *Life in Austral. Backblocks* 36 You can bet your bottom Cobar he will put all his ingenuity into it. **1920** *Bulletin* (Sydney) 15 Jan. 20/2 Western Queensland slang of my day.. 'Cobar', a penny.

2. Special Comb. **Cobar shower,** a dust storm; also as rhyming slang for 'flower'.

1952 J. CLEARY *Sundowners* 105 He could feel the dust falling on him like a dry rain. A Cobar shower, they called this. **1955** N. PULLIAM *I traveled Lonely Land* 374 *Cobar shower*, a dust storm. **1959** S.J. BAKER *Drum* 77 Cobar shower, a flower.

cobba-cobba. /ˈkɒbə-kɒbə/. [a. Bardi *gaba gaba.*] A corroboree. Also *attrib.*

1943 *Bulletin* (Sydney) 8 Sept. 12/3 He could take any new scene or experience, from a mass conversion to a hanging, and reproduce.. a cobba-cooba play. **1953** L. & C. REES *Spinifex Walkabout* 100 'They love their cobba-cobba. Why should we interfere?' We realized that probably only one in twenty thousand Australians had ever witnessed a corroboree.

cobber. [Prob. f. Br. dial. *cob* to take a liking to: see EDD *v.*[2]]

1. An intimate; a companion; a friend. Freq. used as a mode of address. Also *attrib.*

1893 *Worker* (Sydney) 3 Aug. 2/4 He overloads his 'cobber's' ration bags and gives a strange traveller *nil.* **1894** J.W. LONGFORD *Under Lock & Key* 12 The bearer of this stiff has been a good kobber of mine in stir. **1898** *Bulletin* (Sydney) 29 Oct. 15/1 On a racecourse, the other day, saw a gentleman manipulating a purse and sovereigns. Suddenly 'cobber' walks up behind him, 'Nit! Hopscotch on yer paddy-whack, right hook.' Artist disappears. **1902** *Truth* (Sydney) 13 Apr. 1/4 Our 'yeller' cobbers, the Japs. **1908** E.G. MURPHY *Jarrahland Jingles* 18 A man 'oo shakes 'ee's cobber's wife deserves an ounce of lead. **1917** F.J. MILLS *Dinkum Oil* 16 'Sister,' he said, 'You've been a real cobber to me.' **1918** *Kia Ora Coo-ee* May 13/3 'Who goes there?' he roared. 'A bloomin' cobber,' was the reply. **1922** *Bulletin* (Sydney) 29 June (Red Page), Who would not prefer that poetry-in-one-word—'cobber'—to the vapid equivalents 'old bean' or 'old thing' or 'old top' of the Englishman? **1929** *Ibid.* 26 June 14/1 'He was my cobber'—an expressive blend Of 'mate' and 'pal', more definite than 'brother' And somewhat less perfunctory than 'friend'. **1942** T. KELAHER *Digger Hat* 53 For he wasn't much at marching, Or at any sort of drill, But he *was* a dinkum cobber—And we're thinking of you, Bill. **1949** D. WALKER *We went to Aust.* 193 'Cobber' according to Mr Calwell, is not Australian at all, but Yorkshire, eighteenth century. **1957** *Austral. Lett.* (Adelaide) June 19/1 The use of the term 'cobbers' gives away this kind of criticism: it went out of date twenty-five years ago. **1963** D. NILAND *Dadda Jumped* 135 Some jokers go round on their lonesome, but I reckon that does things to a man. He needs a cobber. **1968** J. ALARD *He who shoots Last* 89 'Ya sure went bad me old cobber,' laughed Bill. **1976** *Bronze Swagman Bk. Bush Verse* 65 Come in, old cobber, and swallow a spot. **1982** *Canberra Times* 1 Dec. 12/3 'It appears that in Australia it has become popular to clobber your cobber, and we happen to be your cobber,' he said. 'We don't ever publish in New Zealand details of Australian criminals being deported, or how many Australians are on welfare in New Zealand, because that is not the thing you do to your mate.'

2. Special Comb. **cobber dobber,** one who informs on a colleague (see DOBBER).

1966 S.J. BAKER *Austral. Lang.* (ed. 2) 191 *Cobber-dobber*, one who betrays a friend. **1969** C. CARSTAIRS *Zero Heroes* 45 You rotten cobber-dobber. **1972** A. CHIPPER *Aussie Swearers Guide* 33 If your Grandma's funeral once again falls on Melbourne Cup day, it's a *cobber dobber* who asks the boss if he's ever counted your deceased grandmothers.

Hence **cobberless** *a.*, **cobbership** *n.*

1957 F. CLUNE *Fortune Hunters* 1 His mind was made up, and I was **cobberless.** **1944** S. BROGDEN *Sky Diggers* 107 **Cobbership** and a cool approach to all problems—if there is a more Australian aspect of war it would be difficult to find.

cobber, *v.* [f. prec.] *intr.* To make friends with. Freq. with **up.**

1918 *Kia Ora Coo-ee* June 4/1 I've cobbered up with the bloke on guard here. **1923** J. MOSES *Beyond City Gates* 29 'How's the country down your way?'.. 'Oh, fair,' said Jimmy, cobbering up in true Australian style. **1925** E. MCDONNELL *My Homeland* 30, I struck there an old-aged pensioner... We cobbered. **1929** J.L. MOORE *Canine King* 103 He was once overheard to say.. gazing down at his old dog, 'Ginger, you've cobbered up with an unfortunate poor blighter.' **1935** *Bulletin* (Sydney) 31 July 20/3 The case of the Alsatian that cobbered up with a steer.. reminds me of an equally queer friendship. **1946** F. CLUNE *Try Nothing Twice* 85 I'd cobbered up with a shearer or, rather he'd cobbered up with me when he found I had five bob. **1949** *Bulletin* (Sydney) 12 Jan. 28/2 A school of jackasses chose an overhanging limb near by for their dormitory.. and gradually the birds cobbered-up with us. **1967** R. DONALDSON et al. *Cane!* 194 We've got a bit of cobbering t' do. **1978** W. HOWCROFT *Dungarees & Dust* 3 Old 'Bob the Dog', handyman at the local pub, cobbered up with another boozy character.

cobbera, var. COBRA *n.*[1] and *n.*[2]

cobbler, *n.*[1] [Of unknown origin.]

a. *W.A.* The fresh-water catfish *Tandanus bostocki* of w. Aust., having harmful spiny fins. **b.** The marine fish *Gymnapistes marmoratus* of s. Aust. which has similar fins.

1831 G.F. MOORE *Diary Ten Yrs. W.A.* 10 Nov. (1884) 87 Fished for *cobblers* in the evening. **1832** *Ibid.* 14 Sept. 136 There is another species, somewhat of the nature of an eel, with a sharp spine which it can erect at pleasure; this is caught only in the fresh water, and is called a cobbler. **1847** E.W. LANDOR *Bushman* 394 A flat-headed, tapering fish called a 'cobbler'. This.. has a sharp, serrated bone an inch in length on each side of its head. **1915** *Bulletin* (Sydney) 1 Apr. 13/2 'Cobbler'.. is a corruption. The correct name is 'cobra', bestowed, I presume, on account of the fish's sting being likened to that of the Indian snake. **1948** H.A. LINDSAY *Bushman's Handbk.* 95 There are many fish, despised because of some peculiarity.. which are really excellent eating. The cobbler of Western Australia is one. **1974** T.D. SCOTT et al. *Marine & Freshwater Fishes S.A.* 174 The name 'Cobbler' as applied to this species, should not be confused with the Catfishes of Western Australia, which are commonly named Cobblers. Our species [*sc. Gymnapistes marmoratus*] is often encountered by net fishermen.. and the pain caused by a sting from the spines.. can be very excruciating. **1976** E. WORRELL *Things that Sting* 51 Stinging fish which are well known to fishermen are the.. Fortescues.. and the Cobbler from South Australia. **1983** *West Austral.* (Perth) 19 Sept. 1/4 Cobblers forced the closure of Sorrento beach, north of Perth, yesterday.

cobbler, *n.*[2] [Shortened form of *cobbler's last*, as a pun on *last.*] A sheep which is difficult to shear and therefore often the last sheep to be taken from a pen: see quot. 1898, and also SNOB *n.*[2] Also *attrib.*

1871 *Cornhill Mag.* (London) Jan. 87 The 'Cobbler', or last sheep was seized, and stripped of his rather dense and difficult fleece. **1888** *Bulletin* (Sydney) 8 Sept. 9/3 Shearers call the last and always the worst, sheep in the pen 'the cobbler'. **1898** *Ibid.* 17 Dec. 15/1 *Cobbler* need not be the last or any other sheep in a pen. By *cobbler* shearers mean a dirty, sticky or matted and wrinkly sheep—one that is hard to shear. Two men catching out of one pen naturally avoid bad sheep—i.e., *cobblers*—as long as possible; and pens not being refilled until the last sheep has been caught the last sheep is more often a *cobbler* than any other... The term, I think, comes from the old proverb: 'As dirty as a cobbler'. **1899** *Ibid.* 4 Mar. 14/4 A cobbler is a dirty, matty, hard-to-shear sheep. Anyone who's been in a shed at shearing-time has heard shearers yell out to penners-up, 'Here don't sneak all the — cobblers into my pen!' **1905** *Steele Rudd's Mag.* (Brisbane) July 652 One of the sheep was a big coarse brute with a two-season fleece on him, matted, tangled, and filled with small sticks, thorns, burrs, and the like, and some speculation was rife as to who would get the 'cobbler'. **1910** H. JACKSON *Broken Fleece* 36 From the first off the shears to the 'cobbler'. **1949** *Bulletin* (Sydney) 27 Apr. 14/2 The sheep were clean and free from 'cobblers' which were small burrs that grew on a plant about 9 in. high and were known as 'cobbler's pegs'... The 'cobbler'-wattled sheep was always the last to be shorn, and came to be known as 'the cobbler'. **1965** J.S. GUNN *Terminol. Shearing Industry* i. 15 The last sheep left in the catching pen (because it was difficult to shear) is called the 'cobbler', a play on 'the cobbler's last'... It was a simple transfer to use the term 'cobbler' or 'sandy cobbler' to describe a rough hard sheep at any time. **1974** *Austral. Folksongs* (Folk Lore Council Aust.) 61 The sheep are tall and wiry where they feed on the Mitchell grass, And every second one of them is close to the cobbler class.

cobbler's awl. [Transf. use of *cobbler's awl* the avocet, so called from the shape of the beak.] SPINEBILL.

1843 J. GOULD *Birds of Aust.* (1848) IV. Pl. 61, *Acanthorhynchus tenuirostris*.. Cobbler's Awl, Colonists of Van Diemen's Land. Spine-bill, Colonists of New South Wales. **1861** 'OLD BUSHMAN' *Bush Wanderings* 154 The *Cobbler's Awl* bird was a pretty little bird of a chestnut-brown colour... The beak was long, thin and curved. **1919** *Bulletin* (Sydney) 16 Jan. 24/4 'Cobbler's awl' (spinebill).

cobbler's peg. [Fig. use of *cobbler's peg*: see esp. quots. 1882 and 1949.]

1. Usu. in *pl.* Any of several plants, esp. the annual herbs *Bidens pilosa*, having barbed fruits, and *Erigeron linifolius* (both fam. Asteraceae).

1882 *Proc. Linnean Soc. N.S.W.* VII. 78 A species of *Enigeron* [*sic*] (*canadensis* or *linifolius*). It goes by the name of cobbler's peg, from the ready way in which the erect fragments of old stems penetrate the shoes. **1890** A. MACKAY *Austral. Agriculturist* (ed. 2) 148 Malignant weeds.. are taking the place of so many valuable grasses,.. cobbler's pegs (*Erigeron linifolia*) [etc.]. **1899** *Truth* (Sydney) 19 Feb. 8/3 For the 'brook' is dry and stony And the crop has 'cobbler's pegs'. **1914** H.M. VAUGHAN *Australasian Wander-Yr.* 237 Along the banks of the creeks were flourishing a few coarse and strongly aromatic weeds, mostly owning such expressive names as 'Stinking Roger' and 'Cobbler's Pegs'. **1949** *Bulletin* (Sydney) 27 Apr. 14/2 The sheep were clean and free from 'cobblers' which were small burrs that grew on a plant about 9 in. high and were known as 'cobbler's pegs' because they somewhat resembled the wooden boot-sprig in common use at that time. **1965** *Coast to*

Coast 1963–64 72 It was a dirt track, overgrown with thistles, burrs and cobbler's pegs.

2. *pl.* The pneumatophores of certain mangrove species usu. protruding vertically from the submerged roots.

1896 F.G. Aflalo *Sketch Nat. Hist. Aust.* 259 In the Queensland estuaries . . may be seen . . oysters adhering to the horizontal off-shoots (called 'cobbler's pegs') of the White, Red and Orange Mangroves. **1938** F. Ratcliffe *Flying Fox & Drifting Sand* 44 We . . plodded inland, cursing the cobbler's pegs heartily as we went. [*Note*] Little projections from the surface roots, peculiar to this species of mangrove. **1948** R. Raven-Hart *Canoe in Aust.* 205 The White Mangroves, half-flooded at high tide, with . . the curious stumps which Alan called 'cobbler's pegs', the things that grow up from the roots to get away from the noisome mud into the air.

cobborn, var. Cabon.

cobra /'kɒbrə/, *n.*[1] *Obs.* Chiefly *Austral. pidgin.* Also **cobbera.** [a. Dharuk *gabara.*] The head, skull.

[**1790** J. Hunter *Hist. Jrnl. Trans. Port Jackson* (1793) 408 *Caberra*, the head.] **1831** *Sydney Herald* 14 Nov. 4/1 After a hard fought battle they parted good friends, some of their *cobberas* having sustained considerable damage. **1833** *Currency Lad* (Sydney) 20 Apr. 3 Defendant . . began to deal some ugly thumps on the *cobra* of complainant. **1853** *Moreton Bay Free Press* 8 Feb. 3/3 Mr Horne fired his pistol at them, and so close as to go through the wool of Wickaty Wee's 'cobbera'. **1869** *Adelaide Punch* 25 Mar. 83/2 *Cobra* (head), Caput is believed to be the origin. **1878** J.H. Nicholson *Opal Fever* 100 The cobra of the Scottish chief I pillowed on a bag of beef. **1894** A.B. Bell *Oscar* 17 My colonial, Tim, you've a good old cobbera (head) on yer. **1899** G.E. Boxall *Story Austral. Bushrangers* 243 When all was quiet Gilbert dismounted, turned over Parry's body, and remarked coolly, 'He got it in the cobbera. It's all over with him. Well, I'm sorry for it. He's the bravest trap I've met yet.' **1912** J. Bradshaw *Highway Robbery under Arms* (ed. 3) 24 Up the backbone and on to the cobbora, down the whipping side they fly. **1925** M. Terry *Across Unknown Aust.* 185 Black feller bin hit 'em long cobra. [*Note*] Head.

cobra /'kɒbrə/, *n.*[2] Also **cobbera.** [a. Djaŋadi *gabra.*] A shipworm, a mollusc boring into wood in brackish or sea water and traditionally eaten by Aborigines.

1836 J. Backhouse *Narr. Visit Austral. Colonies* (1843) 366 He was driven by hunger, to eat a species of *Teredo*, or Augur-worm, called by the Blacks, Cobra. **1841** *Colonial Observer* (Sydney) 14 Oct. 10/1 A tree emerging out of the water . . was eaten through with worms called *Coppra.* **1845** C. Hodgkinson *Aust., Port Macquarie to Moreton Bay* 47 A wooden bowl full of cobberra, a long white worm, eaten by them, which is found in wood that has been immersed for some time in the brackish water. **1867** J.R. Houlding *Austral. Capera* 286, I am afraid they will eat me for breakfast some morning, if they run short of bandicoots and cobbera. **1871** J. Baird *Emigrant's Guide Australasia* 220 There is a worm, a variety of which is found on land, and another in the brackish water, called by the colonists the cobra, which plays a prominent part in the affairs of Queensland. **1911** *Bulletin* (Sydney) 7 Dec. 13/4 Jarrah is the only wood that successfully resists *T. navalis*, better known in N.S. Wales as cobra. **1926** *Austral. Encycl.* II. 134 In every sea shipworms (*Teredo*) are represented; those that occur in Australian waters have received locally the name 'cobra'. **1965** *Ibid.* 437 *Cobra*, a name commonly applied to Australian species of shipworms, wood-boring bivalve molluscs of the family Teredinidae, with a small gaping white shell anteriorly and a soft worm-like body. **1978** G. Hall *River still Flows* 7 Each farmer and settler along the river-bank had his rowing boat, usually tied to his own small jetty, or drawn up high and dry on the river-bank, for the cobra or toredo worm quickly honeycombed all submerged planks.

cockatiel. [a. Du. *kaketielje*, prob. a. Pg. *cacatilha*, dimin. of *cacatua* cockatoo.] The crested, predom. grey parrot *Nymphicus hollandicus*, widespread in mainland Aust. and popular as a cage bird in Aust. as elsewhere; *cockatoo parrot*, see Cockatoo *n.*[1] 4; Quarrion; Weero.

1877 C.W. Gedney *Foreign Cage Birds* 57 Cockatiels are natives of South Australia. **1890** G.J. Broinowski *Birds of Aust.* II. Pl. 39, The male Cockatiel is a most attentive husband, and takes his turn on the nest with exemplary punctuality. **1977** W.A. Winter-Irving *Bush Stories* 30 Sometimes grey cockatiels break the silence with their soft intimate call.

cockatoo, *n.*[1] [Spec. use of *cockatoo* crested parrot.]

1. Any of a number of large, noisy, crested parrots, esp. in the genera *Cacatua* and *Calyptorhynchus*. Also with distinguishing epithet, as **black, Major Mitchell's, pink, rose-breasted, sulphur-crested, white** (see under first element).

1770 J. Banks *Jrnl.* 1 May (1896) 267 The trees overhead abounded very much with loryquets and cockatoos. **1793** J. Hunter *Hist. Jrnl. Trans. Port Jackson* 69 Birds . . of the parrot tribe, such as the . . cockatoo. **1809** *Sydney Gaz.* 18 June, *Lost* . . a *cockatoo*, lame a little in the left leg, . . the top of the crest or yellow feathers clipped. **1820** J. Oxley *Jrnls. Two Exped. N.S.W.* 96 A new species of cockatoo or paroquet . . was . . seen, with red necks and breasts, and grey backs. **1843** *Sydney Morning Herald* 16 May 2/5 The prisoner had just finished a sentence of several month's imprisonment for stealing a cockatoo. **1848** R. Marsh *Seven Yrs. of my Life* 179 The cockatoo is the most troublesome bird they have. . . They go in large flocks from field to field, and make great havoc amongst the grain. **1865** G.F. Angas *Aust.* 53 On grand occasions—such as . . during a 'corrobbory', . . the men adorn themselves with the feathers of the emu, the pelican, and the cockatoo. **1888** *Sydney Morning Herald* 24 Jan. 1/5 (Suppl.) The cockatoos, magpies, and butcher-birds can easily be taught to talk. **1894** A.F. Calvert *Aborigines W.A.* 28 Cockatoos are considered another great delicacy, and are often killed with the boomerang. **1935** F. Birtles *Battle Fronts Outback* 32 Thousands of birds . . came . . to drink . . finches, cockatoos and small grey doves. **1953** A.W. Upfield *Murder must Wait* 133 Jet-black cockatoos with scarlet under-wings shrieked. **1983** J. Hepworth *More Birds & Beasties Aust.*, Cockatoo speaks before it thinks, Its voice is rough and raucous.

2. A look-out posted by those engaged in an illegal activity, now esp. the playing of two-up, to give warning of any threat of interruption. Also *attrib.*

1827 P. Cunningham *Two Yrs. in N.S.W.* (rev. ed.) II. 288 It being a common trick to station a sentinel on a commanding eminence to give the alarm, while all the others divert themselves, or go to sleep. Such are known here by the name of 'cockatoo-gangs', from following the example of that wary bird. **1843** *Port Phillip Patriot* 23 Mar. 2/5 Through the promptitude of Alderman Russell in watching the movements of a certain little Cockatoo left in the shop, his bolting was to be 'no go'. **1915** M. Cannon *That Damned Democrat* (1981) 70 Mister 'Andy' Fisher, the Caucus Cockatoo. **1934** *Bulletin* (Sydney) 1 Aug. 36/1 For years those betting on the outers had to employ one or more 'cockatoos' to give warning when a John Hop was spotted. **1943** *Ibid.* 4 Aug. 13/2 'If y' jump up an' down an' wave 'em I'll spot y' in time. Got it?' The cockatoo said he had it, moved off and took up station. **1949** L. Glassop *Lucky Palmer* 3 Years of experience as a 'cockatoo' outside hotels, starting-price betting shops and dice and two-up games had given 'Darky' the ability to turn his head from side to side as if it were moving on ball bearings. **1953** A. Moorehead *Rum Jungle* 52 At the entrance a doorkeeper sits, . . 'the Cockatoo' because he tends to adopt a hunched-up cockatoo-like position from having to sit for such long hours in one place; he checks the credentials of the customers. **1964** G. Johnston *My Brother Jack* 80 There was a big mob of gamblers playing two-up . . with their 'cockatoos' posted all around to keep watch for the police. **1971** P. Kenna *Slaughter St. Teresa's Day* (1972) 23 The cockatoo let me down and I ran into some trouble with the night watchman. **1979** B. Bottom *Godfather in Aust.* 45 A male person in an old Holden car is alleged to act as cockatoo during these meetings.

3. *transf.* and *fig.* (With reference to the cockatoo's habit of sitting on a fence: see Cockatoo *v.*[1] 1.) Freq. *attrib.*

1876 *Austral. Town & Country Jrnl.* (Sydney) 16 Dec. 982/3 Whenever this 'pound' holds cattle of *only one class* you hear the deciding shouts from the cockatoo stockmen, who are doing the 'reviewing' safely on the fence. **1877** *Ibid.* 14 Apr. 584/2 This very trifling matter of a 'cockatoo muster' having been thus concluded . . the fires were lighted and the brands put in. **1909** R. Kaleski *Austral. Settler's Compl. Guide* 65 A top 'cockatoo' rail is put on top.

4. Special Comb. **cockatoo bush,** the widespread shrub or small tree *Myoporum insulare* (fam. Myoporaceae), bearing edible fruits (see quot. 1888), also known as Boobialla b.; **orchid,** Flying duck orchid; **parrot** (or **parakeet**), Cockatiel.

1888 *Proc. Linnean Soc. N.S.W.* III. 532 '**Cockatoo bush**'. . . The berries are edible, though somewhat of a saltish and bitter flavour. They are much relished by birds. ***c* 1910** W.R. Guilfoyle *Austral. Plants* 265 'Cockatoo Blue-berry Bush'. **1975** A.B. & J.W. Cribb *Wild Food in Aust.* 44 *Common boobialla, . . Cockatoo bush*. . . The fleshy fruits are rounded and bluish-purple. **1979** E. Smith *Saddle in Kitchen* 19 Flanked by wattles and scrubby cockatoo bush. ***c* 1910** W.R. Guilfoyle *Austral. Plants* 90 'Large Caleana', or '**Cockatoo Orchid**' (terrestrial orchid), f[lower] dark purplish. **1939** M.B. Eldershaw *My Aust.* 220 Orchids . . with names out of the animal kingdom—the donkey, the cockatoo. **1836** *Sydney Herald* 21 Mar. 2/4 Among the birds we noticed . . black, red-headed and pink cockatoos, . . **cockatoo parrots.** **1842** J. Gould *Birds of Aust.* (1848) V. Pl. 45, The flight of the Cockatoo Parrakeet is even and easy, and is capable of being long protracted. **1888** *Centennial Mag.* (Sydney) 131 The plumed cockatoo parrot, which by reason of its coquettish, fragile beauty, one of the early exploring naturalists named the Wood Nymph. **1926** K. Dahl *In Savage Aust.* 251 Parrots were plentiful, especially the nymph, the 'cockatoo parakeet'. **1962** B.W. Leake *Eastern Wheatbelt Wildlife* 78 Budgerigars and cockatoo parrots or weeros appear in flocks when conditions are very dry further north.

cockatoo, *n.*[2] and *attrib.* [From the name of Cockatoo Island in Sydney Harbour, formerly a prison for intractable convicts.]

1. a. *n. Obs.* A convict serving a sentence on Cockatoo Island; one who has served such a sentence. Also **Cockatoo Islander.**

1841 *Sydney Herald* 14 July 2/5 Cockatoo Islanders. . . A report was forwarded to the proper authority in Sydney, from Cockatoo Island, that two of the convicts . . had effected their escape. **1846** *Bell's Life in Sydney* 26 Sept. 3/1 Robert Hunter, an accomplished Cockatoo, was charged with robbing Mr J.R. Torr, of Miller's Point, of two seals. **1851** H. Melville *Present State Aust.* 88 The Cockatoos are, in fact, the gaol-birds of New South Wales. **1868** *Sydney Punch* 14 Mar. 125/1, I am not an escaped, nor even a reformed Cockatoo-Islander, meditating an autobiography. **1870** M. Cash *Adventures* 123 He's the bravest man that you could choose from Sydney men or Cockatoos. . . This name was applied to a body of desperate men, who were imprisoned on Cockatoo Island. **1888** J.C.F. Johnson *Austral Christmas* 49 In the bush in those days, when so many old 'Derwenters' and 'Cockatoo Islanders' were to be met with, Craig's past record would not have greatly militated against him.

b. *attrib. Obs.*

1845 *Sydney Morning Herald* 7 Jan. 2/5 *Cockatoo men*. . . The total number of prisoners on Cockatoo Island under sentence yesterday was two hundred and fifty-three. **1848** *Guardian* (Sydney) 2/5 In connexion with the removal of these Cockatoo Gentry. **1864** *Sydney Punch* 18 June 28/2 Like a Cockatoo Convict weaving cabbage-tree hats. **1900** C. White *Hist. Austral. Bushranging* I. 216 From the very first of Gardiner's road adventures in the West he was associated in the police and press reports with another notorious criminal named Piesley, who was also an old Cockatoo hand. **1911** A.L. Haydon *Trooper Police Aust.* 71 Jackey Jackey was now sentenced to a life term and became a 'Cockatoo bird'.

2. a. *n.* A small farmer; orig. with reference to tenant farmers, brought from Sydney and settled in the Port Fairy district. Also **cockatoo farmer, selector, settler.**

1845 *Standard* (Melbourne) 13 Aug. 3/2 *The Port Fairy Special Survey.*—Most of the settlers on Mr Atkinson's special survey, either have or are about to flit; it appears that the agreement between 'Cockatoo settlers' and their landlord, was merely verbal. **1849** *Argus* (Melbourne) 6 Feb. 2/4 The harvest has fairly commenced, and the *cockatoo farmers* are in the height of their glory. **1853** F.J. Cockburn *Lett.* (1856) 32 The Colonial term for a small cultivator is 'Cockatoo', as the Cockatoos scrape the outside of the trees for grub. **1855** W. Howitt *Land, Labor & Gold* I. 340 A mischievous cockatoo settler. Most agricultural settlers are thus styled by the squatters, because, I suppose, they look upon them, with their enclosures, as plunderers and encroachers on their wild woods, settling down upon them, as the cockatoos do on the ripening corn. **1865** 'SPECIAL CORRESPONDENT' *Transportation* 10 A number of cockatoo farmers have recently sprung up—men who raise sufficient produce for the consumption of their families. **1869** J. MARTINEAU *Lett. from Aust.* 45 The Selector (or 'Cockatoo', as he is nicknamed) . . obtains a seven years' lease of his 640 acres. **1883** R.E.N. TWOPENY *Town Life Aust.* 244 A 'cockatoo' is a selector who works his piece of land out in two or three years, and having done nothing to improve it, decamps to select in a new district. **1897** J.D. HENNESSEY *New-Chum Farmer* 1 Hire yourself out to a dairyman, take a contract with a rail-splitter, sign articles with a cockatoo selector, but don't touch land without knowing something about it. **1900** *Bulletin* (Sydney) 31 Mar. 31/3 These cockatoos are just budding into landed aristocrats. **1904** L. LAWSON *Lonely Crossing* 31 And take the tightest pinch of all From dire misfortune's screw; And humbly barrack for a job The hated cockatoo. **1910** *Huon Times* (Franklin) 12 Nov. 2/4 The cockatoo farmer could buy and sell some honorable members. **1930** *Bulletin* (Sydney) 3 Sept. 21/1 The squatters called the selectors 'cockatoos', and the selectors called the squatters 'crows'. **1953** H.M. EASTMAN *Mem. of Sheepman* 3 The term 'cockatoo' was said to have been given by the blacks to the new settlers then selecting land on the stations. The blacks, knowing that tame cockatoos were fed on wheat, and seeing wheat being grown . . came to the title 'That one cockatoo', now shortened as we know to 'cockie' in language of more recent years. **1963** F. HARDY *Legends Benson's Valley* 242 The Delahuntys were not bad employers as Australian cockatoos went in the hungry thirties; but they were nearly as poor as the men they exploited. **1967** C. SEMMLER *World of Banjo Paterson* (1967) 43 'Acres be d--d!' Billy would scornfully reply; '. . D'ye think we were blanked cockatoo selectors! Out there we reckon country by the hundred miles.' **1976** B. SCOTT *Compl. Bk. Austral. Folk Lore* 168 You cockatoos, you never need fret, for to pay you out I'll never forget.

b. *attrib.* Of or relating to small farming.

1863 W. MILNE Notes on Journey S. Eastern District 9 Jan. 28 Tomorrow we have arranged that he should drive us up to *his Cockatoo* tenants. **1869** F. ALGAR *Hand-Bk. Qld.* 8 To the small agriculturalist, or 'cockatoo' class, the tillage leases offer unusual advantages. **1873** G. WALCH *Aust. Felix* 21 A squatter—of the Cockatoo persuasion. **1880** 'ERRO' *Squattermania* 185 From the cocatoo [*sic*] country above Stirling. **1890** 'R. BOLDREWOOD' *Colonial Reformer* II. 170 And so you believe in these cockatoo chaps? Now, what's the good of 'em? . . All the crop they'll ever get out of that land you may put in your coat pocket.

3. Special Comb. **cockatoo fence,** a fence improvised from logs and branches; **squatter** *hist.*, see quot. 1862.

1861 *Austral. Settler's Handbk.* 13 A **cockatoo fence** . . consists of forked sticks driven into the ground, and saplings, or young trees laid across them. A second and shorter row is requisite, making it a two railed fence. **1867** J.R. HOULDING *Austral. Capers* 269 Miserable makeshift huts and outbuildings, cockatoo fences and temporary drains. **1882** A.J. BOYD *Old Colonials* 37 When we puts up a saplin' fence, it's called a cockatoo fence; that's 'kase its so handy for the cockatoos to roost on when they'm busted 'emselves with corn. **1890** 'LYTH' *Golden South* 120 The fields were divided by open rails or cockatoo fences, *i.e.* branches and logs of trees laid on the ground one across the other, with posts and slip rails in lieu of gates. **1903** *Bulletin* (Sydney) 3 Sept. 17/2 *Re* cockatoo fences, I heard them so called in '58. All the old clearing leases in the Illawarra district were fenced in with what we now call dog-leg fences, at that time called cockatoo fences. **1926** *Aussie* (Sydney) Aug. 10/2 The 'cockatoo fence', so much favoured by the free selectors. **1930** 'BRENT OF BIN BIN' *Ten Creeks Run* (1952) 73 The old cockatoo fences, perfunctorily topped, wouldn't stop a milking cow. **1973** H. LEWIS *Crow on Barbed Wire Fence* 118 We followed an old cockatoo fence through close scrub. **1862** C. MUNRO *Fern Vale* I. 47 One or two settlers of minor importance, and dignified with the title of 'stringy bark' or '**cockatoo**' **squatters**. **1863** *Bell's Life in Sydney* 2 May 3/2 A number of 'cockatoo squatters' . . are located at no great distance from Goat Island.

cockatoo, *v.*[1] [f. COCKATOO *n.*[1]]

1. *intr. Obs.* To perch on a fence: see COCKATOO *n.*[1] 3.

1876 *Austral. Town & Country Jrnl.* (Sydney) 16 Dec. 982/2 The correct thing, on first arriving at a drafting yard, is to 'cockatoo', or sit on the rails, high above the tossing horn-billows, and discuss the never-ending subject of hoof and horn. **1894** E. TURNER *Seven Little Australians* (1912) 209 But everybody else had gone to 'cockatoo'—to sit on the top rail of the inclosure and look down at the maddened creatures: so at length he fastened his bridle to a tree and proceeded gingerly to follow their example.

2. *intr.* To act as a look-out: see COCKATOO *n.*[1] 2.

1954 L. EVERS *Pattern of Conquest* 216 You'd better stay down and cockatoo for us today. **1974** *Warrumbungle Bk. of Verse* (1978) 20 The fettler's son is keeping nit By a knot hole in the wall Cockatoo-ing just in case, The Coppers pay a call. **1982** LOWENSTEIN & HILLS *Under Hook* 16, I used to cockatoo for them—watch for the police.

cockatoo, *v.*[2] *Obs.* [f. COCKATOO *n.*[2] 2.] *intr.* To farm on a small scale. Freq. as *vbl. n.*

1875 *Austral. Town & Country Jrnl.* (Sydney) 4 Sept. 383/2 A farm! Fancy three hundred acres in Oxfordshire, with a score or two of bullocks, and twice as many black-faced Down sheep. Regular cockatooing. **1876** J.B. STEPHENS *Hundred Pounds* 184 The Government under which I 'cockatooed'. **1880** 'ERRO' *Squattermania* 292, I shall think seriously of bidding good-bye to cockatooing. **1892** *Truth* (Sydney) 17 Apr. 1/4 And I know in Asia Minor, where old Adam used to farm, No cockatooing party ever worked the squatter harm.

cockatooer. *Obs.* COCKATOO *n.*[2] 2 a.

1852 MRS C. MEREDITH *My Home in Tas.* II. 137 'Cockatooers' . . are not . . a species of bird, but human beings; who rent portions of this forest from the proprietors . . and vainly endeavour to exist on what they can earn. **1867** *Colonial Monthly* Dec. 242 The poor—terribly poor, 'cockatooers' (as the very small farmers are called). **1872** G.S. BADEN-POWELL *New Homes for Old Country* 456 In all parts of Australia the antagonism existing between squatters and 'free selectors', 'cockatooers', continually forces itself upon the attention. **1891** J. FENTON *Bush Life Tas.* (1964) 91 For in those middle days, there were many 'cockatooers', with more money than prudence.

cockeye. Shortened form of COCKEYED BOB. Also *attrib.*

1910 *Bulletin* (Sydney) 18 Aug. 13/1 A strong 'cockeye' struck us from the N.E., making further progress impossible. **1927** *R. Comm. on Wireless* 1617 When a squall which we call a 'cock-eye' comes along, it does as much damage as a big storm. **1941** K.S. PRICHARD *Moon of Desire* 36 Things were at their worst, with the heat and cock-eyes brewing—everybody's nerves on edge. **1949** I.L. IDRIESS *One Wet Season* 147 A thundering crash and blackness drove over the town with a howl of wind and hissing rain as the Cock-eye burst. **1954** N. BARTLETT *Pearl Seekers* 170 'Cock-eye' clouds clung to the sea rim, and not a breath of wind stirred the mainsails. **1959** *Bulletin* (Sydney) 4 Mar. 16/1 It's cockeye season in Australia's Nor'-west.

cockeye bob. Altered form of COCKEYED BOB. Also *attrib.*

1926 *Bulletin* (Sydney) 25 Feb. 1/1 Cockeye-bob . . seems to have come from the native word 'kikobor'. What the native word means I do not know, but 'cockeye-bob' seems to be the nearest the white man can get to the pronunciation of the native name. *Ibid.* 25 Mar. 24/1 'Kriz' . . attributes the origin of the term 'cockeye-bob' to the native word 'kikobor'. Old North-Westralians relate that it originated on a pearling lugger whose captain and owner was named 'Bob'. His sight was not of the best, and his blackboy diver, on seeing a miniature cyclone on the skyline approaching, used to warn his skipper by singing out 'Cock eye, Bob!' **1938** X. HERBERT *Capricornia* 128 A cockeye bob roared out of the north and tore the front veranda. **1944** 'S. CAMPION' *Pommy Cow* 264 Looks like the Wet's gonna start with a cock-eye bob—they generally come out of a clear sky. **1953** J.K. EWERS *With Sun on my Back* 94 The period of the cyclone and the 'cock-eye bob' when it is unsafe to venture out. **1960** *N.T. News* (Darwin) 9 Feb. 1/7 A Nightcliff Tornado Distress Fund has been opened . . to help families left homeless by Sunday's 'Cockeye Bob' blow. **1978** M. DOUGLAS *Follow Sun* 11 An early 'cock-eye-bob' or cyclone could sink us or put us on a reef.

cockeyed bob. Chiefly *W.A.* and *N.T.* [Of unknown origin; but see prec. (quots. 1926).] A sudden, violent, but short-lived storm or squall.

1894 *Age* (Melbourne) 20 Jan. 13/4 In some places even on the approach of an ordinary thunderstorm or 'Cock-eyed Bob', they clear off to the highest ground about. **1903** M.S. SMITH *W. Austral. Pearl-Shelling Industry* 1 The fleets again dispersed to seek safe anchorages and snug havens from the 'cock-eyed bobs'. **1915** N. DUNCAN *Austral. Byways* 83 Off Ninety Mile Beach, near Broome, the pearl-fishers call them Cockeyed Bobs. **1941** K.S. PRICHARD *Moon of Desire* 97 As swiftly and disastrously as a cock-eyed bob, this situation had blown up and overtaken him. **1951** *Bulletin* (Sydney) 17 Jan. 12/1 A cockeyed-bob is a local storm, sometimes only a few hundred yards across, and, while it can do quite a fair amount of damage, it couldn't be termed a tornado. It can spring up without warning and end as suddenly, and it can be either completely dry or it can bring a deluge. **1960** *N.T. News* (Darwin) 9 Feb. 3/1 Finally the 'cockeyed Bob' itself cut a twisting swathe through the housing areas. **1977** T.A.G. HUNGERFORD *Wong Chu* 36 The pearlers . . anchored in the bay sometimes, to escape the cock-eyed-bobs that sprang up so suddenly on those treacherous coasts. **1981** *Weekend Austral.* (Sydney) 15 Aug. 13/2 A cockeyed bob, the West Australian term for an unpredictable wind.

cockie, var. COCKY *n.*[1] and *n.*[2]

cockney. [Of unknown origin.] A young SNAPPER: see quot. 1906.

[**1874** *N.S.W. Rep. R. Comm. Fisheries* (1880) 1288 Juveniles rank the smallest of the fry, not over an inch or two in length, as the 'cock-schnapper'.] **1906** D.G. STEAD *Fishes of Aust.* 126 Up to about 4 or 5 inches in length, the young fry of the Snapper . . are very often known as 'Cockneys'. . . Beyond the 'Cockney' stage and up to a weight of about a pound and a half, the Snapper is known as Red Bream. . . Later on in life . . this species is known to the fishermen first as 'Squire' and then as 'School Snapper'; while beyond this stage, we get what is known as the 'Old-Man Snapper'. **1951** T.C. ROUGHLEY *Fish & Fisheries Aust.* 77 The cockney and red bream stages are usually found in the estuaries.

cockrag. A loincloth, esp. as worn by an Aboriginal.

1964 T. RONAN *Packhorse & Pearling Boat* 46 Joe, clad in Malay-style sarong with a grey flannel shirt hanging down outside it . . at night put on the cockrag and joined the blacks in their corroboree. **1971** K. WILLEY *Boss Drover* 144 Proper naked buggers—not even cockrag. **1981** NGABIDJ & SHAW *My Country of Pelican Dreaming* 82 Wallambain threw away his woomera and cock rag and jumped in.

cockroach. A hard, dark-coloured lump (of brown sugar).

1903 J. FURPHY *Such is Life* 229 The prince bounded out through the front door, with a triumphant grin on his brown face, and an enormous cockroach of black sugar in his hand. **1921** G.A. BELL *Under Brigalows* 41 Stacks of sugar. . . She and Mamie used to search the bins for hard, brown lumps, called 'cockroaches' by bush children.

cockspur. [Transf. use of *cockspur*, referring to the spiny flower-head.] Any of several plants, esp. the naturalized annual herb *Centaurea melitensis* (fam. Asteraceae), having thistle-like flower-heads with short slender spines, and occurring in all States but not N.T.; see also *Chinese burr* CHINESE.

1891 E.H. HALLACK *W.A. & Yilgarn Goldfields* 13/2 Raspberry jam-trees, silver-grass, and cockspur, with good soil, are now passed. **1935** W. GRAY *Days & Nights in Bush* 16 Cockspur, . . sturt pea . . cover the plains, valleys and hillsides. **1942** E. ANDERSON *Squatter's Luck* 14 Cockspur, or Saucy Jack, I jest cuts back. **1981** G.M. CUNNINGHAM et al. *Plants Western N.S.W.* 720 Maltese cockspur is a widespread and common plant, invading weak pastures and forming dense stands over wide areas.

cocky, *n.*[1] Also **cockie.** [f. COCKATOO *n.*[1] 1 + -Y.]

1. COCKATOO *n.*[1] 1. Also **cocky-bird.**

1834 G. BENNETT *Wanderings N.S.W.* I. 244 The reaper's song might be, 'Fly not yet, little cockies.' **1844** *Colonial Lit. Jrnl.* (Sydney) 18 July 62/2 And I have on the wattle there A speaking Cocky-bird,—And all who pass the Punt declare The like they never heard. **1885** M.A. BARKER *Lett. to Guy* 125 They lay poisoned grain about for the 'pretty cockies', who sometimes drop, apparently out of the sky, dead at your feet. **1900** *Pastoral Times* (Deniliquin) 16 June 2/7 As I was lying on deck I heard the old familiar screech of a 'cockie'. **1911** ST. C. GRONDONA *Collar & Cuffs* 63 The sulphur crested white cocky is seldom seen in more than a half-dozen at the time. **1934** W.A. OSBORNE *Visitor to Aust.* 79 These white 'cockies' can be taught to speak with clear articulation. **1943** *Bulletin* (Sydney) 11 Aug. 12/4 Sully's got an ancient cockatoo that has two feathers at the most. I remarked that cocky would be in for a miserable time when the cold westerlies started. **1958** F. HARDY *Four-Legged Lottery* 66 I'm practising drawing animals and birds lately. Could I come up tomorrow and draw the cocky? **1977** X. HERBERT *Dream Road* 39 George raked four cockies off the vane with a boomerang. **1983** *Austral.* (Sydney) 14 Oct. 9/4, I estimate there are 200 cockies to every kangaroo on the western plains.

2. Special Comb. **cocky apple,** the tree *Planchonia careya* (fam. Lecythidaceae) of W.A., N.T., Qld., and elsewhere in the tropics, bearing an egg-shaped greenish fruit with edible flesh; the fruit.

[**1908** S.W. JACKSON *Field Trip Notebk.* 198 Then I saw the Cockatoo apple tree growing (Careya australis).] **1936** J. DEVANNY *Sugar Heaven* 13 Over the range were the swamps full of horny pandanus, the shining red and scarlet leaves and the green of the cocky apple. **1965** *Austral. Encycl.* I. 218 The name cocky apple is often given to the tropical tree *Planchonia careya* (syn. *Careya australis*), presumably because cockatoos eat the seeds from its drupaceous fruits. **1975** X. HERBERT *Poor Fellow my Country* 275 The . . escape system under the fence still operated for those venturesome enough to go get the cocky-apples. **1981** D. LEVITT *Plants & People* 24 Flowering of Cocky Apple . . shows that it is time to catch turtles.

3. *fig.* In the collocation **cocky('s)-cage,** applied *attrib.* or *absol.* to the mouth or tongue: unpleasantly furred, usu. as a result of an excessive consumption of alcohol; hence **cocky-caged** *a.*

1967 *Kings Cross Whisper* (Sydney) xxxii. 1/2 It will be available in the form of pills which will . . give cocky-cage mouth. **1971** D. IRELAND *Unknown Industr. Prisoner* 8 His tongue was still cocky-caged from the night before, his huge pink belly tight as a drum. **1974** BUCKLEY & HAMILTON *Festival* 183 A mouth like the bottom of a cocky's cage. **1975** *Bronze Swagman Bk. Bush Verse* 53 Head pounding, mouth a cockie's cage.

cocky, *n.*[2] and *attrib.* Also **cockie.** [f. COCKATOO *n.*[2] 2 a. + -Y.]

A. *n.* Chiefly used of a small farmer but now often applied to a substantial landowner or to the rural interest generally: see quots. 1969 and 1974. Also **cocky farmer.**

1871 *Austral. Town & Country Jrnl.* (Sydney) 14 Jan. 58/4 Which prevented good time being made, and led to one horse, ridden by a young cockey, being killed. **1873** Tasmanian Non-State Rec. 103/11 10 July, With you I do not believe the Cockies are so easily driven off good land. **1883** C. PROUD *Murray & Darling Trade* 27/1 That is one of the lines set by a cocky (selector), who came over from his hut in a boat when the water was up. **1891** *Fortnightly Rev.* (London) 547 'Cockies', 'supplementing' their income as petty proprietors by wage-work. **1899** *Austral. Mag.* (Sydney) Mar. 42 'Cockie' was a contemptuous title by which the big farmers distinguished themselves from the little. **1904** *Bulletin* (Sydney) 14 Sept. 39/1 The Callipo shed is not popular among shearers' cooks owing to most of the stands being occupied by cocky farmers from the Downs. **1910** C.E.W. BEAN *On Wool Track* 64 A 'cocky' is a small farmer. He usually selects himself a three-hundred- or five-hundred-acre holding, clears it, fences it, pays for it, sows wheat in it—and then goes to bed to wait for his crop. The next morning he gets up and finds the paddock white with cockatoos grubbing up his seed. He is there to plough and sow and reap—cockatoos. And that, they say, is how he got the name of a cockatoo farmer—a cocky. **1918** *Huon Times* (Franklin) 28 May 2/7 We're all too ready to accept such designations as 'cocky' and 'hayseed'. **1934** T. WOOD *Cobbers* 140 Cocky-farmers, men who work a few hundred acres apiece, and give their name to a gate made from two bits of stick and a length of barbed wire. **1941** OUTHWAITE & CHOMLEY *Wisdom of Esau* 7 It was war to the knife in those days between the squatter and the 'cockie'. **1952** J. CLEARY *Sundowners* 231 Wattle Run, with its fifty thousand acres and its twenty-five thousand sheep, was not a cocky's farm. No, she had meant the cockies with their couple of hundred acres, the men who did all the work themselves. **1965** G. MCINNES *Road to Gundagai* 244 'Cocky' farmer . . really meant, in European terms, a peasant yeoman, although no Australian would ever admit it. **1968** F. ROSE *Aust. Revisited* 30 These small dairy or 'cocky' farmers were and still are the most backward part of the white Australian community. **1969** B. GARLAND *Pitt Street Prospector* 10 Some of those big Cockies don't know how much land they own, or how many sheep they've got. **1974** *New Press* (Perth) I. ii. 6/1 The cockies' organisations, the Farmers' Union and the Pastoralists and Graziers' Association. **1981** A. WILKINSON *Up Country* 105 Everyone agrees it is splendid to see the 'cocky' (farmer) crack it for a quid for once.

B. 1. *attrib.*

1896 *Bulletin* (Sydney) 25 Apr. 27/4 Your 'road-mending' farmer is all over N.S.W. The members are put in by cockie 'road-menders'. **1900** *Tocsin* (Melbourne) 20 Sept. 6/2 We were being led the wrong way by one of the party, who was a 'cockie shearer'. **1911** R.G.S. WILLIAMS *Austral. White Slaves* 97 The Labor Party determined to make a bold bid for the 'cocky' vote. **1915** J.P. BOURKE *Off Bluebush* 67 His wife and kids is waitin' for a dozen lengthy years On their cocky-patch. **1930** V. PALMER *Passage* (1957) 258 These cockie fruitgrowers are damned hard to satisfy. **1941** C. BARRETT *Aust.* 54 It's not too bad being a cocky sheep farmer in Riverina. **1959** H.G. LAMOND *Sheep Station* 51 Small selectors who were trying to be pastoralists and who had just graduated from the cocky class. **1977** R. EDWARDS *Austral. Yarn* 110 The miners and prospectors, mainly from Victoria had to take jobs on cocky farms, and that sort of thing.

2. Special Comb. and collocations: **cocky chaff,** wheat chaff; **country,** a district chiefly devoted to small farming; **cocky's delight,** *cocky's joy*; **cocky('s) gate,** see quot. 1935; **cocky('s) hours,** dawn to dusk; **cocky's joy,** treacle or golden syrup; **cocky's mile,** an idiosyncratic estimate of distance.

1903 *Bulletin* (Sydney) 22 Oct. 17/2 Mixed some oats through a bag of '**cocky chaff**', and turned it out in a corner of a small paddock for my hack. **1913** W.K. HARRIS *Outback in Aust.* 193 We boiled the billy about 9.30 p.m., and threw ourselves down on some bags of 'cocky chaff' (wheat husks). **1948** J.K. EWERS *For Heroes to live In* 99 Harvesters bit off the wheat heads, sifted the grain and sent the cocky-chaff streaming out in a following cloud. **1974** W. ROEDIGER *We Survived* 12 The chaff from around the wheat, which was blown out of the winnower, was always carefully saved. . . It was known as cocky chaff, and as far as nutriment was concerned its value was just about nil. **1982** M. WALKER *Making Do* 80 They used to come in a . . wooden barrel holding about a hundred dozen eggs, packed in cocky chaff. **1943** *Bulletin* (Sydney) 4 Aug. 13/4 Larry, exiled on foot in the **cocky country**, was looking for a job. **1967** G. JENKIN *Two Yrs. Bardunyah Station* 9 People also came from as far away as the cocky country on the West Coast. **1978** D. STUART *Wedgetail View* 45 Been cookin' . . up an' down the country, from the Fitzroy to the cocky country. **1902** *Bulletin* (Sydney) 5 Apr. 32/2 **'Cockie's Delight'**, better known, perhaps, as 'Bullocky's Joy', occupies a prominent position on the table, and may be called the cockie's 'staff of life'. **1916** A.I. MACLEOD *Hack's Brat* (1920) 38 He produced a half-loaf of bread and a tin of 'Cocky's Delight'. . . He cut a thick slice of bread which he smeared generously with treacle. **1918** R.H. KNYVETT *Over there with Australs.* 158 Molasses or 'golden syrup' called 'bullocky's joy', sometimes 'cocky's delight' because it is the chief covering for slices of bread with the bullock-driver or cocky farmer. **1926** *Bulletin* (Sydney) 11 Nov. 22/2 The new Pommy storekeeper knit his brows when the hatter included in his supply order: '2 tins of cocky's delight and a bottle of Mallee marmalade.' How was he to know that treacle and tomato sauce were indicated? **1926** A.A.B. APSLEY *Amateur Settlers* 138 Typical Australian **'cocky' gates.** **1927** T.S. GROSER *Lure of Golden West* 120 On to a Bush track which led through a 'cocky gate'. **1935** R.B. PLOWMAN *Boundary Rider* 196 Some of these were what is known as 'cockies' gates. . . These gates consist of several wires and a piece of wood. At one end the wires are fixed to a gate-post. At the other they are attached to an upright stick at intervals to correspond with those on the gate-post at the opposite end. In between are usually two sticks or droppers to keep the wires apart. **1977** *Ink No. 2* 35 'The first time we've had a cocky gate out front,' he laughed as he drove through. . . He stopped the car, went back and pulled the strands of wire across the opening again. **1982** R. ELLIS *Bush Safari* 49 We drove through mulga and blue-bush country, every now and then opening a cocky gate as we passed through the large paddocks. **1899** *Bulletin* (Sydney) 12 Aug. 14/4 **'Cockies' hours'** are supposed to be 'from jackass to jackass'. **1926** *Ibid.* 14 Jan. 22/3 With a big herd the owner probably has to get down to cocky hours of labor. **1935** *Red Star* (Perth) 20 Sept. 3/3 Those who are already working 'cockies' hours' have to add another 24 hours or so to their working week. **1902** *Bulletin* (Sydney) 4 Oct. 17/1 He has to fetch in cows, . . milk, snatch some damper and **cocky's joy.** **1904** C.W. JOHNSTON *Out-Back Homestead* 69 A pound a week and tucker, Fresh mutton now and then, And 'cockies' joy' for butter, The fare of station men. **1911** C.E.W. BEAN *'Dreadnought' of Darling* 206 Occasionally jam, but more often golden syrup (which goes by the name of 'cocky's joy' because it is cheaper than jam and is therefore supposed, not without reason, to be the delight of the cockatoo farmer). **1918** N. CAMPBELL *Dinky-Di Soldier* 28 And they'll do you well on cocky's joy, an' damper, an' the rest. **1928** L.A. SIGSWORTH *Various Verse* 1 Young mutton chops afrizzle on the grill, and 'cocky's joy' as black as a gin. **1937** *Bulletin* (Sydney) 28 Apr. 20/4 There is no trade secret about cockies' joy being used to give animals sealskin-like coats. As long as I can remember the stock fodder in the Queensland sugar belt has been chop-chop (cut up sugar cane tops) *plus* molasses. **1948** *Ibid.* 18 Feb. 22/1 He shoved his head through the kitchen window and snatched a piece of bread and cocky's joy out of me 'and. **1967** MEREDITH & ANDERSON *Folk Songs Aust.* 13 Porridge and golden syrup—'cocky's joy', as we called it—for breakfast. **1986** *Daily Tel.* (Sydney) 13 Jan. 4/6 At night, there will be an 1830s-style meal at Gardner's Inn. The menu includes wild game broth, pigeon pie, roast mutton, spotted dick pudding and damper with cocky's joy (golden syrup). **1917** *Bulletin* (Sydney) 12 Apr. 24/4 Between Belgrave and Emerald a **cocky's mile** is about 10 furlongs; from Croydon to Lilydale it is rarely less than 12 furlongs. **1948** H.A. LINDSAY *Bushman's Handbk.* 104 Be suspicious of distances given; the proverbial 'cocky farmer's mile' is most unreliable.

cocky, *v. intr.* To farm in a small way. Chiefly as *vbl. n.*

1895 *Worker* (Sydney) 6 July 3/4 You know Sam Jones . . is going to do a bit of cockying on his own. **1898** *Ibid.* 15 Jan. 8/2, I am learning some of the troubles of cockieing in the back country. **1903** *Bulletin* (Sydney) 20 June 35/1 Dad is a grafter . . but he's a fool. He wouldn't be 'cockying' on the fringe of eternal debt and starvation if he wasn't. **1904** *Ibid.* 12 May 16/4 The ranges near Brisbane, a 'cockying' and dairying district only 20 miles from the Q. metropolis. **1909** *Ibid.* 22 Apr. 13/4 Cockying here won't make any Jimmy Tysons. **1918** *Ibid.* 30 May 24/3 Come to Flanders if you want to see dinkum cockying. **1926** *Ibid.* 18 Feb. 24/4, I have had many a good night's sleep in a stripper box . . whilst cockying in the Victorian mallee. **1941** K. TENNANT *Battlers* 52 His wife's usual scheme to get him a job 'cockying' for one of her uncles or cousins would come to nothing again. **1943** G. CASEY *Birds of Feather* 6 Cockying was tough enough since wheat and wool had gone to glory but it was a proper life. **1946** A.J. HOLT *Wheat Farms Vic.* 150 Boys these days haven't got the guts to go cockying. **1973** P. ADAM SMITH *Barcoo Salute* 140, I was cockying until then, but with the depression and then the drought, I went broke like lots more.

cockydom. *Obs.* The community of small farmers.

1904 *Bulletin* (Sydney) 28 Apr. 16/4 In the very near future cockydom will be down to the primitive aborigine stage. **1905** *Ibid.* 17 Aug. 17/1 Victorian cockydom is quite delirious over the prospect of a good season. **1908** *Ibid.* 21 May 14/2 When this dry spell passes . . there will be an unholy squaring up of accounts throughout cockiedom. **1923** *Ibid.* 5 July 22/3 'E.W.' should advise N.S.W. North Coast cockydom to leg-rope every ibis it can catch.

coconut. *Aboriginal English.* [See quot. 1980 (2).] An Aboriginal who lives in a manner perceived by others as repudiating Aboriginal identity; JACKY JACKY b.

1980 *N.S.W. Parl. Papers* (1981) 3rd Sess. IV. 1798 When the Premier . . sends non-Aboriginal people out into the country, they talk to people that we call coconuts. . . They are assimilated black people who sit about the towns and all they are proud of is how many white friends they have. *Ibid.* 1799, I was interested in your description of people to whom you referred as coconuts. . . They are brown on the outside and white underneath.

cod. [Transf. use of *cod* the Atlantic fish *Gadus callarias.*] Any of several fish, some unrelated to the Atlantic cod, incl. the *Murray cod* (see MURRAY 2). Also **codfish.**

1821 T. GODWIN *Descr. Acct. Van Diemen's Island* 9 Fish are caught in abundance . . those most known are skate, mullet, cod. **1825** *Austral.* (Sydney) 8 Dec. 2 Procured a cod-fish from a creek of the river Macquarie. **1833** C. STURT *Two Exped. Interior Southern Aust.* II. 35 During our stay on the Pondebadgery Plain, the men caught a number of codfish, as they are generally termed, but which are, in reality, a species of perch. **1847** G.F. ANGAS *Savage Life & Scenes* I. 92 The cod of the Murray . . are taken with rude hooks. **1854** W. HOWITT *Boy's Adventures* 354 On the Campaspe we saw natives fishing for what they call cod, but which is a sort of bream. **1881** *Proc. Linnean Soc. N.S.W.* VI. 114 *Lotella Callarias*. . . 'Cod' of Melbourne Fishermen. **1930** C.M. YONGE *Yr. on Great Barrier Reef* 216 The water round the margins of the reefs abounds with a variety of coral or rock 'cod', a popular name given to a number of very different fish, none of which has any relationship to the true cod. **1962** N. MONKMAN *Quest Curly-Tailed Horses* 206 There is one menace in the sea that frightens me—the giant groper. It is an enormous cod.

coffee. Used *attrib.* in Special Comb. **coffee palace** [in Br. use for a coffee house from 1879 (see quot. 1880)], a temperance hotel; **shop, tent,** a place of refreshment, usu. a sly grog shop (see SLY GROG 2).

[**1880** *Argus* (Melbourne) 9 Jan. 6/4 We had no doubt that the **coffee palaces** would have a good influence in promoting temperance and checking drunkenness, and they ought to be encouraged.] **1884** *Sands & McDougall's Melbourne & Suburban Directory* 658 *Melbourne coffee palace*—Coffee Taverns Co. (Limited) . . 89 Bourke-st east. **1893** F.B. BOYCE *Drink Problem Aust.* 107 The Melbourne Coffee Palace was opened in Bourke Street . . in 1882, and it was then claimed as the first large building specially erected for the purpose in these Colonies. . . It has 180 bedrooms. **1921** E.F. TREGASKIS *Santa Claus' Message* 8 B.B. had visited the 'Corfie Palis', as the sign announced it, a place which much belied its name, for it did not resemble a palace in any land. It was built of galvanised iron and stringy bark, and coffee was never seen on the premises. There was a tradition that a traveller could procure a cup of tea, if he waited long enough. They certainly dispensed hop beer, and other liquid refreshment. **1922** *Daily Mail* (Sydney) 12 Jan. 3/3, I can't remember ever having been locked out of a coffee palace because I was mad with drink. **1947** E. GEORGE *January & August* 68 A young bushman . . had come out of the Grand Coffee Palace. **1963** X. HERBERT *Disturbing Element* 11 We were about to go on . . a glorious journey of the entire railway system of West Australia, travelling free, with stopovers at the bigger centres in fascinating places called Coffee Palaces. **1965** G. MCINNES *Road to Gundagai* 277 It was a disgrace that his Dear Old Mother should have to stay at a hotel, let alone a temperance hotel or 'coffee palace' as they were known. **1971** P. HASLUCK *Open Go* 85 In my young day we arrived at night to drive away to a 'coffee palace' in a horse-drawn cab through gas-lit streets. **1978** B. KENNEDY *Silver, Sin, & Sixpenny Ale* 27 Alfred Dunn, a highly successful Melbourne architect, was commissioned to design the Coffee Palace . . in the quaint belief that there were many who would prefer 'the quiet home-life of a well-conducted and high-class Coffee Palace' to the perils of licensed hotels. **1852** Tas. Non-State Rec. 56/1 6 Oct., Several **Coffee Shops** on the way, Coffee 6d. per pint, meals 2s. 6. Most of them are sly grog sellers. **1855** W. HOWITT *Land, Labor & Gold* II. 39 It was, no doubt, intended for the so-called coffee-shop at the bottom of the hill, which, like most of these places, is in reality a sly grog-shop. **1853** *Austral. Gold Digger's Monthly Mag.* v. 165 Sighting a **coffee-tent,** we were delighted enough to have a good supper, and soon after, folding our blankets around us, we lay on the floor, and slept in peace. **1855** W. HOWITT *Land, Labor & Gold* II. 279 At some miles from each other, there are two, so-called coffee-tents, but, in fact, grog-shops. **1857** *Bell's Life in Sydney* 14 Feb. 1/3 Swear to the man that keeps the coffee-tent.

coffee-room. *Obs.* [Spec. use of *coffee-room* the public dining-room of an hotel: see OED.]

1. The better appointed of two dining-rooms in an hotel. Also as quasi-*adv.*

1947 M. RAYMOND *Smiley gets Gun* 138 Naturally the Quirks must have the best, so they stayed coffee-room—and not dining room, where the residents ate at a long table covered with newspaper instead of a cloth. **1959** H. LAMOND *Sheep Station* 51 The Keystone . . ran two tables: coffee-room for the social aspirants; dining-room for those who were hut men and ate in the kitchen on stations.

2. *fig.*

1936 *Bulletin* (Sydney) 30 Dec. 20/1 In bush changes a noticeable one is the passing of the coffee-room bagmen. These old chaps, gentlemen once, would sooner camp on the creek and go hungry than go to the hut. They were 'inside' men, by gad, sir!

coil, *v. Obs.* [Prob. fig. use of *coil* to roll or curl up.] *intr.* To (lie down to) sleep.

1830 *Launceston Advertiser* 11 Jan. 3 This . . is . . the last aggression these Bandits will be suffered to perpetrate, and we are certain their capture must take place immediately, if the numerous parties detached in pursuit be not too fond of *coiling*. **1841** *Geelong Advertiser* 13 Feb. 2/3 A flock of ewes, heavy with their first lambs, were 'coiled' near an adjoining hut. **1873** M. CLARKE *Holiday Peak* 82 Nobody says anything to him if he 'coils' in the front parlour all afternoon. **1896** —— *Austral. Tales* 51 A distinguished barrister, after plugging his ears in vain, was compelled one sultry night to take his blankets and 'coil' on the wood heap in order to escape from the roaring of Mr Mountain's fitful diapason. **1902** R. BRUCE *Reminisc. Old Squatter* 148 W'en ther crimson sun's a-boilin' On a swagman an' his drum, All 'e thinks about is coilin' Underneath a crimson gum. **1905** A.B. PATERSON *Old Bush Songs* 28 A few had taken quarters and were coiling in their bunks.

coil, *n. Obs.* [f. prec.] A sleep.

1849 F.R. GODFREY *Extracts Old Jrnls.* 14 Oct. (1926) 27 We were all very tired and determined to have a good 'coil' this morning; but were awakened at daybreak. **1892** G. PARKER *Round Compass in Aust.* 58 Where is he? Gone to to have a coil.

coiler. [f. COIL *v.*] A loafer or idler; a tramp.

1846 *Hogg's Weekly Instructor* IV. 211/2 Coilers are people in Australia who have been improvident or unfortunate, and who, on retiring, not voluntarily, from town gaieties into the bush, become hangers-on at sheep and cattle stations. **1848** *Britannia* (Hobart) 6 Apr. 3/1 A jetty coiler was sent to the house of correction for three months, under the Vagrant Act. **1857** *Vic. Parl. Papers* (1856–57) III. no.48 41 There is a class that are called 'coilers', and those men live upon a very little; they go begging about. **1891** J. FENTON *Bush Life Tas.* (1964) 37 It was my lot to be resting on its bank one day. . . Some stockriders passed. 'Who is that cove?' asked one of them. 'Only some blessed coiler' replied another; and thence-forward the stream was known as Coiler's Creek. **1973** J. MURRAY *Larrikins* 202 *Coiler*, an idler who sleeps on wharves.

coit, var. QUOIT.

colane /kəˈleɪn,ˈkɒleɪn/. [a. Wiradhuri *galayn*. See also GRUIE.] *Emu apple* (a), see EMU *n.*[1] 3.

1903 *Proc. Linnean Soc. N.S.W.* XXVIII. 410 Of *Owenia acidula*, . . the 'Colane', there is a pretty legend told by the aborigines of the Bogan. **1931** M. TERRY *Hidden Wealth* 325 We came across a clump of trees called 'grooi' or 'colain', the only specimens known to local people as existent in the Kimberleys but identical with others in Queensland. **1981** G.M. CUNNINGHAM et al. *Plants Western N.S.W.* 451 Colane usually occurs as scattered single trees or in small clumps. **1981** J. JESSOP *Flora Central Aust.* 197 *Gruie, colane, gooya, sour apple, emu apple*. . . There are a number of vernacular names but none seems to have achieved very widespread use.

Cold Country. *Obs.* A jocular name for Great Britain. Also *attrib.*

1906 *Bulletin* (Sydney) 24 May 15/3 He could tell on sight whether any man he met came from Queensland, N.S. Wales, Victoria, Tasmania, or the Cold Country. **1911** *Ibid.* 17 Aug. 13/2 Before the rabbit and fox and other Cold Country importations got in their fine work, the cat was the pet curse of the blue-nose settlers. **1912** *Truth* (Sydney) 22 Dec. 1/7 How delightful it was to visit the Cold Country to hear the English language spoken in all its purity. **1918** *Ibid.* 5 May 15/8 The Cold Country clinahs, who are wofully ignorant of Australian affairs. **1936** *Bulletin* (Sydney) 1 Jan. 19/4 In the Cold Country a bird is hung by the tail-feathers until it drops.

cold footer. *Obs.* [Prob. orig. U.S., as was *to get (or have) cold feet* (see OEDS *cold, a.* 19).] A cowardly soldier; one who, although eligible for active service, fails to enlist. Also **coldfoot.**

1916 'MEN OF ANZAC' *Anzac Bk.* 102 He was generally considered by all those who knew of him in the squadron to be a 'cold-foot' and his nickname was appropriately 'Icy'. **1916** F.R. CORNEY Let. 31 Oct., I would like to get back again for the battalion's sake as soon as I can, as I would not like anyone to think that I was a 'cold-footer'. **1918** *Poems by Austral. Soldiers* 15 An' the cold-footers screwed with a sneerin' frown At our push uv a 'undred strong. **1919** *Worker* (Brisbane) 29 May 6/4 These rampant females . . scoured their neighbours' hen-roosts for white feathers to post to the 'slackers' and 'cold-footers'. *Ibid.* 13/5 Some of these young ladies were rather fond of using the terms, 'cold feet', 'shirkers' etc., towards those who did not enlist. **1919** 'SCOTTY'S BROTHER' *Desert Trail* p. vi, A malignant minority even went so far as to call them 'cold-footers out on a picnic'—an outing which these damnable stay-at-homes took care not to sample. And as for cold feet in the desert—I never saw them till they were cold in death. **1920** *Aussie* (Sydney) July 15/2 The only persons to whom he showed any animosity were the 'cold-footers' in Australia, represented by *Me Brother Wot Stayed at 'Ome*. **1948** H.W. CRITTENDEN *Rogues' Paradise* 35 Part of the valiant mob who called the Diggers, among even less complimentary epithets, 'six-bob-a-day-murderers', and whom in turn the Diggers described categorically as 'cold-footers'. **1950** F.J. HARDY *Power without Glory* 255 'I am only doing what every able-bodied man should do: go away and fight for his country'. . . 'Well, why don't you go?' . . 'You be quiet, you cold-footer,' an old lady remarked patriotically.

Also **cold-footed** *a.*

1916 'MEN OF ANZAC' *Anzac Bk.* 108 If Jessie could see me now, would she turn me down for some cold-footed well-groomed fellow? **1918** *Truth* (Sydney) 28 July 6/6 We New Zealanders know that there are no cold-footed Australians in the outfit. **1919** C.H. THORP *Handful of Ausseys* 163 Muttering blasphemies against all '--s who are spongin' on their Governmints an drawin' ten an' a zack a day while they dodge a trip to the firin' line, the cold-footed --s'.

coldie. [f. *cold (beer* + -Y.] COLD ONE.

1953 *Tobruk to Borneo* (Perth) Dec. 12, I took a couple of coldies to augment [his] supply. **1968** B. HUMPHRIES *Wonderful World Barry McKenzie*, What I need are a few swift coldies! **1971** *Bulletin* (Sydney) 4 Dec. 11/2 What's more he goes to a garden party at Buckingham Palace, takes along his own coldies, gets boozed, passes out in the shrubbery, then wanders inside and actually meets the Queen. **1976** *Overland* lxv. 7 Bet they're downin' a few coldies. **1981** Q. WILD *Honey Wind* 84 May Father, Son and Holy Ghost keep your oven full of roast help you fill the fridge with coldies bless the young and soothe the oldies. **1982** R. ELLIS *Bush Safari* 144 A muffled voice . . enquired if there was any chance of cracking a coldie.

cold one. A glass, bottle, or can of chilled beer.

[**1944** *Aust. Week-End Bk.* 25, I think I'll go and have a beer. A nice long cold one.] **1962** MARSHALL & DRYSDALE *Journey among Men* 54 You will find the inevitable bottles and cans discarded along the way, where someone has taken, wrapped in wet paper, a few 'cold ones for the road'. **1968** *Swag* (Sydney) ii. 23/1 'You better head for the Star. It's as good a drop as any. . . ' Neither of us spoke again until we were seated before two long cold ones. **1979** B. HUMPHRIES *Bazza comes into his Own*, What say youse and me adjourn to the nearest rubbidy and sink a few cold ones.

collar. [Prob. f. *collar* to take possession of, master.] Paid employment; a job.

1896 *Worker* (Sydney) 11 Apr. 1/3 Work was . . easily obtainable here—every day's Kalgoorlie *Miner* had a column or so of ads for miners, and men found no difficulty in getting into 'collar'. **1903** *Bulletin* (Sydney) 1 Oct. 17/3 There isn't much in bush work, save a 'collar' here and there. **1903** J. FURPHY *Such is Life* 181 Soft collar we got here—ain't it? **1927** J. MATHIEU *Backblock Ballads* 1 As I've written for a collar To a place called Bundaleer, Where we beat all records holler, In the shearing line one year.

collared sparrowhawk. The bird of prey *Accipiter cirrocephalus*, having a rufous mark round the neck, widespread in Aust. and also occurring in New Guinea; SPARROWHAWK a.

1842 J. GOULD *Birds of Aust.* (1848) I. Pl. 19, *Accipiter torquatus* . . Collared Sparrow Hawk. **1945** C. BARRETT *Austral. Bird Life* 38 The swoop of the collared sparrowhawk . . has justly been likened to the flight of an arrow. **1984** M. BLAKERS et al. *Atlas Austral. Birds* 98 The Collared Sparrowhawk lives in New Guinea and Australia.

collar-proud. [Transf. use of *collar-proud*, (of a horse) restive when in harness.] Resentful of constraint.

1919 C. DREW *Doings of Dave* 168, I never seen a man so collar proud. **1924** LAWRENCE & SKINNER *Boy in Bush* (1980) 25 She was a pearl beyond price, was Miss Ethel. So she seemed to me then. Now she's a termagant as ever was: in double 'arness, collar-proud. **1930** K.S. PRICHARD *Haxby's Circus* 162 The holiday had lasted long enough, she said. It had run from a fortnight to a month. Everybody was beginning to get collar-proud.

Collins Street. Also **Collins-street.** [The name of a principal business street in Melbourne.] Used *attrib.* as a Victorian equivalent of PITT STREET.

1938 *Bulletin* (Sydney) 12 Jan. 20/1 They're Collins-street bushies most likely. **1960** *Ibid.* 27 Apr. 18/1 Cooee is translated 'Yoo-hoo', a Collins Street squatter is a drugstore cowboy. **1967** *Ibid.* 4 Nov. 16/1 Despite the jibes, there are relatively few Pitt or Collins Street farmers. **1973** *Ibid.* 10 Feb. 6/2 The Sydney papers called them 'Pitt Street' farmers, the Melbourne papers, 'Collins Street' farmers. **1980** H. STEPHENSON *Cattlemen & Huts High Plains* 18 Sunburned, young, Collins-street bushmen, clad in khaki shorts, and full of excitement over their first acquaintance with pack-horses.

colonial, *a.* and *n.* Now chiefly *hist.*

A. *adj.*

1. Of, belonging to, or characteristic of one of the Australian Colonies, or of these Colonies collectively; Australian, usu. as distinct from British.

1793 D. COLLINS *Acct. Eng. Colony N.S.W.* (1798) I. 298 The *Daedalus* was considered as a colonial ship. **1804** *Sydney Gaz.* 11 Nov., The approach to maturity of our Colonial youth. **1808** *Ibid.* 6 Nov., For sale also, a quantity of Colonial leather and soap, English boot-legs and twine. **1808** *To Viscount Castlereagh* 7 The Colonial Police . . easily took cognizance of the character and conduct of every individual in the community. **1819** *Sydney Gaz.* 17 Apr., It is a matter of colonial pride that the Sabbath is most decently and decorously observed. **1824** *Hobart Town Gaz.* 1 Oct., Colonial Timber may at any time be purchased of an inhabitant of this town. **1834** J.D. LANG *Hist. & Statistical Acct. N.S.W.* II. 114 Mitchell . . has . . *reformed* the colonial nomenclature, by retaining the native name of any remarkable locality whenever it can be ascertained. **1834** M. DOYLE *Extracts Lett. & Jrnls. G.F. Moore* p. v, Grown on our colonial soil in Western Australia. **1835** *Colonist* (Sydney) 25 June 201/3 We should be sorry to throw any obstacles in the way of respectable settlers going beyond the colonial boundary with their flocks and herds. **1836** J. BACKHOUSE *Extracts from Lett.* (1839) iv. 12 We engaged at Dapto a black native . . to be our guide. . . His colonial name was Tommy. **1838** *Tegg's N.S.W. Pocket Almanac* 12 *August* . . is a fit season for sowing cabbages, . . turnips, and Colonial or New Zealand spinach. **1844** *Colonial Lit. Jrnl.* 4 July 26/1 This system of vilifying every thing colonial has been carried to a ridiculous extent. **1846** *Melbourne Argus* 16 June 2/4 Plans, it is true, were furnished me by the colonial Architect for a commodious building. **1849** A. HARRIS *Emigrant Family* (1967) 12 Our knowledge of colonial '(*Anglicè*, Australian)' matters is tolerably sound. **1860** 'LITTLE JACOB' *Colonial Pen-Scratchings* 94 Edward and Cary were daily getting more colonial, and more reconciled to their new country. **1861** W. WESTGARTH *Aust.* 32 The present colonial population of Australia, numbering nearly 1,100,000, is probably much greater than the aboriginal population has ever attained to. **1862** 'W.T.G.' *Quite Colonial* (*c* 1948) 16 Before I've done with you, you'll be quite Colonial. . . What I mean by the expression , is for a man to become hardy and fearless, not easily upset by trifles, and ready to turn his hand to anything and everything that's not dishonourable. **1871** *Emigrant's Wife* I. 127 *Colonial*, that is Australian, theatres are somewhat peculiar. **1872** MRS E. MILLETT *Austral. Parsonage* 260 The convict hospital contained no accommodation for women. . . The colonial surgeon, who resided at the depôt, was from home. **1873** W. THOMSON-GREGG *Desperate Character* I. 23 It was really marvellous what a subject of congratulation it used to be with some people, that they had become 'quite colonial'—in their own estimation, of course—as if there was something to be ashamed of in the fact of one's being a recent importation from 'home'. **1874** J.T. FALLON *Murray Valley Vineyard* 13 In a few years . . the wines would obtain a good name, and we would have our colonial hock, claret and burgundy. **1890** 'R. BOLDREWOOD' *Squatter's Dream* 125 Having contracted the colonial preference for cognac, our *vin ordinaire.* **1898** R. RADCLYFFE *Wealth & Wild Cats* 101 Colonial politics are essentially parochial, and Colonial statesmen more or less glorified vestrymen. **1909** C. SHELDON *Chewin' Rag* 33 My word! Sandy's as sharp as a 'nife, but he's as streit as a di. . . Blest if I can get a word good enuf, 'colonial' isn't in it. Sandy's so streit. **1922** M.E. JERSEY *Fifty-One Yrs.* 248 This was a very stirring introduction to Colonial life. (The words 'Colony' and 'Colonial' are now taboo, but before Federation the present Australian States were called 'Colonies' and 'Colonial' was freely used by everyone!) **1939** G. DIGBY *Down Wind* 183 What is known in Australia as Colonial Whisky. It is one of those beverages which has to be drunk quickly, or it will corrode the glass.

2. Inferior in some respect, as provincial, lacking polish or cultivation, coarse, vulgar, etc.

1808 *Sydney Gaz.* 25 Sept., The paltry insignificant editor of a paltry insignificant half-sheet colonial news paper. **1832** *Colonial Times* (Hobart) 19 June, The phrase is *too flash and Colonial.* **1842** *S. Austral. Mag.* Aug. 439 There are many who say, 'we must be colonial', meaning thereby, less refined in thought and feeling, and who look upon coarse manners as more suitable to the life of an emigrant. **1845** *Colonial Lit. Jrnl.* (Sydney) 27 Feb. 131/1, I wish you would abolish the use of the word 'Colonial' at any rate with regard to literature, and call it either 'Australian' or 'National'. Depend upon it that Australia will never be more than a cipher among the nations, until her sons assume to themselves national characteristics. **1855** W. HOWITT *Land, Labor & Gold* II. 15 We saw a well-dressed, though a colonial looking man. **1862** *Meliora* (London) V. 76 However good at home, some were apt to think they must be *colonial* out there. To be *colonial* they thought was to be low, drunken and reckless. **1863** R. HENNING *Lett.* (1952) 61 They were nice-looking girls; one of them I thought pretty. They were natives, and a little colonial, as might be expected. **1869** J. MARTINEAU *Lett. from Aust.* 21 The word 'colonial' is often used to express disparagement; 'colonial manners', for instance, is now and then employed as a synonym for roughness. **1873** W. THOMSON-GREGG *Desperate Character* II. 251 The master . . was never very choice in his language, but was terribly 'colonial' when roused. **1891** H. NISBET *Colonial Tramp* I. 216 The soul of an atheist who is very positive in his opinions goes into the body of a colonial bullock—that is why these awful beasts of burden enjoy blasphemy so much. **1898** R. RADCLYFFE *Wealth & Wild Cats* 21 Poor prospectors . . produce the inevitable tin of Colonial jam, which bears as much resemblance to 'whole-fruit jam' as train-oil does to butter. **1905** *Steele Rudd's Mag.* (Brisbane) Jan. 75 We . . are content to imitate the customs of old degenerate nations, and to let our individuality be obscured by the detestable word 'colonial'. **1915** *Truth* (Sydney) 11 Apr. 5/3 It is sheer insolence or gross ignorance of 'London Scottish' to apply the term 'colonial' to Australians, and it affords me surprise that so bounderish and obviously condescending a new-chum has been able to make any friend. **1920** *Bulletin* (Sydney) 8 July 26/4 'Only Colonial muck in stock: unable to fulfil your order', the dinkum Aussie wrote. **1944** F. BRUNO *Sa-eeda Wog!* 16 It became commonplace for enraged warriors to scream, when challenged in a correct and soldierly manner: 'Argh!! Go and --' etc., and even more, etc. In receipt of which undoubted colonial answer would come the satisfied reply: 'Pass, Kiwi.' **1960** D. MCLEAN *Roaring Days* 139 Flaming Ned gave him a 'colonial' reply: 'Lord Flamin' Muck, eh!' he snorted. 'Y' can stick 'em in the two end stalls and go to flamin' hell afterwards, for all I care!' **1979** W.D. JOYNT *Breaking Road for Rest* 3 The word Australian was seldom if ever used and the word Colonial was anathema. 'Don't speak Colonial' was levelled at us if we used slang words or behaved in any other way as 'young gentlemen'.

3. Of, belonging to, or characteristic of Australia before Federation.

1916 *Bulletin* (Sydney) 16 Mar. 22/2 They placed Tom on the 'colonial sofa' in our front room. **1938** W. DENNING *Capital City* 22 Interested parties had seen . . the old colonial homestead at Duntroon. **1941** C. BARRETT *Aust.* 57 The old Colonial name for Australia's only crane has been displaced by 'brolga', an aboriginal word; but 'native companion' pleases me better. **1951** G. FARWELL *Outside Track* 109 The traveller constantly comes upon Colonial town houses, public buildings, churches, homesteads. **1971** *Bulletin* (Sydney) 14 Aug. 40/2 The colonial dream of a better new world, developing alongside the concept of Britain as Home (although they were going in different directions) no doubt shaped or gave thrust to many feelings that came to be Australian. *Ibid.* 27 Nov. 28/1 A small community banding together to revive the colonial era with folk museums and restored timber buildings. **1973** *Ibid.* 27 Jan. 34/1 His home, a large and airy colonial mansion of the 1870's on Sydney's North Shore. **1978** M. WALKER *Pioneer Crafts Early Aust.* 39 Many of the newcomers built in split wood and two varied strands were warped into another variation—Australian colonial. **1980** *Westerly* i. 10 We stopped at a pub by a crossroads. It had had a plastic facelift recently but its solid old colonial lines were still detectable. There was some fine wrought iron on the balcony and the stonework in the foundation was expert.

4. In collocations: **colonial ale, aristocracy, aristocrat, beer, -born** *a.*, **-bred** *a.*, **-built** *a.*, **cloth, dray, government, language, life, -made** *a.*, **parlance, phrase, phraseology, price, produce, slang, society, tobacco, twang, tweed, vessel, wine, wool.**

1853 *Guardian* (Hobart) 2 July 3/5 **Colonial Ale** . . is a rich pale ale of good flavour. **1857** *Illustr. Jrnl. Australasia* III. 109 The young men nearly poisoned themselves with their first draught of colonial ale. **1869** *Colonial Soc.* (Sydney) 25 Feb. 9 *Infallible recipe*—To soften the brain and deteriorate the complexion.—Take Colonial ale until the desired effect is produced. **1886** D.E. BANDMANN *Actor's Tour* 91 The colonial generation of today prefers . . a mug of colonial ale . . to the best drama in existence. **1894** A. ROBERTSON *Nuggets in Devil's Punch Bowl* 191 'Did you ring, mate?' the boy said. 'Yes, I'll take a glass of colonial ale.' **1832** *Colonist* (Hobart) 7 Sept. 3/3 There exists, both in New South Wales and in Van Diemen's Land, a **colonial aristocracy**, composed of the Government officers and members of the Legislative Councils, *not chosen by the settlers, but 'nominated' by the Government.* **1838** *Colonist* (Sydney) 21 July 2/2 The circumstances of this colony are unquestionably favourable to the existence of a Colonial Aristocracy. **1842** *Colonial Observer* (Sydney) 15 Oct. 541/3 R.N. is about to lead to the Hymeneal altar the daughter of one of our colonial aristocracy. **1861** J.D. LANG *Qld., Aust.* p. xix, The proposal of the colonial aristocracy . . was well received. **1875** G. WALCH *On Cards* 3 The Director of the theatre rigidly excludes colonial aristocracy, shoddy princes, wool-kings and all. **1842** *Colonial Observer* (Sydney) 9 Mar. 177/1 The feeble political orator of five feet high—the would-be **Colonial aristocrat.** **1846** *Atlas* (Sydney) II. 394/2 Colonial aristocrats might take for their motto, *non sum qualis eram.* **1831** *Sydney Herald* 2 May 3/4 Bones And Kendall . . are supplying Public House and Private Families, with **Colonial Beer.** **1833** *N.S.W. Mag.* (Sydney) 127 It has long been the fashion to plead . . that colonial beer was not fit to drink. **1841** *Morning Advertiser* (Hobart) 17 Sept. 3/3 We are glad to see a taste for colonial beer increasing. **1854** W. SHAW *Land of Promise*

113 If the emigrant wishes to avoid excruciating torments, let him abstain from the pungent colonial beer. **1869** *Colonial Monthly* June 291 The first money I had ever earned . . and it was twopence . . literally the price of a glass of beer. Yes, but Colonial Beer. **1886** D.M. Gane *N.S.W. & Vic.* 51 The colonial beer, an insipid drink, is looked upon as poison by those who can afford a bottle of Bass. **1892** *Truth* (Sydney) 7 Aug. 1/7 But how can one with blood so blue, Be comfortable here Amongst these low, degraded things, Who drink colonial beer. **1915** A.T.M. Johnson *Austral. Life* 55 'What ales do you keep?' 'Only She Oak. . . ' 'What is that?' 'C'lony'l Beer. . . ' 'Oh! Colonial Beer. Well give me a glass. . . ' 'Aint got no glasses; sell it by the pot.' **1835** *Colonist* (Sydney) 16 Apr. 2/1 Would the **colonial-born** children be warranted to say to those born and still living in England. **1840** *Port Phillip Gaz.* 18 Jan. 4 The most respectable and influential of the 'English, Irish, and Colonial-born'. **1852** W. Hughes *Austral. Colonies* 112 The colonial-born portion of the Australian population—that is, the white natives of the different colonies—are distinguished by the same general spareness of form, and pallidness of complexion, which characterises the people of the United States. **1862** C. Aspinall *Three Yrs. Melbourne* 150 A little colonial born-and-bred boy or girl of British parentage. **1886** P. Clarke *'New Chum' in Aust.* 105 Colonial-born servants should be the natural remedy for the unsatisfactory state of this portion of the labour-market. **1890** 'Mrs A. Macleod' *Austral. Girl* (1894) 104 'You are, perhaps, colonial-born?' 'I am an Australian,' answered Stella. **1906** L. Becke *Settlers Karossa Creek* 9 Kendall and his two sturdy, colonial-born sons. **1827** P. Cunningham *Two Yrs. in N.S.W.* I. 333, I had two dogs with me that had acquired the habit of snake-killing—one being a fine pointer newly from England, and the other a **colonial-bred** kangaroo dog. **1835** *Colonist* (Sydney) 1 Jan. 2/2 Transfer a colonial bred schoolmaster from his respectable academy. **1884** *Austral. Tit-Bits* (Melbourne) 3 July 14/11 A parade of imported and colonial bred trotters will add to the attractions. **1808** *Sydney Gaz.* 15 May, The Mercury **colonial built** vessel . . had not arrived when the Venus left. **1839** *Tasmanian* (Hobart) 22 Feb. 57/1 The very fine new colonial-built barque. **1906** L. Becke *Settlers Karossa Creek* 53 Being a light, colonial-built whaler, she did her work gallantly. **1811** *Sydney Gaz.* 5 Jan., Constables and Night Watch are to receive **Colonial Cloth** sufficient for a Watch Coat. **1829** *HRA* (1917) 1st Ser. X. 369 The Colonial Cloth made in the Government Factory at Parramatta has been found of great use. **1842** *Colonial Observer* (Sydney) 19 Nov. 621/2 If any distinguishing dress were used, it should be colonial cloth. **1856** 'Old Colonist' *How to Farm & Settle in Aust.* 9 The **colonial dray** forms the most complete vehicle for the road carrier. **1978** M. Walker *Pioneer Crafts Early Aust.* 115 Emigrants were advised to hold their money until arrival in Australia and then to purchase a colonial dray, dearer than the English model but superior in all respects, to serve a variety of functions, loads and track conditions. **1808** *To Viscount Castlereagh* 87 On the conduct of Major Johnston, or the other members of the new **Colonial Government,** during their administration, I do not mean to trouble your Lordship with any remarks. **1828** L.E. Threlkeld *Statement* 21 The Colonial Government ought to contribute in some way or other towards the support of Aborigines. **1853** *Visit to Aust. & Gold Regions* (S.P.C.K.) 30 The colonial government consequently exhausted its funds, and was compelled to borrow from the sister colony. **1871** *Austral. Handbk.* 44 The payments required by the Colonial Government. **1918** C.H. Northcott *Austral. Social Dev.* 45 The colonial and home governments both gave assistance to intending settlers. **1828** *Tasmanian* (Hobart) 15 Aug. 4 If you know of any person wanting a situation who is a proficient in the **Colonial language,** you will do me a great service by recommending them to me, as I am resolved that my children shall not remain ignorant of the dialect of the land they live in. **1833** *Jrnls. Several Exped. W.A.* 196 A person uninitiated in the mysteries of colonial language. **1851** J.F.L. Foster *New Colony Vic.* 17 A shepherd may abscond, or, in the colonial language, 'bolt'. **1843** J.F. Bennett *Hist. & Descr. Acct. S.A.* 122 (*heading*) Sketch of Adelaide and surrounding villages—**colonial life** and manners. **1852** J. West *Hist. of Tas.* I. 214 The tendency of colonial life is to annul the prejudices of European society, and to yield to every man the position which may be due to his talents and virtues. **1857** D. Puseley *Rise & Progress Aust., Tas., & N.Z.* 127 The great feature in colonial life, so far as our experience goes, appears to be that of *deception.* **1887** 'Australian' *Our Homes* 11 It is a pity that reliable information cannot be obtained in the old country about colonial life! **1830** Tas. Colonial Secretary's Office Rec. 1/15 141, These latter shoes are part of the 197 Prs. procured from the Commissariat Department at Sydney (**Colonial Made**) in September last year. **1843** *Sydney Morning Herald* 25 May 4/3 Our goods are neat, and cheap, and well-assorted,—Colonial-made, or carefully imported. **1857** 'Old Yet Young Colonist' *One Mode* 9 He is one of our colonial-made lawyers, and has been reared in our own colony. **1879** *Illustr. Austral. News* (Melbourne) 31 Oct. 171/1 This firm now uses very little imported tweed, as it is found that the colonial-made article can be made up and sold at a price to compete with that obtained from England. **1843** J.F. Bennett *Hist. & Descr. Acct. S.A.* 47 Barracouta. . . [*Note*] In **Colonial parlance** so called, from a supposed resemblance to that fish. **1851** J. Henderson *Excursions & Adventures N.S.W.* 69 High winds, called in colonial *parlance*, 'Brick-fielders'. **1862** H. Brown *Vic. as I found It* 105 A glass, containing about a quarter of a tumbler of brandy, or in colonial parlance, a nobler [*sic*] was placed before me. **1880** J.B. Stevenson *Seven Yrs. Austral. Bush* 89 In colonial parlance, 'humping our swags', we struck out for the ranges. **1832** J. Henderson *Observations Colonies N.S.W. & Van Diemen's Land* 38 The settler must . . receive an order to select a grant of land. . . He must then procure an order to take possession of it, or in **colonial phrase,** to 'Locate'. **1852** W.H. Hall *Practical Experience* (ed. 2) 50 Ten shillings a day, with board and lodging, or, to make use of a colonial phrase, 'the run of his knife'. **1874** A. Trollope *Harry Heathcote* 133 In colonial phrase, he was a 'lag', having been transported. **1909** E. Waltham *Life & Labour in Aust.* 62 By the forcible use of colonial phrases and stock whips. **1846** C.P. Hodgson *Reminisc. Aust.* 303 Its duration amounted in **colonial phraseology,** to a 'Sundowner'. **1859** W. Burrows *Adventures Mounted Trooper* 29 Several people had been 'stuck up'—which, in colonial phraseology, means robbed. **1833** J. King *Information Van Diemen's Land* 15 If they happen not to have any article that is wanted, they procure it, and charge the consumer a profit upon the **colonial price.** **1853** Mrs C. Clacy *Lady's Visit to Gold Diggings* 22 We were getting initiated into colonial prices. **1857** 'Returned Digger' *Six Yrs. in Aust.* 13 If I get a good colonial price for it, that is, three or four hundred per cent. on what it cost. **1819** *Sydney Gaz.* 23 Jan. 3/2 British manufactures and **Colonial produce.** **1828** *Tasmanian* (Hobart) 22 Aug. 1 Well washed Wool, and all other kinds of Colonial Produce will be taken in Payment. **1839** *Ibid.* 4 Jan. 3/2 Premises are most eligible for a wholesale or commission business, as Colonial produce can be received from the back. **1848** C. Cozens *Adventures of Guardsman* 136 The mode of transit of colonial produce from the interior to the Sidney market is very slow, tedious, and often difficult. **1866** H. Parkes *Speeches* 15 May (1876) 205 The great grievance . . is the imposition of Custom duties on colonial produce crossing the frontier. **1840** *S. Austral. Miscellany* June 178 The animals were what in **colonial slang** is termed 'planted' (i.e. concealed). **1845** *Atlas* (Sydney) I. 398/3 Such trickery on the part of a common convict, would, in the technical language or colonial slang of this country be denominated *scheming.* **1870** C.H. Allen *Visit to Qld.* 183 There are certain native terms that are used by the whites also as a kind of colonial slang. **1888** A. McLean *Harry Bloomfield* 13 We followed our guide, after receiving our first lesson in colonial slang. **1842** *Tasmanian Jrnl. Nat. Sci.* I. 10 The diffusion of scientific information might be immediately conducive to the advantage of **Colonial society.** **1863** J. Bonwick *Wild White Man* 16 Amidst the convulsions of colonial society. **1874** J.T. Fallon *Murray Valley Vineyard* 25 With the change in colonial society in the year 1852 . . the colonial wine industry was nearly destroyed. **1892** 'R. Boldrewood' *Nevermore* II. 211 A few of the South Yarra notables dropped in, not quite accidentally, to Mrs Vernon's afternoon tea, whose manner and appearance rather altered Estelle's preconceived notion of colonial society. **1829** *Sydney Monitor* 12 Jan. 1460/2 There is not only five thousand pounds of colonial *leaf* tobacco in the Colony altogether, but little **Colonial Tobacco** of any kind. **1843** *Port Phillip Patriot* 5 Jan. 1/5 On Sale at the stores . . colonial tobacco. **1851** J. Henderson *Excursions & Adventures N.S.W.* 295 Colonial tobacco cost from one shilling and six pence to two shillings per pound, and was an indispensible article, for men will do little work without it. **1875** Campbell & Wilks *Early Settlement Qld.* 3, I gave every man, woman, and child a pipe and a small nugget of colonial tobacco. **1915** A.J. Dawson *Rec. N. Freydon* 149 There was threepence for a packet of cigarettes ('colonial' tobacco), the first I had ever smoked. **1859** R.H. Horne *Austral. Facts & Prospects* 67 A different explanation must be given of the vulgarity, illiterateness, public chattering, and **colonial twang** in the speech. **1871** *Austral. Town & Country Jrnl.* (Sydney) 10 June 718/2 We hear of our wines having a 'colonial twang', or having a 'stalky flavour', or some other equally suggestive title. **1894** *Bulletin* (Sydney) 6 Jan. 6/3 Whether the 'colonial twang' dies out of Australian mouths, or grows and strengthens and is improved, on the American system, the fact will remain that it was never at the beginning anything better than the twang of cockney vulgarity. **1843** *Sydney Morning Herald* 23 May 3/3 It is generally understood that many gentlemen intend to appear at Government House, at the Levee, in **colonial Tweeds.** **1850** *Bell's Life in Sydney* 12 Jan. 1/2 His dress of colonial tweed, and jaunty cabbage-tree hat, proclaimed him to be of that anomalous class of Australian colonists—the Squatter. **1860** J. Norton *Condition Colony N.S.W.* 15 A demand sprang up for the Colonial tweeds in both Scotland and England. **1890** 'R. Boldrewood' *Colonial Reformer* III. 129 The shining-faced giant, in a wondrous suit of colonial tweed. **1904** *Advocate* (Burnie) 5 Oct. 2/4 Colonial tweeds, colonial blankets, colonial furniture are all synonyms of inferiority. **1925** *Aussie* (Sydney) May 6/1 In days now far away . . he donned rough 'colonial tweeds'. **1793** D. Collins *Acct. Eng. Colony N.S.W.* (1798) I. 319 Every one was expecting our **colonial vessel,** the Francis. **1808** *Sydney Gaz.* 11 Sept., Yesterday afternoon arrived the colonial vessel Governor Hunter, from King's Town, with coals and cedar for Government. **1834** M. Doyle *Extracts Lett. & Jrnls. G.F. Moore* 145, I sent a few lines to you by Hobart Town, in a small colonial vessel. **1862** J. Bonwick *J. Batman* (1867) 37 John Lancey, pilot, had commanded one of the colonial vessels. **1831** *Sydney Herald* 7 Nov. 4/2 The *Palambam* is taking home a pipe of **Colonial wine.** **1843** *Colonial Observer* (Sydney) 15 Feb. 821/1 Several parties . . are in the habit of making colonial wine. **1850** *Illustr. Austral. Mag.* (Melbourne) Sept. 236 Several samples of colonial wine from the Swiss vineyard, Geelong, were exhibited. **1868** *Pasquin* (London) 16 May 450 South Australia spread rheumatism and insanity all over New Holland with her sour ditch water, christened 'colonial wine'. **1873** A. Trollope *Aust. & N.Z.* I. 116 Sometimes praise is expected for colonial wine which a prejudiced old Englishman feels that he can hardly give with truth. **1897** 'Old Housekeeper' *Austral. Plain Cookery* 19 *Colonial wines*, of the drier order, bought from good manufacturers, may be safely put upon your table before any company whatever. **1905** *Truth* (Sydney) 9 Apr. 1/7 The N.S.W. Wine Association has resolved that in future no more 'Colonial' wine shall be sold, but only 'Australian'. **1915** A.J. Dawson *Rec. N. Freydon* 149 Finally there was fourpence for a glass of colonial wine in a George street wine-shop. **1956** *Bulletin* (Sydney) 28 Nov. 13/3 A local citizen of good repute bought a glass one day. . . Next morning in court the magistrate asked what he'd had. Told that it was 'colonial wine', he snorted, 'Lunatic soup would be a better name for it!' **1834** *Hobart Town Mag.* May 122 Perceive the increase and improvement of our **Colonial wool.** **1841** *Morning Advertiser* (Hobart) 29 Oct. 2/2 Colonial wool in England has become an object of much interest, and there are many more manufacturers who would use it, but at present will have nothing to do with it, on account of the very careless manner in which it is got up.

5. In special collocations: **colonial bill,** a promissory note in the name of an individual, circulating as currency; **convict,** one serving a sentence for a crime committed in an Australian Colony; **currency,** any unofficial medium of exchange, esp. that consisting of colonial bills (see also Currency 1); **dollar,** Holey dollar; **fever** (chiefly *Vic.*), a typhoid-like disease; also *fig.* (see quot. 1876); **fund(s),** monies assigned to civil administration; **goose,** a boned leg of mutton stuffed with sage and onion; **oath,** a strong oath; in the phr. **my colonial oath,** intensive form of *my oath* (see Oath); **offence,** a crime committed by a transported convict in an Australian Colony; **oven,** see quot. 1941; **pine, (a)** Cypress pine; **(b)** Hoop pine; **prisoner,** *colonial convict*; **robert,** a shilling; **secretary,** in an Australian Colony, the official responsible for domestic affairs; the chief minister (see Premier 1); **sentence,** the punishment inflicted upon a *colonial convict*; **style,** a manner thought of as distinctively Australian; a nineteenth-century Australian style of building, furniture, etc.; **treasurer,** in an Australian Colony, the official responsible for internal finance; **youth,** a young person, born in Australia of immigrant descent; (*collect.*) young persons of this category.

1803 *Sydney Gaz.* 26 June, Several forgeries of **Colonial Bills** have lately made their appearance, some of which are backed with the name of responsible inhabitants, which are also counterfeit. **1809** *Ibid.* 20 Aug., Lost, a Black leather Pocket Book, with a number of Colonial Bills. **1819** J.H. VAUX *Mem.* II. 124 He there took from his pocket several colonial bills. **1843** *Colonial Observer* (Sydney) 18 Mar. 892/4 He was not aware whether they were English or **Colonial convicts** who were detained. **1846** STUART & NAYLOR *Norfolk Island* 20 June (1979) 41 A gang of ninety-six colonial convicts (though until a few weeks past consisting of English and colonial indiscriminately). **1873** A. TROLLOPE *Aust. & N.Z.* II. 112, 240 are imperial convicts,—convicts who have been sent out from England. . . And there are 119 colonial convicts,—convicts with whom the colony is charged, as being representatives of colonial crime. **1804** *Sydney Gaz.* 28 Oct., The **Colonial Currency**, as established by the General Order of the 19th November, 1800. **1807** *Ibid.* 5 July, Grain was once considered as a legal tender for a debt contracted, and was therefore one species of colonial currency. **1811** *Ibid.* 8 June, Payment to be made in sterling money or colonial currency. **1819** W.C. WENTWORTH *Statistical, Hist., & Pol. Descr. N.S.W.* 208 The whole of them who had any real, or apparent pretensions to responsibility, became with one accord bankers; issuing small promissory notes . . merely on the strength of their credit. . . This 'Colonial currency', as it was termed, soon experienced that depreciation in the market . . which it was natural to expect from the doubtful circumstances of many of its issuers. **1824** E. CURR *Acct. Colony Van Diemen's Land* 6 No one however can define the true value of colonial currency. **1820** *N.S.W. Pocket Almanack* 72, 1813 . . The **colonial dollar** substituted in the place of the local currency, July 1. **1821** *Sydney Gaz.* 5 May, Colonial Dollars, from which a Portion of Silver has been taken round the Centre, whereby the Hole is made considerably larger. **1825** *Howe's Weekly Commercial Express* (Sydney) 25 July 1 The Spanish Dollar will be received, as heretofore, at Five Shillings; the Colonial Dollar, at Three-fourths of the Spanish Dollar. **1852** J. WEST *Hist. of Tas.* I. 76 The colonial dollars were mutilated to prevent their exportation. **1857** *Illustr. Jrnl. Australasia* III. 214 The angel of death . . cut down many victims. The most fatal diseases were fever and dysentery. The former, known as **colonial fever,** was most dangerous. **1862** 'W.T.G.' *Quite Colonial* (*c* 1948) 19, I hope he is not going to have an attack of colonial fever, poor fellow. **1872** MRS E. MILLETT *Austral. Parsonage* 256 Influenza, or colonial fever as it is sometimes more correctly called. **1873** W. THOMSON-GREGG *Desperate Character* I. 20 'Colonial fever'—a convenient term by which the Melbourne faculty was wont to designate any affection [*sic*] it could not diagnose more exactly. **1876** J.A. EDWARDS *Gilbert Gogger* 189 The new chum has evidently caught the colonial fever, or in plain English, he is humbugging his maternal relative. **1896** J.M. PRICE *Land of Gold* 76 A malignant form of colonial fever, presenting many of the characteristics of typhoid, was very prevalent during the hot months of last summer. **1933** J. VERCO in *S. Australiana* (1963) Sept. 77 'Colonial Fever' . . was the local name for 'Typhoid Fever' during the days of initial ignorance. **1810** *Sydney Gaz.* 17 Mar., He shall receive an Allowance of Five Shillings per Day out of the **Colonial Fund.** **1816** *Hobart Town Gaz.* 15 June, His Honor the Lieutenant Governor has been pleased to appoint Thomas Archer . . with the usual Salary attached to that Office; to be paid from the Colonial Funds. **1830** Tas. Colonial Secretary's Office Rec. 1/12 126, Prepare a warrant for the transfer of that amount from the Colonial Fund to the Military Chest. **1849** *Britannia* (Hobart) 19 July 3/2 The Lieutenant-Governor makes payment of the public money from the colonial funds. **1882** J. SCHLEMAN *Life in Melbourne* 6 A haunch of kangaroo, flanked by a '**colonial goose**'. **1906** *Home Cookery Aust.* (ed. 2) 43 Colonial Goose. Ingredients—Leg of mutton, 1 onion, 2 oz. butter, 1 egg, 1 lb. bread crumbs, 3 sage leaves, pepper and salt to taste. Mode—Remove the bone of the leg of mutton. Mince the onion very finely. Mix with bread crumbs, sage, pepper, salt, and butter, bind with the egg, well beaten up. Bake from 1½ to 2 hours. **1962** *Bulletin* (Sydney) 3 Feb. 43/2 The . . babbler had a feed of cold cuts all prepared—from ham to colonial goose. **1859** H. KINGSLEY *Recoll. Geoffry Hamlyn* II. 94 'Oh my -- (**colonial oath!**)' said the other; 'oh my -- 'cabbage tree!' **1873** W. THOMSON-GREGG *Desperate Character* I. 66 The gaffer wound up his oration with a colonial oath, like the brandy of the same manufacture, uncommonly black and strong. **1887** A. NICOLS *Wild Life & Adventure* 401 My colonial oath! Here is a bully blow-out, boss. **1894** M. GAUNT *Dave's Sweetheart* 28 They do say Black Anderson had a hand in it, and I'll take my colonial oath they ain't far out. **1913** J. BEUKERS *Humour & Pathos Austral. Desert* 58 Whew, my colonial oath, but it's as hot as blazes to-day, chaps. **1947** M. RAYMOND *Smiley gets Gun* 99 'And stay away from that boozer and any other boozer, or you're liable to get hurt.' 'My Colonial Oath!' agreed Smiley fervently. **1963** R.H. CONQUEST *Spurs are Rusty Now* 41 She'll teach you things! Readin', writin', history—my colonial oath! **1838** T.H. JAMES *Six Months S.A.* 43 They have been re-sentenced since their first arrival for **colonial offences.** **1869** T. ATKINS *Reminisc.* 124 Both he and his wife had been convicts, and had been whipped for colonial offences. **1867** 'S. MCTAVISH' *Chowla* 9 A. Simpson & Son, patentees and manufacturers of the **colonial ovens.** **1885** 'OLD HOUSEKEEPER' *Austral. Housewives' Man.* 13 Usually the kitchen . . is merely a back room with a colonial oven in it. **1905** E.C. BULEY *Austral. Life* 16 A large colonial oven, with wood fire on top and beneath it, is used for roasting. **1928** B. CRONIN *Dragonfly* 142 He drew some hot water from the kettle on the wide colonial oven. **1941** *Bulletin* (Sydney) 27 Aug. 17/4 Successor to the camp oven was that one-time pride of the kitchen the colonial oven. It was an oblong box with a full-length door in front. Three-sixteenth—or quarter-inch wrought-iron plate for top and bottom, thinner sheet round back and sides. Open fire on top for boiling or stewing, extra fire underneath when roasting or baking. **1962** O. PRYOR *Aust.'s Little Cornwall* 67 Some women cooked their family pasties in camp ovens; others used colonial ovens, each with a fire of mallee roots on top and underneath. **1984** P. CUFFLEY *Chandeliers & Billy Tea* 148 Customers were able to buy the old-style colonial oven, a simple box-like construction which when bricked into a fireplace had the fire burning on top. **1848** H.W. HAYGARTH *Recoll. Bush Life* 147 The dresser, made of **colonial pine,** was as clean and white as snow. **1904** J.H. MAIDEN *Notes on Commercial Timbers N.S.W.* 24 *Cypress pine*. . . In the western districts this timber is often known simply as 'colonial pine'. **1913** W.K. HARRIS *Outback in Aust.* 94 Later on we entered a forest of graceful, sea-green colonial Pine. **1926** *Qld. Agric. Jrnl.* XXV. 437 *Araucaria Cunninghamii* . . Colonial Pine. **1843** *Melbourne Times* 1 Apr. 2/3 On Sunday morning he inspected the **colonial** or second convicted **prisoners.** **1849** T. ROGERS *Corresp. relating to Dismissal* 127 No 'old hands', *i.e.*, colonial prisoners, were to be permitted to leave the settlement station. [N.Z. **1869** R.P. WHITWORTH *Grimshaw, Bagshaw & Bradshaw's Comic Guide to Dunedin* 39 Shall we invest in two **Colonial Roberts** in a seat each in the stalls?] **1885** *Australasian Printers' Keepsake* 71, I paid, as he discovered he hadn't 'the colonial Robert' upon him that he thought he had. **1917** *Truth* (Sydney) 16 Dec. 1/8 It takes 13 bright Colonial Roberts to get your name in the 'Herald's' Roll of Honour. **1810** *HRA* (1916) 1st Ser. VII. 259, I . . submit that the Gentleman now holding this Office should henceforth be denominated **Colonial Secretary,** with a Suitable Salary. **1821** *Sydney Gaz.* 6 Jan., *His Majesty* has been pleased to appoint *Frederick Goulburn* . . to be Colonial Secretary. **1837** *Rep. Select Committee Transportation* 2 A day is appointed for the colonial secretary . . to go on board and what is called 'muster the convicts'. **1845** M. COLLISON *S.A.* 10 The Executive Council is composed . . of the four principal officers of the Government, namely the Governor, the Colonial Secretary, the Advocate General and the Surveyor General. **1873** A. TROLLOPE *Aust. & N.Z.* I. 232 Mr Parkes . . was premier and colonial secretary. **1898** M. DAVITT *Life & Progress* 424 The Colonial Secretary (who is the 'Home Secretary' of a colony) visits this prison periodically. **1811** *Sydney Gaz.* 16 Feb., Henry Melsom (now under **Colonial Sentence** at Newcastle). **1818** T.E. WELLS *M. Howe* (1945) 30 An old mischievous Bush robber under Colonial Sentence to the Coal River. **1835** J. BACKHOUSE *Extracts from Lett.* ii. (1838) 68 The time spent on Norfolk Island, under a colonial sentence, is not reckoned as any part of an original sentence. **1852** *Guardian* (Hobart) 29 Sept. 3/2 It was found he had received a colonial sentence of transportation for life, for burglary. **1838** *S. Austral. Rec.* (London) 8 Aug. 83/3 The rest of the party bushed it in true **colonial style.** **1855** R. CARBONI *Eureka Stockade* 22 Bottles are handed out burning hot—the necks of two bottles are knocked together!—Contents drunk in colonial style. **1874** *Illustr. Sydney News* 19 Dec. 15/1 It was considered that while the time allowed was too long for the colonial style, it was too short for the English. **1948** F. CLUNE *Wild Colonial Boys* 107 'He'll be a great rider, that boy!' said Jack the Native. 'I can tell by the way he sits and holds himself—in the real colonial style.' **1948** R. RAVEN-HART *Canoe in Aust.* 200 One of the Banks had chosen a definitely 'colonial' style of architecture for their new building, with a triangular pediment above two-storey stone pillars. **1950** J. MORRISON *Port of Call* 184 It was a big two-storeyed building in old colonial style, with flanking stonework, a slate roof blotched with lichens . . and a spacious tiled promenade along two sides. **1951** G. FARWELL *Outside Track* 109 An individual type of architecture—loosely termed Colonial style—expresses Hobart's character. Basically, of course it is Georgian English. **1972** *Bulletin* (Sydney) 5 Aug. 15/1 The architect involved . . turned out a handsome design in the 'colonial' style. **1981** E. POTTER *Scone I Remember* 83 The home had been built in true colonial style with the original shingle roof sloping in one plane to cover dwelling and stone-flagged verandah. **1826** *Colonial Times* (Hobart) 6 May, **Colonial Treasurer**. This Officer, together with the Receipt and Custody of all Public Money, is charged with the Collection of the Quit rents, and other Sources of internal Revenue. **1845** *Sydney Morning Herald* 8 Aug. 4/1 The Colonial Treasurer will put up to Auction, at the Colonial Treasury, in Sydney, the licenses to occupy . . the following portions of land. **1852** *Argus* (Melbourne) 22 Jan. 2/4 The Government have called for tenders . . for the purchase of gold received by the Colonial Treasurer. **1871** *Illustr. Sydney News* 21 Jan. 114/1 The election . . resulted in the return of the Hon. George Lord, the colonial Treasurer. **1834** J.D. LANG *Hist. & Statistical Acct. N.S.W.* I. 176 Contests . . between the **colonial youth** and natives of England, or . . between *currency and sterling*. **1845** J.O. BALFOUR *Sketch of N.S.W.* 6 The colonial youths have nearly all a consumptive appearance. **1851** H. MELVILLE *Present State Aust.* 40 There are few of the colonial youths that are not expert swimmers. **1867** J. BONWICK *J. Batman* 4 Mr John Batman, unlike Mr Faulkner, was a colonial youth. **1869** M. CLARKE *Peripatetic Philosopher* 46 All about town at night I saw more 'colonial youth'.

B. *n.*

1. A person born in Australia of immigrant descent.

1827 P. CUNNINGHAM *Two Yrs. in N.S.W.* I. 9 New South Wales (or *Australia* as we colonials say). **1847** *Abolitionists & Transportationists* 16 In literature colonials are so chaste, You scarce know what to say, to please their taste. **1869** J. MARTINEAU *Lett. from Aust.* 106 Most of the population are natives of the colony, real colonials, and not emigrants from the old country. **1875** G. WALCH *On Cards* 6 We've house and home and tucker, as the colonials say. **1880** *Bulletin* (Sydney) 3 Apr. 5/1 Sir Alfred Stephen is a colonial—a native of Tasmania. **1883** R.E.N. TWOPENY *Town Life Aust.* 245 A white man born in Australia is a 'colonial'. **1884** *Austral. Tit-Bits* (Melbourne) 24 July 5/2 He was not a colonial, but had lived so long in Victoria that he called himself one, and was proud of it. **1886** D.M. GANE *N.S.W. & Vic.* 40 The colonial . . is a person born in the colony of British parents, and influenced to a large extent by companionship with persons from the old country, but lacking the broad and less confined views of the old English settlers. **1897** *Western Champion* (Barcaldine) 9 Feb. 12/2 Now, to be called a new chum was most infernally irritating, as I thought I was the dead spit of a colonial. **1912** *Truth* (Sydney) 25 Feb. 12/4 At a large works recently erected not far from my abode, a new-chum Scotchman will get preference to a colonial. **1918** A.G.N. WALL *Lett. Airman* 106, I am the only colonial in this flight, and one of them told me the other day that 'he'd hardly have suspected it'. Rather an ambiguous compliment! **1930** 'BRENT OF BIN BIN' *Ten Creeks Run* (1952) 24 The solitary conditions of the boundaries of the back runs and the taciturnity of the colonials restricted his life. **1946** K.S. PRICHARD *Roaring Nineties* 110 He could never quite forget that he was an Englishman and she a colonial—as proud of being the daughter and grand-daughter of pioneers as if she were a princess in her own right. **1959** H.H. WILSON *Golden Age* 163 I'm sick of explaining to everybody over here that I'm not a colonial. I'm Australian, and proud of it. **1980** *Southerly* ii. 180 You know, Marcel Proust? He giggles. For Christ sake . . I may be a colonial but I'm not a bloody moron.

2. Shortened form of *colonial ale, beer.*

1853 G.B. EARP *What we did in Aust.* 171 No man can open his mouth, and swallow anything, even a glass of 'colonial', in a public-house, under sixpence. **1856**

H.B. STONEY *Vic.* 83 A considerable number had but recently arrived in the colony, and were not, therefore, properly colonized to immoderate draughts of '*colonial*'. **1869** *Colonial Soc.* (Sydney) 28 Jan. 3 Afterwards went into a public-house and ordered a pot of colonial. **1880** *Illustr. Austral. News* (Melbourne) 31 July 138/3 Your popular politician never gets wound up and set going more effectually than by the inspiring influence of a pint of good colonial. **1883** *Bulletin* (Sydney) 22 Oct. 22 We drink, in a long beaker of the best 'colonial', long life and good health to the editor. **1891** *Quiz* (Adelaide) 23 Jan. 7/3 Smith contented himself with a glass of 'colonial'. **1901** *Truth* (Sydney) 24 Feb. 8/2 A man from the country last week had a pint of the vile stuff called colonial, and it put him dead to sleep.

3. *absol.* In the collocation **my colonial**: shortened form of *my colonial oath* (see COLONIAL *a.* 5).

1873 J.C.F. JOHNSON *Christmas on Carringa* 6 If you was really to say . . will you take a pint of sheaoak . . I'd say, I'd say . . my colonial! **1888** —— *Austral Christmas* 82 My colonial! can't I! just you try me, that's all. **1901** *Truth* (Sydney) 9 June 5/8 My colonial, you were blank shikkered last night. **1911** 'S. RUDD' *Bk. of Dan* 139 Oh, my colonial, . . it makes good readin', all right. **1917** *Truth* (Sydney) 21 Jan. 1/7 Riots at Cologne. My Colonial! **1936** I.L. IDRIESS *Cattle King* 117 'Anything doing on the Darling?' 'My colonial! A gold-rush—two of 'em.' **1959** H. MYERS *Regions of Courage* 183 'Aren't you having one?' 'My colonial. Soon as I chuck up a brownie for Bob.' **1968** D. O'GRADY *Bottle of Sandwiches* 30 My colonial. . . Sorry I'm a day late, but things kept croppin' up.

colonial experience, *n.* and *attrib. Hist.*

A. *n.*

1. First-hand knowledge of the conditions of life in (outback) Australia; training in self-reliance, esp. in station management and in the skills necessary on a sheep or cattle station.

1838 N.L. KENTISH *Pol. Econ. N.S.W.* 17 These letters could be restricted to the perusal of Gentlemen of Colonial experience. **1839** *Tasmanian* (Hobart) 25 Jan. 32/2 *Wanted*, one who perfectly understands the management of sheep, has had Colonial experience. **1847** *Maitland Mercury* 20 Nov. 2/5 The knowledge and practical experience of agriculturists from the other side of our globe is of little advantage in too many respects when brought to bear on Australian affairs in general, rural in particular. There is such a topsy-turvey reverse in almost everything, that no-one need wonder why 'colonial experience' is an article or an attribute in constant demand; and a pretty mess even colonial experience frequently makes of it. **1858** R. ROWE *Peter Possum's Portfolio* 93 Even leaves in Australia possess 'colonial experience', and are anything but green. **1864** *Sydney Punch* 3 Dec. 224/2 Being murdered by a blackfellow may be regarded as the *ne plus ultra* of 'colonial experience'. **1870** E.B. KENNEDY *Four Yrs. in Qld.* 10 Squatters are by no means so anxious to have 'new chums' on their stations, for the purpose of learning colonial experience, as is supposed. **1879** S.W. SILVER *Austral. Grazier's Guide* 11 There is one guide, and one only. . . Such a mentor is known in all lands by the name of Experience. In Australia his style and title has long been changed to that of 'Colonial Experience'. **1894** E.H. CANNEY *Land of Dawning* 58 All Englishmen are more or less idiots whom three years' Colonial experience may possibly redeem. **1904** *Emu* III. 172 Camped out there with sheep, gaining 'colonial experience'. **1920** *Ibid.* XIX. 318 When the rabbits spread over the Castlereagh country, I was doing colonial experience on a station in that district. **1929** 'OLD STOCKMAN' *Sensational Cattle-Stealing Case* 30 Having been for some years, learning colonial experience, on our uncle's station near Adelaide. **1948** G. FARWELL *Down Argent Street* 25 A touch of colour added by a young Englishman out for 'colonial experience' to use a term applied to those in parental disfavour at home. **1965** L. HAYLEN *Big Red* 69 His subaltern who had been with him in India was now with him on the station getting colonial experience. **1975** M. THORNTON *It's Jackaroo's Life* 18 By the late 1840s many young migrants were arriving in Australia with the intention of seeking their fortunes. The first requirement . . was to get what became known as colonial experience.

2. A (British) youth living and working on an (Australian) sheep or cattle station in order to learn the necessary occupational skills: see JACKEROO *n.* 2.

1868 C.W. BROWNE *Overlanding in Aust.* 36 He is usually a man that has been employed on a run as a superintendant, overseer, 'colonial experience', or something of that nature. **1873** *Illustr. Sydney News* 29 Aug. 14/3 He is the butt of old hands, who . . call him the 'Colonial Experience', instead of Mr So and So, as he thinks they ought to do. **1890** R.S. BROWNE *Romances Gold Field & Bush* 27 William . . said to a young 'Colonial Experience', 'Miles, I want you to drive over to Hughenden.' **1892** *Western Champion* (Barcaldine) 21 June 13/2 First of all came the manager . . with his wife and daughter in a buggy, escorted by a couple of 'colonial experiences' on horseback. **1931** LAWSON & BRERETON *H. Lawson* 215 My friends discovered me and consigned me, as a 'colonial experience', to a very far-back station under a spirit-breaking dog of a manager. **1938** F. RATCLIFFE *Flying Fox & Drifting Sand* 122 When I was in Bundaberg forty years ago there was a 'colonial experience' named Thompson.

B. *attrib.* (in sense of *n.* 2).

1886 P. CLARKE *'New Chum' in Aust.* 295 A planter put a new 'colonial experience' man on to 'boss' a gang of black ladies. **1891** T. BATEMAN *Valley Council* 3 His colonial-experience man came over yesterday in a blue funk. **1897** J.J. MURIF *From Ocean to Ocean* 143 A 'colonial experience' gentleman was there, but he was on the sick list. **1900** R. BRUCE *Benbonuna* (1904) 71 Like the general run of 'colonial experience' young men, he would prove nothing better than a useless 'horse-killer'. **1927** A. CROMBIE *After Sixty Yrs.* 31 The Colonial experience boys . . served one year without pay and one year at 10s. per week. **1968** W.N. SCOTT *Some People* 112 He told all the other mozzies about this new chum colonial experience man he'd just spotted. **1976** B. SCOTT *Complete Bk. Austral. Folk Lore* 130 The Colonial Experience Man, he's there, of course, Shiny boots and leggings, boys, just off his horse.

Hence **colonial experienced** *a.*, **colonial experiencer** *n.*

1873 *Illustr. Sydney News* 16 Apr. 18/4 A large section of land should be most carefully selected by a **colonial-experienced** surveyor. **1879** S.W. SILVER *Austral. Grazier's Guide* 13 The '**colonial experiencer**', the 'jackâroo', or 'cadet', as he is variously designated in different colonies, always lodges with the proprietor or the resident manager. **1891** M. ROBERTS *Land-Travel & Sea-Faring* 62 As I lived in the house, not at the men's hut, I was something like what is known in the bush as a 'colonial experiencer'. **1900** *Bulletin* (Sydney) 13 Oct. 14/4 The manager was enlightening the raw 'colonial-experiencer'. **1906** A.B. PATERSON in C. Semmler *World of Banjo Paterson* (1967) 20 They would all start next day for civilization—Charlie to resume the management of Mr Grant's stations, Carew to go with him as 'colonial-experiencer'. **1918** C. FETHERSTONHAUGH *After Many Days* 90 Tom offered to take me . . to get a knowledge of cattle and cattle work while helping him in a general way—in other words to take me on as 'colonial experiencer', nowadays called Jackeroo. **1964** J.S. MANIFOLD *Who wrote Ballads?* 86 The jackaroos . . were usually educated young men studying the art and mystery of station management; sometimes they included a 'colonial-experiencer' or 'pommy jackaroo'. **1975** M. THORNTON *It's Jackaroo's Life* 18 Quite often the colonial experiencer had some capital behind him and intended eventually to get his own run.

colonialize, *v. Obs. trans.* COLONIZE. Also as *pa. pple.*, and *fig.*

1852 F. LANCELOTT *Aust. as it Is* II. 162 Too many of the merchants and traders . . delight in what is called 'colonializing the fresh arrivals right off the reel'—that is, taking advantage of their ignorance of colonial matters, and legally cheating them of all they possess. **1854** 'H.J.L.' *Travels & Adventures*, Having colonialised his dress he secures his swag and prepares for a start into the Country. **1859** J.D. MEREWEATHER *Diary Working Clergyman* 24 To look about him for a year until he became colonialised. **1882** A.J. BOYD *Old Colonials* 233 A tendency to suicide, when under a cloud, is also amongst the pleasant traits of character in our colonialised 'Chinkie'. **1889** *Bulletin* (Sydney) 15 June 13/4 Chaffs our 'style', yet tries to prig it And colonialised become, But in all he does (you twig it), He's a brand new chum. **1890** A.S. DAY *Democrat* 18 When yer been colonialised ye'll know not to ax questions until after yer been properly recommended.

colonially, *adv. Obs.* Locally, i.e. in the Australian Colonies.

1835 H.W. BUNBURY *Early Days W.A.* 16 Aug. (1930) 18 These are all men colonially sentenced, in addition to their former transportation, so are the very *élite* of the English blackguards. **1836** *Hobart Town Almanack* 73 The long wooden sofa-seat as it is colonially called. **1845** C. GRIFFITH *Present State & Prospects Port Phillip* 12 A strong southerly wind, colonially called a Brickfielder. **1854** J. CAPPER *Aust.* 62 The 'new chum', as a fresh settler is colonially termed. **1859** H. KINGSLEY *Recoll. Geoffry Hamlyn* II. 95 A native, colonially convicted. [*Note*] A man born in the colony, of European parents, convicted of some crime committed in the colony. **1862** 'W.T.G.' *Quite Colonial* (*c* 1948) 17 Eugene . . had what is colonially termed 'a down' upon the speaker . . a spite against him. **1872** MRS E. MILLETT *Austral. Parsonage* 121 'Traps', as the vehicles resembling dog-carts are colonially called. **1889** J.H.L. ZILLMANN *Past & Present Austral. Life* 51 'Is it true that you are only a *colonially* ordained clergyman?' Colonially being pronounced *Kah*-lonially with a great and scornful emphasis on the first syllable.

colonist.

1. *Hist.* Prior to Federation: a non-Aboriginal inhabitant of a British Colony in Australia; one taking part in the founding of a Colony (see quots. 1790 and 1833); a settler.

1790 J. HUNTER *Hist. Jrnl. Trans. Port Jackson* 17 July (1793) 455 As the good land could not at present be cultivated by the colonists, it was reserved for the first settlers that should come out. **1796** 'SOCIETY OF GENTLEMAN' *New & Correct Hist. New Holland* 35 The colonists were inclined to hold the spears of the natives very cheap. **1803** G. BOND *Brief Acct. Colony Port Jackson* 4 Their unwillingness to associate and connect themselves with the colonists is manifest. **1821** *Sydney Gaz.* 27 Jan., This state of the law . . affects not only the liberty, property, and civil rights of the Emancipated Colonists, but also . . the property of the Emigrant Colonists. **1833** W.H. BRETON *Excursions* 46 By 'Settlers', I mean the farmers only: and by 'colonists', the whole of the free inhabitants. **1834** J.D. LANG *Hist. & Statistical Acct. N.S.W.* II. 148 That spirit of irreconcileable enmity to all standing timber . . is almost uniformly evinced by the Australian colonists. **1839** T.L. MITCHELL *Three Exped. Eastern Aust.* (rev. ed.) II. 16, I met at the foot of this hill a colonist, a native of this country. **1842** *Sydney Morning Herald* 1 May 1/3, I boldly claim the title of a true Australian Colonist, being a freeholder of its soil. **1852** *Illustr. Austral. Mag.* (Melbourne) Jan. 6 Even native born Australian colonists call Old England 'home'. **1880** *Illustr. Austral. News* (Melbourne) 31 Dec. 250/1 About the pleasantest thing to the mind of a colonist is the recollection of home. **1889** J.H.L. ZILLMANN *Past & Present Austral. Life* 53 There are . . among some of the oldest and wealthiest of our colonists those of whom it may be said 'his father was sent out'. **1891** *Sydney Morning Herald* 3 Mar. 3/6 The colonist is really regarded by the usage of the term as a person who is in some respects inferior, who does not enjoy the same advantages and is not quite entitled to the same privileges as the members of the empire. **1898** M. DAVITT *Life & Progress* 6 'W.A.' (as the colonists familiarly call their province) was a Crown colony. **1910** *Advocate* (Burnie) 3 Jan. 2/3 The deceased had been a colonist for 85 years. **1917** *Huon Times* (Franklin) 23 Jan. 4/3 An old man . . stated he was over 80 years of age, and was a colonist of 62 years standing. **1964** J.S. MANIFOLD *Who wrote Ballads?* 43 The free settlers had a lien on the word 'colonists'.

2. *transf.*

1920 J.H. MAIDEN *Weeds N.S.W.* 70 'Wild Verbena or Vervain', 'Purple-Top or Weed' . . is a very old Australian colonist, and now it is found practically over the settled parts of Australia.

3. In the collocation **old colonist,** one whose standing in the community derives from the length of the period of residence in Australia. Also *attrib.*

1828 H. DANGAR *Index & Directory River Hunter* 33 This regulation . . was a very proper one in reference to the *old colonists*. **1831** H. MELVILLE *Hist. Van Diemen's Land* 23 May (1835) 130 One of the most staunch of the leaders on this occasion, was an old 'Colonist'. **1843** *Sydney Morning Herald* 10 Nov. 2/1 Surprise that the Governor should have passed over all the old colonists, to confer the office on a gentleman who is almost a stranger. **1844** *S. Austral. Odd Fellows' Mag.* July 140, I had begun to consider myself an old colonist, having been then four years in the province. **1850** *Monthly Almanac* (Adelaide) 47 Of the features comprising the physiognomy of Colonial Society, no one stands out in bolder relief than does the Old Colonist. **1855** P. SAUNDERS *Two Yrs. Vic.* (1863) 36 The old colonists have an expression of face that beats *Punch's* pictures of the Yankee. It combines the malicious and keen look of the rat with the cunning of the fox, and their great delight is to perform the operation of what is called *shaving a new chum.* **1858** T. McCOMBIE *Hist. Colony Vic.* 76 He was under the guidance of the old colonist aristocracy of Sydney. **1862** G.T. LLOYD *Thirty-Three Yrs. Tas. & Vic.* 449 The term 'old colonists' applies to the original 'Merchants and Settlers', whose enterprise early led them to the colonies; six tenths of whom were composed of officers of the army and navy, and others; gentlemen of talent and high character. Ticket-of-leave farmers, emanicipists, and such . . do not rank under the above heading. **1882** *Bulletin* (Sydney) 20 May 11/2 At a banquet given to an old colonist at Wagga, prior to the usual trip home, the *menu* was in French. **1898** 'OLD CHUM' *Fragments Old Sydney* 20 In the Old Sand Hills Cemetery . . lie many old colonists. **1909** *Truth* (Sydney) 25 July 1/6 You could not kill some of our old colonists with a ten pound axe. **1918** *Huon Times* (Franklin) 5 July 2/5 An example of harsh treatment towards an old colonist has just been brought to light.

4. In special collocations: **colonists' cement** (see quot.); **colonist's clock,** the bird *Dacelo novaeguineae* (see KOOKABURRA).

1847 *Atlas* (Sydney) III. 62/3 What is the colonists' patent cement? . . The **colonists' cement** is just cow or bullock hide cut into thongs. **1847** *Moreton Bay Courier* 29 May 4/3 They are most absurdly named laughing-jackasses, though some designate them the **colonist's clock**, and the natives, *cucaburra.*

colonize, *v. Obs. trans.* To render (a person) colonial, i.e. Australian, in character or outlook. Freq. as *past pple.*

1849 *Bell's Life in Sydney* 26 May 3/1 'Ma,' said a young lady to her mother the other day, 'What is Emigration?' Mother—'Emigration, dear, is a young lady going to Australia.' Daughter—'What is Colonizing, Ma?' Mother—'Colonizing, dear, is marrying there and having a family.' **1851** *Empire* (Sydney) 25 June 3/2, I bowled him out with a piece of damper in his hat. I told him of it, and would you believe it, he blushed? He's not colonized yet. **1854** W. SHAW *Land of Promise* 326 There are men in the colonies always on the look out to fleece the inexperienced 'griffin', nor is a man considered *colonized* till he has been occasionally over-reached by the more experienced. **1856** H.B. STONEY *Vic.* 83 A considerable number had but recently arrived in the colony, and were not, therefore, properly colonized to immoderate draughts of '*colonial*'. **1857** *Moreton Bay Free Press* 23 Dec. 2/5 She soon became 'colonised' after I engaged her—that is to say, she rapidly became lazy, careless, sluttish in the house, dressy out of it, insolent and unbearable. **1867** 'COLONIST' *Life's Work* 36 Neither Jane nor her father were at present sufficiently colonized to attempt the celebrated Australian 'Co-oee'. **1873** W. THOMSON-GREGG *Desperate Character* I. 204 You're a new chum, you must remember; and a man doesn't get colonised in a day. **1891** 'R. BOLDREWOOD' *Sydney-Side Saxon* (1925) 64 You'll get colonized after a bit, like all the rest of us. **1904** *Truth* (Sydney) 15 May 5/3 The longer a man has been in Australia, if it be sufficiently long for him to have become 'colonized' . . the more remote become his chances of employment. **1916** *Ibid.* 1 Oct. 12/3 The pommies . . who won't pay for the theatre, are colonised, and well colonised . . they are worse than Australians. **1940** J.A. BROOK *Jim of Seven Seas* 67, I did not take kindly to this job, being by now well colonized, and my blood thin and susceptible to keen frost.

Hence **colonization** *n.*, accommodation to life in Australia.

1850 *Monthly Almanac* (Adelaide) 7 He is soon reconciled to this unexpected disbursement by congratulations on the prospect of his rapid 'colonization'.

Colony. Also **colony.**

1. Prior to Federation: one of the British Colonies in Australia or the Australian Colonies collectively; those taking part in the founding of a Colony (see quot. 1788 and cf. COLONIST).

1788 J. HUNTER *Hist. Jrnl. Trans. Port Jackson* (1793) 301 Before the colours were hauled down, I assembled my small colony under them. **1792** R. JOHNSON *Address to Colonies N.S.W. & Norfolk Island* p. iv, The colony already begins to spread, and will probably spread more and more every year, both by new settlements formed in different places under the crown, and by a number of individuals continually becoming settlers. **1794** G. THOMPSON *Slavery & Famine* II. 4 There is not such a thing on the colony as a set of stairs, except in the Governor's house. **1804** *Concise Hist. Eng. Colony N.S.W.* p. xv, It is now eighteen years since the first establishment was made in New South Wales; and the colony is already England in miniature. **1811** G. PATERSON *Hist. N.S.W.* 94 The settler to benefit that colony, the *bona fide* settler, who should be a man of some property, must go thither from England; he is not to be looked for among discharged soldiers, ship-wrecked seamen, or quondam convicts. **1820** H.G. BENNET *Let. to Earl Bathurst* 20 It has now risen from the degraded state of a penal settlement, to the station of a colony, peopled by many thousand free Englishmen. **1832** J. HANSON *Let.* 2 The Town of Perth is at present the capital of the Colony. **1833** W.H. BRETON *Excursions N.S.W.* 101 We may now be supposed to have quitted the colony, properly so called, as no actual *locations* are permitted on this side of Liverpool. **1836** *Cornwall Chron.* (Launceston) 17 Dec. 1 A new Colony has been planted on the south east of New Holland, between the new Province of South Australia and the south east corner of New South Wales. **1840** *Port Phillip Gaz.* 1 Feb. 2 Adelaide, the pet colony of the Home Government. **1853** J. SHERER *Gold Finder Aust.* 10 Although your father might have been my Lord of England-all-over, it goes for nothing in this equalising colony of gold and beef and mutton. **1861** 'OLD BUSHMAN' *Bush Wanderings* 229, I never had a day's illness in the colony. **1874** C. DE BOOS *Congewoi Correspondence* 3, I hate the word 'colony' and fellow-colonist. **1876** J.A EDWARDS *Gilbert Gogger* 151 We are *only* a colony, and are not supposed to be able to grow anything . . as good as the mother country can. **1880** *Bulletin* (Sydney) 31 Jan. 1/1 To-day we send broadcast throughout the colonies the first number of *The Bulletin.* **1891** *Bohemia* (Melbourne) 4 June 4 He found that the Governors from the other Colonies were to take precedence of him at the guzzle. **1901** *Advocate* (Burnie) 6 Feb. 2/3 The old name of 'colony' has been dropped . . and the word 'State' substituted.

2. After Federation: used loosely of Australia as a former British colony or as one of a number of former British colonies.

1910 *Huon Times* (Franklin) 5 Mar. 4/6 A few words . . to those seeking homes in the colonies. **1917** C.E.W. BEAN *Lett. from France* 230 You know the way it makes you wince, if ever you have lived in Australia or New Zealand or Canada, to hear people talk of 'the colonies' or 'the colonials'. **1955** N. PULLIAM *I traveled Lonely Land* 64 It's time this country *quit* being a bloody colony, my word it is. **1978** B. OAKLEY *Ship's Whistle* (1979) 31 All the fools, all the crackpots, they all come out here to the colonies.

colour. *Mining.* Also **color.** [U.S. *color* a trace of gold: see Mathews.]

1. A trace or particle of gold; in opal-mining, esp. in *pl.*, an indication of the presence of opal.

1859 [see sense 2]. **1869** R.B. SMYTH *Gold Fields & Mineral Districts* 607 When only very minute particles of gold are found in a 'prospect' the miner is said to have got the 'color'. **1881** J.C.F. JOHNSON *To Mount Browne & Back* 24 In most cases not even a 'color' was obtained, and none bottomed on good prospects. **1898** D.W. CARNEGIE *Spinifex & Sand* 89 Wherever we tried a 'dish of dirt', colours were sure to result. **1903** J. MARSHALL *Battling for Gold* 67 We went out . . to find, if possible, even a colour, but were unable to see the slightest trace of gold. **1921** K.S. PRICHARD *Black Opal* 168 Roy O'Mara's bottomed on opal there. . . Got some pretty good colours, and we're goin' to peg out. **1933** J. TRURAN *Where Plain Begins* 70, I can get a colour every time I use the dish, but there's never enough to make it worth a man's while. **1944** K.S. PRICHARD *Potch & Colour* Foreword, The chips opal-miners put in a small bottle and call 'potch and colour'—poor and fiery opal, that is. **1949** H.C. JAMES *Gold is where you find It* 63 All he really expected was to find the same old colours of gold, and maybe a few tiny nuggets. **1960** V. CARELL *Naked we are Born* 37 That old diggin's got no colour left an' they got to find 'nother place to dig. **1975** L.H. CLARK *Rouseabout Reflections* 18 Any man with gumption who trekked out Hurst-bridge way, Could get eight colours to the dish, and make the washing pay. **1982** R. HALL *Just Relations* 391 Colour just a bit too deep for the miner.

2. In the phr. **to raise the** (or **a**) **colour,** to find a trace of the mineral sought, usu. gold.

1859 W. KELLY *Life in Vic.* I. 222 They had not, to use a current phrase, 'raised the colour'. **1881** G.C. EVANS *Stories* 90 They had been very unfortunate at the new diggings, having sunk three holes without raising the color. **1886** H. FINCH-HATTON *Advance Aust.* 160 He may toil for ten hours a day and not raise the colour, while his neighbour in the next claim . . is getting an ounce of gold to the dish. **1915** N. DUNCAN *Austral. Byways* 72 I'll raise the color this afternoon! I'll strike it tomorrow! **1930** T.S. MARSHALL *Mem. Victorian Fire Service* 9 John Chinaman had forestalled us . . so that we could scarcely raise the 'colour' anywhere. **1944** M.J. O'REILLY *Bowyangs & Boomerangs* 28 All the other claim-holders seemed to be in the same boat, as they couldn't raise a colour either. **1977** J. DOUGHTY *Gold in Blood* 72 After sinking a trench . . and bottoming on green 'country' without raising a colour, we gave it up.

coloured, *ppl. a.* Applied to Aborigines, and others wholly or partly of non-white descent.

1816 *Hobart Town Gaz.* 8 June, The under-mentioned Prisoners having absented themselves . . —Matthew Keegan; Peter Franks (a coloured man); and Wm. Lee, a boy. **1828** *Van Diemen's Land Corresp. Military Operations* 17 Apr. (1831) 4 The increasing spirit of resentment manifested by the coloured inhabitants of this colony. **1832** J. BISCHOFF *Sketch Hist. Van Diemen's Land* 192 No unnecessary harshness may be exercised in order to confine the coloured inhabitants within the boundaries which you have fixed. **1838** *S. Austral. Rec.* (London) 11 July 77/2 There is no other instance in the history of the world of a European people sitting down among coloured tribes without bloodshed, violence and injustice. **1848** *Port Phillip Herald* 6 Jan. (Suppl.), A colored boy . . applied for a warrant to apprehend two aboriginal boys. **1857** J. NORTON *Austral. Essays* 31 The unenlightened among the native-born should, like their coloured brethren of the soil, see in this nothing. **1862** E. STRICKLAND *Austral. Pastor* 60 They were welcomed . . by two black women and a coloured girl. **1880** J. BONWICK *Resources Qld.* 72 The Coloured Labour question is the vexed one in connection with sugar. **1903** *Bulletin* (Sydney) 23 May 17/1 We were fined, each 25s. and costs. . . Then the colored gentleman threw down a tenner. . . 'Take it out of that!' He was a real 'white' nigger. **1911** W.G. SPENCE *Hist. A.W.U.* 58 A *colored* census taken in 1898 showed that there were 24,366 colored aliens in Queensland. **1919** *Smith's Weekly* (Sydney) 1 Mar. 8/2 It is long since a flogging was imposed in any of the Eastern States, but in Westralia the other day a Judge gave a coloured man the lash, in addition to long imprisonment. **1935** DAVISON & NICHOLLS *Blue Coast Caravan* 188 In speaking to them, of themselves, the expression 'coloured people' was used. The term, apparently, was acceptable to them, but when they spoke of themselves they used the term 'Australian'. **1957** F. CLUNE *Fortune Hunters* 119 The word 'coloured' is used to describe those of mixed race, and 'full-bloods' to describe those of native race. **1965** R.H. CONQUEST *Horses in Kitchen* 107 Cinder was a coloured Australian . . and he spoke with the soft tone of the northern blacks. **1977** T. RONAN *Mighty Men on Horseback* 76 He is no longer a 'blackfellow' or even a 'coloured man' but more formally an 'Aboriginal'.

comb.

1. The lower, fixed, and toothed part of the cutting-piece of a shearing machine.

1887 *Australasian* (Melbourne) 12 Mar. 495/3 Mr Wolseley stated that he had different combs for shearing such sandy sheep. **1891** R. WALLACE *Rural Econ. & Agric.* 379 The cutter . . moves from side to side 4,000 times per minute over the comb, which rests upon the skin of the sheep. **1916** H.B. SMITH *Sheep & Wool Industry* 33 The shearing machine works on the horse-clipper principle—a cutter with three teeth running from side to side over a flat comb. **1950** H.G. BELSCHNER *Sheep Managem.* 93 The machine is a metal comb over which is driven a cutter, the whole being held in a hand piece. **1966** R. ANDERSON *On Sheep's Back* 89 Each checks his shearing handpiece; puts in fresh combs and cutters. **1984** *Age* (Melbourne) 16 May 3/4 The comb is the leading edge of the shearing handpiece and rakes the wool onto the blade.

2. With distinguishing epithet: **narrow comb,** a comb of the standard breadth of 63.5 mm.; also *attrib.*; **wide comb,** a comb of greater breadth; also *attrib.*

1980 *Austral.* (Sydney) 8 July 9/8 The Sunbeam Corporation has an agreement with the union to sell only **narrow combs** in Australia. **1981** *Ibid.* 19 Dec. 5/8 If I worked as hard with wide combs as I used to with the narrow combs . . I would shear approximately 40 sheep a day more with the wide combs, and easier. **1982** *Advertiser* (Adelaide) 11 Dec. 3/2 It will cause widespread confusion throughout the industry with shearers not knowing whether it is a wide or narrow-comb shed, depending on the whim of the wool-grower. **1983** *Sydney Morning Herald* 31 Mar. 3/4 Six of his shearers were attacked by narrow-comb shearers in a hotel last year. **1981, 1982** [**wide-comb:** see *narrow comb*]. **1983** *Bulletin* (Sydney) 4 Jan. 24/3 The hard-nosed union line is . . that wide combs will break down their award conditions and create unfair competition between shearers. **1984** *Canberra Times* 6 June 1/2 Union to abide by wide-comb decision.

Hence **narrow-comber** *n.*, **narrow-combing** *vbl. n.*, **wide-comber** *n.*, **wide-combing** *vbl. n.*

1984 *People Mag.* (Sydney) 7 May 38 You can hear New Zealand wide-combers accused of nearly every sin bar baby-killing. *Ibid.* 39/1 Standard-gaugers say the bigger combs are too hard to push through dense merino fleece and hurt shearers' wrists—a questionable claim, since I could not find one narrow-comber who'd admit to even trying wide gear. *Ibid.* 39/3 No man labours as hard or lives as rough as the 40-hour-a-week shearer, whether he's wide-combing, narrow-combing or biting the wool off.

combine. A combine seed drill: see quot. 1966. Also **combine drill.**

1966 F. WHEELHOUSE *Digging Stick* 30 When the Australian farmer uses the word 'Combine' he means the grain and fertiliser drill combined with the tyne cultivator in one implement. The term 'Combine' used in Australia is not to be confused with the American Combine, which is a wheat harvesting machine. **1975** M. THORNTON *It's Jackaroo's Life* 89 *Combine* in Australia—an implement for planting seed, a drill. **1979** J. BIRMINGHAM et al. *Austral. Pioneer Technol.* 24 The 'combine' drill which sowed seed and fertiliser together, and added cultivator tines to prepare the seedbed and bury the seed.

combo. Also **kombo.** [f. *comb(ination* + -O, earlier than and independent of the U.S. use for a partnership.] A white man who lives with an Aboriginal woman, often within an Aboriginal community; a white man who sexually exploits Aboriginal women. Also *attrib.*, esp. as **comboman,** and as quasi-*adv.*

1896 W.H. WILLSHIRE *Land of Dawning* 72 The *Sydney Bulletin* . . not only reaches the combos and stockmen of Central Australia, but it reaches lepers on isolated islands, [and] lighthouse-keepers. **1899** *Bulletin* (Sydney) 11 Mar. 4/3 The recently-introduced Q. Aborigines Protection Act compels all and sundry (excepting station-managers of the genus 'combo') to either marry or get rid of their dusky Kitties and Pollies. **1901** *Truth* (Sydney) 16 June 5/7 The word Combo . . is a term applied to any white man who consorts or cohabits with gins or lubras. **1907** *Ibid.* 7 Apr. 10/6 (*heading*) Concupiscent combo-land. The nauseated Northern Territory. **1912** *Bulletin* (Sydney) 8 Feb. 13/3 The word 'Combo' . . meant . . a man who associated with the Binghis above what was considered the correct thing; *i.e.*, one who, not content with having a lubra about *his* camp, lived for longer or shorter periods entirely in the camps of black brother—and sister. **1917** *Truth* (Sydney) 18 Feb. 5/2 *The 'Combo'*, the white man, save the name, who exists on the prostitution of gins. **1928** *Bulletin* (Sydney) 19 Sept. 25/4 In Westralia a 'combo' is a degraded white who lives with native women. **c 1934** C. SAYCE *Comboman* 240 You're only a Comboman: That's what yer are. A Comboman. You're only the 'usband of a *lubra*. **1938** X. HERBERT *Capricornia* 36 Once a man went combo he could never again look with pleasure on a white woman unless he blacked her face. **1938** F. BLAKELEY *Hard Liberty* 186 The 'Combo' is . . a wandering outcast—a white man who lives with the Natives and upon them. **1954** H.G. LAMOND *Manx Star* 76 He knew the etiquette of a combo's camp. **1973** D. WOLFE *Brass Kangaroo* 33 'I won't worry till you leave me for a nice white girl.' 'I won't. I don't want a white girl. . . ' 'You combo.' **1981** K. GARVEY *Rhymes of Ratbag* 24 In society's eye he's rated A lowly combo shunned and hated.

Also **comboing** *vbl. n.*, **comboism** *n.*

1938 X. HERBERT *Capricornia* 194 A lean and faded-looking man, become so through excessive drinking and **comboing.** **1907** *Truth* (Sydney) 7 Apr. 10/8 **Comboism** should be wiped out. **1909** *Bulletin* (Sydney) 6 May 13/2 'Combo-ism' is the order of the day. Everyone (more or less) has a sable 'companion'.

come, *v.*

1. Obs. In the phr. **to come it (on),** to inform (upon someone).

1812 J.H. VAUX *Mem.* (1819) II. 163 *Come it*, to divulge a secret; to tell any thing of one party to another; they say of a thief who has turned evidence against his accomplices, that he is *coming* all he knows, or that he *comes it as strong as a horse.* **1841** B. WAIT *Lett. from Van Dieman's Land* (1843) 266 When the party has a *down* upon either *pal's* (mate) *coming it*, (informing against them,) the *trickster* (a false swearer) makes oath. **1844** *Parramatta Chron.* 24 Feb. 2/3 She began . . threatening to 'come it' on a man . . with whom . . she had been concerned in the theft. **1882** *Sydney Slang Dict.* 10 He . . came it on Joe for fencing the prad. **1893** J. DEMARR *Adventures in Aust.* 175 He replied that some one had been '*coming it on me*' (informing on me). **1899** J. BRADSHAW *Quirindi Bank Robbery* 16 He was promised a very light sentence if he would come it on his mate.

2. In the phr. **to come at,** to agree to do (something), to accept (a situation, etc.); to 'try (something) on'. Freq. in negative contexts.

1911 A. WRIGHT *Gambler's Gold* (1923) 118 Punters were watching for a move that the stable was backing. . . It came at last; the word went round that — was 'coming at' Gorki. **1919** W.H. DOWNING *Digger Dialects* 17 *Come at*, undertake. **1922** A. WRIGHT *Colt from Country* 119 Knocker had 'whispered' to one or two likely-looking 'guys', and urged them to 'come at' horses he named, but the fish did not bite. **1945** C. MANN *River* 111 Without Skipper he'd have to come at some other work. **1957** D. NILAND *Call me when Cross turns Over* 92 No, Barbie, he wouldn't come at it. I know him. **1962** MARSHALL & DRYSDALE *Journey among Men* 169 You can't eat that stuff! . . I just couldn't come at it, thanks all the same. **1969** D. NILAND *Dead Men Running* 92 He wants to give me fourpence each for them. In perfect order, they are, the whole ten of them. What's he coming at? **1977** J. O'GRADY *There was Kid* 39 Although often short of food on the farm, our father said that he hoped we would never have to 'come at nardoo bread', or porridge. **1977** R. BEILBY *Gunner* 120 Whaddya comin' at? Get off our backs, will ya! **1984** *Age* (Melbourne) 18 Sept. 17/6, I was a great advocate of Hawke's. . . I went to Canberra deliberately to see him. I spent a week there, but watching him at a distance I just couldn't come at it.

comeback.

1. A boomerang which returns to the thrower. Also **comeback boomerang.**

1878 R.B. SMYTH *Aborigines of Vic.* I. 329 The boomerangs . . from the north-east coast in my collection are not 'come-back' or 'play' boomerangs. **1901** *Bulletin* (Sydney) 2 Mar. 15/1, I am a pretty fair boomerang-thrower, except with the 'returner'. Can any reader inform me as to how Westralian 'comebacks' (kylies) are thrown. **1924** HORNE & AISTON *Savage Life in Central Aust.* 82 In all my travelling among the blacks I have not seen the return boomerang used. . . The comeback—so called—was lighter than the ordinary 'Kirra'. **1927** M. DORNEY *Adventurous Honeymoon* 53 The come-back boomerang, is used mostly for show, although it might sometimes be thrown in among a flock of birds when it will come back if it doesn't hit anything. **1959** E. WEBB *Mark of Sun* 61 He took two 'come-back' boomerangs out of his waist-belt. They were three feet from tip to tip, and about three inches wide.

2. A sheep three-quarters merino and one-quarter crossbred; the wool of the breed. Also *attrib.*

1891 R. WALLACE *Rural Econ. & Agric.* 360 When a pure Merino ram is put to a cross ewe the produce is termed a 'come-back' or 'quarter-back'. **1896** *Bulletin* (Sydney) 11 Jan. 27/2 His youngsters have a pet sheep, of the comeback denomination. **1905** *Shearer* (Sydney) 2 Dec. 3/2 Wools fine in quality, free, sound, and in good condition were in exceptional request, whilst bright, free, comeback and crossbreds created keen bidding. **1910** *Truth* (Sydney) 13 Mar. 11/6, I 'ave a 'arf a million sheep—crossbreds and comebacks, too. **1928** C.E. COWLEY *Classing Clip* 108 With the larger crossbred clips two main divisions will be necessary: *comeback* and *crossbred.* **1939** M. MORRIS *Dark Tumult* 145 'Twon't be merino in the future—it'll be all come-back wool. **1942** E. ANDERSON *Squatter's Luck* 16 Fer comeback ewes 'n' weaners too Th' breed's th' best ye'll get. **1965** G. MCINNES *Road to Gundagai* 260 These were mostly high-class merinos mingled with a few cross-bred or come-backs.

comic cuts. Rhyming slang for 'guts'. Also *ellipt.* as **comics.**

1945 *Newsreel* (Launceston) May 4 Patients feel the pills doing them good even before they reach the 'comic cuts'. **1950** *Austral. Police Jrnl.* Apr. 111 *Comic cuts*, abdomen ('guts'). **1958** F.B. VICKERS *Mirage* 55 'Never drink this well water,' he said. 'It makes you crook in the comics.' **1971** F. HARDY *Outcasts of Foolgarah* 76 Do you get a burning pain that starts in your comic cuts and rises to your throat? **1977** F.A. REEDER *Diary of Rat* 63, I got a bit crook in the comic cuts and had to run for the latrine about ten times a day.

commission. [Abbrev. of *Housing Commission* (in some States).] Used *attrib.* of government-owned housing, etc., for people on low incomes.

1926 *Canberra Community News* 11 June 9 Recently I was severely 'ticked off' . . for building a small fireplace in my shanty with Commission bricks. **1944** A.J. & J.J. MCINTYRE *Country Towns Vic.* 40 The shack-dwellers could not afford to live in commission houses, in spite of the rebate system. **1960** *N.T. News* (Darwin) 5 Feb. 1/8 The commission homes here were about eight squares. **1974** M. GILLESPIE *Into Hollow Mountains* 20 Working-class teenagers haven't much else to do but dropout, out of the concrete commission flat and out of the classroom. **1979** P. ADAMS *More Unspeakable Adams* 92 If we lived in a house, even a commission house, it wouldn't be so bad. **1981** B. GREEN *Small Town Rising* 12 The families of the two aborigines . . were above suspicion, for they lived in Commission homes in the town.

common. Also in *pl.* [Transf. use of *common* communally owned or shared land.]

1. Unenclosed Crown land available as public pasture; sometimes, as in Br. use, an area specifically reserved, but freq. unallocated land adjacent to settlements.

1808 *Sydney Gaz.* 29 May, Fifty Acres of excellent land. . . Four acres much elevated immediately contiguous to an extensive Common. **1811** *Ibid.* 30 Nov., The Farm . . commands a common of 10,000 Acres. **1830** *Sydney Monitor* 30 Oct. 3/2 It was to be reserved as *common* for the use of the village of Parramatta. **1831** *Sydney Herald* 25 Apr. 3/1 A large common of 3000 acres is about to be laid off . . for the benefit of the settlers. **1843** *Adelaide Observer* 18 Nov. 7/1 He could see no objection to the Waste Lands in the settled districts being used as commons. **1887** W.H. SUTTOR *Austral. Stories Retold* 105 The back country was used as a common by the frontage proprietors. **1904** *Bulletin* (Sydney) 25 Feb. 35/1 Two horses drawing a wood-dray across the common. **1930** A.E. YARRA *Vanishing Horseman* 87 The last haul they made was several hundred head of fat stock that had been grazing right on the Commons . . while the owner arranged for grass country for them. **1977** W.A. WINTER-IRVING *Bush Stories* 19 The town common, a huge area of about eight hundred hectares or more, taking in most of the waterhole and contained by a fence.

2. Special Comb. **common ranger**: see quot. 1899.

1899 *Bulletin* (Sydney) 8 Apr. 14/3 Even in the bush exists the desire for titles. . . The bank-clerks are 'bankers', the herdsman is 'common ranger', the bum is 'sheriff'. **1956** T. RONAN *Moleskin Midas* 196 Cooling, the Bank Inspector, was there, and Sid Stangate the common ranger. They were down at the stockyard with Drage, running through the horses.

common fringe-myrtle: see FRINGE-MYRTLE.

Commonwealth. [Shortened form of *Commonwealth of Australia.*] The federated States and Territories of Australia; the government of this federation. Also *attrib.*

1891 *Quiz* (Adelaide) 17 Apr. 6/2 Deakin, it is stated, is the real godfather of the term 'Australian Commonwealth'. **1898** *Austral. Handbk.* 121 'The Commonwealth' shall be taken to mean the Commonwealth of Australia as constituted under this Act. **1899** *North-Western Advocate* (Devonport) 23 Jan. 2/7 The island colony will benefit materially by having a year or two's independence before being merged into the Commonwealth. **1901** F.J. GILLEN *Diary* 9 May (1968) 73 Today the Duke of Cornwall is to open the Commonwealth Parliament. **1901** *Truth* (Sydney) 12 May 2/6 All hail 'The Commonwealth'. Drink Nicoll's Dandelion Ale. **1905** *Nat. Rev.* (London) May 544 There is consequently no party, and no leader in the Commonwealth, in 1905, not pledged to the 'White Australia' policy. **1915** J.P. BOURKE *Off Bluebush* 38 As I lie with my head on your lap, I do not care one Commonwealth rap What may hap! Not-one-blooming-young-Commonwealth-rap! **1934** *Manifesto* (Austral. Labor Party Qld.) 6/1 Labor would . . lag behind the political constitution of the Commonwealth, and would correspond in its structure to the parochial state of things prevailing before Australian nationhood was achieved. **1956** A.C.C. LOCK *Tropical Tapestry* 215 After the six Australian States had federated and formed the Commonwealth, there was no Australian flag. **1965** D. MARTIN *Hero of Too* 319 The past, present and future of Tooramit, the friendliest, most progressive town of its size in the Commonwealth, the strong, sound heart of the wheat bowl. **1978** F. DALY *A to Z Politics* 8 The Whitlam Government in line with its general policy substituted the name Australia for Commonwealth . . e.g. Parliament was designated Parliament of Australia. **1986** *Canberra Times* 18 Feb. 13/1 The Commonwealth is in a position of special strength and it has an overall responsibility to the community at large.

compo. [f. WORKERS') COMP(ENSATION + -O.]

1. A payment or series of payments made under a workers' compensation scheme. Also *attrib.*

1949 *Coast to Coast 1948* 108 What if I am—dusted? What d'you think I'll do? Get outback, take me compo, and nose around till I strike some of the shiny stuff they call gold. **1950** H.C. WELLS *Earth cries Out* 124 'But, Dick, he's set on you goin' to college.' 'Yes, and it'll cost more than his compo for me alone.' **1959** K.S. PRICHARD *N'Goola* 73 His mates thought it a good joke when Tony told them about the accident. 'He after da compo,' Augustino laughed. **1963** B. HESLING *Dinkumization & Depommification* 63, I had to wear crutches, honest. I was knocked down by a tram. Me claim wasn't heard for eighteen months. I had to wear crutches till I'd won me compo. **1966** *Realist* (Sydney) xxii. 20/2 The compo claims on false teeth had reached about their limit. **1982** *Access* Mar. 23 Then he claimed he'd injured his back, and got Compo for it! **1986** *Canberra Times* 22 Feb. 10/3 (*heading*) Court upholds widow's compo.

2. In the phr. **on compo,** in receipt of workers' compensation.

1941 K. TENNANT *Battlers* 291 'If you *do* slice your hand, they put you on compo. . . ' Seeing them puzzled, she explained: 'Compensation money while it heals.' **1958** G. COTTERELL *Tea at Shadow Creek* 244 You're not in our union. If you were we'd have you put on compo. **1965** F. HARDY *Yarns of Billy Borker* 136 Well, every time a ship came into Newcastle, some of the crew would pay off on compo. **1978** R.H. CONQUEST *Dusty Distances* 7, I ruined me back workin' as a ganger on the railways so they've super-ed me out on compo.

concertina, *n.* and *attrib.* [Fig. use of *concertina.*]

A. *n.*

1. a. A side of mutton. **b.** A sheep with wrinkles or folds in its skin.

1897 *Bulletin* (Sydney) 7 Aug. (Red Page), Ribs of Mutton—'Concertina'. Ancient, and very common throughout Australia. **1945** S.J. BAKER *Austral. Lang.* 80 *Concertina*, a side of mutton. **1970** J.S. GUNN in W.S. Ramson *Eng. Transported* 65 *A concertina*, a slang term for a wrinkly sheep is now also a side of lamb in some places.

2. See quot. 1981.

1966 S.J. BAKER *Austral. Lang.* (ed. 2) 68 *Concertinas*, a type of leggings with wrinkles in them. **1981** G. MITCHELL *Bush Horseman* 40 Most stockmen . . preferred to make their own and produced soft, short leggings with turned-down tops. They were very comfortable and were adjusted beneath the swell of the calf by two straps at the top which held them in place during hard riding. Because these leggings wrinkled in the centre, they were known as 'concertinas'.

B. *attrib.* (in senses 1b. and 2).

1905 *Shearer* (Sydney) 4 Mar. 6/2 A lot of the shearing done by Harry Livingstone is of 'concertina' merinos, and not plain bodied crossbreds. **1917** *Bulletin* (Sydney) 18 Oct. 24/2 A tall, amiable-looking giant, speeding-up, ripped a concertina wether with the machine, leaving a 6 in. slash. **1947** E. HILL *Flying Doctor Calling* 19 There are leggings, spring-side or concertina—concertina are the most comfortable, but if you get them wet you can't take them off for six weeks so spring-side are recommended. **1975** R. EDWARDS *Austral. Traditional Bush Crafts* 82 R.M. Williams describes concertina leggings as, 'A stockman's style that is as old as Australia and one of the best'.

conchie, var. CONSHIE.

Condamine /ˈkɒndəmaɪn/. [The name of a town in Queensland.] A type of animal bell originally made at Condamine. In full **Condamine bell.**

1925 M. GILMORE *Tilted Cart* 103 The Condamine bell in Queensland . . was as famous there as Mennicke's bell in New South Wales. The first Condamine bell was made from a pit saw; in later years it was made from circular and from crosscut saws as well. Horses and cattle alike wore it. Its note was so penetrating that in time it would render horses deaf. As far as I recollect it, it had a hard steely sound something like a hammer-clink on an anvil. **1926** K.S. PRICHARD *Working Bullocks* 295 Dick Hayes tinkled the condamine he was carrying round to start events. **1950** J. SORENSEN *Collected Poems* 85 The smith is lost to the Condamine River, Gone is the humpy where he used to dwell, But the song and the clamour of his busy hammer Ring on through the land in the Condamine bell. **1961** J.J. JONES *Condamine Bells* 4 To make the Condamine bell, the smith heated a saw blade, folded the steel and rivetted the joints together. . . The Condamine Bell has a special shape; it was like a diamond with the top and bottom points cut off, and, more important, it had a distinctive and penetrating sound. This sound came not only from the shape of the bell, but also the quality of the steel from which it was made; from the steel which once formed the cross-cut saws. **1969** R. OTTLEY *Brumbie Dust* 60 Around their necks we buckled 'Condamine' horse bells. The clanging of these brass bells will carry over a distance of anything up to five miles if the wind is in the right direction. **1978** D. STUART *Wedgetail View* 115 Each camel belled with a Condamine. **1981** A. MARSHALL *Aust.* 112 The Condamine bell, first made by a part Chinese, has a note that sent horses deaf in time, it was said. Yet it was not a loud note but it was prolonged.

condenser. *Hist.* [Spec. use of *condenser* an apparatus which converts vapour to liquid.] An apparatus by which water is made potable through distillation. Also *attrib.*

1894 F. HART *Miner's Handbk.* 19 The great drawback to the rapid development of the field has, up to the present, been the scarcity of fresh water; but this want has now been, in a great measure, overcome . . by the provision of a public condenser; not to mention that every mine on which machinery has been erected is in a position to supply itself by means of its own condenser, an apparently unlimited supply of salt water having in almost every instance been encountered at no very great depth from the surface. **1929** W.J. RESIDE *Golden Days* 277 There are no condensers, and *few prospectors* in W.A. now. **1937** L.R. MENZIES *Gold Seeker's Odyssey* 138 The Government erected a condenser and sold the water at cost price. **1940** G. MORPHETT *Simple Story Rural Dev.* 4/1 For six weeks I kept the condenser going, the children helping with the firewood. **1944** R. BEDFORD *Naught to Thirty-Three* 197 A condenser where water was sold at the price of beer. **1946** K.S. PRICHARD *Roaring Nineties* 161 There was great indignation when a rumour went round that condenser holders were talking of putting up the price of water. **1964** CASEY & MAYMAN *Mile Midas Touched* 119 Boring revealed only highly mineralized, unsuitable water. Government and private condensers helped solve the immediate problem. **1981** A.B. FACEY *Fortunate Life* 54 They used to be big condenser contractors on the Goldfields.

Hence **condensing** *vbl. n.* and *ppl. a.*

1939 A. GASTON *Coolgardie Gold* 115 As the number of condensing plants increased the price of water came down. **1940** G. MORPHETT *Simple Story Rural Dev.* 4/1 The neighbors used to say, 'When you start condensing you get the rain.'

conditional, *a. Hist.*

a. In special collocations: **conditional emancipation, pardon,** a remission of (a convict's) sentence, subject to varying territorial stipulations but always precluding return to the British Isles until the expiration of the term of the original sentence.

1792 D. COLLINS *Acct. Eng. Colony N.S.W.* (1798) I. 228 One of those convicts who left England in the *Guardian*, and who, from their meritorious behaviour before and after the disaster that befel that ship, received **conditional emancipation** by his Majesty's command. **1798** *HRA* (1914) 1st Ser. II. 208 A convict, shall receive conditional emancipation, that is to be made free in this country and have permission to become a settler. **1800** *Ibid.* 491, I gave him a conditional emancipation. . . By this kind of pardon you will discover that he is as completely exil'd from his native country as he ever was. **1803** *Ibid.* IV. 302 Having given him a Conditional Emancipation to perform the duties of Engineer and Artillery Officer. **1811** *Sydney Gaz.* 19 Jan., Free Women . . including . . those who are free by Absolute Pardon or Conditional Emancipation. **1829** *Launceston Advertiser* 6 July 2 Let each man according to his sentence, receive a ticket of leave or conditional emancipation. **1794** D. COLLINS *Acct. Eng. Colony N.S.W.* (1798) I. 391 James Ruffler, and Richard Partridge (convicts for life), received a **conditional pardon,** or (as was the term among themselves on this occasion) were made free on the ground, to enable them to become settlers. **1810** *Sydney Gaz.* 30 June, All those under Sentence of Transportation to whom Absolute or Conditional Pardons or Tickets of Leave were granted. **1822** J.T. BIGGE *Rep. State Colony N.S.W.* 120 A conditional pardon contains a declaration of the governor, under his hand and official seal, that the unexpired term of the convict's sentence is conditionally remitted to him; and the condition is expressed to be, that he shall continue to reside within the limits of the government of New South Wales during the space of the original sentence, under pain of incurring all the penalties of re-appearing in Great Britain, for and during the term of his original sentence or order of transportation; or as if the remission had never been granted. **1826** *Colonial Times* (Hobart) 12 Aug., The following Men will receive Tickets of Leave; and if after serving One Year in the Field Police, they shall produce Testimonials of good Behaviour, they will obtain Conditional Pardons. **1840** *S. Austral. Rec.* (London) 4 July 4 The instrument called an Emancipation, or Conditional Pardon, should be given to each on landing—making them perfectly free, except as to leaving the colony. **1852** MRS C. MEREDITH *My Home in Tas.* I. 41 After remaining the allotted number of years in the ticket-of-leave class, the deserving convicts . . received a 'conditional pardon', which permitted them the range of the Australian colonies; and to some was granted a 'free pardon'. **1865** 'SPECIAL CORRESPONDENT' *Transportation* 56 South Australian law prohibits the landing of conditional pardon holders. **1872** MRS E. MILLETT *Austral. Parsonage* 243 It was customary for convicts who had served a portion of their sentence to receive what was called a conditional pardon, by which they were free to leave the colony, and to land in ports of any part of the world, those of Great Britain and Ireland alone excepted.

b. In the collocation **conditional pardon man.**

1845 *Observer* (Hobart) 26 Sept. 3/4 On the subject of the Conditional pardon men. **1859** M. MACKAY *Natives' Institution King George's Sound* 9 The eldest girl in the Annesfield Asylum . . is engaged to be married in six weeks from this time . . to a well-conducted, sober, industrious conditional-pardon man. **1865** 'SPECIAL CORRESPONDENT' *Transportation* 57 Conditional-pardon men . . are placed in the most awkward situation of any of the criminal class,—for, though perfectly free to leave the penal colony, there is only the port of Sydney open to them.

condolly /ˈkɒndəli/. *Obs.* [a. Gaurna *kondali* whale.] Whale blubber.

1893 S. NEWLAND *Paving Way* 31 'Frying-down pots'—huge iron boilers in which the fat, technically called 'condolly', or blubber, of the whales is melting. **1894** *Proc. R. Geogr. Soc. Australasia: S.A.* (1899) 42 There was a strong smell of 'condolly' pervading the atmosphere, accompanied by a subtler odor that appeared strongest near the suspended figure, and not devoid of that fragrance so frequently found where soap is absent. **1919** S. NEWLAND *Band of Pioneers* 39 There was a strong odour of 'condolly' (blubber), but the aboriginal luxuriates in ointment that makes itself known.

conjuror. *Obs.* KORADJI.

1846 'COLONIAL MAGISTRATE' *Remarks on Probable Origin* 10 Although the word *Priest* does not appear in the vocabulary of the Natives—the words *Doctor* or *Conjuror* is [*sic*] applied to those old men who assume the guidance in *Coroborees*. **1878** R.B. SMYTH *Aborigines of Vic.* I. 103 Threlkeld mentions a bone—*Mur-ro-kun*—which is obtained by the Ka-ra-kul, a doctor or conjuror. **1886** E.M. CURR *Austral. Race* I. 45 It is an universal belief of the Blacks that a conjuror, wizard, or doctor (as bushmen commonly call and I shall continue to call that personage) . . can charm.

conkerberry /'kɒŋkəbɛri/. Also **coongaberry, konkleberry, koonkerberry.** [Prob. a Majuli *gaŋgabiri*.] Either of two species of the genus *Carissa* (fam. Apocynaceae), esp. *C. lanceolata*, the spiny shrub or small tree of W.A., N.T., and Qld., having edible fruits.

1888 *Proc. Linnean Soc. N.S.W.* III. 495 *Carissa ovata* . . 'Kunkerberry' of the aboriginals of the Cloncurry River (North Queensland). **1948** H.A. LINDSAY *Bushman's Handbk.* 58 The koonkerberry is a shrub with thin spines and a milky juice carrying a sweet little berry like a sultana grape. **1949** H.G. LAMOND *White Ears* 60 A sandhill ridge thick with coongaberry and gooya apples. **1954** B. MILES *Stars my Blanket* 139 The conkerbury bush, which has little grape-like nuts—'good tucker' to the blacks. **1961** W.E. HARNEY *Grief, Gaiety & Aborigines* 24 Prickly Conkerberri (black-currant) bushes. **1969** R. LAWRENCE *Aboriginal Habitat* 58 The Konkleberry . . matured quickly after rain, but the harvest lasted for a few weeks only. **1974** S.L. EVERIST *Poisonous Plants Aust.* 63 *C[arissa] lanceolata*: Conker Berry or Conkle Berry, occurs in north-western Queensland and the Northern Territory. **1982** ELLIOT & JONES *Encycl. Austral. Plants* II. 464 Conkerberry. . . A stunted shrub found in stony terrain often in thickets. A useful plant to the Aborigines.

connie, var. COONIE.

connie, *n.*[1] Chiefly in Melbourne. [f. *con(ductor* + -Y.] A bus or tram conductor.

1933 'TRAMWAY WORKERS' *Shock Brigader* 6 A happy young connie from Kew Called some streets, but omitted a few. **1942** *Survey Sentinel: 2/1 Austral. Army Topogr. Survey Co.* 1 Jan. 2 Another tram arrives. . . Drivers have lost their connies. **1969** P. ADAM SMITH *Folklore Austral. Railwaymen* 207 Passengers often ask the conductor to wake them up on long runs. This passenger said to the old connie, 'Throw me off at Gladstone.'

connie, *n.*[2] [f. *corn(elian* + -Y.] A type of playing marble. Also **connie agate.**

1966 S.J. BAKER *Austral. Lang.* (ed. 2) 284 Marbles of one kind and another are known to Australian children as . . *connies, connie agates.* **1972** *Bulletin* (Sydney) 6 May 63/3 He managed to win a few 'birdcages', bottle-os, connie agates and other middle-class marbles.

conshie. Also **conchie.** [Abbrev. of *consc(ientious.*] A conscientious person. Also **conch, concho,** and *attrib.*

1969 A. BUZO *Front Room Boys* (1970) 20 'All right, you blokes, let's get on with the work, eh?' . . 'Righto, Thomo, righto, You're a bit of a conch this morning, aren't you?' **1970** R. BEILBY *No Medals for Aphrodite* 14 One lousy stripe, and as soon as you tried to do the right thing you were a 'military maniac' or 'Army-happy' or, worst of all, a 'conshie'. **1972** R. MAGOFFIN *Chops & Gravy* 106 *Concho*, a conscientious person. **1974** D. WAUGH *Master White Grass* 15 Mentioned in dispatches for work alone behind the Jap. lines. He tried not to show it. Clean and consci. **1980** G.F. BREWER *On Breadline* 17, I was a 'conchie' worker, but we were still up to our neck in debt as it was, even before the floods came. **1980** F. MOORHOUSE *Days of Wine & Rage* 302 Some Australians . . have a suspicion of swots, 'conchies', people who work hard for their effect.

consolidated, *ppl. a.* In special collocations: **consolidated miner's right,** see quot. 1869; **run,** *Qld., obs.*, a holding of adjacent tracts of pasture land, the combined area of which does not exceed 200 square miles (see also RUN *n.*[2]); **school,** a rural school formed by the amalgamation of two or more small schools.

1869 R.B. SMYTH *Gold Fields & Mineral Districts* 616 A **consolidated miner's right** may be taken out for all the land held by a mining company on payment of a sum equal to that which would be paid for all the miners' rights that the consolidated right represents. **1882** M. SHOLL *Handy Bk. Tasmanian Mining* 111 Consolidated miner's rights are issued to companies or co-operative partners equal to the number of miners' rights by virtue of which their claims are held. **1863** *Act* (Qld.) 27 Vic. no. 17 Sect. 29, Where the licensee or lessee shall have two or more runs adjoining each other not exceeding in the aggregate two hundred square miles he may apply to the commissioner to register the same as a **consolidated run.** **1880** J. BONWICK *Resources Qld.* 34 Several *Runs* may be secured by the same party . . provided they be adjacent, and not exceeding a total of 200 square miles, or only 128,000 acres in the *Consolidated Run.* **1897** *Act* (Qld.) 61 Vic. no. 25 Sect. 60, In the case of two or more conterminous runs held by the same pastoral tenant, the whole shall be dealt with as one run (hereinafter called a 'consolidated run'). **1920** *W. Austral.* (Perth) 15 Nov. 7/7 Toodyay . . is the first district in the State to gain the distinction of having a **consolidated school** opened in its midst. This is a class of school which marks a forward step in the advanced system of education obtaining in Western Australia. **1927** G.S. BROWNE *Educ. in Aust.* 266 The consolidated school in a central position will eventually take the place of a group of one-teacher schools. **1940** *Educ. Studies & Investigations* (Austral. Council Educ. Research) 217 The consolidated school is to be preferred to a group of small rural schools. **1962** *Bulletin* (Sydney) 27 Oct. 3/3 Tasmania set the pace in area (or 'consolidated') schools. **1970** R.T. FITZGERALD *Secondary School at Sixes & Sevens* 97 Cohesion between primary and secondary stages has traditionally existed, namely in area and consolidated schools.

consultation. [Euphem. use of *consultation* the seeking of advice.] A sweepstake (see quot. 1890); a lottery.

1880 *Bulletin* (Sydney) 21 Feb. 7/3 Sydney Cup Consultation, 1880. 2000 Members at One Pound each. **1890** J. HASLAM *Glimpse Austral. Life* 103 In connection with all big races there is carried out by the fraternity what are called consultations. They get fifty thousand subscribers at one pound each, and divide the winnings, less ten per cent., among those individuals who are lucky enough to draw numbers with a horse's name. **1936** *S.A. Rep. R. Comm. Lotteries* 20 He also informed us that never less than 92 per cent. of the tickets in small consultations with a first prize of £6,000 were purchased in Queensland. **1947** *Romantic Career G. Adams (Tattersall)* (rev. ed.) 21 Tattersall changed over from 'horse race' consultations to 'cash' consultations, with the sole exception of its greatest sweep, the £50,000 first prize event on the Melbourne Cup. **1966** *Courier-Mail* (Brisbane) 5 May 3/11 A Scottish couple . . yesterday won first prize in a Queensland consultation, the Scarborough art union.

Hence **consult** *v. trans.*

1880 *Bulletin* (Sydney) 3 Apr. 2/3 Mr T.F. Whistler . . successfully consulted Mr Ned Jones . . re the Sydney Cup—£950.

contingent vote. *Hist.* A form of preferential voting introduced in Queensland in 1892; a vote cast under this system.

1892 *Act* (Qld.) 56 Vict. no. 7 Sect. 22, Electors may give contingent votes. **1899** *North-Western Advocate* (Devonport) 22 Feb. 2/5 Under the Hare-Clark system, or even under Queensland's contingent vote, the result would certainly have been altered. **1919** C.A. BERNAYS *Qld. Politics during Sixty Yrs.* 296 Frequently a member had during the existence of a Parliament represented a minority of the electors. An attempt was now made to put an end to that by introducing what was known as the 'contingent vote'.

conversation-lolly. [f. *conversation* + LOLLY 1: cf. *conversation lozenge*, OEDS *conversation* 11.] A sweet inscribed with a (sentimental) motto: see quot. 1902. Also *ellipt.* as **conversation.**

1901 *Bulletin* (Sydney) 19 Jan. 32/1 He . . purchased silk handkerchiefs and perfume and conversation-lollies at the store. **1902** *Ibid.* 13 Dec. 21/4 He never did anything much except bring me . . conversation-lollies, with 'What about the ring?' 'Be my loved one', 'Love the giver', 'You are very sweet', etc., on them. **1972** J. JONES *Memories Golden Gate* 6 Southern made sweets included conversations, humbugs and happy moments, containing a lot of hot chilli liquid.

convict, *n.* and *attrib. Hist.* [Spec. use of *convict* a condemned criminal serving a sentence of penal servitude: see OED *sb.*[1] 2.]

A. *n. Hist.*

1. One sentenced in the British Isles to a term of penal servitude in an Australian Colony.

1787 *Hist. Botany Bay New Holland* p. i, Names of the Ships, and Number of Convicts embark'd on board each ship. **1791** A. PHILLIP *Copies & Extracts Lett.* 5 Nov. (1792) 126 The first settler was a convict, whose time being expired, a hut was built and one acre and an half of ground cleared for him at Parramatta. **1801** *Gen. Orders issued by Governor King* 11 June (1802) 48 The Governor for the time being is allowed such a number of convicts, victualled from the Stores, as he may judge necessary for his domestic purposes. **1808** *To Viscount Castlereagh* 91 We find it necessary that a colony and civil government should be established in the place to which such convicts shall be transported. **1826** *Monitor* (Sydney) 19 May 2/3 The decent term of *Prisoner*, had been substituted by Macquarie, for the degrading one of *Convict*, as the latter designation had in its turn taken place of the old British appellation of *Felon*. **1827** P. CUNNINGHAM *Two Yrs. in N.S.W.* II. 118 An individual transported to Van Dieman's Land for piracy, who had been emancipated for meritorious conduct there, obtained a verdict with £50 damages against a libeller, who had attempted to malign his character by spitefully spouting the opprobrious epithet of 'd--d convict!' in his teeth. **1834** G. BENNETT *Wanderings N.S.W.* I. 262 Most of the stations are solely under charge of assigned servants, (convict is an obsolete word in the colony). **1838** W. BLAND *N.S.W.: Examination* 84 Squatters, mostly convicts holding tickets-of-leave, or having become free by servitude. **1842** *Austral. & N.Z. Monthly Mag.* 48 *Convicts* . . prisoners of the crown . . will be allowed to enter the police, receiving immediate certificates of pardon upon the following conditions. **1846** *Moreton Bay Courier* 11 July 4/4 Any convict who may have served three entire years without any record of misconduct appearing against him, will be eligible for a ticket-of-leave. **1849** G.F. ANGAS *Descr. Barossa Range* 8 No convicts are transported to this place, for South Australia is not a penal colony. **1872** MRS E. MILLETT *Austral. Parsonage* 66 Depôts . . to which convicts are drafted after serving a portion of their sentence in the Fremantle gaol. **1888** 'R. BOLDREWOOD' *Robbery under Arms* (1937) 6 Government men, as the convicts were always called round our part. **1975** J.D. RITCHIE *Aust. as once we Were* 31 The Aborigines who witnessed the convicts' agonies showed disgust at the punishments.

2. *fig.*

1859 'EYE WITNESS' *Voyage to Aust.* 19 The last dinner taken on British soil is the only comfortable one you will take until you return or die; in short, you are the convict of your own choice, and those with a young family leaving home for Australia would be kindly visited if the undertaker had to receive the money paid to the shipping agents.

B. 1. *attrib.*

1793 W. TENCH *Compl. Acct. Settlement* 25 A dozen farthing candles stuck around the mud walls of a convict-hut. **1829** D. BURN *Bushrangers* (1971) 44 Without encroaching on the convict brood, 'Who left their country for their country's good!' **1835** *Colonist* (Sydney) 23 Apr. 3/4 The prevalence of a convict-morality has been so extensive and so debasing in this colony. **1837** J. MUDIE *Felonry of N.S.W.* 145 Convict prisoners before the supreme court may utter the most atrocious calumnies. *Ibid.* 195 The convict swains . . usually apply for permission to go to the factory in quest of a fair helpmate. **1838** *S. Austral. Rec.* (London) 14 Nov. 116 One universal *esprit de corps* animates and pervades the whole convict body, uniting them like Freemasons in one silent, deep-rooted sentiment of hostility to the free settler, or, as they profanely call them, the b-- emigrants. **1839** *Sydney Standard* 22 July 2/3 The feelings and wishes of convict parents have no right to be considered or consulted upon the question of education. **1840** J.P. JOHNSON *Plain Truths* 44 The occupation of the first class is making convict clothing. **1841** *Port Phillip Patriot* 22 Apr. 4/4 A curious and not a very unfavourable specimen of convict poetry. **1843** *Sydney Morning Herald* 22 Aug. 2/2 He would re-brand the colony with that convict-stigma which made it so long an object of loathing. **1846** *Atlas* (Sydney) II. 553/3 The people of New South Wales will not suffer themselves to be deceived, by canting tirades against convict pollution. **1855** G.H. WATHEN *Golden Colony* 142 He swore a deep convict oath. **1856** J. BONWICK *Bushrangers* 13 We must .. introduce the reader to the convict homes of Macquarie Harbour and Port Arthur. **1869** J. MARTINEAU *Lett. from Aust.* 115 In New South Wales a considerable proportion of the population is of convict descent. **1870** J. BONWICK *Curious Facts* 154 The children were brought up by thirty resident convict nurses. **1878** G. WALCH *Australasia* 12 The salt breezes may blow across Port Arthur at the present time, untainted by convict breath. **1879** 'RECENT SETTLER' *Emigration to Tas.* 40 The standard of morality in Tasmania is decidedly lower than in England; attributable, most probably, to the fact of the convict element having predominated so greatly in former years. **1891** H. NISBET *Colonial Tramp* II. 274 The worst of the convict-floggers, also insane now, was dying when I saw him. **1892** G. PARKER *Round Compass in Aust.* 129 As a refutation of any unusual emphasis of the 'convict taint', it may be noted that the most moral, religious, law-abiding, and arcadian of the Australian colonies, is Tasmania. **1935** F. CLUNE *Rolling down Lachlan* 7 The convict iron-gang roadmenders wore fetters.

2. Comb. **convict boy, -built** *a.*, **class, clerk, gang, labour, labourer, -made** *a.*, **mechanic, population, shepherd, stock-keeper, woman.**

1833 *N.S.W. Mag.* (Sydney) 248 **Convict Boys** may be procured as apprentices on board ships. **1834** J.D. LANG *Hist. & Statistical Acct. N.S.W.* II. 170 The Carters' Barracks—an establishment in which convict-boys are taught mechanical employments. **1837** *Rep. Select Committee Transportation* 67 Convict boys, 16 or 17 years old .. had arrived in the last ships. **1839** *S. Austral. Rec.* (London) 9 Oct. 246 The new colony will throw their **convict built** importance entirely into the shade. **1913** H. LAWSON *Triangles of Life* 179 The old convict-built log fence. **1914** H.M. VAUGHAN *Australasian Wander-Yr.* 109 The old convict-built church of St. John's, with a quaint clock-tower, still remains. **1927** *Melbourne Univ. Mag.* Sept. 90 A stone structure, obviously 'convict-built', arrested our attention. **1837** J. BACKHOUSE *Narr. Visit Austral. Colonies* (1843) 464 Servants of the **convict class**, are amongst the greatest drawbacks upon domestic comfort, in these Colonies. **1840** *Tasmanian Weekly Dispatch* (Hobart) 10 Apr. 7/2 It is wonderful so many, particularly of the convict class, have escaped sickness and death. **1855** J. BONWICK *Geogr. Aust. & N.Z.* (ed. 3) 63 The population is nearly one-half of the convict class. **1874** J.J. HALCOMBE *Emigrant & Heathen* 59 The convict class, not being replenished by fresh arrivals from England, steadily diminished. **1827** P. CUNNINGHAM *Two Yrs. in N.S.W.* II. 297 As these lists are at present made out by a **convict-clerk**, the difference of half-a-crown will make a man either saint or fiend. **1837** J. MUDIE *Felonry of N.S.W.* 249 The convict clerks are often entrusted by their masters with the entire conducting of their business. **1846** *Tasmanian Jrnl. Nat. Sci.* II. 25 There was a small cottage .. occupied by the convict clerks. **1832** BACKHOUSE & TYLOR *Life & Labours G.W. Walker* 22 Feb. (1862) 40 J.B. had an interview with the Governor on the subject of gaining access to the prisons and **convict** or chain-**gangs.** **1846** *Narr. Voyages N.S.W.* 10 At East Maitland, is a garrison of a few soldiers, to look after the convict gang. **1851** *Illustr. Austral. Mag.* (Melbourne) Mar. 159 Among the convict gangs of Tasmania, there prevails an extent of vice and infamy, not exceeded, perhaps never equalled, in the worst ages of pagan darkness. **1878** G. WALCH *Australasia* 14 The convict gangs file past the garden. **1827** *Third Rep. Select Committee Emigration* 394 The demand for **convict labour** has risen so much that we are not likely to obtain much of it. **1835** *Colonist* (Sydney) 15 Jan. 1/1 The abundance of convict-labour in this colony has reduced the wages of all free persons. **1845** *Atlas* (Sydney) I. 241/1 'All went merry as a marriage bell' whilst, in the natural order of things, convict labour was employed in preparing hitherto unsettled lands for settlement and sale. **1854** W. SHAW *Land of Promise* 3 The colony is indebted to convict labour for these and other stupendous monuments of industry. **1872** MRS E. MILLETT *Austral. Parsonage* 18 The work was carried out entirely by convict labour—the only manner in which such an undertaking could ever have been effected in so thinly peopled a colony. **1879** 'RECENT SETTLER' *Emigration to Tas.* 55 A grand trunk road from north to south of the island was originally constructed by convict labour. **1890** MRS R.D. DOUGLAS *Romance at Antipodes* 163 St. James' Church was built by convict labor. **1951** G. FARWELL *Outside Track* 109 The massive sandstone blocks .. could not have been hewn without cheap convict labour. **1824** E. CURR *Acct. Colony Van Diemen's Land* 105 Government, so far from having a superfluity of **convict labourers**, is unable to supply the number voluntarily required by the settler. **1832** J. BISCHOFF *Sketch Hist. Van Diemen's Land* 78, I consider the condition of the convict labourers in New South Wales as infinitely superior to that of the agricultural labourers of this country. **1840** A. RUSSELL *Tour through Austral. Colonies* 108 Farmers usually get convict labourers assigned to them by government. **1852** S. MOSSMAN *Voice from Aust.* 3 The gold-digger .. now travels comfortably along the **convict-made** roads. *c* **1906** L. BECKE *Settlers Karossa Creek* 145, I .. set off along the old convict-made road that led to the beach. **1910** *Bulletin* (Sydney) 8 Sept. 13/4 There were then no roads north of the convict-made ways about Port Macquarie. **1837** J. MUDIE *Felonry of N.S.W.* 28 The secresy [*sic*] as well as co-operation of the **convict mechanics** was secured by means of rum. **1844** *Sydney Morning Herald* 13 Apr. 2/4 An order has been issued to withdraw all convict mechanics now employed in the Colonial Departments. **1863** C. GIBSON *Life among Convicts* II. 217 The condition of a convict mechanic was even better than that of a domestic servant. **1834** J.D. LANG *Hist. & Statistical Acct. N.S.W.* II. 1 The whole of the **convict-population** .. were employed on account of the Government. **1838** T.H. JAMES *Six Months S.A.* 164 The convict population of Sydney is a great annoyance to the respectable emigrants from England. **1846** *Tasmanian Jrnl. Nat. Sci.* II. 148 The free population has increased 515 per cent., while the convict population has advanced only 242 per cent. **1850** *Irish Exile* (Hobart) 9 Mar. 2/3 The moral depravity of the convict population. **1861** L.A. MEREDITH *Over Straits* 8 Many of us would have preferred competence *without* a convict population, to wealth *with* it. **1834** J.D. LANG *Hist. & Statistical Acct. N.S.W.* II. 111 The **convict-shepherd** or overseer in charge .. brought us a bucket. **1839** T.P. BESNARD *Voice from Bush* 21 To the convict *shepherd* .. who has the most lambs after weaning season, I give a premium. **1856** J. FROST *Horrors Convict Life* (1973) 61 The convict shepherd was subsequently taken up on a charge. **1833** W.H. BRETON *Excursions* 108 It would be an interesting point to ascertain the effect on the **convict stock-keepers.** **1838** T. WALKER *Month in Bush Aust.* 19 Rough enough it is .. amongst unmarried convict stock-keepers and shepherds. **1851** H. MELVILLE *Present State Aust.* 353 The evidence adduced against them was entirely that obtained from convict stock-keepers. **1827** P. CUNNINGHAM *Two Yrs. in N.S.W.* II. 271 The usual number of **convict-women** proceeding out in one vessel seldom exceeding ninety. **1835** *Colonist* (Sydney) 21 May 161/1 He .. was actually cohabiting with a convict-woman illegally at large. **1845** C.J. BAKER *Sydney & Melbourne* 143 There were no fewer than 1205 convict women within its walls. **1856** J. BONWICK *Bushrangers* 22 The chief officers were living in open and shameless concubinage with the convict women.

3. Special Comb. **convict barrack(s),** BARRACK *n.*[1] 1 a.; **chaplain,** a clergyman appointed to minister to the spiritual needs of convicts; **colony,** an Australian Colony regarded primarily as a place of penal servitude; **constable,** a convict appointed as an officer of the peace; so **constabulary; days,** the period 1788–1868, during which convicts were transported to Australia; **department,** the government department responsible for the management of the convict population; **establishment,** the buildings and personnel of a convict station; **overseer,** a convict in government or assigned service appointed to supervise convict labourers; **police,** a force of *convict constables*; **servant,** an assigned convict; **settlement,** *convict colony*; *convict station*; **settler,** one transported as a convict who has subsequently taken up land in Australia; **ship,** a ship in which convicts are transported from Britain to Australia; **slave,** a convict servant; **station,** a place at which convicts are confined; STATION 1 a.; **system,** the transportation of convicts and treatment of them during confinement. See also PENAL, PRISONER.

1819 *HRA* (1917) 1st Ser. X. 96 The New **Convict Barrack** is a Commodious Spacious Building... It is Surrounded by a very high Stone Wall and is Calculated to Contain between Five and Six hundred Men. **1837** *Rep. Select Committee Transportation* 2 The convicts are kept on board ship until some necessary arrangements are made on shore for their reception and distribution; the place where they are received is called the Convict Barracks. **1838** W. MOLESWORTH *Rep. Select Committee Transportation* 9 The male convicts are, subsequently, removed to the convict barracks; the females to the penitentiaries. **1845** J.O. BALFOUR *Sketch of N.S.W.* 52 The Courts, the Convict Barracks, and the Legislative House are large brick buildings, quite destitute of any pretensions to architecture. **1852** G.C. MUNDY *Our Antipodes* III. 246 The Military Barracks—(in New South Wales and Van Diemen's Land the adjective is necessary to distinguish the cantonments from the convict barracks). **1844** F.R. NIXON *Pioneer Bishop Van Diemen's Land* 30 Dec. (1953) 41 The Bishop wished particularly to ordain all the **convict chaplains** himself. **1862** E. STRICKLAND *Austral. Pastor* 38 He .. appointed him to discharge the duties of convict chaplain at Hobart Town. **1822** J.T. BIGGE *Rep. State Colony N.S.W.* 147 He has thought, and often repeated, that New South Wales was a **convict colony.** **1827** P. CUNNINGHAM *Two Yrs. in N.S.W.* I. 12 The idea of Australia being a *convict* colony has .. hitherto deterred many worthy individuals from emigrating thereto. **1838** *Cornwall Chron.* (Launceston) 15 Sept. 1 We must .. admit that we are—as Lord Althorp most classically entitled us—a 'convict Colony'. **1847** J.B. ATKINSON *Penal Settlements* 9 Other colonies, free and convict, have since been settled in Australia and Van Diemen's Land. **1853** *Inquirer* (Perth) 8 June 3/1 You are now in a convict colony—is it not dreadful? **1867** J. BONWICK *J. Batman* 41 Both were convict colonies, under Government control. **1834** J.D. LANG *Hist. & Statistical Acct. N.S.W.* II. 267 This delicate task was entrusted by the military commandants to **convict-constables.** **1835** H. MELVILLE *Hist. Van Diemen's Land* 172 No man habited as a magistrate, would be touched by a convict constable. **1839** J. DIXON *Condition & Capabilities Van Diemen's Land* 82 He submits to the rule of convict constables, because such constables alone are suited for such a society. **1856** J. BONWICK *Bushrangers* 10 A charge supported only by two convict constables. **1835** *True Colonist* (Hobart) 27 Nov. 4/1 The subject of the **Convict Constabulary.** **1838** A. MACONOCHIE *Thoughts on Convict Management* 124, I believe the convict constabulary to be most vexatiously officious, both as regards the free and the bond. **1892** 'J. MILLER' *Workingman's Paradise* 92 That's .. a little island and in the **convict days** hard cases were put on it. **1897** *Bulletin* (Sydney) 28 Aug. 21/1 Yet another of the 'old hands' who connect the convict-days with the present has gone. **1972** *Ibid.* 26 Feb. 47/1 The research, which traces the lot of Australian women from convict days to votes for petticoats, comes up with few lights or sidelights. **1842** *Sydney Morning Herald* 2 Aug. 2/6 Three of the convicts attached to this branch of the **convict department.** **1845** J. FRANKLIN *Narr. Hist. Van Diemen's Land* 54 A new officer, to be called the Comptroller-General of Convicts .. was to unite in his own person the powers, if not the labours, of the various subdivisions of the convict department. **1852** R. MORGAN *Life & Adventures W. Buckley* 151, I was paid off by the Convict Department. **1827** *HRA* (1920) 1st Ser. XIII. 471 For the support and maintenance of the **Convict Establishment.** **1841** *Colonial Observer* (Sydney) 18 Nov. 54/2 A person employed in the convict establishment at Hyde Park. **1847** *Maitland Mercury* 29 Sept. 3/1 Instructions have been received in England for the abolition of all the convict establishments, Hyde Park Barracks, the Factory, Cockatoo Island, &c. **1851** H. MELVILLE *Present State Aust.* 88 There are .. some remains of the former convict establishments. **1873** A. TROLLOPE *Aust. & N.Z.* II. 96 The head convict establishment is at Fremantle. **1829** *Sydney Monitor* 16 Feb. 1500/2 Fulton, a convict servant of our **convict overseer** .. was tied up. **1835** *Cornwall Chron.* (Launceston) 13 June 1 A convict overseer complained to a Magistrate .. that *the free British Subject!! the British Sailor!!!* was insolent. **1846** L.W. MILLER *Notes of Exile Van Dieman's Land* 300 The superintendent, convict overseer and clerk now combined to render my life as wretched as possible. **1856** J. BONWICK *Bushrangers* 21 The brutality and injustice of convict overseers were the chief cause of such inflictions. **1865** J.F. MORTLOCK *Experiences of Convict* 68 Driven in gangs to heavy field work .. and mercilessly flogged at the caprice of convict overseers, selected for superior brutal energy. **1838** *Rep. Select Committee Transportation* 26 Mar. 127 'There are a great many convicts employed as Constables?'—'Yes, a .. great many... ' 'How do you find the **convict police**

behave?'—'Very well, I do not think free men would have done the duty that they did.' **1849** T. ROGERS *Corresp. relating to Dismissal* 63 Acts of brutal violence could be practised by the convict police on the men in gangs. **1888** R. CROOKE *Convict* (1958) 115 The Comptroller General . . assembled a posse of convict police. **1790** R. CLARK Jrnl. 15 Feb. 133 My other **convict servants.** **1796** D. COLLINS *Acct. Eng. Colony N.S.W.* (1798) I. 486 John Smith, a seaman belonging to the Indispensable, was shot . . by a convict-servant of his. **1802** *Gen. Orders issued by Governor King* 6 Feb. 80 A convict servant belonging to an officer is this day ordered to receive 100 lashes and remain in the Gaol gang 1 year, for gross abuse to his master (an officer), and refusing to sleep on his Farm. **1808** *Sydney Gaz.* 18 Sept., The following Convict Servants have absconded from the employ of their respective masters. **1821** S. MACARTHUR ONSLOW *Some Early Rec. Macarthurs* (1914) 369 Compelled to dwell in a bark hut, with convict servants, and surrounded by gumtrees, the Emu, and Kangaroo of the Forest. **1825** B. FIELD *Geogr. Mem. N.S.W.* 445 The settlers' convict-servants (stockmen and sheep watchmen) do little but drone about their filthy turf-huts, and have as much milk, fish, mutton and flour, as they can eat and drink. **1836** 'W. R--s' *Fell Tyrant* 46 On your arrival at Port Jackson you are advertised in the papers when those who want convict servants apply for you. **1843** *Sydney Morning Herald* 10 May 2/8 Having caused a convict servant to be tied up all night under the dripping of a cask of brine. **1849** *Bell's Life in Sydney* 29 Sept. 3/5 Immediately upon his landing, his better half was ready with a petition to the governor to have him assigned to her as a convict servant, and, as she had qualified as a householder, the assignment was made to her as a matter of course. **1854** J. MITCHEL *Jail Jrnl.* 222 Enter convict-servant with a mockery of dinner. **1873** J. BONWICK *M. Howe* 127 The men of the woods relied not a little upon the sympathy of convict servants, who, while not approving of the robbery of their masters, had no wish to assist Jack Ketch, as they said. **1890** 'R. BOLDREWOOD' *Squatter's Dream* 21 Old Morgan had taken it up with five hundred head of cattle and two or three convict servants. **1831** J.G. POWELL *Narr. Voyage Swan River* p. x, The trade and number of emigrants to the **Convict Settlements** will be reduced. **1836** J.F. O'CONNELL *Residence Eleven Yrs. New Holland* 87 The connection of adult blacks with the convict settlements imparts to them all the vices of the convicts. **1851** *Empire* (Sydney) 2 Dec. 423/3 The first convict settlement in this locality was situated at a place called Red Bank. **1872** 'RESIDENT' *Glimpses Life Vic.* 14 Men . . had served their time in the convict settlements. **1882** W. COOTE *Hist. Colony Qld.* 2 Fifty-four years after that, the first convict settlement was planted at Brisbane. **1792** P.G. KING Jrnl. Norfolk Island Oct. 50 The **Convict Settlers** are all doing very Well, and are at present the most industrious description of Settlers. **1816** *HRA* (1917) 1st Ser. IX. 237 It will be unnecessary even to Victual Emancipated Convict-Settlers for any Length of time. **1826** *Ibid.* (1919) 1st Ser. XII. 379 Granted to Individuals 177,500 Acres of Land, principally to Convict Settlers. **1835** G. ARTHUR *Defence of Transportation* 107 The market upon which the convict settlers had originally depended for the purchase of their farm produce, was the Commissariat. **1812** E.H. BARKER *Geogr., Comm., & Pol. Essays* 193 The appearance and regulations of a **convict ship** are as singular as the novel punishment of transportation. **1815** H.C. ANTILL in G. Mackaness *Fourteen Journeys Blue Mountains* 25 Apr. (1950) iii. 84 An Orderly Dragoon arrived with despatches from England brought by the *Indefatigable*, convict ship. **1822** T. REID *Two Voyages N.S.W. & Van Diemen's Land* 87, I think the allowance of spirits to the soldiers composing the guard in a convict-ship is too much by half. **1834** J.D. LANG *Hist. & Statistical Acct. N.S.W.* II. 10 When a convict-ship arrives in Sydney harbour, it is the practice of Government to reserve as many of the convicts . . as are required for the public service. **1842** H. PARKES *Stolen Moments* 82 The breeze springs up, the white sails dip Into the shadowy night; And gallant rides the convict-ship. **1858** J.B. MARSDEN *Mem. S. Marsden* 29 The convict-ship, which has now become a reformatory school, was rivalled in its horrors only by the slave ship. **1869** F. ALGAR *Hand-Bk. Qld.* 3 The last convict-ship has been despatched, and in a few years the whole convict element will become totally absorbed. **1829** D. BURN *Bushrangers* (1971) 23 Kindness! I was your husband's **convict slave**—true, an unruly one. **1838** *Rep. Select Committee Transportation* p. xx, Transportation, though chiefly dreaded as exile, undoubtedly is much more than exile; it is slavery as well; and the condition of the convict slave is frequently a very miserable one. **1840** *S. Austral. Rec.* (London) 8 Aug. 86 The laws of New South Wales . . being expressly adapted to a community of convict slaves, are wholly unfit for the new society of Englishmen, who regard free institutions as their birthright. **1841** *Geelong Advertiser* 23 Jan. 2/2 Sir George Gipps may favor a few friends or sycophants, by giving them convict slaves, to enable them to reap a fortune by the mere saving of wages. **1834** *Perth Gaz.* 8 Nov. 387 The propriety of petitioning the Home Government that this [*sc.* Albany] should be made a **Convict Station.** **1854** H.B. STONEY *Yr. in Tas.* 4 The double or most severe convict station. **1857** J. ASKEW *Voyage Aust. & N.Z.* 228 Goat Island was once famous as a convict station or prison. **1898** G.J. DE WINTON *Soldiering Fifty Yrs. Ago* 73 Like all the early settlements in New South Wales, Port Macquarie had been a convict station. **1909** F. COOMBE *School Days Norfolk Island* 14 They are ugly and forbidding indeed, for these are the remains of the convict station that was established here more than a hundred years ago. **1834** *New Brit. Province S.A.* 134 The great natural advantages of Australia had been counteracted by the moral evils of the **convict system.** **1844** *Duncan's Weekly Register* (Sydney) 5 Oct. 173/3 The Colonial Secretary said he had no intention of becoming the apologist of the convict system. **1847** *Port Phillip Herald* 2 Mar. 2/4 The moral and social influences of the convict system and the contamination and vice which are inseparable from it, are evils for which no mere pecuniary benefits would serve as a compromise. **1856** W.H.G. KINGSTON *Emigrant's Home* 5 The crimes of Australia have been the result less of the convict system than of the neglect of religious and moral duties by free settlers. **1869** F. ALGAR *Hand-Bk. Qld.* 2 There is no reason whatever why Western Australia, at last free from the evils of the convict system, instead of being a byeword and a reproach in the history of Australian colonization, should not take a prosperous and honourable rank amongst the Australian communities.

convictism. *Hist.*

1. *Convict system*, see CONVICT *n.* 3; the use of an Australian Colony as a place of penal servitude.

1834 *Colonist* (Hobart) 18 Mar. 2/2 It did not take away, if he might be allowed to use such an expression, 'convictism'. **1838** T.H. JAMES *Six Months S.A.* 39 There is nothing which so strongly recommends the new Colony of South Australia, as its entire freedom from convicts and *convictism*. **1843** *Sydney Morning Herald* 4 Nov. 2/1 It will be many years before the spirit of convictism will have evaporated. **1851** *Irish Exile* (Hobart) 8 Feb. 3/1 Convictism has been the incubus which has restrained the energies of the people. **1852** J.D. LANG *Austral. Emigrant's Man.* p. xii, 'We will have independence of England, rather than convictism',—this is in every mouth not sold to sycophancy. **1875** J. FORREST *Explorations in Aust.* 304 West Australia . . had at last freed herself from the shackles of that curse of convictism. **1889** J.H.L. ZILLMANN *Past & Present Austral. Life* 61 A person . . whose life had been completely spoilt by the degrading associations of 'convictism'. **1897** J.J. KNIGHT *Brisbane* 10 Convictism hung like a pall over Moreton Bay (or Brisbane) from 1824 to 1839, roughly speaking. **1905** *Truth* (Sydney) 7 May 1/4 'Colonel' Davis, from Vandemonia . . has more intimate and precise notions about convictism than he has about Federalism. **1945** J.A. ALLAN *Men & Manners in Aust.* 19 Convictism was neither a shameful 'birthstain'—as Lord Beauchamp called it—nor a sentimental romance. **1965** G. MCINNES *Road to Gundagai* 116 Though convictism had been finally abolished in 1852, the Emigrant Ship still meant Transportation for Life.

2. The convict population (of an Australian Colony).

1847 *Port Phillip Herald* 7 Jan. (Suppl.), A very considerable immigration of exclusively male convictism, undiluted by any admixture of free and untainted persons, has been going on from Van Diemen's Land and from England. **1850** *Illustr. Austral. Mag.* (Melbourne) Sept. 171 It is argued that Van Diemen's Land takes every opportunity, covert, or open, of shifting her convictism, by means of tickets of leave, to the great Australian continent. **1859** F. SINNETT *Acct. 'Rush' Port Curtis* 44 Respectable Sydney men . . regard the influx of Victorians here as a safeguard against the sum of scoundrelism which comes to the surface . . when the New South Welch hive swarms . . and which tells how much our sister colony is still affected by the virus of convictism. **1862** A.J. ALEXANDER *Alexander's Colonial Guide* 6 In New South Wales, also, the old leaven of convictism cannot be said to have yet died out. **1865** 'SPECIAL CORRESPONDENT' *Transportation* 62 Tasmania more nearly resembles the case of Western Australia, for she was but the conduit-pipe through which the stream of convictism was diffused. **1870** *Austral. Jrnl.* (Melbourne) May 499/1 Convictism had established a tacit right to converse in whispers.

convincing ground. *Obs.* A place at which prize or grudge fights are held.

1830 *Sydney Monitor* 14 Aug. 2/2 The place of punishment '*the convincing ground*'. **1848** *S. Austral. Register* (Adelaide) 25 Nov. 3/5 A meeting took place at an early hour on the 'convincing ground' near Kooringa between Jemmy Dunn the Burra miner and John Jones the Sydney native. **1867** *Sydney Punch* 26 Oct. 181/2 A mill took place on Monday last, at the convincing ground, Pitt street between two well known parties, the Barham Pet and Tom G—better known as the Sporting Chairman. **1941** S.J. BAKER *Pop. Dict. Austral. Slang* 19 *Convincing Ground*, the site for a grudge fight. **1951** I.L. IDRIESS *Across Nullarbor* 19 For this was the Convincing Ground. Those were the bare-knuckle days, 'kinged' over by the grim 'grass fighters'.

cooba /'kubə/. Also **couba, cuba.** [Prob. f. a N.S.W. Aboriginal language.] Any of several plants of the genus *Acacia* (fam. Mimosaceae), esp. *A. salicina* of drier mainland Aust.; WIRRA *n.*[2] See also *native willow* NATIVE *a.* 6 a., *willow wattle* WILLOW 2.

1878 'R. BOLDREWOOD' *Ups & Downs* 46 A deep reach of the river, shaded by couba trees. **1889** J.H. MAIDEN *Useful Native Plants Aust.* 115 *Acacia salicina* . . called 'Cooba' or 'Koobah' by the aboriginals of Western New South Wales. . . This is another tree which is rapidly becoming scarce, owing to the partiality of stock to it. **1901** *Proc. Linnean Soc. N.S.W.* XXVI. 209 *Acacia salicina*. . . Cooba appears to be the aboriginal name for this tree, but there is a growing tendency in the west to pronounce the name Cuba. **1913** W.K. HARRIS *Outback in Aust.* 149 Open plains timbered with box, boree, and cuba . . are met with. **1947** W.A.W. DE BEUZEVILLE *Austral. Trees for Austral. Planting* 125 Native Willow or Cooba . . a very beautiful and useful tree for shade, shelter and soil binding. **1965** *Austral. Encycl.* III. 38 Cooba, the aboriginal name and still the vernacular for the pendulous and mainly riparian inland tree *Acacia salicina*. **1981** G.M. CUNNINGHAM et al. *Plants Western N.S.W.* 371 Cooba. . . Shrub, or more commonly a small or large tree, to 20 m. high, with willow-like drooping branches and deep-green foliage.

cooboo /'kubu/. *W.A.* [Poss. a. Yinjibarndi *kubu* small.] An (Aboriginal) baby.

1929 K.S. PRICHARD *Coonardoo* (1961) 10 Their skins darken with exposure to the air and sunshine, so that by the time they are toddling, the cooboos are as bronzed and gleaming as pebbles lying on the red earth. **1931** D.B. O'CONNOR *Black Velvet* 12 In the heat of the sun she exposed her cooboo. **1932** K.S. PRICHARD *Kiss on Lips* 101 All day her baby's crying had irritated Rose. The cooboo had wailed and wailed as she rode with him tied to her body. **1958** *Overland* xii. 8 The cooboo first saw the light of day under a tree.

cooee /'kui, ku'i/, *n.* and *int.* [a. Dharuk *guwi*.]

1. Orig. a call used by an Aboriginal to communicate (with someone) at a distance; later adopted by settlers and now widely used as a signal, esp. in the bush (see quots. 1827 and 1845); a name given to the call.

1790 D. SOUTHWELL Corresp. & Papers, *Coo-ee, cō-ee, cō-eé, cō-é*, to come. **1793** J. HUNTER *Hist. Jrnl. Trans. Port Jackson* 149 We called to them in their own manner, by frequently repeating the word *Co-wee*, which signifies, come here. **1827** P. CUNNINGHAM *Two Yrs. in N.S.W.* (rev. ed.) II. 23 In calling to each other at a distance, the natives make use of the word *Coo-ee*, as we do the word *Hollo*, prolonging the sound of the *coo*, and closing that of the *ee* with a shrill jerk. **1831** *Independent* (Launceston) 24 Dec. 3/1 'The soft cooey' (just such an one as a gentleman might give). **1832** J. BACKHOUSE *Narr. Visit Austral. Colonies* (1843) 41, I . . heard the V.D. Land cry of Cooey, borrowed from the Aborigines. **1833** *N.S.W. Mag.* (Sydney) I. 12 Vane heard a distant 'cooi' or 'comba' (call), which his practised ear at once recognised as proceeding from a native. **1834** *Perth Gaz.* 7 June 298 Soon afterwards a native coo-ee (call) was heard. **1841** G. ARDEN *Recent Information Port Phillip* 98 The natives of every part of the country use the word 'cooee' in calling to one another. **1844** *Duncan's Weekly Register* (Sydney) 20 July 44/3 A white man's .. 'cooey' attracted their attention. **1845** C. GRIFFITH *Present State & Prospects Port Phillip* 65 The cooey is a call in universal use amongst the settlers and has been borrowed from the natives. The performer dwells for about half a minute upon one note, and then raises his voice to the octave. It can be heard at a great distance. **1866** *Austral. Monthly Mag.* (Melbourne) II. 93 'Coo'ey, coo'ey, coo'ey!' As that sound, so familiar all over the Australian bush, met his ear, Chick looked round him. **1872** MRS E. MILLETT *Austral. Parsonage* 85, I have been even told of a man having brought home to London a colonial wife who, alarmed at being separated from her husband by a crowd in Fleet Street, successfully hazarded a *coo-ee* to let him know in what part of that thoroughfare she was bewildered. **1878** R.B. SMYTH *Aborigines of Vic.* II. 20 The well-known call *Coo-ee*, used when the natives hail each other in the bush, is universally adopted in the bush, and this speaks strongly in its favour. **1887** A. MACKAY *Stirrup Jingles* 22 Merciful God! Have pity on me! Cooee! Cooee! Cooee-ee-ee! **1901** H.A. STUART *Bards of Burwood* 1 And the slopes of Gundalooey, echo back the bushman's coo-ee, That will tell Britannia's foemen that we come. **1915** *Truth* (Sydney) 17 Oct. 7/8 Cooees are used almost exclusively by Anglo-Australian spectators at test matches in England; and nowhere else in earnest; least of all in Australia. **1917** M.W. JAMES *'Coo-ee' Call* 1 And here's to the Sound—how we love it—Australia's National Call. 'Coo-ee!' 'Coo-ee!' Australia's National Call. **1924** *Sydney Morning Herald* 21 July 9/1 Australians, who had bought up every available Australian flag, shrieked 'coo-ees' above the din. **1934** WARBURTON & ROBERTSON *Buffaloes* 76 She gave a long, low cooee, which only the Australian aboriginal can give effectively, and in a few moments there was a faint answer. **1944** *Bulletin* (Sydney) 17 May 12/3 I've been bushed myself and also in searches for bushed mates, and I'm blowed if I ever heard the bush 'ring with cooees'. **1951** D. CUSACK *Say no to Death* (1959) 10 'Coo-ees', 'Whackos' and wolf calls burst out in a sustained chorus of recognition and welcome. **1965** G. MCINNES *Road to Gundagai* 183 I'll hump my bluey and I'll shout a 'Coo-ee'. **1980** T.A. ROY *Vengeance of Dolphin* 74, I stood up, cupped my hands to my mouth and gave a 'Coo-ee' to let her know I was on my way. **1982** R. ELLIS *Bush Safari* 187 We gave a loud 'Coo-ee', but no one appeared, although there were several four-wheel drive vehicles outside.

2. *fig.*

1894 W. CROMPTON *Convict Jim* 28 An' the river is a banker, an' its current's running strong, An' I don't think I'll be waiting for Death's cooee very long. **1897** *Bulletin* (Sydney) 26 June 13/1 At last week's Parliamentary cooey in Brisbane (Q.), Ex. Lamington extended his royal hand to Bully Palmer but Bully 'wasn't looking'. **1917** M.W. JAMES *'Coo-ee' Call* 9 They bless the day when first he heard His little Wife's 'Coo-ee'.

3. In the phr. **within cooee,** within earshot; within reach, near.

1836 R. PORTER *Hist. Story* 12 He lay there some time, unable to rise, but had eventually managed to crawl within coo-ee of the camp. **1869** *Bushmen, Publicans, & Politics* 4 Others may finish their last day's march within 'cooey' of assistance from some station or chance traveller. **1871** *Austral. Town & Country Jrnl.* (Sydney) 11 Feb. 184/3 Our party spreading within cooey of each other. **1887** *Boomerang* (Brisbane) 24 Dec. 16/2, I could not detect an inch of sound unoccupied ground within cooeè of the gold. **1890** *Quiz* (Adelaide) 4 Apr. 3/1 An old fellow .. prided himself on being a dead shot... The egotistical old rascal thought no one else could come within coo-ee of him. **1908** 'P. WARREGO' *Diary New Chum* 49 He has become a woman hater, never goes within coo-ee of a female if he can help it. **1918** R.H. KNYVETT *Over there with Australs.* 125 Remember, too, that the Turks were always better equipped and supplied—it was so easy with their chief city of Constantinople just within 'coo-ee'. **1928** A. WRIGHT *Good Recovery* 63 Within cooee of the house .. stood the shearing-shed. **1948** H.W. CRITTENDEN *Rogues' Paradise* 208 No heretic gets within 'coo-ee' of the guild meetings. **1956** E. LAMBERT *Watermen* 144 If I ever see you within coo-ee of my boat again, I'll drown you. **1963** A.E. FARRELL *Vengeance* 188 There are some white men who come into contact with the native that should never come within coo-ee of them. **1979** C. KLEIN *Women of Certain Age* 60 However, there is a certain satisfaction to be got from standing knee-deep in wildflowers on your own land, no other dwelling within cooee. **1984** *Nat. Times* (Sydney) 6 July 50/2 Holland was our only hope within cooee of winning an Olympic gold medal at Montreal.

4. Special Comb. **cooee bird,** the large cuckoo *Eudynamys orientalis*, the Indian koel, a summer visitor from s.e. Asia to n. and e. Aust.

1912 *Bulletin* (Sydney) 22 Feb. 14/1 The coo-ee bird, a fruit-eating nuisance in Queensland... Even those familiar with this bird will fail to distinguish its call, at a distance, from the human coo-ee. **1946** *Ibid.* 13 Nov. 28/3 In this particular part of coastal S.Q. .. are Koels, Cooee-birds in local parlance. **1954** C. BARRETT *Wild Life Aust. & New Guinea* 127 The 'coo-ee bird'—a popular name for this cuckoo.

cooee /'kui/, *v.* [f. prec.] *intr.* To utter a 'cooee'. Also *trans.*

1824 *Austral.* (Sydney) 18 Nov. 3 The little girl told them .. that he intended some mischief, and that he was coo-ing for some of his tribe. **1827** W.J. DUMARESQ in G. Mackaness *Fourteen Journeys Blue Mountains* (1950) 83, I was obliged to exert my lungs and cooey out for my companion, who *cooeyed* in return, and by the sound of his voice I was enabled to find my way back to the road. **1833** *Colonist* (Hobart) 25 Jan. 3/2 A fourth was taken at daybreak next morning, *'cooe'*-ing for his companions. **1838** *Hobart Town Almanack* 93 About half-an-hour after we *cooeed*, and were speedily answered by the men. **1842** *Colonial Observer* (Sydney) 27 Aug. 426/1 Whenever they approached each other's waterholes, they always cooeyed to give notice of their approach. **1847** *Moreton Bay Courier* 17 July 4/1 When a person cooies .. he should stoop low and cooie along the ground. **1869** E.C. BOOTH *Another England* 66 Come along into dinner, for I hear the mistress cooeeing me. **1875** J. FORREST *Explorations in Aust.* 188 Got my gun and coo-eyed to Pierre. **1890** *Truth* (Sydney) 3 Aug. 7/3 She went to the door, and cooeyed, but the mountain only echoed back her cry. **1909** J.C.L. FITZPATRICK *When we were Boys Together* 25 Standing upon London Bridge he 'cooeyed' lustily enough to wake the dead. **1917** M.W. JAMES *'Coo-ee' Call* 14 A Clock from which issues a Blackfellow with a Boomerang in his hand to 'Coo-ee' the hours and half-hours and so announce the time. **1923** J. MOSES *Beyond City Gates* 109 The crowd cheered, hoorayed, and coo-eed as the Governor handed the medal to the horseman. **1930** J.S. LITCHFIELD *Far-North Memories* 53 It was always advisable to cooee loudly when nearing any habitation. **1948** I.L. IDRIESS *Opium Smugglers* 186 When it grew late I looked for him, then cooeed. **1972** M. GILBERT *Personalities & Stories Early Orbost* 36 Just when she had given him up for drowned, Dad coo-eed to her from downstream. **1979** R. MACKLIN *Journalist* 33 At first he had not seen her. Liz had thought to coo-ee as he seemed in danger of blundering into other tables.

Hence **cooeeing** *vbl. n.* and *ppl. a.*

1845 J.O. BALFOUR *Sketch of N.S.W.* 17, I shall never forget the cooing, shouting, roaring, cracking of nulla-nullas. **1849** F.R. GODFREY *Extracts Old Jrnls.* 16 Sept. (1926) 24 After half an hour spent in coo-ee-ing, Cooke and I tossed up, and he had to swim across and get the canoe. **1881** *Adventures of Strollers Otway Ranges* 8 So one is told off to do the cooee-ing for the lost children. **1885** G. DARRELL *Sunny South* 38 There's no one else within cooeeing distance. **1912** J. BOWES *Comrades* 195 Let's keep up the cooeeing. **1955** STEWART & KEESING *Austral. Bush Ballads* 119 He heard the long-drawn cooeeing shout of Trooper Gilbert's men. He cooeed back with feeble force, and soon they gathered round.

coohoy nut /'kuhɔɪ nʌt/. *Hist.* [f. *coohoy* (prob. f. a Qld. Aboriginal language) + *nut.*] The nut of the rainforest tree *Floydia praealta* (fam. Proteaceae) of s.e. Qld. and n.e. N.S.W.; the tree itself.

1886 *Trans. & Proc. R. Geogr. Soc. Australasia N.S.W.* (1888) 242 Our dinner consisted of a few coohoy nuts, so named by the aborigines. The nut is perfectly round, and about 6 inches, in circumference, with a thin shell. .. The nut needs no preparation, only roasting till nicely browned. If eaten raw it resembles the uncooked English potato. **1890** A.J. VOGAN *Black Police* 198 Some *coohoy* nuts give promise of a good 'square meal', at last. **c 1910** W.R. GUILFOYLE *Austral. Plants* 210 *Helicia praealta* .. 'Tall Queensland Nut Tree' .. or 'Coohoy' .. N.S.W. and Q'land. **1924** *Bulletin* (Sydney) 6 Nov. 24/3 The Coo-hoy nut is also good eating, and it merely wants a brown roasting to be fit for a hungry man's meal.

Cook. *Obs.* Shortened form of CAPTAIN COOK *n.*

1899 *Truth* (Sydney) 14 May 3/1 The Cap'en, he merely squinted around, cursory-like, and I'm hanged if his name don't stick to that job, too. How do I mean? Why, if a chap just glances at a thing don't we still say he has 'a Cook' at it? **1910** L. ESSON *Woman Tamer* (1976) 70 Soon's we had a cook at the engines, gorblime, we were pinched, five of us.

Cooktown orchid. [f. the name of a coastal town in n. Qld.] The epiphytic orchid *Dendrobium bigibbum* (fam. Orchidaceae) of n. Qld. and Torres Strait islands, the floral emblem of Queensland, having showy, usu. lilac flowers.

1956 A.C.C. LOCK *Tropical Tapestry* 268 One of the most common species, *Dendrobium phalaenopsis*, is so named on account of the resemblance of its flowers to moths. Because they are plentiful in the country west of Cooktown, they have earned the name of Cooktown orchids. **1972** DOUGLAS & OLDMEADOW *Across Top* 183 High above us clusters of the famous Cooktown orchids were clinging to the bark of paper-bark trees. **1973** H. HOLTHOUSE *S'pose I Die* 82 It was in this limestone country that the Cooktown orchids grew at their best, and before long my fernery was a mass of their mauve blooms. **1984** K.A.W. WILLIAMS *Native Plants Qld.* II. 2 The Cooktown Orchid was declared the Floral Emblem of Queensland in November 1959... This beautiful species is rapidly becoming endangered in the natural habitat as poachers continue to gather large numbers of plants for illegal sale.

coola, var. COOLER, KOALA 1.

coolabah, var. COOLIBAH.

coolah grass /'kulə gras/. [f. Punthamara *gulaa* + (Eng.) *grass.*] Any of several grasses (fam. Poaceae), esp. the introduced *Panicum coloratum*, a summer-growing tufted perennial of N.S.W., Vic., and Qld., and the widespread native *P. prolutum*. See also COOLY.

1847 D. BUNCE *Australasiatic Reminisc.* 20 Apr. (1857) 168 The *Panicum Leavinode* [*sic*] is the plant from which the natives make their bread, and is called by the blacks of Liverpool Plains, *coola grass*. **1938** C.T. WHITE *Princ. Bot. Qld. Farmers* 202 Grasses with wide-spreading, much-branched seed-heads, such as .. *Panicum prolutum*, Coolah Grass. **1981** G.M. CUNNINGHAM et al. *Plants Western N.S.W.* 118 Many forms of coolah grass exist and these differ in habit, size, hairiness and colour.

coolamon /'kuləmən/. Also **coolimon, coolaman, kooliman.** [a. Kamilaroi *gulaman.*]

1. A vessel of wood or bark (but see quot. 1857) used by Aborigines to hold water and other liquids, but also for a variety of other purposes (see quots. 1926 and 1943); PITCHI. See also YANDY *n.*

1845 L. LEICHHARDT *Jrnl. Overland Exped. Aust.* 27 May (1847) 269 Three koolimans (vessels of stringy bark) were full of honey water, from one of which I took a hearty draught, and left a brass button for payment. **1846** *Sydney Morning Herald* 4 Feb. 2/7 When a party dies a stage is immediately erected... The body is placed upon this, and .. small fires are kept burning at the two ends of the stage, and one underneath it. A large 'coulamon' receives the matter thus extracted by the heat, and the tribe close round and greedily consume, and rub their persons with this horrible extract. **1846** C.P. HODGSON *Reminisc. Aust.* 227 Water in wooden 'coolamen', (or hollow excressences [*sic*] lopped off the sides of trees). **1851** J. HENDERSON *Excursions & Adventures N.S.W.* II. 151 The *coolaman* is their jug, or jar, for carrying water. It is a large knot of a tree cut off from it, and hollowed out, a handle of cord being fastened across it. **1857** F. DE B. COOPER *Wild Adventures* 40 Cooliemans (Cameleroi dialect)—vessels for holding water, frequently gourds. **1862** W. LANDSBOROUGH *Jrnl. Exped. from Carpentaria* 83 The gins .. had their coolamans filled with rats. **1875** CAMPBELL & WILKS *Early Settlement Qld.* 45 A coolaman left by some lazy old gin. **1881** A.C. GRANT *Bush-Life Qld.* I. 179 A drink of honey and water was now offered me in a *cooleman*, which I also politely accepted. **1895** G. RANKEN *Windabyne* 260 Toby, getting up the horses one morning, got a glimpse of a little dusky nymph dipping her 'coolamin' in a .. tarn. **1899** J. MATHEW *Eaglehawk & Crow* 88 Water-vessels, such as koolimans (made of a hollow knot of a tree or from the bend of a limb). **1909** F.E. BIRTLES *Lonely Lands* 203 A favourite dish of theirs is a mixture of iguana and leaves, served in 'coolamons' (native dishes). **1920** *Smith's Weekly* (Sydney) 28 Aug. 9/4 The assistant holds the coolamon under a branch while Binghi with his nulla nulla knocks a couple of drops of water into it at a time. **1926** A.A.B. APSLEY *Amateur Settlers* 107 The babies are carried in a rude sort of cradle, called a 'coolimon'. **1930** 'BRENT OF BIN BIN' *Ten Creeks Run* (1952) 267 He always did run to corpulence—a pot on him like a coolamon. **1943** *Bulletin* (Sydney) 11 Aug. 13/3 In the Pilbara district (W.A.) . . abo. gins . . partly fill the coolamons with mullock from the old workings, and by a process known as yandi-ing . . separate from the mullock particles of tin. **1944** M.J. O'REILLY *Bowyangs & Boomerangs* 47 A lubra with a 'Coolamon' could clean more tin by dry process in a day than a white man could do by the same process in a week. **1949** H.E. THONEMANN *Tell White Man* 30 A coolamon is about two feet long and is just a piece of wood with a long hole scooped out of the centre for a piccaninny to lie in. They are used for carrying other things, like cakes and flour. **1959** E. WEBB *Mark of Sun* 59 There was nothing to do but watch the lubras . . squatting in the dirt yandying seeds in their wooden coolamons. **1974** B. ROLAND *No Ordinary Man* 156 The fat contented babies in their coolimons, the wooden cradles slung on the mother's hip. **1980** B. SCOTT *Darkness under Hills* 70 The top of the mountain was shaped like a coolamon.

2. *fig.*

1891 M. ROBERTS *Land-Travel & Sea-Faring* 197 The water-holes, or as they call them in that part of Australia, cooliman holes, gave out.

cooler /'kulə/, *a.* and *n. Austral. pidgin. Obs.* Also **coola, coolie.** [a. Dharuk *gulara.*]

A. *adj.* Angry.

c **1790** W. DAWES Grammatical Forms Lang. N.S.W., *Gūlara*, angry. **1830** R. DAWSON *Present State Aust.* 75, I murry cooler (angry). **1839** T.L. MITCHELL *Three Exped. Eastern Aust.* II. 4 The Myalls were coming up ('murry coola' i.e. *very angry*) to meet us. **1845** J.O. BALFOUR *Sketch of N.S.W.* 18, I . . was told that they did not like my interference, and that they would become 'coolie'; in other words, that there would be enmity between them and me. **1849** A. HARRIS *Emigrant Family* (1967) 253 Baal I coula (angry). **1876** J.A. EDWARDS *Gilbert Gogger* 115 Baail that fellor—something fool; yarraman plenty cooler.

B. *n.* Anger.

1841 *Port Phillip Patriot* 4 Oct. 4/1 They . . then went away, saying, 'we will return in two or three days, when cooler (white man's wrath) is all gone.'

Coolgardie /kul'gadi/. [The name of a gold-mining town in W.A.]

1. a. Used *attrib.* in Special Comb. **Coolgardie safe,** a safe for keeping foodstuffs cool (see quot. 1925); also **Coolgardie foodsafe.**

c **1924** MAW & JORDAN *Hints Pioneering Homemakers* 5 *Coolgardie safes*—All sizes, both straight and sloping sides, galvanised frames, covered with hessian. **1925** *Makeshifts & Other Home-Made Furniture* (New Settlers League Aust.) 40 To make a Coolgardie safe, build a frame from strong packing cases, and put a shelf about 2 ft. from the ground, and another on top 5 ft. from the ground. Cover the frame with hessian, putting a door on one side. On top, place a kerosene tin cut in half lengthwise. Keep this filled with water, and, hanging from it over the sides of the safe, put strips of hessian, towelling or flannel. Make gutters of pieces of tin to go around the bottom of the safe, making them all slope toward one corner. Here let the water drip into a tin underneath. This water may be used again. Keep in a breezy place. **1926** *McEwan's Catal.* 43 Coolgardie Safe, wood, painted white. Trays for water at top and bottom are galvanized iron . . hessian sides, 21s.; white towelling sides, 25s. 6d. each. **1939** M. MORRIS *Dark Tumult* 58 Philip . . was finishing off a Coolgardie safe which he had made out of two large cases and some pieces of sacking. **1945** E. MITCHELL *Speak to Earth* 191 Wet overalls in a warm wind are like a 'Coolgardie safe'. **1953** *Sydney Morning Herald* 15 Aug. 7/2 As its name implies, the Coolgardie safe originated on the Western Australian goldfields. **1956** V. COURTNEY *All I may Tell* 18 Perth of 1911. Refrigeration as we know it was practically unknown. Ice was hard to get and most people went through the summer with a Coolgardie safe and water bag. **1959** *Meanjin* 293 Everything spoke of a man of simple tastes and exacting habits: a single bed made up with military efficiency . . a coolgardie food-safe. **1969** P. ADAM SMITH *Folklore Austral. Railwaymen* 82 When we got to Jessops Wells a fettler came over with a bottle he'd kept cool—well off the boil anyway—in a coolgardie safe. **1977** W.A. WINTER-IRVING *Bush Stories* 97 The ice chest was a lot cooler than the Coolgardie safes we used to keep meat fresh for a day or so, and to provide a change from salt meat. **1978** M. RICHARDSON *Your own Resources* 158 A Coolgardie safe may represent a good short-term alternative, especially for keeping dairy foods. **1982** M. WALKER *Making Do* 61 We had Coolgardie safes. Why they call them that I don't know. They were in use on the Victorian goldfields long before Coolgardie was discovered.

b. In other Special Comb. **Coolgardie cooler,** a refinement of the Coolgardie safe (see quot. 1977); **shampoo,** see quot.; **stretcher** (or **bunk**), a makeshift bed; also **Coolgardie camp stretcher.**

1972 N. KING *Nickel Country* 91 With its tongue flicking in and out, it always headed for the **Coolgardie cooler** where it knew eggs were kept. **1975** R. BEILBY *Brown Land Crying* 203 A Coolgardie cooler had been positioned beside the outer entrance to utilise draughts between window and door. **1977** B. FULLER *Nullarbor Lifelines* 38 Later, the Coolgardie Cooler came into general use. This had double walls of fine-mesh wire netting, usually placed from two to eight centimetres apart. The space between was filled with charcoal kept wet through percolation. **1984** N. HOUGHTON *Beech Forest* 8 Coolgardie coolers were another popular device made by the settlers. **1908** J.A. BARRY *Luck of Native Born* 48 They did as they saw all others around them doing, stripped mother-naked outside their tent, and gave themselves first a scrubbing with Ned's big clothes-brush, then a rub down with a coarse towel—a process locally known as a '**Coolgardie shampoo**'. **1944** M.J. O'REILLY *Bowyangs & Boomerangs* 39 Sitting on **Coolgardie stretchers** were two old miners. **1948** M. UREN *Glint of Gold* 244 He made a raft out of a small tarpaulin wrapped around a Coolgardie stretcher. **1949** I.L. IDRIESS *One Wet Season* 85 Scotty insisted on carrying him into the homestead and making him comfortable on a spare Coolgardie bunk. **1981** M. CRITCH *Our Kind of War* 81 The canvas hold-all contained . . four sheets, towels, pillowslips, a folding Coolgardie camp stretcher, a folding canvas chair.

2. A Coolgardie safe.

1936 M. HERRON *Seed & Stubble* 95 There is a cold fowl and trimmings in the 'Coolgardie'. **1945** E. GEORGE *Two at Daly Waters* 32 To keep food cool we had a home-made Coolgardie—a frame covered with hessian, and with long strips of flannel hanging over the sides and resting in water to syphon and keep the hessian wet and cool. **1955** J. MORRISON *Black Cargo* 204 The ash-dusted stove with kettle and frying-pan standing at one side . . the coolgardie with its moist drapings. **1972** J. HIBBERD *Stretch of Imagination* (1973) 8 Relax, pal, while I repair to the Coolgardie and knock up a snack. **1978** *Bronze Swagman Bk. Bush Verse* 10 Coolgardies swung and spread their hessian-scented breath.

coolibah /'kuləba/. Also **coolabah.** [a. Kamilaroi (and related languages) *gulubaa.*] Any of several myrtaceous trees, esp. the bluish-leaved *Eucalyptus microtheca* of W.A., N.T., Qld., N.S.W., and S.A., a fibrous-barked tree yielding a heavy durable timber and occurring in seasonally inundated areas. See also *flooded box* FLOODED. Also *attrib.*

1883 E. PALMER *Plants N. Qld.* (1884) 14 *E. microtheca* . . The Coolibar or flooded box found on all Gulf waters, often in flooded ground, of a crooked growth, about 30 feet high. **1893** 'TIMES SPECIAL CORRESPONDENT' *Lett. from Qld.* 60 The timber, of course, when seen close at hand is strange. Boree and gidyah, coolibah . . are the unfamiliar names. **1900** *Proc. Linnean Soc. N.S.W.* XXV. 86 It is mostly a crooked tree; and it is from this feature that the aboriginal name 'Coolabah' is derived. **1903** A.B. PATERSON *Waltzing Matilda* (*song*), Once a jolly Swagman camped by a Billabong, Under the shade of a Coolibah tree. **1913** W.H. OGILVIE *Overlander* 67 Are the bullock-teams still bending through the coolibahs to Bourke? **1929** *Bulletin* (Sydney) 2 Jan. 19/4 The dog had planted the mob in the shade of a big coolabah and was giving them a smoke-oh. **1936** A.W. UPFIELD *Wings above Diamantina* 270 The coolibahs—strange, shapeless trees of which not one inch of wood was straight. **1949** H.G. LAMOND *White Ears* 28 The corellas threw snowy mantles of their own white bodies over coolibah-trees. **1951** G. FARWELL *Outside Track* 34 Beneath the weight of the swag his body was bent as an old coolibah. **1956** *Bulletin* (Sydney) 24 Oct. 12/3 The jackeroos were sitting by a coolibah-shaded waterhole, waiting for their quartpots to boil. **1963** X. HERBERT *Larger than Life* 112 Out of the few gnarled coolibahs that fringed the water-hole a flock of galahs flew up. **1973** M. STEEL *Red Rover* 28 Some old coolabahs made a friendly fire.

coolie, var. COOLER.

coolie, /'kuli/, *n.*[1] *Obs.* [a. Wemba *guli* man.] A name given by white Australians to the consort of an Aboriginal woman; also applied, usu. in *pl.*, to Aboriginal men in general.

1842 *Melbourne Times* 3 Dec. 3/1 About ten days since an aboriginal woman died at the station of Mr Allen of the Pyrenees and was laid by her coolie and others of the tribe upon a piece of bark and burned. **1843** *Portland Mercury* 24 May 3/3 About a fortnight since a lubra was killed by her coolie assisted by several others of his tribe at Port Fairy. **1845** *Portland Gaz.* 12 Aug. 3/5 It is said that a white man, whose name has been furnished us, but which we decline publishing, has been cohabiting with a black woman for some time past, but she . . left him to join her Coolie and her tribe. **1847** T. McCOMBIE *Austral. Sketches* 6 He talks of having gone out with his rifle and shot the black coolies by dozens. **1848** *Elector* (Sydney) 27 July 7/2 There are 'gunyas' for coolies, and cannibals wild, Who to tend his vast flocks from their homes were beguil'd. **1850** *Britannia* (Hobart) 12 Sept. 3/4 Although thus stealthily borne away, she was not neglected by the coolies of her tribe, for fourteen black fellows . . were . . in pursuit. **1856** J. BONWICK *W. Buckley* 64 The lubra may now and then get a tap with a waddy for want of assiduity in procuring her coolie a good dinner. **1870** —— *Last Tasmanians* 61 These afterwards told their *Coolies* or husbands. **1886** *Once a Month* (Melbourne) Jan. 21 'Nora,' I said, 'you must be mother now to this little white lubra. You and your coolie,' i.e. husband, 'must come and live at my station.'

coolie /'kuli/, *n.*[2] *Obs.* [Var. of *collie*: see OED 1.] A sheep-dog, a collie. Also **coolie dog.**

1848 H.W. HAYGARTH *Recoll. Bush Life* 44 Here the watchman, after tying up near the folds several of his 'coolie' dogs, who will awaken him on the approach of a 'warragle', or native dog, his only cause of alarm. **1874** C. DE BOOS *Congewoi Correspondence* 128 They was real handsome dogs, more liker coolie than a real downright bush warrigal. **1888** 'R. BOLDREWOOD' *Robbery under Arms* (1937) 473 There was no fear of any other horse overhauling him, any more than a coolie dog or a flying doe kangaroo. **1891** M. ROBERTS *Land-Travel & Sea-Faring* 72 Their dogs are always collies—called by the way in the bush coolies—they come very often from good imported strains.

coolimon, var. COOLAMON.

coolly, var. COOLY.

cool-safe. [Abbrev. of *Coolgardie safe*, with pun on *cool.*] *Coolgardie safe*, see COOLGARDIE 1 a.

1924 *Anthony Hordern Catal.* 421 The 'Cold Cap' Collapsible Cool Safe, made of strong galvanized iron. The perforated zinc sides are covered with White towelling. **1930** K.S. PRICHARD *Haxby's Circus* 144 An old miner knocked up a cool-safe for her. **1941** —— *Moon of Desire* 18 Along the veranda, on which the cool-safe stood, its hessian sides dripping under the flow of water from strips of flannel set in an iron tray above. **1958** P. COWAN *Unploughed Land* 125 He looked with little purpose among the food they had stored in the cupboards and the cool-safe. **1962** E. LANE *Mad as Rabbits* 133 He'd bought himself a buggy-load of harness, and Mother a cool-safe—doors hanging ajar and hessian side-covering missing. **1979** W.K. BECKINGHAM *Red Acres* 24 The 'Coolgardie Safe' or 'Cool' Safe kept food a little longer in the heat in the days before country people had refrigerators, which in our case was until 1949.

cooly /'kuli/. *Obs.* Also **coolly.** [a. Wiradhuri *gooloo.*] The edible seed or seeds of *native millet* (see NATIVE *a.* 6 a.), and prob. also COOLAH GRASS.

1848 T.L. MITCHELL *Jrnl. Exped. Tropical Aust.* 90 The *Panicum laevinode* of Dr Lindley seemed to predominate, a grass whereof the seed ('Cooly') is made by the natives into a kind of paste or bread. Dry heaps of this grass, that had been pulled expressly for the purpose of gathering the seed, lay along our path for many miles. **1888** *Proc. Linnean Soc. N.S.W.* III. 536 'Native Millet'. .. The seed used to be called 'Cooly' by western New South Wales aboriginals.

coon. [Transf. use of *coon* a Black.] An Aboriginal. Freq. as a term of abuse.

1899 *Truth* (Sydney) 9 July 2/2 The mate will never be able to exert his authority over the coon after having been in the same chain-gang with him. **1905** *Ibid.* 24 Dec. 1/7 Australia is a elova fine place for coons, and the blacker and uglier they are the better they seem to be treated. **1924** *Bulletin* (Sydney) 28 Aug. 22/4 At Brewarrina I have seen upwards of 50 coons in the water at the one time, gins and piccaninnies included. **1935** H.H. PARRY *Girl of West* 49 It was like a tribal war; the coons were lying thick upon the field. **1941** *Bulletin* (Sydney) 23 Apr. 16/2 Some passing nigs had arrived at his camp with a sick camel. When it petered out the coons vanished on walkabout. **1958** O. RUHEN *Naked under Capricorn* 94 You've got this tribe of coons in your hand—it wouldn't pay a man to push you out. **1976** C.D. MILLS *Hobble Chains & Greenhide* 97 Don't trust a coon that holds the butt-end of his spear towards you. **1980** R. DAVIDSON *Tracks* 34 A mate includes anyone who is not a .. coon, boong, nigger. **1984** P. READ *Down there with me on Cowra Mission* 22 But they couldn't see that they were hurting me by just using .. 'coon'.

coongaberry, var. CONKERBERRY.

coonie /'kuni/. Also **connie, coondie, cundy.** [Prob. f. a N.S.W. Aboriginal language.] A stone suitable for use as a missile.

1941 S.J. BAKER *Pop. Dict. Austral. Slang* 21 *Cundy*, a small stone. **1968** S. GORE *Holy Smoke* 13 All I needeth is me shanghai here, and a few of these big coonies that's layin' around, and I'll get stuck into it. **1978** W. LOWENSTEIN *Weevils in Flour* 378 One of our blokes threw a great big connie at a policeman who stuck his head out. **1981** D. STUART *I think I'll Live* 316 He hoys me with his right hand, then he heaves this coondie over the fence. .. I went inside and takes the paper off this rock.

coorie, var. KOORI.

coota. Also **couta.** Shortened form of BARRACOUTA.

[N.Z. **1911** *N.Z. Truth* (Wellington) 1 Apr. 6 Hampton said that the 'couta were rotten and stinking.] **1933** D. MACDONALD *Brooks of Morning* 65 Scattered shoals leaped in terror out of the sea with the 'coota through and after them. **1947** MRS A.H. GARNSEY *Romance Huon River* 169, I have seen men standing on the end of a jetty when a shoal of these fish was about, swishing their sticks backwards or forwards in the water and throwing the 'coota' up onto the jetty. **1951** D. COLLINS *Vic.'s my Home Ground* 7 This peculiarly clad but adventurous character was Fisherman Collins, outward bound after the 'coota and crays.

Cootamundra wattle /kutəmʌndrə 'wɒtl/. [f. the name of a town in central N.S.W., referring to the area of the plant's natural occurrence + WATTLE 1.] The N.S.W. shrub or small tree *Acacia baileyana* (fam. Mimosaceae), having pale bluish-grey foliage, now widely planted and naturalized elsewhere (see quot. 1959). Also *ellipt.* as **Cootamundra.**

[**1887** *Trans. & Proc. R. Soc. Vic.* (1888) 170 *Acacia baileyana* .. he found this rare species only near Cootamundra.] **1902** *Proc. Linnean Soc. N.S.W.* XXVII. 198 *Acacia Baileyana* .. (Cootamundra Wattle) is fairly plentiful. **1915** *Bulletin* (Sydney) 2 Sept. 26/2 The silver wattle (Cootamundra or baileyana) .. is beautiful when the greenish-blue tops are sprouting. **1934** J.W. AUDAS *Native Trees Aust.* 92 The widely-known Cootamundra Wattle, a native of New South Wales, is probably the most popular of all the wattles. **1942** C. BARRETT *From Bush Hut* 108 It is mid-July, and the cootamundras are turning from silver-green to gold. **1959** A.E. BROOKS *Austral. Native Plants* 2 *Cootamundra Wattle*, .. found naturally in only a restricted area near Temora and Cootamundra .. is spreading into the bushland in some areas from garden specimens. **1965** G. MCINNES *Road to Gundagai* 84 The .. flower bed between the cootamundra and the peach tree. **1974** *Southerly* i. 50 The bush wattle grew abundantly out there, and flowered earlier than the Cootamundra trees found in the town. **1979** C. KLEIN *Women of Certain Age* 36 She saw sarsaparilla scrambling over stumps, and everywhere the fluffy yellow of Cootamundra wattle.

cop. Used *attrib.* in Special Comb. **copman, copperman** (both *obs.*), a policeman; **shop** [used elsewhere but recorded earliest in Aust.], a police station.

1898 *Bulletin* (Sydney) 4 June (Red Page), A policeman is a 'johnny' or a '**copman**' or a 'trap'. ***c* 1907** C.W. CHANDLER *Darkest Adelaide* 16 Right here Sergeant Radford and a copman appeared on the scene. .. The copmen had come on the scene in the nick of time to save the little fellow being strangled. **1914** E. DYSON *Spats' Fact'ry* 109 There was a John in the nex' room, a copman. **1916** *Truth* (Sydney) 5 Nov. 12/3 Yet he for the copperman (Flannagan) sent. **1941** S.J. BAKER *Pop. Dict. Austral. Slang* 20 *Copman*, a policeman. *Copperman*, a policeman. **1966**—*Austral. Lang.* (ed. 2) 142 The now-obsolete *copman* and *copperman*. **1941**—*Pop. Dict. Austral. Slang* 20 **Copshop**, a police station. **1968** K. DENTON *Walk around my Cluttered Mind* 106 The collapsed pile of the old cop-shop *was* Turkey Creek. **1969** W. MOXHAM *Apprentice* 7 He hadn't worn it to the cop shop. **1970** B. OAKLEY *Salute Great McCarthy* 30 MacGuiness is at the copshop, a charge has been laid.

cop it sweet, to: see SWEET *a.*[2] 2 b.

copper-burr. Any of several spiny-fruited plants, esp. small shrubs of the genus *Sclerolaena*, formerly *Bassia*, (fam. Chenopodiaceae) of all mainland States.

1932 M.R. WHITE *No Roads go By* 45 The flats were sprinkled with .. copper-burr. **1966** A. MORRIS *Plant-life W. Darling* 60 Station people call all Bassias 'Copperburrs'. **1972** V. SERVENTY *Singing Land* 80 Some of the sands have a lime content .. and here the copperburr or bassia may grow. **1982** G.B. EGGLETON *Last of Lantern Swingers* 46 The copper-burr has vicious little needle-like brown spikes about half-an-inch in length, and sheep dogs need to be fitted with leather footguards before they can be worked in this country.

copper-head. [Transf. use of *copperhead* a North American snake.] The venomous snake *Austrelaps superbus* of s.e. Aust. Also **copper-head(ed) snake.**

1878 F. MCCOY *Prodromus of Zool. Vic.* (1885) I. i. Pl. 2, The Copper-head Snake. .. I have adopted the popular name 'copper-head' for this snake from a well-known vendor of a supposed antidote for snake-bites. **1888** *Centennial Mag.* (Sydney) 14 The hill crow-shrike is plentiful; so is the copper-headed snake. **1906** *Bulletin* (Sydney) 12 July 16/1 The diamond snake, which gave Paul's Tasmanian friend such a close call, is known as the copper-headed snake in Victoria, and is called the superb snake in N.S.W. **1976** E. WORRELL *Things that Sting* 14 The Copperhead has a thickset body and usually has the scales around its lips edged with cream. **1983** *Canberra Chron.* 16 Mar. 18/1 At the moment the peak feeding time for trout seems to coincide with that of the tiger snakes and copperheads.

coppertail. *Obs.* [Fig. use of *copper* as contrasting in value with *silver*: see SILVERTAIL.] A person of small social pretension or standing. Also **coppertop.**

1887 *Bulletin* (Sydney) 12 Nov. 4/1 In their thoughts and expressions they betray the demoralisation wrought in the 'copper-top' and 'silver-tail' era. **1901** *Ibid.* 28 Sept. 15/1 'Silvertails' congregate at one end of the room, 'Coppertails' at the other, and the line of demarcation is rarely crossed. **1955** N. PULLIAM *I traveled Lonely Land* 374 *Coppertail (prole)*, one of the *hoi polloi*.

Also **coppertailed** *ppl. a.*

1890 A.J. VOGAN *Black Police* 116 The genus termed in Australian parlance 'silver-tailed', in distinction to the 'copper-tailed' democratic classes.

coral. [Attrib. use of *coral*, with reference either to habitat or to a fancied resemblance.] Special Comb. **coral cod** (or **trout**), the marine blue-spotted fish *Plectropoma maculatum* (fam. Serranidae) of waters off W.A. and Qld., including the Great Barrier Reef; the similar related fish *Cephalopholis miniatus*; **fern,** any of several slender ferns with forked fronds of the genus *Gleichenia* (fam. Gleicheniaceae) of all States and N.Z., New Caledonia, and s.e. Asia; (chiefly *Qld.*) the scrambling tropical fern ally *Lycopodium cernuum* (fam. Lycopodiaceae); **pea, (a)** any of several climbing or trailing plants of the genus *Kennedia* (fam. Fabaceae), with red or purple flowers, esp. *K. rubicunda* (also **dusky coral pea**) of e. Aust. and *K. prostrata* (see RUNNING POSTMAN); **(b)** FALSE SARSAPARILLA; also **purple coral pea; tree,** any of several trees of the genus *Erythrina* (fam. Fabaceae) of n. and central Aust., bearing bright red or yellowish flowers.

1928 S.E. NAPIER *On Barrier Reef* 81 Many **coral cod** .. were caught. **1936** T.C. ROUGHLEY *Wonders Great Barrier Reef* 9 Some fish from the reef .. red emperor and coral trout. **1963** B. CROPP *Handbk. for Skindivers* 118 The coral cod is commonly called a coral trout. **1972** *Bulletin* (Sydney) 5 Aug. 50/3 They serve food that is quite superb .. barramundi, coral trout. **1983** *Ecos* xxxv. 5/1 Until a few years ago, only three commercially important Australian fish were known to change sex: barramundi, coral trout, and threadfin salmon. **1984** *Canberra Chron.* 25 Jan. 19/4 A lot of evening meals along the coast .. are made up of small fillets of nanygai, coral cod. **1898** E.E. MORRIS *Austral Eng.* 98 **Coral-Fern**, name given in Victoria to *Gleichenia circinata.* **1909** *Emu* VIII. 222 The reeds and coral fern growing at the entrance of the Tarwin River. **1938** C.T. WHITE *Princ. Bot. Qld. Farmers* 211 In some places the Coral Ferns (*Gleichenia circinnata* and *G. dicarpa*) are very abundant. **1973** J. MORRISON *Austral. by Choice* 118 At the bottom there was a wide belt of swampy country given over to paperbarks and coral fern. **1985** N. & H. NICHOLSON *Austral. Rainforest Plants* 42 Coral fern makes a pretty ground cover for moist or poorly drained soils in sun or shade. **(a) 1896** *Melburnian* 28 Aug. 53 The trailing scarlet kennedyas, aptly called the 'bleeding-heart' or '**coral pea**'. **1923** *Census Plants Vic.* (Field Naturalists' Club Vic.) 38 *Kennedya—rubicunda* .. Dusky Coral-pea; *prostrata* .. Scarlet Coral-pea. **1942** C. BARRETT *Austral. Wild Flower Bk.* 44, Dusky coral pea, with its dark-red flowers and long, tough rambling stems. **1956** T.Y. HARRIS *Naturecraft in Aust.* 172 Dusky Coral Pea is a trailing plant occurring on the sandy soils of the coast of Queensland, New South Wales, and Victoria. It has dark, trifoliate leaves and deep-red elongate flowers. **(b) 1914** E.E. PESCOTT *Native Flowers Vic.* 35 The thick roots of this species, Hardenbergia monophylla, the 'Purple **Coral Pea**', have a certain medicinal value as a blood purifier. **1942** C. BARRETT *From Bush Hut* 60 Purple coral-pea festooned a sapling. **1981** A.B. & J.W. CRIBB *Wild Medicine in Aust.* 76 Quite possibly the imaginary virtues of the coral pea, if trusted strongly enough by those who drank the infusion, were as effective as the more pharmacologically valuable true colonial sarsaparilla. **1848** T.L. MITCHELL *Jrnl. Exped. Tropical Aust.* 218 One thorny tree or shrub .. had a leaf, somewhat like a human hand, and a pod containing two peas of a bright scarlet colour, about the shape and size of a French bean. .. This proved to be a new species of Erythrina, or **coral tree. 1859** F. FOWLER *Southern Lights & Shadows* 101 The crimson Coral Trees seem to light the pathways. **1885** *Illustr. Austral. News* (Melbourne) 19 Dec. 226/4 Exclamations of admiration are directed not alone to the view, but also to a tree close at hand, covered with bunches of crimson pea-shaped flowers. This is the coral tree .. which being deciduous, like the bottle tree and cedar, has no leaves at present, but allows its gaudy flowers to bloom in unhidden splendor. **1917** *Bulletin* (Sydney) 12 Apr. 24/4 Coral trees .. are natives of the North Coast of N.S. variety about 'our 'arbour'. **1948** R.A. PEPPERALL *Emigrant to Aust.* 25 'Yes, but the Blue Mountains beat them in (Sydney) 8 Aug. 24/4 The correa flower .. is commonly known as Tennant *Battlers* 8 Beside the stones two great coral trees lifted naked grey branches that showed, instead of leaves, clusters of flowers, curved blades of scarlet around the stamens, as though a flock of fiery-coloured Hesling *Dinkumization & Depommification* 22 Coral-trees sprouting vermilion flowers like dangerous plumbing leaks across my windows. **1970** J.V. MARSHALL *Walk to Hills of Dreamtime* 149 *Coral tree* .. light-weight wood, followed by red-brown pods sometimes poisonous. **1985** M. STEWART *Autobiogr. of my Mother* 81 The coral trees round the chooks' yard.

cord. Abbrev. of *corduroy road* (see CORDUROY B).

1898 *Bulletin* (Sydney) 26 Feb. 14/1 He once started from Waratah to the '13-Mile', the whole distance on 'cords', with a newchum. Godkin left with 75 lb., the towny with about 30 lb.

corduroy, *n.* and *attrib.* [U.S., from the resemblance to the ribbed appearance of *corduroy*: see OED(S *sb.* 3.]

A. *n.*

1. A pathway across swampy ground, made of logs or slabs laid transversely and side by side; the logs or slabs so used: see esp. quot. 1920 (2).

1861 [see *corduroy road*]. **1875** R.P. WHITWORTH *Cobb's Box* 4 Over hill and dale, gully and flat, mudhole and 'corduroy'. **1901** *Papers & Proc. R. Soc. Tas.* (1902) p. xxxii, The track along the plains sadly wants attention in many places, a bit of corduroy here and there. **1908** C.H.S. MATTHEWS *Parson in Austral. Bush* 59 'Corduroy' is made by laying side by side large pine-logs, roughly flattened with the axe on their upper surface, and covering them with soil or gravel. **1911** E.J. BRADY *King's Caravan* 233 After the corduroy came the ascent of a hill. **1915** *Bulletin* (Sydney) 18 Feb. 14/2 When I arrived they were trying to skid one of the jinkers over some 'corduroy' they'd laid. **1920** C.C. DUGAN *Old Tasmanian Road* 23 With a jump and a thump and a bump, bump, bump, Over the corduroy. **1920** *Land of Lyre Bird* (S. Gippsland Pioneers' Assoc.) 94 Corduroy was pretty largely used by the settlers in the early days to keep them out of the mud, and the forests of saplings of all kinds through which the roads ran afforded abundance of material for the work. Spars of six or eight inches in diameter were cut into lengths of eight or ten feet and laid close together, transversely to the road, along the worst stretches. . . A better system of corduroy was adopted by the Shire Councils later on, of splitting slabs of about four inches by nine and ten or twelve feet long out of the big timber, and laying them on longitudinal bed logs. **1938** X. HERBERT *Capricornia* 416 They had trodden cinders and corduroy all the way across to the spot in the railway yards where they had kept the tricycle hidden. **1945** E. GEORGE *Two at Daly Waters* 38 At King's River the corduroy had washed away, and there was a mile of flood-waters to cross. . . Without the corduroy it was rough crossing over the stones and through the deeper pools. **1975** X. HERBERT *Poor Fellow my Country* 373 Suddenly they were in dense scrub, bumping over timbered corduroy. **1978** R.H. CONQUEST *Dusty Distances* 54 A corduroy, for the benefit of readers, is a causeway made across swampy ground or shallow rivers by laying logs transversely side by side. . . In later years, the corduroy was one of Australia's secret weapons in the war against Japan, in New Guinea and other Pacific areas.

2. *transf.*

1956 S. GORE *Overlanding with Annabel* 59 The only way to deal with this kind of road hazard is to dig all sand from around the wheels so that it will not grip and bind, then laying spinifex, bushes or matting of some kind under the back wheels, reverse the car out . . and when back on firm ground make another rush at the sand, which will meanwhile have been prepared by laying more 'corduroy' all along in front.

B. *attrib.* Used in various Comb., esp. **corduroy road,** to denote this method of construction or the material used.

1861 L.A. MEREDITH *Over Straits* 160 Corduroy roads of logs were being laid down in some places on the line, because stone for 'road-metal' was scarce. **1863** *Jrnls. & Rep. Two Voyages Glenelg River* 26 June (1864) 12 With the felled trees they have made a corduroy road over the mud. **1869** 'E. HOWE' *Boy in Bush* 177 'Corduroy' causeways of tree-trunks across swampy places. **1880** 'OLD HAND' *Experiences of Colonist* (ed. 2) i. 74 Where the stream was shallow and rapid, an attempt had been made to erect a corduroy bridge over it. **1889** J.L. HUNT *Bk. of Bonanzas* 71 The course of true love began to partake of the nature of a 'corduroy' road in the wet season. **1898** G. DUNDERDALE *Bk. of Bush* 33 Their bullock-drays were often bogged in Elizabeth Street, and they made a corduroy crossing over it with red gum logs. **1901** *Truth* (Sydney) 28 July 5/2 As an orator George is as jolty as a bullock dray going over a corduroy crossing. **1909** G.W. SMITH *Naturalist in Tas.* 93 The culverts were frequently broken in, the 'corduroy' logs were mostly rotten and full of holes. **1918** *Aussie: Austral. Soldiers' Mag.* Feb. 7/2 An' wot about the stiff Fritzes? They use them for making corduroy roads! I tell yer it's the dinkum straight wire, compree? **1928** *Bulletin* (Sydney) 18 Apr. 21/3 The corduroy road is disappearing, much to the relief of man, beast and vehicle. **1934** WARBURTON & ROBERTSON *Buffaloes* 104 We cleared a track through the mangroves on the bank, and having got sufficient timber, we made a corduroy path for some yards into the river. **1944** M.J. O'REILLY *Bowyangs & Boomerangs* 162 Just imagine what it was like on a dark, rainy night trudging along the corduroy track with a couple of hurricane lamps to show the way. **1957** V. PALMER *Seedtime* 123 Donovan drove out over the corduroy road to the mills. **1972** M. GILBERT *Personalities & Stories Early Orbost* 49 He built the corduroy road on the Cabbage-Tree-Tabbara Road. **1982** M. WALKER *Making Do* 130 It had a corduroy bottom, that's wood in the bottom of it to stop you from sinking down in the sand. He broke the wagonette's axle.

corduroy, *v.* [f. prec.] *trans.* To surface (a pathway, etc.) with logs or slabs laid transversely and side by side.

[N.Z. **1868** DILKE *Greater Brit.* I. 340 The highway is 'corduroyed' with trunks of tree fern.] **1879** 'AUSTRALIAN' *Adventures Qld.* 94 Bogs and swamps have not been corduroyed, or in any way altered. **1898** C.L. MORGAN *Rabbit Question in Qld.* 107 Gateways to be corduroyed on either side for a distance of 16 ft. with 18 ft. lengths of 8 in. approved timber, falling from the sill level to 6 in. below the surface of the ground in the length of corduroying. **1911** E.S. SORENSON *Life in Austral. Backblocks* 184 One teamster I remember 'corduroyed' a bog on the Tatham Road with smothered bullocks. **1920** *Land of Lyre Bird* (S. Gippsland Pioneers' Assoc.) 62 The path leading from the gate to his house was also corduroyed with tree ferns. **1932** I.L. IDRIESS *Prospecting for Gold* 21 A hundred yards of creek-bed had to be corduroyed (a road of logs made across it). **1944** A. MARSHALL *These are my People* 7/2 We used logs to corduroy the miles of mud we called roads in the horse and buggy days. **1976** J.H. TRAVERS *Bull Dust on Brigalow* 46 He had up to five tethered together by this method and had them corduroying sandy patches on the road close to Borroloola.

Hence **corduroyed** *ppl. a.*, **corduroying** *vbl. n.*

1946 A.J. MARSHALL *Nulli Secundus Log* 89 We found a muddy, **corduroyed** track. **1898 corduroying** [see CORDUROY *v.*]. **1982** R. ELLIS *Bush Safari* 24 After we managed to dig down and jack up the ute, this timber, in lengths of about 60 centimetres, was placed underneath the wheels and along the wheel tracks, giving, in effect, a made 'road' about 12 metres long. This is known as 'corduroying'.

cordy. [Prob. f. *cord*, in allusion to the epaulettes of a dress uniform: see quot. 1945 where the reference is in a military context and to servants.] A member of the Corps of Staff Cadets at the Royal Military College, Duntroon.

[**1945** *Weekend Mag.* 25 Nov. 2 How would you like to be waited on by 1000 people—or should I say Kordies?] **1964** *Woroni* (Canberra) 9 July 8/1 *Blues Undo Cordies.* After indifferent form in our last two matches Uni. played constructive football to defeat R.M.C. at Duntroon. **1972** *Enobesra* (Canberra) 70 *Cordy*, member of CSC. **1980** C. LEE *Bush Week* 2 Cordies were very regimental, and one day we were told they would make up the cream of Australia's New Army. **1981** *Canberra Times* 18 Sept. 2/6 Changing the guard at Yarralumla Palace would become the top tourist attraction in Canberra, says the task force, with the red-coated RMC band marching down Lady Denman Drive with a smartly outfitted detachment of 'cordies' from Duntroon behind them. **1984** *Ibid.* 18 Aug. 1/1 *Cordies forget the 60s in aid of Bush Week.* About 60 Duntroon cadets marched on the Australian National University yesterday in what looked like a return to the student-cadet confrontations of the 1960s.

corella /kəˈrɛlə/. [a. Wiradhuri *garala.*]

1. a. Either of two predom. white, crestless cockatoos of the genus *Cacatua*, *C. sanguinea* (see *little corella* LITTLE 2) and *C. tenuirostris* (see *long-billed corella* LONG 2). **b.** (Occas.) MAJOR MITCHELL COCKATOO.

1859 H. KINGSLEY *Recoll. Geoffry Hamlyn* II. 77 He had a bird, a white corrella, which could talk and whistle. **1861** 'OLD BUSHMAN' *Bush Wanderings* 161 We had a species of small cockatoo, which we called the *Corella.* **1900** *Bulletin* (Sydney) 16 June 15/1 Galahs and carellas mostly strip the bark off the limbs in which they have their nests. **1924** L. ST. C. GRONDONA *Kangaroo keeps on Talking* 128 Corellas—pink crested—and galahs . . are all good talkers. **1944** J.J. HARDIE *Cattle Camp* (ed. 3) 30 See these dead trees! . . The corellas killed them! Stripped every leaf of them. **1970** *Matilda* (Winton Tourist Promotion Assoc.) 14 White corellas flow across the baked claypan. **1975** X. HERBERT *Poor Fellow my Country* 59 They were corellas, pinkish white cockies with flashes of crimson under wings.

2. Special Comb. **corella pear,** a variety of pear grown in S.A. (see quot. 1975).

1975 *Bulletin* (Sydney) 26 July 50/1 The Corella pear is grown only in South Australia, and is almost manufactured. Cross pollination is done by hand and the beautiful red blush is created by a cold-storage technique. The pear is named after a red-coloured parrot found in South Australia. **1984** E. ROLLS *Celebration of Senses* 68 The little green Corella pear . . grew from a seedling in the Barossa Valley in South Australia.

cork. [f. the resemblance of a bark or wood to the bark of the cork oak *Quercus suber.*] Used *attrib.* in Special Comb. **cork-bark,** any of several shrubs or trees having a thick, rough, and corky bark, esp. of the genus HAKEA; **tree** (or **wood**), any of several trees or shrubs having light and porous wood or rough corky bark, esp. of the genera *Duboisia* (fam. Solanaceae), *Erythrina* (see *coral tree* CORAL), and HAKEA; also **corkwood tree.**

1890 'LYTH' *Golden South* 196 The timber is good,—the jarrah, pine, cajeput, **cork-bark.** **1898** D.W. CARNEGIE *Spinifex & Sand* 198 Clumps of cork-bark trees. **1936** C.T. MADIGAN *Central Aust.* 85 The hakea, or cork-barks, are gnarled-trunked trees, with ribs of cork up the black stems, and long cylindrical foliage. **1972** *Austral. Lapidary Mag.* Sept. 8/2 Abundant 10-feet-high flat narrow leaf, shadeless hakea, called 'cork bark', because of their cork-like bark. **1981** D. STUART *I think I'll Live* 108 Aromatic with resinous smell of spinifex and eucalypts, . . corkbark, all on the heated breath of summer. **1788** J. WHITE *Jrnl. Voyage N.S.W.* 23 Jan. (1790) 117 Some few had shields made of the bark of the **cork tree.** **1845** C. HODGKINSON *Aust., Port Macquarie to Moreton Bay* 4 The popular names of the most remarkable brush trees are as follow . . Lightwood, Sassafras, Corkwood. **1861** J.M. STUART *Explorations in Aust.* 2 Apr. (1865) 264 The last seven miles was sandy soil, with spinifex and scrub, which was mostly young cork-tree. **1889** E. GILES *Aust. twice Traversed* I. 66 A tree that I know only by the name of the corkwood tree. The wood is soft, and light in weight and colour. **1901** J.H. MAIDEN *Plants reputed to be Poisonous* 25 *Duboisia myoporoides* . . 'Corkwood' . . was believed by the late Baron von Mueller to be poisonous to stock. **1911** ST. C. GRONDONA *Collar & Cuffs* 71 Corkwood, or, as it is sometimes called, flametree, has for bark a coarse kind of cork. **1935** DAVISON & NICHOLLS *Blue Coast Caravan* 239 The cork-wood-tree, with its large leaves and large yellow flowers with shiny black centres that turn red as they die. **1952** N. GOREY *Alice* 20 The gnarled corkwoods (hakea) with their cylindrical foliage, deep cream clusters of tiny flowers, and unusual seed pods. **1976** N.V. WALLACE *Bush Lawyer* 124 We mustered over the plains and through the mulga by cabbage tree, cork tree, and bloodwood. **1984** *Rydges* Dec. 109/1 The 'new' crops of pharmaceutical interest—Duboisia (corkwood) [etc.].

corkscrew.

1. Used *attrib.* in the names of flora: **corkscrew grass,** any of several grasses (fam. Poaceae), esp. the perennial *Stipa nitida* and related species, occurring in all States, bearing sharp pointed fruits with spirally twisted awns; **palm,** SCREW PINE.

1872 [**corkscrew grass**] A. MCFARLAND *Illawarra & Manaro* 118 There are many varieties of grass seed; but the one which causes the most trouble is, from its spiral shape, locally known as the 'corkscrew'. **1897** L. LINDLEY-COWEN *W. Austral. Settler's Guide* 79 The chief pasture plants are corkscrew and silver grass, which are very fattening. **1930** *Bulletin* (Sydney) 20 Aug. 21/4 In many parts of N.S.W. and Queensland . . corkscrew grass . . is very tenacious of life and flourishes often when drought has killed all else. It is so called on account of its seeds, which . . will penetrate the outer skin at the slightest touch, and then beginning a slow rotary movement, work into the flesh out of sight after the manner of a tick. **1959** C. & E. CHAUVEL *Walkabout* 33 The plain itself was dotted with . . corkscrew grass. **1974** *Austral. Folksongs* (Folk Lore Council Aust.) 61 Shearin' on the western plains where the fleece is full of sand, And the clover-burr and corkscrew-grass is the place to try your hand. **1862** J. McKinlay *Jrnl. Exploration Interior* 7 June 104 The creeks and the river have lots of **cork-screw palms** in and near them. **1887** Mrs D.D. Daly *Digging, Squatting, & Pioneering Life* 53 Wind rustling through the slender leaves of a clump of corkscrew palms. **1935** F. Birtles *Battle Fronts Outback* 78 The pandanus, or corkscrew palm, branches like a tree, the palm heads being on the ends of the bare limbs. The fruit, in shape, is like a large pineapple, but is hard and woody to taste. The natives roast them and eat the inner portions.

2. *Surfing.* See quot. 1963. Also **corkscrew shoot.**

1931 *Surf: All about It* 36 *Corkscrew shoot.* Ever tried to do a corkscrew? It's one of the higher flights of surfing. **1963** J. Pollard *Austral. Surfrider* 46 For the expert body surfer, a number of fancy slides have been worked out over the years. In the *corkscrew*, the surfer's body makes a complete turn as he goes down the slope of a greenback.

Hence **corkscrewing** *vbl. n.*

1956 S. Hope *Diggers' Paradise* 166 It needs a great deal of practice, and yet more practice if you want to show off by 'corkscrewing' and shooting a 'beacher' on your back.

cormorant. *Obs.* [Spec. use of *cormorant* an insatiably greedy or rapacious person: see OED 2.] A name for a squatter who displays greed in the acquisition of land. Also **cormorant squatter.**

1875 Campbell & Wilks *Early Settlement Qld.* 25 The vicissitudes the early pioneers—or rather cormorant squatters—had to sustain. **1876** J.B. Stephens *Hundred Pounds* 186, I *was* a squatter then: not a cormorant, by any means; I am afraid I partook rather of the nature of a cockatoo. **1881** T. Archer *Hist., Resources, & Future Prospects Qld.* 3 In these old times . . the 'cormorant' squatter ranged at will over the face of the land. **1892** *Truth* (Sydney) 22 May 4/3 The *bona fide* selectors in the Forbes district were two days behind the capitalistic cormorants. **1893** *Antipodean* (Melbourne) 44 A handful of cormorants, squatters, and unprincipled speculators.

corn.

1. Usu., as in U.S., applied exclusively to maize or Indian corn but formerly also used, as in Br. English, to refer to grain crops generally. Freq. *attrib.*

1804 *Sydney Gaz.* 11 Nov., The Rent of the Premises will be received in the following proportions, viz. One half in Pork; One fourth in Wheat and Corn; and the remaining fourth in Money. **1807** *HRA* (1916) 1st Ser. VI. 144 The fine River of the Hawkesbury . . is a great benefit to that principal part of our Corn Settlement. **1809** *N.S.W. Pocket Almanack* 44 The custom of sowing wheat on corn ground full of weeds and rubbish is ruinous to the farmer. **1826** *Monitor* (Sydney) 8 Sept. 134/3 Corn is grown only *for the bakers*—there is consequently, among the wheat growers, little straw. **1827** *Ibid.* 13 Sept. 639/3 The overstocked state of the Corn Market tended materially to its depression. Wheat was rather dull of sale and declined a trifle in price. Maize met a quick demand. **1830** *Sydney Monitor* 6 Jan. 3/2 Mr Robert Cooper, the distiller, has commenced making bread from corn meal, which he disposes of at the reasonable sum of one penny per lb. **1832** *Hill's Life N.S.W.* (Sydney) 9 Nov. 3, 70 acres wheat, corn, and potatoes. **1833** *Colonist* (Hobart) 26 Nov. 2/2 The Government filling the stores when wheat is low and plentiful . . would relieve the market, and always be a check upon monopolists and 'corn badgers'. **1834** G. Bennett *Wanderings N.S.W.* I. 203 The settlers in Australia, as in America, call wheat, barley, &c. grain; and when Englishmen speak of corn-fields, they consider he [*sic*] alludes to maize, which is alone called corn in this country. **1847** A. Harris *Settlers & Convicts* (1953) 4 Few persons who have tasted the deliciousness of a corn-doughboy eaten with the salt pork which constitutes so large a portion of their animal diet, will consider their taste altogether perverted. **1849** C. Sturt *Narr. Exped. Central Aust.* I. 13 Its rich and lovely valleys . . became the happy retreats of an industrious peasantry; its plains were studded over with cottages and cornfields. **1860** 'Lady' *My Experiences in Aust.* 172 It is not usual, except on a journey, to feed horses with corn in the Bush; the grain used, when such sumptuous diet is considered necessary, is maize or Indian corn—not oats, which do not thrive in this country. **1887** W.S.S. Tyrwhitt *New Chum in Qld. Bush* 114 The word 'corn' in Australia means maize. **1901** *Bulletin* (Sydney) 4 May 14/1, I camped with a corn-cocky on the Gilbert River. **1915** *Ibid.* 5 Aug. 24/3, I have been on a dairy farm and on a corn plantation. **1944** E.H. Burgman *Educ. Austral.* 16 Parrots opened the husk at the top of the cob of maize (or 'corn', as we always called it). **1945** F. Cork *Tales from Cattle Country* 51 Among racing enthusiasts in the Outback you will hear much talk about 'corn-feds' and 'grass-feds' that is confusing to the uninitiated. 'Corn-feds' are horses prepared for the regular meetings—training solidly and being fed on such hardening foods as chaff, oats, and corn. The picnic gallopers must be 'grass-feds' unless drought conditions preclude 'grass-fed' meetings, in which case picnic races are held under 'corn-fed' conditions. **1970** N.A. Beagley *Up & Down Under* 73 The maize crop was ripe and pickers were wanted there. The name for their seasonal occupation was, in Aussie language, 'Corn Snatching'.

2. Special Comb. **corn-bird,** *golden-headed fantail warbler*, see Golden *a.* 3.; *bush lark*, see Bush C. 3.

1911 J.A. Leach *Austral. Bird Bk.* 142 Golden-headed Fantail-Warbler, . . Corn (Barley) Bird. **1917** *Bulletin* (Sydney) 16 Aug. 22/3 Bush-lark (or corn-bird). **1941** *Ibid.* 25 June 16/1 The corn-bird, more technically golden-headed fantail warbler.

Corner. With **the.** A name for the area in which the borders of N.S.W., Qld., and S.A. meet. Also **Corner Country.**

1891 *Quiz* (Adelaide) 20 Mar. 7/2 The great jaw man of the Corner. **1920** *Bulletin* (Sydney) 9 Dec. 20/2 Pulled up for the night at the camp of an old boundary-rider in 'the Corner' (far nor'-west N.S. Wales). **1927** *Ibid.* 1 Sept. 26/3 Menindie, on the Darling, has been a watering-place for outbackers ever since the first white man went into 'the corner'. **1937** W. Hatfield *I find Aust.* 101 This was the time of the Birdsville annual races, and the Annandale camp was the first of those to ride in for the yearly get-together of the 'Corner', as they called the district. **1949** G. Farwell *Traveller's Tracks* 21 In the extreme north-west corner, where the border fences of three states meet—the 'Corner Country' they call it. **1952** A.M. Duncan-Kemp *Where Strange Paths go Down* 8 The desert nomads who inhabit that portion of south-western Queensland and the north of South Australia known affectionately by its scattered white residents as 'The Corner'. **1959** E. Webb *Mark of Sun* 51 Drovers coming through with stock from The Corner, or the Territory, were the only visitors. **1967** I.L. Idriess *Opals & Sapphires* 45 It is west of the Darling, enclosed by the Queensland and South Australian border, often called 'the Corner Country'. **1972** J. O'Grady *It's your Shout, Mate!* 72 'I was out in the Corner country one time,' he said. 'You know where that is?' 'No. I'm afraid I don't.' 'Out where Queensland an' New South an' South Aus. meet. On the Corner, see.' **1985** E.W. Docker *Clear Runway* 8 Mostly Nancy was headed somewhere west of Darling, into that boundless region known as the 'Corner Country'.

Hence **Cornerman** *n.*, an inhabitant of the Corner.

1949 *Bulletin* (Sydney) 7 Dec. 13/4 As a 'corner-man'—I've spent quite a slice of my life in that conjunction of three States around Tibooburra and parts adjacent—a man is neither Cornstalk, Croweater nor Bananalander.

cornstalk. *Obs.* [Fig. use of *cornstalk*: see quots. 1827 (1) and 1853.]

1. A nickname for a non-Aboriginal native of Australia. Also **cornstalker.**

1827 P. Cunningham *Two Yrs. in N.S.W.* II. 116 We have . . English and Colonial born, the latter bearing also the name of *corn stalks* (Indian corn), from the way in which they shoot up. **1827** *Monitor* (Sydney) 5 July 496/1 'Corn-stalks for ever' and blue ribbons are the distinguishing symbols of the Currency backers. **1832** *Currency Lad* (Sydney) 22 Sept. 3 Eleven rounds were fought . . and placed the star of the 'corn stalk' once more ascendant over that of the 'rose'. **1834** G. Bennett *Wanderings N.S.W.* I. 341 The Australian ladies may compete for personal beauty and elegance with any European, although satirized as 'corn-stalks' from the slenderness of their forms. **1845** *Cumberland Times* (Parramatta) 11 Oct. 3/1 In the cross-examination, poor old Judy denied that she had struck either defendant or his brother (both of them stout, tall corn-stalks). **1852** G.C. Mundy *Our Antipodes* I. 45 Cornstalk is the national nickname of the Australian white man. **1853** H.B. Jones *Adventures in Aust.* 170 The children born in Australia are, from their lanky appearance and extreme leanness, called 'corn stalks'; they have the appearance of poplars, shorn of their branches. **1866** *Austral. Monthly Mag.* (Melbourne) Nov. 203 All native Tasmanians called cornstalks. **1869** M. Clarke *Peripatetic Philosopher* 15 Your up-country cornstalk . . has not brains enough to be imaginative. **1873** W. Thomson-Gregg *Desperate Character* I. 170 'Corn-stalk! . . What's that, pray?' 'That's the name they give white natives over here.' **1898** *Truth* (Sydney) 10 July 4/3 The 'corn-stalker' from Australia and the smart and sturdy Canadian. **1916** *Ibid.* 1 Oct. 12/1 Why should the Pommies call the Australians Cornstalks when they are glad to get money from what they call Cornstalks? **1921** E. Wells *Fragments* 12 Call them 'oversea soldiers', or down-under men. . . Call them Cornstalks. **1928** H.C. Perry *Son of Aust.* 69 The two young giants attracted universal attention as they took their walks abroad together and they were everywhere spoken of as fine specimens of the Australian type then being bred in the great outback—the type which came to be spoken of as 'Cornstalks'. **1966** C. McGregor *Profile Aust.* 29 Today one is less impressed by the unique appearance of Australians (they are 'cornstalks' no longer) than by their similarity to the people of other western nations.

2. A nickname for a non-Aboriginal person, native to or resident in New South Wales. Also *attrib.*

1851 J. Henderson *Excursions & Adventures N.S.W.* II. 205 Next day, four young men, natives of the colony and excellent swimmers and divers, as all the *Cornstalks* are, went down to recover the bodies, if possible. **1859** W. Burrows *Adventures Mounted Trooper* 170 'Sydney Bill, the native' . . was . . a 'cornstalk', or native of Sydney, though of English parents. **1876** J.A. Edwards *Gilbert Gogger* 189 He is a cornstalk. The natives of New South Wales are so called, because they do not in the least resemble a cornstalk, being mostly short, stout men: but this country is full of these contrarities. **1881** J.C.F. Johnson *To Mount Browne & Back* 13 It is a question that often arises in the 'men's hut'—which are the best fellows, the 'cornstalks', the 'gumsuckers', or the 'croweaters', while the Central Australian or Border man is also discussed under the at first bewildering name of 'overland fisherman'. **1888** R. Thomson *Austral. Nationalism* 85 How does New South Wales stand in the matter with Victoria? Simply that Victoria has on every occasion, when the Cornstalks wanted coin, stood to them with a free and generous hand. **1891** M. Roberts *Land-Travel & Sea-Faring* 85 We . . crossed the Murray from the land of the Victorian 'gum-suckers' to that of the New South Wales 'cornstalks'. **1899** H. Lawson *Autobiogr. & Other Writings* (1972) 42, I have called him 'Cornstalk' for want of another nickname. . . There was a good deal of Indian corn grown in the old districts of New South Wales; hence, I suppose, the nickname. **1903** *Bulletin* (Sydney) 16 July 17/2 The old Cornstalk town of Windsor is a weary, sleepy, drowsy place. **1919** *Aussie* (Sydney) Apr. 3/2 Diggers of the Yarra tribe . . like to chiack the Cornstalk variety about 'our 'arbour'. **1948** R.A. Pepperall *Emigrant to Aust.* 25 'Yes, but the Blue Mountains beat them all,' declared a 'Cornstalk'. ''New South' is the first and still the best State.' **1960** D. McLean *Roaring Days* 38 One of the young fellows . . was a tall dark-haired young cornstalk . . trying to work his way through Sydney University. **1981** A.J. Burke *Pommies & Patriots* 56 New South Wales Corn Stalks.

coroborey, var. Corroboree.

correa /ˈkɒriə/. Formerly also **corroea.** [The plant genus *Correa* was named by English botanical painter and engraver Henry Andrews (*Botanist's Repository* (1798) I. Pl. 18) after the Portuguese statesman and botanist José Francesco Correia da Serra (1750–1823): see quot. 1984.] Any shrub of the chiefly s.e. Austral. genus *Correa* (fam. Rutaceae), bearing decorative, often bell-shaped, flowers.

[**1807** Banks Papers 25 Sept. XX. 259 A Corroea, which grows at the Grose, with green flowers, I found with red ones. **1814** R. Brown *Gen. Remarks Bot. Terra Australis* 14 *Correa*, . . extending to the south end of Van Diemen's Island.] **1833** H.W. Parker *Rise, Progress, & Present State Van Dieman's Land* 142 The green corroea (corroea virens) is one of the most remarkable shrubs. **1847** G.F. Angas *Savage Life & Scenes* I. 155 We penetrated thick woods, amongst which the elegant *corea*, then in blossom, attained a considerable height. **1859** H. Kingsley *Recoll. Geoffry Hamlyn* III. 177 The scarlet correa lurked among the broken country. **1918**

Bulletin (Sydney) 8 Aug. 24/4 The correa flower .. is commonly known as 'correa bells'. **1956** T.Y. Harris *Naturecraft in Aust.* 157 One group in this family has fused petals forming a tube. These are the Correas whose bell-shaped flowers make them look rather like Heaths, but their soft, strongly scented leaves are very like many other members of the Boronia family. **1984** *Canberra Chron.* 1 Feb. 16/1 Correa was named after Jose Francesco Correia de Serra (1750–1823), a Portuguese botanist who published several papers on the family rutaceae.

corroboree /kəˈrɒbəri/, *n.* Formerly with much variety, as **coroborey, corrobbaree, corroboree, corrobara, corroberee, corrobori, corrobory**, etc. [a. Dharuk *garaabara.*]

1. An Aboriginal dance ceremony, of which song and rhythmical musical accompaniment are an integral part, and which may be sacred and ritualized or secular, occasional, and informal. Hence loosely, in extended senses, esp. with reference to a meeting or assembly, or to festivity generally. Also *attrib.*

***c* 1790** W. Dawes Grammatical Forms Lang. N.S.W., *Car-rib-ber-re*, another mode of dancing. **1793** J. Hunter *Hist. Jrnl. Trans. Port Jackson* 213 They .. would apply to us for .. marks of our approbation of their performance; which we never failed to give by often repeating the word *boojery*, which signifies good; or *boojery caribberie*, a good dance. **1811** *Sydney Gaz.* 19 Jan., In the center [*sic*] of the ball-room were the Royal Initials in chrystal .. with a transparent painting .. being the representation of our Native Race .. a striking full-sized figure, drawn in one of the most animated attitudes of the *corrobori* pointed with his *waddy* at the Church of St. Philip. **1819** *Ibid.* 9 Jan., A Corrobora, or Native Dance. **1825** B. Field *Geogr. Mem. N.S.W.* 433 The *corrobory*, or night-dance, still obtains. This festivity is performed in very good time, and not unpleasing tune. The song is sung by a few males and females who take no part in the dance. One of the band beats time by knocking one stick against another. The music begins with a high note, and gradually sinks to the octave, whence it rises again immediately to the top. **1825** *Austral.* (Sydney) 29 Dec. 4 The Corrobory, or Annual Feast of the Aboriginal Natives, usually takes place about this time of the year. **1826** S. Macarthur Onslow *Some Early Rec. Macarthurs* (1914) 455 Let me give you some account of one of our native dances—a 'Corroboree' as they call it, when it is not unusual for two or three hundred to collect, to paint and deck themselves with green boughs, and in sets perform various grotesque figure dances, in most excellent time, which is given by others who sit apart and chant a sort of wild cadence. **1833** H.W. Parker *Life, Progress, & Present State Van Dieman's Land* 6 Aborigines assembled, (as some suppose for the purpose of holding a *corrobery*, or general meeting). **1834** *Perth Gaz.* 6 Sept. 351 A desire to make his arrival here a cause of *corroboree* (rejoicing) to the black man. **1837** W.B. Ullathorne *Catholic Mission Australasia* 46 At full moon, they hold solemn religious dances in the woods beneath her beams, called *corobarees*, in which they mimic their own wars, and the natural habits of the kangaroo and emu. **1839** W.H. Leigh *Reconnoitering Voyages* 141 One of the native *Corrobbarees*, or war songs and war dances, which are performed at the full of the moon. **1840** A. Russell *Tour through Austral. Colonies* 273 He was making a corroborry on another, (naming a young man) which he was sure would make him *very angry*. **1843** C. Rowcroft *Tales of Colonies* III. 164 In the meantime a monosyllabic 'corrobara' had taken place between our guide and the chief of the sable community. **1849** C. Sturt *Narr. Exped. Central Aust.* I. 83 We returned to the camp with a numerous retinue of men, women, and children, who treated us to a corrobori at night... However rude and savage a corrobori may appear to those to whom they are new, they are in truth, plays or rather dramas, which it takes both time and practice to excel in. Distant tribes visiting any other teach them their corrobori, and the natives think as much of them as we should do of the finest play at Covent Garden. **1857** J. Askew *Voyage Aust. & N.Z.* 83 Thirty or forty .. of both sexes, may be seen occasionally on the banks of the Torrens, near the gaol, throwing the spear, and dancing a coroborey. **1867** 'Clergyman' *Aust. as it Is* 59 Messages are very frequently sent to all the members of a tribe .. to attend a 'corrobora', or meeting of the whole tribe. **1872** 'Resident' *Glimpses Life Vic.* 23 It is probable that the real meaning of the corroboree has never been revealed to white men. **1879** 'Australian' *Adventures Qld.* 38 He placed his pipe in his mouth, and threw himself on to his back, relapsing into a merry *corrobboree*, into which he introduced some of the principle events of the day, with a considerable amount of self-laudation for his exploit in spearing his uncle... Bony having *corrobboreed* himself into a first-rate humour again, sat up and had some more tea and damper, and mutton fat. **1884** J.T. Hinkins *Life amongst Native Race* 34 The mounted black police .. invited the Murray Blacks to a corrobbaree held by them in a dell. **1889** J.H.L. Zillmann *Past & Present Austral. Life* 132 The story was a grand joke among the blacks for many a day. It became, no doubt, the theme for 'a corroberee'. **1896** B. Spencer *Rep. Horn Sci. Exped. Central Aust.* I. 35 The term corrobboree is usually applied indiscriminately by white people to any one of the so-called dances of the aborigines; but there are in reality two very distinct classes of corrobborees... One set may be called ordinary corrobborees, such as are held at any time, and which women and children may watch; but in addition to these there is another and very distinct series, which may be spoken of as sacred quapara, which no woman or child is permitted to see, and which are intimately connected with certain Totemic subdivisions of the tribe, members of which alone can take part in them, though members of others, provided they have undergone the ceremonies admitting them to manhood, are allowed to watch wholly or in part. **1925** M. Terry *Across Unknown Aust.* 101 Their explanation is that a 'corroboree' (native dance) must be attended, or a 'walk-about' taken for their health. **1937** G.H. Sunter *Adventures Trepang Fisher* 127 Around the dancing-ground were a dozen or so fires, to give light to the corroboree. **1950** I. Shackcloth *Call of Kimberleys* 223 They were holding a great corroboree he said, in honour of Guirella's brave killing of the white man. **1963** R. Stow *Tourmaline* 171 People began to clap, in corroboree fashion, in time to the crash of the bell and the great shattering chords of the guitar. **1965** J. Iggulden *Dark Stranger* 126 Because he had seen at once the dreary corroboree those two smart darkies had arranged, anger soon dismissed the pleasure. **1970** J. Cleary *Helga's Web* 237 Trees .. danced like corroboree blacks beyond the street lamps. **1980** L.G. Fogarty *Kargun* 7, I give my corroboree Hopping around like roos Nature taking necessity in food Stamping down my feet by my murrie brothers Dancing till sun alights the clap sticks. **1986** *Sydney Morning Herald* 8 Mar. 6/4 Aborigines .. are planning an appropriate 'celebration', presumably a corroboree, which will last six days. The Pope will arrive towards the end.

2. *transf.*

1833 *Perth Gaz.* 24 Aug. 135 Several natives .. expressed some alarm when they perceived the preparations .. for the parade. They were given however to understand, that it was only a corrobora; it seemed to amuse them greatly to find that we had also our corroboras. **1834** G. Bennett *Wanderings N.S.W.* I. 210 The following is a definition of a clergyman, as once given by one of the aborigines: 'He, white feller, belonging to Sunday, get up top o' waddy, pile long corrobera all about debbil debbil, and wear shirt over trowsel.' **1834** J.D. Lang *Hist. & Statistical Acct. N.S.W.* II. 93 Parrot, macaw, and cockatoo—Straining their imitative throats... Right gladly hold corrobory. **1838** *Cornwall Chron.* (Launceston) 3 Mar. 34 Mr Sky .. on Saturday last made .. a 'corrobory' about the goods and chattels of which he had been deprived by his wicked wife. **1871** 'D. Dingo' *Austral. Rhymes & Jingles* 16 They wound up the day with a full-dress corroborree, And kicked up a terrible shindy and bobbery. **1888** 'R. Boldrewood' *Robbery under Arms* (1937) 297 Billy the Boy raises the most awful corroboree of screams and howls, enough for a whole gang of bushrangers, if they went in for that sort of thing. **1897** *Bulletin* (Sydney) 17 July 10/4 A luncheon corroborree where the speakers vied in laying on the color of panegyric. **1901** *Truth* (Sydney) 20 Apr. 4/5 If Parliament were summoned it would refuse to pass the accounts for the Commonwealth corroboree without ejecting from office the Ministers responsible for that shameful exhibition of drunkenness, rowdiness, and gluttony. **1913** *Ibid.* 12 Oct. 3/4 (*heading*) Cockfighting corobboree cracked up. **1934** E. Storey *Eve's Affairs* 15 The only signs of life are the barking of dogs, roosters crowing, and a corroboree of birds I fancy must be magpies. **1952** H.E. Boote *Sidelights Two Referendums* 9 The monthly corroboree of the Artists' Union on Saturday night. A nice little crowd there, and the beer flowing. **1963** F. Flynn *Northern Gateway* 91 Next morning the islanders were amazed to see the white man making a 'corroboree' all by himself. It was the first Mass on Bathurst Island. **1971** *Bulletin* (Sydney) 13 Nov. 13/1 Of all the strange indigenous corroborees that take place in Melbourne, the Melbourne Cup is unquestionably the best.

3. Comb. **corroboree dance, ground, song, stick.**

1839 T.L. Mitchell *Three Exped. Eastern Aust.* (rev. ed.) I. 114 They .. assumed the attitudes of the **corrobory dance.** **1845** J.O. Balfour *Sketch of N.S.W.* 15 The corroborry dance commences to the shouting of old women and the beating of sticks. **1878** R.B. Smyth *Aborigines of Vic.* I. p. xli, White paint is nearly always adopted for the corrobboree dance. **1898** D.W. Carnegie *Spinifex & Sand* 421 Near the spring in the scrub was a cleared **corroboree ground**, twenty feet by fifty yards, cleared of all stones and enclosed by a fallen brush-fence. **1944** *Bulletin* (Sydney) 29 Mar. 13/3 What is known in the N.T. as the Ruined City has been an abo. corroboree ground from the day that the first native ceremony was held in the North. **1845** L. Leichhardt *Jrnl. Overland Exped. Aust.* 1 May (1847) 237 Brown tunes up his **corroborri songs**, in which Charley, until their late quarrel, generally joined. **1961** *Bulletin* (Sydney) 11 Nov. 30/1 With the passing of the overlander, a piece of Northern Territory history has gone into the melting pot... Who will not miss the sight of the wide-hatted drover drifting his cattle along .. and the lonely cry of the native stockboy circling the cattle at night, droning a corroboree song to quieten them? **1980** B. Scott *Darkness under Hills* 22 Bunya chanted a few lines from the corroboree song about the big turtle. **1878** R.B. Smyth *Aborigines of Vic.* II. 294 The dancers .. commence by beating time simultaneously with their **corrobboree-sticks** (short pieces of green wood which give out a loud ringing sound when struck).

corroboree /kəˈrɒbəri/, *v.*

1. *intr.* To perform a corroboree.

1790 D. Southwell Corresp. & Papers, *Că-rāb-bă-răi*, to dance. **1826** R. Dawson *Private & Confidential* 11 They corroberied again & again till we were all tired. **1836** Backhouse & Tylor *Life & Labours G.W. Walker* 13 Apr. (1862) 241 A number of men and boys began to corrobberry. **1847** *Port Phillip Herald* 11 Feb. (Suppl.), When our blacks corroboreed, the others, not to be outdone in compliments, treated us to a similar ceremonial. **1854** W. Howitt *Boy's Adventures* 306 The dance on that day being of a peculiar kind, called gaygip, at which time they corrobery before images carved curiously in bark. **1884** E. Palmer *Notes Austral. Tribes* 4 When tribes met at certain places, such as large lagoons in another's hunting-ground, they did so with the permission or consent of the owner of that place; and when the particular mission they were on was fulfilled—as, for instance, a *Bora* meeting or general gathering to corrobory, they separated and each went to their own home. **1886** E.M. Curr *Austral. Race* I. 90 As the Englishman dines over most things, so the Australian corroborees on public occasions. **1908** P. Stewart *Austral. Tales & Verses* 11 And blacks, who ever feared, Corroboried and joyed aloud. **1916** S. Conigrave *Reminisc.* 6 A gentleman coming to see papa on business was surprised at hearing the blacks corroboring that moonlight night. **1928** *Bulletin* (Sydney) 5 Jan. 31/2 No matter how many holidays they had for races and so forth they had to have a walkabout at least once a year. They chose some secluded part of the run, where they threw off the clothes of civilisation and hunted and corroboreed as in the good old days. **1932** I.L. Idriess *Lassiter's last Ride* 107 Some of the tribes who corroboreed there were notoriously hostile. **1951** C. Simpson *Adam in Ochre* 143 Only two men of all who corroboreed were decorated in the same way. **1976** C.D. Mills *Hobble Chains & Greenhide* 25 A few of us had our 'toes in the ashes', and were smoking and yarning; the boys on watch were quietly corroboreeing to the bullocks who were well settled.

2. *transf.*

1844 *Sydney Morning Herald* 12 Dec. 4/4 The mosquitoes from the swamps corroboreed with unmitigated ardour. **1881** A.C. Grant *Bush-Life Qld.* I. 44 They had almost finished their meal before the new quart 'corroborreed', as the stockmen phrased it. **1882** *Bulletin* (Sydney) 16 Sept. 9/1 The bull-dog faced gentlemen .. corroboreed together to clean out the faithful during three revolutions of the earth last week to crack with their after-dinner wine. **1930** J.S. Litch-

FIELD *Far-North Memories* 62 We told him that Dirty corroboreed in Latin hymn tunes.

Hence **corroboreeing** *vbl. n.*; also *transf.* and *attrib.*

1833 BACKHOUSE & TYLOR *Life & Labours G.W. Walker* 5 Dec. (1862) 171 The arrival of a fresh party of blacks has produced a good deal of excitement at Wybalenna, which shews itself in the constant corrobberrying that is kept up. **1844** *Port Phillip Gaz.* 6 July 3 Inflammation of the lungs, a disease at one time raging among them . . to a serious extent, and arising from the effects of their corrobarying in the night air. **1856** H.B. STONEY *Vic.* 213 The menura imitates the note of almost every other bird in the bush, and resorts periodically to favourite well-beaten 'corroborying places', where it practises certain extraordinary antics. **1860** G. BENNETT *Gatherings of Naturalist* 184 Each bird forms for itself three or four 'Corroboring places', as the sawyers call them. **1902** R.C. PRAED *My Austral. Girlhood* 180 Captain Sherborne was an ungodly man, who encouraged the Blacks in corroboreeing, and was given to unsabbatical recreations. **1945** X. HERBERT *Capricornia* (ed. 6) 39 After a while the corroboreeing drove him mad. He shouted to the mourners to stop their row. **1956** T. RONAN *Moleskin Midas* 167 His boys were sodden from all day gossiping and all night corroboreeing, the lubras in even worse case.

corroboree frog. [See quot. 1953.] The small frog *Pseudophryne corroboree* of mountainous s.e. N.S.W.

[**1953** *Proc. Linnean Soc. N.S.W.* LXXVIII. 180 *Pseudophryne corroboree*. . . The specific name was suggested by the resemblance of the dorsal pattern of *P. corroboree* to the body paintings used by some Australian aboriginal tribes in their corroborees.] **1968** V. SERVENTY *Southern Walkabout* 28 Here live the brilliant black and yellow corroboree frogs. **1976** M.J. TYLER *Frogs* 159 The corroboree frog . . bears spectacular black and yellow stripes along its body. . . Spending much of its life hidden away beneath sphagnum moss, it is difficult to comprehend the purpose of such brilliance. **1986** *Sydney Morning Herald* 15 Jan. 13/3 The beautiful black-and-gold corroboree frog lives above the treeline in the Snowy Mountains and the ACT's Brindabella Range. Its breeding spots are snowdrifts in winter.

cossie /ˈkɒzi/. Also **cozzie.** [f. *(bathing) cos(tume* + -Y.] A swimming costume.

1926 'J. DOONE' *Timely Tips New Australs.*, *Cossie*, a seaside term applied to a swimming costume. **1931** *Surf: All about It* 49 Where's y'r cossy? Didn't y' come here to swim? **1959** D. HEWETT *Bobbin Up* 34 A mob of kids, cozzies and towels tucked under their arms. **1960** R. PULLAN *Hardskins* 20 'We went in the nuddie. You ever do that, Nick?' 'No.' 'You wouldn't think a bathing cossie made so much difference. You feel . . sort of light and real gay.' **1975** *Bulletin* (Sydney) 4 Oct. 30/1 Annette Kellerman our first great swimming star has given her racing cossies and other bits and pieces to the Sydney Opera House Archives of Theatrical Memorabilia. **1986** *Daily Mirror* (Sydney) 6 Jan. 1 (*heading*) Man in woman's cossie stabs two.

cotton. Used *attrib.* in Special Comb. **cotton bush,** any of several plants, usu. shrubs of the genus *Maireana* (fam. Chenopodiaceae), having a cotton-like appearance (see quot. 1981), esp. the spiny plant of mainland Aust. *M. aphylla*, often dominant in drier Austral. shrublands; any of several other plants having a similar resemblance to cotton; also *attrib.*; **tree, (a)** any of several plants, esp. the small tree with yellow flowers *Hibiscus tiliaceus* (fam. Malvaceae) of N.S.W., Qld., N.T., and s.e. Asia; **(b)** KAPOK TREE.

1861 *Burke & Wills Exploring Exped.* 6 Saltbush and **cottonbush** plentiful in the hollows. **1878** R.B. SMYTH *Aborigines of Vic.* I. 281 About ten feet of string, made from the native cotton-bush, and worn round the arm. **1885** P.R. MEGGY *From Sydney to Silverton* 13 Bastard blue-bush, and cotton-bush, of the last named of which the sheep are apparently very fond. **1898** D.W. CARNEGIE *Spinifex & Sand* 425 It is a stony cotton-bush flat, and on it numerous white clay-holes of water. **1935** H.H. FINLAYSON *Red Centre* 32 Of the hosts of smaller plants, the . . bluebush, cotton-bush . . are at all times the subject of . . attention, since it is to them that one looks chiefly for horse-feed. **1976** N.V. WALLACE *Bush Lawyer* 115 Country of cottonbush and gidgee, lignum and wild tobacco. **1981** G.M. CUNNINGHAM et al. *Plants Western N.S.W.* 265 Cottonbush has become the dominant shrub in many communities it formerly shared with bladder saltbush. . . White cotton-like clusters . . are often seen on the branchlets; these growths (from which the common name of the plant was derived) are galls caused by small grubs. **1815** *Govt. & Gen. Orders* 9 Dec., That noxious Plant called the **Cotton Tree** (though not possessed of any of its valuable Qualities) is suffered to extend itself over large Portions of rich soil. **1821** *Austral. Mag.* 241 A Constant Reader Also wishes to enquire . . whether the cotton tree, which grows so spontaneously in this Colony, might not be made useful if collected and properly manufactured. **1845** L. LEICHHARDT *Jrnl. Overland Exped. Aust.* 5 June (1847) 282 We observed a cotton tree (Cochlospermum), covered with large yellow blossoms, though entirely leafless. **1878** R.B. SMYTH *Aborigines of Vic.* I. p. lix, Some of their canoes formed of the trunk of the cotton-tree (*Cochlospermum*) are hollowed out. **1918** G. WHITE *Thirty Yrs. Tropical Aust.* 70 Beautiful flowering trees—one with a large yellow flower, called locally the cotton-tree. **1934** J.W AUDAS *Native Trees Aust.* 174 Its usual name of Cotton Tree is derived from the silky fibre that surrounds the seeds. **1983** MORLEY & TOELKEN *Flowering Plants Aust.* 96 *C[ochlospermum] heteroneurum*, cotton tree, occurs in Western Australia in sandstone areas.

couba, var. COOBA.

coucal. Shortened form of *pheasant coucal* (see PHEASANT 2).

1822 J. LATHAM *Gen. Hist. Birds* III. 239 Giant Coucal . . Inhabits New-Holland. **1931** J. DEVANEY *Earth Kindred* 22 The coucal whoops and the wonga calls. **1956** A.C.C. LOCK *Tropical Tapestry* 243 A coucal flew awkwardly and perched on a fence post, giving us a good look at its brown and black plumage.

count, *v.* [Spec. use of *count* to number.] *trans.* With **out**: to count (sheep or cattle as they leave a pen or paddock, esp. sheep after shearing). Freq. *absol.*

1874 *Australasian Sketcher* 31 Oct. 119/3 The fleece is taken off entire, and the shorn sheep is turned by the shearer into the 'count-out pen', whence the sheep are counted out by the overseer three times a day. **1883** *Illustr. Austral. News* (Melbourne) 28 Nov. 194/3 He asks us to see him 'count out', and consequently we return to the shearing floor, watching him from the windows as he lets the sheep out into the big receiving yard. **1888** 'R. BOLDREWOOD' *Robbery under Arms* (1937) 92 We counted the mob out. **1890** —— *Colonial Reformer* III. 107 The grown cattle were of course pen-branded. By nightfall every one was marked very legibly and counted out. **1938** *Bulletin* (Sydney) 26 May 21/2 Whats the biggest mob of sheep counted out in the one run? Anything over 10,000 gives a man eyestrain and most counters will block such a mob once or twice to give their optics a spell. **1942** W. GLASSON *Our Shepherds* 11 The sheep . . were mustered and counted out of their several paddocks. **1949** *Bulletin* (Sydney) 23 Feb. 14/2 We were down-country after a mob, and, waiting to count out, sought the pub. **1955** H.G. LAMOND *Towser* 89 The last of 216,879 sheep went down the shute . . was counted out and, with its mob, was driven away.

Hence **counting out** *vbl. n.* and *attrib.*, esp. as **counting-out pen,** a pen, usu. that into which sheep are placed after being shorn, the sheep being counted as they leave it.

[N.Z. **1874** J.A.H. CAIRD *Sheepfarming in N.Z.* 23 A small door for each shearer to put his shorn sheep out of the shed, and into the counting out pens.] ***c* 1914** H.B. SMITH *Sheep & Wool Industry* 34 When the shearer has shorn the sheep, he lets it go into another pen, which is known as a counting-out pen, because it is in these pens that the overseer counts the number of sheep each shearer has shorn. **1965** *Tracks we Travel* 90 The sheep started to go down to the counting-out pens. **1975** B. FOLEY *Shearers' Poems* 2 The wool appeared much dimmer Than it had ten years before And 'counting out' was difficult With 'shornies' jaw to jaw. **1980** P. FREEMAN *Woolshed* 20 On completion of shearing, the sheep is dispatched unceremoniously down a sloped ramp into 'counting-out' pens, where the particular shearer's tally of shorn sheep is counted at the welcome 'smoko' and lunch breaks.

count, *n.* [f. prec.]

1. The number of sheep shorn by a shearer and counted at the end of a day; the number of stock mustered and counted. Also with **out** and *fig.*

1895 J. KIRBY *Old Times in Bush* 147 The shearer did not care how much wool he left on the sheep, all his look out was, 'the count'. . . He would not scruple to leave half an inch long ridges of wool on the sheep, so long as he could get paid for the shearing. **1911** H.G. TURNER *First Decade Austral. Cwlth.* 127 In the Committee stage it was shelved by a 'count out' of the House. **1938** *Bulletin* (Sydney) 26 May 21/2 Biggest count-out I ever saw was 24,000, but over a friendly glass or two I've heard of counts of up to 50,000. **1944** *Ibid.* 19 Apr. 12/1 Although not a gun as far as pace was concerned—his tally . . was rarely more than 120 a day—the negro's sheep could easily be picked out in the yard after each count-out. McFowler 'pinked' every sheep and never drew blood.

2. Special Comb. **count muster** (*fig.* in quot.), a count; **(out) pen,** *counting-out pen*, see COUNT *v.*

1891 'R. BOLDREWOOD' *Sydney-Side Saxon* (1925) 1 Well, the old man's having a regular **count-muster** of his sons and daughters, and their children and off-side relatives, that is by marriage. **1874 count-out pen** [see COUNT *v.*] **1894** A. ROBERTSON *Nuggets in Devil's Punch Bowl* 7 'Boys,' he said, 'I've had a dream! I'll never shear another sheep! . . Good-bye all,' he said; then slid into the count-out pen, vaulted two fences, got his saddle and swag. **1894** *Western Champion* (Barcaldine) 16 Jan. 12/1 Mates don't like my name put down, And watch the blessed monkeys fill my count pen with a frown. **1978** M. WALKER *Pioneer Crafts Early Aust.* 153 The fleece is taken off entire, and the shorn sheep is turned by the shearer into the 'count-out pen', whence the sheep are counted out by the overseer three times a day.

counter lunch.

1. a. A midday meal served in the bar of an hotel or public house; orig., to attract custom and so at no cost to patrons, now usu. cheap but substantial. Also *attrib.*

1880 *Bulletin* (Sydney) 14 Aug. 10 (Advt.), H. Donaldson's Mercantile Hotel and Luncheon Rooms. . . Free counter lunch. **1897** *Worker* (Sydney) 25 Sept. 4/4 The labourer is worthy of his beer, And goes where he can get it pure and bright; At Fitz.'s fine Hotel the best of beer they sell And the counter lunch is always a delight. **1898** *Truth* (Sydney) 3 Apr. 4/5 The free counter lunch represents the 'jollity and fatness' of the times. **1904** C.W. JOHNSTON *Out-Back Homestead* 37 And he walloped in punch after punch, Till all that was left of the swaggy Wouldn't make a good counter lunch. **1905** *Truth* (Sydney) 14 May 3/7 The Domain dosser had got loose on the counter lunch, and was poking it into his interior by the waggonload when the barman objected. 'Gor blyme this isn't a blanky tucker 'ouse,' he remarked. **1912** *Ibid.* 15 Sept. 10/4 And, of course, counter lunches are unknown in England. ***c* 1918** D.H. MEIKLE *Humorous Verses* 6 Now they've barred the counter lunches, So I 'ear in evry pub. **1936** *Bulletin* (Sydney) 2 Sept. 21/4 Dad . . had lingered long at the counter lunch bar. **1946** F. CLUNE *Try Nothing Twice* 53 Sumptuous counter lunches were free with beer in those days. **1955** *Overland* v. 5 I've just had a chicken counter lunch and a couple of pots up at the pub. **1960** G. TAYLOR *Crop Dusters* 93 It's hot and there's plenty of it. Irish stew. Counter-lunch stuff from the pub. **1969** B. GARLAND *Pitt Street Prospector* 5 Lunches from the counter-lunch bar. **1972** J. O'GRADY *It's your Shout, Mate!* 44 They told me counter lunches were invented in Victoria. 'Some bloke bunged it on as bait. To get customers away from his opposition, see. Then every publican got into the act. . . Victorian counter lunches are indeed 'bigger and better'. And astonishingly cheap.

b. Similarly **counter tea**: see quot. 1972.

1971 D. WILLIAMSON *Removalists* (1972) 56 Er . . I . . er . . wasn't expecting you home, so I haven't cooked any tea. Why don't you go and have a counter tea with the boys? **1972** J. O'GRADY *It's your Shout, Mate!* 45, I also discovered evening meals served in bars, called, to my delight, 'counter tea'.

2. *fig.*

1908 *Bulletin* (Sydney) 23 Jan. 15/2 The black cockatoo knows exactly where to bite through the bark to find his breakfast, although there may be no evidence to the eye of man which might lead him to suspect the existence of so much as even a counter lunch.

country.

1. *Obs.* An Australian Colony; after Federation, (rarely) an Australian State.

1833 *Launceston Advertiser* 7 Mar. 2 The Colonists of

one country [*sc.* N.S.W.] were trampled upon by a haughty ruler. **1836** *Cornwall Chron.* (Launceston) 2 Jan. 1 In this country [*sc.* Tasmania] we have a felon police riding rough-shod over the liberties and rights of free British subjects. **1839** *Port Phillip Patriot* 19 Aug. 3 Australia Felix, a country larger than England . . is thus thrown open. **1841** *Geelong Advertiser* 21 Aug. 3/1 A new and thinly populated country like Port Phillip. **1842** J. GOULD *Birds of Aust.* (1848) II. Pl. 13, I found that in New South Wales, and every country in Australia within the same latitude, it [*sc.* the Welcome Swallow] arrived much earlier and departed considerably later than in Van Diemen's Land. **1843** *Portland Mercury* 4 Jan. 1/3 Van Dieman's Land, a country previously enjoying abundant and cheap labour. **1845** J. GOULD *Birds of Aust.* (1848) II. Pl. 70, South Australia is the only country in which this rare species [*sc.* the Red-throated Pachycephala] has yet been discovered. **1860** *S. Austral. Advertiser* (Adelaide) 2 July 2/5 The exodus to the Snowy is setting in, and notwithstanding the Government of Victoria will fight hard to secure their own country the benefits to be derived from the labor of their own people, they will find New South Wales running them very closely in the race of competition. **1901** *Tocsin* (Melbourne) 3 Jan. 1/4 In Memoriam. *Perished.* January 1st, 1901, *Our Country, Victoria*, Slain on the Altar of the False God 'Federation', Whose name is Bondage, the High Priest of Mammon. ***c* 1907** C.W. CHANDLER *Darkest Adelaide* 45 Some people think this is a fine country [*sc.* S.A.] since Tom Price and his Labor Party got on top. **1911** *Bulletin* (Sydney) 26 Oct. 13/4 It is Westralia's rotten luck that it is . . one of the lightest stock-carrying countries on earth.

2. The traditional territory of an Aboriginal people; TOWRI. See also quot. 1962. Also *attrib.* as **countryman** (see quot. 1983).

1843 J.F. BENNETT *Hist. & Descr. Acct. S.A.* 59 They are divided into tribes, each tribe having its own district of country or hunting ground. **1877** *Jrnl. Anthrop. Inst.* (London) VII. 291 Often . . have I heard a native say to another, this is my country, yours is Cànturbi (a place near New Nursia) go away. **1897** W.E. ROTH *Ethnological Studies* 160 The aboriginal will speak to this Being. . . 'Do not touch me. I belong to this country.' **1903** *Folklore* (London) XIV. iv. 340 Our Billie and Maggie went, with our permission, to their own country, and have not returned yet. **1912** SPENCER & GILLEN *Across Aust.* II. 499 You countryman along of this boy? **1927** *V & P* (W.A.) I. no. 3 47, I do not like the police; I think they killed my countrymen. **1931** A.P. ELKIN *Understanding Austral. Aborigine* (Morpeth Booklet no. 2) 12 The spirit-home aspect of a man's 'country' also explains the . . frequent refusals of old people to leave it. . . They merely say . . 'This my country.' **1937** G.H. SUNTER *Adventures Trepang Fisher* 93, I heard of an old lubra who had run a trepang camp. . . I will call her Milly. Her country, I remember, was Port Essington. **1955** M. DURACK *Keep him my Country* (1966) 75 This was his 'little country', the place from which he sprang. **1962** D. LOCKWOOD *I, Aboriginal* 31 We all belong to the Alawa tribe and the Roper River district, but every man among us owns a particular plot of tribal ground which he calls 'My Country'. **1975** J.P. ROBERTS *Mapoon Story* ii. 4 The child's own country, its home where it will in the future have the right to hunt and roam, is . . determined not by the place of actual birth, but by the locality where its soul has been held captive. **1977** J. & P. READ View of Past 11 June (1978) 189 (typescript), I bin look where he shootem that man you know. . . I know him too, poor feller. . . This one, this old man, oh, he's my countryman. **1983** B. SHAW *Banggaiyerri* 235 *Countryman*, person(s) with whom one has an especially close and usually life-long association/camaraderie that is cemented continually through ritual, mutual visiting and responsibilities towards each other. **1984** *Aboriginal Hist.* VIII. 36 They differ little from younger people of other descendants . . who have never lived in their ancestral countries.

3. Orig. *S.A. Mining.* [Br. dial. (chiefly Cornish) *country* the rock in which a lode of ore occurs: see OED 11.] The material surrounding a lode of ore. Also **country rock.**

1848 *S. Austral. Register* (Adelaide) 26 Apr. 4/4 The country—that is the ground in which the ore lays. **1853** A. MACKAY *Great Gold Field* 63 The rock on each side of the lode, technically called the 'country', is at first steatite or soapstone. **1863** J.B. AUSTIN *Mines S.A.* 18 A large quantity of the ore consists of what is called 'smalls' and this, as well as much of the other Ores, is so coated with the 'country',—or soil in which it is found,—that it would escape observation. **1873** R.P. WHITWORTH *Lost & Found* 24 His experienced eye told him we had found the right kind of country. **1880** J. BONWICK *Resources Qld.* 101 A promising vein in a good *country* may pass into stone like adamant. **1898** D.W. CARNEGIE *Spinifex & Sand* 127 The country rock lying immediately above the reef is the 'hanging wall', and that immediately below, the 'foot wall'. **1904** *Advocate* (Burnie) 9 Aug. 3/3 Rich ore was obtained for about 10 ft., when a 'horse' or fault of country occurred. . . After 17 ft. of driving through the 'country' a change occurred, rich stuff containing black oxide and native copper being entered. **1911** E.D. CLELAND *W. Austral. Mining Practice* 24 Often separated from the adjacent country rock by a thin seam of clay—or 'dig'. **1915** J.P. BOURKE *Off Bluebush* 108 Oh, I know a place where the gold went down, The spot where the 'country' broke. **1931** C.B. SMITH *Austral. Gold Prospectors' Handbk.* 45 The country rock is the rock which forms the walls of the reef.

4. A rural land-holding; land suitable for this purpose.

1855 N.L. KENTISH *Question of Questions!* 40 They might locate on any 'country' they chose to 'take up', *i.e.*, to select to any extent. **1863** R. HENNING *Lett.* (1952) 63 Mr Devlin is away on an expedition looking for country. **1864** *Ibid.* 72 By the new Land Act, whoever just puts his stock on a new piece of country and then puts in his tenders for it to Government has the right of occupying that country as a sheep-run. **1870** *Sydney Morning Herald* 2 July 3/6 Block of unstocked country, securely fenced; capabilities, 15,000 sheep. **1889** *Braidwood Dispatch* 11 Dec. 2/2 The rabbit pest in Balranald district is becoming very alarming, and unless steps are taken at once to kill the vermin the country will have to be abandoned. **1903** *Bulletin* (Sydney) 17 Sept. 16/2 Your station stock are often on *my* country! **1916** T. WARLOW *By Mirage & Mulga* 2 It'll also give us twelve months in which to form our own country and knock it into shape. **1917** A.B. PATERSON *Saltbush Bill* 10 But when the mustering time came on old Laban acted straight, And gave him country of his own outside the boundary gate. **1923** J. ARMOUR *Spell of Inland* 25 The Wilsons . . are seventy miles away. . . That is why we have made such a friend of George. His country joins ours, so we see him occasionally. **1929** 'OLD STOCKMAN' *Sensational Cattle-Stealing Case* 31 We will start back to Adelaide as soon as the rain ceases and secure this country. **1939** A.B. PATERSON in C. Semmler *World of Banjo Paterson* (1967) 41 His country bounded on a block taken up by a gentleman named Castles. **1939** J.G. PATTISON *'Battler's' Tales Early Rockhampton* 125, I made the mistake of removing the cattle from the brigalow to the coast, and also of letting the country go for £500. **1957** D. NILAND *Call me when Cross turns Over* 136 He's got some country to rabbit. He'd like a mate. What about me? Will I be in it?

county. [Transf. use of *county* a territorial division of Great Britain, serving as a divisional unit for administrative, judicial, and political purposes.]

1. One of a number of territorial divisions delineated in each Australian Colony but lacking the administrative functions of the British model. Also *attrib.*

1804 *Sydney Gaz.* 9 Sept., Charged with feloniously Stealing out of the dwelling house . . he was Committed to the County Gaol at Sydney. **1820** C. JEFFREYS *Van Dieman's Land* 49 Van Dieman's Land is divided into two counties, Buckingham and Cornwall. **1827** P. CUNNINGHAM *Two Yrs. in N.S.W.* I. 74 The inhabited parts of the colony cultivated by free people may be divided into four. *First*, the old settled division, comprehending the county of Cumberland (in which Sydney lies). **1828** H. DANGAR *Index & Directory River Hunter* 41 The assigning of boundaries to parishes, as well as counties, belongs to the land commissioners. **1830** *Extracts Lett. Swan River* III. 17 The territory [*sc.* W.A.] is to be progressively divided into counties, hundreds, townships, and sections. Each section to contain one square mile of 640 acres, each township 25 sections, each hundred 4 townships, and each county 16 hundreds. **1835** *Cornwall Chron.* (Launceston) 9 May 3 A request of Captain Forster to the County Magistrates, to be more particular in forwarding communications for the 'Black Book'. **1841** *Kerr's Melbourne Almanac* 52 The following are the boundaries of the Town of Melbourne, as defined in the *Government Gazette*, of April 1, 1840:- *Parish of North Melbourne*—County of Bourke. . . *Parish of South Melbourne*—County not named. **1851** H.R. RUSSELL *Short Descr. Austral. Colonies* 3 The settled districts of New South Wales Proper are divided into 21 counties, but a great number of squatters have located themselves beyond these boundaries, occupying above one hundred millions of acres. **1853** S. SIDNEY *Three Colonies* (ed. 2) 290 South Australia has been divided into counties, which are more recognised as distinctive boundaries than in the other colonies. **1855** H. CAPPER *Austral. Colonies* 9 The colony is divided into counties of which twenty-two are officially described, and also sixteen squatting districts, the whole being divided again into thirty-one electoral districts, for returning members to the legislative assemblies. **1884** *Austral. Tit-Bits* (Melbourne) 19 June 3/2 The libel case . . comes off before Judge Cope and a jury in the County Court on Monday. **1973** W.G. WALKER *Gloss. Educ. Terms* 32 *County* . . geographical division of a state, of little importance for local government or education.

2. In local government: a territorial division delineated for a specific purpose; see esp. quots. 1919, 1955 and 1962. Freq. *attrib.*

1892 *NSWPD* 1st Ser. LXI. 2579/2, I should like to see a measure of local self-government brought down which would provide not only that there should be municipalities, shires, and boroughs in New South Wales, but that a large portion of the county of Cumberland, should be incorporated into a Sydney county council, or a county council, to which body should be given large powers of local self-government over the metropolitan area. **1898** *Daily Tel.* (Sydney) 23 Sept. 7/2 The Prospect and Sherwood Council . . passed a resolution . . on the desirability of forming a 'county council to embrace Parramatta and the surrounding districts'. **1919** *Act* (N.S.W.) no. 41 Sect. 561 (1), The Governor may, by proclamation, constitute as a county district for local government purposes any groups of wholes and parts of municipalities or shires, or of both municipalities and shires, and may, by proclamation, alter the boundaries of county districts. **1935** *Ibid.* no. 42 Sect. 39, The Sydney County District and the Sydney County Council, constituted under this Part, shall, respectively be deemed to be a county district and a county council. **1955** G.F. ANDERSON *Fifty Yrs. Electricity Supply* 145 The Gas and Electricity Act constituted a county district under the name of 'The Sydney County District'. The Sydney County District consisted of the areas in which the Undertaking supplied electricity direct to customers. **1959** *N.S.W. Parl. Papers* (1959–60) 2nd Sess. III. 647 Proposals for the constitution of county districts for abattoir purposes . . were under consideration. **1962** A. & R. BLUETT *Local Govt. Handbk.* 184 One of the many purposes the creation of county councils serve is the destruction of aquatic pests, mainly water hyacinth. **1978** F.A. LARCOMBE *Advancement Local Govt. N.S.W.* 256 The county council system, from the administrative and local government aspects has much to commend it. The selection of a function and its fitting to an appropriate area is a sound approach to an efficient administration.

Cousin Jack, *n.* and *attrib.* Orig. *S.A.* [f. the Br. dial. use of *cousin* as a familiar term of address or designation, esp. in Cornwall, hence *Cousin Jan, Jacky* a nickname for a Cornishman.]

A. *n.* A man, usu. a miner, of Cornish descent.

1863 J.B. AUSTIN *Mines S.A.* 103 Things are managed better in Cornwall, and though we are apt sometimes to laugh at 'Cousin Jack' we might occasionally gain some useful lessons from him. **1869** *Pasquin* (London) 20 Mar. 760 The noble army of Discoverers, Promoters, Directors, Secretaries, and Cousin Jacks. **1871** 'IOTA' *Kooroona* 161 The speakers were for the most part 'Cousin Jacks', but, nevertheless, they would do their best. **1890** A.J. VOGAN *Black Police* 70 Born a 'Cousin Jack' (a Cornishman). **1895** *Worker* (Sydney) 21 Dec. 2/1 Both were natives of the colony, though Jack generally passed for 'Cousin Jack', which, of course, he was by descent and rearing. **1902** *Truth* (Sydney) 2 Mar. 1/7 A Cousin Jack, with a load aboard, ambled aimlessly into an open cut 30 ft deep. **1915** *Ibid.* 13 June 3/6 *What about Cousin Jack?*. . . What, for instance, of the brave Cornishmen? **1934** A. MELROSE *Song & Slapstick* 127 From overseas the Cousin Jacks Of Cornwall steadily made tracks. **1945** O. PRYOR *Cousin Jack Cartoons* 11 Give me da job, Captain. I am Cousin Jack. **1962** —— *Aust.'s Little Cornwall* 189 In many cases the Cousin Jacks lived and worked under conditions which were tough by any standards. **1972** N. KING *Nickel Country* 63 Both of my grandfathers were 'Cousin Jacks'. One was a young Cornish tin miner who arrived in Australia to work in the copper mines at Kapunda in South Australia. **1980** M. MCADOO *If only I'd Listened* ('Michael

Llewelyn'), The Cousin Jacks used to wear those stiff-fronted shirts, and down 'ere on the front of them there was a little tab they buttoned to the fly of the pants.

B. *attrib.* passing into *adj.* Cornish.

1896 E. DYSON *Rhymes from Mines* 178 She was killed with a slab from a Cousin Jack cake. **1908** —— *Missing Link* 90 He dragged to the ground a heroic Cousin Jack miner who was climbing the verandah post. **1929** W.J. RESIDE *Golden Days* 329 These two miners were noted for their 'Cousin Jack' pasties which they carried to work inside their 'flannel' for 'crib'. **1948** G. FARWELL *Down Argent Street* 21 There were nuggety men in shirt sleeves and tight moleskin trousers, mostly with beards or fierce Cousin Jack whiskers. **1973** A. BURNETT *Wilful Murder in Outback* 47 He was a fund of Cousin Jack humour. **1975** B. FULLER *Ghan* 55 The wheel-barrows used were unusual in build. Sometimes called 'Cousin Jack barrows', they had no sides and were without feet. **1982** M. WALKER *Making Do* 71 My mother was good at cakes and Cousin Jack pasties... The filling was all nicely seasoned, carrots sliced up. She rolled the pastry all out, then put the filling in, rolled over the top, got the end banged into shape, then went over it with her fingers and curled it all around the edges.

Hence **Cousin Jinny** (or **Jenny**), the wife of a miner.

1909 W.G. SPENCE *Aust.'s Awakening* 49 Come on, you Cousin Jinnies; bring me the stones and I will fire them. **1914** *Bulletin* (Sydney) 29 Oct. 13/2 Thirty women laid hold of and court-marshalled three non-unionists. Thirty Cousin Jinnies .. condemned them to be ducked in a convenient waterhole. **1962** O. PRYOR *Aust.'s Little Cornwall* 39 We can be damned thankful that women don't usually unite for a common purpose. Those Cousin Jennies up at Moonta showed us what can happen if they do.

couta, var. COOTA.

cove. [Survival of Br. criminal cant *cove* fellow, 'chap': see OED(S *sb.*[2] Used elsewhere but apparently most freq. in Aust.]

1. A man, a 'bloke' or 'chap'.

[**1812** J.H. VAUX *Mem.* (1819) II. 164 *Cove* .. when joined to particular words, as a *cross-cove*, a *flash-cove*, a *leary-cove, etc.* .. simply implies a man of those several descriptions.] **1828** *Tasmanian* (Hobart) 15 Aug. 41 My friend's eldest son .. replied, 'I have dropped my *thimble*.' His father chid him roundly calling him 'a careless *cove*'. **1832** *Hill's Life N.S.W.* (Sydney) 6 July 4 The politest cove that ever ruled a 'lush crib', the landlord of the 'Pig in Petticoats'. **1839** *Port Phillip Patriot* 20 Mar. 5/1 Ah James Turton my jolly old *cove*, drunk again, eh! **1843** *Dispatch* (Sydney) 25 Nov. 2/4 An oyster-barrow, opposite the barrack wall, kept by an out-and-out knowing-*cove*. **1853** S. SIDNEY *Three Colonies* (ed. 2) 356, That cove with the specs is a first-class swell in Melbourne. **1865** *Sydney Punch* 30 Dec. 668/2 The daughters of Australia rambled both with, and all over the various attractive coves in the harbour, and admired the swells on the shores of the stormy Pacific. **1869** *Adelaide Punch* 4 Mar. 64/2 A cove comes up, and offers to shout for the lot, and we let him. **1873** S.H. BANKS *Vice & Victims Sydney* 4 Look Joe! I'm blowed if that ai'nt the cove that was on the bench this morning, and he's a nipping it like we are! **1891** *Truth* (Sydney) 15 Feb. 7/4 The 'blokes' or 'coves', as the males are impartially styled. **1900** *Bulletin* (Sydney) 10 Mar. 15/2 Local 'coves' especially have to be extra careful when they become teachers, so as not to be accused of 'frill'. 'Outlanders' have more latitude. **1913** H. LAWSON *Triangles of Life* 244 There came a man, or a chap, to the shed where Bob and Jim shore—or rather, a cove, in the vague sense of the term. **1920** *Ross's Monthly* May 5/1 For our little Prince is a mere 'bloke' since the glorious war of gold. 'E's a Democrat of Democrats—at least, that's wot we're told 'E's a 'cove', a 'guy', a 'feller'—why 'e's ev'rythink that's right. **1932** I.L. IDRIESS *Prospecting for Gold* 73 Claims have been worked out and abandoned until some 'heady' cove came along, noticed a wash-store here and there where the bottom should be. **1955** P. WHITE *Tree of Man* 251 Not a bad cove, for a dago. **1965** G.H. FEARNSIDE *Golden Ram* 19 Because of freight charges, we pay more for our beer in the country than them coves in the City. **1978** D. STUART *Wedgetail View* 30 He was a good sort of a cove; quiet.

2. *Obs.* The owner or manager of an establishment, esp. of a sheep station.

[**1812** J.H. VAUX *Mem.* (1819) II. 164 *Cove*, the master of a house or shop.] **1837** *Rep. Select Committee Transportation* 21 Apr. (1838) 32 You must not go on as you have done with the cove; that is the master, the masters are called coves by the convicts. **1845** T. MCCOMBIE *Adventures of Colonist* 47 He asked if it was far to the home-station of his master. 'Not very far,' replied the shepherd. 'Will the gentleman have retired?' inquired Dr Arabin. 'Let me see—will the cove have gone to bed, Jim?' **1849** A. HARRIS *Emigrant Family* (1967) 51 What sort of a lad is this cove of yours? **1869** *Illustr. Sydney News* 23 Dec. 318/2 'The cove—the old man!' explained his companion. 'Well, bless your ignorance! what you swell coves 'ud call the master.' **1873** C.H. EDEN *Fortunes of Fletchers* 98 'The cove' (the elegant term generally used for 'the employer') would see a fellow rot. **1879** 'OLD HAND' *Experiences of Colonist* 3 The party consisted of eleven men, one boy, one overseer and the master, or 'cove', as he was called. **1880** R. ROWE *Roughing It* 3 The roofs were not shingled like that of the 'cove's' house, but thatched. **1889** *Bulletin* (Sydney) 20 Dec. 20/3 Yes, I'm the Cove, the Squatter said. **1914** *Ibid.* 22 Oct. 13/4 The cove who runs the shed is rather a particular sort and doesn't allow slumming, so you may take it that the sheep were well shorn. **1916** J. FURPHY *Poems* 42 'Are you the Cove?' He spoke the words As Freeman only can. The squatter freezingly inquir'd, 'What do you mean, my man?'

3. *transf.*

1903 *Bulletin* (Sydney) 11 Apr. 16/4 Dad isn't going to kill that pig he spoke about now. It's gettin' better, an' Mr Mooney, th' hoss doctor, says it didn't have cancer at all. But there's another cove lookin' a bit multy, so I s'pose he'll kill it. **1920** *Ibid.* 24 June 20/2 A brumby (no unbranded cove under seven years old merits the term) is a grown horse and hits the ground much harder than a 'green' thing.

covie. Also **covey.** [Br. slang *covey* (dimin. of COVE): see OED *sb.*[3]] COVE 1; also used as an affectionate mode of address.

1835 *True Colonist* (Hobart) 21 Jan. 2/4 These 'Covies' were very 'jolly', and endeavoured to 'bounce out of it', but it was 'no go'. **1846** L.W. MILLER *Notes of Exile Van Dieman's Land* 265 Tell you what, my covey, if you want these ere .. take 'em. **1853** C.R. READ *What I heard, saw, & Did* 130 You understand, my old covey, don't ye? **1855** R. CARBONI *Eureka Stockade* 9 By this time two covies—one of them generally an Irishman—had stripped to their middle, and were 'shaping' for a round or two. **1864** *Sydney Punch* 30 July 74/2 Them 2 Hoffices of Justice Sum rum coveys worked therein. **1892** *Bulletin* (Sydney) 26 Mar. 19/2 Here's the bleedin' push, me covey—here's a bastard from the bush! **1914** *Truth* (Sydney) 30 Aug. 5/5 Robert Shannon, a mild-mannered young covie .. looked as if he wouldn't injure the proverbial flea. **1916** *Ibid.* 25 June 1/8 And he is doing quite the grand, This covie from Australia.

cow.

1. Used *attrib.* in Special Comb. with reference to dairy-farming: **cow bail,** BAIL *n.*; **cocky,** a dairy farmer; see also COCKY *n.*[2]; so **cockydom, cockying** *vbl. n.*; **cockyism; farm,** a dairy farm; so **farmer; juice,** milk; **kick,** a violent sideways kick; also as *v. trans.* and *intr.*; so **kicker; paddock,** a paddock in which cows are confined; **spanker,** a dairy farmer; one who works on a dairy farm; so **spanking** *vbl. n.*; **time,** milking time.

[N.Z. **1851** E. WARD *Jrnl.* 12 May (1951) 180 The **cow bails** in the stockyard are fastened up.] **1936** M. FRANKLIN *All that Swagger* 370 He whitewashed the dairy and cowbails. **1979** DUSTY & LAPSLEY *Walk Country Mile* 37, I sat in the cowbail doing the milking. **1902** *Bulletin* (Sydney) 12 July 16/2 The **cow-cocky** is the most awful and wonderful of the genus—especially the young rooster. **1911** *Ibid.* 12 Oct. 14/1 Having no sympathy with those cow-cockies who sweat their children, I would like to describe how a dairy farm can be run. **1917** A.L. BREWER *'Gators' Euchre* 18 Strawberry .. had kicked her with the full force of a pore cow-cocky's blucher-booted hoof. **1934** C. MACKNESS *Young Beachcombers* 161 Cows and chooks are early risers, and cow-cockies and chook-raisers have to be. **1938** F. RATCLIFFE *Flying Fox & Drifting Sand* 67 'They are cow cockies' kids,' the teacher told me. 'They were up at nine last night washing churns, and up again at four this morning fetching in the milkers.' **1955** *Bulletin* (Sydney) 7 Sept. 12/1, I worked for a cow-cocky during the depresh and I still recall vividly his reaction when he caught me dozing once just after midnight. **1960** *Encounter* (London) May 26 The smaller brothers of the sheep-man, the wheat-cocky and cow-cocky, have absorbed his style. **1972** K. WILLEY *Tales Big Country* 173 We just can't stir up Holy Joe (the State Premier, Mr Bjelke-Petersen) and his cow-cocky government to do anything about it. **1974** D. O'GRADY *Deschooling Kevin Carew* 22 Kevin told him that he had the cultural *nous* of a cow-cocky. **1980** D. HEWETT *Susannah's Dreaming* (1981) 16 Cow cockies! All alike, always prayin' for rain. **1911** *Bulletin* (Sydney) 16 Mar. 14/4 When the Big Scrub began to take to dairying he .. took up land, and descended into **cow-cockeydom.** *Ibid.* 28 Dec. 13/3 The close-fistedness of Cow-cockydom is exemplified on a trip down the Richmond River (N.S.W.). **1936** *Ibid.* 16 Dec. 20/1 The stockman who rides without leggings is usually found in **cow-cockying** country. **1964** P. ADAM SMITH *Hear Train Blow* 85 They built slab huts with a 'ground' floor. They took work where they could find it .. and the women and children milked the cows while the father went shearing, fencing—anything to try to make ends meet, for cow-cockying never did. **1916** *Bulletin* (Sydney) 2 Mar. 48/1 Some time back I wrote that **Cow-Cockyism** and Cow were the end of Log Paddock. **1910** *Ibid.* 20 Jan. 15/1 She didn't waste time talking to blokes or coves, and any that came to the **cow-farm** were warned off. **1937** *Ibid.* 30 June 21/1 The rush starts for cow-farm jobs. **1913** *Ibid.* 3 Apr. 15/1 It isn't always the **cow farmer**. Sometimes it is the agriculturist devoted to onions, and on occasion it is the squatter whose speciality is poultry. **1938** F. BLAKELEY *Hard Liberty* 273 One cow-farmer .. tells me that he averages eighty pounds per month. **1903** *Truth* (Sydney) 25 Jan. 1/5 'Killed by a **cow juice** cart', is the heading used by a country paper, to chronicle the death of a little girl recently killed by a milk cart. **1906** *Ibid.* 18 Feb. 1/6 Even at Katoomba the cow-juice vendors know how to adulterate the product. **1941** *Action Front: Jrnl. 2/2 Field Regiment* Nov. 5 That cow-juice was pretty high by mid-day. **1936** J.C. DOWNIE *Galloping Hoofs* 100 After a few '**cowkicks**' and rearing once or twice, he began trotting round the yard. **1947** V.C. HALL *Bad Medicine* 36 The little red mule whipped a slicing 'cow-kick' that grazed its own ear. **1911** 'S. RUDD' *Bk. of Dan* 30 Dan just **cow-kicked** Snowy in the empty stomach and temporarily disabled him. **1927** —— *Romance of Runnibede* 39 The nuggetty grey shook his head violently and cow-kicked under the shaft at his tormentor. **1945** *Bulletin* (Sydney) 3 Jan. 13/1 There is only one way to mount a vicious horse with safety: its head must be held in to the rider by the near-side rein to prevent 'cow-kicking', biting or striking. **1964** B. WANNAN *Fair Go, Spinner* 138 The boss of the mustering camp scratched his head when it came to finding suitable mounts for Pat and finally decided to try him out on Lasher, whose name was bestowed because of his prowess as a '**cow-kicker**'. **1908** *Bulletin* (Sydney) 24 Dec. 14/3 He had a fairly-large dam in the **cow paddock** .. and on it he ran a cranky boat. **1931** V. PALMER *Separate Lives* 125 The shady creek-bend in the corner of the cow-paddock where the grass grew fat and sweet. **1939** FRANKLIN & CUSACK *Pioneers on Parade* 122 He crossed the orchard, vaulted the rabbit fence and made for the ram-paddock beyond the cow-paddock. [N.Z. **1906** *N.Z. Truth* (Wellington) 11 Aug. 3 The king of Okoia **cow-spankers.**] **1919** *Smith's Weekly* (Sydney) 5 Apr. 9/6 The young cow-spankers of Albion park can now devote all Sunday spare time to the Australian national sport of two-up. **1896** *Bulletin* (Sydney) 14 Nov. 27/3 There is nothing in **cow-spanking**... My first job was at a place where they milked 120 cows. Talk about slavery! **1905** *Ibid.* 12 Oct. 14/4 She sent Brown to a cow-spanking friend on the South Coast to purchase a milker... He chose a paunchy poley old enough to have a vote. **1906** *Ibid.* 18 Oct. 44/2 Five o'clock! Nearly **cow-time** again. **1913** *Ibid.* 9 Jan. 14/2, I had 35 cows to milk, and between 'cow-times' was expected to work in the paddock, grubbing, etc. **1922** *Ibid.* 9 Mar. 22/1 He separates the milk, and between 'cow times' follows the plough.

2. [Cf. Br. slang *cow*, used derogatorily of a woman: see OED(S *sb.*[1] 4.] A term of abuse applied to any person, situation, or thing to which the speaker takes, or pretends to take, exception; often used good-humouredly. Cf. BASTARD *n.*

1864 C.R. THATCHER *Colonial Minstrel* 14 Called each one of them [*sc.* bullocks] an old cow, Whilst blows thick and fast he kept dealing. **1894** *Bulletin* (Sydney) 10 Feb. 8/4 Late hangman Jones did not consider Deeming 'a cow', The Bulletin is informed. **1901** *Ibid.* 7 Dec. 30/2 In the whole range of a bullock-driver's vocabulary there is no word that expresses his blistering scorn so well as 'cow'. **1903** *Advocate* (Burnie) 10 Jan. 3/3 Never called him a 'Boer' nor an 'old cow'. **1904** *Bulletin* (Sydney) 7 Jan. 16/2 The worst that Australians can call anything, living or dead is a cow. N.B.—This is a fair cow of a day—with a violent dust-storm, flies, heat. **1905** *Ibid.* 2 Nov. 15/3 A horse has been known to commit suicide and a dog to run amok after being called a cow. **1911** E. DYSON *Tommy Hawker* 12 The baby .. yelled passionately. 'Pore little cow, he's starvin',' said Snifter. **1913** *Bulletin* (Sydney) 6 Nov. 22/3 The Buckley's Chance mine .. was a cow. **1916** O. HOGUE *Trooper Bluegum at Dardanelles* 168 One Light Horseman was heard to observe as a bomb exploded over his head: 'These Turks are clumsy cows; they'll be killing some of us if they ain't more careful!' **1922** *Bulletin* (Sydney) 12 Oct. 22/3 The emu is a brainless cow. **1924** H.E. RIEMANN *Nor'-West o' West* 95 'Nothing—more nor less—here nor there—than a cow of a life,' said Fakir Bill wrathfully. **1934** 'E.N. SPEER' *Destiny* 236 There's that old cow Dan. Come here, Dan, and have a spot with an Old Contemptible! **1943** *Bulletin* (Sydney) 1 Dec. 12/4 You take cups of tea with George the cook in his 'cow of a galley' under the port paddle-box, where baking bread's 'a proper cow' and cutting down a sheep's 'a cow altogether'. **1955** *Khaki Bush & Bigotry* (1968) 123 He's a cranky, unreasonable, old cow. **1978** H.C. BAKER *I was Listening* 128 It's a cow not to be able to read.

cowal /'kaʊəl/. [Prob. f. a Qld. Aboriginal language.] See quot. 1910.

1882 C. LYNE *Industries of N.S.W.* 213 The homestead .. is situated .. not far from .. the shores of a lake which in this part of the Colony is called, in the language of the aborigines, a 'cowall', or 'cowell'. **1899** *Western Champion* (Barcaldine) 25 July 3/2 Then over a choppy jump up, and across a cowal, and over melon holes, and down a gibber go-down. **1905** *Shearer* (Sydney) 22 Apr. 8/4 All the creeks and cowals are full. **1910** C.E.W. BEAN *On Wool Track* 251 If one gets bogged in a creek or a cowal (which is a small tree-grown, swampy depression often met with in the red country), the other will never leave him there. **1911** —— *'Dreadnought' of Darling* 18 The only place where the road was made was where it happened to cross a 'cowal'—a swamp left in a depression of this low undulating red country. **1934** J. DEVANNY *Out of Such Fires* 220 They [*sc.* the horses] could be trusted not to move far from the little shade afforded by the cowal. **1966** S.J. BAKER *Austral. Lang.* (ed. 2) 40 *Cowal*, a swamp left in a depression of low undulating red country.

cowanyoung /'kaʊənjʌŋ/. *N.S.W.* [Prob. f. a N.S.W. Aboriginal language.] The marine fish *Trachurus declivis* of s. Aust. See also JACK MACKEREL.

1897 *Proc. Linnean Soc. N.S.W.* XXII. 761 The true 'Cowanyoung' being .. the adult Yellowtail (*Trachurus declivis*) or some closely allied species. **1953** *Bulletin* (Sydney) 26 Aug. 12/2 There's a school of scad—or cowanyoung—just outside the breakers. **1965** *Austral. Encycl.* IV. 84 Jack mackerel (*Trachurus novaezelandiae*), the cowanyoung of New South Wales and the horse mackerel of South Australia and Tasmania.

cowry pine, var. KAURI PINE.

cowslip orchid. The terrestrial orchid of s.w. W.A. *Caladenia flava* (fam. Orchidaceae), bearing bright yellow flowers.

1926 J. POLLARD *Bushland Man* 207 They plucked .. cowslip orchids. **1934** W.A. OSBORNE *Visitor to Aust.* 154 No botanical knowledge will be necessary to appreciate the native orchids (.. small spider, cowslip, stag's head). **1967** B.Y. MAIN *Between Wodjil & Tor* 97 Clumps of spider orchids, cowslip orchids and the solitary, yellowish-green Jack-in-the-boxes .. were now in flower.

cozzie, var. COSSIE.

crab. [Shortened form of *crab-shell*: in sense 1 in punning allusion to an artillery shell, in sense 2 a boot.]

1. In the phr. **to draw the crabs.**

a. To attract enemy fire.

1918 *Ca ne fait Rien: 6th Battalion A.I.F.* 8 Mar., J.D. Johnston .. being in command of those horrible people who draw the crabs, the T.M.B. **1920** *Aussie* (Sydney) May 11/1 The fact that the fires, generally synchronising with changing over of Brigades did not 'draw the crabs' on the front line arrangements, seems to disprove the theory of Fritz agents. **1932** L. MANN *Flesh in Armour* 260 The Tommy captain lit a cigarette and I lit my pipe. The young wench reckoned we would draw the crabs. **1943** S.W. KEOUGH *Around Army* 46 Nick off, you Alicks, or you'll be drawin' the crabs. **1943** J. DEVINE *Rats of Tobruk* 65 They backed a truck, which usually drew the 'crabs' (enemy fire) more quickly than anything. **1949** F.J. HARTLEY *Sananandа Interlude* 27 Some of the Australians, not knowing how close the enemy were, became a little too venturesome, and 'drew the crabs'. **1953** G.H. FEARNSIDE *Bayonets Abroad* 222 Our noisy neighbours would 'draw the crabs'; in other words, attract counter-battery gunfire and aerial bombardment. **1966** A.R. CHISHOLM *Familiar Presence* 54 There was often a trench-mortar installed just near our post, and at distressingly frequent intervals it would go off with an ear-shattering bang, until it 'drew the crabs' and was removed to another spot. **1978** H.C. BAKER *I was Listening* 169 What were you trying to do—draw the crabs on the camp?

b. *transf.* To attract unwanted attention, esp. from the police.

1959 *Bulletin* (Sydney) 23 Dec. 16/1 Most shearers are .. down on men who 'draw the crabs' through bringing excessive grog to the huts. **1959** D. HEWETT *Bobbin Up* 41 We don't like 'em under age, draws the crabs. **1963** W.E. HARNEY *To Ayers Rock & Beyond* 23 My mate, who was proud of the fact that he had the inside knowledge on Sunday drinking, whispered into my ear that I should wait for him on a fixed spot at a certain time one Sunday afternoon. 'Don't make it too conspicuous,' he added, 'we don't want to draw crabs on the publican.' **1974** *Bulletin* (Sydney) 16 Mar. 17/2 When Prime Minister Whitlam last week told rural members of the Federal Parliamentary Labor Party that they should have expected the abolition of the superphosphate bounty because it was 'in the Coombs report', he really drew the crabs. **1978** D. STUART *Wedgetail View* 90 Just let any bastard talk about underground accidents in a humorous sort of a fashion, an' he's likely to get put back in his place double quick. It's always on, underground, an' I s'pose no one wants to draw the crabs by talking light an' funny about it.

2. In *pl.* A pair of boots.

1896 *Bulletin* (Sydney) 21 Mar. 27/1 If you wear new crabs—I mean boots—out of the shop, instead of having 'em wrapped up, there's several points gained. **1905** *Ibid.* 13 Apr. 19/1 If a bootless man happens along, as is sometimes the case in Victoria, he is offered a 'tucker' job; and a real good-natured cocky has been known to throw in a pair of his own cast-off 'crabs'. **1919** V. MARSHALL *World of Living Dead* 85 I'll, moochin' round about it, wear the crabs from off me feet.

crabhole. [Fig. use of *crab-hole* a hole made or inhabited by a crab.] **a.** A hole in the ground of small diameter, made by a terrestrial crustacean (see LAND CRAB); a collapsed hole caused by the burrowing of the animal; any hole resembling this. **b.** Chiefly *s. Aust.* A depression in heavy clay soils, a form of GILGAI. Also *attrib.*

1847 *Maitland Mercury* 28 Aug. 4/4 The Wimera [*sic*] country, especially the low part of it, is at present an immense lake. A great part of it is 'crab-hole' country, or 'dead men's graves', which at present look like so many islands. **1848** *Ibid.* 16 Dec. 4/1 A stockman in the employ of Mr Lucas, who is engaged in removing his stock down the Murrumbidgee towards Adelaide, was nearly killed through his horse putting its foot into a crab hole while at full speed, and throwing its rider with considerable force against the root of a tree. **1849** *Aust. Felix Monthly Mag.* 176 The water rapidly runs down the comparatively steep sides of the crabholes and collects in the bottom of them. **1855** W. HOWITT *Land, Labor & Gold* I. 327 Crab-holes, or Frog-holes, as they are called in some districts, from land crabs and frogs frequenting them when they hold water, are small pools or quagmires some few yards across. **1862** J.A. PATTERSON *Gold Fields Vic.* 213 After crossing the crab-holes in the basalt, the road lay over fine plains. **1878** MRS H. JONES *Broad Outlines* 111 Crabholes, as we call them, are not the most delightful undulations in the world. **1889** E. GILES *Aust. twice Traversed* I. 256 Here we found a clay crab-hole. These holes are so-called in parts of Australia, usually near the coasts, where freshwater crabs and crayfish bury themselves in the bottoms of places where rain water often lodges; the holes these creatures make are tubes of two, three, or four feet deep, whose sides and bottom are cemented, and which hold water like a glass bottle; in these tubes they remain till rain again lodges above, when for a time they are released. **1897** J.J. MURIF *From Ocean to Ocean* 163 'Gilguy' denotes small patches of mixed 'Biscay' and 'devil-devil' ground—possibly dried up clay pans. And 'crab-holes' are roundish openings like rabbit burrows, but going straight down in the soil. **1915** A.T.M. JOHNSON *Austral. Life* 102 His horse had accidently plunged into a 'crabhole'. [*Note*] A hole formed by the decay of a stump of a tree, or tuft of prairie grass. **1929** K.S. PRICHARD *Coonardoo* (1961) 181 All day children .. played in the crab-holes, sailing an old square box for a boat. **1939** WADHAM & WOOD *Land Utilization Aust.* 25 These soil areas usually carried forest or consisted of types which are known locally as 'crab holes' or 'puff banks'. In areas of the latter kind, the whole countryside may be thrown into a series of pits or troughs, each of which is two or three feet below the adjacent banks. **1944** C. FENNER *Mostly Austral.* 102 The depressions are miscalled 'crab-holes'. .. Apparently the aborigines recognised them, for the name 'gilgais' has long been applied thereto. .. In New South Wales and Queensland such depressions are called 'melon-holes'. **1977** D. STUART *Drought Foal* 165 The road .. goes across a stretch of crabhole country .. dark soil littered with shapeless lumps of black rock.

Hence **crab-holed, crab-holey** *adjs.*

1874 'REV. F.T.P.' *Thirty-Shilling Horse* 36, I had never seen **crab-holed** land before; but now I saw it, and with much fear and trembling passed through it. **1908** MRS A. GUNN *We of Never-Never* 152 The Open Downs .. one hundred and thirty miles of sun-baked, crab-holed, practically trackless plain. **1872** 'RESIDENT' *Glimpses Life Vic.* 305 There rises before my mind some waste of dreary plains, **crab-holey** and treeless, on which stands a handsome house. **1880** C. PROUD *S.-E. District S.A.* 10 Nearly the whole of Tatiara is 'crabholey' country, with dense forests of mallee growing on it. **1891** 'E.H.' *Advance Aust.* 18, 35 acres only were fit for cultivation, the other portion being inferior, crab-holey, grass land. **1911** 'ROSE BOLDREWOOD' *Complications at Collaroi* 16 He walked slowly across the crab-holey plain. **1944** *Bulletin* (Sydney) 12 Jan. 12/3 Those crab-holey, wind-swept plains. **1972** ANDERSON & BLAKE *J.S. Neilson* 21 He managed to clear six acres for the first season's planting, prepared the crabholey soil with a single furrow plough, and sowed the seed by hand.

crack, *v.*[1] [Prob. spec. use of Br. dial. *crack* to boast, brag: see OED *v.* 6 and EDD *sb.*[1] and *v.* 18.]

1. *intr. Obs.* To feign, pretend. Also *trans.*

1900 *Western Champion* (Barcaldine) 10 Apr. 9/2 'He skied his rockets and cracked a deafun. I guyed a whack. Pads it back here.' .. Now, here is the above translated. .. 'He put his hands in his pocket and would not listen to me. I turned away, walked back.' **1904** L.M.P. ARCHER *Bush Honeymoon* 45, I cracked it was a mate had tied me up for a lark. **1911** E.S. SORENSON *Life in Austral. Backblocks* 258 Experienced diggers usually 'crack hard-up', and the big find is only reported when the responsibility has been passed on to the bank.

2. In the phr. **to crack hardy,** (in times of difficulty or misfortune) to feign equanimity, to put on a brave front, to 'grin and bear it'.

1904 *Emu* IV. 45 A fair number .. were 'cracking hardy'. **1916** C.J. DENNIS *Moods Ginger Mick* 117 Sich wus the dreamin's uv a fool 'oo tried To jist crack 'ardy, an' 'old gloom aside. **1919** E. DYSON *Hello, Soldier* 49 In the West we liked the weather, 'n' we fattened in the mud, Crackin' 'ardy, stewed together, rats an' slurry, men 'n' blood. **1929** 'F. BLAIR' *Digger Sea-Mates* 261 'That's them blanky deck shoes. I kept them on yesterday. Er-cheu! Er-cheu!' 'Crackin' 'ardy,' said he. 'You'll know better next time.' **1935** R.B. PLOWMAN *Boundary Rider* 239 Old Bill himself was a great believer in 'cracking hardy'. **1942** M.L. MACPHERSON *I heard Anzacs Singing* 25 'Crack hardy?' I echoed. 'What does that mean?' 'Grin and bear it,' he translated. 'Don't complain.' **1943** A. DAWES *Soldier Superb* 95 Write bright, cheerful letters to a soldier. .. Be bright, certainly, crack hardy if you like, you can bet your socks he does. **1950** K.S. PRICHARD *Winged Seeds* 185 'I feel it, Pat,' he said quietly. 'You know that. But I've got to crack hardy.' **1956** T. RONAN *Moleskin Midas* 273 Maybe he was cracking hardy himself. Maybe that smile he was talking about yesterday was hiding a few tears. **1971** D. IRELAND *Unknown Industr. Prisoner* 331 They called him Crack Hardy. They meant you might as well crack hardy as put in a sickie. **1973** R. ROBINSON *Drift of Things* 138 He examined my stitched eyebrow and told me there was cow manure in it. 'That should make a good poultice,' I said, cracking hardy. **1979** B. HUMPHRIES *Bazza comes into his Own*, You don't have to act brave or crack hardy with old Bazza McKenzie. I'll ring youse a doctor or something.

crack, *v.*[2] [Spec. use of *crack* to puzzle out, solve: see OED(S *v.* 9 b.]

1. In the phr. **to crack it,** to succeed (in an enterprise, etc.).

1936 W. HATFIELD *Aust. through Windscreen* 199 They had worked alongside men who had 'cracked it' on this field in the early days and kept finds to themselves. **1937** —— *I find Aust.* 165 There were gambling schools . . where you could wager as much as a hundred on the spin of a coin or the roll of a dice. A man 'cracked it' for seven hundred that night. **1951** J. DEVANNY *Travels N. Qld.* 131 'It's not often a bloke gets a chance to see the bower-bird playing in his bower,' Bauman continued, 'but once I cracked it real good.' **1963** L. RICHARDS *Boots & All!* 62 As their last flag was sixteen years ago, Carlton must be wondering when they're going to finally crack it again! **1967** *Kings Cross Whisper* (Sydney) xxxii. 6/3 A lot of mugs have had a go before at this, but 'Whisper' has cracked it for the ridgey didge Australian dictionary. **1973** J. POWERS *Last of Knucklemen* (1974) 75 Tell me somethin' Monk. On the level. You ever cracked it? (*Monk looks embarrassed*) You've never cracked it in your life, you bastard! Have you? **1981** A. WILKINSON *Up Country* 105 Everyone agrees it is splendid to see the 'cocky' (farmer) crack it for a quid for once.

2. *trans. Surfing.* To catch and ride (a wave).

1940 P. KERRY *Cobbers A.I.F.* 10 An' the surf wus runnin' 'owlers—an' the shoots were good 'uns, too When yeh cracked one on the front line, yeh could see right ter the zoo. **1949** C.B. MAXWELL *Surf* 112 Over long years surfmen, swimmers and the 'surfboat happy' . . wondered what it might be like to 'crack the bommy' out there. **1957** 'N. CULOTTA' *They're Weird Mob* 71 Can yer crack a wave? **1963** J. POLLARD *Austral. Surfrider* 68 We cracked a big wave and were riding it when the boat suddenly rocked. **1966** R. MORLEY *Cool Change* 29 I'm not a good mahogany colour, and don't know how to miss a dumper or crack a wave. **1986** *Bulletin* (Sydney) 14 Jan. 30/3 If there were 48 hours in the day I'd be down there cracking a few waves with them.

3. In the phr. **to crack a lay,** (in negative constructions) to 'spill the beans', to 'let on'.

1941 *Air Force News* (Melbourne) 7 June 7 The boys didn't crack a lay—just treated him casual like. **1944** L. GLASSOP *We were Rats* 26 Ya won't crack a lay about playin' against the Royal, will ya? **1968** S. GORE *Holy Smoke* 98 *Crack a lay, not to*, never breathe a word. **1975** G.A.W. SMITH *Once Green Jackeroo* 63 All the time telling me that if I so much as cracked a lay he was gone a bloody million. I never did 'crack a lay', and earned his undying gratitude.

4. In the phr. **to crack on to** (a person), to find (someone) sexually attractive, to pursue with amorous intent.

1955 R. LAWLER *Summer of Seventeenth Doll* (1965) 85 'Just cracked on to the very thing. Piece about eighteen. That young enough for yer?' 'What's she like?' 'Only seen her photo, but she looks terrific.' **1969** A. BUZO *Front Room Boys* (1970) 49 You ought to crack on to her, Vitt, might do all right for yourself. **1979** CAREY & LETTE *Puberty Blues* 5 'Smile!' 'No. He'll think I'm trying to crack onoo him.'

5. In the phr. **to crack a fat**: see FAT *n.*[3]

crack-a-back, *v. Austral. pidgin. S.A. Obs.* [Poss. a. Jangkudjera dial. of Western Desert *kakapaka.*] *intr.* To die.

1867 'S. MCTAVISH' *Chowla* 53 Caracalinga, one of the native chiefs, came to the door of the saloon, and . . spoke as follows:- 'That Plower, he bery bad man; he want um take um ship, make um plenty people cracabac.' **1889** J.J. EAST *Aborigines S. & Central Aust.* 6 It is doubtless this custom of keeping the body so long until it cracks or begins to fall away that the native terms now generally used to signify death, viz., 'tumble down' and 'crack-a-back', originated. **1893** S. NEWLAND *Paving Way* 68 After getting the fish, he told me the old man had 'crack-a-backed' a little before daylight; and as he was a big man in the tribe, he would be paid all the funeral honours befitting his station.

cracker, *n.*[1] [Br. dial. and U.S. *cracker* small cord at the end of a whip which makes it crack.] A strip of silk, horsehair, etc., attached to the tip of a stockwhip to make a cracking sound.

1852 *Four Colonies Aust.* 52 The stockman . . wears a jacket of colonial tweed. . . His whip—the handle about a foot and a half long, and the thong 12 or 14 feet, with a 'cracker' at the end generally made of a piece of silk handkerchief twisted, or better still, of a shred of an old infantry sash—is a terrific weapon. **1859** W. BURROWS *Adventures Mounted Trooper* 133 They close in towards the meeting-place, driving the cattle before them with their 'stock-whips'. . . They are made of hide, plaited into a heavy thong, from nine to fifteen feet in length, the thickest part being about an inch in diameter, at the end of which is a 'tail' or point of green hide, crowned with a cracker of twisted raw silk. **1872** 'RESIDENT' *Glimpses Life Vic.* 62 We were all provided with long stock whips, furnished with loud-sounding crackers. **1873** J.C.F. JOHNSON *Christmas on Carringa* 13 Tommy Banks, his bull-puncher, was over last night for to borrer some silk crackers off of me. **1886** R. HENTY *Australiana* 156 The stock whips are handled, and perhaps fresh crackers put on. **1893** 'OLD CHUM' *Chips* 52, I know of no finer sight than to see a well-mounted stockman 'cutting out' cattle from a mob, the lithe body swaying backwards and forwards and from side to side as the horse gallops, props, turns, and always at the bullock's tail; and that merciless whip, with a short handle about a foot long, heavy and tapering to a point, with a heavy whip some ten or twelve feet long, a long 'tail' and 'cracker' at the end of it, whirling round his head continually, and raining a shower of terrible and well-directed blows upon the beast he is chasing. **1908** W.H. OGILVIE *My Life in Open* 6 Let the heavy stock-whip fall; fourteen feet from keeper to cracker it lies out along the sand. **1913** G. HERVEY *Australs. Yet* 233 Silk Cracker Days!!—the roaring whips are silent now, and dumb The scarlet, stinging, goading strips. **1924** *Bulletin* (Sydney) 24 July 24/4 A neighbour of mine while working cattle had worn the horsehair cracker on his whip back to the knot.

cracker, *n.*[2] [Fig. use of *cracker* thin hard biscuit.]

1. a. A term for the smallest imaginable amount of money; cf. a 'bean', RAZOO. Chiefly in negative contexts.

1934 W.S. HOWARD *You're telling Me!* 300 What about money?. . . We haven't got a cracker. **1941** S.J. BAKER *Pop. Dict. Austral. Slang* 20 *Cracker*, a £1 note. Also, 'without a cracker', penniless, broke. **1942** G. CASEY *It's Harder for Girls* 162 'He's got guts, anyway,' said Sayers. 'I didn't think he was worth a cracker.' **1955** J. MORRISON *Black Cargo* 93 He hardly took a cracker home for a month. **1965** R.H. CONQUEST *Horses in Kitchen* 64 The show went bung; everybody was left without a cracker. **1969** W. DICK *Naked Prodigal* 20, I haven't got a cracker. **1980** *Daily News* (Perth) 22 Dec. 40/1 The pub safe had been knocked off the night before. That left us stranded in Wiluna without a cracker.

b. In the phr. **not worth a cracker,** of no value whatsoever.

1953 T.A.G. HUNGERFORD *Riverslake* 221 Any man without some sort of loyalty to whoever pays his wages isn't worth a cracker. **1973** W. MCNALLY *Man from Zero* 110, I better clear outa the Northern Territory now. . . My life won't be worth a cracker if I don't. **1978** N. HASLUCK *Hat on Letter O* 17 'Tony isn't worth a cracker.' 'He was in the old days. He was pretty tough.'

2. *transf.* A worthless animal.

1946 *Bulletin* (Sydney) 17 July 28/1 Gettin' late in the season for y' t' get sheep now. . . I got three hundred crackers in me river paddock. . . Y' c'n have 'em for nothin'. **1950** *Sydney Morning Herald* 21 July 1/8 A puzzled reader asks: 'What is a cracker?' He sends a report of a cattle sale which says '. . meaty cows to £14; stores from £7 to £10; crackers sold for less'. Well, this sort of cracker is a worn-out cow—bottoms in the cattle world. **1961** J.W. JORDON *Practical Sheep Farming* 21 Older and poorer descriptions in sheep are known as 'crackers', 'tinners' and 'canners'. **1965** E.O. SCHLUNKE *Stores of Riverina* 63 'Ever see such a bunch of old crackers [*sc.* sheep]?' he said, laughing contemptuously. 'Fit for nothing but the meat cannery.' **1982** N. KEESING *Lily on Dustbin* 168 Old cows pretty much beyond their usefulness . . are called 'crackers'.

3. A prostitute; a brothel.

1963 J. NAISH *That Men should Fear* 143 My Aunt Helen worked in a cracker in Munro Street. Worked as a madame or a moll. **1967** *Kings Cross Whisper* (Sydney) xxxiii. 4/4 *Cracker*, a prostitute.

cracker night. [Spec. use of *cracker* firework.] An occasion of (public) festivity celebrated by a display of fireworks, orig. a celebration of Empire Day, later of Commonwealth Day, and now of the Queen's official birthday.

1951 *Bulletin* (Sydney) 2 May 14/3 They . . bought bungers out of their shearing cheques . . and 17 of the boys declared to [*sic*] be 'the crackerest cracker night we ever seen!' **1964** A. STAPLES *Paddo* 83 We tried lighting a fire behind the picture show one Cracker Night, but the manager stopped us. **1965** S.J. BAKER *Ampol Bk. Australiana* 189 'Cracker night' in many parts of Australia is the night of Commonwealth Day (formerly Empire Day), May 24 each year. **1974** M. PAICE *Dolan's Roost* 36 Dobbo couldn't raise much of an interest in cracker night. . . Every year it had been great, saving up to buy fireworks, thinking about the bonfire. **1981** Q. WILD *Honey Wind* 95 One cracker night Thommo and his uncle let off a few plugs of dynamite.

crack of the whip: see FAIR *a.*[1] 3.

cradle, *n.* Gold-mining. [U.S. *cradle* gold-mining apparatus: see Mathews.]

1. A box-like apparatus, mounted on rockers and agitated by hand, in which gold is separated from its surrounding sand, gravel, etc., and retained: see esp. quot. 1852.

1851 *Empire* (Sydney) 20 May 2/2 Now and then a respectable tradesman who had just left his bench or counter, would heave into sight with a huge something in front of his horse which he called a cradle, and with which he was about to rock himself into fortune. ***c* 1852** A. MANN *Goldfields Aust.* 33 A cradle . . is six or eight feet long, open at the foot, and its head has a coarse grate . . fixed upon it. The cradle is placed on rockers. . . The sieve at the head keeps the worse stones from entering the cradle; the current of water . . softens and washes off the earthy matter, which is carried away by the foot of the machine, leaving the gold mixed with sand. **1853** *Bell's Life in Sydney* 22 Oct. 2/4 Cradles, save for domestic purposes, are nearly obsolete, sluicing and 'long toms' carrying the day. **1855** G.H. WATHEN *Golden Colony* 71 The method of washing the earth has been also much modified by time and experience. At first, all was done by the *cradle* or *rocker*, and the tin dish. **1872** 'RESIDENT' *Glimpses Life Vic.* 144, I purchased a cradle and other necessary implements for alluvial digging. **1897** R. NEWTON *Work & Wealth Qld.* 37 The miners set up their cradles, turning the stream a tawny yellow with their wash dirt. **1915** L. ROSS *From Rossiville to Victorian Goldfields* 56 On Bendigo Creek the miners were putting the wash stuff through the 'cradles' to get the gold it contained, and some others were 'panning it'. **1931** W. BARAGWANATH et al. *Guide for Prospectors in Vic.* 87 *Cradle*, a box-like contrivance on rockers for treating washdirt for gold. **1948** M. UREN *Glint of Gold* 78 A cradle is built on rockers. The alluvial is put into a hopper, and the cradle is rocked while the water is poured or pumped into the cradle. The gold is collected on riffles. **1977** B. SCOTT *My Uncle Arch* 9 Dolly it up and run it through a cradle.

2. Comb. **cradle-man, -rocker.**

1851 *Empire* (Sydney) 13 Sept. 151/7 The tents are struck—the tribes of **cradlemen** . . have dispersed. **1852** *Murray's Guide to Gold Diggings* 26 The cradle is placed lengthwise with the river or creek. The *cradle-man*, holding the handle, which gives a sort of barrel-churn motion . . keeps the cradle, when it has been charged with 'dirt', constantly going. **1857** 'ONE WHO KNOWS THEM' *Chinese Question Analyzed* 18 It is well known that the thoughtless way in which puddlers allow their sludge to spread, in districts not frequently visited by wardens, is the cause of a great deal of ground being rendered useless to tub and cradle-men for an indefinite period. **1851** *Guardian* (Hobart) 2 July 4/2 The motley group of diggers and **cradle-rockers** in the creek. **1853** MOSSMAN & BANISTER *Aust. Visited & Revisited* 55 The cradle-rocker of this week was cook next week. **1872** 'TASMANIAN LADY' *Treasures, Lost & Found* 33 Several bucketfuls of soil were conveyed to the creek, where Rupert, excited and restless, established himself as cradle-rocker.

cradle, *v.* [f. prec.] *trans.* To wash (gold-bearing sand, gravel, etc.) in a miner's cradle. Also *absol.*

1851 *Empire* (Sydney) 6 Aug. 19/2 Eaton is to commence cradling on Monday. **1852** J. SHAW *Tramp to Diggings* 254 When gold is mixed with any other rock it is frequently disseminated in such masses as to be recognised at once; but, when mixed with earth, its particles are so small as not to be recognized at all by the naked eye; and, to obtain it, it is necessary to be cradled. **1853** J. SHERER *Gold Finder Aust.* 284 It is good washing dirt, it pays to cradle. **1862** J.A. PATTERSON *Gold Fields Vic.* 12 Wash-dirt had to be carted across the plain to the banks of the river, to be there 'cradled' or 'tommed'. **1896** *Bulletin* (Sydney) 18 Jan. 3/2 When you have to act the Chinaman, a thing you mortal hate, An' cradle out old tailin's—a long day for half-a-weight, Your yarn is slightly altered, an' you think you'll 'give it best'. **1921** W.H. CORFIELD *Reminisc. Qld.* 32 As I puddled the wash-dirt he cradled it. **1932** I.L. IDRIESS *Prospecting for Gold* 100 The dirt left in your race you simply carry to the waterhole and cradle it: 'wet jig' it, or dish it as you prefer.

Hence **cradling** *vbl. n.*

1852 G.B. EARP *Gold Colonies Aust.* 167 Much gold is now lost in Australia by the cradling method. **1852** J.E. ERSKINE *Short Acct. Late Discoveries Gold* 30 The following is a list for a cradling party of four. **1852** F. LANCELOTT *Aust. as it Is* II. 29 The following tools are indispensable to a cradling party.

crammer /ˈkræmə/. *Austral. pidgin.* Also **cramma.** [a. Dharuk *garama.*] *trans.* To steal (something). Also *absol.*

1798 D. COLLINS *Account Eng. Colony N.S.W.* I. 614 *Car-rah-mā*, stealing. **1830** R. DAWSON *Present State Aust.* 75 Black pellow crammer (steal). **1845** D. MACKENZIE *Emigrant's Guide* 220 When a man dies .. a neighbouring tribe is blamed for it, as having '*crammer gourai*' (stolen the fat), by some invisible agency, and thus caused his death. **1849** J.P. TOWNSEND *Rambles & Observations N.S.W.* 102 If he had been a good fellow, and had not 'crammered (stolen) corn'. **1879** 'AUSTRALIAN' *Adventures Qld.* 38 Well, that been *crammer* (steal) my gin good while ago. **1912** J. BRADSHAW *Highway Robbery under Arms* (ed. 3) 21 Do you want to cramma young gin. Suppose you like it, she very good look out yarraman.

cranberry: see *native cranberry* NATIVE *a.* 6 a.

cranky fan. [f. *cranky* erratic + *fan(tail* alluding to the bird's rapid changes of direction as it flies after insects.] The predom. grey, fan-tailed, fly-catching bird *Rhipidura fuliginosa*, occurring widely in Aust., and also in N.Z. and some s. Pacific islands; *white-shafted fantail*, see WHITE *a.*[2] 1 b.

1903 *Emu* III. 27 Dusky Fantail... When flitting from bough to bough it has a rather head-over heels kind of flight; it is from this curious habit it gains the name of 'Cranky Fan'. **1942** E. ANDERSON *Squatter's Luck* 26 Then—pandemonium! Cranky Fan At Whistling Dickie ran, Jostled wrens, throstles, And the twelve apostles! **1981** M. SHARLAND *Tracks of Morning* 80 For producing the prettiest nest of any bird, I give full honours to the white-shafted fantail—the 'cranky fan', as it's commonly known.

crash, *v.* [Abbrev. of Br. naval slang *crash the swede* to get one's head down on the pillow: see Partridge. Used elsewhere but recorded earliest in Aust.] *intr.* To collapse into sleep, esp. following a period of prolonged exertion or alcoholic indulgence.

1943 J.F. MOYES *Scrap-Iron Flotilla* 161 'We crawled into our 'flea bags' and 'crashed'—our first sleep after being on deck continuously for more than thirty-six hours,' a seaman wrote home. **1944** *Buzz: Official Organ H.M.A.S. 'Gympie'* Aug. 3 Crashing in the afternoons. **1945** *Dit* (Melbourne) July 65 The other blokes have 'crashed' on the deck, to be woken when the time comes. **1967** *Kings Cross Whisper* (Sydney) xxxiii. 4/4 *Crash*, to pass out from drinking well but not wisely. **1977** H. GARNER *Monkey Grip* 80, I think I'll just go home and crash.

crawfish, var. CRAYFISH *n.* and *v.*

crawl, *n.* [In joc. allusion to the arm movements of a person swimming the stroke. Used elsewhere but recorded earliest in Aust.] A fast swimming stroke in which the body is prone, the arms reach forward alternately in an overarm action and pull back through the water, and the legs maintain a flutter kick; *Australian crawl*, see AUSTRALIAN *a.* 4. Also *attrib.*

1901 *Arrow* (Sydney) 2 Mar. 4/4 Dick .. will set Hogan and Co. a lively go—especially when he gets fairly moving with that great 'crawl' kick of his. **1910** *Referee* (Sydney) 2 Feb. 8/5 For his dash over 100 yds Healey uses the 'crawl'. **1930** D. HELLMRICH *How to swim Correctly* 14 Dickinson was .. the first swimmer in Australia to use the 'Crawl' in a State distance championship. **1956** T.I. THOMPSON *Pop. Handbk. Swimming* 8 Richard Cavill .. at the turn of this century introduced the vertical thrash of the legs and combined it with the over-arm action in the stroke which was the basis of the modern crawl. **1972** *Swimmer's Handbk.* (S. Austral. Amateur Swimming Assoc.) (rev. ed.) 25 The stroke outlined here is the 'six beat' crawl, used by almost every world champion.

crawl, *v.* [Spec. use of *crawl* to move with a slow or dragging motion: see OED *v.*[1] 2.]

1. *intr.* To move at the pace of grazing sheep: cf. CRAWLER 1 b.

1846 C.P. HODGSON *Reminisc. Aust.* 34 Sheep, under the charge of no piping shepherd, but a rough bearded and rougher clad 'old hand', crawl down the plain. **1961** M. KIDDLE *Men of Yesterday* 60 'Crawling' behind sheep was a job which few except old lags, broken in spirit and diseased in body, accepted kindly.

2. [Used elsewhere but recorded earliest in Aust.] *intr.* To behave (towards someone) in an obsequious manner, to seek to ingratiate oneself.

1880 *Argus* (Melbourne) 9 Feb. 4/6 The Ministers to whom it crawled and truckled have pronounced its condemnation. **1898** *Worker* (Sydney) 12 Nov. 1/2 The old hand voted against the Federal monstrosity while the other fellow crawled to the music of the Barton push! **1902** *Tocsin* (Melbourne) 20 Nov. 2/2 No defence can be offered for crawling to royalty. **1913** H. LAWSON *Triangles of Life* 139 They cannot meet you as man to man, as in Australia; they must either crawl or bully. **1927** K.S. PRICHARD *Brumby Innes* (1974) 93 What are you crawlin' round him for? **1943** *Austral. New Writing* 52 How you going to get that back? Not by crawling, my oath you're not! **1965** *Kings Cross Whisper* (Sydney) Feb. 11/1 Crawl to the boss, dob in your best mate, knock off his wife.

Hence **crawlsomeness** *n.*

1900 H. LAWSON *Over Sliprails* 73 If he grafted harder than we did, we'd be sure to feel indignant about that too, and reckon that it was done out of nastiness or crawlsomeness.

crawler. [Fig. use of *crawler*, prob. orig. a term used by convicts: see quots. 1836 and 1838.]

1. a. *Obs.* An idle or incompetent person; one who avoids work, a loafer or shirker.

1827 *Monitor* (Sydney) 5 July 496/1 Another 'hated a *crawler* from his heart', and would 'work by himself and get half his time to the good'. **1836** C. DARWIN *Jrnl. Researches Geol. & Nat. Hist.* 20 Jan. (1839) III. 527 A 'crawler' is an assigned convict, who runs away, and lives how he can, by labour and petty theft. **1838** *Rep. Select Committee Transportation* 75 The cant name for these among the prisoners themselves was 'the crawlers'. They were scarcely able to work, people whom no settlers wished to employ. **1845** J. TUCKER *Jemmy Green in Aust.* (1955) 62 *Green:* I must sit down and rest a bit. *Holdfast:* I never seed such a rank crawler in all my days. **1848** R. MARSH *Seven Yrs. of my Life* 70 Come along you bloody crawlers, you'll have to walk faster than this tomorrow, with a cart load of stone. **1851** *Empire* (Sydney) 13 Sept. 152/1 They are described as men little likely to be able to keep themselves concealed for any length of time; being what is termed 'crawlers', and men who had never been suspected of courage sufficient to make a bolt. **1853** *Moreton Bay Free Press* 12 Apr. 3/2 The Gold Diggings, and the enormous demand for labour which they create, gradually absorb all the best hard-working men, as well as the *crawlers.* **1857** F. DE B. COOPER *Wild Adventures* 35 The 'blacks' seldom troubled us, and we saw none of them, save a few poor 'crawlers', who hang about the head stations of all the farms. **1869** 'E. HOWE' *Boy in Bush* 83, I was lounging, smoking, in a rocking-chair on a verandah, and could not help feeling that I *must* look very much like 'a crawler'. **1883** E.M. CURR *Recoll. Squatting Vic.* 103 As much of our work was done on horseback, an active man, ill mounted, with difficulty escaped the character of a 'Crawler'. **1894** *Bulletin* (Sydney) 10 Feb. 20/3 It's awful how such crawlers come to shear at Castlereagh. **1895** *Worker* (Sydney) 21 Dec. 6/4 Primed with whisky and the promise of a constant job, the crawler 'volunteered'. **1909** M. FRANKLIN *Some Everyday Folk* 44 The crawlers about these parts nowadays toddle about on bikes or sit like great-grandfathers in sulkies. **1931** 'BRENT OF BIN BIN' *Back to Bool Bool* 265 Flaming crawlers! .. I don't know what to make of the young people to-day. They're born dead. **1934** *Bulletin* (Sydney) 21 Mar. 40/3, I promised myself that if ever I met the crawler I'd flay him alive. **1947** W. LAWSON *Paddle-Wheels Away* 102 A dozen river-men, swearing and shouting, erupted into the bar. 'Where are the 'top-end' crawlers? Come and fight, you dingoes.'

b. *Obs.* A shepherd.

1852 S. MOSSMAN *Voice from Aust.* 13 When .. one of your romantic immigrants .. meets one of our Australian shepherds .. he is rather startled... He encounters a bronze-featured, long-bearded 'crawler', as he is termed. **1854** W. SHAW *Land of Promise* 247 We turn from the proprietors of stock to .. the employed, in colonial lingo called 'crawlers'. **1857** F. DE B. COOPER *Wild Adventures* 50 Fit only for shepherding—the one employment despised by all in a country where the strongest reproach was to be a 'crawler'. **1867** 'CLERGYMAN' *Aust. as it Is* 221 They are now scattered over all the occupied interior, and are mostly debilitated old men, to whom the settlers gave the name of 'old crawlers'. **1878** 'R. BOLDREWOOD' *Ups & Downs* 67 Do I look like a slouchin', 'possum-eating, billy-carrying crawler of a shepherd?

2. *Obs.* A slow-moving animal, usu. one enfeebled by age or disease.

1838 *Colonist* (Sydney) 22 Aug. 2/5 Fat cattle are now not to be seen anywhere—a few 'crawlers' may now and then be observed nipping the leaves of the stunted bush. **1843** *Sydney Morning Herald* 23 Aug. 3/4 The owners of large flocks, who every season, after shearing, select the old and feeble, denominated crawlers. **1849** *N.S.W. Sporting Mag.* 1 Jan. 158 These being what were termed the 'crawlers' of one mob, we concluded the others were not far off. **1857** *Moreton Bay Free Press* 29 Apr. 3/1 There were other horses in the stable, but .. an old 'crawler' occupied the stall next to the damaged side. **1868** C.W. BROWNE *Overlanding in Aust.* 2 The sheep soon lose their condition. Many die, particularly such as are old, or weak, technically termed out here, the 'crawlers'. **1874** C. DE BOOS *Congewoi Correspondence* 20 She's an old milker, and always sticks about the place... This everlastin beast is what we call an old crawler. **1887** A. NICOLS *Wild Life & Adventure* 65 A pen for the 'crawlers'—the halt and the maimed, drafted out from other flocks, and sent here. **1897** *Bulletin* (Sydney) 19 June 28/1 The blue grass is over our rollers, And each one contentedly rides And even the worst of the crawlers, Are stuffing green grass in their hides. **1900** R. BRUCE *Benbonuna* (1904) 66 The bird in question was simply watching a 'crawler' (a sheep too sickly to follow the flock). **1927** 'S. RUDD' *Romance of Runnibede* 159 The stockwhips would ring out, and our voices echo: 'Wherp! Wherp! Woh there... You cock-horned, sneaking crawler!' **1943** *Austral. New Writing* 43 Taking it like a lamb, a crawler!

3. [Used elsewhere but recorded earliest in Aust.] A sycophant.

1888 R. THOMSON *Austral. Nationalism* 122 The cause of these city frauds .. is that you put snobs, title-hunters, society crawlers, and lovers of Tite Barnacles, and of Tite Barnacleism into power. **1891** *Truth* (Sydney) 17 May 2/4 The long list of political crawlers who have sold the people's liberties for the bribes which your exalted position permits you to offer them. **1895** *Worker* (Sydney) 26 Jan. 2/5 The servile station crawlers grin and point and sneer at you. **1898** *Bulletin* (Sydney) 30 July 32/3 Another undesirable specimen is the 'crawler'. Always carrying yarns to the boss about the other men. **1900** *Truth* (Sydney) 20 May 5/5 S is for sergeants, the crawlers brigade. **1901** *Ibid.* 28 Apr. 5/4 (*heading*) The dear Duke. The crawler's carnival. A great grovel. **1910** H. LAWSON *Lett.* (1970) 184 When will they be able to run .. the *Lone Hand* without the assistance of a—well—a crawler and a toady? **1955** D. NILAND *Shiralee* 162 Hammer one nail in a piece of timber and the boss thought you were a slacker.

Hammer two, and your mates slurred you as a crawler. **1968** S. Gore *Holy Smoke* 46 '*O King, live for ever*,' they said, bein' real crawlers. **1971** J. O'Grady *Aussie Etiket* 19 Don't offer to buy him a drink, unless he buys you one first. Otherwise you could be called a 'crawler', or a 'brown nose'. **1973** R. Blair *President Wilson* (1974) 50 *House:* But you like Colonel House. *Edith:* Not necessarily. He's a crawler, or I imagine he is.

4. *Obs.* A snake.

1918 *Bulletin* (Sydney) 12 Dec. 24/2 Dunno if 'H.V.E.' has been sufficiently observant when out snaking. He . . expresses a doubt that the bunda-bunda is a Monaro (N.S.W.) crawler. **1929** P.R. Stephensen *Bushwhackers* 23 Sobbing with a hatred of crawlers; sobbing with the death-lust, they exulted together, thumping the earth-thing.

crawling, *ppl. a.* and *vbl. n.* [f. Crawl *v.*]

A. *ppl. a.* Slow-moving; indolent.

1852 S. Sidney *Three Colonies* 309 Above all, he scorns a 'crawling shepherd'. **1860** 'Lady' *My Experiences in Aust.* 186 The Australian stock-keeper . . has a hearty contempt for . . his more natural brethren, whom he is pleased to denominate 'crawling shepherds'. **1878** 'R. Boldrewood' *Ups & Downs* 8 As for sheep, I hate them, and I hate shepherds, lazy crawling wretches! **1883** E.M. Curr *Recoll. Squatting Vic.* 44 They had never seen . . such a lot of 'crawling sheep'. **1899** *Worker* (Sydney) 21 Jan. 8/1 You hear times out of number about the mean, crawling cockie.

B. *vbl. n.* Obsequiousness.

1891 D. Ferguson *Vicissitudes Bush Life* 152 He regarded it as a sign of toadyism or 'crawling'. **1955** R. Lawler *Summer of Seventeenth Doll* (1965) 84, I don't mind sayin' I'm sorry to him, but that's all the crawling he's gunna get. **1965** *Kings Cross Whisper* (Sydney) Dec. 7/2 Some people might think it's crawling to give a present to the turn and toss, but depends on the present.

cray. Abbrev. of Crayfish *n.*

1909 *Bulletin* (Sydney) 1 Apr. 43/1 The crays when they're past prayin' fer, takes care to let y' know they're due fer burial. Oysters is different. **1935** P. Lawlor *Confessions of Journalist* 216 To him a crayfish became a cray only when it poked its nippers through the clumsy parcel under a drunk's arm. **1945** M. Raymond *Smiley* 7 'She'll roar you up a treat,' insisted Blue. 'She won't if she gits them bonzer crays. Give us some string and bait.' **1956** E. Lambert *Watermen* 46 'Who hasn't bought a ticket for the cray?' he shouted at the bar. **1970** I. Gall *Fishing for Fun of It* 72 Queensland fresh waters are teeming with yabbies, and by that I mean lobsters or crays. **1971** D. Williamson *Removalists* (1972) 27, I can . . grab m'self a cray and half a dozen tubes, . . sit m'self down in front of the box and watch the wrestling.

crayfish, *n.* Formerly also **crawfish.** [Transf. use of *crayfish* any of several fresh-water and marine crustaceans.] Any of several elongated decapod crustaceans, marine or fresh-water, esteemed as food. See also Lobster, *painted crayfish* Painted.

1770 J. Cook *Jrnls.* 23 Aug. (1955) I. 394 Cockles and Clams of Several sorts, many of these that are found upon the Reefs are of a Prodigious size; Craw-fish, Crabs, Musles [*sic*], and a variety of other sorts. **1784** G.W. Anderson *New Collection Voyages* 70 Variety of fish is supplied by the seas in these parts, among which are mullets, cray-fish and crabs. **1824** *Hobart Town Gaz.* 3 Dec., The prisoner had sold the prosecutor two craw-fishes. **1833** J. Backhouse *Extracts from Lett.* (1838) ii. 11 Some of the women went into the water among the large sea-tangle, to take crayfish. **1834** G. Bennett *Wanderings N.S.W.* I. 214 In this colony, cray-fish abound in the sea, and lobsters in the river. **1835** *Sydney Herald* 9 Apr. 3/2 The native lobster or crayfish, will present as good a treat in Sydney, as the most fastidious epicure could hope for in London. **1837** J. Backhouse *Extracts from Lett.* (1839) v. 20, I noticed some cray-fish in the river, of a dark colour, and about the size of those in England. **1839** J. Stephens *Land of Promise* 41 The river Torrens abounds in craw-fish. **1847** G.F. Angas *Savage Life & Scenes* I. 90 For eight months in the year they gather crayfish, which they catch with their toes, and immediately crush the claws, to prevent being bitten. **1854** W. Howitt *Boy's Adventures* 78 There are craw-fish here of a light blue, with rows of prickles all down their backs, or rather down their tails. . . They are large—quite as large as the largest craw-fish in England. **1858** C.R. Thatcher *Colonial Songster* (rev. ed.) 53 The Australian people here brag of their crawfish. **1909** G. Smith *Naturalist in Tas.* 108 In Tasmania the term crayfish is applied to the marine Rock Lobster, . . the term Lobster to the Freshwater Crayfish. **1911** *Bulletin* (Sydney) 30 Mar. 44/2 Some of the tanks are so large that you can spend hours round them shooting ducks. . . In most of them youngsters catch crawfish. **1912** Spencer & Gillen *Across Aust.* 65 The crayfish is identical with the one, which, in Victoria, is known as the yabbie. **1946** T. Aston *Mem.* 19 The boys filled buckets with yabbies or crayfish. **1962** N. Monkman *Quest Curly-Tailed Horses* 185 Out came a gorgeous crayfish, the painted lobster, as it is called by the fishermen of the reef. **1972** B. Reed *Mr Siggie Morrison* 93 Oh, crayfish is Aussie for lobster. I think. Yes, and sometimes you sell lobsters to us and sometimes we sell our crayfish to you. Then you call them lobsters and we call them crays. **1983** *Canberra Chron.* 5 Oct. 19/2 A large dam 'stocked with . . freshwater crayfish (marron)'. **1983** *Fishing Information & Services Handbk.* 5 Rock lobsters (crayfish) are measured along the length of the carapace.

crayfish, *v.* Also **crawfish.** [f. prec.] *intr.* To move in the manner of a crayfish; to retract or 'back down', to act in a cowardly fashion.

1894 H. Lawson *Short Stories* 89 All the other chaps crawfished up and flung themselves round the corner and sidled into the bar after Dave. **1900** —— *Over Sliprails* 63 The steamer was just crayfishing away from a mud island, where she had tied up. **1908** *Truth* (Sydney) 22 Mar. 10/7 The Federal Postmaster-General has 'crayfished'—done the crabwalk, as it were—concerning the alleged confidential conversation. **1915** *Ibid.* 7 Mar. 7/1 In the parlance of political slang, you have been pronounced 'a cock-tail, for crawfishing to Fisher'. **1929** G. Meudell *Pleasant Career Spendthrift* 103 One after another of the investors 'cray-fished' out of the ventures, and we had to return their money! **1930** K.S. Prichard *Haxby's Circus* 194 A bloke . . thought I was goin' to hit him, crayfished . . lay down on the floor, and said I couldn't hit a man when he was down. **1936** W. Hatfield *Big Timber* 242 Dale was his weight, only every ounce of him was bone and sinew. . . He might have 'crayfished' but for the crowd.

Hence **crayfishing** *vbl. n.*

1931 V. Palmer *Separate Lives* 194 The truth, the whole truth, and no cray-fishing, so help me God. **1966** H. Gye *Father clears Out* 203 Such hedging and crayfishing about only postponed the dread business.

creamy. [f. *cream(-coloured* + -Y.]

1. A cream-coloured horse; *spec.* a palomino.

1887 *Tibbs' Pop. Song Bk.* 28 He likes all lively hacks, He's very partial to the creamies. **1902** H. Fletcher *Waybacks Town & Home* 105 Der yer mind Jack Clark comin' ter our place er ridin' er bag o' bones he called er creamy? **1951** J. Devanny *Travels N. Qld.* 103 The breeding of Palominos—otherwise . . 'creamies'—for show purposes was undertaken. **1981** G. Mitchell *Bush Horseman* 21 Palominos and buckskins were called 'creamies'.

2. A person of part-Aboriginal and part-white descent; freq. *spec.* (see quot. 1941). Also as adj.

1912 *Bulletin* (Sydney) 11 Apr. 14/4 Fully 50 per cent. of the children are half-castes—'creamies', as the blacks call them. **1941** *Argus Weekend Mag.* (Melbourne) 15 Nov. 1/3 Slang applied to the aborigines occurs, of course, only in the Far North, where the natives are commonly seen. They are referred to invariably as 'Boongs'. Half-castes are 'halfies', and quarter-castes 'creamies'. **1947** O. Griffiths *Darwin Drama* 34 Women were scarce in Darwin and it was said that, to the lonely sailor, soldier and airman, the 'boongs' and 'creamies' got whiter every day. **1956** T. Ronan *Moleskin Midas* 262 A dozen creamies at the missions and more coming on down the camp all using his name, but he wouldn't let any of them claim him as his father. **1960** J. Walker *No Sunlight Singing* 31 Some o' these creamy bitches . . put on airs as if they was white. **1973** D. Wolfe *Brass Kangaroo* 27 She was a half or three quarter caste aboriginal I thought. We called them 'creamies'. **1975** X. Herbert *Poor Fellow my Country* 52 Now, I'm using the term Black Velvet not simply to apply to fullblood women, but any of obvious Aboriginal strain, 'yeller girls' or 'creamy pieces', as they're called, half and quarter.

creek. Also (rarely) **crick.** [Br. *creek* a narrow inlet in the coastline, an estuary, but also an inlet or short arm of a river, applied in U.S. and other former British colonies to a tributary river or stream: see OED(S *sb.*[1] 2 b. The earliest Austral. uses retain the Br. meaning (see quot. 1793).]

1. A watercourse, esp. a stream or tributary of a river; in Australian use often varying widely in application: see esp. quots. 1805, 1833, 1848, 1849, 1903, and 1955.

[**1793** J. Hunter *Hist. Jrnl. Trans. Port Jackson* 489 It will also be necessary . . to make a dam across the creek, in order to prevent the tides making the water brackish at the lower part of it.] **1795** D. Collins *Acct. Eng. Colony N.S.W.* (1798) I. 422 The husband . . sold a very good farm . . on a creek of the river. **1799** *Ibid.* (1802) II. 185 The creek runs winding between two steep hills, and ends in a chain of ponds. **1804** *HRA* (1921) 3rd Ser. I. 584 There is a small Creek . . that discharges the Water of a beautiful Fall at its head into the main River. **1805** *Ibid.* (1915) 1st Ser. V. 586 A Creek—It's locally applied to all brooks and small Rills that are deeply seated in the Ground and the Sides or Banks very Steep. **1819** *Hobart Town Gaz.* 6 Feb., A Creek, supplied with good water throughout the year, runs through the Farm. **1827** *Monitor* (Sydney) 30 Aug. 619/1 In the interior . . the supply of water depends on the creek and 'water holes'. **1833** W.H. Breton *Excursions* 98 A creek is commonly the bed of a stream, which being partially exhausted during the dry weather, forms only an occasional pond or water-hole. **1834** G. Bennett *Wanderings N.S.W.* I. 197 Crossed a small, insignificant rivulet: this was the river (or, according to the colonial vocabulary, 'creek') which empties itself into the Shoalhaven Gullies. **1844** L. Leichhardt *Jrnl. Overland Exped. Aust.* 10 Oct. (1847) 11 We came to a fine running creek . . and . . reached a creek—which, at this time of the year, is a chain of lagoons. **1846** *Tasmanian Jrnl. Nat. Sci.* II. 132 The term creek . . very generally applied in Tasmania to rivulets. **1848** H.W. Haygarth *Recoll. Bush Life* 127 A creek, which in most other parts of the world signifies a small inlet or arm of the sea, is very differently understood in Australia, where it generally means a valley, or any open space in the forest, with or without water. The use of the word in the colony is in fact very vague, and might well mislead a stranger. 'Which is the way?'—'*Down* the creek.' 'Is Mr so and so at home?'—'No; he's just gone *up* the creek.' 'How shall I find the station?'—'Oh, you can't miss it, it's *in* the creek.' **1849** C. Sturt *Narr. Exped. Central Aust.* I. 7 It may be necessary to warn my readers that a creek in the Australian colonies, is not always an arm of the sea. The same term is used to designate a watercourse, whether large or small, in which the winter torrents may or may not have left a chain of ponds. Such a watercourse could hardly be called a river, since it only flows during heavy rains, after which it entirely depends on the character of the soil, through which it runs, whether any water remains in it or not. **1853** W. Westgarth *Vic.* 219 Ever and anon as you pass along the bush-tracks of this colony, you come to what is called 'a gully', which is simply a hollow, the bed of some temporary rivulet, called by colonial custom a creek. **1861** —— *Aust.* 221 Although they have mostly been denominated 'rivers' by the company's surveyors, there is not one deserving of more than the ordinary appellation of 'creek'. **1862** R. Henning *Lett.* (1952) 45 We had to cross a dreadful creek. These creeks are the great plague of Australian travelling. They are deep river-beds, sometimes narrow, sometimes very wide, often with the sides nearly perpendicular. **1872** Mrs E. Millett *Austral. Parsonage* 43 In this spot the word 'creek' meant only a valley, at the bottom of which ran a stream. **1883** W.J. O'Donnell *Diary Exploring Exped.* 29 Apr. (1884) 5 There is no water for 12 miles down this creek. **1903** *Bulletin* (Sydney) 7 Mar. 16/3 Once watched a creek (a bend of the Lachlan) 'come down', as the bush saying is. It had been dry for months. **1905** *Steele Rudd's Mag.* (Brisbane) Mar. 291 'Flannagan's Only Shirt' sent away in a bucket with a bag over it to be washed at the 'crick'. **1929** C.E.W. Bean *Official Hist. Aust. 1914–18* III. 377 They had found a ditch or 'creek' of stagnant water, waist deep. **1936** F. Clune *Roaming round Darling* 54 An old nincompoop, rotting on a horse, called out for our information: 'You're in the crick.' **1948** R. Raven-Hart *Canoe in Aust.* 22 Our first camp was up a very small creek. . . We should call it a brook in England: it is curious that the American 'creek' should be the Australian word, often pronounced 'crick' as in America. **1955** D. Clark *Boomer* 38 The mother kangaroo drank at a billabong—a long, clear creek fringed by reeds.

1958 J.R. SPICER *Cry of Storm-Bird* 43 This country was interlaced with gullies and creeks with rough, rock-strewn bottoms which had to be taken slowly as the truck lurched from side to side... At one of these creeks there was a waterhole. **1965** *Tracks we Travel* 128, I said creek, but I meant river. **1978** D. STUART *Wedgetail View* 42 The creek .. ran its dry course between the Government buildings and the minute town. **1983** *Canberra Chron.* 19 Jan. 18/1 The stream scene is still fairly grim, with the exception of the very highest mountain creeks and some of the larger coastal streams.

2. Comb. **creek bank, bed, crossing, flat.**

1849 A. HARRIS *Emigrant Family* (1967) 76 The slight sweep of a deep and precipitous **creek-bank. 1935** R.B. PLOWMAN *Boundary Rider* 172 A sudden drop over the washed away edge of a creek-bank found a weak spot in the old buggy. **1956** T. RONAN *Moleskin Midas* 80 In the past month Yates had had two acres of creekbank soil enclosed by a chock-and-log fence. **1978** B. ST. A. SMITH *Spirit beyond Psyche* 166 They lie dormant in the flood debris along the creekbank during winter. **1847** A. HARRIS *Settlers & Convicts* (1953) 134 He was down in a deep **creek-bed** in the mountain. **1907** *Emu* VII. 97 A party of three Grey-tailed Thickheads .. entertained us with their tuneful whistling among the young gums just across the creek-bed. **1936** C. CHEWINGS *Back in Stone Age* p. xiv, The creek-bed, occupying nearly the full width of the pass, was filled with high reeds and deep waterholes. **1955** *Meanjin* 166 Horse and man lurched along the creekbed. **1959** D. STUART *Yandy* 88 He sank the well in the creekbed for soakage water. **1978** —— *Wedgetail View* 61 On rough guttery sidlings and over stony creekbeds. **1853** W. WESTGARTH *Vic.* 143 Many .. vexatious gullies, **creek-crossings**, and patches of swamp, might .. have been greatly improved. **1917** A.B. PATERSON in C. Semmler *World of Banjo Paterson* (1967) 255 A nasty creek-crossing here required Alfred's attention. **1980** *Ecos* xxiii. 29/2 Each culvert or creek-crossing drains an area that looks similar to the last or to one a few kilometres back. **1897** J.J. MURIF *From Ocean to Ocean* 96 A wide, fertile and picturesque **creek-flat**, studded with gums. **1935** DAVISON & NICHOLLS *Blue Coast Caravan* 27 The dark brown of newly-turned fallow in the creek flats. **1978** *Ecos* xvii. 26/1 Most of the trees have been planted on creek flats.

3. Special Comb. **creek claim,** a mining claim which includes, or is confined to, the bed of a creek; **gum,** any of several trees of the genus *Eucalyptus* (fam. Myrtaceae), esp. *E. camaldulensis* (see RED GUM 1); **oak,** *river oak*, see RIVER 2.

1869 R.B. SMYTH *Gold Fields & Mineral Districts* 608 ***Creek claim***, a claim which includes the bed of a creek. **1884** *N.T. Times Almanac* (1886) 84 Any holder of a river or creek claim may construct dams within his claim for the purpose of turning water into his flood-race. **1944** M.W. PEACOCK *Dead Puppets Dance* 22 I've only got a creek claim. If I had a bank claim—including the bank as well as the bed of the creek—I'd sink a shaft. **1891** *Proc. Linnean Soc. N.S.W.* VI. 403 *E. rostrata*, var. '**Creek Gum**', Tarella, Wilcannia. **1898** D.W. CARNEGIE *Spinifex & Sand* 174 In the centre ran a line of large white gums (Creek gums, *Eucalyptus rostrata*), the sure sign of a creek. **1901** *Proc. Linnean Soc. N.S.W.* XXVI. 136 *E[ucalyptus] gunnii* .. was called 'Yellow Gum' on a label by the late Rev. Dr Woolls over 40 years ago... It is also called 'Creek Gum'. **1922** 'J. BUSHMAN' *In Musgrave Ranges* 59 Here and there a sprawling stunted creek gum. **1928** B. CRONIN *Dragonfly* 25 He sought unhopefully for a soakage among the paper-barks and creek gums. **1950** G. FARWELL *Land of Mirage* 212 There are some grand and peaceful waterholes down-river, sheltered by white-boled creek gums and coolabahs. **1872** C.H. EDEN *My Wife & I in Qld.* 190 The time being chiefly occupied .. in making yokes which are formed from the **creek oaks** (*Casuarina quadrivalvis*). **1901** H. LAWSON *Joe Wilson & his Mates* 60 The creek oaks have rougher barked trunks, like English elms, but are much taller.

crescent nail-tailed wallaby: see NAIL-TAILED WALLABY.

crested, *ppl. a.* In special collocations: **crested bell-bird,** the bird *Oreoica gutturalis* of arid and semi-arid Aust., the mature male having a black crest; BELL-BIRD 2; **bronze-wing,** *crested pigeon* (a); **hawk,** the bird of prey *Aviceda subcristata* of n. and e. Aust.; **pigeon,** a pigeon with a crest, esp. **(a)** the wide-spread, predom. grey *Geophaps lophotes*; **(b)** FLOCK PIGEON b.

1896 B. SPENCER *Rep. Horn Sci. Exped. Central Aust.* II. 74 *Oreoica cristata*, **Crested Bell-bird** .. is one of our most widely dispersed birds. **1932** *Bulletin* (Sydney) 11 May 21/3 The tinkling note of the bell-birds, whether the bell-miner of the coastal regions or the crested bell-bird of the interior. **1945** C. BARRETT *Austral. Bird Life* 177 An accomplished ventriloquist .. the crested bell bird. **1975** X. HERBERT *Poor Fellow my Country* 465 The crested bell-birds showed him where the grasshoppers were lurking. [**1854 crested bronze-wing:** J. CAPP *Stanford's Emigrant's Guides* 40 There are about thirty varieties of the pigeon, among which is the crested bronze-winged.] **1945** C. BARRETT *Austral. Bird Life* 64 The crested bronzewing .. usually called 'topknot pigeon'. **1844** J. GOULD *Birds of Aust.* (1848) I. Pl. 25, *Lepidogenys subcristatus* .. **Crested Hawk. 1945** C. BARRETT *Austral. Bird Life* 35 The crested hawk .. is an uncommon species. **1980** *Sydney Morning Herald* 10 June 2/9 Terania Creek forest supports an equally distinctive group of animals. These include .. the Crested Hawk. **1823** J. LATHAM *Gen. Hist. Birds* VIII. 106 **Crested Pigeon** .. at the nape of several elongated, narrow, black feathers, some three inches or more in length, giving the appearance of the crest of the Coly... Inhabits New-Holland. **1838** *Southern Austral.* (Adelaide) 21 July 4/3, I saw .. the crested pigeon of the marshes. **1847** G.F. ANGAS *Savage Life & Scenes* I. 100 When the bronze-wing and crested pigeons come at dusk to drink, the nets are let go. **1849** *Adelaide Miscellany* 11 Oct. 50/1 Two pretty little crested pigeons fluttered out. **1871** *Austral. Town & Country Jrnl.* (Sydney) 8 Apr. 431/4 *The crested pigeon.* This bird is of a large size, its body slate colour, .. the crest being a rich copper colour. **1929** A.H. CHISHOLM *Birds & Green Places* 47 The crested pigeon of the whistling wings. **1973** V. SERVENTY *Desert Walkabout* 36 Ken had to make do with .. two crested pigeons and damper.

crib. [Br. dial. *crib* food, something to eat between meals: see OEDS 6 b.]

1. A light meal or refreshment, packed to be eaten during a break from work; the break itself. Also *attrib.*

1890 A.S. DAY *Democrat* 17 What say about crib time? Ye're right, Bob. The billy and chuck's on that 'ere log. Crib, ho! below! **1892** *Truth* (Sydney) 5 June 4/5 Uniformed minions .. who are supposed to sweep out the offices and chase the flies off the clerks' cribs. **1901** M. VIVIENNE *Travels in W.A.* 249, I happened to be at the Lady Shenton Mine at 'crib' time, and after 'crib' the miners went out with their football .. before beginning work again. **1906** *Bulletin* (Sydney) 6 Dec. 16/2 Each man is supposed to cook for himself .. and carry water and crib to work. **1908** *Ibid.* 8 Oct. 39/2 Kitty Coudray had finished licking the raspberry jam off her crib paper. **1916** A. WILSON *Lays & Tales of Mines* 87 I'll send down a bit of 'crib' at 8 o'clock to keep you going 'til 'knock-off'. **1928** N.F. SPIELVOGEL *Affair at Eureka* 13 Groups of miners still in clay-stained working clothes squatted on the ground, eating their evening 'crib'. **1935** J.K. EWERS *Fire on Wind* 109 At half-past four Grace brought down their crib, and work ceased for ten minutes. **1943** *Coast to Coast 1942* 66 Your mother was packing a couple of apple-pies in your crib. **1954** *Coast to Coast 1953–54* 37 Crib over, the men rolled cigarettes. **1969** P. ADAM SMITH *Folklore Austral. Railwaymen* 5 He sat for midday dinner in the sun with a billy of tea and a hunk of bread and salt beef for crib. **1978** M. PAICE *Shadow of Wings* 115 Although I was near enough to go home for lunch I was carrying my crib in a paper bag.

2. Comb. **crib bag, box, can, house, hut, room, time, tin.**

1898 E. DYSON *Below & on Top* 56 He crowded his usual two-pound 'plaster' of cold fried bacon and bread into his **crib-bag. 1911** *Bulletin* (Sydney) 20 Apr. 14/3 Old Hands carry a cheese-rind in their crib bags. **1937** *Ibid.* 27 Oct. 20/1 Queer things turn up in woolbales... Sometimes thermos-flasks and crib-bags. **1945** G. CASEY *Downhill is Easier* 11 Men on push-bikes with their crib-bags dangling from their handlebars. **1950** —— *City of Men* 282 They came between the dumps and over the dumps, with .. empty dynamite cloth crib-bags swinging as they walked. **1947** *Bulletin* (Sydney) 16 July 29/1 His **crib-box** was perched high in a gum-tree. **1968** K. DENTON *Walk around my Cluttered Mind* 20 At crib-time .. I hadn't the strength to unclip my crib-box or unscrew the top of the vacuum-flask. **1957** *Westerly* i. 33 Miners drinking **Crib cans** clinking. **1965** H. ATKINSON *Reckoning* 25 Men sitting about in the dust-hung darkness, their crib-cans open. **1948** G. FARWELL *Down Argent Street* 67 The **cribhouse** is habitually a place for relaxation... It provides a cleaner lunch-place than the stopes. **1986** *Bulletin* (Sydney) 8 Apr. 36/1 All the men will have access to modern air conditioned **crib huts** close to proper (porcelain) toilet and shower facilities. **1949** *Ibid.* 12 Jan. 29/4 Numerous rats .. overran the **crib-room** on 54 level. **1979** *Sydney Morning Herald* 26 July 1/1 When we came to the crib room—where we have our tea break—we saw the bodies. **1890 crib time** [see sense 1.] **1894** *Western Champion* (Barcaldine) 6 Feb. 3/3 It was nearly 'crib-time' before they got the four shots ready for firing. **1908** *Bulletin* (Sydney) 23 Jan. 15/2 The flies .. used to shut out the sun. This was pleasant while working, but at crib times and at breakfast it was troublesome. **1930** *Ibid.* 20 Aug. 20/2 Crib-time came and .. I had some bread and cheese. **1941** *Ibid.* 8 Jan. 16/2 The fourth is the heaviest-lidded hour of them all. Then the half-hour crib-time. **1956** *Ibid.* 15 Aug. 13/1 'How big is the town you come from?' asked one of the hands .. at crib-time. **1965** H. ATKINSON *Reckoning* 25 Me and the boys want to hear her crib-time tomorrer. **1973** J. WILLIAMS *Tom Collins* 28 *Rigby's Romance* was read eagerly by the miners, discussed during crib-time. **1919** *Smith's Weekly* (Sydney) 8 Mar. 9/5 A pet method is to dump a case of whisky or wine on the wharf so darned hard that a few bottles break. What comes out of the box at the corners belongs to the wharfie, and is caught in a **crib-tin. 1948** G. FARWELL *Down Argent Street* 7 An isolated miner, .. crib tin slung on his handlebars. **1964** P. ADAM SMITH *Hear Train Blow* 127 I'd be hauled up .. into the guard's van and given the run of the crib tins while we rattled homewards.

crick, var. CREEK.

crim, *n.* [Abbrev. of *criminal*, prob. orig. U.S.: see OEDS.] One convicted of a crime. Also *attrib.*

1953 K. TENNANT *Joyful Condemned* 293 When Chigger honoured any crim in the gaol, that was the accolade. **1957** J. WATEN *Shares in Murder* 62 Nobs and crims often rub shoulders. **1967** D. HEWETT *This Old Man* (1976) p. xvii, Snow is no Marxist, but an irreverent anarchistic ex-crim. **1970** J. CLEARY *Helga's Web* 22 You're making it pretty bloody crook, ain't you? Asking me to think like a crim! **1978** H.C. BAKER *I was Listening* 17 Prisoners were crims, even to themselves. **1983** *Open Road* Apr. 7/1 What I hadn't reckoned on is that drink-driving is a criminal offence. I was a crim—not just another blundering motorist.

crim, *v.* [f. prec.] *intr.* To engage in criminal or questionable activities. Also *trans.*, to steal.

1968 *Coast to Coast 1968–70* 81 You've been crimming around just this side of the law for years. **1978** H. HAENKE *Bottom of Birdcage* 39, I give a bunch of 'em y' last birthday... Yair, but y' crimmed 'em from the cemetery so it don't count.

crimean shirt. *Obs.* [f. the name of the Black Sea peninsula, prob. with reference to the warmth of the material.] A coloured flannel shirt formerly popular amongst workers in the bush.

1864 R. HENNING *Lett.* 25 Dec. (1952) 80 Hatless and bootless and trouserless and arrayed only in a Crimean shirt. **1865** *Ibid.* 18 Apr. (1952) 83 Jimmy being gorgeous in new white trousers .. a scarlet Crimean shirt and scarlet cap. **1871** *Austral. Town & Country Jrnl.* (Sydney) 13 May 582/3 Nine crimean shirts, and other articles stolen therefrom. **1879** *Kelly Gang* 124 His dress .. consisted of .. an ordinary flannel singlet, covered by an olive-green Crimean shirt; trousers of a kind known .. as 'coloured moles'. **1887** 'COMMERCIAL TRAVELLER' *Diary Three Months Trip Qld.* 22 An elderly bushman, clad in moleskins and crimean shirt, sat down to the piano. **1895** *Worker* (Sydney) 29 Jun. 4/1 One of those slight, active, little fellows whom we used to see in cabbage-tree hats, Crimean shirts, 'strapped' trousers, and 'lastic sided boots. **1911** A. WRIGHT *Gamblers' Gold* (1923) 70 He wore a Crimean shirt, moleskin trousers with bowyangs round each leg .. and a black billy can was by his side. **1918** A.M. MOORE *Autumn Grey* 45 His gaunt frame clothed in moleskin and soft Crimean shirt. **1936** J.E. HAMMOND *Western Pioneers* 42 The 'Crimean' shirts were made of flannel.

crimson, *a.* Used as a distinguishing epithet in the names of flora and fauna: **crimson chat,** the small nomadic bird *Epthianura tricolor* of mainland Aust., the breeding male having crimson, brown, and white plumage; Tricoloured chat; **finch,** the finch *Neochmia phaeton* of n. Aust., the mature male having predom. crimson plumage; *blood finch,* see Blood; **-flowering gum,** see Flowering gum; **rosella (lowry, parakeet, parrot),** the red and blue parrot *Platycercus elegans* of e. Aust.; *red lory,* see Red *a.* 1 b; **-winged parrot,** *red-winged parrot,* see Red *a.* 1 b.

1943 C. Barrett *Austral. Animal Bk.* 274 The **crimson chat** (*E[pthianura] tricolor*) has a wide mainland distribution, but is absent from North Queensland. It is a beautiful little bird, with nomadic habits. **1965** *Austral. Encycl.* II. 334 The beautiful crimson chat . . is distinguished by the colour from which it gets its name. **1984** M. Blakers et al. *Atlas Austral. Birds* 569 The Crimson Chat lives in acacia scrub and other open sparsely-vegetated areas of the inland, specially near salt lakes. **1842** J. Gould *Birds of Aust.* (1848) III. Pl. 83, *Estrelda phaëton* . . **Crimson Finch.** **1902** *Emu* II. 29 A few days ago I found a nest of the Crimson Finch. **1964** M. Sharland *Territory of Birds* 78 Some Crimson Finches came inquisitively into the pandanus. **1843** [**crimson rosella**] A. McEvey *J. Cotton's Birds Port Phillip* 8 June (1974) 36 Shot two crimson lowries or broadtails Platycercus Pennantii. **1907** *Emu* VII. 96 Crimson Parrakeet . . one of those birds that has been pushed back by settlement. **1932** H. Priest *Call of Bush* 163 Some, like the beautiful mountain-loving Crimson Parrot, are most conspicuously red. **1945** C. Barrett *Austral. Bird Life* 79 The crimson rosella . . rivals the common rosella in colour. **1979** C. Klein *Women of Certain Age* 41 The tiny beep-beep of the great crimson rosellas that haunted the garden. **1781** J. Latham *Gen. Synopsis Birds* I. 299 **Crimson-winged Parrot.** . . All the wing coverts a full crimson. **1845** L. Leichhardt *Jrnl. Overland Exped. Aust.* 24 Feb. (1847) 161 Large flights of the blue-mountain and crimson-winged parrots were seen. **1928** G.H. Wilkins *Undiscovered Aust.* 153 Mountain parrakeets, crimson-winged parrots, and cocka-toos screeched and flashed streaks of colour. **1956** A.C.C. Lock *Tropical Tapestry* 278 A pair of crimson-wing parakeets . . were flushed from a bloodwood tree.

cripples, *pl.* [f. Br. dial. *cripple* a disease of cattle: see OEDS 1 b.] An affliction of cattle, characterized by staggering due to weakness in the hindlegs or incoordination, and resulting from poisoning by plants of the genera *Xanthorrhoea* or *Macrozamia,* or a phosphorus deficiency.

1901 J.H. Maiden *Plants reputed to be Poisonous* 31 The settlers in the vicinity of Jervis Bay inform me that the young shoots of the grass-tree, when in blossom, if eaten by cattle, give them a complaint called 'cripples'. **1910** *Advocate* (Burnie) 6 Jan. 2/7 The disease known as coast disease on King Island was well-known in Australia as cripples, and was due to improper feeding. **1929** *Colonial Times* (Hobart) 1 July 15/6 Lack of minerals in pastures causes innumerable diseases, such as . . 'cripples' . . in Australia.

cro, var. Crow *n.*[2]

crockery. [Joc. use of *crockery* earthenware.] False teeth.

1941 *Bulletin* (Sydney) 17 Sept. 14/1 Bill removed his crockery and stood it tenderly on a flat stone while he champed his corned beef sandwiches on his horny gums. **1967** *Kings Cross Whisper* (Sydney) xxxiii. 4/4 *Crockery,* false teeth.

crocodile. [Prob. joc. formation from *crock* broken-down horse.] A horse.

1897 *Worker* (Sydney) 11 Sept. 1/1 Across a wiry 'cuddy' whom he calls his 'crocodile'. **1898** *Bulletin* (Sydney) 17 Dec. 15/1 Shearing Slang is practically uniform in all Australian sheds. . . Horse = *crocodile* (shortened to *croc*) first applied to slow and old horses; now generalised. The common way of spelling this abbreviation *crock*—might baffle the philologists of 2000. **1966** S.J. Baker *Austral. Lang.* (ed. 2) 66 The old Scottish use of *crock* for a broken-down horse has probably influenced the evolution of the Australian outback slang *crocodile* for a horse.

cronk, *a.* and *n.* Also **kronk.** [Prob. var. of Br. dial. *crank* crooked, distorted, infirm, weak.]

A. *adj.* Dishonest, illegal, 'crooked'; ill, in poor condition; not genuine.

1890 'R. Boldrewood' *Nevermore* (1892) III. 143 From the look of him . . I shouldn't be surprised if there was something 'cronk' about him, for all his gold-buying. **1890** A.S. Day *Democrat* 31, I tell yer, partner Dingy, I's scared over this cronk business. **1891** *Truth* (Sydney) 5 Apr. 6/4 In the 20th George went in savagely, and getting his man on the ropes, dealt it on head and body, and had his man very cronk, all but finished. **1894** J.W. Longford *Under Lock & Key* 10 Well, he changed the cronk cheques all right, and then goes for a stroll round town. **1898** [see Crook 1 a.] **1900** *Truth* (Sydney) 21 Jan. 4/3 What a conscientious corrector of cronk capers on the course you are. *Ibid.* 20 May 5/5 The tucker is still cronk. **1904** L. Lawson *Lonely Crossing* 21 'Is she . . very cronk?' 'Yes, mate,' said Tom, 'she's bad.' **1912** J. Bradshaw *Highway Robbery under Arms* (ed. 3) 55 It would be a moral certainty for me to know a man that did anything cronk. **1922** J. Lewis *Fought & Won* 61 He seemed very anxious for me to close for them [*sc.* the horses]. I was doubtful whether there might not be something 'cronk' about them. **1930** 'Brent Of Bin Bin' *Ten Creeks Run* (1952) 148 Larry said that he was feeling so 'cronk' that he would consult Dr Byng. **1942** F. Clune *Last of Austral. Explorers* 109 Touts were making a fortune selling cronk opal to visitors. **1958** J. Lindsay *Life rarely Tells* 213 Not that I believe in doing anything cronk. **1973** J. Murray *Larrikins* 43 'Cronk' houses where non-existent horses were offered for bets did a healthy run. **1981** K. McArthur *Bread & Dripping Days* 11 Every child had to eat 'what was good for you', even parsnips and Swede turnips if fathers liked them. They were 'kronk' in the children's vernacular of the day.

B. *n.* A criminal.

1899 *Bulletin* (Sydney) 22 Apr. 14/3 Spread from the criminal class there to the 'cronks' elsewhere in Australia. **1913** M. Cannon *That Damned Democrat* (1981) 130 All the rooks and crooks and cronks of society assemble at these places.

crook, *a.* [Abbrev. of *crooked* dishonestly come by, made, obtained, or sold in a way that is not straightforward (see OED(S 3 b.); prob. infl. by (orig.) U.S. *crook* swindler, and by Cronk.]

1. a. Dishonest; illegal; illicitly obtained.

1898 *Bulletin* (Sydney) 17 Dec. (Red Page), *Krook* or *kronk* is bad. **1903** *Sporting News* (Launceston) 3 Jan. 4/1 They were satisfied there was . . 'crook' business in the first place. **1907** A. Macdonald *In Land of Pearl & Gold* 26 Are you a 'crook' claimfinder? **1911** A.L. Haydon *Trooper Police Aust.* 333 One striking feature of the new diggings was the absence of the 'crook' element. **1912** J. Bradshaw *Highway Robbery under Arms* (ed. 3) 30, I told After Dark that my horse was a crook one. **1913** A. Pratt *Wolaroi's Cup* 56 Most stables . . are crook some of the time, but none are crook all of the time. **1923** *Bailey, M.L.A. Exonerated* (Austral. Workers Union) 42 Both things were in your mind, both crook tickets and crook ballot boxes, and the whole thing was crook. **1928** A. Wright *Good Recovery* 121, I got back to Aussie under a crook name and I've been buried in the bush. **1944** *Bulletin* (Sydney) 26 July 12/1 She had been lumbered for trying to pass some crook two-bobs. **1954** M. Neville *Murder & Poor Jenny* 177 Accused him of some crook dealings. **1982** R. Hall *Just Relations* 465, I remember some pretty crook things went on there, did some of them meself.

b. Of circumstances, objects, etc.: bad; inferior; unpleasant; unsatisfactory.

1900 *Western Champion* (Barcaldine) 14 Aug. 13/1 At first all the rations were issued to the cooks, and things were very 'crook'. **1914** *Bulletin* (Sydney) 6 Aug. 51/1 A dead crook-notion stops me wif a jar: 'Wot if Doreen,' I thinks, 'should grow to be A fat ole weepin' willer, like 'er mar?' **1918** *Kia Ora Coo-ee* Apr. 20/1 Gawd struth, it's crook to stay for years. **1936** F. Clune *Roaming round Darling* 53 My cobber, here, used to sing in opera. He's a pretty crook singer, but he'll sing for you. **1939** *Bulletin* (Sydney) 11 Jan. 18/2 When the plough-hand complained of the flies the boss admitted that 'they were crook this season'. **1945** J. Devanny *Bird of Paradise* 24, I do think it's crook that our exemption for tools has been cut down. **1954** J. Waten *Unbending* 68 This is a crook place all right, but it's a bed and tucker. **1959** C. Pearl *So, you want to be Austral.* 64 Oh, England's alright . . but the beer's crook. **1963** L. Glassop *Rats in New Guinea* 217 He says things are crook in Talarook. He's the only soldier on his feet in his weapon pit. **1968** J. O'Grady *Gone Troppo* 9 When the mulga starts to die things are crook all right. **1975** 'N. Culotta' *Gone Gougin'* 25 The leaking tyre was all right. . . 'That Gilgandra galah must've had a crook gauge,' he said. **1986** *Nat. Times* (Sydney) 10 Jan. 4/2 It was pretty crook on the land in the early 1970s.

c. Ill; injured; out of sorts.

1908 *Bulletin* (Sydney) 15 Oct. 14/1 Climb out of bunk, feeling crook—sore head from fever over-night. **1912** *Mercury* (Hobart) 17 Oct. 5/2, I am pretty 'crook'. Lying about here broke me up completely. **1918** C.L. Hartt *Diggerettes* 23 The battalion dag thought he was genuinely crook and fell in on sick parade. **1924** H.E. Riemann *Nor'-West o' West* 109 It's the mongrel caste—shamming crook to get a cheap ride. **1930** *Bulletin* (Sydney) 9 Apr. 19/1 'I'm crook, my word I *am* crook,' wailed Bert. 'I got cancer or 'pendercitis or somethin'.' **1946** A.J. Holt *Wheat Farms Vic.* 90 I'm crook in the guts now. **1955** P. White *Tree of Man* 185 Are the burns bad? We must dress them. Tell me? . . do they feel 'crook'? **1966** *Meanjin* 12 He got taken crook something to do with his guts. **1967** A. O'Toole *Coach from City* 67 Last night had been Terry Byron's birthday party and some of the boys would be bound to be a bit crook. **1978** D. Stuart *Wedgetail View* 33 Life wasn't worth livin', an' maybe it ain't . . when a man's real crook from the grog. **1981** *Woman's Day* (Sydney) 9 Sept. 15/1 He did indeed have a crook knee. He'd been riding on a board and a shark had come up and nipped him.

2. In the phr. **to go crook (at, on).**

a. *Obs.* To act dishonestly.

1906 *Bulletin* (Sydney) 20 Sept. 16/1 His integrity was known; Thoughts of snatching pelf he spurned. At suggestions to 'go crook' Righteous wrath within him burned.

b. To become angry (with), to vent one's anger (upon).

1910 L. Esson *Woman Tamer* (1976) 79 Now, don't go crook, Katie. **1911** L. Stone *Jonah* 190 Yer niver 'ad no cause ter go crook on me, but I ain't complainin'. **1918** *Kia Ora Coo-ee* June 3/2, I can tell you I went dead crook at it at first. **1920** *Character Glimpses: Australs. on Somme* 16 Some brand new reinstoushments . . went crook on him because he had nothing to give them better than hot soup, Bully and Anzac wafers. **1924** *Bulletin* (Sydney) 21 Feb. 22/1 When the shearing cheque is finished and the publican goes crook, All the friends we had diminished, till the last one takes his hook. **1937** G.D. Mitchell *Backs to Wall* 84 If Fritzy stonkers Mitch in the next stunt . . I'll go crook a treat. **1944** M.J. O'Reilly *Bowyangs & Boomerangs* 89 When he was told that his mate was buried boots and all Dad 'went crook' and called the diggers a 'flaming lot of new chums'. **1950** *Coast to Coast 1949–50* 165 What'd you do if you were expelled? . . Y'r old man'd go crook, I bet. **1956** C.D. Mills *Stockwhip & Spur* 42, I ain't been drinkin', curse the luck, So don't be goin' crook. **1966** *Overland* xxxv. 37 Well, don't go crook at me. I'm just the Indian. **1971** *Austral. Roadsports & Drag Racing News* 15 Oct. 10/2 Withers went crook at me because I broke the axle. **1978** H.C. Baker *I was Listening* 56 We rolled him for his overcoat. You ought to've heard him go crook.

c. To deteriorate; to cease functioning adequately.

1919 *Smith's Weekly* (Sydney) 21 June 16/5, I neglected to take an overcoat, although it was at that season when the New England weather might at any moment 'go crook'. **1924** F.J. Mills *Happy Days* 138 Only one rat cort [*sic*], and he wasn't noticed and went crook and hummed. **1959** K.S. Prichard *N'Goola* 58 'Me truck's gone crook on me,' Nugget grumbled. 'Want to fix her.' **1963** D. Attenborough *Quest under Capricorn* 66 The pilot . . yelled at me. 'If the engine went crook now, what d'ye reckon we'd do?' **1963** S. Mussen *Beating about Bush* 36 After four months in Australia I thought I could speak like an Australian. My watch did not *break*; it *went crook on me.*

d. To become ill.

1918 *Kia Ora Coo-ee* June 2/3 What a grafter she is, when she doesn't elect to go 'crook'. **1948** R.A. Pepperall *Emigrant to Aust.* 115, I owed much to his help . . when any of my cows 'went crook'. **1955** N. Pulliam *I traveled Lonely Land* 320 Not a chappie among us went crook. **1976** L. Oakes *Crash Through* 237 The last thing we want is to have you start tonight, not turn in a good performance because you're sick, and then in a day or two go crook again.

3. In the phr. **to be crook on,** to be annoyed by (cf. Crooked).

1955 R. Lawler *Summer of Seventeenth Doll* (1965) 48 You're crook on me because I stayed up there with

Dowdie and didn't walk out with you. **1956** *Overland* vi. 9 They're not crook on you Merv. for actually buying a car. **1957** R. BEYNON *Shifting Heart* (1960) 58 Enjoy meself? When she won't even dance with a man. Look, I'm crook on that. **1967** F. HARDY *Billy Borker yarns Again* 130 The landlords are crook on this. **1982** LOWENSTEIN & HILLS *Under Hook* 42, I was there on duty when the police strike was on. I was crook on it because I couldn't get away.

crooked /'krʊkəd/, *a.* [f. CROOK 2 b.] Annoyed; esp. in the phr. **crooked on,** exasperated by, infuriated with.

1942 *Whizz* (Perth) July 1 You're crooked on parasites and profiteers back home. **1944** L. GLASSOP *We were Rats* 48 Ya oughtn't ter feel crooked on things. I s'pose it's because Bertha's outa town. **1953** G.H. FEARNSIDE *Bayonets Abroad* 9, I thought you was crooked on me! **1953** D. CUSACK *Southern Steel* 29 A bloke'd have to be pretty sour to be crooked at life when he had what he had. **1955** *Bulletin* (Sydney) 5 Jan. 12/4, I *was* crooked on the Old Man when he copped me riding it home and promptly flattened me. **1960** J. WALKER *No Sunlight Singing* 49 The man in charge of the bore was 'troppo' and crooked on blacks and just as likely to shoot them as not. **1967** *Kings Cross Whisper* (Sydney) xxxiii. 8/4 The migrants are also crooked on Australia because the sun has shone only three days in the past three months. **1976** C.D. MILLS *Hobble Chains & Greenhide* 22 She had been betrothed from birth to a young buck. He had picked up another, and was crooked on the world because the old fellas made him take this one. **1978** D. STUART *Wedgetail View* 76 Ah you're just crooked, Col . . 'cos she hasn't got a sister here with her, so's you could have a dash. **1982** R. HALL *Just Relations* 335 It's not you I'm crooked on, he assured Vivien.

crooked maginnis: see MAGINNIS.

croppy. *Hist.* [Transf. use of Br. *croppy* one who has the hair cut short, applied esp. to the Irish rebels of 1798.] Orig. an Irish convict, esp. one transported for participation in the 1798 rebellion; any convict, incl. a convict at large.

1800 *HRA* (1914) 1st Ser. II. 581 Drinking inflammatory and seditious Toasts—'Success to the Croppies' and other improper Expressions. **1802** *Ibid.* (1915) 1st Ser. III. 527 A good character . . is now necessary, as the man who had charge of it was such a determined 'Croppy' that I have sent him away. **1807** *Sydney Gaz.* 22 Feb., This rising of the Croppies as it is called has been more or less in agitation for a long time. **1809** *Hist. Rec. N.S.W.* (1901) VII. 216 Such doings was never known—pardons to the worst of characters, Croppeys, and thieves. **1830** R. DAWSON *Present State Aust.* 294 Take care croppy (convict) no crammer (steal). **1833** W.H. BRETON *Excursions* 234 Settlers are allowed to be present, but not the convicts, whom they call croppies. **1835** J. HOLMAN *Travels* IV. 481 The natives are very useful in giving information . . concerning the bushrangers, whom they call croppies. **1842** *Legends of Aust.* Mar. 49 The lawyer held up three fingers, and replied 'make a light, me croppy—sit down along a mountain.' (Meaning there were three bushrangers close at hand.) **1848** H.W. HAYGARTH *Recoll. Bush Life* 9 Mr Longbow . . was . . robbed of his horse, valise, and all the et-ceteras of his style, by the well-known 'croppies'—'Black Joe' or 'Irish Jim'. **1888** W.T. PYKE *Bush Tales* 14 From the close governmental crop of their hair, convicts are called croppies by the blacks. Blacks hate croppies . . and croppies hate blacks as heartily, because they so often prove the means of their detection. **1902** J.S. HASSALL *In Old Aust.* 35 He also gave me an account of the outbreak of the 'croppies'—so called, perhaps, from their close-cut hair—a number of convicts who were once stationed at Castle Hill. **1911** A.L. HAYDON *Trooper Police Aust.* 13 Risings among the 'croppies', as the convicts were termed.

Cross, *n.*

1. Abbrev. of SOUTHERN CROSS 1.

1872 MRS E. MILLETT *Austral. Parsonage* 173 Without its 'pointers', however, as the two splendid stars are called that accompany it, the Cross would lose much of its attraction. **1885** *Australasian Printers' Keepsake* 126 The Cross and Pointers were high in the zenith. **1902** *Blackwood's Mag.* (Edinburgh) May 640/2 The positions of the Cross will indicate plainly, even to minutes, the divisions of the night. **1911** I.A. ROSENBLUM *Stella Sothern* 34 On bright, starry nights we used to look at the Cross together. **1918** G. WHITE *Thirty Yrs. Tropical Aust.* 71, I was informed that the natives see in the Magellan clouds surrounding the Southern Cross the form of an emu, and have a tradition that the three bright stars of the Cross are an emu's footprint, and the two pointers two blackfellows tracking it. **1944** M.J. O'REILLY *Bowyangs & Boomerangs* 37, I tramped most of the night, keeping in a northerly direction by the aid of the 'Cross'. **1951** E. HILL *Territory* 425 'Call me when the Cross turns over,' you will hear the drovers say. **1969** D. NILAND *Dead Men Running* 57 You could look out and see the five white stars of the cross.

2. With **the**: abbrev. of 'King's Cross', the name of a district of Sydney, N.S.W. noted for its cosmopolitan character.

1945 H.C. BREWSTER *King's Cross Calling* 5 Just where is King's Cross?—or as it is referred to affectionately by those who live there—The Cross. **1956** S. HOPE *Diggers' Paradise* 86 A popular district with bodgies and widgies is 'The Cross'—King's Cross—which is Sydney's little Soho. **1963** *Meanjin* 344 She had recently left her parents' home in the suburbs . . and had taken a room at the Cross. **1965** J. WYNNUM *Jiggin' in Riggin'* 41 They cater for all tastes up here at the Cross. Men and women of both sexes. **1972** *Bulletin* (Sydney) 1 Jan. 38/1 Sex, for many Sydneyites, is the Cross. 'The genitals of Sydney', one of my friends calls it. **1976** D. IRELAND *Glass Canoe* 16 It was better up the Cross. King's, not Southern. **1980** M. WILLIAMS *Dingo!* 59 He took me up to the Cross, the city's playground, and introduced me to the molls working in the coffee bars.

Hence **Crossite** *n.*, a frequenter of King's Cross.

1945 H.C. BREWSTER *King's Cross Calling* 112 The Crossite has . . a complacent belief that he may still sit in his beloved cafe.

cross, *a.* [f. *cross* across (as in *cross-country*).] In special collocations: **cross fence,** a fence delineating a part of an externally fenced area; **track,** a cross-country track (see quot. 1849); in *pl.*, an intersection of such tracks, 'cross-roads'.

1840 *S. Austral. Rec.* (London) 29 Aug. 139, I made choice of the E.S.E. corner of section 256, it being the clearest of timber and the most easily inclosed by **cross fences**, the section being previously fenced. **1900** *Advocate* (Burnie) 27 July 4/2, I had to condemn about 100 of his posts. . . I said 'All right, they will do for cross fence.' **1849** A. HARRIS *Emigrant Family* (1967) 309 The road he had to traverse is a **cross-track**, between districts that have . . little business communication. **1914** *Bulletin* (Sydney) 21 May 24/1 A pub . . we had passed at the cross-tracks. **1948** V. PALMER *Golconda* 242 He had meant to run back . . but at the Belalie cross-track he hesitated.

cross-brand, *v. trans.* To re-brand (an animal): legally, by marking it with the brand of a second or subsequent owner; illegally, by altering the existing brand. Also as *ppl. a.*

1936 W. HATFIELD *Aust. through Windscreen* 59 One suspected cattle-thief . . rode into the police paddock where seventeen head of alleged cross-branded cattle were being held as exhibits. **1950** G.M. FARWELL *Land of Mirage* 171 Many a man who stuck up a gold escort . . had started out as a mere gully-raker, putting his brand on scrubbers, or cross-branding in another man's yard. **1956** T. RONAN *Moleskin Midas* 67 These cattle should have been cross-branded at point of origin, and would have to be done before they went another mile. **1978** D. STUART *Wedgetail View* 25 There'd be work . . as soon as they'd cross-branded the young breeders that were to pay for agistment for the mob.

crow, *n.*[1] [Transf. use of *crow* bird of genus *Corvus.*]

1. Any of several large, glossy, black birds of the genus *Corvus*, having a harsh call, esp. *C. orru* of Aust. and New Guinea and *C. bennetti* of mainland Aust. See also RAVEN.

1770 J. BANKS *Endeavour Jrnl.* 19 June (1962) II. 83 There were vast flocks of Pigeons and crows. **1787** *Hist. Botany Bay New Holland* 19 There are also crows exactly the same as those in England. **1793** J. HUNTER *Hist. Jrnl. Trans. Port Jackson* 69 The common crow is found here in considerable numbers, but the sound of their voice and manner of croaking, is very different from those in Europe. **1824** *Austral.* (Sydney) 16 Dec. 4 No fewer than 70 eagles (besides crows, which also are very mischievous), were destroyed within the short space of four months. **1827** P. CUNNINGHAM *Two Yrs. in N.S.W.* I. 322 We have *crows*, resembling in look and hoarse croaking note the English ravens. **1852** J. MORGAN *Life & Adventures W. Buckley* 65 A crow flying over her dropped something like dry grass, which immediately blazed. **1931** *Bulletin* (Sydney) 14 Jan. 21/3, I have often seen crows . . and other indigenous insectivorous birds lunching off a dead animal. **1945** C. BARRETT *Austral. Bird Life* 222 Often mistaken for the raven and suffering for that bird's misdeeds, the crow (*C. cecilae*) deserves protection in sheep country. **1976** *Ecos* viii. 30/2 Most of us would be quite content to label the large black birds of the genus *Corvus* as crows or ravens. . . He has now established that there are in fact five species involved—two crows and three ravens. They all look very much alike.

2. Special Comb. **crow shrike,** (variously) BUTCHERBIRD, CURRAWONG, MAGPIE *n.*[1]

1878 R.B. SMYTH *Aborigines of Vic.* II. 38 *Crow shrike*, Wooryung. **1905** T. WELSBY *Schnappering & Fishing Brisbane River* 72 He at once pointed out to several flocks of 'churwung' (crow shrikes), or, as they are familiarly called, black magpies. **1922** *Bulletin* (Sydney) 20 Apr. 22/2, I have also seen a magpie (crow-shrike) carry a freshly caught mouse to the top of a pine-tree. **1962** B.W. LEAKE *Eastern Wheatbelt Wildlife* 86 The magpie and currawong or squeaker are closely related to the crow and are really crow shrikes.

3. In the phr. **to stone (spare, starve, stiffen) the crows,** an exclamation of surprise, disgust, exasperation, etc. See also LIZARD 2 and STARVE.

1918 H. MATTHEWS *Saints & Soldiers* 116 'Starve the crows,' howled Bluey in that agonised screech of his. **1919** C. DREW *Doings of Dave* 47 Spare the crows! **1927** F.C. BIGGERS *Bat-Eye* 15 Well, stone the floggin' crows! **1932** J. TRURAN *Green Mallee* 75 Stiffen the crows, Fred, a man oughter do it for yer own sake. **1939** G. DIGBY *Down Wind* 210 'Gawd stone the crows!' he remarked, 'you boys handle an axe like a couple of old wimmen in the fam'ly way.' **1949** I.L. IDRIESS *One Wet Season* 69 'You'd be a real man, anyway,' growled Buckle. . . 'Stone the crows!' demanded Scotty, 'what *am* I then?' **1965** G.H. FEARNSIDE *Golden Ram* 211 Stone the flamin' crows, mate, what's the country comin' to? **1973** H. LEWIS *Crow on Barbed Wire Fence* 212, I stepped out of the train in London on a bitter December evening, and, stone the crows, there was my little Dad . . with an overcoat in his arms—for me. **1977** F.B. VICKERS *Stranger no Longer* 99 'Well, starve the bloody crows,' he exclaimed, stopping to eye me off. **1980** R. DAVIDSON *Tracks* 212 Drink with your cobber ocker stone-the-crows fair-crack-of-the-whip mates.

4. In the phr. **to draw the crow,** to receive the least desirable share (of anything).

1942 *Wog Jrnl.: Mag. 3rd Austral. Infantry Brigade* 25 Dec. 1 To draw the crow is to be detailed for a job while others [rest]. **1944** L. GLASSOP *We were Rats* 207, I reckon with sheilas I always draw the crow. **1952** T.A.G. HUNGERFORD *Ridge & River* 75 Sweet's tone was resigned. 'I always cop the bloody crow.' **1970** R. BEILBY *No Medals for Aphrodite* 169, I knew we'd drawn the crow as soon as I seen this place! **1978** H.C. BAKER *I was Listening* 61 You've drawn the crow, eh, Curl? **1985** N. MEDCALF *Rifleman* 207, I bet I had drawn the crow on some louzy detail.

crow, *n.*[2] Also **cro.** [Prob. abbrev. of CHROMO.] A prostitute.

1950 *Austral. Police Jrnl.* Apr. 111 *Crow*, prostitute. **1953** K. TENNANT *Joyful Condemned* 47 She's in with all the higher-ups. And what does she do? Slugs a guy like a cro on a beat. **1965** E. LAMBERT *Long White Night* 80 'Where do yer think? Get a bit of twot.' 'That big café down on the waterfront. The Universal. The crows hang round there in droves.' **1980** B. HERBERT *No Names* 77 What are you, anyway? A Kings Cross crow. Every Yank in town's been rootin' you.

crowea /'kroʊiə/. [The plant genus *Crowea* was named by English botanist J.E. Smith (*Trans. Linnean Soc. London* (1798) IV. 222), after the English surgeon and botanist James Crowe (1750–1807).] Any shrub of the genus *Crowea* (fam. Rutaceae) of s.w. W.A. and parts of s.e. Aust.

1901 M. VIVIENNE *Travels in W.A.* 61 The delicate pink and white flowers of the crowea hang in loose clusters. **1942** E. ANDERSON *Squatter's Luck* 20 Trigger-flowers, crowea, billyardia vines. **1984** ELLIOT & JONES

Encycl. Austral. Plants III. 118 Croweas are not prone to any pests or diseases.

croweater. [See quots. 1881 and 1934.] A nickname for a non-Aboriginal person resident in, or native to, South Australia. Also *attrib.*

1881 J.C.F. JOHNSON *To Mount Browne & Back* 13, I was met with the startling information that all Adelaide men were croweaters . . because it was asserted that the early settlers of 'Farinaceous Village', when short of mutton, made a meal of the unwary crow. **1892** *Truth* (Sydney) 19 June 4/7 South Australians 'get the hump' when addressed as Croweaters. **1898** *Bulletin* (Sydney) 17 Dec. 7/2 S.A. certainly produces a vast amount of wealth for a province with so little visible means of support, but, all the same, the second biggest debt on earth is a tremendous load for barren Crow-eater Land. **1916** E. & M.S. GREW *Rambles in Aust.* 206 Life was hard in early South Australia, and hence the South Australians remain 'Crow-eaters'. **1920** *Aussie* (Sydney) Oct. 37/2 The only two Victoria Crosses awarded for the Russian affair went to Australians—one 'Crow-eater' and one 'Gum-sucker'. **1934** M. GILMORE *Old Days* 18 It was said that they ate the crows they caught. With the cruelty of the times people called them 'crow-eaters', and they were despised accordingly by those who lived in the altitudes of 'killed meat'. **1940** *Bulletin* (Sydney) 24 July 16/3 We were humpin' our drums through Croweater country. **1963** *Ibid.* 20 July 32/1 At the mention of the word Adelaide or 'crow eaters' a chill goes through the room. **1973** P. MCKENNA *My World of Football* 94 The 'Croweaters' threw one of their forwards into the position while they regrouped. **1986** *Centralian Advocate* (Alice Springs) 15 Jan. 6/2 Jim sandstones the croweaters. Sandstone is being exported from Central Australia to a South Australian construction firm.

Hence **crow-eating** *a.*, **crowland** *n.*

1908 *Truth* (Sydney) 5 July 1/7 In Adelaide . . now it is possible for a man to be tortured to death by **crow-eating** officials. **1915** *First Aid Post: Official Organ 2nd Field Ambulance* 23 June 1/1 Received this week from our 'Croweating' correspondent. **1967** G. JENKIN *Two Yrs. Bardunyah Station* 2 The boss was a native of Queensland . . and pretended to despise the 'Damned Crow-eating custom' of drinking wine. **1976** B. SCOTT *Compl. Bk. Austral. Folk Lore* 257 Twelve hundred thousand bottles there was of every size and shape, Nine hundred thousand old flagoons that held Crow-eatin' grape. **1908** M. VIVIENNE *Sunny S.A.* 74 The Maoris vied with each other to do honour to their white brother from '**crowland**'. For the South Australians have long been known as 'Croweaters'. **1908** *Truth* (Sydney) 6 Dec. 9/7 That strip of land between the Cabbage Garden and Crowland is worth a little casual reference.

crown, *n.* [Attrib. use of *crown* the authority so symbolized.]

1. *Obs.* In Comb. as a euphemistic term for a convict: **crown labourer, prisoner, servant.**

1824 E. EAGAR *Lett.* 41 A settler possessing £200 capital . . will employ and subsist four **crown labourers**, or convicts. **1819** *Sydney Gaz.* 4 Sept., The trial of several **crown prisoners** charged with robbing His Majesty's store. **1824** E. CURR *Acct. Colony Van Diemen's Land* 9 A Crown prisoner in Hobart Town does not perform one third of the daily task of a labourer in this country. **1827** *Tasmanian* (Hobart) 19 July 3 Is he a Crown prisoner; and, if so, how is it that, to adopt the Crown expression, he is upon his own hands? **1832** *Sydney Herald* 30 Jan. 2/4 The most valuable accessions . . still consists . . in our importation of crown prisoners. **1843** *Colonial Observer* (Sydney) 30 Aug. 1270/1 A crown-prisoner . . was consigned . . into the custody of the police. **1851** H. MELVILLE *Present State Aust.* 141 The books are supposed to be registers . . of all the crown prisoners in the island. **1870** J. BONWICK *Last Tasmanians* 190 Mr John Batman is to be employed for some time as Conductor of a party of ten Crown Prisoners. **1815** M. HOOKEY *B. Knopwood & his Times* 25 Apr. (1929) 111 The whole of the **Crown Servants** are to be mustered every afternoon at sunset. **1818** T.E. WELLS *M. Howe* (1945) 17 Howe was assigned, as a Crown Servant to Mr Ingle, a merchant and grazier. **1827** *Monitor* (Sydney) 6 Aug. 566/3 All convicts (or as they are styled in New South Wales, crown servants) should be worked in irons. **1832** *Sydney Herald* 9 Apr. 2/2 Turning all crown servants back to the hands of the Government.

2. Special Comb., in terms pertaining to land tenure: **crown grant,** a grant of land made to an individual; **land,** unalienated land; **(land) commissioner,** see quots. 1848 and 1852; **lease,** an agreement under which crown land is tenanted; the land so held; **purchase (land),** crown land which has been sold or is available for sale; **tenant,** one who leases crown land.

1840 *S. Austral. Rec.* (London) 7 Mar. 90 The question of the validity of **crown-grants** of colonial lands has been mooted. **1880** R. ROSE *Vic. Guide* 7 Having fulfilled the conditions, he will have paid £1 per acre, and be entitled to a Crown grant, without any further payment. **1882** W. SOWDEN *N.T. as it Is* 36 The little Crown-grant township on the south bank. **1918** C.H. NORTHCOTT *Austral. Social Dev.* 64 The crown grants of Australia were less for Agriculture than for pasture . . and were . . a reward for the possession of capital sufficient to employ and care for convict servants. [**1789 crown land:** *HRA* (1914) 1st Ser. I. 127 You are also to reserve to Us proper quantities of land in each township.] **1814** *Ibid.* (1916) 1st Ser. VIII. 329 Quit rents to One Shilling per Acre would by no Means answer the Intentions of Government to raise a Revenue from the Crown Lands, intended to be granted. **1819** *Sydney Gaz.* 8 May, The present very great Scarcity of disposable Crown Lands. **1835** *Cornwall Chron.* (Launceston) 16 May 4 'Crown Land', as it is called . . in fact, is the real property of the Colony. **1841** *Colonial Mag.* (London) IV. 231 The available crown land has long since been alienated. **1848** *Sidney's Austral. Hand-Bk.* 13 The disposition of crown lands (as all the unoccupied lands of the colony are called), after several experiments, was settled into what is commonly called the Wakefield system. **1881** W. ALLEN *Immigration & Co-op. Settlement* 37 Our crown lands are almost gone. **1901** W.G. ACOCKS *Settlers' Synopsis Land Laws N.S.W.* p. viii, 'Crown Lands' means lands vested in Her Majesty and not permanently dedicated to any public purpose, or granted or lawfully contracted to be granted in fee simple under any of the Land Acts. **1968** F. ROSE *Aust. Revisited* 22 Governor Bourke announced in 1836 that anyone could 'squat' on Crown Lands on payment of a licence fee of ten pounds—and all land outside the limits of location was Crown Land. **1978** *Ecos* xv. 27/1 On South Australia's eastern border an area of about 2000 sq km of mallee scrub occupies vacant Crown land. **1846** *Moreton Bay Courier* 5 Sept. 4/3 The days of **Crown Land Commissioners** are numbered. **1848** C. COZENS *Adventures of Guardsman* 123 Each party of border-police was placed under the immediate control of a Crown land commissioner, and generally consisted of four men and horses. One commissioner was appointed to each district beyond the limits of location, i.e. the boundary line laid down as the extent of the police districts. **1852** J.E. ERSKINE *Short Acct. Late Discoveries Gold* 17 Mr Hardy, Police Magistrate at Parramatta, was now nominated in addition 'Crown Land Commissioner' for the Gold Districts, and a force of twelve mounted constabulary was raised, both to enable him to preserve order and to enforce the payment of the license fees. **1857** W. HOWITT *Tallangetta* II. 173 This state of things all over the colony compelled the establishment of Crown Land Commissioners and a mounted police. **1861** C. CAMPBELL *Squatting Question Considered* 4 Crown Land Commissioners were appointed, holding arbitrary power to settle all disputes concerning boundaries on their own judgement. **1862** H. BROWN *Vic. as I found It* 148 The crown Commissioner . . has the responsibility of gathering in the license fee, and of generally superintending the affairs of the gold-fields. **1808** *To Viscount Castlereagh* 10 Tenants under **Crown leases** in the town of Sydney. **1887** W. BANNOW *Emigrant's Hand-Bk.* 139 'Improved lands', or lands on which improvements have been made by purchasers on credit, or crown leases. **1972** ANDERSON & BLAKE *J.S. Neilson* 12 If after six years the land had been fenced and rents duly paid, the selector could ask for a Crown lease. **1842** *Sydney Morning Herald* 3 Aug. 1/8 Part of a **Crown purchase** of 820 acres. **1920** B. CRONIN *Timber Wolves* 47 Crown purchase land is open for selection. **1855** W. CAMPBELL *Crown Lands Aust.* 21 There could have been no great loss to the Revenue had the **Crown-tenants** got all the lands they applied for. **1867** 'CLERGYMAN' *Aust. as it Is* 104 The occupiers of the land—that class of the community called *squatters* or *Crown-tenants*—not being required to purchase the land of which they hold possession, they enjoy the full use and benefit of every farthing of their capital.

crown, *v.* [f. *crown fire* a bushfire which moves through the crowns or tops of trees: see OEDS *crown, sb.* 35.] *intr.* Of a bushfire: to move (rapidly) through the tops of trees. Also as *vbl. n.*

1972 B. FULLER *West of Bight* 142 In windy conditions fires travel fast, flames leaping in explosive balls from tree-top to tree-top, a phenomenon known as 'crowning'. **1981** *Bega District News* 27 Nov. 5/6 A tractor and more men were brought in but the fire crowned under the influence of low humidity and strong Westerly winds.

crown of thorns starfish. [f. a fancied resemblance to Christ's *crown of thorns.*] The spiny, coral-eating starfish *Acanthaster planci* of tropical regions, including the Great Barrier Reef. Also **crown of thorns.**

1964 *Austral. Med. Jrnl.* Apr. I. 592 Usually the 'crown of thorns' starfish is to be found entwined in the branches of living coral, on which it feeds. **1970** *Kings Cross Whisper* (Sydney) lxxx. 5/1 The Premier of Queensland, Mr Ernest Wank, today said that the Crown of Thorns starfish menace had been exaggerated. **1976** E. WORRELL *Things that Sting* 58 The Crown of Thorns Starfish or Sea Star, may grow to a diameter of two thirds of a metre. **1984** *Daily Tel.* (Sydney) 20 Jan. 9/2 Scientists are baffled by the upsurge of activity among the coral-gobbling crown-of-thorns starfish on the Great Barrier Reef.

crow's ash. [See quot. 1981.] The rainforest tree of Qld. and N.S.W. *Flindersia australis* (fam. Rutaceae), having a scaly bark and prickly woody fruits; the timber of the tree, which is yellow and oily. See also TEAK. Also **crow ash.**

1903 *Austral. Handbk.* 279 Other orders . . furnish . . large-sized timber, particularly the following:- . . 'Crow's Ash' (*Flindersia australis*). **1926** *Qld. Agric. Jrnl.* XXV. v. 433 There is a Crow's Ash in Queensland which is called Teak in New South Wales. **1927** *Bulletin* (Sydney) 3 Nov. 27/4 Crow's ash is not known by any other names than 'Flindosy' and teak. **1937** *Ibid.* 30 June 21/4 For 25 years I've lived on the edge of a large block of tropical jungle in which such lofty hardwoods as crow's-ash, silver-ash, crow's-foot-elm and Burdekin plum occur numerously. **1944** J. DEVANNY *By Tropic Sea & Jungle* 128 A variety of Flindersia, called crow's ash in the vernacular, is like a gleaming, golden maple, and comes next to the oaks for beauty. **1949** B. O'REILLY *Green Mountains* 144 Of the vast variety of jungle trees, . . Crow Ash and Lignum Vitae were suitable for fencing, all others used to rot in the ground. **1956** N.K. WALLIS *Austral. Timber Handbk.* 4 Other timbers have special uses, such as crow's ash or colonial teak (verandah floors exposed to weather, and shipbuilding). **1981** A.B. & J.W. CRIBB *Useful Wild Plants Aust.* 134 The origin of the name crow's ash is obscure. However, it is reported that crows eat the seeds and this may possibly have led to the use of the common name.

crowsfoot. Used *attrib.* in Special Comb. **crowsfoot elm,** BOOYONG; **grass,** the naturalized tussock-forming grass *Eleusine indica* (fam. Poaceae) of all mainland States except Vic.; the related *E. tristachya*; also abbrev. as **crowsfoot.**

1909 *Emu* VIII. 238 The heavy and tall timbers were represented by . . **crow's foot elm.** **1926** *Qld. Agric. Jrnl.* XXV. v. 433 There is a Crow's Foot Elm which is also called Booyong. **1934** *Tree Lover* Dec. 2 Crowsfoot Elm . . 'Crowsfoot' may have originated from the shape of the leaves or from the way in which the buttresses are outspread. **1937** D. GLASS *Austral. Fantasy* 72 Crowsfoot elm and kauri pine luxuriate in its depths. **1944** J. DEVANNY *By Tropic Sea & Jungle* 128 Tulip oak, also called crow's foot elm. **1903** G. SUTHERLAND *Australasian Live Stock Man.* (ed. 2) 384 Among the grasses of Riverina . . **crowsfoot.** **1912** R.S. TAIT *Scotty Mac* 28 Licked up the dry crowsfoot and clover. **1966** M. BROWN *Jimberi Track* 49 Up there cattle feed is up the knees—everlastin's, parakelia, crow's foot, all fattenin' feed. **1974** S.L. EVERIST *Poisonous Plants Aust.* 227 Crowsfoot grass is a weed of most warm countries.

crudget: see CRUET.

cruel, *v.* [f. *cruel, a.*, perh. infl. by *to queer (the pitch).*] *trans.* To spoil (an opportunity, etc.); to ruin (the chances of a person or enterprise succeeding).

1899 *Truth* (Sydney) 2 Apr. 4/5 Your brand-new

hanky-panky system of drawing in sections 'cruelled' their chances. **1915** *Bran Mash: Fourth Light Horse* 15 June 2 But th' ··· vet 'e crools me pitch. ***c* 1917** C. THACKERAY *Goliath Joe* 20, I s'pose them coves reckoned my crook eye cruelled their luck. **1930** *Aussie* (Sydney) July 12/2 Felix's Australian accent was responsible for 'crueling' him for talkie work. **1938** X. HERBERT *Capricornia* 374 Do you think the Southern graziers'll stand bein' taxed to bring down beasts to cruel the market for 'em? **1953** T.A.G. HUNGERFORD *Riverslake* 106 'Nice day,' the Pole volunteered. 'If not wind come.' 'Yeah, the wind cruels it,' Carmichael answered. **1965** E. LAMBERT *Long White Night* 138 Earnie nearly cruelled the whole thing by laughing. **1971** D. IRELAND *Unknown Industr. Prisoner* 83 His eagerness for overtime and promotion cruelled him.

cruet. [Prob. altered form of Br. slang *crumpet* the head, as in the phr. *barmy in the crumpet*: see OEDS 4.] Also **crudget.**

1. The (human) head.

1941 S.J. BAKER *Pop. Dict. Austral. Slang* 21 *Crudget*, the head. **1966** —— *Austral. Lang.* (ed. 2) 170 *Cruet*, head. Whence *silly in the cruet*. **1967** *Kings Cross Whisper* (Sydney) xxxiii. 4/4 *Cruet*, head. **1977** R. BEILBY *Gunner* 139 'Where did he get it?' 'Through the cruet.'

2. In the phr. **to do one's cruet,** to lose one's temper.

1976 *Bronze Swagman Bk. Bush Verse* 59 The wife would do her cruet, she would murder me.

cruiser. See quot. 1970.

1966 S.J. BAKER *Austral. Lang.* (ed. 2) 229 Names given to other measures . . *schooner, cruiser*. **1970** N. KEESING *Transition* 202 You Australians call a pint glass a cruiser, a three-quarter-pint a schooner, and a half-pint a middy, all very nautical.

crumpet. [Joc. var. of CRACKER *n.*[2]] In the phr. **not worth a crumpet,** worthless.

1944 L. GLASSOP *We were Rats* 153 He won't be worth a crumpet in action, not worth a bloody crumpet. **1962** A. SEYMOUR *One Day of Yr.* 73 Anzacs . . Ballyhoo. Photos in the papers. Famous. Not worth a crumpet. **1968** J. O'GRADY *Gone Troppo* 51 Three trucks and not one of 'em worth a bloody crumpet. Guts driven out of all of 'em.

crush. [Transf. use of *crush* a crowding together.] In a stock yard: a narrow race or passage through which animals can only pass in single file. Also *attrib.*

[N.Z. **1856** W. ROBERTS in J.H. Beattie *Early Runholding in Otago* 18 Dec. (1947) 43 There was no crush pen or drafting race.] **1872** C.H. EDEN *My Wife & I in Qld.* 69 [It] consists of several yards for drafting . . a lane and a crush . . useful for branding or securing a troublesome . . bullock. **1880** *Blackwood's Mag.* (Edinburgh) Jan. 76/1 The 'crush lane' . . is a lane wide enough to permit only a single bullock or horse at a time to make his way up it. It is used for branding full-grown cattle, and the fences are made of the strongest timber, and are very high. **1887** A. NICOLS *Wild Life & Adventure* 154 He shouted to one of the men, 'open the crush lane', and, before the dazed animal knew where it was, a couple more blows urged it into the narrow space between two fences. **1888** *Centennial Mag.* (Sydney) 181 There were some small yards, and a 'crush' as they call it, for branding cattle. **1909** *Bulletin* (Sydney) 14 Oct. 14/2 Station cattle . . have to be checked in the crush, or they will rush through too quickly and jump on those already in the 'slops'. **1911** E.J. BRADY *King's Caravan* 241 The yard ended in a 'crush', a high-railed passage way leading to the 'dip'. **1922** *Bulletin* (Sydney) 31 Aug. 20/2 Tom was working in his own crush and with shorthorns. **1928** B. CRONIN *Dragonfly* 102 I'm going to round-up some cattle. Want to help me with the crush-gate? **1954** H.G. LAMOND *Manx Star* 259 *Crush*, a fenced lane in a yard—too narrow to allow more than one animal abreast. **1963** J.F. HARLEY *Mantle of Safety* 48, I looked across the yard to the crushes, where a line of bullock rumps were turned towards me. **1981** A.B. FACEY *Fortunate Life* 170 Near where we camped there were large stockyards and a crush for handling and marking.

crusher. See quots.

1965 F. HARDY *Yarns of Billy Borker* 59 Some blokes beat the game, I hear. Only bookmakers—and crushers. What's a crusher? A crusher's a bloke who backs a horse at, say, five to one; then lays it in a bookmaker's bag, at say three to one. **1985** *Sydney Morning Herald* 25 Jan. 1/1 A crusher really is not a racing man at all. His practice is to back a horse at longer odds, having received some sort of information that its price is likely to shrink during the betting, and then to sell his betting ticket to somebody at odds which are lower than those shown on the ticket, but which are still higher than those currently being offered in the ring. A crusher is not regarded in the betting ring as an admirable figure. He is regarded as something of a hanger-on, a scalper of good odds.

crust. [Fig. use of *crust* a scrap of bread.]

1. A livelihood.

1888 G. ROCK *Colonists* 40, I generally manages to crack a tidy crust. **1910** H. LAWSON *Rising of Court* 2 Police court solicitors . . wrangling over some miserable case for a crust. **1918** B. CRONIN *Coastlanders* 140 I'll bet a new bridle he's earned his crust in the country some time or other. **1939** K. TENNANT *Foveaux* 312 'What's y'r old man do for a crust?' . . 'Drives a taxi.' **1946** K.S. PRICHARD *Roaring Nineties* 250 A poor boy willing to do anything for a crust. **1966** J. WATEN *Season of Youth* 83, I told him I was going to write a book one day, a book on real life. 'You still have to earn a crust,' he said. **1978** H.C. BAKER *I was Listening* 8 What y' doing for a crust these days? **1980** M. BAIL *Homesickness* (1981) 153 What some people do for a crust.

2. A vagrancy charge; a vagrant.

1910 L. ESSON *Three Short Plays* (1911) 14 You're qualifying for a stiff for the crust. . . You're likely to bring a Sixer, I'm warning you. **1966** S.J. BAKER *Austral. Lang.* (ed. 2) 147 *Crust*, a vagrancy charge. **1967** *Kings Cross Whisper* (Sydney) xxxiii. 4/4 *Crust*, a vagrant. To be crusted is to be vagged. From the proposal that a person has not enough money to purchase a crust of bread.

crutch, *n.*[1] [Fig. use of *crutch* a support for an infirm person.] See quot. 1965.

1879 S.W. SILVER *Austral. Grazier's Guide* 48 The sheep-washers, armed with a species of crook, called a crutch. **1965** J.S. GUNN *Terminol. Shearing Industry* i. 18 *Crutch*, a mallet-shaped instrument (like a crutch) used to push sheep under in a swimming dip. Improved dips, especially spray dips, have caused this tool to become obsolete.

crutch, *n.*[2] [See CRUTCH *v.*] The hindquarters of a sheep; the removal of wool from this area. Also *attrib.*

1941 *Method Performing Mules Operation* (Austral. Wool Board) 1 Crutch strikes are said to account for over 90 per cent. of the strikes incurred by merino sheep in Australia. **1943** *Bulletin* (Sydney) 27 Oct. 13/2 Ten crutchers doing a full crutch on ewes with a proportion of weaners averaged 597 per man per day for seven days.

crutch, *v.* [f. *crutch* the part of the body.] *trans.* To clip wool from about the tail of (a sheep) to prevent fouling. Also *absol.* and freq. as *vbl. n.*

1913 W.K. HARRIS *Outback in Aust.* 151 'Crutching' is necessary in some districts, when blowflies are prevalent, and consists of cutting away the wool from the hind-quarters of the affected animal. **1924** *Bulletin* (Sydney) 21 Feb. 22/1 For the blowfly's getting busy and there's crutching to be done. **1936** *Ibid.* 11 Mar. 21/2 Thus runs the solemn Law's award: For crutching, wigging, ringing The rate's—so much per hundred. **1943** *Ibid.* 27 Oct. 13/2 Dixon crutched 508 ewes. **1953** *Ibid.* 20 May 12/4 He had agreed to crutch Newie's sheep for him. **1969** L. HADOW *Full Cycle* 199 He's gone off to Duggan's for a couple of days' crutching. **1977** W.A. WINTER-IRVING *Bush Stories* 76, I crutched sheep stricken with blowfly maggots. **1979** 'BLUE SHEARER' *First Clip* 17 I'd like to be an artist, but I don't quite have the 'touch', And I couldn't be a grazier. I never learned to crutch.

Hence **crutcher** *n.*, one who crutches; **crutchings** *n. pl.* (see quot.).

1943 crutcher [see CRUTCH *n.*[2]] **1914** H.B. SMITH *Sheep & Wool Industry* 67 Wool which is shorn from the britch of the sheep a few months before shearing is called '**crutchings**'.

cuba, var. COOBA.

cuckoo. *Obs.* [Transf. use of *cuckoo*: see quot. 1827.] The owl *Ninox novaeseelandiae* (see BOOBOOK).

[**1827** *Trans. Linnean Soc. London* XV. 188 Boobook Owl. . . The note of the bird is somewhat similar to that of the European *cuckoo*, and the colonists have hence given it that name.] **1852** S. MOSSMAN *Gold Regions Aust.* 64 Hark to the distant Mopauk, with its strange note, which the unromantic settler translates into 'more pork', while the man who prides himself on having a 'soul above buttons', calls it the cuckoo. **1879** 'AUSTRALIAN' *Adventures Qld.* 129 He heard a hoarse note, resembling that of the cuckoo, or Australian owl, close to his head.

cuckoo-shrike. [See quot. 1945.] Any of several birds of the genus *Coracina* of Aust. and elsewhere. See also *black-faced cuckoo-shrike* BLACK *a.*[2] 1 b.

1898 E.E. MORRIS *Austral Eng.* 109 Cuckoo-shrike. . . This combination of two common English bird-names is assigned in Australia to the following [etc.]. **1922** M. GILMORE *Hound of Road* 141 A grey cuckoo-shrike threaded the air. **1931** E.A. VIDLER *Our Own Birds Aust.* 50 The *cuckoo-shrikes* are only like the Cuckoos in their flight and their French-grey plumage with black and white. **1945** C. BARRETT *Austral. Bird Life* 196 Cuckoo-shrikes derive their compound name from the fact that their flight is undulating, like that of cuckoos, while they have the bill of a shrike. **1981** G. CROSS *George & Widda-Woman* 88 The calls of . . the cuckoo-shrikes in the tree-tops.

cucumber fish. [See quot. 1852.] HERRING 2. Also **cucumber herring, cucumber mullet.**

1843 *South Briton* (Hobart) Apr. 56 Providence has . . not been over-bountiful in peopling our rivers with the finny tribes, the only fresh water fish of note being the mullet, herring, cucumber fish, as it is severally called. **1852** MRS C. MEREDITH *My Home in Tas.* II. 82 A small delicate fish, called 'cucumber fish', from its peculiar odour. **1881** J.F.V. FITZGERALD *Aust.* 35 The Yarra herring . . , called in Tasmania the cucumber mullet, is almost identical with the English grayling. **1899** *North-Western Advocate* (Devonport) 15 Sept. 2/6 There is no truth in the statement that cucumber mullet are plentiful in the Derwent. **1986** *Canberra Times* 25 May 5/7 Fisheries inspectors at Eden have identified several small fish, now known to be an endangered species, as Australian Grayling or Cucumber herring.

cuddleseat. [Proprietary name.] A type of baby carrier or sling: see quot. 1949 (2).

[**1947** *N.S.W. Post Office Commercial Directory* 880 *Baby Carrier Mfrs.* Cuddle Seat Mfg Co, Cessnock.] **1948** *Our Babies* (Victorian Babies Health Centres' Assoc.) (ed. 7) 56 *The comfortable baby is a cuddleseat baby* because Cuddleseat is scientifically designed to carry babies of from 2 weeks to 2 years with safety and freedom from strain. **1949** *Sydney Morning Herald* 1 May 4/1 The manufacturers of 'Cuddleseat' baby carriers trading as Cuddleseat Manufacturing Co. of Cessnock, New South Wales, hereby notify the trade and the public that they are the registered proprietors under the Trade Marks Act of the Commonwealth of Australia of Trade Mark No. 80931 consisting of the word 'Cuddleseat' registered in respect of 'A carrier device or seat for babies'. **1949** D. WALKER *We went to Aust.* 35 The peculiarly Australian 'cuddleseat' which I believe originated in Sydney but is most popular in Brisbane. This contrivance . . is a form of canvas sling, so that the infant is worn round the shoulders, rather than directly carried. **1961** *Bulletin* (Sydney) 15 Mar. 39/1 Today's teenagers were carried about for the first couple of years of their existence in a cuddleseat.

cuddy. [Transf. use of Br. dial. *cuddy* donkey.] A horse.

1897 *Worker* (Sydney) 11 Sept. 1/1 Across a wiry 'cuddy' whom he calls his 'crocodile' . . in search of shearing work he rides from hut to hut. **1904** L.M.P. ARCHER *Bush Honeymoon* 40 I'd a couple of *cuddies*—one was a grand lady's hack. **1917** A.B. PATERSON *Saltbush Bill* 90 That's an old cuddy of Flanagan's. **1945** T. RONAN *Strangers on Ophir* 123 Cuthbert . . started to ride. With his whip going like a flail and his spurs working like pistons he drove his old cuddy to the lead. **1966** C. MCGREGOR *Profile Aust.* 38 The sunburnt bloody stockman stood And, in a dismal bloody mood, Apostrophised his bloody cuddy; This bloody nag's no bloody good. **1969** W. MOXHAM *Apprentice* 97 This was how he won at Kembla Grange, on a country cuddy.

cudgerie /ˈkʌdʒəri/. [a. Bandjalang *gajari.*] Any of several rainforest trees, esp. *Flindersia schottiana* (fam. Rutaceae) of N.S.W., Qld., and New Guinea, having large pinnate leaves and prickly woody fruits; the timber of this tree, which is pale and durable. See also BUMPY ASH.

1884 A. NILSON *Timber Trees N.S.W.* 80 *F[lindersia] australis.*—Ash; Cugerie. . . A tree attaining a height of 100 feet, and a diameter of 4 feet, with a dark brown rugged and scaly bark. **1903** *Austral. Handbk.* 280 Some of the trees of large size which furnish . . soft wood . . are . . 'Cudgerie' (*Hernandia bivalvis*) [etc.]. **1925** *Bulletin* (Sydney) 24 Sept. 22/4 Cudgerie is a tall, smooth-barked Queensland tree. **1932** R.H. ANDERSON *Trees in N.S.W.* 138 Cudgerie (*Flindersia Schottiana*) is also known as Bumpy Ash owing to the presence of fairly large protuberances along the stem. **1985** P. CAREY *Illywhacker* 117 We would want . . cudgerie for the fuselage.

cue, *n.* Also **kew, q.** [Br. dial. *cue* the shoe of an ox: see EDD *sb.*[1] and *v.*[1].] The shoe of a bullock: see quots. 1935 and 1976.

1902 *Bulletin* (Sydney) 22 Mar. 15/1 Where you can't get the proper cue, old horse-shoes are used, cut in two. **1935** R.B. PLOWMAN *Boundary Rider* 146 Picking up a farrier's tool-box, he brought it round to the rear of the pen and took from it a hammer and nails and a flat piece of steel—a cue. This was just large enough to cover one half of the horny part of the hoof from the cleft to the heel, and was about an inch and a quarter wide. **1958** *Bulletin* (Sydney) 23 Apr. 18/2 'Kews', I gather, were made out of old slippers which were carefully nailed to the bullocks' feet. **1976** C.D. MILLS *Hobble Chains & Greenhide* 110 A 'Q' . . is a plate with a flattened, hollowed heel, and a pointed, turned toe. It is the counterpart of a horse-shoe, and serves the same purpose. **1980** O. RUHEN *Bullock Teams* 211 Practically all the draught bullocks in that stony country had to be fitted with the two-part iron shoes named 'cues'.

cue, *v.* Also **kew.** [f. prec.] *trans.* To shoe (a beast) with a cue.

1902 *Bulletin* (Sydney) 22 Mar. 15/1 Bullocks . . are 'cued' . . but to cue a team you have to build a pen (sort of a crush) and put the comether on 'em. **1933** W.L. OWEN *Cossack Gold* 162 Since much of the North-west is stony country the oxen were 'cued', which is immemorial west of England dialect for shod. . . Turning up a cued hoof you see something resembling the crescent-shaped metal protectors on the toe or heel of a shoe or boot. **1951** E. HILL *Territory* 324 A month or two on the westward trail, he cued his bullocks at Cueing Pen Springs. **1958** *Bulletin* (Sydney) 23 Apr. 18/2 'Kewing', or 'cueing' . . was once applied to the shoeing of bullocks in the Kimberley country of W.A. **1976** C.D. MILLS *Hobble Chains & Greenhide* 110 Working bullocks are always Q-ed when working in stony country—particularly the polers.

Hence **cue-er** *n.*, one who cues; **cueing** *vbl. n.*, esp. as **cueing pen.**

1935 R.B. PLOWMAN *Boundary Rider* 147 The bullock recognized the **cue-er** for a stranger and very properly showed his resentment. **1958** *Bulletin* (Sydney) 23 Apr. 18/2 Most stations in the region had their '**kewing**-pens'. **1976** C.D. MILLS *Hobble Chains & Greenhide* 110 A q-ing pen was, as a rule, made like a crush, with a bail, or head-stock, for impounding the head.

cuff. [With ref. to the *cuffs* and *collars* of a formal shirt.] Used *attrib.* and *absol.* in the collocation **cuff and collar,** white collar (worker).

1896 *Bulletin* (Sydney) 23 May 3/2 You bushmen sneer in the old bush way at the new-chum jackeroo, But 'cuffs-'n'-collers' were out *that day*, and they stuck to their posts like glue. **1899** *Western Champion* (Barcaldine) 22 Aug. 14/1 It's Sunday and I suppose in Hughenden all the cuff and collar push are at church. **1936** J. DEVANNY *Sugar Heaven* 211 The 'silvertails', as the cutters designated the bank clerks and other 'cuff and collar' workers, complained they couldn't get a bath nor a seat at table.

cuffer. *Obs.* [Br. dial. *cuffer* tale, yarn (see EDD *cuff*, *sb.*[3]); cf. *cuff* to tell a tale (OEDS *v.*[1] 4).] A story or yarn; a 'tall story'.

1887 K. MACKAY *Stirrup Jingles* 40 Alright, boss! If a yarn I must spin, Leastways it won't be a cuffer. **1894** W. CROMPTON *Convict Jim* 10 And I see the camp-fire blazing 'neath the overhanging trees, And the boys a-spinning cuffers to the sighing of the breeze. **1904** J. FARRELL *My Sundowner* 62 You're a (bad word) duffer Beside this cove at pitchin' of a cuffer! **1916** *Truth* (Sydney) 16 Jan. 11/1 They were in no way green, and knew something about the art of leg-pulling. . . 'Tommy' does so love to spin a 'cuffer'!

cully. [Survival of Br. *cully* fellow, mate: see OED *sb.* 2.] A mate; used esp. as a mode of address.

1905 *Bulletin* (Sydney) 16 Apr. 19/2 You've noticed maybe, cully, that the bush is always callin'. **1908** *Truth* (Sydney) 4 Oct. 1/7 They're not singing Peter's praises, Yet they dodge around like blazes, Crying, 'Nixey cully, here comes Peter Hush!' **1920** 'J. NORTH' *Harry Dale's Grand National* 125 'Right-oh, cully,' said the man, who was never surprised by any of the eccentricities of his customers. **1929** H.M. NEEDHAM *Morepork* 11 Hark, the friendly greetings passing—'How do, Chawley?' . . 'What o' Cully.' **1958** O. RUHEN *Naked under Capricorn* 184 No we don't, cully. That's where you make the big mistake. **1976** A. BUZO *Martello Towers* 20 Listen, cully, no man's going to lay a heavy chauve trip on the head of *my* woman.

cultivation. Abbrev. of CULTIVATION PADDOCK. Also *attrib.*

1906 *Bulletin* (Sydney) 18 Oct. 44/1 Dave goes to look after his private enterprise of wallaby trapping, and Dad to the 'cultivation' he has already spent months clearing. **1917** M.A. ALLAN *Casket of Memories* 40 More paddocks, one, named 'the cultivation'. **1923** *Austral.* (Sydney) Sept. 6 The gates stayed mended, the cattle never got into the cultivation. **1934** 'S. RUDD' *Green Grey Homestead* 35 The tree with the bees' nest will be cut down and lying across your cultivation fence. **1949** *Coast to Coast 1948* 113 Our mother would smarten herself up after dinner and take the afternoon smoke-oh over to the cultivation, and we would play among the cornstalks. **1960** *Khaki Bush & Bigotry* (1968) 256, I came the short cut across the cultivation.

cultivation paddock. An enclosed piece of a rural property, used for the growing of crops.

1841 *Port Phillip Patriot* 25 Feb. 4 There are also considerable improvements on the Estate, having a . . calf paddock, grass paddock, and cultivation paddock. **1850** *Illustr. Austral. Mag.* (Melbourne) Nov. 327 At a short distance to the left was a considerable cultivation paddock, where an ample harvest had been reaped. **1860** 'LADY' *My Experiences in Aust.* 173 There was a space cleared of trees, some 20 to 30 acres in extent, on the banks of the creek, known as the 'Cultivation Paddock'. **1872** G.S. BADEN-POWELL *New Homes for Old Country* 154 Hay is made from lucerne, oats, barley, or wheat, as the case may be, grown in the 'cultivation paddock'. **1885** MRS C. PRAED *Austral. Life* 112 We composed jointly, and courted the muse as we lay among the pumpkins and Indian corn in the cultivation paddock. **1898** L. LINDLEY-COWEN *W. Austral. Settler's Guide* 767 The cultivation paddock should . . be so arranged as to adjoin three or four grass paddocks. **1919** *Huon Times* (Franklin) 14 Mar. 3/6 Rabbits . . sit up like standing lemonade bottles around a farmer's gate in the anticipation of gaining access to a cultivation paddock. **1934** 'S. RUDD' *Green Grey Homestead* 82 You'll turn your thoughts to the bee's nest in the gully near your cultivation paddock. **1946** *Coast to Coast 1945* 4 He ploughed his stony cultivation paddock. **1973** R. ROBINSON *Drift of Things* 98 Mr Simmonds said that I could exercise him in the soft, ploughed cultivation paddock.

cultural cringe. [Coined by A.A. Phillips (1900–85), literary critic: see quot. 1950.] A phr. alluding to an (Australian) attitude characterized by deference to the cultural achievements of others.

1950 A.A. PHILLIPS in *Meanjin* 299 Above our writers—and other artists—looms the intimidating mass of Anglo-Saxon culture. Such a situation almost inevitably produces the characteristic Australian Cultural Cringe. **1972** *Bulletin* (Sydney) 26 Aug. 38/1 After so many years of cultural cringe, even a modest dose of international recognition is proving difficult to take. **1976** *Ibid.* 3 Apr. 80/3 The Cultural Cringe . . has been going on longer. The Australian Establishment has always cringed before 'sophisticated' European literature and taught it in schools and universities to the exclusion of the local product until very recent years. **1983** *Age Monthly Rev.* June 17/4 If the cultural cringe formula has become a handy missile for the smugger obscurantist provincials to fling at their larger-minded betters, I repent of having coined it. . . It is time to accord the phrase decent burial before the smell of the corpse gets too high. **1984** *Canberra Times* 26 Apr. 8/5 The expatriate view of a derivative and unimportant people is so much an accepted part of our cultural cringe that we are embarrassed or unbelieving about European enthusiasm for things Australian.

Hence **cultural cringer** *n.*

1977 P. ADAMS *Unspeakable Adams* 24 We're a nation of cultural cringers who tug our forelocks at French cooking while bemoaning our lack of indigenous dishes.

Cumberland disease. [See quot. 1877.] A local name for anthrax. Also *ellipt.* as **Cumberland.**

1863 R. THERRY *Reminisc. Thirty Yrs. N.S.W. & Vic.* 264 We were again visited with a most infectious and fatal disease, known as the Cumberland disease, which killed immense numbers of sheep and cattle. **1877** G. MITCHELL *Cumberland Disease* 19 Cumberland Disease—so called from the circumstance of its having made its first appearance in Australia in the county Cumberland, New South Wales. **1890** E.T. TOWNER *Selectors' Guide to Barcoo* 3 There is no foot-rot, no scab, no Cumberland and no grass seed, each one of which annoyances and consequent loss has to be borne in many other districts I could mention. **1902** A. NORTON *Settling in Qld.* 148 Before we reached Coolah we became acquainted with anthrax, commonly called 'Cumberland' disease, after the county of Cumberland where it was wont to kill many cattle and sheep. **1980** O. RUHEN *Bullock Teams* 185 Vaccination of a similar sort offered some control over 'Cumberland disease', a malady named for the district from which it was first reported; it was in fact anthrax.

cumbungi /kʌmˈbʌŋgi/. [a. Wemba *gambaŋ.*] BULRUSH.

1878 R.B. SMYTH *Aborigines of Vic.* I. p. xxxiii, The kumpung, a bulrush almost identical with one found in Switzerland—a species of *typha*—is eaten during the summer either raw or roasted, and the fibres are used for making twine. **1889** *Jrnl. & Proc. R. Soc. N.S.W.* XXIII. 396 Along the marshy grounds of the Murrumbidgee and Lachlan Rivers a plant grows profusely which is locally known as 'Combungie'. **1903** G. SUTHERLAND *Australasian Live Stock Man.* (ed. 2) 384 Cumbangee is the name given to a kind of green plant having a strong resemblance to a leek. **1942** E. ANDERSON *Squatter's Luck* 14 Cumbungi, sir, 's in ther drain, Skeleton's 'ere again. **1974** *Ecos* ii. 26/3 The fertilizer-laden water stimulates a rich growth of water plants, particularly of cumbungi, a bullrush. **1978** C. GREEN *Sun is Up* 74 Eastern swamp hens push long-legged through the cumbungi reeds.

cundy, var. COONIE.

cunjevoi /ˈkʌndʒəvɔɪ/, *n.*[1] Chiefly *N.S.W.* Also **cungeboy.** [Prob. f. a N.S.W. Aboriginal language.] The ascidian or sea-squirt *Pyura praeputialis*, occurring on intertidal rocks in s. Aust., the flesh of which is used as bait. Also abbrev. as **cunji, cunjy.**

1821 S. LEIGH in Methodist Missionary Soc. Rec. 18 Nov., This Cunguwa is a kind of living fungus, which at certain seasons they detach from the Rocks on the Sea Shore. **1834** L.E. THRELKELD *Austral. Grammar* 85 A red sea slug adhering to the rocks, and known to Europeans by the name Kunje-wy. **1895** C. THACKERAY *Amateur Fisherman's Guide* 32 There is one bait which is par excellence the bait for the rocks. It is called generally 'cungeboy'. . . The term corresponds with, and is probably a corruption of the word cungevoi or congewoi in the aboriginal vernacular. **1917** —— *Goliath Joe* 29, I . . fell to chuckin' in lumps er cunjy for 'im to eat. **1945** *Sun* (Sydney) 15 May 4/3 If the congevoi isn't a lower form of animal life, the barnacle is a melon plant, or I'm an onion. **1952** W.J. DAKIN *Austral. Seashores* 341 The cunjevoi band [is] found in the south of Queensland, along the whole length of the coast of New South Wales and the Victorian coast west to Cape Otway. **1967** *Surfabout* (Sydney) IV. ii. 22 Another group surf in a decidedly non-functional manner . . which usually results in rather forceful bodily contact with the cunji.

cunjevoi /ˈkʌndʒəvɔɪ/, *n.*[2] Also **cunjiboy.** [Prob. f. a Qld. Aboriginal language.] The plant *Alocasia macrorrhiza* (fam. Araceae), occurring in moist forests of N.S.W., Qld., and elsewhere.

1845 C. HODGKINSON *Aust., Port Macquarie to Moreton Bay* 225 The root of the Conjeboi, a large-leaved plant, which grows on very moist alluvial land, often flooded, is also eaten. **1851** J. HENDERSON *Excursions & Adventures N.S.W.* 142 *Cungevoi* is the root of a plant .. which grows in brushes, and most plentifully just within their margins. **1871** *Austral. Town & Country Jrnl.* (Sydney) 18 Mar. 330/4 The more powerful stinging-tree and its antidote the congewoi are seldom far apart,—the latter being a large-leaved, unwholesome looking green plant, resembling a gigantic lily. **1888** *Proc. Linnean Soc. N.S.W.* III. 365 *Colocasia macrorrhiza*... I know no aboriginal or colonial name used in New South Wales for this plant, although for Queensland .. 'Cunjevoi' is the one best known. **1901** *Bulletin* (Sydney) 9 Mar. 14/3 The cunjevoi plant which flourishes along the northern N.S.W. rivers is one of the most nourishing plant foods of our coast-blacks. **1916** *Ibid.* 3 Feb. 22/2 There are several remedies for bull-rout 'stings'... A wild lily, the 'cungy-boy' .. is said to take out the sting. **1926** M. FORREST *Hibiscus Heart* 119 The pale, lily-leafed cunjiboy, which makes an animal's mouth and tongue swell and which the natives use for a mustard plaster and as a cure for rheumatism. **1963** I.L. IDRIESS *Our Living Stone Age* 10 In tick-infested areas the mother will carefully search baby's body for these vicious creatures, and in some coastal regions will seek a cunjevoi plant as an antidote to their poison.

cunji, cunjy, abbrev. of CUNJEVOI *n.*[1]

cunmerrie /ˈkʌnməri/. [Prob. f. a Qld. Aboriginal language.] In Aboriginal belief: a huge winged spirit which carries off people and animals.

1946 W.E. HARNEY *North of 23°* 79 Fearful cunmerries, bat-like spirits, out to destroy, so powerful that they can lift a horse with its rider into the air. **1959** D. LOCKWOOD *Crocodiles & Other People* 59 They're especially scared of the cunmerrie, a ghastly, ghostly bird with enormous wings, talons, and beak—a bird that can swoop down on a mob and carry away the fattest bullock.

cunning, *a.* In the phr. **to run cunning,** (of a working dog): see quot. 1914.

1914 R. KALESKI *Austral. Barkers & Biters* 76 He loses his youthful dash and energy, and begins to 'run cunning'—lets the other dog do all the work. **1920** *Bulletin* (Sydney) 6 May 20/2 The alleged tame dingo .. is a heartbreak to the shepherd. He will 'run cunning' when sent round the flock, cutting off a 'wing' of the sheep, which is disastrous to the drover.

Cup. *Horse-racing.*

1. Usu. with **the**: shortened form of *Melbourne Cup*, a handicap race over 3200 m., run annually since 1861, on the first Tuesday in November, in Melbourne. Also *attrib.*

1861 *Argus* (Melbourne) 8 Nov. 5/5 His Excellency visited the saddling paddock during the half-hour preceding the Cup Race. **1864** *Australasian* (Melbourne) 12 Nov. 5/2 The slippery state of the ground made the results of the race for the Cup altogether unreliable. **1865** *Illustr. Melbourne Post* Nov. 166/1 In Melbourne all was bustle and excitement—the crisis, the drought .. seemed to have been entirely forgotten in the all-absorbing topic of the Cup. **1881** R. THATCHER *Travelled Actor* 5 The public love sport as well as play; and 100,000 of them will gather to see their Cup run for. **1893** B. MORANT *Poetry* (1980) 17 And when they're sold at Homebush, and the agents settle up, Sing hey! a spell in Sydney town and Melbourne for the 'Cup'. **1904** *Truth* (Sydney) 6 Nov. 4/4 The horsey section of the community goes off its pannikin at Cup time. **1910** *Huon Times* (Franklin) 2 Nov. 3/5 The Federal Houses are frankly recognising the Cup. There is to be a parliamentary holiday. **1916** 'T.O. LINGO' *Austral. Comic Dict.* 53 *Cup Race*, the Australian Race witnessed by the Australian race. **1935** T. RAYMENT *Cluster of Bees* 271 About the time the famous 'Cup' attracts its hundreds .. I see these bees celebrate the day by many copulations. **1955** N. PULLIAM *I traveled Lonely Land* 229 The words 'Melbourne' and 'The Cup' go together as naturally the world over as the words 'acorn' and 'oak'. **1969** L. HADOW *Full Cycle* 126 It was time to board another ship for Melbourne and the Cup. **1981** *Bulletin* (Sydney) 3 Nov. 65/3 For sheer extravagance last year's Cup was hard to beat.

2. Comb. **Cup day, time, week.**

1876 *Illustr. Austral. News* (Melbourne) 29 Nov. 187/3 The **Cup day** of 1876 will be remembered as one of the most successful. **1886** D.E. BANDMANN *Actor's Tour* 85 From Cup day to Cup day these fair, gentle women break their tender heads about what new and elaborate costume, never before seen, they are to wear at the next great meet. **1889** R.W. DALE *Impressions Aust.* 22 'Cup Day' .. was plainly a national festival. **1898** H. MATTHEWS *Chat about Aust.* 11 Who .. has not heard of Cup Day? **1960** *Bulletin* (Sydney) 23 Nov. 9/2 On Cup Day, New Australian started raddling his front fence. **1971** *Island Authors* 115 'Christ,' laughed a man, 'it's worse than Cup Day.' **1891** 'ROUSEABOUT' *Jackeroo* 66 Many persons resident in various parts of the colonies, who would never think of visiting Melbourne at any other time, find themselves irresistably drawn thither at **Cup time.** **1912** O. WOOD *Cup Week* 12 Do you remember cup times These ten years ago? **1924** W.R. SMITH *In Southern Seas* 1 After having experienced the effects and the after-effects of a fortnight's trip to Melbourne with the idea of finding rest and change at Cup time. **1948** A.J. MCLACHLAN *McLachlan* 107 Melbourne was our Mecca at Cup time. **1967** A.E. DEBENHAM *All Manner of People* 130, I spent a week in Melbourne last Cuptime, and cleared £150. **1983** *Canberra Times* 29 Oct. 7/1 It's Cup time again and this year we're going to give you some help with those betting slips. **1882** *Austral. Stories* (ed. 2) 78 Little debts contracted .. in the '**Cup week**', 'bout the Christmas time before. **1912** O. WOOD (*title*) Cup Week. **1934** P. WIRTH *Life* 44 We played Melbourne to the end of Cup Week. **1955** N. PULLIAM *I traveled Lonely Land* 229 Visitors from all over the continent—and elsewhere, if they can come—descend upon the city for Cup Week by every known means of transportation. **1965** G. MCINNES *Road to Gundagai* 117 Many of the squatters had houses in Melbourne as well as their huge stations, and to these they repaired for Cup Week. **1981** *Bulletin* (Sydney) 3 Nov. 65/3 It is perhaps the not knowing what is going to happen next that keeps Cup week fizzing.

curl. [See quot. 1945.] In the phr. **to curl the mo,** to succeed brilliantly; also as quasi-*adj.*, impressive, outstanding.

1941 S.J. BAKER *Pop. Dict. Austral. Slang* 42 *Kurl*, good, excellent. Also 'kurl-a-mo'. **1944** *Truth* (Sydney) 13 Feb. 4/3 Breasley saw Kintore donkey-lick a field of youngsters in the Federal Stakes, and had salt rubbed into his wound when the Lewis cuddy Valour curled the mo in the Bond Handicap. **1945** S.J. BAKER *Austral. Lang.* 126 *Curl-the-mo* was apparently first used to denote the self-satisfaction of a man who twirled the ends of his flowing moustache. **1957** D. WHITINGTON *Treasure upon Earth* 74 An elbow nudged him on the crowded dance floor later. 'Start getting Josie out,' Mick told him... 'This is going to be a real curl the mo' job.' **1963** *Sunday Mirror* (Sydney) 20 Jan. 43/2 Gilli, with Mulley apparently 'curling the mo' was possied behind them for his challenge. **1966** R. MORLEY *Cool Change* 31 Christ, Tom, you look the toff. Curl the mo feller! **1972** *Bulletin* (Sydney) 12 Aug. 7/3 'The National Language Trust favors preservation of old approval terms,' she said; 'In fact we've given a high 'B' classification to 'curl-the mo'.' **1977** S. LOCKE ELLIOTT *Water under Bridge* 313 Maybe I'll look very curl-the-mo in my uniform, eh?

curlew. Either of two ground-nesting birds of the genus *Burhinus*, esp. *B. grallarius*, formerly widespread in Aust. but no longer found in closely settled areas; *stone curlew, stone plover*, see STONE *n.*[1] 3; WEELO.

1834 G. BENNETT *Wanderings N.S.W.* I. 334 At Paramatta [*sic*] I saw two tame specimens of the lesser *Otis*, or Bustard, the 'Curlew' of the colony. **1844** L. LEICHHARDT *Jrnl. Overland Exped. Aust.* 25 Oct. (1847) 23 The melancholy wail of the curlew .. heard from the neighbouring scrub. **1917** *Bulletin* (Sydney) 28 June 24/4 The blacks were in the habit .. of naming the birds by their call. Instances are .. 'weelo', a curlew [etc.]. **1934** WARBURTON & ROBERTSON *Buffaloes* 72 We almost rode on to a couple of birds I recognized as curlews... They are sometimes called the stone-plover... Their plumage is brown flecked with white, and their eyes are large and yellowish-brown. **1970** K. WILLEY *Naked Island* 141 Once he killed a curlew, which the Aborigines call the devil bird because of its eerie cry as it circles the camps at night.

curly Mitchell: see MITCHELL GRASS 2.

currajong, var. KURRAJONG.

currant. *Native currant*, see NATIVE *a.* 6 a. Also **currant bush, tree.**

1817 J. O'HARA *Hist. N.S.W.* 242 A species of currant, green in its state of maturity, afforded an excellent jelly. **1865** R.J. SHOLL *Jrnl. Exped. Camden Harbour to Glenelg River* 205 We bivouacked under what is here called the currant-tree, about 9 or 10 feet high, greyish striated bark, with twisted branches. The leaf is bright-green, smooth on the upper surface, 5 inches long, and 1 to 1½ inch [*sic*] broad. The fruit has a pleasant acid taste—black when ripe. It is of the size of a very small currant, and, like most Australian fruits, has more stone than flesh. **1879** *Native Tribes S.A.* 224 Fomenting the anus with the previously heated green leaves of the currant tree, in cases of diarrhoea. **1887** W.H. SUTTOR *Austral. Stories Retold* 117 There grows profusely a sickly-looking greenish-yellow shrub, locally misnamed the currant bush. Its fruit is a pea. **1915** *Bulletin* (Sydney) 11 Nov. 22/2 The knubbly roots of the currant-bush .. prized because found where no other fuel is available. **1936** F. CLUNE *Roaming round Darling* 165 The currant or emu bush; needle-leafed, with fruit like black berries, each one the size of a pea—not caviare to emus. **1954** *Coast to Coast 1953–54* 88 The 'wet' was approaching. The native plum-tree and the currant-bush were in flower.

currawong /ˈkʌrəwɒŋ/. Also **kurrawong.** [a. Jagara (and neighbouring languages) *garrawaŋ*.] Any of the three birds of the Austral. genus *Strepera*, having predom. black or grey plumage and a ringing call; *bell magpie*, see BELL *n.* Also with distinguishing epithet, as **black, grey, pied** (see under first element).

1905 [see *crow-shrike* CROW *n.*[1]] **1911** *Bulletin* (Sydney) 26 Jan. 15/2 The pied crow-shrike .. is called by various onomatopoeic renderings of its cry, such as .. corowong. **1916** *Ibid.* 3 Feb. 24/4 The kurrawong, or pied-bell magpie, has a loud, ringing voice. **1918** *Ibid.* 14 Feb. (Red Page), When a bird cheerily shouts *Currawong*, why should a kiddy be asked to pass by that musical word in favor of 'pied bell-magpie'? **1929** A.H. CHISHOLM *Birds & Green Places* 18 Those mountain roysterers which bird-men term bell-magpies, and which bush-dwellers know as currawongs or chilla-wongs. **1948** P.J. HURLEY *Red Cedar* 32 Birds of all kinds found this sanctuary .. larrikin currawongs [etc.]. **1951** D. CUSACK *Say no to Death* (1959) 101 A currawong drifted over, uttering its plaintive yang-yang. **1971** J. O'GRADY *Aussie Etiket* 5 'Skinny bloody sliced bread, an' peanut bloody butter.' 'Aw, feed it to the currawongs, mate.' **1980** A.S. VEITCH *Run from Morning* 37 From outside came the melodious song of a currawong.

currency.

1. *Hist.* A local medium of exchange circulating in the Australian Colonies and discounted against sterling (see also *colonial currency* COLONIAL *a.* 5). Also *attrib.*

1792 D. COLLINS *Acct. Eng. Colony N.S.W.* (1798) I. 246 They would have suffered great difficulties from the want of public money .. had not the commissary .. given them notes on himself... These notes passed through various hands in traffic among the people... They were intended to serve, and became a species of currency which was found very convenient to them. **1806** *Sydney Gaz.* 2 Nov., Whereas the term *Currency*, made use of in this Colony, seems not to have carried its proper Signification in the Small Notes generally circulated; It is hereby declared, that its meaning is only applicable to Money, and not *Barter* in Goods: so that if any Note is made payable in *Copper Coin* or the *Currency* of this Colony, it is to be inferred that *Money only* is the means by which it is to be liquidated. **1811** *Ibid.* 30 Nov., Retail Prices .. in Currency and Copper Coin. **1817** *HRA* (1917) 1st Ser. IX. 216 *Currency* Notes, the nature of which was such that the depreciation in the relative Value, when in comparison with Sterling Money, actually became the chief source of profit and advantage .. to the Issuers of those Notes. **1825** *Austral.* (Sydney) 19 May 2. Our readers will rejoice with us at learning that the present difference between currency and sterling is rumoured on respectable authority as likely to cease in a short time, and be superseded by a coinage of sterling consideration. **1826** *Monitor* (Sydney) 1 Dec. 226/3 All classes are suffering . . principally through the traders not having reduced the price of their goods, at the same time exacting sterling money at currency value. **1827** *Ibid.* 20 Dec. 848/1 Mr R. Cooper . . sells his Colonial gin . . for 8s. 8d. Stg. or 10s. Currency by the single gallon, *cash down.* **1828** *Tasmanian* (Hobart) 22 Feb. 3 From 8s. 6d. to 9s. [per bushel of wheat] could be obtained for it in larger quantities, but this was *currency*, equal to about 7s. 6d. to 7s. 9d. *sterling.* **1830** *Launceston Advertiser* 18 Jan. 4 *Sterling and Currency.* It was a strange omission in the Chamber of Commerce, when they passed the Resolutions declaring the dollar to be worth 5s. currency, not to say a word about its price in sterling. **1838** J. MACLEHOSE *Picture of Sydney* 124 Spanish dollars . . for many years—indeed so late as within the last seven or eight years, circulated as 'currency coin'. **1840** *S. Austral. Miscellany* May 175 The *holey* dollar was the rim, the *dump* the centre struck out of the Spanish dollar,—the former passing for 3s. 9d., the latter for 1s. 3d. currency. **1881** J.F.V. FITZGERALD *Aust.* 56 The balance of trade had caused a scarcity of coin. Private individuals were authorized to issue promissory notes for 5*s.*, redeemable in copper. This 'currency' was soon depreciated to the extent of 25 per cent.

2. A non-Aboriginal person native to Australia. Freq. *attrib.* and passing into *adj.*

1824 [see *currency lad, lass*]. **1825** *Austral.* (Sydney) 29 Sept. 3 At peep of day, several persons . . assembled on a spot of ground suitable enough for witnessing a pulley hauley match between two ladies of the fancy; the one a towny, the other of currency worth. **1826** *Colonial Times* (Hobart) 9 Dec., We hope the phrase *'Currency Youths'* will be no longer given to the native born inhabitants of the Colony. **1826** *Monitor* (Sydney) 3 Nov. 194/2 The parties hied to a certain delectable spot . . where the intrinsic merit of *sterling* and *currency* blood was about to be decided. **1829** R. MUDIE *Picture of Aust.* 355 Those who are born in the colony are called *Currency*, and those of English or European birth, and who have not found their way there in such a manner as to entitle them to the cant name of *Legitimates*, are called *Sterling.* **1833** *Currency Lad* (Sydney) 12 Jan. 2 When . . our European friends . . 'set down' on the banks of our rivers, they are the adopted children of our country; and if not Currency themselves our country is very prolific, and they find it not difficult to coin a few. **1844** MRS C. MEREDITH *Notes & Sketches N.S.W.* 50 The natives (not the aborigines, but the 'currency', as they are termed, in distinction from the 'sterling', or British-born residents) are often very good-looking when young. **1845** T. MCCOMBIE *Adventures of Colonist* 134 Nearly all of the species known as 'currency' are matter-of-fact men, with very few elements of originality in their composition, and ignorant of the pleasure to be derived from the fine arts. **1845** *Bell's Life in Sydney* 22 Nov. 2/6 Some people say that the Currency muster too strong in the City Council, and think it would have been but prudent to have intermixed a dash of Sterling matter. **1872** M. CLARKE *His Natural Life* (1970) 616 The cheerful companion suggests a song, and sings one, in which he expresses his opinion that 'Currency Flash' is the 'style for him'. **1888** 'R. BOLDREWOOD' *Robbery under Arms* (1937) 42 He'd always go to the mischief for the sake of a good horse, and many another 'Currency' chap has gone the same way. **1890** —— *Colonial Reformer* III. 60, I want to show the English lady what a Currency girl can walk away with. **1978** M. WALKER *Pioneer Crafts Early Aust.* 116 The main resource of the colonial and currency men, their collective experience, was of paramount importance to the large number of would-be bullockies. **1985** *Bulletin* (Sydney) 27 Aug. 47/2 The Australian flag should be more than a defaced British ensign. . . 'Currency' need pay no deference to 'sterling'.

3. *transf.*

1827 *Monitor* (Sydney) 27 Apr. 400/2 Horses started neck and neck—currency-bred. **1832** *Currency Lad* (Sydney) 8 Sept. 2 Messrs Marshall and Lowe, the enterprising tradesmen . . built our fine currency steamboat *William the Fourth. Ibid.* 8 Sept. 2 Two brothers, named Coutts, have nearly completed a schooner of ninety tons, at George's River. She is entirely the work of their own hands, with not a timber or a plank, not a strand or a stay, but what is 'Currency'. **1848** *Bell's Life in Sydney* 25 Mar. 1/1 The *older* days . . when one or two horses (imported at a vast expense from the *older* country) could enter the colonial arena, triumphantly bearing away the palm of victory from currency cattle.

4. Comb. **currency boy, lad, lass.**

1834 J.D. LANG *Hist. & Statistical Acct. N.S.W.* I. 388 A **currency boy**, or native of the colony. **1874** C. DE BOOS *Congewoi Correspondence* 55 It's no use a-talking, the Currency boys ain't half the chaps as they useter be when I was a youngster. **1824** *Austral.* (Sydney) 18 Nov. 3 Let the **currency lads** and lasses turn Arcadian shepherds and shepherdesses if they choose. **1827** P. CUNNINGHAM *Two Yrs. in N.S.W.* II. 53 Our Currency lads and lasses are a fine interesting race, and do honour to the country whence they originated. **1833** H.W. PARKER *Rise, Progress, & Present State Van Dieman's Land* 189 Currency lads, as the country-born colonists in the facetious nomenclature of the country are called. **1839** J. MARSHALL *Twenty Yrs. Experience in Aust.* 54 He is a 'currency lad' of the first water. **1844** E. GEOGHEGAN *Currency Lass* (1976) 11 France may pride in her courtly airs and polished graces—to me the blunt sincerity and cordial frankness of a currency lad are far more grateful. **1861** 'OLD BUSHMAN' *Bush Wanderings* 247 As for the young 'currency lads', they are more precocious than the youth at home. **1873** J. BONWICK *Tasmanian Lily* 82 Tom Turner was not a bad specimen of a Colonial lad, more commonly called in Sydney a *Currency lad.* **1899** H. LAWSON *Autobiogr. & Other Writings* (1972) 42, I rather like the old, early day name of 'Currency Lad', applied to the native-born. **1904** *Truth* (Sydney) 15 May 5/3 'Currency lads and lasses', to use the old phrase, have to give way to any new Johnnie or Janie who leaves hold Hingland for hold Hingland's good. **1929** G. MEUDELL *Pleasant Career Spendthrift* 75 The dislike of the 'currency lad' for that which he regarded as his oppressive supervision by the police. **1949** W. LAWSON *Blue Gum Clippers* 30 The *Currency Lass*, a schooner built in Sydney by 'currency lads', as the native youths were called. **1975** X. HERBERT *Poor Fellow my Country* 1076 There was a deliberate policy of disparaging the Currency Lads . . as a sort of bastard breed . . and it still goes on. **1982** *Canberra Times* 11 Dec. 2/5 It was a case of the Pommie officer, who thought he knew it all, versus the currency lad. **1824 currency lass** [see *currency lad*]. **1825** *Austral.* (Sydney) 28 Apr. 3 The 'Currency Lasses' were 'bumpered, three times three', as we hope they always will be. **1831** *Sydney Herald* 8 Aug. 2/2 There is abundance of room for large importations of free female emigrants, without deteriorating the value of our currency lasses. **1839** *Sydney Standard* 18 Mar. 3/3 Currency Lasses.—We believe the lady of our Chief Justice is the first instance of a female born in this colony having arrived at the honour of becoming a woman of title. **1840** *Port Phillip Gaz.* 1 Feb. 2 The answer of the simple *Currency Lass* will suit our purpose, who, when asked if she would like to visit England, said, no! there are so many *thieves* there!! **1843** J. HOOD *Aust. & East* 89, I have not yet seen what I should call a fine woman among the native ladies of Australia, the currency lasses, as they are termed. **1852** G.C. MUNDY *Our Antipodes* III. 294 This young lady might have been produced at the Great Exhibition of this year as a favourable specimen of the 'currency lass' of Australia. **1857** J. ASKEW *Voyage Aust. & N.Z.* 223 Much has been said and written touching the loveliness of the 'currency lasses', or native women of New South Wales. **1890** 'R. BOLDREWOOD' *Colonial Reformer* I. 56 I'm sure everybody says English girls have such lovely complexions and figures, and cut out us poor 'currency lasses' altogether. **1899** *Bulletin* (Sydney) 23 Dec. 32/1 She held them at ease in snow-white hands, For Queen over all was the Currency Lass. **1916** *Truth* (Sydney) 8 Oct. 3/7 The Currency Lass can wield a pen as well as the Currency Lad can shoulder a rifle.

curry. [Prob. fig. use of *curry* spiced dish; but see also KURRAJONG 3.] In the phr. **to give** (someone) **curry,** to make life difficult or 'hot' for (a person), esp. to attack (a person) physically or verbally.

1936 *Bulletin* (Sydney) 6 May 21/1 The cocky seems to worry both through drought that gives him curry And through flood that just as ruthlessly destroys. **1944** *Coast to Coast 1943* 124 She was trying to think up what she was going to say from the platform. 'I'm going to give those old tarts a bit of curry tonight, Ron.' **1962** K. SIMONS *Not with Kiss* 25 'I gave him some curry,' Ollie chuckled volcanically and waved the broomstick like a weapon. **1969** A. BUZO *Front Room Boys* (1970) 53 Let's give the ratbags a bit of curry. **1977** *Sunday Tel.* (Sydney) 30 Jan. 48/1 My old mate Lennie Pascoe gave the Bananalanders some curry yesterday. . . He shattered the first four wickets for only 16 off seven overs. **1986** *Canberra Times* 20 Feb. 1/1 Such actions led the Leader of the Government in the House, Mr Young, to threaten last week to give the opposition a 'bit of curry'.

curse.

1. *Obs.* A jocular name for a swag, esp. in the phr. **curse of God** (or **Cain**).

1921 *Smith's Weekly* (Sydney) 10 Dec. 17/4 A few swag aliases:- Matilda, the drum, bluey, white man's burden, and Curse of Cain. **1926** *Bulletin* (Sydney) 18 Nov. 22/4 An old swaggie with the curse o' God on his shoulders called at our place and asked for a bit of tucker. **1939** *Ibid.* 22 Feb. 21/1 We overtook a genuine old-style swaggie, neatly-rolled 'Curse o' Gawd' slung over left shoulder by a towel . . and fly-corks dancing from hat-brim. **1950** *Ibid.* 26 July 12/1 Humping the curse near Bunbury (W.A.), the Count and I found a pick and shovel. **1965** R.H. CONQUEST *Horses in Kitchen* 44 With the coming of the hoboes in their thousands such picturesque phrases as 'waltzing matilda' and 'humping bluey'—not forgetting 'the curse of Cain' to define a swag—vanished from our language.

2. Ellipt. for PATERSON'S CURSE.

1932 K.S. PRICHARD *Kiss on Lips* 38 'The curse!' 'Patterson's curse?' 'A noxious weed.' **1984** *Sydney Morning Herald* 6 Apr. 18/1 Beekeepers took out a successful Supreme Court writ in South Australia restraining the CSIRO from destroying the Curse because of its importance to the honey industry.

cushion bush. The rounded, coastal shrub *Calocephalus brownii* (fam. Asteraceae) of N.S.W., Vic., Tas., S.A., and W.A., cultivated as an ornamental.

1911 D.A. MACDONALD *Bush Boy's Bk.* 10 On many of the Victorian sea slopes . . the Cushion Bush forms a natural bed. **1919** *Emu* XVIII. 266 Here and there along the sand tea-tree, currant-bush and cushion-bush have established themselves. **1951** G. FARWELL *Outside Track* 55 Cushion bush dark upon the bold reddish dunes. **1971** J.R. GARNET *Wildflowers Wilson's Promontory* 5 The cushion-bush of the foreshore dunes owes its remarkably compact character to this habit of growth. **1984** E. WALLING *On Trail Austral. Wildflowers* 58 The silvery-grey Cushion-bush, a mass of tangled stems of small dull yellow knob-like flowers.

cut, *n.*

1. A part of a mob of sheep or cattle separated out for a purpose. See CUT OUT *v.* 1.

1874 *Illustr. Sydney News* 28 Mar. 7/4 Small cuts are brought into the woolshed yards and after the lambs are drafted out, the ewes are taken to the woolshed to be shorn. **1904** *Bulletin* (Sydney) 28 July 17/2 One of the drovers, advised Taylor to steady the bullocks . . and take 'cuts' of a couple of a hundred at a time to the creek. **1963** M. BRITT *Pardon my Boots* 80 My job was to 'hold the cut'—to hold the bullocks or cows which had been cut out of the mob.

2. a. A job as a shearer.

1895 *Worker* (Sydney) 28 Sept. 4/1 Now and then when doing a tramp, Trying to collar a cut. **1898** *Bulletin* (Sydney) 17 Dec. 15/1 *Cut* stands for shed-job. There are *fine cuts* and *rough cuts.* In the former the boss is particular. In a *rough-cut* he is lenient, and shearers can shear anyhow. **1899** *Ibid.* 19 Aug. 32/2 My mate's sick. . . I want a week's cut. **1913** H. LAWSON *Triangles of Life* 235 Jimmy had told us we'd better come on to the station and have a good tuck-out, and one of us, at least, would get a cut at the 'stragglers'. **1951** S. HICKEY *Travelled Roads* 25 Many of them had Conditional Purchase holdings on which they ran a few hundred sheep, shearing them between 'cuts' at the big stations. **1962** *Overland* xxiii. 4 The groups tended to merge, shouting indiscriminately for each other, arranging 'cuts' for the coming season.

b. A harvest, esp. of sugar cane; a job cutting (cane).

1934 T. WOOD *Cobbers* 191 To talk about shearing, and wool-presses, and cuts of lucerne. **1936** J. DEVANNY *Sugar Heaven* 10 The cut was a sure job even if . . conditions were rotten in the sugar now and the money bad. **1957** D.D. LADDS *We have our Dreams* 3 We've had a good cut this week! **1962** J. NAISH *Cruel Field* 54 'I've come to cut cane,' said Emery. 'I've got a cut, here in Cook's end with Ruf Craig.' **1975** J. DINGWELL *Cane Music* 119 'Then how has the hospital been coping?' . . 'It's pretty busy. . . Floods. . . Also, it's the cut. . . You can always count on extras then. . . Slashes at cane but not always going in the intended direction.'

3. *pl.* A caning or strapping, esp. in the phr. **to get the cuts.**

1915 *Bulletin* (Sydney) 28 Oct. 47/1 'Six cuts yer give him,' roared the whiskers. . . The stick emphasized the last remark by a rapid descent on the meek one's shoulders. **1939** L. MANN *Mountain Flat* 48 School's in, Mr Westfield. Give Ted Sutton the cuts if he's late. **1972** M. GILBERT *Personalities & Stories Early Orbost* 104 Getting 'the cuts' (strap or cane) was preferable to being put in the space under the gallery where the infants sat. **1978** M. PAICE *Shadow of Wings* 99 There was no law against caning, I'd had the 'cuts' plenty of times. **1984** J.J. PAGE *Ross Island 'Mud-Pickers'* 89 The cane was used on the hands—so many for various offences (called the 'cuts').

cut, *v.*

1. *trans.* To shear (a fleece, sheep, etc.).

1873 *Illustr. Sydney News* 27 Sept. 7/1 A man, who in one day, can cut eighty fleeces properly is a very good shearer. **1888** 'R. BOLDREWOOD' *Robbery under Arms* (1937) 114 We had cut our last shed before the first week in December. **1899** *Bulletin* (Sydney) 28 Jan. 14/4 Almost without exception the cobbler is a bad 'un to cut, especially when the men are old hands at the game. **1912** J. BRADSHAW *Highway Robbery under Arms* (ed. 3) 24 The boss gave orders to the boundary rider to bring in 7000 of the heavy wethers to steady down these fliers, who were cutting their two goose eggs daily. **1914** *Bulletin* (Sydney) 30 July 24/1 A couple of years back 250,000 fleeces were cut. **1917** *Ibid.* 6 Dec. 24/2 Shearer Ryan . . 'cut' 2100 woollies in 11 consecutive days. **1926** *Ibid.* 11 Feb. 24/1 None of the swanky shearing team have cut their exes. yet.

2. *trans.* To harvest (sugar cane). Also *absol.*

1936 J. DEVANNY *Sugar Heaven* 9 When a man's a cutter he naturally cuts. **1977** C. MCCULLOUGH *Thorn Birds* 254 How much I earn depends on how much sugar I cut, and if I'm good enough to cut with Arne's gang I'll be pulling in more than twenty quid a week.

Hence **cutting** *vbl. n.*

1957 *Bulletin* (Sydney) 13 Nov. 19/1 The cutting-rate fixed by the cane-inspector . . not being acceptable to the gang, the industrial magistrate was called in to arbitrate. **1977** R. MCKIE *Crushing* (1978) 201 Ridiculous paying those loafers full cutting wages.

cut line. [f. *cut* cleared + LINE 1.] A cleared track through scrub country. Also **cut road.**

1927 J. MATHIEU *Backblock Ballads* 19 And the scurried 'possum wonders In his fork all terrified As the flinty cut line thunders Back the rhythm of his stride. [*Note*] Cut line—Cleared track. **1957** J. HAWKE *Follow my Dust* 67 They were travelling a cut line through the mulga. **1981** P.B. CRESWELL *Granite Peak* 8 Getting the wool down the cut line to Milrose presented quite a problem as the scrub had only been cut back sufficiently far to allow passage of a vehicle without a projecting load. **1981** A. WILKINSON *Up Country* 7 This was the demanding, gate-strewn track called the 'cut road' from Tibooburra.

cut lunch. [f. *cut* sliced.]

1. A packed lunch, usu. of sandwiches. Also **cut tucker.**

1937 *Bulletin* (Sydney) 30 June 21/1 The 'keep' on my first ten-bob-a-week-and-keep effort was breakfast at five-thirty, followed by milking; three hours' paddock work to develop an appetite for a 'cut' lunch eaten on the job. **1949** H.C. JAMES *Gold is where you find It* 63 All he really expected was to find . . a few tiny nuggets. Enough to give him cut tucker and tools to go on slaving and searching. **1972** K. CLIFT *Saga of Sig* 2 We were to report at Victoria Barracks complete with a cut-lunch. **1975** G.A.W. SMITH *Once Green Jackaroo* 156, I must get two cut lunches from the cook. **1980** ANSELL & PERCY *To fight Wild* 110 She's bad, that end of the place. Saw a bandicoot with a cut lunch round his neck out there!

2. Special Comb. **cut-lunch commando,** see quot. 1953.

1952 T.A.G. HUNGERFORD *Ridge & River* 123 Think I got nothin' to do but wait around for a bunch of cut-lunch commandos. **1953** S.J. BAKER *Aust. Speaks* 170 *Cut lunch commandos*, soldiers serving with a home base unit. **1981** J. SAXTON *Something will Come* 206 It may be constructed from my experiences as a cut-lunch Commando, that I am an opponent of the concept of a National Service obligation.

cut-out, *n.*

1. The end of a shearing contract or season; a stoppage during shearing (see quot. 1935).

1896 H. LAWSON *While Billy Boils* 35 One Saturday morning, about a fortnight before cut-out, The Oracle came late to his stand. **1898** *Western Champion* (Barcaldine) 21 June 7/1 The little unpleasantness . . took place at the 'cut out' of Saltern Creek shed. **1904** *Shearer* (Sydney) 1 Oct. 5/3 The rainy weather last week has greatly retarded shearing operations in Victoria, delaying the cut out of some of the Riverina sheds. **1918** *Huon Times* (Franklin) 29 Nov. 3/5 Those were the days when at the Burrawang cut-out the Forbes hotels would be crowded for a week. **1935** *Red Star* (Perth) 16 Aug. 3/2 On going to their huts the shearers were told that the overseer had declared a cut out, although there were already mustered and in the yards 7,000 to 8,000 sheep. **1947** J.W. GORDON *Under Wide Skies* 49 There were dances at the cut-out, and neighbors all came over, Lads and lasses blithely riding from the homesteads small and great. **1950** *Coast to Coast 1949–50* 136 The shearers took the hat round and brought her a present at the cut-out. **1955** *Bulletin* (Sydney) 9 Feb. 12/3, I have seen beer turned-on at the cut-out in old-fashioned style by the owner, and left untouched by independent shearers. **1965** R.H. CONQUEST *Horses in Kitchen* 193 The hot sun came out, quickly drying the sheep, and shearing was resumed. The cut-out came about a week later. **1975** W. HOWCROFT *Old Working Hat* 11 With shearing all completed and the wool sold in advance, The outback shed was emptied for the after cut-out dance. **1977** D. WHITINGTON *Strive to be Fair* 29 They saved their drinking till the cut-out.

2. The eradication of a pest, etc., from a piece of land (see quot. 1978).

1908 *Bulletin* (Sydney) 14 Feb. 14/3 A joy in rabbit-infested country is 'cut-out' on a farm. Not 'cut-out' in a shearing sense but the cut-out of each and every cultivation paddock. **1978** A.E. COSH *Jumping Kangaroos* 4 Wallabies were numerous, and sheltered in the mallee scrub. As the roller went around and around the piece of scrub, the wallabies were herded inwards; and, of course, there would be a day of reckoning when the scrub roller approached the centre. I was very young at the time, but I remember that my father invited neighbours from near and far to join him on the day of the 'cut-out'.

cut out, *v.*

1. *trans.* To separate (an animal or a number of animals) from a mob (usu. of cattle). See also CUTTING OUT.

1844 H. MCCRAE *Georgiana's Jrnl.* 15 Feb. (1934) 110 Mr Jamieson was able to identify some of his own bullocks . . whereupon, he and Captain Reid, with much shouting and cracking of whips, proceeded to 'cut them out' from the mob. **1859** W. BURROWS *Adventures Mounted Trooper* 135 Old horses who have been 'after stock' for several years seem to turn as though on a pivot. . . This is particularly exemplified when 'cutting out', as it is called, a single bullock, as, once separated from the rest of the herd, a bullock always shows a great desire to get back again. **1861** 'OLD BUSHMAN' *Bush Wanderings* 235 Cutting out a wild bullock from a mob in the bush. **1875** R. & F. HILL *What we saw in Aust.* 101 We saw a herd of horses. . . Some were being 'cut out', that is separated from the herd by a skilful rider and driven into enclosures. **1886** R. HENTY *Australiana* 158 Fat cattle are 'cut out' of the smaller mobs on the run. **1892** 'R. BOLDREWOOD' *Nevermore* III. 40 Outlying lots of fat cattle were 'cut out' or separated from the border herds. **1893** *Bulletin* (Sydney) 28 Oct. 3/1 If the Heavenly hosts got 'boxed' now, as mobs most always will, Why who'd cut 'em out like William, or draft on the camp like Bill? **1901** *Ibid.* 7 Dec. 30/3 Well-trained camp-horses had cut out the required number. These the head-drover delivered to the buyer. **1908** W.H. OGILVIE *My Life in Open* 82 Stepping quickly across the yard to cut out a wild-eyed brown mare and guide her into a small yard by herself. **1929** K.S. PRICHARD *Coonardoo* (1961) 154 You would think she knew the bullock as well as Hugh did, the way she cut out that beast, walking beside him, following on his tail, on the fringe of the mob, she shot him out before he realized what had happened. **1945** E. MITCHELL *Speak to Earth* 49 Slowly the strings and mobs of cattle collect. . . The 'fats' are chosen and carefully cut out of the mob. **1955** J. CLEARY *Justin Bayard* 86 She could cut out bullocks, wield a branding iron, shoot like a sniper. **1976** C.D. MILLS *Hobble Chains & Greenhide* 143 A good camp-horse senses the bullock you mean to cut out the moment you sight him.

2. *Shearing.*

a. *trans.* To reach the end of (a contract, the shearing of the available sheep, etc.); to finish shearing in (a shed, etc.). Also *absol.*

1882 *Sydney Mail* 12 Aug. 246/3 Jim and I stopped at Boree shed till all the sheep were cut out. **1883** *Illustr. Austral. News* (Melbourne) 28 Nov. 194/2 It is veritably a carnival of work, and goes on from day to day till the last bales are pressed and despatched, when the shouts and songs of the men proclaim that they have at last 'cut out'. **1892** *Bulletin* (Sydney) 14 May 21/1 Well, that shed is cut out, and here I am on the road again to look for another. **1895** *Worker* (Sydney) 5 Jan. 4/4, I have been using the 'Shepherd' shears, and when we cut out I had shorn over 400 sheep with one pair. **1904** *Shearer* (Sydney) 27 Aug. 8/3, I am getting through over 2,000 per day, and anticipate cutting out on the 26th inst. **1912** J. BRADSHAW *Highway Robbery under Arms* (ed. 3) 23 We started to shear the rams next morning, which we cut out in four days. **1921** G.A. BELL *Under Brigalows* 143 As there were so few sheep left on Currawong Mr Leslie arranged for them to be shorn at a neighbouring station when their own shed was 'cut out'. **1928** C.E. COWLEY *Classing Clip* 95 By the time the catching pens have been 'cut-out' for the first time sufficient wool will be available to fix the classes on a better basis. **1955** E. BARNES *Easier Shearing* p. xii, 'Cutting out' shed after shed and following the shearing season down through central New South Wales. **1963** D. NILAND *Dadda Jumped* 150 I'm a shearer. I come in today from Moombala. We cut-out there first run this morning.

b. *intr.* Of the contract, etc.: to come to an end. Also, of (the shearing at) a shed or station.

1899 *Western Champion* (Barcaldine) 18 July 14/2 During the following week Gobbera Downs 'cut out' and the hotel swarmed with shearers. **1917** A.L. BREWER *'Gators' Euchre* 33 Don't you know I'm always moving about? Thousands of Australians in the same position. Muster's cut out—and a chap has to work. **1936** *Bulletin* (Sydney) 30 Dec. 20/1 When they got a job they did it well; but when the job cut out they were the dickens of a bother to shift from the station. **1948** H. DRAKE-BROCKMAN *Sydney or Bush* 39 Charlie had just cut-out on a small shearing job, and his money was dam' well as good as anybody else's. **1975** R. MACKLIN *Queenslander* 118 Hector Bannerman asked him to stay behind when the shed cut out; the last shed of the season. **1981** P.B. CRESWELL *Granite Peak* 35 As soon as shearing cut out all the white men left the station.

3. *intr.* In various extended uses, to come to an end; to become expended or exhausted.

1882 *Sydney Mail* 15 July 86/2 You and George can take a turn at local-preaching when you're cut out. **1907** *Bulletin* (Sydney) 10 Jan. 15/2 Around Gilgandra (N.S.W.), where the timber has been 'cut out' for years, two men recently averaged 8 to 10 'nines' per day. **1931** W. BARAGWANATH et al. *Guide for Prospectors in Vic.* 6 Quartz-gold should be followed until it 'cuts out'. **1941** D. O'CALLAGHAN *Long Life Reminisc.* 100 We were feeding the child . . and his food was just cut out—none for the next day to eat. **1950** G.M. FARWELL *Land of Mirage* 189 Suppose the feed cuts out, and the cattle have to be pushed over the dry plains. **1954** *Bulletin* (Sydney) 3 Nov. 13/2 The stock in his counter drawer had cut out, but he couldn't tell her he had none when the bundles were in full view on the shelf. **1960** *N.T. News* (Darwin) 22 Jan. 6/4 Jim depends for most of his water on shallow wells. Over the past couple of months some of these wells have almost cut out. **1962** *Bulletin* (Sydney) 3 Feb. 44/2 The grog cut out. The last bottle emptied. Party over.

4. *trans.* To spend (money); chiefly in the phr. **to cut out a cheque,** to spend one's entire earnings on liquor. See CHEQUE.

[N.Z. **1906** *N.Z. Truth* (Wellington) 8 Dec. 1 A young man is reputed to have 'cut out' a cheque for £93 at Hastings.] **1913** *Bulletin* (Sydney) 24 Apr. 14/4 Happy . . cut out his cheque on the way to Casterton. **1916** *Ibid.* 10 Feb. 22/2 When a cheque was 'cut-out', Pat would call the depositer aside. **1918** *Huon Times* (Franklin) 29 Nov. 3/5 One never hears of big cheques being handed over the counter and cut out in booze. The shearers' sense has improved with the times. **1935** R.B. PLOWMAN *Boundary Rider* 120 I'm goin' t' stay 'ere till I cut me cheque out. **1942** W. GLASSON *Our*

Shepherds 12 He would place the balance of his money on the hotel bar and ask to be told when it was 'cut out'. **1962** MARSHALL & DRYSDALE *Journey among Men* 56 Not many pubs today keep a drunks' room. This was a room exclusively reserved for the habituals who hit 'town' once every eighteen months or so with a cheque to cut out. **1984** J. BROWN *Just for Rec.* 54 After the refund we had a fiver left over so . . we proceeded to cut it out over the bar.

Hence **cut-out** *ppl. a.*, **cutter out** *n.*

1876 *Austral. Town & Country Jrnl.* (Sydney) 30 Dec. 1062/1 The once small drove of '**cut out** cattle' looked important and respectable. **1925** *Bulletin* (Sydney) 4 June 24/1, I . . know several reasons why sleepers can be obtained in 'cut out' scrubs where mills cannot operate. **1948** *Ibid.* 31 Mar. 29/1 The Tanker and Battling Ben had tossed their cut-out cheques across the bar. **1950** C.E. GOODE *Yarns of Yilgarn* 83 Through undulating 'cut-out' country, with every few miles some forgotten battery and poppet guarding a silent outcrop. **1873** A. TROLLOPE *Aust. & N.Z.* I. 434, I went out one morning at four a.m. to see a lot drafted out of a herd for sale. . . The owner himself was the '**cutter out**'.

cut-tail. [See quot. 1899.] A tree of the genus *Eucalyptus*, esp. *brown barrel* (see BROWN *a.* 1).

1889 *Proc. Linnean Soc. N.S.W.* IV. 612 *E. amygdalina*, var. (near *E. regnans* . .) . . 'Cut-tail.' **1896** *Ibid.* XXI. 810 *E. fastigata* . . *Vernacular names*. . . The one most in use, where also the tree is best developed, is 'Cut-tail'. **1899** *Ibid.* XXIV. 548 This fine splitting was carried so far that (given a good tree) they would split a piece into such thin portions that one could bend them like the leaves of a book, which it roughly resembled, with the solid part at one end resembling the back of the book. Those pieces were called 'Cut-tail'. . . From the piece itself the name was transferred to the tree, and a splitter would point out to you that such and such a tree is a 'Cut-tail'. **1932** R.H. ANDERSON *Trees of N.S.W.* 115 Cut-tail . . occurs on the coastal ranges. **1986** *Parkwatch* (Vic. Nat. Parks Assoc.) Mar. 17 Montane forest dominated by multi-aged alpine ash and shining gum, messmate, cut-tail and mountain grey gum.

cutter, *n.*[1] [f. CUT *v.* 2.]

1. Shortened form of *cane-cutter* (see CANE 2).

1875 *Illustr. Sydney News* 10 Feb. 3/1 The number of labourers is proportioned agreeably to the quantity of cane needed for the day's work. These are divided into three gangs; the first being termed 'Trashers', who with billhooks divest the canes of all their trash, the second is named 'cutters', who afterwards cut them down exactly level with the ground. **1955** R. LAWLER *Summer of Seventeenth Doll* (1965) 89 You see this feller? Know where he comes from? . . Way up north where the sugar grows. And you want to know somethin' else? He's one of the best cutters. **1962** *Overland* xxiii. 4 A cutter's only as good as his back. **1977** C. MCCULLOUGH *Thorn Birds* 254 The best gang of cutters in Queensland is a gang of Swedes.

2. The blade of a shearing machine.

1891 *Conference Amalgam. Shearers' Union & Pastoralists' Fed. Council* 8 In all sheds where shearing machines are provided, shearers shall pay for cutters and combs a price not exceeding cost. **1894** *Bulletin* (Sydney) 10 Feb. 20/3 They trim away the ragged locks—and *rip* the cutter goes. **1897** *Worker* (Sydney) 14 Aug. 4/1 Cost of shears, oils, oilstones, combs and cutters was £1062 14s. 9d. **1915** *Bulletin* (Sydney) 14 Oct. 24/2 The combs and cutters are invariably 'the tools', and when comb and cutter are screwed on the handpiece Billjim reckons he has 'loaded-up his bog-eye'. **1933** J. TRURAN *Where Plain Begins* 147 The 'expert' . . was responsible for keeping the machines oiled and adjusted and the shearer's 'cutters' in good order. **1965** L. WALKER *Other Girl* 53 The cutters were already beginning to hum and the dust and the wool-ends to fly. **1968** J. O'GRADY *Gone Troppo* 183, I was shearin' outback, by a wayside track; Two sheep the cutter lasted; The Roustabout was a Pommie lout, An' the boss was a hungry bastard.

3. A timber-getter.

1949 J.W.S. TOMLIN *Story of Bush Brotherhoods* 43 An encounter with a solitary 'cutter' (timber-getter). **1953** *Bulletin* (Sydney) 30 Dec. 12/1 In the cutter's-camp out from Lakewood (W.A.), thirsts were once quenched with a potent brew of hop-beer, dispensed in bough-shed shanties. **1976** L.R.M. HUNTER *Woodline* 1 Unlike the navvies, the cutters on the Woodline were generally a stable lot.

cutter, *n.*[2] *Obs.* [Of unknown origin.] In the phr. **to run the cutter,** to buy beer by the billy to drink elsewhere (see quot. 1904).

1904 *Bulletin* (Sydney) 12 May 17/1 At Mount Morgan they don't breast the bar. The average man 'runs the cutter'. One shilling and a billy are presented to the barmaid with the order for 'a 'bob's' worth of beer, and may the Lord strengthen yer arm when yer get 'old o' that pump'. Usually there are seven or eight at the same game and pub., all with billies, and a stranger is cordially invited 'to dip his beak' as he faces them on the footpath. **1911** *Ibid.* 18 May 13/2, I can put 'Jonnel' . . on a fair track to the explanation of the origin of the saying 'running the cutter'. In most parts of Scotland a 'cutter' is the accepted name for a flat flask bottle used by the natives for carrying supplies of lime juice in those savage parts. **1965** *Ibid.* 9 Jan. 30/2 You earned an honest penny on the way from school . . by 'running the cutter' for the miners who lined the gutter outside the Shamrock Hotel and were glad to pay a penny for the services of an agile boy who would keep the three-quart billies, that passed down the line from mouth to mouth, rolling from bar to gullet without pause till the shillings paid for them ran out. **1982** N. KEESING *Lily on Dustbin* 120 'The cutter' was a billy of beer. . . Some wives sent a child for a cutter, which the husband drank at home. . . 'Running the cutter' ceased with the introduction and enforcement of stricter licensing laws at the time of World War I.

cutting grass. [See quot. 1831.] Any of several sedges having sharp-edged and sometimes serrated blades, esp. of the genus *Gahnia* (fam. Cyperaceae).

1831 W. BLAND *Journey of Discovery Port Phillip* 61 They had the misfortune to encounter that species of long grass, which is known in the colony by the name of the 'cutting grass', this was between four and five feet high, the blade of it an inch and a half broad, and the edges exquisitely sharp, and fine enough to inflict a severe wound. **1852** MRS C. MEREDITH *My Home in Tas.* I. 57 The ground . . was chiefly covered with coarse, harsh, reedy plants, some of which are called 'cutting grass', from the extremely sharp edges of the leaves, which cut like glass. **1872** 'RESIDENT' *Glimpses Life Vic.* 57 Rocks, scantily overgrown with cutting grass. **1897** *Papers & Proc. R. Soc. Tas.* (1898) 190 He may try to force a way, inch by inch, by tearing apart the interlaced bines, every now and then getting his face and wrists deeply scored by the saw-like blades of 'cutting-grass' (Gahnia [Cladium] psittacorum). **1908** *Emu* VII. 144 One pair has recently bred in an immense cutting-grass tussock. **1968** G.R. COCHRANE et al. *Flowers & Plants of Vic.* 16/2 The leaves of many sedges will often cause deep cuts, and they are commonly referred to as sword grass or cutting grass. **1981** J. JESSOP *Flora Central Aust.* 513 *G[ahnia] trifida* . . Cutting grass.

cutting out, *vbl. n.*

1. The process of separating an animal, or a number of animals, from a mob preparatory to branding, etc. Also *attrib.*

1848 H.W. HAYGARTH *Recoll. Bush Life* 61 The best exemplification of this faculty is the process of driving, or, as it is called, 'cutting out' a single bullock. **1873** A. TROLLOPE *Aust. & N.Z.* I. 434, I went out one morning at four a.m. to see a lot drafted out of a herd for sale. 'Cutting out' is the proper name for this operation. Two or three men on horseback . . drove some hundreds of them into a selected corner. **1891** *Bohemia* (Melbourne) 11 June 6 A certain farmer owned a collie which he had instructed in the art of 'cutting out'. **1901** *Bulletin* (Sydney) 7 Dec. 30/3 Seeing the hash the sheep-men were making of cutting-out, the drovers set to work. **1922** V. PALMER *Boss of Killara* 95 The eyes of the Cameron boy had brightened at the mention of cutting-out. He could never resist the attractions of a cattle-camp. **1930** M.M.J. COSTELLO *Life J. Costello* 197 His dam had been a wonderful 'cutting out' mare in her day. **1942** *Bulletin* (Sydney) 22 July 13/2 We were cutting out yearlings on the open 'cutting-out flat'. **1977** J. WALLACE *Memories Country Childhood* 90 Even the horses enjoyed camp drafting. 'Cutting out' was so popular that we had to take it in turns.

2. Special Comb. **cutting-out camp,** a camp established for the purpose of cutting out (animals); see CAMP *n.* 3; **horse,** a horse trained for this work; see also *camp horse*, CAMP *n.* 6.

1897 *Bulletin* (Sydney) 11 Dec. 22/4 Andy Ferguson, you may go bail, Is yet boss on a **cutting-out camp.** **1901** *Ibid.* 7 Dec. 30/4 They go into the cutting out camp with a zest. **1930** E.R.B. GRIBBLE *Forty Yrs. with Aborigines* 29 A 'cutting-out' camp was always a very exciting time. **1948** G. PIKE *Campfire Tales* (1981) 13 Thrilling feats of horsemanship performed . . by Billy Glennan, a 'king' on the cutting out camp. **1878** 'R. BOLDREWOOD' *Ups & Downs* 13 No, tell him to get 'Mustang', he's the best **cutting-out horse.** **1895** K. MACKAY *Yellow Wave* 202 'Cutting-out' horses used to be led out to a cattle-camp so broken and 'crutchy' that they could hardly walk without stumbling; but once at work, what wonders they were! **1916** *Bulletin* (Sydney) 11 May 24/2 The novice . . sees the head-stockman's two cutting-out horses. **1944** *Ibid.* 20 Dec. 13/3 In stock work a really good cutting-out horse is nothing else but a trick horse.

Cyclone. [The proprietary name of a range of metal and wire products.] Used *attrib.* in Comb. of (fencing) structures made with metal frames or supports and strong interlocking wire: **Cyclone dropper, fence, gate.**

[**1907** *Austral. Official Jrnl. Patents* (Canberra) 1531 *Cyclone* The essential particular of the Trade Mark is the following:- the word 'Cyclone'. 4156. . . Gates, Fencing Droppers and Loops, Wire Netting and Fencing, and all other Goods included in Class 13.] **1909** R. KALESKI *Austral. Settler's Compl. Guide* 94 Five No. 8 galvanised wires, posts 40 feet apart, four **cyclone-droppers** in between, rabbit-proof wire netting on the bottom. **1976** R. PRESTIDGE *Cataclysm* 2 Then leaves a bewildered Morris, runs over to a **cyclone fence** and starts talking to a cop. **1981** B.J. BROCK *Catharsis* 45 Crackly plane tree leaves Climb cyclone fences. **1912** *Bulletin* (Sydney) 8 Aug. 16/3 The first obstacle was a '**cyclone' gate.** **1925** *Ibid.* 1 Oct. 22/1 Where the station fences cross each sports a 'cyclone' gate. **1935** N. HUNT *House of David* 48 The tree stood in front of a neat cyclone gate, giving access to a drive. **1962** J. HEDGE *Trout Fishing N.S.W.* 102 Turn left here and proceed for 3 miles when a cyclone gate will be seen directly ahead. **1978** D. HUTLEY *Swan* 33 He turned through the Cyclone gates.

cypress pine. [See quot. 1904.] Any of several trees of the genus CALLITRIS, belonging to the cypress fam. Cupressaceae; the wood of these trees, often termite-resistant; *native pine*, see NATIVE *a.* 6 a., PINE 2; see also *colonial pine* COLONIAL *a.* 5. Formerly **cypress (tree).**

1820 J. OXLEY *Jrnls. Two Exped. N.S.W.* 15 A few cypresses and camarinas [*sic*], scattered here and there. **1825** B. FIELD *Geogr. Mem. N.S.W.* 14 A little distant from the river, were several brushes or forests of the common Australian cypress-tree (Callitris Australis). **1836** J. BACKHOUSE *Narr. Visit Austral. Colonies* (1843) 369 The Cypress-pine, *Callitris arenosa*, . . forms a spreading tree, forty feet high, and eight feet round. **1846** C.P. HODGSON *Reminisc. Aust.* 148 The cypress pine is a most splendid fellow; very large, free, and odoriferous. **1852** J. MACGILLIVRAY *Narr. Voyage H.M.S. Rattlesnake* I. 47 Abundance of the cypress-pine . . a wood much prized for ornamental work. **1882** *Austral. Handbk.* 391 The timber known as 'Cypress Pine' is the produce of several kinds of *Callitris*. **1904** J.H. MAIDEN *Notes on Commercial Timbers N.S.W.* 24 Under the general name of cypress pine we include a number of Australian trees which, though not true cypresses, more or less resemble those trees in general appearance. **1928** G.H. WILKINS *Undiscovered Aust.* 23 Among the mulgas in this district had once grown some stately cypress pines. **1956** N.K. WALLIS *Austral. Timber Handbk.* 3 Cypress pine is used in home building, mainly for flooring. **1965** R.H. CONQUEST *Horses in Kitchen* 163 It has a scent all its own and once a man has smelled cypress pine burning on a wintry night, the scent will come back, years and years later, just to tantalize his nostrils and stir his imagination. **1974** N. CATO *Brown Sugar* 51 At first wool was exported . . then the valuable native timbers: red cedar, swamp mahogany, blackbutt and cypress pine.

D

daddy. [Used elsewhere but recorded earliest in Aust.] In the phr. **the** (or **a**) **daddy of (them all, the lot,** etc.), the most notable, the biggest.

1898 W.H. OGILVIE *Fair Girls* (1906) 80 Though shaky in the shoulders, he's the daddy of them all; He's the gamest bit of horseflesh from the Snowy to the Bree. **1901** M. FRANKLIN *My Brilliant Career* 194, I never felt such a daddy of a thirst on me before. **1923** J. MOSES *Beyond City Gates* 105 There were many who wondered that night how Clinker, the daddy of all horsemen, would come out of the battle. **1932** M.R. WHITE *No Roads go By* 162 Then we came to the big sandhill, the Daddy of the lot. **1942** J. DEVANNY *Killing Jacqueline Love* 154 She was the daddy of all liars. **1954** 'B. SINGER' *Have Patience, Delaney!* 78, I been in a lot of wild mix-ups in my time . . but this is sure the daddy of the whole flaming lot. **1961** I.L. IDRIESS *Tracks of Destiny* 80 Of the Territory pioneer women, perhaps the 'daddy' of the lot is Mrs Phoebe Farrar.

dag, *n.*[1] [Br. dial.: see OED *dag, sb.*[1] 3 (in Br. usage more commonly *daglock*).]

1. Usu. in *pl.* A lump of matted wool and excreta hanging from about the tail of a sheep; such a lump cut from a sheep.

1891 *Truth* (Sydney) 12 Apr. 73 Smothered in sheep-dung, and pelting one another with 'dags'. **1897** L. LINDLEY-COWEN *W. Austral. Settler's Guide* 653 *Dags.*—This term is applied to the lumps of manure formed on the wool under the sheep's tail, owing to the animal having scoured through a rush of young grass or other cause. **1899** G. JEFFREY *Princ. Australasian Woolclassing* 51 All the large 'dags' are kept out before placing the locks in a heap ready for pressing. **1902** *Bulletin* (Sydney) 5 July 16/2 Many horses that are not hand-fed hang about the wool-sheds browsing on the sheep-dags that lie several feet deep in places. **1912** J. BRADSHAW *Highway Robbery under Arms* (ed. 3) 38, I followed him and butted him into the wool press, and would have dumped him up with a bail [*sic*] of dags only for the other shearers pleading him off. **1928** *Bulletin* (Sydney) 15 Feb. 21/1 There's easy work an' first-rate pay (and you are hard as nails), Off-sidin' cook, or sortin' dags, or maybe brandin' bales. **1944** *Ibid.* 13 Dec. 12/1 Before autumn crutching was introduced sheep dags were often of great size, particularly during lush seasons. For over 20 years in the men's hut on Barooga station (Riverina, N.S.W.) there hung a 'king' dag weighing 18½ lbs. **1957** D. NILAND *Call me when Cross turns Over* 230 Him, his type are as common as dags in a sheepyard, but you won't come across the likes of me too often. **1977** C. MCCULLOUGH *Thorn Birds* 118 Around the sheep's rear end the wool grew foul with excrement, fly-blown, black and lumped together in what were called dags. **1985** J. HARRISON *Bit of Dag* 65 He got into bed that night and found a pile of dags right at the bottom where the cocky had left them.

2. *fig.*

1956 T. RONAN *Moleskin Midas* 142, I ain't letting one of our prominent local cattlemen, like my friend Mr Yates, be jockeyed out of his lawful due by any sheep-man who ever ate fried dags for his supper. **1977** S. LOCKE ELLIOTT *Water under Bridge* 193 Now just frying dags in grim Rockwell Crescent.

3. In the phr. **to rattle (one's) dags,** to bestir oneself, to hurry.

[N.Z. **1968** G. SLATTER *Pagan Game* 161 I'm not overstruck on that new cop.—Told me to rattle my dags out of there.] **1980** S. THORNE *I've met some Bloody Wags* 96 Hurry up! Get down there 'n bleed him! Rattle your dags!

4. Special Comb. **dag-picker,** one employed in a shearing shed to recover wool from dags; hence **-pick** *v. intr.* and **-picking** *ppl. a.*; **-rattler,** a sheep.

1907 *Bulletin* (Sydney) 26 Sept. 13/2 In the woolsheds along the Murrumbidgee there once worked, as bale-brander, an illiterate fellow, who, on the wool-packs, made excellent caricatures of all the shed identities, from squatter to **dag-picker**. **1933** *Bulletin* (Sydney) 8 Feb. 21/1, I work and whistle on my own . . Dag-pickin' all day long. **1934** *Austral. Ring* IX. cvii. 4 When five quid a month was a dag-picker's pay, And the shearers demanded their dues. *Ibid.*, We've camped with the rats on the Warrego side, Fraternised with the drink-sodden wreck, The dag-picking Doctor who swallowed his pride, And the swanker who swallowed his cheque. **1977** A. THOMAS *Bull & Boabs* (1980) 107 Sheep were ground lice . . and **dag-rattlers.**

dag, *n.*[2] [Transf. use of Br. dial. (esp. children's speech) *dag* a 'dare', a challenge: see OEDS *sb.*[5]]

1. A 'character', someone eccentric but entertainingly so; *hard case*, see HARD.

1875 R. THATCHER *Something to his Advantage* 2 These are 'Charley the Dag', 'Old Daddy', 'the Spring-heeled Immigrant'. **1916** 'MEN OF ANZAC' *Anzac Bk.* 47 Yes, 'Enessy was a dag if ever there was one! **1918** *Aussie: Austral. Soldiers' Mag.* Feb. 6/1 It was hard to recognise in him the race-day 'Dag' who, in pre-war days, used to swing the bag on country courses back South in the Land o' Sun. **1919** C.H. THORP *Handful of Ausseys* 133 There was a dag of a bloke there—a wool-classer, who used to spin some great yarns. **1938** *Point* (Melbourne) I. ii. 11 The 'Dag' or 'hard doer' type of Australian whose exploits are recorded week by week in the Diggers' page of Smith's Weekly. **1942** C.E.W. BEAN *Official Hist. Aust. 1914–18* VI. 1085 Men under strong leaders, have been reduced by some Australian caricaturists to . . a slouching 'dag', intent only on beer, thieving 'skirts' and scoring off nincompoop officers. **1968** D. O'GRADY *Bottle of Sandwiches* 68 He was a bit of a dag, the old Ern. **1975** *Bulletin* (Sydney) 17 May 33/1 By now Prince Leonard had become a bit of a dag. The Press loved him. And the public, while occasionally passing him off as a nut, tended to say good on him, at least he's giving those bloody shiny-bums a run for their money. **1976** J. JOHNSON *Low Breed* 30 'Ah! That cop was a dill,' said one of the others. 'A dag,' the other corrected, pedantically. **1980** S. THORNE *I've met some Bloody Wags* 44 After a while the novelty of grooming him wore off though, and to Jamie's dismay, they clipped him. Streuth, he looked a dag then!

2. A socially awkward adolescent: see quot. 1985.

1966 S.J. BAKER *Austral. Lang.* (ed. 2) 289 *Dag*, a person who is unenterprising, without courage. (Quite distinct from the old use of 'dag' for a 'hard case' or 'character'). **1983** *Sydney Morning Herald* 24 Sept. 32/8 Has it helped them feel more relaxed with the boys in their PD group. 'Well, most of them are dags,' Julie laughs, 'but at least they're easier to talk to.' **1985** *Canberra Times* 8 June 21/1 The sublime agony of adolescence can be squirmingly funny, especially from the outside. The title 'Dags' sums it up so well: the state most of us feel we are in during those teenage years—awkward social cripples, unattractive and consumed by anxieties about appearance, sex and all the rest.

dag, *v.* [Br. dial.: see DAG *n.*[1] 1.]

1. *trans.* To remove dags from (a sheep).

1867 J.C. JORDAN *Managem. Sheep & Stations* 74 Before sheep-washing, every sheep will have to be 'dagged'. The wool about and below the anus will be covered with dung, dried into hard knobs, caused by the scouring which always follows the fresh green feed in spring. Dagging, therefore, means cutting away these filthy and unsightly encumbrances, as a preparatory step towards a thorough cleansing of the fleece. **1904** *Worker* (Sydney) 3 Dec. 10/1 Woolbucks are shorn and dagged and cheques are knockin' down. **1917** *11 CAR* 68 The employee may refuse to dag or drench sheep. **1945** E. MITCHELL *Speak to Earth* 149 Many days were now spent with the sheep in the yards or holding-paddocks, dagging them.

2. See quot. 1965.

1965 G. MCINNES *Road to Gundagai* 260 Most of them were not yet 'dagged'. Dagging, which is the castration of baby rams with a dagging knife, was no pastime for the squeamish.

Hence **dagging** *vbl. n.*

1867 [see sense 1]. **1899** *S.A. Parl. Papers* II. no. 77 102 When our sheep require dagging we go down to the Port McLeay Mission Station and get as many blacks as we want. We do not make any agreement with them, but simply pay them so much a hundred for dagging purposes. **1905** *Shearer* (Sydney) 2 Dec. 4/5 They are prepared to do a bit of dagging in the woolshed or to wash-up and cut wood for the cook, in return for which they get 'their tripes lined', their bags filled, and a few shillings for the track. **1934** T. WOOD *Cobbers* 99 Dagging, in polite terms, is the removal, by shears, of wool which is matted on the thighs by excreta. **1941** *Bulletin* (Sydney) 26 Feb. 17/4 On me way to a daggin' job on Milroy station I'd camped at the Barwon Bridge. **1948** R.A. PEPPERALL *Emigrant to Aust.* 163 'Dagging', that is clipping away the befouled wool, is one of the sheep farmer's most important—if unpleasant—tasks in irrigation areas.

daggers, *pl. Shearing. Obs.* Handshears; see also BLADE 1.

1876 J.A. EDWARDS *Gilbert Gogger* 109, I don't think that calling . . a pair of shears, daggers . . [etc.] and a variety of other terms, with which you, my highly educated Australian native, garnish your conversation, is talking pure English. **1878** 'IRONBARK' *Southerly Busters* 179 I'm able for to shear 'em clean, And level as a die; But I prefer to 'tommy-hawk', And make the 'daggers' fly. **1966** S.J. BAKER *Austral. Lang.* (ed. 2) There are still many old-timers who can remember such terms for handshears as *daggers*.

daggy, *a.*[1] [f. DAG *n.*[1] 1.] Of (the condition of) a sheep or fleece: fouled with dags.

1895 *Worker* (Sydney) 14 Sept. 4/2 There the sheep are hard and daggy, full of mulga sticks and sand. **1915** *Bulletin* (Sydney) 4 Nov. 24/2 He is cramped over foul-smelling, daggy, and often fly-blown sheep. **1919** 'JASON' *Blowfly Pest* 48 A marked consequence of spraying is the absence of daggy sheep. **1944** *Bulletin* (Sydney) 13 Dec. 12/1 Daggy sheep *do* slow down the shearing. **1960** D. MCLEAN *Roaring Days* 42 If we lose this strike the boss'll grind our noses in his daggy wool. **1963** C.H. SMITH *How y' going Mate?* 147 A certain mob of sheep had arrived at the shed in a 'daggy' condition. The men . . refused to shear unless the sheep were cleaned up first. **1978** HANIGAN & LINDSAY *No Tracks on River* 60 Shearing lambs with daggy tails.

daggy, *a.*[2] [f. DAG *n.*[2], but poss. infl. also by *n.*[1] 1.]

1. Chiefly of clothing and personal appearance: unconventional; unkempt. Also *transf.* (see quot. 1982).

1967 *Kings Cross Whisper* (Sydney) xxxiv. 4/3 *Daggy*, to be dirty. Same as warby and scungy. **1972** N. MILES *Opal Fever* 98 'A colour bar in government jobs?' exclaimed Chilla. 'That's a daggy state of affairs.' **1972** A. CHIPPER *Aussie Swearers Guide* 37 *Daggy* is associated often with hairiness, untidiness, disintegration, bodily dirt and waste matter, as in: 'She's married to a *daggy* artist in *daggy* jeans in a *daggy* Paddo flat.' **1974** *Gayzette* (Sydney) 3 Oct. 5/1, I now also dress by preference in 'pre-worn' clothing some of which, in normal likelihoods, might be a bit daggy. **1982** *Access* Aug. 23/1 Because tolerance is encouraged throughout the school, unconformity isn't seen as 'daggy'.

2. Unfashionable; graceless.

1983 F. WILLMOTT *Breaking Up* 22 They get fat real young . . and wear daggy dresses and get their hair cut short. **1986** *Nat. Times* (Sydney) 3 Jan. 7/2, I like to write about daggy people who don't get on, mainly because I was a child like that. I never got a look-in.

dago, *n.* and *attrib.* [Orig. U.S., a corruption of *Diego* Sp. proper name, as applied to a Spaniard; now in general use as a derog. term for a foreigner: see OED(S.]

A. *n.* An immigrant (usu. male) of Latin descent; an immigrant from Europe (exc. the British Isles).

1892 *Bulletin* (Sydney) 19 Nov. 19/1 I've got a down on Dagoes, and a Dutchman I detest; As for Chinkies and Eyetalians and such like I gives 'em best. **1902** *Truth* (Sydney) 6 July 8/3 If the police would give a little more of their time to 'moving on' greasy Dagos who stand in almost every street . . it would be more to their credit than is the harrassing of decent whitemen. **1906** *Bulletin* (Sydney) 26 July 44/2 Albert . . attempts to win partisans by working on their White Australia emotions, and urges them to back him up against 'a Dago'. **1912** *Truth* (Sydney) 4 Feb. 1/1 If a number of competent Frenchmen came to Australia, and opened schools of cookery, what delirious denunciation there would be of so-called Dagos! (To the undiscriminating howler at 'foreigners', all persons from the continent of Europe are either 'Dago' or Dutch). **1916** C. Vaude *Tivoli* 4 It's an Italian-Greek clock. . . You stand and look at it for twenty-four hours and you will see a day go (Dago). **1926** *Aussie* (Sydney) Sept. 57/2 The Dago is a rather queer animal lately imported into Australia. He lives in mobs like sheep, his food consisting mainly of macaroni, garlic, olive-oil and wine. **1935** Davison & Nicholls *Blue Coast Caravan* 225 In Italy he was a foreigner and in Australia he was a 'Dago'. **1946** L. Esson *Southern Cross* 76, I ain't no Dago. I'm Greek. **1946** D. Stivens *Courtship of Uncle Henry* 117 He was a Greek and the shop was called Nicko's. Sometimes people said, 'We'll meet you at the Dago's.' **1955** P. White *Tree of Man* 251 Not a bad cove, for a dago. **1965** C. Johnson *Wild Cat Falling* 43 Who wants a shiftless native when he can get a big up and coming Dago to work for him? **1976** L. Oakes *Crash Through* 243 A Croatian migrant shouting in heavily accented English at a group of Italians: 'Go home, dagoes!' **1981** P. Corris *White Meat* 104 This dago wants to set it up all his way.

B. *attrib.*

1900 *Truth* (Sydney) 4 Feb. 3/3 A Dago organgrinder fell in with a section of larrikins of the Queen. **1901** *Ibid.* 15 Sept. 1/4 The writer has seen dago fruiterers spitting on rags in order to make their apples appear as bright as a reflecting pier glass. **1907** *Ibid.* 17 Apr. 9/7 A Dago push, Lutherans, Moravians, or something of the sort, have got hold of more country than you could ride over in a week. **1926** *Illustr. Tasmanian Mail* (Hobart) 24 Mar. 6/2 The Dago prawn-catchers . . now infest Sydney Harbour. **1931** *Pan-Pacific Worker* 5 Aug. 6/2 The irony of this comparison lies in the fact that Australians generally regard Brazil as 'one of those backward Dago republics'. **1937** V. Palmer *Legend for Sanderson* 31 He had a meet with one of those Dago girls down by the river. **1949** C. Benham *Diver's Luck* 152 A dago pearl buyer what calls himself Florio Damiano what come from some place in Europe where dagoes come from. **1955** D. Niland *Shiralee* 96 He's the colour of a sizzled-up steak and tosses the dago language round like it was his own. **1979** J.J. McRoach *Dozen Dopey Yarns* 101 The Australian farmer developed a deep-seated enmity against these dago-wop bastards who, by working their women, could succeed where a decent Aussie could not.

dairy station. *Obs.* A dairy farm.

1838 T. Walker *Month in Bush Aust.* 10 We next came to an extensive country . . formerly a dairy station and cattle run. **1841** *Port Phillip Gaz.* 16 June 2 Cattle and Dairy Station for Sale. **1843** J.F. Bennett *Hist. & Descr. Acct. S.A.* 96 Others keep what is called 'a dairy station', rearing or killing the calves, and making butter and cheese for the Adelaide market. **1848** H.W. Haygarth *Recoll. Bush Life* 147 It was a dairy station, too, and sixty or seventy fine cows were milked at sunrise every morning, and brought home from the pastures in the evening to suckle their calves. **1863** J.C. Knight *Few Particulars Vic.* 14 There is ample scope for the safe investment of capital in mining; sheep farming, cattle and dairy stations. **1867** W. Milton *Victim Nineteenth Century* 23 The dairy station is about ten miles from the Burra Burra copper mines. **1878** R.B. Smyth *Aborigines of Vic.* II. 183 Tea-tree spring (Dairy station).

daisy bush. Any of many shrubs or small trees of the fam. Asteraceae, esp. of the genus *Olearia*, occurring in all States, N.Z., and New Guinea. Also **daisy tree.**

1835 *Hobart Town Almanack* 68 *Aster tomentosus*, daisy tree. A beautiful shrub with oblong toothed leaves, dusky brown underneath. It is highly ornamental and is covered with blossoms for three or four months in summer. **1843** *Portland Mercury* 28 June 2/2 Shrubs of the handsomest dwarf growing flowering kinds, such as aster tomentosus, gracilis and longifolia (daisy trees). **1898** E.E. Morris *Austral Eng.* 113 Daisy Tree . . two Tasmanian trees, *Astur* [*sic*] *stellulatus*, . . and *A. glandulosus*. **c 1910** W.R. Guilfoyle *Austral. Plants* 270 *Olearia Muelleri* . . 'Mueller's Daisy Bush'. **1942** C. Barrett *Austral. Wild Flower Bk.* 179 Among the Olearias or daisy-bushes are many attractive shrubs, but few of them are found in gardens. More than eighty species are known, so that one's choice of 'native asters' is sufficiently wide. **1959** A.E. Brooks *Austral. Native Plants* 106 Many Daisy-bushes make good garden plants, particularly those with pink or blue flowers. **1973** R. Erickson et al. *Flowers & Plants W.A.* 195 Among the smaller shrubs Daisybushes, *Olearia*, are often prominent when in flower.

daisy cutter. [Used elsewhere but recorded earliest in Aust.] In Services' speech: see quot. 1947.

1923 F.E. Trotter *Tales of Billzac* 20 One of those new wide-spreading shells, 'Daisy cutter'. **1943** J. Binning *Target Area* 120 We knelt in the hard rubble that had been swept bare by a daisy-cutter. **1945** L. Jillet *Moresby's Few* 33 The 'daisy-cutter' carved a clean swath through part of the bush. **1946** A. Green *We were (Riff) R.A.A.F.* 40 The Japs dropped ten 'daisy cutters' which overshot the strip and landed with a terrific thud. . . Their marksmanship as bomb aimers was extremely bad. **1947** O. Griffiths *Darwin Drama* 104 The bombs dropped were mostly anti-personnel bombs which do not make a big crater but explode on impact and throw out fanwise, a spray of shrapnel which mows down everything in its way, and for this reason an anti-personnel bomb is known as a 'daisy cutter'.

dalgite /'dælgaɪt/. *W.A.* Also **dalgyte,** etc. [a. Nyungar *dalgayt*.] Bilby a.

1840 T.J. Buckton *W.A.* 96 Opossums, dalgerts, and other small animals. **1841** G. Grey *Jrnls. Two Exped. N.-W. & W.A.* II. 291 Some of the smaller animals, such as the *dal-gyte*, an animal about the size of a weasel, burrow in the earth. **1842** J. Gould *Birds of Aust.* (1848) II. Pl. 12, This bird [*sc.* the White-breasted Swallow] chooses for its nest the deserted hole of either the Dalgyte (*Perameles lagotis*) or the Boodee. **1872** Mrs E. Millett *Austral. Parsonage* 144 She would not return at dinner-time but rather take pot-luck with her relations on some chance dolghite or opossum. **1899** *Bulletin* (Sydney) 21 Jan. 14/3 The 'dulgite' is the most industrious burrower in W.A. . . He is about nine inches long, with coarse greyish hair, sharp snout, and claws like an Act of Parliament. **1925** *Ibid.* 30 Apr. 24/4 Westralian cockies know the common rabbit-bandicoot by the name 'dalgite'. **1982** *West Austral.* (Perth) 21 Dec. 38/1 Now classified as rare and endangered, the dalgyte was once common in the wheat-belt and arid areas across the continent.

dam. [Br. dial. *dam* the body of water confined by a dam or bank, as distinct from the holding barrier: see OED(S *sb.*[1] 2.]

1. An artificial pond or reservoir for the storage of water, usu. run-off rainwater; Tank *n.*[1] 1.

1843 *Sydney Morning Herald* 24 May 3/4 A large waterhole or dam is now being constructed, which will insure a supply of water during the driest seasons. **1849** *N.S.W. Sporting Mag.* 1 Jan. 173 Dams and tanks, or reservoirs for domestic purposes, are seldom required in his moist climate at home. **1862** J.A. Patterson *Gold Fields Vic.* 266 Miners have laboured to provide for their wants by the construction of dams. . . But these reservoirs are generally small. **1874** J.J. Halcombe *Emigrant & Heathen* 117 The season gives water in the dams or gullies. **1887** K. Mackay *Stirrup Jingles* 49 With little or nothing to eat, I may say, And miles from a tank or a dam. **1893** 'Times Special Correspondent' *Lett. from Qld.* 68 There is but one water-hole or dam that can be relied upon to hold out in drought. **1903** *Bulletin* (Sydney) 3 Jan. 16/2 The shower that fills a cockie's dam isn't necessarily a huge affair. **1918** A.M. Moore *Autumn Grey* 89 Miller walked on to what looked like a mud-hole, but which had once been a brimming dam. **1926** L.C.E. Gee *Bush Tracks & Gold Fields* 64 Pits where dry-blowers had been at work; a dam made years ago by some men who had intended to work a puddling machine. **1948** J.K. Ewers *For Heroes to live In* 33 Her only brother had been drowned in this dam. **1972** Anderson & Blake *J.S. Neilson* 22 Shallow dams with supply drains had to be scooped out to retain the rain water run-off for sheep and cattle, especially in the dry years. **1986** *Sydney Morning Herald* 12 Apr. 1/4 Bill Morley . . travelled back and forth from his property carting the last water from the last wet dam within cooee.

2. Comb. **dam-digger; -maker; -making; -sinker; -sinking.**

1957 F. Clune *Fortune Hunters* 170 The Champion **Dam-digger** raises the dust to finish the job before the rains come. **1979** B. Wannan *Chron. Boobyalla* 54 In the early years of the present century Jack Burble and his son Harry gained an enviable reputation as the best well-sinkers and dam-diggers in the Boobyalla district. **1878** 'R. Boldrewood' *Ups & Downs* 68 He kept the different parties of teamsters, fencers, splitters, carpenters, sawyers, **dam-makers,** well-sinkers, all in hand. **1897** R. Newton *Work & Wealth Qld.* 18 For the rest of the time there is a variety of bush work, fencing, yard-making, **dam-making**. **1897** L. Lindley-Cowen *W. Austral. Settler's Guide* 140 There is always a job of fencing or of dam or tank-making to be had. **1893** D. Lindsay *Jrnl. Elder Sci. Exploring Exped.* 126 Dr Elliot and Mr Wells were over at the **damsinkers'** camp. **1925** *Smith's Weekly* (Sydney) 15 Aug. 15/7 In 1888 Jim Hillier unrolled at the dam-sinker's camp at Thackaringa. **1937** A.W. Upfield *Winds of Evil* 28 Stella Borradale felt concern and sympathy for . . the team of dam-sinkers in their unprotected tents. **1957** F. Clune *Fortune Hunters* 169 He is Australia's Champion Dam-sinker—and also Australia's Champion Shearer. **1883** C. Proud *Murray & Darling Trade* 7/2 During the whole of last year the expenditure on tanks, **dam-sinking**, wells, and similar improvements, was not less than £2,000 a month. **1885** *Adelaide Observer* 25 July 9 Sometimes he gets a job at 'dam-sinking'—as the reservoir-excavation is called. **1904** *Bulletin* (Sydney) 4 Feb. 33/1 Some may relish this dam sinkin', for the pay is fairly high. **1925** C. Le Lievre *Memories Old Police Officer* 23 Get work out back at fencing or dam-sinking. **1979** W.K. Beckingham *Red Acres* 37 The ideal way to sink a dam was the way Les Blight and I used to do it. We had a single furrow dam-sinking plough which we pulled with our twelve horses double-banked. Then we used two three-quarter yard Linke Noack scoops each pulled by six horses. Most farmers did not have as many horses so hired dam-sinkers.

dama, damar, varr. Tammar.

damper. [Spec. use of Br. *damper* something which takes the edge off the appetite: see OED 1b and OED(S 6.]

1. A simple kind of bread, traditionally unleavened and baked in the ashes of an outdoor fire. Also **damper bread, cake.**

1825 B. Field *Geogr. Mem. N.S.W.* 371 We had provided ourselves with but little salt meat; flour for the purpose of making what are termed *dampers* (*i.e.* a flat cake, being merely a mixture of flour and water, baked in wood ashes) forming our chief stock. **1825** *Howe's Weekly Commercial Express* (Sydney) 23 May 3 There is at this moment many a poor settler up the country, buried in the bush . . eating salt pork and dampers with an occasional feast of kangaroo. **1828** *Hobart Town Courier* 23 Aug. 2 On the hearth, which was about one-third of the whole room in dimension, lay a heap of warm ashes, on disturbing which was found a damper, that is, about ten pounds of flour made into a lump of dough. **1833** *Perth Gaz.* 13 July 110 They then went on to the place where the other natives were making dampers. **1838** T.H. James *Six Months S.A.* 145 There was nothing . . that the blacks could be induced to eat; neither the damper bread nor biscuit. **1845** *Sydney Star* 25 Oct. 1/2 William Lawson was a fine old fellow, With red face and frosty poll, And he liked Australian damper Better than the best French roll. **1846** *Moreton Bay Courier* 5 Sept. 3/1 The lady and her lover were discovered by the pursuers seated *tete-a-tete* under a gum-tree, enjoying a comfortable pot of the best bohea, and damper. **1848** *Ibid.* 12 Feb. 3/3 Seven bodies were pointed out which were said to have died from partaking of the damper. **1856** *Jrnl. Australasia* I. 116 Our philological co-partner triumphantly quoted a couplet from Swift to prove that the Dean of St Patrick knew all about a very common article of colonial diet—'*Damper* it was; and all th'unleaven'd bread Lay on their stomachs like a ton of lead.' **1861** J.D. LANG *Qld., Aust.* 168 Mixing up arsenic or corrosive sublimate in the *dampers* or *hominy*, the unleavened wheaten cakes baked in the ashes, or the maize-meal porridge with which the settlers and squatters occasionally treat the natives. **1882** A.J. BOYD *Old Colonials* 195, I enjoyed a hearty meal, although the damper was kneaded by an old black gin and the beef salted by native troopers. **1894** W. CROMPTON *Convict Jim* 28 Death's river's running stronger, I can feel it in my veins, An' I'll soon be making damper on the everlasting plains. **1909** *Bulletin* (Sydney) 30 Sept. 13/2 The white flour of the bushman's life does not often bloom into damper nowadays... The modern substitute is bloated with baking powder, fired in a camp oven, and known as 'powder bread'. **1917** *Ibid.* 5 July 22/2 Why 'damper'? An old writer who lived in N.S. Wales about 1840 says that the name comes from Dampier.. and suggests that the old-time buccaneer invented the tucker. Another accusation is that it is so called because it's the best kind of grub to put a 'damper' on the appetite. **1928** B. SPENCER *Wanderings in Wild Aust.* 353 The real, genuine damper of the bushman is simply a mixture of flour and water, kneaded on a piece of bark and shaped into flat buns, varying in size from a diameter of a few inches to a foot or even more, and quite innocent of anything like yeast or baking-powder. **1946** A. THURIAN *Bush Tea & Overlanders* 18 Time doesn't count, one's job comes first, always fresh the dampers, With fresh-cut beef, post and rail tea, johnny cake that pampers. **1956** A. UPFIELD *Battling Prophet* 22 You know, us old geezers in the old days lived on damper bread and meat. **1964** T. RONAN *Packhorse & Pearling Boat* 46 'How much cream of tartar and soda?' 'We don't want that fancy rubbish, Boss! We likes our dampers blue and heavy; something that will stick to our ribs.' **1981** *Austral. Women's Weekly* (Sydney) 26 Aug. 105 (Advt.), It's a taste of Australia's history—the Damper, made better by White Wings in Matilda's Damper Mix. **1986** *Parkwatch* (Vic. Nat. Parks Assoc.) Mar. 3 Rambles, with billy tea and damper for the participants.

2. *fig.* Also *attrib.*

1852 J. BONWICK *Notes of Gold Digger* 24 A stray kangaroo.. was soon converted into some exquisite soup for mutton and damper diggers. **1895** A.B. PATERSON *Man from Snowy River* 14 They wouldn't earn much of their damper In a race like the President's Cup. **1903** J. FURPHY *Such is Life* 262 You're not worth your damper at this work. **1917** W. LEES *Coaching in Aust.* 9 But oh! they were good days; rough days, quart-pot days, damper days, perhaps. **1936** C.T. MADIGAN *Central Aust.* 94 Damper country is a long way outback now; the motor-car has pushed it even farther beyond the limits of permanent dwellings. **1961** P. WHITE *Riders in Chariot* 382 'You are not worth your damper,' she said once. 'Layin' around!' **1978** TEECE & PIKE *Voice of Wilderness* 42 Asked the time, they would squint at the sun and say, 'She's a damper high', meaning that it was yet forty-five minutes or an hour to sundown. That was the time it took to cook a damper.

3. Comb. **damper-maker, -making.**

1959 *Bulletin* (Sydney) 22 July 18/1 A champion **damper-maker** (ashes-style) along the Dawson River (C.Q.).. refuses to divulge his recipe. **1862** A. POLEHAMPTON *Kangaroo Land* 76, I became initiated into the mysteries of **damper-making**. **1922** 'J. BUSHMAN' *In Musgrave Ranges* 75 The great bush art of damper-making. **1946** F. CLUNE *Try Nothing Twice* 86, I had my first lesson in damper-making, and I've been an expert in charring them and sodding them ever since.

dampiera /dæmpi'ɛərə/. [The plant genus *Dampiera* was named by British botanist Robert Brown (*Prodr. Fl. Nov. Holl.* (1810) 587) after the explorer William *Dampier* (1652–1715), who collected the plant in the late 17th century.] Any plant of the Austral. genus of creepers, herbs, and shrubs *Dampiera* (fam. Goodeniaceae) of all States but most numerous in W.A. The flowers of most species are blue.

1844 L. LEICHHARDT *Jrnl. Overland Exped. Aust.* 22 Oct. (1847) 19 On the banks of Hodgson's Creek, grows a species of Dampiera, with many blue flowers, which deserves the name of 'D. floribunda'. **1942** C. BARRETT *Austral. Wild Flower Bk.* 14 The navigator is commemorated also by *Dampiera*, an Australian genus of many species, one of the prettiest being the blue Dampiera with sky-coloured, yellow-eyed flowers. **1958** *Coast to Coast 1957–58* 138 The sapphire of dampiera matted the shingly earth. **1973** R. ERICKSON et al. *Flowers & Plants W.A.* 170 Species of *Dampiera* such as the Common Dampiera.. have a more intense royal blue flower colour. The generic name honours William Dampier who was the first person to remark on the prevalence of blue-coloured flowers in the flora of 'New Holland'. **1985** *Age Weekender* (Melbourne) 31 May 7/4 With more than 70 species occurring throughout Australia, numerous Dampieras are becoming.. available for cultivation.

dandy. Chiefly *S.A.* An ice-cream container, now usu. small. See also BUCKET *n.* 1, DIXIE.

1954 *Australasian Confectioner* Sept. 80 Dandies, Dixies or Cartons—Large, 8½d. (Adelaide) 9d. (country); Small, 4½d., 5d. **1955** *S. Austral. Shopkeeper* Apr. 17 *It pays to sell the public's favourite—Amscol Ice-Cream* in Cones, Bricks, Dandies, Dairy-chock, Slice Creams and *Fro-Joy Twins*. **1970** J.S. GUNN in W.S. Ramson *Eng. Transported* 64 We should investigate the areas of use of such duplications as.. *dixy, dandy, bucket*.

darg. [Br. dial. (esp. Scot. and northern) *darg* a day's work, a defined quantity or amount of work.] An allotted or fixed amount of work.

1927 F.C. BIGGERS *Bat-Eye* 30 Fillin' our dag we was—wot ain't no play. **1929** D.J. DAVIES *Rev. Coal Question* 22 Another issue raised by Mr McDonald, and contained in the demands laid down in the owners' proposals, is the alleged restrictions of output, or more generally termed the 'darg'. **1934** *Red Star* (Perth) 6 Apr. 3/1 Briefly, the department proposed that the darg be 14 skips for pick bords and 19 for machine bords, and no interference with the darg. **1956** S. HOPE *Diggers' Paradise* 251 'Go slow' is not unknown in Britain, and the similar 'darg' in Australia helps to keep numerous workers in easy employment. **1972** G.C. BOLTON *Fine Country to starve In* 202 The miners reacted by imposing a 'darg', or working strictly to rule so as to spin out the work. **1976** J. HOLMES *Govt. Vic.* 38 Mr Hamer has added a third portfolio to his darg. **1978** *Westerly* iii. 16 It makes me glad I'm a journeyman of literature with my daily darg.

dark, *a.* and *n.*[1]

A. *adj.* As used of Aborigines: a euphemism for BLACK *a.*[1] See DARKSKIN.

1838 T.H. JAMES *Six Months S.A.* 232 Our dark friends were signalizing to their neighbours; shortly afterwards we heard a low 'cooe' from the opposite side of the river; I wished the black boy to answer it. **1843** *Sydney Morning Herald* 17 June 2/8 The dark gentleman stoutly denies the charge, but lays the blame on another one of the tribe. **1848** *Sidney's Austral. Hand-Bk.* 28 At the Wellington Mission House, where black natives are educated, I have heard that cattle and land are given as dower with young dark ladies, to induce white labourers to marry them. **1854** MRS C. CLACY *Lights & Shadows* I. 283 Lilian withdrew.. so as not to disturb the dark woman's silent grief. **1859** H.M. HULL *Experience Forty Yrs. Tas.* 16 The dark ladies smoke as well as their lords. **1863** J. DAVIS *Tracks of McKinlay* 189 Seven or eight dark houris camped close to us by themselves, in a 'mia-mia', but no one knew anything of it till the following morning—rather cool that. **1873** W. EVANS *Diary Welsh Swagman* (1975) 38 A dark native, that is an Aborigine, paid me a visit. **1880** *Bulletin* (Sydney) 15 May 1/1 It is high time that all dark men living under the British flag in New South Wales left the colony. **1888** *Ibid.* 23 June 6/4 Neglected he dies, Save Australia's dark children No one knows where he lies. **1941** K. TENNANT *Battlers* 99 About dusk Sam Little, from the dark people's camp, lounged up. **1950** *Dark People in Melbourne* (Victorian Council Social Service) 1 The greatest obstacles to assimilation are the beliefs and attitudes of white people, which underestimate the potentials of the 'dark people' (to use their own preferred euphemism). **1976** D. IRELAND *Glass Canoe* 69 The Darkfella.. got killed doing a delivery run in his truck. **1984** P. READ *Down there with me on Cowra Mission* 20 He was too strict and too rough with the dark people on the Mission.

B. *n.* An Aboriginal.

1950 *Dark People in Melbourne* (Victorian Council Social Service) 25 Although they would prefer to marry darks, a good number of the dark boys.. cannot provide the amenities which association with whites leads the girls to expect.

dark, *n.*[2] *Obs.*

1. See quot. 1873.

1859 W. KELLY *Life in Vic.* I. 166 Fill us a nobbler—dark; what's yours, mate? **1873** W. THOMSON-GREGG *Desperate Character* I. 39 His companion exclaimed.. 'Two dark, my dear'... The liquor was brandy—colonial brandy—of the darkest hue and most excruciating strength.

2. In the collocation **fourpenny dark,** cheap wine.

1955 N. PULLIAM *I traveled Lonely Land* 204 It's too cold for streetcorners and just right for.. a gallon of fourpenny dark with a mate. **1959** D. LOCKWOOD *Crocodiles & Other People* 22 After a week or so he smells worse than an alcoholic who's been drinking fourpenny-dark. **1967** A.E. DEBENHAM *All Manner of People* 84 There was some money left over, so they spent that.. on cheap wine (better known as 'plonk', 'Nellie', or 'fourpenny dark'). **1980** HEPWORTH & HINDLE *Boozing out in Melbourne Pubs* 16 The legendary drink of the twenties and thirties was the Fourpenny Dark. This was a stoup of nourishing bombo which, in the great days, was served in a mug with a handle on it.

dark cell. *Hist.* See quot. 1831.

1831 *Rep. Select Committee Secondary Punishments* (Great Brit. Parl.) 5 There are two modes of solitary confinement; one is in the dark cells, where light is totally excluded, and bread and water is the diet. **1841** *Corresp. on Convict Discipline* (Great Brit. Parl.) 10 Oct. (1846) 149 For the punishment of women who might have been convicted of a fresh offence, the smaller (dark) cells were intended. **1872** M. CLARKE *His Natural Life* 494 Dora was taken through the Hospital and the Workshops, shown the semaphores, and shut up, by laughing Maurice, in a 'dark cell'. **1881** *Bulletin* (Sydney) 29 Oct. 6/1 He is brought before the Visiting Justice and sentenced to seven days dark cells. Now 'dark cells' in Darlinghurst are quite as dark as a coffin tightly screwd [*sic*] down. **1932** W. RADCLIFFE *Port Arthur Guide* 9 Some of the convicts housed in this prison were of the very worst type; many had committed brutal offences, for which they were confined in a special cell called the 'Dark' or 'Dumb' cell. While in there the prisoner could not hear a sound or see any light whatever until he was released.

darkie, *n.*[1] Also **darkey.** [Perh. infl. by U.S. *darky* a Black: see Mathews.] An Aboriginal. Also *attrib.*

1845 *Parramatta Chron.* 12 Apr. 4/1 Information reaching the settlement, the Military and Police were started in pursuit, but before arriving at the scene of action the Darkies had made themselves scarce. **1854** G.H. HAYDON *Austral. Emigrant* 106 The black protectors had taught the Darkeys to read. **1863** J. DAVIS *Tracks of McKinlay* 352 The darkies are refined up here. **1871** 'OLD BOOMER' *Story of Mathinna* 9 'Twas when Sir John was ruler here, That first I saw my darkey dear, My own Mathinna! **1879** 'AUSTRALIAN' *Adventures Qld.* 20 We must have plenty of ball cartridge for the darkies and rations for ourselves. **1894** *Bulletin* (Sydney) 3 Mar. 18/2 Hordern Bros., of Sydney, recently hired an aboriginal blackfellow to stand in their window as an advt. 'Look here,' said the darkey to John L. Hordern, 'this is disgraceful. You gib me one poun' three days an' you make thousan's out o' me.' **1910** *Ibid.* 25 Aug. 14/3 Some of the coastal natives are fine strapping fellows... I guess these darkies would fight all right if properly trained. **1923** J. BOWES *Jackaroos* 75 The darkey's as sharp as a needle. **1932** C.M. GRAY *Western Vic. in Forties* 7 We thought it well to drive the darkeys away before we lay down for the night, so discharged a pistol, which made them decamp. **1949** B. O'REILLY *Green Mountains* 72 Sometimes we had a dear old darkie, Fanny, to do the washing. **1965** *Overland* xxxii. 39 The darkies have been allowed to go to the white school for ages. **1975** R. HALL *Place among People* 219 If its the darkie woman who comes out first, we grab her. **1981** *Sun-Herald* (Sydney) 4 Oct. 11/7 I'd sell about 360 flagons a week to the darkies—it's a good line, they really knock it over.

darkie, *n.*[2] LUDERICK.

1895 C. THACKERAY *Amateur Fisherman's Guide* 10 Your noble 'darkie' is a fine fighter, and has more pull to the square inch of his surface than a jewfish or cod has to the square foot. **1978** D. VAWR *Ratbag Mind* 15 Vast breeding grounds for mullet, garfish and luderick ('niggers' or 'darkies' to Sydneysiders).

darkie, *n.*[3] See quot. and also DARKUN.

1982 LOWENSTEIN & HILLS *Under Hook* 17 We was a darkie, a midnight shift.

darkskin. *Obs.* An Aboriginal.

1845 *Sydney Morning Herald* 8 Apr. 2/7 We have had another affair with the blacks, close to the township... Lieutenant Cooper .. immediately despatched a sergeant and a file of men from his detachment to the scene of the outrage, but before they could reach the spot the dark-skins were off. **1857** F. DE B. COOPER *Wild Adventures* 29, I was one of about thirty that camped with him in that rally, and we stuck to those scrubs up and down the river till the dark-skins were as scarce as kangaroo-meat in a settlement. **1871** *Austral. Town & Country Jrnl.* (Sydney) 17 June 747/3 Within six miles of the Brunswick we came upon a black camp, having passed a heavy mob of dark-skins on the way. **1911** A. SEARCY *By Flood & Field* 27 Lagoons surrounded by patches devoid of timber, but covered with long grass, which would have made the travelling very trying for anyone but a darkskin.

darkun. [Altered form of *dark one.*] A shift lasting twenty-four hours, worked by a wharf labourer.

1957 T. NELSON *Hungry Mile* 81 Some 25 years back a gang of us refused an order of the Union Co. to come back after the breakfast break for four hours, after doing a 'dark-un' (24 hour shift). **1961** *Sydney Morning Herald* 22 May 2/5 One reason for rank-and-file militancy is that many of those who remember the bad days—the jostling for jobs and the 24-hour 'dark-'uns'—are still in the industry. **1977** *Sunday Tel.* (Sydney) 6 Mar. 7/2 For 12 years as foreman I worked a weekly 'darkun'—a 24-hour shift. These shifts were inhuman.

darl. Abbrev. of 'darling', chiefly as a mode of address.

1930 K.S. PRICHARD *Haxby's Circus* 329 'Oh, darl. don't you bother,' he begged. **1950** —— *Winged Seeds* 56 'You can bet your sweet life on that, darl,' Bill replied. **1966** N. SIDNEY *Beyond Bay* 42 Why can't you just let us be, darl? **1969** A. BUZO *Front Room Boys* (1970) 88 'Come on, let's go...' 'Okay darls, we'll go and have a cocktail first, eh?' **1970** J. CLEARY *Helga's Web* 72 'Darl—' He hadn't called her that for several years: short for *darling*, there had been a time when he had called her nothing else. **1984** *Truckin' Life* VII. iv. 91/3 Newcastle to Gosford is only a short run darl.

Darling. [The name of a river in w. N.S.W.] Used *attrib.* in Special Comb. **Darling lily,** the perennial plant of N.S.W., Qld., N.T., S.A., and Vic. *Crinum flaccidum* (fam. Liliaceae), bearing large creamy or white scented flowers; *Murray lily*, see MURRAY 2; **pea, (a)** any of a small number of species of the genus *Swainsona* (fam. Fabaceae), most being perennial herbs of inland Aust., some of which can cause stock-poisoning; see also SWAINSONA; **(b)** such poisoning, usu. affecting sheep, and characterized by stiffness of limbs, inco-ordination and muscle tremor; also *fig.*, see quot. 1894 (see also PEA *n.*[1]); **shower,** a dust storm; **whaler,** see WHALER *n.*[1] b.

1859 J.D. MEREWEATHER *Diary Working Clergyman* 199 Put into my valise two bulbs of the beautiful **Darling lily.** **1888** *Proc. Linnean Soc. N.S.W.* III. 502 *Crinum flaccidum*... The 'Darling Lily'. This exceedingly handsome white-flowered plant .. has bulbs which yield a fair arrowroot. **1919** *Bulletin* (Sydney) 18 Sept. 20/4 The Darling lily is .. a distinguished vegetable. **1927** *Aussie* (Sydney) Mar. 10/3 The Darling lily, which grows about the Darling River country. **(a) 1863** W.J. WILLS *Successful Exploration Interior Aust.* 128 A disputed question .. as to the effect of the **Darling pea** on horses, some asserting that they become cranky simply from eating that herb. *c* **1872** J.C.F. JOHNSON *Over Island* 1 Miles of the squatter's pest—the purple Darling pea. **1901** J.H. MAIDEN *Plants reputed to be Poisonous* 16 *Swainsona galegifolia* .. 'Darling Pea' .. is a dreaded plant from the great amount of loss it has inflicted on stock-owners. Its effect on sheep is well-known; they separate from the flock, wander about listlessly, and are known to the shepherds as 'pea-eaters', or 'indigo eaters'. **1923** *Aussie* (Sydney) Oct. 37/1 They were both bound for the one little two-pub town out in the Darling-pea zone, called Bungledoo. **1955** *Meanjin* 307 Her thoughts bolted like a horse she had once seen crazed from eating the Darling pea. **1966** J.F. MACADAM *Some Poisonous Plants N.-W.* 73 The most colourful and also the most common of the poisonous plants of the north-west are the Darling peas (*Swainsona* spp.). **(b) 1889** T. QUIN *Well Sinkers* 101 'The man's mad!' .. 'No .. he's got a touch of what we call the **Darling Pea.**' **1894** M. ROBERTS *Red Earth* 246 When you say a man has 'got the Darling pea' you mean that loneliness and desolation—the heat of the sun, and the cursed sameness of the sunburnt plains; the lack of human society; the lack of all the natural outlets of humanity—have made him less than human, that he is mad. **1904** L.M.P. ARCHER *Bush Honeymoon* 76 We had about sixty shepherds, and now and then one would get 'Darling Pea' (become insane), and cut his throat, or hang himself to the wall-plate of the hut. **1918** A.J. CAMPBELL *Renaming Austral. Birds* 29 The Darlin' pea is drivin' men an' cattle off their chump. **1935** C.H. SOUTER *Lonely Rose* 54 My nag got 'Darlin' pea', An' Stumpie took a bail. **1887** *Observer* (Adelaide) 8 Jan. 43/2 The wind at Birdsville is a caution, quite reminding one of the **'Darling Showers'** of old. **1895** *Bulletin* (Sydney) 22 June 3/2, I had pierced the 'Never Never' with a 'bluey' slung behind. And been caught in 'Darling showers' that had driven many blind. **1898** A.S. MURRAY *Twelve Hundred Miles* 35 *A Darling Shower.* Few people know what this is. No rain falls... In the heat of summer you notice a black cloud in the north-west... It is a vast accumulation of dust, whirled into the air, and forced onward by a gale of wind. This dust permeates everything. **1900** *Pastoral Times* (Deniliquin) 3 Mar. 2/5 A Darling shower passed over, but there was only the usual forty drops to the acre. **1905** *Bulletin* (Sydney) 19 Oct. 14/2 He came in at the tail-end of a Darling shower, conveying a goodly portion of the Never-Never country about his person. **1920** J.N. MACINTYRE *White Aust.* 40 He knew 'twas the dread Darling shower, Eftsoon came the winds with their circular sweep, The riot of red leaves in storm gusts that leap, And then—we'd dust for a dower. **1929** *Bulletin* (Sydney) 12 June 23/1 The heat, the 'Darling showers'—Those were the evils of the day. **1936** E. HARRINGTON *Boundary Bend* 17 We might have known this promise, like the rest, Would end in nothing but a Darling Shower! **1951** W. HATFIELD *Wild Dog Frontier* 100 By mid-day that first day after their arrival there was little to observe but the classical Darling Shower, sheep-dust and sand. **1968** H.D. DALGLEISH *Tie my Swag* II. 7 The dust came down .. a 'Darling Shower!' .. The visibility was nil... The dust you breathed up made you ill!

dart. *Obs.* [Fig. use of *dart* repr. U.S. or Br. dial. pron. of *dirt* pay dirt: see quot. 1859 and also *old dart* OLD *a.* 1.] A scheme or dodge; a favoured location, object, or course of action.

1859 W. KELLY *Life in Vic.* I. 218 The digger will not only work to the boundary of his own claim, but into his neighbour's territory, if word comes down from above that the 'dart' is payable. [*Note*] Dart is the designation of stuff worth washing, as contradistinguished from that considered useless. **1882** *Sydney Slang Dict.* 3 *Dart*, object of attraction, or enticing thing or event, or a set purpose. **1882** *Sydney Mail* 26 Aug. 335/1 Our dart is to be off and have a month's start before anybody knows they're [*sc.* the cattle] off the run. **1893** J.A. BARRY *Steve Brown's Bunyip* 79 Surfiss is my dart—roun' about the old tailin's and puddlers. Down below's too risky. **1893** *Antipodean* (Melbourne) 32 I'm a giddy little tart, And I'm up to every dart; You should see me when I go upon the knock-O! **1894** *Bulletin* (Sydney) 3 Feb. 13/1 Formerly, the grasping 'trap', hurrying to get rich and own his little terrace, moved heaven and earth to get on to a 'Chow' beat. Now his 'dart' is a district containing a 'tote' or two, and inhabited by a few Sunday-trading publicans. **1900** *Truth* (Sydney) 10 June 5/3 To pose as the president and thereby be entertained at all up-country gatherings—that's his dart. **1904** L.M.P. ARCHER *Bush Honeymoon* 123 Catch her doin' a stroke of work, only she's 'ard up for opium—*that's her dart!* **1914** E. DYSON *Spats' Fact'ry* 120 'Twas now me dart t' get inter the 'ands iv the John. **1918** L.J. VILLIERS *Changing Yr.* 12 She didn't kid yet long—er bloomin' dart Ud git yer goin' till yer 'ad a rat.

Darwin. [The name of the capital city of the Northern Territory.] Used *attrib.* in Special Comb. **Darwin blonde,** see quot. 1947; **rig,** male attire required by etiquette on semi-formal occasions in Darwin (see quot. 1967); **stubby,** a beer bottle having a capacity of 2.25 litres (see STUBBY 1).

1947 O. GRIFFITHS *Darwin Drama* 34 At Bagot Compound for Aborigines a big proportion of the inmates were half-caste girls, referred to as **'Darwin blondes'** many of whom were not unattractive. **1964** *N. Austral. Monthly* Sept. 23 Mr Nott will perhaps be best remembered for his insistence on the **'Darwin rig'** for formal affairs here. **1964** K. WILLEY *Eaters of Lotus* 12 Almost his first act as Administrator was to do away with such nonsense as cummerbands and monkey jackets. He decreed 'coats off' at Government House functions. 'Darwin rig' was to be official wear in future. **1967** *Darwin, Way of Life* (N.T. Admin.) 3 For semi-formal wear, including some receptions at Government house, men adopt what has become famous as 'Darwin Rig' .. long-sleeved white shirt, tie, long trousers, and dark shoes, but no coat. **1984** M. BOZIC *Gather your Dreams* 36 They appeared every morning dressed in their immaculate 'Darwin Rig' shorts, long white socks and open-necked shirts. **1972** J. O'GRADY *It's your Shout, Mate!* 87 'Try a **Darwin stubby** while you're there. See if you can drink it down in one go.' 'That should not be too difficult,' I said. 'You reckon? They're not the same as our stubbies. A Darwin stubby holds forty ounces.' **1975** *Bulletin* (Sydney) 28 June 66/1 Oddly enough all the tasters were keen on the NT Draught. This came in a 76 oz bottle, a true whopper, lovingly known in the North as the Darwin Stubbie. **1975** K. WILLEY *Ghosts of Big Country* 163 Few visitors went anywhere without their 'calling-card', usually consisting of one or more 'Darwin Stubbies', huge, flagon-like containers of local make, each holding the equivalent of three normal-sized bottles. **1980** J. WOLFE *Crocodile Soup* 17 'Darwin stubbies' are oversize bottles each holding half a gallon of beer. **1984** *N.T. News* (Darwin) 18 Sept. 2/4 The Territory has wallowed for too long in the reputation as Australia's hardest drinking community, highlighted by such insidious promotions as the Beercan Regatta and the Darwin Stubbie.

Darwinian. An inhabitant of Darwin.

1928 M.E. FULLERTON *Austral. Bush* 96 At Port Darwin .. the Darwinians. **1968** K. DENTON *Walk around my Cluttered Mind* 171 Darwinians considered the rest of the country to be full of prissy English.

dash. [Spec. use of *dash* capacity for prompt and vigorous action: see OED *sb.*[1] 9.] In the phr. **to have done (one's) dash,** to have exhausted (one's) energies, to have had (one's) chance.

1910 L. ESSON *Woman Tamer* (1976) 82 'So you want to give me the chuck—me for—Bongo Williams...' 'Yes, you've done your dash, Chopsey.' **1915** C.J. DENNIS *Songs of Sentimental Bloke* 119 *Dash, to do one's*, to reach one's Waterloo. **1928** A. WRIGHT *Good Recovery* 137 'What about Norma?' asked Trevot... 'You've done y' dash there as well.' 'Surely you don't mean to tell me that she has fallen to your charms?' sneered Trevot. **1930** K.S. PRICHARD *Haxby's Circus* 283 You've done your dash, Max, thrown up the sponge .. and can't do your work. **1966** G.W. TURNER *Eng. Lang. in Aust. & N.Z.* 152 *Dashing* seems to be a shortened form of *pan dashing*, extracting gold with a pan... It is tempting to wonder whether the expression 'he's done his dash' meaning 'he is played out', 'he has done all he can' is connected with the goldminer's dashing. **1969** G. JOHNSTON *Clean Straw for Nothing* (1971) 134 If you were watching me earlier you'll know I've done my bloody dash. Their daughter has danced me right into the ground. I'm completely bloody well whacked. **1972** D. IRELAND *Flesheaters* 9 No shoelaces for you, Mr Nobbs! You've done your dash. Any more running away and you'll be confined to pyjamas for a week. **1973** C. EAGLE *Who could love Nightingale?* 272 'Keep going,' she said. 'Keep going.' 'I've done my dash, Marg, in every sense of the words.'

dasyure /'dæzijʊə/. [a. mod. L. *Dasyurus* f. Gr. *δασύς* hairy + *οὐρά*, tail, the name of the genus.] Any of several carnivorous marsupials, now usu. those of the genus *Dasyurus* (see *native cat* NATIVE *a.* 6 b.) of Aust. and New Guinea.

1839 *Proc. Zool. Soc. London* 134 In the Thylacine and Ursine Dasyure .. the condyle of the lower jaw is placed low down. **1913** C.G. LANE *Creature-Life* 114 Although Dasyure is their correct name, these animals are always known to bush-dwellers as native-cats. **1926** A.S. LE SOUEF et al. *Wild Animals Australasia* 323 The dasyure, keeping low, ran forward. **1935** D.G. STEAD *Rabbit in*

Aust. 17 A wall of forest . . containing carnivorous animals like the Dasyures or Native Cats.

date. [Cf. BLOT.] The anus; the vagina. Also *attrib.*

[**1919** W.H. DOWNING *Digger Dialects* 18 *Date*, a word signifying contempt.] **1961** M. CALTHORPE *Dyehouse* 214 In your bloody date! What do you think we are? **1971** B. HUMPHRIES *Bazza pulls it Off*, I hear tell the French tarts . . don't say no to robbing the occasional date locker. **1973** 'HOGBOTEL & FFUCKES' *Snatches & Lays* 25 The Australian lady emu, when she wants to find a mate, Wanders round the desert with a feather up her date. **1973** R. EDWARDS *Austral. Bawdy Ballads* 26 His doodle broke off and stayed in her date.

Hence **date** *v. trans.*, to 'goose' (a person).

1972 D. HEWETT *Bon-Bons & Roses* (1976) 52 Remember when I got that plumber in to unblock the sink? I was up on a chair fixing the new curtains and he comes up behind, and dates me. Large as life. Without a word of a lie. He dates me. Cheeky mug. And what did he say? 'Thought you might like *your* plumbing interfered with too, Madam.'

dead, *a.* In special collocations.

1. In the sense of 'without life': **dead heart,** the arid interior of Australia; **house,** see quot. 1855; **marine** [see OED *marine, adj.* 4 b. and *sb.* 4 d.], an empty (beer) bottle; **meat ticket,** an identity disc; **men's graves** *pl.*, mounds in heavy clay soils, often separated by depressions; a form of GILGAI; **wood fence** *Tas.*, see quot. 1852; **wool,** wool taken from a dead sheep.

1906 J.W. GREGORY (title) The **dead heart** of Australia. **1908** *Bulletin* (Sydney) 10 Dec. 40/1 Night in the Great Dead Heart. Moonrise on the Australian Desert. **1926** *Illustr. Tasmanian Mail* (Hobart) 18 Aug. 6/2 The 'dead heart' of Australia has been very much alive lately. **1938** F. BLAKELEY *Hard Liberty* 128 Why not bury that sickening phrase—the Dead Heart of Australia? **1942** *Bulletin* (Sydney) 3 June 12/4 There seems no reason why it shouldn't grow in what is erroneously called the 'Dead Heart'. **1950** G.M. FARWELL *Land of Mirage* 19 Others failing to understand the volatile temperament of this land, echo J.W. Gregory's term, 'the dead heart', little realising that he applied it only to Lake Eyre. **1971** *Bulletin* (Sydney) 28 Aug. 43/1 London is a more tangible reality to most Australians than the Dead Heart of their country. **1982** *Weekend Austral. Mag.* (Sydney) 6 Nov. 4/5 Restored by good February rains, this is at the moment no dead heart. **1855** P. SAUNDERS *Two Yrs. Vic.* (1863) 126 In the interior and at the diggings . . almost every public house has a room very appropriately called the **dead house**. This room generally has but one window high up in the wall. . . All those who get mad drunk, or insensibly drunk, are deposited in the dead house where they are locked up until the morning. **1875** MRS N. WOOD *Waiting for Mail* 111 Jim . . went into the bar, drank himself stupid, and was carried off to an out-building characteristically named 'the Dead House'. **1888** 'R. BOLDREWOOD' *Robbery under Arms* (1937) 430 He was snoring in a back room, and like a man in the dead-house of a bush shanty, not likely to wake before sunrise. **1916** *Bulletin* (Sydney) 10 Feb. 22/2 There was a 'deadhouse' attached to the pub, and into this the drunks and disorderlies were emptied for the night. **1922** A. WRIGHT *Colt from Country* 114 But I'm right mate. I ain't shikkered, only on the verge, that's all. Another pint, as you say, and it'd be me f'r th' dead-house. **1944** M.J. O'REILLY *Bowyangs & Boomerangs* 39 It was the usual thing at that time for hotels, especially in mining towns, to have a room set apart in the back yard for customers who became obstreperous. These rooms were usually called 'deadhouses'. **1864** *Drinkamania* 5 Or sail the ever restless deep, On snow crest wave is seen, Now and again to slyly peep, Its head—a '**Dead Marine**'! **1883** C. PROUD *Murray & Darling Trade* 27/1 The only indication of civilization for many miles along this weary track were the 'dead marines' which were always in most profusion in the vicinity of the grog shanties. **1901** *Truth* (Sydney) 13 Jan. 1/4 A 'Noose' inkslinger wants the 'dead marines' of the Commonwealth junketings preserved in the Art Gallery. Yes, and labelled 'The taxpayer had to pay! pay! pay!' **1907** A. SEARCY *In Austral. Tropics* 110 When a bottle becomes a dead marine, and it has a label, it is an excellent plan to run a knife through the label two or three times. **1920** *Smith's Weekly* (Sydney) 13 May 17/5 The drier the road outback the more thickly the dead marines strew the sides. **1928** *Bulletin* (Sydney) 1 Feb. 25/1 The dead marine is put to all sorts of uses out back. I have seen many a grave in village cemeteries neatly surrounded with inverted empties. . . One, which probably belonged to a temperance family, was enclosed with ginger-beer bottles. **1938** *Ibid.* 26 Jan. 20/4 The commonsense solution of Darwin's dead-marine problem would be the starting of a local brewery. **1952** *Ibid.* 2 Jan. 16/2 'Let's have the bottle back, will y'?' A week later Norm returned the dead-marine. **1960** *N.T. News* (Darwin) 12 Jan. 7/3 The need to declare the Katherine River low-level bridge camping area a reserve is becoming more urgent. Judging by the number of 'dead marines' it is the site of regular drinking orgies. **1973** J. MORRISON *Austral. by Choice* 128 Joe told me to . . carry out the dead marines and stack them in the yard. [N.Z. **1917** MILLER *Camps, Tracks & Trenches* (1939) 15 **Dead Meat Tickets** (identity discs).] **1920** T. CARLYON *Sons of Southern Cross*, Every second Australian had pawned his 'dead-meat ticket'. **1921** E. WELLS *Fragments* 10 This flash dead meat ticket was worn by me on a fine gold chain. **1970** R. BEILBY *No Medals for Aphrodite* 42 Discoloured 'dead-meat-tickets' swinging from a greasy cord round his neck. **1833** J. BACKHOUSE *Narr. Visit Austral. Colonies* 4 May (1843) 147 The soil is strong, and stands in remarkable ridges, called in this country, '**Dead-mens-graves**'. **1847** *Maitland Mercury* 28 Aug. 4/4 The Wimera country, especially the low part of it, is at present an immense lake. A great part of it is 'crab-hole' country, or 'dead men's graves', which at present look like so many islands. **1855** W. HOWITT *Land, Labor & Gold* 28 May I. 328 Akin to these Crab-Holes are the Dead-men's Graves. They are oblong heaps of earth distributed over certain extents of these low, volcanic plains, which for all the world present the appearance of a graveyard. **1855** G.H. WATHEN *Golden Colony* 14 Large flat areas, hundreds or even thousands of acres in extent, are covered with oval mounds and corresponding hollows,—resembling a vast graveyard of giants. Such tracts are known as 'Dead Men's Graves' or 'Bay of Biscay Land'. **1872** 'RESIDENT' *Glimpses Life Vic.* 93 This dead level is occasionally varied by a tract of country known as Bay of Biscay ground, where the soil rises in countless small mounds, called 'dead men's graves', which resemble tiny solid waves. **1891** J. FENTON *Bush Life Tas.* (1964) 154 There were wet, marshy flats to pass through on what was called 'holy ground', or 'dead men's graves', with knotty gum stumps and little hillocks standing in the water. **1901** 'R. BOLDREWOOD' *In Bad Company* 482, I was walking the horses over a curious formation of small mounds, provincially known as 'dead men's graves'. **1844** Tas. Non-State Rec. 103/2, The **dead wood fence** might reach considerably further up the hill. **1852** G.C. MUNDY *Our Antipodes* III. 180 The 'deadwood' fence is one almost peculiar to Van Diemen's land. It is nothing more than the trees of the clearing piled into a sort of wooden wall. **1861** L.A. MEREDITH *Over Straits* 17 Each lessee surrounds his 'lot' with brush or deadwood fences. **1910** *Emu* X. 128 The rough dead-wood fences which are the first attempts at property enclosure. **1980** HOLTH & BARNABY *Cattlemen of High Country* 177 Ned Kelly worked on this dead-wood fence they put along there. **1899** *Bulletin* (Sydney) 16 Sept. 15/2 A sheep, killed lately . . was found with its paunch stuffed with wool. The poor beast had apparently nibbled **'dead' wool** in order to ease its hunger. **1906** *Ibid.* 22 May 15/1 Among queer occupations have never seen 'dead-wool-pickers' mentioned. I have come across many ancient battlers out West busily gathering the fleeces from drought-stricken sheep. Run-holders give £1 a bale for the wool. **1928** C.E. COWLEY *Classing Clip* 139 Dead-wool has a considerable commercial value. **1954** B. MILES *Stars my Blanket* 220 'Mr Prescott, . . he's a dead-wool picker. . . ' 'It's best to let 'em get real rotten first, then all you needs to do is pick 'em up and shake 'em, and the inside'll all fall out neatly. . . I sends all my dead wool to the scourers.' **1977** J. WALLACE *Memories Country Childhood* 115 With wool prices so high at that time, dead wool was valuable.

2. In the sense of 'absolute, complete, unrelieved': **dead beat,** one who is down in luck (not necessarily in the orig. U.S. sense of *loafer*); **bird** *horse-racing*, a certainty; also *fig.*; **frost** *obs.*, a total failure; **knowledge** *obs.* [Br. dial. (see EDD)], deceitfulness, cunning; **nark,** a spoil-sport.

1892 *Truth* (Sydney) 8 May 7/1 Misery and wretchedness were never better exemplified than in the case of those class of unfortunates known as '**dead-beats**'. **1901** *Ibid.* 9 June 3/4 It was hardly good form to allow the wearers of the Royal uniform to loaf about the city as dead-beats—accepting 'shouts' and not being in a position to say, 'Fill 'em up again.' **1911** *Bulletin* (Sydney) 1 June 14/2 The dead-beat was close to the end of things when his mate visited him in hospital. **1911** A. NEEDHAM *Radicals* 32 Drifted, stranded, hopeless wrecked ones—so we call you all 'dead-beats'. **1928** G.H. WILKINS *Undiscovered Aust.* 12 There were many inquiries from 'dead-beats' looking for a job. **1889** A.G. TAYLOR *Marble Man* 18 At night he will be robbing the poor-box to back a **'dead-bird'** at the Carrington. **1889** *Illustr. Austral. News* (Melbourne) 9 Nov. 18/3 A 'dead bird' signifies that a horse is considered certain to win, the analogy being taken from pigeon shooting, the scorer calling 'dead bird' when the bird is shot dead. **1892** *Bulletin* (Sydney) 29 Oct. 7/3 Our war-cry is heard—We have each a 'dead-bird' And a notion absurd That its going to do it. **1906** *Gadfly* (Adelaide) 28 Feb. 17/1 Partridge didn't prove a 'dead bird' . . in the race for Nora Kerin's hand and heart. **1911** L. ESSON *Three Short Plays* 43 We discussed horse-racing. 'Jugger' Reynolds gave me a tip—a deadbird. **1942** F. CLUNE *Last of Austral. Explorers* 113 Donald simply had to wait to see the Cup. Wherever he went in Melbourne the talk was of dead birds—certs for the big race. **1951** D. STIVENS *Jimmy Brockett* 47 One of these days we'd strike a race with most of 'em in it and then we'd be betting on a dead bird. **1980** BRENNAN & WHITE *Keep Billy Boiling* 84 The two Jacky boys, suspended housemen with their little turned up hats, red-coloured checkered coats, bandy legs . . , useless devils with their cigarettes and 'Dead Birds' (certain bets). **1884** *Austral. Tit-Bits* (Melbourne) 3 July 13/1 We have known many Sydney successes a **dead frost** in Melbourne. ***c* 1906** L. BECKE *Settlers Karossa Creek* 97 Mary will tell mother, and mother will tell father, and your surprise will be a dead frost. **1925** *Illustr. Tasmanian Mail* (Hobart) 26 Aug. 9/2 The shoot had been a 'dead frost'. **1905** *Shearer* (Sydney) 15 July 3/1, I remember once meeting an old swaggie—a genuine '**dead knowledge** man'—on the Darling. *Ibid.* 2 Dec. 4/5 They have grown hoary in beggary, falsehood, cunning, 'generalship', servility, 'dead knowledge' and debauchery, and are a curse and a menace about stations, as after 'planting' or drinking their pension money, they are perfectly willing to accept charity. **1908** *Bulletin* (Sydney) 23 Jan. 14/2 An old swaggie—a genuine 'dead-knowledge man'—on the Darling told me how some years previously he had wanted a letter written, and . . determined to master the art. **1906** E. DYSON *Fact'ry 'Ands* 27 Up to yeh, too, fer a **dead nark.** ***c* 1907** C.W. CHANDLER *Darkest Adelaide* 62 Occasionally one [*sc.* prostitute] gets run in on the elastic charge of loitering. Then her fallen sisters fight shy of the particular pitch from which the unlucky one was 'pinched'. They seek out a spot on the beat of a copman who is not a 'dead nark'. **1908** *Austral. Mag.* (Sydney) 1 Nov. 1252/1 The 'push' adopted 'dead' as their general utility word. . . You were a 'dead nark' when you spoiled the other fellow's game. **1975** X. HERBERT *Poor Fellow my Country* 526 'According to them . . I'm . . a Dead Nark. . . ' 'Well . . it means . . well, a spoil-sport.' 'That's the Australian meaning. The English dictionary meaning is a Police Informer.'

dead finish.

1. The shrub or small tree of the drier parts of W.A., S.A., Qld., N.T., and N.S.W. *Acacia tetragonophylla* (fam. Mimosaceae) which can form tangled prickly thickets; any of several other shrubs or trees of similar habit.

1880 *Proc. Linnean Soc. N.S.W.* V. 10 From the flowers of one, *A[cacia] farnesiana* . . called 'Dead-finish' on the Darling Downs, a delicious perfume is distilled. **1881** W. FEILDING *Austral. Trans-Continental Railway* 28 Cut a 'dead finish' sapling for a pole, and spent all morning in fitting it. **1891** *Proc. Linnean Soc. N.S.W.* VI. 138 *Acacia tetragonophylla* . . A 'Dead finish'. Timber very hard, heavy, tough and close-grained. **1911** ST. C. GRONDONA *Collar & Cuffs* 70 'Never-tire', which grows vigorously in the driest years, and 'dead finish' . . are . . desert shrubs, the last being, in reality, a prickly-undergrowth. **1938** *Bulletin* (Sydney) 24 Aug. 21/1 Queensland's 'dead-finish' . . bears no resemblance to the Westralian tree of the same name. It is an acacia growing to a height of 20 ft. and is a valuable fodder tree with a fernlike leaf and a habit of growing dense thickets in which cattle often take shelter, to the exasperation of stockmen in a round-up. Hence its name. **1948** G. FARWELL *Down Argent Street* 31 There is only the kark of the crows settling upon stunted mulga and dead finish. **1959** H. MYERS *Regions of Courage* 183 How they can get along on mulga, bush hay, water, the bit of nutriment in the grass, and other edibles such as dead-finish has me beat. **1963** *N. Austral. Monthly* Dec. 11

'Dead finish', so named because when it dies that is the end of all other plants, is a small tree of the Basalt Country (Acacia basalticus) with fine dark green pinnate leaves which are usually in pairs. **1973** D. WOLFE *Brass Kangaroo* 25 Once I asked him the name of a small scrubby tree about ten feet high... 'That's fucking Dead Finish, the bastard.' **1981** M. SHARLAND *Tracks of Morning* 71 'Dead-finish' is a native pidgin term for certain plants which have adapted themselves to the blasting heat of summer in Australian deserts where, also, they become skeletonised by hungry cattle and camels. One kind particularly—an ugly, thorn-armored acacia—seems always to be hovering between survival and extinction.

2. *transf.* The limit, the end.

1881 A.C. GRANT *Bush-Life Qld.* I. 201 'He's the dead finish—go right through a man,' rejoins Sam, rather sulkily. **1894** G. BOOTHBY *On Wallaby* 294 Grog shanties or 'dead finishes' as they are often termed, are the curse of the bush, and in no other colony are they so bad as in Queensland. **1902** E.B. KENNEDY *Black Police Qld.* 9 Planting and hoeing cane was deadly enough work for the white man, but trashing!—this proved the 'dead finish'. **1918** C. FETHERSTONHAUGH *After Many Days* 205 Another bit of slang that originated at Gayndah was 'the dead finish'. Now it is 'the limit' or 'above the odds'. **1925** A. WRIGHT *Boy from Bullarah* 128 She'd try to make me drop the business, but I'm going to play my part to the dead finish. **1930** V. PALMER *Passage* (1957) 171 I'll show him he's come to a dead-finish as far as I'm concerned. **1950** G. FARWELL *Surf Music* 145 The mate, peering.. at tumbling seas, said.., 'Be the dead finish of all of us, way we're going.' **1956** *Truth* (Sydney) 29 Jan. 37/6 'She's the dead finish,' he said.. and in some indescribable way we knew he had paid the woman who was just entering his life the highest compliment in his power. **1980** ANSELL & PERCY *To fight Wild* 110 If some do-gooder had come along and shoved the poor old buggers in a nice clean home, that would have been the dead finish of them.

dead-set, *a.* and *adv.*

A. *adj.* Genuine; absolute.

1965 F. HARDY *Yarns of Billy Borker* 119 I'm a real crusader against acid stomach, got a dead-set cure for it: Quick-Eze. **1979** CAREY & LETTE *Puberty Blues* 10 'Here comes Darren.' 'What a deadset doll.'

B. *adv.* Truly; really.

1979 CAREY & LETTE *Puberty Blues* 9 Have me lunch. Deadset, I'm not hungry, I just had a curried chop in Home Science. **1980** ANSELL & PERCY *To fight Wild* 30 All muddled up, but dead-set worried I'd sleep again and miss part of the next tide. **1984** *Sunday Tel.* (Sydney) 15 Apr. 60/4 Whenever I get the chance to watch Parramatta I'll go and see them just to watch Grothe. Dead set I'm in love with him.

dead-un. A loser, esp. a racehorse which is deliberately restrained from winning.

1896 N. GOULD *Town & Bush* 225 He has a remarkable way of scenting a 'dead un', or of finding out a non-starter. **1900** *Truth* (Brisbane) 6 May 4/2 This paper thought that Martin had backed a dead un, as it thought the gentlemen were coming in but they didn't. **1904** *Bulletin* (Sydney) 24 Nov. 19/1 The 'dead 'un' he had in view romped home at ten to one, unbacked. **1933** S. GRIFFITHS *Rolling Stone on Turf* 49 Well, I'm damned!.. Another bloody dead 'un has come home on me! **1977** *Sun-Herald* (Sydney) 24 July 57/6 No matter how you analyse the performance of a suspected 'dead-un' there is really only one person who knows absolutely for sure—the man holding the reins. **1982** *Nat. Times* (Sydney) 1 Aug. 14/4 'You hear a lot about dead 'uns *after* the race', said Beirne, 'but 99 per cent of it is sour grapes.'

deaf adder. DEATH ADDER 1.

1827 P. CUNNINGHAM *Two Yrs. in N.S.W.* I. 338 Our *deaf adder* resembles, in its short, puffy, repulsive appearance, the blow-adder of America. **1845** C. HODGKINSON *Aust., Port Macquarie to Moreton Bay* 212 The Death Adder is extremely sluggish in its habits, and rarely moves out of the way of persons approaching it; I am therefore inclined to think, that the original popular name assigned to this reptile, must have been Deaf Adder. **1846** C.P. HODGSON *Reminisc. Aust.* 170 A deaf adder was observed, creeping on a poor quail which crouched on the ground, fascinated. **1871** *Austral. Town & Country Jrnl.* (Sydney) 1 Apr. 391/4 A youth.. came across a deaf-adder some fifteen inches long, having two perfect heads, one of them being where the tail should be. **1880** 'OLD HAND' *Experiences of Colonist* (ed. 2) ii. 34 At last a deaf adder (the most poisonous of all the snake tribe) slipped out of the piece of wood, and fell writhing into the hot ashes. **1911** I.A. ROSENBLUM *Stella Sothern* 74 A large death-adder lay within a foot of his hind legs... Deaf-adder is the old bushman's name for the snake. **1930** HIVES & LUMLEY *Jrnl. of Jackaroo* 113 The deadly 'deaf' or 'death' adder.. is so venomous that its bite is usually fatal in as short a time as half an hour.

deal, *v. Obs.*

1. In the phr. **to deal it out** (to someone), to attack, esp. verbally.

1901 *Truth* (Sydney) 10 Mar. 4/7 Mr Norton began by dealing it out to E.H. Stobo. *Ibid.* 12 May 4/7 The refulgent orators 'deal it out strong' to Australian politicians. **1902** *Ibid.* 30 May 5/3 Among the straw hat push are some fistic fellows, who know how to '*deal it out*'. **1904** *Bulletin* (Sydney) 1 Dec. 40/1 He used to surround a good deal of liquor and then go down to the camp and 'deal it out' to the little woman for spite. **1926** *Illustr. Tasmanian Mail* (Hobart) 17 Nov. 6/3 It is certainly very inconsiderate of the pushes not to give the police fair warning when they are going to 'deal it out'.

2. In the phr. **to deal out stoush,** to assault violently: see STOUSH *n.* 1.

1900 *Truth* (Sydney) 27 May 5/3 The undesirable denizens of such places as Woolloomooloo or 'the Rocks'.. delight in *dealing out stoush* for their own special delectation. **1917** 'D. DELANEY' *White Champion* 152 The more beer Mr Burton drank the more voluminous became his explanations of Jack Redwood's inherited capacity for dealing out 'stoush'. **1918** C.L. HARTT *Diggerettes* 65 Burly One: 'I jes' bin dealin' out stouch to a bloke 'as talked a lot of rot about Billy Hughes. Wot do *you* think about Billy Hughes?' **1939** K. TENNANT *Foveaux* 247 Strikers.. pounced into the tram compartments and began dealing out 'stouch' to the terrified passengers. **1973** J. MURRAY *Larrikins* 84 To 'bondi' someone, especially a policeman, became a very transitive verb, with boots, bottles and all, as the push were 'dealing out stoush'.

deaner, var. DEENER.

death. *Shearing. Obs.* In the phr. **to wait for a death,** see quot. 1965.

1898 *Bulletin* (Sydney) 17 Dec. 15/1 Hanging round a shed until someone is sacked—*waiting for a death.* **1904** *Shearer* (Sydney) 13 Aug. 7/3 Evidently the writer had been doing a loaf, probably waiting for a death, and the shearers tumbled to his game and told him to quit, and of course he didn't like it. **1965** J.S. GUNN *Terminol. Shearing Industry* ii. 25 The old custom of unemployed shearers waiting round a shed in case someone is sacked was called 'waiting for a death'.

death adder.

1. Any of the three species of venomous snake of the genus *Acanthophis* of Aust., New Guinea, and nearby islands, esp. *A. antarcticus* of s. and e. mainland Aust.; DEAF ADDER.

1833 W.H. BRETON *Excursions* 264 The death, or deaf adder is an ugly creature. **1846** *Cumberland Times* (Parramatta) 3 Jan. 4/4 Shun it [*sc.* rum] as you would a black snake or a death adder: one glass leads to two, two to three, and so on. **1853** J. SHERER *Gold Finder Aust.* 29 Snakes are numerous, and the most deadly amongst them is the death-adder, which never moves aside on the approach of the pedestrian. **1859** J.D. MEREWEATHER *Diary Working Clergyman* 134 A woman somewhere near here.. was bitten in the ankle by a death adder. **1915** N. DUNCAN *Austral. Byways* 41 The death-adder, he's a slow, stupid beast—lies still and bites when you tread on him. **1921** *Bulletin* (Sydney) 7 Apr. 20/2 The prevailing term 'death-adder', has doubtless been adopted.. but I was present 50 years ago at a meeting of the Linnean Society to which 'deaf-adder' was suggested as a substitute for the Early-Victorian 'claw-tail' and 'back-stinger'. **1935** F. BIRTLES *Battle Fronts Outback* 25 It was a death-adder. These creatures, in flood-time, invariably seek shelter under drovers' pack-saddles. **1948** H.A. LINDSAY *Bushman's Handbk.* 108 The death adder.. does not strike until the tail-tip is touched. **1973** V. SERVENTY *Desert Walkabout* 24 The death adder.. has a thorn-like tail which is twisted and turned in an enticing fashion.

2. *fig.* See quots. 1962 and 1963. Also *attrib.*

1951 E. HILL *Territory* 3 The bagmen of today, the 'old death-adders Major Mitchelling around' were the young men of yesterday. **1953** *Sydney Morning Herald* 3 Jan. 6/4 'Death adders', old outback gossips. **1962** MARSHALL & DRYSDALE *Journey among Men* 56 These solitary men are usually known as *hatters.* Some of them go under the name of death adder men, for it is reckoned they will bite your head off if spoken to before noon. **1963** X. HERBERT *Larger than Life* 21 Lone prospectors, for all their propensity for living in solitude, are not usually of the retiring type, as witness the lavish good fellowship they invariably show when they make a strike, and that truculent misanthropy of their disappointed age which earns them such names as 'mad-hatter', 'death-adder', 'scrub bull'. **1970** K. WILLEY *Naked Island* 79 He was a dried-up runt, sandy-haired, with a turned-down slash of a mouth—a real old death adder, as they say in the bush.

death bone. BONE *n.* 1.

1899 *Proc. Linnean Soc. N.S.W.* XXIV. 330, I discovered the curious bone ornament or implement now to be described. It is made from the fibula of a kangaroo, is 9¾ inches in length, well polished... Three uses have been suggested for it, viz., netting needle, 'death bone' or 'pointer', and 'nose bone'. **1933** *Bulletin* (Sydney) 19 Apr. 20/3 Even the semi-civilised Binghi of today is not proof against the old belief in the death-bone. **1955** F. LANE *Patrol to Kimberleys* 212 *Death-bone,* also known as the 'pointing-bone'. It is the most feared item in the aborigine witch doctor's 'charm-bag'. **1962** V.C. HALL *Dreamtime Justice* 144 The death-bone might be pointed, and the necessary words sung.

death seat. In a trotting race: the position on the outside of the leader from which overtaking is difficult.

1982 *Weekend Austral.* (Sydney) 7 Aug. 44/8 Prince Jade sat behind a different leader (Rhonda's Al), with Local Honored in the 'death seat'—from where he faded while Prince Jade got a miracle rails run in the final stages to win. **1983** *Sydney Morning Herald* 5 Feb. 54/6 Popular Alm (9–2 on) had to produce one of the great runs of his career to beat Gammalite (12–1) by one and a half metres after being forced to sit in the death seat for most of the race. **1984** *Sunday Independent* (Perth) 17 June 89/5 He was the first pacer to break 2 min. on a country track in Australia... I sat in the death seat with him and we cruised home.

debil debil. *Austral. pidgin.* Also **debbil debbil, debble debble, dibble dibble.**

1. DEVIL DEVIL 1.

1834 G. BENNETT *Wanderings N.S.W.* I. 210 The following is a definition of a clergyman as once given by one of the aborigines: 'He, white feller, belonging to Sunday, get up top o' waddy, pile long corrobera all about debbil debbil, and wear shirt over trowsel.' **1838** *Austral. Mag.* (Sydney) 78 The *debil-debil,* they say, will not leap over the bark, and cannot walk under it! **1844** *Port Phillip Gaz.* 18 May 4 Debil debil send him white feller here. **1852** F. LANCELOTT *Aust. as it Is* I. 28 They believe in the existence of an evil spirit, which they call 'Dibble-dibble', and propitiate by offerings. **1859** J.D. MEREWEATHER *Diary Working Clergyman* 131 In this camp at Poon Boon I saw a case of leprosy on the hips and back of a black girl: the natives call it 'debil-debil'. **1875** CAMPBELL & WILKS *Early Settlement Qld.* 29 They are extremely superstitious, and everything strange to them, even to the flying of a large night-bird, is set down to 'debbil debbil'. **1883** E.M. CURR *Recoll. Squatting Vic.* 275 This spirit the whites have taught the Blacks to call *debble-debble* (the devil). **1898** *Bulletin* (Sydney) 5 Nov. 15/1 To prevent the niggers bathing in it and polluting the water, which was all the station relied upon for drinking and household purposes, they were told debbil-debbil was in it. **1921** *Ross's Monthly* May 21/2 True, the word 'spirit' is followed later by 'debbil-debbil', the true native word for death, or anything they do not understand. **1935** B.E. PHELPS *Austral. tells England* 54 They were afraid that the spirit of the departed would haunt them. Their word covering the matter was 'debbil-debbil'. **1949** G. FARWELL *Traveller's Tracks* 93 He had recently helped to lay the debil-debil a little girl in the hostel complained was frightening her. **1959** D. LOCKWOOD *Crocodiles & Other People* 59 The boss drover must know that his night-watch is all right, that he hasn't been thrown from his horse or foully murdered by one of the evil debbil-

debbils which, according to the native stockmen, haunt parts of the stockroutes. **1968** LINKLATER & TAPP *Gather no Moss* 44, I called to him to help me, but he was sullen and very defiant, refusing to touch the body, and insisting that if he did a debil debil would torment him. **1983** G.E.P. WELLARD *Bushlore* 120 The fire in the entrance [to a mia mia] is a must. Apart from being useful to cook on, it also prevents any debble debble coming in during the night.

2. GILGAI a. Also *attrib.*, esp. as **debil debil country.**

1882 A.J. BOYD *Old Colonies* 189 There only remained six miles more of level country, with a little tract of 'debbil-debbil', and we should stretch our weary limbs in Cardwell. **1913** *Bull. N.T.* vii. 13 Next day we bumped on unceasingly, crossing what is commonly known as 'debill-debill' country, where the earth in dry seasons is hard and seared with cracks . . and covered with a growth of coarse canegrass. **1927** M. DORNEY *Adventurous Honeymoon* 75 At this time of the year . . the swamps had completely dried up and the ground was so fearfully rough and lumpy that driving over it was torture, even although we went as slowly as possible in low gear. We frequently heard this kind of ground referred to outback as 'debil-debil country'. **1937** *Bulletin* (Sydney) 30 June 21/4 Of all the country I've ridden over I give the belt to 'debil-debil' as the most dangerous over which to give a horse its head. . . The greatest patch of 'debil-debil' I've seen was out from the channels of the Diamantina (s.w. Qld.). For every mound there seemed to be a dozen holes. **1946** D. BARR *Warrigal Joe* 16 It's debil-debil country all the way to the coast. **1951** E. HILL *Territory* 294 The mob goes drifting down through . . black soil 'debil-debil' or hard-baked holes hidden in long grass. **1955** M. DURACK *Keep him my Country* (1966) 24 The wild broken debil-debil country, treacherous under the innocent covering of the drying pea bush. **1979** H. PURVIS *Outback Airman* 22 It transpired that we'd landed in an area known locally as 'debble-debble country'—the terrain consisting of conical lumps of earth not visible because of high grass.

deciduous beech: see BEECH.

deckie. [f. *deck(-hand* + -Y.] A deck-hand.

1966 P. PINNEY *Restless Men* 21 There's a few other deckies will be laid off. It'll be harder to find another boat right now. **1984** *Canberra Chron.* 23 May 27/2 His deckie was his son Matthew John, who is only six years old. **1984** *Bulletin* (Sydney) 7 Aug. 148/4 A fisherman who wanted to hire a female deckhand . . approached the Commonwealth Employment Service in his search for a woman 'deckie'.

deener. *Obs.* Also **deaner, deenar.** [Br. slang *deaner* shilling (prob. ult. identical with L. *denarius*, F. *denier* a coin of low denomination), formerly esp. freq. in Aust. and N.Z.: see OEDS.] A shilling.

1882 *Sydney Slang Dict.* 10 A bludger and his mot 'ticed a cully into the 'Deadhouse', and . . buzzed him for three caser and a deaner. **1896** *Bulletin* (Sydney) 18 Apr. 3/2 I've got a deener—would you like a carrot stew? **1899** W.T. GOODGE *Hits! Skits! & Jingles* 150 And his naming of the coinage Is a mystery to some, With his 'quid' and 'half-a-caser' And his 'deener' and his 'scrum'. **1920** C.L. HARTT *More Diggerettes* 47 You being one of the old Battalion, I'll have to give you a deener's worth for a sprat. **1924** *Aussie* (Sydney) Nov. 78/1 'Just a deener, Dig,' he whined. 'I ain't nippin' fer anything big. On'y a bob, mate.' **1933** 'TRAMWAY WORKERS' *Shock Brigader* 19 His first passenger tendered a very doubtful-looking coin, to which 'Woozie' remarked—'This deener's no good!' **1943** *Coast to Coast 1942* 117 But pop'll take these 'ere skins ter town in the car come Saturdee and all I'll see of the greenbacks'll be a sprat or a deener. **1949** D. WALKER *We went to Aust.* 194 'Deenar' for a shilling must have come straight from the Yugoslav dinar. **1957** D. WHITINGTON *Treasure upon Earth* 54, I don't mind giving 'em a couple of deaners, but I won't attend meetings. **1965** H. PORTER *Cats of Venice* 111 She's a hard cruel world. They'll be out after a deener. **1979** K. GARVEY *Absolutely Austral.* 19 On the grog till they do every deener, Stony broke and regretful next day. **1983** *Canberra Times* 18 Oct. 20/3 The deener went to the NSW Aborigines Protection Board, presumably as a finder's fee; the zac as often as not stayed in the thrifty housewife's purse.

deep, *a.* In special collocations: **deep lead,** an alluvial deposit of gold in the (now subterranean) bed of an ancient river (see quot. 1888 and LEAD *n.*[1]); **leader,** one who mines a deep lead; **noser,** a long glass of beer; **sinker, (a)** *obs.*, *deep leader*; **(b)** a long glass of beer; **sinking** *vbl. n.*, the mining of deep leads.

1858 *Colonial Mining Jrnl.* Sept. 9/1 The **deep leads** on Ballaarat. **1867** R.L.M. KITTO *Goldfields of Vic.* 8 The older deposits are found in what are called deep *leads*; these exist in various parts of Victoria. **1870** 'COLONIST TWENTY YRS. STANDING' *Vic., Brit. 'El Dorado'* 110 The bed of this old river, or 'deep lead', technically called by the miners 'drift' or 'wash-dirt', or washing stuff—is generally composed of clay, gravel, quartz, stones and sand. **1888** *Illustr. Austral. News* (Melbourne) 1 Aug. 16/3 'Alluvial' gold mining includes . . 'deep lead' mining, where the concealed auriferous gravel deposits of ancient river beds are reached by sinking costly shafts. **1931** W. BARAGWANATH et al. *Guide for Prospectors in Vic.* 87 *Deep lead*, buried river bed over 100 feet below surface. **1898** *Bulletin* (Sydney) 16 July 15/2 Outside Ballarat . . was an old whim-horse, pensioned by some lucky **deep leader. 1945** A.W. UPFIELD *Death of Swagman* 9 At the only hotel he drank a couple of **deep-nosers** with the licensee. **1952** —— *New Shoe* 88 From the bar door issued Dick Lake. 'Good-day-ee! How's it for a deep noser?' **(a) 1858** *Colonial Mining Jrnl.* Oct. 23/2 There were plenty of men whose faces would be familiar to the **deep-sinkers** at Ballaarat. **1859** *Ibid.* Mar. 106/1 The deep sinkers keep plodding on through rock, drift, water and law. **1868** J. BAIRD *Emigrant's Guide Australasia* 171 The diggers were of diverse kinds—surfacers, shallow-sinkers, deep-sinkers, and quartz crushers—some being all these in turn. **(b) 1877** *Pilgrim* (Sydney) 1st Ser. vi. 64 These misguided mortals spend in '**deep sinkers**' . . that money which their landladies are daily sighing for—and sighing for in vain. **1879** D. MAYNE *Westerly Busters* 26 Farewell to Tonkin's snug little parlour, Where oft' I played euchre with 'Woolwashing Sam', For a couple of D.Bs., or a brace of 'deep-sinkers', While quiet old George sat munching his scran. **1886** F. COWAN *Aust.* 32 *Long-sleever, Bishop Barker*, and *Deep-sinker*, synonyms of Yankee Schooner. **1898** *Bulletin* (Sydney) 23 Apr. 32/4 'Blow me blue!' says Bill the Pinker, 'Can't yer give us a deep-sinker? Ain't yer got a cask o' beer behind the screen?' **1904** *Truth* (Sydney) 13 Nov. 1/4 To see if any loitering drinker Should dare imbibe a last 'deep-sinker'. **1955** N. PULLIAM *I traveled Lonely Land* 286, I met the Boss and some of the friends and neighbors, and as the day faded into evening we had a couple of 'deep sinkers'. **1853** *Austral. Gold Digger's Monthly Mag.* iv. 155 There was not much gravel nor **deep sinking. 1856** S.C. BREES *How to farm & settle in Aust.* 56 Deep-sinking was connected with the later practice of 'bottoming'. **1861** T. M'COMBIE *Austral. Sketches* 133 There are four methods of obtaining the auriferous metal—surface washing, deep sinking, puddling and quartz crushing. **1868** J. BAIRD *Emigrant's Guide Australasia* 171 The aim of deep sinking is to reach the deposits of the precious metal imbedded in ancient watercourses—in diggers' parlance 'leads'—which are situated, in some cases, at the depth of betwixt 200 and 300 feet below the existing surface. **1872** 'TASMANIAN LADY' *Treasures, Lost & Found* 148 'These surface diggings are quickly worked out.' 'Why, as to that, there's a company just formed that means to try deep-sinking.' **1876** 'EIGHT YRS.' RESIDENT' *Queen of Colonies* 141 The major part of the claims on deep sinking are not worked until a few have been proved. **1928** M.E. FULLERTON *Austral. Bush* 17 Easy methods of gold-getting went. The era of deep sinking and of quartz-crushing for gold was upon Victoria.

Deep North. Applied to Queensland, by analogy with U.S. *Deep South* and with reference to a supposedly similar conservatism.

1972 *Bulletin* (Sydney) 26 Aug. 46/3 Perhaps the author thinks that with our 'Deep North' of Queensland, there is little hope for a crocodilian future. *Ibid.* 4 Nov. 24/1 Outside the Deep North, students and staff are also arguing out and evaluating the types of educational experiences most relevant to being an architect today. **1981** *Ibid.* 22 Dec. 32/2 They say down south that we're from the Deep North, that the heat warps our brains. **1982** *Ibid.* 25 May 32/1 Queensland has recently been dubbed the Deep North—a deliberate and conscious analogy to America's Deep South. . . Queensland is regarded as authoritarian and conservative in comparison with other states. **1985** *Ibid.* 30 July 58/1 In the Deep North it is well-known that a blood-thirsty socialist and, more than likely, a communist tries to hide behind every peanut and pumpkin scone.

de facto. [Spec. use of the L. phr. *de facto* in fact (as opposed to *de jure* by law); in Br. use *adj.* or *adv.*] A common-law spouse.

1952 *Bulletin* (Sydney) 22 Oct. 12/4 The help, plump, 40 and *de facto* to Albert, with whom she had spent 17 far-from-peaceful years after leaving her husband. **1957** J. WATEN *Shares in Murder* 71 Milly's de facto, Eddie Conger, will be invaluable. **1960** *Bulletin* (Sydney) 12 Oct. 16/3 In that land of multifarious matrimony and divorce the same press that rather preens itself on being laconic longwindedly translates our snappy 'de facto' into 'great and good friend'. **1977** E. MACKIE *Oh to be Aussie* 24 De fact of de matter is dat the only time it's decent to be a de facto is when you're not really enjoying it. **1978** *Southerly* ii. 173 Mostly Normie lived alone but periodically his de facto would move back. **1978** *Westerly* iii. 6 A series of de factos—it became a pattern, just as others change lovers every six months, every three years I changed my de facto—or was changed by her. **1986** *Income Tax Return Form S* (Austral. Taxation Office), Your spouse's or de facto spouse's name? . . Date you were married or started living together as de factos?

delver. [Spec. use of (prob. U.S.) *delver* one who digs.] See quot. 1972.

1919 *Pastoral Rev.* 16 Aug. 759 This delver is being used extensively throughout Queensland and N.S.W. . . for cutting Couchgrass and Bulrushes out of bore drains. **1972** R. MAGOFFIN *Chops & Gravy* 106 A delver is a boat-type apparatus hauled along the boredrain (formerly by horses, now by tractor) to remove weeds, rubbish and slush.

Hence **delving** *ppl. a.*

1972 R. MAGOFFIN *Chops & Gravy* 106 *Delving*, the process of cleaning or dredging a boredrain.

demo. [f. *dem(onstration* + -O. Used elsewhere but recorded earliest in Aust.: see OEDS.] A demonstration; a public display of interest in a cause, usu. a procession or mass-meeting. Also *attrib.*

1904 *Truth* (Sydney) 11 Sept. 7/2 *A dig at demos.* On a charge of distributing certain handbills advertising a 'Monster Democratic Demonstration'. **1966** A. HOPGOOD *Private Yuk Objects* 7, I know these demos. back home have been worrying some of you. **1969** *Bulletin* (Sydney) 3 May 13/3 At last week's 'student-worker' demo in Sydney, almost all of the police controlling the manifestation kept their cool. **1975** A. O'GRADY *Sugar-Coated Comfortable* 22 A demonstration? What were you at that demo for? **1979** S. MORAN *Reminisc. of Rebel* 15 Every time I appeared at a demo I was immediately arrested. **1986** *Canberra Times* 21 Feb. 3/4 (*heading*) Police condemn policy shift on demo arrests.

democrat. A deep crimson variety of apple, grown chiefly in Tas.

1931 *Tasmanian Jrnl. Agric.* 1 Nov. 173 Amongst all the apples which have ben raised in Tasmania, Tasma, or Democrat, is the most popular throughout Australia. The variety originated as a chance seedling some 25 to 30 years ago at an orchard belonging to Mr J. Duffy, of Glenlusk, in the Glenorchy district. The apple was first known as 'Duffy's Seedling', and later as Democrat but when it was recognised that another variety was in existence under this name, it was subsequently renamed Tasma. **1936** *Austral. Writers' Ann.* 77 Ruddy Democrats, Golden Pippins and gaily striped Rome Beauties. **1947** MRS A.H. GARNSEY *Romance Huon River* 172 The political parties—Senators and Democrats. The latter have little flavour but bright colour and sell well in Sydney. **1961** HYAMS & JACKSON *Orchard & Fruit Garden* 184 *Democrat*, production of this locally [*sc.* Tas.] raised late-season variety is in the vicinity of 1,000,000 bushels. **1969** S.G. HARRISON et al. *Oxford Bk. Food Plants* 54 'Democrat' (a very dark crimson Australian apple). **1978** A.F. SIMMONS *Man. Fruit* 30 Democrat . . Discovered about 1900. To avoid confusion with an American variety called Democrat, the name in New Zealand has now been changed to Tasma.

demon. [Spec. use of *demon*, as applied to 'one who seems more than human in the rapidity, destructiveness, etc. of his play or performance, as a *demon* *bowler*': see OED 3.] A police officer, esp. a detective.

1889 BARRÈRE & LELAND *Dict. Slang* I. 304 *Demons* (Australian), prison slang for police. **1891** *Truth* (Sydney) 17 May 3/4, I only wish I had one of them button-hole cameras you see advertised—the demons use them I believe. **1892** K. LENTZNER *Dict. Slang-Eng. Aust.* 20 *Demons*, prison slang for police. 'The *demons* put pincher on me,' I was apprehended. **1900** *Truth* (Sydney) 21 Jan. 1/7 The blind-coppers could be converted into New South Wales detectives. They'd probably be as effective as our present 'demons'. **1901** *Ibid.* 29 Sept. 7/3 If a Demon or a Crusher Ikes him by the frog and toad (That are slang, but you'll excuse me, It means: 'Coming up the road'.) ***c* 1907** C.W. CHANDLER *Darkest Adelaide* 7 Mr Bludger told me that the Adelaide demons had a quick and ready eye for strange faces. So to prevent any prying inquisitiveness on the part of the John Hops we decided to meet in Whitemore-square. **1941** K. TENNANT *Battlers* 96 The showers were 'demons', or plain-clothes detectives. **1962** K. SIMONS *Not with Kiss* 133 The cockatoo burst in white-faced, with the words, 'Jeez, the demons.' The constables were young. **1968** L.H. EVERS *Fall among Thieves* 68 Before she can stall, the demons lob and put the arm on her. Now she's really in the crush. **1971** J. O'GRADY *Aussie Etiket* 20 Uniformed cops are generally known as 'wallopers', and cops in plain clothes are called 'demons'. **1977** T. RONAN *Mighty Men on Horseback* 45 Demons were flown up from the south to make enquiries. **1978** H.C. BAKER *I was Listening* 19 You're clear away with the dough before the demons can get near.

depasturing licence. *Hist.* See quot. 1841.

[**1836** *Act* (N.S.W.) 7 Gul. IV. no. 4 Sect. 2, Hold a valid license from the Government of New South Wales for depasturing cattle and other animals.] **1841** *Rep. Select Committee S.A.* p. xv, It is a practice long established in New South Wales and Van Diemen's Land, and which will, no doubt, be equally followed in South Australia, for the owners of cattle and sheep to occupy large tracts of land under what are called Depasturing Licences, by which they are entitled, in consideration of a very moderate annual payment, to graze their flocks and herds over Land of which the ownership still remains with the Crown. **1846** *Melbourne Argus* 12 June 2/3 The Colonial Secretary laid upon the table a return of the number of Depasturing Licenses issued for Crown Lands beyond the boundaries of location, and the names of their respective holders. **1847** *Moreton Bay Courier* 26 June 3/2 Considerable sums .. still due to the Government for depasturing licenses. **1851** H. MELVILLE *Present State Aust.* 24 Squatters pay rentals of £10 per annum for depasturing licences, which comprehend a sufficient track of land whereon four thousand sheep may run, or an equivalent number of cattle or horses.

derro. Also **dero.** [f. *der(elict* + -O.] A vagrant, esp. one dependent upon alcohol.

1971 *Southerly* ii. 136 'Just a derro on the meth,' the old men said, the old men on the shop-steps and windows. **1974** M. GILLESPIE *Into Hollow Mountains* 31 The Green Van is a parks and gardens wagon the pigs use to round up the street deros. **1975** *Bulletin* (Sydney) 24 May 25/1 Port and beer are the favourite poisons of the Australian dero. **1978** S.J. SPEARS *Early Works* 44 Without me, you'd be just another derro without no job. **1986** H. GARNER *Postcards from Surfers* 67 Bloody Barney, he tells me, Don't you dare bring those hooers of yours back here, you old dero.

derry. [Prob. shortened form of *derry down*, used joc. for DOWN *n.* 2; perh. infl. by Br. dial. *derry* noise, disorder: see EDD and OED *deray*.] In the phr. **to have a derry on,** to have a prejudice against.

[**1882** *Sydney Mail* 5 Aug. 206/4 They'd keep him [*sc.* a stolen stallion] there for a year .. and when the 'derry' was off, he'd take him over himself.] **1883** *Bulletin* (Sydney) 19 May 7/4 A few years ago some well-to-do young settlers got 17 years each, in West Australia, for shooting, among certain wild cattle, an antiquated working bullock which had strayed amongst the mob. The owner had a 'derry' on them, and the relics of a barbarous law did the rest. **1893** J.A. BARRY *Steve Brown's Bunyip* 199 It's them coves as gets you to sign things... Them's the coves as we've got a derry on. **1899** *Worker* (Sydney) 11 Feb. 4/4 The Bulletin has a terrible 'derry' on Labor-member Sleath. **1900** H. LAWSON *Verses Pop. & Humorous* 185 It's cruel when the p'leece has got a derry on a bloke. **1925** *Bulletin* (Sydney) 18 June 22/3 Most bushmen have a derry on the catfish, and when they catch it throw it away with a curse. **1936** *Ibid.* 4 Nov. 21/2 Everybody seems to have an unreasoning derry on centipedes. **1947** *Ibid.* 20 Aug. 29/1 But why *have* y' got such a derry on swaggies, Tom? **1955** N. PULLIAM *I traveled Lonely Land* 226 Melbourne's always had a silly derry on us. **1968** S. GORE *Holy Smoke* 46 The Chaldeans .. had a derry on the Christians anyhow, for mucking up all their forecasts, like Daniel did.

Derwenter. *Hist.* [f. *Derwent* the name of a river in Tas., on the banks of which stood a penal settlement.] An ex-convict from Tasmania.

1827 *Monitor* (Sydney) 16 Mar. 349/2 The Derwenters were as scantily provided with Spirituous Liquors as ourselves, previous to the late arrivals. **1852** *Austral. Gold Digger's Monthly Mag.* ii. 53 He found her .. with a dirty cap half concealing a black eye, a short pipe in her mouth, and barely sober enough to utter these memorable words, 'I'm a *Derwenter*, and I don't care who knows it.' **1862** *Meliora* (London) V. 68 The one prominent cause of crime there was the presence of runaway convicts and expirees, known commonly as Van Demonians, or Derwenters, as Hobart Town stands upon the river Derwent. **1879** *We 5: Bk. for Season* 11 It was one eternal Orgie, and amongst it all the Derwenters, as thay [*sic*] were called in those days, were the quietest. **1880** 'ERRO' *Squattermania* 61 Port Arran... It's a quiet little place .. with a good many Derwenters in it (ticket-of-leave men from Tasmania); they are generally called old hands out here, and like that name best. **1884** 'R. BOLDREWOOD' *Old Melbourne Memories* 176 The only denizens of that period were an odd pair of sawyers, generally 'Derwenters' as the Tasmanian expirees were called. **1896** M. HORNSBY *Old Time Echoes Tas.* 175 'The Derwenters' were set on by the Victorians in consequence of their crimes on the goldfields, the country roads, and in Melbourne. ***c* 1899** 'SANDALWOOD NUTT' *Tarragal* 4 His father had an old 'Derwenter', Jack Smith by name, who was a good bush carpenter. **1918** C. FETHERSTONHAUGH *After Many Days* 384 A chap .. used to come over from the valley to duff Andrew's cattle; he had been an old Derwenter.

Derwent jackass. *Tas. Grey butcherbird*, see GREY *a.* Also **Derwent jack.**

1898 G. DUNDERDALE *Bk. of Bush* 140 Even the Derwent Jackass, the hypocrite with the shining black coat and piercing whistle, joins in the public outcry. **1903** *Bulletin* (Sydney) 8 Oct. 16/2 The 'Jackass', or 'Derwent jackass' (Kingfisher) sings just between sunset and dusk. **1931** *Ibid.* 29 Apr. 21/2, I suggest that the bird the Frenchmen saw was the Derwent jackass, and not the kookaburra. **1945** A. RUSSELL *Bush Ways* 120 The Derwent Jack, or grey butcher-bird .. cunning, knavish, joyous and melodious.

desert. Used *attrib.* in Special Comb. **desert gum,** any of several trees of the genus *Eucalyptus* (fam. Myrtaceae), occurring in drier Aust., esp. *E. eudesmioides* of w. W.A., *E. gongylocarpa* of w. central Aust., and GHOST GUM; **kurrajong,** see KURRAJONG *2;* **oak,** any of several trees of drier Aust., esp. *Acacia coriacea* (fam. Mimosaceae) of W.A., N.T., Qld., N.S.W., and S.A., and *Allocasuarina decaisneana* (fam. Casuarinaceae) of W.A., S.A., and N.T.; the timber of these trees; **pea, rose,** *Sturt's desert pea, rose*, see STURT; **sandstone,** see quot. 1872.

1893 D. LINDSAY *Jrnl. Elder Sci. Exploring Exped.* 7 The fine growth of *Eucalyptus eudesmioides* (**desert gum**). **1901** *Proc. Linnean Soc. N.S.W.* XXVI. 327 *E. intertexta* .. often known as Desert Gum. **1915** *Bull. N.T.* xiv. 7 A small quartzite ridge was crossed with .. desert gum. **1926** J.M. BLACK *Flora S.A.* iii. 422 *E[ucalyptus] eudesmioides* .. Desert Gum. A medium-sized or tall tree, sometimes reduced to a small mallee, with smooth silver-grey bark. **1956** T.Y. HARRIS *Naturecraft in Aust.* 137 Ghost or Desert Gum—*E[ucalyptus] papuana.* A graceful, willow-like tree with smooth, gleaming white bark, except at the extreme base. It is found in arid areas of Queensland, the Northern Territory, Western Australia, and in Papua. **1898** D.W. CARNEGIE *Spinifex & Sand* 254 We saw the first **desert oak**, standing solitary sentinel on the crest of a ridge. **1920** *Smith's Weekly* (Sydney) 28 Aug. 9/4 Desert oak (Casuarina decaisneana) .. has water in both its stem and roots. **1927** SPENCER & GILLEN *Arunta* 4 A 'desert oak'. [*Note*] The tree to which this most inappropriate name has been given is *Casuarina Decaisneana*; it may reach a height of thirty or forty feet and is often found growing, as its popular name implies, in sterile, desert country. **1934** C. SAYCE *Comboman* 132 The huge desert-oak posts on which the main gates of the yard swung. **1957** F. CLUNE *Fortune Hunters* 35 We boiled the billy at mid-day beneath a clump of desert oaks, which keened mournfully in the breeze. **1968** W. HILLIARD *People in Between* 76 Spinifex-covered land, broken in places by fine stands of stately casuarinas, better known as 'desert oaks', despite little resemblance to the true oak. **1972** V. SERVENTY *Singing Land* 81 Sturdier and longer lasting is the desert oak, a casuarina well-fitted to its environment. **1983** *Overlander* Nov. 28/3 They were wadi (desert oak) posts. **1864** *Illustr. Sydney News* Sept. 4/3 The plant is the **desert pea** of Sturt and abounds in the interior of the Australian continent. **1875** R. THATCHER *Something to his Advantage* 8 A semi-desert covered with shrubs of the lovely desert pea. **1898** G. GARNET *Barrier Bride* 70 The gorgeous desert-pea, also known as the Sturt pea, because it was discovered by the intrepid explorer, who was the first white man that ever trod these central wastes. **1917** C.H. SOUTER *To many Ladies* 19 The desert pea's a flowerin' down To Balaklava South, As red—there's nothin' ain't as red. **1929** K.S. PRICHARD *Coonardoo* (1961) 152 Trails of the desert pea spilt new bright blood beside the track. **1949** G. FARWELL *Traveller's Tracks* 91 Stony rises strewn with wild flowers after rain and with flamboyant Desert Pea. **1968** J. WOODBERRY *Come back Peter* (1974) 57 The glorious crimson of the desert pea. **1952** A.M. DUNCAN-KEMP *Where Strange Paths go Down* 90 The purple, yellow-eyed blossoms of the **Desert rose**, which grew in scattered masses throughout the plains country. **1963** O. RUHEN *Flockmaster* 57 She found, in a glade shaded by the river-gums, a desert rose blooming. **1872** *Jrnl. & Proc. R. Soc. N.S.W.* (1903) XXXVII. 147 Horizontal beds of coarse grit and conglomerate... I have called this upper conglomerate series '**Desert Sandstone**', from the sandy barren character of its disintegrated soil, which makes the term particularly applicable. **1880** J. BONWICK *Resources Qld.* 36 The *Desert Sandstone* will be left for the last comer. **1888** *Jrnl. & Proc. R. Soc. N.S.W.* XXII. 290 All round the Australian coast, proceeding northwards, say from the latitude of Brisbane there occurs at intervals, and in patches of different sizes, a peculiar formation which goes by the name of Desert Sandstone. It varies much in colour and in character. **1906** W.G. COX *Irrigation* 40 It is partly concealed by nearly horizontal tablelands of what is called 'Desert Sandstone'. **1927** SPENCER & GILLEN *Arunta* 2 Thin stratum of rock, called Desert Sandstone. **1967** R.O. CHALMERS *Austral. Rocks* 307 'Desert sandstone'. The formation to which earlier geologists gave this picturesque name is the 'duricrust' which .. is the ferruginous siliceous surface deposit Tertiary in age that covers so much of the surface of arid Australia.

detached, *ppl. a. Hist.* Of a convict or party of convicts: separated for a particular purpose from the main body.

1821 *Regulations respecting Assigned Convict Servants* 30 June 15 No Stock-owner should allow his detached stockmen to keep Hunting Dogs. **1825** *HRA* (1916) 1st Ser. VIII. 505 Convicts in Detached Parties draw their rations for a week in advance. **1826** *Ibid.* (1919) 1st Ser. XII. 757 The Officers in Command of Penal Settlements and detached Stations. **1835** *Colonist* (Sydney) 16 July 228/3 It would tend much to the public welfare, if H.M. Government would not permit overseers of road gangs to send out detached gangs to repair *some* parts of the road, without a responsible person being in charge of the detached parties. *Ibid.*, The road-gang is properly stationed near the stockade .. and the detached party near the township of Bungonia .. and scarce a day passes but one may observe either one or more passing along the road from the chief gang to the detached party. **1849** *Hobart Town Gaz.* 8 May, On route from the Prisoners' Barracks, Hobart, on the 1st instant, to the detached party at Mount Wellington.

deuce, *a.* Of a shearer: capable of shearing two hundred sheep in a day.

1915 *Bulletin* (Sydney) 18 Nov. 24/4 The fastest jumbuck-barber on a board .. is often known as a 'gun', or a 'deuce artist'. **1961** *Ibid.* 3 Feb. 44/2 The young picker-upper .. boasted, 'I picked for seven 'deuce merchants' on my own last year .. and swept each time they let go.'

Hence as *v. trans.*, to shear two hundred (sheep) in a day.

1939 J. SORENSEN *Lost Shanty* 14 Come tell me is the current rumour true, That recently you 'deuced them' at Murgoo? **1975** B. FOLEY *Shearers' Poems* 9 We're shearing here at Kylie And the frost is on the grain The 'molley dooker' is deucin 'em And the Kiwi's draggin' the chain.

deucer.

1. [See prec.] A shearer capable of shearing two hundred sheep in a day.

1923 *Bulletin* (Sydney) 22 Nov. 22/2 In the blade-shearing days the fastest barber was the 'ringer'; later, he was the 'gun'; nowadays he is a 'deucer'. **1953** *Sydney Morning Herald* 3 Jan. 6/4 'Deucer', a man who can shear 200 or more sheep a day.

2. A double shift (but see also quot. 1979).

1953 D. CUSACK *Southern Steel* 138 'He's doing a deucer,' Landy explained. 'The snipe on the 12 to 4's sick.' **1979** G. STEWART *Leveller* 56 If any of the firemen were sick or injured you were called upon to work a 'Deucer' (two hours of his watch each).

devil.

1. *Tasmanian devil*, see TASMANIAN *a.* 2.

1807 Banks Papers 12 Nov. XX. 177, 2 skulls of an Animal called the Devil. **1825** J.H. WEDGE *Diaries* (1962) 10, I understand the Devils did great mischief when Capn. Wood had his sheep there. **1828** *Hobart Town Courier* 28 June 4 The hunting of those singular and destructive animals called devils . . affords better sport than the best fox in Christendom. **1829** R. MUDIE *Picture of Aust.* 176 The *bear-opossum*, or devil (*dasyuris ursinus*) . . lives among rocky mountains. **1841** *Morning Advertiser* (Hobart) 17 Sept. 2/4 Ten shillings for each Devil or other vermin that destroys Sheep. **1846** N.L. KENTISH *Work in Bush Van Diemen's Land* 29 The disgusting animal more nearly resembling a small wild mastiff dog, than any other species, called 'devil', with its double row of teeth. **1850** W. GATES *Recoll. Van Dieman's Land* 200 There is also a species of wild dog or wolf. . . The 'devil', as he is called there . . is a small black animal, with a thick head and a bushy tail, about the size of a common cat. **1871** *Saint Pauls* (London) Apr. 313 'Did you never hear of the Tasmanian devil?' . . 'The devil . . is . . in appearance something between a polecat and a bear, but in kind a poucher, like the opossum or the kangaroo. **1880** R. ROWE *Roughing It* 11 He had to cross a lonely ridge, covered with evergreen beeches and musk-trees, and in a hollow, he came upon a 'devil' (*dasyurus ursinus*) devouring the carcass of a sheep. **1916** T. WARLOW *By Mirage & Mulga* 45 About noon we sighted three devils . . and we tried to get above them so as to drive them on to the open, level country. **1981** *Woman's Day* (Sydney) 14 Oct. 65/1 Unique to Tasmania, the devils are marsupial. . . Tasmanians are proud of their devil—ugly and short-tempered though it is.

2. In the collocation **devil on the coals,** a small damper. See also BEGGAR.

1862 A. POLEHAMPTON *Kangaroo Land* 76 Instead of damper we occasionally made what are colonially known as 'devils on the coals'. . . Only a minute or so is required to bake them. They are made about the size of a captain's biscuit, and as thin as possible, thrown on the embers and turned quickly with the hand. **1900** *Western Champion* (Barcaldine) 28 Aug. 3/3 He had laughed me to scorn for drinking tea with milk, and had been unsympathetically mirthful over my ineffectual effort to make 'damper', or the tasty 'devils on the coals'. **1903** H. TAUNTON *Australind* 45 By the time the water had boiled . . the 'devils-on-the-coals' had been cooked, as well as a rasher or two of bacon.

3. In phr.: **devil's grip,** a condition of sheep characterized by a skin fold behind the shoulders that traps moisture and increases the risk of fly-strike; **guts** *obs.*. *devil's twine*; **pool** *obs.*, a game of chance; **twine,** DODDER-LAUREL.

1930 BILLIS & KENYON *Pastures New* 219 They would suffer a *damnosa hereditas*, like the **'devil's grip'**, left behind on many an Australian flock by the wrinkly rams from Vermont. **1961** J.W. JORDON *Practical Sheep Farming* 9 It stems from a weakness in constitution, and results in an unattractive conformation. Devil's Grip is a narrow depression circling round the sheep's body practically in the girth position. **1888** *Proc. Linnean Soc. N.S.W.* III. 496 *Cassytha filiformis*. . . This and other species of *Cassytha* are called 'Dodder-laurel'. The emphatic name **'Devil's guts'** is largely used. **1892** *Truth* (Sydney) 17 Apr. 2/7 Hon. members can then relieve the monotony of their duties by such innocent recreations as **devil's pool,** dominoes, draughts, penny 'Nap' and 'Three-up'. **1894** *Bulletin* (Sydney) 17 Mar. 9/3 The thing that makes us giggle and our temper often cool Is to see 'em get the 'black 'un' when they're playing devil's pool. **1956** T.Y. HARRIS *Naturecraft in Aust.* 183 **Devil's Twine,** another semi-parasite, in which the leaves are reduced to very fine scales, is found forming great twining masses over the branches of trees and shrubs. **1962** N.C.W. BEADLE et al. *Handbk. Vascular Plants Sydney & Blue Mountains* 133 *Cassytha* . . Devil's Twine.

devil devil. Orig. *Austral. pidgin.* [Reduplicative form of *devil*, indicating intensity, magnitude.]

1. In Aboriginal belief: an evil spirit; a manifestation of evil; evil itself; DEBIL DEBIL 1. Also *attrib.*

1831 TYERMAN & BENNET *Jrnl. Voyages & Travels* II. 156 A man . . was found lying on the ground . . to drive out the devil-devil—the reduplication of the term signifying the great devil. **1834** G. BENNETT *Wanderings N.S.W.* I. 126 They were afraid, if they buried them, the *Buckee*, or devil devil would take them away. **1842** *Austral. & N.Z. Monthly Mag.* 92 They believe in the imaginary existence of a class which . . they call *yahoo*, or, when they wish to be anglified, *Devil-Devil*. **1846** 'COLONIAL MAGISTRATE' *Remarks on Probable Origin* 10 Q. What do Black-fellows mean by *Devil Devil?* A. Devil Devil is, its all over small pox-like. **1857** F. DE B. COOPER *Wild Adventures* 28 The darkies do say that those jungles are haunted, and full of 'devil-devils'; but Bill, the native here, can tell us more about that. **1871** *Austral. Town & Country Jrnl.* (Sydney) 29 Apr. 528/4 Great is their dread of this invisible monster, whose name is Boorong, or Devil-devil. **1880** J.B. STEVENSON *Seven Yrs. Austral. Bush* 131 There were two or three Stockmen and quite a mob of blacks, all eager to catch sight of the mysterious 'devil-devil'. **1893** D. LINDSAY *Jrnl. Elder Sci. Exploring Exped.* 57 Much alarmed when she saw . . the 'devil devil', as the camel is generally supposed to be by the natives. **1923** T. HALL *Short Hist. Downs Blacks* 25 They believed in magic and Devil-Devil. **1930** E.R. GRIBBLE *Forty Yrs. with Aborigines* 87 The poor fellows, in their anxiety to propitiate the evil spirits or 'devil-devil'. **1977** T. RONAN *Mighty Men on Horseback* 80 This motor bike bloke reckon white fellers don't know anything about this Devil-Devil business. Only he don't call it Devil-Devil he call it 'Dreamtime'. I never heard that name before. **1979** M. HEPPELL *Black Reality* 84 Devil-devils . . are commonplace and matter-of-fact explanations and causative agents for everything from puffed eyes (the bite of a flying devil-devil) to afternoon naps (putting a person to sleep against his will is common).

2. GILGAI a. Freq. *attrib.*, esp. as **devil devil country.**

1844 L. LEICHHARDT *Jrnl. Overland Exped. Aust.* 6 Nov. (1847) 32 Rich black soil, which appeared several times in the form of ploughed land, well known, in other parts of the colony, either under that name, or under that of 'Devil-devil land', as the natives believe it to be the work of an evil spirit. **1860** *Trans. Philos. Inst. Vic.* 192 Here, we . . first came upon 'devil devil' flats. There is an old, and a more recent, description of this singular surface; the former being furthest from the sea. It is evidently produced by some kind of worm which builds flat-topped hillocks upon the original surface. An experienced horse can generally step from one to another; but what annoys both horse and rider, is the circumstance that the old variety is generally covered with rich strong grass, rendering the uneven surface invisible. **1864** *Port Denison Times* 17 Sept. 2/4 Ascending out of this swampy gully there extends a swamp composed of what is known to the initiated as 'devil-devil' country. **1870** E.B. KENNEDY *Four Yrs. in Qld.* 20 'Devil devil' . . is simply one formation of holes and hillocks, in some districts of great depth and size. **1897** J.J. MURIF *From Ocean to Ocean* 163 'Devil-devil' . . is applied to clay, pure and simple, or silty soil similar to 'Biscay', but with this difference, that in contracting after rains, in the quick-drying rays of fierce tropical sun it cracks, while the 'Biscay' becomes distressingly bumpy. **1912** J. BOWES *Comrades* 144 The hitherto easy country . . had given way to a class commonly known as 'devil-devil' country. It was full of holes and hillocks, covered with rushes and coarse grass, while here and there were pandanus clumps and mangrove belts. **1922** R.L. JACK *Northmost Aust.* II. 480 This turned out to be marshy 'devil-devil' country—probably a lake in wet weather—a network of boggy ditches, with the intervening dry stools of clay covered with coarse rank grass, through which it was very difficult to push one's way even on foot. **1927** M.H. ELLIS *Long Lead* 128 There will be a deep black-soil washout every three yards. . . All 'devil devil' is bad, but Flinders grass 'devil devil' is the king of its species. **1933** *Bulletin* (Sydney) 20 Dec. 34/1 The alternation of wet seasons or flooding on the one hand and of droughts on the other induces characteristic alternations of depressions and rises in heavy soil. These have received various local names of which melonhole, gilgai, Bay of Biscay, devil-devil and crab-hole are the most frequently met. **1936** W. HATFIELD *Aust. through Windscreen* 79 There is a queer ground formation where the ranges give place to the high plains, known thereabouts as devil-devil country. (There are other kinds of devil-devil country, the term seeming to suffice for anything unusual.) **1943** *Bulletin* (Sydney) 8 Dec. 12/4 Viewed from surrounding hills or the sand dunes which separate it from the sea, southern Queensland's 'paddymelon-hole country' appears as a fine series of flats level enough for a landing ground. . . Tufts of coarse grass separated by channels 18 inches deep and a foot wide, which have evidently been cut during the rainy seasons, leaving miniature islands between, convert it into real 'devil-devil' country. **1955** N. PULLIAM *I traveled Lonely Land* 116 Opened the throttle and drove through the devil-devil country.

3. An ant-lion.

1944 J. DEVANNY *By Tropic Sea & Jungle* 178 The ant-lions, or devil-devils, as they are called up there [*sc.* n. Qld.]. **1945** M. RAYMOND *Smiley* 52 The devil-devil is a fantastic creature that digs ant-traps in the sand.

devon. [f. *Devon(shire* the name of an English county.] A large, bland sausage, usu. sliced and eaten cold; FRITZ.

1962 *Austral. Grocer* Aug. 97/3 Devon . . 2s. 9d. **1965** *Kings Cross Whisper* (Sydney) Oct. 11/2 Pull down the meat-safe and there's Devon. **1981** *Choice* Oct. 315/3 Ham, bacon, sausage, devon and frankfurters. **1984** R.L. REID *Healthy Eating in Aust.* 145 Luncheon meat (devon, pork German, Strasburg, etc.) and salami score 9.

dewfish, var. JEWFISH.

dew lizard, var. JEW LIZARD 1.

dhufish, var. JEWFISH.

diamond, *n.*[1] Used *attrib.* in Special Comb. **diamond bird,** PARDALOTE, esp. the *spotted pardalote*, see SPOTTED; **dove,** the small, predom. grey pigeon *Geopelia cuneata* of n. and central Aust.; **firetail,** the finch *Stagonopleura guttata* of s.e. mainland Aust.; JAVA SPARROW; *spotted-sided finch*, see SPOTTED; see also *diamond sparrow*; **-scaled mullet,** the large-scaled mullet *Liza vaigiensis* of n. Aust. and elsewhere in the tropics; **snake,** any of several snakes incl. *carpet snake* (see CARPET) and (*Tas.*) COPPER-HEAD, and esp. *Morelia spilota spilota*, typically black above with pale spots forming more or less diamond-shaped markings; **sparrow,** any of several small finches or finch-like birds, esp. the *spotted pardalote* (see SPOTTED), *zebra finch* (see ZEBRA) and *diamond firetail*.

1827 *Trans. Linnean Soc. London* XV. 238 Pardalotus . . Punctatus. . . We are informed by Mr Caley, that 'this species is called **Diamond Bird** by the settlers, from the spots on its body'. **1833** *Trumpeter* (Hobart) 8 Nov. 227 *To be sold* . . *Birds, in skins*. . . Georgett Bird, Diamond ditto. **1886** W.J. WOODS *Visit to Vic.* 25 Where in all the world can you match the gay adornment of the little Diamond Bird, with its rich, dark crimson tail, and its bright form bespangled with every hue the diamond itself can take? **1891** G.J. BROINOWSKI *Birds of Aust.* VI. Pl. 8, The spotted Diamond-Bird . . displays great activity among the foliage, flitting about in search of insects. **1948** H.A. LINDSAY *Bushman's Handbk.* 21 The diamond bird, a tiny, fearless, charming thing. **1980** B. ROBERTS *Penalty of Adam* 37 A diamond-bird sang its 'pick-it-up, pick-it-up' from the top of the blue gum. **1931** N.W. CAYLEY *What Bird is That?* 86 **Diamond dove** *Geopelia cuneata*. **1945** C. BARRETT *Austral. Bird Life* 67 The diamond dove . . ranges over Australia, excepting the south-eastern coastal districts. **1973** V. SERVENTY *Desert Walkabout* 40 Hundreds of zebra finches and a few diamond doves came to drink. **1976** *Reader's Digest Compl. Bk. Austral. Birds* 237 The smallest member of the pigeon family, the diamond dove . . is essentially a bird of the arid zone. **1945** C. BARRETT

Austral. Bird Life 205 The spotted-sided finch or **diamond firetail** .. popularly known as 'diamond sparrow'. **1984** M. BLAKERS et al. *Atlas Austral. Birds* 592 The Diamond Firetail lives in mallee, eucalypt forest, eucalypt woodland .. and in farmland. **1906** D.G. STEAD *Fishes of Aust.* 79 The **Diamond-scaled Mullet** .. is notable for its large scales and its broad, flat head. **1951** T.C. ROUGHLEY *Fish & Fisheries Aust.* 31 In Queensland, several species of mullet are marketed, including the .. diamond-scaled. [**1805 diamond snake:** *Sydney Gaz.* 20 Oct., A snake of what is in general termed the *diamond* species was killed at the half-way houses on the Parramatta road and when opened a fine parrot was found within it perfectly entire.] **1825** *Austral.* (Sydney) 8 Dec. 4 On Wednesday se'nnight a man who lives in Pitt-street met with a diamond snake in the bush of the largest dimensions ever seen. **1826** J. ATKINSON *Acct. Agric. & Grazing N.S.W.* 27 The diamond snake sometimes attains the length of 13 or 14 feet, and as thick as a man's leg, but its bite is not dangerous. **1829** *Launceston Advertiser* 12 Oct. 2 His most intimate acquaintance .. will drop off one by one, they will shun him as they would a *diamond snake.* **1844** *Guardian* (Sydney) 76/3 Thomas Douglass .. was bitten in the arm by a diamond snake; and, although he cut out the part bitten with a chisel, he expired in an hour and a half. **1845** C. HODGKINSON *Aust., Port Macquarie to Moreton Bay* 210 The Diamond snake .. is beautifully variegated by black and yellow lozenge-shaped marks from whence it derives its name. **1859** J.D. MEREWEATHER *Diary Working Clergyman* 56 This country of Tasmania abounds with very venomous snakes—such as .. the diamond snake. **1906** *Bulletin* (Sydney) 12 July 16/1 The diamond snake .. is known as the copper-headed snake in Victoria, and is called the superb snake in N.S.W. Its scientific name is *Denisonia superba.* **1944** J. DEVANNY *By Tropic Sea & Jungle* 137 A true carpet-snake is not a distinct species but a colour variety of the diamond-snake (*Python spilotes*). **1977** J. CARTER *All Things Wild* 20 On the front verandah I found the cage filled by a large diamond snake, bulging suspiciously in the middle. **1875** P.E. WARBURTON *Journey across Western Interior* 177 Charley's sharp eyes detected some **diamond-sparrows.** **1889** *Proc. Linnean Soc. N.S.W.* IV. 411 *Estrilda guttata...* Locally known as 'Diamond Sparrow'. **1898** D.W. CARNEGIE *Spinifex & Sand* 78, I was overjoyed to hear the twittering of a little flock of Diamond sparrows—a nearly certain sign that water must be handy. **1901** *Emu* I. 136 Chestnut-eared Finch .. locally called 'Diamond Sparrows'. **1948** *Bulletin* (Sydney) 21 Apr. 23/2, I found .. one diamond-sparrow. 'A dyke!' I exclaimed. 'That's what I missed more than anything on the way here—the long low whistle of a dyke.' **1981** E. POTTER *Scone I Remember* 22 Hundreds of diamond sparrows nested in the long golden grass.

diamond, *n.*[2] *Obs.* [Of unknown origin.] A name given to a soldier by Aborigines.

1846 C.P. HODGSON *Reminisc. Aust.* 234 Having heard some soldiers, or 'diamonds' as they call them, were on the road. **1898** J.J. KNIGHT *In Early Days* 36 The blacks vowed they would kill every 'diamond'—that was the name we gave the soldiers.

diamond-cracking, *vbl. n. Obs.* Breaking rocks, i.e., undergoing a sentence of hard labour; so **diamond cracker,** one sentenced to this.

1885 *Australasian Printers' Keepsake* 25 He caught a month, and had to 'white it out' At diamond-cracking in Castieau's Hotel. **1916** *Truth* (Sydney) 2 Apr. 7/4 He will be caught knapping (stones) for the next six months, for which period he has gone to join the diamond crackers at Sammacauleytown.

dibble dibble, var. DEBIL DEBIL.

dibbler /ˈdɪblə/. [Of unknown origin: see quot. 1970 but also OED 3, where it is derived from *dibble* to make a hole with or as with a dibble.] The rare marsupial mouse *Parantechinus apicalis* of W.A.

1850 A. WHITE *Pop. Hist. Mammalia* 166 The *Antechinus apicalis* of Mr Gray .. is called 'the Dibbler' at King George's Sound. **1894** R. LYDEKKER *Hand-Bk. Marsupialia & Monotremata* 168 This pouched mouse .. is known to the settlers of the last-named district [*sc.* King George's Sound] by the name of the 'Dibbler'. **1941** E. TROUGHTON *Furred Animals Aust.* 28 Speckled Marsupial-Mouse or Dibbler. **1970** W.D.L. RIDE *Guide Native Mammals Aust.* 20 Gilbert got several of the little mammals, both at the Moore River and at King George Sound where Aborigines told him that their name for it was 'Dib-bler'. **1974** *Bulletin* (Sydney) 16 Mar. 32/3 Who has heard of the numbat or the dibbler? **1986** *Austral. Geographic* Apr. 23/2 The dibbler, so named by Aborigines at least a century and a half ago, averages 14 centimetres in length, has a sharp, foxy face and a curious speckled appearance due to white flecking in its fur.

dice, *v.* [Fig. use of *dice* to lose by dicing.] *trans.* To discard; to reject; to abandon.

1943 S.J. BAKER *Pop. Dict. Austral. Slang* (ed. 2) 25 *Dice,* to upset, reject, throw away. **1952** T.A.G. HUNGERFORD *Ridge & River* 46, I got a shock, too, the first time I was jumped—I damn' near filled me strides, but by hell, I never diced me gun and took off like a bloody Bondi tram. **1953** —— *Riverslake* 224 'If you decide to put on a strike, and they want me to crawl down, I'm through.' 'Dicing it?' 'Uh-huh.' **1958** *Bulletin* (Sydney) 11 June 19/1 Consider the number of ways an Aussie can be dismissed from his job .. he can be sacked, fired, hoisted... Should he decide to beat the boss to the punch he may snatch it, pull-out, toss it in, dice it. **1963** *Eureka!* (A.N.U.) 9 Os stubbed at his cigarette. 'Well, I'd better push, I suppose, or Hilda'll dice me.' **1965** C. KOCH *Across Sea Wall* 53 He better behave, the fat old bastard, or I'll dice him. **1977** R. BEILBY *Gunner* 219 The army diced us, remember, down on that beach a few nights ago. **1984** *N.T. News* (Darwin) 16 Nov. 30/4, I was filleting the jewie on the side of the boat and somehow managed to drop one fillet... It must have taken all of 10 seconds to dice the fillet.

dick: see DICKHEAD.

dick. [Familiar form of RICHARD.] In the phr. **to have had the dick,** to be finished, to be irreparably damaged.

1974 D. IRELAND *Burn* 85 Now you've had the dick... That's the finish. You're history now. **1976** B. BENNETT *New Country* 34 The cattle trap up there's had the dick.

dicken. Also **dickin, dickon.** [Var. of *dickens* the deuce, the devil.] An interjectional exclamation, usu. expressing disbelief (but see quot. 1966). Also as *n.* and *adj.*, and with **on.**

1894 *Bulletin* (Sydney) 5 May 13/3 'And did yer stouch him back?' 'No.' 'Dicken!' 'Swelp me.' **1898** *Ibid.* 4 June (Red Page), And 'a dickon pitch to kid us' Is a synonym for 'lie'. **1904** L.M.P. ARCHER *Bush Honeymoon* 311 'No dicken (nonsense) now,' said Jim, 'The truth, the whole truth, and nothing but it, old man.' **1916** J.F. NUGENT *Lorblimey* 13 W'en first I see's Lizzie, lorblimey, I swore I'd chuck up th' mob 'n' I'd shicker no more; I wuz never so shook on'r clinah before: *Dicken.* **1918** L.J. VILLIERS *Changing Yr.* 22 Ere's Augus' runnin'; dicken! **1929** H. EYRE *Hilarities* 46 Those were the days when .. we said 'No flies on you', 'Dicken to that', and similar things. So you see it was some time ago. **1936** W. HATFIELD *Aust. through Windscreen* 293 You've got to tie your horse up; feed and water him, and—*groom* the bastard before you get near a bit of picking for yourself! Dicken to that. The infantry'll do me! **1959** M. RAYMOND *Smiley roams Road* 33 'What about pulling the emergency cord?' 'Aw, dicken on. I haven't got the dingbats and I haven't got five quid.' **1966** S.J. BAKER *Austral. Lang.* (ed. 2) 203 Whereas dicken! meaning cut it out! be reasonable! is still known in most parts of Australia, it flourishes quite remarkably in South Australia. Here, depending on the intonation, it can mean 'Yes, of course!' 'Certainly not!' 'Do you really think so?' and 'You don't say!' **1968** S. GORE *Holy Smoke* 52 He rolls his eyes up aloft and starts orf: 'Eh, dickin on it, Lord! How's about givin' a man a fair crack o' the whip... Let the dog see the rabbit?' **1976** N.V. WALLACE *Bush Lawyer* 172 'He's quite a character.' 'What's that?' she queried. 'A hard case,' I said. 'Dicken!' was her comment. This exclamation seems to be peculiar to our state [*sc.* S.A.], where it is accepted as a brief expression of bright accord. **1981** *Sydney Morning Herald* 24 Jan. 35/7 Mr Dutton remembers being laughed at as a boy at school in Melbourne when he used the term 'dicken!' as an expletive rather in the way in which 'my oath' is usually employed. 'A common term in South Australia,' he said, 'but no one in Victoria had ever heard of it.'

dickhead. [f. *dick* penis (cf. *prick*). Used elsewhere but recorded earliest in Aust.] A fool. Also **dick.**

1967 R. DONALDSON et al. *Cane!* 150 Nobody made a dick out of Nigger and got away with it. **1976** D. IRELAND *Glass Canoe* 16, I called him a dickhead, but he doesn't know what he's doing when he's real full. **1978** J. COLBERT *Ranch* 33, I can't wear dick-heads, all you can do is give them a good thump. **1980** *Westerly* iii. 29 You can go and piss off, dickhead. **1983** F. WILLMOTT *Breaking Up* 54 'You're a dickhead,' he said. 'I'd expect a lot more from you.' **1986** *Nat. Times* (Sydney) 10 Jan. 26/2 People outside our group are called jerks and dickheads.

dickin, dickon, varr. DICKEN.

Dickless Tracy. See quot. 1980.

1980 B. HORNADGE *Austral. Slanguage* 197 The only inventive feminine nickname I have come across is *Dickless Tracy* (a woman police officer). **1984** *Sydney Morning Herald* 4 Feb. 37/2 Mangan is one of 18 policewomen at Darlinghurst (out of 136 police) whom one sergeant calls Dickless Tracys.

diddy. Also **didee.** [Prob., in children's speech, altered form of DUNNY.] A lavatory. Also *attrib.*

1958 M. WARREN *No Glamour in Gumboots* 9 The sanitary system was primitive, the 'diddy' being an imposing and conspicuous edifice perched at the back of the house. **1960** M. VIZZERS *She'll do Me!* 54 'D'you know what a dyke is?' he asked. 'In Holland, yes, in Australia, no!' 'It's a country diddy!' 'I don't understand!' 'You know—a dunny!' **1963** D. ROBERT *Look at me Now* 84 The use of 'baby' and 'dainty' language is common. While the men are referring to a spade as a bloody shovel, the women are calling lavatories 'diddies'. **1965** F. HARDY *Yarns of Billy Borker* 56 A barbecue in the backyard and a didee in the house. **1971** —— *Outcasts of Foolgarah* 91 Tom has studied the layout of all sorts of houses and can pick the diddy door at a glance.

didgeridoo /dɪdʒəriˈdu/. Also **didjeridu, didjiridu, didjerry,** etc. [a. Yolŋu Sub-group *didjeridu* (imitative).] An Aboriginal (orig. Arnhem Land) wind instrument, a long, wooden, tubular instrument producing a low-pitched resonant sound with complex rhythmic patterns but little tonal variation; DRONE-PIPE.

1919 *Huon Times* (Franklin) 24 Jan. 4/3 The nigger crew is making merry with the Diridgery doo and the eternal ya-ya-ya ye-ye-ye cry. **1919** *Smith's Weekly* (Sydney) 5 Apr. 15/1 The Northern Territory aborigines have an infernal—allegedly musical—instrument, composed of two feet of hollow bamboo. It produces but one sound—'didjerry, didjerry, didjerry—' and so on ad infinitum... When a couple of niggers started grinding their infernal 'didjerry' half the hot night through, the blasphemous manager decided on revenge. **1924** *Bulletin* (Sydney) 18 Dec. 24/1 Didjeridoo—didjeridoo! A blackfellow blows through a length of bamboo. **1925** M. TERRY *Across Unknown Aust.* 190 The didjiri-du .. is a long hollow tube, often a tree root about 5 feet long, slightly curved at the lower end. The musician squats on the ground, resting his instrument on the earth. He fits his mouth into the straight or upper end and blows down it in a curious fashion. He produces an intermittent drone. **1935** I.L. IDRIESS *Man Tracks* 195 Money ordered Sandy to play the didgereedoo .. his long bamboo blowing tube. **1948** A. MARSHALL *Ourselves writ Strange* 156 An old man approached carrying a hollow limb about 6 foot long and 6 inches in diameter... 'Didjereedoo!' he said. **1951** C. SIMPSON *Adam in Ochre* 7 Nowhere except in and near Arnhem Land would you ever hear the vibrant droning of the wooden didjeridoo. **1960** *N.T. News* (Darwin) 28 Oct. 2/3 Make them a quintet by including the vibrant beat of their own didgeridoo and they would be a sensation. **1962** C. GYE *Cockney & Crocodile* 58 The exhaust pipe of the ute was used as a didgeridoo to make native music at night. **1967** F.T. MACARTNEY *Proof against Failure* 94 The name 'didjeridoo' is probably not an aboriginal one... It was very likely invented in imitation of the sound the instrument makes. **1977** M. TUCKER *If everyone Cared* 87 Now white youths are playing the didgeridoo! **1980** L.G. FOGARTY *Kargun* 7 Colours of purple, red, blue are filling our leaping thunder—feeding my didgeridoo.

dig, *n.*[1] Abbrev. of DIGGER 2.

1916 J.F. NUGENT *Lorblimey* 9 'Doc.' sez, 'No 'ope, Dig., y'r've taken th' knock.' **1920** *Aussie* (Sydney) June

9/3 The puzzled Digs. went home to bed. **1921** *Bulletin* (Sydney) 26 May 16/2 This Dig... was lucky enough to have a mate to take on the Australian girl. **1927** F.C. BIGGERS *Bat-Eye* 41 But tell me! Tell me, dig! I feel 'e died a cobber—true an' game. **1943** A. DAWES *Soldier Superb* 32 'Good on you, Dig,' waved the ridge-bound Australians to homing flights of bombing and fighter craft. **1944** A.S. SMITH *Boys write Home* 194 One of the boys called him 'Dig.' another 'Mate', and the rest of us 'Lord'. When we asked him how we should address him he replied: 'You are all doing fine.' **1954** J. CLEARY *Climate of Courage* 38 G'day, dig. Me ol' mate, me cobber. **1965** G. MCINNES *Road to Gundagai* 25 Often they shouted at us in goodnatured banter, 'Howsit up in the dress circle, dig?' **1972** *Bulletin* (Sydney) 3 June 27/2 'What's going on here, Dig?' the occupant of a passing taxi calls. **1975** X. HERBERT *Poor Fellow my Country* 1149 'Sure you haven't got it all wrong?'.. 'Never so sure of anything in my life, dig. I've been played for the biggest mug this side o' the Black Stump.' **1980** E. BARCS *Backyard of Mars* 209 Frequently, someone in the place wanted to shout us a beer, and inquired whether one of us or both had been at Tobruk or on the Kokoda Trail. They called me 'Dig' and I felt like a fraud.

dig, *n.*[2] [Perh. fig. use of *dig*, with reference to a hole.] See quot. 1962.

1962 'N. CULOTTA' *Gone Fishin'* 48 Shorty talked about 'digs' the name given by fishermen to areas where they can expect to find fish... He talked about mullet digs, and bream digs, and 'nigger' digs. **1980** B. SHACKLETON *Karagi* 19 He learned the haunts and the 'digs' and the moods of prawns on the big river.

digger. [Spec. use of *digger* a miner, esp. one working surface or shallow deposits (see OED 2 a.); orig. U.S. in its application to gold-mining.]

1. A miner on the Australian goldfields. Also *attrib.*

1849 *Bell's Life in Sydney* 3 Feb. 3/4 In sheer self-defence I was obliged to turn digger myself. *Ibid.* 3 Nov. 3/5 (*heading*) The digger's hand-book. **1851** *Empire* (Sydney) 4 Aug. 11/2 It is estimated that the number of diggers at Golden Point must be about 150. **1852** D. MACKENZIE *Gold Digger* 46 Each digger pays monthly to the Government Commissioner a license fee of 30s. **1859** W. KELLY *Life in Vic.* I. 46 The females we almost invariably encountered were either of that strong-minded class who had caught their diggers *in vinculo matrimonii*, or were anxious to encourage diggers' attentions without the bother or conventional ceremony of forging the chain. **1870** *Sydney Morning Herald* 2 July 5/6 The people.. are much above the average of a new rush population; the proportion of bona fide diggers being greater than is ordinarily the case on a new diggings. **1882** W. COOTE *Hist. Colony Qld.* 125 One consequence was, that in Sydney, great distress arose among the wives and families of absent diggers. **1891** *Hist. Bushranging* 47 We were not in uniform; we were in plain clothes. We were not disguised like diggers. **1901** *Truth* (Sydney) 11 Aug. 1/3 They loaf around hotels.. ever on the scout for 'suction', and not one of them would say 'no' to a drink from a Chinaman or a Digger Indian. **1915** *Ibid.* 14 Feb. 1/7 Is the 'flash light' new? Not at all. In the roaring fifties, the lucky diggers lit their pipes with a fiver. **1924** *Smith's Weekly* (Sydney) 31 May 22/7 Once fossicked in a shaft which a couple of diggers had sunk and deserted. **1938** F. CLUNE *Free & Easy Land* 150 'Go back! Go back! Its a duffer,' shouted the disappointed diggers. **1944** M.J. O'REILLY *Bowyangs & Boomerangs* 45 The digger swaggies, whom I met in the early days of the Western Australian goldfields, were a fine type. **1965** F. HARDY *Yarns of Billy Borker* 144 Some diggers turn mean when they strike it rich. **1982** R. HALL *Just Relations* 41 A digger, he was, no sooner had he got enough gold than he was off to have it fashioned into teeth.

2. [Transf. use of sense 1: see quot. 1922.] In the wars of 1914–18 and 1939–45, a (private) soldier from Australia or New Zealand; increasingly, an Australian soldier exclusively; also used in civilian as well as military contexts as a term of address, and freq. shortened to DIG *n.*[1] Cf. COBBER, MATE.

1916 C.A. HEMSLEY Diary 12 Aug., The officer in charge of the parade was addressing the men, and at some kindly expressed sentiment one wag interjected with 'Hear, hear, old digger!' **1918** *Aussie: Austral. Soldiers' Mag.* Jan. 10/2 *Digger*, a friend, pal, or comrade, synonymous with cobbers; a white man who runs straight. *Ibid.* Feb. 2/1 About the origin of this word 'Digger'... It came to France when the sandgropers gave up digging on the goldfields of W.A. and carried on with it on the battlefields. *Ibid.*, I've got the dinkum oil about the origin of this Aussie word 'Digger'. It started when we were first in the Salient. You'll remember we got no stunting there.. but they took the precaution of preventing us from developing gout by giving us 'beaucoup' digging fatigues—repairing aged and decrepit trenches... So the boys took to alluding to each other as 'diggers'. **1919** P. MACGILL *Diggers* 94 The officer who conducted our party spoke of another grave.. which bears on the headstone: '*Here lie two Huns who met a Digger.*' And near it, in terse and forcible language is inscribed on a second headstone: '*Here lies the Digger.*' **1920** *Huon Times* (Franklin) 23 July 2/5 Be on Harvesten; she's a certainty, Digger. **1922** *Bulletin* (Sydney) 8 June (Red Page), 'Digger' is a title coveted and often stolen. It originally meant the infantryman or artilleryman who was always 'digging in' or rebuilding his parapet after enemy fire... It did not mean a staff-officer or any of the A.I.F. serving in Palestine or Egypt. It meant the man in the front line in France, and no one else. It is ridiculous to talk of the 'Digger Prince' or to use the word for A.I.F. men indiscriminately; and it is mere swank when claimed by men who did not dig. There were no 'Diggers' at Gallipoli where we dug most—the word had not come then! **1932** J. MAXWELL *Hell's Bells* 1 When Digger meets Digger the memory goes jogging back to the Peninsula or to the mud and blood and mad ruin of northern France. **1933** C.E.W. BEAN *Official Hist. Aust. 1914–18* IV. 732 It was at this stage that Australian soldiers—in particular, the infantry—came to be known, together with the New Zealanders, as 'the Diggers'. The term had occasionally been heard before, but hitherto had been general only among the New Zealanders, who are said to have inherited it from the gum-diggers in their country. **1940** 'K. BRUCE' *Digger Tourists* 60, I saw some New Zealand diggers helping along some of our fellows. **1945** A.G. BUTLER *Digger* 23 Caius Marius was a dinkum Digger and a leader of Diggers... Queen Boadicea, King Alfred the Great, King Henry V, had an outlook not alien to the Digger Spirit... In his outlook on life, St Paul himself was a Digger; and he followed in the footsteps of a greater than he. **1956** S. HOPE *Diggers' Paradise* 13 Very few New Australians whether British, Balts, Italians or Greeks, see Australia through the rose-coloured spectacles worn by the dyed-in-the-wool Diggers. **1965** G. MCINNES *Road to Gundagai* 28 'My father's a Captain!' I shouted.., 'and you're only a common Digger!' **1968** M. HILLIARD *Excuse me, Mr Sweetenham* 115 Should our sun-tanned Diggers be fighting in Vietnam? **1980** J. WOLFE *End of Pricklystick* 177 An old man was staring at me. 'How are you, Digger?' he grinned.

3. In the collocation **Little Digger**: a nickname for William Morris Hughes (1864–1952), Prime Minister of Australia during the war of 1914–18 (see quot. 1957).

1919 *Morning Post* (London) 11 Feb. 4/5 'The Little Digger.. is running a great offensive...' From the start it was clear that Mr Hughes was confronted with a formidable task. **1938** *Sydney Morning Herald* 26 Apr. 12/6 Many 'Diggers' broke the lines as they marched yesterday to shake hands with a small figure known to them as 'the little Digger', and, as war-time Prime Minister, one of the heroes of those years. **1950** F.J. HARDY *Power without Glory* 278 The 'Yes' forces needed a leader who could exercise influence over the working man... The Labor Prime Minister Hughes could and did. Before the war was over he had earned a nickname, 'The Little Digger'. **1957** W.F. WHYTE *W.M. Hughes* 242 During this visit to France he addressed many units of the Australian Forces, and on several occasions they broke all the rules and mobbed him, carrying him high on their shoulders. They placed a Digger's hat on his head and called him 'the Little Digger'—and by that affectionate name he was to be known to Australian troops for ever after. **1975** *Austral.* (Sydney) 25 Jan. 16/1 The redoubtable Billy Hughes once observed that he trusted only two people—Jesus Christ and the Commonwealth Statistician. (The little Digger incidentally added that he still wasn't too sure about the former.)

4. Special Comb. **digger costume** (or **dress**), see quots.; also **digger's costume; hat,** the felt slouch hat worn as part of the uniform of the Australian soldier; **hunt,** a raid made on a goldfield by police, for the purpose of inspecting miners' licences; also **hunting** *vbl. n.*; **digger-looking** *a.*, having the appearance of a gold miner.

1853 J. SHERER *Gold Finder Aust.* 173 Hundreds of pedestrians in **digger's costume.** **1856** W.W. DOBIE *Recoll. Visit Port-Phillip* 43 They were dressed in the usual digger costume, blue flannel shirts, without coats. **1857** J. ASKEW *Voyage Aust. & N.Z.* 130 They were dressed in the digger's costume—strong boots reaching to the knee, long blue smocks, and black rustic hats. **1859** W. BURROWS *Adventures Mounted Trooper* 5 A man dressed in the usual digger-costume, consisting of a black wide-awake hat, blue shirt, and moleskin continuations, came up to the dray. **1865** *Austral. Monthly Mag.* (Melbourne) I. 203, I had the greatest difficulty in persuading him to dismiss his digger's dress. **1876** 'RESIDENT' *Girl Life in Aust.* 43 The murderer, a short, stout man, in a digger's dress, with swag and paniken over his shoulder, appeared one evening. **1940** T. WOOD *Cobbers Campaigning* 159 Distant lands that saw those **digger hats** before; through Victory, and beyond. **1944** C.S. WATTS *Selected Verse* 84 She watched for her Johnny, smiling Beneath his Digger's hat. **1954** J. WATEN *Unbending* 88 Williams in his khaki uniform and cocked digger hat. **1965** K. SMITH *OGF* 187 Behind him was the transparent figure of Billy Hughes in a Digger hat, smiling with one hand on the boy's shoulder. **1970** *Bulletin* (Sydney) 4 July 10/2 In Sydney you can buy.. genuine Digger hats. **1979** W.D. JOYNT *Breaking Road for Rest* 106 As I was wearing my digger hat the question put me on my guard at once. **1979** D. MAITLAND *Breaking Out* 125 In the fierce, seething heat, both he and Murphy were wearing wide-brimmed, war-surplus Digger hats with wet towels draped over the backs of their necks. **1855** *Melbourne Monthly Mag.* May 63 The **digger-hunt**.. was ordered during the excitement against the license-fee. **1855** R. CARBONI *Eureka Stockade* 95 The diggers were goaded on to take the stand they did by the 'digger-hunt', of the 30th November, which, we are sustained in saying, was a base piece of gold and silver lace revenge. **1855** G.H. WATHEN *Golden Colony* 86 The pursuit and capture of unlicensed diggers, 'man-hunting' or 'digger-hunting' as the miners called it. **1859** W. KELLY *Life in Vic.* II. 79 Digger-hunting in the days of Mr Latrobe was a fortnightly proceeding. **1869** E.C. BOOTH *Another England* 87 'Digger-hunt'.. was the jocose phrase by which the police called riding after men, whom for lack of licences, they chained to logs. **1870** W.B. WITHERS *Hist. of Ballarat* 53 'Digger-hunting', as the collection of the licence fee was called by the men on the gold-fields, continued. **1887** *Illustr. Austral. News* (Melbourne) 25 June (Suppl.) 11/3 What gave rise to this outbreak was the 'digger-hunting' practised by the constabulary, who enforced an extortionate licence fee from the gold diggers. **1905** H. LAWSON *Elder Son* 257 With all its shameful scenes, the digger-hunt begins. **1909** W.G. SPENCE *Aust.'s Awakening* 19 Digger hunting became a pastime for Commissioners and police. **1913** J. SADLEIR *Recoll.* 44 All 'digger hunts'—the name given to the expeditions for the examination of licenses—were conducted under the personal direction of responsible officers. **1940** T. NELSON *Towards Socialism* 15 Brutal 'digger hunts' were engaged in by Troopers urged on by the gold field Commissioners. **1854** W. HOWITT *Boy's Adventures* 272 Six or seven rough **digger-looking** fellows. **1856** W.W. DOBIE *Recoll. Visit Port-Phillip* 45 The rowdy digger-looking company was smoking and imbibing 'nobblers', 'spiders', and other potent colonial drinks. **1872** 'DEMONAX' *Mysteries & Miseries Scripopolis* 6/1 He returned.. bringing with him a digger-looking person.

Hence **diggerish** *a.*, **diggerism** *n.*

1936 N. CALDWELL *Fangs of Sea* 172 In describing his beloved Barrier he got rather carried away and his language became rather **Diggerish.** **1945** A.G. BUTLER *Digger* 35 *Puck of Pook's Hill*—most 'Diggerish' of Kipling's writings. **1918** *Aussie: Austral. Soldiers' Mag.* (Sydney) Dec. 20/1 To use a **Diggerism**, 'it's out on its own' as regards its method of work and style of entertainment. **1945** A.G. BUTLER *Digger* 50 'Diggerism', that sane satisfaction of a social brotherhood, without political rancour, expresses most happily the idea of the social order most capable of realization in Australia. **1965** E. LAMBERT *Long White Night* 31 On the second Alamein reunion after the war, I went along to the Alexandra Hall... Standing under a lamp, looking fixedly through a high window.. was Prim... I knew he would have loved to be inside there, wallowing in that swamp of juvenile *diggerism.*

diggerdom. *Obs.* The society established by the gold-miners.

1855 W. HOWITT *Land, Labor & Gold* I. 47 Diggerdom

is gloriously in the ascendant here. **1876** J.B. STEPHENS *Hundred Pounds* 5 Sandie had adopted as a mate a young man whose innate and ineradicable new-chumism had caused him to be despised and rejected of universal diggerdom. **1880** G. WALCH *Vic.* 22 The *nouveau riche* of Diggerdom had a lordly taste for playing skittles with bottles of champagne for pins.

digging, *vbl. n.* Usu. in *pl.* [Spec. use of *digging(s* a place where digging is carried out: applied to goldfields in California and then Aust.]

1. A goldfield. Also **diggins.**

1851 *Austral. Gold Digger's Monthly Mag.* (1852) ii. 42 Out of one hundred who flock to the diggings, about three may . . do well. **1851** *Empire* (Sydney) 25 Sept. 191/5 Whilst perambulating the 'diggins' yesterday, Mr Cooper showed me a piece of quartz from about four feet below the surface. **1851** J.H. BURTON *Emigrant's Man.* i 93 To the 'Diggings' in New South Wales and Victoria, crowds of persons are now proceeding. **1852** *Moreton Bay Free Press* 25 Mar. 3/3 Accounts from this locality are very conflicting; but . . it has not turned out a profitable 'diggings'. **1854** W. SHAW *Land of Promise* 261 The 'diggins' of New South Wales . . diverted labour from its customary channels. **1856** W.W. DOBIE *Recoll. Visit Port-Phillip* 39 An emigrant ship is no school for good manners or morals, and, in too many instances, female emigrants are pretty well prepared for the innumerable indelicacies of a life in Canvas Town or at 'the Diggins'. **1857** 'RETURNED DIGGER' *Six Yrs. in Aust.* 40 Forest Creek or any other Australian digging. **1861** E.P. RAMSAY-LAYE *Social Life & Manners* 14 On entering the diggings, the country has the appearance of one vast cemetery with fresh made graves, as the diggers leave their holes uncovered with the earth heaped up at the sides. **1884** *Austral. Tit-Bits* (Melbourne) 24 July 5/2 He followed the diggings for love of the rollicking, devil-may-care life. **1894** *Western Champion* (Barcaldine) 12 June 12/2 Nell had followed her father, an old reprobate, from diggings to diggings, where he usually followed the occupation of shanty-keeping, otherwise sly grog selling. **1910** *Bulletin* (Sydney) 8 Sept. 13/4 He . . made a solid wad of money before the diggings fizzled. **1950** *New Settler in W.A.* (Perth) Feb. 71 From Coolgardie onwards the country changed from the tortured, twisted ground of the diggings to open, smiling wheatlands. **1962** E. LANE *Mad as Rabbits* 28 He'd harness his horse to his van and drive off to the goldfields, for 'the diggins' were always somewhere to go when there was nowhere else. **1982** R. HALL *Just Relations* 141 They overlooked pits and hollows still flooded by an outbreak of despair issuing from abandoned diggings.

2. Special Comb. **digging mania,** *gold fever*, see GOLD 3; **party,** a group of gold-miners working together; **population,** that part of the population engaged in gold-mining; **price,** the (usu. inflated) cost of retailed goods on a goldfield; **settlement, town, township, village,** the dwellings, etc., on a goldfield; **times,** the gold-rush era.

1857 W. WESTGARTH *Vic. & Austral. Gold Mines* 10 A vision still haunted me of servants ever seized with a **diggings mania.** **1862** A. POLEHAMPTON *Kangaroo Land* 30 Our captain being on shore, had already detected symptoms of the *diggings mania* amongst the crew. **1851** *Empire* (Sydney) 6 Aug. 18/5 (*heading*) A **digging party.** **1852** *Moreton Bay Free Press* 22 Jan. 2/5 The efforts of those appointed at the public meeting to collect funds to defray the expenses of the digging party, have been successful to a reasonable extent. **1852** *Argus* (Melbourne) 21 Jan. 2/6 Digging parties have commenced working upon the Bell River. **1855** G.H. WATHEN *Golden Colony* 53 A digging party consists of three or four partners or *mates.* **1851** *Empire* (Sydney) 27 Aug. 91/6 A visible thinning of the **digging population** has taken place in some of the richest points of the Turon. **1854** W. SHAW *Land of Promise* 181 Melbourne, unable to meet the excessive demands of its digging population. **1856** H.B. STOREY *Vic.* 104 From the increase of the digging population . . disaffection was on the increase. **1859** F. SINNETT *Acct. 'Rush' Port Curtis* 7 A rumour reaches some centre of digging population that a rich deposit has been discovered. **1851** *Empire* (Sydney) 16 Dec. 470/7 Mr Badgery is the most considerable storekeeper, and accommodates the public at a **digging price.** **1855** W. HOWITT *Land, Labor & Gold* I. 374 Alfred sold him one of his French pipes . . for 1s.—the digging price for the most ordinary dudeens. **1907** *Bulletin* (Sydney) 14 Nov. 14/1 The pitch-forks came to hand at Gulgong, and were duly auctioned at diggings prices. **1861** L.A. MEREDITH *Over Straits* 141 The chief official in a **digging settlement** . . is entitled the Warden. **1880** G. SUTHERLAND *Tales of Goldfields* 46 Butcher's meat was urgently required at the digging settlement. **1862** C. ASPINALL *Three Yrs. Melbourne* 161 There will be a railroad open to Ballarat, one of the most important **'diggings' towns,** containing twenty-five thousand inhabitants. **1901** *Bulletin* (Sydney) 7 Sept. 14/1 He *was* the only 'trier' in that wearied diggin' town. **1881** A.C. GRANT *Bush-Life Qld.* II. 243 John West vowed that his first night passed in the midst of a **digging township** should be the last, if he could help it. **1882** A.J. BOYD *Old Colonials* 146, I remember one instance of good nature in an apothecary on a small far-inland digging township. **1888** J.C.F. JOHNSON *Austral Christmas* 76 An Australian diggings township. **1855** W. HOWITT *Land, Labor & Gold* II. 114 **Digging villages,** with their tents and stores, mark its course for miles, with all their tumbled heaps, tree-stumps and disorderly objects around them. **1861** L.A. MEREDITH *Over Straits* 256 Pause to make a hasty sketch of this exception to the general rule for digging-villages. **1853** *Austral. Gold Digger's Monthly Mag.* v. 173 In these **diggings times** the domestic duties of the family fall wholly to the lot of mamma and her daughters. **1878** P. FOX *Unsuccessful Colonist* 137 After the speculative and feverish excitement of the 'diggins' times, a fearful lull came over business matters in Adelaide.

digging stick. An Aboriginal food-gathering tool made from a piece of wood pointed at each end and used to excavate roots and tubers; KATTA; YAM-STICK.

1841 G. GREY *Jrnls. Two Exped. N.-W. & W.A.* II. 331, I offered to get a spade, but they would not have it; the digging stick was the proper tool. **1847** G.F. ANGAS *Savage Life & Scenes* I. 75 Wandering in search of roots, with her digging-stick in her hand. **1927** SPENCER & GILLEN *Arunta* 15 Armed with digging-sticks and *pitchis.* **1935** H. BASEDOW *Knights of Boomerang* 78 The only implements she possesses are her digging-stick and small bark scoop. **1938** D. BATES *Passing of Aborigines* 138 Haranguing the lightning and brandishing her digging-stick at the scowling skies in a thunderstorm. **1948** C.P. MOUNTFORD *Brown Men & Red Sand* 171 Their digging-stick is a straight branch of mulga, sharpened to a chisel point in the fire. **1963** D. ATTENBOROUGH *Quest under Capricorn* 151 The women began to clear away the earth at the base of a low acacia bush with their long digging sticks, poles of heavy wood pointed at each end. With these they excavated the roots and cracked them open. **1969** A.A. ABBIE *Original Australs.* 75 Women are the main collectors of vegetable food. They always carry a fairly long 'digging-stick', sometimes armed with a stone point, which may also be used for such other purposes as digging out small animals or fighting. **1979** A. WELLS *Forests are their Temples* 27 You mimic hunting now. Spear and canoe and digging stick will soon mean work to you.

diggins: see DIGGING 1.

dill. [Back-formation from DILLY *a.*] A fool or simpleton.

[**1941** H. PERCY *Here's H. Percy* 23 And he wasn't such a big shot in the days before the war; In fact he was a dillpot as the boss would often say.] **1941** S.J. BAKER *Pop. Dict. Austral. Slang* 23 *Dil,* a simpleton or fool. **1943** R. DIXON *Story J.T. Lang* 19 They could be dills, traitors or scoundrels, but so long as their names started with A Lang was satisfied. **1950** *Bulletin* (Sydney) 8 Nov. 13/4 The new-hand was regarded generally as a bit of a dill. **1957** J. WATEN *Shares in Murder* 50 You must think I'm a dill if you expect me to take any notice of it. **1959** D. NILAND *Gold in Streets* 83 He stands there gaping like a bloody dill. **1966** A. HOPGOOD *Private Yuk Objects* 33, I might look a bit of a dill. I mightn't know much. **1977** B. SCOTT *My Uncle Arch* 159 He was the sort of dill that would volunteer to carry the grand piano up three flights of stairs and play it when he got it there. **1984** *Canberra Times* 11 Apr. 1/1 God, I'm a dill.

dilli, var. DILLY *n.*

dillon bush /ˈdɪlən bʊʃ/. [f. Wemba Wemba dial. of Wemba *diliŋ* + (Eng.) *bush.*] The drought-tolerant plant of all mainland States but not N.T., *Nitraria billardierei* (fam. Zygophyllaceae), a rigid spreading shrub bearing edible fruits.

1885 P.R. MEGGY *From Sydney to Silverton* 21 Another succulent shrub known as the 'dillon' bush, the last being the only one of the four which sheep will eat. **1890** A. WOODHOUSE *Man with Apples* 87 All that met his eyes were a few stray patches of blue or dillon bush. **1949** *Bulletin* (Sydney) 16 Feb. 14/1 The paper gets caught on a bit o' dillon-bush an' he falls out o' the saddle an' grabs it. **1983** *Nat. Farmer* (Perth) 22 Sept. 11/1 When the 84 ha. Kerang property was bought in 1956, it grew mainly barley grass, beadbush and dillon bush, and carried less than two sheep to the hectare.

dillwynia /dɪlˈwɪniə/. [The plant genus *Dillwynia* was named by English botanist J.E. Smith (in Koenig, K.D.E. and Sims, J. *Ann. Bot.* (1805) I. 510) after English botanist L.W. *Dillwyn* (1778–1855).] Any shrub of the Austral. genus *Dillwynia* (fam. Fabaceae), usu. having yellow or yellow and reddish flowers, and occurring in all States but not N.T.

1850 *Britannia* (Hobart) 7 Nov. 4/5 The narrow valleys of the interior, neither agricultural nor pastoral, and filled with the dylwinnea. **1930** V. PALMER *Passage* (1957) 50 He had memories of Clem . . fingering the heath-leaved dillwynias. **1942** E. ANDERSON *Squatter's Luck* 28 Dilwynnia, 'Eggs-and-Bacon'. **1958** *Coast to Coast 1957–58* 138 Daviesia and dillwynia thrust out spikes of tiny bounels, rust-red and burnt sienna. **1984** ELLIOT & JONES *Encycl. Austral. Plants* III. 275 Dillwynias usually inhabit sandheath or dry sclerophyll forest communities.

dilly /ˈdɪli/, *n.* Also **dilli.** [a. Jagara *dili* coarse grass, a bag woven of this.] An Aboriginal bag or basket made from woven grass or fibre.

1830 W.J. HOOKER *Bot. Miscellany* I. 254 On examining the depôt, we found a Kangaroo-Net . . a *Dilly*, or luggage-bag, such as females carry, made of the leaves of a species of *Xanthorrhoea*, and strong enough to bear any weight. **1836** J. BACKHOUSE *Extracts from Lett.* (1838) iii. 62 One of the old women was busy, twisting rushes to make a dilly or bag. **1841** *Sydney Herald* 5 May 2/5 Spears, shields, nets, water-utensils, and bags called *dilly*, are generally stuck or hung up on branches of trees around the hut. **1846** *Moreton Bay Courier* 17 Oct. 2/4 [They] proceeded to Mr Gregor's station, where they found two of the blacks filling their 'dillies' with flour. **1849** *Tasmanian Jrnl. Nat. Sci.* III. 109 The rock crystal was found in their dillis as far as the gulf. **1861** J.D. LANG *Qld., Aust.* 352 Observing a *dilly* or native basket (which is usually formed of a strong native grass, very neatly plaited). **1875** CAMPBELL & WILKS *Early Settlement Qld.* 40 The three sable hags, Who had filled with fat beef all their dillies and bags.

dilly, *a.* [Br. dial. *dilly* queer, cranky: see EDD.] Foolish, dotty.

1905 L. BECKE *Tom Gerrard* 91 Maybe you've forgotten that when you busted your last cheque at Hooley's pub in Boorala, and had the dilly trimmings, that it was the parson who brought you back here, you boozy little swine. **1908** *Bulletin* (Sydney) 12 Nov. 39/1, I am 'elpless in me bunk, Oh, I'm dilly an' I'm drunk. **1916** C.J. DENNIS *Moods Ginger Mick* 112, I fergits the playful 'abits uv our foes, An' finds meself a-thinkin' thorts uv good ole Melbourne town, An' dreamin' dilly dreams about ole Rose. **1918** *Aussie: Austral. Soldiers' Mag.* Sept. 7/2 Don't youse blokes reckon a cove's dilly to splice one of them mademoiselles when there's whips of Aussie tarts like these? **1935** K. TENNANT *Tiburon* 26 'Bless you, lady, bless you,' he says, all dilly with joy, see, thinkin' he's on a good thing. ***c* 1943** *Laugh* 15/1 Me cobber, 'arf dilly, 'e's goin' round the passages sayin', 'Puss! puss!' an' 'Come to father!' **1955** P. WHITE *Tree of Man* 285 It is the telephone. It would drive you dilly. **1970** K. SLESSOR *Bread & Wine* 31 One translation which he has pencilled after the Latin words '*ocules languidum tuens*'—'with a dilly look in her eyes'.

dilly-bag.

1. DILLY *n.*

1867 F.J. BYERLEY *Narr. Overland Exped. Northern Qld.* 68 They . . brought them a villainous compound, in some dilly-bags. **1870** E.B. KENNEDY *Four Yrs. in Qld.* 80 'Dilly bags' were hung up to the trees; these are bags made of a sort of grass, and used by the Blacks for carrying ornaments in, such as coloured earths, to paint themselves with, ochre, feathers, necklaces of glass beads, hair nets; also knives made of flint, small tomahawks, etc. **1876** *Queenslander* (Brisbane) 23 Dec. 24/3 'What is there in the dilly-bag?' 'About enough beef and flour for a day's feed, and a pound of tea.'

of the body were found in her dilly-bag. **1902** *Bulletin* (Sydney) 25 Jan. 14/2 The dilly-bag of the Australian aborigine is a structure far in advance of her white sister's perishable reticule. **1915** J. BOWES *New Chums* 77 It is wonderful what a miscellaneous collection of odds and ends a dilly-bag will hold at times. **1930** HIVES & LUMLEY *Jrnl. of Jackaroo* 75 His spouse would follow with two 'dilly-bags', one made from plaited lawyer cane, and the other of bark. These dilly-bags were generally beautifully made, symmetrical in shape and very strong. They were carried on the back, the weight being supported by a strip of lawyer-cane in the form of a sling, which passed round the forehead. **1931** M.M. BANKS *Memories Pioneer Days Qld.* 46 'Dilly-bags' made of rushes, in which the babies slept peacefully. **1948** A. MARSHALL *Ourselves writ Strange* 167 A dilly bag made of plaited pandanus leaves hung suspended between her shoulders from a cord that passed across her forehead. **1962** D. LOCKWOOD *I, Aboriginal* 35 He handed me a crude dillybag made of grass, reeds and fabric. **1978** 'B. WONGAR' *Track to Bralgu* 25, I could hear Kua's teeth rattling with the cold, like the pebbles in a dilly bag. **1980** T.A. ROY *Vengeance of Dolphin* 170 She was carrying a woven string dilly-bag to carry the bones of Turrapini.

2. *transf.* A bag of any sort, usu. small (but see quot. 1969).

1906 E. DYSON *Roaring Fifties* 91 There's tea in the pannikin, an' . . grub in the dilly-bag. **1912** 'IRONBARK' *Ironbark Splinters* 25 Get some dilly-bags for rations, and, perhaps, a second shirt. **1917** *Bulletin* (Sydney) 18 Jan. 24/2 'Bill Bedsox' . . recommends the bushwhacker to wrap up his dillybag of flour in stout white cotton duck to protect it against the attack of mice. **1969** W. MOXHAM *Apprentice* 61 He checked the contents of his dilly bag: saddles, and he had some beauties, skull cap, goggles, whip, black boots . . . , white breeks and towels, lead bag. **1979** D. LOCKWOOD *My Old Mates & I* 142 She always finished last, but she always completed the course, carrying a dillybag, and wearing an old-fashioned dress and hat and long gloves. **1983** C. BINGHAM *Beckoning Horizon* 7 Anyway, we, the indomitable four, decided to clear out. But by the time our dilly-bags were ready, the afternoon light was beginning to fade.

dim-sim /dɪm-'sɪm/. [a. Cantonese *tim-sam* cake or snack.] A small roll of seasoned meat and vegetable encased in a thin dough and steamed or fried.

1961 X. HERBERT *Soldiers' Women* 174 He plied her with *dim-sims* and *sam-sui*, apparently content to rely on the alleged properties of the fare. **1972** *Bulletin* (Sydney) 26 Aug. 6/1 We are also the Dim Sim capital of the world. I wish I could give you conclusive evidence about the origins of the Dim Sim but there is little doubt that it was invented by the Chinese of Little Bourke Street to cater for our very complex palates.

din, ding, varr. GIN.

ding, *n.*[1] [Abbrev. of DINGBAT.]

1. An Italian (immigrant to Australia); a European (immigrant). Also *attrib.*

[**1922** *Bulletin* (Sydney) 17 Aug. 22/1, I once saw a couple of 'ding-bats' (Italians) place a packet of gelignite . . on a rock.] **1940** *Ibid.* 17 July 17/1 I've a yearning These city rags to doff And go where 'dings' are burning The northern paddock off. **1941** S.J. BAKER *Pop. Dict. Austral. Slang* 23 *Ding*, an Italian. **1948** K.S. PRICHARD *Golden Miles* 82 Sling backs to the shift boss got some men their jobs. Dings and dagoes were accused of making a regular practice of getting a job by this means. **1953** G.H. FEARNSIDE *Bayonets Abroad* 84 A little four-foot-nothing Eytie Major had the temerity to slap a six-foot Aussie's face, then ordered us penned up . . like so many sheep, while the Dings ran a fence around us. **1959** H. DRAKE-BROCKMAN *West Coast Stories* 176 The ding asked for this. Serves him bloody well right. **1965** R. STOW *Merry-Go-Round* 93 'The Dings have surrendered,' Kevin O'Hara shouted. 'Aw, they're always surrendering,' Graham said. 'No, this is dinkum, they've signed a treaty or something.' 'Gee,' said Rob. If Italy was really out of the war, then that might be after all the beginnings of peace. **1969** F.B. VICKERS *No Man is Himself* 15 There's a mob of miners out there with a load of grog. He reckons the Aussies and the Dings and the Balts are getting stuck into each other. **1974** N. PHILLIPSON *As Other Men* 35 They're full of Italians. . . Almost ninety per cent of the workers on this mine are dings! **1976** L.R.M. HUNTER *Woodline* 17 'How do you say 'wood' in Italian?' 'Aw!' said Johnny, 'I don't talk that ding language.' **1979** G. STEWART *Leveller* 24 No matter what race, Slav, Greek, Italian, Maltese, they were all Dings.

2. DINGBAT 2.

1943 S.W. KEOUGH *Around Army* 22 It will be no time at all before he is lending his boss a few 'onks' to tide him over till the ghost wanders, for a 'ding' is never broke.

ding, *n.*[2] [Shortened form of *ding-dong* or *wing-ding* noisy party.] A party. Also *attrib.*

1956 *Sydney Morning Herald* 15 Oct. 1/10 In New Guinea a party is called a 'ding'. **1963** F. GRANT *Death on my Wing* 28 It was ding night in a few hours with the grog ration together with any black market liquor that could be bought. **1967** J. HIBBERD *White with Wire Wheels* (1970) 218 Got a bucks' turn on tonight. One of my old schoolmates is signing his life away. Could be a wild ding. **1970** B. OAKLEY *Salute to Great McCarthy* 153 Here is McCarthy's name in the social page. As one of the guests at Miss Andrea Miller's ding at Portsea. **1973** W. MCNALLY *Man from Zero* 17 All the right people will be there. The State Governor, Sir William Morris, the Chief Justices, prominent members of the medical profession. It'll be a real ding!

ding, *n.*[3]

1. Abbrev. of DINGER: the backside; the penis.

1957 'N. CULOTTA' *They're Weird Mob* 106 Been sittin' on our dings the last 'alf hour. **1966** *Meanjin* 400 Stan was nicknamed Dinger because he had the biggest ding of the boys. **1967** *Kings Cross Whisper* (Sydney) xxxix. 8/4 *Too many bums on buses*. . . The surface area of the average Caucasian ding was 542 square inches (male) and 503 square inches (female). **1972** G. MORLEY *Jockey rides Honest Race* 209 You can get fined or sent to gaol for kicking a cat in the ding, but it's okay if it's a three-month old baby.

2. *transf.*

1967 V.G.C. NORWOOD *Long Haul* 34 Geoff inspected the gory 'roo meat. 'I'll give you half a quid for a ding (haunch),' he offered.

ding, *v. Obs.* [Br. dial. *ding* to throw, hurl, shake off: see EDD *v.*[1] 2.]

a. *trans.* To throw (something) away; to abandon (a course of action, etc.).

1812 J.H. VAUX *Mem.* (1819) II. 166 *Ding*, to throw, or throw away; particularly any article you have stolen, either because it is worthless, or that there is danger of immediate apprehension. **1829** *Sydney Monitor* 10 Oct. (Suppl.), The prisoner called out, 'ding that light, or I will blow your brains out'. **1847** A. HARRIS *Settlers & Convicts* (1953) 38, I shall get these boots and ding (throw away) mine. **1875** R. THATCHER *Something to his Advantage* 22 'Chopping Harry', though not wanting in pluck, declared the game to be up, and determined, in his own vernacular, to 'jack up and ding it altogether'. **1885** *Australasian Printers' Keepsake* 71 Declared that he was tired of Melbourne, 'full up of it' and would soon 'ding it altogether'. **1896** E. DYSON *Rhymes from Mines* 74 Ding it? No. Where gold was getting I was on the job, and early. **1903** J. FURPHY *Such is Life* 142 I'm as weak as a sanguinary cat. I must ding it.

b. *spec.* Of a female kangaroo: to discard (a joey) from the pouch (see quot. 1851).

1851 H. MELVILLE *Present State Aust.* 312 When hard pressed in running by the dogs, the mother 'dings her joey', that is, with her forepaws lifts the joey or young one out, and casts it into or alongside a bush or shelter of some kind, here the little thing nestles up and secretes itself; and if the mother escapes, she returns and takes charge of her little beloved. **1861** 'OLD BUSHMAN' *Bush Wanderings* 11 When the love of life overcomes the love of the mother, and she then casts it away to save herself. This, in bush phraseology, is termed 'dinging the joey'. **1869** 'E. HOWE' *Boy in Bush* 125 They saw the doe watching them, and then bounding to pick up once more the Joey she had 'dinged'. **1880** R. ROWE *Roughing It* 27 She put a forepaw into her pouch, and 'dinged the Joey', i.e., threw away her son. **1891** M. ROBERTS *Land-Travel & Sea-Faring* 159 The flying marsupial . . put its fore-paw into its pouch and threw away its young one, or in Australian parlance 'dinged the joey'.

dingbat. [Perh. f. *ding* (as a bell) + *bat*, joc. formation on *bats in the belfry*.]

1. A simpleton; a halfwit.

1918 *Bulletin* (Sydney) 11 Apr. 47/1 Simon stopped the fight outright by purchasing Bill and presenting him as mascot to the Second Battalion of the Fighting Dingbats. **1919** *Socialist* (Melbourne) 21 Mar. 3/4 The authorities issued brooms to the unfortunates to do the sweeping up. The 'dopy' ones, however, were not 'taking any', and after a consultation shouldered the brooms and tossed them over the fence to the 'sane' soldiers, with the remark, 'Here, you blokes are the ones to do this job.' Now, who are the 'lunatics'? *'Dingbat.'* **1946** R.H. CROLL *Smike to Bulldog* 62 The said little 'dingbat' left a note accepting it for £150. **1977** H. GARNER *Monkey Grip* 61 You mean *cartoons*, dingbat. **1980** C. JAMES *Unreliable Mem.* 160 Our office was a transit camp for dingbats. . . It was my first, cruel exposure to the awkward fact that the arts attract the insane.

2. *transf.* An army batman.

1918 *Aussie: Austral. Soldiers' Mag.* Feb. 4/2 He's not a bally Batman he's a Dingbat now, you know, We've changed his blessed monicker for keeps. **1940** *Bulletin* (Sydney) 3 Jan. 35/3 There is a vast difference between a dingbat in the British Army and one in the A.I.F. **1942** *Cry Havoc: H.M.S. 'Kanimbla'* iii. 25 My latest composition 'A Dingbat Sang in Martin Place'. **1943** S.W. KEOUGH *Around Army* 22 The officer importunate Soon finds that he's unfortunate—No dingbat worth his salt would, in his parlance, 'drag him on'. **1944** *Barging About: Organ 43 Austral. Landing Craft Co.* 1 Sept. 12 He is Scottie's dingbat. To hear him bawl out to the other boongs when they happen to collect some of Scottie's washing, is an education.

3. *pl.*

a. Delusions, esp. those characteristic of *delirium tremens*. Chiefly in the phr. **to have the** (or **to be**) **dingbats.**

[N.Z. **1911** *N.Z. Truth* (Wellington) 4 Nov. 6 The Taranaki horse led the big field home and paid a big dividend, which gives me dingbats every time I remember it.] **1920** *Aussie* (Sydney) Oct. 16/2 It was a bender—a dinkum jamboree—menageries of dingbats, tiger-headed snakes an' snake-headed tigers. **1925** A. WRIGHT *Boy from Bullarah* 66 It's enough to give a fellow the dingbats. I suppose you've been soaking this damn stuff. **1929** 'F. BLAIR' *Digger Sea-Mates* 128 'You've got 'em, Lockie,' said Tom. 'Got what, you ape?' 'The dinkum dingbats.' 'He'll have 'em worse after that whisky,' observed Kiley. **1939** M. MORRIS *Dark Tumult* 57 'If I like I can be the best player in Victoria, Australia, Southern Hemisphere, The World, Amen!' 'You've got dingbats,' said Robin. **1947** M. RAYMOND *Smiley gets Gun* 30 'You must be potty,' remarked the redhead. 'You must 'ave the dingbats.' **1957** J. HAWKE *Follow my Dust* 174 He'll be having the ding-bats in no time. Best thing is to wooden him with a shovel. **1970** N.A. BEAGLEY *Up & Down Under* 64 It dawned on me when I saw him in the morning that he was verging on the DT's or, in Aussie terms, 'the ding bats'.

b. As *adj.* Stupid; eccentric.

1950 *Bulletin* (Sydney) 13 Sept. 13/3 'Dingbats,' nodded Hal. 'Been livin' out with ol' Bill too long, I bet.' **1968** D. O'GRADY *Bottle of Sandwiches* 140 Aw, don't be dingbats. Crocs can't climb trees. **1972** *Bulletin* (Sydney) 12 Aug. 7/3 One woman called her husband a skite and a drongo, dingbats, up to putty, and not the full quid. **1981** P. BARTON *Bastards I have Known* 97 If you give a mob of sheep something to be frightened of they'll run like mad, but I've walked quietly into a paddock full of them and they just stand there and gawk at you. . . A mob of ambling shoppers are just as dingbats. **1983** *Weekend Austral. Mag.* (Sydney) 27 Aug. 20/8 Australian slanguage is well stocked with words and phrases to describe those who are a bit slow off the mental mark. . . Not the full quid. Mad as cut snakes. Dingbats, in fact.

dinger. [Perh. in punning allusion to *ring* anus.] The backside; the anus.

1943 J. BINNING *Target Area* 104 'Dinger', by the way, is a word born in the A.I.F. It describes, neatly, the place on which you sit. **1953** T.A.G. HUNGERFORD *Riverslake* 40 'He thinks the sun shines out of its dinger.' 'It's a decent sort of a cat, at that,' Randolph said. **1966** P. PINNEY *Restless Men* 59 'Righto, you fellers. Where's your tickets?' 'Up our dingers,' Loder snarled. **1969** *Kings Cross Whisper* (Sydney) lxxii. 1/3 Their benchmen in supporting roles Would sit upon their dingers. **1978**

L. HORSPHOL *Turn down Empty Glass* 38 I'd tell him to shove his job, huts and all, up his fuckin' dinger!

dingo /ˈdɪŋgoʊ/, *n.* Pl. **dingoes.** [a. Dharuk *diŋgu*.]

1. The native dog, *Canis familiaris dingo* of mainland Aust., typically tawny-yellow, apparently introduced by the Aborigines; *native dingo, dog,* see NATIVE *a.* 6 b.; WARRIGAL *n.* 1; *wild dog,* see WILD 1.

1789 W. TENCH *Narr. Exped. Botany Bay* 83 The only domestic animal they have is the dog, which in their language is called Dingo. **1798** D. COLLINS *Acct. Eng. Colony N.S.W.* I. 614 Tein-go, Din-go, Wor-re-gal = Dog. **1830** R. DAWSON *Present State Aust.* 178, I soon discovered that the native dogs, or dingo, as the natives call them, had made a charge. **1835** J. BATMAN *Settlement in Port Phillip* 29 May (1856) 11 With the cunning peculiar to the Australian dingo, he would not allow them to lay hands on him. **1840** A. RUSSELL *Tour through Austral. Colonies* 184 The runaway telling him he was travelling on a message, the native . . demanded a sight of the dingo (dog), meaning the unicorn in the royal arms of the passport, which every convict on leave carries. **1848** *Maitland Mercury* 12 July 2/5 The dingo, being liberated from his bag, in good trim, and allowed five minutes *law*, was well followed by all hands, stimulated by the glorious harmony of the pack, and after a run of about six miles in fifteen minutes, was killed amidst the death-whoop of the field. **1857** W. HOWITT *Tallangetta* II. 201 Strychnine had now decimated the dingoes, or wild dogs. **1865** *Illustr. Sydney News* 15 July 3/3 One of the greatest pests of the squatter is the dingo, or native dog—a mean contemptible brute. **1875** R. BRUCE *Dingoes* 80 Oft thro' the chilly winter's night . . Where nought is heard save curlew's cry, Or dingo's howl. **1886** P. CLARKE *'New Chum' in Aust.* 214 The dingo is a thief and a coward. **1909** W.G. SPENCE *Aust.'s Awakening* 189 He . . said they ought to be shot down like dingoes. **1914** R. KALESKI *Austral. Barkers & Biters* 16 More nonsense has been talked about the dingo than about any other animal in Australia. **1934** WARBURTON & ROBERTSON *Buffaloes* 42, I saw a big reddish-brown dingo almost as large as a full-grown Alsatian dog, playing with her five cubs. **1949** H.G. LAMOND *White Ears* 94 What's the good of keeping a dog-poisoner if he can't keep the place free of dingoes! **1965** R.H. CONQUEST *Horses in Kitchen* 189 We were like the dingoes in the back paddocks—sleek and contented. **1973** *Meanjin* 255 You men forget to look after yourselves. You're as lean as a dingo after a five year drought. **1980** *Canberra Times* 19 Aug. 7/3 Police at Alice Springs believe that if a dingo took the baby, she may never be found.

2. *fig.* A term applied to a person who displays characteristics popularly attributed to the dingo, esp. cowardice, treachery. Also *attrib.*

1869 'E. HOWE' *Boy in Bush* 2 He [*sc.* a bushranger] may well call himself Warrigal, the sneaking dingo! **1879** *Hist. Berry Ministry* 55 They called him a 'bad bargain', a 'run-down dingo, snapping right and left at everybody'. **1898** *Truth* (Sydney) 14 Aug. 2/5 To teach the people patience and innocence in the midst of craft and cruelty is to furnish the red-mouthed dingoes of society with woolly, bleating lambs. **1901** H.A. STUART *Bards of Burwood* 13 The dingo I never will show;—That is, I won't turn up the yellow. **1909** H.I. JENSEN *Rising Tide* 105 The existing dingoes of civilisation, by which term, I understand (unlike a Queensland politician of the old school who applied it to the tramps and swagmen), the individualists who fatten on the corpses of the working classes. **1915** *Truth* (Sydney) 13 June 10/3 Brutal garrotters continue to ply their evil calling . . and . . the police are continually running these dingoes of society to earth. **1932** J. TRURAN *Green Mallee* 98 Mother's pet delivered a kick under cover of the table. 'Ow, you little dingo,' she muttered angrily. **1947** W. LAWSON *Paddle-Wheels Away* 102 Come and fight, you dingoes. **1955** D. NILAND *Shiralee* 228 This hit-run driver, the dingo of the highway. **1966** A. HOPGOOD *Private Yuk Objects* 21 You bloody dingo. . . Ya could've given him a chance. **1978** C. GREEN *Sun is Up* 7 All politicians are dingoes. **1978** B. ST. A. SMITH *Spirit beyond Psyche* 49 He's not a dinkum RSL man, he's just a yellow, gutless, dingo cur.

3. Comb. **dingo hunter, -hunting, pack, -proof** *a.*, **scalp, scalper, trap, trapper.**

1908 *Emu* VIII. 42 He is a genuine student of the bush, besides being a successful **dingo-hunter.** **1927** J. POLLARD *Rose of Bushlands* 22 As a dingo-hunter he had long been used to moonlight shooting. **1939** *Bulletin* (Sydney) 21 June 21/4 Most capable dingo-hunter I ever came across was a woman. **1962** MARSHALL & DRYSDALE *Journey among Men* 56 The dogger, or dingo hunter, is an almost incredibly skilled bushman. **1862** G.T. LLOYD *Thirty-Three Yrs. Tas. & Vic.* 384 **Dingo** (native fox) **hunting** . . formed one of the principal sources of amusement. **1892** *Bulletin* (Sydney) 19 Mar. 11/1 We swung with the stride of the **dingo-pack.** **1964** 'E. LINDALL' *Kind of Justice* 22 The sheep station had gone down to the dingo packs. **1968** *How Collinsville was Won* (Trades & Labor Council Qld.) 35 Fights broke out . . one against one, and not the sort of dingo pack attack which the scabs themselves had used on previous occasions. **1925** M. TERRY *Across Unknown Aust.* 96 Proper wire-fenced paddocks . . with **dingo-proof** netting. **1939** C. SEMMLER *World of Banjo Paterson* (1967) 41 Part of the run was enclosed by a dingo-proof fence of thirteen wires, with a strand of barbed wire at top and bottom. **1949** G. FARWELL *Traveller's Tracks* 21 Each of them has some twenty miles of dingo-proof fencing to protect against encroaching sandhills. **1898** *Western Champion* (Barcaldine) 11 Jan. 2/2 **Dingo scalps** to the number of 2042 have been received and paid for. **1931** *Bulletin* (Sydney) 21 Jan. 21/4 Bourneman was a **dingo scalper**, a taciturn man. **1963** W.E. HARNEY *To Ayers Rock & Beyond* 40 He was one of those tough and wiry types, who as 'doggers' or 'dingo-scalpers' helped open this land. **1911** ST. C. GRONDONA *Collar & Cuffs* 51 The poor unfortunate turkey had been caught in a **dingo trap.** **1923** J. BOWES *Jackaroos* 81 When I . . ask questions 'e shuts up like a dingo trap. **1927** J. POLLARD *Rose of Bushlands* 123 He rode to Nestor's to get that dingo-trap. **1930** 'BRENT OF BIN BIN' *Ten Creeks Run* (1952) 28, I want to see what the **dingo-trappers** are after. **1955** F. LANE *Patrol to Kimberleys* 9 The talk and laughter of the stockmen and drovers, sheep-shearers, dingo-trappers and prospectors would ring throughout the township. **1963** S. MUSSEN *Beating about Bush* 96 The only other customer in the café was a dingo-trapper.

4. Special Comb. **dingo fence,** a fence erected to exclude dingoes; **-slut,** a female dingo; **stiffener,** one employed to eradicate dingoes.

1914 'B. CABLE' *By Blow & Kiss* 30 The others found Steve waiting for them at the **dingo fence** of the back paddock. **1967** M. SELLARS *Carramar* 15 I'm trying to imagine that eight-foot high dingo fence. Was it 6,500 miles long you said? **1983** *Open Road* Aug. 19/1 The world's longest fence—the dingo fence . . stretches from the Gulf of Carpentaria to the Indian Ocean. **1899** *Bulletin* (Sydney) 4 Feb. 14/1 When a **dingo-slut** produces a litter of pups she leaves them in charge of a mate. **1900** *Ibid.* 12 May 15/1 The ordinary kangaroo dog will not kill a dingo slut. **1938** *Ibid.* 29 June 21/2 A red dingo slut was trapped and shot on a Wilga selection. **1945** *Ibid.* 31 Jan. 14/1 The rewards hung up for **dingo-stiffeners.** Northern Territory offered a measly seven and sixpence per head. **1949** I.L. IDRIESS *One Wet Season* 115 The first three camels he bought cheaply from a wandering dingo-stiffener.

5. In the collocation **dingo's breakfast**: see quots.

1965 K. MCKENNEY *Hide-Away Man* 101 'Here's yer dinner,' he said, adding with a wink 'I already had me breakfast.' 'What was that?' 'Dingo's breakfast. A piss and a look around.' **1976** B. SCOTT *Compl. Bk. Austral. Folk Lore* 380 A dingo's breakfast is a pee and a good look round.

dingo /ˈdɪŋgoʊ/, *v.* [f. prec.] *intr.* To behave in a cowardly manner. Also with **it.**

1942 *Sun* (Sydney) 26 Aug. 4/9 A man who avoids an unpleasant job is said to dingo it. **1951** E. LAMBERT *Sleeping House Party* 335 'Where is Allison?' 'He dingoed at the last minute.' **1960** R.S. PORTEOUS *Cattleman* 161 'Lay orf. . . I'm done.' The man who had backed Ben for a fiver yelled, 'Don't let 'im dingo on ya, mate. Finish 'im off!' **1981** L. MCLEAN *Pumpkin Pie* 24 Habbie could have outrun him, but had been taught never to 'dingo' it and would stand and fight.

dingy, *a.* Of a fleece: see quots.

1891 *Truth* (Sydney) 19 Apr. 7/3 A lady . . who, if passing through the wool-classer's hands, would have been chucked into the *Dingy* bin. **1914** H.B. SMITH *Sheep & Wool Industry* 182 *Dingy*, yellow and discoloured wool, usually very heavy in condition. **1921** L.G. JONES *Flockmaster's Companion* 77 *Dingy* denotes that there is a general deficiency in colour, the fleece being dark yellow, dull and heavy. **1950** H.G. BELSCHNER *Sheep Managem. & Diseases* 695 *Dingy*, a term applied to wool lacking brightness, possibly the result of excessive yolk, unfavourable environment, or presence of external parasites. **1951** *Concerning Wool* (Austral. Wool Board) 99 *Dingy*, wool of poor colour, carrying excessive yellow yolk, which may not scour white. **1970** HARMSWORTH & PAGE-SHARP *Sheep & Wool Classing* 63 Yolk stained, yellowish, dingy, canary stained, green coloured, or fern-stained fleeces should not be blended with white fleeces.

dink, *n.* [Perh. f. Br. dial. *dink* to dandle a baby: see EDD *v.*[1]] A lift on a bicycle, or a horse, ridden by another. Also **double dink,** and, as *adv.*, **double dinkie.**

1934 *Bulletin* (Sydney) 5 Sept. 20/1 Victorian philologists are becoming alarmed over an outbreak in the State schools of a new form of slang. Two words in particular have gained great popularity—'dink' and 'pug'. These are, apparently, both used to express a request for a double-bank ride. The fortunate Melbourne schoolkid with a bike, when time comes to go home, is asked by his cobbers for a 'dink'. **1965** L. WALKER *Other Girl* 173 Of course, riding home, double-dinkie on a bronco, was part of it too. **1976** K. BROWN *Knock Ten* 95 'Tell you what, let's get him a bike between us . . ?' He really felt he was a lucky bloke. He said so to me, giving me a ride double-dink after school. **1981** G. MACKENZIE *Aurukun Diary* 25 These two were children who loved a 'double-dink' on my horse behind me, clutching fast to my belt.

dink, *v.* [f. prec.] *trans.* To carry (a passenger) on a bicycle or a horse. Also **double-dink.** See also DOUBLE-BANK 3.

1941 S.J. BAKER *Pop. Dict. Austral. Slang* 23 *Double-dink*, to carry a second person on the top bar of a bicycle. . . Exchangeable terms are 'dink' . . and 'double-bank'. **1942** E. LANGLEY *Pea Pickers* 34 [He] pityingly offered to 'double dink' me. My shame had double damned me, and now, double dinked, I bent over the bar of Kelly's bike and off we went. **1948** *Coast to Coast 1947* 135 The lame one who used to let me dink him home on his bicycle. **1964** P. ADAM SMITH *Hear Train Blow* 186 She suggested we should bring her lunch in each day using Kevin's bicycle for transport. We took it in turns 'dinking' one another. **1968** M.T. CLARK *Spark of Opal* 142 No, she certainly didn't look as though she could ride a bike, or even be dinked. **1979** S. MORRISON *Who's taking you to Dance* 49 'Can you dink me down to the car?'. . . He hops on to the bike seat. **1981** B. DICKINS *Gift of Gab* 22 My mother dinked me on her green pushbike to the dentist's. **1981** B. GREEN *Small Town Rising* 36 After school the cubs rushed for their bikes. The motley crew—some being double-dinked—shot through the town to the park.

dink, *a.* and *adv.* Abbrev. of DINKUM *a.* and *adv.* Also **dinks.**

1906 E. DYSON *Fact'ry 'Ands* 92 'Twasn't fair dink t' go outside ther firm. **1914** —— *Spats' Fact'ry* 89 Whatsa matter with the offer? It's fair dink, I tell yeh. **1918** L.J. VILLIERS *Changing Yr.* 14 'Ooever put the cow outer my name Is square dink fer a cert ter stop a clout. **1919** *Aussie: Austral. Soldiers' Mag.* Jan. 16/2 Gawd spare me days, there was something doing fair dink., Dig. **1974** J. JOST *This is Harry Flynn* 41 The bottle was empty but he sucked at it . . without realising the liquor was gone. 'I have got a secret, true dinks.' **1980** C. LEE *Bush Week* 82 They said he was a traitor. I've got to get down to Melbourne to see if he's dink.

dinki-di, dinkie-di, varr. DINKY-DI.

dinkum /ˈdɪŋkəm/, *n.* [Br. dial. *dinkum* work, a due share of work: see EDD.]

1. *Obs.* Work, exertion.

1888 'R. BOLDREWOOD' *Robbery under Arms* (1937) 35 It took us an hour's hard dinkum to get near the peak.

2. *Hist.* In the war of 1914–18: a member of the 2nd Division of the Australian Imperial Forces (see quots. 1917 and 1919).

1916 *Desert Dust Bin: Official Organ 3rd L.H.F.A.* 3 May 8/1 Anzac Day today. The 'Dinkums' put on blue ribbons. **1917** C.E.W. BEAN *Lett. from France* 224 The sort of Australian who used to talk about our 'tinpot navy' labelled the Australians who rushed at the chance of adventure the moment the recruiting lists were opened 'the six bob a day tourists'. Well—the 'Tourists' made a name for Australia such as no other Australians can ever have the privilege to make. The next shipment were the 'Dinkums'—the men who came over on principle to fight for Australia—the real, fair dinkum Australians. **1918** *Kia Ora Coo-ee* Aug. 19/1, I am absolutely certain that every man in the Londoners will always have a soft corner in his heart for the cheery 'Dinkum'. **1918** F. KNOWLES *With Dinkums* 4 Turn over the pages and let the work itself tell you the real story of the 'Dinkums'. **1919** W.H. DOWNING *Digger Dialects* 19 *Dinkums (the)*, the 2nd Division. Also applied to the New Zealanders.

3. *Obs.* Accurate information, the *dinkum oil* (see OIL *n.* 2).

1916 'MEN OF ANZAC' *Anzac Bk.* 56, I was on the beach one day when a friend met me and asked if I had heard the latest dinkum. **1933** *Bulletin* (Sydney) 22 Feb. 34/2 First time I have a cert I'll pass the dinkum to you.

dinkum /'dɪŋkəm/, *a.* and *adv.* [f. prec.]

A. *adj.*

1. Reliable; genuine; honest; true.

[N.Z. **1905** *N.Z. Truth* (Wellington) 10 Oct. 3 Our sergeant said he would walk from [Palmerston North] to Ashurst to see a 'dinkum go'.] **1908** E.G. MURPHY *Jarrahland Jingles* 168 When up I brings me plumber's kit, An' gives 'em dinkum gabbie. **1916** 'MEN OF ANZAC' *Anzac Bk.* 22 An' 'ere's some er the dinkum coc'nut-ice the tart uster make. **1916** *Bulletin* (Sydney) 10 Aug. 22/3 Someone asked for a cure for mange in horses. The following is certified as being dinkum. **1918** R.H. KNYVETT *Over there with Australs.* 130 One of these spies was only discovered through misuse of a well-known Australian slang word... He was getting a lot of information and seemed to know several officers' names, but he bungled over one of them, and on the officer he was speaking to enquiring, 'Is that dinkum?' he answered: 'Yes, *that's* his name!' There was no further investigation, he was shot on the spot. **1920** *Aussie* (Sydney) Apr. 31/2 'Eh, Padre,' he drawled, 'is that furphy about Christ riding into Jerusalem on the back of a donkey dinkum?' **1924** F.J. MILLS *Happy Days* 149 The Kaiser has abducted himself from his throne. It's dinkum. I just got the telegram! **1927** F.C. BIGGERS *Bat-Eye* 22 Now, sheelahs 'oo 'ave any sort uv decent look Gits plenty blokes, an' some is dinkum, some is crook. **1939** J. SORENSEN *Lost Shanty* 15 With their soft voices sweetly mingling, They sang as only dinkum Angels sing. **1944** C. WILMOT *Tobruk* 211 He was rough, but he was dinkum. **1963** R.H. CONQUEST *Spurs are Rusty Now* 24 They presented me with a saddle. They reckoned I was now entitled to call myself a dinkum Queenslander. **1968** S. GORE *Holy Smoke* 55 'Well, stone the crows!' say the crew. 'His God musta been dinkum after all.' **1974** *Bulletin* (Sydney) 5 Jan. 11/2 Among the 30 foot to 80 foot boats.. is one that sounds almost too dinkum to be true—Gumblossom. **1976** T. SHEPHERD *Children of Blindness* 9 He was a real dinkum bloke. **1978** E. HARDING *A. Marshall Talking* 122, I said, 'If you're dinkum, I'll help you. I'll write you a testimonial or something', because I was pretty sure he was really quite intelligent. **1984** *Sydney Morning Herald* 9 Feb. 1/8 Jim Kable believes that 'dinkum' may come from the Cantonese expression 'din kum', meaning real gold. It would have come he says, from Chinese workers during the gold rush. Below are the Cantonese characters for 'din kum'.

2. In collocations: **dinkum Aussie, digger.**

1920 A. L'HOTELLIER *Green Fields of Paraguay* 12 And we lead the van, for every man Is a **dinkum Aussie**, see; And we never turn back till we've cut a track On the page of history. **1921** F. GROSE *Rough Y.M. Bloke* 26 Another bloke in uniform opened the door and he went to take my 'at as I walked in, but I wasn't 'avin' any, fer it was a dinkum Aussie, and I've lorst 'em like that before. **1934** E.J. BRADY *Doctor Mannix* 228 Henceforward, the Archbishop of Melbourne would be classed as a 'dinkum Aussie' among those who loved Australia for Australia's sake. **1940** A. HASKELL *Waltzing Matilda* 27 The black-and-white magpie is the first 'dinkum Aussie'. **1954** J. WATEN *Unbending* 30 'You'll be a dinkum Aussie soon, Kochansky,' he said. **1972** *Bulletin* (Sydney) 26 Feb. 11/2, I like to think that the Belgravia job was done by dinkum Aussies. **1984** *Canberra Times* 11 Feb. 7/2 The kangaroo is a dinkum Aussie. **1919** *Ross's Monthly* Sept. 13/1 He's a **dinkum Digger**, Billy (but he doesn't wear a crutch)—and what he'll say and what he'll do, it—doesn't matter much. **1920** *Huon Times* (Franklin) 19 Mar. 3/4, I have known dinkum diggers to labor under the impression that they were poets when they were merely sundowners, and sundowners when they were merely poets! **1945** A.G. BUTLER *Digger* 16 The highest compliment that might be paid to the highest in the land would be to acclaim him 'a dinkum Digger'! **1956** S. HOPE *Diggers' Paradise* 11 To hear the dinkum Diggers talk, though, you would imagine that they were a race apart; a people who had inhabited the land for two or three thousand years instead of, in most cases, two or three generations. **1965** E. LAMBERT *Long White Night* 8 They were dinkum diggers and bronzed Anzacs all over again. They were perpetuating the Australian Myth.

3. In the collocation **dinkum oil:** see OIL *n.* 2.

B. *adv.* (also) interrog. and as an asseveration: really; truly; honestly; honourably.

1915 T. SKEYHILL *Soldier-Songs from Anzac* 9, I was sittin' in me dug-out, An' was feelin' dinkum good, Chewin' Queensland bully beef, An' biscuits 'ard as wood. **1917** C.L. DREW *Reminisc. D. Gilbert* 54 It's dinkum good stuff. It'll cure any snake-bite in the world! **1919** —— *Doings of Dave* 58, I gave you credit for having better sense. Dinkum, I did. **1920** H.F. MOLLARD *Humour of Road* 189, I fixed up with the widder dinkum this time, and she's going to marry what's left of me in London when I can hop about a bit. **1924** F.J. MILLS *Happy Days* 120 Yes, the little Digger would go to both poles after a skirt, but believe me, friend, he always treated 'em dinkum. He was out for fun, mind you, but he never forgot that 'e has sisters. **1930** V. PALMER *Passage* (1957) 116 'It was really like that?' 'Yes; dinkum.' **1941** *Coast to Coast* 14 'He wanted one you couldn't open from inside.' 'Dinkum?' the clerk asked. 'On my oath,' the waiter said... 'Jesus!' the clerk said. **1946** 'A. SPENCE' *Mystery of Red Gum* 24 People will be breaking their necks to know you! Dinkum! **1957** V. PALMER *Rainbow-Bird* 5 It's a fact. Dinkum. **1960** L.H. EVERS *Make Way for Tomorrow* 43 'You a Park Ranger?' 'A Park Ranger? No I'm not a Park Ranger.' 'Dinkum?' 'Dinkum.' **1968** *Swag* (Sydney) i. 19/1 Last week he was on with a countess, dinkum. **1975** X. HERBERT *Poor Fellow my Country* 213, I didn't have nothing to do with it... Dinkum. They jes sprung it on me.

C. In the collocation **fair (square, straight) dinkum.**

a. Used with reference to an action, pattern of behaviour, etc., which complies with an accepted code: 'fair play'. Freq. as *exclam.*

1890 A.S. DAY *Democrat* 23 Right ye are partner Dingy, and mind ye, when the job's done, fair dinkum. **1891** 'SMILER' *Wanderings Simple Child* (ed. 3) 129 'Let's have fair dinkum,' yells Tom, and the next moment he was under the table. **1895** *Bulletin* (Sydney) 10 Aug. 7/2 Every sinful calico-jimmy roaming at large is an insult to the doctrine of 'fair dinkum' which all men, rogues or otherwise, hold in respect. **1908** 'FIFTY-THREE YRS.' MINER' *So Long* 116 'Fair dinkum', don't deceive me. **1911** 'S. RUDD' *Bk. of Dan* 34 '*Off! Off!* Let go!' Dan cried, assuming the office of referee. 'Square dinkum!' **1924** J. HARPER *Splashes from Narran* 30 Then Gallant Captain Albert With a love for what is right, Jumped in to see fair dinkum And to try and stop the fight.

b. As adj. phr. in emphatic senses of DINKUM *a.*

1890 *Quiz* (Adelaide) 5 Dec. 6/3 In what Literary Society are the terms, 'That's fair dinkum' and 'Oh, yes, whips' to be heard? **1904** *Sporting News* (Launceston) 5 Mar. 1/3 'Oh, it's straight dinkum. You needn't look like that,' he continued. **1908** T.E. SPENCER *Budgeree Ballads* 83 It's fair dinkum what I'm tellin' yer. **1912** *Truth* (Sydney) 17 Mar. 6/5 Admission was by *ticket only* and one had to be a double-barrelled, A1 at Lloyd's, hall-marked, square-dinkum anti-Home Ruler. **1918** R.H. KNYVETT *Over there with Australs.* 82 They even knew our slang for here was 'The Fair Dinkum' Store', and across the way 'Ribuck Goods'. **1934** *Austral. Ring* IX. cviii. 13 You vow that wrestling bouts are 'fair-dinkum'. **1938** F. CLUNE *Free & Easy Land* 151 After the duffer at Canoona, a fair dinkum gold-mine was found. **1939** FRANKLIN & CUSACK *Pioneers on Parade* 109 It seemed as if Ninny's week-end in the genuinely dinky-di, the really square-dinkum Australian bush was not to be so enjoyable as loyal Australians could wish. **1944** A.S. SMITH *Boys write Home* 120 The message brought to us later from a high officer was a gem—mainly because it was a fair dinkum message. **1952** *Coast to Coast 1951–52* 137 Wonder how much of that hoo-hooing in the back seat is fair dinkum. The way women go on at a funeral makes me sick. **1962** V.C. HALL *Dreamtime Justice* 21 Stabbing a hole in the paperbark, he gave way to the pleasures of anticipation. This was going to be a fair dinkum smoke-oh. **1965** R.H. CONQUEST *Horses in Kitchen* 39 Young bushies believed in fair dinkum stoush; the art of fisticuffs was unknown to them. **1969** F. MOORHOUSE *Futility & Other Animals* 86 The old man was fair dinkum and had to bludge a living. **1974** *Bulletin* (Sydney) 12 Jan. 16/2 The families have refused to talk to Federal officials... 'The people in Canberra', he said, 'aren't fair dinkum.' **1981** Q. WILD *Honey Wind* 126 It's got to be Australia again and not inter-continental-land, that bastardised version of borrowed ideas from abroad. It's got to be fair dinkum. **1983** *Cattleman* (Brisbane) Jan. 10/2 Effectively, this meant no new speculators and only 'fair dinkum' hedgers could enter the market.

c. As adv. phr. in emphatic senses of DINKUM *adv.*

1894 A.B. BELL *Austral. Camp Fire Tales* 115 Now Mr Montmorency own up like a man. Wasn't the half of it carried away before they got them ships? Square dinkum, now how about the Goodwin Sands. **1905** *Steele Rudd's Mag.* (Brisbane) Aug. 750 You promist me fust, you won' make .. er drink nothing nasty... You promist me? Straight dinkum? **1910** *Truth* (Sydney) 13 Mar. 11/6 And now, straight dinkum! d'yever see a bloke in such a twig? **1910** L. ESSON *Three Short Plays* (1911) 9 *Smith*: 'Ain't she er 'igh stepper? 'Ad er barney, Chopsey?' *Chopsey*: 'T'aint nuthin'.' *Smith*: 'Fair dinkum?' **1915** *Honk* x. 1 If you let that collection of old bones pull your pile of rotten wood into my lorry I'll blanky well rub you all over the blanky street. And that's fair dinkum! **1918** L.J. VILLIERS *Changing Yr.* 18 'Ere's fer a bit o' kid done up all sweet. This June is like a fancy line o' frill Fair dinkum white. **1923** J. ARMOUR *Spell of Inland* 9 Yes, I'm the new parson for Angoranna. My name is Robertson. Square dinkum, what do you think of me? **1926** E. CONNOLLY *How E. Connolly bets & Wins* 6 The faces of many racecourse rogues are the only honest features about them—they look rogues, and, fair dinkum, they *are rogues.* **1935** K.L. SMITH *Sky Pilot Arnhem Land* 40 No, fair dinkum, there are two white women at Urapungie Station, four miles away. **1944** A.S. SMITH *Boys write Home* 154 Fair dinkum, Mum, Lieut. Brown deserved a V.C. for what he did that day. **1947** M. RAYMOND *Smiley gets Gun* 9 'Damn!' echoed Blue. 'Oo, you swore!' exclaimed a little girl. 'Damn!' repeated Smiley. 'That's what the master said.' 'Dinkum?' 'Square dinkum! Damn, damn, damn!' **1956** K. HAYLES *Long Reach* 163 'Yu-ah. Fair dinkum we go walkabout,' Othello said. **1964** A. STAPLES *Paddo* 115 He jobs me in front of everyone... Fair dinkum, Mum, I don't know what you use for feelings, because I've never seen any. **1969** B. BREYDOR *You oughta seen Us* 153 'Aussies, eh? Fair dinkum! Beauty, mate!' And laughing loudly he went through a whole string of Aussie slang. **1975** D.J. TOWNSHEND *Gland Time* 54 'Ya know old Burt's just told me he's packin' up in a month?' 'Fair dinkum?' Pinhead was astounded. **1986** *Muse Communique* Apr. 21 On the corner a wire-framed Mirror poster swears *Cancer cure—fair dinkum.*

dinky-di /'dɪŋki-daɪ/, *a.* and *adv.* Also **dinkie-di, dinky-die.**

A. *adj.* DINKUM *a.*

1918 N. CAMPBELL *Dinky-Di Soldier* 5 An' I lines up nex' day with some more o' th' mob, An' they makes me a dinky-di soldier! **1923** *Bulletin* (Sydney) 20 Dec. 24/3 The old dinky-di damper was nothing else but flour, water and salt, mixed as stiff as possible and baked in a hole in the white floury ashes. **1929** 'F. BLAIR' *Digger Sea-Mates* 36 'You're the dinkie-die legpuller, Blair,' said he. **1941** B. PENTON *Think* 47 A Labour Government once appointed an Australian Governor-General... The most dinky-di, republican Aussie did not quite feel it was the real thing. **1945** 'MASTER-SARG' *Yank discovers Aust.* 64 This one was dinkum (which is Aussie for O.K.). When an Aussie wants you to believe him he will say 'That's dinky di', which means it is gospel truth. **1956** S. HOPE *Diggers' Paradise* 237 Apparently, no one but dinky-di Aussies need submit a manuscript however talented he might be. **1965** R.H. CONQUEST *Horses in Kitchen* 123 His best friend in Burgoo Gully was a stock agent who was a dinky-di Englishman. **1972** R. MAGOFFIN *Chops & Gravy* 10 Alan McClure's drawings are dinky-dye stuff too and I am always intrigued by the way in which he so accurately brings my words to life. **1977** F.B. VICKERS *Stranger no Longer* 82 It stuck in his gizzard that a Pom should be the boss of the board in a shearing shed—a dinky-di Aussie domain. **1978** K. GARVEY *Tales of my Uncle Harry* 8, I have striven with all my stubborn jingoistic nature to keep them 'dinkie die Aussie'. **1980** J. HOLMAN *Aussies* 23 Well, we got jobs only for dinki-di Aussies right now, mate, but if you'll try somewhere else, maybe you'll have more luck! **1981** Q. WILD *Honey Wind* 131 Ginger was dinky-di. His voice was broad and rawly accented with an occasionally nasal high-pitched twang of dry, sardonic humour. **1984** *Canberra Times* 12 Feb. 2/1 The gallery has nothing of the ocker oeuvre of Rolf Harris, that dinky-di da Vinci.

B. *adv.* DINKUM *adv.*

1915 G.F. MOBERLY *Experiences 'Dinki-Di' R.R.C. Nurse* (1933) 12 Dinki di, boy, how sadly I miss you. **1933** H.B. RAINE *Whip-Hand* 46 You see this bumper I'm smokin'? Well, Lofty could stand over there and nick off the ash without touchin' the rest of the fag. Dinky di. **1938** F. BLAKELEY *Hard Liberty* 69 'Yes,' said Dick, 'Dinky-die dead drunk, and buried so.' **1968** S. GORE *Holy Smoke* 47 Dinky die—was it three, or wasn't it?

dinner.

1. A meal eaten at mid-day, but not the principal meal of the day; lunch.

1911 A. WRIGHT *Gamblers' Gold* (1923) 110 Work started with the rising sun, and ceased when darkness fell. . . During that time there was a break for dinner and a couple of smoke ohs! At sundown one man would go to the camp to prepare the evening meal. **1914** C. MACKNESS *Gem of Flat* 61 The school lunch-time was supposed to last from half past twelve to two, but it had long been limited to half-an-hour, for all the children brought their 'dinners' with them. **1918** B. REYNOLDS *Dawn Asper* 176 It was nearing noon . . and the family were gathering round the long table for that substantial meal called dinner in the back country. **1954** H.G. LAMOND *Manx Star* 45 Then men pulled up for lunch—or dinner, as they call it in the bush—at a small water-hole. **1963** M. BRITT *Pardon my Boots* 32 By midday—'dinner-time'—we had mustered a small mob and driven them into a corner of the paddock. **1977** J. O'GRADY *There was Kid* 57 Our midday meal was called 'dinner', and the more substantial evening one was always known as 'tea'. It still is in many parts of Australia.

2. In the phr. **to do like a dinner,** to defeat; to outwit (usu. in passive).

1847 A. HARRIS *Settlers & Convicts* (1953) 38 If we don't give the rain time to wash out the horse-tracks we shall be done like a dinner. **1893** WHITWORTH & WINDAS *Shimmer of Silk* 13 If you don't, it's another thing, and of course you're done like a dinner. **1895** A.B. PATERSON *Man from Snowy River* 13 We saw we were done like a dinner—The odds were a thousand to one. **1965** W. DICK *Bunch of Ratbags* 236 Chassa came out from behind the counter and done him like a dinner and threw him out the door. **1973** J. POWERS *Last of Knucklemen* (1974) 60 On two legs I'd do you like a dinner, Horse. Even on one I wouldn't write meself off. **1978** C. GREEN *Sun is Up* 11 Anyway, within a week I had old Splinters Maloney the fishing inspector knocking on me door wanting to see me licence. Of course I was done like a dinner.

3. Special Comb. **dinner camp,** (in stock droving) the mid-day break; the place where such a break is taken; see also CAMP *n.* 3; so **dinner-camp** *v. intr.*; hee also CAMP *v.* 2.

1925 M. TERRY *Across Unknown Aust.* 81 At dinner camp that day (midday). **1937** E. HILL *Great Austral. Loneliness* 90 We dinner-camped at Broken Wagon, a billabong of the Fitzroy. **1938** *Bulletin* (Sydney) 12 Jan. 21/3 We were on dinner camp, and the sheep were quietly resting in the river bed. **1947** W.E. HARNEY *Brimming Billabongs* 107 A place would be chosen as dinner camp, and to this spot the pack-horses would go, to be unpacked by the cook and horse tailer so that we could have dinner as soon as we arrived. **1953** H.G. LAMOND *Big Red* 12 They rested during the middle of the day at their dinner-camp. *Ibid.* 56 The 'roos returned one day to their recognized dinner-camp. **1960** R.S. PORTEOUS *Cattleman* 88 They were stringing the cattle off the dinner camp when the policeman rode up. **1976** C.D. MILLS *Hobble Chains & Greenhide* 26 When I was ringing on the road, we were up at about four o'clock, set off with the bullocks at daylight, and fed them as we tailed them along the outside of the track. We had our two to three hours on dinner-camp, ate, slept, stood our watch, and went back to sleep again. Whoever took the dinner-camp watch had the afternoon off. **1976** L. BEADELL *Beating about Bush* 7, I had purposely made the road close to that scraggy tree with a view to its helping some future traveller to boil his billy and have his 'dinner camp' in the twelve per cent protection it afforded from the blazing summer sun. **1978** K. GARVEY *Tales of my Uncle Harry* 21 One day when we were on the dinner camp, up walks a curvy little cattle bitch. **1980** ANSELL & PERCY *To fight Wild* 120 Luke asked Big Rupert where the crossing was, where they were going to stop for dinner camp (lunch). **1981** G. MACKENZIE *Aurukun Diary* 33 Up over rocky ledge to swamp where we dinner-camped.

dinnyhayser /dɪni'heɪzə/. Also **dinnyazer.** [Of unknown origin.]

1. A knockout blow.

1907 N.F. SPIELVOGEL *Cocky Farmer* 14, I gets a dennyaiser in the eye, and sits down suddenly. **1929** *Aussie* (Sydney) Apr. 52/2 One of them, known as Kangaroo Jack, gave him the k.o. with a dinnyazer on the jaw. **1946** K.S. PRICHARD *Roaring Nineties* 28 He could have laid Frisco out long before he did, got him dancing mad and blowing like a grampus before he let him have a dinnyazer that knocked him. **1984** W.W. AMMON et al. *Working Lives* 85 Sometimes he let his dinnyhazer go with such viciousness that Stevie shook his head.

2. *fig.*

1949 I.L. IDRIESS *One Wet Season* 141 Here . . the teamsters have their 'last drink'. A dinnyhayser, at times. . . They had one hundred and twenty-six bottles of whisky and four dozen cases of beer. They drank the lot in eight days! **1966** D.E. CHARLWOOD *Afternoon of Time* 80 'Gunna be a dinnyhazer of a storm,' said Percy.

dip, *n. Obs.* See quot. 1847. See also DOUGHBOY.

1847 D. BUNCE *Australasiatic Reminisc.* 21 Apr. (1857) 171 Dr Leichhardt ordered the cook to mix up a lot of flour, and treated us all to a feed of dips. These were made as follows:- a quantity of flour was mixed up with water, and stirred with a spoon to a certain consistency, and dropped into a pot of boiling water, a spoonful at a time. Five minutes boiling was sufficient, when they were eaten with the water in which they were boiled. **1888** J.F. MANN *Eight Months with Dr Leichhardt* 40 As the last piece of meat had been consumed . . a small additional amount of flour was issued and made into 'dips'—that is, paste dropped from a spoon into boiling water.

dip, *v.*

1. In the phr. **to dip one's lid,** to raise one's hat as a mark of respect. Chiefly *fig.*

1915 C.J. DENNIS *Songs of Sentimental Bloke* 21 'This 'ere's Doreen,' 'e sez. 'This 'ere's the Kid.' I dips me lid. **1938** F. CLUNE *Free & Easy Land* 104, I dipped my lid as we approached the ruins. **1947** —— *Roaming around Aust.* 7 Below us was a cultivated patch, with a few galvanised iron roofs, showing where some rugged battler was trying to coax Nature to give him a living. I 'dips me lid' to him, whoever he is. **1950** J. CLEARY *Just let me Be* 6 'You still do that. . . Why?' 'What?' 'That dipping your lid when you pass the church.' **1957** R. SINGLETON *March Past* 16 And here I stood and dipped my 'lid', For I could almost swear Six martyred shades of Dorset men Had gathered round him there. **1958** F.B. VICKERS *Though Poppies Grow* 134 I'll walk with Protestant and Roman as I've told you, and dip the lid to no bastard. **1967** *Bulletin* (Sydney) 28 Jan. 17/3 We dips our lids to Charles Higham for his article 'The Anti-Star System'. **1977** P. ADAMS *Unspeakable Adams* 165, I resolve to treat each and every dustbin night as a sort of sacrament, as an opportunity to salute my fellow man. In the immortal words of that beloved Australian poet, C.J. Dennis, I dips me lid. **1984** *Sydney Morning Herald* 9 July (Guide) 16/3 So now three journalists, White, Day and Thomson, own a radio station. Us ordinary journos dips our lids.

2. In the phr. **to dip out (on),** to fail, to miss (an opportunity, etc.)

1952 T.A.G. HUNGERFORD *Ridge & River* 56 There wasn't a man in the section who would dip out on a patrol so long as he could drag one leg after the other. **1965** J. WYNNUM *Jiggin' in Riggin'* 28 I'm prepared to take a small wager you'll sign on and dip out on the American draft. **1973** D. FOSTER *North South West* 17, I dipped out at the uni though. It took me two years to fail first year twice. **1984** *N.T. News* (Darwin) 9 Nov. 26/1 Some of your hopes and wishes hinges on the outcome of this weekend but you have good stars for it so you needn't worry about dipping out.

diprotodon /daɪ'prəʊtədɒn/. [The fossil animal genus *Diprotodon* was named in 1838 by English palaeontologist Richard Owen (see quot. 1838) f. Gr. δι- two, πρῶτος first + ὀδούς tooth, referring to the two prominent incisors in the animal's lower jaw.] An extinct, very large, herbivorous, quadruped marsupial of the Austral. genus *Diprotodon.*

[**1838** T.L. MITCHELL *Three Exped. Eastern Aust.* II. 362 Genus *Diprotodon.* I apply this name to the genus of Mammalia, represented by the anterior extremity of the right ramus, lower jaw, with a single large procumbent incisor. . . This is the specimen conjectured to have belonged to the Dugong, but the incisor resembles the corresponding tooth of the wombat.] **1848** *Maitland Mercury* 8 Mar. 3/2 *The Diprotodon.* The fossil remains . . found at a branch of the Condamine River. **1855** J. BONWICK *Geogr. Aust. & N.Z.* (ed. 3) 33 The Diprotoden [*sic*] was like the Wombat with teeth of the Kangaroo. **1881** R. CRAWFORD *Echoes from Bushland* 23 Contemplating us as if we were resurrected specimens of the diprotodon. **1896** B. SPENCER *Rep. Horn Sci. Exped. Central Aust.* I. 55 In 1836 . . Mitchell . . first discovered the Wellington caves and found in them the remains of a gigantic fossil marsupial, to which in 1838 Owen gave the name of Diprotodon. **1926** K. DAHL *In Savage Aust.* 21 The gigantic 'Marsupial elephant', the Diprotodon. **1978** K. WILLEY *Joe Brown's Dog* 20 Palm trees nodded by the shore and the diprotodon and other marsupial monsters, now extinct, wandered through primaeval jungle. **1986** *Sydney Morning Herald* 18 Sept. 1/6 The diprotodon, a two-tonne precursor to kangaroos, browsed Australia's savannah woodlands during the Ice Age or pleistocene period.

dirt. *Obs.* [Orig. U.S.: see OED *sb.* 3 b. and Mathews.] The alluvial soil or gravel from which gold is separated by washing; wash-dirt. Also *attrib.*

1852 *Murray's Guide to Gold Diggings* 26 The *cradleman* . . keeps the cradle, when it has been charged with 'dirt', constantly going. **1853** MRS C. CLACY *Lady's Visit to Gold Diggings* (1963) 64 Into it I placed about half the 'dirt'—digger's technical term for earth, or soil. **1858** *Colonial Mining Jrnl.* Oct. 29/1 On the whole lead, say a distance of three miles, there are scattered parties sinking and driving for 'blocks' and taking dirt headings. **1889** W.H. TIETKENS *Jrnl. Central Austral. Exploring Exped.* 13 Apr. (1891) 11 Washed several dishes of dirt without any results. **1898** D.W. CARNEGIE *Spinifex & Sand* 89 Wherever we tried a 'dish of dirt', colours were sure to result. **1905** *Bulletin* (Sydney) 14 Dec. 36/1 The gold-yield of the dirt he had tapped was far below tucker-standard.

dirty, *a.* Resentful. Freq. with **on,** resentful of.

1965 *Oz* (Sydney) xxiii. 8 Well Kicker gets a bit dirty on this but I keep him sweet an' we shoot thru an' book in at The Rex. **1972** G. MORLEY *Jockey rides Honest Race* 230 There's Deena talking to her boyfriend. I know he's got a bird out in the car waiting for him. She's gonna get dirty if she finds out. **1976** D. IRELAND *Glass Canoe* 73 They're dirty on me, but they have to agree. **1984** *Age* (Melbourne) 29 Mar. 28/4 Even without losing money I get very dirty on a team for not winning when everything points to its certain success.

discoloured, *ppl. a. Obs.* Of a person: neither Aboriginal nor white.

1913 *Bulletin* (Sydney) 6 Nov. 22/1 There were 2054 indented discolored seamen engaged in the pearling industry at Broome. . . Japanese were in the vast majority. **1926** *Illustr. Tasmanian Mail* (Hobart) 27 Jan. 6/1 Alice Springs, with a white population of 30 or more, and a much larger dark and discoloured one.

dish, *n. Gold-mining.*

1. A vessel in which alluvial soil, gravel, etc., is washed to separate out gold; the quantity of alluvial deposit such a vessel contains.

1851 [see *dish man*]. **1852** *Moreton Bay Free Press* 1 Apr. 3/5 He washed two or three dishes full of earth. **1852** *Guardian* (Hobart) 21 Sept. 3/4 The first dish of earth was taken. . . It produced several good looking bits of gold. **1853** R.S. ANDERSON *Austral. Gold Fields* (1956) 21, 100 specs in a dish is a very fair 'prospect'. **1880** *Bulletin* (Sydney) 21 Aug. 2/2 Eight dwts. are said to have been the result of a dish at the Five-mile Creek near Orange. **1896** *Ibid.* 18 Jan. 3/2 When allus sinkin' duffers, allus bottomin' on 'tish', An' steel from off your pick is all you're gettin' in the dish? Yah! what about the diggin's. **1899** *Ibid.* 7 Oct. (Red Page), Luck is kind, at last, at last! Dishes show a 'splendid streak'. **1908** *Ibid.* 22 Oct. 15/2 Many a digger has located the run of gold by taking a dish of wash from the mouth of womby's tunnel. **1928** M.B. PETERSEN *Jewelled Nights* 65 Sam and Dosey went down to see and they got a 'weight' in two 'dishes'! **1939** A. GASTON *Coolgardie Gold* 41 After blowing off several dishes in a very new-chum style and not seeing colour I was not so sure. **1946** K.S. PRICHARD *Roaring Nineties* 40 Every dish Dinny panned off showed a fat tail of fine gold. **1975** L.H. CLARK *Rouseabout Reflections* 18 Any man with gumption who trekked out Hurst-bridge way, Could get eight colours to the dish, and make the washing pay. **1980** N. KING *Colourful Tales* 29 There were the centrifugal dryblowing machines, like gigantic spinning tops, which enabled a large amount of dirt to be put through but which also threw the gold out, or so the old 'dish-twisters' claimed.

2. Special Comb. **dish man,** a gold-miner who uses a dish; **-washing** *vbl. n.*, the process of separating gold from the surrounding alluvial deposit by washing it in a dish.

1851 *Empire* (Sydney) 20 Aug. 67/3 Mr Esmonds .. imagines that a cradle in full operation, with a party of four or five miners, might obtain two ounces a day, and that the **dishmen**, when in full practice, might on the average obtain eight or ten shillings. **1852** D. MACKENZIE *Ten Yrs. Aust.* 24 **Dish-washing** consists simply in pouring water into the dish upon the clay, keeping it stirred, and gradually washing off the upper particles.

Hence **dishful** *n.*, the quantity of alluvial deposit contained in a dish.

1852 D. MACKENZIE *Gold Digger* 37 A man dug up a tin dishful of slaty-coloured clay, when an individual on the adjoining claim offered £50 for the dishful before it was washed.

dish, *v.* [f. prec.] *trans.* To agitate (a quantity of alluvial deposit) in a dish of water in order to separate out the gold.

1851 *Empire* (Sydney) 27 Nov. 407/3 People are obliged to dish their dirt when they are near enough to the water. **1871** *Austral. Town & Country Jrnl.* (Sydney) 22 Apr. 485/4 The highest yield per dish was 7 gms; several dished only the bare colour. **1905** *Bulletin* (Sydney) 26 Oct. 14/2 Every miner loses more or less gold in dishing, for the dish is not an ideal gold-saver. **1929** *Ibid.* 14 Aug. 25/1 A prospector 'dishing' the stuff would be severely handicapped. **1932** I.L. IDRIESS *Prospecting for Gold* 12 Next day take up the bottom and dish it.

dispersal. [See next.] The clearing of Aborigines from a particular locality; the pursuit and slaughter of Aborigines. Also *attrib.*

[**1836** T.L. MITCHELL *Three Exped. Eastern Aust.* 27 May (1838) II. 103 New and remarkable shrub—Darling tribe again—Their dispersion by the party.] **1902** W. LEES *Aboriginal Problem Qld.* 11 The issue of distinct orders .. that the aboriginals were to be treated on humanitarian lines, with the result that since then not a single 'dispersal', i.e., by bullet, has taken place. **1926** *Bulletin* (Sydney) 4 Feb. 22/2 Mrs McAuley's husband was killed long ago by the blacks near Cairns. The 'dispersal party' which went out rushed the camp of the suspected tribe. **1929** *Ibid.* 9 Jan. 25/3 Touching those incidents of 'dispersals' of the blacks in Queensland half a century ago, there is some not over-creditable history recorded... Some of the 'dispersals' were mere butcheries. **1939** J.W. COLLINSON *Early Days Cairns* 64 The blacks gave trouble... The subsequent police 'dispersal' gave great displeasure to the settlers, through the capture of some of the native children.

disperse, *v. Hist.* [Euphemistic use of *disperse* to scatter.] *trans.* Ostensibly, to drive (Aborigines) away from a particular area; commonly, to seek out and kill (an Aboriginal or a party of Aborigines).

1805 *Sydney Gaz.* 19 May, A party composed of the settlers .. went in quest of the natives .. in order to disperse them. **1865** G.S. LANG *Aborigines of Aust.* 79 It would almost appear to people at a distance, that the principal business of the people at Queensland was to 'disperse' the blacks. **1880** *Queenslander* (Brisbane) 1 May 560/2 When the blacks .. shed white blood .. the native police have been sent to 'disperse' them. What disperse means is well enough known. The word has been adopted into bush slang as a convenient euphemism for wholesale massacre. **1889** J.C. NEILD *Songs 'neath Southern Cross* (1896) 176 Do I remember? I should say I do! It was rough work, and mates we lost a few, Dispersing them there blacks in 'fifty-two. **1890** A.J. VOGAN *Black Police* 142 A young 'sub', new in the force .. used the word 'killed' instead of the official '*dispersed*' in speaking of the unfortunate natives left *hors de combat* on the field. The report was returned to him for correction in company with a severe reprimand for his careless wording... The 'sub' .. corrected his report so that the faulty portion now read as follows: 'We successfully surrounded the said party of aborigines and *dispersed* fifteen, *the remainder*, some half dozen, succeeded in escaping.' **1892** *Truth* (Sydney) 12 June 2/3 He waits until three-fourths of the dangerous 'myalls' have been 'dispersed' by the bullets of the police. **1893** S. NEWLAND *Paving Way* 113 'The Inspector will only briefly state that the aborigines attacked him in the most aggressive manner and were ultimately dispersed, after the force had incurred great risk by its forbearance. That's about the official style, isn't it?' 'I don't write the police reports; my own don't leave quite so much to the imagination,' laughed the other. "Disperse' is a word that admits of a wide interpretation.' **1899** *Truth* (Sydney) 5 Mar. 3/1 The official report only read, 'White woman killed by blacks on Jasper Creek; murderers dispersed.' **1914** J. MATHEW *Ballads Bush Life* 8 The clicking of the triggers Dispersed the camp of niggers, They never looked behind nor tried to pass; 'Twas fun to see the ginnies Snatch up the picaninnies And scamper through the bush across the grass. **1918** C. FETHERSTONHAUGH *After Many Days* 232 My friend told me he waited till the blacks had caught a good big lot of fish .. 'dispersed' them, and collared their fish. **1937** D. GUNN *Links with Past* 42 Walker was asked to disperse the blacks. This he did very effectively. No one knows how many were shot. **1950** G. PIKE *Campfire Tales* (1981) 58 After the murder, most of the Aborigines in the area were 'dispersed' by the Native Mounted Police.

Hence **dispersing** *vbl. n.* Usu. *attrib.*

1892 *Bulletin* (Sydney) 2 Apr. 6/3 He had crossed the Nicholson to a white's camp, when a 'dispersing party' that had been trailing him came up. **1893** E. FAVENC *Last of Six Tales* 39 They had some trouble with the blacks up there lately, and, I suppose it was the first dispersing-match he had ever seen. **1894** H. NISBET *Bush Girl's Romance* 9 The aboriginal owners of the land, except during the *dispersing* seasons, were about as happy as the kangaroos before a grand hunt. **1894** *Bulletin* (Sydney) 23 June 24/1 Blacks always want to jabber late after a dispersing match. **1903** 'BOONDI' *Boondi's Bk.* 37 A 'dispersing' party of native police was winding its way along the bed of a dry creek.

dit. In Services' (chiefly naval) speech: a yarn; a reminiscence. Also *attrib.*

1942 *Rag: H.M.A.S. 'Orara'* 25 Dec. 3 Prowling round the mess-decks listening to the leave dits. **1943** J.F. MOYES *Scrap-Iron Flotilla* Pref., The men gathered in groups in the mess decks to spin 'dits'. **1944** *Dit* (Melbourne) Sept. 3 The two men spinning a dit on the front page of this issue. **1945** *Ibid.* Oct. 152 Ships photographic firms are invited to submit similar photos of dit-spinners. **1956** 'A.B.C.' *What is A?* 35 Just watch two ex-sailors swopping dits and you'll see what I mean! **1960** J. WYNNUM *Pinch of Salt* (1963) 8 The Service had been fun for a year or so after the war—swopping 'dits' with old wingers you hadn't seen in ages. **1984** V. DARROCH *On Coast* 19 *Dit* (R.A.N.), book, movie or story.

div. [Abbrev. of *div(idend.*] A sum of money, esp. as won from a bookmaker.

1891 *Bulletin* (Sydney) 28 Mar. 23/1 He borrowed our div. and a lot beside and came out of the fight top dog. **1892** *Ibid.* 6 Aug. 5/4 Let us go together droving and returning, if we live, Try to understand each other while we liquor up the 'div'. **1900** *Advocate* (Burnie) 1 May 4/2 Clerkies and bookies retired to reluctantly pay out their divs. **1966** J. WATEN *Season of Youth* 32 We were to meet after each race near the merry-go-round and I would give him my takings and he would give me my div.

dividing mate. *Obs.* A partner, orig. on the goldfields, with whom the rewards of an enterprise are equally shared.

1878 'R. BOLDREWOOD' *Ups & Downs* 11 The great Australian custom of 'dividing mates' by which .. fortunes have been made and shared. **1886** H. FINCH-HATTON *Advance Aust.* (rev. ed.) 166 We were known on the diggings as 'dividing mates'. **1916** H.L. ROTH *Sketches & Reminisc. Qld.* 10 They had been 'dividing mates' and he insisted on the partnership with the cob continuing.

dividing range. A series of hills or stretch of high country forming a division between adjacent river systems; a watershed.

1834 J.D. LANG *Hist. & Statistical Acct. N.S.W.* II. 105 We were soon obliged to dismount again to climb up the precipitous side of a steep mountain, to gain the summit of what the colonists call 'a dividing range'. These ranges, which are flanked on either side by deep and sometimes impassable ravines, traverse the country in many places for a great distance, either in a northerly and southerly or easterly and westerly direction. **1846** *Bell's Life in Sydney* 27 June 1/5 Other stations are about being formed further to the northward, beyond the dividing range. **1848** T.L. MITCHELL *Jrnl. Exped. Tropical Aust.* 285 We could return to the foot of the dividing ranges. **1861** C. CAMPBELL *Squatting Question Considered* 4 By the end of 1839, the country was occupied as far as the dividing range. **1869** R.B. SMYTH *Gold Fields & Mineral Districts* 609 *Dividing Range*, a range of hills or mountains or relatively elevated lands which separate creeks or rivers. **1906** *Emu* V. 192 The mountains that traverse the whole of the eastern side of the continent .. are known as the Dividing Range. **1931** L.S. SUGGATE *Aust. & N.Z.* 62 The term 'Dividing Range' frequently appears, and though this is useful as indicating the watershed between the coastal rivers and the West-flowing rivers, there is no proper range, but a series of disconnected plateau blocks. **1962** D.C. MONEY *Aust. & N.Z.* (ed. 2) 11 The line of the Dividing Range, under various names, runs nearly parallel to the coast. **1973** *Official Yr. Bk.* 27 The Great Dividing Range .. extends from the North of Queensland .. and .. terminates in Tasmania.

dixie. Chiefly *Vic.* [Transf. use of *dixie* iron pot.] An ice-cream carton, now usu. small. See also BUCKET *n.* 1, DANDY.

1941 S.J. BAKER *Pop. Dict. Austral. Slang* 23 *Dixie*, an ice-cream carton. **1952** *Australasian Confectioner* Oct. 55 (Advt.), Sennitt's Ice Cream... Packets, Polar Pies, Large Dixie, Small Dixie, Vanilla Slice. **1964** P. ADAM SMITH *Hear Train Blow* 63 Mick charged off with the threepence and bought a Dixie. **1972** G.W. TURNER *Eng. Lang. in Aust. & N.Z.* (rev. ed.) 124 Why should .. a pot or tub of icecream be a *dandy* in Adelaide, a *dixie* in Melbourne and elsewhere a *bucket?*

dizz, *v.* [Of unknown origin.] *trans.* See quot. 1872.

1872 M.B. BROWNRIGG *Cruise of Freak* 55, I ventured upon tasting a *young* mutton bird 'dizzed', that is, cooked in its own fat. **1968** P. ADAM SMITH *Tiger Country* 173 She .. like most old hands in the mutton-bird islands likes them 'dizzed', very young birds fried in their own fat.

djanga /ˈdʒæŋə/. *W.A. Obs.* [a. Nyungar *jaŋa* ghost.] A name applied by Aborigines to a white person. Freq. as *pl.*

1838 *Colonist* (Sydney) 31 Jan. 4/1 The name which they invariably apply to the whites, when talking of the latter among themselves, is 'Djanga', or 'the dead'. **1841** G. GREY *Jrnls. Two Exped. N.-W. & W.A.* I. 261 The Djanga (white men) liked it very much. **1851** *Athenaeum* (London) 24 May 557 The word *Djanga* at Swan River, means the dead; but it is indiscriminately applied to Europeans,—as they are believed to be deceased aborigines.

do, *v.*

1. a. *trans. Obs.* To consume (food or drink), chiefly with reference to alcoholic liquor.

1859 F. FOWLER *Southern Lights & Shadows* 48 A wealthy tavern-keeper who came to England with us used to boast of 'doing' his forty nobblers of brandy a day, a nobbler being in quantity little better than half a wine-glass. **1867** J.S. BORLASE *Night Fossickers* 116, I asked him to come to Poole's shanty and do a chop and a nobbler with me. **1869** *Sydney Punch* 13 Mar. 129/2 Let's come now, boys, and 'do a beer', Long Live the Queen. **1893** *Antipodean* (Melbourne) 95, I cud do a bit of doughboy. **1899** *Western Champion* (Barcaldine) 21

Feb. 3/1 'Can you do a drink,' asked one out-of-work of another in like predicament.

b. To spend (one's available money) completely. Also with **in** and **up.**

1889 *Referee* (Sydney) 19 May 2/1 A young fellow .. rushes to 'do in' every spare fiver or tenner that comes into his possession. **1894** *Bulletin* (Sydney) 20 Jan. 24/1 He could do his cheque up quicker than was ever done before. **1899** *Western Champion* (Barcaldine) 9 May 14/1 These latter are those who, in bush parlance, 'done in their stuff'; that is, knocked down the proceeds of their last spell of toil in some bush township to which their footsteps led them. **1905** *Bulletin* (Sydney) 11 May 17/3, I knew a rabbiter do-in a £146 cheque in five days. **1906** *Ibid.* 30 Aug. 16/4 Met a man back in the Territory who had 'done-in' a station; then had 'done-in' a turn-out of 30 horses, waggonette, saddles, packs; after that had swallowed his rifle. Most of it happened at a shanty where they dispense liquid refreshment at 1s. a time. **1922** A. WRIGHT *Boss o' Yedden* 136 'Done y' dough?' 'Every bean. I'm broke. So long.' **1932** L. MANN *Flesh in Armour* 247 'By Gawd,' said Darky softly, 'thirty-two good francs I've done.' **1943** J. DEVINE *Rats of Tobruk* 78 Two-up was much in favour... A few won large sums and many lost quite a lot, and it was not until the Australians were evacuated from the besieged town that the losers realized with a rude shock that they had 'done all their sugar'. **1956** S. HOPE *Diggers' Paradise* 141 Greyhound racing has become popular 'down under', but a much more spectacular means of 'doing your dough' is the Trots. **1968** S. GORE *Holy Smoke* 26 And there, we read, he *wasted his substance with riotous living.* Meanin' in English, that he done in the whole issue on sheilas and bombo. **1974** *Bulletin* (Sydney) 16 Nov. 32/1 It seemed Young had some good oil on the Adelaide races. Certainly their demeanour was not that of men who were doing their money. **1982** N. KEESING *Lily on Dustbin* 62 When a chosen horse 'runs like a hairy goat' both sexes 'do their dough'.

2. With **over**: to assault physically, to 'rough up'. Also as *vbl. n.*

[N.Z. **1866** *Maungatapu Murders*, Since we are going to do these three people over .. I think we had better prevent him from doing us any harm.] **1944** L. GLASSOP *We were Rats* 76 Somebody took my coat. 'Do this galah over,' he whispered in my ear. 'He's a king-hit merchant.' **1945** 'MASTER-SARG' *Yank discovers Aust.* 17 The enemy or a position has been done over when it has been beaten or taken. **1965** W. DICK *Bunch of Ratbags* 177 Sometimes they'd eject some of the more rowdy ones of our mob and take them to the station and do them over. **1975** L. RYAN *Shearers* 103 Get goin' before the mob does you over too. **1977** B. SCOTT *My Uncle Arch* 13 He gave them such a doing over.

dob, *v.* [Fig. use of Br. dial. *dob* to put down, throw down.]

1. a. *trans.* To inform upon; to incriminate. Usu. with **in.**

1955 *Overland* v. 4 He came to me and dobbed in one of the carpenters for talking. **1961** R. BRADDON *Naked Island* 32 A couple of the Indonesian p.o.w.s have dobbed us in. Told the Nips everything. **1965** *Kings Cross Whisper* (Sydney) Jan. 6/2 You must be able to rattle off the names of five adulterous couples smilingly, dob in your mate's wife innocently. **1968** S. GORE *Holy Smoke* 46 They dobbed 'em in, d' y' see? **1973** J. O'GRADY *Survival in Doghouse* 74, I shut up and let Ray take all the credit. Couldn't dob him in, could I? **1974** M. GILLESPIE *Into Hollow Mountains* 15 Someone else saw him with the wad of notes and dobbed him to the principal. **1979** J. SUMMONS *Lamb of God* 43 He and his mates would've got me after school. They bash you up if you dob on them. **1981** P. BARTON *Bastards I have Known* 16 Helen stuck on a real act and dobbed me in to Mum, screaming about how I had busted her best doll on purpose. **1985** *Canberra Times* 28 May 1/6 N.S.W. police officers of all ranks are being asked to dob in their corrupt colleagues to restore confidence in the force.

b. *trans.* To impose (a responsibility upon).

1968 S. GORE *Holy Smoke* 24 Y' know what happened when I'm in at th' Alice the other day? Some sky-pilot joker tried to dob it on me to go to church! **1981** B. HUMPHRIES *Nice Night's Entertainment* 42 She dropped the broad hint that she'd like to go up to the Elizabethan Theatre at Stratford some time .. and I more or less dobbed myself in.

2. *trans.* [Cf. OEDS *dub, v.*[4]] With **in**: to contribute (money) towards a common cause. Also *absol.*

1956 E. LAMBERT *Watermen* 103 The whole town dobbed in and bought Charlie and Russ a new boat. **1968** G. DUTTON *Andy* 197 The ground crew are dobbing in too. **1978** B. ST. A. SMITH *Spirit beyond Psyche* 56 A few of us are dobbin' in a dollar each, for a wreath, an' flowers. **1979** S.W. DUTHIE *Fidlers Creek* 2 Anyway, we all dob a bit in to buy the outfit.

3. *Australian National Football.* To kick (a goal).

1965 J. DYER *Captain Blood* 100 He dobbed it through the middle. **1981** L. MONEY *Footy Fan's Handbk.* 37 *Terms for a goal.* It's full points! He's dobbed it! .. Right through the centre!

dobber. [f. DOB *v.* 1.] An informant; a tale-bearer. Also **dobber-in.** See also *cobber dobber* COBBER *n.* 2.

1958 *Coast to Coast 1957–58* 201 How's his flipping form? Dobber-in Number One. **1968** G. MILL *Nobody dies but Me* 89 Then you're accused of being unfriendly by the dobbers-in. **1973** J. POWERS *Last of Knucklemen* (1974) 95 Don't look at me, you bastards! I'm no bloody dobber! **1977** G.A.W. SMITH *Riding High* 13 '*Nine neighbours*! .. And every one of 'em a dobber... ' The expression 'dobber' was one that I knew implied contempt and was apt to be applied to tale-bearers and informants. **1983** M. HAYES *Prickle Farm* 119 The Village Dobber had put us in to the local shire council for allowing our goat to become a public nuisance.

docker. *Obs.* [Br. dial. *docker* struggle; also *fig.* 'of hard work, strenuous living, fatigue' (see SND).] In the phr. **to go (in) a docker,** to embark on an enterprise, activity, etc., with vigour, wholeheartedly.

1866 *Sydney Punch* 21 Apr. 794/1 Somebody else was going in a 'Docker' in reforming the time-honoured abuses of this Gothic Establishment. **1868** *Ibid.* 24 Oct. 176/1 He then gave Parkes a wigging .. and went in a 'docker' against the new Col. Secretary. **1871** *Austral. Town & Country Jrnl.* (Sydney) 22 Apr. 506/1 On Thursday morning when coming home at the finish of a good gallop, and going a docker. **1880** 'ERRO' *Squattermania* 190 The common enemy, colonially speaking, 'went in a docker', and .. finally routed and dispersed the combined .. forces. **1888** *Centennial Mag.* (Sydney) 183 'I haven't smelt spirits since last Christmas.' 'And then you went in a docker, eh Dick?' **1895** *Worker* (Sydney) 16 Mar. 3/3 We got a bit older, and my chum went in a docker for teachin' and so on. **1902** E.B. KENNEDY *Black Police Qld.* 216 There they are, the two dogs, going a 'docker' under the scrub.

doctor, *n.*[1] KORADJI. Also *attrib.*

1834 G. BENNETT *Wanderings N.S.W.* I. 190 Krardgee Kibba, or Doctor Stone. **1845** *Sentinel* (Sydney) 29 Jan. 2/6 About half an hour after the body has lain, the Doctor or Priest provides each of the inner class of mourners with a short stick about 6 inches long. **1846** 'COLONIAL MAGISTRATE' *Remarks on Probable Origin* 10 Although the word *Priest* does not appear in the vocabulary of the Natives—the words *Doctor* or *Conjuror* is [*sic*] applied to those old men who assume the guidance in *Coroborees.* **1856** J. BONWICK *W. Buckley* 77 The doctor seized the Mooyum Karr, a piece of oval board with a string attached to it, and with a few hearty, whirring swings would effectually purify the atmosphere from the presence of such malignities. **1878** R.B. SMYTH *Aborigines of Vic.* I. 261 The *Kuldukke*—men-priests, sorcerers, or doctors—are impostors, and rob the poor natives of their food, in order that they may live in idleness. **1886** A.W. HOWITT *On Austral. Medicine Men* 24 The term 'Doctor' or 'Blackfellow Doctor' is always used in Australia for those men in a native tribe who profess to have supernatural powers. **1899** J. MATHEW *Eaglehawk & Crow* 142 The titles of these magicians varied with the community, but by unanimous consent the whites have called them 'doctors', and they correspond to the medicine-men and rain-makers of other barbarous nations. **1900** T. MAJOR *Leaves from Squatter's Note Bk.* 152 The doctor, from his dirty dilly-bag, or medical instrument-case, produces a long string of twisted hair. **1947** W.E. HARNEY *Brimming Billabongs* 34 He knows when the doctor blackfellows are roaming the land. **1962** D. LOCKWOOD *I, Aboriginal* 9 It was one walkabout time .. in the Never-Never Land south of the Roper River that the Medicine Man, the Doctor Blackfellow, tried to kill me. **1979** M. HEPPELL *Black Reality* 84 The actual and purported ministrations of 'doctor blokes' vary widely, but they generally have in common a magical control over a person, the possession of a personal trace of the victim and the various internal 'operations' on the person which eventuate in his death.

doctor, *n.*[2] [Transf. use of *doctor* ship's cook or (U.S.) cook in a logging camp.] One who cooks for shearers, etc., on a station.

1868 C.W. BROWNE *Overlanding in Aust.* 71 Grumbling is contagious in its nature so for this reason alone a good cook, or 'doctor', as he is called, is a necessary individual in camp. **1881** A.C. GRANT *Bush-Life Qld.* II. 140 By watching the cook, he discovered the art of making a damper... He confessed to the 'doctor' the ill success of his own first attempt in the baking line. **1885** *Trans. & Proc. R. Geogr. Soc. Australasia, Victorian Branch* (1887) 62 The cook or 'doctor' is unanimously declared to be worthy of a 'cordon bleu'. **1887** 'OVERLANDER' *Austral. Sketches* 1 All bush cooks are called the doctor. **1921** G.A. BELL *Under Brigalows* 147 Next day came another big dish of stew, and another grumbler got up and went outside with the 'Doctor'.

doctor, *n.*[3] [f. the fig. use in the West Indies and S. Africa for a wind with refreshing or cleansing properties.] In the s.w. of W.A., a cool, refreshing sea breeze, with considerable inland penetration, which brings relief at the end of a hot summer day (see quot. 1971). Also **Albany, Esperance, Eucla, Fremantle, Geraldton, Nullarbor, Perth, Southerly doctor.**

1870 W.H. KNIGHT *W.A.* 14 Soon after, the grateful 'doctor', or sea-breeze, sets in. **1892** F. HART *W.A. in 1891* 121 All along the coast in the summer the regular sea breeze, known by the significant name of 'the doctor', tempers the heat of the sun. **1908** *Bulletin* (Sydney) 19 Mar. 14/2 Even when the Albany 'doctor' didn't blow, the mornings were quite cool. **1913** H.A. HUNT et al. *Climate & Weather Aust.* 18 The invigorating sea-breeze—called the 'Doctor'—blows from the W.S.W. during the afternoon. **1920** BRIGGS & HARRIS *Joysticks & Fiddlesticks* (1938) 108 Every evening .. about five o'clock, a wind springs up from the south. It is called the 'Southerly Doctor'. This wind is remarkably cool, and makes life bearable for the people who live along the east-west railway line from Ooldea to Perth. **1920** *W.A.: Early Vicissitudes* 87 Thanks also to the regularity of the calls of Mr South-West Wind—colloquially termed the 'Fremantle doctor'—the post meridian hours of the warmest days are usually tempered with refreshing zephyrs. **1937** A.W. UPFIELD *Mr Jelly's Business* 57 The 'Albany Doctor' people called it, because the strong cool wind from Albany way swept clear the bodily and mental languors brought on by the heat of the long day. **1946** 'A. SPENCE' *Mystery of Red Gum* 32 The breeze you are now enjoying is called the 'Fremantle Doctor'. It gets up almost every day about noon or just after. On some days it's a real life saver. **1955** *Austral. Meteorol. Mag.* Dec. 61 Those resident from Norseman southwards were definite in maintaining that the 'Esperance doctor' did reach them. *Ibid.*, Further north, the accounts were rather confused, and diverse, some at least clearly identifying the 'doctor' with cold frontal passages. **1956** S. HOPE *Digger's Paradise* 71 The 'Perth doctor' .. blows toward evening off the Indian Ocean. **1962** J. GENTILLI in *World Survey Climatol.* (1971) XIII. 113 The Esperance Doctor passed through Norseman at 6 p.m. **1970** B. FULLER *Nullarbor Story* 15 Later, the breeze known locally as the Esperance Doctor, which blows inland from the coast some 230 miles away, dropped the temperature with a bump and sent me early to bed. **1971** J. GENTILLI in *World Survey Climatol.* XIII. 111 In the southwest, sea-breezes have long been recognized as a distinctive feature of the local climate, so much so that they were given local popular names such as (in the likely chronological order of their adoption) *Fremantle Doctor, Albany Doctor, Geraldton Doctor, Esperance Doctor*, and more recently even *Eucla Doctor*, in each case from the name of the coastal locality near which they cross the shore on their welcome way inland. **1977** B. FULLER *Nullarbor Lifelines* 96 The Nullarbor 'doctor' is a desert wind that blows at the equinoxes. **1983** *Bulletin* (Sydney) 1 Nov. 42/1 The cool south-westerly .. brings so much relief that it's become known as the Fremantle Doctor.

doctor, *n.*[4] [Transf. use of the phr. *to go for the doctor* to seek medical help as a matter of urgency.] In the phr. **to go for the doctor,** to go 'all out', to abandon all restraint.

1949 L. GLASSOP *Lucky Palmer* 74 Go for the doctor. Slap a tenner on it. It's only an even-money shot. **1951** D. STIVENS *Jimmy Brockett* 86 There were three of the bastards and they went for the doctor. **1966** T. RONAN *Strangers on Ophir* (rev. ed.) 81 A jackeroo . . suddenly sat down and started to go for the doctor. With his whip going like a flail and his spurs like pistons he drove his cuddy to the lead. **1976** *Sydney Morning Herald* 20 Apr. 13/1, I decided to go for the doctor rather than let Taras Bulba fight for his head. **1984** *Ibid.* 28 Sept. 9/4 The only hope he has . . is to discredit Mr Hawke. That is why he will go for the doctor in Parliament next week.

dodder-laurel. [Transf. use of *dodder* a twining leafless parasitic plant of the genus *Cuscuta* (fam. Cuscutaceae).] Any of several parasitic perennial climbers of the genus *Cassytha* (fam. Lauraceae) of all States; *devil's twine*, see DEVIL 3. Also **dodder, dodder vine.**

1848 T.L. MITCHELL *Jrnl. Exped. Tropical Aust.* 362 One of the Dodder laurels (*Cassytha pubescens* . .) a species also found near Port Jackson. **1888** *Proc. Linnean Soc. N.S.W.* III. 496 *Cassytha filiformis*. . . This and other species of *Cassytha* are called 'Dodder-laurel'. The emphatic name 'Devil's guts' is largely used. It frequently connects bushes and trees by cords, and becomes a nuisance to the traveller. **1906** *Emu* V. 134 Matted together in parts with the native dodder vine (Cassytha). **1967** B.Y. MAIN *Between Wodjil & Tor* 10 Dodder-laurel, the fuscous strings of which were laced and knotted over and around the bushy boughs. Complete parasites, these leafless strings formed a dense net. **1970** J.V. MARSHALL *Walk to Hills of Dreamtime* 42 A battleground of tree and parasite and vine, with the giant dodders and jikkas choking the life out of all they touched with tourniquet arms.

dodge, *v.* [Br. dial. *dodge* to follow in the track of a person or animal; see EDD.]

1. *trans.* To drive (sheep or cattle). Also *absol.* See also *monkey dodging* MONKEY 5.

1881 A.C. GRANT *Bush-Life Qld.* II. 134 On the road—Aboriginal innocents—a wet night on watch—dodging cows. **1897** L. LINDLEY-COWEN *W. Austral. Settler's Guide* 632 When ewes and lambs are being put in the yard it is better to keep the dogs off and dodge the mob in quietly. **1915** *Pastoral Rev.* 16 Feb. 138 The word 'dodging' is an appellation applied to shepherding, or droving sheep, and is an Australian invention given to the occupation by old-time drovers and shepherds. . . The term has gone out of general use. *Ibid.*, A good steady dog, well under control, is worth all the men you could profitably use to dodge up the stragglers [*sc.* sheep]. **1922** 'J. BUSHMAN' *In Musgrave Ranges* 226 'Dodging along' behind cattle, as it is called, is not hard work. **1936** A. RUSSELL *Gone Nomad* 27 My cattle-camp and sheep-dodging days. [*Note*] Sheep mustering and droving. **1944** J.J. HARDIE *Cattle Camp* (ed. 3) 85 Armstrong and Phillips cut out the Ardwell cattle to one side, while Ken and Dusty moved through the mob, dodging our cows with unbranded calves, and grown cleanskins to where Scotty and Jerry proudly rode the face of the camp.

2. *trans.* To misappropriate (an animal): see PODDY-DODGE.

1956 T. RONAN *Moleskin Midas* 149 For every poddy that's up in the Coronet breakaways there's a dozen blokes trying to dodge it off.

3. In the phr. **to dodge Pompey**: see POMPEY.

dodger, *n.*[1] [U.S. *dodger* a small handbill or circular.] An advertising leaflet, esp. one carrying political propaganda.

1891 *Truth* (Sydney) 10 May 3/4 Receiving a pink 'dodger' in the street last Saturday week it was found on reference to be a 'startler' from the Centenary Hall. **1898** *Bulletin* (Sydney) 2 Apr. (Red Page), A Rockhampton friend sends along a 'dodger', boldly printed on paper of a gorgeous blue and headed 'Swimming Extraordinary'. **1903** *Mercury* (Hobart) 2 Apr. 6/4 Dr McCall protested against the 'dodgers' put about in the interest of Sir Elliott Lewis. **1905** *Shearer* (Sydney) 29 Apr. 3/2 Others . . may offer to distribute 'dodgers'. **1924** A.B. PEIRCE *Knocking About* 144 Handbills, or 'dodgers' as the vernacular had it, were given for distribution to the bell-ringer. **1954** J. WATEN *Unbending* 212 Feathers handed to everyone a printed dodger which read: '*Our local has now a library of the best revolutionary literature.*' **1966** D. NILAND *Pairs & Loners* 135 We talked a printer into doing us several posters and a few hundred dodgers. **1973** L. OAKES *Whitlam PM* 54 Margaret Whitlam spent her days folding dodgers, and her husband spent his nights delivering them.

dodger, *n.*[2] [U.S. *(corn) dodger* small cake of cornbread: see Mathews.] Bread.

1897 *Bulletin* (Sydney) 7 Aug. (Red Page), Loaf of bread—'Dodger'. **1907** *Ibid.* 7 June 14/4 Bread is 'dodger', and that hated weapon, the axe, is 'Douglas'—'swingin' Douglas for a loaf of dodger' being a frequent expression. **1919** W.H. DOWNING *Digger Dialects* 19 *Dodger*, bread. **1950** *Austral. Police Jrnl.* Apr. 112 *Dodger*, gaol bread. **1957** 'N. CULOTTA' *They're Weird Mob* 51 Smack us in the eye with another hunk o' dodger, matey. **1964** T. KENEALLY *Place at Whitton* 91 A couple of rounds of mouldy dodger, and you'll be right! **1968** S. GORE *Holy Smoke* 9 Take the troops a few loaves of home-baked dodger. **1980** HEPWORTH & HINDLE *Boozing out in Melbourne Pubs* 141 None of your sliced bread here, but proper hunks of dodger.

dodger, *a.* [Perh. from prec. (but cf. SNODGER).] Good, excellent.

1941 S.J. BAKER *Pop. Dict. Austral. Slang* 24 *Dodger*, food of any kind. As adj., good, excellent. **1953** D. STIVENS *Gambling Ghost* 3 When we got through the valley mouth everything was dodger. The grass was thick . . and there was plenty of water.

doe. A female kangaroo.

1845 L. LEICHHARDT *Jrnl. Overland Exped. Aust.* 15 Feb. (1847) 155 Brown descried a kangaroo. . . It proved to be a fine doe, with a young one. **1888** 'R. BOLDREWOOD' *Robbery under Arms* (1937) 56 Her eyes had a bright startled look like a doe kangaroo. **1975** L. WALKER *Runaway Girl* 124 'Would it be 'roo shooters?' Drew nodded. 'A dead doe back there,' he said.

doer. [Transf. use of *doer* an animal that does well, thrives: see OED 3.]

1. a. One who earns respect by coping well with the vicissitudes of life (see quot. 1942); a 'character' (see quot. 1919).

1902 J.H.M. ABBOTT *Tommy Cornstalk* 14 He has unconsciously been taught . . how to be comfortable, how to become a good 'doer' under all adverse circumstances. **1919** W.H. DOWNING *Digger Dialects* 19 *Doer*, a person unusually humorous, reckless, undisciplined, immoral or eccentric. **1927** A. WRIGHT *Squatter's Secret* 182 He's a doer, all right. **1942** H.H. PECK *Mem. of Stockman* 67 Billy . . just on 87, is a wonderful man, and despite several broken limbs in the last few years, still cuts out his own cattle for market . . truly a great old doer. **1943** J. BINNING *Target Area* 103 Such a 'doer' he is—always 'crackin' hardy'. **1953** T.A.G. HUNGERFORD *Riverslake* 103 He must've been a bit of a doer in his own country. **1955** F. LANE *Patrol to Kimberleys* 196 A ruddy doer is Reddy. **1977** C. KLEIN *Pomegranate Tree* 55 She talked rough as bags, but she acted pure as the Virgin Mary, she was a doer, that one.

b. In the collocation **hard doer**: an intensive form of sense 1 a.; a 'hard case' (see HARD *a.*).

1910 *Bulletin* (Sydney) 21 Apr. 14/1 The hard-doer explaining that the names of the Apostles have been written on the slips of paper. **1917** *Ibid.* 26 July 24/1 A company of Australians were stationed at Herbertshöte. One afternoon a couple of hard-doers broke camp. **1919** J. ANDREWS *Garrison Ginger* 7 We're the Boys of the Guard, the New Guinea Guard, Hard doers, and fairly hot stuff. **1928** *Bulletin* (Sydney) 29 Feb. 21/1 Give me the real hard-doer; the bloke with a bit of guts. **1939** FRANKLIN & CUSACK *Pioneers on Parade* 31 You couldn't tell her from Mrs Bashton or any of those hard old doers. **1950** A.W. UPFIELD *Widows of Broome* 76 We have some pretty hard doers drinkin' here. **1955** F. LANE *Patrol to Kimberleys* 85 There was some ruddy hard-doers in the lot—blokes who shunned work like it was the plague. **1979** W.D. JOYNT *Breaking Road for Rest* 67 We knew we had some hard 'doers' aboard and for that reason the troop train . . had expressed all the way. **1983** C. BINGHAM *Beckoning Horizon* 22 Many of these men were 'hard-doers', but the majority, whatever their failings, were thoroughly reliable.

c. In the collocation **good doer**: one who thrives; a generous person.

1942 H.H. PECK *Mem. of Stockman* 244 With his happy and kindly nature and general appearance of 'a good doer', he was very popular. **1944** A. TURNER *Royal Mail* 32 He is, in his own words, a 'good doer'. Quick of temper and generous to a fault.

2. *transf.* and *fig.*

1944 K.S. PRICHARD *Potch & Colour* 71 When the mugs were filled . . Bill lifted his old hard-doer of blue-rimmed white enamel, chipped and rusty in every crack. **1976** DRAGE & PAGE *Riverboats & Rivermen* 79 I'd go to the gallery and cook up a batch of what we called 'hard doers', the sweet cakes served up for night time snacks and at change of shifts.

dog, *n.*[1]

1. Used *attrib.* in Comb. with specific reference to the dingo: **dog fence, -net** *v.*, **-netting, -proof** *a.*, **-stiffener.** See also DINGO *n.* 4.

1846 F. DUTTON *S.A. & its Mines* 202 Should the timber not be sufficiently straight for making posts and rails, it will always make a kangaroo or **dog fence.** **1966** J. CARTER *People of Inland* 85 Called officially the Dingo-proof Barrier Fence, it is generally referred to by bushmen as 'the dog fence', and it was installed to protect the shepherds . . from dingoes. **1930** D. COTTRELL *Earth Battle* 176 He . . erected . . a six-foot dog-fence . . and men were sorry for him because no one had ever dreamed of **dog-netting** a great station. **1947** E. HILL *Flying Doctor Calling* 108 Crossing the New South Wales border at the Warri Gate in the **'dog-netting'** fence. **1971** W.G. HOWCROFT *This Side Rabbit Proof Fence* 72 The fence, known as the 'dog-netting', consisted mainly of six feet pine posts placed nine feet apart, with 1½-inch mesh wire netting at the bottom, 4 inch mesh netting above. **1865** *Sydney Punch* 7 Jan. 263/1 Numerous sheep yards, most of them **dog proof.** **1907** *Bulletin* (Sydney) 31 Jan. 14/2, I lived for years on the dog-proof boundary of a large Queensland station. **1927** M. DORNEY *Adventurous Honeymoon* 39 Dog-proof fences . . keep out the dingoes. **1981** A.B. FACEY *Fortunate Life* 82 Charlie had three paddocks fenced in for the sheep, but as these were not dog-proof, he set man-traps outside the fencelines. **1898** D.W. CARNEGIE *Spinifex & Sand* 370 The Government is content to pay, not dreaming that **'dog-stiffeners'** (*i.e.*, men who make a living by poisoning dingoes) carry on so base a trade as bartering tobacco for live dog's tails! **1965** J. BECKETT *New-Chum looks at Qld.* 65 Going out with the 'dog-stiffner' (dingo trapper) I came to know how cunning these dogs can be.

2. *transf.* and *fig.*

a. Used *attrib.* in Special Comb. to connote restriction or deprivation: **dog act,** see quot. 1898; **Collar Act,** the Transport Workers' Act (1928), see quot. 1955; **hole** *obs.*, a squalid dwelling, etc.; **licence (certificate, ticket),** a certificate exempting an Aboriginal from legislation pertaining to Aborigines, esp. that prohibiting the sale of alcoholic liquor to Aborigines; **poor** *a.*, in very poor condition; **window,** see quot.

1898 *Bulletin* (Sydney) 31 Dec. 31/3 There is an Act compelling a publican to refuse drink to an habitual inebriate. This is locally known as the **'Dog Act'**, and to be brought under the Dog Act is a glorious distinction, a sort of V.C. of Northern Territory life. **1948** K.S. PRICHARD *Golden Miles* 375 Since they put me old mate, Shack, under the dog act I been kind of lonesome. **1968** LINKLATER & TAPP *Gather no Moss* 103 He was drinking as men do in their reaction against isolation and monotony, and the police took him to court to show cause why he should not be put under the 'dog act'. **1978** PALMER & MCKENNA *Somewhere between Black & White* 115 That night they were arrested for being drunk. The result was twelve months on the dog act and an £18 fine. **1935** *Workers' Weekly* (Sydney) 16 Aug. 1/2 The Federal Government's threat to apply the **Dog Collar** (Transport Workers') **Act** (work licenses) to break the strike can have no other effect than to make the seamen more determined to struggle for complete victory. **1936** *Austral. Worker* (Sydney) 25 Mar. 8/1 In a minority judgement, Mr Justic Evatt delivered a scathing indictment of the 'Dog Collar Act'. **1953** D. CUSACK *Southern Steel* 255 We knew Japan was getting ready for a Pacific war . . yet the Government put the Dog-Collar Act on the wharfies when they refused to load shipments of pig-iron. **1955** G. HEALEY *A.L.P.* 91 Within one week the Bruce-Page Government had passed a Transport Workers' Act, better known as the 'Dog Collar Act', under which waterside workers were issued licenses which could be withheld or revoked for almost any reason. **1982** LOWENSTEIN & HILLS *Under Hook* 62 Bruce introduced the infamous Transport Workers Bill... All waterside workers had to be licensed... It removed the right to strike and gave the boss almost unlimited powers to sack. Waterside workers called it the 'Dog Collar Act'. **1843** *Satirist & Sporting Chron.* (Sydney) 25 Mar. 3/2 Baker, of the *Crown and Anchor*, is about to remove his licence to a **dog-hole** in Market-street. **1847** A. HARRIS *Settlers & Convicts* 94 The wretched half-frantic women .. staggered away to any doghole where they could find a temporary lurking-place to sleep off the effects of the drink. **1878** 'R. BOLDREWOOD' *Ups & Downs* 30 He forgot the dog-hole he had left in the morning, the fleas, the pigs, the evil habilments of Bob the cook. **1955** F.B. VICKERS *Mirage* 257 Monty wants us to get the **dog licence**—that's the paper they give you... If we had this paper, me and you could have walked into that pub and stood at the bar all day and none of 'em could have said a word to us... We'd be as good as the next bloke so long as we could flash the dog licence. **1963** *Bulletin* (Sydney) 13 Apr. 3/2 The recent amendment to the NSW Aborigines' Protection Act to permit aborigines to drink in NSW hotels without a 'dog licence' abolishes an iniquitous law and will free aborigines from exploitation by sly groggers. **1974** J. HORNER *Vote Ferguson* 161 They were hopeful that they might prevail upon the Chifley government .. for an end to the 'dog licence', as they called the exemption certificates. **1977** K. GILBERT *Living Black* 297 Before the 1967 referendum, before citizenship, Aborigines could receive these exemption cards—dog certificates—which enabled them to enter a hotel. **1980** L.R. SMITH *Aboriginal Pop. Aust.* 124 They could be granted permission to assimilate, in the form of a certificate of exemption or 'dog licence' as it was universally known. **1981** *Nat. Times* (Sydney) 15 Nov. 33/2 She carried a Dog Ticket—an exemption card which, despite the evidence of the photograph, stated that she was a white person since she had married a man whose father was white. That ticket allowed her to visit hotels, to vote and to assert her status as an Australian citizen. The catch was that she was no longer allowed to associate with her Aboriginal mother, father and sister or she would be charged with consorting. **1985** J. MILLER *Koori* 174 A Koori had to 'behave' to get the dog licence then continue with 'acceptable behaviour' in order to keep it. **1888** 'R. BOLDREWOOD' *Robbery under Arms* (1937) 70 She was **dog-poor** and hardly able to drag herself along. **1898** *Worker* (Sydney) 2 Apr. 8/1 All these syndicates are running their properties dog poor, and by the time their leases expire they won't be worth taking over. **1904** *Truth* (Sydney) 31 Jan. 1/8 To use an Australianism, the Jew never gets 'dog poor'. **1940** 'K. BRUCE' *Digger Tourists* 112 I'm as lousy as a bandicoot and I'm getting dog poor carrying the damn chats round with me. **1975** B. FULLER *Ghan* 161 The engines, to use a bushman's opinion, are 'dog poor'. **1978** D. STUART *Wedgetail View* This big stuff should make a quid or two; they'll be dog-poor but they'll fatten quick enough. **1981** J. ROBERTS *Massacres to Mining* 70 In most northern pubs the Aborigines are not welcome in the main bar. Instead they are sent to a small side window, or to a '**dog window**' as it is known, or to a dingy minor bar. In the 330 miles between Alice Springs and Tennant Creek all but one of the pubs has a 'dog window'.

b. In special collocations: **dog's disease,** any of several ailments (see quots.); **jew's harp,** see quot. 1904; also *fig.*; **show,** a dog's chance, i.e. no chance at all.

1890 *Braidwood Dispatch* 30 Apr. 2/2 They complain in the first instance of a pain in the head... It is very similar to the epidemic we had some years ago which went by the names of the 'Temora rot' and the '**dog's disease**'. **1932** L. MANN *Flesh in Armour* 218 Half the platoon had had dog's disease. **1953** S.J. BAKER *Aust. Speaks* 166 *Dog's disease*, malaria. **1967** *Kings Cross Whisper* (Sydney) xxxii. 7/1 *Brewer's asthma*, a very severe hangover. Also brewer's croup. Dog's disease. **1982** N. KEESING *Lily on Dustbin* 77 'Dog's disease' to some people means 'flu, to others gastro-enteritis. **1898** W. DOLLMAN *Bush Fancies* 66 You white-livered son of a gun, you **dog's jew's harp!** **1904** *Bulletin* (Sydney) 7 Apr. 16/4 In the heart of the Out-back .. when sugar runs out 'dogs' Jews' harps' are cooked, *i.e.* dumplings punctuated with currants. **1934** *Ibid.* 14 Feb. 21/2 A queer tucker name is dogs' jew's-harps, by which are known the currant dumplings that are cooked when the sugar is done. **1898** E. DYSON *Below & on Top* 179, I don't think you've got a **dog's show.** **1899** *Truth* (Sydney) 3 Dec. 4/5 This A.J.C. measure for the 'moralization of gambling', has a 'dog's show' of becoming law.

c. As **tinned dog,** canned meat; also **(tin) dog.**

1895 *Bulletin* (Sydney) 17 Aug. 27/2 We gave him some 'tinned dorg' and a drink. **1896** J.M. PRICE *Land of Gold* 109 Comestibles .. took the form of tinned meats, 'tinned dog', as all the various preparations of beef and mutton in the bush are humorously .. designated. **1905** L. BECKE *Tom Gerrard* 251 'Tinned dog', as they termed the New Zealand and American canned beef and mutton they bought from the packers. **1913** W.K. HARRIS *Outback in Aust.* 29 In some of the isolated mining camps .. damper, 'dog', and tea is served up meal after meal. **1916** 'T.O. LINGO' *Austral. Comic Dict.* 15 *Tinned dog*, bushman's pate de fois gras. **1920** A.I. MACLEOD *Hack's Brat* (ed. 2) 15 She carried on a remarkably profitable business, dispensing rice and tinned dog at ruinous prices. **1929** R.D. LANE *Romance Old Coolgardie* 55 Those were the days of tin dog and damper. **1936** J. KIRWAN *My Life's Adventure* 68 These recollections call up .. tinned foods always called 'tinned dog'. **1942** *Bulletin* (Sydney) 25 Mar. 13/2 After a months-on-end diet of damper and 'dog' a slab of the big striding bird comes as a gift from the gods. **1950** C.E. GOODE *Yarns of Yilgarn* 37 Living on tinned dog .. as the settlers called it. **1972** N. KING *Nickel Country* 52 Tinned meat, or 'tin dog' as it was mainly called, must have agreed with some. **1982** R. ELLIS *Bush Safari* 15 Another frugal meal of 'tinned dog', a couple of flats to mend, and straight into our swags.

d. As **tin dog,** an improvised rattle used in driving stock: see quot. 1924.

1924 L. ST. C. GRONDONA *Kangaroo keeps on Talking* 60 If one does not possess a tyke of some description one makes .. a 'tin dog', which .. is evolved by perforating the lids of tobacco tins and threading them on a loop of fencing wire. This makes a horrible din, which,—if efficacious while the novelty lasts,—seems later to amuse, and, finally, to bore the sheep. The jackeroo who invents a tin dog with a bite as well as a bark should be raised to the peerage. **1979** R. EDWARDS *Skills Austral. Bushman* 157 It has been suggested that the lagerphone, with its cluster of beer-bottle tops, is derived from the tin dog.

e. In the phr. **a dog tied up,** an unpaid debt, esp. at an hotel.

1905 *Bulletin* (Sydney) 24 Oct. 14/3 'Scarver'—to flit from town secretly, leaving sorrowing creditors behind... 'Leaving a dog tied up' refers to the debts left by the 'scarverer'. **1906** A.B. PATERSON *Outback Marriage* 178 'Paddy's 'ad a dorg tied hup 'ere' (*i.e.*, an account outstanding) 'this two years.' **1944** L. GLASSOP *We were Rats* 83 'He's left so many dogs tied up all over Australia it's a wonder there're enough of 'em left to hold tin-hare meetings,' said Eddie... 'I'll have you know I pay my debts promptly.' **1962** 'N. CULOTTA' *Gone Fishin'* 124, I says what about me three pound six, I haven't got a dog tied up here, have I? **1977** T. RONAN *Mighty Men on Horseback* 17, I had to live on the cuff till the cheque was made good and by that time I had so many dogs tied up that it took the proceeds to let them go.

dog, *n.*[2] [U.S. *dog* informer, traitor: see OEDS *sb.* 3 e.]

a. An informer; one who betrays colleagues or changes allegiance; chiefly in the phr. **to turn dog (on).**

1848 J. SYME *Nine Yrs. Van Diemen's Land* 273 A man known to give officers information is designated by the epithet 'Dog'. **1863** *Frank Gardiner, or Bushranging in 1863* 14 Some of the lads .. are regular young hands, and might turn dog. **1877** *Vagabond Ann.* 138 'A dog' is the name given to a prisoner who spies on his comrades, or to a warder who is obnoxiously active in searching and reporting every petty case. **1885** *Australasian Printers' Keepsake* 148 The varmint .. turned dog on his mates. **1893** *Western Champion* (Barcaldine) 21 Mar. 1/1 A squatter in the Moree district had a dummy who 'turned dog' and would not transfer at the end of the five years' term. **1896** *Worker* (Sydney) 5 Sept. 3/3 Buttabone camp has broken up, and a great number of the members of it, who ate good Union tucker, turned dog and went into the Buttabone shed at the reduced price. **1902** *Bulletin* (Sydney) 31 May 31/2 A man's mother *never* turns dawg! **1918** *Truth* (Sydney) 13 Jan. 1/7 Which is the more deplorable—the twistings of Billee Hughes or those of the old cobbers who turn dorg on him? *c* **1927** J. BRADSHAW *Highway Robbery under Arms* 35 Goodson .. laid me on to do it and turned dog on me. **1942** L. MANN *Go-Getter* 15 Chris often told himself he could not have turned dog on his employer. **1948** F. CLUNE *Wild Colonial Boys* 374 We all decided we'd rather be hung than turn dog on our mates. **1970** K.E.C. GRAVES *Third Chance* 88 Fred must have turned dog on her. **1979** L. NEWCOMBE *Inside Out* 29 Some of the young fellows couldn't live under the conditions and sought the protection of the authorities, only to be labelled 'dogs' by their fellows and to live a locked-away existence, scorned by crims and screws alike. **1980** M. WILLIAMS *Dingo!* 90 The fact that there were informers in the gaol turned my stomach—I had consoled myself with the belief that at least there'd be no 'dogs' at Grafton. **1984** R. & P. THYER *Streetlight* 57, I wouldn't trust her as far as I could throw her. One day she's going to turn dog on you.

b. *fig.*

1919 *7th Field Artillery Brigade Yandoo* 20 Mar. 136 The weather again 'turned dog on us'. Cold winds and driving rain. **1922** J.N. MACINTYRE *High Explosive* 17 The telegraph line .. was 'turning dog' on us; some days there was no connection—then it would get right, and so on. **1922** 'TE WHARE' *Bush Cinema* 84 The way-back herbalist .. seldom turns dog on the awful concoction which results from brook-lime (hyssop) boiled down with Epsom salts.

dog, *v.*[1] [f. DOG *n.*[2]] *intr.* To change allegiance; with **on,** to betray.

1896 E. DYSON *Rhymes from Mines* 129 I'm not goin' to dog on a *mate*. **1953** T.A.G. HUNGERFORD *Riverslake* 228 Perhaps that was why he was pulling out, though he didn't seem to be the type to dog.

dog, *v.*[2] *intr.* To hunt dingoes: see quot. 1981. Also *trans.*: see quot. 1944. Freq. as *vbl. n.*

1910 C.E.W. BEAN *On Wool Track* 55 A man is generally kept dogging, and the boundary rider gets a few pounds out of occasional scalps. **1923** J. ARMOUR *Spell of Inland* 152 He would be able to take out provisions at the same time to .. some men who were 'dogging' in the back country. **1932** M.R. WHITE *No Roads go By* 95 Every man on the station was doing a little 'dogging' as a side-line, scalps were worth twelve and sixpence each, and the game was keen. **1944** *Bulletin* (Sydney) 23 Feb. 12/1, I ran along to see Robbie and found him dogging a paddock near the road. **1978** D. STUART *Wedgetail View* 135 Spent a couple of years dogging, and if trapping dingoes wasn't real bushman's work, nothing was. **1981** A. GRANT *Camel Train & Aeroplane* 258 Over the border in Western Australia, dogging. [*Note*] Trapping, shooting or poisoning Dingoes or wild dogs to prevent their inroads into sheep flocks, for which they received a Government bounty paid on each scalp.

dogbox. A compartment in a railway carriage without internal access to other compartments; a substandard carriage.

1905 N.F. SPIELVOGEL *Gumsucker on Tramp* 44, I found .. railway cars worse than the worst Australia possesses. The one I came down here in was a dog box. **1928** M. FORREST *Reaping Roses* 50 Wanted to know why the blasted old 'dog-box' of a car had to come at all. **1963** B. BEAVER *Hot Summer* 128 They found a dog-box all to themselves which meant an uninterrupted half-hour between Mundulla and the first-stop. **1973** D. FOSTER *North South West* 93 I'm sitting, actually frozen, in the corner of some mail car going west, while outside my second class dogbox (we're stopped) is a platform.

dogger. [See DOG *v.*[2]] One who hunts dingoes.

1890 A. WOODHOUSE *Man with Apples* 64 He was up in Mallee Country .. catching dingoes. He was a reg'lar dogger. **1927** *Bulletin* (Sydney) 15 Sept. 27/4 The dogger .. had come to the homestead for more traps. **1935** W. GRAY *Days & Nights in Bush* 60 The pastoralists have men on camels that patrol their fences. The term 'dogger' is used for such a man. **1944** *Bulletin* (Sydney) 7 June 13/4 As a dogger f'r the council .. I get a call to go out to Rabbit Crick where there's bin a she-dawg chewin' up the jumbucks. **1952** A.M. DUNCAN-KEMP *Where Strange Paths go Down* 112 Crossing the claypan we came upon .. a dogger, busy laying his dingo bait trails. **1974** E. LINDALL *Search for Tomorrow* 129 Two old doggers raising dingoes in the scrub .. and selling the scalps to local government agents. **1984** *West Austral.* (Perth)

19 Jan 45/4 'A number of large dingoes apparently evaded the former dogger and are still at large,' Mr Grill said.

dog-leg, *a.* [f. *dog-leg*, of a bent form like a dog's hind leg.] Of a fence: made from logs laid horizontally on crossed supports (see quots. 1901 and 1980). Also **dog-legged.**

1836 Tas. Non-State Rec. 103/3 25 Oct., All that portion of Land Bounded on the north by a dog leg and furze fence. **1846** F. DUTTON *S.A. & its Mines* 203 There are the 'ditch and bank', 'American or log-fence', and the 'dog-leg fence'. **1854** W. SHAW *Land of Promise* 147 There are three descriptions of fences, the dog-leg, the kangaroo, and the post and rail; the former, which is in the shape of an X, requires a flying leap. **1879** 'RECENT SETTLER' *Emigration to Tas.* 86 The dogleg fence, formed by crossing two short spars and leaning upon them where they cross, a longer spar and so on. **1901** H. LAWSON *Joe Wilson & his Mates* 99 The clearing was fenced in by a light 'dog-legged' fence (a fence of sapling poles resting on forks and X-shaped uprights). **1907** *Truth* (Sydney) 14 Apr. 1/7 The wind was not strong enough to blow a Tom-cat off a dog-legged fence. **1922** J. LEWIS *Fought & Won* 148 Then we fenced off the peninsula with a dog-leg fence. **1947** J.W. GORDON *Under Wide Skies* 20 And my thoughts drift back to childhood with a sentimental yearning For the old-time dog-leg fences and the sturdy post-and-rail. **1972** ANDERSON & BLAKE *J.S. Neilson* 3 So John Shaw learnt to handle an axe, felling the ancient gum trees and making dog-leg fences of interlaced timber spars. **1980** HOLTH & BARNABY *Cattlemen of High Country* 83 Another early method of construction was the dog-leg fence. Stumps about half a metre high with a V cut in them were placed in the ground at wide intervals. A log was laid with its ends on the Vs and supported at each stump by two poles—the dog-leg—crossed above the log and dug into the ground beside the stump. A second row of logs was laid through the crossed poles.

Hence **dogleg** *v. trans.*, to make (timber) into a dog-leg fence.

1891 E.H. HALLACK *W.A. & Yilgarn Goldfields* 14 One of the wheat paddocks is enclosed by the most valuable fencing material I have ever seen, viz., sandalwood, doglegged and propped to escape the risk of fire.

dogman. [f. *dog* mechanical device for gripping or holding something: see OED *sb.* 7.] A worker who rides on the hook of a crane, or a girder, etc., being lifted by a crane, giving signals to the crane-operator.

1948 *Act* (N.S.W.) no. 38 Sect. 17A (6), 'Dogman' means a person directly responsible for slinging and controlling the movement of loads by a crane used in building work or excavation work, or other work where the loads are not usually at all times in full view of the crane driver. **1958** *Guide Dogmen & Crane Chasers* (N.S.W. Dept. Labour & Industry) 3 It is the responsibility of the Dogman to carry out the work of a crane chaser and, in addition, control loads not usually in full view of the crane driver. **1962** R. CLARK *Dogman & Other Poems* 2 The dogman dangles from the clouds, Astride a beam of swinging air, Unrealized hero of the crowds, Whose upturned faces dimly stare. **1965** L. HAYLEN *Big Red* 42 The shrill whistle of the dogman 150 feet above warns us that he is signalling the winding driver to lower away. **1970** *Sunday Mail Mag.* (Brisbane) 25 Apr. 17/6 Most Sydney men will not raise their eyes beyond ladies' leg level except to see one other phenomenon—the daring dogmen on the skyhooks. **1985** *Canberra Times* 13 Feb. 7/3 BLF dogmen want same 'dirty deal'.

dog watch. *Droving.* [Transf. use of the nautical *dog watch* a short watch of two hours between 4 p.m. and 8 p.m.] A short watch in the early evening.

1935 G. MCIVER *Drover's Odyssey* 63 Only one man at a time could have supper, for the others were required to keep the sheep on the camp during what was known as 'the dog watch'. **1954** T. RONAN *Vision Splendid* 163 You can take over the dinner and dog watches as a full-time job. **1979** C. STONE *Riding Brumbies* 8 The first watch, for only one hour, is kept by one of the cattle-men to allow the other men to have their evening meal. This short watch is always called the 'dog watch'.

dogwood. [Transf. use of *dogwood* a shrub of the genus *Cornus.*] Any of several unrelated shrubs or trees, esp. ELLANGOWAN POISON BUSH, and *Jacksonia scoparia* (fam. Fabaceae) of N.S.W. and Qld.; the wood of these plants. See also STINKWOOD. Also *attrib.*

1828 Tas. Colonial Secretary's Office Rec. 1/14 262, A thick underwood of Dogwood. **1844** L. LEICHHARDT *Jrnl. Overland Exped. Aust.* 23 Oct. (1847) 20 A . . creek . . which, from the number of Dogwood shrubs (Jacksonia), in the full glory of their golden blossoms, I called 'Dogwood Creek'. **1856** *Jrnl. of Australasia* I. 37 Pomaderris apetala, broad-leaved dogwood. **1877** 'ANGLO-INDIAN' *Visit Tas.* 22 The brilliant tints of the young dogwood tree leaf. **1885** *Trans. & Proc. R. Soc. S.A.* VIII. 20 *Eremophila longifolia*—The Dogwood of bushmen, and named by them from the offensive smell which the leaves have when crushed. **1910** *Bulletin* (Sydney) 28 Apr. 14/4 Dog-wood (a valuable cattle fodder). **1920** B. CRONIN *Timber Wolves* 162 Here in Tassie . . Hazel we call dog-wood; your dog-wood we call merry weed. **1933** D. MACDONALD *Brooks of Morning* 181 Any new bush, shrub, or tree is to the timber-man 'a kind of dogwood'. **1971** K. WILLEY *Boss Drover* 118 The men make their boomerangs out of dogwood, a low tree thick enough for a six-inch post. **1981** G.M. CUNNINGHAM et al. *Plants Western N.S.W.* 399 The wood emits a most offensive odour when burning, hence two of its common names, stinkwood and dogwood. **1984** E. ROLLS *Celebration of Senses* 153 Burning Dogwood is as fetid as a company of farts.

dole.

1. *Hist.* Used *attrib.*, with reference to unemployment benefits during the Depression of the 1930s.

1930 *Sydney Morning Herald* 7 June 15/5 Representatives of 15 metropolitan councils yesterday asked the Minister for Labour and Industry (Mr Farrar) to alter the dole system so that men receiving unemployment relief should be allowed to work for it. **1933** J. TRURAN *Where Plain Begins* 230 His mind seemed unable to rise superior to the loss of those dole-tickets. **1934** *Red Star* (Perth) 19 Jan. 3/1 The dole-workers in Victoria won victories in their struggles. **1941** K. TENNANT *Battlers* 24 Men with track-cards . . wander the country in search of work, getting their food-orders from declared 'dole stations' in towns fifty or sixty miles apart. *Ibid.* 17 Thursday all over the West is dole day, when the track men come in to have their cards stamped at the police-station and get their rations to carry them to the next 'dole town'. **1959** D. HEWETT *Bobbin Up* 90, I remember him draggin' home week after week with those blasted dole tickets.

2. Special Comb. **dole-bludger,** one who exploits the system of unemployment benefits by avoiding gainful employment; so **dole-bludgery** *n.*, **dole bludging** *vbl. n.* and *ppl. a.*

1976 *Bulletin* (Sydney) 16 Oct. 20/1 A genuine dole bludger, a particularly literate young man . . explained that he wasn't bothering to look for work any more because he was sick and tired of being treated like a chattel. **1977** *Cattleman* (Rockhampton) June 16/3 Young people are being forced from their country homes because of lack of work opportunities and the only response from these so-called political protectors is to label them as 'dole bludgers'. **1978** *Westerly* iii. 9, I love the boy: a painty, dole-bludging, sink-full-of-dirty-dishes love, reeking of sentiment, but love. **1979** P. ADAMS *More Unspeakable Adams* 88, I, the undersigned, am a rotten dole bludger who is living on the hard-earned taxes of my fellow Australians. **1980** R. DAVIDSON *Tracks* 58 One of the myths concerning Aboriginal people is that they are chronic 'dole bludgers'. **1983** *Canberra Times* 26 July 3/3 He said that dole-bludging was a 'socially useful function', as were communes. **1984** *Austral. Short Stories* viii. 1 He had dole-bludgery down to a fine art: bought the Age every day and memorised the relevant jobs advertised so he could con any Social Services Inspector who came snooping. **1986** *Sydney Morning Herald* 8 Mar. 13/2 Board-riding dole bludgers from the south have swollen the unemployment figures.

doleite. *Hist.* One in receipt of an unemployment benefit, esp. during the Depression of the 1930s.

1963 HARNEY & LOCKWOOD *Shady Tree* 194 The first wave of people who resembled the present-day tourists, except that they had no money, were the train-jumpers and 'doleites' who spread across the countryside during the great depression. **1978** G. HALL *River still Flows* 61 The place was quite crowded with Doleites.

doley. Also **dolie.** [f. *dole* + -Y.] One in receipt of an unemployment benefit.

[**1941** *Argus* (Melbourne) 15 Nov. (Suppl.) 1/4 *Doleys*, soldiers in employment platoons.] **1953** 'CADDIE' *Caddie* 209 You needn't worry about 'im Caddie. 'E's a friend to all us doleys. **1961** W.E. HARNEY *Grief, Gaiety & Aborigines* 21 'Couldn't make out that old fellow the other day,' concernedly from a newly-arrived dolie. **1967** *Realist* (Sydney) xxv. 34/2 Few novels have been written which have had for their sole theme, the unemployed: the 'doleys' of the hungry years. **1978** *Nimbin Newsletter* 24 Apr. 5 Why can't there be cheaper prices for dolies like there are for students? **1982** *Sydney Morning Herald* 5 Apr. 6/6 How do the rest of you poor, frustrated out-of-work 'dolies' feel?

dollar.

1. *Hist.* A Spanish dollar circulating in N.S.W.; see also HOLEY DOLLAR.

1803 *Sydney Gaz.* 21 Aug., The Victorians had however absented themselves carrying off a silver watch, *nine* dollars and several pieces of silver foreign coin. **1810** *Ibid.* 14 Jan., Prompt payment to be made in Government and Paymaster's Bills or Dollars. **1825** *Howe's Weekly Commercial Express* (Sydney) 8 Aug. 3/1 Their Lordships are pleased to direct the dollar to be issued to the troops at 52d. each. **1832** *Colonial Times* (Hobart) 17 July, It is a very fortunate circumstance for this Colony, that the dollar at Sydney is not rated at so high a price as it is here, otherwise, in one month there would be *no* medium in circulation. **1836** *Bent's News* (Hobart) 6 Feb. 2 This Journal . . is only 3s. 3d. per quarter; or three dollars per annum. **1844** C. LYON *Narr. & Recoll. Van Dieman's Land* 27 A kind man, on the road, lent me a dollar to buy food.

2. *Hist.* [Also in Br. slang.] The sum of five shillings.

1902 *Sporting News* (Launceston) 13 Dec. 3/4 All the same, were the race run again, my dollar could go on. **c 1907** W.C. CHANDLER *Darkest Adelaide* 58 'Tell me your lowest price,' I said. . . 'Six bob,' she replied. 'No,' I said. 'Well, then make it a dollar, and that's cheap enough for anything.' **1911** A. WRIGHT *Gamblers' Gold* (1923) 58 Soon Harry's wagers dropped from pounds to dollars. **1941** *Troop Ship News: Newspaper of 'Queen Elizabeth'* 11 Nov. 3 That'll make the tongues of the dollar a day boys hang out. **1963** *Meanjin* 387 Give us another dollar. I won't spend more than a bob of it.

3. Since 1966, and independently of its earlier uses, the standard unit of Australian currency. Also *attrib.*

1963 *Sun* (Melbourne) 5 June 2/3 You can bet a dollar it's a dollar. . . Federal Cabinet will meet in Canberra today to choose a name for Australia's new basic decimal currency unit. And the strong tip is that the name dollar will be chosen. **1966** *Age* (Melbourne) 17 Jan. 3/3 The board is now employing 29 Dollar Jills. . . We hope people . . will call the girls for any information they need about decimal currency. **1971** *Sydney Morning Herald* 26 Jan. 6/3 If you go into countries where inflation really applies, you come back here and feel that the Australian dollar is holding very well. **1974** *Herald* (Melbourne) 17 July 5/3 Pet foods rank 10th, accounting for 2.6 c. of each dollar. **1985** *Canberra Times* 4 Jan. 12/2 The Australian dollar hit a record low against the U.S. dollar yesterday.

dollar bird. [With ref. to a coin-like white spot on each wing.] A predom. brown and blue-green bird, the roller *Eurystomus orientalis*, a summer visitor to n. and e. Aust. and widespread in s. Asia.

1827 *Trans. Linnean Soc. London* XV. 202 In Mr Caley's MSS. are the following notices of this bird. . . The settlers call it *Dollar Bird*, from the silver-like spot on the wing. **1845** L. LEICHHARDT *Jrnl. Overland Exped. Aust.* 15 Feb. (1847) 156 The dollar bird passed with its arrow-like flight from shade to shade. **1893** *Western Champion* (Barcaldine) 24 Jan. 1/2 A period of protection shall be in certain districts . . for the whole year, in respect of the following birds:- . . , dollar birds, [etc.]. **1935** F. BIRTLES *Battle Fronts Outback* 133 There came tumbling and flying overhead a dollar bird; so called . . because it makes a noise like your last dollar going over a marble counter. **1948** P.J. HURLEY *Red Cedar* 160 Dollar birds (larrikins of the skies). **1953** E. MITCHELL *Flow River, blow Wind* 166 Sara looked up at a dollar-bird . . rolling down the bright blue sky. **1977** W.A. WINTER-IRVING *Bush Stories* 43 That evening the dollar birds called loudly.

dolly, *n. Gold-mining.* [Transf. use of Br. dial. *dolly* wooden instrument used in washing clothes: see OED *sb.*[1] 4.]

1. An apparatus for crushing auriferous quartz in order to extract the gold.

1859 W. KELLY *Life in Vic.* II. 67 Numbers of people earning a good livelihood by . . pounding it [*sc.* quartz] in dollies—a simple contrivance, constructed of a rude balance lever, made to act on the stump of a tree, by pulling it down with a rope, and letting it rebound after giving the blow, the blow falling on a common iron grating placed over a hollow in the stump, from which the crushed stuff is taken by means of a hand-hole cut in the side. **1869** R.B. SMYTH *Gold Fields & Mineral Districts* 609 *Dolly*, an instrument used by diggers for dividing and mixing the tough clay or cement with water in the puddling tub. A log of wood shod with iron and suspended from a sapling over a stump, and used in the early days for crushing quartz. **1888** *Illustr. Austral. News* (Melbourne) 26 May (Suppl.) 107/4 The first quartz crushing power would provoke a smile now on the goldfields if any one seriously attempted to work a 'dolly', which consisted simply of a short pole put in the ground, with a good sized sapling fixed across the top of it. **1928** M.E. FULLERTON *Austral. Bush* 161 The quartz-mining era necessarily turned away many of the old diggers, men whose work had been with shovel and windlass, with pan and 'dolly'. **1929** W.J. RESIDE *Golden Days* 279 Under the test of the dolly, the ore lived up to its promise. **1959** D. STUART *Yandy* 15 The thudding of the iron dolly in the dolly pot was a familiar sound, and the quartz in the walled ore paddock grew larger day by day.

2. Special Comb. **dolly pot,** the receptacle in which the auriferous quartz is crushed by the dolly.

1931 A.W. UPFIELD *Sands of Windee* 37 It was . . a dolly-pot used by gold miners to pound up samples of ore to dust, then to flood the dust with water and roughly ascertain the gold content. **1944** M.J. O'REILLY *Bowyangs & Boomerangs* 40 The method is to knap off part of the reef, powder it in a 'Dolly pot', and wash in a gold dish, where values, if any, will show up. **1951** G. FARWELL *Outside Track* 29 He would come back to camp with half a dozen white-faced rocks, tirelessly crushing them in his dollypot. **1977** D. STUART *Drought Foal* 87 They know all about . . prospectors, dolly-pots, panning off, batteries and five ounce crushings.

dolly, *v.* [f. prec.]

1. *trans.* To crush (auriferous quartz) using a dolly. Also *absol.*

1893 A.F. CALVERT *W.A. & its Gold Fields* 32 The reefs are so rich at the surface that some of the alluvial diggers in slack times have earned fair wages by simply dollying the stone. **1896** *Bulletin* (Sydney) 18 Jan. 3/2 There's nothin' beats the diggin's when you have a reef-in' show, An' dollied out your exes from the surface of the blow. **1911** *Huon Times* (Franklin) 17 May 4/3 From less than half a dish of dirt, 76½ oz. of gold was dollied. **1935** J.K. EWERS *Story of Pipe-Line* 35 Bayley and Ford continued to dolly gold from this mine. **1939** I.L. IDRIESS *Cyaniding for Gold* 79 So save the skimmings and later dolly them: to be certain, send a sample for assay. **1944** *Bulletin* (Sydney) 26 July 12/4 George came on a granite boulder with leaders of quartz. He took a sample, dollied it and washed up a few specks of color. **1965** L. HAYLEN *Big Red* 64 He had sunk a shaft and dollied along the river, but that was years ago. **1976** *Tracks we Travel* 127 It's only a narrow reef—nine inches in parts, never more'n twenty; an' shallow—but the gold's thick enough to dolly.

2. *fig.*

1890 A.J. VOGAN *Black Police* 56 I'll get dollied if fayther cotched me back at 'ome. **1937** W. & T.I. MOORE *Best Austral. One-Act Plays* 145 No stone undollied! I'll swear not.

Hence **dollying** *vbl. n.*

1894 A.F. CALVERT *Coolgardie Goldfield* 21 Only the very rich reefs—those that will give a return for dollying—are being worked. **1898** D.W. CARNEGIE *Spinifex & Sand* 60 We found gold sprinkled through the stone like pepper, and by 'dollying' obtained good results. **1929** W.J. RESIDE *Golden Days* 172 Dollying is the process of crushing the stone in a mortar, after which it is washed and panned off to ascertain if it contains gold.

dolly's wax. In the phr. **to be (full) up to dolly's wax,** to be satiated (with food).

1945 S.J. BAKER *Austral. Lang.* 207 Among nursery expressions which have acquired a fairly stabilized currency . . are . . the catchphrase [*sic*], *up to pussy's bow* and *dolly's wax*, to denote a surfeit, especially of food. **1965** B. HUMPHRIES *Nice Night's Entertainment* (1981) 85 Everyone was full up to dolly's wax and I was absolutely stonkered. **1982** N. KEESING *Lily on Dustbin* 17 When my children were small a man, then in his eighties, sat back from our table after lunch and announced, 'I'm full up to dolly's wax!' It had to be explained that dolls once had delicate, modelled wax heads with a neck shaped so that it could be sewn to a stuffed rag body.

Domain. [Spec. use of *domain* the land immediately attached to a mansion: see OED *demesne* 3 c.] The name given to the land surrounding Government House in Sydney which is now a public park. Used *attrib.* of frequenters of the area in Comb. with various nouns denoting **(a)** a soap-box orator; **(b)** a vagrant, esp. as **Domain dosser.** See also YARRA-BANKER.

(a) 1883 *Bulletin* (Sydney) 17 Nov. 20/4 The question of interference with the 'Domain howlers' is a very much wider one than would be understood by the perusal of the brief discussion in the Assembly the other day. **1884** *Liberator* (Melbourne) 21 Sept. 259/2 The Domain 'howlers' as the open air preachers are irreverently dubbed. **1913** *Truth* (Sydney) 14 Dec. 6/6 (*heading*) A glut of domain orators. **1918** J.H.C. SLEEMAN *Queer Qld.* 13 The stump orator, the domain blusterer, exhausts adjectival epithets to denounce the profiteer. **1951** *Bulletin* (Sydney) 17 Jan. 12/3 The Sphinx and the late Dean Maitland were Domain spruikers by comparison. **1956** J.T. LANG *I Remember* 164 There were also the Domain demagogues, who simply wanted a chance to get on to a platform to make wild threats. **1979** S. MORAN *Reminisc. of Rebel* p. v, He was a Domain orator and an outstanding one. **(b) 1891** *Truth* (Sydney) 25 Jan. 2/4 Then followed all the 'black-legs' of the late strike, most of them bearing the stamp of Domain prowlers and scamps. **1895** *Worker* (Sydney) 11 May 2/4 A 'Domain squatter' arrested for vagrancy, was . . much overjoyed at the prospect of not having to doss under the rocks. **1897** *Ibid.* 21 Aug. 1/1 Meet him as a Domain dosser tomorrow and he has an entirely different opinion. **1901** *Tocsin* (Melbourne) 3 Jan. 1/2 In Sydney at this boom time were found . . in one day one thousand homeless 'Domain dossers' coming on the same charity for tickets authorising them to obtain one meal a day for a week. **1902** *Bulletin* (Sydney) 21 June 36/2 The State Labor Farm . . is a satisfactory answer to such Domain gentry as perambulate this city with their wardrobe in a state of disrepair. **1903** 'BOONDI' *Boondi's Bk.* 37 A 'bull-dog' ant hates water worse than a Domain 'dosser' does. **1909** *Bulletin* (Sydney) 30 Dec. 15/3 Squatter-men in the past failed because they weren't able to breed a Domain dosser type of sheep, which could go more than a year without water. **1913** H. LAWSON *Triangles of Life* 110 Imagine a Sydney Domain Dosser in his last stage of dosserdom. **1918** *Bulletin* (Sydney) 28 Nov. 47/1 If the Domain dosser were dumped down in a far-back locality . . he would think he was faced with bitter times indeed. **1933** H.B. RAINE *Whip-Hand* 2 These two Domain dossers were no exception.

Hence **Domainiac** *n.*, **Domainite** *n.*

1903 *Truth* (Sydney) 15 Feb. 1/5 If cleanliness is next to godliness many **Domainiacs** have wandered far from grace. *Ibid.* 28 June 1/6 A Domaniac asserted, on Sunday last, that the . . dead King of Servia was a democrat. **1918** *Ross's Monthly* Dec. 5/1 The efforts to convert the Sydney **Domainites** threaten to become popular, like 'slumming' and other forms of patronage and spiritual pride.

domesticated, *ppl. a. Hist.* Of an Aboriginal: trained to live with (and serve) the colonists: see also CIVILIZED.

1835 *True Colonist* (Hobart) 26 Jan. 2/4 The domesticated blacks who have been Mr R's faithful attendants. **1839** W. MANN *Six Yrs.' Residence* 66 They may be influenced by the introduction of the domesticated natives from Flinders' Island amongst their less civilized brethren in New Holland. **1846** *Sydney Morning Herald* 29 Apr. 3/1 Mr Isaacs . . started . . from his station of the Darling Downs, in company with a domesticated aboriginal to act as a guide.

donah /ˈdoʊnə/. Also **dona.** [Br. slang; a. Sp. *dona* a woman.] A woman; a sweetheart (chiefly *c* 1900 in an urban, working-class context).

[**1859** J.C. HOTTEN *Dict. Mod. Slang* 32 *Dona and Feeles*, a woman and children.] **1874** *Melbourne Punch* 9 July 276/1 'Nobby, 'ere's Nixon with a new dona!' (which, being interpreted meaneth that the young man Nixon is paying his addresses to a fresh sweetheart). **1882** *Sydney Slang Dict.* 1 *Bashing a dona*, beating a woman. **1891** *Truth* (Sydney) 5 Apr. 8/2, I noticed that all the ladies or 'donas' were seated at one end of the room. **1892** *Bulletin* (Sydney) 5 Nov. 17/2 To thus desert his donah old was risky and a sin. **1900** *Truth* (Sydney) 27 May 2/8 Ladies and gentlemen from the swell suburbs and both Society Points, blokes and donahs from the lanes and alleys. **1902** *Ibid.* 3 Aug. 1/4 'Never introduce your donah to a parson', would seem to be a good motto nowadays. **1905** N.F. SPIELVOGEL *Gumsucker on Tramp* 14, I expected to find a rowdy crowd of 'Arries and 'Arriets, of 'blokes' and their 'donahs'. **1919** C.H. THORP *Handful of Ausseys* 178 Some uv you Horstralians still think yer out wiff yer donah 'n liftin' 'er week-end suit-case. **1930** 'BRENT OF BIN BIN' *Ten Creeks Run* (1952) 146 The fury breathed by Dot, of whom he had thought swaggeringly as his mere donah, was disintegrating. **1962** D. MCLEAN *World turned upside Down* 12 He was as handsome a young Australian larrikin as ever dipped his lid to a donah. **1977** D. STUART *Drought Foal* 154 Off to Perth, an' across to Adelaide an' Melbourne by steamer, a couple of donahs with him all the time.

dong, *v.* [Fig. use of *dong* the sound made by a bell or clock, prob. as a play on Br. dial. *ding* to strike, beat.] *trans.* To strike; to hit.

1916 G.I. ADCOCK Lett. (1930) 4 (typescript) A Corporal is charged with striking a Sergeant. . . I feel that the Corporal would have failed his manhood had he not 'donged' him. **1930** L.W. LOWER *Here's Luck* (1955) 126 'Slam him!' I shouted to George. . . 'Dong him!' **1938** X. HERBERT *Capricornia* 84 Shut up, Frank. . . Don't go upsettin' your Ma or I'll dong you one. **1945** I.L. IDRIESS *Horrie Wog-Dog* 14 If ever you bring another pet snake into my sight, I'll dong it and you too! **1962** D. MCLEAN *World turned upside Down* 17 You're a good kid when you want to be, and I hate to dong you, but you know the rules in my bar. **1969** W. DICK *Naked Prodigal* 62 If Ian comes in and asks where's tea I'll dong him. **1982** R. HALL *Just Relations* 113 The publican . . gives young Annie Lang a pat on the bottom as a compliment but she dongs him a beauty.

dong, *n.* [Cf. prec.] A blow; a punch.

1932 L. LOWER *Here's Another* 74 How would they like a dong in the gills with a golf ball? **1941** S.J. BAKER *Pop. Dict. Austral. Slang* 24 *Dong*, a blow, esp. with the fist. **1959** D. LOCKWOOD *Crocodiles & Other People* 52 'Maybe Darwin, here, wanted a fight, too?' one suggested. . . 'Hey, Darwin,' an athletic giant growled at me, 'is you insulted you wasn't arst into the dinner dong?' **1965** *Telegraph* (Brisbane) 5 July 8 *Dong*, poke (punch).

donga. [S. Afr. *donga* a channel or gully formed by the action of water: see OED.]

1. A broad shallow often circular depression most commonly found in dry country.

1902 *Bulletin* (Sydney) 8 Mar. 14/3 The origins of . . 'donga' (a hollow)? **1913** W.M. ANDERSON *Rhymes of Rouseabout* 38 I've chucked my canteen down a donga. **1924** *Austral. Museum Mag.* Jan. 19 Scattered over the plain for about twelve miles westward of Ooldea, are slight depressions having the appearance of shallow lake beds, where the soil is softer and the low monotonous blue bush gives place to thick rank grasses and clumps of stunted scrub. These . . 'dongas' . . watered only in times of heavy rain, must seem a veritable haven of refuge to the animal life of the plains. **1943** *Coast to Coast 1942* 158 Brilliant flowers in the dongas after it had rained. **1968** V. SERVENTY *Southern Walkabout* 90 The Nullarbor is unbelievably flat. . . Particularly interesting are hollows called by the locals 'dongas'. These are possibly places where caverns have collapsed and soil has collected. With the deeper soil, grows a more lush vegetation. **1975** L.H. CLARK *Rouseabout Reflections* 100 Down in the donga by the Northern Run, A poor old swaggie hung himself. **1984** M. BLAKERS et al. *Atlas Austral. Birds* 467 Fire and grazing by rabbits have destroyed the vegetation of many dongas.

2. A makeshift or temporary dwelling: see quot. 1972.

1900 *Truth* (Sydney) 28 Jan. 7/4 And dossed in dongas ev'ry night Daown in the old Dermain! **1941** *Through: Official Jrnl. Signals 8th Austral. Division* Dec. 27 The great number of mosquito proof 'Dongas' erected on the beach. **1956** *Sydney Morning Herald* 15 Oct. 1/10 In New Guinea a party is called a 'ding' and a house a 'donga'. **1960** L.H. Evers *Make Way for Tomorrow* 75 You're welcome to come and stay in my donga for as long as you like. **1972** G.W. Turner *Eng. Lang. in Aust. & N.Z.* (rev. ed.) 22 *Donga*, a 'gully', expanding its meaning to include any kind of shelter . . seems likely to be traceable to the battlefields of the Boer War. **1973** J. O'Grady *Survival in Doghouse* 18 Dave has a little old electric stove in his donga—the kind that you just plug in. **1986** *Canberra Times* 22 Apr. 1/5 'Remote area nurses' . . are based in scorching dustbowls where they sizzle in 'dongas'—aluminium demountable shacks—that pass for houses.

donk.

1. Abbrev. of *donkey*, an ass; now used elsewhere but perh. orig. Austral.

1907 *Bulletin* (Sydney) 17 Jan. 40/1 The donkey is now much used in the Australian interior. . . The donk.'s constitution is of iron. **1918** *Aussie: Austral. Soldiers' Mag.* Jan. 4/1 It sorter gets yer thinkin' when the night's as dark as pitch, An' yer donks get mad an' stubborn, an' yer packs they wants a 'itch. **1935** R.B. Plowman *Boundary Rider* 56 'Orses be —! I've give 'er six of the best donks in me team. **1949** I.L. Idriess *One Wet Season* 15 A team of fifty-eight donks would haul a load up to ten tons. **1956** A. Marshall *How's Andy Going?* 186 About every ten minutes a Man Who Understood Donkeys came along. 'Ah, a donk!' he would say with an impressive familiarity. **1975** X. Herbert *Poor Fellow my Country* 57 There's an old chap works a donkey-team down inside. . . He's got a lot of donks.

2. Abbrev. of *donkey-engine* a small, usu. subsidiary, engine.

1960 *Meanjin* 10, I thought that if I throttled back the engines a bit, with a few more revs in the starboard donk to keep the wing up, she'd be nose-heavier and wouldn't yaw. **1964** K. Tennant *Summer's Tales* 63 'The engines must be attended to; I'm the engineer,' he told her. 'Engineer be buggered,' she said. 'Bloody donk driver.' **1977** W. Moore *Just to Myself* 83 He took the head off and decided the donk had to come out. **1981** P. Barton *Bastards I have Known* 61 He lifted the engine cover and peered around the donk.

donkey. *Obs.* [Transf. use of *donkey* a beast of burden.] A swagman's bundle of belongings; Swag *n.* 1.

1872 C.H. Eden *My Wife & I in Qld.* 17 They all chaffed us about our swags, or donkeys or drums, as a bundle of things wrapped in a blanket is indifferently called. **1912** *Mod. Dict. Eng. Lang.* 779 *Donkey* . . same as *drum*. **1945** S.J. Baker *Austral. Lang.* 102 A *drum* . . is the equivalent of *swag* . . *donkey*.

donkey-lick, *v.* [f. *donkey* a horse + *lick* to defeat.] *trans.* To defeat (an opponent, etc.) resoundingly. Also **donkey-wallop.**

1890 *Bulletin* (Sydney) 22 Mar. 8/1 He sold for a hundred and thirty, Because of a gallop he had One morning with Bluefish and Bertie, And donkey-licked both of 'em bad. **1903** *Sporting News* (Launceston) 5 Dec. 1/3 Melrose gave Miss Time 15 yds . . and 'donkey-licked' her. **1916** *Truth* (Sydney) 16 Jan. 1/5 The disorganised Lib. rabble at Drummoyne only accentuates the fear of the Labs. that they'd be donkey-licked if they sent a candidate of their own. **1919** *Smith's Weekly* (Sydney) 5 July 5/2 Being one of the best ponies of the day for his inches he of course 'donkey-licked' the opposition whenever his connections put their money in. **1958** F. Hardy *Four-Legged Lottery* 42 'Who won the footie?' 'Ah, Richmond got donkey-licked. Played bad all day.' **1971** *Sunday Sun* (Brisbane) 17 Oct. 14/2 Only last week I donkey licked the local kindy kids at drop the hankie. **1975** X. Herbert *Poor Fellow my Country* 897 Pat snarled at him, 'Get donkey-walloped!' **1984** *Sun-Herald* (Sydney) 20 Sept. 65/1 Hawthorn donkey-walloped Essendon in last year's one-sided grand final by 83 points.

donkey orchid. [See quot. 1942.] Any of several terrestrial orchids of the genus *Diuris* (fam. Orchidaceae) of all States but not N.T., esp. *D. longifolia*.

1926 J. Pollard *Bushland Man* 207 They plucked . . donkey orchids, leek orchids. **1942** C. Barrett *Austral. Wild Flower Bk.* 132 Some of the many kinds of *Diuris* or double-tails are called 'donkey orchids', with reference to the broad, spreading petals which are not unlike a toy donkey's ears. **1949** D. Walker *We went to Aust.* 184 The donkey orchid, a ridiculous little thing with long ears like an ass, but more comely. **1967** B.Y. Main *Between Wodjil & Tor* 97 Donkey orchids opened their gentle faces amongst the twigs and branchlets under the jam trees. **1978** L. White *Memories of Childhood* 1 All the small orchids; spiders, donkeys, yellows, enamels.

donkey-vote. In a preferential system of voting: a vote recorded by unthinkingly allocating preferences according to the order in which candidates' names appear on the ballot-paper; such votes viewed collectively.

1962 *Meanjin* 356 Would you care to comment on the fact that your surname begins with the letters 'Ab-'? Yes, I see no reason to believe that the alphabetical system for candidates' names will be abandoned on ballot-papers. That being the case . . it seems that I shall always be at the top of the list. . . If I take you correctly sir, you are subtly stressing the importance of the 'donkey vote'? **1963** *Current Affairs Bull.* (Sydney) 25 Nov. 16 The 'donkey vote' is an accepted political term to describe electors who vote straight down the ticket irrespective of parties or merits of candidates. **1968** G. Mikes *Boomerang* 113 The donkey-votes mostly affect elections for the Senate. **1972** J. Mackerras *Austral. Gen. Elections* 245 Australian elections are marked by a factor known as the 'donkey vote'. People who cast such votes simply number their ballot-papers from top to bottom. **1984** *Sun-Herald* (Sydney) 11 Mar. 168/1 Remember Rev. Fearless Fred Nile getting the number one spot on the Upper House ballot papers for his Call to Australia group at the last election. God's work, said Fred, to help him get the donkey vote.

dook /duk, djuk/, *v.* Also **duke.** [f. *dook*, var. *duke* hand.] *trans.* To give.

1954 T. Ronan *Vision Splendid* 119 Did I ever give you that tenner you duked me at the Border Races? **1955** D. Niland *Shiralee* 154 How are you off for lettuce? . . I can dook you a caser if it's any good to you. **1958** T. Ronan *Pearling Master* 126 Jazz, whenever he was holding, always duked a few bob to the Salvos. **1966** D. Niland *Pairs & Loners* 112 He dooked me a couple of quid and said he'd do his best for us. **1977** T. Ronan *Mighty Men on Horseback* 14, I duked Paris a couple of quid. **1978** H.C. Baker *I was Listening* 41 You . . just dooks yerself a good hand from the bottom of the pack.

doorknock. An appeal in which agents for a (charitable) cause go from house to house soliciting contributions; a campaign in support of a political party run similarly. Also *attrib.*, esp. as **doorknock appeal.**

1958 *Sun* (Melbourne) 27 May 17/1 All set for 'Campaign Door-knock'. . . With the Lord Mayor . . are some of the girls who helped pack kits for Anti-Cancer Campaign collectors. **1958** *Age* (Melbourne) 2 June 1/3 Operation Door Knock, in aid of the anti-cancer campaign would far exceed the £100,000 target according to early reports the chairman of the campaign (Mr Don Chipp) said last night. **1963** *War Cry* (Melbourne) 7 Dec. 5/5 Divisions three and four channelled their interests into the door-knock. **1965** *Bulletin* (Sydney) 9 Jan. 9/3 The most recent example was the failure of the Foundation for Aboriginal Affairs to raise £150,000 in a door-knock appeal in Sydney. **1965** *War Cry* (Melbourne) 28 Aug. 6/1 Wherever door-knocks have been conducted on a proper basis there have flowed into the corps, and into the lives of individual participants in the appeal, countless streams of blessing. **1971** *Bulletin* (Sydney) 2 Jan. 4/2 They are not over-enthusiastic about 'special' doorknock days? **1979** *Mercury* (Hobart) 5 July 5/3 The climax of the appeal is a doorknock held this Sunday. **1984** *Canberra Times* 26 July 18/4 The doorknock appeal on Sunday will see teams in all suburbs.

doover. /ˈduvə/. Also **doovah.** [Poss. repr. Yiddish pronunc. of Hebrew *davar* a word or thing.] A thingummyjig; but see quots. 1945, 1959, and 1972.

1940 *Artilleryman: Official Newspaper 2/1 Field Regiment* 6 May 8 Which may be due to the fortnight's 'Douvre' and its attendant change of scenery. **1941** *Wiry: Mag. Second Sixth Field Regiment* Feb. 1 You men of Doover, hear the Call! Sleep on ye men, we take the torch. **1943** J. Binning *Target Area* 139 We introduced them to the word 'doover'. Everything is a 'doover'. If you are looking for an oil can or a piece of soap, you wonder where you put the 'doover'. **1945** 'Master-Sarg' *Yank discovers Aust.* 17 A doover is anything at all and takes the place of the old 'gadget'. Strictly it seems to mean a slit-trench or other funk hole. **1959** E. Lambert *Glory thrown In* 8 Beneath the camouflage nets and the roofs of dug-outs ('doovers' the Australians called them) the industry of war proceeded. **1965** K. Tennant *Summer's Tales* 216 Polished like the doovers on a Nubian princess's charm bracelet. **1968** S. Gore *Holy Smoke* 77 See, they was humpin' along all these other doovers as well as the tucker. **1972** K. Clift *Saga of Sig* 62 Tubby Allen . . was ensconced in a 'doover'—a rough dugout with a piece of truck canvas and camouflage netting. **1977** R. Beilby *Gunner* 269 A large crowd from the Battalion had celebrated after a three-day 'doover', one of those maddening mimic training battles.

dormouse possum. *Pygmy possum*, see Pygmy.

1926 *Bulletin* (Sydney) 25 Feb. 24/1 The dormouse opossum is not as rare as correspondents seem to believe. **1949** B. O'Reilly *Green Mountains* 24 A tiny night rambler in our timber is the dormouse possum, the smallest of our marsupials. . . He sleeps through the winter in a nest deep in a hollow tree.

Dorothy Dix. [f. *Dorothy Dix*, pseud. of E.M. Gilmer (1870–1951), U.S. journalist and writer of a popular question-and-answer column.]

1. A parliamentary question asked of a Minister by a member of the party in government to give the Minister the opportunity to deliver a prepared reply. Also **Dorothy Dixer,** and *attrib.*

[**1941** *Through: Official Jrnl. Signals 8th Austral. Division* Dec. 4 Rarely is it we can slip by our Dorothy Dix (the censor).] **1963** *Austral. Financial Rev.* (Sydney) 31 Oct. 16/2 Queensland Senator Dame Annabelle Rankin may have been posing a 'Dorothy Dix' (political jargon for a planted question) to Senator Sir William Spooner. **1965** Schaffer & Corbett *Decisions* 307 It is possible that the question was a 'Dorothy Dix'. **1970** C.A. Hughes *Govt. Qld.* (1980) 144 In all Parliaments . . questions referred to by members as 'Dorothy Dixers' are part of the establishment. **1974** Blazey & Campbell *Political Dice Men* 90 Whitlam, in answer to a Dorothy Dix question, on April 11, roundly attacked Snedden's economic policy. **1979** B. Delaney *Narc!* 107, I was asked to prepare a 'Dorothy Dixer' for Senator Murphy—a question with a corresponding reply. **1983** G.G. Roper *Labor's Titan* 94 Hall was then asked a 'Dorothy-Dixer' as to whether Brookfield had placed the documents in his hand.

2. *Cricket.* Rhyming slang for a 'six'.

1979 *Age* (Melbourne) 2 July 9/5 He still laughs loudly about hitting a 'George Moore' (to the boundary) and a 'Dorothy Dix'—or 'Dorothy' for short—over the fence. **1983** Hibberd & Hutchinson *Barracker's Bible* 131 Cosier had eight Georgie Moones and two Dorothy Dixers in his knock of 65.

Hence **Dorothy Dixish** *a.*, pre-arranged; lacking spontaneity.

1977 D. Jaensch *Govt. S.A.* 87 Each sitting day opens with question time, sometimes prolonged and lively, more often monotonous and increasingly 'Dorothy Dixish'.

dose. *Obs.* [Joc. use of *dose* a quantity of medicine.] With **the:** alcoholic liquor.

1829 *Cornwall Press* (Launceston) 24 Feb. 11/2 This woman has for years been much addicted to the *dose*, in the manner of which too many examples are before us. **1831** *Independent* (Launceston) 10 Sept. 3/2 The debasing effects of that greatest curse to the colony '*the dose*' has occurred. **1839** *Port Phillip Patriot* 20 Mar. 5/1 He . . came by death, from falling into the river very drunk! *Another* victim to the *dose*!

double, *a.*

1. *Hist.* Used during the convict period in collocations to denote a degree of severity of punishment or sentence: **double cat-o'-nine-tails,** see quot. 1838; **convict,** a transported convict found guilty of a second offence in the colony and sentenced to more severe punishment; so **-convicted** *a.*, **conviction** (see also SECOND, SECONDARY *a.*[1]); **irons,** see quot. 1843; also **iron** *v. trans.*, **ironed** *ppl. a.* See also DOUBLY.

1838 *Rep. Select Committee Transportation* 12 Feb. 38 That which was used at Macquarie Harbour is what is called a thief's cat, or a **double cat-o'-nine-tails**; it did not comprise more than the usual number of tails, but each of those was a double twist of whipcord, and each tail contained nine knots; it was a very formidable instrument indeed. **1839** *Tasmanian* (Hobart) 8 Feb. 45 Was the cat with which the floggings were inflicted at Macquarie Harbour of the same description as the ordinary cat-o'-nine-tails?—No .. that which was used at Macquarie Harbour is what is termed a thief's cat, or a double cat-o'-nine-tails. **1827** [**double convict**] P. CUNNINGHAM *Two Yrs. in N.S.W.* II. 140 The unpleasant dilemma of rubbing his immaculate shoulders against a man who had been sullied by a double conviction. **1836** J.F. O'CONNELL *Residence Eleven Yrs. New Holland* 35 The Phoenix was .. made a receiving ship for double convicts, sentenced to penal settlements. **1843** *Sydney Morning Herald* 7 Sept. 2/8 Now, there is another class of double convicted felons—that is, those who, after being in this ironed gang, are again found guilty of robbery. **1854** H.B. STONEY *Yr. in Tas.* 48 It remained strictly a double convict station: no communication being allowed, except through the Government, until 1841. **1802** *N.S.W. Gen. Orders* 19 Oct. (1806) 7 Every Person who may be absent after that Date will, when apprehended, be punished with 500 lashes and kept in **double-irons** in the Gaol Gang during the remainder of their Terms of Transportation. **1811** *Sydney Gaz.* 30 Mar., *Sayd*, a Moorman, who effected his escape .. by jumping overboard in the night (although in double irons) .. has been many times advertised as a Runaway. **1819** J.H. VAUX *Mem.* I. 186, I continued to labour in double irons .. for about a month. **1827** H. HELLYER Diary 19 July, Threaten to double iron him if they can find him. **1829** *Sydney Monitor* 24 Oct. (Suppl.), A man who was brought before the bench, charged .. with swindling .. was seen at the bar in *double irons*. **1835** *True Colonist* (Hobart) 22 Dec. 3/3 Mr Bryan still continues in prison, double ironed. **1841** *Colonial Observer* (Sydney) 14 Oct. 9/2 Serving their sentences out in gaols, in road gangs, and in double irons! **1843** B. WAIT *Lett. from Van Dieman's Land* 245 On arriving at the place of rendezvous we found eighty or more all invested with double irons... Two rings or bazzles, for the leg, with a chain between them about two feet in length, and weighing about eight pounds.

2. In other miscellaneous collocations: **double board(ed)** *a.*, see quot. 1882; **dipping** *vbl. n.*, see quots. 1981 and 1983; **dissolution** (orig. *Vic.*), the simultaneous dissolution of the upper and lower houses of a parliament preparatory to an election; **drummer,** the black and yellow cicada *Thopha saccata* of s. and e. Aust. (see quot. 1903); see also UNION JACK; **dump,** see quot. 1974; also *attrib.* and as *v. trans.*; see also DUMP *v.* 1; **fleece** *a.*, see quot. 1920.

1882 ARMSTRONG & CAMPBELL *Austral. Sheep Husbandry* 174 There are many descriptions of sheds that find favour with our squatters; some consisting of shearing boards on either side, with the sheep in the middle of the shed; others, with the board in the centre and the sheep on each side. These are called single and **double-boarded** sheds. **1908** W.H. OGILVIE *My Life in Open* 36 In a 'double board' shed the pens [containing the sheep] are in the middle. **1981** *Bulletin* (Sydney) 6 Oct. 26/1 That phenomenon known as **'double dipping'** whereby the individual taxpayer is given tax concessions aimed at encouraging him to provide for his own retirement only to turn that into a non-income producing asset and put himself on the pension. **1983** *Ibid.* 22 Mar. 24/1 The practice of taking retirement benefits in the form of near tax-free lump sums has been compounded by the practice of turning such lump sums into assets and then going on the age pension. 'Double dipping', as this practice is known, has played havoc with the pension system since the Fraser Government abolished the asset test on pensions. **1985** *Canberra Times* 4 Dec. 2/4 The situation will allow double-dipping on a massive scale as retiring members of the workforce dispose of the money and then take up age pensions and other welfare benefits. **1880** *Argus* (Melbourne) 2 Feb. 4/6 Mr Service's remarks with regard to the proposed **double dissolution** clearly set forth the advantages which are expected to flow from the adoption of that principle. *Ibid.* 2 July 6/2 The phrase, 'The double dissolution', refers to the provisions by which, when the two houses disagree upon any particular measure... They .. are liable to be dissolved, and to be compelled to appeal to their constituents themselves. **1899** *Progress* (Brisbane) 29 Apr. 10/2 The provision for a double dissolution in the event of deadlocks sends both houses to the same constituents and enables an effective control to be exercised over them such as obtains in no other country. **1901** *Advocate* (Burnie) 13 Mar. 4/3 For the first time in these southern climes the power to effect a double dissolution is granted. **1931** *Century of Journalism* 386 In the event of .. a deadlock occurring, a simultaneous dissolution of both Houses (a 'double dissolution', as it came to be called) should take place. **1955** G. HEALEY *A.L.P.* 56 The Cook Government lasted a little more than a year, Sir Ronald Munro Ferguson, then Governor-General granting it the first double dissolution in the history of the Commonwealth. **1974** BLAZEY & CAMPBELL *Political Dice Men* 11 The May 1974 election was historic... It was the first time a double dissolution had been precipitated by the Senate. **1983** *Canberra Times* 4 Feb. 1/5 The basis for the double dissolution was the rejection by the Senate of 13 Bills relating to Sales tax. **1895** *Proc. Linnean Soc. N.S.W.* X. 528 From the way in which his musical apparatus projects this Cicada is called the **'Double Drummer'** by the Sydney boys; and the female without this development is called the 'Single Drummer'. **1903** *Agric. Gaz. N.S.W.* XIV. 340 Though the male is well known as the 'Double Drummer' on account of the large swollen covers over the drums, it is also known as the 'Union Jack' and the 'Washerwoman'. **1926** *Austral. Museum Mag.* Oct. 405 Of all the arboreal songsters none is so noisy nor so deafening as the insect the children call the Double Drummer, and which naturalists know as *Thopha saccata*. **1951** CUSACK & JAMES *Come in Spinner* 105 There came the piercing crackle of a cicada. 'He's a double-drummer.' **1956** S. HOPE *Diggers' Paradise* 207 The bodies of Double Drummers contained a mysterious acid believed to have uncanny healing properties. **1974** R. MCKIE *Mango Tree* 18 He had talked to her about .. the Double-drummer he had caught in the garden. **1936** [**double dump**] E. SCOTT *Aust. during War* in *Official Hist. Aust. 1914–18* XI. 575 In the process of double-dumping two bales are placed end to end in a machine, subjected to great pressure, and whilst in the compressed state bound together by steel bands or wires. **1952** *Coast to Coast 1951–52* 170 It's been a long road for most... Bitter struggles 'on the outer' for all the wretched scraps of jobs .. sulphur, superphosphates .. double-dump wool. **1955** J. MORRISON *Black Cargo* 76 Long before the war we was agitating for the abolition of double-dumps. **1974** J. GABY *Restless Waterfront* 237 A wool press is sometimes called a dump. When a bale that had been hand-pressed in the shearing shed went into our hydraulic presses, it was subjected to a pressure of four tons per square inch and was pressed or dumped down to half its original size. During the war .. two station-pressed bales were pressed together or double-dumped so that two ships could lift the wool ordinarily carried by three. **1920** *Bulletin* (Sydney) 29 Jan. 22/2 Every year on big stations there are a few bales of two years' growth, and it is branded **'Double fleece'**.

double, *v. trans.* Abbrev. of DOUBLE-BANK 3.

1950 H.C. WELLS *Earth cries Out* 116 The bicycle ride when Dick 'doubled' her home about midnight. **1982** P. RADLEY *Blue-Checker Corker* 121 Monte .. spun his bike round madly in the empty waiting room. 'Come on, Kylie! I'll doubleya home if you're game.'

Hence **double** *n.*, **doubler** *n.*, a lift on a bicycle or horse.

1943 *Bully Tin* (Baronta) 3 Oct. 3 The latter offered to give his visitor a 'doubler' on his iron steed. **1947** M. RAYMOND *Smiley gets Gun* 173 'Come on I'll give you a double.' Smiley proudly perched himself on the rump of the sergeant's horse and, clinging to the man's rawhide belt, called greetings to everyone he saw. **1975** R. MACKLIN *Queenslander* 3 Come on... I'll give you a doubler home on the bike.

double-bank, *v.* [Transf. use of *double-bank* to double, orig. of rowers either in pairs or two to an oar.]

1. *trans. Mining. Obs.* See quot. 1869.

1869 R.B. SMYTH *Gold Fields & Mineral Districts* 609 Double-Bank—To take up a claim parallel with and adjoining another claim in which has been found an auriferous reef or lead; with the object of getting the underlie of the reef, or a bend in the lead or some portion of the washdirt. **1899** G.R. NICOLL *Fifty Yrs.' Travels* 40 Ten feet was the frontage each man was allowed, and no one could 'double-bank' his claim.

2. *trans.*, becoming *absol.* [In Br. use but apparently more common in Aust.] To yoke on (a second team of bullocks or draught-horses) in circumstances where one is inadequate. Also as *vbl. n.*

1863 R. HENNING *Lett.* (1952) 56 Some of the bad creeks, where they 'double-bank the bullocks', as it is called: that is, put the whole team, thirty yokes perhaps, on to each dray to drag it over. **1879** 'AUSTRALIAN' *Adventures Qld.* 45 Hooking on two or three teams of bullocks—'double-banking', as it is technically called—to one dray, is commonly resorted to in difficult places, such as steep banks, deep sand, or bog. **1897** A.F. CALVERT *My Fourth Tour W.A.* 56 Some of the teamsters 'double-bank' as they call it, by putting on a mate's complement of horses, and then going back for the waggon that has been left behind. **1908** W.H. OGILVIE *My Life in Open* 57 There is nothing for it but to get help and 'double bank'. **1924** J. NISBET *Scraps* 6 Half-way up the hill were the drivers with two teams all of a string on one dray, 'double banking' over the stiff pinch. **1933** W.L. OWEN *Cossack Gold* 124 The teams were often bogged, so had to double-bank. This meant yoking both teams to one wagon. **1956** R.G. EDWARDS *Overlander Songbk.* 125 And when the rain it comes at last, the roads they are like glue, It's dig her out, or double-bank to find the balance due. **1979** W.K. BECKINGHAM *Red Acres* 37 The ideal way to sink a dam was the way Les Blight and I used to do it. We had a single furrow dam-sinking plough which we pulled with our twelve horses double-banked.

3. *trans.*, becoming *absol.* To carry (a second person) on a horse or bicycle. Also with horse as obj.

1876 *Queenslander* (Brisbane) 1 Jan. 12/3 Down goes the mare, dead beat... So we unpacked her, and double-banked my other mail-horse. **1888** 'R. BOLDREWOOD' *Robbery under Arms* (1937) 172 'We must double-bank my horse,' whispers Jim, 'for a mile or two till we're clear of the place.' **1912** J. BOWES *Comrades* 199 Tony's horse was given to him, while the other two boys 'double-banked' on Sam's. **1930** *Bulletin* (Sydney) 8 Jan. 20/4 His sister .. somehow got him on to a horse .. and double-banking to hold him on, she took him to Dr Pirie's surgery at Liverpool. **1934** C. MACKNESS *Young Beachcombers* 41 We own one horse .. a big draught, aged about twenty, very wobbly in the legs. If we double-banked him, he couldn't bite us, for he hasn't a tooth left. **1956** D. ROWBOTHAM *Town & Country* 69 Prue, the tomboy and the second-born, was double-banking on the old plough-horse with John Henning. **1960** M. VIZZERS *She'll do Me!* 83 When Herb wheeled his bicycle through the gates he stopped and said to Mary: 'Hop on Mary, I'll double-bank yer.' **1968** *Kings Cross Whisper* (Sydney) lii. 8/3 He double banks him on the bar of his pushbike down the main street. **1975** X. HERBERT *Poor Fellow my Country* 774 It was a picnic affair, with something like a dozen going along, counting those tots double-banking with grown-ups.

4. *transf.*

1948 G. MEREDITH *Lawsons* 23 With petrol restrictions there was double-banking now, two or even three families to a car.

double dink: see DINK *n.* and *v.*

double-gee. Chiefly *W.A.* [a. Afrikaans *dubbeltjie*, prob. f. *dubbel* double + *-tjie*, dimin. suffix, but poss. alteration of *duiweltjie* little devil.] **a.** The naturalized annual South African herb *Emex australis* (fam. Polygonaceae) of all mainland States, bearing a fruit with three rigid spines; the fruit itself; *Cape spinach*, see CAPE; *prickly jack*, see PRICKLY; *spiny emex*, see SPINY; TANNER'S CURSE; THREE-CORNERED JACK. See also *bull head* BULL *n.*[3], GOATHEAD. **b.** Any of several other plants bearing a similarly spiny fruit; the fruit of these plants.

1872 MRS E. MILLETT *Austral. Parsonage* 102 A poor

barefooted child . . refusing to stir another step forward 'because of the double gees'. **1902** *Proc. Linnean Soc. N.S.W.* XXVII. 541 *Emex australis*. . . In Western Australia it is known as 'Doublegee'. **1920** J.H. Maiden *Weeds N.S.W.* 12 The solid-angled fruits of the Cat's Head (*Emex australis*) and the Double Gee (*Tribulus terrestris*) present a sharp penetrating point to the feet of animals from all aspects. **1943** *Coast to Coast 1942* 69 It was hard work getting through the sand and stones and double-gees. **1955** *Bulletin* (Sydney) 28 Sept. 12/4 One theory says 'double-gee' comes from *dubbeltge-doorn*, Afrikaans for Devil's thorn; another is that it derives from the same language, but the word is *duiveltje*, meaning 'little devil'. **1977** Kleinschmidt & Johnson *Weeds Qld.* 178 In Queensland, spiny emex is also known as double gee, cape spinach, bullhead and goathead. **1984** S. Macintyre *Militant* 33 On your knees picking peas, Kneeling in the double-gees.

double-header. A double measure of an alcoholic drink.

1898 *Bulletin* (Sydney) 19 Mar. 3/2 The 'double-header''s out, And it's no one's turn to shout, And 'School's out!' **1926** M. Forrest *Hibiscus Heart* 160 'He doesn't drink, does he?' 'No: not more than any of us! Has a wad *occasionally* . . sometimes a double-header . . but I've never seen him helpless.' **1937** *Bulletin* (Sydney) 6 Jan. 21/1 Sam's next rum was a double-header. **1943** S.W. Keough *Around Army* 36 The O. in C. will need a big double-header to get his jangled nerves back to normal. **1947** *Bulletin* (Sydney) 19 Mar. 28/1 The rather warby-looking man with the sad expression and the faded blue eyes shuffled into Flanagan's shanty pub and ordered 'a double-header o' the strongest whisky y' got'.

doubly, *adv. Hist.* In special collocations: **doubly convicted, ironed,** *double convicted, ironed,* see Double *a.* 1.

1840 *Sydney Herald* 31 Aug. 6/4 It appears that in 1837, a batch of those **doubly-convicted** from Norfolk Island, and from chain-gangs, were assigned to the trustees of the late Dr Redfern. **1843** *Sydney Morning Herald* 23 Dec. 2/3 The Doubly Convicted Offenders' Bill was read a third time, and passed. **1847** A. Marjoribanks *Travels N.S.W.* 104 Doubly convicted felons—that is, prisoners transported from this country convicted of new crimes there, are now all sent to Van Diemen's Land. **1851** J. Henderson *Excursions & Adventures N.S.W.* 108 Port Macquarie . . was . . a *dépôt* for doubly convicted felons, or those who had, after being transported from the mother country, been tried and convicted in New South Wales. **1846** L.W. Miller *Notes of Exile Van Dieman's Land* 323, I stood before him (**doubly ironed** and handcuffed). **1856** J. Bonwick *Bushrangers* 26 Those brought up . . were Walker, Pennel, McKan, Jones, Ferguson, and a carpenter who was not doubly ironed like the rest.

dough-banger. A cook.

1891 *Truth* (Sydney) 3 May 7/4 *Poor Joe the dough-banger* has still the tea and a heavy day before him. **1904** *Bulletin* (Sydney) 15 Sept. 39/1 The time was come that we should elect our cook. . . Nine doughbangers fer the one job. **1929** *Aussie* (Sydney) Oct. 24/1 In other days when shearers elected their own cooks at nearly all big sheds, the doughbangers stood for selection like a candidate for Parliament. **1943** S.W. Keough *Around Army* 15 He makes inquiries and finds that all the dough-bangers have been promoted to lance-jacks, and that they're sitting around awaiting the arrival of some new privates to order to make the bread. **1953** H.M. Eastman *Mem. of Sheepman* 45 You with the dough-banger's cap, what about it? . . Are you a cook? **1963** *N. Austral. Monthly* Nov. 13/1 Road cooks . . were running under an alias when they classed themselves as dough-bangers.

Hence **dough-banging** *vbl. n.*

1911 E.S. Sorenson *Life Austral. in Backblocks* 88 Dough-banging does not develop the muscles in the manner that bush-whackers used to imagine.

doughboy. [Also Br. dial., nautical slang, and in other (former) Br. colonies.] A flour dumpling, usu. boiled or fried.

1827 H. Hellyer Diary 19 July, I just ate a little salt pork and a 'doughboy', i.e. a pudding made of flour and water boiled hard. **1848** *Bell's Life in Sydney* 4 Mar. 1/1 The sifting bag was had recourse to for the ingredients necessary to manufacture a brace of 'dough boys' being the only treat compatible with the fallen fortunes and present resources of the kitchen. **1853** I. Chamberlayne *Austral. Captive* 54 The mistress told me I was to make some *doughboys* and a *Yorkshire pudding* for the men's dinners. **1855** W. Howitt *Land, Labor & Gold* I. 124 A suet pudding, called a doughboy. **1861** *Burke & Wills Exploring Exped.* 8, I gave him a piece of cold doughboy I had with me for lunch. **1874** C. De Boos *Congewoi Correspondence* 67 He runs as smooth aser doughboy down a blackfeller's throat. **1888** G. Rock *Colonists* 7 Breakfast . . consists of fried chops and 'dough boys', the latter being simply flour mixed to a paste with water, and fried in the same pan and dripping which cooked the chops. **1900** *Bulletin* (Sydney) 31 Mar. 31/1 You get to the end of those directions—and get a fresh batch to lie on your mind like a sod-dened [*sic*] doughboy. **1911** S. Locke *Mum Dawson* 18 'Get away,' she said, spiking the dough boy in the soup and pinning it with the fork. **1937** D. Gunn *Links with Past* 138 On Sundays . . they got doughboys with black sugar, and vinegar spread over them. **1958** W.E. Harney *Content to Lie* 30 His idea of solid food was to make dough boys each Saturday. **1978** M. Walker *Pioneer Crafts Early Aust.* 151 Cooking for shearers was testing work for the self-opinionated connoisseurs of damper, meat, 'dough boys', Johnnie cakes, brownies . . were harsh critics. **1983** *West Austral.* (Perth) 31 Dec. 15/2 We hadn't eaten all day and when we asked for a meal, the farmer boiled us up some doughboys in a kerosene tin.

Douglas. [Proprietary name.] An axe. Also *attrib.*

[**1896** *Australasian Ironmonger* Mar. 30 D. Sharp's superior axes manufactured from the best refined cast steel by the Douglas Axe Mf'g. Co. East Douglas, Mass. U.S.A.] **1905** *Shearer* (Sydney) 17 June 6/3 The squatter presents him to 'Douglas' (the axe!). **1911** *Bulletin* (Sydney) 21 Dec. 15/2 I've had 'Douglas' in my hands for about 15 years . . and nominate *dry* belar as the hardest to fall and log off. **1914** *Ibid.* 16 Apr. 22/3 A pair of German girls (sisters) earn the elusive pin-money . . by swinging 'douglas' for the Mildura firewood supply. **1929** C.H. Winter *Story of 'Bidgee Queen* 106 An' you graft at 'Swinging Douglas' an' you chop the limbs away. **1937** *Bulletin* (Sydney) 29 Sept. 21/4 A Gippsland Douglas-swinger . . climbed 95 ft. up a fair-sized mountain-ash. **1943** *Ibid.* 20 Jan. 13/2, I find myself wielding the weapons in the same manner as I wielded Douglas and banjo. **1966** H. Gye *Father clears Out* 98 The scholars . . could have passed with honours in such subjects as milking, swinging Douglas, panning off.

douligah /'duləgə/. [a. Dhurga and Dharawal *duligaal*.] See quots.

1918 *Bulletin* (Sydney) 4 Apr. 24/1 The existence of 'douligahs' the wild men covered with hair . . was firmly believed in . . on the N.S. Wales South Coast 30-odd years ago. **1922** 'Te Whare' *Bush Cinema* 8 Most of the South Coast, N.S.W., full-blooded aboriginals still believe in the existence of a wild man covered with hair, whom they call 'douligah'. This party is said to inhabit mountain ranges; but he used to come down at night to the camps below.

Dover. *Obs.* Also **dover.** [Proprietary name.]

1. A clasp-knife.

1870 B.L. Farjeon *In Austral. Wilds* 39 He gave me a knife—a first-rate Dover. **1879** 'Australian' *Adventures Qld.* 7 Now, Mr Frank, out with your 'dover' and pitch in, sir. I'm sorry we have nothing better to offer you than some 'New England tongue', a bit of damper, and Johnny-cake. **1892** A. Cameron *Aust. Felix* 14 If I could whip my dover round damper and salt junk like you, sonny, I'd take a contract. **1905** A.B. Paterson *Old Bush Songs* 126 You've only to sport your dover and knock a monkey over—There's cheap mutton for the Wallaby Brigade.

2. In the phr. **to flash one's Dover,** to open one's clasp knife, spec. to begin a meal.

1872 M. Clarke *His Natural Life* (1970) 616 Hang up your moke, my young Ducrow, sit down, and flash your Dover. **1873** J.C.F. Johnson *Christmas on Carringa* 16 Ses he ther's mutton and damper, And on the fire there's tea, So, flash yer dover hearty, For ther's heaps for you and me. [*Note*] Flash your dover—Draw out your knife, so called from the maker's name, 'Dover' on the orthodox bush knife of twenty-five to thirty years ago. **1881** *Bulletin* (Sydney) 26 Mar. 8/3 Who'd think now, to see you a dinin' in state With lords and the devil knows who, You were 'flashin' your dover' six short months ago, In a lambin' camp on the Paroo? **1942** *Ibid.* 26 Aug. 12/2 To 'flash your Dover' was to get to work with your clasp-knife on salt beef and damper, the urban cognomen coming from the trade-mark on the blade.

3. *transf.* Food.

1885 *Australasian Printers' Keepsake* 75 Returned with half a loaf of bread, part of a shoulder of mutton, and some cold potatoes. He roared exultingly—'Here's the sanguinary dover for you—now let us have a blooming pint!' **1887** K. Mackay *Stirrup Jingles* 40 At a pound a week and my dover, Along of a joker named Jack.

4. In the phr. **the run of one's dover,** board and lodging.

[**1852** W.H. Hall *Practical Experience* 50 Ten shillings a day, with board and lodging, or, to make use of a colonial phrase, 'the run of his knife'.] **1929** G. Meudell *Pleasant Career Spendthrift* 247 A salary of £90 a year and the 'run of his dover', meaning his board and lodging. **1942** *Bulletin* (Sydney) 26 Aug. 12/2 In Sydney 80 years ago an employer hiring a man would offer pay at '£30 a year and the run of your Dover', meaning that rations were thrown in.

dowak /'daʊæk/. *W.A.* Also **dowuk.** [a. Nyungar *dowak*.] A wooden club used by Aborigines: see quot. 1962.

1841 G. Grey *Jrnls. Two Exped. N.-W. & W.A.* II. 265 With the dow-uk, a short heavy stick, they knock over the smaller kinds of game. **1848** A.C. & F.T. Gregory *Jrnls. Austral. Explorations* 12 Oct. (1884) 23 We had made an exchange of part of a handkerchief for a quantity of 'noolban', some dowaks, and dabbas. **1875** J. Forrest *Explorations in Aust.* 39 The blood-thirsty villains . . threw three dowaks. **1891** *Proc. Linnean Soc. N.S.W.* VI. 42 The gouge resembles the implement used by the Grey Ranges natives. . . So much slighter an instrument . . could not produce the effects ascribed to the heavier weapon from West Australia. In the last-named province it is called *Dow-ak* or *Dhabba*. **1894** A.F. Calvert *Aborigines W.A.* 24 The equipment of the Blackboy consists of his kiley (boomerang), hatchet, and dow-uk (a short heavy stick), which are stuck in his belt of opossum fur. **1962** B.W. Leake *Eastern Wheatbelt Wildlife* 55 As a boy I remember how a couple of aborigines, when moving from one place to another . . the male would carry a bundle of spears, dowak, which was a waddy about thirty inches long and one and a quarter inches thick sharpened slightly at one end.

down, *n.* [Br. criminal cant: see quot. 1812.]

1. *Obs.* A suspicion; a taint of illegality.

1812 J.H. Vaux *Mem.* (1819) II. 168 *A down* is a suspicion, alarm, or discovery. **1826** Tas. Colonial Secretary's Office Rec. 1/10 215, He touched Dunne and said—Dunne you must get up there is a bit of a down. **1841** B. Wait *Lett. from Van Dieman's Land* (1843) 266 The *cove*, when he discovers any *down* (suspicion) resting upon himself, always makes complaint of having some property *lifted*, and applies for a resident *trap*, who takes the *down* off the place, and all again is *whist*. **1845** *Star* (Parramatta) 22 Feb. 2/1 A man named Thomas Cleghorn, was committed on Monday, for stealing a bag of feathers, which he had been seen taking from a cart in the Market-place. He attempted in his defence to take the *down off*, by saying that they had merely been given to him to hold by some unknown *bird of passage*. **1849** A. Harris *Emigrant Family* (1967) 53 'I know of four or five young cattle now, that never felt the heat of a brand yet.' 'And no down?' rapidly inquired Beck. . . 'Not a bit of a down,' responded the stockman emphatically.

2. A strong objection (towards a person, etc.); a grudge. Freq. in the phr. **to have a down on** (or **against**).

1828 *Hobart Town Courier* 2 Feb. 3 When the ill-disposed, the sheep-stealers, runaways and others, know from the public prints that there is what is called a *down* upon them . . their plans of theft and robbery become paralized. **1835** *Cornwall Chron.* (Launceston) 11 Apr. 2 Now supposing Mr A. . . is fallen in with by a party of our truly trust-worthy constables, one of whom we will suppose for argument sake, has, what in this Colony is termed '*a down*' upon him. **1845** *Star* (Parramatta) 12 Apr. 2/1 He considered his frequent introductions to the watch-house as being merely the result of spite on the part of the Police, whose practices he had so shown *up*, that they had got a *down* upon him. **1855** R. Carboni *Eureka Stockade* 11 From that day, there was a 'down' on the name of Rede. **1862** 'W.T.G.' *Quite Colonial* (*c* 1948) 17 Eugene .. had what is colonially termed 'a down' upon the speaker, that is to say, a spite against him. **1869** 'E. HOWE' *Boy in Bush* 191 It's strange the down black fellows have on black fellows. **1889** H. EGBERT *Pretty Cockey* 73 If he once gets 'a down' on any one, he will often, as a matter of course, do his level best to lag him, or even hound him to the gallows. **1904** A.B. PATERSON *Rio Grande's Last Race* 39 And people have an awful down Upon the district and the town. **1918** V. MARSHALL *Jail from Within* 15 She had a 'down' on the force. Her eldest son had been 'pinched' a month before. **1927** *R. Comm. Moving Picture Industry* 840 A man who had done a great deal of good in this city—was known to have a 'down' on pictures. **1935** R.B. PLOWMAN *Boundary Rider* 191 He has a down on the fowls because they fly up to peck at the scraps of food near the front part of his cage. **1955** N. PULLIAM *I traveled Lonely Land* 227 Sydney's always had a down on Melbourne—just jealous of us, you know. **1982** N. KEESING *Lily on Dustbin* 96 Dad says mum's a bit hard on the newcomer. Why 'have a down' on her? .. She's not 'a bad sort'.

down, *adv.*

1. a. In the phr. **to go** (**come**, etc.) **down,** to travel from the country to a capital city.

1806 *Sydney Gaz.* 31 Aug., Who asked him (tho' he, M'Nanimy, was going towards Parramatta), if he had *met* Blundell *going down* to Sydney. **1837** *Rep. Select Committee Transportation* 119 A ticket-of-leave constable was sent down to Sydney in charge of the prisoner. **1843** *N.S.W. Monthly Mag.* Feb. 83 Mr Editor—Having to Sydney come down From my hut in the bush, to spend Christmas in town. **1846** *Moreton Bay Courier* 25 July 2/3 These men coming down from the bush, indulged in vicious habits on the road, and when sickness overtook them came to Brisbane for relief. **1857** J. ASKEW *Voyage Aust. & N.Z.* 251 There was a young man .. who was in a dreadful state of alarm about going down. **1888** H.S. RUSSELL *Genesis Qld.* 194 Dalzell and Milne both going down, *i.e.* to Sydney, reversing the usual term to the metropolis. **1903** *Truth* (Sydney) 18 Jan. 8/2 The city is still thronged with the bronzed and wiry pioneers from 'out back', who come down to the capital for a holiday once a year. **1929** K.S. PRICHARD *Coonardoo* (1961) 55 Jessica would like to go down—as soon as possible. **1936** W. HATFIELD *Aust. through Windscreen* 98 I'm taking black patients to the clinic at Darwin. V.D. cases. They are desert niggers that come in on to the stock-route when cattle are going down.

b. In the phr. **to come down,** (of a watercourse) to flood, to be in spate.

1868 C.W. BROWNE *Overlanding in Aust.* 7 Whole plains are inundated with water almost instantaneously by the 'coming down' of the Darling. **1875** CAMPBELL & WILKS *Early Settlement Qld.* 18 Before he could get to the other side, the creek came down a 'banker', overturned his dray, and swept it away. **1890** 'R. BOLDREWOOD' *Colonial Reformer* III. 215 In a week or more it would 'come down' in might and majesty, when the freshets at the head waters should have time to gather forces and swell the yellow tide. **1903** *Bulletin* (Sydney) 7 Mar. 16/3 Once watched a creek (a bend of the Lachlan) 'come down', as the bush saying is. It had been dry for months. **1936** I.L. IDRIESS *Cattle King* 309 Rain was steadily falling. . . Then, from north-east, from north, from north-west, thousands of creeks 'came down'. **1951** —— *Across Nullarbor* 17 The river is still a long way ahead, but the news here is that 'she' is definitely 'coming down'. **1976** K. BROWN *Knock Ten* 106 The river's come down! She's down a banker! **1983** C. BINGHAM *Beckoning Horizon* 2 There you could hear the river 'come down' in the wet season.

2. *Obs.* In the phr. **down the country,** to or towards a (capital) city.

1827 P. CUNNINGHAM *Two Yrs. in N.S.W.* II. 122, I knew him also to have lately come down the country in a direction which I was about to take on the morrow. **1842** *Hunter River Gaz.* 8 Jan. 3/5, I hear he has gone down the country and made clear off. **1847** A. HARRIS *Settlers & Convicts* (1953) 180 A party of free men had come here in their way down the country. **1848** H.W. HAYGARTH *Recoll. Bush Life* 31 Being 'down the country'—is the phrase by which, in 'the bush', a visit to the capital is signified. **1851** MRS R. LEE *Adventures in Aust.* 346 We have many incongruous terms; such as going down the country, for going to the capital. **1862** C. MUNRO *Fern Vale* I. 90 After being up in the bush a while one likes to get down the country a bit, just to see what's going on, and to spend one's money. **1874** J.J. HALCOMBE *Emigrant & Heathen* 14, I had come down the country to Morpeth.

3. a. Of someone or something from the country: in town.

1843 *Sydney Morning Herald* 25 May 3/1 Our wool being all down, we have little else to export, until the salting season commences. **1912** *Bulletin* (Sydney) 23 May 47/2 It was in North Sydney .. when I was down with a cheque. **1919** E.S. SORENSON *Chips & Splinters* 67 He was down from Texas Station with a cheque for recreation, And he seemed to own creation by the way he put on side.

b. Of a watercourse: in flood.

1946 L. REES *Austral. Radio Plays* 195 You mightn't get through. The creeks are down, we heard.

4. a. In the phr. **down south,** in a more southerly part of the country; freq. with ref. to the urban populace of (esp.) Melbourne and Sydney.

1893 F.W.L. ADAMS *Australs.* 36 Every one overworks, trying to do as much under this devouring sun as they would do 'down south' or in chill and foggy England. **1903** *Advocate* (Burnie) 25 July 4/2 People down south. **1920** *Land of Lyre Bird* (S. Gippsland Pioneers' Assoc.) 129 It was one immense district to the south of McDonald's Track, vaguely known as 'Down South'. And the nearest we could get to locating a man anywhere from Korumburra to Kongwok was to say he was 'somewhere down south'. **1934** C. MACKNESS *Young Beachcombers* 13 Two down South at school—do you think we can manage it? **1943** *Georges Gaz.* (Melbourne) Nov. 4 Perhaps this will let some of the folks down South know. **1947** F. CLUNE *Roaming around Aust.* 182 The trouble is that taxpayers 'Down South' are not interested in developing our 'Empty North'. **1968** J. O'GRADY *Gone Troppo* p. x, Would be tourists from 'down south', on their way to the islands to get sunburnt. **1977** E. MACKIE *Oh to be Aussie* 131 It came from a place out west. Mother gave it to me when I passed the Intermediate down south. That's an exam.

b. *fig.* See quots.

1916 'MEN OF ANZAC' *Anzac Bk.* 47 Along comes the bloomin' officer, so 'Enessy sticks 'is lighted bumper down south into 'is overcoat pocket. **1967** *Kings Cross Whisper* (Sydney) xxxiv. 4/3 *Down south*, the pocket, i.e. in the direction of the pocket.

5. With ellipsis of preposition, so that **down** stands for 'down at' (or 'to').

1911 I.A. ROSENBLUM *Stella Sothern* 32 I'll just see if she is down the bail-yard. **1912** L. ESSON *Time is not yet Ripe* 39 Are you going down the bay on Sunday? **1918** *Huon Times* (Franklin) 15 Feb. 3/3 Down the coast, at Milton, on the Boyne .. they had some magnificent horses. **1927** K.S. PRICHARD *Brumby Innes* (1974) 65 Here, you, Polly, take Mickina down camp. **1946** A.J. HOLT *Wheat Farms Vic.* 79 Many of the menfolk do not use the latrine, being more content to go 'down the paddock'. **1969** A. BUZO *Front Room Boys* (1970) 48 Been down the pub for lunch? **1972** R. MAGOFFIN *Chops & Gravy* 23 He'd been having a bit of a party down the back with some of the boys. **1975** R.J. MERRITT *Cake Man* (1978) 26 There's work still down the city. **1981** B.J. BROCK *Catharsis* 55 We haul plankton from the jetty Down Marion Bay. **1984** *Canberra Times* 14 Mar. 19/4 The only asset I had that was worth anything was a block of land down the coast.

down country, *a.*, *adv.*, and *n.*

A. *adj.* Of or pertaining to the more closely settled districts.

1846 *Cumberland Times* (Parramatta) 10 Jan. 4/4 A fire was soon made, a Royal George slung to boil the beef, some flour rubbed up, and leather jackets made, and we made a night of it, having been joined in the course of the evening by two or three down country teams. **1853** W. WESTGARTH *Vic.* 112 The bullock-driver enlivened the kitchen with endless yarns about his last down-country excursion with the season's wool-clip. **1896** T. HENEY *Girl at Birrell's* 114 These were mostly sons of down-country selectors or sheep farmers and settlers on a smaller scale. **1914** *Bulletin* (Sydney) 8 Jan. 22/3 Shearers and 'down country' men (everything's 'down' from here) 'take their colonial' that where foxes are thick snakes grow beautifully less. **1943** *Ibid.* 15 Dec. 13/3 Entering town I saw the down-country buyer's car pull out on its return trip. **1945** *Ibid.* 17 Jan. 15/3 Sam returned from his down-country trip to find his offsider a changed man. **1975** X. HERBERT *Poor Fellow my Country* 1012 Soon he was . . known for his dry wit in down-country pubs. **1979** B. HARDY *World owes me Nothing* 32 He was a big shot from one of those down-country schools.

B. *adv.* In or towards the more closely settled districts. Cf. *down the country* DOWN *adv.* 2.

1875 CAMPBELL & WILKS *Early Settlement Qld.* 28 Mr Hargrave, to whom I had sold the station on my way down country. **1880** J.B. STEVENSON *Seven Yrs. Austral. Bush* 138 Having settled with the squatter, he pockets his hard-earned wages, humps his swag, and starts down country. **1896** T. HENEY *Girl at Birrell's* 181 George had proposed a servant, and she thought it was due to her dignity that she should have such an assistant; but any girl worth having would have to be selected 'down country' and sent up by coach, all of which took considerable time. **1913** *Bulletin* (Sydney) 24 Apr. 14/4 After Happy had cut out at his Wimmera shed he made 'down country'. He cut out his cheque on the way to Casterton, but was lucky enough to strike another shed shorthanded. **1920** C.H. SAYCE *Golden Buckles* 54 If one of them does for a white man, he only gets about a year in a Government camp down country, petted by the ladies and missionaries, and fed on the best of tucker. **1923** J. BOWES *Jackaroos* 18 Teams .. going down country laden with wool. **1929** *Bulletin* (Sydney) 27 Mar. 23/3 Mitchell imported a horde of boys from down-country and set them to work. **1932** J. TRURAN *Green Mallee* 14 Some day we'll get the better o' the scrub an' 'ave a few good years; then we'll be able to go an' live down country, where there's no sandy-blight or dust-storms.

C. *n. Obs.* A closely settled district, spec. that adjacent to Sydney.

1869 MRS W.M. HOWELL *Diggings & Bush* 253 At last we came to the Blue Mountains. They form the boundary between 'up the country' and the 'down country'.

downer. *Obs.* Shortened form of SUNDOWNER.

1913 W.K. HARRIS *Outback in Aust.* 145 'Garn!' the 'downer snapped viciously, 'Why don't yer mind yer own business?' **1920** *Land of Lyre Bird* (S. Gippsland Pioneers' Assoc.) 26 He had walked along from the head to the butt of an old 'downer'.

down under, *adv.* and *n.*

A. *adv.* In, at, or to the (British) antipodes, freq. with ref. to Australia exclusively.

1886 J.A. FROUDE *Oceana* 92 We were to bid adieu to the 'Australasian'. . . She had carried us safely *down under.* **1898** T. HAYDON *Sporting Reminisc.* 105, I do not wish it to appear that I in any way unduly belaud a most marked and much-to-be-admired characteristic of our friends, 'down under'. **1902** R.C. PRAED *My Austral. Girlhood* 1 After thirty years of civilised existence, that wild youth 'down under' comes back to me in all its unforgettable charm. **1915** *Honk* x. 2 Both of whom have trained professional bruisers 'down under'. **1918** *Kia Ora Coo-ee* Mar. 13/3, I knew him 'down under' five years ago, a tall, rugged, smiling faced Australian. **1921** E. WELLS *Fragments* 6 Do you think the folk down under ever felt conscious that someone far away was singing to them. **1943** W.G. HARDING *American looks at Aust.* 171 The many oddities with which nature has endowed the continent 'down under'. **1955** F. LANE *Patrol to Kimberleys* 84 There was nothin' here 'down under' 'cept mobs of abos, 'roos, and dingoes. **1967** M. SELLARS *Carramar* 14 I've got beyond the stage of imagining you are a lot of wild and woolly natives Down Under. **1974** *Bulletin* (Sydney) 12 Oct. 48/2 This newspaper displays old-fashioned northern hemisphere snobbery—the same attitude that applied to Australia the patronising term 'down under'. **1981** *Across Country* xii. 17/1 Back in the States telling his co-entertainers that there's gold 'down-under' waiting to be picked up.

B. *n.* Australia (and New Zealand). Freq. preceded by **from** (or **of**). Also *attrib.*

[N.Z. **1905** *N.Z. Truth* (Wellington) 11 Nov. 3 The men from down under.] **1915** *Honk* x. 5 (*heading*) News from down under. **1918** *Kia Ora Coo-ee* May 4/2 Billjim, just arrived from 'Down Under', met a cobber in the unit he was attached to. **1921** E. WELLS *Fragments* 12 Call them 'oversea soldiers', or down-under men. . . Call them Cornstalks. **1933** C.H. HOLMES *We find Aust.* 27 When the peoples of other lands flocked to this continent of 'down under'. **1934** 'E.N. SPEER' *Destiny* 234 He was not handicapped by overbearing English mannerisms and a narrow English outlook, which the 'down-under' people dislike. **1953** *Futurian Soc. News* Oct. 6 *Sydney* *sends Greetings to U.S. Convention*. . . 'Hello all fans. Greetings from Down Under.' **1956** S. HOPE *Diggers' Paradise* 9 To augment the sparse population of what we call Down Under. **1968** G. FULLBROOK *House called Kangaroo* 7 They had both decided that Adelaide was not their idea of Down-Under. **1979** L.G. PLATT *Survival 3* 177 The Who's Who of disreputable despicable and deviously dastardly drongos of down under.

dowuk, var. DOWAK.

drack, *a.* and *n.* Also **drac.** [Of unknown origin.]

A. *adj.* Dreary; unprepossessing.

1945 S.J. BAKER *Austral. Lang.* 127 *Sope* is an old larrikin word . . the direct antithesis of *bonzer*. . . *Drack* and *bodger* are modern equivalents. **1949** R. PARK *Poor Man's Orange* 180 He was always stuck with drack types like Dolour Darcy. **1951** D. CUSACK *Say no to Death* (1959) 86 He tried to close his mind to the beds so horribly close together, but the room oppressed him. 'Pretty drack, isn't it?' he asked. **1953** T.A.G. HUNGERFORD *Riverslake* 94 The Causeway's all right—a damned sight better than the turns up at the Albert Hall. Anyway, it's a football dance, not just one of those drac turns they slap on for the locals. **1967** F. HARDY *Billy Borker yarns Again* 136 'What airline are you travelling on?' 'Qantas.' 'What? The worst service in the world—drack sorts for hostesses, poor service, drunken pilots.' **1969** T.M.A. GRAHAM *Paper Men* 111 Love in the mornings is drac, isn't it? **1972** A. CHIPPER *Aussie Swearers Guide* 38 *Drack sort*, opposite of *good sort*. . . A *drack sort* often has a mind of her own, refuses to be segregated at parties, and complains bitterly when asked to polish a car, scrape a boat, or watch footie in the rain.

B. *n.* An unattractive or unwelcome person, esp. a woman; also, a policeman.

1960 S. WOODFIELD *A for Artemis* 34 It was the police chief. It was as much as I could do to stop yelling, 'Quick Bill, the dracks are in.' **1966** B. BEAVER *You can't come Back* 26, I thought she was going to kiss it [*sc.* my hand] or maybe bite it like another silly drack I knew once did. **1977** W. MOORE *Just to Myself* 13 She was a bit of a drac, but we put up with her.

draft, *n.* Also **draught.** [Spec. use of *draft* the detachment or selection of a party from the main body (esp. military).]

1. An animal or number of animals separated from the main flock or herd for a particular purpose.

1813 *N.S.W. Govt. & Gen. Orders: Food & Transport*, Riding on any of the Animals in the Drafts or Teams in any of the Towns of Sydney, Parramatta, or Windsor. **1833** Tas. Non-State Rec. 103/11, I should have been happy to have made a Draft of your sheep had they been fit for the knife , and if you can assure me that a Draught can be made fit for slaughter my Drover shall be with you. **1843** *Sydney Morning Herald* 26 Dec. 2/3 There are now about 10,000 sheep, from which drafts are taken at convenient opportunities to undergo the melting process. **1857** F. DE B. COOPER *Wild Adventures* 68, I had the cattle mustered, and the draft . . ready for the road. **1871** *Austral. Town & Country Jrnl.* (Sydney) 22 Apr. 487/2 The latter mob consisted of 500 for the Melbourne market, and were an even and weighty draft. **1894** A.A. MACINNES *Straight as Line* 214 If the Mostyns' horses were put into the market, the culls would fetch more than the best drafts from other stations. **1920** *Bulletin* (Sydney) 12 Aug. 20/2 A returned-soldier settler noticed that a couple of his draughts were looking very seedy and were not eating. He sent for a vet. **1936** E.W. COX *Evol. Austral. Merino* 107 The first rams used were Fisher bred—very fine woolled. They were used for a long time, and two more drafts of the same blood were bought at later dates. **1946** *Bulletin* (Sydney) 28 Aug. 28/3 Smithie held his jumbucks outside the contract shed till word came to take the end pens, and from there he was soon shoving his first draft into the building.

2. *fig.*

1965 J. WYNNUM *Jiggin' in Riggin'* 37 There's only one other explanation, I reckon. She must have got a draft to another rubbitty.

draft, *v.* Also **draught.** [f. prec.] *trans.* To divide (a flock or herd of animals) into smaller lots, according to age, sex, etc.; esp. with **out** (or **off**), to separate (a particular division of animals) from the main body.

1837 *Colonist* (Sydney) 18 May 163/2 We never attempted to draft Coleman's and Grover's cattle, we got no directions. **1848** H.W. HAYGARTH *Recoll. Bush Life* 19 The cattle, numbering perhaps upwards of a thousand, have to be driven into the enclosures, and 'draughted', or subdivided. **1849** A. HARRIS *Emigrant Family* (1967) 138 He had got the diseased sheep draughted away from his own. **1867** 'CLERGYMAN' *Aust. as it Is* 53 A mob of young heifers and some bulls were drafted out from old Mr Peterson's herd of cattle to stock the district which was to be taken up. **1879** 'AUSTRALIAN' *Adventures Qld.* 110 The sheep were drafted into four flocks. **1891** 'R. BOLDREWOOD' *Sydney-Side Saxon* (1925) 118 I'll draft the good ones out of the mob and send 'em down with him. **1899** G. JEFFREY *Princ. Australasian Woolclassing* 38 If the sheep are properly drafted, that is, the different sexes, ages, and culls, etc. kept by themselves for the purpose of being shorn separately, the work of the Wool Classer is very much simplified. **1900** *Bulletin* (Sydney) 10 Mar. 31/2 I've seen many a one as would muster a cattle paddock an draft out the strangers before puttin' 'em in the yard. **1925** M. TERRY *Across Unknown Aust.* 143 Each stockyard is divided into a number of 'pens', perhaps a dozen, one leading to another through heavy wooden gates. . . Thus steers may be drafted (separated) from bulls and calves from their mothers. **1939** J.G. PATTISON *'Battler's' Tales Early Rockhampton* 113 He drafted off the best of the herd to take with him, and left all of what 'Banjo' calls the Goulburn roans and polled ballys. **1952** *Bulletin* (Sydney) 16 July 17/3 Every year it is the old man's practice to lamb-down a mob of ewes on the rough flat, and every year it is my job to draft off the woollies as they lamb, and shove them on to the top-dressed country. **1968** W. GILL *Petermann Journey* 43 Some protesting calves were being drafted from their anxious mothers. **1980** ANSELL & PERCY *To fight Wild* 49 Then you have to take them all off to a yard somewhere and draft off your bulls.

Hence **drafter** *n.*

1848 H.W. HAYGARTH *Recoll. Bush Life* 68 The chief share of the danger falls upon the draughter, who has to go amongst the cattle. **1876** *Austral. Town & Country Jrnl.* (Sydney) 16 Dec. 982/3 They [*sc.* the cattle] behave better; though all the while keeping the drafters incessantly popping at the fence by truculent charges. **1880** J.B. STEVENSON *Seven Yrs. Austral. Bush* 115 A small number of cattle having been driven into the pen, the drafter (usually the super or overseer) enters.

drafting, *vbl. n.*

1. The process of separating an animal or group of animals from the main body.

1845 D. MACKENZIE *Emigrant's Guide* 130 The cattle being now secured in the yard . . we draft them. . . Drafting consists in separating those that we want for any particular purpose from those which we do not want, and which, therefore, are turned out into the bush (woods). **1848** H.W. HAYGARTH *Recoll. Bush Life* 67 The most laborious work connected with cattle farming in Australia is that of 'draughting', or separating and classing a herd, which is necessary at certain times of the year, especially when any are to be sold, or removed to fresh pastures. **1872** C.H. EDEN *My Wife & I in Qld.* 69 [It] consists of several yards for drafting . . a lane and a crush . . useful for branding or securing a troublesome or colonially a 'rowdy' bullock. **1886** H. FINCH-HATTON *Advance Aust.* (rev. ed.) 63 Drafting on the camp, or 'cutting out' as it is generally called, is a very pretty performance to watch. **1938** X. HERBERT *Capricornia* 299 The drafting, or Cutting Out, began. Oscar and Sam Snigger and Charles Ket forced a wedge in the mob, and rode in looking for Clean Skins, or unbranded beasts, and for Hornies, or beasts with ingrowing horns. **1963** M. BRITT *Pardon my Boots* 81 We reached the yard at the same time as the station ringers. The cattle were let out of the yard, and the drafting began.

2. Special Comb. **drafting gate,** a gate at the end of a race designed to close one outlet at the same time as it opens that through which the drafter wishes to direct an animal (see quot. 1882); SWING-GATE; **pen,** a small *drafting yard*; **yard,** an enclosure from which or into which animals are drafted; in *pl.*, the set of pens, yards, races, etc., in which animals are contained and managed, esp. in drafting.

1882 ARMSTRONG & CAMPBELL *Austral. Sheep Husbandry* 177 A second gate hung on the inside of the race will act as a **drafting-gate,** and, when not in use, will, when closed, leave the race secure. **1897** L. LINDLEY-COWEN *W. Austral. Settler's Guide* 633 The erection of these yards will require the following material: 15 gates 6 ft. wide (except the draughting gate) [etc.]. **1922** V. PALMER *Boss of Killara* 152 He found Folkard sitting on top of a post working the drafting-gate. **1950** *Bulletin* (Sydney) 30 Aug. 12/4 Barney was on the drafting-gate . . and the jummies weren't running very well. They fought the dogs, balked in the race, and charged out of the forcing-yard. **1958** J.R. SPICER *Cry of Storm-Bird* 75 Tim and three aboriginals . . were in the largest yard keeping the cattle up to the smaller yards which led to the race and the drafting-gate. **1854** *Illustr. Sydney News* 29 Apr. 33/1 The stockyards are very commodious . . and there are four large yards with **drafting pens** sufficiently extensive to accommodate upwards of 1000 head. **1880** J.B. STEVENSON *Seven Yrs. Austral. Bush* 115 First of all the cattle are driven into what is called the 'receiving yard', which is the largest subdivision. From this they are drafted in small numbers into the 'lane', which is an oblong enclosure, and serves as a feeder for the 'drafting pen', where the work of separating the different ages, etc., is performed. **1832** *Sydney Herald* 4 June 1/2 There are erected upon the Estate Men's Huts, Stock, **Drafting . . Yards.** **1848** H.W. HAYGARTH *Recoll. Bush Life* 68 A cattle enclosure is usually subdivided into five yards: two of them facing the entrance are large, the three others are smaller; the former are known as receiving, and the latter as 'draughting' yards, all of which communicate with one another. **1867** J.C. JORDAN *Managem. Sheep & Stations* 70 It is taken from a rough sketch of a set of drafting yards on an extensive and well managed station in the Western District of Victoria. **1882** ARMSTRONG & CAMPBELL *Austral. Sheep Husbandry* 178 Round rails and posts have been proved to make the best fences for drafting yards. **1894** A. ROBERTSON *Nuggets in Devil's Punch Bowl* 130 After breakfast Alec's father rode to the drafting-yards, where some fat sheep were on the point of starting for the Melbourne market. **1928** C.E. COWLEY *Classing Clip* 157 On any sheep-holding serviceable drafting-yards are necessary. **1935** N. HUNT *House of David* 90 The dogs worked the sheep into the drafting yards. **1980** P. FREEMAN *Woolshed* 18 Well-designed drafting-yards that allow the proper storage, movement and handling of the sheep destined to be shorn.

drag the chain: see CHAIN *n.*[1] 3.

dragoon bird. [See quot. 1860.] *Noisy pitta*, see NOISY.

1860 G. BENNETT *Gatherings of Naturalist* 210 The beautiful little Dragoon Bird . . is seen strutting about. . . It has received its colonial appellation from its peculiar gait as it hops along the ground, carrying itself quite erect. **1893** *Western Champion* (Barcaldine) 24 Jan. 1/2 A period of protection shall be in certain districts . . for the whole year, in respect of the following birds . . dragoon birds (pittas) [etc.] **1931** *Bulletin* (Sydney) 29 July 20/3 The dragoon bird taunts the pedestrian by emphatically calling 'Walk to work!' **1949** C. BENHAM *Diver's Luck* 83 The dragon bird . . loudly calls long before the dawn.

draining, *vbl. n.* Used *attrib.* with **pen, yard,** etc., to designate an enclosure in which animals are held after being dipped, etc., until surplus liquid has drained off into a reservoir.

1879 S.W. SILVER *Austral. Grazier's Guide* 67 The sheep . . emerge saturated and staggering upon the battens of the draining yard. **1886** R. HENTY *Australiana* 216 The sheep was . . plunged into cold water and at once held under, a strong flow or jet of cold water being turned completely but slowly round under it, and then permitted to swim out into draining pens. **1960** M. HENRY *Unlucky Dip* 20 Bob turned his head to stare through the rails of the draining-pen at the slowly breathing sides of the cattle that had gone through the dip. **1965** J.S. GUNN *Terminol. Shearing Industry* i. 25 In the older 'dips' and also in modern 'sheep showers', this is an adjoining draining pen to which sheep go after treatment with the 'wash' or 'dip'.

drake. [Var. of Br. *drawk* a kind of grass growing as a weed among wheat: see OED *sb.*] Any of several native or naturalized grasses (fam. Poaceae) growing as a weed in wheat fields; the seed of the grass among wheat grains.

1796 D. COLLINS *Acct. Eng. Colony N.S.W.* (1798) I. 466 The wheat being almost every where mixed with a weed named by the farmers Drake. **1807** Banks

Papers 20 Jan. XX. 334, I noticed wheat, oats and Drake (Lolium) to be all growing promiscuously together. **1810** *Sydney Gaz.* 17 Nov., Owing to the imperfect manner in which the wheat previous to grinding has been cleared of the drake, or grass seed that sometimes grows among it. **1825** Tas. Non-State Rec. 61/2 30 Oct., Weeding the wheat of drake. **1841** *Port Phillip Patriot* 1 Apr. 2/6 That pest to wheat lands, commonly called rye grass, but colonially known as drake. **1871** *Austral. Town & Country Jrnl.* (Sydney) 29 Apr. 519/2 There will be few self-sown crops this season, as the experience of last year proved them a failure, as little else grew from them but grass and 'drake'. **1917** *Bulletin* (Sydney) 15 Feb. 22/2 In Northern Victoria . . local wheat agents . . have found two grains of drake to one of wheat in some bags. **1930** A.J. EWART *Flora Vic.* 200 *L[olium] temulentum* . . Darnel or Drake. . . A weed of pastures, cultivation, and waste places found throughout Victoria, native to Europe and Asia, and recorded as naturalized in . . 1878.

draught, var. DRAFT *n.* and *v.*

dray. [Extended use of *dray* a low cart without sides used for carrying heavy loads.]

1. Any two-wheeled cart; see also *bullock dray* BULLOCK *n.* 1.

1827 P. CUNNINGHAM *Two Yrs. in N.S.W.* I. 294, I have seen four bullocks, in yokes, draw a heavy dray with 24 *cwt.* of wool along one of our indifferent roads with the most perfect ease. **1846** *Lett. from S.A.*, Mrs T. rode on a cart or dray drawn by four oxen. **1852** W. HUGHES *Austral. Colonies* 143 An ordinary dray, drawn by eight bullocks, will generally carry to Sydney or Melbourne . . about fifteen or twenty bales. **1854** J. CAPPER *Aust.* 62 The ordinary conveyance used in Australia for the transport of goods of every kind is the 'dray', a rude but strongly built bullock-wagon. **1872** C.H. EDEN *My Wife & I in Qld.* 31 A horse-dray, as known in Australia, is by no means the enormous thing its name would signify, but simply an ordinary cart on two wheels without springs. **1874** J.J. HALCOMBE *Emigrant & Heathen* 35 The drays are large two-wheeled carts, very strongly built, with low sides, and made to open, if necessary, before and behind. **1882** MRS J.C. STANGER *Journey from Sydney* 29 The horse drays were, at that time, with single shafts, just like the small brewer's dray in use in England. **1903** *Bulletin* (Sydney) 31 Jan. 16/1 At times when the drays have been late, I have 'rung' the ration tea into 'the house', and no one was any wiser. **1915** *Ibid.* 4 Nov. 26/4 Before pole-drays appeared many families navigated themselves in drays drawn by a bullock. . . Then followed the horse dray and the spring-cart. **1926** 'J. DOONE' *Timely Tips New Australs., Dray*, in Australia this word denotes the springless type of cart generally being equipped with a tipping attachment.

2. Comb. **dray man, road, track.**

1831 *Sydney Herald* 5 Dec. 3/3 Kate O'Hearn . . deeply in love with a **drayman.** **1844** *Sydney Morning Herald* 6 Aug. 2/6 John Price, a licensed drayman, was also fined 10s., with 2s. 6d. costs, for riding on his dray in the public streets. **1852** J.D. LANG *Austral. Emigrant's Man.* 9 They must just make the best bargain they can with some carrier or drayman to convey them to the mines. **1868** J. BAIRD *Emigrant's Guide Australasia* 39 In the morning I breakfasted at Wybong Creek, close to a company of draymen returning with supplies of tea, sugar, &c., for the year, to some sheep station, three or four hundred miles away. **1882** G. RANDALL *Aust. for Industrious* 31 He obtained a situation as drayman or carter soon after landing. **1948** *Bulletin* (Sydney) 16 June 23/3 'I hear you want a dray-man,' the prospect said to Sampson, the road contractor. **1843** *Sydney Morning Herald* 17 May 2/6 The land was sworn to be worth 7s. 6d. per acre, although there were no improvements, and no **dray road** into it. **1857** D. BUNCE *Australasiatic Reminisc.* 203 My distances from Mr Ewer's station . . are estimated at straight lines, which in a dray road might occasionally be doubled. **1876** *Willmett & Co.'s Cooktown Almanac* 16 Distance from Townsville, by dray road, 100 miles. **1822** E.C. SOMMERLAD *Land of Beardies* 45 A dray-road cannot be taken, without overcoming great engineering difficulties, to Maitland direct from this place. **1843** *Sydney Morning Herald* 4 Nov. 4/4 The poor bullocks and their drivers travelling upon the **dray tracks**, for roads I will not so misname them. **1864** 'E.S.H.' *Narr. Trip Sydney to Peak Downs* 9 Our road lay then for twelve miles through a dense brigalow scrub with but a single dray track. **1898** D.W. CARNEGIE *Spinifex & Sand* 58 On the 22nd we were surprised at cutting a freshly made dray-track. **1920** *Land of Lyre Bird* (S. Gippsland Pioneers' Assoc.) 57 At Mr Dunlop's the dray track entered the lordly forest, and after penetrating the scrub country for about nine miles became a mere pack-track.

dreadnought. [Transf. use of *dreadnought* the name of a class of battleship.]

1. *Obs.* A glass of beer.

1909 *Bulletin* (Sydney) 17 Feb. 13/2, I have discovered the longest long beer in the Commonwealth, longer than the 'long sleever', deeper than the 'Dreadnought', and bulkier than the beers of Bourke. **1934** *Ibid.* 21 Feb. 10/2 This is a thin glass holding a quart which is affectionately referred to by its intimates as a 'dreadnought'.

2. *Obs.* A river boat.

1911 C.E.W. BEAN *'Dreadnought' of Darling* 19 He fancied he had been told the name of the boat that ran there was the *Yanda.* Did the Citizen know if she was a comfortable boat? 'Why, she's a *Dreadnought*!' exclaimed the Citizen hopefully. 'You'll be all right in her, I reckon.' **1934** F.H. BROWN *Songs of Plains* 35 There wasn't much peace for a dreadnought's crew, When the guts of the Darling had fallen through. **1936** I.L. IDRIESS *Cattle King* 118 Stores came up-river in the 'dreadnoughts' which returned downstream loaded with wool.

3. One who can shear more than three hundred sheep in a day.

1982 P. ADAM SMITH *Shearers* 278 The dreadnought shouts that the Apaches are in and the tomahawks out. Translation: . . a man who can shear up to three hundred a day shouts that he is hacking the animal about. **1982** *Sydney Morning Herald* 23 Oct. 29/4 The mighty men who could knock up a tally of 300 a day are dreadnoughts.

dreaming, *vbl. n.*

1. DREAMTIME 1; esp. as manifested in the natural world and celebrated in Aboriginal ritual; the spiritual identification of an individual with a place, species of plant or animal, etc.; a place, species, or being so regarded; the spiritual significance of a place. Also *attrib.*

1943 W.E. HARNEY *Taboo* 199 Their religion, wherever it came from in the past, is now bound up in those 'dreamings', the traditional sites and memorials of the great deeds of the culture heroes of the past. **1948** C.P. MOUNTFORD *Brown Men & Red Sand* 23 In the beginning, or the 'Dreaming Times' as old Nantawana poetically described the creation period. **1948** A. MARSHALL *Ourselves writ Strange* 198 My dreaming different. It near old camp, long time ago. Near running water. White people, he call it 'Dreaming'. We call it 'Maraiin'. When I die, I go longa my Maraiin, long running water. **1951** E. HILL *Territory* 346 Laws, legends, languages, the corybantic corroborees, every tribal rite and belief belong to 'blackfella dreamin'. **1952** MILLER & RUTTER *Child Artists* 22 Every member of the tribe was allotted at birth by a process of divination, not only a section of his country that was his spirit home—his *'dreaming'*—but his particular relatives in the plant and animal world. **1955** M. DURACK *Keep him my Country* (1966) 75 The goanna would be his 'dreaming', and this his spirit place. **1961** M. KIDDLE *Men of Yesterday* 9 At all times he was close to the time of dreaming, because the rocks and trees, the creeks and water-holes had all played their parts in the legends. **1964** D. LOCKWOOD *Lizard Eaters* 66 The place was now a sacred Dreaming, a totemic centre of great significance in the tribal culture. **1970** R. ROBINSON *Altjeringa* 17 Every waterhole, plain, river, rock, billabong is our dreaming. **1973** *Bronze Swagman Bk. Bush Verse* (1974) 9 The black men have their legends and the Dreaming but here am I with nothing! No God—and none to care, if they could see—Poor fellow me! **1978** 'B. WONGAR' *Track to Bralgu* 23 The rain comes from the Dreaming, the same as everything else, but sometimes it feels too lazy to travel, and then the dancing and singing helps to wake it up. **1979** W.E.H. STANNER *White Man got no Dreaming* 24, I can recall one intelligent old man who said to me, with a cadence almost as though he had been speaking verse: White man got no dreaming, Him go 'nother way. White man, him go different. Him got road belong himself. **1983** D. BELL *Daughters of Dreaming* 22 At other points we would drive quietly so as not to disturb the dreamings who had passed through this area. **1985** I. & T. DONALDSON *Seeing First Australs.* 207 Discussing the history of [Canberra] and being shown archaeological sites and nineteenth century pictures of old Aborigines . . Gurrmanamana said that once, long ago, Aborigines had lived here and that they would have known these attributes of the land which still existed somewhere, but that now, in his own words, 'This country bin lose 'im Dreaming.'

2. Special Comb. **dreaming path, site, track,** a place or route of dreamtime significance.

1978 *Transcript of Proc. Alywarra Land Claim* 2 Oct. 45 It will be the . . transparency showing Dreaming tracks in the claim area. **1979** *N.S.W. Parl. Papers* (1980–81) 3rd Sess. IV. 756/2 That is a line where the old people go and the young fellows are in the middle. . . The line goes up in the mountain and that track is sacred, that is a dreaming track. **1983** D. BELL *Daughters of Dreaming* 33 They went on to accuse men of breaches of the Law ranging from the non-maintenance of dreaming sites to misrepresenting . . women's role. *Ibid.* 50 Their 'countries' are ill-defined, sprawling tracts of land, cross-cut by dreaming tracks. **1983** *Canberra Times* 26 Oct. 23/2 Several Dreaming paths go through or close to MMparntwe [*sic*], which is Alice's other name.

dreamtime. [Translation of ALCHERINGA.]

1. In Aboriginal belief: a collection of events beyond living memory which shaped the physical, spiritual, and moral world; the era in which these occurred; an Aboriginal's consciousness of the enduring nature of the era; ALCHERINGA. See also DREAMING. Also *attrib.*

[**1878** R.B. SMYTH *Aborigines of Vic.* I. 126 There are the dreamers, who direct and control the movements of the tribe until their divinations are fulfilled or forgotten.] **1896** B. SPENCER *Rep. Horn Sci. Exped. Central Aust.* I. 50 They say that in what they call the Alchèringa (or as Mr Gillen appropriately renders it the 'dream times'), a certain noted warrior journeyed to the east. **1905** K.L. PARKER *Euahlayi Tribe* 6 Byamee, in the first place, is to the Euahlayi what the 'Alcheringa' or 'Dream time' is to the Arunta. **1938** D. BATES *Passing of Aborigines* 24 A patriarchal or 'dreamtime' father. **1958** R. ROBINSON *Black-Feller White-Feller* 42 This was a song of the 'dreamtime' when Narait screamed down from the paperbarks and told the blacks how they could live in the desert. **1963** D. ATTENBOROUGH *Quest under Capricorn* 159 Although the Dreamtime was in the past, it is also co-existent with the present, and a man, by performing the rituals, can become one with his 'dreaming' and experience eternity. It is to seek this mystical union that the men enact the ceremonies. **1972** M. CASSIDY *Dispossessed* 6 Deep in his 'dream-time' Paddy-boy hugged the memory of Paddy-jack. **1972** W.E. HARNEY *Brimming Billabongs* 17 We knew that at this time all our tribe would be facing the dreamtime centre and thinking of the absent ones, and in this thought we wished to join. **1977** P. POPESCU *Last Wave* 50 The earth, the sky and all living beings had been created by spirits during the so-called Dreamtime, which incorporated all their major myths and miraculous happenings. The Dreamtime was bygone and prehistoric, and yet it was present still, because it had a flow of its own, separated from the time of normal daily activities. **1980** N. WATKINS *Kangaroo Connection* 6 'What does Djugubra mean?' Charles asked. . . 'Dreamtime or long ago, before whiteman live out here and they tell stories with hands only.'

2. *fig.* A 'fool's paradise'; a 'period of grace'.

1985 H. GARNER *Postcards from Surfers* 11 Remember that seminar we went to about investment in diamonds?. . . S'posed to be an investment that would double its value in six days. We went along one afternoon. They were obviously con-men. Ooh, setting up a big con, you could tell. . . Anyway, look at this in today's *Age.* 'The Diamond Dreamtime. World diamond market plummets.' Haw haw haw. **1986** *Bulletin* (Sydney) 4 Mar. 30/1 The federal Labor caucus has emerged from the dreamtime it granted Burke's reelection campaign and urged Aboriginal Affairs minister Clyde Holding to bring down his model land rights package.

3. Special Comb. **dreamtime track,** see DREAMING 2.

1934 *Oceania* V. 173 The importance of the 'dreamtime' tracks is seen in the custom of approaching sacred totemic and heroic sites by the actual path believed to have been followed by the hero or ancestor.

dredgy, *a. Mining. Obs.* Also **dredgey.** [f. *dredge* ore of mixed quality: see OED *sb.*[2] 3; cf. EDD *dredgy-ore.*] Of ore: of mixed quality and productivity.

1865 *Wallaroo Times* (Kadina) 28 June 2/4 The western lode . . is looking well, the leader of ore being fully eighteen inches wide in the back of level, the remainder is dredgy as before. **1866** *Ibid.* 17 Nov. 2/4 Lode large but dredgey. **1875** *Yorke's Peninsula Advertiser* (Moonta) 6 Aug. 3/2 Dredgy portions of stuff . . passing over the end of the sieve. **1890** H.Y.L. BROWN *Rec. of Mines S.A.* (ed. 2) 23 About 78 tons of ore have been raised but it is very dredgy and requires machinery to dress it.

dress, *v. Obs.* [Br. dial. *dress* to apply a lotion to sheep to kill parasites: see EDD 9.] *trans.* To treat (a sheep afflicted with scab). See also *sheep dressing* SHEEP 2.

1831 *Sydney Monitor* 19 Oct. 3/2, I am a shearer, and have at different times had a great many scabby sheep pass through my hands, but have seldom *drest* any for the scab. **1843** *Sydney Morning Herald* 4 Oct. 4/2 My sheep had been dressed about six weeks; they had been scabby. **1858** T. MCCOMBIE *Hist. Colony Vic.* 91 They were dressing sheep at Muston's Creek. **1874** C. DE BOOS *Congewoi Correspondence* 50 The sheep there was terribly scabby, and no mistake. Well, he hired us to dress 'em, and the way we set about it was a caution to all sheep never to get scabbed.

dressing shed. At swimming pools, sports grounds, etc.: a changing room.

1917 *St. Kilda Ann.* 25 Dressing sheds are now provided on the beach. **1957** 'N. CULOTTA' *They're Weird Mob* 66, I found the dressing sheds and followed other people who were paying money to enter. **1958** E.O. SCHLUNKE *Village Hampden* 228 'We got a new dressing-shed out of him,' Townshend boasted.

dried out: see DRY *v.*

drift. *Mining.* A deposit of sand, gravel, etc., left by (flood) water: see quot. 1860. Also *attrib.*

1852 *Empire* (Sydney) 20 Feb. 699/3 Whence comes the drift matter which now finds profitable employment for the miners at Sheep Station Point? Is it the wash from the Hills? **1856** S.C. BREES *How to farm & settle in Aust.* 45 Deep-sinking was connected with the later practice of 'bottoming', in which the mass of the 'drift', that was previously wont to be washed in its entirety, was passed over, excepting a small quantity immediately adjacent to the rock or bottom on which it rested. ***c* 1860** 'AURIFERA' *Victorian Miners' Man.* 102 *Drift* . . earth and rocks which have been drifted by water, and deposited over a country while submerged. It lies under alluvium and over secondary rocks. **1871** *Austral. Town & Country Jrnl.* (Sydney) 22 Apr. 495/2 Gold has been obtained in the drift, but no signs of the bottom have yet been met with. **1888** 'R. BOLDREWOOD' *Robbery under Arms* (1937) 254 They'd come on a drift in their claim, and were puddling back. **1916** H.L. ROTH *Sketches & Reminisc. Qld.* 5 An isolated pocket in which the drift had duffered out. **1931** C.B. SMITH *Austral. Gold Prospectors' Handbk.* 37 Often at the foot of a hill or base of a mountain you will come across a large deposit of soil and stones which has been washed down by the rains of time immemorial. This 'drift' should be carefully examined.

drive, *n.*[1] *Mining.* [f. *drive* to excavate horizontally (see OED *v.* 10); as *n.* apparently chiefly Austral. and N.Z.] A tunnel excavated horizontally.

[**1846** F. DUTTON *S.A. & its Mines* 281 Allowed by the different proprietors to direct the sinking of shafts and driving of levels.] **1857** C.E. GLASS in *Fresh Evidence Early Goldmining Publications* (Austral. Lang. Research Centre, 1966) 11 A main drive shall be carried along the course of such lead or gutter. **1858** C.R. THATCHER *Colonial Songster* (rev. ed.) 72 Poor Sing-Hi 'd gone there, but put up no prop, And the top of the drive had come down on him whop. **1870** 'COLONIST TWENTY YRS.' STANDING' *Vic., Brit. 'El Dorado'* 115 A 'drive' is a small tunnel, in this case boxed in with wood. **1874** *Adelaide Observer* 26 Dec. (Christmas Suppl.) 13/1 He got half killed by a fall of 'mullock' in a drive. **1885** A. SMITH *Sad but True Story* 4, I am in the upper drive in the middle mine. **1896** H. LAWSON *While Billy Boils* (1975) 5 They lowered the young bride, blindfolded, down a golden hole in a big bucket, and got her to point out the drive from which the gold came that her ring was made out of. **1921** K.S. PRICHARD *Black Opal* 55 Watty crawled off through a drive he was gouging in. **1948** —— *Golden Miles* 74 From every drive and crosscut, men crawled to the stopes, and along to the plat for crib.

drive, *n.*[2] *Timber-getting.* [Transf. use of (chiefly N. American) *drive* mass of logs driven downstream.] The falling in one mass of a number of trees which have been partially cut through, the impetus or 'drive' being given by the felling of a larger tree (or one uphill of the others) against them.

[N.Z. **1899** J. BELL *In Shadow of Bush* 83 The smaller trees . . had been 'scarfed', or cut partly through in readiness, and skilfully, so that each, when struck, might again in its turn strike and bring down another. The noise of a fall or drive of this kind is like thunder.] **1904** *Bulletin* (Sydney) 15 Sept. 40/4 We chop all the trees from the back, and only half way through; each cut has to be made so that when the tree goes it will knock the tree below it; in fact to use the scrub term, we are 'choppin' a drive'. **1909** R. KALESKI *Austral. Settler's Compl. Guide* 97 Take the trees in a face, about every half acre or more, as may suit you, knocking them down with a 'driver'. . . When you think you have enough for a 'drive' pick a large tree with a big head above the last one; nick him first in the front, then in the back. He will fall against the one below him and knock him over, that one will knock the next, and so till they are all down. **1949** B. O'REILLY *Green Mountains* 101 In the felling of a rain forest, much chopping may be saved . . by the use of the 'drive' system.

Hence **driver** *n.*[1], see quot.; **driving** *vbl. n.*

1909 driver [see DRIVE *n.*[2]]. **1909** *Bulletin* (Sydney) 26 Aug. 15/2 **Driving** is the making use of falling trees to assist in felling others. **1949** B. O'REILLY *Green Mountains* 101 Driving is a science which is not learned in a day or in a season. Every tree must have its cut faced so that when the pressure comes on, it will fall on the one ahead.

driver, *n.*[2] *Shearing.* A leather strap attached to a set of hand-shears: see quot. 1965.

1905 *Shearer* (Sydney) 23 Dec. 7/5 Half of their time is taken up in fixing fresh 'knockers', 'drivers', and 'dummies' on their shears. **1912** J. BRADSHAW *Highway Robbery under Arms* (ed. 3) 25 He was the king of all shearers in a long, heavy drag, no drivers, with two fingers right up in the bows of the shears. **1959** H.P. TRITTON *Time means Tucker* 31 There is a band of leather from the heel of one blade (of shears) to the back of the other. This is the 'driver', and its purpose is to prevent the hand from slipping forward onto the blades. **1965** J.S. GUNN *Terminol. Shearing Industry* i. 25 *Driver*, a leather strap on hand shears. This fits firmly round the handle and over the back of the shearer's hand, thus allowing more drive to be given to a blow while preventing the hands from slipping over the blades. **1975** L.R. SMITH *Memories of Hall* 80 The final adjustment was for a strap to be fixed to the spring on one side of the shears, extended across to the opposite side and secured firmly in a position which fitted comfortably over the shearer's hand. This was called '*The Driver*'.

drone-pipe. DIDGERIDOO.

1946 D. BARR *Warrigal Joe* 53 'Didgerydoo,' Dan explained for the benefit of the jackeroo and Bob Greely, who had never before heard the 'music' of the drone-pipe. **1952** R.M. BERNDT *Djanggawul* 310 Drone pipe, didgeridoo: hollow wooden musical instrument into which a man blows to provide an accompaniment to singing and dancing. **1958** R. ROBINSON *Black-Feller White-Feller* 43 Songs accompanied by the drone-pipe and bone-sticks or by boomerangs quivered together. **1963** I.L. IDRIESS *Our Living Stone Age* 177 (*caption*) A call to corroboree on his 'drone-pipe' echoes through the bush. **1969** A.A. ABBIE *Original Australs.* 173 The *didjeridu*, also known as 'drone pipe', 'bombo pipe' and 'bamboo pipe'.

drongo. [Transf. use of *drongo* the name of a bird. Perh. infl. by its earlier use as the name of a racehorse (running between 1923 and 1925): see quots. 1924 and 1946.] A fool or simpleton, a 'no-hoper' (orig. of a Royal Australian Air Force recruit). Also **drong** and *attrib.*

[**1924** *Argus* (Melbourne) 1 Nov. 24/5 Drongo is sure to be a very hard horse to beat. He is improving with every run.] **1941** *Somers Sun* 2 July 2 When you are called Drongo, ignore it. **1942** A.J. MCINTYRE *Putting over Burst* 3 I'm just a flamin' drongo, Just a lowdown useless wart. **1944** *Barging About: Organ 43 Austral. Landing Craft Co.* 1 Sept. 6 All the tribes of Oz did gather together, even the tribes of . . Drongoes, Dopes and Dills. **1946** *Salt* (Melbourne) 8 Apr. 22 Drongo was the name of a horse who failed to win a race. . . The horse retired in 1925 and after that anybody or anything slow or clumsy became a Drongo. **1952** P. PINNEY *Road in Wilderness* 72 Only thing you drongoes can think of is beer, beer, beer, and a sheila on the side. **1960** N. CATO *Green grows Vine* 46 'What a drongo,' said Mitch. 'Dron-go?' said Maria. 'A dill—a no-hoper.' **1966** D. NILAND *Pairs & Loners* 135, I didn't waste time like some drongo salesman who can't tell when the customer really means no. **1968** G. MILL *Nobody dies but Me* 14 It's very likely we're the cleanest bunch of drongs in the entire R-bloody-double-A.F. **1973** H. WILLIAMS *My Love* 89 He said it was a job for drongoes, rubbing down cars one after another. **1981** P. RADLEY *Jack Rivers & Me* 25 'What's a bodgie, Connie?' 'A drongo who's younger than a grub but thinks he's old enough to have a widgie.'

droob. Also **drube.** [Prob. f. U.S. *droop* a fool, a 'drip'.] An unprepossessing person, usu. male.

1933 H.B. RAINE *Lash End* 33 There's a drube out there wanting to see you. **1945** S.J. BAKER *Austral. Lang.* 156 *Drube*, a term of contempt for a person. **1949** R. PARK *Poor Man's Orange* 181 A sick feeling entered Dolour's heart when she saw Harry standing there, his hands thrust into his pockets like packages, and a little, saliva-stained fag stuck on his lower lip. Of all the nice boys going to Luna Park . . she had to draw this droob. **1974** J. JOST *This is Harry Flynn* 29 You're not normal boy. . . You're a mug, a droob, a weak mess of shit! **1983** *Weekend Austral. Mag.* (Sydney) 27 Aug. 20/8 Australian slanguage is well stocked with words and phrases to describe those who are a bit slow off the mental mark, who are—well, to put it bluntly, drongos, galahs, lardheads, droobs.

Hence **drooby** *a.*

1972 J. SEARLE *Lucky Streak* 50 'These are . . decent!' . . 'You look pretty drooby in them. . . ' 'They're just for work.' *Ibid.* 51 Just a minute, pet . . (to Colin, pointing to his shoes). Those ones are getting a bit drooby. **1981** *Sunday Mail* (Brisbane) 25 Oct. 18/5 The party was rotten—drooby creeps, spooks, twits, bores etc.

drooping, *a. Obs.* In the names of plants having pendulous branches or foliage: **drooping gum,** any of several trees of the genus *Eucalyptus* (fam. Myrtaceae); **tea-tree,** any of several trees of the genus *Melaleuca* (fam. Myrtaceae).

1842 *Geelong Advertiser* 21 Mar. 2/2 A species of Eucalyptus known by the appellation of **drooping gum,** of a dwarf and crooked disposition. **1862** J. MCKINLAY *Jrnl. Exploration Interior* 16 June 110 Beautiful drooping gums, papery-bark trees, and various others. **1899** *Proc. Linnean Soc. N.S.W.* XXIV. 629 *E*[*ucalyptus*] *squamosa* . . is the 'Drooping Gum' of Woolls, near Duck River. **1845** L. LEICHHARDT *Jrnl. Overland Exped. Aust.* 12 Feb. (1847) 144 The **drooping tea-tree** (Melaleuca Leucodendron?) . . was generally the companion of water, and its drooping foliage afforded an agreeable shade. ***c* 1864** J. REID *Adventures Austral. Traveler* 5 Huts . . thatched with grass and the bark of the drooping tea tree.

drop, *n.*[1] [f. *drop* to give birth to.] The number of lambs or calves born on a station in a season.

1838 *S. Austral. Rec.* (London) 11 July 75 His annual drop should be . . 40,000 lambs. **1903** *Truth* (Sydney) 31 May 1/8 Mr J.H. Pengilley . . has a splendid drop of early lambs (March drop) this year, and . . he intends to try and get another drop this season. **1978** D. STUART *Wedgetail View* 5 A new windmill, tanks and troughs, a good drop of calves, and a steady future.

drop, *n.*[2] *Australian National Football.* Used *attrib.* in Special Comb. **drop punt** (or **pass**), a kick in which a ball held vertically is dropped on to the foot (as in a punt).

1963 *Footy Fan* (Melbourne) I. i. 18 Kick a long drop-kick or stab, a short or long drop-pass. *Ibid.* ii. 18 *Drop punt*, the long seam should be in line with the target and the ball held almost vertically with the top end slightly away from the body. The fingers should be evenly spread and the top of each middle finger should be near the lacing. **1964** J. POLLARD *High Mark* 26 This is the alternative to the stab and, in today's more hurried game, seems to be more popular. . . Richmond's Jack

Dyer is given credit for having developed the drop-punt. **1973** P. McKenna *My World of Football* 42, I personally prefer to rely on the drop-punt, other forwards have their own favourite style. **1982** G. Atkinson *Everything about Austral. Rules Football* 162 The drop-punt . . is commonly attributed to Jack Dyer (Richmond VFL) and he was certainly using it, almost alone, in the mid to late 30s and throughout the 40s.

dropper. [Spec. use of *dropper* that which descends or falls away.]

1. *Mining.* [Poss. U.S.: see OED 5 d.] A vein which diverges or drops away from the main lode. Also *attrib.*

***c* 1860** 'Aurifera' *Victorian Miners' Man.* 102 *Dropper-strings*, small spurs of a vein. **1891** *Hist. Wedderburn Gold Fields* 35 The leaders are barren, except at the intersections with the indicator, or of nearly vertical thin quartz veins, called 'droppers' by the miners. **1911** E.D. Cleland *Austral. Mining Practice* 13 Occasional small patches—or 'droppers' of ore run out from the main body. **1931** W. Baragwanath et al. *Guide for Prospectors in Vic.* 31 At Maldon also piths are associated with gold in the 'dropper' veins.

2. A vertical batten placed at regular intervals between the posts of a wire fence to keep the wires braced.

1897 L. Lindley-Cowen *W. Austral. Settler's Guide* 236 The droppers for six wires can be obtained in the colony from W.D. Moore & Co., Fremantle. **1913** *Bulletin* (Sydney) 8 May 16/3 Any wire fence (plain or barb) without droppers will slacken. **1937** W. Hatfield *I find Aust.* 82 He was on a contract for . . lightning fence, as they call it, eighty posts to the mile, strung with three steel wires fairly low down and one about three feet six from the ground, all strained to tuning-fork pitch and held by floating bracers about four to the panel known as 'droppers'. **1943** H.G. Lamond *From Tariaro to Ross Roy* 108 Steel wire took the place of the old soft iron wire; droppers and kindred fencing improvements became common. **1964** *Overland* xxx. 21 'D' you know what a Mallee gate is, Bob?' 'Yes, it's a short loose panel, just droppers and wires.' **1973** J. Morrison *Austral. by Choice* 73 It was a good fence, taut and true, the work of a craftsman: posts still unweathered, black iron droppers, and five bright wires, three plain and two barbed. **1978** C. Green *Sun is Up* 99 And strong! He could throw a strainer post that would hold the *Queen Mary* up onto a truck as though it was a dropper.

3. A lambing ewe.

1937 D. Gunn *Links with Past* 204 One man . . would be in charge of the lambing ewes, called the 'droppers'.

dropping, *vbl. n.* and *ppl. a.* [f. *drop* to give birth to.]

A. *vbl. n.* A lambing; also with **down,** and *attrib.*

1839 *S. Austral. Miscellany* Oct. 20 The lambs of the first dropping month in the colony will produce in August next. **1843** J.F. Bennett *Hist. & Descr. Acct. S.A.* 98 Many flockmasters regulate the lambings so as to have three droppings in two years. **1872** G.S. Baden-Powell *New Homes for Old Country* 169 Another man . . shepherds out the flock of ewes, and performs all functions connected with 'dropping down'.

B. *ppl. a.* In lamb.

1943 H.G. Lamond *From Tariaro to Ross Roy* 26 The wet flock, as the lambing ewes were known, was a science in itself. Each flock of lambers was sub-divided into three or four smaller flocks: green, dropping, middle and bigger lambs.

Droughtmaster. A breed of cattle having not less than ⅜ or more than ½ Brahman blood and bred to withstand dry conditons. Also **droughtmaster bull.**

1958 *Pastoral Rev. & Graziers' Rec.* 19 Aug. 987/1 Mr De Landelles also awarded the ribbons in the new section provided for Droughtmasters, a name given to cattle that are regarded as a well balanced cross between red British breeds and Brahmans, that carry enough Brahman blood to make them a good beef breed for tropical surroundings. **1973** *Droughtmaster* (Droughtmaster Stud Breeders' Soc.) 3 Droughtmasters are a beef breed evolved equally from *Bos indicus* and British beef cattle. **1977** *Cattleman* (Rockhampton) June 15/2 Droughtmaster bulls have played a valuable role in maintaining production in the large breeding herd. **1980** H. Lunn *Behind Banana Curtain* 104 He believes the Droughtmaster—a breed developed in Australia to have high heat tolerance and tremendous walking abilities—is the ideal beast for central Australia.

drove, *n.* [Not excl. Austral. but of local significance.]

1. A herd or flock being driven as a body, esp. over great distances. Also *attrib.*

1829 H. Widowson *Present State Van Diemen's Land* 159 As soon as a drove is brought up, two or three quiet working bullocks lead them into the yard. **1839** *Southern Austral.* (Adelaide) 20 Nov. 4/4 The benefits expected from the overland route from New South Wales, by which large droves of cattle had already reached South Australia. **1847** *Moreton Bay Courier* 29 May 3/2 Mr Patrick Bogue arrived overland yesterday, from Penrith, New South Wales, with a drove of horses. **1868** C.W. Browne *Overlanding in Aust.* 1 Sending down large droves of sheep or cattle, overland, for sale at any of the colonial markets. **1874** *Illustr. Sydney News* 30 Jan. 11/1, I engaged with a man to take over a drove of cattle from Maneroo to the Victorian side. **1877** 'Capricornus' *Land Law of Future* 6 Droving reserves shall be confirmed, and such drove roads as may cross the territory shall be created permanent reserves of the full width of existing drove roads. **1886** P. Clarke *'New Chum' in Aust.* 256, I took a drove of cattle through 'black-country', but never found them trouble me. **1926** A.A.B. Apsley *Amateur Settlers* 118 Drove routes over the roadless, unmapped cattle country. **1958** O. Ruhen *Naked under Capricorn* 190 'That fellow's doing more mustering than droving,' he said. 'I picked up the tracks of a shod horse. It turned a little mob of cattle back to the drove, maybe eight or nine.'

2. The driving of a herd or flock.

1935 N. Hunt *House of David* 127 Rowel now engaged a reliable drover and outfit and, superintending from time to time himself the 'drove', he brought . . those Queensland shorthorns on to his run. **1973** H. Lewis *Crow on Barbed Wire Fence* 51 They had told me, over the camp fire, of great 'droves' over the route to Adelaide from Central Queensland, with cattle and horses.

drove, *v.* [See prec.] *trans.* To drive (a herd or flock), esp. over a great distance. Also *absol.*

1847 A. Harris *Settlers & Convicts* (1953) 205, I drafted off two-thirds of the herd and drove them out along with the sheep. **1851** *Bell's Life in Sydney* 29 Mar. 6/2, I drove a little, as a boy. **1876** 'Capricornus' *Colonisation* 21 They like no life better than finding new runs and droving stock to them. **1900** *Bulletin* (Sydney) 3 Feb. 32/2 I've shore for stations, West and South, and drove, and 'overlanded'. **1905** *Ibid.* 11 May 16/2, I was helping to 'drove' 25,000 ewes from the Darling to the Northern Territory. **1933** A.J. Cotton *With Big Herds in Aust.* 83 By the methods described, cattle can be droved seven to eight miles a day. **1940** E. Hill *Great Austral. Loneliness* (ed. 2) 124 She droved cattle overland for 2000 miles. **1956** A.C.C. Lock *Tropical Tapestry* 225 At one stage he and his brother drove cattle to the Bendigo goldfields. **1963** F. Flynn *Northern Gateway* 139 Some beasts might be droved to Daly River Mission. **1976** G. Hall *Rhymes from Rivers* 17 For twenty long years I have drove round the runs, Met bushfires and freshes and floods.

drover. [See Drove *n.*]

1. One who drives a herd or flock, esp. over a great distance.

1841 *Port Phillip Patriot* 4 Oct. 3/3 To be a cattle-jobber or a sheep-drover . . would alike sully the purity of a Barrister's Wig. **1844** *Duncan's Weekly Register* (Sydney) 25 May 601/2 The whole sum expended, including superintendence, shearing, woolbagging . . drover's wages . . would not have exceeded £2,000. **1868** S. Leighton Austral. Jrnl. & Notes NLA MS 360/4 99 He was for some time a 'drover' which signifies in this country a much higher employment than in England—a drover is entrusted with many hundred head of sheep or cattle or horses to take right across country on a journey of several weeks duration perhaps from Sydney to Melbourne, or from Adelaide to New South Wales. **1869** *Colonial Monthly* Aug. 431 We'll call them 'drovers', because that is the accepted term nowadays; but I deem the old term of overlanders much more respectable, euphonious, and appropriate. **1880** P.R. Gordon *Drover's Guide* 9 Every drover in charge of travelling sheep in New South Wales must be provided with a 'travelling statement', signed by the owner. **1887** W.S.S. Tyrwhitt *New Chum in Qld. Bush* 172 Drovers are wanted to take sheep and cattle to market when fat, to bring store cattle from one place to another to stations where the principal business is fattening for market, and in bad seasons to take them travelling for grass. **1914** C.H.S. Matthews *Bill* 97 With a mob of 1000 Bullocks there will be about ten drovers. **1926** A.A.B. Apsley *Amateur Settlers* 118 The drovers are a fraternity. **1943** H.G. Lamond *From Tariaro to Ross Roy* 106 The drover-in-charge . . was a good cattle-man, of a well-known cattle family. **1960** *N.T. News* (Darwin) 5 Jan. 1/4 White drover Mick Daly and full-blood aboriginal girl Gladys Namagu were married in St. Mary's. **1976** B. Scott *Compl. Bk. Austral. Folk Lore* 188 I'll tell you all about the time that I became a drover.

2. In special collocations: **drover's dog,** one who earns no respect, a drudge; the dog itself, applied in similes; **drover's outfit, plant,** the personnel and equipment employed by a drover; Plant *n.*[2]

1947 F. Clune *Roaming around Aust.* 30 Taxi-cabs were scarce in Perth. I was told they had been 'Yanked' by the Yanks. In consequence I got as poor as a **drover's dog**, chasing around on foot. **1978** J. Colbert *Ranch* 37 The other Harry has got a head like a drover's dog and always wears a hat. **1978** T. Davies *More Austral. Nicknames* 44 *The drover's dog*, never stops working. **1983** *Age* (Melbourne) 4 Feb. 4/6, I am not convinced the Labor Party would not win under my leadership. I believe that a drover's dog could lead the Labor Party to victory the way the country is. **1984** *Canberra Times* 2 Dec. 1/5 Mr Hayden would not comment on whether Labor would have done any better with him as leader. He did, however, make reference to a comment he made early last year when he was replaced as leader by the Prime Minister, Mr Hawke. 'The drover's dog will win again but it looks a bit clapped out this time,' he said. **1912** J. Bowes *Comrade* 91 A **drover's 'outfit'** was expected at the station during the course of a few days to 'overland' the bullocks to Adelaide. This meant driving the cattle right across the continent, a big undertaking, often occupying twelve months. **1923** —— *Jackaroos* 103 Had drifted into the town with a drover's outfit. **1979** D. Lockwood *My Old Mates & I* 2 The first time I used it was with a drover's outfit on the Barkly Tableland. **1935** K.L. Smith *Sky Pilot Arnhem Land* 157 One day we pulled up for dinner not far from a **drover's plant.** **1946** A.W. Noakes *Life of Policeman* 62 Several drovers' plants happened to meet at the hotel. **1954** T. Ronan *Vision Splendid* 201 Get the Johns to start on some of your pet drovers' plants before they look at the bagmen's turnouts.

droving, *vbl. n.* [See Drove *n.*]

1. The driving of a herd or flock, esp. over a great distance; the occupation of being a drover. Also *attrib.*

1871 *Austral. Town & Country Jrnl.* (Sydney) 22 Apr. 491/2, I am aware that the necessary steps are intended to be taken by the Survey Department for opening new droving-roads. **1875** *Illustr. Sydney News* 19 Jan. 2/3 The inspectors of stock throughout the colony have received instructions from the Chief Inspector . . to examine the various droving roads and tracks throughout their respective districts. **1879** S.W. Silver *Austral. Grazier's Guide* 12 The young man . . is initiated in the mysteries of . . rail-splitting, stock-riding . . droving. **1886** H. Finch-Hatton *Advance Aust.* (rev. ed.) 67 Droving . . becomes a regular profession, and there are numbers of men who make a living . . by nothing else. **1909** *Bulletin* (Sydney) 28 Oct. 13/3 It's not always easy to steady a big mob and make them feed again. . . Of course, they *can* be stopped. They can be 'rung' and worried into a confused mass; but that's bad droving. **1956** A.C.C. Lock *Tropical Tapestry* 142 Droving is a wonderful life for those who enjoy open air; and the pay is high. **1978** D. Stuart *Wedgetail View* 6 What cattle were left . . would be scarcely worth the droving next year.

2. Special Comb. **droving hand,** one employed by a drover; **plant,** *drover's plant*, see Drover 2.

1930 *Bulletin* (Sydney) 1 Jan. 20/1 To the old **droving-hand** there is some interest in the . . news that the Canadian Government is shifting 300 reindeer. **1937** W. Hatfield *I find Aust.* 106, I went down with the last mob of fat cattle for the season from Glengyle, getting my three pounds a week as a full-blown droving hand. **1902** H. Lawson *Children of Bush* 234 Andy had charge of the **'droving-plant'** (a tilted two-horse waggonette, in which we carried the .. horse-feed). **1923** *Bulletin* (Sydney) 20 Dec. 24/3 Every droving plant carries a cook. **1942** *Ibid.* 6 May 12/1 He was a horse-tailer in a big droving plant. **1962** C. GYE *Cockney & Crocodile* 77 We met a droving plant, two stockmen like black editions of Tom Mix or Wyatt Earp. **1978** R.H. CONQUEST *Dusty Distances* 11 He's a boss drover, boy. Owns one of the biggest droving plants in western Queensland.

drube, var. DROOB.

drum, *n.*[1] [Perh. with ref. to the usually cylindrical shape of a swag.] A swagman's bundle of possessions; SWAG *n.*[1]. See HUMP *v.* 2 a.

1866 W. STAMER *Recoll. Life of Adventure* I. 304 Our ci-devant millionaire would .. 'humping his drum', start off for the diggings to seek more gold. **1868** C.W. BROWNE *Overlanding in Aust.* 64 He is 'humping his drum' (i.e. travelling) looking up a job, and walks into the travellers hut. **1872** C.H. EDEN *My Wife & I in Qld.* 17 They all chaffed us about our swags, or donkeys or drums, as a bundle of things wrapped in a blanket is indifferently called. **1881** J.C.F. JOHNSON *To Mount Browne & Back* 19, I pushed on for the diggings, distant thirty-five or forty miles according to circumstances; 'humping your drum' it is fifty at least. **1894** *Bulletin* (Sydney) 14 Apr. 24/3 With a strong right arm and a willing hand, He shouldered his 'drum' to the Thirsty Land. **1906** *Ibid.* 27 Sept. 16/3 What would the 'waler' do without his nosebag, or without the corn-sack to cover his 'drum'? **1915** A. WRIGHT *Sport from Hollowlog Flat* 51 Eight o'clock next morning saw the same ten depositing their 'drums' on the verandah. **1924** LAWRENCE & SKINNER *Boy in Bush* 236 'But a swaggy is a tramp?' 'It is. It is one who humps it. If he's got a pack, it's his swag. If he's only got a blanket and a billy, it's his bluey and his drum.' **1943** C. SHAW *Warrumbungle Mare* 48 'The place is crook enough,' said he, Enlisting for the scrap, 'But, strike me, think what life would be *Drum-humpin' with a Jap!*' **1954** *Bulletin* (Sydney) 16 June 12/4 Pack-horse is the accepted mode of swag-transport up there, and the swag has more individuality than any back-humped drum. **1976** B. SCOTT *Complete Bk. Austral. Folk Lore* 168 Home, it's home I'd like to be, not humping my drum in the sheep country.

drum, *n.*[2] [Prob. transf. use of *drum* musical instrument used to give a signal, perh. infl. by DRUMMER *n.*[2]]

1. A reliable piece of (inside) information. Freq. in the phr. **to give** (or **get**) **the drum.**

1915 DREW & EVANS *Grafter* 139 It beats me how the punters get the drum. **1922** C. DREW *Rogues & Ruses* 88, I got the drum on the way out to the races. **1937** K.S. PRICHARD *Intimate Strangers* 262 If I give my punter the drum from the field, you can't blame me, can you? **1949** L. GLASSOP *Lucky Palmer* 15 Got the drum about this one. My brother heard about it from the owner. This is one what won't get tossed. **1955** D. NILAND *Shiralee* 97, I don't want to be quizzy, Mac, but, if it's a fair question, what's the drum? **1964** R. PARKER *Boy on Chain* 39 'Before they get you in there,' he said, nodding at the warden's door, 'thought I might give you the drum, sort of.' **1973** J. O'GRADY *Survival in Doghouse* 56 I've given him the drum on vegetables—spuds in their jackets, frozen beans, and a tin of mushrooms. **1986** *Canberra Times* 25 Apr. 1/4 He had got the drum that they [the police] wouldn't lock us up.

2. In the phr. **to run a drum,** (of a racehorse) to perform as tipped.

1942 *Truth* (Sydney) 31 May 2/4 Ridden by McMenamin, Vanity Fair was always an unprofitable quotation, more especially when she subsequently failed to 'run a drum'. **1945** S.J. BAKER *Austral. Lang.* 174 A horse that *runs a drum* performs and wins as tipped. **1957** 'N. CULOTTA' *They're Weird Mob* 76 'Pat what does it mean when somebody says ''e never run a drum'?' 'Means 'e wasn't in the hunt.' 'There is hunting in Australia?' 'Racehorses, I'm talkin' about. If 'e's with the tail-enders, 'e never run a drum.' **1962** S. GORE *Down Golden Mile* 261 'Backed Sweet Friday for a spin,' replied Tug. 'But it never run a drum.' **1978** J. HEPWORTH *His Bk.* 113 Warrego Willie went like a hairy goat—never even looked like running a drum.

drum, *n.*[3] [Spec. use of *drum* (usu. disreputable) house, lodging-place, etc.: see OEDS *sb.*[1] 9 e.] A brothel.

1879 D. MAYNE *Westerly Busters* 27 Farewell to the 'drums' where resided the 'Good Thing'. **1882** *Sydney Slang Dict.* 3 *Drum*, or *Crib*, house of ill repute. **1899** *Truth* (Sydney) 5 Feb. 5/8 The horrible, openly offensive, flaunting Chinese drums .. are allowed to carry on their revolting trade of child prostitution. **1912** M. CANNON *That Damned Democrat* (1981) 138 There were a few drums in the immediate suburbs, such as Carlton .. and the city end of Fitzroy. **1944** L. GLASSOP *We were Rats* 101 'I found one. Comin' round?' 'Found what?' I asked. 'A drum,' said Eddie. 'Comin'?' 'My oath,' said Gordon, 'I don't mind dallying on the couch of purple passion.' **1951** CUSACK & JAMES *Come in Spinner* 254 'Don't I have all the responsibility for getting the right type of girls and keeping them in decent condition?' 'I'll hand it to you there, Grace. This place has the rep. for being one of the safest drums in the town.' **1963** C. ROHAN *Down by Dockside* 41 Each one of these houses was that dreariest, dullest, loneliest and ugliest institution in the whole history of harlotry—the one-woman drum. **1978** L. HORSPHOL *Turn down Empty Glass* 126, I know you're running a drum and a sly-grog shop.

drum, *v.* [f. DRUM *n.*[2]] *trans.* To give information to (someone); to warn. Also with **up.**

1919 V. MARSHALL *World of Living Dead* 30 He impressed on me the exact location of the maternal abode, and proceeded to 'drum me up' with the message. **1949** L. GLASSOP *Lucky Palmer* 229 Jimmy Daley .. drummed me Herb's on his way here now to get his money or he's going to summons you. **1955** R. LAWLER *Summer Seventeenth Doll* (1965) 27 I'm drummin' you for the last time, you touch my cupboard again and I'm off down to Russell Street. **1976** *Bronze Swagman Bk. Bush Verse* 32 This school's orright, we're drummin' yer. **1978** H.C. BAKER *I was Listening* 171 I'm drummin' you, if the Nips come, I'm goin'.

drum country. See quots. See also DRUMMY.

1927 M. TERRY *Through Land of Promise* 82 Some country, like the Georgina River in Queensland, is of very bad repute. Strange cattle do not camp well in that part and only too often make a rush during the night. It is called 'drum country', because a certain hollow ring in the ground enlarges sound. **1970** V. HALL *Outback Policeman* 41 The plain consisted of what is known as 'drum country' having some peculiar property of the soil almost as if it were hollow beneath the surface, so that the stamp of a horse's foot was magnified as enormously as a stroke on a huge drum.

drummer, *n.*[1] Predom. *N.S.W.* [f. U.S. *drum* any of various fish able to make a drumming noise.] Any of several marine fish of the fam. Kyphosidae taken for sport, esp. the rock blackfish *Girella elevata* of N.S.W., Vic., and Tas. and the silver drummer *Kyphosus sydneyanus* of coastal s. Aust. incl. Tas., and N.Z.

1880 *Proc. Linnean Soc. N.S.W.* V. 408 *Girella elevata* .. *'The Drummer'* .. Port Jackson. **1895** C. THACKERAY *Amateur Fisherman's Guide* 21 At the mouth of Lake Macquarie and within coo-ee of Reid's Mistake, a bumbora will be found, and .. drummer, groper [etc.]. **1906** D.G. STEAD *Fishes of Aust.* 91 Such well-known fishes as .. the Drummer (*Kyphosus sydneyanus*). **1948** F.D. MARSHALL *Let's go Fishing* 69 The true drummer is known as silver drummer in New South Wales. The black drummer or rock blackfish is found only in New South Wales. **1963** B. HESLING *Dinkumization & Depommification* 11 Sydney—a place where I once fished for drummer and gathered pippies within a mile of the Town Hall. **1978** N. COLEMAN *Austral. Fisherman's Fish Guide* 119 The flesh of the drummer has a reasonable texture but is weedy in taste.

drummer, *n.*[2] *Obs.* [U.S. *drummer* commercial traveller: see OED 2.]

1. a. A commercial traveller.

1886 P. CLARKE *'New Chum' in Aust.* 124 It is possible you may have to share them with a 'drummer'—that is, a commercial traveller—or a 'swagsman'. **1892** *Quiz* (Adelaide) 1 July 7/1 In the Far North, amidst the saltbush and general parch .. a drummer arrived and ordered breakfast. **1895** *Western Champion* (Barcaldine) 29 Jan. 5/1, I was a smart young 'drummer' then in Queensland's sunny clime. **1902** *Truth* (Sydney) 5 Oct. 4/7 A commercial traveller or 'drummer' in the employ of Service and Co. **1910** *Ibid.* 9 Jan. 1/5 He was a drummer with plenty of mag. **1914** *Bulletin* (Sydney) 1 Jan. 24/4 A 'commercial' was busy writing in a room where two old 'merinos' were talking jumbuck, and nothing but jumbuck. The drummer stood it for an hour and a half.

b. One who 'humps his drum'; a swagman.

1898 *Bulletin* (Sydney) 31 Dec. 14/3 The broken-down old drummer, grown cranky from the sun. **1945** S.J. BAKER *Austral. Lang.* 102 *Bender* (1885) and *drummer* (*circa* 1890) were once popular terms for tramps of slightly better class than the sundowner.

2. *Obs.* [Prob. joc. use of sense 1.] The slowest shearer in a shed.

1897 *Worker* (Sydney) 11 Sept. 1/1 'The ringer' is the 'cove' who takes the biggest cheque away, And 'drummer' marks the man who gets in silver coin his pay. **1898** *Bulletin* (Sydney) 17 Dec. 15/1 *Drummer* is not necessarily the slowest shearer in the shed. He's more often the laziest, and gets the least money on pay-day. .. The man with the smallest amount of sheep to his credit on out-out day used to be drummed out of the shed by the rouseabouts. **1906** W. DEAN *Home & Camp* 13 Tom Brown, a shearing drummer, On horseback came. **1915** *Bulletin* (Sydney) 18 Nov. 24/4 The shearer at the tail-end of the list is 'the drummer'. **1929** C.H. WINTER *Story of 'Bidgee Queen* 57, I have shorn in a shed or two—always in the drummer's place. **1937** D. GUNN *Links with Past* 246 Next morning then, towards the shed The jovial shearers go, The mighty ringers swiftly tread The drummer's crawling slow. **1959** H.P. TRITTON *Time means Tucker* 42 It's not every man that is drummer in four sheds running. **1965** J.S. GUNN *Terminol. Shearing Industry* i. 26 *Drummer*, this word also refers to a type of shearer but is not used very often now.

drummy, *a.* Of earth or rock: hollow-sounding; apparently unstable. See also DRUM COUNTRY.

1899 *Bulletin* (Sydney) 12 Aug. 14/1 The real terror is the man who's been reefing 10 or 20 years, and who, after sounding a 'drummy' place overhead, casually remarks: 'It'll stand while we get them two shots in.' **1948** G. FARWELL *Down Argent Street* 65 He .. prods cautiously at a jagged rock leaf overhead. 'Drummy patch there. Want to watch that, son.' The heavy fragments flake off, thud at their feet. **1951** E. HILL *Territory* 294 The mob goes drifting down, through the pindan .. 'drummy' country, a crust over limestone where their own hoofs with a sound of drums terrify the cattle. **1980** O. RUHEN *Bullock Teams* 80 Some sites made bullocks uneasy—'drummy ground' for instance, where hollows underneath, perhaps old limestone caves or pressure tunnels .. magnified sounds and could start the bullocks rushing in the night.

dry, *a.* and *n.*

A. *adj.*

1. In special collocations denoting a lack of water: **dry camp** [orig. U.S. (see OEDS)], a camp without water; also as *v. intr.*; **country,** country with a very low rainfall; also *attrib.*; **farmer** [orig. U.S. (see OEDS)], one who farms in dry country, also **farming; feed,** dry grass, etc.; **heart,** central Australia; see also *dead heart* DEAD 1; **season, spell,** a period of low rainfall or drought; **stage,** a part of a journey which is through waterless country; also **dry-staging** *vbl. n.*; **track,** a track through waterless country (see also TRACK *n.* 2 a.).

1897 A.F. CALVERT *My Fourth Tour W.A.* 271 They are fortunate if they do not have to make a '**dry camp**' by sundown. A dry camp means that a teamster must go on with his waggon, or if the horses are too exhausted to drag the load, that they must be unyoked, driven to water, and brought back again to where the freight was left. **1905** *Nineteenth Century* (London) Nov. 818 It is an unwritten law that the traveller must never go past water in the afternoon, unless he is certain of reaching another spring, or waterhole, before sundown. A breach of this law brings its own punishment, for a 'dry camp' is not a pleasant experience. **1926** A.A.B. APSLEY *Amateur Settlers* 127 On one or two nights we had a 'dry camp'. **1937** W. HATFIELD *I find Aust.* 227 Galahs at sunset are sure indication of water. They never make 'dry camps'. **1938** F. BLAKELEY *Hard Liberty* 214 We had dry-camped the night before, and there were twenty-two miles to go with very little water in our bags. **1954** *Bulletin* (Sydney) 15 Sept. 12/2 The oldest-established routine incidental to the droving of cattle .. is the 'pint-pot wash'. On a dry camp—and all overlanding camps are dry in W.Q.—the morning wash takes the form of a splash over the face with what water two cupped hands will hold. Your cobber acts as valet. **1959** D. LOCKWOOD *Crocodiles & Other People* 89 We had wanted to get to the Flying Fox that night for a fresh-water camp, but these delays meant that we would probably have to dry-camp at the side of the road. **1878** 'R. BOLDREWOOD' *Ups & Downs* 161 That capacity for sustaining a high rate of speed for hours together peculiar to '**dry-country** horses'. **1885** P.R. MEGGY *From Sydney to Silverton* 135 He knew many squatters in the dry country who would be only too glad to get rid of their leases at a sacrifice. **1909** R. KALESKI *Austral. Settler's Compl. Guide* 13 My former remarks . . apply to dry-country farming. **1926** A.S. LE SOUEF et al. *Wild Animals Australasia* 213 This species is a dry-country animal, and is apparently confined to western Australia. **1938** F. RATCLIFFE *Flying Fox & Drifting Sand* 246 Copley is like all the dry-country towns. . . Permanent beautification was limited to a few pepper trees. **1913** *Truth* (Sydney) 23 Feb. 1/7 Niel Nielsen wants the Government to import a number of **dry farmers** from 'Murka. **1911** *Ibid.* 12 Mar. 1/8 A 'dry farming conference' is being held in Adelaide just at present. The dry farms are doing rather better than usual this year, owing to the unusual rainfall. **1925** J.A. COLLUM *New Settlers' Handbk.* 113 It is the intention to allocate a proportionate area of conveniently situated 'dry' land to each holder of irrigated land, thus affording splendid opportunities for mixed irrigated and dry farming. **1936** F. CLUNE *Roaming round Darling* 113 An Experiment Farm was started to carry investigations with regard to cereals under dry-farming conditions. **1951** G. FARWELL *Outside Track* 101 There is an extensive dry farming area inland. **1965** G. MCINNES *Road to Gundagai* 62 In the semi-desert region known as the Mallee . . pioneer dry farmers strove to grow wheat inside the ten inch isohyet. **1934** C. SAYCE *Comboman* 219 Though no rain had fallen for nine months, there was still **dry feed** to be found some miles off the Great North Stock Route, and they came upon a Government bore at long intervals. **1949** G. FARWELL *Traveller's Track* 72 Between Goyder's Lagoon and Birdsville there's nothing except a bit of dry feed, y' know. **1953** H.G. LAMOND *Big Red* 221 'There's a fair bit of dry feed,' Brown continued. 'That mulga's old and sweet. They should do well on it.' **1960** *N.T. News* (Darwin) 8 Jan. 3/2 Parts of the Barkly Tableland still carry useful dry feed. **1935** T. RAYMENT *Cluster of Bees* 156 His experience, gained in the '**dry heart**' of Australia, has helped me to uncover the secrets of the 'Queen of Diggers', on the beautiful shores of Port Phillip. **1972** *Bulletin* (Sydney) 25 Nov. 43 (*caption*) Brett Whitely had never been to Mount Olga, a group of red stones surging out of the desert at Australia's dry heart. **1837** J. MUDIE *Felonry of N.S.W.* 51 It was afflicted for three years with the calamitous visitations of 'the **dry seasons**'. **1841** *Omnibus & Sydney Spectator* 27 Nov. 68/4 The river at the present time has much less water in it than it had the last dry season. **1843** W. PRIDDEN *Aust.* 45 By *dry season*, or *wet season*, in Australia, we are not to understand, as in England, a *dry* or *wet summer*, but a series of *dry* or *wet years*. **1849** A. ANDREWS *Sketch of Colony W.A.* 4 The nearest approach to drought at Western Australia since the foundation of the colony, can only be called a 'dry season'. **1859** J.D. MEREWEATHER *Diary Working Clergyman* 37 The Campaspie has the characteristics of other Australian rivers: in the dry season it is but a chain of seemingly stagnant water-holes, during the rains it is a raging, rushing torrent. **1884** G. RANKEN *Dry Country* i. 6, 140,000 sheep had been kept without loss all through three dry seasons. **1890** W.F. BUCHANAN *Aust. to Rescue* p. xxiv, That country is subject to dry seasons. There is lots of water along the frontage, but none permanently at the back, and the selectors may come on to the front. **1898** A.S. MURRAY *Twelve Hundred Miles* 9 Sturt in 1828–9, *it being a dry season*, proved conclusively Oxley's error. **1910** *Huon Times* (Franklin) 21 Dec. 3/4 Suppose that you were struck with a dry season; suppose you had no rain up there for a month. **1938** F. BLAKELEY *Hard Liberty* 81 To-day dry seasons are called 'droughts', and before six months have passed the small man's stock are dying. . . None of the big runs is in trouble. . . They only call 'the drought' a dry spell. **1908** *Bulletin* (Sydney) 21 May 14/2 When this **dry spell** passes . . there will be an unholy squaring up of accounts throughout cockiedom. **1910** *Huon Times* (Franklin) 23 Feb. 2/3 The protracted dry spell which has been experienced in these quarters is now beginning to tell upon the water supply. **1914** 'B. CABLE' *By Blow & Kiss* 170 The 'dry spell' showed no signs of breaking. Everyone still spoke of it as 'the dry spell' and none were willing to call it 'the drought'. **1933** C.H. HOLMES *We find Aust.* 149 To move from one area to another cheating the 'dry-spell' demon. **1953** H.G. LAMOND *Big Red* 209 They only come during a dry spell in the west. **1908** MRS A. GUNN *We of Never-Never* 150 He faces its seventy-five-mile **dry stage,** sitting loosely in the saddle, with the same cheery, 'So long, chaps.' **1916** *Bulletin* (Sydney) 24 Aug. 22/1 The . . sprint with 900 fat bullocks over a 97-mile dry stage makes cattle-punchers raise their lids whenever it is recalled. **1923** *Ibid.* 4 Jan. 22/2 If you want cattle to camp you must feed and water them well and not overdrive them. If you have a long dry stage to do, start early and let them get over the bad part as soon as possible. **1931** 'L. KAYE' *Tybal Men* 51 At the end of a long dry-stage which saw the casks empty in the wagon, was a little water. **1937** M. TERRY *Sand & Sun* 143 Weary with so much dry-staging, they complained of loneliness for their folk. **1948** C.P. MOUNTFORD *Brown Men & Red Sand* 133 One of his camels, after three and a half days' dry stage, drank forty-three gallons! **1954** T. RONAN *Vision Splendid* 148 The Farquharson Brothers put up an all-time world's record with a dry stage of a hundred and thirty-four miles with bullocks. **1978** D. STUART *Wedgetail View* 3 The seven hundred mile track . . led down over stone country and plains of soft, easy going, by pool and well and dry stage. **1941** *Bulletin* (Sydney) 1 Oct. 14/1 'These blokes', said Dusty, 'who skite about the **dry tracks** they've struck mostly talk through their hats. . . They've had to do a bit of a perish, walk perhaps 10 or 15 mile on a hot day without a drink. As the years go by the distance gets longer and the day hotter.' **1957** J. HAWKE *Follow my Dust* 83 He is more independent of the pastoralist than the pedaller, being free to camp where he wishes and follow dry tracks from which other men on foot shy away. **1982** D. HARRIS *Drovers of Outback* 82 If I was on a dry track I would travel at night time and when I reached water would spell the mob for a day.

2. Of sheep during shearing: not sufficiently wet (after rain) to prevent shearing.

1894 *Bulletin* (Sydney) 20 Jan. 9/4, I can recall many instances of *some* shearers voting 'wet sheep' while at the hut, and immediately afterwards, under the boss's eye, voting 'dry sheep'. **1911** *Ibid.* 2 Mar. 14/2 It was decided to approach a shearer who was known to be a 'rousies' man'. The result of the vote . . was a majority of one for 'wet sheep'. . . But on the Monday our man deserted us, and the verdict was 'dry sheep'. **1939** *Ibid.* 26 Apr. 20/4 It had been a dry run with a cut-out certain on Friday unless unexpected rain fell. **1956** C.D. MILLS *Stockwhip & Spur* 49 They shedded that night, as the crimson sun set, Their fleeces were dry, but the bellies were wet. Said the boss of the board, 'We must give them a fly,' So they put in their paper, and voted 'em dry. **1975** B. FOLEY *Shearers' Poems* 9 Yesterday was wet at Kylie And at 'smoko' took the vote The Kiwis' tickets said dry The Aussies 'where's the boat'? **1984** P. READ *Down there with me on Cowra Mission* 43 When it's wet, they vote on it. They vote 'em wet or dry, see. The rep comes along and he gives them all a ticket. You shear two sheep then you cast a vote. Say there's ten votes and nine votes 'dry' then they shear 'em.

B. *n.*

1. With **the:** (in northern and central Australia) the dry season, the winter.

1908 MRS A. GUNN *We of Never-Never* 219 It was August, well on in the dry. **1922** *Bulletin* (Sydney) 6 Apr. 20/4 At the end of the dry, when the first few showers fall, 'Send it down, Hughie!' is the heartfelt exclamation of every eager bush-watcher. **1929** H. MACQUARRIE *We & Baby* 173 A kind of parking area for crocodiles during the 'dry'. **1935** K. SMITH *Sky Pilot Arnhem Land* 246 Travelling in the Never Never during the 'dry' is a constant fight against nature. Only the aeroplane has defeated the waterless plains. **1945** J. DEVANNY *Bird of Paradise* 14 A tractor caught by the 'wet' in some areas in the rain forests must remain there till the 'dry'. **1955** J. CLEARY *Justin Bayard* 172 'Thinking of coming down there later in the Dry. Wanna have a booze-up.' 'You can always have a drink at the homestead,' Blanche said. **1964** B. WANNAN *Fair Go, Spinner* 13 This was followed by a flood which washed away everything that had survived the 'dry'. **1970** P. SLATER *Eagle for Pidgin* 45, I noticed the grass was yellowing and realised the Dry had started. **1980** B. SANSOM *Camp at Wallaby Cross* 13 'The Dry' has always been the time of wages while the Wet has stood for a time of lay-off for at least a proportion of the hands on each station. **1984** *Palmerston Herald* 16 Nov. 6/5 Jackie says they all stuck their necks out and . . took out loans on the 'never-never' to buy tractors. . . They would farm during the 'Dry' and get casual work during the 'Wet'.

2. A tract of waterless country (of a specified distance).

1908 MRS A. GUNN *We of Never-Never* 151 Leaving no time for a 'spell' after the 'seventy-five mile dry'. **1937** E. HILL *Great Austral. Loneliness* 103 They changed and glowed . . on the 'forty-mile dry' to Louisa Downs. **1950** A. GROOM *I saw Strange Land* 7 From the lovely Aghadaghada Waterhole . . an old camel pad led out over the 'eighty miles dry'.

dry, *v.* In the phr. **dried out,** (of land) parched; (of people) driven off drought-stricken land.

1902 *Bulletin* (Sydney) 5 Apr. 14/4 For the first time on record Teryawynia station-homestead, on the lower Darling, is 'dried out'. The country has been held for about 48 years. **1932** M. TERRY *Log Bk.* 23 July, No sign of blacks anywhere about—evidently dried out. **1981** G. PIKE *Campfire Tales* 51 The Kennedys packed everything on two wagonettes and driving their sheep, they went on the track in search of grass and water, as many pioneers who were 'dried out' were forced to do.

dryandra /draɪ'ændrə/. [The plant genus *Dryandra* was named by British botanist Robert Brown (*Trans. Linnean Soc. London* (1810) X. 211 pl. 13), after Swedish botanist Jonas *Dryander* (1748–1810), librarian to Joseph Banks.] Any plant of the genus of shrubs and small trees *Dryandra* (fam. Proteaceae) of s.w. W.A., the flower-heads of which are often large and showy.

1827 *HRA* (1923) 3rd Ser. VI. 579, I observed on these Hills an arborescent species of Dryandra. **1834** *Perth Gaz.* 10 May 283 Three species of dryandra, the latter forming small upright growing trees. **1902** *Emu* II. 68 Sheltered gullies or pockets carrying 'stinkwood', dryandra and peppermint scrubs. **1941** C. BARRETT *Aust.* 116 Dryandras, related to the Banksias. **1965** R. STOW *Merry-Go-Round* 30 The water was hidden behind dense thickets of dryandra. **1985** *Canberra Times* 16 Oct. 25/4, I go for a contemplative walk in my garden for the next hour or so and talk to my dryandras.

dry bible. [f. *dry* + *bible* the omasum of a ruminant (from the resemblance of the folds to the pages of a book): cf. Br. dial. *bible-tripe* (EDD).] A condition of cattle characterized by dryness of the omasum (third stomach), an affliction which may result from any of several causes, esp. as occasioned by drought.

1917 *Bulletin* (Sydney) 12 July 24/1 The disease called 'dry bible' . . was simply a manifestation of second-hand poison. **1931** MRS E.P. HALFORD *Pioneers of Yesterday* 22 As the season advanced and the grass got dry and hard, it caused some of the cattle to get 'dry bible', and several of them died of it. **1942** E. ANDERSON *Squatter's Luck* 32 When in a drought the waterholes ran dry, And of 'dry bible' half the herds would die. **1982** N. KEESING *Lily on Dustbin* 163 *Dry bible*, a condition of cattle in which one or more of their stomachs becomes immovably jammed with food. . . By extension, something utterly exasperating can cause the exclamation, 'Wouldn't it give you the dry bloody Bible!'

dry-blow, *v.*

1. *trans.* To separate (particles of a mineral, esp. gold) from the earth, sand, etc., in which it is found, using a current of air. Also *absol.* and with the area treated as obj.

1894 *Bulletin* (Sydney) 5 May 7/3 On Coolgardie now there are fully 4000 men, most of whom are dry-blowing, and I don't believe there are 20 making much more than full tucker, while most of them are not even getting the colour of gold. **1896** J.M. PRICE *Land of Gold* 73 Most of the alluvial workings round Coolgardie and its neighbouring 'fields' have been 'dry blown' over and over again. **1927** M. TERRY *Through Land of Promise* 290 He began to dry-blow in the breeze. Luck was with him, for a few enticing colours lay among the residue. **1946** W.E. HARNEY *North of 23°* 202 With their wooden dishes, they can dry-blow the precious metal from the earth in which it lies. **1965** B. JAMES *Collecting Austral. Gemstones* 83 Where there was no water he learned to dry-blow his gold, using the wind to get rid of the dirt and gravel. **1978** O. WHITE *Silent Reach* 113 The only tin that comes out of that country is what the gins . . dry blow by hand out of a coolamon.

2. *fig.*

a. To wash perfunctorily.

1911 A.L. HAYDON *Trooper Police Aust.* 333 It was usual for travellers to 'dry blow' each other—that is, knock the dust off each other with a handkerchief and wipe their faces with a hat. **1928** R.M. MACDONALD *Opals & Gold* 132 In our camp dry-blowers played for gold for six days in the week and on the seventh washed or 'dry-blowed' their clothes. **1946** K.S. PRICHARD *Roaring Nineties* 51 Water was too precious to spare for a bath, or shower, or clean clothes. A dry blow, or lick-and-promise swipe of face and hands with a wet rag, was all any man could allow himself.

b. To recount or tell.

1950 K.S. PRICHARD *Winged Seeds* 18 Dinny started dry-blowing his reminiscences as if Young Bill . . had never heard them before.

Also as *n.*, a perfunctory wash.

1907 *Bulletin* (Sydney) 7 Nov. 14/2 Did a dryblow many a time during the liver-rousing shanghai trips . . water was *terrible* scarce.

dry-blower.

a. One who uses the method of dry-blowing to separate particles of a mineral, esp. gold, from the surrounding earth, sand, etc.

1894 W.H. BARKER *Gold Fields W.A.* 101 The distance of the true reef from the blow accounts for the inability of the dry-blowers to find the locality in which the rich slug was hidden. **1896** J.M. PRICE *Land of Gold* 71 The 'dry-blower', with his rough primitive method of 'winnowing', as it were, the alluvial ground. **1898** R. RADCLYFFE *Wealth & Wild Cats* 17 The bars were always packed full with dry-blowers of copper-coloured visage. **1913** G. HERVEY *Australs. Yet* 20, I have seen the grim dry-blowers tramping store-ward for their mail. **1919** *Smith's Weekly* (Sydney) 15 Mar. 2/3 Two dryblowers have done a 'perish' into town from away beyond 'Dead Finish'. **1928** R.M. MACDONALD *Opals & Gold* 118 The working tools of the dry-blower are as simple or as complicated as the individual likes. The idea is to pass as much sand through a current of air as is possible. The wind blows the sand away and the gold contents, however fine, fall straight. **1936** J. KIRWAN *My Life's Adventure* 58 They were amazed to see the place a hive of busy dryblowers, most of whom were getting gold. **1946** K.S. PRICHARD *Roaring Nineties* 36 Shouts of 'Slug O!' and the surge from adjacent claims when a dryblower picked up a lump of gold, kept excitement at fever heat. **1975** L. WALKER *Runaway Girl* 78 Old dry-blowers like Pete the Prospector never stop looking.

b. An apparatus used for dry-blowing: see quot. 1928. Also *attrib.*

1897 A.F. CALVERT *My Fourth Tour W.A.* 146 The gullies and flats below the low hills have been turned over and put through the 'dry-blower'. **1928** R.M. MACDONALD *Opals & Gold* 119 'The dry-blower', as generally approved of, consists of a series of sieves mounted on an inclined plane on a frame which allows of their being shaken. A bellows attachment worked by every stroke of the 'shaker' supplies wind, and a hopper is surmounted into which the sand is shovelled. **1936** F. CLUNE *Roaming round Darling* 196 Tom worked the dryblower, a sort of wheelbarrow with a bellows and an arrangement of sieves. Earth . . is shovelled into the top sieve. The bellows are then pumped and the earth is blown away and gold remains—*sometimes.* **1941** D. O'CALLAGHAN *Long Life Reminisc.* 134, I decided to put the pack saddles on the camels and my dry blower gold shaker. **1950** G.S. CASEY *City of Men* 98 The Australian miner had invented a simple and wonderful machine, the 'dryblower'. **1972** B. MYATT *Austral. & N.Z. Gemstones* 31 The dry-blower is a combination of a rocking rifle-box and a bellows. **1981** A.B. FACEY *Fortunate Life* 66 The winnower had sieves and a fan; the sieves were on rockers that worked from side to side like a dryblower.

dry-blowing, *vbl. n.* The process by which a current of air is used to separate particles of a mineral, esp. gold, from the material in which it is found; see quot. 1881. Also *attrib.* and *fig.*

1881 J.C.F. JOHNSON *To Mount Browne & Back* 26 'Dry blowing' . . is conducted as follows:- The operator proceeds to sweep the bottom . . of all its superincumbent deposits . . which he places in an ordinary miner's tin dish till that receptacle is about three parts full. He then begins to throw the dirt into the air with a movement somewhat similar to that of a cook tossing pancakes. The wind carries the finest dust away, and the tossing brings the larger fragments of stone to the top, from whence they are swept with the hand. . . This action is continued till all the dirt but some fine sand and very small particles of stone are left. . . To finally separate gold from dirt he raises the dish to a level with his mouth and blows the dross over, leaving the prospect of more or less of the much-prized metal exposed on the tin. **1898** D.W. CARNEGIE *Spinifex & Sand* 7 A part of the timber had already been cleared to admit of 'dry-blowing' operations—a process adopted for the separation of gold from alluvial soil in the waterless parts of Australia. **1911** L.C.E. GEE *Gen. Rep. Tanami Goldfield* 9 About 60 men were on the field, some 30 of them being engaged in dry-blowing. **1939** A. GASTON *Coolgardie Gold* 76 Several different kinds of dryblowing machines were at work, but the shaker and Steve Lornern's patent dryblower were the most popular. The shaker dryblower came in some time later. It is the most perfect dryblowing goldsaver ever invented. **1955** A. UPFIELD *Cake in Hat Box* 70 Parties still doing a bit of dry-blowing, you know. **1967** K. TENNANT *Tell Morning This* 50 Miss Montrose, who realized she had struck pay-dirt at last after much dry blowing at Grandma's conversation, clicked her tongue to express sympathy and interest. **1972** B. MYATT *Austral. & N.Z. Gemstones* 30 Over much of central Australia water is not normally available for the recovery of alluvial gold and a process known as dry-blowing has been devised to meet this difficulty. **1983** *Canberra Times* 3 Dec. 15/2 Where gold prospectors worked without water supplies, the painstaking dry-blowing process of separating dirt from gold had to be used.

dry digging. Usu. in *pl.* [Orig. U.S.] A place, removed from running water, where gold is found on or near the surface. See DIGGING.

1851 S. RUTTER *Hints to Gold Hunters* 10 Some, bolder than the rest, tried digging deep holes on the plains (called in general, dry diggings, in contradistinction to those mentioned on the banks of rivers). **1851** *Empire* (Sydney) 22 Aug. 75/5 Since my removal hither, many have been at work on the dry diggings on the tops of the hills. **1852** *Ibid.* 21 Feb. 702/6 The Turon . . both in its bed and its dry diggings . . is yet wondrously rich. **1853** MOSSMAN & BANISTER *Aust. Visited & Revisited* 255 The dry diggings are those places where quartz containing gold has cropped out on the surface, and been disintegrated, crumbled to fragments of pebbles and dust, by the action of water, the atmosphere, or some other cause. **1854** F. ELDERSHAW *Aust. as it really Is* 244 The prodigious wealth and extent of our auriferous mountain ranges, our *dry diggings*, as they are called. **1881** J.C.F. JOHNSON *To Mount Browne & Back* 21 Mr Ashwin . . had experience in . . the Queensland dry diggings. **1980** J. WRIGHT *Big Hearts & Gold Dust* 19 There's a place called th' dry diggin'. . . Th' years of wind an' rain had eroded away th' old mullock heaps leavin' th' gold slugs lyin' on th' surface.

Hence **dry dig** *v. intr.*; also as *vbl. n.*

1851 *Bell's Life in Sydney* 23 May 2/4 We found located down the creek, from 500 to 700 people, divided into parties from three to eight each, busy dry digging. **1852** W. HUGHES *Austral. Colonies* 277 No inconsiderable portion of the Australian gold . . has been procured . . by means of dry-digging . . with no other implement than the pick-axe or the crowbar.

dry fiddle, *v. intr.*, DRY-BLOW 1. Also as *vbl. n.*

1881 J.C.F. JOHNSON *To Mount Browne & Back* 26 'Dry blowing' . . is sometimes called 'dry fiddling'. **1976** B. SCOTT *Complete Bk. Austral. Folk Lore* 79, I then had four weeks 'dry fiddling' on the Gilbert, and made an average 4 ozs. per week.

dry horrors.

1. Delirium tremens.

1913 H. LAWSON *Triangles of Life* 1 He had a touch of the 'dry 'orrers', as One-Eyed Bogan said. **1915** N. DUNCAN *Austral. Byways* 86 It was 'a case of the dry horrors' with him (said he); and he was vastly disgruntled with our news that the tavern was closed up.

2. *transf.* Malaria.

1936 K.L. SMITH *Sky Pilot's Last Flight* 193 No-one who has not experienced it can imagine the effect of malaria in its worst form. The bushmen sometimes call it the 'dry horrors'.

dry ration. *Obs.* See quot. 1876.

1846 *Portland Guardian* 15 Sept. 3/4 The cost of shearing is from 2s. 6d. to 2s. 9d. per score with dry rations. **1876** 'EIGHT YRS.' RESIDENT' *Queen of Colonies* 290 The squatters . . had no difficulty in obtaining as many as they required by simply finding them . . a 'dry-ration', that is beef and flour and tobacco, without any tea or sugar, and a very small amount of clothing.

dry-shell, *n.* Pearl shell exposed at low tide.

1959 D. STUART *Yandy* 84 S'pose we go for dryshell, what about licence?

dry-shell, *v. intr.* To gather dry-shell; also as *vbl. n.*

1936 N. CALDWELL *Fangs of Sea* 246 There used to be a lot of dry shelling. . . That is, by those who could not afford a lugger. **1937** E. HILL *Great Austral. Loneliness* 36 Tommy Clark . . dry-shelling on the reefs with an old lubra . . picked up the Southern Cross, jewel of a century. **1970** P. SLATER *Eagle for Pidgin* 162, I know he spent a year here dry-shelling. **1978** M. NIXON *Rivers of Home* 17, I nosed around, and found a man preparing to sail out 'dry-shelling'.

Also **dry-sheller** *n.*

1912 *Bulletin* (Sydney) 19 Dec. 15/1 Dry-shellers (men who gather pearl-shell at low tides), bêche-de-mer fishers and beachcombers in general are ruled out.

dry-stack, *v. Mining. trans.* See quots. 1931 and 1932. Freq. as *vbl. n.*

1931 C.B. SMITH *Austral. Gold Prospectors' Handbk.* 28 Should your creek be dried up, and you know that the ground is worth working, a good plan is to build a strong dam, dig a series of races along your claim and pile the ground up between the races. This practice is called dry-stacking. **1932** I.L. IDRIESS *Prospecting for Gold* 96 Dry-stacking means loosening ground with the pick, preparing it, throwing away the stones, cutting a race, and when a storm comes and the gully 'runs', rushing the dirt through. **1946** W.E. HARNEY *North of 23°* 13, I still think of those days when the 'old man' went out dry-stacking tin on the Tate.

dub. [Shortening of pronunc. of *W.C.*] A lavatory.

1943 'MRS E.F. BOSWORICK' *Amateur* 9 Privy's a new name to us out here, bein' as we was all brought up to call it the Dub. **1966** D. NILAND *Pairs & Loners* 88, I was in the dub dying when a flattened cigarette packet came sliding under the door. **1979** E. SMITH *Saddle in Kitchen* 16 The archaic pit-style dub stood some distance from the house on the bank of Ego Creek.

dubbo /ˈdʌboʊ/. [The name of a country town in N.S.W.] A jocular name for a person who appears something of a country bumpkin. Also *attrib.*

1973 D. FOSTER *North South West* 17 You've only got to look at all the bushwacking, nestfeathering dubbos we get for Education ministers. **1979** CAREY & LETTE *Puberty Blues* 46 'Sprung!' cried Jeff Basin, the local dubbo. **1980** B. HORNADGE *Austral. Slanguage* 172 In Sydney these days a person (particularly if from the country) who is a bit dense or otherwise considered objectionable is branded a *dubbo.* **1984** *Sydney Morning Herald* 15 Oct. (Guide) 15/4 (*caption*) Sylvester Stallone as Rocky. . . He's shaken off his dubbo image.

duchess, *v.* [f. *duchess* a woman of high rank.] *trans.* To entertain (esp. a visiting dignitary) lavishly and with ceremony; to give 'red carpet treatment' to. Also as *vbl. n.*

1956 J.T. LANG *I Remember* 64 On arrival in England he was 'duchessed' in a manner that no Australian Prime Minister has ever been 'duchessed' before or since. *Ibid.* 179 Now, to my amazement, I found that the Prince of Wales was being 'duchessed' in Australia. He was being given no opportunity to see the real Australia. He was surrounded by flunkeys. **1969** L. HAYLEN *Twenty Yrs.' Hard Labor* 134 Cables from London, telling us about the Labor delegation . . being 'duchessed' in the Commons or on the lawns at the Palace, didn't exactly send the Labor benches into transports of delight. **1976** *Sun-Herald* (Sydney) 27 June 38/2 It cannot be said that Malcolm Fraser was 'duchessed' during his memorable stay in Peking. **1982** *Bulletin* (Sydney) 15 June 25/1 The duchessing by Johnny-come-latelys who are beating their path now to the ALP Federal camp is met with a healthy degree of cynicism.

duck.

a. In the phr. **ducks and drakes,** rhyming slang for 'the shakes'.

1967 *Kings Cross Whisper* (Sydney) xxxiv. 4/4 *Ducks and drakes*, the shakes. From over-indulging. **1968** J. ALARD *He who shoots Last* 135 Ya got da bloody ducks an' drakes. **1978** B. ST. A. SMITH *Spirit beyond Psyche* 209 Don't forget you c'n get the ducks an' drakes from drinkin' too much grog.

b. In the phr. **ducks and geese,** rhyming slang for 'police'.

1950 *Austral. Police Jrnl.* Apr. 112 *Ducks and geese*, police. **1967** *Kings Cross Whisper* (Sydney) xxxiv. 4/4 *Ducks and geese*, police. Shortened to 'ducks and'.

duck-bill. PLATYPUS 1. Also *attrib.*

[**1798** Banks Papers 5 Aug. XIX. 49 An Amphibious Animal of the Mole Kind . . ; it has exactly the Bill of a Duck.] **1802** *Ibid.* 14 Aug. VIII. 106 What I most want to know is the mode of generation of the Duck bill & the Porcupine Ant Eater. **1803** *Ibid.* 8 Apr. VIII. 121 Our greatest want here is to be acquainted with the manner in which the Duck Bill Animal & the Porcupine Ant Eater which I think is the same Genus breed. **1833** W.H. BRETON *Excursions* 256 The ornithorynchus paradoxus, called also platypus, duck-bill, or water-mole, is one of the most singular animals in existence. **1844** C. LYON *Narr. & Recoll. Van Dieman's Land* 37 The duck-bill mole has long excited the scepticism and astonishment of naturalists. **1848** H.W. HAYGARTH *Recoll. Bush Life* 119 The ornithorhynchus paradoxus, called also the platypus, duckbill, and watermole by the colonists. **1880** J. BALLANTYNE *Our Colony* 92 Among other animals may be mentioned . . the platypus or duckbill, but better known as the water-mole. **1898** *Bulletin* (Sydney) 15 Oct. 14/3 When the young of the duckbill platypus are hatched out, they are quite blind. **1913** E.W. HOWE *Travel Lett.* 156 The duck-bill has a bill like a duck, fur like a mole, webbed feet, and is about as large as a terrier dog. **1920** *Smith's Weekly* (Sydney) 10 Apr. 9/2 The strangest land-traveller I ever struck was a platypus taken from its native river and placed in a lake over a mile away. The duckbill was afterwards found dead in a patch of scrub. **1928** M.E. FULLERTON *Austral. Bush* 112 The 'duckbill', as he is called, makes some attempt at a pouch. **1944** C. BARRETT *Platypus* 14 'Water-mole' is completely out of fashion, though 'duck-bill' is still used occasionally.

duck-billed, *a.* Used as a distinguishing epithet in various Comb. designating the platypus, as **duck-billed animal, mole, platypus, water-mole.**

1799 G. SHAW *Naturalist's Miscellany* X. Pl. 386, The Duck-billed Platypus. **1803** Banks Papers 7 Aug. VIII. 127 The duck billed mole I should have sought. **1837** *Lit. News* (Sydney) 21 Oct. 105, I sought the burrows of those shy animals, the 'water-moles' the ornithorynchus paradoxus of the naturalists, known also as the platypus or duck-billed animal. **1852** A. MACKAY *Great Gold Field* (1853) 42 In this water hole, I saw several 'duck-billed platypi' or 'duck-billed moles' as they are called by the colonists, paddling about. **1863** F. ALGAR *Handbk. to Colony Vic.* 8 Other remarkable animals are the duck-billed water-mole, or *Platypus Anatinus*, and the *Echidna*. **1872** A. MCFARLAND *Illawarra & Manaro* 148 The *ornithorhynchus*, or duck-billed animal, may be seen swimming. **1916** E. & M.S. GREW *Rambles in Aust.* 23 Unfortunately some of the most interesting cannot be kept in captivity. This applies, for instance . . to the curious duck-billed platypus. **1928** B. SPENCER *Wanderings in Wild Aust.* 152 The name 'ducked-billed mole', originally given to Echidna's close ally the Platypus, is entirely inappropriate. It has, apart from the most beautiful fur, no resemblance whatever to a mole, and its bill, though flattened out, is covered, when it is alive, with a soft, almost velvety, leather-like material, studded over with numberless delicate sense organs, whose functions are probably akin to those of both touch and smell. **1935** F. CLUNE *Rolling down Lachlan* 240 In a chain of ponds near Wallerawang . . he found the duck-billed platypus. **1956** S. HOPE *Diggers' Paradise* 202 Australia is the home of some primeval marsupials such as the duck-billed platypus which is a harmless looking water-mole with a shovel-beak, and surprisingly equipped aft with a spitefully sharp and venomous toe. **1984** *Daily Tel.* (Sydney) 16 Aug. 3/1 David Attenborough's camera has caught many of the world's rarest and shyest creatures, but . . he gave up on Australia's duck-billed platypus.

duckhouse. In the phr. **(one) up against** (one's) **duckhouse,** used allusively of a person's misfortune or disadvantage: see quots.

1933 N. LINDSAY *Saturdee* 7 You think you hid me cap, so that's one up agen your duckhouse. **1941** S.J. BAKER *Pop. Dict. Austral. Slang* 26 *Duck-house, up against one's*, a phrase used to describe some setback to a person's plans: e.g., 'that's one up against your duckhouse', that baffles you, that makes you think. **1968** S. GORE *Holy Smoke* 52 He says, 'That's one up against your duckhouse, Jonah!' **1972** *Bulletin* (Sydney) 12 Aug. 7/1 Who, today, ever . . tells you to put something up against your duckhouse? **1981** *Sydney Morning Herald* 21 Nov. 45/1 National Trust needed to preserve historic Australian idioms, e.g. 'Shove that up against your duckhouse.'

duck-mole. *Obs.* PLATYPUS 1.

1819 *First Fruits Austral. Poetry* 9 Sooty swans are once more rare, And duck-moles the Museum's care. **1844** C. LYON *Narr. & Recoll. Van Dieman's Land* 87 It has lately been proved that these duck-moles not only lay eggs, but suckle their young. **1886** F. COWAN *Aust.* 20 The Tambreet: Duck-mole: Platypus: Ornithorhynchus: furclad, duck-billed and web-footed, sun-abhorring, water-haunting, and earth-burrowing: half-bird, half-beast! **1920** *Land of Lyre Bird* (S. Gippsland Pioneers' Assoc.) 49 The platypus, or duck-mole, is found in the creeks.

duck-shove, *v.*

a. *intr. Obs.* In a business: to act unethically. Also as *vbl. n.*

1870 *Notes & Queries* 4th Ser. VI. 111 'Duck-shoving' . . is the term used by our Melbourne cabmen to express the unprofessional trick of breaking the rank, in order to push past the cabman on the stand for the purpose of picking up a stray passenger or so. **1937** L. MANN *Murder in Sydney* 97 He's big enough now not to have to duck-shove or not so openly.

b. *trans.* To evade (responsibilities); to avoid (an issue). Also *absol.* and freq. as *vbl. n.*

1942 *Ack Ack News* (Melbourne) Apr. 3 If it has been the habit to indulge in this form of 'duck shoving' responsibility, the stultifying of initiative will bear fruit at the critical moment. **1949** J. MORRISON *Creeping City* 34 Mishkin had already decided that this was no time for the truth. . . 'Why should I want to sell out, Bob?' 'Never mind the duck-shoving. . . Would you?' **1969** *Sunday Mail* (Brisbane) 31 Aug. 5/1 Some Cabinet Ministers said that most local authorities were 'duck shoving' on the State's litter problem. **1972** *Bulletin* (Sydney) 10 June 11/1 The matter of who or what banned 'Our Man in Canberra' . . is a typical bit of ABC duck-shoving. **1977** *Sun-Herald* (Sydney) 3 Apr. 15/3 All the Public Service duck-shoving will not change the basic arguments. **1982** *Sydney Morning Herald* 9 Aug. 1/6 Mr Wran said retrospective billing was totally unacceptable. . . 'This sniping and duck-shoving between county councils and the Electricity Commission should also cease,' he said.

Hence **duck-shover** *n.*

1898 E.E. MORRIS *Austral Eng.* 128 A cabman who did not wait his turn on the station rank, but touted for passengers up and down the street in the neighbourhood of the rank, was termed a *Duck-shover.* **1937** L. MANN *Murder in Sydney* 97 He can be pretty nasty if he likes. He's a bit of a duck-shover. **1943** *O-Pip: 'P' Battery Austral. Field Artillery* Aug. 1 If there's anything I can't stand its a duck-shover on mess parades.

Duco /'djukoʊ/. Also **duco.** [Proprietary name.] A kind of paint, used esp. on the body of a motor-car; an application of such paint.

1927 *Austral. Official Jrnl. Patents* (Canberra) 106 *Duco* 44,667. Paints, lacquers, varnishes, and enamel paints, and pyroxylin finishes and thinners. E.I. Du Pont De Nemours and Co., Wilmington, New Castle, Delaware, United States of America, manufacturers. **1928** *Open Road* 25 Nov. 43/2 Motor cars Painted and Varnished, also sprayed with 'Duco', under the personal supervision of the proprietor. **1931** *Ibid.* 30 Apr. 8/1 Duco or paint—5½ day service. **1953** *Wheels* May 97 *Smash repair specialists.* Panel Beating. Duco Spraying. **1958** P. COWAN *Unploughed Land* 101 He looked idly at the still serviceable duco, thin over the bonnet. **1966** A. HOPGOOD *Private Yuk Objects* 4 If I was as dirty as you, mate, I'd need a re-duco! **1978** O. WHITE *Silent Reach* 173 Why did they give it a one-coat spray job over the original white duco and fix it with bodgie number plates? **1985** *New Idea* (Melbourne) 3 Aug. 91 It was a hot day so I threw a blanket over the car to keep the sun off the duco.

duff, *v.* [f. DUFFER *n.* 1.]

1. *trans.* To steal (stock).

1859 *Gippsland Guardian* 6 May 41 To allow every man who has managed to duff together a mob of cattle. **1862** *Western Post* (Mudgee) 13 Dec. 2/5 It would not be advisable to duff any more cattle. **1868** *Colonial Soc.* (Sydney) 3 Dec. 7 The soil a race of cattle-stealers rears; In 'duffing' trained. **1880** 'ERRO' *Squattermania* 73 Any fat cows to duff up your road, Mac? **1888** *Bulletin* (Sydney) 10 Mar. 14/1 We'll duff the squatter's cattle in the darkness of the night. **1899** G.E. BOXALL *Story Austral. Bushrangers* 190 Sheep could be duffed as well as cattle. **1918** C. FETHERSTONHAUGH *After Many Days* 102 All I heard them say was they were going to duff Tyson's calves. **1938** F. CLUNE *Free & Easy Land* 50 Never in the wilds of Texas or Arizona were a thousand cattle duffed at one go. **1978** H.C. BAKER *I was Listening* 77 Complaining to the police that his stock was being duffed.

2. To pasture (stock) illicitly on another's land; to steal (grass).

1900 *Albury Banner* 2 Feb. 16/4 The want of a camping ground with water is sadly felt . . by the wheat carters, causing some of the big teamsters to duff their horses and bullocks into Mr Sloan's for water. **1968** L. BRADEN *Bullockies* 109 As with most teamsters, the grass was 'duffed' at farms where the owner did not live. **1976** C.D. MILLS *Hobble Chains & Greenhide* 124 If the bullocky did 'duff' 'em on the grass' at times . . it was amply repaid by the 'bit of loading at the station, George'.

Hence **duffed** *ppl. a.*

1934 C. SAYCE *Comboman* 141 He's certainly here and so are half a dozen duffed cattle.

duffer, *n.* [Transf. use of *duffer* one who deals in counterfeit goods; that which is counterfeit or 'no good'.]

1. One who steals stock (and alters brand marks). See also CATTLE DUFFER.

1844 *Sydney Morning Herald* 28 Mar. 2/7 Some line of defence might be adopted which is not known by the 'duffers' (cattle stealers) of other districts. **1848** *Bell's Life in Sydney* 11 Mar. 1/1 The negligence of the proprietor of stock in looking after his own—thus affording increased opportunities to the ever wary 'duffer'. **1849** *Ibid.* 21 July 1/3 'Duffers', a title as expressive as could be found for those who live on the thick Fat of the land by cattle stealing. **1867** *Pasquin* (London) 2 Feb. 9 The ancient and modern anti-squatters—dogs and duffers—have restored the waste land to its former peaceful simplicity. **1890** A.J. VOGAN *Black Police* 264 Cattle thieves, or 'duffers', as we call them. **1902** *Bulletin* (Sydney) 25 Jan. 14/2 A number of owners . . only visit their stock once a week or so. 'Duffer' takes them to first sale-yard and sells. Purchaser paddocks them for the night; 'duffer' takes them away again, and puts them where he got them. **1919** *Smith's Weekly* (Sydney) 26 Apr. 19/4 There are still a few clever cattle and sheep 'duffers' in Queensland. **1930** HIVES & LUMLEY *Jrnl. of Jackaroo* 136 'Duffing' . . meant appropriating calves belonging to other squatters, by rounding them up and marking them with the brand of the 'duffer'. **1948** F. CLUNE *Wild Colonial Boys* 130 There's no duffers about these parts game to lift a mob of thirty horses. **1965** R.H. CONQUEST *Horses in Kitchen* 89 That veteran cattleman . . had been a bit of a duffer himself in his youth. **1979** D. LOCKWOOD *My Old Mates & I* 53 There were duffers and duffers. Those who knocked-off a fat killer for the table lived and were let live. **1984** *Age* (Melbourne) 30 June 17/3 Some time during the night of 7–8 May a group of duffers drove their truck onto Mr Wheelhouse's 50-hectare farm at Mooroopna, near Shepparton, and stole 28 Hereford steers worth about $13,000.

2. a. An unproductive mine or claim. Also *attrib.* See also RANK DUFFER.

1855 *Ovens & Murray Advertiser* (Beechworth) 20 Jan. (Suppl.) 6/2 No one is game to run the risk of sinking two or three 'duffers' in the ridges and gullies. **1859** 'EYE WITNESS' *Voyage to Aust.* 17 Should it [*sc.* the claim] turn out bad and give no yield of gold after three or four washings, it is given up and it then bears the name of a shiser or duffer. **1864** J. ROGERS *New Rush* 55 Tho' *duffers* are so common, And golden gutters rare. **1873** W. THOMSON-GREGG *Desperate Character* I. 122 The second shaft—was also off the 'run' of the gold, and what the diggers termed a 'duffer'; *anglicè*, a blank. **1892** *Western Champion* (Barcaldine) 16 Feb. 14/1 They had bottomed several 'duffers', and were now engaged in sinking a shaft which was to be the 'last try'. **1907** C. MACALISTER *Old Pioneering Days* 187, I soon found that like many another field the Turon was much of a lottery—it had plenty of 'duffers' and 'stringers' as well as jewellers' shops. **1915** 'ALPHA' *Reminisc. Goldfields* i. 106 We took some time washing up, during which John Chinaman discovered that he had bought a 'duffer' claim. **1936** J. KIRWAN *My Life's Adventure* 77 It was sold for about £150,000. When opened up that mine, too, proved a duffer! **1955** STEWART & KEESING *Austral. Bush Ballads* 81 He sunk a duffer on the Flat In comp'ny with three more. **1972** N. MILES *Opal Fever* 18, I haven't had much luck on the last four 'duffers' I've sunk.

b. An unproductive goldfield; the rush to such a goldfield. Also *attrib.*, as **duffer rush.**

[N.Z. **1869** R. WAITE *Narr. Discovery W. Coast Goldfields* 15 Those first arrivals chose to call the expedition a duffer rush.] **1873** R.P. WHITWORTH *Lost & Found* 23 Jim was .. too old a stager to be taken in by these 'storekeepers' rushes', which, nineteen times out of twenty, were the most unmitigated 'duffers'. **1876** 'EIGHT YRS.' RESIDENT' *Queen of Colonies* 168 Rockhampton owes its existence to a 'duffer rush'. **1879** 'AUSTRALIAN' *Adventures Qld.* 107 He had before seen the evils of a rush to a field that had turned out a 'duffer'. **1884** G. WIGHT *Qld.* 76 The wretched state of matters .. that succeeded when the diggings proved for a time, at least, to be a 'duffer'. **1889** *Bulletin* (Sydney) 21 Dec. 23/2 A duffer-rush broke out one day, I quite forget where at—(It doesn't matter, anyway, It didn't feed a cat). **1892** *Missing Friends: Adventures Danish Emigrant Qld.* 187 He told me he had been on the spot the previous day, and .. it was a 'duffer', but still there would be a rush. **1904** *Shearer* (Sydney) 10 Sept. 4/4 The Woolgar, Mulgrave and Hodgkinson fields are duffers, or tucker-claims at best. **1941** D. O'CALLAGHAN *Long Life Reminisc.* 46, I stuck pretty well to the Flat, except rushing [*sic*] away to some duffer rush for a day or two. **1947** F. CLUNE *Roaming around Aust.* 177 In other words, the great Kimberley Goldfield turned out to be a 'duffer'! **1955** STEWART & KEESING *Austral. Bush Ballads* 81 A duffer-rush broke out one day, I quite forget where at.

3. One who pastures stock illicitly: see DUFF 2.

1911 *Huon Times* (Franklin) 25 Feb. 3/2 Last year an Act was passed which is intended to make an end of the 'grass duffers'. These people run their cattle on the forest areas, and not content with sneaking the grass, start bush fires when it appears necessary to secure a new growth of grass.

duffer, *v.* [f. DUFFER *n.* 2.]

1. a. *intr. Mining.* Of a mine, etc.: to prove unproductive; to peter out. Usu. with **out.**

1880 *Austral.: Monthly Mag.* (Sydney) V. 61 The party then .. put down another shaft which 'duffered out'. **1888** *Boomerang* (Brisbane) 7 Apr. 9/4 That hall is going up this year—unless the Eidsvold 'duffers'. **1895** *Worker* (Sydney) 30 May 3/4 The flat duffered out, and everybody but these two left it. **1916** H.L. ROTH *Sketches & Reminisc. Qld.* 5 The diggers found no gold, as Wawn and his mate had only struck an isolated pocket in which the drift had duffered out. **1940** I.L. IDRIESS *Lightning Ridge* 160 In a couple of months Tom's claim duffered out. **1952** C. SIMPSON *Come away, Pearler* 135 Billy's tin show must have duffered out by now. **1980** J. WRIGHT *Big Hearts & Gold Dust* 26 Never try to find where gold come from... Git stuck inta it where ya know it is, and when it duffers out, pack ya swag an' go some place else.

b. *trans.* In passive: to be unsuccessful in the search for gold. Also *intr.*, to fail to find gold.

1890 'R. BOLDREWOOD' *Miner's Right* 58 'So you're 'duffered out' again, Harry,' she said. **1895** *Worker* (Sydney) 5 Oct. 2/5, I acknowledge it is hard lines for a man who has got on a lead to be duffered out for want of funds. **1899** *Bulletin* (Sydney) 28 Jan. 3/2 We wish for luck—and duffer out, Or bottom on to payin' stuff.

2. *transf.* and *fig.*

1895 *Worker* (Sydney) 21 Dec. 6/3 All the stores had stopped our tucker since our luck had duffered out. **1906** *Bulletin* (Sydney) 24 May 14/1 Old Jonas sheared away like fun, Until the shearing duffered out.

duffing, *vbl. n.* [f. DUFF *v.*]

1. The action or practice of stealing stock (often involving the alteration of brand marks). Also *attrib.*

1865 *Tumut & Adelong Times* 23 Mar. 3/1 A very lucrative business in the cattle-duffing at Kiandra. **1869** *Bushmen, Publicans, & Politics* 6 The *duffing* of a foal or calf far from being considered a crime, is but a proof of smartness. **1881** H.W. NESFIELD *Chequered Career* 306 'Duffing' is a term used when cattle or horses are illegally branded, or have their brands changed. **1888** 'R. BOLDREWOOD' *Robbery under Arms* (1937) 32 'It's a 'break',' he said, almost in a whisper. 'There's a 'duffing-yard' somewhere handy.' **1900** C.H. CHOMLEY *True Story Kelly Gang* 22 Until the whole of the professional 'duffing' population was .. safely under lock and key in the gaols .. the police felt it would be futile to hope for a full measure of law and order in the district. **1918** C. FETHERSTONHAUGH *After Many Days* 102 There was no 'duffing' of other people's calves. **1930** HIVES & LUMLEY *Jrnl. of Jackaroo* 136 In these days what was called 'duffing' was very prevalent among the more unscrupulous of the smaller squatters. **1960** R.S. PORTEOUS *Cattleman* 16 When it came to duffing he had few equals. A faint or blotched brand he regarded as a challenge to his artistry, a cleanskin a direct invitation. **1968** *Swag* (Sydney) i. 20 A country jury, sometimes consisting of men who have indulged in a bit of duffing themselves, are often reluctant to convict one of their own breed. **1973** H. HOLTHOUSE *S'pose I Die* 48 There were several runs that were well known as duffing stations. **1984** *Age* (Melbourne) 30 June 17/3 Cattle, sheep and horse duffing is alive, well and booming in Victoria.

2. The practice of pasturing animals illicitly.

1959 H.P. TRITTON *Time means Tucker* 17 Our horses were in good order, as there was always good feed in the paddocks alongside the route. It was a simple matter to undo the top wire, throw a bag over the next one, and, being old campaigners, they would step over unconcernedly. This was known as 'grass duffing'.

dugite /'djugaɪt/. Also **dukite.** [a. Nyungar *dukayj.*] A predomin. grey, olive, or brown venomous snake, the elapid *Pseudonaja affinis* of s.w. Aust. Also *attrib.*, as **dugite snake.**

1873 J.B. O'REILLY *Songs Southern Seas* 106 If a spirit of evil Ever came to this world its hate to slake On mankind, it came as a Dukite Snake. **1936** *Bulletin* (Sydney) 3 June 21/2 The boss had killed a big dugaight or dukite, South Westralia's tiger-snake. **1950** *Ibid.* 8 Nov. 12/2 The only poisonous snake around Perth that I know of that will attempt to enter a house is the dugite. **1977** H. BUTLER *In Wild* 89 A Dugite or brown snake .. looks like any other of the common brown snakes in Australia, and is one of the Brown Snake family.

dugong grass. Any of several marine flowering plants (seagrasses), esp. of the fam. Potamogetonaceae and Hydrocharitaceae, eaten by the dugong.

1905 T. WELSBY *Schnappering & Fishing Brisbane River* 142 There is no good drift fishing in these coloured banks, for the dugong grass tears your bait away. **1930** C.M. YONGE *Yr. on Great Barrier Reef* 193 Wide flats of 'dugong grass' on the south-east reef flat. **1944** J. DEVANNY *By Tropic Sea & Jungle* 7 He'd been stranded while feeding on the dugong grass. **1955** V. SERVENTY *Aust.'s Great Barrier Reef* 15 While seaweeds are algae and therefore simple plants, there are true flowering species in the sea. These cling close to land and the most interesting in the Reef area is known as Dugong Grass.

duke, var. DOOK.

dukite, var. DUGITE.

dulachie, var. TOOLACHE.

dummy, *n.*

1. *Hist.* [Spec. use of *dummy* one who is the tool of another.] One commissioned to select a block of Crown land on behalf of another not entitled to do so. Also *attrib.*, esp. as **dummy selector.**

1865 *Australasian* (Melbourne) 24 June 11/5 The different grades employed in this profitable occupation [*sc.* dummyism] may be divided into the substantial dummy, the hired dummy, and the speculative dummy. **1867** 'CLERGYMAN' *Aust. as it Is* 130 The rights to three millions of acres of the best land in Victoria were driven through an Act by card shuffling, dodging—making use of what, in colonial phrase, is called 'dummies'. **1872** 'RESIDENT' *Glimpses Life Vic.* 295 Men who hired themselves out as 'dummy' selectors. **1882** *Bulletin* (Sydney) 15 July 8/2 He, the Land Shark, Dummy Bummer, Cunning, wriggling schemer, up to All the wrinkles of the Land Act. **1891** A.F. SPAWN *New Homes in Irrigation & Fruit-Growing Colonies Vic.* 34 To enable the squatter to still keep control of large holdings, thousands of acres were taken up by squatters' dummies. **1895** J.T. RYAN *Reminisc. Aust.* 391 A great portion of the richest soil in New South Wales was selected by dummies. **1906** *Bulletin* (Sydney) 15 Nov. 17/2 A white 'dummy' has been found to hold a station near the Alligator River for a syndicate of Chows. **1920** W. MCGUFFIN *Austral. Tales of Border* 179 Rafferty fell in with a station employee... He was a dummy selector for the squatter there. **1932** *Bulletin* (Sydney) 20 July 29/3 The dummy selector is extinct, but he is niched among the immortal bush characters of other days. **1944** M.W. PEACOCK *Dead Puppets Dance* 46 'He's no dummy.' 'No squatter's man.' **1959** H.G. LAMOND *Sheep Station* 59 'How about those Ootooloo blocks?' .. 'They're contiguous... That means one man can hold them both without the need of a dummy.' **1980** P. FREEMAN *Woolshed* 92 Conditional purchasers of particular allotments were sometimes 'dummies' who allowed eventual takeover by already wealthy landowners.

2. Chiefly *Vic. Hist.* [Orig. U.S.: see Mathews.] The leading car of a pair of cable tramcars, in which the driver operates the controls: see quots. 1965 and 1967.

1900 *Bulletin* (Sydney) 19 May 19/2 He sat on the dummy of a tram next to an old Irish laborer. **1910** *Truth* (Sydney) Dec. 4 7/1, I was on the 'dummy', as the front outside seat of the car is called. **1926** 'S. WESTLAW' *White Peril* 224 He chose a tram-ride to the beach. .. An unmistakable figure 'hopped on' to the dummy in front of Dick. **1939** P. MCGUIRE *Austral. Journey* 283 There are not many cable-cars left, but they still come through Bourke Street, with their open-air 'dummies' in front, to which you precariously cling. **1965** G. MCINNES *Road to Gundagai* 65 The dummy was essentially a hollow square of seats on wheels, in the centre of which stood the driver or 'gripman' with two levers at his disposal. **1967** F.T. MACARTNEY *Proof against Failure* 7 The cable tram, which was in use in Melbourne from 1885 until the 1930s, consisted of 'the dummy' in front and a detachable car behind. The dummy was quite open except for its roof. In a space between the side seats the driver worked levers which passed through a continuous slot midway between the rails to grip or release a cable. **1971** J. HETHERINGTON *Morning was Shining* 269 A cable tram overtook me and went lurching past. The destination board on the dummy said *Melbourne.*

dummy, *v. Hist.* [f. DUMMY *n.* 1.] *intr.* To act for another; spec. to select land, ostensibly for oneself but in reality as the agent of another not entitled to do so. Also *trans.* (see quot. 1878).

1878 *Austral.: Monthly Mag.* (Sydney) I. 426 Spoiled with the reckless waste of the 'good times', with their territory dummied, and the dummys' profits spent, they have eaten their cake. **1883** *Bulletin* (Sydney) 7 July 13/1 A 'cute N.S.W. squatter somewhere in the Riverine district sent all the way to a Melbourne Asylum for a cripple to dummy for him. **1891** 'ROUSEABOUT' *Jackeroo* 138 'Did you want him to dummy, uncle?' she asked. 'Yes, my dear,' said Old Crusham. 'There's 640 acres must be secured near Brand's.' **1930** 'BRENT OF BIN BIN' *Ten Creeks Run* (1952) 23 He had dummied for Larry Healey's on Monaro in '61 when the Free Selection Act came in. **1941** OUTHWAITE & CHOMLEY *Wisdom of Esau* 4 Men gathered together by Mallock .. to dummy for Harlin, whose run, held now as leasehold, was to be thrown open for selection under the Act. **1960** *Encounter* (London) May 24 They .. financed likely colonials who knew the ropes to dummy for them on the leases.

Hence **dummied** *ppl. a.*

1878 MRS H. JONES *Broad Outlines* 266 The dummied land was all forfeited .. and thrown open again for re-selection. **1884** *Adelaide Observer* 13 Sept. 30 It is proposed to lease, 5,000 acres of dummied land. **1920** *Bulletin* (Sydney) 1 Apr. 20/3 The squatter usually held a mortgage over the dummied selection. Even then he was not always safe.

dummying, *vbl. n. Hist.* The practice of employing one entitled to select land as the agent of one not so entitled. Also *transf.* (see quot. 1946).

1873 A. TROLLOPE *Aust. & N.Z.* I. 101 The . . system is generally called dummying,—putting up a non-existent free-selector,—and is illegal. **1876** 'EIGHT YRS.' RESIDENT' *Queen of Colonies* 85 'Dummying' . . means that various friends and servants were employed to select the maximum quantity of land allowed each individual under the Act, and then to hand them over to the squatter under a power of attorney prepared for that specific purpose. **1888** *Illustr. Austral. News* (Melbourne) 1 Aug. (Suppl.) 12/4 Capitalists, chiefly by 'dummying', obtained possession of the bulk of the land made available for section blocks. **1900** J.C.L. FITZPATRICK *Good Old Days* 137 It was in Phillip's time that dummying was born, then known by the euphemistic term of an 'imposition'. **1909** W.G. SPENCE *Aust.'s Awakening* 246 Mr Carruthers, when leader of the Opposition, must have known of the 'dummying' carried on by Willis. **1930** A.E. YARRA *Vanishing Horsemen* 110 If he hadn't been too good for the old man over the dummying business he might have raised the money. **1946** K.S. PRICHARD *Roaring Nineties* 394 Tributors suspected of dummying for the company began to move ore from dumps claimed by the alluvial diggers. **1968** F. ROSE *Aust. Revisited* 29 One method the squatters used was known as 'dummying', whereby anyone, including his own children, could be paid to take up land in their name and then return it to him after a year. **1976** N.V. WALLACE *Bush Lawyer* 32 A scathing article . . named Mr Hutchison as one given to 'dummying', the practice of some squatters who were unable to obtain further Government land grants. To circumvent this restraint, they took up available land in the name of a shepherd or other hired hand.

dummyism. *Hist.* The practice of dummying.

1865 *Australasian* (Melbourne) 24 June 11/5 Dummyism has made gigantic strides here since the first introduction of this land lottery. **1874** *Illustr. Sydney News* 19 Sept. 2/3 It has also been the means of introducing 'dummyism' on the squatters' part, they taking advantage of every *ruse* to prevent their holdings from being . . rendered valueless for grazing purposes. **1882** W.B. CHRISTIE *Our Land Laws* 2 In common with all others on the station, from the proprietor to the cowboy, [I] became a Dummy in the earliest stages of Dummyism. **1892** *Truth* (Sydney) 19 June 2/7 An effort should be made to stamp out dummyism, which is still rampant in the land. **1895** *Worker* (Sydney) 23 Feb. 1/5 They tried to secure the whole with a system of dummyism, persecuting and annoying the selectors.

dump, *n.*[1] *Hist.* [Br. *dump* rough-cast leaden counter used by children in games.]

1. A coin struck from the centre of a Spanish dollar, circulating in N.S.W. from 1813 at a face value equal to one quarter of a dollar.

1816 W.C. WENTWORTH Miscellanea 1816–45 6 Mar., Two Hundred Pounds' a tempting Sum But whence my Heroes must it come Not from your pockets I declare A sum so great was never there. . . Down with your Dumps and let me see. **1821** *Sydney Gaz.* 5 May, A Number of *bad dollars* and *dumps* having lately been offered in Payment at the Bank of New South Wales. **1823** *Hobart Town Gaz.* 11 Jan., The time fixed for the reception of the 'Dumps' at this Office will expire on the 25th Instant. **1824** *Austral.* (Sydney) 9 Dec. 4 A practice was . . introduced of punching out a portion from the centre of the Spanish dollar. . . The centre-bit, or *dump*, which was the classical term in New South Wales, passed for 1s. 3d. **1827** P. CUNNINGHAM *Two Yrs. in Aust.* I. 44 He only solicits the loan of a *dump* on pretence of treating his sick *gin* to a cup of tea. **1827** *Monitor* (Sydney) 30 Aug. 619/3 Plenty of dumps for the overseer. **1834** J.D. LANG *Hist. & Statistical Acct. N.S.W.* II. 299 The said children are baptized . . at a *dump* or quarter-dollar a head. **1840** *S. Austral. Miscellany* May 175 The *holey* dollar was the rim, the *dump* the centre struck out of the Spanish dollar—the former passing for 3s. 9d., the latter for 1s. 3d. currency. **1849** A. HARRIS *Emigrant Family* (1967) 213 Selling it in the bush at a dump (1s. 3d.) a glass. **1879** 'DOCTOR DORIC' *Unsophisticated Rhymes* 12 Worshipping the Dolar [*sic*] or the Dump. **1890** J. JOUBERT *Shavings & Scrapes* 72 During a drunken spree he sold his property for a bottle of rum and a 'dump'.

2. a. *transf.* A small coin; a small amount of money; money in general.

1825 *Austral.* (Sydney) 1 Dec. 3 She had filched from him many a dump. **1828** *Tasmanian* (Hobart) 6 June 2 They will doubtless export large quantities . . in exchange for tobacco, tea and sugar, in lieu of paying away our dumps. **1829** E.G. WAKEFIELD *Let. From Sydney* 13 These men, all round, declared their innocence, and called Heaven to witness that they had not wronged me of a 'dump'. **1833** *Currency Lad* (Sydney) 9 Mar. 3 He was startled in the night by a noise in his room, when he discovered his chest was minus the dumps. **1846** *Cumberland Times* (Parramatta) 31 Jan. 3/3 Our races will be . . a splendiferous affair; the prospects of the colony being brightening, people are laying down their *dumps*. **1853** W. WESTGARTH *Vic.* 175 This occasioned an issue of small fragments of gold or 'dumps', representing a pound in the proportions fixed by the act.

b. *fig.* In negative contexts.

c **1892** J. CAMERON *Fire Stick* 175, I don't value the two darkies' lives as worth a dump. **1899** *Truth* (Sydney) 26 Mar. 4/6 A lot of irrelevant hogwash, about which neither the public nor I care a dump. **1904** *Ibid.* 13 Nov. 1/4 What folks may say I do not care a dump. **1955** STEWART & KEESING *Austral. Bush Ballads* 12 His life's not worth a dump. **1962** D. MCLEAN *World turned upside Down* 13 He laughed so often you'd never think he was worth a dump as a fighter. **1981** *Sun-Herald* (Sydney) 13 Dec. 97/1 From now on you can have your three pronged Australian pace attack. . . I wouldn't give you a tuppeny dump for it.

dump, *n.*[2] [f. DUMP *v.* 2.]

1. DUMPER 1.

1935 *Bulletin* (Sydney) 9 Jan. 11/3 It gave the Duke of Gloucester his first experience of a dump, in the Mooloolaba surf, and he didn't like it. **1959** H. DRAKE-BROCKMAN *West Coast Stories* 20 There was no slope for the crest to slide down on; it was going to topple in a bone-crushing dump.

2. DUMPER 3. Also *attrib.*

1974 J. GABY *Restless Waterfront* 237 A wool press is sometimes called a dump. **1980** P. FREEMAN *Woolshed* 155 They installed a giant dump-press to dump or compress the wool bales prior to loading on the wagons.

dump, *v.*

1. *trans.* To compress (a bale of wool). Also as *vbl. n.*

1849 *Portland Gaz.* 9 Mar. 3/5 Wool packed by the spade turns out very badly. . . It cannot be compressed, or as it is usually termed 'dumped', so well as that packed by the lever or screw. **1857** W. WESTGARTH *Vic. & Austral. Gold Mines* 124 The bale was now 'dumped' in a hydraulic press. **1872** C.H. EDEN *My Wife & I in Qld.* 98 It is always repressed or 'dumped' as it is called, by hydraulic pressure on its arrival in port. **1884** A.W. STIRLING *Never Never Land* 155 Other men pick up the fleeces, fold them and put them in bales, when they are pressed, and sometimes 'dumped', that is, subjected to hydraulic pressure to make carriage easier. **1890** E.T. TOWNER *Selectors' Guide to Barcoo* 40 Greasy Wool, properly dumped. **1912** J. BRADSHAW *Highway Robbery under Arms* (ed. 3) 38, I followed him and butted him into the wool press, and would have dumped him up with a bail [*sic*] of dags only for the other shearers pleading him off. **1980** P. FREEMAN *Woolshed* 41 The wool bale was often subjected to the final process of 'dumping', which was carried out in the Sydney or Melbourne wool stores.

2. *trans.* Of a wave: to break suddenly and violently into shallow water, throwing (a surfer) down, often against the bottom. Also *absol.*

1932 R.W. THOMPSON *Down Under* 57 One has to learn to distinguish between the breaker that will carry one in on its crest and the wave that will 'dump'. **1940** P. KERRY *Cobbers A.I.F.* 10 An' 'e rode it like a mermaid, an' wus flyin' on the crest, When it dumped 'im down the mine, an' pounded wildly on 'is chest. **1942** A.L. HASKELL *Waltzing Matilda* 141 Sometimes the surfer is dumped, bumped and rolled along the bottom, as I know to my cost. **1949** C.B. MAXWELL *Surf* 10 Being 'dumped', the experience of being overwhelmed by some hollow-fronted top-heavy green peril. **1969** D. CUSACK *Half-Burnt Tree* 3 He was . . dumped against the gravelly bottom, twisted by a cross-current. **1976** H.F. BRINSMEAD *Under Silkwood* 57 They spent more time under the waves than on top. . . Dumped over and over, they had sand in mouth, eyes and nose.

dumper.

1. *Surfing.* A wave which crashes down as it breaks suddenly and violently, driving the surfer towards the bottom.

1920 A.H. ADAMS *Australs.* 185 A dumper is a badly behaved breaker . . that instead of carrying you on its crest gloriously right up the beach till you ground on the sand, ignominiously breaks as it strikes the shallow water and deposits you, smash! in a flurry of sand and water, any side up. **1931** *Surf: All about It* 34 Dumpers are hollow-fronted waves whose crests curl over and break in front of their bases. **1940** P. KERRY *Cobbers A.I.F.* 10 Johnny Jones from Tumbarumba was a new one at the game, An' 'e got on to a dumper, fer 'e thought all waves the same. **1949** C.B. MAXWELL *Surf* 10 Not all tall waves are dumpers. **1954** P. GLADWIN *Long Beat Home* 209 'Not that one,' he yelled. 'It's a dumper.' . . He saw the wave's crest, instead of sliding, arch enormously and hang, and hurl her down and crash on her. **1963** J. POLLARD *Austral. Surfrider* 42 Dumpers occur when the slope of the beach is steep and sandbanks have formed. **1975** *Bulletin* (Sydney) 31 May 12/1 Mr Whitlam may feel he is standing in the surf with a big dumper coming up. **1979** D. MAITLAND *Breaking Out* 155 All I could think of was a big fifteen-foot surf, a big dumper, breaking and crashing over at Bondi.

2. *transf.* and *fig.*

1939 *Bulletin* (Sydney) 6 July 21/2 The next capping-rail squatter who tells me 'they don't breed 'em like they useter' when speaking of the young Aussie is inviting a dumper. **1969** D. CUSACK *Half-Burnt Tree* 1 It might also be the dumper that would finish things for him. **1986** *Bulletin* (Sydney) 7 Jan. 78/1 Most of the new-wave floats of the 1970s nickel boom were killed in the dumpers or went industrial.

3. A wool-press.

1948 R. RAVEN-HART *Canoe in Aust.* 53 The hydraulic 'dumper', which squashes two bales of wool into the size of one.

dumpling. [See quot. 1888.] *Apple berry*, see APPLE 3; the fruit of this plant. Also **dumplings.**

1888 *Proc. Linnean Soc. N.S.W.* III. 491 'Apple Berry.' The berries are acid and pleasant when fully ripe. From their shape children call them 'dumplings'. **1921** *Aussie* (Sydney) Jan. 12/2 'Dumplings' . . *Billardiera Scandens.* **1956** T.Y. HARRIS *Naturecraft in Aust.* 182 Dumplings, with yellow flowers and bright-blue or yellowish-green elongate fruits, is frequently seen in coastal bush in the eastern States.

dumpty. [Prob. joc. formation on DUNNY.] An outside privy. Also **dumpty-doo.**

1965 N. LINDSAY *Bohemians of Bulletin* 131 There was revealed to us the immense importance Lou attached to an early morning visit to the privy. . . Mrs Stone had warned us of this ritual by saying, 'Don't go to the dumpty till Father . . has his turn there.' **1965** R.H. CONQUEST *Horses in Kitchen* 85 Find yourself a shady spot behind the dumpty-doo, eat the bananas and do some hard thinking. **1970** P. AMOS *Silver Kings* 37 'I can't find Dad. . . ' 'Perhaps he's in the dumpty,' she said . . and he walked across the yard to the lavatory. **1970** N.A. BEAGLEY *Up & Down Under* 98 In this hotel, as in all country hotels and homes, there are no water-flushed sanitary toilets, so the 'dumpty' is usually down the garden path in the backyard. **1978** *Sunday Sun* (Brisbane) 19 Sept. 4/2 Brisbane City Council has made sure of it by plonking a collection of 18th Century dumpty-doos smack in the middle of the festival amusement area.

dungaree settler. *Obs.* A name given to a poor settler: see quot. 1826. Also **dungaree chap.**

1826 J. ATKINSON *Acct. Agric. & Grazing N.S.W.* 29 The early Settlers, and the lower orders of the present—who are technically termed in the Colony *Dungaree Settlers*, from a coarse cotton manufacture of India which forms their usual clothing. **1827** *Monitor* (Sydney) 9 Mar. 339/2 Be they sinners gentle or simple, Squire Settlers or Dungaree Settlers. **1836** 'W.R--s' *Fell Tyrant* 46 There are four sorts of settlers, the Swell settler, that is the rich, the Dungaree, the Souge, and the last and poorest of all is the Stringybark settler. **1847** A. HARRIS *Settlers & Convicts* (1953) 4 The poor Australian settler (or, according to colonial phraseology, the Dungaree-settler; so called from their frequently clothing themselves, their wives, and children in that blue Indian manufacture of cotton known as *Dungaree*). **1849** S. & J. SIDNEY *Emigrant's Jrnl.* 184 In the early days of the colony of New South Wales, there lived on the Hawkesbury River an old Dungaree settler, by name Tim Kennedy. **1864** *Illustr. Sydney News* 16 June 10/1 This hamlet . . consisted then, whatever it may be now, of about a dozen little huts or shanties inhabited by what were termed 'Dungaree' or 'Stringybark settlers'. **1880** *Melbourne Christmas Ann.* 2 Byron's 'Address to the Ocean' Would fall rather flat on these 'dungaree' chaps.

dunnart /'dʌnat/. [a. Nyungar *danart.* The name was first applied by John Gilbert to the fat-tailed *Sminthopsis crassicaudata.*] Any of the narrow-footed marsupial mice of the terrestrial genus *Sminthopsis* (fam. Dasyuridae) of all States and New Guinea. See also *marsupial mouse* MARSUPIAL 1, POUCHED MOUSE.

1928 *Pop. Names for Marsupials* (Public Library, Museum, & Art Gallery W.A., Museum Leaflet no. 1), *Sminthopsis murina* . . Dunnart. **1941** E. TROUGHTON *Furred Animals Aust.* 36 The local name of Fat-tailed Dunnart has been advocated for Western Australia. **1967** B.Y. MAIN *Between Wodjil & Tor* 85 Other marsupials, e.g. the little dunnart (*Sminthopsis crassicaudata*) appear to be able to subsist in small broken pieces of bushland. **1982** *Bulletin* (Sydney) 13 Apr. 82/1 Dartling from beneath a stone A dunnart caught The quick eye of a hooded bird.

dunny. [f. Br. dial. *dunnekin* privy: see EDD.]

1. Orig. an unsewered outside privy; now used loosely of any lavatory.

[**1843** *Satirist & Sporting Chron.* (Sydney) 25 Mar. 3/2 There is not space sufficient whereon to erect a '*dunniken*'.] **1933** N. LINDSAY *Saturdee* (1936) 40 Who kidded he wasn't home; only hidin' in the dunny? **1947** —— *Halfway to Anywhere* 72 'What are you doing there?' . . 'On'y goin' out to the dunny,' mumbled Waldo. **1957** *Overland* x. 11 We used ter have a snake in the dunny—lav., sir. **1960** C. YOUNGER *Less than Angel* 41 With your conscience you'd stick out like a country dunny. **1963** B. HESLING *Dinkumization & Depommification* 116 Two cops, according to the inquiry, booked nearly two hundred 'pervs' a year from this one dunny. **1967** F. HARDY *Billy Borker yarns Again* 151 They wouldn't wake up if an Adelaide River dunny fell on 'em. **1972** *Daily Mirror* (Sydney) 12 Oct. 4/5 I hope all yer chooks turn into emus and kick yer dunny down. **1978** R. MACKLIN *Newsfront* 91 Three hands of poker behind the dunny is their idea of a hard day's work. **1979** D. LOCKWOOD *My Old Mates & I* 147 My first silly question at the homestead, which I thought might be equipped, was 'Where's the loo, Jack?' 'There you are, mate,' he had said, and waved his arm outside at the spectacular cattle country. 'Biggest bloody dunny in the world.' **1982** P. ADAM SMITH *Shearers* 232 As late as September 1980 I saw 'pit dunnies', blowfly-filled holes in the ground covered with a rough wooden board with a hole for the backside to squat on, no cover.

2. Special Comb. **dunny can,** a removable receptacle in a privy; **cart,** a vehicle for the collection and disposal of human excrement, etc.; **man,** one who mans such a vehicle. See also SANITARY.

1962 J. DALTON *Walk back with Me* 102 'I'll say he wasn't cut out for the buildin' trade,' Grist growled. 'The little rat couldn't make a good **dunny can**.' **1965** J. IGGULDEN *Dark Stranger* 6 Swanno calls me Duncan and somehow he makes it sound like dunny-can, and that kills them. **1963** B. HESLING *Dinkumizatin & Depommification* 52 Tom snorted. 'You're as class-conscious as a bloody squatter! What's it matter whether he built dingo fences, or even worked the **dunny cart**?' **1968** *Kings Cross Whisper* (Sydney) li. 2/1 The speed limit for sanitary trucks—better known as night carts and dunny carts—is to be raised. **1980** C. JAMES *Unreliable Mem.* 50, I often watched the dunny cart from the front window. As it slowly made its noisome way down the street, the dunny men ran to and from it with awesome experience. **1962** H. PORTER *Bachelor's Children* 280 Early in December, one found a card on the lavatory seat: *Enjoy Christmas as best you can, And don't forget the* **dunny man.** **1969** *Kings Cross Whisper* (Sydney) lxvi. 5/5 Most modern cities in the world just don't have any dunny men. They have this new-fangled thing called sewerage. **1972** D. IRELAND *Flesheaters* 5 The dunnyman in his heavy loaded truck looked tired as the motor ground up the hill to the depot where the nightsoil would be buried. **1977** W. MOORE *Just to Myself* 15 The dunny man was Uncle Perce.

durry. [Of unknown origin.] A cigarette.

1941 S.J. BAKER *Pop. Dict. Austral. Slang* 26 *Durry,* a cigarette butt. **1972** N. MILES *Opal Fever* 17 'Here, can't even roll a durrie with these bandages on.' 'Quit bitchin'. I ought to make you go without a smoke.' **1976** S. WELLER *Bastards I have Met* 80 Here's Crot slumped in the saddle, shirt out, feet out of the irons, reins on the horse's neck and a durry stuck to his lip. **1977** N. MANNING *Us or Them* (1984) 6 *Steve*: (stubbing out his cigarette) Waste of a good durry! **1982** *Sydney Morning Herald* 18 Sept. 1/5 Cigarettes, also known as durries, lungbusters and backnails are still smoked behind the toilet block after school.

dusky, *a.*

1. As used of Aborigines: a euphemism for BLACK *a.*[1]

1847 *Moreton Bay Courier* 16 Oct. 3/2 *The blacks in Gippsland* These 'dusky warriors' are 'playing up' pretty lively in Gippsland. **1852** *Moreton Bay Free Press* 27 May 2/5 The annual distribution of blankets to the blacks in the Brisbane District took place in the Police-yard. . . There was a strong muster of the dusky children of the forest on the occasion. **1867** A.K. COLLINS *Waddy Mundoee* 21 Waddy Mundoee watched the faces of the dusky warriors around him. **1876** 'CAPRICORNUS' *Colonisation* 23 You may well peer through the leafy screen of brigalow, dusky warriors of the Kamilaroy. **1886** R. HENTY *Australiana* 18 A white man . . must be well tutored by his dusky brother. **1898** *Bulletin* (Sydney) 21 May 14/1 Several dusky Kitties have lately donned a wedding-ring. **1910** W.C. WALL *Sydney Stage Employee's Pictorial Ann.* 74 The dusky people were invited to the show. **1925** *Smith's Weekly* (Sydney) 21 Feb. 20/5 The Australian abo. is seldom credited with the capacity for using his brains to make money. But one dusky dogger showed his white brother points. **1935** 'D. LAURIER' *Two Men from Northern Rivers* 14 One of the 'dusky' gentlemen limped as he proceeded to his wurly. **1961** *Bulletin* (Sydney) 8 Feb. 15/1 The dusky handmaidens appeared carrying the marrowbones, the opening course of every 'never never' banquet.

2. Special Comb. **dusky coral pea,** see *coral pea* CORAL; **flathead,** the dark brownish estuarine fish *Platycephalus fuscus* of e. Aust., valued as food; **robin,** the predom. brown, insectivorous bird *Melanodryas vittata* of Tas.

1906 D.G. STEAD *Fishes of Aust.* 197 The Common or **Dusky Flathead** . . is very abundant along the coast of New South Wales. **1984** *Canberra Chron.* 11 Apr. 27/1 The last of the summer dusky flathead which are still taking lures. **1842** J. GOULD *Birds of Aust.* (1848) III. Pl. 8, *Petroica fusca* . . **Dusky Robin.** **1945** C. BARRETT *Austral. Bird Life* 175 The dusky robin . . is the largest . . of Australian robins. **1976** *Reader's Digest Compl. Bk. Austral. Birds* 361 The dusky robin often nests in niches in fire-blackened trees.

dust.

1. [U.S., *dust* ellipt. for *gold dust*: see Mathews.] Granular gold; gold dust.

1851 *Empire* (Sydney) 22 May 3/2 Away, away to the Bathurst ground, Where the 'dust' is brightly shining. *Ibid.* 16 Aug. 55/5 The Bondicar has left since our last report with nearly £30,000 of dust. **1853** R.S. ANDERSON *Austral. Gold Fields* 11 The weekly arrival by escort and mail is 3,500 ounces of dust and nuggets. **1854** *Bell's Life in Sydney* 11 Feb. 2/2 The Major's Creek gold is granular, and what is commercially termed 'dust'. **1855** R. CARBONI *Eureka Stockade* 121 The only thing which I saved was a little bag, containing some Eureka dust, and my 'Gold-licence'. **1886** D.M. GANE *N.S.W. & Vic.* 135 A party of men would come down from the 'diggings' to Melbourne, or what was then 'Canvas Town', with nuggets and dust of considerable value. **1928** M.E. FULLERTON *Austral. Bush* 80 Many a poor miner tramping . . from the field with his 'dust' or nuggets on him.

2. *fig.*

a. Flour.

1878 'IRONBARK' *Southerly Busters* 90 A mildewed crust or a pint o' dust Or a mutton cutlet fried. **1895** *Worker* (Sydney) 19 Oct. 1/3 The 'whaler's' home is . . near enough to some squatter to go for a pannikin of 'dust' (termed flour in the squatter's books). **1900** *Bulletin* (Sydney) 22 Dec. 14/4 In N.Q. . . the white has to tramp hundreds of miles . . existing on salt-junk and a pannikin of dust. **1912** 'IRONBARK' *Ironbark Splinters* 45 The stations gives no 'pints o' dust', Nor sugar, beef, nor tea, An' Murrumbidgee-whalin' ain't The game it used to be. **1913** W.K. HARRIS *Outback in Aust.* 146 All the greatest . . celebrities of the day were 'on the wallaby' . . and had called at his particular station for the proverbial free pannikin of 'dust' (flour). **1923** *Bulletin* (Sydney) 16 Aug. 24/3, I have used some queer recipes for making the pint of 'dust' rise when jazzing with Matilda around the bush. **1930** *Ibid.* 5 Feb. 25/1 The swaggies padded on the hoof. . . But old-time custom said I must Bestow on each a pint of 'dust'.

b. Tobacco.

1903 *Bulletin* (Sydney) 13 Aug. 14/2 'Dust', in the Emperor Edward's free hotel, means the tobacco dust accumulated in the pocket. Remand prisoners . . are, on admittance, often requested to feel their pockets for 'dust'.

3. A miners' term for silicosis. Also *attrib.* See also DUSTED.

1937 H.E. GRAVES *Who Rides?* 53 He . . like nearly every other goldminer had contracted the 'Dust'. This meant that having breathed an atmosphere of fine, gritty dust for years, his lungs had become affected and . . he was now suffering from the deadly miners' phthisis. **1955** *Overland* iii. 17 For twenty years I have hewn the coal, For a man has to earn his crust; And now 'long service reward' has come—The doctors have called it 'dust'. **1959** R. BURNS *My Brain knows Best* 16 We'd want something more than dust money to get others out as well. **1978** S. BALL *Muma's Boarding House* 108 He had seen the curse of silicosis—known by miners as 'dust'—and was obsessively convinced that he and all his mates had it and were to die of it.

4. Special Comb. **dust-hole (of the (British) Empire),** Tasmania.

1847 *Melbourne Argus* 9 Nov. 4/3 It will be strange indeed if the outcry against pollution, even in the 'dust-hole of the empire' does not open the eyes of the British Government to the . . necessity of having some consideration for the Colonies. **1848** *Guardian* (Hobart) 1 Mar. 2/5 Well may we be called *the Dust-hole*—in every sense—of the British Empire. **1851** *Britannia* (Hobart) 17 Feb. 3/2 Freed from its present reproach as emphatically denounced in the House of Lords as the 'Dust-hole of the British Empire'. **1852** *Guardian* (Hobart) 28 Aug. 3/4 Notwithstanding Van Diemen's Land being . . termed the 'dust hole' by our Victorian moralists. **1858** T. MCCOMBIE *Hist. Colony Vic.* 177 The colony still continued the 'dust-hole' of the empire.

dusted, *ppl. a.* Suffering from silicosis.

1942 *Mulga* (Alice Springs) 22 Dec. 2 When a miner says he is 'dusted' you realise his lungs are affected. **1948** K.S. PRICHARD *Golden Miles* 119 Dusted miners were cut out of the Workers' Compensation Act. **1950** C.E. GOODE *Yarns of Yilgarn* 68 The Government had transplanted about a hundred 'dusted' miners there. **1957** D. WHITINGTON *Treasure upon Earth* 96 'He's dusted,' Mick whispered. 'South Coast coal. . . If you opened him up you'd find two lumps of coke where his lungs ought to be.' **1966** *Realist* (Sydney) xxiv. 21 My old man was a Kalgoorlie miner. He formed the first I.W.W. local in Kal, and he died dusted. **1969** L. HADOW *Full Cycle* 237 They'd found him in his bunk one day, been dead a long time, died alone, just another dusted miner. **1973** R. ROBINSON *Drift of Things* 162 This miner told me that he was 'dusted', that is, he had silicosis of the lungs. **1978** S. BALL *Muma's Boarding House* 108 I'm dusted. There's nothing to be done about it; I'll die of the dust like all of my mates.

dwarf. Used *attrib.* in Special Comb. **dwarf apple,** the shrub or small tree of N.S.W. *Angophora cordifolia* (fam. Myrtaceae); **grass-tree,** *small grass-tree,* see GRASS-TREE 1 b.; **gum,** any of several small gum trees (see GUM *n.* 1); **honeysuckle** *obs.*, any of several small shrubs of the genus *Banksia* (see BANKSIA).

1911 A. MACK *Bush Days* 31 Through all the changing seasons, the **dwarf apple** spreads its beauty on that windy hill—an emblem for its lovers of eternal hope and courage. **1914** H.M. VAUGHAN *Australasian Wander-Yr.* 72 The handsome Dwarf Apple (*Angophora* *cordifolia*) . . was successfully propagated from some seedpods brought to Europe by Sir Joseph Banks. **1933** H.J. CARTER *Gulliver in Bush* 17 My introduction to that wonderful plant, *Angophora cordifolia*, popularly misnamed the dwarf apple. **1945** *Coast to Coast 1944* 138 The low scrub had been the very devil. The botanist said it was a species of angophora; locally it was called dwarf apple or more commonly bungally. **1832** G.F. MOORE *Diary Ten Yrs. W.A.* 29 Sept. (1884) 141, I have two, or perhaps three acres ready for the plough, that is, cleared from black boys (**dwarf grass trees**), which are grubbed out of it. **1834** *Hobart Town Almanack* 132 The dwarf grass tree (*Zanthorrhoea humilis*) . . abundant about York-town. **1852** W. HOWITT *Land, Labor & Gold* I. (1855) 159 There are here many shrubs and flowers quite new to us. There are some beautiful geraniums, dwarf grass-trees [etc.]. **1911** J. MOORE-ROBINSON *Rec. Tasmanian Nomenclature* 40 *Grass Tree Hill* . . was so named from the dwarf grass tree (*Xanthorrhoea minor*), which grows in abundance near the saddle of the ridge separating Risden from Richmond. **1796** D. COLLINS *Acct. Eng. Colony N.S.W.* (1798) I. 557 In the body of the **dwarf gum** tree are several large worms and grubs. **1834** *Colonist* (Hobart) 13 May 3/3 The timber in the Derwent . . principally of the dwarf gum . . looked at a distance like the mimosa. **1869** M. CLARKE *Peripatetic Philosopher* 51 A blazing sun. The white and red heaps of mullock cropping up among the dusty dwarf gums. **1915** *Bull. N.T.* xiv. 10 Two species of dwarf gum having miniature leaves and seeds. **1826** J. ATKINSON *Acct. Agric. & Grazing N.S.W.* 19 At certain seasons of the year, the **dwarf honeysuckle** . . yields an immense quantity of beautiful transparent honey. **1890** 'MRS A. MACLEOD' *Austral. Girl* (1894) 107 The sterner green of the dwarf honeysuckle, whose pointed leaves when ruffled by the wind show their silver under-lining like pale buds that never blossom.

dynamite. Baking powder. Also *attrib.*

1898 *Bulletin* (Sydney) 1 Jan. 14/2 Perhaps the most necessary article on the track is baking-powder. Dampers and johnnie-cakes without 'dynamite' ruin cast-iron livers and galvanised digestions. **1905** *Shearer* (Sydney) 17 June 6/2 The squatter gives him a pint of 'dust', a 'banjo' of mutton, and a pinch of 'dynamite' (baking-powder). **1907** *Bulletin* (Sydney) 11 Apr. 14/3 A scram-bag . . is the very embodiment of life, even if it only contains 'dust' and 'dynamite'. **1923** *Ibid.* 16 Aug. 24/3 Apart from the real dynamite (baking powder), carbonate of soda is the cheapest and best. **1955** N. PULLIAM *I traveled Lonely Land* 354 'What's a damper?'. . . 'Bread, in a way. Flour, salt, water, a little dynamite if you've got it.' **1972** F. BLAKELEY *Dream Millions* 59 Damper is made with baking powder that causes much belching—the common term outback is dynamite bread!

E

eagle hawk. A large bird of prey, usu. the *wedge-tailed eagle* (see WEDGE-TAILED).

1805 *Sydney Gaz.* 16 June, An *eagle hawk* rose from the spot with a large *viper* focused within its talons. **1827** *Monitor* (Sydney) 29 Oct. 727/2 The Eagles (improperly called Eagle Hawks) in the interior, are surprisingly bold. **1842** J. GOULD *Birds of Aust.* (1848) I. Pl. 1, *Aquila fucosa* .. Wedge-tailed Eagle... Eagle Hawk, Colonists of New South Wales. **1846** C.P. HODGSON *Reminisc. Aust.* 164 The Eagle Hawk is a monster indeed, the monarch of the feathered tribes. **1856** H.B. STONEY *Vic.* 212 In the interior, the wedge-tailed eagle, or eagle-hawk, is well known as destructive to lambs. **1896** F.G. AFLALO *Sketch Nat. Hist. Aust.* 143 The Wedge-Tailed Eagle (*Aquila audax*), or, 'Eagle-Hawk' of Victoria .. is easily approached when gorged from a recent feed. **1905** A.B. PATERSON *Old Bush Songs* 69 He'd never make one of them angels, With faces as white as chalk, All wool to the toes like hoggets, And wings like an eagle-hawk. **1928** M.E. FULLERTON *Austral. Bush* 122 The wedge-tailed eagle, and the eagle hawk, a smaller bird. **1934** W.A. OSBORNE *Visitor to Aust.* 82 The wedge-tailed eagle or eagle-hawk is a magnificent creature. **1978** L. WHITE *Silent Reach* 122 A pair of hunting eagle hawks, soaring, dipping and wheeling above the expanse of bleached buffel grass.

ear-bash, *v. trans.* To subject (a person) to a torrent of words. Also *absol.*

1944 L. GLASSOP *We were Rats* 205 Are you going to sit there ear bashing all night? **1946** *Strictly Personal* (Ministry Post-War Reconstruction) 4 He was ear-bashing me the other day because he can't get this or that. **1962** *Texas Q.* 57 They adjourned, and everybody went on earbashing him. **1968** S. GORE *Holy Smoke* 43 Just like you hear 'em ear-bashin' each other in Parliament to this day. **1977** R. CLOSE *Of Salt & Earth* 167, I ear-bashed him with sales-talk that would not have shamed a Rolls-Royce. **1981** *Sydney Morning Herald* 31 Jan. 16/2 Conferring awards on writers is usually a mistake. It encourages them to earbash instead of getting on with their writing.

Hence **ear-bashed** *ppl. a.*, **ear-bashing** *vbl. n.*

1978 H.C. BAKER *I was Listening* 107 An **earbashed** victim groaned as he worked alongside the garrulous one. **1945** G. POWELL *Two Steps to Tokyo* 190 He had been getting an **ear-bashing** from that worthy gentleman.

earbasher.

1. One who talks incessantly; a bore.

1941 E. LOCKE *From Shore to Shore* (1944) 25 Listen to the champ 'earbasher's' din. **1943** *Barrage: Mag. Headquarters R.A.A. 7th Austral. Division* 30 Aug. 10 The Prince of Ear Bashers Sgt. Baldy Borsmann... Motto: Blah Blah Blah. **1951** D. COLLINS *Vic.'s my Home Ground* 23 Ear-bashers there are—and what an expressive word that is, and to the best of my belief as Australian as bonzer—but they generally got something to bash about. **1966** J. SMITH *Ornament of Grace* 19 All Indians are like that. Tiresome over-educated earbashers. **1973** *Kings Cross Whisper* (Sydney) clv. 16/1 He's found some little rippers in the time he's been in the club .. earbashers, con-men, no-hopers, mugs. **1984** *Sunday Independent* (Perth) 26 Feb. 16/6 Now he's a middle-aged, overweight earbasher who drinks too much and hustles old acquaintances for hours.

2. *fig.*

1967 F. HARDY *Billy Borker yarns Again* p. v, Many new yarns from this most renowned 'ear basher' of modern Australian fiction.

ear-biter. *Obs.* A cadger: see BITE *n.* 1 and *v.*

1899 *Truth* (Sydney) 30 Apr. 5/1 Holiday spirits and careless generosity made them soft marks for the ear-biter. **1913** A. PRATT *Wolaroi's Cup* 38 The 'whisperers' and 'ear-biters' began to assail me. **1934** *Bulletin* (Sydney) 17 Oct. 21/2 No .. earbiters anxious to give you a moral for the lars'.

early, *a.* and *n.*

A. *adj.*

1. Used with reference to the earliest period of white settlement in Australia.

1847 G.F. ANGAS *Savage Life & Scenes* II. 213 With this soil the early settlers were accustomed to manure their gardens. **1857** J. ASKEW *Voyage Aust. & N.Z.* 130 Liardit, a Frenchman and one of the early colonists. **1864** H. JONES *New Valuations* 8 Early settling has some pleasing recollections for the old colonists. **1874** J.T. FALLON *Murray Valley Vineyard* 22 This gentleman, an early settler in New South Wales, was one of its early benefactors. **1905** *Bulletin* (Sydney) 21 Dec. (Red Page), He was a great man in Mudgee in the early days. **1921** *Smith's Weekly* (Sydney) 17 Sept. 17/4 Gins were useful rouseabouts for the early settlers on the 'northern rivers'. **1931** J.H.M. ABBOTT *King's School* 39 The style of Australian architecture known as Early Colonial—one of those plain, solid and unpretentious edifices that retired civil servants and military officers used to build for themselves in the old town when it wasn't as yet much over thirty years of age and was the social centre of Australia. **1945** J.A. ALLAN *Men & Manners in Aust.* 137 The early Australian was forced to make his own amusements. **1973** *Bulletin* (Sydney) 27 Jan. 5/3 The majority of the early settlers .. carved a living out of the country with their bare hands. **1981** A.B. FACEY *Fortunate Life* 129 The early settlers and travellers dug a large hole at this spot.

2. In collocations: **early Nancy,** any of several plants of the genus *Wurmbea* (fam. Liliaceae), esp. the small, bulbous-rooted perennial *W. dioica* of all States, but not N.T.; **shed,** a shearing shed which is operative in the early part of the season; **spring grass,** any of several spring and summer grasses of the genus *Eriochloa* (fam. Poaceae), esp. the annual or short-lived perennial forage plant *E. pseudoacrotricha* of all mainland States.

1914 E.E. PESCOTT *Native Flowers Vic.* 91 The small white flower called '**Early Nancy**' is one of the lilies, and is known as Anguillaria dioica. **1944** A. MARSHALL *These are my People* 201 Say diggers, do you remember picking the ham and eggs .. the early nancy? **1967** B.Y. MAIN *Between Wodjil & Tor* 70 Springing up amongst them were purple-speckled Early Nancy flowers. **1978** B.P. MOORE *Life on Forty Acres* 41 The first of the lilies is Early Nancy .. whose dainty stems of white starlike flowers rise by the hundreds in the short grass. **1901** *Bulletin* (Sydney) 27 June 14/4 Strike-camps have been formed at Cobham and other **early sheds**. **1912** J. BRADSHAW *Highway Robbery under Arms* (ed. 3) 23, I had agreed to shear .. at Nochleccha, as it was an early shed. **1895** F. TURNER *Austral. Grasses* I. 27 *Eriochloa punctata* .. '**Early Spring Grass**'. **1903** *Austral. Handbk.* 280 The following are looked upon by pastoralists with the greatest favour .. 'Early Spring grass' [etc.]. **1970** N.T. BURBIDGE *Austral. Grasses* III. 94 *Early Spring Grass.* A tufted perennial grass which is possibly not long-lived.

B. *n. pl.* The early years of white settlement in a given area.

1933 C. FENNER *Bunyips & Billabongs* 65 The interesting story of the wild adventurers who lived on this remote island in the 'earlies' is not our subject. **1935** G. MCIVER *Drover's Odyssey* 1 Away back in the 'earlies' I was staying at the Royal Hotel. **1937** E. HILL *Water into Gold* 47 So much for the Murray in the earlies, when the river-mists of antiquity rolled away. **1945** A. RUSSELL *Bush Ways* 151 The story of the Finke River country in 'the earlies' would make an undying saga of adventure. **1946** D. BARR *Warrigal Joe* 62 Things have changed a bit since I was knockin' around in the earlies. **1955** N. PULLIAM *I traveled Lonely Land* 45 In The Earlies men moved in mobs from one shearing to another. **1981** G. PIKE *Campfire Tales* 223 A splendid old pioneer station owner .. came to Queensland in 'the earlies'.

early gluyas: see GLUYAS.

earth tank: see TANK *n.*[1] 1.

Eastern, *a.* Also **eastern.**

1. Of, pertaining to, or situated in, the eastern part of the Australian continent. In special collocations: **Eastern Australia** *hist.*, the Colony of New South Wales; **Colony, State** (usu. in *pl.*) Australia, excluding Western Australia and (occas.) South Australia; also *attrib.*; **Stater,** an inhabitant of an *Eastern State*; **Standard Time,** see quot. 1942.

1829 E.G. WAKEFIELD *Let. from Sydney* 1, I have to give you .. my opinion of **Eastern Australia**, and of the prospects which this penal settlement offers to emigrants. **1830** T.J. MASLEN *Friend of Aust.* p. x, The continent is called 'Australia'; the eastern half, commonly called New South Wales, is called 'Eastern Australia'; the western, or New Holland, 'Western Australia'. **1840** *Sydney Herald* 28 Sept. 2/2 This settlement [*sc.* Port Macquarie] is *now*, not the 'metropolis of Eastern Australia', but .. it may be some years hence, the third town (Melbourne being the second) in New South Wales. **1841** H.S. CHAPMAN *New Settlement Australind* 27 New South Wales, sometimes called Eastern Australia, on the eastern coast. **1841** 'R.R.' *Aust., Van Dieman's Land, & N.Z.* 7 Eastern Australia .. is divided into nineteen distinct counties. **1865** 'SPECIAL CORRESPONDENT' *Transportation* 33 The 'tother side', as they call the **eastern colonies.** **1878** G. WALCH *Australasia* 47 Perth .. is sometimes enlivened by 'talent' from the Eastern Colonies—as they term South Australia, Victoria, and New South Wales. **1907** *Truth* (Sydney) 20 Jan. 7/2 The Agriculturalists of W.A. are beginning to feel the pinch of competition with the pioneers of the **Eastern States.** **1919** *Smith's Weekly* (Sydney) 1 Mar. 8/2 It is long since a flogging was imposed in any of the Eastern States, but in Westralia the other day a Judge gave a coloured man the lash. **1936** *Post Office Guide* (Melbourne) 444 The standard time for the Eastern States of Australia (Queensland, New South Wales, Victoria and Tasmania) is in advance of that of the places shown. **1937** A.W. UPFIELD *Mr Jelly's Business* 89 Bony's investigations were not progressing as rapidly as the Western Australian Police Chief considered that his eastern States reputation demanded. **1971** *Bulletin* (Sydney) 23 Oct. 21/1 How could the Perth financial world cope with a three-hour time lag with the eastern states. **1984** *Weekend Austral. Mag.* 26 May 24/6, I was raised in the West Australian belief that everything evil, rapacious and sinful in Australia was in 'the Eastern States'—and you have to be a West Australian to be able to produce the tone of voice that conveys the loathing, suspicion, fear and frightfulness 'the Eastern States' phrase creates in the State Of Excitement. **1952** *Bulletin* (Sydney) 9 Apr. 13/2 Mention has often been made by **eastern-Staters** in *The Bulletin* of the bloodwood-tree. **1959** D. HEWETT *Bobbin Up* 14 They'd never wanted her to marry Len. 'One of them flash Eastern Staters,' her father grumbled. **1960** *N.T. News* (Darwin) 5 Feb. 2/1 In common with the majority of eastern staters, I had never visited the West Australian capital. **1967** *Kings Cross Whisper* (Sydney) xliv. 1/5 He persuaded crayfish dealers to put the nips into eastern Staters by shipping pots of crays here. **1942** C.F. LASERON *Direction Finding* 20 **Eastern Standard Time** as referred to in Australia is that adopted for Tasmania, Victoria, New South Wales and Queensland. It is based on the 150th meridian of east longitude, and is therefore 10 hours ahead of Greenwich time. **1969** *Post Office Guide* (Melbourne) 339 Local time in South Australia, the Northern Territory and Broken Hill is half an hour behind Eastern Standard Time. Local time in Western Australia is two hours behind Eastern Standard Time. **1971** D. WILLIAMSON *Don's Party* (1973) 32 As Western Australian time is two hours behind Eastern Standard Time results are not expected from Western Australian until about ten o'clock tonight.

2. In the names of animals: **eastern grey kangaroo,** see GREY *a.*; **rosella,** the parrot *Platycercus eximius* of s.e. Aust.; NONPAREIL PARROT; **spinebill,** the small, long-billed honeyeater *Acanthorhynchus tenuirostris* of s.e. and e. Aust.

1931 N.W. CAYLEY *What Bird is That?* 145 **Eastern Rosella** *Platycerus eximius.* **1945** C. BARRETT *Austral. Bird Life* 79 No parrot has received greater publicity than the common eastern rosella. **1948** R. RAVEN-HART *Canoe in Aust.* 192 Eastern Rosellas, very gay in crimson and blue and orange-yellow. **1981** A. WILKINSON *Up Country* 129, I am even 'bombed' regularly as I ride for the cows by a furious eastern rosella mother. **1945** C. BARRETT *Austral. Bird Life* 155 The **eastern spinebill** . . , nicknamed 'cobbler's awl', commonly visits gardens. **1978** B.P. MOORE *Life on Forty Acres* 96 The dainty little Eastern Spinebill . . with the long, needlelike bill and habits recalling rather a large hummingbird. **1986** *Your Garden* Jan. 34 Birds abound there, and if you want to verify what New Holland Honeyeaters or Eastern Spinebills prefer . . a visit there will delight you.

Easterner. One from or belonging to an eastern State.

1941 *Bulletin* (Sydney) 24 Sept. 15/2 One tyke . . was paddling in a swamp and had its paw nipped by a gilgie —or yabbie, as you easterners call 'em. **1944** R. BEDFORD *Naught to Thirty-Three* 193 The old settlers' objections to giving immediate political power to the Easterners was based on sound premises. **1956** V. COURTNEY *All I may Tell* 14 Native-born Western Australians who profited most by the coming of t'other siders, as the Eastern Staters were referred to, were the most critical. . . It was almost as if the Easterners belonged to another land.

ebero, var. EBORO.

ebony, *a.* [Cf. U.S. use with reference to a Black (OED(S 4 b.).] Black; Aboriginal. Also *absol.*, as a nickname.

1862 *Bell's Life in Sydney* 1 Feb. 3/2 Old Ebony has kindly been admitted by his captor as a *'sleeping* partner'. **1903** *Truth* (Sydney) 4 Jan. 1/3 Warrigal, the ebony slugger(?), is in the heavyweight division. **1907** *Ibid.* 7 Apr. 10/8 A Northern Territory ebony damsel . . dwells on a tinfield with a European. **1909** *Bulletin* (Sydney) 6 May 13/2 You get Miss Ebony at every meal hour. **1912** *Ibid.* 29 Feb. 44/2 The ebony ones get *carte blanche.* **1916** S.A. WHITE *In Far Northwest* 105 My ebony-hued friend . . went to the end of the cleared space and began to dance.

eboro /ˈɛbəroʊ/. *Obs.* Also **ebero, ebroo.** [a. Margu *eboro.*] DIDGERIDOO.

1845 L. LEICHHARDT *Jrnl. Overland Exped. Aust.* 16 Dec. (1847) 534 They tried to cheer us up with their corrobori songs, which they accompanied on the Eboro, a long tube of bamboo, by means of which they variously modulated their voices. **1846** J.L. STOKES *Discoveries in Aust.* I. 394, I here saw the only musical instrument I ever remarked among the natives of Australia. It is a piece of bamboo thinned from the inside, through which they blow with their noses. It is from two to three feet long, is called *ebroo*, and produces a kind of droning noise. **1890** J. EDGE-PARTINGTON *Album Pacific Islands* i. 363 Musical instrument of bamboo called 'Ebero' Port Essington.

echidna /əˈkɪdnə/. [The genus name *Echidna* was first applied to this animal by French naturalist G. Cuvier (*Tableau Elementaire des Animaux* (1798) 143), a. Gr. *ἔχιδνα* viper, alluding to the tongue, which resembles that of a snake.] The egg-laying mammal *Tachyglossus aculeatus* of Aust. and New Guinea, which has a long muzzle and spiny back, and eats ants and termites; (occas.) any of several other animals, living or extinct, of the same family, Tachyglossidae; ANTEATER 1; HEDGEHOG; *native hedgehog, porcupine*, see NATIVE *a.* 6 b.; PORCUPINE; *spiny anteater*, see SPINY.

1815 W.E. LEACH *Zool. Miscellany* 90 Porcupine Echidna . . Inhabits New Holland. **1832** J. BISCHOFF *Sketch Hist. Van Diemen's Land* 29 The native porcupine or echidna is not very common nor so large as that found in America. **1861** 'OLD BUSHMAN' *Bush Wanderings* 54 We had a curious species of hedgehog or anteater . . the *Echidna* or *Spiny Ant-eater* of naturalists. **1888** *Sydney Morning Herald* 24 Jan. (Centennial Suppl.) 1/5 The echidna, or Australian hedgehog. **1907** *Bulletin* (Sydney) 17 Jan. 15/3 'Prooshan's' failure to catch echidna (otherwise porky) at breakfast. **1935** M. GILMORE *More Recoll.* 218 A spiky thing which I had not seen before but which was an echidna. **1955** D. CLARK *Boomer* 70 Once, as a gift, he had brought Maudie an extraordinary creature: an echidna, or a kind of small porcupine with a long bird's bill, out of which flicked a red, wormlike tongue. **1963** X. HERBERT *Larger than Life* 6 He held out his gift, saying 'You want 'im porkypine?' The echidna were taken eagerly. **1970** W.D.L. RIDE *Guide Native Mammals Aust.* 191 One species of monotreme which formerly occurred in Australia is now confined to New Guinea and some of the islands near by. This is *Zaglossus*, the Long-Beaked Echidna, which is fairly common in Australian fossil deposits. **1972** ANDERSON & BLAKE *J.S. Neilson* 41 The children saw . . echidnas burrowing noiselessly in the sand. **1980** J. WOLFE *End of Pricklystick* 79 She looked like an echidna that has just heard of a place where thousands of ants are waiting to be licked up.

economic conscript. *Hist.* A name applied to an unemployed person who enlisted during the war of 1939–45.

1950 J. CLEARY *Just let me Be* 153 There were a lot of other blokes like me. Mr Calwell gave us a name—'economic conscripts'. He'd been angry when the Cabinet Minister came out with that remark, even though he knew it was true: it reduced the sacrifice of Andy Jenkins and Bluey McKenna and all the others who had gone, to something that had been bought for five bob a day. **1975** G.H. FEARNSIDE *Half to Remember* 11 Others were jobless and found employment with the Army, thereby earning themselves the sobriquet of 'economic conscript'.

Edgar Britt. [The name of Edgar *Britt* (b. 1913), Austral. jockey: see also JIMMY BRITTS.] Rhyming slang for 'shit'.

1969 A. BUZO *Front Room Boys* (1970) 22 He raced out to the john for an Edgar Britt. **1971** F. HARDY *Outcasts of Foolgarah* 28 'I want to go for a Jerry Riddle and an Edgar Britt,' Little Tich whispered, suddenly caught short. 'A what?' 'A piddle and a shit.' **1979** B. HUMPHRIES *Bazza comes into his Own*, With all them coppers on me tail I very nearly done an Edgar Britt in me strides. **1983** B. DAWE *Over here, Harv!* 101 'Jeez,' said Wooffer. 'You give me the Edgar Britts, sometimes.'

educated, *ppl. a. Hist.* Of a convict: fitted by some training or experience prior to transportation for employment in a clerical or professional capacity. See GENTLEMAN CONVICT.

1830 *HRA* (1922) 1st Ser. XV. 832 'Educated Convicts' as they are termed . . includes those transported for *Forgery.* **1831** *Ibid.* (1923) 1st Ser. XVI. 10 'Educated Convicts' . . on their arrival in the Colony were usually sent to Wellington Valley. **1834** J. BACKHOUSE *Extracts from Lett.* (1838) ii. 50, I was surprised to find only two of the educated prisoners acting as teachers. **1834** 'EMIGRANT' *Party Politics Exposed* 4 The educated prisoners were . . occupied in manual labour apart from the other class. **1836** J. BACKHOUSE *Extracts from Lett.* (1838) iii. 81 A depôt for that description of educated prisoners, denominated 'specials'. **1837** W.B. ULLATHORNE *Catholic Mission Australasia* 20, I do not mean to say that he is of the educated class—these are sent to Port Macquarie. **1851** H. MELVILLE *Present State Aust.* 159 Educated convicts are sometimes transported from the mother country.

egg-and-bacon: see EGGS-AND-BACON.

eggs-a-cook. [From a Cairo street cry: see quot. 1921.] A piece of armed services' badinage: applied *attrib.* to the Third Australian Division and its members (see quot. 1979); see also quot. 1918 (2).

1918 *Aussie: Austral. Soldiers' Mag.* Jan. 8/1 It was the day after the Eggs-a-cook Division's 'stunt' in front of Ypres. *Ibid.* 10/2 *Eggs-a-cook*, an Egyptian dish, also known as '2 for ½', and now used to express that which is expensive and barely worth while. **1921** C.E.W. BEAN *Official Hist. Aust. 1914–18 War* I. 218 Australians and New Zealanders carried with them for years strange tags of 'Arabic' and broken English, such as . . 'Eggs-a-cook', 'oringhes', 'Boots-i-clean'—calls of the Cairo urchins who sold eggs or oranges, or who blacked boots. **1940** *Digger Yarns: Cream of Aussiosities*, Among the eggs-a-cook signallers, there was a classic joke at the expense of the O.C. **1979** W.D. JOYNT *Breaking Road for Rest* 119 Our new 3rd Australian Division, nicknamed the 'Eggs Is Cooked Division', because its colour patch was in the shape of an egg, reminding us of the Arab boys in Egypt trying to sell us cooked eggs and shouting 'Eggs Is Cooked!'

eggs-and-bacon. Any of several leguminous shrubs bearing yellow and reddish-brown flowers, the colours of which suggest those of eggs and bacon. Also **bacon-and-egg(s), egg-and-bacon,** and *attrib.*

1942 E. ANDERSON *Squatter's Luck* 28 Dilwynnia, 'Eggs-and-Bacon'. **1964** E. LANE *Our Uncle Charlie* 47 The yellow-and-brown egg-and-bacon creeper growing beside the track. **1977** D. STUART *Drought Foal* 6 Miles of the brown and gold flowers of bacon-and-egg bushes, cat's paws and kangaroo paws. **1978** B.P. MOORE *Life on Forty Acres* 145 The bees . . being most active in spring when the native legumes with brownish-yellow flowers (collectively known as 'eggs and bacon') are in bloom. **1979** WRIGLEY & FAGG *Austral. Native Plants* 182 *Bossiaea* . . are mostly small shrubs with yellow and brown pea-flowers, and provide a significant part of the 'bacon and eggs' element of the Australian bush. **1981** J.A. BAINES *Austral. Plant Genera* 118 *Daviesia*. . . One of the many . . papilionaceous plants known generally as Eggs-and-bacon. **1985** *Age* (Melbourne) 20 Sept. (Suppl.) 7/1 Gaudy yellow and red masses of egg-and-bacon bushes.

eight. In the phr. **eight, ten, two, and a quarter,** a week's ration of food as issued to a hand by an employer on a rural property: see quot. 1937. See also TEN.

1937 W. HATFIELD *I find Aust.* 84 Rations per man per week were eight pounds of flour, ten pounds of meat, two pounds of sugar and a quarter-pound of tea. Eight-ten-two-and-quarter, it was known. **1978** K. GARVEY *Tales of my Uncle Harry* 72 In those days the squatters had all the money and men like Stevo and me had to exist on 8, 10, 2 and a ¼.

eighteen. A keg of beer which holds eighteen gallons (now seventy-nine litres).

1918 G. DALE *Industr. Hist. Broken Hill* 117 The procession proceeded to the goods stations, loaded some foodstuffs and five 'eighteens' of beer, and started back to the mine. **1942** G. CASEY *It's Harder for Girls* 218 'What sort of a party?'. . . 'Over at Syd's place. We got an eighteen, and plenty o' bottles coming over.' **1968** *Kings Cross Whisper* (Sydney) xlvii. 5/4 Bertie the publican had to get 24 extra eighteens up on the train on Friday. **1971** F. HARDY *Outcasts of Foolgarah* 194 'Two eighteens, twenty dozen hot dogs,' Molly counted to herself, a hostess to the finger tips. **1980** B. HORNADGE *Austral. Slanguage* 230 When beer started to appear in steel kegs of nine or eighteen gallon capacity, the word *keg* was quickly dispensed with and they were (and are) simply referred to as *nines* or *eighteens.*

eight hour. Used *attrib.* or in the possessive, usu. in *pl.* [With reference to the slogan 'eight hours' labor, eight hours' recreation, eight hours' rest': see quot. 1876.]

1. Used in various industrial contexts with reference to the campaign waged during the latter half of the nineteenth century for the mandatory institution of an eight-hour working day. Also *ellipt.* for *eight-hour day, eight-hour movement*, etc.

1858 *Illustr. Jrnl. Australasia* IV. 271 Melbourne in 1845, and Melbourne in 1855 . . were two different places. Parks, universities, and 'eight hours labor commemorations' were unknown. **1870** *Eight Hours Hist.* 2 In September, 1858, the ironworkers of Melbourne secured the Eight Hours. **1876** *Illustr. Austral. News* (Melbourne) 4 Oct. 154/4 Below this again is inscribed in very large letters the words now so well known—'Eight hours' labor, eight hours' recreation, eight hours' rest'. **1892** ROYDHOUSE & TAPERELL *Labour Party N.S.W.* 41 He participated in the strike of 1873 for the 'eight hours'. **1896** W.E. MURPHY *Hist. Eight Hours' Movt.* 60 The Eight Hours' at its birth owed nothing to Parliament, and still less to the press. **1903** *Truth* (Sydney) 17 May 4/5, I still see you and your thugs . . at Trades' Hall and Eight-Hours' functions. **1909** W.G. SPENCE *Aust.'s Awakening* 510 The Operative Stonemasons of Melbourne moved in the matter early in 1856, and .. successfully launched the eight hours. **1914** R. KALESKI *Austral. Barkers & Biters* 13 Form a union, and insist upon proper wages and eight hours. **1917** *Shire & Municipal Rec.* (Sydney) X. Dec. 202, I do hope that my action won't mean that I will be marching in the next Eight-hour procession. **1973** J. MURRAY *Larrikins* 22 The introduction of an eight-hour day in response to the slogan, '8 hours work, 8 hours play, 8 bob-a-day'.

2. Comb. **eight-hour(s') movement, principle, system.**

1856 *Argus* (Melbourne) 13 May 5/1 The inauguration of the **eight hours movement**, now in operation among the various operative trades in this city, was celebrated yesterday by a procession of workmen. **1858** *Colonial Mining Jrnl.* Oct. 30/3 Supposing the 'eight hours movement' obtained on the diggings. **1866** *Queenslander* (Brisbane) 10 Feb. 4/7 The object of the meeting was to consider the propriety of procuring a banner to celebrate the Eight Hours' Movement. **1870** *Eight Hours Hist.* 1 Many of the men who took an early part in the Eight-Hours movement in Victoria had been engaged in some of the trade disputes in the old country. **1886** R.C. SEATON *Six Lett. from Colonies* 35 The eight hours movement many years ago became law in Victoria. **1896** W.E. MURPHY *Hist. Eight Hours' Movt.* 66 What scheme stands so great a chance of success as the Eight Hours' movement? **1870** *Eight Hours Hist.* 3 They would perpetuate the honour and dignity of labour, and the **Eight-Hours principle.** **1911** *Huon Times* (Franklin) 25 Oct. 3/2 Lyden was one of the party who were supposed to have infringed the eight hour principle. **1856** *Argus* (Melbourne) 22 Apr. 5/5 The procession of today may tend to lead the public to believe that a general strike had taken place for the obtainment of the **Eight-Hour system.** **1859** P. JUST *Aust.* 147 These latter had agitated for .. an 'eight hours' system. **1870** *Eight Hours Hist.* 1 The 21st of April, 1870 .. the fourteenth anniversary of the triumph of the Eight Hours system. **1896** W.E. MURPHY *Hist. Eight Hours' Movt.* 59 A custom prevailed under the long ten-hour system of providing a 'spell', or cessation of work for a quarter of an hour, at 11 o'clock in the forenoon, and again at three in the afternoon, which was called 'smoko'. It was on one of these occasions, in midsummer of 1855 .. that James Stephens first spoke of the Eight Hours' system. **1922** C. DALEY *Early Squatting Days* 14 The minimum wage, the Wages Board, the Arbitration Court, even the eight hours system, were beyond the ken of worker and employer alike.

3. Special Comb. **eight-hour(s') day,** a working day of eight hours' duration; the day on which the introduction of this is celebrated; **demonstration,** an assembly in support of the introduction of an eight hour day; a procession commemorating its introduction; **man,** one who supports the principle of, or works, an eight hour day.

[**1887 eight-hour day:** *Blackwood's Mag.* (Edinburgh) May 677/1 In Australia .. they thirst for unlimited beer, and uphold the 'eight hours a-day' principle.] **1892** *Bulletin* (Sydney) 18 June 10/1 Eight-hours' Day is not a regular Melbourne holiday. It is only gazetted annually in the hopes of its being abolished. **1897** *Tocsin* (Melbourne) 9 Oct. 3/3 Sydney's Eight Hours Day passed off successfully. **1902** *Bulletin* (Sydney) 7 June (Red Page), We have instituted Eight-hours Day, the Melbourne Cup, and Hospital Saturday, and have neglected .. to make the land independent of droughts. **1909** W.G. SPENCE *Aust.'s Awakening* 510 A clause fixing an eight-hour day. **1911** *Huon Times* (Franklin) 26 Apr. 3/1 The demonstration held in connection with the eight hours day festivities. **1919** *Bulletin* (Sydney) 21 Aug. 22/2 At the Eight-hour Day Sports in Orange (N.S.W.). **1942** F. CLUNE *Last of Austral. Explorers* 108 The gougers were in festival mood for Eight-hour Day. **1956** J.T. LANG *I Remember* 159 Early in October, 1855 the union conducted the first strike in the city for the 8-Hour Day. **1973** [see sense [1]]. **1869** E.C. BOOTH *Another England* 151 The '**eight-hours' demonstration**' is one of the most interesting gatherings in Victoria. **1892** 'E. KINGLAKE' *Austral. at Home* 69 There is also a labour carnival known as the Eight Hours' Demonstration, which demands the cessation of all business on the day on which it is held. **1905** *Truth* (Sydney) 23 Apr. 2/3 The Eight Hours' Demonstration paraded the streets of Melbourne on April 10. **1896** W.E. MURPHY *Hist. Eight Hours' Movt.* 93 The **Eight Hours' men** early learned that the landed interest retarded settlement and agricultural prosperity in a primary degree. **1905** *Shearer* (Sydney) 14 Jan. 8/3 How can the A.W.U. claim bush cooks as being eight hours' men when, by the very nature of their occupation, they have to work all hours to keep things going?

elastic-side. Usu. in *pl.* Also **'lastic-side.** A boot without laces and having a piece of elastic inset into each side; part of the traditional Australian bush costume.

1891 *Truth* (Sydney) 1 May 2/4 Every week some eight is spent on 'elastic sides' or blucher. **1896** *Worker* (Sydney) 21 Mar. 1/3 She wore an ill-fitting print frock, and a pair of 'men's 'lastic sides' several sizes too large for her. **1898** G.T. BELL *Coolgardie* 85 My boots—an enormous pair of elastic-sides. **1921** 'J. O'BRIEN' *Around Boree Log* 30 There I see the boots in order—''lastic-sides' we used to wear—With a pair of 'everlastin's' cracked and dusty here and there. **1936** J. MATHESON *Day Dreams* So pull you 'lastic side off, Joe. **1954** *Bulletin* (Sydney) 16 June 12/4 An old bushman .. spat between his elastic-sides. **1968** *Southerly* i. 6 The pair of new elastic-sides was white with dust. **1976** C.D. MILLS *Hobble Chains & Greenhide* 1 A four-roomed galvanised iron bungalow, peopled with ringers garbed in moleskins and ''lastic sides'. **1978** C. GREEN *Sun is Up* 46 A bushman from the toes of his 'lastic-sides to the crown of his regulation hat.

elder. A person of recognized authority in an Aboriginal community.

1879 J. CAMPBELL *Norfolk Island* 29 If the case be of a serious character, and the contending parties are unwilling to submit to the decision of the magistrates, a jury, consisting of 7 Elders is summoned, and the whole case being submitted to them, their decision is final. **1885** A.W. HOWITT *Jeraeil* 301 After due consultation by the elders, their decision was announced to a general assembly of all the men; and the headman now in his turn sent the message forward by one of his own people. **1963** I.L. IDRIESS *Our Living Stone Age* 132 Next in line aspiring to this Supreme Council were the Elders, those who had successfully passed all degrees. **1978** 'B. WONGAR' *Track to Bralgu* 35 He reminds me of a tribal elder, serene and calm.

elder colony. *Obs.* A name given to New South Wales.

1832 *Sydney Herald* 17 May 2/2 The Government of Van Diemen's Land has in several instances, exercised a degree of political wisdom, which the Elder Colony has neglected. **1833** *Colonist* (Hobart) 7 May 3/3 The Act .. recently promulgated in the elder colony. **1843** *Sydney Morning Herald* 2 May 2/2 The whole population of the Swan River settlement does not exceed that of one of our Sydney Wards, their example is a standing reproach to the supineness of the elder colony. **1849** A. HARRIS *Emigrant Family* (1967) 140 Mushrooms plentiful in South Australia; not so much so in the elder colony. **1858** T. MCCOMBIE *Hist. Colony Vic.* 69 The colonists of Australia Felix care little for what has long been considered the great question by the elder colony.

elegant parrot. The small, predom. green parrot *Neophema elegans* of s.w. and central s. Aust., having blue markings on the wings and between the eyes.

[**1841** J. GOULD *Birds of Aust.* (1848) V. Pl. 38, *Euphema elegans* .. Elegant Grass-Parakeet.] **1937** R.H. CROLL *Wide Horizons* 51 Another native of the Inland, commonly called the Elegant Parrot. **1976** *Reader's Digest Compl. Bk. Austral. Birds* 290 The elegant parrot raises four or five young in a nest in a tree hole.

elephant beetle. [From a fancied resemblance.]

1. Any of several weevils, esp. some species of *Orthorrhinus.*

1890 *Agric. Gaz. N.S.W.* I. 278 Some of the most destructive insects with which the fruitgrower has to contend are the so-called elephant beetles, which pass their early stages in the limbs and branches of the orange, apricot, peach, and vine. **1935** *Bulletin* (Sydney) 27 Feb. 21/1 The little animal that pulled the splinter out .. was a wattle-borer, or elephant beetle. **1968** H. FRAUCA *Bk. of Insects* 102 Curculionidae. .. Popularly these beetles are known as Weevils and also as Elephant Beetles on account of the head structure.

2. The scarab beetle *Xylotrupes gideon* of Qld.

1891 *Quiz* (Adelaide) 9 Jan. 15/3 Flying foxes and elephant beetles made evening hideous as they disputed possession of stray bits of the anatomy of mine host. **1907** W.W. FROGGATT *Austral. Insects* 159 The Queensland Elephant Beetle .. in the larval state feeds upon decaying vegetable matter. **1949** D. WALKER *We went to Aust.* 60 The elephant beetles of northern Queensland are 10 inches long and fight to the death. **1984** *Mercury* (Hobart) 23 May 1/3 (*caption*) The elephant beetle, or in scientific terms, xylotrupes gideon, has dumb-founded museum staff simply because they don't know how it moved from the warmth of Queensland to the cooler climate of Queenstown, on Tasmania's West Coast.

elkhorn. [Transf. use of *elk('s)-horn*, the fern *Platycerium alcicorne.*] Any of several epiphytic or lithophytic ferns of the genus *Platycerium* (fam. Polypodiaceae), esp. *P. bifurcatum* of N.S.W. and Qld. Also **elk's-horn.**

1835 J. BACKHOUSE *Narr. Visit Austral. Colonies* (1843) 240 A fine patch of the Elks-horn Fern, *Acrosticum alcicorne*, retains its native station on a rocky point. **1881** *Proc. Linnean Soc. N.S.W.* VI. 736 'Elk's-horn', ferns that are common throughout the Colony. **1926** A.S. LE SOUEF et al. *Wild Animals Australasia* 250 One was searching among the elk-horn and orchids. **1935** DAVISON & NICHOLLS *Blue Coast Caravan* 125 There was life feeding upon life; elkhorns, orchids, and staghorns, drooping festoons high up under the roof of the jungle. **1959** M. RAYMOND *Smiley roams Road* 196 Figs hung with mossy vines and decorated with staghorns and elkhorns.

Ellangowan poison bush /ɛlən'gaʊən pɔɪzən bʊʃ/. [f. the name of Mt. *Ellangowan* in s.e. Qld.] The shrub of drier mainland Aust. *Eremophila deserti* (fam. Myoporaceae), sometimes poisonous to stock; *turkey bush*, see TURKEY *n.*[1] 5. See also DOGWOOD.

1889 J.H. MAIDEN *Useful Native Plants Aust.* 135 'Ellangowan Poison-bush' of Queensland. .. It is reported from Ellangowan, Darling Downs, Queensland, that out of a flock of 7,000 sheep .. 500 succumbed to eating this plant. **1897** L. LINDLEY-COWEN *W. Austral. Settler's Guide* 591 *Myoporum deserti* .. 'Ellangowan' poison bush of Queensland; 'Dogwood' of New South Wales. Considered most dangerous when in fruit. **1947** *Qld. Agric. Jrnl.* LXIV. 83 To camp mobs of sheep or cattle where Ellangowan poison bush is growing generally leads to heavy losses. **1979** K.A.W. WILLIAMS *Native Plants Qld.* I. 202 Ellangowan Poison Bush .. is a small much branched shrub.

elvan. *Obs.* Also **elvin.** [Br. dial. *elvan* 'the name given in Cornwall to intrusive rocks of igneous origin, so hard as to resist the pick': see OED.] See quot. 1852.

1845 M. COLLISSON *Miner's Man.* 19 The floors are also found in the granite and elvan. **1852** A. MACKAY *Great Gold Field* 20 Nov. (1853) 62 The rock through which the miners have to tunnel is a dark compact trap of the hardest description called by the miners 'elvan'. **1872** *Yorke's Peninsula Advertiser* (Moonta) 5 Nov. 2/6 The ground consists of a dark elvin containing stains of green carbonates. **1883** *Mining Chron.* (Melbourne) 2 Jan. 11/1 The face shows hard slate and elvan bars.

emancipate, *v. Hist.* [Spec. use of *emancipate* to release from legal restraint.] *trans.* To discharge as free (a convict who has received a conditional or absolute pardon).

1787 *Hist. Rec. N.S.W.* 25 Apr. (1892) I. ii. 90 Full power and authority to emancipate and discharge from their servitude any of the convicts .. who shall, from their good conduct and a disposition to industry, be deserving of favour. **1798** D. COLLINS *Acct. Eng. Colony N.S.W.* (1802) II. 138 Stephenson had been emancipated for his orderly behaviour. **1820** H.G. BENNET *Let. to Earl Bathurst* 7 Limitations .. have been imposed on the power of the governor to pardon or emancipate convicts. **1821** T. GODWIN *Descr. Acct. Van Diemen's Island* 15 Those who are virtuously and industriously disposed, are emancipated from bondage. **1844** *Duncan's Weekly Register* (Sydney) 5 Oct. 175/1 The Queen might choose to emancipate the convicts transported from this colony.

emancipate, *a.* and *n. Obs.* [f. prec.]

A. *adj.* EMANCIPATED.

1829 *Sydney Monitor* 12 Jan. 1458/2 A panel of 2000 persons, fit for Jurors could be obtained, and in about the like proportion of Emigrants, Colony born and Emancipate Settlers.

B. *n.* EMANCIPIST.

1838 W. BLAND *N.S.W.* 58 The brutal crimes of irresponsible overseers, superintendents, and magistrates, inflicted on defenceless, starved, and wretched convicts, emancipates, or simply paupers. **1848** *Britannia* (Hobart) 20 July 4/1 A diabolical effort was made to antagonise the free population and the emancipates.

emancipated, *ppl. a. Hist.* [f. EMANCIPATE *v.*] Of a former convict: discharged as free having been granted a conditional or absolute pardon, or (loosely) having completed the sentence imposed.

1803 *Sydney Gaz.* 26 Mar., The quantity of ground allowed to such emancipated convicts as the Governor may think proper to settle is as follows. For every male—30 acres. **1803** *HRA* (1915) 1st Ser. IV. 106 Respecting the List of Settlers, and Emancipated People. **1810** *Ibid.* (1921) 3rd Ser. I. 445 All applications made for Grants of Lands by Settlers or Emancipated Convicts are to be transmitted to me. **1822** J.T. BIGGE *Rep. State Colony N.S.W.* 68 They have .. been placed on a level with the emancipated and free convicts of their own sex. **1826** *HRA* (1922) 3rd Ser. V. 51 Edited by a time expired Convict, and printed and published by an emancipated Felon. **1834** J.D. LANG *Hist. & Statistical Acct. N.S.W.* II. 68 An emancipated convict-settler .. lived .. down the river. **1839** *Sydney Herald* 9 Jan. 2/5 The prisoner said he was 'emancipated' having received the Governor's letter, informing him that he would recommend him for a conditional pardon. **1847** H.P. FRY *Let. to Householders Hobarton* 22 No invidious feeling of animosity exists between the Emancipated and those who have never been convicts. **1865** 'SPECIAL CORRESPONDENT' *Transportation* 51 The delicacy is with those of the emancipated population. **1921** J.T. SUTCLIFFE *Hist. Trade Unionism Aust.* 28 The peculiar condition under which convict, indentured and emancipated labour were utilized in production.

emancipation. *Hist.* [f. EMANCIPATE *v.*] The act of discharging as free a convict who has received a conditional or absolute pardon; a document certifying this.

1793 *Hist. Rec. N.S.W.* (1893) II. 50 Such convicts as become settlers, either on emancipation or upon the expiration of the term for which they have been transported. **1794** D. COLLINS *Acct. Eng. Colony N.S.W.* (1798) I. 391 Some warrants of emancipation passed the seal of the territory and received the lieutenant-governor's signature. The objects of this indulgence were, Robert Lidaway, who received an unconditional pardon; and William Leach, who was permitted to quit this country but not to return to England during the unexpired term of his sentence of transportation. **1803** *HRA* (1915) 1st Ser. IV. 173, I judged it necessary and advisable to give Mr Bellasis an Emancipation, or Pardon, conditionally on his not leaving this Territory. **1804** *Ibid.* V. 220 Among the Emancipations sent by the Endeavour, I observe several Names whom I did not recommend. **1810** *Sydney Gaz.* 17 Mar., Those Persons to whom he has promised Emancipations will receive them at the Secretary's Office. **1822** J.T. BIGGE *Rep. State Colony N.S.W.* 119 Conditional pardons, or emancipations, were not to be granted to convicts for life until they had been 10 years in the colony; nor to convicts for limited terms, until they had resided at least two-thirds of their original sentences. **1827** P. CUNNINGHAM *Two Yrs. in N.S.W.* II. 299 When an individual has enjoyed the privilege of a ticket of leave for two years, and maintained an unimpeachable reputation during that time, emancipation might follow as a matter of course. **1838** W. BLAND *N.S.W.* 12 Convicts .. became free, either by ticket, emancipation, pardon, or expiration of their respective sentences. **1840** *S. Austral. Rec.* (London) 4 July 4 The instrument generally called an Emancipation, a Conditional Pardon, should be given to each. **1846** C. CHISHOLM *Emigration & Transportation* (1847) 38, I was sent here as a *lifer*. I am now on my Ticket—not yet received my emancipation. **1865** 'SPECIAL CORRESPONDENT' *Transportation* 40 A convict whose period of emancipation is deferred until he obtains employment.

emancipationist. *Obs.* [f. prec.] EMANCIPIST.

1850 W. GATES *Recoll. Van Dieman's Land* 196 If .. they have succeeded in keeping out of punishment .. they are allowed emancipations, and are then called Emancipationists, having the full privilege of citizenship, and the full freedom of the island.

emancipist. [f. EMANCIPATE *v.*]

1. A convict who has been pardoned or whose sentence has expired.

1822 J. RITCHIE *Evidence to Bigge Reports* 6 Nov. (1971) II. 212 Those persons who came under sentences of Transportation, but have become free by Pardon or Service of the Term, and designated 'Emancipists'. **1825** *HRA* (1919) 1st Ser. XII. 81 It is quite clear that the Emancipists .. have gained an ascendancy, to which their opponents are not likely to offer any effectual Counterpoise. *Ibid.* 82, I can discover no just or reasonable ground for treating the Emancipists, as a Body, with indiscriminate contumely. **1827** *Tasmanian* (Hobart) 7 June 4 In this Colony .. a large proportion of the Population consists of Emancipists (cidevant Convicts). **1832** *Currency Lad* (Sydney) 15 Sept. 1 We have lately witnessed the desire of a few to perpetuate the distinctive titles of emigrant and emancipist. **1834** 'EMIGRANT' *Party Politics Exposed* 11 The great body of Emigrants .. repudiate even the implied *wish* to detract from, or perpetuate the recollections of, the former state of the Emancipists. **1841** *Van Diemen's Land Papers Legis. Council* no. 26 53 Very many emancipists and ticket-of-leave men marry free women. **1846** *Moreton Bay Courier* 12 Sept. 2/2 Emancipists, who have received free or conditional pardons, are also entitled to vote, when otherwise qualified. **1847** A. MARJORIBANKS *Travels N.S.W.* 150 The second class in society consists of those who have once been prisoners, and are now free; they are termed *emancipists*. **1853** E. MACKENZIE *Emigrant's Guide Aust.* 108 Many are 'emancipists'—that is, those who were originally convicts. **1869** J. MARTINEAU *Lett. from Aust.* 115 The line of separation is no longer strictly preserved .. between free settlers and emancipists. **1881** J.F.V. FITZGERALD *Aust.* 54 This unhappy division between them [*sc.* 'Exclusionists'] and the 'Emancipists' lasted until the cessation of transportation. **1918** C.H. NORTHCOTT *Austral. Social Dev.* 38 As the sentences of the short-term convicts expired, they became freedmen, or, in the language of the settlement, 'emancipists'. **1948** F. CLUNE *Wild Colonial Boys* 14 Macquarie's benevolent regime .. under which convicts were encouraged to become 'emancipists'—free men and property owners. **1972** C. PEARL *Brilliant Dan Deniehy* 4 There was social conflict between the Emancipists, who had been convicts, and the Exclusives .. who had not.

2. Comb. **emancipist class, party.**

1823 *HRA* (1922) 4th Ser. I. 462 This general union and harmony between the Emigrant and **Emancipist Classes** continued unabated and undisturbed until the end of the year 1819. **1825** *Ibid.* (1917) 1st Ser. XI. 894 It would be proper to admit the Emancipist Class of the Colonists to a participation of the privilege of sitting in Juries. **1834** G. BENNETT *Wanderings N.S.W.* I. 91 The influence of the emancipist class of the New South Wales population is great. **1845** *Sydney Morning Herald* 20 Sept. 2/2 Take steps for bringing immediately from Van Diemen's Land such labourers *from the emancipist class* as they may deem requisite. **1835** G. ARTHUR *Defence of Transportation* 93 There is .. no **emancipist party** in Van Diemen's Land. **1839** *Sydney Standard* 4 Feb. 2/4 We do not write thus .. to give unnecessary offence to the Emancipist party. **1841** *Port Phillip Patriot* 10 June 4/3 According to the declaration of the Governor .. the emancipist party no longer predominate.

emigrant, *n.* and *a.*

A. *n.*

1. One who leaves another country to settle in Australia by choice; in early use (like SETTLER 1) freq. contrasted with CONVICT. Cf. IMMIGRANT 1, MIGRANT.

1820 C. JEFFREYS *Van Dieman's Land* p. iv, He has no hesitation in recommending emigrants to the banks of the Derwent and Tamar Rivers. **1823** *Hobart Town Gaz.* 4 Jan., The Author's design is to guide Emigrants from the delusive path of fancy, to the rational bourne of probability. **1824** *HRA* (1917) 1st Ser. XI. 413 The practice of allowing six Months Rations to Emigrants, upon their first arrival in the Colony, is still continued. **1827** P. CUNNINGHAM *Two Yrs. in N.S.W.* I. 5, I give a decided preference to New South Wales, as an eligible asylum for an agricultural emigrant. **1832** *Hill's Life N.S.W.* (Sydney) 23 Nov. 2 The emancipists and their children on the one side, and the emigrants and their children on the other, were hostile to each other. **1838** *S. Austral. Rec.* (London) 14 Nov. 116 One universal *esprit de corps* animates and pervades the whole convict body, uniting them like Freemasons in one silent, deep-rooted sentiment of hostility to the free settler, or, as they profanely call them, the b-- emigrants. **1839** W. BLAND *N.S.W.* 52 According to Mr James Macarthur .. the circumstances of being an emigrant .. is *prima facie*, if not positive proof of respectability. **1849** J.P. TOWNSEND *Rambles & Observations N.S.W.* 168 Convicts often address an emigrant thus—'Oh, you great fool! *we* came out here because we could not help it; but you .. were *lagged* with your own consent!' **1859** W. BURROWS *Adventures Mounted Trooper* 147 If the men are emigrants, and not 'old hands', as the convicts are called, they may be seen poring over the letters they have received from home. **1863** P. SAUNDERS *Two Yrs. Vic.* 7 The boa does not crush the rabbit more effectually than the Colony of Victoria does the emigrant. **1881** W. ALLEN *Immigration & Co-op. Settlement* 48 Emigrants from the old country .. might find their way into all parts of the interior.

2. Comb. **emigrant barracks, depot, ship.**

1840 *S. Austral. Rec.* (London) 18 July 34 We left the quarantine ground and went to the **emigrant barracks**, in Sydney. **1841** *Morning Advertiser* (Hobart) 12 Aug. 3/3 Extensive emigrant barracks have been erected. **1848** J. BYRNE *Twelve Yrs.' Wandering Brit. Colonies* I. 281 The emigrant barracks, where new arrivals in bounty ships, who have come out at the Government expense, are housed for a few days. **1853** W. WESTGARTH *Vic.* 351 The officials at the emigrants' barracks .. have been at some pains to provide respectable first engagements for .. fastidious inmates. **1848** *Sydney Daily Advertiser* 12 July 2/3 **Emigrant Depot**. . Great anxiety .. to provide suitable places in the interior for the reception of newly arrived immigrants. **1856** W.H.G. KINGSTON *Emigrant's Home* 127 Irish orphan girls .. are sent at once to the Emigrant Depôt .. and are never allowed to go and live at public-houses. **1857** F. DE B. COOPER *Wild Adventures* 25 Formerly the prisoners' barracks, but now served the purpose of an emigrant depôt. **1837** *Cornwall Chron.* (Launceston) 9 Sept. 2 Two **emigrant ships** and two convict ships have made an addition of 1400 persons to our population. **1840** *S. Austral. Gaz.* (Adelaide) 16 Apr. 2 *A Pennant above a ball*—Denotes an Emigrant ship. **1848** *Sydney Daily Advertiser* 5 June 2/2 His proposal to withdraw two out of every three emigrant ships from Port Jackson would have sacrificed the interest of Sydney. **1856** W.W. DOBIE *Recoll. Visit Port-Phillip* 39 An emigrant ship is no school for good manners or morals. **1859** J.D. MEREWEATHER *Diary Working Clergyman* 1 The passengers of the emigrant ship and myself all went to the little church at Port Adelaide. **1877** J. VICARS *Tariff, Immigration, & Labour Question* 9 A decent and steady young fellow lately arrived by emigrant ship. **1892** *Missing Friends: Adventures Danish Emigrant Qld.* p. vi, I found myself on board an emigrant ship bound for Queensland. **1926** A.A.B. APSLEY *Amateur Settlers* 63 That Victorian picture of the Irish emigrant ship. **1965** G. MCINNES *Road to Gundagai* 115 Though convict days had been left far, far behind, the era of the Emigrant Ship was still with us.

B. *adj.* In collocations: **emigrant colonist, girl, labour, labourer, settler.**

1821 *Sydney Gaz.* 27 Jan., This state of the law, in its consequences, affects .. a very considerable part of the property of the **Emigrant Colonists.** **1834** *Sydney Herald* 24 Feb. 2/1 We are confident that the whole body of Emigrant Colonists feel disgusted. **1839** S. BUTLER *Hand-Bk. Austral. Emigrants* 152 We totally deny that there is any difference of opinion between the great bulk of the emigrant colonists of New South Wales and the witnesses examined. **1837** *Cornwall Chron.* (Launceston) 19 Aug. 2 Except that little foolery with the **Emigrant girls**—nothing can be said prejudicial to his general official efficiency. **1854** W. SHAW *Land of Promise* 109 The freshness and roseate complexion of the 'emigrant girls' .. contrasts strongly with the sallow, and acclimated style, of the 'Currency Lasses'. **1838** *Southern Austral.* (Adelaide) 30 June 4/2 The Commissioners proceeded with confidence to increase the supply of **emigrant labour.** **1840** *S. Austral. Rec.* (London) 7 Nov. 293 To provide means for a continued importation of emigrant labour is necessarily a consideration. **1835** R. TORRENS *Colonization of S.A.* 16 If the **emigrant-labourer**, who accepts a free passage to the new colony, will be a slave and a villain, as the Reviewer asserts, then he will not be in a condition to run away from his owner. **1850** J.W. MELVIN *Emigrant's Guide to Colonies* 23 The Emigrant labourer need not entertain any ridiculous fears respecting the blacks or bush-rangers. **1826** *Monitor* (Sydney) 27 Oct. 187/3 Mr Farquharson a respectable **emigrant settler** convicted of sheep stealing. **1835** *Colonist* (Sydney) 23 July 237/2 A respectable emigrant settler . . lodged at Barnes' for the night. **1835** G. ARTHUR *Defence of Transportation* 108 Tenders were then invited—the emigrant settlers competed with the emancipist settlers—and wheat was offered at from six to seven shillings per bushel.

emigrate, *v. intr.* To leave another country by choice, with the intention of settling in Australia. Cf. IMMIGRATE 1.

1796 'SOCIETY OF GENTLEMEN' *New & Correct Hist. New Holland* 65 Persons induced to emigrate hither, are recommended, before they quit England, to provide all their wearing apparel for themselves, family and servants. **1820** C. JEFFREYS *Van Dieman's Land* 5 Those who emigrate . . and . . wish still to enjoy British laws, with British manners and comforts, will find the settlements in Van Dieman's Land, and New South Wales . . suited to their expectations. **1832** *Colonial Times* (Hobart) 9 May, I paid a heavy purchase in the very act of emigrating here, fully equal to the value of the land. **1848** H.W. HAYGARTH *Recoll. Bush Life* 161 If he now emigrates, he must do so with the intention of making a long residence in the country, or of adopting it as his permanent home. **1859** W. KELLY *Life in Vic.* I. 4 They constrained him to emigrate to South Australia.

Hence **emigrating** *ppl. a.*

1861 F. ALGAR *Handbk. to Colony Qld.* 3 The advantages which it offers to the emigrating classes of the mother country. **1852** D. MACKENZIE *Ten Yrs. Aust.* 4 A mania originating in the townland speculations of South Australia . . seized the colonists and the emigrating public.

emigration.

1. The action of leaving another country by choice to settle in Australia. Cf. IMMIGRATION 1.

1820 C. JEFFREYS *Van Dieman's Land* 78 The southern parts of this island . . hold out every possible inducement to emigration. **1822** J.T. BIGGE *Rep. State Colony N.S.W.* 155 How far the late emigrations of free settlers to New South Wales and Van Dieman's have relieved the pressure, I have not any means of determining. **1824** *HRA* (1921) 3rd Ser. IV. 572 The reputation of the climate of these Colonies for Sheep has been the main-spring of Emigration. **1832** *Sydney Herald* 5 Mar. 2/1 The Legislative Council has been deeply engaged for some time in devising a scheme for promoting emigration. **1839** *HRA* (1924) 1st Ser. XX. 71 An Association for promoting the Emigration of a superior class of Laborers and Artizans to the Australian Colonies. **1852** G.B. EARP *Gold Colonies Aust.* 208 In the Australian colonies there is a land fund, which is annually set apart for the purpose of procuring emigration from the mother country.

2. Special Comb. **emigration agent,** one employed to promote emigration to the Australian Colonies and to assist with settlement; **fund** *S.A.*, a fund accumulating from the proceeds of land sales used to provide financial assistance for emigrants to the Colony (see quot. 1848).

1833 H.W. PARKER *Rise, Progress, & Present State Van Dieman's Land* 221 One of the colonial newspapers, in speaking of parties living in London who advertise themselves as '**Emigration Agents**', says, 'they had much better turn their attention to obtain a livelihood by some more honest and creditable species of industry, than by deceiving, way-laying, entrapping, and kidnapping their fellow-countrymen.' **1840** *Port Phillip Gaz.* 21 Mar. 2 We received a communication from Mr James, emigration agent at Sydney. **1848** J. STEPHENS *Voice from Aust.* 5 If any of you . . wish to cast in your lot with me and my fellow-colonists . . go to one of the Emigration Agents, whom they have appointed at the principal seaports and inland towns of England, Ireland, Scotland, and Wales. **1849** J.P. TOWNSEND *Rambles & Observations N.S.W.* 236 Such emigrants were well-cared-for on their arrival by Mr Merewether, the emigration agent. **1835** R. TORRENS *Colonization of S.A.* 83 The minimum price of public land should be fixed sufficiently high, to create an **emigration fund. 1840** *S. Austral. Rec.* (London) 7 Nov. 293 As the emigration fund is now managed, the money paid for passage to emigrants is lost now and for ever to the colonists. **1848** J. BRICE *S.A. as it Is* 5 All the proceeds of the land sales goes into what is called an Emigration Fund, and . . the money is sent over to the English Government, for them to send out as many male and female servants, labourers, tradesmen, &c. of certain trades or callings, as the money sent will pay for. **1849** S. & J. SIDNEY *Emigrant's Jrnl.* 162 As for capital, it is always growing on the sheeps' backs without let or hindrance, except the want of shepherds; and, with land for sale in farm-lots, shepherds will arrive on the emigration fund fast enough.

emperor. [See quot. 1906.] **a.** Any of several tropical or sub-tropical fish, esp. of the fam. Lethrinidae. **b.** *Red emperor*, see RED *a.* 1 b. Also **emperor bream.**

1906 D.G. STEAD *Fishes of Aust.* 130 A closely-allied species [to the Yellow-mouthed Perch] is known in Queensland as 'Emperor', on account of its glorious colouration. **1951** T.C. ROUGHLEY *Fish & Fisheries Aust.* 75 The best-known of the emperor breams is the sweet-lip or red-mouthed emperor, one of the commonest fish caught by both professional fishermen and anglers on the Great Barrier Reef.

empty north: see NORTH 2.

emu /'imju/, *n.*[1] Formerly also **emeu.** [Prob. a. Pg. *ema* applied to any of various ostrich-like birds; now restricted to the Austral. sense.]

1. The flightless bird *Dromaius novaehollandiae*, widespread in mainland Aust., up to 2 m. tall and having exposed blue skin on the neck and long grey-brown feathers on the back; CASSOWARY 1; *New Holland cassowary*, see NEW HOLLAND 2.

[**1789** W. TENCH *Narr. Exped. Botany Bay* 123 The bird which principally claims attention is, a species of ostrich, approaching nearer to the emu of South America than any other we know of.] **1803** *Sydney Gaz.* 26 June, Two young Emues, procured at King's Island were sold to a Master of a Vessel for Seven Guineas. **1817** *Hist. N.S.W.* (1818) 53 A bird of the ostrich genus. . . It has obtained the name of the New South Wales Emu. **1827** P. CUNNINGHAM *Two Yrs. in N.S.W.* I. 320 At particular periods of the year the emus are bedded round the rump with a prodigious quantity of fat, which is melted down and much esteemed by the settlers. **1846** *Moreton Bay Courier* 19 Sept. 4/2 We saw the foot of an emu cut very carefully and accurately into the bark of a tree. **1862** G.T. LLOYD *Thirty-Three Yrs. Tas. & Vic.* 77 The Emu of Tasmania . . is much smaller and darker in plumage than that of Australia. **1865** G.F. ANGAS *Aust.* 97 The largest bird peculiar to Australia is the emeu or New Holland cassowary. **1872** MRS E. MILLETT *Austral. Parsonage* 203 The kangaroo is one of the supporters of the arms of Australia, his fellow-helper . . being an emu, light-heeled creatures both of them, to which the motto 'Advance Australia' seems thoroughly suitable. **1872** G.S. BADEN-POWELL *New Homes for Old Country* 345 The Emeu is still pretty common. **1888** *Sydney Morning Herald* 24 Jan. 1/5 The emu, which is very much like an ostrich, must be regarded as the representative bird of Australia. **1897** R. NEWTON *Work & Wealth Qld.* 69 The emu's chief weakness is curiosity. **1920** J.J. GLADSTONE *Tragedy of Gallipoli* 36 There's the emu, fond emblem of our land. **1935** H. BASEDOW *Knights of Boomerang* 159 A large plume of emu-feathers. The central, cylindrical part . . contained a sacred Tjuringa belonging to the totem ancestors of the emu. **1942** *Southerly* iii. 14 And who shall say on what errand the insolent emu Walks between morning and night on the edge of the plain. **1962** MARSHALL & DRYSDALE *Journey among Men* 169 He heard that we were about to eat emu. . . 'You can't eat that stuff!' he cried, 'it's bloody muck.' **1964** M. SHARLAND *Territory of Birds* 140 The Emu lays its eggs on the ground and when incubating sits as low as possible. **1978** 'B. WONGAR' *Track to Bralgu* 23 So many things we tried to teach Nulumb, but it was like teaching an emu to fly. **1982** *Weekend Austral. Mag.* (Sydney) 6 Nov. 4/4 Beside a dirt road, a run-down emu like a broken feather duster.

2. *attrib.* Of, obtained from, or relating to the emu.

1794 D. COLLINS *Acct. Eng. Colony N.S.W.* (1798) I. 380 To barter with the natives, and procure emu feathers from them. **1829** *Sydney Monitor* 16 Feb. 1498/4 Two rosewood stands, 18 inches high by 6 inches, to hold Emu eggs. **1841** *S. Austral. Mag.* (Adelaide) July 4 Its [*sc.* S.A.'s] mimic representation of the 'Wild Sports of the West' in the Emu or Kangaroo hunts of the interior. **1870** E.B. KENNEDY *Four Yrs. in Qld.* 113 Emu oil is said to possess wonderful properties. **1875** J. FORREST *Explorations in Aust.* 236 Windich said he had seen emu tracks. **1883** E.M. CURR *Recoll. Squatting Vic.* 346 After the emu-hunt I went to Melbourne. **1975** R. BEILBY *Brown Land Crying* 50 Emu eggs, skilfully incised like cameos, pale green and pearly white. **1976** *Reader's Digest Compl. Bk. Austral. Birds* 25 The famous 'Emu War' of 1932, when an army detachment with two Lewis guns attempted to exterminate the emus.

3. In the names of flora and fauna: **emu apple, (a)** the small tree of central Aust. *Owenia acidula* (fam. Meliaceae); its edible apple-like fruit with bitter red flesh; COLANE; GOOYA; GRUIE; MOOLEY APPLE; *sour apple*, see SOUR; see also *sour plum* SOUR; **(b)** any of several other similar plants, esp. *Petalostigma quadriloculare* (fam. Euphorbiaceae); the fruit of these plants; also *attrib.*; **berry,** any of several plants, esp. the small twiggy shrub of tropical and subtropical Aust. *Grewia retusifolia* (fam. Tiliaceae), bearing small edible fruits; the fruit of these plants; **bush, (a)** any of many woody shrubs usu. of the mainland Austral. genus *Eremophila* (fam. Myoporaceae), some species of which bear fruits eaten by the emu; FUCHSIA BUSH; see also *turkey bush* TURKEY *n.*[1] 5; **(b)** PITURI; **wren,** either of the two small, long-tailed birds of the genus *Stipiturus*, *S. malachurus* of s.e. and s.w. Aust., and *rufous-crowned emu wren* (see RUFOUS).

1881 *Proc. Linnean Soc. N.S.W.* VI. 740 *Owenia acidula* or '**Emu Apple**' . . mostly confined to the brigalow scrubs in the neighbourhood. **1901** *Brisbane Courier* 27 July 9/4 One of the 'boys' sighted three turkeys feeding round an emu apple tree. **1911** ST. C. GRONDONA *Collar & Cuffs* 69 The emu apple is a very pretty, compact little tree, with fresh evergreen foliage, and a large red fruit, muchly sought after by blacks and emus, and even by bush children, who eat it with sugar. **1932** J. MCCARTER *Pan's Clan* 155 Animal life began to wend towards the shade of fence posts and emu apple bushes, following the release of the sheep. **1956** A.C.C. LOCK *Tropical Tapestry* 147 Emu apple trees . . belong to the *Petalostigma* group, the small leaves being ovate and bright green in colour. After its white, clustered flowers have bloomed, it breaks into purple fruit, the size of a large plum. They are bitter, but emus like them, from which the tree derives its common name. **1977** G.W. LILLEY *Lengthening Shadows* 91 From time to time they chewed the emu apple, the bitter acid of which to some extent refreshed them. **1902** *Emu* II. 31 Emus . . live in very poor country, and seem, from their droppings, to live principally on cranberries, or **Emu berries**, as they are called. **1914** E.E. PESCOTT *Native Flowers Vic.* 81 Styphelia Sonderi is a brilliantly scarlet species with large flowers. . . Its seeds are produced in the form of succulent red berries, which are sweet and well flavoured; they are much relished by emus, and on that account the plant is often called the emu-berry bush. **1974** M. TERRY *War of Warramullas* 151 Emu berries . . grow in dozens on a small bush. These small fruits are red and brown. **1981** D. LEVITT *Plants & People* 35 Emu Berry (*Grewia retusifolia*). . . The small berries were picked and eaten, seeds and all. They are about the size of a currant . . and . . are popular with women and children. **(a) 1885** P.R. MEGGY *From Sydney to Silverton* 57 Jolting over trunks, scrunching along in the scrub, smashing through the **emu bush** . . the party managed to survive without accident. **1892** *Trans. & Proc. R. Soc. S.A.* XV. 205 Cattle, although very destructive to some of the shrubby trees, such as Emu-bush or Bitter-bush (*Heterodendron oleaefolia*) . . are otherwise not nearly so destructive as sheep. **1900** *Proc. Linnean Soc. N.S.W.* XXV. 596 *Eremophila longifolia* (Emu-bush, because the emus eat the fruit). **1901** K.L. PARKER in M. Muir *My Bush Bk.* (1982) 103 A few pendulous meamei, emu bush, for the sake of their bright orange berries, which, bursting open, show crimson seeds. **1921** *Bulletin* (Sydney) 12 May 24/2 *Re* the cure of gonorrhoea by a gin. . . The blacks of the Bogan, Lachlan and Paroo rivers all swear by a scrub called emu-bush. **1936** F. CLUNE *Roaming round Darling* 165 The currant or emu bush; needle-leafed, with fruit like black berries, each one the size of a pea—not caviare to emus. **1944** A. MARSHALL *These are my People* 185 Grampian lillies pushed their way through clumps of emu bush. **1972** S.H. COURTIER *Dead if I Remember* 9 A mixture of emu-bush and needlewood, making the inside quite dark. **(b) 1968** W. HILLIARD *People in Between* 118 A branch from the '**emu bush**' (*Duboisia Hopwoodii*). **1974** M. TERRY *War of*

Warramullas 63 Aborigines once used to poison emus with pituri. Perhaps for that reason one colloquial name for it, among Centralian bushmen, used to be 'emu bush'. [**1827 emu wren:** *Trans. Linnean Soc. London* XV. 224 Soft-tailed Flycatcher... 'This bird,' Mr Caley observes, 'is called *Emu Bird* by the colonists'.] **1834** J. BACKHOUSE *Narr. Visit Austral. Colonies* (1843) 210 A little bird with open feathers, like those of the Emu, in its tail, whence it has obtained the name of the Emu Wren. **1859** H. KINGSLEY *Recoll. Geoffry Hamlyn* III. 4 The emu wren, a little tiny brown fellow .. flitting from bush to bush. **1860** G. BENNETT *Gatherings of Naturalist* 213 The delicate little Emeu Wren .. is now very rare. It was also named the Cassowary Bird by the colonists. **1902** *Emu* II. 71 *Stipiturus malachurus* (Emu Wren). These feathered pygmies were very abundant. **1964** M. SHARLAND *Territory of Birds* 143 The Weebill is said to be Australia's smallest bird. If we were to disregard the length of a bird's tail .. then the Weebill would .. be challenged by the tiny but elegant Emu-wren.

4. Special Comb. **emu dance,** an Aboriginal dance (see quot. 1832); **eye,** *emu stone*; **hunting** *vbl. n.* the pursuit of emus (with dogs) as sport; **parade,** an assembly, esp. of soldiers, for the purpose of picking up litter; **stone,** AUSTRALITE.

1832 J. BACKHOUSE *Narr. Visit Austral. Colonies* (1843) 82 In the **emu dance** they placed one hand behind them, and alternately put the other to the ground and raised it above their heads .. imitating the motion of the head of the emu when feeding. **1937** E. HILL *Great Austral. Loneliness* (1940) 27 Australites, or obsidianites, or meteorites... The blacks know them as 'warragetti milki'—**emu-eyes. 1827** P. CUNNINGHAM *Two Yrs. in N.S.W.* I. 308 A very useful breed for **emu-hunting. 1870** E.B. KENNEDY *Four Yrs. in Qld.* 112 Emu hunting is great fun, either with or without dogs. **1941** T.I. MOORE *Emu Parade* 12 Halters of futility Drag us upon **emu parades**, the Army wasting Prodigal hours while soldiers, eager for the fighting, Billions of butts in hand, bob on to victory! **1943** *Signals* (Melbourne) Christmas 43 We'll never outlive the memory of the .. daily emu parades. **1951** E. LAMBERT *Twenty Thousand Thieves* 417 *Emu parade*, a line of men to clean up an area in camp. **1986** *Sydney Morning Herald* 24 Mar. 3/8 They had worked in their allotted leisure time, including all-day 'emu parades' to gather wind-blown litter, and had dug out large amounts of old machinery and building materials embedded in thick ice. **1902** *Geol. Survey Bull. no. 67* (W.A.) vi. 79 They [*sc.* obsidianites] have been called '**Emu-stones**' in this State [W.A.]. **1946** C. FENNER *Gathered Moss* 101 They [*sc.* australites] are sometimes also called 'emu-stones', because emus swallow them.

emu /'imju/, *n.*[2] [See EMU-BOB.] See quot. 1966.

1966 S.J. BAKER *Austral. Lang.* (ed. 2) 237 *Emu*, a racecourse lounger who picks up discarded betting and tote tickets in the hope of finding one which has not been cashed. **1983** *Sydney Morning Herald* 23 Jan. 50/7 There was an epidemic of emus at Rosehill yesterday... 'Perhaps it is a sign of the recession times but I have never seen so many emus picking up discarded tote tickets at a race track .. ' Candrick said. **1984** *Age* (Melbourne) 20 Mar. 50/8 He picks up all the old betting tickets. They call them emus.

emu-bob, *v. intr.* To pick up pieces of timber, roots, etc., after clearing or burning; to collect litter. Also *trans.* (with an area as obj.)

1926 *Bulletin* (Sydney) 25 Feb. 24/1 While in Parilla (S.A.) stump-picking, or 'emu-bobbing' as the old hands termed it, I came across several of the little chaps [*sc.* opossom dormouse]. **1941** T.I. MOORE *Emu Parade* 12 Emu-bobbing, bending, down the line of huts We march at morning, picking up the litter. **1944** *Bulletin* (Sydney) 19 July 12/3 We were emu bobbing on contract and were close to finishing the 200-odd acres. **1949** *Ibid.* 1 June 11/2 As near as we could make it by stepping out the boundaries, we'd emu-bobbed about 400 acres. **1957** *Ibid.* 18 Sept. 19/4, I emu-bobbed five acres of 'Hungry's' back-paddocks. The big logs I rolled together with a crowbar. It took all day to get some where they were wanted then there was all the small stuff to gather up in armfuls; *real* emu-bobbing this.

Hence **emu-bobber** *n.*, **emu-bobbing** *vbl. n.*

1920 *Bulletin Bk. Humorous Verses* 187 A score of '**emu-bobbers**' came a-tramping from the Bland. **1959** H.P. TRITTON *Time means Tucker* 58 'Stick-pickers', or 'emu-bobbers' whose job was to pack the timber in heaps. **1948** *Bulletin* (Sydney) 19 May 23/1 We had inspected an **emu-bobbing** contract, battled the owner to a price and were set to start. **1959** H.P. TRITTON *Time means Tucker* 58 Emu-bobbing, for the benefit of the bush, is picking up the fallen timber. At a distance a group of men bending head-down and tails-up look very much like a flock of emus. **1978** M. WALKER *Pioneer Crafts Early Aust.* 85 The children played an integral part, gathering firewood in billy carts, home-made barrows and throwing the gathered Mallee roots onto the horse and dray, at the weekends. This occupation possessed the honorary title of 'Emu bobbing'. **1981** K. GARVEY *Rhymes of Ratbag* 174 I've .. Done a stint at emu-bobbing On the wide Nor'western plains.

enamel orchid. Either of the two orchids (fam. Orchidaceae) of s.w. W.A. *Elythranthera brunonis* and *E. emarginata* having glossy flowers of (respectively) purple and pink. Also *absol.* as **enamel.**

1951 R. ERICKSON *Orchids of West* 78 Outside the fence grows yet another orchid, a lovely Purple Enamel Orchid. The wax-like flowers would grace a queen's table. **1967** B.Y MAIN *Between Wodjil & Tor* 97 Purple enamel orchids glittered in the sunlight. **1978** L. WHITE *Memories of Childhood* 1 All the small orchids; spiders, donkeys, yellows, enamels.

endowment. CHILD-ENDOWMENT. Also *attrib.*

1933 J. TRURAN *Where Plain Begins* 140 What wi' the dole an' the endowment money, I'll guarantee there's a lot o' coves gettin' more sittin' on their tails than ever they made when they were workin'. **1945** J. DEVANNY *Bird of Paradise* 60 The endowment money .. was the big factor... We could see the children thriving. **1950** A. GROOM *I saw Strange Land* 107 There were several adopted orphans; and 240 people received Government rations and endowment. **1978** K. GILBERT *People are Legends* 11, I can't get me welfare cheque no more Nor me 'dowment, the man at the general store Gits me cheque 'n me 'dowment now.

en-suite, *n.* [f. Fr. *en suite, adv.* so as to form a suite; used in Br. English as *a.* and *adv.*] An en-suite bathroom; a bathroom leading off a bedroom.

1970 *Austral. Home Beautiful* Aug. 64 Walk-in robes adjoin a compact en-suite in this house. **1971** *Canberra Times* 17 Feb. 3/2, I shall broadcast the proceedings of the House of Representatives, yea, even of the Senate, into thine house, and into thy bedchamber, and into thy en-suite. **1984** *Ibid.* 14 Nov. 47/4 Extra large master bedroom with BIR and ensuite. **1986** *Nat. Times* (Sydney) 21 Feb. 14/4 An *en-suite* (with spa bath) for every bedroom.

entire. [Abbrev. of *entire horse.*] A stallion.

1848 *Observer* (Melbourne) 14 Sept. 205/4 Horses—The show of Entires took place at the Bazaar on Tuesday last. **1871** *Austral. Town & Country Jrnl.* (Sydney) 25 Mar. 363/4 See the very small entires with very large heads. **1891** D. FERGUSON *Vicissitudes Bush Life* 8 She'll have some foals by this time, but then they'll not be much worth, as they'll be got by some scrubber of an entire. **1929** K.S. PRICHARD *Coonardoo* (1961) 32 Mumae had bought a new stallion while she was away and Hugh was anxious to weed out crocks and old entires. **1961** *Bulletin* (Sydney) 3 May 51/2 It was through this happy association of Rocky with Lame Lass that the fact of his being an 'entire', which is to say a stallion, was discovered.

Enzed. Also **N.Z.** [Repr. pronunciation of the initial letters of *New Zealand.* Used elsewhere but recorded earliest in Aust.] A popular name for a New Zealander, esp. a New Zealand soldier; New Zealand. Also *attrib.*

1915 'LANCE-CORPORAL COBBER' *Anzac Pilgrim's Progress* (1918) 54 An' our Light Horse, the spry N.Z.'s, and the English boys, you bet. **1919** A. WRIGHT *Game of Chance* 63 Had to come at the mare from En zed. **1921** *Aussie* (Sydney) Aug. 17/1 The Aussies and Enzeds found each other on the battlefield. **1930** *Listening Post* (Perth) Jan. 15 Canadians, Enzeds and Diggers were present. **1944** *Sa-eeda Wog* 16/1 In answer to the challenge the Enzed one-pipper in charge yelled 'Waipukurau!' and drew a volley in reply. **1949** G. BERRIE *Morale* 71 A few .. were passed as fit .. : the remainder were shipped to Southhampton .. and they included an Enzed who protested strongly. **1977** C. MCCULLOUGH *Thorn Birds*, I swear that mare has the hardest mouth in En Zed.

Hence **Enzedder** *n.*, a New Zealander.

1933 H.B. RAINE *Whip-Hand* 19 Forty or more of the finest ships afloat sailing out one by one filled with Aussies and Enzedders! **1943** *Mulga* (Alice Springs) 10 Aug. 2 'En Zedders' First Used Word Digger. **1955** N. PULLIAM *I traveled Lonely Land* 57 New Zealand is variously the Quaky or the Shaky Island .. and its inhabitants are Enzedders, among other things. *Ibid.* 117 Australian girls? Ugly and unco-operative in comparison to the Enzedders. **1970** R. BEILBY *No Medals for Aphrodite* 166 The Aussies and Enzeders are into it again. **1978** P. ADAM SMITH *Anzacs* 287 Theo Ford remembers that 'by the end of 1917 we were all, Aussies and En-Zedders alike, calling one another 'Digger''.

epacris /ə'pækrəs/. [f. Gr. *ἐπί* upon + *ἄκρις* dative of *ἄκρου* summit, from the habitat of some species, orig. given to plants now otherwise classified, by the European naturalists J.R. and G. Forster (*Characteres Generum Plantarum* (1776) 19). The name was first applied to the modern genus *Epacris* by Spanish botanist A.J. Cavanilles (*Icon. et Descr. Plant* IV. (1797) 25).] A shrub (or occas. small tree) of the mainly s.e. Austral. genus *Epacris* (fam. Epacridaceae), some of which bear attractive tube-shaped flowers. See also HEATH.

1805 *Curtis's Bot. Mag.* (London) XXII. 844 (*heading*) Rigid Epacris. **1825** B. FIELD *Geogr. Mem. N.S.W.* 422 All the other indigenous trees and shrubs, that I have seen are evergreens .. the exquisite epacris, the curious grevillea. **1845** *Colonial Lit. Jrnl.* 13 Feb. 106/2 Wild cotton, epacris, and rose. **1852** J. BONWICK *Notes of Gold Digger* 6 The modest cup of the beautiful epacris. **1871** *Austral. Town & Country Jrnl.* (Sydney) 7 Jan. 18/4 A few tall crimson spikes of Epacris. **1890** 'MRS A. MACLEOD' *Austral. Girl* (1894) 108 She discovered a whole range-side of early epacris. The brief blossoming season of the region was yet two months off, yet here were acres of this radiant native heath. **1971** G. WISEWOULD *Outpost* 148 The lesser growth .. of 'heath'—the white, pink and red epacris—which is the first to flower starting in mid-June, early winter. **1986** *Canberra Times* 30 Jan. (Suppl.) 11/5 Depending on the time of year, even the less knowledgable gardener will find the 'familiar' growing in the park as nature intended .. kunzea .. and epacris.

eremophila /ɛrə'mɒfələ/. [The name *Eremophila* was given in 1810 by the British botanist Robert Brown (*Prodr. Fl. Nov. Holl.* 518), from the Gr. *ἐρῆμος* desert and *φιλο-* loving, referring to the arid habitat of members of the genus.] Any shrub or small tree of the large genus of mainland Aust. *Eremophila* (fam. Myoporaceae), esp. prevalent in dry inland W.A., and bearing usu. tubular or bell-shaped flowers. See also *emu bush* (a), EMU *n.*[1] 3, POVERTY BUSH.

1935 H. BASEDOW *Knights of Boomerang* 78 The workers carry the honey from the mulga ('acacia') and eremophila blossom to the favoured ants. **1948** C.P. MOUNTFORD *Brown Men & Red Sand* 93 Nearby were the terra-cotta sand-hills, dotted with .. the eremophilas. **1971** J.N. HUTCHINSON *N.W. Austral. Wildflowers* 14 Eremophilas are hardy shrubs which survive under severe conditions.

erky, *a.* [Prob. f. *erk*, orig. a naval rating, later a term of contempt.] Disagreeable, unpleasant.

1959 D. HEWETT *Bobbin Up* 119, I don't like this stew. It's erky. **1960** K. SMITH *Word from Children* 43 It boiled over and ran down the sides of the stove. It looked all erky, too.

escort. *Hist.*

a. *Gold escort*, see GOLD 3. Also *attrib.*

1852 *Murray's Guide to Gold Diggings* 38 The escort came in yesterday from the 'diggings' with £70,000 worth of gold. **1853** J. SHERER *Gold Finder Aust.* 64 The private escort arrived in town .. bringing 32,000 ounces. **1859** P. JUST *Aust.* 42 The escort was established on the 30th of September; and upon that date .. 123,835 ounces were conveyed to town. **1872** 'QUIRIS' *Port Darwin* 17 The escort carried away .. 11,060 oz. **1882** A.J. BOYD *Old Colonials* 184 The help of the black troopers is often very acceptable to the escort. **1894** *Bulletin* (Sydney) 28 Apr. 9/3 Coolgardie road again blocked for want of water. The escort horses had only two drinks in 130 miles. **1915** A.T.M. Johnson *Austral. Life* 107 He .. finished his escapades by smashing the 'Escort' at Deep Creek Hill.

b. The consignment carried by a gold escort.

1859 *Colonial Mining Jrnl.* Feb. 93/1 Our last escort is about 2000 ozs.—an increase on the previous one. **1870** *Sydney Morning Herald* 5 July 2/4 We shall soon be able to make up a pretty good escort of gold got in the Valley, as for months past had it not been for Major's Creek, Bell's Creek, and other places round about, we should have shown very poor escorts.

Esky. Also **esky.** [Proprietary name.] A portable insulated container in which food and drink is kept cool.

1953 *Hardware Jrnl.* Nov. 95 The Esky Auto Box is one of the fastest selling lines ever to come out of the Malley's stables... It's a portable ice refrigerator, big enough to take a man-sized family picnic lunch plus six nice cold bottles! **1962** *Austral. Official Jrnl. Patents* (Canberra) 1997 *Esky* A170,377. 2nd Nov., 1961. Cooling apparatus and equipment inclusive of portable ice boxes. Malleys Ltd. **1965** *Oz* (Sydney) May 6/2 Joan Sutherland staggers out of smoking bush with an esky full of Millers New slung over her back. **1973** *Australasian Post* (Melbourne) 18 Jan. 37 Use the word 'Esky' lightly—and you'll get a lightweight imitation. Esky—the registered trade-mark of Malley's original steel ice-box. Yet somehow the name of our product became the name of the game. **1976** A. Buzo *Martello Towers* 30 Look, why don't we take the boat up river with an esky full of booze and knock off a few oyster leases. **1980** C. Kelen *Punks Travels* 50 On the beach below me the browning girls wait manacled up in bikinis next to full eskies. **1982** A. Jute *Festival* 38 Under the table was a styrene cooler, in the vernacular .. an 'esky' and a status symbol judged by the number of 'tinnies' of beer it would hold.

Esperance doctor: see Doctor *n.*[3]

establishment. *W.A. Obs.* [Joc. use of *establishment* a public institution.] With **the:** a local name for the Fremantle Gaol.

1857 M.B. Hale *Transportation Question* 8 The men commit some offence against ticket-of-leave discipline, and are committed again to the Establishment. **1865** 'Special Correspondent' *Transportation* 32 The men .. are removed to Fremantle Gaol... They are not detained long, however, at the 'establishment', or 'college', as it is termed. **1872** *Mission Life* (Perth) 1 Aug. 466 The population consisting mostly of convicts, Government officials connected with the 'Establishment'—as by an amusing euphemism the prison is styled. **1878** G. Walch *Australasia* 47 The large gaol, or 'establishment', as they politely term it. **1891** J.J. Roche *Life J.B. O'Reilly* 69 The great white stone prison which represents Fremantle's reason for existence. It was 'The Establishment'. **1897** Z.W. Pease *Catalpa Exped.* 114 Mr Breslin was invited to inspect the prison, 'The Establishment', as they call it in the colony.

eucalypt. Abbrev. of Eucalyptus.

1877 F. von Mueller *Introd. Bot. Teachings* 7 The vernacular name of Gum-trees for the Eucalypts. **1888** *Sydney Morning Herald* 24 Jan. 1/6 Next to the cedar, for usefulness, are the various kinds of hardwood, being mostly eucalypts and myrtaceous trees. **1928** G.H. Wilkins *Undiscovered Aust.* 57 The ordinary trees of the Australian bush: eucalypts, acacias, and hakeas. **1934** W.A. Osborne *Visitor to Aust.* 64 *Eucalypts.* Originally and well named Aromadendron, the genus obtained its present name in 1788 from the lid or cap which so well covers the young blooms. **1954** J. Waten *Unbending* 12 The remarkable flora and fauna in Australia, the eucalypts, the white cockatoos and black swans, wombats and kangaroos. **1965** G. McInnes *Road to Gundagai* 14 They sent out a strange and daring perfume of eucalypt. **1984** *Canberra Times* 12 Dec. 25/3, I think that I shall never hum a tune as lovely as a gum. A tune can be a dreadful clamour While every eucalypt has glamour.

eucalyptic, *a.* Of or pertaining to the eucalyptus. Also **eucalypti, eucalyptian,** and *fig.*

1838 *Tegg's N.S.W. Pocket Almanac* 13 The poles should be made from stringy bark or other *Eucalyptic* trees. **1855** W. Howitt *Land, Labor & Gold* II. 279 The eternal sameness of the eucalyptic forests. **1866** *Sydney Punch* 17 Nov. 203/2 We'll leave the mud-built city far behind us And dwell beneath the eucalyptic shade. **1870** A.L. Gordon *Bush Ballads* 8 When the gnarl'd knotted trunks Eucalyptian Seem carved like weird columns Egyptian. **1872** Mrs E. Millett *Austral. Parsonage* 43 Another kind of eucalyptic tree, commonly called in the colony the red gum. **1892** 'A.M.' *From Aust. & Japan* 19, I shouldn't be very sorry to grow grey in the midst of this eucalyptic cloisterdom. **1899** *Truth* (Sydney) 5 Mar. 3/1, I am one of the people—just a simple, plain, blunt, ordinary eucalypti sort. **1945** J.F. Blight *Old Pianist* 7 Perhaps alone he understood A world of eucalyptian hills.

eucalyptol. A common (and formerly scientific) name for the volatile oil cineole, a principal component of pharmaceutical-grade eucalyptus oil.

1884 *Pall Mall Gaz.* (London) 28 July 12/2 Any preparation from which the slightest odour of eucalyptol is diffused. **1899** *Bulletin* (Sydney) 9 Dec. 20/2 He .. boiled young gum leaves in the hope they might yield eucalyptol. **1920** Baker & Smith *Research on Eucalypts* (ed. 2) 357 *(heading)* Cineol (or Eucalyptol). **1977** R. Genders *Scented Flora* 75 Eucalyptol (or cineol) is present in the essential oil of a number of plants.

eucalyptus. Pl. **eucalypti.** [f. Gr. εὖ well *(adv.)* καλυπτός and covered, referring to the bud and the operculum which covers it before the flower opens; the genus was named by the French botanist Charles Louis L'Héritier (*Sertum Anglicum* (1788) 18), from specimens of *Eucalyptus obliqua* collected at Adventure Bay, Tas.]

1. a. Any tree of the genus *Eucalyptus.* See Gum tree 1. Also *attrib.*

1801 *HRA* (1915) 1st Ser. III. 175 The trees very lofty, mostly blue gum (Eucalyptus). **1807** Banks Papers 20 Jan. XX. 335 The genus Eucalyptus must be revised, and fresh specimens collected. **1814** R. Brown *Gen. Remarks Bot. Terra Australis* 15 Mr Caley has observed within the limits of the colony of Port Jackson nearly 50 species of Eucalyptus, most of which are distinguished, and have proper names applied to them, by the native inhabitants, who from differences in the colour, texture, and scaling of the bark, and in the ramification and general appearance of these trees, more readily distinguish them than botanists have as yet been able to do. **1837** J. Backhouse *Extracts from Lett.* (1839) v. 13 There were scattered eucalypti. **1839** J. Stephens *Land of Promise* 62 The timber trees principally consist of various species of *Eucalyptus*, commonly called gum-tree. **1846** *Moreton Bay Courier* 8 Aug. 3/2 Eucalyptus trees flourish luxuriantly. **1868** *Illustr. Sydney News* 16 Jan. 294/1 A Mr Ramel has patented in Victoria eucalyptus cigars made from the leaves of gum trees. **1920** *Huon Times* (Franklin) 22 Oct. 4/5 When twilight greys the light and shadows deepen the green, the Eucalyptus trees gain new beauty. **1927** R.S. Browne *Journalist's Memories* 259 Ring-barked eucalypti figured numerously. **1933** C.W. Peck *Austral. Legends* (ed. 2) 202 Eucalypti turned their leaf-edges to the sun. **1948** F. Clune *Wild Colonial Boys* 77 The eucalyptus forest, growing tall and thick on the eastern coastal slopes. **1958** C. Koch *Boys in Island* 16 They wait, the dead-quiet eucalyptus gullies, the damp bracken hollows.

b. Ellipt. for *eucalyptus oil.* Also *attrib.*

1960 B. Harney *Cook Bk.* 88 The red young tips of the gum tree, plucked off and eaten, relieve pain in the stomach. The basic ingredient, 'crude eucalyptus', is the medicine. **1982** R. Hall *Just Relations* 84 She placed the cat in the open box of eucalyptus drops... The cat purred from its bed of lollies.

2. Special Comb. **eucalyptus leaf,** Gumleaf b.; **oil,** any of several volatile oils of trees of the genus *Eucalyptus* valued for medicinal and germicidal properties; Eucy.

1971 *Bulletin* (Sydney) 15 May 25/1 He's also a dab hand at blowing American and Australian tunes on the **eucalyptus leaf** and throwing boomerangs. **1876** E. Cooper *Forest Culture & Eucalyptus Trees* 60 We have in Australia a resource of our own in the **Eucalyptus oil.** **1891** J. Fenton *Bush Life Tas.* (1964) 29 Grilling in front of the fire by means of a forked stick, prepared for the occasion out of a sapling, redolent of the fumes of eucalyptus oil. **1911** *Huon Times* (Franklin) 9 Dec. 2/5 Clennett and Brown are going to lay down a plant for distilling Eucalyptus oil. **1913** *Emu* XII. 270 Comfortable homesteads, with neat gardens, eucalyptus oil factories, and a macadamised road. **1924** *New Settlers' Handbk. Vic.* 21 Among the by-products are tan-barks, eucalyptus oil. **1935** T. Rayment *Cluster of Bees* 560 Mr Cope, a South Australian distiller of eucalyptus-oil. **1983** Lassak & McCarthy *Austral. Med. Plants* 46 Without any doubt eucalyptus oil is Australia's most important and best known contribution to medicine.

euchre, *v.* [See next.] *trans.* To destroy.

1974 *Austral.* (Sydney) 12 Oct. 19/2 He sits in the mayoral car ('So many dials and buttons! I hope I don't euchre this thing').

euchred, *ppl. a.* [Transf. use of U.S. *euchred* outwitted, orig. in the card game.] Exhausted, finished, 'at the end of one's tether'.

1932 W. Hatfield *Ginger Murdoch* 194, I always think of you there that time absolutely euchred, cryin' like hell. **1935** I.L. Idriess *Man Tracks* 267 We're euchred; not a breath of wind. **1946** K.S. Prichard *Roaring Nineties* 47 I've got to get water for me horses at the next tank, or we're euchred. **1951** I.L. Idriess *Across Nullarbor* 36, I believe we're euchred. Can't find a way out of this tangle at all. **1962** *Overland* xxvii. 7, I can hardly see... I'm euchered. **1973** J. Morrison *Austral. by Choice* 83 This man has worked hard in Australia for forty years, but he's euchred now... All he asks for is the old age pension. **1975** D.E. Kelsey *Shackle* 40 'We are euchred,' the poor fellow replied.

Eucla doctor: see Doctor *n.*[3]

eucy /'juki/. Also **eucky, euky.** Abbrev. of *eucalyptus oil* (see Eucalyptus 2). Also **eucy oil.**

1977 *Overland* lxvi. 7 That eucy is the real McCoy, not that diluted stuff you buy... When she's moppin' the floor .. put just a couple of drops in the water. Makes the house smell good. **1978** W. Lowenstein *Weevils in Flour* 48 The next day I'm back on the eucky with the old man. **1982** M. Walker *Making Do* 75 I've got the eucalyptus bottle, which was my mother's old favourite for us kids when we had colds. The eucy oil seems to alleviate the rough voice and the rough children. **1984** *Sun News Pictorial* (Melbourne) 2 Aug. 3/3 Arthur said 'euky oil' could cure anything from a runny nose to tired feet—and, naturally, his brew was the best at the princely sum of $1 a bottle.

eugari, var. Ugari.

Euraustralian. See quot. 1936. Also as *adj.*

1936 *Publicist* (Sydney) i. 15/1 The Aboriginal blends perfectly with the European to make a superior new type of human being, the Euraustralians. **1963** X. Herbert *Disturbing Element* 82 Handsome Euraustralian people are amongst the most beautiful of the human species. **1983** *Bulletin* (Sydney) 1 Nov. 80/2 The 'Old People' .. would never get their rights without the loving efforts of those of what I called the New Aboriginal Race, the Euraustralians.

Eureka. [a. Gr. εὕρηκα used as the name of a lead in the Ballarat goldfield.]

1. A clash between gold-miners and the police and military at Ballarat in 1854, now a symbol of republicanism. Also *attrib.*

[**1853** Mrs C. Clacy *Lady's Visit to Gold Diggings* 207 About seven miles to the north of Ballarat, some new diggings called the Eureka have been discovered.] **1906** *Gadfly* (Adelaide) 20 June 8/1 Dyson's first-hand knowledge of the Eureka days. **1948** F. Clune *Wild Colonial Boys* 204 Insurrection is in the air. The word 'Eureka' is frequently heard. **1965** D. Martin *Hero of Too* 29 Ghosts of gold miners, ghosts of Eureka, ghosts of mangled but indomitable men. **1978** B. Oakley *Ship's Whistle* (1979) 35 *Alf*: A mob of diggers heading our way. *Horne*: Oh no, not another Eureka!

2. Special Comb. **Eureka flag,** a blue flag bearing a white cross with a star at the end of each arm, first raised at the *Eureka stockade*; Southern Cross 2 a.; **stockade,** the site of the clash; so **stockader.**

1896 *Ballarat Courier* 1 May 4/5 He enclosed to me a fragment of the **Eureka flag,** given to Mrs Clendinning by Dr Alfred Carr who was doing .. general medical duties of the camp at that time. **1945** *Tribune* (Sydney) 17 July 4/4 When he began to interrogate old Ballarat diggers who had seen the Eureka flag, he found that 'some thought it was blue, some white, one actually had seen a black flag'. **1947** *Meanjin* 107 We've been accustomed to think vaguely of the Eureka flag as simply four or five silver stars on pale blue silk. **1963** L. Fox *Strange*

Story Eureka Flag 20 The Eureka flag is . . important not only in relation to the historic fight at the Stockade, but also as one of a number of Southern Cross flags which have been symbols of the aspirations of our people. **1966** F. CAYLEY *Flag of Stars* 70 The Eureka Flag, which originally measured about twelve feet by eight feet, has been variously depicted as having (on a blue ground) an elegant silver cross with silver stars, or alternatively as having a very simple white cross with white stars. **1973** *Bulletin* (Sydney) 17 Feb. 5/3 The 'Eureka' flag is the natural and obvious choice. **1976** *Ibid.* 21 Aug. 6/1 The Eureka Stockade flag was the symbol of resistance against oppressive legislation enacted by the alleged peers of . . the miners. This flag should enjoy an honored place in the history of this country. **1854** *Argus* (Melbourne) 11 Dec. 5/4 John Badcock, a constable at Ballarat, was present at the **Eureka Stockade** on Sunday morning when it was charged. **1855** R. CARBONI *Eureka Stockade* 57 The Council of the Eureka Stockade never gave or hinted at any order to stop the usual work on the gold-field. **1856** H.B. STONEY *Vic.* 136 He died from the effects of wounds received on the 3rd instant, while bravely leading his company in storming the Eureka stockade. **1859** R.H. HORNE *Austral. Facts & Prospects* 31 It was at Warranga that the great émeute occurred on the question of licence-fees, and heralded the Eureka stockade affair, which took place not very long after. **1904** *Bulletin* (Sydney) 25 Feb. 16/2 An old Eureka Stockader . . was sinking a shaft at Ballarat when he broke into a drive where there were six dead Chinamen. **1955** G. HEALEY *A.L.P.* 8 General dissatisfaction among the miners led to bloodshed at Eureka on Sunday morning 3rd December, 1854, when twenty miners and six soldiers lost their lives in the so-called Eureka Stockade.

euro /'jurou/. Chiefly *S.A.* and *W.A.* Formerly also **uro, yura.** [a. Adnyamadhanha *yuru.*] The reddish, short-haired macropod *Macropus robustus erubescens*, a sub-species of the WALLAROO, of drier Aust. west of the Great Dividing Range.

[**1841** C.G. TEICHELMANN *Aborigines S.A.* 8 They say, the milky way is a large river. . . The darker spots in it are water lagoons, in which monsters called *yura* are living.] **1855** J. BONWICK *Geogr. Aust. & N.Z.* (ed. 3) 199 The Euro, by Lake Torrens, reaches six feet in height. **1863** J.B. AUSTIN *Mines S.A.* 44 The uro, or huro, is a variety of the kangaroo distinguished chiefly, for its skin being covered with hair, while the common kangaroo has a wooly [*sic*] kind of fur. **1896** B. SPENCER *Rep. Horn Sci. Exped. Central Aust.* II. 14 *Macropus robustus*. . . This is the 'Wallaroo' of Queensland and the inland parts of New South Wales and the 'Euro' of South Australia. **1900** R. BRUCE *Benbonuna* (1904) 86 Loosely-furred euros. **1934** *Bulletin* (Sydney) 17 Jan. 20/4 Winnie, our pet euro (Westralian rock kangaroo), had a liking for softgoods. **1975** D. STUART *Walk, trot, canter & Die* 40 A good night camp, with a fat euro, the sturdy hill-kangaroo falling to the spear of one of the men.

European. *Obs.* [Spec. use of *European* one of European extraction who lives elsewhere: see OED(S.] A (British) immigrant to Australia, as distinct from an Australian-born descendant of an immigrant; a non-Aboriginal inhabitant of Australia. Also as *adj.*

1832 *Currency Lad* (Sydney) 1 Dec. 2 We commenced our political career with the expressed determination of publishing the sentiments of the Currency Lads. Whether we do so or not, we leave our countrymen to determine. Many Europeans were surprised at the intemperance, as they termed it, of our last leader. **1840** *S. Austral. Gaz.* (Adelaide) 23 July 7 The great question at issue in the present correspondence—whether the aboriginal inhabitants or the European preliminary purchasers have the first right of selection from the waste lands of the province—is one of bare justice. **1842** *Sydney Morning Herald* 1 Aug. 1/3 Have the Aboriginal Blacks such a prescriptive right to the soil of Australia as to have been extinguished by the occupancy of Europeans? **1843** W. PRIDDEN *Aust.* 122 One day, fired with a wish to emulate his betters, the black man assumes the costume of an European, likes to be close-shaved, wears a white neck-cloth, and means to become entirely 'a white fellow'. **1850** *Britannia* (Hobart) 31 Oct. 2/3 Cambridge Ploughing Match. . . *Native Ploughman*: Samuel Joseph, 1st prize. *European*: John Lee, 1st prize. **1855** G.H. WATHEN *Golden Colony* 20 Above the aboriginal scrub, however, appear the towers and public buildings of the European city. **1869** *Bushmen, Publicans, & Politics* 5 We allude to the country-born Europeans, or as we generally style them, Natives. **1878** R.B. SMYTH *Aborigines of Vic.* I. 51 That there are instances, occasionally, of culpable negligence should not warrant us in stating that the affection of the Aboriginal parents for their children is less than that of the best educated amongst Europeans. **1880** *Bulletin* (Sydney) 4 Sept. 13/2 The narrative does not state whether 'Charlie' was a European or a blackfellow.

exclusionist. *Hist.* [Spec. use of *exclusionist* one who would exclude another from some privilege: see OED.] One opposed to the integration of ex-convicts into Australian society. Also *attrib.*

1826 *Monitor* (Sydney) 30 June 53/2 We rejoice that the impotent folks, yclept 'The Exclusionists', are not the only persons who can live in the style and adopt the manners of gentlemen. **1827** P. CUNNINGHAM *Two Yrs. in N.S.W.* II. 118 One subdivision of the emigrant class . . is termed the *exclusionist* party, from their strict exclusion of the emancipists from their society. **1835** *Colonist* (Sydney) 22 Jan. 29/2 Neither threw himself into the hands of the emancipists, like Sir Thomas Brisbane at the close of his government, nor into those of the exclusionists, as General Darling is asserted to have done. **1843** W. PRIDDEN *Aust.* 237 The *exclusionists*, who were free settlers, refused to associate at all with those that had ever been convicts. **1852** J. WEST *Hist. of Tas.* II. 152 Mr W.C. Wentworth, turned the artillery of his wrath against the exclusionists. **1881** J.F.V. FITZGERALD *Aust.* 54 Negro blood does not more rigorously exclude from society in New York, than did the smallest taint of convictism from the social circle of the 'Exclusionists'. **1967** D. HORNE *Southern Exposure* 10 The division between 'exclusionists' (those who had no convict blood) and 'emancipists' . . was maintained.

exclusive. Chiefly in *pl. Hist.* [f. *exclusive, a.* of a class of society disposed to resist the admission of outsiders: see OED 9.] EXCLUSIONIST. Also as *adj.*

1836 *Colonist* (Sydney) 28 Jan. 27/4 Our *Pure Merino*, our *Exclusive* contemporaries, who have been abusing the Governor. **1841** *Port Phillip Patriot* 10 May 2/7 A gentleman, a member of the Melbourne Club, and moreover one of the 'Exclusives'. **1841** *Morning Advertiser* (Hobart) 3 Sept. 3/2 Must the *exclusives* come to Launceston for justice? **1841** *Launceston Courier* 18 Oct. 2/3 To-morrow is the day appointed for revising and settling the Jury List; an occasion, which for many years past, has given rise to much vigorous contention between the 'liberals' and 'exclusives'. **1904** *Truth* (Sydney) 29 May 7/3 Was it that the 'exclusives' were toadies enough to go to Government House, knowing well Macquarie's partiality for the 'birthstained'? **1962** B. BEATTY *With Shame Remembered* 115 Bitter quarrels were frequent between the emancipists and the 'exclusives' throughout Macquarie's term of office.

Executive Council. The constitutional body, in an Australian Colony (later State) or, since 1901, in the Commonwealth, responsible for the implementation of the laws.

1825 *Sydney Gaz.* 22 Dec., *The Governor* takes this Opportunity to notify, that *His Majesty* has been pleased to constitute an *Executive Council* for this Government. **1839** *Sydney Standard* 7 Jan. 2/4 The Executive Council should continue as at present, in order that the colony might be fairly represented in the Legislative Council. **1845** M. COLLISSON *S.A.* 10 The administration of the affairs of the colony is at present vested in a Governor, conjointly with a Legislative Council and an Executive Council. **1857** *Royal S. Austral. Almanack* 31 The political administration of South Australia includes several phases. The province was at first governed exclusively by the Governor and Executive Council. **1859** *Qld. Govt. Gaz.* 10 Dec. 2/2 It is expedient that an Executive Council should be appointed to advise and assist you. **1873** A. TROLLOPE *Aust. & N.Z.* I. 245 The Upper House, or Legislative Council, in Sydney is dignified and conservative. . . The Executive Council consists of the Governor and seven ministers—one of whom must be in the Legislative Council. **1900** *Act* (G.B.) 63 & 64 Vict. no. 12 Sect. 62, There shall be a Federal Executive Council to advise the Governor-General. **1934** F.A. BLAND *Planning Modern State* 6 Constitutionally, the members of the Executive Council are chosen and summoned by the Governor or Governor-General. **1946** W. DENNING *Inside Parliament* 43 The Executive Council exists merely to rubber-stamp decisions made by the Cabinet. **1973** *Bulletin* (Sydney) 27 Jan. 12/2 As recently as 1956 the Governor of Tasmania insisted that he had the right to refuse to accept the advice of the Government of Tasmania and act contrary to Executive Council advice in the terms of his British Instructions. **1986** *Canberra Times* 23 Apr. 2/4 Sir Ninian presided at a meeting of the Federal Executive Council at Government House.

Hence **Executive Councillor** *n.*, a member of the Executive Council.

1825 *AJCP* 851 C.O. 380/140 fo. 88, The persons so appointed by you shall be to all intents and purposes Executive Councillors within our said Territory. **1840** *Tasmanian Weekly Dispatch* (Hobart) 21 Feb. 7/2 Mr Gregory is suspended as an Executive Councillor.

exile. *Hist.* One convicted and imprisoned in Britain, and sent to the Port Phillip District on a conditional pardon which prevented return to Britain until the expiration of sentence. See also PENTONVILLE. Also *attrib.*

1844 *HRA* (1925) 1st Ser. XXIII. 700 The result of our deliberations on the subject is first of all to convince us that there is no sufficient reason why the better class of Prisoners, who have served the prescribed period of secluded punishment at Parkhurst and Pentonville should be transported as Convicts at all. We apprehend that they may with equal advantage to Society at large and with greater benefit to themselves be sent to Australia as Exciles [*sic*]. That is, it appears to us that this class of persons should leave this Country with Free pardons qualified only by the condition of their not returning hither until the expiration of their Sentences. *Ibid.* XXIV. 60 The formation of a labour Depot to be recruited by Prisoners sent from this Country as Exiles, not as Convicts. **1845** *Portland Gaz.* 1 Jan. 3/2 In the absence of the ordinary means of obtaining free immigration, it will be beneficial to the province of Port Phillip to receive the class of men from the Pentonville Penitentiary, denominated 'Exiles'. **1847** *Port Phillip Herald* 7 Jan. (Suppl.), The British Government has sent from England nearly 500 exiles from the Pentonville and Parkhurst prisons. **1848** *Maitland Mercury* 26 July 2/4 Now, if the squatters got exile labour, and paid wages—not in money, but with the stripes and triangles . . what would become of the business of these establishments? **1851** *Empire* (Sydney) 24 Jan. 2/3 The perfection of the social system has been attained when the relation of Master and Servant has become that of Squatter and 'Exile'. **1852** G.B. EARP *Gold Colonies Aust.* 100 The convict system ceased in New South Wales in 1839; but 'exiles', as they were termed, *i.e.* men who had passed their probation at home, were forwarded till 1843. **1871** *Illustr. Sydney News* 15 May 80/1 Conditionally pardoned Convicts . . were known by the name of 'exiles'. **1882** W. COOTE *Hist. Colony Qld.* 78 In this part of the then colony, the friends of the 'exiles', the mild term then in fashion, were in the ascendant. **1911** A.L. HAYDON *Trooper Police Aust.* 368 The outlying settlers were those most in favour of the employment of 'exiles', as the felon immigrants were termed.

Hence **exile** *v. trans.*; **exileism** *n.*, the practice of sending prisoners to Australia on conditional pardon; the prisoners so treated.

1847 *Port Phillip Herald* 7 Jan. (Suppl.), The experiment of **exiling** the inmates of Pentonville Prison has been attended with perfect success. **1862** BACKHOUSE & TYLOR *Life & Labours G.W. Walker* 517 A new scheme of Transportation was projected. The convicted offender . . was . . to serve, first a year of probationary discipline. . . Next, a three years' term of hard labour . . and lastly to be 'exiled' to Tasmania. **1847** *Maitland Mercury* 20 Oct. 2/1 **Exileism**, as at present contemplated by the Whig Ministry, is, in fact, only deferred transportation. **1848** *Ibid.* 29 Apr. 3/2 One public writer in the colony has raised his voice against this threatened influx of exileism. **1849** *Britannia* (Hobart) 22 Feb. 4/3 The last act in the moral masquerade of Exileism has been performed. **1850** *Sydney Morning Herald* 28 Sept. 2/4 Since 1848, when he voted in favour of exileism, the circumstances of the colony had changed.

experience. *Obs.* Shortened form of COLONIAL EXPERIENCE *n.* 1. Also *attrib.*

1872 G.S. BADEN-POWELL *New Homes for Old Country* 156 The storekeeper is usually some youth getting his 'experience', and he takes charge of the store and books, and lends a hand generally on the run. ***c* 1892** J. CAMERON *Fire Stick* 62 A prostrate Unionist . . was being belaboured by a big lump of a lad, the youngest of the experience men. **1897** *Bulletin* (Sydney) 2 Oct. 32/2 When young Wilkins . . began his course of 'experience' on Serano, he naturally thought the knowledge of how to crack a stockwhip was the very first requisite of a bush education. **1913** *Ibid.* 16 Jan. 14/2 He was out on a station for experience, and he wasn't imported goods either. We were on the road with sheep. The fence on one side of the 'break' for a couple of panels was not too safe for the first night's camp; so 'Sydney' was sent ahead and told to 'brush up' the wire at the back of the canvas. . . When we arrived Sydney was still hard at work 'brushing up' the fence. But not with timber and small boughs. He had a tin of polish.

expert, *n.*

a. One responsible for the maintenance of machinery, esp. in a shearing-shed. Also *attrib.*

1910 C.E.W. BEAN *On Wool Track* 195 The expert (the man in the engine-room). **1923** J. MOSES *Beyond City Gates* 25 The binder is out of order; I can't get the expert chap to fix it up. **1928** L.A. SIGSWORTH *Various Verse* 2 The experts 'smooge' to the shearers, too, and the pen men stand in awe. **1933** J. TRURAN *Where Plain Begins* 147 The 'expert' . . was responsible for keeping the machines oiled and adjusted, and the shearer's 'cutters' in good order. **1953** *Bulletin* (Sydney) 4 Mar. 12/3 Declaring shearing 'off' for the day, they stopped the engine, assaulted the 'expert', menaced the boss of the board and remained in undisputed command of an idle shed. **1969** J. CARTER *Four-Wheel Drive Swagman* 105 An 'expert' in the bush is a sort of Mr Fixit to a shearing team. **1979** HARMSWORTH & DAY *Wool & Mohair* 150 The *expert* is in charge of the machinery. His duties are to drive the engine, attend to the overhead gear and hand pieces, and sharpen the shearers' combs and cutters. **1980** P. FREEMAN *Woolshed* 20 The introduction of machine shears meant that an 'expert' was often employed to sharpen the shearer's handpieces on the grinder.

b. *transf.* The manager of a team of shearers.

1967 G. JENKIN *Two Yrs. Bardunyah Station* 66 But for the lowly rouseabout there is no battle—only work and a bit of skylarking when the boss-of-the-board (known usually as the 'Expert' or the 'Super') isn't looking. **1977** J. DOUGHTY *Gold in Blood* 37 They got into trouble with the 'expert' (usual name for the team manager) for arriving late to work.

expert, *v.* [f. prec.] *intr.* To maintain the machinery in a shearing shed. Chiefly as *vbl. n.*

1944 A.E. MINNIS *And All Trees are Green* 97 'I suppose he does the boss of the boarding himself?' 'Yes, and the woolclassing *and* the experting.' **1952** *Bulletin* (Sydney) 12 Nov. 13/1 Many a man is capable of doing his own classing as well as 'experting', and shearing or crutching a few hundred sheep himself. **1960** *Ibid.* 23 Mar. 16/3 My brother had been 'experting' in sheds for years. **1969** J. CARTER *Four-Wheel Drive Swagman* 105 'Experting' is a trade in which you can be specially trained at places like the School of Sheep and Wool. **1980** P. FREEMAN *Woolshed* 20 At Kingsvale and most small sheds, the shearer himself did the 'experting'.

expiree. *Hist.* An ex-convict; one whose term of sentence has expired. Also **expiree convict.**

1829 *Sydney Monitor* 15 Aug. (Suppl.), *Expirees*, or those who have served the full period of their sentences, are to all intents and purposes . . restored to all constitutional privileges. **1835** G. ARTHUR *Defence of Transportation* 46 Should the emancipist, or expiree, or ticket-of-leave labourer, be placed on the same footing with the immigrant labourer? **1843** *Sydney Morning Herald* 19 Oct. 2/3 Expiree convicts . . landed in the district of Port Phillip from Van Diemen's Land. **1845** *Observer* (Hobart) 2 Dec. 2/5 It is proposed to give grants of land to *expirees.* **1855** G.H. WATHEN *Golden Colony* 179 In the towns the force was almost worthless. Its ranks had been supplied by *expiree* convicts from Van Diemen's land; but these robbed the citizens whom they were paid to protect. **1865** 'SPECIAL CORRESPONDENT' *Transportation* 41 None of the expirees who have become employers of labour would take a free man so long as they can obtain a 'ticketer'. **1883** E.M. CURR *Recoll. Squatting Vic.* 40 Labourers (almost all old gaol-birds and expiree convicts). **1894** J.K. ARTHUR *Kangaroo & Kauri* 6 A few ticket-of-leave men and some expirees are still to be met, but the monstrous evil of convict importation has long ceased to exist. **1904** *Bulletin* (Sydney) 17 Nov. 40/1, I found food for reflection in the autobiography of an old Sydney-side expiree. **1962** B. BEATTY *With Shame Remembered* 114 An 'expiree' was a convict who had served his term of imprisonment.

extended claim. See quot. 1869.

1869 R.B. SMYTH *Gold Fields & Mineral Districts* 610 *Extended claim*, a block or frontage claim, the extent of which has been increased by the annexation to the original claim of an additional area of ground or length of lead, or by the amalgamation of one or more claims with the original claim. **1881** A.C. GRANT *Bush-Life Qld.* II. 253 The discoverers of a new and payable field are entitled to a certain reward, sometimes in money, and at others in extended claims, or both. **1882** T.F. DE C. BROWNE *Miners' Handy Bk.* 22 *An extended claim.* Regulation 39 deals with this class of claim, which may be any area not less than *three* acres nor more than *twenty-five* acres of 'old and abandoned ground'. **1931** C.B. SMITH *Austral. Gold Prospectors' Handbk.* 62 The following claims must be registered within twenty-eight days after possession is taken:- . . Extended alluvial claim. Sluicing claim.

extra-colonial, *a. Obs.* Outside an Australian Colony.

1835 *Van Diemen's Land Monthly Mag.* Sept. 6 We need to apologise to all extra-colonial readers. **1860** *S. Austral. Advertiser* (Adelaide) 5 July 1/4 *Extracolonial circulation of the 'Advertiser' and 'Chronicle'.*—These papers are now regularly transmitted to various places . . in Great Britain and Ireland, India, Cape of Good Hope, Mauritius, the Australian Colonies, &c., &c., &c. **1865** 'W.R.L.' *Our Wool Staple* 11 For the benefit of extra-colonial readers, it is deemed advisable to introduce the following pages with a few words of explanation.

-ey, var. -Y.

eye. [Transf. use of *eye* mass of ore in a mine, hence 'plum', tit-bit left to the last: see OED(S *sb.*[1] 16 b.]

a. The most desirable piece of land in a holding; esp. in the phr. **to pick (out) the eyes** (see quot. 1889).

[**1849** *S. Austral. Register* (Adelaide) 2 June 4/1 Mr Fisher wished the witness to explain what was meant by the technical term 'picking out the eyes of a mine'.] **1865** *Australasian* (Melbourne) 24 June 11/5 As the day advanced, and sections were taken up, and the 'eye picked from the area', numbers would return and groups form again. **1867** 'CLERGYMAN' *Aust. as it Is* 107 Good land is . . usually found in streaks and patches. . . The getting hold of these streaks and patches has been called 'picking the eyes out of the country'. **1876** 'CAPRICORNUS' *Colonisation* 38 The £20,000 got for the land sold, 'the eyes of the run', is spent long ago. **1886** W.J. WOODS *Visit to Vic.* 26 Since the squatter had no security of tenure, he was liable after the expense of fencing and stocking his 'run', to find the eyes of it picked out by the free-selectors. **1889** R.W. DALE *Impressions Aust.* 197 Free selectors 'picked out the eyes' of the runs, to use the Australian phrase. They selected the most valuable parts of a run; sometimes they selected those parts which gave value to all the rest—for example, the parts where the sheep or the cattle found water. **1899** MRS A. HAY *Footprints* 45 Owing to . . the 'free selector', who walks into the run and picks the eyes of it, squatting has become anything but a lucrative occupation. **1910** *Huon Times* (Franklin) 28 Sept. 2/5 The property that had just been left was not an 'eye' of that locality. **1919** *Smith's Weekly* (Sydney) 15 Mar. 15/3 Old-time selectors used to complain bitterly of how the eyes were picked out of the country by obliging surveyors in the interests of the big pastoralist. **1930** A.E. YARRA *Vanishing Horsemen* 75 Owners who were . . employers of the 'dummy' method of land grabbing, and likely to be annoyed if Bruce were successful at the ballot; 'picking the eyes out' of their grazing country. **1968** F. ROSE *Aust. Revisited* 29 'Peacocking' or 'picking the eyes out of the run' was another way of getting round the law. **1975** X. HERBERT *Poor Fellow my Country* 786 The general idea is they'll pick the eyes out of the land, and that you're helpin' 'em.

b. *transf.*

1981 SANDERCOCK & TURNER *Up where, Cazaly?* 213 There is much interstate resentment against Victoria's ability to 'pick the eyes' out of Australian football.

F

face.

1. The front of a bushfire.

1876 R.P. Falla *Knocking About* (1976) 65 For some days a large bush fire has been raging . . and on Tuesday night it had a face of fifteen miles. **1925** M. Terry *Across Unknown Aust.* 206 The wind took the flames to the river. . . When the 'face' got to the river the wind changed slightly, making the fire creep along the banks.

2. In a camp muster: the side of the mob which is being worked. Also *attrib.*

1932 J.J. Hardie *Cattle Camp* 95 Ken and Dusty moved through the mob, dodging out cows with unbranded calves, and grown cleanskins to where Scotty and Jerry proudly rode the face of the camp. **1943** *Bulletin* (Sydney) 7 Mar. 13/3 About a thousand head were being held on 'camp' while the best of them were being cut out to go on the road, and The Breaker was on a youngster working on the 'face' of the camp. **1975** G.A.W. Smith *Once Green Jackaroo* 82 Two 'face riders' appeared, and steered the beast into the waiting mob of cut-outs.

3. *Surfing.* The wall of a wave.

1963 B. Johnson *Surf Fever* 24 The head dip is usually only done on fast waves with a good high face (a good wall). **1963** *Surfabout* (Sydney) I. v. 20 John Williams . . drives across the face of a tube at Burleigh Heads. **1967** *Ibid.* IV. iii. 11 Fred 'Squeaky' Tucker really moves along the face of the wave on his mini.

face plaster. An alcoholic drink.

1941 K. Tennant *Battlers* 173 It was Uncle who insisted that, as Snow was just out of hospital, they should all stop at the first hotel and get him a 'face plaster'. **1970** J.S. Gunn in W.S. Ramson *Eng. Transported* 50 *Face plaster*, alcoholic drink.

factory, *n.* and *attrib. Hist.*

A. *n.* A prison for the confinement of female convicts, esp. that at Parramatta, N.S.W. In full, **female factory.**

1806 *Sydney Gaz.* 13 July, Catherine Eyres . . ordered to the Factory at Parramatta for the term of six months. **1811** *Ibid.* 6 July, The Female Convicts . . are to be sent direct . . to the Factory at Parramatta. **1819** W.C. Wentworth *Statistical, Hist., & Pol. Descr. N.S.W.* 18 The public institutions are an Hospital, a Female Orphan House . . and a factory, in which such of the female convicts as misconduct themselves, and those also who upon their arrival in the colony are not immediately assigned as servants to families, are employed in manufacturing coarse cloth. **1826** *Austral.* (Sydney) 5 Jan. 4/1 To the care of the lady of that delightful mansion, ycleped the 'female factory'. **1827** *Tasmanian* (Hobart) 17 May 2 Mr Lowes tendered, to the Government of this Colony, his distillery at the Cascade . . as a building adapted to the uses of a Female Factory. **1832** *Colonial Times* (Hobart) 21 Aug., The lass I adore, the lass for me, Is a lass in the Female Factory. **1838** *Cornwall Chron.* (Launceston) 11 Aug. 2 When . . refractory females, who refuse to work for their masters and mistresses, are sent in to the factory as a place of punishment, it turns out to be more a party of pleasure. **1844** *Colonial Times* (Hobart) 5 June, A Female Factory, where the 'fair *im*penitents' are to be converted into cloth-weavers. **1848** *Sidney's Austral. Hand-Bk.* 27 Any man can go to the factory at Parramatta, have the convict women mustered in a row, and, on his selecting the one that meets his fancy, have her assigned to him for the remainder of her term, as soon as the marriage ceremony has been performed. **1856** V. Pearce *Life* 4, I took from 'Paramatta Female Factory', two women for domestic purposes at Bathurst. **1861** T. Bunbury *Reminisc. Veteran* II. 281 One interesting looking girl . . had . . been out in service four different times, but had always, after a few months, been returned to the factory for correction. **1873** 'Lady in Aust.' *Memories Past* 9 The servant was . . eventually sentenced to two years' imprisonment in the female factory. **1895** *Bulletin* (Sydney) 17 Aug. 13/4 Mrs Mood, who died at Parramatta last week, had for 70 years resided there, having arrived when only 22 years of age, as matron of the female convicts' 'factory'. **1913** J.C.L. Fitzpatrick *Good Old Days of Molong* 89 The 'factory' at Parramatta . . was really a depot in which female prisoners were kept—it was only a 'factory' in the sense that the licentious amongst the officials of the day used it for immoral purposes and turned out of it women of loose character. **1930** 'Brent of Bin Bin' *Ten Creeks Run* (1952) 47 His wife was supposed to have been born in the 'Female Factory' at Parramatta.

B. *attrib.*

1829 *HRA* (1922) 1st Ser. XV. 4 The winter clothing being entirely composed of Factory Cloth. **1832** *Sydney Herald* 9 Jan. 3/2 Mary James, a coiner of new oaths and impudent phrases, was ordered factory discipline for six weeks. **1836** J.F. O'Connell *Residence Eleven Yrs. New Holland* 55 The above is a faithful picture of too many 'factory weddings'. **1840** *Tasmanian Weekly Dispatch* (Hobart) 14 Aug. 6/3 Alice Reedy was ordered 12 months to the factory crime class. **1843** *Duncan's Weekly Register* (Sydney) 16 Dec. 335/2 The bringing into competition the Factory women with the free females of the Colony by taking in washing and needlework was a very paltry concern. *c* **1891** J. Gardiner *Twenty-Five Yrs. on Stage* 39 This man had been a convict before him, but they got on very well together until a 'factory girl' had been hired by him.

fadge. [Br. dial. *fadge* loosely packed sack of wool, etc.: see OED(S *sb.*[1] and EDD.] An unpressed pack of wool containing less than a bale.

1914 H.B. Smith *Sheep & Wool Industry* 183 *Fadges*, Australian wool-brokers call any bale or parcel of wool under 200 lb. in weight, and which is too large to be called a sack, a fadge. **1921** L.G. Jones *Flockmaster's Companion* 81 *Fage*, an irregular package of wool, any that is not in shipping order. **1928** C.E. Cowley *Classing Clip* 166 In this section (the bags) will often appear consignments of wool known as *fadges*. This is a quantity of wool of much greater weight than a bag and contained in a receptacle made of a number of bags sewn together to form a kind of pack. **1953** S.J. Baker *Aust. Speaks* 60 *Fadge*, a butt of a bale or two bags sewn together, usual weight 60 lb. to 150 lb.

fair, *a.*[1] [Spec. use of *fair* equitable: see OED(S *a.* 10.] Used to qualify various nouns or collocations which themselves signify an opportunity for displaying or exerting oneself, one's talents, etc., and so indicating that that opportunity is equitable, reasonable, socially just.

1. *Obs.* In the collocation **fair show**, an equitable opportunity; a reasonable choice.

1884 *Austral. Tit-Bits* (Melbourne) 25 Dec. 18/1 We have given you a fair show, and we find that you don't care about working. **1897** *Tocsin* (Melbourne) 25 Nov. 9/1 Give the working man a fair show.

2. In the collocation **fair go.**

a. An equitable opportunity; a reasonable chance.

1904 *Bulletin* (Sydney) 14 Apr. 29/1 A 'fair bonus' is a real trier, a fair go, or a bit of a don. **1912** *Huon Times* (Franklin) 17 Apr. 3/2 He did not know if he was to have opposition, but if so let them have a fair go, and he would be satisfied at the election decision. **1918** C. Fetherstonhaugh *After Many Days* 118 Forth agreed that it would be a fair go if I rode the colt. **1927** R.S. Browne *Journalist's Memories* 290 The Queenslanders did not get 'a fair go'. **1948** M. Uren *Glint of Gold* 39 'Gives yer a fair go, the Warden does,' was the considered judgment of the miners. **1960** D. McLean *Roaring Days* 100 Anyone's entitled to a fair go, even an abo, or a policeman. **1972** *Bulletin* (Sydney) 22 July 10/3 Australia has always been a dedicatedly capitalist country with socialist principles such as 'fair go' being used as a cover for laissez-faire individualism. **1986** *Canberra Times* 10 Mar. 3/3, I still believe the average Australian believes in a fair go.

b. *spec.* An equitable contest.

1911 'Rose Boldrewood' *Complications at Collaroi* 79 We shall have a 'fair go', and the best side will win. **1920** *Huon Times* (Franklin) 14 Dec. 2/5 'It's all right; so Mr Gilmore says, if it's a fair go.' . . 'I never said that. . . What I said was that a man may strike in self-defence.' **1927** R.S. Browne *Journalist's Memories* 285 Chaffed by a 'common bullocky' whom he fought, a really fair 'go'.

c. As *adj.* Equitable, egalitarian.

1935 *Red Star* (Perth) 4 Oct. 2/4 Comrades seem to have a lot of the carefree 'fair go Aussie' left in them, and this is another version of rotten liberalism. **1964** B. Beaver *Hot Men* 80 'I and my kind were here before this game was invented.' 'And you'll be here long after the dam is built, too,' the controller went on in his fair-go tones. **1973** *Bulletin* (Sydney) 13 Jan. 41/1 It has the potential to eradicate a most disgraceful aspect of Australia's so-called 'fair-go' society. **1974** D. Ireland *Burn* 110 The good old fair-go Aussies.

d. As *exclam.* In the game of two-up: an indication to the spinner that all bets are laid, and an appeal for fairness.

1911 L. Stone *Jonah* 215 The spinner handed his stake of five shillings to the boxer, who cried, 'Fair go!' **1925** A. Wright *Boy from Bullarah* 17 The spinner stood waiting, while the players noisily made their wagers, and then again the voice of the ring-keeper rang out. 'Fair go! Set a quid.' **1942** *Sun* (Sydney) 26 Aug. 4/9 From two-up comes the expression 'Fair go, spinner', which is a request for a fair deal. **1943** H.M. Murphy *Strictly for Soldiers* 17 So the kip you gather tightly, Watch the pennies put on lightly By the ringer, who then bellows: 'Fair go, spinner, let 'em go.' **1977** R.E. Gregory *Orig. Austral. Inventions* 117 The coins are tossed by the spinner from a flat piece of wood called a 'kip'. . . When all the bets are laid, the boxer calls, 'Come in, spinner', or 'Fair go, spinner', and the coins are tossed aloft.

e. Hence as *exclam.* in other contexts: 'Steady on!' 'Be reasonable!'.

1938 *Smith's Weekly* (Sydney) 31 Dec. 4/1 When the laugh had gone on long enough, he would silence it by his opening words, 'Fair go, mob.' **1945** 'R. Rene' *Mo's Mem.* 144 People sometimes ask me where I get my expressions like 'Strike me lucky', 'you little trimmer', 'fair go', 'you beaut', 'I'm a wakeup to you' and 'struth'. They are just ordinary Australian sayings . . household words. **1953** A.W. Upfield *Venom House* 6 Aw! Fair go, Inspector. **1958** H.D. Williamson *Sunlit Plain* 163 Fair go. . . Don't hang around here, trying to pick off my customers. **1960** L.H. Evers *Make Way for Tomorrow* 63 A course in practical politics and lunch cooked at the same time, fair go, matey. **1963** R. Stow *Tourmaline* 123 'He can stay there and the ants can eat him alive,' said Deborah, 'for all I care.' 'Fair go,' said Horse, a bit shocked. **1968** E.M. Noblet *Winds that Blew* 9 'Fair go. Fair go,' Austin begged. **1971** *Bulletin* (Sydney) 20 Feb. 22/1 Fair go, Glen Innes. Let us learn to live and socialise with these people. **1982** R. Hall *Just Relations* 27 Fair go! How can I ask a thing like that?

3. a. [Used elsewhere but recorded earliest in Aust.] In other fanciful collocations: **fair crack of the whip, fair suck (of the sauce bottle),** an equitable opportunity; a reasonable chance.

1924 *Truth* (Sydney) 27 Apr. 6/3 *Fair crack of the whip*, just treatment. **1929** K.S. Prichard *Coonardoo* (1961) 158 Gale laughed. 'I'll see you get a fair crack of the whip now, Mr Watt.' **1944** L. Glassop *We were Rats* 2 The Lord's had a fair crack of the whip and He's missed the bus. It's surfing for me. **1964** P. Adam Smith *Hear Train Blow* 120 Give the gentlemen of the open road a fair crack of the whip, Bill. It's a hard row they hoe.

1972 *Bulletin* (Sydney) 21 Oct. 45/2 Humphries . . goes down under a knuckle sandwich, his mouth and detached teeth so reddened you can see he's had more than a fair suck of the sauce bottle. **1980** R. DAVIDSON *Tracks* 212 To drink with your cobber ocker stone-the-crows fair-crack-of-the-whip mates. **1983** *Weekend Austral. Mag.* (Sydney) 27 Aug. 20/8 In short, Drongo didn't give the punters a fair crack of the whip . . the stupid drongo.

b. As *exclam.* 'Give (someone) a chance!'.

1966 A. HOPGOOD *Private Yuk Objects* 47 Oh, fair crack of the whip! How corny can ya get! **1968** G. DUTTON *Andy* 116 'Shut up, youse animals,' shouted the sergeant. 'Fair crack of the whip, Sarge.' **1972** J. HIBBERD *Stretch of Imagination* (1973) 7 Fair crack of the whip. 89 degrees of quicksilver already. **1976** J. JOHNSON *Low Breed* 198 'Fair suck!' said Gavin, 'If you haven't had a beer for six months you don't walk up to the bar and order half a shandy.' **1976** J. HIBBERD *Three Pop. Plays* 56 'You must be perfect.' . . 'I will be in a few months. Fair crack of the whip.' **1981** P. BARTON *Bastards I have Known* 9 The barker tried to kick me off, but yells from the crowd, 'Fair crack of the whip mate, give the kid a go' . . persuaded him to hand the snake to me.

fair, *a.*[2] [Prob. an amelioration of *fair* expressing moderate commendation, 'pretty good': see OED(S *a.* 11 c.]

1. Thorough-going; absolute.

1903 *Sporting News* (Launceston) 16 May 3/7 Some of his mates in the air were—in the vernacular of the 'talent'—'fair butes'. **1912** S. LOCKE *Dawsons' Uncle George* 79 They all have the idea that Sydney's a fair petunia of a place. **1950** K.S. PRICHARD *Winged Seeds* 40 'How do I look?' she queried. . . 'A fair treat,' Bill said softly. **1967** M. SELLARS *Carramar* 69 This cow is a fair swine. **1978** J. DINGWALL *Sunday too far Away* 42, I reckon, if he can't cook, he's going to be a *fair bastard* to get rid of.

2. In the collocation **fair cow**: used of a person, situation, etc., to which the speaker takes, or pretends to take, the strongest exception. See also COW *n.* 2.

1904 *Bulletin* (Sydney) 7 Jan. 16/2 The worst that Australians can call anything, living or dead, is a cow. N.B.—This is a fair cow of a day—with a violent dust-storm, flies, heat. **1916** O. HOGUE *Trooper Bluegum at Dardanelles* 278 Merry Christmas, Abdul; you're a good sport anyhow, but the Hun is a fair cow. **1929** K.S. PRICHARD *Coonardoo* (1961) 155, I had a fair cow of a horse called Grasshopper. **1936** N. CALDWELL *Fangs of Sea* 244 It had been a fair cow of a day at the factory. **1948** R. RAVEN-HART *Canoe in Aust.* 103 They tried to work that regulator, and jammed it, and gave me a fair cow of a job. **1963** F. HARDY *Legends Benson's Valley* 171 Rich people . . can only eat three meals a day and sleep in one bed. Can't spend all their money. Must be a fair cow. **1973** J. GREENWAY *Down among Wild Men* 225 It is a bloody fucking shit of a road, a *fair cow.* **1978** J. DINGWALL *Sunday too Far Away* 41 He's going to be a fair cow to get rid of.

fair, *adv.* [Br. dial. *fair* completely: see OED(S *adv.* 9 c.] Entirely; absolutely.

1888 G. ROCK *Colonists* 39 Now then, no larks, ye know; fair horney, my covie. **1892** 'R. BOLDREWOOD' *Nevermore* 37 Trevanion and party of Number six, Growlers' Gully were 'fair on it'—had struck it rich, and no mistake in miners' parlance. **1898** *Bulletin* (Sydney) 4 June (Red Page), I haven't seen noted the common expression, 'fair into my tomahawk', meaning 'it -- suits me'. **1919** A. THOMAS *Moments of Leisure* 47 That fair bowled me over. **1932** K.S. PRICHARD *Kiss on Lips* 274 'I'm fair gone on her, Bill,' he said. **1950** —— *Winged Seed* 50 Fair gives you the creeps. **1966** H. GYE *Father clears Out* 181 A cow . . will come home, and in a most flagrant manner, deposit a pat fair bang in the bail.

fairy, *n.*[1]

1. In the names of birds: **fairy martin,** the predom. black and white insect-eating bird *Hirundo ariel*, widespread in Aust., having a red-brown crown, and building a mud nest shaped more or less like a bottle; *blue martin* (a), see BLUE *a.*; BOTTLE-SWALLOW; see also MARTIN; **penguin,** the small penguin *Eudyptula minor*, which breeds on coasts of s. Aust. and New Zealand; *little penguin*, see LITTLE 2; **wren,** any bird of the genus *Malurus*, all of which are small and long-tailed, the breeding males of most species having brightly coloured plumage.

1842 J. GOULD *Birds of Aust.* (1848) II. Pl. 15, The **Fairy Martin** . . although enjoying a most extensive range, appears to have an antipathy to the country near the sea. **1896** B. SPENCER *Rep. Horn Sci. Exped. Central Aust.* II. 108 Fairy Martin . . were seen skimming over the water and flying across our camp. **1945** C. BARRETT *Austral. Bird Life* 167 The fairy martin or bottle-swallow . . is noted for the retort-shaped mud nest with a long, spouted entrance. **1970** P. SLATER *Eagle for Pidgin* 56 A long-winged bird which braked at a cluster of mud bottle-nests plastered on to a wall. It shoved its head inside a bottle, paused, then flicked away again to the daylight. . . 'Fairy martin, Ned. It must have chicks.' **1848** J. GOULD *Birds of Aust.* VII. Pl. 85, *Spheniscus undina* . . **Fairy Penguin.** **1890** G.J. BROINOWSKI *Birds of Aust.* I. Pl. 1, The distinguishing peculiarities of the Fairy Penguin . . consist in its lesser size, it being considerably the smallest of the *Spheniscidae* yet discovered. **1951** R. DORIEN *Venturing to Aust.* 28 There they were! Little shapes of the fairy penguins clustered together, for all the world like groups of human beings lingering on the way home. **1983** *Bulletin* (Sydney) 6 Sept. 23/1 Phillip Island, home of the fairy penguins. **1928** *Ibid.* 25 Apr. 23/1 Mrs Daisy Bates . . records that the **fairy** or blue-cap **wren** and his mate . . are known to many tribes of natives by the euphonious names of *Miril Yiril Yiri* and *Minning Minning.* **1975** X. HERBERT *Poor Fellow my Country* 1293 A pair of fairy wrens, called *Biaiuk*, the male vivid blue, the female russet, arrived, to peep from branches, to twitter faintly, fluttering wings at each other. **1984** SIMPSON & DAY *Birds of Aust.* 325 The fairy-wrens are well-known for the beauty of the male's plumage.

2. Special Comb. **fairy floss,** a confection of spun sugar, usu. pink; candy floss. Also *attrib.*

1945 H. ARTHUR *Flicka Daze* 66, I . . ate another piece of fairy floss. **1956** E. MITCHELL *Black Cockatoos* 40 They threaded their way past stands . . past the Fairy Floss makers, and the canvas snake pit. **1961** X. HERBERT *Soldiers' Women* 81 Ate fairy-floss from the booth like nostalgic exiles from fairyland. **1986** *Canberra Times* 9 Mar. 9/3 After the Canberra show, the Braidwood one might seem a bit like a burp after a feast of fairy floss.

fairy, *n.*[2] [Abbrev. of *fairy tale.*] A tall story. Also **fairy twister.**

1892 *Bulletin* (Sydney) 20 Aug. 21/2 Between the acts they treat him While he's swapping 'fairy twisters' with the 'girls behind their bars'. **1895** *Western Champion* (Barcaldine) 4 June 1/4 And so, the awful, beg pardon, Alpha snake yarn was a 'fairy'. **1896** *Ibid.* 17 Mar. 1/4, I do not believe this 'fairy' though. **1897** *Worker* (Sydney) 17 Aug. 4/2 Some bushmen pride themselves upon their story-telling powers, and . . don't stick at a 'fairy' when an impression is to be made around the camp fire.

fake, *v.* [Spec. use of (orig. criminal cant) *fake* to tamper with for the purposes of deception.] *trans.* To change (the brand) on a stolen beast. Also **brand-fake.**

1888 'R. BOLDREWOOD' *Robbery under Arms* (1937) 149 A horse-brand . . had been 'faked' or cleverly altered. **1899** G.E. BOXALL *Story Austral. Bushrangers* 355 The manner in which brands might be 'faked' was endless, and when it was impossible to 'fake' a brand it was 'blotched' or burned over, so that the original design could not be recognised. **1909** E. WALTHAM *Life & Labour in Aust.* 39 They could artfully alter, or, as it is termed in bush language 'fake' the brands. **1914** C.H.S. MATTHEWS *Bill* 23 'Cattle-duffing' . . means stealing cattle, sometimes young unbranded calves, sometimes full grown cattle already branded. The bushrangers used to 'fake' the brands on the latter so that their owners couldn't recognise their own. **1918** C.E. BOSWORTH *Shoe & Leather Trade* 29 Graziers say the only means they have of quickly picking out their cattle in a round-up is by heavily branding; moreover, it is a check on 'faking' by cattle thieves. **1940** W. HATFIELD *Into (Great?) Unfenced* 211 Taken here in the heart of the property, brand-faking.

Hence **brand faker** *n.*

c **1906** L. BECKE *Settlers Karossa Creek* 150 The sons of the settlers, who were all more or less cattle stealers and horse and cattle 'brand fakers'. **1935** M. GILMORE *More Recoll.* 64 A brand faker was one who could change one letter into another, as a D, into a B . . or who doubled the letters.

fall, *n.*[1] *Obs.* [Br. dial. *fall* portion of growing underwood ready to fell: see EDD *sb.* 5.] A group of trees.

1847 A. HARRIS *Settlers & Convicts* (1953) 29, I had found a fall of timber (as a group of trees is termed). **1849** —— *Emigrant Family* (1967) 309 He had traversed it often to some falls of cedar. **1857** F. DE B. COOPER *Wild Adventures* 45 A 'fall' of trees to suit us was soon found. **1962** B. BEATTY *With Shame Remembered* 199 If one chance to light upon a 'fall' of cedar, none of the others will attempt to cut even a tree out of the group.

fall, *n.*[2]

1. A strip of leather at the end of the plaited lash of a stockwhip: see quot. 1983.

1888 H.S. RUSSELL *Genesis Qld.* 349 A stock-whip with a long green-hide fall. **1909** *Anthony Hordern Catal.* 749 Kangaroo or White Hide Stock Thongs, Fine Plaited, Snake Shaped, Plaited Bellies, Turks Head at Keeper, With Fall and Silk Lash. **1912** G.H. GIBSON *Ironbark Splinters* 10 He could sit on a buckin' brumbie like a nob in an easy-cheer, An' chop his name with a green-hide fall on the flank of a flyin' steer. **1924** *Anthony Hordern Catal.* 873 Bullock Thongs, with falls on, round belly. **1932** J.J. HARDIE *Cattle Camp* (1944) 61 Quick as lightning, he cuts the new kangaroo-hide fall off his whip, winds it round and round his finger. **1956** C.D. MILLS *Stockwhip & Spur* 11 Good plaited thong and tapered fall, The deftly braided lash, With bluntened rowels of honest steel We'll halt the scrubbers' dash. **1969** L. BRADEN *Bullockies* 103, I made myself a beauty once; fourteen feet long plus the fall. The fall is the single strand after the plait. **1983** R. EDWARDS *Whipmaking* 6 The fall is a strip of leather attached to the end of the whip. The end of the whip gets a lot of knocking around so it is better to have a fall that can be replaced rather than let the plaited end take the damage.

2. See quot.

1940 J.A. BROOK *Jim of Seven Seas* 59, I think the most dexterous feat executed by the stock rider is the crack of the whip called 'the fall'. To perform this act he lays out the full length of his whip to the rear on the ground. He then raises the short, eighteen-inch handle over his head, and with one fell swoop will bring the full length of the whip right over to the front, and make the extreme end of the lash strike any pre-selected spot in front of him the full length of the whip away.

fall, *v.* [Br. dial. *fall* to fell (trees): see OED(S *v.* 51 c.] *trans.* To fell (a tree).

1793 P.G. KING Jrnl. Norfolk Island 31 Dec. 110 Falling an Acre of Wood From 10s. to 13s. per day. **1822** *Hobart Town Gaz.* 9 Mar., All persons are hereby warned against falling or carrying away timber, or otherwise trespassing on my Farm. **1828** *Tasmanian* (Hobart) 29 Aug. 3 An assigned servant of Captain Ritchie's was killed at his Stock Run . . while falling timber. **1847** A. HARRIS *Settlers & Convicts* (1953) 44 The little chaps at nine and ten years of age could take their axe and fall a moderate sized tree. **1851** *Empire* (Sydney) 5 Aug. 14/5 By falling the swamp oaks, they formed a bridge over the water. **1885** *Illustr. Austral. News* (Melbourne) 25 Nov. 202/2 'Falling' a tree, though hard, is a little better. Having put in the front 'carve', on the side the tree is to fall, the back one, which is usually a little higher than the front, is commenced and the tree is cut across. **1899** H. LAWSON *Autobiogr. & Other Writings* (1972) 42 We 'played the wag', or, as we had it, 'wagged it', from school, to 'go and fall a tree'—working long hours with blunt axes or tomahawks. **1918** *Huon Times* (Franklin) 13 Dec. 2/6 We have got a right to fall scrub and keep it in order. **1930** A.E. YARRA *Vanishing Horsemen* 20, I had to borrow money to pay scrub-cutters to fall mulga on the back part of the run. **1944** E.H. BURGMANN *Educ. Austral.* 40, I have felled ('fallen', we would say) a tree down the mountain side. **1948** *Bulletin* (Sydney) 7 July 23/1 The boss wanted to know could he fall a tree. **1965** J. BECKETT *New-Chum looks at Qld.* 52 Soon I was picking cotton on contract and falling scrub at so much per acre. **1972** B. FULLER *West of Bight* 133 Why, in the south-west, the term should be 'falling' and not 'felling' I cannot say, but so it is.

Hence **fallen** *ppl. a.*; **faller** *n.*, a tree feller.

1808 *Sydney Gaz.* 11 Sept., A capital and extensive farm at George's River, comprising 160 acres, 20 clear, and 6 **fallen** timber. **1828** *Tasmanian* (Hobart) 23 May 3 The inconvenience of passing amongst fallen timber and cultivated land. **1906** *Bulletin* (Sydney) 26 Apr. 14/1 In my own maize patch in the fallen scrub I have dozens of stalks 12 ft. high. **1793** D. COLLINS *Acct. Eng.*

Colony N.S.W. (1798) I. 331 To each [timber] carriage were annexed two **fallers** and one overseer. **1827** *Monitor* (Sydney) 5 July 495/3 He had beat 'Jem Somebody, the crack-faller on the Plains'. **1900** *Bulletin* (Sydney) 13 Oct. 14/1 Moreton Bay figs and spurway trees have spurs at the base which make it impossible to fall them stump-high. The faller therefore cuts steps up the spurs. **1927** T.S. GROSER *Lure of Golden West* 103, I have made little mention of the 'Bush-gangs'—the 'fallers', the 'haulers', and the 'loaders'. **1938** F. RATCLIFFE *Flying Fox & Drifting Sand* 100 The axe-beats of the 'fallers' in the scrub above us sounded. **1958** P. COWAN *Unploughed Land* 86 He's a faller. Won a few prizes for log-chops. **1980** J. WOLFE *End of Pricklystick* 27 Only thing that can go wrong is a sudden gust of wind, or a pocket of rotten wood the fallers don't know about.

fall in, *v. Obs. intr.* To make a mistake.

1894 A.B. PATERSON *Singer of Bush* (1983) 221 If I can't get a copper, by Jingo, I'll stop her, Let the police fall in, it will serve the brutes right. **1903** J. FURPHY *Such is Life* 291, I would n't advise you to count upon the institution as a neat and easy escape from the Adamic penalty. You might fall-in. *c* **1907** C.W. CHANDLER *Darkest Adelaide* 81, I go in strong for racing, yet a bet I never lose; I smile upon a bookie, and the tip he can't refuse; Then twenty pounds to nothing is the entry that he makes, And I really can't fall in you knows because I risk no stakes. **1910** L. ESSON *Woman Tamer* (1976) 74, 'I was dead innocent, they'll all tell you that. . . ' 'How did you fall in? . . ' 'Got rung into the pool somehow.' **1922** C. DREW *Rogues & Ruses* 164 I've fell in meself before to-day and I know that it hurts real bad.

Also as *n.*

1902 *Sporting News* (Launceston) 27 Sept. 1/2 With one 'fall in' to their credit, the punters made a mad rush for Benedict . . and again were disappointed.

falling, *vbl. n.* [f. FALL *v.*]

1. The cutting down of timber; felling.

1804 *Sydney Gaz.* 2 Sept., A labouring man who was employed in falling on Livingston's Hill, near Parramatta, was unfortunately killed by a tree which fell in a direction probably contrary to the poor man's expectation. **1833** *Perth Gaz.* 2 Nov. 173 It has been found expedient to alter and define more fully the regulations hitherto existing relative to the Falling of Timber on Crown Reserves. **1885** *Illustr. Austral. News* (Melbourne) 25 Nov. 202/2 In 'falling' . . the tree can go only one of two ways. **1960** *Khaki Bush & Bigotry* (1968) 227 Just doin' a bit of scrub fallin'.

2. Comb. **falling axe, gang.**

1792 P.G. KING Jrnl. Norfolk Island 16 Jan. 16 The Settlers . . are totally destitute of many necessaries . . particularly **Falling Axes.** **1822** *Hobart Town Gaz.* 22 June, Cross-cut and pit saws, . . falling axes. **1828** *Tasmanian* (Hobart) 19 Sept. 3 Solomon, accused of murdering one of his companions . . by inflicting several blows on the head with a falling axe. **1849** A. HARRIS *Emigrant Family* (1967) 168 Common Australian falling axe (forged only in the colony). **1927** *Bulletin* (Sydney) 21 July 27/2 It is only in the 'falling' axe that the knob is a nuisance at times; but for downward chopping it is a decided advantage. **1825** *Austral.* (Sydney) 13 Jan. 2 The numerous road gangs, **falling gangs,** . . are at this moment in the greatest requisition by the settlers. **1920** B. CRONIN *Timber Wolves* 111 They each have charge of a falling gang.

false sarsaparilla. The twining purple-flowered perennial *Hardenbergia violacea* (fam. Fabaceae) of e. Aust., sometimes confused with *sweet tea* (see SWEET *a.*[1]) which it resembles in leaf and habit; *coral pea* (b), see CORAL; SARSAPARILLA a.

1896 J.H. MAIDEN *Flowering Plants & Ferns N.S.W.* 55 *Hardenbergia monophylla* . . Vernacular name—We know of none except 'False Sarsaparilla'. **1933** C.W. PECK *Austral. Legends* (ed. 2) 112 Big cold boulders were lying under . . the clustered true and false sarsaparilla. **1956** T.Y. HARRIS *Naturecraft in Aust.* 172 False Sarsaparilla is a twining plant with dark-green leaves and small purple flowers. . . It is very attractive to bees. **1978** B.P. MOORE *Life on Forty Acres* 41 The False Sarsaparilla (*Hardenbergia violacea*), a sprawling and clambering legume that seems to grow best amongst the sandstone flakes.

family reunion. An immigration policy which makes specific provision for immigrants who have relatives already resident in Australia. Also *attrib.*

1972 *Bulletin* (Sydney) 25 Nov. 21/2 Emphasis in immigration changed from government recruitment to 'family reunion' and retaining immigrants already here. **1974** *Austral. Financial Rev.* (Sydney) 9 Oct. 2/2 Family reunion will still remain the central policy theme. **1976** *Canberra Times* 21 May 13/1 Some widening of the present 'family reunion' categories will be permitted. **1978** *Sydney Morning Herald* 13 June 3/7 Mr MacKellar said that a substantial part of the migrant intake was brought in for family reunions and other compassionate reasons. **1981** *Austral. Financial Rev.* (Sydney) 3 Nov. 3/4 On the family reunion side the Government made some concessions last week making it easier for brothers and sisters of non-dependent children of resident migrants to settle in Australia. **1984** G. BLAINEY *All for Aust.* 97 It is not a way of winning friends to point out that the family-reunion scheme strongly favours Asian immigrants. **1985** *Canberra Times* 24 Jan. 1/3 His wife and daughter have been on the Australian list for family reunions for some time.

fancy. *Obs.* In the collocation **the fancy,** the criminal class.

1832 *Sydney Monitor* 22 Aug. 4/2 The offence was of a serious nature, notwithstanding that many gentlemen, termed *the Fancy*, might make light of being transported for seven years. **1848** *Port Phillip Herald* 18 Jan. 2/4 About six o'clock on Friday evening the 'Fancy' indulged themselves with another specimen of fistic science, at the back of the Gaol. **1848** T.L. MITCHELL *Jrnl. Exped. Tropical Aust.* 396 A tolerable pun for one of 'the fancy', of which class we had rather too many in the party. **1882** *Sydney Slang Dict.* 8 *The talent*, low gamblers, sharpers, larrikins and their girls, confirmed prostitutes, and 'the fancy' generally who frequent their resorts. **1903** *Truth* (Sydney) 31 May 3/5 The thieves dealt an unfortunate peeler a blow with an iron bar, and in the expressive language of the 'fancy', laid him out!

fang, *n.*[1]

a. A pressing request for a loan or gift, esp. in the phr. **to put the fangs in** and varr.; the loan or gift so secured.

1919 W.H. DOWNING *Digger Dialects* 22 *To put in the fangs*, to demand money, etc. **1924** A.W. BAZLEY et al. Gloss. Slang A.I.F. (typescript) 23 *Put the fangs in*, to request a favour or loan. **1932** L. MANN *Flesh in Armour* 250 They were all short of cash. . . 'I'll stick the fangs in him all right,' Tich averred. **1952** T.A.G. HUNGERFORD *Ridge & River* 218 'Give me a smoke,' Wallace suggested. 'If there's one thing I like, it's to sink the fangs into an officer.' **1967** *Kings Cross Whisper* (Sydney) xxxiv. 4/5 Whereas a snip is only a small loan a fang is a large bite.

b. Special Comb. **fang artist,** one who is skilled at securing loans etc.

1972 A. CHIPPER *Aussie Swearers Guide* 24 *Fang Artist*, applied to (a) a glutton, (b) a constant borrower, or (c) a lecher.

fang, *n.*[2] [f. the name of Juan *Fangio* (b. 1911), racing driver.] A drive in a motor vehicle at high speed.

1969 A. BUZO *Front Room Boys* (1970) 20 If I were one of the back room boys, you wouldn't see me here before noon. I'd be down by the pool or out for a fang in the Jag.

fang, *v.*[1]

1. *trans.* To induce (someone) to give (money or goods) by begging or borrowing, esp. in an exploitative manner.

1967 *Kings Cross Whisper* (Sydney) xxxiv. 4/5 *Fang*, to borrow from a person. **1969** *Ibid.* (Sydney) lxxvii. 10/3 Fang your neighbours for their gardening implements. (Extra points if you score a rotary hoe or late model motor mower.) **1975** *Daily Tel.* (Sydney) 10 July 2/3 What if they'd fanged us for **$800 million?** **1979** *Herald* (Melbourne) 3 Mar. 41/1 He fanged me for a brick and next thing I know he's shot through all the way to Darwin.

fang, *v.*[2] [f. FANG *n.*[2]] *intr.* To drive a vehicle at high speed. Also *trans.* with the vehicle as obj.

1969 A. BUZO *Rooted* (1973) 36 Let's hop in the B and fang up to the beach. **1981** *Bulletin* (Sydney) 10 Nov. 43/3 We pick up sheilas, get drunk, steal cars, fang 'em (drive them fast) . . anyfink! **1984** *Nat. Times* (Sydney) 14 Sept. 14/4 They've had half a dozen drinks and, you know, they want to impress the girls and their mates at how fast they can fang their car around the corner.

fan palm. a. Any palm of the genus *Livistona* (fam. Arecaceae), occurring in mainland Aust. and elsewhere: see CABBAGE TREE 1 a.; **b.** The lowland rainforest palm *Licuala ramsayi* (fam. Arecaceae) of n.e. Qld. and elsewhere, having leaf blades divided into many-ribbed segments. Also *attrib.*

1834 J.D. LANG *Hist. & Statistical Acct. N.S.W.* II. 163 The species of palm most frequently met with in the low grounds of Illawarra is the fan-palm or cabbage-tree. **1849** W. CARRON *Narr. Exped. Rockingham Bay & Cape York* 69 The women . . shaded themselves with large fan-palm leaves. **1862** J.M. STUART *Explorations in Aust.* 10 July (1865) 388 The fan palm . . leaf very much resembles a lady's fan set on a long handle, and, a short time after it is cut, closes in the same manner. **1896** B. SPENCER *Rep. Horn Sci. Exped. Central Aust.* I. 161 The fan-palm, for example (*Livistona Mariae*), is limited to a single colony along the Finke gorge and a small tributary, the Palm Creek. **1935** DAVISON & NICHOLLS *Blue Coast Caravan* 241 There were a great number of fan palms. . . These . . large, pale green disks, overlapping each other in varying degrees, made delightful patterns. **1948** H.A. LINDSAY *Bushman's Handbk.* 59 The fan-palms of the area have an edible heart (terminal bud) in the centre of the young leaves. **1962** V.C. HALL *Dreamtime Justice* 38 The inky shadow of the fan palms. **1980** *Ecos* xxiv. 6/3 (*caption*) Fan palms, *Liguala ramseyi*, dominate a tract of lowland tropical rainforest in northern Queensland.

fantail. Any bird of the genus *Rhipidura* of Aust. and the s. Pacific region, insect-eating birds which habitually spread their tail feathers, esp. WILLY WAGTAIL and CRANKY FAN. Also **fantail(ed) flycatcher.**

1773 W. WALES *Jrnl.* 10 May in J. Cook *Jrnls.* (1969) II. 786 The last I shal mention is the Fan-Tail. Of these there are different sorts, but the body of the most remarkable one is scarce larger than a good Filbert, yet spreads a tail of most beautiful plumage full ¾ of a semicircle, of, at least, 4 or 5 Inches radius. **1827** *Trans. Linnean Soc. London* XV. 247 Mr Caley thus observes . . '*Fantail*—There is something singular in the habits of this bird. It frequents the trees and bushes, from whence it suddenly darts at its prey, spreading out its tail like a fan.' **1841** *S. Austral. Rec.* (London) 2 Jan. 10 The nest of the fan-tailed fly-catcher, shaped like a wine-glass or egg-cup, with a long stem. **1892** 'MRS A. MACLEOD' *Silent Sea* I. 153 There was silence for a little time, broken only by the notes of a fantail in the garden, who sang as if his small heart was too full of joy to go to sleep at his accustomed hour. **1931** J. DEVANEY *Earth Kindred* 14 The fantail busy at his wee webbed house. **1980** M. WILLIAMS *Dingo!* 201 Over me fantail fly-catchers danced.

fantail banger: see BANGER.

fan-tailed cuckoo. The predom. blue-grey and rufous cuckoo *Cuculus pyrrhophanus* of e. and s.w. Aust. Also **fantail cuckoo.**

1801 J. LATHAM *Gen. Synopsis Birds* Suppl. II. 138 Fantailed C[uckow]. . . Inhabits *New Holland.* **1911** A. MACK *Bush Days* 64 The rollicking note of the pallid cuckoo, and the sad wail of his cousin, the fantail cuckoo. **1976** *Reader's Digest Compl. Bk. Austral. Birds* 296 Caterpillars are the main food of the fan-tailed cuckoo.

fantail(ed) flycatcher: see FANTAIL.

fan-tan, *n.* and *attrib.* [a. Chinese *fan .t'an* repeated divisions; used elsewhere but recorded earliest in Aust.]

A. *n.* The name of a Chinese gambling game (see quot. 1937).

1870 *Sydney Morning Herald* 4 July 3/1 The table was crowded with Chinamen eagerly staking their money in a game of 'Fantan'. **1891** H. NISBET *Colonial Tramp* I. 101 It is not the Chinese I object to. . . His Fan-tan is a game of chance. **1898** G.T. BELL *Coolgardie* 8 At the large tables were a number of Chinkies playing Fan Tan. **1917** C.L. DREW *Reminisc. D. Gilbert* 85 Once inside, where Fan-Tan was being played, the scene baffled description. **1933** H.B. RAINE *Lash End* 120 He could just get glimpses of four Chinese faces, whose owners were playing their beloved game of fan-tan. **1937** E. FLYNN *Beam Ends* 164 Fan-Tan is .. a straight out gamble that requires no skill. A handful of beans is taken .. and placed under a metal cover... Bets are laid on four little squares bearing the numbers one, two, three, and four; certain odds being given on certain numbers. The croupier lifts the metal cover and begins to extract the beans four at a time... Those who have bet on the correct number remaining win, while the house collects the rest.

B. *attrib.*

1872 'DEMONAX' *Mysteries & Miseries of Scripopolis* 42/2 We now made for the fan-tan establishment. **1888** M.M. BALLOU *Under Southern Cross* 199 Melbourne has its Chinese quarter... It is situated in Little Burke Street .. and forms a veritable China-Town with its joss-house, opium-dens, lottery cellars, 'fantan' cafés. **1899** *Bulletin* (Sydney) 18 Feb. 15/2 An eminent Chinese physician, being suspected of 'putting away' a fan-tan swindle, had to be rescued by the police. **1917** C.L. DREW *Reminisc. D. Gilbert* 85 There were plenty of Fan-Tan joints in Sydney then. **1937** E. FLYNN *Beam Ends* 164 There, masquerading as business premises, are to be found large numbers of Fan-Tan joints to satisfy the cravings of those inveterate gamblers, the Chinese.

fantass /'fæntæs/. [a. Arabic *fințās* water tank (pl. *fanāțīs*).] A water-container, as carried by a camel. Also **fantassy.**

1916 G.M. BERRY *Rep. G.O.C. Light Horse Brigade* 14 Nov. 2 A good deal of damage is done to saddlery by leaky fantasses. **1919** O. HOGUE *Cameliers* 134 Three weeks' trek .. necessitated merely the prearrangement of depots at two particular points for replenishing the .. water fantasses. **1923** H.S. GULLETT *Austral. Imperial Force* in *Official Hist. Aust. 1914–18* VII. 365 At Shellal alone arrangements were made to fill and load on to camels every hour 2,000 fantasses, each containing ten or twelve gallons of water. **1934** F. REID *Fighting Cameliers* 8 Soon we were issued with the full equipment that was to be our property so long as we remained in the Camel Corps. This consisted of rifle with two hundred and forty rounds of ammunition, and, on one side of the saddle, and held in position by leather straps which fitted over the front and rear of the saddle, a galvanized-iron fantass to hold five gallons of water. **1976** G.F. LANGLEY *Sand, Sweat & Camels* 146 Let us also be thankful that thro' all the bad desert days we had 'fantassies', as well as water bottles. **1984** *Daily Tel.* (Sydney) 20 Mar. 4/3 First priority are fantassies, elliptical-shaped metal containers which used to hold five gallons (23 litres) of water. These were specially constructed to hang off camel saddles.

f.a.q. /ɛf eɪ 'kju/, *a.* [Acronym f. the initial letters of *fair average quality*.]

1. In the grading of wheat: of fair average quality (see quot. 1956).

1908 *S.A. Parl. Papers* II. no. 20 16 None of this cocky chaff .. is in the f.a.q. sample. **1922** *Daily Mail* (Sydney) 18 Jan. 4/5 Agents are interpreting the order to mean that f.a.q. wheat cannot be consigned to Alexandria. **1926** *Bulletin* (Sydney) 4 Feb. 22/1 He farmed his land by methods new, And every bag was f.a.q. **1956** CALLAGHAN & MILLINGTON *Wheat Industry Aust.* 349 In those early days a method was evolved that came to be known as the f.a.q. system... The system was adopted in Victoria in 1891, by New South Wales in 1899 and by Western Australia in 1905... The 'quality' in f.a.q. refers not to the baking quality of the flour the wheat will produce but to its milling value. The actual determination of the f.a.q. is organised by the Chamber of Commerce in each State. **1976** *Bulletin* (Sydney) 31 July 64/1 For a long period after the war the Australian Wheat Board marketed basic qualities of wheat—FAQ (fair average quality) and premium wheat.

2. *transf.* Average.

1930 E. SHANN *Econ. Hist. Aust.* 311 It is impossible, however, to 'bear' a land boom by selling f.a.q. land for future delivery. **1945** *Bulletin* (Sydney) 12 Sept. 13/2 Mention the Barrier Reef to any f.a.q. southern-dwelling Australian and the usual reaction will be something about having heard it's a good place for a winter holiday. **1948** A.J. MCLACHLAN (*title*) McLachlan: an f.a.q. Australian. **1960** C. CLIFT *Walk to Paradise Gardens* 32 You're far too collected and nice to be an f.a.q. product of such a theatrical environment. **1971** P. HASLUCK *Open Go* 87 There are now trees in what was largely a tree-less plain, lawns and gardens on what was an f.a.q. sheep run. **1986** *Bulletin* (Sydney) 15 Apr. 110/3 On the whole I would say f.a.q. of its type with interesting possibilities as the show moves along.

far, *a.* [Spec. use of *far* remote.]

1. Used as an intensifier with nouns which themselves denote isolation, with reference to places extremely remote from major centres of population: **far bush, interior.**

1843 *Sydney Morning Herald* 27 July 2/7 In the **far bush** the poor settlers are in a miserable condition, should sickness overtake them. **1849** 'BUSHMAN' *Sidney's Austral. Handbk.* 64 The boiling system is only useful to get rid of scabby sheep; and of fat wethers when there is no demand for mutton in the market to which they have been driven from the far bush. **1851** J. HENDERSON *Excursions & Adventures N.S.W.* I. 143 Settlers would not .. be able to procure men to go out into the far bush. *Ibid.* II. 7 It cannot be expected that there is much of interest or variety to relate in the life of a squatter in the far bush. **1854** G.H. HAYDON *Austral. Emigrant* 185 They were happy days too, those Sundays in the far bush. **1859** J.D. MEREWEATHER *Diary Working Clergyman* 60 He sold these horses, and went into the far bush. **1890** J.I. WATTS *Family Life S.A.* 167 He was a gentleman, a son of an Edinburgh physician, and .. did not shine as a hutkeeper in the far bush. **1843** *N.S.W. Monthly Mag.* Apr. 177 South Australians with their corn at the door .. may be able to ship it to this colony at less expense than that at which your farmers convey it to Sydney from the **far interior.** **1850** *Illustr. Austral. Mag.* (Melbourne) July 71 The colonists have for several years been steadily advancing into the far interior to the west and north. **1857** W. WESTGARTH *Vic. & Austral. Gold Mines* 23 Almost inaccessible wilds of the far interior. **1880** J.B. STEVENSON *Seven Yrs. Austral. Bush* 173 Many wild escapades .. used to take place in the far interior. **1890** 'R. BOLDREWOOD' *Squatter's Dream* 95 An Australian lady, whose husband lives in the far interior, in the *real* bush. **1907** F. TURNER *Anderson's Man. Farm* 131 Creeping Salt-Bush .. is found from the coast to the far interior.

2. Used with a noun which denotes a place in a particular direction: **far north,** the northern-most part of a particular State (or Colony); **west,** the western regions of New South Wales and Queensland; (less frequently) Western Australia; also *attrib.*; so **far-western** *a.*

1849 *Bell's Life in Sydney* 13 Oct. 3/1 Mr Bilyard (late of North Australia) .. this gentleman having come from the '**far north**'. **1857** F. DE B. COOPER *Wild Adventures* p. iii, Few seem to touch upon the far North, and none give an idea .. of the actual life upon the interior boundaries of the Colony. **1864** R. HENNING *Lett.* (1952) 68 The 'far-north' here is like the far-west in America. **1880** *Bulletin* (Sydney) 14 Feb. 3/3 Every one who has been in the far north knows 'George the Greek'. **1898** *Ibid.* 21 May 14/1 The recent appointment in Queensland of an Aborigine's Protector has caused quite a boom in the mixed matrimonial market in the Far North and the Never-Never. **1925** M. TERRY *Across Unknown Aust.* 32 There are only two seasons in the Far North, the 'wet' and the 'dry'. **1951** G. FARWELL *Outside Track* 170 No wonder there was little profit from grazing the Far North in those exacting days. Yet they went through with it; and they peopled the North. **1962** N. MONKMAN *Quest Curly-Tailed Horses* 170 Always, with a feeling of being released from a noisy squabbling prison, we left the cities to return .. to our camps in the tropical jungles of the Far North. **1980** ANSELL & PERCY *To fight Wild* 51 The climate is too hot in the Far North to use horses. **1841** *Sydney Herald* 2 Oct. 2/6 It has been observed, by we distant settlers of the '**Far West**' .. that a considerable number of emigrants have lately arrived in the metropolis... Would it not be an act of justice .. were the Government to forward a number of the disengaged emigrants to the principal inland towns say—Yass, Bathurst, Berrima, Goulburn, &c. **1870** E.B. KENNEDY *Four Yrs. in Qld.* 148 Such districts in the 'far west' as the 'Warrego', 'Paroo', down the 'Darling', etc. **1896** *Bulletin* (Sydney) 4 Apr. 22/2 Far western fleeces are light. **1897** *Ibid.* 20 Nov. 7/2 The Far-West Aboriginal. The Westralian Government is making another vigorous effort to get at the local aboriginal. **1903** *Ibid.* 3 Jan. 16/1 The boss of one far-western station (Poolamacca) drove in through the dust to Broken Hill. **1936** W. HATFIELD *Aust. through Windscreen* 132 It would .. prevent the cases of rickets .. which the diligent workers under the Far West Children's Health Scheme come across. **1925** M. TERRY *Across Unknown Aust.* 47 The word 'gun' is used in the Far West to describe anyone specially proficient at his work, hence 'gun' drover or 'gun' shearer. **1959** *Bulletin* (Sydney) 23 Dec. 16/1 One far-west shearing-contractor .. carries in his truck two refrigerators filled with beer and rum.

far-back, *a.* and *n.*

A. *adj.* Remote from a major centre of population; OUTBACK *a.*

1851 'SQUATTER' *Let. to Squatters N.S.W.* 9 Did you inform them that they never need hope to hear the innocent prattle of childhood in the far back bush, whither you were leading them? **1879** S.W. SILVER *Austral. Grazier's Guide* 43 From 18s. to £1 per week is the general average; higher rates, of course, ruling in the far back districts. **1889** A.B. PATERSON *Aust. for Australs.* 19 At present the far back land has little value except what the owners add to it. **1897** *Bulletin* (Sydney) 18 Sept. 31/2 Alice Springs .. is about the most interesting far-back township in Australia. **1911** C.E.W. BEAN *'Dreadnought' of Darling* 77 Out on these far-back Darling stations .. the man lives in a solitary log-hut. **1920** J.N. MACINTYRE *White Aust.* 27 We far back bush people are doing more for the progress of outback Australia than all the people of the cities. **1931** LAWSON & BRERETON *H. Lawson* 215 A very far-back station. **1964** H.M. BARKER *Camels & Outback* 42 The easy-going ways of those far back places.

B. *n.* A region remote from a major centre of population; OUTBACK *n.*

1898 D.W. CARNEGIE *Spinifex & Sand* 143 Should we find auriferous country in the 'far back', it was not my intention to stop on it. **1926** *Spectator* (London) 11 Sept. 370/1 It [*sc.* Australia] is no longer a pioneering country, except in the far-back.

farewell, *v.* [Spec. use of *farewell* to take leave of, bid or say goodbye to.] *trans.* To take leave of (a person who is departing from a place, job, etc.), usu. in a fairly formal manner (but see quot. 1942).

1897 *Bulletin* (Sydney) 30 Jan. 10/4 Some Kanakas in Bundaberg (Q.) farewelled Parson Eustace, the other day. **1903** *Truth* (Sydney) 16 Aug. 1/7 Dean Pownall's daughter was farewelled at Wagga on Wednesday, prior to taking up mission work in China. **1906** *Gadfly* (Adelaide) 18 Apr. 18/2 Last night the Semaphore shivoo'd at the Ward Street Hall to farewell popular Canon Swan. **1937** F. CLUNE *Dig* 234 He had farewelled Commander Norman at the Albert River. **1942** —— *Last of Austral. Explorers* 125 The manager welcomed and farewelled them with a tot of rum. **1944** A. TURNER *Royal Mail* 9 May found us farewelling the Lamberts, transferred to Toodyay. **1950** 'B. JAMES' *Advancement of Spencer Button* 130 The staff farewelled Mr Goodman at an afternoon-tea. **1960** *N.T. News* (Darwin) 19 Jan. 7/3 John Healy was farewelled by residents of the mining township. **1969** A. CLARK *Austral. Adventure* 50 We had a reception for two hundred to 'farewell' the Lydmans. **1975** B. DAWE *Just Dugong at Twilight* 61 So they shook his little hand And farewelled him with a band.

Hence **fareweller** *n.*

1942 F. CLUNE *Last of Austral. Explorers* 120 The escorting farewellers were beginning to feel the strain.

farewell, *n.* [f. prec.]

1. An occasion organized to mark a person's departure. Also *attrib.*

1880 *Argus* (Melbourne) 6 Feb. 5/5 Mr George Danell will take his farewell benefit this evening at the People's Theatre, when 'The Forlorn Hope' will be performed for the 37th and last time. **1904** *Truth* (Sydney) 28 Aug. 7/2 *Farewelling footballers.* The National Sporting Club has decided to entertain the English Football Team at a farewell smoke concert. **1945** *Queanbeyan Age* 16 Mar. 1/1 A public farewell will be tendered Rev. H.R. Arthur. **1961** *Meanjin* 402 Calnan attended the farewells of all the bank managers who'd been there when he arrived. **1983** P. ADAM SMITH *When we rode Rails* 93 With the solid railway stations came station masters who .. were solid citizens. Most took a prominent part in the affairs of the town and in the event of their being transferred to another town were always tended a 'farewell' presentation.

2. *fig.*

1974 B. JUDDERY *At Centre* 123 Before 1973 public servants commonly styled them the 'farewell departments'—good for a sinecure, or at worst a routine job that required little serious effort and less serious thought, but offering scant opportunity to the man or woman of ambition or, for that matter, social conscience.

farinaceous, *a. Hist.* [Joc. use of *farinaceous* consisting or made of flour.] Used in various Comb. with reference to Adelaide: see quot. 1873.

1872 W.C. TAYLOR *Jottings on Aust.* 2 Adelaide wheat is very fine, and has led to the city being called by the Melbournites 'the farinaceous village'. **1873** A. TROLLOPE *Aust. & N.Z.* II. 184 Adelaide . . has . . been nicknamed the Farinaceous City. . . The colony by the sister colonies is regarded as one devoted in a special manner to the production of flour. Men who spend their energies in the pursuit of gold consider the growing of wheat to be a poor employment. **1881** J.C.F. JOHNSON *To Mount Browne & Back* 13 It was asserted that the early settlers of 'Farinaceous Village', when short of mutton, made a meal of the unwary crow. **1937** D. GLASS *Austral. Fantasy* 96 Adelaide . . is sometimes christened 'City of Churches', or lightly termed 'Farinaceous Village'. **1965** *Austral. Encycl.* I. 116 Adelaide was once called a 'farinaceous village'.

farm.

1. **a.** Used generally and unspecifically as elsewhere, but esp. of a comparatively small landholding used primarily for the cultivation of crops.

1803 G. BOND *Brief Acct. Colony Port Jackson* 12 Trotman . . was sent . . to a settler's farm for turnips. **1808** 'GENTLEMAN JUST RETURNED FROM SETTLEMENT' *Acct. Eng. Colony Botany Bay* 10 The first settler in this country who declared himself able to live on the produce of his farm, without any assistance from the stores, was James Ruse. **1821** T. GODWIN *Descr. Acct. Van Diemen's Island* 7 At Pitts-water there are about thirty-five farms well cultivated. **1834** J.D. LANG *Hist. & Statistical Acct. N.S.W.* II. 17 One of the best-regulated farms or rather estates in the colony, is that of Colonel Dumaresq. **1841** *Port Phillip Patriot* 13 Sept. 4/6 The undersigned has for sale some herds of cattle, together with flocks of sheep, with right of stations; also several farms. **1847** A. HARRIS *Settlers & Convicts* (1953) 72 Like almost all the old settlers he had a great many farms, as well as cattle and sheep stations . . ; he also as usual, had at the home farm his smithy, flour-mill, tailors', shoemakers', harness-makers' and carpenters' shops, tannery, cloth-factory, tobacco sheds; besides stables, dairy, barn, wool-sheds, brick-kilns, saw-pits. **1861** C. CAMPBELL *Squatting Question Considered* 22 If farmers, who don't know how to make a living by farming, are anxious to obtain little stations to improve their income, let the owners of the farms and the stations toss up which takes both, for I presume the squatter would also not object to have a farm at a convenient distance. **1873** A. TROLLOPE *Aust. & N.Z.* I. 35 You may free-select a nice little farm of 80 acres of agricultural land, or 160 of pastoral. **1911** *Truth* (Sydney) 14 May 1/7 In the Tamworth district, a lucerne farm of 17 acres was sold at £85 an acre. **1927** T.S. GROSER *Lure of Golden West* 154 My home for several years was in the hot far North. A station there is bigger than what is ordinarily called a 'farm'. In the Southern and more settled parts of Australia, anything up to 5,000 acres may be spoken of as a farm; anything above that, up to tens of thousands of acres, would be classed as a station. In the great North of Western Australia, however, as in Queensland, stations often ran to well over a million acres. **1946** M. TRIST *What else is There?* 44 'Out at your station?' 'Oh, it's not a station,' Grandmother answered. 'Well, farm then. . . ' 'It's not a farm. . . ' 'Well, what do you call it? Selection?' 'Certainly not!' exclaimed Grandmother. 'My place is no selection!' 'Well, what is it? . . ' 'Well, I'm blest if I know. . . It's just a few hundred acres, or is it a few thousands?' **1951** *Bulletin* (Sydney) 13 June 14/4 He worked on the farm after that, eventually taking up a bush-block for himself.

b. Special Comb. **farm constable,** see quot. 1847; **hut,** a farmer's dwelling; **overseer,** a farm manager; **settler,** a farmer; **station,** a holding used primarily for the cultivation of crops.

1834 N.S.W. Magistrates' Deposition Bk. 17 Dec., I then went over to Mr Donald McIntyre's farm and told the **farm constable** there to search the huts. **1847** A. HARRIS *Settlers & Convicts* (1953) 82 The farm-constables . . are prisoners of the crown actually serving their sentence, who have been authorised to act ostensibly for the purposes of convict restraint on the farm. **1849** —— *Emigrant Family* (1967) 103 Grimsby, after getting over the principal part of his servitude as a farm constable. **1907** C. MACALISTER *Old Pioneering Days* 16 The 'farm-constables' in charge of the prisoners were often impudent ruffians who caused more evil than they suppressed. **1823** *First Fruits Austral. Poetry* (ed. 2) 17, I have been musing what our Banks had said And Cook, had they had second sight, that here . . on this south head Should stand an English **farm-hut.** **1828** *Tasmanian* (Hobart) 18 July 3 The farm hut of Mr George Stokell . . having been intentionally set on fire. **1847** A. HARRIS *Settlers & Convicts* (1953) 9 A gentleman, through misfortunes reduced to the inferior condition of a **farm overseer.** **1847** J.D. LANG *Phillipsland* 114 The cottages of her farm-overseer and servants are close at hand. **1879** *Native Tribes S.A.* 108 A farm overseer was . . appointed. **1847** E.W. LANDOR *Bushman* 108 The **farm-settlers** generally are young men of good birth. **1848** *Britannia* (Hobart) 23 Mar. 2/5 Every farm-settler is now adding a vineyard to his estate. **1839** *Southern Austral.* (Adelaide) 10 May 2/2 Every useful requisite for a Dairy and **Farm Station.** **1843** *S. Austral. Mag.* (Adelaide) Nov. 292 The intermediate farm-stations southward to Encounter Bay. **1856** H.B. STONEY *Vic.* 11 Hundreds who have gone to the Fields . . gladly returned to the cattle and farm stations.

2. A nickname given to Monash University, Melbourne (see quot. 1982).

1963 *Age* (Melbourne) 8 Mar. 18/3 By 1968, it is estimated that 12,000 students . . will be down on 'the farm'. This not-unsuitable nickname has been bestowed by Melbourne University students on the 250-acre campus at Clayton. **1964** *Bulletin* (Sydney) 2 May 24/2 Now the only people who call Monash 'The Farm' are those who want to be derisive. **1964** *Sydney Morning Herald* 28 Aug. 2/9 Melbourne University is known as 'The Shop' and Monash as 'The Farm'. **1982** *Age* (Melbourne) 22 May (Suppl.) 7/2 It is a far cry from the opening, in 1961, with 363 students, when Monash was called 'The Farm' because cows grazed on campus and rabbits, hares and foxes were a common sight.

3. Australia, or the Australian economy, esp. as supposed to be under the control or influence of foreign investors.

[**1963** J. McEwen as quoted in *Countryman* (Melbourne) 25 Apr. 1/1 We . . are mostly established farmers. If we earn enough annual income we can live comfortably. If we don't, we could still live comfortably by selling a bit of the farm every year, and that is pretty much the Australian situation—we are not earning enough and we are selling a bit of our heritage every year.] **1973** L. OAKES *Whitlam PM* 237 Australia became more jealous about the ownership of its resources, controls on foreign investment were tightened, and plans were laid to expand the Australian Industries Development Corporation to help 'buy back the farm'. **1975** *Sun-Herald* (Sydney) 3 Aug. 7/5 The Minister for Minerals and Energy . . revealed . . his plans to 'buy back the farm' in less than three years. **1985** *Canberra Times* 29 Aug. 2/6 Australia will again either incur further net debt abroad or be forced to sell off a bit more of the national 'farm' to foreigners.

farmer.

1. Used generally and unspecifically as elsewhere, but esp. of one whose principal occupation is the cultivation of crops.

1809 *HRA* (1916) 1st Ser. VII. 201 The average crops of the Colony are *generally more* than the consumption and would be considerably increased if the Farmer had any means of disposing of the surplus. **1822** J. DIXON *Narr. Voyage N.S.W. & Van Dieman's Land* 34 You there observe corn, barley, etc. thriving well, under the management in general, of only very indifferent farmers. **1828** *Austral. Q. Jrnl. Theol., Lit. & Sci.* Jan. p. x, Contrast the condition of the wretched Settler at the Cape, with that of the jolly farmer on the Hawkesbury. **1840** *Port Phillip Gaz.* 8 Jan. 4 The continuation of bad weather during the last month has very much retarded the operations both of the farmer and the sheep holder. **1849** G.B. WILKINSON *Working Man's Handbk. S.A.* 18 She is now the satisfied wife of a large farmer and sheep-owner. **1873** A. TROLLOPE *Aust. & N.Z.* I. 33 Generally throughout Australia, the farmer is a small man as opposed to the squatter, who is a great man and an aristocrat. **1883** R.E.N. TWOPENY *Town Life Aust.* 244 The term 'farmer' is applied exclusively to the agriculturist, and a squatter would be very much offended if you called him a sheepfarmer. **1901** W.T. REAY *White Aust.* 20 The man who holds much land, runs sheep or cattle upon it, and is, therefore reputedly wealthy, is colloquially alluded to as a 'squatter'. His neighbour, on a small area, even though engaged in precisely similar pursuits, and putting only a fragment (if any) of his holding under cultivation, is called a 'farmer'. The distinction is really more social than industrial. **1922** *Daily Mail* (Sydney) 20 Jan. 5/2 He will actively support the move to induce the graziers and farmers and settlers to form a new party with a new name. **1930** BILLIS & KENYON *Pastures New* 21 The farmer was . . a man with a few if any grazing stock, who made his living by agriculture. **1945** E.W. CAMPBELL *Hist. Austral. Labour Movt.* 95 The Hon. A.K. Trethowan, President of the Farmers' and Settlers' Association . . Colonel Alfred Spain, of the Graziers' Association. **1968** G. MIKES *Boomerang* 120 You must never refer to a grazier as a farmer. A farmer is a lower type of human. **1970** *Bulletin* (Sydney) 18 Apr. 35/2 It is easily the most difficult club in town to join . . and there was a time when neither Catholics nor graziers who grew a bit of quiet corn in a far paddock (thus becoming 'farmers', not 'graziers') stood a chance.

2. See COLLINS STREET, PITT STREET, QUEEN STREET.

farming, *vbl. n.*

1. Used generally as elsewhere, as in 'dairy-farming', but esp. of the cultivation of crops. Also *attrib.*

1824 E. CURR *Acct. Colony Van Diemen's Land* 106 The turf hut in which they reside during their labours will serve afterwards to contain the farming men and stock-keepers. **1838** *S. Austral. Rec.* (London) 13 June 66, I think our colony will be more engaged in woolgrowing for the first few years than in farming. **1845** *Sydney Morning Herald* 30 Dec. 2/7 There is no doubt that a system could be devised, as in England, by which farming and grazing could be combined with advantage. **1852** S. MOSSMAN *Voice from Aust.* 28 He feels himself qualified and inclined to follow farming or grazing. **1890** *Braidwood Dispatch* 29 Mar. 2/3 The farming class of Australia, . . reclaiming the land and spending their days tilling the soil, producing the necessaries that all classes require.

2. Special Comb. **farming overseer** *obs.*, a farm manager; **station,** *farm station* FARM 1 b.

1833 *Launceston Advertiser* 9 May 1 Wanted, a situation, as **Farming Overseer**, by a respectable middle aged man, well versed in Farming. **1839** *Tasmanian Weekly Dispatch* (Hobart) 29 Nov. 1/2 A Young Man . . is desirous of obtaining a situation as Farming Overseer. **1838** *S. Austral. Rec.* (London) 11 July 84 There appears no danger to be apprehended from them [*sc.* Aborigines] in establishing sheep or **farming stations** at any point on the great tract through which we passed.

farmstead. [Spec. use of *farmstead* a farm with the buildings upon it.] A farm-house.

1823 *Hobart Town Gaz.* 26 July, The farmstead is a neatly finished residence. **1916** *Truth* (Sydney) 5 Mar. 11/6 Zam-Buk has such a wide range of usefulness that it should be kept handy in every Australasian home, workshop, farmstead, [etc.] **1941** *Bulletin* (Sydney) 19 Feb. 20/1 Stevens was doing a bit of a starve when he struck a farmstead. **1953** A.W. UPFIELD *Venom House* 4 Here and there were small neat farmsteads.

far-out, *a.* Remote from a major centre of population; OUTBACK *a.*

1879 S.W. SILVER *Austral. Grazier's Guide* 9 It was wonderful upon what indifferent mental pabulum the 'far-out squatter' managed to subsist. **1888** 'R. BOLDREWOOD' *Robbery under Arms* (1937) 462 The far-out squatters . . were stocking up new country in Queensland. **1890** —— *Colonial Reformer* III. 133 They had seen quite enough of this far-out life. **1910** *Bulletin* (Sydney) 15 Sept. 13/3 If a far-out track gets a bad name it is shunned until the scarcity of labor sends wages to balloon altitudes. **1923** *Ibid.* 1 Nov. 24/4 A 'night horse' yarded all night on the far-out stations . . can be used to run up the mob in the morning. **1935** N. HUNT *House of David* 126 Far 'out'—places remote from the southern and eastern capitals. **1950** A. GROOM *I saw Strange Land* 1 The transceiver—the two-way radio and telephone transmitter and receiver—has become the speedy messenger . . and far-out homes may talk several times a day with Alice Springs.

farther-back, var. FURTHER-BACK.

farther-out, var. FURTHER-OUT.

farthest-out, var. FURTHEST-OUT.

fat, *a.*[1] [Spec. use of *fat* containing much fat.] In collocations: **fat cake** [orig. Br. dial.], see quots. 1852 and 1888; **jack,** a tallow candle; *fat cake*; **lamp,** an improvised lamp which burns animal fat (see quot. 1886).

1826 *Monitor* (Sydney) 15 Dec. 245/3 He who has fed upon corn for six-months, can eat a '**fat cake**', with a true epicurean relish. **1827** *Ibid.* 12 July 507/1 The carcase divided, gave each a good share, and 'a screech in the pan', 'a pot of soup', 'a fat cake' .. were the delicacies which such a God-send would plentifully afford. **1845** L. LEICHHARDT *Jrnl. Overland Exped. Aust.* 24 May (1847) 265 It was the Queen's birth-day, and we celebrated it with what .. we were accustomed to call a fat cake, made of four pounds of flour and some suet, which we saved for the express purpose. **1852** MRS C. MEREDITH *My Home in Tas.* II. 59 That favourite bush dainty, a 'fat cake' .. was hot and brown .. (its composition being that of pie-crust, with abundance of dripping or 'fat' kneaded into it). **1855** W. HOWITT *Land, Labor & Gold* I. 126 A fat-cake is the same thing as a leather-jacket, only fried in fat. **1888** J.F. MANN *Eight Months with Dr Leichhardt* 15 Our daily allowance of flour .. was made into a fatcake, that is, it was mixed up solely with fat, no water being used in the composition, and was cooked in the frying pan. **1962** O. PRYOR *Aust.'s Little Cornwall* 166 The Cornish miners of Moonta were singing carols by the light of '**fat jacks**'—tallow candles—stuck on the front of their safety hats. **1982** PAGE & INGPEN *Aussie Battlers* 22, I can make .. Fat Jacks which is damper fried in mutton fat. **1883** E.M. CURR *Recoll. Squatting Vic.* 34 The fire, the vapour, the odour of the '**fat lamp**', the scalding hot tea and reeking mutton, were neither pleasant nor inviting. **1886** H. FINCH-HATTON *Advance Aust.* (rev. ed.) 41 The inside of the hut was illuminated by a fat-lamp; a simple contrivance in the form of a jam tin full of fat with a fragment of tweed trousers stuck through a hole in the top for a wick. **1888** H.S. RUSSELL *Genesis Qld.* 340 By the fat-lamp light I was struck by his appearance. **1901** *Bulletin* (Sydney) 9 Feb. 15/1 'Where's that fat-lamp, Jim?' .. 'Pitched it away... It's only an old fruit-tin.' **1928** *Ibid.* 16 May 21/1 The venerable fat lamp, alias 'slushy' and 'greasy', is still used in hundreds of N.S.W. farmers' barns.

fat, *a.*[2] and *n.*[1] [Spec. use of *fat* fattened for slaughter.]

A. *adj.* In collocations: **fat cattle, stock.**

1855 *Illustr. Sydney News* 21 Apr. 187/2 Mrs George Lang's first auction of **fat cattle** was held .. at Camperdown. **1872** G.S. BADEN-POWELL *New Homes for Old Country* 150 Here we have the breeding both of 'store' and 'fat' cattle. **1890** 'R. BOLDREWOOD' *Squatter's Dream* 3 'Muster for fat cattle', as the important operation was termed. **1901** *Bulletin* (Sydney) 7 Sept. 14/1 A noted cattle duffer .. met with a travelling mob of fat cattle. **1937** W. HATFIELD *I find Aust.* 106, I went down with the last mob of fat cattle for the season. **1844** *Sydney Morning Herald* 29 July 2/6 Not one moment's delay is occasioned to travellers or teams, or **fat stock**, in passing this hitherto enormous obstacle. **1855** R. CALDWELL *Gold Era Vic.* 90 The fat stock, wool, &c., will pay the last instalments. **1890** 'R. BOLDREWOOD' *Squatter's Dream* 29 A dealer in fat stock might have taken the whole lot to market .. without rejecting a beast. **1892** *Braidwood Dispatch* 21 Dec. 2/4 At the Homebush fat stock sales yesterday 1180 cattle were yarded. **1927** *R. Comm. on Wireless* 2868 Sales of wool, fat and other stock.

B. *n.*

a. Usu. in *pl.* (but see quot. 1923) or (in *attrib.* use) as a collect. sing. Sheep or cattle ready for slaughter.

1888 A.P. MARTIN *Oak-Bough & Wattle-Blossom* 127 Our 'fats' had been collected from three different stations. **1890** A.J. VOGAN *Black Police* 262, I have taken several mobs of 'fats' (fat bullocks) from the Never Never Land to Sydney—a distance of about fifteen hundred miles. **1894** *Bulletin* (Sydney) 27 Oct. 23/2 It only cost a trifle to drive 'fats' to the great Victorian markets. **1903** *Ibid.* 22 Oct. 36/1 We were taking down 'fats' from the head of the Brisbane for a large firm of butchers. **1915** *Ibid.* 11 Feb. 22/2 One unfortunate cowpuncher .. with 1200 fats, was stuck on one camp for 17 days. **1923** *Ibid.* 29 Mar. 22/2 The saddler, when assisting the butcher to yard a killer, threw a nigger's null-nulla at the 'fat'. **1942** H.H. PECK *Mem. of Stockman* 123 The farthest out of the Queensland runs .. regularly sent fats to Melbourne. **1946** *Bulletin* (Sydney) 6 Feb. 12/1 The bullock .. was almost ready for the fat market. **1962** *Ibid.* 3 Mar. 36/2 They were 'cutting out' the fats on Carpentaria Downs. **1976** N.V. WALLACE *Bush Lawyer* 125 The cattle camp grew as we mustered the fats.

b. *transf.*

1912 *Bulletin* (Sydney) 11 Apr. 13/4 Only saw turkey-droving once. That was 26 years ago, when I ran into a mob of prime fats travelling from Tumut to Wagga (N.S.W.).

fat, *a.*[3] and *n.*[2] [Spec. use of *fat* affluent.]

A. *adj.*

1. a. *Obs.* Capitalistic.

1896 *Bulletin* (Sydney) 28 Mar. 10/2 Anti-Sweating League has discovered a woman who earned at the rate of 6s. 9d. for 66 hours' work, and has been cut by the sweater, so that her earnings for the same time would be 4s. 'Let 'em sweat', says the Fat ring in the Leg. Council. **1906** *Gadfly* (Adelaide) 14 Mar. 5/1 According to the Fat Person's fancy picture of him the Australian socialist is a wild-eyed, frantic person, who breathes anarchy.

b. *Obs.* In the collocation **fat man,** a capitalist; also *attrib.*

1893 *Bulletin* (Sydney) 24 June 21/2 And, musing then upon the old-time lags, May doubt, perhaps, if they were more to blame Than modern Fat Man who, unpunished, drags A country's honour through a slough of shame. **1894** *Ibid.* 1 Dec. 16/1 The Fatman party in Vic. Assembly received a nasty pill from Labor-member Cook. **1895** *Worker* (Sydney) 5 Jan. 3/1 The more experience I have of the Fat Man and all his ilk the more I am convinced of his being an ass. **1899** *Tocsin* (Melbourne) 12 Jan. 7/1 Fatman's Dream. Let us corner up the sunbeams Lying all about our path, Get a trust on wheat and roses, Give the poor the thorns and chaff. **1903** *Truth* (Sydney) 26 July 1/6 This is the season when the fat man smiles in anticipation of his half-yearly divvies. **1905** *Bulletin* (Sydney) 5 Oct. 14/4, I have found a Fatman's ideal worker. He is working on a Vic. Western District station for 12s. a week. **1911** R.G.S. WILLIAMS *Austral. White Slaves* 68 The Trades Hall officials .. mention no names when referring to the 'bloated capitalist' or the 'fat man'. **1916** J. FURPHY *Poems* 12 That Fatman, dining at his club, On costly wet and sumptuous grub.

2. In the collocation **fat cat** [spec. use of (orig. U.S.) *fat cat* a wealthy and hence privileged person], a term applied to a person in one of the more highly paid grades of the public service (carrying the assumption that they are overpaid and underproductive); also *transf.*, and *attrib.*

1973 *Bulletin* (Sydney) 25 Aug. 67/3 There are radicals in the government who would really like to reduce the incomes of the various fat-cat groups. **1974** *Ibid.* 5 Jan. 23/3 With recession approaching .. wage demands are being refuelled by government handouts at the 'fat cat' level. **1975** *Ibid.* 7 June 13/1 The number of second division (over $20,600 salary) positions has grown to 31. There are 19 branches, headed by these fat cats as Labor Minister Cameron would call them. **1976** *Ibid.* 11 Sept. 27/3 The ABC has been accused of being a pretty fat cat when it comes to staffing news bulletins or whatever. **1984** *Canberra Times* 29 Apr. 4/6 Staff of the National Library are by no means in the fat-cat class.

Hence **fatmanity** *n.*, capitalism.

1897 *Tocsin* (Melbourne) 28 Oct. 3/3 The present crowd of fawning parasites of Fatmanity.

B. *n. Obs.* A capitalist.

[N.Z. **1905** *N.Z. Truth* (Wellington) 16 Sept. 1 A representative of fat proposed that he and his fellow fats [etc.]. **1906** *Gadfly* (Adelaide) 25 Apr. 5/2 Suggestions have been made to turn the Territory into a black-labour colony for the benefit of the Fat.] **1908** *Truth* (Sydney) 5 Apr. 9/4 And it isn't quite apparent why the Fats love Hingland so, Didn't Mother 'lag' their parents in the days not long ago? **1914** *Bulletin* (Sydney) 9 Apr. 3/2 Lo, Fat is loyal and loveth the Crown, But his greater desire is for many half-crowns! **1916** *Ross's Monthly* Oct. 1/1 Fat is prone to babble to discontented wage-slaves that there is plenty of room at the top. **1921** *Industr. News* (Sydney) 1 May 1/1 Quite so, fat, that has always been our lot.

fat, *n.*[3] [f. *fat* distended.] A (sexual) erection; esp. in the phr. **to crack a fat,** to have an erection.

1967 J. HIBBERD *White with Wire Wheels* (1970) 224 By Christ, if he races her off, it'll be the last fat he cracks. **1968** B. HUMPHRIES *Wonderful World of B. McKenzie*, Pommy sheilas? Aw, they're apples I s'pose—but the way I feel now I don't reckon I could crack a fat! **1969** A. BUZO *Front Room Boys* (1970) 21 You'd get a fat as you went in and it'd take about twenty minutes to have a squirt. **1971** B. HUMPHRIES *Bazza pulls it Off*, Come off it Bazza you old bastard you're too flamin' shicker to crack a fat now. **1976** R. DREWE *Savage Crows* 88 When he'd cracked a fat against her... 'Hey Stiffy,' she'd whispered in his ear, and giggled.

fattening, *ppl. a.* [Spec. use of *fattening* making fat.] Used with various nouns denoting place, with reference to the suitability of pasture for stock being prepared for slaughter for human consumption: **fattening country, paddock, run, station.**

1875 *Austral. Town & Country Jrnl.* (Sydney) 6 Feb. 223/4 It's first-class **fattening country;** I dare say you saw that if you noticed any mobs as you came along. **1942** H.H. PECK *Mem. of Stockman* 79 Kidman had a great preference for good fattening country in contrast to purely breeding country. **1909** M. FRANKLIN *Some Everyday Folk* 17 There was no lack of fodder that season, and even the lanes and byways would have served as **fattening paddocks.** **1923** 'J. NORTH' *Son of Bush* 26 The fattening paddocks supported hundreds of head of cattle. **1946** J.G. EASTWOOD *More about Cairns* 23, I had had plenty of boat pulling at the 'fattening paddock' on the Richmond River. **1848** T.L. MITCHELL *Jrnl. Exped. Tropical Aust.* 15 That country is considered excellent as a **fattening run** for sheep. **1890** 'R. BOLDREWOOD' *Colonial Reformer* II. 100 Rainbar was an out-and-out fattening run. **1847** *Port Phillip Gaz.* 24 Mar. 3 The improvements are extensive and complete, for either a **fattening,** dairy, or jobbing **station.** **1870** *Sydney Morning Herald* 2 July 3/6 Fattening station, Lachlan frontage, securely fenced. **1897** T.W. BEILLEY *Australasia's Goldfields* 58 The author .. possessed .. a magnificent fattening station .. having on it over 4,000 cattle. **1936** *Bulletin* (Sydney) 27 May 21/4 Several properties .. sent their store cattle to their own fattening stations nearer southern markets.

feather foot. *Aboriginal English.* KURDAITCHA 4.

1966 M. BROWN *Jimberi Track* 78 Ralph was thinking: Might be featherfoots watchin' me that side! **1980** *N.S.W. Parl. Papers* (1980–81) 3rd Sess. IV. 1666 At Kinchela we had a feather foot, a Kadachi man, and he came to do the programme... Normally Aborigines are frightened of these people.

fed. [Abbrev. of *federal(ist).*]

1. *Hist.* One who supports federation; FEDERALIST a.

1899 *Progress* (Brisbane) 10 June 1/2 The anti-feds, who were so much distressed by the delusion that in some way the people of Australia were going to pay something towards the maintenance of bounties on Victorian grown beet sugar, will be relieved in their minds when they learn that the factory is to be closed.

2. a. [Transf. use of U.S. *fed* member of the Federal Bureau of Investigation.] A police officer.

1966 P. COWAN *Seed* 2 The car began to gain speed... 'Better take it easy. The feds might pick us up.' **1972** *Ten Award Winning Stories* 29 No, he wouldn't wait that long for his dough. He would dob us in to the Feds. **1976** D. IRELAND *Glass Canoe* 76 The Great Lover's got his eyes peeled and a paddy waggon comes round the corner with its lights out. 'The feds!' he yells. And goes for his life.

b. [Transf. use of U.S. *fed* official of the federal government.] A member of the federal parliament; a member of a federal political party.

1978 *Bulletin* (Sydney) 11 Apr. 14/1 At the moment they're leaving it all to Joh, whom they can trust to see that the Feds don't pull any swifties. **1980** *Sun-Herald* (Sydney) 24 Feb. 50/5 My impression is that purges are not on. The Queensland branch is very cocky. It has the cash, and the Feds (according to them) cannot get hold of it. **1980** *Sydney Morning Herald* 11 Dec. 6/5 Mr Hills has resorted to rule No. 2 in the State politicians' handbook to justify this situation. Rule No. 2 says: If you can't blame The Feds blame your predecessor.

federal, *a.*

1. *Hist.* Of or pertaining to the association of the Australian Colonies in a federal union.

1835 *True Colonist* (Hobart) 4 Dec. 6/1 A *Federal* Union amongst all the Austral-Asian Colonies, will be most beneficial and desirable. **1849** *Britannia* (Hobart) 2 Oct. 2/2 Another object contemplated by the bill, was a federal union of the colonies . . a General Assembly of the whole union. **1859** R.H. Horne *Austral. Facts & Prospects* 212 The grand and final question of a Federal Union. **1889** *Austral. Handbk.* 462 The opening of the year 1886 was characterised by the meeting of the first Federal Council at Hobart. **1892** *Bulletin* (Sydney) 7 May 6/3 The irrational and barbarous property-vote could be made no worse by the establishment of the Federal Legislature. **1899** *North-Western Advocate* (Devonport) 23 June 2/7 Making reference to the federal referendum in New South Wales. **1901** *Truth* (Sydney) 17 Feb. 1/1 *Fellow-citizens*: Now that you are surfeited with Federal 'Flapdoodle'. **1944** G. Cockerill *Scribblers & Statesmen* 105 Lyne was a thorough going Protectionist. . . Further, he was a 'State rights' man, whose support for the Federal movement was only nominal.

2. Of or pertaining to the Commonwealth of Australia as distinct from the States which constitute it.

1901 *Truth* (Sydney) 23 June 4/2 Fixed firm in the Federal trap, New South Wales is already beginning to feel its iron teeth. **1917** *Huon Times* (Franklin) 16 Nov. 2/3 He has been in confabulation with members of the Federal Cabinet. **1919** C.A. Bernays *Qld. Politics during Sixty Yrs.* 532 The Federal pact, so far as Queensland is concerned, was entirely the doing of the North and the Centre. **1955** G. Healey *A.L.P.* 43 Another trend which, by 1905, was becoming noticeable was the 'Federal' attitude of Federal politicians of all parties. **1973** L. Oakes *Whitlam PM* 60 The Menzies Government, Whitlam said, had breached the Federal-State Housing Agreement. **1983** *Open Road* Apr. 2/1 NSW is burdened with an inadequate road system, yet this financial year will receive back for roads only about 22 per cent of total State and Federal fuel tax revenue collected from NSW motorists.

3. In collocations: **federal election, government, parliament.**

1910 *Huon Times* (Franklin) 19 Feb. 2/1 The **Federal elections** are approaching. **1971** D. Williamson *Don's Party* (1973) 15 Polling closed tonight at eight o'clock and the counting of votes for the 1969 Federal Election has begun. **1896** C.E. Lyne *Life H. Parkes* 545 The main trunk lines of railway to be at the service of the **Federal Government.** **1911** R.G.S. Williams *Austral. White Slaves* 78 There will be nothing left to the States that the Federal Government would take as a gift after April next. **1935** *Red Star* (Perth) 19 Apr. 3/2 We have received a small Federal Government bounty amounting to 3d. a bushel. **1942** *Welcome to Aust.* 20 The Federal Government . . looks after such national interests as defence, communications, tariffs and immigration. **1972** *Bulletin* (Sydney) 5 Aug. 16/3 Aborigines throughout Australia have found common cause in the federal government's removal of the Aboriginal embassy from the lawns of Parliament House. **1898** *Ibid.* 19 Feb. 6/3 It has been decided to leave the fixing of the capital to the **Federal Parliament.** **1899** *North-Western Advocate* (Devonport) 26 June 2/4 The Federal Parliament must meet within six months after the Queen's Proclamation. **1911** H.G. Turner *First Decade Austral. Cwlth.* 140 Transferred to the Federal Parliament. **1954** J. Waten *Unbending* 85 He had been given the opportunity of . . entering the Federal Parliament.

4. In special collocations: **Federal capital,** Canberra, the capital city of the Commonwealth of Australia; **Capital Territory,** that part of N.S.W. ceded to the Commonwealth of Australia as the site of Canberra and its immediate environs, since 1938 known as the Australian Capital Territory; **House,** either of the two federal Houses of Parliament; **Territory,** the Australian Capital Territory; in *pl.*, the Australian Capital Territory and the Northern Territory.

1898 *Bulletin* (Sydney) 19 Feb. 6/3 The remnant of the Cabbage-tree Mob has risen to announce that it will do all it knows to prevent any Federation unless N.S. Wales receives a special bribe by the establishment of the **Federal capital** in its territory. **1899** *North-Western Advocate* (Devonport) 9 Jan. 3/1 It is thought also that the fixing of the site for the federal capital should be left in the hands of the Federal Parliament. **1900** *Truth* (Sydney) 28 Jan. 1/2 Having filched away the Federal Capital from the Mother Colony. **1911** A. Marshall *Sunny Aust.* 67 We went through the site of the proposed Federal capital, which has no name yet but the Yass-Canberra site. **1942** *Welcome to Aust.* 20 Canberra, Federal Capital, the new city built to be the centre of Federal Government, was designed by Walter Burley Griffin. **1913** *Bulletin* (Sydney) 6 Nov. 22/3 I've been in the **Federal Capital Territory** . . for three months. **1917** *Huon Times* (Franklin) 20 July 2/5 It is proposed to close absolutely the construction work in the Federal Capital territory. **1911** *Ibid.* 30 Sept. 2/4 Seeing that this political machine for the time being dominates both **Federal Houses.** **1961** *Bulletin* (Sydney) 8 Feb. 15/1 The most vocal members of the Federal House are apt to come from pastoral stock. **1917** *Ibid.* 1 Mar. 22/4 This season the **Federal Territory** . . was over-run by the sow thistle. . . It might be better known to the city folk as 'cocky weed', for it is often gathered for tame cockatoos. **1927** *R. Comm. on Wireless* 2941 East Lake in the Federal Territory. **1955** N. Pulliam *I traveled Lonely Land* 62 Officially, Australia is the Commonwealth of Australia, composed of six states and the federal territories.

federalist.

a. *Hist.* One who supports the introduction of federation.

1898 *Bulletin* (Sydney) 25 June 20/1 Anti-Federalists in S.A. Assembly . . were sacked by their constituencies. **1899** *North-Western Advocate* (Devonport) 23 Jan. 2/7 Leave the most ardent federalist in doubt. **1907** *Bulletin* (Sydney) 14 Feb. 14/4 There are eighty of us, good Federalists, in a mining camp 100 miles from railway. . . Our Australia won't give us a mail.

b. One who supports the strengthening and extension of Commonwealth powers; one who seeks to preserve the federal character of the Constitution.

1944 G. Cockerill *Scribblers & Statesmen* 134 Former 'State-righters' became earnest Federalists. **1954** T. Ronan *Vision Splendid* 124 Besides, I'm a Federalist. I don't believe in restriction of trade between states. **1978** L. O'Charley *Anatomy of Strike* 44 I'd forgotten you are a federalist.

Hence **federalistic** *a.*, inclined to federalism.

1891 E.H. Hallack *W.A. & Yilgarn Goldfields* 27 Talk about federation and the small part intercolonially the colony must, from her position, necessarily play, it might with safety be recommended that a more federalistic form of government ought here to exist.

federate, *v. Hist.*

1. *intr.* To enter into a federal association.

1894 *Bulletin* (Sydney) 25 Aug. 6/2 If Australia is going to federate at all it is almost certain that it must start with a machine-made Constitution. **1899** *Austral. Tit-Bits* (Sydney) 25 Feb. 38/2 Oh! do not let us longer wait, Now's the time to federate.

2. *trans.* To bring under the control of the Commonwealth government.

1898 *Bulletin* (Sydney) 9 Apr. 7/1 Many of the residents of Sydney . . are apprehensive lest . . the railways be federated.

Hence **federated** *ppl. a.*, **federating** *ppl. a.*

1899 *North-Western Advocate* (Devonport) 17 May 2/5 Our relationship to Federated Australia vastly enhances the question of education. **1900** *Advocate* (Burnie) 8 Dec. 1/8 When the Commonwealth comes into existence the federating colonies will drop the name of 'colonies' and be henceforth designated as 'States'.

federation.

1. The association of the Australian Colonies in a federal union; the formation of the Commonwealth of Australia on 1 January 1901. Also *attrib.*

***c* 1875** *Me an' George* 45 If there's no patriotism, no unselfishness, no natural nobility, no good at all in Australians, why are you appealin' to them to 'make sacrifices' for the sake of federation? **1882** *Bulletin* (Sydney) 13 May 9/2 We are to have Federation at last. J. Henniker Heaton is the donor. **1883** *Adelaide Observer* 27 Oct. 6 We can plant the first grand stepping stone of the united federation throne, to be erected somewhere in central Victoria. **1888** *Plea for Separation* 17 Nationalism alone will bring Australian Federation, but Separation will come almost simultaneously. **1891** *Bohemia* (Melbourne) 4 June 4 Scott bucked violently just before the Federation banquet in Sydney, because he found that the Governors from the other colonies were to take precedence of him at the guzzle. **1901** *Truth* (Sydney) 9 June 4/4 Federation, as now consummated and carried on in Melbourne, is a constitutional comedy and a financial farce. **1903** *Ibid.* 15 Mar. 1/6 Federation is now spelt 'Damnation' by many erstwhile enthusiasts. **1919** C.A. Bernays *Qld. Politics during Sixty Yrs.* 532 There was a substantial majority in the South against Queensland entering the Federation. **1936** E. Scott *Aust. during War* in *Official Hist. Aust. 1914–18* XI. 5 The Australian federal movement did not emanate from war . . and it is that difference which denotes the making of the federation of Australia as arising from causes unlike those which produced other important federations. **1955** G. Healey *A.L.P.* 29 In 1901—Federation year. **1965** J. Iggulden *Dark Stranger* 195 We're the hottest piece of news since federation. **1978** L. O'Charley *Anatomy of Strike* 155 Thirty six proposed constitutional amendments since federation.

2. Abbrev. of *Federation wheat.* Also *attrib.*

1901 *Agric. Gaz. N.S.W.* XII. 429 Federation and Purple Gown were from the same cross. **1916** *Jrnl. Dept. Agric. Vic.* Feb. 75 None of his many successful crossbred wheats have enjoyed such a wide measure of popularity as Federation. Indeed, during the last six years the golden yellow characteristic of old-time Australian harvest fields has been gradually changed to a dull bronze through the ever-increasing popularity of Federation wheat. . . Federation is a short, erect-growing variety of moderate stooling capacity, with broad, semi-erect, light-green foliage. **1928** R.G. Stapledon *Tour in Aust. & N.Z.* 38 'Federation' is still of course a most important variety in Australia. **1931** *Century of Journalism* 345 As the result of that assiduous labour, Farrer produced a bewildering variety of wheats, suitable for all sorts and conditions of soil and climate, the most valuable of them all being his famous 'Federation'. **1984** P. Cuffley *Chandeliers & Billy Tea* 194 The 1890s saw superphosphate fertilisers being applied. . . Seed drills . . when allied to the new Federation strain of wheat, resulted in a new life for the industry. **1986** *Canberra Times* 2 Feb. 18/6 Farrer's first commercial variety, Federation, released in 1901, dominated Australian wheat production for more than two decades.

3. Special Comb. **Federation style,** a name given by Bernard Smith (b. 1916), art historian, to a style of domestic architecture flourishing between 1895 and 1915; **wheat,** an early maturing variety of wheat developed by William Farrer (1845–1906) and released in 1901 (see quot. 1956).

1969 B. Smith in *Hist. Studies* XIV. 90 The Australian house called Queen Anne has little in common with the English domestic brick architecture of the first decade of the eighteenth century. . . My own nomination would be **Federation style**. For it was born within the context of a discussion about the nature of an Australian style which parallels the political discussion that led to the foundation of the Commonwealth. **1973** B. & K. Smith *Archit. Character Glebe* 107 The Federation style makes its appearance in Glebe in fairly pure forms around 1893. **1984** *Multilist Realtor* (Sydney) 20 Sept. 49/2 Federation style 2 br with ornate ceilings, fireplaces can be restored, big lounge and separate dining. **1901 federation wheat** [see sense 2]. **1905** *Agric. Gaz. N.S.W.* XVI. 465 For the country and plains to the west of Warialda, Gunnedah, Narromine, Forbes and Wagga I know of no bread-wheat which is likely to be more suitable than Federation (1 or 2). **1948** E.H. Collis *Lost Yrs.* 88 His best-known creation was 'Federation' wheat, which transformed growing conditions in New South Wales, Victoria and South Australia, while his 'Florence' wheat proved particularly adapted for Queensland. **1956** Callaghan & Millington *Wheat Industry Aust.* 275 This new variety was released in 1901 and named Federation to mark the foundation of the Australian Commonwealth, a political event very dear to the heart of Farrer.

Hence **federationist** *n.*

1888 *Plea for Separation* 12 Separationists are essentially Federationists.

feed. [Spec. use of (esp. Br. dial.) *feed* pasture, green crops.] (Natural) vegetation, esp. grasses, suitable as food for stock; Picking. See also *green feed, pick* Green 2, *sheep-feed* Sheep 2.

1847 *Bell's Life in Sydney* 16 Jan. 3/4 The country

however, is looking beautiful just now, the feed being most abundant. **1851** *Empire* (Sydney) 16 Apr. 2/4 On the Upper Murray, where there is good feed, a number of settlers have driven their starving flocks and 'sat down' upon the runs of their more fortunate neighbours. **1855** R. HENNING *Lett.* (1952) 18 A place called Gerar, where 'feed'—as they always call grass here—was plentiful. **1862** J. MCKINLAY *Jrnl. Exploration Interior* 3 June 102 The feed in general is very dry, except in the neighbourhood of the creeks or lagoons. **1874** C. DE BOOS *Congewoi Correspondence* 142 When the first rain comes and there'ser springer young grass, the paddies come back again in hunderds on to the burnt feed. **1884** *Adelaide Observer* 9 Aug. 35 The drovers' account of the state of the road for feed along the Darling is not of a cheering description, but I never knew stock-drovers to 'blow' about the grass being too good. **1891** *Quiz* (Adelaide) 6 Mar. 7/1 There was no water on the land and no feed, except saltbush. **1915** *Bulletin* (Sydney) 14 Jan. 22/4 Feed has come on rapidly, and now . . the usually dry northern parts of S. Aus. are offering to paddock the suffering stock from the usually moist southern region. **1931** B. CRONIN *Bracken* 35 'We've never had real feed this winter,' the boy replied. 'It's more fern and prickly-mosses than grass.' **1944** A. MARSHALL *These are my People* 105 There's feed in his paddock six inches high. **1950** A.W. UPFIELD *Bachelors of Broken Hill* 163 Ned tells me that the feed your way is knee-high and dry as tinder. **1960** *N.T. News* (Darwin) 12 Feb. 7/5 Re-growth of feed will occur almost everywhere in the Alice Springs district following recent widespread rain. **1978** D. STUART *Wedgetail View* 4 By sundown the cattle were all watered and most of them were out on dry feed south of the pool, a wide stretch of feed east of the river. **1983** *Canberra Times* 24 May 3/1 At this time of the year there was usually standing dry feed left.

feeding, *vbl. n.* [Br. dial. *feeding, vbl. n.* pasturage.]

1. Used *attrib.* with reference to the pasturing of stock. Cf. GRAZING.

1856 W.W. DOBIE *Recoll. Visit Port-Phillip* 102 The flocks are brought in by the shepherds from their several feeding stations, one by one, to the home-station, to undergo the processes of washing and shearing. **1875** J. FORREST *Explorations in Aust.* 207 We saw a beautiful piece of feeding country. **1935** R.B. PLOWMAN *Boundary Rider* 41 Beyond the feeding range of the township stockgrass and saltbush and other feed became plentiful.

2. *transf.* and *fig.*

1869 'Q' *Peripatetic Philosopher* 41 The Wimmera district is noted for the hordes of vagabond 'loafers' that it supports, and has earned for itself the name of 'The Feeding Track'. I remember an old bush ditty, which I have heard sung when I was on the 'Wallaby': Hurrah! hurrah! for the feeding track, I've left the Avoca behind my back, Hurrah! hurrah! for the feeding track, Hurrah! hurrah! for the Wimmera.

feed-shed. An out-building in which fodder is stored.

1941 *Bulletin* (Sydney) 7 May 17/3 In the feed-shed he tackled his son. **1948** *Ibid.* 21 Apr. 22/1 Just then the hand came out of the feedshed. **1960** *Ibid.* 18 May 19/1 The trucks coming into the feed-shed had been running over it. **1963** X. HERBERT *Disturbing Element* 67 We had to camp the night in the feed-shed with the rats and eat linseed oil cake. **1965** H. ATKINSON *Reckoning* 8 Looked . . at the dairy, the feed-shed, the cattle grazing on the flat.

Felician. *Obs.* Shortened form of AUSTRAL FELICIAN.

1848 *Omnibus & Sydney Spectator* 6 Nov. 42/2 It appears he is quite delighted with his trip, and has made the *Felicians* happy by the promise of a visit every year, during his stay in the colony.

fellmonger, *v.* [f. *fellmonger, n.* one whose occupation is the removal of wool from sheepskins.] *trans.* To remove (the wool) from a sheepskin. Also *absol.*, and with 'skin' as obj. Freq. as *vbl. n.* and *ppl. a.*

1847 *Maitland Mercury* 27 Oct. 1/2 *Fellmongering Establishment.* The undersigned . . found it advisable to *open* an *establishment* of the above nature in Maitland. **1851** *Illustr. Austral. Mag.* (Melbourne) July 26 Fellmongering and Boiling-down establishments next contribute their rich and fertilizing streams—more invigorating, however, to our mother-earth than to the nicer constitutions of her human family. **1871** *Austral. Town & Country Jrnl.* (Sydney) 28 Jan. 106/1 The remaining class was devoted to fellmongered wool, but there were no entries. **1872** G.S. BADEN-POWELL *New Homes for Old Country* 29 Fellmongering is a peculiar industry. Sheepskins are rotted by damp or other means, and the wool, thus easily separated from them, is washed and packed for the market. **1882** ARMSTRONG & CAMPBELL *Austral. Sheep Husbandry* 248 Fellmongering should be done at or as soon after shearing time as possible, so as to allow of the fellmongered wool being sent to market with the general clip. **1899** G. JEFFREY *Princ. Australasian Woolclassing* 112 Green skins, if fellmongered soon after being taken from the carcase need not be soaked. **1912** *N.S.W. Parl. Papers* II. 118 'Wool-scouring and fellmongering' shows a decrease in the number of hands employed. **1924** E.C. SNOW *Leather, Hides, Skins* 59 The Census of Production of 1907 gave the number of sheep and lambskins fellmongered in England and Wales and Ireland as 8,928,000. **1946** *Pastoral Rev. & Graziers' Rec.* 16 Sept. 784 He will carry out research work of fundamental importance to certain fellmongering problems in this country. **1957** H. PHILLIPS *Survey Fellmongering N.Z. & Aust.* 16 State abattoirs do not fellmonger.

fellmongery. [f. prec.] **a.** An establishment in which wool is removed from sheepskins. **b.** The process involved.

1880 R. ROSE *Austral. Guide: S.A.* 10 There are 60 tanneries and fellmongeries . . and, in addition to these, there are numerous large wool-washing works. **1899** G. JEFFREY *Princ. Australasian Woolclassing* 108 Fellmongery . . here refers to taking the wool off the skin. **1957** H. PHILLIPS *Survey Fellmongering N.Z. & Aust.* 16 There are more separate fellmongeries in Australia than in New Zealand.

fellow. *Austral. pidgin.* Also **fella, feller.** [Transf. use of *fellow* man.]

1. See quots.

1856 W.W. DOBIE *Recoll. Visit Port-Phillip* 91 The flattering compliment meant for my brother and myself, that 'there was no gammon along o' two fellow Dobie'. **1870** C.H. ALLEN *Visit to Qld.* 182 'Fellow' is a very important word in their English vocabulary, and expresses number; as 'six fellow yarraman', six horses; 'big fellow waddy', a large quantity of wood; 'little fellow waddy', a small quantity. **1872** 'RESIDENT' *Glimpses Life Vic.* 195 Three fellow potato. The word 'fellow' was always used as an additional qualification of the noun; as for instance 'fine fellow horse', or 'big fellow river', which meant simply 'a fine horse', or 'a big river'. **1884** A.W. STIRLING *Never Never Land* 93 Everything is a 'fellow'; 'one fellow bob', the black calls a shilling; 'me got three fellow gin', meaning 'I have three wives' and so on. **1953** L. & C. REES *Spinifex Walkabout* 125 The homestead itself is . . two-storeyed—as the natives say 'him two-fella house'.

2. Chiefly *attrib.* in quasi-adj. (or adv.) phr.: **good fellow,** excellent; **proper fellow,** properly.

1935 K.L. SMITH *Sky Pilot Arnhem Land* 50 To Dan everything that flew, or walked, or creeped, or swam was '**good fellow** tucker'. **1947** W.E. HARNEY *Brimming Billabongs* (1963) 92 They told me that this boss of theirs was a 'good fellow man'. **1968** S. GORE *Holy Smoke* 16 Make 'im goanna too, and snake—goodfeller tucker longa you binjy, eh? **1977** *Up Beat* Aug. 7, Him goodfella, but jus' keep 'im 'way from me. **1951** I.L. IDRIESS *Across Nullarbor* 145, I can assure Mrs Melang back in Norseman that the meal was '**proper feller**' appreciated. **1963** —— *Our Living Stone Age* 30 They would . . seriously paint the doll, boy or girl, with stripes of red or yellow ochres, 'dressing' them thus for various corroborees; all had to be done 'proper feller'.

felon. In occasional use in Australia during the period of transportation as a synonym for CONVICT. Used *attrib.* in Special Comb. **felon colony, constable, constabulary, overseer, police:** see CONVICT B. 3.

1851 *Illustr. Austral. Mag.* (Melbourne) Oct. 210 A narrow jealousy of what we had been pleased, in our virgin purity, to stigmatise as the '**Felon Colony**'. **1853** J. SHERER *Gold Finder Aust.* 167 Although Victoria has never had the penal stigma upon it, yet it is so close in the neighbourhood of the felon colonies, that it now affords shelter to a large share of their population. **1835** H. MELVILLE *Hist. Van Diemen's Land* 217 Three witnesses were **felon constables**, John Boswood, a convict attaint, being a prisoner for life. **1837** *Cornwall Chron.* (Launceston) 1 July 1 People . . have been stopped in the streets at night when walking peaceably in them, and *charged* by the felon constables with the commission of a crime. **1839** W. MANN *Six Yrs.' Residence* 125 The felon-constables . . were actively employed in preventing them, and put some of the most respectable inhabitants in the watch-house. **1846** *Britannia* (Hobart) 12 Nov. 2/4 Supported by the perjured evidence of felon constables. **1856** J. BONWICK *Bushrangers* 92 He . . brooked not the gentle influence of felon constables. **1835** H. MELVILLE *Hist. Van Diemen's Land* 268 It . . will serve to shew the villainy practised by the **felon constabulary.** **1837** *Cornwall Chron.* (Launceston) 3 June (Suppl.) 5 This is an awful country to live in no wonder the newspapers so unanimously deprecate the *felon* constabulary system. **1835** *Ibid.* 14 Nov. 2 All the bolstering of the *Courier*, will never make British free subjects believe, that under any circumstances they are liable to be scourged by **felon overseers**, at the caprice of the Subaltern of a marching regiment. **1844** C. LYON *Narr. & Recoll. Van Dieman's Land* 25 Several hundred prisoners . . were again subject to the caprice of felon overseers. **1834** *True Colonist* (Hobart) 25 Nov. 2/3 Procure a dollar to shut the eyes of any of the **Felon Police**, who may observe an *impropriety.* **1836** *Cornwall Chron.* (Launceston) 3 Mar. 33 In this country we have a felon police riding rough-shod over the liberties and rights of free British subjects. *Ibid.*, Are the *free* Colonists to be *made* to pay an immense sum to maintain a thrice and oftener convicted felon Police? **1849** T. ROGERS *Corresp. relating to Dismissal* 125 Bransom was, in felon police parlance, a 'parson's man'.

felonize, *v. Obs. trans.* To taint (with the human degradation associated with a penal settlement). Also as *ppl. a.*

1827 *Monitor* (Sydney) 20 Apr. 388/2 The sight of human woe and degradation continually before our eyes, will gradually impress upon our imaginations the feelings of gaolers, and *felonise* as it were every conception of our minds. **1841** *Geelong Advertiser* 6 Feb. 2/2 My Lord . . your liberal measures for the division of this colony from the felonized colony of New South Wales.

felonry. *Hist.* [See quot. 1837.] The convict and ex-convict population, conceived of as a class.

1837 J. MUDIE *Felonry of N.S.W.* p. vi, The author has ventured to coin the word *felonry*, as the appellative of an *order* or class of persons in New South Wales. **1837** H. WATSON *Lecture on S.A.* 6 The 'felonry of New South Wales', as the emancipated convicts have been called, form a distinct class. **1838** *Austral. Mag.* (Sydney) 111 The governor himself in those days deigned to hold occasional converse with one of the 'Felonry'. **1839** *Port Phillip Patriot* 24 Apr. 3/3 They [*sc.* capitalists in New South Wales] have a Felonry, we have not; we would raise a *Yeomanry*, they having none, are determined to prevent such a class in Australia Felix if possible. **1845** *Atlas* (Sydney) I. 241/2 Men . . said their worst of the 'Felonry of New South Wales', and by way of mending the matter, the sister island has been made to groan under the Felonry of Van Diemen's Land. **1847** *Port Phillip Herald* 2 Mar. 2/4 He would then ask them if they intended to nip their brightest prospects in the bud—to convert this province into a receptacle of British felonry, and themselves so many unpaid gaolers. **1849** *Perils, Pastimes, & Pleasures of Emigrant* 62 His tales of the *Felonry* of this colony would make you shudder or weep. **1882** J. ALLEN *Hist. Aust.* 86 In the early part of 1849 . . meetings were held in Melbourne to protest against this attempt to deluge that part of the colony of New South Wales with the felonry of Great Britain. **1904** *Truth* (Sydney) 28 Feb. 1/2 The curse of the felonry planted here by Phillip. **1913** *Ibid.* 29 June 12/3 *Felonry in Victoria.* Convicts or 'Exiles'? **1939** FRANKLIN & CUSACK *Pioneers on Parade* 12 Felonry, of whatever virtue, was taboo in the pioneerage, but descendants of free settlers, however humble or undesirable, were recognized. **1945** J.A. ALLAN *Men & Manners in Aust.* 164 At Port Arthur the chief use of public worship was the enabling of the felonry to carry on surreptitious conversations.

female factory: see FACTORY.

fence, *n.*[1]

1. a. Used *attrib.* in Special Comb. **fence country,** fenced (hence settled) country, 'civilization'; also as *adj.*; **strainer,** STRAINER.

1940 W. HATFIELD *Into (Great?) Unfenced* 63 '*Mister* Barton, an' you're sweet. See?' Harry winked. 'What, Sir an' all?' 'Oh, he's not quite **fence-country.** No. Don't lap it round too thick. Might think you're swingin' on his foot. Mister'll do.' **1976** C.D. MILLS *Hobble Chains & Greenhide* 182, I wanted to be in Sydney for Christmas... 'I'm gonna miss you all and I hate to go. Yet I'm glad to be goin' back to see my people again.' I didn't realize as I said it, how much I would miss them and the life I had led once I hit the 'fence country' again. **1944** *Bulletin* (Sydney) 12 Apr. 12/2 Whenever he appeared with a shanty hung on his eye—and that was not seldom. Never did he attribute it to an upflung bit of firewood or a slipped **fence-strainer.** **1955** P. WHITE *Tree of Man* 268 How very plain and boring they were, especially the father when explaining the workings of a fence-strainer or the ailments of cows.

b. In the phr. **outside the fences,** beyond settled country.

1937 W. HATFIELD *I find Aust.* 101 When the Annandale stock camp rode into town, Jack Gaffney, the manager, gave me a job right away. Over here in the cattle-country, managers were called by their Christian names... I approached him and asked was he Mr Gaffney... 'There's no handles out in this country. You're outside the fences now. Jack Gaffney's my name.'

2. In the phr. **over the fence,** objectionable; unacceptable; 'beyond the pale'.

1918 *Kia Ora Coo-ee* May 4/2 'It's over the blinking fence,' cried one chap, and he voiced the general opinion. **1927** K.S. PRICHARD *Brumby Innes* (1974) 77 It's over the fence, Brum, the way you been carrying on. Way you been treating Nyedee. I've shut my eyes to it, over and over again. And I've warned you. **1950** —— *Winged Seeds* 62 After all, it was 'over-the-fence' for Wally and his cobbers to talk about any women in a bar as they had done. **1964** *Sydney Morning Herald* 18 Sept. 11/1 Some publications which unduly emphasize sex were 'entirely over the fence', the Chief Secretary, Mr C.A. Kelly, said yesterday. **1972** A. CHIPPER *Aussie Swearers Guide* 79 A man who drinks lemonade or milk in a *rubbity* (pub) is *over the fence.*

fence, *n.*[2] Shortened form of *rabbit-proof fence* (see RABBIT-PROOF *a.* 1). Also *attrib.*

1930 E. ANTONY *Hungry Mile* 36 The days I steered the hunchies through the sandhills 'down the fence'. **1937** A.W. UPFIELD *Mr Jelly's Business* 175, I thought Lucy Jelly was sweet on the Fence-rider. **1954** I.L. IDRIESS *Nor'-Westers* 113 When we moved on.. 40 miles out to stations or 'roo shooters' camps, or to 'the Fence' (rabbit-proof fence), and thus the news would spread.

fencer. [Used elsewhere but recorded earliest in Aust.]

1. One whose occupation is the erection of (rural) fences.

1827 P. CUNNINGHAM *Two Yrs. in N.S.W.* II. 167 Carrying up with you three fencers, if you can obtain them, to secure crops by a good four-rail fence. **1830** *Sydney Monitor* 12 May 4/3 Governor Darling sent *fencers* upon the land, and they fenced off such portion as His Excellency was pleased to claim. **1849** S. & J. SIDNEY *Emigrant's Jrnl.* 5 We hired an old fencer at 10s. a week and his grub. **1881** W.E. ABBOTT *Notes Journey on Darling* 60 The station-buildings are erected, stock bought, and fencers and tank-sinkers set to work in all directions. **1892** ROYDHOUSE & TAPERELL *Labour Party N.S.W.* 30 He was for eight years a drover, and was also, by turn, miner, fencer, tank sinker, and shearer. **1935** R.B. PLOWMAN *Boundary Rider* 90 Arthur, another stockman, was already helping to get the horses out, assisted by Sam, a fencer. **1943** *Bulletin* (Sydney) 8 Dec. 13/2 Jim the fencer had collected his cheque from the station after six months' solid toil, and proceeded to the nearest bush pub. **1960** *N.T. News* (Darwin) 16 Feb. 1/1, 36-year-old fencer is still alive after 14 days lost. **1981** A. WILKINSON *Up Country* 167 Leonard, a fencer.. had set up camp, with his dogs, just outside a small.. mining settlement.

2. In the collocation **fencer's tea**: see quot.

1942 W. GLASSON *Our Shepherds* 12 The ration supplied to each shepherd was extremely meagre and restricted... ¼ lb. tea, commonly called 'fencer's tea' because of its absence of leaf and preponderance of 'posts and rails'; 1½ lb. dark treacly sugar... 1 lb. of coarse salt; 10 lbs. of flour... 12 lb. of meat.

fencing, *vbl. n.* Used *attrib.* in Special Comb. **fencing camp,** the accommodation, personnel, etc., of a party of fencers; **wire,** heavy-gauge wire used in making fences; also in metaphorical comparisons.

1913 [**fencing camp**] *Bulletin* (Sydney) 6 Nov. 24/2 The most common subject of conversation in any bush camp, whether it's sheep, cattle, scrub cutters', fencing or any other.. is horse: racehorse, stock horse,.. pack horse,.. the take-down horse, the wool-team horse and, of course, the bucking horse. **1917** *Ibid.* 15 Feb. 24/4 A deputation from the fencing camp approached the boss for a change of tucker. **1858** *Royal S. Austral. Almanac* 27 (Advt.), *R.H. Crittenden, iron merchant,* Dealer in Ploughs, **Fencing Wire,** &c. **1897** L. LINDLEY-COWEN *W. Austral. Settler's Guide* 31 The sum in hand should be sufficient to buy tools, plough horses, fencing wire, clothing and sundries for the first twelve months. **1914** 'B. CABLE' *By Blow & Kiss* 20 He's as tough as fencin'-wire. **1921** W.H. PHIPPS *Bush Yarns & Town Sketches* 41 While the fat on the second slice is flaming on the grid of fencing wire. **1922** V. PALMER *Boss of Killara* 145, I thought you had nerves like fencing-wire, Delia. **1944** E.M. ANDERSON *Typist Tales* 106 He saw.. a table-top waggon loaded with fencing wire. **1946** *Bulletin* (Sydney) 18 Sept. 29/1 The cocky uses fencing-wire; the townie gets most things done with the yard of string and a good lick.

fern.

1. *spec. Obs.* BRACKEN.

1834 *Hobart Town Almanack* 129 *Pteris esculenta*.. is known.. among the European inhabitants of the colony by the name of fern. **1841** *Port Phillip Gaz.* 7 Aug. 3 There are many gum trees on portions of the island, with quantities of fern growing under them. **1897** L. LINDLEY-COWEN *W. Austral. Settler's Guide* 217 In fern (bracken) country ring-barking appears to be of doubtful benefit.

2. Special Comb. **fern-gully,** a small valley or ravine, esp. in an area of moist forest, characterized by a high incidence of tree ferns; **hook** (or **slasher**), a long-handled arcuate tool used for cutting bracken; **tree,** *tree fern,* see TREE; also *attrib.*, esp. as **fern tree gully.**

1889 A. BRASSEY *Last Voyage India & Aust.* 318 We crossed a large river, the Nepean, passing through some charming **fern-gullies.** **1903** *Emu* II. 177 A ramble in a fern gully. **1911** *Huon Times* (Franklin) 9 Dec. 2/2 Visitors to this meeting will enjoy one of the grandest drives in Tasmania, principally through fern gullies. **1932** J. TRURAN *Green Mallee* 71 They told him of.. silent fern-gullies in the Dandenongs. **1949** J. MORRISON *Creeping City* 8 You pay sixpence to go in and have a gig at his fern-gully and fishponds and smoodging nooks. **1951** D. COLLINS *Vic.'s my Home Ground* 60 That run through the fern gullies, stopping at little stations which are only a signboard, hugging the river, lost in the green shade, must have been a joy. **1980** J. WOLFE *End of Pricklystick* 9 A thousand lyre-birds sang from deep, dark fern-gullies. **1920** G. SARGANT *Winding Track* 155 Muscles were hardened to the **fern hook**.. cutting off the young bracken. **1931** B. CRONIN *Bracken* 53 Full of weeds, Martin. Full of bracken-fern. Get the fern-hook to work, man. **1952** *Bulletin* (Sydney) 27 Aug. 16/4 'Don't let him see a mattock, either,' the neighbor continued, 'or a fern-slasher.' **1958** P. COWAN *Unploughed Land* 56 The boy swung the fern hook. **1788** J. HUNTER *Hist. Jrnl. Trans. Port Jackson* (1793) 326 The **fern-tree** which is very plentiful is good for hogs. **1811** G. PATERSON *Hist. N.S.W.* 429 Black and white mottled Fern tree was found at the head of Lane Cove, by Colonel Paterson, about five years since. **1838** *Cornwall Chron.* (Launceston) 22 Sept. 1 Those who have only seen the sickly semblance of the graceful fern-tree where they are cultured by the hand of man, can ill form an idea of them in their native splendour. **1848** J. SYME *Nine Yrs. Van Diemen's Land* 61 The fern tree.. the most elegant production of nature in the island, growing many feet high, with a splendid top. **1866** *Illustr. Sydney News* 16 May 12/1 One of the most lovely features in Australian scenery.. is.. the Fern-Tree Gullies. **1880** 'ERRO' *Squattermania* 220 He.. finally deposited him in a gloomy fern-tree gully for the night. **1884** 'R. BOLDREWOOD' *Old Melbourne Memories* 147 Picnics to fern-tree gullies.. were successfully carried out. **1948** F. CLUNE *Wild Colonial Boys* 612 It was wild country, the rugged ranges covered with stringybark and peppermint-gum scrubs and fern-tree forests.

fern root. *Obs.* The edible root of the ferns *Blechnum indicum* (see BUNGWALL) and *B. orientale* (fam. Blechnaceae) of tropical Aust. and elsewhere.

1788 *HRA* (1914) 1st Ser. I. 31, I also found the root of fern, or something like the fern root that had been chewed by one of the natives. **1811** G. PATERSON *Hist. N.S.W.* 106 These wood natives make a paste formed of the fern-root and the ant bruised together. **1825** B. FIELD *Geogr. Mem. N.S.W.* 59 Their women and children.. have been employed during the day in procuring fern-root, which they call *dingowa.* **1845** C. HODGKINSON *Aust., Port Macquarie to Moreton Bay* 225 The fern root.. is rendered edible by beating it on a stone into a sort of paste. **1888** R. CROOKE *Convict* (1958) 79 The fern root, which is by no means a bad substitute for the potato was to be found in abundance. **1899** J. MATHEW *Eaglehawk & Crow* 89 Fern roots and the Australian yam.. are perhaps the most common edible vegetables.

fettler. [Spec. use of Br. dial. *fettler* navvy: see EDD *fettle, v.* to repair, maintain, etc., esp. sense 7.] One of a party of workers responsible for the maintenance of a section of railway track.

1887 *V & P* (N.S.W. L.A.) VI. 441 Number and Classification of Persons employed in the Engineer for Existing Railway Branch, year 1886.. Fettlers.. 1177. **1890** *Braidwood Dispatch* 30 Apr. 4/1 Mrs Condon, wife of a fettler at Locksley, is seriously ill. **1900** *Bulletin* (Sydney) 29 Sept. 14/4 Beyond Drummond Range, C.Q., the goats.. swarm about railway-fettlers' camps. **1935** R.B. PLOWMAN *Boundary Rider* 160 Then.. at a group of fettlers' cottages.. no fewer than twenty people.. turned out for the service. **1945** J. DEVANNY *Bird of Paradise* 158 Railway extra gangs are flying fettlers, groups of approximately twenty-five men. They do the big jobs on the lines that are beyond the powers of the four-men fettler gangs. **1964** *Mount Isa Mail* 13 Feb. 3/3 Railway engineers, fettlers and gangers could have given valuable information. **1980** M. DUGAN *Early Dreaming* 18 Today, technology is taking away the necessity for fettlers (railway gangs) on the Transcontinental Railway. **1983** P. ADAM SMITH *When we rode Rails* 154 Permanent-way men.. are known as.. fettlers in Tasmania, New South Wales and Queensland.

Also **fettling gang.**

1937 *Bulletin* (Sydney) 4 Aug. 21/2 Why do swagmen shy clear of fettling gangs? **1938** X. HERBERT *Capricornia* (ed. 6) 63 Oscar stood on the track conversing with members of the fettling gang.

fever bark. [See quot. 1926.] The tree *Alstonia constricta* (see BITTER BARK). Also **fever tree.**

1888 *Proc. Linnean Soc. N.S.W.* III. 361 *Alstonia constricta*.. 'Fever-bark' or 'Bitter-bark' tree. **1926** *Bulletin* (Sydney) 14 Jan. 22/3 The 'fever'-tree.. is the native quinine.. commonly known on the North Coast of Bananaland as 'bitter bark'. **1977** R. MCKIE *Crushing* (1978) 151 A fever bark from which the blacks made medicine.

few. [Used elsewhere but recorded earliest in Aust.] Esp. in the phr. **to have a few (in),** to have (or to have had) a few alcoholic drinks.

1903 *Truth* (Sydney) 12 Apr. 1/6 Senior-sergeant: 'You're charged with being drunk.' Female: 'Guilty on a false oath!' As she had a few in at the time she was sent to the cells. **1912** M. SWEENEY *Melbourne's Armageddon* 22 He was 'havin' a few' with a couple of mates, down in a slum hotel. **1937** W. HATFIELD *I find Aust.* 95 Twelve western cattlemen with money in their pockets can make a two-pub town look quite lively... 'Last man to Dingo Charlie's has to shout for the house!'.. I considered myself a cattleman, now, and with a few across my chest, found I could kick up my quota of the din. **1954** N. BARTLETT *Pearl Seekers* 122 Naughton, with a few in, used to walk into Farquhar McCrae's store-cum-bank and say: 'Give me some money, Farquhar.' **1968** D. O'GRADY *Bottle of Sandwiches* 159 We repaired to the rubbity.. intending to have a quiet few before wandering out to the camp. **1975** *R.A.N. News* (Sydney) 28 Nov. 3 Statistics prove that there is always a first time for the social drinker to become involved in an accident, even after years of experience of driving 'with a few in'.

fibro. Abbrev. of FIBRO-CEMENT. Freq. *attrib.*

1946 M. TRIST *What else is There* 167 The house was a dishevelled structure of brick, weatherboard and fibro. **1952** *Bulletin* (Sydney) 16 Apr. 16/2 The stream of ants was making its way down the skirting-board along the outside wall of my fibro home. **1959** J. CLEARY *Strike me Lucky* 114, I got the Rolls out of the fibro garage. **1964** C. KUNRATHY *Impudent Foreigner* 142 In Europe they never build of fibro, it would not suit the climate. **1965** K. SMITH *OGF* 83, I felt better already with familiar things around me: the long line of pretty, well-painted fibro boxes . . , the neat paling fences, every lawn cut. **1972** *Bulletin* (Sydney) 5 Aug. 16/2 The mother of Australian parliaments continued to spread backwards and sideways . . a labyrinthine muddle of fibro, weatherboard and corrugated iron infested by rust, dry rot and white ants. **1975** R.J. MERRITT *Cake Man* (1978) 18 Inside a house on a mission for Aborigines. It is night. The walls are wooden below, fibro on top. **1986** *Sydney Morning Herald* 12 Apr. 3/2 The small courthouse has the stateliness of a fibro fishing shack.

fibro-cement. A mixture of asbestos and cement compressed into sheets for use as a building material; asbestos cement. Also *attrib.*

1918 G. WHITE *Thirty Yrs. Tropical Aust.* 202 The church is of fibro-cement. **1929** A. SMITH *Austral. Home Carpenter* 91 You can build a seaside or mountain week-end cottage or garage *with Fibro Cement Sheets.* **1955** P. WHITE *Tree of Man* 409 There were the homes in fibro-cement. **1964** K. TENNANT *Summer's Tales* 166 She came from the Old Country at the turn of the last century, to a land where there were no fibro-cement cottages, no hospitals, no ballet.

fiddle-back blackwood. [f. *fiddle-back* with reference to the wavy grain of wood traditionally used in the making of violins: see OEDS *fiddle, sb.* 8 d.] Figured timber obtained from BLACKWOOD, characterized by a wavy grain and highly prized as a cabinet timber.

[**1902** *Papers & Proc. R. Soc. Tas.* (1903) 35 One of the most beautiful ornamental timbers, the Blackwood (*Acacia melanoxylon*). . . Some of it is called locally 'fiddle-back', from the resemblance of its grain to that of the back of a fiddle.] **1908** J. MANN *Suitability Australasian Timber* 4 Many trees have naturally a very handsome grain. . . The Fiddle-back, Mottled, and Dark-coloured Blackwood of Victoria and Tasmania . . are examples. **1920** *Land of Lyre Bird* (S. Gippsland Pioneers' Assoc.) 36 'Fiddleback' blackwood was beautifully marked, the grain being wavy in appearance with longitudinal ripples of alternately dark and light shades, and of great commercial value. **1928** M.E. FULLERTON *Austral. Bush* 104 Fiddle-back blackwood in a rough brush or log fence does seem rather an ignoble use for a wood now prized by the best furniture makers. **1945** *Bulletin* (Sydney) 6 June 14/2, I had a closer look at the 'curly lightwood'—the best piece of fiddleback blackwood I ever struck.

fiddler. [See quot. 1857.] Any of several fish of the genus *Trygonorhina*, as *T. fasciata* of N.S.W. and s. Qld.; BANJO 4. Also **fiddler ray.**

1857 J. ASKEW *Voyage Aust. & N.Z.* 229 There is a large flat fish called 'the fiddler', found in shoal water, where there is a muddy bottom. . . In shape it resembles a fiddle. **1885** *Adelaide Observer* 18 Apr. 29 Rays and sharks undescribed, namely, the common shovel-nosed 'fiddler' [etc.]. **1906** D.G. STEAD *Fishes of Aust.* 233 Amongst the Rays the following are of interest . . the 'Fiddler' (*Trygonorrhina fasciata*) [etc.]. **1978** N. COLEMAN *Austral. Fisherman's Guide* 34 The fiddler ray inhabits both the sandy sea floor and algae-covered reefs in both shallow and deeper waters, offshore and in estuaries.

fiddley-did. *Obs.* Rhyming slang for 'quid', the sum of one pound; a one-pound note; also *ellipt.* as **fiddley**, and *attrib.*

1941 S.J. BAKER *Pop. Dict. Austral. Slang* 28 *Fiddley*, a £1 note. **1951** E. LAMBERT *Twenty Thousand Thieves* 417 *Fiddley-did*, rhyming slang for a quid. **1955** *Overland* iii. 16 A score in the guts, gentlemen! I want twenty fiddlies. Come on you tail punters, twenty quid in the centre! **1959** *Bulletin* (Sydney) 9 Dec. 20/1 The price of this breed? Forty fiddlies for day-olds! **1965** F. HARDY *Yarns of Billy Borker* 94 Paid a hundred thousand fiddley-dids for a billiard table. **1968** D. O'GRADY *Bottle of Sandwiches* 6 We had to fork over eight hundred fiddly-bloody-dids for her. **1977** R. BEILBY *Gunner* 81 He would 'like to be home right now, putting a couple of fiddleydids on a little horse'.

field, *n.*[1] Shortened form of GOLDFIELD 1.

1856 H.B. STONEY *Vic.* 10 The Fields are not now worked in the selfish mania that characterized the onset, but rather as an occupation; the digger is not now, as at first, the sole gainer. **1859** R.H. HORNE *Austral. Facts & Prospects* 37 A third field broke out at a few miles' distance, and I was obliged to write for assistance. **1878** G. WALCH *Australasia* 35 The rush set in, and the Dunstan and other familiar fields drew thousands of eager diggers from the failing Victorian workings. **1891** 'OLD TIME' *Convict Hulk 'Success'* 9 Gold had been discovered, and everyone was rushing off pell-mell, helter-skelter to the fields. **1906** *Gadfly* (Adelaide) 20 June 22/1 The salvation of Jim Done . . begins with his contact with the roaring cosmopolitanism of the fields. . . He is finally dangerously wounded at the Stockade on Eureka Hill. **1923** *Bulletin* (Sydney) 4 Jan. 24/4 The natives said the rockholes their [*sic*] 'never died', but scarcity of water depopulated the field more than once during the days of the first alluvial finds. **1936** *Ibid.* 6 May 21/1 The 'fields' put a bit of money into W.A.'s pocket, and its ambitions soared accordingly. **1948** K.S. PRICHARD *Golden Miles* 14 Sally wondered whether she had been right to send Dick to a public school in Adelaide where the mine managers sent their sons, while Tom and Lal had grown up on the fields with nothing but a state school education. **1972** N. KING *Nickel Country* 62 Many of the old personalities of the goldfields . . talk nostalgically of their days on the 'fields. **1983** *West Austral.* (Perth) 21 Nov. 64/2 Power line a key in Fields growth. The new power line between Muja and Kalgoorlie is expected to be instrumental in bringing many gold prospects in the Goldfields into production.

field, *n.*[2] [Fig. use of *field* the horses, excluding the favourite, in a race: see OED *sb.* 10 a.] The accepted standards of behaviour; esp. in the phr. **to come back to the field,** to relinquish delusions of grandeur; to 'return to the fold'.

1944 L. GLASSOP *We were Rats* 82 'Don't worry,' said Bert. . . 'The poor bastard's hopeless. He'll come back to the field.' **1954** T.A.G. HUNGERFORD *Sowers of Wind* 4 Young Mark Flannery should come back to the field. **1984** *Sun-Herald* (Sydney) 11 Mar. 96/1 Whenever a comparative newcomer enjoys quick success at some facets of racing, his seniors tag him as 'a lucky, young upstart who will quickly come back to the field'.

field police. Chiefly *Tas. Hist.* [Spec. use of *field* the country as opposed to a town.] A police force deployed to maintain law and order outside closely settled districts; *border police* see BORDER 3.

1825 *Hobart Town Gaz.* 17 Dec., A Band of Constables shall be forthwith formed, to consist of Thirty Men, to be constantly employed in the Pursuit of Runaway Convicts. . . The Constables of the Field Police will each receive an ample Allowance of Rations and Slop Clothing. **1827** *Tasmanian* (Hobart) 11 Oct. 2 A Correspondent at New Norfolk, says that the Field Police are doing some good in that neighbourhood, by apprehending runaways and detecting robberies. **1828** *Ibid.* 22 Feb. 3 The military parties are stationed in the most sequestered spots, whilst the field police occupy those huts immediately contiguous to the main road. **1832** *Colonist* (Hobart) 2 Nov. 3/2 The supineness of the Field Police gives the people cause to suspect that *they are* in league with the smugglers and grog-sellers. **1838** *Colonist* (Sydney) 19 May 4/2 He established a field-police; and convicts in the service of masters in the interior were restrained from congregating in public-houses. **1844** *Colonial Times* (Hobart) 1 Sept., In order to relieve the minds of the inhabitants of the interior of the colony, it is recommended, that a well mounted field police of twenty-five will be necessary. **1862** BACKHOUSE & TYLOR *Life & Labours G.W. Walker* 278 The adult natives were also regarded and made use of as citizens, sixteen of the most active and intelligent having been organized by the police magistrate at Port Phillip into a field police.

field umpire. *Australian National Football.* The umpire or umpires in overall control of a game (see quot. 1965).

1885 D.E. MCCONNELL *Austral. Etiquette* 640 The Goal Umpires shall be the sole judges of goals, and . . in case of doubt may appeal to the Field Umpire. **1925** *Laws of Football* (Australasian Football Council) 10 The controlling body shall appoint for each match a field umpire, who shall have full control of the play. **1953** H. BUGGY *Let's look at Football* 58 The field umpire shall instruct the timekeepers to add 'Time on' by blowing his whistle and waving his arms to the timekeepers. **1965** A. SCOTT *Man. Austral. Football* 66 Before the game, the field umpire should speak with the goal umpires, boundary umpires, and the time-keepers, to make sure that they understand each other's signals. **1971** B. ANDREW *Austral. Football Handbk.* 87 There are five umpires in Australian Football and the field Umpire is in sole control of the game, and awards penalties in accordance with the Laws. His whistle is all-powerful. **1982** G. ATKINSON *Everything about Austral. Rules Football* 92 A field umpire was appointed for the first time in the Melbourne v. Carlton (Victoria) game on 1st July 1886, as the umpires 'at the extremities are unable to note closely what takes place so far from them'.

fifty, *n.*[1] *Obs.* (The punishment of) fifty lashes.

[**1827** 'PINDAR JUVENAL' *Van Diemen's Land Warriors* 30 To every *private volunteer*, the sum Of *fifty lashes* on his naked b--m.] **1830** *Sydney Monitor* 14 Aug. 2/3 To have a knife or other weapon in their possession after work-hours is sure to be punished with *fifty*. **1837** *Rep. Select Committee Transportation* (1838) 37 A convict has passed me in the street, and said in passing, 'No more fifties now, you bloody old tyrant.' What do you mean by 'fifties'?—Fifty lashes. **1852** J. WEST *Hist. of Tas.* I. 105 The magistrate said 'give him fifty'—an easy compromise with the hangman.

fifty, *n.*[2] *N.S.W.* [Abbrev. of *fifty-fifty*.] See quot. 1978.

1971 F. HARDY *Outcasts of Foolgarah* 76 Five schooners of fifty, thanks, love. **1974** BUCKLEY & HAMILTON *Festival* 55 He said he would have his usual middy of fifty. **1978** R. MCLELLAND *Outback Touring* 121 In New South Wales some pubs have both old and new beer on tap. . . A 'fifty' is a 50–50 combination of new and old, i.e. half a glass from one tap and half from the other.

fig. *Obs.* [Spec. use of *fig* a small piece of tobacco.] The unit by which tobacco was customarily sold: see quots. 1846 and 1852.

1834 N.S.W. Magistrates' Deposition Bk. 12 Nov., I gave him 7 figs of Tobacco for the Shepherds. **1846** MRS C. MEREDITH *Notes & Sketches N.S.W.* 104 The term 'fig of tobacco', so general here, will not be understood at home. . . That kept here for general use is 'Negro-head', and comes in large kegs, packed closely in layers of twisted rolls, about eight inches long,and one inch broad; each of these being technically termed a 'fig'. **1852** F. LANCELOTT *Aust. as it Is* II. 87 All the tobacco is uncut, and retailed in square sticks, called figs, each weighing about an ounce. **1859** J. LANG *Botany Bay* (1885) 55 He served out to each person . . a 'fig' (one ounce) of colonial tobacco. **1871** *Austral. Town & Country Jrnl.* (Sydney) 17 June 748/1 Two pounds of sugar, no tea, and a fig of tobacco, a week. **1921** D. GRANT *Through Six Gaols* 118 Do you think it would be safe for me to back you with two figs? **1930** HIVES & LUMLEY *Jrnl. of Jackaroo* 67 Nearly a whole 'fig' of tobacco.

figbird. The fruit-eating bird *Sphecotheres viridis* of n. and e. Aust., related to the orioles. The male is predom. green and grey, the female brown.

1898 E.E. MORRIS *Austral Eng.* 144 Fig-bird . . *Sphecotheres maxillaris* . . Yellow-bellied, *S. flaviventris.* **1900** A.J. CAMPBELL *Nests & Eggs Austral. Birds* 82 The Sphecotheres or Fig Birds appear to have affinity to the Orioles. **1937** *Bulletin* (Sydney) 9 June 21/2 The oriole or fig bird, familiar to owners of mulberry-trees in eastern N.S.W. and Queensland, is another of Australia's feathered mimics. **1976** *Reader's Digest Compl. Bk. Austral. Birds* 548 Outside the breeding season figbirds move around in flocks, seeking food trees.

fighting-stick. *Obs.* A name given by settlers to an Aboriginal weapon: see quot. 1878.

1878 R.B. SMYTH *Aborigines of Vic.* I. p. xlv, The *Kounung* of the Victorian natives . . is not a club, but a fighting-stick. It is sharpened at both ends, and, whether used as a missile or a dagger, is a dangerous weapon. **1883** F. BONNEY *On Some Customs Aborigines* 7 Then throw fighting sticks or boomerangs at the young men, which they ward off with their shields (*oolumburra*).

Fiji. In the phr. **an uncle in** (or **from**) **Fiji** and varr., an imaginary financial backer.

1902 H. FLETCHER *Waybacks Town & Home* 6 'Ain't yer got an uncle in Fiji?' demanded Dads, with scorn. 'Ain't yer got two hundred quid to give to the honest man who will trust you to the same amount?' **1906** T.E. SPENCER *How M'Dougall topped Score* 50 Before he breathed his last, says he, Remember, though I'm leaving you, That coves with uncles in Fiji Are frauds who are deceiving you. **1914** H. LAWSON *Collected Prose* (1972) I. 716 They were both spielers... Their game was anything weaker or stupider than themselves that had cash or property, and when they were in Sydney their uncles lived in Fiji. **1916** 'T.O. LINGO' *Austral. Comic Dict.* 13 'Uncle in Fiji'—Arms, Thimble and Pea. A non-existent old gentleman of benevolent aspect and capacious bankbook, who, nevertheless is often the cause of landing people in gaol. **1943** L. MANN *Go-Getter* 139 He was as much a mug as a way back deceived in the existence of a rich uncle in Fiji. **1928** A. WRIGHT *Good Recovery* 9 I'm beginning to think that rich uncle is like the one from Fiji, eh, Lance?

financial, *a.* Financially solvent. See also UNFINANCIAL.

1899 *Bulletin* (Sydney) 30 Dec. 14/3 No outback station refuses to sell rations; very few refuse to *give* when coin is not forthcoming... Stop the rations.. and only 'financial' travellers will venture out, and these.. can refuse work until offered suitable wages. **1910** *Ibid.* 8 Dec. 13/3 She.. married a repulsively ugly but very financial old Chow gardener. **1935** *Ibid.* 2 Jan. 25/1 Now the warm weather's here we should be more financial: once again we will be able to pawn our overcoat. **1957** D. NILAND *Call me when Cross turns Over* 132 He only worked when he needed money, or felt the itch for a change. When he was financial he came to Tambourine and had a good lay-off. **1959** H. LAMOND *Sheep Station* 122 The men had about six weeks' work behind them: they should be well chequed-up. They should be financial. **1973** F. PARSONS *Man called Mo* 4 The Mo character was never financial enough to be a business man. He was the down-trodden employee, but never the employer.

find. [Spec. use of *find* a discovery of archaeological remains, minerals, treasure, etc.]

a. The finding of a deposit of gold or of an area potentially rich in gold; the location of the find.

1851 S. RUTTER *Hints to Gold Hunters* 10 In about a year and a half or two years from the first *find*. ***c* 1852** A. MANN *Goldfields Aust.* 11 Gold had been picked up among the Bathurst mountains... A shepherd.. sold some hundreds of pounds worth.. and he was constantly dogged by his fellow labourers to discover the 'find', the locality of which he would not divulge. **1856** *Moreton Bay Free Press* 10 Mar. 3/1 Mr J.G. Rossiter of the Darling Downs, had brought down a sample of gold which had been found during the week... Water is abundant, and the 'find' is said to be of a productive character. **1858** T. MCCOMBIE *Hist. Colony Vic.* 218 The great 'finds' of gold were.. first discovered on the old Golden Point. **1872** 'RESIDENT' *Glimpses Life Vic.* 147 News of the first lucky finds spread rapidly. **1896** J.M. PRICE *Land of Gold* 73 It is scarcely possible to give any adequate idea of the state of feverish excitement to which the news of a new 'find' arouses the small prospectors and diggers. **1955** A.C.V. BLIGH *Golden Quest.* 17 There was little mining or fossicking, as everyone was searching for slugs. Barely earning wages, we travelled to many small finds.

b. The gold obtained from the find.

1853 J. SHERER *Gold Finder Aust.* 58 Many instances might be adduced of large 'finds' having been made out of such holes. **1888** A.P. MARTIN *Oak-Bough & Wattle-Blossom* 144 It represented the only result of a strong man's hard toil for many weeks, and, as nuggets go, it was considered by no means a bad 'find'.

fine, *v.* [Br. dial. *fine up* to clear.] *intr.* With **up.** Of the weather: to clear; to become fine.

1926 *Bulletin* (Sydney) 11 Feb. 24/1 What cares the cook if it don't fine up? It's he who'll ring the shed. **1966** S.J. BAKER *Austral. Lang.* (ed. 2) 350 *Bogaduck weather* for heavy rain and *to fine up* (of weather) to become fine, are other Australianisms.

fine-woolled, *a.* Also **fine-wooled.** Of sheep: having wool of fine fibre.

1819 *Sydney Gaz.* 12 June, Some fine woolled Rams of the Spanish Breed. **1829** H. WIDOWSON *Present State Van Diemen's Land* 142 To whom credit is due for introducing the fine-woolled sheep husbandry in Tasmania, I know not. **1839** *S. Austral. Rec.* (London) 12 June 194/3 The natural pastures upon which the fine-wooled sheep feed and multiply. **1843** J.F. BENNETT *Hist. & Descr. Acct. S.A.* 95 Many thousands of fine wooled sheep were driven over by the New South Wales Settlers, and disposed of to the South Australians. **1849** S. & J. SIDNEY *Emigrant's Jrnl.* 35 Buy fine woolled sheep, nothing else pays. **1852** S. MOSSMAN *Voice from Aust.* 11 Our plains and valleys.. furnish excellent pasture for fine-woolled sheep. **1865** Tas. Non-State Rec. 103/1, I have to go to Mr Gibson's today to look at some fine Wooled Sheep. **1936** E.W. COX *Evol. Austral. Merino* p. ix, There were fine-woolled sheep in Spain before the Christian era.

finger. *Obs.* [Prob. joc. use of *finger* policeman: see OEDS *sb.* 10 b.] See quot. 1898.

1897 *Worker* (Sydney) 11 Sept. 1/1 His boss he gives some funny names, when he can't hear the joke, He calls him 'joint' and 'finger', and he sometimes calls him 'bloke'. **1898** *Bulletin* (Sydney) 1 Oct. 14/3 In a shearing-shed: The boss is the 'finger'. **1920** *Ibid.* 15 Jan. 20/2 Some Western Queensland slang of my day:.. in the shearing-shed the boss was the 'finger'.

finger cherry. a. The elongated cherry-like fruit of the shrub or tree of Qld. and New Guinea *Rhodomyrtus macrocarpa* (fam. Myrtaceae). **b.** The shrub or tree.

1902 *Truth* (Sydney) 23 Nov. 4/8 Children and animals have become suddenly blind after eating wild berries known as finger cherries. **1908** E.J. BANFIELD *Confessions of Beachcomber* 23 The finger cherry.. (*Rhodomyrtus macrocarpa*), possesses the flavour of the cherry guava, but has a most evil reputation. **1929** *Bulletin* (Sydney) 9 Jan. 25/2 The finger cherry (so called on account of its articulations, which give it a digital appearance),.. is common in parts of N.-E. Queensland. **1948** H.A. LINDSAY *Bushman's Handbk.* 142 Another highly dangerous vegetable is found in the scrub of northern Queensland; it is the finger cherry. Somewhat like a small, elongated, reddish loquat in appearance. **1967** G.J. HENRY *Girro Gurrl* 58 Some said it caused blindness, but the aboriginal always ate the finger cherry or bush loquat. The fruit.. was considered a bush delicacy. **1982** K. MCARTHUR *Bush in Bloom* 64 The notorious Finger Cherry, Wannaki of the Aborigines. The fruit of this tree, if eaten, can send people blind.

finger-talk. [Spec. use of *finger-talk* sign language using the fingers.] A sign language used by Aborigines. Also *attrib.*

1936 'L. KAYE' *Black Wilderness* 166 Talk to him, Kombi... He might have a word or two of your lingo. Anyway you've both got hands for finger-talk. **1947** V.C. HALL *Bad Medicine* 147 Menikman glanced back and shot up a hand in a 'finger-talk' question. **1962** D. LOCKWOOD *I, Aboriginal* 121 Finger-talk is also constant among men who speak the same tongue. It not only saves unnecessary speech but has the added advantage that evil spirits cannot hear it. **1976** C.D. MILLS *Hobble Chains & Greenhide* 173 He waved to me in 'finger-talk' that he was set.

Hence **finger talk** *v. intr.*

1956 T. RONAN *Moleskin Midas* 48 There's blacks ahead. I was finger talking with one old King and he is bringing two singers.

fire, *n.* [With reference to the colour.] Used *attrib.* in the names of flora and fauna: **fire fish,** any of several reef-dwelling fish of the fam. Scorpaenidae, esp. the red fire fish *Pterois volitans,* having stripes of scarlet and other colours; BUTTERFLY COD; **tail,** any of several finches of the genera *Emblema* and *Stagonopleura,* having red upper tail-coverts; esp. *S. bella* of s.e. Aust. incl. Tas.; also **fire-tailed finch; tree,** any of several trees, usu. so-called from their flame-coloured flowers (but see quot. 1972), incl. the W.A. *Christmas bush* b. (see CHRISTMAS).

1906 D.G. STEAD *Fishes of Aust.* 195 The Red **Fire-Fish** is remarkable for the tremendous elongation of the rays and spines of the fins. **1928** S.E. NAPIER *On Barrier Reef* 125 What is this gay galleon... He is the fire-fish. **1967** M. SELLARS *Carramar* 15 The ballerina of the reef is the fire fish, an iridescent miracle of living opal. **1976** E. WORRELL *Things that Sting* 51 Butterfly cod from the coral reefs can cause painful injuries with the spines on their backs and fins. The pain can be so intense that some island people call them 'Fire Fish'. **1845** J. GOULD *Birds of Aust.* (1848) III. Pl. 78, *Estrelda bella.* Fire-tailed Finch.. **Fire-tail,** Colonists of Van Diemen's Land. **1872** 'TASMANIAN LADY' *Treasures, Lost & Found* 126 The little firetail. [*Note*] A bird which derives its name from a bright red spot beneath the tail, the rest of the plumage being brown. **1931** J. DEVANEY *Earth Kindred* 15 The firetail flock from twenty angles Shot for the low lantana tangles. **1980** M. DUGAN *Early Dreaming* 42, I was given special dispensation for access.. to out-of-bounds bush areas to note the daily progress of a fire-tailed finch's nest. **1985** P. CAREY *Illywhacker* 561 The window was full of little firetails and the background had been painted with the dun-khaki that is the firetail's dominant colour so that as the little birds flew to and fro their bodies disappeared and only their ember-red tails showed, like flying sparks. **1851** *Illustr. Austral. Mag.* (Melbourne) June 357 The *nuytsia floribunda,* whose flame-coloured blossoms have acquired for it the name of the **fire-tree,** exhibits the curious phenomena of a parasitical plant trailing along the ground. **1862** R. HENNING *Lett.* (1952) 44 We picked branches of fire-tree; it bears a most beautiful crimson blossom and keeps some time in water. **1889** J.H. MAIDEN *Useful Native Plants Aust.* 600 *Stenocarpus sinuatus*.. 'Fire Tree' (on account of the brilliancy of its flowers). **1901** M. VIVIENNE *Travels in W.A.* 65 A handsome painting of the Nutsyia fire-tree, or Christmas-bush, also demanded notice. **1933** C.W. PECK *Austral. Legends* (ed. 2) 116 This fire-tree is a Brachychiton, and it is the same genus as the Queensland bottle-tree. **1972** V. SERVENTY *Singing Land* 81 One of the striking trees of the desert country, with bright green foliage and bell-shaped fruits, is the desert poplar, sometimes called.. fire tree, since it grows vigorously after fire, sending up a long, spindly trunk.

fire, *v. trans.* Esp. of Aborigines: to set fire to (the natural vegetation of an area), for the purpose of trapping animals or maintaining grassland (see quots. 1852 and 1882).

1835 *True Colonist* (Hobart) 14 Feb. 2/4 Caution them against the old system of firing the Bush. **1843** C. ROWCROFT *Tales of Colonies* III. 281, I suppose it's the natives that have fired the country. **1852** J. MORGAN *Life & Adventures W. Buckley* 100 Natives.. hunt round a kind of circle into which they force every kind of animal and reptile to be found; they then fire the boundary, and so kill them for food. **1853** A. KINLOCH *Murray River* 22 To improve the feed.. recourse is often had to firing the country. **1882** W. SOWDEN *N.T. as it Is* 33 The natives and the teamsters periodically fire the grass to secure a succulent growth immediately after the late rains.

fire-brand, *v. Obs.* [Prob. independent of the obs. Br. use: see OED *sb.* 3.] *trans.* To mark (an animal) with a branding iron.

1825 Tas. Non-State Rec. 61/2 2 Dec., Firebranded the lambs. **1832** *Colonial Times* (Hobart) 9 May, Highly improved Ewes, fire-branded on the 14th instant with the letter F on the left cheek; also.. one hundred Sheep, pitch branded with the letters MF. **1890** 'R. BOLDREWOOD' *Squatter's Dream* 47 'Every sheep of mine will be legibly fire-branded.'.. 'He'll fire-brand too,' said Hawkesbury, 'in the same place.'

fire-plough, *n.* and *attrib.*

A. *n.* An implement which cuts a furrow wide enough to form a fire-break: see quot. 1926.

1907 *Bulletin* (Sydney) 25 Apr. 14/2 The 'fire-plough', devised by C.P. Bell, manager of Westland station, near Longreach (Q.).. will cut a furrow up to 11 ft. wide—enough to keep back a fire except in heavily-grassed country. **1920** J.N. MACINTYRE *White Aust.* 9 The cutting of the road over the roughest of the 'devil-devil' ground with a fire plough was to cost me at least £200. **1926** A.A.B. APSLEY *Amateur Settlers* 130 A fire-plough is drawn by some fifteen horses, and is a wide metal scoop on a timber frame, after the fashion of a snow-plough. **1935** F. Birtles *Battle Fronts Outback* 267 There was a good surfaced road right across . . blacksoil plains. This had been made by the use of fire-ploughs drawn either by donkeys or tractor power. **1954** T. Ronan *Vision Splendid* 156 Old Jack took the lead straight along after the recently passed fireplough.

B. *attrib.* Made by means of a fire-plough.

1930 D. Cottrell *Earth Battle* 291 The fire-plough roads were creeping in a mighty cross through the heart of The Block. **1927** M. Terry *Through Land of Promise* 116 There was a well-marked fireplough track for guidance. **1972** R. Magoffin *Chops & Gravy* 59 The car was still racing at ninety miles an hour along the fireplough road.

fire-plough, *v.* [f. prec.] *trans.* To form a fire-break on (land). Also *absol.*

1925 M. Terry *Across Unknown Aust.* 41 One station, which has the homestead in the centre of the run (property), has the ground fire-ploughed like a wheel, with many tracks radiating from the homestead right to the boundary. **1926** A.A.B. Apsley *Amateur Settlers* 130 Track leading from Wave Hill to Soakage Creek 'fire-ploughed' most of the way. **1971** W.A. Winter-Irving *Beyond Bitumen* 65, I spent three weeks camped out fire ploughing with a friend.

Hence **fire-ploughed** *ppl. a.*

1935 I.L. Idriess *Man Tracks* 133 Natives showed him Moody's camel pads following a fire-ploughed track leading to a boundary-rider's camp. **1954** T. Ronan *Vision Splendid* 153 They strung the cattle along a freshly fire-ploughed road to within a mile of the next bore.

fire-stick. A stick used to light a fire; usu. a smouldering stick carried by Aborigines when travelling, but see quot. 1920. Also *attrib.*

1804 *Sydney Gaz.* 11 Nov., These accidents . . are frequently attributed to the . . heedlessness of the natives in transporting fire sticks from place to place. **1820** J. Oxley *Jrnls. Two Exped. N.S.W.* 236 The third . . threw his firestick at me, and next a waddie. **1830** R. Dawson *Present State Aust.* 77 We get it fire-stick (firebrand) to make fire. **1847** G.F. Angas *Savage Life & Scenes* I. 96 The women, when mourning, singe off their hair with a small fire-stick. **1859** W. Burrows *Adventures Mounted Trooper* 105 They . . came back with firesticks to throw upon the bark roof of the hut. **1870** J. Bonwick *Last Tasmanians* 162 Several rushes were heard, and the firesticks of the people were seen in the gloom. **1893** D. Lindsay *Jrnl. Elder Sci. Exploring Exped.* 116 Blackfellows, especially the women, always carry firesticks when moving about, for the purpose of signalling, burning out game, or for the camp fire. **1920** *Land of Lyre Bird* (S. Gippsland Pioneers' Assoc.) 141 They made fire with their firesticks of 'jealwood'. . . The method of raising fire with them was very simple—a piece of wood about 1½ inches in diameter was split in half, a countersunk hole made on the flat side, and groove cut from that to the edge of the piece of wood, and then a small round piece of similar wood fitted at the end into the countersunk hole. The small piece of wood was then turned with the hands after the manner of a drill. This caused a friction, and in a very short time this began to smoke. The little black particles were run down the groove on to some very fine bark and then blown into a flame. **1929** K.S. Prichard *Coonardoo* (1961) 101 The old women wandered about carrying fire-sticks to warm them. **1938** D. Bates *Passing of Aborigines* 221 Four seasons—had passed in her travels and never in all that time was her firestick allowed to go out; for it is forbidden to women to make fires. **1962** C. Gye *Cockney & Crocodile* 88 Ten men seize fire-sticks from the small dying fires, dance to the women and plunge the sticks into the women's fire until they burn fiercely. **1978** 'B. Wongar' *Track to Bralgu* 21 There will be no matches there. . . I'll make fire with fire sticks. **1984** B. Dixon *Searching for Aboriginal Lang.* 21 It was nicely printed in Brisbane and had an attractive cover with an Aboriginal firestick design.

firewater. [Spec. use of *firewater* any strong liquor; orig. U.S. and prob. a translation of an Indian word: see Mathews.] Any strong alcoholic liquor, esp. as supplied to Aborigines.

1853 *Austral. Gold Digger's Monthly Mag.* v. 187 Wretches are always found ready to take their cash and give them firewater. **1867** J. Bonwick *J. Batman* 75 'Twould be a heinous sin to taint their unadulterated palates with baleful firewater. **1898** *Worker* (Sydney) 15 Jan. 8/1, I will see what alteration there is in this God-forgotten country since the days when Johnny McDonald used to sell 'firewater' to King Tubo and his numerous dark subjects. **1930** Hives & Lumley *Jrnl. of Jackaroo* 8 There were seldom any disputes or wrangling, although quantities of 'fire-water' were consumed during the morning. **1972** M. Cassidy *Dispossessed* 27 'You like fire water, eh?' and he made a drinking sign with one hand.

fireweed. [Spec. use of *fireweed* any of various weeds that spring up in burnt areas; orig. U.S.: see Mathews.] Any of several shrubs or herbs of the genus *Senecio*, esp. *S. lautus* and *S. linearifolius*, and also *Arrhenechthites mixta* (both genera fam. Asteraceae) which rapidly appear after fire.

1910 *Advocate* (Burnie) 6 Jan. 4/2 'Bullage'—a very bad species of 'fireweed' . . allowed to come up thickly. **1914** H.M. Vaughan *Australasian Wander-Yr.* 111 Most noticeable of all was the fire-weed, a native golden-rod somewhat resembling our own gaudy ragwort. . . Its local name derives from the circumstances that the fire-weed always springs up in abundance in the clearings made by Bush fires. **1931** B. Cronin *Bracken* 61 When first scrubbed and burned off it was remarkably free from fern or fireweed. **1972** *Ten Award Winning Stories* 41 He brushed through a patch of dolly-bush and fire-weed that had taken over after a burn the year before. **1983** *Macarthur Advertiser* (Sydney) 20 Sept., In a vase with other flowers, fireweed looks innocent and unobtrusive, but it's driving farmers and their cows mad.

fire-wheel tree. [See quot. 1913.] The tree of e. N.S.W. and e. Qld. *Stenocarpus sinuatus* (fam. Proteaceae) which is grown as an ornamental for its striking red flowers. Also **wheel of fire tree.**

1913 F. Sulman *Pop. Guide Wild Flowers N.S.W.* 6 The genus Stenocarpus . . is best known by the Fire Wheel Tree, a handsome species with a very distinctive wheel-like arrangement of scarlet flowers, each resembling those of the Waratah. **1949** B. O'Reilly *Green Mountains* 15 A glorious 'Wheel of Fire' tree in full bloom had smashed into the middle of the road, scattering its blood-red blossoms. **1956** T.Y. Harris *Naturecraft in Aust.* 156 The Firewheel-tree of Queensland . . has large handsome sinuate leaves and brilliant red flowers arranged in the form of wheels. **1983** *Heritage Aust.* II. ii. 14 The border of the window is filled with splendid examples of Australian wild flowers— . . stenocarpus (fire-wheel).

first, *a.*

1. In special collocations referring to the British colonization of Australia: **first fleet,** the eleven British ships under the command of Arthur Phillip which arrived in Australia in January 1788; also *transf.* (see quot. 1945), and *attrib.*; **fleeter,** one who came to Australia aboard one of the ships of the first fleet; a descendant of a first fleeter; **settler,** one of the earliest non-Aboriginal residents of a particular area.

1791 P.G. King Jrnl. Norfolk Island 12 Nov. 6 The far greater part of those Convicts who left England in the **First Fleet** in 1788 . . conduct themselves with Honesty. **1817** *Hobart Town Gaz.* 11 Oct., Mrs Marsha Jones, wife of Edward Jones, baker. They both arrived in the first fleet and were the first couple married in that Colony. **1834** J.D. Lang *Hist. & Statistical Acct. N.S.W.* I. 26 The little fleet . . designated by the colonists of New South Wales the first fleet, set sail from Portsmouth on the 13th of May 1787 . . arrived at Botany Bay on the 18th, 19th, and 20th January, 1788. **1868** *Sydney Punch* 1 Feb. 74/2 Boast that your family, quite the *elite*, Came in with the Conqueror, viz., the 'first fleet'. **1896** *Bulletin* (Sydney) 4 July 10/1 'A first fleet family.'—Noah's in the Ark. **1908** *Ibid.* 24 Dec. 14/4 The rabbit is everywhere and always. He came out with the first fleet. **1945** *Ibid.* 24 Jan. 13/4 Some of the arrivals by Westralia's First Fleet had to learn the selection of edible fish the hard way. **1948** R. Raven-Hart *Canoe in Aust.* 204, I ought to qualify that 'First Fleet' statement: to be of this elite one's ancestor must, of course, have been an officer or a civil servant; but it is notorious that the common soldiers of that Fleet very rarely had children, and the convicts never. **1968** *Kings Cross Whisper* (Sydney) lviii. 2/4 Descendents of people who arrived in Australia with the first fleet have formed their own society. **1986** *Bulletin* (Sydney) 11 Mar. 52/2 Your item . . drives a wedge between First Fleet migrants and those arriving later. **1826** *Monitor* (Sydney) 1 Sept. 123/2, I am, Sir, Yours, &c. *An Old Hand, but not a* **First Fleeter.** **1842** *Geelong Advertiser* 14 Feb. 3/1 *The First Fleeters.*—The Government have ordered a pension of one shilling a day to be paid to the survivors of those who came by the first vessel into the colony. The number of these really 'old hands' is now reduced to three. **1847** *Bell's Life in Sydney* 11 Sept. 2/6 John Limeburner, the last of the *first fleeters*, as they are called in this Colony, died at Longbottom on Thursday last week, at the advanced age of 104 years. **1863** R. Therry *Reminisc. Thirty Yrs. N.S.W. & Vic.* 70 But for this promptitude on the part of Phillip in removing the convicts known by the name of the 'First Fleeters' to the site on which Sydney now stands . . Australia might have been lost to the empire. **1888** P.L. Buddivent *Centennial* 16 The poor '*first-fleeters*' . . camped 'neath the blue gum trees. **1913** *Bulletin* (Sydney) 1 May 16/2 The N.S.W. stock returns for 1788 showed five bunnies—first-fleeters. **1934** M. Gilmore *Old Days* 185 In the days of the first-fleeters . . the hills and shores of Sydney Cove were sheets of flowers. **1952** *Bulletin* (Sydney) 6 Aug. 17/1 Don't know if the hare, like the rabbit, was a 'First Fleeter', but it certainly made better time crossing the Divide than did its cousin. **1961** *Ibid.* 10 May 4/4 How long will it be before 'First Fleeters'—descendants of those who arrived with Governor Phillip—manage to work up the same sort of snobbery about their status as America's Pilgrim Fathers have? **1983** J. Hepworth *Great Austral. Cities*, When the First Fleeters clanked ashore To Sydney Town in Seventy Eight, They threw a rorty party As the way to celebrate. Available bum and lashings of rum Led to lots of fornication. No wonder that the city's known As the birthplace of our nation. **1790** *Extracts Lett. Arthur Phillip* 12 Feb. (1791) 3 The draining . . would be a work of time, and not to be attempted by the **first settlers.** **1790** *Copies & Extracts Lett. Governor Phillip* 17 June (1792) 111 We, as first settlers, labour under some inconvenience from not being able to employ the convicts in agriculture on the spot where the provisions and stores are landed. **1791** *Ibid.* 5 Nov. (1792) 126 The first settler was a convict, whose time being expired, a hut was built and one acre and a half of ground cleared for him at Parramatta. **1803** *Sydney Gaz.* 9 Oct., The improvident method taken by the First Settlers on the sides of the Hawkesbury and Creek; in cutting down Timber. **1834** J. Roberts *Two Yrs. at Sea* 60 Many were the hints and reproaches thrown out against the first settlers who had arrived there before them, for not having planted, and sown seeds around their temporary location [W.A.]. **1838** R. Gouger *S.A. in 1837* 61 Upon . . the blue-mountain parrot and lemon-crested cockatoo, the first settlers frequently regaled before beef and mutton were imported into the colony. **1852** J. Morgan *Life & Adventures W. Buckley* 126 The confidence . . placed in my future exertions to benefit the first settlers, gratified me exceedingly. **1859** W. Fairfax *Handbk. to Australasia* 145 They had purchased in London, of course, before the first settlers had landed [in S.A.]. **1861** N.W. Pollard *Homes in Vic.* 4 Liberty . . which has taken so many centuries to come to maturity in the mother country, was imported here by our first settlers. . . The people of Victoria have even out-run the parent country. **1899** G. Jeffrey *Princ. Australasian Woolclassing* 17 Little more than one hundred years ago . . the first settlers in New South Wales kept their few sheep for mutton purposes. **1977** R. McKie *Crushing* (1978) 148 Duncan, Bosworth, Dean, Parr and plain Smith. They were all first settlers along this part of the coast.

2. In other collocations: **First Australian,** an Aboriginal; **preference,** see Preference.

1952 R.M. & C.H. Berndt *First Australs.* 11 Let us introduce you to an Australian minority—the Aborigines, the First Australians, who before the coming of the white man occupied the whole of this Continent and its immediate islands. **1953** *Sydney Morning Herald* 3 Jan. 6/1 Screams of protest followed, in the course of which it was proposed that the aborigines should be known as 'First Australians'. . . [L]ate in the year, two books were published, each with the title 'First Australians' and dealing with the aborigines. It is not impossible that the term may have come to stay. **1965** G. McInnes *Road to Gundagai* 124 Boys, I want to introduce you to a great man. Doctor Uniapon is head of the Leper Mission at Yarrabunga in the Northern Territory. He is also one of the First Australians. We who have built a great democracy in this young land of ours are apt to forget that his people were here twenty thousand years before we came.

first-timer. One who is serving a first sentence in prison. Also *attrib.*

1881 *Bulletin* (Sydney) 8 Oct. 9/3 In Darlinghurst . . No. 1 yard contains men convicted three times or more. No. 2, twice-convicted men; No. 3, what is called 'first-timers'. **1903** *Ibid.* 25 Apr. 17/1 In a 'first-timers' prison 12 acres of cabbage garden outside the walls are cultivated by prisoners. **1921** D. GRANT *Through Six Gaols* 48, I was, in the language of gaols, a 'first-timer'. According to the generally accepted idea, as a 'first-timer' I should be guarded by the authorities from contamination with [*sic*] men who had grown old in crime. **1949** J.F. DWYER *Leg-Irons on Wings* 52, I would be taken to Goulburn Gaol, where all 'first timers' . . served. **1978** H.C. BAKER *I was Listening* 39 Nathan's a first-timer in quod, isn't he?

fishbone fern. [Fig. use of *fishbone*, from the resemblance of the shape of the frond of the fern to the skeleton of a fish.] Any of several ferns, esp. the hardy, common *Blechnum nudum* (fam. Blechnaceae) of e. Aust. incl. Tas., and those of the genus *Nephrolepis* (fam. Nephrolepidaceae), esp. *N. cordifolia* of n. Aust. and elsewhere. Also *ellipt.* as **fishbone.**

1923 *Census Plants Vic.* (Field Naturalists' Club Vic.) 2 *Blechnum discolor* . . Fishbone Fern. **1941** C. BARRETT *Aust.* 26 Maidenhair grows thickly along the creek . . but tree-ferns have gone and only common 'fishbones' flourish. . . The young fronds of this poorman's fern . . are tinted rose-pink and salmon-red. **1986** *Your Garden* Jan. 20 Some ferns can become problem plants in eastern Australia; one example being *Nephrolepis cordifolia*, the fishbone fern.

fishing, *vbl. n. Obs.* Used *attrib.* in Special Comb. **fishing station,** WHALING STATION; a place for catching fish; **weir,** a barrier built across a watercourse (by Aborigines) to trap fish.

1836 H. CAPPER *S.A.* 24 Sept. (1837) 11 The Island [*sc.* Kangaroo Island] commands good harbours which are well adapted for **fishing stations**, refitting whalers, &c. **1840** *S. Austral. Gaz.* (Adelaide) 20 Feb. 1 Various Fishing Stations have been established in or near to several of the Inlets or Bays of this Province for the purpose of killing and taking Whales. **1845** *Portland Guardian* 15 Mar. 3/1 Captain Underwood has been in negotiation with Sir George Gipps for a lease of the island for two years as a fishing station. **1845** L. LEICHHARDT *Jrnl. Overland Exped. Aust.* 9 Sept. (1847) 396 A very conspicuous foot-path led us through heaps of cockle shells to a fishing station of the natives. **1880** J. BONWICK *Resources Qld.* 117 There are no fishing stations beyond the Queensland boundary. [**1698 fishing weir:** W. DAMPIER *New Voyage round World* I. (ed. 3) 465 Their only food is a small sort of Fish, which they get by making Wares of stone, across little Coves, or branches of the Sea: every Tide bringing in the small Fish, and then leaving them for a prey to these people, who constantly attend there to search for them at low water.] **1845** L. LEICHHARDT *Jrnl. Overland Exped. Aust.* 13 July (1847) 330 We crossed two creeks, with good water-holes, in one of which was a fishing weir. **1867** F.J. BYERLEY *Narr. Overland Exped. Northern Qld.* 5 A great many fishing weirs were observed in the channels of the river, from which it would appear that the blacks live much . . on fish.

fish spear. A spear used by Aborigines to catch fish.

1845 L. LEICHHARDT *Jrnl. Overland Exped. Aust.* 27 May (1847) 269 Dillis, fish spears . . and several other small utensils, were in their camp. **1849** A. HARRIS *Guide Port Stephens* 89 The fish-spear is jagged in such a manner that, being once driven in, it will not draw out, but brings the fish out with it, and is then extracted by force. **1854** *Moreton Bay Free Press* 3 Jan. 4/1 He had met the black fellow with a fish spear in his hand. **1878** 'R. BOLDREWOOD' *Ups & Downs* 51 First walked a tall, white-haired old man, carrying a long fish-spear, and but little encumbered with wearing apparel. **1935** F. BIRTLES *Battle Fronts Outback* 102 He would now and then grab his fish-spear. It had four eighteen-inch prongs of sharpened wood, fixed to the shaft by means of bloodwood gum.

fit, *v.* [Br. *fit* to visit (a person) with a fit penalty; now apparently obs. outside Aust.: see OED *v.*[1] 12.] *trans.* To fix upon (a person) the responsibility for having committed a criminal offence by securing (or contriving) sufficient evidence to ensure a conviction.

1882 *Sydney Mail* 2 Sept. 374/2 When he gets in with men like his old pals he loses his head, I believe. . . He'll get 'fitted' quite simple some day if he doesn't keep a better look-out. **1914** E. DYSON *Spats' Fact'ry* 22, I thought I'd fitted yeh. Now do a bunk. **1919** V. MARSHALL *World of Living Dead* 12 Stretch—two drags—coomyerlative. Three, charges agin' me—righteous, vag, an' resisting. Fitted on first two, turned up on third. **1941** S.J. BAKER *Pop. Dict. Austral. Slang* 28 *To fit* (a person), to secure evidence sufficient for his conviction for a crime. **1977** T. RONAN *Mighty Men on Horseback* 26 They tried to fit him for horse and cattle stealing. **1978** H.C. BAKER *I was Listening* 185 He's a copper now. Give him his due—he didn't try to fit anything on me. **1986** *Canberra Times* 2 Apr. 1/1, I feel that they are now determined to fit me on something.

five-corner. Usu. in *pl.* Chiefly *N.S.W.* [See quot. 1834.] The fruit of any of several shrubs of the genus *Styphelia* (fam. Epacridaceae), esp. *S. triflora* of N.S.W. and Qld.; any of the shrubs themselves. Also *attrib.*

1826 J. ATKINSON *Acct. Agric. & Grazing N.S.W.* 19 The native cherry, five corners, jibbong, and others, are mere tasteless berries. **1834** G. BENNETT *Wanderings N.S.W.* I. 337 Sold in the shops under the popular name of '*five corners*': this name, no doubt, was applied to it on account of the *calyx* projecting in five points above the fruit. **1847** *Heads of People* (Sydney) 6 Nov. 29 Industrious urchins, who like ants have been out after 'five-corners'. **1854** F. ELDERSHAW *Aust. as it really Is* 43 Geebungs, Five-Corners, Lillypillies . . are . . well-recognized delicacies among the rising Anglo-Australian generation. **1888** *Proc. Linnean Soc. N.S.W.* III. 547 *Styphelia triflora* . . 'Five Corners'. These fruits have a sweetish pulp with a large stone. **1896** H. LAWSON *In Days when World was Wide* 158 Of the box-covered hills where the five-corners grew. **1907** J.K. CHISHOLM *Speeches & Reminisc.* 112 The students of the College occasionally strayed into the grounds to gather 'five corners', . . a wild fruit I fancy, more relished by youngsters in those days than now. **1918** *Bulletin* (Sydney) 1 Aug. (Red Page), Fifty or sixty years ago the ground near Sydney in the vicinity of Centennial Park, Randwick and Botany was covered with five-corner and geebung bushes. **1928** W. ROBERTSON *Coo-ee Talks* 32 He then forced her to eat of the magic five-corners, seeds which deadened all fear in the person who ate them. **1942** E. ANDERSON *Squatter's Luck* 23 Sappy five-corners. **1982** K. McARTHUR *Bush in Bloom* 93 Five-corners . . is a flower of mid-winter.

five islands. *Austral. pidgin. Obs.* [Transf. use of a name formerly given to the Illawarra district, N.S.W.: see quot. 1836.] Biscuits.

1836 J. BACKHOUSE *Narr. Visit Austral. Colonies* 16 Apr. (1843) 376 While in Moreton Bay, we were surprised by hearing the Blacks call biscuits, Five Islands. This we learned, arose from some men who, several years ago, were driven from the part of the Illawarra coast called the Five Islands having held up biscuits to the blacks and said, Five Islands, in the hope of learning from them the direction of their lost home. The Blacks, however, mistook this for the name of the biscuits and hence have continued to call them by this name. **1882** W. COOTE *Hist. Colony Qld.* 33 They made him understand they wanted 'bread', 'bacca' and 'five allan'. **1891** *Proc. R. Soc. Qld.* VIII. 41 Four men in an open boat were blown to sea from the neighbourhood of Illawarra, or the Five Islands, in New South Wales. After being adrift for twenty-one days they were wrecked on Stradbrooke. . . Pamphlett, Finnigan, and another—were well received by the blacks. . . The blacks used to call ship's biscuits 'Five Islands', which I have always understood to refer to this occurrence.

five-wire fence. A fence having five horizontal members made of wire.

1909 E. WALTHAM *Life & Labour in Aust.* 40 He would cut through the strands of a 5-wire fence with the palm of his bare hand. **1913** *Bulletin* (Sydney) 8 May 16/3 A small swag couldn't be pushed through a five-wire fence. **1914** 'B. CABLE' *By Blow & Kiss* 220 He leaped a log as high as a five-wire fence. **1942** W. GLASSON *Our Shepherds* 3 It was a five-wire fence . . of No. 4 gauge. **1945** *Bulletin* (Sydney) 24 Oct. 13/4 The five-wire fence . . tore him from his mount. **1953** A.W. UPFIELD *Venom House* 157 Old Blaze chuckled and declared he preferred a blacks' wurlie to a house, and in the greatest storm would choose a five-wire fence to the shelter of Venom House.

fizgig. Also **phizgig.** [Prob. transf. use of *fizgig* frivolous woman, one who gads about.] A police informer.

1895 C. CROWE *Austral. Slang Dict.* 29 *Fizgig*, a spy for a detective. **1899** *Truth* (Sydney) 2 Apr. 2/2 Constable Webster is what is known in 'professional' circles as a 'fizgig', and on that account ready to swear to anything. **1901** *Tocsin* (Melbourne) 25 July 3/2 Advanced opinions sufficed to make a man the . . prey of unlimited fizgigs, pimps, and false informers. **1909** C. CROWE *Inquiry Agent* 57 The Commission . . asked an ex-convict, who was himself induced into an attempt to rob a bank, to define the term 'fizgig': . . 'A 'fizgig' is in most cases a man who has recently come out of gaol . . engaged by any individual member of the detective force either at a salary . . per week, or a small sum for each individual job. He either puts up or pre-arranges.' **1913** 'D. DELANEY' *Captain of Gang* 94 If ye think I'm goin' to keep company with a fiz-gig, Joe Butt, you're very much mistaken. 'Twas you that brought Greening and the police here. **1952** C. SIMPSON *Come away, Pearler* 151 Now nobody saw you . . except Moong Soo and Lily Choon. I talked to Clover about Lily, and she doesn't think she's likely to be a fizgig. Had too much trouble with the police herself. **1957** J. WATEN *Shares in Murder* 25 It would now be his job to get a lead on the culprit through one of the fiz-gigs. **1980** A.S. VEITCH *Run from Morning* 43 You can't get nowhere without good contacts. Phizgigs don't come out of automatic bloody dispensers! **1984** *Sun-Herald* (Sydney) 29 Jan. 47/1 We described him as a rather big crim and also a 'fiz gig'—an interesting word that means a grass, an informer.

fizz: see FIZZER *n.*[2]

fizz, *v.* [Fig. use of *fizz* to effervesce.] *intr.* Of stock: to behave in a lively or rebellious manner, to be difficult to control. Also as *n.* (see quot. 1968).

1966 S.J. BAKER *Austral. Lang.* (ed. 2) 62 *Fizz*, to move rapidly and erratically, originally applied to a lively bull in a yard. **1968** LINKLATER & TAPP *Gather No Moss* 31 A 'rush' was the term used to describe the headlong flight that the westerns of a later day called a stampede. Strings of cattle often break out of a mob and cause trouble. In proper droving language this is only a 'fizz'. **1976** C.D. MILLS *Hobble Chains & Greenhide* 183 She was a mite touchy when I rode her, and fizzed a bit until I got her warmed up, but soon settled down again.

fizzer, *n.*[1] [f. FIZZ *v.*] See quot.

1927 J. MATHIEU *Backblock Ballads* 41 My horse beneath me swerved around, And like a frightened 'fizzer' fled. [*Note*] Fizzer—Untameable brumby.

fizzer, *n.*[2] Also **phizzer.** [f. FIZGIG.] A police informer. Also **fizz.**

1943 S.J. BAKER *Pop. Dict. Austral. Slang* (ed. 3) 32 *Fizgig*, a stool pigeon. *Fizz*, as for 'fiz-gig'. **1950** *Austral. Police Jrnl.* Apr. 112 *Fizz-gig, or Fizzer*, a police informant. **1957** J. WATEN *Shares in Murder* 25 He had turned more criminals into police spies than any other officer Fields had ever known. No one had more fizzes in his hands than Brummel. **1969** B. GARLAND *Pitt Street Prospector* 71 Chow soon had a wealth of information on . . where the fizzers were situated. **1974** *Bulletin* (Sydney) 15 June 27/1 [The] police commissioner . . told Cairns 'you are wasting your time studying. Your job is to get phizzers.' **1975** LATCH & HITCHINGS *Mr X* p. vi, How a crim becomes a 'fizzer', or police informer. **1985** *Austral. Short Stories* x. 83 'See any drugs over there?. . . We catch twenty a week,' he lied. 'Mostly through fizzers.'

fizzer, *n.*[3] [Transf. use of *fizzer* a firework which fails to explode; perh. infl. by *fizzle* a failure or fiasco.] A failure or fiasco.

1957 R.S. PORTEOUS *Brigalow* 101 Good old Carson, I thought. You may be a bit of a fizzer, but you'll do me. **1969** W. DICK *Naked Prodigal* 236 We all went to a New Year's Eve party in Goodway, but it was a fizzer. **1975** *Bulletin* (Sydney) 29 Nov. 25/1 The greatest bloody fizzer in the history of Australian politics. **1981** *Austral. Roadsports & Drag Racing News* 27 Feb. 6/1 The Funny Car match . . was something of a fizzer, as both cars were shut down at the first start.

fizzy, *a.* [See FIZZ *v.*] Of stock: rebellious, difficult to control.

1975 D. STUART *Walk, trot, canter & Die* 52 How are you on the real rough horses, or in a yard with fizzy cattle? **1976** C.D. MILLS *Hobble Chains & Greenhide* 175 One old mare was very fizzy, and too old to try and break.

flag.

1. *Australian National Football.*

a. In the phr. **to raise** (or **bring up**) **both flags,** to score a goal (as opposed to a behind), thus causing the goal umpire to signal the event by raising a small flag in each hand.

1908 *Clipper* (Hobart) 27 June 2/2 Ward skyscraped to some tune, and Cook had a try for goal, both flags being raised. **1960** *N.T. News* (Darwin) 12 Jan. 8/3 Bedwell sent it on to P. Marrego who raised both flags. *Ibid.* 5 Jan. 8/5 Cooper snapped a neat handpass to Potts when he got into trouble and Potts brought up both flags.

b. A pennant awarded to the team which wins a competition.

1969 A. HOPGOOD *And Big Men Fly* 3, I promised our supporters that this year I'd get 'em a flag. **1980** *Sporting Globe* (Melbourne) 22 July 1 Controversial ex-president of Carlton, George Harris believes the Blues will fail to win this year's flag. **1983** HIBBERD & HUTCHINSON *Barracker's Bible* 79 The winners of a premiership receive a special pennant which has emblazoned on it the year of victory. This flag is usually hoisted on the occasion of the first home game for the victors in the following season.

2. *Obs.* The sum of one pound; a one-pound note.

1943 S.J. BAKER *Pop. Dict. Austral. Slang* (ed. 3) 32 *Flag,* a banknote, especially £1. **1950** *Austral. Police Jrnl.* Apr. 112 *Flag,* £1. Half a flag is 10s. **1955** *Bulletin* (Sydney) 5 Jan. 12/1 Recognised price for a healthy, weaned kid was four-bob, 7s. 6d. for a nanny at the flapper-stage, half-a-flag to twelve-and-a-break for a young milker.

3. In the phr. **to fly the flag**: see quot. 1975.

1975 *Bulletin* (Sydney) 26 Apr. 45/2 Pig .. asks Gulcher why he doesn't fly the flag; that is, appeal the case to a higher court in the hope of having the sentence reduced. **1980** B. HORNADGE *Austral. Slanguage* 81 His cell mate asks him will he appeal against the severity of the sentence to a higher court (*to fly the flag*) and the aggrieved one says that he will.

flag fall. An initial hiring charge incurred as the flag of a taximeter is lowered and the meter engaged.

1931 *N.S.W. Govt. Gaz.* II. 1306 'Flag Fall' means the amount of fare recorded by a taximeter immediately upon the flag being lowered to set the taximeter in motion at the commencement of a hiring. **1954** *Taxi News* Feb. 16/3 Every taxi meter shall .. be so constructed that when set in motion by the driver it registers the prescribed fare at flag fall and each part of a mile. **1978** *Gregory's Sydney Pocket Guide* 6 Charges are .. based on a flat rate flag fall and a metered charge per mile.

flag-flapper. One who, though overtly patriotic, avoids active service.

1918 *Ross's Monthly* July 1/2 *Aghast*—what some wartime flag-flappers (and other flappers) would feel like in the presence of the Real thing. **1919** *Worker* (Brisbane) 26 June 9/3 The flag-flappers .. called you heroes when you enlisted. **1954** J. WATEN *Unbending* 249 You bloody cowardly flag-flappers; you stay-at-home fighters.

flagon-wagon. A vehicle used to transport alcoholic liquor to an Aboriginal settlement.

1982 *Bulletin* (Sydney) 7 Dec. 47/1 The 'flagon-waggon' on the grog-run to an isolated settlement, where some people would pay exorbitant prices, has been part of Central Australian culture since the white man introduced alcohol last century. **1985** *Canberra Times* 11 Aug. 5/1 The flagon wagons run less regularly up and down the road.

flame.

1. The brilliant flashes of red found in some opal; an opal gem so characterized. Also **flame opal.**

1932 I.L. IDRIESS *Prospecting for Gold* 245 'Fire' or 'flame', in a stone is the most valuable colour as 'harlequin' is the most prized pattern. **1967** K. LLOYD *Black Opal* 24 He carefully edged away the ironstone covering gradually revealing the gem. 'It's a 'flame',' Agnes cried. **1974** P. HALL *Sun & Grey Shadow* 28 From the highest ridge they gouged black opal... Harry knew the patternings, deep in the gem. Pinpoint and Harlequin and Flame. **1974** B. MYATT *Dict. Austral. Gemstones* 134 Flame opal describes a precious gem in which the colour occurs as red bands or streaks, similar to flickering flames.

2. Special Comb. **flame robin,** the flycatcher *Petroica phoenicea* of s.e. Aust.; formerly also **flame-breasted robin, flame bird; tree, (a)** the chiefly deciduous tall tree of coastal e. Aust. *Brachychiton acerifolius* (fam. Sterculiaceae) occurring from Illawarra N.S.W. to n. Qld. and cultivated for its conspicuous red flowers; *Illawarra flame tree,* see ILLAWARRA 1; **(b)** *coral tree,* see CORAL.

1842 [**flame robin**] J. GOULD *Birds of Aust.* (1848) III. Pl. 6, *Petroica phoenicia* .. Flame-breasted Robin. **1849** C. STURT *Narr. Exped. Central Aust.* II. 24 App. *Flame-breasted Robin* .. has .. a breast of red, approaching to a flame colour. **1891** P.D. LORIMER *Songs & Verses* (1901) 178 Startling the nesting flame-bird, where it lurks. **1902** *Emu* II. 11 The Flame-breasted Robin .. comes thus far inland. **1942** C. BARRETT *From Bush Hut* 74 The scarlet-breasted species, the flame robin. **1977** *Ecos* xi. 22/1 Flame robins prefer open country, so .. the fire probably altered the habitat to the species' advantage. **1860** G. BENNETT *Gatherings of Naturalist* 355 The **Flame-tree** of Illawarra (*Brachychiton acerifolium*) is of slender growth, lofty, and .. denuded of branches, except at the summit. **1871** *Austral. Town & Country Jrnl.* (Sydney) 13 May 592/4 Growing side by side with the flame tree of Australia. **1888** *Centennial Mag.* (Sydney) 319 Orchards sheeted in white and pink, with a gorgeous flame-tree keeping guard. **1920** *Bulletin* (Sydney) 8 Jan. 20/2 If the flame- or coral-tree .. is any harder to kill than the white ti-tree .. I will hand in the belt. **1931** J. DEVANEY *Earth Kindred* 22 The passionate flame-trees flare Patches of scarlet. **1948** J. FAIRFAX *Run o' Waters* 30 The scarlet torch-lines of the flame trees .. skirt your little lanes. **1953** L. & C. REES *Spinifex Walkabout* 156 Another leafless, black-stemmed tree was the native flame, with its red bells. **1967** G.J. HENRY *Girro Gurrl* 29 The flame tree .. looks for all the world like a candle on a Christmas tree. **1981** A. WILKINSON *Up Country* 68 Tiny, bright green parrots sip nectar from the flame trees.

flaming fury. An outdoor earth-closet, so-called because the contents were periodically doused with an inflammable liquid and ignited.

1960 *N.T. News* (Darwin) 5 Feb. 5/3 Only one dilapidated flaming fury is provided for the present nine people. **1966** *Kings Cross Whisper* (Sydney) xxvi. 3/1 Once they were just thunder boxes, flaming furies, dunneys, shouses, dykes or crappers. **1975** K. WILLEY *Ghost of Big Country* 143 Less privileged residents .. lived at Parap, Winnellie, Nightcliff, and other areas in encampments of .. huts which dated from the second World War... Toilets were of the 'flaming fury' type and dysentery was more or less endemic. **1982** *N.T. News* (Darwin) 13 Dec. 7/2 We have heard of a famous Territory dunny that was known far and wide in the post-war years as 'The Blue Room'... for a 'flaming fury' it was something out of the ordinary.

flank. *Australian National Football.* An outside position; a player in an outside position.

1931 J.F. MCHALE et al. *Austral. Game of Football* 60 The wings and half-forwards should adopt the same tactics as the halfbacks when the ball is coming down *via* the flanks. **1963** L. RICHARDS *Boots & All!* 217 *Half-back flank,* an ideal back flank should be around about the six-foot mark, vigorous, dashing and a strong mark and kick. **1973** P. MCKENNA *My World of Football* 108 The flank is usually referred to as the 'graveyard' of football, but played by an expert it can become the most dangerous position in a team's attack.

flanker.

1. A beast that travels on the flank of a drove; a stockman who rides on the flank of a drove to prevent straggling. See DROVE *n.* 1.

1843 R.D. MURRAY *Summer at Port Phillip* 233 There is a flanker .. who seems inclined to part company from the 'mob'. **1904** *Bulletin* (Sydney) 8 Dec. 36/4 There was a sufficient number of them to drive even such a mob as was on that plain. Flankers, leaders and tailers, plenty there. **1957** J.M. HOSKING *Aust. First & Last* 30 With the cattle dog under the tucker cart and the flankers swinging wide, And my horse just wanting to gallop fast, I settle down for a ride. **1960** I.L. IDRIESS *Wild North* 204 Often some startled beast would make a wild get-away from the flank, to be rounded back instantly by superb horsemanship on the part of both flanker and horse.

2. *Australian National Football.* See quot. 1968 and FLANK.

1968 EAGLESON & MCKIE *Terminology Austral. Football* ii. 5 *Flanker,* a popular variant recorded by informants in reference to a player occupying outside positions, normally the half-back and half-forward outside positions. **1973** J. DUNN *How to play Football* 45 The flanker, like the key position player, is there either to feed the forward line or score himself. **1973** P. MCKENNA *My World of Football* 108 A good flanker relies on his anticipation, elusiveness and cunning.

flannel flower. [From the appearance of the bracts: see quot. 1895.] Any of several annual or perennial plants of the genus *Actinotus* (fam. Apiaceae), esp. the bushy *A. helianthi* bearing conspicuous bracts which are soft, white, and woolly; the flower of these plants.

1888 *Sydney Morning Herald* 24 Jan. (Suppl.) 1/6 The 'flannel flower' (Actimotus [*sic*] helianthi) .. which is found in sandy places, is of the parsley tribe. **1895** J.H. MAIDEN *Flowering Plants & Ferns N.S.W.* 9 The 'Flannel Flower'—a rather unpoetical designation, but a really descriptive one... It is .. in allusion to the involucre, which looks as if it were snipped out of white flannel. **1918** K.L. PARKER *Walkabouts of Wur-Run-Nah* 32 The white feathers .. sprang up again as flowers, so soft that they are called 'Flannel Flowers'. **1926** S.F. CASHMORE *N. Coast Verses* 20 And the flannel-flower with her starry crown, Our own State's marguerite. **1948** E.H. COLLIS *Lost Yrs.* 101 The flannel flower is shrinking back before the advance of population. **1968** A. D'OMBRAIN *Fish Tales* 8 Creamy white flannel flowers spread in great patches through the bush. **1979** C. KLEIN *Women of Certain Age* 70 Everywhere she looked there were flannel flowers, their pale grey petals the only soft shape in a harsh terrain.

flashjack.

1. One whose behaviour or dress is characterized by flamboyance and showiness; a 'swell'.

1898 *Bulletin* (Sydney) 16 Apr. 14/1 Years ago, before the days of paddocks, the 'Flash Jack' was in evidence on every cattle-station, in white moles, cabbage-tree hat, silk neckerchief, and long spurs, and slouching on the back of a raking brumby. **1905** A.B. PATERSON *Old Bush Songs* 26, I can do a respectable tally myself whenever I like to try, But they know me round the back blocks as Flash Jack from Gundagai. **1934** A. RUSSELL *Tramp-Royal* 41 It would savour too much of 'swank', and Tuck is well content to 'leave that kind of talk to Flash Jacks'. **1960** C. YOUNGER *Less than Angel* 124 We don't like flash jacks hanging round our girls. Stick to the tarts, son.

2. *Bridled nail-tailed wallaby,* see NAIL-TAILED WALLABY.

1913 W.K. HARRIS *Outback in Aust.* 130 The 'Flash Jack' is very similar in appearance to the kangaroo known as the 'Blue Flier', but does not grow so large. **1923** *Bulletin* (Sydney) 2 Aug. 24/2 Some .. have confused the paddy-melon with a smaller marsupial known as the flash-jack. **1941** E. TROUGHTON *Furred Animals Aust.* 186 Specimens in the Museum collection are from as far south as Wagga, in 1896, where it was locally known as 'Flash Jack' (quite a good name because of its swift actions).

flash jane. A name given to the female equivalent of FLASHJACK 1.

1932 K.S. PRICHARD *Kiss on Lips* 174 Smellin' so as you'd look round to see if a flash Jane from the city was about. **1950** —— *Winged Seeds* 54 You never saw such flash janes: twins with ginger hair.

flat, *n.*[1] [Spec. use of *flat* a piece of level ground.]

a. A stretch of level ground, esp. adjacent to a watercourse (or former watercourse) and of alluvial formation; hence, such a stretch of ground as a source of alluvial gold: see quots. 1855 (1) and 1869. See also *river flat* RIVER 1.

1799 D. COLLINS *Acct. Eng. Colony N.S.W.* (1802) II. 165 In the bottoms of the vallies and upon the damp flats. **1814** *HRA* (1916) 1st Ser. VIII. 167 The Trees being thin and light, the flats clear of Timber. **1829** *New Monthly Rev.* (London) June 499 Farther up the river, the party found the flats to become more extensive. **1834** G. BENNETT *Wanderings N.S.W.* I. 259 The numerous lagoons and flats, swamps or marshes, (for by all these names they seem equally known), had a fresh green appearance, occasioned by the young reeds springing up, which are greedily devoured by cattle and horses. **1840** J.P. JOHNSON *Plain Truths* 8 In the low lands, or to use a Colonial phrase, the flats. **1840** *S. Austral. Rec.* (London) 23 May 268 Amidst the monotony of the Australian bush, a river occasionally intervenes, on the banks of which really good soil is found; for the water way being dammed up with trees, the nucleus of muddy fords, the banks are constantly overflowed in the rainy season; alluvial deposits are formed; these gradually rise till the river's course is so checked as to turn it into other channels, and such low islands colonially termed 'Flats' of fertility are left to mark its former path, and tempt the new settlers to believe, that the productive powers of this deep black land are inexhaustible. **1842** *Sydney Herald* 26 Mar. 3/2 The next object of inquiry was about a small flat occupied by a Chinaman, who with another had a vegetable garden on the banks of the river. **1844** *Colonial Lit. Jrnl.* (Sydney) 18 July 62/2 And after rain a creek will rush Inundating the flat. **1852** J.D. LANG *Austral. Emigrant's Man.* 48 Where I have employed the word Flat in speaking of the former, I should use the epithet Plain, when alluding to the . . latter—a distinction to which their vastly greater size, and total exemption from timber, entirely justifies them. **1855** *Ovens & Murray Advertiser* (Beechworth) 3 Feb. 5/4 The flats and low grounds, many of which were too wet to be worked last summer, continue to be selected by the miners. **1855** W. HOWITT *Land, Labor & Gold* II. 239 Broad levels, which we should call meadows or plains, are flats. **1869** R.B. SMYTH *Gold Fields & Mineral Districts* 611 *Flat*, a low even tract of land, generally occurring where creeks unite, over which are spread many strata of sand and gravel, with the usual rich auriferous drift immediately overlying the bed-rock. **1880** C. PROUD *S.-E. District S.A.* 26 The swamp land is entirely different from the ordinary drain lands—the 'flats' as they are called. **1892** E.B. KENNEDY *Out of Groove* 30 Nothing could they see but a dank and lurid mist which was creeping over the 'flats' on which they were standing. **1914** C.H.S. MATTHEWS *Bill* 85 The country we were racing through was mostly little flats a quarter to half a mile across. **1927** 'S. RUDD' *Romance of Runnibede* 26 Mother sighed, seating herself near the open window that looked out on to the home paddock flat. **1943** *Bulletin* (Sydney) 8 Dec. 12/4 Viewed from surrounding hills or the sand dunes which separate it from the sea, southern Queensland's 'paddymelon-hole country' appears as a fine series of flats level enough for a landing ground. **1963** I.L. IDRIESS *Our Living Stone Age* 58 The two cunning old horses had been coming to that grassy flat to feed. **1978** D. STUART *Wedgetail View* 3 By the time the flat was clear of the stragglers, the main line of the mob was walking satisfactorily in single file across the soft ground.

b. With distinguishing epithet, as **apple-tree flat,** such a stretch of ground as characterized by its predominant form of vegetation.

1827 H.S RUSSELL *Genesis Qld.* 19 May (1888) 91 Descending without much difficulty to an apple-tree flat, the valley gradually expanded. **1840** J. GOULD *Birds of Aust.* (1848) II. Pl. 3, I found it [*sc.* the tawny-shouldered podargus] breeding on the . . Apple-tree (*Angophora*) flats of Yarrundi, near the Liverpool Range. **1853** J. CAPPER *Emigrant's Guide to Aust.* (ed. 2) 8 Lightly covered with a tree, so closely resembling the apple-tree of the west, that colonists name these pastures apple-tree flats. **1880** J. BONWICK *Resources Qld.* 36 Such phrases as 'Box forest', 'Iron-bark ranges', 'Apple-tree flats' . . have all had their own respective associations in the minds of those interested in the pastoral or agricultural capabilities of land.

flat, *n.*[2] [Spec. use of Br. slang *flat* one who is easily taken in.] A gullible person or dupe, esp. a recent immigrant. See also SHARP.

1812 J.H. VAUX *Mem.* (1819) II. 174 *Flat*, in a general sense, any honest man, or *square cove*, in opposition to a *sharp* or *cross-cove*; when used particularly, it means the person whom you have a design to rob or defraud. **1832** *Hill's Life N.S.W.* (Sydney) 16 Nov. 4 O! what a mob of *flats* and *sharps* Was crowded on the ground! **1842** *True Colonist* (Hobart) 25 Nov. 2/4 She has been encouraged in the most extraordinary manner, and in her list of *flats* exhibits the names of several respectable married as well as single ladies. **1845** J. TUCKER *Jemmy Green in Aust.* (1955) 43 The Londoners are the sharpest in business. . . It's no use to take them for flats. **1849** A. HARRIS *Emigrant Family* (1967) 32 There are some who are emigrants, and some who are freed-men: the emigrants are flats, and the others are sharps. **1861** J.T. COCKERELL *Scenes behind Curtain* 25 It was agreed by all three that he was only a *flat*, that is, a new comer. **1866** *Sydney Punch* 30 June 41/2 Look on this picture, villain, and on that, And thank your stars you were not born a flat. **1881** R. CRAWFORD *Echoes from Bushland* 55 There are avenues to wealth and power not open to flats, but accessible equally to all men of pluck and noûs. **1900** *Truth* (Sydney) 25 Feb. 4/8 All the Sydney aristocrats, Guns and mugs and sharps and flats. **1909** A. WRIGHT *Rogue's Luck* 196 As the breed of 'flats' grows less in the cities, the 'sharps' who prey on them are forced to travel far afield in search of plunder. **1956** R.G. EDWARDS *Overlander Songbk.* 63 At ten o'clock we'd then toss up to see who was to shout, And if there were but three of us, we did it 'odd man out'; And should there chance to be a flat, he'd certain to be stuck, And he'd often wonder to himself why he always had bad luck. **1971** H. ANDERSON *Larrikin Crook* 6 He was . . depending for a living on his skill in exploiting the 'flats' who appropriately enough gather on that part of the racecourse known as the flat.

Hence **flatcatcher** *n.*, see quot. 1882; **flat-catching** *vbl. n.*, indulging in sharp practice.

1877 *Vagabond Ann.* 136 You have to be a bit of a magsman, a pincher, a picker-up, a **flatcatcher**, a bester. **1882** *Sydney Slang Dict.* 4 *Flatcatchers*, those who 'work' by false pretences and by fraud. **1849** A. HARRIS *Emigrant Family* (1967) 245 **Flat-catching** is out of season.

flat, *n.*[3] *Horse-racing.* [Transf. use of *flat* level piece of ground at the end of some racecourses.] A level and undeveloped enclosure for spectators; the area in the centre of a racecourse.

1846 *Bell's Life in Sydney* 27 June 2/3 After a rapid transit from the flat (not flats) of Campbellfield to . . Bathurst, our Racing Reporter reached . . Wellington. **1880** *Bulletin* (Sydney) 11 Sept. 2/3 On the 'flat', a green-robed lady with a roulette table occasioned some excitement by 'landing' a red-bearded monte-player 'a domino in the kisser'. **1893** *Ibid.* 4 Mar. 19 Have you ever, when you went to see the races, Taken notice of the people on the flat? **1920** 'J. NORTH' *Harry Dale's Grand National* 167 The crowds on the lawn and the outer and the flat took up the cheering. **1971** [see FLAT *n.*[2]].

Hence **flatite** *n.*, one who patronizes the flat.

1896 *Bulletin* (Sydney) 19 Dec. 20/3 Flatites don't, as a rule, run to binoculars, so a board, on which starters' numbers and riders' names are legibly exhibited, should be provided by the rich A.J.C. for the multitudinous shilling patrons. **1933** S. GRIFFITHS *Rolling Stone on Turf* 2 The first Melbourne Cup I can clearly recall is the race won by Chester in 1877. . . In those days the flatites after each race used to swarm on to the running-track in order to get a close view of the weighing out of jockeys and to talk with friends 'inside'.

flat, *n.*[4] See quot. 1950.

1902 *Bulletin* (Sydney) 31 Mar. 31/2 A half plug of 'flat' . . mysteriously disappeared. **1950** *Austral. Police Jrnl.* Apr. 112 *Flat*, fine cut flake tobacco.

flat, *a. Two-up.* Of coins after spinning: landing flat, not rolling on impact. Also *absol.*

1911 A. WRIGHT *Gambler's Gold* (1923) 57 Quickly the coins are up and down. One fell a flat tail. **1925** —— *Boy from Bullarah* 17 'Heads ten bob!' That was Router's first bet, and the fall of two 'flat' tails left him with but half of his purloined capital. **1934** *Austral. Ring* IX. cviii. 13 He angled for the 'flat'. 'Watch the penny as I spin it—make it vanish in the air.' **1950** F.J. HARDY *Power without Glory* 323 He threw the pennies high . . and three times they came down heads. He spun a fourth time, all eyes looked upwards, then down again as the pennies reappeared . . and thudded on the canvas. 'Flat tails!'

flat, *adv.*

1. Usu. in the phr. **flat as a strap** (or **tack**), **flat to the boards,** at the limit of one's powers or resources.

1955 *Bulletin* (Sydney) 14 Dec. 12/4 Mo walked on to the board . . and saw an old pen-mate . . who soon told him he was flat as a strap to get the bare ton. **1963** M. BRITT *Pardon my Boots* 83, I seemed to have been going extra fast just then—'flat to the boards'. **1972** R. MAGOFFIN *Chops & Gravy* 106 *Flat*, up against it, hard pressed. **1976** C.D. MILLS *Hobble Chains & Greenhide* 48 They were no trouble for they headed home 'flat to the boards', and Dicky was hard put to it to keep in the lead. **1977** J. WALLACE *Memories Country Childhood* 101 Every night after work he would gallop ('flat as a tack', the men said) the thirteen miles over the range into town. **1983** *Sydney Morning Herald* 13 June 25/4 'I rode her in the Brisbane Cup and she went disgracefully,' Quinton said. 'She was as flat as a tack after the hard run.'

2. In the phr. **flat out like** (or **as**) **a lizard (drinking),** fully extended.

1935 *Bulletin* (Sydney) 23 Oct. 21/4 'Flat out like a lizard drinking' is a well-worn bush phrase. **1938** F. CLUNE *Free & Easy Land* 227 Dirty Dora was as flat out as a drinking lizard. **1952** *Meanjin* 208 I've been flat out like a lizard since eight o'clock this morning. **1958** O. GRAY *Drive Hard Bargain* 10 You must be flat out, like a lizard drinking. **1972** *Bulletin* (Sydney) 12 Aug. 7/3 I'm afraid I'm too busy, I'm flat out like a lizard drinking. **1981** P. BARTON *Bastards I have Known* 12 Both flat out like lizards drinking, we were soon neck and neck.

flatette. A small flat or apartment.

1945 S.J. BAKER *Austral. Lang.* 133 *Flatette*, a small flat, also appears to be indigenous. **1949** *Argus* (Melbourne) 8 June 16/4 Brisbane business girl urgently requires Flatette. **1951** *Age* (Melbourne) 5 May 12/2 Business lady requires furn. or unfurn. Flatette. **1955** *Ibid.* 7 Apr. 44/3 Flatette, S.C., kitchenette, bathroom. . . Accom. 2 adults. **1960** *Ibid.* 9 Jan. 38/5 *Flatette* vacant . . suitable business lady. **1965** C. KOCH *Across Sea Wall* 222 The flatette I've rented for us in the Cross. **1980** *Express* (Brisbane) 28 May 4/1 Granny flats are usually small self-contained flatettes built underneath or attached alongside an existing house.

flathead.

1. [See quot. 1974.] Any of many bottom-dwelling marine and estuarine fish, esp. of the fam. Platycephalidae, having a flattened head and body, and valued as food. Also with distinguishing epithet, as **dusky, long-spined, rock, sand, tiger** (see under first element).

1790 J. HUNTER *Hist. Jrnl. Trans. Port Jackson* (1793), *Paddewah*, a fish called a flat-head. **1827** *Tasmanian Almanack* 142 Flat-heads, 1s. 3d. [per dozen]. **1832** J. BACKHOUSE *Narr. Visit Austral. Colonies* (1843) 38 Numbers of fish called Flat-head and Rock Cod were taken. The former is firm, and resembles in figure the Bull-head of English rivers, but weighs about 1½lb. **1852** G.C. MUNDY *Our Antipodes* I. 392 The flathead is half buried in the sand at the bottom, but bites freely. **1876** 'RESIDENT' *Girl Life in Aust.* 206 Do you remember the speckled flounders (flatheads) in the Chinamen's baskets, what low ugly fish they were? **1901** O. OSBORNE *Golden Jubilee* 4 Like flathead new chums came in shoals. **1918** 'J. SCOTT' *How, when & where to catch Fish* 22 Probably the best known fish in New South Wales is the flathead, and it easily heads the list as regards numbers caught by hand-line fishermen. **1951** T.C. ROUGHLEY *Fish & Fisheries* 132 The family of flatheads is more richly represented in Australian waters than in those of any other country, for round the coast of Australia there are about 37 species. . . The three commonest species of flathead—the dusky, tiger, and sand flathead—can be readily distinguished. **1974** T.D. SCOTT et al. *Marine & Freshwater Fishes S.A.* 165 The fishes of this family, known as flatheads, are familiar to those with the barest knowledge of our fishes. As the popular name implies, the head is broad and flattened, being much broader than deep. **1984** *Canberra Chron.* 2 May 19/3 There are plenty of fish in the estuaries, particularly bream and flathead.

2. *Qld.* LUNGFISH.

1880 A.C.L.G. GÜNTHER *Introd. Study Fishes* 357 Locally, the settlers call it [*sc. Ceratodus*] 'Flat-head', 'Burnett- or Dawson-Salmon', and the aborigines

'Barramunda'. **1906** D.G. STEAD *Fishes of Aust.* 229 The Australian Lung-Fish (*Neoceratodus forsteri*) . . is a native of the Mary and Burnett Rivers in Queensland. . . By many Queenslanders this species is known as 'Barramundi'. . . Other names are 'Flathead' and 'Burnett salmon' or 'Mary-River salmon'.

flat-top. An unenclosed, flat-decked railway freight car.

1966 M. BROWN *Jimberi Track* 12 They clambered onto the flat-tops in their bits-and-pieces of cast-off clothing, tugging their blankets and billycans, for they loved nothing so much as travel, and there was nothing in their eyes to match the train. **1973** R. ROBINSON *Drift of Things* 368 Ralph went to the railhead and booked a couple of 'flat-tops' for our six trucks on the next train out of Alice Springs.

flax. *Native flax*, see NATIVE *a.* 6 a.

1824 *Hobart Town Gaz.* 24 Dec., The flax which may be seen growing spontaneously on all the hills, and in nearly all the vales of Tasmania. **1838** *S. Austral. Rec.* (London) 11 July 84 Some fine specimens of flax growing in the valley in great abundance. **1841** *Sydney Herald* 28 Jan. 3/3 As the common flax grows wild in the bush in Australia, it is highly probable that it might be rendered a valuable article of produce and export. **1855** 'RUSTICUS' *How to settle in Vic.* 65 *Flax*, this plant is an annual, and is indigenous to Australia. **1928** J. POLLARD *Bushland Vagabonds* 151 The blue wild flax.

flea. Used allusively in the phr. **to flog** (or **hunt**) **a flea (over),** apparently with reference to ground being so bare of vegetation that a flea being driven across it would be visible.

1866 *Cornhill Mag.* (London) Dec. 741 The vast natural meadow was, as one of the stockmen feelingly observed, 'as bare of grass as the palm of your hand'; while another gravely professed his belief 'that you could hunt a flea across it with a stock-whip'. **1903** J. FURPHY *Such is Life* 165 The famine was sore in the land. To use the expression of men deeply interested in the matter, you could flog a flea from the Murrumbidgee to the Darling. **1944** *Bulletin* (Sydney) 11 Oct. 13/3 A little concerned over the feed shortage on my own slopes, I entered the new settler's rails to find that one could flog a flea over any of his paddocks. **1964** B. WANNAN *Fair Go, Spinner* 79 You could flog a flea across the paddocks, go home to dinner, and come back and *still* find him.

fleas and itches. Rhyming slang for 'the pictures', the cinema.

1967 *Kings Cross Whisper* (Sydney) xxxiv. 4/5 *Fleas and itches*, movies. Pictures, a hangover from the bughouse days. **1968** D. O'GRADY *Bottle of Sandwiches* 60 When not too tired, a man was able to visit . . the open-air fleas-n' itches.

flick. *Surfing.* With **off** and **out**: see quots. 1963.

1963 B. JOHNSON *Surf Fever* 33 *Flick off*, a method of manoeuvring the board whereby the rider is able to pull off the wave before it breaks. **1963** J. POLLARD *Austral. Surfrider* 19 If you bring your board up from the bottom of a wave and over the top you do a 'flick out'. **1979** CAREY & LETTE *Puberty Blues* 28 Sit on the sandhills in the blazing sun from dawn to dusk to watch their flick-outs and drop-ins.

flick pass. [Spec. use of *flick pass* a quick pass.]

1. *Australian National Football.* See quot. 1963 (2).

1936 E.C.H. TAYLOR et al. *Our Austral. Game Football* 23 *The Flick Pass*, this method . . consists of holding the ball in one hand and hitting it with the other hand outstretched. **1963** *Footy Fan* (Melbourne) I. vii. 10 He considers the reaction of the umpires to the flick pass makes it a risky proposition in play. **1963** L. RICHARDS *Boots & All!* 81 Len Smith must also go down in football history for inventing a new style of hand-ball—even though it borders on a throw—he was the first coach to wake up to the fact that the flick pass could be used. His players started using lightning-fast passes in which the ball was hit with the open hand, a more accurate and far quicker method than the ordinary hand pass with the punch or the clenched fist. **1965** A. SCOTT *Man. Austral. Football* 15 The flick pass, in which the ball is struck with a 'backhand' motion with the open palm of the hitting hand, makes it difficult for the striking hand to hit the ball. **1982** *Bulletin* (Sydney) 28 Sept. 36/3 The return to fashion and subsequent prohibition of the flick pass, a device roughly equivalent to a backhand handball.

2. *fig.* In the phr. **to get the flick pass,** and as **flick-pass** *v. trans.*: see quots.

1983 *Canberra Times* 19 Aug. 8/3 He had recalled the dinner when he heard Mr Ivanov 'got the flick pass'. *Ibid.* 31 Aug. 25/6 (*caption*) The Princess of Wales . . flick-passes her son to a nanny.

flier, var. FLYER.

flimsy. *Obs.* [Survival of Br. slang *flimsy* a bank-note: see OED *sb.* 1.] A bank-note.

1845 *Parramatta Chron.* 19 Apr. 3/2 He . . admitted the finding the *flimsies*, but made the rather *flimsy* excuse that having got the 'kites' he considered he had a right 'to fly them'. **1853** J. SHERER *Gold Finder Aust.* 73 Them chaps will finger a rare bunch o' flimsie's now. **1879** *Kelly Gang* 11 With flimsies, gold and silver coin, The threepennies, and all, Amounting to two thousand pounds, They made a glorious haul. **1897** *Bulletin* (Sydney) 25 Sept. 3/2 We'd all been taking flimsies and were giving change in tin. **1915** *Truth* (Sydney) 8 Aug. 4/2 A Filthy Fish Shop. *And a fine of three flimsies*. . . A fine of £3 with 6s. costs was imposed. **1930** A.E. YARRA *Vanishing Horseman* 220 The white man . . gave him a punch for trying to snatch a bundle of flimsies out of his hand.

Flinders grass. [Prob. from the name of Matthew *Flinders* (1774–1814), English explorer.] Any of several annual or short-lived perennial fodder grasses, esp. of the genus *Iseilema* (fam. Poaceae) occurring in all mainland States except Vic.; *Barcoo grass*, see BARCOO A. 2.

1886 *N.T. Times Almanac* 5 Mitchell, blue, barley, Flinders, umbrella, and tuft grass are all well represented. **1903** E. PALMER *Early Days N. Qld.* 237 'Anthistiria membracea', called the Flinders or Barcoo grass, is an annual of a reddish colour, found all over the western plains. **1918** G. WHITE *Thirty Yrs. Tropical Aust.* 25 Producing in good seasons great quantities of the beautiful Flinders grass. **1926** A.A.B. APSLEY *Amateur Settlers* 101 Various kinds of grass lands, some of which was long and thin with sharp pointed ends called 'spear' grass, some extraordinary thick and high called 'Mitchell', and 'Flinders' grass, which the kangaroos like. **1938** C.T. WHITE *Princ. Bot. Qld. Farmers* 200 The value of the Flinders Grasses lies in their peculiar habit of growing extremely palatable and nutritious in the form of standing hay, in this respect differing from practically all other grasses. **1955** H.G. LAMOND *Towser* 104 Flinders grass lay in scarlet blankets on the ground as it emitted an odour of drying hay. **1963** F. FLYNN *Northern Gateway* 190 During the Wet the stock are left entirely to themselves. They put on condition feeding on lush Flinders and Mitchell grasses—and on the young spinifex clumps which have not yet become too coarse. **1975** X. HERBERT *Poor Fellow my Country* 429 No more knee-deep Flinder's grass growing on the little flats that wound between the hummocks of raised ground as when only the kangaroo as herbivore roamed the land.

flindosa /flɪnˈdoʊzə, flɪnˈdaʊzə/. [Corruption of *Flindersia* a genus of trees, from the name of Matthew *Flinders* (1774–1814), English explorer.] CROW'S ASH. Also **Flindosy, Flindozy.**

1861 *Catal. Natural & Industr. Products N.S.W.* 49 *Flindersia australis.* Cedrelaceae. Ash, Beech, and Flindosa. . . A large sized tree of very general occurrence in the Northern districts. . . Timber valuable for staves. **1905** J.H. MAIDEN *Forest Flora N.S.W.* 156, I believe it to be one of the trees which has passed under the name 'Flindosa'. The origin of this name I have been unable to trace, and would suggest that it is a timber-man's rendering of *Flindersia*. **1916** *Bulletin* (Sydney) 4 May 22/3 The coastal bullocky's 'Flindozy' (for Flindersia). **1927** *Ibid.* 3 Nov. 27/4 Crow's ash is not known by any other names than 'Flindosy' and teak. **1977** *Austral. Encycl.* III. 54/2 *F. australis* is . . known generally throughout Queensland as 'crow's ash', but in some places as 'flindosy', an unfortunate corruption of the generic name.

floater, *n.*[1] [f. *float* loose rock or an isolated mass of ore: see OED *sb.* 20 a.; also as *float mineral, ore, quartz.*] A piece of ore detached and removed by water or erosion from the main body. Also *attrib.*

1881 G.C. EVANS *Stories* 300 (Empties the water out of the tub . . and endeavours to find some gold in the gravel.) 'Two specks and a floater. Pshaw.' **1903** J. FURPHY *Such is Life* 158 The surrounding country had been prospected for a few floaters. **1916** *Bull. N.T.* xxi. 8 'Floaters' of considerable size have been found on the slopes of the ridges under the outcrop of the reefs. **1932** I.L. IDRIESS *Prospecting for Gold* 184 A floater is a piece of stone which has broken from a reef and either fallen, been washed away, or blown away. **1941** D. O'CALLAGHAN *Long Life Reminisc.* 144, I only took that lease up for the floaters. I then took up another 12 acres lease, just south and joining that floater lease. **1944** M.J. O'REILLY *Bowyangs & Boomerangs* 128 The first indication that ground was opal-bearing was the finding of what were known as 'floaters'. Floaters were pieces of opal broken away from the pocket, through erosion or some other cause, come to the surface. **1955** D. CLARK *Boomer* 141 That's a floater . . that is—a chunk o' quartz rock with gold showin'. An' I'll bet yer there's plenty more of it upstream of where I found this 'un. **1973** D. WOLFE *Brass Kangaroo* 22 The stone resembled a battered piece of mother of pearl fused on to the side of a rock. . . 'A floater, eh?' . . 'You find floaters where the opal level outcrops on the side of a hill.' **1977** J. DOUGHTY *Gold in Blood* 237 Some of the patches of floaters, he told us, were good enough to crush.

floater, *n.*[2] *S.A.* [Transf. use of Cockney slang *floater*: see quot. 1864.] A dish consisting of a meat pie floating in pea-soup: see quot. 1976.

[**1864** J.C. HOTTEN *Dict. Mod. Slang* (rev. ed.) 135 *Floater*, a small suet dumpling put into soup.—*Whitechapel.*] **1915** *Pepper Box* Dec. 1 Say, matey, give me two pies and a floater. **1945** J. HOLMES *Is it Dinkum?* 8 To the pie cart for a 'floater' (a plate of peas and pie). **1971** J. O'GRADY *Aussie Etiket* 61 South Australians especially during their short winters, are fond of a thing called a 'floater'. **1976** M. POWELL *Down Under* 58 You haven't lived if you've never eaten one of Harry's floaters. It's a bowl of pea-soup so thick that the spoon will stand upright in it; floating on the top is a real meat pie, stuffed full of meat, a liberal dousing of tomato ketchup on top. **1978** J. HEPWORTH *His Bk.* 44 It was many a mortal year since he had been able to sink a fang into the soothing savory pie-and-pea-soup sog of the dreaded 'floaters' which are Adelaide's pride. **1982** M. WALKER *Making Do* 86, I didn't waste much time in partaking of a floater (plate of pea soup and a pie).

floater, *n.*[3] *Two-up.* A coin which fails to spin.

1944 E. LOCKE *From Shore to Shore* 27 If they leave the ring we bar 'em; we bar the floaters, too. **1976** L.R.M. HUNTER *Woodline* 16 'Bar 'em! They're floaters!' someone called. . . 'Heads again!' (and with a groan), 'it's just raining bloody heads!' **1977** R. BEILBY *Gunner* 299 Slight shock put Gunner off his toss so that the coins drifted up sedately, not turning. 'Floater,' several voices shouted. 'Barred,' shouted the ringie. **1983** HIBBERD & HUTCHINSON *Barracker's Bible* 81 In two-up, a coin which doesn't spin properly is known as a 'floater'.

floating station. *Pearling.* The mother ship of a pearling fleet. Also *attrib.*

1897 *V & P* (Qld. L.A.) II. 1320 Floating stations . . enable between fifty and sixty boats to keep constantly at work on the pearling grounds. **1902** *Cwlth. Parl. Papers* (1901–2) II. 1069 When did the floating-station system commence here [*sc.* Queensland]?—About 1891, the vessels came from West Australia. **1913** *Ibid.* III. 644 Divers on the floating stations, in order to secure a better price for their shell, transferred a lot of it to divers on the shore stations. **1918** G. WHITE *Thirty Yrs. Tropical Aust.* 61 Shelling operations have been carried on from 'floating stations' instead of from shore bases—schooner of some 100 tons being used as a parent or store ship. **1949** C. BENHAM *Diver's Luck* 9 The fleet of luggers came flocking around the floating station. **1982** M.A. BAIN *Full Fathom Five* 71 Clarke had been . . the brains behind the concept that emerged of establishing floating stations with a mother schooner controlling a fleet of luggers.

flock. *Obs.*

1. Used *attrib.* in Special Comb. **flock-holder, -owner,** a sheep farmer; **station,** a sheep farm.

1825 *HRA* (1921) 3rd Ser. IV. 319 He rapidly

becomes a large **Flock-holder.** **1837** *Perth Gaz.* 30 Sept. 981 The improvement effected by the system of crossing, generally adopted of late years by the flock-holders. **1847** G.F. ANGAS *Savage Life & Scenes* I. 193 He then repaired to the station of a neighbouring flock-holder, whose hut-keeper returned with him to the premises, which they carefully examined. **1853** J. SHERER *Gold Finder Aust.* 279 One of the largest flock-holders informs me. **1829** R. GOUGER *Let. from Sydney* 84 There is no chance of an alteration favourable to the **flock-owner.** **1839** *Tasmanian* (Hobart) 4 Jan. 6 The clip this year has more than realised the expectations of flock owners. **1847** *Maitland Mercury* 20 Nov. 2/3 We hear that about Scone, and other parts, flockowners have been obliged to shear in the grease, from want of water; this will account for the large proportion that has already reached Maitland in grease. **1871** *Austral. Town & Country Jrnl.* (Sydney) 21 Jan. 75/4 Indeed there are few flockowners who have not suffered very serious loss. **1843** D.G. BROCK *Recoll.* 22 Port Gawler is evidently the most desirable port for ships to take in wool, as the bulk of the **flock stations** lie away to the north.

2. Occas. applied to a group of kangaroos.

1835 T.B. WILSON *Narr. Voyage round World* 243 On perceiving a flock of kangaroos . . he walked . . towards them. **1845** L. LEICHHARDT *Jrnl. Overland Exped. Aust.* 23 Apr. (1847) 227 Two flocks of kangaroos passed me. **1847** G.F. ANGAS *Savage Life & Scenes* I. 203 We observed numerous kangaroos. They frequently appeared in flocks of eight or ten at a time, and gave constant sport to the dogs.

flock pigeon. Either of two species of pigeon that habitually form flocks.

a. The nomadic, predom. brown pigeon *Phaps histrionica* of inland n. Aust.; HARLEQUIN BRONZE-WING.

1851 J. HENDERSON *Excursions & Adventures N.S.W.* II. 178 The flock pigeon is of a lead colour, frequents the brushes, and is generally found in large flocks of several hundreds, and sometimes thousands. **1948** *Austral. Bushcraft* (Austral. Army Educ. Service) 18 The flock pigeon, found on the plains of inland Queensland. **1959** H. LAMOND *Sheep Station* 93 Before the country had been settled, flock pigeons were in unbelievable swarms. They cast huge shadows and blotted out the sun as they gathered and flew to water. **1964** M. SHARLAND *Territory of Birds* 15 The Flock Pigeons, a plains bird which . . has derived a new lease of life from the bores that have been drilled in numbers during recent years.

b. The predom. grey pigeon *Lopholaimus antarcticus* of rainforests in e. Aust.; *crested pigeon* (b), see CRESTED; see also TOPKNOT PIGEON.

1845 C. HODGKINSON *Aust., Port Macquarie to Moreton Bay* 33 Large numbers of the crested flock-pigeon were feeding on this fruit. **1890** G.J. BROINOWSKI *Birds of Aust.* III. Pl. 3, This bird, more commonly known among settlers as the 'Flock Pigeon' is found . . along the north-eastern sea coast. **1948** P.J. HURLEY *Red Cedar* 161 Flock-pigeons come in large numbers every year to feed on the cork trees which are in abundance here. **1965** *Tracks we Travel* 44 Four or five flock pigeons had been wheeling about the Moreton Bay fig. **1982** H.J. FRITH *Pigeons & Doves Aust.* 134 Throughout the range of the Topknot Pigeon, the name Flock Pigeon is used, perhaps more commonly than is Topknot Pigeon. This is undesirable because of the pre-emption of 'Flock Pigeon' by *Phaps histrionica*.

flogger. [In allusion to the whip or cat-o'-nine tails; in sense 1, because the coat is tailed.]

1. A morning-coat. Also *attrib.*

1905 N.F. SPIELVOGEL *Gumsucker on Tramp* 11 A top hat and 'flogger' are signs of a certain amount of—what shall I say—affluence. **1906** E. DYSON *Fact'ry 'Ands* 125 Mills had been seen at large in a flogger coat. **1915** *Bulletin* (Sydney) 6 May 22/4, I found myself in the Hobart Domain listening to a soul-saver in a rusty flogger and a black eye. **1971** F. HARDY *Outcasts of Foolgarah* 10 Little Tich . . unrecognisable in a black flogger-tail coat, grey trousers, pointed toes.

2. *Australian National Football.* A set of streamers in the colours of a team attached to a rod and waved by supporters.

1972 *Bulletin* (Sydney) 5 Aug. 30/2 In Melbourne, most sports-mad of the cities, a VFL Grand Final can draw 100,000 to the Cricket Ground. 'Floggers' have been outlawed this season but the crowds make up for it by flogging their vocal chords. **1973** P. MCKENNA *My World of Football* 90 The carnival atmosphere, the tier after tier of packed stands encircling the MCG, the cheer squads with their long club banners and until recently the highly colourful floggers and run-throughs. **1976** C. EAGLE *Four Faces* 70 Children trailed over their shoulders the limp besoms of black and white streamers known as 'floggers'. **1981** *Age* (Melbourne) 28 July 38/8 There you'd be in your decorated coat, a few badges, and a flogger on a stick, and there they'd be. **1983** K. DUNSTAN *Footy* 31 *Floggers.* Bundles of shredded paper attached to a stick.

flood-bird. [See quot. 1894.] CHANNEL-BILLED CUCKOO.

1887 *Illustr. Austral. News* (Melbourne) 20 Aug. 155/1 They were caught on the Diamantina River and only appear in times of great floods. . . The natives call them flood birds. **1894** E.H. CANNEY *Land of Dawning* 8 Natives . . in the vicinity of Cooper's Creek . . when they heard a bird known in those parts as the 'Flood-bird', whose presence always preceded rain and flood . . would fall flat upon their faces. **1931** J. DEVANEY *Earth Kindred* 68 Yesterday the flood-bird flew with harsh boding cries.

flooded, *ppl. a.* Used in collocations to designate species of trees which are characteristically found in a wet habitat, esp. periodically inundated alluvial flats and river banks: **flooded box,** the tree *Eucalyptus microtheca* (see COOLIBAH); **gum,** any of several trees of the genus *Eucalyptus* (fam. Myrtaceae) growing in moist places, esp. the tall tree of e. N.S.W. and e. Qld. *E. grandis*, also known as *rose gum* (see ROSE), the spreading tree of s.w. W.A. *E. rudis*, and (*obs.*) *E. camaldulensis* (see RED GUM 1).

1839 T.L. MITCHELL *Three Exped. Eastern Aust.* (rev. ed.) II. 49 Clumps of trees of the **flooded box.** **1848** *Atlas* (Sydney) IV. 56/3 Flat country lightly timbered by a species of flooded box. **1867** F.J. BYERLEY *Narr. Overland Exped. Northern Qld.* 26 The flats . . timbered with flooded box and tea tree. **1883** E. PALMER *Plants N. Qld.* 14 *E. microtheca* . . The Coolibar or flooded box found on all Gulf waters, often in flooded ground, of a crooked growth, about 30 feet high. **1819** *Sydney Gaz.* 26 June, To the Productions of the country . . may now be added great Quantities of . . the **Flooded Gum.** **1832** *Currency Lad* (Sydney) 10 Nov. 1/4 Her floor timbers are of iron bark, first futtocks flooded gum. **1843** J.F. BENNETT *Hist. & Descr. Acct. S.A.* 41 In alluvial flats, and along the banks of streams and rivers, is found what is termed the flooded gum—a majestic-looking tree, with a short thick stem, with immense branches spreading all around, and the smaller boughs drooping towards the ground. **1858** A.C. & F.T. GREGORY *Jrnls. Austral. Explorations* 4 May (1884) 40 A narrow belt of flooded-gum lined either bank. **1874** *Illustr. Sydney News* 30 May 14/3 E. rostrata, which is . . known in various parts of Australia as Flooded Gum, White Gum or Red Gum. **1926** M. FORREST *Hibiscus Heart* 280 Satin-white boles of flooded gums. **1948** P.J. HURLEY *Red Cedar* 154 'Flooded Gums' (*Eucalyptus grandis*) have grown to seventy feet in height in six years. **1978** *Ecos* xvii. 25/3 Plantations of flooded gum . . could lose up to 40% of trees through cockatoo attack.

flossy. *Obs.* [Prob. f. U.S. slang *flossy* saucy, showy: see OEDS *flossy* and also *floosie*.] A prostitute.

1899 B. MORANT *Poetry* (1980) 50 Scanty stock of gold—Scanty! yet the whole d--d lot Publicans and Flossies got. **1903** *Truth* (Sydney) 18 Jan. 1/6 An irate Flossie hit a Chow on the head with a large lump of road metal, and drew the 'claret'. **1914** *Ibid.* 15 Feb. 1/7 A group of Saturday night flossies were surfing on Sunday morning. One of the plumpest was carried off by a shark.

flour-bag, *a. Austral. pidgin.* [With reference to the colour.] Of hair: white.

1857 F. GERSTAECKER *Two Convicts* 35 In the corrupt language used as a means of communication between white and black . . 'flour-bag' means 'white'. **1859** H. KINGSLEY *Recoll. G. Hamlyn* II. 36 An old lady . . with a head as white as snow, topping her black body (a flourbag cobbler, as her tribe would call her). **1889** *Centennial Mag.* (Sydney) 595 Blackfellows' hints of an 'old man with flour-bag beard', have been reported. **1893** E. FAVENC *Last of Six Tales* 38 That old nigger with the white hair has been after me all night—the old buck who was potted in the head. He comes along every night now with his flour-bag cobra all over blood. **1927** M.H. ELLIS *Long Lead* 107 Francis had particular faith in the thews and muscles of one dignified old 'flour bag fella' (old gentleman with white hair and beard). **1955** DEAN & CARELL *Dust for Dancers* 95 Her aged old father, whose hair was pure white or 'flour bag', as the natives say. **1975** X. HERBERT *Poor Fellow my Country* 1426 They unpacked, with no more conversation than a couple of jests about their age, 'Flour-Bag', as they called themselves, with reference to the white in their hair.

flour gold. [With reference to the fineness of flour.] See quot. 1869.

1869 R.B. SMITH *Gold Fields & Mineral Districts* 611 *Flour-gold*, the finest alluvial drift-gold. **1896** J.W. ROBERTS *Mining Industry N.S.W.* 11 Everywhere I got good prospects of flour gold by dollying, and the coarse exception was a splendid prospect. **1935** F. BIRTLES *Battle Fronts Outback* 143 It was flour-gold, in ironstone capped quartz, and . . assays of samples had shown good results. **1979** B. SCOTT *Tough in Old Days* 31 We heard of 'flour' gold that was so fine it would float out of your dish, of grassroots gold that lay just below the surface of certain kinds of country.

floury baker. [See quot. 1895.] The cicada *Abricta curvicosta* of s.e. Qld. and coastal N.S.W., having a covering of easily detachable hair-like scales resembling flour in appearance; BAKER. Also **floury miller.**

1895 *Proc. Linnean Soc. N.S.W.* X. 530 The whole of the insect is black on the upper surface, but covered with fine silvery white hairs which form little white spots here and there, looking as though it had been dusted with flour. From this circumstance it has received from the Sydney children the rather appropriate name of the 'Floury Miller'. **1903** *Agric. Gaz. N.S.W.* XIV. 418 A well-known 'locust', to the Sydney boys is popularly known as the 'Floury Miller', or the 'Baker'. **1905** *Bulletin* (Sydney) 28 Dec. (Red Page), There's heaps of different kinds of locusts, heaps! . . Greengrocers, and floury bakers [etc.]. **1951** CUSACK & JAMES *Come in Spinner* 106 'Mine's a Floury Baker . . and mine's a Black Prince!' Young Jack and Andrew held up their fists for her to peep at frosted fawn body and tan-and-black. **1981** *Sydney Morning Herald* 19 Dec. 29/2 So we missed them—greengrocer, black prince, double drummer, floury miller—where had they gone? **1982** N. KEESING *Lily on Dustbin* 95 His ambition is to capture a rare 'cherry nose' or an even rarer 'floury baker'.

flowering gum. Any of several species of GUM TREE noted for their beauty while flowering, esp. the widely-cultivated small tree *Eucalyptus ficifolia* (fam. Myrtaceae) of s.w. W.A. See also *scarlet gum* SCARLET. Also **red-** (or **crimson-**)**flowering gum.**

1905 *Emu* V. 79 Where the crimson-flowering gums (Eucalyptus ficifolia)—perhaps the most beautiful and ornamental of Australian trees—bloom in varying shades of red. **1935** T. RAYMENT *Cluster of Bees* 54 The rosy blossom of the red-flowering gum, *Eucalyptus calophylla*, is so abundant that it effectively eclipses the green of the foliage. **1942** C. BARRETT *Austral. Wild Flower Bk.* 20 The handsome red flowering gum belongs to southwestern Australia as a wild tree: it has been extensively cultivated in the eastern States, being favoured especially for street planting. **1948** A. MARSHALL *Ourselves writ Strange* 287 Red flowering gums, trees I had imagined only grew in their natural state in Western Australia, were exclamations of colour. **1963** X. HERBERT *Disturbing Element* 40 We might be lying chewing the sweet seeds of knobby-grass under a scarlet flowering gum . . in poor arid Groperland. **1981** *Access* Dec. 6/2 Any tree of outstanding aesthetic significance; e.g. *Eucalyptus ficifolia* (Flowering Gum) at the Metropolitan Golf Club, Oakleigh.

Flowery-Lander. *Obs.* [f. *Flowery Land*, a name for China.] A Chinese immigrant.

1851 *Empire* (Sydney) 21 Mar. 3/4 The sulky Mantchoo was consequently sentenced to be imprisoned for one month, which will give him an opportunity of nursing the 'rheumatism' so prevalent among these 'Flowery Landers'. **1888** J. FREEMAN *Lights & Shadows Melbourne Life* 101 The flowery-lander would get the fowls for four shillings.

flow-on. *Industrial Relations.* The wider application

of a wage increase, or improvement in working conditions, awarded to one sector of the community (see quot. 1981); the increase or improvement itself. Also *attrib.*

[**1951** *73 CAR* 337 It was contended that it did not follow that whatever was done in regard to margins for tradesmen in the Metal Trades award would flow into other awards. **1967** *Age* (Melbourne) 12 Dec. 11/1 They appealed to the Arbitration Commission and unions to ensure that the increases did not flow on to other awards.] **1969** *Sydney Morning Herald* 4 Dec. 1/4 All the professional engineers had received was a 'flow-on' of the metal trades decision. **1973** *Ibid.* 14 Dec. 9/1 The State Government will not move at present to seek an automatic flow-on of a 17½ per cent holiday pay loading to all employees under State awards. **1976** *Ibid.* 27 Nov. 4/2 Workers under N.S.W. awards to get flow-on wage rise. **1978** *Ibid.* 14 June 13/3 Workers under State awards were granted the 1.3 per cent flow-on on Monday from the national wage decision last Wednesday. **1981** SHEEHAN & WORLAND *Gloss. Industr. Relations Terms* (ed. 2) 31 *Flow-on*. . The process by which a wage increase in one section of the wage community is applied to other sectors for the purpose of maintaining a given community wage structure. **1985** *Canberra Times* 5 Nov. 1/5 A small number of actions in strategic areas also had the potential for wide flow-on that could make the system unworkable.

flute, *n.* In the phr. **to be** (or **get**) **on the flute,** to monopolize a conversation, to 'hold the floor'. Also **to hold** (or **pass**) **the flute.**

1896 T. HENEY *Girl at Birrell's* 23 'You've got the flute properly to-night, Graham,' returned the other. 'You can gas for all hands.' **1898** *Bulletin* (Sydney) 17 Dec. (Red Page), An incessant talker is a *skiter* or a *fluter*, and a request to him *to pass the flute* or the *kip* is to allow someone else to 'do a pitch'. **c 1907** C.W. CHANDLER *Darkest Adelaide* 7 The young fellow had the flure, and was, as Mr Bludger informed me, fairly 'on the flute', square an' all. **1920** A. WRIGHT *Rogue's Luck* 59 Cut it out, Chilla; ring orf. Gor blime, oncet you get on th' flute about th' good ole days. **1934** J.C. LEE *Boshstralians* 35 'Squashy's on the flute now,' whispered Hegarty. 'Knows all about the petticoats, he does,' acknowledged Benson. **1955** STEWART & KEESING *Austral. Bush Ballads* 278 He never tired while he 'held the flute' of telling what he could do.

flute, *v. Obs.* [f. prec.] *intr.* To hold forth. Also **fluter** *n.*

1898 [see FLUTE *n.*]. **1915** *Truth* (Sydney) 18 Apr. 2/6 It may have suited Premier Holman, when 'fluting' against the totalisator to 'deplore the drinking habits of the working classes'. **1959** D. NILAND *Big Smoke* 178 Where's Phil the Fluter now?

flute-bird. *Obs.* The bird *Gymnorhina tibicen* (see MAGPIE *n.* 1).

1862 H. KENDALL *Poems & Songs* 53 The echu's songs are dying with the flute-bird's mellow tone. **1919** *Bulletin* (Sydney) 16 Jan. 24/4 'Flute-bird' is good for the black-backed magpie.

fluted gum. *Obs.* [See quot. 1833.] GIMLET.

1833 *Jrnls. Several Exped. W.A.* 214 We named them cable or fluted gum, being considerably twisted. **1855** R. AUSTIN *Jrnl. Interior W.A.* 9 Patches of gnaleruk (fluted or cable-gum of Roe), a singular species of eucalyptus, with smooth, glossy bark, and three spiral channels along the trunk, which make it resemble a twisted clustered column growing on the loamy soil. **1897** L. LINDLEY-COWEN *W. Austral. Settler's Guide* 215 Fluted gum, or gimlet wood (*E. salubris*).

fly, *n.*[1]

1. Used *attrib.* in Special Comb. **fly blight** *obs.*, an eye infection, supposed to have been transmitted by flies; **bog,** jam; treacle; **cork,** one of a number of pieces of cork dangling from a wide-brimmed hat to keep flies from the wearer's face; **door,** a door fitted with a *fly screen*; **flapper,** a piece of fine material attached to the hat of a person or the harness of an animal to keep flies away; **loo,** see quot. 1910; **net,** **(a)** *fly veil*; **(b)** a piece of fine netting or mesh used to protect the person or a structure from flies; see also quot. 1924; **fly-netted** *ppl. a.*, (of a structure) protected by fly screens; **-proof** *a.*, protected against flies; so **-proofed** *ppl. a.*; **screen,** a frame in or over which fine netting or mesh is stretched, fitted to an aperture to permit ventilation but prevent the entry of flies; also *attrib.*; **veil,** a piece of finely meshed material hanging from a hat brim to protect the wearer's face from flies; **wire,** fine wire mesh used to make fly screens; also *attrib.*, made from or equipped with fly wire; so **-wired** *ppl. a.*; **-wiring** *vbl. n.*

1851 *Empire* (Sydney) 12 Dec. 459/4 **Fly blight** is a curse under which every second person suffers. **1855** W. HOWITT *Land, Labor & Gold* I. 247 The flies and the fly-blight! . . Some people altogether lose their sight. . . It is the little black devil [*sc.* fly] which causes it here. **1918** *Aussie: Austral. Soldiers' Mag.* Feb. 6/2 Back in the wagon lines we get butter, rooty, rice an' **flybog.** **1943** *Bulletin* (Sydney) 29 Sept. 13/1 Have heard jam called 'fly-bog' as often as treacle. **1944** J. DEVANNY *By Tropic Sea & Jungle* 214 Sometimes you take a tin of flybog (treacle), with you as a luxury. **1968** S. GORE *Holy Smoke* 27 Not even a tin of fly-bog of a Sunday's tea—that's if they *had* jam in them days. **1939** *Bulletin* (Sydney) 22 Feb. 21/2 We overtook a genuine old-style swaggie, neatly-rolled 'Curse o' Gawd' slung over left shoulder by a towel . . and **fly-corks** dancing from hat-brim. **1981** P. RADLEY *Jack Rivers & Me* 90 Now me and Maggie and Big Myrt are swaggies and come on humpin' our blueys, and wearing old hats with fly-corks swinging round the edge. **1900** *Albury Banner* 5 Jan. 16/4 Having then got our **fly doors**, we can set at nought those 'creeping things with horrid wings'. **1904** *Bulletin* (Sydney) 28 Jan. 17/2 A Cobar publican put a 'fly' door to the bar one summer evening when the flies were ravenous. **1949** J. CLEARY *Long Shadow* 53 He could see the room beyond but dimly through the wire screen of the fly-door. **1980** *Southerly* iii. 295 Bob Maher flung open the fly-door. **1853** J.R. GODLEY *Extracts Jrnl. Visit N.S.W.* 16 Flies . . defile everything. Everybody in the interior wears a short veil, or rather **fly-flapper**, made of net, round his hat, to keep them off the face. **1893** *Adelaide Observer* 28 Oct. 34/3 The horses . . seemed to feel it so they ploughed along with bent down heads, hardly troubling to shake their fly-flappers and disperse the black masses clustering at each eye. **1910** *Bulletin* (Sydney) 21 Apr. 15/2 **Fly-loo** is very simple. If there be six thirsts to quench, six pieces of lump sugar are put on the bar, Mr Pub, as referee explaining that he on whose sugar a fly first alights must pay. But five of the pieces have at a former date been damped with whisky, and as a fly is teetotal it alights on the sixth one. **1917** C. DREW *Reminisc. D. Gilbert* 97 The game of Fly Loo is a sweepstake. **1911** *Bulletin* (Sydney) 16 Feb. 13/2 A . . tin-fossicker ambled in, wearing his big straw hat, decorated with a **fly-net.** **1913** W.K. HARRIS *Outback in Aust.* 144 To travel with out fly-nets, corks on strings from round the brim of the hat, or a bush in hand, means torture to the average 'Bushie'. **1924** F.J. MILLS *Happy Days* 123 A tall elderly gentleman, with an umbrella and a cork flynet, approached us. **1927** *Bulletin* (Sydney) 7 July 24/3 Fly-nets are not to be had at every small store outback. **1937** A.W. UPFIELD *Mr Jelly's Business* 106 Through open **fly-netted** doors and windows came drifting the soft distinct night-sounds. **1948** V. PALMER *Golconda* 59 A butcher began work in a small, fly-netted enclosure. **1848** T.L. MITCHELL *Jrnl. Exped. Tropical Aust.* 380, I fancied myself . . sun-proof, **fly-proof** and water-proof. **1925** *Makeshifts & Other Home-Made Furniture* (New Settlers League Aust.) 19 A double layer of strong net tacked to the frame of windows inside will make them fly-proof. **1933** W. HATFIELD *Desert Saga* 235 They were on the fly-proof veranda. **1938** A. UPFIELD *Bone is Pointed* (1966) 50 The fly-proofed veranda along the south side of the house. **1946** A.J. HOLT *Wheat Farms Vic.* 168 One-half of the houses are fly-proofed. **1929** A. SMITH *Austral. Home Carpenter* 49 Renewal of **fly-screen** windows and doors. **1932** *Bulletin* (Sydney) 2 Nov. 21/4 The fly-screens outside my laboratory windows have been in places criss-crossed with chalk. **1960** G. TAYLOR *Crop Dusters* 198 The Italian stood aside, holding the fly-screen door open. **1963** X. HERBERT *Disturbing Element* 75 The wards were . . shaded . . by wide verandas and flyscreens. **1890** A. WOODHOUSE *Man with Apples* 81 Few of his most intimate associates would have easily recognized Maurice Dalby in the billycock hat, **fly veil**, leggings and general bushman's garb. **1897** J.J. MURIF *From Ocean to Ocean* 36 Procured a fly-veil here. Should have had one before this: my eyes are already sore from the . . irritating flies. **1917** *Truth* (Sydney) 15 Apr. 1/8 He exchanged his hard-hitter for a soft hat and flyveil. **1940** E. HILL *Great Austral. Loneliness* (ed. 2) 46 Snowy the Poet . . writing bush verses under a fly-veil as he thrashed along. **1925** *Makeshifts & Other Home-Made Furniture* (New Settlers League Aust.) 19 If **fly-wire** can be bought by the yard and nailed outside the window frame, it serves the purpose better. **1935** K.L. SMITH *Sky Pilot Arnhem Land* 94 In the mustering camps and on the road, it is rarely possible to have fly-wire butchers' shops. **1960** G. TAYLOR *Crop Dusters* 100 Beer had condensed outside the glass in the dry wind that idled through the fly-wire on to the wide, shaded veranda. **1962** *N.T. News* (Darwin) 13 Jan. 3/4 Immediate fly-wiring of all wards, kitchens, and other areas not yet closed to mosquitoes and flies. **1969** J. PACKER *Leopard in Fold* 57 He pushed open the fly-wired door of the back verandah. **1973** R. ROBINSON *Drift of Things* 330 The homestead was dinky-di, a real Northern Territory homestead. It was built on tall, tree-post supports. You lived mainly beneath it. Here it was always cool. The house itself was fly-wired in and one rarely went upstairs. **1975** *Meanjin* 168 He pushed open the flywire door and went. **1980** ANSELL & PERCY *To fight Wild* 137 Sitting on Luke's verandah, fly wire all round, clean floor, no dust, no flies.

2. a. [With *on* now also used elsewhere.] In the phr. **(there are) no flies on** (or **about**), (there is) no lack of alertness, astuteness, competence or energy in (a person); no fault to be found with.

1845 C. GRIFFITH *Present State & Prospects Port Phillip* 78 The person who excites their greatest respect is the man who is alive to their attempts (or, as they express it themselves, *who drops down to their moves*), and the highest encomium they can pass on such an one is, that *there are no flies about him.* **1845** S. SIDNEY *Three Colonies* (1953) 163, I saw the swell I mentioned: and I tell you There are no flies about him, my good fellow. **1848** H.W. HAYGARTH *Recoll. Bush Life* 101 'It's lucky we got them,' said Amos, 'there were no flies about that black bull.' [*Note*] This expression is very common in Australia, and is apparently borrowed from the American 'no snakes'. It denotes admiration or triumph. Anything particularly good is said by the class of men we are here describing to have 'no flies' about it. **1859** J. LANG *Botany Bay* (1885) 62 Whether he had faked the swag or not, he was a tip-top nob, and no flies about it. **1864** *Sydney Punch* 3 Sept. 115/1 All right, mate; there's no flies about you, I see. **1904** L.M.P. ARCHER *Bush Honeymoon* 134 Sandy's a *silvertail.* There ain't no flies on Sandy fer grit. **c 1907** C.W. CHANDLER *Darkest Adelaide* 81 I'm a simple little barmaid, and there ain't no flies on me; I'm as chipper as they make 'em, so are all my family. **1932** L. MANN *Flesh in Armour* 305 They admitted, though, there were few flies on him. **1950** 'B. JAMES' *Advancement Spencer Button* 44 'No flies on May!' 'Oh Fred!' 'No flies!' It was Fred's favourite expression of excellence. **1954** I.L. IDRIESS *Nor'-Westers* 85 No, there were no flies on Mrs Thompson. Any pellet at all that was not cleaned properly she put aside. **1977** R. BEILBY *Gunner* 131 Sure, captain, we can take it. There's no flies on us—but you can bloody well see where they've been. **1984** *Sun-Herald* (Sydney) 29 Jan. 136/5 No flies on officials out at the SCG. That's why members now have coded plastic card keys which they must pop into the computer before turnstiles click open to let them in.

b. In the (exclam.) phr. **no flies (about),** no possible doubt (about), no fuss.

1858 C.R. THATCHER *Colonial Songster* (rev. ed.) 39 Hurrah, my brave pals, ye may all nobblerize, There's plenty more grog in the camp, and no flies. **1859** J. LANG *Botany Bay* (1885) 47 To use a popular expression current that day in the police-office—'Whether he had faked the swag or not, he was a tip-top nob and no flies about it.' **1873** J.C.F. JOHNSON *Christmas on Carringa* 5 There ain't no flies about that . . *that's* real beer. **1882** *Sydney Slang Dict.* 6 *No flies*, emphatic in the affirmative. **1890** A.J. VOGAN *Black Police* 139 He could talk 'bullock' and 'no flies'. **1895** *Worker* (Sydney) 26 Jan. 3/2 He was speculator, storekeeper, and gambler, and made no more flies about robbing his own countrymen than he did the 'White Devils'. **1950** [see sense 2 a.].

3. In the phr. **(to drink) with the flies,** (to drink) alone, usu. in a public drinking place.

1911 *Truth* (Sydney) 10 Dec. 3/4 No person is allowed to 'shout', so each one, 'with the flies', Absorbs his Jimmy Woodser, while the watchful wowser spies. **1912** *Ibid.* 16 June 4/6 While he was having his 'Jimmy Woodser', Pearce came into the parlor—also in search of liquid; but though the accused apparently came in with the intention of *drinking with the flies* he did not do so, but asked him (Murphy) to wet his neck with him.

1926 M. FORREST *Hibiscus Heart* 135 The slanging he knew he probably deserved for letting the rum lure him to 'drink with the flies'. **1940** *Digger Yarns: Cream of 'Aussiosities'*, Blimey, Bin drinkin' with the flies again, and the blighters are bringin' 'im 'ome. **1959** D. HEWETT *Bobbin Up* 102 Vic was drinking with the flies. . . Little groups of workers nattered and argued and hung over the bar, but they gave Vic a wide berth. **1963** D. WHITINGTON *Mile Pegs* 177 'Have a drink?' the larrikin invited. 'Or do you prefer drinking with the flies?' **1980** B. HORNADGE *Austral. Slanguage* 237 There are always the solitary types who drink alone or who 'drink with the flies'.

fly, *n.*[2] [Fig. use of *fly* act of flying.] In the phr. **to have a fly, to give (it,** etc.) **a fly,** to make an attempt, to take a chance, to 'have a go'.

1915 *Bulletin* (Sydney) 5 Aug. 24/1, I myself have had a fly after a fox in a green-timber paddock on a 6-h.p. cycle. **1918** C.J. DENNIS *Digger Smith* 68 Jim mightn't come back 'ome, yeh know. You 'ave a fly; yeh're sure to score; Besides, all's fair in love an' war. **1925** A. WRIGHT *Boy from Bullarah* 21 Seein' a quid that he had missed layin' near him on the floor, I picked it up and gave it a fly. **1934** A. MELROSE *Song & Slapstick* 7 If I summon my courage and scatter this verse Will you be indulgent and 'give it a fly'. **1956** C.D. MILLS *Stockwhip & Spur* 49 Their fleeces were dry, but the bellies were wet. Said the boss of the board, 'We must give them a fly.' **1971** G. MORGAN *We are borne On* 87 In my first two spins I lost three pounds, so I decided to give another pound a fly. **1982** PAGE & INGPEN *Aussie Battlers* 85, I couldn't see any future but tending someone else's sheep and cows, so me and my brother Ivan decided to give it a fly on our own account.

fly, *v. Australian National Football. intr.* To jump high in an attempt to take a mark. Also as *ppl. a.*

1960 *N.T. News* (Darwin) 23 Feb. 1/1 The high flying tribesmen of Maningrida settlement in Arnhem Land are after your blood . . on the Australian Rules field. **1963** L. RICHARDS *Boots & All!* 68 Dick stood about 5 ft. 11 in. in his socks, and on top of this he had very long arms, which gave him a decided advantage as a rover, because he could fly for marks against bigger men. **1965** *Sydney Morning Herald* 2 Aug. 15/5 Eastern Suburbs' John Grey . . flies head and shoulders over four other players in an attempt to mark in the Australian Rules match. **1967** *Austral.* (Sydney) 24 Apr. 12/5 Peter Hudson, Hawthorn's star full-forward recruit from Tasmania flies in front of his opposing full-back . . to mark in the VFL game at Princes Park in Melbourne. **1969** A. HOPGOOD *And Big Men Fly* 44 There's the bounce. And the big men fly! **1986** *Mercury* (Hobart) 27 Mar. 40/2 (*heading*) Big men will fly on TV.

fly-blown, *ppl. a.* [Transf. use of *fly-blown* putrid, hence spoilt, 'ruined'.] Ruined financially; penniless. Also **fly-blowed.**

1853 C.R. READ *What I heard, saw, & Did* 51 Being 'fly-blown' is a colonial term for being 'done *up*'. **1873** J.C.F. JOHNSON *Christmas on Carringa* 21 Look here, mate, you might as well do me a good turn for I'm reg'lar fly-blowed. **1889** H. EGBERT *Pretty Cockey* 36 When he was fly-blown, he was taken by an ex-attorney, with whom he had been boozing, to one of Watson's stations, to look for a job. **1898** *Bulletin* (Sydney) 17 Dec. 15/2 Hard-uppishness a shearer confesses when he says he's . . *fly-blown*. **1912** J. BRADSHAW *Highway Robbery under Arms* (ed. 3) 56 Them chumps . . blow to one another . . what they are going to do when the shearing is over and they are dead fly-blown. **1931** W. HATFIELD *Sheepmates* 161 Sit in, some o' yous that ain't flyblown. **1948** J. FURPHY *Buln-Buln & Brolga* 50 An' on'y thirteen shillin's in my pocket! About as near flyblowed as a man could wish to be. **1966** T. RONAN *Once there was Bagman* 25 They'd been on that Katherine railway job, living from pay to pay, and when it shut down they were flyblown. **1971** K. WILLEY *Boss Drover* 150 After some days he was broke with a hang-over—'fly-blown', he called it. **1985** W.W. AMMON et al. *Working Lives* 105 All my money's going to keep the payments up on the plant. I'm broke—flyblown.

flyer. Also **flier.** [Spec. use of *flyer* one who or that which moves with exceptional speed.]

1. An exceptionally fast kangaroo, usu. young and esp. female. See also *blue flyer* BLUE *a.*, FLYING DOE.

1826 J. ATKINSON *Acct. Agric. & Grazing N.S.W.* 24 The animals of this kind [*sc.* kangaroos] that are not quite full grown are termed flyers; they are exceedingly swift. **1834** G. BENNETT *Wanderings N.S.W.* I. 287 The males of this species are called by the colonists 'foresters', the females 'flyers'. **1848** H.W. HAYGARTH *Recoll. Bush Life* 118 A young male or female kangaroo, called in the colony 'a flyer'. **1871** *Austral. Town & Country Jrnl.* (Sydney) 7 Jan. 24/2 Among them were several flyers, of various sizes, and one large old man kangaroo. **1884** A.W. STIRLING *Never Never Land* 40 Lady . . sighted a 'flyer' or three-parts grown kangaroo. **1888** 'R. BOLDREWOOD' *Robbery under Arms* (1937) 70 He had as much chance of coming up with her as a cattle dog of catching a 'brush flyer'. **1893** C.H. BARLEE *Humorous Tales & Sketches* 8 What can be more exhilarating than a burst of twenty minutes across respectable country, at the tail of a brace of good dogs, after a regular flyer. **1939** J.G. PATTISON *'Battler's' Tales Early Rockhampton* 74 In an exciting chase, one flyer was brought down. **1955** D. CLARK *Boomer* 27 First were the 'fliers', unmated doe kangaroos, fleet, irresponsible creatures.

2. A fast shearer; the fastest shearer in a shed, RINGER *n.*[1] 2 a.

1908 W.H. OGILVIE *My Life in Open* 42 The 'ringer' or flier of the shed. **1912** J. BRADSHAW *Highway Robbery under Arms* (ed. 3) 24 After 'Smoko' the bell was rung, and the fliers were at it again red-hot. **1949** *Bulletin* (Sydney) 23 Feb. 14/4 The flier rung at Yanco, Eden Plains and Pompadour.

flying, *ppl. a.* Used as a distinguishing epithet in the names of animals: **flying mouse,** the mouse-sized gliding marsupial *Acrobates pygmaeus*, the feathertail glider, of e. and s.e. Aust.; **possum** (or **squirrel**), any of several tree-climbing marsupials, esp. those that glide through the air using flaps of skin between the fore and hind limbs as 'parachutes'.

1811 D.D. MANN *Present Picture N.S.W.* 50 **Flying Mice** are likewise found, in considerable numbers, in this country, of a very handsome appearance, and . . of the Opossum species. The tail of this interesting little animal resembles a feather. **1861** 'OLD BUSHMAN' *Bush Wanderings* 50 The Flying Mouse is certainly the most beautiful little animal in the colony. **1885** A.W. HOWITT *Jeraeil* 316 The novice . . may eat the males of . . the brushtail and the flying mouse. **1945** *Bulletin* (Sydney) 3 Oct. 13/3 A pygmy glider it was, *Acrobates pygmaeus* to scientists, flying mouse to bush folk. **1788** [**flying possum**] *HRA* (1914) 1st Ser. I. 31 At the foot of one tree we found the fur of a flying squirrel. **1792** R. ATKINS Jrnl. 26 June, The bats and flying squirrels . . traverse the air by means of membranous instead of feathered wings. **1805** J. TURNBULL *Voyage round World* III. 151 Amongst the four footed animals might be reckoned the flying squirrel, and the guana, all of which serve as food for the natives. **1827** P. CUNNINGHAM *Two Yrs. in N.S.W.* I. 156 The flying squirrels are of a beautiful slate colour with a fur so fine that although a small animal, the hatters would give a quarter-dollar for every skin. **1829** R. MUDIE *Picture of Aust.* 171 There is another class to which the colonists give the names of . . squirrels, flying-opossums, [etc.]. **1833** W.H. BRETON *Excursions* 261 The flying squirrel, often called the flying oppossum . . is . . the petaurus Australis (Sciurus). **1845** R. HOWITT *Impressions Aust. Felix* 114 Flying squirrels, or tuans, in hollow gum trees. **1847** G.F. ANGAS *Savage Life & Scenes* 75 The flying opossums, or Phalangers, are also nocturnal in their habits. **1856** *Moreton Bay Free Press* 8 Jan. 3/1 The flying squirrel; this animal the size of a Skye terrier, will, in descending from a high tree, extend its flight to 100 yards. **1886** P. CLARKE *'New Chum' in Aust.* 302 These same flying opossums and flying foxes do an immense deal of harm to fruit-trees. **1916** *Emu* XV. 260, I found a Powerful Owl . . having in its talons the body of a black 'flying squirrel' (Phalanger). **1936** J.R.B. LOVE *Stone-Age Bushmen of Today* 71 While searching the hollow trees the women often will find . . a pair of the lovely little flying opossums or 'flying squirrels'. **1986** *Sydney Morning Herald* 13 Feb. 6/1 The forests contained great numbers of flying possums, such as the feathertail glider and the greater glider.

flying doctor.

1. A medical practitioner who uses radio communication and travels by aircraft to provide services to patients in places which are remote and without readily accessible medical services; orig. with reference to the service provided by the Australian Inland Mission from Cloncurry, Qld., established in 1928. Also *attrib.*

1920 *Inlander* July 80 A Flying Doctor could be planted down at Winton immediately. **1922** *Ibid.* June 20 The outlying areas must have more nurses stationed here and there before Flying Doctors can do their part satisfactorily. **1929** *Ibid.* Nov. 50 Other countries have been watching this first 'Flying Doctor' experiment. **1932** I.L. IDRIESS *Flynn of Inland* (1965) 178 The first flying doctor had increased the ordinary 'radius' of the A.M.S. to four hundred miles, saved valuable lives, alleviated untold suffering, and brought a feeling of security to that particular portion of the Inland which the people had never experienced before. **1936** *Beyond Furthest Fences* (Austral. Inland Mission) 9 With Cloncurry, Queensland, as his base, the A.I.M. Flying Doctor casts a mantle of safety over an outback area. **1936** W. HATFIELD *Aust. through Windscreen* 140 We were joined by Dr Fenton, the Flying Doctor of the North who is always getting into hot water through his reckless readiness to go anywhere, any time, to carry medical aid to the sick or injured. **1950** G.M. FARWELL *Land of Mirage* 85 The Flying Doctor's plane can reach a place like Mungerannie by direct flight in three hours. **1960** *N.T. News* (Darwin) 22 Jan. 4/6 Mrs Peter Gunning . . immediately sent out an emergency call over the Flying Doctor radio network. **1965** E. LAMBERT *Long White Night* 136 She was a Flying Doctor nurse. **1976** J.H. TRAVERS *Bull Dust on Brigalow* 40 It was run by the Presbyterian Church with two Bush Nurses in charge. There was no other habitation and these two brave women with a pedal wireless and an occasional visit from the Flying Doctor attended to any casualties from the big holdings which were hundreds of square miles in area. **1983** J. HEPWORTH *Extraordinary Austral. Landmarks*, If you break a leg out Back o' Bourke, Or get gout on the parched Paroo . . Don't fly for the doc, that's not the lurk, Flying doctors fly to you!

2. Comb. **flying doctor base, service.**

1939 J.W. COLLINGS *8000 Miles by Air* 3, I naturally wasted no time in becoming acquainted with the service on this my first visit to a fully established **Flying Doctor Base.** **1951** G. FARWELL *Outside Track* 131 He was notifying the Flying Doctor Base three hundred miles away that we were in the air again. **1968** S. GORE *Holy Smoke* 64 First we visited the Flying Doctor base, where constant watch is maintained in the radio-room for emergency signals from the outback stations. **1939** J.W. COLLINGS *8000 Miles by Air* 6 At the same time, I imagined what must have been the condition of things before the advent of our **Flying Doctor Service** at Wyndham. **1957** V. PALMER *Seedtime* 143 They were more interested in . . the creation at Golconda of a headquarters for the Flying Doctor Service. **1969** A. BUZO *Front Room Boys* (1970) 112, I mean, you're a man of stature, Robbo. . . You ran the flying doctor service in the outback. I believe you, but Jacko reckons you're all crap. **1983** *Canberra Times* 26 Oct. 23/4 Even the Flying Doctor service was refused access.

flying doe. A young female kangaroo, characteristically fleet of foot. See also FLYER 1.

1846 *Tasmanian Jrnl. Nat. Sci.* II. 372 The grey kangaroo. . . The swiftest runner is the female of the first year before having young, and of the second year with her first young; at this age her speed is so great, that she is termed the 'Flying Doe'. **1850** *Bell's Life in Sydney* 22 June 3/2 A *flying doe* is no exaggeration, for fly they seem to, taking immensely high and quick bounds. **1861** 'OLD BUSHMAN' *Bush Wanderings* 3 When hard pressed, an 'old man', or 'flying doe' will clear nearly ten yards at a spring. **1890** J.I. WATTS *Family Life S.A.* 186 A young buck or a flying doe when kept for some days is very good eating, but an 'old man' is only fit for a cannibal. **1906** W.A. HORN *Notes by Nomad* 77 She was clean thorough-bred, with a beautiful head, And as fleet as a blue 'flying doe'. **1952** B. BEATTY *Unique to Aust.* 26 In bush parlance the old male kangaroo is called an old man, the young female a flying doe and the offspring until eight or ten months old, a joey.

flying duck orchid. [From the fancied resemblance of the appearance of the flower to that of a duck in flight.] Either of the widespread terrestrial orchids *Caleana major* and *Paracaleana minor*; also *P. nigrita* (fam. Orchidaceae) of s.w. W.A. Also **flying duck.**

1914 E.E. PESCOTT *Native Flowers Vic.* 87 A pretty purplish-brown orchid . . known as the 'Cockatoo' or 'flying duck'. **1973** R. ERICKSON et al. *Flowers & Plants*

W.A. 55 Flying Duck Orchid . . is an inconspicuous plant of the jarrah forest and swamp margins between Moora and Ravensthorpe. **1981** M. CAMERON *Guide Flowers & Plants Tas.* 108 Pollination is effected as the insect struggles out of the body cavity. This interesting mode of pollination occurs also in *Caleana major*, the Flying Duck Orchid.

flying fox. [Fig. use of *flying fox* fruit bat.] An overhead cable and apparatus for the transport of materials, supplies, etc., esp. over difficult terrain. Also *attrib.*

1901 M. VIVIENNE *Travels in W.A.* 210 What is here called the 'Flying Fox' . . has an iron bucket on a single rope of twisted wire. **1916** H. LAWSON *Collected Verse* (1969) III. 360 The 'flying foxes' glide in on the cable, Behind rock buttresses out of sight. **1935** DAVISON & NICHOLLS *Blue Coast Caravan* 131 The 'flying fox', a contrivance of pulleys and wires that enabled the banana bunches to be drawn up from hill-side plantations. **1944** A.S. SMITH *Boys write Home* 132 Sheer down this side of the mountain is the R.A.E.-built 'flying fox', a really magnificent achievement, for the speedy transport of supplies from the top to the bottom. **1957** D.D. LADDS *We have our Dreams* 3 The flaming flying-fox wire's nearly busted through. **1982** *Sydney Morning Herald* 13 Mar. 6/6 In earlier years cabin owners constructed flying foxes from the escarpment to carry materials and supplies down to the beach.

flying fox camp. [f. *flying fox* fruit bat + CAMP *n.* 4.] A place where flying foxes congregate; a congregation of flying foxes.

1903 *Truth* (Sydney) 8 Mar. 1/7, 50 guns attacked a flying fox camp on the upper Orara, and killed about 2000. **1903** *Bulletin* (Sydney) 1 Oct. 17/1 The fruit bats, popularly known as flying foxes . . do not hibernate. . . There are a number of well known 'flying fox camps' in the County of Cumberland. **1928** M. FORREST *Reaping Roses* 229 In the timber they passed a flying fox camp where the noisome bird-beasts hung in dark clusters. **1937** C. WARBURTON *White Poppies* 78 A medley of discordant sounds reached their ears. 'A flying-fox camp—listen to the brutes!' **1970** W.D.L. RIDE *Guide Native Mammals Aust.* 178 A visit to a flying fox camp is a remarkable experience.

flying gang. A team of railway maintenance workers.

1897 J.J. MURIF *From Ocean to Ocean* 29 The same night Diamond and I reached Lake Eyre cottages where were the husbands and others, a 'flying gang' of navvies. **1933** R.B. PLOWMAN *Camel Pads* 243 Temporary homes for the fettlers, 'flying gangs', as they were called. Each flying gang has thirty miles of line in its 'length', with three groups of cottages. **1969** P. ADAM SMITH *Folklore Austral. Railwaymen* 10 The elite of all maintenance men is the Flying Gang, a group of specialists, experienced fettlers under a ganger who are rushed to wherever their skill is needed.

fly-moth. *Obs.* An insect that destroys cereal grain; an infestation of these insects.

1805 *Sydney Gaz.* 13 Oct., The destruction occasioned by the Fly Moth to the Wheat in Stacks. **1806** *Ibid.* 6 July, The destruction previously occasioned by the Fly Moth or Hessian Fly. **1825** T. KENT *Let. to B. Field* 68 An insect, denominated the *Fly-moth*, was observed to be generated in the grain produced in the settled districts, before it was removed from the field. **1838** *S. Austral. Rec.* (London) 12 Dec. 139/3 Finish wheat harvest, and take care that the stacks are of moderate size. . . If housed in barns they should be well ventilated to prevent fly-moth.

Flynn. [The name of Errol *Flynn* (1909–1959), Australian-born actor with a reputation as a playboy.] In the phr. **to be in like Flynn,** to seize an opportunity; to be actively or impetuously engaged; to be successful.

1959 E. FLYNN *My Wicked, Wicked Ways* 290 A new legend was born, and new terms went into the national idiom. . . A G.I. or Marine or sailor went out at night sparking and the next day he reported to his cronies, who asked him how he made out, and the fellow said, with a sly grin, *'I'm in like Flynn.'* **1963** T.A.G. HUNGERFORD *Shake Golden Bough* 219 You're in like Flynn, and there's no turning back. **1965** J. WYNNUM *Jiggin' in Riggin'* 36 'What's our chance of picking up a cab this time of day?' 'Knowing my form, not so hot. But there should be any number around the Quay. Sooner or later one will stop within grasp. Then I'll be in like Flynn—maybe quicker.' **1972** *Bulletin* (Sydney) 19 Aug. 6/1 He's got a great big grin And a great big chin. Give him half a chance, He'll be in like Flynn. **1980** B. HORNADGE *Austral. Slanguage* 190 Another expression for sexual intercourse that is distinctly Australian is *in like Flynn*, derived from the well publicised sexual prowess of the Australian-born movie star Errol Flynn. **1981** P. BARTON *Bastards I have Known* 6 Bert had been barred from the Unley hospital but he was 'in like Flynn' through the window one night. **1984** *Nat. Times* (Sydney) 26 Oct. 5/1 All the political heavies covering the campaign . . were in like Flynn.

fly-speck. [Joc. use of *fly-speck* tiny stain made by the excrement of an insect.]

1. *Obs.* Used *attrib.* in Special Comb. **Fly-speck Isle,** Tasmania; so **Fly-specker** *n.*, a Tasmanian.

1906 *Gadfly* (Adelaide) 25 Apr. 9/3 Tasmania has lost its oldest inhabitant. . . He had inhabited the Flyspeck Isle since 1828. **1912** *Truth* (Sydney) 30 June 1/5 Vandemonians appear to be rather proud of that particularly black page in the history of their little island; but of course the poor 'fly-speckers' haven't much diversion.

2. A minute particle of gold. Also *attrib.*

1932 I.L. IDRIESS *Prospecting for Gold* 105 If you get 'fly specks' in your dish, then try all over the place, higgledy-piggledy. **1939** —— *Cyaniding for Gold* 32 That contained just as much gold, in an exceedingly fine state—all 'fly speck' gold in fact. **1977** J. DOUGHTY *Gold in Blood* 86 The wash looked as if it could carry gold, but after putting a few runs of it through the shaker without finding as much as a 'fly-speck' I lost heart.

fog. *Obs.* Used *attrib.* in Special Comb. **Fog Land,** England, the British Isles; **town,** London.

1907 *Bulletin* (Sydney) 7 Feb. 15/2 An English chap and fast shearer . . used to go 'home' to **Fogland** every year. **1914** H.M. VAUGHAN *Australasian Wander-Yr.* 61 'Fog Land' often denotes the British Isles, and the 'Big Smoke' stands for London. **1906** *Gadfly* (Adelaide) 20 June 17/1 Writes my **Fogtown** correspondent:- ' . . all the South Australians . . who happened to be wandering loose about London just then gathered themselves into a bunch.'

Also **fogwards** *adv.*

1906 *Gadfly* (Adelaide) 13 June 17/1 There departed fogwards on last week's English mail the Misses Clowes.

follow, *v. trans.* Used in phr. of an itinerant pursuing a specified avocation: (of a gold or opal miner) **to follow the colour, diggings, game**; (of a shearer or swagman) **to follow the sheds**; (of a swagman) **to follow the luck, rivers.**

1890 A.J. VOGAN *Black Police* 35 The true prospecting and working miner, who has 'followed the diggings' since the Canoona rush or the Palmer field excited the mining world, is a veritable Admirable Crichton. **1915** *Bulletin* (Sydney) 14 Oct. 24/4 Tell me a profession with more *aliases* than the swagmans? Here are a few: 'Waltzin' Matilda', . . 'followin' the luck', 'carryin' the swag' . . 'followin' the sheds'. **1921** *Ibid.* 17 Nov. 20/2 My dad who 'followed the diggings' tells me that to call a man 'Joe' on the Vic. rushes was the surest way of buying a fight. **1922** J. LEWIS *Fought & Won* 105 Some of them were good miners who had been 'following the game' for many years in Queensland. **1940** I.L. IDRIESS *Lightning Ridge* 148 Some of the old sundowners of the old Murrumbidgee Whaler brotherhood, those who 'followed the rivers' all their lives were characters. . . We 'casuals' always felt embarrassed, when in the society of these Knights of the Road. **1948** M. UREN *Glint of Gold* 28 Both had been following the colour most of their life. **1957** *Overland* ix. 9 They were mates of long standing and had followed the sheds all the way down through Queensland. **1979** D. STIVENS *Demon Bowler* 94 'We'd have given you a better game if that young fellow hadn't moved on,' they said. 'Following the sheds,' said one.

follower. *Australian National Football.* Either of two players who, with the rover, do not have fixed positions and so follow play. See RUCK *n.*

1876 T.P. POWER *Footballer* 11 Followers—Be always on the ball and don't hold it too long. Practise the punt and drop-kicks with both feet. **1894** J.M. MACDONALD *Thunderbolt* 87 He kicked it among the 'followers' on both sides, hoping that Andrew Loughman, the graceful, dashing follower, would get hold of it. **1930** W.S. SHARLAND *Sporting Globe Football Bk.* 42 A ruck is comprised of two followers and a rover. **1963** L. RICHARDS *Boots & All!* 82 At 6 ft. 1 in. he wasn't exceptionally tall for a follower, but he had an exceptionally high spring and his burly 14½ stone carved space in the packs for him. **1964** *Footy Fan* (Melbourne) II. xii. 33 A ruck consists of two followers—tall, heavy, strong, fast men—and a rover—a fast, clever player. They are a team within a team. **1971** B. ANDREW *Austral. Football Handbk.* 67 The Rover plays near the Follower to whom the ball is being kicked.

footballer. *Obs.* A prison warder: see quot. 1921.

1919 V. MARSHALL *World of Living Dead* 33 He'd left his mark on a couple of the pet 'footballers' when they come at the kickin' game down in the Parramatta basement. **1921** D. GRANT *Through Six Gaols* 51 One day while at work in the shop I heard a warder's name mentioned and noticed that the term 'footballer' was applied to him. I discovered that this title had been conferred upon him for his well-known habit of kicking prisoners.

footie, var. FOOTY.

footman. *Obs.* [Spec. use of *footman* one who travels on foot: becoming obs. *c* 1900 in Br. use.] A swagman.

[**1890** 'R. BOLDREWOOD' *Squatter's Dream* 277 A 'footman' (as a person not in possession of a horse is termed in Australian provincial circles).] **1900** H. LAWSON *On Track* 76 If it was a footman (swagman), and he was short of tobacco, old Howlett always had half a stick ready for him. **1902** *Bulletin* (Sydney) 8 Feb. 32/3 Of footmen there are two classes. First, the non-horsey man. . . Next the man who, through bad luck, or bad liquor, has for the time being, parted from his horses. **1906** *Ibid.* 26 July 16/2 The bush-horse rug is . . not often carried by footmen, being a heavy article. **1911** E.S. SORENSON *Life in Austral. Backblocks* 68 Nearly everywhere in country parts the term 'traveller' is more often heard than 'swagman'. It is applied to the footman, as though he were the only genuine species of the order that has a habit of moving about. **1938** F. BLAKELEY *Hard Liberty* 18 A sign-writer footman told Taylor that he had a scheme that would stop travellers killing sheep on the back portion of his run.

foot-rot, *v. trans.* To treat (sheep) suffering from foot-rot. Also **foot-rotting** *vbl. n.*

1870 E.B. KENNEDY *Four Yrs. in Qld.* 7, I asked one man if he had seen or done anything in the Bush, 'Oh yes, I did some 'foot rotting',' was the languid reply. **1898** G. DUNDERDALE *Bk. of Bush* 107 Bez . . took a job at foot-rotting sheep on a station. **1902** E.B. KENNEDY *Black Police Qld.* 37, I was first drafted on to a sheep station, which was situated some miles inland from the township of Gladstone, to do some 'foot rotting'. **1980** G. ROBINSON *Decades of Duntroon Bastard* 189 A holding cradle . . was a most useful invention which made handling sheep generally, and 'foot-rotting' in particular, much easier work.

footwalk, *v. Austral. pidgin. intr.* To travel on foot. Also as *adv.*, on foot.

1946 W.E. HARNEY *North of 23°* 172 Natives went footwalk to Barraloola for assistance through the mud of the rainy season. **1952** *Bulletin* (Sydney) 17 Dec. 12/1 Rosie, our housegirl, recently received a filial visit from her son. He 'footwalked' direct overland from the Daly River to Darwin. **1963** F. FLYNN *Northern Gateway* 138 He is known to have 'footwalked' far to the south and way over into West Australia during his younger, more adventurous days. **1984** K. BENTERRAK et al. *Reading Country* 109 So we went down the beach . . all the way, footwalk.

Hence **footwalker** *n.*

1937 M. TERRY *Sand & Sun* 22 A footwalker appeared over a sandhill. . . After the footwalker a string of camels. **1951** E. HILL *Territory* 301 For ten years there were only occasional horsemen and 'footwalkers' along the Murran-ji.

footy, *n.* and *attrib.* Also **footie.** [f. *foot(ball* + -Y.]

A. *n.* The game of football, esp. Australian National Football; a football.

1906 *Bulletin* (Sydney) 20 Sept. 44/1 They copped 'im on the square, watchin' the 'footy'. **1916** G.C. COOPER Diary 1 Feb., Mounted parade during morning, played 2nd L.H. footy again—this time resulted in a draw of 3 all. **1934** F.E. BAUME *Burnt Sugar* 58 It all sounds pretty cronk to me, especially the dressing-up and the black shirts and all that. I'd rather go for a swim or play footie. **1949** *Coast to Coast 1948* 101 Having . . a year of abstinence from beer, footie, two-up, and the dogs, he felt at least he should get value for money from the suit. **1958** F. HARDY *Four-Legged Lottery* 25 Tom Roberts would take his son to the Australian Rules football. Young Jim . . was a keen follower of the footie. He barracked for Richmond. **1966** A. HOPGOOD *Private Yuk Objects* Pref., I'm an Australian, mate. . . That means I can have three meals a day, watch the telly every night, go to the footy or the races . . and generally get a good spin out of life. **1972** *Bulletin* (Sydney) 14 Oct. 44/1 Footy is King in Melbourne, and its reign never runs down. **1978** B. ST. A. SMITH *Spirit beyond Psyche* 209, I just don't reckon he's a *real man*. . . He's not alive, no interest in the footy, the gees, or in sheilas. **1981** C. WALLACE-CRABBE *Splinters* 89 Some brightly besweatered children ran larruping along the footpath, one of them bouncing a footy. **1984** *Nat. Times* (Sydney) 6 July 29/6 At last art viewing has become as popular if slightly less meaningful than footy.

B. *attrib.*

1923 *Aussie* (Sydney) Sept. 28/1 And the old school's gravelled playground, where we often barked our knees, Near the wider 'footie' oval ringed around with hills and trees. **1960** *N.T. News* (Darwin) 23 Feb. 1/1 A social committee of three white men and six natives has been set up to handle the footy fund. **1961** *Bulletin* (Sydney) 22 Mar. 28/1 He bought a pair of footy-boots. **1966** *Ibid.* 19 Nov. 40/1 A genuine coat of arms for the city of Melbourne would depict a nest of beer cans, a meat pie, a footy guernsey, and a TAB ticket. **1972** *Ibid.* 14 Oct. 44/1 The footy fans of Victoria and the game they make must constitute one of the social phenomena of this age. **1978** D. WILLIAMSON *Club* p. vii, His mastery of ocker footy lingo is so word perfect you'd swear he was given Ron Barassi's old athletic support for his first birthday. **1979** J.J. MCROACH *Dozen Dopey Yarns* 158 The sort of chap trained in public speaking at an early age, his first gig possibly a country footy club thank-you to the R.S.L. committee for keeping the urinals unclogged. **1981** B. DICKINS *Gift of Gab* 6 Silly Cyril blinks as Old Baldy pins a sprig of wattle to his Fitzroy footyhat.

forcing, *vbl. n.* Used *attrib.* in Comb. of enclosures so designed as to compel the movement of stock confined therein in a particular direction: **forcing pen, yard.**

1935 G. MCIVER *Drover's Odyssey* 7 The men . . were busy constructing **forcing pens** of boughs and logs to cross the sheep to the north side of the river. **1936** *Bulletin* (Sydney) 9 Sept. 20/2 A winner among discordant bush noises is the Barcoo dog—an elaboration of a baby's rattle that some genius long ago invented for scaring sheep up into the forcing pens and down the drafting race. **1857** *Moreton Bay Free Press* 5 Jan. 3/2 The animals are generally too wild to be punted, and the only way is to force them into the river and compel them to swim. For this purpose the mobs are driven into a strongly-fenced paddock, covering about half an acre, which is called the '**forcing yard**', and all other means of exit are closed, except a narrow passage called the 'tan' which slopes towards the river, and terminates at a perpendicular bank. **1871** *Austral. Town & Country Jrnl.* (Sydney) 22 Apr. 491/3 The sheep . . would be divided into two lots in the receiving yard, and one-half put into the forcing yard. **1882** ARMSTRONG & CAMPBELL *Austral. Sheep Husbandry* 139 A small forcing-yard must be formed at the mouth of the lane by fencing off a corner of the yard. **1890** 'R. BOLDREWOOD' *Squatter's Dream* 164 There had been an old forcing-yard built at the spot for the purpose of swimming cattle and horses over the river. **1957** D. NILAND *Call me when Cross turns Over* 28 Out of the forcing yard, into the race leading to the van, surged the bullocks. **1960** M. HENRY *Unlucky Dip* 17 The usual activity was going on in the forcing and drafting yards.

forest. [Spec. use of *forest* tract of land covered with trees and undergrowth, sometimes intermingled with pasture.]

1. *Obs.* A tract of open, well-grassed land, with occasional trees or stands of trees; see OPEN *a.*[1] 1. In early use usu. *attrib.* as **forest land** (see esp. quot. 1805).

1805 *HRA* (1915) 1st Ser. V. 586 Forest Land—is such as abounds with Grass and is the only Ground which is fit to Graze; according to the local distinction, the Grass is the discriminating Character and not the Trees, for by making use of the Former it is clearly understood as different from a Brush or Scrub. **1809** *N.S.W. Pocket Almanack* 36 From this Month's middle to the next Month's end, Let Forest Land, well worked, with wheat be sown. **1819** *HRA* (1917) 1st Ser. X. 191 A sufficiency of Grain produced on the High Grounds and Forest Lands. **1827** *Monitor* (Sydney) 13 Sept. 640/2 Let what rain will come now, there will not be one-third of a crop of wheat in any forest land in the country. **1831** *Acct. Colony Van Diemen's Land* 98 To this practice among the natives of burning the bush in order to circumvent and enclose their prey, may be attributed the general openness of the forest land in the island, and its usefulness for pasture. **1832** *Sydney Herald* 27 Feb. 1/3 *A small farm*, . . an extensive back run of Forest and Swamp, affording abundance of grass and water in every extreme of seasons. **1839** *S. Austral. Rec.* (London) 11 Sept. 232 The forests, although very extensive, are not thickly wooded, or encumbered with brush or underwood. **1840** *Ibid.* 29 Aug. 139 We ploughed . . about forty acres of forest land, quite from its natural state. **1844** C. WILKES *Narr. U.S. Exploring Exped.* II. 178 There are many continuous miles of waste lands, which by the inhabitants are called 'forests'. These are very different from what we understand by the term, and consist of gum trees (Eucalypti), so widely scattered that a carriage may be driven rapidly through them without meeting any obstruction, while the foliage of these trees is so thin and apparently so dried up as scarcely to cast a shade. **1849** A. HARRIS *Emigrant Family* (1967) I. 24 The clear ground changes only into fine open forest, with scarcely a tree to the acre. **1868** J. BAIRD *Emigrant's Guide Australasia* 223 The forest, or bush, is tame, uniform, forever the same endless waste of gum-trees, making all but shepherds and stockmen miserable, and many of *them* too, we should find, were they to favour us with their experience; the scrub only is beautiful; that is, the dense vegetation that grows on the alluvial banks of rivers and creeks.

2. Used *attrib.* in the names of flora and fauna, usu. having the more usual meaning of trees and undergrowth combined: **forest kangaroo** *obs.*, *grey kangaroo* (a), see GREY *a.*; **mahogany** *obs.*, a tree of the genus *Eucalyptus* (fam. Myrtaceae), esp. *E. resinifera* (see *red mahogany* RED *a.* 1 a.); **oak,** the tree *Allocasuarina torulosa* (fam. Casuarinaceae) of e. N.S.W. and Qld., having slender drooping branchlets and red timber; the wood of the tree; **red gum,** the tall tree *Eucalyptus tereticornis* (fam. Myrtaceae) occurring in e. Aust. from e. Vic. to n. Qld., usu. in open forest, and also in New Guinea; the wood of the tree.

1817 J. MYERS *Life Voyage & Travels Capt. J. Myers* 196 We met several of the **Forest Kangaroos.** **1826** J. ATKINSON *Acct. Agric. & Grazing N.S.W.* 23 The Kangaroos are of four kinds, viz. the buroo or forest kangaroo; the wallabee, or brush kangaroo [etc.]. **1848** J. SYME *Nine Yrs. Van Diemen's Land* 62 The forest kangaroo is quite a large animal. . . Its enormous tail is much esteemed for the rich soup it makes. **1862** G.T. LLOYD *Thirty-Three Yrs. Tas. & Vic.* 64 First in the list stands the fine forest kangaroo, so called from its frequenting the open park grounds. **1913** C.G. LANE *Creature-Life* 30 The kangaroos I have photographed while camping in and exploring the mountainous districts of Victoria are examples of a large, heavily-built species usually known in the bush as Forest-kangaroos, because of their distinct preference for well-wooded localities. **1830** R. DAWSON *Present State Aust.* 243 The timber . . is generally useless, consisting chiefly of what are called **forest-mahogany** and blood-wood. **1845** C. HODGKINSON *Aust., Port Macquarie to Moreton Bay* 40 The grassy flats were principally wooded by that species of Eucalyptus called Forest Mahogany. **1880** J. BONWICK *Resources Qld.* 37 Peppermints are often content with inferior ground, like . . the Forest Mahogany &c. **1904** J.H. MAIDEN *Notes on Commercial Timbers N.S.W.* 12 The red or forest mahogany of New South Wales. **1819** W.C. WENTWORTH *Statistical, Hist., & Pol. Descr. N.S.W.* 46 Full sized gums and ironbarks . . with the beefwood tree, or as it is generally termed, the **forest oak** . . are the usual timber. **1829** R. MUDIE *Picture of Aust.* 137 The forest oak (*Casuarina torulosa*) of which the bark has some resemblance to that of the cork oak. **1839** H. CAPPER *S.A.* (rev. ed.) 47 *Forest oak.* In appearance this tree very much resembles the Scotch fir. The grain is peculiar, but the wood is not valuable, as it soon decays; it makes good shingles, and may be nailed without boring with a gimlet. **1845** *Sydney Morning Herald* 26 Apr. 2/6, I travelled for many miles without seeing a single forest-oak (*Casuarina torulosa*), which forms, almost universally, a sort of underwood to the larger trees of the genus Eucalypti, in the forests of New South Wales. **1854** J. CAPPER *Aust.* 36 Forest-oak is suitable for tool-handles, bullock-yokes, &c. **1893** J. DEMARR *Adventures in Aust.* 81 Here for the first time we saw the forest oak intermingled with the gum tree. **1938** C.T. WHITE *Princ. Bot. Qld. Farmers* 153 The Red Oak or Forest Oak (*C. torulosa*) is very common on better-class forest country throughout coastal Queensland and New South Wales. It is one of the principal fuel timbers of the State, and great quantities of it are used by bakers, being the favoured bread-baking fuel of coastal Queensland. **1983** *Victorian Timber News* Apr. 8/2 Forest Oak (Casuarina torulosa), which has red heartwood with very large darker rays (fine texture). **1899** *Proc. Linnean Soc. N.S.W.* XXIV. 468 Ordinary **Forest Red Gum** (*Eucalyptus tereticornis*). **1904** J.H. MAIDEN *Forest Flora N.S.W.* II. 1 'Forest Red Gum' . . is . . usually found in open forest country, hence I recommend the adoption of the prefix 'Forest' to Red Gum, the name by which it is very commonly known, with the view to save confusion. **1905** P. MACMAHON *Merchantable Timbers of Qld.* 20 *Eucalyptus tereticornis* is Blue gum in Brisbane, but Forest Red Gum in Sydney. **1930** E. MAXWELL *Afforestation Southern Lands* 273 This other Red Gum, the Forest Red Gum, will grow under conditions that the River Red Gum will not. **1957** *Forest Trees Aust.* (Cwlth. Forestry & Timber Bureau) 86 Forest red gum . . extends beyond the shores of Australia to the drier parts of Papua. **1979** *Ecos* xix. 32/4 Koalas have been linked with some 60 species. Forest red gum . . , grey gum . . seem most favoured.

forest devil. A mechanical contrivance used to clear land by pulling out trees and stumps.

1885 F.A. BOYD *Farmer & Settler's Guide* 9 Where . . stumps have to be removed we would recommend a 'Forest Devil'. **1896** A. MACKAY *Austral. Agriculturist* (rev. ed.) 54 In stump-extracting and tree-falling machines, sometimes termed 'forest devils', we have most excellent results from the application of lever power. **1897** L. LINDLEY-COWEN *W. Austral. Settler's Guide* 228 A . . more expeditious means of clearing is by means of a tree-puller or 'forest devil'. Several of these machines, both for horse and man power, have been invented and perfected in this colony, and will be found satisfactory in every way. **1915** F.C. SPURR *Five Yrs. under Southern Cross* 112 So rapidly have the plough and the 'forest devil' cleared the ground. **1919** *Jrnl. Dept. Agric. S.A.* Dec. 440 During the first 18 months we used Brown's forest devil to grub trees, and without hesitation I can say that it is the most thorough grubbing machine which we have put into operation. The process is slow, necessitating very heavy hand work; but through this slowness, the height of pull on the trees can be regulated very much better, and with ordinary care only a few trees should be broken off. **1934** J.S. NEILSON *Autobiogr.* (1978) 96 My next job was grubbing and I was working a forest devil. **1974** M. WILLIAMS *Making of S. Austral. Landscape* 162 Brown's Forest Devil (a lever system worked by two men). **1979** P. PAVY *Bush Surgeon* 4, I was put to felling giant-sized mallee scrub and heaving the roots out with an antique system of levers called a 'forest devil'.

forester. *Obs.* [See quot. 1826.] *Grey kangaroo* (a), see GREY *a.* Also *attrib.*

1804 R. KNOPWOOD in J.J. Shillinglaw *Hist. Rec. Port Phillip* 17 June (1879) 122 Thos. Salmon, my man, killd a very large kangaroo—a forester. **1826** J. ATKINSON *Acct. Agric. & Grazing N.S.W.* 24 The forester is the largest of the common kinds [of kangaroo], frequently weighing 150 lbs. It is seldom found in an open country, delighting in forests that have occasional thickets of brush. **1833** W.H. BRETON *Excursions* 251 Forester. Found in forest land. **1845** R. HOWITT *Impressions Aust. Felix* 273 A boomer, or large forester kangaroo. **1853** J. SHERER *Gold Finder Aust.* 27 Of the kangaroos there are several varieties, from the forester, standing six feet high, and weighing from 100 lbs. to 140 lbs. down to the size of a common English mouse. **1871** *Austral.*

Town & Country Jrnl. (Sydney) 7 Jan. 18/4 The little red brush kangaroo, and the grey forester, skipping away in all directions. **1898** W. REDMOND *Shooting Trip* 28 Some old 'foresters' are magnificent-looking animals standing fully five and in some cases over six feet high.

form, *v.* [Spec. use of *form* to make, to bring into existence.]

1. *trans.* To establish (a sheep or cattle station, etc.).

1837 *Colonist* (Sydney) 8 June 188/2 The absolute necessity of forming a Post and that without delay, for the purpose of intercepting runaways and bushrangers. **1840** *S. Austral. Rec.* (London) 11 July 18/1 Our sole intention, when we first formed our dairy establishment in connexion with our cattle station, was to tame the cattle. **1849** R.J. MANN *Emigrant's Guide Aust.* 60 Comparatively little expenditure is required to form a sheep or cattle station. **1855** H. HUME *Brief Statement* 32 Collins arrived at Port Phillip, and proceeded to form a settlement. **1866** *Colony of Qld. as Field for Emigration* 9 Often he has to drive this stock over a thousand miles of country, or more, before he reaches his destination. He has then to form his station, and to organise his establishment. **1879** 'AUSTRALIAN' *Adventures Qld.* 1 Those who pulled safely through were generally rewarded by some fair one, who felt proud of being the mistress of a station formed by her husband. **1893** S. NEWLAND *Paving Way* 47 A number of us are going . . to New South Wales with the intention of bringing cattle over to South Australia to form runs in the country round about here. **1916** T. WARLOW *By Mirage & Mulga* 2 It'll also give us twelve months in which to form our own country and knock it into shape. **1942** H.H. PECK *Mem. of Stockman* 105 He took up, formed and stocked many of the best stations in western Queensland. **1946** J.G. EASTWOOD *More about Cairns* 81, I . . received rations for the camp where Cairns now is, but before it was formed.

2. *trans.* To construct (a road). Also as *vbl. n.* and *ppl. a.*

1846 N.L. KENTISH *Work in Bush Van Diemen's Land* 30 The only serious objection to the *forming* of the road . . is a 'bluff', or projecting mass of rock. **1865** 'SPECIAL CORRESPONDENT' *Transportation* 20 The traveller can proceed to Perth . . along a good road, formed by convict labour. **1924** MRS H.A. DOUDY *Magic of Dawn* 27 Wagoners, with bullock teams, were carting stone to form a roadway. **1939** J.W. COLLINSON *Early Days Cairns* 140 A road had been formed, of mangrove mud, which gave a good surface when set. This formed road turned a corner into Abbott Street.

formation road. See quot.

1973 R. ROBINSON *Drift of Things* 55 We are on a dirt 'formation' road. This is a high, mounded road with a ditch on either side and you drive along on one side of the mound. Mr Goldsmith says that the roads are made like this because of the wet weather.

fortescue. [Of uncertain origin, but see quot. 1874.] The fish *Centropogon australis* of e. Austral. coasts, having venomous spines that can inflict painful wounds.

1874 E.S. HILL in J.E. Tenison-Woods *Fish & Fisheries N.S.W.* (1882) 49 The scorpion or Fortescue . . for its number and array of prickles . . enjoys in this country the *alias* 'Forty skewer' or 'Fortescure'. **1880** *Proc. Linnean Soc. N.S.W.* V. 439 *Pentaroge marmorata*. . . '*Fortescue*' of the Sydney Fishermen. **1895** C. THACKERAY *Amateur Fisherman's Guide* 78 Such rarities as the boxfish and the dangerous fortescue are often caught in the Spring and Summer. **1906** D.G. STEAD *Fishes of Aust.* 195 The Fortescue (*Centropogon australis*) . . is most abundant on the coast of New South Wales, and is known to occur along the coasts of Queensland and Victoria. **1915** *Bulletin* (Sydney) 6 May 22/4 The fortescue, found in the rocky shallows and among the oyster-beds of coastal lakes. **1962** 'N. CULOTTA' *Gone Fishin'* 60 There won't be any floods an' sticks an' leaves an' empty tins an' broken bottles an' stingrays an' fortescues an' bullrouts an' bloody crabs. **1977** *Austral. Encycl.* III. 98 The fortescue rarely attains a length of 15 centimetres.

forty. *Obs.* Usu. in *pl.* [Of unknown origin.] A sharper, a swindler; orig. a member of a gang in Sydney (see quots. 1876 and 1882). Also **forty thieves,** and *attrib.*

1876 *V & P* (N.S.W. L.A.) VI. 856 What class of men are these 'Forties'—what is their occupation? They are a band of thieves. Some ten years ago, before the Industrial Schools Act came into operation, a number of youngsters were on the streets; they used to sleep about the wharves, lived on thieving, and were ready to snap up anything they came across. I do not know how they came to be christened 'The Forties', but when they grew up to be men the name stuck to them, and they continued their old habits. They prowl about all night, go to one of these places about 4 or 5 o'clock in the morning, and sleep till 1 or 2 in the day. **1882** *Sydney Slang Dict.* 8 *The Forties*, the worst types of 'the talent', who get up rows in a mob, often after midnight and sometimes assault and rob, either in barrooms or the streets. Name originated with a gang in Sydney under 'Dixon the dog hanger', 'King of the Forties'. **1895** J.T. RYAN *Reminisc. Aust.* 219 Mr E. Deas Thompson was the Colonial Secretary who lowered the duty on spirits to 3s. per gallon . . and the 'Forty Thieves' at once found themselves up a tree. **1899** *Austral. Tit-Bits* (Sydney) 6 May 196/1 A gang of men . . existed in New South Wales in the old, bad days of convicts, bushrangers, and doctored rum . . known as the 'Forties', and were men who carried on illicit distilling and smuggling. **1902** *Bulletin* (Sydney) 5 Apr. 15/1 There is an allied class known as buskers, jugglers, 'forties', two-up men, tramp-journalists, tinkers, raffle promoters. **1904** L.M.P. ARCHER *Bush Honeymoon* 144 A small array of bookmakers, with a slight sprinkling of the 'forty' element. **1910** C.E.W. BEAN *On Wool Track* 226 A few sharpers with a slight knowledge of shearing often get into a big shed, and get a 'school' going—a nightly gamble. They are regularly called 'forties'—the forty thieves—and they sometimes make a pile out of young shearers. **1927** M.M. BENNETT *Christison of Lammermoor* 194 Their numbers swelled with rowdies and 'forties'—gambling sharpers who travelled from shed to shed making five pounds by cheating for every five shillings they earned. **1955** N. PULLIAM *I traveled Lonely Land* 376 *Fortie*, a crook, double-crosser. **1966** T. RONAN *Strangers on Ophir* (rev. ed.) 76 With chequemen rolling in from three watersheds and the locals spending the money they had saved since Christmas with the usual percentage of spielers and forties, rogues and vagabonds to watch.

forward pocket: see POCKET.

fossick, *v.* [Br. dial. *fossick* to obtain by asking, to 'ferret out'; cf. *fursick, fussick* to potter over one's work, *fussock* to bustle about quickly: see EDD.]

1. *intr.* To search or pick about for gold on the surface, usu. in a desultory or unsystematic way and often on an abandoned or unattended claim. Also with **about, around.**

1852 *Austral. Gold Digger's Monthly Mag.* ii. 49 It is far better to spend time thus rationally and pleasantly, than . . fossick in the holes of absent diggers. **1852** W. STRUTT *Austral. Jrnl.* (1958) i. 27 Today the diggers were mostly occupied with domestic matters, or strolling about fossicking. **1857** 'RETURNED DIGGER' *Six Yrs. in Aust.* 41 Those wily diggers have done very well who have been 'fossicking', as it is termed, that is to say, going about the deserted holes and heaps of refuse, and washing the soil over again in the tub and cradle. **1861** H. EARLE *Ups & Downs* 350 They had been fossicing in old holes, but had found nothing. **1873** J.C.F. JOHNSON *Christmas on Carringa* 23 Old Dan Rourke, the 'hatter', who was always fossicking about early and late, high day and holiday, in his surface claim at the bottom of the rise . . was just thinking of 'knocking off work' for the night. **1890** 'R. BOLDREWOOD' *Miner's Right* 35 'We must go and fossick for a bit now,' I said. 'Just for enough to make the pot boil: but we won't take any more of your tucker.' **1914** C. MACKNESS *Gem of Flat* 10 He sank shafts that were often 'duffers', or fossicked in the creek-bed. **1924** *Smith's Weekly* (Sydney) 31 May 22/7 Once fossicked in a shaft which a couple of diggers had sunk and deserted. **1934** WARBURTON & ROBERTSON *Buffaloes* 15 After the line was completed the Chinese, instead of settling on the land like the whites might have done, went prospecting and fossicking. **1946** K.S. PRICHARD *Roaring Nineties* 37 He prospected twenty miles out, as far as Red Hill and specked alluvial. We fossicked along the ridge. **1965** N. LINDSAY *Bohemians of Bulletin* 154 In my home town I had known many of his type; who spent their later days fossicking in the worked-out diggings. **1976** F.R. ST. JOHN *Verse in Retirement* 8 He walked the busy roadway Beside the mullock heap And fossicked in the spillway Along Ned Stringer's creek. **1979** *Sydney Morning Herald* 17 Oct. 13/4 Those wishing to fossick on private land declared as a fossicking area must first obtain the landowner's permission. To fossick in a Crown fossicking area, they must obtain a licence from the Department of Mineral Resources and Development.

2. *intr. transf.* To search or rummage for something.

1853 *Wanderer* (Adelaide) June 75 Usage has extended the term beyond gold matters. If a man were to take a log of fire-wood from a neighbour's heap . . it would be said he had been fossicking. **1859** W. KELLY *Life in Vic.* I. 179 Fossicking means picking, prying, or examining minutely. **1871** *Emigrant's Wife* II. 24, I goes over to where he had thrown it, and takes out my knife and stoops down to fossick among it. **1884** *Goldfield's Reminisc.* 120 Fossicking for information was 'No go'. Many parties there divided their gold, and sold it to storekeepers in the back gullies of the district. **1911** A. SEARCY *By Flood & Field* 27 A third, as the result of his fossicking, returned with a large iguana. **1930** V. PALMER *Passage* (1957) 177 He had been fossicking in the pool where the money-cowries were, putting his fingers into the small clefts and occasionally jerking out the precious shells of creamy enamel with their single band of gold. **1943** A.E. MANDER *Our Sham Democracy* 40 A 'Good Local Member' . . does not need to fossick for information about public affairs. **1956** B.J. RAYMENT *My Towri* 13 Both chatting freely and fossicking through the very thick leafy foliage searching for an odd fruit that may have been missed. **1964** P. WHITE *Burnt Ones* 51 On one occasion . . they were fossicking through a cupboardful of junk which provoked a joint hilarity. **1965** D. MARTIN *Hero of Too* 110 Stumbled across a female lyre bird, fossicking in the leafy undergrowth. **1975** *Southerly* ii. 181 This is he who approached an octogenarian fossicking in the tin marked 'Litter Please' outside Federation Café. **1978** C. RUHEN *Crocodile* 82 Bob hauled himself up into the boat . . and fossicking in a bag, found a can of beer.

3. *trans.* To search (a place); to find (something) through searching or rummaging about. Also with **out, up.**

1858 C.R. THATCHER *Colonial Songster* 19 Next morning I well fossicked it, And washed the bottom out; The tub turned out a pennyweight, And I began to doubt. **1886** *Bulletin* (Sydney) 26 June 15/2 Who is it fossicks out a pain, So Dr Pills can come again. And with her *tête-à-tête* remain? The lady! **1888** 'SPECIAL CORRESPONDENT' *Barrier Silver & Tin Fields* 22 Green fossicked out from the surface several hundred tons of good ore. **1891** D. FERGUSON *Vicissitudes Bush Life* 160 He fossicked up some white tablecloths. **1894** *Bulletin* (Sydney) 16 June 20/1 'P'raps you've got some rakings?' 'Eh?' 'Rakings—dust—let's try yer pipe-pockets.' We fossicked out pockets and linings and got fluff, and devils dust, and tobacco-scraps enough to fill two pipes. **1914** 'B. CABLE' *By Blow & Kiss* 289 She could hardly have found a man so hard to fossick anything from. Scottie was not given to gossip. **1926** *Bulletin* (Sydney) 14 Oct. 24/4 A South Coast (N.S.W.) butcher . . wore a silver watch and chain he had fossicked out of the inside of a slaughtered cow. **1935** R.B. PLOWMAN *Boundary Rider* 198 The belated visitor gratefully followed the manager to the kitchen where he proceeded to fossick out some food. **1956** R.G. EDWARDS *Overlander Songbk.* 95 I've loafed upon the Lachlan and fossicked Lambing Flat. **1964** 'E. LINDALL' *Kind of Justice* 3 He didn't count the groups of aborigines . . poking around the worked-out dumps of mined earth, fossicking a few miserable stones for hours of trouble.

Hence **fossicking** *vbl. n.* and *ppl. a.*

1852 *Argus* (Melbourne) 14 Jan. 2/6 Let them immediately return, or commence what is called surface-washing, or fossicking. **1853** C.R. READ *What I heard, saw, & Did* 18 Knives that had been used for *fossicking, nuggeting,* &c. outside, were inside used for carving. **1853** W. WESTGARTH *Vic.* 258 One kind of robbery peculiar to the gold-fields was carried on extensively, and particularly at night. This was the extracting of auriferous matter from holes that were known to be rich, or where some promising material had just been met with. These depredations were termed 'fossicking'. **1855** R. CARBONI *Eureka Stockade* 3 The holes all around, three feet in diameter, and five to eight feet in depth, had been abandoned; we jumped into one, and one of my mates gave me the first lesson in 'fossiking'. **1859** W. KELLY *Life in Vic.* I. 234, I was highly edified . . at the conduct of three under-sized fossicking coons, who discussed the nature of 'their shout' with the gravity of veteran topers. **1861** T. M'COMBIE *Austral. Sketches* 60 A number of idle and disorderly fellows had introduced a practice which was termed 'fossicking'. They skulked about the sly grog tents during the day . . watching such claims as were returning large returns to their owners. In the dead hour of midnight they issued forth and stole the auriferous earth. **1862** J.A. PATTERSON *Gold Fields Vic.* 67 Father and son are following farming as sedulously as they had before done fossicking. **1867** 'CLERGYMAN' *Aust. as it Is* 155 Fosacking [*sic*] is the term given to the employment of those who go about searching for gold . . exposed on the surface of the ground. **c 1882** T.F. DE C. BROWNE *Miners' Handy Bk.* (ed. 2) 21 *A fossicking claim*, Regulation 38 provides for this class of claim, which can only be occupied in 'old and abandoned ground'. **1896** E. DYSON *Rhymes from Mines* 42 'T was old Flynn, the identity, told us That the creek always ran pretty high. But that fossicking veteran sold us, And he lied as his quality lie. **1899** *Bulletin* (Sydney) 1 Apr. 14/4 Steve tumbled over a fossicking hen as we went through the bar door. **1915** *Ibid.* 3 June 47/2 The gullies with their sordid and ghastly tragedies, strangely connected nearly always with mysterious fossicking mates. **1920** B. CRONIN *Timber Wolves* 42 A nice, quiet life of trapping along the coast, with here and there a bit of fossicking. **1951** G. FARWELL *Outside Track* 33 Years of fossicking in this uninhabitable country had preceded his discovery of the lode. **1980** R. SHEARS *Gold* 125 Fossicking is defined as 'the gathering of minerals as a recreation without any intention to sell the minerals or use them for a commercial or industrial purpose'.

fossick, *n.* [f. prec.] The act of fossicking. Also *attrib.*

[N.Z. **1898** H.B. VOGEL *Maori Maid* 332 Ngaia only laughed, and picking up the axe followed her husband, not, however, until she had made a close fossick for any further gold there might be.] **1904** *Bulletin* (Sydney) 17 Nov. 19/1 Brother Coverdale has been doing a 'fossick round'. **1969** B. GARLAND *Pitt Street Prospector* 26 Aw, just having a bit of a fossick; thought I might pick up a stone or two.

fossicker. Also **fossiker.** [f. FOSSICK *v.*]

1. One who fossicks for gold.

1852 *Argus* (Melbourne) 14 Jan. 2/6 These fossickers are a race of people, resembling drones in a community of bees, collecting their soil from the cells or holes which have been dug and abandoned by more industrious workmen, and occasionally stealing from other holes during the temporary absence of their industrious proprietors. **1852** *Austral. Gold Diggers' Monthly Mag.* ii. 53 *Fossiker.*—We understand that this digger's term has got into town, and is used as a provocative of a most scandalous character. Nothing so excites the ire of our gentle fair ones of Melbourne and of Geelong, as to say that their sweethearts are fossickers. **1853** C.R. READ *What I heard, saw, & Did* 149 He said the man was what they called a *night fossicker*, who slept, or did nothing during the day, and then went round at night to where he knew claims to be rich, and stole the stuff by candle light. **1859** W. KELLY *Life in Vic.* I. 203 They would be in a position to commence a hole on their own account, and ascend on the social ladder from the non-commissioned grade of fossickers to the rank of diggers. **1869** R.B. SMYTH *Gold Fields & Mineral Districts* 612 *Fossicker*, is to the miner as is the gleaner to the reaper. Picks the crevices and pockets of the rocks. **1891** 'SMILER' *Wanderings Simple Child* (ed. 3) 3, I felt that I had the makings of something nobler than a 'fossicker' inside my clothes. **1897** *Antipodean* (Melbourne) 36 It is contrary to strict etiquette and accepted professional usage for one fossicker to go sneaking around another fossicker when the latter is panning off. **1907** *Truth* (Sydney) 7 Apr. 10/8 About the best fossicker I ever saw was a Northern Territory ebony damsel, who dwells on a tinfield with a European. **1926** *Bulletin* (Sydney) 11 Feb. 22/3 A friendly nig . . would bring to the tent of the fossicker small pieces of gold specked by him. **1944** *Ibid.* 15 Mar. 12/2 A fossicker in the Victorian Alps was prospecting country between Mt. St. Bernard and Mt. Jim. **1972** T. KENEALLY *Chant of Jimmie Blacksmith* 120 Old fossickers . . kept maps in their head and nuggets in gunnysacks under the floor. **1980** R. SHEARS *Gold* 125 The weekend prospector is classified as a fossicker.

2. *transf.*

1853 *Wanderer* (Adelaide) June 75 If one in want of a dinner called at his neighbour's tent at mutton time he would be a 'fossicker'. **1874** C. DE BOOS *Congewoi Correspondence* 115 There's no mistake about the Treasurer bein a first-rate fossicker. My word! Why if he was on a tucker diggins I believe he'd fossick good wages in the old drives.

fossicking knife. An implement used to poke out or pry for nuggets of gold.

1853 J. SHERER *Gold Finder Aust.* 284 We came to a pipe-clay which is the bottom, we must now use a 'fossicking knife', and, scraping the pipe-clay, we see a bit of gold stick out. **1854** W. HOWITT *Boy's Adventures* 243 They have a butcher's knife at their waist, in a leathern case, called a fossicking-knife, to pick out nuggets. **1861** T. M'COMBIE *Austral. Sketches* 87 They are usually provided with a 'fossicking' knife, a small trowel and a miner's pickaxe. **1893** 'OLD CHUM' *Chips* 21 The man in digger's dress—blue serge blouse, moleskin trousers, and cabbage-tree hat, with his 'fossicking knife'.

fountain. [Spec. use of *fountain* constant source of water.] A cast-iron urn in which water is heated on an open fire or solid-fuel stove. Also *attrib.*, as **fountain kettle.**

1876 'RESIDENT' *Girl Life in Aust.* 59 A chain and hook holds the fountain, a constant supply of boiling water being required for tea. **1916** J.B. COOPER *Coo-oo-ee!* 11 Over the kitchen fire a fountain kettle hung with boiling water. **1962** D. MCLEAN *World turned upside Down* 99 Mr Boyd had taken down a tub which had been hanging on a nail in the wall, placed it in front of the warm stove and begun to fill a bucket from the huge black iron urn, called a fountain, which stood on top of the stove.

four-railer. FOUR-RAIL FENCE.

1851 *Bell's Life in Sydney* 19 Apr. 1/4 Clearing the four-railer like a bird. **1900** *Bulletin* (Sydney) 22 Sept. 14/4 She jumped a four-railer into a lane. **1923** M.B. PETERSEN *Jewelled Nights* 161 Nothing she can't do on horse-back . . and she skims a four-railer as if she were merely stepping over a match-box!

four-rail fence. A fence having four wooden rails as its horizontal members. Also **four-railed fence.**

1819 *Sydney Gaz.* 17 Apr., Surrounded with substantial Four-rail Fences, with or without a Range for a limited number of Cattle. **1829** *Sydney Monitor* 16 May 1603/2 Capt Wentworth possesses the beautiful estate at Tongabbee, . . upon which there was in 1822, not less than *thirty miles* of four railed fence. **1844** *S. Austral. Odd Fellows' Mag.* July 141 Here and there stood a cottage, with its enclosure for poultry, and its garden of flowers, terminating the long four-railed fences, through which might be seen the waving corn, now arrived at half its growth. **1849** S. & J. SIDNEY *Emigrant's Jrnl.* 162 Get the stuff for a good substantial three or four rail-fence of iron or stringy bark wood. **1858** R. ROWE *Peter 'Possum's Portfolio* 95 What a dismal substitute is an Australian four-rail fence for an English hedge. **1911** *Huon Times* (Franklin) 25 Nov. 5/3 The defendant leapt over a four-railed fence from a paddock into the roadway. **1936** J.E. HAMMOND *Western Pioneers* 84 The building of the old-fashioned four-rail fences, all constructed of split timber, employed a large number of hands.

fourteen years' man. *Hist.* A convict sentenced to fourteen years of penal servitude.

1834 *Perth Gaz.* 14 June 304 Fourteen years' men, four years in the Gangs, four years to be mustered weekly if living in Town; and monthly, if in the Country; and the remainder of their time annually. **1840** *Tasmanian Weekly Dispatch* (Hobart) 15 May 5/3 A Government ticket may be given to fourteen years men. **1849** J. PATTISON *N.S.W.* 16 Seven-year men received their tickets at the expiry of four years; fourteen-years men after six years' servitude.

foxie. Also **foxy.** [f. *fox(-terrier* + -Y.] A fox-terrier.

1906 E. DYSON *Fact'ry 'Ands* 246 Like er bally foxie after er rat. **1933** *Bulletin* (Sydney) 13 Sept. 21/1 The first dog I loved lived long—a fat old foxie older than I. **1942** *Ibid.* 13 May 13/1 Our foxies treed a possum in a loaded orange-tree. **1959** H. DRAKE-BROCKMAN *West Coast Stories* 134 Two dogs that never left his side—a kelpie called Sneezer and a foxie called Flick. **1966** M. BROWN *Jimberi Track* 114 A little foxie came out and sniffed at his feet. **1952** A. MARSHALL *Aust.* (1981) 147 I'll bet you had a half-bred sheepdog. . . And you would have a foxie, too.

fracture. Also (erron.) **fracteur.** [Transf. use of *fracture* the act of breaking.] (An) explosive. Also *attrib.*

1897 *Bulletin* (Sydney) 21 Aug. 3/2 The 'fracteur smoke hangs thickly and we breathe it till it dies. **1929** W.J. RESIDE *Golden Days* 247 There were sufficient detonators, powder and 'fracture' to blow up all Coolgardie. **1944** J. DEVANNY *By Tropic Sea & Jungle* 212 Before, a prospector who'd discovered a lode and wanted to sink on it could apply to the Mines Department and receive a certain amount of free fracture. **1966** J. CARTER *People of Inland* 271 The hole was needed so that 'fracture' (gelignite) could be placed within the rock. **1972** N. MILES *Opal Fever* 82 'You've got fracture an' fuse, haven't you?' 'Yes. I've brought the detonators too. . . ' At the sight of the plug of gelignite Bill was waving about, one of the miners grumbled: 'I'd use two sticks of fracture, just to make sure.' **1977** B. SCOTT *My Uncle Arch* 68 If you put a charge of fracteur in you shatter any opal in a quarter of a mile radius.

frame. [U.S. *frame* emaciated animal: see OEDS *sb.* 9 b.] An emaciated beast.

1903 J. FURPHY *Such is Life* 200 By the way, there's four of your frames left—out near those coolibahs. **1934** *Bulletin* (Sydney) 10 Oct. 21/4 No poorer or weaker old frames ever travelled the Birdsville stock route. **1946** A.J. HOLT *Wheat Farms Vic.* 127 You raise and kill a decent beast yourself and divide it with your neighbour. When it comes for his turn to kill he picks out some rangy old frame with only hair on it.

freckle.

1. See quot. 1967. Also *fig.*

1967 *Kings Cross Whisper* (Sydney) xxxiv. 4/5 *Freckle*, anus. **1968** B. HUMPHRIES *Wonderful World Barry McKenzie*, You can put it up your *freckle* if you don't flamin' like it. **1978** —— *Nice Night's Entertainment* (1981) 180, I too believed that the sun shone out of Gough's freckle. **1983** *Sydney Morning Herald* 19 Mar. 37/4 It is not only a sailor who has *dooks* and *lugs*, a *belly-button* and a *freckle*.

2. Special Comb. **freckle puncher,** a male homosexual.

1968 B. HUMPHRIES *Wonderful World Barry McKenzie*, Kevin huh? Sounds like a flamin' freckle puncher!! **1979** —— *Bazza comes into his Own*, You mean instead of talkin' like a sky pilot, he talks like a raving freckle-puncher?

free, *a. Hist.*

1. Of one formerly a convict: released from penal servitude; FREED. Freq. as **free convict.**

1792 D. COLLINS *Acct. Eng. Colony N.S.W.* (1802) I. 238 The people employed about the stores, if not free, should at least have been so situated as to have found it their interest to resist temptation. **1804** *Sydney Gaz.* 5 Aug. 1/1 Whether the Person is Free, off the Stores by Certificate, or at Public labour. **1822** J.T. BIGGE *Rep. State Colony N.S.W.* 68 They have established themselves in the town of Sydney, and at once been placed on a level with the emancipated and free convicts of their own sex. *Ibid.* 120 The certificates issued by the secretary attest . . that by reason of the expired service, the said party is restored to all the rights of a free subject. **1831** *Sydney Monitor* 13 Aug. 3/5 By such illiterate ignorant beings, the very term *free* is construed (particularly among a prisoner population) as a power given them exclusively of being lazy, impertinent, and licentious. **1836** *Tegg's Monthly Mag.* I. 5 He had also soon after he became free obtained a grant of a town allotment. **1837** *Colonist* (Sydney) 18 May 163/2, I am a stockman; I have been free about three years. **1837** *Rep. Select Committee Transportation* 13 The pardoned convict or the free convict enjoys all the political rights of the free emigrants . . from the date of the governor's pardon. **1846** H. EASY *Horrors of Transportation* 9 At that time, Van Dieman's Land was not overpopulated with free convicts, as it now (1846) is. **1847** *HRA* (1925) 1st Ser. XXVI. 8 Any person, who, having been transported to this Colony, had become free. **1849** S. & J. SIDNEY *Emigrant's Jrnl.* 323 It was no unusual thing to find a blacksmith, not yet free, the owner of 100 or 150 head of good cattle, for whose run he of course paid.

2. a. Applied as a distinguishing epithet to a settler in an Australian Colony who had not been transported as a convict: see esp. quots. 1824, 1844, and 1854.

1795, 1804 [see *free settler*]. **1815** *HRA* (1916) 1st Ser. VIII. 489 Persons, *who have been once Convicts*, can never be restored to *a full* participation in the Rights and Privileges of Free British Subjects. **1824** E. CURR *Acct. Colony Van Diemen's Land* 11 In Van Diemen's Land, a line of demarcation has ever existed between convicts and free persons, which the future acquisition of their freedom has never enabled them to overstep. **1838** *Colonist* (Sydney) 24 Jan. 3/1 The parties concerned in the foregoing are respectable, free (not freed) persons. **1839** *Sydney Standard* 7 Jan. 2/4 We would invest every man . . with the privileges of a Burgess, provided he came free, and has continued free in the colony. **1840** *Sydney Herald* 25 Sept. 2/7 On Monday last a free black, who had been acting for some time past as a hired servant to Mr Gannon . . was committed to take his trial. **1844** *Colonial Times* (Hobart) 10 July, The community is composed of three classes, the *free*, the *freed*, and the *bond*. **1854** J. MITCHEL *Jail Jrnl.* 231 She took an early occasion of informing me that she 'came out free'; which in fact is the patent of nobility in Van Diemen's Land. **1887** W.H. SUTTOR *Austral. Stories Retold* 144 Some of the men in the same service had 'come out free'. **1898** *Western Champion* (Barcaldine) 20 Dec. 1/3 What d'ye mean, Mr Goodyer, in asking Dr Thursby for a ticket for me? What business is it of yours whether I'm free or bond?

b. In collocations: **free emigrant, immigrant, native, settler.**

1827 P. CUNNINGHAM *Two Yrs. in N.S.W.* II. 133 A body of proprietors . . the greater portion of whom are **free emigrants**. **1838** *Cornwall Chron.* (Launceston) 17 Feb. 26 It is certainly very unjust that a gentleman felon should be made to work in the service of a blackguard free emigrant. **1856** W.H.G. KINGSTON *Emigrant's Home* 6 Western Australians . . arranged to receive a certain proportion of free emigrants with the bond. **1867** 'CLERGYMAN' *Aust. as it Is* 222 There was more crime committed by free emigrants than by old convicts. **1841** *Port Phillip Patriot* 10 June 4/3 The population of New South Wales consists of four classes; the **free immigrants** and their progeny; the convicts; the convicts who have become free through pardon or expiry of their term of service; and the progeny of the convict immigrants—persons who have always been free, but have a 'taint' in their blood. **1842** *Colonial Observer* (Sydney) 16 Nov. 612/3 One half of the whole number of the City Councillors, are not native-born Australians at all, but free immigrants from the mother-country. **1865** *Illustr. Sydney News* 16 Mar. 5/1 The number of virtuous free immigrants was not sufficiently large to check the contaminating influence of the convict element. **1819** *Sydney Gaz.* 18 Sept., Hannah Harris, herself, a **free native** of this Territory. **1848** *Guardian* (Hobart) 12 Feb. 3/1 Ellen Brown a free native—not a black one—drunk and disturbing the peace of her father-land, fined 5s. **1795** *HRA* (1914) 1st Ser. I. 679 To the Civil, Military, **Free Settlers,** and People serving in the Stores. Flour . . 6 lbs. Beef . . 4 lbs. 10 oz. **1804** *Sydney Gaz.* 10 June, He came to this Colony under the auspices of Government, a Free Settler, in the latter part of 1801. **1813** *N.S.W. Pocket Almanack* 63 Reports to state the age, description, and country of the deceased; whether free settler, free or conditionally pardoned convict; free by servitude, or then a convict. **1820** *Sydney Gaz.* 5 Aug., The Free Settlers, who have lately been promised Cattle from the Government Herds, are required with their sureties to execute the usual Bonds. **1830** T. BETTS *Acct. of Colony Van Diemen's Land* 27 The free settlers will not, generally, associate with the emancipists. **1831** H. SAVERY *Quintus Servinton* III. 186 When married men were joined by their wives, . . the latter, in capacity of free settlers, claimed their husbands to be assigned to them, thus virtually removing many of the pains of transportation. **1838** *S. Austral. Rec.* (London) 14 Nov. 116/3 One universal *esprit de corps* animates and pervades the whole convict body, uniting them like Freemasons in one silent, deep-rooted sentiment of hostility to the free settler, or, as they profanely call them, the b-- emigrants. **1840** *Ibid.* 22 Feb. 65/1 The free settlers consist chiefly of persons whose former station was that of farmer, merchant, or officer. **1856** W.H.G. KINGSTON *Emigrant's Home* 5 The crimes of Australia have been the result less of the convict system than of the neglect of religious and moral duties by free settlers. **1865** 'SPECIAL CORRESPONDENT' *Transportation* 42 The few free settlers of Western Australia were benefited at the outset by the convict system. **1876** 'CAPRICORNUS' *Colonisation* 15 The increase of live stock flowing westward, and the pressure of the leading free settlers towards the frontier, told of what was coming. **1939** FRANKLIN & CUSACK *Pioneers on Parade* 12 Felonry, of whatever virtue, was taboo in the pioneerage, but descendants of free settlers, however humble or undesirable, were recognised. **1971** *Bulletin* (Sydney) 1 May 18/1 At first convicts hated free settlers, and then Aussie workmen hated Pommy bastards who might pinch their jobs.

3. In collocations which may be used either exclusively as in sense 2, or to include sense 1: **free colonist, female, labour, labourer, man, overseer, people, population, servant, woman.**

1832 *Hill's Life N.S.W.* (Sydney) 9 Nov. 1 The increase of **free Colonists**, by the late numerous discharges within the Colony, of Soldiers of good character. **1833** *Colonist* (Hobart) 9 July 4/4 He most improperly *classifies* the free colonists. He distinguishes the *free* from the *freed*(!). **1838** *Cornwall Chron.* (Launceston) 3 Mar. 33 Are the *free* Colonists to be *made* to pay an immense sum to maintain a thrice and oftener convicted felon Police? **1848** W. WESTGARTH *Aust.* 151 The 'free colonists' included those who were originally convicts but had become free by servitude. **1852** S. MOSSMAN *Voice from Aust.* 5 Convict pioneers who assisted us in clearing the wilderness, have become absorbed in our army of free colonists. **1854** S. SIDNEY *Gallops & Gossips* 28 In the first place, understand young gentleman, we are divided into at least three sets, but you have only to do with two, the Free Colonists and the Emancipists. **1837** W.B. ULLATHORNE *Catholic Mission Australasia* 28 The government . . has been sending out ship-loads of **free females. 1843** *Duncan's Weekly Register* (Sydney) 16 Dec. 335/2 The bringing into competition the Factory women with the free females of the Colony by taking in washing and needlework was a very paltry concern. **1847** R. WELCH *Convict & Free Labour* 29 If one thousand convict women were transported, there would be required at the same time 4,000 free females. **1832** J. BACKHOUSE *Narr. Visit Austral. Colonies* (1843) 66 One of them . . has put up about 17 miles of post and rail fence, at the rate of £70 per mile, by **free** and £60 by convict **labour. 1839** *Sydney Standard* 15 Apr. 2/3 Free labour is at an extravagant premium. **1848** J.C. BYRNE *Twelve Yrs.' Wanderings* I. 211 Of free-labour, the principal introduction took place in the year 1841, when no less than 32,625 persons were landed in the colony. **1855** J. BONWICK *Geogr. Aust. & N.Z.* (ed. 3) 24 The introduction of free labour was an advantage to the settlement. **1805** *Sydney Gaz.* 3 Nov., Wanted immediately, several **Free Labourers** to work in the yard of J. Underwood and Company. **1842** *Colonial Observer* (Sydney) 2 Feb. 142/2 To the free labourer . . transportation would be the death blow of his hopes. **1791** P.G. KING Jrnl. Norfolk Island 11 Nine **Freemen** . . had served their Terms of Transportation and . . were permitted to become Settlers. **1789** D. COLLINS *Acct. Eng. Colony N.S.W.* (1798) I. 74 Several convicts . . signified that the respective terms for which they had been transported had expired, and claimed to be restored to the privileges of free men. **1807** *HRA* (1916) 1st Ser. VI. 151 There are now One Hundred and Sixty-Six Free Men holding Land who have not come here under the Sentence of the Law. **1811** *Sydney Gaz.* 19 Jan., The whole of the Free Men on and off the Stores, including such as came free into the Colony, such as have become free from their Sentences of Transportation having expired, and such as are free by Absolute Pardon or Conditional Emancipation. **1825** *HRA* (1917) 1st Ser. XI. 607 The rapidly increased numbers of Freemen by emigration has almost merged the convict character of the Colony. **1830** *Ibid.* (1922) 1st Ser. XV. 789 The qualification which they laid down as necessary to constitute Special Jurymen . . was calculated to admit None but Freemen. **1839** *Sydney Standard* 7 Jan. 2/5 At the expense of this colony, they can transport hundreds as free men. **1847** R. WELCH *Convict & Free Labour* 21 There are three methods of procuring it, by convict assignment, by the emigration of free men from Great Britain, and by the introduction of Coolies from some of the neighbouring countries. **1858** T. MCCOMBIE *Hist. Colony Vic.* 73 A majority were expirées, until the large free immigration of 1841 and 1842 gave the freemen an enormous preponderance. **1865** 'SPECIAL CORRESPONDENT' *Transportation* 41 A strong cliqueism pervades the whole penal class against the free man. **1880** *Bulletin* (Sydney) 31 Jan. 4/1 The ordinary felon's new year meant not merely a year nearer the grave as did the freemen's; but a year which only came to be wasted. **1894** *Ibid.* 10 Mar. 13/1 The Pentridge prison convicts . . are allowed cushions to sit upon while breaking stones. Contractors who employ free men don't often provide them with cushions. **1834** J.D. LANG *Hist. & Statistical Acct. N.S.W.* I. 356 A party of eight or ten convict-labourers, under the charge of a **free overseer. 1842** *Geelong Advertiser* 24 Oct. 4/3 Every master to maintain a free overseer, or to superintend his prisoner servants himself. **1857** P.J. MURRAY *Not so Bad* 65, I had only five free overseers with 1,500 or 2,000 men. **1789** J. HUNTER *Hist. Jrnl. Trans. Port Jackson* (1793) 346 A plan had been concerted among the convicts, to surprize me, with the rest of the officers, marines and **free people**. **1795** D. COLLINS *Acct. Eng. Colony N.S.W.* (1798) I. 432 To the settlers who arrived in the *Surprise* he allowed five male convicts; . . to settlers from free people, two; to settlers from prisoners, one. **1802** *HRA* (1915) 1st Ser. III. 473 There are many who have obtained their free pardons and emancipations, or who have expiated their sentence of the law, or are otherwise ranked as free people. **1827** P. CUNNINGHAM *Two Yrs. in N.S.W.* I. 74 The inhabited parts of the colony cultivated by free people may be divided into four. **1827** *Tasmanian* (Hobart) 18 Oct. 2 We wish to learn what the particular grievances are that the **free population** labour under, that could be avoided. **1846** *Tasmanian Jrnl. Nat. Sci.* II. 148 The free population has increased 515 per cent., while the convict population has advanced only 242 per cent. **1851** H. MELVILLE *Present State Aust.* 182 How many thousands of convicts are there mingled among the free population? **1862** BACKHOUSE & TYLOR *Life & Labours G.W. Walker* 265 They published two christian addresses; one to the free, the other to the prisoner population of the Colony. **1808** *Sydney Gaz.* 28 Aug., On Tuesday night John Brazil, a **free servant** of Mr Thompson, at Hawkesbury, was found murdered. **1831** *Sydney Monitor* 13 Aug. 3/5 We are perfectly satisfied with prison-labour. . . We, all of us, have brought out more or less of these *Free Servants*, and we have found them invariably not only a great expense, but a source of injury. **1843** C. ROWCROFT *Tales of Colonies* III. 260 Give them the same high wages which are obtained by good free servants in the colony. **1847** R. WELCH *Convict & Free Labour* 16 Reformatory effects are shown by a convict becoming a free servant, and then a small settler. **1791** D. COLLINS *Acct. Eng. Colony N.S.W.* (1798) I. 181 There were also eight **free women** (wives of convicts) and one died. **1829** *Sydney Monitor* 23 Feb. 1512/1 Ann Baker, a free woman, was sentenced by the Police Magistrate on Saturday for 'being found at her old tricks in the street', to one month's hard labour in the 3rd class factory. **1836** J.F. O'CONNELL *Residence Eleven Yrs. New Holland* 47 The government of the convicts at this institution is intrusted [*sic*] principally to a female, whose title is 'The Matron'. The matron must be a free woman, not a freed transport, but a person whose character has never been endorsed by a judicial tribunal.

4. In special collocations: **free colony** (as distinct from a penal colony), a Colony which was not founded as, and has not been used as, a place of penal servitude; **settlement, (a)** *free colony*; **(b)** part of a penal colony which is not, or is no longer, used as a place of penal servitude. See PENAL.

1828 *Murray's Austral-Asiatic Rev.* i. 33 Government . . aim to make this not only a **free Colony**, but one of the highest order of Colonies under the Crown. **1835** *Colonist* (Sydney) 22 Oct. 338/3 In marking out a *highway* to the Twelve-shillings-an-acre free colony of Southern Australia, Major Mitchell has, perhaps unconsciously, been performing a signal service to the *highwaymen* of Eastern Australia. **1843** J.F. BENNETT *Hist. & Descr. Acct. S.A.* 11 A proposition was . . made to form a new and free colony in some other part of Australia which should be beyond the pale of convict contamination. **1857** M.B. HALE *Transportation Question* 17 The progress of the two free colonies has been more rapid than that of the two penal settlements. **1867** J. BONWICK *J. Batman* 13 Mr Batman, a free man, of free descent, was desirous of laying the foundations of a free colony here in 1827. **1882** J. ALLEN *Hist. Aust.* 85 Although nominally forming an integral part of New South Wales, until formally separated from it in 1851, it cannot be too confidently affirmed that Victoria was always a free colony. **1832** J. HENDERSON *Observations Colonies N.S.W. & Van Diemen's Land* 17 Smaller indulgences should be (within, or near the penal settlement), allowed them after their sentences had been completed, and similar to what they would have been entitled to in the **free settlements. 1836** J. BACKHOUSE *Extracts from Lett.*

(1839) iv. 7 The first commandant of the penal settlement of Port Macquarie, (now a free settlement). **1840** *Port Phillip Gaz.* 12 Feb. 2 Two distinct causes may be assigned for these examples of successful colonization [*sc.* South Australia and Port Phillip]—The first, originates in the difference between the results of a *penal* and a *free* settlement. **1843** *Sydney Morning Herald* 12 June 3/1 He is not a native candidate, and consequently has no claim on the score of nationality, he being a native of Norfolk Island when it was a free settlement. **1849** J. KINGSMILL *Advice to Prisoners* 12 A conditional pardon . . entitles the individual during the remainder of his sentence to migrate to any of the Australian free settlements. **1875** CAMPBELL & WILKS *Early Settlement Qld.* 15 Shortly after . . the commandant was relieved . . by a Police Magistrate and Brisbane was proclaimed a free settlement.

5. In the phr. **free by servitude,** (one who has been) released, having served the full sentence imposed: see quots. 1847 and 1848.

1813 *N.S.W. Pocket Almanack* 63 State the age, description, and country of the deceased; whether free settler, free or conditionally pardoned convict; free by servitude, or then a convict. **1818** *Hobart Town Gaz.* 3 Jan., Several Females . . appeared at the General muster who state themselves to have become Free by Servitude. **1824** E. CURR *Acct. Colony Van Diemen's Land* 59 A great part of them are occupied by persons of a very inferior class, mostly emancipated convicts, or such as are become free by servitude. **1829** *Launceston Advertiser* 2 Nov. 2 On Thursday last, George Pennington (free by servitude) was brought before the Police Magistrate, charged with stealing. **1844** *Sydney Morning Herald* 8 Jan. 2/4 *David Fleming*, free by servitude was acquitted of a charge of robbery. **1847** A. HARRIS *Settlers & Convicts* (1953) 47 A convict free by servitude (so convicts are designated whose term of sentence has expired). **1848** C. COZENS *Adventures of Guardsman* 163 The 'free by servitude', he who has served his full sentence, is required to show his 'certificate of freedom'.

free, *n. Australian National Football.* Abbrev. of 'free kick'. Also as *v. intr.*

1859 G. ATKINSON *Everything about Austral. Rules Football* (1982) 197 In case of infringements, captain may claim free from where breach occurred. **1908** *Clipper* (Hobart) 19 Sept. 2/2 From the kick-off Abel played grandly; Teddy Russell put in a good bit of graft. Webb freed to Abel, Webb ditto to Molross. Free to Webb. **1931** J.F. MCHALE et al. *Austral. Game of Football* 77 Received an enormous number of 'frees'. **1960** *N.T. News* (Darwin) 5 Jan. 8/5 A very dubious free to Marcellus gave them a sixer to make it 4.1 to 3.2.

freebooter. *Obs.* [Spec. use of *freebooter* one who goes about in search of plunder, esp. a pirate.] A runaway convict; BUSHRANGER 1.

1817 *Hobart Town Gaz.* 16 Aug., All who attempt to establish themselves in the Woods as Free-Booters will meet the same Fate as those men who have lately tried it. **1839** *Sydney Herald* 29 May 2/5 New South Wales is once more assuming an alarming aspect: her freebooters are abroad, while her troopers repose in quietude at head-quarters. **1855** G.H. WATHEN *Golden Colony* 147 News of the escape of these formidable and blood-stained freebooters. **1866** *Sydney Punch* 3 Mar. 739/2 Such a *rara avis* in horseflesh would be a real blessing to 'bobbies' in pursuit of those merry freebooters who roam unmolested over the Arcadian plains of the interior. **1888** 'R. BOLDREWOOD' *Robbery under Arms* (1937) 493 How the last members of this well-known, long-dreaded gang of freebooters had actually perished can only be conjectured. **1900** C. WHITE *Hist. Austral. Bushranging* 101 The free-booters . . were exceedingly pleased with this prize, which they declared was 'just what they wanted'.

free-born, *a. Obs.* Used as a distinguishing epithet to deny association with convicts and convictism, esp. of one born in an Australian Colony. Also *absol.*

1825 *Austral.* (Sydney) 17 Mar. 1 The Governor has been pleased to approve of the following Appointments: William Eagleton (free born) to be a constable. **1835** *Sydney Herald* 5 Jan. 2/1 It will give much satisfaction to the Emigrants and free-born of Australia, to learn, that the cause of virtual representation has experienced a triumph at Swan River. **1846** E. KEMP *Voice from Tas.* 34 Wholly indifferent, in the mean time yet, sirs, As to the interests of the free born settlers. **1849** A. HARRIS *Emigrant Family* (1967) 92 Beck was understood to be a free born native. **1858** —— *Secrets* (1961) 78 He would then be assigned to her as her convict servant, she being free-born and the law requiring some free person always to have custody of the convict. **1889** J.H.L. ZILLMANN *Past & Present Austral. Life* 50, I am one of the oldest free-born white natives of the youngest of the group of our Australian colonies, though at the time of my birth, Queensland, as it is now called, was still a dependency of New South Wales.

freed, *ppl. a. Hist.*

a. Of one formerly a convict: restored to the possession of civil liberties, having served a sentence imposed or obtained a remission thereof.

1829 *Tasmanian Almanack* 97 Governor Macquarie and Lieutenant Governor Sorell promote the objects of the emancipated (or, as the Right Hon. William Huskisson says, *freed*) Colonists. **1833** *N.S.W. Mag.* (Sydney) 316 Divided into its aboriginal inhabitants, the free, the freed, the emancipist, the ticket of leave, and the prisoners. **1836** J.F. O'CONNELL *Residence Eleven Yrs. New Holland* 47 The matron must be a free woman, not a freed transport, but a person whose character has never been endorsed by a judicial tribunal. **1852** W. HUGHES *Austral. Colonies* 170 Distinction between the 'free' and the 'freed' is . . becoming weakened.

b. In collocations: **freed convict, man.**

1832 J. BUSBY *Authentic Information N.S.W. & N.Z.* 13 A degree of trust . . cannot be committed to a convict, or a **freed convict.** **1837** J. MUDIE *Felonry of N.S.W.* 220 The whole body of the freed convict portion of the population. **1844** *Colonial Observer* (Sydney) 10 Oct. 4/1 The Corporation was to provide police for the restraint of convicts, and ticket-of-leave holders, and freed convicts. **1847** *HRA* (1925) 1st Ser. XXVI. 1 The desire shown by the Settlers there to receive and employ Exiles and freed Convicts. **1830** *Ibid.* (1922) 1st Ser. XV. 791 Much has been said of the equal Right to protection and legal privileges of the Freemen and **Freedmen.** **1835** 'IMPARTIAL OBSERVER' *Illustr. Present State N.S.W.* 8 All natives at a certain age, and freedmen . . shall receive a proportional grant of land. **1845** M. COLLISSON *S.A.* 11 The police force is maintained in its present strength principally to repress the outbreaks of runaway convicts and freedmen from the neighbouring colonies. **1849** A. HARRIS *Emigrant Family* (1967) 32 There are some who are emigrants, and some who are freed-men: the emigrants are flats, and the others are sharps. **1852** S. & J. SIDNEY *Emigrant's Jrnl.* 43 Free or *freedmen* settlers . . were, if they required, victualled and clothed from the public store for eighteen months from the time of their going on their grants. **1871** C.L. MONEY *Knocking about N.Z.* p. viii, Those who—freedmen of the rolling Australian plains—have slept uncanopied beneath the South Cross.

freedom. *Obs.* Shortened form of *certificate of freedom* (see CERTIFICATE).

1847 A. HARRIS *Settlers & Convicts* (1953) 153 Free men do not like being continually called upon by prison constables to 'show their freedom'. **1848** J.C. BYRNE *Twelve Yrs.' Wanderings* I. 167 The free immigrant has nothing of the kind to produce, if required by any prying constable to 'show his freedom'.

freedom of contract. *Hist.* The right (of an employer) to hire non-union labour and to set conditions of employment. Also *attrib.*

1891 *Australasian Pastoralists' Rev.* 15 Aug. 217 The following was agreed to:- 'That employers shall be free to employ and shearers shall be free to accept employment whether belonging to Shearers' or other unions or not, without favour, molestation, or intimidation on either side.' This is the definition of 'freedom of contract' by the Pastoralists' Federal Council of Australia. **1900** H. LAWSON *Over Sliprails* 62 We got back, and the crew had to reload the wool without assistance, for it bore the accursed brand of a 'freedom-of-contract' shed. **1909** W.G. SPENCE *Aust.'s Awakening* 441 From 'freedom of contract' to compulsory collective bargaining is a far cry. **1918** C.H. NORTHCOTT *Austral. Social Dev.* 79 The employers were ready to fight for 'freedom of contract', and would have nothing to do with organised labour.

free grant. *Hist.* The granting of the freehold of a tract of unalienated land; the land so granted. Also *attrib.*

1817 *Hobart Town Gaz.* 24 May, To Be Sold, A Free Grant Farm, situated at Crawfish Point, in the District of Queensborough. **1833** *Austral. Almanack* 100 Non-commissioned officers and privates, discharged from the service *for the purpose of settling in the Colony*, will be allowed *Free Grants* to the following extent; viz. Serjeants . . 20 Acres. Corporals and Private Soldiers . . 100 ditto. **1835** F.C. IRWIN *State & Position W.A.* 46 The system of free grants, which was the first adopted in Western Australia, is decidedly injurious to the prosperity of a settlement. **1839** *S. Austral. Rev.* 15 Until recently all the unappropriated lands were bestowed on emigrants *by free grant.* **1843** C. ROWCROFT *Tales of Colonies* I. 23 At that time, when land was granted, it was a free grant, or gift, from the Crown to the emigrant. **1849** A. HARRIS *Guide Port Stephens* 208 In the year 1831 Lord Ripon's Regulations for the abolition of free grants and the sale by auction of all Crown lands, were first promulgated in the colony. **1857** M.B. HALE *Transportation Question* 20 Upon the first formation of the colony, the grants were entirely free; and, when free grants were no longer made, the land was sold at a very low rate indeed.

freeman's key. *Obs.* [f. Br. slang *(to drink, lush at) Freeman's Quay* to drink at another's expense, with ref. to the name of a wharf near London Bridge at which free beer was distributed to porters, etc.: see Hotten, *Dict. Mod. Slang* (1859) and Partridge.] Used allusively with reference to a set of circumstances in which a consumer does not pay for, or is able to defer payment for, alcoholic liquor.

1891 *Truth* (Sydney) 29 Mar. 7/5, I must explain that getting in on the *nod* is the same as on the 'never never', 'Freeman's key', 'the ready'. **1915** 'ALPHA' *Reminisc. Goldfields* i. 51 He . . usually went on the spree every second month, and while in that state lost more than he made, the house being freeman's key for a time, until he again sobered up, after having had what he declared 'a regular soaker'.

free pardon. ABSOLUTE PARDON.

1794 D. COLLINS *Acct. Eng. Colony N.S.W.* (1798) I. 387 Richard Blount, for whom a free pardon had some time since been received. **1808** *To Viscount Castlereagh* 8 Even granting a free pardon to those convicts he should think worthy of so great a boon. **1819** J.H. VAUX *Mem.* I. 190 His clerk, having received a free pardon from Governor King, was about to quit the colony. **1832** J. BACKHOUSE *Narr. Visit Austral. Colonies* (1843) 20 A further continuance in good conduct, would open the way for a free pardon, which would liberate those who received it, to return to their native land. **1839** *Tasmanian* (Hobart) 8 Feb. 43/4 Pleased to grant to Edward Newman . . (holding a conditional pardon) a free pardon, and to John Bradkin . . (holding a ticket-of-leave) a conditional pardon. **1856** J. BONWICK *W. Buckley* 11 He had obtained a free pardon from Colonel Arthur, August 25th, 1835. **1875** CAMPBELL & WILKS *Early Settlement Qld.* 56 The Government offered a large reward and a free pardon for . . information.

free-select, *v. Hist. trans.* To acquire (a tract of land) under a free selection scheme. See also SELECT. Also *absol.*

1861 H. PARKES *Speeches* 6 Mar. (1876) 138 Those who free-selected land would enter upon it under conditions enforcing them to its improvement. **1871** *Austral. Town & Country Jrnl.* (Sydney) 4 Mar. 266/4 McAteer has free selected 1200 acres of land. **1872** A. MCFARLAND *Illawarra & Manaro* 133 An application to free-select should preclude all competition for the land. **1879** S.W. SILVER *Austral. Grazier's Guide* 6 Forty acres . . is the smallest . . 640 acres is the largest quantity which can be 'free selected', as the colonial phrase runs, or 'occupied as a conditional purchase', in more official language.

Hence **free-selected** *ppl. a.*, **free-selecting** *ppl. a.* and *vbl. n.*

1863 *Frank Gardiner, or Bushranging in 1863* 16 Which brought them in a few moments to the door of a partly constructed hut, on the **free selected** block of James Sinclair. **1862** *Bell's Life in Sydney* 27 Sept. 3/2 Easier to get a living by **free selecting** than by working for wages. **1869** *Colonial Soc.* (Sydney) 18 Mar. 2 He tightly pinched his tiny prize—a free-selecting man! **1873**

A. TROLLOPE *Aust. & N.Z.* I. 101 Anything to them was better than a free-selecting cattle-stealer at their gates. **1890** 'R. BOLDREWOOD' *Colonial Reformer* III. 133 Free-selecting here might be very well for some people; it didn't suit them.

free selection. *Hist.* A scheme under which the freehold of a tract of unalienated rural land, of a size suitable for small farming, could be acquired on terms favourable to the buyer; the land so acquired. See also SELECTION.

1859 *Bell's Life in Sydney* 21 May 1/1 The right of purchase of farms, surveyed or unsurveyed, without competition, and without delay, by persons willing to settle upon and improve them, and generally known as 'Free Selection', I have ever held to be a principle of essential importance. **1862** H. BROWN *Vic. as I found It* 164 The cry was raised, 'Unlock the lands to the people'... In 1860, the land was thrown open... The main feature of the system being, free selection at one pound an acre, one half only of the allotment being paid for at the time of purchase. **1865** *Sydney Punch* 3 June 431/1 Free Selection's a swindle, a cheat, and a sin, And the squatters may win if they keep their tongues in, And triumphantly grin, as they pocket their tin. **1872** A. MCFARLAND *Illawarra & Manaro* 7 If there be any 'Free-selections' they must be confined to the base and slopes of the mountains. **1876** 'CAPRICORNUS' *Colonisation* 6 When free selection became law in New South Wales, a generation had passed since squatting first became an institution. **1882** *Three L's* 291 'Free selection' and 'deferred payments' were two things which the farmers really required. **1895** *Bulletin* (Sydney) 26 Jan. 24/1 He tramped his free-selection, morning, afternoon and night. **1911** 'ROSE BOLDREWOOD' *Complications at Collaroi* 282 Another of my experiences was to take up a homestead lease of three thousand acres with .. an old schoolfellow. These homestead leases are much the same as free selections. **1919** *Huon Times* (Franklin) 21 Jan. 2/5 Farms had been allotted to 156 men, free selection of Crown lands to 43, and remissions of rent to 41 Crown selectors. **1928** M.E. FULLERTON *Austral. Bush* 17 'Free selection' is a comparative term; it did not mean exactly free grants of land to persons by the Crown. The government terms, however, were easy. **1956** R.G. EDWARDS *Overlander Songbk.* 81 On my little free selection I have acres by the score Where I unyoke the bullocks from the dray. **1968** F. ROSE *Aust. Revisited* 28 Premier John Robertson .. led the way in New South Wales by proposing a policy of 'free selection before survey' which became law in 1861.

free selector. A small farmer who acquires a tract of land under a free selection scheme (but see quot. 1867). See also SELECTOR 2.

1864 J. ROGERS *New Rush* 22 Free selectors we shall be! Deserting mineralogy, Retir'd to farms six foot by three—Free selectors we shall be! **1867** 'CLERGYMAN' *Aust. as it Is* 131 The wife of his overseer said to me, that the infant at her breast, and the rest of her children, were 'free selectors'—that is the owner of the station had made use of their names in picking up the best parts of the run, not for the land itself, but to remain in undisturbed possession of the grazing land adjoining. **1872** G.S. BADEN-POWELL *New Homes for Old Country* 456 In all parts of Australia the antagonism existing between squatters and 'free selectors', 'cockatooers', continually forces itself upon the attention. **1873** A. TROLLOPE *Aust. & N.Z.* I. 34 If one is to believe the Queensland squatter .. 'free-selectors', or small farmers, do deal in beef, but they steal the cattle from the large cattle-runs. **1886** W.J. WOODS *Visit to Vic.* 26 A free-selector is one who has selected an agricultural allotment for purchase in fee simple. **1890** J. HASLAM *Glimpse Austral. Life* 19 The Free-selectors' Bill in the mother colony has cost the squatters thousands upon thousands of pounds to buy out what they term the minions of those wretches who have selected the water-holes of the squatters' runs, and defied, in accordance with the law, the squatters. **1896** H. LAWSON *In Days when World was Wide* 51 And ere I left I swore I'd win The free-selector's daughter. **1920** W. MCGUFFIN *Austral. Tales of Border* 180 When the boundary riders noticed the advent of a free selector on the run instead of the 'dummy', the matter was promptly reported to the squatter, who felt very much annoyed at one of the farming class settling on the land. **1951** G. FARWELL *Outside Track* 92 New homesteads are pencilled in, small shacks marked 'Free Selector', new pubs and grog shanties.

freezer.

1. An animal bred to be slaughtered for export as frozen meat. Also *attrib.*

[N.Z. **1889** WILLIAMS & REEVES *Colonial Couplets* 21 Be they [*sc.* sheep] freezers or crawlers or wethers or ewes.] **1897** R. NEWTON *Work & Wealth Qld.* 22 (*caption*) 'Freezers' for the meat works. **1925** *Pastoral Rev.* 16 Dec. 1114 Freezer Lamb Competitions. **1947** H. DRAKE-BROCKMAN *On N.-W. Skyline* 71 At present only ten per cent. of all cattle passing through the Wyndham meat-works are 'chillers'. 'Freezers' provide forty per cent; the remaining fifty per cent. are merely 'boners'—fit for boiling down into bovril and bone-dust.

2. FREEZING WORKS.

1933 J. TRURAN *Where Plain Begins* 12 Rabbits were worth a shilling a pair that winter: the 'freezer' up at Blayney would take any number of them at that price.

freezing works. An abattoir at which animal carcasses are prepared and frozen for export.

1881 *Queenslander* (Brisbane) 12 Nov. 635/1 Being specially suitable from its position for raising stock for the large Meat Preserving and Freezing Works about to be erected at Townsville. **1891** R. WALLACE *Rural Economy & Agric.* 464 For the shipment of the Queensland supply, freezing works are in process of construction in Brisbane, Rockhampton, and Townsville. **1899** R. SEMON *In Austral. Bush* 50 'Freezing works' have been erected in Brisbane .. and here the meat is prepared and made ready for shipment to Europe. **1925** *Pastoral Rev.* 16 Jan. 71/1 Sir Philip went on to say that there are 53 freezing works in the Commonwealth of Australia. **1942** H.H. PECK *Mem. of Stockman* 94 These were treated at the Deniliquin freezing works.

Fremantle doctor: see DOCTOR *n.*[3]

freshy. Also **freshie.** [f. *fresh(water* + -Y.] A fresh-water crocodile.

1964 B. CRUMP *Gulf* 28 Best professional croc-shooter .. would say, '.. me and Andy Meikin shot four hundred and eighty freshies and nine fourteen-foot salties in the Normanby one trip.' **1969** J. DINGWELL *One String* 109 The freshies rarely got to eight feet, but the flesh-eaters reached ten. **1970** D. BAIRD *Incredible Gulf* 96 Joh Dimmock, a dark-haired young man with several days' growth of beard and no shirt on, is discussing the crocodile situation. 'I got forty-three freshies last week. They're there if you know where to look.' **1972** K. WILLEY *Tales Big Country* 174 'What we have got,' Percy said, 'is a bunch of ragged-pants New Australians wiping out the harmless freshwater crocodile with nets. The freshie is protected everywhere else, but not in Queensland.' **1985** *Age* (Melbourne) 3 Aug. (Saturday Extra) 15/1 There are no recorded attacks by 'freshies' on humans.

friar bird. [See quot. 1841.] Any of the four species of the honeyeater genus *Philemon* of n. and e. Aust., New Guinea, and nearby islands, having bare facial skin, esp. the *noisy friar bird* (see NOISY). Formerly also **friar.**

1790 J. HUNTER *Hist. Jrnl. Trans. Port Jackson* (1793) 410 Wir-gan, A bird called fryar. **1827** *Trans. Linnean Soc. London* XV. 324 Mr Caley has the following observations on these birds. '*Friar.*—A very common bird about Paramatta... It repeats the words 'poor soldier' and 'four o'clock' very distinctly.' **1841** J. GOULD *Birds of Aust.* (1848) IV. Pl. 58, Its bare head and neck have .. suggested the names of 'Friar Bird', 'Monk', 'Leather Head', etc. **1881** E. DAVIES *Story Earnest Life* 380 The friar bird has a bald head. **1890** G.J. BROINOWSKI *Birds of Aust.* IV. Pl. 25, Every inhabitant of New South Wales knows the Leather Head, or Friar Bird, or at any rate has heard its peculiar note. **1909** *Bulletin* (Sydney) 28 Oct. 13/2 Leatherheads .. are notoriously free from face herbage. Why the alternative name of these sinstained fowl should be friar-birds passes my comprehension. **1918** *Ibid.* 2 May 24/3 The bobala has probably more *aliases* than any other Australian bird, being variously known as friar bird, monk, pimlico, four o'clock, poor soldier and leatherhead. Bobala is Binghi's name for him. **1928** C.G. LANE *Adventures in Big Bush* 276 The great drab-feathered friar-bird. **1945** C. BARRETT *Austral. Bird Life* 162 'Friar' and 'leatherhead' .. refer to the appearance of the head, which is naked and ink-black. **1965** *Austral. Encycl.* IV. 217 The friar-birds are brown above and whitish below, with pointed, silver-white feathers on the breast. All are very noisy.

frib. [Prob. Br. dial.: cf. *fribble* trifling thing (OED *sb.* 2.); *frip* anything worthless or trifling (EDD); *frib* small, dirty lock of wool (DAE).] Usu. in *pl.* A small tuft of wool matted with grease, either under a sheep's legs or on the edge of the shorn fleece.

1805 *Sydney Gaz.* 9 Sept., This wool when sorted produced .. Prime Wool .. choice locks .. Fribs. **1879** S.W. SILVER *Austral. Grazier's Guide* 55 Small cut locks, or 'fribs' .. fall out and pass between the battens of the wool-table on to a heap of 'locks' below. **1900** [see FRIBBY *a.*]. **1921** L.G. JONES *Flockmaster's Companion* 77 *Fribs* are second cuts caused by indifferent shearing. **1961** *Bulletin* (Sydney) 3 Feb. 44/2 The old piece-picker went on: 'I picked for ten guns on me own and not a frib in the broken.'

fribby, *a.* and *n.*

A. *adj.* Characterized by the presence of fribs (see prec.).

1900 A. HAWKESWORTH *Austral. Sheep & Wool* 180 A fleece is said to be fribby when a great number of second cuts or fribs fall out when it is shaken or in the process of rolling. **1921** L.G. JONES *Flockmaster's Companion* 77 A fleece is called *fribby* when there are an excessive number of fribs adhering to it. **1929** H.B. SMITH *Sheep & Wool Industry Aust. & N.Z.* (ed. 3) 209 *Fribby*, short locky pieces of wood such as second cuts and small black yolky locks from crutch and under fore-legs of sheep.

B. *n.* See quot.

1951 *Concerning Wool* (Austral. Wool Board) 100 *Fribby*, wool containing an excessive amount of second cuts and sweat points.

frilled lizard. The agamid lizard *Chlamydosaurus kingii* of n. and n.e. Aust., having a layer of loose tissue around the neck that can be erected when the animal is alarmed. Also **frill lizard, frill-neck, frill-necked lizard, frilly.**

1841 G. GREY *Jrnls. Two Exped. N.-W. & W.A.* I. 94 We fell in with a specimen of the remarkable frilled lizard (*Chlamydosaurus Kingii*). **1899** R. SEMON *In Austral. Bush* 183 The weird-shaped 'frilled-lizards', .. tree animals which, when attacked, hotly defend themselves with their sharp teeth. **1901** *Bulletin* (Sydney) 23 Nov. 32/1 Yer don't like chuckin' yer swag off all of a sudden to run down a frill-neck. **1904** M. WHITE *Shanty Entertainment* 67 There is nothing so naturally exhilarating as to watch a good big buck goanna making love to a frill-necked lizard on the wing. **1928** M.E. FULLERTON *Austral. Bush* 135 The frilled lizard (Queensland) .. when angry or excited shoots out a frill-like membrane from the neck. **1936** C.P. CONIGRAVE *North Aust.* 164 The very handsome but ferocious-looking frilled-necked lizard .. when enraged, throws out a beautifully-coloured frill that looks like an Elizabethan ruffle round the creature's neck. **1945** M. RAYMOND *Smiley* 36, I thought bees could let go o' their stings like frill lizards let go o' their tails. **1957** *Bulletin* (Sydney) 16 Jan. 13/3 Frill-necked jew-lizards seem to have a dire effect on the domestic cat. We had a portly tom in the country that became a 'frilly'-addict. **1958** E. SALTER *Will to Survive* 86 Something darted under his feet... A lizard. A poor harmless frilly. **1976** C.D. MILLS *Hobble Chains & Greenhide* 162, I saw this dusky imp Pluto approaching Ned with a 'frilly' that he had found. **1978** J. ROWE *Warlords* 135 She radiated so much irritation that she reminded him of a small angry frilled lizard. **1981** P. BARTON *Bastards I have Known* 25 Sleepy lizards are pretty slow but in this new environment old Barney was getting about like a frillneck.

fringe. An area of sparse settlement bordering the arid inland region of Australia. Also *attrib.*, esp. as **fringe country**.

1902 *Bulletin* (Sydney) 13 Sept. 16/1 Government men stationed on 'The Fringe' are mostly in their right place... The 'Fringe' civil servant, being king of his tin-pot village, generally has an overweening conceit of his own abilities. **1944** J.H. PICK *Aust.'s Dying Heart* (ed. 2) 89 The fringe Country, that is, roughly, the ten- to fourteen-inch rainfall country, has .. proved to be highly dangerous country to develop. **1961** *Meanjin* 264 He had come from the cattle country to the edge of the Desert, and had found the fringe country to his liking.

fringed lily. Any of several perennial herbs of the genus *Thysanotus* (fam. Lilaceae) bearing purple or blue flowers the three broad segments of which are fringed, esp. *T. tuberosus*; also with distinguishing epithet, as **twining fringed lily** (see quot. 1978). Also (esp. formerly) **fringed violet.**

1819 *First Fruits Austral. Poetry* 3 Th' Australian 'fringed Violet' Shall henceforward be my pet! **1834** G. Bennett *Wanderings N.S.W.* I. 219 The delicate and beautiful orchideous plant called 'fringed violet' by the colonists, the *Thysanotus junceus* of botanists, was particularly abundant: its elegant lilac-coloured flowers, in clusters of from three to six upon the same stalk were very conspicuous. **1846** C.P. Hodgson *Reminisc. Aust.* 155 My delicate friend, the fringed violet, whose beautiful purple flowers supported on delicate round stems, and fringed with webs of finest texture, just peep above the grass. **1860** 'Lady' *My Experiences in Aust.* 46 The *Fringed Violet*, a most exquisite little thing, of the *Iris* tribe, I fancy. **1870** E.B. Kennedy *Four Yrs. in Qld.* 145 The fringed violet grows in the grass on the forest land. **1901** M. Vivienne *Travels in W.A.* 61 The thysanotus, or fringed lily, is a remarkable satiny-looking flower, and has a habit of climbing. **1928** J. Pollard *Bushland Vagabonds* 151 The fringed lily, a fragile mauve bloom with three petals, the sides of which were fringed. **1933** C.W. Peck *Austral. Legends* (ed. 2) 207 It is a lily, We know it as Thysanotus or Fringed Violet. **1942** C. Barrett *Austral. Wild Flower Bk.* 61 The common fringed lily grows abundantly on sandy heaths and grasslands. **1948** H.A. Lindsay *Bushman's Handbk.* 53 *Fringed 'violet'.* Very pretty mauve flower with three petals, like a clover leaf, each fringed with delicate hairs. **1977** D. Stuart *Drought Foal* 6 Fringed lilies and spikes of blue hovea. **1978** B.P. Moore *Life on Forty Acres* 43 The less spectacular Twining Fringed Lily (*T. patersonii*), with smaller flowers on twisting stems.

fringe-dweller. An Aboriginal who lives on the outskirts of a town. Also *transf.* and *fig.*

1959 *Fringe Dwellers* (Dept. Territories) 6 Most of these people are 'fringe dwellers'—people living merely on the fringes of Australian towns, of the larger Australian society, of the Australian economy. **1965** *Realist* (Sydney) xx. 2 The huts of the Cape Town slum-dwellers are rather like the tin shacks of our Aboriginal 'fringe-dwellers'. **1976** N. Cato *Mister Maloga* 12 In the early 1860s, apart from the fringe-dwellers living in a camp . . there were hundreds of Aborigines still living in Barnah Forest. **1976** C. Forsyth *Governor-General* 65 He began drifting with the Aboriginal fringe dwellers and soon . . he was equating with them. **1980** M. Dugan *Early Dreaming* 3 Looking over my shoulder, I see I am a fringe dweller of the atomic society. . . As opposed to that lowering shadow of the future . . my shelter is the cool green shadow of Longtime. **1984** P. Read *Down there with me on Cowra Mission* 133 They referred to them as fringe dwellers, because the Aboriginal stations would be set up on the outskirts of town. **1986** *Nat. Times* (Sydney) 21 Feb. 7/1 A gossipy article . . sent . . a number of political fringe-dwellers—staff, journalists, and public servants—into a state of shock.

fringe-myrtle. [Prob. with reference to the long hairs (awns) of the calyx.] Any of several shrubs of the chiefly w. Austral. genus *Calytrix* (fam. Myrtaceae), typically having clusters of attractive, starry flowers, esp. the widely cultivated *C. tetragona*, also known as **common fringe-myrtle.**

1866 J. Lindley *Treasury of Bot.* 508 *Fringe-Myrtles*, a name given by Lindley to the Chamaelauciaceae. **1923** *Census Plants Vic.* (Field Naturalists' Club Vic.) 49 *Calytrix tetragona* . . Common Fringe-myrtle. **1942** C. Barrett *Austral. Wild Flower Bk.* 173 Common fringe-myrtle . . has long been associated with the Grampians, but it ranges throughout Australia, excepting only the north. **1967** N.A. Wakefield *Naturalist's Diary* 27 The sandstone outcrops carried an outstanding display of fringe-myrtle (*Calytrix*), with its masses of flowers either rich pink or pure white. **1984** E. Walling *On Trail Austral. Wildflowers* 35 Dusky pink fringe-myrtle.

fritz. Chiefly *S.A.* [Transf. use of *Fritz*, nickname for a German, with reference to *German sausage*.] A large, bland sausage; Devon. Also **pork fritz,** and *fig.*

1914 *Truth* (Sydney) 8 Nov. 7/7 Pork fritz manufacturers have become alarmed, and some are . . advertising that their commodities are really made from pork and veal. **1965** *Kings Cross Whisper* (Sydney) vi. 3/2 Four slices of slightly mouldy pork-fritz. **1966** S.J. Baker *Austral. Lang.* (ed. 2) 347 South Australia . . *yard of fritz*, a tall man. **1972** G.W. Turner *Eng. Lang. in Aust. & N.Z.* (rev. ed.) 123 Sausages in South Australia . . retain German names . . and the same influence is seen in the now standard use of *fritz* for a German sausage. **1981** P. Barton *Bastards I have Known* 114 With a half-eaten hunk of fritz. **1982** N. Keesing *Lily on Dustbin* 121 During the 1914–18 War . . the humble German sausage (sometimes known as Fritz) a staple for sandwiches then as now, had to be amended. First it was called 'Belgian' sausage, then in many places 'Devon' sausage.

frog. [f. *frog* french (letter).] A condom. Also **froggie.**

1952 T.A.G. Hungerford *Ridge & River* 23 Having a bath and a shave, getting into clean clothes, whacking a froggie into the kick, to lare up at the dance. **1969** A. Buzo *Front Room Boys* (1970) 40 'Jees I forgot the frog,' he said. . . I was disgusted. I put my pants back on and told him to take me home immediately. **1981** C. Gorman *Night in Arms of Raeleen* (1983) 45 Nine is gettin' yer length in, with a frog on, and both fully stripped, and ten is gettin' yer end in, with no frog, and both fully stripped.

frogskin. *Obs.* [From the colour.] A one-pound note; the sum of one pound; Toadskin. Also **frog.**

1907 *Clipper* (Hobart) 28 Dec. 4/3 'I'll give yer a quid for yer old red shawl,' and I 'olds out a frogskin. 'The man's mad,' sez she to 'erself, 'but a quid's a quid.' **1919** *Aussie: Austral. Soldiers' Mag.* (Sydney) Jan. 2/1 The Prince pushed his frame in and risked ten 'frogs' and won. **1919** C. Drew *Doings of Dave* 104 You shove a couple of frogskins on him, and I'll go ten bob with you. **1936** A.B. Paterson *Shearer's Colt* 15 That bag full of frogskins (pound notes). **1944** *Austral. New Writing* 36 You come back here tomorrow night . . and it's two frogskins for you and drinks all round! **1949** R. Park *Poor Man's Orange* 102 'How much they sting yer for it?' 'Half a frog.'

front, *n.* [Deteriorated use of *front* effrontery, impudence (rare in standard English after 1850): see OED *sb.* 4.] Effrontery. Formerly with indefinite article.

1896 H. Lawson *While Billy Boils* 20 'Well, I'll be blessed!' I says. 'I'll see you further first. You have got a front.' **1936** 'Sweeney, Ex-Crook' *I Confess* 61 'Front' is the slang term indicating presence, demeanour, poise, manner. Without it, the confidence man will not go far. **1958** F. Hardy *Four-Legged Lottery* 87 Must get back to the game. Some of these bastards have more front than Myers; might get their hand caught in the tin. **1975** *Bulletin* (Sydney) 26 Apr. 46/1 According to Jimmy, the Limp had front (boldness and self-confidence). **1981** C. Gorman *Night in Arms of Raeleen* (1983) 30 That guy's got more front than the National Bank.

front, *v.* [Spec. use of *front* to confront, orig. in Austral. Services' speech.]

1. *trans.* To appear before (a court, etc.); to confront.

1941 *Argus* (Melbourne) 15 Nov. (Suppl.), *Fronting the Bull*, facing a charge. **1943** K. Tennant *Ride on Stranger* 65 Mr Litchin was . . making frantic signs to Beryl who fronted him much in the manner of a ruffled kitten. **1950** *Austral. Police Jrnl.* Apr. 112 *Front, to*, to appear before. 'Front' the court. **1968** D. O'Grady *Bottle of Sandwiches* 28 A man feels a galah fronting a new boss and putting the bite on him for the price of a gallon of juice.

2. *intr.* To make an appearance, to 'turn up'. Also with **up.**

1968 J. Alard *He who shoots Last* 3 Look like doin a drag wen I front tomorrow. **1968** D. O'Grady *Bottle of Sandwiches* 102, I had to front up at the office. **1973** *Kings Cross Whisper* (Sydney) cl. 6/1 Speiler Wilson and Stalky Robson haven't fronted this Saturday. The only time they've ever missed the first schooner. **1978** D. Ball *Great Austral. Snake Exchange* 36 He knew he was afraid to front up. **1982** H. Knorr *Private Viewing* 68 Now she's gone to Canberra to see her parents. So I'm going to Tassie to mine. They get a bit worried if you don't front up now and then.

frontage.

1. Used in the standard sense of land abutting on a river or stretch of water, but acquiring special prominence because of the importance, esp. in rural areas of comparatively low rainfall, of access to water. See also *river frontage*, River 1. Also **water frontage,** and *attrib.*

1832 J. Backhouse *Narr. Visit Austral. Colonies* (1843) 27 He has about a mile of frontage on the Clyde, which at this season of the year is little more than a chain of pools—called here lagoons. **1838** *Tegg's N.S.W. Pocket Almanack* 71 In general, each lot will consist of 640 acres. But if a section, with water frontage does not contain the full quantity, the section behind it will be added to the lot. **1839** 'Friend To Truth' *True Picture Aust.* 19 Unless the farmer can secure a 'frontage' to his ground, that is, a river running along some part of it, he has little prospect of success. **1845** C.J. Baker *Sydney & Melbourne* 41 The frontage on both sides of the Yarra Yarra . . has been sold by the government in small allotments at high prices. **1854** *Moreton Bay Free Press* 4/5 The Farm has a large frontage to Doughboy and Bulimba Creeks, and a permanent supply of good fresh water can always be depended on. **1870** *Sydney Morning Herald* 2 July 3/6 Profitable station, Lachlan frontage, with permanent back water. **1880** J.B. Stevenson *Seven Yrs. Austral. Bush* 126 There was a large frontage of open downs. **1891** 'R. Boldrewood' *Sydney-Side Saxon* (1925) 2 A big block of country that laid back from the frontage runs on the Logan. **1912** *Truth* (Sydney) 24 Nov. 3/6 Beautiful water frontages good enough for home sites. **1927** A. Crombie *After Sixty Yrs.* 40 Not a blade of grass . . anywhere upon the Lachlan frontage. **1936** *Bulletin* (Sydney) 8 Jan. 19/1 Nearing the hot season the emus used to come in from the north on to the frontage country and join forces in a mob of about 40. Every billabong on the 45 miles of the station's river frontage was the week-end home of a mob. **1945** *Ibid.* 2 May 12/1 The boss put me on ploughing a piece of frontage where the sheila passed on her way for the cows. **1949** J. Morrison *Creeping City* 141 Clavering came upon Smith while the latter was rabbit-proofing his fence on the frontage.

2. *Mining.* Used *attrib.* in Special Comb. **frontage claim,** a tract of land of specific measurement in front, but (initially) of otherwise indefinite dimension (see esp. quots. 1869 and 1870); **lead,** an auriferous deposit subject to *frontage claims*; **system,** the division of an area into *frontage claims.*

1869 R.B. Smyth *Gold Fields & Mineral Districts* 612 **Frontage Claim,** a claim, the lateral boundaries of which are not fixed until the lead has been traced through it. **1870** W.B. Withers *Hist. Ballarat* 126 Two kinds of claim have for some years been in existence, one called 'block' and the other 'frontage' claims. The block claim is a fixed area, with bounds ascertained from the first; the frontage is a claim with a given width on a lead or gutter, with boundaries changeable as to direction according to the course of the lead. **1871** *Austral. Town & Country Jrnl.* (Sydney) 17 June 751/2 There is not a legal frontage claim on the gold-field, as none have their boundaries defined by six pegs. **1874** *Illustr. Sydney News* 25 July 5/4 Amongst the most important measures agreed to by the Mining Board is one regulating the taking up and tenure of frontage claims. ***c* 1882** T.F. de C. Browne *Miners' Handy Bk.* (ed. 2) 18 A 'frontage claim' shall mean a claim . . in new alluvial ground (other than block claims), where the auriferous deposit is not less than 150 feet in depth from the surface, as proven by the depth of a prospecting claim or ordinary block claim. **1890** 'R. Boldrewood' *Miner's Right* 31 When a 'frontage claim' is blocked off . . anyone can take up or seize upon the 'block off it'. **1858** *Colonial Mining Jrnl.* Nov. 44/1 The Mining Board have . . under consideration a code of laws applicable to **frontage leads.** ***c* 1882** T.F. de C. Browne *Miners' Handy Bk.* (ed. 2) 11 On a frontage lead the block claim is exactly the same size that a frontage claim for the same number of miners is, when 'blocked off'. **1858** *Colonial Mining Jrnl.* Oct. 28/3 The amount of litigation in connection with this lead is great, some of the claims being under the **frontage,** and others the block **system.** **1859** *Ibid.* Mar. 106/1 The frontage system is only applicable where a gutter has been defined. **1862** J.A. Paterson *Gold Fields Vic.* 178 Early necessity and practical sagacity led to the adoption of extensive areas under the frontage system, which secured to the country a prescribed length of the gutter . . with a considerable extent of land on each side of it, the lines following the windings of the ancient watercourse.

c **1882** T.F. DE C. BROWNE *Miners' Handy Bk.* (ed. 2) 17 Shepherding in connection with the frontage system is now wholly abolished.

frontier. [U.S. *frontier* that part of a country which forms the border of its settled or inhabited regions: see OED(S 4 b. and Mathews.] An area of newly or sparsely settled country, remote from closely settled districts, esp. as marking either the limit of settlement or habitable country. Also *attrib.*

1840 *S. Austral. Rec.* (London) 19 Sept. 179 We trust that during the ensuing session Sir George and his councillors will look to the evil effects of the rum-selling system on the frontiers, which are inhabited, generally speaking, by the most lawless portion of our lawless population. **1844** *Sydney Morning Herald* 9 Apr. 2/2 The stations beyond the frontier [will] be abandoned—and the entire colony impoverished. **1847** *Atlas* (Sydney) III. 3/1 They were acquainted with the stations that had recently been formed on the frontier of the colony. **1854** W. HOWITT *Boy's Adventures* 35 We saw many of them near the Murray, on the Sydney frontier. **1864** *Sydney Punch* 2 July 44/1 Why is the Shoalhaven district like a frontier town? Because it is all Berry, and, of course, that has a resembling sound to Albury. **1876** 'CAPRICORNUS' *Colonisation* 21 Among the old stocked stations, the talk is mainly of the price of wool and fat bullocks... Towards the sparsely-peopled frontiers the topic is of new country. **1887** A.W. HOWITT *Notes on Songs* 328 It is curious to note how words are carried by settlers from one part of Australia to another, and even by wild blacks who have visited their friends on the frontier settlement. **1893** J.A. BARRY *Steve Brown's Bunyip* 51 'Yes, I'm from out back,' said a dark, wiry little man, as he dismounted from his horse at a Queensland frontier-township hotel. **1930** D. COTTRELL *Earth Battle* 97 The vast interminable gossip, which is the 'newspapers' of the outlands and the frontiers, commented upon H.B.'s madness in attempting to water lands that could not be watered. **1962** *N.T. News* (Darwin) 4 Jan. 11/5 You would think in a frontier town there would be a wide-awake dynamic spirit.

front verandah: see VERANDAH.

fruit, *n.*[1]

1. Used *attrib.* in Special Comb. pertaining to commercial fruit-growing: **fruit block,** a fruit farm; **cocky,** a fruit farmer; **property,** a fruit farm.

1939 P. MCGUIRE *Austral. Journey* 258 William stayed on at Mildura .. but the population fled and the **fruit-blocks** which had grown along the river front were falling back into the wilderness. **1947** M. MORRIS *Township* 28 The wandering air .. flowed over the fruit-blocks and the channels and the straight, dusty roads towards the sleeping township. **1980** *Southerly* iii. 336 He swept his arm around to include Wendy, the house and the fruit block. **1982** M. WALKER *Making Do* 6 When I first came on to the Murray I was six years old, and the family shifted down the river and got to Mildura to start a fruit block. **1910** *Bulletin* (Sydney) 13 Jan. 14/2 These fences are prime breeding grounds for sparrows, codlin moths and other tireless foes of the **fruit** and grain **cockies**. **1925** *Smith's Weekly* (Sydney) 18 Apr. 13/6 A grower himself.. he .. can tell the fruit cocky back home when it is his own fault that his stuff doesn't get top price. **1935** J.K. EWERS *Fire on Wind* 184 It was not to be expected that these two sons of a fruit-cocky would last long. **1968** W.N. SCOTT *Some People* 121 An old bloke up on Buderim Mountain had the arthritis so bad his bananas caught it off him, and all the other fruit-cockies got suckers from him to save having to bend by hand. **1973** H. LEWIS *Crow on Barbed Wire Fence* 81 Hugh was excited about a fruit cocky he had been having a series of talks with. **1946** A.M. LAPTHORNE *Mildura Calling* 45 'Blockie' .. originally referred to the owner of a block of land comprising ten or more acres, but is now used for smaller land-holders of **fruit properties.**

2. *fig.* In the phr. **fruit for (or on) the sideboard,** abundant riches, esp. as resulting from gambling; one who is viewed as a source of 'easy' money.

1953 T.A.G. HUNGERFORD *Riverslake* 128 He was not afraid that they would ever wake up to it .. not the poor dopes who came back week after week to buy the fruit for his sideboard. **1966** S.J. BAKER *Austral. Lang.* (ed. 2) 157 *Fruit for the sideboard*, easy money. **1968** A. BUZO *Norm & Ahmed* (1973) 8 Some of our blokes were easy pickings for those bastards. Fruit on the sideboard. That's what they were. **1982** *Sydney Morning Herald* 6 Mar. 13/7 No political party in Australia, least of all the Liberals, has the courage to stop giving public money to people who do not need it. The political consequences of playing Robin Hood by depriving the most articulate political force in Australia of some fruit on the sideboard would be catastrophic.

fruit, *n.*[2] *Austral. pidgin.* The amount of ore held by a fruit tin: see quots.

1953 J.K. EWERS *Sun on my Back* 81 When a fruit-tin was full it was taken to Dan Thompson's store where it was weighed... I asked one blackfellow who was digging for pug how much tin he got a week and he replied, 'Three or four fruits.' Thus, at Moolyella, a new standard of measurement had been evolved—a 'fruit'. **1973** J. GREENWAY *Down among Wild Men* 254 Every man Jack of the community .. had to collect every day one 'fruit' (a thirty-ounce fruit can) of tantalite yandied from surface iron with a magnet. No fruit, no bloody food for you.

fruitologist. [f. *fruit* + *-ologist* one who professes a science.] A fruiterer; a greengrocer.

1958 G. COTTERELL *Tea at Shadow Creek* 26 Mr Tontelli said that he was a fruitologist. He had several fruitariums in the city. **1958** *Bulletin* (Sydney) 19 Mar. 16/2 We have lubritoriums, fruitologists, paintologists, and now I see, in an ad. for a large department-store, a 'toyteria'. **1959** *Times* (London) 30 Oct. 13/4 In my own country I purchased fruit regularly from a 'fruitologist'. Yours faithfully, *Allen Brown*, Australia House, Strand. W.C.2.

fry. [Spec. use of Br. dial. *fry* used of various kinds of offal, usu. eaten fried.] (A) lamb's liver. Freq. as **lamb's fry.**

1847 E.W. LANDOR *Bushman* 158 The tempting savour.. arose from the large dish of sheep's fry. **1925** *Commonsense Cookery Bk.* (N.S.W. Public School Cookery Teachers' Assoc.) 42 *Liver and bacon. Ingredients.*—1 lamb's fry, ¼ lb. fat bacon... *Method.*—1. Wash liver and soak in warm salted water. **1968** E. PAGRAM *Never had it so Good* 67, I went to the meat counter and asked for a chicken and some liver. I came away with a 'chook' and some 'lamb's-fry'. **1973** J. O'GRADY *Survival in Doghouse* 47, I get a leg, and a fry, and a heart, and half-a-dozen chump chops. **1975** J. ROMERIL *Floating World* 26 Lamb's fry! I wouldn't be surprised to learn this lot came over with MacArthur (*sic*).

frying-pan, *attrib.*

a. Special Comb. **frying-pan brand,** a crudely applied brand used by a cattle thief to efface the rightful owner's brand; also *ellipt.* as **frying-pan.**

1857 F. DE B. COOPER *Wild Adventures* 104 This person was an 'old hand' and got into some trouble .. by using a 'frying-pan brand'. He was stock-keeping in that quarter, and was rather giving [*sic*] to 'gulley raking'... He ran in three bullocks belonging to a neighbouring squatter, and clapt his brand on the top of the other so as to efface it. **1916** *Truth* (Sydney) 17 Dec. 4/5 There used to be many jokes made, when Patterson was Premier of Victoria, about what was called 'the frying-pan brand'. What was meant by this was that somebody, supposed to be acting on Patterson's behalf, had allegedly added cattle to Patterson's flocks, by the simple expedient of taking other men's cattle, and obliterating the brands on them with a red-hot frying-pan. **1951** E. HILL *Territory* 310 Those well away from police patrols .. were content with the good old Frying Pan, a blotch.

b. Of criminals: petty; small-time.

1865 J.F. MORTLOCK *Experiences of Convict* 90 Some, unarmed, prowl about, watch the inmates of a dwelling away [*sic*], and then pilfer. These are called 'frying-pan' bushrangers, being looked upon with much contempt. **1966** T. RONAN *Strangers on Ophir* (rev. ed.) 46 Oh, just a frying-pan fighting man who blew in from Coronet.

fuchsia bush. [From a fancied resemblance of the flower of the plant to that of the ornamental shrub.] *Emu bush* (a), see EMU *n.*[1] 3; (*spec.*) *Eremophila maculata* (see *native fuchsia* NATIVE *a.* 6 a.). Also **fuchsia tree.**

1883 F. BONNEY *On Some Customs Aborigines* 7 His bed, made of the small branches of a fuchsia bush. **1916** S.A. WHITE *In Far Northwest* 25 It was dotted over with .. bright flowering fuchsia trees (Eremophila). **1936** *Bulletin* (Sydney) 9 Dec. 20/2 The 'fuchsia' bush of s.-w. Queensland .. attains luxuriant growth and, mixed with other herbage, has good fattening properties. **1982** M. WALKER *Making Do* 117 The undergrowth is fuchsia bush, which is quinine bush.

fuck truck. *Shag-wagon*, see SHAG *n.*[2] Also *attrib.*

1979 R.D. JONES *Walking Line* 19 The boys wearing blue singlets in their striped fuck trucks yelled & pressed down on the horns but fifi kept going. **1982** *Meanjin* 395 How did you adapt your fuck-truck style of driving to a foreign car?

fuckwit. A nincompoop, a dimwit. Also *attrib.*

1969 A. BUZO *Front Room Boys* (1970) 89 Ooh, temper! Well, ta-ta for now, fuckwit. **1970** D. WILLIAMSON *Coming of Stork* (1974) 5 'I'm a trainee marketing executive...' 'You're a fuckwit.' **1977** *Southerly* i. 48, I object to trendy words like fuckwit and avoid it even in Scrabble. **1979** *Meanjin* 464 It sounded like a load of fuck-wit shit to me. **1980** F. MOORHOUSE *Days Wine & Rage* 79 The present government consists of the finest set of fuckwits seen since federation. **1985** *Canberra Times* 25 Aug. 20/2 He had contempt for police and more than once .. had called them fuckwits.

Also **fuckwitted** *a.*

1973 D. WILLIAMSON *Coming of Stork* (1974) 152 That fuckwitted agent of yours is really driving me right off my brain.

full, *a.*[1] [Scot. dial. *fou, fow, full* drunk (cf. *full* replete).]

a. Inebriated; drunk.

c **1848** 'SICK MAN' *Voyage Sydney to S.A.* 7 We stopped, of course, at almost every public-house until we were full. **1873** 'DEMONAX' *Mysteries & Miseries* 14 Two ales with Young Cautious .. (I began to feel 'full' at this stage). **1899** *Austral. Tit-Bits* (Sydney) 18 Mar. 95/3 When 'Billy' was full he would retire to a familiar lamp post, and leaning against it sleep off his weakness, and then shaking his tail would return to the hotel for a 'reviver'. **1909** *Truth* (Sydney) 18 Apr. 1/8 Maybe you got full on swankey, Rum an' cloves, or various gins. **1918** *Bulletin* (Sydney) 1 Aug. 22/4 Two bullockies went into the township to get well shickered. They succeeded. Each man was fuller than the other. **1924** F.J. MILLS *Happy Days* 95 A drunkard appears on the screen. He is very 'full'. A deep voice, 'I'd give 'im a quid for 'alf 'is complaint.' **1942** *Aust. Week-End Bk.* 169 This bloke's not crook, he's full. **1956** E. LAMBERT *Watermen* 75 Rafferty .. seemed to immerse his nose in the beer. 'Wait till he gets full,' Len promised Hugh. **1962** *Meanjin* 326 Listen, you're too bloody drunk to drive—you're full. **1978** D. STUART *Wedgetail View* 64 He set down four bottles of muscat... 'There we are, enough to get full on, if you're in the mood.' **1980** C. LEE *Bush Week* 19 We were all pretty well full when the van rolled into Mittagong.

b. [Spec. use of, and elaboration upon, *full as a tick* full to repletion: see OEDS *tick, sb.*[1] 1 c.] In the phr. **full as a tick** and varr., extremely drunk.

1892 *Dialect Notes* I. 210 *Full as a tick*, drunk [Aust.]. Used also of fulness of any kind. **1907** *Truth* (Sydney) 27 Jan. 1/6 Unfortunate women derelicts .. can always get as full as a tick for the asking. **1909** A. WRIGHT *Rogue's Luck* 32 You was full as er tick. **1917** *Bulletin* (Sydney) 1 Nov. 24/2 Blue-bottle tick and .. bush tick .. are one and the same insect. It has a grip like the Hun's on Belgium when it first takes hold, but eventually falls off—literally 'full as a tick'. **1941** S.J. BAKER *Pop. Dict. Austral. Slang* 30 *Full as an egg (goog, tick)*, completely drunk. **1944** F. JOHNSON *F. Johnson's Laugh* 58 One night my husband came home as drunk as Chloe .. as full as a boot, in fact! **1944** K.S. PRICHARD *Potch & Colour* 175 Charley would not drink with him. 'No thanks, Joe,' he said. 'I'm full—full as a tick.' **1948** V. PALMER *Golconda* 66 Full as a tick, he was, when he come—full and trying to buy into a fight. **1959** J. WYNNUM *Down Hatch* 40 He walked groggily across the restaurant towards the appropriate door and Trunky .. noted that Dusty was making very heavy weather of it. 'Dusty's sloshed to the gills,' he grinned. 'As full as a bull,' confirmed Watts with finality. **1959** *Bulletin* (Sydney) 30 Dec. 45/1 I'm going to get full as a State school, whittled as a penguin, cacko, blind sleeping drunk. **1966** P. COWAN *Seed* 115 They reckon there's a lot of .. drinking these days. When I was your age I was full as a boot every weekend. **1970** N. KEESING *Transition* 98 Full as a boot, lad, full as a boot: Well, Christ, why shouldn't I be? **1971** B. HUMPHRIES *Bazza pulls it Off*, A bloke'd have to be full as a bull's bum to come at that!

1972 *Ten Award Winning Stories* 29 Old Cooper the accountant from Carney's was full as a boot. **1981** P. RADLEY *Jack Rivers & Me* 156 They're so full of rum if any of the . . genteeler ladies take seconds they'll get full as farts. **1983** *Daily Tel.* (Sydney) 2 Apr. 3/6 The saying 'as full as a Bourke Street tram' is soon to take on a new meaning in Victoria, where alcohol may soon be served to passengers as the rails sing by.

c. In the phr. **full as a goog,** extremely drunk; replete with food. See GOOG.

1941 [see sense b.]. **1950** 'B. JAMES' *Advancement Spencer Button* 95 Well, old Foll was in that bar, as full as a goog. **1959** D. NILAND *Gold in Streets* 147 'When'd he get in?' ''Bout an hour ago,' she lied. 'Full as a goog, I s'pose?' **1966** *Realist* (Sydney) xxiv. 18/1 Ginger was bringin' him home in the spring cart, full as a goog, been drinkin' whisky. **1981** P. RADLEY *Jack Rivers & Me* 132 We sat under the oleanders eating liquorice all-sorts. . . 'God, I'm full as a goog,' Connie said. **1982** N. KEESING *Lily on Dustbin* 140 Standard compilations of colloquial speech give 'full as a goog' as a term for drunkenness. . . Several women, however, gave 'full as a goog' as a term meaning replete with food. **1982** LOWENSTEIN & HILLS *Under Hook* 27 The seamen'd stagger back to their ships. . . I've seen them like monkeys climbing up this single hawser rope, full as a goog.

full, *a.*[2] *Obs.* [Survival of Br. *full* sated, weary of; obs. exc. in 'modern colonial slang' as *full up*: see OED *a.* 4 c.]

a. Usu. with **of**: surfeited (with), disgusted (with), 'fed up'.

1871 *Austral. Town & Country Jrnl.* (Sydney) 21 Jan. 89/2 People are beginning to get 'full' about pony races. **1880** *Bulletin* (Sydney) 26 June 3/1 The Brisbane public are getting very 'full' of bookmakers. **1911** *Ibid.* 8 June 14/1 Gilligan was about full of the shed, and wanted the sack. **1913** C.J. DENNIS *Backblock Ballads* 88 I'm full Of that crook mob!

b. Also with **up.**

1881 J.C.F. JOHNSON *To Mount Browne & Back* 17 Most of the returning diggers will be almost too 'full up on digging' to care about taking much trouble in prospecting on the back track. **1885** *Australasian Printers' Keepsake* 71 Declared that he was tired of Melbourne, 'full up of it' and would soon 'ding it altogether'. **1895** *Bulletin* (Sydney) 13 Aug. 27/1 For 12 months straight-off I take nothing stronger than billy-tea, and then I get full-up. **1899** *North-Western Advocate* (Devonport) 8 Nov. 3/1 Mr Nichols said he was 'getting full up of this sort of game'. . . He felt inclined to resign. **1910** *Advocate* (Burnie) 12 Feb. 3/1 As he was full up of the — place; he was 'not going to work his guts out'. **1926** E. MCKENZIE-HATTON *Moluscut* 38 Disheartened and weary, they were just about 'full up', but our cheery songs had helped them to 'stick it out'.

full, *a.*[3] [Abbrev. of *full-blood.*] Qualifying an ethnic designation: of unmixed race.

1879 G. TAPLIN *Folklore S. Austral. Aborigines* 125 Agnes Bates was a full native of South Australia. **1920** *Bulletin* (Sydney) 22 Sept. 13/2 A daughter . . married a full Chow. **1930** D. COTTRELL *Earth Battle* 24 Her skin darkened until she might have been taken for a 'full black'. **1945** E. GEORGE *Two at Daly Waters* 106 Micky and Nancy were full blacks and the baby was a half-caste. **1979** C. GREEN *Burn Butterflies* 18 Settled in the Barossa. Your full kraut cockie. Lutheran; couldn't speak a word of English.

full-blood. [Spec. use of *full-blood* a person of unmixed race.] An Aboriginal. Also *attrib.*

1895 A. MESTON *Qld. Aboriginals* 12 A grand total of 114 full bloods. **1912** *Bulletin* (Sydney) 30 May 15/2 A boundary-rider (full-blood) complained to me last week that his leg was very bad. **1944** A. MARSHALL *These are my People* 76, I gets a job buildin' sheds and they puts a full-blood on to help me. **1957** F. CLUNE *Fortune Hunters* 119 The word 'coloured' is used to describe those of mixed race, and 'full-bloods' to describe those of native race. **1978** D. STUART *Wedgetail View* 18 With a full-blood woman in tow, he'd be greatly handicapped. **1980** L.G. FOGARTY *Kargun* 33 The half caste says you Queensland banana benders you pie eaters and the full blood says, where is our identity going down or up. **1981** A.B. FACEY *Fortunate Life* 140 Six part-blooded Aboriginals and two full-bloods.

full board: see BOARD 2.

full forward. *Australian National Football.* Any of three players who constitute the full, as distinct from the half forward line; *spec.* the centrally positioned player. Also *attrib.*

1928 G. MORIARTY *Teaching Game of Football* iii. 4 The full forward is your goal kicker; shepherd him and play to him. **1931** J.F. MCHALE et al. *Austral. Game of Football* 66 The pocket full forwards contribute by straying right back on to the boundary line. **1936** E.C.H. TAYLOR et al. *Our Austral. Game Football* 55 The half-forwards must be very careful not to encroach in the full-forward line. **1959** PARNELL & ANDREW *Austral. Football* 45 The tall strong full forward prefers the ball to be kicked high to him while the smaller player prefers it to be kept low. **1967** *Austral.* (Sydney) 24 Apr. 12/5 Peter Hudson, Hawthorn's star full-forward recruit from Tasmania flies in front of his opposing full-back. **1973** J. DUNN *How to play Football* 66 It does not matter whether the full-forward is an amateur with a church seconds team or a VFL professional; he must get his share of goals or help the other forwards to a serving.

full mouth, *a.* and *attrib.* Of an adult sheep: having its full complement of eight incisors.

1855 Tas. Non-State Rec. 103/4 8 June, The Wethers must be from 6 Tooth to full mouth or they will not suit my purpose. **1867** *Ibid.* 103/6 30 Oct., Drop Mr Harrison a line and say that the *1000* full mouth wedders will require to be sold. **1897** L. LINDLEY-COWEN *W. Austral. Settler's Guide* 652 *Full mouth,* a term applied to a sheep that has its full complement of eight permanent incisors fully developed. **1961** J.W. JORDON *Practical Sheep Farming* 22 Four year old sheep—eight permanent teeth called eight tooth sheep or 'Full Mouth'.

full points, *pl. Australian National Football.* The six points awarded for a goal; a goal. Also **full-pointer.**

1960 *N.T. News* (Darwin) 5 Jan. 8/5 Hobson sent the ball right in for Cooper to grab it off hands and run in for a clever full-pointer. **1981** L. MONEY *Footy Fan's Handbk.* 37 *Terms for a goal.* It's full points! He's dobbed it! . . Right through the centre!

full-woolled, *a.* Of sheep: having twelve months (or more) growth of wool.

1916 *Bulletin* (Sydney) 31 Aug. 22/4 O'Shea . . killed and dressed 140 full-woolled ewes. **1930** D. COTTRELL *Earth Battle* 33, I undressed fifty-one full-woolled wethers at Sunda's Plain last month in a two-hour run! **1975** R.O. MOORE *Sunlit Plains Extended* 31 It was only a small hole . . and the whole of the surface was completely covered with dead full woolled sheep!

fummy. [Prob. f. *foumart* polecat, in standard use but also widespread in Br. dial.] A domestic cat.

1901 *Truth* (Sydney) 27 Oct. 1/7 Charged at the Water with saturating a cat with kerosene and setting poor fummy aflame. **1912** *Ibid.* 5 May 9/7 *Amy's pussy.* Peregrinating Persian Cat. *The fummy flits to Flora.* **1947** F. CLUNE *Roaming around Aust.* 99 Port Headland should be named 'Catville', judging by the scores of fummies I heard yelling there. **1959** *Bulletin* (Sydney) 16 Dec. 18/1 The fummy we inherited with the house occasionally stalks up the hill, playing at being a tiger, and returns with a young kitten-rabbit. **1966** A.R. CHISHOLM *Familiar Presence* 79 A female cat was, in schoolboy language, a 'fummy'—a useful word that does not seem to have been replaced by any single term since it fell into disuse. **1978** H.C. BAKER *I was Listening* 29 The big 'fummy' would stand up, spit defiance, then take off in undignified flight.

function. [Spec. use of *function* religious or public ceremony, social gathering conducted with form and ceremony.] An organized social gathering, not necessarily characterized by great ceremony: see quots.

1910 *Truth* (Sydney) 28 Aug. 6/1 *Frosty female function.* (National Council of Women biennial meeting.) *Ibid.* 25 Sept. 5/8 The little *friendly farewell function* extended him by a few of his friends. **1912** *Ibid.* 28 Apr. 7/7 They are to be seen at every 'hop', function, or side-show in the place. **1935** K. TENNANT *Tiburon* 61 She . . teaches sewing, runs school functions, makes cakes for school picnics. **1972** *Bulletin* (Sydney) 15 Apr. 35/2 Big pop festivals are pretty much a thing of the past in the United States at the moment. . . Local authorities are jacking up and the kids themselves are getting sick of badly-organised functions and functions that turn violent. **1984** *Tourist: Ansett Airlines Mag.* Jan. 12 This two-storey . . restaurant seats 140, caters in fine style for all functions.

funnel web. [Transf. use of the U.S. name for a spider of the fam. Agelenidae.]

1. a. Any of many venomous spiders of the genera *Atrax* and *Hadronyche* (fam. Hexathelidae), some of which make a web with a funnel-shaped entrance. **b.** *spec. Atrax robustus* of N.S.W., having a potentially fatal bite; *Sydney funnel web,* see SYDNEY 2.

1933 *Bulletin* (Sydney) 15 Mar. 21/3 Three people have been killed recently from the bite of a spider, known as the atrax or funnel-web spider. **1955** *Ibid.* 2 Nov. 12/2 A friend tells me that garden-wasps are the only known counter to funnel-web spiders. **1971** *Ibid.* 23 Oct. 20/3 'The Venomous Australians' shows doctors . . fighting to save the life of a small boy bitten by a funnel-web. **1976** E. WORRELL *Things that Sting* 24 There are several species of Funnel-webs. The deadliest species is the Sydney Funnel-web. **1978** E. SLOAN *Kangaroo in Kitchen* 154 He pulled in the corpse of the spider. . . 'Does look like a funno, doesn't it?' . . If it was a funnel web, I asked him, did that mean there were others breeding in the area? **1981** *Woman's Day* (Sydney) 9 Sept. 75/1 Another silly and misleading story has it that the funnel web leaps or pounces upon humans.

2. *transf.* and *fig.*

1986 *Sydney Morning Herald* 8 Mar. 1/8 Sydney's Most Feared Q.C. The funnel-web of Phillip Street.

furfy, var. FURPHY.

furnisher. *Mining. Obs.* See quot. 1869.

1859 *Colonial Mining Jrnl.* Feb. 90/3 The old party have a disagreement between themselves and furnisher. . . The furnisher has I believe, taken proceedings. **1862** J.A. PATTERSON *Gold Fields Vic.* 319 Deep-sinking . . brought into existence . . a class known as 'furnishers', who are now disappearing from the older fields. They furnished the machinery, or portions of it, receiving in exchange a certain interest in the company, and hence their name. **1869** R.B. SMYTH *Gold Fields & Mineral Districts* 612 *Furnisher,* a capitalist who by erecting machinery for, or otherwise assisting a party of miners working a claim, becomes entitled to a share of the profits.

furphy /'fɜfi/. Also **furfy, furphey.** [f. the name of a firm, J. *Furphy* & Sons Pty. Ltd., operating a foundry at Shepparton, Vic., and manufacturing water-carts, etc., the name *Furphy* appearing on such carts.]

1. A rumour or false report; an absurd story: see quot. 1915 (1), but see also quot. 1965.

1915 R. GRAVES *On Gallipoli* 9 To cheer us then a 'furphy' passed around. . . 'They're fighting now on Achi Baba's mound.' [*Note*] *Furphy,* slang for rumour. In Egypt the various rumours were brought into the camps by the drivers of the water carts. As these water carts were branded Furphy, it is easy to see the origin of the slang meaning. **1915** *First Aid Post: Official Organ 2nd Field Ambulance* 30 June 1/1 Furphys are scarce today owing to the Turks capturing . . our wireless. **1916** 'MEN OF ANZAC' *Anzac Bk.* 134 Wanted—man with active imagination to supply furfies to the Beach, where the supply is running short. **1917** *All abaht It* (London) (1919) Feb. 23 He who brings us wild furpheys. **1918** *Kia Ora Coo-ee* Apr. 15/2 Every time he told a tale, the boys said, 'It's a furfy.' **1918** *Aussie: Austral. Soldiers' Mag.* Jan. 3/1 A Tassie indignantly urges us to deny the furphy that Tasmania is seeking a separate peace. **1918** *Two Blues: Mag. 13th Battalion A.I.F.* 24 Dec. 3 We were asked by a reader the derivation of the word 'furphy'. In our Australian camps all we now call 'Furphies' were called 'Latrine Wireless Messages' and later 'Latrines'. In Victorian camps, water carts made by Furphy were used as sanitary carts—hence 'Latrines' become 'Furphies'. **1931** *Bulletin* (Sydney) 12 Aug. 20/4 Adelaide's morning paper has revived the furphy of frogs being found alive after having been hermetically sealed up in rocks for thousands of years. **1943** S.W. KEOUGH *Around Army* 17 One of the proudest distinctions that can be attained by one of the ordinary troops in the ranks is that of 'furphy king'. The noun is apt, too, for he holds court for those who come looking for information. **1964** G. JOHNSTON *My Brother Jack* 307

You go barmy trying to sort out the furphies that go around. **1965** *Austral. Encycl.* IV. 235 Furphy worked for 20 years in Shepparton, and it was there that he turned in a serious way to writing, first as a contributor of paragraphs and articles to the Sydney *Bulletin* under the pen-name 'Tom Collins', which was in those times a synonym for idle rumour; it was an amusing coincidence that during World War I his real name, Furphy, came to mean the same thing. **1975** X. HERBERT *Poor Fellow my Country* 26 To make a denial would be to deprive the community of one of its favourite furpheys. **1986** *Sydney Morning Herald* 8 Mar. 1/4 The Premier described the rumours of changes to the legislation as a great furphy that had got out of control.

2. A water-cart. Also **furphy tank.**

1938 *Bulletin* (Sydney) 2 Feb. 20/1 A rotund citizen up our way went to fill his furphy-tank at the creek and, with the first bucketful he tipped in, fluked a fair-sized eel. **1959** C.V. LAWLOR *All This Humbug* 171 Ungarie became accustomed to the sight of vehicles of all kinds carting water. Most of them were trucks carrying farm petrol or fuel tanks, or 400-gallon water tanks. There were also many 'Furphies' drawn by horses. **1964** P. ADAM SMITH *Hear Train Blow* 88 On the little iron tank of the furphy was a plaque with the motto engraved, 'Good, better, best, never let it rest, until your good is better and your better best.' **1971** W.A. WINTER-IRVING *Beyond Bitumen* 65 An hour to fill the Furphy, an hour home and an hour to pump it into the kitchen tank.

further-back, *adv.* Also **farther-back.** Compar. formed on FAR-BACK *a.* Also *absol.* as *n.*

1887 'OVERLANDER' *Austral. Sketches* 71 Taking up some of that wretched country further back and forming a pastoral company. **1903** *Advocate* (Burnie) 20 Oct. 4/5 The tram would . . cause settlement to go further back. **1920** *Huon Times* (Franklin) 16 Nov. 4/1 Crown land can still be bought but as it is being constantly alienated from the Crown the intending settler has, as time goes on, 'to go further back'. **1928** M.E. FULLERTON *Austral. Bush* 41 He went into the 'farther back', caught and mastered a 'brumby'.

further-out, *adv.* and *a.* Also **farther-out.** Compar. formed on FAR-OUT *a.*

A. *adv.* Also *absol.* as *n.*

1895 A.B. PATERSON *Man from Snowy River* 117 He came from 'further out', That land of heat and drought. **1905** *Bulletin* (Sydney) 12 Jan. 17/1 It is the moneyed people who ride in private conveyances Further-Out. **1905** *Truth* (Sydney) 23 Apr. 7/5 The magsman talks 'em into shout To drink and sorrows drown. There's joy because from 'Farther Out' The Bills have come to town. **1909** *Bulletin* (Sydney) 4 Nov. 13/2 Just now the Mighty Plains of Further Out are good to see. . . A Mulga mate of mine writes to say that there are wonderful expanses made yellow with everlastings and 'billy-buttons'. **1912** *Ibid.* 20 June 15/4 Back country-men . . grow to be part and parcel of Farther Out. **1915** W.J. WYE *Souvenirs Sunny South* 39 A message arrived from a mate further out, And so in response to a special request, I left Goodiwindi and rode to the West. **1929** C.H. WINTER *Story of 'Bidgee Queen* 42 When the 'further out' has known The benison of rain. **1976** C.D. MILLS *Hobble Chains & Greenhide* 122 Let's think of how they suffered On the tracks to Further Out, With a scrub-and-water ration, Through the months of blazing drought.

B. *adj.*

1908 *Bulletin* (Sydney) 9 Apr. 15/1 It's time *The Bulletin* shut down on those urban outbackers who can't write a Further-Out par without referring to . . 'Jimmie Pannikin'. **1909** *Ibid.* 14 Oct. 15/1 She used to hold Bible-classes for a week or two at a time, at mail-changes, fishermen's camps, steamer woodgetters' camps, and such Farther-Out settlements. **1937** W.R. GLASSON *Musings in my Saddle* 84 When leaving Bourke for such 'further out' and distant places as Wanaaring or Hungerford we travel northwards by a level road. **1956** T. RONAN *Moleskin Midas* 148 The big movements of cattle to settle the farther-out country were now in their closing stages.

furthest-out, *adv.* and *a.* Also **farthest-out.** Superl. formed on FAR-OUT *a.*

A. *adv.* Most remote from a major centre of population; more so than FURTHER-OUT.

1917 A.B. PATERSON *Saltbush Bill* 26, I own without a doubt That I always see a hero in the 'man from furthest out'. **1964** B. WANNAN *Fair Go, Spinner* 156 A bushman from 'farthest out' was visiting his sister who lived near Melbourne.

B. *adj.*

1917 A.B. PATERSON *Three Elephant Power* 123 He had been for many years pioneering in the Northern Territory, the other side of the sun-down—a regular 'furthest-out man'.

Fusion. *Hist.* A name given to the alliance of the non-Labor free trade and protectionist groups formed in 1909. Also *attrib.*

1909 *Sydney Morning Herald* 28 May 8/2 The Fusion. How it stands on protection. **1910** *Bulletin* (Sydney) 21 Apr. 6/1 (*heading*) The fall of the Fusion. **1911** H.G. TURNER *First Decade Austral. Cwlth.* 215 Mr Deakin's seventeen followers, including two Senators, passed a formal resolution, approving of the Fusion, by twelve votes to three. **1978** F. DALY *A to Z Politics* 63 The Liberal Party of Australia was founded by Robert Gordon Menzies in 1944. Unlike its preceding non-labor parties (Fusion Liberal Party, Nationalist Party and United Australia Party) it was the first conservative party to develop a grass-roots organization in each State operating under the same Federal Constitution. **1979** J. BARRETT *Falling In* 66 When Protectionists and Free Traders combined in 1909, their 'Fusion' government amended the Defence Act to prescribe compulsory junior cadet training.

Hence **Fusionist** *n.*

1910 *Bulletin* (Sydney) 24 Mar. 8/1 One of the worst disasters that is perpetually striking the Fusionists is the man with the long memory. **1911** R.G.S. WILLIAMS *Austral. White Slaves* 21 Brought about the downfall of the Fusionists in April, 1911. **1946** F.C. BROWNE *They called him Billy* 78 The Fusionists had selected Cole, a man notable for his good works in Glebe.

fuzzy-wuzzy. *Hist.* [Transf. use of *fuzzy-wuzzy* a soldier's nickname for a Sudanese warrior: see OED *fuzzy* 5.]

1. A name given by Australian soldiers to an indigenous inhabitant of New Guinea during the war of 1939–45. Also *attrib.*

1942 *WogJnrl.: Mag. Headquarters 3rd Austral. Infantry Brigade* 25 Dec. 2 The Fuzzy Wuzzies carried them to save their lives. **1943** *Mulga* (Alice Springs) 16 Dec. 2 He also disliked 'Fuzzy Wuzzy' as a term for Papuans and New Guinea natives. **1944** G. HAMLYN-HARRIS *Through Mud & Blood* 47 We turned under our ground sheets, well satisfied with 'fuzzy-wuzzy postmen'! **1945** G. POWELL *Two Steps to Tokyo* 220 Think of that comradeship shown by the fuzzy-wuzzies on this island. **1949** F.J. HARTLEY *Sananada Interlude* 27 The 'Fuzzy Wuzzies' carried out Ham Morton. **1974** D. IRELAND *Burn* 59 What were the little fuzzy-wuzzy girls like, eh?

2. Special Comb. **fuzzy-wuzzy angel,** one who gave assistance to Australian Service personnel, esp. as a stretcher-bearer.

1942 *WogJrnl.: Mag. Headquarters 3rd Austral. Infantry Brigade* 25 Dec. 1 *The fuzzy wuzzy angels* (By an unknown wounded Australian soldier). **1943** L.M. HANBURY *Fragments* 7 And God will be the artist, and this picture He will paint, Of a fuzzy wuzzy angel with the halo of a saint. **1944** G. HAMLYN-HARRIS *Through Mud & Blood* 63 The 'fuzzy-wuzzy angels' come over bearing the stretchers on which sufferers are lying between life and death. **1945** *Aust. Week-End Bk.* 168 Those dusky, smiling heroes—the 'fuzzy-wuzzy angels'. **1974** D. WAUGH *Master White Grass* 159 The native population, known to war correspondents and sociologists as 'fuzzy wuzzy angels'. **1977** M. TUCKER *If everyone Cared* 161 My husband . . was . . sent to Papua-New Guinea, part of the cleaning-up operations to send the Japanese back home. His praise for the 'fuzzy-wuzzy angels' was great.

G

gaff, *v.* [Br. slang *gaff* to gamble with cards, dice, etc.; not attested in Br. use after 1828: see OED *v.*[2]] *intr.* To gamble, esp. by tossing coins. Freq. as *vbl. n.*

1812 J.H. VAUX *Mem.* (1819) II. 176 *Gaff*, to gamble with cards, dice, etc., or to toss up. **1849** A. HARRIS *Emigrant Family* (1967) 329 Replenishing his funds by 'gaffing' with the settler's men he met with 'on the spree'. **1882** *Sydney Slang Dict.* 4 *To gaff*, to toss and play for money. **1888** 'R. BOLDREWOOD' *Robbery under Arms* (1937) 52 The youngsters, havin' so much idle time on their hands, take to gaffin' and flash talk. **1897** *Western Champion* (Barcaldine) 23 Feb. 5/4 The hours of idleness are devoted to the mysteries of 'gaffing'. **1903** J. MARSHALL *Battling for Gold* 25 Despite all the 'gaffing' (gambling), no more orderly or law-abiding crowd of men . . ever lived. **1911** A. WRIGHT *Gamblers' Gold* (1923) 115, I blued me cheque drinkin' an' gaffin'. **1946** K.S. PRICHARD *Roaring Nineties* 147 The racket of gaffing over the spinning pennies went on into the small hours.

Hence **gaffing school,** a group of gamblers; a place where gamblers meet: see SCHOOL 3.

1899 J. BRADSHAW *Quirindi Bank Robbery* 43 His share came to 11 . . of these new £5 notes. He answered, 'Ribuck I know what to do; I will pass them off at a gaffing school all at once.' **1909** A. WRIGHT *Rogue's Luck* 216 Ken mixed with *habitues* of gaffing schools, and the army of battlers who, somehow, exist on the sport of horseracing. **1911** *Bulletin* (Sydney) 19 Jan. 13/4 Generally we knocked off at about 5 p.m., and then to the gaffing 'school' we took ourselves 'heading them' till dark.

galah /gəˈla/. Formerly also **galar, gillar,** etc. [a. Yuwaalaraay (and related languages) *gilaa.*]

1. The grey-backed, pink-fronted cockatoo *Cacatua roseicapilla*, formerly of n. Aust. and now widespread; *red-breasted cockatoo*, see RED *a.* 1 b.; *rose-breasted cockatoo*, see ROSE. Also *attrib.*

1862 J. MCKINLAY *Jrnl. Exploration Interior* 6 May 88 A vast number of gulahs, curellas, macaws . . here. **1867** F.J. BYERLEY *Narr. Overland Exped. Northern Qld.* 3 The creek received the name of Galaa Creek, in allusion to the galaa or rose cockatoo (*Cacatua Rosea*). **1872** MRS J. FOOTT *Sketches Life in Bush* 14 The Galah parrot feeds on its fragrant petals. **1884** A.W. STIRLING *Never Never Land* 169 Flocks of rose-breasted cockatoos, called by the colonists gillars (I spell the name as it is pronounced) are to be met with everywhere. **1886** P. CLARKE *'New Chum' in Aust.* 233 Not far off a large flock of the rose-crested galar—a grey and rose parrot, well known by bird fanciers—is feeding. **1889** F. CRAWFORD *Native Companion Songster* 21 Hark! hark! to our whips, as they echo afar, And start from her nest the rose-crested galar. **1902** *Truth* (Sydney) 21 Dec. 1/7 The sunburnt residents at that God-forsaken outpost of civilisation were subsisting on stewed galah and curried crow. **1913** W.K. HARRIS *Outback in Aust.* 42 Instead of being asked whether you will have roast beef or mutton, you will have 'goat or galah' shouted in your ear. **1922** M. GILMORE *Hound of Road* 40, I have seen a galah measure distance, head on one side, exactly like a tradesman. **1931** D.B. O'CONNOR *Black Velvet* 30 The tropic sun looked down On cars as gaudy as galahs. **1936** *Publicist* (Sydney) iv. 8 About 160 miles as the galah flies. **1941** K. TENNANT *Battlers* 54 That store ain't done enough business in ten years to feed a galah. **1962** *Texas Q.* 162 The afterglow in the east was as pink as the breasts of the circling galahs. **1969** A. GARVE *Boomerang* 27 'The galah's an Aussie parrot,' Dawes said. 'Never stops talking.' **1976** N.V. WALLACE *Bush Lawyer* 124 Mobs of corellas and galahs screamed down on the waterholes at evening time.

2. *fig.* A fool, a nincompoop. Also *attrib.*

1938 H. DRAKE-BROCKMAN *Men without Wives* (1955) 103 That Rienzi. . . A black-eyed nasty-tempered galah. **1951** E. LAMBERT *Twenty Thousand Thieves* 160 Yair, and I got better ideas than some of the galahs that give us our orders. **1960** R.S. PORTEOUS *Cattleman* 201 The bloke on the other end of the line is only some useless galah tryin' to sell a new brand of dip. **1962** MARSHALL & DRYSDALE *Journey among Men* 91 A clue to the possible origin of the slang usage of 'galah'. In Malaya *gila* (pron. gee-la) means mad; hence *orang gila*, a madman. **1963** J. DUFFY *Outsville Pub* 45 'I put *all* my money on *Crazy Boy*,' he said. 'You stupid galah,' snarled Mack. **1968** G. DUTTON *Andy* 22 You two galahs chatter too much. **1971** J. O'GRADY *Aussie Etiket* 30 You would be the greatest bloody galah this side of the rabbit-proof fence. **1978** M. PAICE *Shadow of Wings* 123 A bloke feels a galah being laid up like this. **1982** *Bulletin* (Sydney) 16 Feb. 35/1 It was once the done thing . . for a galah DJ to put down country music and its performers.

3. Comb. **galah pie.**

1932 J.J. HARDIE *Cattle Camp* (1944) 31 Galah pie is not too bad! **1962** MARSHALL & DRYSDALE *Journey among Men* 169 One old country dish, and a very good one too, was galah pie.

4. Special Comb. **galah session,** a period allocated for private conversation, esp. between women on isolated stations, over an outback radio network; also *transf.*, a long chat.

1956 H. HUDSON *Flynn's Flying Doctors* 119 At the Cloncurry Base I listened in to the 'Galah Session', as menfolk call it, also known as the Gossip Session, but officially Intercommunication Between Outposts. **1963** F. FLYNN *Northern Gateway* 188 The women's radio hour, held regularly night and morning and referred to everywhere as the 'Galah Session'. It is a special time set aside for lonely station women to chat on whatever subject they like. **1968** F. ROSE *Aust. Revisited* 267 *Galah session*, a period in the day when the transceiver (pedal) radio of inland Australia can be used for private conversations between distant stations or settlements. **1969** A. GARVE *Boomerang* 26 For hours the three men chatted. . . It was Dawes who said at last, ' . . I reckon this galah session's gone on long enough.' **1976** B. NORMAN *Bush Pilot* 81 Storm clouds built up during the day and wandered around the country pouring rain on the parched land and giving the 'Galah Session' on the radio plenty to talk about.

galley. [Transf. use of *galley* ship's kitchen.] A crudely-shielded outdoor cooking fire.

1955 H.G. LAMOND *Towser* 21 A few sheets of tin made a wind-break for a fire . . which Jack and all his class termed a 'galley'. **1977** V. PRIDDLE *Larry & Jack* 8 Old Tom always used an outside fire, known by all bushmen as a galley. Just a few bush saplings supporting a few sheets of iron. That was Tom's kitchen.

gallon licence. See quot. 1880. Also *attrib.*

1880 *Act* (W.A.) 44 Vict. no. 9 Sect. 9, A gallon license shall authorise the licensee to sell and dispose of any liquor in any quantities not less than one gallon, not to be drunk on the premises in which such liquor is sold: Provided that such liquor shall consist of but one description of liquor, and be delivered and shall be taken away from the premises at one and the same time, and not by instalments, at the time of sale. **1911** R.S. HAYNES *Licensing Act* 67 Holders of gallon licenses who send round to their customers soliciting orders should be extremely careful not to hawk liquor for sale to persons who have not previously sent orders. **1928** *W.A. Govt. Gaz.* 26 Oct. 2438/1 The Licensing Court . . have authority to grant a Gallon License. **1943** *Jest: Digestion Good Humor* 46 The publican, the grocer with the gallon licence, and the shanty-keepers knew this idiosyncracy of Stingcroft's. **1953** *Bulletin* (Sydney) 30 Dec. 12/1 Thirsts were once quenched with a potent brew of hop-beer, dispensed in bough-shed shanties. Then the company employing the cutters acquired a gallon-licence. **1962** G. CASEY *Amid Plenty* 7 'Don't fergit, I got a gallon licence too.' 'I'm off the grog.' **1966** T. RONAN *Once there was Bagman* 8 He . . found me a gallon-licence store where, with the right introduction, beer would be bought a bottle at a time.

gallows. A structure consisting of two uprights and a crosspiece, from which the carcass of a slaughtered animal is hung, esp. to remove the hide. Also *attrib.*

1847 A. HARRIS *Settlers & Convicts* (1953) 159 Another convenience it must contain is what is called 'the gallows' for hauling up a beast that has been slaughtered, to take the hide off. **1848** H.W. HAYGARTH *Recoll. Bush Life* 15 What is usually known as a gallows . . is simply formed by two saplings, about twenty feet high, forked at the top, on which is laid a strong cross piece, to which the carcase of the animal is pulled up by means of a windlass. **1874** J.J. HALCOMBE *Emigrant & Heathen* 103 That universal accompaniment of a settler's homestead, the stock-yard, with the gallows at one corner. **1890** 'R. BOLDREWOOD' *Colonial Reformer* III. 50 Close to the side of the house was a stockyard, comprising the 'gallows' of the colonists, a rough, rude contrivance. **1898** *Bulletin* (Sydney) 8 Jan. 32/1 They . . took the end of the rope which he passed to them, put it once round the gallows-post. **1928** L.A. SIGSWORTH *Various Verse* 18 There's a 'gallows' out on the pine trees' fringe, with a gambrel-wire attached; I fancy it swings a dressed sheep as I look. **1955** M. DURACK *Keep him my Country* (1966) 95 The butcher's gallows stood out eerily against the rising yellow moon. **1960** *Khaki Bush & Bigotry* (1968) 222 'What'd he use the gallows for?' . . 'He started killin' his own beef.' **1977** W.A. WINTER-IRVING *Bush Stories* 8 A killing pen and gallows.

galvanized, *a.*

1. In the collocation **galvanized iron** [not exclusively Austral. but of special significance because of the extensive use of the material in Aust.], iron coated with zinc to protect it from rust, used esp. in (corrugated) sheets as a building material. Also *attrib.*

1860 *S. Austral. Advertiser* (Adelaide) 2 July 2/4 *Labour market*, Galvanized Iron Workers, 12s. to 14s. **1887** A. NICOLS *Wild Life & Adventure* 65 The store and the wool-shed . . were covered in with sheets of galvanized iron. **1898** C. BOND *Goldfields & Chrysanthemums* 23 The Grand Hotel is built of galvanised iron, which is much used for houses here. **1913** W.K. HARRIS *Outback in Aust.* 57 The place was a rambling old mixture of brick, slabs, weatherboards, and galvanised iron. **1918** R. KNYVETT *Over there with Australs.* 28 They live in galvanised-iron humpies with dirt floors. **1926** A.J. GOLDSMITH *Reminisc. Old Engineer* 5 Most of the houses bringing big rents were only a few sheets of galvanised iron. **1934** R.H. MILFORD *Aust.'s Backyards* 176 To quote Lawson: 'God may forgive the man who introduced galvanised iron into Australia—but I never will!' **1944** M.J. O'REILLY *Bowyangs & Boomerangs* 53 A string of camels, loaded with corrugated iron roofing or galvanised iron tanks. **1972** *Bulletin* (Sydney) 19 Aug. 12/3 Australia was built on meat pies, sausages and galvanised iron.

2. *fig.* In the collocation **galvanized burr,** the low, spreading shrub *Sclerolaena birchii* (fam. Chenopodiaceae) of Qld., N.T., S.A., and N.S.W., bearing a hard spiny fruit.

1934 *Bulletin* (Sydney) 20 June 22/3 Now they [*sc.* graziers] have a new pest—galvanised burr. It resembles roly-poly, but is the colour of galvanised iron. **1935** *Know your Weeds* (N.S.W. Dept. Agric.) 18 Galvanised Burr (*Bassia Birchii*) . . native to Australia. Fairly widely distributed over western New South Wales. . . The inconspicuous flowers are very numerous . . and later develop into a hard spiny, burr-like fruit. **1952** *Bulletin* (Sydney) 19 Nov. 13/3 Hundreds of acres of grazing land are densely covered by what is known locally as 'galvanised-burr', a greyish-green and very prickly pest. **1983** *Bingara Advocate* 7 Dec., Because it is a native plant, galvanized burr is, unfortunately, not susceptible to biological control by the techniques accepted for introduced weeds.

galvo. [f. *galv(anized iron* + -O.] *Galvanized iron*, see GALVANIZED 1.

1945 S.J. BAKER *Austral. Lang.* 266 *Galvo*, galvanised iron. **1973** D. STUART *Morning Star, Evening Star* 97 A canoe that you'd made with your own hands from a sheet of galvo. **1979** BAGLIN & AUSTIN *Galvo Country* 5 Galvo is an intrinsic part of Australia's heritage. **1983** *Bulletin* (Sydney) 24 May 54/2 It's clear what Utzon's Opera House needs instead of those neo-Islamic tiles is more sheets of rusting, flapping galvo. **1986** *Nat. Times* (Sydney) 17 Jan. 22/3 It was a small place .. made of vertical galvo with pitched roof of galvo.

gammon, *n.* [Orig. Br. criminal cant: see quot. 1812. Used as elsewhere but of interest because sense 2 is attested chiefly in pidgin: see OED *sb.*[4] and *v.*[4]]

1. *Obs.* Guile; deceit.

1812 J.H. VAUX *Mem.* (1819) II. 176 *Gammon*, flattery; deceit; pretence; plausible language; any assertion which is not strictly true, or professions believed to be insincere, as, I believe you're *gammoning*, or, that's all *gammon*, meaning, you are no doubt jesting with me, or, that's all a farce. To *gammon* a person, is to amuse him with false assurances, to praise, or flatter him, in order to obtain some particular end; to *gammon* a man *to* any act, is to persuade him to it by artful language, or pretence; to *gammon* a shop-keeper, &c., is to engage his attention to your discourse, while your accomplice is executing some preconcerted plan of depredation upon his property; a thief detected in a house which he has entered, *upon the sneak*, for the purpose of robbing it, will endeavour by some *gammoning* story to account for his intrusion, and to get off with a good grace; a man who is, ready at invention, and has always a flow of plausible language on these occasions, is said to be a *prime gammoner*; to *gammon lushy* or *queer*, is to pretend drunkenness, or sickness, for some private end. **1827** P. CUNNINGHAM *Two Yrs. in N.S.W.* II. 233 As the person they palm the robbery upon is always some simple country fellow, with but little *bounce* or *gammon* in his composition, he gets confused, blushes, stammers, and contradicts himself. **1830** R. DAWSON *Present State Aust.* 179 They never like to be accused of gammon. **1838** D. WAUGH *Three Yrs.' Practical Experience N.S.W.* 36 There is an immense deal of slang in the language of the country—'cove', 'gammon', 'plant', are as familiar as household words.

2. Chiefly *Austral. pidgin.* Nonsense; pretence; 'humbug'.

1837 *Colonist* (Sydney) 22 June 205/1 He replied, that he thought it was all gammon that master had told him about the Creation, for who was there who saw God create man! **1839** T.L. MITCHELL *Three Exped. Eastern Aust.* (rev. ed.) II. 79 Piper's watchword .. when taking up his carabine, usually was 'Bell gammon soldiers' .. meaning, 'Soldiers are no joke'. **1844** *Atlas* (Sydney) I. 4/3 Oh, our Governor's one who, without any gammon, Makes scarcely a secret of worshipping Mammon. **1849** J.P. TOWNSEND *Rambles & Observations N.S.W.* 100 A favorite expression is 'gammon'. When anything is narrated to them which they do not credit, they grin and shake the forefinger in the manner of reproof, and ejaculate, 'Too much gammon belonging to you, massa; too much altogether.' **1861** J.D. LANG *Qld., Aust.* 394 They threatened without executing their threatenings, and the black fellows knew well that it was only *gammon.* **1891** MRS J.I. WATERHOUSE *Bowled Out* 156 'None of your gammon, young man,' said Mr Beaumont, coolly. **1898** *Truth* (Sydney) 21 Aug. 1/3 Laying on the gammon, not with a trowel, but with a big shovel. **1922** R.L. JACK *Northmost Aust.* II. 590 Billy protested his sincerity in the words, 'No gammon-gammon no good.' **1937** M. TERRY *Sand & Sun* 211 'I'll show them it's all gammon,' Ben sang out. **1976** B. SCOTT *Complete Bk. Austral. Folk Lore* 274 But there's no gammon in this yarn, for every word is true, How maidens four waged deadly war with an old man kangaroo.

gammon, *v.* [f. prec.]

1. *trans. Obs.* To deceive, fool, or cheat (a person, etc.).

1812 [see GAMMON *n.* 1]. **1827** P. CUNNINGHAM *Two Yrs. in N.S.W.* II. 232 All these *innocent* rogues .. laugh and vaunt .. how they have gammoned you over. **1831** *Sydney Herald* 25 July 3/2 William Gammon for endeavouring to gammon his master. **1843** *Colonial Observer* (Sydney) 26 Apr. 981/2 Deceased was 'gammoned' by Chapman to go into the Brush .. to shoot paddy-melons for him. **1853** C.R. READ *What I heard, saw, & Did* 185 He being able to talk to them in their native tongue, gammons them with all sorts of stories about murders and thieves at the diggings. **1867** *Sydney Punch* 6 Apr. 150/2, I was told by the giggling maid-of-all-work that 'some one must have been a gammonin o' me, 'cos missus was gone too!' **1873** J.C.F. JOHNSON *Christmas on Carringa* 16 Oh, stow that, Jimmy .. you don't gammon Mr Verner with that rot. **1890** MRS H.P. MARTIN *Under Gum Tree* 153 He won't gammon me again, I'll bet. **1892** *Bulletin* (Sydney) 10 Sept. 19/2 Bob's gammoning the Chow .. he'll wake .. in a minute.

2. *intr.* To pretend; also *trans.* to feign (illness, etc.).

1812 [see GAMMON *n.* 1]. **1826** *Monitor* (Sydney) 2 June 20/1 Nothing but peace and fidelity marked the conduct of these good-natured, easily-pleased Tribes. We have often been delighted at the unreserved *belief of our word* .. taking what we said for truth and gospel until our foolish stockmen with their misplaced love of the ludicrous, related to them such arrant falsehoods, that now they will answer you in an interrogative tone '*gammon you?*' **1845** J. TUCKER *Jemmy Green in Aust.* (1955) 62 'Twelve months slangs.' .. 'Vot do you means by slangs?' .. 'Oh, gammon you don't know? I mean twelve months in irons.' **1847** *Bell's Life in Sydney* 11 Dec. 2/6 Mac in the street .. *gammoning* drunkenness, rocked to and fro. **1869** P.A. TAYLOR *Colony of Qld.* 11 They often gammon to be ill, but we take a whip and tickle them up a bit, and then they soon get well. **1882** A.J. BOYD *Old Colonials* 125 You'll see a dozen fellows pokin' round, gammoning to be out for a stroll. **1894** A.B. BELL *Austral. Camp Fire Tales* 101, I gammoned as I could never tear myself away from her lovely presence, and Julia believed me. **1902** *Truth* (Sydney) 4 May 7/5 You tell 'm lie—you gammon. **1916** *Bulletin* (Sydney) 23 Nov. 24/1 They arranged that he .. should gammon sickness. **1947** W.E. HARNEY *Brimming Billabongs* 7 Let's gammon we are old men and talk big. **1962** *N.T. News* (Darwin) 11 Jan. 11/4 She thought I was only gammoning. I walked away with the rifle about 15 feet and turned round. **1972** S. SHEAHAN *Songs from Canefields* 38 He never looked up at the leaves hanging dense—Gammoned a while to be fixing the fence. **1985** B. ROSSER *Dreamtime Nightmares* 68 We used to gammon hunt.

Hence **gammoner** *n.*, **gammoning** *ppl. a.* and *vbl. n.*

1812 [see GAMMON *n.* 1]. **1916** *Truth* (Sydney) 17 Dec. 5/1 He should be a good 'guffer', or, as it used to be customary to say, a good '**gammoner**'. **1918** *Ibid.* 6 Jan. 6/6 That oily, blather skiting gammoner .. sets out to give .. political advice. **1846** C. ROWCROFT *Bushranger Van Diemen's Land* III. 4 We shall have time enough to read that **gammoning** paper afterwards.

gang. *Hist.* [Spec. use of *gang* party of workmen.] A detachment of convicts under the supervision of an overseer detailed to a particular branch of public labour: see e.g. quot. 1842. Also with distinguishing epithet, as **battery, carrying, chain, gaol, government, iron, ironed, loan, penal, probation, public, punishment, respite, road, town, working,** etc. (see under first element).

1789 J. HUNTER *Hist. Jrnl. Trans. Port Jackson* (1793) 370 The overseers, or the greatest part of any gang, should have reason to complain of the idleness of any one man belonging to that gang. **1799** *HRA* (1914) 1st Ser. II. 352 The necessity of keeping up our artificer gangs for various essential purposes. **1813** *Van Diemen's Land Govt. & Gen. Orders* 14 Apr. (1814) 11 The Prisoners being now distributed into Gangs .. are not upon any occasion whatever to be taken from those Gangs, or their employment changed, but by the express direction of the Lieut. Governor. **1822** J.T. BIGGE *Rep. State Colony N.S.W.* 26 The gangs vary from 30 to 60 each; and as their work proceeds, they remove their huts, which are always constructed of the branches and bark of the eucalyptus, from one station to another. **1835** *Colonist* (Sydney) 16 July 228/3 Scarce a day passes but one may observe either one or more passing along the road from the chief gang to the detached party. **1842** *Tasmanian Jrnl. Nat. Sci.* I. 287 The dockyard gang is scarcely less laborious than the carrying, the men being frequently immersed in water to the neck while securing naval timber to the launches. **1847** 'COLONIST' *Remarks Transportation Question* 5 That great evils have been the result of the Gang system upon the convict, I at once admit. **1853** J. CAPPER *Emigrant's Guide to Aust.* (ed. 2) 13 For three days we were yoked to draw timber, twenty-five in a gang. **1865** 'SPECIAL CORRESPONDENT' *Transportation* 32 The others are .. formed into road-gangs—'probation parties' should rather be said, for the convicts are treated with no little deference, and so coarse a word as 'gang' is never used in connection with them.

gang-gang /ˈgæŋ-gæŋ/. [a. Wiradhuri *gang gang* (onomatopoeic).] The predom. grey cockatoo *Callocephalon fimbriatum* of s.e. Aust., the mature male having a red head and crest. Also **gang-gang cockatoo.**

1833 C. STURT *Two Exped. Interior S.A.* I. p. xxxviii, Upon their branches, the satin bird, the gangan, and various kinds of pigeons were feeding. **1834** G. BENNETT *Wanderings N.S.W.* I. 287 Many of the Grey cockatoos, with red crests, known by the native name of 'Gang, gang', were seen. **1851** J. HENDERSON *Excursions & Adventures N.S.W.* 96 At Shoalhaven, I saw that singular bird, called the 'gangang', grey and red, and having a crest or top-knot. **1860** *Sydney Mail* 27 Oct. 3/3 The shrill grating cry of the Gang gang. **1890** G.J. BROINOWSKI *Birds of Aust.* III. Pl. 20, The discordant grating cry of the Gang-gang .. is an experience in ugly sounds not easily forgotten. **1925** *Bulletin* (Sydney) 23 Apr. 23/2 The blacks usually named a bird from its call, and good examples are .. gang-gang (cockatoo) [etc.]. **1939** FRANKLIN & CUSACK *Pioneers on Parade* 135 The gang-gangs .. were a pest, devouring every berry as it ripened. **1950** *Bulletin* (Sydney) 18 Jan. 12/3 The only time gang-gang cockatoos are really quiet is when they are dining. **1982** R. HALL *Just Relations* 145 A pair of gang-gangs squawked cheerily, took to air scattering olive and scarlet among the branches.

gaol gang. *Hist.* Also **jail gang.** A punishment gang; one to which a convict is sentenced, esp. for an offence committed in a colony, to be confined in gaol when not engaged in hard labour in irons. See also GANG.

1796 D. COLLINS *Acct. Eng. Colony N.S.W.* (1802) II. 3 The most notorious .. were formed into a gaol gang. **1802** *Gen. Orders issued by Governor King* 6 Feb. 80 A convict servant .. is this day ordered to receive 100 lashes and remain in the Gaol gang 1 year, for gross abuse to his master. **1802** *N.S.W. Gen. Orders* 19 Oct. (1806) 7 Every Person .. will when apprehended, be punished with 500 lashes and kept in double-irons in the Gaol Gang during the remainder of their Terms of Transportation. **1804** *Sydney Gaz.* 29 July, Every Prisoner off the Store, who does not attend that Muster, will be committed to the Gaol Gang for Twelve Months. **1814** L. MACQUARIE *Let.* 20 Sept. (1821) 82 The Governor .. directed .. the immediate establishment of Gaol Gangs at the Towns of Parramatta, Windsor, and Liverpool. **1819** J.H. VAUX *Mem.* 105 My condition in the jail-gang was deplorable enough. **1821** *HRA* (1917) 1st Ser. X. 484 You are to form a Gaol Gang, who are to be worked in Irons, be employed on all the most heavy and disagreeable Labour, and always sleep in the Gaol. **1827** P. CUNNINGHAM *Two Yrs. in N.S.W.* I. 46 The jail-gang straddling sulkily by in their jingling leg-chains,—tell a tale too plain to be misunderstood. **1843** *HRA* (1925) 1st Ser. XXIII. 133 The Gaol Gang to attend at Divine Service. **1865** J.F. MORTLOCK *Experiences of Convict* 74 Punishment gaol gangs, heavily cross-ironed, worked in the stone quarry.

garage sale. [Used elsewhere but recorded earliest in Aust.] A sale of miscellaneous unwanted household goods, usu. for the benefit of a householder but sometimes to raise funds for a charitable cause.

1973 *Canberra Times* 25 Aug. 29/8 *Garage* sale, furniture, odds and ends... Must sell. **1973** *Centralian Advocate* (Alice Springs) 6 Dec. 27/4 *Garage* sale, stereo with speakers, camp stretchers .. miscellaneous items. **1979** *Canberra Times* 7 July 33/5 *Garage* sale (indoors for warmth!) .. going O/seas, everything must go. **1983** *Open Road* Feb. 12/3 Bumper sticker on a car doing a slow crawl down a suburban street: 'Caution. This car stops for garage sales.'

garbage. Used *attrib.* in Special Comb. **garbage man,** one employed to collect and dispose of (domestic) refuse; **tin,** the receptacle in which (domestic) refuse is put for collection, a dustbin.

1944 *Austral. Week-End Bk.* 108 The mule-drawn lorry of the '**garbage man**' was drawn up at the rear of the camp. **1959** *Bulletin* (Sydney) 21 Jan. 18/2, I think the garbage-man has won, by-law or no by-law. **1907** *Ibid.* 5 Dec. 15/3 Saw a number of fat sheep eating out of **garbage-tins.** **1959** *Ibid.* 21 Jan. 18/2, I left my garbage-tin inside the front fence, according to our council by-laws.

garbo. [f. *garb(age* + -O.]

1. *Garbage man*, see GARBAGE.

1953 S.J. BAKER *Aust. Speaks* 105 *Garbo*, a garbage man. **1963** J. O'GRADY *Things they do to You* 196 Putting beer bottles out for the garboes to take away. **1971** F. HARDY *Outcasts of Foolgarah* 1 There they were . . sorting their bottles at the garbage dump . . pursuing their chosen career as scavenging labourers (self styled Garbos for short). **1976** A. STRETTON *Furious Days* 149 The smelly garbo who had just been handling the animals, suddenly kissed me in front of the press corps. **1985** *Canberra Times* 8 Sept. 2/5 Garbos on the job: only a matter of time before one of them becomes a road-accident statistic.

2. Rubbish; garbage. Esp. *attrib.*

1970 *Kings Cross Whisper* (Sydney) lxxxiv. 8/3 He is alleged to have flogged the bottles to highly-placed employees of city and suburban council garbo rounds. **1973** J. O'GRADY *Survival in Doghouse* 12 He came back with a ten-gallon plastic garbo bin. **1978** R. WALLACE-CRABBE *Feral Palit* 24 Thought is rubbish, garbo, it has got no purpose.

Garden State. The State of Victoria. See also CABBAGE GARDEN.

1914 *Bulletin* (Sydney) 9 Apr. 22/2, I write from the Garden State. But the garden is a bit wilted just now . . and I start to find the *Argus* disappearing off the verandah in the arms of a northerly gale. **1946** *Vic. Garden State* (Victorian Railways Commissioners) 1 Victoria Garden State of Australia. Here is a fertile and progressive State. **1976** *Age* (Melbourne) 29 Nov. (Suppl.) 1/2 Come into the Garden State. **1982** *Bulletin* (Sydney) 21 Sept. 12/2 Victoria may be the Garden State . . but we all know what you put on gardens.

garfish. [Transf. use of Br. *garfish* the long-snouted fish *Belone vulgaris.*] Any fish in the fam. Hemirhamphidae, having a long snout. See also BEAKIE. Formerly also **guard-fish.**

1699 W. DAMPIER *New Voyage round World* (1703) III. 125 Here are also Skates . . and Garfish. **1786** *Hist. Narr. Discovery New Holland & N.S.W.* 10 The sea-fish seen here were . . guard-fish, bonatos, etc. **1827** *Tasmanian Almanack* 142 Guard Fish, 6d. **1851** J. HENDERSON *Excursions & Adventures N.S.W.* II. 204 The most delicious fish of all is the Guard-fish. It is the size of a small herring. **1865** G.F. ANGAS *Aust.* 109 The principal fish with which the colonial markets are supplied are the schnapper, . . garr-fish [etc.]. **1873** F. DE CASTELNAU *Edible Fishes Vic.* 15 *Hemiramphus Melanochir*, which is the *garfish* of the colonists . . is remarkable by the extraordinary length of its lower jaw. It is good for the table. **1901** *Tocsin* (Melbourne) 9 May 5/3 A bent old woman was . . carefully storing for her evening meal sundry dead gar-fish abandoned . . by fishermen of the previous night. **1948** F.D. MARSHALL *Let's go Fishing* 141 The sea garfish enter bays and estuaries in early summer. **1973** *Gregory's Fishing Guide* (ed. 8) 73 In our waters there are at least 18 species of garfish. **1984** *Canberra Times* 28 Apr. 13/4 We used to stand and pull in garfish with breadcrumb bait.

gash. [Spec. use of Br. slang *gash* something superfluous, extra.] A second helping of food.

1943 S.J. BAKER *Pop. Dict. Austral. Slang* (ed. 3) 34 *Gash*, a second helping of food; any surplus or residue (R.A.N. slang). **1946** R.D. RIVETT *Behind Bamboo* 93 'Gash', as the Perth boys called second helpings. **1955** N. PULLIAM *I traveled Lonely Land* 377 *Gash*, a second helping of food. **1972** W. WATKINS *Don't wait for Me* 32 He didn't have to beg the cook for left over scran—gash, the crew called it.

gastric brooding frog. Either of two species of aquatic frog of the genus *Rheobatrachus* occurring in e. Qld.: see quot. 1983.

[**1974** *Science* (N.Y.) 6 Dec. 946 Gastric Brooding: Unique Forum of Parental Care in an Australian Frog. . . The recently described leptodactylid frog *Rheobatrachus silus* of Queensland, Australia, exhibits a unique form of parental care. The female carries embryos and young in the stomach, propulsively ejecting the juveniles.] **1981** *Animal Behaviour* (London) Feb. 280 (*heading*) Oral birth of the young of the gastric brooding frog *Rheobatrachus silus.* **1983** M.J. TYLER *Gastric Brooding Frog* 1 The Gastric Brooding Frog, *Rheobatrachus silus*, of Queensland, Australia, is one of the most bizarre species of animal in the world. It is not much to look at, but it is unique in the Animal Kingdom in its habit of swallowing its fertilised eggs, converting its stomach to a uterus, and finally giving birth to fully formed young through its mouth. **1985** *Austral.* (Sydney) 4 Nov. 3/3 The bizarre mouth-breeding, gastric-brooding frog, originally dismissed as a hoax by the scientific world, is threatened by the continued logging of Queensland's rainforests.

gather, *v. trans.* To apprehend (a person) legally, to arrest.

1968 J. ALARD *He who shoots Last* 60 Da coppers might arrive any time now and gather us. **1975** *Bulletin* (Sydney) 26 Apr. 45/3 'The Limp was lucky he wasn't gathered because those Goulburn jacks are bad bits of furniture. . . ' To be 'gathered' or 'lumbered' is to be arrested.

gay. *Obs.* Abbrev. of *gay and hearty*, rhyming slang for 'party'.

1965 *Kings Cross Whisper* (Sydney) May 7/1 The mere mention of . . gay, booze-up, turn, rort, do, will have his ears pricked like fish-hooks. **1967** *Ibid.* xxxv. 6/1 *Gay*, a . . party from rhyming slang, gay and hearty. **1968** *Swag* (Sydney) ii. 38 The most important point is whether or not the lounge will accommodate a gay. In other words, can 200 people, 200 drinking, singing, fighting . . dancing, chundering people fit into the lounge?

gay house. *Obs.* [f. *gay, a.* living by prostitution: see OED 2 b.] A brothel.

1903 *Truth* (Sydney) 20 Dec. 4/8 Most serious allegations have been made . . such as the bribery of harlots in brothels. . . £40 worth of champagne having . . found its way into a gay house. ***c* 1907** C.W. CHANDLER *Darkest Adelaide* 54 He neither drank, smoked, nor gambled and made every post a winning post and, as for going into a gay house, the thought never entered his head. **1908** *Truth* (Sydney) 3 May 1/4 It was alleged that he had been taken down in a gay house for $22 worth.

gazob /gəˈzɒb/. *Obs.* [Prob. f. U.S. slang *gazabo* fellow, 'guy', itself prob. a. Sp. *gazapo* sly fellow.] A fool; a bumbler.

1906 E. DYSON *Fact'ry 'Ands* 162, I thought barrer-pushin' was er game fer gazobs? **1914** —— *Spats' Fact'ry* 51 He butted into some gazob in the street. **1915** C.J. DENNIS *Songs of Sentimental Bloke* 42 Ar! but 'e makes me sick! A fair gazob! **1924** *Truth* (Sydney) 27 Apr. 6/3 *Gazob*, a foolish person. **1966** S.J. BAKER *Austral. Lang.* (ed. 2) 135 Fools of one kind or another . . *gazob, gimp, gup*, [etc.].

g'day, var. GOOD DAY.

geebung /ˈdʒibʌŋ/. Also formerly **geebong, jibbong.** [a. Dharuk *jibuŋ*.]

1. The fruit of any of several shrubs or small trees of the genus *Persoonia* (fam. Proteaceae), predom. of s.w. W.A. and s.e. Aust., having an edible fleshy layer around the stone; the plant itself. Also *attrib.*

***c* 1790** W. DAWES Grammatical Forms Lang. N.S.W., Mān mangun tyiung, we will gather tyibungs. **1826** J. ATKINSON *Acct. Agric. & Grazing N.S.W.* 19 There are no indigenous fruits worth mentioning: the native cherry, five corners, jibbong, and others, are mere tasteless berries. **1834** G. BENNETT *Wanderings N.S.W.* I. 331 The yellow flowers of the native 'Jibbong', (*Persoonia sp.*). **1845** *Colonial Lit. Jrnl.* 13 Feb. 106/2 Just then a gay butterfly, large as his hand! On her beautiful wings sail'd along, Her colours set off by the glistening sand, And she staid on a neighbouring geebong. **1852** W. HUGHES *Austral. Colonies* 74 The *geebung* (or *jibbong*), a kind of plum . . is much relished by the juvenile population of Sydney. **1888** P.L. BUDDIVENT *Centennial* 12 New Holland's birds are mating dear, beneath the Gee-Bung tree, The Lyre birds are wooing dear, then why not you and me. **1902** R.C. PRAED *My Austral. Girlhood* 50 The geebung was not quite so nice—its fruit was slimy and rather sickly, yet not unpalatable. **1918** *Bulletin* (Sydney) 1 Aug. (Red Page), Fifty or sixty years ago the ground near Sydney in the vicinity of Centennial Park, Randwick and Botany was covered with . . geebung bushes. **1935** T. RAYMENT *Cluster of Bees* 368 The neat operations of the blue-banded bees when visiting the prickly geebung. **1978** E. SIMON *Through my Eyes* 127 The nut of the Geebung was chewed . . for teeth and for indigestion. **1981** L. MCLEAN *Pumpkin Pie* 123 He was going to look for 'geebungs', a small green berry, favoured by some, unpalatable to others.

2. *transf.* [First used by D.H. Deniehy (1828–1865), writer: see quot. 1859.] A derogatory term, app. applied first to an Australian-born person whose interests are primarily material; then (cf. 'Philistine') to one who is uncultured, unsophisticated. Also *attrib.*

1859 *Southern Cross* (Sydney) 12 Nov. 12/3 Born and bred—(the *geebung* is always a native)—where pecuniary success is with the majority, the only test of worth, intelligence, and respectability—the object of all honour and the aim of life, the Geebung's first business is to make money. **1874** C. DE BOOS *Congewoi Correspondence* 109 You know morer these things than I do, seein as I'm only a poor old geebung, as ain't up to the ins and outser politics. **1880** *Bulletin* (Sydney) 25 Sept. 4/4 C.M.G. does not and never did mean 'Crawling Multiform Geebung'. **1892** *Truth* (Sydney) 26 June 4/4 The mills owned by the geebung gods of the Pastoralists Union. *Ibid.* 7 Aug. 5/5 Some of the 'bong-tong' ladies of our geebung aristocracy. **1899** *Progress* (Brisbane) 17 June 1/1 We ain't a-gettin' frightened by the Geebungs any more! **1972** M. GILBERT *Personalities & Stories Early Orbost* 87 Some geebungs got in before us They took up every bed And when . . whiskey got to work We were bunged out in the shed.

geek, *n.* [f. Br. dial. *geek, v.* to peep, peer, spy; to look at intently: see EDD.] A look, usu. in the phr. **to have a geek at.** Also as *v. intr.*

1919 W.H. DOWNING *Digger Dialects* 25 *Geek* (vb. or n.), look. **1954** T.A.G. HUNGERFORD *Sowers of Wind* 190 There's a circus down by the dance-hall, a Jap show. . . What about having a geek at that? **1968** D. O'GRADY *Bottle of Sandwiches* 31 We had a geek at the stuff. **1981** P. BARTON *Bastards I have Known* 159 There was a lot of grass I wanted to have a geek at on the other side of a lot of hills—not only in Australia, but around the world.

gee-man. [f. *gee, v.* to encourage (the public) to patronize side-shows at a fair.] One who encourages the public to patronize side-shows at a fair; AMPSTER.

1941 K. TENNANT *Battlers* 141 In the show world a 'gee-man' . . is the man who goes out in the crowd and touts for custom with such inspiring cries as: 'Come along now. Come and have your fortune told.' **1966** S.J. BAKER *Austral. Lang.* (ed. 2) 143 A *geeman* or *amster* . . is a decoy who works with a sideshow operator to induce the public to spend its money.

gemfish. [See quot. 1974.] The marine fish *Rexea solandri*, having an elongated body and occurring in coastal waters of s. Aust., and N.Z.; HAKE.

1974 *Bulletin* (Sydney) 12 Oct. 23/2 A N.S.W. fish called 'hake' is felt to suffer by public confusion with 'flake' and is to be renamed 'gemfish'. **1976** *Ecos* ix. 4/1 Fishable stocks off the New South Wales coast that include . . jack mackerel, and possibly gemfish. **1979** GOODE & WILLSON *Orig. Austral. & N.Z. Fish Cookbk.* 74 Bought whole or in fillets, gemfish is medium oily and is best if grilled, baked, fried in batter or poached.

general store. [Used elsewhere but recorded earliest in Aust.: see OED(S *general, a.* 7 b.] A shop stocking a wide range of miscellaneous goods, usu. including clothing, foodstuffs, hardware, etc. See also STORE 2.

1827 *Tasmanian* (Hobart) 4 Oct. 3 G.W. Robson . . has . . opened a General Store, to which he invites the attention of the Public, where all kinds of Groceries will be sold on the most reasonable terms. **1834** *Trumpeter* (Hobart) 14 Feb. 352 James Shaw . . will open in the course of a few days, a General Store . . where will always be on sale, a general assortment of merchandize of every description, suitable for the consumption of private families, settlers in the interior, and seafaring persons. **1845** *Sydney Morning Herald* 25 Aug. 1/3 *Gundagai General Store.* The settlers on the Murrumbidgee, and adjoining neighbourhood, can be supplied with every description of store goods, at the above establishment, at very reasonable prices, for cash. **1854** J. CAPPER *Aust.* 88 A general 'store' whether in one of the capitals, or in a rural town, or at the diggings, presents an equally motley appearance. **1892** *Missing Friends: Adventures Danish Emigrant Qld.* 188 There was nobody at all who had anything for sale at the 'rush', and I determined to go out and build a hut and start a general store and shanty. **1935** DAVISON & NICHOLLS *Blue Coast Caravan* 32 We made some purchases in a 'general store' of the kind in vogue before country stores became 'emporiums'. **1978** K. GILBERT *People are Legends* 11, I can't get me welfare cheque no more Nor me 'dowment, the man at the general store Gits me cheque 'n me 'dowment now.

Hence **general storekeeper** *n.*

1840 *Port Phillip Gaz.* 1 Aug. 1 *M. Cashmore* . . will in a few days, commence business as a General Storekeeper in Elizabeth-street. **1871** 'IOTA' *Kooroona* 160 One was a miner, another a shoemaker, a third a general storekeeper. **1886** *N.T. Times Almanac* 125 Armstrong and Bryden, Importers and *General Storekeepers*, Stock and Station Agents. . . Full Stocks of General Stores and Station Requisites at Reasonable Rates.

general useful, generally useful: see USEFUL.

gentle Annie.

1. [Common in N.Z. from the 1870s.] A jocular name for a steep incline.

1913 W.K. HARRIS *Outback in Aust.* 108 Driving across creeks with 'Gentle Annies' (the coach-drivers and 'bullocky's' term for a stiff pull up a sandy ridge) on the other side is very trying to the nerves of elderly lady passengers. **1930** BILLIS & KENYON *Pastures New* 62 He did not tackle McKillop's Omeo track, with its 'Big Pinches' and 'Gentle Annies', but went round to Yass, where he learnt there were 20,000 cattle ahead of him.

2. See quot.

1965 *Coast to Coast 1963–64* 154 It was . . raining, that soft rain mother used to call Gentle Annie.

gentleman convict. *Hist.* A convict with either a liberal education or some training requiring literacy (acquired prior to transportation), and so fitted for employment in a clerical or professional capacity. See EDUCATED.

1830 T.P. MACQUEEN *Thoughts Present Condition of Country* 33 That most useless class, generally designated as *gentleman convicts*, persons guilty of minor cases of forgery, of breaches of trust as merchant's clerks, etc. **1832** H. MARTINEAU *Homes Abroad* 63 He was a gentleman convict;—a young man who had gamed away his little fortune, and then taken to swindling, for which he had been transported. **1833** H.W. PARKER *Rise, Progress, & Present State Van Dieman's Land* 132 The class of convicts, called 'gentlemen convicts', educated men, who have fallen from their high estate. **1837** *Rep. Select Committee Transportation* 114 Now, with regard to the assignment of those persons who are called gentlemen convicts, how are they assigned?—A great deal depends upon the description of gentleman, but if he happens to be a fellow that has been in a lawyer's office, then there are great exertions made to get him because those sort of persons are considered particularly valuable as clerks; and if he is a person of pretty good education, who can speak French and can draw, he is generally applied for as a teacher in a school. **1841** *HRA* (1924) 1st Ser. XXI. 318 Pardons granted to Educated Convicts, or to those who in the Colony are familiarly called 'Gentlemen Convicts'. **1849** *Perils, Pastimes, & Pleasures of Emigrant* 66 They seldom put these gentlemen convicts or Felon-*swells*, as we call 'em, to any hard work like ganging. **1851** J. HENDERSON *Excursions & Adventures N.S.W.* 111 Port Macquarie, ever since it ceased to be exclusively a penal settlement, has been used as a *depôt* for what are called 'specials'; that is, special, or *gentlemen*-convicts, and for invalids.

George Street. *Obs.* Also **George-street.** [The name of a major street in central Sydney.] Used *attrib.* in various Comb. to indicate an uninformedly urban perception (of rural matters).

1907 *Bulletin* (Sydney) 11 Apr. 14/3 It places us in the same niche as the George-street nomad, to whom a tucker-bag would be as much a superfluity as a conscience would be to a sweater. **1911** *Ibid.* 19 Jan. 13/4, I . . suggested that the sufferer should disguise himself as a bushman. . . Reft of his bowler hat, umbrella, boiled shirt, patent leather boots and other accessories, the George-street wattle-hunter looked the part fairly well. **1912** *Ibid.* 12 Sept. 18/3 'Machete' is but a carpet bushman, or George-street backblocker, or something similar. **1939** *Ibid.* 8 Mar. 21/2, I . . met with much ridicule from George-street bushmen.

Georgina gidgee: see GIDGEE *n.*[2] 2.

Geraldton doctor: see DOCTOR *n.*[3]

Geraldton wax. [f. the name of a town on the w. coast of W.A.] The shrub of s.w. W.A. *Chamelaucium uncinatum* (fam. Myrtaceae), occurring on coastal land between Geraldton and Perth, and widely cultivated as an ornamental (see quot. 1956). Also *attrib.*, esp. as **Geraldton wax plant.**

1920 *Jrnl. & Proc. R. Soc. W.A.* VI. 42 Geraldton Wax-plant, Ornamental shrub. **1930** H. REDCLIFFE *Yellow Cygnet* 229 Through the air was flung a bushland odour, sweet and pungent, diffused from honey blossoms of the Geraldton wax-flower. **1939** M.B. ELDERSHAW *My Aust.* 219 The Geraldton Wax Plant, with its delicate pink five-petalled flowers. **1956** F.B. VICKERS *First Place to Stranger* 152 In the centre of it grew a Geraldton wax tree. The Geraldton wax is a native that grows round the Geraldton district some three hundred miles north of Perth; and in its native state is no more than a straggly shrub, and is called wax because of its tiny, flowers—the petals of which seem to be made of wax. **1986** *Your Garden* Jan. 10 (*caption*) Kangaroo Paw . . in vibrant rust beside traditional pink Geraldton Wax flowers.

geri /ˈdʒɛri/. Also **gerri.** [Abbrev. of *geriatric.*] An elderly person.

1977 *Sydney Morning Herald* 5 Apr. 7/1 Geris (short for geriatrics) is applied by the young to anyone over 40, and has replaced 'oldies'. **1982** N. KEESING *Lily on Dustbin* 50 'Geris' are geriatric patients but *also* may be rigid and unpopular senior nurses. **1984** *Sydney Morning Herald* 3 May 14/3 Enrol now in training schemes for the care of our growing legion of gerris.

German brick. See quots.

1915 *Bulletin* (Sydney) 2 Sept. 26/4 At Niagara (W.A.) there is a township built of 'German bricks', *i.e.* clayey loam which is first puddled then dumped into boxes (18 in. x 9 in. x 9 in.), and left in the sun to dry. **1962** O. PRYOR *Aust.'s Little Cornwall* 66 The best walls were built of 'German bricks' made by placing wet earth lime-stone rubble and straw or long grass in moulds nine inches by fifteen and allowing them to dry.

German wagon. Any of a range of open, all-purpose, (usu. horse-drawn) wagons.

1934 'S. RUDD' *Green Grey Homestead* 67 The Lukins, and Miskins, and Abrahams . . for years have been sending their kids per horse, and per milk-cart and German waggon to school at the township. **1939** *Bulletin* (Sydney) 25 Jan. 20/4 The old German wagon can be included with the bullock-dray on the list of Australia's vanishing vehicles. **1945** C.A. PRICE *German Settlers S.A.* 14 The German wagon was in general use. **1981** P. CUFFLEY *Buggies & Horse-Drawn Vehicles* 102 It seems the name German waggon was applied to a range of designs some bearing little resemblance to the classic style.

gerri, var. GERI.

gerrund, gerun, varr. JERRAN.

get, *n.* [f. (orig. U.S.) *to get* to be off, to 'clear out'.] A hasty departure, esp. in the phr. **to do a get.**

1898 *Bulletin* (Sydney) 28 May 31/2 Their inquisitiveness . . compelled Jim to kill his stud-sluts and growing stock, and do a timely 'get'. **1900** *Advocate* (Burnie) 6 July 1/8, I am writing this by the firelight. We might have to 'do a get' tomorrow. **1909** M. FRANKLIN *Some Everyday Folk* 31 Thanks, I must do a get and put the pony in. **1917** C.L. DREW *Reminisc. D. Gilbert* 100 I'm pickin' your bloke to do a get first. **1957** N. ELLISON *Flying Matilda* 15 While he's explaining we do a get. **1963** A. UPFIELD *Madman's Bend* 55 Musta done a get after bashing up his wife.

get, *v. trans.* With **up.**

1. To prepare (wool) for sale. Also as *vbl. n.*

1835 *True Colonist* (Hobart) 16 Oct. 1/2 He is in possession of *valuable information*, connected with '*getting up the wool*', which he will engage to increase its value. **1845** *Sydney Morning Herald* 11 Oct. 3/1 Sheepwashing and getting up of wool is a subject which every individual in this colony is deeply interested in. **1866** Tas. Non-State Rec. 103/1, This Season of the year when the getting up of the wool . . is the Principal part of Sheep farming. **1880** J. BONWICK *Resources Qld.* 49 The latest European and American modes of treatment are in exercise, especially in the washing and getting up of fleeces. **1899** G. JEFFREY *Princ. Australasian Woolclassing* 46 Most competent Woolclassers hold satisfactory references . . from Woolbrokers, as to their skill in getting up a clip. **1916** H.B. SMITH *Sheep & Wool Industry* 90 He would have had the wool skirted better and his low sorts got up and attended to in a proper manner.

2. *intr.* To be successful in an endeavour, orig. of a racehorse. Also *trans.* in the phr. **to get** (someone) **up,** to engineer (someone's) success (see quot. 1986).

1904 H. FLETCHER *Dads Wayback* 100 When ther public fancies yer nag's chance, an' puts ther beans on, ther books gives yer ther office, an' that prad don't quite get up that time; though he runs close. **1949** L. GLASSOP *Lucky Palmer* 48 The way you bet you're up for a bundle if the favourite gets up. **1958** F. HARDY *Four-Legged Lottery* 176 Snozzle Purtell timing his run, getting up in a punishing photo finish. **1974** *Austral.* (Sydney) 6 Nov. 22/5 (*heading*) Rival owner sorry Leilani didn't get up. **1983** *Sun-Herald* (Sydney) 9 Oct. 9/1 'I can't think of one confronting feature film that has criticised our society and got up,' he says. **1986** *Sydney Morning Herald* 14 June 33/3 Virtually the last words Barrie said to me were, 'Well, we've got to get Brereton up.'

3. In the interrogative phr. **(are you) getting any?,** 'is your sex-life satisfactory?'

1941 S.J. BAKER *Pop. Dict. Austral. Slang* 124 The jocular greeting between man and man, *gettin' any?* . . draws such set replies as, *climbing trees to get away from it! got to swim under water to dodge it!* and *so busy I've had to put a man on!* **1963** J. NAISH *That Men should Fear* 82 Hey there, Hans, gettin' any, kid? **1967** *Kings Cross Whisper* (Sydney) xxxv. 6/1 *Getting any*, a customary greeting usually answered by: 'Knockin' it back with sticks.' **1971** A. BUZO *Roy Murphy Show* (1973) 103 Morning, Col. Getting any? That's the stuff. **1984** *Nat. Times* (Sydney) 6 July 5/1 The Prime Minister's informal contact runs to occasional en-route card games lasting for hours with several press favorites—Hawke plays fiercely to win—and social banter of the 'are yer gettin' any' kind.

get up. The preparation and presentation of wool for sale.

1899 G. JEFFREY *Princ. Australasian Woolclassing* 75 The small Farmer who keeps his few hundred sheep, is in no way exempt from the necessity of paying proper attention to the 'get up' of his wool. **1916** H.B. SMITH *Sheep & Wool Industry* 131 The pressing of the wool plays a very important part in the get-up of a clip. **1928** C.E. COWLEY *Classing Clip* 15 Much valuable information obtained regarding the 'get-up' of the clip for sale. **1930** BILLIS & KENYON *Pastures New* 191 Asked to advise as to the 'get up' of certain Victorian clips.

'Ghan /gæn/. Also **Ghan.**

1. Shortened form of AFGHAN. Also *attrib.*

1911 *Bulletin* (Sydney) 10 Aug. 14/2 Menzies (W.A.) . . confessed shamefacedly to two Jap laundries and numerous 'Ghan camel-drivers. **1913** W.K. HARRIS *Outback in Aust.* 21 While the 'Ghans were out one morning rounding up the camels, he put a piece of pig in their camp oven. **1915** N. DUNCAN *Austral. Byways* 107 'We used to think,' Jerry chuckled, 'that we couldn't get along without the 'Ghans.' **1923** J. ARMOUR *Spell of Inland* 62 He thought he would see what was going on in what was called 'Ghan town. The wives and children of the 'Ghans peered at him from behind doors and windows. **1938** F. BLAKELEY *Hard Liberty* 137 Afghan, Turk, or Arab, they were all 'Ghans'. **1946** K.S. PRICHARD *Roaring Nineties* 183 I'd like to see a bloody 'Ghan move me off a water hole—or washin' his feet in water I had to drink. **1950** G.M. FARWELL *Land of Mirage* 14 Our buggy jolted over the railway line, past 'Ghan Town' with its lovely mosque. **1957** *Austral. Lett.* (Adelaide) Nov. 21 Mohammed Hassen was another Ghan that bred good camels. **1975** D. STUART *Walk, trot, canter & Die* 95 Never had any time for 'Ghans as camel-men, meself.

2. A nickname for a train running on the Central Australian Railway, originally between Port Augusta and Oodnadatta.

1933 F.E. BAUME *Tragedy Track* 21 This train, once known as the Ghan, because it was largely patronised by Afghans going to the then railhead of Oodnadatta, to-day is making history. **1952** A.C.C. LOCK *Travels across Aust.* 265 The famous 'Ghan', the prince of all the picnic trains in Australia. **1955** N. PULLIAM *I traveled Lonely Land* 288, I was told the word 'ghan' is the aboriginal for smoke. If that's so, the little train is well named, for certainly it belches out plenty of smoke. **1963** SINGLETON & BURKE *Railways of Aust.* 101 Historically 'The Ghan' was the carefree, meandering son of the inland, threading its way round salt pans and creeping across the hard burnt earth of Australia's red heart on the 757 miles from Port Augusta to Alice Springs. **1965** *Advertiser* (Adelaide) 30 Mar. 4/7, I claim to be the first person to name the 'Ghan' the Afghan Express. I was a porter at Quorn station the first morning the train ran. There were very few passengers, but among them were two big Afghans wearing native dress. I made the remark that it should have been called the Afghan Express, and ever after that morning it became known as the 'Ghan'. **1975** B. FULLER *Ghan* 3 Later, when a passenger through-train began running to Alice Springs, this became known as 'The Flash Ghan'. **1979** D. LOCKWOOD *My Old Mates & I* 127 The 'Ghan, the marvellous old train named after the Afghan camel teamsters. **1984** *Austral.* (Sydney) 16 Jan. 1/3 The Ghan, which operates between Adelaide and Alice Springs, has been cancelled until further notice.

ghilgai, var. GILGAI.

ghittoe /ˈgɪtoʊ, ˈdʒɪtoʊ/. Also variously, as **jhitu, jidu, jitto.** [a. Dyirbal and Warrgamay *jidu.*] Either of the two rainforest tree species of the genus *Halfordia* (fam. Rutaceae) of N.S.W., Qld., New Guinea, and New Caledonia, yielding a tough and flexible timber easily burnt when green; the wood of these trees. See also *kerosene wood* KEROSENE 2.

1909 F.M. BAILEY *Comprehensive Catal. Qld. Plants* (ed. 2) 81 Halfordia scleroxyla. . . Kerosene-tree, 'Ghittoe' of Herberton natives. **1927** *Bulletin* (Sydney) 17 Mar. 24/2 Contract scrubfallers usually stipulate that all jhitu may be left standing. **1930** V. KENNEDY *By Range & River* 73 Ghittoe for the making of fishing rods. **1945** J. DEVANNY *Bird of Paradise* 24 The wood was that remarkable product known variously among bushmen as jitter, jitto and ghito. So saturated with resin is it that when splinters were laid upon the wet mud and a match put to them they flamed up instantly. **1984** B. DIXON *Searching for Aboriginal Lang.* 86 A special long stick called *gugulu* . . was made from the hard Jidu tree (*Halfordia scleroxyla*) carefully shaped and polished smooth.

ghost. See quot. 1967.

1967 *Kings Cross Whisper* (Sydney) xxxv. 6/1 *Ghost*, a creditor. One who haunts for repayment. Usually publicans and bookies. **1968** J. ALARD *He who shoots Last* 87 Ruffy asked: 'Why d'ya calls people wot ya owes money ta ghosts, Ragged?' 'Because I always get such a nasty fright when one appears in view.'

ghost gum. The tree of n. Aust. *Eucalyptus papuana* (fam. Myrtaceae), the bark of which is smooth and white. See also *desert gum* DESERT, WHITEWASH GUM.

1935 H.H. FINLAYSON *Red Centre* 32 The most beautiful picture of the Central vegetation . . is of the dainty ghost gums with chalk-white stems. **1946** A. THURIAN *Bush Tea & Overlanders* 18 The ghost-gums shine like silver and stretch their spectral arms. **1955** N. PULLIAM *I traveled Lonely Land* 351 The ghost gums along the bone-dry river courses were so startlingly white they looked almost phosphorescent in the blistering heat. **1979** J. JOST *Kangaroo Court* 29 An area shaded by the thin, olive-grey leaves of an unusually large white-trunked ghost gum.

giant, *a.* Used as a distinguishing epithet in the names of flora and fauna: **giant earthworm,** any of several long earthworms, esp. *Megascolides australis* of Gippsland, Vic.; **lily,** see GIGANTIC LILY; **perch,** the n. Austral. fish *Lates calcarifer* (see BARRAMUNDI a.); **stinging tree,** the large rainforest tree *Dendrocnide excelsa* (fam. Urticaceae) of N.S.W. and Qld., bearing large, heart-shaped leaves covered with virulent stinging hairs; formerly **nettle (tree).**

1886 F. COWAN *Aust.* 18 The **Giant Earthworm**: six feet long: the Anaconda of the Annelids. **1977** *Austral. Encycl.* II. 305 Claimed to be the world's largest [earthworm] is the Gippsland giant earthworm, *Megascolides australis*, which has reached a length of about 3.7 metres. **1896** F.G. AFLALO *Sketch Nat. Hist. Aust.* 214 The . . **Giant Perch** (*Oligorus gigas*) of the Fitzroy . . is one of the finest of . . perches. **1906** D.G. STEAD *Fishes of Aust.* 25 At least two other fishes in Queensland, viz.: the Giant Perch and the Lung-fish, are also known in parts by the name of Barramundi. **1962** MARSHALL & DRYSDALE *Journey among Men* 103 There was not much use setting a night line for the giant perch, the so-called barramundi, with so many small crocodiles about. **1980** H.W. CUMMINGS *Confessions of 'Mud Skipper'* 237 The local name 'Barramundi' refers to the Giant Perch (lates Calcarifer). **1836** [**giant stinging tree**] J. BACKHOUSE *Narr. Visit Austral. Colonies* (1843) 363 In the forests, the Giant Nettle, *Urtica gigas*, forms a large tree. **1886** F. COWAN *Aust.* 16 The Giant Nettle-tree: a hive of bees in every leaf. **1909** *Emu* VIII. 252 Got badly stung on the face by the giant or large-leaved stinging-tree. **1938** C.T. WHITE *Princ. Bot. Qld. Farmers* 157 The Giant Stinging Tree (*Laportea gigas*) attains the dimensions of a very large tree.

gibber /ˈgɪbə/. Formerly also **gibba.** [a. Dharuk *giba.* See also KIPPER *n.*[1]]

1. A stone; a rock or mass of stone; a boulder. In early use applied chiefly to a large outcrop of rock or boulders (see quots. 1833, 1847, 1850 and GIBBER-GUNYAH); now used spec. for *gibber-stone*, and colloq. for a stone of any size. Also *attrib.*

1790 D. SOUTHWELL Corresp. & Papers, *Kee-bah*, a stone. **1833** *Currency Lad* (Sydney) 13 Apr. 2 As the hour appointed for the combat approached, all the 'lads' from the 'gibbers [*sc.* The Rocks, a district of Sydney] and Cockle-bay' repaired to a spot in the latter place where the mill was to '*come off*'. **1847** A. HARRIS *Settlers & Convicts* (1953) 87 Under the 'gibbers' (overhanging rocks) of the river. **1850** *Australasian Sporting Mag.* 92 The great velocity and ease with which these creatures [*sc.* rock wallabies] ascend or descend the huge gibbas, is truly astonishing. **1874** C. DE BOOS *Congewoi Correspondence* 11 Like a footsore horse picking his way amongst the ghibers on a stony range. **1887** S. NEWLAND *Far North Country* 7 For twelve miles the country may be described as stones with some soil still left in the crevices. . . 'Gibbers' they are called in New South Wales and Queensland. **1895** *Bulletin* (Sydney) 21 Dec. 14/2 They crippled a policeman, laid out a local citizen with a large 'gibber' in the waistcoat. **1907** *Truth* (Sydney) 24 Feb. 12/4 It isn't every man who can kill an infuriated bull with a gibber. **1924** HORNE & AISTON *Savage Life Central Aust.* 2 The sand blow polishes the coppery-looking surface until it is far smoother than any water-worn stone would be. Gibber or 'gibba' is the name given by the blacks and adopted by the whites for these stones, and 'the gibbers' is the term used to denote the wind-swept plains. **1933** F.E. BAUME *Tragedy Track* 55 That low, red, stony patch, with streaks of gibbers radiating from it, is the beginning of 'The Granites'. **1945** M. RAYMOND *Smiley* 66 He reached for a stone. 'Don't chuck any gibbers!' shouted Smiley. **1966** B. BEAVER *You can't come Back* 81 No harm in that, I thought . . kill two sparrows with one gibber. **1973** A. BURNETT *Wilful Murder in Outback* 41 We reached the gibber lands at the dog proof fence. **1979** *Southerly* iii. 275 The next stone was plain, what the schoolboys of my generation called simply a 'gibber'.

2. Special Comb. **gibber country, plain,** an arid stony area of low relief in which the stones sometimes form a surface layer; **stone,** a rounded, weather-worn stone, usu. siliceous, of arid, inland Australia.

1894 *Argus* (Melbourne) 1 Sept. 4/2 Our track led across what is called the **gibber country.** **1897** *Tocsin* (Melbourne) 23 Dec. 6/2 We went about twenty miles further, through, first, sandy, and then 'gibber' country. **1909** F.E. BIRTLES *Lonely Lands* 221 At Charlotte Waters I was out on to the 'gibber' country; big, open, stony plains stretched away as far as the eye could see—the 'Stony Desert' of the early explorers. **1944** C. FENNER *Mostly Austral.* 97 Among other interesting features of the gibber country are the sandhills. **1956** H. HUDSON *Flynn's Flying Doctors* 210 We came to Gibber country, wide extended treeless plains covered with millions of stones about the size of human heads. **1963** S. MUSSEN *Beating about Bush* 94 We came to the gibber country, like an ocean of small red pebbles. Not a tree, not a bush, not a blade of grass. **1968** J. O'GRADY *Gone Troppo* 146 Wild white horses that gallop on the sea. . . I'd sooner ride a camel in the gibber countree. **1896** B. SPENCER *Rep. Horn Sci. Exped. Central Aust.* I. 12 Nothing could be more desolate than a **gibber plain** when everything is bare and dry, and the outline of the distant horizon is indistinct with the waves of heated air. **1914** S.A. WHITE *Into Dead Heart* 55 All that remained would be the bare gibber plain. **1932** I.L. IDRIESS *Flynn of Inland* (1965) 1 A gibber plain bearded with tufts of spinifex. **1944** C. FENNER *Mostly Austral.* 96 The characteristic gibber (boulder) plains and the tent-hills of this part of South Australia. **1983** *Open Road* Aug. 19/1 There's also a good variety of flora and fauna, and fascinating country, ranging from gibber plains to swamps. **1914** *Emu* XIV. 99 The table-land country . . is covered with loose **gibber stones.** **1932** I.L. IDRIESS *Flynn of Inland* (1965) 127 The country is strewn with gibber stones and suggests a gigantic cobble pavement. **1962** I. SOUTHALL *Woomera* 39 Polished gibber stones as small as peas, as large as pumpkins and as huge as barrels.

gibber-gunyah /gɪbə-ˈgʌnjə/. [f. GIBBER + GUNYAH.] A shallow cave used as a dwelling or for shelter; *rock shelter*, see ROCK *n.* 3.

1836 *Tegg's Monthly Mag.* (Sydney) I. 136, I found the shepherd . . safely ensconced from the scorching heat of the sun under the shade of a commodious *gibba gunya.* **1847** G.F. ANGAS *Savage Life & Scenes* II. 271 Caves, formed by projecting masses of rock, called by the natives 'Giber Gunyah'; *i.e.* stone or rock house. **1849** A. HARRIS *Emigrant Family* (1967) 268 It was one of the class of natural excavations called, in the phrase of the colony, Ghibber Gunyahs. **1863** R.W. VANDERKISTE *Lost—but not for Ever* 210 Our home is the gibber-gunyah, Where hill joins hill on high. **1893** *Trans. & Proc. R. Soc. S.A.* XVII. 21 Cave-shelter, or *Gibber-gunyah* hearths. **1947** *Bulletin* (Sydney) 11 June 28/3, I came on a gibber-gunyah at the foot of Dark Gully.

gidday, var. GOOD DAY.

gidgee /ˈgɪdʒi/, *n.*[1] Chiefly *W.A.* Also **gidgie,** etc. [a. Nyungar *giji.*] An Aboriginal spear. Also as *v. trans.* (see quots. 1847 and 1979).

1845 J. BRADY *Descr. Vocab. Native Lang. W.A.* 21 *Gidji*, a spear. **1847** E.W. LANDOR *Bushman* 191 He *gidgied* Womera through the back, because Womera had *gidgied* Domera through the belly. **1857** W.S. BRADSHAW *Voyages* 107 Their war weapons are of three kinds, a spear or gigie, the kilie or bomerang. **1878** *Catal. Objects Ethno-Typical Art Nat. Gallery, Melbourne* 46 *Gid-jee*, hardwood spear, with fragments of quartz set in gum on two sides and grass-tree stem. Total length, 7 feet 8 inches. **1960** H.H. WILSON *Where Wind's Feet Shine* 31 Joe knew all about fish, and could throw a gidgie quicker'n you could see! **1965** C. JOHNSON *Wild Cat Falling* 12 What say we catch gilgies? I've got a gidgee hidden down the river bank. **1979** H. WILSON *Skedule* 192 Mr Brent gidgied a section of bakewell tart which had bounced off his plate. **1983** *West. Austral.* (Perth) 17 Dec. 3/4 A boy was rushed to hospital yesterday afternoon with the head of a three-pronged spear embedded in his stomach. . . He accidentally fell on a 'gidgee'.

gidgee /ˈgɪdʒi/, *n.*[2] Formerly also **gidgea, gidyea,** etc. [a. Wiradhuri (and related languages) *gijir.*]

1. Any of several trees of the genus *Acacia* (fam. Mimosaceae) of drier inland Aust., esp *A. cambagei*, the foliage of which at times emits an odour often considered disagreeable; the wood of these trees. Also *attrib.*

1862 W. LANDSBOROUGH *Jrnl. Exped. from Carpentaria* 73 Western wood acacia . . is called gidya in some places of Australia. **1887** S. NEWLAND *Far North Country* 8 Hanging myself in a gidea tree. **1892** *Bulletin* (Sydney) 28 May 18/2 The gidya ripped your moleskins, and the mulga rent your shirt. **1898** *Ibid.* 8 Jan. 14/1 Gidgea tea . . gives you the 'barcoo' for a week after. **1901** *Proc. Linnean Soc. N.S.W.* XXVI. 326 About half-way between Condobolin and Dandaloo it [*sc. Acacia Oswaldi*] is known by some as Gidgea, its value for stockwhip handles having probably caused it to be confused with the Bourke species of the same name, *A. Cambagei*, which is famous over most parts of the colony among stockmen. **1908** C.H.S. MATTHEWS *Parson in Austral. Bush* 244 'Gidgea'—a tree which in damp weather has a peculiar odour, rather more offensive than that of boiling cabbages. **1917** *Birth* Nov. 1 A wurley built of gidgea boughs and wheat bags on the bank of a dry creek in Central Australia. **1929** K.S. PRICHARD *Coonardoo* (1961) 151 Gidgee, round, dark-green and glossy-leafed. **1936** F. CLUNE *Roaming round Darling* 177 Harry says gidgee is a barometer. 'Always smells when the rain is in the offing.' **1948** C.P. MOUNTFORD *Brown Men & Red Sand* 8 Spotted round the flats were some picturesque stands of gidya trees (*Acacia cambagei*). **1949** H.G. LAMOND *White Ears* 1 The perpetual gidyea . . covered the whole of Western Queensland. **1955** *Bulletin* (Sydney) 18 May 13/1 Gidgee-wood gives off terrific heat and produces fierce red coals, which should be used sparingly when cooking in a camp-oven. **1956** A.C.C. LOCK *Tropical Tapestry* 108 'Is that gidgee or boree?' Hobbs pointed to a tree. 'Gidgee,' Alan replied. 'Anything that looks like gidgee out here you call gidgee. It makes no difference.' **1967** E. HUXLEY *Their Shining Eldorado* 316 A dead-flat plain dotted with thickets of twisty-trunked, untidy little gidyea trees. **1979** D.R. STUART *Crank back on Roller* 158 No mulga, no gidgee . . not a bloody thing for a camel.

2. With distinguishing epithet, as **Georgina gidgee,** the small tree *A. georginae* of e. N.T. and the Georgina R. basin in n.w. Qld., sometimes poisonous to stock.

1900 *Proc. Linnean Soc. N.S.W.* XXV. 596 There is an Acacia with a strong smell . . on the Georgina River, and evidently to distinguish it from the original Gidgea (or Gidgee as it is often spelt) of Bourke to Charleville this tree is called Georgina Gidgee (*Acacia georginae*). **1975** *Bulletin* (Sydney) 18 Jan. 48/3 Several thousand cattle die every year in the Northern Territory and north-west Queensland after eating a shrub called Georgina gidyea, or gidgee.

gig, *v.* [Br. dial. *gig* to laugh in a suppressed manner, to laugh at, taunt: see OED *v.*[4]]

a. *trans.* To mock or make fun of (a person); to stare mockingly at (a person). Also *intr.* and as *vbl. n.*

1891 *Truth* (Sydney) 15 Mar. 2/1 His name was written as co-respondent, and the judge rebuked him . . and the people gigged him. **1916** *Ibid.* 5 Mar. 12/7 It was deemed advisable to have her appear in court in woman's dress, so as to avoid having her 'gigged at' by the police and pressmen. **1919** *Aussie: Austral. Soldiers' Mag.* Jan. 2/2 The cook's mate had seen five deer there. . . Gunner visioned himself dragging home a good fat buck. What a gutzer it would be for those who'd gigged him! **1924** 'S. RUDD' *Me an' Son* 238 He was always giggin' me when I was shearin' against him. **1953** R. PARK *Power of Roses* 164 A girl don't want people giggin' her when she's just starting to branch out. **1963** J. POLLARD *Austral. Surfrider* 31 They don't usually try to catch waves as big as the best boy board riders, and sometimes receive a little 'gigging' from the boys. **1972** D. IRELAND *Flesheaters* 108 'Are you gigging me?' 'Never. I wouldn't do that.'

b. *intr.* To stare.

1967 K. TENNANT *Tell Morning This* 393 'Let's have some light on it,' his host muttered. 'Can't waste our whole bloody life gigging out windows.' **1959** S.J. BAKER *Drum* 112 *To gig (at)*, to stare.

gig, *n.*[1] [f. prec.]

a. An inquisitive look.

1924 C.J. DENNIS *Rose of Spadgers* 65 'Is this 'ere coot,' I arsts, 'well knowed to you?' The parson takes another gig. 'Why yes.' **1949** J. MORRISON *Creeping City* 8 You pay sixpence to go in and have a gig at his fern-gully and fishponds and smoodging nooks. **1965** J. O'GRADY *Aussie Eng.* 42 'Gig' is also heard sometimes in the sense of 'look'. For example, 'Have a gig at this.' **1978** C. GREEN *Sun is Up* 37 We drove out through the back gate and down the road to 'get a gig at it'.

b. [Cf. FIZGIG.] One who pries; a busybody.

1953 K. TENNANT *Joyful Condemned* 70 She hadn't asked him to bring any women poking about. This was her flat until Julie came out of gaol. 'Just gigs,' Rene commented silently. 'Slumming.' **1967** *Kings Cross Whisper* (Sydney) xxxv. 6/1 *Gig*, stickybeak. **1975** LATCH & HITCHINGS *Mr X* 147 The bloke's mate had been what the crims called a gig—and had gone along for a look at a robbery he knew his brother would be involved in. **1975** *Bulletin* (Sydney) 26 Apr. 46/2 There were Mortons nearby (Morton Bay Figs; gigs, meaning busybodies). **1984** *Ibid.* 19 June 69/1 Fifty percent of the Drug Squad's arrests are based on information received and woebetide a user, supplier or anyone else who becomes a dog, a gig or as the police term it, a Moreton Bay.

gig, *n.*[2] [Br. dial. *gig* a fool, a singular character: see EDD *sb.*[4] and OED *sb.*[1] 5.] A fool, a figure of fun.

1943 J. DEVINE *Rats of Tobruk* 31 We had a saying that any one who did anything so silly as to get caught by a booby trap was a 'gig'. **1945** *Chocolate & Green* (Sydney) July 50 The brainium contains the brain, if any, but in the case of 'gigs' . . may be a complete vacuum. **1954** *Coast to Coast 1953–54* 172 A man? Why, he was just an old gig. Like one of those silent squirts that hang round lanes on betting days and pimp to the jacks for a plug of tobacco. **1967** *Kings Cross Whisper* (Sydney) xxxvii. 6/1 You reckon you're not the one who makes a gig of himself with a skinful of slops. **1968** D. O'GRADY *Bottle of Sandwiches* 46, I felt a bit of a gig not having any bait. **1977** R. BEILBY *Gunner* 235 Blokes . . making gigs of themselves all over the Middle East. **1984** W.W. AMMON et al. *Working Lives* 83 They'll laugh and talk about it till everybody knows what a hopeless gig I am.

gigantic lily. The plant *Doryanthes excelsa* (fam. Agavaceae) of N.S.W. coastal forests and heathlands, bearing a large red flowerhead on a scape 2 to 4 m. tall; the related *D. palmeri* of n. N.S.W. and s. Qld., bearing red-brown flowers on an elongated panicle. Also **giant lily.**

1813 *N.S.W. Pocket Almanack* 49 The Dorianthus, or Gigantic Lily . . begins to flower about the latter end of September . . and continues . . 120 days from the first bursting of the bud. **1829** R. MUDIE *Picture of Aust.* 156 The gigantic lily . . well merits its name; for though it has all the habits of a lily, it is eighteen or twenty feet high. **1846** *Bell's Life in Sydney* 12 Sept. 3/4 Here proudly luxuriates the queen of Australia's flora, as if scorning to breathe the air of any other than that of her native soil—the doryanthes excelsa, or gigantic lily. **1871** *Austral. Town & Country Jrnl.* (Sydney) 1 July 12/1 The Australian gigantic or torch lily, which bears an immense head of crimson flowers on a stout stem about fifteen feet in height. **1914** H.M. VAUGHAN *Australasian Wander-Yr.* 71 A magnificent flowering plant that can be observed amongst the gorges of the National Park or the Bulli Pass, is the Giant Australian Lily. **1933** C.W. PECK *Austral. Legends* (ed. 2) 22 One of the most wonderful of Australian flowers is the New South Wales variety of Gymea or Gigantic Lily. **1942** C. BARRETT *Austral. Wild Flower Bk.* 64 Giant lilies are related to the aloes, and the big, bright-green leaves, each a mass of fibre, are much like those of some aloes. **1956** T.Y. HARRIS *Naturecraft in Aust.* 237 Totally Protected Native Plants Banned from Sale in New South Wales. . . Northern Giant Lily—*Doryanthes palmeri.*

giggle.

1. Used *attrib.* in Special Comb. **giggle house,** a psychiatric hospital; also *fig.*; **juice,** intoxicating liquor.

1919 W.H. DOWNING *Digger Dialects* 26 **Giggle-house**, lunatic asylum. **1943** *Troppo Tribune* (Mataranka) 10 May 2 Holds the belt as being the greatest 'log' in the 'Giggle House'. **1955** D. NILAND *Shiralee* 28 What a ratbag situation, what a story to make the hens in the giggle-house laugh. **1975** J. GIBBS *Bitch called Tracy* 172 Zelma decided she had better have it out with Bob so that they could complete the trip without all ending up in the gigglehouse. **1978** W. LOWENSTEIN *Weevils in Flour* 174 The Giggle House, an old asylum . . became a famous place for travelling unemployed. **1982** *Weekend Austral. Mag.* (Sydney) 27 Nov. 14/5 The classic story of that beautiful poet, John Clare, who had himself locked up in the giggle-house for nearly a quarter of a century. **1940** *Action Front: Jrnl. 2/2 Field Regiment* Oct. Ode to Beer . . o **giggle juice** divine! **1944** *Biscuit Bomber Weekly: Mag. 1st Austral. Air Maintenance Co.* 18 Nov. 1 Trust Blue to get amongst the giggle-juice!

2. Used *attrib.* in Comb. with nouns denoting items of (often ill-fitting) clothing issued as fatigue dress to personnel of the Australian army during the war of 1939–45: **giggle frock, hat, pants, suit.** Cf. GLAMOUR.

1940 *Action Front: Jrnl. 2/2 Field Regiment* 1 Apr. 4 That extra-large Giggle hat. **1940** *Men may Smoke* (Sydney) Dec. 17 Having just struggled into my giggle pants. **1941** *Argus* (Melbourne) 15 Nov. (Suppl.) 1/3 Throughout Australia one of the best Australian slang words of the war has now become 'official'—the 'gigglesuit'. **1943** H.E. BEROS *Fuzzy Wuzzy Angels* 62 No one would believe that a man could be low enough to pinch a giggle hat. **1943** *Georges Gaz.* (Melbourne) Nov. 6 The giggle frock which our Lieutenant had graciously lent me. **1943** S.W. KEOUGH *Around Army* 63 The new recruit has got into his giggle suit, turned up the spare 18 inches of sleeves and legs. **1963** J. O'GRADY *Things they do to You* 29, I was one of the smartest privates ever to wear a giggle-suit. **1975** S. O'LEARY *To Green Fields Beyond* 12 Chrysalis soldiers in their ill-fitting giggle suits and floppy cloth hats.

gilgai /ˈgɪlgaɪ/. Also **ghilgai, gilgie.** [a. Wiradhuri and Kamilaroi *gilgaay*.] **a.** Terrain of low relief on a plain of heavy clay soil, characterized by the presence of hollows, rims, and mounds, as formed by alternating periods of expansion during wet weather and contraction (with deep cracking) during hot dry weather; DEBIL DEBIL 2; DEVIL DEVIL 2. **b.** A hole or hollow in such terrain; *melon hole*, see MELON 1; also **gilgai hole.** See also BAY OF BISCAY, CRABHOLE, *dead men's graves* DEAD 1.

1867 F.J. BYERLEY *Narr. Overland Exped. Northern Qld.* 44 The party camped on a small tea-tree 'Gilgai', or shallow water-pan. **1881** W.E. ABBOTT *Notes Journey on Darling* 12 At the blackfellows' tanks the clay excavated is still seen beside the waterholes, while in the gilgies there is no appearance of any embankment, the ground all round being perfectly level. **1897** J.J. MURIF *From Ocean to Ocean* 163 'Gilguy' denotes small patches of mixed 'Biscay' and 'devil-devil' ground—possibly dried up clay pans. **1898** *Bulletin* (Sydney) 1 Jan. 3/2 Slowly o'er the salt-bush ridges see the moving cattle feed; Ne'er a gilgi-hole they break for, not a clay-pan do they heed. **1900** *Ibid.* 9 June 14/3 Gilgai is the name given to a hole, or collection of holes (found in brigalow scrubs more especially). They are filled with water in a wet season, and will hold for a considerable time. **1911** E.J. BRADY *Bells & Hobbles* 34 A-plunging through the gilgas, a-ploughing up the track. **1922** V. PALMER *Boss of Killara* 117 A swarm of finches fluttered around a dried-up gilgai, seeking water. **1942** F. CLUNE *Last of Austral. Explorers* 101 Gough Senior went for water to some gilgie holes, farther down the creek. **1944** C. FENNER *Mostly Austral.* 102 The depressions are mis-called 'crabholes'. . . Apparently the aborigines recognised them, for the name 'gilgais' has long been applied thereto. **1949** H.G. LAMOND *White Ears* 56 Every ghilgai was full; every creek was running. **1952** *Bulletin* (Sydney) 21 Jan. 13/3 The rain came. Before it, the gilgai holes were dry, dusty depressions. Within a week they were fairly teeming with small black and brown crabs. **1964** T. RONAN *Packhorse & Pearling Boat* 157 It was just dark when the old packhorse floundered into a gilgai (small billabong). **1977** J.A. MABBUTT *Desert Landforms* 131 The Australian Aboriginal word *gilgai*, for a small waterhole, has been applied to various forms of hummocky microrelief on clay-rich soils. **1982** BARKER & GREENSLADE *Evol. Flora & Fauna* 3 The gilgai microrelief, where small changes (2 cm.) in the level of the surface can redistribute rainfall and produce different vegetational assemblages.

gilgaied, *a.* Of soils: characterized by the presence of gilgai holes.

1968 B. WILSON *Pasture Improvement Aust.* 248 The 'brigalow' is a term given to various types of forest . . which are developed mainly on deep gilgaied clay soils. **1976** *Ecos* vii. 24/3 Other soils, like the undulating 'gilgaied' clays, are unattractive to the engineer and agriculturalist alike.

gilgie /ˈdʒɪlgi/. *W.A.* Also **jilgie.** [a. Nyungar *jilgi*.] Either of the two small fresh-water crayfish of s.w. W.A. *Cherax crassimanus* and *C. quinquecarinatus*.

1937 A.R. GRANT *Memories of Parliament* 29 I'm not sure how to spell 'gilgies', but they are a small fresh water crayfish, caught in the same way as crabs. **1938** D. BATES *Passing of Aborigines* 70 The place where once she had gathered *jilgies* and vegetable food with the women. **1941** *Bulletin* (Sydney) 24 Sept. 15/2 One tyke . . was paddling in a swamp and had its paw nipped by a gilgie—or yabbie, as you easterners call 'em. **1951** *Ibid.* 2 May 14/1 I've spent a lot of time in areas where yabbies abound—we call them gilgies in W.A. **1965** A.W. UPFIELD *Lure of Bush* 124 A . . gilgie, a miniature crayfish, partly emerged from its hole, in which position it remained as if daring the fish to make a dash. **1973** W.G. WALKER *Gloss. Educ. Terms* 5 In this water lurked jilgies, black armoured monsters of freshwater crayfish, whose heavy claws could pinch hard on small fingers. **1986** *Bulletin* (Sydney) 7 Jan. 89/1 With them came three wonderful yabbies' tails, or as we Sandgropers know them, gilgies.

gillar, var. GALAH.

gill bird. WATTLE BIRD.

1854 *Illustr. Sydney News* 28 Feb. 162/1 The gill or wattle bird is pleasing in its plumage. . . Under each eye descends a bright red wattle. **1896** F.G. AFLALO *Sketch Nat. Hist. Aust.* 118 One of the most remarkable groups of honey-eaters is that of the Wattle Birds, to which, if I am not mistaken, belongs the 'Gill Bird' dear to Sydney pot-hunters. **1901** 'A. FERRES' *Free Selector* 105 The gill bird pipes his weird, strange song. **1916** *Bulletin* (Sydney) 12 Oct. 24/1 Cannot something be done to prevent the wholesale slaughter of gillbirds in N.S. Wales? **1944** L. WELSH *Kookaburra* 8 'Drink up,' the gill-birds say. 'Drink up!' **1965** *Austral. Encycl.* IV. 294 Gill-birds, a term that used to be freely applied, mainly in New South Wales, to the large honeyeaters known as wattle-birds. . . Both names derive from the birds' possession of fleshy wattles (or gills) at the corners of the beak.

gills, *pl. Obs.* [f. Br. slang *gill* a chap or cove, app. obs. by mid-19th cent.: see OED *sb.*[1] In the collocation **his gills**, a jocular designation for a (self-important) person, 'his nibs'.

1899 J. BRADSHAW *Quirindi Bank Robbery* 37 Riley came round to tell me to go to the closet, as his gills would be going to cover up his horse in a few minutes. **1914** E. DYSON *Spats' Fact'ry* 79 Up comes his gills, the junior partner, Duff.

gimlet. [Fig. use of *gimlet* boring tool: see quot. 1950.]

a. The slender tree of s.w. W.A. *Eucalyptus salubris* (fam. Myrtaceae), the trunk of which is characteristically twisted, shiny, and bronze-coloured. Also *attrib.*

1891 E.H. HALLACK *W.A. & Yilgarn Goldfields* 16 The gimlet gum, the upper branches of which partake of the gimlet twist, with its red, smooth bark throwing off when bent streamers which wave in the wind. **1904** *Emu* III. 218 The . . gimlet gums (E. salubris) . . held sway. **1921** W.H. PHIPPS *Bush Yarns* 87 Flimsy buildings clumsily constructed of hessian cloth and gimlet-wood saplings. **1936** J. KIRWAN *My Life's Adventure* 71 He set alight a gimlet tree and the flames made a roaring sound. **1946** K.S. PRICHARD *Roaring Nineties* 26 Thickets of gimlet, dark-leafed, with a natural screw down their slim bronze trunks. **1950** C.E. GOODE *Yarns of Yilgarn* 51 There was a thicket of red gimlets (gum trees which get their name from their twisted trunks). **1979** J. WILLIAMS *White Rivers* 80 Clumps of smooth-trunked gimlet bore into a cloudless sky.

b. With distinguishing epithet, as **silver-topped gimlet,** the smaller *E. campaspe* of s.w. W.A. which also has a twisted or fluted trunk.

1953 *New Settler in W.A.* (Perth) Jan. 9 There are two distinct trees called gimlets, the common gimlet (Eucalyptus salubris) and the silver-topped gimlet (E. campaspe). **1967** B.Y. MAIN *Between Wodjil & Tor* 1 A mopoke calling . . from its roost on a dead branch in a silver-topped gimlet.

gimme. [Transf. use of *gimme* acquisitiveness, greed: see OEDS.] An acquisitive woman.

1930 L.W. LOWER *Here's Luck* (1955) 61 She kissed me on the ear. She was a gimme, but twenty years of life fell from me. **1966** G. BARRY *Bed & Bored* 122 He doesn't want to leave his knock-kneed, buck-toothed, brass-eyed gimme for a while!

gin /dʒɪn/. Formerly also **din, ding, jin.** [a. Dharuk *diyin.*]

1. An Aboriginal woman or wife. Also *attrib.*

1790 R. CLARK Jrnl. 15 Feb. 133, I heard the crying of children close to me I asked them for to go and bring me there (Dins) which is there [*sic*] woman. **1793** W. TENCH *Compl. Acct. Settlement* 202 The letter y frequently follows d in the same syllable: thus the word which signifies a woman is *Dyin*; although the structure of our language requires us to spell it *Dee-in.* **1800** *Hist. Rec. N.S.W.* II. 414 William Fuller saw a Blanket which he had lent to John Wimbow on one of the Native Gins or Women. **1818** W. LAWRY Lett. 9 Oct., Their festivals are generally followed by hostilities occasioned generally by some young men making too free with their Dins or females of another Clan. **1826** *Monitor* (Sydney) 20 Oct. 178/1 *Gins* were running hither and thither, ever and anon aiding by an unseen blow, their favoured warriors. **1826** R. DAWSON *Private & Confidential* 11 During the dance I observed the women (married women are called 'Jins') standing in a circle by themselves. **1835** *Sydney Herald* 9 Mar. 2/1 Paragraph-mongers . . know as much of this Colony, or the merits of the case as an aboriginal *gin* does of the Court of St. James. **1846** C.P. HODGSON *Reminisc. Aust.* 367 'Gin', the term applied to the native female Blacks; not from any attachment to the spirit of that name, but from some (to me) unknown derivation. **1848** H.W. HAYGARTH *Recoll. Bush Life* 104 The female or 'gin' (the pronunciation of the *g* is soft, though perhaps the determined etymologist would choose to derive the word from γυνή). **1851** H. MELVILLE *Present State Aust.* 348 They were much attached to their 'gins' or wives, and treated them kindly, and they were equally fond of their 'piccaninnies' or young children. **1864** J.D. LANG *Qld., Aust.* 372 'The black fellow and his jin' . . is their name for the constellation Gemini. **1867** *Sydney Punch* 23 Feb. 104/1 He saw once more the dark-eyed gin Taking a bange at noon; she clasped his hand, and begged a bit Of baccy as a boon. **1878** R.B. SMYTH *Aborigines of Vic.* I. 63 All the gins stand naked, except an apron of emu feathers round their waists, and cords made of stringybark round their heads. **1881** *Bulletin* (Sydney) 26 Mar. 8/3 Oh! don't you remember Black Alice, Sam Holt—Black Alice so dusky and dark—That Warrego gin with the straw through her nose, And teeth like a Moreton Bay shark. **1883** *Ibid.* 7 July 6/3 Near Braidwood are five of the original proprietors of the soil of N.S.W. They have their ancient jins with them. We spell it with a j, because the English people have got into the habit of pronouncing them with a hard g. **1891** *Truth* (Sydney) 19 Apr. 3/3 My wife is dying, I've left her there In the hut for a while in the old gin's care. **1894** R. CALDWELL *In our Great N.-W.* 45 Her dark-eyed princess daughters too Were known to all as 'gins', And they helped the white man at his toils, And helped him in his sins. **1900** *Truth* (Sydney) 20 May 6/3 Around Widgiemooltha a black gin is a part of a prospector's camp furniture—a luxury he never attempts to conceal. **1902** *Ibid.* 23 Nov. 1/4 'All is fair in love'—except the black gin! **1914** C.H.S MATTHEWS *Bill* 104 All day long the 'gins' (i.e. women) keep up an incessant wailing and howling. **1923** T. HALL *Short Hist. Downs Blacks* 3 Darby (whose wife was a Macintyre River gin, and a black virago). **1929** K.S. PRICHARD *Coonardoo* (1961) 58, I don't want you to go mucking round with gins. But I'd rather a gin than Jessica. **1942** E. ANDERSON *Squatter's Luck* 40 Who much delighted in His sooty piccanin, And thin, rococo gin. **1947** *Bulletin* (Sydney) 4 June 28/1 'As skinny as a black gin' used to be a proverb . . but nowadays it is surprising how fat a gin may become when attached to a station where the hand-out of tucker is liberal. **1948** P.J. HURLEY *Red Cedar* 95 An old gin from a black's camp sat on a seat near a big spreading fig-tree. **1957** P. WHITE *Voss* (1960) 182 He went down to the gunyas, and cursed the black gins that were squatted there. **1962** H.J. FRITH *Mallee-Fowl* 126 Gins are . . cunning, and when the crocodile charges one, another slips in and removes the eggs. **1975** R. THROSSELL *Wild Weeds & Wind Flowers* 221 Even after a small electric oven was installed, she still liked to do her 'gin cooking' over the open fire in the sitting room. **1977** T.A.G. HUNGERFORD *Wong Chu* 31 It's like the gins used to say up on the station when I'd tell them it was time they stopped going walkabout. No more, Missus. **1978** D. STUART *Wedgetail View* 76 Hardy ole bastard; great man on a rough horse, bash a nigger as soon as look at him, terrible hard on niggers he was, an' awful fast after them young gins, too.

2. *transf.*

1833 W.H. BRETON *Excursions* 254 The flying gin (gin is the native word for woman or female) is a boomah, and will leave behind every description of dog. **1916** H.A. ABERDEEN Lett., As soon as we landed [in Freetown, Sierra Leone] black jins swarmed around us selling oranges, bananas & cocoanuts. **1954** H.G. LAMOND *Manx Star* 74 'An' he done th' lot on wine, women an' song?' 'On gins, gee-gees and grog,' Wilson corrected.

3. a. Used *attrib.* to designate a white man who sexually exploits an Aboriginal woman, or the activity of so doing.

1902 *Bulletin* (Sydney) 27 Dec. 15/1 Camp-robberies . . were almost always due to nigs. being encouraged around camps by 'gin-mashers'. **1912** *Ibid.* 15 Feb. 14/1 The word 'combo' . . means a 'gin banger', which, in turn, means a white man who descends to domestic association with the female aboriginal. **1925** *Ibid.* 6 Aug. 24/1 The news was brought to the gin-stealer by a boy. **1937** Austral. Archives CRS F3 8/30, What official would undertake to separate 'genuine' prospectors from the other sort who are merely what is vulgarly known as 'gin hunters'? **1946** W.E. HARNEY *North of 23°* 77 In those old days we had the eternal clash of 'gin burglar' versus 'gin shepherd'. **1947** O. GRIFFITHS *Darwin Drama* 40 Certain low types of white men visited the southern shore of Melville Island and there held 'gin rorting' parties. They would fill the Aborigines and the gins with methylated spirits and ravage the gins. **1949** H.G. LAMOND *White Ears* 9 You calls yersel' a white man! You! You all-same blackfellow-combo, murlonga, gin man! **1955** D. NILAND *Shiralee* 135 He hated the ignominy of capitulating to a harlot, and a black one at that. Macauley, the gin-jockey, they could say. **1956** T. RONAN *Moleskin Midas* 149 Alec Drage had allowed gin-stealing as one of the permissible reasons for Dolman to use his whip on Yates. *Ibid.* 225 Why would blokes like Frank Heritage, who'd been a pretty good gin-cuddler in his day, turn round and get married? **1958** W.E. HARNEY *Content to Lie* 46 The down-trodden's day will come soon, then you 'gin-burglars' will have to respect the rights of the weak. . . Yes, on that day, both you and I, my friend, will have to pay more for the 'girls' than we do today. **1960** J. WALKER *No Sunlight Singing* 160 'I've been wondering what're your thoughts on the colour question—female—to do or not to do, as it were?' Bob put on a thoughtful look. 'Well,' he said with deliberation, 'I'm not exactly a gin-burglar, you know. I have to be persuaded.' **1960** M. HENRY *Unlucky Dip* 148 The Old Letch now, Bob—used to be the biggest gin-jockey in the North in his time, they say. **1963** *Bulletin* (Sydney) 23 Mar. 15/1 The Daly River . . for 80 years has been a refuge for happy-go-lucky hermits with a taste for OP rum and what Territorians call 'gin burglary'. **1965** *Austral.* (Sydney) 5 Feb. 10/7 The popularity of gin burglary is reflected in the staggering proportion of half-castes among Hall's Creek's tiny (200 to 300) population. *Ibid.* 10/8 Resistance to a gin burgling expedition would have been unheard of in the Hall's Creek of 10, or even five years ago. **1965** R. STOW *Merry-Go-Round* 186 'I like them,' the boy said. 'There's some nice boong kids at school.' 'He's gunna grow up to be a gin-jockey,' said Alan. **1971** *Bulletin* (Sydney) 9 Jan. 37/1 As late as 1928, a report to the Federal Government spoke of 'carloads of men from bush townships and construction camps bent on 'ginsprees', in other words, drink and prostitution orgies'. *Ibid.*, On the South Australian northern frontier, the settler's pastime of 'ginbusting' caused so much concern that it led to the introduction of welfare legislation in 1899. **1971** K. WILLEY *Boss Drover* 45 Now and then you would meet fellows who . . would go from station to station, scrounging feeds and hanging about the blacks' camps looking for girls. They were known as combos, murlongers, or gin burglars. **1974** N. PHILLIPSON *As Other Men* 122 He could provide a little summary justice on that gin-humping crud. **1975** X. HERBERT *Poor Fellow my Country* 31 The trouble was there were the white women to reckon with. Eventually they'd come looking for their men, find them Gin Jockeying, as they say, empty out their black rivals. **1977** T.A.G. HUNGERFORD *Wong Chu* 91 Your old man's grandfather was a gin-jockey, wasn't he? **1977** D. STUART *Drought Foal* 188 You're a thoroughgoin' gindozzler, an' in a year or two you'll be a red-hot combo. **1980** P. PEPPER *You are what you make Yourself* 40 Grandfather told us the white men had 'gin-hunts'—come down on their horses to get the women in the camps. *Ibid.* 113 We have 'gin-men' come round for a young girl, hanging about lookin' for a dark girl.

b. gin shepherd, gin shepherder: see main entry.

4. In special collocations: **gin's piss,** beer deemed to be of inferior quality; **gin's sister,** see quot.

1972 J. O'GRADY *It's your Shout, Mate!* 43 Yeah, but

you come from England. That's **gin's piss** country. Any kind o' beer'd be better than that English muck. **1978** D. BALL *Great Austral. Snake Exchange* 29 The beer was jin's piss. **1878** R.B. SMYTH *Aborigines of Vic.* I. 64 *Djeet-gun* is the superb warbler; the *eering* the *emu wren*; the former is called the '**gins' sister**', the latter the 'black-fellows' brother'.

gina-gina /ˈdʒɪnə-dʒɪnə/. *Austral. pidgin.* Chiefly *W.A.* Also **jinna-jinna.** [a. Mantjiltjara dial. of western desert *jua jina.*] A kind of dress worn by an Aboriginal woman: see quot. 1955.

1927 *Bulletin* (Sydney) 7 Dec. 11/4 A gina-gina .. almost black with dust and grease, showed her bony legs and feet. **1932** K.S. PRICHARD *Kiss on Lips* 235 Dirty and weather-beaten, in a gina-gina she had made and dyed herself. **1944** M.J. O'REILLY *Bowyangs & Boomer-angs* 77 All lubras and boys working around the institution were compelled to wear either gin-a-gins (a long one-piece dress), or trousers. **1955** F.B. VICKERS *Mirage* (1958) 187 The jinna-jinna dress was a shapeless scarlet colored bag with holes in it for neck and arms. It had no trimmings, no finish, except the turned-in hems. **1969** L. HADOW *Full Cycle* 253 [An] Aboriginal woman .. disappeared on silent feet .. her shapeless gina-gina a blur of blue. **1977** F.B. VICKERS *Stranger no Longer* 170 The economics of getting something better than the rag of a jinna-jinna, and something better in your stomach than a slice of meat and damper washed down with black tea, is real enough.

ging. [Prob. onomatopoeic.] A catapult.

1903 *Bulletin* (Sydney) 17 Dec. 35/1 He had in his pocket a 'ging' with a shop-made wire prong, a 'ging' of marvellous power and deadly accuracy. **1915** N. LINDSAY *N. Lindsay's Bk. II.* 79 He had even knocked a parrot with his 'ging', but the parrot is an indomitable bird. **1933** —— *Saturdee* 152 Peter took out his ging to make a show of catapulting a stone at a non-existent bird. **1950** *Arna* (Sydney) 5 He put the ging back in his hip-pocket, and practised whipping it out and loading and shooting as fast as he could. **1965** C. JOHNSON *Wild Cat Falling* 12 'What're we going to do?' 'Go after birds and rabbits. We got some gings.' **1968** S. GORE *Holy Smoke* 14 Young Dave only lets fly with one shot outa his ging, and the big bloke's stonkered. **1980** W.H. O'ROURKE *My Way* 286 In my boyhood days, every boy had a 'shanghai', or 'ging', as it was more generally known, and no bird was safe.

ginger, *n.* [Abbrev. of *ginger ale*, rhyming slang for 'tail'.] In the phr. **on one's ginger,** close behind, 'on one's tail'. Also *fig.*

1967 *Kings Cross Whisper* (Sydney) xxxv. 6/1 *Ginger ale*, bail. Tail. Shortened to ginger when meant tail. 'I got the coppers on my ginger.' **1971** F. HARDY *Outcasts of Foolgarah* 76 The legal-eagles are on our ginger. **1977** D. STUART *Drought Foal* 224 I'd hate to have a coupler blokes as smart as them two, right on me ginger.

ginger, *v.* [Prob. back-formation f. *gingerly* with extreme caution, with stealth.] *trans.* Esp. of a prostitute: to steal from (a man's person or clothing). Also as *n.*

1945 S.J. BAKER *Austral. Lang.* 139 A prostitute who robs a man by taking money from his clothes is known as a *gingerer*... *To ginger* and *gingering* are associated terms. **1950** *Austral. Police Jrnl.* Apr. 114 *Ginger*, the theft from a man's person or clothing in a brothel, usually carried out by a second prostitute who is working in league with her more active partner. **1953** K. TENNANT *Joyful Condemned* 5 'I've just gingered the copper. Give him his pants back when he gets too noisy.' .. 'Gingering', or robbing prospective clients, was considered low taste, but after all the man was a copper. **1961** X. HERBERT *Soldiers' Women* 306 Call the cops and prove it for yourself. They'd like to do business with the gal who gingered Plug for his roll. **1978** H.C. BAKER *I was Listening* 18 The two conspirators 'gingered' his unoccupied trousers for their contents.

Hence **gingered** *ppl. a.*, stolen by gingering.

1978 H.C. BAKER *I was Listening* 18 In Nug's pocket was found the gingered eight pounds.

ginger beer.

1. *Obs.* A euphemism for an alcoholic drink.

1843 *Satirist & Sporting Chron.* (Sydney) 25 Mar. 3/2 If old Smith .. does not leave off visiting Taylor's Public House, and drinking *ginger beer*, we must tip it home to him in character next week. **1898** *Bulletin* (Sydney) 19 Mar. 14/2 An old whaler .. had the usual ('gingerbeer', I suppose), and straightway became a 'corpse'.

2. [Orig. Br. nautical slang.] Rhyming slang for 'engineer', spec. a member of the Royal Australian Engineers.

1941 S.J. BAKER *Pop. Dict. Austral. Slang* 31 *Gingerbeers*, the Aust. Engineer Corps. **1951** E. LAMBERT *Twenty Thousand Thieves* 149 And minefields! The Ginger Beers have laid so many mines they've lost trace of some of 'em! **1970** R. BEILBY *No Medals for Aphrodite* 83 'Who are these people, sergeant?' 'Couple of Gingerbeers, sir. Picked 'em up along the track. Said they blew the pass and lost their truck.' **1982** J.J. COE *Desperate Praise* 86 This type of job normally fell to the Engineers, but our officer .. volunteered us to give the 'ginger beers' a hand.

gink. [Prob. f. Br. dial. *geek* to peep, spy, stare about: see EDD.] A scrutinizing look.

1945 R.S. CLOSE *Love me Sailor* 227, I kept staring so that he could get a gink at me wide awake. **1961** —— *With Hooves of Brass* 121 Get a gink at that chin, mates! **1962** S. GORE *Down Golden Mile* 205 Come up to my camp on the way home in the morning and have a gink at it then. **1968** —— *Holy Smoke* 47 Old misery guts takes a gink at Shad, Mesh and Ab.

gin shepherd.

1. A white man who cohabits with an Aboriginal woman. Also **gin shepherder.**

1929 K.S. PRICHARD *Coonardoo* (1961) 30 Sam Gears had been known as 'a gin shepherder' for some time and a family of half-castes swarmed about his verandahs. **1958** W.E. HARNEY *Content to Lie* 35 'Twas here, on one cold night I witnessed my mate going for his life down a lignum 'pad', with an irate 'gin shepherd' (a white man who lives with a native woman) on his heels.

2. One who seeks to prevent the sexual exploitation of Aboriginal women by white men.

1946 [see GIN 3 a.]. **1954** T. RONAN *Vision Splendid* 111 The reason why most of them left was that 'the Missus was too much of a gin shepherd'.

Hence **gin shepherding** *vbl. n.*

1945 S.J. BAKER *Austral. Lang.* 197 *Gin-shepherding* and *going on a gin spree*, taking to the bush in search of an aboriginal woman. **1946** K.S. PRICHARD *Roaring Nineties* 191 I'm not going to have you mixed up with his gin-shepherding. **1971** K. WILLEY *Boss Driver* 46 The practice of separating the women from the combos was known as 'gin shepherding'.

give, *v.*

1. [See OED *give, v.* 59 f.] In the phr. **to give in,** to give (something) in addition; to 'throw in'.

1849 *Belfast Gaz.* (Port Phillip) 1 June 3/1 Those possessed of runs capable of running more than 100,000 sheep ought to have sold a few head, and 'given in' the remainder of their runs to those who wanted them badly. **1864** J.D. LANG *Qld., Aust.* 171 It is often difficult to dispose of a large flock or herd of cattle at all, unless the run *is given in* with them. **1886** MRS C. PRAED *Miss Jacobsen's Chance* I. 157 Don't you be led away by that professional manner of his. It's the regulation thing, given in gratis with the prescription. **1939** J.G. PATTISON *'Battler's' Tales Early Rockhampton* 123, I put in an offer of 17s. 6d. per head for all branded stock, calves to be given in. By this offer I secured a clean run at the clean skin cattle.

2. [Br. dial.: see EDD *best, a.* 3 and OED *give, v.* 39.] In the phr. **to give** (someone, something) **best,** to acknowledge defeat by (a person, set of circumstances, etc.).

1888 'R. BOLDREWOOD' *Robbery under Arms* I. 94, I could hardly stand for laughing, till the calf gave him best and walked. **1895** *Worker* (Sydney) 9 Feb. 3/2 Give it best, old man. You're only busting yourself for nothing. **1900** R. BRUCE *Benbonuna* (1904) 174 Giving the dinner 'best' (in colonial parlance) .. he seated himself in one of the unwieldy armchairs. **1902** —— *Reminisc. Old Squatter* 141, I concluded that what little fun I might derive from hunting the poor wretches was more than counterbalanced by my feelings of compunction afterwards, and I soon, in bush parlance, 'gave the thing best'. **1914** C.H.S. MATTHEWS *Bill* 128 Tommy 'gave me best' and I was declared winner. **1978** H.C. BAKER *I was Listening* 139 Suddenly, Kevan threw up his hands. 'I give you best!' .. a schoolboy expression used in an adult fight.

3. [Fig. use of *to give away* to give as a present: see OEDS *give, v.* 54 h.] In the phr. **to give** (something) **away,** to abandon (an activity, etc.); to 'give up'.

1948 *Khaki Bush & Bigotry* (1968) 98 *Andy*: How's the garden going, Ot? *Ot*: Give it away. **1953** T.A.G. HUNGERFORD *Riverslake* 191 'You're stung,' Murdoch said flatly, 'you're on the skids. You want to give it away when you start raving after a quiet night like we had tonight!' **1964** K. WILLEY *Eaters of Lotus* 4 The impossibility of owning a home in Darwin has been one of the big factors leading people after perhaps two, three, or ten years here to 'give it away' and go south. **1969** L. HADOW *Full Cycle* 142 You'd have to work; and give the grog away. **1977** V. PRIDDLE *Larry & Jack* 16 He'd given away some of the nasty tricks he got up to when he was a young man. **1981** P. BARTON *Bastards I have Known* 69 It just wouldn't work... The lunch gong sounded and everyone gave it away.

gladdy. Shortened form of 'Gladiolus', a plant bearing spikes of colourful flowers. Also *attrib.*

1947 M. MORRIS *Township* 193 A proper garden with old-fashioned flowers like stocks and 'snaps' and in the summer 'gladdies' with tall, flowering, scarlet spikes. **1967** D. HEWETT *This Old Man* (1976) 99 Gladdies in summer. I always did like them pretty things. **1969** *Listener* (London) 24 Apr. 588/1 On a good night she reaches the gallery and when all the absurd phallic blooms have found their place, Edna leads the audience in the Gladdie Song. **1972** *Daily Mirror* (Sydney) 12 Oct. 4/2 She's still with the gladdies and 'Excuse I' and The Trip. **1980** *R.A.N. News* (Sydney) 13 June 5 Gladdies and curlers and slippers and things. These are Australian we're all proud to sing. **1982** B. HUMPHRIES *Dame Edna's Bedside Companion* 100 In the spring unsuspecting lawn-squatters run the terrible risk of being 'goosed' by an upwardly mobile gladdy.

glamour. *Obs.* Used *attrib.* in Comb. with reference to dress uniform issued to personnel of the Australian army during the war of 1939–45 (cf. GIGGLE 2).

1941 *Argus* (Melbourne) 15 Nov. (Suppl.) 1/4 *Glamour gowns*, khaki dress uniforms. **1942** *Action Front: Jrnl. 2/2 Field Regiment* Dec. 5 A glamour suit to save battle dress. **1943** *Troppo Tribune* (Mataranka) 8 Feb. 3 Monday morning looked a certainty for 'Glamour' Parade. **1945** *Chocolate & Green* (Sydney) July 6 The officers, resplendent in what we have learned to call glamour suits.

glass.

1. *Obs.* In the phr. **glasses round,** a drink for everyone present.

1858 A. PENDRAGON *Queen of South* 209 The trooper .. went so far as to offer a bet of 'glasses round' to the foreman of the jury. **1871** *Illustr. Sydney News* 23 Dec. 210/3 No wonder old Jonas was in good humour, and occasionally stood 'glasses round' for us all. **1879** 'AUSTRALIAN' *Adventures Qld.* 8 I'll bet you 'glasses round' you'll be tight before the yokes is off your bullocks.

2. In the phr. **glass of lunch, steak,** etc., a glass of beer.

1968 J. O'GRADY *Gone Troppo* 112 At the moment, he's having a glass of lunch. **1969** A. BUZO *Front Room Boys* (1970) 48 'Been down the pub for lunch? .. ' 'Yeah, had a glass of steak with Barry Anderson.'

glassy. Also **glassey.** [Fig. use of *glassy* highly-prized marble.] With **the:** someone (or something) prized or admired. Also as *adj.* in the phr. **glassy marble.**

1905 *Steele Rudd's Mag.* (Brisbane) June 553 That girl'll do you bad every time; she's the real glassy, an' no mistake. **1915** C.J. DENNIS *Songs of Sentimental Bloke* 42 'E's jist the glarsey on the soulful sob, 'E'll sigh and spruik, an 'owl a love-sick vow. **1951** CUSACK & JAMES *Come in Spinner* 300 Low profits and quick turnover, and this is the glassy marble.

glory box. A box in which a woman accumulates her trousseau; 'bottom drawer'; the trousseau itself. Also *attrib.*

1915 L. STONE *Betty Wayside* 244 It was her glory box, containing all her treasures that she had gathered together against such a day as this. **1934** F.S. Hibble *Karangi* 110 They came to gossip and to rave over the glory-box, being frank in their envy. **1956** 'A.B.C.' *What is A?* 22 A Glory Box, alias a Hope Chest, alias the Little Bottom Drawer, is both a figurative and material possession, generally filled with nick-nacks, bits and pieces, and a few odds and ends of lacy unmentionables. **1966** B. Beaver *You can't come Back* 118 That's my glory-box... I'm saving up things so I can get married and get away from here. **1976** D. Hewett *Golden Oldies* (1981) 40 He jilted my Ellie, her glory box ready, doilies and supper cloths, embroidered shams. **1984** P. Cuffley *Chandeliers & Billy Tea* 97 Ladies .. turned out .. beautiful lace, dozens of doilies, and scores of eccentric needleworked knick-knacks. Much of it went into 'glory boxes' and was rarely if ever used.

glue-pot. A wet and muddy section of a road or track in which a vehicle may become bogged. Also *attrib.*

1875 R.P. Whitworth *Cobb's Box* 4 The wild gorges, deep swamps, and terrible 'glue pots' of Gipps Land. **1898** G.H. Haydon *Sporting Reminisc.* 249 Bullock drays would be bogged in some 'glue-pot' hole. **1901** C. Wright *Historic Melbourne* 36 Travelling by Cobb's coaches in the country districts before the time of railways .. through the 'glue pots' as the seas of mud were called. **1914** T.C. Wollaston *Spirit of Child* 66 Hand to it, lad, on the glue-pot track. **1923** J. Moses *Beyond City Gates* 46 I've struck some bogs, and 'glue pot' clogs. **1942** H.H. Peck *Mem. of Stockman* 140 The road trip to Melbourne, 150 miles, over the famous 'glue-pot' took four days. **1966** J. Pollard *One for Road* 7 From Glenrowan to Winton, the going was rough, the famous 'glue-pot' having to be negotiated. This 'glue-pot' is about half a mile long, and is usually about two feet deep in sticky mud.

gluyas /'glujəs, 'glaɪjəs/. [The name of H.I. *Gluyas*, a wheat-farmer of S.A., who selected and distributed the variety.] A drought-resistant Australian variety of wheat (see quot. 1956). Also **early gluyas.**

1928 R.G. Stapledon *Tour in Aust. & N.Z.* 39 'Nabawah,' 'Gluyas' .. are important varieties in Western Australia. **1932** C.E. Goode *Grower of Golden Grain* 10 'Tis not the time to wreath the brow with spray of Gluyas green. **1956** Callaghan & Millington *Wheat Industry Aust.* 262 Early Gluyas .. was for 30 years, from 1910 onwards, a leading variety in the drier areas of Australia and .. was only displaced by its own progeny.

gnamma hole /'næmə hoʊl/. Also **namma hole.** [f. Nyungar *ŋama* + (Eng.) *hole.*] A hole (commonly in granite) in which rainwater collects: see esp. quot. 1948; *rock-hole*, see Rock *n.* 3.

[**1842** G.F. Moore *Descr. Vocab. Aborigines W.A.* 164 *Water*, standing in a rock—Gnamar.] **1893** D. Lindsay *Jrnl. Elder Sci. Exploring Exped.* 116 Northeast of the station there was a fine 'gnamer' rockhole and well of good water. **1896** *Bulletin* (Sydney) 18 Apr. 3/2, I don't want no blasted gnamma-holes—give me a Melbourne tap. **1897** A.F. Calvert *My Fourth Tour W.A.* 141 The hole widened out from its narrow neck like a demijohn, and it appeared to be replenished from a 'soak' or spring. Such reservoirs, more commonly known as 'namma holes', occur here and there all over the back country. **1901** M. Vivienne *Travels in W.A.* 339 Native wells or 'namma holes' have saved many a prospector from death by thirst, and men well used to the Bush soon know how to find them. **1911** A.L. Haydon *Trooper Police Aust.* 317 A large 'gnamma hole' is capable of holding 20,000 gallons. **1929** W.J. Reside *Golden Days* 132 The 'gnamma' or natural water-holes were full of water. **1929** K.S. Prichard *Coonardoo* (1961) 28 His eyes, namma holes in viscid orbits, glittered at her, as he swung his naked feet. **1935** I.L. Idriess *Man Tracks* 22 There comes an occasional year when rain falls, which fills the gnamma holes—holes in granite rocks. **1948** M. Uren *Glint of Gold* 34 Gnamma holes are holes in rock with an impervious bottom and walls, and generally with a narrow neck. Natives enlarge the necks sufficiently to get their arms into the holes and dip out the water. The rock covering prevents the water from evaporating. **1972** N. King *Nickel Country* 37 A remarkable feature of this arid country is the number of granite outcrops which appear at intervals. On nearly every patch of rock is a cavity called a gnamma hole which holds water... It is not known how they were formed; some say by natives in by-gone ages, while others say they are natural formations caused by weathering processes and chemical change.

gnow /naʊ/. *W.A.* Formerly also **ngowa, ngow-oo.** [a. Nyungar *ŋaw.*] *Mallee fowl*, see Mallee 6.

1840 J. Gould *Birds of Aust.* (1848) V. Pl. 78, In these close scrubby woods small open glades occasionally occur, and here the Ngöw-oo constructs its nest. **1851** J. Henderson *Excursions & Adventures N.S.W.* II. 177 The Native, or Mountain Pheasant, called *ngow-oo* by the blacks. **1855** R. Austin *Jrnl. Interior W.A.* 9, I passed a gnow-ow or native pheasant's nest. **1864** *Jrnls. & Rep. Two Voyages Glenelg River* 38 Of birds .. the 'ngowoo' or native pheasant (leipoa ocellata) .. may be mentioned. **1872** Mrs E. Millett *Austral. Parsonage* 223 There is, however, amongst edible birds none that can at all compare with the one known to natives as the *Ngowa*, and to naturalists as the *Leipoa*. **1885** M.A. Barker *Lett. to Guy* 124, I have been given some emeu's eggs for you, and some 'Gnow's' eggs. **1962** H.J. Frith *Mallee-Fowl* 3 In Western Australia the native name 'gnow' has been adopted, and in Victoria 'lowan'. Mallee-fowl is chiefly a New South Wales name.

go, *n.*[1]

1. See *fair go* Fair *a.*[1] 2.

2. [Used elsewhere but recorded earliest in Aust.]

a. In the phr. **to give** (something) **a go,** to make an attempt to perform (a task, feat, etc.), often incautiously; to 'have a crack (or shot) at'.

1908 *Bulletin* (Sydney) 17 Dec. 14/1, I gave her a 'go' for half-a-mile; And then when her pedigree I'd seen, I bought her, and christened her 'Bidgee Queen. **1919** *Ibid.* 13 Nov. 20/3 The bullock-dray was well bogged, and the conductor seemed at the end of his resources. Knowing something of the game I offered to 'give 'em a go', and he handed me the persuader. **1929** C.E.W. Bean *Official Hist. Aust. 1914–18* III. 519 Australian troops were always ready to accept a risk if the object seemed worth achieving. 'Give it a go' expressed their attitude in facing many a dangerous project. **1941** A.E. Clarke *Man nobody Understood* 43 He was asked point blank if he would undertake the cook's job. 'Yes, I'll give it a go,' said Mica Fred. **1950** *Bulletin* (Sydney) 5 Aug. 12/2 It was a hungry track, and when we sighted a homestead off the main road a bit Mat decided to give it a go. **1962** J. Mackenzie *Austral. Paradox* 106 In Australia still, 'give it a go' and 'near enough' are recognised traits. **1977** R. Beilby *Gunner* 20 'I'll give it a go,' he called back.

b. In the phr. **to give** (someone) **a go,** to give (someone) the opportunity to attempt (a task, feat, etc.); to give (someone) a 'fair go'.

1937 J.M. Harcourt *It never Fails* 45 All right, we'll give you a go. You ought to be all right. **1943** E.J. Kahn *G.I. Jungle* 74 We would .. yell, 'Give 'em a go, Yank!'—a war cry the Aussies sometimes addressed to us. **1957** D. Whitington *Treasure upon Earth* 128 'If the Prime Minister can't fix it, who can?' 'Give him a go. You know the mob who have to be satisfied at a time like this.' **1969** L. Hadow *Full Cycle* 8 He said .. 'O.K. Give's a go, mate,' and got up yawning. **1978** L. Randall *Austral. Family Plays* 69 Hell, he only left here about 10 minutes ago. Give him a go, he's not driving a jet. **1982** *Weekend Austral. Mag.* (Sydney) 13 Nov. 16/2 He gave that [*sc.* shearing] away, too, 'to give the young blokes a go'.

3. In the collocation **open go,** an unimpeded opportunity, a 'free rein'.

1918 *Twenty-Second's Echo: Mag. 22nd Battalion A.I.F.* 15 May 3 We did not get an open go in the way of food nor medical attention. **1928** L.A. Sigsworth *Various Verse* 2 The organiser kids to them through most of his 'mass address'; He lets them chip—but their brains are dulled, and gives them an open go. **1945** J.E. Allan *Men & Manners* 33 During 'Whitehall's long distraction' they had, in twentieth-century Australian slang, 'an open go'. **1953** *Bulletin* (Sydney) 1 Apr. 12/1 The little township in the Queensland far west was holding its one-day Bushman's Carnival, and an 'open go' had been unofficially declared. **1959** D. Stuart *Yandy* 142 There were practically no whitefellers prospecting, and certainly none out on the new ground, and the blackfellers knew there was an open go ahead of them. **1971** P. Hasluck *Open Go* 2, I found that I could range further afield if my 'open go' took the form of making suggestions, asking questions, or raising doubts rather than asserting what should be done.

4. In the phr. **from go to whoa,** from start to finish.

1971 D. Ireland *Unknown Industr. Prisoner* 54 Usually he talked from go to whoa. **1978** R.H. Conquest *Dusty Distances* 21 The entire audience would shout encouragement from go to whoa. **1983** *Truck & Bus Transportation* Aug. 48/2 The organ-type brake pedal sits several inches off the floor on a metal box which causes an unusually high and awkward lift from 'go' to 'whoa'.

go, *n.*[2] Abbrev. of Goanna 1.

1904 *Bulletin* (Sydney) 12 May 16/2 The eye can detect no difference in the 'bingy' of the go. when he emerges from his winter quarters .. and the same 'bingy' when it wobbles away from the interior of a dead bullock. **1919** *Smith's Weekly* (Sydney) 15 Mar. 2/1, I opened a big 'go.' some time back, and found his very simple digestive apparatus alive with thin leech-like worms. **1942** C. Barrett *From Bush Hut* 15 The old go's oil no good at all for snakes. **1954** —— *Wild Life Aust. & New Guinea* 118 The 'go' (a bushman's name for the big lizard) has an uncanny way of detecting the presence of eggs. **1969** L. Hadow *Full Cycle* 139 If there's any blue this time, I'm heading north like a go up a tree.

go, *v.*[1] With **through.**

1. a. *trans. Obs.* To rob (a person).

1882 *Sydney Slang Dict.* 4 Go through (or run the rule over) a Man—To rob a man in a haunt or the street. **1896** *Worker* (Sydney) 25 Apr. 4/2 He dextrously 'went through' the three mates and left 'em as closely fleeced as the sheep they had shorn last season.

b. *Obs.* To shear.

1910 *Bulletin* (Sydney) 8 Sept. 13/2 A chap that I knew to be among the best and fastest sheep-shearers in Australia invited me to watch him and some mates 'go through' a shed of Angoras. **1911** *Ibid.* 25 May 13/3, I have seen Wilson day after day go through 140 or 150 rough 'wrinklies'.

2. *intr.* To make a speedy departure, esp. to avoid fulfilling an obligation. Cf. *shoot through* Shoot *v.* 3.

1943 S.J. Baker *Pop. Dict. Austral. Slang* (ed. 3) 35 *Go through*, to desert from a northern base to the south. War slang. **1945** 'Master-Sarg' *Yank discovers Aust.* 17 When a man has 'been pegged' he has been charged with a military offence—which may be that he has 'gone through' or been absent without official leave. **1951** E. Lambert *Twenty Thousand Thieves* 222 He shrugged. 'I'll probably have to go through meself again.' He said it as though going A.W.L. was as casual a thing as shaving. **1952** *Coast to Coast 1951–52* 169 It can mean one of two things. Either you're being admitted to the Union—the Waterside Workers' Federation of Australia—or you're, well, just 'going through' .. knocking off before time, beating the whistle. **1977** B. Scott *My Uncle Arch* 113 The first few times she went through on him nearly broke his heart.

go, *v.*[2] [f. *go, n.* a fight or argument: see OED(S *sb.* 4 b.] *trans.* To fight or take to task (a person, etc.).

1938 *Bulletin* (Sydney) 21 Apr. 20/1 Bill developed a cheque, a thirst and a grouch. Riding in to the homestead he decided to 'go' the boss .. collect his cheque and drift. 'Going' the boss would make Bill's name big in the district. **1945** *Ibid.* 17 Jan. 14/1 The boss goes the cook, and the cook goes his dawg. **1947** E. Hill *Flying Doctor Calling* 15 Big long horned fellers out there, you've got to be quick or they'll go yer! **1955** R. Lawler *Summer Seventeenth Doll* (1965) 33 This strikes Dowd as bein' funny, see, and he starts to laugh. Well, that did it. Roo went him and it was on, cane knives and the lot. **1969** F.B. Vickers *No Man is Himself* 170 Don't come the duchess of bloody Perth stuff with me. I knows you bin on with Fraser... So come clean. Is your old man goin' him? **1977** J. O'Grady *There was Kid* 74 In the words of our father, he would 'go yer'... I told myself that that rooster would get an unpleasant surprise if he 'went me'.

go, *v.*[3] In the phr. **to go off.**

a. Of a person or premises: to be raided by the police force.

1941 S.J. Baker *Pop. Dict. Austral. Slang* 31 *Go off*, when an hotel or club is raided by the police for permitting gambling or after-hours drinking, it is said to 'go off'. **1949** L. Glassop *Lucky Palmer* 5 Clarrie, he ain't gone off in six months. Must sling to the cops. Wonder how much he pays 'em. **1953** K. Tennant *Joyful Condemned*

12 The nice thing about this place . . is that it's never raided. Number Ten went off last week, and the Vice Squad are always in and out of the place two doors down. **1977** J. RAMSAY *Cop it Sweet* 41 *Go off*, the raiding of premises taking part in illegal activities. **1982** *N.T. News* (Darwin) 3 Apr. 33/5 Among those who 'went off' that night was one Harry David, who had a fruit and veg. business in Tennant Creek. **1984** *Bulletin* (Sydney) 10 July 49/2 Mona last went off in December 1983 when she was charged under her real name, Lucy Domingo, and fined $200 for having been the keeper of a brothel.

b. Of a racehorse: see quot. 1941.

1941 S.J. BAKER *Pop. Dict. Austral. Slang* 31 When a horse is expected or 'fixed' to win a race it is said to 'go off'. **1949** L. GLASSOP *Lucky Palmer* 176 A bloke who's got a mare like Laughin' Water is extra welcome. Let's know when she's goin' off. **1976** S. WELLER *Bastards I have Met* 104 They had a real hot-pot ready to go off and they played it very cagey.

c. To be stolen.

1953 T.A.G. HUNGERFORD *Riverslake* 151, I wondered if you'd mind my wireless while I'm in Sydney? If I leave it in my room it'll go off. **1963** F. HARDY *Legends Benson's Valley* 44 There's been a lot of wood goin' orf from yards round the town lately.

goak. [Prob. altered form of *joke*, influenced by Br. dial. *goak* var. *gowk* fool, simpleton: see EDD.] A jest; a practical joke.

1869 *Lictor* (Sydney) 16 Dec. 339 Mr Alderman Andrews made an *impromptu* 'goak', which we cordially endorse. Let us have no 'free selection' among our visitors. If we are to entertain them at all, let us shew that we recognise not only the officer, but the *sailor*. **1888** *Illustr. Austral. News* (Melbourne) 11 Feb. 26/4 Two sundowners, with the contemptuous insolence of their class, call upon our wandering artist to take their portrait. This is supposed to be a 'goak'. The photographer pays no heed to these sneers. **1931** *N.T. Times* (Darwin) 9 Jan. 8/1 Aussie can best be described in the words of Josh Billings: 'This is a 'goak'!'

goal. *Australian National Football.* Used *attrib.* in Special Comb. **goal sneak,** a player adroit at scoring goals, esp. one who takes the opposition unawares; a full-forward; **square,** a rectangle in front of the goal (see quot. 1968); **umpire,** one of two umpires who judges when a goal or behind is scored.

1881 [**goal sneak**] *Devon Herald* (Latrobe) 14 Sept., Crooks and Henry as goal snicks had their time fully taken up. **1894** J.M. MACDONALD *Thunderbolt* 88 The local goal-sneak . . turned round and made a flying drop at the coveted space between the posts. **1900** B. KERR *Silliad* 21 Full well the unerring goal-sneak's fame was known. **1964** *Footy Fan* (Melbourne) II. ii. 30 Hawthorn and Victorian full-forward John Peck, last year's winning 'goalsneak' with 75 in the bag. **1969** *Sporting Globe* (Melbourne) 9 July 2/2 Rooky Carlton goalsneak Doug Baird impressed me. **1982** G. ATKINSON *Everything about Austral. Rules Football* 203 Goal-sneaks . . watch the ball and play for it. **1959** PARNELL & ANDREW *Austral. Football* 35 It is very poor forward work to crowd the **goal square.** **1968** B. HOGAN *Follow Game* 3 Two straight lines are drawn at right angles to the goal line for a distance of 10 yards from each goal post. The outer ends of these lines are joined by another straight line to form a rectangle 10 yards by 7 yards. This rectangle is often referred to as the 'goal square'. **1971** B. ANDREW *Austral. Football Handbk.* 85 Five players of the one team flying for a Mark and packing up the goal square. **1876** T.P. POWER *Footballer* 1 Umpires are appointed, goal and field, a **goal umpire** standing between the goal-posts at each end, and deciding as to goals, and the field umpire following the ball, throwing it in out of bounds. **1885** D.E. MCCONNELL *Austral. Etiquette* 640 The Goal Umpires shall be the sole judges of goals, and of cases of the ball going behind goals, and in case of doubt may appeal to the Field Umpire. **1931** J.F. MCHALE et al. *Austral. Game of Football* 44 A position might arise when a goal umpire is unable to give the decision. **1965** A. SCOTT *Man. Austral. Football* 67 At the end of each quarter, the two goal umpires should compare their score-cards to make sure they agree. **1971** B. ANDREW *Austral. Football Handbk.* 87 Two Goal Umpires indicate when goals or behinds have been scored after receiving the 'All Clear' from the Field Umpire.

goanna /goʊ'ænə/. Formerly also **gohanna.** [Altered form of *iguana* any of several large lizards.]

1. A monitor, any lizard of the genus *Varanus*, typically large and fast-moving; GUANA; IGUANA, *tree lizard*, see TREE. See also BOBTAIL.

1831 G.A. ROBINSON in N.J.B. Plomley *Friendly Mission* 12 July (1966) 376 The *kie* or rat had torn up the ground in quest of the goanna's eggs. **1848** *Maitland Mercury* 25 Oct. 2/4 The body was floating on its back, naked with a large gohanna lying on it. **1890** A.J. VOGAN *Black Police* 307 A 'gohanna', as old Williams calls the iguana-like lizards. **1908** *Bulletin* (Sydney) 16 July 14/3 The gohanna is a whale on hen fruit. **1926** A.S. LE SOUEF et al. *Wild Animals Aust.* 279 The great monitor lizard, or goanna. **1932** R.W. THOMPSON *Down Under* 153 Goannas also were numerous. Strange reptiles, sometimes six feet long, and exactly like small crocodiles. **1949** H.G. LAMOND *White Ears* 56 Carney lizards and goannas were reeking in rich oils from a surfeit of grasshoppers. **1962** H.J. FRITH *Mallee-Fowl* 109 The goanna, large and strong, can chase the bird from the mound and dig in and destroy the eggs. **1972** *Bulletin* (Sydney) 30 Dec. 8/1 He had found a goanna . . and offered the foundling beaten egg yolks in a silver egg-cup. Goanna swallowed cup and all. **1980** *Sydney Morning Herald* 13 Oct. 3/4 His Aboriginal employee has told him that though he will keep working, he will go back to goanna hunting for food.

2. Comb. **goanna fat, oil.**

1926 M. FORREST *Hibiscus Heart* 139 A trooper . . was cleaning his boots with **goanna fat.** **1930** 'BRENT OF BIN BIN' *Ten Creeks Run* (1958) 30 Do you think goanna fat mixed with wombat grease would take the freckles off your nose, Milly? **1963** I.L. IDRIESS *Our Living Stone Age* 9 Baby's first few baths, especially in the more arid lands, are given with soft, warm ashes lovingly rubbed over the skin, then goanna fat—which, by the way, has long been believed to contain medicinal properties by some white folk also—is rubbed well in for protection against heat, cold, and especially vicious flies and numerous biting insects. **1895** *Bulletin* (Sydney) 3 Aug. 28/1 Dave had a bottle of **'Goanna' oil** ready to keep his [boots] soft with. **1932** R.W. THOMPSON *Down Under* 154 Goanna Salve is an ointment of which the principal constituent is goanna oil, made from the fat of the goanna—a specific for rheumatism. **1944** C. BARRETT *From Bush Hut* 15 You'll not mind me tellin' you, sir, that goanna oil's best for a cold, and splendid for bullant stings. **1955** M. DURACK *Keep him my Country* (1966) 6 'Goanna oil,' he says, 'lizard in a bottle side of the stove, strain off the oil,' he says, 'cure fever, rheumatism, stricture, everything.' **1968** R. HILL *Bush Quest* 55 The old bushmen have a panacea, applicable to man or beast, for almost every ill short of the death spasm. 'Rub in a bit of goanna oil, mate, that'll fix her.'

3. Rhyming slang for 'piano': cf. 'joanna'.

1918 *7th Field Artillery Brigade Yandoo* Jan. 97 Did you know the 7th has a Y.M.C.A. now? Rather! We have got a 'gohanna' too. **1952** C. MACINNES *June in her Spring* 40 I've been fishing with him once or twice. . . He also plays the goanna. **1965** F. HARDY *Yarns of Billy Borker* 39 Grabbed the grand goanna and lowered it down in a lifeboat, see. They get ashore, load the piano on a truck and hides it.

goat.

1. In the phr. **goat and** (or **or**) **galah,** used *attrib.* of a hotel, town, etc., to indicate a low level of amenity.

1924 V. PALMER *Black Horse* 69 It was a little bit of a township near the Warrego. . . Smaller than this, wasn't it Jack? . . A lot smaller. What they call a goat-and-galah township back there, Mrs Baker. **1945** *Bulletin* (Sydney) 7 Mar. 12/4 We dropped in at a goat-or-galah pub in a little western N.S.W. town. My cobber . . called for boiled eggs. A bowl of about a dozen was set in front of him. 'Strewth!' he exclaimed, 'I on'y wanted a couple.' 'That's all right,' the waitress smiled reassuringly, 'you won't get more than two good 'uns out of that lot!' **1949** E. NAPIER *Winter is in July* 168 Some men may intend deliberately to drink their savings; others will avoid the 'goat-and-galah' Bush-pubs until parched. **1951** J. DEVANNY *Travels N. Qld.* 167 Some . . were of the 'goat and galah' variety, the generic name given to pubs that supplied food of redoubtable nature.

2. In the collocation **hairy goat,** a horse which performs badly in a race. Also *transf.*

1941 S.J. BAKER *Pop. Dict. Austral. Slang* 34 *Hairy goat, run like a* (used esp. of horses), to perform badly in a race. **1956** J.T. LANG *I Remember* 150 It was a 'hairy goat' but Smithy decided it would be better to ride the 'hairy goat' than not have a mount. **1965** J. BEEDE *They hosed them Out* 192 Our skipper, from the time we got near the enemy coast, flew like a hairy goat. **1969** O. WHITE *Under Iron Rainbow* 110 If there'd been a few hairy goats galloping around and a couple of bookies standing on whisky cases it'd have looked like the bloody Roebourne races. **1978** J. HEPWORTH *His Bk.* 113 When the barrier flew up Warrego Willie went like a hairy goat—never even looked like running a drum.

goathead. [Prob. from the fancied resemblance of the spiny fruit of the plant to the horned head of a goat: cf. *bull head*, see BULL *n.*[3]] The shrub of all mainland States except Vic. *Sclerolaena bicornis* (fam. Chenopodiaceae), the fruits of which have two stout spines; any of several other similar plants, esp. DOUBLE-GEE. Also **goatshead,** and *attrib.*

1945 M. RAYMOND *Smiley* 17 A bindyeye—not the small, common kind, but a goatshead with four ugly barbs. **1952** A.M. DUNCAN-KEMP *Where Strange Paths go Down* 89 The bindi-eye, or useless Goatshead Burr. **1962** N. MONKMAN *Quest Curly-Tailed Horses* 179 On the Barrier islands I always go barefooted, but my feet were now soled with a mass of 'goat's heads', a most viciously spiked seed. **1974** S.L. EVERIST *Poisonous Plants Aust.* 410 *Emex australis* . . is known as goathead or bullhead but both these names are also applied to other plants with large spiny fruits. **1980** J. FITZPATRICK *Bicycle & Bush* 145 It made the machine harder to pedal and was consequently used only in areas where he encountered the more vicious 'goatshead'.

goburra /'goʊbərə/. *Obs.* [Prob. f. an Aboriginal language, but poss. an abbrev. form of KOOKABURRA.] KOOKABURRA. Also *attrib.*

1862 H. KENDALL *Poems & Songs* 123 Wild goburras laughed aloud Their merry morning songs. **1867** *Illustr. Sydney News* 16 Apr. 154/3 A brotherhood of chuff-headed goburras, those lusty laughing spirits of the bush, sat on the branches. **1891** P.D. LORIMER *Songs & Verses* (1901) 165 'Tis the Goburra choir—they still are filling Their happy lives with joy. **1904** *Truth* (Sydney) 20 Nov. 3/2 If a giant goburra had perched on the Lord Mayoral chair to guy the councillors, it couldn't have got in its condemnatory croaks so effectively. **1907** *Bulletin* (Sydney) 31 Oct. 15/3 The goburra has been called the 'settler's clock', but he should be altogether an unreliable one. Jacko is apt to go off at any time. **1918** *Barrack: Official Organ Imperial Camel Corps* 1 Feb. 3/2 Laughing goburras perched on the old split rail fence.

God's trousers. See quot. 1900.

1900 *Bulletin* (Sydney) 17 Feb. 14/2 The up-to-date larrikin doesn't really curse now, but has invented curious out-of-the-way expressions. . . The strangest I have heard is 'God's trousers!' . . 'God's trousers!' serves as verb, adjective and noun. It also does duty as curse and interjection. **1954** P. GLADWIN *Long Beat Home* 209 God's trousers, I don't get the chance.

goffer. [f. the name of *Goffe* and Sons Ltd., a Br. manufacturer of mineral waters; orig. Br. naval slang.] A soft drink.

1945 *Dit* (Melbourne) June 29, 1 'goffer' (lemon flavour). **1972** R. POLLARD *Cream Machine* 35, I pay, plunge the steel spike, and the top foams. They call them 'goffers'. **1982** J.J. COE *Desperate Praise* 132 *Goffer*, soft drink. Naval slang adopted by diggers whilst aboard the troopship HMAS Sydney en route to Vietnam.

gohanna, var. GOANNA.

go-in. [Transf. use of *go-in* attack or onslaught upon: see OED *go-in* and *go, v.* 80 f.] A battle; a fight; a row.

[**1871** *Austral. Town & Country Jrnl.* (Sydney) 11 Feb. 166/4 Both parties have stated their intention of having a 'go-in' at the Commissioner . . for damages.] **1900** *Advocate* (Burnie) 6 July 1/8 We started to march on the morning of the first 'go-in' at 3.30 a.m. . . We had a real good 'go-in'. **1917** Tas. Non-State Rec. 103/11 2 May, We are on the eve of another big 'go-in'. **1939** J. CAMPBELL *Babe is Wise* 312 Didn't we have some ding-dong go-ins. **1953** K. TENNANT *Joyful Condemned* 257 That had been the result of Jess's 'go-in' with Nance, and Jess was lucky to get only six months for malicious wounding. **1968** *Swag* (Sydney) i. 5/2 We had a bit of a session—a 'go in' as they call it. **1981** A.B. FACEY *Fortunate Life* 61, I heard him say to Mum that her brother was a dirty scoundrel. She didn't like this and they had a real go-in.

going, *pres. pple.* [Used elsewhere but recorded earliest in Aust.] In the phr. **how are you going?** a conventional greeting; cf. 'how's things?'

1958 O. RUHEN *Naked under Capricorn* 118 'Why, hullo, Charlie,' Ben said. 'How are you going?' **1968** H.D. DALGLEISH *Tie my Swag* I. 1 'How ya goin'?' called Bill from behind the big bar—'I'm goin' to Hell!' said Muldoon—'it's not far.' **1968** D. O'GRADY *Bottle of Sandwiches* 151 G'day. Owyezgoin'? **1973** F. MOORHOUSE *Austral. Stories* 58 Bob said, 'Giday, how ya going?' **1979** D. MAITLAND *Breaking Out* 62 Walking, talking, irreverent identity crises hanging on the flyscreen door with a case of chilled beer, a howyergarnmate—orrite?

gold. *Mining.* In Comb. and Special Comb. chiefly *Hist.*

1. In the phr. **to be (up)on gold**: (of a claim) to contain auriferous material; (of a miner) to be mining auriferous material.

1871 *Austral. Town & Country Jrnl.* (Sydney) 4 Mar. 271/3 Several claims are upon good gold. **1892** 'R. BOLDREWOOD' *Nevermore* II. 244 He saw the windlass and shaft of Number Six, above which floated a red flag, the well-known signal, brought here by Californian miners, that the claim was 'on gold'. **1893** J.A. BARRY *Steve Brown's Bunyip* 72 No life can equal that of a digger's if he be 'on gold', even moderately so; if not, none so weary and heartbreaking. **1898** D.W. CARNEGIE *Spinifex & Sand* 7 Right enough for the lucky ones 'on gold', and for them not a life of ease! **1911** *Bulletin* (Sydney) 19 Jan. 13/4 Roughly, there were 2000 men on the rush, and a fair percentage were on gold. **1939** A. GASTON *Coolgardie Gold* 53, I was on a little gold but thought I could do better in some of the abandoned claims. **1946** K.S. PRICHARD *Roaring Nineties* 335 If a man was on gold, nobody bothered about his manners or who his father was. **1977** J. DOUGHTY *Gold in Blood* 85 There were very few men 'on gold' those days.

2. Comb. **gold country** [U.S., see Mathews], **find, finder, finding, hunter** [U.S., see Mathews], **hunting** [U.S., see Mathews], **seeker** [U.S., see Mathews], **seeking.**

1851 *Empire* (Sydney) 15 Aug. 51/1 The earliest and most certain information from the **Gold Country.** **1872** 'RESIDENT' *Glimpses Life Vic.* 115 The gold-country is usually undulating. **1893** *Braidwood Dispatch* 7 June 2/5 Information . . respecting the Tid River **gold-find**, stating that payable gold has been found on the supposed old river bed. **1917** *Bulletin* (Sydney) 1 Feb. 22/1 Bathurst . . royal mail-coach . . opened its service . . at the time of the big goldfinds, early in the '70s. **1981** A.B. FACEY *Fortunate Life* 12 A railway the Government was building from Kalgoorlie to another gold find. **1851** *Empire* (Sydney) 10 July 3/4 Mr Stewart . . and party, amongst whom is the **gold finder** McGreggor, have been successful in finding some beautiful specimens of gold. **1852** G.B. EARP *Gold Colonies Aust.* 130 The camp of the goldfinders was called the city of Ophir. **1937** H.E. GRAVES *Who Rides?* 20 A tried and knowledgeable gold-finder. **1851** *Bell's Life in Sydney* 31 May 1/3 Disgust against **gold-finding.** **1853** S. SIDNEY *Three Colonies* (ed. 2) 376 We have done very little here for six weeks past in gold-finding, though we have worked hard. **1885** N.W. SWAN *Couple of Cups Ago* p. xii, So back to gold-finding, this time at Sandhurst. **1926** S. WESTLAW *White Peril* 311 To others belongs more honour than I deserve . . to Jim Johnstone for his black-tracking and gold-finding work. **1851** *Empire* (Sydney) 18 Aug. 59/1 The very picturesque style of habiliment affected by our **gold-hunters.** **1852** *Austral. Gold Digger's Monthly Mag.* iii. 10/2 How many a fine dream upon his bark bedstead has the gold hunter had of finding the 'original nugget'. **1851** 'OMEGA' *Gold in Aust.* 6 The raging fever for **Gold hunting**, in nine case out of ten, would perhaps invite him to the Diggings. **1852** *Murray's Guide to Gold Diggings* 48, 10 lb. of gold, the produce of one fortnight's gold-hunting. **1853** W. WESTGARTH *Vic.* 45 These soils . . are usually safe from the troubled scenes of gold-hunting. **1885** N.W. SWAN *Couple of Cups Ago* p. xi, Fortune, throughout his many months of gold hunting declined to smile on him. **1852** J. BONWICK *Notes of Gold Digger* 12 The delight of the **gold seeker**, when he first drops upon a good pocket of nuggets. **1855** N.L. KENTISH *Question of Questions!* 76 The fraternity of Gold-diggers in general, and of Gold-finders in particular, (also to that most comprehensive class in the whole world, the Gold-seekers). **1888** G. ROCK *Colonists* 5 Gold-seekers were flocking there from all parts of the world. **1943** *Bulletin* (Sydney) 18 Aug. 13/2 Even in the 'fifties goldseekers overlanding from S.A. to Ballarat found game so scarce that they had to shoot crows to survive. **1852** F. LANCELOTT *Aust. as it Is* I. 302 Numbers were disheartened, and abandoning **gold seeking** in despair, returned to Sydney. **1853** J. SHERER *Gold Finder Aust.* 39 The great game of gold-seeking. **1863** F. ALGAR *Handbk. to Colony N.S.W.* 6 The diggings in New South Wales were soon eclipsed by the much greater richness of those in Victoria, to which the great bulk of the gold-seeking population have since flocked.

3. Special Comb. **gold broker, buyer,** one who deals in gold; **cart,** a vehicle for the transport of gold; **colony,** an Australian Colony in which gold has been discovered; **commissioner,** an officer responsible for the issue and administration of *gold licences*; **digger** [U.S., see Mathews], a gold-miner, DIGGER 1; **digging** *vbl. n.*, **(a)** [U.S., see Mathews], gold-mining, also *attrib.*; **(b)** [U.S., see Mathews], a place where gold is found or mined; **escort,** an armed party responsible for the protection of gold being transported from the diggings; the vehicle used for this purpose; ESCORT a., *government escort*, GOVERNMENT B. 4; also *attrib.*, and **escorting** *vbl. n.*; **fever** [U.S., see Mathews], an over-riding urge to search for gold; the excitement associated with this; so **fevered** *ppl. a.*; **hole,** a hole excavated in the search for gold; **licence,** a permit to dig for gold, later *miner's right*, see MINER *n.*[2]; **mania** [U.S., see Mathews], *gold fever*; **police,** a force under the command of a *gold commissioner*; **rush,** an influx of people to a newly discovered goldfield; such a goldfield; also **rushing** *vbl. n.*; **show,** a trace of gold; COLOUR 1; **warden,** a judicial officer responsible for the maintenance of law and order on a goldfield; **washer,** one who mines alluvial gold; **washing** *vbl. n.*, **(a)** the process of separating alluvial gold from its surrounding materials; **(b)** [U.S., see Mathews], usu. in *pl.*, the site of an alluvial gold deposit.

1854 W. SHAW *Land of Promise* 94 **Gold-brokers** seem to vie with each other in auriferous exhibition. **1855** G.H. WATHEN *Golden Colony* 41 A class which has been called into existence by the gold discoveries—I mean the gold-brokers. **1892** T. BRACKEN *Dear Old Bendigo* 12 The principal gold brokers were located on View Point. **1852** *Moreton Bay Free Press* 24 June 3/5 One of the resident . . **gold buyers** on those diggings is Mr Abraham Solomons. **1853** J. SHERER *Gold Finder Aust.* 318 The gold-buyer . . was likewise a storekeeper. **1853** *Moreton Bay Free Press* 1 Mar. 3/4 The driver of the **gold cart** will have enough to do. **1859** R.H. HORNE *Austral. Facts & Prospects* 9 There rattled along three small, very strong gold-carts. **1978** B. OAKLEY *Ship's Whistle* (1979) 24 In the bush, by the Bendigo road. The gold cart has come to grief, and it's getting dark. **1862** C. ASPINALL *Three Yrs. Melbourne* 33 This may naturally be expected in a new **gold colony.** **1865** 'SPECIAL CORRESPONDENT' *Transportation* 12 Many is the immigrant who has landed at Freemantle with the full assurance that he had reached the rich and prosperous gold colonies. **1869** 'SPECIAL REPORTER' *Hist. Launceston & Western Railway* 3 The gold colony soon began to feel and to draw upon its own resources; and almost as by the hand of magic, the country from Melbourne to the Murray, and from west to east, became opened up. **1852** J. SHAW *Tramp to Diggings* 255 Mr Hardy, a **gold commissioner**, has stated . . that any man might earn his ten shillings a day. **1863** *Bell's Life in Sydney* 4 July 3/2 Neither police nor gold-commissioner honoured us with their presence. **1865** MRS A. CAMPBELL *Rough & Smooth* 70 Papa . . asked for shelter, telling her who he was, which the small regulation cap all gold commissioners were obliged to wear confirmed. **1872** 'RESIDENT' *Glimpses Life Vic.* 150 A troop of horsemen, among whom were several gold-commissioners and police officers. **1936** F. CLUNE *Roaming round Darling* 86 Grenfell was appointed gold commissioner, and the newly formed town was called after him. **1852** *Moreton Bay Free Press* 1 Jan. 2/2 Bathurst **gold-digger's** first class 'hole'. **1853** A. MACKAY *Great Gold Field* 23 The laborious gold digger, who endures any amount of toil and privation in the pursuit of gold. **1862** BACKHOUSE & TYLOR *Life & Labours G.W. Walker* App. 4 The occupation of the gold-digger is nearly allied to that of the gambler. **1890** A. WOODHOUSE *Man with Apples* 53 That slit made by the gold digger's knife when he entered the tent and tried to rob Maurice's father. **1909** W.G. SPENCE *Aust.'s Awakening* 18 There was no life more free and independent than that of the gold digger. **1963** I.L. IDRIESS *Our Living Stone Age* 156 The discovery and rich returns from the Empress, New Anniversary, and Gadfly made all men's mouths water, no matter whether we were gold-diggers, tin-scratchers, or silver-gougers. **(a) 1851** *Empire* (Sydney) 1 Aug. 3/1 **Gold digging** is no child's play. **1854** G.W. WALKER *Friendly Counsel* 8 Gold-digging is a lottery in which there are, it is true, some prizes, but many more blanks. **1862** A.J. ALEXANDER *Alexander's Colonial Guide* 11 Gold digging is still attractive, and sometimes paying, but not always so, and machinery now does a great part of the work. **1870** C.H. ALLEN *Visit to Qld.* 130 The Church of England is not . . much in favour amongst the gold-digging class. **1888** G. ROCK *Colonists* 8 Prospecting ventures and gold-digging pursuits. **1926** G. BLACK *Hist. N.S.W. Political Labor Party* i. 11 The gold-digging days. **(b) 1850** *Monthly Almanac* (Adelaide) 60 In the **Gold Diggins** the price of meat is . . high. **1853** *Visit to Aust. & Gold Regions* (S.P.C.K.) 37 A productive gold 'digging' has yet to be discovered. **1860** 'LADY' *My Experiences in Aust.* 125 Most of the bad characters I fancy are to be found in the immediate vicinity of the large towns, and the gold-diggings. **1888** 'R. BOLDREWOOD' *Robbery under Arms* (1937) 227 Here was the first Australian gold diggings in full blast. **1892** *Braidwood Dispatch* 17 Dec. 6/1, I was out in the gold-diggings. **1913** *Bulletin* (Sydney) 6 Feb. 15/4 The native-yam workings . . resemble an old alluvial gold diggings. **1935** F. CLUNE *Rolling down Lachlan* 121 On this road are the remains of the old gold-diggings. **1852** *Moreton Bay Free Press* 24 Aug. 3/3 A notice appears in the Government Gazette . . notifying that a **gold escort** will leave Tamworth for Sydney. **1859** R.H. HORNE *Austral. Facts & Prospects* 13, I suddenly found myself, after about a fortnight's residence in Victoria, the commander of a gold escort. **1882** A.J. BOYD *Old Colonials* 177, I travelled from Georgetown to Cardwell on one occasion with the Gold Escort. **1891** *Braidwood Dispatch* 25 Mar. 2/5 The first gold escort left Pambula to-day for Sydney and Merimbula with over 200 oz. of gold. **1917** W. LEES *Aboriginal Problem Qld.* 26, I was driving the gold escort from Bargo Brush to Campbelltown. **1918** *Bulletin* (Sydney) 30 May 22/3 Gold-escorting nowadays in Westralia has hardly any . . thrill. **1936** F. CLUNE *Roaming round Darling* 47 The gold escort came through in the early fifties, an added attraction to the bushrangers of the district. **1972** ANDERSON & BLAKE *J.S. Neilson* 41 Drive north-east to cut the former gold-escort track. **1851** *Empire* (Sydney) 5 Aug. 15/2 The **Gold fever** has now considerably abated. **1861** L.A. MEREDITH *Over Straits* 5 Then the gold-fever broke out . . and raged furiously. **1875** CAMPBELL & WILKS *Early Settlement Qld.* 58 He took the gold-fever and went to the diggings. **1884** *Goldfield's Reminisc.* p. vii, The exciting times of the first dozen years of our gold fever. **1894** *Bulletin* (Sydney) 31 Mar. 9/3 In one week over 1400 gold-fevered passengers left Melbourne for Westralia. **1901** *Twentieth Century Impressions W.A.* 32 In 1894, like many others, he contracted the 'gold fever', and came to Western Australia. **1923** H. LEAF *Under Southern Cross* 68 Many prospectors contract what is known as the 'gold fever' from which they may never recover. **1946** K.S. PRICHARD *Roaring Nineties* 70 You've got the gold fever, too, Alf. I can see it in your eyes. **1980** *Sydney Morning Herald* 13 Oct. 2/7 It was windy, wet and wintry this weekend in Wedderburn, the Victorian town where gold fever has struck twice in three months. **1852** J.E. ERSKINE *Short Acct. Late Discoveries Gold* 22 The weather . . set in cold and wet, which . . retarded the digging by flooding the banks of the creek, and filling the **'gold holes'**. **1862** C. ASPINALL *Three Yrs. Melbourne* 182, I was driving . . through some very rough Bush-road, which also was full of gold-holes. **1851** *Empire* (Sydney) 7 Aug. 22/7 The fund from **gold licenses** alone must, by this time amount to no inconsiderable sum. **1852** *Ibid.* 18 Feb. 690/3 Will the British Ministry expect to find a sufficient profit from convictism and gold licenses to pay the expense of whole regiments of soldiers? **1855** R. CARBONI *Eureka Stockade* 41 A regular volley of revolvers and other pistols now took place, and a good blazing-up of gold licences. **1851** J.C. HAWKER Diary 19 Dec., Owing to the fearful **gold Mania** both Miners and Smelters are leaving in hundreds for the Melbourne gold diggings. **1854** W. SHAW *Land of Promise* 64 One of the great disadvantages attending the gold mania has been the partial cessation of educational labours. **1861** J.D. LANG *Qld., Aust.* 127 Gold mania had affected multitudes, both of the mining population at all the existing diggings, and even of the more staid inhabitants of the colonial towns. **1853** *Moreton Bay Free Press* 22 Mar. 3/3 The **gold police** have now taken up the pursuit, and it is hoped that the ruffians may soon be in the hands of justices. **1911** A.L. HAYDON *Trooper Police Aust.* 40 What were known as the Gold Police came into force in the early fifties. . . In 1859 the Gold Police as a separate body disappeared. **1873** [**gold rush**] A. TROLLOPE *Aust. & N.Z.* I. 29 Gold rushing is of all pursuits . . the most alluring and the most precarious. **1893** G. TREGARTHEN *Austral. Cwlth.* 158 The gold-rush had introduced many unruly spirits. **1911** *Bulletin* (Sydney) 19 Jan. 13/4 The Westralian gold rushes of the early '90s never had a lynching. **1928** M.E. FULLERTON *Austral. Bush* 3 Pioneers of the gold rush period. **1935** F. CLUNE *Rolling down Lachlan* 186 When the gold-rush broke out in 1861. **1948** —— *Wild Colonial Boys* 165 Just before the goldrush, a long drought had parched the land. **1923** M.B. PETERSEN *Jewelled Nights* 210 'E's found a **gold show** on Long Plains. **1974** D. STUART *Prince of my Country* 64 They're on a bit of a gold show and this particular day Bill's down the shaft. **1867** J. BONWICK *J. Batman* 89 Like a rush to a new diggings before the arrival of a **gold** commissioner, or **warden** each new comer to Port Phillip grasped at what he could. **1895** A.C. BICKNELL *Travel & Adventure Northern Qld.* 38 A gold warden is appointed to each of the gold districts. **1897** R. NEWTON *Work & Wealth Qld.* 39 He hurries off to the township where the Gold Warden resides. **1901** *Bulletin* (Sydney) 2 Feb. 14/3 There is in Q. a gold-warden . . whose casual deed of daring was worth a few hot-blooded, impulsive V.C.'s. **1851** W.B. CLARKE *Researches Southern Goldfields N.S.W.* (1860) 16 The profits of the **gold washers** at present have not been great. **1852** *Murray's Guide to Gold Diggings* 41, I rode slowly up the valley, visiting several gold-washers on my way. **(a)** **1850** W.B. BROWN *Narr. Voyage London to S.A.* 16 Gold . . has recently been found in the beds of the Torrens and Onkaparinga Rivers, and **gold-washing** has already commenced. **1853** J. SHERER *Gold Finder Aust.* 34 The water . . was applied, as long as it lasted, for gold-washing. **1854** MRS C. CLACY *Lights & Shadows* I. 228 The leather belt, with fossicking-knife or hatchet—the swags, large tin gold-washing dishes. **1858** *Colonial Mining Jrnl.* Sept. 1/1 We . . having used one of Hart's Patent Gold Washing Machines . . certify to the advantages we have derived from its use. **(b)** **1851** *Empire* (Sydney) 20 Aug. 67/3 On Sunday night last, 24 strangers were lodged in Mr Macallum's huts, 5 miles from the gold washings. **1872** A. MCFARLAND *Illawarra & Manaro* 86 In some places gold-washings have been established.

4. *fig.* Used *attrib.* in Special Comb. as an emblem of privilege or affluence: **gold lace,** uniformed officialdom; also *attrib.*; **pass,** a warrant entitling the bearer (usu. a politician) to free travel on public transport systems; also *transf.*, and *attrib.*; **top,** champagne; also *fig.* and *attrib.*

1841 *Port Phillip Patriot* 21 Oct. 2/4 We have received from William's Town a communication addressed to 'the **gold lace** fraternity, *alias* the crown and anchor button mob'. **1851** *Empire* (Sydney) 17 Oct. 266/4 Runaways, . . at the sight of the gold lace, decamp with their tools. **1855** R. CARBONI *Eureka Stockade* 31 It is his policy ever to keep friendly, with red-coats and gold-lace, at one and the same time as with blueshirts and sou'-westers. **1867** *Essay on Politics in Verse* 4 Our local hero . . Blackguards 'gold-lace'. **1919** C.A. BERNAYS *Qld. Politics during Sixty Yrs.* 200 He has 'M.L.A.' attached to his name and a **gold** railway **pass** attached to his watch-chain. **1956** *CPD* (H. of R.) X. 2481 Recommendations which it is appropriate to handle administratively . . include such things as air and rail travel, the abolition of the gold pass, visits to the Australian territories. **1960** *Realist* (Sydney) iii. 26 We're politicians, after a manner of speaking. If the game was fair dinkum, we'd be travelling first class with a gold pass on the motor train. **1973** *Bulletin* (Sydney) 25 Aug. 13/3 A parliamentarian or senator is entitled to a life gold pass after having served in the Parliament for 20 years or for seven Parliaments. **1984** *Canberra Times* 17 Mar. 7/4 We didn't invent the gold pass. Politicians have passes to everything that moves in Victoria. **1984** *Age* (Melbourne) 22 Mar. 4/3 Building workers on the Arts Centre project remained off the job yesterday in support of their claim for a lifetime gold pass to performances at the centre. **1885** *Australasian Printers' Keepsake* 139, I cracked too much about the '**gold-top**' champagne (speaking candidly, gentlemen, ordinary fizz). **1896** T. HENEY *Girl at Birell's* 245 He stood rather in awe of his son-in-law, who was to him a swell, a squatter, a gold-top. **1901** *Truth* (Sydney) 8 Dec. 5/4 With the uncorking of a dozen or more of full-sized 'gold top', asked them to drink to 'our happy union'. **1928** N.F. SPIELVOGEL *Affair at Eureka* 31 Men smoked their pipes and listened, while waiters in felt slippers moved along the aisles with trays of cocktails . . and 'gold-top'. **1977** R. EDWARDS *Austral. Yarn* 30 There were mitred napkins, hors d'oeuvres of every sort, and gold tops showing above the napkins, which some said was . . sparkling cider—but in the end everyone praised the champagne.

golden, *a.*

1. Used in special collocations, esp. with reference to an apparent abundance of gold: **golden colony** *hist.*, Victoria; **fever** *hist.*, *gold fever*, see GOLD 3; **hole** *hist.*, a highly productive mining claim; also *attrib.*; **land** *hist.*, Australia, esp. Victoria; **mile,** see quot. 1971; **West,** Western Australia.

1857 W. WESTGARTH *Vic. & Austral. Gold Mines* 11 Streamed over as from an open gaol to the all-attractive shores of the **golden colony.** **1870** W.B. WITHERS *Hist. Ballarat* 44 There came . . drawn by the fame of the golden colony, some of the most accomplished . . artistes. **1851** *Empire* (Sydney) 18 July 2/3 Bathurst is made again. The delirium of **golden fever** has returned with increased intensity. **1875** G.M. NEWMAN *N.T. & its Gold-Fields* 9 The golden fever became contagious through the land. **1855** J. CHARLESWORTH *Visit to Diggings* 5, I had a **golden hole,** and did not know it until months afterwards. **1855** R. CARBONI *Eureka Stockade* 8 Gravel Pits, famous for its strong muster of golden holes. **1871** *Austral. Town & Country Jrnl.* (Sydney) 21 Jan. 71/1 Two more golden holes have been bottomed. **1892** 'R. BOLDREWOOD' *Nevermore* I. 94 A 'golden-hole man' and the half-owner of one of the richest claims on the field. **1896** H. LAWSON *While Billy Boils* 5 They lowered the young bride, blindfolded, down a golden hole in a big bucket, and got her to point out the drive from which the gold came that her ring was made out of. **1852** *Austral. Gold Digger's Monthly Mag.* ii. 39 The southern mines sustained the honour of the **golden land** when the western fields began to fail. **1854** *Bell's Life in Sydney* 23 Dec. 1/3 He left England certain of making a fortune in the Golden Land. **1863** J. BONWICK *Wild White Man* 2 William Buckley was to be one of these first unsuccessful settlers of the golden land of Victoria. **1901** M. VIVIENNE *Travels in W.A.* 210 From this place one has a glorious view of the other great mines on the **Golden Mile**, so-called on account of the marvellous quantity of gold that has been and is still being extracted from its depths—Lake View, Great Boulder, Ivanhoe, Boulder Perseverance, and Golden Horseshoe. **1906** *Gadfly* (Adelaide) 21 Mar. 3/1 The stars look down on the Golden Mile and the pubs. of Boulder Block. **1911** E.D. CLELAND *Austral. W. Mining Practice* p. xvi, Mines on what is now known as the 'Golden Mile' began to show results. **1938** W. HATFIELD *Buffalo Jim* 34 'That'll see you pretty well to the Mile.' 'The Mile?' 'Kalgoorlie. They call it the Golden Mile.' **1948** M. UREN *Glint of Gold* 24 Hannan's Find became Kalgoorlie, the Golden Mile, the richest square mile of auriferous ground in the world. **1971** C. SIMPSON *New Aust.* 557 The Golden Mile lies between Kalgoorlie and Boulder and is an extraordinarily rich auriferous reef area that is actually about two miles long and a third of a mile wide and has been mined to thousands of feet. **1984** *Canberra Times* 12 May 25/1 Kalgoorlie's famous Golden Mile has again lived up to its reputation as the richest stretch of dirt on Earth. **1897** *Worker* (Sydney) 13 Feb. 2/2 Men flocking in for another year's 'yacker' in the '**Golden West**'. **1901** *Illawarra Mercury* (Wollongong) 31 Jan. 2/6 Mr Ewing after finishing his articles with Mr Woodward as a solicitor, struck out for the 'Golden West'. **1903** *Westminster Gaz.* (London) 28 Jan. 9/2 They [*sc.* men from the Eastern States] looked upon the golden West as a wilderness to be exploited, and left as soon as possible. **1917** *Bulletin* (Sydney) 9 Aug. 24/1 The snake-wood tree . . bedecks the auriferous belts of the Golden West. **1948** M. UREN *Glint of Gold* 27 Because of successive gold discoveries, Western Australia came to be called the 'Golden West'.

2. With reference to privilege or affluence: **Golden Casket,** a State lottery in Queensland (see quot. 1955); **fleece** *hist.*, wool, esp. as perceived as the source of national wealth; **lace** *hist.*, *gold lace*, see GOLD 4; **top** *hist.*, *gold top*, see GOLD 4.

1916 *Telegraph* (Brisbane) 25 Nov. 3/6 Queensland's **Golden Casket** Art Union. Australian Soldiers' Repatriation Fund. (For returned sailors and soldiers.) **1917** *Ibid.* 15 June 3/3 As is well known, the Golden Casket Art Union was held for the purpose of augmenting the repatriation fund. **1942** A.L. HASKELL *Waltzing Matilda* 194 The Golden Casket is a lottery that was inaugurated in 1916 for patriotic purposes. **1955** N. PULLIAM *I traveled Lonely Land* 75 In Queensland the lottery operates under the unusual name of the 'Golden Casket'. It was started during World War I to raise funds for some sort of patriotic effort and subsequently was taken over by the government, under which it has continued to flourish, producing the money to build and maintain the large and numerous hospitals of Queensland. **1957** D. NILAND *Call me when Cross turns Over* 50 It was just like winning a prize in the Golden Casket, only better. **1837** *Sydney Herald* 29 June 2/2 Australia's '**golden fleece**'. **1848** *Port Phillip Herald* 30 Mar. 2/2 Our staple commodity, the 'golden fleece', has increased its export during the past year. **1852** *Empire* (Sydney) 6 Jan. 543/3 The stillness which so long reigned around, was broken in upon by the passage through the town of teams carrying the golden fleece of Australia to the metropolis. **1879** 'AUSTRALIAN' *Adventures Qld.* 116 The shearers arrived and took off the 'golden fleeces'. **1890** J. SADLER *Lyrics & Rhymes* 33 Land of the Golden Fleece! Give me thy plenty, happiness, and peace! **1914** J. FERGUSON *White Aust.* 10 So we will sing till the echoes ring, To the land of the golden fleece. **1927** 'JULIET' *Devotion* 15 Australia had settled down to more solid prosperity after the golden nugget had been replaced as a source of natural wealth by the golden fleece, and subsequently by the addition of the golden grain. **1855** R. CARBONI *Eureka Stockade* 24 Who dares to teach the **golden-lace** . . how to shoot? **1903** J. FURPHY *Such is Life* 87 Illicit snake-juice for them, and **golden top** for the other fellow.

3. As a distinguishing epithet in the names of flora and fauna: **golden-headed fantail warbler,** the small warbler *Cisticola exilis* of Aust. and elsewhere; TAILOR-BIRD; see also *corn-bird* CORN 2; **perch,** the yellowish or white fresh-water fish *Macquaria ambigua* (fam. Percichthyidae, formerly classed in Percidae) of s.e. Aust. and prob. introduced into W.A. and N.T.; CALLOP; YELLOWBELLY; see also *Murray perch* MURRAY 2; **shoulder,** the parrot *Psephotus chrysopterygius* of Cape York Peninsula, Qld., having yellow median wing coverts; see also ANTHILL PARROT; also **golden-shouldered parrot** (or **parakeet**); **wattle,** the heavily flowering small tree *Acacia pycnantha* (fam. Mimosaceae) of N.S.W., Vic., and S.A., popularly regarded as the floral emblem of Australia; PYCNANTHA WATTLE; **(breasted) whistler,** the bird *Pachycephala pectoralis* of s. and e. Aust., the male having yellow on the neck and underparts; *white-throated thickhead*, see WHITE *a.*[2] 1 b.

1911 J.A. LEACH *Austral. Bird Bk.* 142 **Golden-headed Fantail-Warbler.** **1917** *Bulletin* (Sydney) 19 July 24/4, I plump for the little tit-warbler . . and the barley-bird or golden-headed fantail-warbler (*Cisticola exilis*) as the two smallest Australian birds. **1952** B. BEATTY *Unique to Aust.* 52 The Golden-headed Fantail Warbler, after building its coned nest, sews on leaves using cobwebs and gossamers for thread and its beak for a needle. **1964** M. SHARLAND *Territory of Birds* 96 Three Golden-headed Fantail Warblers . . were living in the rank grass fringing the garden. **1847** G.F. ANGAS *Savage Life & Scenes* I. 92 The **golden perch** are driven out of the rushes. **1873** F. DE CASTELNAU *Edible Fishes Vic.* 9 The most important of the Murray fishes, after the cod, is the *golden perch*. . . It unites beauty of colours to the good quality of its flesh. **1906** D.G. STEAD *Fishes of Aust.* 97 The Golden Perch or 'Yellow-belly' . . is abundant in all the western rivers of New South Wales. **1911** *Bulletin* (Sydney) 30 Mar. 44/2 Some of the tanks are so large that you can spend hours round them shooting ducks. A few contain yellow-belly (golden perch). **1935** F. BIRTLES *Battle Fronts Outback* 161 Yellow-belly, or golden-perch, up to a few pounds in weight, bit readily. **1951** T.C. ROUGHLEY *Fish & Fisheries* 147 The name 'callop' has been customarily used for this fish in South Australia over a long period of years, whereas in New South Wales it was until recently referred to as golden perch or yellowbelly, in Victoria frequently as freshwater bream, and in Queensland and Western Australia as Murray perch. **1985** *Sydney Morning Herald* 6 Feb. 6/4 When trees fall into the river, they provide a natural shelter for . . golden perch and other fish. [**1859 golden shoulder:** J. GOULD *Birds of Aust.* Suppl. (1869) Pl. 64, Golden-backed Parrakeet. . . This bird is in every way a true *Psephotus*. . . It is allied both to the *P. pulcherrimus* and *P. multicolor*, but differs from them, among other characters, in the rich-yellow mark on the shoulder.] **1865** —— *Handbk. Birds Aust.* II. 65 Golden-shouldered Parrakeet. **1928** G.H. WILKINS *Undiscovered Aust.* 143 The beautiful golden-shouldered parrots, which make their nests in deserted anthills, were disappearing fast. **1946** W.E. HARNEY *North of 23°* 75 Above flashes in the sunlight that marvel of colour and flight, the golden shoulder. **1970** P. SLATER *Eagle for Pidgin* 41 Something rare, like golden-shouldered parrots, brings up to three thousand dollars a pair. **1975** *Bulletin* (Sydney) 22 Feb. 20/2 The more exotic parrots, such as Golden Shoulders and Superbs, fetch $10,000 a pair. **1980** M. GRANT *Barrier Reef* 9 He pronounced them Golden Shoulders, certainly one of the rarest and most expensive birds in the world, found only in the narrow strip of dry Savannah grassland in the far north of Australia where they live on termite mounds. **1985** P. CAREY *Illywhacker* 587 The last-recorded golden-shouldered parrot was destined to take its species into extinction, to breathe its last breath in the honey-sweet embrace of a beautiful woman. **1850** J.B. CLUTTERBUCK *Port Phillip* 32 Few . . of the native Australian flowers emit any perfume except the **golden** and silver **Wattle.** **1878** R.B. SMYTH *Aborigines of Vic.* II. 173 Golden-wattle . . Acacia pycnantha. **1890** *Sydney Mail* 14 June 1300/1 A 7 lb. bag of the seed of the South Australian Golden or Broad-leaved Wattle. **1918** C.E. BOSWORTH *Shoe & Leather Trade* 37 Two wattles used for tanning are locally known as golden wattle and green wattle. **1921** A.J. CAMPBELL *Golden Wattle* 28 In September the Golden Wattle . . with its stiff eucalypt-like leaves . . is in full flower. **1946** A.H. CHISHOLM *Making of Sentimental Bloke* 8 *Acacia pycnantha*, the golden wattle, perhaps the most decorative and fragrant member of the whole large group. **1963** X. HERBERT *Disturbing Element* 40 Chewing the sweet seeds of knobby-grass under a scarlet flowering gum or golden wattle. **1985** *Canberra Times* 15 Aug. (Suppl.) 11/1 The broad-leafed golden wattle is generally recognised as the Australian national emblem. **1917** [**golden whistler**] *Bulletin* (Sydney) 16 Aug. 22/3 Golden-breasted whistler (also called white-throated thick-head). **1942** C. BARRETT *From Bush Hut* 25, I heard the golden whistler's song. **1948** P.J. HURLEY *Red Cedar* 141 That glorious rollicking songster, the Golden Whistler. **1976** *Reader's Digest Compl. Bk. Austral. Birds* 375 Golden whistlers are common in dense forests.

goldfield. [Used elsewhere but recorded earliest in Aust.]

1. A place in which gold is found and mined. Also *attrib.*

1851 J.H. BURTON *Emigrant's Man.* ii. 123 You may suppose a gold-field a most original sight: at a distance it can only be compared to an immense army, encamped in myriads of tents of all shapes, sizes, and colours. **1851** *Empire* (Sydney) 2 Aug. 6/4 The tide of emigration from England to the Gold Fields will have set in. **1853** MOSSMAN & BANISTER *Aust. Visited & Revisited* 21 Their flocks and herds had been cropping the very grass which grew upon the 'gold fields'. **1861** C. CAMPBELL *Squatting Question Considered* 14 We have been deteriorated by the presence of gold-fields, where concubinage . . has infected our population. **1876** *Willmett & Co.'s Cooktown Almanac* 26 The gold-fields of the far north very soon became of such importance as to demand the appointment of a gold commissioner. **1883** R.E.N. TWOPENY *Town Life Aust.* 245 When speaking of a goldfield a colonist says 'on'. Thus you live 'on Bendigo', but 'in' or 'at' Sandhurst—the latter being the new name for the old goldfield town. **1903** *Bulletin* (Sydney) 11 Apr. 16/1 It was at a Goldfields Mission, In the land of Sand and Sin, That a wandering apostle Asked the Groper miners in. **1911** *Huon Times* (Franklin) 1 Feb. 4/3 The Yilgarn gold field requirements were also before both Houses. **1926** A.J. GOLDSMITH *Reminisc. Old Engineer* 5 We arrived in Melbourne in the goldfield days, to find living very rough. **1937** H.E. GRAVES *Who Rides?* 18 Kalgoorlie . . with its little-sister town of Boulder . . forms the principal gold-mining area of Western Australia. These two towns are The Goldfields as distinct from many minor goldfields. **1950** G. CASEY *Wits are Out* 290 The goldfield outback is served by slow trains and fast motor-trucks. **1978** B. OAKLEY *Ship's Whistle* (1979) 31 Seventy thousand men out on the goldfields and five hundred troopers to watch 'em. I'm not raising the licence fee.

2. In the collocation **goldfields scavenger,** a whirlwind.

1903 J. MARSHALL *Battling for Gold* 85 (*caption*) 'Willy Willy' or Goldfields Scavenger. **1929** W.J. RESIDE *Golden Days* 341 Goldfields residents also knew of the 'Willy-willy', or, as it was sometimes called 'the Goldfields Scavenger'.

goldfielder. [Chiefly Aust.: see prec.] One who works or resides on a goldfield.

1903 *Westminster Gaz.* (London) 28 Jan. 9/2 The goldfielders began to clamour for separation, and talked rather wildly of setting up a Government of their own in the interior and using Esperance Bay as a port. **1920** *Referee* (Sydney) 11 Feb. 13/5 The coastal swimmers received a great shock at the skill and power shown by the Goldfielders. **1929** W.J. RESIDE *Golden Days* 5 The author is indebted to all old Goldfielders. **1936** J. KIRWAN *My Life's Adventure* 113 J.H. Curle, a mining engineer . . was amongst the early day goldfielders. **1950** G.S. CASEY *City of Men* 49 The holidaying goldfielder starts off pretty scornful of the seventh-story [*sic*] miners in city office buildings.

goldfish. In Services' speech: tinned fish. Also *attrib.*

1942 T. KELAHER *Digger Hat* 24 You're sick of eating 'goldfish', bully beef and army stew. **1943** *Troppo Tribune* (Mataranka) 4 Jan. 3 Goldfish and onions to swell out the waist. **1945** G. POWELL *Two Steps to Tokyo* 146 'Goldfish' . . are tinned sardines of the large variety. **1962** MARSHALL & DRYSDALE *Journey among Men* 104 'Tell us about your part in that rather disagreeable goldfish business during the war, Dom.' . . 'It was not goldfish,' said Dom quietly. 'The fish is *Nematalosa erebi*, a so-called bony bream. It is, in fact, a true herring—one of the soft-rayed clupeoid fishes.' **1974** L. WEDLICK *Sporting Fish* 18 Returned servicemen need no introduction to the hairback herring, having met it during World War II as a canned herring. They were known in army language as 'goldfish'.

gonce /gɒns/. *Obs.* Also **gons.** [Of unknown origin.] Money.

1899 *Bulletin* (Sydney) 1 July 32/2 Yes, I'm doin' pretty middlin' And I'm layin' up the gonce. **1902** *Truth* (Sydney) 25 May 2/2 You're a glutton for the 'gonce'—gonce in Australia meaning gold. **1905** *Shearer* (Sydney) 18 Nov. 4/2 How much of our 'gonce' has gone to line the pockets of a crowd of human leeches who don't care a tinker's d-- for us or our troubles? **1906** *Truth* (Sydney) 8 Apr. 8/1 God gets all the glory and Booth gets all the 'gonce'. **1916** *Ibid.* 29 Oct. 7/3 It doesn't matter to me much from whence they sprang; they are here, and they have got the 'gonce'. **1918** J.A. PHILP *Jingles that Jangle* 52 We hadn't copped the gons yet. **1930** J.S. LITCHFIELD *Far-North Memories* 8 Old dad can't spare any time for frills; but he's got the gonce all right. He's worth more than most of the first-class travellers on this boat. **1941** S.J. BAKER *Pop. Dict. Austral. Slang* 32 *Gons*, money.

good, *a.*

1. In the collocation **good on you** (**her, him,** etc.): an expression of approbation, 'well done!'.

1907 *Truth* (Sydney) 11 Aug. 1/7 Good on them! Another ship captain . . has been fined £100 for landing a smelful alien on our shores, to contaminate the country. **1920** A.I. MACLEOD *Hack's Brat* (ed. 2) 14 'MacLure will stay here to start the mine.' 'It ain't moonshine, then?' 'No—it's a jolly good speck.' 'Good on yer!' howled Watty. **1922** A. WRIGHT *Boss o' Yedden* 117 'Miss Goulder warned the train in time, but the bridge went up.' 'Good on her,' cried Tom, admiringly. **1935** DAVISON & NICHOLLS *Blue Coast Caravan* 232 There was an Australian present. . . Following each anecdote he clicked his tongue and said, 'Good on you!' **1958** F.B. VICKERS *Though Poppies Grow* 55 'I was in the R.A.A.F. for four years.' 'Good on you.' **1968** H.D. DALGLEISH *Tie my Swag* I. 36 His approbation hit the spot. . . 'By Cripes! Good on yer, mate!' **1975** J. ALDRIDGE *Untouchable Juli* 181 'Good on you, Dad,' my young brother Tom (our family moralist) shouted down the table. 'How many times must I tell you not to use that Australian expression in this house.' **1982** R. HALL *Just Relations* 265 'Good on you Uncle', shouted Billy. 'Good on you Uncle', other voices encouraged him.

2. [Perh. f. U.S. *to feel good* to feel in good spirits or health: see OED(S *good, a.* 3 c.] In good health, well.

1934 T. WOOD *Cobbers* 27 He said he was good, which means his health was, and added that it was a bonza day. **1950** 'B. JAMES' *Advancement Spencer Button* 165 'How is he?' said Mr O'Leary one day when Carlyle was about seven or eight months old. 'Good,' said Spencer. . . 'He's active—never saw such a wonderful crawler.' **1960** J. GLENNON *Heart in Centre* 231 'How have you been?' he said. 'Me? Oh, good.' 'Sleeping well?' 'Never better.' **1977** E. MACKIE *Oh to be Aussie* 7 The most the Aussie will do, if well disposed towards you is to ask you 'howyergoin?' In answer to this *never* say more than 'Good thanks!' and hang the grammar! **1979** *Westerly* i. 7 'Hello. . . How are you?' 'Good thanks. How about you?'

3. In the phr. **to come good,** to fulfil an expectation or aspiration; (of a situation, etc.) to ameliorate.

1946 A. THURIAN *Bush Tea & Overlanders* 13 There had come good the chance to class some sheep. **1956** F.B. VICKERS *First Place to Stranger* 121 What's the good of howling about it? It'll come good if you stick it. **1960** M. VIZZERS *She'll do Me!* 83 Australia would 'come good' again. Brighter times were ahead. **1972** J. HIBBERD *Stretch of Imagination* (1973) 45 The elements have come good. This augurs well for the ensuing festivities. **1977** B. SCOTT *My Uncle Arch* 135 He came good, when we put it on him for a job without any argument. **1981** D. STUART *I think I'll Live* 8 Righto, Kek, come good with a quid or two, these blokes don't put it in the book for strangers like us.

good day. Also **g'day, gidday, gooday.** [Elliptical form of *(may you) have a good day*: see OED *good, a.* 10 c. and *good day*.] A familiar greeting, used freq. and at any hour.

1857 *Illustr. Jrnl. Australasia* III. 66 Not one of them spoke to me, except to give me an occasional 'Good day, mate'. **1862** A. POLEHAMPTON *Kangaroo Land* 99 A man . . greeted me after the fashion of the Bush, with a 'Good day, mate!' **1872** H. HEAD *Under Cloud* 27 The 'good-day' mates of these old chums Seemed very strange to me, For though I'd been three years from home, They had been spent at sea. **1882** *Rec. Castlemaine Pioneers* 31 Mar. (1972) 47 'Good day, mate,' was the salutation of a blue-shirt. 'Good day, mate,' we echoed, 'are you from the diggings?' **1898** G.T. BELL *Coolgardie* 47 Not much ceremony enters into the salutation—a gruff 'Good day, mate'. **1919** R.J. CASSIDY *Gipsy Road* 87 Out in the Bush every stranger bids him 'Good day' . . but here nobody says 'Good day', instead the men and women pass him with stony, unrecognising stares. **1928** *Bulletin* (Sydney) 19 Dec. 20/1 He had little to say—Just a quiet 'G'day'. **1939** *Southerly* i. 17 Slowed down his car beside the tin and bag humpy to exchange his usual 'good-day' with the old man. **1948** R.A. PEPPERALL *Emigrant to Aust.* 57 An exchange of 'Good'ay' on his part and a pedantic 'Good evening' on mine. **1959** D. STUART *Yandy* 53 Ernie said 'Gooday' and pointed to the small fire behind the siding shed where the billy was boiling. **1963** D. ATTENBOROUGH *Quest under Capricorn* 26 'G'day,' we said, slipping into the vernacular. 'Yer right?' 'Ball o' muscle,' he replied with gusto. . . 'If I felt any better I couldn't stand it.' **1973** *Overland* lvii. 46 'G'day,' I said. 'G'day,' the fella answered. 'G'day,' said Benny. **1974** D. STUART *Prince of my Country* 135 'Righto, gooday, young David' . . he answers, wondering why such a well spoken man says 'Gooday' only for a greeting. . . 'Gooday' is for daytime or anytime. If you meet a bloke at midnight you still say 'Gooday'. **1981** P. CORRIS *White Meat* 19 'Gidday,' he said, 'pleased to met you.' **1985** *Canberra Times* 25 Nov. 2/2 You can get pretty sick of people saying 'G'day' in New York these days.

good man. *Obs.* A convict whose behaviour in custody is exemplary: see BAD 1.

1788 D. COLLINS *Acct. Eng. Colony N.S.W.* (1798) I. 43 A convict who had been looked on as a good man (no complaint having been made of him since his landing, either for dishonesty or idleness). **1837** *Rep. Select Committee Transportation* 9 May (1838) 117 They go out perhaps 30 in a gang . . under the charge of a convict who is considered an active sort of a man, and perhaps better dressed than the others, and he passes as a good man. **1847** A. HARRIS *Settlers & Convicts* (1953) 108 Being paid by the piece, men acquire a habit of working so eagerly . . if they are what are called 'good men'. **1850** W. GATES *Recoll. Van Dieman's Land* 124 If we continued to be good men till our probation of two years was expired, we should have tickets-of-leave.

good-o, *a., absol.*, and *adv.* Also **good-oh** and without hyphen.

A. *adj.* In a satisfactory or proper state, 'all right'.

[N.Z. **1905** THOMSON *Bush Boys* 34 That was real good-o.] **1914** 'B. CABLE' *By Blow & Kiss* 246 They're good-oh. . . Chock full of ginger yet. **1931** O. WALTERS *Shrapnel Green* 14 Don't you worry. It'll be good-o. **1938** C.P. CONIGRAVE *Walk-About* 186 'You must be mad to come to a place like this. . . ' 'Garn, it's good-o.' **1946** *Southerly* ii. 75 'Tastes goodoh, eh?'. . 'Tastes absolutely bonzer. . . ' 'I'm out to get stonkered good and proper.' **1961** *Bulletin* (Sydney) 11 Nov. 30/3 It turned the meat black and a southern analyst said it wasn't fit for human consumption, but we reckoned it was good-oh. **1970** P. AMOS *Silver Kings* 157 He had always said . . to the union leaders, 'You scratch my back, I'll scratch yours and we'll all feel good-o.' **1982** *Down to Earth News: Confest 82* 28, I reckon it was real good-oh. Ace, even.

B. *absol.* Used as an exclamation, expressing assent or approbation.

1918 *Kia Ora Coo-ee* Aug. 5/2 'Fish for dinner to-day, Jack.' 'Good O! What sort?' 'Mafish.' **1919** W.A. CULL *At all Costs* 132 'You are going away in an hour.' 'Goodo!' I exclaimed. **1930** M.B. PETERSEN *Monsoon Music* 80 'You'd better make tracks and get to Narooma before we do—you may prove handy there.' 'Good-o.' **1937** H.E. GRAVES *Who Rides?* 111 She assented shyly . . with that silly, 'Oh, good-oh', which passes for 'Yes' in Western Australia. **1949** D. WALKER *We went to Aust.* 193 Whatever you say to anyone it's an even bet that they will counter with the cryptic remark 'good-o'. **1963** X. HERBERT *Disturbing Element* 168 Good-o. I'll see you there after school, eh? **1970** C. NOLAN *Bride for St. Thomas* 57 'Good-oh,' I said, over-loudly, trying to get closer to the retreating wall, 'Right-oh, bonzer.'

C. *adv.* Satisfactorily, properly, well.

1920 C.H. SAYCE *Golden Buckles* 120 The mills are working good-O.

good oil: see OIL *n.* 2.

goog /gʊg/. [Abbrev. of GOOGIE.]

1. An egg.

1941 S.J. BAKER *Pop. Dict. Austral. Slang* 32 *Goog*, an egg. **1953** T.A.G. HUNGERFORD *Riverslake* 210 He'll scone the Bastard with that goog. **1958** *Bulletin* (Sydney) 3 Sept. 18/1 Washed eggs aren't accepted. . . Retailers want clean googs, but they'd sooner have dirty ones than washed ones. **1959** D. NILAND *Big Smoke* 91 'Hey, Spider, he likes them googs. Where's another?' Mr Halley stopped his third egg. **1968** S. GORE *Holy Smoke* 13 A man'd be fried like a goog sunny side up in that outfit. **1981** P. BARTON *Bastards I have Known* 29 We half filled the tub with water, chucked in a handful of soap powder, and gingerly tipped in about 120 googs.

2. In the phr. **full as a goog**: see FULL *a.*[1] c.

googie /'gʊgi/. [f. Scot. dial. *goggie* child's word for an egg: see SND *googie*.] An egg. Also *transf.* and *fig.*, esp. in the collocation **golden googie,** a coin, a 'golden egg'; in *pl.* riches. Also **googie egg.**

1903 *Truth* (Sydney) 5 Apr. 5/2 At the show he will . . boast of the golden 'googies' he has in his 'kick'. **1905** *Ibid.* 27 Aug. 1/7 Patrick . . gets swindled out of 300 lovely golden googies by a cheque forger. **1907** *Ibid.* 7 Apr. 11/1 We are owing the grocery 1s. 10d. a dozen for 'fresh googies', and when you come to crack 'em in the morning—phew! The shell parts and they fairly snarl at one. **1914** *Ibid.* 13 Dec. 7/6 (*heading*) The bean tree. Golden googies grew thereon. **1945** S.J. BAKER *Austral. Lang.* 207 Among nursery expressions which have acquired a fairly stabilized currency in this country are *googy-egg* for an egg [etc.]. **1958** M.D. BERRINGTON *Stones of Fire* 78, I shall love to teach you Australian. . . Googies are eggs. **1968** B. HUMPHRIES *Nice Night's Entertainment* (1981) 113 Beryl popped an empty egg-shell upside-down in my egg-cup and I pretended I was surprised to find no googie egg inside. **1981** B. DICKINS *Gift of Gab* 2 Two holy eggcups . . that once supported my daddy's googy egg when he was a tin-lid.

goolie /'guli/, *n.* [Prob. f. a N.S.W. Aboriginal language.] A stone.

1924 *Truth* (Sydney) 27 Apr. 6/3 *Gooley*, a stone. **1941** S.J. BAKER *Pop. Dict. Austral. Slang* 32 *Gooly*, a stone or pebble. **1949** *Coast to Coast 1948* 34 He could . . hurl goolies, gibbers, and plain bluemetal with devastating accuracy. **1960** D. IRELAND *Image in Clay* (1964) 28 Garn, get out of it, before I let fly with a goolie. **1978** R. MCLELLAND *Outback Touring* 99 *Gibber plains*, 'ironstone' cobbles or 'goullies' cover the surface like an armour coating.

goolie /'guli/, *v.* [f. prec.] *trans.* To throw.

1982 *Nat. Times* (Sydney) 3 Jan. 49/1 He catapulted out of doors, shot towards the swimming pool and goolied the box into the chlorinated depths.

goom /gʊm, gum/. [Poss. transf. use of Jagara (and neighbouring languages) *guŋ* fresh water.]

a. Methylated spirits (as drunk by a derelict).

1967 *Kings Cross Whisper* (Sydney) xxxv. 6/1 *Goom*, methylated spirits. **1978** K. GILBERT *People are Legends* 2 What else is there for me? Except a bottle full of Goom. A fire, an old gum-tree? **1982** *Meanjin* 453 Goom! What a name for methylated spirits.

b. Abbrev. of GOOMY.

1984 P. CORRIS *Winning Side* 172 You can't inform on your own, Dick. If you do the place'll be finished for sure. No one'll touch it except the *gooms*.

goomy /'gʊmi, 'gumi/. Also **goomee.** [f. prec.] One addicted to drinking methylated spirits.

1973 K. GILBERT *Because White Man'll never do It* 97 Right at the bottom of the pile are the 'goomies'. These are the Aboriginal alcoholics, the metho drinkers. **1977** —— *Living Black* 93 My uncle was a goomee and when he died it really broke me up. Seeing those people having to go down to the back lane to drink a bottle of meths and the next morning his mate found him dead beside him. **1981** D. STUART *I think I'll Live* 112 'Meself,' he used to say, 'meself, I'm a bit of a goomy,' and you two blokes sound just like him; can't keep your minds off your bellies. **1984** P. CORRIS *Winning Side* 161 He took a big gulp of wine and then remembered, and had a small sip. Lennie had been a *goommee*, a bad one, but he'd reformed with a lot of help.

goon, *n.*[1] *Services' speech.* Abbrev. of GOONSKIN. Also *attrib.*

1941 *Men may Smoke* (Sydney) June 7 Goon trousers. **1946** *They wrote it Themselves* (W.A.A.A.F.) 19 A W.A.A.A.F. refers to her overalls or *jeans* . . as *goons* or goonskins.

goon, *n.*[2] [Prob. f. altered pronunc. of *flagon*, but see also GOOM.] A flagon (of wine).

1982 *Sydney Morning Herald* 13 Nov. 30/2 Tim Stanford started off drinking with 'the goon'. It's a flagon of moselle or riesling. **1983** *Ibid.* 23 Nov. 1/1 Three flagons of port (known as goons) have been consumed noisily by about 8.30.

goondie, var. GUNDY *n.*[1]

goonskin. [f. *goon* simpleton, after a character called Alice the *Goon* in the 'Popeye' series by E.C. Segar (1894–1938), American cartoonist; also used of a flying suit in R.A.F. slang.] In Services' speech: see quot. 1942. Also *attrib.*

1940 *Muzzle Blast* (Sydney) Sept. 7 Stitch in time saves goonskin button. **1942** *Southerly* i. 14 *Giggle Suit* (*Australian.*) Also *Goon Skins*, loose and ill-fitting fatigue dress. The *goon* is a clumsy and shapeless character in the 'Popeye' comic strip. **1946** [see GOON *n.*[1]].

gooseneck. See quot. 1972. Also *attrib.*

1970 *Matilda* (Winton Tourist Promotion Assoc.) 18 The men who once lived in the saddle, Have put leggings and goosenecks away. **1972** J. BYRNE *Horse Riding Austral. Way* 22 Australia is unique in its styles of saddle . . *The Gooseneck Poley Saddle.* Used by the majority of horse breakers . . a very deep seated saddle, with a short built in surcingle to attach the girth to; also fitted with a ring either side just behind the flap, to use with a cinch girth.

gooya /'guja/. [a. Yuwaalaraay *guuya.*] *Emu apple* (a), see EMU *n.*[1] 3. Also *attrib.*

1949 H.G. LAMOND *White Ears* 60 The two dogs came upon the flock of goats feeding on a sandhill ridge thick with coongaberry and gooya apples. **1955** —— *Towser* 82 A clump of gooya, or emu apple, stood out on a small plain.

gordo /'gɔdoʊ/. [Abbrev. of Sp. *gordo blanco* lit. 'fat white', a variety of grape known in the industry as 'muscat gordo blanco'.] A popular variety of grape.

1907 *Jrnl. Dept. Agric. Vic.* V. 714 Our raisin growers may have trouble in suiting their Gordos with a stock. **1913** W.K. HARRIS *Outback in Aust.* 70 The great standby of the Mildura settlers has been the lexia, or pudding raisin, commonly known in Mildura as the 'gordo', a term contracted from the Spanish name of 'gordo blanco', meaning the 'fat white' grape. **1946** A.M. LAPTHORNE *Mildura Calling* 51 Gordos are generally picked, packed and sent away fresh to the Melbourne markets, or dried in clusters without dipping. **1970** J.S. GUNN in W.S. Ramson *Eng. Transported* 60 Vocabulary of the dried fruits industry . . *gordo*, 'variety of large muscatel.'

go-slow. [Used elsewhere but recorded earliest in Aust.: see OEDS.]

a. A form of industrial protest in which employees work to rule or at a deliberately slow pace. Also *attrib.*, and formerly **go-slow strike.**

1917 *Sydney Morning Herald* 23 Aug. 6/8 If New South Wales is going to progress in the future . . this 'go-slow' policy which has been preached amongst our people for years past must be put an end to. **1923** *Aussie* (Sydney) Apr. 16/2 It is easiest . . for the employer to forget that the men he reviles as red-raggers and 'go slow' gospellers are mainly the same men that kept his capital and profits secure eight years ago. **1923** C.F. THWING *Human Australasia* 59 Another form, or cause, of the strike is found in what is known as the 'go-slow' or 'lazy' strike. It represents a desire to lessen the output. **1948** H.W. CRITTENDEN *Rogues' Paradise* 80 Thanks to the pernicious teachings of Clan demagogues and Communist quislings, go-slow is now a fixed principle of Australian trade union philosophy. **1951** S. PARANJPYE *Three Yrs. in Aust.* 85 This is due to the international 'go slow' policy of the trade unions. **1956** J.T. LANG *I Remember* 254 He had made many speeches about 'go-slow' in the railways.

b. One who takes part in such a protest.

1926 G. BLACK *Hist. N.S.W. Political Labor Party* iv. 15 Jobs for go-slows and incompetents.

Hence **go-slowism** *n.*

1917 *Byron Bay Rec.* 18 Aug. 4 The engineers are demanding that in the workshops go-slowism shall be accepted.

gouge, *v. Mining. intr.* To dig in order to secure a mineral deposit, esp. in opal-mining; also *trans.*, to prize (a stone) out of the surrounding material (see also quot. 1971).

1902 [see *gouging, vbl. n.*]. **1906** *Bulletin* (Sydney) 15 Feb. 15/1 We've sunk and we've driven and paddocked and gouged for scarcely a color a week. **1930** V. PALMER *Passage* (1957) 245 A nuggetty little fossicker . . held one of the leases on the silver-lead mountain and was gouging for ore. **1960** D. MCLEAN *Roaring Days* 62 We gouged them from a white clay below the band. **1971** J.S. GUNN *Opal Terminol.* 21 *Gouge*, to cut carefully under the roof searching for a seam of potch so that full scale cutting of the drive can begin.

Hence **gouging** *vbl. n.* and *attrib.*

1902 *Chambers's Jrnl.* (Edinburgh) Mar. 175/1 In the 'back blocks' of New South Wales opal is abundant, and 'gouging'—the term given to opal-mining—is the chief pursuit of every man on the western side of the Darling River. **1932** I.L. IDRIESS *Flynn of Inland* (1965) 233 He sends down a sheath-knife, a 'spider', or a gouging pick. **1944** M.J. O'REILLY *Bowyangs & Boomerangs* 128 Success at opal gouging depended more on luck than any class of mining. **1971** J.S. GUNN *Opal Terminol.* 21 *Gouging-pick*, short-handled pick, chisel nosed at both ends of the head, which can be used in a confined space. **1975** 'N. CULOTTA' *Gone Gougin'* 56 Would any of us recognize an opal if we found one? They were called 'nob-bies' . . and were coated with sandstone, and digging for them in a drive was called 'gouging', and one had to listen for a 'clink'.

gouge, *n. Mining.* A hole, freq. off a drive or shaft; a cavity made by a gouger.

1921 K.S. PRICHARD *Black Opal* 253 We'd better get down and clear out some of the mullock. . . The gouges are fair choked up. **1958** M.D. BERRINGTON *Stones of Fire* 49 The shaft . . had a small gouge in one end.

gouger. *Mining.* An independent miner who works a surface deposit, now usu. an opal miner. See also *opal gouger* OPAL 1.

1898 *Barrier Weekly Post* (Broken Hill) 17 Sept. 13 The reason assigned for the absence of the gouger from this hill is the extreme hardness of the ground not altogether the absence of opal. **1906** *Bulletin* (Sydney) 27 Dec. 14/3, I struck a copper-gougers' camp lately. **1921** *Ibid.* 18 Aug. 22/3, A gouger on the Lightning Ridge (N.S.W.) opal field was struck by a fall of earth. **1925** M. TERRY *Across Unknown Aust.* 66 The 'free-lance' copper-gouger. **1945** *Aust. Week-End Bk.* 81 At Coober Pedy the opal 'gougers' all live underground. **1948** V. PALMER *Golconda* 53 Tell me any gold-field that has better prospects for the gouger. **1961** *Bulletin* (Sydney) 15 July 8/1 It is a truism among miners in the north that the real bonanzas are invariably found by the small man—the gouger. **1979** D. LOCKWOOD *My Old Mates & I* 144 Several big mines were producing gold, copper, tin and wolfram, and Chinese gougers were active.

Gouldian finch. [f. the name of English natural history artist Elizabeth *Gould* (1804–1841), first applied as the specific epithet *Gouldiae* by her husband, English naturalist John Gould (1844 *Birds of Aust.* (1848) III. Pl. 88): see quot. 1976.] The n. Austral. finch *Erythrura gouldiae*, brilliantly coloured and a popular cage-bird.

1844 J. GOULD *Birds of Aust.* (1848) III. Pl. 88, *Amadina gouldiae* . . Gouldian Finch. **1903** *Emu* II. 150 *Poephila mirabilis* (Gouldian Grass-Finch). . . This most beautiful of all Finches is found in Northern Australia. **1933** W.L. OWEN *Cossack Gold* 131 Among decorative birds was the 'Nor'-wester', the local name for the polychromatic Gouldian finch whose tiny frame shines with all the colours of the kaleidoscope and more. **1976** *Reader's Digest Compl. Bk. Austral. Birds* 543 Of all Australian grass finches the Gouldian finch is the most striking. Its beauty inspired the naturalist, John Gould, to name the bird *gouldiae* in honour of his wife, who drew many of the birds illustrating his books.

gouty stem tree. *Obs.* [From the swollen or bulging appearance of the trunk.] BAOBAB. Also **gouty tree.**

1838 J.L. STOKES *Discoveries in Aust.* 21 Mar. (1846) I. 158 We found here [*sc.* Compass Hill] the gouty-stem tree of large size, bearing fruit. **1855** J. BONWICK *Geogr. Aust. & N.Z.* (ed. 3) 205 The Bottle tree, 40 feet high, is a Sterculia, so bulging out as to be called the Gouty tree. **1865** G.F. ANGAS *Aust.* 120 The baobab or gouty-stem tree. The trunks of these trees, resembling enormous yams, are filled with abundance of mucilage. **1875** C.H. EDEN *Aust.'s Heroes* (ed. 3) 109 Upon the bark of the gouty tree being cut, it yielded in small quantities a nutritious white gum. **1880** *Argus* (Melbourne) 7 Feb. 4/7 The gouty stem tree (Adansonia Gregorii) . . is closely related to the baobab of Central Africa. **1908** *Bulletin* (Sydney) 3 Dec. 15/2 On the plains of the Northern Territory there are numbers of the gouty-stem tree.

government, *n.* and *attrib.* [Of Austral. significance because of the proliferation of Comb. and Special Comb., perh. reflecting the nature of the role played by colonial governments in the settlement of Australia.]

A. *n.*

1. Freq. without article. The governing power in a (penal) colony, the body of instrumentalities responsible for the administration of a (penal) colony; the administrative arm of (colonial, state, or federal) government.

1793 S. MACARTHUR ONSLOW *Some Early Rec. Macarthurs* (1914) 45 Where Mr Macarthur had been the greater part of his time . . on account of the employment he holds under Government. **1795** *Ibid.* 50 These labourers are such as have been convicts, and whose time of transportation has expired. They then cease to be fed at the expence of Government. **1810** *Sydney Gaz.* 21 Jan. 3/3 The Hours of Labour for Working Gangs in the Employ of Government will be as follows. **1820** C. JEFFREYS *Van Dieman's Land* 97 Government having thought it advisable to form another settlement, or town, called George Town . . Launceston has been suffered to go considerably to decay. **1834** J.D. LANG *Hist. & Statistical Acct. N.S.W.* II. 10 When a convict-ship arrives in Sydney harbour, it is the practice of Government to reserve as many of the convicts . . as are required for the public service. **1841** *Tasmanian Jrnl. Nat. Sci.* (1842) I. 414 Government has not recognised *Tasmania* as the name of that island improperly denominated Van Diemen's Land. **1850** W. GATES *Recoll. Van Dieman's Land* 166 Had the money in my pocket belonged to Government, I could have taken it without compunctions. **1872** MRS E. MILLETT *Austral. Parsonage* 331 The frequent reference in West Australia to the word 'Government', and the manner in which it was alluded to, might have led one to suppose it was an imaginary creature whose character varied with that of each person who spoke of it. **1888** 'R. BOLDREWOOD' *Robbery under Arms* (1937) 230 The Government hadn't time to get a lock-up, with cells and all the rest of it, so they had to do the chain business. **1911** 'S. RUDD' *Bk. of Dan* 49 Tambooroora was the average sort of agricultural township where Government purchased support with a few public buildings and an equal distribution of J.P.-ships. **1934** J.C. LEE *Boshstralians* 38, I was in the Government in those days, doing relief duty, and necessarily away from home a goodish bit.

2. a. In the phr. **returned to** (or **sent back to**) **government**: (of a convict assigned to private service) returned to official custody.

[**1801** *HRA* (1915) 1st Ser. III. 254 If any person cannot support or employ the prisoners they have taken off the stores they are to be returned to Government labour.] **1834** *Austral. Almanack* 140 Convicts returned to Government, without complaint . . may be immediately re-assigned. **1835** J. LHOTSKY *Journey from Sydney* 12 Road Parties are formed by probationary Convict Servants, returned to Government by their masters. **1843** *Colonial Observer* (Sydney) 5 Apr. 933/1 Assignees returning their convict servants to government, will be required in future to pay . . the expence of their conveyance to Sydney. **1847** A. HARRIS *Settlers & Convicts* (1953) 138 A female prisoner . . had been giving her mistress what they here technically term 'cheek', and was sentenced to some months confinement and to be returned to Government. **1848** S. & J. SIDNEY *Emigrant's Jrnl.* 125 If a man wanted twice flogging he was of no use to me; I sent him back to Government. **1858** N.L. KENTISH *Treatise on Penal Discipline* 24 The runaway's indulgence shall be cancelled, and he returned to the Government to work in a Road-gang.

b. In the phr. **in government,** in official custody (as opposed to private service).

1827 Tas. Colonial Secretary's Office Rec. 1/23 404, I understand this man is now in Government. **1845** *Cumberland Times* (Parramatta) 15 Nov. 4/4 Tim was an honourable sort of fellow, and whilst he continued in Government, could never bring himself to make any direct advances, towards improving the good will which Mary evidently entertained for him. **1865** S. BENNETT *Hist. Austral. Discovery* 434 Instead of desiring to be assigned to private persons . . it became the almost universal desire of the convicts to be 'in government', as they termed it.

B. *attrib.*

1. Owned, funded, administered, or in the service of the government (of a Colony, later a State, or the Commonwealth).

1790 R. CLARK Jrnl. 20 May 168 They sowed two bushels of barley at the Government Farm. **1798** D. COLLINS *Acct. Eng. Colony N.S.W.* I. 513 The artificers are indulged with the use of government tools. **1805** *HRA* (1915) 1st Ser. V. 272 A Quantity of Beer being brewed at the Government Brewery at Parramatta. **1813** *Van Diemen's Land Govt. & Gen. Orders* 14 Apr. (1814) 11 The Lieut. Governor further directs that no person whatsoever will presume to employ the Government Bullocks or carts, for any other than Government purposes, without the express permission of the Lieut. Governor, expressed through the Inspector of Public Works. **1817** *Hobart Town Gaz.* 18 Oct., Much Injury having been done in the Government Brick Fields, by Cattle and Carts being driven through them, all Persons are cautioned against trespassing. **1822** *Ibid.* 5 Oct., The Government District Schoolmasters will make returns of Children under their Instruction. **1827** *Diary Officer 16th (Queen's) Lancers* 10 Aug. (1894) 205 The Government gardener has orders to supply me with a variety of seeds peculiar to the island. **1827** *Tasmanian* (Hobart) 18 Oct. 3 Charged with stealing a quantity of Government timber, at North-West Bay. **1832** *Currency Lad* (Sydney) 1 Dec. 3 The Government dead-cart or hearse. **1848** T.L. MITCHELL *Jrnl. Exped. Tropical Aust.* 41 Mr Kennedy was absent, having set off that morning . . on two government horses. **1853** *Visit to Aust. & Gold Regions* (S.P.C.K.) 180 Government clerks have given notice of resignation. **1857** *Queen v. Beaton* 31, I am blamed for breaking down the Government enclosure, and taking this cow from it. **1862** C. ASPINALL *Three Yrs. Melbourne* 90 The gardens were laid out by . . the Government botanist. **1872** 'TASMANIAN LADY' *Treasures, Lost & Found* 88 The ore . . was . . transferred to the boxes of the Government carts, in which it was to be taken to Melbourne. **1873** *Austral. Handbk.* 48 The effects of government emigrants dying on the voyage to South Australia, and having no near relatives in the colony, are publicly sold by the Government auctioneer at Adelaide. **1882** J. WOOD *'Neath Southern Skies* 48 The Government railways (and, be it observed, nearly all the railways in the Colony come within this category) run their trains at a rate of speed which for slowness would send a Midland Railway official into the nearest district asylum. **1882** A.J. BOYD *Old Colonials* 246 It is a wearing life, that of a schoolmaster, and especially when a man is not a Government teacher. **1887** 'COMMERCIAL TRAVELLER' *Diary Three Months Trip Qld.* 27 One might imagine that instead of travelling on a Government highway, 'chaos had come again'. **1891** W.H. THOMES *Life at Gold Mines Ballarat* 52 The assembled miners did not dare to interfere, for fear their licenses would be forfeited by the Government commissioner. **1901** *Bulletin* (Sydney) 2 Nov. 16/1 Have visited a couple of Govt. agricultural farms. **1904** *Ibid.* 1 Sept. 17/1 A gang of Government rabbiters. ***c* 1906** L. BECKE *Settlers Karossa Creek* 104 'Toby', the Government black tracker. **1911** *Bulletin* (Sydney) 23 Feb. 14/1 The S.A. Government Vet. has added to his weird collection a lamb with only one eye set in the middle of its forehead. **1923** M.B. PETERSEN *Jewelled Nights* 188 He had been in the laboratory when the Government Assayer had been making experiments with this gas. **1930** A.E. YARRA *Vanishing Horsemen* 18 Tamporina, the official king of the Government blacks' reserve, was committing sorcery—making rain. **1931** *Bulletin* (Sydney) 25 Nov. 20/3 The fact that Queensland has a Government water-diviner . . doesn't settle the question whether water-divining is a reliable business. **1934** WARBURTON & ROBERTSON *Buffaloes* 9 There were . . three government hotels in Darwin. **1937** A.W. UPFIELD *Mr Jelly's Business* 166 Mr Thorn . . walked north along the Government track beside the Fence. **1949** B. O'REILLY *Green Mountains* 182 The new business . . made a telephone a necessity and here again we had to help ourselves. . . Fifteen miles of private line had to be constructed to the nearest Government wire. **1951** *Bulletin* (Sydney) 2 May 15/1 At the timber depot . . the scrubcut sleepers awaited inspection and judgement by the Government 'passer'. **1960** *Ibid.* 23 Nov. 8/3 Annually the Darwin Wet is advertised in advance by the migrations of wily Government shiny-pants and wheeling kite-hawks. **1962** C. GYE *Cockney & Crocodile* 136 In the evening the Government Dogger came to dinner. He wanders here and there, shooting, trapping and poisoning the dingoes that worry the sheep. **1963** X. HERBERT *Disturbing Element* 73 It was a government hospital, built to serve a railway junction that hadn't expanded. **1973** R. HALL *Poems from Prison* 33 There's an iron grille fence painted Government green. **1975** L.H. CLARK *Rouseabout Reflections* 98 Should our Queen pen a letter, her armies and navy may bear it, it's true; But the back-o'-Bourke postie, the government rover must still get it through.

2. a. *Hist.* As a euphemism for 'convict'; also *ellipt.* as *adj.* (see quot. 1872); **b.** Of or relating to the apprehension or detention of a criminal.

1803 *Sydney Gaz.* 6 Nov., The Government Workmen are busy in walling in a channel for the run of water which crosses the Row at the lower end in rainy seasons. **1813** *HRA* (1916) 1st Ser. VII. 746 The Government Stockmen are to be kept Constantly with their respective Herds. **1816** *Hobart Town Gaz.* 1 June, The Government Mechanics and Labourers will be exempted from Work on Tuesday next. **1825** *London Mag.* May II. 62, I never saw any woman with the government cloathing on. **1833** *Launceston Advertiser* 24 Jan. 446 The late daring outrage committed down the Tamar, by the government sawyers. **1840** A. Russell *Tour through Austral. Colonies* 126 These worthies are very indignant at the name of convict being applied to them. *Government people* is the appellation most suited to their fancy. **1846** C. Rowcroft *Bushranger Van Diemen's Land* I. 12 This party . . were clothed in the government dress of convicts suits of yellow. **1849** *Britannia* (Hobart) 13 Dec. 4/3 Foster had his yellow clothes in his hand, and said, 'if you have got any blunt, I will leave the government slops for it'. **1850** C.A. King *Life* 23 What gave me the greatest amount of uneasiness was wearing the government clothes—a brand as conspicuous as that of Cain's. **1851** H. Melville *Present State Aust.* 295 There may be, among the Government hands, or rather among those men that have just received their indulgences, a difficulty in obtaining work. **1864** J. Armour *Diggings, Bush & Melbourne* 16 Philip drunk said that his wife Nancy—an old 'government lady' I had every reason to believe—would be as good as a mother to me. **1872** M. Clarke *His Natural Life* 574 The major part of them had been 'government' themselves, and resented the fact that one of their number had been raised up to rule over them. **1874** C. De Boos *Congewoi Correspondence* 165 Bullocks'll do as much if you've goter good driver as keeps 'em up to the mark, and don't let 'em get into the old Government pace. **1894** *Bulletin* (Sydney) 9 June 21/1 Incontinently thrown—yes, *thrown*, for I moved slowly and looked round for my cab!—into the Government Coach—Black Maria. **1933** C. Woodward *Peeps into Gaols* 35 The Police Court cells, or, as the 'crooks' would say . . the 'Government cooling chambers'. **1979** A.J. Burke *Bite Pineapple* 2 Peter . . had just served three months in a government boarding house for desertion.

3. Comb. **government cattle, dam, domain, emigrant, emigration, farm, flock, garden, ground, herd, hut, immigrant, immigration, job, land, paddock, reserve, road, run, school, sheep, stock, store, well.**

1794 G. Thompson *Slavery & Famine* ii. 5 Here is a large park, called Cumberland Park, where the **government cattle** are put to graze. **1808** *HRA* (1916) 1st Ser. VI. 439 They are giving away and disposing of Government Cattle to their own party. **1821** T. Godwin *Descr. Acct. Van Diemen's Island* 8 Some distance from the road are the fine Emu plains, occupied chiefly by the government cattle. **1838** *S. Austral. Rec.* (London) 13 Jan. 30 Stephen has been after the government cattle nearly to the head of the gulf. **1887** Mrs D.D. Daly *Digging, Squatting, & Pioneering Life* 61 The few Government cattle we had, were turned out here. **1901** *Bulletin* (Sydney) 4 May 32/2 Watson and I were . . pulling some sheep out of a **Government dam** they had got bogged in. **1954** *Ibid.* 30 June 12/3 Years ago the Government dam near Malcolm (W.A.) was stocked with freshwater fish. **1958** G. Casey *Snowball* 28 The Government Dam was the inland town's beach and playground, its courting-place and secret rendezvous. It was just a big waterhole, about seventy-five yards square. **1813** *N.S.W. Pocket Almanack* 72 **Government Domain**—No cattle of any description but those belonging to Government are to be permitted to graze or feed thereon. **1822** J.T. Bigge *Rep. State Colony N.S.W.* 44 An inclosure of a tract of hilly land contiguous to it, comprising near 3,000 acres . . is occupied by the draught cattle and horses in the use of government. . . This tract is called the government domain. **1839** J. Marshall *Twenty Yrs. Experience Aust.* 19 Ten acres of land along the river Torrens are reserved for a government domain. **1847** *Atlas* (Sydney) III. 49/1 The privilege of using the Government Domain as a place of recreation. **1860** 'Lady' *My Experiences in Aust.* 32 This same Government Domain is in my estimation the great ornament and attraction, I had almost said redeeming feature, of Sydney. It was laid out during General Macquarie's government. . . It is situated on one of the small bays of the harbour, and commands many beautiful views of different points and headlands. **1854** W. Shaw *Land of Promise* 40 '**Government emigrants**' have likewise come under the animadversion of the colonist. **1856** W.H.G. Kingston *Emigrant's Home* 146 As you came out as a Government emigrant, I conclude that you had not much money. **1865** G.E. Sargent *Frank Layton* 11 You might go out as a government emigrant. **1840** *S. Austral. Rec.* (London) 14 Mar. 109 There will in all probability be no funds out of which the expenses of **government emigration** can be defrayed, after the end of 1839. **1859** 'Eye Witness' *Voyage to Aust.* 3 Single females . . should try to get out by the Government Emigration . . as they will then have good protection. **1891** *Aust. Handbk.* 94 Government emigration entirely suspended. **1791** S. Macarthur Onslow *Some Early Rec. Macarthurs* (1914) 40 The **Government Farm** did not this year in grain return three times the seed that had been sown. **1809** *HRA* (1921) 3rd Ser. I. 247, I have prepared an Inclosure at the Government Farm. **1821** *Ibid.* IV. 390 Set about establishing a small Government Farm at George Town, as an experiment. **1831** Tyerman & Bennet *Jrnl. Voyages & Travels* II. 144 We passed some fields of barley about a foot high, on government-farms. **1843** *HRA* 1st Ser. XXII. 509 Produce of every description, which may be grown on the Government Farms. **1882** A. Tolmer *Reminisc.* II. 20 After reaching Adelaide, I sent her to the Government farm. **1900** *Advocate* (Burnie) 17 Aug. 2/3 The establishment of a Government farm, which term we use in preference to an experimental farm. **1937** A.W. Upfield *Mr Jelly's Business* 43 Reaching the entrance to the Government farm, he could have turned the car. **1802** *Gen. Orders issued by Governor King* 16 Mar. 84 Ewes lately given to Settlers from the **Government flock** to breed from, have been thus purchased, killed and sold. **1811** *HRA* (1916) 1st Ser. VII. 398 They may be farther accommodated with a Proportion of Sheep from the Government Flocks. **1858** J.B. Marsden *Mem. S. Marsden* 59 The wool of the government flocks and the flesh of the wild cattle was already sufficient to provide both food and raiment for the convicts without any expense to the parent state. **1806** *N.S.W. Gen. Orders* 15 Mar. 187 A quantity of very fine Acorns being saved from the Oaks in the **Government Gardens**, at Sydney. **1817** *Hobart Town Gaz.* 5 July, The fence newly erected round the Government Garden having been injured by Cats running against it. **1832** J. Backhouse *Narr. Visit Austral. Colonies* (1843) 23 We walked to the Government-garden, which is situated on the beautiful banks of the Derwent. **1838** *HRA* (1923) 1st Ser. XIX. 376 He was quite right in having the Clearing of the Streets taken to the Government Garden for the Purpose of Manure. **1845** *Sydney Morning Herald* 7 May 3/3 The Government Gardens, as they are called, are a favourite resort of many of the citizens, and constantly visited by strangers. **1852** *Four Colonies Aust.* 20 The favourite portion of the Domain . . is that which constitutes the Government Gardens. **1956** F.B. Vickers *First Place to Stranger* 276, I had to go into Perth . . so I strolled into the Government Gardens. **1798** D. Collins *Acct. Eng. Colony N.S.W.* I. 506 Not more than a third of the **government-ground**, and a fifth of the ground belonging to individuals, was in any state of cultivation. **1838** D.L. Waugh *Three Yrs.' Practical Experience N.S.W.* 45 Three-fourths of the stock of this colony are grazed on government ground for nothing. **1843** *Teetotal Advocate* (Launceston) 7 Aug. 1/5 The Estate . . with an unlimited back run on government ground. **1803** *HRA* (1915) 1st Ser. IV. 307 Toongabbee will remain some time Fallow and be benefitted by the **Government Herds** manuring it. **1813** *Ibid.* (1921) 1st Ser. I. 18 The Marine Settlers are . . to receive one Cow each from the Government Herds. **1823** *Ibid.* (1917) 1st Ser. II. 99 It is no longer necessary to issue Cattle to Settlers from the Government herds. **1829** *Extracts Lett. Swan River* 22 Nov. (1830) II. 36 These bullocks will be obtained from the Government herds, at an average of £2 each, thus standing, on delivery, 18s. per head. **1841** *HRA* (1924) 1st Ser. XXI. 336 The small number of Convicts required for the custody of the Government Herds. **1812** *Rep. Select Committee Transportation* 19 Feb. (1838) 31 There were houses which were called **Government-huts**, which by the superintendent of convicts were appropriated to their purpose. **1825** *Austral.* (Sydney) 12 May 4 He became acquainted with the prisoners at the bar, and resided with them in the government hut. **1831** *Acct. Colony Van Diemen's Land* 117 A Government hut with a party of military has . . been stationed on the upper part of the plains. **1838** R. Gouger *S.A. in 1837* 20 Ten acres of land, close to the town . . are reserved as the government domain; and upon these the government-hut is now standing. **1849** A. Harris *Guide Port Stephens* 22 Estimate Australian society by 'the Rocks' at Sydney and the government huts of the interior. **1840** *S. Austral. Rec.* (London) 14 Mar. 110 Receiving and rationing **government immigrants** at the public cost until they obtain situations. **1841** G. Arden *Recent Information Port Phillip* 71 The first vessel containing government immigrants, as also the first ship with bounty immigrants, supplied the chief want of the distressed colony. **1841** *Port Phillip Patriot* 16 Aug. 2/5 The late Dowager Duchess, Countess of Sutherland, had influence sufficient to procure the sending of a **Government immigration** ship to a neighbouring port. **1845** *Star* (Parramatta) 22 Feb. 1/1 We are now threatened with a fresh experiment in Government Immigration, in the very questionable shape of *Exiles*. **1891** *Austral. Handbk.* 93 Government Immigration is now entirely suspended. **1905** *Truth* (Sydney) 12 Mar. 3/2 Should he apply for a **Government job**, and be 40 years of age, he is told that he is too old. **1905** *Bulletin* (Sydney) 6 July 36/1, I was serving my time to the building trade, and we were doing a Government job. **1919** *Smith's Weekly* (Sydney) 5 Mar. 5/2, I am the Government Job. By me are all things Australian made that are made. **1926** S. Westlaw *White Peril* 105 The other winked. 'Government job, you know. He's here till he finishes it.' Dick, who knew something about Government jobs himself, refrained from comment. **1985** *Canberra Times* 24 Nov. 20/6, I always wanted a government job and this is very secure. **1792** R. Atkins Jrnl. 21 May, The lands here [*sc.* Parramatta] are **Government lands** that is, lands cultivated for the maintenance of the Colony. **1822** *Launceston Advertiser* 6 July 2 Government Lands generally, do not earn their various expenses which they cost to the Crown. **1838** T. Walker *Month in Bush Aust.* 17 His improvements (on government land) are of course not much or many. **1846** G.H. Haydon *Five Yrs. Experience Aust. Felix* 13 The price of government land outside the town boundaries, is £1 per acre. **1859** J.D. Mereweather *Diary Working Clergyman* 34 Attended a government land sale. The land is put up in lots, varying from two roods to six hundred acres. **1897** L. Lindley-Cowen *W. Austral. Settler's Guide* 151 There are no good roads to Government land that is open for selection. **1910** *Huon Times* (Franklin) 31 Dec. 4/5 There is no Government land available or very little. **1822** *Hobart Town Gaz.* 24 Aug., Strayed or stolen from the **Government Paddock** . . two Working Oxen. **1841** *Hunter River Gaz.* 25 Dec. 2/5 The immigrants will arrive in the steamer this morning, and will be accommodated in tents pitched in the Government paddock at East Maitland. **1851** H. Melville *Present State Aust.* 321 Cricket is a game much played in Van Diemen's Land. . . The ground is in the Government paddock, within sight of the city. **1856** H.B. Stoney *Vic.* 85 We halted in the Government Paddock, having completed a distance of thirty-two miles. **1859** W. Kelly *Life in Vic.* II. 85 The Government Paddock—the head-quarters of the police establishment. **1831** R. Robison *Case of Captain Robison* 50 Mr Mackay . . had made use of the **government reserve** (land) at Nelson's Plains, for his private purpose. **1839** *Port Phillip Gaz.* 25 Dec. 2 This delightful spot admirably calculated for a Dairy Farm . . adjoins a Government Reserve, abounding with the richest and best pasturage, and is only five miles from town. **1856** H.B. Stoney *Vic.* 28 On a Government reserve, in Swanston-street, has been lately completed a magnificent building of white sandstone, as a Public Library and National Gallery. **1881** G. Walch *Vic.* 156 The Government reserve known as the Kamarooka and Egerton State Forest. **1914** N.F. Spielvogel *Gumsucker at Home* 15 The miners 'jumped' a big Government reserve and built their houses on it. **1930** *Bulletin* (Sydney) 2 Apr. 23/3 Bordering the bush track through the Government reserve on the way to Minnamurra Falls (N.S.W.) there are some giant stinging-nettle trees. **1963** X. Herbert *Disturbing Element* 74 An extensive government reserve . . was watered by a permanent creek. **1971** W.G. Howcroft *This Side Rabbit Proof Fence* 79 A strange old character known as the 'Roarer' had a camp in a patch of thick scrub on a Government Reserve. **1834** J.D. Lang *Hist. & Statistical Acct. N.S.W.* II. 160 The remainder of the route to Illawarra is a mere bush-road, there being no regular **Government road**. **1849** A. Harris *Emigrant Family* (1967) 137 Some of his bullocks being on the Government road. **1888** *Tasmanian* (Hobart) 1 Sept. 21/1 The Government road party are making poor progress. . . I have still to man-pack everything three miles of a dreadful track. **1901** *Bulletin* (Sydney) 5 Oct. 17/1 A certain corn-and-pig Macleay cockie wants a Govt. road, so that two 'verticles' can pass without 'coinciding'. **1918** B. Reynolds *Dawn Asper* 39 The girl watched him ride away across the home-paddock and out towards Government road. **1930** L.W. Lower *Here's Luck* (1955) 49 The postman . . was usually as regular in his movements as a government road-mender. **1796** P.G. King Jrnl. Norfolk Island Apr. 273 Several Swine have been bought from Phillip Island . . and put into the **Government Run** on this Island. **1825** *HRA* (1921) 3rd Ser. IV. 319 Have not suffered his Flocks to encroach on the Government Run which adjoins his Farm. **1847** *Maitland Mercury* 18 Sept. 3/3 One of 43 acres, and the other of 53 acres, are valuable as forming excellent sites for an inn or public-house, as well as from their enjoying the privileges of the government run in the rear. **1872** MRS E. MILLETT *Austral. Parsonage* 159 The usual feeding-ground of the cattle belonging to the Pensioners and other towns-people of Barladong was what was called the 'Government run', a phase which denoted all such bush in the vicinity as had not been appropriated to private holders. **1829** H. WIDOWSON *Present State Van Diemen's Land* 25 The . . gentleman has been lately appointed superintendant of the **government schools.** **1837** *Elliston's Hobart Town Almanack* 86 Of what are called 'Government schools' the number at present is, I believe about thirty. **1852** *Four Colonies Aust.* 21 Parramatta contains . . a government school. **1881** A.C. GRANT *Bush-Life Qld.* II. 287 She qualified as a Government school-teacher, and, through Stone's influence, got herself appointed to the little Government school in the township near his property. **1897** L. LINDLEY-COWEN *W. Austral. Settler's Guide* 107 Three miles from Quandinning Daylerking is passed. There is a Government school there. **1917** T.J. BRIGGS *Life & Experiences Successful W. Austral.* 17 During the time I lived at the Half-way House I attended the Government school at Fremantle. **1967** D. HORNE *Educ. Young Donald* 22 My father was only a teacher at the government school. **1801** *Gen. Orders issued by Governor King* 1 May (1802) 40 A large body of Natives . . have attacked and killed some of **Government sheep.** **1842** *Colonial Observer* (Sydney) 8 Oct. 524/4 The Government sheep are slaughtered almost openly. **1888** H.S. RUSSELL *Genesis Qld.* 225 What Government sheep we saw were leggy, coarse-woolled brutes. **1803** *HRA* (1915) 1st Ser. IV. 302 Sent over 18,535 pounds of Salt Pork, part from **Government Stock** and part purchased from Settlers. **1811** *Proc. of Gen. Court-Martial Lieut.-Col. G. Johnston* 29 All the Governor's provisions come from the Government stock. **1817** *Hobart Town Gaz.* 27 Dec., Government Stock will be ready on the 10th of January to Issue . . to such Settlers as have Orders to receive Cattle from Government. **1846** *Moreton Bay Courier* 19 Sept. 3/2 He will be instructed to act as pioneer for the cutting of roads from this place to the new settlement to facilitate the removal of Government stock. **1875** CAMPBELL & WILKS *Early Settlement Qld.* 6 The late John Kent, Esq.—then a commissary-general, and as such having full control over the Government stock. **1800** *HRA* (1915) 1st Ser. III. 3 Competition will do that which the **Government Store** and arbitary Power of the Government to regulate Price must do now. **1816** *Ibid.* (1917) 1st Ser. IX. 121 Blaxland had been struck off the List of those persons who were allowed to furnish Meat to the Government Stores. **1825** *London Mag.* May II. 56 Fat beasts come to Sydney for the government stores. **1840** A. RUSSELL *Tour through Austral. Colonies* 83 Two natives . . were recently executed in front of the government stores for murder. **1887** MRS D.D. DALY *Digging, Squatting, & Pioneering Life* 54 There was a large Government store, from which rations allowed to officers and men were drawn. **1900** J.C.L. FITZPATRICK *Good Old Days* 207 Alongside of the church was another brick building, used as Government stores or granary. **1875** P.E. WARBURTON *Journey across Western Interior* 142 The **government well** was quite dry. **1887** S. NEWLAND *Far North Country* 8 Near the Government well of fresh water. **1924** LAWRENCE & SKINNER *Boy in Bush* 231 By mid-day they camped . . at the Three-mile Government well. **1936** F. CLUNE *Roaming round Darling* 267 It cost sixpence a drink for your horse in the government well. **1981** A.B. FACEY *Fortunate Life* 70 Many settlers had trouble getting permanent water for their properties and had to cart water from Government wells miles away.

4. Special Comb. **government bill** *obs.*, a promissory note issued in payment for commodities purchased by a government instrumentality; **billet,** a position in the public service, esp. one which is well-paid and undemanding; **blanket,** a blanket issued by a government instrumentality, esp. to an Aboriginal; BLANKET 1; **bore,** a bore owned and maintained by a government instrumentality for use by travelling stock; **bounty,** BOUNTY 1; reward, subsidy; **bream,** *red emperor*, see RED *a.* 1 b.; **camp,** a police outpost, esp. on a goldfield; a place for the detention of Aborigines; **cottage** (chiefly *Tas.*), a small residence for the accommodation of a visiting official; **(gold) escort** *obs.*, *gold escort*, see GOLD 3; **gang** *hist.*, a detachment of convicts assigned to public labour; see GANG; **hours** *pl.*, **(a)** the daily period which a convict was required to work at public labour; **(b)** public service office hours; **labour** *obs.*, (of a convict) forced labour on public works; **labourer** *obs.*, a convict assigned to public labour; the employee of a government instrumentality; **man,** a convict (see quot. 1827); a public servant; **mark** *obs.*, a brand or stamp identifying government property; **ration,** a dole (of foodstuffs); RATION *n.* 1 c.; **resident,** a representative of the Crown in a settlement remote from a centre of government; (chiefly *N.T.*) the principal resident representative of a government in a territory administered by that government; **servant,** a convict; a public servant; **settlement, station,** an outpost, esp. as established for agricultural purposes or to promote Aboriginal welfare; a community of Aborigines established and maintained by a government instrumentality; **stroke** (orig. of a convict; now freq. of a public servant), a deliberately slow pace of working; also **stroker,** one who works in this way; **tank,** a dam owned and maintained by a government instrumentality to provide water for travelling stock; **town, township** *obs.*, a settlement established and laid out by a government instrumentality; **woman** *obs.*, a female convict; **work,** public labour, esp. as performed by convicts; **works** *pl.*, constructions as roads, etc., for public use.

1808 *Sydney Gaz.* 18 Dec. Payment to be made in Paymasters' or **Government Bills.** **1811** *Ibid.* 13 Apr. 2/2 Prompt payment to be made in Government or Paymasters' Bills or Dollars. **1826** *Monitor* (Sydney) 23 June 42/2 The expression, '*depending upon Government bills*', means in fact, depending upon English husbandry, in lieu of commercial husbandry, and marine speculations. **1870** E.B. KENNEDY *Four Yrs. in Qld.* 7 A certain class of men . . come back to Brisbane, and either get a **Government 'billet'**, or go home. **1880** *Bulletin* (Sydney) 29 May 1/2 He would, while offering £50 for 'a billet', have had sufficient sense to say nothing about a 'Government billet'. **1899** *Ibid.* 21 Jan. (Red Page), Deafness stood in the way of a possible Government billet. **1944** G. COCKERILL *Scribblers & Statesmen* 26 Why not be wise before it is too late, and get into a Government billet? **1839** T.L. MITCHELL *Three Exped. Eastern Aust.* (rev. ed.) II. 335 Having a superfluity of **government blankets**, I have taken the liberty of giving her one. **1843** *N.S.W. Monthly Mag.* Feb. 52, I find . . in the course of the annual distribution of the Government blankets, that the number of children . . very little exceeds that of *parents*. **1881** *Bulletin* (Sydney) 18 June 12/1 The official responsible for the non-delivery of Government blankets to the Penrith blacks ought to be exposed. **1924** J. HARPER *Splashes from Narran* 15 Shouldering his swag, one well-worn Government blanket, he lit out. **1943** *Jest: Digestion Good Humor* 5 The policeman, with a native trooper standing by a big pile of government blankets, had the recipients fairly straightened out. **1899** *Bulletin* (Sydney) 9 Sept. 17/1 The Richmond . . **Govt. bore** gives splendid water. **1924** *Smith's Weekly* (Sydney) 16 Aug. 23/5 The water from the Government bore at Tilcha, Yandama station (N.S.W.), is charged with gas. **1934** C. SAYCE *Comboman* 219 There was still dry feed to be found some miles off the Great North Stock Route, and they came upon a Government bore at long intervals. **1950** G.M. FARWELL *Land of Mirage* 203 No Government bores when I went through. Didn't need 'em. We went from waterhole to waterhole. **1963** R.H. CONQUEST *Spurs are Rusty Now* 30 It was hard country at the time, dry as a bone, but there were Government bores at fairly regular intervals. **1836** *Tegg's Monthly Mag.* I. 6 The **Government bounty** might not be sufficient to pay the passage money to Australia. **1842** *Colonial Observer* (Sydney) 16 Feb. 158/4 The total indifference of our immigrationists to the moral and religious character of the individuals selected for the Government Bounty. **1851** H. MELVILLE *Present State Aust.* 104 Some individuals do not like to receive Government *bounty*. **1948** J.K. EWERS *For Heroes to live In* 222 'I don't see how I'll be able to pay them out of this harvest.' 'There's the government bounty,' Charlie reminded him. 'What's the good of that? Fourpence halfpenny a bushel isn't going to make any difference.' **1948** C.P. MOUNTFORD *Brown Men & Red Sand* 172 Grief . . always followed the visits of trespassing doggers, who shot the dogs of the natives in order to collect the Government bounty paid for dog scalps. **1963** O. RUHEN *Flockmaster* 32 The Government bounty of a pound or two, set upon the ordinary dingo, did not tempt them into the business of destroying dogs. **1896** F.G. AFLALO *Sketch Nat. Hist. Aust.* 225 The so-called arrow-marked **'Government Bream'**. **1955** V. SERVENTY *Aust.'s Great Barrier Reef* 40 Another interesting food fish is the Government Bream or King Snapper. **1962** J. MACKENZIE *Austral. Paradox* 230 Someone soon caught a government bream—so-called because of the brown, broad arrow marking reminiscent of convict dress. **1978** N. COLEMAN *Austral. Fisherman's Fish Guide* 44 Displaying the colours which were responsible for it being named the 'Government bream', after the early settlement arrowhead signature depicting government property. **1841** *Geelong Advertiser* 7 Aug. 1/4 The **Government camp,** Corio. **1855** R. CARBONI *Eureka Stockade* 66 They had been sticking up some three or four tents, called the Eureka Government Camp. **1861** E.P. RAMSAY-LAYE *Social Life & Manners* 16 We walked to the government camp, where divine service was performed. **1875** G.M. NEWMAN *N.T. & its Gold-Fields* 13 After the removal of the Government camp from Yam Creek to that prison-looking den named Shackles. **1920** C.H. SAYCE *Golden Buckles* 54 If one of them does for a white man, he only gets about a year in a Government camp, down country, petted by the ladies and missionaries, and fed on the best of tucker. **1829** *Hobart Town Almanack* 44 At the township . . is erected a **Government cottage,** the residence of a military officer, stationed here with a detachment of troops. **1841** 'LADY LONG RESIDENT N.S.W.' *Mother's Offering to Children* 157 There was the government cottage; the public buildings; the officers' quarters. **1851** H. MELVILLE *Present State Aust.* 233 There is a Government cottage, in which His Excellency resides when he visits the town. **1855** *Illustr. Sydney News* 10 Mar. 3/1 Directions have been issued for having Government Cottage put into a state of thorough repair. **1882** J.I. WATTS *Memories Early Days S.A.* 70 Glenelg in 1842 . . contained a government cottage then called a custom house. **1852** *Murray's Guide to Gold Diggings* 38 We have a **'government escort'** or conveyance, bringing every week into town from the gold-field, a *ton* of gold. **1867** 'CLERGYMAN' *Aust. as it Is* 159 The 'Government gold escort', a four-wheeled vehicle, drawn by four horses, in which are seated armed policemen, is intrusted with the conveyance of the gold to the capital. **1872** 'TASMANIAN LADY' *Treasures, Lost & Found* 46 The Government escort for conveying the gold to Melbourne consisted of about a dozen mounted and well-armed troopers, with officer and sergeant. **1913** J. SADLEIR *Recoll.* 46 The Government Gold Escorts were instituted in the very earliest digging days. **1808** *Sydney Gaz.* 22 May, A search to be made to discover whether any of the **Government gangs** were absent. **1820** H.G. BENNET *Let. to Earl Bathurst* 67 They endeavour to run away from their masters and after having committed all sorts of offences are frequently returned to the government gang. **1829** J. ATKINSON *Distilling & Brewing N.S.W.* 3 Land must be cleared and enclosed, working cattle broke in . . and the government gangs . . must be drained of every man capable of performing agricultural labour. **1840** A. RUSSELL *Tour through Austral. Colonies* 240 Government gangs in New South Wales are to be seen daily employed at the improvement of roads. **1847** *Transportation Question Considered* 29 The most reformatory position in which a convict can be placed is private service, and . . the most pernicious one is a Government gang. **1851** H. MELVILLE *Present State Aust.* 215 The men that are serving under the modern regulations, prefer remaining in the Government gangs. **1809** *N.S.W. Pocket Almanack* 8 Persons secreting or employing such servants during **Government hours** will be punished for a breach of public orders. **1887** MRS D.D. DALY *Digging, Squatting, & Pioneering Life* 55 The office hours were from ten to four, the ordinary Government hours. **1802** *HRA* (1915) 1st Ser. IV. 325 Settlers have been in the habit of employing those who have left **Government Labour.** **1823** *Ibid.* (1917) 1st Ser. XI. 81 The Government Men hitherto assigned to Overseers are to be immediately recalled to Government Labour. **1836** G. LOVELESS *Victims of Whiggery* 14 At the government farm I continued until I was exempted from government labour. **1807** *Sydney Gaz.* 5 Apr., A charge of employing *John Campbell*, a **Government labourer**, without demanding his certificate or pass. **1822** J.T. BIGGE *Rep. State Colony N.S.W.* 21 All the government labourers and convicts, at this period, were allowed to leave their work at three o'clock every day. **1839** *Sydney Standard* 7 Jan. 2/4 The stock of government labourers remains stationary. **1846** 'SQUATTER' *Visit to Antipodes* 97 Government labourers were . . getting 17s. 6d. a day, while the South Australian Company were only paying 12s. **1797** D. COLLINS *Acct. Eng. Colony N.S.W.* (1802) II. 25 A **government man** allowed to officers or settlers in their own time. **1801** *HRA* (1915) 1st Ser. III. 113, I have been obliged to rent a large farm to employ the Government men on.

1808 *Sydney Gaz.* 18 Dec., Mrs Cox's Government man has run from her employ. **1814** L. MACQUARIE *Let.* 10 Sept. (1821) 86 Those Government Men who have the indulgence of cultivating ground, and rearing stock .. frequently become receivers of stolen grain and provisions. **1820** *HRA* (1921) 3rd Ser. III. 404, I had a Govern. man on the store and one quart of spirits a week but about six months ago both were discontinued. **1827** P. CUNNINGHAM *Two Yrs. in N.S.W.* II. 117 Convicts .. when fairly domiciliated .. are .. spoken of under the loyal designation of *government-men*, the term *convict* being erased by a sort of general tacit compact from our Botany dictionary. **1839** 'FRIEND TO TRUTH' *True Picture Aust.* 51 The richest men in the country, and the best liked men, are the old convicts, Government men. **1843** *Colonial Observer* (Sydney) 11 Jan. 737/3 Mr Therry is .. a mere '*Government-man* to Sir George Gipps',—a mere placeman and place-hunter, a man who subsists entirely on his Government pay. **1850** C.A. KING *Life* 15, I will tell you what I do with my government men, I feed and clothe them well, and if they deserve it I flog them well. **1869** MRS W.M. HOWELL *Diggings & Bush* 47 There are hundreds of government men here (convicts) who are now honest, good men. **1882** A.J. BOYD *Old Colonials* 253 The life of the 'independent teacher' appears to be far more 'dependent' than that of the Government man. **1888** 'R. BOLDREWOOD' *Robbery under Arms* (1937) 38 The Government men used to hide the cattle and horses there in old times. **1902** *Bulletin* (Sydney) 13 Sept. 16/1 Government men stationed on 'The Fringe' are mostly in their right place... The 'Fringe' civil servant, being king of his tinpot village, generally has an overweening conceit of his own abilities. **1910** *Huon Times* (Franklin) 12 Mar. 2/4 The Government man usually stepping in long after and advising all and sundry how the thing ought to be done. **1912** A. BERRY *Reminisc.* 180 Some of these Government men are still in my service to the present day, and some are my tenants. **1920** *Smith's Weekly* (Sydney) 1 May 9/6 Money-lenders are only too pleased to 'assist' the Government man. **1813** *N.S.W. Pocket Almanack* 58 The Superintendant of the Government Herds is enjoined to continue .. to renew the **Government Mark** on all cattle, if by time or accident obliterated. **1822** J.T. BIGGE *Rep. State Colony N.S.W.* 45 From the want of the usual government mark, and the difficulty of impressing it upon every description of the purchased tools, some loss has been occasioned. **1848** *Britannia* (Hobart) 7 Sept. 2/5 Identification now had become impossible by reference to the government marks alone. **1801** *HRA* (1916) 1st Ser. VI. 202 The Expense of supporting them by **Government Rations.** **1840** *True Colonist* (Hobart) 24 Jan. 4/2 [Assigned servants] are very expensive servants at the Government rations and slops, in return for their labour. **1878** MRS H. JONES *Broad Outlines* 194 The usual Government rations for the aborigines had not arrived at the nearest police station. **1912** A. BERRY *Reminisc.* 180 When they misbehaved or became contumacious we put them on Government rations. **1948** H. DRAKE-BROCKMAN *Sydney or Bush* 54 Here was Thursday and he had only a Government ration of food and a striped 'nigger' blanket and he'd promised to take Jess to the pictures Saturday night! **1950** A. GROOM *I saw Strange Land* 107, 240 people received Government rations and endowment. **1985** I. WHITE et al. *Fighters & Singers* 73 We never got government ration in those days. **1842** *Austral. & N.Z. Monthly Mag.* 28 The church service is .. read at Freemantle and Albany by the **government residents.** **1845** E.J. EYRE *Jrnls. Exped. Central Aust.* II. 197 The police .. were sent by the Government Resident to see what number of natives were at the camp. **1870** *S.A. Parl. Papers* (1870–71) II. no. 25 3 Consider it your duty to proceed, under the instructions of the Government Resident, to any part of the settlement. **1880** *Austral. Handbk.* 81 A 'Government Resident' and other necessary officers are to be appointed by the Governor. **1887** MRS D.D. DALY *Digging, Squatting, & Pioneering Life* 7 A Government Resident was appointed in 1864. **1890** *Quiz* (Adelaide) 16 May 2/1 Many months ago *Quiz*, discussing the question of the appointment of a Government Resident, suggested that the Ministry need not look further than Mr J.G. Knight. **1897** J.J. MURIF *From Ocean to Ocean* 181 The Government Resident presided over a large gathering. **1918** G. WHITE *Thirty Yrs. Tropical Aust.* 98 The first step was to abolish the Government Resident, who had hitherto sufficed to conduct affairs, and administer justice, and appoint an Administrator with the title of His Excellency and absolute and autocratic powers. **1802** *HRA* (1915) 1st Ser. III. 644 A proportion of **Government servants** are employed. **1803** *Sydney Gaz.* 7 Aug., Patrick Shannon exhibited a complaint against John Hunter his Government servant. **1810** E. BENT Let. 3 Apr. 105 The Government Servants work only till three o'clock in the day and never on Saturdays or Sundays. **1819** *Sydney Gaz.* 17 Apr., The prisoner was Mr Hall's government servant. **1834** G. BENNETT *Wanderings N.S.W.* I. 91 Some of the lower orders contrive to get government servants assigned to them. **1839** *Port Phillip Patriot* 3 A certain Dr Thomson has manoeuvred in some very peculiar manner, so as to obtain from the Sydney Government some five or six White Slaves. He calls them Government servants. **1854** MRS C. CLACY *Lights & Shadows* I. 42 Colney was Government servant to a settler. **1905** *Bulletin* (Sydney) 23 Mar. (Red Page), So presently the Govt. servant is unable to do more than his task, becomes incompetent to meet responsibility. **1907** *Ibid.* 4 Apr. 15/3 Pine Creek (N.T.) .. is now a one-horse village. No one there but Government servants, a pub, saddler and storekeeper. **1926** *Smith's Weekly* (Sydney) 5 June 21/3 In W.A. a Government servant can own half-a-dozen hotels by choosing sites when townships are surveyed. **1940** E. HILL *Great Austral. Loneliness* (ed. 2) 249 The 'Trans' and its people are a little world sufficient for themselves, a remarkable colony of government servants... With .. week-end dances at Cook, and a weekly shopping orgy on the 'Tea and Sugar' train that brings their water and supplies. **1946** F. CLUNE *Try Nothing Twice* 63 My career as a government servant had ended. I didn't get the sack. I just left. **1837** *S. Austral. Rec.* (London) 8 Nov. 3 We then went forward on the sand for about three miles, to the **government settlement**, where there still remain many capital huts, made of brush wood, by the first people who came here, before the site of the city of Adelaide was determined on. **1861** J.D. LANG *Qld., Aust.* 359 A place called *Umpie Bung*, or the dead-houses, where there had once been a government settlement. **1959** A. UPFIELD *Bony & Black Virgin* 213 The abos would rather starve than go and live in a government settlement and fatten on plenty. **1977** V. PRIDDLE *Larry & Jack* 132 Old Wambo, his faithful old aboriginal stockman was taken away to a Government Settlement to spend the evening of his life with his own people. **1825** *Austral.* (Sydney) 12 May 4 Sarah Brown .. saw the prisoners at the bar at a **government station** at .. the Cowpastures. **1835** J. LHOTSKY *Journey from Sydney* 9, I stopped at Cawdor, an old Government station. This is one of the places, which are called in the Colony, 'wateringplaces'. In such the government men .. stop with their teams, and cook their provisions. **1843** *Portland Mercury* 15 Mar. 4/3 Friendly relations .. had been established with the aborigines on the Murray, at a very early period after the formation of a government station at Mooninde. **1846** *Moreton Bay Courier* 21 Nov. 2/4 Charged with having aided and abetted other blacks in spearing cattle at the Government station. **1878** R.B. SMYTH *Aborigines of Vic.* I. 258 On the Government Stations in Victoria .. considerable numbers of Aborigines are now located. **1886** E.M. CURR *Austral. Race* I. 40 It is noticeable on the Government stations, on which the Blacks have been collected and well fed for over twenty years, that the females who have grown up on them have entirely ceased to show this disparity of stature. **1950** *Dark People in Melbourne* (Victorian Council Social Service) 7 Any dark person who is in need may be admitted to the Government Station at Lake Tyers. **1957** J. HAWKE *Follow my Dust* 194 The owner of Narndee Station had bought all the mules from the Government station, and his men had mustered the mules into Government camel yards to be broken before being taken to Narndee. **1842** *Geelong Advertiser* 7 Mar. 2/3 The men are employed on the public works; but we are sorry to say that they do not appear to be of much use, apparently from the want of an active overseer. The '**government stroke**' is soon learned; and the proficiency of the new hands appears to exceed that of the oldest gang in the colony. **1844** *Colonial Times* (Hobart) 10 Sept., The men rebelled... Armed constables were again despatched to coerce them .. and the men returned sullenly, to the 'Government stroke'. **1847** Z.P. POCOCK *Transportation & Convict Discipline* 8 Gangs of men .. were seen .. some resting on their shovels, some riding in hand carts, some lying on the ground smoking their pipes .. having acquired what was emphatically termed 'the Government stroke', as descriptive of the slovenly and tediously measured way in which they learned to work. **1856** W.W. DOBIE *Recoll. Visit Port-Phillip* 47 Government labourers, at ten shillings a-day, were breaking stones with what is called 'the government stroke', which is a slow-going, anti-sweating kind of motion. **1869** W.M. AKHURST *House Jack Built* 13 Lots of show—but real work—no, We can't think of that affordin' Come and do a little of the Government stroke, Come and do a little of the Government stroke, Quite as gay as actual play, And first-rate pay accordin'. **1880** *Bulletin* (Sydney) 17 July 4/4 The Government stroke! The *Hansard* reporters have worked over fourteen hours a day during the last eight months. **1901** *Truth* (Sydney) 8 Sept. 5/6 The 'Government stroke' .. is having a fair run... Men with their coats and vests off, and their sleeves rolled up, were standing about doing—what think you? Nothing. **1912** *Bulletin* (Sydney) 19 Sept. 16/4 Recently I saw the 'Government Stroke'... A decent-looking length of hardwood required chipping at one corner. Two men stood over it, pointing in an interested way, and discussing procedure generally... Two other chaps .. cross over and give their evidence about the piece of cedar. The barrow man .. saunters across and joins in. **1936** C.P. CONIGRAVE *N. Aust.* 84 We are inclined .. to be facetious in regard to the so-called 'Government stroke', and to believe generally that any work .. under Government supervision takes more time and costs more than that done by private enterprise. **1943** E. MERCIER *Giggles* 13 There appear to be two occasions when the Government stroke is not noticeable in a Government department—when it is hounding a private citizen for money, and when it is trying to pass a liability on to another department. **1958** R. WARD *Austral. Legend* 117 The colloquial expression 'Government Stroke' first became common in Victoria. **1979** B. SCOTT *Tough in Old Days* 74 The uninitiated, watching a gang of navvies at work, will speak scornfully of the 'Government stroke', and think they are watching lazy men. **1892** *Truth* (Sydney) 7 Feb. 4/4 Mr Dibbs .. bluntly declared that if the '**Government Strokers**' didn't like the present arrangements they could clear out at once, for thousands of others were ready to fill their billets and submit to the terrible inconvenience of being paid *a fine fat 'screw'*. **1911** ST. C. GRONDONA *Collar & Cuffs* 98, I didn't see them at work in the yards, but I was told they were real Government strokers. **1894** A.F. CALVERT *Coolgardie Goldfield* 40 **Government tanks** here quite dry. **1905** *Bulletin* (Sydney) 26 Oct. 15/2, I lately passed a Government tank... It is let to the present 'caretaker' at a few pounds a year. There are hundreds of acres of good fenced-in land included with the tank. **1920** H.F. MOLLARD *Humour of Road* 41 A Government tank, for travelling stock, .. the long troughs being capable of watering hundreds of sheep at one time. **1933** J. TRURAN *Where Plain Begins* 138 Their talk at first was of the commonplaces of the day's journey; the state of the Government tanks; the feed, or lack of feed, along the stock-routes. **1946** K.S. PRICHARD *Roaring Nineties* 46 He was going to water his horses at the first government tank. **1982** *Aboriginal Hist.* VI. 12 We used to .. all end up back there at old Carowra Government Tank, that's where we used to get our government rations. **1827** W.J. DUMARESQ in G. Mackaness *Fourteen Journeys Blue Mountains* (1950) ii. 93 As the *town* of Bathurst is exclusively a **government town**, every tenement in it is occupied by government officers. **1843** *Colonial Observer* (Sydney) 12 July 1157/1 The new wooden bridge leads across from the government township to a new town. **1846** G.F. DAVIDSON *Trade & Travel Far East* 129 The township of Maitland is divided into two towns or villages, called East Maitland and West Maitland. The former has been fixed upon as the site of the town by Government, and the latter by the public... The Government town is three miles further up the river. **1848** J.C. BYRNE *Twelve Yrs.' Wanderings* I. 148 Parramatta, Maitland East and West, Windsor, Newcastle .. are all **government townships,** established and laid out by the executive. **1853** J. ALLEN *Jrnl. River Murray* 37 Swan Hill is a Government township, situated on the Victoria side of the river. **1834** J. MUDIE *Vindication* 8 She was Mr Larnach's **Government woman.** **1844** *Sydney Morning Herald* 31 Dec. 2/6 Two government women, one assigned to Dr Forster, and the other to Dr Cartwright, were on Saturday last, each sentenced to two months' imprisonment in the third class of the Female Factory for drunkenness and disorderly conduct. **1854** *Illustr. Sydney News* 11 Nov. 356/2 A government woman .. is the proper phrase for a female prisoner, the word convict being always applied and accepted in bad part and as a term of reproach. **1882** *Austral. Stories* (ed. 2) 88 Some trouble he got into, while he was wardsman at the stockade, along of a Government woman there. **1803** *Sydney Gaz.* 17 July, Thomas Higgins .. for neglect of his **Government work** was sentenced to receive twenty-five lashes. **1810** *Ibid.* 28 Jan., All Persons possessed of such Free or Conditional Pardons are hereby required .. to surrender the same .. on Pain of being immediately apprehended and set to Government Work. **1822** J.T. BIGGE *Rep. State Colony N.S.W.* 21 Those who are now permitted to remain out of barrack, are compelled to work the whole of the day, but are allowed to employ themselves after the hours of government work, and on the whole of Saturdays, for their own benefit. **1825** *London Mag.* May 53 A man as can work can get a Government day's work done in 4 hours. When he his [*sic*] doing his Government work for his master, he gets no wages only his clothing. **1901** *Advocate* (Burnie) 9 Nov. 3/3 'The breakwater was built very slowly . . ?' 'It was.' 'That very fact gives strong presumptive evidence of Government work.' **1822** J.T. BIGGE *Rep. State Colony N.S.W.* 39 The first of these individuals acts as superintendent of the **government works** at Windsor. **1847** R. WELCH *Convict & Free Labour* 19 Until convicts were assigned in New South Wales, they were employed on Government and Colonial works.

government house.

1. a. The official residence of the principal representative of the Crown in each Colony (now State); since Federation, also the official residence of the Governor-General of Australia. Also *attrib.*

1788 *HRA* (1914) 1st Ser. I. 48 The ground marked for Government House is intended to include the main guard. **1791** S. MACARTHUR ONSLOW *Some Early Rec. Macarthurs* (1914) 40 One day . . when I happened to dine at Government House, a melon was produced weighing 30 lbs. **1799** D. COLLINS *Acct. Eng. Colony N.S.W.* (1802) II. 207 The foundation of the walls of a government house at Parramatta was laid. **1820** C. JEFFREYS *Van Dieman's Land* 51 The Government House occupies the centre of the main street; and is, if not a superb, a very comfortable dwelling. **1834** J.D. LANG *Hist. & Statistical Acct. N.S.W.* I. 276 Government-House is merely a large and rather ancient cottage. **1846** *Atlas* (Sydney) II. 110/3 They say there will be no balls at Government-house in Sir Charles Fitzroy's reign. **1860** 'LADY' *My Experiences in Aust.* 35 Government House . . is the only building in Sydney or its environs which can give the young Australians any idea of 'the stately homes of England'. **1883** J. WILLIS *Summer Holiday Vic. & N.Z.* 20 One of the pleasantest retreats . . is to be found . . adjacent to the £100,000 worth of ugly architecture known as Government house. **1899** *Austral. Tit-Bits* (Sydney) 25 Feb. 34/2 Francisco Miranda . . was hospitably entertained by the Government House party both in Melbourne and Sydney. **1918** *Bulletin* (Sydney) 1 Aug. 48/1 The factory girls weren't keen on the invitation to Government House. **1950** A.W. UPFIELD *Bachelors of Broken Hill* 26 We met . . at a reception at Government House in Brisbane. **1978** B. OAKLEY *Ship's Whistle* (1979) 42 It is not Government House, Mr Horne, but it is roomy enough for the single person.

b. *transf.* The principal residence on a sheep or cattle station.

1884 J. BAKER *Diary & Sketches Journey S.A.* 23 Were well recd. by acting Manager (Napier) & had 'Government House' to ourselves. **1895** *Adelaide Observer* 9 Nov. 33/4 We arrived at Murnpeowie, one of the finest stations in the North, the capacious stone buildings including a splendidly built Government House of eight rooms, woolshed for over fifty shearers, men's quarters, large store, &c. **1913** W.K. HARRIS *Outback in Aust.* 2 'Government House' (the owner's or manager's residence) on a big sheep station. **1936** A.W. UPFIELD *Wings above Diamantina* 77 Heading this class trilogy on the average station is the owner, or the manager, and his family. They reside in what is termed 'government house', the main residence on the property. **1946** L. REES *Austral. Radio Plays* 199, I don't travel a clean shirt in me swag, and me trousers is all worn through. I don't ever ask to go in to the Govermint 'Ouse. **1950** *New Settler in W.A.* (Perth) 50 There is an almost feudal character about these stations, with their many outbuildings grouped about 'government house'. **1967** G. JENKIN *Two Yrs. Bardunyah Station* 2, I . . walked through the trees towards 'Government House'. The homestead was a huge stone house encircled by verandahs. **1982** M. WALKER *Making Do* 105, I would be cooking in the manager's house on a station, which was always called Government House.

2. A dwelling built and maintained at public expense, esp. in a newly established town or to provide low-cost accommodation.

1827 P. CUNNINGHAM *Two Yrs. in N.S.W.* I. 147 Few except the government houses are worthy of much notice, being chiefly small detached cottages of brick or wood, presenting no very imposing appearance. [**1943** *First Interim Rep.* (Cwlth. Housing Comm.) 10 The demand for government dwellings will be greater than the supply. **1945** *Ann. Rep.* (S.A. Housing Trust) 6 Out of a total of 645 Government-sponsored houses sanctioned for South Australia, 200 had been completed.] **1950** *Canberra Times* 5 June 4/4 There are 2,644 applicants awaiting Government houses. **1969** *Bulletin* (Sydney) 22 Feb. 32/3 Paul Hasluck now moves from a small Government house in the Canberra suburb of Deakin . . to Yarralumla. **1970** *Tomorrow's Canberra* (Nat. Capital Dev. Comm.) 128 In 1966 the cost per square of a government house in Canberra was $713, in Sydney $617, and in Melbourne $730. **1983** *Canberra Chron.* 7 Sept. 1/2 Some of the fibro houses have been removed and the blocks sold for private building, some have been replaced with attractive brick-veneer government houses and some have been bought by tenants. **1985** *Canberra Times* 24 July 37/8, 68 Government houses, Florey. Sub-contractors and suppliers are invited to submit quotes for the above project.

Governor.

1. The principal representative of the sovereign in an Australian Colony (later State); formerly an abbreviation of GOVERNOR-GENERAL 1, GOVERNOR-IN-CHIEF, LIEUTENANT GOVERNOR 1. See also *State Governor* STATE 2 b.

1793 J. HUNTER *Hist. Jrnl. Trans. Port Jackson* 244, I called them Phillip Islands, after Arthur Phillip, the governor of New South Wales. *c* **1795** G. BARRINGTON *Voyage to Botany Bay* 49 Considerable buildings have been erected for the governor, the lieutenant-governor, the judge-advocate, and the greatest part of the officers. **1803** *N.S.W. Gen. Orders* 11 Jan. (1806) 23 When any Persons, either Male or Female, are sent to any of the different Settlements as a punishment, they are on no pretence whatever, to be allowed a Pass from thence, without the *Governor's* permission. **1814** *Govt. & Gen. Orders* 5 Feb., *The Governor* has observed, with Regret, the Reluctance of the *settlers* in general throughout this Colony, in coming forward to supply His Majesty's Stores with *grain* in the present alarming season of scarcity. **1829** *Rules & Regulations Managem. Aborigines* 8 The Governor wishing to hold a Public Conference with all those Tribes of the *Natives of New South Wales* who are in the Habit of resorting to the British Settlements . . requests that they will assemble and meet Him. **1845** C.J. BAKER *Sydney & Melbourne* 16 Australia Felix is a province of New South Wales, and is governed by a 'superintendent', resident at Melbourne, and acting under the immediate orders of the Governor of the Colony. **1851** *Illustr. Austral. Mag.* (Melbourne) Aug. 101 Separation has been finally effected. . . His Honor the Superintendent of the District of Port Phillip has become His Excellency the Governor of the Colony of Victoria. **1861** F. ALGAR *Handbk. to Colony Qld.* 5 Queensland enjoys a complete system of self-government. The administration of its affairs is vested in the Governor, the Legislative Council, and the Legislative Assembly. **1886** F.A. HAGENAUER *Rep. Aboriginal Mission Ramahyuck, Vic.* 6 Sir Henry Loch, Governor of Victoria, sent me a letter of introduction to the Governor of Queensland . . and to the Surveyor-General of the same colony. **1892** *Bulletin* (Sydney) 18 June 15/1 Miss Grace Norman, daughter of the Governor of Bananaland, is said to be engaged to a W.Q. squatter. **1927** A.W. PEARSE *Windjammer 'Prentice* 60 The Governor's box was given him at the theatre. **1955** N. PULLIAM *I traveled Lonely Land* 62 The monarch appoints, as her personal representatives, a Governor-General for Australia and, in addition, a Governor for each Australian state. **1972** *Bulletin* (Sydney) 21 Oct. 34/3 The roles of Queen Elizabeth's Australian representatives, the six governors and the governor-general, are threefold—constitutional, ceremonial and what has come to be described as charismatic.

2. *Hist.* In the collocation **Governor's Court**: see quot. 1819.

1812 *HRA* (1916) 1st Ser. VII. 673 There should be established two Courts in the Settlement, one the Supreme Court, the other the Governor's Court. **1819** W.C. WENTWORTH *Statistical, Hist., & Pol. Descr. N.S.W.* 30 The Governor's Court consists of the Judge Advocate and two inhabitants of the colony, appointed by precept from the governor, and takes cognizance of all pleas where the amount sued for does not exceed £50 sterling, (except such pleas as may arise between party and party at Van Dieman's Land) and from its decisions there is no appeal. **1820** H.G. BENNET *Let. to Earl Bathurst* 38 The governors court is composed of the judge-advocate, and two merchants of the town of Sydney. **1852** J. WEST *Hist. of Tas.* I. 63 The civil, called the 'Governor's Court', was instituted by George III in virtue of his prerogative. It consisted of the judge advocate, and two inhabitants chosen by the governor: it was empowered to decide in a summary manner all pleas in relation to property and contracts, and it granted probates of wills.

Governor-General.

1. *Hist.* A title bestowed on a Governor of the Colony of New South Wales whose jurisdiction extended also to other Colonies.

1827 P. CUNNINGHAM *Two Yrs. in N.S.W.* II. 312 New South Wales and Van Dieman's Land are under the jurisdiction of a governor-general, who resides in the former, with a lieutenant-governor under him for each colony. **1849** *Britannia* (Hobart) 2 Oct. 2/3 They should address the Governor-General for that purpose, it being intended to confer that office upon one of the governors of the colonies. **1861** A. KINLOCH *Lett. from S.A.* 11 A similar report for the information of His Excellency the Governor-General of Australia. **1873** A. TROLLOPE *Aust. & N.Z.* I. 205 In 1856 . . responsible government was established in New South Wales. . . This happened during the reign of Sir William Denison. . . He, however, still kept the title of Governor-General of Australasia, which was not borne by his successor.

2. The principal representative of the sovereign in the Commonwealth of Australia.

1898 *Austral. Handbk.* 122 The Queen may from time to time appoint a Governor-General, who shall be Her Majesty's Representative in the Commonwealth. **1903** *Truth* (Sydney) 5 Apr. 7/5 Our Governor-General and family . . come to camp down near Circular Quay for a month or two. **1941** B. PENTON *Think* 47 A Labour Government once appointed an Australian Governor-General. . . The most dinky-di republican Aussie did not quite feel it was the real thing. **1972** *Bulletin* (Sydney) 21 Oct. 34/3 Constitutionally . . the governor-general is the commander in chief of the Australian armed forces; he opens and closes Federal Parliament; he may grant pardons to criminals; and must give his assent to acts of parliament. **1973** *Ibid.* 24 Feb. 15/3 Gough says Mick Young would make an ideal Governor-General. He's the only man who knows what to do with the Yarralumla shearing shed. **1986** *Canberra Times* 15 Mar. 2/4 The Gurindji tribe . . petitioned the Governor-General, seeking some of their tribal land.

Governor-in-Chief.

Hist. A title formerly bestowed on the Governor of an Australian Colony; in full **Captain-General and Governor-in-Chief.**

1787 *HRA* (1914) 1st Ser. I. 2 We . . do constitute and appoint you the said Phillip to be our Captain-General and Governor-in-Chief in and over our territory called New South Wales. **1816** *Hobart Town Gaz.* 7 Sept., His excellency the Governor in Chief having been pleased to extend Conditional Emancipations to the undermentioned Persons . . they may be received . . at this Office. **1820** C. JEFFREYS *Van Dieman's Land* 166 From the subordinate nature of the government of Van Dieman's Land, all grants of land must be made by the Governor in Chief at Port Jackson. **1824** E. CURR *Acct. Colony Van Diemen's Land* 104 A regulation was lately made by the new Governor in Chief, Sir Thomas Brisbane, requiring every person . . to enter into a bond. **1832** *Sydney Herald* 20 Feb. 4/3 His Excellency Major-General Richard Bourke, Captain-General and Governor-in-Chief of the Territory of New South Wales and its Dependencies, and Vice-Admiral of the same. **1851** H. MELVILLE *Present State Aust.* 203 Van Diemen's Land is even yet only a lieutenancy, the Governor-in-Chief being stationed in New South Wales. **1860** *S. Austral. Advertiser* (Adelaide) 3 July 2/4 His Excellency the Governor-in-Chief could not with propriety preside at a meeting where the Judges of the Supreme Court of the province were to be censured, although the Head of the Executive and Her Majesty's representative may with the most perfect propriety. **1881** J.F.V. FITZGERALD *Aust.* 76 Sir William Dennison . . and Sir Charles Fitzroy were styled 'Governors-General'; they were supposed to have some sort of pre-eminence over the other Governor. Sir John Young (Lord Lisgar) succeeded . . in May, 1861, with the title of 'Governor-in-Chief': this has continued to be the style.

govie, var. GUVVIE.

Goyder's line. *S.A.* [From the name of G.W. *Goyder* (1826–1898), Surveyor-General of South Australia.] A line north of which the annual rainfall is less than 355 mm., and the land in consequence unsuitable for wheat-farming. Also **Goyder's line of rainfall.**

1873 A. TROLLOPE *Aust. & N.Z.* II. 195 The surveyor-general, Mr Goyder, has drawn an arbitrary line across the map of South Australia, which is now known as Goyder's line of rainfall. **1887** MRS D.D. DALY *Digging, Squatting, & Pioneering Life* 107 On past 'Goyder's line of rainfall'. **1899** *North-Western Advocate* (Devonport) 4 Jan. 4/1 Definite information in regard to the South Australian harvest is not yet available, but . . the crops within Goyder's rainfall line are good. **1948** A.J. MCLACHLAN *McLachlan* 98 An old Surveyor-General, basing, no doubt, his opinions on nature, had long ago laid down a line known as 'Goyder's Line', outside of which it was unsafe to embark on cultivation, owing to the paucity of the rainfall. **1952** A.C.C. LOCK *Travels across Aust.* 216 'How near we are to Goyder's line of rainfall.' This 'line' . . was a geographic reference to a part of the State where, through various causes, the rainfall rapidly diminished. **1967** R. HAWKER *Emu in Fowl Pen* 162 The country slowly growing drier all the way, to well beyond Goyder's line, which indicated a settled and predictable rainfall.

Grabben Gullen pie /græbən gʌlən 'paɪ/. [f. the name of a town in N.S.W.] See quot. 1899.

1899 *Bulletin* (Sydney) 2 Sept. 14/2 'Grabben Gullen pie' . . is properly . . a pumpkin scooped out and stuffed with 'possum. **1980** B. HORNADGE *Austral. Slanguage* 207 Another old timers' dish was the Grabben Gullen Pie, also known as Possum Pumpkin Pie.

graft, *n.* [Br. dial. *graft* work of any description: see EDD.] Work of any sort, esp. demanding work. Also *attrib.*

[N.Z. **1853** J. ROCHFORT *Adventures of Surveyor* 47, I could make more money by 'hard graft', as they call labour in the colonies.] **1873** J.C.F. JOHNSON *Christmas on Carringa* 15 My name is Jim, the Cadger, I'm a downy cove you see, 'Hard graft', it ain't my fancy. **1892** 'J. MILLER' *Workingman's Paradise* 104 I've been out of graft for months and haven't got any money . . and there's no chance of another job. **1895** *Worker* (Sydney) 30 Mar. 4/2 They're soon at their graft, and things are running along smoothly, from the publican's point of view. **1897** *Ibid.* 25 Sept. 1/1 When nice, genteel work's denied you tackle harder kind of graft; Take to fencing, shearing, ploughing. **1904** L.M.P. ARCHER *Bush Honeymoon* 278 Writing is *hard graft* to me. I'd rather dig post-holes any day. **1908** *Clipper* (Hobart) 19 Sept. 2/2 From the kick-off Abel played grandly; Teddy Russell put in a good bit of graft. **1913** H. LAWSON *Triangles of Life* 137 'I've been used to hard work' (they call 'graft' work in England). **1918** *Kia Ora Coo-ee* Aug. 17/2 They do graft, those A.M.C. chaps; no soft jobs in a hospital. **1949** C. BENHAM *Diver's Luck* 31 Each one of us was in good trim, and all did their graft, so by that evening the work was done. **1973** F. PARSONS *Man called Mo* 2 'Graft' was one of his [*sc.* Mo's] favourite words. It meant anything that could help him. **1981** H. LINDSAY *Echoes H. Lawson* 19 Home is a suddenly-strange and old-fashioned farmhouse away to hell in a lousy hard-graft valley nobody ever heard of.

graft, *v.* [Br. dial. *to graft* to do work of any description.] *intr.* To work; to labour strenuously.

[**1859** J.C. HOTTEN *Dict. Mod. Slang* 47 *Graft*, to go to work.] **1890** *Argus* (Melbourne) 9 Aug. 4/2 You graftin' with him? **1892** *Bulletin* (Sydney) 20 Feb. 14/2 What are you doing now, Paddy Magee? Grafting, or spelling now, Paddy Magee? **1896** *Ibid.* 9 May 3/2 Ho! their barrackers yell louder, And they graft like nigs to crowd her. **1902** J. MATHEW *Austral. Echoes* 90 The next to sing was Dick the digger, A man who 'grafted' like a nigger. **1915** *N.S.W. & its Germans* 72, I would make them all graft, and I would see that they earned enough to pay for their tucker. **1920** *Ross's Monthly* Dec. 7/2 As long as men must graft for grub 'twill always be the same. **1924** *Aussie* (Sydney) Feb. 24 When the weather is hot . . Then I'd much rather not Remain grafting in town. **1946** M. FRANKLIN *My Career goes Bung* 214 At home grafting away like fury.

Hence **grafting** *ppl. a.*

1980 *Sydney Morning Herald* 24 Apr. 32/3 The mountain men—Penrith Rugby League team—knuckled to a grafting 26–14 win against Cronulla-Sutherland in the Tooth Cup match at Leichhardt Oval last night.

grafter. [f. prec.] One who works hard.

1891 *Truth* (Sydney) 11 Jan. 1/7 Is your husband a good hard 'grafter', or is he lazy and slack? **1895** *Worker* (Sydney) 31 Aug. 3/5 All grafters should take note of the fact that the inclusion of a 7s. minimum rate would have obviated the necessity of a strike for it. **1903** *Bulletin* (Sydney) 20 June 35/1 Dad is a grafter . . but he's a fool. He wouldn't be 'cockying' on the fringe of eternal debt and starvation if he wasn't. **1918** *Kia Ora Coo-ee* June 2/3 The Primus is the hardest grafter in the army. **1926** M.M. KNOWLES *Meg of Minadong* 10 Their 'old man' had been not only what was termed a hard grafter, but a shrewd, farseeing settler. **1944** M.J. O'REILLY *Bowyangs & Boomerangs* 46 The dinkum 'grafter', forced to carry his swag in search of a job, deserves all the help that can be given him. **1953** 'CADDIE' *Caddie* 12 He was a grafter and worked out in the bush six days a week. **1981** *Austral.* (Sydney) 3 June 14/1 *A grafter* in Trevor Chappell or a dasher in Martin Kent?

gramma. [Of unknown origin.] A variety of pumpkin having a sweet, fibrous flesh. Also *attrib.*

1964 P. WHITE *Burnt Ones* 183 'But why pick on a poor pumpkin? If it had been a gramma,' she said. **1976** G. HALL *Rhymes from Rivers* 14 We have porridge and potatoes, Scones and gramma pie. **1982** N. KEESING *Lily on Dustbin* 116 Although the Americans invented pumpkin pie, we adapted it, and gramma pie is its close cousin. **1985** *New Idea* (Melbourne) 8 June 79/1 Gramma, or bugle pumpkin, is the variety traditionally used for Pumpkin Pie.

Granny, *n.*[1]

1. A nickname for *The Sydney Morning Herald.* Also **Granny Herald.**

1851 *Press* (Sydney) 189/2 'My Grannie O,' (which we beg to submit as a very good cognomen for the *Herald* and its antiquated and obsolete notions on the subject of Government). **1900** *Truth* (Sydney) 18 Feb. 1/5 'Granny' gets hold of some prodigious hunks of news occasionally. **1931** *Century of Journalism* 239 The *Herald* has long been affectionately—and sometimes contemptuously—known as 'Granny', the nickname being supposed to refer to its age, its allegedly conservative methods and the untiring energy with which it has always dealt out advice, comment and criticism. **1940** A. HASKELL *Waltzing Matilda* 176 The dean of papers is the *Sydney Morning Herald*, 'Grannie', an organ of conservative views and amazing respectability. **1950** J. CLEARY *Just let me Be* 241 'You're beginning to talk like some old spinster,' Harry said. 'You'll be writing letters to Granny Herald next.' **1967** *Kings Cross Whisper* (Sydney) xxxv. 6/1 *Granny*, The Sydney Morning Herald.

2. *transf. Obs.* A nickname given to other daily newspapers.

1884 *Adelaide Punch* 25 Apr. 2/2 Every day the old dame of Grenfell Street is becoming more feeble and ridiculous. Last Wednesday Mr H. Gawler wrote complaining of some aspersions Granny had cast upon his father. **1890** *Quiz* (Adelaide) 4 Apr. 2/1 It is not often that *Quiz* agrees with the *Register*. . . Granny has hit the right nail on the head. **1905** *Tocsin* (Melbourne) 3 Nov. 6/1 According to the 'Argus', 'an old man died in London at the age of eighty one'. When a young man dies at the age of 81, we wish Granny would ring up the 'Tocsin' and let us know about it. **1906** *Gadfly* (Adelaide) 20 June 21/1 Granny *Register* made a great fuss over her seventieth birthday.

granny, *n.*[2]

a. Abbrev. of GRANNY SMITH.

1944 C.S. WATTS *Selected Verse* 13 Cast-off clothes and greasy bacon, and . . 'Grannies! Ten a bob!' **1959** *Sydney Morning Herald* 9 Oct. 2/8, I want some big Grannies. **1979** *Mercury* (Hobart) 3 Sept. 11/1 The Yugoslav freighter . . unloaded 42,000 cases of Grannies.

b. In the phr. **she'll be Grannies,** all will be well: see APPLE 4.

1963 B. BEAVER *Hot Summer* 115 'She'll be Grannies,' cackled the ragged informant. 'And I know the girls will be in it because they tipped me off to tell you.'

Granny Smith. [f. the name of Maria Ann *Smith* (*c* 1801–1870), cultivator of the apple.] A variety of apple, green-skinned and especially suitable for cooking.

1895 *Agric. Gaz. N.S.W.* VI. 900, I think that the Sturmer Pippin, Stewarts, Granny Smith's Seedling . . would be worth a trial. **1913** H. MCEWIN *Fruitgrower's Handbk.* (ed. 2) 32 *Granny Smith*, succeeds well in New South Wales, where it is a leading favourite as a shipper and long keeper. **1924** J. FARRELL *Apple Culture in Vic.* 142 *Dates of Blooming* . . Granny Smith 19–10. **1936** *Austral. Writers' Ann.* 77 Cleopatras, sweet as Egypt's golden queen; Statesmen; Granny Smiths, green and tart and useful. **1947** MRS A.H. GARNSEY *Romance Huon River* 172 Granny Smiths, Rome Beauties and Jonathons. **1971** D. IRELAND *Unknown Industr. Prisoner* 252 From his pocket he took an apple, a large, green Granny Smith. **1985** *Sydney Morning Herald* 23 Feb. 109/4 Granny Smith, of Granny Smith Apple fame, grew her apples on a farm near North Road and Threlfall Street, Eastwood, in the 1860s.

grant. *Hist.* Between 1788 and 1831 (when the practice ceased): the granting to an individual (emancipated convict, settler, marine officer, etc.) of a tract of Crown land; the tract of land so granted; the document or deed in which the conditions of the grant are stated.

1793 J. HUNTER *Hist. Jrnl. Trans. Port Jackson* 531 To Philip Schaffer, . . one hundred and forty acres; called in the grant, the *Vineyard*. **1804** *HRA* (1921) 3rd Ser. I. 246 The Parties will become entitled to Grants at the New Settlement of Port Dalrymple. **1808** *To Viscount Castlereagh* 8 To the settlers at large, grants of land and stock, and assistance from the public stores, afforded the unlimited means of reward and encouragement. **1817** *Hobart Town Gaz.* 31 May, All Settlers and Stock-owners who hold Certificates of Occupation or Written Authority for occupying as Grazing Ground, Land not their own Grant or Property . . are forthwith to exhibit their Certificate. **1821** T. GODWIN *Descr. Acct. Van Diemen's Island* 16 The grant . . to the ordinary class of emigrants, is usually from 600 to 800 acres. **1824** *Australasian Pocket Almanack* 82 In the Grants is contained a proviso, that the grantee, his heirs and assigns, shall . . procure to be assigned to his or their service . . one transported convict for every 100 acres of the said land. **1826** J. ATKINSON *Acct. Agric. & Grazing N.S.W.* 33 It was formerly the custom to give grants of from 30 to 60 acres to all convicts who had served their term without being convicted of any misdemeanour. **1827** P. CUNNINGHAM *Two Yrs. in N.S.W.* II. 157 In searching for a suitable grant, it is a great point to fix upon a place where the land *round* it is all so indifferent that no new settler is likely to place himself near you . . enabling you thus to have a free run for your stock for miles without being encroached on. **1829** *Hints Emigration New Settlement Swan & Canning Rivers* 6 At the expiration of seven years . . so much of the whole Grant as shall still remain in an uncultivated or unimproved state, will revert absolutely to the Crown. **1844** *Colonial Times* (Hobart) 2 June, To Let . . Three Thousand Acres of the finest Grazing Land in the colony, well known as the grant to Francis Smith Esq. **1848** J. SYME *Nine Yrs. Van Diemen's Land* 117 A gentleman . . walked . . a thousand miles before he fixed upon his land, and his grant thus chosen was certainly a thousand pounds more valuable than if taken in an inferior situation. **1857** D. BUNCE *Australasiatic Reminisc.* 31 Jericho was merely a small hamlet, consisting, at the time of our visit, of eight houses and of three grants, and no more. **1860** 'LADY' *My Experiences in Aust.* 24 In time these grants became very valuable.

grantee. *Hist.* The recipient of a grant of land.

1800 *HRA* (1914) 1st Ser. II. 514 You assign to each grantee, the service of any number of them [*sc.* convicts] that you may judge necessary. **1814** *Ibid.* (1916) VIII. 393, I have had Certain Conditions Inserted, respecting the Clearing and improving of the Lands so granted, which are required to be performed before the Grantees Can Sell. **1825** *Ibid.* (1917) XI. 443 The lands will be held by the Grantee free of all Quit rents. **1830** *Launceston Advertiser* 4 Jan. 2 No restraint should apply to any grantee as respects the disposal of such ground. **1841** *Van Diemen's Land Chron.* (Hobart) 23 July 4/3 In fact, it was formerly a condition to obtaining a grant of land, that the grantee should support so many convict servants. **1847** E.W. LANDOR *Bushman* 375 The original grantees have clung to their lands with desperate tenacity. **1848** *Britannia* (Hobart) 10 Oct. 2/2 The present possessor of the property, a son of the original grantee, wishes to sell. **1853** S. SIDNEY *Three Colonies* (ed. 2) 87 Persons desirous of becoming grantees without purchase might obtain land in satisfying the governor that they had the power and intention of expending in the cultivation of the land a capital equal to half the estimated value of it.

grape. [Prob. infl. by the expression *sour grapes*.] In the phr. **a grape on the business**: see quot. 1941.

1941 S.J. BAKER *Pop. Dict. Austral. Slang* 32 *Grape on the business, A* (of a person), one who is a blue stocking, a wallflower or a drag on cheery company. **1944** L. GLASSOP *We were Rats* 9 I've got nobody to go with. All the girls'll be going with their boy friends and I don't want to be a grape on the business. **1946** A. MARSHALL *Tell us about Turkey, Jo* 62 She hasn't got a bloke. She is a grape on the business.

grape-cocky. [See COCKY *n.*[2]] One who grows grapes, esp. for the dried-fruits industry.

1941 *Bulletin* (Sydney) 28 May 16/2, I lands a job helpin' one of them grape-cockies stack lucerne. **1968** S. GORE *Holy Smoke* 62 These grape cockies think to themselves, Strewth, it's us that's doin' all the hard yakka round the joint.

grape-snatching, *vbl. n.* Grape-picking. Also *attrib.*

1952 *Bulletin* (Sydney) 9 Jan. 16/2 A gang of us congregated in a Mildura boarding-house waiting for the grape-snatching to start. *Ibid.* 2 Apr. 17/1 A temperance advocate joined our grape-snatching gang in Mildura. **1982** J.A. SHARWOOD *Vocab. Austral. Dried Vine Fruits Industry* 22 Unwilling *casuals* . . take on *grape-snatching*, only because there is no other work.

grass. In the phr. **on the grass**: see quot. 1941.

1885 *Australasian Printers' Keepsake* 93 I'm *on the Grass* (worse luck!) for now I find I dare not shift. I'm tethered to this state. **1941** S.J. BAKER *Pop. Dict. Austral. Slang* 51 *On the grass*, free, at large. A criminal is 'on the grass again' after being released from gaol. **1955** N. PULLIAM *I traveled Lonely Land* 383 *On the grass*, out of jail.

grass-fed, *a.* and *n.*

A. *adj.* Of a horse: inexperienced; not trained as a racehorse. Of a race(-meeting): organized for such horses. Also *transf.*

1878 G. WALCH *Australasia* 28 In the heyday of his grass-fed youth while being ridden just beyond the Sapling Camp he had inadvertently grazed with his hoof an unwary snake. **1891** *Truth* (Sydney) 5 Apr. 2/4 There are plenty of intelligent, honest, educated men in the ranks of Labor who are well enough 'grass fed', but can't stand corn. **1934** J.C. LEE *Boshstralians* 132 Walgett's holdin' a grass-fed meetin' that day. **1973** R. ROBINSON *Drift of Things* 92 There was a grass-fed race meeting coming up and Mr Simmonds wanted to try out his horses.

B. *n.* A horse which has not been trained as a racehorse: see quot. 1945.

1940 E. HILL *Great Austral. Loneliness* (ed. 2) 125 Horses are hacks and grass-feds from the drovers' plants and the stations. **1945** F. CORK *Tales from Cattle Country* 51 Among racing enthusiasts in the Outback you will hear much talk about 'corn-feds' and 'grass-feds' that is confusing to the uninitiated. 'Corn-feds' are horses prepared for the regular meetings—training solidly and being fed on such hardening foods as chaff, oats, and corn. The picnic gallopers must be 'grass-feds' unless drought conditions preclude 'grass-fed' meetings, in which case picnic races are held under 'corn-fed' conditions. **1973** D. STUART *Morning Star, Evening Star* 9 A one-day meeting for grassfeds, when every station for a couple of hundred miles sends in its best.

grass-fighter. One who fights 'with no holds barred'.

1951 I.L. IDRIESS *Across Nullarbor* 19 Those were the bare-knuckle days, 'kinged' over by the grim 'grass fighters'. **1953** H.G. LAMOND *Big Red* 283 *Grass-fighter*, bare-knuckle man. Prize-ring rules, or no rules at all. **1957** D. NILAND *Call me when Cross turns Over* 220 Fascination was the grass-fighter. No two-minute rounds and a minute spell for him. Just a start and a finish, short or long, and a matchless endurance to see that he was the one left standing at the end. **1965** R.H. CONQUEST *Horses in Kitchen* 123 He reckoned any good Australian grass-fighter, fast on his feet, could skittle a shillelagh man in no time.

Also **grass-fighting** *vbl. n.*

1978 D. STUART *Wedgetail View* 99 Professional pug, yes, he makes money . . though it's a pretty crook way of making a quid. But grass fighting; hell . . it's crazy.

grasshopper. *fig.* A nickname for a tourist, esp. one visiting Canberra.

1955 S. RUDD *Far & Near* 67 Pioneer tourists are nicknamed the 'Grasshoppers', by the country folk, who state that they fly into a town, devour all there is to eat, drink and see and then fly out again. **1969** L. HAYLEN *Twenty Yrs.' Hard Labor* 204 The private member has, however, his visitors from the electorate. Now . . they arrive in such numbers that they have come to be called 'the grasshoppers'. **1972** *Sydney Morning Herald* 3 Nov. 6/3 At last the politicians are gone from Parliament and have dispersed to their electorates for the federal campaign. King's Hall . . has been taken over by 'grasshoppers'—an old Canberra nickname for tourists. **1976** C. FORSYTH *Governor-General* 117 He picked his way past a group of tourists de-bussing. . . Grassies, short for grasshoppers, they were called in Canberra because of their habit of descending on the national capital in plague proportions.

grass parrot. Any of various parrots that habitually frequent grassy country, esp. species of *Psephotus* and *Neophema*. Also **grass parakeet.**

1840 J. GOULD *Birds of Aust.* (1848) V. Pl. 47, Swift Lorikeet . . in its style of colouring and in its more lengthened and slender tail . . is beautifully intermediate between the Grass Parakeets and the *Trichoglossi*. **1841** *Proc. Zool. Soc. London* VIII. 147 Three new species of small Grass Parrakeets (*Euphema*). **1862** J.A. PATTERSON *Gold Fields Vic.* 213 The road lay over fine plains . . wooded with box . . amid which grass parrots . . flitted. **1867** F.J. BYERLEY *Narr. Overland Exped. Northern Qld.* 21 Large flocks of . . budgerygars or grass parrots. **1932** H. PRIEST *Call of Bush* 163 The sweet little Grass Parakeets, or Lovebirds . . frequently dart up in small coveys. **1954** C. BARRETT *Wild Life Aust. & New Guinea* 135 Popularly known as the 'grassie', or 'grass-parrakeet', the familiar little red-backed parrot enlivens gum-tree paddocks. **1962** B.W. LEAKE *Eastern Wheatbelt Wildlife* 77 The handsome mulga or grass parrots came from further north or from the Eastern Goldfields. **1972** J. HIBBERD *Stretch of Imagination* (1973) 19, I can see her now . . on a wicker chair . . under a pergola of everlastings . . enjoying the sunsets over Lake Hindmarsh . . feeding a grass parrot or two.

grass roots, *pl. Mining.* [Prob. f. *grass* earth's surface: see OED *sb.*[1] 9 b.] The surface of a mine. Also *attrib.*

1932 I.L. IDRIESS *Prospecting for Gold* 264 *'Grass roots'*, a term used where a working is started from, or worked up to, the surface. **1979** B. SCOTT *Tough in Old Days* 31 We heard of . . grassroots gold that lay just below the surface of certain kinds of country.

grass-tree.

1. a. Any of many small trees of the fam. Xanthorrhoeaceae, usu. of the genus *Xanthorrhoea*, having a crown of grass-like leaves; BLACKBOY 2 a.; YACCA 1. See also XANTHORRHOEA.

1794 G. THOMPSON *Slavery & Famine* ii. 12 Their spears are made of the stem of the grass tree. **1805** J.W. LEWIN *Prodromus Ent.* 19 We found . . the larvae of this Tinea in a decayed stump of the grass tree of the colonist. **1834** G. BENNETT *Wanderings N.S.W.* I. 62 It is named *'grass-tree'* by the colonists for its long pendent grassy foliage, and *'yellow gum tree'* from secreting a quantity of yellowish gum. **1840** T.J. BUCKTON *W.A.* 32 The remarkable forms of the *Kingia Australis* (grass-tree). **1843** *S. Austral. Mag.* (Adelaide) Nov. 334 The grass-tree . . is one of the most useful of the indigenous productions to the Australian native. It is the sole means he has of obtaining fire, by friction of its dry, pithy stalk. **1875** CAMPBELL & WILKS *Early Settlement Qld.* 30 Collecting as much sticks and grass-tree as would boil my pot of tea. **1880** C. PROUD *S.E. District S.A.* 17 There are thousands of the peculiar-looking grass-trees, with their bright-green quill-like branching leaves shooting out of their short, black trunks. **1914** H.M. VAUGHAN *Australasian Wander-Yr.* 214 On the railway banks grew thousands of the curious grass-trees, or 'Black-fellow's Spear'. **1926** W.A. CAWTHORNE *Kangaroo Islanders* 71, I tell yer it's the heart of the grass-tree. Yer chops all the leaves away and gees it a smart rap, and the heart jumps out beautiful; yer can live upon it by the week. **1952** B. BEATTY *Unique to Aust.* 111 The Grass tree is of immense commercial value because of the resin or gum it yields. **1979** DOUGLAS & HEATHCOTE *Far Cry* 38 The grasstrees' stems were like lizard bodies, with the fine geometric 'Grass' flaring out over the brown skirt of old dead grass hanging down like a native's ceremonial dress. **1981** A.B. FACEY *Fortunate Life* 20 The blackboy is a native grass-tree that grows in the Western Australian bush.

b. With distinguishing epithet: **small grass-tree,** any of several smaller species of grass-tree, esp. (in e. Aust.) *Xanthorrhoea minor*, having a tuft of leaves less than 1 m. tall topped by a slender scape of similar height; *dwarf grass-tree*, see DWARF.

1844 L. LEICHHARDT *Jrnl. Overland Exped. Aust.* 23 Oct. (1847) 21 The first appearance of the small grass-tree (Xanthorrhaea). **1923** *Census Plants Vic.* (Field Naturalists' Club Vic.) 17 *Xanthorrhoea minor*, Small Grass-tree. **1972** *Lal Lal Blast Furnace* (Forests Comm. Vic.) 3 An unusual flora feature of the Reserve is the density of *Xanthorrhoea minor*, or small grass tree.

c. Special Comb. **grass-tree gum,** the resin exuded by any of several species of grass-tree, rich in picric acid, usu. red, and formerly much used as an adhesive; BLACKBOY 2 b.; *yacca gum*, see YACCA 2. See also YELLOW GUM 1 a.

1835 J. BACKHOUSE *Narr. Visit Austral. Colonies* (1843) 288 He used a spear in fishing, made of a long stick, with four, long, wooden prongs attached to it, by means of string and Grass-tree Gum. **1847** G.F. ANGAS *Savage Life & Scenes* I. 93 The tea-tree spear which is barbed with sharp quartz or glass, cemented . . by grass-tree gum and sand, of which they form a kind of glue. **1883** *Bulletin* (Sydney) 19 May 14/3 Between Milton and Moruya 200 men are employed gathering grass-tree gum, which fetches £80 per ton in the English market. **1890** *Proc. Linnean Soc. N.S.W.* V. 429 The term grass-tree 'gum' is of course scientifically untenable, as it is insoluble in water; it is soluble in spirit and is a true resin. **1900** *Bulletin* (Sydney) 28 Apr. (Red Page), Years ago . . the gathering of grass-tree gum was a promising industry round Sydney-side. **1914** *Ibid.* 17 Sept. 22/2 With a tommyhawk, or, rather, a half-handled 'Douglas', the gum is chipped off. . . Whether grass tree gum from the mainland is used . . I don't know. **1973** V. SERVENTY *Desert Walkabout* 27 Near the coast blackboy or grass tree gum was used as an adhesive.

2. Any of several species of the chiefly Tasmanian genus *Richea* (fam. Epacridaceae), having prickly grass-like leaves, esp. *R. dracophylla* and *R. pandanifolia.*

1833 J. BACKHOUSE *Narr. Visit Austral. Colonies* (1843) 159 The Broad-leaved Grass-tree, *Richea Dracophylla*, forms a striking object; it is very abundant, and on an average, from ten to fifteen feet high; it is much branched, and has broad, grassy foliage. **1878** W.W. SPICER *Handbk. Plants Tas.* 125 *Richea pandanifolia* . . Giant Grass Tree. **1909** G.W. SMITH *Naturalist in Tas.* 53 In the sub-Alpine zone we meet with a number of species of the almost exclusively Tasmanian genus *Richea* . . popularly known as the Grass-trees. **1933** C.W. PECK *Austral. Legends* (ed. 2) 228 The jet-black king had chosen a burnt patch on the side of a Richea . . his colour and that of the grass-tree making him almost invisible. **1942** C. BARRETT *Austral. Wild Flower Bk.* 159 It [*sc. Richea pandanifolia*] is called 'grass tree', despite its palm-like appearance. **1968** V. SERVENTY *Southern Walkabout* 54 The giant grass tree or 'pandanni'.

grazier. [In Br. use apparently uncommon and applied chiefly to one who raises cattle for market.] One who raises sheep or cattle; in early use distinguishing one who raises stock from a crop-farmer, in later use denoting a land-holder whose interests are substantial. See also *cattle grazier* CATTLE 2, PASTORALIST, *sheep grazier* SHEEP 2.

1804 *HRA* (1915) 1st Ser. IV. 462 Forms the most inviting and extensive country for the comfort and benefit of the cultivator and grazier. **1814** S. KITTLE *Concise Hist. N.S.W.* 141 When he commenced grazier, the price of mutton and beef fluctuated from 2s. 6d. to 3s. per lb. and now he can supply the market at 9d. per lb. **1828** *Austral. Quarterly Jrnl. Theol., Lit., & Sci.* Jan. p. x, Contrast the condition of the wretched Settler at the Cape, with that of the jolly farmer on the Hawkesbury, or the opulent grazier and wool grower, of Bathurst, or Argyle. **1843** *Sydney Morning Herald* 21 June 3/2, I . . in my last letter, divided the various classes of the colonists into two great ones, namely the graziers and the farmers. It would have made the illustration plainer, if I had supposed both these classes to reside in Sydney, as all the graziers *used* to do, and as many of them do *now*, and that their grazing and farming concerns were managed by *overseers*. **1849** S. & J. SIDNEY *Emigrant's Jrnl.* 50 These large squatters, or graziers, as they call themselves, have, perhaps, five, ten, or twenty . . stations . . scattered over different parts of the colony. **1872** 'CAPRICORNUS' *Bush Essays* 41 Whatever the Australian selector may profess to be . . he is nearly always more a grazier than anything else. The grass is the resource most readily available. **1884** A.W. STIRLING *Never Never Land* 19 'Is it a crime, Sir,' began the hon. member, 'to be a squatter? Is it a Sin, Sir, to be a grazier?' **1892** 'E. KINGLAKE' *Austral. at Home* 116 In official returns . . the name 'squatter' is not used, there he is called grazier or pastoral lessee, but squatter is the only term for him in colloquial use. **1918** C.H. NORTHCOTT *Austral. Social Dev.* 51 The physical geography of the country has made a distinction between the farmer and the grazier, who exist side by side in permanent rivalry. **1919** *Bulletin* (Sydney) 1 Mar. 6/3 Many a small selector, buying a few poddy calves here and there, or a few store beasts and fattening them, has blossomed in a few years into a rich grazier. **1927** *Ibid.* 20 Jan. 22/3 In Australia the grazier is a person of financial and social tonnage. **1935** F. CLUNE *Rolling down Lachlan* 111 What a difference between a grazier and a cocky. The former prefers to keep shade wherever possible; the other begrudges even the mere hint of it from fence-posts and wires. **1953** *Bulletin* (Sydney) 7 Jan. 12/2 The son of a grazier seeking political honours . . was a suitable representative, as his people had 'made their money off the sheep's back'. **1958** E.O. SCHLUNKE *Village Hampden* 19 The expensive sports-coat his wife made him buy so that he will look like a grazier instead of a farmer. **1968** G. MIKES *Boomerang* 120 You must never refer to a grazier as a farmer. A farmer is a lower type of human. You may call them pastoralists; in fact a pastoralist is a higher kind of grazier. **1981** Q. WILD *Honey Wind* 69 Too much rain this year, Harry, all the graziers have got to get webbed feet fitted to their Mercedes. **1984** *People Mag.* (Sydney) 7 May 39/1 Greedy graziers with a long range strategy to cut pay rates.

grazing, *vbl. n.* [Not necessarily excl. Austral. but of local significance because of the importance of the grazing industry.] Used *attrib.* in Special Comb. **grazing country,** land suited to or used for the raising of sheep or cattle; **district,** an area in which sheep or cattle raising is the principal industry; **establishment, farm,** a rural property on which sheep or cattle raising is the principal activity; also **farmer,** one who owns such a property; **paddock,** an enclosure in which sheep or cattle pasture; **property,** *grazing farm*; **run, station,** *grazing farm*; an area of pasture detached from the principal landholding; see also RUN *n.*[2] 1 a., STATION 2 a.

1831 *Acct. Colony Van Diemen's Land* 117 Part of this fine **grazing country** has now been located and converted into profitable sheep and cattle walks. **1892** *Braidwood Dispatch* 7 Dec. 6/1, 3421 acres . . of first class agricultural and grazing country. **1963** *Bulletin* (Sydney) 14 Sept. 29/2 Ways will have to be found for incorporating permanent kangaroo-controls into the standard management practices of the grazing country. **1831** *Acct. Colony Van Diemen's Land* 84 The road continues through a fine **grazing district.** **1845** E.J. EYRE *Jrnls. Exped. Central Aust.* I. 34 Our whole route today, had been through a fine and valuable grazing district. **1891** H. NISBET *Colonial Tramp* I. 130 The chief grazing district of Victoria. **1835** *Colonist* (Sydney) 30 July 243/3 Widely-scattered **grazing establishments** in the interior. **1843** *Portland Mercury* 1 Mar. 3/5 Several other gentlemen of large capital may be daily expected, who will commence agricultural operations and form grazing establishments on an extensive scale. **1867** 'CLERGYMAN' *Aust. as it Is* 1 A shepherd's hut . . formed one of the numerous out-stations of a large grazing establishment. **1810** *Sydney Gaz.* 23 June, Wanted . . a careful man to take the charge of a **Grazing Farm** with about 100 Head of Horned Cattle. **1827** *Hobart Town Gaz.* 17 Mar., To Be Sold, That excellent Grazing Farm, called the Hermitage of 1000 acres, with an unlimited run. **1861** C. CAMPBELL *Squatting Question Considered* 24 There will always be a degree of insecurity attached to the tenure of grazing farms. **1877** 'CAPRICORNUS' *Land Law of Future* 18 £2000 would . . tell to great advantage on a grazing farm. **1901** *Bulletin* (Sydney) 28 Dec. 31/2, I had done a two-days' 'perish' for mutton . . but hoped to have my wants supplied at the homestead of a handy grazing-farm. **1927** T.S. GROSER *Lure of Golden West* 154 A mere pocket-handkerchief block of 25,000 or 50,000 acres would be a 'small man's' block, and be called a grazing farm or selection. **1855** 'RUSTICUS' *How to settle in Vic.* 104 The undisputed occupation of the **grazing farmer** or squatter, as he has hitherto been termed. **1861** C. CAMPBELL *Squatting Question Considered* 6 Squatters should be 'grazing farmers', holding lands on certain fixed principles. **1897** R. NEWTON *Work & Wealth Qld.* 19 These grazing farmers are squatters on a small scale. **1925** J.A. COLLUM *New Settlers' Handbk.* 89 Every person engaged in the occupation of—Dairy farmer, wheat, maize or cereal grower, sugar-grower, fruit-grower, grazing farmer [etc.]. **1827** P. CUNNINGHAM *Two Yrs. in N.S.W.* II. 167 A good stock-yard and **grazing-paddock** for your working bullocks, should follow as speedily as possible. **1845** D. MACKENZIE *Emigrant's Guide* 120 One of my grazing-paddocks is formed by running a straight fence from one angular point to another. **1857** J. ASKEW *Voyage Aust. & N.Z.* 56 The land on both sides . . is fenced off into large grazing paddocks. **1880** *Argus* (Melbourne) 24 Jan. 8/6 *Grasmere grazing paddocks*, one mile from Dandenong. **1934** C. SAYCE *Comboman* 178 From stations in Central Australia, mobs of cattle and horses are sent down to Adelaide every year. The cattle are either put on local grazing paddocks to fatten up for market or are immediately killed for beef. **1876** 'CAPRICORNUS' *Colonisation* 12 **Grazing properties** had been formed on which for over thirty years the labours and earnings of thousands of people were sunk. **1890** 'R. BOLDREWOOD' *Colonial Reformer* III. 244 Annexed, irrevocably, an area which reduced the value of the grazing property by about one-third. **1930** M.M.J. COSTELLO *Life J. Costello* 191 This was an excellent grazing property, consisting, for the most part, of Mitchell grassed plains and downs dotted by picturesque clumps of Gydia. **1955** J. MORRISON *Black Cargo* 151 She comes from a poor little grazing property deep in the mallee scrub over the New South Wales border. **1982** *Austral. Women's Weekly* (Sydney) 10 Feb. 22/1 A bleak northern tablelands grazing property in N.S.W. **1826** J. ATKINSON *Acct. Agric. & Grazing N.S.W.* 136 These roads . . have generally been formed by people who have . . taken possession of a **grazing run** beyond the occupied part of the country. **1848** S. & J. SIDNEY *Emigrant's Jrnl.* 72 At present, the grazing runs in New South Wales which the Government has at its disposal, are all situated at least 500 miles from Sydney, the only real market for wool or stock in any quantity. **1834** J.D. LANG *Hist. & Statistical Acct. N.S.W.* II. 121 The sheep and young horses were sent, under charge of a hired overseer and two convict-servants, to form a **grazing station** at the distance of thirty miles. **1844** *HRA* (1925) 1st Ser. XXIII. 439 A Grazing Station belonging to Messrs Smith and Osbrey. **1881** T. ARCHER *Hist., Resources, & Future Prospects Qld.* 4 Articles produced on a grazing station are . . comparatively easily brought to market.

greasy.

1. One who cooks for an assemblage of employees, esp. on a sheep or cattle station; an army cook.

1873 J.C.F. JOHNSON *Christmas on Carringa* 1 Bill . . was our *chef d'cuisine* . . in the vernacular, cook or 'greasy'. **1918** *Twenty-Second's Echo: Mag. 22nd Battalion A.I.F.* 15 Oct. 2 Someone suggested that the German had been a 'greasy' who was being boiled to extract the grease. **1936** *Bulletin* (Sydney) 18 Nov. 20/4 The best-informed man on any station is invariably the cook. . . The camp greasy, though he seldom sees any outsiders . . always . . knows what is going on at the other end of the run. **1943** S.W. KEOUGH *Around Army* 19 In base camps, barracks, and other pleasant places where military life, in terms of scran, approximates civvy spheres, it amounts almost to a sacrilege to refer to the lordly being who presides over the kitchen as a greasy. **1953** T.A.G. HUNGERFORD *Riverslake* 148 'God, cooks aren't people!' Carmichael retorted. . . 'I'm going to write a book about greasies one day!' **1980** B. HORNADGE *Austral. Slanguage* 205 It is not without justification that outback cooks from the earliest time earned the nickname of *greasy*.

2. A shearer.

1939 *Bulletin* (Sydney) 14 June 20/1 When the mob lined up at Drill Park the greasies found that one of the two learners was a cocksure little beggar. **1943** *Ibid.* 3 Nov. 12/1 A bunch of greasies downed handpieces in a Longreach shed. **1955** *Ibid.* 9 Mar. 12/1 He went as a piece-picker, but, like all bushmen, commented on the quality of the cooking, whereupon the reigning poisoner asked how Dad would go cooking for 88 greasies. **1956** F.B. VICKERS *First Place to Stranger* 134 When those five greasies get moving they'll shear a lot of sheep. **1977** —— *Stranger no Longer* 49 There's ten of us greasies to shear 'em. That's five thousand a man if a man gets his cut.

great Australian adjective: see *Australian adjective* AUSTRALIAN *a.* 4.

great brown kingfisher. *Obs.* The kookaburra *Dacelo novaeguineae*. Also **great brown kingsfisher, great kingfisher.**

1782 J. LATHAM *Gen. Synopsis Birds* I. 609 Great Brown Kingsfisher. This is the largest species [of kingfisher] yet known, and is in length eighteen inches. **1788** J. WHITE *Jrnl. of Voyage N.S.W.* (1790) 137 We not long after discovered the great brown King's Fisher. **1822** J. LATHAM *Gen. Hist. Birds* IV. 10 Great Brown Kingsfisher . . the note compared to human laughter, which should give the idea of cheerfulness; hence called the Laughing Bird, or Laughing Jack-Ass. **1844** J. GOULD *Birds of Aust.* (1848) II. Pl. 18, I recollect shooting a Great Brown Kingfisher in South Australia in order to secure a fine rat I saw hanging from its bill. **1860** G. BENNETT *Gatherings of Naturalist* 177 The Great Brown Kingfisher of naturalists, called by the blacks *Gogera* or *Gogobera*, probably from its note resembling the sound of the word. **1893** *Western Champion* (Barcaldine) 24 Jan. 1/2 A period of protection shall be in certain districts . . for the whole year, in respect of . . great kingfisher (laughing jackass).

greater glider. The large gliding possum *Petauroides volans* of e. mainland Aust. See also SQUIRREL 1. Also **great glider,** and formerly **greater flying phalanger.**

1943 C. BARRETT *Austral. Animal Bk.* 66 Largest of all the 'flying squirrels' is the greater or taguan flying phalanger (*Petauroides volans*); a beautiful creature with dusky black or dark-grey, soft, silky fur, and a long, pendulous tail, cylindrical and bushy. **1956** T.Y. HARRIS *Nature-craft in Aust.* 75 The Great Glider Possum of the coastal highlands of eastern Australia is noted for the jewel-like glow of its eyes when the light from a torch is focussed on them. **1965** *Austral. Encycl.* VII. 235 In the greater glider (*Schoinobates volans*, meaning 'flying rope-dancer') head and body average 17 inches in length and the slender furry tail 20 inches. **1983** R. STRAHAN *Compl. Bk. Austral. Mammals* 134 The abundance of the Greater Glider in undisturbed forests is in strong contrast to its absence from pine plantations and its paucity in regenerated forest.

great grey kangaroo. *Grey kangaroo* (a), see GREY *a.* Also **great kangaroo.**

1836 *Proc. Zool. Soc. London* 188 When sitting in a state of repose the *great Kangaroo* throws the tail behind him. **1841** 'R.R.' *Aust., Van Dieman's Land, & N.Z.* 6 The great kangaroo is the largest quadruped of Australia. **1850** J.B. CLUTTERBUCK *Port Phillip* 35 The great *grey* Kangaroo, a saltatory animal, and gregarious in its habits. **1894** J.K. ARTHUR *Kangaroo & Kauri* 12 Near your home you will probably have the kangaroo, called also the 'Great Kangaroo', the Boomer, and the Forester. **1980** C. ALLISON *Hunter's Man. Aust. & N.Z.* 34 The great-grey or 'forester' kangaroos (there are two sub-species) prefer the more timbered coastal slopes and the open western forests.

great kingfisher: see GREAT BROWN KINGFISHER.

Great South Land: see SOUTH LAND.

Greek. In the collocation **the Greek's:** a small café.

1946 M. TRIST *What else is There* 144 She caught up with Mamie and Teddy outside the Greek's. 'How about an ice-cream?' asked Teddy. **1953** T.A.G.

HUNGERFORD *Riverslake* 234 Sometimes they eat at the Greek's, down at the Kingston shops. **1963** D. NILAND *Dadda Jumped* 140 We went to the Greeks for a feed. **1971** *Bulletin* (Sydney) 8 May 47/3 By the late 'twenties the cafe-soda bar (later milkbar) had spread across Australia. Every suburb and town had a 'Greeks' named the New York, the Miami, the California, the Niagara, the Astoria, the Florida, the Regal, the Manhattan. **1976** *Ibid.* 17 July 44/1 Until the service stations started putting on food the only way to get a meal at night in a country town was usually to 'pop down to the Greeks'. **1977** A. SYKES *Five Plays* 234 Should be out celebrating. What about a feed at the Greeks?

green.

1. Used as a distinguishing epithet in the names of flora and fauna: **green ant,** *green tree-ant*; **head,** the predom. metallic bluish-green ant *Rhytidoponera metallica*; **leek,** any of several predom. green parrots; **mallee, (a)** the small tree *Eucalyptus viridis* (fam. Myrtaceae) of inland e. mainland Aust., having narrow green leaves; **(b)** (occas.) a similar tree, as *E. oleosa*; **monday,** GREENGROCER; **parrot** (or **parakeet**), any of several predom. green parrots (cf. *green leek*); **snake,** any of several snakes sometimes having a greenish hue, as the *green tree-snake*; **tree-ant,** the ant *Oecophylla smaragdina* of n. Aust. and elsewhere, having a green body and living in trees, where it makes nests from leaves; *green ant*; **tree-snake,** the tree-snake *Dendrelaphis punctulata* (fam. Colubridae) of n. and e. Aust. and New Guinea, some specimens of which have green upperparts; **wattle,** any of several trees of the genus *Acacia* (fam. Mimosaceae), esp. *A. decurrens* of e. N.S.W. and naturalized elsewhere; also *attrib.*

1843 J.L. STOKES *Discoveries in Aust.* (1846) I. 429 Found ourselves under a tree covered with large **green ants.** **1865** J.R. SHOLL *Jrnl. Exped. Camden Harbour to Glenelg River* 221 The green-ant is about half an inch long, of a light arsenic green. **1872** C.H. EDEN *My Wife & I in Qld.* 148 Bulldogs, green ants and heaven knows how many different kinds. The latter are tree-ants. **1956** A.C.C. LOCK *Tropical Tapestry* 279 Big green ants' nests, made of leaves of trees marvellously welded together until they were as big as footballs, hung from some of the limbs. **1879** *Queenslander* (Brisbane) 20 Sept. 365/2 You . . find you have pitched your bed on or near a nest of '**green-heads**' or soldier ants. **1900** *Western Champion* (Barcaldine) 30 Oct. 13/1 She can work a mob o' greenheads on a common dinner plate. **1917** *Bulletin* (Sydney) 27 Dec. 24/2, I stood over a greenhead's nest with one doorway, and tried to make sense out of what the greenies were up to. **1936** *Austral. Writers' Ann.* 32 The greenhead is a mean sneak . . a pariah of the ant tribe . . whose vicious stab is usually the first intimation you get of its presence. **1845** *Bell's Life in Sydney* 18 Jan. 3/4 A most extraordinary bird of the parrot species, commonly called the **green leek**, a native of New South Wales. **1848** H.W. HAYGARTH *Recoll. Bush Life* 139 The sorts [of parrot] which . . are most 'fancied' are the green leek, the king parrot, [etc.]. **1889** *Proc. Linnean Soc. N.S.W.* IV. 418 *Trichoglossus concinnus* . . known as 'Green-leek' and 'Musk-paroquet'. **1917** *Bulletin* (Sydney) 7 June 24/4 Another rare parrot is the green leek, or superb parrot. . . The common green, or swift parrot . . is very often styled 'green leek', though the real Simon Pure is a very different bird. **1945** M. RAYMOND *Smiley* 9 He opened the dilly-bag and disclosed a young greenleek parrot. **1948** P.J. HURLEY *Red Cedar* 179 Loquat trees were loaded with Blue Mountain parakeets and Green Leek parrots. **1900** *Proc. Linnean Soc. N.S.W.* XXV. 301 *Eucalyptus viridis*. . . A Mallee of dense growth, the stems usually 2–3 inches in diameter, though occasionally measuring 20 feet in height. . . The name '**Green Mallee**' refers to the vivid lustreless green of the leaves. **1926** J.M. BLACK *Flora S.A.* iii. 418 A form [of *Eucalyptus oleosa*] . . growing in the scrub near Pinnaroo . . is only 1–2 m. high and is locally called 'Green Mallee'. **1947** W.A.W. DE BEUZEVILLE *Austral. Trees* 181 *Green Mallee* (*Euc. viridis*) . . occurs naturally in dry inland New South Wales. . . Very hardy and quick growing. **1984** E. WALLING *On Trail Austral. Wildflowers* 45 Branches of the Green Mallee tree were used for whips. **1895** *Proc. Linnean Soc. N.S.W.* X. 528 *Cyclochila Australasiae* . . **Green Monday** . . is our commonest Sydney Cicada. **1903** *Agric. Gaz. N.S.W.* XIV. 337 This cicada is very variable in its colouration, and the green and yellow forms are popularly called 'Green Mondays' and 'Yellow Mondays'. **1970** J.S. GUNN in W.S. Ramson *Eng. Transported* 60 We must not forget those marvellous names for cicadas such as . . *lamplighter, green Monday*, and *double drummer*. **1793** J. HUNTER *Hist. Jrnl. Trans. Port Jackson* 69 There are a great variety of birds in this country; all those of the parrot tribe, such as the macaw, cockatoo . . **green parrot.** **1832** J. BACKHOUSE *Narr. Visit Austral. Colonies* (1843) 30 Green Parrots . . are great pests in gardens. . . Green Parroquets . . frequent farm yards. **1845** J. GOULD *Birds of Aust.* (1848) V. Pl. 24, *Platicercus flaviventris* . . Green Parrot, Colonists of Van Diemen's Land. **1861** 'OLD BUSHMAN' *Bush Wanderings* 165 The commonest of all the paroquets is the *Green Paroqueet*, which in shape and habits rather resembles the blue mountaineer. **1806** *Sydney Gaz.* 16 Mar., A beautiful **green snake** made its appearance on a summer house. **1807** *Ibid.* 8 Feb., A green snake was killed last Friday on the South Head Road. **1844** *Duncan's Weekly Register* (Sydney) 16 Nov. 246/1 The Green Snake is usually found in scrubby grounds or thickly wooded places. **1893** *Western Champion* (Barcaldine) 7 Feb. 1/1 A Boy named Alfred Bachelor was bitten by a 'green snake' at Cabbagetree, Ipswich district. **1845** L. LEICHHARDT *Jrnl. Overland Exped. Aust.* 16 June (1847) 291 It was at the lower part of the Lynd that we first saw the **green-tree ant**; which seemed to live in small societies in rude nests between the green leaves of shady trees. **1908** E.J. BANFIELD *Confessions of Beachcomber* 253 Sipping . . cordial compounded of the larvae of green-tree ants ('book-gruin'), acidulous and pippy. **1928** *Victorian Naturalist* XLV. 132 Captain Cook was the first white man to observe Green Tree-ants, or, at least, their nests. **1936** T.C. ROUGHLEY *Wonders Great Barrier Reef* 176 'Hell has no fury like a woman scorned,' wrote Congreve early in the seventeenth century. The green tree-ant was obviously not known then. **1975** K. WILLEY *Ghosts of Big Country* 129 Once when I was ill I ate green tree-ants, which taste strongly of eucalyptus and are used by the Maillis as an emetic. **1869** G. KREFFT *Snakes of Aust.* 24 The **Green Tree Snake**, in a state of excitement, is strongly suggestive of one of the popular toys of childhood, by the peculiar white marks which become visible when its skin is distended. **1933** C.W. PECK *Austral. Legends* (ed. 2) 227 Sleek tiger-cats lay in wait for the pretty green tree-snake. **1973** V. SERVENTY *Desert Walkabout* 73 It was a green tree-snake about three feet long, a harmless species. **1984** B. DIXON *Searching for Aboriginal Lang.* 99 He soon despatched it, with one blow from a sharp caneknife, and identified it as a green tree snake. **1814** *HRA* (1916) 1st Ser. VIII. 223, I beg to turn my Ideas to the **Green Wattle** Bark. **1828** *Tasmanian* (Hobart) 13 June 4 While green wattle blooms on the face o' yon mountain, I'll love thee sincerely—I'll love evermore. **1834** G. BENNETT *Wanderings N.S.W.* I. 85 A few trees of the 'green wattle' (*acacia decurrens*), profusely governed by golden blossoms. **1844** *Swan River News* June 48/1 The common green wattle . . is found plentifully on the alluvial flats of the Swan. **1851** *Empire* (Sydney) 26 Apr. 8/2 Greenwattle bark, 60s. to 75s. good samples are very much inquired after. **1881** *Proc. Linnean Soc. N.S.W.* VI. 771 Now the terms Black and Green Wattle are applied almost universally to the two varieties of *Acacia decurrens.* **1921** A.J. CAMPBELL *Golden Wattle* 28 The fine Green or King Wattle (*A. normalis*) is native of the region of sandstone Sydney. **1982** ELLIOT & JONES *Encycl. Austral. Plants* II. 40 *Acacia decurrens* . . Green Wattle. . . Leaves suitable as a dyeing material. Cultivated as a glasshouse plant in Europe. Has also been called *A. normalis.*

2. Used to designate a class (or area) of vegetation: **green drought,** the phenomenon of new but insubstantial growth (of forage), promoted by rain during or after a drought and unsupported by standing dry feed; **feed,** forage (grown to be) fed fresh to livestock; **pick,** new growth (of forage) promoted by rain; **shoot,** new growth (of vegetation) immediately after a fire.

1980 *Sydney Morning Herald* 5 Sept. 1/7 The rain has to be heavy, to sink into the earth, to push up grass with guts—not the water-filled junk around some areas now, after last week's sprinkling. That's a '**green drought**'. **1983** *Canberra Times* 24 May 3/1 Because of the extended drought, there was no such hayed-off feed. The green feed was succulent for stock but contained little nutritive value. Graziers refer to this situation as a 'green drought'. **1876** 'EIGHT YRS.' RESIDENT' *Queen of Colonies* 202 The sorghum, or Chinese sugar-cane, is a small species of sugar-cane which is propagated from seed. It is a most excellent **green feed**, for which purpose it is alone grown. . . Market-gardeners . . cut it when four to five feet high and sell it in bundles as 'green-stuff'. **1891** W.H. TIETKENS *Jrnl. Central Austral. Exploring Exped.* 28 There is the most luxuriant green-feed for the camels. **1898** L. LINDLEY-COWEN *W. Austral. Settler's Guide* 769 Green feed, such as maize, sorghum, etc., may be used with advantage in the summer. **1923** *Austral.* (Sydney) May 57 He soon had plenty of 'green feed' flourishing where the ground had been bare. **1956** T. RONAN *Moleskin Midas* 250 Cattle which had survived three years of drought, now further weakened by the scouring effect of unaccustomed green-feed, were getting bogged everywhere. **1982** D. HARRIS *Drovers of Outback* 69, I went out to the Crows Nest to check for feed. I found good dry feed but a lot of green feed in it. **1966** J. CARTER *People of Inland* 13 Kidman usually managed to get his sheep or cattle under some rain, so they could have a decent feed of young '**green pick**' before moving on again. **1980** *Sydney Morning Herald* 22 Oct. 1/6 Despite its patchy nature, the rain . . was enough to spark a glimmer of hope among farmers. . . It would produce a green pick for hard-pressed stock. **1983** *Canberra Times* 24 May 3/1 At this time of the year there was usually standing dry feed left . . to bolster the green pick that came through with autumn rain. **1953** H.G. LAMOND *Big Red* 197 As the shooters knew, a **green shoot** always followed a burn of spinifex. **1959** D. LOCKWOOD *Crocodiles & Other People* 70 'Get a green shoot after fire's been through this stuff,' he explained. . . On the way back a fortnight later I found the small, charred circles with a green shoot already an inch high.

3. Used with various nouns to denote youth or immaturity: **green hand,** one who lacks experience; **lamb,** a very young lamb; **skin,** the hide of a freshly slaughtered sheep.

1872 *Illustr. Sydney News* 13 Apr. 55/1 Should any infatuated **green hand** decline the 'spell' and continue to work while the others rest, he becomes a marked man. **1882** J.I. WATTS *Memories Early Days S.A.* 56 The poor patient animals . . are often terribly cut about by 'green hands'. **1900** *Bulletin* (Sydney) 13 Jan. 32/2 Over the whirr and roar and hum all day long, and with iteration that is childish and irritating to the intelligent greenhand, float unthinkable adjectives and adverbs. *c* **1907** W.C. CHANDLER *Darkest Adelaide* 8 He did not know any old ones [*sc.* prostitutes] that had a vacancy for a protector, and thought perhaps that I would have to take on a green hand—one that had just joined the ranks of public women. **1888** *Bulletin* (Sydney) 10 Mar. 14/2, I went a lambing down to fetch home the **green lambs**; But I couldn't find 'em green—for lambs are mostly white. **1913** M.A. MCMANUS *Reminisc. Maranoa District* 69 She was driving some sheep with very young or 'green' lambs, as they are called. **1943** H.G. LAMOND *From Tariaro to Ross Roy* 26 The wet flock, as the lambing ewes were known, was a science in itself. Each flock of lambers was sub-divided into three or four smaller flocks: green, dropping, middle and bigger lambs. **1845** *Portland Gaz.* 3 June 2/5 **Green skins** are not to be purchased from the butchers, owing to all being contracted for. **1914** H.B. SMITH *Sheep & Wool Industry* 183 *Green skins*, . . sheep-skins fresh from the slaughter-house.

greenback.

1. *Obs.* [Transf. use of U.S. *greenback* a legal tender note.] A one-pound note.

1919 C.A. BERNAYS *Qld. Politics during Sixty Yrs.* 16 He did not understand the futility of flooding Queensland with 'greenbacks' without a gold backing. **1945** *Aust. Week-End Bk.* 29 £200 . . a hundred greenbacks apiece. **1967** J. WYNNUM *I'm Jack, all Right* 11, I also happen to have a roll of greenbacks big enough to choke a horse.

2. GREENIE 2.

1963 *Bulletin* (Sydney) 23 Nov. 13/2 The roaring greenbacks can make the blood sing, but they can also break a limb or gulp the swimmer in a rip. **1963** J. POLLARD *Austral. Surfrider* 20 Just out a little further are the 'green-backs', the unbroken waves.

green ban. [Used elsewhere but recorded earliest in Aust.] A prohibition (esp. as imposed by a trade union) which prevents construction work from proceeding on a site within a green belt; a similar prohibition made to protect a building, site, etc., of natural or cultural significance. See also *black ban* BLACK *a.*[4] 2. Also *attrib.*

1973 P. THOMAS *Taming Concrete Jungle* 43 A unionist coined a happy phrase for such bans to save natural bush and park. 'They're not black bans,' he said;

'they're green bans.' **1974** Blazey & Campbell *Political Dice Men* 227 By 1974 the Green Bans had halted $300,000,000 worth of 'developments', and had become the most controversial issue within N.S.W. **1976** *Bulletin* (Sydney) 27 Nov. 18/3 Unions will provide the industrial muscle but the left will also try to reconvene the coalition workers, middle-class conservationists and intellectuals which proved so effective for the 'green ban' movement. **1977** E. Mackie *Oh to be Aussie* 32 Sydney history... Some builders' labourers wouldn't pull *down* what they were *paid* to pull down because what would go *up* would be even worse than what would come *down* so a lot of people were *stood* down while others were sent up... Green bans were altruistic. **1981** Sheehan & Worland *Gloss. Industr. Relations Terms* 9 They are generally known as 'black bans' but where they have been placed on projects because of environmental factors, they are known as green bans. **1981** *Bulletin* (Sydney) 24 Feb. 38/1 The effects of the green bans—which at one stage were blocking an estimated $3000-million worth of development—are beginning to reveal themselves.

green cart. See quot. 1982.

1935 D.G. Stead *Rabbit in Aust.* 14 We were suitable for cargo for the 'green cart', or for whatever other vehicle is used to take us to the mental hospital. **1959** D. Hewett *Bobbin Up* 110 You're mad, that's what's up with you. They'll come for you in the green cart one of these days. **1975** *Overland* lxii. 27 The green cart will come for me, and I'll disappear into Callan Park. **1982** L. Keesing *Lily on Dustbin* 164 *Green cart*, vehicle allegedly sent to convey mad people to the asylum. 'He wants to look out, they'll be sending the green cart for him next.'

greengrocer. The cicada *Cyclochila australasiae*, when green. See also *yellow monday* Yellow 1.

1905 *Bulletin* (Sydney) 28 Dec. (Red Page), There's heaps of different kinds of locusts, heaps! .. Greengrocers, and floury bakers, and yellow Mondays. **1951** Cusack & James *Come in Spinner* 106 'Mine's a Greengrocer—look!' Durras opened his hand carefully, showing a cicada with iridescent wings folded back on a body of delicate green. **1968** V. Serventy *Southern Walkabout* 10 The yellow monday or greengrocer. **1985** *Northern Herald* (Sydney) 10 Jan. 1/2 There are several species of noisy cicada about Sydney but the prime culprit, the Greengrocer, may be undergoing a natural cycle.

greenhide, *n.* and *attrib.* [In Br. use from 1577 (see OED *green, a.* 9 c.) but of special significance in Aust.: see quot. 1980.]

A. *n.*

1. The untanned hide of a beast; untanned hide, rawhide.

1809 *Sydney Gaz.* 18 June, For Sale .. Leather both English and colonial... No expence is spared to manufacture it from the Green Hide to the Shoe or Boot. **1827** *Monitor* (Sydney) 20 Aug. 593/1 *Two-pence* Sterling per Pound, will be paid for all *green hides* delivered at this Warehouse, if perfect. **1845** D. Mackenzie *Emigrant's Guide* 135 The hide is kept to be cut up for ropes. In this colony everything is held, tied, or mended with green hide. **1862** J. McKinlay *Jrnl. Exploration Aust.* 6 July 122 We tried some green hide .. in our soup of this morning, and being pickled in salt when taken from the bullock, it imparted quite an agreeable flavour. **1881** A.C. Grant *Bush-Life Qld.* I. 27 A long-handled whip with a thong of raw salted hide, called in the colony 'greenhide'. **1890** A.J. Vogan *Black Police* 254 The rafters and purlieus, are ingeniously kept in position by neatly fastened strips of 'green hide' (raw leather). **1909** M. McConnel *Memories Days Long gone By* 16 To save the springs of the phaeton they were bound up with 'green hide', *i.e.*, the untanned hide of a bullock cut up in strips, not elegant in appearance, but answering the purpose well. **1934** W. Hatfield *River Crossing* 29 The comfortable bed of laced green-hide. **1978** M. Nixon *Rivers of Home* 35 One never saw a cotton rope such as we have nowadays, for ropes, too, were handmade, plaited or twisted from lengths of greenhide. **1980** P. Freeman *Woolshed* 28 For stringybark and greenhide will never, never fail yer, Stringybark and greenhide is the mainstay of Australia.

2. *transf.* See quot.

1918 *Huon Times* (Franklin) 24 Dec. 3/3 Away in the misty past the Greenhides were a society of young bucks who dwelt on the neighboring stations, where they maintained English traditions and always dressed for dinner, but when they came to town they put off all restraint.

B. *attrib.*

1. Of or pertaining to greenhide.

1847 A. Harris *Settlers & Convicts* (1953) 125 The beast's hide was cut through in all directions with the green-hide lash of the heavy bullock whip. **1865** *Sydney Punch* 28 Jan. 288/2 Why does a bullock-driver resemble jealousy?—Because he is a green-hide (green-eyed) monster! **1880** *Blackwood's Mag.* (Edinburgh) Jan. 76/2 A strongly plaited green-hide halter was now slipped over the head. **1888** H.S. Russell *Genesis Qld.* 349 Having a stock-whip with a long green-hide fall, I made a rude *tourniquet*. **1895** *Bulletin* (Sydney) 17 Aug. 17/4 A selector named Gimblett, aged 23, returned home and found that his 19-year-old wife had suicided by hanging herself with a greenhide strap. **1910** *Huon Times* (Franklin) 23 Mar. 4/4 He had given her a thrashing with a greenhide whip. **1922** *Smith's Weekly* (Sydney) 8 July 17/5 Greenhide workers .. plait whips, bridles, halters and ropes, and sell them to stockmen and drovers. **1946** *Bulletin* (Sydney) 21 Aug. 28/2 Greenhide experts are few these days. **1954** T. Ronan *Vision Splendid* 60 He shifted a greenhide-and-bush-timber bunk on to the store verandah. **1978** D. Stuart *Wedgetail View* 24 They were seated .. on rough bush-timber chairs strung with greenhide thongs.

2. *fig.* Strong, sinewy.

1918 C.J. Dennis *Backblock Ballads* 29 He was tall and tough and stringy, with the shoulders of an axeman, Broad and loose, with greenhide muscles; and a hand shaped to the reins.

3. Comb. **greenhide bucket, rope.**

1888 'R. Boldrewood' *Robbery under Arms* (1937) 227 Winding up **greenhide buckets** filled with gravel from shafts. **1895** *Bulletin* (Sydney) 17 Aug. 9/3 Most of the leases around .. are still in the windlass-and-greenhide-bucket stage of development. **1920** A.I. Macleod *Hack's Brat* (ed. 2) 8 She asked an exorbitant price for them, which included a windlass and the usual greenhide bucket. **1843** *Sydney Morning Herald* 8 Sept. 2/7 He took a **green hide rope** with him to tie up the horse in the bush. **1852** G.C. Mundy *Our Antipodes* I. 290 Green hide rope, an article used here in various departments georgic and bucolic, is formed of long narrow strips cut from the raw skin of an ox. The epithets 'green' and 'raw' are synonymous. **1881** A.C. Grant *Bush-Life Qld.* I. 226 Fitzgerald .. takes the noose end of a long, thin, but exceedingly strong greenhide-rope, and dexterously lassoes a yearling scrub bull. **1923** *Bulletin* (Sydney) 18 Oct. 22/2, I would like the cattle-duffers and poddy dodgers of the Council to give their views on the merits of twisted and plaited green-hide ropes. **1960** M. Henry *Unlucky Dip* 17 A sort of desperate tug-of-war was going on: Brown and Donegan pulling on a greenhide rope while Everett ('not a bushman's backside' Bob recalled grimly) tugged spasmodically and ineffectually at the end.

4. Special Comb. **greenhide station,** a primitively appointed station; one at which rough-and-ready methods are employed.

1942 *Bulletin* (Sydney) 16 Dec. 12/1 On our greenhide station, when abo. camps were numerous, we ran out of shot. **1944** *Ibid.* 6 Dec. 12/2 On our greenhide station the customary preliminary to boarding a bucking broncho was to grab the near end.

greenhood. Any of many species of the genus of terrestrial orchids *Pterostylis* (fam. Orchidaceae) of Australasia and the s.w. Pacific, having a hooded greenish flower.

1914 E.E. Pescott *Native Flowers Vic.* 86 The 'greenhoods' belong to the genus Pterostylis; they are usually greenish in colour, and the upper portion of the flower is shaped like a hood, covering the rest of the flower. **1941** C. Barrett *Aust.* 27 At the base of a very old white gum nodding greenhoods abound. 'Parrot-beaks' they are to children who gather them. **1958** *Coast to Coast 1957–58* 138 Glossy greenhoods under the bushes. **1967** B.Y. Main *Between Wodjil & Tor* 76 Clumps of single-flowered green-hood orchids sprouted and opened their bird-beak flowers. **1985** *Age* (Melbourne) 20 Sept. (Suppl.) 7/1 Many varieties of greenhoods are like scattered, tiny gems in a sea of muted green.

greenie. Also **greeny.** [f. *green* + -Y.]

1. Any of several predom. green birds or animals.

1890 *Quiz* (Adelaide) 19 Sept. 6/2 Two Hindmarsh young gentlemen went out with a gun .. shot a little 'greenie'. **1908** *Emu* IX. 183, I soon detected the notes of a *Zosterops* in the mangroves which I knew were not those of *Z. gouldi*, our familiar 'Greenie' of the south-west. **1917** *Bulletin* (Sydney) 9 Aug. 24/4 He hasn't tasted the green-pigeon... The wonga's flesh is white but very dry and tasteless compared with the 'greenie'. **1917** *Ibid.* 27 Dec. 24/2, I stood over a greenhead's nest with one doorway, and tried to make sense of what the greenies were up to. **1929** A.H. Chisholm *Birds & Green Places* 209 The larger 'blueys' (rainbow lorikeets) and 'greenies' (scaly-breasts). **1933** *Bulletin* (Sydney) 4 Jan. 21/4 As to the frog's persistency, I can vouch for that. I once saw a big 'greeny', who used to come up on the table at nights. **1947** M. Raymond *Smiley gets Gun* 33, I wisht I 'ad a gun .. and then I'd pot ten greenies and me mother'd make parrot pie.

2. *Surfing.* A large unbroken wave; Greenback 2.

1940 P. Kerry *Cobbers A.I.F.* 12 About 'alf a mile from shore, Where 'e was loafin' on the greenies, an' lookin' out fer more. **1941** H.D.A. Joske *Life to Live* 25 'Greenies'—the name given along the coast to that extra big wave which takes the unwary by surprise. **1964** B. Humphries *Nice Night's Entertainment* (1981) 77 The surf was *fantastic.* You should have seen those greenies.

3. One who supports a Green ban; a conservationist.

1973 *Nation Rev.* (Melbourne) 28 Sept. 1572/1 The local greenies have despaired of stopping the dreaded post office tower by indirect means. **1978** *Truckin' Life* II. vii. 77 There is a nice old barney going on involving .. the motor industry and the 'greenies' over the question of vehicle emission controls. **1979** Douglas & Heathcote *Far Cry* 90 Even though our bush is all shades of smoke and cocoa and pink and blue grey, with only the tiniest touches of true green, our conservationists are called 'Greenies'. **1982** *Down to Earth News* Dec. 1 The 'greenies' and 'hippies' are on the move again. **1983** *Bushdriver* Mar. 11 Generally, I have no time at all for 'greenies'—at least not the type that don't wash, don't shave, don't work and don't make any real contribution to Australia. **1985** J. Miller *Koori* 218 Since I believe in Koori land rights and no dams on the Franklin River, that makes me a black, greenie, pinko.

green slip. *S.A. Obs.* A portion of Crown land remaining unalienated as a result of a discrepancy between the size of section into which the land was surveyed, and that into which it was divided.

1838 *Southern Austral.* (Adelaide) 3 Nov. 3/1 The Treasurer, could he have known these tenders were for the green slips, would not have received the deposit, because the regulations were not complied with. **1839** *S. Austral. Rec.* (London) 8 May 187 The supplemental slips of 54 acres (called 'Green Slips') appear still to occasion some ill-feeling. **1839** *S. Austral. Gaz.* (Adelaide) 7 Nov. 2 In reference to those portions of land usually called 'Green Slips' .. the Resident Commissioner is of opinion that they never have been thrown open to general selection and tender, and that therefore no valid claims upon them exist. **1840** *Ibid.* 20 Aug. 2 The Council .. ordered that the limits of the City of Adelaide should be extended .. so as to include the following sections and green slips contiguous or adjacent to the outer boundary of the park lands.

grevillea /grəˈvɪliə/. [The plant genus *Grevillea* was named by the British botanist R. Brown (in Knight, J. (1809) *Proteeae* 120) after the botanist C.F. *Greville* (1749–1809), Vice-President of the Royal Society.] Any shrub or tree of the large, chiefly Austral. genus *Grevillea* (fam. Proteaceae) many of which are cultivated as ornamentals. See also Spider flower. Also *attrib.*

[**1814** R. Brown *Gen. Remarks Bot. Terra Australis* 36 That section of *Grevillea* having a woody capsule.] **1825** B. Field *Geogr. Mem. N.S.W.* 422 All the other indigenous trees and shrubs, that I have seen, are evergreens .. the curious grevillea. **1836** J. Backhouse *Extracts from Lett.* (1839) iv. 8 Four species of Grevillea, one of which had brilliant scarlet blossoms. **1875** P.E. Warburton *Journey across Western Interior* 66 The body was brought back to the depôt and buried under a grevillia [*sic*] tree. **1888** *Sydney Morning Herald* 24 Jan. 2/1 There are several classes of the Grevillea to be found, and in some instances they are cultivated. **1914**

E.E. PESCOTT *Native Flowers Vic.* 75 Grevilleas . . frequently . . are called 'comb' or 'tooth-brush' flowers, owing to their peculiar similarity to those articles. **1928** R.H. CROLL *Open Road Vic.* 104 That gay scarlet Grevillea which Von Mueller named after Queen Victoria. **1931** M.M. BANKS *Memories Pioneer Days Qld.* 78 The grevillea produces an uncommon flower of dark bronze, mixed with gold, full of honey and beloved by bees. **1958** *Coast to Coast 1957–58* 138 The grevillea bushes bore a fleece of snowy blossom. **1979** DOUGLAS & HEATHCOTE *Far Cry* 47 Paintings of grevilleas with their strange un-English flowers. **1982** R. HALL *Just Relations* 453 The plants themselves tell their own saga, geraniums among grevillea, honeysuckle behind the wattle.

grey, *n.* [Orig. Br. slang; of unknown origin but see OED *grey, sb.* 10.] A coin having two heads or two tails; in the game of two-up, esp. a coin with two tails. Cf. NOB.

1812 J.H. VAUX *Mem.* (1819) II. 179 *Gray*, a half-penny, or other coin, having two heads or two tails, and fabricated for the use of gamblers. **1895** *Bulletin* (Sydney) 16 Feb. 21/2 'Grey', a spieler's double-headed coin. **1898** *Western Champion* (Barcaldine) 11 Jan. 4/5 He had been playing 'two-up' on the racecourse, and took a man down for 23s. by 'ringing-in a grey' (a two-tailed penny) on him. **1906** A.G. LESLIE *Rifle Sketches* 59, I might have suspected the existence of a grey or a nob, which my sons tell me are cant terms for pennies with two heads or tails. **1918** *Twenty-Second's Echo: Mag. 22nd Battalion A.I.F.* 1 June 4 We rung the 'grey' on them this morning. Once I get to England I'll lose no chance of introducing Australia's national game. **1941** D. O'CALLAGHAN *Long Life Reminisc.* 59 There was plenty of two-up played there and a fair amount of nob and gray spinning. **1946** K.S. PRICHARD *Roaring Nineties* 152 Some of them had been fleeced by spielers 'ringing in the nob', a two-headed penny, or 'the grey', a penny with two tails. **1975** L. RYAN *Shearers* 153 *Greys*, double tail pennies.

grey, *a.* Used as a distinguishing epithet in the names of flora and fauna: **grey box,** any of several trees of the genus *Eucalyptus* (fam. Myrtaceae), usu. having a rough, grey bark, esp. *E. moluccana* of e. N.S.W. and e. Qld.; the wood of these trees; also *attrib.*; **butcherbird,** the woodland bird *Cracticus torquatus*, widespread in Aust., having black, grey, and white plumage; DERWENT JACKASS; JACKASS 2; **-crowned babbler,** the bird *Pomatostomus temporalis* of n. and e. Aust. and s. New Guinea, having a grey stripe on the crown; YAHOO *n.*[2]; see also HAPPY JACK; **currawong** (or **magpie**), the predom. grey or black bird *Strepera versicolor* of s. Aust. incl. Tas.; **gum,** any of several trees of the genus *Eucalyptus* having a predom. grey bark, esp. *E. punctata* of e. N.S.W. and s.e. Qld.; the wood of these trees; **handlewood,** any of several trees esp. *Aphananthe philippinensis* (see *axe-handle wood* AXE-HANDLE 1); **ironbark,** any of several ironbark trees having a greyish bark, esp. *Eucalyptus paniculata* of near-coastal N.S.W.; **kangaroo, (a)** the eastern grey kangaroo *Macropus giganteus* of e. Aust., having silvery-grey fur; FORESTER; *forest kangaroo*, see FOREST 2; GREAT GREY KANGAROO; **(b)** *western grey kangaroo*, see WESTERN; **mangrove,** *white mangrove*, see WHITE *a.*[2] 1 a.; **nurse,** the shark *Odontaspis arenarius* of e. and s. Aust. coasts, usu. having a grey back; also **grey-nurse shark**; **teal,** the small, nomadic, predom. grey duck *Anas gibberifrons* of Aust. and s.w. Pacific; **thrush,** the predom. grey woodland bird *Colluricincla harmonica* (fam. Muscicapidae) of Aust. and e. New Guinea; *whistling dick*, see WHISTLING; also **grey shrike-thrush.**

1878 R.B. SMYTH *Aborigines of Vic.* II. 160 **Grey box**—Boo-loitch. **1884** A. NILSON *Timber Trees N.S.W.* 71 *E[ucalyptus saligna]*—Grey Gum . . Grey Box—A tall tree with a smooth silvery-grey shining bark. **1891** *Proc. Linnean Soc. N.S.W.* VI. 393 *Eucalyptus hemiphloia*. . . Sample from Wagga Wagga, N.S.W. . . Tree locally known as 'Grey Box'. **1911** *Bulletin* (Sydney) 14 Sept. 13/4, I beg to name grey box as being a harder timber than black wattle. **1935** *Honey Flora Vic.* (Vic. Dept. Agric.) (rev. ed.) 8 When heating Grey Box honey to reliquefy it . . care should be taken that the temperature does not rise beyond 150° Fahr. **1956** A. UPFIELD *Battling Prophet* 37 Three ancient gums held his attention. . . They were actually grey box. The bark was softly grey. **1986** *Trees & Natural Resources* Mar. 8 In the Wimmera . . Grey box (*Eucalyptus microcarpa*) and Black box . . were found on the best wheat land. **1902** *Emu* I. 82 **Grey Butcher Bird** . . *Cracticus cinereus* is a true 'Butcher Bird' in its habits, and has apparently the same propensity for 'spitting' its prey on thorns as its English namesake. **1929** A.H. CHISHOLM *Birds & Green Places* 136 Mockery is authenticated in the cases of the oriole, . . the grey butcher-bird, [etc.]. **1945** A. RUSSELL *Bush Ways* 120 The Derwent Jack, or grey butcher-bird . . cunning, knavish, joyous and melodious. **1976** *Reader's Digest Compl. Bk. Austral. Birds* 573 Adult grey butcherbirds live in permanent territories. **1928** G.H. WILKINS *Undiscovered Aust.* 31 Soon after we established our camp two groups, the one of **grey-crowned babblers**, and the other of Apostle-birds, came and made their home with us. **1948** R. RAVEN-HART *Canoe in Aust.* 99 A band of street-urchin birds, quarrelling . . and chasing each other. . . Bevan called them 'Cat-birds'—a more official name is Grey-crowned Babbler but another popular name fits them even better, 'Yahoo', both imitating their call and suggesting their behaviour. **1983** *Sun* (Sydney) 17 Aug. 17 Another 25 species have either a restricted distribution or are rare. They include the grey-crowned babbler, [etc.]. **1889** [**grey currawong**] *Proc. Linnean Soc. N.S.W.* IV. 404 *Strepera cuneicaudata*. . . Local names, 'Rain-bird' and 'Grey Magpie'. **1906** *Bulletin* (Sydney) 13 Sept. 17/2 My landlady was liberal with native 'game', from kangaroo-rat to the hedgehog, or grey magpie. **1928** R.H. CROLL *Open Road Vic.* 102 From boyhood memories we dug up many names for these handsome birds. 'Peter Kling' was one. . . 'Grey magpie' was another and 'grey jay' a third. **1945** C. BARRETT *Austral. Bird Life* 217 The grey currawong is at home in humid ranges and hills of the eastern states. **1965** *Austral. Encycl.* III. 149 In Western Australia the grey currawong is generally known as the 'squeaker'. **1984** M. BLAKERS et al. *Atlas Austral. Birds* 643 The Grey Currawong was reported to be retreating from the wheatbelt of the South-West Region in the 1940s but has since begun to return. **1837** *Colonist* (Sydney) 350/2 The trees used in the colony for domestic purposes are . . **grey gum**, fencing, building, etc. **1845** C. HODGKINSON *Aust., Port Macquarie to Moreton Bay* 85 Grassy forest land, heavily wooded by . . grey gum. **1880** J. BONWICK *Resources Qld.* 37 The Grey Gum looks for granite. **1894** *Proc. Linnean Soc. N.S.W.* IX. 377 *E. resinifera*, locally known as the 'Grey Gum'. **1904** J.H. MAIDEN *Notes on Commercial Timbers N.S.W.* 17 Grey gums (*Eucalyptus punctata* . . also *Eucalyptus propinqua*) . . largely used as an ironbark substitute for railway sleepers. **1913** *Bulletin* (Sydney) 2 Oct. 24/1 With regard to the 'faking' of timber . . I assert that slaty gum is passed as grey gum, and grey gum goes as ironbark. **1948** P.J. HURLEY *Red Cedar* 96 Trees for commerce . . gnarled old grey-gums. **1979** *Ecos* xix. 32/4 Koalas have been linked with some 60 species. Forest red gum (*Eucalyptus tereticornis*), grey gum (*E. punctata*), and manna gum (*E. viminalis*) seem most favoured. **1926** *Qld. Agric. Jrnl.* XXV. 438 *Aphananthe Philippinensis* . . **Grey Handlewood. 1947** I.H. BOAS *Commercial Timbers Aust.* 219 Grey handlewood . . is used for axe handles and engineers' handles. **1981** W.D. FRANCIS *Austral. Rain-Forest Trees* (rev. ed.) 73 *Streblus brunonianus* . . Whalebone Tree, Axe-handle Wood . . Grey Handlewood. . . Some specimens of *Aphananthe philippinensis* very closely resemble specimens of this species. **1900** *Proc. Linnean Soc. N.S.W.* XXV. *E. paniculata* . . the **Grey** or White **Ironbark** of the coast. **1909** R. KALESKI *Austral. Settler's Compl. Guide* 33 *Ironbark*, the white or grey, is the hardest and most durable of Australia's hardwoods. **1963** C. BURGESS *Blue Mountain Gums* 56 '*Grey ironbark*' . . has a typical 'ironbark' . . but of a greyish colour. **1980** L. FULLER *Wollongong's Native Trees* 49 Grey ironbark (*Eucalyptus paniculata*) . . reliable and worth growing. **1793** W. TENCH *Compl. Acct. Settlement* 171 The large, or **grey kanguroo**, to which the natives give the name of Pa-ta-ga-ràn. **1822** G.W. EVANS *Geogr., Hist., & Topogr. Descr. Van Diemen's Land* 7 Besides the small quadrupeds already mentioned, they observed the grey and red kangaroo. **1845** *Atlas* (Sydney) I. 258/1 The grey kangaroo . . has very thin hair in summer, while in winter the coat is thick and woolly. **1855** J. BONWICK *Geogr. Aust. & N.Z.* (ed. 3) 199 The Kangaroos have 28 teeth. . . There is the grey of Tasmania and the red of North Australia. **1953** H.G. LAMOND *Big Red* 11 A grey kangaroo sat in a huddled position at the foot of a gidyea tree. **1984** *Qld. Country Life* (Brisbane) 14 June 44 Grey kangaroos in the Goondiwindi wheatgrowing region. **1926** *Qld. Agric. Jrnl.* XXV. 440 Avicennia officinalis . . **Grey** or white **Mangrove. 1985** *Sydney Morning Herald* 14 Dec. 16/6 A square kilometre of grey mangrove forest contributes about 600 tonnes of leaf litter a year to the estuarine food chain. **1852** G.C. MUNDY *Our Antipodes* I. 390 If the '**grey nurse**' or old solitary shark be hooked, the cable is cut. **1901** *Bulletin* (Sydney) 14 Sept. 16/3 At Watson's Bay, Sydney, was recently caught a 'grey-nurse' shark. **1934** T. WOOD *Cobbers* 223 Even I got a fish: a grey-nurse shark. . . He had seven rows of teeth. **1951** *Bulletin* (Sydney) 18 Apr. 14/2 It's not a dog-shark; it's a young grey-nurse and they're man-eaters. **1977** R. MCKIE *Crushing* (1978) 44, I hope a shark gets you. . . A bloody big sixteen-foot Grey Nurse. **1900** A.J. CAMPBELL *Nests & Eggs Austral. Birds* 1039 The **Grey Teal** . . has a more extensive habitat than the chestnut-breasted. **1948** R. RAVEN-HART *Canoe in Aust.* 39 Grey Teal, showing white diamonds below the wings as they flew. **1974** J. BYRNE *Duck Hunting Aust. & N.Z.* 185 Although most inland billabongs in Australia support a small population of Grey Teal, large flocks move about over much of the continent in a highly erratic manner. **1980** *Ecos* xxiii. 24 Black duck and grey teal together make up about 80% of hunters' bags each duck-shooting season in south-eastern Australia. **1861** 'OLD BUSHMAN' *Bush Wanderings* 138 The common **Gray Thrush** is a dull-looking bird, of a uniform ash-gray colour. **1945** C. BARRETT *Austral. Bird Life* 138 That general favourite down south, the grey thrush. **1949** B. O'REILLY *Green Mountains* 111 Those staunch bushmen's friends, the grey thrushes, followed our lunch fires for months. **1968** D. FLEAY *Nightwatchmen* 3 Grey Thrushes treated us to the magic of their mellow outbursts. **1976** *Reader's Digest Compl. Bk. Austral. Birds* 379 The grey shrike-thrush is well named *harmonica*, for it is among the world's most pleasing songbirds. . . In eastern Australia the bird is often called simply the grey thrush—a misleading name because it is not a member of the thrush family.

grey billy. [Prob. f. Br. dial. *bully* a rounded stone: see EDD *sb.*[3]] A hard, strongly cemented silcrete of a greyish or cream colour; BILLY *n.*[3]

1942 M.L. MACPHERSON *I heard Anzacs Singing* 54 'Gray Billy?' 'Uh-huh. You have to dig right through that before you come to the opal.' **1961** F. LEECHMAN *Opal Bk.* 112 The quartzite boulders . . were called Grey Billy or Grey Bullies by the old miners; some were Cornishmen and the term 'bully' for a big round stone is well known in Cornwall. **1967** R.O. CHALMERS *Austral. Rocks* 33 These siliceous rocks should properly be referred to by the scientific term *silcrete* but Australian geologists will probably always cling affectionately to the colloquial term 'grey billy' or 'billy'. **1973** V. SERVENTY *Desert Walkabout* 62 The hard silica capping of the breakaways. . . Called 'grey billy' this breaks to a sharp cutting edge and is suitable for a variety of purposes from cutting flakes to stone axes.

greycoat. *Obs.* A prisoner.

1902 *Bulletin* (Sydney) 31 May 31/2 The Spider, Rajah Riley, Pincher Wilson, and three other greycoats comprised the representatives of the bond, and compared very favorably with the six freemen, amongst whom was the gaol wood-carter. **1907** *Ibid.* 17 Jan. 40/1 Corpse-watchers guard the doom-cell in 'B' wing all the night; The sleepless 'grey-coats' mumble and start in sudden fright.

grey death. See quot. 1967.

1967 *Kings Cross Whisper* (Sydney) xxxv. 6/1 *Grey death*, weak prison stew. The cause of many prison 'rally ups'. **1968** J. ALARD *He who shoots Last* 125 Dey locks y'up at four in the arvo until da grey death lobs on ya plate in da mornin'. **1979** L. NEWCOMBE *Inside Out* 27 The food was atrocious. In particular the evening meal. . . In 1957 they called it the Grey Death. *Ibid.* 32 The riot over the 'Grey Death' involved everybody in the boys' wing.

grid, *n.*[1] [Br. slang *grid* bicycle: see OED(S *sb.* 7.] A bicycle.

1927 A. WRIGHT *Squatter's Secret* 118 Sorry about your grid. . . It's a good bike. **1942** G. CASEY *It's harder for Girls* (1944) 125 Here, you go on, on my grid, an' I'll do the walking. **1965** G. MCINNES *Road to Gundagai* 122 'Where's the grid?' 'My bike!' 'Yeah, the old mangle; isn't this where we left it?'

grid, *n.*[2] In an opening in a fence: a set of rails above a shallow trench, so spaced as to prevent the passage of stock.

1930 *Bulletin* (Sydney) 16 July 20/2 The grids . . are fast outnumbering the licensed public gates. **1964** *Mount Isa Mail* 19 May 7/5 All the Grids on the Gregory to Almora section of the . . Road would be completed.

grill. A person of southern European descent: see quot. 1967 and GREEK.

1957 J.M. HOSKING *Aust. first & Last* 123 We call them New Australians now; once we called some Dagoes, Others Balts and Squareheads, Pongoes, Grills and Rice and Sagoes. **1967** *Kings Cross Whisper* (Sydney) xxxv. 6/1 *Grills*, Greeks. From the ability of industrious Greeks to control country town cafes. **1970** J.S. GUNN in W.S. Ramson *Eng. Transported* 53 *Grill*, 'Southern European'.

grip. *Obs.* A job; employment.

1903 *Bulletin* (Sydney) 24 Sept. 16/2 For myself, I must be goin'—yes I must be movin' quick; For I've got a 'grip' with sheep that are a-comin' up from Vic. **1906** E. DYSON *Fact'ry 'Ands* 243, I had t' do it 'r resign me grip on ther spot. **1914** —— *Spats' Fact'ry* 77 The whole bloomin' fact'ry got a bit ratty erbout it, 'n' was thinkin' iv givin' the grip brusher, 'n' goin' into co. with the unemployed. **1915** C.J. DENNIS *Songs of Sentimental Bloke* (1936) 63 Ferever yappin' like a tork-machine About 'The Hoffis' where 'e 'ad a grip. **1955** N. PULLIAM *I traveled Lonely Land* 377 *Grip*, a regular job.

gripman. [U.S. *gripman* operator of a cablecar: see Mathews.] The driver and operator of a cable-drawn tram.

1894 *Bulletin* (Sydney) 10 Feb. 9/4 Any tram-man having a shop in his family is ignominiously 'fired'. The gripman or conductor whose industrious wife runs a green-grocery or lolly-stall is a comparatively independent individual. **1901** *Advocate* (Burnie) 9 May 3/2 The gripmen and conductors on the trams. **1916** C. VAUDE *Tivoli* 25 Does the old gripman still shout out 'Mind the curve'? **1965** G. MCINNES *Road to Gundagai* 66 Gripmen tended to be taciturn and morose, and when asked whether the next stop was the Hospital or Domain Road were apt to point to an enamelled sign which read, 'Do Not Talk to the Gripman'. **1967** F.T. MACARTNEY *Proof against Failure* 7 He was then no longer a bus-driver but a 'gripman', as the driver of a cable tram was called.

grog, *n.* [Generalized use of Br. *grog* drink of spirits (usu. rum) and water.]

1. Alcoholic liquor of any kind; a drink of an alcoholic beverage. See also SLY GROG 1 a. Also *attrib.*

1832 *Currency Lad* (Sydney) 22 Sept. 2 A parcel of young 'bloods', generally termed 'cocks of the first water', with more grog aboard than brains, appeared to have assembled for the express purpose of creating a disturbance. **1840** J.P. JOHNSON *Plain Truths* 55 Their grog, or bull, as it is termed, is a small quantity of boiling water put into a cask, out of which all the spirits have been drawn, or at any rate only leaving the dirt at the bottom. **1843** *Teetotal Advocate* (Launceston) 29 May 2/3 The history of grog indeed—thereby meaning all intoxicating liquors. **1844** *Bee of Aust.* (Sydney) 2 Nov. 3/1 With lots of brandy, rum and gin, To lull each doubt to sleep, sirs. Ah! Fisher's sure the day to win; For grog to him's so cheap, sirs. **1858** C.R. THATCHER *Colonial Songster* (rev. ed.) 39 Hurrah, my brave pals, ye may all nobblerize, There's plenty more grog in the camp, and no flies. **1880** *Argus* (Melbourne) 19 Jan. 7/2 It is stated that the Bulli (N.S.W.) grog strike has been concluded by a compromise. Nobblers are again being supplied at three-pence by the publicans, but for 'long-sleevers' they charge fourpence. **1907** *Truth* (Sydney) 20 Jan. 3/1 Annie Hill . . and Ruby Moore . . were charged with sly-grog selling. The 'grog' in this instance was *a large bottle of champagne*. **1909** *Bulletin* (Sydney) 3 June 13/2 Travelling to Marble Bar with grog—bottled beer, whisky and brandy. **1938** X. HERBERT *Capricornia* 256 'Sorry—I've knocked your grog over. Let's buy you another. . . What you drinking?' 'Double whiskey.' **1945** W.E. HOLT *Your Friend Ben* 24 As we approached Cana, one informed the other. . . 'This is where Jesus and His friends came to a wedding, and when the grog gave out He fixed things for 'em.' **1963** R. MCGREGOR-HASTIE *Compleat Migrant* 16 'Well, mate, you want some grog, right?' You deny this. Rum's the last thing you could take on a hot summer's day. 'Grog's anything yer drink, mate,' explains the friend. **1971** *Bulletin* (Sydney) 27 Nov. 48/3 His heaven is described as a beer garden with free grog of all types and naked angels who'd be in anything. **1974** *Ibid.* 4 May 31/3 His office suite in Parliament House used to be quite famous for an indoor cricket match played noisily around the grog fridge with a screwed up paper ball. **1986** *Centralian Advocate* (Alice Springs) 5 Feb. 1/1 Mr Forrester agreed that the main 'grog problem' on the town camps was caused by the licensed stores.

2. In the phr. **on the grog,** engaged in a drinking bout or session.

1959 *Never kill Dolphin* (Writers' Guild Qld.) 185 It's Christmas Eve and they're all on the grog. **1960** M. HENRY *Unlucky Dip* 46 You'll have to watch the niggers, Boss. . . They won't miss a chance to get on the grog if they can get hold of it. **1963** M. BRITT *Pardon my Boots* 43 All three were what is known as 'on the grog', or just reluctantly leaving it. **1969** A. BUZO *Rooted* (1973) 44 Hammo had been on the grog and he didn't give way to his right. **1976** B. SUTTON *Comrade George* 2 When Paddy and Lofty were on the grog they recognised no masters. **1979** K. GARVEY *Absolutely Austral.* 19 On the grog till they do every deener, Stony broke and regretful next day.

3. Special Comb. **grog artist,** a heavy drinker (see also ARTIST); **seller,** an (unlicensed) retailer of alcoholic beverages; also **selling** *vbl. n.*, the (unlicensed) retailing of alcoholic beverages; **shanty,** a roughly constructed (unlicensed) public house, esp. on a goldfield; also *attrib.*; **tent,** a tent on a goldfield for the unlicensed retailing of alcoholic beverages.

1965 *Kings Cross Whisper* (Sydney) Oct. 6/2 Your correspondent, being a **grog-artist** of merit and renown, is also the World Champion Hangover Sufferer. **1978** B. ST. A. SMITH *Spirit beyond Psyche* 48 Quiet, the lot of youse! He's got a point. Jim ain't much of a grog-artist, but pour a few beers inter him an' he's a real bush-lawyer. **1827** *Colonial Times* (Hobart) 21 July, Last week, Mrs Jillett, a notorious **grog seller** at the Green Ponds, was convicted. **1842** *Austral. & N.Z. Monthly Mag.* 39 There is no class of individuals more useful to society than respectable innkeepers; but the class of low grog-sellers which abound throughout these colonies, are the plague spots of society. **1855** *Illustr. Sydney News* 23 June 328/1 Some time since the licensed publicans organized a society to watch after the grog-sellers, who have now, in self-defence, betaken themselves to the watching of the hotels as regards their violations of Sunday trading and night licenses. **1863** P. SAUNDERS *Two Yrs. Vic.* 70 The sole resource of the digger . . would seem to be drinking ardent spirits, either in his own tent or that of the grog-seller. **1870** W.B. WITHERS *Hist. Ballarat* 38 Unlicensed at first, the grog-sellers got licensed afterwards. **1907** *Truth* (Sydney) 17 Mar. 1/3 The last prospect a grog-seller probably looks forward to is being killed by cold water. **1934** C. SAYCE *Comboman* 225 He wondered whether the grog-seller knew about his marriage. **1968** LINKLATER & TAPP *Gather no Moss* 84 Inevitably, there was gambling, too, and soon a peaceful camp would be alive with drunks fighting and cursing, and easy victims for the grog-sellers' hangers-on. Men got into debt, and health suffered. **1829** *Launceston Advertiser* 14 Sept. 3 On Saturday last, Mrs Townsend was indicted for selling liquor without a license. . . Mr William Duncan was next on the list for the offence of **grog-selling.** **1840** *Tasmanian Weekly Dispatch* (Hobart) 10 Apr. 7/1 Charged by Mr Swift with grog-selling. **1848** J.C. BYRNE *Emigrant's Guide* 37 The profits of grog-selling even in a legitimate way were some years since perfectly enormous, and are even now considerable. **1859** F. SINNETT *Acct. 'Rush' Port Curtis* 83 M.T. had surrounded himself with compatriots and Italians, who were all evidently quite new to the business of grog-selling. **1889** H. EGBERT *Pretty Cockey* 60 How many large fortunes, thought he, had been made during those years, by grog-selling, land-sharking, and other questionable means. **1858** *Colonial Mining Jrnl.* Dec. 59/3 **Grog-shanties** are super-abundant. **1871** *Austral. Town & Country Jrnl.* (Sydney) 8 Apr. 422/4 Even in the vicinity of Brisbane grog shanties still exist, and several convictions have taken place. **1874** *Adelaide Observer* 26 Dec. (Christmas Suppl.) 12/1 The 'grog shanties', with their glaring canvas signs, . . '*The Digger's Rest*', and '*The Puddlers' Flat Hotel*'. **1890** A.J. VOGAN *Black Police* 34 The half digger, half speculator . . haunts the grog-shanties at night, and spies for chances to make some 'unearned increment' from the whisky-wagging tongues of the true workers on the field. **1897** *Western Champion* (Barcaldine) 9 Feb. 12/2, I struck a bush hotel or grog shanty about sundown, and feeling tired I thought I'd stick out the night there. **1913** W.K. HARRIS *Outback in Aust.* 39 We discovered that it had in its time been a 'grog-shanty', and a night or two previous had been visited by sundowners. **1928** E. FOREMAN *Hist. & Adventures Qld. Pioneer* 33 *Grog shanties.* When the road was first opened from Brisbane to Gympie there was not a licensed public house the whole distance, but my word! **1945** *Bulletin* (Sydney) 30 May 12/1 The two hefty wheat-lumpers got into an argument in the unlicensed grog-shanty. **1969** F.B. VICKERS *No Man is Himself* 23 Outside Don Fraser's bough grog-shanty . . hard liquor drunk out of jam tins. **1982** P. JAMES *Stories Central Qld.* 7 Grog shanty towns sprouted and decayed like mushrooms in those days of alluvial gold. **1852** *Guardian* (Hobart) 10 Jan. 3/6 The Commissioner received intelligence of a **grog-tent.** **1853** J. SHERER *Gold Finder Aust.* 78 Here is a grog-tent; the haunt of the low and the lawless. **1857** *Bell's Life in Sydney* 14 Feb. 1/3 You say there was a grog-tent where you stopped. **1864** J. ARMOUR *Diggings, Bush & Melbourne* 25 He . . crossed the road to a grog tent for a drink.

grog, *v.*

1. *intr.* To drink an alcoholic beverage. Also *trans.* (see quot. 1978).

1959 R. BURNS *Mr Brain knows Best* 79 You'd be enlisting with the no-hopers, the types you see getting into crutch kicking fights when they've been grogging at the football. **1969** P. ADAM SMITH *Folklore Austral. Railwaymen* 87 The boys were grogging—this is thirsty country up here with a constant over the century heat in summer and a week at a time at over 110 degrees. **1978** K. GILBERT *People are Legends* 42 A *real man* don't grog away money.

Hence **grogging** *vbl. n.* and *attrib.*

1965 D. ELLIS *Screw Loose* 122 What 'appens on New Year's Day, besides grogging and what-not? **1980** B. SANSOM *Camp at Wallaby Cross* 50 The point is that grogging restrictions have become very sensitive indicators of the political state of Territory communities.

2. With **on**: to engage in a protracted drinking session. Also as *vbl. n.* and *attrib.*

1951 E. LAMBERT *Sleeping House Party* 31 We were over with Helen and John and Paul, grogging on regardless. **1958** G. COTTERELL *Tea at Shadow Creek* 204 It's murder, really. It's like everywhere in the bush. If you don't grog on, you're an outcast. **1965** K. SMITH *OGF* 59 Once an Australian's been a boss he can never go back to where he was. He can do his dough in the poker machines, grog on twice as hard and swear twice as much, but he'll always be up the other end of the bar by himself because once you outpace the mob they never trust you again. **1967** M. HORNER *Austral. One-Act Plays: Bk. 3* 29, I suppose it's the grogging-on that bothers you? There isn't much of it. **1969** A. GARVE *Boomerang* 141 If I want to grog on, I'll bloody well grog on. **1974** D. IRELAND *Burn* 49 'And there sits a man could drink the likes of you mob under the table.' 'He can grog on. Well that is a help,' Mary says. **1976** K. CLIFT *Soldier who never grew Up* 181 In his . . 'grogging-on' experiences he'd heard of a drink called 'White Lady' which consisted of a jigger of neat gin poured over a dollop of ice-cream. **1978** B. ST. A. SMITH *Spirit beyond Psyche* 20 You an' me, like, when we retire, we can go down t' the RSL of an arvo an' grog on regardless.

3. With **up**: to drink, usu. to excess. Also as *ppl. a.*

1956 J.E. MACDONNELL *Commander Brady* 249 Now don't forget. Nobody grogged-up. Nobody rortin' it up with them Yanks. Behave yerselves. **1957** R. BEYNON *Shifting Heart* (1960) 53 Well . . ah look, I'm grogged-up anyway: you talk in circles, I'm bushed altogether. **1963** *Meanjin* 177 You just couldn't discuss with a man. So you had to get in bed with him. Grogged up half the time. That was how she had copped the twins, after she had said never ever. **1968** *Coast to Coast 1967–68* 107 Sometimes . . Mr Philip, if he felt like grogging up with the locals, would drive him in. **1977** K. GILBERT *Living Black* 303 When a man grogs up his kids' food money you straighten him out.

grog-up. A drinking party or session. Also **grog-on.**

1959 D. HEWETT *Bobbin Up* 31 The noise and abuse at one of Hazel's regular grog-ups was worse than usual. **1962** A. SEYMOUR *One Day of Yr.* 77 Day of salute to the fallen, day of grief. . . It's just one long grog-up. **1965**

D. MARTIN *Hero of Too* 197 Trapped like a careless idiot after a grog-up. **1967** J. HIBBERD *White with Wire Wheels* (1970) 194 We're all going up to the hills for a grog-on tomorrow. Just to give the Valiant a try-out. **1974** *Telegraph* (Brisbane) 8 Nov. 4/4 (*heading*) School grog-ups. **1978** WARD & SMITH *Vanishing Village* 123 Apex-wise, the service work that we do is probably not as enjoyable as it used to be, but a lot of them used to be grog-ons, there wasn't much service done.

groper /'groʊpə/, *n.*[1] [Var. of *grouper* any of several fish of the fam. Serranidae.] Any of several fish, esp. *Promicrops lanceolatus* (fam. Serranidae), a large marine species of n. Aust. and elsewhere in the Pacific and Indian Oceans; *Queensland groper* QUEENSLAND 2. See also *blue groper* BLUE *a.*

[**1789** W. TENCH *Narr. Exped. Botany Bay* 129 A species of grouper, to which, from the form of a bone in the head resembling a helmet, we have given the name of a light horseman.] **1833** W.H. BRETON *Excursions* 160 Fish are plentiful, and the most abundant are snappers . . gropers, etc. **1852** G.C. MUNDY *Our Antipodes* I. 392 We saw a Black spearing the rock-cod and groper. **1854** *Moreton Bay Free Press* 14 Mar. 3/3 The crew of the ketch Sarah . . caught an immense fish called a 'Groper', weighing about 290 lbs. **1874** *N.S.W. Rep. R. Comm. Fisheries* (1880) 16 The gruper . . popularly called in this country blue or black groper—no doubt from the fact of these fishes groping in and out of the caverns and crevices of rocks in search of crustaceae. **1897** R. NEWTON *Work & Wealth Qld.* 75 The groper, a gigantic variety of rock cod, is met with in bays and tidal waters. **1928** *Bulletin* (Sydney) 27 June 23/4 An outsize groper caught near Burketown (N.Q.) recently turned out to be a ladies' marine store. Amongst a lot of articles stored in its stomach were a gold watch, a gold brooch, stockings and a pair of shoe heels. **1945** J. DEVANNY *Bird of Paradise* 90 The monster 'groper' or estuary cod. **1948** F.D. MARSHALL *Let's go Fishing* 73 Groper . . are called blue pigfish in Queensland. **1979** A.J. BURKE *Bite Pineapple* 5 An old groper took a man holus bolus near the Victoria Bridge.

Groper, *n.*[2] and *attrib.* [Abbrev. of SAND-GROPER.]

A. *n.* A nickname for a non-Aboriginal person native to or resident in Western Australia, esp. an early settler or a descendant of an early settler.

1899 *Bulletin* (Sydney) 1 July 7/2 Apparently the Old Gropers who govern Westralia have decided to throw in their lot with the Provincialists. **1903** *Westminster Gaz.* (London) 28 Jan. 9/2 Fierce jealousies arose between the gold-hunters and the sandalwood gropers, as the new people contemptuously termed the old. **1907** *Truth* (Sydney) 7 Apr. 10/7 West Australia was a long time awakening to the awful treatment that was meted out to the blacks by the Gropers. **1918** *Ibid.* 6 Jan. 13/3 The Gropers, prior to the discovery of Coolgardie, were, to put it plainly, merely a community of white aboriginals with primitive ideas concerning morality and sanitation. **1929** W.J. RESIDE *Golden Days* 125 Many of the 'Gropers' (early settlers) of the West, awakened from their lethargy, felt as though they had been rudely shaken by a mighty earthquake. **1936** J. KIRWAN *My Life's Adventure* 134 The energetic and enterprising mining community described the Western Australians as 'Gropers'. **1950** *New Settler in W.A.* (Perth) Oct. 15 In the South African War, Australian soldiers were called 'Cornstalks', 'Gropers', and so on, according to their State of origin. **1966** J.E. WEBB *Alms for Oblivion* 36 'I've heard Sir John is a Groper. What is a Groper?' 'All the ole settlers is Gropers, an' 'e's one.' **1979** W.D. JOYNT *Breaking Road for Rest* 47 A local 'groper' (the name given to the West Australian born at the time) assured me that it took many years of grazing and cultivation before land could grow crops, or even grass.

B. *attrib.*

1900 *Truth* (Sydney) 20 May 6/2 The settlers in the North-West are almost entirely composed of the old groper group, and many of them are wealthy. **1903** *Bulletin* (Sydney) 11 Apr. 16/1 It was at a Goldfields Mission, In the land of Sand and Sin, That a wandering apostle Asked the Groper miners in. **1913** *Ibid.* 9 Jan. 13/2, I have . . known of several attempts to take them to the Eastern States, but the pangs of leaving their 'Groper state have been too much for them. **1948** *Ibid.* 5 May 22/3 There used to be a night-well on the way to Jerramungurup (s.-w. W.A.). Originally an abo drinking place it was enlarged by Groper teamsters to a capacity of about 100 gallons. **1956** V. COURTNEY *All I may Tell* 26 James was one of those 'Groper' types who rose above the narrowness of so many of the early Western Australians, although he was a staunch State Righter to the end. **1963** X. HERBERT *Disturbing Element* 37 The *jilgie* in Groper lingo is the yabbie of the T'other-siders.

Hence **Groperdom** *n.*, **Groperism** *n.*

1900 *Bulletin* (Sydney) 13 Jan. 7/2 (*heading*) The moan of old **groperdom**. **1903** *Truth* (Sydney) 29 Mar. 1/4 Hackett—by far the ablest man in Groperdom—managed to dissuade you from political suicide. **1907** A. BUCHANAN *Real Aust.* 54 The *West Australian* occupies a unique position. It is the accented mouthpiece of '**groperism**'; that is to say, of those privileged few who came to the State in early days, and monopolised as much of the earth as seemed worthy of their attention.

Groperland. A nickname for the State of Western Australia.

1900 *Bulletin* (Sydney) 14 July 6/1 The Parochialists of Groper Land have girded up their intelligence for the fray. **1901** *Truth* (Sydney) 16 June 5/7 Slavery in the west. The gangrene of Groperland. ***c* 1907** W.C. CHANDLER *Darkest Adelaide* 29 The husband cast longing glances towards Western Australia. . . The upshot of those longing glances was that the husband sold out and set sail for Groperland. **1930** E. ANTONY *Hungry Mile* 7, I ploughed the sand in Groperland, I poisoned prickly pear. **1959** H. DRAKE-BROCKMAN *West Coast Stories* 2 Hail, groperland! Australia West! Of earth's fair places thou art best. **1963** X. HERBERT *Disturbing Element* 40 Wild flowers of loveliness, variety and profusion to be found nowhere else on earth but in poor arid Groperland.

Hence **Groperlander** *n.*, a Western Australian.

1906 *Bulletin* (Sydney) 13 Sept. 17/1 A Groperlander . . has been gathering facts about big Australian grape vines. **1919** *7th Field Artillery Brigade Yandoo* Mar. 142 The Groperlanders . . will be associated with us. **1945** S.J. BAKER *Austral. Lang.* 186 *Western Australians* . . groperlanders.

ground, *n.*[1] Used *attrib.* in Special Comb. **ground-berry,** the edible fruit of any of several small, often prostrate, shrubs of the genera *Acrotriche* and *Astroloma* (both fam. Epacridaceae); any of the plants themselves; **parrot** (or **parakeet**), any of several parrots typically seen on the ground (cf. GRASS PARROT), now usu. spec. *Pezoporus wallicus* of heaths and grassland in s. Aust.; see also *swamp parrot* SWAMP *n.*; also *fig.*; **thrush,** any of several birds typically seen on the ground, esp. *Zoothera dauma* (fam. Muscicapidae) of e. Aust., in size, shape, and plumage resembling the song thrush of Britain, and the species of *Cinclosoma* (fam. Orthonychidae) of s. and central Aust.; see also *mountain thrush* MOUNTAIN, QUAIL-THRUSH.

1849 *Bell's Life in Sydney* 13 Oct. 1/1 The most luxuriant crops of **ground-berries**. **1888** *Proc. Linnean Soc. N.S.W.* III. 489 *Astroloma humifusum* . . Commonly called 'Ground-berry'. In Tasmania the fruits are often called 'Native Cranberries'. **1902** J.S. HASSALL *In Old Aust.* 18 Outside the school grounds, the younger boys often went picking ground-berries and 'five-corners'. **1933** C.W. PECK *Austral. Legends* (ed. 2) 211 He had not ever been taught how to prepare . . Astrolomas or Ground berries. **1953** *Bulletin* (Sydney) 4 Nov. 13/4 A tastier and more sizeable titbit was the 'ground-berry'. **1794** G. SHAW *Zool. New Holland* 10 The **Ground Parrot** . . differs from all the rest of its tribe in never perching on trees, but constantly frequenting low and sedgy places, running along the ground in the manner of a rail. **1827** *Trans. Linnean Soc. London* XV. 278 *Psittacus Pulchellus* . . Mr Caley says . . —The settlers call it Ground Parrot. It feeds upon the ground. *Ibid.* 286 *Pezoporus Formosus* . . 'What is called the Ground Parrot at Sydney inhabits the scrubs in that neighbourhood.' **1841** J. GOULD *Birds of Aust.* (1848) V. Pl. 38, *Euphema elegans* . . Elegant Grass-Parrakeet. . . Ground Parrakeet of the Colonists. **1849** C. STURT *Narr. Exped. Central Aust.* II. 41 (*App.*) The Ground Parrot . . has a dark green plumage mottled with black, and has a patch of dull red over the bill. **1853** MOSSMAN & BANISTER *Aust. Visited & Revisited* 63 Flocks of the ground-parrakeet, feeding by the way-side as plentifully as sparrows in England. **1855** M. SPENCER et al. *Aunt Spencer's Diary* (1981) 52 The ground parrot, a very pretty bird—like a parrot in plumage, beak and head, though not much larger than a swallow. It builds on the ground and is very tame. **1857** *Illustr. Jrnl. Australasia* III. 195 The beautiful ground-parrakeet darted from beneath one's feet, his brilliant plumage flashing in the beams of the morning sun. **1874** J.J. HALCOMBE *Emigrant & Heathen* 32 Ground parrots, with their gorgeous crimson, green, and blue plumage. **1905** *Shearer* (Sydney) 3 June 2/2 The 'cocky', . . 'ground parrot', . . or whatever name he is known by. **1952** B. BEATTY *Unique to Aust.* 52 The Ground Parakeets comprise three species, the best-known being the Budgerigar, which is now a popular house pet. **1980** H.W. CUMMINGS *Confessions of 'Mud Skipper'* 74 There had been an Air Force camp during war time . . and some of the 'Ground Parrots' . . had relieved their boredom by shooting .303 bullets through the ship's side. **1840** J. GOULD *Birds of Aust.* (1848) IV. Pl. 4, Spotted **Ground-Thrush** . . *Cinclosoma Punctatum* . . gives a decided preference to the summits of low stony hills and rocky gullies. **1855** R. AUSTIN *Jrnl. Interior W.A.* 20 The natives returned to camp with . . two cinnamon coloured ground thrushes (*cinnamonus cinclosoma*). **1903** *Emu* II. 164 Ground-Thrush (*Geocichla lunulata*). Very common in the Otways. **1978** B.P. MOORE *Life on Forty Acres* 95 The Ground Thrush (*Zoothera dauma*) is . . a true thrush that occurs widely in eastern Australia and New Guinea.

ground, *n.*[2] *Obs.* [Br. dial. *ground* a piece or parcel of land; OED records this as obs. in the singular from *c* 1733 (see *sb.* 10 b.) but see also EDD *sb.* 4, 'a field; a piece of land enclosed for agricultural purposes'.]

1. A piece of land suitable for cultivation or for grazing stock; see also BACK GROUND 1.

1792 D. COLLINS *Acct. Eng. Colony N.S.W.* (1798) I. 234 The settlers late belonging to the Sirius, whose grounds had, on a careful survey by Mr Grimes, been found to intersect each other. **1804** *HRA* (1915) 1st Ser. V. 27 It also may be adviseable to discriminate between those who hold Grounds by Grant or Lease, and those who occupy Farms without either. **1807** *Ibid.* (1916) 1st Ser. VI. 146 The ignorance of those who possess Grounds and never knew the practical part of Agriculture. **1820** C. JEFFREYS *Van Dieman's Land* 59 The ground Mr Miller cultivated had been for some time before occupied as stock yards for cattle and sheep. **1831** *Sydney Herald* 25 Apr. 1/4 Lot II. A House And Ground. **1831** *Returns Relative to Settlement Swan River* 7 Ten or Twelve of the leading men of the Settlement having occupied their Grounds . . declared themselves fully satisfied. **1835** 'IMPARTIAL OBSERVER' *Illustr. Present State N.S.W.* 46 She and her husband were *Squatters*, the name given in the Colony to persons who cultivate unoccupied Ground, belonging therefore, as they say to Government.

2. *Gold-mining.* A goldfield, a piece of land being worked for gold; a claim. Esp. in the phr. **on the ground.**

1851 *Empire* (Sydney) 4 Aug. 11/2 There were a great many purchasers of gold on the ground. **1852** *Austral. Gold Digger's Monthly Mag.* iii. 79 Persons desirous of changing their ground, were required to notify the same to the Commissioner. **1853** *Ibid.* v. 192 Mr Selwyn, our Government Geologist, is on the ground. **1858** *Colonial Mining Jrnl.* 2 Sept. 2/2 He has, nevertheless, permitted the ground to be temporarily worked by a party of farm miners. **1876** 'EIGHT YRS.' RESIDENT' *Queen of Colonies* 135 Nash . . had at last found what for many long years he had been in quest of—a payable piece of ground. **1888** 'R. BOLDREWOOD' *Robbery under Arms* (1937) 250 Ours was a middling good claim, too; two men's ground.

ground, *n.*[3] [Spec. use of *ground* the soil of the earth, obs. elsewhere exc. in *Mining*: see OED *sb.* 16.] Used *attrib.* in Special Comb. **ground floor,** an earthen floor; **tank,** an excavation sited to retain rain-water, a dam.

1894 H. LAWSON *Short Stories* 28 The kitchen has 'no floor', or rather an earthen one called a '**ground floor**'. **1964** P. ADAM SMITH *Hear Train Blow* 85 They built slab huts with a 'ground' floor. **1973** R. ROBINSON *Drift of Things* 127, I asked at an isolated homestead if I could put my horses in the paddock and camp by the **ground tank**. **1975** L.A. POCKLEY *Handbk. for Jackeroos* 73 The most universal method of stock watering is from ground excavations or 'ground tanks', sited to catch water from an adequate run off area.

Group. *W.A. Hist.* Abbrev. of GROUP SETTLEMENT. Also *attrib.*

1922 [see GROUP SETTLEMENT]. **1927** T.S. GROSER *Lure of Golden West* 29 The conditions attached to 'Groups' are as follows:– A settlement under the 'Group' system is arranged. . . A 'Group' consists of twenty settlers. **1946** 'A. SPENCE' *Mystery of Red Gum* 56 When they first arrive they are put on to Groups. That is, a group of houses something like those you have seen, under the supervision of a foreman. **1956** V. COURTNEY *All I may Tell* 44 It is to the credit of Mitchell's opponent, Philip Collier, that he recognized the genuineness of Mitchell's attempt to make the Groups a great enterprise. **1965** *Tracks we Travel* 148 You don't have to worry about interest and paying off a mortgage, like those poor devils on the Groups.

grouper.

1. *W.A. Hist.* Shortened form of GROUP SETTLER.

1926 A.A.B. APSLEY *Amateur Settlers* 164 Each Grouper as a rule working. **1927** T.S. GROSER *Lure of Golden West* 33 The 'Groupers' come out without any capital at all.

2. A member of one of the 'Industrial Groups', factions formed within trade unions by the Australian Labor Party to support Labor policies and oppose Communist influence; (loosely) a member of a right-wing faction of the Australian Labor Party; a member of the Democratic Labor Party.

[**1947** *Argus* (Melbourne) 7 Apr. 2/4 Sixteen industrial groups had been formed in unions following the decision by the 1946 Victorian ALP conference to combat anti-Labour, Liberal and Communist influences.] **1955** *Sydney Morning Herald* 27 Apr. 1/1 Last year the groupers altered the rules to give two delegates for every 250 members from a State electorate council. **1956** *Daily Tel.* (Sydney) 5 Apr. 3/5 The Groupers . . practically drove Communism out of the Australian trade union movement. **1956** J.E. WEBB *So much for Sydney* 26 Cynics will go on thinking that the sudden change was prompted . . by disgust with the proceedings of the A.L.P. Industrial Groups ('Groupers' to them). **1970** R. MURRAY *Split* 19 The 'Groupers', as the ALP Industrial Group members and their supporters became known. **1973** L. OAKES *Whitlam PM* 72 In October, 1954, Evatt brought the internal Labor Party fight between his supporters and the Catholic social movement and the Groupers out into the open with a press statement headed 'Labor Unity in Australia'. **1974** BLAZEY & CAMPBELL *Political Dice Men* 60 The Federal Labor Party was undergoing its worst split and the Labor party in Victoria had been virtually destroyed by the strength of the 'groupers' during 1954–55. **1975** *Bulletin* (Sydney) 22 Nov. 17/1 It is true that Kerr was something of a 'grouper', or anti-communist Labor man at one stage, but that is really only a serious indictment in extreme left circles. **1985** *Sydney Morning Herald* 24 Apr. 5/5 He said that activities of the 'groupers' meant that he and his mates spent the best years of their political lives in the wilderness.

groupie. *W.A. Hist.* [f. GROUP (SETTLER + -Y.] GROUP SETTLER.

1926 A.A.B. APSLEY *Amateur Settlers* 195 Some of the Groupies . . were clever carpenters. **1934** *Red Star* (Perth) 24 Aug. 4/2 One of the many groupies who are compelled to seek sustenance work was employed. **1939** J.T. MCMAHON *Bushies' Scheme in W.A.* 15 The Group Settlements were recently established. I accompanied the pastors on a look round for Catholic children among the 'groupies'. **1946** 'A. SPENCE' *Mystery of Red Gum* 30 'The government will buy it to divide into small holdings for the 'Groupies'.' . . 'Who are the 'Groupies', Steve?' 'People sent out by the government to take up farming. Chiefly English.' **1972** M.L. SKINNER *Fifth Sparrow* 119 Few of the 'groupies' knew anything about farming at all and the raw land daunted and frustrated them. **1983** J.K. EWERS *Long enough for Joke* 111 The Collie miners were earning good money; the groupies were earning only sustenance.

Group Settlement. *W.A. Hist.* A scheme developed in the 1920s for establishing settlements of British immigrants in the underdeveloped s.w. of Western Australia; such a settlement. Also *attrib.*

1922 *West Austral.* (Perth) 4 Aug. 8/2 Dealing with Group Settlement the Premier said there were 26 groups and the work was past the experimental stage. **1926** A.A.B. APSLEY *Amateur Settlers* 163 The Group Settlements in south-west Australia go through a number of phases. **1927** T.S. GROSER *Lure of Golden West* p. x, The 'Group Settlement' scheme in the south-west, inaugurated only five years ago by Sir James Mitchell. **1935** *Red Star* (Perth) 12 July 4/3 Over 18 months ago he left the group settlements after being subject to a foreclosure by the bank. **1956** V. COURTNEY *All I may Tell* 43 His greatest gamble, however, was Group Settlement, and it proved disastrous. **1979** J. WILLIAMS *White River* 11 The Group Settlements of Western Australia were a topsy-turvey place.

Group Settler. *W.A. Hist.* A member of a Group Settlement.

1926 A.A.B. APSLEY *Amateur Settlers* 198 Other Group Settlers spent with considerably less sense. **1935** *Red Star* (Perth) 5 Apr. 3/1 Recently a meeting of group settlers was held here. **1965** *Tracks we Travel* 139 Several of the Group Settlers had abandoned their farms after the first two or three years.

grouse, *a.* [Of unknown origin.] Very good of (its) kind; highly desirable. Freq. with the intensive **extra.**

[**1924** *Truth* (Sydney) 27 Apr. 6/3 *Grouse*, something good.] **1944** L. GLASSOP *We were Rats* 5 You know them two grouse sheilas we've got the meet on with tomorrer night? **1948** R. RAVEN-HART *Canoe in Aust.* 43 Australians grouse wildly ('winge', they would say: the word 'grouse' is an adjective in Australian slang, and means 'excellent') about their post-war beer. **1953** G.H. FEARNSIDE *Bayonets Abroad* 38 The D Company boys were not unappreciative. . . 'George . . that was grouse!' . . 'No, no!' he said quickly. 'It vas not Grouse—it vas *Strauss!*' **1953** T.A.G. HUNGERFORD *Riverslake* 168 The Balt's got a grouse sister! **1963** D.H. CRICK *Martin Place* 29 We're going over to Manly next Sunday arvo. There's a grouse fun parlour over there. Pinballs, shooting galleries, picture machines. **1965** E. LAMBERT *Long White Night* 81 Rosa! Me mate Johnny here reckons you're a real grouse hunk of woman. **1965** J. O'GRADY *Aussie Eng.* 38 Beaut. Wonderful. Our beer is 'extra grouse'. **1967** *Kings Cross Whisper* (Sydney) xxxvii. 9/2 'Whisper's' super colossal, humdinger, extra grouse, beaut competition for all the family. **1973** *Austral. Rodsports & Drag Racing News* 2 Mar. 7/1 The car was a striking 'red pepper' (a grouse tomato red which everyone liked). **1975** D.J. TOWNSHEND *Gland Time* 7, I dunno why you won't let the White Leghorn move in here with ya. She'd keep the place in bloody grouse shape. **1979** D.R. STUART *Crank back on Roller* 97 She's a grouse sort of a joint, this bloody Ceylon; do me. **1981** P. BARTON *Bastards I have Known* 85 If the city mob didn't reckon it was all that grouse in the hills they would keep away and leave all that much more free space for us.

grouse, *n.* [Prob. f. prec.] In prison speech: a cigarette, superior in quality to prison issue; also *pl.* and as *adj.*

1968 J. ALARD *He who shoots Last* 125 Da stuff's like gold in here. . . Gees, it's da grouse weed too—we gits a coupla ounces a week, but boob weed is like smokin' horse dung. **1971** J. MCNEIL *Chocolate Frog* (1973) 17 'I was kind of hopin' somebody might lob from court with a grouse cigga. . . ' 'Hey? Oh, yeah . . a grouse'd go well, all right. . . ' 'Like, a tailor-made, I mean.' **1974** ADAMSON & HANFORD *Zimmer's Essay* 53 'You got any grouse?' . . 'You bring any smokes in with you?'

grouter. [Of unknown origin.] A fortuitous circumstance; an unfair advantage; in the game of two-up, an opportune bet, esp. one made as a run of heads or tails ends. Esp. in the phr. **to come in on the grouter, to run a grouter.** Also *attrib.*, as **grouter bet, grouter bettor.**

1902 *Truth* (Sydney) 6 Apr. 7/2 For Chamberlain with cast-iron cheek Has come in on 'the grouter' And told us that our statesmen are Of the grimy outer outer. **1916** *Battery Herald: Jrnl. 14th Field Artillery* 9 Oct. 8 The B.S.M. hopped on the grouter . . spinning tails about six times in succession. **1918** *Port Hacking Cough* (Sydney) 14 Dec. 11 The orderly sergeant, grouter seeking, chanced upon a meek looking person shaving. **1921** F. GROSE *Rough Y.M. Bloke* 147 Find out when it is best for an investor to 'get in on the grouter' in the national game of two-up? **1931** O. WALTERS *Shrapnel Green* 26 I'll bet you a dollar, and then You might . . get in on the grouter again. **1944** G.H. FEARNSIDE *Sojourn in Tobruk* 69 This woman is coming in on the grouter. She's blackmailing me. **1946** K.S. PRICHARD *Roaring Nineties* 152 Sometimes a successful bettor twisted, after backing heads, and backed tails. 'Catching the grouter', that was called. But a grouter bettor could only have one or two bets a night. **1949** L. GLASSOP *Lucky Palmer* 174 A real grouter bet, gents. . . Any tailie who missed out on that run of heads can come in on the grouter now. **1963** J. POLLARD *Austral. Surfrider* 53 The man closest to the peak of the wave has the right of way. He is in the best position to take it, so give him a go. Too often there is someone 'coming in on the grouter', the bloke on the 'slop' trying to steal your wave. **1965** L. GLASSOP *We were Rats* (ed. 3) 19 'O.K., Spike. Only I gotta have the blonde, see? You take the chance on her cobber.' 'Suits me, Mick. Ya never know. I might come in on the grouter.' **1968** S. GORE *Holy Smoke* 51 He decides he'll run a grouter on the Lord, and took his bait. **1976** L.R.M. HUNTER *Woodline* 65 Scotty has managed to 'come in on the grouter'; with a borrowed pound he is now betting tails although he had not bet on any one of the previous throws. **1977** R. BEILBY *Gunner* 296 By coming in on the grouter he had augmented the remaining pound of the two Whiteside had given him. **1977** D. STUART *Drought Foal* 142 That bloody grouter bettor came in on the seventh pair of heads.

grouter, *v.* [f. prec.] *trans.* To acquire (something) fortuitously; to take advantage of (a situation, etc.); see quot. 1967.

1918 G.C. COOPER Diary 24 Feb., Drew rations, also two lots of Canteen; 'groutered' some NZ Canteen Stores. **1967** *Kings Cross Whisper* (Sydney) xxxv. 6/1 *Grouter*, to come in on the tail end of a game of chance and clean up.

grow, *v. Aboriginal English.* In the phr. **to grow** (someone) **up,** to bring up; to rear.

1938 V.E. TURNER *Good Fella Missus* 91 You won't . . leave me?. . . You growed me up. **1961** W.E. HARNEY *Grief, Gaiety and Aborigines* 16 He recounted in his soft drawl how the manager had 'grown up' a copper-skinned native girl. **1962** D. LOCKWOOD *I, Aboriginal* 35 If I thought that my testing time was now ended I was soon disillusioned. Marbunggu, tribally appointed to 'grow me up' like a Christian Godfather, laid down the law. **1963** HARNEY & LOCKWOOD *Shady Tree* 95 More than sixty years ago at Charters Towers, while my mother toiled to keep the family going, it was Beattie who became responsible for me and, as the natives say, 'grew me up'. **1975** J.P. ROBERTS *Mapoon Story* i. 7 My father reared Jerry's father. . . My father grew him up. **1977** J. & P. READ View of Past 5 Apr. (1978) 249 (typescript) That's all, my old boss. He grow me up. Poor feller, my old boss.

Hence **grower-up** *n.*

1943 W.E. HARNEY *Taboo* 155 Accordingly he claimed Sarah. . . Claimed her by the right of a feeder, or as the natives say, a 'grower up'.

grub. WITCHETTY 2.

1793 J. HUNTER *Hist. Jrnl. Trans. Port Jackson* 516 The natives were known to eat a grub which is found in the small gum-tree. **1805** J.H. TUCKEY *Acct. Voyage to Establish Colony Port Phillip* 180 That they scruple not to eat lizards and grubs, as well as a very large worm found in the gum-trees, we had ocular demonstration. **1844** D.G. BROCK Jrnl. 30 Sept. 26 This is used as a spade—to throw away the soil from beneath trees, to discover the Holes formed by . . a large white colored grub—which grub is highly esteemed . . and if the Native is hungry he does not wait to boil it but down it goes all alive and writhing. **1852** J. MORGAN *Life & Adventures W. Buckley* 34 They brought with them several large fat grubs, which they found buried in decayed trees, and more particularly about the roots. **1894** A.F. CALVERT *Aborigines W.A.* 28 Grubs, which are extremely palatable, are procured from the grass-tree; and likewise in an excrescence of the wattle tree. They are eaten either raw or roasted, but seem to be greatly improved by cooking. I am told they have a nut-like flavour. **1955** F. LANE *Patrol to Kimberleys* 214 The blacks prefer bush tucker—lizards, snakes, etc. Grubs are eaten raw; other foods are merely scorched in hot ashes. For the most part, the aborigines like their meat underdone.

grudge match. [Cf. Br. *grudge fight* (see OEDS *grudge, sb.* 6.).] A game or contest in which there is bitterness or personal antipathy between the opponents. Also in shortened form, as **grudgie.**

1973 P. McKenna *My World of Football* 173 Imagine the interest that would be injected into Sydney football if Collingwood and Richmond played one of their annual 'grudge matches'—as part of the normal season on the Trumper Oval. **1973** *Kings Cross Whisper* (Sydney) clii. 4/2 To see the stoush which this day is between Easts an' Saints and the beats have been tellin' everybody . . that the game's a 'grudgie' because one a Easts' lot was found in bed with one of the Saints' wives. **1985** *Good Weekend* (Sydney) 20 Apr. 8/2 They were both with the Storemen and Packers. Now they go to grudge matches between their football teams.

gruie /'grui/. [a. Kamilaroi *garui.*] *Emu apple* (a), see Emu *n.*[1] 3. Formerly also as **gruie-colaine,** a compound formed from the Kamilaroi and Wiradhuri names (see Colane).

1888 *Proc. Linnean Soc. N.S.W.* III. 534 *Owenia acidula* . . Aboriginal names are . . 'Gruie-Colaine', [etc.]. **1889** J.H. Maiden *Useful Native Plants Aust.* 49 'Gruie-Colaine.' The sub-acid fruit of this tree relieves thirst. It is eaten both by colonists and aboriginals, and is of the size of a small nectarine. **1897** K.L. Parker *Austral. Legendary Tales* 16 Red is the fruit of the grooees. **1912** *Emu* XII. 74 Passed several beautiful gruie or Emu apple trees. **1931** M. Terry *Hidden Wealth & Hiding People* 325 We came across a clump of trees called 'grooi' or 'colain', the only specimens known to local people as existent in the Kimberleys but identical with others in Queensland. **1938** C.T. White *Princ. Bot. Qld. Farmers* 217 Associated with the various species of Wattles and beelah are other trees such as . . Emu Apple or Gruie.

grunter. [Spec. use of *grunter* any fish that makes a grunting noise.] Any of many fish of the fam. Teraponidae, usu. fresh-water species, incl. *Bidyanus bidyanus* (see *silver perch* Silver 1) and the spangled grunter *Leiopotherapon unicolor*, widespread in Aust.

1906 D.G. Stead *Fishes of Aust.* 123 The Silver Perch . . in many parts of western New South Wales . . is familiarly-known as 'Grunter'. **1944** J. Devanny *By Tropic Sea & Jungle* 73 A grunter weighing a pound and a half. **1951** T.C. Roughley *Fish & Fisheries Aust.* 149 The silver perch . . has frequently been referred to as 'grunter' because of the grunting noise it makes when captured. **1969** J. Pollard *Austral. & N.Z. Fishing* 289 Grunter . . take their name from the peculiar internal noises they make when breathing and it is by this noise rather than by scientific reasoning that they are grouped. They have defied attempts to classify them. Most grunter are perch. **1971** P. Bodeker *Sandgropers' Trail* 86 We saw orange spotted grunter perch. **1973** V. Serventy *Desert Walkabout* 100 These fish [*sc.* spangled perch] are . . known as grunters because of the noise they can make with their swim bladders. **1982** R. Ellis *Bush Safari* 85 The spangled grunter, an edible fish that grows up to 15 centimetres long.

guana *Obs.* Also **guaner, guano.** [Aphetic form of *iguana.*] Goanna 1.

1699 W. Dampier *New Voyage round World* (1703) III. 124, I think my Stomach would scarce have serv'd to venture upon these *N. Holland* Guano's, both the Looks and the Smell of them being so offensive. **1786** *Hist. Narr. Discovery New Holland & N.S.W.* 10 The guana of New Holland. **1827** P. Cunningham *Two Yrs. in N.S.W.* I. 330 Our *guanas* are generally of a dirty brown colour, and seldom exceed four feet long. **1839** W.H. Leigh *Reconnoitering Voyages* 95, I must, I think be very hungry indeed before I should relish a guano. **1842** *Hunter River Gaz.* 8 Jan. 3/4 There is a woman here who is possessed of a very large guana, which she has so far succeeded in taming that it leaves her residence in the morning and returns in the evening with the greatest regularity. **1847** E.W. Landor *Bushman* 157 The whole country swarms with lizards . . but the most common are the Iguana, or Guana. **1859** H. Kingsley *Recoll. Geoffry Hamlyn* II. 45 Well, I've eaten guaners myself. **1861** 'Old Bushman' *Bush Wanderings* 205 The guano is a large species of tree-lizard. **1872** Mrs E. Millett *Austral. Parsonage* 180 The lizard which the colonists call the 'bob-tailed' guana, or in colonial pronunciation 'gew-anna'. **1880** J.B. Stevenson *Seven Yrs. Austral. Bush* 42 We had a comical adventure with a large iguana, or, as they are shortly called, 'guana. **1896** A. Mackay *Austral. Agriculturist* (rev. ed.) 214 Poultry in this country have many enemies, including . . guanos.

guard-fish: see Garfish.

gub. Also **gubb.** Abbrev. of Gubba.

1971 K. Gilbert *End of Dreamtime* 9 They called me, Kalari, a 'Pommy' and 'Gub', laughed at my speaking, laughed when I tried to join in their song and dance. **1976** T. Shepherd *Children of Blindness* 76 He had . . scorned and verbally lacerated Pete for wanting to become a white man, a Gub, as he sneeringly referred to them. **1977** K. Gilbert *Living Black* 91 If the black women have a relationship with a gub, we get shot down by the rest of the blacks so it's very hard for them to relate to anybody else except black men. **1978** M. Kamien *Dark People of Bourke* 5 There is some dispute among Aborigines and white Aboriginologists as to the exact derivation of the word 'Gub'. Some Aborigines said that it came from 'government' and others that it came from 'garbage'. It is widely used by Aborigines throughout New South Wales as a collective term for whites. Like the white Australian vernacular 'bastard' its use covers a wide emotional spectrum, from hatred to affection. **1981** P. Corris *White Meat* 100 You said your name was Tickener mate. Now it's Hardy. We don't like gubbs who hang around bullshitting us. **1984** P. Read *Down there with me on Cowra Mission* 135 Now even can't get down to the place because the gubbs have moved in with them white goats and . . they've got twelve foot high fences.

gubba. [Of unknown origin.] Also **gubbah, gubbar, gubber.** A name given by Aborigines to a white person.

[**1949** B. O'Reilly *Green Mountains* 72 She told uncanny tales drawn from aboriginal lore of ghosts and devils, which came under the general heading of 'gubba'. When telling her gubba stories, she talked deep down in her throat.] **1963** *Bulletin* (Sydney) 13 Apr. 8/1 Any aborigine living in New South Wales who is over the age of 18 can go into a hotel and have a drink like any 'gubbar' (white man). **1971** K. Gilbert *End of Dreamtime* 7 Now we wander crying and the gubbahs go on lying:- O Land of hope and glory! Southern stronghold of the free! **1975** *Bulletin* (Sydney) 18 Jan. 44/3 He makes him repulsive, frightening, and human, putting one of our stereotypes live on stage for probably the first time—our own white trash, the black man's gubba. **1975** R.J. Merritt *Cake Man* (1978) 12 A gubba never had a social welfare cheque in his whole life. 'Gubba', that's Kuri lingo for whitefella. **1977** K. Gilbert *Living Black* 161 We go to school, that means the gubbah is trying to wipe out the tribal law. **1983** *Sydney Morning Herald* 14 Feb. 7/8 There are two Aboriginal words for the races in Moree. One is 'murri', an Aboriginal word for themselves, which is quite acceptable. The other, for whites, is 'gubber', which is derogatory.

gudgeon. [Transf. use of *gudgeon* a fish of the genus *Gobius.*] A small fish of any of several genera of marine, estuarine, or fresh-water fish of the fam. Eleotridae.

1793 W. Tench *Compl. Acct. Settlement* 176, I shall not pretend to enumerate the variety of fish which are found; they are seen from a whale to a gudgeon. **1832** *W. Austral. Colonial News* (Perth) 28 July 4 Talking Colonial Politics and fishing for—*Gudgeon.* **1878** R.B. Smyth *Aborigines of Vic.* I. 203 Amongst the fish commonly taken by the blacks are . . the gudgeon or trout of colonists (*Galaxias ocellatus* and *G. attenuatus*). **1906** D.G. Stead *Fishes of Aust.* 184 The simple and convenient term 'Gudgeon' is made to apply to the whole of the known species—as well as, I am sorry to add, several others of a totally different character, which have no right to the name whatever. **1974** L. Wedlick *Sporting Fish* 19 The river gudgeon found in the Murray River is often confused by anglers with the young Murray cod.

guernsey. [Spec. use of *guernsey* 'thick, knitted, closely fitting vest or shirt, generally made of blue wool, worn by seamen': see OED(S 2 a.]

1. *Obs.* A kind of shirt, esp. as worn by a gold-miner.

1850 *Monthly Almanac* (Adelaide) 9 In their place appear the sober Guernsey—the humble moleskin—the strong fossil shaped colonial Blucher. **1852** F. Lancelott *Aust. as it Is* I. 140 The usual male attire is a pair of common slop trowsers, a blue guernsey . . a broad-brimmed cabbage-tree hat. **1888** G.O. Preshaw *Banking under Difficulties* 8 The head of the house in Highland bonnet, blue guernsey, long boots. **1891** C.H. Chambers *Thumb-Nail Sketches Austral. Life* 214 McGee darted to the wagon, returning presently, guernsey, breeches, and boots his sole attire. **1892** 'Mrs A. Macleod' *Silent Sea* I. 288 Well, and he left all that behind him, and ran away for what? To scrape dirt underground till his guernsey pours over wid sweat.

2. A football jersey, esp. the (usu.) sleeveless shirt worn by an Australian National Football player. Also **football guernsey.**

1925 *Bulletin* (Sydney) 30 Apr. 22/4 The majority was with an urchin who 'wasn't takin' any chance with a snake in a football guernsey'. **1945** *Aust. Week-End Bk.* 43 His football guernsey isn't striped so darkly. **1958** E.O. Schlunke *Village Hampden* 211 The women knit the players' guernseys. **1969** A. Hopgood *And Big Men Fly* 12 Drop-kick your way to fame and fortune in number 10 guernsey. **1973** K. Dunstan *Sports* 228 On this cushion was the most cherished article in all Collingwood—the No. 1 black and white Collingwood guernsey. **1975** T. Schurmann *Shop!* 13 He should have been wearing a Pinchinilla guernsey, as he was certainly on their side. **1978** *Overland* lxxii. 16, I left it in the tram. . . Had me guernsey, boots and jockstrap in it. Sheila clippie found it.

3. In the phr. **to get** (or **to be given**) **a** (or **the**) **guernsey,** to win selection (for a team); *fig.* to win selection, recognition, or approbation.

1918 E.J. Rule *Jacka's Mob* 26 Sept. (1933) 319, I was told I'd be given a 'guernsey' this time in the line, which was welcome news; I'd missed the 8 August show, and did not want to miss this one. *c* **1920** 'Hamer' *Search for Bonzer Tart* 72 The infamous conduct of the referee awarding a penalty against the Eastern Glebes roused him once more. 'Yah! Get a guernsey!' he yelled disgustedly. **1957** D. Whitington *Treasure upon Earth* 177 The executive won't give me a guernsey for the Senate. **1959** J. Wynnum *Down Hatch* 112 Looks like this Tribal in Sydney Harbour gets the guernsey. **1975** *Bulletin* (Sydney) 22 Feb. 12/1 Doug was the next man on the NSW Liberal Country Party ticket . . and if everything goes according to the rules . . then he should be the one to get the guernsey for Canberra. **1978** J. Hepworth *His Bk.* 175 The papers weren't going to give Jack Lang a guernsey, no matter how brilliant he might be. **1979** *Age* (Melbourne) 2 July 9/2 'To get a guernsey'. . . Originally it was a great honour to be selected for a VFL team. Now it means to be invited, selected or included in just about anything. **1980** I. Warden *Worst Of* 45 John Stephenson chose a verse entirely preoccupied with lamentation in which the alleged solaces of faith do not get a guernsey.

Guildford grass. [f. the name of a town in W.A. (see quot. 1948).] The S. African perennial herb *Romulea rosea* (fam. Iridaceae) naturalized in s. Aust. See also *onion grass* Onion 1.

1909 A.J. Ewart *Weeds* 58 *Romulea* . . *cruciata* . . The Guildford or Onion Grass. **1948** *Bulletin* (Sydney) 26 May 22/1 Early in Westralia's history a well-meaning pastoralist introduced . . Guilford grass—the pest takes its name from the district in which it first appeared. **1978** L. White *Memories of Childhood* 7 The delicate pink flowers of guildford grass clustered about my mother's fingers.

guinea-flower. [See quot. 1968.] Any of many plants of the large, chiefly Austral. genus *Hibbertia* (fam. Dilleniaceae) of all States, bearing showy, usu. gold or yellow, flowers. Also *attrib.*

1923 *Census Plants Vic.* (Field Naturalists' Club Vic.) 45 *Hibbertia densiflora* . . Silky Guinea-flower. **1933** C.W. Peck *Austral. Legends* (ed. 2) 200 A tangle of Hibbertia, or Guinea-flower vine. **1968** G.R. Cochrane et al. *Flowers & Plants Vic.* 28 There is no brighter display on Australian heathlands than that provided by the various guinea-flowers, popularly so called from their flat, regular, golden blooms. **1981** *Bulletin* (Sydney) 7 July 55/3 One by one they died . . even the hibbertia, or guinea flowers, which, normally, you couldn't kill with an axe.

guiver, var. Guyver *n.*

Gulf.

a. Used *attrib.* with reference to the hinterland of the Gulf of Carpentaria, esp. in the Comb. **Gulf Country.**

1867 *Australasian* (Melbourne) 3 Aug. 134/5 It is the unanimous opinion of the squatters that this year's lambing is the best they have had since the Gulf country was first opened. **1872** *Punch Staff Papers* 62 The Gulf country, and the Great Australian Bight . . are fertile paradises compared to the district between Albany and Perth. **1893** E. Favenc *Last of Six Tales* 50 The new super. was a young man from the South, and Tranter was an old Gulf hand. **1917** *Bulletin* (Sydney) 26 Apr. 24/1 The Gulf disease which horses suffer from in Carpentaria is also prevalent in Kimberley (W.A.). **1920** J.N. Macintyre *White Aust.* 196 There is an old saying, and a true one, 'Once a Gulfman, always a Gulfman'. **1927** M.H. Ellis *Long Lead* 17 Out of rations in the Gulf country. **1942** H.H. Peck *Mem. Stockman* 125 Farther out, right up to the gulf country. **1951** J. Devanny *Travels N. Qld.* 7 The extent of country reticulated by these rivers is enormous and generally known as the Gulf Country. **1975** R. Edwards *Austral. Traditional Bush Crafts* 93 The Gulf knot is used for attaching reins to the bit without the use of a buckle. In north-west Australia it is known as a Kimberley knot. **1978** C. Ruhen *Crocodile* 10 The stationmaster wistfully recalled the time of the great desert drives when the cattle herds of two thousand or more were raced down over the Carpentaria gulflands.

b. Gulf fever, malaria.

1901 P.D. Lorimer *Songs & Verses* 13 The Gulf fever, as it is called, is of a very malignant character. **1903** E. Palmer *Early Days N. Qld.* 73 Poor Walker died of Gulf fever in 1866, at a miserable shanty on the Leichhardt River. **1911** E.J. Brady *King's Caravan* 269 He was not the only man I met coming down from the North to shake off Gulf fever.

Hence **Gulfer** *n.*, see quot. 1977; **Gulfite** *n.*, one who lives in the Gulf Country.

1977 B. Scott *My Uncle Arch* 55 It seems that once every eight years this cloud comes down from Arnhem Land and rains on them from a very great height. They call this cloud the Gulfer out there, because it isn't so much a cloud as part of the Gulf of Carpentaria, and it brings all its contents with it. You've heard of those fishes that rain out of the sky in Western Queensland haven't you? Well, these are normally only the fringe of the **Gulfer**. The real middle of it has dugongs, turtles, and all kinds of other wildlife. **1963** *N. Austral. Monthly* Dec. 31/1 When I came to the Gulf Country to take up work . . I was to become a permanent '**Gulfite**'. **1976** B. Norman *Bush Pilot* 203 It isn't often that the womenfolk on the stations get together for a talk about the things that women talk about, but when they do they make up for lost time. And the Gulfites seem to be particularly good at it.

gully. [Extended use of *gully* ravine, small gorge: see OED(S *sb.*[1] 2.]

1. a. A ravine; an eroded watercourse; an elongated water-worn depression; a (small) valley. See also *fern-gully*, Fern 2. Also *attrib.*

1798 J. Hunter *Hist. Jrnl. Trans. Port Jackson* 525 They came to a hollow, in which they found some very good water; here they stopped near an hour: after passing this gully, and a rocky piece of ground, the soil grew better. **1820** J. Oxley *Jrnls. Two Exped. N.S.W.* 64 Small holes of water were found in almost every gully. **1827** *Monitor* (Sydney) 26 June 472/2 These are the men who detected and secured the infamous cattle-stealers and bushrangers, 150 miles beyond Abercromby's River, (which is 60 miles from Bathurst) *playing at cards, on a sheet of bark, in a Gulley*! **1827** P.P. King *Narr. Survey Intertropical & Western Coasts* I. 195 In the gullies, Mr Cunningham reaped an excellent harvest, both of seeds and plants. **1833** C. Sturt *Two Exped. Interior Southern Aust.* II. 236 The sides of the hills became more broken, and valleys, or gullies, more properly speaking, very numerous. **1840** *S. Austral. Rec.* (London) 10 Oct. 238 In the valleys (or gullies as they are called here) there is very good pasturage for cattle or sheep. **1853** A. Mackay *Great Gold Field* 28 The word 'gully' seems to be a general term for all hollows or valleys from the slightest perceptible undulation to the deepest ravine. **1855** W. Howitt *Land, Labor & Gold* II. 239 A gully, to my mind, is a deep, narrow ravine torn out by a watercourse. But here the broadest and smoothest valleys, or any dimple amongst the hills, is a gully; broad levels, which we should call meadows or plains, are flats. **1859** H. Kingsley *Recoll. Geoffry Hamlyn* II. 28, I crossed the river. A gully, deep at first, but getting rapidly shallower. **1871** 'Iota' *Kooroona* 40 'What is a gully?' enquired Edith. 'A very ugly name for a valley or a ravine; for both are called gullies here, indiscriminately.' **1886** J.F. Conigrave *S.A.* 80 The market gardens range from three or four acres in the rich peaty bottoms of gullies up to thirty, and even fifty acres. **1887** A. Nicols *Wild Life & Adventure* 139 A rough gully, containing patches of thick scrub, where the game could be completely surrounded. **1899** *Bulletin* (Sydney) 21 Jan. (Red Page), We two bullocked in a rough, wet gully for a fortnight—felling trees, making a track for the bullocks, and 'jacking' logs to it over stumps and boulders. **1918** H. Dinning *Byways on Service* 89 Should Gallipoli be garrisoned, Australian terms, not to be found in the dictionary, will stick; scrubs, creeks, and gullies, dignified with the names of heroes who commanded there, will abound. **1921** *Bulletin* (Sydney) 10 Mar. 22/3 A recipe for making a gully dam. **1935** F. Birtles *Battle Fronts Outback* 169 Little groups were scattered about down in their quiet gullies, busily painting themselves and their boomerangs. **1948** F. Clune *Wild Colonial Boys* p. xix, Rounding up wild cattle . . and droved 'em up hill and down gully, through creek and over plain. **1960** *Bulletin* (Sydney) 16 Mar. 19/3 The paling-splitter . . may be flushed in an odd gully or two . . catering for a Macquarie Street farmer with some fancy bull-oak shingles. **1966** G.W. Turner *Eng. Lang. in Aust. & N.Z.* 57 The word *valley* has fallen from use in Australia and . . is replaced by *gully*. **1981** K.M. Old et al. *Eucalypt Dieback* 11 Hopkins . . singled out several diebacks which were insufficiently studied. These included high altitude dieback, gully dieback and regrowth dieback, all located in Tasmania.

b. *fig.*

1975 *Nat. Times* (Sydney) 30 June 26/1 Wheeler has crossed a few dry gullies in his career. **1977** V. Priddle *Larry & Jack* 100 There must be a showdown and I know as an old man who has been up plenty of dry gullies, these boys with a fair go, will belt anyone who has drunk beer in that bloke's bar. **1982** *Bulletin* (Sydney) 6 Apr. 80/3 'Life is interesting,' he muses. 'I've crossed a few dry gullies in my time.'

2. a. *spec.* A gully in which alluvial gold is sought.

1852 *Austral. Gold Digger's Monthly Mag.* ii. 38 The gold of the Californian gulches and Australian gullies is not found in veins. **1852** J. Bonwick *Notes of Gold Digger* 17 Occasionally a rush gives animation to a gully. **1853** A. Mackay *Great Gold Field* 4 The diggings are all in the hollows of undulating table lands called there 'gullies'. **1853** J. Sherer *Gold Finder Aust.* 176 The gold is found principally in what they call gullies, like as if there had been some running water in them at some time. **1855** G.H. Wathen *Golden Colony* 184 At the Diggings every gully and 'flat' was infested with 'sly grog-tents'. **1872** 'Quiris' *Port Darwin* 10 In this gully I obtained the best prospect. **1862** J.A. Patterson *Gold Fields Vic.* 66 The gullies at the head of Kangaroo Flat have still gold to be got out. . . About them linger several old 'fossickers'. **1870** *Sydney Morning Herald* 4 July 2/4 The gullies, where our alluvial workings are situated, are in such a miry and swampy state that it is dangerous to work under ground, and shafts in spite of slabbing are insecure. **1892** T. Bracken *Dear Old Bendigo* 16 Old gullies gaped, and worked-out claims appeared in all their mullocky ugliness. **1926** L.C.E. Gee *Bush Tracks & Gold Fields* 64 Along the edge of the gully and dotted here and there, curious old tin shanties, and at long intervals an old man working a shaker. **1975** *Southerly* ii. 195 The sides of the gully had a mined-over look, resembling fresh mullock heaps.

b. *fig.*

1872 'Demonax' *Mysteries & Miseries* 17 He is rich. Unlike the run of typos, his 'case' is full, and he's got in a good 'gully'.

gully-rake, *v.*

1. *intr.* To muster unbranded cattle from country not readily accessible (see quot. 1900); to appropriate illegally cattle so mustered. Chiefly as *vbl. n.*

1847 A. Harris *Settlers & Convicts* (1953) 144 Gully-raking . . derives its name from the circumstance of cattle straying away . . and forming wild herds which chiefly congregate down in the wild grassy gullies of the mountains. . . The gully-rakers eventually driving them out and branding all the young ones, and any others they can manage, with their own brands. **1857** F. de B. Cooper *Wild Adventures* 104 He was stock-keeping in that quarter, and was rather giving [*sic*] to 'gully raking'. . . He ran in three bullocks belonging to a neighbouring squatter, and clapt his brand on the top of the other so as to efface it. **1874** *Illustr. Sydney News* 30 Jan. 11/1 My rascally mate . . had been doing a bit of 'gully-raking'—the genteel term for cattle-stealing. **1900** T. Major *Leaves from Squatter's Note Bk.* 11 A large number of wild cattle were to be found in the scrubby ranges, and could only be yarded by gully-raking. **1950** G.M. Farwell *Land of Mirage* 167 The plain fact about rustling—as they call cattle-lifting, poddy-dodging, or gully-raking over the other side—is that after all it is only droving, with an extra note of gambling and suspense. **1961** M. Kiddle *Men of Yesterday* 66 A certain amount of gully-raking and cattle-duffing—when the brands were 'duffed' by a new one being superimposed on the first—was considered normal colonial practice. **1976** B. Scott *Complete Bk. Austral. Folk Lore* 274 Her father, who was absent with his gully-raking sons, Was busy duffing cattle on the nearest squatters' runs.

2. *Gold-mining. intr.* To search for surface gold. Also as *vbl. n.*

1881 J.C.F. Johnson *To Mount Browne & Back* 21 The principal work done on it . . has been mere gully-raking or surfacing in the bed of the creek. **1932** I.L. Idriess *Prospecting for Gold* 3 Where men are 'gully raking' in the ranges. **1947** F. Clune *Roaming around Aust.* 177 Most of the gold . . was got in patches, by 'gully-raking', that is, on the surface. **1967** I.L. Idriess *Opals & Sapphires* 67 The fossicker goes 'gully-raking' into old gullies and worked-out creeks, and into old workings.

gully-raker. *Obs.* [f. prec.]

1. A cattle-thief; one who engages in gully-raking.

1840 *Colonist* (Sydney) 17 Oct. 3/1 The slanderous expressions used . . were the epithets of 'gulley-raker' and 'cattle-stealer'. **1845** *Atlas* (Sydney) I. 241/2 The security enjoyed in the absence of any kind of roads, by gully-rakers, bushrangers *et hoc genus omne*. **1854** S. Sidney *Gallops & Gossips* 74 Some of the Highland black cattle imported by the Australian Company, after being driven off by a party of Gully Rakers (cattle stealers), had escaped into the mountains and turned quite wild. **1874** *Illustr. Sydney News* 30 Jan. 3/1 Mr Cooper seems to be the only member of the Assembly whose knowledge of free selectors is so limited as to induce a belief that none but cattle-duffers and gully-rakers can join their ranks. **1895** *Bulletin* (Sydney) 21 Dec. 27/4 To strongholds where the wild mobs hide The gully-rakers go. **1919** *Ibid.* 18 Sept. 20/1 At Kiandra (N.S.W.) I once lobbed into the camp of a gully-raker. **1944** *Ibid.* 22 Nov. 12/3, I was having some corned mutton and damper at an old gully-raker's camp. **1950** G.M. Farwell *Land of Mirage* 171 Many a man who stuck up a gold escort or a Cobb & Co. coach had started out as a mere gully-raker, putting his brand on scrubbers, or cross-branding in another man's yard.

2. A stockwhip.

1873 *Illustr. Sydney News* 5 July 11/1 At first crack of the stockman's 'gully-raker', as his long-thonged whip is termed, the cattle fly in all directions. **1881** A.C. Grant *Bush-Life Qld.* I. 40 The driver appealing occasionally to some bullock or other by name, following up his admonition by a sweeping cut of his 'gully-raker', and a report like a musket-shot. **1913** W.K. Harris *Outback in Aust.* 85 The stockwhip . . has undergone many alterations of taste and fashion . . from the redoubtable old 'gully raker' to the exaggerated thong affixed to a hunting crop. **1945** E. Mitchell *Speak to Earth* 71 The scrub in the gullies was impenetrable and they used a great heavy stockwhip called a 'gully-raker'.

gum, *n.* and *attrib.*

A. *n.*

1. Abbrev. of Gum tree 1.

1805 *Sydney Gaz.* 16 June, With my dog and my gun to the forest I fly, Where in stately confusion rich gums sweep the sky. **1814** *HRA* (1916) 1st Ser. VIII. 169 Thinly wooded with small Gums. **1819** W.C. Wentworth *Statistical, Hist., & Pol. Descr. N.S.W.* 46 Full sized gums and ironbarks . . are the usual timber. **1824** *Hobart Town Gaz.* 1 Oct., Colonial Timber . . Gum, for heavy buildings. Stringy Bark, for general work. **1832** *Colonial Times* (Hobart) 21 Mar., The felled timber consisted of . . gum and apple tree, so that it was a perfectly mixed forest. **1838** *S. Austral. Rec.* (London) 11 July 75 There are three trees of great use, the gum, pine, and stringy bark. **1847** *Moreton Bay Courier* 22 May 2/2 The country was wretched, presenting all the usual characteristics of coast country—grass-tree, gum, tea-tree scrubs, etc. **1851** *Bell's Life in Sydney* 1 Mar. 1/4 A forest of the monotonous, shadeless gum. **1864** *Sydney Punch* 22 Oct. 170/2 Here are grisly gums. **1878** *Illustr. Australian News* (Melbourne) Sept. 154/1 What the oak and the elm are to the Briton the gum and the wattle are to the Australian. **1898** *Proc. Linnean Soc. N.S.W.* XXIII. 786 *Eucalyptus pilularis* . . Before the term 'Gum' was restricted to those Eucalypts which have smooth or nearly smooth bark, it was called 'Black-butted Gum'. **1915** *Forestry Question in N.S.W.* (Austral. Forest League) 3 The species popularly termed 'gums' are of great economic importance in Australia and abroad. **1942** C.H. GRATTAN *Introducing Aust.* 31 All the eucalyptus trees are loosely called 'gums'. **1948** B. CRONIN *How runs Road* 68 We know them all affectionately as 'gums', albeit the botanists admit the name only to those species whose bark on trunk and branches is smooth to the base. **1955** F. LANE *Patrol to Kimberleys* 41 There are three hundred and sixty-five varieties of gum—one for every day in the year. **1966** B. BEAVER *You can't come Back* 40 Nothing but gums for miles both sides of the line. **1970** *Meanjin* 56 The tangle of gums and scrub crowded into almond trees and shrubs that remained from a formal garden. **1974** A. BUZO *Coralie Lansdowne says No* 61, I . . sat on the beach and looked at the outline, the rocks and gums.

2. With distinguishing epithet, as **apple, blue, brittle, cabbage, cider, creek, desert, flooded, flowering, fluted, forest red, ghost, grey, lemon-scented, manna, mountain, Murray red, poplar, red, ribbon, river, rose, salmon, scarlet, scribbly, shining, snappy, snow, spotted, Tingaringy, water, white, whitewash, yellow, York,** etc.: see under first element.

B. 1. *attrib.*

1827 *Tasmanian* (Hobart) 1 Nov. 3 Manifest of the cargo on board the ship Harvey . . 86 pieces cedar, 256 gum planks. **1839** W.H. LEIGH *Reconnoitering Voyages* 92 The natives ascend the trees by means of a hardened gum stick, which they thrust into the bark and hold on by it. **1841** *Port Phillip Patriot* 15 Mar. 4/3 Here and there patches of the gum scrub shewed themselves. **1844** *Colonial Times* (Hobart) 28 May, On Sale . . Dry She Oak and Gum Wood. **1847** G.F. ANGAS *Savage Life & Scenes* I. 49 The gum bushes, of which this scrub is composed, were from 3 to 10 or 12 feet high, and grow close together, forming one vast copse; and the soil is little better than a loose light sand. **1856** J. BONWICK *Bushrangers* 85 The hills are covered with enormous Gum and Stringy bark forests. **1862** J.M. STUART *Explorations in Aust.* 28 May (1865) 355 Followed them for three miles, crossing a gum and grass plain. **1872** 'RESIDENT' *Glimpses Life Vic.* 36 Numbers of tall straight gum-saplings grew close at hand. **1880** J.B. STEVENSON *Seven Yrs. Austral. Bush* 36 A few sheets of gum bark laid upon some saplings. **1882** *Three L's* 135 Three or four stools made out of gum slabs. **1891** H. NISBET *Colonial Tramp* I. 206 The gum-trunks are very massive. **1926** L.C.E. GEE *Bush Tracks & Gold Fields* 73 An awning, supported by gum sticks. **1934** W.A. OSBORNE *Visitor to Aust.* 66 Joists made of gum hardwood are assured of a long life. **1952** J.R. SKEMP *Memories Myrtle Bank* 70 The hill at the back of the hut . . was allowed to grow up again in 'gum-boughs' as the bushmen always call young eucalypts. **1968** D. O'GRADY *Bottle of Sandwiches* 36 We were waiting in an old hollow gum-stump. **1969** D. CUSACK *Half-Burnt Tree* 46 Hungry for the meat that they would grill over a fire of gumwood that smelt like incense.

2. Comb. **gum flat, forest.**

1846 *Moreton Bay Courier* 28 Nov. 3/2 There are also numerous apple-tree and **gum flats.** **1860** J.M. STUART *Explorations in Aust.* 13 May (1865) 179 It is a small narrow gum flat which receives the drainage from this low range. **1899** *Western Champion* (Barcaldine) 25 July 3/2 He spun up a blind gully, then over a gum flat, and up a boree spur, on to a spinifex tableland. **1908** W.H. OGILVIE *My Life in Open* 3 Miles and miles of twisted mulga, stony ranges, gum flats, brigalow plains. **1843** J. GOULD *Birds of Aust.* (1848) III. Pl. 12, The thickly-wooded **gum-forests** of the mountain districts. **1855** R. AUSTIN *Jrnl. Interior W.A.* 6 Steering by compass N.E. by E. over open undulating sandy plains, and through gum forest. **1863** J. BONWICK *Wild White Man* 45 Romantic love scenes are not altogether unknown in Gum forests. **1872** 'RESIDENT' *Glimpses Life Vic.* 9 The shores were covered with close gum-forests. **1914** H.M. VAUGHAN *Australasian Wander-Yr.* 18 To get 'bushed' is to become lost in the gum-forests.

3. Special Comb. **gum creek,** a creek bed of drier Aust. (see quot. 1896); **grub** *obs.*, WITCHETTY 2; **nut,** the inedible, woody, seed-bearing capsule of the gum tree; also *attrib.*; **tips** *pl.*, the young, often red, growing shoots of the gum tree.

1860 J.M. STUART *Exploration of Interior* 4 Crossed the bed of a large **gum creek,** but no water. **1875** P.E. WARBURTON *Journey across Western Interior* I. 199 We followed the gum creek through the range and ran it up to its head. Not a drop of water! **1888** W.H. WILLSHIRE *Aborigines of Central Aust.* 4 Alice Springs telegraph station . . is situated on a fine gum creek, the Todd. **1889** E. GILES *Aust. twice Traversed* I. 192 We crossed a kind of dry swamp or water flat, being the end of a gum creek. **1896** B. SPENCER *Rep. Horn Sci. Exped. Central Aust.* I. 74 They gave rise to what have always been termed by the early explorers 'Gum creeks', that is sandy beds which only contain water, if at all, at rare intervals, but along the sides of which grow a line of gum trees (*Eucalyptus rostrata*). **1923** J. ARMOUR *Spell of Inland* 13 In a valley below ran a gum creek, with hundreds of cockatoos swarming among the trees. **1840** T.J. BUCKTON *W.A.* 83 The **gum-grub,** or *grungru*, is by some gastronomists considered a great dainty. **1852** F. LANCELOTT *Aust. as it Is* I. 51 The gum-grub, a milk-white maggot, about 5 inches long, and as thick as a man's forefinger. **1916** M. GIBBS *Gumnut Babies* 4 On all the big Gumtrees there are **Gum-Nut** Babies. **1928** J. POLLARD *Bushland Vagabonds* 48 Other sounds were few—a leaf fluttering down; a gum-nut thudding on the gravel soil. **1958** P. COWAN *Unploughed Land* 176 There were the mudlarks, and he drew her attention to one of their cup-shaped nests fitted to a high bough, like an oversized gum-nut. **1965** L. WALKER *Other Girl* 154 Small things slid in and out under the fallen bark, and a dead gumnut fell. **1979** C. KLEIN *Women of Certain Age* 14 He was the most angelic baby, like a little brown gumnut. **1984** M.K. VAUGHAN *Wombat Stew* 24 Any bush cook knows you can't make a spicy stew without gumnuts. **1942** *Troppo Topics* 21 Dec. 5 With two bottles of beer apiece and plenty of **gumtips.** **1954** J.E. MACDONNELL *Jim Brady* 37 The smell of grass and gum-tips. **1962** E. LANE *Mad as Rabbits* 125 Until I went back to school I picked fresh gumtips every day to put on her grave. **1965** H. ATKINSON *Reckoning* 139 White box posts with saplings nailed to them had once held the shade of a verandah, probably ferns from the creek nearby, laced with branches of gum tips. **1979** E. SMITH *Saddle in Kitchen* 19 Brownish red gumtips . . substituted for flowers and looked attractive in a pair of old brass vases. **1985** *Melbourne Winners Weekly* 11 Nov. 21/2 Young gum tips suck up water from vases quicker than other plants.

gumleaf.

a. The leaf of a gum tree.

1803 *Sydney Gaz.* 21 Aug., An Animal whose species was never before found in the colony . . has a false belly like the opposim [*sic*] and its food consists solely of *gum leaves* in the choice of which it is excessively nice. **1844** L. LEICHHARDT *Jrnl. Overland Exped. Aust.* 20 Nov. (1847) 47 About fifteen pounds of flour were scattered over the ground. We all set to work, to scrape as much of it up as we could, using the dry gum leaves as spoons. **1858** *Bell's Life in Sydney* 16 Oct. 4/3 A lighted torch of gum leaves. **1862** A. POLEHAMPTON *Kangaroo Land* 107, I did not . . feel the want of anything more luxurious than a gumleaf-stuffed mattress. **1926** A.A.B. APSLEY *Amateur Settlers* 166 The fire built up and lit, the sticks, gum-leaves and 'blackboy' for this purpose being, as a rule, dried and laid ready the night before. **1941** *Bulletin* (Sydney) 9 Apr. 16/2 Bushmen working in bull-ant country always light a few gumleaves and twigs on any nearby nests so that they can work undisturbed.

b. A gumleaf used to make musical sounds, serving as a resonator when cupped in the hands and blown upon.

[**1921** G.A. BELL *Under Brigalows* 129 Begged Gore to give the ladies a tune on 'the leaf'.] **1939** *Bulletin* (Sydney) 11 Jan. 19/3 The gumleaf can be added to the jew's-harp as a bush musical instrument that's outdated. **1959** D. NILAND *Big Smoke* 45 Used to play a gumleaf in a vaudeville show that did the country towns. **1964** P. ADAM SMITH *Hear Train Blow* 106 Almost to a man they played the gumleaf, getting a variety of tones and pitches from different leaves. **1965** A.W. UPFIELD *Lure of Bush* 102 The tinkling of the piano, the organ-notes of the accordian, and the tin wailing of the gum-leaf broke into the beautiful melody of 'The Blue Danube'. **1977** D. WHITINGTON *Strive to be Fair* 32 They . . played haunting tunes on gum leaves.

Also **gumleaf band** *n.*

1951 D. COLLINS *Vic.'s my Home Ground* 107 They played for us on their gumleaves, lovingly, with a kind of tenderness. Odd though it may seem, I'd never heard a gumleaf band before. **1954** *Dawn* July 18 (*caption*) Members of the Wallaga Lake Gum Leaf Band at Bega Show. **1957** R.S. PORTEOUS *Brigalow* 38 Night-time in a mustering camp is a time for . . listening to someone playing the mouth-organ or perhaps all joining in with a gum-leaf band.

gummy. [f. *gum* + -Y.]

1. A sheep that has lost or is losing its teeth, esp. a six-year-old sheep.

1871 *Austral. Town & Country Jrnl.* (Sydney) 22 Apr. 487/2 Fat sheep are sent to the butcher; gummies and thin-woolled sheep are culled, and sold to beginners. **1910** H. JACKSON *Broken Fleece* 92, I have seen scores of ewes, not 'gummies' either, cutting fleeces of pocket handkerchief dimensions. **1933** *Bulletin* (Sydney) 6 Sept. 24/1 One young breeding ewe is worth three old 'gummies'. **1948** R.A. PEPPERALL *Emigrant to Aust.* 101 At many sales will be found a line of 'Gummies', aged ewes with broken or uneven teeth which renders proper mastication difficult. **1959** H.G. LAMOND *Sheep Station* 66 Within a few days Jack Campbell was a stock-owner with his own mob of sheep on the road towards his own property. . . 'You've been took down, Boss. . . They're a lot of old gummies what's past breedin' age.' **1961** J.W. JORDAN *Practical Sheep Farming* 21 At six years they may have lost all their teeth. They are then known as 'gummies', and become a liability to the sheep farmer.

2. Any of several sharks of the genus *Mustelus*, esp. the widespread *M. antarcticus* (see quot. 1898). See also SWEET WILLIAM. Also **gummy shark.**

1893 *Funk's Stand. Dict.*, *Gummy*, a galeoid shark. **1898** E.E. MORRIS *Austral Eng.* 185 The word *Gummy* is said to come from the small numerous teeth, arranged like a pavement, so different from the sharp erect teeth of most other sharks. **1922** F.C. GREEN *Fortieth* 19 One man puts forward the claims of a dog he once had that would catch 'gummy' sharks. **1937** *Bulletin* (Sydney) 25 Aug. 21/4 In the last 12 months the consumption of gummy shark has increased in Melbourne by over 200 p.c. . . Of course, you don't ask for gummy fillets. 'Sweet William' is the moniker. **1951** *Ibid.* 18 Apr. 14/2 Fish-café blokes rush the trawlers for gummy-shark. **1963** D.G. STEAD *Sharks & Rays Austral. Seas* 108 The name of Gummy is applied to it because of the rhombic, pavement-like teeth, which . . give the impression of toothless gums. **1967** V.G.C. NORWOOD *Long Haul* 43 A species of small cat-shark called a 'gummy' is as popular in Australia as cod or haddock are in Britain. **1983** *Austral. Fisheries* June 28/1 Continued assessment of the gummy shark fishery indicates the shark stock may not be in such bad shape as previously thought.

3. A toothless person; an old person.

1907 *Truth* (Sydney) 30 June 9/5 In the train—upon the dummy, And across the billiard baize, From the 'kiddie' to the 'gummy', We discuss the toeball craze. **1939** *Bulletin* (Sydney) 19 July 20/2 Located these past 40 years anywhere other than the Cabbage Garden, it makes me wonder to hear present-day Gummies raving about the iniquitous blackberry. **1941** *Ibid.* 17 Sept. 14/1 Old Bill had been a 'gummie' for over eighteen months, and when he collected his uppers-and-lowers from the travelling dentist there was no prouder man in Saltbush.

gumsucker. A nickname for a native-born, non-Aboriginal Australian; a Victorian. Also *attrib.*

[**1827** P. CUNNINGHAM *Two Yrs. in N.S.W.* I. 201 The acacias are the common wattles of this country. . . From their trunks and branches, clear transparent beads of the purest Arabian gum are seen suspended in the dry spring weather, which our young currency bantlings eagerly search after and regale themselves with.] **1840** G.T.W.B. BOYES Diary 2 June, These colonial chaps, Gumsuckers as they are not inappropriately called are my aversion—puffed up with success of his father . . without education or manners. **1849** *Britannia* (Hobart) 7 June 3/1 Convicted mainly on the evidence of the butcher's clerk, a lad of 12, and a smartish specimen of the genus 'gum-sucker'. **1852** W. HOWITT *Land, Labor & Gold* 29 Sept. (1855) I. 26 Bitten twice by the over 'cute 'gum-suckers', as the native Victorians are called. **1865** *Austral. Monthly Mag.* (Melbourne) I. 308 A young lady, vulgarly yclept a 'Gum-sucker', or more euphoneously a 'native lass' arose. **1865** J.F. MORTLOCK *Experiences of Convict* 222 Both Sydney and Melbourne boast of establishments dignified by the term University; being on a par with English public schools. The attempt to educate, as at Cambridge or Oxford, young 'gumsuckers' savours of the absurd. **1872** MRS E. MILLETT *Austral. Parsonage* 168 A sort of sweetmeat or lollipop, whence the *soubriquet* 'gum-suckers', as applied to the young colonists, owing to their habit of never passing a wattle-tree without putting a piece into their mouth. **1883** R.E.N. TWOPENY *Town Life Aust.* 245 A white man born in Australia is a 'colonial', vulgarly a 'gum-sucker'. **1885** *Australasian Printers' Keepsake* 20 Our colonial lads showed their right to the appellation of 'Gum-sucker' by chewing the transparent lumps that depended from the silver wattles. **1892** *Truth* (Sydney) 19 June 4/7 Victorians feel jerky when styled Gumsuckers. **1905** N.F. SPIELVOGEL *Gumsucker on Tramp* 40, I trink two glass Gomsucker beer, I get head top. I trink twenty glass Deutscher beer, not so bad. **1915** *Bulletin* (Sydney) 18 Mar. 13/1 Oh, therefore, I do thank my stars, son of Gumsucker-folk, For that I am, whate'er I am, a mere Australian bloke. **1955** STEWART & KEESING *Austral. Bush Ballads* 298 I've a truthful reputation, boss, as you can well believe, For a native-born gumsucker isn't given to deceive. **1963** *Gumsucker's Gaz.* (Melbourne) July 2 'Gumsucker' was an old nickname by which Victorians were known (it was used a quarter of a century before Victoria became a state). Later it was applied to Tasmanians and Queenslanders, then to Australians as a whole. **1968** A. CLIFFORD *Send her down, Hughie* 51 We learned that Victorians are called gumsuckers.

gum tree. [Spec. use of *gum tree* gum-exuding tree.]

1. a. Any tree of the large, chiefly Austral. genus *Eucalyptus* (fam. Myrtaceae), the dominant tree genus of Austral. forests and woodlands. **b.** *spec.* Any of many species of *Eucalyptus* distinguished by having a smooth bark (see quot. 1860). **c.** Any of several other usu. myrtaceous trees, as *Angophora*. **d.** The wood of any of these trees. See GUM *n.* 1. Also *attrib.*

1789 A. PHILLIP *Voyage to Botany Bay* 107 The gum-tree is highly combustible. **1804** *Sydney Gaz.* 15 July, Those stains were occasioned by the gum tree. **1820** J. OXLEY *Jrnls. Two Exped. N.S.W.* 3 Ill-grown gum and stringy bark trees (all of the eucalyptus genus). **1827** *Monitor* (Sydney) 30 Mar. 363/1 The white majestic Gum trees in our valley, have acquired a sacred character in my regard, as the symbolic pillars of an august temple formed by the Deity! **1827** P. CUNNINGHAM *Two Yrs. in N.S.W.* I. 200 The gum trees are so designated as a body from producing a gummy resinous matter. **1839** H. CAPPER *S.A.* (rev. ed.) 39 The river, its course being indicated by a belt of magnificent gum trees growing along its banks. **1846** *Moreton Bay Courier* 5 Sept. 3/1 The lady and her lover were discovered by the pursuers seated *tête-à-tête* under a gum-tree, enjoying a comfortable pot of the best bohea, and damper. **1852** J. MACGILLIVRAY *Narr. Voyage H.M.S. Rattlesnake* I. 54 The usual monotonous gum-trees. **1860** G. BENNETT *Gatherings of Naturalist* 358 The *Eucalypti*, commonly called Gum-trees by the colonists, have smooth bark, which is shed annually in long strips; among these, the Peppermint . . and others are classed. The species with rough, fixed bark, as the . . Stringy-Bark, Box, and others, are not named gum-trees, but are designated by the above appellations. The *Eucalypti* are thus popularly divided into two distinct classes. **1864** *Illustr. Sydney News* 15 Oct. 7/1 The gaunt bare gum trees . . their stately limbs upon its banks . . present one of the most picturesque and romantic scenes in the Colony. **1877** *Illustr. Austral. News* (Melbourne) 3 Oct. 154/1 In this suburb of Melbourne many of the old gum trees still remain which, within living memory, have afforded shelter to the black aboriginal tribes. **1889** F. CRAWFORD *Native Companion Songster* 21 And tall gum trees shadow The Stockman's last bed. **1902** R.C. PRAED *My Austral. Girlhood* 115 It was in the middle of a big gum-tree paddock—those were 'iron-bark' gums. **1914** H.M. VAUGHAN *Australasian Wander-Yr.* 214 The tall straggling gum-trees are thickly interspersed with the 'cabbage-tree' and the bangalow palms. **1928** B. SPENCER *Wanderings in Wild Aust.* 151 The popular name 'gum tree' was given first to an American tree, quite unlike any Australian 'gum tree'. **1936** *Publicist* (Sydney) i. 16/1 The unsymmetrical gum trees, leaf-edge to the sun. **1938** C.T. WHITE *Princ. Bot. Qld. Farmers* 186 The name 'gum-tree', as applied to Eucalypts generally originated from the amount of dark, gumlike matter that exudes from the tree or is found in cracks in the timber. On exposure to the air it becomes dry and brittle. Such plant juices are known technically as kinos. They are generally impregnated with dark colouring matters, and are used in medicine and in the dyeing and tanning industries. **1947** M. MACLEAN *Drummond of Far West* 15 On some of the larger of these dry water-courses, however, grow stately gum trees, drawing moisture from far below the surface. **1956** N.K. WALLIS *Austral. Timber Handbk.* 2 Over 90% of the timber trees of Australia consist of hardwoods mainly of the genus *Eucalyptus* (gum trees). **1972** *Bulletin* (Sydney) 30 Dec. 41/2 Rod is a 30-year-old junior executive with a clinker brick house in the North Shore gum tree belt, a dissatisfied wife and trouble in the office. **1980** M. DUGAN *Early Dreaming* 11 Stories of picnics in the bush . . and of adventures among the gumtrees.

2. [f. U.S. *up a tree* entrapped, in a 'fix' (see OED *tree, sb.* 7), *'possum up a gum tree* in great difficulties (see OED(S *gum-tree* 2).] In the phr. **up a gum tree,** in another place, another state of mind; 'treed', cornered; in a state of confusion; in a predicament.

1851 J. HENDERSON *Excursions & Adventures N.S.W.* I. 64 My convicts were always drinking rum, I often wished they were up a gum-tree. **1863** R. THERRY *Reminisc. Thirty Yrs. N.S.W. & Vic.* 459 When required on the day of election at the polling-booth, they [*sc.* half-castes] may probably be found up a gum-tree, chasing an opposum, or cooking a kangaroo. **1882** J.I. WATTS *Memories Early Days S.A.* 10 A tame opossum . . was in the habit of indulging in frequent nightly excursions amongst the furniture on the rafters, doubtless fondly imagining itself to be 'up a gum tree'. **1919** A. THOMAS *Moments of Leisure* 88 You might find hit heasy to kid th' Sydney girls up a gum tree. **1945** G. CASEY *Downhill is Easier* 87 They wanted to know whether or not we'd been kidded up a gum-tree, and they shouted and roared a lot about it. **1955** N. PULLIAM *I traveled Lonely Land* 227 My Sydney cobbers were going to fix it so I'd be up a gum tree the first time I opened my mouth in Melbourne. **1960** J. WYNNUM *Pinch of Salt* (1963) 17 They can talk me all the way up a gumtree and down again. **1967** R. DONALDSON et al. *Cane!* 67 He's pissed off to Cairns. That tit he met last year's gottim uppa gumtree. **1982** *Nat. Times* (Sydney) 15 Aug. 12/2 It was not until the analyst sent back his magnificent document . . that we realised we were up the original gum tree.

3. *transf.* Used *attrib.* and derogatorily in various contexts: see quots.

1845 R. HOWITT *Impressions Aust. Felix* 298 If a poor fellow . . is caught trespassing . . on Crown land, he is summoned before the monarch of the Gum-tree-court. **1968** B. MOLONEY *Mem. Abominable Showman* 25 Overseas stage-folk often asked, 'Who's that great comic, Rene, you've got out there, and why don't we see him?' . . There was always the little doubt whether his 'gum-tree flavour' would be appreciated. **1983** *Weekend Austral.* (Sydney) 10 Sept. 5/4 Fifty traditional Australian paintings of a group sometimes irreverently called the Gum Tree School.

gum-wattle. *Obs.* Any of several species of *Acacia* (fam. Mimosaceae) yielding quantities of gum (see quot. 1839).

c **1810** *Trans. Linnean Soc. London* (1827) XV. 261, I have known large flocks of these birds come occasionally into the small trees (*Gum-wattle*) about Government House. **1839** *S. Austral. Rec.* (London) 11 Sept. 232 The gum wattle . . seldom exceeds 12 or 14 feet in height; it yields an immense quantity of gum, and the bark is used for tanning and various medicinal purposes. **1840** *Ibid.* 14 Mar. 109 Every wave of a blossom-covered gum wattle fills our hut with its colour. **1853** S. SIDNEY *Three Colonies* (ed. 2) 371 Encamped, having for beds the branches of the gum wattle, as soft and luxurious as a bed of down.

gun, *n.*[1] and *attrib.* [Spec. use of *(big, great) gun* one eminent in anything: see OED(S *sb.* 7 b.]

A. *n.*

1. A shearer who has a consistently high daily tally (of sheep shorn); an expert shearer. Also **gun shearer.**

1897 *Worker* (Sydney) 11 Sept. 1/1 To shear a thou. or more a week, which is but seldom done, Will gain a shearer high respect and the title of a 'gun'. **1898** *Bulletin* (Sydney) 17 Dec. 15/1 A *gun* means, generally speaking, a man who can shear over 200 per day, though in some parts—Monaro mountains, for instance—where high tallies are unknown, an 80-a-day man is a *gun*. **1905** *Steele Rudd's Mag.* (Brisbane) July 651 'The Nuggett' was stout . . and blasphemous; once in the far past a 'gun' shearer and ringer of many a leading shed. **1906** J. BARBOUR *Pencillings on Wallaby* 10 The second man is going strong -A famous gun outback—But, do his best, he stands no chance Beside the Queensland crack. **1912** R.S. TAIT *Scotty Mac* 21 Me, a gun shearer's cook, boundary-ridin'! **1924** *Bulletin* (Sydney) 24 Apr. 22/2 When Stumpy was ringer at Burnima, a back country 'gun', Wild Rorty, got a pen there. **1930** *Aussie* (Sydney) May 27/3 'Gun' . . only superseded the expression 'ringer' when machine shearing was 'in'! Never heard 'gun' in a blade shed! **1940** I.L. IDRIESS *Lightning Ridge* 152 The 'gun shearer' there was a two hundred-a-day man. **1944** A.E. MINNIS *And All Trees are Green* 68 He told me it wasn't a bagman's camp when I put it on him this afternoon—me, that was a gun shearer years before he was dropped. **1949** *Bulletin* (Sydney) 23 Feb. 14/3 As to 'gun' shearers . . it was about the times of Carbine and Musket that many good race-horses were named after various types of firearms, hence, if a horse showed a turn of speed, it was said, not always kindly, that he must be a 'gun', and the term came to be applied to the fast shearer. **1965** R.H. CONQUEST *Horses in Kitchen* 191 The oldest shearer in the shed was The Gun. It was only an honorary title—a mark of respect—as he had ceased to be a gun many years earlier. **1975** B. FOLEY *Shearers' Poems* 1 In 1951 I went north as a shedhand in a shearing team. The same year I obtained a learner's pen and although it will not be found in the Guiness Book of Records I was acknowledged 'The Slowest Gun in the West'. **1984** *People Mag.* (Sydney) 7 May 40/1 Des Bourke . . would be shearing's loss. He's a gun with a best tally of 247 in a day and a fine reputation as a trainer.

2. *transf.*

1913 *Bulletin* (Sydney) 13 Mar. 13/2 'Ginger's' tally . . of 600 to 900 chaff bags sewn per day . . is worthy of the most enthusiastic disbelief. . . The highest tally for one day (10 hours) was 480, and my mate taking turns with me was considered to be one of the 'guns' of the West. **1955** STEWART & KEESING *Austral. Bush Ballads* 282 To those chopping guns you mention Lachlan Jack can give you a mile!

B. *attrib.*

1. Pre-eminent (in an occupation or activity); exceptionally talented or skilled.

1916 *Bulletin* (Sydney) 27 Jan. 22/3 Young . . had the reputation amongst 'gun' sheep men of being the fastest lamb-marker in Australia. . . He could keep eight catchers busy. **1939** *Ibid.* 20 Dec. 17/4 A 'gun' fencer . . operated around the Western Riverina. **1941** K. TENNANT *Battlers* 216 Most of the gun pickers'll make for Waldo's. **1957** D. NILAND *Call me when Cross turns Over* 131 He was a gun potato-digger and pea-picker. **1971** *Sydney Morning Herald* 29 Oct. 14/9 He was N.S.W.'s gun batsman last summer with 782 runs at an average of 55.86. **1976** C.D. MILLS *Hobble Chains & Greenhide* 10 One of our 'gun' bronco horses named 'The Ache' was temporarily out of action. **1977** T.A.G. HUNGERFORD *Wong Chu* 22 He would always begin roaring with laughter even before I had begun. Then, I didn't know why, except to think that I was a gun entertainer. **1979** K. DUNSTAN *Ratbags* 17 So maybe the Yabba was for the gun rabbit skinner.

2. Comb. **gun (cane) cutter, drover.**

1922 *Bulletin* (Sydney) 19 Oct. 22/2 We've settled all the shearing and post-hole tallies; now what about the **gun cane-cutter**? **1925** *Ibid.* 15 Jan. 24/3 What about a 'gun' cutter? . . The phrase is in common use on the canefields, a 'gun' among canecutters being the equivalent of a 'ringer' in the shearing-shed. **1972** K. WILLEY *Tales Big Country* 171 She spoke nostalgically of Bluey, the 'gun' cutter of them all. . . 'He'd take a bag of beer to work with him of a morning and put a bottle at the end of every sixth row, and he'd cut more cane than anyone around.' **1977** B. SCOTT *My Uncle Arch* 62 When my Uncle Arch was cutting cane in North Queensland . . he was the gun cutter in the area. **1923** *Six Austral. One-Act Plays* (1944) 18 The old bloke'll pull them through. He's the big **gun drover** of the North. **1939** *Bulletin* (Sydney) 8 Feb. 21/2 Where are the old-time gun drovers of years gone by? **1961** G. FARWELL *Vanishing Australs.* 51 You heard tales of 'gun' drovers still in the saddle, of famous ones now passed away.

gun, *n.*[2] [Prob. transf. use of Br. slang phr. *in the gun* drunk.] In the phr. **in the gun,** in bad favour; likely to attract criticism or punishment.

1924 R. DALY *Outpost* 36 They've got you in the gun, all right. There have been half-a-dozen Residents there in the last few years, and every man-jack of them has gone out to it. **1940** P. KERRY *Cobbers A.I.F.* 21 Even if we wus returnin', an' the flamin' war wus won, An' our gory deeds were 'istory, why I'd still be in the gun! **1953** T.A.G. HUNGERFORD *Riverslake* 220 We should jack up right now, and put him properly in the gun. **1966** B. BEAVER *You can't come Back* 114 Just don't get caught there by any drivers or we'll all be in the gun. **1969** *Kings Cross Whisper* (Sydney) lxxviii. 2/3 Home boaties in gun. War was today declared on all backyard boat builders in Australia. **1982** LOWENSTEIN & HILLS *Under Hook* 105 Everybody seemed to have the wharfies in the gun, we were no good, people didn't want to know us.

Gundaroo /gʌndəˈru/. *Obs.* [The name of a town in s.e. N.S.W.] Used *attrib.* in Special Comb. **Gundaroo bullock, mutton,** see quots.

1899 *Bulletin* (Sydney) 6 May 14/3 A native bear is not . . a 'Grabben-Gullen bullock'; it is mostly known in the South as a 'Gundaroo bullock'. *Ibid.* 3 June 14/3, I was myself in Yass court-house when some members of a Gundaroo family were tried for having supposed stolen mutton in their possession, but they produced testimony that the salted meat . . was native bear. Ever since native bear has in that locality been 'Gundaroo mutton'.

gundy /ˈgʌndi,ˈgʊndi/, *n.*[1] Also **goondie.** [a. Wiradhuri and Kamilaroi *gunday* stringybark, a hut made therefrom.] GUNYAH 1.

1876 *Austral. Town & Country Jrnl.* (Sydney) 2 Dec. 902/1 There were a dozen 'goondies' to be visited, and the inmates started to their work. Each blackfellow at the reveillé caught up a few waddies. **1901** K.L. PARKER in M. Muir *My Bush Bk.* (1982) 87 Then came a little winsome brownie girl wanting to work for Innerah—'boss woman' . . and live in the big goondie too. **1927** M. DORNEY *Adventurous Honeymoon* 53 The few gins who hadn't run away were hidden in the gunyahs or gundhies (called wurleys in Central Australia) which are their huts built of a few branches leaning against one another or against a tree and are so low that it is impossible to assume anything like an erect position inside. **1956** T. RONAN *Moleskin Midas* 158 Miserable rats waiting outside a blackfellow's gundy for the buck to send out the gin when he's done with her himself. **1965** F.G.G. ROSE *Wind of Change* 143 The following is the distribution of the Aborigines in the camp according to gundies (*wilja*). **1980** S. THORNE *I've met some Bloody Wags* 82 My mate Tom and I went there after a busy afternoon bending the elbow around at his gundy.

gundy /ˈgʌndi/, *n.*[2] [Of unknown origin: see quots.]

a. In the phr. **no good to gundy,** no good at all; positively disadvantageous.

1906 *Bulletin* (Sydney) 19 Dec. 14/1 *Re* . . origin and meaning of . . 'No good to gundy'. 'Gundy' is a corruption of a Welsh word meaning to steal, shake, pinch, or hook, and the expression simply means that a thing is not worth stealing. **1907** *Ibid.* 19 Dec. 14/2 The origin of the expression 'No good to Gundy'. Gundy is an abbreviation of Gundagai and the phrase originated way back in 1852—the year of the big flood. . . A bullocky . . disentangling a few codfish from his whiskers . . looked towards the blank that had been Gundagai, and remarked sadly, that ''Tweren't much good to Gundy.' **1908** *Ibid.* 2 Jan. 14/4 'No good to Gundy'. . . This is the only explanation of its origin I could discover: A mounted constable was bringing a darky named Gundy down to Bathurst for trial. . . In the same carriage were some young men who procured much whisky at Wellington . . and when one of the boys playfully held the bottle about a foot in front of the aboriginal's nose and begged of him to [*sic*] 'Do have a drop', Gundy threw one black foot in the air, and deftly kicking the bottle of whisky through the carriage window, yelled 'No plurry good to Gundy.' **1908** *Truth* (Sydney) 30 Aug. 1/7 A temperance fanatic many years ago lectured at Gundy. . . The cold tea advocate was going to shut up every hotel in the land. 'What!' yelled the audience in united voice, 'shut up our pub.' 'Precisely,' replied the ranter. 'Be hanged,' chorused the crowd, 'that's no good to Gundy.' **1915** *Ibid.* 24 Jan. 11/8 Five or six drinks *ain't no good to Gundy.* **1950** E.M. ENGLAND *Where Turtles Dance* 131 All the coves fightin' and boozin' it away on payday . . no homelife. . . Just cards and races and booze—and fightin'. No good to Gundy! **1955** N. PULLIAM *I traveled Lonely Land* 324 'Just another Canb'ra,' they tell you. 'Worthless, absolutely no good to Gundy.' **1968** S. GORE *Holy Smoke* 35 'She's a real gig,' he reckons. 'But they don't! This is no good to gundy,' they say.

b. In the phr. **good enough for Gundy**: see quot.

1949 C. BENHAM *Diver's Luck* 151 When yer got a job ter do yer wants ter do it prop'ly, none o' yer, 'That's near enough', or 'That's good enough for Gundey'.

guneah, var. GUNYAH.

gungurru /gʌngəˈru/. Also **gungunnu.** [Prob. a. Mirniŋy *gaŋurru.*] A small tree of s.w. W.A., of the genus *Eucalyptus* (fam. Myrtaceae), usu. *E. caesia*, cultivated as an ornamental.

1949 S. KELLY *Forty Austral. Eucalypts* 20 The vernacular name 'Gungurru' is of Aboriginal origin, and therefore wholly Australian. It applies to one of the loveliest of our ornamental trees. **1954** *Jrnl. Agric. W.A.* 105 Gungunnu (*Eucalyptus caesia* . .). For the want of a good descriptive common name for this handsome mallee I have used the name which Richard Helms stated was used by the aborigines of the Fraser Range district. **1976** C. EAGLE *Four Faces* 33 The gungurru in flower . . the long-stalked gumnuts of last year's flowering mingling with the powdered buds and the pink-red flowers. **1982** *Jrnl. R. Soc. W.A.* LXV. iii. 95 Gungurru is clearly not *Eucalyptus caesia* and there is little doubt that its true identity is *E. woodwardii.* **1984** *Age* (Melbourne) 1 May 22/6 Gungurru, *E. caesia*, which the honeyeaters adored.

gunna. [Not excl. Austral.: cf. OEDS *gonna.*] Repr. colloq. pronunc. of 'going to'.

1950 J. CLEARY *Just let me Be* 11 They could feel the sun hot on their backs. . . 'It's gunna be a beaut again today,' Harry said. **1962** A. SEYMOUR *One Day of Yr.* 11 Thought you was gunna do all them dishes for me. **1963** J. O'GRADY *Things they do to You* 79, I dunno what you're gunna do about it. **1969** —— *O'Grady Sez* 57 'Cheers.' 'Gunna have another one?' 'Well, I don't suppose it would hurt us.' **1978** T. DAVIES *More Austral. Nicknames* 71 *Mrs Gunner*, she's the female equivalent of The Gunner, the fellow who's forever gunna do this or gunna do that. **1983** *Truck & Bus* July 126/3, I want answers outa you, Crackers. More than answers—I want them spuds replaced! What are yer gunna do about it?

gunyah /ˈgʌnjə/. Also **gunya** and formerly with much variety as **guneah, gunneah, gunnie, gunyer,** etc. [a. Dharuk *ganya.*]

1. A temporary shelter of the Aborigines, usually made of sheets of bark and/or branches; any makeshift shelter or dwelling. Cf. HUMPY, MIA-MIA, WILTJA, WURLEY.

[*c* **1790** W. DAWES Grammatical Forms Lang. N.S.W., *Mau-gon-yai-ra*, at his house.] **1803** J. GRANT *Narr. Voyage N.S.W.* 96 The native . . led us . . very near a *gunnie*, or house, which he made us understand was the place of his birth. **1817** J. OXLEY *Jrnls. Two Exped. N.S.W.* (1820) 117 He threw down with apparent fierceness the little bark guneah which had sheltered him and his family during the night. **1818** *N.S.W. Mag.* (Sydney) (1834) II. 59 We agreed to . . rest for the night in our native *gunnya*, or bower, formed of myrtle-branches. **1827** *Monitor* (Sydney) 5 July 496/1 A sheet of bark was stripped, and a *gunyah* rigged while others were looking about them. **1830** R. DAWSON *Present State Aust.* 70 The poor natives . . soon made me one of their gunyers, (bark huts). **1833** *Austral. Almanack* p. xv, Nor cease their revels till the morning gun Booms o'er the waves to greet the rising sun; Then to their *gunneahs*, sullenly repair, Like wolves retreating to their caverned lair. **1845** L. LEICHHARDT *Jrnl. Overland Exped. Aust.* 14 June (1847) 290 We saw a very interesting camping place of the natives, containing several two-storied gunyas, which were constructed in the following manner: four large forked sticks were rammed into the ground, supporting cross poles placed in their forks, over which bark was spread sufficiently strong and spacious for a man to lie upon; other sheets of stringy bark were bent over the platform, and formed an arched roof. **1860** 'LADY' *My Experiences in Aust.* 203 Even while they remained in our paddock they would change the site of their little bark huts or *gunneyahs* every eight or ten days. **1874** J.J. HALCOMBE *Emigrant & Heathen* 114, I galloped as fast as my good horse could carry me to the *gunyeh.* **1880** 'ERRO' *Squattermania* 53 A blacksmith's shop, in size and appearance very much like a black fellow's gunzah. **1888** P.L. BUDDIVENT *Centennial* 11 The aborigines were black, and dearly fond of ease, And in a state of nature, lived in 'gunyahs' 'neath the trees. **1897** *Proc. R. Soc. Vic.* 6 The old women, and mothers of the boys erect a gunyah . . composed of forked saplings, rails and boughs. **1908** *Bulletin* (Sydney) 8 Oct. 15/2 The black-fellow has a habit of leaving used-up gunyahs and mia-mias scattered promiscuously over the landscape. **1919** *Huon Times* (Franklin) 28 Oct. 4/7 They had had need of no other dwelling than a gunya made with three sticks in the form of a triangle with a few sheets of bark leaning against two sides of it. **1927** M. DORNEY *Adventurous Honeymoon* 43 (*caption*) A gunyah—the unpretentious dwelling of the Australian nigger. **1935** B.E. PHELPS *Austral. tells England* 52 When the travelling aborigines made a camp, tent-shaped 'gunyahs' of bark were set up; they were about three feet in height, and were set around a place where the fire was made. **1948** R. RAVEN-HART *Canoe in Aust.* 47 They could go off alone or with a friend to build 'gunyahs', shelters after the aboriginal model. **1963** I.L. IDRIESS *Our Living Stone Age* 103 How miserable it must be, we thought, within those wretched gunyahs still miraculously standing against this fury of wind and rain. **1975** DONALDSON & JOSEPH *Wilderness* 1 Gunyahs, crude bough dwellings thatched with straw and bark, each with its smouldering fire of dung and sticks and roots.

2. *transf.* and *fig.*

1827 *Austral.* (Sydney) 27 Mar. 2/3 At my friend L--'s *gunha*, the native name for house, our breakfast table was never without beefsteaks, roast wild duck, fried bream and potatoes, besides the more usual accompaniments of pancakes, eggs, cream, and bread superior to any out of Sydney. **1845** R. HOWITT *Impressions Aust. Felix* 145, I again found a cast-down gunyia, or bark-peeler's hut. **1846** *Portland Guardian* 14 Aug. 4/1 In hopes at the gloomin my gunee to see, Where the lass of Australia is waiting for me. **1847** A. HARRIS *Settlers & Convicts* (1953) 32 An occasional little column of smoke curling slowly up from where they were freshening the fire at some sawyer's gunyah in a gully. **1857** F. DE B. COOPER *Wild Adventures* 76 Gunyie . . a hut or dwelling: a word frequently used by bushmen, instead of the vernacular. **1860** G. BENNETT *Gatherings of Naturalist* 114 The name given by the natives to the burrow or habitation of any animal is *guniar*, and the same word is applied to our houses. **1875** CAMPBELL & WILKS *Early Settlement Qld.* 10 Three miles further up the creek we came upon a gunyah occupied by a hut-keeper. **1888** 'R. BOLDREWOOD' *Robbery under Arms* (1937) 32 Go to that gunyah, just under the range where that big white rock is, and you'll find tea and sugar and something to eat. **1911** *Truth* (Sydney) 18 June 5/6 (*heading*) The Guv's gunyah. Deserted Government House. **1928** B. CRONIN *Dragonfly* 192 Voices . . roused him to seek temporary hiding in the cane-grass and blade-grass gunyah summerhouse which Nye had built . . at a corner of the homestead plot. **1946** *Bulletin* (Sydney) 7 Aug. 29/4 The track crossed a bridge near our gunyah.

gunyang /ˈgʌnjæŋ/. [a. Ganay *gunyaŋ.*] Any of several plants, esp. the shrub *Solanum vescum* (fam. Solanaceae) of s.e. Aust. and Tas., bearing a green to ivory-coloured globular berry. See also *kangaroo apple* KANGAROO *n.* 5.

1855 J. BONWICK *Geogr. Aust. & N.Z.* (ed. 3) 204 The Gunyang fruit of the Gipps Land sand ridges is of the taste and size of a Cape gooseberry, on a sort of nightshade shrub 6 feet high. **1878** R.B. SMYTH *Aborigines of Vic.* I. 213 Fruits of *Solanum vescum* (the Gunyang of our natives). **1888** *Proc. Linnean Soc. N.S.W.* III. 544 *Solanum aviculare* . . 'Gunyang' or 'Koonyang' of the Gippsland and other aboriginals. . . Its large fruit resembles that of the potato. **1981** G.M. CUNNINGHAM et al. *Plants Western N.S.W.* 589 Gunyang [*sc.* fruit] globular, to 3 cm diameter, green to ivory.

gurnet. *Obs.* [Var. of *gurnard* a fish of the fam. Triglidae: see quot. 1898.] Any of several marine fish of fam. Triglidae and Scorpaenidae.

1828 *Hobart Town Courier* 9 Feb. 3 No fish were caught except a few gurnet. **1880** *Proc. Linnean Soc. N.S.W.* V. 437 *Centropogon scorpaenoides* . . The '*Gurnet*' of the Melbourne Market. **1898** E.E. MORRIS *Austral Eng.*

187 The word *Gurnet* is an obsolete or provincial form of Gurnard, revived in Australia.

gurry. *Tas.* [Transf. use of *gurry* fish offal, of unknown origin and chiefly U.S.: see OED 4 and Mathews.] The stomach contents of the mutton-bird *Puffinus tenuirostris*, after removal of oil for commercial use.

1975 *Linguistic Communications* xiii. 88 The gurry go to the bottom. **1982** *Victorian Naturalist* XCIX. 52 Patches of oil and gurry were seen in much of the rookery. [*Note*] Gurry is a birding term for the partly-digested stomach contents, exclusive of the oil, of muttonbird nestlings. The killed nestlings are squeezed to empty their stomach contents through their bills.

gutless, *a.* [Used elsewhere but recorded earliest in Aust.] In the collocation **gutless wonder,** one who lacks courage or determination.

1955 D. NILAND *Shiralee* 64 'You're a gutless wonder, Christy,' he gibed. 'What's holding you back?' **1960** D. IRELAND *Image in Clay* (1964) 92 Don't you talk back to your father like that, you soft-bellied, mealy-mouthed, gutless wonder! **1969** W. DICK *Naked Prodigal* 50, I reckon in a one-out blue I'd do him, he's such a gutless wonder. **1978** R. MACKLIN *Newsfront* 50, I always knew you were a gutless wonder. **1982** H. KNORR *Private Viewing* 29 'Try!' it mimicked. 'Why, you gutless wonder, your generation doesn't know what trying is!'

guts.

1. [Used elsewhere but recorded earliest in Aust.] Information, the facts (of a matter); freq. in the collocation **good guts.**

1919 W.H. DOWNING *Digger Dialects* 27 *Guts*, the substance or essential part of a matter; information. **1946** R.D. RIVETT *Behind Bamboo* 7 The news is the kernel and guts of everything. **1953** T.A.G. HUNGERFORD *Riverslake* 166 'Hear about the blue?' . . 'A bit—what's the guts of it?' **1965** G.H. FEARNSIDE *Golden Ram* 18, I had a long yarn with Johnny Nash before he went. . . I got his guts. **1975** 'N. CULOTTA' *Gone Gougin'* 72 'We'll go to the cop shop an' see if that mob . . were havin' us on about that Miner's Right lurk. . . ' 'Righto, matey. We'll organise the grog. You front the wallopers an' get the good guts.'

2. In the phr. **to come** (or **give**) **(someone's) guts,** to divulge incriminating information, to inform.

1953 K. TENNANT *Joyful Condemned* 295 The sullen, big oaf, baited and jeered at by everyone, a man who had 'come his guts to the coppers', was almost driven desperate. **1959** D. HEWETT *Bobbin Up* 135 She's in the manager's office half the day, with her legs crossed so you can see everythin' she's got, givin' him all our guts. **1966** E.J. WALLACE *Sydney & Bush* 141 'The police are outside.' Bill thought: 'A pinch? Me? Come me guts? A top-off? Strike! I'll tell 'em it was a stranger, like.'

3. *Two-up.* The ring in which the spinner operates; CENTRE 3 (bets being placed either in the centre or as side-bets).

1941 *Wagflagger: Mag. Signals 6th Austral. Division Abroad* Sept. 7 Toss up pennies bright and clean. . . 'Some money in the guts.' **1946** *Austral. New Writing* 36 The ring or gutz now needs a pound, for the original ten bob is doubled. **1953** T.A.G. HUNGERFORD *Riverslake* 129 There's one hundred and forty quid in the guts—get it set before you bet on the side. **1955** *Overland* iii. 16 A score in the guts, gentlemen! I want twenty fiddlies. Come on you tail punters, twenty quid in the centre! **1974** *Warrumbungle Bk. of Verse* (1978) 20 Another swy in the guts boys For two-up is the game.

4. In the phr. **(as) rough as guts**: (of a person) lacking in refinement or sophistication.

1966 B. BEAVER *You can't come Back* 118 I'm shy all right, but I'm not smooth. . . I'm rough as guts. **1968** F. HARDY *Unlucky Australs.* 11 The old Territorian is a good bloke, rough as guts but his heart's in the right place. **1972** A. CHIPPER *Aussie Swearers Guide* 48 Her teas are like Bush picnics. *Rough as guts.* **1978** *Southerly* iii. 260 The rough-as-guts but dinkum workers in bars he would have to tape in order to support his—and her—style of living.

gutser, var. GUTZER.

gutta-percha tree. [Transf. use of *gutta-percha* a tree yielding a rubbery juice: see OED.] The small tree of Qld. and N.T. *Excoecaria parvifolia* (fam. Euphorbiaceae), having an irritant milky sap. Also **gutta-percha.**

1883 E. PALMER *Plants N. Qld.* (1884) 15 Excoecaria parviola [*sic*] . . The gutta-percha tree; grows all over the Gulf waters and also on the Mitchell River. **1897** J.J. MURIF *From Ocean to Ocean* 145 Bright green-leaved guttapercha trees are numerous. . . When a branch is broken, a thick milky substance exudes. Scratches made on one's hands or face by its thorny projections become very painful and take a long time to heal. **1927** M.H. ELLIS *Long Lead* 76 Poor land growing gutta percha trees. **1947** H. DRAKE-BROCKMAN *On N.-W. Skyline* 74 Stiff little gutta-percha trees (examined in war time for their rubber possibility, but discarded as too meagre on output). **1962** T. RONAN *Deep of Sky* 163 Avenues of gutta-percha . . form an archway of branches.

gutter.

1. *Mining.* The lowest part or deepest channel in a former watercourse, where auriferous matter is likely to be most concentrated: see quot. 1856.

1853 W.H. ARCHER Papers NLA MS 266/5 28 Aug., We are forced to sink a new shaft on the hillside of our claim to follow up the gutter if we can get at it again without being smothered with water. **1854** *Illustr. Sydney News* 14 Oct. 292/3 The fortunate owners when they bottom on the gutter generally 'shout' champagne for all hands in the immediate neighbourhood. **1855** R. CARBONI *Eureka Stockade* 10 The Eureka gutter was fast progressing down hill towards the Eureka gully. **1856** 'OLD COLONIST' *How to Farm & Settle in Aust.* 58 The idea generally pervading the mind of the miner is to this effect, that there is a lead, or particular direction of the main charge or accumulation of gold formed by the in-pourings in former times from the surrounding country. This lead takes a very irregular and wholly uncertain direction. It is not found in directions at all conformable to the lines of the lowest level of the present valleys. 'The gutter' is a term applied to a supposed central line of this lead, into which, as into a groove or ditch, the main mass of the gold had been brought together. **1857** W. WESTGARTH *Vic. & Austral. Gold Mines* 126 When at a depth of 200 feet a 'lead' is struck, the practised miner searches for the 'gutter', and if he is fortunate in finding it, his hands may come back to him filled with solid gold. **1862** H. BROWN *Vic. as I found It* 244 Those who took the chance of sinking a hole on the outside of what had appeared to be the gutter were rewarded by finding that the stream had taken a bend towards them, and that their hole brought them exactly on the run of gold. **1881** J.C.F. JOHNSON *To Mount Browne & Back* 25 It may be that the 'gutter' is a very narrow one and nothing but a line of shafts across the flat, with drives between covering the whole width. **1892** *Bulletin* (Sydney) 16 Apr. 11/4 E'en tho they'd worked the field as Chinese do, Had 'bulled' each shaft and scraped out every gutter. **1932** I.L. IDRIESS *Prospecting for Gold* 12 Alluvial gold often runs in a 'lead', or a 'gutter'. That is, it may run in a more or less broken 'line', perhaps only one foot wide, down the centre of a creek. **1939** A. GASTON *Coolgardie Gold* 137 We drove a cross-cut from boundary to boundary, but after six weeks' work we gave it up as a duffer. Good gold was being got within 50 yards of us, but we were just off the gutter. **1977** J. DOUGHTY *Gold in Blood* 83 The deep cut I had driven through the claim was finished, and though I sank various holes on either side of it, trying to strike another 'gutter', my efforts were futile.

2. A nickname for the Darling River. Also **Gutter of Australia.**

1937 A.W. UPFIELD *Winds of Evil* 179 'You're a stranger to this district.' 'Yes. I've come over from The Gutter for a change.' **1957** J. HAWKE *Follow my Dust* 83 The Darling River having been called The Gutter of Australia, the Murray River, of which it is a tributary, may rightfully be referred to as The Great Australian Drain. **1963** A. UPFIELD *Madman's Bend* 73 This Darling River, sometimes called the Gutter of Australia.

gutzer, *n.* Also **gutser.**

a. A (heavy) fall; a collision; *fig.*, a 'let down' or disappointment; a failure.

1918 *Aussie: Austral. Soldiers' Mag.* Oct. 7/1 'What do you boys mean, exactly, when you refer to a gutzer?' . . 'It means a 'thud'.' . . 'A fall-in.' . . 'A bad sort of failure.' **1919** R.T. WYATT *Digger on 'Durham'* 23 We regret to inform our patrons that our stock of cigarettes is far from large and they should place their orders early to avoid gutzers. **1919** *Aussie: Austral. Soldiers' Mag.* Jan. 2/2 The cook's mate had seen five deer there, so he said. . . Gunner visioned himself dragging home a good fat buck. What a gutzer it would be for those who'd gigged him! **1933** N. LINDSAY *Saturdee* (1936) 231 Snowey . . threw himself recklessly off it and landed such a gutzer that he knocked all the wind out of himself. **1937** L. MANN *Murder in Sydney* 71 'I'm going to make a splash, too.' 'Mind it isn't a gutser.' 'Oh, no. I'm doing quite well for myself.' **1979** B. SCOTT *Tough in Old Days* 135 Smashes were known colloquially as 'gutzers', and it was a lucky and skilful driver who did not have at least one a week.

b. In the phr. **to come a gutzer,** to fail as a result of miscalculation, to 'come a cropper'.

1918 N.P.H. NEAL *Back to Bush* 10 The man who came to the war to get away from a nagging wife came a horrible—gutzer, didn't he? **1918** *Aussie: Austral. Soldiers' Mag.* Dec. 23/1 The best nut-worker sometimes comes a gutzer. Private Pepperpot, who is a keen admirer of the fair sex, will tell you if this is true or not. **1919** C.H. THORP *Handful of Ausseys* 201 The doctors are gettin' wise an' yer liable ter cum a gutser. **1928** *Bulletin* (Sydney) 5 Sept. 27/1, I quick woke up to 'ow much 'e knew, 'E came a gutzer an' no mistake, An' I bet it 'urt 'im. **1940** *Ibid.* 7 Aug. 16/3 These practical jokers sometimes come a gutser. **1955** D. NILAND *Shiralee* 98 'It was me that come the gutser.' 'How?' 'Because she didn't want the kid. . . I take it off her hands and put it on my own back.' **1960** R.S. PORTEOUS *Cattleman* 245 Start dishin' out presents with strings attached to 'em and you'll end up comin' a big gutser with the strings tangled round your own legs. **1967** D. HEWETT *This Old Man* (1976) 88 You'll come a gutser if you arst George to put 'is hand in 'is pocket. They don't come any meaner than our Georgie. **1970** R. BEILBY *No Medals for Aphrodite* 233 Only this time you come a gutser, did you? This one was a decent sheila who wouldn't stand for your mucking about. **1983** *Canberra Times* 23 Oct. 2/3 'The Opposition,' raged Mr Dawkins during Wednesday's Question Time in the House of Representatives, 'has come an absolute gutser on this one!'

c. In the phr. **to bring** (someone) **a gutzer,** to engineer (someone's) downfall.

1939 FRANKLIN & CUSACK *Pioneers on Parade* 218 You didn't tell him! Of all the poor soft mugs you're the softest. You let slip the chance to bring him a gutser. **1964** E. LANE *Our Uncle Charlie* 35 Skitchem became entangled in his legs and—as Uncle himself would say—'brought him a gutzer', flinging him to the floor like a bag of potatoes.

gutzer, *v. intr.* To fail miserably.

1924 *Aussie* (Sydney) Feb. 42/2 Most of our time was spent in trying to invent some excuse to get us a few days' leave in London, but no matter what excuse we put up, we always 'gutzered'. **1944** *Barging About: Organ 43 Austral. Landing Craft Co.* 1 Sept. 16, I have tried him with a lot of other tales but gutzered because someone else had thought of them first. **1960** S. WOODFIELD *A for Artemis* 117, I made some terrible mistakes in my daily work, but this was the worst. I gutzered. **1976** S. WELLER *Bastards I have Met* 3 He bought a pub in Charters Towers and gutzered.

guvvie. Also **govie.** [f. GOV(ERNMENT HOUSE 2 + -Y.] GOVERNMENT HOUSE 2. Also as **guvvie flat.**

1984 *Canberra Times* 8 Apr. 9/3 House: Brick veneer guvvie, South Gowrie. **1985** *Ibid.* 15 Apr. 20/2 Probably the most attractive govie in this suburb. **1986** *Ibid.* 9 Apr. 3/1 (*heading*) Pets get the push in guvvie flats blitz.

guy a whack, *v. phr. Obs.* [Prob. joc. formation on Br. dial. and slang *guy* act of decamping: see OED *sb.*[2] 3 b.] *intr.* To decamp, to take (oneself) off, to abscond.

1882 *Sydney Slang Dict.* 5 Hoop (or Hook) it, or Guy Avack—To run. **1892** J. MURRAY *Larrikins* (1973) 40 The Tempe blokes just slopped one each And then they guyed a whack. **1900** *Western Champion* (Barcaldine) 10 Apr. 9/2 'I guyed a whack. Pads it back here.' . . Now, here is the above translated. . . 'I turned away, walked back.' **1912** J. BRADSHAW *Highway Robbery under Arms* (ed. 3) 28 We would then guy a whack, and go to our virtuous camp. **1915** *Truth* (Sydney) 10 June 1/7 Madam Melba is on the eve of returning to the old country. . . There are many who would (like Melba) guyawhack if they had the wherewithal (like Melba).

guy-a-whack, *n.* [f. prec.] The act of decamping or absconding; one who does this.

1899 *Truth* (Sydney) 17 Sept. 4/5 At the slightest scent of troubles, Why, it does a 'duck' and doubles, By a process pusillanimous that's known as guy-a-whack! **1903** *Ibid.* 5 Apr. 5/2 The *greatest curse of Sydney* is its innumerable spielers, guns, buncosteerers, guya-whacks, and confidence men. **1916** *Ibid.* 2 Apr. 10/2 For woman, lovely woman, skipped-the-gutter, did a guy-a-whack, vanished, and vamoosed. **1922** A. WRIGHT *Colt from Country* 131 'Lookin' fer th' guy what had y' in tow all day?' he asked. 'Yes,' moaned Yalty. 'Where is he?' . . 'Done er guy whack, I expect,' he grunted.

guyver, *n.* Also **guiver, gyver.** [Used elsewhere but recorded earliest in Aust.] An affectation of speech or behaviour, esp. empty or ingratiating talk, persiflage.

1864 C.R. THATCHER *Colonial Minstrel* 13 I'll give you the sack pretty quick, If my wife you offend with your guiver. **1896** *Truth* (Sydney) 7 June 1/3, I knew it was merely gyver, so my answer was straight an' blunt. **1905** *Ibid.* 28 May 5/5 (*heading*) Great anti-gambling guiver. **1916** V.G. DWYER *Conquering Hal* 136 'You've got a real little bushwoman's soul. . . That's why you've got no guyva about you. We can't stand guyva in the Bush, you know.' "Guyva'! . . What's that? . . ' 'Guyva,' he said, 'is—well, its just—guyva, see?' **1919** E. DYSON *Hello, Soldier* 15 But the parsons and the poets couldn't teach him to discourse When it come to pokin' guyver at a pore, deluded horse. **1929** C.H. WINTER *Story of 'Bidgee Queen* 48, I didn't like 'is guiver an' 'is 'igh-falutin rot. **1947** V. PALMER *Cyclone* 68 'I can earn money when I want to,' he said defensively. 'Pity that doesn't happen every day.' He flushed to the eyes, a sudden assurance coming to him. 'Chuck that cheap guyver, Con.' **1955** *Overland* iv. 10 Within the ring a horse cavorts. Buck on, you beaut! I'd give a fiver To see you smash snakeheaded through Palings, poons, illywhack and guyver. **1977** D. STUART *Drought Foal* 32 Pity they can't find something better to do than all this guiver.

guyver, *v. Obs.* [f. prec.] *trans.* To abuse (a person) verbally.

1882 *Bulletin* (Sydney) 17 June 10/2 Larrikin mob guyvored a Sydney Chinese storekeeper.

gympie: see GYMPIE HAMMER.

gympie /'gɪmpi/. [a. Gabi (and other s.e. Qld. languages) *gimbi.*] Any of several trees of the genus *Dendrocnide* (fam. Urticaceae), esp. the shrub or small tree *D. moroides* of n. N.S.W. and Qld., the hairs of which inflict an extremely painful recurring sting. See also STINGING TREE. Also *attrib.*

1895 A. MESTON *Geogr. Hist. Qld.* 55 *Gympie*, the Mary River blacks' name for the stinging tree. **1908** S.W. JACKSON Field Trip Notebk. 92, I saw 'The Gympies' growing all up the mountain side today. It is a nettle which grows about 12 feet high. **1929** *Bulletin* (Sydney) 9 Oct. 23/4, I nominate gympie as the lightest timber in Australia. **1949** B. O'REILLY *Green Mountains* 103 The Gympie stinging tree, or Gympie Gympie, as it is called by the blacks, is readily identified by its huge dinner plate leaves a foot across. The leaves and young stems are hairy with transparent, stinging spines and contact with them is as painful as a scald. **1963** *N. Austral. Monthly* Dec. 17/1 Mention has been made of the nasty stinging tree grown in the Queensland scrubs. Here in Mackay we call it the 'moonlighter', but in the south it is known as the 'gympie'. **1968** L. BRADEN *Bullockies* 85 Gympie Nettles, with their big prickly leaves; stings ache for hours . . and sometimes days, and it is just agony every time you wash yourself in cold water. **1974** S.L. EVERIST *Poisonous Plants Aust.* 516 *Dendrocnide excelsa* . . is often known as *Gympie* in southern Queensland and New South Wales but this common name is generally restricted nowadays to shrubby species, mainly *D. moroides.*

Gympie hammer. *Mining.* [Also U.S.; of unknown origin.] A lightweight hammer used in hand-drilling; a single-jack. Also *ellipt.* **gympie.**

1945 S.J. BAKER *Austral. Lang.* 94 *Gympie work*, single-handed hammer and drill work (a Queensland use). **1946** K.S. PRICHARD *Roaring Nineties* 248 A bit of gym, which was what they called the gold they got out of a mine with the Gympie hammer. **1975** D. STUART *Walk, trot, canter & Die* 96 A swag . . mattress an' piller an' all; pick an' shovel, Gympie hammer an' yards an' yards o' steel. **1977** J. DOUGHTY *Gold in Blood* 215, I got drills and gympie to work then and used dynamite, taking care to make the charges light. **1977** D. STUART *Drought Foal* 158 Swing a Gympie hammer down at the bottom of the underlay. **1982** R. BROMBY *Rails to Top End* 15 The tools he writes, were of a type which 'few men could readily use with success: they consisted of cross-cut saws, adzes, axes, picks, shovels, hand drills, jumper drills, Gympie hammers'.

gyver, var. GUYVER *n.*

H

ha-ha. [Cf. LAUGHING JACKASS 1.] Used *attrib.* in Special Comb. **ha-ha pigeon (bird, duck),** the kookaburra *Dacelo novaeguineae.*

1938 F. CLUNE *Free & Easy Land* 257 The Ha Ha pigeons (Kookaburras) of Woothakata can Ha Ha without fear and trembling. **1962** MARSHALL & DRYSDALE *Journey among Men* 169 In the settled areas Italian migrants have begun to put themselves on the wrong side of the law by eating .. kookaburras ('ha ha pigeons') and, in fact, almost everything in feathers. **1969** P. ADAM SMITH *Folklore Austral. Railwaymen* 128 They .. even shot 'Ha-Ha birds' and magpies until I stopped them. **1970** J.S. GUNN in W.S. Ramson *Eng. Transported* 50 In certain areas along the Murray River the kookaburra is also called a *ha-ha duck* because some migrants eat them.

hair-trigger. *Obs.* TRIGGER PLANT.

1852 MRS C. MEREDITH *My Home in Tas.* II. 71 The *Stylidium*, or as we named it, the 'Hair-trigger', is common all over the colony. **1898** E.E. MORRIS *Austral Eng.* 189 Hair-trigger .. a Tasmanian name for any plant of genus *Stylidium.* Called also Trigger-plant.

hairy goat: see GOAT 2.

hairy Mary. See quots. 1936 and 1979.

1936 J. DEVANNY *Sugar Heaven* 41 The 'hairy Mary', fine prickles which clothed leaves and cane, penetrated every pore of the cutters' arms and hands. **1963** D. ROBERT *Look at me Now* 114 Each carried a long cane knife. The arm of one was bandaged. He probably had an infection caused by a growth called 'Hairy Mary' which works into the skin and sets up an irritation. **1976** S. WELLER *Bastards I have Met* 7 I'd barked my hands on the rocks, just about up to the elbows, the hairy-mary got in and they festered and the insides had blisters like hen's eggs. **1979** B. SCOTT *Tough in Old Days* 110 There is a substance, called by cutters 'Hairy Mary', which coats the underside of the young leaves and the top of the stalk with what looks for all the world like velvet.

hairy-nosed wombat. Either of two wombats of the genus *Lasiorhinus* of s. and e. Aust., having fine hairs on the snout.

1867 *Illustr. Sydney News* 18 July 205/1 The broad-faced or hairynosed wombat .. of South Australia. **1926** A.S. LE SOUEF et al. *Wild Animals Australasia* 295 The hairy-nosed wombat has been killed out over a large part of its range. **1972** *Bulletin* (Sydney) 30 Dec. 40/3 The audience .. was convulsed by the unintentional humor of the Tourist Commission's choice, 'The Hairy-Nosed Wombat', because a series of zoologists stomped into frame, elaborated on the doings of the hairy-nose with enough worried intensity to be talking about the infiltration of the countryside by Vietcong, then stomped off. **1981** *Woman's Day* (Sydney) 9 Sept. 95/2 The Hairy-nosed Wombat is one of the world's rarest mammals. The survivors, perhaps as few as 40, are threatened by cattle grazing in their last remaining colony in Queensland. **1983** *Sydney Morning Herald* 15 Oct. 32/5 Identifying S.A.'s State pet as the hairy-nosed wombat.

hake. [Transf. use of *hake* a gadoid fish.] GEMFISH.

1951 T.C. ROUGHLEY *Fish & Fisheries Aust.* 128 In the Sydney fish market it [*sc.* the king barracouta] is known as 'hake'. **1974** *Bulletin* (Sydney) 12 Oct. 23/2 A N.S.W. fish called 'hake' is felt to suffer by public confusion with 'flake' and is to be renamed 'gemfish'.

hakea /'heɪkiə/. [The plant genus *Hakea* was named by H.A. Schrader (1797) (*Sert. Hannov.* 27 Pl. 17) after the Hanoverian patron of botany Baron C.L. von *Hake* (1745–1818).] Any shrub or small tree of the large Austral. genus *Hakea* (fam. Proteaceae) of all States, characterized by spidery inflorescences and woody fruits with winged seeds. See also *cork-bark, cork tree* CORK, NEEDLEWOOD.

1827 *HRA* (1923) 3rd Ser. VI. 579, I observed on these Hills .. several Species of Hakea. **1844** *Sydney Morning Herald* 12 Dec. 4/4 We found .. a graceful pendulous hakea. **1855** J. BONWICK *Geogr. Aust. & N.Z.* (ed. 3) 203 The Hakea is like the Banksia. **1887** W.H. SUTTOR *Austral. Stories Retold* 117 The prickly hakea. **1896** B. SPENCER *Rep. Horn Sci. Exped. Central Aust.* I. 47 Patches of rugged stemmed Hakeas with stiff spike-like leaves. **1928** G.H. WILKINS *Undiscovered Aust.* 57 The ordinary trees of the Australian bush: eucalypts, acacias, and hakeas. **1936** C.T. MADIGAN *Central Aust.* 85 The hakea, or cork-barks, are gnarled-trunked trees. **1967** B.Y. MAIN *Between Wodjil & Tor* 33 Amongst the long, wiry leaves of hakeas sprouted hands of bird-beaked woody fruits. **1985** *Age* (Melbourne) 20 Sept. (Suppl.) 7/1 Shrubs, such as the beautifully adorned grevilleas and spiky hakeas, sometimes form dense patches of bush.

half.

1. *pl. Obs.* [Cf. Br. dial. and U.S. *to (the) halves* so as to have a half-share in the profits: see OED *half, sb.* 7.]

a. In the phr. **on (the) halves, for halves:** see quot. 1845.

1829 *Launceston Advertiser* 4 May 5 From One to Two Hundred Head of *cattle*, will be taken on the halves, on one of the best runs on the Island. **1836** *Cornwall Chron.* (Launceston) 1 Oct. 3 *Wanted* .. on one of the best runs in the Colony .. from forty to fifty head of female Cattle, on the halves. **1845** D. MACKENZIE *Emigrant's Guide* 106 A sheepowner .. will have no difficulty in meeting a respectable stockholder, who will receive and graze his sheep on what is called *halves*; that is the grazier receives yearly one-half of all the wool, and one half of the increase from the flock. ***c* 1852** A. MANN *Goldfields Aust.* 61 It is usual to buy sheep and stock, and entrust them to a respectable stockholder, who pastures and tends them for *halves*—that is .. he takes half the wool and increase, the owner receiving the other half. **1896** N. BARTLEY *Austral. Pioneers* 53 He bound the tenants to grow a certain area of cane, which he crushed for them 'on the halves'.

b. Used *attrib.* in Special Comb. **halves man,** one who farms 'on halves'.

1900 *Albury Banner* 5 Jan. 16/3 Farmers, selectors, and halves-men seem to care very little about comfort in their small shantys, as long as they get plenty of black billy, tough burnt chops, and half-baked bread.

2. *Australian National Football.* Used *attrib.* in Special Comb. **half-back,** any of the three positions on the line between the centre-line and the full-back line; a player occupying one of these positions; **-back flank** (or **flanker**), a player occupying either outside position on the half-back line; **-forward,** any of the three positions on the *half-forward line*; **-forward flank** (or **flanker**), a player occupying either outside position on this line; **-forward line,** the line between the centre-line and the full-forward line.

1931 J.F. MCHALE et al. *Austral. Game of Football* 60 The backs should kick wide in order to allow the **half-backs**—or very often the centre wings, because the back men may kick right over the half-back lines—to receive the ball on the run. **1936** E.C.H. TAYLOR et al. *Our Austral. Game Football* 34 Half-Back, Centre .. should be a very good high mark and excellent kick, and able to move off the mark. **1982** G. ATKINSON *Everything about Austral. Rules Football* 203 Half-backs—You are the van-guard of the citadel. Defend the rear-guard to the death! Mind your marking and kick at once. **1963** L. RICHARDS *Boots & All!* 217 **Half-Back Flank**, an ideal back flank should be around about the six-foot mark, vigorous, dashing and a strong mark and kick. *Ibid.*, He is also the perfect example of post-war half-back flankers because as soon as he grabbed the ball he was on the move. **1973** J. DUNN *How to play Football* 78 Obviously, a half-back flanker has to defend. He is pitted against a half-forward flanker and basically his job is to stop his opponent from slicing open the defence for a goal feast. **1973** P. MCKENNA *My World of Football* 103, I don't suppose any young player likes to look up the team sheet and find that he is picked to play in the back pocket or a half back flank; you never win games off your own boot from there. **1876** T.P. POWER *Footballer* 11 Centres and **half-forwards**—Keep your places and kick at once. Never run unless the coast be very clear. **1931** J.F. MCHALE et al. *Austral. Game of Football* 60 The wings and half-forwards should adopt the same tactics as the half-backs when the ball is coming down *via* the flanks. **1936** E.C.H. TAYLOR et al. *Our Austral. Game Football* 34 Half-Forward Left .. a big man, not too slow, who can take his turn in the ruck. **1963** L. RICHARDS *Boots & All!* 36 At South one day Jack Hamilton wasn't getting a kick at full-back... He was being murdered, so Jock decided to shift him to a **half-forward flank.** **1964** *Footy Fan* (Melbourne) II. ii. 19 After making a name for himself as an elusive half forward flanker, Hassa got his chance to play pivot in 1961. **1982** *Austral.* (Sydney) 7 Aug. 44/3 Admirers of Carlton's jack-in-the-box half-forward flanker, Peter Bosustow, call him 'Mr Magic' and 'Mr Wonderful'. His detractors call him a mug lair and a show pony. **1963** L. RICHARDS *Boots & All!* 105 He knew how to make position on the **half-forward line.**

3. In the phr. **half your luck**: exclam. form of 'I wish I had a half of your luck'.

1933 H.B. RAINE *Lash End* 60 'From now on, Marie and I will be seen together very frequently. Get me?' 'Half your luck, son.' **1935** DAVISON & NICHOLLS *Blue Coast Caravan* 2 Strangers .. said: 'Half your luck!' when they heard where we were going. **1957** D. NILAND *Call me when Cross turns Over* 205 It was good-o, but half your luck, Barbie. **1963** X. HERBERT *Disturbing Element* 159 Cyril delighted me with his frank comment on her: 'Half your luck, old chap!'

half-axe. [Fig. use of *half-axe* a small axe.] A youth.

1938 *Bulletin* (Sydney) 12 Jan. 21/2 When I was a half-axe .. me ole man had given me a boyproof watch. **1963** I.L. IDRIESS *Our Living Stone Age* 76, I was only a 'half-axe', as the bushmen say, midway between boy and man. **1976** B. NORMAN *Bush Pilot* 14 Young men, including me—'half-axes' as we were known then. **1978** G. HALL *River still Flows* 110 In Dad's young days, to call any young half-axe a 'sissy' was the worst possible insult... Now the young feller was wearing much the same as his girlfriend.

half-blood. HALF-CASTE (but see quot. 1959). Also *attrib.*

1952 *Bulletin* (Sydney) 19 Mar. 15/4, I remarked to Townie, a half-blood aboriginal yardman, that he, no doubt, didn't feel the heat. **1959** E. WEBB *Mark of Sun* 112 Anyone with twenty-five per cent of aboriginal blood in him is legally classified as a half-blood under Queensland law.

half-bred, *a.*

a. Of sheep: see quots.

1819 *Sydney Gaz.* 12 June, Three Half-bred Merino Rams. **1891** R. WALLACE *Rural Economy & Agric.* 265 The half-bred sheep, being the various crosses between Merino ewes and long-woolled rams. **1959** S.J. BAKER *Drum* 116 *Half-bred sheep*, orig. a sheep by a longwool ram from a merino ewe; now loosely applied to the type.

b. HALF-CASTE *attrib.*

1891 'R. BOLDREWOOD' *Sydney-Side Saxon* (1925) 118 All those half-bred brats of his are sure to give him the slip as they get older. **1901** *Bulletin* (Sydney) 28 Dec. 31/2 Only the last of six persons met proves to be a 'clean white', and the other five are half-bred and drunk—*i.e.*, it was in Western Queensland.

half-caser. *Obs.* A half-crown. See also CASER. Freq. **half-a-caser.**

1882 *Sydney Slang Dict.* 2 *Half a-caser*, half-a-crown. **1891** *Truth* (Sydney) 10 May 3/4 The solicitude he showed over the little half-crowns of the youths who plunge to that extent on the horse of their fancy, made very evident the sorrow he felt that their two-and-a-tanner was not devoted to the Centenary Hall collection plate. The way he hung and lingered over these half-casers was most interesting. **1894** H. LAWSON *Short Stories* 5 He had 'had' three 'blanky fellers' for some tucker and 'half a caser' by pretending to be 'barmy'. **1895** *Worker* (Sydney) 12 Jan. 1/4 The Maori helped us up, and we had a drink with him at the expense of one of the half-casers. **1908** C.H.S. MATTHEWS *Parson in Austral. Bush* 69 Why, I put half a caser in his bloomin' collection every time I came to church! **1914** —— *Bill* 248 It was not up to him—Bill—to pay the grouser half-a-caser (i.e. half a crown).

half-caste. Formerly also **half-cast.** [Spec. use of *half-caste* one of a mixed race.] One of mixed Aboriginal and non-Aboriginal parentage or descent. Freq. *attrib.*

1836 *Colonist* (Sydney) 7 July 211/4 They often kill their half-cast offspring. **1844** L. LEICHHARDT *Jrnl. Overland Exped. Aust.* 31 Dec. 90 Brown thought that one of them looked like a half-caste. **1855** J. BONWICK *Geogr. Aust. & N.Z.* (ed. 3) 196 Half castes are generally destroyed. **1876** *Austral. Handbk.* 204 Many of them are 'half-castes', the offspring of marriages between the sealers and aboriginal women. **1888** 'R. BOLDREWOOD' *Robbery under Arms* (1937) 28 The boy was a half-caste that father had picked up somewhere; he was as good as two men any day. **1892** J. FRASER *Aborigines N.S.W.* 3 A black woman likes to have children by a white father, for the half-caste son has the qualities of a superior race. **1914** M. O'HALLORAN *W. Austral. Police Man.* 30 Q. – What does the term 'half-caste' mean? A. – It means any person being the offspring of an aboriginal mother and other than an aboriginal father. **1921** *Ross's Monthly* Nov. 3/1 Ruby, the half-caste gin, is a wonderfully well-drawn character. **1938** A. UPFIELD *Bone is Pointed* (1966) 52 I've known lots of fine blackfellers and more 'n one extra good half-caste. **1945** E. GEORGE *Two at Daly Waters* 106 Micky and Nancy were full blacks and the baby was a half-caste. **1957** F. CLUNE *Fortune Hunters* 119 The old-fashioned term 'halfcaste', as applied to persons of mixed Aboriginal and European descent, is going into the discard. **1978** D. STUART *Wedgetail View* 30 He had this half caste piece . . a good looker. **1986** *Centralian Advocate* (Alice Springs) 15 Jan. 10/3 What I want to know is where the half-caste kids are going to drink now.

half-civilized, *a. Obs.* Of an Aboriginal: living outside colonial society, or incompletely assimilated into it. See also CIVILIZED.

1819 *Sydney Gaz.* 17 Apr., The poor half civilized native. **1865** S. BENNETT *Hist. Austral. Discovery* 220 They had the misfortune to fall in with two half civilised blackfellows from Botany Bay. **1870** C.H. ALLEN *Visit to Qld.* 186 'Native troopers' . . are half-civilised 'blacks' from another colony, so as to be quite free from all sympathy with the tribes of that district. **1887** 'COMMERCIAL TRAVELLER' *Diary Three Months Trip Qld.* 35 A big half civilized blackfellow . . killed him. **1900** T. MAJOR *Leaves from Squatter's Note Bk.* 155 This rough, honest old sea-dog . . with the assistance of two half-civilized black boys, managed to work his station.

halfie. [f. HALFCASTE + -Y.] HALF-CASTE.

1941 *Argus* (Melbourne) 15 Nov. (Suppl.) 1/3 Slang applied to the aborigines occurs, of course, only in the Far North. . . Half-castes are 'halfies', and quarter-castes 'creamies'. **1942** *Ack Ack* (Melbourne) Jan. 3 Some run by 'Halfies', some by whites, some by Chinese. **1960** J. WALKER *No Sunlight Singing* 175 Say, Les, what's the drill with these halfies? . . That dance I went to th' other night. There was all colours there – black, white, brown and brindle.

half-masters. A pair of trousers too short for the wearer.

1924 F.J. MILLS *Happy Days* 112 Those trousers . . were what was known as half-masters. There was a space of three inches between the bottom of each leg and top of each boot. **1943** A. STEWART *Let's get Cracking* 55 My Malayan-issue trousers – weird garments which looked like bell-bottomed 'half-masters' when turned down.

half-time school. *Hist.* See quot. 1912.

1873 H. PARKES *Speeches* 5 Aug. (1876) 379 The half-time school means that the teacher goes to one place where there are 8 or 10 children and teaches them for three days, and then rides on to another place 30 miles distant and teaches another group there for three days. **1874** *Illustr. Sydney News* 19 Dec. 11/3 As instancing one benefit which the half-time bush schools in the interior confer upon the settlers there, it is only necessary to say that in many places where children have to travel a mile or two to the teacher's residence, parents have been compelled to dispense with the daily education from fear of danger to which female children are exposed from ruffianly shepherds and tramps. **1889** R.W. DALE *Impressions Aust.* 121 Wherever twenty children between the ages of six and fourteen are residing within an estimated radius of ten miles from a central point, and can be collected in groups of not less than ten children in each, 'two half-time schools shall be established, and one teacher is to divide his time equally between them'. **1899** *Bulletin* (Sydney) 14 Jan. 14/1 In a New England farming-district were two half-time schools. **1912** *Cwlth. of Aust. for Farmers* (Dept. External Affairs) 92 In still more thinly-peopled areas, half-time schools are to be found, *i.e.*, schools which are visited alternately by the one teacher, while itinerant teachers visit the scattered settlers in the 'back blocks'. **1916** E. & M.S. GREW *Rambles in Aust.* 178 'Bush' children have 'Provisional' or 'Half-time' schools, provided for them.

halves, on (the): see HALF 1.

ham and beef shop. A shop that specializes in the sale of cooked meats. Also *attrib.*, and *ellipt.* as **ham and beef.**

1905 *Truth* (Sydney) 23 Apr. 1/7 The small goods in a Leichhardt ham and beef shop have a row every morning while settling the question as to who is the oldest inhabitant. The German sausage that has sat in a window for about three weeks . . should be dipped in Condy's fluid and buried. **1907** *Ibid.* 18 Aug. 1/7 The ham and beef shopman will persist in doctoring his goods with boric acid preservatives. **1933** F. CLUNE *Try Anything Once* 134, I got a cab and drove to Redfern where I knew my brother Jack had had a ham-and-beef shop. **1949** R. PARK *Poor Man's Orange* 8 It was as much part of Surry Hills life as the picture-show or the police station, the ham and beef or the sly-grog shop. **1959** D. NILAND *Big Smoke* 114 That old hen would be either going to church or to the ham-and-beef for a headache powder. **1967** F.T. MACARTNEY *Proof against Failure* 9 There were few 'delicatessens', known more humbly then as 'ham and beef shops'. **1977** H. GARNER *Monkey Grip* 149 An hour later I was in Lesley's Ham and Beef Shop.

ham and egg. a. In the collocation **ham and egg daisy,** *poached egg daisy*, see POACHED. **b.** *pl.* Any of several yellow-flowering plants.

1932 M.R. WHITE *No Roads go By* 230 Patches of ham-and-egg daisies, or Soldier's Buttons as bush folk call them. . . These flowers are really more like poached eggs than anything else, with their yellow lopsided centre and setting of white. **1935** T. RAYMENT *Cluster of Bees* 176, I sit down beside the 'Ham and Eggs' of the school-children. **1944** A. MARSHALL *These are my People* 201 Say diggers, do you remember picking the ham and eggs. **1948** G. FARWELL *Down Argent Street* 87 Thick with wild flowers; paper-petalled white everlastings, yellow ham-and-eggs.

hambone. [Prob. transf. use of *ham-bone* inferior actor: see OEDS 2.] A striptease performed by a male.

1966 C. MCGREGOR *Profile Aust.* 64 In March 1964 the citizens of Sydney were shocked when a medical student did a 'hambone'—a male striptease which continues until the man is stark naked—in front of a packed audience of freshers during a Sydney University orientation week; what they did not know was that the 'hambone' had been a popular entertainment at parties in the exclusive suburbs of the North Shore for many months beforehand! **1972** *Bulletin* (Sydney) 21 Oct. 45/3 It is not repeated—during the hambone nor the mass Percy-pointing event that follows. **1972** L. IRISH *Time of Dolphins* 99 People were yelling things like 'hambone'. His pants were coming down, that was it, and everyone was jumping to have a look.

hammer. [Abbrev. of *hammer and tack*, rhyming slang for 'back'.] In the phr. **to be on** (someone's) **hammer,** to be in hot pursuit of (a person, etc.); to hound or pester.

1942 *Truth* (Sydney) 31 May 12/2 Someone 'drums' me there's two 'Jacks' on me 'hammer'. **1955** D. NILAND *Shiralee* 42 The child was on his hammer from the moment he woke. **1962** K. SIMONS *Not with Kiss* 12 'What about these rumours! If the Company is going to sell out, the men have a right to know. . .' 'Look, everyone here has been on my hammer. . . I don't know.' **1975** L. RYAN *Shearers* 5 The shearing committee will be on your hammer later. **1986** *Canberra Times* 20 June 2/3 Things have really gone bad . . when a peaceful demonstrator can't even break a few windows on a foreign embassy without someone getting on her hammer.

hammer-and-tap. A method of drilling rock by hand. Also *attrib.*

1977 J. DOUGHTY *Gold in Blood* 243 We went to work with gympie and drill, 'hammer-and-tap', and bored and fired our first cut. **1978** D. STUART *Wedgetail View* 75 Well, we can both use jackhammers, an' we've done a bit of hammer and tap, an' pick an' shovel, axe work. **1982** M. WALKER *Making Do* 68 There were miners doing 'hammer and tap' demonstrations, with two men on top of a waggon, with a great piece of stone, belting it with a double-header hammer and drill.

hand, *n.*[1] *Hist.* [Cf. *for one's own hand* for one's own interest: see OED *hand, sb.* 27.]

1. In the phr. **on** (or **upon**) **one's own hands**: (of a convict) permitted to work for one's own interest or benefit, as distinct from being assigned to public labour or into private service.

1801 *HRA* (1915) 1st Ser. III. 254 Several settlers and others who have been allowed to take prisoners off the stores have abused that indulgence by receiving payment from the prisoners to allow them to be on their own hands. **1803** *Sydney Gaz.* 7 Aug., Patrick Shannon exhibited a complaint against John Hunter, his Government servant, for intending to defraud him of nine days pay, at the rate of Ten shillings per week, for allowing him the indulgence of being on his own hands. **1810** *Ibid.* 17 Feb., Those who take prisoners off the Stores shall not permit them to go upon their own hands, under penalty of 2s. 6d. per diem for every day the prisoner shall be absent from their service. **1818** *Hobart Town Gaz.* 3 Jan., All Female Prisoners not assigned to Service, and who are allowed to be at large on their own Hands, must have regular Tickets of Leave. **1827** *Colonial Times* (Hobart) 27 Jan., In no instance . . do we approve of rewarding the labourer by placing him on his own hands for any portion of the day, to work or amuse himself. **1834** J.D. LANG *Hist. & Statistical Acct. N.S.W.* II. 47 The assigned servant . . was naturally enough desirous of being *on her own hands*, as the wife of a free mechanic.

2. In the phr. **on the hands of the government**: (of a convict) in official custody; also *transf.*: see quot. 1874.

1829 *HRA* (1922) 1st Ser. XV. 309 The Number of female Convicts who remained on the hands of the Government. **1874** J. FORREST *Explorations in Aust.* (1875) 339 A source of employment for paupers on the hands of the Government.

hand, *n.*[2] *Shearing.* Used *attrib.* in Special Comb. **hand-piece,** the part of a shearing machine that is held in the hand, the shearing attachment; **(-blade) shearer,** one who uses manually operated shears; **(-shearing) shed,** a shed in which the shearers use manually operated shears.

1912 R.S. TAIT *Scotty Mac* 9 The **hand pieces** are adding their chatter to the din. **1933** J. TRURAN *Where Plain Begins* 148 Perspiring men in flannel singlets . . wrestled with the big, merino wethers . . running the whizzing 'handpieces' along their bellies. **1943** *Bulletin* (Sydney) 3 Nov. 12/1 My Queensland paper has it that a bunch of greasies downed handpieces in a Longreach shed because they thought they'd catch something from a few jummies with scabby mouths. **1956** *Ibid.* 5 Dec. 12/4 The young learner-shearer was having a rough time... A slip of the handpiece and there was one dead sheep. **1904** *Shearer* (Sydney) 30 July 1/3 **Hand** and machine **shearers.** **1910** *Bulletin* (Sydney) 22 Dec. 44/2 Very few new hand-shearers are turned out now from any but cocky sheds. **1949** G. FARWELL *Traveller's Tracks* 100 Eighty-four years old Jim Huxley, one of the original hand-blade shearers. **1904** *Shearer* (Sydney) 15 Oct. 8/5 Until this year this place was a **hand shed,** but Mr Chomley, wishing to be up to date, installed the latest pattern of the Wolseley sheep-shearing machine. **1910** *Bulletin* (Sydney) 22 Dec. 44/2 Men follow machine sheds or hand sheds. **1919** *Ibid.* 23 Jan. 24/2 In some hand-shearing sheds a couple of stands are set apart for learners.

handball. *Australian National Football.* HANDPASS *n.*

1859 C.C. MULLEN *Hist. Austral. Rules Football* (1959) 11 Handball will only be allowed if the ball is held clearly in one hand and punched or hit out with the other. **1900** B. KERR *Silliad* 31 Now Titus Green burst through the bustling throng And by nice handball brought the ball along. **1931** J.F. MCHALE et al. *Austral. Game of Football* 48 Handball is where the ball is clearly held in one hand and punched with the closed fist of the other hand. **1936** E.C.H. TAYLOR et al. *Our Austral. Game Football* 23 The wonderful display of handball exploited by the Footscray team when that club defeated Essendon.. in 1924. **1963** L. RICHARDS *Boots & All!* 81 Len Smith must also go down in football history for inventing a new style of hand-ball—even though it borders on a throw. **1982** *Bulletin* (Sydney) 28 Sept. 36/3 Standard handball.. punching an oval ball with the clenched fist.

Also as *v. intr.*

1963 *Footy Fan* (Melbourne) I. vii. 10 He is able to handball with both hands.

handle. Chiefly *S.A.* and *N.T.* A measure of beer; the glass (having a handle) in which it is contained.

[N.Z. **1909** *N.Z. Truth* (Wellington) 29 May 7/3 Did he have 'a handle' of beer every time, or just a drop o' Scotch?] **1943** *Bulletin* (Sydney) 14 Apr. 27/4 As no bottles can be bought for love or money Mum and the girls and the little wife go to the hotels. And do they drink it from nice dainty little glasses? Not on your life—from handles and schooners, and some will order pints if they can get them. **1956** S. HOPE *Diggers' Paradise* 231 In South Australia.. a middy is called a 'handle'. **1966** H. PORTER *Paper Chase* 201 In Adelaide.. I pick up the local expressions.. handle, schooner, middy and butcher as names for beer-vessels. **1978** M.J. BURTON *Bush Pub* 58 Give us three handles with a dash of rum. **1982** *Bulletin* (Sydney) 28 Sept. 28/2 They troop in at the end of the day for a 'handle' (pot or middy) costing $1—living in Darwin is not expensive.

handpass, *n. Australian National Football.* A pass in which the ball is held in one hand and struck with (usu. the clenched fist of) the other hand.

1931 J.F. MCHALE et al. *Austral. Game of Football* 56 *Handpass,* the ball may be held in one hand and hit with the open palm of the other hand, not necessarily with the clenched fist. **1960** *N.T. News* (Darwin) 5 Jan. 8/5 Cooper snapped a neat handpass to Potts. **1963** L. RICHARDS *Boots & All!* 81 His players started using lightning-fast passes in which the ball was hit with the open hand, a more accurate and far quicker method than the ordinary hand pass with the punch or the clenched fist. **1973** J. DUNN *How to play Football* 41 The handpass, therefore, is tremendously important in football, and almost as important as the kick itself.

handpass, *v. Australian National Football. intr.* To deliver a handpass. Also as *vbl. n.*

1960 *N.T. News* (Darwin) 5 Jan. 8/6 Sparks marked well within kicking distance but foolishly handpassed to Lew Fatt. **1963** *Footy Fan* (Melbourne) I. xiii. 13 Hand passing is now divided into two categories—the conventional and the modern. **1971** B. ANDREW *Austral. Football Handbk.* 43 Players *must* learn to punch the ball with either hand—and to be able to handpass in any direction.

hand-throw, *v. trans.* To cast (a beast) to the ground preparatory to branding.

1921 *Bulletin* (Sydney) 15 Sept. 22/4, 107 fat calves.. were hand-thrown ('scruffed'). **1931** *Ibid.* 29 July 21/3 To hand-throw 300 nuggety calves before breakfast might be considered a good morning's work.

hang, *v.*

1. a. *trans.* Usu. with **up**: to tether (a horse). Also *intr.*

1859 W. KELLY *Life in Vic.* I. 49 In Melbourne there are posts sunk in the ground almost opposite every door, with rings and latches for affixing the bridles to them... Fastening your horse to one of these posts is termed 'hanging him up'. **1869** J. MARTINEAU *Lett. from Aust.* 90 Let your horse stand quietly grazing—'hung up', as the phrase is, to a tree. **1871** *Austral. Jrnl.* Aug. 663/2 Hang up your moke, my young Ducrow, sit down. **1888** 'R. BOLDREWOOD' *Robbery under Arms* (1937) 191 They thought we didn't tumble I expect; but I seen their horses hung up outside. **1902** H. LAWSON *Children of Bush* 192 Several saddle-horses, which had been 'hanging-up' round the verandah, were galloping wildly down the road in clouds of dust. **1916** J.B. COOPER *Coo-oo-ee!* 164 An Australian 'hangs' his horse to a fence. **1928** R.H. CROLL *Open Road Vic.* 19 A typical country market. There is no mistaking the appointed day: horses are 'hung up' in long lines on the fences of the reserves. **1962** J. MARSHALL *This is Grass* 60 Why didn't you hang up your horse outside?

b. *intr.* With **up**: to stop work, esp. in shearing. Also as *vbl. n.*

1891 H.W. HARRIS *Shearers or Shorn* 5 In decreeing this present 'hanging up' of the mine of unionist labour, the unionist leaders seem to have acted as though they were frightened that calm deliberation would too glaringly expose their present errors in the past. **1896** *Worker* (Sydney) 11 Jan. 3/4 Was ordered to hang up by Mr Stokes, the person over the board, which rather surprised me, as I had not been 'chipped' at, taking good care from the start to do my work well. **1962** *Sydney Morning Herald* 24 Nov. 12/3 A shearer putting in a wet ticket, after a majority dry vote, can 'hang up' and go to the huts without dismissal. **1975** L. RYAN *Shearers* 123 The greasies have hung up. Why can't we?

2. In the phr. **to hang (it) out,** to endure (hardship, etc.), to hold out.

1890 'R. BOLDREWOOD' *Colonial Reformer* II. 130 As long as they have their grub and their wages they'll hang it out. **1914** T.C. WOLLASTON *Spirit of Child* 65, I think I'll *hang it out a bit longer*! **1923** J. ARMOUR *Spell of Inland* 125 Their water bags.. were almost empty, but George knew where there was a pool of water in the rocks about ten miles on, and they would easily 'hang out' until then. **1936** C.T. MADIGAN *Central Aust.* 258 It is one of the driest seasons.. and the.. brave people of the north.. slowly say, 'I think I'll hang it out a bit longer.' **1946** K. TENNANT *Lost Haven* 132 The old punt had broken down at last. He had been hoping against hope that it would hang out until the war ended, but the luck was against him.

hanging, *vbl. n. Obs.* A perquisite. Usu in *pl.*

1847 *Guardian* (Hobart) 8 Sept. 3/5 A friend at our elbow, acquainted with Colonial *slang,* tells us, that the *hangings* have been monstrous heavy!!! **1849** A. HARRIS *Emigrant Family* (1967) 199 There was hangings to it, lad. She gave old Tom such a bang-up new Spanish bladed pocket-knife; one of them the old Jew sells for three bob. **1862** *Bell's Life in Sydney* 2 Aug. 2/5 This fortunate gentleman, in addition to his 'screw' and the 'hangings', holds a military license for the purpose of dispensing the blessings of 'grog for the million'. **1899** L. BECKE *Old Convict Days* 63 While the flogger was fixing me up [to the triangles] he said to me quietly, 'Is there any hangings to it?' meaning had I anything to give him to lay it on lightly.

happy family. [From the bird's gregarious habit.] APOSTLE. Occas. as collective.

1901 *Emu* I. 113 Variously known as 'The Happy Family', 'The Twelve Apostles' and 'Seven Sisters'.. my particular flock numbers twelve usually. **1904** *Bulletin* (Sydney) 24 Mar. 17/2 The happy family, or grey-crowned Pomatastomus.. is a trifle smaller than the 'twelve apostles'. **1938** F. BLAKELEY *Hard Liberty* 179 The cock-a-whizzle is found in all mulga country; it belongs to the group of 'Happy Family' and 'Twelve Apostles'—always good camp birds.

Happy Jack. Either of two babblers, the *grey-crowned babbler* (see GREY *a.*) and the *white-browed babbler* (see WHITE *a.*[2] 1 b.), both of which live in groups; APOSTLE b.

1921 'J. O'BRIEN' *Around Boree Log* 31 Happy Jacks (alias Gray-crowned Babblers) are brown with white markings. **1925** *Bulletin* (Sydney) 1 Jan. 24/4 'Happy Jacks' foraged for scraps thrown out. **1953** A. RUSSELL *Murray Walkabout* 103 Hardly had we settled down in camp when we had a visit from a company of gambolling white-browed babblers, or 'happy jacks'. **1961** *Bulletin* (Sydney) 29 Mar. 42/1 A flock of Happy Jacks ran merrily and noisily up and down the bimble-box trees.

harbour. In the collocation **our harbour** (freq. **'arbour**), Sydney Harbour.

1880 *Bulletin* (Sydney) 20 Mar. 1/3 Gentle Reader,—What do you think of our Harbour? And having mastered this time-honoured question, tell me what do you think of our Circular Quay? **1883** R.E.N. TWOPENY *Town Life Aust.* 19, I suppose that nearly everyone has heard of the beauties of Sydney Harbour—'our Harbour', as the Sydneyites fondly call it. **1902** *Sporting News* (Launceston) 29 Nov. 1/3 The genial Sam will vacate 'Our Arbour' and all the beauty spots of Sydney. **1914** N.F. SPIELVOGEL *Gumsucker at Home* 111 Sydney folk ask your opinion about 'our 'Arbour', Ballarat folk about 'our lake', and Warrnambool folk about 'our breakwater'. **1925** S. HICKS *Hullo Australs.* 242 'Our 'arbour' as its owners humorously and lovingly call it is indeed a veritable marvel. **1940** A. HASKELL *Waltzing Matilda* 136 Sydney.. is dominated by the Harbour, 'our Harbour' as it is so proudly called. **1960** S. WOODFIELD *A for Artemis* 118 You Aussies are the bloody limit. You can't see any further than 'Our 'Arbour'. **1965** G. MCINNES *Road to Gundagai* 71 So the battle raged. 'Our 'Arbour, Our Bridge and Our Bradman' was the Melbourne jibe at Sydney.

hard, *a.* In miscellaneous collocations: **hard case** [transf. use of U.S. *hard case* hardened criminal (OED(S *a.* 7)], a character; one who does not conform; an incorrigible (drinker, liar, eccentric, etc.); **hitter,** a bowler hat; **labour** [used elsewhere but recorded earliest in Aust.], physically hard labour imposed on a convict; also *attrib.*; **stuff** [used elsewhere but recorded earliest in Aust.], spirituous liquor; **timer,** one who has experienced hard or difficult times; **tucker,** lean rations; **word** [Br. dial. in various senses (see OEDS 6 b.)], an importunate request, esp. in the phr. **to put the hard word on.**

1892 *Truth* (Sydney) 8 May 3/7 What a study were those faces! Many of them real '**hard cases**'. **1897** J.J. MURIF *From Ocean to Ocean* 27 A dozen or so miles from Hergott, I met a 'hardcase' of the bush. **1904** C.W. JOHNSTON *Out-Back Homestead* 51 *Ned Allardyce* was accredited with being the hardest case on, or within miles of, Ryan's Creek. **1908** 'FIFTY-THREE YRS.' MINER' *So Long* 75 'Well,' she said to Jack, 'you are a 'hard case'. I don't know how to take you.' **1919** C.H. THORP *Handful of Ausseys* 84 There was a barmaid, quite a hard case and a sport, in one of the hotels. **1936** N. CALDWELL *Fangs of Sea* 89, I well knew the old fisherman, a real hard case. **1965** R.H. CONQUEST *Horses in Kitchen* 144 The Australian stock-horse is also a 'hard case', but you don't appreciate this until you've known him for a good many years. **1976** N.V. WALLACE *Bush Lawyer* 172 'He's quite a character.' 'What's that?' she queried. 'A hard case,' I said. **1892** 'J. MILLER' *Workingman's Paradise* 156 He turned and looked at her as he passed; he had a short beard and wore a '**hard hitter**'. **1898** *Worker* (Sydney) 1 Jan. 7/1 The tie beams there.. are today laden with portmanteaux, fashionable hard-hitters. **1917** *Truth* (Sydney) 15 Apr. 1/8 He exchanged his hard-hitter for a soft hat and flyveil. **1943** *Bulletin* (Sydney) 20 Oct. 13/2, I met them out on the desert prospecting, always in thick clothes and a felt hat and not seldom the old 'hard-hitter'. **1966** A.R. CHISHOLM *Familiar Presence* 80 What is now called a 'bowler' used to be a 'hard-hitter' or a 'pee-wee'. **1982** J. ANDERSON *Winners can Laugh* 19 In his frock coat and black 'hard hitter' his was an overwhelming presence. **1803** *Sydney Gaz.* 10 July, They will on conviction be put to **Hard Labour** for six months. **1844** *Duncan's Weekly Register* (Sydney) 20 Jan. 386/1 Sentenced to twelve months hard labour in irons. **1851** *Irish Exile* (Hobart) 18 Jan. 3/1 Mr P. O'Donohoe arrived here on Wednesday evening last, and was 'classed' on Thursday morning, for a hard labour party. **1832** *Hill's Life N.S.W.* (Sydney) 6 July 4 Lots of swizzle, **hard stuff**, two waters, heavy wet, 'weed', and long steamers, were the *last act.* **1851** *Empire* (Sydney) 22 Oct. 282/6 'Please sir, can we have three glasses of hard stuff?' 'No—got none—can have three pints of ale.' **1888** 'R. BOLDREWOOD' *Robbery under Arms* (1937) 40, I can stand what any other man can, and without the hard stuff, either. **1892** 'J. MILLER' *Workingman's Paradise* 114 On a seat in the rain, near a lamp, was a poor devil of a woman, a regular **hard-timer** . . sleeping with her head hung over the back of the seat like a fowl's. **1944** J. DEVANNY *By Tropic Sea & Jungle* 215 Some hard-timers don't even bother about an oven—cook everything in the ashes. **1932** M. TERRY *Out Back* 2 Good honest work, **hard tucker**—with plenty of it. **1932** J. MCCARTER *Pan's Clan* 138 Heat, flies, hard tucker, an' on yer flamin' own from mornin' till dark. **1959** H. DRAKE-BROCKMAN *West Coast Stories* 196 We'd lived for a fortnight on kangaroo and bungarra, cooked blackfeller fashion in the coals . . hard tucker, but good solid strengthening tucker. **1918** J.A. PHILP *Jingles that Jangle* 23 An Irish friend to whom I was reading the proof of this preface gave me 'the **hard word**'. **1923** *Austral.* (Sydney) Apr. 56 An old tart breasts up ter 'im an' puts th' 'ard word on 'im. 'Shout's a drink, ol' sport,' gurgles th' nimp' du pave. **1937** A.W. UPFIELD *Winds of Evil* 44, I came along on the look out for work. . . I . . put the hard word on Mr Borradale for a job. **1939** K. TENNANT *Foveaux* 359 The landlord tried to make love to her, or, as she termed it, 'put the hard word on her'. Linnie was no stranger to the hard word. **1953** D. CUSACK *Southern Steel* 144 Trouble about you is you've got the Middle East superiority complex. I bet you put the hard word on plenty of girls in between the fighting. **1969** F.B. VICKERS *No Man is Himself* 3 He caught her putting the hard word on some bloke on Saturday night. It seems the bloke knocked her back. **1985** H. GARNER *Postcards from Surfers* 68, I can go into any one of them and get myself a fuck, without having to *fight* for it. I never put the hard word on you, did I Watto, in all those years?

hardenbergia /hadən'bɜgiə/. [The Austral. plant genus *Hardenbergia* was named by English botanist G. Bentham (*Enu. Pl. Huegel* (1837) 40) after Countess Franziska von *Hardenberg*, an Austrian patron of botany.] Any species of the genus of trailing or climbing plants *Hardenbergia* (fam. Fabaceae). See also FALSE SARSAPARILLA.

1879 'OLD HAND' *Journey Port Phillip to S.A.* 19 The scarlet Kennedia and the purple hardenbergia climbed over the verandah. **1948** P.J. HURLEY *Red Cedar* 28 Robes of richest purple where hardenbergias grew. **1981** *Wild Food Recipes* (Univ. Qld. Bot. Club) II. 24 *Hardenbergia tea.* Made in the same manner as ordinary tea, however more dried leaves are required to get a strong flavour. **1984** E. WALLING *On Trail Austral. Wildflowers* 11 The purple Sarsaparilla or *Hardenbergia* (one of the plants with a botanical name as familiar as the common one).

hard-gut mullet. [With reference to a large, hard lump in the gut of the fish.] A young *sea mullet* (see SEA). Also abbrev. as **hard-gut.**

1874 *N.S.W. Rep. R. Comm. Fisheries* (1880) 12 The smaller Australian varieties [of mullet] consist of—*Mugil argentens*, or hard-gut [etc.]. **1896** F.G. AFLALO *Sketch Nat. Hist. Aust.* 232 The Sydney Sea Mullet keep well out in the offing, wherein they differ from the younger generation known as Hard Gut mullet, which frequent the estuaries and generally keep inshore. **1965** *Austral. Encycl.* IV. 82 During January and February 'hard-gut' mullet (young sea mullet) are caught in great numbers.

hardwood. The relatively hard wood of any of many genera of Australian trees, esp. of the genus *Eucalyptus* (see EUCALYPTUS); a tree having such wood; *spec.* the wood of an angiosperm (see quots. 1957 and 1984). Also *attrib.*

1842 *Sydney Herald* 12 Apr. 3/3 The forests . . abound with rosewood, cedar, and hardwood, of a very fine description. **1853** J. SHERER *Gold Finder Aust.* 61 The earnings of hard-wood sawyers can scarcely be estimated. **1864** J. ARMOUR *Diggings, Bush & Melbourne* 13 The hut was roomy; the walls were formed of hardwood slabs. **1872** W.H. THOMES *Bushrangers* 101 The bunch of bones landed on the hard-wood floor. **1882** *Austral. Handbk.* 391 The greater part of the timber termed 'Hardwood' is the produce of various kinds of Eucalypts. **1919** R.T. BAKER *Hardwoods of Aust.* 1 The line of demarcation between a 'hard-' and 'soft-' wood is rather vague as it is not based on figures, for many a wood is easily worked with a chisel and saw and is yet classed as hard, whilst another kind will offer great resistance to cutting tools. **1955** K. SHERROTT *Your House* 15 *Hardwood* means any Australian wood of the eucalypt group, or any other timber known locally as hardwood. **1957** *Forest Trees Aust.* (Cwlth. Forestry & Timber Bureau) 16 The forest trees of Australia may be arranged conveniently into two broad categories, 'hardwoods' and 'softwoods'. Hardwoods, also known as 'broad-leaved' plants, include all the woody plants except the conifers. **1978** B. ST. A. SMITH *Spirit beyond Psyche* 131 To carry his swag along the hardwood railroad sleepers that snaked off into the Queensland bush. **1984** D.J. BOLAND et al. *Forest Trees Aust.* (rev. ed.) 650 Hardwood. Wood from trees classified botanically as angiosperms. The term does not denote the relative hardness of the wood, though it is sometimes used in this sense.

hardyhead. Any of several small marine and freshwater fish of the fam. Atherinidae, often occurring in schools.

1881 *Proc. Linnean Soc. N.S.W.* VI. 38 *Atherina pinguis* . . *'Hardyhead'* of Sydney Fishermen. **1936** T.C. ROUGHLEY *Wonders Great Barrier Reef* 207 Small fishes known as 'hardyheads', which grow to . . about four inches, frequently congregate in shoals so dense that they lie like a solid mass in the water. **1977** J.M. THOMSON *Field Guide Common Sea & Estuary Fishes* 107 Not unlike small mullet, the hardyheads are often called silversides from the broad silver stripe which many of the species carry along the sides.

hare-wallaby. [From the resemblance of the wallaby to the European hare: see quot. 1841.] Any of several small wallabies of the genera *Laborchestes* and *Lagostrophus* of mainland Aust. Also with distinguishing epithet (see *spectacled hare-wallaby* SPECTACLED).

[**1841** J. GOULD *Birds of Aust.* (1848) I. Pl. 12, The name of Hare Kangaroo has been given to this species [*sc. Lagorchestes leporoïdes*], as much from the similarity of its form, its size, and the colour and texture of its fur, as from its habits assimilating in many particulars to those of that animal.] **1896** B. SPENCER *Rep. Horn Sci. Exped. Central Aust.* I. 109 At Mount Sonder we had obtained specimens of the hare-wallaby (*Lagorchestes conspicillatus var. leichardtii*). **1935** H.H. FINLAYSON *Red Centre* 62 Of the smaller herbivorous marsupials, two of the most interesting are the hare wallabies. **1962** MARSHALL & DRYSDALE *Journey among Men* 65 Ivan, the ex-kangaroo shooter, was out after hare wallabies and the euro. **1983** R. STRAHAN *Compl. Bk. Austral. Mammals* 195 The distribution of all hare-wallabies has declined severely since European settlement.

harlequin. A highly prized form of opal (see quot. 1974); a stone of this type. Also *attrib.*

1873 C. ROBINSON *N.S.W.* 62 Opals. . . Amongst polished stones are some of the harlequin class. **1932** I.L. IDRIESS *Prospecting for Gold* 245 A pattern stone, if the colours are bright, is the most valuable, and of all patterns the Harlequin is, perhaps, the most prized. **1960** D. MCLEAN *Roaring Days* 62 The opal is the most beautiful of all gems, and the most beautiful opal is the harlequin. . . It's a round stone covered with little angular surfaces as if it has been cut by a master hand; these surfaces flash every colour known to nature in a constantly changing, shimmering mosaic. **1967** K. LLOYD *Black Opal* 81 From the space that he uncovered on the stone he identified it as a 'harlequin' black opal of considerable value. **1974** B. MYATT *P. Hamlyn Dict. of Austral. Gemstones* 134 Harlequin opal shows a mosaic-like pattern of colour in angular, roughly rectangular or rounded patches of about equal size.

harlequin bronzewing. FLOCK PIGEON a. Also **harlequin pigeon.**

1841 J. GOULD *Birds of Aust.* (1848) II. Pl. 66, *Peristera histrionica* . . Harlequin Bronzewing. **1845** L. LEICHHARDT *Jrnl. Overland Exped. Aust.* 20 June (1847) 296 Large flocks of Peristera histrionica (the Harlequin pigeon) were lying on the patches of burnt grass on the plains. **1849** C. STURT *Narr. Exped. Central Aust.* II. App. 43 Phaps Histrionica . . *The Harlequin Bronze-wing* . . has a white and black head, the crown being white, and its back is a rusty brown. **1962** MARSHALL & DRYSDALE *Journey among Men* 73 The harlequin bronzewing, or flock pigeon . . declined mysteriously and was thought to be on the verge of extinction.

harness-cask. [Transf. use of *harness-cask* shipboard container in which salt meat is kept.] A container in which salt meat is stored prior to use.

1848 T.L. MITCHELL *Jrnl. Exped. Tropical Aust.* 39 The dray—already there with the harness casks. **1888** 'R. BOLDREWOOD' *Robbery under Arms* (1937) 16 The steer was cut up and salted and in the harness-cask soon after sunrise. **1921** G.A. BELL *Under Brigalow* 211 The 'duffers' were suspected of replenishing their own 'harness' casks from their neighbours' herds.

hash. Used *attrib.* to designate a cheap eating house, boarding house, etc., or one who works in such an establishment.

1892 *Truth* (Sydney) 15 May 1/5 'D'ye love me Bill?' the hash girl said, While out with her Waterloo mash. **1896** H. LAWSON *While Billy Boils* 48 The landlady of a hash-house where I was stopping in Albany. **1898** *Worker* (Sydney) 8 Jan. 8/1 The high rate of house rents in Sydney is largely responsible both for the doss-houses and the cheap hash-foundries. **1898** *Bulletin* (Sydney) 9 July 15/1, I 'put up' in a hash-mosque lately. . . I . . said I was willing enough to fire the old man out, if she gave me the management of the hash-tower. **1903** *Truth* (Sydney) 18 Jan. 1/6, I boarded at a hash-house where they serve out undercut steak at 6d. a time. *Ibid.* 24 May 1/8 A thirty bob per week clerk was bundled out of his boarding-house . . for failing to pay his board bill. Being a bit sweet on the hashman's daughter he felt extremely hurt. **1905** *Ibid.* 2 July 1/3 Many of our book-writers would rather, if given the choice, be editor of the bill of fare in a hash-tower. **1911** *Bulletin* (Sydney) 23 Nov. 43/1 His bill of fare is less changeable than that of a hash-house. **1912** *Ibid.* 25 Apr. 44/1 There comes a time in the life of every right-thinking male person when the hash-tower revolts him, and when life in an hotel looks ghastlier the closer it is seen. **1933** H.B. RAINE *Whip-Hand* 40 You ought to be on the stage, or in a circus, instead of jugglin' dishes in a hash-house. **1943** S.W. KEOUGH *Around Army* 19 It is axiomatic that a bab. should either have had absolutely no experience of cooking or experience confined to hashhouses. **1945** *Atebrin Advocate: Mag. 2/4 Austral. Armoured Regiment* Jan. 2 They want a drum of Range fuel at the hash foundry or there'll be no tea.

hashmagandy. Also **hash-me-gandy.** [f. prec., perh. infl. by *salmagundi* mixture of meats, etc.]

1. A stew.

1919 W.H. DOWNING *Digger Dialects* 28 *Hashmagandy*, an insipid and monotonous army dish. **1945** S.J. BAKER *Austral. Lang.* 81 For stews our only original contributions appear to be *hash-me-gandy* and *mulliga stew.*

2. Special Comb. **hashmagandy bag,** see quot.

1944 *Bulletin* (Sydney) 23 Feb. 12/3, I wonder if any Murray fisherman these days ever uses a 'hashmagandy' bag. First you got hold of one of those old-fashioned open-wove potato sacks. Then from any handy boiling-down works a couple of bucketfuls of cooked-to-rags mutton; or, failing that you cooked a similar quantity and quality of rabbit. Hung over the stern of the moored flattie such a bag, given an occasional shake, discharged a stream of tasty meat particles. . . The modern angler would probably call it 'burley', but present-day mixtures of bran and pollard and soaked bread can never come near the old 'hashmagandy' as a fish-enticer.

hat, *n.* In the phr. **to throw** (one's) **hat in (first),** to declare an intention with a view to ascertaining the response, to 'test the water'.

1953 'CADDIE' *Caddie* 248 As he walked in through the back door I said: 'Hadn't you better throw your hat in first?' **1960** R. TULLIPAN *Follow Sun* 53 There is, I suppose, a need to throw my hat in where you're concerned, Julie. **1975** X. HERBERT *Poor Fellow my Country* 343 It was Fay McFee again, declaring in her brassy contralto that she supposed she ought to throw her hat in first, but didn't have one. **1981** *Weekend Austral. Mag.* (Sydney) 25 Apr. 18/6 This week the builder returned with a big smile: 'Should I throw my hat in first?' he asked, as his only concession.

hat, *v.* [Back-formation f. HATTER.] *intr.* To live a solitary life, esp. as a gold-miner; *transf.*, to fossick.

1868 *Wallaroo Times* (Kadina) 4 Mar. 6/3 A German named Jacob . . had been 'hatting' in Splitters Gully, Whipstick. **1891** *Age* (Melbourne) 25 Nov. 6/7 Two old miners have been hatting for gold amongst the old alluvial gullies. **1900** H. LAWSON *On Track* 88 He 'hatted' and brooded over it till he went ratty. **1902** —— *Children of Bush* 38 When a man drops mateship altogether and takes to 'hatting' in the Bush, it's a step towards a convenient tree and a couple of saddle-straps buckled together. **1913** —— *Triangles of Life* 216 No, it wasn't drink. They reckoned he'd been 'hatting' it too long. **1980** *Canberra Times* 18 Aug. 7/1 On the Victorian gold fields he averages 85 gms. a day by 'hatting', searching through the tailing heaps left by the original gold diggers.

hatter. [Prob. f. the phr. *(one's) hat covers (one's) family*, used of one who is alone in the world (see OED *hat, sb.* 5 c.); later infl. by the phr. *mad as a hatter*.]

a. *Mining.* A miner who works independently (rather than in partnership).

1853 J. ROCHFORT *Adventures Surveyor* 66 The Bendigo diggings are suitable for persons working singly. . . Such persons are called 'hatters'. They live alone, in a tent often not more than six feet long, three feet high, and three feet wide. **1862** J.A. PATTERSON *Gold Fields Vic.* 317 The 'hatter' is a solitary man who disdains the company of 'mates', and with his own tub and cradle works for his own hand wherever his fancy leads him. **1873** 'DEMONAX' *Mysteries & Miseries* 37 He used to go wandering about in the gullies, and was a 'hatter'; which signifies a person who lives by digging in the gullies. **1890** MRS H.P. MARTIN *Under Gum Tree* 28 A 'hatter', that is to say, a man who has lived by himself until his brain has been turned. **1898** *Bulletin* (Sydney) 30 July 3/2 He was sixty-six, a corrugated hatter, An' he said he'd bin a miner from his birth. **1913** *Ibid.* 2 Oct. 22/4 The solitary digger often found it necessary to sink to a greater depth than that from which he could conveniently throw up dirt. He therefore put down a hole of a certain diameter, and reducing its dimensions, left a bank on which he could deposit the dirt temporarily. This made the excavation look like a gigantic inverted hat—hence the term hatter. **1923** *Aussie* (Sydney) Dec. 55/1 Tim Pottinger, the hatter, whose camp is on the old alluvial workings down near the dredge. **1944** M.J. O'REILLY *Bowyangs & Boomerangs* 111 Danny was what was known as a 'Hatter', that is, a lone prospector. He only had the one camel to carry his swag, tools, and tucker. **1962** *Gumsuckers' Gaz.* (Melbourne) Oct. 4 A 'hatter' was a gold fossicker who preferred to live as a hermit and work on his own, was very secretive usually and regarded as an eccentric. **1978** M. WALKER *Pioneer Crafts Early Aust.* 104 Some of the solitary prospectors became known as 'hatters'—their isolation had severed their connection with mankind.

b. A rural worker pursuing a solitary occupation; a single man; a misanthrope; an eccentric.

c **1872** J.C.F. JOHNSON *Over Island* 2 'Hatter', in bush phraseology, is a man who shepherds or lives by himself. **1892** *Bulletin* (Sydney) 9 July 21/3 Where the God forgotten hatter dreams of city-life and beer. **1898** *Ibid.* 15 Jan. 14/2 *Hatter*, one who travels alone and camps alone. Either 'ratty', or has money, or does it to avoid bad society, which is about the only society going in the bush. **1901** *Ibid.* 7 Sept. 14/3 Twelve Russian and Scandinavian settlers reside there, seven married and five hatters. **1911** *Ibid.* 23 Nov. 43/1 The average boundary-rider is a hatter more by compulsion than preference. **1925** C. LE LIEVRE *Memories Old Police Officer* 24 Men of this kind were called 'hatters', in consequence of living the solitary lives they did. Most of them were well-educated Englishmen, and chose the lives of a recluse in the bush for reasons best known to themselves. **1942** F. CLUNE *Last of Austral. Explorers* 98 They came to a Government artesian bore. . . The bore-keeper was a 'hatter'. **1956** B. BEATTY *Beyond Aust.'s Cities* 114 It was . . on a hut door, the home of a 'hatter' (one of those individuals who live a lone existence away from civilisation and their fellow man), that I saw the surprising invitation: 'Any woman coming around while I am away please wait, as I want a wife.' **1965** D. MARTIN *Hero of Too* 149 She looked a scarecrow, a frump, an incurable hatter. **1977** G.W. LILLEY *Lengthening Shadows* 22 Boundary-riders on the big Queensland sheep runs . . were a varied lot. The married men were more or less normal but the single tended to be hatters, that is, somewhat queer, the monotonous and solitary life they led tended to make them so.

c. *transf.*

1893 D. LINDSAY *Jrnl. Elder Sci. Exploring Exped.* 23 No sign of the lost brute [*sc.* a camel], which is, I find, a regular 'hatter', always poking away by himself. **1945** E. MITCHELL *Speak to Earth* 113 Fences meant nothing to two of those eighteen-month steers. A white one—'a bit of a hatter, always on his own', Mr Herbert described him—was the first to jump back into the Kurrajong.

have, *v.* In the phr. **to have** (someone) **on,** to engage (someone) in a fight, contest, etc.

1941 S.J. BAKER *Pop. Dict. Austral. Slang* 34 *Have (someone) on*, to be prepared to fight a person; to accept a challenge to a contest or fight. **1962** S. GORE *Down Golden Mile* 137 What! I'm as good as some o' you young jokers. I'll have any one of yer on—old and all as I am. **1979** *Sun-Herald* (Sydney) 30 Dec. 4/7 If I had another 50 rounds I would really have these bastards on. **1980** *Ibid.* 6 Apr. 24/2, I never picked fights, but if someone picked one with me, I'd have them on.

Hawkesbury Rivers, *pl.* [f. the name of a river in N.S.W.] Rhyming slang for 'shivers'.

1941 S.J. BAKER *Pop. Dict. Austral. Slang* 35 *Hawkesbury Rivers*, the shivers. **1951** D. STIVENS *Jimmy Brockett* 141, I got the Hawkesbury Rivers while I was undressing. My hands shook. **1962** D. MCLEAN *World turned upside Down* 12 Danny would have been the first to admit that he was as game as Ned Kelly in most things, but girls gave him the Hawkesbury Rivers.

hay, *v. trans.* With **off**: to dry (standing grass, etc.). Chiefly as **hayed-off,** *ppl. a.*, dried while standing.

1948 *Bulletin* (Sydney) 24 Nov. 29/2 Sudden heat and a dry westerly hayed-off Mac's oats and he put the binder in. **1976** C.D. MILLS *Hobble Chains & Greenhide* 136 That's Mitchell, good feed, 'specially when its hayed-off like it is now. **1983** *Canberra Times* 24 May 3/1 At this time of the year there was usually standing dry feed left . . to bolster the green pick that came through with autumn rain. Because of the extended drought, there was no such hayed-off feed.

hay burner. [Also U.S.: see Mathews.] A jocular term for a horse. Formerly **hay motor.** Also *attrib.*

1900 E.L. HOLMES *Pioneer Motor Car Trip* 8 We had matched against us a pair of iron grey 'hay motors', but we . . beat them badly into Cootamundra. **1920** *Character Glimpses: Australs. on Somme* 28 What's the idea of socking our hard earned jack in that hay burner? **1942** *Bulletin* (Sydney) 29 Apr. 12/3 Even the quietest bottle-oh's hayburner is apt to 'see red' when he sees red. **1959** *Tobruk to Borneo* (Perth) June 8 A row of hay burners lined up for a match trot and gallop. **1969** P. ADAM SMITH *Rails go Westward* 14 Within a few months agitation began for horse-drawn railways . . what has been called 'the hay burner railway'. **1979** S.W. DUTHIE *Fidlers Creek* 9 This particular Saturday is the Tooley Bend Handicap and they are all going for a hay-burner called Irish Belle.

hazel. [Transf. use of *hazel*: see quot. 1920.] Either of the two shrubs or trees *Pomaderris aspera* and *P. apetala* (fam. Rhamnaceae) of e. Aust., having rough, wrinkled leaves.

1827 G.W. BARNARD in *HRA* (1923) 3rd Ser. VI. 267, A Shrub . . I shall call the 'Hazel' to which it has a similitude, is found commonly in the Creeks of V.D. Land; it has an appearance between the 'Curryjong' and the 'Hazel'. **1881** *Illustr. Austral. News* (Melbourne) 27 July 138/3 The graceful blackwoods and the pungent hazel scrub are here in abundance. **1889** J.H. MAIDEN *Useful Native Plants Aust.* 590 *Pomaderris apetala* . . called 'Hazel' in Victoria. **1920** *Land of Lyre Bird* (S. Gippsland Pioneers' Assoc.) 38 Of the different scrub timbers above mentioned the hazel was the most largely represented. . . The leaves were like those of the English Hazel, with clusters of small brown sweet smelling flowers. . . The wood was tough and good to burn. **1956** A. MARSHALL *How's Andy Going?* 12 Through the fragrant hazel . . she sped. **1973** D. WOLFE *Brass Kangaroo* 195 A dense under-forest of blackwoods, hazel, musk and other mountain species.

head, *n.*[1] *Two-up.*

1. In *pl.* A fall of the coins in which the heads face upwards; a bet that the coins will fall this way; a call declaring this.

1897 *Worker* (Sydney) 18 Dec. 3/4 Hey, bar that toss! Heads it is! **1918** J.A. PHILP *Jingles that Jangle* 34, I dreamt I saw Ted Theodore a-handling a 'kip' And a-yellin' 'Heads a dollar'. **1919** H.B. FLETCHER *Boundary Riders Egypt* 47 Look at those scamps; not two minutes in the Holy Land, and they are backing heads. . . Anyhow, I will bet you a sovereign they are heads. **1925** A. WRIGHT *Boy from Bullarah* 17 'Heads ten bob!' That was Router's first bet, and the fall of two 'flat' tails left him with but half of his purloined capital. **1944** G.H. FEARNSIDE *Sojourn in Tobruk* 24 It is just like a game of two-up. . . A man can have a run of heads and get out while he's still winning. **1972** D. SHEAHAN *Songs from Canefields* 31 When Sarg'n-Majors that used to roar The 'heads' and the two-up kings—Have called at the heavenly Q-M's store And signed for their golden wings. **1977** R. BEILBY *Gunner* 299 'Bar that spin! All bets stand!' . . 'Heads're right!'

2. Comb. **head backer, bettor.**

1925 A. WRIGHT *Boy from Bullarah* 18 From all around the ring **head backers** rose to gather in their winnings, and stake again on the next spin. **1954** T. RONAN *Vision Splendid* 230 Any of you head-backers got a bob or two to pay for my boot leather? **1946** *Austral. New Writing* 36 Taily wanted for a dollar . . there y' are, mate, **head bettor** over here. **1953** T.A.G. HUNGERFORD *Riverslake* 130 The head-betters [*sic*] . . now tumbled to the run of tails, and before long the game began to peak.

head, *n.*[2] A rogue, a sharper.

[N.Z. **1908** *N.Z. Truth* (Wellington) 2 There were a few 'heads' up from Christchurch.] **1918** *Euripidean: Troopship Souvenir* 6 Cold foot was a gentlemanly epigraph; 'ead . . those . . Johns addressed me as. **1919** A. WRIGHT *Game of Chance* 32 Is this dinkum? . . or are you puttin' a tale over on me? Your mate looks like a 'head' to me. **1924** *Bulletin* (Sydney) 21 Feb. 22/1 Yes, you'll find it quickly dwindles, with the girls and 'heads' you meet, When they work their little swindles and they throw you in the street. **1947** W.E. HARNEY *Brimming Billabongs* (1963) 115 They trap us, the station people, who are the justices of the peace, call us a 'head' or a 'rogue', and send us to jail. **1958** E. WORRELL *Song of Snake* 20 Don was disliked by whites. They called him a 'head', which is a way of saying he knew too much of white man's way for his comfort. **1964** P. ADAM SMITH *Hear Train Blow* 125 When the 'head' gave up and went back to the van, the guard motioned me to put the window up.

head, *v.*[1] [Spec. use of *head* to get ahead of so as to turn back: see OED(S *v.* 13 b. and c.] *trans.* To get ahead of (a travelling, often stampeding, mob of sheep, cattle, etc.) so as to arrest its progress.

1846 *Bell's Life in Sydney* 17 Jan. 3/3 The defendant driving a mob of cattle, and Jones being apprehensive of receiving an injury from them—not being able to reach a fence, from the position of that part of the road—'headed them', as it is termed, which so irritated Kennedy that he struck at him with his whip. **1867** 'CLERGYMAN' *Aust. as it Is* 52 None can compete with them as horsemen in the mustering of cattle and in 'heading' mobs of wild horses. **1888** 'R. BOLDREWOOD' *Robbery under Arms* (1937) 35 Father headed 'em, and turned 'em towards the peak. **1891** —— *Sydney-Side Saxon* (1925) 104 It'll take some galloping to wheel that poley brindle's mob, and if they once break there's no headin' 'em! **1923** *Austral.* (Sydney) June 11 The dog is racing to head them again. He keeps well out from the woollies. Wide-working is a test of his worth. **1938** D. BATES *Passing of Aborigines* 53 At last the galloping drovers 'headed' them again.

head, *v.*[2] *Two-up.*

1. a. In the phr. **to head them** (also **'em**), to play the game of two-up; to toss the coins so that they fall with the head side upwards. Also **to head it**.

1902 *Truth* (Sydney) 14 Sept. 1/6 The life of the Domain dosser is indeed hard. He is not allowed to even 'head 'em'. **1915** C.J. DENNIS *Songs of Sentimental Bloke* 15 An' spen's me leisure gittin' on the shick, An' 'arf me nights down there, in Little Lon., Wiv Ginger Mick, Jist 'eadin' 'em, an' doing in me gilt. **1925** A. WRIGHT *Boy from Bullarah* 19 A demand was made that he should lay odds that he would 'head' them again. **1928** M. FORREST *Reaping Roses* 96 Taught him to play 'two up', and to 'head it' with anybody. **1937** W. HATFIELD *I find Aust.* 79, I saw Fritz lose fifty pounds in one pop at 'two-up'. At this game, so long as the player can 'head them' he can keep on playing, doubling his stake. **1943** J. BINNING *Target Area* 47 'She's done it again. She's headed 'em ten times.' 'You mean to say your granny plays two-up.' **1959** *Never kill Dolphin* (Writers' Guild Qld.) 68 There was the old man on the mat with the tail-backers all round him and Shorty heading them again and again. **1981** *N.S.W. Parl. Papers* (1980–81) 3rd Sess. IV. 1970/2, I was playing two-up. . . I got barred because I headed them twice.

b. *transf.*

1945 'MASTER-SARG' *Yank discovers Aust.* 75 '*Headed 'em*', got a homer or pulled off some other good thing.

2. As ppl. (and n.) phr. in the collocation **heading them**: the playing of two-up; the spinning of two coins so that they fall head side upwards. Also *ellipt.* as **heading.**

1871 *Austral. Town & Country Jrnl.* (Sydney) 10 June 730/2 The course was soon deserted, save by a select circle of the 'heading-em' brotherhood. **1887** K. MACKAY *Stirrup Jingles* 58 Then an hour was devoted to blowing And drinking and handling the 'kip', For at 'heading' these shearers were knowing, And at talk creation could whip. **1890** *Truth* (Sydney) 16 Nov. 7/3 At the other end of the park a number of young men were engaged in the popular *pastime of 'heading 'em'*, a gambling game played with pennies. **1901** *Ibid.* 11 Aug. 3/5 The unlawful game of 'heading 'em'. **1913** H. LAWSON *Triangles of Life* 244 He kept away from drink, cards, dice, and headin' 'em. **1930** HIVES & LUMLEY *Jrnl. of Jackaroo* 8 On Sunday mornings there would be a 'school' in the back yard of the hotel, when the game of 'heading them' would be indulged in for high stakes. **1959** A. VON BERTOUCH *February Dark* 69 'I see that we might just as well take up heading 'em for a living,' said Peter. 'Heading 'em?' said Helen. 'Two-up,' said Max. 'Tossing coins.'

headings, *vbl. n. pl. Gold-mining.* [Spec. use of *heading* top layer: see OED 12.] See quot. 1869.

1859 *Colonial Mining Jrnl.* May 145/2 Their wash-dirt principally consists of the pipeclay found in the old drives, together with 2 feet of headings. **1869** R.B. SMYTH *Gold Fields & Mineral Districts* 613 *Headings*, coarse gravel or drift overlying the washdirt. **1873** W. THOMSON-GREGG *Desperate Character* II. 82 We mostly hire some fellow to help us hawl up the mullock, and get the headings out. **1887** 'OLD GOLD DIGGER' *Gold Digger's Guide* 8 Where the bottom is only up to 5 or 6 feet in depth . . one man can throw back as much headings as two men could do by pulling it up, always taking into consideration that no tight ground exists from the surface to the wash dirt. **1921** E.F. TREGASKIS *Santa Claus' Message* 5 During the dry spells he sought old tailings and headings. **1941** D. O'CALLAGHAN *Long Life Reminisc.* 27 They threw a lot of headings (that is, dirt which lies above the wash dirt). . . Headings as a rule are not payable to treat.

head serang: see SERANG.

head-station. *Home-station*, see HOME *attrib.*[2] b.

1835 J. LHOTSKY *Journey from Sydney to Austral. Alps* 97 This time of year is the conclusion of sheep-shearing, where the persons employed in it (free and bond), were returning home, or to the head-stations. **1842** *Sydney Morning Herald* 1 Aug. 1/6 On the head station is a good substantial Cottage, with Garden in front; also, a Paddock. **1846** C.P. HODGSON *Reminisc. Aust.* 37 The Main Hut, or the Head Station, so called from its being the master's own residence. **1848** H.W. HAYGARTH *Recoll. Bush Life* 14 The head station, at which the owner or superintendent resides, is generally so situated as to be as nearly as possible equidistant from the several sheep stations, to which frequent visits are necessary. **1860** 'LADY' *My Experiences in Aust.* 170 In no part of a bush establishment is the progress of neglect so rapid and so visible as at a head station. . . This term of *head* or *home* station is applied to the residence of the proprietor or manager of a grazing establishment. **1880** R. ROWE *Roughing It* 4 He and his father helped the men in building . . the permanent 'head-station' at Broadoaks—a weatherboard bungalow, with a verandah on a brick foundation. **1898** *Western Champion* (Barcaldine) 18 Jan. 6/3 There is no public road passing the Head Station. **1913** *Bulletin* (Sydney) 6 Mar. 16/2 As she was about to become a mother, the boss decided to send her to the head station, where she would have the benefit of the station gins' attention. **1937** D. GUNN *Links with Past* 11 On arrival at Wyaga, we found the head station house was a bark hut with an earth floor, but there was a good woolshed. **1955** H.G. LAMOND *Towser* 28 Gooya, the out-station, was a small replica of the head station, minus any staff not needed. **1978** R.H. CONQUEST *Dusty Distances* 55 They established an out-station, naming it after their home town. . . Over the range into the Dawson and Callide Valleys, and from there to Gracemere, where they established their head-station.

heady. *Two-up.* [f. HEAD *n.*[1] + -Y.] A person reputedly skilled in spinning the coins so that they fall head side upwards; one who bets on the coins so falling.

1950 F.J. HARDY *Power without Glory* 323 Big Bill spun first. He was considered to be one of the best 'headies' in Queensland. **1946** *Austral. New Writing* 37 Tail better here . . heady over there, mate.

heaps. In the phr. **to give** (someone) **heaps,** to oppose (an adversary, team, etc.) with vigour.

1978 *Sydney Morning Herald* 26 Sept. 2/1 *Good luck Kangaroos (and give 'em heaps)* Tooths KB is proud to sponsor the 1978/79 Kangaroo tour of Great Britain and France. And wish players and officials good luck in their quest to keep the Ashes. **1979** *Bulletin* (Sydney) 9 Oct. 6/3 Keep up the great work, Max Harris. Give 'em heaps. Stuff it up their pinched and arid little nostrils. **1982** *Sunday Mail* (Brisbane) 5 Sept. 80/5 Punters give Malcolm heaps. . . Malcolm Johnston was booed after champion galloper Kingston Town was beaten into fourth place . . at Randwick yesterday.

heart-leaf poison. [See quot. 1853.] Any of several shrubs of the genus *Gastrolobium* (fam. Fabaceae) poisonous to stock, esp. (*W.A.*) *G. bilobum* of s.w. W.A. and (*Qld.*) *G. grandiflorum* of central and n. Aust. Also **heart-leaf poison bush** (or **plant**).

[**1853** E. SAUNDERS *Our Austral. Colonies* 4 There are very few horses, cattle, or sheep in the settlement, in consequence of there being a plant called 'heart-poison' (so-called because the leaf is in shape like a heart) which is very destructive to them.] **1865** 'SPECIAL CORRESPONDENT' *Transportation* 14 Whole districts are overrun with strong quick-growing bushes, the juices of which are fatal to animal life. . . Four are commonly pointed out. These are the York-road, the heart-leaf, the rock, and the box-scrub. **1897** L. LINDLEY-COWEN *W. Austral. Settler's Guide* 42 Heartleaf poison is found in patches. **1916** *Bulletin* (Sydney) 16 Mar. 22/4 The sudden and deadly effect of the 'heart leaf' poison plant. **1944** *Ibid.* 5 July 13/2 Queensland seems to lead Australia in the number of poison plants; perhaps the deadliest of all is the heartleaf poison bush (*Gastrolobium grandiflorum*). **1977** W.A. WINTER-IRVING *Bush Stories* 46 There is a quite attractive looking but poisonous bush. . . The ringers call the bush 'Heart leaf poison bush'. During the dry season cattle are tempted by the green foliage and will eat it, and die from it. **1984** *West Austral.* (Perth) 7 Nov. 48/2 Heartleaf, one of Australia's most toxic plants, contains high levels of sodium fluoroacetate, the active component in 1080 poison.

heath. [Transf. use of *heath*, from the similarity of habitat.] Any of several plants occurring in heathland, usu. of the fam. Epacridaceae, and esp. of the genus *Epacris* including the shrub of s.e. mainland Aust. *E. impressa*, the floral emblem of Vic.; *native heath*, see NATIVE *a.* 6 a. See also EPACRIS.

1849 J.P. TOWNSEND *Rambles & Observations N.S.W.* 28 This open ground produced many specimens of 'the beautiful genus *Epacris*, which may be called the Heaths of Australia, being nearly allied to them, and perhaps superior in beauty' (Sir William Hooker). **1853** MOSSMAN & BANISTER *Aust. Visited & Revisited* 270 Occasionally small tufts of the dry yet beautiful heaths of Australia. **1884** 'R. BOLDREWOOD' *Old Melbourne Memories* 92 Several species of epacris (heath) grew there. **1931** *Victorian Naturalist* XLVIII. 152 'Heath'—locai name for *Melaleuca* (*Melaleuca pubescens*), and *M. squarrosa.* **1970** K.E.C. GRAVES *Third Chance* 91 On the heaths which had blazed through the winter, the last scarlet and carmine bells lingered. **1984** E. WALLING *On Trail Austral. Wildflowers* 11 It is still winter when the . . heath comes into flower. Tall slender stems with tiny bells clustering closely to them wave gently beneath a thin canopy of gum trees.

heavy, *a. Obs.* In the collocation **heavy gold**: see quot. 1869.

1855 R. CARBONI *Eureka Stockade* 10 A party of Britishers had two claims; the one, on the slope of the hill, was bottomed on heavy gold. **1869** R.B. SMYTH *Gold Field & Minerals Districts* 613 *Heavy gold*, gold in large particles. Sometimes called 'shotty gold', when it has the appearance of gun-shot. **1886** J.W. ANDERSON *Prospector's Handbk.* 120 *Heavy Gold (Australia)*, gold of the size of gun-shots.

heavy, *n.* Usu. in *pl.*

1. *Surfing.* A large wave.

1962 *Austral. Women's Weekly* (Sydney) 24 Oct. (Suppl.) 3/2 *Heavy*, a big wave. **1964** *Surfabout* (Sydney) I. vi. 20 Cyclonic weather . . had an enormous effect and influence on the North Narrabeen surf. . . The cyclonic pattern produced big-day heavies. **1965** I. HAMILTON *Persecutor* 180 A few of them were hoods but most of them really did get out on boards among the heavies booming in from the Pacific.

2. A person of influence or importance.

1973 A. BROINOWSKI *Take One Ambassador* 85 'Wow,' said Andy. 'This Fujita must be a real heavy.' ' . . I beg your pardon?' 'Fujita is a very important man?' **1976** J. HOLMES *Govt. Vic.* 23 Cabinet 'heavies' have multiple portfolios which keep them constantly in the parliamentary eye.

heavy, *v. trans.* To harass (a person), to put pressure on. Chiefly in *pass.*, and also as *vbl. n.*

1974 M. GILLESPIE *Into Hollow Mountains* 31 The Free Store harbored a few criminals from time to time . . and we got heavied by the police a few times. **1979** R.M. ELLINGHAUS *Coping with Bust* 5 Your first impulse on being heavied may well be, 'Who the hell does this bastard of a cop think he is?' **1986** *Sydney Morning Herald* 14 June 33/5 Heavying doesn't mean you ask someone to do something and tell them they're a mug if they don't. Heavying is 'I want you to do this but if you don't do it, there's a penalty.'

hedgehog. *Obs.* ECHIDNA.

1827 P. CUNNINGHAM *Two Yrs. in N.S.W.* I. 317 Our *porcupine*, or Australian hedgehog, serves for another native dish. **1855** F.J. COCKBURN *Lett.* (1856) 120 From its burrowing abilities, and short, sharp spines, it is sometimes called a hedge-hog, but it is not like either porcupine or hedge-hog. **1860** G. BENNETT *Gatherings of Naturalist* 147 The Porcupine Ant-eater of Australia (*Echidna hystrix*) (the native Porcupine or Hedgehog of the Colonists). **1906** *Bulletin* (Sydney) 13 Sept. 17/2 My landlady was liberal with native 'game', from kangaroo-rat to the hedgehog.

hedgewood. [Transf. use of *hedge-wood* trees or timber grown in hedgerows.] A plant of arid Aust. forming dense thickets; perh. BULWADDY (see quot. 1951). Also *attrib.*, and formerly **hedge-tree.**

1861 J.M. STUART *Explorations in Aust.* 29 May (1865) 299 We have again met with the mulga. . . Amongst it is the hedge-tree. **1883** E. FAVENC *Rep. Country N.T.* 3 After crossing this branch we got into thick mulga and hedgewood scrub. **1897** J.J. MURIF *From Ocean to Ocean* 147, I led Diamond to a hedgewood tree. **1951** E. HILL *Territory* 299 Hedgewood, allumbo, the 'bulwaddi'. . . These gnarled dark woods are the hardest timber on earth—when very old it will break and burn, but it never bends.

heeler. Abbrev. of *blue heeler* BLUE *a.* Also *attrib.*

1914 R. KALESKI *Austral. Barkers & Biters* 36 These speckled heelers are like a small thick-set dingo. **1931** F.D. DAVISON *Man-Shy* (1962) 31 It produces blue- and red-speckled prick-eared dogs called 'heelers'. **1937** *Bulletin* (Sydney) 11 Aug. 20/2 In the kelpie and the cattle 'heeler' Australia possesses two of the most intelligent and useful working dogs of the world. **1948** R. RAVEN-HART *Canoe in Aust.* 27 What Jack called a 'heeler', a Queensland cattle-dog trained to bark and nip at the heels of cattle. **1954** C. BARRETT *Wild Life Aust. & New Guinea* 46 The cattle-dogs called 'heelers' originated from a cross between dingo and merle. **1980** HOLTH & BARNABY *Cattlemen of High Country* 103 Mountain cattlemen also need a heeler dog to push lagging cattle along a highway.

heifer. Used *attrib.* in Special Comb. **heifer paddock,** an enclosure in which calves are isolated from their mothers until weaned; also *fig.* a girls' school; **station** *obs.*, see quot. 1849.

1845 D. MACKENZIE *Emigrant's Guide* 120 Without a weaning or **heifer paddock**, you will be obliged to allow your calves to continue sucking their mothers for a whole year. **1849** R.J. MANN *Emigrant's Guide Aust.* 30 The stock-farmer . . requires . . to prepare a wheat paddock, a large heifer paddock, and a small paddock near the huts for the riding horses and working bullocks. **1885** MRS C. PRAED *Austral. Life* 50 Next year I shall look over a heifer-paddock in Sydney and take my pick. NB.—Heifer-paddock in Australian slang means a ladies' school. **1955** N. PULLIAM *I traveled Lonely Land* 233 Basketball here is mainly an indoor game. Mostly it's just played in the heifer paddocks—oh, pardon me, I mean in the girls' schools. **1839** D. MACKELLAR *Austral. Emigrant's Guide* 10 When the increase of the cattle are ready for weaning, a **heifer station** is established at a considerable distance from the home station, at which a stock-yard is erected. **1849** J.P. TOWNSEND *Rambles & Observations N.S.W.* 182 The squatter has need of many stations distinct from each other. He has first his 'sheep station', then his 'breeding station' for cattle, then his 'heifer station', where young heifers are kept until they are old enough to be transferred into the breeding herd. **1851** J. HENDERSON *Excursions & Adventures N.S.W.* II. 50 Two or three heifer stations were formed.

hell. In the phr. **hell, west and crooked,** all over the place; in disarray.

1951 E. HILL *Territory* 295 One big stampede to unnerve them, and the cattle are off every night, 'hell, west and crooked'. **1966** D. NILAND *Pairs & Loners* 48 You'll never see me again. I'm off hell, west and crooked for any old where. **1970** V. HALL *Outback Policeman* 43 Everything went 'hell, west and crooked' as the mob divided at the tree.

helmet orchid. [See quot. 1984; cf. *helmet-flower* (OED *helmet, sb.* 9).] Any of several dwarf ground orchids of the genus *Corybas* (fam. Orchidaceae), occurring in all States but not N.T., and from s.e. Asia to N.Z.

1923 *Census Plants Vic.* (Field Naturalists' Club Vic.) 19 *Corysanthes unguiculata.* Small Helmet-orchid. **1942** C. BARRETT *Austral. Wild Flower Bk.* 135 There are about fifty species of helmet orchids, delightful little wild flowers, often growing in extensive colonies. **1950** *Bulletin* (Sydney) 6 Sept. 4/3 It is the helmet orchid That will not lift itself Higher than a fallen leaf. **1961** J. HYETT *Bushman's Harvest* 7 This particular patch of Helmet Orchids blooms every year. **1984** D.T. & C.E. WOOLCOCK *Austral. Terrestrial Orchids* 56 Helmet orchids. . . The helmet is formed by an erect dorsal sepal, usually enlarged, concave, and bending forward as a hood, and a large labellum.

helmeted honeyeater. The rare honeyeater *Lichenostomus melanops cassidix*, occurring in a small area e. of Melbourne (Vic.), and a faunal emblem of Vic.

1867 J. GOULD *Birds of Aust.* Suppl. (1869) Pl. 39, Helmeted Honey-eater. . . The *P[tilotis] cassidix* differs from *P. auricomis* in its much larger size, in the dark olive-black colouring of its upper surface, wings, and tail. **1900** A.J. CAMPBELL *Nests & Eggs Austral. Birds* 400 The Helmeted or Leadbeater Honeyeater is perhaps the rarest and the most splendid bird of its genus. **1911** LUCAS & LE SOUEF *Birds of Aust.* 385 The Helmeted Honey-eater. . . Crown of head and nape dull yellow, feathers of the crown forming a crest or helmet-like elevation. **1945** C. BARRETT *Austral. Bird Life* 158 Rarest of all our many species of honeyeaters . . the helmeted honeyeater (*M[eliphaga] cassidix*). **1968** R. HILL *Bush Quest* 9 The territory of the helmeted honeyeater, which surely must be one of the most localised birds in Australia. **1983** *Sun* (Sydney) 17 Aug. 17 At similar peril are the regent and helmeted honeyeaters.

Henare /'hɛnəri/. [Maori form of 'Henry'.] A Maori; the typical Maori. Cf. HORI.

1921 *Smith's Weekly* (Sydney) 1 Jan. 9/3 Henare made his first aeroplane flight at Palmerston North (N.Z.) the other day. **1933** *Bulletin* (Sydney) 12 July 21/1 Binghi could probably lick Henare at tree-climbing any day in the week, but the old-time Maori had a technique which was safe if slow. **1936** *Ibid.* 19 Feb. 20/1 When Henare's aged grandfather died his tangi and funeral were the largest in the history of Taupo. **1942** *Ibid.* 23 Sept. 12/1 The country storekeeper had repeatedly billed Henare for his account, but without any result. At last he wrote asking what the Maori intended to do. **1958** *Ibid.* 17 Sept. 18/3 Henare was up before the Beak for beating his wife.

he-oak. *Obs.* [f. the pronoun *he* (see quots. 1855 and 1857) + OAK 1. Cf. SHE-OAK.] Any of several trees of the fam. Casuarinaceae.

1792 *Hist. Rec. N.S.W.* (1893) II. 799 There are two kinds of oak, called the he and the she oak, but not to be compared with English oak. **1828** *Tasmanian* (Hobart) 9 May 2 The poor man put upon his fire, a log of wood, about 80 inches long, of the he or she-oak kind. **1855** J. BONWICK *Geogr. Aust. & N.Z.* (ed. 3) 202 The Casuarinae, or He and She Oak, have no leaves, but long knotted twigs at the end of branches. The He oak is Cas. stricta, or upright; the She oak is C. tortulosa [*sic*], or bending. **1857** D. BUNCE *Australasiatic Reminisc.* 33 The trees forming the most interesting groups were the *Casuarina torulosa* she-oak; and *C. stricta*, he-oak. . . *C. stricta*, or he-oak, has been named in contradistinction of the sexes, as if they constituted one dioecious plant, the one male and the other female, whereas they are two perfectly distinct species. **1868** *Colonial Monthly* Sept. 68 Here and there, I saw a few thickets of black-oak; or, as some call it, he-oak. **1898** E.E. MORRIS *Austral Eng.* 325 The word *He-Oak* is applied sometimes to the more imposing species of *She-Oak*. **1909** E. ASH *Austral. Oracle* 21 Stooping to cut a nice he-oak sapling.

herbs. The horsepower of an engine, esp. of a motor vehicle; also *fig.*

1957 R. STOW *Bystander* 116 'I think you're beaut. . . You're the nicest boy in this car,' she said. Derek said sardonically, 'Go on, give him the herbs. Bet he doesn't even notice you're there.' **1961** *Age* (Melbourne) 20 May 17/2 One teaser I want explained . . is . . 'herbs' for a car's horse power. **1967** *Kings Cross Whisper* (Sydney) xxxv. 6/2 *Herbs*, reference to power in a motor vehicle. **1975** D.J. TOWNSHEND *Gland Time* 140 Them glands have given him more herbs than a tractor. **1977** W. MOORE *Just to Myself* 80 Got plenty of herbs. Get in and I'll take ya for a drag.

herd. *Obs.* [Spec. use of *herd* a company of animals of any kind: see OED *sb.*[1] 2.] Used formerly of a number of kangaroos, etc., feeding or travelling together; now replaced by MOB *n.* 2 or 'flock'.

1831 *Acct. Colony Van Diemen's Land* 62 Herds of kangaroos were seen in the plains, but they quickly bounded away. **1833** *Perth Gaz.* 21 Sept. 152 We arrived at extensive downs where we saw numerous herds of kangaroos. **1843** W. PRIDDEN *Aust.* 101 A herd of kangaroos. **1884** W.H.G. KINGSTON *Adventures in Aust.* 172 A whole herd of these wombats came sniffing round me. **1885** MRS C. PRAED *Austral. Life* 7 In the daytime, the only audible signs are the stampede of a herd of kangaroo, or the rustle of a wallabi or dingo stirring the grass. **1926** A.S. LE SOUEF et al. *Wild Animals Australasia* 19 A herd of kangaroos.

herring. [Transf. use of *herring* an edible sea fish.]

1. *W.A.* **a.** *Obs.* BONY BREAM. **b.** TOMMY ROUGH.

1832 G.F. MOORE *Diary Ten Yrs. W.A.* 14 Sept. (1884) 136 Fish, which are very numerous in the river about and below Perth . . of the kind *called* herrings, but do not look very like them; they make a noise when out of the water, and on that account are also called trumpeters. **1840** *S. Austral. Rec.* (London) 10 Oct. 229 In Swan River there is great abundance of a fish of the herring tribe, of a flatter description, and broader than those in the English seas. **1882** J.E. TENISON-WOODS *Fish & Fisheries N.S.W.* 107 It is known there [*sc.* Swan River] as the 'herring', quantities being smoked with *Banksia* wood or sawdust and sold. **1969** J. POLLARD *Austral. & N.Z. Fishing* 813 Many World War II servicemen have strong memories of this fish [*sc.* tommy ruff] as it was often served to them interminably in cans as Perth herring. Western Australian anglers mostly call it 'herring'. **1980** N. COLEMAN *Austral. Sea Fishes* 152 When the 'herring' (an inaccurate term) are 'on', people turn out in their hundreds.

2. The Australian grayling *Prototroctes maraena*, a fresh-water fish of s.e. Aust.; CUCUMBER FISH; *native herring* (b), see NATIVE *a.* 6 b.

1841 *Port Phillip Patriot* 1 Apr. 4/1 A stream . . abounding in black-fish, herring and lobsters. **1848** *Port Phillip Herald* 25 Apr. 2/3 There could not be less than one hundred and fifty rods on the river, and the gross 'take' of herring may be estimated at eighty dozen. **1878** R.B. SMYTH *Aborigines of Vic.* I. 203 Amongst the fish commonly taken by the blacks are . . the herring (*Protroctes maroena*). **1906** D.G. STEAD *Fishes of Aust.* 52 The Australian Grayling (*Prototroctes maroena*) . . in Tasmania, where it is common . . is known under a multiplicity of names, but chiefly as 'Herring' and 'Cucumber Mullet'. **1921** *Bulletin* (Sydney) 16 June 26/3 In many rivers of Tasmania there is a lively little fish, usually called 'herring'.

Hewie, var. HUGHIE.

Hexham grey. [f. the name of a town on the Hunter River near Newcastle, N.S.W.] The widespread, dappled grey mosquito *Aedes alternans*, the largest biting mosquito in Australia; SCOTCH GREY.

1889 'SALTBUSH' *Sydney to Croydon* 4 The famous swamps, rendered memorable as the breeding-grounds of the well-known and duly appreciated 'Hexham Greys', those noted mosquitos. **1948** P.J. HURLEY *Red Cedar* 38 Two breeds of 'mossies' mobilised themselves . . along the soaked and sunny sidewater. They were big 'Hexham Greys' and little black blighters. . . The 'Greys' easily won on noise. **1981** L. MCLEAN *Pumpkin Pie* 15 He was almost eaten alive by mosquitoes at a place called Hexham, where he said the mossies were the biggest, and blood thirstiest he had ever met. They were called 'Hexham Greys'.

hickory. [Transf. use of *hickory* a North American tree of the genus *Carya*, yielding a tough timber.] Any of several trees, usu. of the genus *Acacia* (fam. Mimosaceae), yielding a tough, close-grained timber; the wood of these trees. Also **hickory wattle.**

1840 *S. Austral. Rec.* (London) 27 June 356 Various shrubs—as the tea-tree, hickory (which may be called a tree) . . were abundant. **1882** A.J. BOYD *Old Colonials* 25 The scrubs were full of hickory, while silky oak was getting scarce. **1884** 'R. BOLDREWOOD' *Old Melbourne Memories* 35 The beautiful umbrageous blackwood, or native hickory, one of the handsomest trees in Australia. **1889** J.H. MAIDEN *Useful Native Plants Aust.* 350 *Acacia aulacocarpa* . . 'Hickory Wattle'. Wood hard, heavy, tough, and dark-red; useful for cabinet-work. **1911** *Bulletin* (Sydney) 2 Nov. 13/1 The North Queensland hickory is the hardest wood. **1934** W.A. OSBORNE *Visitor to Aust.* 62 The visitor, therefore, when he hears such terms as . . box, hickory, and others must not expect striking resemblances to the originals. *Ibid.* 64 The Hickory Wattle is used for axe handles, but is not equal to imported American hickory. **1944** J. DEVANNY *By Tropic Sea & Jungle* 130 The fine-grained, golden-tinted hickory. **1978** B.P. MOORE *Life on Forty Acres* 46 The Hickory wattles (*A. implexa*) . . thrive only in the hardest places on the ridge and adjacent stony slopes.

hide. [Ellipt. use of *thick hide*: see OEDS *sb.*[1] 2 c. Used elsewhere but recorded earliest in Aust.] Impertinence; effrontery.

1902 *Truth* (Sydney) 9 Feb. 4/2 Last week I had a caligraphic cut at what I called, for want of a better name, your 'hide', a word which, in Australian 'slanguage', signifies a tough moral, or rather immoral, article. **1918** *Ibid.* 10 Mar. 6/8 Wake up and cut out this pommy stuff, otherwise . . the average person will want an interpreter to understand these imported mediocres who only have hide and leather lungs to recommend them. **1936** 'SWEENEY, EX-CROOK' *I Confess* 55 He also has temerity (commonly called 'hide'). **1951** *Bulletin* (Sydney) 27 June 13/1 Oily Jackson's hide was equalled only by his gift for magging his way out of things. **1979** K. DUNSTAN *Ratbags* p. xx, If they've got the hide to do this, then I've got the hide to photograph it.

hidey. [f. *hide(-and-seek* + -Y.] The game of hide-and-seek.

1957 A. MARSHALL *Aust.* (1981) 73 'Kick the Tin' was a version of 'Hidey' with a race back to the tin when the person who was 'he' found anyone. **1978** M. WALKER *Pioneer Crafts Early Aust.* 85 The girls played less vigorously—tiggy touchwood, hidey, domestic games, mothers, fathers and naughty children.

hieleman /'hiləmən/. Also with much variety, esp. formerly as **yeelaman, yelaman.** [a. Dharuk *yili-maŋ.*] An Aboriginal shield made from bark or wood; SHIELD.

1793 W. TENCH *Compl. Acct. Settlement* 191 Their shields are of two sorts: that called *Il-ee-mon*, is nothing but a piece of bark, with a handle fixed in the inside of it. **1798** D. COLLINS *Acct. Eng. Colony N.S.W.* I. 585 Of shields they have but two sorts. One, named E-lee-mong, is cut from the bark of the gum tree. **1805** *Sydney Gaz.* 22 Dec., He considered the heel-a-man or shield an unnecessary appendage, as the hand was sufficient to put aside and alter the direction of any number of spears. **1820** J. OXLEY *Jrnls. Two Exped. N.S.W.* 237 In the camp were several spears . . there were also some elamongs (shields). **1830** W.J. HOOKER *Bot. Miscellany* I. 254 On examining the depôt, we found a Kangaroo-Net . . a *Dilly*, or luggage-bag . . two *Eillmans*, or shields, of the wood of *Urtica Gigas*, or the *Tree Nettle*, as light as cork. **1839** T.L. MITCHELL *Three Exped. Eastern Aust.* (rev. ed.) II. 349 There is . . much originality in the shield or *hieleman* of these people. **1848** H.W. HAYGARTH *Recoll. Bush Life* 113 The heeloman is a sort of shield, made of the toughest wood procurable, about three feet in length, and six inches in breadth at the centre, whence it gradually tapers off to a point at either extremity. The handle is in the middle, and is merely a small aperture, just large enough to admit the hand. **1852** G.C. MUNDY *Our Antipodes* I. 221 The hielman, or shield, is a piece of wood, about two and a half feet long, tapering to the ends. **1861** *Bell's Life in Sydney* 30 Nov. 4/3 Lo! yeelamans splinter and boomerangs clash. **1878** R.B. SMYTH *Aborigines of Vic.* II. 5 *Heileman*, a shield. **1889** E.B. KENNEDY *Blacks & Bushrangers* 60 He was able to point out and name to Tim spears, woomeras, yelamans, boomerangs, stone tomahawks, and nullah-nullahs. **1923** T. HALL *Short Hist. Downs Blacks* 17 *Helimon or shield* . . was used for precisely the same purpose as that of our ancient European warriors. It was made out of stinging tree wood, which was very light and soft, but tough. **1930** HIVES & LUMLEY *Jrnl. of Jackaroo* 83 The shield, or 'heeliman', was roughly elliptical in shape, and made of soft wood—usually that obtained from the flanged buttresses of a fig or cotton tree.

High Court. The federal supreme court established by the Constitution as the final arbiter of constitutional questions and final court of appeal from State and federal courts. In full **High Court of Australia.**

1900 J.H. SYMON *Austral. Cwlth. Bill* 4 From the High Court appeals lie to the Privy Council. **1903** *Act* (Cwlth. of Aust.) no. 7 Sect. 5, All writs and process issued from the High Court . . shall be dated as of the day on which they are issued. **1911** H.G. TURNER *First Decade Austral. Cwlth.* 112 A test action by the Government of New South Wales against a trades union connected with the brewing industry was brought before the High Court of Australia. **1918** *Huon Times* (Franklin) 11 Oct. 3/1 During the hearing of a case in the High Court, Melbourne, some months back. **1971** *Bulletin* (Sydney) 27 Nov. 17/2 The High Court is one of the great courts of the common law world. Its legal standing is higher than that of the U.S. Supreme Court, which is mainly concerned with constitutional or federal law. **1978** F. DALY *A to Z Politics* 53 The High Court comprises a Chief Justice and six other judges appointed by the Governor-General on the recommendation of the Government. **1986** *Canberra Times* 15 Mar. 2/2 After . . such a battle in Parliament there would have been the High Court challenge.

hill. With **the.**

1. An uncovered area of rising ground for spectators at a sporting event:

a. At Flemington Racecourse, Melbourne.

1872 'RESIDENT' *Glimpses Life Vic.* 399 A crowd numbering some thirty thousand persons is seen moving to and fro on the hill. **1888** A.P. MARTIN *Oak-Bough & Wattle-Blossom* 105 Behind the grand stand was a hill—the 'hill' famous in Gordon's poems and in the annals of Melbourne racing. **1892** *Truth* (Sydney) 17 Apr. 5/5 Williams was a bookmaker . . one of the smaller fry who pursue the business on 'the hill'. **1900** *Advocate* (Burnie) 8 Nov. 4/2 People who go to the hill do not make nearly so much litter or give us half so much trouble as . . the grandstand.

b. In front of the scoreboard at the Sydney Cricket Ground.

1925 S. HICKS *Hullo Australs.* 246 The Hill is occupied by thousands of barrackers . . who are sure they understand cricket better than the umpires. **1932** R.W. THOMPSON *Down Under* 225 The knowledge of cricket possessed by the average Australian was far in advance of that of the average Englishman. The crowd on the 'hill' understood all the finer points. **1936** *Publicist* (Sydney) i. 15/2 A ferocious howl emitted from that more vulgar part of the Ground known as 'The Hill'. **1979** K. DUNSTAN *Ratbags* 14 So too was the Hill at the S.C.G. **1986** *Canberra Times* 20 Jan. 1/1 (*heading*) The Hill disappearing under sea of alcohol.

2. Broken Hill, a mining town in N.S.W.

1948 G. FARWELL *Down Argent Street* 1 The place which had been named . . by the station people on Mount Gipps the 'broken hill', because of its hog-back silhouette against the sky, and by cynics and baffled prospectors the 'hill of mullock' . . came at last to be called, casually and with spare affection, just The Hill. **1951** I.L. IDRIESS *Across Nullarbor* 22 We're due in the Hill tomorrow. **1979** D.G. POSTLETHWAITE *Home to Hill* 14 A rock hound who visited the hill, Picked up a round black stone.

Hence **hillite** *n.*

1902 *Sporting News* (Launceston) 11 Oct. 1/5 Withdraw Grand Flaneur at the very last moment, much to the disgust of the hillites and others, who were not slow in significantly showing their disapproval. **1936** *Publicist* (Sydney) i. 15/2 Why do the Hillites pick on poor inoffensive footballers? **1957** F. CLUNE *Fortune Hunters* 21 The people of Broken Hill have a strong community spirit. . . The Hillites even have a lingo of their own. **1974** *Bulletin* (Sydney) 9 Nov. 47/1, I recall a formal Hillite (shorts, singlet, nose-cover, pie, beer-can) coming to us down on the slope, on all fours, asking 'Whadderyez gettin' interyez there?' **1984** P. JARRATT *Aussie* 121 In the summer of 1984, the Hillites seemed to have found a new hero in the brash young allrounder, Greg Matthews.

hill crow-shrike. *Obs.* The Tasmanian race of the *grey currawong* (see GREY *a.*).

1888 *Centennial Mag.* (Sydney) 14 Up on the sand-hills a few wallaby are seen, and the hill crow-shrike is plentiful. **1846** J. GOULD *Birds of Aust.* (1848) II. Pl. 44, *Strepera arguta* . . Hill Crow-Shrike. **1902** *Emu* II. 98 Large companies of Hill Crow-Shrikes.

hill kangaroo. WALLAROO.

1902 F.S. BROCKMAN *Rep. Exploration N.-W. Kimberley* 4 Between the Chamberlain and the Charnley Rivers we saw no game, except a few hill kangaroos in the sandstone ridges. **1935** H.H. FINLAYSON *Red Centre* 58 The lower slopes of the ranges are the stations of the short-limbed, broad-chested, sturdy, hill kangaroos or euros (*Macropus robustus*). **1962** V.C. HALL *Dreamtime Justice* 121 The guide was still moving with the ease and grace of a hill-kangaroo.

hipper. A pad of soft material arranged so as to protect the hip of a person sleeping on hard ground; a hollow made in the ground to serve this purpose. Also **hipper-hole.**

1875 R. BRUCE *Dingoes* 134 Feather beds as aids to sleep By none are here possessed; And he is lucky who obtains One sheepskin for a hipper. **1898** *Bulletin* (Sydney) 6 Aug. 14/4 Have never seen anything written about the swaggie's 'hipper'—a piece of anything soft, such as 'possum-skin, piece of cocoa-nut fibre, bit of blanket or a horsehair pad to put under the hip when lying on hard ground. **1904** *Ibid.* 11 Feb. 16/1 The 'hipper' . . is worn round the hips at night, generally consists of a marsupial fur or a stuffed strip of bagging and is a great saver of the hip bone. **1925** M. TERRY *Across Unknown Aust.* 68 Adopted dried sheepskins as 'hippers' to ease the hardness of the stony ground. **1932** J. MCCARTER *Pan's Clan* 252 Chil Blane . . stretched . . to allow his right thigh to sink into the 'hipper', a hollow he had scooped out of the ground and which enabled his body to rest more peacefully. **1938** F. BLAKELEY *Hard Liberty* 223 In this old camp the ground was dry and nice and soft, and just the place in which to scoop out a hipper-hole. **1940** I.L. IDRIESS *Lightning Ridge* 130 The stars don't use a 'hipper' but the drover does if the ground be hard. **1969** R. OTTLEY *Bates Family* 23 Each had three empty wheat sacks, sewn together for a 'hipper', spread on the ground underneath them.

hit-out. *Australian National Football.* In a ball-up, or after a throw-in from the boundary: the striking of the ball towards a team-mate.

1931 J.F. MCHALE et al. *Austral. Game of Football* 69 The importance of the 'hit-out' at the centre has been stressed. **1936** E.C.H. TAYLOR et al. *Our Austral. Game Football* 58 A successful 'hit out' means that the ball is at once transferred to your half-forward line, or perhaps beyond it, while if your ruck fails, your team is immediately compelled to defend its goal. **1964** *Footy Fan* (Melbourne) II. xv. 3 If he did not get the hit-outs from his own followers, he certainly 'sharked' plenty from the opposition. **1969** A. HOPGOOD *And Big Men Fly* 43 It's gone forty yards. At least forty yards! What a hit-out!

Hence **hitter-out** *n.*

1931 J.F. MCHALE et al. *Austral. Game of Football* 72 Stalwart 'hitters out'.

hoary-headed grebe. The bird *Poliocephalus poliocephalus* of Aust. incl. Tas., having a black or grey head, with narrow white plumes in the breeding season.

1843 J. GOULD *Birds of Aust.* (1848) VII. Pl. 82, *Podiceps poliocephalus* . . Hoary-headed Grebe. **1890** G.J. BROINOWSKI *Birds of Aust.* I. Pl. 3, In spite of its head-feathers, the Hoary-headed Grebe exhibits the same powers of diving as others of the tribe. **1945** C. BARRETT *Austral. Bird Life* 52 The hoary-headed grebe . . sometimes called 'Tom Pudding'. **1968** R. HILL *Bush Quest* 1 All the grebes were there: hoary headed, with their 'spiny' cheeks showing up well. **1976** *Reader's Digest Compl. Bk. Austral. Birds* 29 (*caption*) The head of the hoary-headed grebe looks hoary only in the breeding season.

Hobart trumpeter. *Obs.* The fish *Latris lineata* (see TRUMPETER *n.*[1] 1).

1892 *Bohemia* (Melbourne) 7 Jan. 19 From Tasmania they get the famed Hobart trumpeter, as well as other finny denizens.

hobble, *n.* [Fig. use of *hobble* a rope, strap, etc.] In the phr. **to snap one's hobbles,** to die.

1911 *Bulletin* (Sydney) 5 Oct. 16/1 His mates in the tunnel variously informed me that Uncle Dick had . . 'snapped his hobbles', 'run a bye', 'heaved the sponge', [etc.]. **1980** ANSELL & PERCY *To fight Wild* 30 The only real consciousness was riveted on the one thing: water . . and staying alive long enough to reach it. I wasn't going to snap my hobbles while there was still the faintest chance.

hobble, *v.*

1. *trans.* With **out**: to put (a horse, etc.) out to rest, fettered so as to prevent straying. Also *absol.*

1849 S. & J. SIDNEY *Emigrant's Jrnl.* 162 Young bullocks are almost always broken in at plough. . . When they have done working, they are hobbled out; that is their fore feet are confined in a kind of handcuff, colonial [*sic*], called hobbles. **1870** E.B. KENNEDY *Four Yrs. in Qld.* 26 Take your horses down to the water before hobbling them out, and take a pannikin with you. **1888** 'R. BOLDREWOOD' *Robbery under Arms* (1937) 83 Wait till I hobble out Bilbah. **1893** E. FAVENC *Last of Six Tales* 71 He had hobbled his horses out and was lighting a fire. **1909** A.R. RICHARDSON *Early Memories Great Nor-West* 38 Take a good brisk canter for a couple of miles in the dark and then off-saddle and hobble out in a quiet place. **1935** R.B. PLOWMAN *Boundary Rider* 249 We'll show you where to hobble out the horses. **1976** B. SCOTT *Complete Bk. Austral. Folk Lore* 86 The swarthy stockman, hobbling out his parboiled Bucephalus, and stretching himself for a noontide siesta.

2. *fig.* See quots. Also as *vbl. n.*

1958 W.E. HARNEY *Content to Lie* 48 Here we all camped and waited in a time that was known to all as 'Hobbling out'—waited till the next mustering season—then off we would go once more. **1958** *Overland* xiii. 3 We naturally all got paid off. They used to call it 'hobbling out'. **1963** HARNEY & LOCKWOOD *Shady Tree* 79 Camooweal was the 'hobbling-out' place for the drovers and the stockmen for hundreds of miles around. To 'hobble-out', in the patois of the stock-routes, simply meant that the horses were being rested while their human owners caught up on a bit of back drinking.

hobble chain. Also **hopple chain.** [Chiefly Austral.: see OEDS *hobble, sb.* 3.] A length of chain or other material used to fetter an animal.

1901 M. FRANKLIN *My Brilliant Career* (1966) 52 The sound of camp-bells and jingle of hobble chains . . had come to these men. **1928** 'BRENT OF BIN BIN' *Up Country* 272 He remembered the hobble-chains behind the old stable. **1946** W.E. HARNEY *North of 23°* 75 Out of the distance comes the jingle of hopple chains and the tinkle of bells.

hod. [Prob. a. Arabic *hod* a pool.] An oasis.

1918 G.C. COOPER Diary 10 Aug., Left Oghratina and went out looking for a Hod—after riding all the morning, we found it—we waited up at Hod-el-Bakieh; others went on to Hod-el-Oghra, and waited there all day, had a good night's sleep. *c* **1919** C. DUGUID *From Suez Canal to Gaza* 8 The next day the Regiment pitched camp in the hod. **1931** 'D. BLACK' *Red Dust* 12 The only shelter, an occasional *hod.*

hoddie. [f. *hod(man* + -Y.] A bricklayer's labourer, a hodman.

1952 *Bulletin* (Sydney) 23 Apr. 17/4 Our hoddie recognised the new bloke the moment he stepped on the scaffold. **1978** H.C. BAKER *I was Listening* 60 He had been a hodcarrier, and hoddies either died young or lived forever.

hoe, *v.* In the phr. **to hoe in(to),** to begin (a task, activity, etc.) with energy and enthusiasm; to 'dig in'.

1935 R.B. PLOWMAN *Boundary Rider* 119 'Us blokes' . . not averse to using the backs of our hands to wipe our mouths, 'hoe into the scran'. **1939** I.L. IDRIESS *Cyaniding for Gold* 86 The local cow . . took a lick; fancied the salty taste and hoed in for breakfast. **1980** ANSELL & PERCY *To fight Wild* 74 Up to fifty [wallabies] get onto the lawn the manager is trying to grow round his house, all at once, all hoeing into the one poor little patch of green.

Hogan's Ghost. [An unexplained euphemism for *Holy Ghost.*] An expletive; also, rhyming slang for 'toast'.

1930 *Listening Post* (Perth) Aug. 22 And a sleepy voice would answer From the dug-out 'Hogan's Ghost!' **1968** D. O'GRADY *Bottle of Sandwiches* 101 All of us well-fortified with a before-sunrise Saturday morning breakfast of bacon, cackleberries, Hogan's ghost, and two quarts of tea. **1977** J. O'GRADY *There was Kid* 65 'Caesar's ghost', or 'Hogan's ghost' meant that our father's exasperation was nearing the explosive level.

hoist, *v.* In the phr. **to hoist one's bluey (drum, Matilda,** etc.), to (set off on a) journey as a swagman.

1897 *Worker* (Sydney) 18 Sept. 3/3 That highly intelligent shearer had to hoist 'Matilda' a sadder, and let us hope a wiser, man. **1912** *Bulletin* (Sydney) 15 Feb. (Red Page), Next day a mulga coaxes him to pack; He hoists his drum, and ambles down the track. **1947** *Ibid.* 16 Apr. 28/2 After hoisting our blueys over most of the State we felt ready to take it easy.

holding, *pres. pple.* Possessing money, in funds. Esp. in the phr. **(how) are you holding?**

1924 *Truth* (Sydney) 27 Apr. 6/3 *Holdin'*, possessing money. **1934** *Bulletin* (Sydney) 7 Nov. 10/1 Think not I'm throwing 'biting' hints, Nor how you're 'holding' seek to know. **1944** *Gabber: Qld. Lines of Communication Army Trade Training Depot* Oct. 4 Are you holding? . . Let me have ten bob then. **1950** G.M. FARWELL *Land of Mirage* 120 Stiffen the crows, if it isn't Slim! How're you holding, son? **1966** J. WATEN *Season of Youth* 72 'How are you holding?' he asked. I didn't have much I told him. But I thought I had enough. **1977** R. BEILBY *Gunner* 237 'Which reminds me, how're you holding?' 'Holding?' . . 'I'm putting the bite on you,' Gunner explained gently. **1980** J. ANDERSON *Impersonators* 93 His message was: *how are you holding?* . . 'Oh,' she said . . 'how am I holding for money? I'm quite all right.'

holding, *vbl. n.* Used *attrib.* in Special Comb. relating to the confinement of stock, as: **holding paddock, pen, yard,** an enclosure in which stock is kept for some particular purpose.

[N.Z. **1933** *Press* (Christchurch) 28 Oct. 17/7 **Holding paddock,** a small paddock, close to yards, woolshed, or mustering hut, for holding (not feeding) sheep.] **1934** *Bulletin* (Sydney) 16 May 38/4 At midday the cattle, mad with thirst, broke out of the holding paddock. **1941** *Coast to Coast* 22 Wiggins said some steers had got out of his holding paddocks. **1960** R.S. PORTEOUS *Cattleman* 35 Instead of running in the saddle horses each morning, he and Biddy put up a small holding paddock and improved the yards. **1981** A.B. FACEY *Fortunate Life* 168 The cattle would be put into holding paddocks. The firms that handle the sale of cattle have these paddocks and the cattle stay there until they are sold and shipped away—disposed of. [N.Z. **1923** *N.Z. Jrnl. Agric.* 20 Mar. 144 The **holding-pens** in the shed . . should never be too large.] **1965** J.S. GUNN *Terminol. Shearing Industry* i. 32 *Holding pen*, one of the small pens or yards in which sheep are held, usually within the shed, under shelter, while awaiting shearing. **1929** *Bulletin* (Sydney) 22 May 23/1 No vestige remains of the **holding-yards** close by, Where the must'rers and dogs yelped a tune. **1956** T. RONAN *Moleskin Midas* 64 He learned that Andy Kerr had finished building a holding yard on Lloyd's Creek. **1960** *N.T. News* (Darwin) 8 Jan. 1/3 Holding yards with a capacity for 1000 to 1100 head are being built at the 10-mile. They cover two square miles. **1982** *More & Better Lambs* (Agri-man Prime Lamb Seminar) no. 10 5 These two examples both show holding yards made of low density fencing such as pig netting.

hole.

1. Shortened form of WATERHOLE 1 a. and c.

1843 *Sydney Morning Herald* 26 Aug. 3/3 The River Page has been constantly running several weeks; a rather unusual state of things, as previous to these late soakings, it was totally destitute of water (except here and there a hole) for nearly four years. **1848** T.L. MITCHELL *Jrnl. Exped. Tropical Aust.* 69 He took us through scrubs, having in the centre those holes where water usually lodges for some time after rain, where some substratum of clay happens to be retentive enough to impede the common absorption. **1850** *Illustr. Austral. Mag.* (Melbourne) Dec. 421 The beds of those rivers which for long intervals are destitute of running water, exhibit a series of holes or ponds in which large quantities of water are still retained. **1872** *Mission Life* (Perth) 1 Aug. 470 In a vain search for water. One 'hole' after another proved to be dry. **1910** *Bulletin* (Sydney) 6 Jan. 14/4 Murranji Waterholes is one of Australia's most dismal spots. The holes from which the place takes its name are in the centre of the 100 mile dry stage. **1950** G.M. FARWELL *Land of Mirage* 212 It was on one of these very holes, forty feet deep and permanent, that Burke and Wills both met their deaths.

2. *Gold-mining.* An excavation made in the ground by a miner.

1851 *Empire* (Sydney) 5 Aug. 15/1 If our hole keeps as good as it seems, we will make £3 per day each, for some time. **1852** A. MACKAY *Great Gold Field* 22 Oct. (1853) 10 Many of the holes have turned out very rich. **1855** R. CARBONI *Eureka Stockade* 6 My hole was next to the one which was jumped by the Eureka mob, and where one man was murdered in the row. **1864** J.G. MOON *Tarrangower, Past & Present* 3 They were sinking and slabbing a hole. **1872** 'QUIRIS' *Port Darwin* 10 Holes Nos. 4 and 8 . . will . . prove payable, considering we obtained half an ounce to two ounces to the load, all rough nuggetty gold. **1888** G.O. PRESHAW *Banking under Difficulties* 45, I put down a hole close to our own tent. **1894** A.F. CALVERT *Coolgardie Goldfield* 78 On his arrival at Hannan's he thought it was necessary to put a hole down somewhere, and by a wonderful accident sunk fair on the gold. **1905** *Horlick's Mag.* (London) Feb. 180/1 Reaching a logged-up hole on the flat, I returned for a moment to hide behind it and reconnoitre. **1921** E.F. TREGASKIS *Santa Claus' Message* 5 During dry spells he sought old tailings and headings among the abandoned holes, and had them carted to the sluice boxes. **1960** D. MCLEAN *Roaring Days* 124 There's many a record of placer gold being above the reef, so I took over and sank that hole another twenty feet.

holey dollar. Also **holy dollar.** A coin, circulating as official currency between 1814 and 1828, which was that part of a Spanish dollar remaining after a circular piece (see DUMP *n.*[1] 1) had been struck from its centre; *colonial dollar*, see COLONIAL *a.* 5; RING DOLLAR. Also *attrib.*

1840 *S. Austral. Miscellany* June 175 The *holey* dollar was the rim, the *dump* the centre struck out of the Spanish dollar, the former passing for 3s. 9d., the latter for 1s. 3d. currency. **1849** J.P. TOWNSEND *Rambles & Observations N.S.W.* 11 It used to be the practice to cut the centre out of a dollar, and the middle piece was called 'a dump', and the remainder of the original coin 'a holey dollar'. To such shifts, in the early days of the colony, were people driven for small change! **1857** D. BUNCE *Australasiatic Reminisc.* 59 Our first change for a pound consisted of two dumps, two holy dollars, one Spanish dollar, one French coin, one half-crown, one shilling, and one sixpence. **1948** R. RAVEN-HART *Canoe in Aust.* 199 'Holy dollar' . . is a pun: it was a silver dollar from the centre of which a 'dump' worth ⅓, had been punched out, to meet the needs for smaller change. **1981** *Bulletin* (Sydney) 20 Jan. 103/1 Probably the best-known of the valuable Australian coins are the holey dollars . . by Governor Lachlan Macquarie. These are now worth $10,000 or more. **1982** *Austral. Financial Rev.* (Sydney) 5 Feb. 40/4 The holey dollar market appeared to ease in one sale last year when a big buyer who spent over $100,000 on holey dollars at the sale appeared to exhaust himself.

hollow, *a.* In the collocation **hollow log**: used allusively with reference to a statutory authority's ability to retain its funds instead of having to pay them into consolidated revenue.

1982 *Nat. Times* (Sydney) 31 Oct. 15/1 Was he planning to do a Wran, keeping all charges steady while he emptied the hollow log? 'We left the Treasury in a hollow log situation but that has eroded considerably since.' **1983** *Bulletin* (Sydney) 12 July 27/1 They all had good reason for remembering this 'heated' meeting: it was the first confrontation between the Treasury officials and Wran's advisers over the idea of drawing funds from the State's 'hollow logs'—a process which saw some $230 million scooped from the cash reserves of statutory authorities to support the State's capital works program. **1985** *Canberra Times* 11 Sept. 2/4 Canberra's cash-rich hollow logs, to adopt the phrase used for such bodies in Victoria and N.S.W., are the sort of trading enterprises run by all State Governments.

holts. [Var. of Br. dial. *in holds* at grips: see OED(S *hold, sb.*[1] 2 b. and *holt, sb.*[2] 1.] In the phr. **in(to) holts,** in conflict, at grips.

1902 *Truth* (Sydney) 17 Aug. 1/7 A few Cooma parsons nearly got into 'holts' on Sunday night. **1907** *Bulletin* (Sydney) 24 Jan. 40/2 Hendry swore Matthew did it on purpose, and, but for the timely arrival of Dad on the scene, they would very likely have got into 'holts'. **1911** *Huon Times* (Franklin) 29 July 2/6 He did not know what the quarrel between them was, but they were in holts when he saw them. **1922** A. WRIGHT *Boss o' Yedden* 37 Men were in holts, wrestling and punching. **1947** *Bulletin* (Sydney) 17 Dec. 37/2 During one of Bombo's periodic walkabouts he got into holts with a brown snake. **1958** H.D. WILLIAMSON *Sunlit Plain* 250 'You got too much respect for the law.' 'Don't want to get into holts with it, anyhow.' **1964** H.M. BARKER *Camels & Outback* 41 The blackfella hit the cook over the head with his bucket and the next thing they were in holts. **1973** R. ROBINSON *Drift of Things* 377 At an English Association evening, I got into holts with a young university student over Christopher Brennan. **1976** B. SCOTT *Compl. Bk. Austral. Folk Lore* 373 You should've been here last night. Two wogs bunged on a blue. One of them got into holts with some young lair from Inala, but his china wouldn't back him.

Holy City. A nickname for Adelaide, the capital city of South Australia. Cf. CITY OF CHURCHES.

1908 M. VIVIENNE *Sunny S.A.* 36 Adelaide is frequently described as the 'Holy City'. **1909** *Truth* (Sydney) 2 May 9/2 There is not another city in the whole of the Commonwealth that can boast such a large and variegated collection of canines than can Adelaide. . . It is time someone took a hand in ridding the Holy City of one of its chief pests.

Holy Cross toad. [See quot. 1956.] CATHOLIC FROG.

1891 *Proc. Linnean Soc. N.S.W.* VI. 265 '*Notaden bennettii*', the 'Catholic frog' or, as I have heard it called, the 'Holy Cross toad'. **1925** *Bulletin* (Sydney) 9 July 22/3 The 'Catholic frog' or 'Holy Cross toad' of the dry interior, which disappears during a drought, but re-appears in thousands when the weather breaks. **1956** T.Y. HARRIS *Naturecraft in Aust.* 55 The Holy Cross Toad is readily identified by the crude warty cross of black with orange and whitish spots on its green back.

holy dollar, var. HOLEY DOLLAR.

Holy Land. *Obs.* A nickname for Tasmania.

1888 C.D. FERGUSON *Experiences of Forty-Niner* 373 The well understood slang of the 'Holy Land', as Van Diemen's Land or Tasmania is called. **1889** *Bulletin* (Sydney) 5 Oct. 8/2 In the rouse-abouts' hut .. they always spoke of the Cabbage Garden as 'Port Phillip', of the Holy Land as 'tother side.

home, *n.*[1] and *attrib.*[1] [Spec. use of *home* native land: see OED(S *sb.*[1] 6 and 11 b.]

A. *n.* Applied to the United Kingdom, esp. England, orig. by colonists and later by their descendants.

1808 *To Viscount Castlereagh* 24 The Government at home, and their instructions to the Governor. **1822** *N.S.W. Agric. Soc. Prospectus* 10 We trust that .. we shall be .. thought worthy of the patronage of the Government here, and at home. **1831** J.G. POWELL *Narr. Voyage Swan River* 164 It will be long before the native of Sydney or Hobart Town will be readily received into good society 'at home'. **1836** J. BACKHOUSE *Extracts from Lett.* (1839) iv. 7 Almost every body in this land calls Great Britain *home*, and speaks with desire respecting returning thither. **1852** *Illustr. Austral. Mag.* (Melbourne) Jan. 6 Even native born Australian colonists call Old England 'home'. **1857** J. ASKEW *Voyage Aust. & N.Z.* 92 The young child so soon as it can lisp a word, is told something about England, and taught to call it *home*. **1865** *Austral. Monthly Mag.* (Melbourne) I. 279 They don't understand us at 'home'. **1880** *Argus* (Melbourne) 2 Jan. 6/4 The advent of the New Year—1880—took place last night, not in a cold sheet of white, as most New Years do at home, but in a warm robe of silvery, clear moonlight. **1893** F.W.L. ADAMS *Australs.* 41 Ten years ago England was spoken of affectionately as the Old Country or Home. Now it is 'home' or more sarcastically ''ome'. The inverted commas make all the difference, and the dropped 'h' contains a class contempt. **1916** E.F. HANMAN *Twelve Months with Anzacs* 1 Deep down in our hearts, we knew that England, dear old England—Home—needed us and was hailing us now as her sons, her supports! **1929** G. MEUDELL *Pleasant Career Spendthrift* 237 Home to 90 per cent of Australians is a Sydney or Melbourne slum, or a decayed mining town, or the wide and dreary bush, yet they talk glibly of England as 'Home'. **1960** M. VIZZERS *She'll do Me!* 98 We still talk about England as Home here. My wife and I do, and we were born and bred out here. **1965** G. MCINNES *Road to Gundagai* 115 The description of England (it never seemed to be Scotland or Ireland) as Home was not an affectation then, though it was on the way to becoming one. **1975** X. HERBERT *Poor Fellow my Country* 1063 'A condition that's giving us a bad name throughout the world, and particularly at Home.' 'You mean Britain?' 'Of course.' 'But you're Australian born.' 'To me Britain is spiritual home.'

B. *attrib.*

a. English; British.

1858 T. MCCOMBIE *Hist. Colony Vic.* 334 The first number was issued on the 1st October, 1850, and was about the size of a home magazine. **1862** G.T. LLOYD *Thirty-Three Yrs. Tas. & Vic.* 2 Educated home-folks would make themselves ridiculous to colonial post-masters and their subordinates by directing their letters 'Mr So-and-So, Van Diemen's Land, Australia'. **1935** B.E. PHELPS *Austral. tells England* 210 Our Home girls could never hold a candle to the Australian Mountain girls for riding. **1943** *Bulletin* (Sydney) 29 Sept. 13/4 Till 1840 jarrah was called mahogany. But the Swan Riverites found that the Home folk were accepting the name all too literally.

b. Special Comb. **home authorities, government,** the British government; the Colonial Office; **sentence** *hist.*, a term of transportation from the United Kingdom to an Australian Colony.

1851 H. MELVILLE *Present State Aust.* 135 The **home authorities** determined to interfere with local arrangements respecting convicts. **1852** J. MORGAN *Life & Adventures W. Buckley* 125 It was more than I had reason to expect from any governor, without a previous reference to the home authorities. **1830** H. SAVERY *Quintus Servinton* III. 172 Representation, after representation had continued to be made in allusion to him, to the **Home Government. 1840** *Tasmanian Weekly Dispatch* (Hobart) 21 Feb. 7/1 *Orders* have been received from the Home Government to place Mr Gregory and Mr Spode, in the Executive Council. **1865** 'SPECIAL CORRESPONDENT' *Transportation* 58 Were labour alone wanted, much more than is now received could be obtained from the home Government. **1888** *Plea for Separation* 23 Our invertebrate statesmen are afraid of displeasing the 'Home' Government. **1901** *Brisbane Courier* 1 July 5/7 Lord Brassey .. suggested that the home Government should concert measures with the Commonwealth Government for the raising of an Imperial Yeomanry. **1848** C. COZENS *Adventures of Guardsman* 165 Whenever any convict incurs a sentence to an ironed gang, the treadmill, or cell, the term of punishment .. is added to his original or **home sentence. 1848** *Britannia* (Hobart) 11 May 4/1 The practice of having men under home-sentence acting as headboroughs in the interior townships .. is an outrage.

home, *attrib.*[2] and *n.*[2] [Spec. use of *home* dwelling-place. For the *attrib.* use see OED(S *sb.*[1] B. 2, for the *n.* OEDS *sb.*[1] 2.]

A. *attrib.*

a. Used to denote relative proximity to the *home station* (see sense b. below).

1823 *Hobart Town Gaz.* 26 July, The farmstead is a neatly finished residence, having .. home-yards fenced in for cattle-stock. **1825** B. FIELD *Geogr. Mem. N.S.W.* 445 Cisalpine settlers .. whose home-runs are now hemmed in by neighbouring grantees. **1843** C. ROWCROFT *Tales of Colonies* II. 104 My home flocks of merinoes had got dispersed in the bush. **1849** A. HARRIS *Emigrant Family* (1967) 140 Cattle having been drafted off from the home herd, had been sent to Manaroo.

b. Special Comb. **home paddock, (a)** a paddock adjacent to a homestead or *home station*; **(b)** *fig.*, familiar territory; **station,** the principal residence on a large stock-raising property, together with the associated buildings and establishment (yards, accommodation for employees, etc.); HEAD-STATION; also *attrib.*

(a) [N.Z. **1866** M.A. BARKER *Station Life N.Z.* (1874) 66 The country outside the **home paddock** is too rough.] **1872** MRS E. MILLETT *Austral. Parsonage* 125 She was asked, she said, to look after the sheep in a home paddock for part of a day. **1881** W. FEILDING *Austral. Trans-Continental Railway* 31 Remained in Camp 28 washing our goods and 'spelling' the horses in the good grass of the home paddock of this station. **1897** *Bulletin* (Sydney) 2 Jan. 28/2 Abdul Khan .. had camped just outside the home paddock overnight. **1919** V. PALMER *Prisoner* (1924) 39 There's five hundred cattle in the home paddock. **1942** W. GLASSON *Our Shepherds* 11 The sheep .. were mustered and counted out of their several paddocks .. then all were assembled in the home paddock closest to the trucking yards. **1978** L. WHITE *Silent Reach* 121 In front lay what had been, at the turn of the century, five thousand acres of lush home paddock. **1981** A. WILKINSON *Up Country* 157 As the time of her confinement grew near we put her in the home paddock. **(b) 1920** *Emu* XIX. 292 They had been liberated from their **'home paddock'. 1951** CUSACK & JAMES *Come in Spinner* 37 'Don't try and tell me you don't like a bit of gossip?' 'Too right .. but not in the home-paddock.' **1965** R.H. CONQUEST *Horses in Kitchen* 116 Broke and exhausted, they returned to the home paddock swearing that they'd reach the Big Smoke, for sure, the following year. **1827** *Monitor* (Sydney) 12 June 433/3 This Farm is situate near the Cowpastures, and is well qualified for a **Home Station. 1834** J.D. LANG *Hist. & Statistical Acct. N.S.W.* I. 348 Supplies of flour, etc., are forwarded .. from the proprietor's home-station. **1845** *Portland Gaz.* 7 Oct. 4/1 Defendant ordered Rutherford to move Payne's sheep, which were unyarded round the home station hut. **1857** *Illustr. Jrnl. Australasia* III. 171 They rarely, it is true, attacked the home stations of the settlers, but shepherds were cut off in every part of the settlement, and numbers of sheep were stolen. **1863** R. THERRY *Reminisc. Thirty Yrs. N.S.W. & Vic.* (ed. 2) 241 The *home*, or *head station*, is generally applied to that portion of the run on which stands the hut occupied by the owner or superintendent of the whole property. **1872** W.M. HUGO *Hist. First Bushmen's Club* 383 A 'men's hut' at a home station is the home of the bullock-driver, the ploughman, the boundary-rider, the carpenter, and of the other men—from one to forty—who may be employed on the station. **1891** D. FERGUSON *Vicissitudes Bush Life* 30 On the station several men were employed throughout the year—a bullock driver, two bushmen, and the home-station shepherd. **1898** *Worker* (Sydney) 15 Jan. 8/1 A boundary rider from the home station has a ride round once every few weeks. **1930** BILLIS & KENYON *Pastures New* 22 A run in those pioneering days .. consisted of the home station, where the owner or his superintendent resided, and several huts placed at convenient spots for feed and water. **1958** E. SALTER *Will to Survive* 20 The three properties .. have been bequeathed to his three sons, Jock as the eldest inheriting Marrabri, the home station. **1961** M. KIDDLE *Men of Yesterday* 58 At even the roughest home station some essential crops had to be tended.

B. *n.*

1. A house; a house and its material embellishments: see esp. quot. 1924. Also *attrib.*

1848 *HRA* (1925) 1st Ser. XXVI. 691 The ill advised method, by which tenure of our homes is to be obtained. **1861** N.W. POLLARD *Homes in Vic.* 4 Place before our countrymen in the old country, a picture of the homes which we already enjoy, and to which their pioneer relatives .. are ready to assist them to share. **1867** 'CLERGYMAN' *Aust. as it Is* 45 The squatter homes will always be found to bear the aspect of thriving little villages. **1872** A. MCFARLAND *Illawarra & Manaro* 56 The homes of Illawara .. are chiefly in the cottage style. **1885** N.W. SWAN *Couple of Cups Ago* 68 The new home stretched out amongst the blossoming shrubs. **1892** *Truth* (Sydney) 5 June 6/6 The terrible distress in so many toiler's 'homes', was strongly animadverted on. **1922** *Daily Mail* (Sydney) 6 Jan. 7/6 On general averages you only sell your Home once in a lifetime. **1924** A. GASK *Secret of Garden* 27 My word, but wasn't it a gorgeous home! Beautiful and costly furniture everywhere, carpets into which you seemed to sink ankle-deep with your feet, pictures and statuary just as if one was in an art saloon and everything suggesting of the utmost money could buy. **1937** W. POLLOCK *So this is Aust.* 155 They call houses homes in Australia. **1947** F. CLUNE *Roaming around Aust.* 107 Its name was 'Holm Park', a colonial home built of stone, with wide verandas. **1959** D. HEWETT *Bobbin Up* 189 She thought of the Housing Commission home with the bare floors and the scanty furniture. **1961** *Bulletin* (Sydney) 14 Oct. 29/1 Don't let's sell houses, let's sell 'dream' homes. **1971** *Ibid.* 1 May 66/2 Most people still prefer to live in homes rather than home units, but the number of units is rising. **1978** J. ANDERSON *Tirra Lirra* 28 Additions to their house making it 'the best home in the street'. **1981** B. HUMPHRIES *Nice Night's Entertainment* 83 Beryl had given the home a good going over with the Flytox so we wouldn't have to race the blowies to our dinner. **1986** *Nat. Times* (Sydney) 21 Feb. 14/4 The former fitter-and-turner .. has built a huge home on the Brisbane River.

2. Special Comb. **home-unit,** a flat or apartment, usu. one owned by the occupant; also *attrib.*

1949 *Sydney Morning Herald* 4 May 13/2 Commands *glorious views* of Elizabeth Bay and is *ideal for the erection* of a block of *modern home units.* **1961** *Bulletin* (Sydney) 8 July 27/3 No matter how you look at them, a home unit is not, in the Australian sense at least, a home. **1967** C. RUHEN *Wild Beat* 18 The tall block of home-units on the opposite side of the street. **1973** *Bulletin* (Sydney) 13 Jan. 16/2 The development manager of Sydney-based Home Units Australia, the nation's biggest home unit developer, is quietly optimistic about prospects. **1977** *Drag Show* 10 The scene is the living room of Holly Brown's home unit in an eastern suburb of Sydney. **1979** H. WELLER *Lip Service* 75 Always, after months, the terror will return in some creature of legendary loathsomeness nurtured among the labyrinths between our white-washed super-clean home units. **1984** *Sydney Morning Herald* 10 Nov. 10/5 (Advt.), Live in the lap of luxury with one of Hordern Place's top of the range 2 bedroom home units that provide panoramic and spectacular City and Harbour views.

home, *adv.*

1. [See HOME *n.*[1]] To England (from Australia).

1791 *Hist. Rec. N.S.W.* (1893) II. 784 There are in the bay with us two ships .. which afford us an excellent opportunity of writing home. But, why should I say *home*? What is England, or Ireland, or Scotland to me now? **1810** *Sydney Gaz.* 7 Jan., The 102d (or New South Wales) Regiment is to be held in readiness to embark for England on the shortest notice.—An Opportunity of sending them home will certainly occur in the course of a very few weeks. **1825** *Howe's Weekly Commercial Express* (Sydney) 19 Sept. 3 The greatest part of the cedar, which was sent home hence on the Surry, had been purchased by the contractors for Windsor Castle. **1851** *Empire* (Sydney) 10 May 4/3 The phrase 'going home' . . is still the current equivalent amongst us Australians for departure for England. **1867** G. WALCH *Fireflash* 11 He elected 'to try wool-broking in Sydney for a short time, and if that didn't pay he'd marry some colonial girl with money and take her home, and make a lady of her'. **1877** *Free Trade Papers* x. 2 If we don't sell, we can't buy what we want from other people. The wool goes home, but the butter and cheese are consumed in the colony. **1883** A.J. CAMPBELL *Nests & Eggs Austral. Birds* p. xxi, 'Bin home too, and along France.' It appears he had been to England as servant to some squatter's family. But fancy an aboriginal stating he had been '*home*'. **1892** 'E. KINGLAKE' *Austral. at Home* 85 All good Australians hope to go to England when they die. Not only does everybody, now-a-days, go 'home' when able to do so, but many stay there. **1906** W. HORNE *Tas. as 'Home'* 9 'The world is growing smaller every day', and the Australian businessman takes a run 'home' (as the United Kingdom is affectionately termed), with little more concern than English people visit Scotland. **1942** A.L. HASKELL *Waltzing Matilda* p. xxi, England is automatically referred to as Home, even in such a common paradox as 'I have never been Home.' **1952** J.R. TYRRELL *Old Bk.* 35 She was still afloat to take me from here to London and Edinburgh when subsequently I made a trip 'home' for Angus and Robertson's. **1969** G. JOHNSTON *Clean Straw for Nothing* (1971) 74 The only really happy person on the deck . . is a middle-aged Australian. . . He has been saving for years for his trip Home. . . He wept when we raised the Lizard and saw the green Cornish folds beyond, and wept again for the Isle of Wight and the Dover cliffs.

2. [In Br. usu. *home and dry*: see OED(S *home, adv.* 2 and 3 b.] In the phr. **home and dried,** having safely and successfully completed (a task, journey, sporting contest, etc.); apparently certain to do so. Also **home and hosed, home on the pig's back** (or **ear**), and varr.

1918 *Kia Ora Coo-ee* Oct. 14/1 All being home and dried, 'Shorty' went over to the 'Q. Emma's' to borrow a bit of 'buckshee' sugar. **1919** A. WRIGHT *Game of Chance* 65 If Muski's as good as you say, he's 'ome an' dried. **1930** V. PALMER *Passage* (1957) 74 You've done it this time, Lew! Home and dry on the pig's back. **1936** A.B. PATERSON *Shearer's Colt* 54 The Gunner's vocabulary seemed to be limited to two sentences: 'She's home and dried', and 'She'll lob in'. **1944** J. HOLMES *Punter*, Soon out of sight, 'home and dried', as it were. **1945** C. MANN *River* 52 He's a monty! We always were lucky. He's home on the pig's ear. **1948** H. DRAKE-BROCKMAN *Sydney or Bush* 207 The chap advised no one to sell. Hang on, he said. It's going to rise. Home on the pig's back we are—talk about a merry Christmas! **1948** K.S. PRICHARD *Golden Miles* 76 'Kittiwake ought to win the hurdle, Saturdee.' . . 'Garn, wot are yer givin' us? Daisy Bell's home and dried on the pig's back.' **1955** N. PULLIAM *I traveled Lonely Land* 378 *Home and dried*, very easy to do. **1959** E. LAMBERT *Glory thrown In* 219 'Look!' he yelled to Christy. 'A and C Companies home and hosed!' **1960** J. WYNNUM *Pinch Salt* (1963) 52 He was 'ome an' 'osed, if you ask me. **1960** *N.T. News* (Darwin) 23 Feb. 10/4 Wallabies were home and hosed, 30–5. **1967** F. HARDY *Billy Borker yarns Again* 18 Don't tell a soul: number six, Hairy Legs, is home and hosed. **1969** H. PORTER *Eden House* 55 'Sign now and . . you'll be in the millionaire bracket. You'll be free to do anything you want to. . . ' 'Anything I want to. . . ' 'You'll be home on the pig's back, Maxine.' **1973** D. FOSTER *North South West* 96 Unless of course I happen to know some people in the district: then I'm home and hosed. **1981** *Sunday Mail* (Brisbane) 9 Aug. 57/6 Ideal Planet, having the second start of his career, was 'home and hosed' until Black Shoes came with her unbeatable challenge.

homeland. Used *attrib.* in Special Comb. **homeland centre,** OUT-STATION 3 (see quot. 1978); **movement,** the practice of Aboriginal people forming out-stations on their traditional lands. Also **homelands.**

1978 H.C. COOMBS *Kulinma* 150 The descriptive term 'outstation' is increasingly used for such settlements, reflecting probably the use of this term for settlements around Elcho Island which for many years had been serviced by Harold Sheppardson. However, the term somewhat misrepresents the Aboriginal conception of them, for each clan appears to consider its settlement as existing in its own right and not as an off-shoot from a larger unit, although some sense of affiliation with the central unit continues. The Yirrkala community now refers to these settlements in English language contexts as '**homeland centres**'. This phrase probably reflects more accurately the Aboriginal conception. **1979** M. HEPPELL *Black Reality* 3 Why are so many remote Aborigines leaving government and mission settlements to set up small homeland centres away from European influence? **1979** *Identity* Nov. 35/3 The outstation or **homeland movement** . . is alive and well across the north and centre of Australia. **1980** *Aboriginal News* ix. 28//1 This movement to outstations, also frequently called the 'decentralisation' or 'homelands' movement, has been gaining momentum since 1972.

homer. In the war of 1939–45: a wound of sufficient severity to ensure the recipient's repatriation.

[N.Z. **1942** *2nd N.Z. Exped. Force Times* 5 Oct. 5 He wagged his stumps at me. 'Look at me. . . I've got a homer.'] **1945** 'MASTER-SARG' *Yank discovers Aust.* 17 *A homer*, a wound which sends a man home. **1952** T.A.G. HUNGERFORD *Ridge & River* 173 He'll get a homer out of it—perhaps Australia. **1970** R. BEILBY *No Medals for Aphrodite* 164 Yeah. Looks like a homer. He's all bust up in the crutch. I fixed 'im up a bit, but he's bleeding badly. **1977** —— *Gunner* 87 She's apples. Now you just lie back an' take it easy. Ya got a homer, mate, you arsey bastard.

homestead, *n.*[1] [Spec. use of *homestead* house with its dependent buildings, esp. a farmstead: see OED(S 2.] A house, usu. the principal residence on a rural property (but see quot. 1878).

1822 J. DIXON *Narr. Voyage N.S.W. & Van Dieman's Land* 73 When he has received his grant and pitched on the spot for his homestead, he ought to take as many necessaries as will serve him for a long time into the country. **1833** *Trumpeter* (Hobart) 20 Aug. 136 The homestead affords all the comforts of a Norfolk farm house. **1838** *Aboriginal Claims Discussed* 7 The neighbouring woods will furnish abundance of suitable timber, and comfortable cottages and homesteads . . may easily be erected. **1847** A. HARRIS *Settlers & Convicts* (1953) 71 Every quarter of a mile or less a homestead alone at the river's edge, or embosomed in a rich orchard. **1852** S. MOSSMAN *Voice from Aust.* 10 There is no lack of snug farms with post and rail fences and well-built homesteads . . around Port Fairy. **1868** J. BAIRD *Emigrant's Guide* 38 Standing at the door of a comfortable homestead in the outskirts. **1878** *Squatter's Plum* 36 For a distance of 14 miles the visitor will see deserted claims and abandoned homesteads of miners, who once resided there. **1884** *Austral. Tit-Bits* (Melbourne) 25 Dec. 14/1 The hut that Jack occupied was about a mile from the homestead or residence of the squatter. **1901** *Bulletin* (Sydney) 28 Dec. 31/2, I . . hoped to have my wants supplied at the homestead of a handy grazing-farm. **1922** J.H. BIRDWOOD *Visit Aust. & N.Z.* 35 The house, a comfortable, rambling old Queensland homestead—is built of wood, with long low rooms and deep verandahs. **1930** D. COTTRELL *Earth Battle* 22 There was . . no one to take them to in the untidy, low-roofed homestead. **1943** H.G. LAMOND *From Tariaro to Ross Roy* 21 Candles . . were the illuminants of the homestead—the 'big' house, or 'gov'ment' house as it was known in the bush vernacular. **1957** F. CLUNE *Fortune Hunters* 91 Liddle's homestead (a hut) was near a good spring of permanent water. **1965** R.H. CONQUEST *Horses in Kitchen* 135 One homestead I know in the central-western stock country has eight bedrooms, and each bedroom has wall-to-wall carpets. There is a billiard-room, study and library; a huge lounge, dining-room, breakfast-room, and sunroom for winter months. **1986** *Sunday Examiner* (Launceston) 30 Mar. 49/3 The homestead, which was built in 1898, had been converted into flats.

homestead, *n.*[2] *Hist.* [U.S. *homestead* lot of (rural) land adequate for the maintenance of a family: see OED 3 and Mathews.]

1. A small rural land-holding, esp. as (variously) designated in land acts of the Australian Colonies (but see also quot. 1954). Also *attrib.*

1832 *Hill's Life N.S.W.* (Sydney) 17 Aug. 1 *The quid-pro-quo estate*; consisting of 1,000 acres . . will be divided into four homesteads, for the convenience of purchasers. **1841** *Launceston Courier* 22 Feb. 1/3 One of the most complete homesteads that has for a long time been offered to the public . . contains about 650 acres of land, all of the very best description, having a marsh frontage on the Macquarie river. . . It comprises a lately erected and beautifully situated Family Residence, with garden, stables, and outhouses of every description, barns, stockyard—in short, a complete farming establishment. **1845** *Portland Gaz.* 30 Sept. 3/4 It is Sir George Gipps's intention, should the Secretary of State leave to him the arrangements respecting Homesteads, to make them consist of only 160 acres and to be paid for by equal instalments of £20 per annum for 8 years. **1857** M.B. HALE *Transportation Question* 28 This estate . . has a fine stream running through the midst of it, and a more than average proportion of good land, and has also upon it five small farms or homesteads. **1871** *Austral. Handbk.* 40 Heads of families and persons of 21 years of age are allowed to select as 'homesteads' lots not exceeding 80 acres of agricultural or 160 acres of pastoral land. . . No person is allowed to acquire more than one 'homestead' allotment. **1886** P. FLETCHER 'Hints to Immigrants' in P. Fletcher *Qld.* 9 A 'Homestead' . . is an agricultural farm the area of which must not exceed 160 acres. **1919** *Smith's Weekly* (Sydney) 1 Mar. 6/3 Gleeson . . took up a selection near Wollar in 1861. To this block, known as Coomealla homestead, he added from time to time, until he had acquired a small squattage. **1936** E. SCOTT *Aust. during War* in *Official Hist. Aust. 1914–18* XI. 515 Pastoralists were informed by their city agents that there would be no sale for their wool, and were advised to hold it back at their homesteads. **1954** A. UPFIELD *Death of Lake* (1956) 5 The great homestead . . which comprised eight hundred thousand acres . . was populated by sixty thousand sheep. **1965** G. MCINNES *Road to Gundagai* 136 Expert in the ways of running a small homestead in the Australian bush.

2. Comb. **homestead block, farm, selection, selector, settlement, settler.**

1890 *Quiz* (Adelaide) 9 May 2/1 *Quiz* has never lost his mental balance in gushing on the subject of **homestead blocks.** **1898** *Tocsin* (Melbourne) 3 Mar. 3/3 The Government are charging Sale Village Settlers at the rate of £30 an acre for their homestead blocks. **1972** ANDERSON & BLAKE *J.S. Neilson* 12 In 1876 he had acquired his homestead block and an adjoining one in what was now the parish of Booroopki. **1981** A.B. FACEY *Fortunate Life* 132 The paddock was a homestead block of one hundred and sixty acres. **1897** L. LINDLEY-COWEN *W. Austral. Settler's Guide* 261 The **homestead farm** settler . . will be content with a single furrow plough and a couple of good horses. **1898** *Austral. Handbk.* 92 Village sites in connection with homestead farm areas may be proclaimed. Such sites shall consist of allotments of one acre each. Each homestead farm selector may select one such village allotment without payment. **1907** *W. Austral. Selector's Guide* (W.A. Lands Dept.) 11 Any person not already holding more than 100 acres within the State, if the head of a family, or a male of 16 years or over, may select a Free Homestead Farm of from 10 to 160 acres. **1952** J.F. HADDLETON *Katanning Pioneer* 75 Twenty years ago there were a number of small farmers who had taken up homestead grants limited to 160 acres which the Government termed a free homestead farm. The conditions were £1 on application, and if the specified improvements were done . . 40 acres cleared and ring-fenced with three wires, the selector paying £7 which was the cost of survey and Crown grant deed, the land became freehold. **1880** J. BONWICK *Resources Qld.* 75 The **homestead selection** cannot be more than 80 acres within the homestead area. **1887** W. BANNOW *Emigrant's Hand-Bk.* 60 Special provision is also made in certain cases for acquiring freeholds, not exceeding 160 acres, at 2s. 6d. per acre, after personal occupation for five years. This is commonly called Homestead Selection. **1921** J.P. OSBORNE *Nine Crowded Yrs.* 19 In 1895 . . Carruthers had passed a Bill creating new forms of land tenure called Settlement Leases and Homestead Selections. **1934** 'S. RUDD' *Green Grey Homestead* 10 You'll hear of a block of good land open for homestead selection, and you'll find out all about it from the storekeeper. **1981** H. HANNAH *Together in Jungle Scrub* 10 The first selections were all what they called homestead selections and were very cheap to take up, only cost about five or six pounds. **1880** R. ROSE *Austral. Guide: Qld.* 13 The Government always favours the **homestead selector**, as it desires the settlement of the land in moderate sized farms by responsible parties. **1898**

Austral. Handbk. 88 The homestead selector taking up 640 acres valued at £1 per acre would . . be required to deposit £6 13s. 9d. **1877** 'CAPRICORNUS' *Land Law of Future* 7 The leaders of thought elsewhere have by no means overlooked the advantages of '**homestead settlement**'. **1859** R.H. HORNE *Austral. Facts & Prospects* 105 The great majority will be respectable small farmers and **homestead settlers.**

3. Special Comb. **homestead area,** a district reserved for small land-holdings; the land-holding itself; **clause** *Qld.*, see quot. 1870; **lease,** an agreement setting out the terms of tenure of a homestead; the land so held.

1879 *Queenslander* (Brisbane) 26 Apr. 539/1 Certain areas are proclaimed as '**Homestead areas**'; you can select by 'conditional purchase' even in a homestead area. **1880** R. ROSE *Austral. Guide: Qld.* 13 The homestead areas, which are limited to 80 acres for each person, are always of the best agricultural land. **1898** *Austral. Handbk.* 92 Homestead areas may be proclaimed in the South-West Division or in the Eastern or Eucla Division, if within forty miles of a railway. **1910** *Huon Times* (Franklin) 21 May 6/4 A 'homestead area' upon which he would have to reside for five years continuously and make improvements to the value of £1 per acre annually. **1870** C.H. ALLEN *Visit to Qld.* 72 The '**Homestead Clause**' . . allows any one who is head of a family, or is of the age of twenty-one years to enter upon 80 acres of agricultural land, or 160 acres of pastoral land, open to selection, on payment annually, for five years, at the rate of ninepence an acre for the former, and sixpence for the latter, description of land. **1873** A. TROLLOPE *Aust. & N.Z.* I. 35 You may free-select a nice little farm of 80 acres of agricultural land, or 160 of pastoral . . under the homestead clause;—but . . you are bound down to residence. **1889** *Braidwood Dispatch* 25 Sept. 2/3 The amendments made by the Legislative Council in the Crown Lands Bill . . which relate to the extension of **homestead** and pastoral **leases** by way of compensation for improvements were first considered. **1891** *Austral. Handbk.* 100 No holder of a pastoral lease is to be entitled to hold a homestead lease. **1897** L. LINDLEY-COWEN *W. Austral. Settler's Guide* 6 The area of a homestead lease shall not be less than 1,000 acres, or more than 3,000 acres in second class land, nor less than 1,000 acres nor more than 5,000 acres in third class land. **1902** *Bulletin* (Sydney) 7 June 17/1 A S.A. farmer crossed the border into N.S.W. . . and took up a 10,240-acre homestead lease. **1911** 'ROSE BOLDREWOOD' *Complications at Collaroi* 282 Another of my experiences was to take up a homestead lease of three thousand acres with . . an old schoolfellow. These homestead leases are much the same as free selections.

homesteader. [Orig. U.S.: see OED(S.] A small farmer (see HOMESTEAD *n.*[2] 1).

1897 *Bulletin* (Sydney) 19 June 9/4 Great game in 'goldfields homesteads' at Gympie. Some of the homesteaders pay 1s. an acre rent to Govt. and sub-let to Chinese lettuce . . man for 10s. an acre. **1934** 'S. RUDD' *Green Grey Homestead* 56 It'll be a damp, drizzling day, a day when homesteaders turn their hands to plaiting green-hide into rope and reins, or to ring-barking. **1938** W. DENNING *Capital City* 26 Around Canberra is shaggy tableland not possessing great economic value, though a few homesteaders get a living from it. **1977** M. TUCKER *If everyone Cared* 94 The farmers and homesteaders . . got together and protested. **1983** K.W. MANNING *In their Own Hands* 142 They were 'gentlemen farmers' . . but in an era when planters did not do much manual work, they worked as hard as many a homesteader.

hominy. Also **ominny, ominy.** [U.S. *hominy* maize meal boiled with milk or water: see Mathews.] A gruel or thin porridge made from maize meal, esp. as part of a prison diet. Also *attrib.*

1827 P. CUNNINGHAM *Two Yrs. in N.S.W.* II. 72 If a sentimental shoplifter, fresh run from the trade, is heard pathetically descanting upon the sorrows of sour *smiggins* (cold-meat hash), and the horrors of *homony* (maize pudding), the old voyageur will facetiously remind him of the 'hundred hungry days' of yore. **1830** *Monitor* (Sydney) 14 Aug. 2/4 The cook brings in a kind of *ominy* (made of maize meal and water boiled together). **1836** J.F. O'CONNELL *Residence Eleven Yrs. New Holland* 47 Indian corn meal stirred in boiling water, called in American hashy pudding, or mush, in Australian hominy, makes the breakfast. **1847** *Gleaner* (Sydney) 4 Dec. 252 Convert the meal into ominny, Hawkesbury cakes, and bread. **1877** *Vagabond Ann.* 169 The meal, made into what they call 'hominy' here, is very good '*scuddgeroo*', and is wholesome and fattening. **1906** *Bulletin* (Sydney) 5 July 17/1 Yer feeds on, strike-me-dilly, hominee an' best o' skilly, Up be Pentridge on ther Model Lodgin' Farm. **1910** *Huon Times* (Franklin) 9 Apr. 4/2 Discussing their life in gaol, the men complained bitterly of the food, more especially of the hominy. **1918** V. MARSHALL *Jail from Within* 30 A tin of tasteless hominy which, as yet, I could not touch. **1921** D. GRANT *Through Six Gaols* 35 They develop what is known among prisoners as 'a hominy stomach'. That is, they suffer from a gastric trouble that is most unpleasant. **1968** J. ALARD *He who shoots Last* 128 Breakfast (hominy-ground corn) was served at seven.

honey. Used *attrib.* in the names of flora and fauna: **honey(-pot) ant,** an ant of any of several genera, including *Melophorus* and *Camponotus*, able to store a honey-like liquid in its distended crop; *honey-bag ant* HONEY-BAG 2; **flower,** the shrub *Lambertia formosa* (fam. Proteaceae) of e. N.S.W., having nectar-rich flowers; *mountain devil* (b), see MOUNTAIN; **-parrot,** LORIKEET; **possum** (formerly **mouse**), the small nectar-eating possum of s.w. W.A. *Tarsipes rostratus*.

1896 B. SPENCER *Rep. Horn Sci. Exped. Central Aust.* I. 87 We went out into the Mulga scrub in search of **honey ants.** **1937** A.W. UPFIELD *Mr Jelly's Business* 64 He saw the grey-and-black honey ants taking down into inconspicuous holes their loads of honey, which they crammed into the mouth of the store ants in their caves deep in the earth. **1963** D. ATTENBOROUGH *Quest under Capricorn* 150 These were honey-pot ants. The workers labour in the bush, collecting honey-dew exuded by the desert plants . . and . . they feed it to newly emerged workers in the nest until they become so distended that they cannot move. **1968** E.L.G. WATSON *Journey under Southern Stars* 28, I have bought honey-ants from native girls. The living ant is held in the fingers and the abdomen bitten off. The taste is delicious, like honey with a slight formic-acid flavour. **1973** V. SERVENTY *Desert Walkabout* 88 Honeypot ants . . those extraordinary insects. **1861** *Sydney Mail* 6 July 3/3 The *Lambertia formosa*, by some called **Honeyflower**, is only found in sandy soil. **1888** *Proc. Linnean Soc. N.S.W.* III. 521 *Lambertia formosa* . . 'Honey flower' or 'Honeysuckle' . . obtains its vernacular name on account of the large quantity of a clear honey-like liquid the flowers contain. **1914** H.M. VAUGHAN *Australasian Wander-Yr.* 72 Another very striking plant was the Honey Flower. **1972** M. GILBERT *Personalities & Stories Early Orbost* 82 They ate fruit out of the bush . . geebung and what they called honey flowers. **1888** *Centennial Mag.* (Sydney) 129 Thousands of **honey parrots**, the light of the spring sun glancing from their lustrous wings. **1929** A.H. CHISHOLM *Birds & Green Places* 18 A terrified flock of honey-parrots. **1923** [**honey possum**] *Austral. Zoologist* III. 148 The *Tarsipes* are known throughout the district as 'Honey Mice'. **1926** J. POLLARD *Bushland Man* 278 I'm going after the honey-mouse and the pigmy flying-'possum—two fairy-like dwellers of the big timber. **1976** *Bulletin* (Sydney) 2 Oct. 42/3 The tiny honey possums which suck nectar from the banksias. **1983** R. STRAHAN *Compl. Bk. Austral. Mammals* 173 The long, pointed snout and brush-tipped tongue with which the Honey-possum probes flowers are its most obvious specialisations for an exclusive diet of nectar and pollen.

honey-bag.

1. The honeycomb or hive of the wild bee: see SUGAR BAG 1.

1928 B. SPENCER *Wanderings in Wild Aust.* 499 To secure what the natives call a 'honey-bag'. This is the honeycomb of the native bee that makes its rough hive in a hollow tree or bough. **1983** C. BINGHAM *Beckoning Horizon* 11 A young Aborigine climbing high on a river gum for a wild bee hive ('the honey bag', which we harvested in kerosene tins).

2. Special Comb. **honey-bag ant,** *honey ant*, see HONEY.

1896 B. SPENCER *Rep. Horn Sci. Exped. Central Aust.* II. 386 The honey-bag ants were found hanging in clusters to the roof of the chambers by the feet, their large globular bodies looking like bunches of grapes. **1932** *Bulletin* (Sydney) 13 Jan. 21/2 Far-northern blacks make use of two kinds of ants, the green and the honey-bag.

honey cart. [Cf. U.S. *honey-bucket*; OEDS *honey, sb.* 7.] *Sanitary cart*, see SANITARY.

1970 J.S. GUNN in W.S. Ramson *Eng. Transported* 50 *Honey cart*, or *17-door sedan*, sanitary cart. **1971** *Bulletin* (Sydney) 3 July 13/1 A honey cart is the dear little vehicle that the airlines use to empty the aircraft lavatories.

honeycomb. *Obs.* Used *attrib.* in Special Comb. **honeycomb ground,** land having an uneven surface. See CRABHOLE. Also **honey-combed,** *ppl. a.*

1849 W. CARRON *Narr. Exped. Rockingham Bay & Cape York* 54 During the day's journey, we passed over some flats of rotten honeycomb ground, on which nothing was growing but a few stunted shrubs. **1853** MOSSMAN & BANISTER *Aust. Visited & Revisited* 129 A coarse sandy clay, full of shallow hollows, in which water remains for a time. . . This . . description of country is what the colonists term 'honeycomb' ground, and is very unsafe to ride over. **1861** T. M'COMBIE *Austral. Sketches* 79 The land [was] what is termed 'honey-combed' and covered by dwarfed ungainly trees.

honeyeater. [Transf. use of *honey-eater* an African bird, the honey-guide.] Any bird of the fam. Meliphagidae of Aust. and nearby, having a brush-tipped tongue for feeding on nectar and other foods. Also with distinguishing epithet, as **black-headed, helmeted, Keartland, Lewin, New Holland, painted, pied, red-headed, regent, scarlet, singing, spiny-cheeked, warty-faced, white-bearded, white-cheeked, white-eared, white-fronted, white-gaped, white-naped, white-plumed, white-throated, yellow, yellow-faced, yellow-plumed, yellow-spotted, yellow-tufted** (see under first element). Also *attrib.*, and formerly also **honey-bird, honey-sucker.**

1790 J. COOK *Collection Voyages round World* VI. 2034 There are four species that seem to belong to the trochili, or honey-suckers of Linnaeus. **1813** J.W. LEWIN *Birds N.S.W.* 15 Blue Face Honeysucker. . . This Species are fond of pecking traverse Holes in the Bark, between which and the Wood they insert their long Tongues in search of small Insects, which they draw to them with great dexterity. **1822** J. LATHAM *Gen. Hist. Birds* IV. 208 None of them, although the tongue be cloven into two filaments, are at all fringed on the edges, as is the case with very many of the Honey-eaters. **1832** BACKHOUSE & TYLOR *Life & Labours G.W. Walker* 27 July (1862) 76 Numbers of Honey-eaters—small birds about the size of a wren—were hopping from branch to branch in those trees where the flowers were expanding. **1841** *Port Phillip Patriot* 9 Aug. 4/2 Honey-eaters on restless wings. **1854** W. HOWITT *Boy's Adventures* 36 The honey birds . . suck the flowers like humming birds. **1886** F. COWAN *Aust.* 20 *The Honey-suckers*, feather-tongued, Australia's humming-birds. **1913** F. SULMAN *Pop. Guide Wild Flowers N.S.W.* 22 The Banksia spikes, with their abundance of honey, attract many visitors, among them the Honey-suckers. **1934** T. WOOD *Cobbers* 191 A hermit . . nearly persuaded me that the only life was to . . lie . . among the roots of the bread-fruit trees, and . . listen to the honey-birds. **1948** P.J. HURLEY *Red Cedar* 33 The coral trees . . brought along the honey-eaters of all kinds. **1974** N. CATO *Brown Sugar* 33 Honey-eaters called and chattered among the flowering poinciana. **1976** *Reader's Digest Compl. Bk. Austral. Birds* 602 The diversity of Australian birds is exemplified by honey-eaters. With 66 species, they are the largest Australian family. **1986** *Canberra Times* 16 Apr. 19/2 The annual honeyeater migration is one of the highlights of the bird-watchers year.

honeysuckle. [See quot. 1895.] Any of several trees or shrubs bearing nectar-rich flowers, esp. of the genus *Banksia* (see BANKSIA); the wood of these trees; *native honeysuckle*, see NATIVE *a.* 6 a. Also with distinguishing epithet, as **dwarf, red, white** (see under first element), and *attrib.*

1803 *Sydney Gaz.* 26 June, Timber in this Colony includes Box, Honeysuckle, Cedar. **1810** *Ibid.* 21 July, Stolen. . . Nine large Pieces of well-seasoned Honeysuckle. **1825** B. FIELD *Geogr. Mem. N.S.W.* 144 A body of honeysuckle (banksia integrifolia) brush. **1834** G. BENNETT *Wanderings N.S.W.* I. 61 The *Banksia* genus (or honeysuckle, as all the species are indiscriminately termed by the colonists). **1845** R. HOWITT *Impressions Aust. Felix* 231 This tree the Australians call Honeysuckle; little short of blasphemy. **1861** 'OLD BUSHMAN'

Bush Wanderings 32 A fire of honeysuckle cones and other rubbish. **1878** R.B. SMYTH *Aborigines of Vic.* I. p. xxxiii, He [*sc.* the Victorian Aborigine] .. made sweet drinks of the flowers of the honeysuckle. **1895** J.H. MAIDEN *Flowering Plants & Ferns N.S.W.* 31 'Honeysuckle' is so called because the spikes of flowers are often full of honey, which the aborigines used to consume either by passing them over their tongues, or by soaking in water, when a sweetish liquid would be obtained, which was drunk either before or after fermentation. **1931** M.M. BANKS *Memories Pioneer Days Qld.* 77 The honeysuckle tree, a native Banksia, has dense, cylindrical, honey-coloured spikes amongst its silver-lined foliage. **1936** M. FRANKLIN *All that Swagger* (1980) 40 The children .. plucked the chookies of the banksia—misnamed honeysuckle. **1962** E. IRVIN *Early Inland Agric.* 13 Many honey-suckle trees (Banksia) .. dotted the river sandhills.

hooded, *ppl. a.* Used in the names of birds distinguished by the dark colour of the head or crown, esp. of the mature male: **hooded dotterel,** the wading bird *Charadrius rubricollis* of coastal s. Aust. incl. Tas., and inland salt lakes of s.w. Aust; **parrot,** the parrot *Psephotus dissimilis* of the N.T.; see also ANTHILL PARROT; **robin,** the widespread black and white bird *Melanodryas cucullata*; *pied robin*, see PIED.

1848 J. GOULD *Birds of Aust.* VI. Pl. 18, *Hiaticula monacha.* **Hooded Dottrel.** **1887** *Illustr. Austral. News* (Melbourne) 21 Dec. 218/1 The pretty hooded dottrell—seldom seen in Victoria—existed in large numbers along the beach. **1903** *Emu* II. 209 *Aegialitis cucullata* (Hooded Dottrel) .. plentiful on the sandy beaches. **1945** C. BARRETT *Austral. Bird Life* 102 The hooded dotterel .. patrols the sea beaches of Southern Australia. **1985** *Age* (Melbourne) 13 Sept. (Suppl.) 6/3 The sea birds are always fascinating: white-faced herons in the shallows .. dainty hooded dotterels and crested terns. **1929** A.H. CHISHOLM *Birds & Green Places* 98 The golden-shouldered and **hooded parrots,** of northern Australia, bore into the earthern homes of termites (white ants). **1964** M. SHARLAND *Territory of Birds* 37 Along the Stuart Highway between Pine Creek and Katherine there are small numbers of the Hooded Parrot in the flowering eucalypts; they are attractive birds and uncommon as parrots go. **1896** B. SPENCER *Rep. Horn Sci. Exped. Central Aust.* II. 77 *Melanodryas bicolor* .. **Hooded Robin** .. were very tame and easily approached. **1945** C. BARRETT *Austral. Bird Life* 175 The hooded or black-and-white robin .. is found throughout the mainland, North Queensland excepted. **1962** B.W. LEAKE *Eastern Wheatbelt Wildlife* 90 The hooded robin, the male of which is black and white and the female just grey.

hooer. [Prob. repr. dial. pronunc. of *whore.*] A term of abuse; used with varying degrees of strength and applied to a person of either sex. Cf. BASTARD.

1937 E. PARTRIDGE *Dict. Slang & Unconventional Eng.* 403 *Hoor, hooer, hooa or hua*, a sol. pronunciation of *whore.* **1952** T.A.G. HUNGERFORD *Ridge & River* 31 Cranky old hooer! White thought. .. Always on the bloody job. **1968** D. O'GRADY *Bottle of Sandwiches* 191 'What's it famous for?' .. 'Rum, you higorant hooer. Any idiot knows that.' **1977** T.A.G. HUNGERFORD *Wong Chu* 52, I got slime all over me from these dirty hooers. **1985** N. MEDCALF *Rifleman* 121 Anyone would think you were professional pox-doctors, checking the hooers in Palmer Street!

hook. A riding spur.

1920 B. CRONIN *Timber Wolves* 41, I touches my horse with the hooks and away we goes, helter-skelter across the button-grass. **1968** W. GILL *Petermann Journey* 23 Horses being what they are, there comes the time when, mounted on a strange animal, a touch of the 'hook' becomes a necessity.

hoon. [Of unknown origin.] A lout; an exhibitionist; a man who manages a prostitute.

1938 X. HERBERT *Capricornia* 338 'You flash hoon,' he went on. 'Kiddin' you're white, eh?' **1962** R. TULLIPAN *March into Morning* 45 'You're a witty hoon.' The sergeant dismissed Dixon with a glare. **1968** *Swag* (Sydney) iv. 26/3 Bugger me dead if the little hoon of a landlord doesn't turn up with two coppers. **1969** *Kings Cross Whisper* (Sydney) lxxii. 6/2 A hoon sent his new girl-friend to walk the streets. **1977** R. BEILBY *Gunner* 157 That bastard run ya down, the bloody hoon! **1980** M. WILLIAMS *Dingo!* 59 The Yanks were still there but the girls had a whisper that the American Army was shifting to Brisbane. The brothels would go with them. Bill thought we should follow the girls. 'We can be hoons, mate!' he laughed. 'A couple of Terry toons!' I didn't say much, there was a stigma to being a bludger, living off the proceeds. **1982** *Canberra Times* 27 Jan. 17/5 Sydney .. the city which had invented the word bludger .. was just starting to use the word hoon, successive terms for the same occupation.

hoop. [Transf. use of *hoop* coloured band on a jockey's blouse.] A jockey.

1941 S.J. BAKER *Pop. Dict. Austral. Slang* 36 *Hoop*, a jockey. **1945** W. NOONAN *Surprising Battalion* 33 The 'hoop' told us that these girls take their job seriously. **1956** *Truth* (Sydney) 29 Jan. 16/5 However, punters weren't the only ones who took exception to Mulley's riding as immediately the hoop was dismounted, he was invited into the stewards sanctum and asked to explain his exhibition. **1969** W. MOXHAM *Apprentice* 27 Guy Moreton was tops as a trainer in his heyday. He's schooled some crackerjack horses as well as hoops. **1984** *Bulletin* (Sydney) 18 Dec. 66/1 Now Moore and Higgins two of the best hoops in the history of racing.

hoop pine. [From the bark hoops (see quot. 1969) which remain conspicuously on the forest floor after the wood has decayed.] The tall conifer *Araucaria cunninghamii* (fam. Araucariaceae), of near-coastal N.S.W. and Qld., and New Guinea; the pale-coloured softwood timber of the tree; *colonial pine* (b), see COLONIAL *a.* 5; *Moreton Bay pine*, see MORETON BAY.

1861 J.D. LANG *Qld., Aust.* 118 Timber exists; cedar, cowrie, and hoop pine. **1903** *Austral. Handbk.* 280 Some of the trees of large size which furnish .. soft wood .. are .. 'Dundathu Pine' (*Agathis robusta*), 'Hoop Pine' (*Araucaria Cunninghamii*). **1920** B. CRONIN *Timber Wolves* 21 Didn't see how they were going to keep up the supply of Norway pine for their matches... Their substitute is Queensland hoop pine. **1936** *Publicist* (Sydney) i. 14/2 Australia contains the most wonderful natural timber in the world (including Hoop Pine and Bunya Pine). **1949** *Bulletin* (Sydney) 2 Mar. 14/4 Had the good fortune to travel through the last great stand of hoop-pine in Southern Queensland the other day. **1956** N.K. WALLIS *Austral. Timber Handbk.* 3 Hoop pine is used for joinery, cabinet work, butter boxes, and for plywood, much of the latter being exported to other States. **1969** T.H. EVERETT *Living Trees of World* 25 The Richmond-river-pine or hoop-pine .. the latter name deriving from its bark, which has horizontal cracks in encircling bands. **1981** A.B. & J.W. CRIBB *Useful Wild Plants Aust.* 109 Butter very readily picks up taints so the timber used for the boxes had to be virtually odourless; hoop pine is such a timber.

hooray /'hureɪ/, *exclam.* [Var. *hurrah* a shout.] A conventional form of farewell, 'good-bye'.

1898 *Bulletin* (Sydney) 4 June (Red Page), In many places the salutation 'good-day' or 'good-night' is simply 'Hooray!' **1941** K. TENNANT *Battlers* 164 She gave Snow's arm a squeeze as she rose to go. 'Hooray for now, Snow.' 'Hooray,' Snow responded. **1945** *Atebrin Advocate: Mag. 2/4 Austral. Armoured Regiment* Jan. 2 Hooray David! **1953** 'CADDIE' *Caddie* 255 Well, hooray, see you anon. **1965** P. TODHUNTER *Aust. under Scalpel* 84 The way they treated me as a chum embarrassed me, and when they said 'T'rah' and even 'Hooray' (a farewell completely new to me) when I departed I was sure they were talking to someone else. **1969** E. O'CONNER *Second Helping* 163 'Hooray!' called Mrs Bridson, waving from the doorway of her ancient hotel. **1977** V. PRIDDLE *Larry & Jack* 10 As George moved to go, Tom said: 'Hooray George, promise now, you will come back and see me before you leave.'

hooroo /'huru/. Also **hurroo, ooroo.** HOORAY.

1906 *Bulletin* (Sydney) 22 Nov. 44/4 Hurroo. See yer ter-morrer. **1916** *Truth* (Sydney) 23 Jan. 10/5 Page said, 'Well, too-ra-loo; I'm getting off here.' 'Hoo-roo,' he replied. **1938** A. UPFIELD *Bone is Pointed* (1966) 86 Well, I must get along. I may see you all again soon. Hooroo! **1945** —— *Death of Swagman* 92 'See you sometime.' 'Yep. In the ruddy pub, prob'ly. Hooroo!' **1963** F. HARDY *Legends Benson's Valley* 145 'Hooroo, Charlie,' Betty called after him. 'Goodbye, Betty,' he answered without looking round. **1967** D. HEWETT *This Old Man* (1976) 21 Ooroo, Laurie. You there, love? **1970** J. CLEARY *Helga's Web* 288 Hooroo, sport. It's a shame about Helga, but I wouldn't lose too much sleep about it. **1982** *Bulletin* (Sydney) 6 July 88/3 Anyhow, hopefully we'll see y' again, hoo roo.

hooshter /'hʊʃtə/. *Hist.* [Transf. use of *hooshter* a command or shout (of encouragement) to a camel.] One who rides a camel, esp. a member of the Imperial Camel Corps.

1917 *Barrack: Offical Organ Imperial Camel Corps* 1 Sept. 2/2 *The camelier's lament.* Out east with the 'Hooshters'. **1978** P. ADAM SMITH *Anzacs* 235 He remained with the 'hooshters' until April 1918 when the camel corps was disbanded, its members forming the 5th Light Horse.

hoot. [N.Z. slang *hoot* money, a. Maori *utu* payment, recompense.] Money.

[N.Z. **1864** *Saturday Rev.* iii. 12 We shall soon have no 'hoot' to pay the piper.] **1881** G.C. EVANS *Stories* 265 Why the very stuff you are now drinking has been bought with 'hoot', obtained from stolen goods. **1889** *Bulletin* (Sydney) 13 July 20/1 Two years without spell on the back-blocks, While hoarding each cent of the 'hoot'. **1898** *Australasian Suppl. Webster's Internat. Dict.* 2024 *Hoot* (Maori *utu* vengeance), payment; reward; recompense; rate of wages. (*Slang. N.Z.*). **1938** X. HERBERT *Capricornia* 301 On the construction you could make a pot of hoot in no time. **1962** H. PORTER *Bachelor's Children* 185 He's got plenty of hoot; has shares in everything from here to Perth. **1966** *Kings Cross Whisper* (Sydney) July 8/1 Here in Kings Cross cabbage means money, and so does hoot. **1977** *Sun-Herald* (Sydney) 24 July 111/1 It's about a QC and his wife, who live in Point Piper and obviously have lots of hoot.

hop, *n.*[1] [Used elsewhere, but chiefly Austral. and N.Z.]

1. Usu. in *pl.* Beer; esp. in the phr. **on the hops,** engaged in a drinking session.

1930 *Bulletin* (Sydney) 1 Jan. 11/4 The proprietor provided a beer party, and the riot that arose out of the hop-drinking led to the school's first raid. **1956** S. HOPE *Diggers' Paradise* 233 The result was that several rounds of Drambuie were ordered in succession before they again 'got stuck in the hops', the Digger's expression for beer swilling. **1966** D. NILAND *Pairs & Loners* 102 I'm on the hops and yakking away and neither is any trouble to me. **1969** W. MOXHAM *Apprentice* 25 When Gus was on the hops he smashed everything in sight. **1972** J. HIBBERD *Stretch of Imagination* (1973) 14, I was in a sad state .. all psychological .. the hops were having their desired effect.

2. Special Comb. **hophead,** a heavy drinker.

[N.Z. **1942** *2nd N.Z. Exped. Force Times* 17 Aug. 16 Private Harry Hophead.] **1957** D. NILAND *Call me when Cross turns Over* 31 A terror for the grog, my old woman, a real hophead. **1960** E. NORTH *Nobody stops Me* 177 Rat-hole shelters for the plonk merchants and hopheads.

Hop, *n.*[2] Abbrev. of JOHN HOP. Also *attrib.*

1916 *Truth* (Sydney) 19 Nov. 1/7 The shooting of our Bluebottles in Sydney is wretched, that is, more honored in the 'breech' than the Hopp-servants. **1923** D.H. LAWRENCE *Kangaroo* 310 'Police!' snarled Jack. 'Bloody Johnny Hops. They couldn't hold a sucking pig in their hands, unless somebody hung on to its tail for them. It's our boys who've got things in hand. And handed them over to the Hops.' **1933** *Bulletin* (Sydney) 8 Feb. 12/3 The Hops were taking the shattered body out of the water. **1959** S.J. BAKER *Drum* 118 *Hop*, a policeman.

hop, *v.*

a. *intr.* With **in(to)**: to begin on (a meal, activity, etc.) with alacrity. Also in the phr. **to hop in for one's chop** etc., to seize an opportunity.

1939 J. CAMPBELL *Babe is Wise* 307 An' hop in, 'cause if you don't you'll just have to see how fast you c'n run. **1968** S. GORE *Holy Smoke* 21 Come on, you Adam, hop in for your chop. Good peller tucker orright! **1971** B. HUMPHRIES *Bazza pulls it Off*, 'You're not tryin' to kid me youse invited me all the way up here for a chin wag!'

'Course she didn't you stupid drongo cut the cackle and hop into the horsecollar!' **1976** B. BENNETT *New Country* 50 Niggers got to hop in for their chop while the hoppin's good. **1980** ANSELL & PERCY *To fight Wild* 65 The crows and kites . . used to hang about the camp, on the look-out, and if I was away for any length of time, would hop into any fresh meat left hanging up. **1982** R. HALL *Just Relations* 27 Time you woke up to yourself. Hop in for your cut.

b. *trans.* To attack (a person, meal, etc.).

1945 R.S. CLOSE *Love me Sailor* 160 Did you see young Ernie hopping into Christenson? **1958** G. CASEY *Snowball* 207 'All right, kid, hop into your tucker,' Plugger ordered briskly.

hop-bush. [Transf. use of *hop*, from the bitter leaf or hop-like winged fruit of the plant.] Any shrub or small tree of the widespread genus *Dodonaea* (fam. Sapindaceae), the bitter fruits of which have been used as a substitute for hops; any of several other plants, esp. the shrub *Daviesia latifolia* (fam. Fabaceae), with leaves used similarly. See also *native hop* NATIVE *a.* 6 a., *wild hop* WILD 1. Also **hop scrub**.

1853 W. HOWITT *Land, Labor & Gold* 15 Jan. (1855) I. 201 The country was covered with hop-scrub up to their very heads. **1883** F.M. BAILEY *Synopsis Qld. Flora* 82 The capsules of many *Dodonaeas* are used for hops, and thus the shrubs are known as hop-bushes in Queensland. **1893** S. NEWLAND *Paving Way* 238 Undulating sandhills, well grassed and clothed with box-wood, hop-bush. **1900** *Bulletin* (Sydney) 21 Apr. 14/3 The men . . found horse-bells tied to hop-bush twigs. **1904** *Proc. Linnean Soc. N.S.W.* XXIX. 692 *Daviesia latifolia* . . (Hop Scrub). **1915** *Bull. N.T.* xiv. 10 Two species of hopbush (dodonea) are found on the limestone and metasomatic limestone areas between Frog Valley and Tanami. **1924** J.A. REID *Pioneer Grazier* 6 Further out from the river is a considerable amount of hop-bush on the sandy country. This is not an edible scrub, but the blossom is very similar to that of brewers' hops, and it has been reported to have been used for that purpose. **1932** J. TRURAN *Green Mallee* 104 The little green parrots rose from his path, whirring into the safety of the hop-scrub. **1977** *Ecos* xiii. 18 Goats eliminated shrubs like hopbush. **1984** E. WALLING *On Trail Austral. Wildflowers* 24 Hop bushes with clear green leaves and rusty-red papery fruits.

hop-over. *Obs.* The action of 'going over the top', of leaving a trench (to attack an enemy). Also *transf.*

[**1917** W.D. JOYNT *Breaking Road for Rest* 9 Sept. (1979) 123 At eleven o'clock, just as I was turning in, I got orders to proceed to the front line and reconnoitre the position where we would have to 'hop over' when the time came.] **1918** *Aussie: Austral. Soldiers' Mag.* Jan. 10/2 *Hopover*, a departure from a fixed point into the Unknown, also the first step in a serious undertaking. **1919** *7th Field Artillery Brigade Yandoo* 20 Mar. 135 The Yanks made the initial hopover. **1932** *Whiz-Bang* (Brisbane) 1 July 15 We are warning our readers that should they wish . . to start a 'hop-over' with Harry, all they will need to do is to ridicule Australians. **1933** H.B. RAINE *Lash End* 166 'Feels like it did in France, just before a hop-over,' he reflected. 'Only this time it might be knives instead of guns!' **1978** P. ADAM SMITH *Anzacs* 324 Norman Young wrote again to his mother on 25 September [1918]: 'The excitement of recent days has been tremendous. Look up the papers that refer to the stunt of 18 September and you will get a small—very small—idea of what we call 'a hop-over'.

hopper. [Spec. use of *hopper* an animal characterized by hopping.] A kangaroo.

1879 *Queenslander* (Brisbane) 5 July 27/3 The late invasion by the marsupials of the settled districts induced the settlers to wage a war of extermination against the 'hoppers and jumpers'. **1897** *Tocsin* (Melbourne) 4 Nov. 8/3 We could . . get near these bloomin' hoppers, and shoot the bloomin' lot. **1942** T. KELAHER *Digger Hat* 22 The flat Is now dotted with the 'hoppers' who have lately . . come in from the scrub to flog the frontage of its feed.

hopping mouse. Any of several mice of the genus *Notomys* (fam. Muridae) of drier Aust., having long hind legs and a rapid hopping gait; JERBOA; *kangaroo mouse*, see KANGAROO *n.* 5.

1941 E. TROUGHTON *Furred Animals Aust.* 319 This beautiful little hopping-mouse is at once recognized by the distinct pouch-like skin-pocket on the throat. **1972** ANDERSON & BLAKE *J.S. Neilson* 41 Smaller creatures too lived by these oases—the tiny hopping mouse, the fat-tailed pouched mouse. **1977** *Ecos* xiv. 11/1 Two species of hopping mouse of Australia's arid zone can survive without water on a diet of dry seed.

hopple chain, var. HOBBLE CHAIN.

Hori /'hɒri/. [Maori form of 'George'.] A nickname for a Maori. Cf. HENARE.

1922 *Smith's Weekly* (Sydney) 19 Aug. 17/5 As Hori was notoriously lazy, it was a mystery how he managed to get the birds. **1944** *Bulletin* (Sydney) 8 Nov. 13/3, I struck Hori along the bush road, cranking vigorously at his ancient T model. . . I continued on into town, returning two hours later. The Maori was still cranking away, but with noticeably less vigor. **1950** *Ibid.* 20 Sept. 13/4 Hori was annoyed with his 16-year-old son Hatti. 'He won't cut his toenails,' the old Maori complained.

horizontal scrub. [See quot. 1888.] The small tree or shrub *Anodopetalum biglandulosum* (fam. Cunoniaceae), of central, w., and s. Tas., the interlocking trunks and branches of which may form an almost impenetrable thicket. Freq. *ellipt.* as **horizontal.**

1875 *Papers & Proc. R. Soc. Tas.* (1876) 96 A tall and tangled growth of wireweed (*Bauera*) and cutting-grass, with horizontal scrub (*Anodopetalum*). **1888** R.M. JOHNSTON *Systematic Acct. Geol. Tas.* 6 The Horizontal is a tall shrub or tree. . . Its peculiar habit—to which it owes its name and fame—is for the main stem to assume a horizontal and drooping position after attaining a considerable height, from which ascend secondary branches which in turn assume the horizontal habit. From these spring tertiary branchlets, all of which interlock, and form . . an almost impenetrable mass of vegetation. **1904** *Advocate* (Burnie) 7 Mar. 4/5 Even worse than horizontal, which everybody knows is bad. **1940** *Bulletin* (Sydney) 28 Feb. 16/1 A belt of dense-growing scrub known as 'horizontal'. Tough, wiry and seldom thicker than a man's arm, this scrub grows stark upright and so dense that pine logs have been rolled over its top without breaking through the mass. **1959** *Westerly* i. 17 You'll be walking along on what you think's the ground and find yourself twelve feet up in the air, on a platform of horizontal. **1967** V.G.C. NORWOOD *Long Haul* 74 Obstructed by an interwoven mat of horizontal scrub. **1980** *Habitat Aust.* Aug. 24 Scrub species, such as the infamous *Anodopetalum biglandulosum*, more commonly known to intrepid bushwalkers as horizontal scrub.

horned dragon. *Mountain devil* (a), see MOUNTAIN.

1930 *Bulletin* (Sydney) 26 Mar. 21/3 The most formidable looking thing in the bush is the thorny devil (*Moloch horridus*), which is also called the horned dragon. **1968** G. MIKES *Boomerang* 160 The horned dragon . . grows to seven inches in length and its appearance is really fearsome; but it is a gentle and harmless creature often kept as a pet.

horny. [Scot. dial.: see OEDS B. 3.]

1. A bullock.

1901 *Bulletin* (Sydney) 30 Nov. 32/1, I am getting tired of roving Round those hornies in the lead, And I'm tired, sick tired of droving On the stock-routes bare of feed. **1909** *Ibid.* 28 Oct. 13/3 One loud crack . . is sometimes sufficient to cause a thousand restive 'hornies' to stop feeding and to walk. **1927** *Ibid.* 6 Jan. 22/4 A withering dry spell . . had wiped off every horny of the Coolumbooka sawmill teams. **1932** J. MCCARTER *Pan's Clan* 109 Might have to leave right away for Camooweal t' pick up nine hundred head of hornies, then deliver 'em in New South Wales. **1943** *Bulletin* (Sydney) 7 Mar. 13/3 The bullock-muster was on. . . Suddenly the colt dropped his head and bucked into the milling mob of 'hornies'. **1976** C.D. MILLS *Hobble Chains & Greenhide* 43 Nugget gave me a spell after smoke-oh, and I went to the crush to deal with the 'hornies'.

2. Special Comb. **horny-steerer,** a bullock-driver.

1905 *Bulletin* (Sydney) 27 July 16/4 A bullock-driver is called a bullocky, a bovine-puncher, an ox-persuader, a horny-steerer. **1943** S.J. BAKER *Pop. Dict. Austral. Slang* (ed. 3) 40 *Horney-steerer*, a bullock driver.

horse.

1. Used *attrib.* in Special Comb. which have a local significance but may not be excl. Austral.: **horse-duffer,** a horse thief; **-duffing** *vbl. n.*, horse-stealing; see DUFFING 1; **-hunt** *v. intr.*, to attempt to round up strayed or wild horses; so **-hunt** *n.*, **-hunting** *vbl. n.*; **paddock, (a)** an enclosure for horses, usu. small and for horses in regular use; **(b)** a large paddock on a horse-raising property; **plant,** a team of working horses; **planter** *obs.*, a horse-thief; **-police** *hist.*, a force of mounted police; so - **policeman; station,** a property used primarily for raising horses; **-sweating** *vbl. n., obs.*, see quot. 1922; **-tailer,** one responsible for the care of working horses; so **-tailing** *vbl. n.*; **yard,** a yard for the temporary detention of horses.

1892 'R. BOLDREWOOD' *Nevermore* II. 39 So you've dropped down to it at last, my flash **horse-duffer,** have you? **1963** A. LUBBOCK *Austral. Roundabout* 161 Horse- and cattle-duffers. **1882** *Sydney Mail* 1 July 6/3 Poaching must be something like cattle and **horse duffing**—not the worst thing in the world itself, but mighty likely to lead to it. **1891** MRS J.I. WATERHOUSE *Bowled Out* 179 The horse-duffing episode and his one act of breaking out of prison fill the list of his crimes. **1910** *Bulletin* (Sydney) 17 Mar. 14/1 Horse and cattle-duffing was not looked upon as a crime. **1936** M. FRANKLIN *All that Swagger* 92 Cattle- and horse-duffing became staple industries in the wilds of Monaro. **1848** H.W. HAYGARTH *Recoll. Bush Life* 61 Cattle-hunting in Australia is excellent sport . . with less speed than in **horse-hunting.** **1926** J. POLLARD *Bushland Man* 48 The few words at the Stroner home with regard to the horse-hunt had placed him in a false position. **1911** *Huon Times* (Franklin) 7 June 4/3 He had told him that he was going horse-hunting at Corella. **1919** *Smith's Weekly* (Sydney) 1 Mar. 6/3 He . . worked at Muntarungy, horse-hunting at 8s. a week. **1955** A.C.V. BLIGH *Golden Quest* 143 He was out horse-hunting with Jack. **1963** X. HERBERT *Disturbing Element* 7 He came horse-hunting with Phillip and me, and out in the bush ate jilgies and bardies. **1839** *Port Phillip Gaz.* 4 Dec. 3 This allotment is admirably adapted for a **Horse** or Cattle **Paddock**, and on an eligible order being made, it will be immediately enclosed with a substantial three-rail fence. **1849** A. HARRIS *Emigrant Family* (1967) 373 The well-stocked horse-paddock . . furnished him with a steed. **1874** A. TROLLOPE *Harry Heathcote* 26 The horses . . roamed in the horse-paddock—a comparatively small enclosure, containing not above three or four hundred acres—and were driven up as they were wanted. **1893** 'OLD CHUM' *Chips* 47 A 'horse paddock'—an enclosure fenced by posts and rails to keep in a few horses for immediate use on an emergency. **1919** *Emu* XIX. 40 A pair of these birds built a nest in the horse-paddock. **1937** W. HATFIELD *I find Aust.* 59 The 'horse-paddock' near the homestead was eight miles by eight, and that wasn't a big 'paddock'. **1963** M. BRITT *Pardon my Boots* 23 Stretching in front of the house was the horse paddock. This reminded me of an English park, except that the grass was dry and the scattered trees were gums. **1930** D. COTTRELL *Earth Battle* 103 In addition to Big Harry's teams, six other '**horse plants**' dragged plough and scoop in the slow piling of dam and tank. **1946** C.T. MADIGAN *Crossing Dead Heart* 113 We saw a horse plant approaching the waterhole from the opposite direction. **1980** ANSELL & PERCY *To fight Wild* 121 They rode off to catch up with the rest of their horse plant that was spreading out a bit. **1841** *Port Phillip Patriot* 28 Oct. 2/6 George Kilpatrick, the notorious **horse 'planter'** . . was . . committed to take his trial for stealing a grey mare. ***c* 1891** J. GARDINER *Twenty-Five Yrs. on Stage* 115 These landlords many of them are 'horse-planters'. **1905** *Bulletin* (Sydney) 15 June 35/4 A horse-planter told me . . that scalps are worth £5 each. **1838** L.E. THRELKELD *Ann. Rep. Mission to Aborigines, Lake Macquarie* 2 The engagement . . took place betwixt the **Horse police**, commanded by Major Nunn, and the Aborigines in the interior. **1849** A. HARRIS *Emigrant Family* (1967) 48 Give my constables and horse-police a night's quarters. **1854** C.A. CORBYN *Sydney Revels* 126 Andreas Brown, a horse-policeman. **1855** *Illustr. Sydney News* 7 Apr. 156/3 Some of the horse-police ran up with carbines but could not get a shot at it. **1842** R.G. JAMESON *N.Z., S.A., & N.S.W.* 113 Gentlemen from the interior, who have left their inland **horse**, sheep, or cattle **stations**, for the purpose of transacting business.

1845 C. Hodgkinson *Aust., Port Macquarie to Moreton Bay* 93, I next passed a horse station belonging to the Company, and rode through a large troop of mares and foals feeding in a flat. **1897** J.J. Murif *From Ocean to Ocean* 70 The supplies for Arltunga goldfields, the mica fields, neighboring horse-station and cattle ranches . . all pass through here. **1930** 'Brent Of Bin Bin' *Ten Creeks Run* (1952) 2 He had . . started a horse station with some first-class blood at Ten Creeks. **1887** S. Newland *Far North Country* 33 When horse-stealing, horse-swindling and **horse-sweating** are put down . . then the 'spieler' must reform or seek pastures new. **1922** *Bulletin* (Sydney) 23 Feb. 22/1 In the old days in N.S. Wales the law—in practice if not by Act of Parliament—made a distinction between horse-stealing and horse-sweating. . . Borrowing a horse without the owner's knowledge or consent, and turning it adrift at the end of the ride, was called 'sweating'; and though it was punishable by law, the penalty was usually light. **1924** *Smith's Weekly* (Sydney) 6 Dec. 23/6 Horse-sweating was one time common in many parts of N.S. Wales. **1913** W.K. Harris *Outback in Aust.* 100 I've had some experience as '**horse-tailer**' for drovers. **1920** *Bulletin* (Sydney) 25 Mar. 22/2 The best horsetailer I ever knew was on a large Queensland cattle-run. **1923** *Ibid.* 22 Nov. 22/3 His daily routine as I have known it has been: Horse tailing, 5.30 a.m. till 6.30. **1925** M. Terry *Across Unknown Aust.* 195 One usually takes a black boy to help with the saddles and horse-tailing. **1942** L. & K. Harris *Lost Hole Bingoola* 197 Horsetailer. The man who has charge of the stock horses on a cattle station, in the far interior usually an Aboriginal. **1949** G. Farwell *Traveller's Tracks* 17 Horse-tailing is virtually extinct in these days of mechanical transport and agriculture. **1963** M. Britt *Pardon my Boots* 65 Henry was the 'horse-tailer', the man who looks after the horses, brings them to camp every morning, makes and mends hobbles, and gives a hand in the yards when necessary. **1978** R.H. Conquest *Dusty Distances* 11 'He might give you some horse-tailing work.' 'What's that?' 'You'll help to look after the horses on droving trips—dozens of 'em and most of 'em wild.' **1981** D. Stuart *I think I'll Live* 303 Just let me settle down in a nice quiet job, outcamp man, or horsetailer for a drover, station cook, anything slow. **1931** A.W. Upfield *Sands of Windee* 26 In the **horse-yards** is a light-draft gelding with white forefeet. **1932** J. Truran *Green Mallee* 76 They made a temporary horseyard in one corner of the ploughed ground. **1947** *Bulletin* (Sydney) 21 May 29/2 Monkeystrap was packing away the damper and jerk in the sun when the manager walked past making for the horseyards.

2. [Transf. use of *dead horse* the type of that which is no longer of use: see OED *horse, sb.* 18.] In the collocation **dead horse.**

a. An undischarged debt.

1847 A. Harris *Settlers & Convicts* 327 From the constant practice among settlers of ill-using free men in point of rations, it often happens that men run away leaving jobs half finished; in other cases it is the consequence of a dishonest endeavour on the part of the labourer, after having largely overdrawn his account, to get rid of the debt; they call working out such a debt, *riding the dead horse.* **1899** *Truth* (Sydney) 30 July 5/5 The men start to work under difficulties. They have a 'dead horse' to work off when they get there. . . By the times the Government advances have been met, men have at the end of six months the paltry amount of £5 saved. **1903** *Bulletin* (Sydney) 30 July 17/1 He had to work off the 'dead horse' before he could get credit for the pants he didn't want. **1907** A. Searcy *In Austral. Tropics* 21 The reason of Robinson's settling at Port Essington, and leading the life he did, was because he had a 'dead horse' to work off. **1978** L. Horsphol *Turn down Empty Glass* 42 Until we finish up findin' ourselves having to work for naught. Now if there's one thing I don't fancy, it's workin' out dead horses.

b. Rhyming slang for 'sauce'.

1940 *Puckapunyal: Official Jrnl. 17th Austral. Infantry Brigade* Oct. 2 How would the Q.M. go if he was faced with an order like this . . a couple of pounds of stammer and stutter with a bottle of dead horse. **1968** *Swag* (Sydney) i. 24/3 A pie is called a dog's eye. . . 'Two dogs, one with dead 'orse,' was a favorite catchcry. **1980** J. Wolfe *Crocodile Soup* 141 'Hey George, where's the dead-horse?' (sauce). 'There's a bastard out there thinks it's Christmas!'

3. In the phr. **to sell a horse,** to organise or participate in a simple game of chance or lottery: see quots. 1899 and 1964.

1899 *Austral. Tit-Bits* (Sydney) 8 Apr. 130/1 Selling Horses. (An Australian Game.) No, this title does not refer to the selling of that noble animal 'the friend of man', but merely to a curious game that is played in some Australian pubs., when a few meet to pass a convivial hour or two, to settle the question as to who will bear the expense of the drinks. . . The 'modus operandi' of the game is as follows:- Assuming the 'crowd' to be six, and the amount to be pooled to be sixpence each man, a half-dozen matches will be procured, and one of the party will be the seller and the rest the purchasers. The seller will take the matches and, concealing them behind his back, will produce a certain number in his closed hand. Then he will go round the purchasers asking them how many 'horses' they will buy. If, for example, the seller offers for sale three 'horses' and buyer No. 1 states three, then No. 1 will be 'stuck' for sixpence, will receive the six matches, and in his turn become seller. If buyer No. 1 states a number not agreeing with the 'horses' offered for sale, then he escapes, and the rest of the purchasers will be invited to buy in a similar fashion. . . The 'art of the game' is always to dodge stating the correct number of horses for sale, and if you are a smart hand at this you can score many a free drink at the game of 'selling horses'. **1935** *Frontier News* Apr. 4/3 We 'sold a horse' for the honour of getting supper ready, and another for the privilege of washing up. **1964** T. Ronan *Packhorse & Pearling Boat* 234 'Selling a horse' is a very simple substitute for the cards and dice and, when there are fourteen in the party, much quicker. The barman collects the two bobs and, on a scrap of paper, writes down a number between fifty and a hundred. Then the party forms up in a group, someone starts counting at any number between one and ten, and whoever calls the figure the barman has written down scoops the pool. **1978** W. Lowenstein *Weevils in Flour* 247 They usually gave the job to the man who was there first, or they sold a horse—the boss wrote down a number and then you'd number off.

horse-collar swag. A long, thin swag, carried around the neck. Also **horseman's swag, horse-shoe swag.**

[N.Z. **1873** Pyke *Wild Will Enderby* 3 He proceeded forthwith to arrange his blankets in the form known to the initiated as 'horse-collar swag'.] **1880** 'Erro' *Squattermania* 215 Giving a hitch to his horse-shoe swag, he strode off. **1888** J. Potts *One Yr. Anti-Chinese Work Qld.* 10 He had a horse-collar swag around him in scarf fashion. **1891** *Bohemia* (Melbourne) 26 Nov. 6 Snail-like the swagman carries his house across the plains. . . He is the typical unthrift of modern times, for does he not, especially if he . . carries a 'horse collar swag', *stand in the midst of his goods!* **1898** *Bulletin* (Sydney) 19 Mar. 14/2, I saw an old whaler—must have been nearing 60—not an ounce of flesh on him . . with a horse-collar swag 85 lb. weight. **1956** *Ibid.* 15 Feb. 12/2, I watched him weaving carefully across the roadway to pay his debt, half-empty bottle in one hand and his thin horseman's-swag in the other.

horse mackerel. [Spec. use of *horse-mackerel* any of several fish allied to the mackerel.] Any of several marine fish, esp. Jack mackerel and the Austral. bonito *Sarda australis*, abundant along the e. coast of Aust.

1793 W. Tench *Compl. Acct. Settlement* 176 Grey-mullet, bream, horse-mackarel [*sic*]. **1880** *Proc. Linnean Soc. N.S.W.* V. 558 *Auxis Ramsayi* . . '*Horse Mackerel*' of the Sydney Fisherman. **1896** F.G. Aflalo *Sketch Nat. Hist. Aust.* 229 The 'Horse Mackerel' (*Pelamys*), is exceedingly abundant at certain seasons in and around Port Jackson. **1906** D.G. Stead *Fishes of Aust.* 163 The Horse-Mackerel [*sc. Sarda chilensis*] . . put in an appearance on the coast of New South Wales, and it is also known from the Victorian coast. **1924** Lord & Scott *Synopsis Vertebrate Animals Tas.* 59 (Trachurus novae zealandiae) This fish is known in New South Wales as the 'Cowanyoung' but often referred to as the 'Horse Mackerel' in Tasmania. **1935** Davison & Nicholls *Blue Coast Caravan* 220 Kingfish (horse mackerel, they are called farther south). **1965** *Austral. Encycl.* IV. 84 Jack mackerel (*Trachurus novaezelandiae*), the cowanyoung of New South Wales and the horse mackerel of South Australia and Tasmania.

horseman's swag: see Horse-collar swag.

horseradish tree. [See quot. 1889.] The shrub or tree *Codonocarpus cotinifolius* (fam. Gyrostemonaceae) of drier Aust., the bark and leaves of which have a pungent taste. See also *mustard tree* Mustard, *native poplar* Native *a.* 6 a.

1886 F.A. Hagenauer *Rep. Aboriginal Mission Ramahyuck, Vic.* 47 You can see . . the horseradish tree. **1889** J.H. Maiden *Useful Native Plants Aust.* 164 *Codonocarpus cotinifolius* . . called . . 'Horse-radish Tree', owing to the taste of the leaves. **1904** *Proc. Linnean Soc. N.S.W.* XXIX. 142 One of the most remarkable trees in the interior . . is known locally [*sc.* s.w. N.S.W.] as the 'horse-radish tree'. **1972** V. Serventy *Singing Land* 81 One of the striking trees of the desert country, with bright green foliage and bellshaped fruits, is the desert poplar, sometimes called horseradish or fire tree.

horse-shoe swag: see Horse-collar swag.

hospital. Used *attrib.* of sheep: diseased. Also, of a paddock, etc.: reserved for such sheep.

1855 W. Howitt *Land, Labor & Gold* I. 192 The squatters are killing off first what they call their hospital flocks—the scabbiest sheep, and those worn to skeletons with foot-rot. **1881** A.C. Grant *Bush-Life Qld.* II. 87 They had passed some miles back a small gunyah and yard temporarily occupied by a flock of 'hospital' sheep, shepherded by an old black gin. **1934** *Bulletin* (Sydney) 14 Nov. 22/3 Some owners run a 'hospital' paddock, into which the ailing ones [*sc.* sheep] are drafted. **1966** S.J. Baker *Austral. Lang.* (ed. 2) 47 A sheep which is put on its own because of illness is a *hospital sheep.*

hostie /'hoʊsti/. [f. *(air) host(ess* + -Y.] A female flight attendant.

1960 'N. Culotta' *Cop This Lot* 27 'That hostie's a slashin' line,' Dennis said. **1967** *Ringo: 2nd Battalion Royal Austral. Regiment* xvi. 22 Anyway, the . . hostie belted up the aisle of the aircraft to tell the crew. **1971** B. Humphries *Bazza pulls it Off*, I got this Qantas hostie up into me sheilah trap and uncoiled the old one eyed trouser snake. **1972** *Bulletin* (Sydney) 19 Aug. 41 (*caption*) Doing their bit for licit love, Qantas has agreed to keep their hosties on after they sort themselves into connubial bliss. **1981** *Sydney Morning Herald* 28 Apr. 1/2, I have been talking to the hosties since last Thursday and they are not concerned about Qantas picking up passengers here and there.

hostile, *a.* Angry. Also with **on** and in the phr. **to go hostile (at).**

1937 E. Partridge *Dict. Slang & Unconventional Eng.* 408 *Hostile*, . . angry, annoyed; esp. *go hostile*, to get angry: Australian and New Zealand military. **1941** S.J. Baker *Pop. Dict. Austral. Slang* 36 *Hostile*, angry, annoyed. Also 'go hostile at', express annoyance (towards someone). **1957** *Overland* ix. 5 She's hostile about the money she's getting. **1960** *Ibid.* xviii. 5 A bloke comes to steal my chooks. He knows I'm hostile on it, and I'll do something about it. **1962** D. Cusack *Picnic Races* 176 Nobody really blames her but they go pretty hostile on the bloke. **1973** F. Huelin *Keep Moving* 83 We don't want to get hostile about it. Yous got your ideas and I've got mine. Let it go at that.

hot box. An insulated container for keeping food hot (see also quot. 1982).

1925 *Makeshifts & Other Home-Made Furniture* (New Settlers League Aust.) 32 The principle of the Hot Box is . . to surround the central vessel (with food in it) with a non-conductor of heat, so that the heat is retained for a long time. **1936** *Bulletin* (Sydney) 6 Nov. 21/2 The 'hot box' used by countless bush housewives. A tea-chest is padded inside with paper 2 in. thick and lined with hessian. Into this is piled screwed-up paper and straw; a lid is lined similarly, and fitted. All Mrs Bushie has to do when she wants to give dad a hand with the milking is to put the tea in boiling water about lunch-time and sink the pots in the box. **1982** J.J. Coe *Desperate Praise* 133 *Hot box*, hot meal contained in insulated 'esky'.

hot coffee. *Obs.* (A show of) antagonism; a display of anger.

1885 *Australasian Printers' Keepsake* 121 He was an Englishman—one of the worst sort—overbearing, ignorant, and impudent, and between him and me there usually was hot coffee. **1905** *Shearer* (Sydney) 20 May 8/5 On the say-so of the Toowoomba 'rag' Tom Mann recently got 'hot coffee' from the Charter's

Towers miners for calling the adulterous Dunsford, M.L.A. a fool. **1915** *Truth* (Sydney) 26 Sept. 3/1 Like all such 'trimmers' and 'twicers', however, he is beginning to get 'hot coffee' from both sides.

hot pot. *Horse-racing.* [f. *hot* heavily backed + *pot* favourite: see OED *hot, a.* 8 e. and *pot, sb.*[1] 9 c.] A heavily-backed favourite. Also *transf.*

1904 *Sporting News* (Launceston) 16 Apr. 3/1 Baden Powell was made a hot pot for the Flying Stakes . . but he failed to come on. **1969** *Sporting Globe* (Melbourne) 9 July 22/5 A southern 'hot-pot'—Lord Setay—dismally let his supporters down at Albion Park last Saturday night.

hottie. Also **hotty.** *Obs.* [f. *hot (shot* + -Y.] A 'hot shot'; someone of importance.

1910 L. ESSON *Woman Tamer* (1976) 78 How is it, Katie? What's up? Blime, you've cleaned the knives. Cake? 'Struth, we are hotties. Boronia? Are you expecting the gawd Mayor for tea? **1911** *Bulletin* (Sydney) 23 Nov. 13/4 Micko, from Collingwood, may be a 'tug' or a 'crook' or a 'rough-up' or a 'hotty', but if you called him a larrikin he'd look at you and wonder. **1922** 'J. NORTH' *Black Opal* 29 We've had hotties like you in Australia before.

hot wind.

1. An extremely hot, dry wind, blowing periodically from the interior during summer.

1791 Macarthur Papers 18 Mar. XII., We have need of cooling fruit in the warm season—particularly when the hot scorching winds set in—but which however are followed by what is termed the Sea Breeze, and this keeps down the temperature of the air, but when they are overpowered by the hot wind the heat is excessive. **1804** *Sydney Gaz.* 2 Dec., The *hot winds* that prevailed in the early part of last week have in numerous instances been found prejudicial to the eyes. **1825** M. HINDMARSH *Lett.* (1945) 19 The failure [of the wheat crop] was occasioned by the Hot Winds which are very prevalent in the latter end of Novr. and Decr. **1834** J.D. LANG *Hist. & Statistical Acct. N.S.W.* II. 186 The phenomenon of the hot winds of New South Wales is utterly inexplicable in the present state of our knowledge of the interior of the continent of Australia. **1841** G. ARDEN *Recent Information Port Phillip* 31 Those northerly winds which in the summer season are distinguished as the 'hot winds', are far less frequent and injurious at Port Phillip than elsewhere. **1855** G.H. WATHEN *Golden Colony* 89 The hot wind is in fact the Simoom of Australia, and results apparently from the same cause as that of Africa, namely, radiation from the scorched lands of the interior. **1869** 'E. HOWE' *Boy in Bush* 79, I have been in glass-works, and close by the mouths of blast-furnaces, but the heat of an Australian hot wind is worse than theirs. **1888** W.T. PYKE *Bush Tales* 17 As the hot wind moans and whistles through the trees, birds drop dead from the branches, shrivelled fruit and sere leaves fall from the orchard trees, while shrubs and plants have the appearance of bundles of sticks. **1908** W.H. OGILVIE *My Life in Open* 62 The blue-grass has long since withered and blown away in the hot winds. **1923** W.J. BROWN *Who Knows* 5 There came three days of hot winds. The air seemed to come straight out of hell. **1937** L.R. MENZIES *Gold Seeker's Odyssey* 138 The heat was terrific with the hot wind blowing sand in gusts across our faces.

2. Comb. **hot-wind day.**

1862 C. ASPINALL *Three Yrs. Melbourne* 6, I . . found it to be rather refreshing to the eye . . on a 'hot wind' day. **1869** J. MARTINEAU *Lett. from Aust.* 37 It must be depressing . . on a hot-wind day in summer. **1885** 'OLD HOUSEKEEPER' *Austral. Housewives' Man.* 19 When we have hot-wind days boards are hot, everything is hot. **1920** H. HANSELL *Everlastin' Ballads* 42 I'm for pullin' the Empire to bits for a pot o' beer on a hot wind day.

house.

1. The principal residence on a rural property (as distinct from accommodation provided for employees); prob. perpetuating a distinction made in penal settlements (see HUT *n.* 2 and 3, and also quots. 1788 and 1812). Also *attrib.*

[**1788** J. HUNTER *Hist. Jrnl. Trans. Port Jackson* (1793) 310 Two sawyers were sawing timber to build me a house; two men were employed in building huts. **1812** *HRA* (1916) 1st Ser. VII. 583 A few Houses for the Civil and Military Officers . . and a few Huts for Convicts.] **1832** *Colonial Times* (Hobart) 25 Apr., There is a new House . . a good Hut for the men, and other Outhouses, on the Grant. **1833** *Trumpeter* (Hobart) 19 July 102 There is an excellent dwelling-house, and a good hut for servants. **1852** BACKHOUSE & TYLOR *Life & Labours G.W. Walker* (1862) 134 Two missionaries . . staying a while at the various settlers houses, visited all the huts of working men throughout the neighbourhood. **1873** M. CLARKE *Holiday Peak* 82 Dudley is a great man. . . He is called the '— boss', and lives in the 'house', in contradistinction to the 'hut'. **1876** J.B. STEPHENS *Hundred Pounds* 17 When a squatter speaks of a very respectable man, he means a man whom he *might* ask in to the house for a glass of grog, but whom he would forthwith relegate to 'the hut' for his supper and his night's quarters. **1880** J.B. STEVENSON *Seven Yrs. Austral. Bush* 32 The principal hut, or as it is called in the bush, 'The House', was constructed of what is known as wattle and dab, with a thatched roof. **1903** *Bulletin* (Sydney) 21 Feb. 17/1 At Merungle I saw house-tea vilified; we got a box by mistake in the hut. **1921** M.E. FULLERTON *Bark House Days* 117, I was a favorite with the men, being even then a reader of the newspapers. I constituted myself the medium by which the huts were supplied with the weeklies as soon as the house was finished with them. **1937** W. HATFIELD *I find Aust.* 175 Anyone from the 'house' coming out to eat with the men and sleep on the ground around cattle is looked upon with suspicion. **1943** H.G. LAMOND *From Tariaro to Ross Roy* 20 Candles were the only illuminant then—candles in the house; slush lamps in the hut. **1973** J. MORRISON *Austral. by Choice* 116 Across the garden I had got a glimpse of the long verandah of the House; coloured lights, moving figures: the Boss and his wife, the Overseer, one of the jackeroos, guests from a neighbouring station.

2. Special Comb. **house gin (girl, lubra),** a female Aboriginal employed as a domestic servant; **man,** one whose social status secures him accommodation in the house (rather than in the huts); **paddock,** an enclosure, usu. for horses, adjacent to the house; **people,** see *house man.*

1890 A.J. VOGAN *Black Police* 144 We can see the dark-skinned, brightly dressed aboriginal '**house gins**'. **1913** *Bulletin* (Sydney) 6 Mar. 16/2 Scraggy was the house gin on an outstation. **1934** *Ibid.* 7 Mar. 21/4 Nellie, the house lubra, hitched up her Mother Hubbard and showed us women the scar. **c 1947** *Home Building Inland* (Flying Doctor Service Aust.) 13 Aboriginal house girls can only do simple jobs. **1947** E. GEORGE *January & August* 23 Left his white silk shirt in the middle of the floor in his room for Jackson's house lubra to wash. **1948** H. DRAKE-BROCKMAN *Sydney or Bush* 117 Fetched the car down to pick up the kid . . who'd been to the beach with the house-gin. **1952** *Bulletin* (Sydney) 17 Dec. 12/1 Rosie, our housegirl, recently received a filial visit from her son. **1954** T. RONAN *Vision Splendid* 135 It was Desert Mary, now promoted to house lubra, who carried his swag over to his room. **1969** F.B. VICKERS *No Man is Himself* 10 How did she come by an outfit as good as that? Not out of the two or three dollars a week she'd earn working as a house-gin on a station. **1936** W. HATFIELD *Aust. through Windscreen* 64 Find out where he stayed at Whereisit Downs. If he's a **house man** ask him in. If he isn't, tell him he can go down to the kitchen for tea and take his swag over to the hut. **1894** *Bulletin* (Sydney) 20 Oct. 23/2 The **house-paddock** slip-rail edges a side-slope leading down to 'the crossing'. **1902** *Ibid.* 12 July 36/1 Harvest-time: Dave and Joe and Bill carting barley off the house-paddock. **1938** F. CLUNE *Free & Easy Land* 112 He was a wonderful navigator, but no bushman. He would get lost in the house paddock unless he had a companion. **1948** P.J. HURLEY *Red Cedar* 63 A couple of saddle horses are enjoying their midday freedom in a 'house-paddock', rolling or drinking. **1964** P. ADAM SMITH *Hear Train Blow* 50 Billy was the best of all the horses that came and went in our house paddock. **1977** J. O'GRADY *There was Kid* 42 There was a small open verandah on one side of the house. From it you could see across the 'House Paddick', fenced with barbed wire. **1891** *Truth* (Sydney) 15 Mar. 7/3 In a general way, the hybrid between **house-people** and the hut is, *ex officio*, a Jackeroo.

house of accommodation. *Obs.* ACCOMMODATION HOUSE.

1804 *Sydney Gaz.* 12 Aug., Halted at a distant house of *accommodation.* **1843** *Church in Aust.* (Soc. Propagation Gospel) 31 Aug. (1845) ii. 40 This morning I rose early . . to walk to Ipswich, which is about sixteen miles distant from Owen's house of accommodation. **1853** MOSSMAN & BANISTER *Aust. Visited & Revisited* 133 A place called the 'Black-dog Creek', where there is a house of accommodation. **1879** *Kelly Gang* 15 They built a small house, which was kept as a shanty or house of accommodation. **1885** *Adelaide Observer* 22 Aug. 10/2 Coondambo is . . the site of a store, Post Office, and house of accommodation. **1896** H. LAWSON *While Billy Boils* 311, I fully expected to have found a house of accommodation of some sort on the way. **1917** H.H. RICHARDSON *Fortunes Richard Mahony* (1930) 33 Complaining of a mouth like sawdust, Purdy alighted and lumped across the verandah of a house-of-accommodation. **1928** 'BRENT OF BIN BIN' *Up Country* 146 They started a house of accommodation in the most unlikely place for patrons, and their neighbours had a sage intuition that it was a sly grog-shanty and fly-trap for the unwary.

House of Assembly. The lower legislative house in the States of South Australia and Tasmania.

1853 *S. Austral. Register* (Adelaide) 9 Aug. 3/4 With reference, then, to the three provinces remote from Sydney, at present the nominal capital of Australia, my belief that the existence of a general Senate, independent of and possessing higher powers than the local Houses of Assembly sitting in Adelaide, Melbourne, and Hobart Town, would prove beneficial. **1873** A. TROLLOPE *Aust. & N.Z.* I. 240 Sir James Martin carried the House of Assembly with him. **1886** M. KERSHAW *Colonial Facts & Fictions* 133 One lot of deadheads I travelled with turned out to be honourable members of the House of Assembly. **1890** *Quiz* (Adelaide) 4 Apr. 1/1 Nine of the principal electoral districts of the colony will have decided who are to be their representatives in the House of Assembly. **1910** *Walch's Tasmanian Almanac* 59 *House of Assembly* (30 Members) . . continues for three years from the day of the return of the writs; it can, however, be dissolved by the Governor whenever he shall deem it expedient. **1937** E.T. EMMETT *Short Hist. Tas.* 76 The Act provided for an elective Legislative Council of fifteen members, and a House of Assembly of thirty. **1948** G. SAWER *Austral. Govt. Today* 17 The lower houses in Tasmania and South Australia are called Houses of Assembly. **1956** F.C. GREEN *Century Responsible Govt.* 18 The House of Assembly or Lower House is also known as the 'People's House'.

House of Representatives. The lower legislative house of the Federal Parliament.

1898 *Austral. Handbk.* 122 The Legislative powers of the Commonwealth shall be vested in a Federal Parliament, which shall consist of the Queen, a Senate, and a House of Representatives. **1918** C.H. NORTHCOTT *Austral. Social Dev.* 27 In every Australian State and in the Commonwealth, there are two legislative houses. One of these, known in the States by the term Legislative Assembly, and in the Commonwealth as the House of Representatives. **1933** A.N. SMITH *Thirty Yrs.* 97 Voting for the House of Representatives showed a further cleavage between the Ministerialists and the Opposition. **1978** F. DALY *A to Z Politics* 54 The House of Representatives or Lower House is the legislative body directly chosen by the people of Australia to represent their interests. **1986** *Canberra Times* 15 Mar. 3/2 The Departments of the House of Representatives and the Senate were logically separate.

hovea /'hoʊviə/. [The Austral. plant genus *Hovea* was named by the British botanist Robert Brown (in Aiton (1812) *Hort. Kew.* ed. 2, VI. 275) after the Polish botanist A.P. *Hove* (*fl.* 1785–1798).] Any shrub of the genus *Hovea* (fam. Fabaceae), having pea-flowers which are usu. purple or blue, some species being cultivated as ornamentals.

1926 A.A.B. APSLEY *Amateur Settlers* 207 Decorated with a jar full of Hovea—a bright blue kind of pea flower. **1946** *Victorian Naturalist* LXII. 229 Looper caterpillars . . trouble my garden in the Dandenong Ranges, where they attack . . the Hoveas. **1958** *Coast to Coast 1957–58* 138 In the early spring her wild garden was purple with hovea. **1981** *Bulletin* (Sydney) 21 Apr. (Suppl.) 25/2 Purple hovea beside our feet.

how, *adv.* In the phr. **how are you going?** and varr., 'how are you?', a conventional greeting.

1930 V. PALMER *Passage* (1957) 182 Well, how's it going, Peter? Getting the wind up? **1957** 'N. CULOTTA' *They're Weird Mob* 75 ''Ow yer goin' Nino?' 'Orright mate,' I said. **1968** D. O'GRADY *Bottle of Sandwiches* 24

We said, 'G'day, mate. How ya goin'?' **1977** E. MACKIE *Oh to be Aussie* 7 The most the Aussie will do, if well disposed towards you is to ask you 'howyer-goin?' In answer to this *never* say more than 'Good thanks!' and hang the grammar! **1978** P. ADAM SMITH *Anzacs* 94 Private W.S. Percival of the 15th Battalion told of 7 August, after the futile but desperate attack on Hill 971... Clumsily turning the man over, he shouted, 'How's she going, mate?' There was no answer. He yelled, 'Strike me pink the poor bugger's just about outed.'

boy. A game of chance, resembling bingo, in which playing cards are used. Also *attrib.*

1965 *Courier-Mail* (Brisbane) 2 Mar. 15/2 A hoy evening which the Royal Society of St. George planned to hold at St. George House. **1969** *Sunday Mail* (Brisbane) 24 Aug. 3/3 Police said that bingo, or hoy, which was played in the same way, was illegal in Queensland. **1970** *On Guard* (Broken Hill) Apr. 7 Wednesday, April 8th, Hoy and How Afternoon in Mica St Hall. **1974** *QPD* 4 Apr. 3564, I know that pensioners love to play bingo and hoy. The game used to be called yahoo or hoy before bingo was made legal. Pensioners love to play hoy a couple of days a week. **1978** H. HAENKE *Bottom of Birdcage* 49, I go to the Hoy 'n Euchre, up the Catholic Hall.

Hoyt's. [f. the name of *Hoyt's* Theatre in Melbourne.] In the phr. **the man outside Hoyt's,** the commissionaire outside Hoyt's Theatre in Melbourne in the 1930s; also *fig.* (see quot. 1953).

1953 S.J. BAKER *Aust. Speaks* 133 *Hoyt's, the man outside*, a mythical person who starts all false rumours; the source of stolen property which an innocent (!) receiver is found to have in his possession. **1961** F. HARDY *Hard Way* 85 Struth, it's funny enough for a fat bludger dressed up like the man outside Hoyt's to come into a prison cell in the middle of the night. [*Note* Uniformed announcer outside Hoyt's theatre in Melbourne who wears a most elaborate uniform.] **1966** H. PORTER *Paper Chase* 64 Hoyt's de Luxe (where the commissionaire, hoarsely and non-stop, brays himself into fame and the Australian vernacular as The Man Outside Hoyt's). **1975** *Sydney Morning Herald* 5 July 9/4 We might be better off to abandon pre-selections and elections, and choose our politicians by having the Governor (or the man outside Hoyts) stick pins into the telephone book.

Hughie. Also **Hewie.** [Of unknown origin.] The 'rain god', esp. as invoked in the phr. **send it** (or **her**) **down Hughie.** Also *transf.* as **send 'em up Hughie** (see quot. 1981).

1912 *Bulletin* (Sydney) 5 Dec. 15/2 *Re* the shearer's 'Send it down, Hughie!' .. when needed rain is threatening. I first heard the expression in Narrandera (N.S.W.)... I believe that it originated in that district, by reason of a Mr Huie .. an amateur meteorologist, who had luck in prophesying rain... Hence, 'Send it down, Huie'. **1922** *Ibid.* 6 Apr. 20/4 At the end of the dry, when the first few showers fall, 'Send it down, Hughie!' is the heartfelt exclamation of every eager bush-watcher. **1936** M. HERRON *Seed & Stubble* 32 'Send it down, Huey! Send it down!' he sang as he bowled along. Mrs Riley stood where he had left her, gazing unseeingly at the rain. **1946** K.S. PRICHARD *Roaring Nineties* 43 Miners and prospectors would turn out and yell to a dull, dirty sky clouded with red dust: 'Send her down! Send her down, Hughie!' **1956** C.D. MILLS *Stockwhip & Spur* 48 Send her down Hughie, the rouse-abouts roared, In an obscene petition addressed to our Lord. **1970** S.H. COURTIER *No Obelisk for Emily* 172 'Send it down, Hughie; send it down,' she said. I stared, for it was many years since I had last heard the old bushman's invocation to the mythical Hughie when rain was wanted badly. **1981** *Nat. Times* (Sydney) 20 Dec. 26/4 Incoming waves may be assessed, and sometimes the ancient cry will rise during a lull: 'Send 'em up Huey!' Meaning: push some waves in. Some surf scholars believe Huey to be a corruption of Jupiter Pluvius. **1985** *N.T. News* (Darwin) 19 Apr. 37/1 Who would have expected such a flushing so late in the year? Hewie pulled the chain over the whole of the Top End and every river .. responded with massive flooding.

hum, *n.* [f. the *v.*]

1. An habitual borrower; a cadger. Also *attrib.*

1915 J.P. BOURKE *Off Bluebush* 190 If you cannot be a spendthrift, be a hum. **1919** V. MARSHALL *World of Living Dead* 70 This type consists of the 'hum', the unskilled derelict or derelict-to-be who stands upon the 'pub' corner kerb, 'bites' all and sundry, and, at regular intervals, succeeds in getting lumbered for 'vag'. **1921** *Aussie* (Sydney) July 40/2 In one of the Aussie re-inforcement camps in England were two tough Diggers... They were 'hum' experts, their speciality being smokes and drinks. **1934** F.H. BROWN *Songs of Plains* 26 The flies may grow dopey and stick to you close As a hum or a mother-in-law. **1936** *Listening Post* (Perth) May 7 There's a chap .. a pretty miserable sort of poor coot .. a hum or something. **1966** D. NILAND *Pairs & Loners* 81 Charley was talking, 'There's some blokes on the track you just can't get along with .. hums, crawlers, top-offs, twisters.' **1983** WHITE & HALLIWELL *Dole Bludger's Handbk.*, Two professional hums .. took an oath at Bendigo no more work they would do.

2. In the phr. **on the hum,** engaged in cadging.

1932 C. HADE *Ebeneezer* 8 At 'run-the-rule' or a two-up school he took the bun—Half his time hungry—always on the hum.

hum, *v.* [Prob. spec. use of *hum*, abbrev. of *humbug* to impose upon, take in: see OED *hum, v.*[2]]

1. *trans.* To cadge (a cigarette, etc.). Also *intr.*

1913 *Bulletin* (Sydney) 30 Jan. 15/2 He has promised to 'hum' a stamp to post this at the first town we strike. **1915** J.P. BOURKE *Off Bluebush* 77 Got no coin to treat a pal! Got no face to hum! **1916** *Bostall Boshter* (Bostall Heath, England) 22 Feb. 1 'How to hum tobacco' by Old Soldier. **1938** X. HERBERT *Capricornia* 257 You old blowbag! You're only humming for a drink. Nick off home. **1944** *Barging About: Organ 43 Austral. Landing Craft Co.* Nov. 11 He's never got a cigarette He hums them all from 'Stuey'. **1983** WHITE & HALLIWELL *Dole Bludger's Handbk.*, If we've luck we'll hum our cheques and shoot the man that works.

2. *trans.* To work one's way through (a town) begging.

1918 A. WRIGHT *Breed holds Good* 148 The travellers have 'hummed' the towns with varying success. **1935** *Bulletin* (Sydney) 30 Jan. 21/4 Where other 'Bidgee whalers 'hummed' a town for booze, Mick 'hummed' it for tea, going from house to house with his plea: 'Missus, could y' spring a cup o' tea?'

Hence **humming** *vbl. n.*

1913 W.K. HARRIS *Outback in Aust.* 47 What'll happen to *us* if you town-ies start on the 'humming' game? **1922** *Bulletin* (Sydney) 13 July 22/4 The 'beer-hum' who for six pints of beer swallowed six young mice .. didn't feel inclined for the beer. It cured his 'humming', too.

hummer, *n.*[1] *Obs.* A name given to an Aboriginal ceremonial object; BULLROARER.

1887 *Proc. R. Geogr. Soc. Australasia, S.A. Branch* 29 Occasionally the 'hummer' is used, but not frequently; probably because it is considered too sacred to be seen by women or young men. **1903** *Bulletin* (Sydney) 3 Sept. 16/2 The 'bull-roarer', or 'gooanduckyer' .. is merely what was known in my boyhood days as a 'hummer'.

hummer, *n.*[2] [f. *hum, v.*] One who makes a practice of cadging.

1916 *Battery Herald: Jrnl. 14th Field Artillery* 9 Oct. 9 *Hummers.* During the week our old friend 'Duke Mullins' was caught napping. As usual .. he put the .. sting for a fag. **1929** C.H. WINTER *Story of 'Bidgee Queen* 100 But one blazing day in summer, Came a battered-looking 'hummer'. **1945** S.J. BAKER *Austral. Lang.* 108 *Hummer, poler* and *bot-fly* are additional synonyms for a cadger.

hump, *n.*[1] [f. the *v.*]

a. *Obs.* An arduous walk, carrying a load on one's back.

[N.Z. **1863** J.G. WALKER Jrnl. 27 Jan. 4 It was a precious hump [over the hill].] **1890** 'R. BOLDREWOOD' *Miner's Right* 46 We get a fair share of exercise without a twenty mile hump on Sundays.

b. A swagman.

1955 D. NILAND *Shiralee* 51 'I tell you, them humps out there, they want shootin'.' 'Oh, well some like to have fun.' Macauley hoisted the swag. 'So long.'

hump, *n.*[2] A camel.

1935 H. FINLAYSON *Red Centre* 120 We were heading for a camp in the Everard forty miles away, with a string of twenty-two 'humps'. **1976** C.D. MILLS *Hobble Chains & Greenhide* 82 In common with all cameloid ruminants 'Humps' are mainly top-feeders and revel in such timbers as gidyea, mulga [etc.]. **1978** D. STUART *Wedgetail View* 65, I see old Dotty Stanley once .. with a pair o' camels; it was the first time he'd ever had humps, an' he wasn't too sure of 'em.

hump, *v.* [Transf. use of *hump, v.* to make humped.]

1. a. *trans.* To carry (a load, etc.), esp. on one's back. Also *fig.*

1851 *Empire* (Sydney) 4 July 4/1 No sooner is the Commissioner seen on the creek than .. those who have not paid may be seen 'humping' their cradles to some secluded spot. **1851** *Ibid.* 30 Aug. 104/1 Removed all our things about four miles up the creek, having to hump (carry) them principally on our backs. **1858** C.R. THATCHER *Colonial Songster* (rev. ed.) 72 The Chinese were running about in shoals, Humping the heading that comes from the holes. **1873** W. THOMSON-GREGG *Desperate Character* I. 178 'I'll hump the windlass and stand.' 'Hump them! .. what in the world do you mean?' 'Well, carry them on my back; if you must have English for it.' **1887** A. NICOLS *Wild Life & Adventure* 283 The horse was done for, and he had 'humped this bloomin' lot five miles through them scrubs.' **1903** *Advocate* (Burnie) 25 May 4/1 They had been—when at work on the property—driven to 'hump' their rations. **1908** *Bulletin* (Sydney) 16 Apr. 43/1 Take up your cross and hump it—what tho' the way be long. **1919** *7th Field Artillery Brigade Yandoo* Sept. 160 He humps his gladstone bag from Tempe station. **1926** L.C.E. GEE *Bush Tracks & Gold Fields* 34 He used to 'hump' wood and water. **1965** D. MARTIN *Hero of Too* 326 What did she mean, and what did it take? He knew the answer: to hump your cross till it broke your back. **1968** S. GORE *Holy Smoke* 14 You got yer sword and yer spear, and yer shield that that other mug's humping for yer. **1980** J. WRIGHT *Big Hearts & Gold Dust* 16 Stringy corn beef we'd humped in our tucker bag for the last hundred miles.

b. *trans.* Freq. with **it**: to travel on foot, carrying one's bundle of possessions.

1891 M. ROBERTS *Land-Travel & Sea-Faring* 84, I packed my clothes in a rough kind of 'swag', or bundle, and 'humped' it down to Albury. **1902** *Truth* (Sydney) 25 May 1/5 If he, like you, don't like it, like you, he'll have to lump it, and 'hump' it off 'Home' again as you are doing. **1908** *Bulletin* (Sydney) 29 Oct. 13/2 We humped the lonely road to Sydney city 'on our pad'. **1921** *Ibid.* 3 Mar. 22/2, I have humped it, ridden and coached it between Winton and Boulia (Qld.). **1924** LAWRENCE & SKINNER *Boy in Bush* 236 'But a swaggy is a tramp?' 'It is. It is one who humps it.'

2. a. In the phr. **to hump one's swag (bluey, drum, knot, Matilda),** to travel on foot carrying, esp. on one's back, a bundle of possessions.

1851 *Empire* (Sydney) 17 Oct. 266/4 The Messrs Owen .. are 'humping the swag' to the washing hole, and doing fairly; but the labour is immense. **1853** *Moreton Bay Free Press* 19 July 3/5 A correspondent of the *Empire* .. passed through all the stages of the digger's life, and 'humped his swag' many a weary mile. **1867** *Austral. Monthly Mag.* IV. 37 Men .. humped their swag, and departed to seek the fortune which some did find. **1870** E.B. KENNEDY *Four Yrs. in Qld.* 14 They might hear of a station where shearers were wanted .. and after 'humping their drum' for many hot dusty miles, find there was no room for them. **1878** *Squatters' Plum* 15 He soon finds that, though he is said to be on the wallaby, or on the tramp, or humping his drum, his self-respect is fast deserting him, for, under these new terms, lies hidden the incontestable fact that he is but a beggar, seeking food and shelter from unwilling givers. **1891** *Truth* (Sydney) 1 Feb. 5/3 Some time in September 1890, they packed their traps, and humping 'bluey', set out with cheerful faces. **1902** *Ibid.* 17 Aug. 1/8 It isn't all beer and skittles humping 'Matilda' at the best of times. **1918** A.M. MOORE *Autumn Grey* 49, I guess you're one of them cranks from the University .. humping the bluie for a whim. **1930** E. ANTONY *Hungry Mile* 6 O'er muddy plain and sandy waste I've humped the ancient drum. **1937** *Bulletin* (Sydney) 10 Mar. 20/2 Humping their knots west of Condoblin (N.S.W.), Bluey and Dutch discovered a mob of wethers. **1951** G. FARWELL *Outside Track* 19 The shearer nowadays does not hump his bluey from one station to the next; he is more likely to arrive by car. **1965** G. McInnes *Road to Gundagai* 183 No longer will I roam From my own Australian home I'll hump my bluey and I'll shout a 'Coo-ee' Back to Croa-jinga-linga-linga-long. **1976** B. Norman *Bush Pilot* 208 He was unable to get a lift home so he decided to hump his bluey the sixty miles to the mission. **1977** D. Stuart *Drought Foal* 155 Hardest bloody work there is, humpin' the drum. **1980** N. King *Colourful Tales* 87 The rough track . . was full of motor cars, buggies . . while a considerable number of men 'humped Matilda'.

b. *fig.* To strive (towards the achievement of a goal).

1891 *Extracts from 'Worker'* (Qld. Patriotic League) 14/3 Australia's a big country, An' Freedom's humping bluey, An' Freedom's on the wallaby—Oh, don't you hear 'er cooey. **1893** D. Healey *Cornstalk* 78 He realized that humping 'bluey' after fame is a weary journey. **1952** H.E. Boote *Sidelights Two Referendums* 25 England has declared war on Germany. Progress is humping bluey now, for many a long day, perhaps.

humper.

a. *Obs.* One who carries a heavy load.

1851 *Empire* (Sydney) 12 Dec. 459/4 This is profitable digging certainly, yet the work is exceedingly laborious, the humpers having to walk twenty-three and a-half miles each day, and to carry on the average one and a-half cwt. of clay for upwards of eleven miles of that distance.

b. A swagman.

1944 C. Shaw *Sheaf of Shorts* 96 Who was I, a lonely humper of a bluey. **1945** *Bulletin* (Sydney) 12 Dec. 13/1 A fairly well set-up humper of bluey.

humpty-doo, var. Umpty-doo.

humpy /'hʌmpi/. Formerly chiefly *Qld.* [a. Jagara (and neighbouring languages) *yumbi.*] A temporary shelter of the Aborigines (see quot. 1853); *transf.*, any makeshift or temporary dwelling, esp. one made with primitive materials. See also Gunyah.

1846 C.P. Hodgson *Reminisc. Aust.* 238 A 'Gunyia' or 'Umpee'. **1853** *Moreton Bay Free Press* 13 Dec. 4/6 These *humpeys* or *gunyahs*, as they are called, are constructed by placing a few young boughs or saplings tightly in the ground, in a semi-circular form, the upper parts are then woven or fastened together, and the framework of the structure is thus completed. **1862** C. Munro *Fern Vale* I. 2 If we succeed in forming a station, as soon as we can get up a decent sort of a 'humpie', and comfortably settled, I will come and fetch you. **1866** *Colony of Qld. as Field for Emigration* 37 One of the first works which the settler has to perform is the erection of his umpie, or dwelling. **1870** C.H. Allen *Visit to Qld.* 73 He would build his small wooden 'humpy', in which his wife and children would reside during his long journeys to the interior. **1881** W. Feilding *Austral. Trans-Continental Railway* 42 Mr Bell . . has not as yet built even a 'humpy', and moves about his camp with his cattle. **1893** S. Newland *Paving Way* 326 The 'humpy' proved to be an excavation in the broken side of the hill, the entrance being closed by slanting timbers covered with earth. **1903** *Bulletin* (Sydney) 7 Feb. 16/2 See a little bare galvanised-iron 'humpy' at the end of a small winding dusty track. **1919** *Huon Times* (Franklin) 17 Oct. 4/2 The tent gives place to the humpy; the humpy gives place to the home of the settler's dreams. **1936** J. Devanny *Sugar Heaven* 44 He went under the shower in the tiny sackcloth humpy, attached to the outside wall, which constituted their bathroom. **1940** *Bulletin* (Sydney) 15 May 16/1 Old Baldy wasn't too shook on the pair of Uni. undergrads. who pitched their natty tent close to his own humpy on the Murray. **1954** T. Ronan *Vision Splendid* 50 Mr Toppingham decided that 'humpie' must be onomatopeia. No word in any civilized tongue could describe those erections. **1960** *N.T. News* (Darwin) 12 Feb. 3/6 She was taken back . . to her old life in a squalid humpy outside Hall's Creek. **1969** A.A. Abbie *Original Australs.* 242 When school is over the children change back to their old rags and scamper back to their parents' *wurleys* or humpies—'humpy' is a flexible English term used to describe the patchwork iron, wood and canvas constructions made in imitation of the white man's huts. **1984** B. Dixon *Searching for Aboriginal Lang.* 45 He visited every group of Aborigines—those on missions and cattle stations, and odd little groups that no one else had ever heard of, living in a tumbledown humpy by the mouth of a river, or camping by the workings of a deserted tin mine.

hunchy. A camel. Also *attrib.*

1919 R.J. Cassidy *Gipsy Road* 58 Some of the best 'hunchy' persuaders in Never-Never Land are Australians. **1930** E. Antony *Hungry Mile* 7 I've steered the 'hunchies' the desert thro'. **1931** Lawson & Brereton *H. Lawson* 200, I went out west to the Camel Country, Back o' Bourke, where turbaned Abdul Mahommed steers his ungainly lopsided 'hunchies' through the glittering sands.

hungry, *a.*

1. Niggardly; grasping; mean.

1855 W. Howitt *Land, Labor & Gold* II. 314, I asked two men who were resting with their cart by the roadside whose station that was?—'Hungry Scott's', was the reply. **1876** 'Resident' *Girl Life in Aust.* 53 'Do you prefer dinner or meat tea on their arrival?' 'Which do you say, my dear?' he said, turning to me. 'I should think a hungry tea would be the easiest to manage.' **1891** 'R. Boldrewood' *Sydney-Side Saxon* 166 'I was never to say stingy about a trifle of rations like 'hungry Jackson',' he said once. **1948** K.S. Prichard *Golden Miles* 74 'There's some hungry bastards', the men said, 'makin' big money on their ore, and never give the poor bugger boggin' for 'em a sling back.' **1964** H.M. Barker *Camels & Outback* 70 They spoke disdainfully of teamsters who looked carefully after their teams and called them 'hungry-gutted', a reference to their anxiety to make money. **1980** B. Hornadge *Austral. Slanguage* 157 In the last century the derogatory term *hungry* was universally applied to anyone who was mean, or grasping. It was a particular term of abuse for station owners who refused to give food to swagmen.

2. Special collocations: **hungry mile,** a stretch of Sussex Street, Sydney, frequented by unemployed wharf-labourers in search of work; **quartz** [see OED *hungry* 6 c.], quartz with a very low yield (see quot. 1853); **track,** a stretch of country in which an itinerant has difficulty in obtaining work and sustenance.

1930 E. Antony *Hungry Mile* 5 They toil and sweat in slavery, 'twould make the devil smile, To see the Sydney wharfies tramping down the **hungry mile**. **1957** T. Nelson *Hungry Mile* 75 The stretch along Sussex Street was called the 'Hungry Mile' by the wharfies . . a very apt title indeed. **1960** R. Tullipan *Follow Sun* 173 I'm going to the Hungry Mile to be a wharfie. **1967** *Kings Cross Whisper* (Sydney) xxxv. 6/2 *Hungry Mile*, a length of Sussex Street in Sydney frequented in the early days by out of work men. **1974** J. Gaby *Restless Waterfront* 245, I never thought I'd get a job on those wharves. I pounded the old Hungry Mile, but I couldn't get a look-in. **1853** A. Mackay *Great Gold Field* 19 Samples, selected on account of their unpromising appearance, called '**hungry quartz**', yielded 13 dwts. per ton, while samples selected as favourable gave 35 ounces to the ton. **1887** *N.T. Times Almanac* 129 If no gold is found, henceforth the reef has a bad name as hungry quartz. **1895** *Bulletin* (Sydney) 26 Oct. 7/4 Eight weeks on a **hungry track**. Got a week's work at last for a blacksmith cocky—*such* a nice man. . . Have just got my wages—a pair of good pusher boots (second-hand) and a 2d. stamp. **1939** *Southerly* i. 23 Grumble monotonously about the hungry track, the poor cockies, the infrequency of handouts. **1941** K. Tennant *Battlers* 33 The unwanted, crouched in little groups on the edge of the gutter, talking and smoking and comparing 'handouts' and 'bites' and good towns and 'hungry tracks'. **1950** *Bulletin* (Sydney) 5 Aug. 12/2 It was a hungry track, and when we sighted a homestead off the main road a bit Mat decided to give it a go.

hunting, *vbl. n. Obs.* Used *attrib.* in Special Comb. **hunting ground,** a stretch of country which is the hereditary possession of an Aboriginal community; **smoke,** a cloud or column of smoke rising from a fire lit by Aborigines to drive game towards hunters.

1830 *Van Diemen's Land Correspondence* 15 Mar. (1831) 55 The Natives are as tenacious of their **hunting-grounds** as settlers are of their farms. **1843** J.F. Bennett *Hist. & Descr. Acct. S.A.* 59 They are divided into tribes, each tribe having its own district of country or hunting ground. **1851** H. Melville *Present State Aust.* 114 Squatters take possession of the hunting grounds, the natives to whom they belong have no land to call their own. **1861** J.D. Lang *Qld., Aust.* 168 A tribe which has been driven from its own hunting-grounds by European intrusion has no place to retreat to. **1890** W.F. Buchanan *Aust. to Rescue* 22 Each tribe of blacks has its hunting-ground. **1875** P.E. Warburton *Journey across Western Interior* 207 Nothing was to be seen . . except several '**hunting smokes**' in different directions. **1898** D.W. Carnegie *Spinifex & Sand* 226 Presently a smoke, their first hunting-smoke of the day, rose close to us. **1935** I.L. Idriess *Man Tracks* 311 No big gathering of the tribes was there . . though numerous hunting-smokes revealed their vicinity.

huntsman spider. [Spec. use of *huntsman*, from the hunting habits of the spider, which stalks and pounces on its prey.] Any of many spiders of the fam. Heteropodidae (Sparassidae) (esp. of the genus *Isopoda*), members of which are typically large, flat-bodied spiders which dwell under the bark of trees; Tarantula; Triantelope. Also *ellipt.* as **huntsman.**

1936 K.C. McKeown *Spider Wonders Aust.* 68 This . . power of the eyes of spiders to reflect light is strongly present in the large Huntsman Spiders. **1967** *Sunday Mail Mag.* (Brisbane) 9 Apr. 2/5 There was the Huntsman spider who adopted us and took up residence behind a painting in the living-room. **1978** N. Coleman *Look at Wildlife Great Barrier Reef* 35 The huntsman is a ground-dwelling spider which may grow to almost 70 mm across the leg span. **1986** *Canberra Times* 29 Jan. 21/2 Huntsman spiders can also cause alarm by their sneaky behaviour and huge size. *Isopoda, Delena* and *Olios* are common genera in the ACT, and all have a tendency to lurk behind curtains and towels, or to scurry across the wall during dinner parties.

Huon pine. [From the name of a river in s. Tas.] The conifer *Lagerostrobus franklinii* (fam. Podocarpaceae) of s. and w. Tas., having weeping foliage and occurring in damp forests; the durable softwood timber of the tree; *Macquarie Harbour pine*, see Macquarie Harbour. Also *attrib.*

1810 *Derwent Star* (Hobart) 3 Apr. 2 The Body was placed in a Shell of Huon pine wood. **1820** C. Jeffreys *Van Dieman's Land* 28 Huon Pine (so called from the river of that name where it was first found) . . resembles the common pine, in shape and colour; but bears a very different leaf; and its wood has a peculiar smell, which has the effect of destroying insects. **1827** *Hobart Town Courier* 24 Nov. 2 The wood called Huon Pine has been already often sent here [*sc.* London]. **1849** *Britannia* (Hobart) 2 Oct. 2/4 Three very excellent cricket bats, made of Huon Pine. **1865** G.F. Angas *Aust.* 173 The Huon pine is used for all building and domestic purposes, and is a very superior wood. **1879** *Illustr. Austral. News* (Melbourne) 2 Aug. 122/1 Planked with Kauri and Huon pine. **1903** *Tasmanian Timbers* (Tas. Lands & Survey Dept.) 24 Huon Pine (*Dacrydium franklinii*) . . named after Sir John Franklin. **1956** B. Beatty *Beyond Aust.'s Cities* 84 Along both its banks dense forests of myrtle, sassafras, blackwood, leatherwood and Huon pine. **1967** E. Huxley *Their Shining Eldorado* 169 Once the Huon valley had its Huon pines, finest of the few kinds of native conifer. **1978** N. Evers *Tas. Paradise & Beyond* 43 You boil down the shavings . . and you'll get Huon pine oil that is just the shot for rheumatism. **1983** *Sydney Morning Herald* 3 Feb. 13/1 Huon pines can live for more than 2,000 years.

hurl, *v. intr.* To vomit. Also as *n.*, the act of vomiting; vomit.

1964 B. Humphries *Nice Night's Entertainment* (1981) 78 I've had liquid laughs in bars And I've hurled from moving cars. **1967** F. Hardy *Billy Borker yarns Again* 63 Calling for Herb, see, that's one of the many euphemisms for vomit, others include spue, burp, hurl, the big spit, the long spit, throw. **1971** B. Humphries *Bazza pulls it Off*, A bastard tucks away a few jars of ice-cold it's only in his Ned Kelly for a few jiffs, and then when he has a decent hurl it comes out all . . different somehow.

hurroo, var. Hooroo.

hurry-scurry. At a country race-meeting: a final event for horses unplaced in previous races.

1878 G. Walch *Australasia* 33 He asked Harry if he could let him have Tearaway to ride in the Hurry-

Skurry. **1932** K.S. PRICHARD *Kiss on Lips* 176 There was none of the usual barney and belting on the hurry-scurry. **1969** A. FADDEN *They called me Artie* 12 The final race of the day was a consolation event for beaten horses, known as the 'Hurry-Scurry'.

hurry-up. [f. the vbl. phr. *to hurry up.*] A spur to action, esp. in the phr. **to give** (someone) **a bit of hurry-up.**

1916 O. HOGUE *Trooper Bluegum at Dardanelles* 171 We were giving Abdul a 'bit of hurry-up' . . at Quinn's. **1917** *Byron Bay Rec.* 15 Sept. 9, I think they were still giving the Huns a bit of 'hurry-up' further up the line. **1924** A.W. BAZLEY et al. Gloss. Slang A.I.F. (typescript), *Hurry up*, vigorous banter; forced to travel with greater rapidity than was intended. **1954** H.G. LAMOND *Manx Star* 164 If those men are in position we'll give 'em some hurry-up. **1965** *Tracks we Travel* 128 The young bloke's giving him a bit of hurry-up. **1986** *Canberra Times* 26 May 3/1 (*heading*) A hurry up for late ratepayers.

hut, *n.*

1. *Obs.* An Aboriginal dwelling.

1770 J. COOK *Jrnls.* 29 Apr. (1955) I. 305 We found here a few Small Hutts made of the bark of trees in one of which were four or five small children. **1789** 'OFFICER' *Authentic & Interesting Exped. Botany Bay* 27 Their huts are formed of boughs and covered with bushes and earth. **1793** J. HUNTER *Hist. Jrnl. Trans. Port Jackson* 60 In the woods . . we sometimes met with a piece of the bark of a tree, bent in the middle, and set upon the ends, with a piece set up against that end on which the wind blows. This hut serves them for a habitation, and will contain a whole family. **1820** C. JEFFREYS *Van Dieman's Land* 128 The huts made by the natives of Van Dieman's Land, approach . . the principles of regular architecture. **1836** R. PORTER *Hist. Story* 11 These gunyahs, or huts, were formed by sticking forked sticks in the ground, putting a sapling across, and leaning against them sheets of bark stripped from the white box. **1849** C. STURT *Narr. Exped. Central Aust.* 233 We passed several native huts. . . They were all arched elliptically by bending the bough of a tree at a certain height from the ground, and resting the other end on a forked stick at the opposite side of the arch. A thick layer of boughs was then put over the roof and back, on which there was also a thin coating of red clay, so that the hut was impervious to wind or heat. **1901** G. WHITE *Across Aust.* 16, I found two well-made blacks' huts shaped like a Kaffir kraal, well thatched and waterproof.

2. *Obs.* A building for the accommodation of a convict (or convicts).

1793 J. HUNTER *Hist. Jrnl. Trans. Port Jackson* 303 The huts were building at the distance of one hundred feet from each other, and each hut was to contain ten convicts. *Ibid.* 316 Three women lived at present in tents, I put them into the storehouse, until they could build huts for themselves. **1824** E. CURR *Acct. Colony Van Diemen's Land* 106 The turf hut in which they reside during their labours will serve afterwards to contain the farming men and stock-keepers. **1825** B. FIELD *Geogr. Mem. N.S.W.* 31 The remainder of the town . . is entirely occupied by the prisoners . . who have each a small but neat hut, constructed of split-wood, lathed, plastered and white-washed, with a garden attached. **1833** W.H. BRETON *Excursions* 315 The huts of the convicts are seldom notorious for cleanliness or comfort. **1834** *HRA* (1923) 1st Ser. XVII. 338 A Tub of Water and a drinking vessel, together with one or more Tubs for Wine, is however to be placed in each Hut previous to the Evening Muster.

3. A dwelling, esp. in the country, not necessarily either temporary or mean (see e.g. quots. 1841 and 1864); such a dwelling as provided for the accommodation of assigned convicts and, later, of employees; also **men's hut**. Also *attrib.*

1803 *Sydney Gaz.* 19 Mar., She saw two men approach a hut in which one of Mr Declamb's men-servants then was. **1816** *Hobart Town Gaz.* 3 Aug., Lately, Matthew Keegan, a Bush Ranger, paid a visit to a Stock-keeper's hut at Pit Water. **1823** *Ibid.* 4 Jan., There is a capital Cow-yard and Calves-pen, with Men's Hut and considerable fencing on this Farm. **1836** *Hobart Town Almanack* 69, I succeeded in hiring a hut of two apartments in one of the principal streets [of Hobart]. **1841** *Port Phillip Gaz.* 20 Mar. 6 [On] the Cattle Station . . is a comfortable Hut, containing five rooms . . also two huts for stockmen and servants. **1843** *S. Austral. Odd Fellows' Mag.* Oct. 43 At this spot a community of Germans have settled, and formed a kind of village of picturesque huts, with high pointed roofs and gable ends. **1856** W.W. DOBIE *Recoll. Visit Port-Phillip* 70 One large hut, called 'the men's hut', is usually set apart for the working-men engaged in various jobs on the station, and who are without the encumbrances of wives or families. **1860** 'LADY' *My Experiences in Aust.* 142 He entreated us to come to his cottage, or hut, as all bush dwellings are called, though this deserved a better name. **1864** H. JONES *New Valuations* 28 Nearly all the huts are of stone, and well built by competent masons. **1873** M. CLARKE *Holiday Peak* 82 Dudley is a great man. . . He is called the '— boss', and lives in the 'house', in contradistinction to the 'hut'. **1900** *Tocsin* (Melbourne) 6 Sept. 5/1 Imagine a log or slab structure, having one door and no window; a long table, surrounded with benches, down the middle; and the rest of the space, all around except at the door and fireplace, occupied by rough shelves, partitioned after some fashion into six or seven feet lengths, tier above tier from the mud floor to the springing of the roof. You will then have a fair conception of the hut that the squatter provides for the bushworkers. **1911** E.M. CLOWES *On Wallaby through Vic.* 103 The shearers live—that is, sleep and eat—in what is known as 'the Hut', a long narrow structure with bunks at either side, in two tiers, each bunk just long enough to hold a man. **1921** G.A. BELL *Under Brigalows* 118 A 'men's hut', as the stockmen's quarters were called. **1935** *Red Star* (Perth) 16 Aug. 3/2 On going to their huts the shearers were told that the overseer had declared a cut out. **1952** *Bulletin* (Sydney) 30 Jan. 15/1 We were snatching grapes in Mildura and camped in a two-room hut on the property. **1956** F.B. VICKERS *First Place to Stranger* 233 The accommodation he provided for the shearing team to live in was up to the standard laid down by the Hut Accommodation Act. **1965** R.H. CONQUEST *Horses in Kitchen* 16 Until about sixty years ago the men's quarters were referred to as the hut. The hut at the head station was known as the big hut, and those on the boundaries were known as boundary huts.

4. Comb. **hut-mate.**

1827 *Monitor* (Sydney) 5 July 496/1 Five matched themselves together, as hut-mates, for each of the four huts. **1843** *Parramatta Chron.* 30 Dec. 4/3 The hut-mate of the unfortunate man who was killed had a very narrow escape with his life. **1874** J.J. HALCOMBE *Emigrant & Heathen* 60 Evening and morning brought the hut-mates together again. **1879** 'AUSTRALIAN' *Adventures Qld.* 150 He . . inwardly vowed that he would never again take a situation where it would be necessary for him to have hut-mates. **1916** *Bulletin* (Sydney) 5 Oct. 22/2 He had been Kellar's hut-mate for a year or so. **1944** *Ibid.* 10 May 13/1 Old Jim had a handsome grey cat as his hut mate.

5. Special Comb. **hut-man,** a person, esp. a shepherd, who is accommodated in a hut; a HUT-KEEPER; also *transf.* (see quot. 1936).

1826 *Monitor* (Sydney) 19 May 2/2 The distant Woods of the Colony, where neither the Clergyman nor the Missionary penetrates to remind the poor Hutmen and lonely Settlers, either of the difference between the Sabbath and the week-day, or, that they have Souls which may be lost for want of consideration. **1839** *S. Austral. Rec.* (London) 1 Nov. 255 The hutman of No. 2 station had been down. **1849** R.J. MANN *Emigrant's Guide Aust.* 34 They will find it no hardship . . to live in the open air the life of a shepherd, or stock-keeper, or that of a hutman. **1936** W. HATFIELD *Aust. through Windscreen* 64 It was policy to have a policeman in the house, as an ally against the cattle-thieves. 'But,' said a manager once to me, 'they're really hut men, below the rank of sub-inspector. Yet what can you do?' **1959** H.G. LAMOND *Sheep Station* 51 The Keystone . . ran two tables: coffee-room for the social aspirants; dining-room for those who were hut men and ate in the kitchen on stations.

hut, *v. Obs.* [Prob. back-formation f. HUTTER, but cf. HAT.] *intr.* To live alone.

1888 *Centennial Mag.* (Sydney) 499 Sauerkraut had worked his claim with varying success, always hutting, or in other words living alone.

hut-keep, *v.* [Back-formation f. HUT-KEEPER.] *intr.* To perform the duties of a hut-keeper.

1840 J. GUNTHER Jrnl. 14 Dec. 44 On my road I called at a Shepherd's hut where a Scotchwoman was hut-keeping as they call it. **1853** S. SIDNEY *Three Colonies* (ed. 2) 380 At this, as well as at every other station I have called at, a woman 'hutkeeps', while the husband is minding the sheep. **1859** W. BURROWS *Adventures Mounted Trooper* 101 A young colonist . . was hut-keeping on a station near the Murray river. **1870** 'JACKAROO' *Immigration Question* 6, I shall shepherd and hut-keep to the end of my days. **1891** D. FERGUSON *Vicissitudes Bush Life* 148 The shepherd for whom he was hutkeeping was tending a flock of ewes.

Hence **hutkeeping** *vbl. n.*

1841 *Geelong Advertiser* 13 Dec. 2/5 Reardon returned, but Captain Webster refused to let him have any other work than hut-keeping. **1853** W.J. WILLS *Successful Exploration Interior Aust.* 12 Feb. (1863) 17 We have engaged as shepherds at £30 per annum each, and rations. . . We take the hut-keeping and shepherding in turns. **1891** D. FERGUSON *Vicissitudes Bush Life* 47 When you are well spelled after your long tramp, I may get the Coni to give you a job at hut keeping.

hut-keeper. One who takes care of a hut, esp. as occupied by convicts or employees (e.g., shepherds, shearers, etc.), providing for the occupants and attending to certain menial tasks.

1794 G. THOMPSON *Slavery & Famine* ii. 8 Those who are not fortunate enough to be selected for wives . . are made hut-keepers. **1802** D. COLLINS *Acct. Eng. Colony N.S.W.* II. 285 Among the lower classes were many old men, unfit for anything but to be hut-keepers, who were to remain at home to prevent robbery, while the other inhabitants of the hut were at labour. **1805** *Sydney Gaz.* 5 May, A party of natives visited the Government stock farm at Seven Hills . . launching several spears at the hutkeeper. **1826** *Hobart Town Gaz.* 11 Nov., A band of natives . . attacked the shepherd's hut of Mr Gilles, at the Elizabeth River, robbed it of every article, and beat the hut-keeper, a harmless old man. **1830** *HRA* (1922) 1st Ser. XV. 502 It has been customary to allow Men, who from lameness or debility were incapable of Labour, to act as Hut Keepers to parties of the Convicts. **1842** *S. Austral. News* (London) 15 Aug. 28/2 The principal work of the hut-keeper, is to sweep out the sheep-pen every morning, as soon as the sheep leave it, during dry weather, or shift the hurdles every day to fresh or clear ground during wet weather. . . Cooking the victuals for the shepherd and himself is the remainder of his work. **1849** T. ROGERS *Corresp. relating to Dismissal* 141 Before a month both these men were in billets: one as hut-keeper to the police, and the other as a policeman. **1867** A.K. COLLINS *Waddy Mundoee* 27 The hutkeeper bustled about, and soon laid before her the simple repast. ***c* 1891** MRS P. MARTIN *Coo-ee* 278 Mick . . had been hut-keeper to a party of shearers. **1910** *Bulletin* (Sydney) 29 Sept. 13/3 For indolent habits and downright laziness the Outback hut-keeper ranks second only to a Domain dosser. **1930** BILLIS & KENYON *Pastures New* 252 A barbarous murder has just been committed . . by the blacks, four of them having attacked a hut keeper . . in the service of Major Davidson and disembowelled him to obtain the kidney fat. **1961** M. KIDDLE *Men of Yesterday* 60 Besides attending to the hurdles the hut-keeper cooked for the shepherds and himself. . . But as well as this, at night the hut-keeper was supposed to sleep in the watchbox with a carbine by his side to guard the flocks. **1982** PAGE & INGPEN *Aussie Battlers* 22 A hut-keeper is different from what he was when I was young. I just look after the shearer's quarters, cook their grub and so on.

hutter. [f. HUT *n.* 3, poss. infl. by HATTER.] One who prefers to live alone.

1878 F.W. FENTON *This Side Up* 8 The few 'hutters' who vegetated on Boggy Creek, earning a few shillings a week in working ground that had been turned over and over again. **1880** 'ERRO' *Squattermania* 257 He went off through the bush to his own hut, where he lived by himself, being what is colonially known as a hutter. **1937** D. GUNN *Links with Past* 207 After a time . . shepherds' huts were made larger and better. . . If the country was very good, two flocks were camped at the same locality, which meant two single men could live together, but still there were many old hutters who preferred to be alone.

hyena. Prob. *obs.* [Transf. use of *hyena*, from a fancied resemblance to a carnivore of the fam. Hyaenidae.] *Tasmanian tiger*, see TASMANIAN *a.* 2; *opossum hyena*, see OPOSSUM *n.* 3. Also **hyena opossum.**

[**1805** *Sydney Gaz.* 21 Apr., The form of the animal is that of the hyaena, at the same time strongly reminding the observer of the appearance of a low wolf dog.]

1810 *HRA* (1921) 3rd Ser. I. 771 The only animal unknown on the Continent is the Hyaena Opossum. **1811** D.D. MANN *Present Picture N.S.W.* 49 Latterly . . a species of the Hyena has been found at Port Dalrymple, which is extremely ferocious in appearance, has a remarkably large mouth, is striped all over, very strongly limbed, and its claws strong, long and sharp. This animal is . . of the Opossum kind, having, like the generality of subjects found in New Holland, a false belly. **1833** J. BACKHOUSE *Narr. Visit Austral. Colonies* (1843) 122 The animal, called in this country the hyena and the Tiger, but which differs greatly from both, also kills sheep. **1846** N.L. KENTISH *Work in Bush Van Diemen's Land* 29 Besides mankind, these timid creatures (wallabies) especially the young, have formidable enemies in the 'tiger', or 'hyaena' (which animal is more of the character of the jackall). **1852** J. WEST *Hist. of Tas.* I. 322 The Tiger or Hyaena of the colonists (*Thylacinus cynocephalus* . .) is a very powerful animal, about the size of a large dog, with short legs. It is of a tawny or brownish yellow color, with numerous black bands arranged transversely along the back, from the shoulders to the tail; hence the erroneous names tiger and hyaena, given to it by the early settlers. **1880** J.J. JONES *Openings for Emigrants* 57 In the fastness of this wild and uncultivated country the hyaena, or native tiger, is found, and also the native devil, both of which used formerly to be so destructive to sheep. **1900** *Advocate* (Burnie) 1 June 2/4 A large hyena was captured . . at South Montagu, lately; it measured six feet two inches from tip to tip. **1919** *Huon Times* (Franklin) 14 Mar. 2/7 Plaintiff used to assert that a wild hyena was killing his sheep.

I

ibis. [Transf. use of *Ibis* a genus of large grallatorial birds.] Any of three species of long-legged wading birds of the genera *Plegadis* and *Threskiornis*, occurring in Aust. and elsewhere. Also with distinguishing epithet, as **straw-necked, white** (see under first element), and *attrib.*

1836 *Sydney Herald* 21 Mar. 2/4 Among the aquatic birds we recognised the . . white crane, and Ibis. **1897** MRS L. RAWSON *Austral. Cook & Laundry Bk.* 41 The Ibis . . has a very objectionable odour, and consequently is little used. **1927** *Bulletin* (Sydney) 21 Apr. 24/4 The ibis is the yabbie's greatest enemy, and should be a welcome guest on every irrigation farm. **1948** J. FAIRFAX *Run o' Waters* 110 The ibis, long-necked, curious, and vaguely concerned, stared down in wonderment, occasionally uttering sharp hoarse cries. **1964** H.P. TRITTON *Time means Tucker* (rev. ed.) 27 Ibis, swans and pelicans abounded. **1986** *Sydney Morning Herald* 26 Apr. 6/4 Grain farmers recognise the value of ibis birds which are native to the area and which are important in controlling locust plagues.

iceberg. One who makes a practice of swimming regularly during the winter in unheated water.

1932 L. LOWER *Here's Another* 12 One of the toughest surfs I've experienced this winter. All the Icebergs agreed. **1943** S.J. BAKER *Pop. Dict. Austral. Slang* (ed. 3) 41 *Iceberg*, one who swims regularly in winter time. **1964** T. RONAN *Packhorse & Pearling Boat* 80, I admit that I did not join the icebergs who favoured cold showers even on the bitterest winter mornings. **1974** G. LEHMANN *Spring Day in Autumn* 174 I'm a regular swimmer myself, right in the middle of winter. They reckon I'm the oldest iceberg in Sydney. **1986** *Good Weekend* (Sydney) 26 Apr. 60/2 The Bondi Icebergs . . begin their season on Sunday, May 4, at their freshwater pool in South Bondi. Hardy male swimmers are welcome.

ice-block. A confection of flavoured and frozen water, a water-ice.

1948 C.B. MAXWELL *Cold Nose of Law* 45 Her father . . had given her a paper-wrapped ice-block, a brilliant green water-ice. **1966** S.J. BAKER *Austral. Lang.* (ed. 2) 290 *Ice-block*, a small block of coloured and sweet-tasting ice on a stick. **1970** J.S. GUNN in W.S. Ramson *Eng. Transported* 64 We should investigate the areas of use of such duplications as *lolly/iceblock*.

Icy-pole. Also **icy-pole.** [Proprietary name.] An ice-block.

1932 *Austral. Official Jrnl. Patents* (Canberra) 1067 *Icypole* 59,348. Ice cream, ice cream sherbert, water ice and frozen fruit juices. *Peters American Delicacy Company (Vic.) Ltd.* **1968** M. HILLIARD *Excuse me, Mr Sweetenham* 16 'An icy pole for me, sir, thanks.' 'One icy pole. . . ' 'Cherry flavour, sir.' **1978** B. ST. A. SMITH *Spirit beyond Psyche* 151 Ann's voice was muffled by the icy-pole she was licking. **1986** *Austral. Short Stories* xiii. 12 The worst they can do is not make up their minds whether to have a lemonade icypole or a raspberry one.

identity. [Spec. use of *identity*; prob. orig. N.Z. (see quot. 1874).] One who is a well-known and long standing resident of a place; a local 'character'. Esp. in the collocation **old identity.**

[**1862** C. THATCHER *Dunedin Songster No. 1* 18 (*title*) The old identity.] **1874** A. BATHGATE *Colonial Experiences* 26 The term 'old identities' took its origin from an expression in a speech made by one of the members of the Provincial Council, Mr E.B. Cargill, who, in speaking of the new arrivals, said that the early settlers should endeavour to preserve their old identity. . . [An Austral.] comic singer [C.R. Thatcher] helped to perpetuate the name by writing a song. **1886** R.P. WHITWORTH *Velvet & Rags* 22 All the old identities were glad to see me. . . What a place for old identities Bathurst used to be. . . The same old faces year after year; they never appeared to grow older or to die out. **1895** *Bulletin* (Sydney) 3 Aug. 13/3 An old Parramatta identity and a native of the town, Andrew Payten, died of heart-disease last month. **1913** *Truth* (Sydney) 4 May 4/3 (*heading*) Mosman identity of 76 seeks a divorce. **1919** C.A. BERNAYS *Qld. Politics during Sixty Yrs.* 14 An old identity informed the writer that when Macalister rose to speak only brickbats would stop him. **1938** F. CLUNE *Free & Easy Land* 76 An old identity, an Irishman, had turned up his toes. **1943** *Austral. New Writing* 16 The title of respect with which the bush canonizes its masters—an old identity. **1960** *N.T. News* (Darwin) 19 Feb. 9/4 When he's had one or two too many these days local identity Cyril Waalks walks. **1969** A. BUZO *Rooted* (1973) 77, I was in the pub having a quiet beer with a few Werris Creek identities, when this bloke came up and started picking a blue. **1980** F. MOORHOUSE *Days Wine & Rage* 302, I remember a local identity was picked up for driving under the influence after the picnic races.

-ie: see -Y.

ignore. In the phr. **to treat with ignore,** to disregard the presence or advice of someone or something. Also *transf.* and *fig.*

1936 *Bulletin* (Sydney) 6 July 26/1 The habit of 'treating with ignore' our own industrial experience is quite wrong. **1942** *Sun* (Sydney) 26 Aug. 4/9 In one battery, if a man was overruled he was 'treated with ignore'. **1946** A. MARSHALL *Tell us about Turkey, Jo* 202 At first he treats me with ignore, then he answers me back, then he just looks at me. **1965** K. SMITH *OGF* 78 Ain't you got any manners? A man says something to you by way of conversation and you treat him with ignore. **1975** *Sydney Morning Herald* 1 July 7/4 With gathering speed downhill, the train treated Wollstonecraft with ignore. **1983** *Ibid.* 27 May (Metro) 3/3 When you ask politely for room to pass, you can be treated with cold ignore.

iguana. *Obs.* [Transf. use of *iguana* any of several large lizards.] GOANNA 1.

1801 M. FLINDERS *Observations Coasts Van Diemen's Land* 21 Amongst other reptiles, are poisonous snakes, and some brown iguanas. **1836** E.K. THOMAS *Diary & Lett. M. Thomas* 25 Dec. (1925) 60 We took a walk round the lagoon, and saw a large iguana basking in the sun. It was about three feet long, in form like a lizard, with a long pointed tail and of a beautiful light brown, in some parts approaching to gold colour. **1854** W. HOWITT *Boy's Adventures* 74 The great lizard Iguana would astonish you. It is like a little crocodile, and runs up the trees. **1862** W. LANDSBOROUGH *Jrnl. Exped. from Carpentaria* 82 They had no rations, excepting an iguana and a few mussels. **1886** W.J. WOODS *Visit to Vic.* 39, I found . . a repulsive-looking reptile, not much less than six feet long, with a dark-brown, scaly hide, and the yawning jaws of a crocodile. It was an Iguana. **1901** *Brisbane Courier* 3 Aug. 15/4 The Iguana—or, as it is more commonly called, the 'Goanna'—is very plentiful. **1914** H.M. VAUGHAN *Australasian Wander-Yr.* 240 The iguana, or lace monitor . . is, at least to the 'new chum', most alarming in his attitude and aspect. **1942** W. GLASSON *Our Shepherds* 23 For lumbago and all rheumatic pains iguana oil was freely 'rubbed in'.

ijjecka, var. ADJIGO.

Illawarra /ɪləˈwɒrə/. [The name of a coastal district south of Sydney, N.S.W.]

1. Used *attrib.* in Special Comb. **Illawarra flame tree,** *flame tree* (a), see FLAME 2.

1902 *Proc. Linnean Soc. N.S.W.* XXVII. 578 During the year of heaviest flowering the Illawarra Flame-tree, *Sterculia acerifolia* . . is almost leafless. **1942** *Bulletin* (Sydney) 7 Jan. 17/3 Rivalling the Illawarra flame-tree in brilliance of hue. **1953** D. CUSACK *Southern Steel* 9 The jacaranda and the Illawarra flame-tree mingled their misty blue and bush-fire red. **1980** L. FULLER *Wollongong's Native Trees* 90 Illawarra flame tree can be found in most rainforest communities on the escarpment.

2. A popular breed of dairy cattle developed in the Illawarra district. Also **Illawarra (milking) Shorthorn.**

1911 *N.Z. Jrnl. Agric.* May 274 The breed . . known as the Illawarra Milking Shorthorn, a dairy type of Shorthorn evolved on the south coast districts of the State from a Shorthorn-Ayrshire foundation, but now bred for about thirty years to a Shorthorn dairy type. **1923** J. MOSES *Beyond City Gates* 155 Browsed the 'Illawarras', representatives of the dairy herds of the great, rich districts. **1962** *Daily Mercury Centenary Story Mackay* 40 Illawarra Milking Shorthorn bulls comprised his herd which aimed at 250 milkers. **1972** D. SHEAHAN *Songs from Canefields* 38 A red Illawarra hangs out by the creek Her udder is big—she's fat and she's sleek. **1981** A. WILKINSON *Up Country* 155 The red heifers actually belonged to one of Australia's own breeds, the Illawarra shorthorn. These mature into monumental milkers.

illywhacker /ˈɪliwækə/. Also **illywacker.** [Of unknown origin.] A small-time confidence trickster.

1941 K. TENNANT *Battlers* 145 An illy-wacker is someone who is putting a confidence trick over, selling imitation diamond pins, new-style patent razors or infallible 'tonics' . . 'living on the cockies' by such devices. . . A man who 'wacks the illy' can be almost anything, but two of these particular illy-wackers were equipped with a dart game. **1943** S.J. BAKER *Pop. Dict. Austral. Slang* (ed. 3) 41 *Illywhacker*, a trickster or spieler. **1975** H. PORTER *Extra* 15 Social climber, moron, peter-tickler, eeler-spee, illy-wacker. **1985** P. CAREY *Illywhacker* 245 'What's an illywhacker?' . . 'A spieler . . a trickster. A quandong. A ripperty man. A con-man.'

Hence **illywhack** *n.*, the patter of an illywhacker.

1955 *Overland* iv. 10 Within the ring a horse cavorts. Buck on, you beaut! I'd give a fiver To see you smash snakeheaded through Palings, poons, illywhack and guyver.

imbo /ˈɪmbəʊ/. [f. *imb(ecile* + -O.] A gullible person, esp. the victim of a criminal.

1953 S.J. BAKER *Aust. Speaks* 125 Australia's underworldsters have commemorated the services of their victims by calling them any of these assorted terms: . . *imbo* [etc.]. **1974** J. MCNEIL *How does your Garden Grow* 78 Top idiots. Imbos. **1981** P. RADLEY *Jack Rivers & Me* 50 'What *is* an imbo, Connie? Please?' 'If you don't know what imbeciles are far be it from me to tell you.'

immigrant.

1. One who has come to Australia from another country by choice and with the intention of settling. Cf. EMIGRANT *n.* 1, MIGRANT 1. Also *attrib.*

1838 *HRA* (1923) 1st Ser. XIX. 290 This has been a great disappointment to many immigrants. **1844** *Sydney Morning Herald* 18 Jan. 4/3 All married families, whether immigrants or the old colonists, I should be disposed to receive. **1862** F. SINNETT *Acct. Colony S.A.* 11 A sudden and excessive influx of ill-selected immigrants . . was causing great embarrassment. **1880** *Bulletin* (Sydney) 22 May 2/4 All the single female immigrants per Clyde were engaged within a quarter of an hour after hiring commenced. Another contingent of 'slaveys' arrives within ten days. **1895** *Ibid.* 5 Jan. 24/1 Dan was a young immigrant, just out from the sod. . . His brogue was rich enough to make an Irishman laugh. **1912** *Truth* (Sydney) 26 May 3/6 You don't own the street, *you dirty immigrant.* **1926** A. EDEN *Places in Sun* 55 Some of them recent immigrants. **1939** J.T. MCMAHON *Bushies' Scheme in W.A.* 37 The 'Big Brother' assumes a paternal interest in some immigrant boy, promising to care for him when out of employment, and to guard him while in it. **1970** *Bulletin* (Sydney) 21 Mar. 47/1 Some of my closest friends are immigrants. **1979** W.D. JOYNT *Breaking Road for Rest* 48 The men turned out to be English immigrants, newly arrived in the country.

2. One who moves from one Australian Colony or State to settle in another.

1845 *Portland Gaz.* 1 July 2/2 About 70 immigrants are expected to arrive at Geelong per the schooner David from Hobart Town. **1847** *Port Phillip Gaz.* 6 Feb. 3 Tenders for the conveyance of 500 Immigrants from Van Diemen's Land, to the Wharf, Geelong. **1902** *Bulletin* (Sydney) 28 Oct. 36/2 The culprit is frequently a new-chum or an immigrant from the Paroo country, where bush fires are unknown.

3. *transf.* A species of bird, etc., introduced into Australia.

1925 *Bulletin* (Sydney) 1 Oct. 24/2 Quarrians, rosellas, green-leeks and red-backs, all very numerous on the N.S.W. tablelands, are now eagerly searching for nesting-places which they have carelessly let fall into the hands of immigrants. **1936** *Ibid.* 15 Apr. 20/2 The house-sparrow, aptly termed 'the rat of the air', is certainly Australia's most successful bird immigrant.

4. Comb. **immigrant barracks, depot, ship.**

1842 *Sydney Morning Herald* 2 Aug. 2/3 The admission into the **Immigrant Barracks,** and the temporary maintenance there of. . labourers with families. **1848** *Sydney Daily Advertiser* 12 July 2/3 A better place could not be selected to form an **immigrant depot**. **1859** J.D. MEREWEATHER *Diary Working Clergyman* 234 Went to the Immigrant Dépôt, and saw thirty young women, who have just arrived. **1841** *Port Phillip Patriot* 21 Oct. 2/2 The *Agricola*, an **immigrant ship** from London and Cork. **1853** *Moreton Bay Free Press* 15 Feb. 3/3 The *Florentia*, the next immigrant ship, is daily expected. **1873** J.C.F. JOHNSON *Christmas on Carringa* 21, I come out in one of the fust reg'lar immigrant ships as come to Sydney. **1879** 'AUSTRALIAN' *Adventures Qld.* 42 Grosse . . had arrived at Brisbane in a German immigrant ship.

5. In the collocation **immigrants' home,** an establishment in which newly-arrived immigrants are given temporary accommodation.

1852 J. MORGAN *Life & Adventures W. Buckley* 150, I was soon afterwards appointed assistant to the storekeeper at the Immigrants' Home, Hobart Town. **1853** W.J. WILLS *Successful Exploration Interior Aust.* 12 Feb. (1863) 18 We preferred the Immigrant's Home, a government affair, just fitted up for the accommodation of new-comers, where you pay a shilling a night, and find yourself. **1889** *Illustr. Austral. News* (Melbourne) 1 Oct. 18/2 The Immigrants' Homes were first originated for the purpose of housing newly arrived immigrants, so that people who required servants could easily engage them. **1977** F.B. VICKERS *Stranger no Longer* 10 When our ship docked at Fremantle, us twenty-eight chaps who were bound for the Immigrants' Home were lined up in single file.

immigrate, *v.*

1. *intr.* To come to Australia from another country with the intention of settling. Cf. EMIGRATE.

1837 *Lit. News* (Sydney) 9 Dec. 180 Those Gentlemen who immigrated on the faith of the Home Government Regulations of 1827. **1950** *Sun* (Sydney) 15 Sept. 14/4, I sent a translation of my diploma, saying that I am a qualified pharmacist, to Canberra, and the Immigration Department replied with an authorisation to immigrate. **1966** *Austral.* (Sydney) 23 Feb. 2/10 He had been inundated with people asking how they could immigrate to Australia. **1982** *Sydney Morning Herald* 13 Dec. 2/1 Prospective immigrants . . must get 60 points under the department's point system before they are allowed to immigrate.

2. *Obs.* To move from one Australian Colony to live in another.

1889 J.H.L. ZILLMANN *Past & Present Austral. Life* 92 Moonlight and his gang . . were for the most part a band of 'larrikins' that immigrated from the Melbourne side and started as bush-rangers in the neighbouring colony of New South Wales.

Hence **immigrating** *ppl. a.*

1896 *Bulletin* (Sydney) 17 Oct. 10/4 As the immigrating Chows did not report themselves to the police, the Government and its officials took no cognisance of this increase in the pig-tailed population.

immigration.

1. The action of coming to Australia from another country with the intention of settling; [also U.S.: see Mathews] the body of immigrants. Cf. EMIGRATION 1.

1824 *HRA* (1921) 3rd Ser. IV. 567 The chief of the Immigration being directed to Van Diemen's Land. **1837** *Perth Gaz.* 7 Jan. 825, I hope that the representations which have been sent home within the last year, with regard to the true state and prospects of the Colony, will tend to produce a fresh stream of Immigration. **1843** *HRA* (1925) 1st Ser. XXIII. 96 A Committee has been appointed by the Legislative Council on the subject of Immigration. **1855** *Illustr. Sydney News* 2 June 279/2 The stream of immigration still continues to pour in as briskly as ever. **1862** F.H. NIXON *Population* 4 An almost unanimous verdict has been given in favour of increased and abundant Immigration to Victoria from the Mother Country. **1881** T. PRESTON *Chinese Question* 24 Unrestricted Chinese immigration would be as a slow but subtle poison. **1912** *Register* (Adelaide) 28 Mar. 4/3 By various means the facilities to immigration will be increased or made easier. **1893** *Age* (Melbourne) 12 May 4/7 It is absurd to imagine that any voluntary immigration will take place. **1965** *Canberra Times* 6 July 3/5 This high figure for British immigration to Australia is only temporary. **1984** *Age* (Melbourne) 8 Dec. 5/2 A major issue was whether immigration would increase to further speed up population growth.

2. Special Comb. **immigration agent,** one employed to promote immigration and to assist with the settlement of immigrants; **department,** the (government) department responsible for the implementation and administration of an immigration policy; **lecturer,** one employed to promote the advantages of immigration to Australia; **society,** an organization established to encourage immigration and to provide assistance to immigrants.

1841 *Morning Advertiser* (Hobart) 5 Aug. 1/3 The regulations of the Bounty system are laid down in the Government Notice of the 14th May, 1840, and by these the **Immigration Agent** will be governed. **1851** C.P. FORD *Emigrant Family* 9 The immigration agent seemed to think that there was nothing extraordinary in what was to be done. **1872** J.L.A. HOPE *In Quest of Coolies* 12 The Immigration Agent in Brisbane is . . bound to see that, on arrival, all the men fully understand their agreements. **1880** *Bulletin* (Sydney) 7 Feb. 3/1 Mr W.J. Harris, speaking at Monday night's anti-immigration meeting, said that immigration agents at home went about wearing beaver hats, frock coats, and white ties. **1913** *Ibid.* 30 Jan. 15/2 Two youthful and inexperienced Londoners, stranded in Sydney through a blind faith in immigration agents, last June wandered towards Israel with their payable property, and then trained it to Wagga. **1842** *Aust. & N.Z. Monthly Mag.* 47 This excess arises from an increase of. . £1,200 for the **immigration department.** **1848** *Sydney Daily Advertiser* 19 July 2/3 The Surgeon Superintendent will be required to satisfy himself of the respectability of the hiring party . . by reference to the officer of the Immigration Department. **1912** *Bulletin* (Sydney) 19 Sept. 16/1 Mohomed . . wrote . . to the Immigration Department. **1961** *Ibid.* 8 Feb. 8/4 The Immigration Department . . allows Asian workers to enter Australia on temporary permits to take up 'approved' employment. **1980** *Sydney Morning Herald* 15 Feb. 3/3 The Immigration Department estimates that there are up to 70,000 illegal immigrants in Australia. **1868** *Coalition between Squatters & Free Selectors* 7 In 1861 . . the two well known gentlemen (Mr Dalley and Mr Parkes) were immediately instructed to start for England, as '**Immigration Lecturers**'. **1899** *Bulletin* (Sydney) 15 Apr. 31/4 'Majah' Lyons was recently in the old country as immigration-lecturer. **1847** *Maitland Mercury* 24 Nov. 3/2 In consequence of. . the organization of several **immigration societies**, chiefly in Port Phillip, who pay emigrants' passages, the stream of emigration from Van Diemen's Land . . is diverted to that district. **1854** BACKHOUSE & TYLOR *Life & Labours G.W. Walker* 29 June (1862) 536, I have mentioned the Immigration Society. The Government furnishes Bounty Tickets for each adult emigrant.

imperial convict. *W.A. Hist.* A convict the cost of whose penal servitude was met by the British as distinct from the Colonial government.

1873 A. TROLLOPE *Aust. & N.Z.* II. 112, 240 are imperial convicts,—convicts who have been sent out from England, and who are now serving under British sentences, or sentences inflicted in the colony within twelve months of the date of their freedom. **1875** J. FORREST *Explorations in Aust.* 334 It has been for me to preside over the latter stages of the existence of the Imperial convict establishment in Western Australia. **1880** *Bulletin* (Sydney) 31 Jan. 4/3 Bull, an old Imperial Convict, was installed as executioner. **1885** *V & P* (W.A. L.C.) no. 25 5 It would be liberal to offer to the Colony the same sum per head for the Imperial Convicts as the Colony has paid for Colonial Convicts, viz; £42.

imported, *ppl. a.* Immigrant. Also *absol.*

1849 A. HARRIS *Emigrant Family* (1967) 198 The inferior portion of the imported free population sympathises. **1891** 'SMILER' *Wanderings Simple Child* (ed. 3) p. v., The author all the way through takes every opportunity to have a passing slap at the imported element, which naturally forms a large proportion of the humanity which gather on a new mining rush. **1910** *Bulletin* (Sydney) 10 Nov. 13/2, I had to fall back on an assisted immigrant, who was journeying to nowhere in particular. Now, I've found most 'importeds' have a failing, and mine had his. **1913** *Ibid.* 16 Jan. 14/2 He was out on a station for experience, and he wasn't imported goods either. **1917** *Truth* (Sydney) 15 July 12/2 As long as imported people come out here *to be good Australians* I have no fault to find with them.

improve, *n.* In the phr. **on the improve,** showing signs of betterment.

1959 S.J. BAKER *Drum* 119 *Improve, on the*, improving in health or proficiency. **1965** H. PORTER *Cats of Venice* 144 Had a bout of Bronchitis but on the improve. **1971** *Bulletin* (Sydney) 11 Dec. 50/3 Back to Australia. It now appears that things are on the improve, you little bottler! **1982** *Weekend Austral.* (Sydney) 17 Apr. 44/6 Channel 10 said 'Canberra is on the improve, and could prove too good.' **1984** *West Austral.* (Perth) 4 Jan. 92/5 Regal Martin on the improve. . . Three-year-old Regal Martin showed improvement with a smart trial over 800 m. on the wood fibre track at Ascot yesterday morning.

improve, *v.* [U.S. *improve* to bring land under cultivation: see Mathews *v.* 1., and also OED(S *v.*[2] 2 b. for the older and more general meaning of which this is a spec. use.]

1. *trans.* To bring (land) into agricultural or pastoral use; to clear, fence, provide with buildings, etc., so making more productive and more valuable.

1834 H. MELVILLE *Two Lett. Van Diemen's Land* 4 Mr Auley. . may dispose of his grant—without ever having seen it, without ever having improved it. **1839** *Port Phillip Gaz.* 30 Oct. 3 The lands of Australia Felix, which belong by the law of nature and of man, to the industrious public who has sought, located and improved them. **1870** *Sydney Morning Herald* 5 July 3/1, 2000 acres (half of which is cleared, but not otherwise improved) were offered. **1894** W.H. BARKER *Gold Fields W.A.* 52 As in Victoria, Tasmania, and New Zealand, so in Western Australia; the aboriginal is being improved off the face of the earth. **1905** *Bulletin* (Sydney) 19 Oct. 40/2 The land is half-cleared (improved they call it; Nature forgive them).

2. *trans. Obs.* To increase (the quality or yield of stock or of animal produce).

1820 *Hobart Town Gaz.* 2 Dec., Settlers, improving Wool on an extensive Scale, are requested to take this Opportunity of pointing out any Facilities which they consider might be afforded them. **1833** *Trumpeter* (Hobart) 19 Nov. 242 The Proprietors of Cows wishing to improve their breed, may do so, by sending them to Mr Rawling's highly-improved Bull.

Hence **improver** *n.*, **improving** *vbl. n.*

1824 *Hobart Town Gaz.* 9 July, The very best shipments of the oldest **improvers** in New South Wales fetch from 1s. 3d. to 2s. **1956** K. TENNANT *Honey Flow* 113 The **improving** and clearing and ring-barking went on until the foothills of the enclosing ranges were almost bare of trees save ring-barked, dead skeletons.

improved, *ppl. a.* [U.S.: see Mathews.] Of land: brought into agricultural or pastoral use; made more productive.

1839 *Sydney Standard* 1 Apr. 3/3 Did not include . . the sale of improved lands. **1848** H.W. HAYGARTH

Recoll. Bush Life 11, I was better off than many, for we had purchased an 'improved station'. **1870** *Sydney Morning Herald* 5 July 3/1 O'Connell's Plains . . is a very fine piece of country, but having no land open for free selection; though improved land can be had at a moderate rental. **1879** S.W. SILVER *Austral. Grazier's Guide* 10 He buys a partially improved run, with huts, paddocks, and stackyards [*sic*], with flocks of sheep and herds of cattle ready broken and acclimatised to the district. **1890** 'R. BOLDREWOOD' *Colonial Reformer* III. 40 There is never so much money to be made at comfortable, highly improved stations. **1910** *Bulletin* (Sydney) 6 Jan. 14/2 The Government dared not place the whole cost of improvement against the improved blocks. **1925** J.A. COLLUM *New Settlers' Handbk.* 53 He should buy an improved or partly improved farm. **1979** *Sydney Morning Herald* 5 Sept. 6/3 Could it not be that the country man even more than the town man needs generous areas of national parkland, bush and wilderness as islands of normality in our over-'improved' countryside? **1986** *Canberra Times* 5 Mar. 18/4 The growth of the wheat industry and the spread of improved pasture in inland Australia provided ideal conditions for the great 20th-century galah boom, but the factors that contributed to the success of the galah around Canberra since the 1940s remain obscure.

improvement. [U.S.: see OED(S 2 a. and b.]

1. The bringing of land into agricultural or pastoral use; the provision of fences, buildings, etc., associated with this process; the increasing of productivity. Also *attrib.*

1834 H. MELVILLE *Two Lett. Van Diemen's Land* 4 No improvements were being made on Mr Auley's grant. **1848** H.W. HAYGARTH *Recoll. Bush Life* 14 The huts, paddocks, and various other 'improvements', as they are generally called, are often spread out here and there, over a large space of ground. **1855** W. HOWITT *Land, Labor & Gold* II. 248 These encroachments they coolly call *improvements*, and put in a claim for them. **1864** H. JONES *New Valuations* 6 Twenty years ago the land which is now occupied by my home station, outbuildings and my improvements, was a solitude, only trodden by the wild savage. **1880** R. ROSE *Austral. Guide: S.A.* 7 The improvements . . consist in erecting a dwelling-house or farm-building, sinking wells, constructing water-tanks or reservoirs, putting up fencing, draining, or clearing or grubbing the said land. **1890** 'R. BOLDREWOOD' *Colonial Reformer* I. 175 Jedwood rode over 'the run', among his flocks and herds, his men and his 'improvements', his dams, his wells, his fences, his buildings, his fields, and his teams. **1925** J.A. COLLUM *New Settlers' Handbk.* 55 The most carefully erected improvements will not improve the quality of the land. **1925** *Pastoral Rev.* 16 Feb. 147 While pasture improvement may not be a question which comes under the definition of agriculture, it is very directly associated with it. **1934** 'S. RUDD' *Green Grey Homestead* 65 The Crown Lands ranger has been along taking stock of your improvements, and giving you advice on the making of farms and farmers. **1956** *Westerly* i. 13 Schemes for the reduction or abolition of income taxation have often been proposed . . to compel owners to carry out the improvement clauses in their pastoral leases. **1979** *Sydney Morning Herald* 3 Sept. 6/6 Governments in Australia have regarded clearing of timber as 'improvement' of land.

2. *transf. Obs.* An increase in the value or quality (of sheep or cattle).

1835 *Cornwall Chron.* (Launceston) 21 Feb. 3 The proprietor . . paid the greatest attention towards the improvement of his cattle. **1837** *Perth Gaz.* 30 Sept. 981 The improvement effected by the system of crossing, generally adopted of late years by the flock-holders.

3. Special Comb. **improvement lease** [U.S.; see Mathews], IMPROVING LEASE; the land so held.

1895 *Act* (N.S.W.) 58 *Vict.* no. 18 Sect. 26 (*heading*) Improvement leases. **1910** *Bulletin* (Sydney) 7 Apr. 14/3 The Hay (N.S.W.) Land Board recently wrestled with some Improvement Leases totalling 31,000 acres. **1912** 'IRONBARK' *Ironbark Splinters* 124 Little Bo-Peep she sought her sheep On the neighbours' Improvement Leases: She found 'em (how hard!) in another chap's yard, *With his tar-brand on their fleeces!*

improving lease. *Obs.* An agreement by which the occupation of land is subject to the carrying out by the lessee of specified improvements.

1823 *Hobart Town Gaz.* 4 Oct., To be Let, upon an improving Lease, a small Farm. **1832** *Colonial Times* (Hobart) 9 May, A part of the Farm is let to an industrious tenant on an improving lease, and progressively increasing rent. **1843** *Duncan's Weekly Register* (Sydney) 18 Nov. 249/3 Mrs Chisholm is now at Illawarra selecting farms, upon improving leases for a number of families. **1857** Tas. Non-State Rec. 103/4 9 Oct., I intend to let it on an improving lease.

imshi /ˈɪmʃi/, *v. imp.* Also **imshee.** [Services' speech of the war of 1914–18, f. the colloq. (Egyptian) Arabic. Chiefly Austral.] 'Be off'; 'go away'. Also as *v. intr.*

1916 'MEN OF ANZAC' *Anzac Bk.* 135 It is enough. *Imshee!* [*Note*] Imshee is the Arabic for 'go away'. The Australasian Corps, which had so far employed it only to street hawkers in Cairo, used this war cry on April 25. **1918** R.H. KNYVETT *Over there with Australs.* 83 The first Egyptian word we learned was '*Imshi!*' literally, 'Get!'—but it generally required the backing of a military boot to make it effective. **1921** C.E.W. BEAN *Official Hist. Aust. 1914–18* I. 217 Australians and New Zealanders carried with them for years strange tags of 'Arabic' and broken English, such as 'Imshi Yallah' (Go away). **1933** H.B. RAINE *Lash End* 34 These coves come in and think they can see a bloke soon's they swing the door open. Will I tell him to imshi? **1947** F. CLUNE *Roaming around Aust.* 170 Without any preambles he imshies below the horizon—'leaving the world to the darkness and to me'. **1966** J. WATEN *Season of Youth* 129 You must leave. Imshee and what not.

in, *adv.* Following a verb of motion either expressed or implied, esp. **come**: within the bounds of the settled districts; at a (sheep or cattle) station; in town.

1798 D. COLLINS *Acct. Eng. Colony N.S.W.* (1802) II. 80 Wilson . . lately came in from the woods. **1805** *Sydney Gaz.* 7 July, *The natives*, after giving up the Principal [*sic*] in the late Outrages, having generally expressed a Desire to *come in*, and many being on the Road from Hawkesbury and other Quarters to meet the Governor at Parramatta, *no molestation* whatever is to be offered them. **1839** N.M. TAYLOR *Jrnl. Ensign Best* 6 Mar. (1966) 201 Two of the Men who took the Bush a day or two ago were brought in this morning but *Dignum* is still out. **1849** J.P. TOWNSEND *Rambles & Observations N.S.W.* 76, I had an opportunity of comparing the appearance of blacks, three parts wild, with those who had 'come in', or become partially civilised. **1855** G.H. WATHEN *Golden Colony* 34 The broad 'cabbage-tree' hats and bushy beards of the settlers 'in from the Bush' might attract the notice of the newly arrived. **1865** G.S. LANG *Aborigines of Aust.* 69 When they saw that I wished to make peace, it was painful to see their eagerness to be allowed to 'come in' before the arrival of the black police. **1906** J. PARSONS *Thirty-Six Yrs. amongst Criminals* 37 When the 'backblockers' first came in they purchased a new suit of clothes and made a great show for a few days. **1919** *Bulletin* (Sydney) 9 Oct. 20/2, I was coming in for a spell after 'rousin'' at a run of sheds in the West. **1937** W. HATFIELD *I find Aust.* 104, I met a man who said he was going back again *out-back*! He had come in with store cattle from one of the huge holdings in the Northern Territory, following the course of the Georgina River. **1945** E. GEORGE *Two at Daly Waters* 56 Myalls from other parts of the country came in on walkabouts. **1950** A. GROOM *I saw Strange Land* 10 My wood-cutting camp was . . seventy miles west of the homestead. I rose one hot morning to find that nearly one hundred and fifty natives had 'come in' during the night. **1960** *N.T. News* (Darwin) 22 Jan. 6/4 Visitors to Borroloola recently were old-timer Jack Shadforth and Arthur Alpin, both of whom were in for rations. **1968** LINKLATER & TAPP *Gather no Moss* 84 A group who had been tank-sinking on Brunette Downs started in with good cheques for a rest and a change of diet.

in, *prep.* [Spec. use of *in it* partaking, sharing: see OED(S *prep.* 27.] In the phr. **to be in it,** to take part (in an activity, etc.), usu. with some enthusiasm.

1928 A. WRIGHT *Good Recovery* 37 'It's a queer business,' ventured Trilet, 'and if I am to be in it, I want to know the strength of it.' **1945** 'MASTER-SARG' *Yank discovers Aust.* 17 'To be in it' means to take part in a battle. **1957** D. NILAND *Call me when Cross turns Over* 136 He's got some country to rabbit. He'd like a mate. What about me? Will I be in it? **1965** J. O'GRADY *Aussie Eng.* 47 He wanted to turn on a blue, but I wouldn't be in it. **1973** J. POWERS *Last of Knucklemen* (1974) 74 Tarzan's checkin' to see if any of the engineers are gonna be in it. **1982** R. HALL *Just Relations* 129 Naturally they'd all be in it. They'd hitch a ride down the Yalgoona road with the cheese delivery.

inclusions, *pl.* Soft furnishings as included in the purchase price of a residence.

1970 *Canberra Times* 7 Nov. 31/1 Built on concrete slab. Double carports, quality inclusions. **1974** *Ibid.* 9 Nov. 27/4 Quality inclusions with carport under main roof line. **1978** *Ibid.* 4 Nov. 31/1 An excellent family home for the buyer looking for value, top quality finish and inclusions. **1981** *Ibid.* 4 Nov. 38/7 This is a *solid brick* builders own home with quality inclusions. **1985** *Ibid.* 13 July 5/3 An upgraded kitchen, good quality inclusions and tasteful decor.

incorrigible. *Obs.* A recalcitrant convict.

1827 P. CUNNINGHAM *Two Yrs. in N.S.W.* I. 149 From . . the lazy habits of the *incorrigibles* who are sentenced to this labour, the produce does not at all correspond with what may be expected. **1849** T. ROGERS *Correspondence relating to Dismissal* 72, I would not believe a word he says; he is an incorrigible. **1912** A. BERRY *Reminisc.* 180 We managed our convicts chiefly by moral influence as we had no police. Occasionally we had troubles with incorrigibles.

indent. *Hist.* [Spec. use of *indent* official list.] A document recording the names of a party of convicts transported to Australia and transferring a property in these convicts to the relevant governor, usu. detailing name, date of trial, sentence, etc.

1802 *HRA* (1915) 1st Ser. III. 564 Frauds . . have been practised . . by making an alteration in the indents sent out with the convicts, and thereby shortening the periods by which certain of them were sentenced to transportation. **1803** *Ibid.* IV. 282 The indents cannot be given up . . being the only guide or official document I have for the convicts' terms of transportation. **1812** *Ibid.* (1916) 1st Ser. VII. 615 The regular Indents . . frequently do not arrive until long after the Landing of the Convicts. **1820** *Ibid.* (1917) 1st Ser. X. 333 The Ship Indefatigable . . which arrived here with Male Convicts . . did not bring out, as is usual, any Indents or Deed Poll, whereby the respective Sentences of those Persons can be ascertained. **1828** *Ibid.* (1922) 1st Ser. XIV. 116 To bring under your Notice the very defective nature of the 'Indents' of Convicts sent out from England and Ireland. **1837** *Rep. Select Committee Transportation* 2 The list, or Indent as it is called, containing the names and a short description of the convict, the place where he was tried . . and the term of his transportation. **1841** *Geelong Advertiser* 29 May 2/4 There is a possibility of some error having occurred in the writing or printing of the indents. **1965** L.L. ROBSON *Convict Settlers Aust.* 241 The convict records consolidated as 'Convict Indents' . . vary from little more than lists of convicts' names in the early years to much fuller descriptions after 1825.

indented, *ppl. a. Hist.* [Spec. use of *indented* bound by a formal agreement.] Of a convict: assigned into private service.

1804 *HRA* (1915) 1st Ser. IV. 480 There is now a great demand for indented convicts. **1809** *Ibid.* (1916) 1st Ser. VII. 148 Using various threats (among which to take our Indented Servants from us). **1810** *Sydney Gaz.* 28 July, Female Convicts, whom it is His Excellency the Governor's intention to distribute among the Settlers, as indented Servants. **1816** *Hobart Town Gaz.* 30 Nov., All Persons are hereby Cautioned against Employing Robert Manders, Carpenter, as he is my indented Servant, from the 6th of August last, for twelve months.

Indian. *Hist.* A name formerly applied to an Aboriginal. Also *attrib.*

1770 J. BANKS *Jrnl.* 28 Apr. (1896) 263 Our boat proceeded along shore, and the Indians followed her at a distance. **1788** R. CLARK Jrnl. 19 Feb. 125 The indians had gone to the number of twenty over to the island. **1814** M. FLINDERS *Voyage Terra Australis* I. p. xcviii, Learning from two Indians that no water could be procured at Red Point, we accepted their offer of piloting us to a river. . . These men were natives of Botany Bay. **1823** *First Fruits Austral. Poetry* (ed. 2) 16 This must be the place Where our Columbus of the South did land; He saw the Indian village on that sand, And on this rock first met the simple race Of Australasia. **1829** H. WIDOWSON *Present State Van Diemen's Land* 187 The natives of Van Diemen's Land are unlike any other Indians, either in features, their mode of living, hunting, etc. **1844** *Dispatch* (Sydney) 27 Jan. 2/3 We trust a good collection of Kangaroos, Wild-dogs, Oppossums, Wallabi, Native bears, Emus, Cockatoos, Parrots, and wild Indians, will be got together to welcome the strangers. **1847** T. McCombie *Austral. Sketches* 124 Black sod is the most opprobrious term that you can apply to an Indian. **1872** Mrs E. Millett *Austral. Parsonage* 127 The 'aborigines', as they are now styled . . Captain Cook would in his older time have called 'Indians'.

indications, *pl. S.A. Mining. Obs.* [Also U.S.: see OEDS *indication* 2 b.] Evidence of the presence of ore in sufficient quantity to make mining profitable.

1846 F. Dutton *S.A. & its Mines* 281 Several sections with mineral indications have . . been surveyed by Government. **1847** *S. Austral. Register* (Adelaide) 9 June 2/1 Sydney Company's mine . . is now being explored but without decided success at present; the 'indications' however are said to be good. **1848** *Ibid.* 27 Dec. 3/4 Spending capital upon 'indications' far fetched and dear bought. **1865** *Wallaroo Times* (Kadina) 15 Feb. 2/4 New Cornwall Mine—Present indications are encouraging.

indicator. *Mining.* [Used elsewhere but recorded earliest in Aust.: see OEDS 2 c.] A geological pointer to the presence of gold: see quot. 1932.

1894 *Miner's Handbk.* (Vic. Dept. Mines) 5 Where the gold ceases is usually near and above the line of reef or vein whence it was derived. . . 'Indicators' or small veins of pyrites, ironstone, and often thin bands of peculiar slate, intersected by small quartz veins, should . . be carefully looked for. **1896** J. Holt *Virgin Gold* 83, I have said nothing about the magnificent reefs at Bendigo, the 'indicator' at Ballarat East; the various layers of basalt in the Ballarat West field. **1931** W. Baragwanath et al. *Guide for Prospectors in Vic.* 31 The discovery of 'specimens' (gold attached to quartz) . . attracted the attention of the miners and led them to follow certain belts of strata where such specimens were more abundant than elsewhere. These . . were named indicators. **1932** I.L. Idriess *Prospecting for Gold* 189 Some reefs have 'indicators'. A trail of a particular kind of stone which only occurs with the gold in that reef, will lead right up to the gold. **1966** *Prospectors' Guide* (Vic. Dept. Mines) 37 It was natural that a great deal of importance was attached to 'indicators' by the early prospectors. They were the first indication that any kind of useful clues might be found to assist in a better understanding of the location of gold shoots. *Ibid.* 54 These black slates of the Indicator belt are known as The Indicator, the Pencil Mark, and the Black Seam; the two last-named are comparable with The Indicator in regard to deposition of gold. **1979** *Australasian Post* (Melbourne) 3 May 2/4 An important key to making a strike is to find mineral 'indicators', which are thin veins of bright mica-bearing material sandwiched in the rock. The places where these 'indicators' intersect with quartz reefs are where coarse gold is usually found.

indigo. [Spec. use of *indigo* plant of the genus *Indigofera* yielding a blue dye.] **a.** Any of several plants of the genus *Indigofera* (fam. Fabaceae), esp. the widespread *I. australis* of all States, having pinnate leaves and (usu. purple) flowers; *native indigo*, see Native *a.* 6 a.; *wild indigo*, see Wild 1. **b.** (Rarely) any of several species of *Swainsona* (fam. Fabaceae), esp. *S. galegifolia.*

1825 B. Field *Geogr. Mem. N.S.W.* 181 We penetrated through a barren forest of box, abounding in brushes of the native indigo (indigofera australis). **1834** G. Bennett *Wanderings N.S.W.* I. 115, I remarked the Indigo shrub . . abundant, and I was told that indigo of good quality has been prepared from it at Bathurst. **1861** J.D. Lang *Qld., Aust.* 189 Indigo is indigenous in Australia, and could be cultivated. **1901** J.H. Maiden *Plants reputed to be Poisonous* 14 *Indigofera australis* . . 'Australian indigo', closely allied to the indigo of commerce (*Indigofera tinctoria*), but not to be confused with *Swainsona*, commonly called 'indigo' in this colony. **1903** G. Sutherland *Australasian Live Stock Man.* (ed. 2) 387 Among the sheep in the Darling River district, the 'indigo-eaters' in the flock are like the most abandoned opium-eaters. **1942** C. Barrett *Austral. Wild Flower Bk.* 50 Its lilac or blue flowers, borne in short racemes, are so attractive that many an indigo plant is despoiled of its early summer beauty. **1981** A.B. & J.W. Cribb *Useful Wild Plants Aust.* 70 Of the native species of *Indigofera*, none has been significant as a dye source. In the early days of European settlement here, vigorous attempts were made to find native dyes, and the Australian indigo was one of the earliest plants investigated.

Indon /ˈɪndɒn/. Abbrev. of 'Indonesian'. Also as *adj.*

1972 J. Hibberd *Stretch of Imagination* (1973) 37 The Indon and Kanaka we will civilize. **1982** *Age* (Melbourne) 30 June 10/6 (*heading*) End Indon arms aid, inquiry told. **1983** *Nat. Times* (Sydney) 13 May 2/2 Intriguing is the request recently made by the Indonesian Government to the Department of Foreign Affairs in Canberra. The Indons want to know the sleeve measurement of the Prime Minister, Bob Hawke.

indulge, *v. Hist. trans.* To grant (a convict) some mitigation of the conditions under which a sentence is being served. Chiefly in *pass.*

1805 *Sydney Gaz.* 14 July, Several of the Prisoners under Sentence of the Law . . have been indulged with Permission to be off the Stores on Tickets of Leave. **1832** J. Backhouse *Narr. Visit Austral. Colonies* (1843) 19 They would in the course of a proper time, be indulged with a ticket-of-leave. **1840** *S. Austral. Rec.* (London) 4 July 3 This person, it appears, was transported for fourteen years: his wife followed him to the colony and established a shop, and he was indulged with an exemption from labour. **1849** J.P. Townsend *Rambles & Observations N.S.W.* 221 When a 'lifer' had held a ticket-of-leave for six years, and could produce good testimonials to character, he was further indulged with a conditional pardon.

indulgence. *Hist.* A mitigation of the conditions under which a convict's sentence is served.

1794 D. Collins *Acct. Eng. Colony N.S.W.* (1798) I. 391 Some warrants of emancipation passed the seal of the territory and received the lieutenant-governor's signature. The objects of this indulgence were, Robert Lidaway . . and William Leach. **1803** *Sydney Gaz.* 28 Aug., A Situation wanted, Michael Hares from an Indulgence granted him is desirous to engage as an *accomptant* in a Mercantile situation. **1814** L. Macquarie *Lett.* 10 Sept. (1821) 86 Those Government Men who have the indulgence of cultivating ground, and rearing stock . . frequently become receivers of stolen grain and provisions. **1828** *Tasmanian* (Hobart) 12 Dec. 4 Married men, or men of particular good conduct . . are permitted the indulgence of sleeping out of Barracks. **1837** *Cornwall Chron.* (Launceston) 26 Aug. 1 Certain it is, that the indulgence of a 'Ticket-of-leave' to a prisoner tradesman in a comfortable assigned service, is a disadvantage to him. **1847** *Maitland Mercury* 22 Sept. 4/5 A general muster of all prisoners of the crown holding tickets of leave . . when all persons holding the indulgence are required to attend personally. **1849** T. Rogers *Corresp. relating to Dismissal* 154 It had been the custom at Norfolk Island to grant an *indulgence* to such prisoners as performed the office of hangman. **1858** N.L. Kentish *Treatise on Penal Discipline* 24 The runaway's indulgence shall be cancelled, and he returned to the Government to work in a Road-gang.

informal, *a.* Of a vote or ballot paper: invalid. Also as quasi-*adv.* in the phr. **to vote informal.**

1948 R. Raven-Hart *Canoe in Aust.* 66 The official (not slang) uses of 'to be financial' for to have paid one's dues, and of 'informal vote' for our invalid vote were . . novelties. **1963** R. McGregor-Hastie *Compleat Migrant* 64 Alas, your vote for him does not count. It is called an 'informal vote'. **1984** *Courier-Mail* (Brisbane) 5 Dec. 4/7 Saturday's large informal vote was, I hope, the start of a strong and healthy reaction against trivialised TV democracy. *Ibid.*, I voted informal for the first time in my life, and did it with a clear conscience.

inked, *ppl. a.* [Obscurely f. *ink.*] Intoxicated.

1898 *Bulletin* (Sydney) 1 Oct. 14/3 To have a whisky is to 'oil up'; . . to get drunk is to get 'inked'. **1910** *Ibid.* 20 Jan. 15/1, I was witness to a brawl in a pub yard . . between five inked-up Hindus and two half-inked white Australians. **1918** *Aussie: Austral. Soldiers' Mag.* Oct. 11/2 Digger (rescued by cobbers in an inked condition): 'Hey, cobber—hic—'old on a bit.' **1940** *Bulletin* (Sydney) 19 June 16/1 Got home from the town well-inked one Sunday morning. **1947** N. Lindsay *Halfway to Anywhere* 181 Are you on for getting properly stonkered on beer? . . How much you got for buying enough to get inked on. **1969** P. Adam Smith *Folklore Austral. Railwaymen* 85 Driver found well and truly inked and lying down to it.

inkweed. The tropical American perennial herb *Phytolacca octandra* (fam. Phytolaccaceae) of all mainland States but not N.T., having a fruit which is purplish-black when ripe and yields a red juice.

[N.Z. **1906** T.F. Cheeseman *N.Z. Flora* 1085 *Phytolacca octandra* . . Ink-plant; Poke-weed.] **1909** *Emu* VIII. 278 Red-winged Lories . . feeding . . on the introduced ink-weed. **1920** *Bulletin* (Sydney) 24 June 20/2 'What is it?' I demanded. 'Ink-weed, miss.' . . I crushed some of the dark red berries, and the documents were despatched in their full British glory. **1933** H.J. Carter *Gulliver in Bush* 73 Most gorgeous were the satin bower-birds and the regent-birds, of which both sexes used to display themselves at dawn—feeding on inkweed and wild raspberries at the edge of the jungle. **1981** A.B. & J.W. Cribb *Useful Wild Plants Aust.* 222 Inkweed is closely related to the American pokeweed, well-known in herbal medicine; the pokeweed has been introduced to Australia but is uncommon.

inky, *a.* [f. Inked.] Intoxicated. Also **inky-poo.**

1907 *Truth* (Sydney) 28 Apr. 9/7 He was 'inky', but was happy, for he roared with mad refrain, 'Salley Stiggins, show your pegs and drink your beer!' **1915** *Bulletin* (Sydney) 22 Apr. 24/2 Smith was 'inky'; he was screwed; in sober earnest, he was 'foo'. **1929** W.J. Reside *Golden Days* 372 You turned the old camp upside down and made us inky-poo. **1955** A. Upfield *Cake in Hat Box* 5 'Doc in town?' asked Silas of the licensee. 'Yes, but he's inky-poo. Be out to it till morning.' **1965** R. Fair *Treasury Anzac Humour* 38 Well, he . . was very particular about the rum issue. . . The offsider . . was usually a bit inky.

Inland. [Spec. use of *inland* interior part of a country.] With **the:** the sparsely populated interior of Australia; the outback; the inhabitants of this region collectively. Also *attrib.*

1912 *Messenger Presbyterian Church N.S.W.* 29 Nov. 764/3 The '*Australian Inland Mission*'. . . The Presbyterian Church is launching an enterprise which it is fondly hoped . . will be of the utmost importance to the national well-being of the continent. **1923** J. Armour *Spell of Inland* 5 The spell of the Inland settles upon train, passengers and officials. **1932** I.L. Idriess *Flynn of Inland* (1965) 180 As to the outer Inland he found great areas of it completely transformed under motor transport. **1935** R.B. Plowman *Boundary Rider* 4 There are certain qualifications necessary for the man who has to knock about the Inland, whether he be stockman, teamster, swagman. **1948** H.A. Lindsay *Bushman's Handbk.* 23 When a drought breaks over the Inland, the most striking result is the ringing frog chorus. **1951** G. Farwell *Outside Track* 11 Snaring birds was simply a means of reaching the vastness and the silences of the Inland. **1956** H. Hudson *Flynn's Flying Doctors* 194 The Country Women's Association . . holds its meetings through the Flying Doctor network, with all the Inland listening. **1972** C. Duguid *Doctor & Aborigines* 134 It was the coldest trip that I have ever made through the Inland.

inlander. Freq. with initial capital. [Spec. use of *inlander* one who dwells in the interior of a country.] One who lives in the sparsely populated interior of Australia.

1911 E.S. Sorenson *Life in Austral. Backblocks* 282 There is one thing about the inlander that favourably impresses itself upon those who have to look after a city's water supply, and that is his careful use of the liquid. **1913** *Inlander* Nov. 3 Surely, if any man deserves our friendship the Inlander more than deserves our very best. This man . . silently makes his way where few have trodden. **1925** *Makeshifts & Other Home-Made Furniture* (New Settlers League Aust.) 70 A scheme for the inlander . . a call from the inland. **1930** *Bulletin* (Sydney) 13 Aug. 21/4 Many inlanders of the Ma State would be glad to see some of the nonpaying railways scrapped. **1932** I.L. Idriess *Flynn of Inland* (1965) 166 A great turnout that for fleeting moments brings the breath of companionship to many lonely Inlanders. **1956** H. Hudson *Flynn's Flying Doctors* 119 Although separated by immense distances, these Inlanders have developed a keener community spirit and a more intimate interchange of ideas than some suburban dwellers. **1962** *N. Austral. Monthly* Feb. 29/2 A Mission which would concentrate on making the Christian Gospel a reality to inlanders.

inside, *a.* and *adv.*

A. *adj.*

1. a. Of or pertaining to a (comparatively) closely settled part of Australia.

1864 R. HENNING *Lett.* (1952) 73 When Biddulph first took up Exmoor it was the very outside run northwards. . . Now it is quite an inside station, every bit of country is taken up for several hundred miles round it. **1879** *Queenslander* (Brisbane) 19 Apr. 492/4 At any of the large stations upon the 'inside' borders . . they work hard and the life is rough enough. **1881** A.C. GRANT *Bush-Life Qld.* II. 171 Stations were formed for nearly a hundred and fifty miles outside John's run, and he began to regard himself as quite an inside squatter. **1899** *Bulletin* (Sydney) 24 June 16/1 Anybody ever comment on difference of status between 'inside' and outback policemen. Inside, commoners; out-back, toffs—who mix only with squatters and such. **1913** W.K. HARRIS *Outback in Aust.* 48 While the 'Inside' man has enjoyed almost uninterrupted prosperity, the 'Outback' pioneers have many ups and downs. **1922** *Bulletin* (Sydney) 23 Mar. 22/4 She had never seen a train. One expects to find such cases in the back country, but with 'inside' people it is hard to understand. **1923** *Ibid.* 4 Jan. 22/2 I've had over 40 years of droving, with both 'inside' and 'outside' stock.

b. In the collocation **inside country.**

1902 *Blackwood's Mag.* (Edinburgh) May 639 We can always make tucker shootin' kangaroos and emus . . an' if any man wants a cheque bad, for a spell or anything, he can always go shearing inside country. **1910** C.E.W. BEAN *On Wool Track* p. viii, City-bred Australians go very little into the 'outside' country . . or if they do, they return to the 'inside' country where life is easier and profits are as large. **1928** R.M. MACDONALD *Opals & Gold* 181 We were still in 'inside country', as the vast grazing land between the railway's far-flung terminals and the coast is termed. **1949** G. FARWELL *Traveller's Tracks* 16 The Darling is something of a frontier. . . It separates the familiar and well settled Inside Country from the far west, the great and mysterious Outside. **1954** T. RONAN *Vision Splendid* 148 Queensland! The wonderful 'inside' country from which most of the men he knew had come. **1980** S. THORNE *I've met some Bloody Wags* 115 He was a prime example of 'mulga madness'. Given a good drench and put on a small lush block in the 'inside country' he would be a new man.

2. Having some expectation of accommodation in the house (as distinct from the huts) of a sheep or cattle station.

1936 *Bulletin* (Sydney) 30 Dec. 20/1 These old chaps, gentlemen once, would sooner camp on the creek and go hungry than go to the hut. They were 'inside men, by gad, sir!' and if they couldn't put their legs under the manager's table they spread them under the coolibah.

B. *adv.*

1. Within a more closely settled part of Australia. Also as quasi-*n.*

1909 *Bulletin* (Sydney) 28 Oct. 13/3, 1000 head of fat bullocks . . from the Northern Territory . . going 'inside' for sale. **1924** *Ibid.* 15 July 38 With nose-bags well-filled—I had been good cobbers with the poisoner—we started for 'Inside'. **1937** W. HATFIELD *I find Aust.* 104 He had come in with store cattle from one of the huge holdings in the Northern Territory, following the course of the Georgina River, and he said he didn't like going any farther 'inside'. **1954** H.G. LAMOND *Manx Star* 259 *Inside*, back-country men refer to 'inside' near the coast or city. **1965** G.W. BROUGHTON *Turn again Home* 50 'Inside', as men in the North called all the southern part of Australia. **1976** C.D. MILLS *Hobble Chains & Greenhide* 21 The other tracks had lined out straight for country 'inside'. **1984** *Good Weekend* (Sydney) 20 Oct. 24/1 The Charnleys think they have been out west long enough and next year they will take their two children 'down inside', somewhere east of Bourke.

2. In the house of the owner or manager of a sheep or cattle station.

1930 *Bulletin* (Sydney) 5 Mar. 25/1 Among the allegedly 'silvertail' jobs of Outback is that of station book-keeper. Its lucky possessor lives 'inside'.

intercolonial, *a. Hist.* Existing, conducted, etc., between two or more Australian Colonies.

1841 H.S. CHAPMAN *New Settlement Australind* 40 Steam . . in a very few years will be established, at all events for inter-colonial, if not for European intercourse. **1855** G.H. WATHEN *Golden Colony* 202 The squabble has, in fact, all the threatening aspect of the commencement of inter-colonial warfare. **1863** *Bell's Life in Sydney* 6 June 2/1 This emanation of intercolonial sagacity. **1866** *Austral. Monthly Mag.* (Melbourne) II. 154 (*heading*) Intercolonial musical festival. **1873** A. TROLLOPE *Aust. & N.Z.* I. 343 Who would willingly multiply such barriers, and accumulate the sure means of intercolonial irritation? **1882** *Illustr. Austral. News* (Melbourne) 5 Aug. 122/3 The intercolonial ploughing match . . was . . one of the most important events . . that has ever taken place in Victoria. **1892** *Truth* (Sydney) 22 May 3/2 'Victoria, New South Wales, and South Australia are provoked by one another's border taxation.' . . Intercolonial taxation will be abandoned. **1900** *Ibid.* 4 Feb. 6/2 The last intercolonial match of the season has ended in a victory for New South Wales.

Hence **intercolonially** *adv.*

1891 E.H. HALLACK *W.A. & Yilgarn Goldfields* 27 Talk about federation and the small part intercolonially the colony must, from her position, necessarily play.

intermediate, *a. Hist.*

a. Of a tract of land: lying between a part of the country which is settled and one which is not yet settled.

1847 *Britannia* (Hobart) 26 Aug. 4/3 The lands of New South Wales are to be divided into the settled, the intermediate, and the unsettled districts. **1847** *Port Phillip Herald* 9 Sept. 2/4 The settled district of Geelong is equal to an average-sized English county. . . This is saying nothing of the intermediate district, the limits of which remain to be defined, and which, to all intents and purposes, will be a mere extension of the settled district. **1852** W. HUGHES *Austral. Colonies* 127 In the settled districts, the lease is enjoyable for one year only; in the intermediate, for eight years; in the unsettled (or ultra-frontier) lands—which are those of the greatest extent—for the term of fourteen years. **1855** G.H. WATHEN *Golden Colony* 212 All the lands in the colony were divided into three classes,—the *settled*, or that around the towns, the *intermediate*, and the *unsettled*. **1882** W. COOTE *Hist. Colony Qld.* 74 The colony of New South Wales was divided into 'settled' 'intermediate' and 'unsettled' districts.

b. Of a person: living in such a part of the country.

1902 *Bulletin* (Sydney) 8 Feb. 32/4 The intermediate man, neither out-backer nor 'inside man' . . is met with about Winton, Cloncurry, the Birdsville district . . [etc.].

interstate, *a.* and *adv.*

A. *adj.*

1. Chiefly since Federation: existing, conducted, etc., between two or more Australian States.

1900 *Advocate* (Burnie) 24 Apr. 2/5 It is provided by the Bill that all inter-state duties must be repealed by the end of two years. **1910** *Huon Times* (Franklin) 24 Sept. 2/2 The allegations made were unjustifiable and born of an inter-State jealousy. **1920** H.F. MOLLARD *Humour of Road* 72 Interstate barriers will go down before trade. **1943** M. LAMB *Red glows Dawn* 5 As far back as 1924 the Inter-State Australian Labour [*sic*] Party Conference agreed. **1958** *Bulletin* (Sydney) 9 July 16/4 Let us now praise inter-State transport-drivers! **1963** V.B. CRANLEY *27,000 Miles through Aust.* 145 Australia is so afraid of disease—witness the strict interstate plant control. **1980** C. LEE *Bush Week* 54, I hitched a lift with a truckie in an interstate hauler. **1986** *Canberra Times* 15 Mar. 16/5 For details of interstate buses in and out of Canberra, telephone Ansett Pioneer.

2. Of a person, etc.: in or belonging to an Australian State other than that in which one is normally resident; 'out-of-state'.

1903 *Emu* II. 138 Mr J.W. Mellor, on behalf of the two inter-State visitors. **1911** H.G. TURNER *First Decade Austral. Cwlth.* 19 Prominent officials, and distinguished interstate visitors. **1927** *R. Comm. on Wireless* 3098 Reception at Tumut from Sydney and Interstate stations. **1948** *Bulletin* (Sydney) 24 Mar. 28/2 Tasmania's oldest apple-tree . . has attracted inter-State visitors for many years. **1957** J. WATEN *Shares in Murder* 78 'Who were the blokes?' 'Some interstate business men.' **1960** *N.T. News* (Darwin) 19 Feb. 9/5 Anyone found driving with an interstate licence was regarded as 'driving without a licence'. **1972** *Bulletin* (Sydney) 29 July 34/1 Our first Preview Pack is now available *for interstate and country members.* **1977** D. WILLIAMSON *Club* (1978) 23 Some interstate club might offer you money.

B. *adv.* In, into, or from an Australian State other than that in which one is (normally) resident. Also as quasi-*n.*

1957 J. WATEN *Shares in Murder* 110 Stan's away interstate. **1960** J. GLENNON *Heart in Centre* 85 'Jerry Franklin is going away next Sunday.' 'Back home?' 'Interstate somewhere.' **1965** K. SMITH *OGF* 124 Would any Australian businessman go interstate without a living allowance. **1971** *Bulletin* (Sydney) 9 Jan. 41/1 About 500,000 Australians . . are going to be transferred interstate or to the country this year. **1977** D. WILLIAMSON *Club* (1978) 24 When you decide to go interstate and make some money you'll need our signature. **1985** *Canberra Times* 2 Sept. 3/3 Police said . . the man they are seeking had only recently arrived in Adelaide from interstate. **1986** *Ibid.* 15 Mar. 9/4 House for sale. . . Owner moving interstate.

invalid gang. *Hist.* A detachment of convicts unfit for hard work.

1832 BACKHOUSE & TYLOR *Life & Labours G.W. Walker* (1862) 47 We arrived at Deep Gully, where the huts of an Invalid Gang are situated. . . Many of them are labouring under debility or indisposition, the result of intemperance, others are cripples or superannuated. **1846** L.W. MILLER *Notes of Exile Van Dieman's Land* 342 Miller, you look very ill. You cannot be able to perform such heavy work, and I shall shift you to the invalid gang. **1848** R. MARSH *Seven Yrs. of my Life* 118 There was what was called the invalid gang; picking up brush, &c.

Irish-Australian. A person of Irish descent normally resident in Australia. Also as *adj.*

1907 *Westminster Gaz.* (London) 17 Sept. 1/3 The . . Irish-Australian baronet. **1916** *Truth* (Sydney) 26 Mar. 3/4 Michael Dwyer . . was, as all Irish-Australians know, banished from his native country. **1932** J. MAXWELL *Hell's Bells* 7 A lumbering, carefree Irish-Australian, with a heart of gold. **1946** A.H. CHISHOLM *Making of Sentimental Bloke* 55 A scholastic but breezy Irish-Australian lawyer. **1958** F. HARDY *Four-Legged Lottery* 101 O'Donnell was an Irish Australian. **1966** *Bulletin* (Sydney) 22 Jan. 13/3 It is not easy for an Irish-Australian to pay tribute to a Pom. **1971** *Ibid.* 24 Apr. 58/2 (*caption*) At Waverly Cemetery, Sydney, in 1966 Irish Australians celebrate the 50th anniversary of the Easter Uprising.

iron, *n.*

1. *Hist.* Used *attrib.* in Special Comb. to denote a fetter: **iron collar,** a band of iron worn round the neck; **iron gang,** IRONED GANG; see also *single iron* SINGLE *a.*, *double irons* DOUBLE *a.* 1; also *attrib.*

1791 D. COLLINS *Acct. Eng. Colony N.S.W.* (1798) I. 165 To make it a chearful day to every one, all offenders who had for stealing Indian corn been ordered to wear **iron collars** were pardoned. **1792** *Ibid.* 199 She [*sc.* a convict] was detected . . and was ordered to wear an iron collar for six months as a punishment. **1793** P.G. KING *Jrnl. Norfolk Island* 86, I ordered the culprits to be punished with Twenty-five Lashes; to wear an Iron Collar and to keep in the Penitentiary for Two months. **1833** *Sydney Herald* 23 Sept. (Suppl.) 1/1 She was sentenced . . to wear the iron collar—and to have her head shaved. **1829** *Sydney Monitor* 3 Jan. 1453/4 A large party of prisoners destined for **iron gangs** at remote parts of the interior, left the Sydney Gaol. **1831** *Sydney Herald* 16 May 4/1, 56 men were forwarded from the gaol . . to be distributed among various iron gangs. **1832** J. HENDERSON *Observations Colonies N.S.W. & Van Diemen's Land* 14 The second punishment is, the iron-gangs, where the prisoners are worked in chains, on the roads, in large parties. **1836** J.F. O'CONNELL *Residence Eleven Yrs. New Holland* 72 Iron gangs labor under heavy guards of soldiers in clearing tracts of land in the interior, all wearing gyves, proportioned in weight to their crimes. **1839** T.P. BESNARD *Voice from Bush* 17 Lately the Governor has sent some iron-gangs to make a road through the plains. **1847** A. MARJORIBANKS *Travels*

N.S.W. 71 Iron-gangmen not allowed to be hut-keepers, cooks, or other occupations, as such is considered an indulgence. **1848** *Heads of People* (Sydney) 12 Feb. 132 The prisoners on Cockatoo Island . . are serving iron gang sentences. **1851** *Empire* (Sydney) 30 Dec. 519/3 Upon examining them he found they were branded with an iron gang mark. **1882** MRS J.C. STANGER *Journey from Sydney* 15 At the bottom of Soldier's Pinch is another cluster of huts belonging to the iron-gang Station. **1900** W. DELAFORCE *Life & Experiences Ex-Convict Port Macquarie* 19 He was thereupon caught by the collar and taken off to the watchhouse, and was sentenced to two months in the iron gang.

2. Used *attrib.* in Comb. to distinguish a structure made wholly or partly of sheets of (corrugated) iron.

1859 W. BURROWS *Adventures Mounted Trooper* 45 The men no longer live in tents, but have also a good row of iron houses. **1861** L.A. MEREDITH *Over Straits* 267 Leaving the iron-roofed station we again galloped and galloped all afternoon. **1882** W.B. CHRISTIE *Our Land Laws* 14 Iron houses having portable frames sprang up all over the country. **1882** W. SOWDEN *N.T. as it Is* 11 You can't see much of Cooktown from the offing—only (besides some iron stores) a handsome snow-white villa. **1887** MRS D.D. DALY *Digging, Squatting, & Pioneering Life* 51 The iron roof was shaded by bark. **1897** *Bulletin* (Sydney) 13 Nov. 31/1 In the same old iron shanty, looking bold as bold can be, There's a tow-haired girl a-serving, and I know she's fancy free. *Ibid.* 11 Dec. 29/1 Dusty patch in baking mulga—glaring iron hut and shed. **1922** 'J. BUSHMAN' *In Musgrave Ranges* 49 The glitter of iron roofs in the sun. **1941** C. BARRETT *Aust.* 105 The little iron-roofed farmhouse was a furnace in summertime. **1950** V.E. TURNER *Ooldea* 6 It was a sandy basin with sandhills surrounding some remains of iron huts. **1963** X. HERBERT *Disturbing Element* 5 Our little weatherboard and iron houses used . . to quiver to the thunder of Mother's pianoforte. **1983** *Sydney Morning Herald* 30 Apr. 32/7 His modest fibro and iron home in the township was bought on an eight-year term loan with repayments of $245 a month.

3. *fig. Obs.* [See quot. 1899.] In the collocation **good iron,** deserving of approbation. Freq. as *exclam.*

1894 E. TURNER *Seven Little Australians* (1912) 54 'Good iron,' Pip whistled softly, while he revolved the thing in his mind. **1895** *Bulletin* (Sydney) 9 Feb. 15/4 Oh, she's good iron, is my little clinah; She's my cobber an' I'm 'er bloke. **1899** *Ibid.* 22 Apr. 14/3 'Ringer' and 'good iron' are both derived from the game of quoits. . . 'Good iron' corresponds to 'good ball' at cricket. **1908** *Austral. Mag.* (Sydney) Nov. 1250/2 'Good iron', a very approbatory ejaculation, comes from quoits, the players in the old days being wont to call the phrase after the manner of 'good ball' of the cricketers. **1916** J.B. COOPER *Coo-oo-ee!* 305 'Good iron, Martin!' replied one man, followed by murmurs of approval throughout the bar. **1936** M. FRANKLIN *All that Swagger* (1980) 267 'Sure, it's come-aisy, go-aisy,' Grandfather remarked. 'And that is 'good-iron wingey!' till there's a stoppage in the come-easy part,' added William. **1941** S.J. BAKER *Pop. Dict. Austral. Slang* 35 *Good iron*, . . (something) good, pleasant, desired. **1965** J.S. GUNN *Terminol. Shearing Industry* ii. 10 In the early days when men were isolated at the sheds, quoits was a popular game. . . Iron rings were used, and the one who beat the rest was the 'ringer'. This term 'ringer' and 'good iron' for the shed's best shearer suggests an origin.

iron, *v. trans.* To knock (someone) down. Usu. with **out.**

1953 S.J. BAKER *Aust. Speaks* 104 *To iron*, to attack or fight (a person) i.e. *to flatten* him. **1963** *Footy Fan* (Melbourne) I. iv. 5 Murray's public image does not bring him off-the-field abuse other than from the supporter of some player he may have ironed out. **1969** *Sporting Globe* (Melbourne) 12 July 10/3 Rollinson was 'ironed out' in a centre clash by a big Collingwood ruckman. **1973** J. POWERS *Last of Knucklemen* (1974) 20 All right, he's a tough old guy. He's ironed a few fellers out. **1984** *Sunday Independent* (Perth) 9 Sept. 86/3 He was absolutely ironed out . . with a shirt-front bump that you could feel in the press box.

ironbark.

1. Any of several trees of the genus *Eucalyptus* (fam. Myrtaceae) having a characteristic thick, hard, deeply furrowed, usu. black bark and occurring in e. Aust.; the wood of these trees. Also with distinguishing epithet, as **broad-leaved, grey, narrow-leaved, red, silver-leaved, white** (see under first element), and *attrib.*

1799 D. COLLINS *Acct. Eng. Colony N.S.W.* (1802) II. 145 A sort of gum tree, the bark of which along the trunk is that of the iron bark of Port Jackson. **1827** P. CUNNINGHAM *Two Yrs. in N.S.W.* I. 98 Houses in Paramatta are . . roofed . . with iron-bark shingles. **1843** *Satirist & Sporting Chron.* (Sydney) 11 Feb. 2/3 The Australian was ushered into the ring by a body of his countrymen, stalwart and sturdy-looking as the iron-bark trees of their native forests. **1852** G.C. MUNDY *Our Antipodes* I. 156 The Ironbark, with its tall, black, upright, and rugose trunk. **1864** *Illustr. Sydney News* 16 June 10/1 In a piece of iron bark scrub . . we were stopped by three bushrangers. **1881** C.F. CHUBB *Fugitive Pieces* 20 Hearts that were harder than ironbark. **1904** J.H. MAIDEN *Notes on Commercial Timbers N.S.W.* 8 Ironbark is the king of New South Wales hardwoods. **1935** F. CLUNE *Rolling down Lachlan* 11 The main shaft was an ironbark log. **1974** N. PHILLIPSON *As Other Men* 114 A rough-hewn slab of ironbark that served as the doorstep.

2. *fig.* (Something) hard, unyielding; of notable quality. Freq. *attrib.* passing into *adj.*

1833 *Currency Lad* (Sydney) 30 Mar. 2 We would advise all such iron bark politicians . . to resume the strains of Orpheus of old and 'fiddle to the trees!' **1845** *Star* (Sydney) 25 Oct. 1/2 Braveo Billy! You're a right good, proper mark; There's no stringy stuff about you, You're the real iron-bark. **1894** *Western Champion* (Barcaldine) 2 Jan. 2/1 The tucker at Charley's was not quite up to the Café Royal Style; salt junk about six months old and ironbark damper. **1907** *Truth* (Sydney) 14 July 1/8 'Girls are not like they were in my young days,' said an elderly ironbark lady seated in an Abbotsford tram. **1982** P. RADLEY *My Blue-Checker Corker* 93 In Allsopp annals there was never a greater knighthood than to be dubbed a Jack Robertson. It was the pinnacle. The ironbark of the bush.

3. Special Comb. **ironbark pumpkin,** a variety of pumpkin having an exceptionally tough skin. Also *ellipt.* as **ironbark.**

1849 A. HARRIS *Guide Port Stephens* 96 Pumpkin . . especially the iron-bark species, as large as a bucket, and, literally in favourable seasons and soils, covering the ground. **1867** J.R. HOULDING *Austral. Capers* 416 A tunderin grate big iron-bark pumpkin wud come rattlin down. **1917** *Bulletin* (Sydney) 4 Oct. 22/3 The best substitute for tobacco is crushed pumpkin seeds, ironbark preferred, sprinkled with a very small quantity of rum. **1943** *Signals* (Melbourne) Christmas 43 Iron-bark pumpkin to attack with knives that were never sharp enough. **1966** J. WATEN *Season of Youth* 29 He was an enthusiast for pumpkins . . the grey-blue ironbarks, Queensland blues. **1974** B. KIDMAN *On Wallaby* 96 Ironbark pumpkins . . made a welcome addition to our ration food.

ironed gang. *Hist.* A detachment of convicts assigned to hard labour in fetters; *iron gang*, see IRON *n.* 1. See *chain gang* CHAIN *n.*[1] 1. Also *attrib.*

1832 *Currency Lad* (Sydney) 6 Oct. 1 Superintendents of ironed gangs. **1834** *HRA* (1923) 1st Ser. XVII. 316 Repair of the old roads as well as the construction of new by means of the ironed Gangs only. **1839** *Sydney Standard* 21 Jan. 3/2 *Thomas Skinner*, stealing from the person, twelve months to an ironed gang. **1841** *Sydney Herald* 4 Jan. 2/5 He was appointed constable to the ironed-gang stockade, but allowed to reside at home. **1848** C. COZENS *Adventures of Guardsman* 109 A kind of small penal settlement, where prisoners suffering under a local sentence to an 'ironed gang' . . were sent. **1852** G.C. MUNDY *Our Antipodes* III. 320 A convict of an ironed gang, working on the roads near Bathurst, was flogged for having in his possession a lump of rough gold.

ironshot. BUCK-SHOT (*attrib.* in quots.).

1902 *Blackwood's Mag.* (Edinburgh) May 643 We plunged into a clump of gidgyas, and in a few minutes burst out on the ironshot plain. **1916** A.I. MACLEOD *Hack's Brat* (1920) 3 The whole sandy, iron-shot slopes near him dotted with spasmodic groups of dry saltbush.

ironstone.

1. A hard, sedimentary rock rich in iron oxides (see quot. 1967). Freq. *attrib.*

1843 *Sydney Morning Herald* 12 July 2/6 Large masses of iron ore, or iron-stone, as the colonists call it. **1869** *Illustr. Sydney News* 13 May 184/2 Stony in places, as also are the ridges, quartz and iron stone cropping out in places. **1891** *Braidwood Dispatch* 4 Feb. 2/5 A new discovery has been made . . about one mile south-east of the Crystal Hill Prospecting Claim. . . A shaft on an iron stone lode, showing peacock ore on the surface for a long distance. **1912** T.E. SPENCER *Bindawalla* 98 Crossed the ironstone ridge at a gallop. **1935** F. BIRTLES *Battle Fronts Outback* 146 Under the blazing sun the hard ironstone soil became as hot as the Hobs of Hades. **1948** G.W. LEEPER *Introd. Soil Science* 43 'Ironstone gravel' or 'buckshot' . . varies greatly in size, shape (round or angular), hardness, and chemical composition. . . In the great majority of cases this gravel is absent from the parent material, so it is clear that it has been formed in the soil. **1967** R.O. CHALMERS *Austral. Rocks* 30 *Ironstone*, as the term is used in England, Europe and America, strictly applies to shales heavily impregnated with siderite. . . There are beds of this rock . . in the Sydney district. However more generally in Australia, this name popularly applies to sandstones, siltstones, and shales that are coloured various shades of brown, red and purple, and are hard, due to the amount of iron oxide present. **1978** D. STUART *Wedge-tail View* 2 Swirl shuffled her front hooves on the ironstone pebbles, and he heeled her hard to get her moving.

2. *Tas. Obs.* An igneous rock, prob. dolerite, used in the construction of buildings and roads.

1852 MRS C. MEREDITH *My Home in Tas.* I. 161 The walls of our cottage were to be built of the common 'iron-stone' of the country. **1863** F. ALGAR *Handbk. to Colony Tas.* 9 A stone, commonly called 'Ironstone', a species of trap, and admirably adapted for road-making exists everywhere in vast quantities.

iron tree. IRONWOOD. Also *attrib.*

1830 W.J. HOOKER *Bot. Miscellany* I. 241 They [*sc.* fig-trees] had immediately vegetated, and thrown out their parasitical and rapacious roots, which adhering close to the bark of the *Iron Tree*, had followed the course of its stem downwards to the earth. **1853** W. WESTGARTH *Vic.* 253 The punch of an iron tree waddy upon the skull of an aboriginal lubra. **1861** J.D. LANG *Qld., Aust.* 82 The specimen . . had fortunately attached itself to an iron-tree—the hardest and heaviest species of timber in the district. **1886** F.A. HAGENAUER *Rep. Aboriginal Mission Ramahyuck, Vic.* 47 You can see . . the iron tree. **1979** R. DUFFIELD *Rogue Bull* 69 The 'iron tree' . . is a scrawny, rubbery-looking plant which in the Hamersleys grows out of the sheer face of perpendicular rock, in seeming defiance of nature.

ironwood. [Spec. use of *ironwood* the hard wood of any of various trees: see OED.] Any of several trees yielding a particularly hard, heavy timber, esp. *Acacia estrophiolata* and *A. excelsa* (fam. Mimosaceae), and *Erythrophleum chlorostachys* (fam. Caesalpiniaceae) of n. Aust.; the wood of these trees. Also *attrib.*

1802 G. BARRINGTON *Hist. N.S.W.* 479 They . . made fast a club of iron wood, which the cannibals had left in the boat. **1834** *Perth Gaz.* 10 May 283 We saw the first specimens of the large glaucus [*sic*]-leaved acacia or wattle, so common in the York District, and called by the settlers iron wood. **1885** *Once a Month* (Melbourne) June 455 What is called the ironwood-tree is an acacia. The wood is so hard as to render it useless for fencing. **1891** 'OLD TIME' *Convict Hulk 'Success'* 25 One of the convicts was badly hurt through having had his head dashed by the other repeatedly on the iron-wood floor. **1901** *Brisbane Courier* 2 Aug. 7/6 The ironwood . . is a little too much for even the phenomenal digestive apparatus of the camel. **1919** *Bulletin* (Sydney) 30 Oct. 24/4 The ironwood, or 'dead finish', tree of Southern and Western Bananaland is a surer destroyer of axes than the yellow-box. **1935** H.H. FINLAYSON *Red Centre* 31 Ironwood (*A. estrophiolata*), widely spread over all the sand country. . . The leaf is small and narrow but the foliage is profuse, and the tree has a rounded compact top which throws the densest shade to be got in the Centre. **1963** I.L. IDRIESS *Our Living Stone Age* 119 He presented a brand-new shield of fire-hardened iron-wood, guaranteed to turn the impact of the heaviest spear and club. **1970** D. STIVENS *Horse of Air* 113 A brilliant green ironwood (*Acacia estrophiolata*). With its rounded top it looked like a topiarized English oak strayed from a Home County estate. **1984** *Advertiser*

(Adelaide) 27 June 1/3 The ironwood tree . . forlorn on the perimeter of farming land.

irrigation. Used *attrib.* in Comb. to denote that the productivity of the land is dependent upon an artificially engineered water supply, as **irrigation block, colony, farm, settlement.**

1891 *Bohemia* (Melbourne) 24 Dec. 10 Let him be content with a three hundred and twenty-acre selection, and if that is too much, let him settle down on a ten-acre **irrigation block.** **1910** *Huon Times* (Franklin) 7 Sept. 2/7 The Mackenzie-Mead delegation, wandering in search of experts in intense culture to settle on irrigation blocks. **1890** *Braidwood Dispatch* 1 Feb. 5/1 We understand that overtures have been made to the government of this colony for the establishment of an extensive **irrigation colony** by Messrs Chaffey Bros. **1891** A.F. SPAWN *New Homes in Irrigation & Fruit-Growing Colonies Vic.* 34 Large holdings are being cut up into irrigation colonies. . . The first to make a move in this direction were Messrs Young Brothers, founders of the Young Brothers' Irrigation Colony, located in the suburbs of Horsham on the Wimmera river. **1911** *Huon Times* (Franklin) 11 Jan. 4/7 It is rushing the men with a little capital about the State, showing them the irrigation colonies that are going concerns. **1927** *Bulletin* (Sydney) 21 Apr. 24/4 The ibis is the yabbie's greatest enemy, and should be a welcome guest on every **irrigation farm.** **1972** *Ibid.* 26 Feb. 58/3 The fruit growers on small irrigation farms are the worst off. **1920** H.S. TAYLOR *Pioneer Irrigationists' Man.* lxx. 3 The Australian **irrigation settlements** are still in their infancy. **1926** A. EDEN *Places in Sun* 63 Mildura is one of the oldest irrigation settlements in Australia. **1953** *Bulletin* (Sydney) 4 Feb. 13/3 Three swaggies came across a broken-down lorry . . destined for a distillery at one of the Murray irrigation settlements. **1960** N. CATO *Green grows Vine* 3 She would be setting off for a season of grape-picking in an irrigation settlement.

island. Used *attrib.* in Special Comb. **island continent,** mainland Australia; **State,** Tasmania.

1835 *Sydney Herald* 19 Mar. 2/1 The establishment of a New Colony in Southern Australia, is so much connected with the interest of the settlements now existing on the same **Island-Continent**, that it would at any time excite great sensation in the inhabitants of those Colonies. **1839** *S. Austral. Gaz.* (Adelaide) 11 July 3 He will be ready to attempt the transit from the head of Spencer's Gulf to Port Essington, across the centre of our mysterious island continent. **1891** 'SMILER' *Wanderings Simple Child* (ed. 3) p. iv, The coast line of the island continent. **1927** 'VIATOR' *From up along Down Under* 330 When the Island-Continent is populated. **1983** *Bicentenary '88* (Austral. Bicentennial Authority) Nov. 6/2 Jessie Ackermann's book *Australia from a Woman's Point of View* . . 'reveals frankly and fearlessly 'things as they are' in the Island Continent'. **1910** *Huon Times* (Franklin) 12 Nov. 6/4 He left Tasmania to take part in the rushes of the fifties, and was ready to do fight for the **Island State.** **1917** *Ibid.* 6 Nov. 5/2 The volunteer crews of the boats that kept our Island State linked up with the Mainland.

Israelite. A member of the Christian Israelite sect: see BEARDIE.

1852 *Murray's Guide to Gold Diggings* 17 Amongst the miners now at work is a party of Israelites. **1851** *Empire* (Sydney) 9 Sept. 135/5 A party of Israelites, Beardies, Southcotarians or by whatever signification they may be known . . left for Sydney with 75 oz. of clean gold. **1967** F.T. MACARTNEY *Proof against Failure* 13 Music was provided by a brass band, consisting of the male members of a sect who . . were known as the Israelites, but we boys called them the Beardy-bucks.

itchy grub. Any of many caterpillars capable of causing skin irritation, esp. the PROCESSIONAL CATERPILLAR.

1940 *Bulletin* (Sydney) 4 Dec. 16/2 Of all the miscellaneous assortment of wogs that bountiful Nature inflicts on her sons, the 'itchy grub' is the most insidious. A harmless-looking hairy caterpillar, about two inches long, it leaves an invisible irritant behind that lingers long after it has gone. **1960** *Ibid.* 6 July 16/3 Quite a swag of Australian birds often have 'itchy grubs' on their menu. **1973** C. AUSTIN *I left my Hat in Andamooka* 100 One gum tree in the caravan park was infested and campers were warned not to camp under it because this 'itchy grub' as it is called, on coming into contact with the skin, can cause intense irritation or even a serious infection.

itinerant teacher. A peripatetic teacher employed to visit, and supervise the schooling of, children living in areas remote from a school; orig. (*N.S.W.*) a teacher serving in two small half-time schools.

1866 *Act* (N.S.W.) 30 *Vict.* no. 22 Sect. 12, In districts where from the scattered state of the population or other causes it is not practicable to establish a public school the Council of Education may appoint itinerant teachers under such regulations as may be framed by them for that purpose. **1908** *Bulletin* (Sydney) 12 Mar. 12/2 A feature of the Queensland back-blocks is the itinerant teacher. . . Families remote from civilisation are visited, the children taught for a day or two, and set work for the teacher's next coming, frequently a year after. **1925** J.A. COLLUM *New Settlers' Handbk.* 109 For the benefit of families outside the areas visited by itinerant teachers, tuition by correspondence . . is carried out. **1956** B.J. RAYMENT *My Towri* 60 The Itinerant Teacher not only relieved the outback mother of a tiresome burden but also gave that personal touch which makes such a vast difference to the outback child. **1963** *Cwlth. Office Educ. Bull.* xxviii. 4 There are now several itinerant teachers who make brief annual visits to the homes of all correspondence children in the North-West and West Kimberley districts.

ivorywood. [See quot. 1965.] The tree *Siphonodon australis* (fam. Celastraceae), of near-coastal and seasonally dry vine forests of e. Qld. and n.e. N.S.W.; the wood of the tree.

1887 *Colonial & Indian Exhib. Rep. Col. Sect.* 429 Ivory-wood. **1903** *Austral. Handbk.* 280 Some of the trees which furnish wood suitable for carving or engraving purposes . . 'Ivory Wood' (*Siphonodon australe*). **1965** *Austral. Encycl.* II. 310 The ivorywood . . possesses a fine-textured, hard, ivory-coloured wood excellent for carving.

J

jabiru /dʒæbəˈru/. [Transf. use of *jabiru* a large wading bird *Jabiru mycteria*, of the stork family.] The large wading bird *Ephippiorhynchus asiaticus*, having glossy greenish-black and white plumage and red legs and occurring along the n. and e. coasts of Aust., in New Guinea, and in s. Asia; *policeman bird*, see POLICEMAN.

1847 L. LEICHHARDT *Jrnl. Overland Exped. Aust.* 194 We saw a Tabiroo [*sic*] (Myceteria) and a rifle bird. **1860** G. BENNETT *Gatherings of Naturalist* 197 The Jabiru is partial to salt-water creeks and lagoons. **1865** G.F. ANGAS *Aust.* 98 The mycteria, or jabiru, is a fine bird, standing nearly as high as the crane; it has a large, powerful beak, with glossy green and white plumage and bright-red legs. **1889** R.B. ANDERSON tr. Lumholtz's *Among Cannibals* 96 He threw down to me two large young of the gigantic wader Jabiru (*Mycteria australis*). **1896** W.H. WILLSHIRE *Land of Dawning* 3 The wild aboriginals are as shy and as wily as the 'Jabiru' (Xenorhynchus Asiaticus). **1925** *Bulletin* (Sydney) 23 Apr. 23/2 The blacks usually named a bird from its call. .. Galah and jabiru (our one stork) are a few of the survivals. **1937** G.H. SUNTER *Adventures Trepang Fisher* 226 Jaberoo .. are something like geese to eat. **1945** C. BARRETT *Austral. Bird Life* 25 While emu, brolga, and bustard are widely known, the jabiru or black-necked stork (*Xenorhynchus asiaticus*) is familiar to the great majority of Australians only as a zoo bird. **1965** G. MCINNES *Road to Gundagai* 125 Polygonum swamps over which the long legged jabiroo flew creating on its way. **1979** D. LOCKWOOD *My Old Mates & I* 11 A solitary jabiru .. stalking its prey, occasionally jumping ludicrously and jabbing at fish with its monstrous bill.

jacana. [Spec. use of *jacana* any bird of the fam. Jacanidae, having long claws enabling it to walk on floating aquatic plants.] LOTUS BIRD.

1921 S.A. WHITE *Bunya* 8 That strange bird, the jacana, was espied running over the waterlily leaves, being able to do this owing to its remarkably long toes. **1938** C.P. CONIGRAVE *Walk-About* 69 Over the large, dinner-plate lily leaves that floated on the surface ran comb-crested jacanas or parras (*Hydralector gallinaceus*), a bird with outsize feet and thin legs, twelve inches long. **1951** E. HILL *Territory* 22 Little jacana, the 'Jesus-bird', walks on the water-lily leaves. **1970** J.V. MARSHALL *Walk to Hills of Dreamtime* 38 A family of long-legged jacaras [*sic*] were walking single file across the billabong.

Jack, *n.*[1] Also **jack.** [Shortened form of LAUGHING JACKASS 1, assimilating with the proper name *Jack*.] A nickname for a kookaburra; JACKO *n.*[1]; JACKY *n.*[1]

1898 E.E. MORRIS *Austral Eng.* 216 The bird is generally called only a *Jackass*, and this is becoming contracted into the simple abbreviation of *Jack*. **1901** *Advocate* (Burnie) 21 Feb. 2/4, I brought one of these birds (the Laughing Goburra) over from Victoria a few weeks ago... A snake falling in 'Jack's' way, it was interesting to watch. **1916** *Bulletin* (Sydney) 20 Jan. 22/1 Can any Abo. brother truthfully say that he has seen a laughing Jack kill a venomous snake? **1922** A.D. MICKLE *Wee Dog* 11 Never was a madder jollification than that of the 'jacks' in the great gums. **1936** *Bulletin* (Sydney) 1 July 21/4 Kookaburras would never go for the giant worms... We have .. put them .. not 19 ft. from a Jack; but he would not have them. **1949** B. O'REILLY *Green Mountains* 136 Mention of Australian birds should begin with the kookaburra. Jack is like the 'digger'—the gamest of his tribe. **1954** C. BARRETT *Wild Life Aust. & New Guinea* 120 'Old Jack', the kookaburra, may have faults, but he has always been a general favourite.

Jack, *n.*[2] [Cf. prec.] Abbrev. of JACKEROO *n.* 2.

1904 L.M.P. ARCHER *Bush Honeymoon* 211 Dad had two *Jacks*, who did the out-station work with the help of men about the place. **1967** G. JENKIN *Two Yrs. Bardunyah Station* 29 'How does that soliloquy of Macbeth's go in Act I Scene 7, Jack?' .. (Jack stood for Jackaroo).

Jack, *n.*[3] *Two-up.* [Of unknown origin.] A counterfeit penny having a head on both sides.

1936 'SWEENEY, EX-CROOK' *I Confess* 100 The 'double-headed' penny or 'Jack' as it is generally known. **1967** *Kings Cross Whisper* (Sydney) xxxv. 6/3 *Jack*, a double-headed penny in two-up.

Jack, *n.*[4] [Abbrev. of *Jack (McNab*, rhyming slang for 'scab'.] A member of the Permanent and Casual Waterside Workers' Union.

1947 J. MORRISON *Sailors belong Ships* 29 An air of strained expectancy pervades the great bleak shed. In the outer divisions—'Jacks', 'Seconds', 'Unattached', 'Blanks'—the bell is hardly heard over the babel of four thousand voices. **1955** —— *Black Cargo* 25 In defeat, Federation men have no alternative but to associate with Jacks at work, but there are hotels in Flinders Street into which no Jack would ever dare to venture. **1982** LOWENSTEIN & HILLS *Under Hook* 88 The Permanent and Casual Waterside Workers' Union (popularly known as Jacks or scabs).

Jack, *n.*[5] Also **jack.** [Abbrev. of *jack in a box*, rhyming slang for 'pox'.] Venereal disease; an attack of venereal disease.

1954 T.A.G. HUNGERFORD *Sowers of Wind* 3 Penicillin'll take care of that! They reckon they just pump you full of it, and bingo! No more jack! **1960** J. IGGULDEN *Storms of Summer* 297 Some rotten poxy bitch of a chromo dobbed them in... They reckon she was rotten with the jack so they never paid her. **1971** *Kings Cross Whisper* (Sydney) cxvii. 5/2 Suffering from an overdose of the jack. **1974** *Gayzette* (Sydney) 14 Nov. 14/2 No worries about jack in this one. A virgin, no worries. **1979** D.R. STUART *Crank back on Roller* 199 Ah, the poor bastard got a jack in Tassie before we'd been in camp a month... Fuck a dog on a chain, the bloody fool. **1985** N. MEDCALF *Rifleman* 73 Got malaria, beri-beri, malnutrition and probably a dose of jack.

jack, *v.* [Spec. use of *jack up* to give up suddenly: see OED *v.*[1] 3 b.] *intr.* With **up:** to refuse to participate or co-operate; to show disapproval. Freq. with **on.**

1898 'R. BOLDREWOOD' *Romance of Canvas Town* 253 The half-used plates and dishes were to me as things loathsome... So, as a man, a gentleman, and a squatter, I 'jacked up' at the cookery. **1936** M. FRANKLIN *All that Swagger* 470 Grandfather always took Grandma with him everywhere until she jacked up. **1953** T.A.G. HUNGERFORD *Riverslake* 163 'Would you have jacked up because Bellairs took the Balt's money?' Randolph demanded savagely. **1965** K. SMITH *OGF* 80 The retail fruiterers jacked up on us today. The wife is goin' to be real crooked on me when she sees how much I take home this afternoon. **1972** *Bulletin* (Sydney) 15 Apr. 35/2 Local authorities are jacking up and the kids themselves are getting sick of badly-organised functions and functions that turn violent. **1973** *Kings Cross Whisper* (Sydney) cliii. 6/1 He carries on belting away till the neighbors come out and jack up on him. **1978** H.C. BAKER *I was Listening* 177 Now you're on the point of jacking up on me. **1984** *Sunday Tel.* (Sydney) 1 Apr. 58/1 Higgs was the easiest touch I've met. I reckon anyone could get a minimum of three 'accounts' with him before he jacked up.

Hence **jacked up** *ppl. a.*, disenchanted, 'fed up'.

1981 D. STUART *I think I'll Live* 5 The local sheilahs .. they're jacked up to the eyebrows.

jack, *a.* [f. *jack up* to give up: see prec.] Disenchanted; tired of (a person, activity, etc.), 'fed up with'. Esp. in the phr. **to be jack of.**

1889 J.L. HUNT *Bk. of Bonanzas* 79 We've hed two ov them trips already, an' we'er getting Jack about the business. **1892** *Bulletin* (Sydney) 10 Dec. 24/2 I'm jack o' them practical jokes They ain't neither pleasure ner profit. **1908** E.G. MURPHY *Jarrahland Jingles* 58 And Brim's in London on his 'ace', Of Andrew Barr a trifle 'jack'. **1914** E. DYSON *Spats' Fact'ry* 61 Afore I got jack of it. **1944** J. DEVANNY *By Tropic Sea & Jungle* 155 Too much of it makes you jack of it quick. **1963** A.E. FARRELL *Vengeance* 19 An' not before time, neither... I'm jack o' this joint! **1971** *Bulletin* (Sydney) 8 May 11/1 A number of ALP parliamentarians believe that more and more people are getting 'jack' of both strikes and the ACTU president, Mr R.J. ('Bob') Hawke. **1986** *Austral. Geographic* Apr. 68/1 'The missus might get jack of it and clear out for the city,' observed one miner, 'but most of them come back.'

jackaburra /ˈdʒækəbʌrə/. [Blend of LAUGHING JACKASS 1 + KOOKABURRA.] A kookaburra.

1917 *Bulletin* (Sydney) 22 Feb. 24/4 There is a flock of Jackaburras near my place. **1944** *Ibid.* 4 Oct. 15/4 The jackaburra has not varied the landing technique inherited from his laughing ancestors.

jackaroo, var. JACKEROO *n.* and *v.*

jackass.

1. Abbrev. of LAUGHING JACKASS. See also JACKO *n.*[1], JACKY *n.*[1]

1805 J. GRANT *Jrnl.* 17 May 76 Will send you where they flog Jack-asses. **1827** P. CUNNINGHAM *Two Yrs. in N.S.W.* I. 232 The loud laughter of the *jackass* summons us to *turn out*, and take a peep at the appearance of the morning. **1845** D. MACKENZIE *Emigrant's Guide* 193 At dawn you will be awakened by a bird called the 'Jackass', which then sets up a long-continued horse-laugh. **1859** W. KELLY *Life in Vic.* I. 250 Set it out by the fragment of jackass-pie (the poor bird, not the animal, mind you). **1879** A.P. MARTIN *Easter Omelette* 22 Loud from the fork of a gum squaaked, deep-mouthed, the earsplitting jackass. **1898** *Bulletin* (Sydney) 5 Mar. 14/3 The jackass flew off, evidently glad to be rid of his encumbrance. **1903** 'BOONDI' *Boondi's Bk.* 36 From the tree-tops shrieked the 'jackass', Screamed the kookaboora's cry. **1918** B. REYNOLDS *Dawn Asper* 125 Take him down and show him the jackasses' nest. **1937** *Bulletin* (Sydney) 7 July 20/3 Like most chatterers, the jackass hogs all the publicity for his tribe. **1943** C.E. GOODE *Bridge Party at Boyanup* 25 A jackass laughed from a mountain ash near a sleeper cutter's camp. **1966** S.J. BAKER *Austral. Lang.* (ed. 2) 300 The common appellation *laughing jackass* dates from 1798 or earlier (.. this *jackass* is probably a mutilation of the French *jacasse*, a magpie, a name which seems to have been bestowed on the kookaburra by early French observers round these coasts; the verb *jacasser* means to chatter, to cackle). **1979** B. MARTYN *First Footers S. Gippsland* 138 Jackasses had awakened and were breakfasting at the roots of fallen trees.

2. *Tas.* *Grey butcherbird*, see GREY *a.*

1880 L.A. MEREDITH *Tasmanian Friends & Foes* 110 We, too, have a 'jackass', a smaller bird, and not in any way remarkable, except for its merry gabbling sort of song. **1901** *Emu* I. 82 Cracticus cinereus .. Grey Butcher Bird .. the common name for the bird being the 'Jackass'. **1931** *Bulletin* (Sydney) 6 May 21/3 The 'jackass' of Tassie is the grey butcher-bird.

3. *fig.* In the phr. **(from) jackass to jackass** and varr., (from) dawn to dusk.

1899 *Bulletin* (Sydney) 12 Aug. 14/4 'Cockies' hours' are supposed to be 'from jackass to jackass'. **1902** *Ibid.* 5 July 16/1 From jackass-laugh to dingo-cry We're grubbing giant trees. **1903** *Ibid.* 24 Dec. 36/4 He worked from 'jackass to jackass', going to the bush at daylight and coming back when he could no longer see to work. **1904** *Ibid.* 10 Nov. 18/4 The jackass and the mopoke are supposed to be the earliest and the latest of our birds. 'From jackass to mopoke' is a saying used by bushmen to designate hours worked for a slave-driving cocky. **1909** *Ibid.* 6 May 13/2 You get Miss Ebony at every meal hour. In fact the only topic from jackass to jackass is ebony girl. **1912** *Ibid.* 11 Jan. 44/4, 15 bob a week and tucker—jackass to jackass and Sundays off. **1930** *Ibid.* 29 Jan. 25/3 The kookaburra used to be known in N.S.W. as the settlers' clock, and the working day was from 'jackass to mopoke', which was generally interpreted as 'from dawn to dark'. **1978** W. LOWENSTEIN *Weevils in Flour* 361 Hours? From jackass to jackass! You never run out of work till just about sundown and you was on the move at four or five o'clock when you got up and fed your horses.

jackass-fish. The marine fish *Nemadactylus macropterus*, widely distributed in Austral. waters and having a distinctive elongated ray of the pectoral fin. See also MORWONG. Also **jackass morwong.**

1886 *Proc. Linnean Soc. N.S.W.* I. 880 *Chilodactylus macropterus* . . is known as the 'Jackass-fish'. **1906** D.G. STEAD *Fishes of Aust.* 119 The Jackass-Fish is generally confounded by amateur fishermen, and many others, with the Morwong. **1951** T.C. ROUGHLEY *Fish & Fisheries Aust.* 97 The morwong and the jackass-fish are grouped together . . in New South Wales under the name of 'morwong'. **1962** 'N. CULOTTA' *Gone Fishin'* 87 Funny thing about morwong. There's another fish like it that used to be called jackass fish. Nobody'd eat it. **1967** D.F. MCMICHAEL *Treasury Austral. Wildlife* 178 The term jackass fish, applied to one of the Australian morwongs, doubtless originated from the dark shoulder stripes, like those of a donkey, on the grey ground colour. **1983** *Canberra Chron.* 23 Nov. 19/1 Dave Gill . . fished out of Bermagui . . 15 jackass morwong.

jackeroo /dʒækəˈru/, *n.* Also **jackaroo.** [a. Jagara *dhŭgai-iu* wandering white man.]

1. Orig. *Qld. Obs.* A white man living beyond the bounds of close settlement.

1845 *Bell's Life in Sydney* 4 Jan. 4/1 The Jackeroos all smoke their pipes and sit still. **1853** H.B. JONES *Adventures in Aust.* 210 Here and there you may notice a squatter, or as they are called by Sydneyites, a 'Jacky Rue', who has ridden from Wellington or Bathurst, or perhaps five or six hundred miles, to have an interview with his merchant or agent. **1875** CAMPBELL & WILKS *Early Settlement Qld.* 18 A black-fellow . . warned me . . that their intention was first to spear all the commandants, then to fence up the roads and stop the drays from travelling, and to starve the 'jackaroos' (strangers). **1888** H.S. RUSSELL *Genesis Qld.* 207 Limestone in 1840 . . stands out as the handselled resting-place for the 'jackeroos'! By this wild name the 'jumped up' white men beyond the range had been reported by the blacks from tribe to tribe. [**1896** B. SPENCER *Rep. Horn Sci. Exped. Central Aust.* II. 71 Perched on a dead branch, the black-throated Crow-Shrike often kept up a continous carol for over an hour. . . They are generally described as 'jackeroos' by the residents of the north.] **1896** *Bulletin* (Sydney) 18 Apr. 27/3 The word 'jackeroo', a station new-chum, comes also from the old Brisbane blacks, who called the pied crow shrike (*Stripera [sic] graculina*) 'tchaceroo', a gabbling and garrulous bird. They called the German missionaries of 1838 'jackeroo', a gabbler, because they were always talking. Afterwards they applied it to all white men.

2. A young man (usu. English and of independent means) seeking to gain experience by working in a supernumerary capacity on a sheep or cattle station (see COLONIAL EXPERIENCE *n.* 1); a person working on a sheep or cattle station with a view to acquiring the practical experience and management skills desirable in a station owner or manager; COLONIAL EXPERIENCE *n.* 2.

1870 'JACKAROO' *Immigration Question* 5 A species of Pariah, or Anglo-Bedouin, or whatever category the Jackaroo proper may be presumed to come under, ought perhaps to be the last to offer any remarks upon a political question affecting a country in which he can have little interest. . . A philanthropic friend got me upon an inland station as a 'jackaroo', and a jackaroo I shall remain to the end. **1873** *Austral. Town & Country Jrnl.* (Sydney) 5 July 18/4 It's very hard on the poor man. . . You won't want no hands from shearing to shearing, except two or three Jackeroos. **1876** J.A. EDWARDS *Gilbert Gogger* 156 *Jackeroo*, small swell, or half loafer, half gentleman; sometimes used to denote a young gentleman gaining colonial experience. **1878** 'IRONBARK' *Southerly Busters* 9 Young gentlemen getting their 'colonial experience' in the bush are called 'jackeroos' by the station-hands. The term is seldom heard except in the remote 'back-blocks' of the interior. **1892** *Truth* (Sydney) 17 Apr. 3/3 Jackaroo is the term applied to those flash ha-ha sort of gentlemen just out from home—generally some relation to the manager, and who, of course, must get a good screw for doing nothing. **1893** *Bulletin* (Sydney) 16 Dec. 19/1 There are jackeroos *and* jackaroos—Bolder was of the latter. His father, a curate in England, had almost famished to provide £100, the premium of his son's apprenticeship. **1898** R. RADCLYFFE *Wealth & Wild Cats* 48 A hard-up miner or 'Jackaroo', as they call gentlemen miners. **1906** *Bulletin* (Sydney) 28 June 14/2 New chums were originally called Johnny Raws. From that it got to Jacky Raw. And from Jacky Raw to Jackeroo is but a slip of the tongue. **1911** C.E.W. BEAN *'Dreadnought' of Darling* 78 In the bachelors' quarters there will probably live . . one or two 'jackeroos'—young Australians, or sometimes young Englishmen, learning the work of a sheep run by taking an ordinary part in it. **1925** *Aussie* (Sydney) Apr. 52/3 It was said that the term jackeroo originated from the fact that one of the earliest of the brand was named Jack Carew. **1933** C.E.W. BEAN *Official Hist. Aust. 1914–18* IV. 666 (*footnote*) Lieut. E.C.P. Thomas, 33rd Bn. Jackeroo; of 'Vermont', Amby, Q'land. **1948** B. CRONIN *How runs Road* 31 The fastidious Britisher, serving his apprenticeship as a jackaroo. **1960** *N.T. News* (Darwin) 5 Feb. 8/7 Jackeroos required. . . Applicants should supply full personal details and experience, particularly experience as stockmen, transport drivers, bulldozing and grading, station engineering, bookkeeping, storekeeping, butchering and milking. **1974** F. STEVENS *Aborigines in N.T.* 37 A 'jackeroo' was defined in the Cattle Station Industry (N.T.) Award, 5.3 as a person 'employed with a view to becoming an owner, overseer, manager, etc.' **1977** D. WHITINGTON *Strive to be Fair* 38 Jackaroos are, or were, sweated labour. The legend is that they are social equals with the station owners, and are virtually treated as belonging to the family. Because of this, they receive only about half the pay of a station hand, and are liable for duty at any time. **1984** B. DIXON *Searching for Aboriginal Lang.* 123 We were in full swing when the jackeroo—white lad training to be a manager somewhere, someday—came and said we'd better break it up.

jackeroo /dʒækəˈru/, *v.* Also **jackaroo.** [f. prec.] *intr.* To work as a jackeroo. Freq. as *pres. pple.*

1875 *Austral. Town & Country Jrnl.* (Sydney) 28 Aug. 343/3 A year or two more Jackerooing would only mean the consumption of so many more figs of negro-head, in my case. **1900** *Bulletin* (Sydney) 8 Dec. 21/1 He was jackerooing on Mistral Creek. **1909** *Ibid.* 14 Jan. 14/2, I was jackerooing there in 1900–01–02. **1926** *Ibid.* 14 Jan. 24/2 While . . jackerooing a few years ago I was called to the woolshed. **1934** E. STOREY *Eve's Affairs* 152 Mr Shepherd, whom David had jackerooed for, rode up to our door. **1948** *Bulletin* (Sydney) 24 Mar. 28/4 A jackeroo was expending a lot of time and sweat 'maggoting' on fly-struck sheep out Cobar way. . . They have to work harder now than when I was jackerooing. **1959** K.S. PRICHARD *N'Goola* 105 He could jackeroo on Yienda for a year or so—or until he made up his mind where he was going to take up land. **1973** J. POWERS *Last of Knucklemen* (1974) 57, I was jackerooing in Queensland—bummin' an' odd-jobbin' about. **1981** *Bulletin* (Sydney) 29 Sept. 64/3 Alas there is no time what with horses and young Old Etonians learning to jackaroo.

Hence **jackerooing** *vbl. n.*

1900 T. MAJOR *Leaves from Squatter's Note Bk.* 22 A young friend . . was learning colonial experience—afterwards termed 'Jackarooing'. **1958** J.R. SPICER *Cry of Storm-Bird* 9 Carrying on with the jackarooing. I was learning to be a manager. **1965** G. MCINNES *Road to Gundagai* 257 Harry Laing, a cousin of the Kininmonths . . had come out to do a spot of desultory jackarooing.

jacket, *v. Obs.* [Transf. use of *jacket* to swindle, betray: see quot. 1812.] *trans.* To inform on (someone).

[**1812** J.H. VAUX *Mem.* 181 *Jacket*, to jacket a person . . is more properly applied to removing a man by underhand and vile means from any birth or situation he enjoys.] **1825** *Austral.* (Sydney) 10 Feb. 3 Maurice Welsh . . knew that Griffiths had a spite against the prisoners; heard Griffiths say frequently, he would *jacket* him. **1849** A. HARRIS *Emigrant Family* (1967) 30 It's not allowed, I suppose; but nobody cares about that. Nobody need 'jacket' (*inform against*) himself. **1852** *Empire* (Sydney) 27 Feb. 723/5 Whelan . . was continually 'jacketing' him about giving rations to the black gins. **1888** J.C.F. JOHNSON *Austral Christmas* 48 I'm blessed well sure it was him as blowed the gaff an' jacketted me to the 'cove' about them three bottles of grog I brought out from the township.

jackie, var. JACKY *n.*[1] and *n.*[4]

jack-jumper. [f. the name *Jack*, in names of animals sometimes signifying *small* (OED *sb.*[1] 37) + JUMPER *n.*[1]] JUMPER *n.*[1] Also *attrib.*

1921 *Bulletin* (Sydney) 7 Apr. 20/3 The publican directed my attention to some small, dark-green ants, known, I believe, as jack-jumpers. **1980** J. WOLFE *End of Pricklystick* 64 There's jack-jumper ants live in the flowers [*sc.* ragwort] . . and sometimes you get stung on the hand.

jack mackerel. [Transf. use of *jack* as used in the names of fish: see OED *jack, sb.*[1] 30.] Either of the fish *Trachurus novaezelandiae* (see YELLOWTAIL) and *T. declivis* (see COWANYOUNG).

1950 *Rep.* (Dept. Commerce & Agric., Fisheries Division) 7 At the conference of Commonwealth and State Fisheries Officers in 1947, steps were taken to introduce uniform names for certain species of fish common to more than one State. One of the new names was Scad, previously known as horse mackerel or cowanyoung. From the marketing point of view the name Scad was not satisfactory and in addition had to compete with a closely related species known as jack mackerel in the United States. To help the Australian pack compete with the American pack on the same markets, the Division after consultation with the canners, State Fisheries Departments, C.S.I.R.O. Fisheries Division and others, was instrumental in having the species renamed jack mackerel. **1951** T.C. ROUGHLEY *Fish & Fisheries Aust.* 59 The jack mackerel is . . found in abundance on the south coast of New South Wales and through Bass Strait to the east and west coasts of Tasmania. **1965** *Austral. Encycl.* V. 115 The original jack mackerel is *T[rachurus] symmetricus* of California, but when, in 1950, Australia began to export *T. novaezelandiae* as a food-fish, that species was officially designated jack mackerel. **1974** K. PULLEY *Marine Fishes Austral. Waters* 99 They feed on squid, small fishes and some that are not so small, such as jack mackerel. **1980** *Ecos* xxiv. 28/2 Jack mackerel is not considered a good table fish in Australia.

Jacko, *n.*[1] [f. JACK *n.*[1] + -O.] A kookaburra.

1907 *Bulletin* (Sydney) 31 Oct. 15/3 The goburra has been called the 'settler's clock', but he should be altogether an unreliable one. Jacko is apt to go off at any time. **1941** S.J. BAKER *Pop. Dict. Austral. Slang* 38 *Jacko*, a kookaburra. **1955** N. PULLIAM *I traveled Lonely Land* 381 *Laughing jackass*, one nick-name for the kookaburra. . . Other names are: jacky, jacko [etc.].

Jacko, *n.*[2] *Hist.* [Joc. use of the proper name *Jack* + -O.] In the war of 1914–18: a nickname for a Turkish soldier; the Turkish army. Cf. ABDUL 1. Also as *adj.*

1916 'MEN OF ANZAC' *Anzac Bk.* 126 By jingo! how your bloomin' grit Must make old Jacko dance. **1917** *Barrack: Official Organ Imperial Camel Corps* 1 July 6/2 Italians capture twenty towns Five thousand 'Jackos' killed. **1918** *Kia Ora Coo-ee* Apr. 18/2 We spotted a Jacko, with a big bulge on his left side, sneaking away. **1919** O. HOGUE *Cameliers* 267 They wished that every Turk had been a Hun; For they rather like old 'Jacko'. **1937** WISBERG & WATERS *Bushman at Large* 162 Dig for your bloody lives. Jacko's liable to rush us any minute now! **1949** G. BERRIE *Morale* 43 There's a Jacko general out there trying to tell them something, and they think he's talking French.

Jack Rice. [The name of a racehorse which ran successfully in hurdling and steeplechasing events between 1915 and 1919.] In the phr. **a roll (pile,** etc.) **Jack Rice couldn't jump over**: see quot. 1945.

1945 S.J. BAKER *Austral. Lang.* 107 A man well supplied with cash . . may even be fortunate enough to have *a roll Jack Rice couldn't jump over.* Jack Rice was a racehorse noted for his performances over hurdles. **1954** T. RONAN *Vision Splendid* 119 I'm on a tenner a week here, danger money for handling explosives, and I'm running a penny game at night. I've got a roll Jack Rice couldn't jump over. **1960** 'N. CULOTTA' *Cop this Lot* 82 Man walks around with a roll in 'is kick Jack Rice couldn' jump over, an' 'e's not worth a zac. **1970** J. CLEARY *Helga's Web* 297 'I never seen twenty thousand in cash before. Somehow you'd think it'd amount to a pile Jack Rice couldn't jump over.' Helidon wondered who Jack Rice was; then remembered it was a famous hurdle horse with a prodigious leap. **1972** *Bulletin* (Sydney) 12 Aug. 7/2 You never hear now of a punter . . having a roll Jack Rice couldn't jump over.

Jack Shay. *Obs.* Also **Jack Shea,** without initial capital(s), and as one word. [Perh. f. *jack* black (leather) drinking vessel or container (see OED *sb.*[2] 2) + *O')Shea* Irish surname, as rhyming slang on /teɪ/, obs. and Irish pronunc. of *tea.*] A tin vessel holding a quart (cf. QUART-POT 1) used for brewing tea and incorporating a smaller vessel for drinking. Also *attrib.*

1879 'AUSTRALIAN' *Adventures Qld.* 17 He . . never, by any chance, irritated her, unless he had previously swallowed at least five inches of strong rum out of a 'Jack Shea'. Not that that small quantity (a good quart) of alcohol affected his brain. **1881** A.C. GRANT *Bush-Life Qld.* I. 209 Hobbles and Jack Shays hang from the saddle-dees. *[Note]* A tin quart-pot, used for boiling water for tea, and contrived so as to hold within it a tin pint-pot. **1893** *Antipodean* (Melbourne) 109 On the left [of the saddle] was suspended a tin 'Jack Shay' quart-pot. **1900** *Bulletin* (Sydney) 22 Dec. 14/4 Cookson . . wagered that he would put, at 80 yds., four shots out of five in the bottom of a Jack-Shay pint. **1923** J. BOWES *Jackaroos* 238 Jackshay, a quart pot with a deep-sided lid. The lid acts as a cup. A jackshay was the bushman's kettle and teapot combined in one. It was a good substitute for the billycan, which in time ousted it. **1926** M. FORREST *Hibiscus Heart* 133 A magpie, head on one side, perched on the jack shay. **1936** *Bulletin* (Sydney) 29 Jan. 21/4 How many could tell you whether a 'Jack Shea' was a pug, a movie star, a fencer or a quart-pot?—the last has it. **1943** H.G. LAMOND *From Tariaro to Ross Roy* 42 That was just about the time the Jack Shea quart-and-pint was being introduced.

Jack Shepherd. *Obs.* Also **Jack Sheppard.** [Prob. quasi-proper name indicating familiarity or contempt: see OED *jack, sb.*[1] 35.] A rogue. Also *attrib.*

1841 *Morning Advertiser* (Hobart) 1 Oct. 2/1 This town has been invested with a new denomination of juvenile Jack Shepherds, commonly called *Bricks,* who to the reproach of the police and their parents, have been permitted to commit acts. **1844** *Duncan's Weekly Register* (Sydney) 12 Oct. 181/3 They richly merit to become the slaves which their children, will infallibly be, if, unhappily, the designs of these Political Jack Shepherds should succeed. **1846** *Britannia* (Hobart) 1 Oct. 4/3 The convict Comptroller-General must have felt it, no doubt, together with all the probation Jack Sheppard Nix my Dolly lockers-up, to be an abominable nuisance. **1847** *Ibid.* 8 Apr. 2/3 A certain Jack Sheppard audacity suited only to a convict police.

Jack the painter. *Obs.* A coarse green tea, so named because of its staining properties.

1852 G.C. MUNDY *Our Antipodes* I. 329 Another notorious ration tea of the bush is called 'Jack the painter'. This is a *very* green tea indeed, its viridity evidently produced by a discreet use of the copper drying pans in its manufacture. **1855** W. HOWITT *Land, Labor & Gold* I. 254 Jack-the-painter tea, that is, a green preparation of leaves of some kind, which taste like a mixture of copperas and verdigris, and leave a green scum on the infusion. **1875** R. BRUCE *Dingoes* 130 And each man has a bright tinpot Of drink above attainder, Brewed of dried leaves and water hot—They call it Jack, the painter, Because an odor it has got Far worse than rank Bohea. **1902** —— *Reminisc. Old Squatter* 36 Several chests of 'Jack the Painter' (tea) which had a delightful odour, similar to that to be found in the oil and colour warehouse. **1937** D. GLASS *Austral. Fantasy* 89 'Jack the Painter', which extra potent version was apt to leave its mark around the drinker's mouth.

jack up. [f. the vbl. phr. *to jack up*: see JACK *v.*] A dispute; a refusal to co-operate (esp. with an employer or superior).

1948 *Khaki Bush & Bigotry* (1968) 94 By gee, if I'm not on the next draft I'm telling you there's going to be the biggest jack-up you ever saw. **1953** T.A.G. HUNGERFORD *Riverslake* 163, I seen the day when there would've been a jack-up over it. **1983** *Canberra Times* 22 Apr. 2/7 Those miners who took arms against authority and staged the first Australian 'jack-up'.

Jacky: see *Jacky Winter* JACKY *n.*[2]

Jacky, *n.*[1] Also **jackie.** [f. JACK *n.*[1] + -Y.] A kookaburra.

1898 *Bulletin* (Sydney) 10 Sept. 14/4, I have four tame 'jackies' which roam about a large garden. **1901** *Ibid.* 12 Oct. 3/2 Jocund jackies roar with mirth among the messmate-trees. **1918** *Aussie: Austral. Soldiers' Mag.* Feb. 12/1 There's the 'Jackies' laugh and the 'Coo-ee' call. They echo and ring in the hearts of us all. **1931** *Bulletin* (Sydney) 20 May 21/4, I happened on only one kookaburra. . . This jackie had adopted a small flock of sheep as his companions. **1948** J. FAIRFAX *Run o' Waters* 115 The kookaburra we saw in circumstances more damaging to his prestige. A very angry Willy Wagtail . . sped across the river, perched at times on Jacky's back, pecking at the back of his neck. **1964** *N. Austral. Monthly* Sept. 12 A small brown snake . . with a jackass (kookaburra) in pursuit. . . Jacky juggled it around for a while until he got its head in his beak.

Jacky, *n.*[2] [Attrib. use of *Jacky,* dimin. form of *Jack,* in names of animals signifying *small*: see OED *sb.*[1] 37.] Special Comb. **Jacky lizard,** the small, grey, mainly arboreal dragon lizard *Amphibolurus muricatus* of e. Aust.; **Winter,** the small, predom. grey-brown and white flycatcher *Microeca leucophaea,* widespread in mainland Aust. and also found in n.e. New Guinea; *brown flycatcher,* see BROWN *a.* 1; PETER PETER; POST-BOY; also abbrev. as **Jacky.**

1967 H. COGGER *Austral. Reptiles* 38 The lining of the mouth is brightly coloured in some species. In . . the **Jacky Lizard** (*Amphibolurus muricatus*) it is bright yellow, and is believed to have the function of scaring a potential enemy. **1977** *Southerly* iii. 337 He was holding a jackie lizard by the tail, letting its feet run on his open palms. **1978** B.P. MOORE *Life on Forty Acres* 106 The smallest but perhaps the most attractive of the local dragons is the Jacky Lizard . . an agile and handsomely patterned species about a foot in length. **1889** *Proc. Linnean Soc. N.S.W.* IV. 407 *Micraeca fascinans* . . locally known as '**Jacky Winter**'. **1898** E.E. MORRIS *Austral Eng.* 218 Jacky Winter. . . The name has been ascribed to the fact that it is a resident species, very common, and that it sings all through the winter, when nearly every other species is silent. **1906** *Bulletin* (Sydney) 2 Aug. 3/2 Sharp-eyed Jacky of the city, you bring back those good old days . . Jacky Winter then we called you. **1911** A. MACK *Bush Days* 11, I heard a cheery voice at my ear, and there was Jacky Winter sitting on the rail, dressed in his very neatest grey coat and white vest. **1925** E. MCDONNELL *My Homeland* 68, I have often noticed Jacky in the Sydney parks, where the little Aussie has to battle with the pommy pest—the English house sparrow. **1926** *Aussie* (Sydney) Jan. 7/3 A Jacky Winter crying, 'Peter, Peter, Peter' . . with joyous repetition. **1932** A.H. CHISHOLM *Nature Fantasy in Aust.* 161 During the cooler months . . we hear that blithe 'Jacky-Jacky-Jacky' issuing from a fence-post, a stump, a telephone wire, or a favourite old tree; and thus came the names 'Jacky Winter' . . and 'Stumper', familiar now to school-children in many parts of Australia. **1945** C. BARRETT *Austral. Bird Life* 171 Was ever small bird more happily named than 'Jacky Winter'? **1962** MARSHALL & DRYSDALE *Journey among Men* 169 In the settled areas Italian migrants have begun to put themselves on the wrong side of the law by eating willy wagtails, jacky winters, kookaburras . . and, in fact, almost everything in feathers. **1964** M. SHARLAND *Territory of Birds* 145 The 'Jacky Winter', a sleek and friendly little brown flycatcher, is known and liked in many bushland patches and southern gardens. . . I met 'Jacky' in many places. **1981** G. CROSS *George & Widda-Woman* 161 The ugly immigrant starlings, mynahs, sparrows and the fruit-pecking bul-buls, drove away our own sweet Jacky Winters.

Jacky, *n.*[3]

1. Abbrev. of JACKY JACKY. Also *attrib.*

1890 *Adelaide Observer* 15 Feb. 15/3 We have very few friends as it is, but those we have will feel inclined to shun us after reading the Jackey correspondence. **1922** *Smith's Weekly* (Sydney) 12 Aug. 19/1 Nowadays, Binghi is insulted if alluded to as 'Jacky'. **1936** J.C. DOWNIE *Galloping Hoofs* 6 That black was the most persistent I have ever met, and . . knowing 'Jacky' as I did, I knew it would not be long before there was a tribe following me. **1954** T. RONAN *Vision Splendid* 190 Most of the Territorians'd sooner get a Jacky to take the edge off their horses. **1968** F. ROSE *Aust. Revisited* 226 They get my back up because of their attitude towards the Aborigines. . . Jackie's all right, provided you treat him decently. **1973** K.J. GILBERT *Because White Man'll never do It* 18 As the blacks are quick to point out, you don't get to be a councillor unless you are a good jacky who is totally under the manager's thumb. **1975** R.J. MERRITT *Cake Man* (1978) 34 You know what, Rube . . about me, I ain't never stuck up no white man, and I ain't done not one thing in my whole life is brave. All my life, all I ever done was be a jacky-boy. **1985** J. MILLER *Koori* 156 The popular Press of Australia makes a joke of us by presenting silly and out-of-date drawings and jokes of 'Jacky' or 'Binghi', which have educated city-dwellers and young Australians to look upon us as sub-human.

2. In the phr. **to sit up (settle in,** etc.) **like Jacky,** to sit up straight; to display an ingenuousness (supposedly characteristic of an Aboriginal).

1941 S.J. BAKER *Pop. Dict. Austral. Slang* 42 *Jacky, sit up like,* to behave, sit up straight. **1950** E.M. ENGLAND *Where Turtles Dance* 102 She's settled in like Jacky and might take some shifting now. **1958** P. COWAN *Unploughed Land* 182 'Arriving in state today,' he said. 'Sitting up here in the front like Jacky.' **1971** F. HARDY *Outcasts of Foolgarah* 57 Take a look at the no-hopers sitting up like jackey at a football match. **1981** G. CROSS *George & Widda-Woman* 47 Out came a tram from the Arcade with George stuck up in front like Jacky. **1982** R. HALL *Just Relations* 336 Course I'm only an old bushman sittin up on my little mountain like Jacky; and you've travelled the world.

jacky, *n.*[4] Also **jackie.** [f. JACK *n.*[2] + -Y.] JACKEROO *n.* 2.

1945 *Bulletin* (Sydney) 24 Oct. 12/1 The new jackie was an all-wool, double-weft know-all. **1957** *Ibid.* 24 July 16/2 It took an effort to break myself in to the idea of jilleroos replacing jackies on stations.

Jacky Howe. [f. the name of *John* Robert *Howe* (?1861–1920), a champion Queensland shearer of the 1890s.] A (navy or black) sleeveless singlet worn esp. by shearers, rural workers, etc. Also as *adj.* and **Jackie Howe'd.**

1930 *Bulletin* (Sydney) 9 Apr. 19/2 It took nine bars of soap to wash his 'Jacky Howe' flannel. **1936** J. DEVANNY *Sugar Heaven* 39 'Some chaps work in a Jackie Howe and shorts –.' 'What on earth is that?' 'A Jackie Howe? This.' He indicated the athletic singlet he wore. **1949** R. PARK *Poor Man's Orange* 122 He had finished his tea and was sitting in his Jackie Howe, which is a singlet with the sleeves out of it, and called after a famous shearer of the blade days. **1952** A.C.C. LOCK *Travels across Aust.* 77 They could eat their meals arrayed in a 'Jacky Howe' open-neck type of singlet. **1954** *Bulletin* (Sydney) 24 Feb. 13/3 He was able to stride bowyanged and 'Jackie Howe'd' to his place on the board. **1976** S. WELLER *Bastards I have Met* 27 Sweeney was in a 'jacky howe' and shorts. **1980** A.S. VEITCH *Run from Morning* 150 He was wearing . . a blue singlet of the kind the shearers once called a Jacky Howe. **1983** P. KILVINGTON *P. Kilvington* 36 That's Stew in his Jackie Howe in 'Dimboola 1980' opposite.

Jacky Jacky.

a. A nickname for an Aboriginal; the typical Aboriginal.

1845 *Portland Gaz.* 1 July 3/2 Jacky Jacky suddenly turned round and slipped a large jagged spear in his wamera. **1848** *Guardian* (Hobart) 6 May 3/4 The hootings and yells of the Jacky Jackeys. **1872** 'RESIDENT' *Glimpses Life Vic.* 24 'Jacky-Jacky' roamed over the country. **1885** *Australasian Printers' Keepsake* 26 The white-folk wallaby, in numbers vast, Fill all the valleys where my fathers sprang When Jacky Jacky hurled his boomerang. **1901** *Truth* (Sydney) 10 Mar. 1/6 This should have provided evening dress clothes for all the blacks; yet the arrow-branded blanket is still served out to Jacky Jacky. **1922** *Smith's Weekly* (Sydney) 12 Aug. 19/1 Jacky-Jacky christened the birds mostly from their cries and calls. **1960** *Realist* (Sydney) ii. 10 White men that call us all 'Jacky-Jacky' are no good white men.

1977 J. BARKER *Two Worlds* 59 Now that I was able to read I found that the *Bulletin* and newspapers were full of derogatory stories about blacks and 'Jacky Jacky'. **1980** L.G. FOGARTY *Kargun* 28 Are they told that Jacky Jackys and Marys are going to be killed Tell the abo child the true history.

b. COCONUT.

1974 C. BUCHANAN *We have bugger All*, Bullymen do not like Aboriginals to be strong and stand together fighting for land rights. But they do like Jacky Jackys.

Jacky Raw. Altered form of *Johnny Raw* (see JOHNNY 2).

1906 *Bulletin* (Sydney) 28 June 14/2 New chums were originally called Johnny Raws. From that it got to Jacky Raw. And from Jacky Raw to Jackeroo is but a slip of the tongue. **1908** *Austral. Mag.* (Sydney) Nov. 1251/2 A 'jackeroo' (a new chum on a station out for colonial experience) is supposed to be 'Jacky Raw' with a kangaroo's tail to it as it were. **1962** D. MCLEAN *World turned upside Down* 79 What th' ell's th' matter with you today? Y' moonin' about like a jacky raw.

jaffle /'dʒæfəl/. [Transf. use of a proprietary name: see quot. 1965.] A sandwich, with a savoury or sweet filling, sealed and toasted (freq. over an open fire) in a jaffle-iron, a long-handled device consisting of two (usu.) saucer-shaped moulds, hinged and locking together.

1950 *Hardware Jrnl.* May 50 A 'Jaffle' is actually a sealed, toasted sandwich. **1965** *Austral. Official Jrnl. Patents* (Canberra) 1542 *Jaffle* A180,630. 28th May, 1963. Toasters. Hi-Craft Manufacturing Co. Pty. Ltd. **1974** B. HUMPHRIES *Nice Night's Entertainment* (1981) 143 Kicking around the tip with the old mattresses and jaffle irons. **1981** C. WALLACE-CRABBE *Splinters* 97 'Aren't you eating with us, Nigel?' . . 'No way. . . I had a couple of jaffles and a malted earlier.'

jail gang, var. GAOL GANG.

jakeloo, *a.* Also **jakealoo, jakerloo.** [Joc. formation on (orig. U.S.) *jake*: see quot. 1924.] All right, in good order; 'fine'.

1919 W.H. DOWNING *Digger Dialects* 29 Jake-aloo. **1924** A.W. BAZLEY et al. Gloss. Slang A.I.F. (typescript), 17 *Jakerloo* or *jake*, 'jake' was in use before the war, in Australia by drivers & others to indicate that the load and harness were secure and everything ready for a start. It was also used to indicate that all was well with the speaker. The addition of the last two syllables appear to have been made in the A.I.F. abroad; perhaps . . to [rhyme] with 'Bakerloo' the name of the underground railway that connected Waterloo station with Baker Street, both in London. **1927** F.C. BIGGERS *Bat-Eye* 10 These dancin' stunts was jakeloo—a bloke Jist prats 'is frame in, an' selects a girl. **1949** C. BENHAM *Diver's Luck* 39 When everything's jakeloo I rake the fire out er me oven an' claps in me bread. **1965** G. MCINNES *Road to Gundagai* 123 Jakeloo! Let's have the names then, *and* the addresses. **1968** S. GORE *Holy Smoke* 80 The least you could do now is give some sorta guarantee that me and me Mum and Dad'll be jakealoo, when the invasion starts.

jam, *n.*[1] Shortened form of RASPBERRY JAM. Also **jam-tree, jam-wood,** and *attrib.*

1837 *Perth Gaz.* 977 Jam-wood . . grows in such abundance over the mountain range. **1844** J. GOULD *Birds of Aust.* (1848) IV. Pl. 22, In Western Australia the nest . . is usually constructed in a dead jam-tree. **1855** R. AUSTIN *Jrnl. Interior W.A.* 15 Grassy land . . timbered with jam, sandal-wood, and tuart-trees. **1872** *Mission Life* (Perth) 1 Aug. 465 All the jam trees are in their chief beauty in September. **1897** L. LINDLEY-COWEN *W. Austral. Settler's Guide* 49 Sheep will feed down the shoots of jam and keep the cultivable ground clean. **1905** *Rep. W.A. R. Comm. Immigration* p. ix, Had cultivated all classes of land, forest, jam, york gum, and sand plain. Got best results off jam country. **1925** *Bulletin* (Sydney) 1 Jan. 22/2 Jamwood fills the mill with the smell of crushed raspberries. **1933** W.L. OWEN *Cossack Gold* 197 The women fight with waddies of 'jam' or other hardwood. **1960** *Bulletin* (Sydney) 20 July 18/1 The best jam-tree I've dropped wouldn't have yielded 9 in. boards. **1968** V. SERVENTY *Southern Walkabout* 102 The jam, or raspberry-jam tree, is a wattle found growing through much of the South-West [of W.A.] particularly in good soil. Early settlers christened it from the raspberry-jam smell of its freshly cut wood. **1973** *Meanjin* 251 The jam scrub he disliked because it looked regimented, like so many open umbrellas standing in rows or ordered clumps.

jam, *n.*[2] Affectation; pretentious display; 'side'. Freq. in the phr. **to put on jam.** Also *attrib.*

1882 *Sydney Slang Dict.* 5 *Jam (Putting on)*, assuming fast airs of importance. **1884** *Austral. Tit-Bits* (Melbourne) 19 June 14/3 Jam is a drug in the English market. So it is here—if you go down Collins street in the afternoon you can get tons of it for nothing. **1905** *Truth* (Sydney) 12 Mar. 7/1 It's style as has the name; Jam & side are awl the go, fur Them as works upon the game. **1924** LAWRENCE & SKINNER *Boy in Bush* 237 'Jam and dog both mean 'side'?' 'Verily.' **1936** F. CLUNE *Roaming round Darling* 250 They seem to be a community of jam-swappers *de luxe.* **1951** D. STIVENS *Jimmy Brockett* 30 Sadie put a bit of jam on when she talked, but not too much. **1973** F. MOORHOUSE *Austral. Stories* 112 'Marian, clear the table please,' she asked with an intonation the children called 'putting on jam'. **1980** B. HORNADGE *Austral. Slanguage* 92 Anyone who adopts an affected speech or manner in Australia is said to be *putting on the jam*, a saying which probably had its origin back in the nineteenth century when jam was a luxury.

jamberoo /dʒæmbə'ru/. [Altered form of U.S. *jamboree*, perh. infl. by the place-name in N.S.W.] A spree: see quot. 1909.

1889 J.L. HUNT *Bk. of Bonanzas* 83 Jones was on the 'Jamberoo' the other night, and . . he was zig-zagging along the pathway home. **1901** *Truth* (Sydney) 17 Nov. 7/4 But, alas and alack, on the morning On which they were going to be wed, His darling went out on a Jamberoo, And was dumped in the 'nick' instead. **1904** *Ibid.* 4 Sept. 1/1 A prolonged gerrymandering jamberoo. **1908** T.E. SPENCER *Budgeree Ballads* 127 We'll go and see the town, and have a jamberoo. **1909** F.E. BIRTLES *Lonely Lands* 115 It was here I met a party of station hands out on what is termed locally a 'shivoo'. In other parts this function is called a jamberoo, a beano, a bender. **1955** N. PULLIAM *I traveled Lonely Land* 380 *Jamberoo*, a gay party.

jammy, *a.* [f. JAM *n.*[2]] Affected.

1911 A. SEARCY *By Flood & Field* 291 A new chum fellow with notions of city decorum, and not a little 'jammy'. **1966** H. PORTER *Paper Chase* 67 The landlady's 18 year old daughter, a head-tosser with a jammy accent.

japanning, *vbl. n. Obs.* [Perh. with reference to the *japanned* or glossy black finish of a cash-box.] The act of stealing a cash-box.

1902 *Bulletin* (Sydney) 31 May 31/1 Pincher Wilson . . undergoing a sentence of two years for 'japanning', known to the initiated as cash-box or till-snatching, was a gambler. **1904** *Truth* (Sydney) 16 Oct. 7/1 Paddy Toole, serving two years' for 'japanning' (thieving a cash-box).

jarrah /'dʒærə/. [a. Nyungar *jarily.*]

1. The (usu. tall) tree of s.w. W.A. *Eucalyptus marginata* (fam. Myrtaceae), valued for its hard, durable, reddish-brown wood; the wood itself; *native mahogany*, see NATIVE *a.* 6 a.; SWAN RIVER MAHOGANY. See also MAHOGANY 1. Also *attrib.*, esp. as **jarrah wood.**

1846 *Portland Guardian* 18 Sept. 3/3 As a ship-building timber the Jarrah is not only firm-grained, remarkably free from defect, and naturally durable, but seems to be proof against the salt-water worm which is so destructive even to well-seasoned English oak. **1847** E.W. LANDOR *Bushman* 277 She was built partly of deal, and had only her lower streaks of jarra wood, which does not float. **1855** *Further Corresp. Convict Discipline & Transportation* (Great Brit. Parl.) 27 Jan. (1856) 97 The upper tier of cells ceiled with jarra boarding. **1868** J. BAIRD *Emigrant's Guide Australasia* 71 The Jarrah timber, of which there is an inexhaustible supply. **1873** A. TROLLOPE *Aust. & N.Z.* II. 102 It may be that after all the hopes of the West-Australian Micawbers will be realised in jarrah-wood. **1891** E.H. HALLACK *W.A. & Yilgarn Goldfields* 12 Jarrah blocks exported to Melbourne and Sydney for the purpose of woodpaving the streets of those cities. **1902** *Timber Industry & Forests N.S.W.* 2 We have reason to believe that West Australia possesses some 14,000 square miles of jarrah tree country (*Eucalyptus marginata*). **1915** N. DUNCAN *Austral. Byways* 39 A devil-may-care little locomotive, which ate jarrah-wood for breakfast. **1933** J.L. GLASCOCK *Jarrah Leaves* 81 On the long solid jarrah table, crisp and newly-baked loaves lay cooling. **1934** T. WOOD *Cobbers* 57 Every one was built from floor to roof of jarrah. . . When newly cut it is red in colour, but time and polish and housewifely care give it the sheen and lustre of mahogany. **1949** D. WALKER *We went to Aust.* 172 Jarrah is a lovely red wood that seasons darkly but is nothing much to look at as a tree. **1964** G. GELBIN *Australs. have Word for It* 95 A tough, stringy old woman with skin like polished jarrah. **1981** A.B. FACEY *Fortunate Life* 298 We settled into the house . . which was four-roomed, weather-board lined with dressed jarrah board.

2. Special Comb. **jarrah-jerker,** see quot. 1980; **Jarrahland,** the State of Western Australia.

1965 H. PORTER *Cats of Venice* 110 An unmistakable Australian—Joe Blow the Sandgroper; the **jarrah-jerker** doing his dough. **1980** E. & J. TRAUTMAN *Jinkers & Jarrah Jerkers* 1 The descriptive term 'jarrah-jerker' was one term coined to cover all men who 'worked the bush'. **1911** A.S. STEPHENS *Pearl & Octopus* 136 **Jarrahland** jingles. **1928** *Bulletin* (Sydney) 25 Apr. 25/3 One of the strangest things about the abo. is his absence from the sou'-west portion of Jarrahland.

Java sparrow. [f. the resemblance of the finch to the Java sparrow *Padda oryzivora.*] *Diamond firetail*, see DIAMOND *n.*[1]

1855 R. AUSTIN *Jrnl. Interior W.A.* 49 We shot . . four small finches, resembling, but smaller than Java sparrows. **1935** F. BIRTLES *Battle Fronts Outback* 32 A series of wells for travelling stock. . . Thousands of birds . . came to them to drink; shell-parrots, tom-tits, Java sparrows. **1978** D. STUART *Wedgetail View* 41 Empty waterbag, and the start of thirst but the Java sparrows had shown where the water was.

javelin fish. [See quot. 1965.] Any of several marine fish of n. Aust. of the genera *Pomadasys* and *Hapalogenys* (fam. Haemulidae), incl. *Pomadasys hasta.*

1896 F.G. AFLALO *Sketch Nat. Hist. Aust.* 225 Of perches, there are . . the Javelin-fish (*Pristi poma hasta*), Hussar (*Genyoroge amabilis*). **1906** D.G. STEAD *Fishes of Aust.* 123 The Queensland Trumpeter . . is also known in Queensland as the 'Javelin Fish'. **1965** *Austral. Encycl.* V. 123 Javelin-fish . . is regarded as a good food-fish. One of the spines of the anal fin is enlarged to form a stout spike, from which the fish takes its popular name. **1971** P. BODEKER *Sandgropers' Trail* 96 It fought well, a one and one half-pound black spotted javelin fish with tall erect dorsal spines and a loud croaking voice.

jay. [Transf. use of *jay* a noisy bird with striking plumage.] Any of several birds, usu. having a loud call, including the *grey currawong* (see GREY *a.*), and CHOUGH. Also **jay bird.**

1836 J. BACKHOUSE *Narr. Visit Austral. Colonies* 438 Some of the birds of V.D. Land abound; such as the Piping Crow . . the Jay or Black Magpie, *Coronica fuliginosa.* **1853** J. SHERER *Gold Finder Aust.* 39 The voice of the bell-bird, or the cry of the jay. **1918** *Bulletin* (Sydney) 14 Feb. (Red Page), Bush Canaries, Jay-birds. **1981** A.B. FACEY *Fortunate Life* 90 The rosella . . was . . destructive on cereal crops and fruit, as was the jay bird.

jeerun, var. JERRAN.

jelly blubber. A jelly-fish.

1980 C. JAMES *Unreliable Mem.* 171 At Sans Souci baths I dive-bombed a jelly blubber for a dare. **1981** G. CROSS *George & Widda-Woman* 9 We could not swim there, because of the sharks and the jelly blubbers.

jelly leaf. [See quot. 1897.] *Paddy's lucerne*, see PADDY.

1888 *Proc. Linnean Soc. N.S.W.* III. 391 'Paddy Lucerne'. . . In some parts of this colony the plant bears the name of 'Jelly leaf'. **1897** L. LINDLEY-COWEN *W. Austral. Settler's Guide* 537 *Sida rhombifolia* (. . jelly leaf in Queensland. Synonym—*Sida retusa*) . . when old, hard and dry, but when young mucilaginous, which characteristic accounts for Queensland vernacular. **1920** J.H. MAIDEN *Weeds N.S.W.* 58 It sometimes goes by the name of 'jelly-leaf', on account of its mucilaginous character, which causes it to be nibbled by stock.

jemmy. *Obs.* [Altered form of EMIGRANT *n.* 1, by analogy with JIMMY 1.] An emigrant.

1850 W.B. BROWN *Narr. Voyage London to S.A.* 9 They call all government emigrants New Jemmies, and all passengers New Chums, both of which names are now used by the colonists to all new comers. **1880** 'OLD HAND' *Experiences of Colonist* (ed. 2) ii. 7 With these expirees I had two immigrants, or Jemmys as they were called. **1897** H. HUSSEY *Colonial Life & Christian Experience* 61 The word 'emigrant' was considered too long for ordinary use, and, as a substitute, the term 'Jemmies' was usually applied: thus, 'There's another batch (or lot) of 'Jemmies'.'

Jemmy Low: see JIMMY LOW.

jerboa. *Obs.* [Transf. use of *jerboa* a small rodent of arid regions.] HOPPING MOUSE.

1845 J.H. BROWNE *Jrnl. Sturt Exped.* 11 Oct. in *S. Australiana* (1962) Mar. 51 The Jerboa is [a] beautiful little animal about as big [as] a large mouse but formed like a Kangaroo with a very long tail with a brush at the end. **1849** C. STURT *Narr. Exped. Central Aust.* I. 317 Mr Browne had well nigh captured a jerboa, which sprang from under my horse's legs. **1852** W. HUGHES *Austral. Colonies* 80 Among smaller animals of this continent are the native cat . . jerboas, ant-eaters, and a few others. **1896** B. SPENCER *Rep. Horn Sci. Exped. Central Aust.* I. 75 In the jerboa burrows (*Hapalotis mitchelli*) there was never more than one adult.

jerran /'dʒɛrən/, *a.* Chiefly *Austral. pidgin. Obs.* Also **gerrund, gerun, jeerun, jerrund, jirrand.** [a. Dharuk *jiran*.] Afraid. Also as *n.*, a coward.

[*c* **1790** W. DAWES Grammatical Forms Lang. N.S.W., *Tyérun kamarigál*, the kamarigals are afraid.] **1798** D. COLLINS *Acct. Eng. Colony N.S.W.* I. 549 A man who would not stand to have a spear thrown at him, but ran away, was a coward, jee-run. **1827** P. CUNNINGHAM *Two Yrs. in N.S.W.* II. 38 'Come on, white fellow—black fellow no *jirrand*' (afraid). **1829** *Sydney Monitor* 12 Dec. 4/2 The Black . . endeavoured to turn the whole into a joke and called out, 'what for you so *gerrund* (frightened)?' **1839** T.L. MITCHELL *Three Exped. Eastern Aust.* (rev. ed.) I. 64 'What for you jerran budgerry whitefellow?' . . Meaning; why are you afraid of a good white man? **1841** 'LADY LONG RESIDENT N.S.W.' *Mother's Offering to Children* 213 Too much *gerun* me: (meaning frightened). **1847** A. HARRIS *Settlers & Convicts* (1953) 122, I began to feel rather 'jerran' as the blacks say (i.e. timorous). **1867** A.K. COLLINS *Waddy Mundoee* 12 I'm a bit jerrund to stay out at Crowther's with nobody but my mate. Them darkies are knockin' about, I know. **1879** 'AUSTRALIAN' *Adventures Qld.* 38 My word! that fellow *cobborn gerrand*! **1888** 'R. BOLDREWOOD' *Robbery under Arms* (1937) 386 When I saw the mob there was I didn't see so much to be jerran about. **1896** *Bulletin* (Sydney) 18 Apr. 27/1 From Botany came the once familiar . . 'jerran' frightened.

jerry, *v.* [f. U.S. slang *jerry, a.*, in the phr. *to be jerry* to be 'wise' to: see OEDS *a.*[2]] *intr.* To understand; to realize. Also *trans.* and with **to**, and as *n.* in the phr. **to take a jerry to.**

1894 J.W. LONGFORD *Under Lock & Key* 12 The bearer of this stiff has been a good kobber of mine in stir, and as he jerrys to the lingo in this stiff, he will be able to explain everything. **1917** *Bulletin* (Sydney) 15 Feb. 22/3 An old Riverina squatter . . lost a thousand pounds' worth of rams before he jerried that musty ensilage was the murderer. **1919** *Aussie: Austral. Soldiers' Mag.* Feb. 15/1 As for decorations . . he was heard to remark that if his pals heard of his getting one they were to jerry that there had been a comb-out and that he had been unlucky. **1924** *Ibid.* Feb. 6/1 ' 'Ave sense!' snorted Jimmy. 'Don't yer jerry w'y I reneged?' **1926** *Bulletin* (Sydney) 18 Feb. 22/1 Oh, we called him 'Mister Bent', but *he* jerried what we meant! **1938** X. HERBERT *Capricornia* 232 'Use y' bit o' brains,' he says, 'an take a jerry to y'self.' **1945** C. MANN *River* 26 Y' know what, Sandy, I've just taken a jerry to y'. Never struck me before. You got your woman here. Y'r in love with that bloody gun. **1955** N. PULLIAM *I traveled Lonely Land* 380 *Jerry*, to understand. **1967** *Kings Cross Whisper* (Sydney) xxxv. 6/3 *Jerry*, to be awake up. From the prophet Jerimiah who knew all. **1975** *Bulletin* (Sydney) 26 Apr. 44/2, I should've jerried when the guy gave me the tug.

jerryang /'dʒɛriæŋ/. [a. Dharuk *jiraŋ*.] *Little lorikeet*, see LITTLE 2.

1843 J. GOULD *Birds of Aust.* (1848) V. Pl. 54, *Trichoglossus pusillus* . . Jerryang, Aborigines of New South Wales. **1890** G.J. BROINOWSKI *Birds of Aust.* III. Pl. xli, The Jerry Gang or Little Lorikeet . . is dispersed over the same localities as *Trichoglossus concinnus* (musk lorikeet). **1925** *Bulletin* (Sydney) 23 Apr. 23/2 The blacks usually named a bird from its call. . . Jerryang (green lorikeet), gang-gang (cockatoo) . . are a few of the survivals.

Jerusalem screw. [f. *screw* a prison warder.] See quot. 1978.

1972 J. MCNEIL *Old Familiar Juice* (1973) 82 Our favourite provo, a bastard named Hunter, a bloody Jerusalem screw if there ever was one. **1978** E. HARDING *A. Marshall Talking* 57 The most brutal warders were always called Jerusalem Screws—and this was from the first war where the British in Palestine trained some Australians in the way to break really tough prisoners; the name had stuck.

jew. Abbrev. of JEWFISH.

1902 *Bulletin* (Sydney) 7 June 16/2 Have frequently caught 'jews' by throwing a jag-hook on to the nest. **1906** *Truth* (Sydney) Apr. 22 1/7 'Tis rough when persons have to chew Instead of schnapper, full-grown 'Jew'. **1928** 'S. RUDD' *Romance of Runnibede* 35 Many a huge cod, and swags of jew were hauled out of it. **1962** *Meanjin* 53 This one hanging out in the hole I'm fishing is a real beauty—coupla hundred pound, I'd say. The fifty pound jew was just a sparrer's fart to him. **1978** K. GARVEY *Tales of my Uncle Harry* 19 Little jews are tastier than all the big cod and yellow-belly.

jewel beetle. Any of many brightly-coloured beetles of the fam. Buprestidae. Also *attrib.*

1933 H.J. CARTER *Gulliver in Bush* 18 Here with delight came the capture of our first jewel-beetles. [*Note*] *Stigmodera grandis, S. goryi, S. affinis.* **1945** *Coast to Coast 1944* 138 Great creamy sprays of blossom—happy haunts of the big jewel-beetle. **1952** A.M. DUNCAN-KEMP *Where Strange Paths go Down* 148 Quaint jewel beetles were there too, long-legged living emeralds who made their tunnels in the saltpan and sapphire country. **1970** P. SLATER *Eagle for Pidgin* 1 Jewel beetle grubs bored into trees and wrecked them for timber companies.

jeweller's shop. *Mining.* A rich deposit of gold (or opal).

1853 *Guardian* (Hobart) 3 Dec. 3/2 The greatest activity is now displayed in opening new spots, not only in the vicinity of the 'jeweller's shops', but also, higher up the Buninyong Gully. **1857** J. D'EWES *China, Aust. & Pacific Islands* 77 In a part of the diggings named the Canadian Gully, some claims had yielded such a large amount of gold that they were styled the 'Jeweller's Shops'. **1862** J.A. PATTERSON *Gold Fields Vic.* 2 'The jewellers' shops' of former days had long ago been rifled of their golden stores, and . . the flats of Bendigo no longer offered such 'piles' to the lucky miner. **1887** *Illustr. Austral. News* (Melbourne) 25 June (Suppl.) 10/2 Some of the claims were not inappropriately called 'jewellers' shops', and as much as 90 lb. weight of gold has been taken out of a single hole. **1907** C. MACALISTER *Old Pioneering Days* 187 Like many another field the Turon was much of a lottery—it had plenty of 'duffers' and 'stringers' as well as jewellers' shops. **1939** J.N. BARCHAM *Nothing is ever Lost* 3 Why, them 'jewellers' shops' ain't shops at all. It's only a name the miners give to terrible rich patches of alluvial. **1960** D. MCLEAN *Roaring Days* 62 When you strike what you call the 'steel band' of hard sandstone you know you're on the last layer before the opal dirt. A jeweller's shop might be under your feet. **1965** F. HARDY *Yarns of Billy Borker* 142 A jeweller's shop is what they call a mineral formation in rock. Minerals forming a bugh—B-U-G-H—a hole in the rock; looks beautiful, glistens like a jeweller's shop. And that mineral can be pure gold.

jewfish. Also **dewfish, dhufish.** [Transf. use of *jewfish* any of various fish, chiefly of the fam. Serranidae.] Any of several large, edible, marine fish, esp. *Glaucosoma hebraicum*, found only in the coastal waters of W.A., *Johnius diacanthus*, and MULLOWAY; any of several eel-tail catfishes; JEW; JEWIE.

1803 J. GRANT *Narr. Voyage N.S.W.* 159 We caught . . a species of jew fish. **1844** L. LEICHHARDT *Jrnl. Overland Exped. Aust.* 17 Nov. (1847) 40 The jew-fish has the same distoma in its swimming bladder, which I observed in specimens caught in the Severn River. **1851** J. HENDERSON *Excursions & Adventures N.S.W.* II. 204 The Jewfish is also an inhabitant of salt water; it attains a great size, and is excellent when salted. **1870** E.B. KENNEDY *Four Yrs. in Qld.* 126 Jewfish . . are very handsome: the inside of their mouth is orange colour. **1877** *Proc. Linnean Soc. N.S.W.* II. 233, I was astonished to find that a *Sciaena* was amongst the most common fishes of Moreton Bay. . . It is called *Dew-fish*, on account of its beautiful silvery grey colour. . . At Sydney this fish is common, and . . it is generally called *Jew-fish.* **1888** 'R. BOLDREWOOD' *Robbery under Arms* (1937) 209 Even the Jewfish weren't bad with their skins off. **1896** F.G. AFLALO *Sketch Nat. Hist. Aust.* 233 The Jewfish is . . the 'King-fish' of Melbourne. But indifferent eating, even in the young stage known as 'Silver Jew', it is nevertheless served in . . Sydney fish-shops under the sobriquet of 'schnapper cutlets'. **1917** C. THACKERAY *Goliath Joe* 45, I s'pose I'd cort about nineteen dozen fish includin' catfish. They called a catty a jewfish up there. **1921** *Bulletin* (Sydney) 12 May 24/2 At McKenzie Island (Q.) . . newly-caught dew fish were hung under the verandah. **1932** R.W. THOMPSON *Down Under* 243 Of all Australian fish, I like the Jew fish the best to eat. **1948** F.D. MARSHALL *Let's go Fishing* 76 One of the best tablefish, the jewfish (also known as dewfish, butterfish . .) grows up to 120 pounds in weight. **1951** T.C. ROUGHLEY *Fish & Fisheries Aust.* 151 The freshwater catfish . . is appreciated as food by most country people, who frequently know it as 'jewfish'. **1960** *N.T. News* (Darwin) 16 Feb. 2/3 The Jew Fish in these waters is often called the Eel-tailed Catfish as its tail is much the same as that of the freshwater eel. **1977** J. O'GRADY *There was Kid* 52 Sandgropers are not like us 'from the East'. . . They spell jewfish 'dhufish'. **1980** W.H. O'ROURKE *My Way* 195 Another fishing matter led me into an argument in the North [of W.A.]. The mulloway, or kingfish, is known there as jewfish, or 'jewy'.

jewie. Also **jewy.** [f. JEW(FISH + -Y.] JEWFISH.

1917 C. THACKERAY *Goliath Joe* 25 But about ther jewy. Yes! We got some more fish I needn't bother about. **1930** *Bulletin* (Sydney) 25 June 21/4, I was trying to catch a couple of jewies in a waterhole near Mitchell (W.Q.). **1945** C. MANN *River* 3 He hooked a tremendous jewy. **1965** *Tracks we Travel* 173 We might get a couple of bream or jewie for breakfast. **1984** *N.T. News* (Darwin) 16 Nov. 30/4, I was filleting the jewie on the side of the boat.

jew lizard. Formerly also **dew lizard.** [Fig. use of *Jew*, in allusion to the lizard's bearded appearance.]

1. BEARDED DRAGON.

1845 C. HODGKINSON *Aust., Port Macquarie to Moreton Bay* 43 My black companions . . killed an opossum and a large dew-lizard. **1849** *Tasmanian Jrnl. Nat. Sci.* III. 105 Chlamydophorus (the Jew-lizard of the Hunter). **1879** 'OLD HAND' *Experiences of Colonist* 22 The jew lizard stuck out his spiny whiskers. **1886** F. MCCOY *Prodromus Zool. Vic.* (1890) II. xiii. Pl. 121, The Jew Lizard . . is easily distinguished by the beard-like growth of long, slender spines round the throat and paratoids. **1891** *Braidwood Dispatch* 21 Jan. 2/4 Someone brought into the meeting a large live Jew lizard, which during the service was set free amongst the congregation. **1900** *Bulletin* (Sydney) 1 Sept. 14/3 It doesn't seem to have occurred to the gohanna-eaters to try the ugly jew-lizard as a viand. **1927** 'S. RUDD' *Romance of Runnibede* 51 An inoffensive jew lizard . . lay sleeping on a log. **1934** S. KING *Molly's Yr. in Camp* 25 We found a Jew Lizard's nest, with twenty eggs in it, about the size of an English cherry. **1944** P.C. NEASBEY *Blokes I Knew* 50 Enough land and you could just about run two jew-lizards to the acre. **1962** B.W. LEAKE *Eastern Wheatbelt Wildlife* 105 The jew lizard has always been the rarest of all goannas and lizards in the Eastern Wheatbelt. Its colour is greyish brown and it grows to a length of one foot. **1978** K. GARVEY *Tales of my Uncle Harry* 84 You don't see many Jew lizards about the bush these days.

2. *fig.* Also *attrib.*

1895 *Worker* (Sydney) 14 Sept. 4/2 A jewlizzard-looking angel is the manager. **1930** 'BRENT OF BIN BIN'

Ten Creeks Run (1952) 91 You don't mean to say the ould jew lizard is quoite as mean as that!

jewy, var. JEWIE.

jhitu, var. GHITTOE.

jibbong, var. GEEBUNG.

jidu, var. GHITTOE.

jig, *v. trans.* To play truant from (school).

1977 J. RAMSAY *Cop it Sweet* 50 *Jig*, run away, play truant. **1979** *Nat. Times* (Sydney) 3 Nov. 25/4 A group from Leichhardt High 'jig' school at the shops, taking care to avoid the police. . . If you can't nick off sometimes you can find a place to hide, and jig it in the toilets or the change rooms. **1983** *Sydney Morning Herald* 26 July 1/3 'I used to jig school almost every day because I just hated the place, and did not like the teachers very much either,' Sarah said.

jigger, *n.*[1] [Spec. use of *jigger* any of numerous contrivances: see OED(S *sb.*[1] 5.]

1. In prison speech: an improvised radio receiver.

1953 K. TENNANT *Joyful Condemned* 293 He was offered . . a wireless concealed in the false bottom of a treacle tin, a beautiful job, the coil wire being part of an old scrubbing-brush, and most of the rest stolen from the fuse-box outside the cell. A complete jigger such as this was worth at least five pounds money, or forty-eight ounces of tobacco. **1967** B.K. BURTON *Teach them no More* 155 We could make jiggers right under the noses of the screws. **1978** H.C. BAKER *I was Listening* 36 They were listening to their 'jiggers'. A jigger, I learned, was an ingeniously devised miniature radio, made from scraps, on the principle of the first crystal sets. The main materials seemed to be an empty toothpaste tube and a few metres of fine copper wire.

2. A device for administering an electric shock, usu. illegally during a horse race.

1953 *Bulletin* (Sydney) 7 Oct. 13/1 The stewards put me in the sweat-box, fanned me and me gear to see if I've got a 'jigger', and after a long inquiry paid out. **1958** F. HARDY *Four-Legged Lottery* 172 'A jigger job? What do you mean by that, Jim?' He told me. A jigger is a battery. It is not used in the actual race. A horse is 'hit with it' on the training tracks . . usually on the morning of the actual race. They rub a mixture called Penetaine on the horse's sides. This acts as a conductor. In the actual race, the jockey hits the horse with the spurs or the whip at the same point of the track, and the sensation is like that of the battery. **1972** *Sunday Sun* (Brisbane) 26 Nov. 1/2 Battery operated jiggers are being used on mentally retarded children . . to bring them into line. The electric shock treatment is followed by . . lollies if they behave. **1973** *Sunday Mail Mag.* (Brisbane) 25 Feb. 14/1 Occasionally, a blue spark would flash forth as a recalcitrant beast was touched with the 'jigger' (a battery-operated device carried over the shoulder and imparting an electric shock through an insulated rod held in the hand). **1982** J. ANDERSEN *Winners can Laugh* 99 Hand held devices were designed just to make a sound similar to that made by the painful jigger used only in track gallops. When the horse heard the sound during a race it anticipated a coming shock and accelerated in order to avoid it.

3. See quot. 1981. Also **jigger root.**

1954 *Bulletin* (Sydney) 29 Sept. 12/2 Why . . should dry, fibrous roots that could be smoked with no injury but much pretence of pleasure be universally known as 'jigger'? **1981** L. MCLEAN *Pumpkin Pie* 99 One of them produced a box of matches, broke off a piece of root from an old apple tree gum, and set alight to it. These roots have holes running through them. . . You would draw the smoke through just like a cigarette. This was called smoking 'Jigger Root'.

jigger, *n.*[2] [f. JIG.] A truant.

1983 *Sydney Morning Herald* 26 July 1/3 Sarah was sent to Ormond where she and the 39 other school children there have one thing in common: they are chronic 'jiggers', or truants.

jilgie, var. GILGIE.

jill. Abbrev. of JILLEROO.

1974 J. DINGWELL *Cattleman* 87 Noel came in with a pacific: 'She's a first-class jill on a station.'

jilleroo. /dʒɪlə'ru/. Also **jillaroo.** [Joc. formation on JACKEROO *n.* 2.] A female station-hand. Also as *v. intr.*, to work as a jilleroo.

1943 S.J. BAKER *Pop. Dict. Austral. Slang* (ed. 3) 42 *Jillaroo*, a land girl (War slang). **1944** *Land Army Gaz.* (Brisbane) Mar. 5 Here's to the Jillaroos of the Army. **1944** *Sun* (Sydney) 1 June 3/5 On the job at the ram sales today was small, fair, 19-year-old Jean Adams 'Jilleroo', from Uardry Station, near Hay. . . She does all the work usually done by a Jackeroo. **1957** *Bulletin* (Sydney) 24 July 16/2 It took an effort to break myself in to the idea of jilleroos replacing jackies on stations. **1962** J. MACKENZIE *Austral. Paradox* 225 This was a busy, lively family in which two of the daughters—jilleroos—and one son—a jackeroo—help with the cattle and the cane. **1970** *Sunday Mail Mag.* (Brisbane) 15 Aug. 7/3 Isabel has been jillarooing all over Australia for the last four years. **1973** H. LEWIS *Crow on Barbed Wire Fence* 214 Our eldest daughter at twenty-two went alone to Australia to check up on some of my tales and worked as a jilleroo on an up-country sheep station in South Australia. **1982** *Canberra Times* 23 Oct. 28/5 *Jillaroo.* Must be competent rider. Some sheep, and housework. **1984** *Age* (Melbourne) 2 June 2/6 She reckoned she learnt it while jillarooing in the outback. **1986** *Nat. Times* (Sydney) 7 Mar. 2/3 'Jackaroos are really trainee managers, but jillaroos rarely become station managers,' she said. 'Most bushmen wouldn't accept taking orders from women.'

jim. *Obs.* Also as *pl.* [Abbrev. of *Jimmy O'Goblin*, rhyming slang for 'sovereign'.] The sum of one pound; a sovereign.

1889 *Bulletin* (Sydney) 6 July 5/4 Won fifty 'jim' it all got 'blown', In 'arf a week I spent it. **1901** *Truth* (Sydney) 31 Mar. 5/5 Brown wanted to know where we got the 'shikker', and he told him that he paid for it with a 'half-jim', and that he got 5s. change. **1917** C.L. DREW *Reminisc. D. Gilbert* 141 'She's up another half a jim!' returned the sharp, putting the necessary money in. **1921** W.H. PHIPPS *Bush Yarns* 80 Dropped half-a-sovereign in the plate. . . I thort th' good old priest wud drop dead. . . He first picked up that half er jim as ef it were dirt. **1930** A.E. YARRA *Vanishing Horsemen* 221 The racehorse they have just bought in Bourke for fifty jim.

Jim Gerald. Rhyming slang for 'Herald', applied to newspapers bearing that name.

1956 *Overland* vi. 17, I see there's a bloke who claims to be thirty-third cousin of the Tsar, and says he's an authority on Russia, writing his memoirs for the Jim Gerald. **1974** *Bulletin* (Sydney) 2 Nov. 57/2 Melbourne's evening newspaper was, and sometimes still is, called the Jim Gerald (Herald) which would simply confuse the Cockneys.

jimmigrant, var. JIMMYGRANT.

Jimmy.

1. *Obs.* Abbrev. of JIMMYGRANT.

[N.Z. **1850** D. MCLEAN Papers VIII. 177 The 'Jimmies' usurpers of the soil.] **1859** H. KINGSLEY *Recoll. Geoffry Hamlyn* II. 154 'Why, one,' said Lee, 'is a young Jimmy (I beg your pardon, sir, an emigrant).' **1878** *Austral. Town & Country Jrnl.* (Sydney) 6 July 27/2 The country was worth living in, not like it is now, over-stocked with 'jimmies'—a lot of useless trash. **1913** *Truth* (Sydney) 22 June 7/7 *Weedy Jimmygrants.* The class of English chawbacon at present being imported into the Commonwealth to 'go on the land' belong to the 'weedy order'. . . Certainly many of the Jimmies look a bit on the 'weedy' side, but appearances are sometimes deceptive. **1915** *Ibid.* 28 Mar. 5/2 The 500 home-bolting 'Jimmies' (as he calls them) who were pining for the bacon and bread or slice of suet pudding which was all they knew of meat.

Also **jimmygration** *n.* [f. IMMIGRATION].

1908 *Truth* (Sydney) 27 Dec. 1/4 One of those Jimmygration Leagues wants to get the reservists from India out here.

2. *pl.* Abbrev. of JIMMY BRITTS.

1945 *Certo Insana: 5th Austral. Division Signals* 3 All the staff have got the Jimmys. **1955** D. NILAND *Shiralee* 50 Men was growlin' crook tucker, gettin' the jimmies, an' all that, they said. **1958** F.B. VICKERS *Mirage* (ed. 2) 121 A bloke who's got the jimmies bad is very quick on the trigger.

Jimmy Britts, *pl.* Also **Jimmy Brits.** [f. the name of *Jimmy Britt* (1879–1940), an American-born boxer.] With **the:** rhyming slang for 'shits'. Cf. EDGAR BRITT. Also *fig.*

[**1941** S.J. BAKER *Pop. Dict. Austral. Slang* 15 *Brits up, have the*, to be afraid, alarmed.] **1954** J. CLEARY *Climate of Courage* 292 Malaria and the jimmy britz have sucked him dry. **1959** D. NILAND *Gold in Streets* 169 Strike a light Danno, you gimme the jimmy britts at times. **1960** J. WYNNUM *Sailor Blushed* (1962) 10 'You gimme the Jimmy Brits,' grunted Lofty, darting a left fist into Tony's eye. **1972** D. CRICK *Different Drummer* 37 He gave me a touch of the Jimmy Brits. **1975** L. RYAN *Shearers* 120 'Gees!' Sandy exclaimed in awe. 'Has he got the jimmy brits!'

jimmygrant. Also **jimmigrant, Jimmy Grant.** Rhyming slang for IMMIGRANT 1.

[N.Z. **1845** E.J. WAKEFIELD *Adventure in N.Z.* I. 337 The profound contempt which the whaler expresses for the 'lubber of a *jimmy-grant*', as he calls the emigrant.] **1859** J.D. MEREWEATHER *Diary Working Clergyman* 4 Speaking contemptuously of some newly-arrived immigrants ('Jimmy Grants', I think, was the slang term she applied to them). **1878** J.H. NICHOLSON *Opal Fever* 113 We met i' the forest a motley new chum, Isn't it odd, by the by, how few come So far out west as Springsure Plains? I suppose the poor jimmygrunts haven't the brains. **1887** W.H. SUTTOR *Austral. Stories Retold* 144 Looked upon the 'Jimmygrants' (with an expletive)—as newcomers were called—as intruders, and to be treated with hatred and contempt. **1893** J. DEMARR *Adventures in Aust.* 45 Anyone who had been in the colony for some length of time would know a newly-arrived 'jimmygrant' at once. **1907** *Truth* (Sydney) 26 May 1/4 Most of the 'Jimmy Grants' arrived so far look like Dukes in disguise. **1912** *Bulletin* (Sydney) 15 Aug. 15/2 A newly arrived 'Jimmy Grant' passed a paddock of dead, ring-barked timber. . . 'Crikey!' he howled, 'have all those trees been struck by lightning?' **1916** W.C. WATSON *Mem. Ship's Fireman* 61 As I hailed from the Old Dart, I, of course, in their estimation, was an immigrant, hence the curl up of the lip. But 'pommy-grant' or 'jimmygrant', they always had a helping hand for me. **1920** H.J. RUMSEY *Pommies* Introd., In the early seventies . . the colonial boys and girls . . ready to find a nickname, were fond of rhyming 'Immigrant', 'Jimmy-grant', 'Pommegrant'. **1948** F. CLUNE *Wild Colonial Boys* 67 More and more Crown land was taken up by the ever-arriving 'jimmygrants' who had government help and favour. **1963** X. HERBERT *Disturbing Element* 91 He still wore the heavy clumsy British type of clothing of the day. When we kids saw people on the street dressed like that we would yell at them: 'Jimmygrants, Pommygranates, Pommies!'

Jimmy Low. *Qld. Obs.* [See quot. 1904.] The tree *Eucalyptus resinifera*, also known as *red mahogany* (see RED *a.* 1 a.). Also **Jemmy Low.**

1882 *Austral. Handbk.* 391 'Jemmy Low' . . is a very large tree, and much in demand for fencing. **1894** *Proc. R. Soc. Qld.* X. 99 *E. resinifera*—a name which to-day is reserved for the Jimmy Low. **1904** J.H. MAIDEN *Forest Flora N.S.W.* I. 67 In Queensland it [*sc. Eucalyptus resinifera*] is often called 'Jimmy Low', after the late Mr James Low, of Maroochie River, a locality for some of the finest specimens in that State. **1926** *Qld. Agric. Jrnl.* XXV. 439 *Eucalyptus resinifera* . . Jimmy Low (Queensland).

Jimmy Woodser. [f. *Jimmy Wood*, the name of a character in the poem of that name (see quot. 1892, 1) by Barcroft Boake, and perh. the name of an actual person.] One who drinks alone in a public bar; a drink taken on one's own. Also **Jimmy Woods,** and as *v. intr.*

1892 B.H. BOAKE in *Bulletin* (Sydney) 7 May 17/3 Who drinks alone, drinks toast to Jimmy Wood, sir. [*Note*] A man who drinks by himself is said to take a 'Jimmy Woodser'. *Ibid.* 2 July 7/3 Dear Bulletin—A 'Jimmy Woodser' may mean a solitary drink (or a solitary drinker) in some places . . but in the Western district of Victoria, if a man takes a drink by himself, he is said to 'go Ballarat'. **1898** *Critic* (Adelaide) 16 Apr. 5/3 If I'm feelin' thirsty now; Which is frequent I'll allow, For I've got a sort o' thirst that never dies; I sneak in all alone An' quench it on me own—Take a lonely Jimmy Woodser with the flies. **1903** *World's News* (Sydney) 11 Apr. 14 They lack the moral courage to enter a populous tap-room and call aloud for a 'Jimmy Woodser', because long-standing public opinion regards the solitary imbiber with a certain degree of contempt. **1908** *Bulletin* (Sydney) 10 Dec. 21/1 The long sleever that cheers and the Jimmy Woodser that inebriates. **1916** *Truth* (Sydney) 17 Sept. 6/8 The Wowser and Jimmy Woodser began closing hotels and crying around street corners for Conscription. **1923** J. MOSES *Beyond City Gates* 65 It's not a Jimmy Woodser 'Cause I've got me cobber here. **1940** *Digger Yarns: Cream of 'Aussiosities'*, Old Bill Dickson was a Jimmiwoodser. Whenever Bill had a bob, he made a bee-line for the nearest pub, and enjoyed its worth on his 'ownsome'. **1952** C. SIMPSON *Come away, Pearler* 136, I should have had a beer, too, instead of that nobbler of gin—I'm still thirsty! . . You won't think too badly of me if I stop and have a Jimmy Woodser. **1967** *Kings Cross Whisper* (Sydney) xxxv. 6/3 *Jimmy Woodser*, to drink by oneself. **1972** D. SHEAHAN *Songs from Canefields* 74 And see old Jimmy Woodzer in a corner by himself Telling stories to the bottles that are standing on the shelf. **1981** L. McLEAN *Pumpkin Pie* 87 We were told that any man drinking alone in a bar was referred to as having a 'Jimmie Woodser'. Apparently there had been a Jim Woods who was a loner.

jim-rags, *pl. Obs.* [Var. of Br. dial. *jamrags* rags, tatters, shreds: see EDD.] Small pieces, 'smithereens'. Esp. in the phr. **to kick** (one) **to jim-rags** and varr.

1894 H. LAWSON *Short Stories* 65 If yer starts playin' any of yer jumpt-up pranktical jokes on me . . I'll kick yer to jim-rags, so I will! **1899** *Austral. Mag.* (Sydney) Apr. 77 Me and you ain't goin' to fight, Andy. . . If you try it on I'll knock you into jim-rags!

jims, *pl. Obs.* Abbrev. of 'jim-jams' delirium tremens.

1894 G.H. GIBSON *Ironbark Chips* 55 Cure him of D.T.s and 'jims'. **1906** E. DYSON *In Roaring Fifties* 168 Only a touch o' the jims.

jin, var. GIN.

Jindyworobak /dʒɪndi'wɒrəbæk/. [Prob. f. an Aboriginal language.] A member of a literary group formed in 1938 by the poet R.C. Ingamells (1913–1955), to promote Australianism in art and literature. Also *attrib.*

[**1929** J. DEVANEY *Vanished Tribes* 240 *Jindy-worabak*, to annex; to join.] **1938** R. INGAMELLS *Conditional Culture* 4 'Jindyworobak' is an aboriginal word meaning 'to annex, to join', and I propose to coin it for a particular use. The jindyworobaks, I say, are those individuals who are endeavouring to free Australian Art from whatever alien influences trammel it, that is, to bring it into proper contact with its material. **1941** *Southerly* iii. 29 This illustrates the kind of delusion of the Jindyworobak mind which sees the corroboree as a literary rite. **1943** *Meanjin Papers* Winter 33 How little competent poetic analysis, discussion of rhythm, texture, poetic integrity has gone on in this country since the Jindyworobaks and others started screeching about National Resurgence and What Poetry Should Be About. **1948** *Jindyworobak Rev.* 31 The Jindyworobaks desire supremely that the Australian imagination shall be the fruitage of an Australian perception. **1966** H. PORTER *Paper Chase* 176, I blunder through this group quickly, and just as quickly through the Jindyworobak group of poets. Indeed, several meetings with Rex Ingamells, the Jindyworobak high priest . . a quiet fanatic intent on making aborigines fashionable. **1974** D. O'GRADY *Deschooling Kevin Carew* 60 'I'll admit I'm sounding like a Jindyworobak.' . . He intoned 'Did-ji-ri-doo—Did-ji-ri-doo' to the amusement of three . . students on their way to the oval. **1979** B. ELLIOT (*title*) The Jindyworobaks.

Jinga, var. JINGY.

jingera /'dʒɪndʒərə/. [The name of a town in s. N.S.W.] Remote and mountainous bush-covered country. Also *attrib.*

1870 *Illustr. Sydney News* 13 Apr. 379/3 Here and there set among the thickly wooded ridges . . pieces of pasture land of small extent upon which the 'Jingera squatter' or 'gully-raker' locates himself. . . The real occupation of the Jingera squatter is to 'spot' the cattle-drove wandering about out-lying stations, or straying among the gullies, to 'tail off' the cows heavy with calf, and run them home to lonely mountain gulches, where feed is plentiful. **1977** G.C. JOYNER *Hairy Man of S. Eastern Aust.* 20 It was supposed to be in the Tinderry mountains, and what is known as the 'jingera' behind—the wild, rough country.

Jingie, var. JINGY.

jingle.

1. *Hist.* A covered two-wheeled carriage.

1862 C. ASPINALL *Three Yrs. Melbourne* 122 Gentlemen who have lived in India will persist in calling this vehicle a jingle. . . It is a kind of dos-a-dos conveyance, holding three in front, and three behind, it has a waterproof top to it . . and oilskin curtains to draw all round. **1869** J. MARTINEAU *Lett. from Aust.* 16 There are plenty of street-cars, or jingles as they are called, which are like Irish cars with the seat turned breadthways instead of lengthways, and with a covering to keep off sun and rain. **1881** *Austral. Handbk.* 213 Waggonettes have superseded the car or 'jingle', and are a great improvement upon them. **1981** A.S. VEITCH *Roses & Boronia* 51 There was a line of cabs waiting, what the townsmen called 'jingles'.

2. Money in small coins, change.

1906 E. DYSON *Fact'ry 'Ands* 99 Ther Elder dug in 'n' brought up er 'andful iv jingle. **1941** S.J. BAKER *Pop. Dict. Austral. Slang* 39 *Jingle*, money. **1958** *Bulletin* (Sydney) 11 June 19/1 If he is a youngish man, his pockets are lined with coin, oof, dough, sugar or hay. If he is getting on in years his pockets will hold jingle.

jingling johnny.

1. *Sheep-shearing.* **a.** One who uses hand shears. **b.** *pl.* A set of hand shears.

[N.Z. **1934** *Press* (Christchurch) 20 Jan. 15/7 *Jingling Johnnies*, old time slang term for hand shearers.] **1941** S.J. BAKER *Pop. Dict. Austral. Slang* 39 *Jingling johnnies*, hand shears. **1965** J.S. GUNN *Terminol. Shearing Industry* i. 33 *Jingling Johnny*, originally a swagman or bagman but in many districts this was also another name for a hand-shearer.

2. LAGERPHONE.

1963 *Gumsuckers' Gaz.* (Melbourne) Aug. 10 Interesting to those who play the lager-phone, or jingling johnnie, is the information that hand shears were also called *jingling johnnies.*

Jingy /'dʒɪndʒi/. *W.A. Obs.* Also **Chingah, Chingi, Jinga, Jingie.** [a. Nyungar *jiŋa.*] A devil or evil spirit. Also *attrib.*

1837 G.F. MOORE *Evidences Inland Sea* 48 One . . was considered by our guide to be the peculiar residence of a 'Chingah', (a spirit) which he described as having large head and horns. **1847** E.W. LANDOR *Bushman* 208 They have some indistinct ideas about Chingi, the Evil Spirit. **1851** MRS R. LEE *Adventures in Aust.* 243 Everybody believed in an evil spirit, which haunts dark caverns, wells, and gloomy plains; that its name is Jinga, and that they are afraid of him at night. **1857** W.S. BRADSHAW *Voyages* 116 To drive away Chingie the evil spirit. **1872** MRS E. MILLETT *Austral. Parsonage* 58, I heard a native speak of them as 'Jingy birds', that is, Satan's birds, Jingy being the name of the evil spirit. *Ibid.* 289 A yearly feast held in honour of the evil spirit, and called on that account the 'Jingy corobbery'. **1901** M. VIVIENNE *Travels in W.A.* 337 They greatly fear an evil spirit, Jingie.

jinker, *n.* [Var. of Scot. dial. *janker* long pole on wheels used esp. for carrying logs.]

1. A wheeled conveyance used for moving heavy logs, etc.: see quot. 1889. Also **timber jinker,** and *attrib.*

1889 A. BRASSEY *Last Voyage India & Aust.* 238 We followed a double team of sixteen horses drawing a timber-cart composed of one long thick pole between two enormous wheels some seven or eight feet in diameter. Above these wheels a very strong iron arch is fastened, provided with heavy chains, by means of which and with the aid of an iron crowbar used as a lever, almost any weight of timber can be raised from the ground. The apparatus is called a 'jinka'. **1897** *Bulletin* (Sydney) 15 May 28/1, I have seen the Gippsland jinkers hauling paves for London streets. **1916** J.B. COOPER *Coo-oo-ee!* 1 Along the tracks heavy timber-jinkers groaned on their way to the Ironbark Sawmill. **1935** DAVISON & NICHOLLS *Blue Coast Caravan* 54 Earth was ploughed deep by the wheels of the timber jinkers. **1951** D. COLLINS *Vic.'s my Home Ground* 87 Back at Echuca I sat for a space in the morning sunshine on an old timber jinker with solid wooden wheels. **1960** E. O'CONNOR *Irish Man* 302 He saw a jinker carrying four huge logs wrapped about with sturdy chains. In front of the jinker stood ten horses. **1980** M. WILLIAMS *Dingo!*, Watch the crouching jinker driver bring his haul across the bridge.

2. A light, two-wheeled, horse-drawn cart. Also *attrib.*

1916 *Bulletin* (Sydney) 28 Dec. 24/3 A small boy was sitting in a jinker drawn up at the roadside. **1921** K.S. PRICHARD *Black Opal* 6 The . . homemade jinker, whose body was painted a dull yellow, came last of the vehicles on the road. **1926** 'S. WESTLAW' *White Peril* 102 'Jinker'—which is in common use in Australia means a light, two-wheeled, horse-drawn vehicle which holds two or three people. **1946** *Bulletin* (Sydney) 16 Jan. 13/4 Old Charlie pensioned his horse and jinker in favor of a vintaged Ford. **1976** C.D. MILLS *Hobble Chains & Greenhide* 140 Clarabelle . . jogged a jinker load of mates with you on exciting bird-nesting forays.

jinker, *v.* [f. prec.] *trans.* To convey (a log, etc.) using a jinker.

1903 R. BEDFORD *True Eyes & Whirlwind* 240 Waiting for a fine day to jinker those trees out of the bush. **1908** L.S. CURTIS *Hist. Broken Hill* 24 House after house had been 'jinkered' over the rough road and dumped down on the 'Hill'. **1938** F. CLUNE *Free & Easy Land* 267 Walnut logs jinkered down the hills.

jinna-jinna, var. GINA-GINA.

jirrand, var. JERRAN.

jitto, var. GHITTOE.

jockey.

1. *pl.* Horizontal wooden poles used to hold a bark roof in place: see quot. 1905.

1905 *Bulletin* (Sydney) 2 Mar. 17/1 The logs which 'anchor' the roof—known as 'riders' and 'jockeys'. The first-named are perpendicular, in pairs; and the ends overlapping the ridge are loosely held together with wooden pins, to allow their spread to conform to the roof-angle and lie close to the bark when the weight of the jockey comes on their loose ends—those nearest the eaves. The jockeys are laid horizontally across these lower ends, and are held in position by wooden pegs driven into the underlying rider. **1911** E.S. SORENSON *Life in Austral. Backblocks* 26 It was roofed with stringy-bark, the latter being hung with greenhide and held down with poles ('riders' and 'jockeys') pegged together. **1945** S.J. BAKER *Austral. Lang.* 78 *Jockeys* are logs laid horizontally across the riders at their lower ends.

2. One who acts as an assistant to a carrier, taxi-driver, etc. Also as *v. intr.*

1910 STEPHENS & O'BRIEN Materials Austrazealand Slang Dict. 26 *Brewer's jockey*, (Melbourne) a man who rides about with the driver of a brewer's waggon helping him load and unload on the chance of a share of the drinks which fall to the lot of a brewer's man. **1945** S.J. BAKER *Austral. Lang.* 140 A jockey is a taxi-driver's accomplice who pretends to be a passenger in order to encourage legitimate travellers to pay extortionate fares to secure the taxi. **1973** J. POWERS *Last of Knucklemen* (1974) 58 One of the cattle stations used a helicopter for spottin' stray cattle. I jockeyed for the pilot. **1978** J. COLBERT *Ranch* 25 Quite a few truck drivers drink at the pub and sometimes they need a jockey the next day to help them loading. **1986** *Good Weekend* (Sydney) 19 Apr. 11/1 He left at 14 and got a job as a jockey on two fruit trucks at the Victorian markets.

jockey spider. [From the resemblance of the striking colours of the female to those of a jockey's blouse.] RED-BACK. Also *ellipt.* as **jockey.**

1922 *Bulletin* (Sydney) 16 Mar. 20/4 The red-back or jockey spider (*Latrodectus hasselti*) is being discussed by the country medicoes of N.S.W. **1942** C. BARRETT *On Wallaby* 30 An infant bitten by a 'jockey', to give the little horror one of its nicknames, died six hours later.

1956 S. HOPE *Diggers' Paradise* 203 The little red-back . . also known in some quarters as the jockey spider.

joe, *n. Hist.* [Prob. from the name of Charles *Joseph* La Trobe (1801–1875), Lieutenant-Governor of Victoria, but see quot. 1859.]

1. A policeman, trooper, etc., esp. one charged with the implementation of licensing regulations of the Victorian goldfields; a cry warning of the approach of such a person.

1854 *Illustr. Sydney News* 28 Oct. 234/3 Some of the police . . were now ordered to fall back on the hotel for its protection if necessary. The Joe!, Joe! soon began and some boys threw stones at the windows. **1855** W. HOWITT *Land, Labor & Gold* I. 427 The well-known cry of 'Joe! Joe!'—a cry which means one of the myrmidons of Charley Joe, as they familiarly style Mr La Trobe. **1859** W. KELLY *Life in Vic.* I. 191 Joe is a term of opprobrium hurled after the police ever since the diggings commenced, but the derivation is still a mystery. Some commentators trace it to the Christian name of Mr Latrobe; but this is an error; the ex-governor was never personally unpopular, except with the editor of the *Argus*. **1868** *Wallaroo Times* (Kadina) 4 Nov. 3/4 The stupid and formerly incessant cry of 'Joe' is seldom heard. **1892** F.A. HARE *Last of Bushrangers* 11 Whenever a policeman or any other Government servant was seen they raised a cry of 'Joe-Joe'. I never heard the origin of the word. **1906** E. DYSON *In Roaring Fifties* 108 'Jo!' was the favourite epithet hurled at the troopers and all representatives of constituted authority. **1915** L. ROSS *From Rossiville to Victorian Goldfields* 82 It had become the usual practice among the miners to shout 'Joe, Joe, Joe', when a blue-coat appeared on the creek, and this note of warning was repeated from one to the other till it rang all over that part of the field. **1928** N.F. SPIELVOGEL *Affair at Eureka* 6 The Police Commissioner and his troopers ('Joes' in digger parlance) were all powerful, and often used their power with harshness and brutality.

2. *transf.* A term of derision or abuse, esp. as applied to one whose appearance, dress, etc., is not that of a miner.

1857 *Illustr. Jrnl. Australasia* III. 65 'Did you go down dressed as you are now?' 'I did.' . . 'Then I'll be bound . . that you are annoyed because they called 'Joe' after you.' **1872** 'RESIDENT' *Glimpses Life Vic.* 137 A friend . . lately arrived . . ventured one day among the diggings, wearing the conspicuous tall hat, which he had always been used to wear at home. He was instantly assailed by cries of 'Joe, Joe'. **1886** *Lantern* (Adelaide) 11 Dec. 6 'Yes, I ain't got no blank objection to be interviewed, Joe.' (The familiar term 'Joe', I may mention, is a diggings fashion—my name is not Joseph.) **1921** *Bulletin* (Sydney) 17 Nov. 20/2 My dad who 'followed the diggings' tells me that to call a man 'Joe' on the Vic. rushes was the surest way of buying a fight.

joe, *v. Hist.* [f. prec.] *trans.* To taunt (a person) by calling out 'Joe'; to jeer. Also *absol.* and as *vbl. n.*

1854 R. CARBONI *Eureka Stockade* 26 Aug. (1855) 16 A mob soon collected round the hole; we were respectful, and there was no 'joeing'. **1855** *Illustr. Sydney News* 6 Jan. 3/3, I am sorry that the childish and cowardly system of 'Joeing' still continues. **1855** R. CARBONI *Eureka Stockade* 103 The Ballaarat diggers . . considered themselves luckily cunning to have got off safe, and therefore could afford to 'joe' again. **1858** C.R. THATCHER *Colonial Songster* (rev. ed.) 7 The swell that in London rides through Rotten-row, Is admired and bowed to by many you know; But if he were to ride down the Ballarat-road, I rather think he would be jolly well 'joed'. **1867** *Essay on Politics in Verse* 6 Now smash a state, now mould a crinoline, Now 'joe' a bell-topper. **1882** A.J. BOYD *Old Colonials* 160 If a bank manager even wore a coat he would be 'joed'. **1903** W. CRAIG *My Adventures* 255 In security they 'Joe'd' and jeered the police to their hearts' content. **1918** C. FETHERSTONHAUGH *After Many Days* 24, I am afraid we boys used to join in 'Joe-ing' him when he happened to come to the wharf. **1955** H. ANDERSON *Colonial Ballads* 47 If they were out for licences we'd stand and joe the traps.

Joe Blake.

1. Rhyming slang for 'snake'.

1905 J. MEREDITH *Learn to talk Old Jack Lang* (1984) 12, I saw a lot of *Joe Blakes*, but don't know if they were dinkum or just the after effects of the grog. **1927** M. TERRY *Through Land of Promise* 123 I'll bet you what you like there are Joe Blakes in this camp. **1934** F.H. BROWN *Songs of Plains* 30 An old goanna . . That bit the Jo-Blake's head in halves. **1946** D. STIVENS *Courtship of Uncle Henry* 150 We decide to settle accounts with Mr Joe Blake. **1963** *N. Austral. Monthly* Dec. 13, I understand the common Joe Blake to which we refer as a grass snake isn't a snake at all—it's a worm! **1970** J. O'GRADY *So sue Me* 14 Along would come the Joe Blake, nearly as stupid as a chook. **1981** P. BARTON *Bastards I have Known* 21 I'd never heard of anyone actually being bitten by a 'joe blake' in the hills.

2. *pl.* Rhyming slang for 'the shakes'; delirium tremens.

[N.Z. **1942** *2nd N.Z. Exped. Force Times* (Johnny Enzed) 41/6 The Joe Blakes.] **1944** A. MARSHALL *These are my People* 155 You feel nothin' when you're on a bender. . . You get the Joe Blakes bad after a few weeks. **1963** J. CANTWELL *No Stranger to Flame* 39 'What's up Dot?' Lou Keller said, grinning. 'Why the Joe Blakes.' **1967** *Kings Cross Whisper* (Sydney) xxxv. 6/3 *Joe Blakes*, shakes, horrors, rats, delirium tremens. **1971** W.G. HOWCROFT *This Side Rabbit Proof Fence* 85 As Phil arrived, a shooter suffering from a bad attack of the morning after 'Joe Blakes' was trying to take aim.

joes, *pl.* [Of unknown origin.] An attack of revulsion or depression.

1910 L. ESSON *Three Short Plays* (1911) 8 Yer giv 'er man ther joes. **1915** C.J. DENNIS *Songs of Sentimental Bloke* 41 They smooge some more at that. Ar, strike me blue! It gimme Joes to sit an' watch them two! **1942** L. MANN *Go-Getter* 97 'The weather's bad enough to give a man the joes.' The innuendo was that she was giving him the joes also. **1947** M. RAYMOND *Smiley gets Gun* 207 'You look as if you've got the joes reel bad,' she commented. Smiley blurted out the whole story. 'Oh, well don't drop yore bundle,' advised his mother cheerfully. **1955** N. PULLIAM *I traveled Lonely Land* 227 Give a bloke the joes, my word it would.

joey, *n.*[1] [Of unknown origin.]

1. A young possum. Also **joey possum.**

1828 *Trumpeter* (Hobart) 3 Oct. 3 A young opossum (perhaps two or three days old) was put to a cat which had two kittens. . . It is really amusing to see the kittens crawling about with Joey clinging to one of their backs. **1859** W. BURROWS *Adventures Mounted Trooper* 81 The 'joeys', as the young ones [of the common opossum] are called, seldom come out of the pouch. **1898** *Truth* (Sydney) 20 Feb. 2/8 A 'possum's called a 'Joey' up around New England way. **1898** E. DYSON *Below & on Top* 289 That 'possum in the big blue gum . . has two joeys, and she has gone mad. **1899** *Tocsin* (Melbourne) 2 Mar. 1/1 The frontispiece, representing a procession of 'possums with their joeys ascending a gum tree. **1928** W. ROBERTSON *Coo-ee Talks* 19 Give her wattle blossom, and a joey 'possum, She's a good Australian piccaninny. **1948** *Bulletin* (Sydney) 24 Mar. 28/4 Those joeys must have been at least a month old. When the young possum is born it is a tiny, hairless, ugly creature. **1958** *Ibid.* 13 Aug. 18/3 By the time he had got outside with its supper of bread and jam the possum was waiting for him. After she had finished eating she took another lot for her joey. 'Been coming here for 17 years,' said our host. 'We reared her from a joey.' **1973** S. & K. BREEDON *Wildlife Eastern Aust.* 43 The possums throw the half-eaten leaves to the ground; the joeys rush back to their mothers, climb on their backs and hold on with claws and teeth.

2. A young kangaroo or wallaby. Also **joey kangaroo.**

1839 W.H. LEIGH *Reconnoitering Voyages* 94 The wallaba . . are of the kangaroo species. . . The young of this animal is called by the islanders a joè. **1845** J.A. MOORE *Tasmanian Rhymings* (1860) 15 He was a 'joey', which, in truth, Means nothing more than that the youth Who claims a kangaroo descent, Is by that nomenclature meant, Just in the way that sheep were lambs, When they were following their dams. **1862** G.T. LLOYD *Thirty-Three Yrs. Tas. & Vic.* 73 The little shapeless pimple . . is in reality no other than the Joey kangaroo in its truly wonderful and peculiar embryo state. **1873** W. THOMSON-GREGG *Desperate Character* II. 78 They soon fell in with another of the marsupial inhabitants; and just in time for dinner, too—a half-grown joey, just the right size for cooking. **1886** P. CLARKE *'New Chum' in Aust.* 220 The Joey takes its rise in the pouch and draws its nourishment from its very commencement from its mother's milk. **1896** *Bulletin* (Sydney) 8 Feb. 26/2 'Practical' bushmen don't see births, and, because they only find the joey in the pouch, assert that it never was anywhere else. **1911** C.E.W. BEAN *'Dreadnought' of Darling* 117 People who have tamed an occasional 'joey' told us that the kangaroo is an intelligent pet. **1921** *Bulletin* (Sydney) 12 May 26/2 It's nearly time the lie about the kangaroo throwing her joey to the dogs when hard pressed, in order to save her own life, was squashed. **1940** J. POLLARD *Out of West* 106 The low booming of a frogmouth perched in a tree made the joey squat for an instant with ears twitching. **1956** 'N. SHUTE' *Beyond Black Stump* 72 There was generally a little kangaroo hopping about Laragh homestead, a joey brought in by one of his stockmen. **1970** *Meanjin* 332 Only the little china joey from the kangaroo's pouch obstinately refused to smash and was swept up whole into the dustpan. **1980** C. ALLISON *Hunter's Man. Aust. & N.Z.* 35 A doe takes thirty-five to thirty-eight days in gestation. To give birth to the joey—which will weigh about less than a gram—she merely drops out of the mob for a few hours. **1984** *Courier-Mail* (Brisbane) 30 June 26/2 A joey wallaby about 30 cm. high hopped and propped not three metres away.

3. a. Any young creature.

1874 R.W. MAYNE *Two Visions* 39 And parrots numerous, trainable to talk—the best for this, the Parrot-Cockatoo, familiarly called 'Joey' from his cry. **1902** *Bulletin* (Sydney) 8 Mar. 3/2 He employed a hundred blacks, Who were out a-branding joeys now upon the lone Paroo. *Ibid.* 20 Dec. 16/4 Natural, perhaps, that people who live to have a squeaking 'joey' in a cage should be deaf to less insistent songsters. **1904** *Ibid.* 25 Feb. 36/1 Why, a joey—a kid—to be branded. **1906** D.G. STEAD *Fishes of Aust.* 211 The Joey is very common along a great portion of the New South Wales coast attaining a length of about 4 inches. **1913** C.G. LANE *Creature-Life* 36 It is strange that the term 'joey' is usually applied by bush-folk to any young creature, whether beast or bird, common to Australia; a young opossum, parrot, 'native bears', cockatoo—all may be called 'joey'. The juvenile kangaroo also rejoices in the same title. **1944** *Bulletin* (Sydney) 6 Dec. 12/2 When I was a joey-tailer on our greenhide station the customary preliminary to boarding a bucking broncho was to grab the near end.

b. A baby or young child.

1887 *All Yr. Round* (London) 30 July 67 'Joey' is a familiar name for anything young and small, and is applied indifferently to a puppy, or a kitten, or a child. **1905** *Steele Rudd's Mag.* (Brisbane) June 565 Jane has started drinking beer; has a Joey ev'ry year, 'Anging on 'er ragged skirt. **1948** K.S. PRICHARD *Golden Miles* 75 'No y'r don't, Smiler,' she ses, 'y'r not walkin' out with my Ruby. A girl never knows when she'll be bringin' home a joey if she goes with you.' **1959** D. NILAND *Gold in Streets* 46 Got the wife down with another joey. **1968** S. GORE *Holy Smoke* 42 Along comes young Daniel, not much more'n a joey at the time, but pretty shrewd for his age.

c. In the phr. **to get a joey in the pouch,** to become pregnant; also **with a joey in the pouch,** pregnant.

1957 D. NILAND *Call me when Cross turns Over* 227 Dorry's boy-friend had blown through. She's in a spot. Nobody wants to take her on with a joey in the pouch. **1968** W. GILL *Petermann Journey* 14 An' you can stuff that bloody muck I bought off you. Ma's got another joey in th' pouch, that's how good it is.

joey, *n.*[2] [f. JOE *n.* 1 + -Y.]

1. JOE *n.* 1.

1869 'E. HOWE' *Boy in Bush* 219 Policemen lounged about, striving to look unconscious of the 'Joey!' which the miners found time to shout after them in scorn. **1898** G. DUNDERDALE *Bk. of Bush* 108 At last I threatened to denounce him as a 'Joey'—he was in plain clothes—and have him killed by the crowd. **1953** 'CADDIE' *Caddie* 140 Kneeling down behind the bar counter we could pour ourselves a glass of ginger-ale. . . A whistled Joey from a barmaid was the danger signal. **1976** B. SCOTT *Complete Bk. Austral. Folk Lore* 64 If you do join the Joeys, I hope you'll be shot. I'd shoot the hull blessed lot of 'em if I had my way.

2. *Obs.* A recent arrival on a goldfield; an inexperienced miner. See JOE *n.* 2.

1864 E. WARDLEY *Confessions Wavering Worthy* 171 As we threaded our way, with peering and new-chummish curiosity, through the mammon-worried labyrinth . . we were hailed as Joeys, and asked if we wanted a feather-bed, or a 'sophy'. **1895** *Worker* (Sydney) 9 Feb.

3/2 He had had but three weeks' experience of colonial life. In digging parlance he was a 'joey'.

joey, *n.*[3] Shortened form of WOOD-AND-WATER JOEY.

1949 *Bulletin* (Sydney) 14 Dec. 42/4 The old Joey seemed to think that now Marks might just as well go and cut his throat.

John.

1. [Abbrev. of *johndarm*, a. F. *gendarme*; used elsewhere but recorded earliest in Aust.: see OED(S *John* 1 c.] A police officer.

1898 *Worker* (Sydney) 8 Jan. 8/2 There was not a sign when the 'Johns', as the police are called in that neighbourhood, passed along. **1907** *Bulletin* (Sydney) 25 Apr. 14/1 A John read out the charge—Drunk an' disorderly, language, *and* resistin'. **1914** A. WRIGHT *In Last Stride* 73 The water Johns will be after us in a jiffy. **1923** *Bulletin* (Sydney) 7 June 22/2 At kookaburra call next morn the local John came round. **1932** W. HATFIELD *Ginger Murdoch* 76 Fancy calling a John 'Mister', as if they were like other people. 'Trooper' or 'Sergeant', that was the way they should be referred to. **1944** *Bulletin* (Sydney) 8 Mar. 12/3 Hobbs was still backing off with excuses as the town John walked round the corner. **1955** R. LAWLER *Summer of Seventeenth Doll* (1965) 28 Yez'll be laughing the other side your face once the johns git after yer! **1982** R. HALL *Just Relations* 144 He took possession of the book. . . The johns'll get it if we leave it here.

2. In Special Comb. with a second element forming a quasi-name: **John Bull,** rhyming slang for 'full', intoxicated; **Dunn** *obs.*, **(a)** rhyming slang for 'one' (pound, etc.); **(b)** [perh. infl. by *johndarm*, see JOHN 1] a police officer; **Hop** [prob. formed on JOHN 1] rhyming slang for 'cop', a police officer.

1967 *Kings Cross Whisper* (Sydney) xxxv. 6/3 **John Bull**, full, inebriated. **1979** B. HUMPHRIES *Bazza comes into his Own*, Where am I! . . Musta got John Bull and dropped off. **1895** *Western Champion* (Barcaldine) 31 Dec. 9/5 A profitable profession it seemed, too, judging from the cool way they talked of '**John Dunns**' (£1), 'thick 'uns' (sovs.), 'canarys' (half-sovs.), 'finn' (£5), &c. **1905** *Shearer* (Sydney) 4 Mar. 4/1 It would be interesting to know how many 'working-men' in this country . . are in receipt of three 'John Dunns' per week *all year round.* *Ibid.* 23 Dec. 7/5 Some of the lads had facetiously christened him 'The Mad Sardine', but he was much better known to the 'John Dunns' and shanty-keepers by the former name. **1908** *Truth* (Sydney) 25 Oct. 1/4 Wowsers who are interesting themselves in trying to get policemen Sunday off, assume that the John Dunns want to go to church to put a thrum in the plate. **1913** *Bulletin* (Sydney) 6 Feb. 15/1 The mute, inglorious cobber 'keeping nit' for the coming of John Dunn. **1941** S.J. BAKER *Pop. Dict. Austral. Slang* 39 *John Dunns*, policemen. [N.Z. **1905** *N.Z. Truth* (Wellington) 12 Aug. 4 An incident occurred which . . robbed **John Hop** of his glory.] **c 1907** C.W. CHANDLER *Darkest Adelaide* 7 Mr Bludger told me that the Adelaide demons had a quick and ready eye for strange faces. So to prevent any prying inquisitiveness on the part of the John Hops we decided to meet in Whitemore-square. **1910** *Bulletin* (Sydney) 21 Apr. 14/3 A hardened criminal . . was fined 10s. . . for referring to a policeman as a 'John Hop'. **1917** *Ibid.* 14 June 24/3 There was no lock-up but that did not worry our ingenious John Hop. **1934** T. WOOD *Cobbers* 122 This country is that stiff with 'don'ts' that if you blow your nose in the wrong pozzy some John Hop will come along and shove you in the cooler! **1953** *New Settler in W.A.* (Perth) Apr. 5 Hell-for-leather's the word, mate. The Johnops are around. **1965** G. MCINNES *Road to Gundagai* 123 We were off like the wind and the constable, who had earned himself the title of 'The Friendly John Hop' for life went back to the station. **1981** G. CROSS *George & Widda-Woman* 51 A couple of John-Hops arrived to investigate the accident.

Johnny.

1. a. Abbrev. of JOHNNY-CAKE *n.* Also **johnny on the coals.**

1893 *Western Champion* (Barcaldine) 7 Nov. 12/1 Now I'm mixing up a 'Johnny' on a Barcoo billybong. **1895** *Worker* (Sydney) 14 Dec. 4/1 My tucker-bags were full of dainties, such as cake—And nothing like the johnnies on the coals that shearers make. **1905** *Steele Rudd's Mag.* (Brisbane) May 451 When bread is wanted for immediate use a few 'Johnnies' are baked on the coals. **1923** *Bulletin* (Sydney) 20 Dec. 24/3, I have made good johnnies by mixing flour, salt, a little sugar and water, lighting a good fire of light stuff on a flat, even surface, then brushing the fire clean away and baking the thin Jacks on the bare, hot ground. **1932** I.L. IDRIESS *Flynn of Inland* (1965) 3 He wished he had a dip of treacle to sweeten the last Johnny. **1948** —— *Opium Smugglers* 43 While Dick knocked up a few johnnies on the coals for the evening meal, we started to boil the water.

b. *Obs.* [Shortened form of *John Chinaman.*] A Chinese immigrant; a generic name for the Chinese.

1886 D.M. GANE *N.S.W. & Vic.* 69 A spare and weazen-looking Johnny was standing by, ready to recharge the pipes, when called upon, with a fresh supply of the inspissated juice of the white poppy. **1887** *Bulletin* (Sydney) 2 July 8/1 'Tis 'Johnny's' happy hunting ground The Celestial spitoon. **1891** H. NISBET *Colonial Tramp* I. 101 'Johnny' in Victoria is a model of cleanliness and industry, and as the times go, honest also.

c. *Obs.* Abbrev. of *Johnny Raw* (see sense 2).

1895 A.B. PATERSON *Man from Snowy River* 10 But maybe you're only a Johnnie And don't know a horse from a hoe? **1898** *Truth* (Sydney) 4 Sept. 3/6 The collar outrageous and covert coat show Young Johnnie just come out by the last P and O. **1904** *Ibid.* 15 May 5/3 'Currency lads and lasses', to use the old phrase, have to give way to any new Johnnie or Janie who leaves hold Hingland for hold Hingland's good. **1946** G.E.L. WATSON *But to what Purpose* 98, I was still conspicuous of being such a mere 'Johnnie', as Englishmen were then called.

d. *Obs.* Abbrev. of *Johnny Government* (see sense 2).

1900 *Bulletin* (Sydney) 6 Jan. 15/1 The disheartened villager says 'It's all for Johnny'—meaning a benevolent Govt., to whom they owe over £80,000.

Hence **Johnniedom** *n.*, England.

1904 M. WHITE *Shanty Entertainment* 26 Fancy Fred was English and A 'Simon Pure' of Johnniedom. **1906** *Truth* (Sydney) 28 Oct. 5/6 He had a very haw-haw voice and the high-pitched intonation peculiar to well-to-do Johnniedom.

2. In Comb. with a second element, freq. forming a quasi-name: **Johnny all sorts** *obs.*, a dealer in (secondhand) goods; such a shop; **Government** *obs.*, an agency responsible for the administration of public affairs; such agencies collectively; **jumper,** MUDSKIPPER: **Raw** [spec. use of *Johnny Raw* novice], a newly-arrived immigrant; **Russell** *obs.*, rhyming slang for 'bustle', esp. in the phr. **on the Johnny Russell** (see quot. 1897); **Turk,** a Turkish soldier; the Turkish army; **Warder** *obs.*, a vagrant, esp. one habitually intoxicated (see quot. 1880); **Woodser,** JIMMY WOODSER.

1887 S. ELLIOTT *Fifty Yrs. Colonial Life* 49, I . . displayed my goods in the open air. They consisted of tents, cradles, blankets, shovels, hobbles, tin dishes; in fact, I kept one of those popular shops, a '**Johnny all sorts**'. **1901** *Tocsin* (Melbourne) 19 Sept. 7/3 Usually, he would succeed somewhere in obtaining a gift, which he would forthwith sell to a Johnny-All-Sorts. **1914** *Truth* (Sydney) 1 Mar. 2/5 The ways of '**Johnny Government**' are really very funny at times. **1937** E. HILL *Water into Gold* 156 'Johnny Government' was an enemy, to be side-tracked and duped. **1915** *Bulletin* (Sydney) 24 June 26/1 That little lung-breathing fish called the **Johnnie-jumper**, or mud-skipper . . can climb a vertical mangrove tree with ease. **1976** B. NORMAN *Bush Pilot* 236 He fairly skipped along the top of the water like a 'Johnny jumper'. **1840** *Temperance Advocate* (Sydney) 11 Nov. 4/2 Why man you are a regular **Johnny-raw** to be in Sydney two months, and not know how to do business yet. **1841** *Port Phillip Patriot* 21 Jan. 3/1 A new chum . . returning from town, encountered two men on the road, who perceiving they had a 'Johnny Raw' to deal with, invited him to come a nearer way home. **1854** C.A. CORBYN *Sydney Revels* 120 These 'ere 'our correspondents' keeps the pot boiling, a writing long twisters to the papers which 'ood make a Johnny Raw 'spect that the roads were lined with gold. **1898** *Bulletin* (Sydney) 3 Sept. 15/1 The man who . . asserted . . that bell-birds sing or 'bell' at night is probably a Johnny Raw whom some Cornstalk has 'soaped' by putting a horse-bell on, say, a heifer, and then awakening Johnny at 1.40 a.m. to listen to 'the Australian bell-bird'. **1906** *Ibid.* 28 June 14/2 New chums were originally called Johnny Raws. **1975** M. THORNTON *It's Jackaroo's Life* 20 Johnny Raw, the original title of new chum. **1897** *Bulletin* (Sydney) 7 Aug. (Red Page), *Battling* . . struggling—On the **Johnnie Russel. 1910** STEPHENS & O'BRIEN Materials Austrazealand Slang Dict. 11 'On the Johnny Russell' as a variant for battling is merely a rhyming slang arrangement of 'on the bustle'. **1941** S.J. BAKER *Pop. Dict. Austral. Slang* 43 *Johnny Russell*, rhyming slang for bustle. **1916** E.F. HANMAN *Twelve Months with Anzacs* 90 'Hullo!' say the men, '**Johnny Turk** is not expecting us, we shall get ashore unnoticed.' **1918** R.H. KNYVETT *Over There with Australs.* 126 Evidently Johnny Turk could not understand the Australian disregard for conventionality. **1928** 'C. DENISON' *Glimpses* 92 'Johnny Turk' sent over a few light shells once or twice and killed a man. **1936** N. CALDWELL *Fangs of Sea* 234 Johnny Turk twice put him out of action: wounded at the landing . . and at Lone Pine. **1965** R.H. CONQUEST *Horses in Kitchen* 183 Three times in three days Johnny Turk shot the feathers off my hat. **1983** *Bulletin* (Sydney) 17 May 18/1, I am responsible for his reference to 'Johnny Turk'. My father always referred to the brave Turks in this way, as did other Australians who were there. In no way did this denigrate the enemy. **1872** *Punch Staff Papers* 218 On the kerbstone sat one of those amiable old ladies who are popularly known as '**Johnny Warders**'. She was very drunk. **1876** *V & P* (N.S.W. L.A.) VI. 866 Their usual lodgers are the poor characters that knock about the town—Johnny Warders—they have to put up with the outside of the house. **c 1879** *Ye Prodigal* 89 Sydney is by no means to be disregarded as an asylum for men who have seen better days. Some who are now mere 'Johnny Warders' have been worth many thousands. **1880** *Bulletin* (Sydney) 4 Dec. 4/2 The title 'Johnny Warder' applied to vagrants of a certain description, had its origin from the fact that a man named John Ward, who kept a public house in Sussex-street many years ago, used to allow persons of that class to congregate and sleep in a large room adjoining his hotel. **1882** *Sydney Slang Dict.* 5 *Johnny Warder*, an idle drunkard who hangs about public-house corners looking for a drink. **1895** C. CROWE *Austral. Slang Dict.* 40 **Johnnie Woodser**, taking a solitary drink at the bar. **1899** *Truth* (Sydney) 21 May 5/6, I think I'll have a tiddly Johnny Woodser. **1902** *Ibid.* 17 Aug. 8/4 'Hey, mate,' said a punter, 'there's Ginger doing a Johnny Woodser on his own!' **1943** H.E. BEROS *Fuzzy Wuzzy Angels* 19 You could bet he was a Johnny Woodser soaking Jungle Juice.

johnny-cake, *n.* and *attrib.* [Transf. use of U.S. *johnny-cake* a flat cake of corn bread.]

A. *n.* A small, usu. thin, damper.

1827 *Monitor* (Sydney) 12 July 507/1 The carcase divided, gave each a good share, and 'a screech in the pan', 'a pot of soup', 'a fat cake', 'a johnny-cake', or 'fritters', alias 'pancakes', were the delicacies which such a God-send would plentifully afford. **1848** *Bell's Life in Sydney* 4 Mar. 1/1 Just put down a *Johnny Cake* in the smouldering embers. **1862** R. HENNING *Lett.* (1952) 46 Tom lit a fire and made some beautiful 'Johnny cakes'—thin soda cakes which are baked in about ten mintues and are the best bread you ever ate. **1875** R. & F. HILL *What we saw in Aust.* 110 Mr Sandys proposed that he should make some 'Johnny cakes', that is baby-dampers, in the shape of captain's biscuits, though somewhat larger. **1887** A. NICOLS *Wild Life & Adventure* 107 Mike skimmed the fat from the water . . and mixed it with some flour in a tinned dish to make a stiff paste for the 'johnny cakes'. **1899** R. SEMON *In Austral. Bush* 66 We even baked a sort of cake on particularly festive occasions, the 'Browny' or 'Johnny cake' of the Australians. Its production is based on the same principle as that of the damper, but the dough is made rich by adding some sugar, suet, and, if possible, some currants and raisins. **1919** *Smith's Weekly* (Sydney) 19 Apr. 14/3 Even the swagman, with no utensils, can provide you with an appetising variety of bread. With a good fire he will turn out damper, brownie, johnnycakes, flapjacks, and biscuit-on-the-coals. **1933** W.L. OWEN *Cossack Gold* 124 A damper . . must be buried in the ashes. A johnny-cake is made of the same dough, rolled into a ball, and thrown upon the fire. . . Its name is, apparently, derived from the 'Journey Cake' of the early American settlers. **1944** M.J. O'REILLY *Bowyangs & Boomerangs* 124 'Johnny cakes' may be all right for humans, but they are not much use to keep condition on horses. **1960** *N.T. News* (Darwin) 4 Mar. 5/3 The only food they took with them was a few pieces of cooked beef, some Johnny Cakes. **1978** K. WILLEY *Joe Brown's Dog* 8 She could . . cook damper and johnny-cakes, and make a decent meal out of very little.

B. *attrib. Obs. fig.* Of an illicit activity: petty, small-time.

1903 *Bulletin* (Sydney) 2 May 17/2 The bush spieler . . often owns a 10th-rate racehorse or a 'johnnycake' book, with which he takes down the public. **1911** *Huon Times* (Franklin) 21 June 4/3 One of the deputation said that this had been a case of 'Johnny Cake' bushranging, which no one had taken seriously. **1930** A.E. YARRA *Vanishing Horsemen* 58 Somerville who seemed to have become sober with remarkable suddenness, booked several bets with those who had seen 'johnny-cake' speilers at work before.

Johnstone River hardwood. [f. the name of a river in n.e. Qld. + HARDWOOD.] The tall, rainforest tree *Backhousia bancroftii* (fam. Myrtaceae), occurring along the lower Johnstone and Russell Rivers, and yielding a very hard, close-grained timber. Also **Queensland Johnstone River hardwood,** and *attrib.*

1905 P. MACMAHON *Merchantable Timbers of Qld.* 54 Queensland Johnstone River hardwood. *Backhousia Bancroftii*. . . Found in the neighbourhood of Johnstone River, in Northern Queensland, and it is coming into favour for carriage-finishing. **1909** *Emu* VIII. 269 Numbers of dead, ring-barked scrub trees, known locally as Johnstone River hardwood. **1936** *Bulletin* (Sydney) 8 July 21/4 One of Australia's most peculiar timbers is the Johnstone River hardwood, much prized as fuel in the Innisfail (N.Q.) district, to which parts it is peculiar. **1978** R.J. BRITTEN *Around Cassowary Rock* 94 A couple of wild scrub hens . . far up in the topmost branches of a big Johnstone River hardwood tree.

Johnstone's crocodile. [f. the name of explorer and police officer R.A. *Johnstone* (1843–1905), after whom the Johnstone River (Qld.) was also named.] The narrow-snouted fresh-water crocodile *Crocodylus johnstoni*, occurring only in coastal and near-coastal n. Aust. Also **Johnston crocodile, Johnstone crocodile, Johnstone River crocodile.**

1925 M. TERRY *Across Unknown Aust.* 230 The other, commonly misnamed alligator, is the . . Johnstone's crocodile. **1935** F. BIRTLES *Battle Fronts Outback* 75 These 'Johnstone' crocodiles are comparatively harmless. They grow up to a length of about twelve feet. **1943** *Bulletin* (Sydney) 7 July 12/3 In an anabranch of the Copperfield (N.Q.) my mate and I stumbled on about a score of Johnston crocodiles. **1953** L. & C. REES *Spinifex Walkabout* 199 This is a Johnston croc—freshwater type, y' know, more or less harmless. **1965** *Austral. Encycl.* III. 130 Johnstone's crocodile, *Crocodilus johnstoni* . . (which is named after a former sub-inspector of police) is restricted to the freshwater streams of northern Australia. **1969** J. DINGWELL *One String* 109 Up Toppers called the fresh-water Johnstone crocodile an alligator to differentiate from the flesh-eating estuarine fellow, but actually there were no alligators in Australia, only crocs. **1986** *Woman's Day* (Sydney) 24 Feb. 6/3 Val had been told by old crocodile shooters that some Johnson [*sic*] River crocodiles grew to nearly four metres long and should be regarded with caution.

joint. *Obs.* [Recorded by Partridge as chiefly Cockney.] A chap.

1897 *Worker* (Sydney) 11 Sept. 1/1 His boss he gives some funny names, when he can't hear the joke, He calls him 'joint' and 'finger', and he sometimes calls him 'bloke'. **1917** C. THACKERAY *Goliath Joe* 71, I tell you wot I'd do to the bloke wot interdooced trout to Australia. I'd give him a Docker twist of ten years' penal, like I would the other joint wot brought the foxes. **1922** A. WRIGHT *Colt from Country* 131 He's one of the hottest joints at the game.

joker. [Br. slang use of *joker* jester, merry fellow, now chiefly Austral. and N.Z.]

1. A fellow, a chap.

1810 *Sydney Gaz.* 20 Oct., Six jokers on horseback were standing stock still, Like as many dragoons that were learning to drill. **1887** K. MACKAY *Stirrup Jingles* 40 At a pound a week and my dover, Along of a joker named Jack. **1892** *Bulletin* (Sydney) 17 Dec. 19/1 Jim you know was not a croaker . . Said he loved me like a brother, but 'twas rough upon a joker. **1907** G. EDEN *Bush Ballads* 82 Beside us sat a joker toying idly with the poker. **1942** A.J. MCINTYRE *Putting over Burst* 9 I'm a quiet sort of joker, And I love to work in peace. **1959** *Bulletin* (Sydney) 17 June 16/1 Only in Australia would you hear a joker say 'Where yer bloody been yer drongo?' **1965** G.H. FEARNSIDE *Golden Ram* 18 You think us married jokers have got no lives of our own. **1978** D. HUTLEY *Swan* 54 There's nothing as stupid as an older joker with long hair.

2. *transf.*

1914 R. KALESKI *Austral. Barkers & Biters* 37 Try the black sheep-dog called the barb. This joker shoos frightened cattle along nicely. **1915** J. BOWES *New Chums* 55, I could stand one sort at a time, but when these jokers [*sc.* fleas and mosquitoes] combine forces, they drive me silly. **1918** *Bulletin* (Sydney) 12 Sept. 22/2 It is the green turtle that is chiefly used for food. The shell variety . . is the joker that provides the ladies with combs and other fal-lals.

jollo. [f. *joll(ity* + -O.] A spree; a party.

1907 *Truth* (Sydney) 6 Jan. 11/8 On the day of the jollo there was a trifling dispute about the nightman omitting to empty the pans at the hall, of which witness was the caretaker. **1916** *Ibid.* 17 Dec. 11/3 He ceased living with her, especially after she had gone on a 'jollo', as he expressed it, to Cook's River with a man. **1917** *Ibid.* 14 Jan. 7/6 (*heading*) The Lancashire lass and O'Malley o' Nimitybelle come to town for Xmas jollo. **1938** F. BLAKELEY *Hard Liberty* 60 Sometimes these good-night parties were bottle parties also. . . A sleeping miners' camp would be selected for the jollo. **1952** C. SIMPSON *Come away, Pearler* 112 Laughs and banter came from the hold. . . Gympie was pleased at the mood created by what he called a 'bit of a jollo'. **1955** N. PULLIAM *I traveled Lonely Land* 306 My mother used to ask some of the chappies in for a little week-end jollo—like a touch of home, you know. **1966** S.J. BAKER *Austral. Lang.* (ed. 2) 230 Australians have a fair selection of terms to describe drinking and drinking bouts, such as . . jollo [etc.].

jollytail. Chiefly *Tas.* Any of several small fresh-water fish of the genus *Galaxias*, esp. *G. attenuatus* common in coastal streams of s. and s.e. Aust. incl. Tas.

1892 P.L. SIMMONDS *Commercial Dict. Trade Products* (rev. ed.) Suppl. 463/2 *Jolly-tail*, a small fresh-water fish of Australia . . highly esteemed as a delicacy for the table. There are several species. **1906** D.G. STEAD *Fishes of Aust.* 50 In Tasmania, these fishes [*sc.* Australian Minnows] are often familiarly known under the designation of 'Jollytails'. **1926** *Tasmanian Mail* (Hobart) 17 Feb. 6/2, I was once perched on a partly submerged log fishing for 'jollytails'. **1951** T.C. ROUGHLEY *Fish & Fisheries Aust.* 157 The jollytail is widely distributed throughout Australia, but . . it does not appear to have been found anywhere in sufficient concentrations to encourage its exploitation as a source of whitebait. **1985** *Mercury* (Hobart) 30 May 4/7 The jollytail . . lives in fresh water then migrates to spawn in estuaries.

jonick /ˈdʒɒnɪk/, *a.* Also **jonic, jonnic, jonnik.** [Var. of Br. dial. *jannock* fair, straightforward: see OED *a.*] Fair; genuine; honest; true. Also as *adv.* See also DINKUM *a.* and *adv.*

[**1854** S. SIDNEY *Gallops & Gossips* 89 'The swell's all right'; 'He's *jammock*'; 'He won't split'.] **1874** C. DE BOOS *Congewoi Correspondence* 173, I don't harf like the way as Brown served us. . . I don't think as he acted jonick. **1897** J. FARRELL *How he Died* 61, I know what's Jonnik, coves, and no mistake. **1900** *Truth* (Sydney) 1 Apr. 1/6, I know that I now myself feel far from 'jonick' . . whatever that means. **1927** F.C. BIGGERS *Bat-Eye* 7 An' wot I'm tellin' now is jonick stuff. **1945** S.D. RAILTON *Southern Cross* 28 Marty gimme th' oil you wanted to see me. . . That jonnic? **1953** T.A.G. HUNGERFORD *Riverslake* 166 'Got the knife right into him.' 'Jonic?' 'Jonic!' **1984** W.W. AMMON et al. *Working Lives* 65 It's not bloody bullshit, I tell you. It's jonnick.

joss. [Br. dial. *joss* foreman, employer, 'boss': see OEDS.]

a. A person of influence or importance; a boss.

1919 *Ross's Monthly* Jan. 19/1 Despite all the smirks of your josses . . you're snug as a bug in a rug, with your One Big Union of Bosses. **1919** *Smith's Weekly* (Sydney) 1 Mar. 10/2 Josses should never talk about one another. Each joss is more successful when he talks about himself; most successful, when he lets his priesthood or his press do all the talking. **1948** V. PALMER *Golconda* 28 'Then why don't you go to the Golconda Mining Company?' asked Donovan slyly. 'Tilburg Kloss is there, a big joss from down south.' **1956** *Coast to Coast 1955–56* 36 A big joss among the young bucks and gins.

b. *fig.*

1922 F.C. GREEN *Fortieth* 71 The Australian is unconventional, and surrounded by others, whose 'josses' are tradition and convention, he is proud of it.

josser. [f. *joss* Chinese idol, esp. as in *joss-house* temple.] A clergyman.

1887 J. FARRELL *How he Died* 22 The Reverend josser . . hammering the pulpit. **1889** BARRÈRE & LELAND *Dict. Slang* I. 507 *Josser* . . a priest. . . Australian slang designated those who ministered in them [*sc.* joss-houses] *jossers*, and then extended this term it had created to mean ministers of any religion. **1941** S.J. BAKER *Pop. Dict. Austral. Slang* 40 *Josser*, a parson. **1973** G. ROSE *Clear Road to Archangel* 35 The old josser, all black robe and beard and upside-down hat and silver cross, addressed himself to me. In German.

journo /ˈdʒɜnoʊ/. [f. *journ(alist* + -O.] A journalist.

1967 *Kings Cross Whisper* (Sydney) xxxv. 6/3 *Journo*, journalist. **1969** T.M.A. GRAHAM *Paper Men* 149 The quiz kid journo. **1971** *Bulletin* (Sydney) 14 Aug. 50/3 The taxi-driver is all things to all journos. **1981** C. WALLACE-CRABBE *Splinters* 50 Smashed out of his mind he was when some creeping journo got onto him. **1986** *Bulletin* (Sydney) 15 Apr. 90/3 They accepted a view, vigorously put by the journo who was to interview him, that Irving deserved obscurity.

jug-handle. See quot. 1958.

1958 J.R. SPICER *Cry of Storm-Bird* 115 To aid mounting, the rider often twisted a short strap on the right side of the pommel, a fixture that came in very useful when dealing with a lively horse. . . The strap in question was known as a 'monkey' or 'jug-handle'. **1976** C.D. MILLS *Hobble Chains & Greenhide* 31, I was unashamedly swinging on the jug-handle, and showing a foot of daylight every buck.

juju tree. [Abbrev. of *jujube* tree of the genus *Ziziphus.*] A tropical tree of the genus *Ziziphus* (fam. Rhamnaceae), bearing an edible fruit.

1960 E. O'CONNER *Irish Man* 136 Saw a patch of burnt country, a ju-ju tree, gnarled and bent by the wind. **1962** *N. Austral. Monthly* Jan. 21, I was asked for the 'Sunday name' of the China apple or Juju tree. I couldn't think of the name but Mr Dan Corney tells me it is Zixphus jujuba.

July fog. *Obs.* See quot. 1893.

1893 F.W.L. ADAMS *Australs.* 167 The 'July fog' (the dead season when no shearing is done). **1927** J. MATHIEU *Backblocks Ballads* 1, I don't succumb to swagging, July fogs, or charcoal tarts. **1982** P. ADAM SMITH *Shearers* 405 *July fog*, the dead season when no shearing is done.

jumbuck /ˈdʒʌmbʌk/. [Of unknown origin: orig. in *Austral. pidgin* and poss. an alteration of an English word (see e.g. JUMP UP *v.*).]

1. A sheep.

1824 Methodist Missionary Soc. Rec. 26 Jan., To two Brothers of mine, these monsters exposed several pieces of human flesh, exclaiming as they smacked their lips and stroked their breasts, 'boodjerry patta! murry boodjerry!—fat as jimbuck!!' i.e. good food, very good, fat as mutton. There is no doubt of their cannibalism. Pray for me, and for them. **1841** *Port Phillip Patriot* 19 July 4/5 The villains laughed at and mocked us, roaring out 'plenty sheepy', 'plenty jumbuck', (another name of theirs for sheep). **1847** *Melbourne Argus* 22 Oct. 2/2 Shearing is the great card of the season, and no settler being the owner of jumbucks can give a straight answer upon any other, than this all absorbing topic. **1854** W. HOWITT *Boy's Adventures* 129 He did not know what jumbucks were, he candidly said so. 'Why, sheep man, sheep! They are jumbucks in this country.' **1863** C. HARPUR Kangaroo Hunt 32 Jimbuc is an aboriginal name of a little shag-haired species of Kangaroo. . . The jimbuc is the least elegant in its form, and the dullest in its nature, of all the Kangaroo kinds. . . The Blacks of the Hunter call the sheep jimbuc, no doubt from a resemblance . . arising out of the hairy shagginess of the one and the woolliness of the other. **1869** *Adelaide Punch* 25 Mar. 83/2 *Jumback* or *jimbuck* (sheep), is a corruption of *himbuck*, a name originally applied to the horse. On the introduction of *yarraman jumbuck* found its way to the sheep-yard where it has since steadfastly remained. **1883** *Illustr. Austral. News* (Melbourne) 28 Nov. 194/3 Now the 'jumbucks' have all been penned up in the immense 'sweating pen'. **1891** *Truth* (Sydney) 26 Apr. 3/7 He's punished less who roundly robs the nation Than he who 'nabs' a jumbuck from a station. **1896** *Bulletin* (Sydney) 18 Apr. 27/2 The word 'jumbuck' for sheep appears originally as jimba, jombock, dambock, and dumbog. In each case it meant the white mist preceding a shower, to which a flock of sheep bore a strong resemblance. It seemed the only thing the aboriginal imagination could compare it to. **1913** W.K. Harris *Outback in Aust.* 44 If a 'jumbuck' strays into your backyard you must impound it. **1921** *Aussie* (Sydney) Sept. 7/3 They fight the bush and the land, play football, shear sheep, kill bullocks, freeze jumbucks and stand to attention for 'Gorsave'. **1932** *Bulletin* (Sydney) 10 Feb. 21/4 What do they know of jumbucks that only Pitt-street know? **1952** T.A.G. Hungerford *Ridge & River* 89 You back with the jumbucks, eh? .. You was talkin' about shearin' jus' before you dozed off! **1969** L. Hadow *Full Cycle* 205 'I feel sorry for those poor sheep,' she said again. 'Why? Nobody here feels sorry for a jumbuck.' **1981** P. Barton *Bastards I have Known* 57 My favourite was a little grey mare that .. knew more about handling sheep than most sheep dogs. She sensed the first day I was on her that I was a novice with the jumbucks.

2. Special Comb. **jumbuck barber,** Barber *n.*, so, **jumbuck barbering** *vbl. n.* and *attrib.*

1913 *Bulletin* (Sydney) 24 Apr. 14/3 You have no earthly of securing a partner if you are not a jumbuck barber. **1915** *Ibid.* 1 July 22/2, I was quite young at the time, earning a few bob picking-up at a shed. Jumbuck-barbering looked easy enough. *Ibid.* 28 Oct. 22/4 A jumbuck-barber always refers to himself as a 'shearer man'. **1918** *Kia Ora Coo-ee* May 5/3 To test the clippers two jumbuck barbers fastened on to a couple of Palestine merino kings. **1926** *Bulletin* (Sydney) 14 Jan. 24/3 With a board of 16 shearers a jumbuck-barbering firm this season cut out 105,000 sheep.

jummy. [f. Jum(buck + -y.] Jumbuck. Also *attrib.*

1943 *Bulletin* (Sydney) 3 Nov. 12/1 My Queensland paper has it that a bunch of greasies downed handpieces in a Longreach shed because they thought they'd catch something from a few jummies with scabby mouths. **1946** *Ibid.* 20 Nov. 29/2 More than one casual stroller was upset in a flying tangle as Ned made a dive for the next woolly, though the jummie barber was usually the last to become aware of it. **1950** *Ibid.* 30 Aug. 12/4 Barney was on the drafting-gate .. and the jummies weren't running very well.

jump, *v.*[1] [U.S. *jump* to take possession of without legal procedure: see Mathews *v.* 2.]

1. *trans. Mining.* To occupy or take summary possession of (a claim), in the absence of the former occupant or by resort to legal technicalities.

1852 *Empire* (Sydney) 16 Jan. 578/5 In some instances, parties have 'jumped' claims .. that is, taken possession of claims not registered, and worked in them for two days without being disturbed by the owners, and hence acquiring a right of ownership to them. If the owners of the claims order them out before they have been two clear days at work, they must decamp; but if not their two days' working and possession entitles them to keep the claim. **1856** *Jrnl. Australasia* I. 116 Jumping claims .. he insisted, was a practice not unknown at the time when Shakespere gave his Antony and Cleopatra to the stage, as in that drama occurs the expression—'Our future lies Upon this *jump*.' **1859** W. Kelly *Life in Vic.* I. 212 Any other person possessed of a license might jump the claim... Jumping is the technical term for ejecting an unlicensed digger—the person ejecting literally jumping into the hole. **1874** *Adelaide Observer* 26 Dec. (Christmas Suppl.) 12/1 Whilst lying ill, his claim had been jumped by a couple of 'tother siders', who actually took nearly £1,000 a piece out of it. **1892** *Missing Friends: Adventures Danish Emigrant Qld.* 187 He was satisfied to return to Ravenswood before anyone could jump his claim there. **1915** 'Alpha' *Reminisc. Goldfields* i. 98, I was bound to continue working on the claim, as had I not done so, it would have been jumped. **1936** J. Kirwan *My Life's Adventures* 77 'The golden hole' from which the rich specimens came was covered with a strong plate and sealed. The mine was 'jumped' on the plea that the regulations were not complied with, but the 'jumpers'' claim was not upheld... When opened up .. the one that remained was worthless! **1950** C.E. Goode *Yarns of Yilgarn* 79 A fair amount of secrecy was observed... As times were bad, thousands were out combing the Fields. We didn't want our claims jumped! **1977** V. Priddle *Larry & Jack* 21 The mining business is very flat at the moment and all the fossickers are down and out more or less. We hear of them fighting between themselves, jumping claims and doing anything to get a quid.

2. *transf.* To occupy or take possession of (a tract of land) in this manner.

1880 *Argus* (Melbourne) 20 Jan. 6/3 He resolved to jump the selection, and took advantage of the temporary absence of my son. **1890** J. Joubert *Shavings & Scrapes* 70 Field of Mars common—some 6800 acres of land .. had been 'jumped' by some very rough people—old convicts, runaway sailors, and jail-birds—who eked out a living by stealing timber and boating firewood to Sydney. **1907** *Truth* (Sydney) 24 Feb. 2/4 We denounced the audacious attempt on the part of Manager W. Anderson to 'jump' a valuable section of 'the people's heritage', the land known as Tamarama Bay.

3. *fig.*

1868 *Sydney Punch* 29 Aug. 117/2 It has been reserved to an individual of Sydney to arrive at similar 'blushing honors' without either process being employed. In other words, he has 'jumped another's claim'. **1891** H. Nisbet *Colonial Tramp* II. 281, I noticed a singular colonial habit while I was going by train, that I did not exactly admire, the 'jumping' of seats. **1926** L.C.E. Gee *Bush Tracks & Gold Fields* 58, I wonder does a lazy pheasant ever try to 'jump' another one's mounds? **1930** V. Palmer *Passage* (1957) 163, I planned to start a Tourist Service... Someone else will hop in and jump the claim if we don't. **1956** R.G. Edwards *Overlander Songbk.* 61, I *shepherded* that girl, sir, And soon got in such a flame, That I fancied every fellow there Was going to *jump my claim.*

Hence **jumpable** *a.*, **jumped** *ppl. a.*, **jumping** *vbl. n.* and *attrib.*

1884 'R. Boldrewood' *Old Melbourne Memories* 114 The Heifer station was what would be called in mining parlance 'an abandoned claim', and possibly '**jumpable**', to use another effective expression with which the goldfields have enriched the Australian vernacular. **1858** *Colonial Mining Jrnl.* Nov. 45/2 Some quartz crushed from some **jumped** ground between the Welshman's and New Chum Claim. **1855** R. Carboni *Eureka Stockade* 11 For the commissioners, this **jumping** business was by no means an agreeable job. **1873** *Australasian Sketcher* (Melbourne) 17 May 19/1 'Jumping' of claims .. is, taking possession of them on the plea that they are illegally held by the parties working them.

jump, *v.*[2] In the phr. **to jump** (a horse, etc.) **over the bar,** to trade one's horse for liquor.

1895 *Bulletin* (Sydney) 27 Apr. 24/1 Oh! when a landlord has your cheque, Think what a hopeless fool you are, You poor, degraded spineless wreck, To jump your crock across the bar. **1906** *Ibid.* 12 July 17/1 A man could do in his cheque and then jump his horse over the bar, and be a 'real good bloke', but he who at the tail of a spree, sold his swag for ale, was a waster, a fool, and several other things. **1920** *Smith's Weekly* (Sydney) 28 Aug. 9/4 A man might 'swamp his cheque and jump his horses over the bar', but he won't part with his bundle. **1923** *Aussie* (Sydney) Dec. 11/1 We had 'jumped our horses over the bar', in other words, handed over our nags to the publican so as to wipe off the slate. **1936** *Bulletin* (Sydney) 30 Dec. 20/2 Many a one of them was given an old saddle, a pack-saddle and a pair of pensioned horses just to get rid of him. That he jumped 'em over the bar at the first bush pub didn't matter. **1957** Stewart & Keesing *Old Bush Songs* 229 My horses all sold—they'd jumped over the bar—And I got the dirty kick-out.

jumper, *n.*[1] Any of several smaller species of ant of the genus *Myrmecia*, many of which are capable of jumping and of inflicting a painful sting; Jack-jumper. Also **jumper ant.**

1845 C. Hodgkinson *Aust., Port Macquarie to Moreton Bay* 51, I was severely bitten by the stinging-ants, called Jumpers, which leap like grasshoppers, and inflict a sharp pain. **1903** *Bulletin* (Sydney) 31 Jan. 36/1 There were big and little ants .. black joeys, red joeys, jumpers. **1936** *Austral. Writers' Ann.* 31 The jumper is a fanatic. He doesn't wait for a declaration of hostilities. **1939** L. Mann *Mountain Flat* 181 He lit a match and looked at the ground to see if there were any jumper ants. **1959** *Overland* xv. 14, I was nearly eaten alive by jumper ants and leeches. **1968** L. Braden *Bullockies* 86 Three boys frantically scratching themselves. They had dug up a jumper-ant's nest and were in great pain. **1971** J. Carter *Wild Country* 111 Small bulldog ants are called jumpers because of their zig-zag or skipping movements. **1972** K. Willey *Tales Big Country* 151 Then there's jumper ants. Those blokes will leap six feet in the air to get at you and they've got teeth like a crocodile's.

jumper, *n.*[2] *Hist.* [Spec. use of *jumper* loose outer jacket or shirt worn by seamen, labourers, etc.: see OED(S *sb.*[2]] A smock-like outer garment, distinctive in Australia as part of the conventional attire of a gold-miner.

1852 R. Cecil *Gold Fields Diary* (1935) 15 We saw a digger in his jumper and working dress walking arm in arm with a woman dressed in the most exaggerated finery. **1852** *Austral. Gold Digger's Monthly Mag.* i. 13 The jumper of a lucky digger produces the same flutter in the female circle, which the red coat of a soldier used to do. **1853** W.J. Wills *Successful Exploration Interior Aust.* 12 Feb. (1863) 21 What they call a jumper here .. is a kind of outside shirt, made of plaid, or anything you please, reaching just below the hips, and fastened round the waist with a belt. **1862** C. Munro *Fern Vale* I. 48 He was dressed in the usual bush costume .. a loose woollen frock, barely covering his hips, made so as, in putting on and taking off, to require slipping over the head, and as a garment of constant use .. elegantly designated 'a jumper'. **1873** R.P. Whitworth *Lost & Found* 21 Men with big beards, clad in red and blue jumpers. **1881** T. Bastard *Autobiogr. 'Cockney Tom'* 44 Our ball comes off next week... No diggers will be allowed in except they wear a silk jumper or dress coat. **1888** *Illustr. Austral. News* (Melbourne) 1 Aug. (Suppl.) 9/2 Beneath the mud-bespattered digger's 'jumper' there often beats a generous heart. **1903** W. Craig *My Adventures* 256 Even unofficial visitors to the field were allowed no peace until they had donned the orthodox serge jumper and 'billy cock' or cabbage tree hat. **1921** M.E. Fullerton *Bark House Days* 117 He wore a grey 'jumper' reaching to the knees.

jumper, *n.*[3] *Mining.* [f. Jump *v.*[1] 1.] One who jumps another's claim; *claim jumper*, see Claim 3.

1854 *Guardian* (Hobart) 25 Mar. 3/4 Some Scotchmen jumped a hole... The Commissioner .. decided in favour of the jumpers. **1871** *Austral. Town & Country Jrnl.* (Sydney) 4 Feb. 143/3 This claim is not yet lawfully blocked off, but an enterprising party of jumpers have blocked it off. **1895** A.F. Calvert *W.A. & Welfare* 105 There are several species of the genus 'jumper' in the mining world. **1898** E. Dyson *Below & on Top* 144 His nose .. had been badly battered by a blow from a shovel in an encounter with a 'jumper' at Deadman's Rush in '52. **1922** J. Lewis *Fought & Won* 107 The objection raised by the jumpers was that we had not properly pegged out. **1950** K.S. Prichard *Winged Seed* 28 The reshuffle of claims didn't bring the jumpers much luck, anyhow. **1969** E. Waller *And There's Opal* 25 If I get a couple of roo carcases and dump them down the shaft, it should keep the 'jumpers' out.

jumping snake. Any of several lizards of the fam. Pygopodidae of mainland Aust.

1919 *Bulletin* (Sydney) 6 Nov. 22/1 Tom Ward .. describes a reptile known to Westralians .. as the 'jumping snake'. **1954** C. Barrett *Wild Life Aust. & New Guinea* 180 'Jumping snake' and 'saltbush snake' are popular names for scaly-foot, which timid people who have met with it declare is so aggressive that it jumps at anyone who disturbs it.

jump up, *v. Austral. pidgin.*

1. *intr.* To come back to life; esp. in the phr. **to jump up whitefellow,** to be reincarnated as a white person.

1826 *Monitor* (Sydney) 29 Dec. 259/3 One of them saw the eye of the deceased glisten, and imagining he might still 'jump up' (to use their own expression, for they are horribly afraid of the resurrection of a dead corpse) he beat the skull till it parted. **1836** *Aborigines of Aust.* 9 White people are their ancestors returned to them, and after they die they will '*jump up white man*'. **1843** *Sydney Morning Herald* 2 Nov. 4/3 He was perfectly aware of the fate which awaited him; but appeared to have the notion that he would soon 'jump up, white fellow'! **1847** J.D. LANG *Cooksland* 416 Convict-servants . . had persuaded them, in the convict slang of the times, that 'black-fellows, when they died, would *jump up*, or rise again white-fellows'. **1851** *Athenaeum* (London) 24 May 557 A native who was executed at Melbourne consoled himself by saying—'Never mind, I jump up white fellow.' **1866** *Australasian* (Melbourne) 22 Sept. 774/4 They had a superstition that black people went at death to some of the islands, and 'jumped up' white people. **1878** R.B. SMYTH *Aborigines of Vic.* II. 280 It was . . discovered that the natives believed that unless they were buried there was no future existence for them—that they would never 'jump up' again. **1886** E. PALMER *Concerning Some Superstitions N. Qld. Aborigines* 2 They knew nothing of what blacks call 'devil devil' or 'jump up whitefellow', nor did they entertain any foreign religious ideas whatever except their own native traditions. **1927** M.M. BENNETT *Christison of Lammermoor* 109 One old gin wanted to claim Munggra as a defunct brother who had 'jumped up white fellow'.

2. *intr.* To come; to appear.

1845 D. MACKENZIE *Emigrant's Guide* 241 The black fellow returned . . to complain that the young potatoes did 'not yet jump up'. **1848** H.W. HAYGARTH *Recoll. Bush Life* 108 In talking to a black . . to come, or appear, is to 'jump up'. **1853** *Visit to Aust. & Gold Regions* (S.P.C.K.) 162 The black fellow . . went to his instructor, and told him with much chagrin that the potatoes had not yet 'jumped up', and inquired if they would 'jump up' in two days more. **1857** F. GERSTAECKER *Two Convicts* 35 In the corrupt language used as a means of communication between white and black . . 'flour-bag' means 'white'; 'jump up', to come, to appear.

jump-up, *n.* [Prob. infl. by prec.]

1. An elevated, step-like obstacle on an ascending road or track; a sudden, steep rise; an escarpment. Also *attrib.*

[**1844** MRS C. MEREDITH *Notes & Sketches N.S.W.* 70 The main portion of the road is *bad* beyond an English comprehension; sometimes it consists of natural step-like rocks protruding from the dust or sand, one, two, or three feet above each other, in huge slabs the width of the track, and over these '*jumpers*', as they are pleasantly termed, we had to jolt and bump along as we best might.] **1847** *Maitland Mercury* 27 Oct. 2/4 Here and there are also to be found, by way of variety, a few of what are expressively termed 'jumps up', and other numerous obstacles. **1849** A. HARRIS *Emigrant Family* (1967) 366 He went . . up the smooth hill-sides and the rocky jump-ups. **1864** 'E.S.H.' *Narr. Trip Sydney to Peak Downs* 9 The water was rapid but only three feet deep, the opposite shore being soft and sandy, with a few 'jump up ridges' to get to the level. **1896** D. STEWART *Thousand Miles & More* 65 Crossing Lake Carey you ascend steep 'jump ups'. **1925** M. TERRY *Across Unknown Aust.* 197 The edge of the Barkly Tableland . . the 'Jump-up', as the edge was known. **1928** B. SPENCER *Wanderings in Wild Aust.* 867 At 11.40 we came to what is locally known as a 'jump-up', that is, a sudden rise, usually short and very steep, leading on to the high ground that in these parts forms really the line of watershed separating the belt of coastal country, from the great central area. **1935** H.H. FINLAYSON *Red Centre* 39 Isolated rock outcrops ranging from the little granite 'jump-ups' . . to huge tors. **1945** T. RONAN *Strangers on Ophir* 38 By sheer sense of locality he threaded his way through gullies and ridges until he once more was able to climb the jump-up. **1959** H. DRAKE-BROCKMAN *West Coast Stories* 157 Buncher turned the wheel sharply to avoid a jump-up in the track. **1962** *N. Austral. Monthly* Feb. 14 Along a valley, until the Churchill 'Jump-up'. This is a very steep hill. **1967** L. BEADELL *Blast Bush* 26 A huge wild dingo silhouetted against the blue sky on the jump-up. **1981** *Austral. Women's Weekly* (Sydney) 26 Aug. 43 Rolling grasslands give way to 'jump-up country', isolated flat-topped mountains, stark against the sky. Red sandhills undulate away to the north. **1985** *Overlander* Jan. 55 Sandy Thomas had warned of the 'jump-ups' on the early stages of the trail.

2. a. See quot.

1859 W. BURROWS *Adventures Mounted Trooper* 101 A young colonist . . was in the habit of giving the black near him a feed of 'jump up' as they call it; this stuff consists of flour and water boiled into a paste, and sugar put into it, and from the bubbles rising to the surface when boiling, they call it 'jump up'.

b. A raising agent.

1915 *Bulletin* (Sydney) 20 May 22/3 How to make a damper. . . One large bag of flour, plenty of 'jump up' and water to mix with.

junga. /'dʒʊŋə, 'dʒʌŋə/. [a. Yinjibarndi *junga.*] PARAKEELIA.

1932 I.L. IDRIESS *Flynn of Inland* (1965) 141 It held . . the parakelia, the 'chunga' (milk) and 'junga' (water) plant of the natives. **1984** W.W. AMMON et al. *Working Lives* 151 There was a plant there called junga or parakeelya. It is very sappy and keeps the sheep from needing water till late in the summer.

jungle-fowl. [Transf. use of *jungle-fowl* an East Indian bird of the genus *Gallus.*] *Scrub fowl*, see SCRUB *n.* 5. Also **jungle-hen.**

1842 J. GOULD *Birds of Aust.* (1848) V. Pl. 79, I came to a mound of sand and shells, with a slight mixture of black soil. . . On pointing it out to the native and asking him what it was, he replied, 'Oooregoora Rambal', Jungle-fowls' house or nest. **1863** G.W. EARL *Handbk. for Colonists Tropical Aust.* 89, I do not know how the name of Jungle-Fowl came to be conferred on this singular bird, for it is altogether unlike the Jungle-Fowl of India, but I believe the Port Essington colonists were guilty of the misnomer. **1889** R.B. ANDERSON tr. Lumholtz's *Among Cannibals* 96 The melancholy note of the jungle-hen. **1907** A. SEARCY *In Austral. Tropics* 71 We also bagged some jungle fowl, a good table bird. **1931** *Bulletin* (Sydney) 19 Aug. 21/3 If there were a prize for the biggest nest among the world's birds the jungle-fowl of North Queensland would have a walk-over. **1964** M. SHARLAND *Territory of Birds* 64 Here was a mound, six feet high and thirty-five feet in circumference, built by the Jungle Fowl. And in it the bird had laid eggs which, like those of the turtle, would be hatched by the sun's warmth. **1973** S. & K. BREEDON *Wildlife Eastern Aust.* 70 The Jungle Fowl is terrestrial and more often heard than seen. Its trumpeting call is one of the most characteristic of the rainforest.

jungle juice. [Used elsewhere but recorded earliest in Aust.] Orig. in Services' speech in New Guinea: any crude alcoholic drink.

1942 H.E. BEROS *Fuzzy Wuzzy Angels* (1943) 18 An epidemic hit the camp, it travelled fast and loose, It was started by a liquid with the name of Jungle Juice. **1944** *Tropic Spread: Mag. 18th Austral. Advanced Ordnance Depot* Aug. 7, I was able to obtain a 44 gallon drum of jungle juice. **1945** 'MASTER-SARG' *Yank discovers Aust.* 17 *Jungle juice*, an alcoholic drink concocted out of jungle ingredients. **1957** F. CLUNE *Fortune Hunters* 196 They were marked, 'Medicines with Care'. This did not deceive the bullockies. They camped for a week until all the jungle-juice was consumed. **1965** *Coast to Coast 1963–64* 78 Crikey, Bert, this calls for a drink—and no bloody jungle-juice, either! Remember that time at Salamana? The bloody coconut-juice with the currants in? **1968** G. DUTTON *Andy* 268 The Americans had two bottles of bourbon and one of jungle juice made from fermented coconut milk and surgical alcohol.

K

kadaitcha, kaditcha, varr. KURDAITCHA.

kadoova /kəˈduvə/. *Obs.* [Of unknown origin.] In the phr. **to be off one's kadoova,** to be mentally unbalanced.

1889 BARRÈRE & LELAND *Dict. Slang* 94 A man had tried to prove a man wrong who said he was *off his kadoova*. **1946** D. STIVENS *Courtship of Uncle Henry* 72, I reckoned then Thompson was a bit off his kadoova. **1966** S.J. BAKER *Austral. Lang.* (ed. 2) 136 In earlier times, the state of being stupid was described .. as being *off one's kadoova*.

kai /kaɪ/. [a. *kai*, *v.* to eat, and *n.* food, widespread in Polynesian languages and adopted in its reduplicated form *kai-kai* in Pacific pidgins.] Food.

[N.Z. **1845** E.J. WAKEFIELD *Adventure in N.Z.* I. 265 The determination of the natives not to move until all the *kai* was exhausted.] **1872** 'RESIDENT' *Glimpses Life Vic.* 253 'Kai! me get that fellow [*sc.* an iguana] out quick,' said the native. **1945** *Action Front: Jrnl. 2/2 Field Regiment* May 13 Does that mean that the 'kai' will be three times as good? **1946** *Austral. New Writing* 50 A long-snouted pig grunting always for 'kai'.

So, in reduplicated form, **kai-kai,** food, a meal. Also **ki-ki.**

[N.Z. **1807** J. SAVAGE *Some Acct. N.Z.* 75 *Kiki*, food.] **1893** *Antipodean* (Melbourne) 82 An hour for 'ki-ki' and 'Smoke, oh!' in the middle of the day. **1918** *Bulletin* (Sydney) 17 Oct. 24/2 With .. our far northern abos .. 'kai-kai' was the only word I heard them use for tucker; but this was evidently taken from the Melanesian dictionary. **1944** *Ibid.* 19 July 13/1 Arrows were pointed with tridents made of umbrella ribs. With this outfit Charlie Kanaka and his mates obtained many a good kai-kai of mullet and barramundi. **1969** E. WALLER *And there's Opal* 8 We may as well swing the billy and have some kai kai. **1970** *Coast to Coast 1967–68* 48 No, she didn't say tucker. The kanakas said kai-kai. And I guess the word spread.

kai-yai /ˈkaɪ-jaɪ/, *a.* Also **ki-eye.** [Prob. transf. use of U.S. slang *ki-yi* dog.] Used *attrib.* as **kai-yai bones:** see quots.

1953 J.K. EWERS *With Sun on my Back* 177 That night, back at the homestead, we had rib-bones grilled over an open fire... 'Ki-eye' bones they call them up there. **1976** C.D. MILLS *Hobble Chains & Greenhide* 95 We grilled the 'kai-yai' bones for lunch. These are the short ribs, and a really epicurean delicacy.

kakka /ˈkækə/. *W.A.* Also **cacker, cakker.** [Of unknown origin.] An undersized crustacean, esp. a marine crayfish. Also *attrib.*

1965 *R.A.N. News* (Sydney) 30 Apr. 2 'Any kakkas?' .. (A kakka is an undersize crayfish). **1969** *W. Coast Fisherman* May 1 A rise in numbers of lobsters following the clamp-down on 'cakkers'. **1983** *Sunday Independent* (Perth) 21 Aug. 47/1 Cacker-catchers .. are generally recognisable by the size of their buckets, and their habit of indiscriminately slaughtering as many undersized fish and crustaceans as they can.

Kanaka /kəˈnækə/, *n.* and *attrib. Hist.* [a. Hawaiian *kanaka* man.]

A. *n.* A Pacific islander, esp. one brought to Australia to work as an indentured labourer in the sugar and cotton industries of Queensland.

1836 J.F. O'CONNELL *Residence Eleven Yrs. New Holland* 75 The Kanakas (South Sea Islanders) discharged from American and English whalers, at Sydney, supply the Sydney whalers with half their crews. **1851** *Illustr. Austral. Mag.* (Melbourne) June 333 Spirits and wines are not permitted to be given to the Kanakas. **1876** 'EIGHT YRS.' RESIDENT' *Queen of Colonies* 96 This town [*sc.* Maryborough] has of late acquired a somewhat unenviable notoriety in connexion with the Polynesian trade, some of the people interested in sugar growing having used great exertions to replace the white labourers by Kanakas. **1879** *Truth* (Sydney) 11 Dec. 5/1 If a man loved his neighbour as himself, he might have to love a Chinaman or a Kanaka, or perhaps a member of Parliament, and then the absurdity of the thing becomes apparent at once. **1899** *Progress* (Brisbane) 4 Feb. 9/2 It is Queensland's difficulty and Queensland's shame; and the re-introduction of Kanakas in 1892 remains the darkest blot in our legislative record. **1905** *Truth* (Sydney) 29 Jan. 1/3 It will, with increased sugar planting, be impossible to obtain a sufficiency of labor unless the *kanoodling kanaka* is retained. **1919** C.A. BERNAYS *Qld. Politics during Sixty* 161 The soft-eyed, odoriferous, and gentle kanaka .. was alleged to be the one and only prop of our greatest agricultural industry. **1939** J.W. COLLINSON *Early Days Cairns* 78 The final repatriation of the kanakas took place after the establishment of the Commonwealth in pursuance of the White Australia policy. **1957** V. PALMER *Seedtime* 47 He was a planter come down from Papua... There would have been no one but kanakas to nurse him as he lay in his bungalow up there. **1980** *Westerly* i. 6 'You're a Solomon Islander eh?' I said. 'That's right, both sides. Course I was born here, and so was me mum, but me dad was a kanaka.'

B. *attrib.*

1. Of or pertaining to a Pacific islander employed as a labourer in Australia, or to this as a practice.

1881 W. FEILDING *Austral. Trans-Continental Railway* 51 The native constable and our Kanaka lad (Walter) .. got drunk. **1886** *Bulletin* (Sydney) 9 Jan. 13/3 North Queensland don't like to be preached at about the kanaka trade. **1892** *Ibid.* 16 Apr. 6/4 The Registrar-General will keep quiet and cook the death-records, then there will be no more Kanaka 'scandals'. **1894** *Ibid.* 24 Mar. 9/1 The Kanaka-catcher up to date has just returned to Brisbane with his phonograph and his magic-lantern, which helped to lure 88 recruits. **1906** *Ibid.* 5 Apr. 15/4 Mean cockies .. expect white men to work for Kanaka wages. **1956** J.T. LANG *I Remember* 35 In Queensland they had the Kanaka problem with the sugar cane industry. **1959** *Meanjin* 143 About the time the kanaka-workers appeared my grandmother left us.

2. Comb. **Kanaka labour, labourer.**

1882 J. ALLEN *Hist. Aust.* 213 **'Kanaka' labour** was a mild form of slave labour. **1892** A.K. LANGRIDGE *Qld. Kanaka Labour Traffic* 3 The Kanaka labour trade was unmitigated slavery. **1894** J.G. PATON *Kanaka Labour Traffic* 19 The Kanaka Labour Traffickers. **1904** L. HOPKINS *On the Hop* p. xli, When the Kanaka labour system was in full swing, life in the South Sea Islands was insupportable. **1927** J. LYNG *Non-Britishers in Aust.* 100 Continue with Kanaka labour. **1887** MRS D.D. DALY *Digging, Squatting, & Pioneering Life* 24 Planters left their estates in the care of their **Kanyaka** [*sic*] **labourers** for a time.

3. Special Comb. **Kanaka question,** the subject of the use of Kanaka labour in Queensland as a matter of debate, controversy, etc.

1901 *Brisbane Courier* 1 July 7/1 He confessed he did not hold any very strong opinions on the Kanaka question until he visited the Bundaberg district. **1948** H.I. JENSEN *Dan Green* 16 We conversed freely on politics, the kanaka question and many other matters.

4. Prefixed by **anti-**: opposed to the employment of Kanakas in Queensland.

1883 T. ARCHER *Alleged Slavery in Qld.* 10 The journal you quote (one of the most rabid of the Anti-Kanaka papers). **1898** M. DAVITT *Life & Progress* 253 Mr Griffith .. was .. an anti-Kanaka man.

Kanakaland. *Obs.* A nickname for Queensland. Also *attrib.*

1892 *Bulletin* (Sydney) 31 Dec. 9/1 The wholesale perfidy and corruption of the present Kanakaland Parliament. **1894** *Ibid.* 3 Nov. 11/1 More slave-scandals in Kanakaland. The dog returneth to its vomit. **1898** *Tocsin* (Melbourne) 14 July 16/1 In Kanakaland the white workers are at last displacing coloured labour. **1903** *Bulletin* (Sydney) 17 Sept. 35/4 Queensland, Chowland, Kanakaland—it is all one. **1942** F. CLUNE *Last of Austral. Explorers* 124 Donald .. reached Port Mackay, the metropolis of Kanakaland.

Hence **Kanakalander,** a resident of Queensland.

1903 *Bulletin* (Sydney) 17 Sept. 35/1 The limp Kanakalander gloomily looks up from his lounge. **1945** S.J. BAKER *Austral. Lang.* 186 *Kanakalanders* .. used [of Queenslanders] during the closing decades of the last century when many Pacific island natives were imported.

kanga.

1. Abbrev. of KANGAROO *n.* 1.

1917 *Bulletin* (Sydney) 15 Feb. 24/4, I have had many opportunities of measuring the jump or stride of the kanga. **1959** A. UPFIELD *Bony & Mouse* 12 The dog chased the kanga over the fence. **1965** R.H. CONQUEST *Horses in Kitchen* 170 That kanga's our white hope. Call the dog off! **1981** A.J. BURKE *Pommies & Patriots* 66 The machine gun is being used to kill as many as a thousand kangaroos at a time and approximately five million kangas are being destroyed annually in the 1980s.

2. [Abbrev. of *kangaroo* rhyming slang for 'screw'.] **a.** Money. **b.** A prison warder.

1953 S.J. BAKER *Aust. Speaks* 133 *Kangaroo*, a warder, by rhyme on 'screw'; also used in the abbreviated form, *kanga*. **1969** A. O'TOOLE *Racing Game* 6 On account of you being a mighty bloke, and sending Ape that kanga without asking any questions, we're all agreed on one thing. You're getting the biggest share. **1978** E. HANGER *2D & Other Plays* 44 Your daughter's got a bit of kanga, but, hasn't she?.. Kanga?.. Cash. That's what they say in the bush.

3. See quot.

1975 *Sun-Herald* (Sydney) 20 July 13/2 Her friend .. prefers a bone-shaking ride on a 'kanga'—a jackhammer, to the uninitiated.

4. Special Comb. **Kanga Cricket,** see quot.

1986 *Canberra Chron.* 2 Apr. 1 (*caption*) Nine-year-old Matthew Pampling .. has a mighty swing during a match of Kanga Cricket... Kanga is a fast-developing form of cricket with rules and equipment especially designed for youngsters.

kangaroo /kæŋgəˈru/, *n.* Pl. **kangaroos** but formerly also **kangaroo.** [Extended use of Guugu Yimidhirr *gaŋurru* a large black or grey kangaroo, prob. *spec.* the male *Macropus robustus*.]

1. a. Any of the larger marsupials of the chiefly Austral. fam. Macropodidae (see quot. 1956), having short forelimbs, a tail developed for support and balance, long feet and powerful hind limbs, enabling a swift, bounding motion. **b.** Occas. loosely, referring to any or all of the members of the fam. Macropodidae and Potoroidae: see quots. 1839, 1870, and 1970. **c.** The flesh or hide of the animal. See also WALLABY *n.* 1. Also *attrib.*

1770 J. BANKS *Endeavour Jrnl.* 14 July (1962) II. 94 Kill Kanguru. **1770** J. COOK *Jrnls.* 4 Aug. (1955) I. 367 The Animal which I have before mentioned called by the natives *Kangooroo* or *Kanguru*. **1787** *Hist. New Holland* 71 We found that the animal called kangooroo at Endeavour River, was known under the same name here [*sc.* Van Diemen's Land]. **1788** *HRA* (1914) 1st Ser. I. 31 Near one of these huts we found some of the bones of a kangaroo. **1789** A. PHILLIP *Voyage to Botany Bay* 104 Kangaroos were frequently seen, but were so shy that it was very difficult to shoot them. **1792** *Hist. Rec. N.S.W.* (1893) II. 799 Of the beasts, the kangaroo is found to be the best eating, exactly resembling venison. **1805** *Sydney Gaz.* 13 Oct., Sixty seven large Kangaroos were caught from the first to the 10th of September, and issued from the Store instead of Salt Meat. **1814** *HRA* (1916) 1st Ser. VIII. 167 Found the Kangaroo the dogs must have killed yesterday. **1829** *Ibid.* (1922) 1st Ser. XIV. 591 A foundation for European civilisation in those wilds, of which the Aborigines, the Kangaroo and the Emu have hitherto been the undisturbed possessors. **1838** *S. Austral. Rec.* (London) 11 July 74 There is a good supply of fresh meat; beef and mutton, 1s. per lb.; kangaroo, which is excellent, from 6d. to 1s. per lb. **1839** H. Capper *S.A.* (rev. ed.) 52 Kangaroos are of five different species, viz., the forest, the brush, the wallaby, the kangaroo rat, and the kangaroo mouse. **1846** *Moreton Bay Courier* 8 Aug. 4/3 Fossil remains of an extinct race of animals, apparently a gigantic species of the kangaroo, had been discovered in the neighbourhood of Geelong. **1852** G.C. Mundy *Our Antipodes* I. 302 The caves are the night lodgings of numerous wallabis and wombats, the former a small kind of kangaroo. **1865** *London Soc.* Dec. 446/1 Nearly all the members of the corps of rangers are men of classical education and good birth, who can quote Homer or Virgil as well as they can shoot a kangaroo, or kick a black. **1870** *Illustr. Austral. News* (Melbourne) 28 Feb. 52/4 Of the kangaroo, which is too well known to need description, there are between twenty and thirty species in Australia. **1888** *Sydney Morning Herald* 24 Jan. 1/5 The most representative is the kangaroo class. These animals, by means of long hind legs and a strong tail, move in bounds or long jumps, and with some of them a well-mounted horseman cannot keep pace. **1892** A. Cameron *Aust. Felix* 11 There—on the river bank. . Old men kangaroo! . . No, not kangaroos. **1914** C.H.S. Matthews *Bill* 18 As out of his element as . . a kangaroo in a drawing-room. **1928** W. Robertson *Coo-ee Talks* 71 There has been considerable controversy as to the name of Australia's chief marsupial—the kangaroo. There are, of course, hundreds of native names by which the animal is known, but the name 'Kangaroo' is in the dialect of the old Endeavour River tribe of north Queensland. It was first heard by Captain Cook and his men when they landed at that spot. **1930** *Bulletin* (Sydney) 2 Apr. 25/1 His reins were made of rawhide, his lash of kangaroo. **1939** G. Digby *Down Wind* 258, I do not know whether I am biologically accurate in stating that the kangaroo is in the line of evolution from the deer, but to me it seems fairly obvious. **1944** C. Fenner *Mostly Austral.* 90 They're going to cut down mallee scrub, And live on kangaroo. **1954** T. Ronan *Vision Splendid* 82 The ideal anatomical construction for a drinker is that of the female kangaroo. Two legs and a tail to balance on, and a pouch for the spare bottles. **1956** T.Y. Harris *Naturecraft in Aust.* 76 There is no clear anatomical distinction between a kangaroo, a wallaroo, and a wallaby. In general, 'wallaby' is used for the smaller forms, 'wallaroo' for the stockily-built types of mountain and open forest type of habitat, and 'kangaroo' for the larger forms. **1970** W.D.L. Ride *Guide Native Mammals Aust.* 44 In some parts of Australia, and in particular where great kangaroos are rare, such as in Tasmania, or in the Kimberley, the local people may refer to large wallabies as kangaroos. **1972** *Bulletin* (Sydney) 17 June 9/3 Hunters . . can get seven to eight cents a pound for a kangaroo in Queensland, about double the going price in New South Wales. **1974** *Oceania* XLIV. 216 Modern Guugu Yimidhirr retains the word *gangurru*, which refers to a species of large black kangaroo, now, unhappily, rarely seen in the area. **1983** J. Hepworth *Birds & Beasties Aust., The Kangaroo* Our own unique bipedal bounding marsupial. We put it on our Coat of Arms—and shoot it by the million.

2. With distinguishing epithet, as **brush, bush, eastern grey, great grey, grey, hill, Kangaroo Island, red, western grey**: see under first element.

3. *fig.*

a. An Australian, esp. a member of the armed services or one representing Australia in a sport; Australia as so represented.

1883 Beeston & Massie *St Ivo & Ashes* 8 The battle for the 'ashes' was over, and once more the Englishmen had regained their lost supremacy in the cricket field. Neither Lion nor Kangaroo, however, was satisfied, apparently. **1898** *Truth* (Sydney) 23 Jan. 3/7 The English team of cricketers, lately badly walloped by the kangaroo. **1900** G.F. Chinner *Spray from War Wave* 38 No marvel, then, that 'Tommies' choose To call Australians 'Kangaroos'. **1906** *Truth* (Sydney) 22 July 6/1 The muddied oafs from Auckland also gave the kangaroo a father of a beating. **1949** G. Berrie *Morale* 197 Well, if you bloody Kangaroos aren't sick of the war, I *am*.

b. *pl.* The name of the Australian international Rugby League team; in *sing.*, a member of such a team. Cf. Socceroo and Wallaby *n.* 4.

1933 *Sydney Morning Herald* 27 Oct. 11/2 Widnes attacked early, bustling into the 'Kangaroos' territory. **1937** *Ibid.* 20 Dec. 14/6 The Kangaroos won the third test match against England at Huddersfield to-day by 13 points to three. **1964** *Rugby League News* Oct. 4 Mr W.G. Buckley . . presided at the Kangaroos' Annual Re-Union . . on . . September 20. **1973** *Canberra Times* 17 Sept. 14/8 The Kangaroos, who will leave next Sunday, carry a blend of youth and experience. **1985** *Sydney Morning Herald* 4 Apr. 32/4 When the 1982 Kangaroos left for England Steve Mortimer was considered to be Australia's first-string Rugby League half-back.

c. In the phr. **(to have) kangaroos in the** (**your,** etc.) **top paddock,** (to be) crazy or eccentric.

1908 *Austral. Mag.* (Sydney) Nov. 1250/1 If you show signs of mental weakness you are either balmy, dotty, ratty, or cracked, or you may even have . . kangaroos in your top paddock. **1946** D. Stivens *Courtship of Uncle Henry* 70 Talked like a toff himself, he did, but he had the kangaroos in the top paddock. **1968** S. Gore *Holy Smoke* 59 'Strewth what's wrong with this nut?' says one of 'em. 'Kangaroos in the top paddock, by the seem of it.' **1980** B. Hornadge *Austral. Slanguage* 120 A few have become hermits and solitary bush dwellers avoiding all human contact. Of such men it is said that they *have kangaroos in their top paddock*. **1985** P. Carey *Illywhacker* 53 'And he was a big man too, and possibly slow-witted.' 'Leichhardt?' 'No, Bourke. . . He had kangaroos in his top paddock.'

4. Comb. **kangaroo flesh, fur, hide, hunt, hunter, -hunting, leather, meat, scalp, shoot, shooter, -shooting, skin, stew.**

1806 *HRA* (1915) 1st Ser. V. 643, I have directed that **Kangaroo Flesh** be received into the Stores. **1829** *Hobart Town Almanack* 87 Kangaroo flesh, which was sold at 18d. a pound, and that species of sea weed called Botany bay greens, being the chief support of the inhabitants. **1848** *Emigrant's Friend* 26 The colony at first suffered great hardships, so much so, that eighteen-pence per pound was given for kangaroo flesh. **1872** 'Resident' *Glimpses Life Vic.* 5 We feasted on steaks of kangaroo flesh and damper. **1842** *Colonial Observer* (Sydney) 23 Mar. 198/4 The officer . . obtained from them a belt composed of small **kangaroo fur,** commonly worn by the natives of this coast. **1848** J. Gould *Birds of Aust.* IV. Pl. 35, The nest of this species . . is more neatly built, and is lined internally with opossum or kangaroo fur. **1971** *Bulletin* (Sydney) 13 Nov. 27/2 He . . glances enviously at a Cornelius Furs stand nearby which is doing a booming trade in kangaroo-fur coats. **1828** *Tasmanian* (Hobart) 29 Aug. 3 Cash Price allowed for **Kangaroo** Skins and **Hides. 1911** St. C. Grondona *Collar & Cuffs* 57 Kangaroo hide is also a very useful commodity. **1928** M.E. Fullerton *Austral. Bush* 40 Strips of kangaroo-hide for trace-chains. **1956** B. Beatty *Beyond Aust.'s Cities* 71 The roof is made of kangaroo hide. **1964** 'E. Lindall' *Kind of Justice* 36 His habit of rough cloth trousers held up by a wide, thick kangaroo-hide belt. **1827** *Monitor* (Sydney) 15 Nov. 767/1 Which is the least demoralizing . . the Theatre or the **Kangaroo hunt? 1839** J.G. Johnston *Truth* 27 Man, you would be delighted with a good kangaroo hunt. **1857** W. Westgarth *Vic. & Austral. Gold Mines* 36 A kangaroo hunt, so familiar to the early colonist, is now a remote and difficult pleasure. **1873** A. Trollope *Aust. & N.Z.* I. 37 Squatters . . get up kangaroo hunts and make picnics. **1891** D. Ferguson *Vicissitudes Bush Life* 89 We can have plenty of time to enjoy a kangaroo hunt at Christmas. **1923** T. Hall *Short Hist. Downs Blacks* 19 The day a kangaroo hunt was to take place was looked forward to as a day of great sport and pleasure. **1984** B. Dixon *Searching for Aboriginal Lang.* 79 A song about poking a stick into a hollow log to dislodge the white-tailed rat—good eating. Then one about a kangaroo hunt. **1841** *Port Phillip Patriot* 5 Aug. 2/4 The **kangaroo hunters** of his department. **1862** F.J. Jobson *Aust.* 124 We were joined on the coach by some Kangaroo-hunters. **1897** L. Lindley-Cowen *W. Austral. Settler's Guide* 111 The kangaroo hunters feed the dingoes and enable them to rear all their young. **1828** *Tasmanian* (Hobart) 11 July 3 **Kangaroo hunting** and fowling, although innocent in themselves, are *real crimes* when practised on a Sunday. **1886** D.M. Gane *N.S.W. & Vic.* 173 Many persons imagine there is no risk in kangaroo-hunting. It is a mistake. **1911** *Huon Times* (Franklin) 30 Aug. 3/2 He was kangaroo hunting in the vicinity of the Sleeping Beauty mountain. **1932** C.M. Gray *Western Vic. in Forties* 6 Whilst at our first squattage I went out kangaroo hunting one day with Stephen Ewing. **1972** *Bulletin* (Sydney) 1 Jan. 45/3 The popularity of kangaroo hunting, fist fighting and sodomy rises, following the success of 'Wake in Fright'. **1833** *Trumpeter* (Hobart) 31 Dec. 287 **Kangaroo leather,** for shoe-making purposes. **1845** C. Hodgkinson *Aust., Port Macquarie to Moreton Bay* 50 Light kerseymere trowsers, doubled in kangaroo leather down the legs. **1908** 'P. Warrego' *Diary New Chum* 16 Syd owns a stockwhip made of kangaroo leather, and is very proud of it. **1851** H. Melville *Present State Aust.* 308 In the event of **kangaroo meat** being wanted, he skins the forepart and cuts it off. **1856** J. Bonwick *Bushrangers* 2 As much as eighteen pence a pound was paid for kangaroo meat. **1877** *Austral. Handbk.* 283 In 1808 . . the salt beef and pork gave out, and kangaroo meat had to be the means of subsistence. **1937** W. Hatfield *I find Aust.* 240, I would have hated to be reduced to their mulga flour cakes and kangaroo meat as a diet. **1972** Anderson & Blake *J.S. Neilson* 19 For the hard-up families kangaroo meat helped to fill empty bellies. **1983** *Daily News* (Perth) 11 Aug. 10 The U.S. looks set to support the export of kangaroo meat from Australia. **1885** *Bulletin* (Sydney) 5 Dec. 10/4 **Kangaroo-scalps** are paid for at the rate of 9d. each. **1897** *Western Champion* (Barcaldine) 12 Oct. 3/3 There is a great commotion amongst the scalpers owing to the reduction in price for kangaroo scalps. **1899** *Bulletin* (Sydney) 4 Feb. 32/2 Dad and Dave were away after kangaroo-scalps. **1936** F. Clune *Roaming round Darling* 119 A young grazier . . made up a party for a **kangaroo shoot. 1886** P. Clarke *'New Chum' in Aust.* 215, I knew a **kangaroo-shooter** who employed himself occasionally in killing and salting hams from wild pigs. **1917** C.L. Drew *Reminisc. D. Gilbert* 23 He fitted himself out as a kangaroo shooter; and was well on the road to knocking up a good cheque. **1928** G.H. Wilkins *Undiscovered Aust.* 31 A kangaroo-shooter, and his son, who gained their living by shooting kangaroos for their hides. **1965** L. Walker *Other Girl* 28 Kangaroos are a menace to sheep country. If we don't kill them with cars the professional kangaroo-shooters get them. **1985** *Woman's Day* (Sydney) 1 July 21/2 While I was a kangaroo-shooter I would be away in the bush for weeks at a time. **1886** J.A. Froude *Oceana* 122 Two young English lords on their travels . . who had been up the country **kangaroo-shooting. 1936** W. Hatfield *Aust. through Windscreen* 47 At £1 a head kangaroo-shooting was a profitable enterprise. **1964** A. Staples *Paddo* 22 There was no work and he went out kangaroo-shooting. **1985** *Woman's Day* (Sydney) 1 July 20/2 He went on to do many jobs, including opal mining, professional boxing . . and, finally, kangaroo shooting. **1809** *Sydney Gaz.* 16 Apr. 2/1 On Sunday last arrived the colonial vessel Eliza from the South West coast of this Territory with . . about 1000 **Kangaroo skins. 1822** J. Dixon *Narr. Voyage N.S.W. & Van Dieman's Land* 85 These servants generally make Kangaroo-skin jackets, and shoes of something of the same sort. **1840** J.P. Johnson *Plain Truths* 12 They seldom wear anything on their persons except a kangaroo skin. **1857** J. Askew *Voyage Aust. & N.Z.* 98 Leather made of the kangaroo-skin, always brings the highest price in the market. **1873** J. Bonwick *M. Howe* 66 A rough knapsack of kangaroo skin contained his little property. **1892** J. Fraser *Aborigines N.S.W.* 47 A kangaroo skin, with the hair worn inwards, is a favourite kind of cloak in wet weather. **1953** H.G. Lamond *Big Red* 36 One of the fashion's whims had lately raised the price of kangaroo skins. **1968** G. Dutton *Andy* 127 On the kangaroo skin rug on the floor. **1981** A.B. Facey *Fortunate Life* 147 The men wore kangaroo skin loin coverings, the women had most of their body covered. **1834** M. Doyle *Extracts Lett. & Jrnls. G.F. Moore* 100 Dined on **kangaroo stew. 1847** E.W. Landor *Bushman* 257 Cooked a kangaroo stew for the three shepherds. **1881** E. Davies *Story Earnest Life* 132 Around the camp-fire were several men preparing kangaroo stew, and cockatoo pie and damper.

5. In the names of flora and fauna: **kangaroo acacia,** see *kangaroo thorn*; **apple,** any of several shrubs of the genus *Solanum* (fam. Solanaceae), chiefly of s. and e. Aust., esp. *S. aviculare, S. laciniatum* and *S. vescum* (see Gunyang), bearing an egg-shaped fruit edible when completely ripe; the fruit of these plants; **bush, (a)** PUNTY; **(b)** SANDHILL WATTLE; **fish, (a)** BURNETT SALMON; **(b)** MUDSKIPPER; **fly,** a small and intensely irritating fly, prob. any of several species, poss. incl. *Ortholfersia macleayi* and *Austrosimulium pestilens*; **grass, (a)** the tall, tussocky, perennial grass *Themeda triandra* (fam. Poaceae), widely distributed throughout Aust. and occurring elsewhere; **(b)** (occas.) any of several other similar grasses; **mouse,** HOPPING MOUSE; **paw,** see main entry; **prickly acacia,** see *kangaroo thorn*; **rabbit** *obs., kangaroo rat* (a); **rat, (a)** any of the small macropodoids of the fam. Potoroidae, incl. the BETTONG and POTOROO, most species of which have a fast hopping gait and construct a nest with material carried in the tail; RAT-KANGAROO; **(b)** *transf.* WEET-WEET; **thorn,** the prickly shrub *Acacia paradoxa* (fam. Mimosaceae), of all mainland States but not N.T., naturalized in Tas. and often planted as a hedge; formerly also **kangaroo (prickly) acacia; tick,** either of two ticks having the kangaroo or wallaby as chief host, the argasid tick *Ornithodoros gurneyi* of arid inland Aust., the bite of which can severely affect a human, and the ixodid tick *Amblyomma triguttatum*.

1828 *Hobart Town Courier* 2 Feb. 3 We have had occasion . . to remark the great luxuriance of what is called the **Kangaroo apple**, or New Zealand potato, a species of Solanum common to this country and New Zealand. **1834** J.D. LANG *Hist. & Statistical Acct. N.S.W.* I. 133 *Solanum laciniatum*, the kangaroo-apple, resembling the apple of a potato. **1842** *Tasmanian Jrnl. Nat. Sci.* I. 41 Kangaroo Apple . . has a mealy subacid taste, and may be eaten in any quantity with impunity. **1856** *Jrnl. Australasia* I. 37 Kangaroo apple . . producing in abundance a fruit a trifle larger than a pigeon's egg, which, when ripe, has a rich lemon colour. **1872** M.B. BROWNRIGG *Cruise of Freak* 77 We set sail for Cape Barren and by 12.30 p.m. were at Apple Orchard, so named, because of the kangaroo apples which abound there. **1888** *Proc. Linnean Soc. N.S.W.* III. 544 *Solanum aviculare* . . 'Kangaroo apple', 'Gunyang' . . of the Gippsland and other aboriginals. **1928** M.E. FULLERTON *Austral. Bush* 130 There is the kangaroo-apple, a yellow loquat-looking fruit. **1976** B. LEWIS *Sunday at Kooyong Road* 94 This weed? It is a kangaroo apple; are kangaroo apples really poisonous? **1901** *Proc. Linnean Soc. N.S.W.* XXVI. 318 The Acacias noticed were . . *A. Burkittii* (**Kangaroo Bush**). **1956** T.Y. HARRIS *Naturecraft in Aust.* 194 A light sandy soil in the 10-inch rainfall belt carries fairly large shrubs, such as . . Kangaroo Bush. **1980** G. DUTTON *Wedge-Tailed Eagle* 33 The noise of a horse and cart came. . . I ran around the thick kangaroo bush to see who it was. **1931** *Bulletin* (Sydney) 14 Jan. 21/4 The **kangaroo fish** or mudskipper, found in the mangroves of N.Q., does not always use its gills for breathing. **1971** P. BODEKER *Sandgropers' Trail* 191 Wyndham's waterfront at low tide was literally jumping with mud-hoppers. . . Northerners call them . . kangaroo fish . . because they like to elbow themselves up on mangrove roots to enjoy the sunshine. **1833** C. STURT *Two Exped. Interior S.A.* I. 72 We had left the immediate spot at which the **kangaroo flies** (cabarus) seemed to be collected. **1841** E.J. EYRE *Jrnls. Exped. Central Aust.* 26 May (1845) II. 56 The kangaroo fly (a small brown fly) became very troublesome, annoying us in great numbers, and warning us that rain was about to fall. **1865** S. BENNETT *Hist. Austral. Discovery* 643 The explorers . . were much persecuted by . . a terribly irritating fly called the kangaroo fly. **1902** *Bulletin* (Sydney) 8 Mar. 14/3 The kangaroo-fly . . is of slaty-brown color, somewhat smaller than the common house-fly, and it invariably accompanies the kangaroo. **1936** F. CLUNE *Roaming round Darling* 133 Their life was made miserable by . . a pest called the kangaroo-fly. **1826** J. ATKINSON *Acct. Agric. & Grazing N.S.W.* 20 The principal grasses are, the oak grass, **kangaroo grass**, two sorts of rye grass. **1843** J.F. BENNETT *Hist. & Descr. Acct. S.A.* 43 Of grasses, that named the kangaroo grass, from the animal of that name feeding on it, is the most general. **1859** W. BURROWS *Adventures Mounted Trooper* 151 Kangaroo grass . . is very much sort [*sic*] after by sheep, who will bite it as close to the roots as it is possible for them to reach with their teeth. **1887** W.H. SUTTOR *Austral. Stories Retold* 120 A kind of small cake . . served with fresh nutty kangaroo grass butter and new-laid eggs. **1899** J.C. HAWKER *Early Experiences S.A.* 37 The name kangaroo grass was given from the great height it grew. Many colonists used to call it native wheat. **1924** A.B. PEIRCE *Knocking About* 164 The males wear belts to which are attached tails of kangaroo grass three or four feet in length. **1968** B. WILSON *Pasture Improvement Aust.* 130 Species such as kangaroo grass are very susceptible to grazing and will persist only under conditions of high fire frequency and low grazing pressure. **1971** G. MORGAN *We are borne On* 381 We saw thousands of acres of kangaroo grass up to eight feet high. It must have been some job trying to muster cattle out of it. **1984** B. DIXON *Searching for Aboriginal Lang.* 22 A flock of brolgas dancing over the long green kangaroo grass. **1833** W.H. BRETON *Excursions* 410 The **kangaroo**, or opossum **mouse**, is a mouse formed like a kangaroo. **1854** J. CAPPER *Aust.* 38 The kangaroo-rat and kangaroo-mouse are two varieties of the same species; the former is the size of a rabbit, the latter considerably smaller. **1860** J.H. LEWIS *Stuart's Journey Interior Aust.* p. iv, Stuart and his companion existed . . for more than a month, with but little animal food, and that chiefly kangaroo mice. **1902** *Bulletin* (Sydney) 27 Dec. 15/1 Any of your readers ever see any kangaroo mice . . ? I killed a couple out here (about 250 miles N.E. of Kalgoorlie). **1923** A.G. BOLAM *Trans-Austral. Wonderland* 24 The Kangaroo Mouse (Hapalotis Mitchelli) . . is found well distributed all over the countryside. **1933** R.B. PLOWMAN *Camel Pads* 283 Most interesting . . were the tracks of the brush-tailed kangaroo mice. **1940** *Bulletin* (Sydney) 12 June 17/4 At rare intervals parts of Queensland will be invaded by kangaroo mice. **1839** J.C. HAWKER Diary 33 The Wallaby and **Kangaroo** rat or **rabbit** are a small species of the kangaroo and abound in the scrubs. **1860** 'LADY' *My Experiences in Aust.* 249 The kangaroo rabbit I had . . roasted and stuffed. **(a) 1788** J. WHITE *Jrnl. Voyage N.S.W.* (1790) 182 Every animal in this country partakes, in a great measure, of the nature of the Kangaroo. We have the Kangaroo Opossum, the **Kangaroo Rat**, &c. *Ibid.* 286 The Poto Roo, or Kangaroo Rat. . . The forelegs are short in comparison to the hind. **1793** W. TENCH *Compl. Acct. Settlement* 172 The kanguroo-rat is a small animal, never reaching . . more than fourteen or fifteen pounds, and its usual size is not above seven or eight pounds. It joins to the head and bristles of a rat, the leading distinctions of a kanguroo. **1830** *Sydney Monitor* 28 Apr. 2/2 A Kangaroo rat was found in the belly of a rock diamond snake. **1852** MRS C. MEREDITH *My Home in Tas.* I. 252 The Kangaroo-Rat. . . A very rich gravy soup is often made from it, and a colonial dish called a 'steamer', consisting of the meat and some good bacon finely minced. **1861** 'RESIDENT' *Social Life & Manners* 188 The kangaroo-dog . . gave chase to a Paddy melon or kangaroo rat. I . . did not feel comfortable after having partaken of *rat curry*. **1891** *Quiz* (Adelaide) 11/3 The small species of marsupials, such as kangaroo-rats, are being completely exterminated. **1912** SPENCER & GILLEN *Across Aust.* 110 Desolate though the land was we continually met with little kangaroo-rats (*Bettongia lesueurii*) dodging in and out among the tussocks. **1948** P.J. HURLEY *Red Cedar* 71 We kicked up from grass-tufts kangaroo-rats, fastest things on legs for forty yards. **1960** R.S. PORTEOUS *Cattleman* 211 She knew where to part the grass and disclose the cunningly built nest of a kangaroo rat. **1981** A.B. FACEY *Fortunate Life* 42 The kangaroo rats only come out at night. They are about the size of a house cat. **(b) 1870** J.G. WOOD *Nat. Hist. Man* II. 42, I have seen an Australian stand at one side of Kennington Oval, and throw the '**kangaroo-rat**' completely across it. **1890** J. EDGE-PARTINGTON *Album Pacific Islands* i. 353 Kangaroo rats are play things—the game being to throw them as far as possible along the surface of the ground. **1929** *Austral. Aborigines & South Sea Islanders Implements, Weapons & Curios, Tyrrell's Museum* 5 *Weet weet.* Aboriginal toy or sporting implement . . 23 Weet Weet, or Kangaroo Rat, 2 ft. 3½ in. Queensland. 12s. 6d. **1967** [see WEET-WEET]. ***c* 1856** F. GERSTAECKER *Life in Bush* 9 'And your men?' 'Are looking for you on the beach, or among the **kangaroo thorns**.' **1854** *Hobarton Guardian* 1 Feb. 3/2 The very dangerous character of the kangaroo prickly acacia as a fence in case of fire. **1874** 'SPECIAL REPORTER' *Agric. in S.A.* 21 The only hedges seen are of patchy untended kangaroo acacia, which in this condition are neither ornamental nor useful. **1914** E.E. PESCOTT *Native Flowers Vic.* 45 Of the Wattles with prickly foliage, the 'Kangaroo thorn', Acacia armata, is the best. **1921** A.J. CAMPBELL *Golden Wattle* 42 The Prickly Wattle (*Acacia armata*), or so-called 'Kangaroo Thorn' . . is perhaps the oldest known of Australian Wattles, and was originally gathered by the first explorers. **1935** E. COLEMAN *Come back in Wattle Time* 19 The bushman has bestowed his own peculiarly apt names on certain well-known species . . Prickly Moses, Wait-a-while, Kangaroo-thorn. **1979** WRIGLEY & FAGG *Austral. Native Plants* 161 Kangaroo thorn. . . Excellent hedge species. Very hardy; suitable for road batters and beach-front plantings. **1938** *Austral. Vet. Jrnl.* Apr. 69 The **kangaroo tick**, as a parasite of kangaroos and other native fauna, dogs and occasionally man, is to be found in parts of the north-western division of this State [*sc.* N.S.W.]. **1953** H.G. LAMOND *Big Red* 211 Them kangaroo ticks is comin' out again. . . They on'y come in a dry spell. **1962** MARSHALL & DRYSDALE *Journey among Men* 68 Our only major complaint was the kangaroo ticks. They seemed to inhabit every bush. They dropped down on us, and imperceptibly bored into our hides. **1975** *Bulletin* (Sydney) 1 Nov. 25/1 In N.S.W. and Queensland another kangaroo tick (*Ornithodorus* [*sic*] *Gurneyi*) has caused a few cases of sickness; and there is one recorded instance of temporary blindness. **1984** W.W. AMMON et al. *Working Lives* 188 Another problem is the kangaroo tick. This pest gets on your clothes when you're skinning a roo and buries its head right through and under your skin.

6. Special Comb. **kangaroo bar,** BULLBAR; **bone,** a bone from a kangaroo, used by Aborigines as a tool or as an item of personal adornment; **camp,** a place where kangaroos habitually congregate (cf. CAMP *n.* 3 and 4); **cloak,** a cloak made of kangaroo skin; **closure** [orig. Br. (see OEDS *sb.* 4 b.], see quot. 1936; **corroboree,** *kangaroo dance*; **court** [orig. U.S. (see OEDS *sb.* 4 b.)], an improperly constituted court having no legal standing; **dance,** an Aboriginal ceremonial dance in which the dancers' movements represent those of a kangaroo; **dog (bitch, hound),** a dog used for hunting the kangaroo; (*spec.*) a breed of dog evolved in Aust. from the Scottish deerhound and the greyhound for this purpose; a dog of this breed; **drive,** an operation in which kangaroos are herded, trapped, and slaughtered, or otherwise hunted; **feather,** (in the war of 1914–18), a jocular name for an emu plume worn on the hat of a member of the Australian Light Horse; **fence,** a fence made to exclude kangaroos (see quots. 1852 and 1978); **ground** *obs.*, a place habitually frequented by kangaroos; **hedge** *obs.*, a hedge of *kangaroo thorn* (see sense 5); **jack,** a heavy-duty, lever-action jack, used esp. to lift logs, stumps, etc.; **joey,** a young kangaroo; **knapsack,** a knapsack made from kangaroo skin; so **-knapsacked** *a.*; **land,** Australia; **leap,** a sudden or jolting bound; also *fig.*; **mat,** a floor rug made from kangaroo skin; **net,** a net used by Aborigines to snare kangaroos; **route,** a name for the Sydney-Singapore-London air route, orig. as flown by Qantas Airways Ltd.; **rug,** a rug made from kangaroo skin; **sinew,** a kangaroo tendon used for binding, tying, etc., or for personal adornment; also *attrib.*; **soup,** soup made from kangaroo meat; **spear** *obs.*, a spear used by Aborigines to kill kangaroos; **start,** (of a motor vehicle) a jerking start (see KANGAROO *v.* 2 a.); **steak,** a piece of kangaroo meat cut and cooked in the manner of beef-steak; **steamer,** a stew made from kangaroo meat (see quot. 1864); STEAMER; **tail,** the tail of a kangaroo as an article of food, esp. *attrib.* as **kangaroo-tail soup; tooth,** the tooth of a kangaroo, as used for personal adornment; **Valley,** a name given to Earls Court, a district of London (see quot. 1965).

1969 L. HADOW *Full Cycle* 207 He took a folded handkerchief from the glove box, wet it from the water-bag on the **kangaroo bar**. **1975** R. BEILBY *Brown Land Crying* 274 His vehicle was a late-model bone-white station wagon with plenty of chrome and massive kangaroo-bars forming a protective grid in front of the radiator grille. **1977** B. FULLER *Nullarbor Lifelines* 161 A driver, reckless of his car and his life, occasionally collided with a kangaroo at night, but not often. And, we without fitting a kangaroo-bar, had no trouble whatever. **1842** *Colonial Observer* (Sydney) 23 Mar. 198/4 The officer . . obtained from them a . . nose-piece of **kangaroo bone.** **1845** *Bell's Life in Sydney* 11 Jan. 4/1 Her nose was adorned with a kangaroo bone. **1846** C.W. SCHÜRMANN *Aboriginal Tribes Port Lincoln* 3 A small hole is bored by means of a sharp kangaroo bone. **1879** *Native Tribes S.A.* 213 The root end, which is about as thick as a man's thumb, is pointed, being previously hardened in the fire, and at the taper end a small hole is bored by means of a sharp kangaroo bone. **1969** D.J. MULVANEY *Prehist. Aust.* 169 Examples of crocodile, kangaroo and emu bone arrangements are known, presumably at totemic increase sites. **1878** R.B. SMYTH *Aborigines of Vic.* II. 63 *Burrai gurrai* . . a **kangaroo camp.** **1946** *Service Publication No. 6* (School Public Health &

Tropical Med.) 258 Specimens that he had found in what he considered their natural habitat, a kangaroo camp about twenty miles north of Tibooburra. **1830** S.H. COLLINS *Geogr. Descr. Australasia* 17 Most of them wore **kangaroo cloaks**, which were their only cloathing. **1846** C.P. HODGSON *Reminisc. Aust.* 361 The gins were covered with kangaroo cloaks branded with fantastical figures and signs. **1936** H.D. INGRAM *Australasian Secretarial Principles* 75 **Kangaroo Closure.** A method adopted in Parliamentary committees by which the chairman is permitted to select what amendments he considers are relevant to the question and 'jump over' those he thinks are not worth considering. **1883** A.W. HOWITT *On Some Austral. Beliefs* 11 He .. dreamed for several consecutive nights that he was present at a **Kangaroo Corroboree.** **1898** D.W. CARNEGIE *Spinifex & Sand* 331 The kangaroo-corroboree, in which a man hops towards the musicians and back again, to be followed in turn by every other dancer and finally by the whole lot, who advance hopping together, ending up with a wild yell, in which all join. **1967** *Kings Cross Whisper* (Sydney) xlii. 9/3 Mr Justice Collusion interrupted to point out that he was not running a **kangaroo court** .. and adjourned for lunch. **1974** *Bulletin* (Sydney) 19 Jan. 38/2 The IRA .. has been trying some of its members in 'kangaroo courts', and inflicting harsh punishments. **1982** *Weekend Austral.* (Sydney) 14 Nov. 12 Mr Gough Whitlam stood as a petitioner .. defending his government's role in the East Timor crisis before a kangaroo court. **1984** *Canberra Times* 29 Feb. 1/4 Mr Sinclair made a statement accusing Mr Justice Cross of .. presiding over a 'star chamber' .. 'kangaroo court'. **1833** *Currency Lad* (Sydney) 27 Apr. 3 The **kangaroo-dances** .. of the aborigines. **1849** J.P. TOWNSEND *Rambles & Observations N.S.W.* 98 In these dances they often imitate the motions of animals, the kangaroo for instance... Certain settlers, inspired by rum and water, have adopted the kangaroo dance. **1878** S. TANDY *Children in Scrub* 64 They were hard at work dancing a kangaroo dance. .. One blackfellow, who has a long tail fastened to him, goes about on his hands and knees, and pretends to eat the grass; then he jumps up, as if he were frightened, and imitates as nearly as he can the movements of a kangaroo. The rest of the party pretend to be the dogs and hunters, and run round him in a circle at a short distance. **1898** W.A. SQUIRE *Ritual, Myth, & Customs Austral. Aborigines* 20 At the termination of the tests the kangaroo dance is generally performed; the dancers after fastening to themselves long tails of twisted grass, jump about in imitation of the kangaroo. **1924** A.B. PEIRCE *Knocking About* 164 The monkey or kangaroo dance are the most distinctive. **1805** *Sydney Gaz.* 21 July, Capital **kangaroo dog**—To be sold. **1810** *Ibid.* 14 Apr., Lost, a large Kangaroo Dog, colour pale red and some little white, particularly under the neck. **1823** *Hobart Town Gaz.* 21 June, To be Sold about 1100 feet of seasoned 2 inch Stringy Bark Planks; also 2 excellent Kangaroo Dogs. **1827** *Monitor* (Sydney) 17 Sept. 642/2 Stolen, a black brindled kangaroo bitch, with a white spot on the breast. **1839** W.H. LEIGH *Reconnoitering Voyages* 96 We untied the kangaroo hounds, and they gave it a splendid chace. **1845** C. GRIFFITH *Present State & Prospects Port Phillip* 154 The kangaroo dog .. is a greyhound with a dash of the mastiff. **1850** J.B. CLUTTERBUCK *Port Phillip* 35 On every station .. a large kind of greyhound, a cross of the Scotch greyhound and English bulldog, called the Kangaroo-dog, which runs by sight, is kept for the purpose of their destruction. **1870** *Illustr. Austral. News* (Melbourne) 3 Jan. 7/3 The corded breeches, the boots with spurs attached, the kangaroo dog stretched at his feet, the bridle suspended from the rafters indicate the stockrider rather than the digger. **1888** 'R. BOLDREWOOD' *Robbery under Arms* (1937) 24 My kangaroo dog killed her favourite cat. **1913** R. GRAY *Reminisc. India & N. Qld.* 59 Having a big kangaroo dog with us and revolvers, we secured an old man kangaroo the first afternoon. **1935** M. GILMORE *More Recoll.* 115 Our .. kangaroo-hound (which we never dignified with the name hound) hunted anything that ran, and scratched like a terrier for anything that earthed. **1969** F.B. VICKERS *No Man is Himself* 153, I was holla gutted as a kangaroo dog... I was just about out to it. **1870** C.H. ALLEN *Visit to Qld.* 169 In some places there are what are called '**kangaroo drives**', and then immense numbers are killed. **1885** A.W. HOWITT *Jeraeil* 318 When all was prepared, the men began to shout, as if driving game, to beat the logs and tree stems with clubs and tomahawk heads, and in fact to represent a 'kangaroo drive'. **1893** 'PIONEER' *Reminisc. Austral. Early Life* 147 Twenty or thirty horsemen generally taking a line of country and riding within sight of each other .. driving some fifteen hundred to two thousand kangaroos to a certain point, where there was a line of fence, about eight or nine feet in height, and between two and three miles in length, with an entrance of about a mile in width, and gradually tapering down to a point of a couple of hundred yards, where large pits had been excavated, behind a blind fence, as well as high slaughter yards, into which they were forced, by the horsemen closing in... This was called a 'kangaroo drive'. **1930** *Aussie* (Sydney) 15 May 14/1 One of the preliminaries was a kangaroo drive. A patch of country was encircled by the hunters, who gradually closed upon a narrow valley. There they rushed upon the hunted, and the yelling, dancing lines, the flying and clattering of spears and boomerangs, so confused the animals that dozens were easily killed. **1965** R.H. CONQUEST *Horses in Kitchen* 131 The pioneering days when cattle stampedes and kangaroo drives were the order of the day in northern parts. **1986** *Canberra Times* 30 Aug. 6/2 Graziers had told committee members of kangaroo drives involving indiscriminate shooting. **1916** *Kangaroosilite: On Board 'Wandilla'* Jan. 4 *Stolen.* Brown felt hat as worn by young children, decorated with several '**Kangaroo feathers**'. **1917** *Toorowan Tattler* (Melbourne) Dec. 3 Kangaroo feathers may be worn in the hat if the hat is placed on the head at an angle of 45 degrees. They are not the badge of the Jellicoe Light Horse. **1919** W.H. DOWNING *Digger Dialects* 30 *Kangaroo feathers*, (1) a tall tale; (2) an impossible thing; (3) spring millinery of the Light Horse. **1937** R. Fairbridge *Pinjarra* 189 A good many young women had lost their hearts to some fine upstanding young man with a 'Kangaroo feather in his hat'. **1846** F. DUTTON *S.A. & its Mines* 203 The **'kangaroo' fence** is composed of pieces of timber large and small. **1852** F. LANCELOTT *Aust. as it Is* I. 138 Where timber is plentiful, the 'Kangaroo' fence is preferred before all others, as it keeps out sheep, pigs, and such like quadrupeds; it is formed of pieces of timber, large and small, all cut into equal lengths, either of 7 or 8 feet, and placed close and upright in a trench 2 feet deep and tightly rammed; a rough batten being nailed along the top as a band. **1943** *Bulletin* (Sydney) 1 Sept. 13/4, I helped to repair a kangaroo fence on Lower Crawford station. **1978** M. WALKER *Pioneer Crafts Early Aust.* 28 An early form of hemming in the paddock was the palisade fence, also known as the kangaroo fence, being made up with split trunks, straighter branches and saplings, all being cut to a consistent length, which varied from seven to ten feet (2.1–3 m.). A continuous two to three feet (0.6–0.9 m.) trench was dug and the timbers stood upright; the earth was backfilled and tightly rammed about the uprights. **1833** W.H. BRETON *Excursions* 76 The grounds that enclose the ravines are level .. the **kangaroo ground** being one of the most remarkable. **1835** H. MELVILLE *Hist. Van Diemen's Land* 24 Their fine kangaroo grounds were taken from them. **1861** 'OLD BUSHMAN' *Bush Wanderings* 19 There is a good kangaroo-ground up by the Yarra. **1875** R. & F. HILL *What we saw in Aust.* 236 *Acacia armata* .. as a hedge and well pruned .. forms an impervious fence... Coming originally from Kangaroo Island, the fences thus made are called **Kangaroo hedges.** **1882** E.B. BAYLY *Alfreda Holme* 67 'Here our place begins,' said Mr Raymond, pointing to a dark line of kangaroo hedge on their right. **1911** *Settlers' Handy Pamphlet* (W.A. Lands Dept.) 7 The cost of clearing is greatly reduced by the use of 'jacks', gelignite, and fire. .. When the roots are burned through and the tree falls the roots are run and lifted with a '**Kangaroo**' or 'Wallaby' **jack.** **1977** J. DOUGHTY *Gold in Blood* 209 A kangaroo jack, one of those huge, box-like affairs that weigh about a hundredweight and will lift anything. **1941** W.J. DENNY *Digger at Home & Abroad* 150 The familiar picture .. of units preceded by a **kangaroo joey** .. is not of recent origin. **1957** *Bulletin* (Sydney) 27 Nov. 16/3 In outback Queensland we reared dozens of kangaroo-joeys, with few fatalities. **1838** *Cornwall Chron.* (Launceston) 22 Sept. 2 On Saturday night last, four men, well armed, and with **kangaroo knapsacks**, entered a sawyer's hut. **1839** *Tasmanian* (Hobart) 8 Feb. 46, I was provided with a musket and pistol, and a kangaroo knapsack. **1850** *Irish Exile* (Hobart) 5 Oct. 2/2 A shifting population of blue-shirted, kangaroo-knapsacked labourers. **1982** P. ADAM SMITH *Shearers* 20 The Derwenters were distinguished by their tall hats and kangaroo knapsacks, or Derwent drums as they were called. **1827** *Monitor* (Sydney) 20 Apr. 386/3 Easter Monday .. was signalized among us of **Kangaroo Land**, in the *usual mode* adopted at seasons of joy. **1852** *Austral. Gold Digger's Monthly Mag.* I. 7 The kangaroo land had often been in his thoughts. **1862** *Bell's Life in Sydney* 4 Oct. 4/2 *Kangaroo-land.* By the Rev. Arthur Polehampton. **1900** *Western Champion* (Barcaldine) 24 Apr. 7/5 The Boers, appearing to be struck with panic, bolted into the ravines, hoping the Australians would rush in after them and be slaughtered; but the men from kangaroo land declined the invitation. **1913** *Truth* (Sydney) 19 Oct. 6/3 (*heading*) America and Australia. If 'Hayseed' Came to Kangarooland. **1954** C. BARRETT *Wild Life Aust. & New Guinea* 1 In the old colonial days Australia often was called 'Kangaroo Land'. **1852** *Austral. Gold Digger's Monthly Mag.* III. 98 We have some amazing **kangaroo leaps** in our mineralogical conformations. **1966** J. ALDRIDGE *My Brother Tom* 171 There was no dramatic dog fight, no picture of Tom tearing apart the northern skies with his kangaroo leaps from star to star. **1972** D. MARTIN *Frank & Francesca* 5 Francie gave a kangaroo leap and half fell over the bike. **1980** G. DUTTON *Wedge-Tailed Eagle* 31 We flew over the switch-backs in long kangaroo leaps, over and thump, over and thump. **1861** E.P. RAMSAY-LAYE *Social Life & Manners* 123 My drawing-room was made quite gay with some handsome **kangaroo mats.** **1972** *Bulletin* (Sydney) 15 Jan. 25/3 In one of the 30 or so souvenir stops .. are three Tokyo tourists, flapping kangaroo mats and stroking koalas. **1830** W.J. HOOKER *Bot. Miscellany* I. 253 It is customary for the tribes, when leaving a district, to deposit in such a situation their **Kangaroo-Nets**, *Dillies, Bass-mats*, chissels, and superfluous implements, until their return. **1846** *Moreton Bay Courier* 19 Sept. 4/1 Kangaroo nets, made of the bark of the kooremin (sterculia heterophylla) .. were found in the camps of the natives. **1870** E.B. KENNEDY *Four Yrs. in Qld.* 80 Kangaroo nets, some of them forty yards long, and in mesh and substance like a cricket net, were rolled up in bundles. **1889** —— *Blacks & Bushrangers* 82 They .. made strong kangaroo nets out of a fine flax, which the natives showed them how to prepare. **1923** T. HALL *Short Hist. Downs Blacks* 11 It was the duty of the old women and widows to teach the girls .. to make .. kangaroo and wallaby nets. [**1946** **kangaroo route:** *Sydney Morning Herald* 8 Nov. 6/4 Because of the European winter and the wet season in North Australia the 'Kangaroo' flying boat service between Sydney and the United Kingdom has been modified. **1948** *Ibid.* 7 Aug. 2/7 The Qantas Kangaroo land plane service between Australia and the United Kingdom is to be increased from three to four trips a fortnight.] **1961** *Nation* (Sydney) 12 Aug. 11/2 On the Kangaroo route, the flight to Britain, strange things have been happening. **1971** *Bulletin* (Sydney) 11 Dec. 22/2 The new fare on the Kangaroo route to London will be $600 cheaper than the present economy class rate. **1972** *Ibid.* 4 Nov. 26/3 On the Kangaroo Route there is a natural flow of traffic—immigrants going home on holidays, young Australians 'discovering' Europe—to be tapped. **1981** *Age* (Melbourne) 16 July 5/2 Rising costs and falling revenues on the once-lucrative Kangaroo route to Europe have forced Qantas and British Airways each to drop another service. **1984** *Bulletin* (Sydney) 3 July 146/3 Ward says that the Kangaroo route to London has picked up. **1828** *Hobart Town Courier* 5 July 4, I .. wrapped myself in my **kangaroo rug**, and reposed like a king until day. **1831** *Acct. Colony Van Diemen's Land* 86 My kangaroo rug, composed of the furry skins of 16 of these interesting forest rangers. **1843** C. ROWCROFT *Tales of Colonies* II. 10, I proceeded to eat my supper in great state, the kangaroo rug forming a comfortable carpet. **1852** J. WEST *Hist. of Tas.* II. 205 He now requested to lie on a bed, and that a kangaroo rug might be thrown over him. **1878** R.B. SMYTH *Aborigines of Vic.* I. 123 When evening arrives .. the leader .. stops, throws down his kangaroo rug (*Mogra*), sticks his spears in the ground, and at once commences important duties. **1967** J.M. BROOKS *Opal Witch* 43 A few kangaroo rugs and a couple of aboriginal paintings. **1832** J. BACKHOUSE *Narr. Visit Austral. Colonies* (1843) 84 They also wear necklaces formed of **Kangaroo-sinews** rolled in red ochre. **1844** *Duncan's Weekly Register* (Sydney) 20 July 44/3 Mending his trousers with kangaroo sinews. **1846** *Tasmanian Jrnl. Nat. Sci.* II. 414 The women generally wear a kangaroo skin, likewise the kangaroo sinew belt. **1829** *Cornwall Press* (Launceston) 17 Feb. 8/2 The additional luxuries of **kangaroo soup** and *opossum gravy*!!! **1837** *S. Austral. Rec.* (London) 11 Nov. 14 A tureen of kangaroo soup, is a dish that you would relish even in London. **1856** *Moreton Bay Free Press* 18 Aug. 4/4 Kangaroo-soup, that would have delightfully astonished the palate of a Lord Mayor. **1870** *Lictor* (Sydney) 19 May 23 In some few country hotels, and even occasionally in a city restaurant we find 'Kangaroo soup' .. figuring on the bill of fare. **1898** *Tocsin* (Melbourne) 17 Nov. 3/3 Imagine the excited state of my stomach when the waiter declared the bill of fare to contain 'kangaroo soup'. **1875** CAMPBELL & WILKS *Early Settlement Qld.* 44 One of the gins with a **kangaroo spear**, Had sadly annoy'd Billy Ure in the rear. **1886** R. HENTY *Australiana* 9 He was one of my instructors in the mysteries of Australian bush life, such as throwing . . the kangaroo spear. **1971** D. IRELAND *Unknown Industr. Prisoner* 308 The Mercedes made a few **kangaroo starts** then lurched off up the road. **1983** *Reader's Digest* (Austral. ed.) Aug. 25 A thoughtless motorist creates three times the noise of a more considerate one. You, too, can belong in the latter category if you *don't* burn rubber in kangaroo starts. **1826** *Monitor* (Sydney) 15 Dec. 243/3 The common dinner at Hunter's River is salt pork, or a **Kangaroo steak**, without vegetables, and with dumpling-like bread unleavened. **1843** R.D. MURRAY *Summer at Port Phillip* 257 A kangaroo steak, cooked though it be after the bush fashion—that is to say, in a very indifferent style—is nevertheless a highly savoury morsel. **1854** MRS C. CLACY *Lights & Shadows* I. 35 I'll have some kangaroo steak. **1886** D.E. BANDMANN *Actor's Tour* 90, I had some kangaroo-steak, which was quite as tender as that of an ox. **1898** *Bulletin* (Sydney) 7 May 14/4 Kangaroo-steak was served for breakfast during a visit . . to a Southern hotel. **1932** C.M. GRAY *Western Vic. in Forties* 2 They had prepared their supper of kangaroo steaks and damper. **1954** A. UPFIELD *Death of Lake* (1956) 127 Kangaroo steak on a slab of baking-powder bread. **1981** A.B. FACEY *Fortunate Life* 163 She gave me some kangaroo steak that had been grilled on hot coals. **1833** C.O. BOOTH *Jrnl.* 24 Aug. (1981) 160 Had a capital **Kangaroo Steamer** for B-fast. **1849** J. PATTISON *N.S.W.* 73 There is another very good colonial dish, called kangaroo steamer; which . . is the best parts of animal stewed in its own gravy without water. **1854** *Courier* (Hobart) 12 Apr. 2/4 We . . hauled the boat up, and had a good kangaroo steamer for supper, the first which we had been able to cook during our voyage. **1864** *Colonial Cook Bk.* (1970) 70 Kangaroo Steamer. . . Take the most tender part of the kangaroo . . chop it very fine, about the same quantity of smoked bacon (fat); season with finely-powdered marjoram, pepper, and a very little salt. Let it 'steam', or 'stew', for two hours; then pack or press tight in open-mouthed glass bottles. ***c* 1899** 'SANDALWOOD NUTT' *Tarragal* 28 A treat was in store for them in the shape of a kangaroo steamer, Dick having shot a 'boomer'. **1903** *Bulletin* (Sydney) 1 Oct. 17/1 The menu was . . 'kangaroo steamer', and I was the only guest who didn't beam upon the 'steamer' with joy. **1932** C.M. GRAY *Western Vic. in Forties* 18 Upon one such occasion Bob said he would like much to get a kangaroo steamer. . . This 'steamer' is made of kangaroo flesh minced and mixed with bacon. **1830** R. DAWSON *Present State Aust.* 207 Dinner consisted of a dish of fine perch, and some excellent **kangaroo tail** soup. **1837** *S. Austral. Rec.* (London) 27 Nov. 19 To those who are fond of ox-tail soup, I should recommend a trip to South Australia, to eat kangaroo-tail soup, which, if made with the skill that soups in England are, would as far surpass the ox as turtle does the French potage. **1852** G.C. MUNDY *Our Antipodes* I. 228 He thinks . . in his primeval simplicity, that he has as good right to beef and mutton as John Bull-calf, the Anglo-Australian, has to kangaroo-tail soup. **1862** G.T. LLOYD *Thirty-Three Yrs. Tas. & Vic.* 129 Kangaroo-tails baked in wood ashes. ***c* 1880** R. ROWE *Roughing It* 26 Perhaps you have tasted the kangaroo-tail soup that is sent over to England in tins? **1898** *Bulletin* (Sydney) 12 Nov. 14/4 Kangaroo-tails are now on sale in London. **1911** I.A. ROSENBLUM *Stella Sothern* 135 Kangaroo tail soup and careful nursing soon caused the patient's colour to return. **1934** WARBURTON & ROBERTSON *Buffaloes* 17 On our first night out we shot a kangaroo, and I revealed . . the secret of making kangaroo-tail soup. **1953** H.G. LAMOND *Big Red* 157 I've read of kangaroo-tail soup as a luxury. **1976** N.V. WALLACE *Bush Lawyer* 134 As we were driving along a bush road, the Governor, being English, asked me about kangaroos and particularly kangaroo tail soup. **1833** W.H. BRETON *Excursions* 210 The only ornament that I procured was a string of **kangaroo teeth.** **1856** J. BONWICK *W. Buckley* 77 The youth may adorn his hair with two kangaroo teeth and emu feathers. **1965** H. PORTER *Cats of Venice* 108 Londoners call Earl's Court—you can readily imagine the tone of voice—**Kangaroo Valley**. That's because it's the address of the Australians, the invaders, the temporary, the hit-and-run, cut-and-come-again yahoos, the colonial vagabonds, the loud-mouthed and light-fingered rowdies, the uncouth, irreverent, cock-sure, yankee-ized and so on and so forth so-and-sos. **1971** *Sunday Rev.* (Melbourne) 24 Jan. 463/2 Peter Cook . . suggested that I collaborate with the New Zealand monochromaticist Nicholas Garland on a comic strip set in Kangaroo Valley, and from this collaboration Barry McKenzie was born. **1972** *Daily Mirror* (Sydney) 12 Oct. 4/1 For anyone who wanted to lampoon the Earls Courters, the Kangaroo Valley lot, Bazza would be as good as a feast.

kangaroo /kæŋgə'ru/, *v.* [f. prec.]

1. *intr.* To hunt the kangaroo. Chiefly as *pres. ppl.* and *vbl. n.*

1803 J. GRANT *Narr. Voyage N.S.W.* 91 He had been Kangarooing, had lost his way, and was almost starved. **1821** Macarthur Papers XII. 57, I passed a week very agreeably—inspecting our Cattle, superintending the putting up a Stockyard, and *Kangarooing*. **1833** C.O. BOOTH *Jrnl.* 23 May (1981) 158 Kangaroo'd unsuccessfully and made for Eagle Hawk Neck. **1843** *Portland Mercury* 1 Feb. 2/3 It was usual for some to go out in parties on the Sabbath with guns for the ostensible purpose of Kangarooing, but in reality to hunt and kill these miserable beings. **1853** *Bell's Life in Sydney* 10 Sept. 1/6 It is very interesting to see a native kangarooing. **1866** *Colony of Qld.* 20 'Kangarooing' is an exciting institution, as thoroughly antipodean in every sense of the word as fox hunting is English. **1871** *Austral. Town & Country Jrnl.* (Sydney) 7 Jan. 24/1 There is no sport—a young Australian would say—like kangarooing, with good dogs, a fast horse, and a fair prospect of game. **1885** D.E. MCCONNELL *Austral. Etiquette* 465 A hunting sport, which is essentially Australian, is called 'Kangarooing', and is often indulged in by both ladies and gentlemen. **1900** R. BRUCE *Benbonuna* (1904) 290 No accident could very well have happened to him, unless he has gone kangarooing and come down in a crab-hole. **1914** C.H.S. MATTHEWS *Bill* 117, I went off with some other chaps kangaroo shooting . . and it was not till I was away kangarooing that I decided at last to write. **1949** G. FARWELL *Traveller's Tracks* 168 If you're a good hand with a gun, there's all the kangarooing you want. **1981** A.B. FACEY *Fortunate Life* 81, I went out kangarooing many times and got quite a few.

2. a. *intr. transf.* To leap in a manner resembling that of a kangaroo; (of a motor vehicle) to move forward in jerks. See also KANGAROO-HOP. Also as *vbl. n.*

1867 *Sydney Punch* 30 Mar. 142/1 A daring spirit then initiated a peculiar description of jumping which he called 'Kangarooing'. **1915** *Bulletin* (Sydney) 9 Sept. 26/2 That'll stop any kangarooing, because a horse when about to spring places his front paws together, and he can't do it when the piece of timber is in the way. **1931** D.B. O'CONNOR *Black Velvet* 19 Over logs and rocky ridges, Kangarooing through the gidyas, When he came to gates or fences, Why, he hurdled like a horse. **1968** D. O'GRADY *Bottle of Sandwiches* 136 Kangarooing our way up the track in half-mile jumps. Stop, swear, fill, drive. **1971** C. MCGREGOR *Don't talk to me about Love* 187 The car jerked and kangarooed off into the night.

b. *trans. fig.* To squat over (a lavatory) with one's feet on the seat. Also as *vbl. n.*

1955 D. NILAND *Shiralee* 129 There was a notice on the wall . . 'Craphouse Duties'. . . It ended up with the injunction in snaggled capitals: 'Kangarooing is not allowed.' And in smaller letters: 'Remember others have to sit where you shat.' **1964** A.H. AFFLECK *Wandering Yrs.* 74 Please don't kangaroo the seat, Our breed of crab can leap six feet. **1965** J. O'GRADY *Aussie Eng.* 36 The practice of 'kangarooing the dyke'—squatting on it with your feet on the seat—is reprehensible, and frowned upon by all purveyors of public amenities. **1981** P. RADLEY *Jack Rivers & Me* 6 An accumulation of advice. 'Yeah! Like: 'No use to kangaroo this seat; the crabs here jump fifteen feet'.'

kangarooer. One who hunts kangaroos.

1836 'W. R--s' *Fell Tyrant* 40 This man was a constant visitor at Government House, and was chiefly kept by the commandant as kangarooer, and when his services were required, as flogger. **1846** N.L. KENTISH *Work in Bush Van Diemen's Land* 29 Skins were advertised for, and dealt in by 'kangarooers', by the thousand. **1852** MRS C. MEREDITH *My Home in Tas.* I. 245 Many of the so-called 'kangarooers' are notorious cattle and sheep-stealers. **1892** 'J. MILLER' *Workingman's Paradise* 143 The kangarooers have got good rifles. **1922** E. MERYON *Holland's Tank* 12 No man went out there—not even the kangarooers and 'possumers. **1931** MRS E.P. HALFORD *Pioneers of Yesterday* 30 The kangarooers and others had been using the water from the rock-holes. **1970** P.J. BAILLIE *Bush Ballads* 73 Three kangarooers up the Coast Once shot a tidy pile.

kangaroo-hop, *v. intr.* **a.** To move in a manner resembling that of a kangaroo; to move with an awkward gait; to leap or move in bounds (also *fig.*). **b.** (Of a motor vehicle) to move forward in jerks. See also KANGAROO *v.* 2 a.

1943 *Double Gee* (Kalgoorlie) Christmas 5 Recently when on leave he found himself in an unenviable situation kangaroo-hopping. **1960** H.H. WILSON *Where Wind's Feet Shine* 43 There was Cousin Millie coming down the track from the sandhills, her tight shoes making her look as though she were kangaroo-hopping over burning hot ground. **1967** R. DONALDSON et al. *Cane!* 66 A savage pulse kangaroo-hopped in his ears. **1979** J.J. MCROACH *Dozen Dopey Yarns* 75 She . . rushes past us . . and into a volkswagen. She starts it, jumps it forward about eight feet, stalls, starts again and kangaroo hops. **1980** B. REED *Stigmata* 81 The car had been driven off—kangaroo hopping at first as though the driver couldn't regain his co-ordination. **1981** *Austral. Women's Weekly* (Sydney) 28 Oct. 11/1 Kathleen recently kangaroo-hopped her way across Australia in a tiny Robinson helicopter.

Kangaroo Island kangaroo. [See quot. 1941.] The kangaroo *Macropus fuliginosus fuliginosus*.

[**1852** *Austral. Gold Digger's Monthly Mag.* i. 20 The Sooty Kangaroo, of Kangaroo Island, is of great size.] **1926** A.S. LE SOUEF et al. *Wild Animals Australasia* 177 Gould never actually saw a specimen of the Kangaroo Island kangaroo. **1941** E. TROUGHTON *Furred Animals Aust.* 219 Kangaroo Island Kangaroo *Macropus fuliginosus* . . restricted to Kangaroo Island, off Yorke Peninsula, South Australia, where it inhabits the dense scrub and bushland. **1943** C. BARRETT *Austral. Animal Bk.* 89 The Kangaroo Island kangaroo . . is a coarse-furred, heavily built, slow-moving animal, often called the 'sooty kangaroo' because of its general sombre-brown hue.

kangaroo paw.

1. [See quot. 1926.] Any plant of the genera *Anigozanthos* and *Macropidia* (fam. Haemodoraceae), perennials of s.w. W.A. having distinctive elongated, paw-like flowers, esp. the red-and-green flowering *A. manglesii*, floral emblem of W.A.

1901 M. VIVIENNE *Travels in W.A.* 61 The anygoxanthus (kangaroo paw), a most wonderful flower, was to be seen in many different hues. **1916** *Bulletin* (Sydney) 2 Jan. 24/1 In the Golden West . . on the 'desert' plains . . I have ridden . . over a knee-deep carpet woven of . . crimson, velvet-textured 'kangaroo-paws'. **1926** A.A.B. APSLEY *Amateur Settlers* 207 A curious tufted sedge-like plant called a Kangaroo Paw . . so called from its quaintly shaped flowers so like the paws of a kangaroo. **1936** *Publicist* (Sydney) i. 16/1 Are the Kangaroo Paw still out in King's Park? **1948** E.H. COLLIS *Lost Yrs.* 101 There is the gorgeous Kangaroo Paw, of which there are several species and different colours, scarlet and green, purplish-red, orange, green and the splendid black. **1955** 'M. HILL' *Land nearest Stars* 35 The tall kangaroo paw, very profuse and decorative, strangely prehistoric. **1968** G. MIKES *Boomerang* 150 The most famous of all the flowers is the Kangaroo Paw, Western Australia's floral emblem. The Kangaroo Paw is exclusive to south Western Australia, has very curiously shaped flowers and coloured vestiture of plume-like, interlocked hairs. **1979** *Ecos* xxii. 11/3 Trade in the kangaroo paw, *Anigozanthos manglesii* . . is estimated at 200,000 bunches a year. **1985** *Canberra Times* 15 Dec. 2/7 The audience, most of them other-worldly scholars from the School of Inconsequential Studies who would not know a kangaroo paw from a primrose.

2. [See KANGAROO *n.* sense 3 a.] A name given to tenosynovitis, in the belief that it occurs more commonly in Aust. than elsewhere.

1985 *Med. Jrnl. Aust.* Feb. CXLII. 237 So what are we left with? Obviously a unique Aussie 'disease' which one day no doubt will find its place into [*sic*] the small print of an occupational health medical tome—possibly under the eponym of 'Kangaroo paw'. Perhaps 'Kangaroo poor' would be more appropriate, as that's the likely result of the burgeoning spiral of costs associated with an epidemic which, however it started, could only be perpetuated with the approbation of the medical profession, either through ignorance or avarice or both.

kangarooster. *Obs.* An Australian.

1909 *Truth* (Sydney) 2 May 1/4 The Kangaroosters have arrived back. Their tails aren't even half-mast high. **1922** 'J. NORTH' *Black Opal* 164 The Kangaroosters . . were privileged to view that contest.

kanooka /kəˈnukə/. Also **kanuka.** [Poss. transf. use of Maori *kanuka* the tea-tree *Kunzea ericoides.*] The tree *Tristaniopsis laurina* (see *water gum* WATER); the wood of the tree. Also *attrib.*

1914 E.E. PESCOTT *Native Flowers Vic.* 62 Tristania laurina, the 'Kanuka', is a compact growing shrub. **1926** *Bulletin* (Sydney) 7 Oct. 22/3 Kanooka . . is a hard, heavy, close-grained dark-red wood, found in rocky creeks in East Gippsland (Vic.). **1967** N.A. WAKEFIELD *Naturalist's Diary* 10 The Kanooka . . has stiff lance-shaped leaves and deep yellow tea-tree-like flowers. **1979** DOUGLAS & HEATHCOTE *Far Cry* 78 At Nambour we were camped on the side of a hill near a kanooka forest (a cousin of the eucalypt). **1981** J.A. BAINES *Austral. Plant Genera* 381 *T[ristania] laurina*, Kanooka (apparently Aboriginal, as the Maori name Kanuka is used in NZ for a quite different sp., *Leptospermum ericoides*, and has a first syllable stress, unlike Kanooka of Aust.).

kapok tree. [Transf. use of *kapok tree* the fibre-producing *Ceiba casearia*: see OED(S *kapok*.] Any of several small deciduous trees of the genus *Cochlospermum* (fam. Bixaceae), bearing a fruit containing seeds embedded in soft cottony fibres; *cotton tree* (b), see COTTON. Also **kapok.**

[**1909** F.M. BAILEY *Comprehensive Catal. Qld. Plants* (ed. 2) 42 *Cochlospermum . . Gillivraei* . . yields a useful kapok.] **1933** *Bulletin* (Sydney) 6 Sept. 21/1 The kapok-tree has its habitat among the rocky escarpments of Queensland and certain parts of Centralia. **1970** J.V. MARSHALL *Walk to Hills of Dreamtime* 76 He . . cut from the kapok tree a straight pole. . . He . . collected an armful of fluffy white down from the pods. **1976** C.D. MILLS *Hobble Chains & Greenhide* 41 The flowering kapok.

karara /kəˈrarə/. Also **karrara, kurara.** [Prob. f. a W.A. Aboriginal language.] The plant *Acacia tetragonophylla* (see DEAD FINISH 1). Also *attrib.*

1929 K.S. PRICHARD *Coonardoo* (1961) 117 Hugh and the boys threw themselves in any shred of shade beside a clump of karrara bush, or thicket of mulga. **1942** *Bulletin* (Sydney) 22 July 13/1 Every blackfellow in my mustering team carried on his saddle a koondy—a heavy stick, usually of karara wood, sharpened at each end by charring and scraping. **1966** M. BROWN *Jimberi Track* 32 Everything was different here—no gidgie tree, karara, no quondong of the little round nuts. **1984** W.W. AMMON et al. *Working Lives* 150 The kurara grows mostly in watercourses and, like the spinifex further north, give it a few millimetres of rain and it throws out thousands of new green leaves.

karbeen, var. CARBEEN.

karbi /ˈkabi/. [a. Jagara *kabai.*] The small, dark-coloured, stingless bee *Trigona carbonaria.*

1884 *Trans. Entomol. Soc. London* 149 (OEDS) Of these stingless bees of Australia two varieties only have come under my immediate observation. . . 'Karbi' or 'Keelar' and 'Kootchar' are the names given to them by the natives. . . 'Karbi' gather but little honey. **1932** *Victorian Naturalist* XLVIII. 185 The aborigines were familiar with several species, and . . *Trigona cassiae* . . is known as 'Koochee', and *Trigona carbonaria* . . as 'Koobee', or 'Karbi'. **1948** *Bull. Amer. Museum Nat. Hist.* XC. 22/1 (OEDS) The spiral staircase type of nest was recorded by Hockings . . in the case of an Australian *Trigona* known as 'karbi' or 'keelar' that he believed to be *carbonaria.*

kark, *v.* Also **cark.** [Prob. fig. use of CARK to caw, from the assoc. of the crow with carrion.] *intr.* To die.

1977 R. BEILBY *Gunner* 302 'That wog ya roughed up—well, he karked.' Sa'ad dead! **1980** R. DAVIDSON *Tracks* 105 A need to lay a ghost . . before it was too late (i.e. before I karked in the desert). **1982** N. KEESING *Lily on Dustbin* 50 A 'stiff dunny' is dead or, in other words 'has carked it', and a patient who has 'sloughed off' has disappeared. **1982** *Sydney Morning Herald* 18 Dec. 24/4 We talked parties, weddings, people karking it and the attendant floral arrangements. **1984** *Ibid.* 17 Mar. 37/8 Meanwhile over in London they're flogging off the last of the D'Oyly Carte company's costumes. The tradition that we thought would die hard has carked completely.

karkalla /kaˈkælə/. [a. Gaurna *kargala.*] Any of several species of PIGFACE, incl. *Carpobrotus rossii* of coastal Tas., Vic., S.A., and W.A.

1846 C.W. SCHÜRMANN *Aboriginal Tribes Port Lincoln* 6 The fruit of a species of cactus, very elegantly styled pig-faces, by the white people, but by the natives, called karkalla. **1862** C. WILHELMI *Manners & Customs Aboriginal Natives* 12 The most important and abundant fruit is that of a mesembrianthemum, to which the Europeans have given the somewhat vulgar name of pigfaces, but the natives the more euphonical one of karkalla. **1888** *Proc. Linnean Soc. N.S.W.* III. 529 *Mesembryanthemum aequilaterale* . . 'Pigs' faces.' 'Karkalla' of the Port Lincoln (S.A.) aboriginals. **1984** *Flora Aust.* IV. 27 *Carpobrotus rossii* . . Karkalla. A native species found primarily in coastal areas in S.A., Vic. and Tas.

karri /ˈkæri/. [a. Kalaaku *karri.*] The tall timber tree of s.w. W.A. *Eucalyptus diversicolor* (fam. Myrtaceae), having a straight, smooth-barked trunk and reaching a height of 70 m.; the hard, heavy, red wood of the tree. Also *attrib.*

1866 *S. Austral. Register* (Adelaide) 17 May 3/7 The Karri gum-tree (*Eucalyptus diversicolor*) attains . . stupendous dimensions. **1870** W.H. KNIGHT *W.A.* 38 The Karri (*eucalyptus colossea*) is another wood very similar in many respects to the tuart. **1901** M. VIVIENNE *Travels in W.A.* 132 The karri is an exceptionally quick-growing tree, and when the matured trees are cut down the young trees shoot up at once. **1908** J. MANN *Suitability Australasian Timber* 4 Timbers in which the fibres are straight and even, and relatively less hard and dense, and lighter. . . Such timbers as Karri. **1934** T. WOOD *Cobbers* 81 Karri is king of the bush. . . A giant two hundred feet high, slim and straight and graceful, whose bark is watered silk. **1935** L.J. GOMM *Blazing Western Trails* 135 We were staying in the deep karri country of the extreme South West. **1948** H.A. LINDSAY *Bushman's Handbk.* 13 Jarrah saplings are full of water and so are those of the karri. **1955** K. SHERROTT *Your House* 15 Karri is used to a limited extent for roof-framing. **1975** R. THROSSELL *Wild Weeds & Wind Flowers* 196 Those great white stanchions of the karri, like organ pipes for winds to blow their storm themes on. **1983** P. ADAM SMITH *When we rode Rails* 66 The many little milling lines in the area called the 'Kingdom of the Karri'.

Kathleen Mavourneen, *a.* and *n.* [In allusion to the song 'Kathleen Mavourneen', the refrain of which is: 'it may be for years, it may be forever.']

A. *adj.* Of indeterminate duration.

1903 J. FURPHY *Such is Life* 161 Heaven grant that that parting may be a Kathleen Mavourneen one; and let me have some other class of difficulty to deal with next time. **1927** J.M. WALSH *Man behind Curtain* 75 That fact that you're an habitual criminal will be pressed by the police . . and you'll probably get a Kathleen Mavourneen sentence. **1951** S. HICKEY *Travelled Roads* 38 One hawker owed $75 to his supplier . . and called to tell him he was on a Kathleen Mavourneen (it may be for years, it may be forever) trip to Beirut. **1983** *Sydney Morning Herald* 20 May 16/2 Two on a lengthening list of the Bowen Basin's 'Kathleen Mavourneen' mines whose development could be for years or could be forever.

B. *n.*

a. A gaol sentence of indeterminate duration.

1910 L. ESSON *Three Short Plays* (1911) 16 It's a Kathleen Mavourneen, you know. It may be for years, or it may be for ever. **1919** V. MARSHALL *World of Living Dead* 30 'How much longer yer gotter do?' Jail diction and phraseology are catching. . . 'C176' chuckled mirthlessly, 'Mine's a Kathleen Mavourneen—maybe fer years an' maybe fer ever.' **1978** H.C. BAKER *I was Listening* 41 The judge declared him an 'habitual criminal' and gave him a 'Kathleen Mavourneen' ('It may be for years and it may be forever', as the old song went).

b. *transf.* An habitual criminal.

1917 *Bulletin* (Sydney) 1 Nov. 24/1 The hawk . . spells danger and death to many . . sweet bush singers . . and so he should get a place with the Kathleen Mavourneens. **1941** S.J. BAKER *Pop. Dict. Austral. Slang* 40 *Kathleen Mavourneen* . . an habitual criminal. **1950** *Austral. Police Jrnl.* Apr. 116 *Kathleen Mavourneen*, declared an habitual criminal.

c. *fig.* A swag.

1922 *Smith's Weekly* (Sydney) 28 Jan. 17/4 Swag aliases are . . 'Kathleen Mavourneen' [etc.].

katta /ˈkætə/. *Obs.* Also **kiatta.** [a. Gaurna *kata.*] DIGGING STICK.

1839 *Tasmanian* (Hobart) 5 Apr. 110/3 The only instruments he used were a *katta* (cudgel) and a *joko* (wooden scoop). **1845** E.J. EYRE *Jrnls. Exped. Central Aust.* II. 308 Another weapon . . is the katta, a round chisel-pointed stick, about three feet long. **1846** C.W. SCHÜRMANN *Aboriginal Tribes Port Lincoln* 4 The kiatta or grubbing stick, is a gum or she-oak sapling, five feet long and two inches in diameter. **1847** G.F. ANGAS *Savage Life & Scenes* I. 84 The women dig various roots . . for which purpose they use a stout pointed stick, about five feet long, called a *katta.* **1858** W.A. CAWTHORNE *Legend of Kupirri* 13 The *kuttas* soon at work resound, And women, joking, dig the ground. **1860** *Trans. & Proc. R. Soc. Vic.* 170 The 'katta' is a cudgel or stick, four or five feet long, and one or two inches thick, the lower end of which, when hardened by fire, is sharpened something in the shape of a chisel. This tool is used for digging up roots. **1879** *Native Tribes S.A.* 214 The kiatta or grubbing stick is a gum or sheoak sappling.

kauri pine /ˈkaʊri paɪn/. Also **cowry pine.** [Transf. use of Maori *kauri* the N.Z. tree *Agathis australis.*] Any of three tall, coniferous, rainforest trees of the genus *Agathis* (fam. Araucariaceae), *A. microstachya* and *A. atropurpurea* of n. Qld. and *A. robusta* of n. and s. Qld.; the pale, light, easily worked wood of the tree. Also **kauri,** and *attrib.*

1861 J.D. LANG *Qld., Aust.* 122 The principal timber is Kauri, of large growth and it stands thicker on the ground than in any scrubs I have seen on the Mary. **1879** *Illustr. Austral. News* (Melbourne) 2 Aug. 122/1 She is composite built, with . . Kauri decks and teak fittings. **1901** C. MOYNIHAN *Feast of Bunya* 32 From woody-crowned Maroochie, Where grow the kauri pines. **1918** G. WHITE *Thirty Yrs. Tropical Aust.* 18 The scrub is composed of magnificent trees, whose straight stems run up one hundred feet or more without a branch . . kauri, mahogany. **1930** HIVES & LUMLEY *Jrnl. of Jackaroo* 212 Huge cotton, cedar and cowry pine-trees grew in great numbers. **1937** D. GLASS *Austral. Fantasy* 72 On a rich plateau North Queensland produces a jungle worthy of the most tangled tropics. Crowsfoot elm and kauri pine luxuriate in its depths. **1956** A.C.C. LOCK *Tropical Tapestry* 45 Shortly afterwards another lorry appeared, this one carrying kauri pine logs. **1975** *Ecos* vi. 10/2 Commercial plantations of valuable native timbers like . . kauri pine on cleared rainforest sites.

Keartland honeyeater /kɑtlənd ˈhʌniitə/. [f. the name of G.A. *Keartland* (1848–1926), an ornithologist who accompanied the Horn expedition to central Aust. and collected the type specimen.] The grey-headed honeyeater *Lichenostomus keartlandi* of inland n. Aust., a predom. yellowish-green bird. Also **Keartland's honeyeater.**

1896 B. SPENCER *Rep. Horn Sci. Exped. Central Aust.* II. 65 Keartland's Honey-eater is here burdened with the trouble of rearing young cuckoos. **1903** *Emu* II. 147 Keartland Honey-eater. . . A nest of this Honey-eater was found. **1916** S.A. WHITE *In Far Northwest* 39 These birds turned out to be a variety of the rare Keartland honey-eater (Lichenostomas [*sic*] keartlandi).

kebah, kebarra, kebarrah, varr. KIPPER *n.*[1]

keenly, *a. S.A. Obs.* [Cornish dial. *keenly* (of a mine) promising: see EDD.]

a. *Mining.* Of ore, a lode, etc.: promising; likely to yield the mineral sought.

1849 *S. Austral. Register* (Adelaide) 25 July 3/2 We venture to express an opinion experimentally in favour of a mining log-book . . that 'she's looking keenly'. **1863** J.B. AUSTIN *Mines S.A.* 95 No Ore had been cut, but the country looked remarkably 'keenly', and there were indications which led to the supposition that they were not far from the back of the lode. **1869** *Wallaroo Times* (Kadina) 28 Aug. 5/4 Operations have suspended until . . the present 'keenly' indications shall have changed to bunches of rich copper. **1872** *Yorke's Peninsula Advertiser* (Moonta) 8 Nov. 2/7 Some very 'keenly stone' has already been found on the surface.

b. *transf.*

1872 *S. Austral. Register* (Adelaide) 9 Oct. 3/6 The crops look 'keenly', being refreshed by late rains.

keepara, keeparra, varr. KIPPER *n.*[1]

keet. [Shortened form of LORIKEET.] Any of several small parrots, incl. the *little lorikeet* (see LITTLE 2). Often with distinguishing epithet.

1874 C. DE BOOS *Congewoi Correspondence* 148 The keets and the blue mountaineers seems to be the only birds as don't mind it. **1892** *Bulletin* (Sydney) 30 July 7/3 By day when the 'keets' in the blossom nestled. **1901** *Emu* I. 18 The 'keets do not come to the orchard until the fruit is ripening. **1931** J. DEVANEY *Earth Kindred* 15 The green keets shrill'd and whirl'd away. **1948** J. FAIRFAX *Run o' Waters* 58 A little colony of green 'keets would dive between the forest trees with shrill screams. **1970** V. SERVENTY *Dryandra* 53 Purple-crowned lorikeets is the ornithologist's name, 'keets' to the small boy, or 'Zipp parrots' as they screech across the sky.

keg. [Spec. use of *keg* small barrel or cask.]

1. A barrel of beer.

1896 *Bulletin* (Sydney) 5 Sept. 3/2 We wore our knuckle-dusters, and we took a keg on tap For our friendly game of football with the fellows at the Gap. **1957** 'N. CULOTTA' *They're Weird Mob* 110 We struggled with the kegs, and got them set up on the beach. **1965** J. O'GRADY *Aussie Eng.* 16 Containers run from five-ounce glasses to eighteen-gallon kegs.

2. Special Comb. **keg party,** a party at which a keg of beer (the cost of which is met by subscriptions from the participants) is the principal refreshment.

1950 K.S. PRICHARD *Winged Seeds* 60 They were in demand at all the dances and keg parties of the smart set. **1962** *N.T. Times* (Darwin) 4 Jan. 4/3 Keg and bottle parties blossomed in the suburbs and hardly a street in Darwin did not have lights blazing at midnight. **1964** *Mount Isa Mail* 28 Jan. 1/4 Keg parties where guests 'chipped in' towards the cost of a keg were probably illegal.

kellick. [Var. of Br. *killick* (of unfixed spelling, *killick, killock* being preferred elsewhere): see OED(S *killick*.] A stone; an anchor. Also *attrib.*

1867 J.R. HOULDING *Austral. Capers* 215 Vainly did he implore his jovial companions to up kellick, and land him on the nearest point. **1873** R.P. WHITWORTH *Lost & Found* 44 Left the boat afloat with the German in her, and moored by a kellick rope and a large stone. **1911** A. SEARCY *By Flood & Field* 16, I had no kellick (anchor). **1945** *Buzz Rev.: H.M.A.S. 'Manoora'* 18 Feb. 9 When in walks a bloke with a . . jacket over his arm adorned with the gleaming gold badge of a kellick. **1962** 'N. CULOTTA' *Gone Fishin'* 8 Anglin'. All over the River every weekend. Rowin' backwards. Plonk goes a kellick. Plonk goes a dirty big sinker. Who's got the bottle-opener?

Kelly, *n.*[1] [f. the name of Ned *Kelly* (1857–1880), bushranger.]

1. Used *attrib.* in Special Comb. **Kelly country,** a district in n.e. Victoria in which Ned Kelly and his brothers were active as bushrangers; **gang** *transf.*, see quots. See also NED KELLY *n.* and *v.*

1880 *Argus* (Melbourne) 2 Feb. 5/4 A gentleman . . had come through from Sydney, and stayed for a time to have a look at 'the **Kelly country**'. **1897** *Tocsin* (Melbourne) 4 Nov. 9/1 The buck-jumping contest . . should be a great draw. Already several entries have been received from the Kelly country. **1913** J. SADLEIR *Recoll.* 170 The Mansfield district might easily have become a second 'Kelly Country' with its own independent gang of bushrangers. **1939** G. DIGBY *Down Wind* 197 Not far from Dalbeny was what was known as the Kelly country. **1955** G. HEALEY *A.L.P.* Pref., Our family moved to Whitfield in the King Valley, in the heart of the Kelly country. **1972** *Bulletin* (Sydney) 28 Oct. 48/1 We've called it 'The Kelly Country', though none of the material was actually filmed in Ned Kelly's area. In the wider sense, the Kelly Country means Australia. **1975** K. WILLEY *Ghosts of Big Country* 110 Jim Escreet was reared in the 'Kelly country' of Victoria. **1985** M. STEWART *Autobiogr. of my Mother* 71 She had been a teacher at a bush school near Jerilderie in the Kelly country. **1902** *Truth* (Sydney) 28 Sept. 8/3 English papers have been referring to *our Boer-baiting braves* as **Kelly gangs** owing to their pleasant little ways. **1941** S.J. BAKER *Pop. Dict. Austral. Slang* 41 *Kelly gang*, a term applied to any business firm whose practices are not above suspicion, and esp. to a ruling Government, with reference to tax-grabbing propensities.

2. [Prob. *transf.*] A crow. Also **kelly crow.**

1924 *Smith's Weekly* (Sydney) 23 Feb. 23/5 'Kelly' was found guilty and sentenced to six months in chains on hard food. A chain was attached to the crow's leg and thence to a stake in the ground. **1934** F.H. BROWN *Songs of Plains* 24 Then someone found a 'Kelly' That the boundary-rider shot—It was more or less fermented, Still, it went inside the pot. **1945** *Bulletin* (Sydney) 2 May 12/3 'Kelly' for crow had its genesis in the deeds of the Kelly gang. Birds and bushrangers were addicted to forays; hence 'Those damn crows are *just like the Kellys*'; hence 'Kelly'. The name is indiscriminately applied to crows and ravens. *Ibid.* 11 Apr. 12/2 My theory of the Kelly derivation . . is that it dates from Henry Lawson's 'The Darling River', in which Kelly, the lost Murrumbidgee hatter, is guided home by a crow. **1973** *Southerly* ii. 218 A crow perched in a bloodwood tree, wings part spread, beak agape. 'Look at ole Kelly,' Colin said. 'Poor devil of a bird, he's got heat stroke.' **1981** A.J. BURKE *Pommies & Patriots* 44 In times of frequent drought the Kelly Crows descend on millions of dead cattle like vultures.

3. One whose behaviour is supposed in some way to resemble that of Ned Kelly.

1947 *Bulletin* (Sydney) 11 June 28/1 When he was camped by Naracan Creek a couple of louts bailed him up. . . The amateur Kellies rushed. **1953** S.J. BAKER *Aust. Speaks* 142 *Kelly*, a tram or omnibus inspector. **1980** J. WRIGHT *Big Hearts & Gold Dust* 57 'Kelly's rules,' Sam yelled. That meant that the one who caught the least fish had to clean the lot. **1980** C. JAMES *Unreliable Mem.* 155 The inspectors were called Kellies, after Ned Kelly, and were likely to swoop at any time. A conductor with twenty years' service could be dismissed if a Kelly caught him accepting money without pulling a ticket.

Kelly, *n.*[2] Also **kelly.** [Proprietary name.] A type of axe; (loosely) an axe. Also **Kelly axe,** and *attrib.*

1909 R. KALESKI *Austral. Settler's Compl. Guide* ii. 11, I try every axe on the market, but the only two I care to use are either Plumb's or the black Kelly, the Kelly for choice as the best all-round axe. **1911** *Bulletin* (Sydney) 21 Dec. 15/2 [I] nominate *dry* belar as the hardest to fall and log off. . . A two-foot diameter *dry* belar . . over a wager, knocked out a 'Kelly' and 'Plum' in about three minutes. **1918** *Austral. Official Jrnl. Patents* (Canberra) 784 *W.C. Kelly Perfect Axe* Patented May 7th & April 29th 1889. Made by *Kelly Axe M'f'g. Co.* Charleston, W. Va. USA. **1929** P.R. STEPHENSEN *Bushwhackers* 92 He went and got a Kelly axe, and single-handed he chopped down that Ironbark tree. **1945** D. ROBINSON *Pop's Blonde* 84 'Up the Alley,' roared a big Australian, an ex-kelly swinger from Queensland. **1948** *Harry Peck's Post* (Sydney) Jan. 10 Jennings . . is 'swinging the Kelly' for a crust. **1961** *Bulletin* (Sydney) 12 Apr. 48/1 In the not-so-distant past, too many men on the land were Kelly-happy. The sight of a growing tree fired them with an uncontrollable urge to grab an axe. **1973** R. ROBINSON *Drift of Things* 96 There were two kinds of axes, a 'Plumb' and a 'Kelly'. The Plumb had a more squat blade than the Kelly with its slightly curved sides. **1975** *Bronze Swagman Bk. Bush Verse* 23 The Kelly still rings in the timber. **1983** R. BECKETT *Axemen* 12 Most axemen . . use a standard axe. . . It used to be referred to as a 'Kelly' because it was just that . . the 'Kelly' axe.

kelp fish. [Attrib. use of *kelp*, from the fish's habit of lying among algae and seagrasses.] Any of several marine fish, esp. of the fam. Chironemidae, incl. *Chironemus georgianus* and *C. marmoratus* of s. Aust., and (*Tas.*) *Neoodax balteatus* (fam. Odacidae).

1842 *Tasmanian Jrnl. Nat. Sci.* I. 102 *Odax*, known at Port Arthur by the name of Kelp Fish. **1881** *Proc. Linnean Soc. N.S.W.* VI. 106 *Odax baleatus* . . *'Kelp Fish'* of Tasmania. **1892** *Papers & Proc. R. Soc. Tas.* (1893) 78 While fishing for crayfish recently, on the East Coast, I caught a couple of so-called 'Kelpfish'. **1906** D.G. STEAD *Fishes of Aust.* 147 A very much smaller kind of Rock Whiting . . is the little Rock-Whiting (*Odax balteatus*), known in Tasmania as the Kelp-Fish. **1974** T.D. SCOTT et al. *Marine & Freshwater Fishes S.A.* 232 Kelp Fish. . . This species is quite good eating.

kelpie /ˈkɛlpi/. [f. the name of an individual bitch *Kelpie* a progenitor of the breed: see quot. 1974.] An Australian breed of short-haired, prick-eared dog, noted for its hardiness and ability to tend and work sheep; a dog of this breed. See also BARB.

1895 *Australasian* (Melbourne) 12 Jan. 60/2 There is a little smooth-coated sheep dog with prick ears . . in several parts of Australia called Kelpies. I have seen them at Wagga and other shows. **1904** M. WHITE *Shanty Entertainment* 65 A kelpie . . whined with pain. **1914** R. KALESKI *Austral. Barkers & Biters* 8 She was a prick-eared black and tan bitch named Kelpie (a shepherd's pet name for bitches, and Gaelic for water-sprite) after the mother. **1920** J.B. CRAMSIE *Managem. & Diseases Sheep* 26 It is necessary to have a dog to work sheep, and the Australian 'Kelpie' can be recommended as the most suitable for enduring long journeys in the hot climate. **1933** C.H. HOLMES *We find Aust.* 154 The sheep-dog is known as a kelpie, is smooth-haired and about the size of a Scotch collie. **1937** *Bulletin* (Sydney) 11 Aug. 20/2 In the kelpie and the cattle 'heeler' Australia possesses two of the most intelligent and useful working dogs of the world. . . Both tykes are dinkum Aussies with a strain of dingo in the blood. **1959** D. LOCKWOOD *Crocodiles & Other People* 6 Blackfellows' mongrels, pet kelpies, and tramps living on a town are also worth a pound if you know the trick of dying them dingo-colour. **1974** *Dogs of Aust.* (Kennel Control Council Vic.) 64 Mr King's 'Kelpie' won the first ever sheep dog trial at Forbes N.S.W. about 1872, thus establishing the breed as good workers of sheep. Her fame as a worker spread throughout the country with the result that all her pups were known as Kelpie's pups; thus 'Kelpie' was established as a breed name. **1983** *Bulletin* (Sydney) 28 June 44/2 Exporting kelpies to Scotland is particularly interesting since they are descendants of dogs brought from that country to Australia in the 1860s.

kennedia /kəˈnɛdiə/. [The plant genus *Kennedia* was named by the French botanist E.P. Ventenat (*Jard. Malm.* II. (1805) 104, Pl. 104) after the London nurseryman John *Kennedy* (1759–1842).] Any plant of the genus of climbing or trailing perennials *Kennedia* (fam. Fabaceae), occurring in s.w. W.A. and all other States but not N.T., some species being cultivated for their colourful pea flowers and trifoliolate leaves.

[**1814** R. BROWN *Gen. Remarks Bot. Terra Australis* 21 Among the Diadelphous genera of Terra Australis the most remarkable in habit and structure, namely . . Hovea, Scottia and Kennedia. **1834** G. BENNETT *Wanderings N.S.W.* I. 64 The *Kennedia* is called the 'woodbine' by some of the shepherds in the colony, who use a decoction of its leaves as a lotion for scabby sheep.] **1845** *Florist's Jrnl.* 75 (OED) An early vinery is exactly the place in which to grow Kennedyas. **1859** H. KINGSLEY *Recoll. Geoffry Hamlyn* II. 38 Bring back a wreath of scarlet Kennedia. **1885** MRS C. PRAED *Head Station* I. 221 The road . . threaded rocky gorges, where grew . . beautiful scarlet kennedia. **1926** L.C.E. GEE *Bush Tracks & Gold Fields* 93 The Kennedyea, called after an explorer who died in the Australian wilderness. **1976** *Ecos* vii. 11/1 In the jarrah forest . . the mild fires of prescribed burning produce very little regeneration of nitrogen-fixing plants, particularly wattles and ground-hugging kennedias.

kero /ˈkɛroʊ/. Abbrev. of 'kerosene'. Freq. *attrib.*

1930 *Bulletin* (Sydney) 10 Sept. 22/3 With little stalls and cut-down kero.-tins . . calves can be fed quickly enough. **1948** R.S. CLOSE *Morn of Youth* 64 We boiled a kero tin of sea water on the galley stove. **1958** P. COWAN *Unploughed Land* 93 The dump held bits of old machinery, old tyres, rusty kero tins and the tins and bottles from the house. **1968** S. GORE *Holy Smoke* 94 *You'll* be like them Foolish Virgins, who never had a skerrick of kero left in their lamps to greet the second coming of the Lord! **1977** B. REED *Cass Butcher Bunting* 11 Cats set alight in the phone box the kero tin left charred alongside. **1981** *Bulletin* (Sydney) 21 July 62/3 Exhausting the supply of used kero tins in Central Australia.

kerosene.

1. Used *attrib.* with a second element designating a container for the storage or transport of kerosene subsequently used to improvise a utensil or article of furniture: **kerosene box, (-tin) bucket, case, tin.**

1901 *Advocate* (Burnie) 8 June 4/2 The Duchess sat down on a **kerosene box**, covered with a rug. **1925** *Makeshifts & Other Home-Made Furniture* (New Settlers League Aust.) 8 Stand two kerosene cases on end, about 20 in. apart. On top of each place a half kerosene box. Nail boards across these to form a table top. **1962** E. LANE *Mad as Rabbits* 215 A kerosene-box beside the stove made his kipsie complete. **1901** H. LAWSON *Joe Wilson & his Mates* (1902) 64, I ran down to the creek with the big **kerosene-tin bucket**. **1927** K.S. PRICHARD *Brumby Innes* (1974) 59 Two smoke-blackened kerosene buckets for water on the hearth. **1938** D. BATES *Passing of Aborigines* 212 Two four-gallon kerosene tin buckets. **1948** J.K. EWERS *For Heroes to Live In* 1 Flo came out of the house carrying a kerosene-bucket full of slops. **1975** A. MARSHALL *Hammers over Anvil* 34 Everyone had kerosene buckets in those days. They cut the top off a kerosene tin, then punched two holes—one on each side but dead centre—through which they hooked some wire and curved it to make a handle. Each kerosene tin bucket held four gallons of water. **1903** J. FURPHY *Such is Life* 157 Bendigo Bill, sitting on the same **kerosene-case**, long afterward narrated the episode fully. **1925** [see *kerosene box*]. **1896** M. CLARKE *Austral. Tales* 61 A band of merry boys would have exploded in his back yard, and have banged **kerosene tins** beneath his wedding window. **1899** *North-Western Advocate* (Devonport) 16 Aug. 2/3 The indispensable 'kerosene tin'... There has been some talk of pans being provided by the Town Board .. but even a legal tin may not be more commodious than the kerosene utensil. **1906** *Bulletin* (Sydney) 11 Jan. 15/1 What a multiplicity of uses the kerosene tin is put to in the bush! It is a water bucket and a boiler. The women use it as a copper for their clothes. Cut down, it is used as a baking-dish, wash-bowl, and water-trough for the chickens. The dog and the horse drink out of it. Houses are made of it in some parts, and I have heard they feed the goats on kerosene tins about Byrock, but I cannot vouch for that. **1916** 'T.O. LINGO' *Austral. Comic Dict.* 38 *Kerosene Tin*, the bush conjuror's 'property' which he transforms into four hundred and six different articles for domestic use. **1918** *Huon Times* (Franklin) 9 Apr. 2/5 At Wangaratta the honey is selling .. in kerosene tins from £1 to £1 5s. per tin. **1946** 'A. SPENCE' *Mystery of Red Gum* 212 Kerosene tins seemed to be used for everything. One held a few books, another some tinned food, another some blackboy, and another was full of water. **1956** R. THROSSELL *Day before Tomorrow* (1969) 2 The fire-place is littered with blackened pots, a few empty bottles and an improvised cooking arrangement in a kerosene tin. **1962** O. PRYOR *Aust.'s Little Cornwall* 35 There was a hut with a kerosene-tin oven to warm the pasties. **1981** A.B. FACEY *Fortunate Life* 98 On the farm, having a bath was an ordeal. You had to put the water in an empty kerosene tin and warm it over the fireplace, then you poured it into a bath tub.

2. In the names of highly flammable plants: **kerosene bush,** the small, aromatic shrub *Helichrysum hookeri* (fam. Asteraceae), occurring in mountainous Tas., Vic., and s.e. N.S.W., esp. in swamps and near watercourses; the related *H. ledifolium*; **wood** (or **tree**), GHITTOE.

1965 *Austral. Encycl.* V. 181 The highly resinous *Helichrysum hookeri*, which flares up when ignited, has been called **kerosene-bush** in Tasmania, where it is a common mountain shrub. **1981** M. SHARLAND *Tracks of Morning* 53 Tough, highland plants like kerosene bush .. having dug themselves in among the cavities, have reduced both its size and its stark bareness. **1919** [**kerosene wood**] R.T. BAKER *Hardwoods of Aust.* 63 *Halfordia scleroxyla* .. 'Kerosene Tree.' **1944** J. DEVANNY *By Tropic Sea & Jungle* 18 Take kerosene wood, or jitter, as some people call it. **1948** H.A. LINDSAY *Bushman's Handbk.* 77 In the jungles of Queensland .. there are two ways of starting a fire. Find a ghittoe or 'kerosene-tree' (*Halfordia scleroxyla*) whose wood burns green. **1981** A.B. & J.W. CRIBB *Useful Wild Plants Aust.* Pl. 139, Timber of both species is oily and burns readily when green, hence the common name kerosene wood.

kestrel. [Spec. use of *kestrel* a hovering bird of prey.] *Nankeen kestrel*, see NANKEEN.

1893 *Argus* (Melbourne) 25 Mar. 4/5 The kestrel's nest we always found in the fluted gums that overhung the creek, the red eggs resting on the red mould of the decaying trunk being almost invisible. **1912** *Emu* XII. 113 *Cerchneis cenchroides*. Kestrel. Common. **1953** H.G. LAMOND *Big Red* 283 *Kestrel*, Nankeen kestrel. **1984** M. BLAKERS et al. *Atlas Austral. Birds* 111 The Kestrel inhabits any country where it can hunt over open space, often urban areas, even town centres.

kew, var. CUE *n.* and *v.*

kiatta, var. KATTA.

kick, *v.*[1] In the phr. **to kick the tin,** to contribute money to a cause.

1965 J. O'GRADY *Aussie Eng.* 53 'Kick the tin' .. when it's your turn to buy a round of drinks. **1965** J. WYNNUM *Jiggin' in Riggin'* 40 Your turn to kick the tin. **1969** L. HAYLEN *Twenty Yrs.' Hard Labor* 37 Then Chifley said, 'You are going to have a tough fight in Parkes. I brought you a little aid and comfort.' He gave me £50 for my campaign funds out of his own pocket and said, rather unnecessarily I thought, 'I'm kicking the tin for a few others as well so you needn't mention this.' **1976** *Sunday Tel.* (Sydney) 30 May 34/2 When A.L.P. president Bob Hawke was appealing for money to help pay the Federal election campaign debt of $300,000, the N.S.W. Labor Party was claiming it could not afford to 'kick the tin'. **1982** *Austral.* (Sydney) 11 Aug. 9/1 The Tasmanian Premier would do all (except, presumably, kick the tin) that the Victorian Premier would not do.

kick, *v.*[2] *intr.* With **on**: to maintain momentum; to gain momentum. Also *trans.*

1949 L. GLASSOP *Lucky Palmer* 153 'I knew him when I used to slip ten bob out of the till .. so he could kick on with it.' 'You can often kick on with ten bob,' said 'Lucky' judicially. **1955** R. LAWLER *Summer of Seventeenth Doll* (1965) 48 What about all those times you've carried me—every year when I've run dry down here you've kicked me on. **1965** C. JOHNSON *Wild Cat Falling* 87 I'm doing a fantastic picture I'd like to discuss with you, but got to get this party kicking on first. **1978** N. HASLUCK *Hat on Letter O* 140 'E says to say the pardy's kickin' on like an 'e's stayin' overnight.

kick-off. *Australian National Football. Obs.* In the collocation **kick-off post,** *behind post* (see BEHIND 2).

1859 C.C. MULLEN *Hist. Austral. Rules Football* (1959) 10 Two posts to be called the 'kick off' posts shall be erected at a distance of 20 yards on each side of the goal posts. **1885** D.E. MCCONNELL *Austral. Etiquette* 640 Two posts, to be called the 'kick-off posts', shall be erected at a distance of twenty yards on each side of the goal posts, in a straight line with them; the intervening line between such kick-off posts shall constitute the 'goal line'.

Kidman. [The name of Sidney *Kidman* (1857–1935), grazier.]

1. Used *attrib.* with ref. to large-scale stock-raising.

1946 C.T. MADIGAN *Crossing Dead Heart* 88 Annandale was a typical example of what is often called the Kidman blight on the country. **1949** G. FARWELL *Traveller's Tracks* 88 The country can only be held in large holdings, preferably in the Kidman manner, so that stock can be shifted from one property to another, instead of droving them straight down.

2. In the collocation **Kidman's blood mixture (delight, joy),** golden syrup or treacle.

1935 R.B. PLOWMAN *Boundary Rider* 187 The better class employer added a tin of jam per week, or its equivalent in 'Bullocky's Joy' (treacle) or what was later known as 'Kidman's Delight' (golden syrup). **1945** S.J. BAKER *Austral. Lang.* 200 *Kidman's joy or Kidman's blood mixture*, treacle or golden syrup. Commemorating the late Sir Sidney Kidman, noted squatter. **1980** B. HORNADGE *Austral. Slanguage* 220 Another distinctive Australian product is Golden Syrup... It was known as .. 'Kidman's Joy' or 'Kidman's Blood Mixture'—a somewhat backhanded tribute to Sir Sidney Kidman, the 'Cattle King', whose penny-pinching ways led him to supply the substance to his stockmen in place of the much more expensive jam.

kidstakes, *pl.* [Prob. joc. formation on Br. slang *kid* humbug.] Nonsense; pretence. Also *attrib.* and *v. intr.*

1912 *Huon Times* (Franklin) 9 Mar. 6/3, I thought whirlwinds were kid stakes, just bits of games, but I don't want to see another. **1918** *Our Empire* (Melbourne) 19 Aug. 25 Such women employ the supporting smoke screen of camouflage, or what our soldier boys .. call 'the kid stakes'. **1927** F.C. BIGGERS *Bat-Eye* 7 This 'ere ain't now no kidstakes yarn ter touch yer 'earts. **1935** J.P. MCKINNEY *Crucible* 231 The same old stupidity. The same old 'kid-stakes'! **1950** F.J. HARDY *Power without Glory* 525 Sent him to manage those milk-bars in Brisbane... Kidstaked to him a bit at the finish to sugar-coat the pill. **1959** M. RAYMOND *Smiley roams Road* 127 Smiley suddenly realised that the skyhook must be a joke and he hastily exclaimed: 'It's a lot of kidstakes, isn't it?' **1968** S. GORE *Holy Smoke* 14 I'd say that was just kidstakes.

ki-eye, var. KAI-YAI.

ki-ki: see KAI.

kiley, var. KYLIE.

killer. An animal, esp. a bullock or sheep, selected and killed for immediate consumption.

1897 I. SCOTT *How I stole over 10,000 Sheep in Aust. & N.Z.* 9 'You know the killers, don't you?' .. i.e., the sheep the boss used for his own mutton at the house. **1914** *Bulletin* (Sydney) 18 June 16/4 The 'killers' were run in one Sunday afternoon .. but somehow the slaughtering was overlooked. **1929** K.S. PRICHARD *Coonardoo* (1961) 67 Expecting the buggy from Nuniewarra, Warieda had gone out after a killer, cut up the beast and given everybody in the uloo his or her share. **1932** J.J. HARDIE *Cattle Camp* (1944) 38 We only lost one bullock—he went lame on the rocks, so we used him as a killer. **1960** M. HENRY *Unlucky Dip* 59 The ancient station bullock who decoyed the killers quietly to their slaughter, mooching gloomily by. **1980** ANSELL & PERCY *To fight Wild* 133 Christopher cooked the rib bones from our killer that night.

killing, *vbl. n.*

1. Used *attrib.* in Comb. with reference to the butchering of animals, as: **killing day, gallows, paddock, pen, season, yard.**

***c* 1877** W. ARCHER in R. Stanley *Tourist to Antipodes* (1977) 33 As **killing day** comes round generally not oftener than once a week, fresh meat is regarded as quite a delicacy. **1976** E.H. MCFARLANE *Land of Contrasts* 8 There was one donkey on Durham, its main use being to pull the cart from the slaughter yard to the meat-house on 'killing' days. **1893** E. FAVENC *Last of Six Tales* 97 On the **'killing-gallows'** hung a freshly-slaughtered beast. **1917** A.L. BREWER *'Gators' Euchre* 87 He had not killed the beast at his killing-gallows (nearly every farmer has his own gallows). **1955** *Meanjin* 166 From one end stretched the sheepyards, a crisscross maze of heavynetted fences, with the killing gallows the only vertical line. [N.Z. **1907** W.H. KOEBEL *Return of Joe* 281, I see'd [the dog] after some sheep in the **killing paddock**.] **1922** V. PALMER *Boss of Killara* 77 The fattest bullocks had been brought into the killing-paddock. **1925** M. TERRY *Across Unknown Aust.* 143 There is also the **'killing pen'**, paved with slabs, where the butcher kills his beast. **1937** C. WARBURTON *White Poppies* 253 He noted the killing-pen—a bough shelter had been erected above it; the gallows and windlass used in the hoisting of slain beasts stood out prominently. **1971** W.G. HOWCROFT *This Side Rabbit Proof Fence* 74 A 'judas' sheep—a big, knowing-looking black-faced wether—upon which the boss placed great value .. regularly led his trusting charges up the stairs to their doom in the killing pens. **1939** J.G. PATTISON *'Battler's' Tales Early Rockhampton* 61 My mission was to ride to Laurel Bank in the **killing season** on every Saturday morning to collect a cheque for my father who had the contract to supply the works with cattle. **1956** H. HUDSON *Flynn's Flying Doctors* 140 The stock routes to the coast cannot be used during the Wet, which limits the 'killing' season to six months of the year. **1965** *N. Austral. Monthly* Dec. 3 The town's population is swelled by the influx of three to four hundred slaughtermen, who come from the South for the killing season. **1870** C.H. ALLEN *Visit to Qld.* 139 The **killing-yards** and boiling down houses are on a very extensive scale. **1882** A.J. BOYD *Old Colonials* 214 He has now large killing yards, which may be known by an odour of decayed offal. **1898** *Bulletin* (Sydney) 5 Nov. 31/2 The paddock that they showed me was a one-time killing-yard. **1914** *Ibid.* 19 Feb. 22/2 The local butcher used to send his meat from the killing yard per boat along the Herbert River. **1943** *Ibid.* 20 Oct. 13/4 The three greyhound pups ventured up towards the killing yard. **1954** T. RONAN *Vision Splendid* 101 Now and again the old crow at the killing yard gave out an apathetic car-r-k.

2. Special Comb. **killing sheep,** a sheep selected to be killed for food (esp. for the employees on a station).

1901 *Bulletin* (Sydney) 22 June 32/3 I've seen a native sent on the road with a mob of killing sheep (native name cookinjerry). **1923** *Ibid.* 22 Nov. 22/3 Two or three times a week killing (ration) sheep are required, necessitating another short journey for the night-horse. **1965** R. OTTLEY *By Sandhills* 174 All meat eaten is killed on the station, and some stations graze a flock of 'killing sheep' to add variety to an otherwise continuous diet of beef.

Kimberley /ˈkɪmbəli/. [f. the name of the *Kimberley* Range in n.w. W.A.] Used *attrib.* in Special Comb. **Kimberley (horse) disease** *n. Aust.*, a usu. fatal illness of horses in which liver damage, the cause of which is believed to be the consumption of certain species of *Crotalaria* (fam. Fabaceae), occurs; see also WALKABOUT DISEASE a.; also **Kimberley walkabout (disease)**; **knot,** see quot.; **mutton,** goat meat; **oyster,** *Burdekin duck* (b), see BURDEKIN.

1915 *Bulletin* (Sydney) 18 Feb. 13/3 The 'walkabout' disease of the Northern Territory, the **Kimberley disease** of Westralia and the Birdsville disease of Queensland have been identified as one and the same. **1928** B. CRONIN *Dragonfly* 153 My horse was sick... He's got the walk-about disease. Kimberley disease—if you want the proper name. **1954** *Bulletin* (Sydney) 25 Aug. 12/2 Gardiner has established that the Kimberley (walk-about) horse disease is caused by the animals eating the wedge-leaved rattlepod. **1971** K. WILLEY *Boss Drover* 72 Horses .. would die in hundreds from what we called the Kimberley walkabout. This was a disease which set a horse walking, round and round and up and down, knocking into trees and rocks and never stopping to eat, until in a few hours or days he would literally have walked himself to death. **1978** M. NIXON *Rivers of Home* 42 Kimberley walkabout disease .. is a terrible slow poisoning, which horses can contract after eating the crotalaria plant, the disease itself sometimes not becoming evident for twelve months after ingestion of the plant. **1975** R. EDWARDS *Austral. Traditional Bush Crafts* 93 The Gulf knot is used for attaching reins to the bit without the use of a buckle. In north-west Australia it is known as a **Kimberley knot**. **1953** L. & C. REES *Spinifex Walkabout* 119 You've tasted goat, of course—they call it **Kimberley mutton** up here. **1959** J. CLEARY *Back of Sunset* 167 The roast goat, Kimberley mutton, as it was called. **1945** T. RONAN *Strangers on Ophir* 39 A meat fritter known in the Kimberleys as a 'Burdekin Duck', and on the Burdekin as a '**Kimberley Oyster**'. **1960** B. HARNEY *Cook Bk.* 24 Burdekin's Duck (or Kimberley Oysters).

kinchela /kɪnˈtʃɛlə/. *Shearing. Obs.* Also **kinshela.** [Poss. f. the name of John *Kinsella* (d. 1902), labourer.] An adjustment made to shears to increase the width of the blow: see quots. 1911 and 1937.

1897 *Bulletin* (Sydney) 25 Sept. (Red Page), 'Putting Kinchela on 'em' is evidently inspired by the fact that one Kinchela, some years ago, wrote and published a pamphlet on the art of sharpening and 'keeping' shears. The expression was at first confined exclusively to shear-sharpening but in time came to have a wider application. **1911** E.S. SORENSON *Life in Austral. Backblocks* 233 The blades are pulled back and the knockers filed down, so the shears will take a bigger blow. This is called 'putting Kinchler on them', from the fact that it was first adopted by John Kinsella. **1937** *Bulletin* (Sydney) 14 July 20/1 Bar 'kinshela', no bladesmen sought for artificial aids to pace... 'Kinshela' consisted of putting the bottom blade back so as to obtain a wider cut.

kinder. Abbrev. of 'kindergarten'. Also *attrib.*

1955 *Meanjin* 308 Like Billy in the Kinder. **1959** D. HEWETT *Bobbin Up* 130 It was his version of a particularly sissy 'kinder' song, that offended his rugged masculinity. **1979** P. ADAMS *More Unspeakable Adams* 99 We'll be issuing free of cost, hundreds of thousands of storybooks to mothers' clubs and kinders. **1983** M. LURIE *Seven Bks.* 100 Little Norbert and little Hermione and little all the rest of them, are all tucked nicely away in their kinders and creches and day-care centres.

kindy. Also **kindie.** [f. *kind(ergarten* + -Y.] A kindergarten. Also *attrib.*

[N.Z. **1959** G. SLATTER *A Gun in my Hand* 146 Two kids at school now and the little joker's at a kindy.] **1973** *Courier-Mail* (Brisbane) 4 June 15/6 The State Education Department will provide children in isolated areas with a pre-school education... A scheme for 'kindy by correspondence' would be available by the start of 1974. **1981** P. RADLEY *Jack Rivers & Me* 66 They sound like Kindie-kids. Run, fish, run, here comes the sun, fish. **1984** *Sun-Herald* (Sydney) 17 June 154/3 'Same thing with my kids,' I said. 'I told them almost from kindie that they had to be *dying* before they didn't go to school cos I was working.' **1986** *Canberra Times* 23 Apr. 8/4 The trouble with being a girl .. is that 'everybody thinks that you want to be a kindy teacher. And I hate kids'.

king, *n.*[1] *Hist.*

1. a. A title given by colonists to the male leader of an Aboriginal community; CHIEF; *native chief*, see NATIVE *a.* 5.

1830 G.C. INGLETON *True Patriots All* 27 Nov. (1952) 122 We have to announce the death of his Aboriginal Majesty King *Boongarie*, Supreme Chief of the Sydney tribe. **1847** *Maitland Mercury* 15 Dec. 4/4 The tribe of natives inhabiting the mountains have had for a long time a great *down* upon the king of the Avoca blacks, a most intelligent and useful fellow. **1863** J. BONWICK *Wild White Man* 80 Sometimes one is invested with the name of chief or king, although no extra attention seems ever paid to him, nor is any presumption of power evident. **1880** *Bulletin* (Sydney) 4 Sept. 3/4 'Jemmy', the last king of the Dabee blacks .. whose right to the title of Native King there was therefore none to dispute .. died on Tuesday week. **1895** R.H. MATHEWS *Bora* 415 The effigy of a black fellow composed of sticks and old clothes, like a scarecrow, having round his neck a string from which was suspended a crescent shaped piece of tin resembling the brass plate sometimes given by Europeans to aboriginal 'kings'. **1913** J.C.L. FITZPATRICK *Good Old Days of Molong* 122 The tribe, one and all, left the station after the 'King' was buried. **1930** A.E. YARRA *Vanishing Horsemen* 18 Tamporina, the official king of the Government blacks' reserve, was committing sorcery—making rain. **1956** T. RONAN *Moleskin Midas* 48 There's blacks ahead. I was finger talking with one old King and he is bringing two singers, one for me and one for you. **1978** E. SIMON *Through my Eyes* 78 'King' Billy Ridgeway .. used to wear a brass plate around his neck; it had been given to him when Parliament had made it fashionable to call the elders 'kings'.

b. Special Comb. **King Billy** [prob. in joc. allusion to King William IV (1830–37)], a generic term for an Aboriginal leader; an Aboriginal; **plate,** see quot. 1817.

1847 *Maitland Mercury* 24 July 3/1 We were in conversation with '**King Billy** Boomee'. **1883** *Bulletin* (Sydney) 10 Nov. 6/4 Boomerang, spear, and bow Laid by for ever—lo, Dead is King Billy! **1892** *Ibid.* 14 May 7/3 King Billy was a Myall black Of very early type, He never used a handkerchief His royal nose to wipe. **1906** *Ibid.* 3 May 14/1 But there ain't no tumbling water On the other side o' Bourke, And you'll meet King Billy's daughter When you're goin' back to work. **1919** E.S. SORENSON *Chips & Splinters* 44 It is a libel on the race to take the degenerate King Billy, who loafs about towns, as a criterion, embodying, as he does, the results of rum, opium, tobacco, and other vices of the white man. **1943** G. MCIVER *Bunyip & Other Verses* 43 Of the Bungeluke tribe only one is left—King 'Billy' of those whom he loved bereft. **1960** N. CATO *Green grows Vine* 165 Can you produce a palace, or even an uncle who is a king? King Billy perhaps! King Billy of the River Murray tribes. **1981** Q. WILD *Honey Wind* 42 We'll build a new mining village and throw in a coat and a couple of flagons for King Billy himself. [**1817 king plate:** *Sydney Gaz.* 4 Jan., His *Excellency* .. assembled the chiefs .. confirmed them in the ranks of chieftains to which their own tribes had exalted them, and conferred on them badges of distinction, whereon were engraved their names as chiefs and those of their tribes. **1849** A. HARRIS *Emigrant Family* (1967) 233 He picked up from the ground a brass-plate, of a half-moon shape, such as the settlers give to favourite leading blacks as a distinguishing badge, to be worn slung from the neck by a chain. On it was engraved 'Bondi, King of the Snowy Mountains'. **1894** *Bulletin* (Sydney) 13 Jan. 4/3 The honour of being King Billy fell into contempt when every male member of the Australian aboriginal race began to lay claim to an elaborately engraven brass half-moon of his own.] **1980** *Catal. Fine & Rare Bks.* (James R. Lawson Pty. Ltd.) 14 Dec. 58 An exceptionally fine solid brass king plate or breastplate weighing 14 oz., bearing engraved crown to centre and engraved with figures of an emu and a kangaroo. **1982** *Bulletin* (Sydney) 2 Feb. 64/1 King plates (inscribed neck plates given to the Aborigines) two or three years ago went for $25 to $50. **1982** *Austral. Financial Rev.* (Sydney) 5 Feb. 40/4 The experience in Aboriginal kingplates, brass breastplates awarded by the authorities to tribal elders for keeping the peace, shows that prices can fall away dramatically when another specimen sells for a high price.

2. Special Comb. In the names of flora and fauna: **king brown (snake),** the large, venomous snake *Pseudechis australis*, occurring throughout n. and drier s. mainland Aust.; *mulga snake*, see MULGA *n.*[1] B. 3; **fern,** either of the two large ferns, *Todea barbara* (fam. Osmundaceae) of shady forests in e. Aust., N.Z., and S. Africa, and the tropical *Angiopteris evecta* (fam. Marattiaceae), chiefly of Qld., Malaysia, and Polynesia; **honeysucker** *obs.*, *regent bird*, see REGENT 1; **parrot,** any of several parrots, esp. the predom. scarlet and green *Alisterus scapularis* of coastal and near-coastal mountain regions of e. mainland Aust., and (*W.A.*) the *red-capped parrot* (see RED *a.* 1 b.); **pigeon** *obs.*, WOMPOO PIGEON; **prawn,** a large prawn of the genus *Penaeus* valued as food, *P. plebejus* occurring in the waters of e. Aust., and *P. latisulcatus* in w. and n. Aust. and throughout the Indo-Pacific region; **quail,** the small, wide-ranging bird *Coturnix chinensis*, occurring in near-coastal e. and n. Aust. and through s.e. Asia to China; **snapper,** any of several fish incl. *red emperor* (see RED *a.* 1 b.).

1935 D. THOMSON *In Arnhem Land* (1983) 35 *Pseudechis australis*, the **King Brown Snake** .. a fine showy snake, rich copper-brown .. and about seven feet long and very thick. **1962** *N.T. News* (Darwin) 9 Jan. 2/3 A deadly King Brown snake was killed in the kitchen. **1980** ANSELL & PERCY *To fight Wild* 48 If I was bitten by a king brown out in the bush and didn't get antivenene for six hours I'd be dead anyway. **c 1910** W.R. GUILFOYLE *Austral. Plants* 354 *Todea barbara.* '**King Fern**' or 'Swamp Sponge Fern'. **1934** C. MACKNESS *Young Beachcombers* 122 Admire a graceful king fern. **1955** N.A. WAKEFIELD *Ferns of Vic. & Tas.* 10 Though the Austral King-fern often grows to truly immense proportions, it will also subsist as a tiny plant in small crevices in the rock faces of waterfalls. **1981** G. ELLIS *Hey Doc, let's go Fishing!* 72 Even the huge King ferns, *Angiopteris evecta*, with huge fronds five metres in length, have vanished. **1813** J.W. LEWIN *Birds N.S.W.* 16 **King Honeysucker.** Inhabits Banks of Patterson's River. Frequents thick brushy Woods. **1860** G. BENNETT *Gatherings of Naturalist* 215 The Regent-bird, or King Honeysucker of the colonists (*Sericulus chrysocephalus*). **1803** J. GRANT *Narr. Voyage N.S.W.* 111 Mr Cayley shot a **king parrot.** **1836** J. BACKHOUSE *Extracts from Lett.* (1839) iv. 13 The King Parrots, of scarlet and green, were sitting in flocks, on the post-and-rail fences, in the little settlement of Kiama, where they are very mischievous in the gardens. **1857** W.S. BRADSHAW *Voyages* 87 There are a great variety of parrots, namely .. the king parrot, the walkinger .. and the red-crested. **1887** J.H. WRIGHT *Our Victorian Coalfields* 42 A beautiful king parrot flutters down and rests on a low tree-fern. **1932** J. PRIEST *Call of Bush* 164 The Crimson Parrot, and the flame-breasted King Parrot (*Aprosmictus cyanopygius*) .. shine out as red lamps in any situation. **1951** D. COLLINS *Vic.'s my Home Ground* 72 It seemed almost the perfect barber's shop, with the king parrots and rosellas flashing by to add local colour. **1985** D. FOSTER *Dog Rock* 87 King parrots—the ones that sound like squeaky gates—eat acorns. **1889** R.B. ANDERSON tr. Lumholtz's *Among Cannibals* 214 Up here I saw several nests of the beautiful **king-pigeon** (*Megaloprepia magnifica*). **1929** A.H. CHISHOLM *Birds & Green Places* 156 The 'Bock, bock, buck-oo' of the big whampoo or king-pigeon. **1950** *Fisheries Newsletter* IX. vii. 5 The **King prawns** were going out into deeper water. **1976** *Ecos* ix. 24/3 Moreton Bay, off Brisbane, is the heart of one of Australia's main prawn fisheries. The annual catch of king prawns brings in $2 million or more. **1889** *Proc. Linnean Soc. N.S.W.* IV. 419 *Excalfatoria australis* . . known as '**King-quail**'. **1945** C. Barrett *Austral. Bird Life* 67 The king quail (*Excalfactoria chinensis*), our smallest species of these little game birds. **1976** *Reader's Digest Compl. Bk. Austral. Birds* 143 King quail prefer the densest of grassland habitats. **1951** T.C. Roughley *Fish & Fisheries Aust.* 98 A species closely related to the nannygai and caught in the Great Australian Bight is known commonly as '**king snapper**'. **1955** V. Serventy *Aust.'s Great Barrier Reef* 40 Another interesting food fish is the Government Bream or King Snapper. **1972** *Meanjin* 318 The reef fish included . . government bream, yellow-banded hussars, king snapper.

3. Special Comb. **king post** [transf. use of *king-post* upright post in the centre of a roof-truss], one of the main uprights in a fence, etc.; **tide,** a spring tide; an unusually high tide.

1892 *Bulletin* (Sydney) 30 July 7/3 Nigh a shattered drum and a **king-post** rotting, Are the bleaching bones of the old grey horse. **1975** G.A.W. Smith *Once Green Jackaroo* 139 A complete netting fence was erected. . . This too was attached to a king-post and strained to a float-post at the other end. **1979** D. Stuart *Crank back on Roller* 71 No more king posts to be manhandled into position to make the start of a cattle yard. **1926** M. Forrest *Hibiscus Heart* 261 There was a **king tide** coming in: to-night the full moon would see itself in a vast assemblage of waters, thundering on the trunks of the pandanus, flooding the milk-white beaches. **1949** *Bulletin* (Sydney) 2 Feb. 14/2 It was dark, and right at the top of a 'king' tide, so the visitor to the little seaside holiday resort decided to give the black bream a go. **1960** *N.T. News* (Darwin) 8 Jan. 12/3 Following the blustery weather the King Tides have done nothing towards stabilising the local fishing. **1980** K. Shortt *Echoes of Clarence* 24 Oh! don't be silly Bud . . of course we're moving. Don't forget we're punching a king tide.

king, *n.*[2] Abbrev. of Kingfish.

1939 *Bulletin* (Sydney) 1 Mar. 21/2 He talks about night-angling for kingfish. Our kingies, or the things we call kings, observe early closing hours and don't bite after dark. **1959** *Never kill Dolphin* (Writers' Guild Qld.) 91 He was sore at the hole in the net, and the fact that they had not netted either a barra or a king. **1983** *Canberra Chron.* 15 June 18/3 Tracy, 13, took another big king.

king, *n.*[3] Abbrev. of King-hit *n.*

1952 *Argus Mag.* (Melbourne) 18 Jan. 4/3, I brought him back to the subject of the king-hit again, and he said, 'You've always got to connect with a king. It's no good swinging one and missing.'

king, *v.* Abbrev. of King-hit *v.*

1940 W. Hatfield *Into (Great?) Unfenced* 124 He would slip in now and 'king' him. **1952** *Argus Mag.* (Melbourne) 18 Jan. 4/2 'He kinged me! Me own mate, and he kinged me!' . . King-hits do not always come from strangers. **1957** D. Whitington *Treasure upon Earth* 182 A big and muscular laborer aimed a blow at him, shouting 'King me now, you bastard. I haven't got me back turned.' **1968** D. Niland *Dadda Jumped* 127 If I hadn't been kinged they would never have got out of the room. **1975** *Bulletin* (Sydney) 26 Apr. 45/3 He kinged a floorwalker just to let the bagman off the hook.

King Billy pine: see King William pine.

kingfish. [Transf. use of *kingfish* a fish remarkable for its size or value as food, etc.] Any of several fish, esp. the large, common *Seriola lalandi*, having edible flesh and a yellow caudal fin, and Mulloway. See also Yellowtail.

1825 B. Field *Geogr. Mem. N.S.W.* 22 The bay abounds with what are called in the colony . . king-fish. **1840** *S. Austral. Rec.* (London) 10 Oct. 229 On one occasion they caught so vast a quantity of a species called the kingfish, that the net they were using broke, and the fish were literally driven on shore. **1854** H.B. Stoney *Yr. in Tas.* 103 In the winter season great quantities of the kingfish are driven into the different bays and left on the beach. On the receding of the tide, they are collected by the inhabitants, dried, and salted for market. **1864** *Papers & Proc. R. Soc. Tas.* 65 The Barracouta and Kingfish, closely allied forms, whose speed and ferocity are truly wonderful. **1873** F. de Castelnau *Edible Fishes Vic.* 11 The *king fish*, sometimes . . makes its appearance on the market; the fishmongers often give that name to the *yellow tail*, but I have only seen the true king fish once in two years; it is considered a very great delicacy, and is sold for £2 or £3. **1897** 'Old Housekeeper' *Austral. Plain Cookery* 47 *Kingfish* . . is best trussed round, and boiled in a floured cloth. **1924** Lord & Scott *Synopsis Vertebrate Animals Tas.* 62 *Sciaena antarctica* . . serves to form an interesting commentary on the need for scientific nomenclature. . . In New South Wales this fish is known as the 'Jew Fish'. In Queensland as the 'Dew Fish'. In Victoria and Western Australia as the 'King-fish', and in South Australia as the 'Butter Fish' or 'Mulloway'. **1934** W.A. Osborne *Visitor to Aust.* 102 The king-fish of Sydney, much the same as the amber fish of America, averaging 4 ft. in length, swims in shoals of thousands. **1977** *Commercial Fish Aust.* (Dept. Primary Industry) 22 Yellowtail kingfish are also called simply yellowtail or kingfish. **1983** *Canberra Chron.* 15 June 18/3 They finally managed to salvage a saurie that a hooked kingfish spat our near their boat, caught a kingfish with it, then gutted him to obtain even more sauries.

King George whiting. [See quot. 1974.] *Spotted whiting*, see Spotted.

1968 D. O'Grady *Bottle of Sandwiches* 15 The bay was alive with . . King George whiting, and many other mouth-watering finny pan-fillers. **1974** J.M. Thomson *Fish Ocean & Shore* 126 The King George or spotted whiting (*Sillaginodes punctatus*) ranges from south-western Australia, where the name King George is derived from King George Sound, to the southern coast of New South Wales. **1983** *Ecos* xxxv. 7/3 Only two snapper fillets out of 15 were genuine, and all four King George whitings turned out to be hollow pretenders.

king-hit, *n.* A sudden, damaging blow; a knock-out punch; an unfair punch. Also *fig.*, and *attrib.*

1917 A.C. Panton *Dinkum Oils*, K is the King-hit we'll give to the guy, Who started this war, or we'll want to know why. **1921** E. Wells *Fragments* 14 Guess we'll give 'em the king hit to-night. **1923** *Communist* (Sydney) 16 Mar. 4/1 No doubt Ted will take warning from James and get in on the Queensland Central Executive with his king-hit. **1929** H. MacQuarrie *We & Baby* 84 The king-hit . . would have been a truly awful blow. **1947** O. Griffiths *Darwin Drama* 152 Stone, who had a good reputation for his skill at boxing, immediately registered a 'king hit' on the oriental and, by hitting him on the apple of his throat, knocked him out. **1958** J.R. Spicer *Cry of Storm-Bird* 152 'King-hit, you bastard!' the miner growled. 'I'll kill you, mate!' He swung a heavy left. **1965** L. Haylen *Big Red* 46 He could almost hear Felix who had taught him a bit saying, 'Get in now. Get in for the king hit.' **1966** S.J. Baker *Austral. Lang.* (ed. 2) 126 The true *king hit* is a sudden, cowardly blow designed to end a fight before the opponent can prepare to defend himself. **1974** J. Gaby *Restless Waterfront* 62 You're the two greatest king-hit, stand-over artists on the waterfront. **1985** *N.T. News* (Darwin) 16 Apr. 35/4 The final chapter of the ugly 'king-hit' incident from last month's NTFL grand final will unfold tonight.

king hit, *v.* [f. prec.] *trans.* To punch (a person) suddenly and hard, often unfairly; to knock out.

1959 E. Lambert *Glory thrown In* 150 They stopped us and tried to arrest us. I king-hit the sergeant and we up and off. **1962** Marshall & Drysdale *Journey among Men* 34 They try to climb over the bar to hit you. . . When they've got their hands and feet full of bar you can king-hit them with no trouble at all. **1968** S. Gore *Holy Smoke* 13 Best take this lot . . in case he tries to king-hit yer first time up. **1969** A. Buzo *Front Room Boys* (1970) 118 *Jacko* jumps up and 'king-hits' *Gibbo*, who reels across the floor. **1977** *Drag Show* 45 The stationary boxer . . made a desperate effort to king-hit Soapy with one final blow. **1985** *N.T. News* (Darwin) 17 Apr. 40/1 Nikoletos was reported by goal umpire Peter Hardy after 'king-hitting' McPhee in the first term of the grand final.

Hence **king hitter** *n.*, **king hitting** *vbl. n.* and *ppl. a.*

1952 *Argus Mag.* (Melbourne) 18 Jan. 4/3 King-hit Delaney of Bourke, a man who earned his nickname over the fallen bodies of a score of victims, once gave me the low-down on **king-hitters.** **1974** J. Gaby *Restless Waterfront* 39 Talking about king hitters, the most notorious was a crazy Scot called Jim Woods. **1979** G. Stewart *Leveller* 35 'You **king-hitting** bastard, out the back and fight like a man,' Paddy screamed. **1981** A.B. Facey *Fortunate Life* 224 If you won't withdraw what you said I'm prepared to test you with your king-hitting business.

kingie. [f. *king* (as first element indicating size) + -y.]

1. Kingfish.

1936 N. Caldwell *Fangs of Sea* 90 The immense schools of striped tuna, locally called 'kingies' (kingfish) work into the warmer waters. **1970** I. Gall *Fishing for Fun of It* 16 The kingie probably headed for New Zealand or at least Norfolk Island, for we never, at any stage, saw that rod and reel again. **1985** *Canberra Chron.* 23 Oct. 19/3 He had plenty of berley and live bait for a change, and the kingies in the 10–15 kg. range were up and active.

2. *King prawn*, see King *n.*[1] 2.

1966 P. Pinney *Restless Men* 20 We export our Australian prawns to . . Japan, so that . . the Japs can cut up our Kingies and sell 'em back to us as prawn-flake. **1980** B. Shackleton *Karagi* 23 The school and ground prawners of the estuaries battled to compete with the big 'Kingie' running at about ten to the pound.

King Street. [The name of a street in central Sydney, used in allusion to the hearing of bankruptcy cases in the Supreme Court located there.] In the phr. **up** (or **in**) **King Street,** in financial difficulty.

1864 *Bell's Life in Sydney* 11 June 3/1 Always avoid the society of obstinate 'jolly good fellows' who 'won't go home till morning', for late hours are very expensive, and generally lead to an *early* 'walk up King-street'. **1866** *Sydney Punch* 17 Feb. 721/1 That 'poor man's friend' and Refuge for the destitute, familiarly known as 'Up King Street'. **1887** *Bungendore Mirror* 8 Oct. 2 The speculation would not pay at present and could but land us in King-street. **1895** *Worker* (Sydney) 14 Sept. 1/4 He has been on the high road to fortune, and has been up 'King-Street'. **1934** C. Stead *Seven Poor Men* (1971) 78 They don't sweat their guts out for a chap who buys . . himself a new car when he's up King Street. **1967** S. Shumack *Autobiogr.* 28 They had a good start in life . . but when I met them in 1858 both had been up 'King Street'. **1980** B. Hornadge *Austral. Slanguage* 69 *Up King Street* is an expression fairly widely used for at least the first half of this century to describe any one who was bankrupt or insolvent. The term originated in Sydney where the Bankruptcy Court was located at the top end of King Street.

King William pine. [Prob. f. the name of the *King William* Range in w. Tas.] The coniferous tree *Athrotaxis selaginoides* (fam. Taxodiaceae) of w. and s.w. Tas.; the softwood timber of the tree, being straight-grained, light, and very durable. Also **King Billy pine.**

1903 *Tasmanian Timbers* (Tas. Lands & Survey Dept.) 25 King William pine . . *Athrotaxis selaginoides* . . is so named from the leaf resembling the selaginela, an ornamental tree-moss. **1916** *Bulletin* (Sydney) 10 Aug. 24/2, I move that a D.S.O. be awarded to King Billy pine, which grows on the wet side of Tassy, as the best timber for huts. **1947** Mrs A.H. Garnsey *Romance Huon River* 130 The King William Pine and the more ornamental Celery Top Pine grew in the Upper Huon District. **1956** N.K. Wallis *Austral. Timber Handbk.* 8 King William pine (joinery, pattern making, small boat-building, musical instruments). **1985** *Mercury* (Hobart) 8 Mar. 1/5 The King Billy pine can grow as high as 40 metres and live as long as 1,500 years.

kinshela, var. Kinchela.

kip. *Two-up.* [Perh. f. Br. dial. *kep, v.* to catch; to throw up in the air: see EDD.] A small, flat piece of wood with which the coins are tossed.

1887 K. Mackay *Stirrup Jingles* 58 Then an hour was devoted to blowing And drinking and handling the 'kip' For at 'heading' these shearers were knowing, And at talk creation could whip. **1895** *Bulletin* (Sydney) 16 Feb. 21/2 *Kip*, the short stick used in tossing coins. **1901** *Truth* (Sydney) 3 Feb. 5/5 The pennies are placed on a piece of flat, thin wood, which is termed a 'Kip', and tossed up from it. **1911** L. Stone *Jonah* 215 The spinner placed the two pennies face down on the kip, and then, with a turn of the wrist, the coins flew twenty feet into the air. **1925** A. Wright *Boy from Bullarah* 17 Ronter possessed himself of the kip, and, placing the pennies upon it, spun them high into the air. **1943** H.M. MURPHY *Strictly for Soldiers* 17 So the kip you gather tightly, Watch the pennies put on lightly By the ringer, who then bellows: 'Fair go, spinner, let 'em go.' **1953** A. MOOREHEAD *Rum Jungle* 53 One player held the 'kip'—a thin piece of wood a little wider and longer than a toothbrush—and on this two pennies were poised. **1972** J. O'GRADY *It's your Shout, Mate!* 25 The technique seemed to be to turn the wrist slightly but sharply just as the coins were leaving the 'kip'. **1977** R. BEILBY *Gunner* 297 Gunner waited with the kip at the ready: it was a small rectangle of sweat-darkened wood, smoothed by handling and scored with cross-hatching which gave it a rudimentary but professional look.

kipper /'kɪpə/, *n.*[1] *Hist.* Formerly also with much variety, as **kebah, kebarra, kebarrah, keepara, keeparra, kippa.** [a. Dharuk *gibara* f. *giba* a stone, from the use of a stone as an implement for the ceremonial extraction of teeth. See also GIBBER 1.]

1. a. An Aboriginal male who has been initiated into manhood. Also as quasi-*adj.*

1798 D. COLLINS *Acct. Eng. Colony N.S.W.* I. 580 They were also termed Ke-bar-ra, a name which has reference in its construction to the singular instrument used on this occasion, ke-bah in their language signifying rock or stone. **1841** *Colonial Observer* (Sydney) 14 Oct. 10/4 We went with some of the natives to see the spot where the solemnity of making *kippers* is to take place. **1847** G.F. ANGAS *Savage Life & Scenes* II. 222 The boys were now termed 'Kebarrah', from *keba*, a rock or stone. **1851** J. HENDERSON *Excursions & Adventures N.S.W.* 158 The principal ceremony of the aborigines is that which takes place when they meet to convert .. the boys into young men. This meeting is called a *keepara* .. and the youths are called *keeparas*. **1869** 'E. HOWE' *Boy in Bush* 204 One of them asked, 'Was not the son of Kaludie a kipper?' and then pointed to Harry's mouth, out of which, of course, no tooth had been knocked, black-fellow fashion, at the 'kipper' age. **1885** MRS C. PRAED *Austral. Life* 24 The great mystery of the Blacks is the Bora—a ceremony at which the young men found worthy receive the rank of warriors and are henceforth called *kippers*. **1923** T. HALL *Short Hist. Downs Blacks* 6 Each pole or post bore the distinct mark belonging to each 'Kippa' (or youth), and the Councillors knew which Kippa belonged to the different posts. **1935** DAVISON & NICHOLLS *Blue Coast Caravan* 195 A young man who had been through the Bora-ring was said to be kippa.

b. The ceremony in which such an initiation takes place. Also **kipper ceremony, kipper making.**

1833 *N.S.W. Mag.* (Sydney) I. 11 'Bappo' .. the deity supposed to preside at the celebration of the 'Kebarrah'. **1837** *Lit. News* (Sydney) 28 Oct. 114 There is a remarkable ceremony performed .. with some variation, in many parts of New Holland: here it is called kabarrah. **1847** *Moreton Bay Courier* 21 Aug. 3/1 The natives .. were assembled from all parts of this district .. to the number of at least three hundred, at a place called Waralpa .. to perform the ceremony of kipper-making. **1854** MRS C. CLACY *Lights & Shadows* II. 27 *Kebarrah* .. is the ceremony of installing the boys of the tribe into the dignity of the warrior. **1876** 'EIGHT YRS.' RESIDENT' *Queen of Colonies* 327 Among the customs of our blacks, perhaps the most curious and mysterious is that of kipper making. **1896** W.A. SQUIRE *Ritual, Myth, & Customs Austral. Aborigines* 7 The Bora, Kabbara, Yoolangh or Kipperah, which is of a religious and civil character, is the great educational ceremony of the Murri or Australian race. **1899** R.H. MATHEWS *Folklore Austral. Aborigines* 23 The rocks .. enclosed a large oval or circular space, like the *kackaroo* ring at the keeparra ceremony.

2. Special Comb. **kipper ground, ring,** the place reserved for the holding of an initiation ceremony.

1851 *Empire* (Sydney) 22 Oct. 284/3 Nor are they treated in any manner as men, nor allowed to take to themselves a wife or wives (for Polygamy is allowed among them) until they have their allotted probation at the **Kipper ground.** **1856** J. BONWICK *W. Buckley* 77 He is said to be sent to the Kipper Grounds. **1876** 'EIGHT YRS.' RESIDENT' *Queen of Colonies* 328 '**Kipper rings**' may be seen, where these mysteries are performed and the initiations take place. **1978** K. MCARTHUR *Pumicestone Passage* 39 Both Pamphlet and Finnegan were .. taken to tribal fights, held at rings... That which Finnegan saw could have been at the Redcliffe kippa-ring.

kipper, *n.*[2] [f. the popular assoc. of *kipper* a cured herring with the English.] A sailor in the Royal Navy; an English person.

1943 J.F. MOYES *Scrap-Iron Flotilla* 105 The soldiers were mostly Australians, the nurses were 'Wallabies', 'Kiwis' and 'Kippers'. **1946** *Daily Tel.* (Sydney) 22 Jan. 11/2 Hansen told Mr Goldie, S.M., that the girls called them 'Pommies' and 'kippers'. I understand that in Australia 'kipper' means two-faced and gutless. **1948** H.W. CRITTENDEN *Rogues' Paradise* 172 It is this ignorance that inspires a Royal Australian Navy rating in uniform to publicly describe the British Navy men as 'kippers', and proudly proclaim that he is 'Anti-British'. **1962** J. WYNNUM *Storm in Port* 13 He is a kipper, which is one step worse than an ordinary officer. **1967** —— *I'm Jack, all Right* 17, I tell you this is a terrific opportunity for you—a ruddy kipper—to see something of the real Australia. **1975** *Bulletin* (Sydney) 30 Aug. 63/1 The Australian naval slang-term for a Pommy matelot is—or was—'bloody kipper'... The real derivation .. is on the victualling side. In the days before refrigeration, British ships, both men o' war and merchantmen, stocked up with kippered fish (not necessarily herring) because it kept well and was highly nutritious. **1980** B. HORNADGE *Austral. Slanguage* 165 There is certainly nothing friendly in another (increasingly) common expression directed at Englishmen—a *kipper*.

kipper /'kɪpə/, *v.* [f. KIPPER *n.*[1]] *trans.* To initiate (an Aboriginal male) into manhood.

1873 J.B. STEPHENS *Black Gin* 39 Where of old with awful mysteries and diabolic din, They 'kippered' adolescents in the presence of their kin. **1972** M. CASSIDY *Dispossessed* 174 Murac .. had broken the tribe's law by marrying a girl before he was kippa-ed.

kippy. *Two-up.* [f. KIP + -Y.] SPINNER a.

1946 K.S. PRICHARD *Roaring Nineties* 152 The ring-keeper might object to a spin, on the grounds that the kippy had put a 'gig' on it, or touched the kip with his fingers.

kipsy. Also **kipsie.** [Elaboration of *kip* lodging-house.] A house; a shelter.

1905 J. BUFTON *Tasmanians in Transvaal War* 95 Rigged a kipsie up on truck to keep the wet off. **1909** *Bulletin* (Sydney) 16 Sept. 14/2 Cocky's first rain-water reservoir is usually a barrel, stuck at one corner of the kipsy with a sheet of stringy-bark connecting it with the roof. **1915** C.J. DENNIS *Songs of Sentimental Bloke* 66, I see 'er in me mind be'ind the cups In our own little kipsie, bye an' bye. **1940** H. DRAKE-BROCKMAN *Men without Wives* (1955) 133 Let this kipsy. I'll board for a bit. **1954** T. RONAN *Vision Splendid* 283 Blow me down if he don't get me drunk, take me out to his kipsie, and put me to bed, and then sneak back after my sheila. **1982** R. ELLIS *Bush Safari* 17 Located in a picturesque donga, the living area consisted of something Harry called a 'kipsy' .. a rectangular wooden structure of about 3 by 2.5 by 2 metres, placed on four 200-litre drums under a mulga, and brightly painted green and white. Inside was a bed (with sheets), cupboards, small table, and two chairs—very cosy. The whole thing sat on the back of Harry's Studebaker when he shifted camp.

kiss-and-ride, *attrib.* See quot 1975.

1974 *Sydney Area Transportation Study* III. vi. 8 The statistics include both 'park-and-ride' and 'kiss and ride' passengers. **1975** *Sydney Morning Herald* 16 Jan. 6/7 The alternative is the kiss-and-ride system—the wife drops her husband off at the station or terminal, keeps the car for her own use during the day, and picks him up at night. **1982** *Sun-Herald* (Sydney) 18 Apr. 23/5 Parking areas, kiss'n'ride facilities and bus/ferry interchanges would be the responsibility of local councils.

kit, *v. S.A. Mining. Obs.* [Prob. f. Br. dial. *kit* to pack in a kit or wooden vessel: see OED *v.*[1]] *trans.* To steal (ore). Chiefly as *vbl. n.*

1865 *Wallaroo Times* (Kadina) 9 Dec. 5/2 Three men .. were discharged from the mine minus a good character for stealing or, to use the mining term 'kitting' ores from the company's piles. **1962** O. PRYOR *Aust.'s Little Cornwall* 56 There were dire penalties for 'kitting' as the stealing of ore was known.

kitchen.

1. In the phr. **the rounds of the kitchen,** a severe reproof; a scolding.

1873 J.C.F. JOHNSON *Christmas on Carringa* 4 He had been getting from Mrs M... what he termed 'the rounds of the kitchen', for being such a fool. **1939** J. CAMPBELL *Babe is Wise* 211 An does she gimme the rounds of the kitchen! Pitches into me like I dunno w'at. **1966** S.J. BAKER *Austral. Lang.* (ed. 2) 427 *Reprove (v.)*, give the rounds of the kitchen to (someone).

2. Special Comb. **kitchen tea,** a party given for a bride-to-be to which the (usu. female) guests bring gifts of kitchen equipment.

1934 T. CLARKE *Marriage* 17 Tom Rawlings led me off to see the bride at a 'kitchen tea'... In the centre of affairs was the young bride in whose honour the 'kitchen tea' had been arranged; and it was so called because each guest brought a kitchen utensil as a wedding-gift. **1943** K. TENNANT *Time enough Later* 166 Restrain them from any idea of visitings and junketings and gruesomeness in the form of kitchen teas. **1965** *Sunday Mail* (Brisbane) 28 Nov. 26 Michelle Bowes and Patricia Donovan .. gave the bride a kitchen tea on Friday. **1970** G. GREER *Female Eunuch* 116 The more class the families can pretend to the more they can exact in the way of presents at showers, kitchen teas and the like. **1981** P. RADLEY *Jack Rivers & Me* 120 A kitchen tea in Boomeroo is not a shower tea. That would be like calling the Great Coral Sea Typhoon of World War II summer rain.

kitehawk. The predom. brown, carrion-eating bird *Milvus migrans*, common in n. Aust. and widespread to Europe and Africa.

1909 LINDSAY & HOLTZE *Territoria* 24 There are the .. hawks (eagle, brown, and kite hawks). **1925** *Bulletin* (Sydney) 1 Jan. 24/4 Immediately they located anything edible, the shrill whistling call of the kite-hawk would sound .. and there would be a scurry for the skyline and safety. **1932** W. HATFIELD *Ginger Murdoch* 151 Not a living thing stirred except the tireless kite-hawks wheeling high against the blue. **1963** V.B. CRANLEY *27,000 Miles through Aust.* 18 The kitehawks hovered in the heat over the well-pumps, waiting for some stray lamb. **1979** D. LOCKWOOD *My Old Mates & I* 58 Kitehawks (fire hawks) feeding on the perimeter of a grass fire, swooping on insects, rodents, lizards.

Kiwi, *n. Obs.* [f. KIWI *v.*] A soldier, esp. one with highly-polished accoutrements.

1916 *Astra* (Melbourne) Sept. 1/2 Demands .. are made on them as Kiwi Kids. **1917** *Southern Cross Gaz.: Jrnl. H.M.A.T. 'Thermistocles'* 28 May 3 This army .. consists of soldiers and 'Kiwis'... 'Kiwis' .. Australia's bad bargains are much more easily distinguished by the high polish of their boots.

kiwi, *v. Obs.* [f. the proprietary name of a brand of shoe polish.] *trans.* To polish (shoes); to spruce up (one's appearance). Usu. with **up.** Also *absol.*

[**1910** *Austral. Official Jrnl. Patents* (Canberra) 749 *Kiwi*... *Boot Polish*. 9219... Boot Polishes and all other Polishes.] **1917** *All abaht It* (London) Feb. (1919) 51 Hair sleekly brushed and kiwi-ed up as much as possible. **1917** P. AUSTEN *Bill-Jim* 21 Oh, keep yer job, yer little kiwied Serg. [*Note*] Polished up with Kiwi. **1929** 'F. BLAIR' *Digger Sea-Mates* 112 Whose boots were not bright as a mirror 'Kiwied' to the highest perfection? **1949** G. BERRIE *Morale* 210 Men will shave and wear bandoliers. They don't need to kiwi up specially.

kleiner, var. CLINER.

knap, *v. Gold-mining.* Also **nap.** [Spec. use of Br. (chiefly dial.) *knap* to strike sharply, to tap (esp. stone): see OED *v.*[2] and EDD *v.*[2]] *trans.* To break off (pieces of an outcropping reef) in order to ascertain if gold is present.

1898 W. DOLLMAN *Bush Fancies* 22 We'd been prospecting and hunting for miles, We'd 'napped' full many a reef. **1898** D.W. CARNEGIE *Spinifex & Sand* 127 In prospecting a reef, a miner walks along the strike of the outcrop, 'napping' as he goes, *i.e.*, breaking off with a hammer or pick, pieces of the quartz or ironstone outcrop. **1925** J.E. LIDDLE *Selected Poems* 86 Oft he 'naps' reefs with his pick, if they have 'specks' he may 'costeen'. **1929** W.J. RESIDE *Golden Days* 51 He had found a virgin reef which had never been 'napped' before. **1938** F. CLUNE *Free & Easy Land* 152 Noticing some black boulders knapped them, and put the specimens in his pocket. **1946** K.S. PRICHARD *Roaring Nineties* 59 Dinny went loaming along the ridge for several days before he knapped a rock that showed fine shotty gold. **1980** M. MCADOO *If only I'd Listened* ('Pop Doherty'), Now one Sunday morning he went napping, that is he napped the stones with a little hammer and if they showed any sign of gold, he'd be able to read the country pretty well.

knight. Used ironically in fig. collocations, as: **knight of the blades, of the bright** (or **shining**) **sword,** a shearer who uses hand shears; **of the road, (a)** a bushranger; **(b)** a swagman.

1896 *Worker* (Sydney) 5 Sept. 3/4 If the '**knights of the blades**' and their comrades will resolve to sink all minor issues .. Unionism must soon flourish and become all powerful throughout Australia. **1898** *Ibid.* 26 Feb. 7/2 As 'Knights of the Blade' we may not be as swift as Power or Mick the Ringer, but we are all there from start to finish. **1949** *Bulletin* (Sydney) 23 Feb. 14/4 Another common way to describe the ringer is to say that he 'swung the gate'... Can any old '**knights of the bright swords**' say how that term originated? **1978** M. WALKER *Pioneer Crafts Early Aust.* 151 The 'Knights of the Shining Swords'—the blade shearers. **(a) 1864** *Bell's Life in Sydney* 9 Jan. 2/6 A member of the Fighting Blues .. while out on horseback last week with the ostensible purpose of bushranger-hunting, accidentally stumbled over one of the **Knights of the Road**. **1874** *Illustr. Sydney News* 27 June 6/1 As the precautions taken against recognition on this occasion, were much greater than those usually adopted by 'Knights of the Road', it is scarcely possible that even if arrested the evidence given will be sufficient to insure conviction. **1891** *Braidwood Dispatch* 14 Jan. 2/5 Power the liberated bushranger .. will revisit the scenes of some of his former exploits during his career as 'knight of the road'. **1912** J. BRADSHAW *Highway Robbery under Arms* (ed. 3) 7 The bushranger's song was called for immediately. The young knight of the road cleared his throat. **(b) 1936** I.L. IDRIESS *Cattle King* 351 Gone .. were the picturesque characters of the bush... Numerous similar **Knights of the Road** who had brought countless laughs to the tracks. **1942** *Bulletin* (Sydney) 29 Apr. 13/4 The knight of the road mournfully thudded his bluey down and peered wistfully over the fence. **1959** *Ibid.* 25 Mar. 19/1 The signals left at homestead-gates by itinerants for the information of other knights of the road who may be following. **1978** M. WALKER *Pioneer Crafts Early Aust.* 124 The 'Knights of the Road', the swagmen, travelled from place to place mostly on foot but sometimes pushing a wheelbarrow.

knock, *n. Australian National Football.* The striking of the ball towards a team-mate after a ball-up or throw-in.

1960 *N.T. News* (Darwin) 2 Feb. 8/8 Shields won the knock and Buffs brought the ball down for Frankie Ah Mat to goal. **1964** J. POLLARD *High Mark* 37 Shepherding .. is illegal when .. players are going for the knock in the ruck as the ball is bounced.

knock, *v.*

1. a. *trans.* With **down**: to spend (one's available resources) in a spree or drinking bout; esp. in the phr. **to knock down a (one's,** etc.) **cheque.** See also CHEQUE.

1845 *Sentinel* (Sydney) 15 Jan. 1/6 Inns .. where the profligate or improvident resorts when released from the engagement with his master, and in three or four days 'knock down' [*sic*] the hard earned gains of perhaps six months. **1848** *Port Phillip Herald* 4 Apr. 3/2 Having 'knocked down' whatever money he had saved, he could find no other lodging than where he was found. **1855** G.H. WATHEN *Golden Colony* 35 The diggers returned to Melbourne to 'knock down' their money. **1869** *Colonial Soc.* (Sydney) 14 Jan. 6 In the country townships, about shearing time, he reaps a large harvest by trading upon the indiscriminate generosity of those bushmen who happen to be 'knocking down' their cheques in them. **1876** 'EIGHT YRS.' RESIDENT' *Queen of Colonies* 31 Scores of young men .. after 'knocking down' the few scores or hundreds of pounds given them to make a start in the colony .. here obtain skilful medical treatment and careful nursing. **1889** *Illustr. Austral. News* (Melbourne) 1 May 74/2 Tom and Bill, who have not left the station perhaps for some years, have a chance of once more knocking down their cheques in civilisation. **1912** *Bulletin* (Sydney) 29 Feb. 44/2 The ebony ones get *carte blanche*... To get the true sense of the words 'knocked down', you must go to one of these outposts. There is no doctoring of liquor and no dead house. **1923** *Ibid.* 11 Jan. 22/3 Among a crowd of us busy knocking down our cheques at a bush shanty was one who had just bought a new pair of boots. **1946** *Ibid.* 16 Aug. 28/3 Nowadays a bushman knocking down a cheque .. is a rarity. **1976** J.H. TRAVERS *Bull Dust on Brigalow* 66 After they made payment, they would book up another three months' supply, and then knock the balance down at the local pub.

Hence **knocking down** *vbl. n.* and *attrib.*

1873 A. TROLLOPE *Aust. & N.Z.* I. 172 The knocking down of an imaginary cheque would be dreadful to the publican. **1893** F.W.L. ADAMS *Australs.* 167 The legend of the 'knocking down' of cheques is still current, but the actual thing is becoming rarer and rarer. **1895** *Worker* (Sydney) 9 Feb. 4/2 The knocking-down-cheque trick is fast becoming a matter of the past. **1909** F.E. BIRTLES *Lonely Lands* 57, I was informed it was only Jim-so-and-so knocking down his cheque and that whoever cared to claim relationship with—and there were many—was welcome to assist him in the knocking down process until his fifty or a hundred pounds had been transferred to the publican's pocket.

b. [Spec. use of *knock up* to accumulate.] In the phr. **to knock up a cheque,** to get or accumulate (a total sum) by one's labour.

1890 A.J. VOGAN *Black Police* 258 Here he is, working hard to 'knock up' another cheque. **1908** *Truth* (Sydney) 12 Apr. 11/4 Men .. making for the sugar country where a cheque can be knocked up quickly. **1920** *Bulletin* (Sydney) 11 Mar. 20/4 His beloved gin had, whilst he had been knocking up a cheque to tide them over the honeymoon, allowed a rival to cut him out. **1937** A.W. UPFIELD *Mr Jelly's Business* 32, I knocked up a good cheque there breaking horses. **1949** G. BERRIE *Morale* 102 They had knocked up a cheque on a seven-months job, and they were going to knock it down before they signed on for another.

2. *trans.* With **out: (a)** to extract (payable dirt); **(b)** to earn (a living).

1853 S. SIDNEY *Three Colonies* (ed. 2) 375, I tried surface washing, and knocked out an ounce a day. **1871** *Austral. Town & Country Jrnl.* (Sydney) 18 Mar. 335/1 The first machine we used to knock out over 3 oz. a day in old Long Gully. **1881** A.C. GRANT *Bush-Life Qld.* I. 31 These were part of the Ipswich tribe, and knocked out a precarious living by hunting in the bush and begging in the town. **1896** E. DYSON *Rhymes from Mines* 93 Yet Jo contrived to knock out bread and butter, And something for a dead-broke mate. **1898** G.T. BELL *Coolgardie* 5 Big Flat .. at that time was entirely occupied by Celestials, who were knocking out fair tucker on the neighbouring creeks and old alluvial workings. **1901** *Brisbane Courier* 2 July 4/7 Some of the old residents .. have been knocking out a good thing [from mining]. **1949** I.L. IDRIESS *One Wet Season* 103 There's old-timers still knocking out a crust in the Kimberleys could tell you of those days. **1975** *Bulletin* (Sydney) 30 Aug. 16/3 What about the school-teacher, the young computer programmer or plumber knocking out about $200 a week.

3. [f. *knock out* to stun or kill.] *trans.* To kill (esp. in *pass.*). Also (formerly) *intr.*, to die.

1911 *Bulletin* (Sydney) 5 Oct. 16/1 His mates in the tunnel variously informed me that Uncle Dick had 'kicked the bucket' .. 'knocked' [etc.]. **1920** W.H. DOWNING *To Last Ridge* 177 'Eat, drink and be merry as possible, for to-morrow we may get knocked,' was the prevailing faith. **1931** O. WALTERS *Shrapnel Green* 22 A couple knocked, an' three or four got Blighties. **1944** C. WILMOT *Tobruk* 211 A bloke doesn't mind so much if he gets knocked in a stunt .. but to cop it out in a listenin'-post. **1967** *Kings Cross Whisper* (Sydney) xxxv. 6/3 *Knocked*, to be murdered. Shortened from the American to be knocked off.

4. [f. KNOCKBACK *n.*] *trans.* With **back**: to reject; to rebuff.

1918 *Kia Ora Coo-ee* July 12/1 Have you ever got arrangements completed for your holidays to commence on a Monday at home, and then about six of your fellow workers got sick on the Saturday, and you have been knocked back? **1930** *Bulletin* (Sydney) 19 Feb. 51/1 Not the sort of man we want... I knocked him back. **1935** K. TENNANT *Tiburon* 361 They weren't 'going to give old Ma .. the satisfaction of knocking them back'. **1948** J.K. EWERS *For Heroes to live In* 137 That harvest he kept on knocking back the agents who came out worrying him to sell. **1957** D. WHITINGTON *Treasure upon Earth* 102 We didn't ask her after she knocked us back the first time. **1972** *Bulletin* (Sydney) 12 Aug. 7/3 Some of our male members have had success in reviving the old Australian form of greeting: 'Getting plenty?' 'Knocking it back with a stick.' **1979** B. HUMPHRIES *Bazza comes into his Own*, If you try makin' me a lord I'll more than likely knock it back!

knockabout.

1. An unskilled labourer on a rural property; ROUSEABOUT *n.* a. Also *attrib.*, esp. as **knockabout man (hand, joey).**

1867 *S.A. Parl. Papers* no. 14 28 What were they principally?—Shepherds, and knock-about hands. The usual bush hands. **1869** *Bushmen, Publicans, & Politics* 5 They have .. to serve an often hard apprenticeship, as what is locally known as knock-about men, doing small jobs by weekly labour, shovelling up along fences, sheep-washing, yard work. **1872** W.M. HUGO *Hist. First Bushmen's Club* 268 'William' did send one man named MacDonald to his office yesterday morning, thinking that, though no shearer, he might do for a knock-about hand. **1881** A.C. GRANT *Bush-Life Qld.* I 80 What is called in the bush 'knock-about men'—that is, men who are willing to undertake any work, sometimes shepherding, sometimes making yards or droving. **1893** R. BRUCE *Echoes from Coondambo* 195 So then a job to make a bob I takes as 'knockabout'. **1902** *Bulletin* (Sydney) 13 Dec. 17/1, I was knockabout man at Uoorendah. **1909** E. WALTHAM *Life & Labour in Aust.* 44 We were very dubious as to whether he was the 'Boss' or the Knockabout Joey. **1941** S.J. BAKER *Pop. Dict. Austral. Slang* 41 *Knockabout*, a station 'rouseabout' or handy-man. **1977** D. WHITINGTON *Strive to be Fair* 28 Classing in Tasmania was not as important .. as the knockabout experience in the New South Wales Riverina.

2. A loafer; a tramp. Also *attrib.*

1888 *Centennial Mag.* (Sydney) 234 Here he was, a ragged, hard-up tramp, a 'knock-about' as Talgai called him. **1939** K. TENNANT *Foveaux* 312 If Neicie's husband had been a 'knockabout', Curly could have dealt with him according to the unwritten rules of his own circle. **1958** F. HARDY *Four-Legged Lottery* 117 The prisoners can be divided roughly into three categories. First offenders and 'knock-about men' (semi-criminals who come here at infrequent intervals); hardened criminals; and, thirdly, 'poofters' (homosexuals). **1977** *Bulletin* (Sydney) 26 Apr. 44/3 A knock-about (or knock-around) is what the British might call a lay-about. That is, a guy who is appalled at the idea of an honest day's work.

knockback. [Br. dial. *knock-back*: see OEDS.] A repulse; a rebuff. See also KNOCK *v.* 4.

1915 B. GAMMAGE *Broken Yrs.* (1974) 13 Things are now looking so serious, and the Russians and Allies are getting so many knock backs, that .. I have decided to [enlist]. **1933** L.A. SIGSWORTH *Verse* 10 You get a surly knock back half a mile in off the pad. **1939** *Bulletin* (Sydney) 13 Sept. 16/1, I begged the Shire Council ter give me a decent road, but all I got was knockbacks. **1956** F.B. VICKERS *First Place to Stranger* 194, I knew I was going to get a knock back before she said: 'I'm sorry Owen.' **1967** D. HORNE *Educ. Young Donald* 211 Behind it there lurked the anxiety of a knockback. The girl might not Come Across! **1975** *Bulletin* (Sydney) 1 Feb. 17/2, I called 15 and got 15 knockbacks, with reasons ranging from the old favourite 'Me truck's broken down' to 'Only got one bloke on the job'.

knock-down. [Orig. U.S.: see OEDS.] An introduction (to a person).

1915 C.J. DENNIS *Songs of Sentimental Bloke* 125 *Knock-down*, a formal introduction. **1919** C.H. THORP *Handful of Ausseys* 200 'E gives me a knock-down to 'is tart—yer know 'ow a bloke does when it's 'is cobber—never mentions no names er anything. **1942** M.L. MACPHERSON *I heard Anzacs Singing* 35 When an Australian says he will give you a knock-down it does not mean he is going to apply his fists to you; he is merely going to give you a formal introduction to someone. 'Knock-down' is the antonym, you see, of 'pick-up'. **1947** M. RAYMOND *Smiley gets Gun* 170 'You're the one who can arrange an introduction.' 'I'd like to give you a knockdown to 'er—fair dinkum I would.' **1950** J. MORRISON *Port of Call* 68 You come along wiv us an' I'll give yer a knock-down ter some of the locals. **1966** G. WYATT *Strip Jack Naked* 49 Would you like me to give you a knockdown to her?—or better still .. you can go find her yourself. **1975** R. BEILBY *Brown Land Crying* 169 Old Dinny's too ignorant to give us a proper knock-down, so I do it myself. I'm Mrs Benner, an' this is me daughter, T'rese, Mrs Bonney. **1981** *Sun-Herald* (Sydney) 1 Mar. 97/1 That's a grouse-looking little sheila over there, Sal. Any chance of a knockdown to her later on?

knock 'em down, *a.* Chiefly *N.T.* Torrential. Chiefly in the collocation **knock 'em down rain.**

1946 W.E. HARNEY *North of 23°* 99 With the final storms--'knock 'em down' they call them—it bends to the ground. **1946** A. GREEN *We were (Riff) R.A.A.F.* 31 Towards the end of February, and in early March, the 'knock 'em down rains' flattened the tall spear grass. **1951** E. HILL *Territory* 102 In April the wind changed—'knock-em down rain'—flattening the long grasses till you could see the next hut. **1960** J. GLENNON *Heart in Centre* 240 Another spring had gathered up her remnants of green and departed, followed by a sweltering summer and the 'knock 'em down' rains which flattened the spear grass that had lately flourished.

knocker, *n.*[1] *Obs.* [Of unknown origin.] Common sense, gumption.

1891 *Truth* (Sydney) 15 Mar. 7/3 This kit consisted of a tin can, a tin mug, a blanket, and a good deal of assurance. These, in bush parlance, are *billy, pannikin, bluey, and knocker.* **1900** H. LAWSON *On Track* 120 The old woman might have had the knocker to keep away from the bush while I was in quod.

knocker, *n.*[2] [Spec. use of *knocker* that which knocks.]

1. *Shearing.* See quots. 1941 and 1959.

1895 *Worker* (Sydney) 28 Sept. 4/1 And set to work with my file—Levelled my knockers quickly, and then I rigged them up in style. **1905** *Shearer* (Sydney) 23 Dec. 7/5 Half of their time is taken up in fixing fresh 'knockers', 'drivers', and 'dummies' on their shears. **1937** *Bulletin* (Sydney) 14 July 20/1 The 'knockers' had to be filed away, with the result that the heels of the blades overlapped when closed. **1941** S.J. BAKER *Pop. Dict. Austral. Slang* 42 *Knocker*, a leather pad fixed near the heel of a pair of hand shears to prevent the blade closing too deeply. **1959** H.P. TRITTON *Time means Tucker* 31 Shears do not click. The gullets of the blade are filled with soft wood, or sometimes with cork. These are called 'knockers' and they stop the heels of the blade from meeting. **1974** *Austral. Folksongs* (Folk Lore Council Aust.) 61 As I drove 'em to the knockers, and I chopped away the wool. **1982** P. ADAM SMITH *Shearers* 389 The knockers are really only put on to stop the noise of the blades grinding and clicking, and to stop the shears overlapping at the points.

2. [Cf. Br. slang *on the knocker* on credit (see OEDS 2 e.).] In the phr. **on the knocker,** (payment made) immediately, on demand, 'on the nail'.

1962 J. CLEARY *Country of Marriage* 297 Sid was a man who wanted cash on the knocker. **1965** L. HAYLEN *Big Red* 151 Never knew Tim to owe a penny... Always paid on the knocker. **1967** F. HARDY *Billy Borker yarns Again* 71 Settle our monthly bills dead on the knocker. **1973** J. POWERS *Last of Knucklemen* (1974) 96 Even money. A thousand on the knocker. **1975** *Austral.* (Sydney) 12 Aug. 9/4 He has to pay cash on the knocker for everything he buys, but he has to wait two or three months for payment from the big firms.

knock-off. [Used elsewhere but recorded earliest in Aust.: see OED(S *sb.* 2.] The time set for the day's work to finish. In full **knock-off time.**

1867 J.S. BORLASE *Night Fossickers* 97 By knock-off time I had taken out five pounds' weight of gold. [*Note*] Hour of leaving work. **1905** *Shearer* (Sydney) 25 Mar. 6/4 The N.S.W. civil service .. watch the clock for knock-off time with a sublime faith in that beautiful idea that time, not work means money. **1916** A. WILSON *Lays & Tales of Mines* 87 I'll send down a bit of 'crib' at 8 o'clock to keep you going 'til 'knock-off'. **1943** *Land Girls Gaz.* (Perth) June 1 We set ourselves a certain number [of cases] for the period until knock-off time. **1960** *Bulletin* (Sydney) 10 Aug. 19/2 Walking around the job after knock-off, he found a piece of timber almost cut through. **1981** A.B. FACEY *Fortunate Life* 226 Just before knock off time the new Ganger arrived.

knot. [See quot. 1898; later infl. by *knot* a mass as formed by a knot in string.]

1. In the phr. **to push the knot,** to travel carrying a swag.

1896 *Bulletin* (Sydney) 3 June 14/1 'Push the knot to 'Ungry'—walk to Hungerford. **1898** *Ibid.* 8 Oct. 15/1 *Re* derivation of 'pushing the knot'. When I wore the Order of the Wallaby .. swag was fastened near the ends with the binders, through which was passed the sling, so arranged that the knot came just below the breast and gave a rest for the hand, which thus acquired a habit of pushing the sling outwards from the body as the man neared the end of his tramp. **1905** *Ibid.* 13 Apr. 18/2 Pushing the 'knot' down a Darling tucker track, some time back. **1977** D. STUART *Drought Foal* 167 Hard work pushin' the knot, an' I don't suppose you're in much of a hurry.

2. A swag. Also *attrib.*

1911 *Bulletin* (Sydney) 20 July 13/2, I remember the time when a man could arrive per boot, with his 'knot' up, and obtain a contract for (say) grubbing or fencing. **1926** *Ibid.* 16 Dec. 24/3 The bearer of a light swag is generally looked upon with contempt by the professional waltzer of Matilda, whose 'knot' often weighs anything up to 100 lb. **1941** *Ibid.* 7 May 16/2 Most penurious knot-carriers I have met put night ease ahead of a little extra daytime labor. **1942** *Ibid.* 27 May 12/1 What with escaped aliens, national-register cards and sentries .. you never know when some official is going to spring out and demand to see whether the knot hides a secret radio. **1949** *Ibid.* 6 Apr. 15/4 The knot-humper had been given a feed at the farmhouse. **1955** *Ibid.* 29 June 12/4 Under our knots we were pushing into N.S.W. on the wrong side of Bogan Gate.

knuckle. In the phr. **to go the knuckle** (or **knuckles**), to fight; to punch.

1944 J. DEVANNY *By Tropic Sea & Jungle* 160, I always got on well with the blacks, because I never went the knuckle on them. **1968** S. GORE *Holy Smoke* 46 The biggest jokers among his mob .. able to go the knuckles a bit themselves. **1972** J. HIBBERD *Stretch of Imagination* (1973) 15 That's when you discovered us. Stacked on a turn. Went the knuckle. Dorabella shot through, abandoning her white bloomers on a low bough. **1977** B. SCOTT *My Uncle Arch* 63 They never did go the knuckle on each other over this sheila. **1984** *N.T. News* (Darwin) 13 Nov. 26/3 Katherine went the knuckle against Banks in the NT Football Association—and paid the price.

koala /koʊ'alə/. Formerly also **coola, koolah.** [a. Dharuk *gulawaŋ.*]

1. The arboreal, mainly nocturnal marsupial of e. Aust. *Phascolarctos cinereus*, having a stout body, thick grey-brown fur with a pale underside, large rounded furry ears, a leathery nose, strong claws and a vestigial tail. It feeds largely on the leaves of certain eucalypts, and is the faunal emblem of Qld.; BEAR; MONKEY BEAR; *native bear, sloth*, see NATIVE *a.* 6 b.; SLOTH; *tree-bear*, see TREE. Also *attrib.*, esp. as **koala bear.**

1798 *Hist. Rec. N.S.W.* (1895) III. 821 There is another animal which the natives call a cullawine, which much resembles the stoths [*sic*] in America. **1803** *Sydney Gaz.* 9 Oct., Serjeant Packer of Pitt's Row, has in his possession a native animal .. called by the natives, a Koolah. **1808** *Philos. Trans. R. Soc. London* XCVIII. 305 The koala is another species of the wombat... The natives call it the koala wombat; it .. was first brought to Port Jackson in August, 1803. **1827** P. CUNNINGHAM *Two Yrs. in N.S.W.* I. 317 Our *coola* (sloth or native bear) is about the size of an ordinary poodle dog, with shaggy, dirty coloured fur, no tail, and claws and feet like a bear, of which it forms a tolerable miniature. **1829** R. MUDIE *Picture of Aust.* 170 Of the animals whose teeth more particularly adapt them for gnawing bark, the most remarkable is the *Koala.* **1854** *Trans. Philos. Soc. Vic.* (1855) 68 The koala .. (*Phascolarctos cinereus*) frequents very high trees. **1886** D.M. GANE *N.S.W. & Vic.* 171 In admitting that we shot this koala, we must inform our readers that it was not for the mere satisfaction of bringing it down, but principally for the acquisition of its skin. **1901** 'A. FERRES' *Free Selector* 139 McGuffin gave a koala laugh when the boxing gloves he saw. **1921** M.E. FULLERTON *Bark House Days* 49 The trees .. in the day-time held up aloft the iron-clawed koala. **1937** C. KEARTON *I visit Antipodes* 132 The Koala Bear was first seen by a young explorer who journeyed to the Blue Mountains in 1798. **1955** F. LANE *Patrol to Kimberleys* 214 The name 'koala' means: 'nothing to drink'. These little bears drink nothing. They feed only on eucalyptus leaves. **1970** B. OAKLEY *Salute to Great McCarthy* 69 Koala nose, Beethoven glasses, thermos of coffee in his huge hand. **1984** *Tourist: Ansett Airlines Mag.* Jan. 4 Had enough of Oz tea-towels printed in Hong Kong, boomerangs made in Taiwan, koalas from Japan?

2. *transf.* and *fig.* A person, etc., treated as a protected species.

1942 *CPD* (H. of R.) VII. 1418 Does the Minister for the Army intend to deal with the naughty, nasty people who insist on referring to members of his beloved Militia as Koalas, because, under Australian law you must not shoot at them, and you must not export them. **1953** *Sydney Morning Herald* 3 Jan. 6/2 'Koalas', police or diplomatic cars, immune from being booked for parking offences, and therefore 'protected creatures'.

kobong /'koʊbɒŋ/. *Obs.* [a. Nyungar *koboŋ.*] A totem.

1841 G. GREY *Jrnls. Two Exped. N.-W. & W.A.* II. 228 Each family adopts some animal or vegetable, as their crest or sign, or *kobong*, as they call it. **1843** W. PRIDDEN *Aust.* 100 [The kangaroo] being one of the productions peculiar to Australia, it may be said, from the figures of it to be seen upon the back of every book relating to that country, to have become almost the *kobong* or crest of that southern region. **1851** MRS R. LEE *Adventures in Aust.* 168 Kinchela .. would not eat the former; and when asked why, he said it was 'Kobong', and he must not. **1894** A.F. CALVERT *Aborigines W.A.* 19 Each Australian Native family has its kobong, or crest. Some animal or vegetable is taken as the sign, and in recognition of this the owner of the kobong will never kill the animal to which it refers, should he find it asleep; while his family vegetable can only be gathered under certain conditions, and at special seasons of the year. **1901** M. VIVIENNE *Travels in W.A.* 337 Each family has its kobong, or cognisance, some animal or vegetable for which they have a reverence.

koel /'koʊəl/. [Transf. use of *kōēl* a cuckoo of India.] *Cooee bird*, see COOEE *n.* 4. Also *attrib.*

1903 *Emu* II. 211, I have only come across the Koel about Homestead. **1929** A.H. CHISHOLM *Birds & Green Places* 157 A koel cuckoo .. was rendered almost frantic by imitations of its curious notes. **1956** *Bulletin* (Sydney) 18 Apr. 13/3 A koel had somehow got into our bathroom, and, however gently and coaxingly I tried, there were still frantic flutterings and dashings against walls before it could be cornered and freed. **1976** *Reader's Digest Compl. Bk. Austral. Birds* 300 Although adult koels are mainly fruit-eaters, the nestlings are forced to take whatever is offered by their foster parents, such as insects and caterpillars.

koepanger /'kupæŋə/. [f. Du. *Koepang* (Kupang), the name of a town in w. Timor.] A diver, crew-hand, etc., recruited from or through Kupang to work in the pearling industry; a Timorese. Also *attrib.*

[**1902** *Cwlth. Parl. Papers* II. 1079 The Asiatics are got from three sources: .. (2) Koepang (in Timor). These men sign a 'musterrol' in Koepang before the Dutch authorities for a term of 20 months, at the end of which they have to be returned at employers' expense. **1933** L. KORNITZER *Trade Winds* 18 But these others, Corporal, Japs, Filipinos, Koepang men—they aren't whites?] **1936** T.E.A. HEALY *And far from Home* 57 The Malays, Koepangers and other coloured races conducted their religious services privately. **1937** I.L. IDRIESS *Forty Fathoms Deep* 168 The Japanese .. had almost displaced the Manilamen and Koepanger divers. **1948** *Sun* (Sydney) 12 Feb. 13/4 Having been diving for the past four months in competition with the Malays and Koepangers, he came in to tell us that he did not think much of the Government's idea to gradually supplant the colored divers with white men. **1954** N. BARTLETT *Pearl Seekers* 186 Koepangers from the Netherlands East Indies were the most tractable and most favoured crew boys. **1956** S. GORE *Overlanding with Annabel* 63 Five smartly-dressed Koepangers, pearling lugger hands from Broome, 440 miles away .. had flown in on the bi-weekly plane for a haircut. **1978** O. WHITE *Silent Reach* 160 There's an awful lot of fishin' boats workin' off the coast out there, hull down. Taiwanese, Nips, Koepangers—even bloody Russians.

koie-yan /'kɔɪ-jæn/. *Obs.* [Prob. a. Warrgamay *guriyan.*] The vigorous climbing plant *Faradaya splendida* (fam. Verbenaceae) of rainforest in n.e. Qld., having large leaves and clusters of fragrant white flowers. **1908** E.J. BANFIELD *Confessions of Beachcomber* 270 Another method by which the blacks secure fish in pools left by the receding tide is to scrape off the inner bark of the 'Koie-yan' (*Faradaya splendida*) with a shell. **1914** *Bulletin* (Sydney) 26 Feb. 22/4 Of these [fish poisons] the best is 'koie-yan', a Queensland vine, from which the outer bark is scraped, while the inside is macerated and thrown into the water. **1925** *Ibid.* 19 Feb. 24/4 Koie-yan is a pretty jungle-vine addicted to climbing trees.

kombo, var. COMBO.

konkleberry, var. CONKERBERRY.

kooditcha, var. KURDAITCHA.

kooka. Abbrev. of KOOKABURRA.

1906 *Bulletin* (Sydney) 22 Mar. 14/2 Our kookas fairly cackled with delight at the sight of raw beef. **1920** *Smith's Weekly* (Sydney) 11 Sept. 17/4 Once regarded the kookaburra as a paragon of all the virtues; now I know better... Lay in wait and met a 'kooka' carrying another dead 'un to the gully. **1942** C. BARRETT *From Bush Hut* 29 I've only once seen a kooka with a snake hanging from its beak. **1951** *Bulletin* (Sydney) 17 Oct. 13/2 There are two distinct types of kookas: the big fellow known as the swamp-jackass .. and the common—or—garden variety. **1984** *Age Weekender* (Melbourne) 7 Dec. 4/5 As the sun went down the kookas gave us a grand finale as we toasted the first of the season's great catches—and the first of the memorable outdoor feasts.

kookaburra /'kʊkəbʌrə/. Formerly also with much variety, esp. **kukuburra.** [a. Wiradhuri *gugubarra.*] Either of two Austral. kingfishers, the large, predom. brown and white laughing kookaburra, *Dacelo novaeguineae*, of s. and e. Aust. (introduced into Tas. and s.w. W.A.), having a distinctive loud, laughing call, and the *blue-winged kookaburra* (see BLUE *a.*); GOBURRA. See also LAUGHING JACKASS 1.

1834 G. BENNETT *Wanderings N.S.W.* I. 222 The natives at Yass call the bird 'Gogera', or 'Gogobera', probably from its peculiar note, which has some resemblance to the sound of the word. **1847** *Moreton Bay Courier* 29 May 4/3 They are most absurdly named laughing-jackasses, though some designate them the colonist's clock, and the natives, *cucaburra.* **a 1859** L. THRELKELD Specimens of Lang. Aborigines N.S.W. 130 Laughing Jackass, Kōōkūndi—Kookōōbarra. **1867** *Pasquin* (London) 7 Sept. 198 The cooguburra woke the silent wood. **1871** *Austral. Town & Country Jrnl.* (Sydney) 28 Jan. 99/4 A fellow-countryman of his .. had a cooraburra, or 'laughing jackass', which his friends jeered him about. **1881** *Bulletin* (Sydney) 21 May 8/4 List'ning to the Kookaburra pealing loud his grotesque lay. **1896** *Ibid.* 18 Apr. 27/2 From the Kamil comes the word 'kookaburra' for jackass. **1907** *Truth* (Sydney) 24 Feb. 1/5 It's enough to make a kukuburra forget his chuckle and weep. **1914** H.M. VAUGHAN *Australasian Wander-Yr.* 105 At sunset, the gum-forests rang with the elfin laughter of the kukaburra or laughing-jackass. **1917** *Bulletin* (Sydney) 23 Aug. 22/2 The Murra Warri tribe, between the Warrego and Culgoa rivers, named the brown jackass kugu-burra, of which our kookaburra is doubtless a corruption. **1926** A.A.B. APSLEY *Amateur Settlers* 41 Kuku-burras echoed their evening chorus. **1926** M. FORREST *Hibiscus Heart* 130 On the mountain top the kookaburra were preparing to chortle their farewells to the day. **1935** T. RAYMENT *Cluster of Bees* 63 The sudden swoop of the kookaburra, diving at the haystack for the suspicious mouse. **1944** *Aust. Week-End Bk.* 12 That slapstick comedian, the kookaburra, splitting his sides over his own private joke. **1963** A. UPFIELD *Madman's Bend* 32 The kookaburras watched him conveying meat to the house, their wonderful eyes beady. **1973** D. WOLFE *Brass Kangaroo* 268 The kookaburras .. kill the little birds and eat the young ones in the nests. **1975** *Bronze Swagman Bk. Bush Verse* 24 O carol, carol, magpies gay, While shy koala peeps; Laugh, kookaburra, laugh with glee While little Jesus sleeps.

kooky. [f. KOOK(ABURRA + -Y.] KOOKABURRA. Also **kooky jack** (see JACK *n.*[1]).

1918 L.J. VILLIERS *Changing Yr.* 24 Too flamin' soon we're roused be Kooky Jack. **1930** *Bulletin* (Sydney) 14 May 20/2, I found two kookies—full-grown birds—under a small bush.

koolah, var. KOALA.

kooliman, var. COOLAMON.

koonkerberry, var. CONKERBERRY.

koori /'kʊri/, *n.*[1] Also **koorie** and formerly **coorie, kuri, kurri.** [a. Awabakal (and other n. N.S.W. languages) *guri* man.] An Aboriginal (now used chiefly by Aborigines). Also *attrib.*

1834 L.E. THRELKELD *Austral. Grammar* 87 *Ko-re*, man, mankind. **1845** C. HODGKINSON *Aust., Port Macquarie to Moreton Bay* 54 They .. informed me that the Bellengen corees (black fellows), were belcoula, (not angry). **1892** J. FRASER *Aborigines N.S.W.* 2 The kuri, *or* 'blackman' is usually kind and affectionate to his jin, 'wife'. **1966** M. BROWN *Jimberi Track* 40 At any moment the dogs were liable to be sent racing through the camp, or some koorie or other set screaming. **1970** R. ROBINSON *Altjeringa* 30 These wild Kurris were runnin' out of the scrub. **1973** D. WOLFE *Brass Kangaroo* 306 You should get rid of the white bosses here and let us koories run the station. **1977** K. GILBERT *Living Black* 201 How many Kooris, town or mission, would be prepared to come out here and put up signs saying 'This is an Aboriginal Burial Ground. Keep Off. This is a Sacred Area.' Who'd be in it? **1985** J. MILLER *Koori* 218 Since I believe in Koori land rights and no dams on the Franklin River, that makes me a black, greenie, pinko.

koori, /'kʊri/, *n.*[2] [a. Panyjima *kurri* marriageable teenage girl.] A young Aboriginal woman.

1908 *West Austral.* (Perth) 22 Feb. 12/3 Do you remember .. there was a coorie and two piccaninnies. .. What was her age? About ten or eleven. **1968** D. O'GRADY *Bottle of Sandwiches* 28 The only women around the place were the gins and coories of his Aboriginal stockmen. **1985** MARIS & BORG *Women of Sun* 94 If you were a koori, what chance did you have of finding a job?—except .. cleaning up whitefeller's dirt?

kopi /'koʊpi/. Also **kopai.** [Prob. a. Bagandji *gapi.*] A fine powdery gypsum occurring near salt lakes in arid areas, and used in ritual Aboriginal mourning; a more cohesive, gypsum-rich mass, sometimes a rock, found where opal is mined. Also *attrib.*

1889 *Rec. Geol. Survey N.S.W.* I. 3 There is abundance of earthy gypsum, locally called 'Copi', present in patches over this country. **1897** J.J. KNIGHT *Brisbane* 42 We came on a small tract of 'kopi country' (powdered gypsum). **1898** D.W. CARNEGIE *Spinifex & Sand* 91 An effective method of clearing muddy clay-pan water is by dropping into it a sort of powdery gypsum called 'Kopi' by the natives, which is usually to be found round the margin of the salt lakes. **1915** J.P. BOURKE *Off Bluebush* 97 He rests at the foot of a kopi hill By the old Coolgardie track. **1935** R.B. PLOWMAN *Boundary Rider* 265 That white stuff is kopi to show she is in mourning. **1951** E. HILL *Territory* 19 If you happened to call on a burial, you would see .. women of the dead men .. wearing heavy widows' caps of kopi, black man's plaster of Paris. **1967** G. JENKIN *Two Yrs. Bardunyah Station* 8 Patches of Kopi—a white powder something like talcum which is often two or three feet deep. **1972** N. MILES *Opal Fever* 13 The white kopi mullock-heaps of the opal workings. **1978** D. STUART *Wedgetail View* 92 Lake beds dry and salt-crusted with islands of dirty white kopai country where stunted mallees struggled to survive.

koradji /kə'rædʒi/. Also formerly in a wide variety of unfixed spellings. [a. Dharuk *garaji.*] An Aboriginal having recognised skills in traditional medicine and (freq.) a role in ceremonial life. For words taken from other Aboriginal languages, see BOYLYA and WARRA-WARRA; for those applied by colonists to denote a perceived function or power of such a person, see *clever man* CLEVER 1, CONJUROR, DOCTOR *n.*[1], MEDICINE MAN, *native doctor* NATIVE *a.* 5, PRIEST, SORCERER, WISE MAN, and WIZARD.

1793 W. TENCH *Compl. Acct. Settlement* 232 Yellomundee was a Cár-ad-yee, or Doctor of renown. **1793** J. HUNTER *Hist. Jrnl. Trans. Port Jackson* 523 Having taken leave of their new friends the *Car-ra-dy-gans* (doctors), our party set off. **1805** J. TURNBULL *Voyage round World* I. 85 This operation is performed very simply by their curradiges or wise-men. **1826** L.E. THRELKELD *Austral. Reminisc. & Papers* (1974) I. 50 The doctor, or rather sorcerer .. [*Note*] Called *karakal* by the Awabakal, but known more widely by Europeans as *koraje* or *koradji.* **1829** R. MUDIE *Picture of Aust.* 265 The Carradhys are physicians, as well as performers of ceremonies. **1834** G. BENNETT *Wanderings N.S.W.* I. 155 The kradjee, priest, soothsayer, or physician, (for he appears to exercise the functions of each). **1845** C. GRIFFITH *Present State & Prospects Port Phillip* 163 Their sorcerers, priests, or koragees (as they are called) are the interpreters of .. customary laws. **1851** J. HENDERSON *Excursions & Adventures N.S.W.* II. 107 All belonging to the tribe are equal, unless perhaps the *crodgy*, or doctor, who appears to be a kind of quack and leader of the ceremonies combined. **1878** R.B. SMYTH *Aborigines of Vic.* I. 62 When a lad has to be initiated, he is removed to some remote and secluded spot, and when it is night, the coradjes (priests and doctors), painted and decorated with feathers, &c., begin their operations. **1899** J. MATHEW *Eaglehawk & Crow* 142 The titles of these magicians varied with the community... *Koradji* was the name applied in the neighbourhood of Sydney, and it still holds the ground among Europeans. **1913** *Bulletin* (Sydney) 21 Aug. 18/1 The grave was the property of a Lachlan River chief and 'Karadja' (medicine) man. **1932** *Ibid.* 22 June 20/2 A crajee, or wise man, of a Richmond River clan years ago told me all about the place of unrest and torment where the bad Binghis go. **1937** *Leaves from Diary of Lunatic* 14 Only the Koradjee men (doctors or wizards) could tell where he lay hidden. **1946** A.P. ELKIN *Aboriginal Men High Degree* 19, I have known white persons almost fear the eyes of a *karadji*, so all-seeing, deep and quiet did they seem. This 'clever man' was definitely an outstanding person. **1965** A.W. REED *Aboriginal Words Aust.* 96 *Koradji (coradgee)*, clever man, medicine man, sorcerer.

Kosciusko minnow /kɒziɒskoʊ 'mɪnoʊ/. [See quot. 1906.] The small fresh-water fish *Galaxias olidus*, widespread in e. mainland Aust.

1906 D.G. STEAD *Fishes of Aust.* 50 The Kosciusko Minnow .. is found on the highlands of the Monaro and Snowy River Districts, particularly in the neighbourhood of Mount Kosciusko, the 'roof' of Australia, from which it takes its name. **1933** D. MACDONALD *Brooks of Morning* 115 The clear, cold pinnacle stream, of which the spotted Kosciusko minnow is still the sole occupant.

kukuburra, var. KOOKABURRA.

kunzea /'kʌnziə/. [The plant genus *Kunzea* was named by German botanist H.G.L. Reichenbach (*Conspect. Reg. Veg.* (1828) 175) after the botanist and physician G. *Kunze* (1793–1851), Professor of Botany at Leipzig.] Any shrub or small tree of the genus *Kunzea* (fam. Myrtaceae) of s. Aust., having attractive, fluffy flowers for which some species are cultivated.

1942 C. BARRETT *Austral. Wild Flower Bk.* 149 Some of the Kunzeas are small trees up to about twenty feet high; others never grow out of shrubhood and one lives close to the ground. **1956** E. MITCHELL *Black Cockatoos* 87 In late spring the pink Kunzea flowered in a soft cloud. **1981** *Bulletin* (Sydney) 21 Apr. (Lit. Suppl.) 25/2 Purple hovea beside our feet, Snow daisies and kunzea's foam.

kurara, var. KARARA.

kurdaitcha /kə'daɪtʃə/. Also **kadaitcha, kaditcha, kooditcha.** [Poss. a. Aranda *kerdayje.*]

1. A malignant spirit. Also **kurdaitcha spirit.**

1886 E.M. CURR *Austral. Race* I. 148 It was discovered in 1882, or thereabouts, that the Blacks to the westward of Lake Eyre .. wear a sort of shoe when they attack their enemies by stealth at night. Some of the tribes call these shoes *Kooditcha*, their name for an invisible spirit... The soles were made of the feathers of the emu, stuck together with a little human blood... The uppers were nets made of human hair. The object of these shoes is to prevent those who wear them from being tracked... It is only on the softest ground that they leave any mark, and even then it is impossible to distinguish the heel from the toe. **1901** G. WHITE *Across Aust.* 28 During the night the blackboy rushed up to the fire crying out that the Kadaitcha was out after him with a spear and a firestick. The Kadaitcha is an evil spirit or ghost. **1920** C.H. Sayce *Golden Buckles* 99 'What is a Kadaitcha?' 'Oh—that's a kind of avenging spirit—devil if you like—who deals out stoush to anyone who breaks the rule. He's supposed to enter into one of the niggers, and the poor beggar can't rest till the other chap is avenged.' 'A kind of blood-avenger,' suggested Tynan. 'Yes, something of that kind.' **1936** 'L. Kaye' *Black Wilderness* 108 'Thos' fellers like catch 'm me or Kombi. Fright of this country, me. All same *kaditcha*.' .. '*Kaditcha*' he said in fear, as he trekked not through darkness filled with spearmen merely, but with things supernatural and terrible. The witch doctors and witchcraft of an alien tribe were out there in the night. **1944** M.J. O'Reilly *Bowyangs & Boomerangs* 142 There is one great Spirit, who is everywhere, knowing everything, even to the innermost thought of the Allatunga, or headman. The spirit is called 'Kaditcha'. He controls the elements, sends good or bad seasons, according to the behaviour of the tribe. **1952** A.M. Duncan-Kemp *Where Strange Paths go Down* 151 'Kadaitcha' really means—if one can read the aboriginal's mind—the spirit of evil or anyone sneaking about with evil intent. **1952** A.W. Upfield *New Shoe* 13 A mopoke 'Ma-parked' at him .. and later still a curlew screamed like a kurdaitcha spirit is alleged to do when after an aborigine away from his camp at night. **1953** J.K. Ewers *With Sun on my Back* 171 If the children speak in wide-eyed wonder of 'the Kurdaitcha', it is no more than an environmental equivalent of the white youngsters' 'bogey-man'. **1957** F. Clune *Fortune Hunters* 68 The five murderers and Wong-we, overcoming their fear of the *Kadaitcha* who roam in the night, had sneaked from the camp-fire and escaped into the mulga scrub.

2. A shoe, worn esp. on a mission of vengeance, so made as to leave no trace of the wearer's movements: see quot. 1886. Also **kurdaitcha boot (shoe, slipper).**

1886 [see sense 1]. **1901** G. White *Across Aust.* 28 When a black is about some nefarious purpose he puts on Kadaitcha shoes, made of emu's feathers, and leaving no track. **1933** F.E. Baume *Tragedy Track* 84 The dogs fail to hear the approach of the warriors who have been chosen to wear the trackless kaditcha boot of emu feathers stuck together with human blood and woven into a shoe without toe or heel, so that no one can tell from the tracks how a native is moving. **1952** *Bulletin* (Sydney) 23 Apr. 17/3 They are Kadaitcha slippers, not 'boots'. **1970** K. Willey *Naked Island* 138 Whenever they found a patch of stony ground the party would put on the kadaitchas, spirit shoes of emu and turkey feathers which made the wearers' tracks invisible. **1977** J. Carter *All Things Wild* 61 They seek out their victim by stealth, wearing magic kurdaitcha shoes, fashioned from kangaroo fur string and emu feathers. These leave no tracks.

3. a. A mission of vengeance; the ritual accompanying this. Also *attrib.*

1895 *Proc. R. Soc. Vic.* (1896) 66 The shoes themselves in this district are known by the name of 'Urtathurta', and the occasion on which they were used is spoken of as 'Kūrdaitcha lūma ' (Kūrdaitcha—a bad or evil spirit, and luma, to walk). The wearing of the Urtathurta and going Kūrdaitcha lūma appears to have been the medium for a form of vendetta. **1896** B. Spencer *Rep. Horn Sci. Exped. Central Aust.* IV. 110 When a native for some reason desired to kill a member of another camp or another tribe he consulted the medicine man of his camp, and arrangements were made for a kurdaitcha luma. **1928** —— *Wanderings in Wild Aust.* 261 The Kurdaitcha is only a special one amongst many forms of magic and, like many other things, a great deal of humbug is associated with it. **1938** F.J. Hayter *Deadly Magic* 13 The Pointing Bone and the Pointing Stick serve the same general purpose but the former is usually made use of in cases of tribal reprisal for wrong doing, included in the native term Kurdaitcha. **1940** E. Hill *Great Austral. Loneliness* (ed. 2) 175 Kurdaitcha, the blood vengeance .. extends throughout the whole of unoccupied Central Australia. **1943** *Coast to Coast 1942* 167 'They mean to get him. Last night he found *kaditcha* tracks round his camp. . . ' 'What do you mean? What sort of track. . . ' Dingo made a sound in his throat. 'Call y'self desert bred—*kaditcha*, that's what I said—meaning the shoes abos make themselves out of emu's feathers stuck together with blood and hitched on with a bit of hair string; meaning likewise vengeance; sort of executioner's mask.' **1972** M. Cassidy *Dispossessed* 95 Whatever the cost to himself in labour or in personal feelings he must keep the Kuradaitcha Oath. **1959** L. Rose *Country of Dead* 29 'It seems to have been some tribal affair. You know, the sort of thing that will take Native Affairs weeks to unravel.' 'A kurdaitja killing, then?' **1962** V.C. Hall *Dreamtime Justice* 138 This water country would hold no tracks for the eyes of any men who walked the Kadaitja trail—the mission of revenge.

b. In the phr. **to go kurdaitcha,** to embark on such a mission.

1901 F.J. Gillen *Diary* 23 May (1968) 88 The members of a group fully realise that they cannot go Kurdaitja, that they cannot in fact impart to the feather shoes the magic properties which make them leave no track. **1927** Spencer & Gillen *Arunta* 458 Many will . . confess that they do go Kurdaitcha.

4. One who undertakes a mission of vengeance. Also **kurdaitcha man.**

1927 Spencer & Gillen *Arunta* 458 We have met several Kurdaitcha men who claim to have killed their victim. **1952** *Bulletin* (Sydney) 23 Apr. 17/3 In primitive aboriginal society the kadaitcha man was the official killer. **1953** A.W. Upfield *Murder must Wait* 121 Those prints would be followed back to the tree, where the kurdaitcha put on his great boots and mounted a bike to go back to Mitford. **1961** J.W. Bleakely *Aborigines of Aust.* 61 The sorcerers, known as kadaitcha, seem to work as though members of a secret society. **1982** *Bulletin* (Sydney) 23 Mar. 42/1 The practice among Aborigines—most notably among the Kadaitcha men—of controlling their heart rate, breathing and body temperature.

kuri, var. Koori.

kurrajong /ˈkʌrədʒɒŋ/. Also **currajong.** [a. Dharuk *garajuŋ*.]

1. A name given to any of several plants yielding a useful fibre; spec., any of several such trees of the genera *Brachychiton* (see also Bottle tree) and *Sterculia*, esp. the fodder tree *B. populneus* of N.S.W., Qld., Vic., and N.T.; Ordnance tree. Also *attrib.*

[**1793** J. Hunter *Hist. Jrnl. Trans. Port Jackson* 408 *Carra-duin*, a fishing-line.] **1801** *HRA* (1915) 1st Ser. III. 179 Many parts are covered with a new hibiscus, which the natives use as flax for making their nets and for other purposes. This plant is much superior to the carradgan, which is of the same species. *Ibid.* 415 The cedar and curradjong are more plentiful up the new river than any other part. **1825** B. Field *Geogr. Mem. N.S.W.* 60 The nets used for fishing are made by the men from the bark of the kurrajong (hibiscus heterophyllus) a shrub which is very common in the swamps. **1835** J. Backhouse *Narr. Visit Austral. Colonies* 19 Sept. (1843) 314 One of the trees .. is *Sterculia diversifolia*; it resembles the Oak in form, and the Poplar in foliage. . . It attains to forty feet . . and its bark is so tenacious as to be convertible into cordage; whence it also, is called Corrijong. Its roots are thick and soft, so as to be cooked for food by the natives. The trunk . . is remarkably thick and green. **1847** E.B. Kennedy *Extracts Jrnl. Exped. Central Aust.* 263, I left the horses (all endeavouring to obtain shelter from a solitary Kurrajong tree, which was scarcely capable of affording shade to one). **1874** J.J. Halcombe *Emigrant & Heathen* 58 The chief variety in the foliage is made by the currajong, which, in bark, and in the colour and shape of its leaves, is very like the pear-tree. **1889** E. Giles *Aust. twice Traversed* I. 73 We passed the night under the umbrage of a colossal Currajong-tree. **1895** *Proc. Linnean Soc. N.S.W.* X. 396 (*note*) Among the white people of Australia the name kurrajong is applied to a tree (*Brachychiton*), but the natives in most parts give it a different name and say that kurrajong is white fellow name. It seems to me that the tree obtained its name through a misunderstanding because it yields a fibre that is frequently used by aborigines for making nets. This fibre is called kurrajong by some natives, which seems to have led to the name being applied to the tree. On the other hand, as the Omeo blacks called their bush as well as the fibre kurrajong, such may possibly be the case with the Brachychiton tree in some tribal dialects. **1915** *Bulletin* (Sydney) 15 July 24/3 Let me nominate kurrajong as the best all-round vegetable-friend the dry-country farmer can have. **1931** *Ibid.* 18 Mar. 21/2 Thirty years ago 'kurrajong coffee' was a common beverage in Australia wherever the tree from which it took its name grew. **1948** H.A. Lindsay *Bushman's Handbk.* 8 Right out in what is almost desert . . is another tree with these curious water-filled swellings on the roots; it is the kurrajong. **1956** D. Rowbotham *Town & City* 117 We boiled the billy near a grand old kurrajong. **1970** J.V. Marshall *Walk to Hills of Dreamtime* 153 *Kurrajong*[:] *Brachychiton populneum*, a graceful tree growing to about sixty feet, with oval lobed leaves and green-to-white flowers rich in nectar. The young shoots are often eaten by cattle and used by Aborigines to make dilly-bags. **1986** *Sun-Herald* (Sydney) 26 Jan. 7/3 Kurrajongs are highly prized as feed for livestock during drought. Large trees can take 100 years to grow. At this time of the year they are usually so leafy a cockatoo could fly into them and not be seen.

2. With distinguishing epithet: **desert kurrajong,** the tree of W.A., N.T., and S.A. *Brachychiton gregorii*, occurring in sandy country in drier Aust.

1948 C.P. Mountford *Brown Men & Red Sand* 129 The desert kurrajong (*Brachychiton gregorii*) with its smooth, light-green trunks, and symmetrical heads of lush-green foliage, is one of the most beautiful of the desert trees. **1969** A.A. Abbie *Original Australs.* 74 Ground into flour, as are the seeds of the Desert Kurrajong tree.

3. *Austral. pidgin. Obs.* In the phr. **to give** (someone) **kurrajong,** to hang (someone) with a rope made from kurrajong fibre.

[**1830** R. Dawson *Present State Aust.* 43 They strangled him by a narrow slip of bark, called by the natives *curryjung*.] **1848** *Maitland Mercury* 8 Nov. 2/1 When the white men tried to prevent these outrages the blacks told them plainly that the magistrate would give them curryjong (i.e. hang them). **1851** J. Henderson *Excursions & Adventures N.S.W.* II. 284 Up to the last moment, he thought the threat to 'give him curryjung', that is, to hang him, was 'all gammon'.

kurrawong, var. Currawong.

kurri, var. Koori.

kwee-ai, var. Queeai.

kylie /ˈkaɪli/. Also **kiley.** [a. Nyungar (and other w. Austral. languages) *karli*.]

1. Chiefly *W.A.* Boomerang *n.* 1.

1835 G.F. Moore *Diary Ten Yrs. W.A.* (1884) 358, I am sorry that nasty word 'boomerang' has been suffered to supercede [*sic*] the proper name. Boomerang is a corruption used at Sydney by the white people, but not the native word, which is tur-ra-ma; but 'kiley' is the name here. **1838** J. Backhouse *Extracts from Lett.* (1839) v. 40 As different tribes excelled each other in the manufacture of different weapons, such as spears, throwing sticks (woomeras), kylers (boomrings), shields, and waddies, these formed the articles of exchange. **1842** *Geelong Advertiser* 28 Mar. 1/5 Of all the advantages we have derived from our Australian settlements, none seems to have given more universal satisfaction than the introduction of some crooked pieces of wood shaped like a horse's shoe, or crescent moon; and called boomerang, waumerang, or kilee. **1845** J. Brady *Descr. Vocab. Native Lang. W.A.* 28 Ky-li, a flat curved thowing [*sic*] weapon made plain on one side and slightly convex on the other. **1872** Mrs E. Millett *Austral. Parsonage* 221 The flat curved wooden weapon, called a *kylie* . . the natives have invented for the purpose of killing several birds out of a flock at one throw. **1885** M.A. Barker *Lett. to Guy* 177 There are heavier 'ground kylies', which skim along the ground, describing marvellous turns and twists, and they would certainly break the leg of any bird or beast they hit. **1923** E.J. Stuart *Land of Opportunities* 20 The performance ended with kylie (boomerang) throwing, and many of the men made these curious weapons circle round them three or four times. **1927** M. Terry *Through Land of Promise* 184 The boomerang and kylie are similar to look at, but quite different in action. . . The kylie, used by the hunter, goes straight out and stays out. **1943** *Bulletin* (Sydney) 29 Dec. 13/1 Walking into swamps and lagoons chin-deep to retrieve wild duck brought down by kylie or throwing-stick. **1963** X. Herbert *Disturbing Element* 7 He . . let us teach him how to hunt and fish with a hoop-iron kylie. **1971** K. Gilbert *End of Dreamtime* 24 Whirling high to beating kylies and the thump of stamping feet while didjeridoos are dreeing to the weird outlandish beat.

2. *transf.* See quot. 1945.

1945 S.J. Baker *Austral. Lang.* 176 The small piece of board upon which the two pennies are rested for spinning is called the *kip, stick, bat* or *kiley*. **1955** N. Pulliam *I traveled Lonely Land* 76 The game is played with two pennies, a mattress, a thin piece of wood called a 'kip' (sometimes a stick or a kiley), and amazing dexterity and ardor.

L

laap, var. LERP.

labour. Also **labor.** As **labor. a.** The wage-earning sector of the population, viewed with regard to its political interests. **b.** With initial capital: short for 'Labor Party', from 1918 for 'Australian Labor Party'. Freq. *attrib.*

1870 *Age* (Melbourne) 5 Nov. 2/5 In August last a labor convention was held at Cincinatti to consider the desirability of forming a political party that should be consecrated to 'labor reform'. **1890** *Ibid.* 14 Aug. 4/6 If either of the great principles for which the labor organisations contend were to be threatened, the sympathy of the public would be with the men. **1892** *Ibid.* 5 Mar. 6/7 Two of the labor candidates have now spoken out at Prahran, and we may congratulate them on having been reasonable in their tone. **1911** H.G. TURNER *First Decade Austral. Cwlth.* 198 The Labor Caucus . . submitted the names of twenty-one candidates to an exhaustive ballot. **1926** G. BLACK *Hist. N.S.W. Political Labor Party* ii. 10 My Labor comrades adopted my head-covering, which afterwards was known widely as 'the Labor Hat'. **1934** *Manifesto* (Austral. Labor Party Qld.) 6/1 Labor would . . lag behind the political constitution of the Commonwealth, and would correspond in its structure to the parochial state of things prevailing before Australian nationhood was achieved. **1948** H.W. CRITTENDEN *Rogues' Paradise* 11 The lower half under the 'Labor' banner is the more aggressive and supplies the positive pole of Australian politics. **1964** *Austral.* (Sydney) 30 Dec. 6/7 For Calwell, Labor was always right. **1973** *Age* (Melbourne) 21 May 9/6 Labor's rural rump calls the tune. **1983** *Sydney Morning Herald* 7 Sept. 9/2 N.S.W. provides an excellent example of how Labor can get on with the bush. **1986** *Ibid.* 15 Feb. 6/2 Labor losing hearts and minds beyond the Divide.

2. Usu. as **labour.** *Hist.*

a. Used *attrib.* as a euphemism for KANAKA B. 1.

1872 *Australasian* (Melbourne) 5 Oct. 434/1 Dr Murray, of 'labour-collecting' fame, gets off very well indeed. **1892** J.G. PATON *Slavery under British Flag* 4 Your last Royal Commission brought before the world such a record of kidnapping and crime in one year, by the witnesses of all the six labour vessels whose conduct it enquired into. **1898** *Bulletin* (Sydney) 12 Mar. 14/3 T'other day at Bundaberg (Q.) the cook of a labor-vessel took up his headquarters.

b. With reference to communities established to provide rural work for the unemployed.

1893 *Act* (N.S.W.) 56 Vict. no. 34, An Act to establish and regulate Labour Settlements on Crown Lands. **1894** *Bulletin* (Sydney) 10 Nov. 6/2 The idea of founding labour settlements was conceived by city politicians who had a vague conviction that agriculture was an instinct. **1898** M. DAVITT *Life & Progress* 73 The traveller in South Australia . . should pay a visit to the labour settlements on the Murray River. . . These Labour Villages originated in an unemployed agitation in Adelaide and district in the winter of 1893. *Ibid.* 152 Under the Act of 1893 land . . can be appropriated for purposes of homestead associations, Labour colonies, and village settlements. **1899** *Austral. Tit-Bits* (Sydney) 68/1 Mr William Squire, the manager of Labour Colony at Levingatha [*sic*] Victoria, has been twice suspended. **1917** *NSWPD* 2nd Ser. vol. 69 1930 The object of this bill is to put the finishing touch to two unfortunate settlements which were started in the year 1893 as co-operative labour settlements. **1924** S.H. ROBERTS *Hist. Austral. Land Settlement* 330 At the same time 'labour colonies' were set up for a totally different class of persons, the 'absolutely destitute'.

lace monitor. [See quot. 1962.] The large, tree-climbing monitor *Varanus varius*, widespread in e. mainland Aust.; any lizard of the genus *Varanus* (see GOANNA 1). Also **lace lizard, laced lizard.**

1789 A. PHILLIP *Voyage to Botany Bay* 279 Laced Lizard. . . This beautiful Lizard is not uncommon at *Port Jackson*, where it is reputed a harmless species. **1880** F. MCCOY *Prodromus Zool. Vic.* (1890) II. v. Pl. 41, The present Lace Lizard is generally arboreal, climbing the forest trees with ease. **1914** H.M. VAUGHAN *Australasian Wander-Yr.* 240 The iguana, or lace monitor (*Varannus* [*sic*] *varius*), is, at least to a 'new chum', most alarming in his attitude and aspect. **1932** M.R. WHITE *No Roads go By* 233 Dick Willow, a full-blooded black, was licking his shiny chops after polishing off a large-sized carney, i.e., a lace lizard. **1962** B.W. LEAKE *Eastern Wheatbelt Wildlife* 101 The lace lizard is so called because of the yellow spots all over the body, which is dark green in colour, though less so than that of the bungare. **1968** R. HILL *Bush Quest* 56 The lace monitor is the common goanna of our eastern States. It can be found almost anywhere in lightly timbered country, being largely arboreal in its habits.

Lady Blamey. [f. the name of the wife of *Sir* Thomas *Blamey* (1884–1951), soldier.] See quot. 1972.

1945 *Action Front: Jrnl. 2/2 Field Regiment* May 11 Ernie Stagg wanted to know where his large supply of 'Lady Blameys' would go in the kit layout. **1945** *Chocolate & Green* (Sydney) July 50 With frothing Lady Blameys in their hands. [**1972** *Sydney Morning Herald* 28 Oct. 8/8 Lady Blamey stayed put and continued her welfare work. During this time she gave her name to the 'bottle' drinking glass used by thousands of Diggers. She taught them to slice an empty bottle cleanly in half with the aid of kerosene-soaked string. The string was wound round the bottle, and set alight. When the bottle was hot it was plunged into water and would break cleanly. The men used the lower part for drinking.] **1976** B. NORMAN *Bush Pilot* 71 Fortunately for me I had a silver pewter while they were using 'Lady Blameys' (beer bottles cut in half with the edges rounded).

lady's finger. Also **lady finger.**

1. A tall-growing variety of banana of commercial importance in Aust.; the short, sweet fruit of the plant. Also **lady('s) finger banana.**

1893 MRS C. PRAED *Outlaw & Lawmaker* II. 91 They were sitting . . in the banana grove, whither Elsie had gone on pretext of finding some still ungathered 'Lady's fingers'. **1911** A.J. BOYD *Banana in Qld.* 30 *Lady's Finger* . . has much the appearance as to colour of fruit and flesh as the Cavendish; it is an excellent dessert fruit. **1959** N.W. SIMMONDS *Bananas* 145 The cultivation of the tall 'Lady's finger' banana on the Queensland flats. **1965** *Austral. Encycl.* I. 406 Another variety of some importance is the Lady Finger or Manilla banana. **1981** P. BAXTER *Growing Fruit in Aust.* 164 The main types of banana grown commercially in Australia are the smaller 'Cavendish' . . and the taller sugar banana ('Lady Finger').

2. A variety of grape; the fruit of this, a large, elongated dessert grape. Also **lady('s) finger grape.**

1892 E. REEVES *Homeward Bound* 90 The very finest ladies'-fingers, sweet-waters, and muscatels. **1907** F. TURNER *Anderson's Man. Vegetable Garden* 116 Lady's Finger—The berries of this variety are long, and have a delicious flavour. **1916** C. ROSS *Observations on Grapes* 16 Lady's Finger is largely grown in South Australia, and is a popular late market variety, although coarse and of poor flavour. **1924** L.H. BRUNNING *Austral. Gardener* 198 The following sorts are all suitable for growing for table use in the Home Garden . . Black Hambro, Lady Finger. **1966** H. PORTER *Paper Chase* 17 Bunches of Lady Finger and Black Hambro grapes.

lady's waist. A small, slender, waisted beer glass; the drink contained in this.

1934 *Bulletin* (Sydney) 4 Apr. 20/1 A daintier goblet I never fingered than the hourglass shape of a lady's waist. **1941** S.J. BAKER *Pop. Dict. Austral. Slang* 42 *Lady's Waist*, a gracefully shaped glass in which beer is served; . . the drink served. **1943** *Bulletin* (Sydney) 5 Jan. 12/1 Whatever you think of a Lady's Waist Or a Barmaid's Blush or a Horse's Neck, A bull-whale's Crush or a Slippery Deck, There's nothing solid in what ghosts drink. **1956** S. HOPE *Diggers' Paradise* 232 What is called a 'lady's waist' in some parts of the country is generally known as a 'butcher'. **1980** B. HORNADGE *Austral. Slanguage* 230 The old terms of *lady's waist* (Sydney) and *pixie* (Melbourne) for small glasses appear to have disappeared from the scene. **1985** *Bulletin* (Sydney) 24 Dec. 62/2 The shearers and drovers I met at Coonabarabran drank from the smallest, known as a lady's waist (five ounces)—probably because it was so hot the beer in a schooner would get flat and warm.

lag, *v.* [Spec. use of *lag* to transport to penal servitude: see OED *v.*[3] 2.]

1. *trans.* To transport (a convict) from Britain to a penal settlement in Australia; to sentence (a criminal) to a term of imprisonment.

1812 J.H. VAUX *Mem.* (1819) II. 185 *Lag*, to transport for seven years or upwards. **1827** *Monitor* (Sydney) 27 Apr. 396 Stealing a bit of bread on the road, to satisfy hunger, would have *lagged* him for life. **1839** *Sydney Standard* 6 May 3/1 You do not boast the distinguished honour of having been *lagged* yourself, or of even being the son of a *lag*. **1843** *Colonial Observer* (Sydney) 9 Sept. 1285/1 We find him . . *lagged* and transported, it may be to Norfolk Island. **1853** H.B. JONES *Adventures in Aust.* 105 Our guide . . had been a whipper-in to some hounds before he was 'lagged', somewhere in . . Lancashire. **1859** H. KINGSLEY *Recoll. Geoffry Hamlyn* II. 22 They wouldn't lag a man for that. **1873** A. TROLLOPE *Aust. & N.Z.* II. 21 Now and then good-natured reference is made in regard to some lady or gentleman to the fact that her or his father was 'lagged'. **1891** *Hist. Bushranging* 42 The people lagged at Beechworth no more had revolvers in their hands than you have at present. **1903** J. FURPHY *Such is Life* 287 Why, just now, I saw your two horses in the paddock as I came up; and, if I was to be lagged for it, I couldn't think where I had seen them before. **1908** *Truth* (Sydney) 5 Apr. 9/4 And it isn't quite apparent why the Fats love Hingland so, Didn't Mother 'lag' their parents in the days not long ago? **1916** H.L. ROTH *Sketches & Reminisc. Qld.* 5 The stranger turned out to be a very old man of a class not uncommonly met with in those days—a convict, one who had been 'lagged' for 'lifting' copper boilers, and had been one of the early lot of transports to Moreton Bay District when it was a penal settlement. **1943** J. DEVINE *Rats of Tobruk* 95 Though it had not been his fault he was blamed and 'lagged'. When he got out he managed to get two years for pinching three hundred fowls. **1955** STEWART & KEESING *Austral. Bush Ballads* 8 But in the end they lagged him, Two-and-thirty years in all.

2. a. *trans.* To inform against (a person) with the object of securing arrest and imprisonment.

1832 *Currency Lad* (Sydney) 10 Nov. 3 Morrison had uttered threats that 'if his master turned him in, he would turn *him* in, and lag him'; if he could not *lag* him right, he would do it wrong. **1843** *Sydney Morning Herald* 24 May 2/4 If I can succeed in lagging these fellows, I shall get rid of this contract. **1849** *Argus* (Melbourne) 19 Sept. 2/4 Ireland replied that he was entrusted by Mrs Sutton with the horse, and that if he were to give him up, she might 'lag' him for fourteen years. **1854** C.A. CORBYN *Sydney Revels* 15 When taxed with dishonesty, she threatened to 'lag' Mrs W. **1889** H. EGBERT *Pretty Cockey* 73 If he once gets 'a down' on any one, he will often, as a matter of course, do his level best to lag him, or hound him to the gallows. **1899** J. BRADSHAW *Quirindi Bank Robbery* 34 He lagged Jack Hassett and Tom Brown at Cobar, for a crime which Goodson himself helped to commit. **1910** *Bulletin* (Sydney) 27 Jan. 14/3 The trooper . . tried to lag the drover for it . . but . .

found there was no provision made for such an offence. **1970** K. MACKEY *Cure* 63 Maybe I should split. This flip might just lag me to the jacks.

b. To inform against (a fellow-prisoner).

1968 L.H. EVERS *Fall among Thieves* 177 The rights and wrongs of 'lagging' (reporting fellow prisoners to the authorities) formed the sole topic of debate. **1971** J. MCNEIL *Chocolate Frog* (1973) 32 It ain't just any sort of maggot gets to be a dog . . only those that lag other people . . who co-operate with bastards in uniform . . see?

lag, *n.* [f. prec.]

1. A convict who has been transported to a penal settlement in Australia; any convict. Also *attrib.*

1812 J.H. VAUX *Mem.* (1819) II. 185 *Lag*, a convict under sentence of transportation. **1845** C. GRIFFITH *Present State & Prospects Port Phillip* 76 The old hands are men who, having been formerly convicts, (or *lags* as they are generally termed) have become free by the expiration of their sentences. **1852** G.C. MUNDY *Our Antipodes* III. 259 One or two of them had 'lag' . . indelibly written on their hardened lineaments. **1873** A. TROLLOPE *Aust. & N.Z.* II. 114 It is perhaps something of a disgrace to Western Australia that the other colonies will not receive a stranger from her shores without a certificate that the visitor has not been a 'lag'. **1893** F.W.L. ADAMS *Australs.* 30 The hopeless criminality of the old lineal descendants of the 'lags' gathered together in Wooloomooloo. **1903** *Truth* (Sydney) 5 Apr. 5/3 Botany Bay law, while hampering an outraged husband 'under the ban', aided and abetted the adulterous wife. The old lag law is still law. **1928** N.F. SPIELVOGEL *Affair at Eureka* 5 There were many lags (ex-convicts) from New South Wales and Tasmania. **1930** 'BRENT OF BIN BIN' *Ten Creeks Run* (1952) 143, I didn't come here to be insulted. . . You're the son of a lag yourself. **1939** FRANKLIN & CUSACK *Pioneers on Parade* 208 Primrose woke next morning with a depressing sense of the bottom having fallen out of life overnight. Ah, the lag pedigree! **1963** X. HERBERT *Disturbing Element* 13 Mother's favourite cut at Sylvia in a row was: 'You wife of the son of a lag!'

2. In the collocation **old lag,** an ex-convict; a former prisoner.

1812 J.H. VAUX *Mem.* (1819) II. 193 *Old lag*, a man or woman who has been transported, is so called on returning home, by those who are acquainted with the secret. **1842** R. DAWSON *Lett. to G. Arnatt* 3 The whole colony is quite ruined, except some of the old lags who came out 30 years ago, and had plenty of land given them. **1853** A. KINLOCH *Murray River* 19 They were probably *ci devant* convicts, or, as they are here termed, 'old lags'. **1876** 'EIGHT YRS.' RESIDENT' *Queen of Colonies* 198 We hope, as the old 'lag' element dies out, that Queenslanders will be equally sensible with their American cousins. **1903** *Truth* (Sydney) 27 Dec. 1/3 Retribution has overtaken the Old-Lag gang in Westralia, bossed by Bigjohn Forrest. **1935** H. MCCRAE *My Father* 73 Ulladulla . . was a convict settlement, populated by timber-getters, old lags, bullock-drivers. **1944** R. BEDFORD *Naught to Thirty-Three* 14 Transportation had ceased twenty years before I was born . . but local tradition fastened the term of 'old lag' to any ancient man or woman of whose history it was ignorant. **1965** *Coast to Coast 1963–64* 96 'Take an old lag,' I began. 'Say he's about sixty . . one of those miserable crooks that are more to be pitied than loathed.' **1977** B. SCOTT *My Uncle Arch* 48 Another old lag . . used to make dud two-bobs for a sideline.

Hence **(old) lagdom,** the convict period; **lag(s')land,** Australia.

1900 *Bulletin* (Sydney) 29 Dec. 15/2 Darlinghurst . . is the pet prison of **Old Lagdom,** which some of the 'Botany Bay Aristocracy', or their convict progenitors, helped to build. **1903** *Truth* (Sydney) 5 Apr. 5/3 On the Statute Book of all the Australian States there are laws which were conceived in the days of convictism and . . are . . legacies of lagdom. **1905** *Bulletin* (Sydney) 6 July 16/2 A relic of old Lagdom was unearthed at West Dapto (N.S.W.). . . Two rust-eaten leg-irons. . . In 1848 Governor Gipps ordered the demolition of all prisoners' stockades or barracks in the locality and wiped away . . the traditions of lagdom. **1858** A. PENDRAGON *Queen of South* 76 What right have such as you to come here, to this island—to our country—to the **lags' land** . . to rob us of our gold? **1878** G. WALCH *Australasia* 47 Steamed away from Albany as if rejoiced to leave Lagsland (as one of our number facetiously termed Western Australia). **1896** *Bulletin* (Sydney) 18 Jan. 9/3 In England, Howard is the name of a philanthropist; in Botany Bay he is the hangman. In England 'all the blood of all the Howards' means one thing; in Lagland, quite another thing.

lagerphone. [Prob. f. *lager* (with reference to the beer-bottle tops employed) + *xylo)phone.*] See quot. 1979.

1956 *People Mag.* (Sydney) 11 Jan. 26/3 The lager-phone, a broomstick and crosspiece studded with beer bottle tops, produces a jingling sound, something like that of a big tamborine, when shaken. **1963** *Gumsuckers' Gaz.* (Melbourne) Aug. 10 Interesting to those who play the lager-phone, or jingling johnnie, is the information that hand shears were also called *jingling johnnies*. **1967** MEREDITH & ANDERSON *Folk Songs Aust.* 17, I played the bush accordion . . Brian the lagerphone. **1979** R. EDWARDS *Skills Austral. Bushman* 157 The lager-phone . . a percussion instrument . . made by loosely tacking rows of bottle tops to a stick, usually a worn-out broom or a stick of similar length with a crossbar at the top. The tops are vibrated by banging the instrument on the floor, and also by 'bowing' it with a serrated stick.

lagger. [f. LAG *v.*]

1. *Obs.* A sailor.

1812 J.H. VAUX *Mem.* (1819) II. 185 *Lagger*, a sailor. **1827** *Monitor* (Sydney) 11 Nov. 759/2 Two urchints as are wenting their malicious tricks upon the done-up *lagger*. **1847** A. HARRIS *Settlers & Convicts* (1953) 50 Old George was always hocussing some poor lagger (sailor). **1849** —— *Emigrant Family* (1967) 93 He had got the title of 'the lagger' (or sailor) among the men.

2. A police informer, esp. a prisoner who informs against a fellow prisoner.

1967 B.K. BURTON *Teach them no More* 17, I knew an old lagger once. He was quite famous. He made little statues out of his mush. Didn't eat breakfast for years. **1968** L.H. EVERS *Fall among Thieves* 30 The 'lagger', the prisoner who complains to authority of another prisoner, must be unreservedly despised. **1971** J. MCNEIL *Chocolate Frog* (1973) 18, I seen Eddie talkin' ter that weak bludger Brown . . yer remember him? He used ter be lagger at Gosford years ago. **1974** *Gayzette* (Sydney) 14 Nov. 13/3 Maitland also houses the cretins, and the laggers.

lagging, *vbl. n.* [f. LAG *v.*] A term of penal servitude; a sentence or term of imprisonment.

1832 *Hill's Life N.S.W.* (Sydney) 16 Nov. 4 All the risques I ran Of *lagging, scragging*, and so forth, To be a *swell-mob-man*. **1843** *Melbourne Times* 13 May 4/1 Charles Rix, just become free from his second *lagging* was charged with a felony. **1857** J. ASKEW *Voyage Aust. & N.Z.* 297 These men had committed crimes, and were doing their lagging with Mr Smith, who appeared to be a very humane man, and they seemed to have easy times of it. **1871** J. BAIRD *Emigrant's Guide Australasia* 33, I am not certain that every individual in two English Houses of Parliament would be the worse for a seven years' 'lagging'. **1898** M. DAVITT *Life & Progress* 176 The 'Tichborne Claimant' . . managed to get on pretty well . . during his 'lagging'. ***c* 1920** *Breakers of Men* (I.W.W. Prisoners Release Committee) 25 It must not be supposed, however, that the men are complaining or really despondent, in other words, are doing their 'lagging' hard. **1968** L.H. EVERS *Fall among Thieves* 8 Had he brought his dinner-party humour into the gaol and left his poetic sensibilites in his 'property' . . then he would have 'done his laggin' standing on his ear', as the saying goes. **1979** L. NEWCOMBE *Inside Out* 106 About six more prisoners made up the van load, some with brand-new 'laggings' (prison slang for sentences) and others remanded to a later date.

lagoon. [In Br. use applied only to an area of salt or brackish water; in U.S., infl. by Sp. *laguna*, applied also to an area of fresh water: see DAE.] An expanse of fresh water, usu. shallow but of indeterminate extent: see quots. 1805 and 1878.

1797 *Hist. Rec. N.S.W.* (1895) III. 765 Walked 8 miles and came to a river, where we met fourteen natives, who conducted us to their miserable abodes in the wood adjoining to a large lagoon. **1801** M. FLINDERS *Observations Coasts Van Diemen's Land* 19 The fresh-water lagoon, at the back of the beach near Low Head, is the most convenient place we met with. **1805** *HRA* (1915) 1st Ser. V. 586 Some local Expressions that have obtained in this Colony . . *A Lagoon*—Is a large Pond of Stagnant water; Although in many places the water does not Stagnate being supplied with Springs. **1814** *Ibid.* (1916) 1st Ser. VIII. 177 At the end of todays Journey is a Lagoon of good Water. **1827** *Hobart Town Courier* 17 Nov. 1 The first cove on the left next Cape Raoul called Safety Cove, is . . well watered by a small stream and a large fresh water laggoon. **1839** W.H. LEIGH *Reconnoitering Voyages* 103 The fresh water lagoon, as it is called, is in the vicinity of the salt one. **1849** C. STURT *Narr. Exped. Central Aust.* I. 7 A lagoon is a shallow lake, it generally constitutes the back water of some river, and is speedily dried up. **1863** J. MORRILL *Sketch of Residence* 24 There are a great many Aligators . . particularly in one large fresh water lagoon. **1878** J.H. NICHOLSON *Opal Fever* 32 In some parts of this vast colony [of Queensland] two buckets of water and a frog would be called a 'lagoon'. **1912** J. BOWES *Comrades* 75 The lagoon, as luck would have it, was a permanent water-hole. **1925** M. TERRY *Across Unknown Aust.* 150 In its broad interpretation the term 'lagoon' is used, by the Australian bushmen, to denote a large shallow depression in the ground, containing water, adjacent to a water-course, but not actually in its bed, i.e. not directly filled by the stream. **1965** R.H. CONQUEST *Horses in Kitchen* 133 In the early days of pastoral development, when squatters had to depend on rivers, waterholes and lagoons for water, stock losses were alarming in time of drought. **1978** E.L. HARPER *King of Ballyhoo* 14 Way out in the Never-Never, by an eight mile long lagoon—In a shack of dereliction, neath a blood-red rainless moon.

lair, *n.* and *a.* Also **lare.** [Back-formation from LAIRY.]

A. *n.*

a. One who displays vulgarity, esp. in dress or behaviour; a show-off; a larrikin.

1923 C.E. SAYERS *Jumping Double* 60 A hit behind the ear from one of those back street lairs. **1940** P. KERRY *Cobbers A.I.F.* 17 Put 'em up, yeh lousy lair! An' take wot's comin' to yeh. **1956** K. TENNANT *Honey Flow* 188 When Blaze and Big Mike were working around in boiler suits, they were men. When they dressed best, they looked cheap lares, the type you see leaning against the hotel or the general store. **1957** D. WHITINGTON *Treasure upon Earth* 39 'He's got little sideboards, and parts his hair in the middle and brushes it down very flat.' 'Sounds like a dead lair,' Mick growled. **1963** 'C. ROHAN' *Down by Dockside* 51 Poor Vic Hodges was what we called a lair. . . She had her hair dyed an astonishing shade of blonde. **1974** *Bulletin* (Sydney) 16 Mar. 44/3 By decking himself out in a frilled shirt . . and still pretending to be your friendly neighbourhood pub lair he is losing his way. **1979** C. KLEIN *Women of Certain Age* 128 'Old crocks in cars, they ought to be coralled. . . ' 'Along with young lairs. Like you.' **1983** T.A.G. HUNGERFORD *Stories Suburban Road* 117 He used to wear gold cuff-links in the coat sleeves of his blue serge suit: I suppose he was what we used to call a lair.

b. In the collocation **mug lair,** a term of abuse applied to a person supposed to be both stupid and vulgar. Also *attrib.*

1965 *Oz* (Sydney) xxiii. 8 Now I reckon any bloke that goes for your technical apparatus is a mug lair mongrel! **1974** J. GOODWOOD *Last Gamble* 98 There was real venom in his parting words. 'You're just a mug lair poofter.' **1978** S. BALL *Muma's Boarding House* 141 Larry's a real mug lair—been training his boy since he could walk and reckons he's a world beater. **1982** *Austral.* (Sydney) 7 Aug. 44/3 Admirers of Carlton's jack-in-the-box half-forward flanker . . call him 'Mr Magic' and 'Mr Wonderful'. His detractors call him a mug lair and a show pony.

B. *adj.* Vulgarly flamboyant.

1971 *Bulletin* (Sydney) 10 Apr. 37/3 There are four broad styles of Australian automobile decor—Domestic, Functional, Speed and Lair.

lair, *v.* [f. prec.] *intr.* To behave in the manner of a lair. Usu. with **up.**

1928 L.A. SIGSWORTH *Various Verse* 2 The 'babbling brook' will let the guns lare up in the shearers' mess. **1940** P. KERRY *Cobbers A.I.F.* 25, 'I wonder 'ow me missus is,' sez Corporal Billie Brown. 'I bet she's lairin' up a bit, an' gettin' round the town.' **1958** H.D. WILLIAMSON *Sunlit Plain* 12 And him lairing up with a lot of bull about what he said to the fencing contractor and what the fencing contractor was too frightened to say to him.

1972 J. JONES *Memories Golden Gate* (rev. ed.) 6 When we kids had grown up to young manhood some of us 'laired up' in Assam silk suits, fine quality Panama hats, coloured 'flyaway' ties and brown shoes or boots, or even white buckskin ones. **1983** A.F. HOWELLS *Against Stream* 1 Earning something in the vicinity of three pounds ten shillings a week . . I could still afford to lair up a bit, get on the scoot occasionally with my mates.

lairize, *v.* [f. LAIR *n.*] *intr.* LAIR *v.* Also (rarely) as *n.*

1953 K. TENNANT *Joyful Condemned* 22 You came lairizing round at our place like you owned it. **1960** *N.T. News* (Darwin) 5 Feb. 10/2 All they seem to think of these days is lairizing around in ten-gallon hats, flash, colored shirts, gabardine riding breeches and polished riding boots chasing a bit of fluff. **1967** *Kings Cross Whisper* (Sydney) xxx. 4/3 'The boys in the local brigades are getting very toey, indeed,' a Country Fire Authority official said. 'They haven't had a chance for a good lairise.' **1968** D. IRELAND *Chantic Bird* 178 A kid on a bike, lairising, leaned right over in front of me. **1974** *Bulletin* (Sydney) 5 Jan. 33/3 'Lairising around' in London he acquired his wife, Sadie. **1981** *Ibid.* 19 May 65/1 The crew raced for stretchers, first aid kits, splints. The mountain men looked on impassively. 'He was lairising,' they said.

lairy, *a.* Also **leary, leery.** [Transf. use of Cockney slang *lairy* knowing, 'fly': see OED(S *lairy, a.*[2] and *leery, a.*[2]] Flashily dressed; showy; socially unacceptable.

1898 *Tocsin* (Melbourne) 15 Sept. 3 Height, about 5 ft. 6½ in.; style 'lairy'. Shop made suit, tight fit and cheap. Flower in slouched hat, well over eyes. 'Silk' rag around neck. **1899** *Bulletin* (Sydney) 1 Apr. 26/2 The dressy larrikin . . is the 'leary one'. ***c* 1907** C.W. CHANDLER *Darkest Adelaide* 7/2 Sitting on the seat with him was a nice specimen of the Australian larrikin. Not so leery, perhaps, as his prototypes of Melbourne and Sydney, but a choice specimen of his class nevertheless. **1916** C.J. DENNIS *Moods Ginger Mick* p. x, An' that is orl there wus to Mick, wiv orl 'is leery ways. **1949** L. GLASSOP *Lucky Palmer* 142 You ought to see the rug I got for Bunny. All done in my colours, red, green and gold. Classy eh? Some of the boys reckon it's too lairy, but I reckon it's a beaut. **1959** D. HEWETT *Bobbin Up* 3 Shirl looked down . . at the tattoo on her forearm, '*Shirl loves Roy*'. . . They'd done it for a lairy joke. **1967** F.T. MACARTNEY *Proof against Failure* 41 We thought it rather daring to put an arm round a girl, and to do so in daylight slouching along the street, as is common now, was considered 'lairey'—a term for larrikin behaviour. **1976** S. WELLER *Bastards I have Met* 11 A big flash car pulled up and a bloke stepped out, dressed in a lairy shirt. **1979** B. MARTYN *First Footers S. Gippsland* 106 He was a stout fleshy chap wearing a dazzling tie and fancy waistcoat. He was popularly described as a 'bit lairy'.

Hence **lairiness** *n.*

1965 D. MARTIN *Hero of Too* 318 By no means all Queenslanders are lairs, nor is every politician, but all Queensland politicians are, or endeavour to be, lairs. . . Their lairiness is of the type that captures the national imagination.

la-la. A euphemism for 'lavatory'.

1963 B. HESLING *Dinkumization & Depommification* 116 Couldn't you last out to the Wentworth? Even Judge Willis said on the bench that he wouldn't be game to risk a visit to the Lang Park la-la. **1964** A.H. AFFLECK *Wandering Yrs.* 41 For the next few hours Lord Stonehaven and I, beating a track to and from the lala, compared visits as we passed like ships in the night. **1977** J. O'GRADY *There was Kid* 56 There are many euphemisms for dunnies, such as . . loos, la-las, toots. **1984** *Canberra Times* 28 Apr. 13/4 Once we were caught in a hurricane that caused a small amount of damage, including knocking over someone's outside dunny. The lady in whose house we were sheltering was laughing fit to burst. 'Ho! Ho! There goes old Fitz's la-la!'

lamb. Used *attrib.* in Special Comb. **lamb-catcher,** one who assists a *lamb-marker*; **-marker,** see *-marking*; **-marking** *vbl. n.* the marking of an ear of a lamb with the owner's brand; the completing of other processes, as castrating male lambs, docking, etc., at the same time (see quot. 1975).

1882 ARMSTRONG & CAMPBELL *Austral. Sheep Husbandry* 139 The required number of **lamb-catchers** have been employed and despatched, under the overseer, with from 50 to 60 hurdles, for the purpose of arranging the yards in the paddock. **1965** A.W. UPFIELD *Lure of Bush* 148 For an hour at a time Watts kept moving up and down the line of lamb-catchers, followed by Ralph with ear-markers and tar-brush. **1891** *Truth* (Sydney) 22 Mar. 7/1 His brother, a union shearer, was slushing for the **lamb-markers. 1916** *Bulletin* (Sydney) 27 Jan. 22/3 Young . . had the reputation amongst 'gun' sheep men of being the fastest lamb-marker in Australia. **1928** L.A. SIGSWORTH *Various Verse* 18 A tar drum tells of the lost lamb-marker's art. **1882** ARMSTRONG & CAMPBELL *Austral. Sheep Husbandry* 136 Successful **lamb-marking** is one of the most important items in the management of a station. **1903** *Bulletin* (Sydney) 30 July 17 Lamb-marking is now general in the Milparinka-Tibooburra district. **1916** *Ibid.* 6 July 22/3 'M.J.'s' lambmarking record . . is nothing to ring the church bells about. **1930** *Ibid.* 2 Apr. 23/3 During lamb-marking on a n.-w. Queensland station a ewe lamb showed on one ear a perfect replica of the station tarbrand. **1948** R. RAVEN-HART *Canoe in Aust.* 72 'Lamb-marking', the cutting off of the tails, the castrating of the male lambs, and the clipping of a notch into the left or right ear for ewes and males respectively. **1955** *Meanjin* 49 Lamb-marking! All you got to do is catch 'em and hold 'em on a board while they git their tails cut off. **1975** M. THORNTON *It's Jackaroo's Life* 90 *Lamb-marking*, castration; however, the term is used to cover a series of operations undertaken in conjunction with castration, including ear-marking, tailing, mulesing, drenching, inoculating, ear-tagging, jowlsing. **1985** *Town & Country Mag.* 15 July 7/3 Rapley's . . popular lamb marking cradles come in single or multi and can also be adapted to suit handler's needs.

lamb down, *v.* [Br. *lamb (down)* to tend (ewes) at lambing time; app. rare as OED records only 1850 and 1851: see OED *v.* 3 and, for sense 2, OED *v.* 4.]

1. a. *trans.* To tend (ewes) at lambing time. Also *absol.*

1848 S. & J. SIDNEY *Emigrant's Jrnl.* 31, I have known two little fellows, under ten years of age, sons of a settler, lamb down a flock of 1,000 ewes. **1851** *Illustr. Austral. Mag.* (Melbourne) Sept. 169 An Australian squatter, in the midst of the miseries of lambing down his sheep under a more than usual infliction of 'bolters', bad weather, native dogs. **1888** *Bulletin* (Sydney) 10 Mar. 14/2 And next I went a lambing down to fetch home the green lambs; But I couldn't find 'em green—for lambs are mostly white. **1952** *Ibid.* 16 July 17/2 Every year it is the old man's practice to lamb-down a mob of ewes on the rough flat, and it is my job to draft off the woollies as they lamb, and shove them on to the top-dressed country. **1959** H. LAMOND *Sheep Station* 67 Anyone would think you was lambin' down 'bout eighty thousan' ewes 'stead o' a pint-pot mob like this.

b. *trans. Obs.* To accommodate (ewes) at lambing time; to provide accommodation for (a client). Also *absol.*

1863 R. HENNING *Lett.* (1952) 53 Biddulph bought the station in question . . and Palmer asked him to let him 'lamb-down', as it is called, on some part of his country as he (Palmer) had no place of his own. Biddulph gave him leave to go on this new station for a few months, and then the fellow claimed it on the ground of prior occupation. **1873** M. CLARKE *Holiday Peak* 21 As the Three Posts was to Trowbridge's, so was Trowbridge's to the Royal Cobb. . . True, that Trowbridge's did not 'lamb down' so well as the Three Posts, but then the Three Posts put fig tobacco in the brandy casks, and Trowbridge's did not do that.

2. *fig.*

a. *trans.* To inveigle (a client, esp. a shearer or shepherd) into spending accumulated earnings on liquor. Esp. in *pass.* Also *transf.* (see quot. 1879).

1850 *Bell's Life in Sydney* 12 Jan. 2/6 There are such things as roadside public houses . . and shepherds and shearers, in about three days are quietly *lambed down.* **1869** *Australasian* (Melbourne) 17 July 72/5 *To lamb-down*, that is, to make drunk and incapable—of course originated with some shepherd. **1878** 'IRONBARK' *Southerly Busters* 24 He got upon the spree, And publicans was awful cheats For soon 'lamm'd down' was he. ***c* 1879** *Ye Prodigal* (Sydney) 54 He proved that he had very considerably more money than brains; and the [gambling] Ring, not taking long to discover the fact, he was 'lambed down' to a very respectable tune. **1889** H. EGBERT *Pretty Cockey* 36 He landed in Sydney, some months ago, with several hundred pounds in his pocket, got on the spree, and was lambed down inside of a fortnight. **1906** G.M. SMITH *Days of Cobb & Co.* 71 He got a call girl up from town Who was good at cracking jokes, A thing quite indispensible To lambdown bushy blokes. **1918** C. FETHERSTONHAUGH *After Many Days* 390 Why, there's Christians . . that would lamb you down and skin you for your last penny—not that I was ever lambed down. **1947** W. LAWSON *Paddle-Wheels Away* 165 'I want one [*sc.* a pub] here. We're entitled to a licence at Tilliba.' 'And you'll lamb down your own hands, eh?' **1959** H.P. TRITTON *Time means Tucker* 78 Pitt had been lambed-down at the Pig and Whistle shanty, near Guntawang.

b. *trans.* To squander (one's accumulated earnings) on liquor. Also *absol.*

1899 F. CRAWFORD *Native Companion Songster* 11 'I'll cash your cheque and send you on.' He stopped, and now his money's gone—Lambed down. **1890** *Argus* (Melbourne) 9 Aug. 4/5 The old woman, of course, thought that we were on gold, and would lamb down at the finish in her shanty. **1935** A. FRANCIS *Then & Now* 43 This was a rough and rowdy place where bushmen 'lambed' down their cheques. **1980** P. FREEMAN *Woolshed* 72 'Oh, stay!' old Ryan said, 'and slip your blanket off, and have a nip; I'll cash your cheque and send you on.' He stopped, and now his money's gone—Lambed down.

Hence **lambed-down** *ppl. a.*, **lamber-down** *n.*

1889 F. CRAWFORD *Native Companion Songster* 11 A man whom you could plainly see Had just come off a drunken spree, **Lambed down. 1914** *Bulletin* (Sydney) 9 Apr. 22/1 And out in Piker's bar The eyes of many 'lambed-down' men resemble each a star. **1880** 'ERRO' *Squattermania* 168 What thrown over the pick and sluice-box, and gone among the '**lambers-down**' [*sc.* sheep-farmers]? **1882** *Bulletin* (Sydney) 10 June 1/1 The Press has been full of reports from the Criminal Courts and Coroners' inquests, in which the 'lamber down' has figured with remarkable splendour.

Lambert's wren. [Applied as the specific epithet *Lamberti* in 1825 by ornithologists N.A. Vigors and T. Horsfield (*Trans. Linnean Soc. London* (1827) XV. 221) after English naturalist A.B. *Lambert* (1761–1842), Vice-President of the Linnean Soc. London.] VARIEGATED WREN. Also **Lambert's (superb) warbler.**

1841 J. GOULD *Birds of Aust.* (1848) III. Pl. 24, *Malurus lamberti* . . Lambert's Wren. . . Lambert's Superb Warbler is a species with which we have been long acquainted. **1921** S.A. WHITE *Bunya* 8 The chattering song of Lambert's wren was heard on every side. **1928** B. SPENCER *Wanderings in Wild Aust.* 96 Lambert's Warbler . . is also striking on account of the presence of a patch of cinnamon-brown, edged with deep cobalt-blue, on the top of its head.

lambing. Used *attrib.* in Comb. with reference to the provision made for the accommodation of ewes at lambing time, as **lambing camp, paddock, station, yard.**

1851 *Illustr. Austral. Mag.* (Melbourne) Sept. 171, I have to go to a lambing station the first thing in the morning. **1879** S.W. SILVER *Austral. Grazier's Guide* 30 Before the month of May or June . . good 'lambing-stations', as they are called, will need to be provided for the expectant ewes. **1881** *Bulletin* (Sydney) 26 Mar. 8/3 You were 'flashin' your dover' six short months ago, In a lambin' camp on the Paroo? **1888** 'R. BOLDREWOOD' *Robbery under Arms* (1937) 78 We were out at the back making some lambing yards. **1891** D. FERGUSON *Vicissitudes Bush Life* 149 Lambing stations were put each under the charge of an efficient manager. **1907** *Bulletin* (Sydney) 12 Sept. 14/4 With paddocked sheep, if tucker-bags Runs low . . You 'aven't Buckley's show to strike A (lurid) lambin' camp. **1948** J.K. EWERS *For Heroes to Live In* 17 He walked with her one evening out to the lambing paddock. The air was loud with the bleating of the young lambs. **1965** A.W. UPFIELD *Lure of Bush* 149 Many times did they come upon a great flock of sheep being taken to or brought from the lambing camp.

lambing down, *vbl. n.* [f. LAMB DOWN *v.*]

1. The tending of ewes about to lamb. Also as *ppl. a.*

1864 'E.S.H.' *Narr. Trip Sydney to Peak Downs* 20 The

grass was all eaten by the lambing-down flocks. **1874** *Illustr. Sydney News* 28 Mar. 7/4 The very great mistake of early lambing down is often committed from an erroneous opinion that the flocks can be shorn earlier. **1910** C.E.W. BEAN *On Wool Track* 215 When sheep are lambing men are sent into the paddocks to see that everything goes smoothly. This process is called 'lambing down'. By a gentle metaphor the words have been transferred to the assistance which in the old days it was customary for publicans to give to men who came in to get rid of a cheque.

2. a. The process of spending one's earnings on liquor. Also *attrib.*

1870 W.H. KNIGHT *W.A.* 76 The man comes into the town for the confessed purpose of 'lambing down', as it is called. He places his money in the hands of a publican, and instructs him to let him know when the amount is reduced to what he reckons will be sufficient to carry him back to his district or home. **1873** J.B. STEPHENS *Black Gin* 51 It is the Bushman come to town . . Come to spend his cheque in Town, Come to do his lambing down. **1890** *Argus* (Melbourne) 7 June 4/2 The paying off of drovers, the selling off of horses, the 'lambing down' of cheques.

b. The process of inveigling a shearer, shepherd, etc., into spending his entire resources on liquor. Also as *ppl. a.*

1882 *Bulletin* (Sydney) 10 June 1/1 The business of 'lambing down' has of late exhibited a singular briskness. . . One of the most singular circumstances which successive inquests have brought to light, is the inherent capacity of the 'lambing down' publican to tell when a man has had more drink than is good for him. **1886** *Once a Month* (Melbourne) June 489 The periodical spree, when they submitted themselves to the 'lambing-down' process at the hands of the tender publicans. **1898** G. GARNET *Barrier Bride* 135 He had married a strapping Irish wench, with a shrewd eye for business, and was now running the 'Lambing Inn', a bush shanty notorious for the 'lambing down' of shearers or miners with big cheques. **1914** *Bulletin* (Sydney) 15 Jan. 22/1 Every bush-pub isn't the bush-pub of lambing-down literature.

3. Comb. **lambing down shanty, shop.**

1894 *Bulletin* (Sydney) 13 Jan. 74 Close the swagger's port of departure—the **lambing-down shanty. 1904** *Ibid.* 13 June 16/2 A lambing-down shanty in real life. **1889** F. CRAWFORD *Native Companion Songster* 9 A filthier place you'd not find in a week—A regular **'lambing down' shop. 1895** J. KIRBY *Old Times in Bush* 150 A bush pub at the time I am writing about (the forties) served as a kind of 'labor depôt' as well as 'lambing down shop'.

lamb poison. [See quot. 1981.] Any of several shrubs or herbs of the genus *Isotropis* (fam. Fabaceae), apparently sometimes toxic to stock.

1897 L. LINDLEY-COWEN *W. Austral. Settler's Guide* 591 *Isotropis juncea* . . 'Lamb poison.' Suspected. **1926** *Poison Plants W.A.* (W.A. Dept. Agric.) 25 The Lamb Poisons are said to be dangerous to lambs, and to some extent to sheep also, but apparently not to other stock. **1981** G.M. CUNNINGHAM et al. *Plants Western N.S.W.* 398 Wheeler's lamb-poison has a scattered distribution. . . As its name suggests, it has been suspected of poisoning stock, although no definite evidence is available.

lamb's fry: see FRY.

lambswool. The shrub of s.w. W.A. *Lachnostachys eriobotrya* (fam. Verbenaceae), having a white, woolly flowering panicle and felt-like leaves.

1926 J. POLLARD *Bushland Man* 127 This . . is the wild violet; this is 'lamb's wool'. **1939** M.B. ELDERSHAW *My Aust.* 219 Among the more modest are . . a flower called Lambswool. **1973** R. ERICKSON et al. *Flowers & Plants W.A.* 187 Lambswool . . is a grey shrub with linear leaves and open panicles of white flowers.

Laminex. Also **laminex.** The proprietary name of a hard, durable, plastic laminate used esp. as a surfacing material; any similar surface. Also *attrib.*

1945 *Austral. Official Jrnl. Patents* (Canberra) 2226 *Laminex.* 83,123. Articles (included in this class) moulded, cast or otherwise formed from or incorporating synthetic resin or similar moulding material and including laminated sheets, blocks, tubes, rods, gear wheels and other goods comprising superposed sheets of fabric, paper or other material impregnated with synthetic moulding material. **1952** *Austral. House & Garden* Dec. 76 Kitchen Aid can create just the kitchen for you . . with Formica, Laminex or Lino bench tops. **1953** *Ibid.* Jan. 2 Laminex is the registered name of the wonder surfacing material that is made only in Australasia by Laminex Pty. Ltd. *Ibid.* July 91 Furniture becomes inspired with the sheer beauty of Laminex. **1968** M.T. CLARK *Spark of Opal* (1973) 137 The boys sat at the table, spreading the sandwiches on the Laminex top. **1969** F. MOORHOUSE *Futility & Other Animals* 62 Into the bright, laminex and detergent kitchen. **1971** *Bulletin* (Sydney) 15 May 51/2 All night we talked ardently Of Revolution, traced new histories Along the wet beery laminex. **1985** M. LEUNIG *Ramming Shears*, Hey look, wow! Hey fabuloso! Under these pine boards. Genuine fifties Laminex with silver flecks. *Woooowee*!!

lamington. [Prob. f. the name of Charles Wallace Baillie, Baron *Lamington* (1860–1940), Governor of Queensland (1895–1901).]

1. A square of sponge cake coated in chocolate icing and desiccated coconut. Also *attrib.*

1909 *Guild Cookery Bk.* (Holy Trinity Church Ladies Working Guild) 66 Quarter lb. butter, 1 cup icing sugar; beat to cream; 2 tablespoons of cocoa, mixed with 2 tablespoons boiling water. Mix all well together, and put over the Lamington. **c 1919** *'All in One' Recipe Bk.* (Disabled Men's Assoc. Aust.) 438 *Lamingtons* [recipe follows]. **1938** F. CLUNE *Free & Easy Land* 171 Baked us lamingtons lined with cream. **1956** D. ROWBOTHAM *Town & City* 49 The lamingtons were a real luxury. **1962** C. GYE *Cockney & Crocodile* 28, I had to be shaken awake at 3 p.m. to partake of tea and lamingtons—those square sponge cakes rolled in chocolate sauce and dusted with coconut which are a national dish in Australia. **1977** E. MACKIE *Oh to be Aussie* 45 If you like Lamingtons you can even buy a *special Lamington tin*—and bake your own. **1981** *Bulletin* (Sydney) 13 Jan. 74/1 Another great antipodean delicacy called the Lamington. Allegedly named after the man who broke the world record for running from Sydney to Perth carrying a dog, the Lamington is a delicious sponge square dipped in melted chocolate and dessicated coconut which progresses through the digestive tract with all the ease of a building block. **1985** *Canberra Chron.* 31 July 4/3 Students set sight on lamington record.

2. Special Comb. **lamington drive,** an organized effort (by a community group) to raise money from the sale of lamingtons.

1979 C. KLEIN *Women of Certain Age* 37 'It's lamington day,' she informed Elissa, full of virtue. 'I made four dozen lamingtons for the lamington drive.' **1984** *Canberra Times* 21 July 25/2 (Advt.) *Fund raising lamington drives.* Pre-cut cake ready to dip—22 dozen per box.

lamplighter. [See quot. 1860.] The cicada *Cyclochila australasiae* (see *yellow monday* YELLOW 1).

1860 G. BENNETT *Gatherings of Naturalist* 271 From the circumstances of these having three ruby-coloured spots in the front of the head, they are called *Lamplighters* by the boys. **1966** S.J. BAKER *Austral. Lang.* (ed. 2) 283 When cicadas are shouting in the summer trees, who but an expert or a child could identify them? There are many types . . *lamplighter* [etc.].

lancewood. [Transf. use of *lancewood* the tough, elastic wood of a W. Indian tree.] Any of several trees, usu. yielding a tough, durable timber, incl. *Acacia shirleyi* of Qld. and N.T., often forming dense stands; such a stand; the wood itself. Also *attrib.*

1861 J.M. STUART *Explorations in Aust.* 3 May (1865) 278 A thick scrub of dwarf lancewood, as tough as whalebone. **1881** W. FEILDING *Austral. Trans-Continental Railway* 38 The Lancewood Range . . is covered with lancewood bushes about 12 feet high, which grow on the bare rock. **1903** *Tasmanian Timbers* (Tas. Lands & Survey Dept.) 28 Lancewood (*Eriostemon squameus*)—a tree of small growth, with wood of a yellow colour, which is fairly tough, and of a very fine grain. **1922** 'J. BUSHMAN' *In Musgrave Ranges* 229 The shaft . . was made of lance-wood. The head of the spear was broad and flat, and was made of red mulga. **1934** WARBURTON & ROBERTSON *Buffaloes* 28 The lancewood is particularly dangerous. In dry spells it sheds its foliage, leaving the branches brittle, hard, and pointed: small stock have frequently been found impaled on them. **1960** E. O'CONNER *Irish Man* 254 You'll always get a good, clean camp in the lance wood . . but it's hungry country and sort of lonely-feeling. **1984** *Courier-Mail* (Brisbane) 30 June 26/4 Lancewood and bendee . . combine with mulga to give a vegetation cover where soil patches remain.

land. Chiefly *hist.*

1. Used *attrib.* in Comb., not always excl. Australian, with reference to the occupation and tenure of land: **land agent, board, boom, boomer, commissioner, court, jobber, -jobbing, mania, order.**

1839 *Southern Austral.* (Adelaide) 2 Oct. 2/5 Messrs O'Halloran, Nixon & Co. The above firm have now commenced business as **Land Agents.** Land selected for Special Surveys or otherwise. **1849** J.P. TOWNSEND *Rambles & Observations N.S.W.* 187 The management of the Crown-lands of the Colony is . . the business of a *land-agent*, who ought thoroughly to understand the pursuits of the occupants of such lands. **1901** W.G. ACOCKS *Settlers' Synopsis Land Laws N.S.W.* 2 If land applied for is in more than one land district the application therefor may be lodged with the Land Agent of either district. **1920** *Huon Times* (Franklin) 19 Nov. 2/5 It is not right that he should be left unassisted by the Government, to fall . . into the hands of some unscrupulous land agent and have foisted on him some useless property. **1930** V. PALMER *Passage* (1957) 26 Fancy a quiet little place like this being turned into a nightmare of land-agent's notices and forty-perch allotments. **1828** *Sydney Gaz.* 12 Jan., The *Governor* has been pleased, under the Authority of the Secretary of State, to form a Board, to be termed the **Land Board,** for the Purpose of assisting Him in investigating such Particulars as may appear necessary to an impartial Decision, on the Applications which may be made for Grants, or to purchase Land. **1829** *Sydney Monitor* 26 Dec. 2/1 He had to pass the *Thing* called here a *land-board*; a species of civil Inquisition. For in lieu of enabling the Governor to give land to Emigrants in proportion to their property, it merely enables keen people, particularly old Colonists, to obtain great quantities of land with either no property or all, or with property quite disproportioned to the amount they really possess. **1831** *Sydney Herald* 4 July 2/2 The Land Board is to be abolished. **1877** 'CAPRICORNUS' *Land Law of Future* 6 The Land Board shall then procure . . a return specifying the sales of station properties. **1891** *Austral. Handbk.* 99 All disputes and claims as to fencing are heard and determined by the local land board. **1910** *Bulletin* (Sydney) 7 Apr. 14/3 The Hay (N.S.W.) Land Board recently wrestled with some Improvement Leases totalling 31,000 acres. **1917** R.D. BARTON *Reminisc. Austral. Pioneer* 19, I was once summoned to appear before the land board to give evidence that I had never had a 'dummy'. **1890** J. HASLAM *Glimpse Austral. Life* 11 Soon after I got fairly settled to work, what is called a **Land Boom** set it [*sic*]. **1925** G. WIRTH *Round World with Circus* 64 Australia was now in a very bad way through the 'Land Boom' failures. **1930** J.A. GURNER *Life's Panorama* 57 In the . . 'eighties, at the time of the Land Boom, began the erection of very tall buildings in the City of Melbourne. **1890** *Truth* (Sydney) 3 Aug. 2/6 As a natural result, that enterprising philanthropist, the **land boomer**, will be found on the war-path over again. **1894** *Bulletin* (Sydney) 6 Jan. 7/3 Land-boomers, according to 'representative' people, were merely artificial swindlers. **1909** C. CROWE *Inquiring Agent* p. iv, Bent, the land-boomer, always trying to make money by hook or crook, could be generous with public money when it came to a matter of finding a fat billet for a loose woman or a notorious convict. **1929** G. MEUDELL *Pleasant Career Spendthrift* 13 Prahran, a council celebrated . . as a graduation college for land boomers. **1971** *Bulletin* (Sydney) 14 Aug. 41/1 Landboomers took that in stride, forming companies to manufacture lifts or provide hydraulic power. **1828** H. DANGAR *Index & Directory River Hunter* 41 The assigning of boundaries to parishes, as well as counties, belongs to the **land commissioners. 1845** T. MCCOMBIE *Adventures of Colonist* 19 The Australian settler may be deprived of his run of stock at the caprice of a Government pimp, called a land commissioner. **1852** A.E. ERSKINE *Short Acct. Late Discoveries Gold* 15 A charge or license-fee of thirty shillings . . was to be paid by every individual applying for permission to search for the precious metals for every calendar month or part of a month, to a Land Commissioner appointed to receive it, who was also to have the power of allotting small portions of Crown land to each worker, and of settling disputes as to conflicting claims, etc. **1877** 'CAPRICORNUS' *Land Law of Future* 7 At the first sitting of the **Land Court** . . the land agent shall read aloud a report. **1889** *Act* (N.S.W.) 53 Vict. no. 21 Sect. 8, There shall be a Land Court, which shall be a Court of Record, and have an official seal... The Land Court shall have power to hear and determine all appeals. **1891** *Austral. Handbk.* 99 All appeals and disputed matters are to be referred by the Minister to a Land Court which is also a Court of Record, and consists of three members, one of whom acts as President. **1935** B.E. PHELPS *Austral. tells England* 167 Mr A.H. Simpson acted as agent for his sons, and defended their case in the Land Court in Gunnedah. **1835** *True Colonist* (Hobart) 27 Nov. 2/4 A celebrated and very successful **Land Jobber**. **1857** D. PUSELEY *Rise & Progress Aust., Tas., & N.Z.* 11 One of these land jobbers left the colony with £150,000—the whole of which he had amassed in the space of six months; and .. in one instance, this individual bought a plot of land and re-sold it within the same hour of the purchase at a clear profit of £10,000. **1882** *Three L's* 289 The squatters and land-jobbers would not bid against each other at the land sales. **1910** *Bulletin* (Sydney) 13 Jan. 14/3 The land jobber .. buys allotments in suburban sub-divisions and sits down tight to wait until other people build expensive residences around his lot, after which he can sell for a considerable unearned increment. **1931** *Century of Journalism* 100 'Town-booming' had been carried to a ridiculous excess; the voice of the 'land-jobber' had been heard in the land. **1945** H.S. ROBERTON *Now blame Farmer* 16 They selected land in the hope that they might 'strike it lucky'... They 'peacocked' the land and held the squatter up for ransom. They selected where it would do the squatter the greatest harm, and then they offered to sell. They were our first land-jobbers. **1809** *Hist. Rec. N.S.W.* (1901) VII. 33 They had for years commenced **land-jobbing.** This went so far as the selling of land before the grant for land was obtained. **1839** *Dublin Rev.* VI. 457 The profits of land-jobbing. **1848** A. MACONOCHIE *Emigration* 5 The sales of Crown Land .. created everywhere a passion for land-jobbing—for buying up land on the speculation of its rising in value. **1854** J. CAPPER *Aust.* 53 The whole attention of the settlers appeared directed to land-jobbing, while agricultural and farming pursuits were utterly neglected. **1882** *Three L's* p. i, The history of farmers' grievances from the days of land-jobbing to the present time. **1844** *HRA* (1925) 1st Ser. XXIII. 343 **Land Mania** was an evil. **1849** J.P. TOWNSEND *Rambles & Observations N.S.W.* 142 Kiama, is a place at which during the height of the land mania, the most absurd prices were given for land. **1857** W. WESTGARTH *Vic. & Austral. Gold Mines* 5 The decline of a speculative movement amongst the colonies, that we are accustomed to term a land mania. **1838** *Southern Austral.* (Adelaide) 23 June 1/4 The Owners and Representatives of Owners of Preliminary or other **Land Orders** .. are requested to meet at My Office .. J.H. Fisher, Colonial Commissioner. **1859** W. FAIRFAX *Handbk. to Australasia* 145 'Land orders' were afterwards sold in London, authorising the holder to select 80 acres of land upon payment of £80. **1876** 'EIGHT YRS.' RESIDENT' *Queen of Colonies* 88 The land orders which immigrants had been unable to use to advantage had nearly all found their way into the hands of the squatters at a great reduction on their actual value, and had by them been made use of in purchasing the best portions of their runs. **1883** *Austral. Handbk.* 111 A Land Order Warrant from the South Australian Government Emigration Office is absolutely necessary to certify the claim to Land Orders.

2. Special Comb. **land council,** a body appointed to represent the interests of Aborigines in Aboriginal land (see quot. 1976); **fund,** the revenue realized from the sale of Crown land; **-grant railway,** a railway built in return for a grant of land; **rights,** the entitlement of Aborigines to possess their traditionally occupied territory (see COUNTRY 4); the acknowledgement of this entitlement; **-shark,** one who speculates in land transactions; also **-sharking** *vbl. n.*

1973 *Cwlth. Parl. Papers* no. 138 41 It is recommended that two Aboriginal **land councils** be set up in the Northern Territory: one for the central region, based on Alice Springs, and the other for the northern region, based on Darwin. **1976** *Act* (Cwlth. of Aust.) no. 191 Sect. 23, The functions of a Land Council are .. to ascertain and express the wishes and the opinion of Aboriginals living in the area of the Land Councils as to the management of Aboriginal land in that area and as to appropriate legislation concerning that land. **1980** *CPD* (H. of R.) CXIX. 615 The Commonwealth Government negotiated .. agreement with the Northern Land Council. **1835** *Colonist* (Sydney) 28 May 170/2 The whole of the **land-fund** appropriated in bringing out virtuous and industrious families from the mother-country, to occupy our waste lands, and to cultivate those that are already located. **1845** *HRA* (1925) 1st Ser. XXIV. 212 No part of the Land Fund should be applied to Immigration. **1847** *Ibid.* XXVI. 47 The Governor was at liberty to draw £3,000 out of the Land Fund every quarter. **1852** W. HUGHES *Austral. Colonies* 107 The colonists .. regard with just indignation the reservation to the Crown of exclusive control over the appropriation of the land fund. **1863** F. ALGAR *Handbk. to Colony Vic.* 3 The land fund .. failed in 1841 .. and affected the inflocking of immigrants from the parent land. **1883** *Victorian Rev.* Aug. 460 If the example be once set on a large scale in Queensland, **land-grant railways** are almost sure to be constructed, whether for good or for evil, in other parts of Australasia. [**1887** *S.A. Parl. Papers* III. no. 34A 5 The Commission deliberated on the .. 'terms, limitations, restrictions, and obligations which the State would require to impose upon capitalists undertaking the construction of the Trans-continental Railway on the land-grant system'.] **1895** K. MACKAY *Yellow Wave* 112 Sir Peter McLoskie, Premier of Queensland and high-priest of land-grant railways and cheap alien labour. **1903** *Advocate* (Burnie) 11 Feb. 2/4 The proposed land-grant railway between Oodnadatta and Pine Creek .. tenders have been invited .. offering 79,000,000 acres of land, free of all taxes for 10 years. **1936** C.P. CONIGRAVE *N. Aust.* 90 A Bill authorizing a land grant railway from Port Augusta to Port Darwin was carried by the South Australian legislature. **1939** J.W. COLLINSON *Early Days Cairns* 107 His mission was to further land grant railways. **1964** *Anthropol. Forum* Nov. 294 What is at issue here is the actual acknowledgment of Aboriginal **land rights** as having any contemporary relevance at all. **1967** *Smoke Signals* Mar. 26 The concern for Aboriginal land rights, based as it is on the moral rights of the original occupiers of the land, the social need for Aboriginal self-respect and a sense of security and belonging in a situation of rapid social change; and the desperate need for economic capital by Aborigines, necessarily involves a concern for mineral rights. **1970** *Ibid.* Dec. 9 Although land rights is seen as a major pre-requisite in the advancement of Aborigines, there is an unanswered ambiguity in the proposals that are frequently made. **1976** *Bulletin* (Sydney) 16 Oct. 16/3 For land rights to have any meaning to these people, the title to the land which belongs to any one group must be given immediately and directly to the group through its traditional leader. **1984** *Age* (Melbourne) 16 Aug. 11/2 Nearly 24 per cent of the Northern Territory population is Aboriginal (or 29,088 people) and they have been granted about 32 per cent of the Territory in land rights. **1986** *Canberra Times* 3 Mar. 2/7 Aborigines in Western Australia have stated they will not give up their land-rights aspirations. **1836** *Sydney Herald* 4 July 2/7 When these allotments are put up for sale, those persons on the spot, who would become purchasers, cannot contend against the **land-sharks.** **1844** *Simmonds's Colonial Mag.* III. iv. 376 The emigrant .. will generally find many of the *land-shark genus* to welcome him. **1855** G.H. WATHEN *Golden Colony* 214 'Unlock the lands!' cried the Melbourne townsman, as he .. handed over two or three hundred pounds to some 'land-shark', for a few square yards of land in the suburbs. **1874** 'SPECIAL REPORTER' *Agric. in S.A.* 24 The land has been obtained by the present holders by purchase from agents, who, previous to the coming in force of the present Land Act, held the soil in monopoly. These agents are commonly called land-sharks. **1890** *Truth* (Sydney) 21 Sept. 4/7, I withdraw the remark implying that there is anything piscatorial about the hon. member. There is too much of the 'land-shark' about him. **1914** *Ibid.* 19 July 3/2 Bananaland has for years been the boodlers' Paradise .. and the land shark flourishes. **1929** G. MEUDELL *Pleasant Career Spendthrift* 16 Owning his own home was a craze in those parlous and perilous days of land sharks. **1840** D. BURN *Vindication Van Diemen's Land* 45 All the **land-sharking** put together will make land very cheap. **1841** *HRA* (1924) 1st Ser. XXI. 293 New South Wales has been particularly reproached for the obnoxious practice of 'Land Sharking'. **1889** H. EGBERT *Pretty Cockey* 60 How many large fortunes, thought he, had been made during those years, by grog-selling, land-sharking, and other questionable means.

3. a. In the phr. **(up)on the land,** in(to) a rural occupation, esp. owning or managing a rural property.

1902 *Advocate* (Burnie) 20 Feb. 4/1 Go on the Land! **1911** *Huon Times* (Franklin) 14 Jan. 3/4 Are there no men upon the land who are still struggling to try and get an existence? **1930** BILLIS & KENYON *Pastures New* 50 Not caring for the shackles of the Sydney Government routine, went on the land. **1971** *Bulletin* (Sydney) 8 May 9/1 They are all discussing the miseries of life on the land. **1984** *Ibid.* 24 Apr. 68/1, I was born on the land... I've farmed my own properties.

b. In the phr. **the man on the land,** one who owns or manages a rural property, esp. as representative of those engaged in rural occupations.

1911 *Huon Times* (Franklin) 8 Feb. 3/4 We could not possibly oppose it as advocates for assistance for the man on the land. **1917** *Ibid.* 17 Apr. 2/4 The insincerity of politicians' election addresses when they stump the country promising all sorts of things for 'the man on the land'. **1923** J. MOSES *Beyond City Gates* 23 The 'man on the land', in pursuit of his daily vocation, has much to contend with. **1966** *Kings Cross Whisper* (Sydney) Mar. 8/4 Nonetheless in the grin-and-bear-it tradition of the Australian man on the land, there are no kicks coming from Hunter River marijuana farmers. **1979** *Cattleman* (Rockhampton) Feb. 11/2 The Australian man on the land places unique demands on all his machinery, particularly his multi-purpose workhorse—the farm car.

land crab. Any of several small, fresh-water crayfish, esp. of the genus *Engaeus*. Also **land crayfish.**

1844 L. LEICHHARDT *Jrnl. Overland Exped. Aust.* 16 Dec. (1847) 78 Mr Gilbert found a land crab in the moist ground under a log of wood. **1855** W. HOWITT *Land, Labor & Gold* I. 327 Crab-holes, or Frog-holes, as they are called in some districts, from land crabs and frogs frequenting them when they hold water. **1905** *Bulletin* (Sydney) 12 Jan. 16/2 The land crab is one of the pests of South Gippsland. This gentleman is a pinkish yellow creature from two to four inches long, very similar in shape to the yabbie of Northern Victoria... It scoops holes about half an inch in diameter and pushes upward the mud to form a ring of well-worked stiff clay about the top, like the sand around an ant-hill. **1912** SPENCER & GILLEN *Across Aust.* 65 In both Victoria and Tasmania there is a special kind of little crayfish (*chaerops sp.*), popularly known as a 'land crab', which is never found in waterholes, but always burrows in more or less damp ground. **1965** *Austral. Encycl.* III. 92 A number of smaller aberrant members of the same crayfish family (Parastacidae) are the so-called land crayfish. These have a limited distribution in the temperate areas of eastern Australia, being mainly concentrated in Victoria and northern Tasmania.

land mullet. [See quots.] The large skink *Egernia major* of e. Aust.

1945 S.J. BAKER *Austral. Lang.* 214 Various Australian lizards are known in popular speech as the .. *land mullet*, mallee trout, railway lizard and stump-tail. **1956** T.Y. HARRIS *Naturecraft in Aust.* 53 The Land Mullet .. is mullet-like, both in roundness of form and in colouring, with a shiny black back speckled with lighter colours. **1973** S. & K. BREEDEN *Wildlife Eastern Aust.* 89 A few of the fungi are poisonous to animals but others are a valuable food source... A shiny black skink, almost two feet long—the Land Mullet—methodically eats all the tiny white umbrellas from another log. **1979** D.R. MCPHEE *Observer's Bk. Snakes & Lizards Aust.* 136 This species [*sc. Egernia major*] .. receives its vernacular name from the large scales which almost cover the ear openings, adding to the superficial likeness of its head to that of the mullet fish... The Land Mullet is endowed with considerable lung capacity and if antagonized exhales a loud hissing blast.

Landsborough grass. *Obs.* [f. the name of William *Landsborough* (1826–1886), explorer.] FLINDERS GRASS.

1881 T. ARCHER *Some Remarks on Proposed Qld. Trans-Continental Railway* 18 Over all these plains [near Burketown] we rarely lost sight of the Mitchell, blue, and Landsborough grasses. **1890** W.F. BUCHANAN *Aust. to Rescue* 65 The grasses are principally Mitchell, Landsborough or Flinders and blue grass. **1903** *Austral. Handbk.* 280 The following are looked upon by pastoralists with the greatest favour .. 'Landsborough grass' [etc.]. **1923** E. BREAKWELL *Grasses & Fodder Plants N.S.W.* 18 *Iseliema* [*sic*] *membranacea* (Flinders or Landsborough grass). Common in the north-west; less abundant elsewhere in interior.

land train. *Road train*, see ROAD 3.

1963 D. ATTENBOROUGH *Quest under Capricorn* 130 Once or twice we passed a land-train, a line of gigantic trailers, each the size of a large furniture van, stretching for fifty yards and drawn by an immense diesel lorry, the size of a military tank transporter, with twenty-two gears and the speed of a saloon car. **1969** A. GARVE *Boomerang* 61 An enormous land train of three linked trailers drawn by a gigantic diesel truck.

lane. An enclosure in a stock yard from which animals may be fed in small numbers into the appropriate pen (see esp. quots. 1880 and 1890).

1880 J.B. STEVENSON *Seven Yrs. Austral. Bush* 115 First of all the cattle are driven into what is called the 'receiving yard', which is the largest subdivision. From this they are drafted in small numbers into the 'lane', which is an oblong enclosure, and serves as a feeder for the 'drafting pen', where the work of separating the different ages, etc., is performed. **1886** H. FINCH-HATTON *Advance Aust.* (rev. ed.) 70 Five or six men . . go into the receiving yard and jam the cattle up into the corner against the gate of 'the lane'. **1890** 'R. BOLDREWOOD' *Colonial Reformer* II. 113 About fifty head have been run into the drafting lane and are ready for separating. The 'lane' is a long narrow yard about three panels wide and eight in length—a panel of fencing is not quite nine foot in length—immediately connected with the pound or final yard, and leading into it by a gate opening into the latter. **1930** E.R. GRIBBLE *Forty Yrs. with Aborigines* 27 My post during drafting was in the 'check pens'. The two men in the long narrow yard called the 'lane' would let two or three beasts into the check-pen. **1954** H.G. LAMOND *Manx Star* 259 *Lane*, a narrow V-shaped yard up to the crush.

langeel, var. LEANGLE.

lapunyah /lə'pʌnjə/. [a. Gunya *yapanʸ*.] **a.** The tall, smooth-barked tree *Eucalyptus argophloia* (fam. Myrtaceae) of s.e. Qld. **b.** YAPUNYAH. Also *attrib.*

1940 W. HATFIELD *Into (Great?) Unfenced* 41 A strong growth of eucalypts, the common river-gum, and . . lapunyah. **1955** STEWART & KEESING *Austral. Bush Ballads* 108 And still the yellow wattles rose through the thin lapunyah-trees. **1984** D.J. BOLAND et al. *Forest Trees Aust.* (rev. ed.) 514 Queensland Western White Gum, Lapunyah . . *Eucalyptus argophloia.*

lare, var. LAIR.

larrikin. [Br. dial. *larrikin* 'a mischievous or frolicsome youth': see OED(S.]

1. *Hist.*

a. A young, urban rough, esp. a member of a street gang; a hooligan.

1868 W. COOPER *Colonial Experience* 58 Allow me to introduce you to . . one of the most accomplished swindlers ever imported into the colonies. . . Why, you infernal old larrikin! **1870** *Age* (Melbourne) 8 Feb. 3/1 A gang of 'larrikins' . . had been the terror of Little Bourke-street and its neighbourhood. **1872** 'RESIDENT' *Glimpses Life Vic.* 330 The name 'larrikin', whose origin was the subject of a recent discussion in a police court, was pronounced by a constable of abstruse research to owe its derivation to the well-known relaxation called 'larking' to which the youths of most countries are partial. The pranks of the 'larrikin' are, however, neither innocent nor amusing. **1879** *Austral.: Monthly Mag.* (Sydney) II. 523 About six years ago, a gang of 'larrikins' took a servant-girl to the North Shore in a boat. She was violated by the party. **1886** D.M. GANE *N.S.W. & Vic.* 59 The Australian larrikin, a type of humanity of the lowest and most criminal order. **1890** H.A. WHITE *Crime & Criminals* 239 The genus 'larrikin' . . is chiefly composed of lads and young men who have been permitted . . to assume much too formidable a position. . . They may be considered as the 'Thugs' of Australia. . . They are generally known by their peculiar style of dress, viz., the broad-brimmed, low-crowned felt hat, the coat dotted with buttons in every conceivable spot, the tight-fitting bell-bottomed trousers, and the heels of the boots or shoes, which are disproportionately small, being placed almost under the instep, while the uppers are usually studded with brass eyelet-holes. **1892** 'E. KINGLAKE' *Austral. at Home* 109 The female larrikin . . is worse than her correlative of the opposite sex because she has farther to fall. **1898** *Bulletin* (Sydney) 26 Feb. 32/4 The suggested derivation of 'larrikin' from gypsy or Romany 'leary kinchin'—cheeky or precocious youngster is no novelty. **1911** 'R.T.H.' *Ourselves & our Land* 7 The Australian larrikin is supposed to be only one step removed from the jackal. **1922** *Daily Mail* (Sydney) 6 Jan. 1/5 A crowd of youthful larrikins is posing as a 'modern push'. **1963** F. HARDY *Legends Benson's Valley* 98 Past . . the Court House Hotel. The group of larrikins on the corner sniggering and calling out from a safe distance. **1975** *Bulletin* (Sydney) 22 Nov. 30/1 Whitlam, under the shock of his dismissal, revealed some of those characteristics which seem to lie so close beneath his urbane exterior. The larrikin came out in the unseemly attack on the Governor General. **1982** R. HALL *Just Relations* 465, I remember some pretty crook things went on there, did some of them meself. . . Ears? yes, cut off of Abos and Chinks and the like: we was young larrikins.

b. Comb. **larrikin class, element.**

1879 *Kelly Gang* 108 Sympathy and admiration for the Kellys . . by the **larrikin class**, are not only barely disguised in some cases, but openly vaunted in others. **1887** *Illustr. Austral. News* (Melbourne) 15 Oct. 178/2 The young fellows of the larrikin class who are over 16 years . . are rendered liable to be imprisoned and subjected to the discipline of solitary confinement on bread and water. **1890** *Truth* (Sydney) 16 Nov. 7/3 On a seat nearby two young girls, of the larrikin class, were talking earnestly. **1893** *Braidwood Dispatch* 8 Feb. 2/5 An organised body of about thirty boys of the larrikin class made an attack on some vans of fruit being unloaded at a jam factory. . . Whatever they could not carry away the boys scattered wantonly on the street . . and the windows in the factory were smashed. **1877** J. VICARS *Tariff, Immigration, & Labour Question* 22 The hourly and daily surroundings, and the circumstances in which this **'larrikin' element** is placed, exert a very great deal of influence in moulding their habits and modes of life. **1886** P. CLARKE *'New Chum' in Aust.* 262 Brisbane does not contain such a 'larrikin' or socialistic element as Sydney. **1910** *Huon Times* (Franklin) 3 Aug. 2/1 A crowd of young men of the larrikin element were creating a disturbance. **1918** *Ibid.* 7 June 6/1 A disgraceful street fight, reminiscent of the days when the larrikin element predominated in the suburban streets, broke out.

c. Special Comb. **larrikin push,** a street gang; PUSH b.

1890 *Braidwood Dispatch* 5 Nov. 2/6 The larrikin 'pushes' are about again. On Friday night a gang of them assaulted a young lad. **1896** *Western Champion* (Barcaldine) 4 Feb. 1/2 The town at night is virtually in the possession of larrikin 'pushes' who number nearly 100. **1899** *Tocsin* (Melbourne) 19 Jan. 5/4 The hideous crimes occasionally perpetrated by the . . degraded larrikin pushes. **1905** E.C. BULEY *Austral. Life* 84 One of the least agreeable features of the Australian holiday is the prominence of the larrikin 'push'. The larrikin has his equivalent in most big cities, and may not differ much in type from the English Hooligan, the American Tough, or the French Apache. **1946** F. CLUNE *Try Nothing Twice* 5 The streets of Woolloomooloo were paved with blue-metal stones, which came in quite handy for the larrikin 'pushes' in their frequent fights. **1950** F.J. HARDY *Power without Glory* 9 The 80s were . . the hey-day of the larrikin pushes. These groups of youths roamed the streets, mainly at night; breaking windows, knocking on doors, often insulting and molesting people.

2. a. One who acts with apparently careless disregard for social or political conventions. Also *attrib.*, and as *adj.*.

1891 *Truth* (Sydney) 15 Mar. 7/3 Jackeroos . . are such fun, and vary, from the sensible one, in a fair way for promotion, to the larrikin, who will either sling station life or hump the swag. **1891** *Bohemia* (Melbourne) 3 Sept. 21 Roseate hopes are entertained that the experiment may yet produce male and female voters far less larrikin than many of those who—but that has been said often before. **1899** *Truth* (Sydney) 13 Aug. 4/4 Nowadays the Premier is the chief political larrikin of the House. **1904** *Ibid.* 27 Mar. 1/1 A literary larrikin like John Norton. **1944** R. BEDFORD *Naught to Thirty-Three* 144 John L. Sullivan—almost the last of the larrakin fighters. **1955** N. PULLIAM *I traveled Lonely Land* 263 The M.G.'s just the larrikin's motorcar, madam. **1968** *Nation* (Sydney) 25 May 9/1 The peculiar character of political leadership in Australia, with its recurrent tendency to throw up two major personality types: the larrikin, represented . . by Mr J.G. Gorton, and the prima donna, by Mr E.G. Whitlam. **1977** S. LOCKE ELLIOTT *Water under Bridge* 119 Maggie McGhee maintained a reputation for being a card, a wag, or in the local jingo, a larrikin. **1980** *Nat. Times* (Sydney) 5 Oct. 9 Hawke: a larrikin trying to reform. **1984** *Sydney Morning Herald* 9 Feb. 1/7 She . . grins and accepts cheerfully enough the description of being an Australian intellectual larrikin. **1986** *Ibid.* 12 Apr. 1/4 Top surfer Tom Carroll now earns £250,000 a year from promotions and endorsements, the wave of the future for a larrikin sport which has grown respectable.

b. *transf.*

1881 G. WALCH *Little Tin Plate* 28 While larrikin spiders aloft, like youths trammelled in sin, Exhausted their vital resources to keep 'on the spin'. **1884** 'R. BOLDREWOOD' *Old Melbourne Memories* 107 He was . . adjured to cull the herd severely . . to eliminate without delay all the bovine 'larrikins' . . by boiling them down. **1912** *Bulletin* (Sydney) 15 Aug. 15/2 When the inkweed . . is seeding, this harsh-voiced air larrikin darts round with the push, devouring the ripe berries. **1941** *Ibid.* 7 May 16/3 Indian mynahs rarely venture into small gardens, the larrikins from Curryland being content to trill from the housetops. **1942** *Ibid.* 14 Jan. 12/1 Our parrot . . was a happy-go-lucky Blue Mountain larrikin.

3. In the collocation **bush larrikin,** a rural larrikin.

1889 J.H.L. ZILLMANN *Past & Present Austral. Life* 159 There is now the bush 'larrikin' as well as the town 'larrikin', and it would be difficult sometimes to say which is the worse. Bush 'larrikins' have gone on to be bush-rangers. **1896** H. LAWSON *While Billy Boils* 104 About Byrock we met the bush liar in all his glory. He was dressed like—like a bush larrikin. **1950** 'B. JAMES' *Advancement Spencer Button* 26 Mr Rigby went on to paint bush larrikins in gloomier colours still. **1959** V. PALMER *Big Fellow* 115 Donovan, the one-time bush larrikin was distrusted by his party.

larrikiness. *Hist.* A female associate of a LARRIKIN 1 a.

1871 *Collingwood Advertiser & Observer* 22 June 3/5 Evidence was tendered as to the manner of life led by these larikinesses. **1891** *Truth* (Sydney) 1 Feb. 1/3 A contemporary writes of a fine inflicted ' . . on a brace of larrikins and a pair of larrikinesses'. **1892** G. PARKER *Round Compass in Aust.* 224 The slouch-hat, the rakish jib, the drawn features are not to be seen; nor does the young larrikiness—that hideous outgrowth of Sydney and Melbourne civilisation—exist as a class. **1898** *Bulletin* (Sydney) 22 Oct. (Red Page), The larrikiness eats fried fish in bed, and when her larrikin wakes up in the morning he finds he has been sleeping on the bones and the stopper of the vinegar-bottle. **1916** *Truth* (Sydney) 30 July 1/7 Jibe-Belles: Larrikinesses. **1956** J.E. WEBB *So much for Sydney* 10 These children of the new slums are natural recruits for the strange legion of 1955–56 larrikins and larrikinesses called 'bodgies' and 'widgies', and they know enough to realise that they have little to fear from a 'Labor' régime which has abolished the hangman. **1982** N. KEESING *Lily on Dustbin* 104 Cartoons of larrikinesses (or 'donahs') of the 1890s–1900s period show the hats worn by them and other 'flash' girls in a great variety of exaggerated forms.

larrikinism. Behaviour such as characterizes a larrikin.

1870 *Austral.* (Richmond) 10 Sept. 3/3 A slight attempt at 'larrikinism' was manifested. **1873** *Illustr. Sydney News* 10 June 2/2 Larrikinism seems rampant at Sofala. **1887** 'COMMERCIAL TRAVELLER' *Diary Three Months Trip Qld.* 28 This . . is a great place for 'playing larks'—not a harmless and innocent amusement, which the term would seem to imply, but rather the development of the innate spirit of larrikinism which unhappily is so characteristic of the Australian youth throughout the land. ***c* 1905** *Tourists' Guide Geelong* 7 The court of petty sessions, held fortnightly at Drysdale, has occasionally a case of larceny or larrikinism to deal with, the culprit being, as often as not, alien. **1920** *Huon Times* (Franklin) 5 Nov. 2/5 A party of bargemen from Hobart landed there and were guilty of such acts of larrikinism as would disgrace any civilised community. **1935** L.J. GOMM *Blazing Western Trails* 102 The apathy of the police in social questions, one sergeant . . going so far as to argue that there was no 'larrikinism' in Boulder City! **1963** J. POLLARD *Austral. Surfrider* 9 Farrelly is . . intense about the unfairness of the young surfer's reputation for larrikinism. **1968** *Nation* (Sydney) 25 May 9/1 Political larrikinism is well developed in this country. **1972** *Bulletin* (Sydney) 16 Dec. 56/2 Not only is Mathers prodigally verbally gifted, but he is immensely funny, a truly comic writer. How else embody Australian larrikinism? **1983** *Austral.* (Sydney) 29 Oct. 3/3 (*heading*) One of its two artistic directors .. believes it should not lose its essential 'larrikinism'.

larry, var. LARY.

Larry.

1. [Used elsewhere but recorded earliest in Aust.: see OEDS *sb.*[3]] In the phr. **as happy as Larry,** extremely happy.

1905 *Barrier Truth* (Broken Hill) 29 Dec. 1 Now that the adventure was drawing to an end, I found a peace of mind that all the old fogies on the river couldn't disturb. I was as happy as Larry. **1914** R. KALESKI *Austral. Barkers & Biters* 40 This makes her as happy as Larry, and she works A1 till she gets another spell. **1920** W.H. DOWNING *To Last Ridge* 47 McAlister .. got a piece in the leg and went off in a stretcher as happy as Larry. **1941** K. TENNANT *Battlers* 177 They was all as happy as Larry till you came down talking bloody war. **1946** D. BARR *Warrigal Joe* 68 He liked an easy life, and was as happy as Larry when on the wallaby. **1955** D. NILAND *Shiralee* 96 The same old Lucky. Full as a boot and happy as Larry. **1966** G. WYATT *Strip Jack Naked* 18 The cab driver is happy as larry with the bargain. **1978** S. BALL *Muma's Boarding House* 122 They talk like married magpies all night, eat and drink like navvies, and go home as happy as Larry. **1984** B. DICKINS *Crookes of Epping* 13 There are such nights and days of joy, the Crookes are happy as Larry.

2. [Perh. f. Br. dial. *larry* a disturbance, a scolding (see OED *sb.*[1] and EDD *sb.*[1] 2.), infl. by the name of *Larry* Foley (1849–1917), pugilist.] In the collocation **Larry Dooley,** a beating; a disturbance or fracas. Chiefly in the phr. **to give** (someone) **Larry Dooley.**

[**1886** *Daily Tel.* (Sydney) 21 Oct. 5/1 'I'll give you something as soon as you go outside.' Mr Neild ejaculated 'Another Larry Foley,' and Mr Melville replied 'I'll Larry Foley you where you sit.'] **1943** *Coast to Coast 1942* 12, I had driven him back a week before, and that morning I gave him Larry Dooley. **1964** P. ADAM SMITH *Hear Train Blow* 155 Ted and Alan still gave me larry-dooley. **1973** J. MURRAY *Larrikins* 169 The country towns at race time saw the wild boys rampage about, throwing stones on corrugated iron roofs, smashing windows, and creating Larry Dooley, in honour of the boxer named Foley. **1974** *Austral. Folksongs* (Folk Lore Council Aust.) 98 They say, 'Give them Larry Dooley', but they don't care how you feel. **1983** B. DAWE *Over here, Harv!* 5 Mum looked up eventually from the shirt she was ironing and I could see my stocks hadn't gone up at all overnight... 'Oh, have a heart, Mum... You want to ruin my appetite, or something?' 'Huh-huhh!' she said, giving the shirt Larry Dooley and shaking her head.

larry-doo. Abbrev. of *Larry Dooley*, see LARRY 2.

1978 SAW & MILBANK *Back to Back Tango* 21 The sport and games and, hum, gaming and larry-doo that could, just *could* be lined up.

lary. Also **larry.** Abbrev. of LARRIKIN.

1891 *Bohemia* (Melbourne) 3 Sept. 20 The 'lary' who has come to the years of indiscretion. **1907** *Truth* (Sydney) 30 June 9/5 'Oh, yer boshters! Go in South!' Yes the 'larys' all are raving, When they're killing with the mouth. **1970** P. WHITE *Vivisector* 109 Once a mob of larries happened to pass underneath, and he spat.

lash. [Spec. use of *lash* a sudden blow, esp. as infl. by the *v. to lash out*.] An attempt, a 'go'; a fight; fighting. Chiefly in the phr. **to have a lash at** (a person, an object, etc.).

1894 A.A. MACINNES *Straight as Line* 222 The fighting blood was roused within him, and he longed to have a 'lash', as he put it, at the gang. **1915** *Truth* (Sydney) 4 July 6/8 Fighters are wanted at the front, and the average larrikin loves lash. **1918** *Ibid.* 8 Sept. 3/8 If you are looking for a lash, you can always be accommodated at any football match in which Collingwood is engaged, unless you sport the Collingwood colours, and barrack for the home bunch. **1932** J. MCCARTER *Pan's Clan* 133 Stoush-artists from other places, who think they can use their mitts and look for lash, come the proverbial gutzers in Longreach. **1940** *Sentry Go* (Keswick) June 5 He was making the last 'lash at the roll'. **1953** K. TENNANT *Joyful Condemned* 214 If things get any tougher, I guess I'll have a lash at it. **1964** *Mount Isa Mail* 7 Jan. 1/8 Mr Stuart prefers station work but will have 'a lash' at anything offering. **1970** R. BEILBY *No Medals for Aphrodite* 23 Have a lash! Fighting back, no matter how futile that might be. **1976** K. BROWN *Knock Ten* 135, I reckon meself that carting'd be the lash... There's always no end of stuff getting shipped out for construction.

'lastic-side, var. ELASTIC-SIDE.

latchet. [Transf. use of *latchet(t)* the gurnard.] The edible marine fish *Pterygotrigla polyommata*, having large pectoral fins and a reddish-coloured skin.

1951 T.C. ROUGHLEY *Fish & Fisheries Aust.* 130 Originally the sharp-beaked gurnard was known as 'latchet', but this name has come to refer to the more slender species. **1962** 'N. CULOTTA' *Gone Fishin'* 87 One row of boxes contained very strange-looking red fish, with ugly heads, and fins like wings. 'They're gurnard... Those brownish-looking ones are called latchet. Not bad, if you skin 'em.' **1980** N. COLEMAN *Austral. Sea Fishes* 103 The latchet is often caught around reefs by line and is also taken in large numbers by trawling.

lathered, *ppl. a.* [Prob. joc. formation on BLITHERED. Used elsewhere but recorded earliest in Aust.] Drunk.

1910 L. ESSON *Three Short Plays* (1911) 17, I don git lathered on ther takin's, do I? **1945** J.A. ALLAN *Men & Manners* 167 When you have over-indulged in intoxicants .. you may be .. 'lathered' .. but you are never 'drunk'.

latrine wireless. [Formed by analogy with *latrine rumour*: see OEDS *latrine* 2.] In Services' speech: the latrine block (of a barracks, camp, etc.) as a source of rumour; a rumour. Also *attrib.*

1918 *Two Blues: Mag. 13th Battalion A.I.F.* Dec. 3 In our Australian camps all we now call 'Furphies' were called 'Latrine Wireless Messages'. **1931** 'D. BLACK' *Red Dust* 14 The term rumour is one we seldom use, preferring the less polite but more expressive 'Latrine Wireless'. It is nearly always from these places that stories emanate. **1944** J.F. DETTMAN *Here was Glory* 61 No doubt th' latrine wireless will again broadcast, 'fer certain This move will surely be th' dinkum thing. Next week we'll all see action.' **1944** G. MANT *You'll be Sorry* 67 The Latrine Wireless indeed kept us on considerable tenterhooks.

laughing jackass.

1. The kookaburra *Dacelo novaeguineae*. Also **laughing jack** and formerly **laughing bird.**

1798 D. COLLINS *Acct. Eng. Colony N.S.W.* I. 615 Go-gan-ne-gine, Bird named by us the Laughing Jack-Ass. **1804** G. CALEY in A.E.J. Andrews *Devil's Wilderness* (1984) 60 Heard Laughing Jack-Ass, a species of Alcedo. **1833** H.W. PARKER *Rise, Progress, & Present State Van Dieman's Land* 187 The laughing jackass (dacelo gigantea) is remarkable for the noise which it makes, and which, by the imagination of the first settlers was supposed to be like the noise .. a jackass would send forth, could it laugh; hence its name. **1849** W.S. CHAUNCY *Guide to S.A.* 28 The laughing bird .. may also be noticed .. for the peculiar strains in which it indulges. **1852** G.C. MUNDY *Our Antipodes* I. 192 The Laughing Jackass or *Dacelo gigantea* .. with little or no tail, and an enormously disproportionate head and bill—a most ugly and eccentric-looking fellow. **1868** J.R. HOULDING *Austral. Tales* 352 The next morning Wicky was up before the 'laughing jackasses'. **1885** J. HOOD *Land of Fern* 14 Day woke, on the stream I saw its first beam glide, And heard the first notes of the laughing jack's song. **1885** *Australasian Printers' Keepsake* 17 A laughing jackass, perched upon a noble blue-gum tree fronting our door. **1900** *Tocsin* (Melbourne) 2 Aug. 6/2 We determined to look out for a laughing jackass for supper .. we succeeded in bringing down a fat young bird, which we found very palatable, and somewhat resembling roast lamb. **1906** *Gadfly* (Adelaide) 13 June 21/3 The smell of the gumtrees and the sound of the laughing jack. **1926** L.C.E. GEE *Bush Tracks & Gold Fields* 95, I can't let you get back to England till I have shown you a laughing jackass. **1941** C. BARRETT *Aust.* 27 Each season .. a pair of kookaburras nested in a hollow in the old tree's bole... Perhaps that is why we have so many laughing Jacks on the farm. **1956** S. HOPE *Diggers' Paradise* 209 The wonderful lyre bird .. can imitate anything from a laughing jackass (the kookaburra) to the creak of a wagon wheel. **1962** B.W. LEAKE *Eastern Wheatbelt Wildlife* 79 Laughing jackasses were unfortunately brought here from the Eastern States by the W.A. Acclimatisation Society and occasionally appear. **1979** B. WANNAN *Chron. Boobyalla* 27 A superb pendant consisting of a simple circle of rolled gold, studded with seven Australian rubies encircling a kookaburra (laughing jackass) of diamente-encrusted [*sic*] white gold.

2. *fig.*

1874 C. DE BOOS *Congewoi Correspondence* 2, I couldn't believe that Australians would ever send into Parliament such a lot of chattering, laughing jackasses. **1899** *Progress* (Brisbane) 4 Feb. 1/2 Laughing-jackasses of the Press took up the cry with becoming fidelity.

laughing owl. Either of two nightjars, the *spotted nightjar*, see SPOTTED *a.*, and the *white-throated nightjar*, see WHITE *a.*[2] 1 b.

1929 A.H. CHISHOLM *Birds & Green Places* 157 A 'laughing owl', the white-throated nightjar of ornithology. **1964** M. SHARLAND *Territory of Birds* 199 The curtain of night came down .. slow enough to persuade a 'Laughing Owl' to utter its curiously eerie herald to the night. **1976** *Reader's Digest Compl. Bk. Austral. Birds* 312 White-throated nightjars .. are also called 'laughing owls'. Like owls, they fly almost noiselessly—and if they did not emit loud, laughing calls as they sweep silently overhead, an observer would not be aware of their presence.

laughing-side. Usu. *pl.* A jocular name for an ELASTIC-SIDE. Also **laughing side(d) boot.**

1937 *Bulletin* (Sydney) 6 Jan. 20/3 'Laughing-sides' wouldn't last long in a boggy cowyard. **1960** J. WALKER *No Sunlight Singing* 51 The dirty bare ankles .. disappeared into a broken-down pair of 'laughing-side' riding boots. **1968** F. HARDY *Unlucky Australs.* 8 High-heeled elastic-sided boots (which the Aborigines, with their genius for turning their limited vocabulary and pronunciation into poetry, call laughing-sided boots). **1976** C.D. MILLS *Hobble Chains & Greenhide* 107 Dicky .. had acquired a pair of the Trump's old cast-off 'laughin' sides'.

lavender bug. [See quot. 1976.] A bug, prob. a burrowing bug of the fam. Cydnidae.

1944 *Troppo Tribune* (Mataranka) 15 Apr. 2 At the closing of each day Lavender bugs come out to play. **1956** T. RONAN *Moleskin Midas* 156 The light is not so dim as to necessitate lamps with their accompanying swarm of flying ants and lavender bugs. **1976** B. SCOTT *Complete Bk. Austral. Folk Lore* 379 Re '*stinking, stinking wogs*' mentioned in the poem; these are undoubtedly the little beetles known in Innisfail as the '*lavender*' bug, or '*stink*' bug. When distressed these squirt out a corrosive fluid or gas which stings severely, especially if it gets you in the eye. The smell is unmistakable, like bitter almonds raised to the power of ten.

lawn sale. *N.T.* (chiefly in Alice Springs). GARAGE SALE. Also *attrib.*

1974 *Centralian Advocate* (Alice Springs) 21 Mar. 19/5 Lawn sale .. Clothing, toys, baby gear, records, typewriter, bicycle and more. Good buys. **1975** *Ibid.* 10 Apr. 19/3 Lawn sale .. Odds and ends. Household items something maybe for you. **1980** *Ibid.* 9 Oct. 46/7 Bring your leftover lawn sale stuff down to the Sunday Market and sell it there. **1985** *Ibid.* 6 Sept. 27/4 Do you have a houseful of furn. you don't know what to do with and can't be bothered with lawn sales.

lawyer vine. [Spec. use of Br. dial. *lawyer* a long bramble: see OED 3.] Any of several plants, chiefly of tropical and subtropical e. coastal Aust., esp. climbing plants of the genus *Calamus* (fam. Arecaceae), having long, whip-like leaf appendages armed with strong, pointed, recurved hooks; BUSH LAWYER 3. See also WAIT-A-WHILE. Also **lawyer, lawyer cane, lawyer palm.**

1871 *Austral. Town & Country Jrnl.* (Sydney) 18 Mar. 330/4 Lawyers make excellent clothes-lines, lasting for as many years as the hemp lines do months, and being always clean. **1876** 'EIGHT YRS.' RESIDENT' *Queen of Colonies* 117 One [Chinaman] was engaged in making baskets from the split canes of the 'lawyer' vine. **1887**

H. GULLET *Tropical N.S.W.* 10 Here . . is a long, vine-like creeper, throwing about its strong shoots, all armed with sharp hooks pointing backwards. It grows freely by the side of the track, and has an amiable way of hooking the face or eyes of the passing pedestrian or horseman. . . Some admirer of the ways of the learned profession has, with a just appreciation, happily named this aggressive and retentive and unscrupulous plant the 'lawyer vine'. **1889** R.B. ANDERSON tr. Lumholtz's *Among Cannibals* 103 The stem and leaves are studded with the sharpest thorns, which continually cling to you and draw blood, hence its not very polite name of *lawyer-palm*. **1896** J.W. ROBERTS *Mining Industry N.S.W.* 67 Woe betide the wayfarer who gets off the beaten track and finds himself entangled in a web of lawyer-canes and parasitic vines. **1908** 'FIFTY-THREE YRS.' MINER' *So Long* 20 The gully was a 'rough shop', being full of 'lawyer' and 'wait-a-while' vines. **1926** M. FORREST *Hibiscus Heart* 116 The ever-present glossy olive lawyer vine to catch at and imprison one. **1946** D. BARR *Warrigal Joe* 18 A mate of mine was hanged when a lawyer vine looped round his neck. **1962** H.J. FRITH *Mallee-Fowl* 4 The dense lawyer-cane jungle at the top of the Nightcap Ranges. **1984** B. DIXON *Searching for Aboriginal Lang.* 92 Walking in the bush . . plaiting split lawyer vine into a dilly-bag.

lay-by, *n.* A system of payment whereby a purchaser puts a deposit on an article which is then reserved by the retailer until the full price is paid. Freq. in the phr. **on (the) lay-by.** Also *attrib.*

1926 *Smith's Weekly* (Sydney) 9 Oct. 18/2 Farming on the Lay-by. **1927** Memo (Governing Director's Office, Grace Bros. Ltd. Sydney) 29 July, Please arrange for Mr Roach to exchange Lay By 7691 & to credit the full amount. **1938** *Point* (Melbourne) I. ii. 24 He wanted me to buy two tickets for the office dance on the lay-by. **1959** D. HEWETT *Bobbin Up* 10 Lovingly she'd pressed the blue silk dress for her wedding. . . She'd had it on lay-by ever since that night on Bondi Beach. **1967** D. HORNE *Educ. Young Donald* 95 Mum paid off, at two shillings a time, the collection of Shakespeare's plays she had put on the 'lay-by' for me. **1969** *Bulletin* (Sydney) 15 Feb. 4/3 Castlereagh Street swarms with girls assessing the lay-by situation in gear. **1980** S. ORR *Roll On* 59 They still talk of lay-bys and perms. **1984** *Age* (Melbourne) 30 June (Saturday Extra) 7/4 In our circle, the line was drawn at the lay-by (always 'the lay-by'), a sort of half-way house of credit in which you were given the thrill of purchase but denied the pleasure of consumption. Women of this era were for ever putting twin-sets on the lay-by.

lay-by, *v. trans.* To purchase (an article), using the lay-by system. Freq. *absol.*

1969 *Bulletin* (Sydney) 15 Feb. 10/2 The girls from the Rural are lay-bying like crazy. **1979** *Westerly* July 29 The draper's window urges Lay By Now for Xmas in May. **1985** P. READ *Down there with me on Cowra Mission* 29 My mother used to lay-by about six or seven months before Christmas.

lazy strike. *Obs.* GO-SLOW a.: see quot. 1920.

1920 *Argus* (Melbourne) 24 Feb. 6/9 The tramway employees put into force what was described as a 'lazy' strike. . . The men observed the regulations to the letter, limiting the number of passengers standing on the platform and paying strict attention to the speed at turns and crossings. The result was a slowing down of the service, with inconvenience to the passengers. **1923** C.F. THWING *Human Australasia* 59 The 'go-slow' or 'lazy' strike . . represents a desire to lessen the output.

Leach's kingfisher. [The specific epithet *Leachii* was applied by ornithologists N.A. Vigors and T. Horsfield, after English naturalist William *Leach* (1790–1836), founder of the genus *Dacelo*: see quot. 1825.] *Blue-winged kookaburra*, see BLUE *a.* Also **Leach kingfisher.**

[**1825** *Trans. Linnean Soc. London* (1827) XV. 205 [*Dacelo*] *Leachii* . . In honorem Gulielmi Elford Leach, Medicinae Doctoris, Sócietatum Regiae et Linneanae Socii . . ornithologi eximii, qui primùm hoc genus detexit characteribusque illustravit, haec species perpulchra nominatur.] **1848** J. GOULD *Birds of Aust.* II. Pl. 19, *Dacelo leachii* . . Leach's Kingsfisher. **1903** *Emu* II. 151 Dacelo leachii (Leach Kingfisher). . . The various nests I have personally found of these birds have all been holes drilled in the earthen nests of termites. **1917** *Bulletin* (Sydney) 5 July 22/2 Leach's kingfisher is aboriginally known as kitticarrara.

lead /lid/, *n.*[1] [Used elsewhere but recorded earliest in Aust.: see OED *sb.*[2] 6 b.] See quot. 1869 and also *deep lead* DEEP.

1852 *Empire* (Sydney) 16 Jan. 578/5 Experience . . proves that the *chief* deposit of gold is to be found at the turns of the stream on the inner side, in a line or *lead*, as it is termed. **1867** R.L.M. KITTO *Goldfields of Vic.* 63 *Quartz* mining is a much more profitable speculation than *alluvial* mining (except, of course, where a miner is fortunate enough to obtain a claim on a *known lead*, in which case the accumulation of a fortune is only a question of time). **1869** R.B. SMYTH *Goldfields & Mineral Districts* 614 *Lead*, a deep alluvial auriferous deposit or gutter. A lead, correctly defined, is an auriferous gully or creek, or river, the course of which cannot be determined by the trend of the surface, in consequence of the drainage having been altered either by the eruption of basalt or lava, or the deposition of newer layers of sand and gravel. **1880** *Argus* (Melbourne) 5 Feb. 5/7 There is every probability that the Flinders Basin will be the seat of further finds, and a lead discovered of payable gold in this watershed. **1932** I.L. IDRIESS *Prospecting for Gold* 11 Alluvial gold often runs in a 'lead', or a 'gutter'. That is, it may run in a more or less broken 'line', perhaps only one foot wide, down the centre of a creek.

lead /lid/, *n.*[2] [Spec. use of *lead* the front or leading place.]

1. a. The front part of a travelling mob (of sheep, cattle, etc.).

1904 *Bulletin* (Sydney) 8 Dec. 19/3 When cattle have 'rushed' . . the rider has seldom need to urge the good nag beneath him to 'get to the lead of 'em'. **1907** *Ibid.* 11 Apr. 15/3, I collared the spare night-horse and lit out to the old man's assistance. He had the lead blocked on the edge of the scrub when I came up, and was ringing 'em finely. **1950** G.M. FARWELL *Land of Mirage* 92 The lead was moving steadily along in a compact little mob with a check-shirted ringer standing in his stirrups alongside. **1954** T. RONAN *Vision Splendid* 160 Before old Jack and Phar Lap had hunted the last tail bullock off the stone, the lead was lying down full-bellied and contented. **1972** *Bronze Swagman Bk. Bush Verse* (1973) 9 'Twixt the river bank and the myall scrub Where Gold Star wheeled the lead.

b. In the phr. **on the lead,** at the head of a travelling mob.

1919 *Bulletin* (Sydney) 17 July 22/3 A dog on the lead of bolting jumbucks should turn out. By so doing he meets sheep that are breaking behind him. A stockman on the lead of rushing cattle or horses always turns his mount's tail to the herd for the same reason. **1981** A.B. FACEY *Fortunate Life* 168 The cow on the lead had to go back and come over in front of each lot to show them the way.

2. *transf.* A route followed by travelling stock.

1962 MARSHALL & DRYSDALE *Journey among Men* 54 In an odd way they have even affected the landscape, for on the long leads you will find the inevitable bottles and cans, discarded along the way, where someone has taken . . a few 'cold ones for the road'. **1963** R.H. CONQUEST *Spurs are Rusty Now* 50 Judy and I had twelve gallons of water between us when we started on the last dry 'lead', and eleven gallons of it went to the two horses. **1978** D. STUART *Wedgetail View* 5 On a hard track with a mob of cattle that wasted away week after week, crawling down the long leads.

Leadbeater's cockatoo /lɛdbitəz kɒkəˈtu, lɛdbɛtəz kɒkəˈtu/. [f. the name of the nineteenth-century English natural history agent Benjamin *Leadbeater* (see quot. 1831).] MAJOR MITCHELL COCKATOO.

[**1831** *Proc. Zool. Soc. London* 61 Mr Vigors exhibited, from the collection of Mr Leadbeater, an undescribed species of *Cockatoo* from New Holland . . *Plycotolophus leadbeateri.*] **1843** J. GOULD *Birds of Aust.* (1848) V. Pl. 2, *Cacatua leadbeateri* . . Leadbeater's Cockatoo. **1849** C. STURT *Narr. Exped. Central Aust.* II. 39 App. *Leadbeater's Cockatoo* . . frequents the pine forests near Gawler Town. **1865** *Illustr. Sydney News* 15 July 12/1 This, the most elegant of all our cockatoos . . inhabits the barren desolate country stretching from the Wimmera to Western Australia; the dense mallee scrubs is its home. **1896** B. SPENCER *Rep. Horn Sci. Exped. Central Aust.* II. 57 Leadbeater's Cockatoo . . were first seen near Finke Gorge, but were too shy to approach within shot. **1943** C. BARRETT *Austral. Animal Bk.* 225 Known to all Australians as the 'Major Mitchell', the pink or Leadbeater's cockatoo . . is the handsomest of all the species, and the least plentiful.

Leadbeater's possum /lɛdbitəz ˈpɒsəm, lɛdbɛtəz ˈpɒsəm/. [f. the name of the naturalist John *Leadbeater* (*c* 1832–1888), taxidermist at the National Museum, Melbourne, Vic. (see quot. 1968).] The rare possum *Gymnobelideus leadbeateri*, having a grey to greyish-brown back with a dark stripe and a pale underside, restricted to the mountain ash forests of the central highlands of Victoria, and a faunal emblem of that State.

1926 A.S. LE SOUEF et al. *Wild Animals Australasia* 249 Leadbeater's opossum *Genus Gymnobelideus*. . . The one species of this family was restricted to a very small district, that of the Bass River valley, in South-eastern Victoria. **1935** T. RAYMENT *Cluster of Bees* 378 The small graceful Leadbeater's opossum. **1942** C. BARRETT *On Wallaby* 37 Though I prowled by night with a powerful torch, no Leadbeater's possum was seen, only a few ringtails. **1968** V. SERVENTY *Wildlife of Aust.* 30 In 1867 a new possum was found in the forests of south-eastern Victoria. It was named Leadbeater's possum in honour of the taxidermist then at the Melbourne Museum. **1975** *Ecos* v. 26/2 Among the rediscovered species, the Leadbeater's possum and the New Holland mouse have turned out to be relatively common. **1985** *Canberra Times* 24 July 21/3, I hope that Leadbeater's possum has not been officially selected, without anyone telling me, as the faunal symbol of arms control.

leaden flycatcher. [See quot. 1929.] The flycatcher *Myiagra rubecula* of n. and e. Aust. incl. Tas., and New Guinea, having a swift, darting flight.

1908 E.J. BANFIELD *Confessions of Beachcomber* 95 Leaden Fly-catcher, *Myiagra rubecula.* **1917** *Bulletin* (Sydney) 19 July 24/1 The leaden flycatcher makes a noise like . . a frog in the grip of a snake, wherefore it is the 'frog-bird'. **1929** A.H. CHISHOLM *Birds & Green Places* 77 The leaden flycatcher is a shapely and pretty bird. Light-lead colour on the coat, head and chest is set off by pure white on the abdomen in the case of the male, and in the female the leaden hue is relieved by rich rust-red on throat and chest. **1964** M. SHARLAND *Territory of Birds* 160 (*caption*) The Leaden Flycatcher—one of several flycatchers that visit the mangrove flats and melaleuca jungles of the North. **1984** M. BLAKERS et al. *Atlas Austral. Birds* 405 The Leaden Flycatcher breeds in New Guinea and adjacent islands and in Australia.

leader. [Transf. use of *leader* front horse.] One of the leading bullocks in a team: see quot. 1959.

1843 H. CASWALL *Hints from Jrnl.* 33 A two-wheeled dray with a pole, is certainly better than with shafts. . . The shafter should be a large heavy animal. . . Two good leaders are also indispensable. **1874** J.J. HALCOMBE *Emigrant & Heathen* 35 Bullock-drays . . have a strong pole, to which the yokes of the pole-bullocks, and the chain of the leaders, are fastened. **1904** *Bulletin* (Sydney) 15 Dec. 40/1 Eighteen to twenty constitute a team, which includes polers—those nearest the waggon—clampers, body bullocks and leaders. **1939** J. SORENSEN *Lost Shanty* 16 The shafters prop, the leaders pull, The wheels creak dismally. **1948** P.J. HURLEY *Red Cedar* 71 Among those bullockies were two girls . . who were not only able to pick off 'leaders' with their long whips, but push off any prowling philanderers. **1959** H.P. TRITTON *Time means Tucker* 36 A bullock-team is made up in four parts: polers, pin, body and leaders. The leaders are the most important, being the mainstay of the team. **1968** L. BRADEN *Bullockies* 34 A bullock team is comprised of leaders, the pair of which are the brains of the team [etc.].

leaf-cutting bee. [See quot. 1960.] Any of several bees of the fam. *Megachilidae*, using pieces of leaf to construct or line cells for their eggs. Also **leaf-cutter (bee).**

1935 T. RAYMENT *Cluster of Bees* 213 There were wild-flowers to yield nectar for the innumerable wild bees, including . . black leaf-cutters. **1955** *Bulletin* (Sydney) 5 Oct. 12/4 There are more than one species of leaf-cutter bee. **1960** J. CHILD *Austral. Insects* 67 Leaf-cutting bees, Megachilidae. Many bees in this family cut circular pieces of leaf with which they construct a case in which the food supply and egg are deposited.

leangle /li'æŋgəl/. Formerly with much variety, as **langeel, leangil, liangel, liangle, liangra.** [a. Wergaia (dial. of Wemba) *lieŋgel* f. *lieŋ* tooth.] An Aboriginal fighting club with a hooked striking head: see quot. 1845. See also LEONILE.

1841 *Geelong Advertiser* 26 June 2/4 The Aborigines got drunk . . and gave vent to their blood-thirsty passions by quarrelling and fighting with each other. Some of them are frightfully wounded. The liangra, a hatchet-shaped club, is the weapon generally used in such brawls. **1845** C. GRIFFITH *Present State & Prospects Port Phillip* 155 The liangle is . . of the shape of a pickaxe, with only one pick. Its name is derived from another native word, *liang*, signifying tooth. **1861** 'OLD BUSHMAN' *Bush Wanderings* 225 The root of the shey-oak is much used by the Blacks in making their weapons, such as boomerangs, liangels, etc. **1867** G.G. MCCRAE *Mamba* 9 The long leangle's nascent form Forespoke the distant battle-storm. **1878** R.B. SMYTH *Aborigines of Vic.* II. 299 The Murray and Lower Goulburn natives . . use . . the leangle—a peculiar weapon not unlike the miner's pick. **1891** H. NISBET *Colonial Tramp* I. 125 He is attacked singly by his enemies, who each deliver one blow with a 'liangle', as blood must be spilt. **1910** J. MATHEW *Two Representative Tribes Qld.* 122 A weapon called *bokkan*, from *bokka*, a horn or projection, corresponded to the leangil of the Victorians. **1936** *Amer. Anthrop.* (Menasha, Wisconsin) 83 In slightly varying forms, the marpungy is often met with under such names as burrong, langeel, leonile, and bendi, according to district. **1966** W.S. RAMSON *Austral. Eng.* 132 Leangle, 'a club', and wirri, 'a throwing stick', are Victorian.

learner. *Shearing.* One not yet fully trained as a shearer.

1917 *11 C.A.R.* 433 'Learner' means a shearer or intending shearer who has not yet shorn under engagement through three sheds. **1938** *37 C.A.R.* 613 Both sides agree that the current definition of learner limits unduly the amount of training required. I have now inserted a definition by which one who has not shorn 5,000 sheep is still a learner. **1956** *Bulletin* (Sydney) 12 Sept. 13/1 The learner was battling through a penful of tough wethers when the boss appeared. **1965** J.S. GUNN *Terminol. Shearing Industry* i. 35 A learner is not a shedhand or barrower, but a budding shearer who has not yet shorn 5,000 sheep (10,000 in Queensland). **1979** M. RUTHERFORD *Departmental* 42 Shearing was okay. Dad took me everywhere to get me learner's pen but I could never get a run of me own.

leary, var. LAIRY.

lease. [Spec. use of *lease* a piece of land leased.]

a. An area of land used for mining.

1883 *Northern Daily Leader* (Tamworth) (1983) 2 Dec. 6/3 There is no progress being made with the mines owing to the want of machinery, and several leases have been taken up with a view to floating them to Sydney, mostly abandoned leases. **1889** *Goldfields Vic.* 26 The Never-can-tell Gold Mining Company has been recently formed, having purchased two leases on the Dandenong Spur, Long Gully. **1890** *Ibid.* 15 A nice block of stone was crushed from Johnston's lease. **1950** G.S. CASEY *City of Men* 177 Kevin tramped off across the leases until at last he reached the outskirts, where there was just bush and a few old, abandoned 'shows'. **1962** O. PRYOR *Aust.'s Little Cornwall* 65 The mining company . . realized that it would be better to have most of their employees living on the leases than in the towns.

b. An area leased for farming.

1897 *Tocsin* (Melbourne) 9 Dec. 4/1 Those gifts by the State . . are euphoniously termed 'selections', 'leases', and even 'purchases'! **1944** J.H. PICK *Aust.'s Dying Heart* (ed. 2) 85 These leases were completely spelled for over twenty years. Despite this prolonged rest the frontages which were eaten out in the first occupation made absolutely no progress in the way of regeneration. **1960** *N.T. News* (Darwin) 12 Feb. 7/5 Rain extended to Katherine and relieved near-drought conditions on a number of leases there.

leatherhead. [See quot. 1854.] Any of several friar birds, esp. the *noisy friar bird* (see NOISY).

1841 J. GOULD *Birds of Aust.* (1848) IV. Pl. 58, Its bare head and neck have also suggested the names of 'Friar Bird', 'Monk', 'Leather Head', etc. **1845** L. LEICHHARDT *Jrnl. Overland Exped. Aust.* 31 Oct. (1847) 461 A species of Ptilotis . . entertained us at daybreak, as the Leatherhead, with its constantly changing call and whistling did during the day. **1854** W. HOWITT *Boy's Adventures* 27 The leatherhead is a very odd bird. It is as large as a fieldfare, with ash-coloured back and whitish stomach, but the singularity of it lies in the head, which is destitute of feathers, and covered with a brown skin resembling leather—whence its name. **1888** M.M. BALLOU *Under Southern Cross* 217 Now and then the confused utterances of the leather-head were heard, a peculiar bird resembling a small vulture. **1904** *Emu* III. 235 In an orchard close by, Leatherheads . . waged ceaseless war on the ripe figs. **1915** *Honk* ii. 5/2 'Leatherheads' are unknown here [*sc.* Sydney] and one is as much a curiosity here as in London. **1928** M.E. FULLERTON *Austral. Bush* 122 The leatherhead is the foe of the orchardist. **1948** R. RAVEN-HART *Canoe in Aust.* 207 Leatherheads (Noisy Friar-birds) with shiny black helmets like coal-heavers, and a call like 'Pig-aback'. **1981** Q. WILD *Honey Wind* 2 'Hey, you old djurwarag,' she called to the leatherhead feeding among the white blossoms.

leatherjacket.

1. [See quots. 1770 and 1974.] Any of many marine fish of the fam. Monacanthidae, widely distributed in Austral. waters and elsewhere in the Pacific and Indian oceans, having a tough skin.

1770 J. COOK *Jrnls.* 5 May (1955) I. 310 They had caught a great number of small fish which the sailors call leather Jackets on account of their having a very thick skin. **1789** W. TENCH *Narr. Exped. Botany Bay* 129 Soles, leather-jackets, and many other species, all so good in their kind, as to double our regret at their not being more numerous. **1842** *Tasmanian Jrnl. Nat. Sci.* I. 105 *Monacanthus Rudis* . . known at Port Arthur (as well as the *Aleuteres* . .) by the name of Leather Jacket. **1873** F. DE CASTELNAU *Edible Fishes Vic.* 16 The family of *Sclerodermi* or *leather jackets*. . . Many are remarkable by their curious forms and the great beauty of their colours. **1895** C. THACKERAY *Amateur Fisherman's Guide* 3 The fisherman suffers much tribulation when a leatherjacket or tailer bites his line and clears off with his hook. **1935** F. CLUNE *Rolling down Lachlan* 2 Hairy-legged fishermen who sold skinned leather-jackets as butter-fish. **1960** M. VIZZERS *She'll do Me!* 86 It was weird looking, shaped like a parallelogram, with a hard dark skin and a big spike on its back. 'Leatherjacket! Three quarters gut but the rest is good eatin'!' **1974** J.M. THOMSON *Fish Ocean & Shore* 140 Leatherjackets have small fine spines which are modified scales scattered over their bodies giving the body a velvety feeling and providing the name for the group. **1983** *Age* (Melbourne) 19 Sept. 11/1 Mr MacDonald said commercial fish hardest hit by the dieback were . . rock flathead, leatherjacket and calimari.

2. [See quot. 1853.] A thin cake made of a (sometimes leavened) flour and water dough, cooked (usu. with fat) in a pan over a fire.

1843 *Melbourne Times* 11 Mar. 4/6 A damson tart of goodly dimensions, was sent to a baker, to receive the benefit of his oven, upon its return, lo! it had become a gooseberry tart, a veritable leather jacket, unsightly to the eye, tough and sour to the palate. **1846** G.H. HAYDON *Five Yrs. Experience Aust. Felix* 151 A plentiful supply of 'leather jackets', (dough fried in a pan) served to appease us until a damper could be made. **1853** MOSSMAN & BANISTER *Aust. Visited & Revisited* 126 'Leather-jackets', an Australian bush term for a thin cake made of dough, and put into a pan to bake with some fat. The term is a very appropriate one, for tougher things cannot well be eaten. **1855** W. HOWITT *Land, Labor & Gold* I. 126 The leather-jacket is a cake of mere flour and water, raised with tartaric acid and carbonate of soda instead of yeast, and baked in the frying pan. . . A fat-cake is the same thing as a leather-jacket, only fried in fat. **1893** *Antipodean* (Melbourne) 96, I wish I had enough fat to make the pan siss, I'd treat meself to a leather-jacket. **1904** *Bulletin* (Sydney) 7 Apr. 16/4 When the baking powder is used up, unleavened bread is cooked in thin wafers, so that the crust on both sides meets, leaving no room for dough between; this is called 'leather jacket'.

3. Usu. as **leather-jacket.** Any of several trees, sometimes so-called from the toughness of their bark.

1860 G. BENNETT *Gatherings of Naturalist* 325 Another species is named Coach-wood, Leather-jacket, and also Light-wood by the colonists (*Ceratopetalum apetalum*). **1871** *Austral. Town & Country Jrnl.* (Sydney) 18 Mar. 330/4 The bean-tree or leather-jacket with pods 4 in. long. **1937** D. GLASS *Austral. Fantasy* 12 The leaves point long fingers to the ground, and hesitate to fall throughout the seasons. So the bark peels off instead: not only the stringy 'messmate' variety, but iron-bark, leather-jackets, black-butts and all. **1981** Q. WILD *Honey Wind* 124 A big hive of bees hung thick on a leather-jacket eucalypt.

leatherneck. *Obs.* A rouseabout.

1897 *Worker* (Sydney) 11 Sept. 1/1 The 'rouseabout' . . he sneeringly terms 'loppy' and a 'leatherneck'. **1900** *Bulletin* (Sydney) 18 Aug. 14/3 The shearer terms the rouseabout variously a 'loppy', 'bluetongue', 'wop-wop', 'leather-neck', 'crocodile', etc. **1905** *Shearer* (Sydney) 4 Feb. 4/2 What do you know of . . 'loppies', 'leather-necks' and 'blue-tongues'. **1945** S.J. BAKER *Austral. Lang.* 286 *A leatherneck* is a marine in the U.S.; in Australia he is a station handyman.

leatherwood. [See quot. 1969.] The rainforest tree or (occas.) tall shrub *Eucryphia lucida* (fam. Eucryphiaceae) of Tas., yielding a tough timber, and bearing showy, scented flowers from which a pale, distinctively scented honey is made; any of several other trees or shrubs, esp. the related shrubby *E. milliganii* of Tas.; the wood of these trees. See also *pink wood* PINK *a.* Also *attrib.*

1903 *Tasmanian Timbers* (Tas. Lands & Survey Dept.) 27 Leatherwood (*Eucryphia billardieri*) . . is very useful in the manufacture of implements being somewhat akin in nature to the English ash, but stronger. **1923** M.B. PETERSEN *Jewelled Nights* 298 She had decorated both camps with big jars of leatherwood blossom. **1956** B. BEATTY *Beyond Aust.'s Cities* 84 Leatherwood and Huon pine, together with various species of eucalypts, grow from the water's edge to the skyline. **1969** KING & BURNS *Wildflowers Tas.* 36 The name 'leatherwood' was originally given to *Acradenia franklinii*, possibly on account of the toughness of its wood, but by 1903 was being transferred by common usage to the *Eucryphias*, which produce honey. **1975** L.E. & O.B. FAULK *Austral. Alternative* 72 With our toast . . we had 'leatherwood honey', one of the . . flavours of honey for which the island . . is famous.

leave.

1. *Obs.* Of a convict: in the phr. **on leave,** in possession of a ticket of leave.

1811 *Sydney Gaz.* 19 Jan., Those who have received Emancipations or Pardons will be required to produce them, as will also those who are off the Store on leave, be required to produce their Tickets of Leave. **1840** A. RUSSELL *Tour through Austral. Colonies* 184 The runaway telling him he was travelling on a message, the native . . demanded a sight of . . the passport, which every convict on leave carries.

2. Special Comb. **leave pass** [transf. use of *(leave) pass* written authority for Services' personnel to be on leave], 'permission' to be away from home.

1973 J. O'GRADY *Survival in Doghouse* 11 We had a bit of trouble getting leave passes from our wives, and had to make all sorts of impossible promises. **1979** A.J. BURKE *Bite Pineapple* 86 A husband could get a much sought leave pass from kerosene lamps and Home, Sweet Home which lacked colour T.V. and other modern amenities. His excuse was that he was going to the lodge.

lechenaultia, var. LESCHENAULTIA.

leek. Shortened form of *green leek* (see GREEN *a.* 1).

1854 W. HOWITT *Boy's Adventures* 34 We have seen thousands of small green parroquets, which they call leeks. **1902** *Bulletin* (Sydney) 6 Sept. 16/3 A great pest to N.S.W. orchardists is the common 'green-leek' parrot. Just as the fruit is ripening these 'leeks' swoop down upon it.

leek orchid. Any of many terrestrial orchids of the chiefly Austral. genus *Prasophyllum* (fam. Orchidaceae), having a single onion-like leaf and spike of very small flowers.

1914 F. SULMAN *Pop. Guide Wild Flowers N.S.W.* II. 190 *Prasophyllum elatum.* 'Tall Leek Orchid' . . the tallest terrestrial orchid in Australia. **1926** J. POLLARD *Bushland Man* 207 They plucked . . donkey orchids, leek orchids and many others. **1951** R. ERICKSON *Orchids of West* 52

A company of little Leek Orchids has an elfin quality. **1984** D.T. & C.E. Woolcock *Austral. Terrestrial Orchids* 82 Leek orchids . . are well represented in Australia. . . Their distinguishing . . features are the smooth, long leaf, like that of the onion plant [etc.].

leery, var. Lairy.

leg. Used *attrib.* in Special Comb. **leg-iron** *hist.* [used elsewhere but recorded earliest in Aust.], a shackle or fetter for the leg; also *fig.*; so **-ironed** *a.*; **-rope,** a noosed rope used to secure an animal by one hind leg; also *fig.*, and as *v. trans.*

[**1827 leg iron:** P. Cunningham *Two Yrs. in N.S.W.* I. 46 The jail-gang straddling sulkily by in their jingling leg-chains.] **1849** A. Harris *Emigrant Family* (1967) 310 The clank of the leg-iron . . sounded in his ears. **1892** 'R. Boldrewood' *Nevermore* II. 91 Lance found himself early next morning driven off to Ballarat, leg-ironed and hand-cuffed. **1903** *Truth* (Sydney) 5 Apr. 5/3 What was good enough for a leg-ironed community seems now to be good enough for the 'new nation' sprung from its lecherous loins. **1905** *Bulletin* (Sydney) 6 July 16/2 Unearthed at West Dapto (N.S.W.) . . two rust-eaten leg-irons. **1911** R.G.S. Williams *Austral. White Slaves* 72 He was leg-ironed, in accordance with the prison regulations. **1921** *Bulletin* (Sydney) 21 Apr. 25/2 Only two Australian theatrical managements were to be trusted out of leg-irons. **1936** F. Gerald *Millionaire in Memories* 175 One set of leg-irons interested me greatly. Attached to the ankles were great balls of iron that made it impossible for the wearer to lift his feet; he could only shuffle an inch or two at a time. **1849** A. Harris *Emigrant Family* (1967) 129 The **leg-rope** is now passed round his hind legs. **1888** 'R. Boldrewood' *Robbery under Arms* (1937) I. 14 We could milk, leg-rope, and bail up for ourselves. **1898** *Bulletin* (Sydney) 14 Nov. 27/3 Bailing up cows is nice, too. . . When you have got them bailed, its ten to one that the first you go to leg-rope plants her foot in your stomach. **1911** *Truth* (Sydney) 7 May 7/6 (*heading*) Lee leg-roped for lurid language. **1946** F. Clune *Try Nothing Twice* 100 Run that creamy heifer into the bail . . then leg-rope her and milk her—it's easy. **1956** A. Marshall *How's Andy Going?* 2 'He tried to leg-rope it,' Joe explained, 'and the cow let out and got him in the stomach.'

Legacy.

1. An organization dedicated to the care of dependents of deceased Services' or ex-Services' personnel. Also **Legacy Club.**

1923 *Argus* (Melbourne) 31 Oct. 20/3 Mr C.V. Watson . . at the Legacy Club luncheon yesterday, addressed members on the subject of 'The Protection of Industrial Property'. **1932** C. Blatchford *Legacy* 5 'The Spirit of Legacy is Service.' Legacy has been aptly defined as 'A Practical Expression of the Comradeship of the War'. **1936** E. Scott *Aust. during War* in *Official Hist. Aust. 1914–18* XI. 856 A Melbourne club, formed in kinship with that at Hobart, preferred to call itself the Legacy Club. Legacy clubs were afterwards established in Sydney, Canberra, Adelaide, Brisbane, Perth, Geelong, Ballarat, Bendigo and other cities, and they were ultimately federated. . . The peculiar object of the clubs has been to ensure that the children of soldiers who died, whether during or as a result of the war, should have as good a start as if their fathers were able to guide and provide for them. **1944** *Bandicog* (Bandiana) 19 Aug. 2 There are toys to be made for Legacy. **1953** *Old Faithful: Jrnl. 3rd Battalion R. Austral. Regiment* 10 Oct. 1 Legacy is a force for good in the community worthy of your support. **1979** W.D. Joynt *Breaking Road for Rest* 160 The name Legacy was chosen because the members of the new organisation had accepted as a legacy the responsibility of seeing that the ideals which their comrades had died fighting for were maintained in Australia. **1985** *Bombala Times* 18 July 5/1 Legacy held their annual meeting on June 28.

2. Used *attrib.* to designate a recipient of support from Legacy.

1958 *Meanjin* 136 James is a Legacy boy. No one is more pleased at the boy's success than Ned Williams, who has been acting in loco parentis since the lad's father died in action at Gallipoli. **1965** *Legacy* (Legacy Club Adelaide) 6 The Gellibrand Scholarship . . provides Legacy children with post-graduate education overseas. **1969** *On Guard* (Broken Hill) Sept. 7 A letter received by the President of Adelaide Legacy from . . a Legacy Boy.

leger /ˈlɛdʒə/. [f. St. *Leger* the name of a classic horse-race held annually at Doncaster in England since 1776.] A stand or section of a racecourse, usu. at some distance from the finishing-post. Also *attrib.*

1907 *Truth* (Sydney) 20 Jan. 7/8 The iron fence which divides the leger stand from the grandstand on the Mudgee racecourse was the means of cutting off the poor man's beer on the occasion of the Spring Flat races. **1949** L. Glassop *Lucky Palmer* 66 'I'm going round to the Leger.' . . Forcing his way through the crowd in the Leger, the cheaper section of the course, 'Lucky' noticed that Norm Carston . . had Glittering Gold at seven to one.

legislative, *a.* In special collocations: **Legislative Assembly,** the title of a Colonial (later State) legislature, now esp. the lower house of a State parliament; **Council,** the title of a Colonial (later State) legislature, now the upper house of a State parliament.

1823 *Act* (G.B.) 4 Geo. IV. no. 96 Sect. 24, It is not at present expedient to call a **Legislative Assembly** in the said Colony. **1834** *Hobart Town Mag.* May 115 Captain Swanston to the Legislative Assembly . . advocated the appropriation of the colonial revenue to objects of Colonial utility and improvement. **1854** *Vic. Govt. Gaz.* 28 Mar. (Suppl.) 1 There shall be established in Victoria instead of the Legislative Council now subsisting one Legislative Council and one Legislative Assembly. **1859** *Qld. Govt. Gaz.* 10 Dec. 2/2 There shall be within our said Colony of Queensland a Legislative Council and a Legislative Assembly. **1889** *Act* (W.A.) 52 Vict. no. 23 Sect. 3, It shall be lawful for the Governor . . to prorogue the Legislative Council and Legislative Assembly. **1918** C.H. Northcott *Austral. Social Dev.* 27 In every Australian State and in the Commonwealth, there are two legislative houses. One of these, known in the States by the term Legislative Assembly, and in the Commonwealth as the House of Representatives. **1823** *Act* (G.B.) 4 Geo. IV. no. 96 Sect. 33, In the case of the Death, Absence, or permanent Incapacity of any Member or Members of the said **Legislative Council,** the Governor, or Acting Governor . . shall and may appoint some fit and proper person to act in the Place and Stead of such Person. **1825** *Hobart Town Gaz.* 10 Dec., His Majesty Doth hereby . . commit to such Persons, as shall by any Warrant or Warrants . . be constituted and appointed to be the Legislative Council of the said Island of Van Diemen's Land. **1837** *Act* (S.A.) 1 Vict. no. 1 Sect. 1, Be it enacted by His Excellency John Hindmarsh . . Governor and Commander-in-Chief of . . South Australia by and with the advice of the Legislative Council. **1850** *Act* (G.B.) 13 & 14 Vict. no. 59 Sect. 2, There shall be within and for the Colony of *Victoria* a separate Legislative Council. **1854, 1859** [see *Legislative Assembly*]. **1873** A. Trollope *Aust. & N.Z.* I. 245 The Upper House, or Legislative Council, in Sydney is dignified and conservative. . . The Executive Council consists of the Governor and seven ministers—one of whom must be in the Legislative Council. **1890** *Quiz* (Adelaide) 4 Apr. 1/2 The next three years of politics will be a conflict between the Assembly, as representing the will of the people, and the Legislative Council, as the champions of large proprietorship. **1918** C.H. Northcott *Austral. Social Dev.* 27 The other house, called the Legislative Council, is designed to check and criticise the onslaught of 'direct leveling democracy'. **1986** *Canberra Times* 3 Mar. 2/4 The legislation was defeated by the then Liberal-dominated Legislative Council.

legitimacy. *Obs.* See quot. 1827.

1827 P. Cunningham *Two Yrs. in N.S.W.* I. 16 *Legitimacy*, a colonial term for designating the *cause* of the emigration of a certain portion of our population; i.e. having legal reasons for making the voyage. **1836** J.F. O'Connell *Residence Eleven Yrs. New Holland* 34 Legitimacy, in all other parts of the world a coveted qualification, is in New Holland a term of reproach.

legitimate. *Obs.* One who came to Australia as a convict. Also *attrib.*

1827 P. Cunningham *Two Yrs. in N.S.W.* II. 116 We have the *legitimates*, or *cross-breds*,—namely, such as have *legal* reasons for visiting this colony; and the *illegitimates*, or such as are free from that stigma. **1829** R. Mudie *Picture of Aust.* 355 Those who are born in the colony are called *Currency*, and those of English or European birth, and who have not found their way in such a manner as to entitle them to the cant name of Legitimates, are called *Sterling*. **1836** J.F. O'Connell *Residence Eleven Yrs. New Holland* 34 The veracity of this narrative is not so questionable as it might be, were he left to the presumption that the narrator was a *legitimate, legal*, or *sentenced* visiter [*sic*] of Botany Bay.

Leichhardt pine. [f. the name of the Prussian naturalist and explorer F.W.L. *Leichhardt* (1813–?1848).] The tree *Nauclea orientalis* (fam. Rubiaceae) of coastal n. Aust. and elsewhere in the tropical Indo-Pacific region, having large leaves and yielding an edible fruit and a close-grained, yellowish, soft wood. Also **Leichhardt tree,** and *ellipt.* as **Leichhardt.**

1860 F. von Mueller *Essay* 12 The opportunity is an apt one for offering here some remarks on the 'Leichhardt-tree' of the settlers of Rockhampton. **1870** C.H. Allen *Visit to Qld.* 172 We made our 'camp' . . under the thick shade of a splendid Leichhardt tree. **1882** W. Sowden *N.T. as it Is* 55 Leichhardt pine . . is not really a pine at all, but its timber is useful. **1886** H. Finch-Hatton *Advance Aust.* (rev. ed.) 231 Both fig-trees and Leichardt are very handsome. **1908** E.J. Banfield *Confessions of Beachcomber* 252 Dessert . . might be plentiful and varied . . 'Koo-badg-aroo' (Leichhardt-tree, *Sarcocephalus cordatus*), resembling a strawberry in shape, but brown, spicy and hot. **1928** C.G. Lane *Adventures in Big Bush* 281 There had been but one tree . . that had withstood the fiery onslaught, and that tree was a leichardt. **1946** W.E. Harney *North of 23°* 147 These were Leichhardt pines, a large green tree with big leaves and a pod in season that is fairly edible. **1967** E. Kettle *Gone Bush* 241 One of the women . . picked a large leaf from a Leichhardt pine to demonstrate how it could be neatly folded to form a cup. **1975** X. Herbert *Poor Fellow my Country* 1315 There was the red flag fluttering against blue sky high in a dead leichhardt pine.

leipoa /laɪˈpoʊə/. *Obs.* [The bird genus *Leipoa* was named in 1840 by English naturalist John Gould (*Birds of Aust.* (1848) V. Pl. 78), f. Gr. λειπ- stem of λείπειν to leave + ᾠά eggs, referring to the bird 'leaving' its eggs in a mound.] *Mallee fowl*, see Mallee 6.

1840 *Proc. Zool. Soc. London* 126 This new species . . Mr Gould proceeded to characterize . . as a new genus, under the name of *Leipoa*, signifying 'a deserter of its eggs'. **1845** E.J. Eyre *Jrnls. Exped. Central Aust.* II. 274 The eggs of the leipoa, or native pheasant, are found in singular-looking mounds of sand, thrown up by the bird in the midst of the scrubs. **1853** S. Sidney *Three Colonies* (ed. 2) 289 The leipoa, or mound-building bird, improperly named by the colonists the wild turkey, is found in great numbers. **1865** G.F. Angas *Aust.* 96 The leipoa . . is an inhabitant of the dry and desert mallee scrubs of South and Western Australia. **1872** Mrs E. Millett *Austral. Parsonage* 223 There is, however, amongst edible birds none that can at all compare with the one known . . to naturalists as the *Leipoa.*

lemon.

1. Used *attrib.* in the names of flora and fauna: **lemon-breasted flycatcher,** the flycatcher *Microeca flavigaster*, a predom. olive-brown bird with a lemon-yellow belly, occurring in n. Aust. and New Guinea; **-crested cockatoo** *obs.*, *white cockatoo* (a), see White *a.*[2] 1 b.; **gum,** any of several trees, usu. of the genus *Eucalyptus* (fam. Myrtaceae), esp. *lemon-scented gum*; **-scented gum(-tree),** the tree *Eucalyptus citriodora* (fam. Myrtaceae) of e. Qld., having a smooth, sometimes spotted bark and leaves which are strongly lemon-scented when crushed.

1901 *Emu* I. 59 The little **Lemon-breasted Flycatcher** (Microeca flavigaster) has a habit of covering its tiny nest with pieces of bark. **1945** C. Barrett *Austral. Bird Life* 172 The lemon-breasted flycatcher . . builds a smaller nest than any other Australian bird. **1964** M. Sharland *Territory of Birds* 145 This one has two close relatives in northern areas—the Lemon-breasted and Brown-tailed Flycatcher. The first, with a yellow breast, likes the forested country around Darwin. **1832** J. Backhouse *Narr. Visit Austral. Colonies* (1843) 30 **Lemon-crested Cockatoos** . . are . . a great annoyance to the farmer. **1838** R. Gouger *S.A. in 1837* 61 Upon . . the blue-mountain parrot and lemon-crested cockatoo, the first settlers frequently regaled before beef and mutton were imported into the colony. **1840** *S. Austral. Rec.* (London) 3 Oct. 214 The splendid plumage of the birds—the lemon-crested cockatoo, the jet black macaw .. add an oriental grandeur to our plains. **1899** *Proc. Linnean Soc. N.S.W.* XXIV. 467 *E[ucalyptus] tereticornis* .. var. *brevifolia* .. is the 'Orange Gum' or '**Lemon Gum**' of the Port Macquarie district. **1959** E. LAMBERT *Glory thrown In* 34 They say about me that I know and name most of the five hundred varieties of gum. Manna gum, lemon gum, red gum. **1980** B. SCOTT *Darkness under Hills* 45 Downstream was a tall stand of black bean trees, red cedar and lemon gums. **1860** G. BENNETT *Gatherings of Naturalist* 265 The **Lemon-scented Gum-tree** (*Eucalyptus citriodora*) is peculiar to the Wide Bay district [of N.S.W.]... The leaves .. on being bruised, yield a delightful citron-like odour. **1882** *Proc. Linnean Soc. N.S.W.* VII. 338 Lemon Scented Gum extends right up to the waters of Carpentaria. **1928** R.H. CROLL *Open Road Vic.* 7 The slim, graceful lemon-scented gum. **1970** D. STIVENS *Horse of Air* 43 The elegant lemon-scented gum .. with a quicksilver trunk, straight as a gun-barrel for forty feet before it pushes out the first branch. **1985** *Age* (Melbourne) 30 Aug. (Suppl.) 6/1 If you need a large tree or native tree for a large garden *Eucalyptus citriodora*, the lemon-scented gum, which stands outside my lounge window, emits a beautiful lemon scent when the leaves are crushed.

2. In the phr. **to go (in) lemons,** to act with enthusiasm and vigour; to make a fuss.

1872 G.S. BADEN-POWELL *New Homes for Old Country* 186 A boy, as soon as he gets old enough and strong enough to manage a horse, delights in mustering. He will then, in his Australian, 'go in big lemons' whenever he gets the chance. **1886** H.W.H. STEPHEN *Lily's Fortune* 8 Mother Grabbles had not had such a chance for many a year, and 'went in lemons'. **1904** L.M.P. ARCHER *Bush Honeymoon* 338 She'd been *goin' in lemons*, and had eaten two. **1905** J. FURPHY *Rigby's Romance* (1946) 78, I drops like a cock, jumps up agen, an' goes for him lemons. **1943** *Bulletin* (Sydney) 8 Dec. 12/2 A tall bloke in a striped sweater comes up, takes a screw at the bottle an' starts goin' lemons because he was wantin' gin.

3. *pl. Australian National Football.* A break in the game at three-quarter time for refreshment taken on the field.

1960 *N.T. News* (Darwin) 12 Jan. 8/3 At lemons, Wanderers led by 8.11 to 8.6. *Ibid.* 9 Feb. 11/5 Ah Mat snapped a major to leave Buffaloes with a lead of 9.9 to 7.10 at lemons. **1968** EAGLESON & MCKIE *Terminol. Austral. Nat. Football* ii. 21 *Lemons*, three-quarter time.

lemony, *a.* Irritable; aggressive.

1941 S.J. BAKER *Pop. Dict. Austral. Slang* 31 *Go lemony at*, to become angry, express anger towards someone. **1946** D. STIVENS *Courtship of Uncle Henry* 75 He's as lemony as hell when he opens the door. **1955** —— *Ironbark Bill* 5 The heap of stingers get bigger and the mozzies get more lemony. **1963** J. O'GRADY *Things they do to You* 197 You can't blame a man for getting a bit lemony. **1968** S. GORE *Holy Smoke* 35 Oh, blimey, they went real lemony on 'im!

lend, *v. Obs. trans.* To give to another the temporary use of the labour of (a convict in one's charge). See also LOAN GANG.

1827 *Tasmanian* (Hobart) 18 Oct. 2 The Government can either lend or assign the prisoner to a master. **1833** *Launceston Advertiser* 31 Jan. 454 Thirty-four mechanics and labourers .. will be lent to the Contractor by Government for 12 months. **1837** J. MUDIE *Felonry of N.S.W.* 54 General Darling had reclaimed a convict servant who had been *lent*, not assigned, to a free emigrant in Sydney. **1838** *Tegg's N.S.W. Pocket Almanac* 86 Convict Mechanics may be lent, and Labourers during Harvest. **1849** A. HARRIS *Emigrant Family* (1967) 30 If he's a prisoner, the master can lend him, if he likes: it's not allowed I suppose; but nobody cares about that.

leonile /ˈliənil/. *Obs.* Prob. var. LEANGLE, but poss. from a related language.

1894 *Jrnl. Anthrop. Inst.* (London) XXIII. 317 The *Australian Aboriginal weapon*, termed the *leonile, langeel, bendi* or *buccan*... The *leonile* consists, speaking generally, of a more or less long straight handle, or shaft, and a sharp pointed head, of greater or less length, either at right angles to the former, or opposed to the shaft at an angle somewhat greater than a right angle. **1921** *Mid-Pacific Mag.* June 541/1 The boomerang .. appears to possess the greatest affinity to the bent hand clubs, which were very often thrown, and it is certain that the first boomerangs were modifications of the leonile, for intermediate forms of this weapon have been met with.

leopard orchid. Either of two terrestrial orchids (fam. Orchidaceae) bearing a yellow flower with brown markings: in s.e. Aust. applied to *Diuris maculata* of s.e. Aust. incl. Tas., and in W.A. to *Thelymitra fuscolutea* of s.w. W.A., S.A., and Vic.

1923 *Census Plants Vic.* (Field Naturalists' Club Vic.) 21 *Diuris maculata* .. Leopard Orchid. **1939** M.B. ELDERSHAW *My Aust.* 220 Orchids .. with names out of the animal kingdom—the donkey, the cockatoo .. the leopard. **1952** B. BEATTY *Unique to Aust.* 105 The Leopard orchid, a tawny, spotted fellow complete with clawed paws may be found beneath the gum-trees in many parts of Western Australia. **1978** B.P. MOORE *Life on Forty Acres* 41 The taller and attractively spotted Leopard and Tiger orchids (*Diuris maculata* and *D. sulphurea*) in butter yellow and chocolate brown.

leopard-wood. [See quot. 1863.] Either of two trees of the genus *Flindersia* (fam. Rutaceae) having a distinctive spotted trunk and occurring in N.S.W. and Qld., *F. maculosa* of drier country and *F. collina* of rainforest and drier scrub; the wood of these trees. Also *attrib.*, and **leopard tree.**

1863 W.J. WILLS *Successful Explorations Interior Aust.* 130, I have never seen in any other part of the country—the leopard tree (called so from its spotted bark). **1912** *Emu* xii. 8 Various berries and seed-pods including .. old ones of the leopard-wood tree (*Flindersia maculosa*). **1924** J.A. REID *Pioneer Grazier Aust.* 7 The .. homestead was a six-roomed structure, built of locally pit sawn 'leopard wood' weatherboards. **1937** *Bulletin* (Sydney) 1 Sept. 21/1 For bullock yokes there's no timber to equal leopard-wood. **1966** J. CARTER *People of Inland* 57 On the horizon, a ragged line of mulga and leopard trees, vividly green. **1973** V. SERVENTY *Desert Walkabout* 66 While travelling from Mootwingee to White Cliffs we saw some beautiful trees by the side of the road. From a distance they looked like willows, but at close quarters we saw the beautifully spotted bark which identified them as leopard-wood. **1980** *Sydney Morning Herald* 14 Oct. 3/6 The station is 40 per cent red soil, which holds tough leopardwood.

Leperland. *Obs.* A nickname for Queensland.

1896 *Bulletin* (Sydney) 17 Oct. 25/2 Barcoo rot .. extends all over Western Leperland. **1898** *Tocsin* (Melbourne) 28 July 3/4 Outrages by Kanakas and other degraded 'cheap and reliable' coloured aliens are becoming so common in Leperland that they hardly arouse public interest. **1898** *Worker* (Sydney) 20 Aug. 3/3 He had to cross a creek up Leperland way, which is infested with alligators.

leper-line. *W.A. Hist.* See quot. 1977.

1966 S.J. BAKER *Austral. Lang.* (ed. 2) 354 What is known as the *leper line* in Western Australia. **1969** F.B. VICKERS *No Man is Himself* 58 The 20th parallel of south latitude—known locally as the leper-line. **1977** —— *Stranger no Longer* 167 My copy of the Western Australian Native Welfare Act was approved for reprint on 22nd August 1955 .. and section 10 in its preamble *says: In order that the spread of leprosy within the State may be limited the following provisions shall operate .. no person shall cause a native to travel from a place north of the boundary line to a place south of the boundary line*... The 20th parallel of south latitude was the boundary line, more usually referred to as the Leper line.

lerp /lɜp/. Also (esp. formerly) **laap, loap.** [a. Wemba Wemba dial. of Wemba *lerep*.] **a.** The whitish, sweet, waxy secretion produced by insect larvae of the fam. Psyllidae, often in the form of a conical covering of scales; the insect secreting this. Also *attrib.*, esp. as **lerp scale. b.** MANNA 1 a.

1845 *Papers & Proc. R. Soc. Tas.* 25 Mar. (1851) 242, I had no dinner, but I got plenty of lerp. Lerp is very sweet, and is formed by an insect on the leaves of gum-trees; in size and appearance like a flake of snow, it feels like matted wool, and tastes like the ice on a wedding-cake. **1848** W. WESTGARTH *Aust. Felix* 73 The natives of the Wimmera prepare a luscious drink from the laap, a sweet exudation from the leaf of the mallee (Eucalypt dumosa). **1850** *Papers & Proc. R. Soc. Tas.* (1851) 235 Laap, or lerp, the cup-like coverings of Psyllidae found on the leaves of certain Eucalypti. **1856** J. BONWICK *W. Buckley* 50 The Loap, or Manna, causes quite a festival in its season. **1878** R.B. SMYTH *Aborigines of Vic.* I. 212 Another variety of manna is the secretion of the pupa of an insect of the *Psylla* family, and obtains the name of *lerp* among the Aborigines of the northern districts of the colony [of Vic.]. **1907** W.W. FROGGATT *Austral. Insects* 363 Their popular name of 'Lerp Insects' [comes] from the habit of the larvae of many species of forming 'lerp scales', shell-like protective coverings formed from exudations from the insects. **1942** E. ANDERSON *Squatter's Luck* 41 Went to the northern springs For manna—called 'loap'. **1948** W.W. FROGGATT *Insect Bk.* 113 The most typical [lerp insects] of all use the sap of the tree to form lerp scales, under which they hide and feed until they are fully fed... Two different species live on our kurrajong trees. One is a small brown free-living lerp. **1966** G.W. BROUGHTON *Men of Murray* 138 All round us, on the ground, were hundreds of sugary white slabs about the size of a sixpence... The rather rare red-gum manna is now known to be the scale of a small insect of the species known as 'lerp'. **1975** G. BLAINEY *Triumph of Nomads* 154 The aboriginals who daily walked a long way to reach patches of mallee scrub to eat the *laarp* became fat and sleek in the space of six weeks. **1979** WRIGLEY & FAGG *Austral. Native Plants* 63 The sap-sucking larva .. builds an intricate cover around itself which is known as the lerp-scale.

leschenaultia /lɛʃəˈnɒltiə/. Also **lechenaultia.** [The plant genus *Lechenaultia* was named by British botanist Robert Brown (*Prodr. Fl. Nov. Holl.* (1810) 581) after the French botanist J.L.C.T. *Leschenault* de la Tour (1773–1826).] Any plant of the genus of perennial herbs and shrubs *Lechenaultia* (fam. Goodeniaceae), occurring chiefly in s.w. W.A., some of which are widely cultivated for their colourful flowers.

1825 *Curtis's Bot. Mag.* (London) LII. 2600 (OEDS) Handsome Lechenaultia. **1916** L.H. BAILEY *Standard Cyclop. Hort.* IV. 1844 The leschenaultias require special care in watering. **1958** *Coast to Coast 1957–58* 138 Leschenaultia made patches as blue as the sky everywhere. **1972** *Southerly* i. 18 The coffin draped in scarlet with a single bunch of blue leschenaultia, gathered by her friends in the hills. **1985** *Canberra Times* 7 July 2/5 Perth .. is a plain city (becoming increasingly ugly) set in a once beautiful place under a Leschenaultia-blue sky.

leso /ˈlɛzoʊ/. Also **lezo, lezzo.** [f. *les(bian* + -O.] A lesbian. Also as *adj.*

1945 S.J. BAKER *Austral. Lang.* 123 A lesbian is known mainly as a *lezo* and *a lover under the lap.* **1972** *Bulletin* (Sydney) 21 Oct. 45/1 The Tories, trendies, lesos, poofters, four-be-twos and just plain Pommy bastards. **1974** D. HEWETT *Tatty Hollow Story* (1976) 118 What's up with you? Are you leso or something? **1983** *Nat. Times* (Sydney) 22 July 37/3 And *Gay*! What an insult to the poofs and lezzos who made this country what it is today!

Lesueur's rat-kangaroo /ləsɜz ræt-kæŋgəˈru/. [f. the name of the French illustrator and naturalist C.A. *Lesueur* (1778–1846), who sailed on an expedition to the Pacific led by T.N. Baudin.] BOODIE.

1926 A.S. LE SOUEF et al. *Wild Animals Australasia* 235 Lesueur's rat-kangaroo... Islands of Sharks Bay, Western Australia. **1981** *Ecos* xxix. 21/2 Smaller macropods .. such as .. Lesueur's rat-kangaroo, fared less well, becoming scarce or extinct with the disappearance of the long grass in which they had sheltered.

let go, *v. phr. Shearing.* Of a shearer: to release a shorn sheep.

1879 *Austral. Grazier's Guide* 54 Previously to letting go the sheep .. the shearer marks it with a piece of chalk, putting on his own hieroglyph. **1912** J. BRADSHAW *Highway Robbery under Arms* (ed. 3) 24 The eight ringers let go at once, and into the pens they waltzed. **1939** *Land Farm & Station Ann.* 20/3 When shearing started, old Bill cut in as though he had a wager on, while the boys talked about the local races between blows. They were a long way behind when he let go, and when their fleeces did fall the girl proceeded to carry them away. **1961** *Bulletin* (Sydney) 3 Feb. 44/2 The young picker-upper .. boasted, 'I picked for seven 'deuce merchants' on my own last year . . and swept each time they let go.'

Hence **letting-go** *ppl. a.*

1925 *Pastoral Rev.* 16 Jan. 31 C, in the plan, denotes the pens where the sheep are caught for shearing; B the shearing board; and L the letting-go pens. **1956** *Bulletin* (Sydney) 12 Sept. 13/1 Having lost one [*sc.* wether] into the letting-go pen he called out to the boss to pull it out. **1957** L.D. RYAN *Sheep-Shearing Experting* 191 The sheep released and placed down the letting-go race. *Ibid.* 207 *Letting-go-chute*, an inclined surface down which the sheep slide to the counting-out pens after being shorn.

letter-stick. MESSAGE-STICK.

1887 *Proc. Linnean Soc. N.S.W.* II. 621 Mr Palmer exhibited two 'letter-sticks' obtained from the Aborigines of the Gascoigne River district where, as in other parts of Australia, they are used for inter-tribal communication. **1901** M. VIVIENNE *Travels in W.A.* 56 The letter-sticks of the natives, or paper-talk as they now call them, are beautifully marked. **1935** R.B. PLOWMAN *Boundary Rider* 267 The padre delivered the letter-stick. **1959** A. UPFIELD *Bony & Mouse* 84 The short stick . . was about six inches in length, and had been scraped by a quartz or granite chip, scorched by fire and polished by sandstone mixed with saliva. Two encircling cuts gave the stick three divisions, and within two of the divisions, short cuts had been made, the third division untouched. It was, as Bony knew . . a ceremonial letter-stick. **1977** X. HERBERT *Dream Road* 13 George told Prindy he had made up a Letter Stick for sending to the Wise One to say that they two would be going on to the Alice Country.

letter-winged kite. [See quot. 1976.] The bird of prey *Elanus scriptus* of mainland Aust., predom. light to dark grey with white underparts, feeding chiefly on rodents.

1842 J. GOULD *Birds of Aust.* (1848) I. Pl. 24, *Elanus scriptus* . . Letter-winged Kite. **1849** C. STURT *Narr. Exped. Central Aust.* II. 15 App. *The Letter-winged Kite*. . . This beautiful bird was first seen on a creek to the eastward of the Barrier or Stanley's Range. **1891** G.J. BROINOWSKI *Birds of Aust.* VI. Pl. 33, The present species . . was called Letter-winged Kite from the fact that . . the black mark on the upper surface of the wing resembles a V. **1945** C. BARRETT *Austral. Bird Life* 35 Other hawks do their share of destruction, notably the beautiful letter-winged kite. **1976** *Reader's Digest Compl. Bk. Austral. Birds* 117 The letter-winged kite . . in flight . . is clearly distinguished by its underwing pattern—a black line in the shape of a W or an M. **1982** R. ELLIS *Bush Safari* 172 Frank secured some good film of two Letter-winged Kites.

leubra, var. LUBRA.

Lewin /ˈluən/. [f. the name of the naturalist and artist J.W. *Lewin* (1770–1819), author of a work on Austral. birds.] In the names of birds: **Lewin('s) honeyeater,** the bird of forested e. mainland Aust. *Meliphaga lewinii*, having olive-green plumage with yellow neck markings; **Lewin's rail** (or **water rail**), the mottled grey and white bird *Rallus pectoralis*, inhabiting areas of dense vegetation in Aust., New Guinea, and Indonesia.

[**1808 Lewin honeyeater:** J.W. LEWIN *Birds New Holland* 9 Yellow-Eared Honeysucker. . . These birds inhabit the banks of the Hawkesbury and Patterson rivers, frequenting thick bushes.] **1931** N.W. CAYLEY *What Bird is That?* 9 Lewin Honey-eater *Meliphaga lewini* . . also called Yellow-eared Honey-eater and Banana-bird. **1945** C. BARRETT *Austral. Bird Life* 157 The . . Lewin honeyeater . . inhabits humid scrubs. **1967** V.G.C. NORWOOD *Long Haul* 80 A yellow-eared Lewin honey-eater . . swooped across the shallow flow. **1980** L. FULLER *Wollongong's Native Trees* 46 Lewin's Honeyeater . . the only rainforest honeyeater may also [be] found in wet sclerophyll forests and nearby gardens. **1848** [**Lewin's rail**] J. GOULD *Birds of Aust.* VI. Pl. 77, *Rallus lewinii* . . Lewin's Water Rail. **1945** C. BARRETT *Austral. Bird Life* 58 The habits of Lewin's water-rail . . are much the same as those of the common landrail. **1984** *Age* (Melbourne) 7 July 2/3 Hands up all those who knew that Lewin's Rail had disappeared from Western Australia.

lezo, lezzo, varr. LESO.

liangel, liangle, liangra, varr. LEANGLE.

licence. *Hist.* Also **license.**

1. A formal, annually renewable, permission to occupy Crown land for grazing purposes; a certificate of this. See also TICKET OF OCCUPATION. Also *attrib.*

1820 *Hobart Town Gaz.* 2 Dec., The Licenses for Occupation of Grazing Grounds for the Year commencing September 29, 1820, will be delivered at this Office on Saturday, December 9th. **1820** *HRA* (1921) 3rd Ser. III. 575 License of Occupation for Grazing Ground . . has my permission to occupy Pasture Land for grazing Cattle and Sheep . . whilst the same shall remain unlocated. **1839** *S. Austral. Miscellany* Dec. 55 There are four hundred stock-stations, which pay £10 per annum each, as a licence to graze their flocks and herds, for the purpose of raising a revenue to support the police, and to exclude improper characters from obtaining such indulgences. **1842** *Geelong Advertiser* 25 July 3/1 An order has been received to deprive several settlers at Port Fairie [*sic*] of their licenses, owing to circumstances connected with the murder of three black women in that district. **1847** J.D. LANG *Cooksland* 229 In charge of the flocks and herds to the Squatting Station; for which the sum of £10 a-year is payable to the Government for a license, as it is called. **1848** *Moreton Bay Courier* 12 Feb. 3/2 Several applications having been made to the Government by parties who have . . failed . . to take out their licenses for the current year, for the occupation of runs beyond the settled districts. **1853** *Visit to Aust. & Gold Regions* (S.P.C.K.) 83 The squatter pays his licence-fee of ten pounds for liberty to occupy his land for a year.

2. a. Prior to the introduction of the *miner's right* (see MINER *n.*[2]): a permit, renewable monthly, to remove gold. Also *attrib.*

1851 *Illustr. Austral. Mag.* (Melbourne) Nov. 262 The Commissioner has a busy post, issuing licenses, (thirty shillings for the month is charged) receiving gold, and arranging matters brought for adjudication. ***c* 1852** A. MANN *Goldfields Aust.* 14 Gold diggers poured into the district . . each digger paying for license to dig. **1862** H. BROWN *Vic. as I found It* 144 'It is a digger hunt.' 'What are they hunting them for?' 'For their licences.' **1859** W. KELLY *Life in Vic.* I. 104 The license tax (a most odious imposition in the eyes of the diggers) was . . held up to public execration. **1870** W.B. WITHERS *Hist. Ballarat* 94 Provoked hostilities by the peculiarly despotic action taken in the last license-collecting raid.

b. Special Comb. **licence fee,** the fee for a mining permit; **hunt,** an inspection, carried out by police and troopers, to ensure that anyone engaged in gold-mining has a permit; also **-hunting** *vbl. n.*

1851 *Britannia* (Hobart) 26 June 4/5 The diggers who were without means, for the immediate payment of the **license fee.** **1852** J.E. ERSKINE *Short Acct. Late Discoveries Gold* 15 A charge or license-fee of thirty shillings . . was to be paid by every individual applying for permission to search for the precious metals for every calendar month or part of a month, to a land Commissioner. **1859** R.H. HORNE *Austral. Facts & Prospects* 31 It was at Warranga that the great émeute occurred on the question of licence-fees, and heralded the Eureka stockade affair, which took place not very long after. **1862** H. BROWN *Vic. as I found It* 148 The crown Commissioner . . has the responsibility of gathering in the license fee. **1855** R. CARBONI *Eureka Stockade* 13, I was often compelled to produce my licence twice at each and the same **licence hunt.** *Ibid.* 17 Up to the middle of September, 1854, the search for licences happened once a month; at most twice: perhaps once a week on the Gravel Pits, owing to the near-neighbourhood of the Camp. Now, licence-hunting became the order of the day. **1859** W. KELLY *Life in Vic.* 187 Long odds were laid that there would be a 'license hunt'. **1859** P. JUST *Aust.* 139 The judicious measures of the officials . . in respect to licence-hunting had . . done much to re-assure the community. **1906** E. DYSON *In Roaring Fifties* 119 Done's first experience of a license-hunt was largely farcical.

licensed, *ppl. a. Hist.*

1. To whom or for which a permit to occupy Crown land for grazing purposes has been granted.

1839 *Port Phillip Patriot* 27 May 3 No such licensed person, nor his or her Overseer or Manager, shall keep any stock whatever, belonging to any other person. **1841** *Geelong Advertiser* 17 July 2/5 A complaint . . had been preferred against him by Mr William Hamilton, for depasturing cattle on his licensed run. **1842** *Ibid.* 5 Sept. 2/3 Mr William Lee, a much respected settler . . the occupier of a licensed station. **1843** *Sydney Morning Herald* 10 Aug. 2/1 The qualification both of legislation and electors being based upon real estate, the licensed graziers, as such, are of course disqualified for either function, the land they occupy being the property of the Crown. **1851** J.H. BURTON *Emigrant's Man.* ii. 21 There can be little doubt that . . licensed settlers will subside into leaseholders in perpetuity. **1853** *Visit to Aust. & Gold Regions* (S.P.C.K.) 83 There is a wide difference between an agricultural and a pastoral farmer. The former is most frequently the proprietor of the land he cultivates, while the latter is no more than a 'licensed squatter', a tenant at will to the Crown. **1858** T. MCCOMBIE *Hist. Colony Vic.* 185 The licensed occupiers of Crown lands, and the tenant farmers.

2. To whom or for which a permit to remove gold has been granted.

1851 *Empire* (Sydney) 3 Sept. 115/3 A party of three men were dispossessed of their licensed diggings by a number of impudent fellows walking coolly into the hole and commencing operations. **1853** C.J. LA TROBE *Reply to Petition* 20 Aug. 7, I shall be seconded by . . a very great majority of the licensed occupants of the Gold Districts. **1855** R. CARBONI *Eureka Stockade* 110 The extent of claim allowed to each Licensed Miner is 12 feet square, or 144 square feet. **1856** H.B. STONEY *Vic.* 103 The licensed digger was granted a power to change his locality as often as he pleased during the month.

lick. [Spec. use of *lick* a spurt at racing, speed: see OED(S *sb.* 6.] In the phr. **for the lick of one's life,** at a cracking pace.

1915 *Honk* x. 7 Straight for his own lines he goes for the lick of his life. **1936** N. CALDWELL *Fangs of Sea* 216 Out I gets . . for the lick o' me life, grabs some mendin' wire, and 'ops it back. **1954** N. BARTLETT *Pearl Seekers* 177 He cleared out for the lick of his life from Broome, after starting what threatened to become a major international incident. **1966** *Sunday Mail Mag.* (Brisbane) 3 Apr. 6/3 A section of the miners agreed that the happiest solution to the sorry affair would be to lynch Mr Chapple. The little Cornishman got wind of this thinking and . . went for the lick of his life.

lick hole. [f. U.S. *lick* place at which animals lick salt or salt earth: see OED(S *sb.* 2.]

a. A shallow depression in which stock lick for salt which occurs naturally or is supplied. Also **licking hole,** and *attrib.*

1848 T.L. MITCHELL *Jrnl. Exped. Tropical Aust.* 53 Salt wort plants . . were . . efficacious . . as wholly preventing cattle and sheep from licking clay, a vicious habit to which they are so prone that grassy runs in the higher country near Sydney are sometimes abandoned only on account of the 'licking holes' they contain. **1871** *Austral. Town & Country Jrnl.* (Sydney) 22 Apr. 490/4 Cattle depasturing . . in the up-lying 'lickhole' country are more subject to the ailment. **1928** 'BRENT OF BIN BIN' *Up Country* 143 No horse . . was safe . . in the lick-hole country of its myriad spring-heads. Pool found a way with rock-salt to make the lick-holes a trap. **1936** M. FRANKLIN *All that Swagger* 148 A hint without evidence is a snake in the grass, like that boomer you dispatched to-day at the lickhole.

b. *fig.* A public house.

1911 *Bulletin* (Sydney) 16 Feb. 13/2 Some of us . . were anxious to get back to the pub to collect . . so when . . he acknowledged defeat . . we got back to the 'lick-hole'.

Lieutenant-Governor /lɛftɛnənt-ˈgʌvənə/.

1. One who deputizes for the Governor of an Australian Colony (later State), or for the Governor-General; formerly also, in Tasmania, Victoria, and Western Australia before their independence from New South Wales, the principal resident representative of the sovereign.

1787 *HRA* (1914) 1st Ser. I. 3 Our Judge-Advocate in our said territory is hereby required to tender and administer unto you and in your absence to our Lieutenant Governor. **1793** J. HUNTER *Hist. Jrnl. Trans. Port Jackson* 85 He proposed to the lieutenant-governor, that an officer should be sent down the harbour. **1813** *Van Diemen's Land Govt. & Gen. Orders* 23 Feb. (1814) 2

This day His Majesty's Commission appointing Lieut. Colonel Davey of the Royal Marine Force, to be *Lieut. Governor* of His Majesty's Settlements on Van Diemen's Land. **1820** C. JEFFREYS *Van Dieman's Land* 166 All grants of land must be made by the Governor in Chief at Port Jackson, though the recommendation of the Lieutenant Governor as to the land to be presented to settlers arriving out with the sanction of the Secretary of State, is in general attended to. **1832** J. BACKHOUSE *Narr. Visit Austral. Colonies* (1843) 15 He introduced us to the Lieutenant Governor, Col. George Arthur. **1835** H. MELVILLE *Hist. Van Diemen's Land* 52 On the independence of the Colony being declared, the designation of 'His Honor', by which the Lieutenant Governor had hitherto been addressed, was changed to the appellation of 'His Excellency'. **1842** *Austral. & N.Z. Monthly Mag.* 163 The Lieutenant-Governor had made the following appointments:- . . Mr R.S. Bird to be pound-keeper at Perth. **1852** J.E. ERSKINE *Short Acct. Late Discoveries Gold* 19 Mr La Trobe, the Lieutenant-Governor, had sent a surveying party . . into the district. **1891** *Bohemia* (Melbourne) 10 Dec. 5 *Hopetoun* objects to the appointment of a Lieutenant-Governor. **1973** W.G. WALKER *Gloss. Educ. Terms* 74 *Lieutenant-Governor*, (A) official representative of the Sovereign when a temporary vacancy in the office of either Governor-General *q.v.* or Governor *q.v.* occurs; *syns.* Administrator; Deputy Governor.

2. The title given to a deputy State Governor (in some States).

1902 *N.S.W. Govt. Gaz.* I. 374 His Excellency the Lieutenant-Governor . . directs the publication . . of the substance and prayer of a Petition. **1913** *Vic. Govt. Gaz.* 28 Aug. 3975 All the powers and authorities . . have become and are now vested in me as Lieutenant-Governor of the said State. **1934** *S. Austral. Govt. Gaz.* 17 May 1230 His Excellency the Lieutenant-Governor will hold a Levee at Government House on Saturday. **1963** *Austral. Encycl.* IV. 351 The vice-regal representative in each State is . . called the Governor of that State, and he generally has a Lieutenant-Governor as his deputy. **1983** *Sydney Morning Herald* 11 May 12/7 As Chief Justice, Sir Laurence is also Lieutenant-Governor of New South Wales.

life.

1. [Used elsewhere but recorded earliest in Aust.: see OEDS *sb.* 8 d.] A sentence of transportation to Australia and penal servitude for life; imprisonment for life. Freq. *attrib.*

1833 T. BANNISTER *Let. on Colonial Labour* 12 The number of years, for a . . life Convict to serve in the Gangs, before he can get his ticket-of-leave, to be mentioned. **1834** *Perth Gaz.* 14 June 304 Life men, five years in the Gangs. **1841** B. WAIT *Lett. from Van Dieman's Land* (1843) 230, I learned in court, that my sentence is *fourteen years after arrival in V.D.L.*—Mr Watson's is 'life'. **1849** J. PATTISON *N.S.W.* 16 Seven-years men received their tickets at the expiry of four years; fourteen-years men after six years' servitude; and life-men after eight. **1857** *Vic. Parl. Papers* (1856–57) III. no. 48 46, That is the time I am satisfied he got life. **1893** M. JEFFREY *Burglar's Life* 69 My master came to me with the good news that the term life prisoners had to serve to obtain a ticket-of leave [*sic*] had been reduced from twelve to six years.

2. In the phr. **to go for one's life,** to engage (in an activity, etc.) with vigour and enthusiasm. Now chiefly as an exhortation.

1920 H.F. MOLLARD *Humour of Road* 14 You'll have to go for your life now, Jim, if you want your firm's boots to keep walking. You have a keen competitor up against you. **1922** A. WRIGHT *Colt from Country* 18 Go for y' life, and I'll explain as we go. **1940** J. POLLARD *Out of West* 16, I shoved the menu across to him. 'Go for your life,' I said, trying not to sound too patronising. **1958** H.D. WILLIAMSON *Sunlit Plain* 133 'Got a warrant,' was his brief explanation. Eddie nodded. 'Go for your life, son.' **1966** *Meanjin* 282 'Mind if we have a little snort, Eva?' 'Go for your life, Jack.' **1971** P. HASLUCK *Open Go* 2, I could not . . comment on the efficiency of this or that Education Department, but I could go for my life on the aims of education. **1979** *Meanjin* 461 Have some more champagne. Fortunately it's French . . so no hangovers. Go for your life, there's lots more. **1985** *Canberra Times* 15 Aug. 3/8 If you have a Prime Minister like Bob Menzies who, when asked by the British for anything, was accustomed to drop his strides and say 'Go for your life', you must expect the worst.

lifer. [Used elsewhere but recorded earliest in Aust.] One sentenced to transportation to Australia and penal servitude for life; one sentenced to life imprisonment. Also *attrib.*

1827 *Monitor* (Sydney) 29 Oct. 728/1 As the law, affecting male Prisoners of the Crown now stands, 'lifers' have either a very remote, or as it regards 999 out of every thousand of them, no chance whatever of being permitted to marry. **1835** *Colonist* (Sydney) 4 June 177/2 *The Sydney Monitor* . . soon acquired a sufficient degree of piquancy even for the ticket-of-leave men and lifers. **1843** C. ROWCROFT *Tales of Colonies* (1858) 216, I was a lifer. It's bad that; better hang a man at once than punish him for life. **1847** C. CHISHOLM *Emigration & Transportation* 38, I was sent here as a *lifer*. I am now on my Ticket—not yet received my emancipation. **1857** *Vic. Parl. Papers* (1856–57) III. no 48 46, I am satisfied that he is a 'lifer' and that is the reason he absconded. ***c* 1872** J.C.F. JOHNSON *Over Island* 16 The second in command was an old escaped 'lifer' from Port Arthur called Daddy Black. **1892** *Bulletin* (Sydney) 9 Jan. 10/1 The gaol at 'the Pivot' is a sort of Benevolent Asylum for used-up assassins, and in the 'lifer' yard of that drowsy institution you can see groups of mild-looking ancients. **1918** V. MARSHALL *Jail from Within* 59 With hands treated and bandaged by a prison 'lifer', I was told off. **1936** F. CLUNE *Roaming round Darling* 69 The cleanest cells were those of the 'lifers'. **1979** L. NEWCOMBE *Inside Out* 155 Within six months Newcombe and two lifers . . had been transferred to other gaols.

lift, *v.* [Br. *lift* to drive (cattle) away or to market; now chiefly Austral.: see OED(S *v.* 11.] *trans.* To move (stock) from one place to another. Also as *vbl. n.*

1875 *Austral. Town & Country Jrnl.* (Sydney) 27 Feb. 343/2, I haven't lifted a finer mob [of cattle] this season. **1905** *Steele Rudd's Mag.* (Brisbane) July 646, I went out to the Barcoo to lift 20,000 sheep for a Brisbane firm. **1917** A.L. BREWER *'Gators' Euchre* 33 They're lifting cattle from Wave Hill for Alligator Creek. **1923** J. BOWES *Jackaroos* 102 The drovers of the last mob of stores having agreed to lift them and 'drove' them to their destination. **1935** N. HUNT *House of David* 126 The 'lifting' of starving stock on the 'drove' so far 'out' . . was a business too risky to anyone who knew his business. **1975** D. STUART *Walk, trot, canter & Die* 13 He'd gone with a drover to lift a mob further up, and that was that.

light, *n.*

1. *Austral. pidgin. Obs.* In the phr. **to make a light,** to see; to understand.

1834 G. BENNETT *Wanderings N.S.W.* I. 325 My fadder no see white feller trowsers—*if make a light* (see) make get; but no white feller sit down this place when my fadder here. **1849** A. HARRIS *Emigrant Family* (1967) 222, I make a light (I know). **1859** H. KINGSLEY *Recoll. Geoffry Hamlyn* II. 185 'Make a light', in blackfellow's gibberish, means simply 'see'. **1888** W.T. PYKE *Bush Tales* 14 Make a light (look sharp) croppy sit down along there. **1893** S. NEWLAND *Paving Way* 325 First time make-a-light (see) white fellow, then come back yabber (tell).

2. As a mild oath, in the imp. phr. **strike a light.**

1936 A. RUSSELL *Gone Nomad* 44 'Strike a light!' he broke in suddenly. 'See them?' **1953** J.E. MACDONNELL *Wings off Sea* 215 'Strike a light!' answered Tiger. 'The bloody old gawk's gonna fly-off that U S Fury.' **1965** *Kings Cross Whisper* (Sydney) Mar. 5/2 Well, strike a light. We reckon this'd be the first time it's happened in Australia. **1979** K. DUNSTAN *Ratbags* 9 Gawd strike a light.

light, *a.* With **on**: in short supply; under-weight.

1944 L. GLASSOP *We were Rats* 122 'You're a bit light on too, aren't you?' 'Purely a temporary state of poverty, Reynolds old boy.' **1946** A.J. MARSHALL *Nulli Secundus Log* 87 Biscuits became 'light on'; we were limited to half a packet per day. **1960** N. CATO *Green grows Vine* 17 Mike . . never goes crook at yer if your tins is a bit light-on. Only thing he hates to see good fruit left behind on the vine. **1969** A. O'TOOLE *Racing Game* 49 'It'll be round about ten dollars. . . ' 'Won't harm anybody,' I agreed. 'Quite so,' Joe said. . . 'Trouble is, I'm a bit light on myself.' **1977** T. RONAN *Mighty Men on Horseback* 28 She may have been light on for looks. **1984** *Age* (Melbourne) 22 Aug. 5/3 It is largely because Canberra is light-on for events, certainly anything on the scale of the Grand Final or Melbourne Cup, that it makes such a fuss about Budget day.

lightning fence. A wire fence strung from widely spaced posts and therefore quickly constructed; fencing of this kind.

1913 *Bulletin* (Sydney) 13 Mar. 14/3 New settlers in the Vic. and South Aus. mallee run up 'lightning' fences (posts a chain apart and one barb). **1937** W. HATFIELD *I find Aust.* 82 He was on a contract for . . lightning fence, as they call it, eighty posts to the mile, strung with three steel wires fairly low down and one about three feet six from the ground, all strained to tuning-fork pitch and held by floating bracers. **1981** A.B. FACEY *Fortunate Life* 194 The fence consisted of two barbed wires strung from tree to tree. Where the distance between trees was more than five yards, we put a post in. The barbed wire was nailed to the trees and posts. This kind of fence was called a 'lightning fence'.

lightwood. Any of several trees yielding a timber which is light in weight or pale in colour, esp. the shrub or small to medium tree *Acacia implexa* (fam. Mimosaceae) of e. mainland Aust., having a rough, greyish bark and pale yellow flower-heads; the wood of these trees.

1803 *Sydney Gaz.* 26 June, Timber in this Colony includes . . Light-wood. **1805** J.H. TUCKEY *Acct. Voyage to establish Colony Port Philip* 226 Light-wood grows to twenty inches, and from its buoyancy (whence its name), is proper for building small craft and boats. **1827** *HRA* (1923) 3rd Ser. VI. 265 'Light Wood', called so at Hobart, is narrow, rather fine lanceolate in the leaf, wood clear grained, white in the Sap or outer part, and dark chocolate coloured within. **1852** J.D. LANG *Austral. Emigrant's Man.* 15 The extensive plains . . are generally covered with a rich carpet of grass, with a solitary tree here and there, of a species called in the colony *lightwood*, not much larger than an apple-tree. **1868** 'J.A.B.' *Meta of Gaindara* 54 The bushy lightwood everywhere Hath ta'en the place of gum-tree tall. **1884** 'R. BOLDREWOOD' *Old Melbourne Memories* 196 Broad limestone flats upon which rose clumps of the beautiful lightwood or hickory trees. **1928** H.C. PERRY *Son of Aust.* 77 When accident overtook the orthodox bat they made excellent substitutes from the 'lightwood', which grew in the adjacent scrubs. **1935** *Tree Lover* Oct. 5 Blackwood. . . The wood varies in colour from pale to dark reddish brown with a pale coloured sapwood. . . The paler coloured wood, which is also usually lighter in weight, is often known as 'Lightwood' and is regarded as being generally inferior. **1981** L. COSTERMANS *Native Trees & Shrubs S.-E. Aust.* 327 Lightwood . . common and widespread in Vic.–N.S.W. hill country.

lignum.

1. [See quot. 1981.] Any of several plants, usu. of the genus *Muehlenbeckia* (fam. Polygonaceae) and esp. *M. cunninghamii* of all mainland States, a twiggy shrub with slender, tangled stems, often forming dense, almost impenetrable thickets; POLYGONUM 1. Also *attrib.*, esp. as **lignum swamp.**

1872 MRS J. FOOTT *Sketches Life in Bush* 15 The poor animals were glad to munch the roots of salt-bush or lignum. **1893** *Western Champion* (Barcaldine) 27 June 10/1 Down amongst the lignum some are forced to make their bed. **1902** *Emu* II. 100 A 'lignum' swamp. **1904** E.S. EMERSON *Shanty Entertainment* (1910) 10 The Seventy Mile Creek was drowning all its lignum fringes in silent stretches of water. **1932** H. PRIEST *Call of Bush* 57, I once discovered a literary supplement of an English newspaper wedged in lignum bush at a time when I was thirsty for something to read. **1933** *Bulletin* (Sydney) 7 June 21/1 Lignum swamps on the dry Paroo Take the place of the ledger page. **1951** W. HATFIELD *Wild Dog Frontier* 32 The country ahead and all around them a monotonous stretch of dried 'lignum brakes. **1964** W. MOXHAM *Longshot* 16 He hated the lignum, waist high and spiny, as it grew on the river bank. **1981** J.A. BAINES *Austral. Plant Genera* 246 *Muehlenbeckia cunninghamii*, Tangled Lignum, all States (named after Allan Cunningham, who placed the Aust. spp. in the genus *Polygonum*, of which Lignum is a corruption).

2. Abbrev. of LIGNUM VITAE.

1893 D.J. FROST *Crown Lands N.S.W.* 19 Among the timbers which these northern river forests contain are .. lignum .. and hickory.

lignum vitae. [Transf. use of *lignum vitae* a timber tree of the genus *Guaiacum*.] Any of several trees, esp. the tall, rainforest tree *Premna lignum-vitae* (fam. Verbenaceae) of Qld. and n.e. N.S.W., yielding a durable timber; the wood of these trees; LIGNUM 2.

1803 *Sydney Gaz.* 26 Mar., Lignum Vitae, used in sheaves and pins for blocks. **1824** *Hobart Town Gaz.* 1 Oct., Colonial Timber may at any time be purchased of an Inhabitant of this town .. Lignum Vitae, for mill cogs. **1888** *Proc. Linnean Soc. N.S.W.* III. 532 *Myrtus acmenioides* .. 'Lignum-vitae' .. The leaves of these .. are used for flavouring tea in Queensland. **1929** W.D. FRANCIS *Austral. Rain-Forest Trees* 336 *Vitex Lignum-vitae* .. Lignum-vitae, the colonists' name for the tree. **1949** B. O'REILLY *Green Mountains* 144 Crow Ash and Lignum Vitae were suitable for fencing, all others used to rot in the ground. **1986** STANLEY & ROSS *Flora S.-E. Qld.* II. 374 *Premna lignum-vitae* .. Lignum-vitae... Flowers found throughout the year.

likely, *a. Mining.* [Spec. use of *likely* apparently suitable (for a purpose): see OED *a.* 3.] Of rock, country, etc.: promising, likely to yield ore.

1873 W. THOMSON-GREGG *Desperate Character* I. 160 We'll go up the gully a bit; and if I don't think the ground up there looks likely; why, we must just take up an outsider. **1873** R.P. WHITWORTH *Lost & Found* 23 An unsystematic method of shovelling up likely stuff, washing thence the nuggets, and larger bits. **1876** 'EIGHT YRS.' RESIDENT' *Queen of Colonies* 156 If he fancies it is 'likely' quartz he will, as we have said, sink down with a view to finding the reef. **1946** K.S. PRICHARD *Roaring Nineties* 49 He had come on likely country about twenty-five miles north-east of the camp.

lilac. *Obs.* [See quot. 1834.] *White cedar*, see WHITE *a.*[2] 1 a.

1834 G. BENNETT *Wanderings N.S.W.* I. 205 *Melia azedarach* .. the fragrance of the flowers so closely resembles those produced by the tree known in England as the 'lilac', that the same appellation is given to it in this colony. **1886** F. COWAN *Aust.* 17 The Lilac or White Cedar-tree: deciduous: its purple bloom, night-scented, beautiful.

lil-lil /'lɪl-lɪl/. [Poss. a. Wemba *liawil*.] An Aboriginal weapon used both as a missile and in close combat (see quot. 1974).

1878 R.B. SMYTH *Aborigines of Vic.* I. p. xlv, The *Lil-lil* is not so often used as a missile as to strike at and cut the enemy, and may indeed be properly called a wooden sword. **1936** F. CLUNE *Roaming round Darling* 250 We saw every sort of boomerang, from the heavy-ended *lil-lil* to the formidable return-weapon. **1974** M. TERRY *War of Warramullas* 121 Boomerang-shaped clubs were used in eastern and central Australia. The lil-lil, a short, bladed weapon with a curved handle was much used in New South Wales and Victoria for hand-fighting or throwing.

lilly-pilly /'lɪli-pɪli/. Also **lilli-pilli.** [Of unknown origin.] The tree *Acmena* (syn. *Eugenia*) *smithii* (fam. Myrtaceae), having glossy, dark green foliage, occurring in rainforest and sheltered gullies of e. Vic., N.S.W., and Qld., and widely cultivated esp. as a street tree; the purplish to white, edible fruit of the tree. Also *attrib.*

1854 F. ELDERSHAW *Aust. as it really Is* 43 Five-Corners, Lillypillies .. are .. well-recognized delicacies among the rising Anglo-Australian generation. **1888** *Proc. Linnean Soc. N.S.W.* III. 512 *Eugenia smithii* .. 'Lilly-pilly'. Called 'Tdgerail' by the aboriginals of Illawarra .. and 'Coochin-coochin' by some Queensland aboriginals. **1897** MRS L. RAWSON *Austral. Cook & Laundry Bk.* 86 What the children call Lilly Pilly is a bright red berry growing in the scrubs on a very tall, glossy-leafed tree. **1907** G. EDEN *Bush Ballads* 29 Away down in the Gully Where the lillipillies grow. **1936** F. CLUNE *Roaming round Darling* 26 In 1881 King George V planted a lillipilli-tree here. **1947** *Bulletin* (Sydney) 26 Mar. 44/1 Ripe lillipillies dropped on the dry forest bed. **1972** M. GILBERT *Personalities & Stories Early Orbost* 41 Flying foxes could be found hanging in the lilly-pilly jungles. **1982** *Bulletin* (Sydney) 6 July 80/1 The bees that live in the hive in the base of the lilly-pilly near Norwood Street.

lily. In the phr. **like a lily on a dust bin (dirt tin,** etc.), used as an emblem of incongruity.

1943 *Signals* (Melbourne) Christmas 41 Girl sitting on Piano like lily on dirt tin. **1982** N. KEESING *Lily on Dustbin* 14 One woman says to look like a lily on a dustbin (or garbage or dirt bin) is to dress inappropriately for an occasion and/or to wear over-fussy, frilly clothes. Another uses it for a variety of incongruous matters: an informal or poor family meal table might have newspaper instead of a cloth and cracked and battered utensils and one pretty milk jug stands in the centre of it like a lily on a dustbin.

lily-trotter. [See quot. 1934.] LOTUS BIRD. Also **lily-walker.**

1934 *Bulletin* (Sydney) 7 Feb. 21/3 Lotus birds .. are essentially swamp dwellers and get their colloquial name of 'lilly trotters' from their ability to scamper over the wide leaves of the lotus and other water plants. **1945** J. DEVANNY *Bird of Paradise* 114 A lotus-bird, or lily-walker, pattered across the surface of the pond. **1946** D. BARR *Warrigal Joe* 100 Their broad, round leaves forming a green carpet over which comb-crested jacanas or lily-trotters ran nimbly.

lime-juice. *Obs.* [Fig. use of *lime-juice* the juice of the lime used as an antiscorbutic on a long sea voyage.] Used allusively of a recently arrived British immigrant.

1855 G.H. WATHEN *Golden Colony* 39 He is quite green; he has only been here eighteen months; he hasn't got the lime-juice off. **1873** J.C.F. JOHNSON *Christmas on Carringa* 21, I smelt so strong of lime juice that the very cows ud twig me in a moment for a new chum. **1886** W.J. WOODS *Visit to Vic.* 12 The colonials know at sight a stranger from the old country. They call him a 'new chum'. They pretend that there is about him an aroma of the limejuice he has been drinking at sea. **1897** *Jrnl. Pioneers & Old Residents Assoc. Castlemaine* 12 I'll never forget how I was stared at. The diggers cried, 'Look at him; you can smell the lime-juice.'

lime-juicer. *Obs.* [f. prec.] A recently arrived British immigrant. See also LIMEY.

1857 J. ASKEW *Voyage Aust. & N.Z.* 55 The black gins kept calling out as I passed each 'whurlie'—'Ah! white fellow, limejuicer' (which is a term used in all the colonies to newly arrived emigrants). **1859** W. KELLY *Life in Vic.* I. 45, I was unwilling to subject myself to the ordeal of the jeering laugh to which every tired-out 'limejuicer', as we new chums were called, was treated. **1869** *Bushmen, Publicans, & Politics* 5 Another source from which we draw our supply of bush labour is the recent immigrants, uncourteously styled by the older bushman, 'New Chums', or 'Lime Juicers'. **1885** *Australasian Printers' Keepsake* 85 At length the last proof was carried to the printer, and 'young limejuicer' was surlily liberated. **1906** E. DYSON *In Roaring Fifties* 68 They've been hazing you properly, mate. Pea-soupers and lime-juicers are strangers off shipboard.

limewood. [See quot. 1981.] Either of the two trees *Eucalyptus papuana* (GHOST GUM) and *E. aspera* (fam. Myrtaceae) of n. Aust., having a white bark yielding a chalky powder.

1931 M. TERRY *Hidden Wealth* 326 Limewood is a very handsome tree, shapely, with a white trunk and light green foliage; it is very plentiful in the Tanami district. **1936** C. CHEWINGS *Back in Stone Age* 64 The tape-hand is whitened with chalk, or the white substance on the limewood trees (*Eucalyptus papuana*). **1968** A.M. DUNCAN-KEMP *Where Strange Gods Call* p. iii, The Limewoods or white boled Eucalyptus .. are known as (Virgins) Nukka-car, young girls still virgin, uninitiated and untouched. **1981** A.B. & J.W. CRIBB *Useful Wild Plants Aust.* 214 The very white bark of the ghost gum is covered with a fine white powdery layer which comes off on the hand; this is responsible for the less common name of limewood.

limey. [f. LIME(JUICER + -Y. In later use prob. infl. by U.S. *limey* English sailor or ship (see OEDS).] A British immigrant. Also *attrib.*

1888 D.B.W. SLADEN *Austral. Ballads & Rhymes* 31 They'd seen old stagers and limey new chums. **1937** WISBERG & WATERS *Bushman at Large* 92 All you limeys are nutty. **1953** J.E. MACDONNELL *Wings off Sea* 125 Them Limeys sure fan the breeze.

limits, *pl. Hist.* Abbrev. of *limits of location* (see LOCATION 4).

1821 J. WALLIS *Hist. Acct. Colony N.S.W.* 17 The strictest orders were .. given to prevent the convicts from straggling beyond the limits which were marked and known. **1836** *HRA* (1923) 1st Ser. XVIII. 589 Any relaxation will establish a precedent, of which the numerous occupants beyond the limits will not fail to avail themselves. **1841** 'AUSTRALIAN COLONIST' *Resources Aust.* 90 Taking the whole of the unappropriated pastoral lands within the old limits, fully *five* acres will be required to feed a sheep. **1847** *Port Phillip Herald* 5 Jan. 2/7 This system of leases is only to be applied beyond the limits. **1980** P. FREEMAN *Woolshed* 48 The 1836 Squatting Act .. allowed squatting beyond the Limits, providing a license fee of £10 per annum was made for each 'run'.

line.

1. In the collocation **line of road,** a course marked out for a road; the completed road.

1828 *Tasmanian* (Hobart) 9 May 3 Three prisoners in the chain gang at Oatlands, succeeded in slipping off their fetters, while at work in the new line of road at a distance from the huts. **1834** G. BENNETT *Wanderings N.S.W.* I. 202 The new line of road .. was broad, straight, and in excellent condition. **1843** *Sydney Morning Herald* 23 June 2/8 A new, much shorter, and better line of road from New England to the McLeay will sooner or later be discovered and opened. **1853** J. SHERER *Gold Finder Aust.* 21 A heterogeneous stream of human prodigality, pouring itself along a single line of road. **1867** F.J. BYERLEY *Narr. Overland Exped. Northern Qld.* p. x, Cardwell has experienced a check, in consequence of an undue haste in the adoption of a line of road over its Coast Range. **1888** 'R. BOLDREWOOD' *Robbery under Arms* (1937) 95 We kept working by all sorts of outside tracks on the main line of road. **1898** J. RAE *Thirty-Five Yrs. N.S.W. Railways* 5 A survey was .. made from Richmond to the Kurrajong along the Bell's line of road over Mount Wilson to Hartley's Causeway. **1949** *Main Roads* Sept. 15 The building of the main railway to the west during the sixties and seventies of the last century altered the line of road in some places. **1953** *Ibid.* Mar. 73 The new line of road was approved and proclaimed as a Parish Road in the Government Gazette on 18 November, 1840.

2. [Also Canadian and N.Z. from 1828: see OEDS *sb.*[2] 26 e.] Abbrev. of *line of road.* Also *attrib.*

1837 *Perth Gaz.* 25 Mar. 872 In an E.N.E. course from the same point (York), we have now the satisfaction of knowing that .. about eight or ten farmsteads and sheep runs could be formed on that *line.* **1843** *N.S.W. Monthly Mag.* June 283 The new marked line passes through the labyrinth of rocky gullies. **1847** *Atlas* (Sydney) III. 2/2 From *Mongregah* the marked line takes a more northerly course through a portion of poor forest country, to a beautiful reedy lagoon called *Boorambah*, and thence along a succession of water holes, to a sheep station. **1855** H. HUME *Brief Statement* 29 On leaving our sable friends, they pointed out the direct line for Tumut. **1875** CAMPBELL & WILKS *Early Settlement Qld.* 13 A better line *viâ* Drayton was marked, and a day appointed for all the station teams to meet and assist in making the new road. **1890** 'R. BOLDREWOOD' *Miner's Right* 76 The impatient holders of claims on 'the line' frontage. **1936** 'L. KAYE' *Black Wilderness* 13 'Gooran Mahomet's got his camels on the Birdsville track.' 'I thought he might have been up the line,' Lex said. 'He's got some business up there.' **1952** *Main Roads* Mar. 74 All possible routes were investigated, and the existing line, which is to the east of the Centre Ridge, was constructed. **1980** A.S. VEITCH *Run from Morning* 187, I thought .. it might be better if I took him to my place, up the line. I'm very—private there.

3. In the collocation **back line** *obs.*, a rear boundary.

1847 *Britannia* (Hobart) 8 July 2/3 His back line may be Macquarie Harbour. **1849** A. HARRIS *Emigrant Family* (1967) 81 The back line—running just clear of immense masses of broken rock. **1899** *North-Western Advocate* (Devonport) 10 Feb. 4/1 The part of Forest tapped by the Back Line road west has gone ahead wonderfully.

4. *Hist.* Abbrev. of *black line* (see BLACK *a.* 7).

1831 G.A. ROBINSON in N.J.B. Plomley *Friendly*

Mission 5 Nov. (1966) 503 Miles Opening was where the natives got through at the time of the Line. **1835** H. MELVILLE *Hist. Van Diemen's Land* 99 That something was necessary, either to intimidate the blacks, or to capture them, there cannot be a question; and although the 'line' proved a failure, yet it was undertaken with the best intentions. **1870** J. BONWICK *Last Tasmanians* 131 The *Line*, the most formidable part of the Black War, was formed towards the close of 1830. **1886** *Austral. Handbk.* 554 In 1830 an attempt on a gigantic scale called The Line was made to drive the aborigines into a corner of the island.

5. [Poss. transf. use of *line* a department of activity, branch of business: see OED(S *sb.*[2] 28 but also 13 d.] In the phr. **to do a line with,** to behave amorously towards (another).

[**1884** *Austral. Tit-Bits* (Melbourne) 19 June 3/3 'Good morning,' echoed the broker, who thought he could smell a line in shares. 'You sell shares, I suppose?' 'That's our business, sir. Can we do a line with you, sir?'] **1933** N. LINDSAY *Saturdee* 242 'I suppose you're going with Elsie Coote, aren't you?' 'Oh, yes, I'm doin' a line with her,' said Peter. **1941** S.J. BAKER *Pop. Dict. Austral. Slang* 43 *Line with, do a,* to take an amorous interest in a girl or young woman. **1946** K. TENNANT *Lost Haven* 156 Do you know young Len's doing a line with Gran'pa's little angel? **1955** N. PULLIAM *I traveled Lonely Land* 375 *Do a line with*, take a shine to a girl, take a walk with her. **1961** N. GARE *Fringe Dwellers* 286 I'm gunna do a line with the little gel that wants to go to Perth with me.

line-ball. [Fig. use of *line-ball* a ball striking the line and therefore almost out of play.] An indecisive event; a borderline case.

1915 DREW & EVANS *Grafter* 54, I don't know how he'd sling if he had a good winning day. Last day was a line ball. **1919** C. DREW *Doings of Dave* 14 Even then it would only be a line ball. **1951** S. HICKEY *Travelled Roads* 4 Con was clearly a line-ball so decorous conviviality marked his wake.

ling. [Transf. use of *ling* a long, slender fish.] Any of several marine fish, usu. of the fam. Ophidiidae, esp. *Genypterus blacodes*, having a long, tapering pinkish-white body, and the reddish-brown *Lotella callarias*, both of s. Aust.

1895 C. THACKERAY *Amateur Fisherman's Guide* 57 *Tumble-down* is the .. habitat of .. ling. **1906** D.G. STEAD *Fishes of Aust.* 86 The Cod family .. is comparatively unimportant so far as our Australian waters are concerned .. the most important being the Beardie or Ling (*Lotella callarias*). **1933** D. MACDONALD *Brooks of Morning* 181 The rock cod, which is the solace of winter fishermen about Black Rock, is transformed to a ling in Botany Bay .. a long, white, withered fish sold by the yard, soaked by the week, and camouflaged to the sheepsick bush palate under a smoke screen of egg sauce. **1975** *Bulletin* (Sydney) 9 Aug. 17/2 The *ling* (long, pinkish) .. magnificent in both taste and texture. **1984** *Canberra Chron.* 4 July 19/3 Ling, an excellent chunky fish taken offshore along eastern Australia and which in past years has been deliberately and illegally sold as barramundi, is being sold under its own name and is selling well.

lippy. Also **lippie.** [f. *lip(stick* + -Y.] Lipstick.

1955 *Meanjin* 310 Jest .. for fun I put some of Mums [*sic*] lippy on. **1965** H. PORTER *Cats of Venice* 139 'Is there any lippy on the snowy tats?' And she bares her brilliant teeth at Mum like a poster Polynesian. **1976** D. HEWETT *Golden Oldies* 39 Just a wee dab of lippy, dear. Look at that, a picture no artist could paint. **1983** *Sydney Morning Herald* 19 Dec. (Guide) 1/2 On radio, Miss Buttrose sounds as though she is wearing a sun-frock, bit of lippie and a pair of orthopaedic sandals.

liquid, *a.* In special collocations: **liquid laugh,** a vomit; **lunch,** a mid-day meal consisting mainly of an alcoholic beverage, esp. beer.

1964 B. HUMPHRIES *Nice Night's Entertainment* (1981) 78 I've had **liquid laughs** in bars. **1971** —— *Bazza pulls it Off*, All them liquid laughs I had on the boat have left me feelin' weak as piss! **1980** S. THORNE *I've met some Bloody Wags* 89 A 'Get Well' bag—the type airlines usually supply for 'liquid laughs'. **1969** A. BUZO *Front Room Boys* (1970) 21 We used to go down to Jim Buckley's .. for a **liquid lunch.** **1973** *Bulletin* (Sydney) 13 Jan. 28/1 (*caption*) Jonathan Crawford and local girl Chris Coates .. take liquid lunch in the sun. **1980** L. DAVIES *Past Master* 23 He always liked a liquid lunch at the Commercial Hotel over the way.

little, *a.*

1. In special collocations: **Little Brother,** a British youth who emigrates to Australia under the auspices of the *Big Brother Movement* (see BIG BROTHER); **-go** *obs.*, a nickname for the Court of Requests; also **little-go court,** and *attrib.*; **house** [Br. dial. (see EDD *little, a.* 30)], a euphemism for an outside privy; **lunch,** light refreshment eaten during a mid-morning break at school.

1927 J.A.R. MARRIOTT *Empire Settlement* 81 The idea is that a band of well-established Australian citizens, clergymen, government officials, bankers, farmers, etc., should individually undertake to act the part of a Big Brother to an individual **Little Brother** from the homeland. **1932** R.W. THOMPSON *Down Under* 25 Boxing competitions were organised for the 'Little Brothers'. **1959** E. WEBB *Mark of Sun* 101 Any British boy could migrate to Australia as a Little Brother. **1984** *Canberra Times* 9 July 8/1 There are over 100,000 ex-'Little Brothers', their families, friends and other supporters living in Australia. **1837** *Cornwall Chron.* (Launceston) 5 Aug. 3 First, an Under Sherriff of the Supreme Court .. now a **Little-go** Sherriff! *Ibid.* 12 Aug. 3 But for the strictest exactness in matters of accounts carried into the 'Little Go' Court, a system of roguery would take place. **1841** *Port Phillip Patriot* 5 July 2/2 A correspondent informs us that finding some of his customers rather *dreigh* in their payments, he took the liberty of summoning them to the 'little-go' or Court of Requests. **1843** *Melbourne Times* 10 June 3/2 Your carriage hire you must pay or they will put you in the 'Little-go'. **1847** *Port Phillip Herald* 9 Sept. (Suppl.), Some singular cases were tried at the recent Court of Requests. A Pentonville *attaché* of the 'little go', named Whitelaw summoned Mr Francis M'Connell of Collins-street, for damages—the result of a dog bite. **1886** N. ROBINSON *Stagg of Tarcowie* 9 Aug. (1977) 84 Building at the **little house.** **1939** L. MANN *Mountain Flat* 23 A gate led from the first yard into another in which were the pig sty, the hen-house, the tool-shed and what they jocosely called 'the little house'. **1966** *Kings Cross Whisper* (Sydney) xxvi. 3/1 Rural and outer suburban areas where little houses, commonly known as thunder boxes, are most popular. **1982** N. KEESING *Lily on Dustbin* 120 In Queensland 'eleveners' have disappeared in favour of the universal '**little lunch**' to eat during the morning; 'big lunch' is eaten at lunch time.

2. As a distinguishing epithet in the names of birds: **little corella,** the predom. white, crestless cockatoo *C. sanguinea* of Aust., esp. arid regions, and New Guinea; see also CORELLA; **eagle,** the bird of prey *Hieraaetus morphnoides* of mainland Aust. and New Guinea; **falcon,** the bird of prey *Falco longipennis* of Aust. and islands to the north; *white-fronted falcon*, see WHITE *a.*[2] 1 b.; **kingfisher,** the smallest Austral. kingfisher *Ceyx pusillus*, a blue and white bird of coastal N.T. and n. Qld.; **lorikeet,** the small lorikeet *Glossopsitta pusilla* of e. and s.e. Aust., a predom. green bird with a red face; JERRYANG; see also KEET; **penguin,** *fairy penguin*, see FAIRY *n.*[1] 1; **quail,** the small, nomadic bird *Turnix velox* of mainland Aust.; **wattle bird,** either of the two smaller wattle birds, *Anthochaera lunulata* of s.w. Aust., and *A. chrysoptera* (see *brush wattle bird* BRUSH *n.*[1] B. 2); **wood swallow,** the predom. grey-brown bird *Artamus minor* of n. and central Aust.

1948 A. MARSHALL *Ourselves writ Strange* 247 **Little corellas,** those cockatoos with naked blue skin around their eyes, were feeding in the long grass. **1986** *Canberra Times* 5 Mar. 18/5 Canberra's bird gurus were agog several years ago when a hybrid between a galah and its close relative the little corella turned up. **1902** *Emu* II. 10 The **Little Eagle** .. are constant visitors during summer, autumn and winter. **1945** C. BARRETT *Austral. Bird Life* 32 More shy and wary than other species, the little eagle .. preys mainly upon rabbits. **1962** B.W. LEAKE *Eastern Wheatbelt Wildlife* 83 The little eagle and the wedge tailed prefer eating carrion to catching their own food. **1976** *Reader's Digest Compl. Bk. Austral. Birds* 127 The little eagle is a tireless hunter which prefers live prey, but will occasionally eat carrion. **1984** E. ROLLS *Celebration of Senses* 19 Our Little Eagle, a sturdy bird patterned in cream and brown, keeps watch effortlessly by gliding round within the thermals a few hundred metres up. **1841** J. GOULD *Birds of Aust.* (1848) I. Pl. 10, *Falco frontatus* .. **Little Falcon**, Colonists of Western Australia. **1902** *Emu* II. 10 The Black-cheeked Falcon .. and the Little Falcon (*F. lunulatus*) keep Sparrows and all small fry in mortal terror. **1948** J. FAIRFAX *Run o' Waters* 58 The Little Falcon .. a little black demon of incredible speed. **1968** R. HILL *Bush Quest* 64 A drive along the Boulevard can produce such excitements as a little falcon. **1984** E. ROLLS *Celebration of Senses* 17 The Little Falcon, a supreme hunter, could simply lift one foot and pluck the nuisance out of the air. **1843** J. GOULD *Birds of Aust.* (1848) II. Pl. 26, *Alcyone pusilla* .. **Little Kingfisher.** **1945** C. BARRETT *Austral. Bird Life* 144 The little kingfisher .. keeps within the tropics. **1964** M. SHARLAND *Territory of Birds* 202 One also sees the Little Kingfisher perched beside some lagoon or river; it is a dumpy little bird with an abbreviated tail and a round patch of white on each wing which it displays in flight. [**1843 little lorikeet:** J. GOULD *Birds of Aust.* (1948) V. 54 *Trichoglossus pusillus* .. Little Parrakeet.] **1929** A.H. CHISHOLM *Birds & Green Places* 209 The tiny red-faced species, known as the 'gizzie' or little lorikeet. **1935** DAVISON & NICHOLLS *Blue Coast Caravan* 18 The Doctor identified .. little lorikeet, crimson parrot. **1965** *Austral. Encycl.* VII. 25 Three smaller species—the musk, little, and purple-crowned lorikeets—are found mainly in southern Australia. **1978** B.P. MOORE *Life on Forty Acres* 95 Calosoma has been favoured .. by the Little Lorikeet (*Glossopsitta pusilla*). Nomadic and very gregarious, these active and charming little parrots are largely nectar-feeders and they possess a special brush-like tongue for lapping up their food. [**1785** J. LATHAM *Gen. Synopsis Birds* III. 572 **Little Pinguin** [*sic*] .. This species is found among the rocks on the southern parts of *New Zealand*. .. The inhabitants of *Queen Charlotte's Sound* kill the birds with sticks, and, after skinning them, esteem the flesh as good food.] **1844** J. GOULD *Birds of Aust.* (1848) VII. Pl. 84, *Spheniscus minor* .. Little Penguin. **1890** G.J. BROINOWSKI *Birds of Aust.* I. Pl. 1, On some of these islands largely frequented by the Little Penguins, beaten tracks have been formed by them. **1974** C. THIELE *Albatross Two* 128 You can .. say The Little Penguin: Or do as the vulgar do and call him a Fairy. **1841** J. GOULD *Birds of Aust.* (1848) V. Pl. 87, *Hemipodius velox* .. **Little Quail**, of the Colonists. **1903** *Emu* II. 155 *Turnix velox* (Little Quail). .. These little birds seem very plentiful near Port Darwin. **1916** S.A. WHITE *In Far Northwest* 48 We .. flushed a quail or two, which I feel sure was the little quail. **1945** C. BARRETT *Austral. Bird Life* 67 The swift flying little quail. **1962** B.W. LEAKE *Eastern Wheatbelt Wildlife* 79 The white winged triller .. and little quail arrive in August. **1846** J. GOULD *Birds of Aust.* (1848) IV. Pl. 57, *Anthochaera lunulata* .. **Little Wattle-Bird,** Colonists of Swan River. **1861** E.P. RAMSAY-LAYE *Social Life & Manners* 132 Here I heard .. the little *wattle-bird*, like a thrush in appearance, adding its shrill note. **1905** *Emu* V. 79 Together with the Little Wattle Bird .. chased and scolded one another. **1945** C. BARRETT *Austral. Bird Life* 162 The red wattle-bird .. and the little wattle-bird (*A[nthochaera] chrysoptera*) range from southern Queensland to Victoria. **1980** L. FULLER *Wollongong's Native Trees* 46 Little wattlebird .. and red wattlebird .. which are both large nomadic honeyeaters follow blossoming eucalypts and banksias, especially *Banksia ericifolia*. **1842** J. GOULD *Birds of Aust.* (1848) II. Pl. 28, *Artamus minor* .. **Little Wood Swallow.** **1896** B. SPENCER *Rep. Horn Sci. Exped. Central Aust.* II. 108 Little Wood Swallow .. were seen flying about and soaring along the Levi Range. **1945** C. BARRETT *Austral. Bird Life* 202 The little wood-swallow .. ranges over the northern half of the continent. **1964** M. SHARLAND *Territory of Birds* 76 We also saw hundreds of Tree Martins in close formation cleaning up some form of insect life. .. Little Wood-swallows also shared the feast.

littley. [f. *little* + -Y; prob. independent of Br. dial. *littly* small person: see OEDS.] A child.

1965 *Coast to Coast 1963–64* 84, I take a bunch of littlies for Bible lessons, hymns, you know. **1967** B. JEFFERIS *One Black Summer* 122 Can you see Hilary instructing the littlies at Sunday school? **1968** D. O'GRADY *Bottle of Sandwiches* 62 The amount of grog consumed there really separated the boys from the littleys. **1976** K. DENTON *Thinkable Man* 72 Mum used to tell me that when I was a littley I wouldn't hold anyone's hand. **1980** S. THORNE *I've met some Bloody Wags* 109 He .. bundled him in the car with Denise and four other 'littlies' and sped into Collarenebri hospital.

liver. In the phr. **shit on the liver**: see SHIT 2.

lizard.

1. One employed: **(a)** to muster sheep; **(b)** to maintain boundary fences. Also *attrib.*

1897 *Worker* (Sydney) 11 Sept. 1/1 By 'lizards' he means musterers, sometimes he calls them 'snails'. **1898** *Bulletin* (Sydney) 17 Dec. 15/1 Musterers are *lizards* and *snails* (originally applied to slow musterers who couldn't keep up with the sheep and stopped the shearing. Now a general term). **1905** *Shearer* (Sydney) 4 Feb. 4/2 What do you know of .. 'tick-jammers', or of 'lizards' and 'wire inspectors'? **1912** *Bulletin* (Sydney) 30 May 16/3 He does the lizard act along a fence, and pulls up at water by noon. **1925** *Ibid.* 12 Feb. 22/2 A lizard is a boundary rider, from his habit of crawling along fences. **1936** *Ibid.* 29 Jan. 20/4, I have heard boundary-riders referred to by many names. Blue-tongues, lizards .. [etc.]. **1945** S.J. BAKER *Austral. Lang.* 63 Shepherds have been known variously as *lizards, crawlers.*

2. In the exclam. **starve** (or **stiffen**) **the lizards,** an expression of surprise or exasperation. See also CROW *n.*[1] 3.

1927 *Bulletin* (Sydney) 27 Jan. 22/2 'Starve the lizards,' he said, 'there ain't no kangaroos in the West now.' **1944** L. GLASSOP *We were Rats* 204 'God starve the lizards,' said Eddie. 'Another dud.' **1959** M. RAYMOND *Smiley roams Road* 17 Stone the crows and stiffen the lizards. **1965** E. LAMBERT *Long White Night* 89 'Starve the bloody lizards!' breathed Clancy. 'Now I've seen the lot.' **1983** *Weekend Austral. Mag.* (Sydney) 27 Aug. 20/8 Starve the lizards, only a touch better than a poke in the eye with a burnt stick.

3. In the phr. **flat out like a lizard:** see FLAT *adv.* 2. Hence **lizarding** *vbl. n.*, mustering; also *transf.*, lazing.

1908 'G. SEAGRAM' *Bushmen All* 240 This blessed lizarding is bad enough, but wood and water joey is worse. **1975** *Sun* (Sydney) 16 May 13/2 He likes his golf and just lizarding in the sun.

loading, *vbl. n.*[1] [Br. *loading* a load, cargo, but app. now rare: see OED *vbl. n.* 4.] Freight carried by a vehicle; a load.

1862 C. MUNRO *Fern Vale* I. 127 By this time the drays were seen making their approach; and great was instantly the bustle in preparation for the reception of the 'loading'. **1890** 'R. BOLDREWOOD' *Colonial Reformer* II. 144 He had, as early as such loading could be procured, ordered from town great stores of fruit-trees and plants. **1903** *Bulletin* (Sydney) 3 Jan. 16/1 Station-contracting .. is the 'bullocky's' sheet-anchor when loading is scarce. **1921** G.A. BELL *Under Brigalows* 82 The coming of the drays from Rockhampton a couple of times a year with the loading was always a great event on a station. **1936** I.L. IDRIESS *Cattle King* 75 The new combine obtained plentiful loading in busy Wentworth. **1959** A. UPFIELD *Bony & Mouse* 164 The truckers .. had merely rolled into their swags beside the tarpaulin-covered loading. **1976** K. BROWN *Knock Ten* 59 A teamster .. took loading out from the railhead at The Mount to any point .. in the Gulf.

loading, *vbl. n.*[2] A payment in addition to an award wage or salary, in acknowledgement of conditions of employment, degree of skill, a prosperous economy, etc.

1941 *44 CAR* 456 In addition to amounts otherwise payable a special loading at the rate of 3s. per week shall be payable to occupants of any of the callings specified. **1943** *50 CAR* 87 Adult male employees shall each be paid a prosperity loading at the rate of 1s. per day, such amount, unlike the needs basic wage, not to be adjustable. **1952** *73 CAR* 1008 'Loading' means any addition or additions to ordinary rate. **1966** *Sydney Morning Herald* 10 Oct. 2/2 The failure of the unions' claim for 'prosperity loadings' in the General Motors-Holden's case .. shows that the unions need to do a great deal more hard thinking. **1972** *Age* (Melbourne) 14 Dec. 1/7 Victorian painters will receive a 17½ per cent. loading of their three-weeks holiday pay as a Christmas bonus. **1976** Academic Salaries Tribunal Rev. 209 Other members of staff, in addition to professors, should be eligible to receive merit loadings. **1983** J. CARROLL *Austral. Industr. Relations Handbk.* (rev. ed.) 86 Whether or not an employee is entitled to payment of the loading on pro rata annual leave on termination of his employment depends primarily on the terms of the relevant award.

loam, *n.*

1. *pl.* Particles of gold found by loaming (see LOAM *v.*) and indicating the presence and location of a deposit. Also **loam gold.**

1934 S.J. CASH *Prospecting for Gold* 8 Quartz of a sugary nature would .. throw loam gold or 'loams' as it is called, more freely than harder quartz. **1977** J. DOUGHTY *Gold in Blood* 196 Near The Castlemaine outcrop, I had discovered a shed of loam gold. **1982** M. WATTONE *Winning Gold in W.A.* 76 Loams were traced to a shallow reef about 46 cm. under the surface and I ended up recovering 300 oz. of gold.

2. Special Comb. **loam bag,** the bag in which a sample of soil which is to be tested for gold particles is placed.

1896 J. HOLT *Virgin Gold* 42 The prospector, pure and simple .. sets out with his pick and shovel, his dish and his loam-bag. **1931** W. BARAGWANATH et al. *Guide for Prospectors in Vic.* 6 The 'loamer' .. places the 'prospect' in the loam bag, tying the bag tightly with strong cord above and below the sample. **1934** S.J. CASH *Prospecting for Gold* 9 When loaming was first introduced a big dish of loam was carried to the nearest creek to be washed... There was an improvement in the method .. when someone brought the *loam-bag* into requisition.

loam, *v.* Also **loom.** [f. *loam* clay, soil.] *intr.* To search (an area) for a mineral, usu. gold, by washing loam: see quot. 1932. Also *trans.* and as *vbl. n.*

1896 J. HOLT *Virgin Gold* 19 That important branch known as '*loaming*'. **1916** R. MACKAY *Recoll. Early Gippsland Goldfields* 29 The science of loaming was either then unknown, or known to very few. **1932** I.L. IDRIESS *Prospecting for Gold* 264 *Loaming*, a method of prospecting for a metal-bearing vein or mineralized area in which dirt is washed from places chosen systematically around and up the slope of a hill. Presence, absence, and the number of colours in the dish eventually indicate the mineral source. **1934** S.J. CASH *Prospecting for Gold* 7 Very often prospectors are discouraged from further 'loaming' on account of getting a set-back at the first effort to find the deposit shedding the colors. **1946** K.S. PRICHARD *Roaring Nineties* 59 Dinny went loaming along the ridge for several days before he knapped a rock that showed fine shotty gold. **1950** —— *Winged Seeds* 21 'Ye've loomed her north, a bit, Mick?' .. 'Got colours in every dish,' Mick told him. **1966** H. GYE *Father clears Out* 50 Old Tom was to make himself useful about the plant, and loam the surrounding country for the reef. **1977** J. DOUGHTY *Gold in Blood* 47 It is not unusual in waterless country to use dryblower machines to 'loam' up to the gold-carrying portions of a lode or reef.

loamer. Also **loomer.** One who searches for gold by loaming: see LOAM *v.*

1931 W. BARAGWANATH et al. *Guide for Prospectors in Vic.* 6 The 'loamer' digs a small hole to bedrock. **1934** S.J. CASH *Prospecting for Gold* 29 Should he not be successful he has not lost so much as the loamer doing the same class of ground with the wet process. **1977** J. DOUGHTY *Gold in Blood* 180 When a loamer strikes gold he keeps his mouth shut. **1980** M. MCADOO *If only I'd Listened* ('Pop Doherty'), Now those fellows .. could find the source of the gold; they called it 'looming', and oh it was an art because there wasn't much water about. The Cash brothers .. they were famous loomers. **1982** M. WATTONE *Winning Gold in W.A.* 75 John is recognized by Kalgoorlie prospectors as being one of the best loamers that the district has produced.

loan. [Var. of Br. dial. *to take the lend of a person* to take advantage of, to cajole: see EDD *lend, v.* and *sb.*[1] 4.] In the phr. **to get** (or **have**) **the loan of** (someone), to trick (a person); to treat (a person) as a fool.

1903 J. FURPHY *Such is Life* 143 'Jist what I told you!' she replied, with a sunny laugh. 'Think I was tryin' to git the loan o' you?' **1955** R. LAWLER *Summer of Seventeenth Doll* (1965) 95 It's all fellers—Barney wouldn't take a girl to the races with a crowd of fellers. He's havin' a loan of yer. **1967** G. JENKIN *Two Yrs. Bardunyah Station* 64 The chaps were 'having the loan of him'. They gave him a couple of buckets and sent him over to the kitchen to get some steam to start the engine. **1977** R. BEILBY *Gunner* 200 Ya havin' a loan of yaself, Snow. I can just see it. Tom Mix in Pine Gulch.

loan gang. *Hist.* A detachment of artisan convicts employed on public works but made available to settlers: see quot. 1840. See also LEND.

1833 *Colonist* (Hobart) 4 Jan. 2/4 Much as has been said about the Loan-Gang, we are firmly persuaded, that had it not been for this gang, the price of labour would have risen. **1835** H. MELVILLE *Hist. Van Diemen's Land* 259 There is what is termed 'the loan gang', consisting of a parcel of men, the best workmen in the Colony; these men it is understood, are lent on loan to the settlers generally, but this is not the case, these men are for the greater part employed by Government Officers, or men friendly with the chief authorities. **1840** D. BURN *Vindication Van Diemen's Land* 14 The loan-gang .. is formed of artisans employed in government works, who .. are lent .. to assist settlers in building, or other needful improvements. **1852** J. WEST *Hist. of Tas.* II. 240 The artizan, when not adapted for public works, was placed in the loan gang, and lent from time to time, chiefly to the officers of the government, or to such settlers as were deemed worthy of official patronage. **1863** C. GIBSON *Life among Convicts* II. 227 In Van Diemen's Land, all the convicts, who were mechanics, were retained in the service of Government, and placed in the engineer department, the loan-gang, or the police.

loap, var. LERP.

lob, *n.* [Spec. use of Br. dial. *lob* lump (of money): see EDD *sb.*[1] and OED *sb.*[2] 4.] A rich deposit of gold: see quot. 1869. Also **lob of gold.**

[**1858** C.R. THATCHER *Colonial Songster* (rev. ed.) 4 Folks rushed to Bendigo; And went and pitched in Eagle Hawk, Where lobs were made you know.] **1861** H. EARLE *Ups & Downs* 287 The gold perhaps may tempt us the diggings to try, In a hole or fine 'lob' we may see. **1869** R.B. SMYTH *Gold Field & Minerals Districts* 164 *Lob of gold*, a very large quantity or rich deposit of gold contained within a small area. **1873** W. THOMSON-GREGG *Desperate Character* I. 80 At Bendigo, Pat hit upon a 'lob', which produced him a no less sum than nine hundred pounds. **1864** J. ROGERS *New Rush* 5 Imagine future 'lobs' of which they share. **1895** J.W. ANDERSON *Prospector's Handbk.* (ed. 6) 161 *Lob of gold* (Australia), rich gold deposit found in an area of small extent. **1944** M.W. PEACOCK *Dead Puppets Dance* 41 I'm selling out my claim to Ah Kar and another chow. Some people would call me a mug to give it up after striking a lob like this.

lob, *v.* [Transf. use of *lob* to move heavily or clumsily: see OED(S *v.* 3.] *intr.* To arrive, esp. without ceremony; to turn up. Freq. with **in(to), on to, up,** etc.

1911 *Bulletin* (Sydney) 17 Aug. 14/3 I first lobbed on to the 'far Barcoo' .. years ago. **1918** A. WRIGHT *Over Odds* 121, I beat it to the West on my share of Skimmy's roll; only lobbed back two days ago. **1925** *Aussie* (Sydney) Aug. 57/2 The next day we all lobbed up to the local hall. **1934** A. MELROSE *Song & Slapstick* 121 The dust would clear and in old Dan would lob. **1943** S.W. KEOUGH *Around Army* 23 He doesn't take a risk that a few visitors may lob unexpectedly at the last minute and he'll miss out on the good things. **1955** J. MORRISON *Black Cargo* 216 What the hell's a Canadian ship doing—lobbing in Melbourne now? **1965** R.H. CONQUEST *Horses in Kitchen* 47 Any man who lobbed in with an empty tucker-bag was promptly fed. **1977** F.A. REEDER *Diary of Rat* 61 We lobbed there about nine thirty in the morning and went inside to report to the C.O. **1984** *Age* (Melbourne) 6 July 4/2 The Chinese Noodle Shop Restaurant seemed the logical choice, so three of us lobbed there at 8 o'clock.

lobby. Chiefly *Qld.* [f. LOB(STER + -Y.] YABBY 1.

1952 W.J. DAKIN *Austral. Seashores* 183 In Queensland they are known as lobbies (the derivation of this can be guessed)—in that State yabbies are something quite different. **1970** I. GALL *Fishing for Fun of It* 72 Queensland fresh waters are teeming with yabbies, and by that I mean lobbies or crays. **1977** K. MCARTHUR *Bread & Dripping Days* 10 Other lucky families had waterholes or creeks and in those pools were lobbies. Outside Queensland they are called yabbies but in Queensland they are lobbies which pedants call fresh-water crayfish. **1984** H.W. DAVIS *Bachelors in Bush* 51 Harry and me was fishing for them little freshwater lobsters what they call 'lobbies'.

Hence **lobbying,** *vbl. n.*

1977 K. McArthur *Bread & Dripping Days* 10 For a day's lobbying, first a kind mother had to supply meat bones which were well and truly picked over on the way to the creek. **1981** G. Ellis *Hey Doc, let's go Fishing!* 63 Country kids get 'hooked on fishing by the beguiling sport of 'yabbying' or lobbying'.

lobster. [Transf. use of *lobster* a large marine decapod crustacean of the genus *Homarus*.] Any of several crayfish, esp. those having claws the flesh of which is esteemed as food. See also Crayfish *n.*

1826 J. Atkinson *Acct. Agric. & Grazing N.S.W.* 25 Lobsters, crayfish, and prawns, are also found in many places. **1834** G. Bennett *Wanderings N.S.W.* I. 214 In this colony, cray-fish abound in the sea, and lobsters in the river. **1844** *Sydney Morning Herald* 3 May 3/2 The lobster or craw-fishing this season has been unusually unproductive. **1871** J. Baird *Emigrant's Guide Australasia* 72 Fish of excellent quality abound in the inland rivers and creeks, including mullet, perch, the small lobster. **1909** G. Smith *Naturalist in Tas.* 108 In Tasmania the term Crayfish is applied to the marine Rock Lobster (*Panulirus*), the term Lobster to the Freshwater Crayfish (*Astacopsis*). **1972** L. Irish *Time of Dolphins* 109 She rescued the lobsters—why *do* we call them lobsters when they're crays? **1985** *Age* (Melbourne) 19 Mar. 29/2 The light sauce with the dish . . and the freshness and perfect cooking of the crayfish (please let us break the 'lobster' habit; lobsters have claws) were laudable.

local government. *Hist.* Any one of the Colonial administrations as distinct from the *home government* (see Home *n.*[1] B b.).

1835 *Cornwall Chron.* (Launceston) 14 Nov. 1 The Local Government is guilty at the least of an injudicious arrangement of the means placed at its disposal for the benefit of the whole Colony. **1837** *Ibid.* 5 Aug. 2 The protecting influence of *our* Local Government. **1838** W. Bland *N.S.W.* 5 We have been blessed, from the first establishment of the Colony down to the present hour, with an almost *irresponsible* local government. **1841** *Port Phillip Patriot* 11 Oct. 3/1 A choice breed of asses and of Arabian camels appear to be an object well worthy the attention of the local governments of Australia and New Zealand. **1845** *Portland Gaz.* 1 Apr. 4/4 The state of the Great Southern Road is positively a disgrace to the local government.

locatable, *a. Obs.* [f. Locate *v.* 3.] Of land: available for occupation by a settler.

1833 *Launceston Advertiser* 13 June 2 *For sale. A maximum grant*, free from Quit Rent, to be taken where the purchaser may choose from Land yet locatable.

locate, *v. Hist.* [Spec. use of *locate*, not always excl. Austral. but of local significance: see OED *v.* 3, 4, and 5, and Mathews.]

1. [See esp. OED *v.* 5.] *trans.* To allocate (a specified block of land or an entitlement to a specified area of unidentified land), esp. to a settler or for the purpose of grazing stock; to grant.

1811 *HRA* (1921) 3rd Ser. I. 458 No New Town Allotment is to be located to any person whatever in '*George Square*' or in 'Macquarie Street'. **1820** H.G. Bennet *Let. to Earl Bathurst* 4 He may grant pardons, and give tickets of leave to the convicts; he may locate land to the amount of one hundred acres. **1826** *HRA* (1922) 3rd Ser. V. 45 Respecting the Lands, which I considered were located to me previous to my departure for England. **1836** *Bent's News* (Hobart) 26 Mar. 2 Let the British Government rather encourage an industrious peasantry in this Colony, by locating upon the most extensive scale limited grants of land, from 50 to 100 acres. **1848** *Britannia* (Hobart) 10 Oct. 2/2 The Lieutenant Governor will approve of two hundred acres being located to you on Partridge Island. **1851** H. Melville *Present State Aust.* 226 Sir William Denison trusted that his locating the allotment to the captain, would be sanctioned by the home authorities. **1952** J.R. Skemp *Memories Myrtle Bank* 25 The land they had taken, or part of it, was subsequently 'located' to them and they were granted titles to it on relatively easy terms.

2. [See esp. OED *v.* 3 and 4.] **a.** *trans.* To establish (a settler, etc.) in a place suitable for permanent occupation; to settle. Freq. *refl.*

1823 *HRA* (1914) 1st Ser. II. 122 On obtaining the promise of a grant, the settler formerly went and located himself. **1834** H. Melville *Two Lett. Van Diemen's Land* 7 On his arrival he located himself upon a tract of land granted him in consideration of his capital. **1837** *S. Austral. Rec.* (London) 8 Nov. 3 Colonel Light will send to Sydney for assistance, to prevent disappointment to those who come out and expect to be located immediately. **1841** *Port Phillip Patriot* 23 Aug. 4/2 Dr Wilson, of Braidwood, engaged nearly one hundred of the lately arrived emigrants, who are to be located on the Doctor's splendid property, in St. Vincent. **1844** *Colonial Observer* (Sydney) 22 Aug. 163/3 Three resolutions . . locating families on small farms of crown lands. **1848** *Port Phillip Herald* 27 June 2/5 Large landholders will find it their interest to locate a German community on their property. **1849** A. Harris *Emigrant Family* (1967) 150 These wild bushmen and . . the few settlers of the poorest class . . had located themselves thereabouts, without any regular license. **1874** J.J. Halcombe *Emigrant & Heathen* 13 Settlers had located themselves, not in reference to the proximity of a church, but according as the land was better suited for agriculture.

b. *trans.* To establish (a person) in a place for a period of limited or uncertain duration. Freq. *refl.*

1839 *Southern Austral.* (Adelaide) 10 May 4/1 The recent murders were committed by a tribe of natives whom I can assert to have been two months absent from Adelaide. . . I am the owner of the property on which they located themselves during that period. **1839** J. Marshall *Twenty Yrs. Experience Aust.* 18 He tells stories of people losing themselves . . and being compelled to locate themselves for the night beneath a tree. **1845** *Parramatta Chron.* 19 Apr. 2/1 The accused . . was not discovered until . . the following morning, at a public house, where he admitted having located himself for fourteen hours. **1847** *Port Phillip Herald* 11 Mar. 2/6 Prisoners in future to be located at Maria Island. **1848** *Maitland Mercury* 16 Aug. 2/6 *The recently arrived immigrants* . . have been located in the old Military Barracks, where they have been supplied with rations.

3. *trans.* To select (a piece of land as specified in the terms of a grant).

1823 *Hobart Town Gaz.* 4 Oct., New Settlers, or those who have not yet located their Grants. **1829** *HRA* (1922) 1st Ser. XV. 275 The *extended* and *scattered* manner in which the Settlers have located their grants. **1831** *Colonial Times* (Hobart) 1 Oct., Great inconvenience having arisen from granting permission to persons who have located their Grants in situations chosen by themselves, subsequently to remove their Locations to other parts of the Colony, the Lieutenant Governor has been pleased to direct . . that such permission will not hereafter be given. **1839** *Tegg's Handbk. for Emigrants* 11 You intend to locate a maiden tract.

4. [See esp. OED *v.* 4.] **a.** *intr.* To establish oneself (as a settler) in a place.

1827 *Tasmanian* (Hobart) 7 Dec. 2 On coming here, they get land in proportion to their property, on which they can locate with as little expense as at Canada. **1832** J. Henderson *Observations Colonies N.S.W. & Van Diemen's Land* 38 The settler must . . receive an order to select a grant of land . . he must then procure an order to take possession of it, or in colonial phrase, to 'Locate'. **1840** A. Russell *Tour through Austral. Colonies* 66 About 300 Germans have located in the neighbourhood of Adelaide. **1843** *Sydney Morning Herald* 12 Oct. 3/3 Mr Eales, who is the only squatter near the Wide Bay, will . . find anything but a profitable speculation in locating out there. **1855** N.L. Kentish *Question of Questions!* 40 They might locate on any 'country' they chose to 'take up', *i.e.*, to select to any extent.

b. *transf.*

1842 *Portland Mercury* 14 Sept. 3/2 Mr James Allison . . had . . started from Portland on horseback, armed to the teeth, with the dire intention of proclaiming war against the ducks located at Bridgwater. **1843** *Ibid.* 24 May 3/4 It is reasonable to suppose that these insects will locate where they can obtain water.

Hence **locating** *vbl. n.*

1827 *Monitor* (Sydney) 3 Mar. 362/3 His resignation was tendered upon the condition usually granted to public servants, namely a grant of land. For the present 'granting' and 'locating' are at a stand still.

located, *ppl. a. Hist.*

1. Of land: allocated, granted; occupied by settlers. See also Unlocated.

1825 *Hobart Town Gaz.* 8 June, Even those whose sheep and cattle are not numerous, find a difficulty in depasturing on their located grounds. **1825** B. Field *Geogr. Mem. N.S.W.* 151 It will be centrically distanced between the located pasture-lands on Hunter's River, and our future stock stations on Liverpool Plains. **1843** *Portland Mercury* 8 Feb. 3/4 The survey takes in the located part of the township. **1844** *Colonial Observer* (Sydney) 13 June 88/4 The district is every day becoming more thickly located. **1848** J.C. Byrne *Emigrant's Guide* 12 Secure a good master and a comfortable home within the located parts of the colonies.

2. In the collocation **located district,** a district occupied by settlers.

1825 M. Hindmarsh *Lett.* (1945) 20 Government is now about selling all the Crown Lands in the Located Districts which is mostly choice land. **1837** *Perth Gaz.* 5 Aug. 948 The natives in the more densely located districts are very peaceable, as far as regards their intercourse with the white people. **1849** C. Sturt *Narr. Exped. Central Aust.* I. 145 There was an abundance of feed for our cattle: the locality would be of great value as a station if it were near the located districts of South Australia.

locatee. *Hist.* One to whom an allocation of land has been made.

1834 H. Melville *Two Lett. Van Diemen's Land* 6 Numerous instances of the resumption of land . . have taken place, in order to bestow them gratuitously upon other locatees. **1837** *Cornwall Chron.* (Launceston) 17 June 1 The land . . marked on the chart as belonging to the original locatees. **1855** N.L. Kentish *Question of Questions!* 11 Subjecting it, by the conveyance deed, to *certain conditions* binding on each locatee.

locater, var. Locator.

location. *Hist.* [Spec. use of *location*, as infl. by prec.]

1. An allocation or grant of land; the piece of land so allocated.

1813 *HRA* (1921) 3rd Ser. I. 35, I cannot sanction nor confirm some of the Locations you directed Mr Meehan to make. **1822** J.T. Bigge *Rep. State Colony N.S.W.* 114 Governor Macquarie . . has put a stop to several unauthorized locations of land in that town. **1827** *Tasmanian* (Hobart) 1 Nov. 1 *Persons* having chosen *locations* . . are informed that Surveys are now proceeding . . and Locations will be surveyed and marked off. **1832** *Colonial Times* (Hobart) 25 Apr., Lot No. 18—640 acres, Bounded on the north by a location to James Maclanachan. **1839** *Tegg's Handbk. for Emigrants* 11 Your wants as an agriculturalist will depend upon . . the extent of your location. **1853** *Visit to Aust. & Gold Regions* (S.P.C.K.) 84 The capitalist, fresh from home . . looks round for some one who will be willing to part with his established location, for a 'consideration'. **1865** 'W.R.L.' *Our Wool Staple* 9 They were to be accredited cultivators of wool fixed down to particular locations, and subjected to rentals proportioned to the area of their runs.

2. The act of establishing a settler in a place; settlement.

1819 *HRA* (1921) 3rd Ser. II. 411 Preclude my authorizing any extensive location thereon. **1831** *Ibid.* (1923) 1st Ser. XVI. 148 The location of settlers on their lands, when they first come to the Colony. **1839** *Port Phillip Gaz.* 27 Nov. 3 The country around this intended settlement [*sc.* Moreton Bay] . . will shortly be thrown open to general location. **1843** *Sydney Morning Herald* 1 May 2/5 During the first year of our location we were wholly employed in providing the necessaries of life for our establishment. **1850** *Illustr. Austral. Mag.* (Melbourne) Aug. 118 Her father . . had, from his first location in the Bush, carefully abstained from contracting any of those vulgar or *flash* habits. **1865** G.S. Lang *Aborigines of Aust.* 39 The grand foundation of all the evil is the absence of any systematic provision . . for the location of the blacks, when their country is occupied by the whites.

3. Special Comb. **location duty,** an obligation imposed on the occupier of a location by the terms under which the land was allocated; **order,** a warrant authorizing the holder to select and occupy a piece of land on certain stipulated terms.

1832 G.F. MOORE *Diary Ten Yrs. W.A.* 1 July (1884) 122 Here I have as much as I can manage, perhaps more, as the **location duties** are heavy. **1835** *Perth Gaz.* 5 Apr. 470 The location duties [on an estate being offered for sale] have been so far performed as to render it free from any tax for seven years. **1838** *Southern Austral.* (Adelaide) 23 June 4/4 Many of the large landholders [at Swan River] have parted with one-half of a grant to a person who would fulfil the 'location duties', as they are called, by which the proprietor of the land is bound to expend 15s. 6d. per acre within ten years of the time it was located. **1832** *Colonist* (Hobart) 28 Sept. 3/5 It will require . . more than all the casuistry of all the lawyers to prove that **location order** can be substituted for the term *grant.* **1842** *Colonial Observer* (Sydney) 9 Mar. 182/4 The deed of grant is what is called a *location order*, and is similar to the tenure on which a large extent of land is held in this Colony. **1851** H. MELVILLE *Present State Aust.* 335 Many of the 'location orders' have been lost or accidently destroyed. **1891** J. FENTON *Bush Life Tas.* (1964) 26 The possessor of a location order could select Crown land where he pleased, without any risk of competition—but then he had to pay for it dearly.

4. In the phr. **the limits (boundaries, bounds) of location,** the frontier of settlement; *spec.* boundaries delimiting those parts of an Australian Colony within which land is available for alienation. See also BORDER 1 and BOUNDARY *n.*

1837 *Rep. Select Committee Transportation* 23 May (1838) 190 They take their sheep establishments not beyond the limits of the colony, but beyond the limits of location. **1837** *Colonist* (Sydney) 25 May 169/4 The following gentlemen have been appointed Commissioners of Crown Lands in the . . districts . . beyond the boundaries of location. **1838** *HRA* (1923) 1st Ser. XIX. 508 Various outrages . . had taken place in the remote districts of this Colony beyond what are the boundaries of Location. **1839** *Kerr's Melbourne Almanac* (1841) 24 Such land, whenever it may be deemed expedient to extend the boundaries of location, will be liable to be put up to competition at public auction. **1840** A. RUSSELL *Tour through Austral. Colonies* 246 The greater number of settlers go beyond the limits of location. **1840** *Port Phillip Gaz.* 25 Jan. 4 The Brickmakers . . are always close upon the town, and cannot therefore be said to live beyond the bounds of location, a position which can alone demand the protection of a Border Police. **1844** *Dispatch* (Sydney) 6 Apr. 3/3 *The squatters. . .* A meeting of the gentlemen interested in the depasturing of sheep and cattle, beyond the limits of location, will be held on Tuesday next, at the Royal Hotel. **1845** D. MACKENZIE *Emigrant's Guide* 49 There are several people living in a state of concubinage beyond the boundaries of location. **1848** J.C. BYRNE *Twelve Yrs.' Wanderings* I. 279 It is a question if the Aborigines within the bounds of location in New South Wales number . . five hundred persons. **1849** C. STURT *Narr. Exped. Central Aust.* II. 212 They would have attacked the station next the river . . and with their stealthy habits and daring, would have been no mean enemy on the boundaries of location. *Ibid.* 244 South Australia . . contains about 300,000 square miles. . . The limits of location, however, do not exceed 4,000 miles. **1862** E. STRICKLAND *Austral. Pastor* 65 Albury is situated far beyond what are called 'the bounds of location' in the squatting district of the Murrumbidgee; consequently it is not a colonial chaplaincy, and receives no aid from government. **1962** E. IRVIN *Early Inland Agric.* 11 Occupation of the southern districts, 'beyond the boundaries of location', dates from the 1830s. **1972** W.K. HANCOCK *Discovering Monaro* 41 The understaffed Department of the Surveyor-General was quite unable during the 1830s to keep pace with the rapid territorial expansion of the pastoral industry. Crown land that could not be surveyed could not be alienated by any legal process. Hence the much used phrase, 'the limits of location'. **1980** P. FREEMAN *Woolshed* 48 The 'Limits of Location', that had contained the young colony of New South Wales until the 1830s were finally breached by the early explorers and the 1836 Squatting Act which allowed squatting beyond the Limits, providing a license fee of £10 per annum was made for each 'run'.

locator. *Obs.* Also **locater.** One who takes up an allocation of land.

1829 H. WIDOWSON *Present State Van Diemen's Land* 46 February 26, 1827—Orders all locaters of town grants to build their houses in such a way as to leave 60 feet for carriage and foot roads. **1847** *HRA* (1925) 1st Ser. XXV. 563 The Establishments of the licensed Locators of the Crown Lands.

lock, *v.* [Spec. use of *lock* to shut off from: see OED *v.*[1] 4, esp. quot. 1785.] *trans.* With **up**: to shut (land) off from small settlers; to prevent the release of (land). Also as *vbl. n.* See also UNLOCK.

1855 P. SAUNDERS *Two Yrs. Vic.* (1863) 6 The immediate effect of this locking up the land was the enormous prices paid. **1866** 'J.W.T.' *Land Question in Qld.* 13 To lock up our lands in the settled districts for fourteen years would be a disgrace to the science of colonisation. **1889** A.B. PATERSON *Aust. for Australs.* 20 As to the locking-up of land; it is astonishing how far this locking-up system prevails. Nearly every country town in New South Wales is cursed by the proximity of some large estate, which can neither be bought nor leased. **1898** 'OLD COLONIST' *How Constitutional Govt. was Won* 31 Land along the railways, although resumed by the Government 14 years ago, is still locked up, and . . there is no room for the *bona fide* settler in this gigantic colony of Queensland—no room for any but the foreign syndicator, the absentee, the financial institution. **1902** *Bulletin* (Sydney) 31 May 31/2 There are millions of acres of Crown Lands in N.S.W. locked up for no apparent reason. **1947** F. CLUNE *Roaming around Aust.* 146 The best land is all 'locked up' in these big leaseholds. They have the river frontage and all the good land, so there's no chance for small-farming to develop.

locust. [Extended and transf. use of *locust* an insect of the fam. Acrididae.]

1. A winged insect of the fam. Acrididae or Tettigoniidae; applied esp. to those species able to form a destructive, migratory swarm, incl. the plague locust *Chortoicetes terminifera.*

1822 J. DIXON *Narr. Voyage N.S.W. & Van Dieman's Land* 67 A kind of grasshopper, or locust . . spread over the land, and ate up the herbage of the colony. **1834** J. BACKHOUSE *Narr. Visit Austral. Colonies* (1843) 230 The *Tettigoniae*, here called Locusts, of which there are several species, keep up a constant rattle, like that of a cotton-mill, both in the town and out of it. **1874** J.J. HALCOMBE *Emigrant & Heathen* 3 The shrill noise of the tettigonia or locust, whose continuous *whirr*, like that of a scissor-grinder's wheel. **1902** *Bulletin* (Sydney) 19 June 16/2 A chance drift of locusts came along and ate it before the sheep could get a bite. **1960** G. TAYLOR *Crop Dusters* 86 'What will I be doing?' 'Spraying locusts. . . There's a big invasion of them on the Murray at Red Bend.' **1969** *Victorian Yr. Bk.* LXXXIII. 6 The Australian plague locust (*Chortoicetes terminifera*) breeds in plague numbers in inland Australia under certain conditions.

2. A cicada.

1834 J. BACKHOUSE *Extracts from Lett.* (1838) II. 54 The cicadae (here called locusts), of which there are several species, keep up a constant rattle. **1844** MRS C. MEREDITH *Notes & Sketches N.S.W.* 115 Equally annoying with the dust was the loud, incessant, and indescribable noise of myriads of large and curious winged insects, commonly and incorrectly called locusts, but which are totally different from any kind of locusts I ever saw. **1874** *Illustr. Sydney News* 25 July 15/1 No insect is more familiarly known in and about Sydney during the summer months than the cicada or as it is erroneously called 'Locust'. **1905** *Bulletin* (Sydney) 28 Dec. (Red Page), There's heaps of different kinds of locusts . . greengrocers, and floury bakers, and yellow Mondays, and black fiddlers, and double drummers, and black-bottles—heaps! **1956** S. HOPE *Diggers' Paradise* 206 Juveniles rapturously hail a lush cicada season . . 'locusts', as they erroneously call them. **1982** N. KEESING *Lily on Dustbin* 94 It is high summer. Cicadas, popularly called 'locusts', which they are not . . drum insistently from garden trees.

3. *transf.* A tourist.

1972 A. CHIPPER *Aussie Swearers Guide* 41 *Locust*, a popular Australian term for a tourist pest.

log, *n.*[1]

1. Used *attrib.* in (orig. U.S.) Comb. **log fence, fencing, hut.**

1846 F. DUTTON *S.A. & its Mines* 203 There are the 'ditch and bank', 'American or **log-fence**' and the 'dog-leg fence'. **1852** S. MOSSMAN *Voice from Aust.* 10 A brushwood or log fence often serves for a hedge. **1879** 'RECENT SETTLER' *Emigration to Tas.* 85 When the land is first cleared, an ordinary log fence is usually constructed. **1882** ARMSTRONG & CAMPBELL *Austral. Sheep Husbandry* 195 Log Fence . . is a fence seldom used on stations except where clearing or grubbing is done, the logs only being dragged in and built closely together. **1911** *Bulletin* (Sydney) 16 Feb. 14/4 Frill lizards . . frequently are seen resting on a log fence. **1851** H. MELVILLE *Present State Aust.* 109 Yards are commenced; if for sheep, brush fence serves very well for a time,—but for cattle more substantial work, such as **log fencing**, is required. **1920** *Bulletin* (Sydney) 6 May 20/2 About the toughest of all bushwork, not excepting wattle-barking or log-fencing, is burning. **1923** *Ibid.* 18 Jan. 22/2 Jim rode the old fellow to his log-fencing job away in the mountains. **1825** T. KENT *Lett. to B. Field* 45 Another Englishman living in a **log hut** on his farm in Van Diemen's Land. **1837** *Perth Gaz.* 11 Feb. 849 Three public house licenses have been granted; one is kept in a log hut, the others are of turf. **1843** C. ROWCROFT *Tales of Colonies* (1858) 231 Their men were despatched to prepare the rude log-hut which usually forms the first habitation of the new settler. **1887** MRS D.D. DALY *Digging, Squatting, & Pioneering Life* 50 The sleeping apartments were in a large log hut divided by partitions. **1897** L. LINDLEY-COWEN *W. Austral. Settler's Guide* 296 Possibly a tent, a slab-and-dab or log hut, or a tin shanty will be the first home of the new settler.

2. In *pl.* with **the.** A gaol, orig. (see quots. 1796 and 1873) one constructed of logs.

[**1796** D. COLLINS *Acct. Eng. Colony N.S.W.* (1802) II. 2 A strong and capacious Log Prison at each of the towns of Sydney and Paramatta.] **1872** *Austral. Jrnl.* Jan. 327 To-morrow morning, Mac, we'll have all these fellows comfortably in the logs. **1873** *Austral. Town & Country Jrnl.* (Sydney) 2 Aug. 147/1 The aforesaid lockup, popularly known as 'the Logs', from the preponderating quantity of these massive timbers displayed in the floor, the wall, and indeed the ceiling of the edifice. **1885** *Once a Month* (Melbourne) Dec. 430 As many as sixty diggers, handcuffed together like convicts, have been marched to the camp and put in the 'logs'. **1900** *Pastoral Times* (Deniliquin) 6 Jan. 2/5, I knows him becos he shoved me in the logs more 'n once, and it allus dun me good. **1913** *Bulletin* (Sydney) 3 Apr. 15/3 A detective entered the hut, and emerged . . with a pair of odd boots, which . . completely fitted the . . tracks. The scowling man was lodged in the Mitta logs that night. **1928** N.F. SPIELVOGEL *Affair at Eureka* 15 Lalor drew himself up to his full height of 6 ft. 6 in. . . 'Remember your thirty-five friends lying in 'the logs' to-night.' **1948** F. CLUNE *Wild Colonial Boys* 292 They were suddenly seized and handcuffed—then lodged in 'the logs'—a lock-up built of hewn pine trunks.

3. Special Comb. **log-chop,** a wood-chopping competition.

1905 *Bulletin* (Sydney) 31 Aug. 36/1 'I bet on the log-chop,' the one bookmaker reminds the public. **1958** P. COWAN *Unploughed Land* 86 He's a faller. Won a few prizes for log-chops.

4. *fig.* A block-head. Also **log of wood.**

1959 S.J. BAKER *Drum* 124 *Log*, any person regarded contemptuously for his lack of ability, brains and energy. **1961** F. HARDY *Hard Way* 12 On the way to the lift, I remembered with a start that I had forgotten to empty my pockets. What a log of wood I am! **1966** G. BARRY *Bed & Bored* 40 'What do you think about letting everyone in?' Tony asked. 'I don't see why not,' I replied. 'If it gets too crowded we can chuck the logs out later.' **1968** J. ALARD *He who shoots Last* 53 Yer a nice bloody log of wood. **1971** F. HARDY *Outcasts of Foolgarah* 195 You forgot the milk, you bloody log.

log, *n.*[2] *Industrial Relations.* [Spec. use of *log* a record.]

1. A set of claims for an increase in wages, improvement in working conditions, etc., esp. as lodged by a trade union with an industrial tribunal. See also AMBIT. Also **log of claims.**

1911 *5 CAR* 181 The claims of the employees have been framed into a log of wages and conditions. **1912** *6 CAR* 144, I do not rely on the mere fact that the association's log, containing the association's definite requests, was twice sent . . to each of the respondents and rejected. **1914** *18 CLR* 289 That combined statement of altered conditions is usually termed a 'log', and has been so called in this case. **1929** *28 CAR* 321 The awards in question were made upon logs of demands made by the federation. **1937** O. DE R. FOENANDER

Towards Industr. Peace 24 In order to ascertain the upper and lower limits of a dispute, reference must be made to the 'logs' of the parties exchanged at the time of the original dispute. **1948** G. FARWELL *Down Argent Street* 102 When the unions submitted their log of claims for the 1925 Agreement, they asked for increased wages and yet shorter hours. **1958** J.H. PORTUS *Dev. Austral. Trade Union Law* 130 At any early stage the union practice developed of creating disputes by serving a log of claims on a list of employers and producing evidence that the claims sought were rejected. **1974** *Bulletin* (Sydney) 26 Jan. 9/1 The existing two-year award for waterside workers expires on May 5, and a new log submitted by the Waterside Workers' Federation . . is reported to ask for a 32-hour week. **1975** *Ibid.* 5 Apr. 57/3 Miners in a new log of claims are expected to move to have wage adjustments tied to movements in the consumer price index. **1983** D.J. BAILEY *Holes in Ground* 15 In 1920 Queensland miners endorsed a Federal claim. The log included: six hours, bank to bank; a five-day working week.

2. With qualifying element, as **Lygon Street log**: see quot. 1976.

1976 *10 ALR* 473 The log of claims for improved wages and conditions is in the standard form currently used by many trade unions and is described as a Lygon Street log (referring to the Trades Hall, Lygon Street, Melbourne). **1980** MCCALLUM & TRACEY *Cases & Materials Industr. Law* 174 An 'ambit' log of claims. . . This relatively simple form of log (known colloquially as a 'Lygon Street log').

log, *v.*

1. *Mining. intr.* With **up**: to construct a log frame to support a windlass. Also *trans.*

1871 *Austral. Town & Country Jrnl.* (Sydney) 8 Apr. 431/3 They have . . logged up and covered their shaft. **1888** *Tasmanian* (Hobart) 1 Sept. 21/2 Have logged up shaft and made paddock for quartz. **1916** A.I. MACLEOD *Hack's Brat* (1920) 3 The prospectors . . had already started logging up. The little dump-heads, as yet no higher than a few feet, seemed like ant-hills. **1932** I.L. IDRIESS *Prospecting for Gold* 232 Log up and put the windlass on at eight or nine feet.

2. *intr.* Of an animal: to take refuge inside a hollow log.

1920 *Bulletin* (Sydney) 8 Jan. 20/2 Big Murray cod when closely pursued scoot into hollow logs. . . The 'yellow belly' (golden perch), like the hare, 'logs' only in the last extremity. **1943** *Ibid.* 27 Oct. 12/3 When I was a nipper I hunted kangaroo-rats and bandicoots with a cattle-dog and I never knew one to escape him except by 'logging'.

Hence **logged-up** *ppl. a.*

1905 *Horlick's Mag.* (London) Feb. 108/1 Reaching a logged-up hole on the flat, I returned for a moment to hide behind it and reconnoitre.

Logie /'loʊgi/. [f. the name of John *Logie* Baird (1888–1946), British inventor of television.] One of the statuettes awarded annually since 1958 by the magazine *TV Week* for excellence in acting, etc., in a television production. Also **Logie award,** and *attrib.*

1963 *TV Week* (Melbourne) 5 Jan. 3 *Logie votes* are flowing in to the *TV Week* office in their thousands this month. **1968** *Austral.* (Sydney) 30 Mar. 11/4 One of the rites involved in this apotheosis of the mediocre is the annual presentation of the Logies, those squat statuettes named after John Logie Baird. **1971** *Bulletin* (Sydney) 3 Apr. 17/2 Maggie Tabberer, who won a gold Logie for the best national female star on television . . hasn't appeared regularly on TV since her show was dropped. **1981** P. BEILBY *Austral. TV* 13 The first Logie Awards were given only to Melbourne programmes. **1985** *Sydney Morning Herald* 27 Apr. 3/8 *A Country Practice* dominated the 27th annual Logie Awards in Melbourne last night.

log-runner.

1. Either of two ground-dwelling, rainforest birds of the genus *Orthonyx*, the dark-plumaged *O. spaldingii* of the Atherton region in Qld., and the *spine-tailed log-runner*; CHOWCHILLA.

1898 E.E. MORRIS *Austral Eng.* 272 *Log-runner* . . an Australian bird, called also a *spinetail.* **1954** C. BARRETT *Wild Life Aust. & New Guinea* 145 Log-runners, or 'chowillas' [*sic*] as they are called by naturalists, are birds of the rain-forest floor. **1967** V.G.C. NORWOOD *Long Haul* 73, I . . detoured through the brush, disturbing a pair of log-runners.

2. With distinguishing epithet: **spine-tailed log-runner,** the mottled brown bird *Orthonyx temminckii* of e. coastal Qld. and N.S.W., having tail feathers in which the central shaft projects in a spine-like tip.

[**1848** J. GOULD *Birds of Aust.* IV. Pl. 99, The Spine-tailed Orthonyx is very local in its habitat, being entirely confined, so far as I have been enabled to ascertain, to the brushes which skirt the southern and eastern coasts of Australia.] **1909** *Emu* VIII. 242 The southern species, known as the Spine-tailed Log-runner (*O. spinicauda*). As their name implies, their habit is running more than flying. **1929** A.H. CHISHOLM *Birds & Green Places* 20 If the spine-tailed logrunner is neither a mocker nor a dancer, his voice is just as ringing. **1945** C. BARRETT *Austral. Bird Life* 135 Jules Verreaux nearly a century ago published field notes on the southern spine-tailed log-runner.

Lola Montez /loʊlə 'mɒntɛz/. [The name of *Lola Montez* (1818–1861), an Irish dancer and courtesan, who toured Australia in 1855.] A drink with a rum base: see quot. 1859.

1859 F. FOWLER *Southern Lights & Shadows* 52 The following are a few of the names of favourite beverages:- . . A Lola Montez . . Old Tom, ginger, lemon, and hot water. **1981** *Bulletin* (Sydney) 1 Aug. (Red Page), If you murmured 'a Lola Montez', the barman of the fifties handed you over a concoction of Old Tom, ginger, lemon and hot water.

lolly. [Br. dial. *lolly* a sweetmeat, abbrev. of *lollipop.*]

1. A sweet of any kind, esp. boiled. Also *attrib.*

1854 C.H. SPENCE *Clara Morison* II. 102 Fanny ran away to the nearest lolly shop, and all her brothers and sisters followed her. **1859** 'O. KEESE' *Broad Arrow* I. 324 She wouldn't give me any more lollies. **1872** G.S. BADEN-POWELL *New Homes for Old Country* 157 The squatter keeps up a supply of . . 'lollies', dress pieces, shirts, coats, boots. **1883** *Bulletin* (Sydney) 21 Apr. 1/3 The article meant that plaintiff was a looter of children's lollies. **1892** *Ibid.* 20 Feb. 21/1 The babe was not contented, Though his pinafore was scented With oranges, and sticky from his lollies. **1903** *Truth* (Sydney) 4 Jan. 7/4, I gave her 3d. to buy lollies, and told her that if she was in the park tomorrow I'd meet her. **1917** M.A. ALLAN *Casket of Memories* 45 Uncle one evening enquired if they always used the word 'lolly' when they spoke of sweetmeats. **1924** F.J. MILLS *Happy Days* 111 Three helpings of Christmas cake (including two lolly swans and a lolly man). **1933** F.E. BAUME *Tragedy Track* 135 They sucked boiled lollies. **1948** E.H. COLLIS *Lost Yrs.* 31 Reid . . who habitually sucked lollies, was called a clown by his opponents. **1964** P. ADAM SMITH *Hear Train Blow* 62 We bought two navel oranges and a bag of lollies. **1972** *Bulletin* (Sydney) 19 Aug. 51/2 Dad, I wanna lolly. **1981** D. STUART *I think I'll Live* 53 It's as well planned as a Sunday School picnic, all we need is the boiled lollies. **1986** *Canberra Times* 24 Feb. (Suppl.) 2/1 It is one of those programs which is bad for the brain in the same way that lollies are bad for the teeth.

2. Comb. **lolly paper, shop, tin.**

1968 D. IRELAND *Chantic Bird* 13 Plenty of litter with milk cartoons, soft drink cans, **lolly papers,** sandwich crusts. **1972** *Southerly* i. 4 A small whirly-whirly swept down the verandah, lifting dust and lolly papers in a mini-spiral. **1854 lolly shop** [see sense 1]. **1883** J.E. PARTINGTON *Random Rot* 95, I noticed one enterprising man had over his shop, 'The largest lollie shop on earth'. **1899** *Austral. Tit-Bits* (Sydney) 1 July 338/2 'Come out of there and I'll lick . . you,' said the Sydney urchin to some sticks of peppermint in a lolly shop in King Street, Sydney. **1930** *Bulletin* (Sydney) 3 Dec. 2/2, I fell in love with an elderly married lady who kept a lolly-shop. **1949** J. MORRISON *Creeping City* 41 Joe's saying if you don't shut your mouth about his missus and the lolly-shop, Bob, he'll shut it for you. **1974** BUCKLEY & HAMILTON *Festival* 90 Past Mrs Rattles' lolly shop, with quilted Easter eggs in golden foil, and fat doughnuts with red jam eyes. **1901** F. GILLEN *Diary* 3 Aug. (1968) 193 Two Warramunga kiddies . . frequently raid our **lolly tin.** **1908** *Bulletin* (Sydney) 24 Dec. 39/2 There are dozens of bush post offices along the road. These are simply candle boxes, lolly tins, or kerosene tins, nailed to trees and gate posts.

3. Special Comb. **lolly boy,** one who sells refreshments from a tray at a cinema, sports ground, etc.; also *fig.*; **money,** cash given to a child to buy sweets; **-pink** *a.*, shocking pink; **stick,** a boiled sweet on a stick or shaped like a stick; **water,** a soft drink.

1950 F. HARDY *Power without Glory* 460 Above the mumble of five thousand voices could be heard the calls of the drink and **lolly boys** with their trays. **1971** G. JOHNSTON *Cartload of Clay* 45 The lights came on for the interval and the lolly boys were shuffling raucous with their trays. **1980** *Sydney Morning Herald* 4 Nov. 2/8 The former Finance Minister, Mr Eric Robinson . . was prepared to speak his mind and . . was not one of the Prime Minister's lolly boys. **1983** H.M. MILLER *My Story* 10, I soon got a job as a lolly boy during Saturday afternoon football matches. A man named Streeter had the refreshment franchise and he paid young boys a commission of sixpence in the pound to sell lollies, soft drinks and ice cream. **1917** *Truth* (Sydney) 12 Aug. 7/8 The tramways have taken **lolly-money** from the kiddies. **1964** A. STAPLES *Paddo* 71 'They put in their lolly money,' Mac said, 'for me.' **1958** M. WARREN *No Glamour in Gumboots* 214 Joe came, and the post-girl, who produced, as a parting gift, a particularly repulsive boutonnière of **lolly pink** duck feather flowers. **1974** *Meanjin* 21 Her paintings: *Italian Girl Skipping* in the lolly-pink and aqua kitchen. **1980** ANSELL & PERCY *To fight Wild* 18 Now the sun was getting right down, a big, lolly-pink ball turning the brown water into mauve and pink and a kind of gun-metal green. **1911** 'S. RUDD' *Bk. of Dan* 26 'Look,' Dan said, extending his big toe to the infant as though offering it a **lollie stick.** **1925** E. MCDONNELL *My Homeland* 74 'Bull's-eyes' and red and white lollysticks. **1905** J. MEREDITH *Learn to talk Old Jack Lang* (1984) 14, I can . . have a lemonade . . and no one ever laughs at me or calls me sissy because I am drinking **lolly water.** **1943** *Troppo Tribune* (Mataranka) 19 Apr. 2 'Lolly water' is not supplied in sufficient quantity. **1953** J.K. EWERS *With Sun on my Back* 20 Savage green ants! Harney showed me how to hold them by the head, as the blacks did, and suck the pleasantly sharp acid out of the abdomen. They used it to make 'lolly water', he said. **1963** D. NILAND *Dadda Jumped* 185 We bought the girls lollywater. . . We had a couple of hot beers at the booth. **1981** G. MACKENZIE *Aurukun Diary* 161 Her mother could not be persuaded that a packet of biscuits and a bottle of 'lolly-water' (soft drink) was not an adequate dinner for her.

4. *transf.* and *fig.* The head; esp. in the phr. **to do one's (or the) lolly,** to lose one's temper; to lose one's head; to 'do one's nut'.

1951 *New Settler in W.A.* (Perth) Feb. 77 That joint has a clothes line in the front yard so go slow or get your lolly lopped off. **1956** *Truth* (Sydney) 15 Jan. 21/2 Punters were inclined to do their 'lolly' at Alan Burton. **1965** F. HARDY *Yarns of Billy Borker* 77 'She cursed and swore at the moon. And the moon did the lolly'—I slipped into the Australian language again there for a minute. **1978** L. HORSPHOL *Turn down Empty Glass* 82 I'm sorry I did my lolly. **1983** *Weekend Austral. Mag.* (Sydney) 26 Mar. 16/3 In Britain they had seen Richard Carleton's *Nationwide* interview with Hawke in which Hawke did his lolly.

London fog. A nickname for a person who loafs on the job: see quots.

1967 *Kings Cross Whisper* (Sydney) xxxvi. 4/1 *London fog*, any person who will not lift. **1979** S. MORAN *Reminisc. of Rebel* 59 On the Sydney waterfront nearly everyone had a nick-name. The odd worker who didn't pull his weight was always a butt. . . The London Fog (never lifts). **1981** *Nat. Times* (Sydney) 25 Jan. 24/2 A lazy wharfie would be known as 'the Judge' because he was always sitting on a case, and another 'the London Fog' because he would never lift.

long, *a.*

1. Used in special collocations to indicate greater than usual length: **long blow** *shearing*, a stroke of the shears which extends from the tail to the neck; **paddock,** a *stock route* (see STOCK 2); a public road the sides of which are used for grazing; **-sentence(d) man** *obs.*, a convict serving a long sentence; **-sleever,** a tall beer glass; the drink so contained; **'un,** a long beer.

1904 *Shearer* (Sydney) 10 Dec. 4/4 In a shed can be seen all the latest styles—**long blow,** three-quarter blow, and the blow which is a mixture of both. **1910** *Bulletin* (Sydney) 8 Sept. 13/2 A chap . . invited me to watch him and some mates 'go through' a shed of

Angoras. . . All went well until the 'long blow' from shoulder to hindquarters was reached. **1926** *Ibid.* 25 Mar. 22/3 The 'long blow', that is, when the sheep is on its right side and the shearer sweeps the shears up the back from the tail to the neck, is the favorite position. **1943** C. SHAW *Outback Occupations* 29 'This is the long blow, Tom,' you say as the machine lays aside the creaming fleece in fold after fold along the back. **1955** E. BARNES *Easier Shearing* 33 To shear the wool from the first side of the sheep easily and quickly while doing the 'long blow' requires the skill of an artist. **1979** HARMSWORTH & DAY *Wool & Mohair* 154 The last blow starts from the tail and finishes up near the top of the head. This is known as the *long blow* and should be sufficiently over the backbone so as to avoid breaking the fleece when shearing the last side. **1929** *Bulletin* (Sydney) 16 Oct. 25/2 The '**long paddock**' is not the only place in which sheep-owners have had . . cheap feed. **1962** T. RONAN *Deep of Sky* 15 In some places 'the long paddock', i.e. the public road—two chains wide, I think—was not always securely fenced off from the adjacent holdings. **1975** *Bulletin* (Sydney) 24 May 66/2 Drovers came back because there was no agistment left on private properties and the long paddock was the only alternative. **1977** T.L. MCKNIGHT *Long Paddock* 29 The stock may spend many weeks or even months 'hunting for grass' on the 'long paddock'. **1985** *Sydney Morning Herald* 21 June 1/3 Taking sheep into 'the long paddock' is becoming more prevalent as the drought continues. **1840** *Tasmanian Weekly Dispatch* 5 June 4/2 This '**long sentenced man**' . . had . . the power of mustering. **1875** J. FORREST *Explorations in Aust.* 334 The residue of convicts are, many of them, men of the doubly reconvicted class and long-sentence men. **1877** *Pilgrim* (Sydney) Ser. I. viii. (Suppl. no. 2) 18, I should blow the froth from off the festive '**long sleever**'. **1879** *Truth* (Sydney) 31 Dec. 6/3 A decided weakness for 'long-sleevers'. **1896** W. BANNOW *Colony of Vic.* 19 A threepenny glass of beer—'a long sleever', of course. **1902** *Bulletin* (Sydney) 1 Mar. 16/3 A black-tracker . . used to boast that, although he was only as high as 12 'long-sleevers', he could drink 13 inside the hour. *Ibid.* 18 Oct. 14/4 'Long-sleever' comes from the resemblance between a pint-pot and a 'long-sleeved hat'. **1916** *Truth* (Sydney) 19 Mar. 12/4 They adjourned to Dind's Hotel, where Kinder had his usual 'long-sleever'. **1931** LAWSON & BRERETON *H. Lawson* 126 One could procure 'long sleevers' of colonial beer for threepence. **1952** C.J. DENNIS *Random Verse* 13 The scene shifts to Australia, 'where a man can raise a thirst'. (See Kipling) From 'long-sleevers' now they drained the stuff acurst. **1975** X. HERBERT *Poor Fellow my Country* 1144 The priest got out the whisky bottle. Sims had a long-sleever. **1895** *Bulletin* (Sydney) 5 Jan. 3/2 He can't fight; he always gets beaten; he has no science, no constitution, and won't train as long as '**long 'uns**' are plentiful. **1903** *Truth* (Sydney) 1 Nov. 1/5 With beer at 2d. a long 'un almost any man can afford to run for Parliament in Sydney now. **1916** *Kangaroosilite: On Board 'Wandilla'* Jan. 4 'A long 'un' in Melbourne is now called a 'Billy Khaki'. **1934** J.C. LEE *Boshstralians* 31 'Come on, Mag, another long 'un all round,' chirped up Tommy Little impatiently. 'We're dry as dust.'

2. As a distinguishing epithet in the names of flora and fauna: **long-billed corella** (or **cockatoo**), the predom. white bird *Cacatua tenuirostris* of s.e. Aust., having orange-red markings on the head and throat, and a long, curved upper bill; see also CORELLA 1 a.; **-leaved acacia** (or **wattle**) *obs.*, *Acacia longifolia*, see *sally wattle* SALLY 2; **-necked tortoise,** the tortoise of s.e. and e. mainland Aust. *Chelodina longicollis*, occurring in various fresh-water habitats, esp. swamps; also **long-neck(ed) turtle; -spined flathead,** the marine fish *Platycephalus longispinis* of s.e. and w. Aust.; see also SPIKEY; **yam,** the twining plant *Dioscorea transversa* (fam. Dioscoreaceae) of n. Aust.; the long, edible tuber of the plant.

[**1822 long-billed corella:** J. LATHAM *Gen. Hist. Birds* II. 205 *Long-nosed cockatoo.* Psittacus nasicus. . . The general colour of the plumage is pure white, but the whole face or front of the head is rose-colour.] **1847** J. GOULD *Birds of Aust.* (1848) V. Pl. 5, *Licmetis nasicus.* Long-billed Cockatoo. **1891** H. NISBET *Colonial Tramp* I. 121 A *kuurokutch*, or long-billed cockatoo. **1912** *Emu* XII. 117 Long-billed cockatoo . . very rare. **1934** H.G. LAMOND *Aviary on Plains* 57 Those birds with clumsy bills—remember their proper name is 'Long-billed Cockatoo'—pick up those infinitesimally small seeds out of the dust. **1945** C. BARRETT *Austral. Bird Life* 72 The long-billed corella . . is a favourite, ranking first as a talking bird. **1961** M. KIDDLE *Men of Yesterday* 9 The first father of the Western District tribes, so his descendants believed, belonged to the totem of the long-billed cockatoos. **1984** *Sydney Morning Herald* 22 Sept. 12/5 Some farmers in western Victoria resorted to poisoning long-billed corellas which were digging up the seed in recently sown cereal crops. **1820** J. OXLEY *Jrnls. Two Exped. N.S.W.* 103 There were only four different kinds of plants at this terminating point of our journey, viz. the small eucalyptus, the **long-leaved acacia** [etc.]. **1835** *Hobart Town Almanack* 63 *Acacia longifolia?* Long leaved Acacia. A large shrub, with fragrant cylindrical spikes of blossoms. **1856** *Jrnl. Australasia* I. 37 You may now plant . . acacia longifolia, long-leaved wattle. **1794** G. SHAW *Zool. New Holland* 19 Testudo Longicollis. The **long-necked tortoise** . . is a species never before figured or described. . . The neck extremely long, and (as it should seem) always exserted. **1802** —— *Gen. Zool.* III. i. 62 *Long-necked tortoise.* . . Smooth ovate Tortoise, with extremely long neck. . . This species is a native of Australasia or New Holland, and is of the river or fresh-water kind. **1886** F. COWAN *Aust.* 19 The Long-necked Turtle of the inland creeks: reptilian crane. **1943** C. BARRETT *Austral. Animal Bk.* 316 The long-necked tortoise . . grows to a length (the carapace or shell) of up to about 14 inches, while the extension of the flat head and the neck in front of the shell is about 10 inches. **1960** B. HARNEY *Cook Bk.* 65 Freshwater turtles (known as 'Long Neck' turtles) are caught in the swamps where they lie during the dry months of the year. **1906** D.G. STEAD *Fishes of Aust.* 198 The **Long-spined Flathead** is a small, large-bellied species, occurring on the coast of New South Wales. It is not uncommon on sandy patches in deep water off a number of the beaches in the vicinity of Sydney. **1969** J. POLLARD *Austral. & N.Z. Fishing* 203 Long-spined Flathead. . . Another small variety which does not grow much beyond 12 inches in length but yields splendid fillets. **1983** HUTCHINS & THOMPSON *Marine & Estuarine Fishes S.-W. Aust.* 28 Long-spined Flathead. . . Best identified by the characteristic long spine on side of head and colour of caudal fin. **1878** R.B. SMYTH *Aborigines of Vic.* I. 229 *Dioscorea punctata* . . **long yam.** **1965** *Austral. Encycl.* IX. 524 The small, tubers of *D*[*ioscorea*] *transversa* (long yam) are eaten without preparation by aborigines. **1981** D. LEVITT *Plants & People* 41 Long Yam grows in jungles. . . The long, thin root . . can be eaten raw but was usually cooked in hot sand and ashes.

longa, *prep. Austral. pidgin.* Belonging to; near; about; with.

1879 'AUSTRALIAN' *Adventures Qld.* 21 Then mine ask him look out sugar-bag long a me—mine kill him behind *cobra.* **1951** E. HILL *Territory* 108 'Debil-debil piccaninny walkabout longa sit-down,' he informed the astonished tribe. **1955** F. LANE *Patrol to Kimberleys* 215 *Longa*, aborigine pidgin for 'at' or 'with'. Instead of saying the boss is down at the billabong, an aborigine will say: 'Boss longa billabong.' **1968** S. GORE *Holy Smoke* 104 *Longa*, to do with; pertaining to. (Pidgin.)

long service leave. A period of paid leave granted to an employee who has served a specified period of continuous employment: see e.g. quots. 1918 and 1927. Also *attrib.*

1900 *Act* (W.A.) 64 Vict. no. 21 Sect. 29, Public servants shall be entitled to long service leave. **1918** *Act* (Tas.) 9 Geo. no. 69 Sect. 90 (1), Every officer under the age of Sixty-five years, or of or over Twenty years' continuous service in the Public Service shall, for the *bonâ fide* purpose of furlough only, be entitled to . . long-service leave of absence for Six months on full pay, or, at the option of the officer, Twelve months on half-pay. **1927** *N.S.W. Industr. Gaz.* 30 June 1202 Long Service Leave. Four weeks' leave of absence on full pay shall be granted to each employee on the completion of twenty years' service with the Company. **1938** *AR* (N.S.W.) 282 The claim for long service leave is an industrial matter. **1959** O. DE R. FOENANDER *Industr. Conciliation & Arbitration Aust.* 80 In all of the States . . legislation has been enacted to provide for long service leave with pay. **1972** *Advertiser* (Adelaide) 15 Dec. 17/5 The SA Government's long-service leave legislation will come into force on January 1. **1984** *Austral. Financial Rev.* (Sydney) 16 May 1/1, 60 of Australia's largest companies have among them, provisions for annual leave and long service leave payments totalling $1.5 billion. **1986** *Good Weekend* (Sydney) 19 Apr. 12/1 Diabetes and deregistration have left him tired and lonely and dreaming of long-service leave.

long tom.

1. *Gold-mining.* [U.S.: see OED(S 2.] A trough used for washing auriferous material: see quot. 1865. Also **long-tom sluice.**

1852 *Empire* (Sydney) 23 Jan. 602/4 Long-toms are coming into use on the river—they do more work than an ordinary cradle. **1857** W. HOWITT *Tallangetta* I. 272 They turned the water of the dam into the Long Tom, or washing trough, and began washing in good earnest. **1865** J.F. MORTLOCK *Experiences of Convict* 149 They had first dammed the river, a mere brook; they then constructed a 'long Tom' sluice; merely a wooden trough some ten feet in length having at its lower end a compartment lined with tin, perforated in many places, so as to permit the mud and water freely to escape, but to retain in a shallow tray underneath the minutest particles of weightier ore. **1888** *Centennial Mag.* (Sydney) 67 He was working away with a 'long Tom' with his trousers as yellow as a guinea. **1915** 'ALPHA' *Reminisc. Goldfields* i. 30 All along its course from Silver Creek down to the Falls, numberless tubs, cradles, 'Long Toms', sluice boxes and diggers' picks, shovels and other mining utensils were visible. **1965** G.H. FEARNSIDE *Golden Ram* 87 Andy knew about the sluice boxes, or 'long-toms', as many prospectors called them. **1979** J. BIRMINGHAM et al. *Austral. Pioneer Technol.* 37 Such gold was easily separated by . . box-sluicing in a Long Tom.

2. ALLIGATOR PIKE.

1881 *Proc. Linnean Soc. N.S.W.* VI. 241 *Belone ferox* . . '*Long Tom*' of the Fishermen . . Port Jackson. **1908** E.J. BANFIELD *Confessions of Beachcomber* 154 The 'long tom' . . or alligator-pike, which shoots from the water and skips along. **1936** T.C. ROUGHLEY *Wonders Great Barrier Reef* 5 A long, narrow fish came up behind, slowly at first, then with a rush—a needle-toothed garfish [*Note*] Usually called 'long-tom' in Australia. **1963** F. FLYNN *Northern Gateway* 103 Little six-inch fish, which the islanders call Long Toms, skitter along the surface in a series of mad leaps, staying on top of the water for ten to fifteen yards before flopping back below. **1983** HUTCHINS & THOMPSON *Marine & Estuarine Fishes S.-W. Aust.* 22 Like most longtoms it can 'run' across the sea's surface using the tail for propulsion.

Hence **long-tomming** *vbl. n.*, the act of using a long tom.

1856 G. WILLMER *Draper in Aust.* 78, I resolved to try the experiment of 'long-tomming'; and accordingly, without delay, I procured one of the long troughs known in digging parlance as a 'tom'.

lookout. [Transf. use of *lookout* view, prospect, infl. by *lookout* place for keeping watch: see OED(S.] An elevated place from which a particular scenic attraction can be viewed.

1930 M.B. PETERSEN *Monsoon Music* 51 After driving some miles, the party reached the turning to the well-known 'Jimmie's Look Out'. **1960** *N.T. News* (Darwin) 22 Jan. 5/5 Mr Nordsvan said he hoped the mount itself would be developed later as a tourist lookout. **1981** *Meanjin* 153 'This is called Mitchell Lookout,' he said, 'but as you see it is not a Lookout in the Rotary sense.' It was just a shelf of rock.

loom, var. LOAM *v.*

loomer, var. LOAMER.

loppy. [Prob. f. Br. (dial.) *lop* to hang about, to idle: see EDD *v.*[2] and OED *v.*[2] 2; but see also OEDS *loppy, sb.*, which suggests a derivation f. *loppy, a.* flea-ridden.] A rouseabout.

1897 *Worker* (Sydney) 11 Sept. 1/1 The 'rouseabout' . . he sneeringly terms 'loppy' and a 'leatherneck'. **1911** ST. C. GRONDONA *Collar & Cuffs* 85 Five points of rain means a sad shearer and a joyful loppy. **1926** *Smith's Weekly* (Sydney) 24 July 16/3 At Bolgelly . . last shearing season . . male cooks being unobtainable, we voted a woman in. Her presence made a big difference to the general routine, every boggi-rusher and loppie washing and brushing up before meals. **1954** *Bulletin* (Sydney) 24 Feb. 13/2 That opprobious epithet 'loppy' . . all good shed-hands, eating their epicurean four-course meals and lolling between their laundered-linen sheets, sincerely hoped had been forgotten. **1981** K. GARVEY *Rhymes of Ratbag* 76 The loppies all complain a lot Because it didn't rain a spot.

loranthus /lə'rænθəs/. *Obs.* [The plant genus *Loranthus* was named by French botanist N.J. Jacquin (*Enum. Stirp. Vindob.* (1762) 55,230): all Austral. plants once included in this genus are now classified in different genera.] Any of several mistletoes.

1827 A. CUNNINGHAM *Gen. Remarks Vegetation* 18 The genus Loranthus . . is . . sparingly scattered on all the Coasts of Australia, where about eleven species have been recently observed, parasitical upon certain trees. **1834** *Perth Gaz.* 10 May 283 Fine loranthus . . grows parasitically on the wattle trees at the head of the Swan. **1844** L. LEICHHARDT *Jrnl. Overland Exped. Aust.* 3 Oct. (1847) 6 The Loranthus and Myal in immense bushes.

Lord Howe Island woodhen. [f. the name of *Lord Howe Island*, n.e. of Sydney, N.S.W.] The small brown bird *Tricholimnas sylvestris* of Lord Howe Island.

[**1889** *Lord Howe Island* 13 Soon to become extinct on Lord Howe, unless protected, is the Wood-Hen, *Ocydromus sylvestris* . . a curious and stupid bird.] **1977** *Ecos* xi. 18 Lord Howe Island lies about 600 km. off the coast of northern New South Wales. . . It provides refuge for one of the world's rarest birds—the Lord Howe Island woodhen. The entire breeding population of this flightless fowl numbers about 25. **1985** *Parks & Wildlife News* Winter 20 Apart from being small and having a less than spectacular plumage that can only be described as dag brown, its other notable non-attribute is that it can't fly. . . A Lord Howe Island Woodhen.

lorikeet. Any of several small, and usu. predom. green, nectar-feeding parrots most common in n. and e. Aust.; *honey parrot*, see HONEY. Also with distinguishing epithet, as **little, musk, purple-crowned, rainbow, red-collared, scaly-breasted, varied** (see under first element).

1770 J. BANKS *Jrnl.* 1 May (1896) 267 The trees overhead abounded very much with loryquets and cockatoos. **1796** 'SOCIETY OF GENTLEMEN' *New & Correct Hist. New Holland* 38 The country abounds with birds of various kinds, amongst which are many of exquisite beauty, particularly loriquets and cockatoos. **1842** J. GOULD *Birds of Aust.* (1848) V. Pl. 51, The northern coast is the only part of Australia in which this elegant little Lorikeet [*sc. Trichoglossus versicolor*] has yet been discovered. **1877** C.W. GEDNEY *Foreign Cage Birds* 102 *The Blue Mountain Lory*. . . By some writers this bird is called 'Swainson's Lorikeet'. **1890** *Argus* (Melbourne) 7 June 13/4 On the hill-sides the . . lorikeets . . drain the honey-cups and swing and chatter in low undertones. **1934** T. WOOD *Cobbers* 226 We found . . herons and lorikeets. **1952** B. BEATTY *Unique to Aust.* 52 The Lorikeets are small honey-eating birds extracting nectar from flowers or pulp from juicy fruit by means of a brush-like tongue. **1979** C. KLEIN *Women of Certain Age* 43 She saw her mother holding a tray of bread and honey for the lorikeets.

lotus bird. The wading bird *Irediparra gallinacea novaehollandiae* of e. and n. Aust. and southernmost New Guinea, having exceptionally long toes which enable it to walk on aquatic plants; JACANA; LILY-TROTTER.

1870 E.B. KENNEDY *Four Yrs. in Qld.* 114 The lotus bird . . runs along the leaves of the water-lily. **1889** R.B. ANDERSON tr. Lumholtz's *Among Cannibals* 22 The most striking bird on the lagoon is doubtless the beautiful *Parra gallinacea*, which in Australia is called the lotus-bird. **1934** *Bulletin* (Sydney) 7 Feb. 21/3 Sydney naturalists have been agreeably fluttered by the discovery of lotus birds breeding within 30 miles of the Bridge. **1967** *Darwin, Way of Life* (N.T. Admin.) 12 The strange . . lotus bird . . has feet almost as large as its body to enable it to walk over the water-lily pads. **1982** R. ELLIS *Bush Safari* 55 Quite close to camp Jacanas or Lotus-birds ran across waterlilies on their long spider-like feet.

loubra, var. LUBRA.

lounge room. [In Br. use usu. *lounge*.] The sitting-room of a private house.

1917 *Huon Times* (Franklin) 26 Oct. 5/2 A lounge room presents a very cosy and attractive appearance. **1934** S. HOWARD *Forty-Six* 205 He banged on the receiver, then stood for a few seconds before returning to the lounge room. **1944** *Aust.: Nat. Jrnl.* Apr. 48 His mother called him into the good lounge room. **1958** D.S. LESLIE *Green Singers* 35 The drawing-room. . . What they call out here a lounge-room! **1965** P. TODHUNTER *Aust. under Scalpel* 85 All the women wore gloves, and stayed in the 'lounge-room'. **1979** P. ADAMS *More Unspeakable Adams* 92 Paul . . lumbered out to the loungeroom where he switched on the telly.

louse, *v.* [Fig. use of *louse* to search for lice.]

a. *Mining. trans.* To pick over (waste material) looking for pieces of the mineral sought; esp. in the phr. **to louse the dump.** See also NOODLE. Freq. as *vbl. n.*

1934 *Geol. Survey: Mineral Resources 36* (N.S.W. Dept. Mines) 117 Small parcels have been obtained by the method known locally as 'lousing', which is simply picking the material over. **1937** R.H. CROLL *Wide Horizons* 28 Sometimes a man would haul for another for the privilege of 'lousing the dump', an inelegant but extremely expressive way of saying that he is allowed to take away any of the opal which has been unintentionally thrown out with the 'potch' and worthless earth. **1946** K.S. PRICHARD *Roaring Nineties* 97 Meanwhile he did a bit of lousing on the dumps: picked up a nice little nugget now and then. **1950** *Coast to Coast 1949–50* 137 She loused the dumps, sifting the dirt that came up, and she found chips which she bottled and a few nobbies that the buyers bought for a quid or two. **1955** N. PULLIAM *I traveled Lonely Land* 281 Even the women pick over the waste and rubble—this activity is called 'lousing'—and sometimes are lucky enough to retrieve an overlooked beauty. **1967** R.O. CHALMERS *Austral. Rocks* 310 The process of picking over the old [opal] dumps by hand is called 'noodling' at the Ridge, and 'lousing' at White Cliffs and on Queensland fields. **1977** J. DOUGHTY *Gold in Blood* 49 He and young Jimmy toiled . . 'lousing' the stones for nuggets.

b. *trans.* To pilfer (food, etc.).

1957 W.E. HARNEY *Life among Aborigines* 66 Not that the natives wished to 'louse' much—a bush term for minor pilfering of small quantities of food to feed their kin, and as such considered wages.

Hence **louser** *n.*

1948 K.S. PRICHARD *Golden Miles* 27 A louser's always suspected of pimping for the boss.

lousy jack. APOSTLE a.

1933 J. MCCARTER *Love's Lunatic* 220 To-day they did not . . hear the chattering lousy-jacks. **1964** W. MOXHAM *Longshot* 15 The lousy jacks woke Mark on his first morning at Bungandoo. They were making a hell of a racket in the peppercorn over the meat house. **1980** S. THORNE *I've met some Bloody Wags* 69 Lousyjacks are small, grey, ugly, nasty-looking birds, which are found in the west grouped together, continually screeching in an irritating manner.

love-bird. [Transf. use of *love-bird* a small African parrot: see quot. 1842.] BUDGERIGAR.

1837 *S. Austral. Rec.* (London) (1838) 13 Jan. 30 Strictly speaking, there are no real parrots, except the small love birds, the rest are parroquets, cockatoos, and macaws. **1842** R.G. JAMESON *N.Z., S.A., & N.S.W.* 71 There is another species, called the love-bird, which usually associate in pairs, perching so close together, that it is generally impossible to shoot them singly. **1897** E. SOLDENE *My Theatr. & Mus. Recoll.* 227 A pretty sight in Adelaide were the hundreds and hundreds of love-birds flying about. **1935** M. & E. DURACK *All-About* (1940) 26 A scintillant cloud of green lovebirds swoops to drink in the dim grey of the dawn. **1953** H.G. LAMOND *Big Red* 209 'They call them budgerigars *love birds*, so I've heard,' Larry stated suggestively. **1975** *Bulletin* (Sydney) 15 Feb. 48/3 Male budgerigars can manufacture spermatozoa at the age of two months—an attribute which . . has helped them earn the name of love-birds. **1981** A. GRANT *Camel Train & Aeroplane* 128 From the east came flock upon flock of love-birds . . countless thousands flying waterwards in their vivid green.

love creeper. The Austral. twining plant *Comesperma volubile* (fam. Polygalaceae) bearing racemes of (usu. bluish) flowers. Also *ellipt.* as **love.**

1894 J.K. ARTHUR *Kangaroo & Kauri* 26 Among Australian flowering plants, 'Love' is the pet name bestowed on a most beautiful little creeper bearing flowers of a lovely blue. **1942** C. BARRETT *Austral. Wild Flower Bk.* 45 The stems twist spirally and it is difficult to separate the love creeper from its supporting plant without breaking or cutting them. **1947** MRS A.H. GARNSEY *Romance Huon River* 88 Tangled masses of the blue creeper known as 'love'. **1973** J. MORRISON *Austral. by Choice* 74 The whole hillside was speckled with colour: blue love-creeper, yellow leopard orchids [etc.].

lowan /'loʊən/. [a. Wemba (and neighbouring languages) *lauan*.] *Mallee fowl*, see MALLEE 6.

1847 *Port Phillip Herald* 16 Mar. 2/5 The eggs of the Lowan, a bird frequenting the barren plains on and about the Lower Murray. **1853** J. ALLEN *Jrnl. River Murray* 44 A specimen, shown to me by Mr Beveridge, of the Luanna (or Lowan) bird. **1872** 'RESIDENT' *Glimpses Life Vic.* 243 The wild fowl available for the table include the Lowan or mallee bird. **1893** D. LINDSAY *Jrnl. Elder Sci. Exploring Exped.* 42 Tracks of emu, lowan, and kangaroo plentiful. **1912** B. O'DOWD *Bush* 23 Where teal once dived and lowan raised her mound. **1944** *Bulletin* (Sydney) 2 Aug. 14/1 A Vic. Mallee contractor put a dozen Australorp eggs in a Lowan nesting mound last spring. **1962** H.J. FRITH *Mallee-Fowl* 3 In Western Australia the native name 'gnow' has been adopted and in Victoria 'lowan'. Mallee-fowl is chiefly a New South Wales name. **1972** ANDERSON & BLAKE *J.S. Neilson* 41 More than once as a youth he watched the lowans building.

lowey, var. LOWIE.

low-heel. [Perh. infl. by orig. U.S. *round heels*, used transf. of a sexually compliant woman: see OEDS *round, a.* 15 a.] A prostitute; a sexually promiscuous woman.

1939 K. TENNANT *Foveaux* 311 In this crowd of low heels, quandongs and ripperty men, she looked at her ease and yet not one of them. **1941** *Men may Smoke* (Sydney) Feb. 11 Drunk with . . lowheels. **1951** D. STIVENS *Jimmy Brockett* 45 Sheilas generally get round in pairs. If you do see a sort on her own it's an even chance she's a pro or a lowheel. **1965** J. BEEDE *They hosed them Out* 193 My well-bred low-heel declared it was the first time she'd been done on the floor and voted it an exceedingly diverting experience.

lowie /'loʊi/. Also **lowey.** [f. LOW(-HEEL + -Y.] LOW-HEEL.

1953 K. TENNANT *Joyful Condemned* 21 There's many a man thought he was going to stand over some little lowie and now he's either looking through the bars, or else he's mowing the lawn for her. **1967** *Kings Cross Whisper* (Sydney) xxxvi. 4/1 *Lowey*, an immoral young hussy very popular among young knockabouts. **1979** *Sydney Morning Herald* 3 Mar. 13/1 Harkins points out the 'rev heads' (fast driving teenage yobos) and the 'loweys' (equally fast young girls) he knows lolling about outside the Commercial Hotel.

lubra /'lubrə/. Formerly also with some variety, as **leubra, loubra.** [a. s.e. Tasmanian *lubara*.]

1. An Aboriginal woman. Also *attrib.*

[**1829** G.A. ROBINSON in N.J.B. Plomley *Friendly Mission* 18 May (1966) 59 The husband soon followed me, his cheeks wet with tears. Said *leuberer lowgerner unnee* (his wife asleep by the fire).] **1830** *Ibid.* 19 Mar. (1966) 133 Dray told me that the natives had gone away last night and that Woorrady and *lubra* or *lore* went after them. **1836** M. THOMAS *Diary & Lett.* (1915) 70 On the following day, having by some means procured a small curtain ring, she placed it on a finger of her right hand, and coming to the tent held it up exultingly, exclaiming, 'Lubra! Lubra!' which is the word in their language for either husband or wife. **1841** *Geelong Advertiser* 8 May 2/5 Within the last few days, we have been informed, two leubras were killed and eaten, at the Protector's station, near Killembeet. **1843** *Port Phillip Gaz.* 10 June 3 The reward offered for the apprehension of the murderers of the Loubras. **1856** J. BONWICK *W. Buckley* 76 A female friend of ours was once talking with a lubra pensioner. **1872** 'RESIDENT' *Glimpses Life Vic.* 18 The lubras did not follow their lords to the chase. **1889** E. GILES *Aust. twice Traversed* II. 124 For their kindness I gave the pretty lubras some tea and sugar. **1892** *Truth* (Sydney) 1 May 2/7 It was Baldy Black and his Lubra It was Baldy Black and his Gin Who in Hyde Park after midnight dark Created such a din. **1901** *Ibid.* 16 June 5/7 The Sultan of Turkey is not more jealous of his veiled mistresses than is a Westralian station master of his stark naked lubras. **1906** *Ibid.* 28 Oct. 4/2 Young lubras of 10 years are allured to these dens by the cunning, slant-eyed heathen, and while in a comatose condition *openly ravished by scores* of these mongrels. **1916** C. VAUDE *Tivoli* 19 My little Lubra, won't you be my Gin, And in this wild bush new life begin: I'll go catch you plenty 'possum, dress you up in wattle blossom, Lubra, won't you be my Gin. **1922** 'TE WHARE' *Bush Cinema* 38 A tribal fight or disagreement, resulting in fatalities, over some unusually attractive lubra. **1933** *Bulletin* (Sydney) 26 Apr. 11 Never conclude, O moralist omniscient, That lubras three behind a sable gent Denote he's found one consort insufficient For absolute connubial content. **1934** WARBURTON & ROBERTSON *Buffaloes* 67 The lubras! .. their sagging breasts, flat noses, huge mouths, and filthy hair made me feel ill. **1951** E. HILL *Territory* 111 They came straggling back in a dry time .. travelling as a tribe travels .. lubras in the centre carrying .. coolamons. **1962** *N. Austral. Monthly* Jan. 29 A truck full of lubras in neat print dresses, hair sleekly combed, picaninnies in their arms shining with soapy cleanliness. **1964** K. WILLEY *Eaters of Lotus* 86 He brought the first mob of cattle through to Brunette Downs from Queensland in 1883 and built up a number of stations, living 'on corn beef, damper and a lubra' as the saying goes. **1980** N. WATKINS *Kangaroo Connection* 54 'But, what kind of person .. this lubra?' 'An abo woman, and I'm the last person to be interested in bedding down with one.'

2. *transf.* and *fig.*

1950 *Southerly* iii. 142 So we grew gamblers, tough, hard-bitten, taking The lubra of luck for a mistress. **1969** A. HOPGOOD *And Big Men Fly* 40 I'll coach the lubra league or something. **1971** D. WILLIAMSON *Don's Party* (1973) 49 Any man who isn't married with four kids is a lecher in your book, you flop-bellied, breast-sucked old lubra.

Lucky Country, the. [The title of a book by Donald Horne (b. 1921), published in 1964.] A (chiefly ironic) name for Australia; the popular assumption that Australia is 'a land of opportunity'.

1968 K. DENTON *Walk around my Cluttered Mind* 168 We take it for granted that this *is* the Lucky Country, ignoring the fact that when Donald Horne titled his book he was writing in acid. **1972** *Bulletin* (Sydney) 9 Dec. 29/2 The Lucky Country became the luckier country. **1977** P. TENNISON *Heyday or Doomsday?* 18 There is too much ambivalence about the Lucky Country's pride in its 'realism', and its flight from reality. **1982** *Bulletin* (Sydney) 13 July 103/2 The regional security outlook for The Lucky Country is .. almost undeservedly bland and favorable. It doesn't owe much to Australia's efforts or policies. **1984** *Direct Action* (Sydney) 22 Feb. 6/2 The Lucky Country doesn't often find itself in agreement with the Catholic Weekly. **1986** *Bulletin* (Sydney) 28 Jan. 24/1 As a rapidly falling relative standard of living focuses their minds, Australia's educators are wondering how to cope with the loss of the 'lucky country'.

lucky digger. *Obs.* A successful gold-miner.

1852 *Austral. Gold Digger's Monthly Mag.* i. 13 Tom, the lucky digger, is to be bridegroom. **1855** G.H. WATHEN *Golden Colony* 40, I have seen little coteries of friends, evidently men of education, working together breaking stones, while a rough-bearded 'lucky digger' has galloped gaily by, well mounted, over the roads which the others were forming. **1891** E. HULME *Settlers 35 Yrs. Experience Vic.* 15, I was not a 'lucky digger', with the exception of one little patch. **1903** N. CRAIG *My Adventures* 228 He is a lucky digger, and considers himself quite good enough to mate with a scion of Royalty.

lucky shop. *Vic.* See quot. 1982.

1979 *Age* (Melbourne) 19 Dec. 24/4 He was intrigued by the number of people at the so-called 'Lucky Shop' frittering away all kinds of money on undisciplined quadrella betting. **1982** *Sun-Herald* (Sydney) 7 Mar. 144/5 Victoria's TAB (quaintly called lucky shops) now seems to be the place to spend a pleasant Saturday afternoon.

luderick /'ludərɪk/. Formerly also **ludrick.** [a. Ganay *ludarag.*] The largely herbivorous *Girella tricuspidata*, a brown or silvery-green marine and estuarine fish with dark vertical bands, of commercial importance in e. Aust.; DARKIE *n.*[2]; NIGGER 3. See also BLACKFISH.

1886 *Argus* (Melbourne) 13 Mar. 4/2 The ludrick is a rare and fine fish, something like a bream, but striped with dark bands. **1910** J.T. CHAMPSLEY *Austral. Angler's Guide* 89 The Ludrick is very rare in Port Phillip; we have never seen one caught near Melbourne. **1948** F.D. MARSHALL *Let's go Fishing* 65 The blackfish is also known as luderick or black perch. **1963** B. CROPP *Handbk. for Skindivers* 120 The luderick inhabits the estuaries and rocky foreshores. **1985** *Canberra Chron.* 10 July 19/5 The big winter luderick are turning up in the estuaries.

lug-bite, *v. trans. Obs.* To cadge (money, food, etc.): see BITE *n.* and *v.* Also as *n.*

1891 *Truth* (Sydney) 29 Mar. 7/5 Getting in on the *nod* is the same as .. 'the bustle', 'the whisper', 'the lug-bite', 'on the have'. **1902** *Ibid.* 25 May 1/1 'Lugbiting' meaning in the Australian vernacular, cadging—impudent, outrageous begging.

Hence **lug-biter** *n.*

[N.Z. **1905** *N.Z. Truth* (Wellington) 5 He looked so much more like a low-down lug biter than a wool king.] **1911** L. STONE *Jonah* 223 Joe Grant, a loafer by trade and a lug-biter by circumstance, shifted from one foot to another.

lumber, *v.* [Transf. use of Br. slang *lumber* to place (property) in pawn: see quot 1812 and OED(S *v.*[3] Used elsewhere but chiefly Austral.] *trans.* To arrest; to imprison; to punish judicially (see quot. 1827). Chiefly *pass.*

1812 J.H. VAUX *Mem.* (1819) 188 *Lumber, to lumber* any property, is to deposit it at a pawnbroker's or elsewhere for present security; to retire to any house or private place, for a short time, is called *lumbering yourself.* A man apprehended, and sent to gaol, is said to be *lumbered,* to be *in lumber,* or to be in *Lombard-street.* **1827** *Monitor* (Sydney) 2 Aug. 559 He was sentenced to be *lumbered* for six months; i.e. to go on the tread-mill every Saturday. **1885** *Australasian Printers' Keepsake* 39 A benevolent bobby .. had him lumbered along with all the other jolly dogs who had been out on the loose all night. **1895** *Bulletin* (Sydney) 6 July 3/2 Ere we went Homeward again they lumbered me, and then I got twelve years for wounding with intent. **1916** *Truth* (Sydney) 26 Mar. 12/3 Finding that they could not secure the bushrangers while 'bush telegraphs' were allowed to watch and report, the police decided to 'lumber' the telegraphs. **1944** *Bulletin* (Sydney) 26 July 12/1 They saw the constable taking the gipsy into custody... She had been lumbered for trying to pass some crook two-bobs. **1965** R.H. CONQUEST *Horses in Kitchen* 49 Aw, he's in the can at Maitland. He'll catch me up. He got lumbered outside Newcastle. **1981** C. WALLACE-CRABBE *Splinters* 65 Quit it, you stupid buggers, or you'll both get lumbered! They'll be getting the cops in any time. **1984** P. READ *Down there with me on Cowra Mission* 57, I got lumbered. Copper pulled up and asked me my name, where I was going.

lumber yard. *Obs.* [f. *lumber* 'disused articles of furniture and the like, which take up room inconveniently': see OED(S *sb.*[1] 1. Cf. U.S. *lumber house* building in which various things may be stored: see DAE.] See quot. 1837.

1793 D. COLLINS *Acct. Eng. Colony N.S.W.* (1798) I. 324 The lumber yard near Sydney being completed, the convict millwright Wilkinson was preparing his new mill. **1816** *Hobart Town Gaz.* 13 Aug., Broke-out of the Stock Yard in the Lumber Yard at Hobart Town .. Three Working Bullocks. **1831** *Acct. Colony Van Diemen's Land* 17 The Engineer's stores, or Lumber yard, where the blacksmiths, carpenters and other mechanics in the employment of Government are always at work. **1837** J. MUDIE *Felonry of N.S.W.* 28 The lumber-yard, as it was called, was an establishment containing workshops for convict mechanics of various descriptions, in the employ of government, and was also a depot for materials and stores used in the carrying on of the government works. **1845** *Parramatta Chron.* 9 Aug. 2/2 Knew Bishop from having been a fellow-prisoner with him in the Lumber-yard. **1852** J. WEST *Hist. of Tas.* II. 296 The place of promiscuous association was called the lumber yard, and was subject to the dominion of a 'ring'.

lumpy, *a.* Of an animal: afflicted with lumpy jaw (actinomycosis). Also as *n.*

1907 *Bulletin* (Sydney) 6 June 4/4 An old 'lumpy' bullock was missed .. when the herd was removed to fresher fields. **1932** J.J. HARDIE *Cattle Camp* (1944) 20 On every cattle-camp you'll get an odd 'lumpy' or cancered beast. **1942** H.H. PECK *Mem. of Stockman* 33 Some of the biggest Melbourne butchers were buyers for the bullocks, with .. Edmund Tucker whipping in for 'the lumpies'. **1974** B. KIDMAN *On Wallaby* 16 He found some of the beasts were infected with pleuro pneumonia; they were easily recognised by a swelling on the cheek or the neck. These 'lumpies' were shot at once.

lunar. *Obs.* Esp. in the phr. **to take a lunar.** [Shortening of 'to take a lunar observation', Br. slang *to take a sight* to make an observation with an instrument, *transf.* to make a gesture with the fingers in front of the nose similar to the action of doing this: see OED *sight, sb.*[1] 7 b. and c. and OED(S *lunar, sb.* 2. Sense 2 is now used elsewhere but is recorded earliest in Aust.]

1. An offensive gesture (see quot. 1847, 1). Also *transf.* (see quot. 1866).

1847 *Bell's Life in Sydney* 8 May 3/5 This worthy, upon meeting me in the streets lately, saluted me with a *lunar,* by placing his thumb on his nose and extending his fingers. **1847** *Maitland Mercury* 28 July 2/4 Davis's much enduring spirit was driven beyond all bounds by Mrs Tennant and a friend of hers 'taking a lunar' at him as he was returning towards his house. **1866** *Sydney Punch* 7 Apr. 791/2 Is it not just possible that the writer may be 'taking a lunar' at human credulity. **1871** *Austral. Town & Country Jrnl.* (Sydney) 29 July 132/1 He groaned and got excited, made faces, and took 'lunars' at the electors, and called them a lot of blackguards. **1892** F.A. HARE *Last of Bushrangers* 204 They saw .. Mrs Skillian sitting on a log facing them, and her two hands extended from her nose, and taking what is called a 'lunar' at them. **1903** 'BOONDI' *Boondi's Bk.* 31 'Little Geordie' made a 'lunar' behind his back.

2. A look.

1849 A. HARRIS *Emigrant Family* (1967) 16 You go towards 'the Rocky Springs' and 'take a lunar' at them. **1874** E.A. BANKS *Sunshine & Shadow* 46 And talking thus, his nose upturning, He 'takes a lunar' to the sky. **1876** J.A. EDWARDS *Gilbert Gogger* 93 Ikey informed Billy that he and Slimy were going to take a lunar. **1880** *Bulletin* (Sydney) 28 Aug. 12/1 Young ladies .. used to believe there was a man in the moon... What are the fair ones to do now, having no object in view 'when taking a lunar'?

lunatic soup. Alcoholic liquor of poor quality.

1933 *Bulletin* (Sydney) 6 Sept. 42/1 Lunatic soup, as the few fellows who knew him as Darkie called the brandy he drank. **1956** *Ibid.* 28 Nov. 13/3 Next morning in court the magistrate asked what he'd had. Told that it was 'colonial wine', he snorted, 'Lunatic soup would be a better name for it.' **1967** *Kings Cross Whisper* (Sydney) xxxvi. 4/1 *Lunatic soup,* booze of any description. **1986** *Transair* Mar. 9/1 They went about destroying themselves with the lunatic soup crippling their larynx as surely as if they'd downed an economy size tin of paint stripper.

lunette. [Transf. use of *lunette* the figure of a crescent moon.] A usu. curved or crescent-shaped dune, largely of wind-borne material, formed on the lee side of a lake basin in parts of arid s. Aust. and elsewhere, having smooth contours and with the concave edge along the shore.

1940 E.S. HILLS in *Austral. Geographer* Mar. 15 Along the eastern shores of almost every lake and swamp in the plains of northern Victoria there occurs a crescentic ridge of silty clay or clay 'loam', whose smooth and regular outlines, rising above the plains, at once catch the eye in an otherwise monotonous landscape... The present writer can find no record of the occurrence of such land forms in any other part of the world. It is therefore proposed to designate them by a new term—*lunette.* **1977** J.A. MABBUTT *Desert Landforms* 208 Sand lunettes are less stable than clay lunettes. **1982** BARKER & GREENSLADE *Evol. Flora & Fauna* 104 Lunettes occurred throughout the southern half of Australia and could be formed of a wide range of materials, of silt and clay, or sand, with every gradation between the two. It is evident that lunettes have been formed by wind action.

lungfish. [Spec. use of *lung-fish* a dipnoan fish.] The lungfish *Neoceratodus forsteri* of Qld. rivers; BURNETT SALMON. See also *mud fish* MUD 1.

1896 F.G. AFLALO *Sketch Nat. Hist. Aust.* 211 'Barramunda', a name that more properly belongs to the *Ceratodus*, or Lung Fish. **1906** D.G. STEAD *Fishes of Aust.* 25 The Giant Perch and the Lung-fish, are also known in parts by the name of Barramundi. **1919** *Bulletin* (Sydney) 22 May 20/2 The now almost extinct ceratodus, or Burnett salmon, or lung-fish, is the most remarkable fish Australia has. **1926** *Illustr. Tasmanian Mail* (Hobart) 31 Mar. 6/2 Specimens of the Ceratodus, or lungfish, now confined to two or three rivers in Central Queensland. **1952** B. BEATTY *Unique to Aust.* 74 The most outstanding fresh water fish is the famous . . Lung-fish of Queensland which exists nowhere else. **1982** *Bulletin* (Sydney) 26 Jan. 18/2 Dead lungfish, believed to have been killed by water pollution, were discovered in Brisbane's Breakfast Creek.

lurk. [Generalized use of Br. slang *lurk* a method of fraud: see OED(S *sb.*[1])] A profitable stratagem; a dodge or scheme (not necessarily implying fraud); a job (see quots. 1915 and 1958).

1891 *Truth* (Sydney) 15 Mar. 2/1 The young man took thought within his bosom, and he said within his own heart, 'Now, what's his lurk?' **1904** *Ibid.* 31 Jan. 2/3 He's always devising dodges for raising the wind—picnics, bazaars . . and any other 'lurk' for laying hold of loot. **1915** C.J. DENNIS *Songs of Sentimental Bloke* 20, I found 'er lurk wus pastin' labels in a pickle joint. *Ibid.* 125 *Lurk*, a regular occupation. **1917** C.T. O'NEILL *Soldiers' Poems*, They call the roll before yer go—it's no use working lurks; We go an' do about an hour at what we call Physical Jerks. **1927** F.C. BIGGERS *Bat-Eye* 22 Bat-Eye got th' wind uv Ripper's lurk. **1944** L. GLASSOP *We were Rats* 54 The Home Defence Forces—officially known as . . the Australian Military Forces—were what the boys would call 'the lurk'. **1951** E. LAMBERT *Twenty Thousand Thieves* 307 Miserably they performed their duties, cursing the tedium of their comfortless camp. They invented 'lurks'—ways of evading duties. **1958** R. STOW *To Islands* 126 'What's your lurk, mate?' 'Me? Stockman on a mission.' **1963** B. HESLING *Dinkumization & Depommification* 49, I don't know any other door-to-door fried-fish bludger in Sydney. It's a new lurk. **1972** *Bulletin* (Sydney) 25 Nov. 48/2 To soften the financial burden a favorite lurk is to employ the yacht hand as a company 'storeman and packer'. **1978** B. ST. A. SMITH *Spirit beyond Psyche* 208, I told him once t' try the Repat. for war-nerves. I told 'im what a terrible good lurk it was. **1980** *Overland* lxxxii. 7 You'll soon learn the lurks and perks. **1985** N. MEDCALF *Rifleman* 83 This would be a pretty good lurk.

lurkman. One who lives by sharp practice.

1945 S.J. BAKER *Austral. Lang.* 138 We are . . originators of the following terms for various sharpers, tricksters and others who live by their wits: *spieler* . . *lurk man* . . and *amsterdam*. **1978** L. HORSPHOL *Turn down Empty Glass* 32, I felt strangely sorry for the old man. Lurkman he might have been. **1978** W. LOWENSTEIN *Weevils in Flour* 139 You couldn't get a deener where there was no deener to be got. You had to be there where it was, so we became lurkmen. Not bad people but sharp!

lyre-bird. [See quot. 1886.]

1. Either of the two species of ground-dwelling bird of the genus *Menura*, the ALBERT LYRE-BIRD or the more widespread and common *superb lyre-bird* (see SUPERB), *M. novaehollandiae* of forest in s.e. mainland Aust. and introduced into Tas. The bird is noted for its resounding call and remarkable power of mimicry, and for the long, lyre-shaped tail displayed by the male; MENURA; *mountain pheasant*, see MOUNTAIN; *native pheasant* (a), see NATIVE *a.* 6 b.; PHEASANT 1 a. Formerly also **lyre(-tailed) pheasant, lyre-tail(ed) bird.**

[**1824** QUOY & GAIMARD in L. de Freycinet *Voyage autour du Monde: Zoologie* 694 *Ménure*, nommé aussi *oiseau-lyre* et *lyre magnifique*, parce qu'il déploie en lyre élégante les plumes de sa queue.] **1834** G. BENNETT *Wanderings N.S.W.* I. 277 The 'Lyre bird' of Australia. . . The lyre-pheasant is a bird of heavy flight, but swift of foot. **1841** J. GOULD *Birds of Aust.* (1848) III. Pl. 14, The Lyre-bird . . uttering his various cries, sometimes pouring forth his natural notes, at others mocking those of others, and even the howling of the . . Dingo. **1851** MRS R. LEE *Adventures in Aust.* 356 What is the reason I have never met with the Lyre-tail Birds? **1853** S. SIDNEY *Three Colonies* (ed. 2) 282 The shy and curious lyre bird (Menura superba), which is peculiar to Australia, and only found on the south-eastern coast. **1861** E.P. RAMSAY-LAYE *Social Life & Manners* 178 Lyre pheasants . . inhabiting in numbers the most inaccessible parts of the mountain. **1886** J.A. FROUDE *Oceana* 146 We saw a lyre-bird . . the body being like a coot's and about the same size, the tail long as the tail of a bird of paradise, beautifully marked in bright brown, with the two chief feathers curved into the shape of a Greek lyre, from which it takes its name. **1896** C.E. LYNE *Life H. Parkes* 398 And have we no visions pleasant Of the playful lyre-tailed pheasant. **1912** B. O'DOWD *Bush* 15 This lyre-bird on his dancing-mound of song Our mystagogue of some Bacchantic vale. **1931** J. DEVANEY *Earth Kindred* 25 The glad shout of the lyrebird. **1957** M. PAICE *Valley in North* 92 They came unexpectedly upon a lyre-bird preening its feathers in a glade. **1979** B. MARTYN *First Footers S. Gippsland* 66 He . . was carrying a dead lyre bird, that glorious elusive spirit of the bush so martyred for its plumage.

2. *transf.* (Punningly) a liar; a mimic.

1895 G. RANKEN *Windabyne* 234 Boggs and Nipper were certainly unbusiness-like . . and Short blurted out that they were 'lyre birds' of the most pronounced type. **1941** S.J. BAKER *Pop. Dict. Austral. Slang* 45 *Lyre-bird, a bit of a*, one disposed to tell lies. **1969** A. GARVE *Boomerang* 86 'You're like a ruddy lyre bird.' 'Oh, lord—not *more* ornithology! What does that one do?' 'Imitates everything.'

M

Ma: see MA STATE.

macadamia /mækəˈdeɪmiə/. [The plant genus *Macadamia* was named by the botanist F. von Mueller (*Trans. Philos. Inst. Vic.* (1858) II. 72) after the chemist John *Macadam* (1827–1865), Secretary of the Philos. Inst. Vic.] Any rainforest tree of the genus *Macadamia* (fam. Proteaceae) of e. Qld., n.e. N.S.W., and the Celebes, esp. *M. integrifolia* and *M. tetraphylla* which are cultivated for their edible nuts; the nut of these trees; BOPPLE NUT; *Queensland nut*, see QUEENSLAND 2. Also **macadamia (nut) tree,** and *attrib.*

[**1857** *Trans. Philos. Inst. Vic.* (1858) II. 72 *Macadamia* . . a tree of oriental subtropical Australia, with leaves three in a whorl or rarely opposite . . a beautiful genus . . dedicated to John Macadam . . the talented and deserving Secretary of our Institute. **1880** J. BONWICK *Resources Qld.* 82 The Queensland Nut, *Macadamia*, rapidly becoming scarce, is a small scrub tree of alluvial flats, whose fruit is ever welcome, and the wood of which takes a capital polish.] **1927** H.J. RUMSEY *Austral. Nuts* 8 A rather strange feature of the Macadamia is that the nut adheres to the bottom of the exocarp or husk, instead of hanging from the stem like other nuts and the seeds of stone fruit. **1953** L. & C. REES *Spinifex Walkabout* 32 Pineapples, paw-paws . . macadamia or Australian bush-nuts. **1970** *Coast to Coast 1967–68* 4 The butcher-birds and magpies in the macadamia-trees. **1976** *Ecos* ix. 16/1 With the exception of the macadamia nut, no agricultural or horticultural crops came from wild plants in Australia. **1978** S. GOULDSTONE *Austral. & N.Z. Guide Food Bearing Plants* 48 The macadamia nut tree is a beautiful evergreen tree which is indigenous to northern New South Wales and Queensland.

macaroni. Rhyming slang for 'baloney'; nonsense.

1924 LAWRENCE & SKINNER *Boy in Bush* 46 Yes. Jam, macaroni, cockadoodle. We're plain people out hereaways. Not mantle ornaments. **1941** S.J. BAKER *Pop. Dict. Austral. Slang* 45 *Macaroni*, nonsense, foolishness. **1984** A. DELBRIDGE *Aussie Talk* 201 *Macaroni*, nonsense.

macaw. *Obs.* [Transf. use of *macaw* any of several birds of tropical America of the genus *Ara.*] A black cockatoo, prob. PALM COCKATOO.

1793 J. HUNTER *Hist. Jrnl. Trans. Port Jackson* 69 There are a great variety of birds in this country; all those of the parrot tribe, such as the macaw. **1840** *S. Austral. Rec.* (London) 3 Oct. 214 The splendid plumage of the birds—the lemon-crested cockatoo, the jet black macaw . . add an oriental grandeur to our plains. **1862** J. MCKINLAY *Jrnl. Exploration Interior* 6 May 88 A vast number of gulahs, curellas, macaws . . here.

macca, var. MACKER.

machine.

1. *Obs.* A totalizator.

[N.Z. **1889** A.E. WOODHOUSE *N.Z. Farm & Station Verse* (1950) 26 What a lot [of money] you left behind in the 'machine'.] **1893** *Bird o' Freedom* (Sydney) 7 Jan. 7/3 Shortly after the machine opened it was seen that the party behind St. Nipps were backing him. **1903** *Sporting News* (Launceston) 11 July 1/5 His or her investment on the machine, either straight-out or for a place.

2. Abbrev. of *shearing machine* (see SHEARING B. 3). Freq. *attrib.*

1891 *Conference Amalgam. Shearers' Union & Pastoralists' Fed. Council* 20 The strong desire shown by men who have never shorn by machine to get into machine sheds. **1904** *Shearer* (Sydney) 30 July 1/3 Hand and machine shearers and bush-workers generally of every class and section desirous of becoming members of the Machine Shearers and Shed Employees' Union are requested to forward their names to the Secretary. **1910** *Bulletin* (Sydney) 22 Dec. 44/2 Men are often expert machine shearers, and yet novices when it comes to operating on a little flock at home. Men follow machine sheds or hand sheds. **1935** R.B. PLOWMAN *Boundary Rider* 159 The blade-shearer finds it hard to cut through the gritty mass of wool and sticks and sand, and the machine-shearer finds the edge worn off his comb in a few minutes. **1940** *Bulletin* (Sydney) 10 Jan. 16/1 Anyone . . could put up tallies with machines.

Mackenzie bean. [f. the name of the *Mackenzie* River: see quot. 1982.] The trailing creeper *Canavalia rosea* (syn. *C. maritima*) (fam. Fabaceae) of tropical n. Aust. and elsewhere, the immature pod of which may be cooked and eaten.

1845 L. LEICHHARDT *Jrnl. Overland Exped.* 15 Mar. (1847) 180 The scrub is generally an open Vitex. . . The Mackenzie-bean and several other papilionaceous plants . . grow in it. **1847** D. BUNCE *Australasiatic Reminisc.* 21 May (1857) 182 Wommai brought me . . some green and dry pods of the creeping plant to which we had given the name of the Mackenzie Bean, having found it, in the first instance, growing on the banks of that river. **1982** K. MCARTHUR *Bush in Bloom* 25 We call it simply the Beach Bean because that describes it sufficiently for people living near the coast, as here it is a plant of the sand dunes. . . Leichhardt called it the Mackenzie Bean because he found it on the Mackenzie River in Central Queensland. **1986** K. BRENNAN *Wildflowers of Kakadu* 101 McKenzie Bean *Canavalia* sp. . . A distinctive, broad-leafed vine with large, flat seed pods.

macker. Also **macca.** [Of unknown origin.] A recruit in the armed forces; a newcomer.

1944 *H.M.A.S. 'Westralia'* Dec. 5 All the tried and noted 'mackers' from the messes near and far. **1945** *Buzz Rev.: H.M.A.S. 'Manoora'* 18 Feb. 9 'Quite an old hand,' thought we mackers. **1965** J. WYNNUM *Jiggin' in Riggin'* 112 Only a macca in the outfit, too. Only been in half as long as us. **1966** G. WYATT *Strip Jack Naked* 19 How about you maccas having a shot at it?

mackerel. [Transf. use of *mackerel* the marine fish *Scomber scombrus.*] Any of several marine fish, usu. of the fam. Scombridae, esp. *Scomber australasicus*, a silvery-greenish fish of s. Aust. and elsewhere.

1770 J. COOK *Jrnls.* 23 Aug. (1955) I. 394 The sea is indifferently well stock'd with Fish of various sorts, such as . . Mackarel [*sic*]. **1789** 'OFFICER' *Authentic & Interesting Narr. Exped. Botany Bay* 38 Bream and mackerel are the most plenty of any fish, but none are so delicate as those caught in the European seas. **1826** J. ATKINSON *Acct. Agric. & Grazing N.S.W.* 25 The coasts of New South Wales abound with fish; The best kinds are snappers . . and mackarel [*sic*]. **1880** *Proc. Linnean Soc. N.S.W.* V. 555 *Scomber antarcticus* . . 'The Mackerel' of the South-east Coast of Australia. **1906** D.G. STEAD *Fishes of Aust.* 162 The Mackerel (*Scomber colias*) . . of Australia is a fish of considerable value. **1936** T.C. ROUGHLEY *Wonders Great Barrier Reef* 194 One can easily feel sorry for a mackerel or any of the other food fishes as they lie gasping on the deck. **1965** *Austral. Encycl.* V. 436 Though its flesh is apt to decay rapidly (especially if it is not well bled), a fresh mackerel is a sound food-fish. **1974** T.D. SCOTT et al. *Marine & Freshwater Fishes S.A.* 289 The Mackerel is a migratory fish and occurs in large numbers in the open ocean off the coasts of southern Australia.

macnoon, var. MACNOON.

Macquarie Harbour. [f. the name of an inlet on the w. coast of Tas.] Used *attrib.* in the names of flora and fauna: **Macquarie Harbour pine** *obs.*, HUON PINE; **vine,** (chiefly *Tas.*) the twining plant *Muehlenbeckia gunnii* (fam. Polygonaceae) of Tas. and S.A., bearing edible fruit in loose, grape-like clusters; also **Macquarie harbour grape (vine), Macquarie vine.**

1851 *Hobarton Guardian* 8 Jan. 4/2 On Sale . . 150,000 feet of **Macquarie Harbour pine.** **1891** W. TILLEY *Wild West of Tas.* 43 Macquarie Harbour or Huon pine . . grows chiefly about the flats of the rivers. **1831** [**Macquarie Harbour vine**] *Hobart-Town Almanack* 265 The Macquarie harbour grape . . produces its fruit in large bunches, resembling grapes. **1843** J. BACKHOUSE *Narr. Visit Austral. Colonies* p. xxxvi, Macquarie Harbour Vine or Grape. This large climber was introduced into Hobart Town from Macquarie Harbour about 1831 or 1832; but it also abounds in almost every other humid forest in the Colony. **1857** D. BUNCE *Australasiatic Reminisc.* 39 *Polygonum adpressum*, or Macquarie harbor grape vine. . . Its quick growth, dense foliage, and white blossoms, succeeded with clusters of waxy transparent fruit, slightly acid, renders it a desirable ornament. **1891** J. FENTON *Bush Life Tas.* (1964) 174 Covered with its primitive garb of . . Macquarie Harbour vine, and all the mosses and lichens that grow so delicately in the forest shade. **1952** J.R. SKEMP *Memories Myrtle Bank* 67 Sometimes the undergrowth was linked together by vines and creepers—mainly the tough far-reaching ropes of the Macquarie Vine, which, incidentally, bears sweet edible little grapes. **1975** A.B. & J.W. CRIBB *Wild Food in Aust.* 66 Macquarie Vine is a woody, twining plant, sometimes prostrate but often climbing over other plants in moist forests.

Macquarie Island parrot. [f. the name of an island s.e. of Tas.] See quot. 1965. Also **Macquarie Island parakeet, Macquarie parrot.**

1827 P. CUNNINGHAM *Two Yrs. in N.S.W.* I. 326 The Macquarie parrot is the inmate of an island even more bleak and cold than the Orkneys. **1831** *Hobart-Town Almanack* 260 Macquarie island parrot—Pacificus. **1919** *Bulletin* (Sydney) 30 Jan. 24/3 Amongst Australasian birds which have become extinct are the Macquarie Island parrot [etc.]. **1965** *Austral. Encycl.* VII. 28 Unfortunately, the Macquarie Island parakeet (*Cyanoramphus novaezelandiae erythrotis*) is extinct; it was exterminated by sealers seeking food.

Macquarie perch. Also **Macquarie's perch.** [f. the name of a river in central N.S.W.] The freshwater fish *Macquaria australasica* of rivers and lakes in Vic. and N.S.W., valued for its fine flesh.

1906 D.G. STEAD *Fishes of Aust.* 99 Macquarie's Perch attains a length of from 12 to 15 inches. **1938** *Bulletin* (Sydney) 12 Jan. 20/1 The Macquarie perch is making a welcome reappearance in Gippsland streams. **1978** D. VAWR *Ratbag Mind* 27 A perch of sorts, but obviously not the perch I knew. This was a Macquarie. **1984** *Age* (Melbourne) 30 Jan. 1/5 The survival of the Murray cod and Macquarie perch is threatened by silt, filling the deep holes in river beds they inhabit and killing the bottom-dwelling insects they feed on.

Macquarie vine: see *Macquarie Harbour vine*, MACQUARIE HARBOUR.

macrozamia /mækroʊˈzeɪmiə/. [f. Gk. μακρο-, comb. form of μακρός large and *Zamia* a plant genus, a name given by the Dutch botanist F.A.W. Miquel (*Monogr. Cycad.* (1842) 35).] Any plant of the genus *Macrozamia* (fam. Zamiaceae) of e., s.w., and central Aust., typically having stiff, palm-like leaves and cone-bearing seeds edible after treatment (see quot. 1951). See also *wild pineapple* WILD 1, ZAMIA. Also *attrib.*

1871 *Illustr. Sydney News* 30 Sept. 158/4 On the Manning River there grows a noble arborescent Macrozamia . . which attains a height of eight or ten feet, with a splendid canopy of leaves at the top, bearing resemblance to the arborescent fern. **1897** L. LINDLEY-

COWEN *W. Austral. Settler's Guide* 587 The macrozamia is a palm-like plant having a thick stem globose underground, and growing in time to a considerable height. **1903** A.G. CHARLETON *Gold Mining & Milling W.A.* 10 Where the land is scantily forested . . a patch of 'nigger-head' . . often intermixed in the coastal districts with the palm-like Macrozamia. **1951** C. SIMPSON *Adam in Ochre* 138 Between the trees there were often macrozamia palms. These are a good food-palm to the natives, who know that the nuts must be crushed, washed, and baked before they are eaten.

mad, *a.*

1. In the phr. **(as) mad as a (cut) snake,** (or **as a meat axe**), angry; crazy; eccentric.

1917 A.L. BREWER *'Gators' Euchre* 29 When a new-chum gets lost, why in thunder does he lose his head? . . White or colored, they run as mad as snakes. **1920** L. ESSON *Dead Timber* 34 The Boss is as mad as a snake—he was flourishing his greenhide and cursing. **1932** W. HATFIELD *Ginger Murdoch* 30 'But you're mad,' said Mick, 'mad as a cut snake!' **1944** J.J. HARDIE *Cattle Camp* (ed. 3) 53 They're well matched! Mad as snakes—the pair of them! **1946** *Coast to Coast 1945* 252 The cow's mad—mad as a meat-axe! **1951** 'S. MACKENZIE' *Dead Men Rising* 203 Mad as a cut snake . . and there's not a better feller. . . Wedgie was the bravest silly bastard in the whole Aussie Army. **1960** D. IRELAND *Image in Clay* (1964) 79 Strewth, Mary! You're as mad as a meataxe! **1964** D. REIDY *It's This Way* 33 That's Noisy Joyner's; he's as mad as a snake on a chain but clever mad like, if yer get what I mean. **1974** *Bulletin* (Sydney) 19 Jan. 12/3 What got me mad as a meat axe, was when old Grazza did the big rubbish on some of me Aussie mates in London. **1977** R. MCKIE *Crushing* (1978) 38 A great bunch. Mad as cut snakes some of 'em. **1978** R.A.F. WEBB *Brothers in Sun* 66 He often gave others the impression that he was irresponsible. Indeed he was one reason why some people regarded all Brothers as being 'as mad as meat axes'. **1982** T. WINTON *Open Swimmer* 23 He's as mad as a cut snake. **1984** *Weekend Austral. Mag.* (Sydney) 28 July 4/3 John McArthur is ruled out. He was monomaniac, if not as mad as the proverbial meat-axe.

2. In the collocation **mad mick,** rhyming slang for 'pick'.

1919 *Aussie: Austral. Soldiers' Mag.* Jan. 8/1 We were issued with . . 'Mad Micks', as the Diggers call . . picks. **1936** *Bulletin* (Sydney) 4 Mar. 21/1 'Douglas', 'banjo' and 'Mad Mick' have ceased to have any meaning. **1953** T.A.G. HUNGERFORD *Riverslake* 224, I swung a mad-mick there for eighteen months during the depression. **1958** T. RONAN *Pearling Master* 170 Native-born Australians mostly . . called . . a pick a 'Mad Mick'. **1973** F. HUELIN *Keep Moving* 78 Well! I won't buy drinks f'r any bloody ganger, just f'r a chance to swing a mad mick.

made, *ppl. a.* [Spec. use of *made* artificially (as opposed to naturally) constructed: see OED *ppl. a.* 1.]

1. In the collocation **made road** [in Br. use an artificially constructed road], a formed but freq. unsealed road; see also UNMADE.

1827 P. CUNNINGHAM *Two Yrs. in N.S.W.* I. 123 A *made* bush-road is one where the brushes have been cleared, banks of rivers and gullies levelled, and trees notched, on the route, and cuts made on the faces or tops of hills when necessary, the remainder being all left in a natural state. **1852** MRS C. MEREDITH *My Home in Tas.* I. 74 The road by which we had ascended was a 'made' one, and tolerably good. **1886** W.J. WOODS *Visit to Vic.* 21 Colonists distinguish between roads which have been 'made' and such as are mere tracks among the trees cleared of fallen timber. **1893** 'OLD CHUM' *Chips* 82 At this time there were no 'made roads', except from Melbourne to Mount Alexander. **1972** M. CASSIDY *Dispossessed* 24 It was not metalled, had no shining stone surface, and however often the council had the clay rolled it quickly re-formed itself into those queer tiny regular corrugations which characterize all 'made' roads. **1981** A.B. FACEY *Fortunate Life* 44 The road was just a winding track—there were no made roads in those days.

2. *Obs.* In the collocation **made ground,** ground composed in part of drifts of sand, soil, etc., washed from elsewhere; also *fig.*

1871 *Austral. Town & Country Jrnl.* (Sydney) 25 June 778/4 Here springs and the rainfall are carrying away the soil which supports the timber on the flanks of the ranges and spurs, and depositing it, as what miners call 'made ground', in the small hollows which are tributary to the larger plains, and which they gradually assist to form. **1887** H.Y.L. BROWN *Rec. of Mines S.A.* 78 Northwards of where Brady's Gully runs on to the Salt Creek Flats there is a table-land of drift, known to diggers as 'made ground'. **1890** 'R. BOLDREWOOD' *Miner's Right* 277, I had been actuated by the best and purest motives, if such there be within this strangely concocted entity, this jumble of 'made ground' (to use the miner's phrase) that we call humanity.

mado /'meɪdoʊ/. [Prob. f. a Qld. Aboriginal language.] Either of two small marine fish *Atypichthys mado* and *A. strigatus*, commonly found near wharves and inlets of e. Aust.

1906 D.G. STEAD *Fishes of Aust.* 134 The Mado [*sc. Atypichthys strigatus*] is a handsome little fish. **1965** *Austral. Encycl.* V. 458 In colour it is yellowish, with several brown longitudinal bands, which do not form the letters m, a, d, o, as is sometimes averred; the name 'mado' was aboriginal. **1978** N. COLEMAN *Austral. Fisherman's Fish Guide* 139 The mado seems to prefer a somewhat sheltered habitat and is more likely to be found in bays, inlets and estuaries than open water.

mag, *v.* [Br. dial. *mag* to chatter (as in *magpie*): see EDD.] *intr.* To prattle; to talk incessantly. Also *trans.*

1895 [see *magging, vbl. n.*]. **1918** 'LANCE-CORPORAL COBBER' *Anzac Pilgrim's Progress* 82 He's no bully, doesn't mag, Doesn't swank around an' sprag, You will never hear him brag. **1925** A. WRIGHT *Boy from Bullarah* 166 Don't mag so much, Yank. . . Y're always yappin'. **1938** *Bulletin* (Sydney) 23 Nov. 21/4 These blokes maggin' about marks on trunks growin' up with the trees reminds me of the big drought. **1944** 'S. CAMPION' *Pommy Cow* 110 You don't wanna hear me mag about Queensland. **1960** E. O'CONNER *Irish Man* 194 We'll get the billy boiling, while old Carl mags with the boss. **1978** H.C. BAKER *I was Listening* 180 Brash will mag his way in, and mag his way out wherever he goes. **1981** D. STUART *I think I'll Live* 170 Get him talking, an' he'd mag the leg off a campoven.

Hence **magger** *n.*, **magging** *vbl. n.*

1973 *Bronze Swagman Bk. Bush Verse* (1974) 6 One could out-talk all the rest Of **maggers** that I know. **1895** *Worker* (Sydney) 14 Sept. 4/2 You never get a rest From his growling and his **magging.** **1943** *Austral. New Writing* 45 Some magging and arguing, mostly quiet. **1944** 'S. CAMPION' *Pommy Cow* 216 With this sister female under the same roof, he hoped Kate would settle down and embark on one of those magging contests dear to the heart of woman. **1959** E. WEBB *Mark of Sun* 122 People everywhere—and the magging, you never heard anything like the din.

mag, *n.* [See prec.] Talk; a gossip or chat; a 'tale'.

1895 *Worker* (Sydney) 28 Sept. 4/1 When a couple of fast men draw a pen There is always a lot of mag. **1910** *Truth* (Sydney) 9 Jan. 1/5 He was a drummer with plenty of mag. **1914** E. DYSON *Spats' Fact'ry* 122 'I found it in the gutter when you had gone.' 'Likely story,' snorts Elder Odgson. 'Pretty mag,' grins the John. **1945** J. HOLMES *Is it Dinkum?* 6 At last the 'mag' is ended, with her friend she makes a date. **1957** V. PALMER *Rainbow-Bird* 94 All the mag there was about munitions. **1980** D. HEWETT *Susannah's Dreaming* (1981) 8 She wants ter stay and 'ave a bit of a mag with Freddy.

maga, var. MOGO.

maggie. Also **maggy.** [Br. dial.: see OED(S 2 b.] A hypocoristic name for MAGPIE *n.* 1 a.

1901 *Bulletin* (Sydney) 5 Oct. 17/1 *Re* the black-backed Monaro magpies. . . Has 'Gumleaf' . . ever seen two 'maggies' marked alike? **1917** C. THACKERAY *Goliath Joe* 46, I was jest skinnin' a black maggy fer bait fer my 'and-line wen I seen my springer bend. **1934** 'S. RUDD' *Green Grey Homestead* 58 'Maggies' were always warbling and yabbering among its green boughs in summer time. **1951** R. DORIEN *Venturing to Aust.* 74 They were the voices of the black and white magpies, larger than the British magpies, called familiarly 'maggies'. **1975** T. SCHURMANN *Shop!* 71 'Just where did you get this pipe?' . . 'I found it in a maggie's nest.' **1982** T. WINTON *Open Swimmer* 5 He could . . see the scabby trunk above bearing all the open-mouthed maggies that chased them to and from school.

maggotty, *a.* Also **maggoty.** [Br. dial. *maggoty* queer-tempered, fractious, etc.: see EDD.] Angry; bad-tempered. In the phr. **to go maggotty,** to become irritable.

1919 W.H. DOWNING *Digger Dialects* 33 *Maggotty*, angry. **1951** D. STIVENS *Jimmy Brockett* 31, I didn't need to, but I shaved every day and my old man made me maggotty by asking me one day, 'Do you shave up or down?' **1959** 'D. FORREST' *Last Blue Sea* 74 He's down there . . going maggotty about doctors and Japs and boongs. **1967** R. DONALDSON et al. *Cane!* 21 'Watch his hair, fellers,' he cried. 'The wonk gets maggoty if you ruffle et!' **1977** B. SCOTT *My Uncle Arch* 63 Scotty got a bit maggoty about this.

maggy, var. MAGGIE.

maginnis /mə'gɪnəs/. [Of unknown origin.] *Obs.* Also **McGinness, McGinnis, McGuiness.** A (wrestling) hold from which escape is difficult. Freq. *fig.* and esp. in the phr. **to put** (or **clap**) **(the) maginnis on.** Also **crooked maginnis.**

1901 *Truth* (Sydney) 6 Oct. 6/4 And if I see a drunken man I soon gets on his trail; I claps McGinness on to him And hugs him off to jail. **1904** *Ibid.* 13 Nov. 3/3 He was followed by the two accused, one of whom (the colored man) 'put the McGuiness on' witness. **1905** J. FURPHY *Rigby's Romance* (1946) 67, I could see my way to Agnes in a more manly, off-hand way than depending on the sort of crooked maginnis I had on her. **1912** J. BRADSHAW *Highway Robbery under Arms* (ed. 3) 27 The chump may tumble that we played the trick, and put Maginnis on us. **1941** S.J. BAKER *Pop. Dict. Austral. Slang* 46 *McGinnis on, put the*, to render an opponent hors-de-combat, to put on the pressure.

magnetic, *a.* [See quot. 1909.] In the name of a termite, and its nest: **magnetic ant hill (bed, nest),** the wall-like nest constructed by the *magnetic termite*, with the long axis pointing roughly north-south; **termite,** the termite *Amitermes meridionalis* of n. Qld. and N.T.; MERIDIAN ANT.

[**1897 magnetic ant hill:** *Proc. Linnean Soc. N.S.W.* XXII. 727 This is the species which constructs the remarkable 'meridional' or 'magnetic nests' found from near the Bloomfield River, North Queensland, to Palmerston, Port Darwin.] **1909** F.E. BIRTLES *Lonely Lands* 198 They are sometimes called 'magnetic' ant hills, owing to the fact of their pointing due north and south. **1934** WARBURTON & ROBERTSON *Buffaloes* 12 The magnetic ant beds . . were fashioned like huge tombstones. **1966** B. BEATTY *Around Aust.* 62 Some ten miles to the south of Darwin covering an area thirty miles wide, may be seen the unique 'magnetic' anthills. . . They are found nowhere else in the world but in Cape York Peninsula of Queensland, but those of the latter are not as tall as the 'hills' in the Darwin area. **1935** K.C. MCKEOWN *Insect Wonders Aust.* 140 The **Magnetic Termite** . . with a world-wide reputation, builds an amazing nest like a brick wall. **1952** B. BEATTY *Unique to Aust.* 73 The Magnetic Termites of Northern Australia . . build astonishing nests . . with the narrow ends pointing always north and south. **1965** *Austral. Encycl.* VIII. 464 In the nests of the magnetic termite . . food . . is stored in some or most of the galleries and chambers of the mound.

magnificent, *a.* In the names of fauna having a striking appearance: **magnificent (fruit) pigeon,** WOMPOO PIGEON; **spider,** the spider *Dicrostichus magnificus* of e. Aust.

1846 J. GOULD *Birds of Aust.* (1848) V. Pl. 58, *Carpophaga magnifica.* **Magnificent Fruit Pigeon.** **1916** *Bulletin* (Sydney) 23 Nov. 24/2 The 'Big Scrub', towards the Tweed (N.S.W.) and the jungles further north, once teemed with pigeons, among them the . . 'magnificent' . . and 'topknot'. **1949** B. O'REILLY *Green Mountains* 148 An occasional wampoo—that miracle of purple and green, to which the naturalist, in an expansive mood, has given the vernacular name of magnificent fruit pigeon. **1936** K.C. MCKEOWN *Spider Wonders Aust.* 107 Fully justifying the name of **Magnificent Spider** . . about the size of a large Barcelona nut; it is cream-coloured above. . . Along the front edge of the abdomen is an intricate mosaic of fine lines and small salmon-pink dots. **1952** B. BEATTY *Unique to Aust.* 63 The Magnificent spider . . has a beautiful mosaic pattern with a finely sculptured royal crown upon its back.

. .This spider comes out at night to feed upon night-flying moths. **1969** D. CLYNE *Guide Austral. Spiders* 74 *D. magnificus* . . the Magnificent spider—is a rather lumpy-looking spider when at rest.

magnoon /mæg'nun/, *a.* Also **macnoon, magnune, mangoon.** [f. the colloq. (Egyptian) Arabic.] Mad; eccentric.

1917 P. AUSTEN *Bill-Jim* 8 I'll be orl rite nex' wick!—Why kid I ain't magnoon. **1918** *Kia Ora Coo-ee* Apr. 18/2 Poor old Bob Gordon's gone magnune. **1919** O. HOGUE *Cameliers* 5 Admittedly their language, when a camel went mangoon, was simply shocking. **1924** A.W. BAZLEY et al. Gloss. Slang A.I.F. (typescript) *Andey McNoon*, an unqualified idiot. From the Arabic 'Inta machnoon'—a damned fool. **1932** I.L. IDRIESS *Lasseter's Last Ride* 116 A bolting camel travels at an amazing speed. These beasts, gone 'macnoon', covered the ground in giant strides. **1940** *Sentry Go* (Keswick) Aug. 40 A 'Magnoon' Waler is next to ride. **1949** G. BERRIE *Morale* 34 Anyway, I'll chance it. I'll go 'magnoon' if I stop here. **1970** R. BEILBY *No Medals for Aphrodite* 15 Shut up your clowning, you magnoon bastard.

mago, var. MOGO.

magpie, *n.* and *a.* [Transf. use of *magpie* a black and white bird of the crow family.]

A. *n.*

1. a. The black and white bird *Gymnorhina tibicen*, widespread in Aust., occurring also in New Guinea and introduced to New Zealand, having a melodious, carolling call; BREAK O' DAY BIRD; MAGGIE; *native magpie*, see NATIVE *a.* 6 b.; PIPING CROW. **b.** (Occas.) Any of several other birds having black and white plumage. See also ORGAN BIRD.

1792 R. ATKINS *Jrnl.* 13 Nov., We . . made some excellent Soup of 1 Duck 1 Pidgeon 1 Crow & 3 Magpies. **1804** G. CALEY in A.E.J. Andrews *Devil's Wilderness* (1984) 100 A sort of Magpie seems to be an inhabitant of the rocky vallies. **1831** *Acct. Colony Van Diemen's Land* 88 At intervals the magpie, though unseen, filled the valley with its loud but sweet song, or rather bar of music. **1846** *Cumberland Times* (Parramatta) 17 Jan. 3/4 *Lost. On Wednesday last*, from Macquarie Street, *a young magpie*. **1850** *Illustr. Austral. Mag.* (Melbourne) Nov. 329, I was awoke by the warble of the magpie. **1886** W.J. WOODS *Visit to Vic.* 24 The Magpie is very amusing—fussy, inquisitive, impudent, and self-sufficient as an auctioneer. **1891** G.J. BROINOWSKI *Birds of Aust.* VI. Pl. 2, The different species of this genus (*Cracticus*) and of the *Gymnohinae* [*sic*] are very generally confused with one another, and go by the broad appellation of 'Magpie'. **1914** T.C. WOLLASTON *Spirit of Child* 43 Our glorious Magpie stands as the symbol of our love of liberty and manly contest. **1931** M.M. BANKS *Memories Pioneer Days Qld.* 74 The magpie, a shrike thrush by classification, is, like the butcher bird, also pied black and white. **1962** E. LANE *Mad as Rabbits* 9 Jack had an encounter with a fierce nesting magpie that left a long scar on the top of his head. **1983** J. HEPWORTH *More Birds & Beasties Aust.*, Contralto with the brightest beak, Magpie's voice is one in a million. No poofy trill or silvery squeak, But a fullblooded bush carillon!

2. *transf.* Used *attrib.* in the names of birds having black and white plumage: **magpie goose,** the large bird *Anseranas semipalmata*, occurring near fresh water in n. Aust. and New Guinea, having a resonant honking call and the male a conspicuous knob on the head; *pied goose*, see PIED; SEMIPALMATED GOOSE; **lark,** the common, widespread bird *Grallina cyanoleuca* of Aust. and New Guinea having a loud, piping call and building a mud nest; *mud lark*, see MUD 1; *Murray magpie*, see MURRAY 2; PEEWEE 1; *pied grallina*, see PIED.

1861 'OLD BUSHMAN' *Bush Wanderings* 70 As the name denotes, the colour of the **magpie-goose** is pied, dull black and white. **1896** F.G. AFLALO *Sketch Nat. Hist. Aust.* 99 As *Chenopis* is no true swan, so is *Anseranas melanoleuca* no true goose, though it goes by that name. . . I have shot this 'semi-palmated' bird, known locally as 'Magpie Goose', in Cleveland Bay and further north. **1937** *Bulletin* (Sydney) 18 Aug. 21/3 Magpie geese in the N.T. coastal country roost on trees when the 'wet' season is at hand. **1963** D. ATTENBOROUGH *Quest under Capricorn* 30 Nowhere in the world, except in tropical Australia and New Guinea, can you see magpie geese in any number. **1975** K. WILLEY *Ghosts of Big Country* 121 Here is the home and one of the last refuges of the king of Australian wildfowl, the black and white magpie goose. **1843** J. GOULD *Birds of Aust.* (1848) II. Pl. 54, *Grallina australis* . . **Magpie Lark,** Colonists of New South Wales. **1857** W. HOWITT *Tallangetta* I. 18 Then flew past a number of those beautiful black-and-white dove-like birds, called magpie larks. **1870** E.B. KENNEDY *Four Yrs. in Qld.* 117 The magpie-lark is about the size of a thrush, black and white in colour, and whistles beautifully. **1917** *Bulletin* (Sydney) 14 June 24/4 Doesn't he know that the magpie-lark and the peewit are one and the same? **1931** M.M. BANKS *Memories Pioneer Days Qld.* 73 The magpie-lark is a frequenter of gardens in every part of Australia. **1964** M. SHARLAND *Territory of Birds* 37 Lured with cheese, scraps of cake, and a dish of water, the thirty Magpie-larks that gathered near my door . . showed many individual variations in the amount of white or black through their bodies and wings.

3. A nickname for a South Australian. Also *attrib.*

1915 *Truth* (Sydney) 10 Oct. 6/16 *Magpie magsters.*—South Australian Wowserdom worked itself into a fine frenzy. **1955** N. PULLIAM *I traveled Lonely Land* 381 *Magpie*, a person from South Australia.

4. HALF-CASTE.

1982 *Austral.* (Sydney) 30 Aug. 9/7 'It's difficult if you're a 'magpie'. You cop it from both sides,' he says.

B. *adj. Obs.*

1. Of cattle: two-coloured (one colour usu. being white).

1824 *Hobart Town Gaz.* 12 Nov., Impounded, at Iverdon, a magpie Cow, branded S R on the off hip. **1829** *Launceston Advertiser* 2 Nov. 1 Impounded, at Perth . . two three-year-old Steers, one jet black, the other black and white magpie. **1833** *Ibid.* 17 Oct. 3 Impounded . . one brown magpie cow . . one black magpie bullock. **1847** *Port Phillip Gaz.* 8 May 1 Impounded at the Kalkallo Pound . . blue magpie cow. **1884** 'R. BOLDREWOOD' *Old Melbourne Memories* 45, I missed a magpie steer to-day, and I didn't see that fat yellow cow with the white flank.

2. Of convict clothing: black and yellow (see quot. 1850). Also as quasi-*n.*

1841 B. WAIT *Lett. from Van Dieman's Land* (1843) 350 Near the dock, you cannot but observe a mass of beings, dressed in magpie (black and yellow) clothes, with chains coupling the legs together. **1846** L.W. MILLER *Notes of Exile Van Dieman's Land* 349 He then ordered them to be dressed in *magpie* (as a punishment for *our* absconding). **1850** W. GATES *Recoll. Van Dieman's Land* 112 The day after the capture of our friends, we were ordered to be dressed in 'magpie' and changed to another station. . . This 'magpie' suit is intended for chain gangs and doubly convicted prisoners, and is ordered by government as a badge of the deeper disgrace. It is composed of black and yellow cloth, of the same quality as the grey. The left side of the front part of the body, with the front of the left arm and leg, together with the right side of the back part of the body were yellow, whilst the remainder was black. **1865** J.F. MORTLOCK *Experiences of Convict* 105, I . . having made for Hobart Town, knocked at the barrack gate and reported myself a 'bolter'. . . They immediately ordered me to put on a vile, dirty, coarse threadbare cloth suit (no lining, no drawers) of yellow and black, called 'magpie'.

magsman. [Survival of Br. slang *magsman* swindler: see OED.]

1. A confidence trickster.

1877 *Vagabond Ann.* 136 You have to be a bit of a magsman, a pincher, a picker-up, a flatcatcher, a bester. **1888** *Illustr. Austral. News* (Melbourne) 28 Apr. 75/4 The puzzles were of a character that should prove a source of wealth to a smart magsman. **1913** J.B. CASTIEAU *Reminisc. Detective-Inspector Christie* 35 If you do not clear out of this at once I'll 'vag' you, as I know you are a magsman. **1948** R.A. PEPPERALL *Emigrant to Aust.* 142 Bert soon lived down his little affair with the 'Magsman' as Australians term the confidence trickster. **1971** G. MORGAN *We are borne On* 358 A good magsman can draw money at any time from the racing fraternity, often in the way of horse feed or cash, and the good hearted fellow is promised to be told when the good thing is going to win a race. **1975** *Bulletin* (Sydney) 31 May 26/1 My mate was a top-shelf magsman on the phone and could mimic the tone of gruff arrogance . . so characteristic of the cop in my day.

2. A talker; a raconteur.

1935 K. TENNANT *Tiburon* 182 He became very anti-strikers when he discovered that the Magsman was the same Dennis Kelly. **1957** D. NILAND *Call me when Cross turns Over* 68 'He's a quiet one,' Barbie said. 'All right in a dust-up, though.' 'No magsman at all.' **1964** K. WILLEY *Eaters of Lotus* 88 Tex had just challenged all comers for a World Windbagging Championship. He threw down the gauntlet in the public bar after demolishing noted bush magsman Lloyd ('Walkie Talkie') Nelson for the Territory crown. **1974** F. MOORHOUSE *Electrical Experience* 121 Now he would dearly love to be a Bachelor of Arts or a Bachelor of Science. He had been a real magsman in his day. Nothing more than a magsman.

mahleesh /ma'liʃ/, *int.* Also **mahlish, maleesch, malish.** [f. the colloq. (Egyptian) Arabic.] See quot. 1962.

1918 H. DINNING *Byways on Service* 124 If you missed, a consolatory *Malish*! (never mind). **1919** O. HOGUE *Cameliers* 116 The word cannot be translated into English. The nearest approach is 'What matter'. So in days to come Australian settlers, viewing the devastation brought by fires and floods and drought, will grin and exclaim, 'Maleesch.' **1944** L. GLASSOP *We were Rats* 138 Oh well, *mahlish*! We'll get no promotion this side of the Ocean, so cheer up, my lads, bless 'em all. **1962** A. SEYMOUR *One Day of Yr.* 18 Mahleesh. Expression Dad brought back from the Middle East. 'Never mind.' 'Forget it.'

mahogany. [Transf. use of *mahogany* the tree *Swietenia.*]

1. Any of several tree species, esp. of the genus *Eucalyptus* (fam. Myrtaceae), incl. JARRAH, yielding a hard, usu. reddish-brown, timber; the wood of these trees. Also *attrib.*, and with distinguishing epithet, as **red, swamp, white** (see under first element).

1792 *Hist. Rec. N.S.W.* (1893) II. 799 A kind of pine and mahogany, so heavy that scarce either of them will swim. **1805** J.H. TUCKEY *Acct. Voyage to establish Colony Port Phillip* 226 Mahogany runs good to three feet, and by its texture can scarcely be known from the mahogany of Jamaica. **1829** R. MUDIE *Picture of Aust.* 131 *Eucalyptus robusta* is by much the largest of the species. . . This tree has sometimes got the name of mahogany, though it has no relation to the mahogany tree of America in its habits, the colour, or the quality of its timber. **1830** *Extracts Lett. Swan River* 31 Jan. III. 11 The woods are very extensive and contain a large quantity of good timber; the white gum, blue gum, and a very fine species of mahogany, which we use to build with. **1840** *S. Austral. Rec.* (London) 22 Feb. 60 The mahogany is hard, dark, and heavy, and better adapted for the beams and flooring of houses than for furniture. **1853** J. SHERER *Gold Finder Aust.* 176 The Diggings are all covered with wood, fair mahogany. **1880** J. BONWICK *Resources Qld.* 83 The Mahogany of Rockhampton, *Tristania*, has a hard, tough, red wood, with soft bark used sometimes for candles. **1904** J.H. MAIDEN *Notes on Commercial Timbers N.S.W.* 16 Red Mahogany (*Eucalyptus resinifera*) . . is the timber called mahogany, because it reminded the early settlers of the Central American wood. **1918** G. WHITE *Thirty Yrs. Tropical Aust.* 18 The scrub is composed of magnificent trees, whose straight stems run up one hundred feet or more without a branch: cedar, kauri, mahogany. **1948** P.J. HURLEY *Red Cedar* 28 Tall Water Gums . . reared their white arms loftily above lesser stringies, mahoganies. **1972** B. FULLER *West of Bight* 124 The first flour mills in Perth were built entirely of jarrah. . . The pioneers were so impressed by the tree that they called it 'mahogany', a name retained until the early 1860s, when it became known by its Aboriginal name. **1986** *Parkwatch* (Vic. Nat. Parks Assoc.) Mar. 13 Cape Conran is a popular destination where people enjoy camping amongst banksias and mahogany gums 100 metres from an excellent beach.

2. Special Comb. **mahogany beef** (or **shavings**), jerked beef.

1846 *Cumberland Times* (Parramatta) 10 Jan. 4/4 As he had some old mahogany beef, and the other flour, a fire was soon made, a Royal George slung to boil the beef; some flour rubbed up, and leather jackets made. **1922** B. THREADGILL *S. Austral. Land Exploration* 70 The party were without flour, depending on native vegetables, 'mahogany shavings' (jerked beef), and the small amount of euro they could kill.

maidenhair. [Transf. use of *maidenhair* a fern having fine hair-like stalks and delicate fronds.] Any of several ferns of the genus *Adiantum* (fam. Adiantaceae), incl. the European maidenhair *A. capillus-veneris* of scattered parts of mainland Aust., but referring more commonly to other species, esp. *A. aethiopicum*. Also *attrib.*, esp. as **maidenhair fern.**

1867 *Lang. Native Flowers Tas.* 5 Maiden Hair Fern . . concealed love. **1888** *Proc. Linnean Soc. N.S.W.* III. 361 *Adiantum aethiopicum* . . Common 'Maiden-hair fern'. **1893** R. RICHARDSON *Willow & Wattle* 11 Knee-deep lies the maiden hair Which no garden craft hath planted there. **1930** V. PALMER *Passage* (1957) 15 Signboards with announcements of subdivisional sales shooting up daily from sandhills and maidenhair gullies. **1984** E. WALLING *On Trail Austral. Wildflowers* 12 Maiden-hair fern appears in beautiful and extensive patches of pale green, with shining black stems gleaming through the delicate leaves.

maiden's blush. [Transf. use of *maiden's blush* a delicate pink colour.]

1. The small rainforest tree *Sloanea australis* (fam. Elaeocarpaceae), occurring from n.e. Qld. to s.e. N.S.W., often along creeks and in gullies; the wood of the tree.

1884 A. NILSON *Timber Trees N.S.W.* 54 *E[chinocarpus] australis*—Maiden's Blush—A beautiful tree, sometimes attaining a height of 150 feet. . . *Timber* of a delicate rosy tint, close-grained, but soft and easily wrought. **1904** J.H. MAIDEN *Notes on Commercial Timbers N.S.W.* 29 Maiden's Blush (*Echinocarpus australis* . .), a soft, durable brush timber, useful for turnery and ordinary carpentry purposes, it is of a delicate rosy colour when freshly cut. **1936** E. MCDONNELL *Land of Budgeriga* 48 Where 'maiden's blush' and wattle tree Threw shadows in propinquity. **1985** N. & H. NICHOLSON *Austral. Rainforest Plants.* 59 Maiden's Blush . . was named by timber-workers for the colour of its heartwood. . . The young toothed leaves are a beautiful pink, another possible reason for the name.

2. See quots.

1941 S.J. BAKER *Pop. Dict. Austral. Slang* 45 *Maiden's blush*, ginger beer and raspberry. **1966** G.W. TURNER *Eng. Lang. in Aust. & N.Z.* 116 *Maiden's blush*, a drink, either of port and lemonade or rum and raspberry. **1970** W. FEARN-WANNAN *Austral. Folklore* 32 Usually in old-time bushmen's meaning, a drink of rum and raspberry is a Barmaid's Blush. This drink is also known as a 'Maiden's Blush'.

mail, *n.*[1] Used *attrib.* in Special Comb. **mail car,** a motor vehicle used primarily for the conveyance of the mail; **change,** a staging-post on a mail route; also *attrib.*; **driver,** the driver of a horse-drawn vehicle in which the mail is conveyed; **man** [also Br. and U.S. but recorded earliest in Aust.], one who conveys the mail (see quot. 1977); **track,** the route by which the mail is delivered.

[N.Z. **1942** *N.Z. New Writing* I. 55 Martin heard the **mailcar** go past.] **1945** C. MANN *River* 4 Fish . . sent by the mail-car up to town. **1905** *Bulletin* (Sydney) 31 Aug. 16/2 'Crooked Mick', the **mail-change** groom at the Seventeen Mile, had an old 'oss. **1906** *Ibid.* (Sydney) 25 Jan. 39/3 The only habitations are little bark shanties, or tents, called 'mail changes', mostly in charge of hatters, where one gets nothing but a pipe of tobacco or the loan of a firestick to light up with. **1914** C.H.S. MATTHEWS *Bill* 38 About once in thirty miles or so there was a 'mail change', where dad changed his horses for fresh ones. **1935** R.B. PLOWMAN *Boundary Rider* 224 To harness and yoke them in was a task for a superman, for his assistants at the mail-changes were only partly civilized black boys. **1944** *Bulletin* (Sydney) 30 Aug. 13/4 This superb drover worked his epic way till he reached a mail-change on the Ayrshire Downs road, whence he collected a few monkey conductors suffering a holiday. **1891** E.H. HALLACK *W.A. & Yilgarn Goldfields* 15 The part of the track most dreaded by teamsters and **maildrivers.** **1891** 'SMILER' *Wanderings Simple Child* (ed. 3) 33 If mortal skill and pluck and energy can pull a man through difficulties and dangers by road, I'll back the mail-drivers of the Barrier Ranges against all comers, Yankees or what not. **1849** J.P. TOWNSEND *Rambles & Observations N.S.W.* 161 The road . . crosses a height, where it is usual for the '**mail-man**' to pull up his vehicle. **1864** *Bell's Life in Sydney* 21 May 3/1 The mailman, whose duty it was to meet the Wagga Wagga mail at Cootamundry, from Murrumburrah, got drunk. **1911** *Emu* XI. 110 The mailman, Mr F.H. Gillings, arranged to drive me to my destination. **1977** W.A. WINTER-IRVING *Bush Stories* 98 Our only reliable contact with the outside world was the mailman. He was paid by the government to carry the letters; but he also carried a hell of a lot of other things, for which he was subsidised by us and the other people on his round. He would bring flour, potatoes, onions, bags of loose salt to rub into the meat to keep it fresh, pumpkins, sugar, loaves of bread, and barbed wire. He even carried a block of ice a metre long, wrapped in newspaper and stuffed into a sack. . . He also brought a private supply of illegal goods such as rum, gin, beer [etc.]. **1924** H.E. RIEMANN *Nor'-West o' West* 96 He could . . follow the creek until he came to the Nanunabberra River **mail-track.** **1940** G. MORPHETT *Simple Story Rural Dev.* 2 We lived four miles away from the mail track.

mail, *n.*[2] [See BUSH TELEGRAPH and MULGA WIRE.] Information; rumour.

1966 S.J. BAKER *Austral. Lang.* (ed. 2) 77 Along with the variations *mulga mail* (or *wire*), it [*sc.* mulga] can mean a source of rumour. **1975** *Bulletin* (Sydney) 26 Apr. 44/2 His mail was that if I didn't weigh in soon I'd be gathered for sure. **1983** *Sun-Herald* (Sydney) 27 Mar. 66/6 The mail is the Minister for Sport, *Mike Cleary*, is wary of new betting introductions following footie flop. **1984** *Age* (Melbourne) 19 Sept. 38/2, I had never heard of the horse before. I didn't receive any special 'mail' on it, but I've gone to races all my life—money speaks all languages.

mai-mai, var. MIA-MIA.

mainland. The continent of Australia, as opposed to any of the offshore islands and esp. Tasmania. Also *attrib.*

1829 Macquarie Harbour Commandant's Letter-Bk. 20 Aug., One of the gangs sent to the mainland opposite the Settl[t] to cut Timber. **1843** *Adelaide Observer* 26 Aug. 5/1 We understand that Government have it in contemplation to appoint an Official Resident at Kangaroo Island. . . It is well-known that the Island is becoming a place of resort for whaling ships, and that, from its contiguity with the main land, it affords a too ready facility for contraband trading. **1847** G.F. ANGAS *Savage Life & Scenes* I. 183 Nearly opposite to our anchorage was the settlement of Kingscote, where the South Australian Company first established themselves, before they crossed to the mainland. **1878** G. WALCH *Australasia* 12 It seems to scowl in its solitude like an outcast from the mainland. **1910** *Huon Times* (Franklin) 19 Feb. 2/6 They only had to look at the experience of the Mainland States in that regard. **1917** *Ibid.* (Franklin) 6 Nov. 5/2 The volunteer crews of the boats . . kept our Island State linked up with the Mainland. **1926** A.S. LE SOUEF et al. *Wild Animals Australasia* 17 The marsupial wolf and the Tasmanian devil . . have disappeared from the mainland. **1949** D. WALKER *We went to Aust.* 208 Tasmanians always refer to the rest of Australia as 'mainland' with an almost imperceptible lift of the nose. **1962** J.T. LANG *Great Bust* 310 The wowser element on the mainland was always trying to block Tattersalls. **1978** L. HORSPHOL *Turn down Empty Glass* 32 He suggested that I pay a visit to the Cadbury-Fry chocolate factory, posing as a mainland tourist.

Hence **mainlander** *n.*, one who dwells on the Australian mainland.

1910 *Advocate* (Burnie) 8 Jan. 3/2 A number of mainlanders. **1914** HOGAN & GYE *Tight Little Island* 55 There is a strange thing about the Island girl—she almost invariably marries a mainlander. The reason is this—The mainlander is usually a man with his eye to business. **1970** K.E.C. GRAVES *Third Chance* 33 'Comes from over the strait, I believe.' 'Ah! Smart mainlander, perhaps!' **1974** *Bulletin* (Sydney) 7 Dec. 9/1 Tasmanians are known to have this paranoia about 'mainlanders' and anybody north of the Bass Strait is one of those. **1984** *Examiner* (Launceston) 12 Sept. 1 (*heading*) Breweries to spend $5m. to ward off mainlanders.

maisonette. [Transf. use of *maisonette* a small house.] A semi-detached house. Also **maisonette house,** and *attrib.*

1949 *Argus* (Melbourne) 4 June 17/6 Brick Maisonette, mod. 6 rms. in each. **1971** *Bulletin* (Sydney) 8 May 25/3 Joined or semi-detached houses are called 'maisonette houses' in Queensland and South Australia and 'duplexes' in Western Australia and the Northern Territory. **1982** *Advertiser* (Adelaide) 8 Aug. 33/5 Lockleys $46,500 Maisonette style strata unit. Ent. hall/sunroom. Spacious lounge, 2 b.r., large kitchen, laundry.

major. *Australian National Football.* A goal, scored when the ball is kicked between the goal-posts and earning six points.

1951 *Football Rec.* (Melbourne) 8 Sept. 18 They opened with four behinds, and then rattled on sixteen majors. **1960** *N.T. News* (Darwin) 8 Mar. 10/1 Saints . . kicked only two majors and four behinds. **1980** *Ibid.* 19 Jan. 8/5 Tahs swung forward for Vierk to snap another from a sharp angle and at last post a major from a free.

Major Mitchell, *n.*: see MAJOR MITCHELL COCKATOO.

Major-Mitchell, *v. Obs.* [f. the name of T.L. *Mitchell* (1792–1855), Surveyor-General of N.S.W. and explorer.] *intr.* To pursue a zig-zag course, orig. as a method of exploration; to meander; to become lost. Also **Major-Mitchelled** *ppl.a.*, lost.

1900 *Bulletin* (Sydney) 28 July 14/4, I don't mean 'bushman' in its ordinary acceptation; that term is applied to timber-getters in general, except when tracking, mustering, overlanding, or Major-Mitchelling is the subject. **1922** R.L. JACK *Northmost Aust.* I. 295 The Brothers . . after majormitchelling to the north, north-east and north-west, returned on the 27th, having failed to find the Lynd River. **1934** *Bulletin* (Sydney) 2 May 21/2, I don't know what originated the expression, and I don't know if Mitchell himself warranted it; but to Major-Mitchell meant to work in zig-zags, to poke about a lot, avoid a straight line, and, in some cases, a man who was lost was referred to as being 'Major-Mitchelled'. **1951** E. HILL *Territory* 3 The bagmen of today, the 'old death-adders Major Mitchelling around' were the young men of yesterday. **1981** *Bulletin* (Sydney) 1 Sept. 97/3 'To Major Mitchell' is 'to ride a zig-zag course across country'. A phrase of Australian origin. A nice image, but I don't believe it has been used in this country during the present century.

Major Mitchell cockatoo. [As prec.] The predom. pink and white cockatoo *Cacatua leadbeateri*, having a scarlet crest with a central yellow band, and occurring in arid and semi-arid Aust.; LEADBEATER'S COCKATOO; *pink cockatoo*, see PINK *a.*; WEE JUGGLER. Also **Major Mitchell cocky, Major Mitchell's cockatoo,** and *ellipt*, as **Major Mitchell.**

[**1838** T.L. MITCHELL *Three Exped. Eastern Aust.* II. 62 This day, we saw for the first time on the Kalâre, the red top cockatoo (Plycotolophus Leadbeateri).] **1898** E.E. MORRIS *Austral Eng.* 280 *Major Mitchell, n.* vernacular name of a species of Cockatoo. **1927** *Bulletin* (Sydney) 3 Mar. 24/2, I brought a Major Mitchell cockie from the bush and put him in an enclosure. **1945** A.W. UPFIELD *Death of Swagman* 30 A Major Mitchell cockatoo spread its multicoloured crest. **1950** *Bulletin* (Sydney) 27 Dec. 12/3 In some localities the Major Mitchell cockatoo receives its correct name, in others it is a 'wee juggler'. **1962** B.W. LEAKE *Eastern Wheatbelt Wildlife* 78 The Major Mitchell with its delicate white, pink, and red colouring is probably the most beautiful of all the Australian cockatoos. **1973** R. ROBINSON *Drift of Things* 435 You could watch daylight coming . . gradually being suffused with rose like the wings and breast of a Major Mitchell cockatoo. **1982** *Ecos* xxxiii. 13/1 Major Sir Thomas Livingstone Mitchell, the explorer whose enthusiasm for the pink cockatoo led to its being popularly known as Major Mitchell's cockatoo.

Major's line. *Hist.* The route followed by the explorer T.L. Mitchell on his return to Sydney from Portland Bay in 1836.

1853 T.F. BRIDE *Lett. Victorian Pioneers* (1898) 52 We followed the track of those before us . . and in a short distance came on to the Major's line, which was easily recognised at that time. **1883** E.M. CURR *Recoll. Squatting Vic.* 22 The 'Major's line' is a term signifying the track, or line of road, formed by the drays of Major (afterwards Sir Thomas) Mitchell in his explorations. In some localities the track or road which his drays left behind is called 'the Major' to this day. **1886** *Once a Month* (Melbourne) Mar. 233 Settlers began to arrive along the 'Major's line' from the 'Sydney side'—the Major's line being the track by which Major Mitchell returned to Sydney from Portland Bay.

makarrata /mækəˈratə/. Also **makharata, makkarata.** [a. Yolŋu sub-group *makarrata*.] An Aboriginal ceremonial ritual symbolizing the restoration of peace after a dispute; an agreement.

1946 D. Barr *Warrigal Joe* 105 Dan went on to describe the 'makkarata' of Arnhem Land tribes... 'It's a sort of ceremonial ordeal, this makkarata business, and there are rules which all must obey.' **1979** A. Wells *Forests are their Temples* 50 The ancient ceremony of makharata began with calm deliberation. **1980** *Canberra Times* 5 July 2/2 Makarrata, described by the National Aboriginal Conference subcommittee on the subject as 'a coming together after a struggle'. The subcommittee is likely to be right about this meaning because one of its members, Mr Peter Minyipirrwuy, comes from Elcho island [*sic*] in north-east Arnhem Land, where the word is used.

make, *v.*[1] *Mining.* [Spec. use of *make* to extend: see OED *v.*[1] 73 b.]

a. *intr.* Of a mineral deposit: to occur.

1850 *S. Austral. Register* (Adelaide) 14 Nov. 2/5 The ore makes in small bunches or lumps and then disappears. **1863** J.B. Austin *Mines S.A.* 85 It is not improbable that the lodes turning out so well in the Talisker Mine may make in depth in the ground worked by the Campbell's Creek Company. **1880** 'Erro' *Squattermania* 183 He talked largely about the direction of the compass in which the reefs ran, their 'pinching out and making' again, their 'backs' with the dip of their inclination, etc. **1887** H.Y.L. Brown *Rec. of Mines S.A.* 38 The lode has twice pinched out and made again. **1888** *Tasmanian* (Launceston) 1 Sept. 21/3 While writing one of the men informed me the gold had made again in the shaft in flat. **1932** I.L. Idriess *Prospecting for Gold* 189 A patch of golden stone may 'make' anywhere at all in a reef. Often you known nothing about it until your pick 'breaks' gold.

b. *trans.* To yield (a mineral). Also *intr.* See also *to make values* Values.

1932 I.L. Idriess *Prospecting for Gold* 190 A reef may 'make' gold when it strikes a change of country. *Ibid.* 236 Be very careful when on potch and colour—at any moment they may 'make' into a 'stone'. **1939** [see Values].

Hence **making** *vbl. n.*, an occurrence of ore.

1862 J.A. Patterson *Gold Fields Vic.* 17 At Poverty Reef and Nuggetty Reef (Maldon), the stone has been found, not in one unbroken mass, but in separate 'makings'. *Ibid.* 243 'Pockets', 'bunches', or 'makings', as they are variously termed, are perpendicularly placed with relation to each other.

make, *v.*[2] *trans.* To initiate (an Aboriginal male) ceremonially into manhood. Esp. in the phr. **to make a (young) man.** Also as **(young) man-making** *vbl. n.*

1856 J. Bonwick *W. Buckley* 77 Man making is attended with several mysterious and often torturing ceremonies. **1857** —— *Early Days Melbourne* 38 Their ceremonies of man making, when lads are about 14 years old, are similar to those of the American Indians. **1899** *Bulletin* (Sydney) 12 Aug. 14/2 Hardly think 'F.A.R.'.. could really have seen an aboriginal 'man-making' ceremony. **1930** J.S. Litchfield *Far-North Memories* 126, I told Marion how keen I felt to see the 'making-young-man' ceremonial. **1947** W.E. Harney *Brimming Billabongs* 60 It was at the trading time that my uncle gave the sign that I was ready to be made a young man. **1961** *Oceania* XXXII. 82 When a boy reached puberty.. the initiative to 'make him a man' might be taken by one or more of several classes of men. **1979** *Aboriginal Hist.* III. 65 The first of my examples was compared by the late Jack King, father of Archie King, the lone survivor of those who were 'made men' in 1914. **1982** *Ibid.* VI. 10 The most intense period of contact with other Ngiyampaa groups.. came at the end of Eliza's childhood when the last.. 'school for making men' was held in bull oak country in 1914. **1985** I. White et al. *Fighters & Singers* 5 We were following the business... We were making young mans.

make, *n. Mining.* [f. prec.] A deposit or pocket of ore.

1889 *Braidwood Dispatch* 30 Nov. 2/4 Rich gold has again been struck.. and there are indications that the new make of gold has.. been reached. **1887** H.Y.L. Brown *Rec. of Mines S.A.* 36 The fourth lode is similar in character to the third lode. Its features.. indicate that it and the foregoing ones are 'makes' of the same great lode. **1919** *Guide Bk. Prospectors N.S.W.* (ed. 2) 14 Attention is chiefly directed to the mining for Wolfram, which occurs in 'bunches' or 'makes'.

makharata, var. Makarrata.

makings, *pl.* [U.S.: see OEDS *making, vbl. sb.*[1] 8 b.] Paper and tobacco as materials for rolling a cigarette; a hand-made cigarette.

1924 *Aust.* (Sydney) Apr. 8 Drawing the 'makings' from my pocket, I proceeded.. to roll a cigarette. **1935** K.L. Smith *Sky Pilot Arnhem Land* 44 'I say, old man, could you give me the makings?'.. 'Why, sure! I thought you had given up smoking?' **1944** *Aust. Week-End Bk.* 108 Winters was seen smoking a Wog 'makings', which is the lowest form in which tobacco can be introduced to the human lungs. **1958** H.D. Williamson *Sunlit Plain* 17 'Got the makings on you?' Eddie.. handed over a tin of tobacco and papers. **1964** E. Lane *Our Uncle Charlie* 114 He rolled his own, and was always cadging 'the makings'. **1981** P. Corris *White Meat* 34 We drank some beer. I asked Sunday if this was his local. He said it was and borrowed the makings from me. He rolled a cigarette.

makkarata, var. Makarrata.

maleesch, var. Mahleesh.

malga, var. Malka, Mulga *n.*[1]

malgun /mælˈgun, mælˈgʌn/. *Obs.* [a. Dharuk *malgun.*] The ceremonial amputation of the first two joints from the fourth finger of the left hand of a female Aboriginal infant: see quot. 1878.

1798 D. Collins *Acct. Eng. Colony N.S.W.* I. 553 Mutilation of the two first joints of the little finger of the left hand... They name it Mal-gun. **1847** G.F. Angas *Savage Life & Scenes* II. 225 Whilst still infants, the females undergo amputation of the two first joints of the little finger of the left hand. This operation is called 'Malgun'. **1878** R.B. Smyth *Aborigines of Vic.* I. p. xxiii, The practice of mutilating the body prevails in all parts of Australia. In New South Wales, at an early age, the women are subjected to an uncommon mutilation of the first two joints of the little finger of the left hand. This operation is performed when they are very young, and is done under an idea that these little joints of the left hand are in the way when they wind their fishing lines over the hand. This amputation is termed *Malgun.*

malish, var. Mahleesh.

malka /ˈmælkə, ˈmʌlkə/. Also **malga** and now usu. **mulga.** [a. Wemba *malga.*] An Aboriginal shield: see quot. 1856.

1839 T.L. Mitchell *Three Exped. Eastern Aust.* (rev. ed.) II. 269 The malga is a weapon.. but that with which these natives were provided somewhat resembled a pick-axe with one half broken off. **1852** J. Morgan *Life & Adventures W. Buckley* 66 Shields, which they call malka, are used very dexterously in warding off blows from the waddie. **1856** J. Bonwick *W. Buckley* 71 Buckley tells us that the Yarra Blacks called.. the two shields, Malka and Seaugwell... The Malka, to ward off blows, is two or three feet long, and is provided with a handle. **1867** G.G. McCrae *Mamba* 9 And club and malka's embryo shape, Seem'd longing for red wounds to gape. **1878** R.B. Smyth *Aborigines of Vic.* I. p. xlix, The *Mulga*—the wooden shield—is a defence when attack is made by the *Kud-jee-run* or the *Leon-ile. Ibid.* 291 He armed himself, and approached Charley's mia-mia, waddy and malka in hand. **1889** J.H. Maiden *Useful Native Plants Aust.* 349 'Mulga' is the name of a long narrow shield of wood, made by the aboriginals out of Acacia wood. **1944** C. Fenner *Mostly Austral.* 81 From the mulga the blacks made a special implement of war, the mulga, from which the plant got its name.

mallee /ˈmæli/. [a. Wuywurung *mali.*]

1. a. Any of many trees of the genus *Eucalyptus* (fam. Myrtaceae), characteristically small and having several stems usu. arising from a lignotuber, as *E. dumosa, E. socialis* and *E. oleosa*; the wood of these trees. **b.** A vegetation community in drier Aust., characterized by the presence of mallee eucalypts. Also *attrib.*, esp. as **mallee scrub.**

1845 *Standard* (Melbourne) 7 June 2/6 The stock.. are with all possible expedition driven into an almost impenetrable scrub, termed by the natives 'Malley'. **1847** *Port Phillip Herald* 16 Mar. 2/5 The place of habitation of this interesting reptile [*sc.* the Mindai] is the Marlis or as it is perhaps more properly called in Mr Ham's new chart—the Mallee Scrub. **1848** W. Westgarth *Aust. Felix* 27 The Wimmera.. traverses a region of sand and heath, succeeded by jungle and *mallee* scrub... [*Note*] Eucalyptus dumosa. **1859** P. Just *Aust.* 191 The men carry neither spears nor waddies; but each has several yamsticks made of mallee. **1886** P. Clarke *'New Chum' in Aust.* 195 This mallee scrub is one of the worst features of Australian scenery. **1896** B. Spencer *Rep. Horn Sci. Exped. Central Aust.* I. 59 For the first time also we met with *Eucalyptus gamophylla*, one of the Mallee gums, that is, those which have a bole or bossy stem often not conspicuous above the ground from which arise a number of small branches. **1920** Baker & Smith *Research on Eucalypts* (ed. 2) 185 The term 'Mallee' is applied in Australia to those Eucalypts which differ in their mode of growth from other species, by sending out a number of small stems from an expanded root-stock. **1926** A.A.B. Apsley *Amateur Settlers* 46 Mallee is a eucalypt shrub, which grows in this dry country. **1944** C. Fenner *Mostly Austral.* 90 Jack has gone to the mallee, And Mary, she's gone too. They're going to cut down mallee scrub, And live on kangaroo. **1955** 'M. Hill' *Land nearest Stars* 182 This—bush? This withering grass and miserable, sparse malley scrub. **1962** E. Lane *Mad as Rabbits* 31 Here he was, hitting a baby rabbit on the head with a mallee-stick and thinking nothing of it. **1974** N.B. Tindale *Aboriginal Tribes Aust.* 62 The aborigines of the mallee scrub belt.. were collectively known by the Wotjobaluk of the Wimmera as Malikuunditj. It is derived from a species of *Eucalyptus*, generally *E. oleosa*, the water mallee. **1979** Douglas & Heathcote *Far Cry* 18 The chooks were allowed to run free and nested in a big old mallee-gum in the 'garden'. **1981** G.M. Cunningham et al. *Plants Western N.S.W.* 530 Yorrell.. usually a mallee with many fine stems, less commonly a tree.

2. Any of the semi-arid areas of N.S.W., S.A., W.A., and esp. Vic., the principal natural vegetation of which is mallee scrub. Also *attrib.*, esp. as **mallee country, desert, district, land.**

1851 *Empire* (Sydney) 13 Feb. 3/3 The flock masters in the Mallee country.. are compelled to move their flocks. **1854** E.S. Parker *Aborigines of Aust.* 12 The terms *Mallegoondeet* and *Millegoondeet* are very precise in their application, as indicating the men of the *Malle* country, or the inhabitants of the banks of the Murray, which is known for a very considerable portion of its stream, by the native name of *Mille.* **1881** G. Walch *Vic.* 125 At Bael-Bael.. the mallee and rabbit country commences. **1890** *Illustr. Austral. News* (Melbourne) 1 Feb. 6/2 The Mallee districts in particular, which are among the earliest in the colony, have come out well with respect to the average yield and the quality of the grain. **1902** *Bulletin* (Sydney) 28 Jan. 14/3 Nobody knows who made the mallee, but the Devil is strongly suspected. **1909** E. Waltham *Life & Labour in Aust.* 143 The usual miserable barren wilderness termed the Mallee country. **1910** 'Yarran' *Mallee* 3 Less than ten years ago the Mallee was considered the danger zone of agricultural settlement in Victoria. **1924** *New Settlers' Handbk. Vic.* 16 Not so long since the Mallee was looked upon as being more or less a desert. **1941** C. Barrett *Aust.* 13 July brings other kinds of wattles into flower: silver mulga in the Mallee [etc.]. **1952** P. Pinney *Road in Wilderness* 69 You think I love that dirty rabble of tin-roofed shanties I was born in, way out in the Mallee? **1962** H.J. Frith *Mallee-Fowl* 63 The spinifex and mallee desert near Mossgiel, New South Wales. **1983** *Bogong* (Canberra) IV. v. 4 The mallee lands are found in the southern parts of Australia, in a broad band stretching from south-western Western Australia to central New South Wales with a break at the Nullarbor plain. In New South Wales the mallee occurs across the central slopes and western plains. **1985** H. Garner *Postcards from Surfers* 15 Auntie Lorna and my father come from the same town, Hopetoun in the Mallee.

3. Used, with reference to eucalypts of mallee regions and elsewhere, to designate the many-stemmed form typical of the mallee eucalypt. Also *attrib.*

1938 C.T. WHITE *Princ. Bot. Qld. Farmers* 65 In some plants such as certain Eucalypts in Western Australia there is a tree form and shrub (mallee) form of the same species. **1956** T.Y. HARRIS *Naturecraft in Aust.* 192 These many-stemmed Eucalypts characteristic of so much of our inland, are known as Mallees; a general term applied to any species of Eucalypt which grows after this fashion. **1969** S. KELLY *Eucalypts* 53 Little sally . . is often a mallee, whereas black sallee is normally a single-stemmed tree. **1972** N. HALL et al. *Use of Trees & Shrubs in Dry Country* 365 Usually in mallee form and 15–25 feet high it [*sc. Eucalyptus behriana*] sometimes grows as a single stem tree up to 35 feet in height.

4. *fig.* Also *attrib.*

1853 MOSSMAN & BANISTER *Aust. Visited & Revisited* 191 The promontory of his nose being only visible through the scrubs which, from his lips downwards to his chin, were impervious. No Leichardt razor had penetrated there; it was all 'Mallee'. **1867** *Pasquin* (London) 16 Nov. 267 Black people disguised and made ridiculous as mallee Christians—half thieves half methodists.

5. In the phr. **fit as a mallee bull,** 'fighting fit'.

1960 *Overland* xvii. 7 'How's Bubby?' 'Fit as a Mallee bull! Got another tooth.' **1966** *R.A.N. News* (Sydney) 27 May 6 The patient is now fit as a malee [*sic*] bull. **1968** D. O'GRADY *Bottle of Sandwiches* 11 Three raw eggs for breakfast, then a quick jog around the park with a coupla jerseys on, and by the time the footy season gets under way you'll be as fit as a mallee bull. **1981** *Sun-Herald* (Sydney) 14 June 151/4 He looked as fit as a Mallee bull.

6. In the names of birds: **mallee fowl (hen** and formerly **bird)**, the mound-building *Leipoa ocellata*, a mottled grey, brown, and white bird of dry, inland, southern mainland Aust.; GNOW; LEIPOA; LOWAN; *native hen* (b), *native pheasant* (b), see NATIVE *a.* 6 b.; **ringneck (parakeet, parrot),** the parrot *Barnardius barnardi* of e. Aust., a predom. green bird with a green head, blue back, and yellow collar.

1849 [mallee fowl] *Belfast Gaz.* (Port Phillip) 30 Nov. 3/4 Mr White . . has sent to Portland the drawing of 'the Mallee bird', which is peculiar to the Mallee scrub. **1860** G. BENNETT *Gatherings of Naturalist* 174 That elegant creature, the Mallee Bird (*Leipoa ocellata*). **1862** J.A. PATTERSON *Gold Fields Vic.* 15 All between and around is a mass of mallee and whipstick, in the shelter of which that strange bird, the mallee hen, builds her nest from year to year. **1874** R.P. FALLA *Knocking About* (1976) 6 Occasionally the monotony was broken by . . the plaintive cry of the mallee hen. The nests of these birds are most peculiar, they are generally made in a crab-hole and vary from eight to twelve feet in diameter at the base. **1878** R.B. SMYTH *Aborigines of Vic.* I. 346 A beautiful basket (*Mid-jerr*) from the Lower Murray . . is used for carrying the eggs of the *Lowan* (Mallee hen). **1898** W. REDMOND *Shooting Trip* 75 The 'Mallee Hen' is splendid eating, and in appearance is not unlike a hen pheasant. **1901** *Emu* I. 51 In the densest portion of the scrub a Mallee Fowl's egg-mound was discovered. **1929** 'A. RUSSELL' *Bungoona* 74 You're about as cheerful as a Mallee hen with the toothache. **1953** A. RUSSELL *Murray Walkabout* 79 The Australian mallee fowl, that archaic mound-building bird . . is among the bird wonders of the world. **1962** H.J. FRITH *Mallee-Fowl* 4 In this mallee 'scrub' and related areas of the four States, which parts have an annual rainfall of only from five to fifteen inches . . the remarkable mallee-fowl occurs. **1981** B.J. BROCK *Catharsis* 55 Looks like your Mallee Hen's safe, though, And the orchids Now they've made it a park. **1985** *Sydney Morning Herald* 17 Aug. 10/3 Pity the poor, hard-working male mallee fowl, nature's supporter of the feminist cause. **1898 [mallee ringneck]** E.E. MORRIS *Austral Eng.* 341 Mallee Parrakeet—*Platycercus barnardi.* **1912** *Emu* XII. 118 Mallee Parrakeet . . generally becomes vindictive when caged. **1932** H. PRIEST *Call of Bush* 162 Less commonly seen, but no less beautiful, is the Mallee Parrot. . . The scheme of its colouring is green, melting into blue-grey and blue on the wings. **1943** C. BARRETT *Austral. Animal Bk.* 232 The Mallee ringneck . . frequents trees growing along the banks of rivers and creeks. **1984** M. BLAKERS et al. *Atlas Austral. Birds* 278 The Mallee Ringneck occupies the mallee belt of eastern Australia.

7. Comb. in the sense of MALLEE 2: **mallee cocky, farmer, town.**

1902 *Bulletin* (Sydney) 22 Nov. 16/1 You can meet the starved-out **mallee cocky** anywhere in Vic. **1962** *Meanjin* 357 He would never ask the Mallee cockies to help. **1899** *Bulletin* (Sydney) 11 Mar. 14/1 The editor of a way-back Vic. paper was misinformed of the death of a far-out **mallee farmer**, an old identity. **1910** 'YARRAN' *Mallee* 3 To-day the best Mallee farmers are following principles of agriculture as near perfection, when considered in relation to the rainfall and the soil, as any in Europe or America. **1937** E. HILL *Water into Gold* 183 Many of the mallee-farmers made a bigger income clearing their land. **1913** *Bulletin* (Sydney) 9 Oct. 24/3 My brother is a doctor in a **Mallee town.** **1956** *Ibid.* 28 Nov. 13/3 Manangatang (Vic.) . . is the Mallee town . . commonly known as 'The Tang'. **1981** B. GREEN *Small Town Rising* 139 The festival was unusual for a Mallee town.

8. Special Comb. **mallee gate,** a makeshift gate (see quot.); **roller,** a heavy roller used to crush and flatten mallee scrub (see quots. 1926 and 1977); **root,** the large, woody rootstock of any of several species of mallee eucalypt, valued as firewood; **soil,** a brownish, alkaline soil commonly having calcareous concretions in the subsoil; **stump** (usu. *pl.*) *mallee root.*

1964 *Overland* xxx. 21 'D' you know what a **Mallee gate** is, Bob?' 'Yes, it's a short loose panel, just droppers and wires.' **1910** *Jrnl. Dept. Agric. Vic.* 780 **Mallee roller**. . . The accompanying drawings show the usual type of roller in the Mallee districts. The roller itself varies in length from 8 feet to 12 feet, and in diameter from 1 ft. 6 in. to 3 ft. 6 in., and may be either a log, an old boiler, or a specially constructed iron cylinder. **1926** A.A.B. APSLEY *Why & how I went to Aust.* 14 The invention of the mallee roller. . . It was found that by hitching a large iron roller, generally an old boiler with a heavy timber framework, to a team of from ten to twelve horses, the mallee could be crushed and rolled flat on the ground. **1959** C.V. LAWLOR *All This Humbug* 14 The men talked of stump jump ploughs, mallee rollers, ringbarking and other methods of clearing timber. **1977** R.E. GREGORY *Orig. Austral. Inventions* 78 In the case of the mallee and brigalow scrub, it was the Mallee Roller. This was an invention which in its simplest form consisted of a hollow tree trunk with a strong branch through it for an axle. . . These Mallee Rollers were pulled by horses or bullocks and either dragged the trees out . . or smashed them down. **1892** *Bulletin* (Sydney) 27 Aug. 19/1 The two old cronies sat together over a fire of **mallee-root**. **1928** M.E. FULLERTON *Austral. Bush* 172 A Mallee-root fire dullness cannot be, it loosens wit as wine does. **1949** D. WALKER *We went to Aust.* 86 Chopping Mallee root all morning (it is the toughest of all roots in the world, a dark angry red in colour, and if you fail to strike at the right spot, the axe comes back at you as if you had been chopping steel; but it gives out an astonishing heat). **1964** N. PARKER *Mystery aboard Murrabit* 13 Ed was small and gnarled, with unexpected thicks and thins like a mallee root. **1976** B. HUMPHRIES *Dame Edna's Coffee Table Bk.* 96 The mallee root crumbled to ash in the heat As we sat holding hands on the Patterson suite. [*Note*] An ethnic Melbourne fuel. **1920** H.S. TAYLOR *Pioneer Irrigationists' Man.* lxx. 2 The **mallee soils** of Berri may be conveniently grouped into two classes, deep and shallow. **1948** G.W. LEEPER *Introd. Soil Science* 26 Mallee soils and mallee vegetation are not always associated even in Victoria. **1982** BARKER & GREENSLADE *Evol. Flora & Fauna* 3 The variable compaction of calcium carbonate concretions in the so-called 'mallee' soils (calcareous earths . .) can lead to markedly different soil moisture profiles. **1926** A.A.B. APSLEY *Why & how I went to Aust.* 17 **Mallee stumps** which were split with a blunt axe . . make a most excellent fuel. **1976** J. HIBBERD *Three Pop. Plays* 17 Radishes the size of Mallee Stumps.

mallet /ˈmælət/. [a. Nyungar *malat.*] Any of several trees of the genus *Eucalyptus* (fam. Myrtaceae) of s.w. W.A., typically having a bark rich in tannin. Also *attrib.*

1837 G.F. MOORE *Evidences Inland Sea* 49 Here we saw another variety of the *Eucalyptus*, called 'Mallat'. **1897** L. LINDLEY-COWEN *W. Austral. Settler's Guide* 215 Mallet, or fluted gum, or gimlet wood (*E. salubris*). **1922** E. MERYON *Holland's Tank* 153 This mallet bark has brought a lot of lags about the district. **1941** D. O'CALLAGHAN *Long Life Reminisc.* 143 He was the biggest mallet bark stripper at Wagin. **1967** V. SERVENTY *Nature Walkabout* 14 The forest was set aside . . for the mallets, a group of eucalyptus rich in tannins. **1973** G.M. CHIPPENDALE *Eucalypts W. Austral. Goldfields* 91 The term 'mallet' was applied to several tall, smooth-barked trees. **1984** *West Austral.* (Perth) 24 Mar. (Country ed.) 58/2 Mallet wood is one of the strongest and most flexible woods in the country.

Maltese cross. [Transf. use of *Maltese cross* a form of cross.] The right-angled form of the cross-shaped twinned crystals of the mineral staurolite.

1963 *N. Austral. Monthly* Nov. 10 The Staurolites—commonly called 'Maltese Crosses'—are geologically known as 'twin crystals'. **1973** C. AUSTIN *I left my Hat in Andamooka* 142 Were we interested in going out after some 'Maltese crosses'? . . A well-formed ninety degree twin makes a perfect cross and they can be used as attractive charms to hang on a necklace or the tiny ones as earrings.

Maluka /mæˈlukə/. Also **Maluga.** [a. Ngaliwuru *maluga.*] The person in charge; the boss.

1905 MRS A. GUNN *Little Black Princess* 3, I was 'the Missus' from the homestead, and with the Boss, or 'Maluka' (as the blacks always called him), was 'out bush', camping near the river. **1908** —— *We of Never-Never* 340 The tribe mourned for their beloved dead—their dead and ours—our Maluka, 'the best Boss that ever a man struck'. **1928** 'M. MILLS' *Montforts* 238 'You'd better come and see the Maluka.' 'What's that?' ventured Raoul. 'It's aboriginal for headmaster.' **1937** *Oceania* VII. 311 The widespread North Australian term *maluka* or *maluga* implies both status and age. **1954** T. RONAN *Vision Splendid* 55 To the blacks he was just as often Old Man or Maluka as Storekeeper. **1978** R.A.F. WEBB *Brothers in Sun* 173 As one cheerful Aboriginal said, when he saw one of the Brothers scratching his head over a broken-down Gypsy, 'Maluka (Boss), 'im all bugger-up proper. No more little bit, eh!' **1981** *Bulletin* (Sydney) 3 Mar. 35/2 The successful entry was 'The Maluka', the name of a major character in Aeneas Gunn's classic novel 'We of the Never-Never'. It means either 'friend' or 'bossman', and is still a term current in the Territory. **1983** *N.T. News* (Darwin) 1 Jan. 6/4 Anthony Thomas is a quiet self-effacing man. And that is probably the reason the Chief Minister overlooked him in the realignment of responsibilities. A source close to the Maluka told me that he was unaware of the fact that Anthony is a vet.

man. [Spec. use of *man* as the correlative of *master*: see OED *sb.*[1] 10 c.]

1. Used in the possessive pl. in collocations designating accommodation, etc., provided on a rural property for workers (as distinct from that for the owner, manager, etc.).

1826 *Colonial Times* (Hobart) 14 Oct., An Eighty acre Farm, with Cottage, Men's Skilling, a stock-yard and Pig-stye. **1833** *Launceston Advertiser* 3 Oct. 2 On the premises, is a good dwelling house, with barn, men's house, yards, and an excellent garden. **1842** *Colonial Observer* (Sydney) 15 Apr. 960/2 To Be Sold . . a good three-stall stable, hay loft, men's house, piggeries, sheds. **1891** D. FERGUSON *Vicissitudes Bush Life* 3 The men's cook . . had a fire blazing in the hut on my entrance. **1913** W.K. HARRIS *Outback in Aust.* 36 'Government House' hospitality was warmly extended, but in our travelling rig-out we felt more at home in the 'Men's Kitchen', and bunking out under the stars. **1931** A.W. UPFIELD *Sands of Windee* 35 The first place to be inspected was the men's kitchen. **1937** *Bulletin* (Sydney) 28 July 21/4 My mate and I took a job with a cocky in the Bendigo district, and after showing us the 'men's quarters' (a disused calf pen) he took us in to tea consisting of bread, rancid butter and stewed pears.

2. In the collocation **men's hut:** see HUT *n.* 3.

manatee. *Obs.* [Transf. use of *manatee* a large aquatic mammal of the genus *Trichechus*, incl. the West Indian *T. manatus.*] The large, herbivorous marine mammal *Dugong dugon*, the dugong, occurring in coastal waters of n. Aust. and elsewhere.

1698 W. DAMPIER *New Voyage round World* (ed. 3) I. 33 The Manatee . . on the Coast of *New Holland*. This creature is about the bigness of a Horse, and 10 or 12 foot long. **1798** D. COLLINS *Acct. Eng. Colony N.S.W.* I. 409 Mr Cummings . . brought back with him some of the head bones of a marine animal, which . . Captain Paterson, the only naturalist in the country, pronounced to have belonged to the animal described by M. de Buffon, and named by him the Manatee. **1825** B. FIELD *Geogr. Mem. N.S.W.* 291 The manatee, that Dampier describes, was not seen by us, unless on one occasion, when an animal entirely different from the turtle was seen on the surface of the water. **1847** J.D. LANG *Cooksland* 97 The fish, or rather sea-monster, peculiar to Moreton Bay, and the East coast to the northward, is a species of sea-cow or manatee. **1933** C. FENNER *Bunyips & Billabongs* 2 As long ago as 1821 the explorer Hamilton Hume reported the existence in Lake Bathurst of a large animal, supposed .. 'to be a manatee (dugong) or a hippopotamus'.

manchester. [Ellipt. and transf. use of *Manchester wares* cotton goods manufactured at Manchester.] Household linen; the department of a shop in which such goods are sold. Also *attrib.*

1907 *Anthony Hordern Catal.* 60 *Manchester Department.* So called from the majority of the goods included within its scope being of what is popularly known as Manchester manufacture. But the department, as arranged at our store, goes far beyond, for in it will be found, not only fabrics which owe their substance to Cotton, but Linen, Holland, Damask, Flannel, and scores of other materials of domestic and general utility. **1924** *Ibid.* 1 Household Linen Department. Also known as the *Manchester Department*, where will be found every description of *household* and *family linen*, all of the best makes from the World's *celebrated mills.* **1935** *Austral. Woman's Mirror* (Sydney) 2 July 21 Thrifty Housewives should not delay to choose from these Manchester Values. **1953** *Retail Merchandiser* July 28 Mr G.S. Ghent, buyer for the Manchester Department, has retired after twenty-three years' service. **1964** *Ibid.* Mar. 29 Merchandise will include manchester and soft furnishings. **1977** E. MACKIE *Oh to be Aussie* 42 When *he's* finished spending, 'Mum' carries on buying Manchester at the January sales. **1983** *Bulletin* (Sydney) 29 Nov. 90/2 She had just concluded a transaction [in London] and was asked if she would take her purchase with her. 'No,' she said, 'just hold it. I have to go to manchester but I'll be back in a while.' A baffled sales assistant informed madam that it was quite a long way to Manchester... Only Australian shoppers buy their sheets and pillow cases from a manchester department.

maned goose. [f. the mature male bird's 'mane' of elongated, black, hair-like feathers.] *Wood duck*, see WOOD *n.*[1] 3 b. Also **maned duck.**

1845 J. GOULD *Birds of Aust.* (1848) VII. Pl. 3, *Bernicla jubata.* Maned Goose .. Wood Duck, Colonists of New South Wales and Swan River. **1896** B. SPENCER *Rep. Horn Sci. Exped. Central Aust.* II. 110 Maned Goose .. are met with in considerable numbers near the permanent waters. **1948** R. RAVEN-HART *Canoe in Aust.* 39 The rarer Maned Goose, locally Wood Duck, with the wings barred with white. **1974** J. BYRNE *Duck Hunting Aust. & N.Z.* 190 The Wood Duck has a bill which is similar to the bill of a goose but there the resemblance ends. Although it is called the Maned Goose in some areas, this is a misnomer. **1984** *A.N.U. Reporter* (Canberra) 26 Oct. 4 (*caption*) Two Maned Ducks out for a stroll on the banks of Sullivans Creek.

man fern. *Tas.* [Perh. with ref. to a supposedly male characteristic, as size: see *male fern*, OED *male, a.* 2 b.] *Tree fern*, see TREE.

1900 *Bulletin* (Sydney) 30 June 14/3 The fern-tick .. smoodges in the dry seeds of the todia and man-ferns. **1920** B. CRONIN *Timber Wolves* 38 He'll likely mistake you for a man fern. **1952** J.R. SKEMP *Memories Myrtle Bank* 66 Along the creek below the hut was a glen of tree ferns—always called 'man' ferns by the bushman. **1985** *Tasmanian Travelways* Aug. 32 Manferns have taken over a long abandoned carriage from the old Kelly Basin railway line.

mangle. [Fig. use of *mangle* device for pressing water from washed clothes, etc.] A bicycle.

1941 S.J. BAKER *Pop. Dict. Austral. Slang* 45 *Mangle*, a bicycle. **1965** G. MCINNES *Road to Gundagai* 226 It's clear you weren't a bicycle fan in Australia in the Twenties. Oppie was the idol of all, boy and man, who could 'push a mangle'.

mango. Used *attrib.* as an emblem of 'midsummer madness'.

1978 H. LUNN *Joh* 203 Queenslanders call it the Mango Season... It is the season of destruction—of cyclones and floods and whirly-whirlys. **1984** *N.T. News* (Darwin) 22 Sept. 6/2 The season of mango madness is one of many dangers. Who knows what crazy idea a Commissar might come up with while under the influence of the dreaded mango fruit. *Ibid.* 21 Dec. 35/2 It seems 'mango madness', that mystery affliction which hits Darwin during November and December, struck Top End footballers last weekend.

mangoon, var. MAGNOON.

mangrove. Used *attrib.* in the names of fauna: **mangrove (swimming) crab,** *mud crab*, see MUD 1; **heron** (or **bittern**), the predom. grey or brown bird *Butorides striatus* of warmer coastal Aust., and elsewhere in the tropics and sub-tropics; **jack,** the chiefly marine and estuarine fish *Lutjanus argentimaculatus* of n. Aust. and elsewhere; **kingfisher,** the predom. white and blue-green kingfisher *Halcyon chloris sordida* of coastal n. Aust.; **mullet** (chiefly *Qld.*) any of several fish, usu. of the genus *Mugil*, esp. *M. cephalus* (see *sea mullet* SEA); **pigeon,** the bar-shouldered dove *Geopelia humeralis*, occurring near water in n. and e. Aust., and in s. New Guinea.

1930 [**mangrove crab**] C.M. YONGE *Yr. on Great Barrier Reef* 217 The mangrove swimming crab (*Scylla serrata*) and the blue mudcrab (*Portunus pelagicus*) .. are excellent eating. **1935** DAVISON & NICHOLLS *Blue Coast Caravan* 193 He asked if we had ever eaten mangrove crabs. **1968** D. O'GRADY *Bottle of Sandwiches* 62 The Mangrove Crab is a playful little bloke, growing up to a spread of around twelve inches, with claws that can snap a decent-sized stick like it was a toothpick. **1977** *Commercial Fish Aust.* (Dept. Primary Industry) 74 They live in mudflats and tidal estuaries, particularly mangrove-lined shores, sometimes in burrows, hence the name mangrove crab. **1948** [**mangrove heron**] R. RAVEN-HART *Canoe in Aust.* 202 Another 'permanently-folded' heron stumped him, like the Nankeen but bluish .. the Mangrove Bittern. **1955** V. SERVENTY *Aust.'s Great Barrier Reef* 55 The Mangrove Heron looks a little like a dark Reef Heron, but has a much more skulking habit and creeps stealthily over the reef. **1976** *Reader's Digest Compl. Bk. Austral. Birds* 83 The mangrove heron confines its activities to dense stands of mangroves and nearby coastal woodlands. **1951** T.C. ROUGHLEY *Fish & Fisheries Aust.* 69 The **mangrove jack** .. is an inhabitant of the rivers, which it penetrates right into fresh water, its favourite haunt being amongst the mangrove roots. **1969** J. POLLARD *Austral. & N.Z. Fishing* 344 On one point anglers agree—the mangrove jack is not merely a capable opponent, it is a delicious table fish. **1985** *Canberra Times* 24 June 16/5 Over the week this safari captured .. mangrove jacks in mobs. **1945** C. BARRETT *Austral. Bird Life* 144 There are several other northern species: the **mangrove kingfisher** (*Halcyon chloris*) [etc.]. **1965** *N. Austral. Monthly* Dec. 17 The Mangrove Kingfisher stays close to the seafront, but forages largely on the mud. **1884** *Proc. Linnean Soc. N.S.W.* IX. 870 The '**Mangrove Mullets**' of the Brisbane fishermen are *M[ugil] tade* .. and *M. longimanus.* **1905** T. WELSBY *Schnappering & Fishing Brisbane River* 78 Mangrove mullet are the next to appear—about Christmas. **1844** J. GOULD *Birds of Aust.* (1848) V. Pl. 72, It may often be seen among the mangroves in flocks of several hundreds, and hence its colonial name of **Mangrove Pigeon.** **1955** A.C.V. BLIGH *Golden Quest* 219 Mangrove pigeons .. feed on small ripe berries or nuts .. and when cooked make a very good meal.

man-hunting, *vbl. n. Gold-mining. Obs.* See *digger-hunt* DIGGER 4.

1855 G.H. WATHEN *Golden Colony* 86 The pursuit and capture of unlicensed diggers, 'man-hunting' or 'digger-hunting' as the miners called it. **1888** G. ROCK *Colonists* 51 'Man-hunting' has become a recognized pastime of the gentlemen in blue.

Hence **man-hunter** *n.*, see quot. 1855.

1855 W. HOWITT *Land, Labor & Gold* II. 15 The foot police .. generally are the man-hunters, or blood-hounds.

manna. [Spec. use of *manna* a sweet exudation from a plant.]

1. a. The white, sugary, soluble exudation of a tree, usu. of the genus *Eucalyptus* (fam. Myrtaceae), esp. *E. viminalis* and *E. rubida.* **b.** LERP.

1808 *HRA* (1921) 3rd Ser. I. 692 An insect which produces very fine Manna. **1811** D.D. MANN *Present Picture N.S.W.* 51 Manna has also been found near Port Dalrymple, made by the locusts on the trees, from which it drops in very considerable quantities. **1827** P. CUNNINGHAM *Two Yrs. in N.S.W.* I. 203 A species of our eucalyptus produces also the finest manna, and that in very considerable abundance. It is named by Mr Allan Cunningham, the able botanist from Kew, the *eucalyptus mannifera.* **1834** J.D. LANG *Hist. & Statistical Acct. N.S.W.* II. 151 From the lower side of the leaves of the white gum a substance of a whitish colour exudes .. called manna in the colony; but whether its chemical qualities are exactly similar to those of the manna of commerce, I do not know. **1857** W.S. BRADSHAW *Voyages* 115 Manna is abundant in the colony at a certain season of the year, of which the natives are very fond made into cakes. **1878** R.B. SMYTH *Aborigines of Vic.* I. p. xxxiii, He [*sc.* the Victorian aborigine] gathered manna, and made sweet drinks of the flowers of the honeysuckle. **1903** *Bulletin* (Sydney) 31 Jan. 36/1 When, after a wet season, the 'manna' ran down the grey gums, we have sometimes caught froggies and black-caps by creeping up to the tree where they were feasting. **1927** *Ibid.* 21 July 27/2 Victoria has two substances commonly known as manna... One is the dried sweet sap of certain eucalypts... The second kind is found chiefly in the Mallee. Its native name is 'lerp' or 'laap'. It .. is secreted by the pupa of an insect known as *Psylla eucalypti* on the leaves of the mallee scrub. **1969** *Victorian Yr. Bk.* LXXXIII. 10 Lerp insects (Psyllidae) often secrete scale-like coverings (lerps) in the nymph stage, those of *Spondyliaspis eucalypti* on gum leaves being known as 'manna'. **1977** STIRLING & RICHARDSON *Memories of Aberfeldy* 10 All the girls, big and little, went walking, gathering wildflowers .. and manna in the season.

2. Special Comb. **manna gum.**

a. Any of several trees yielding manna, esp. *Eucalyptus viminalis* of s.e. Aust. incl. Tas. Also *ellipt.*

[**1834** G. BENNETT *Wanderings N.S.W.* I. 146 Several of the elegant species of the *Eucalyptus*, the *E. mannifera*, or manna-tree, were seen, having just produced flower-buds; but no manna was yet secreted from the trees.] **1837** *Lit. News* (Sydney) 21 Oct. 108 The lofty and majestic gum-trees, the graceful manna. **1855** J. BONWICK *Geogr. Aust. & N.Z.* (ed. 3) 201 The chief of these are the .. manna, poplar, and mountain Gum trees. **1904** *Bulletin* (Sydney) 4 Feb. 17/1 Manna gums .. supply various birds and insects with snow-white sugar. **1949** J. MORRISON *Creeping City* 21 Giant manna gums, meeting a hundred and fifty feet overhead, shut out the stars. **1982** K. HUENEKE *Huts of High Country* 189 Further up the track we passed under some manna gums... These eucalypts exude a sugary resin which is edible though it may not be enough to save a starving skier.

b. *Obs.* MANNA 1.

1868 J. BAIRD *Emigrant's Guide Australasia* 71 The 'bush' of Western Australia yields a 'manna gum', which is coming into much request.

many-coloured parakeet. *Mulga parrot*, see MULGA *n.*[1] B. 3. Also **many-coloured parrot.**

1847 J. GOULD *Birds of Aust.* (1848) V. Pl. 35, *Psephotus multicolor.* Many-coloured Parrakeet. **1904** *Emu* III. 172 *Psephotus multicolor* (Many-coloured Parrakeet)—These birds were not uncommon a little north of the Gascoyne River early in 1887. **1916** S.A. WHITE *In Far Northwest* 51 They belong to those known as the many-coloured parrot.

Maori /ˈmaʊri/. [See quot. 1974.] The brightly coloured marine fish *Ophthalmolepis lineolatus* of s. Aust. See also *rainbow fish* RAINBOW 2. Also **Maori wrasse.**

1882 J.E. TENISON-WOODS *Fish & Fisheries N.S.W.* 74 Those [Labridae] that are most familiar to the Sydney public are .. the 'Maori' (*Coris lineolatus*) [etc.]. **1906** D.G. STEAD *Fishes of Aust.* 144 Young Maoris are captured in numbers on the small-boy's line, around weedy rocks in the lower parts of our inlets. **1974** T.D. SCOTT et al. *Marine & Freshwater Fishes S.A.* 302 Maori... Head green, with narrow blue lines below the eye, and on the throat, rather resembling the tatto marks of the Maoris, from which the common name is no doubt derived. **1984** *Austral. Gourmet* June-July 59 The choicest of local seafood, such as coral trout, red emperor, maori wrasse.

Maoriland /ˈmaʊrilænd/. [Used elsewhere but

recorded earliest in Aust.: see OEDS.] A name for New Zealand.

1859 *Bell's Life in Sydney* 30 Apr. 2/2 To gallop in Maori-land. **1880** *Bulletin* (Sydney) 7 Feb. 4/1 Maori-land, or Maoritania, is a grand country for the 'show' business. **1909** H.I. Jensen *Rising Tide* 64 In Maoriland wages are high. **1918** *Kia Ora Coo-ee* May 15/2 He started for Maoriland, but Queensland called him back when he reached Melbourne. **1929** G. Meudell *Pleasant Career Spendthrift* 265 It is a crime against nomenclature, against patriotism, against common sense, and above all against aesthetics . . to call Maoriland—New Zealand. **1979** J. Davies *Souvenir Kangaroo Island*, Of all the walls I've painted, and some in Maori land Corrugated iron walls, are tough to understand.

Hence **Maorilander** *n.*

1892 *Truth* (Sydney) 19 June 4/7 A colonist of the 'three islands' is proud to be a Maorilander. **1894** *Bulletin* (Sydney) 7 July 23/4 A Maorilander writes from Coolgardie to report that the Westralians are the dirtiest, laziest, and most disobliging white people he ever came across. **1919** O. Hogue *Cameliers* 50 With a blood-curdling yell the Maorilanders charged with the bayonet. **1951** *Bulletin* (Sydney) 18 July 14/1 Maorilanders inform me that the shellfish is regarded as a luxury in the Shivery Isles.

mapi /'mapi/. [a. Dyirbal (and neighbouring languages) *mabi*.] Boongarry. Also **mappy-mappy.**

1895 *Proc. Linnean Soc. N.S.W.* IX. 573 When engaged in obtaining *D. lumholtzi* . . he seldom saw them at rest. . . The native name is Mapi (Marpee, according to English pronunciation). **1919** *Bulletin* (Sydney) 30 Jan. 22/4 In the southern States the tree-kangaroo of North Q., known locally as 'mappy-mappy', is ignorantly regarded as a myth. *c* **1934** R.M. Crookston Unseen Tragedy of Aborigines 2 An expert tree-climbing native came with us into the scrub to spot, climb for, and chase down Mapi, the tree-climbing 'roo, from his perch on the branches sixty or seventy feet up.

maple. [Transf. use of *maple* a tree of the genus *Acer*.] Any of several trees yielding an attractive, usu. pinkish, cabinet timber, esp. *Queensland maple* (see Queensland 2); the wood of these trees.

1889 J.H. Maiden *Useful Native Plants Aust.* 611 *Villaresia Moorei* . . 'Maple' . . a most excellent wood, white in colour, and durable. **1930** V. Kennedy *By Range & River* 73 Such cabinet timbers as maple, silkwood, cedar. **1975** *Ecos* vi. 10/2 Commercial plantations of valuable native timbers like maple, red cedar, and kauri pine on cleared rainforest sites. **1985** *Age* (Melbourne) 31 Oct. 11/3 We came to a giant maple, about 200 centimetres in diameter.

mappy-mappy: see Mapi.

maramie /'mærəmi/. [Prob. f. a N.S.W. Aboriginal language.] A fresh-water crayfish.

1844 Mrs C. Meredith *Notes & Sketches N.S.W.* 108 The moramies, or crayfish, live in holes in the muddy banks of these pools. **1845** J.O. Balfour *Sketch of N.S.W.* 35 A small crayfish called by the aborigines '*morramma*', is better eating than any shell fish I ever tasted. **1867** F.J. Byerley *Narr. Overland Exped. Northern Qld.* 14 They camped and caught some fish and maramies (cray-fish) by puddling a hole in the creek. **1951** J. Devanny *Travels N. Qld.* 195 A real delicacy . . was a small crayfish: maramie to the Aborigines.

marara /mə'rarə/. [Prob. f. a Qld. Aboriginal language.] Either of two large rainforest trees of the fam. Cunoniaceae, *Pseudoweinmannia lachnocarpa* and the rose-leaf marara *Caldcluvia paniculosa* (*Ackama paniculata*), both of e. Qld. and N.S.W.; the wood of these trees.

1884 A. Nilson *Timber Trees N.S.W.* 124 *W[einmannia] rubifolia*—Marara . . *timber* close-grained and tough, but easily wrought. **1909** F.M. Bailey *Comprehensive Catal. Qld. Plants* (ed. 2) 169 'Merrany' or 'Marara' of Nerang. Wood light-pink; useful for making planes, mallets, and chisel-handles. **1981** H. Hannah *Together in Jungle Scrub* 19 To start with they lived in a big marara tree. They've got big spurs on the hips. They felled that and they used it until they got a hut built.

marble.

1. *Obs.* In the phr. **to pass (chuck,** etc.) **in one's marble,** to die; to give up. See Alley 1.

1908 *Austral. Mag.* (Sydney) Nov. 1250/1 Instead of dying you can . . 'pass in your marble'. **1911** *Bulletin* (Sydney) 5 Oct. 15/1 On one was a man who had just handed in his marble; on the other was his drunk and morbid friend, bemoaning the loss of his pal. **1918** *Passed by Censor: Souvenir Austral. Naval & Military Exped. Force New Guinea* Christmas 7 Verily hath the Hun chucked in his marble. **1927** F.C. Biggers *Bat-Eye* 33 An' we was beat. We chucked our marble in an' 'ad ter wait. **1951** D. Stivens *Jimmy Brockett* 304 I'm not going to pass in my marble just yet! **1961** G. Farwell *Vanishing Australs.* 77 He drank his way through to that second afternoon and then went into a coma, and it was some time before the coves he was shouting woke up that he'd really passed in his marble. **1972** J. Hibberd *Stretch of Imagination* (1973) 24 What if I pass in my marble like this?

2. a. In the phr. **to make** (or **keep**) **one's marble good,** to ingratiate oneself; to improve one's position. See Alley 2.

[N.Z. **1909** *N.Z. Truth* (Wellington) 15 May 7 He 'made his marble good', he alleged, by paying up a score he owed.] **1928** L.A. Sigsworth *Various Verse* 2 And the classers keep their marbles good with 'guns', for they have pull. **1950** B. James *Advancement Spencer Button* 162 You can't get that class any time—that bloody Button's got them all the time. He's trying to make his marble good, all right. **1964** *Sydney Morning Herald* 10 Aug. 2/6 'He's making his marble good with the boss' meant, and I daresay still means, that he is polishing up his brain-sweat in manoeuvring for a better or softer job.

b. In the phr. **one's marble is good,** one is in a favourable position.

1966 D. Niland *Pairs & Loners* 80 My marble's good there for a cushy job and a few quid picking apples and pears.

3. *Horse-racing.* The number drawn by a jockey which determines the horse's position on the starting line.

1924 'S. Rudd' *Me an' Son* 90 To see who were th' rider ov Sardinia, an' what was his marble. **1964** *Sydney Morning Herald* 10 Aug. 2/5 A good marble in the racing game can be a lower number giving the inside running, and a good marble in Sydney today can mean a hundred thousand quid.

marbled frogmouth. The bird *Podargus ocellatus* of e. Qld. and N.S.W., having red, brown, and white marbled plumage. Formerly also **marbled frogsmouth.**

1898 E.E. Morris *Austral Eng.* 155 The mouth and expression of the face resemble the appearance of a frog. The species are . . Marbled F[rogsmouth].—*P[odargus] marmoratus* [etc.]. **1913** *Emu* XII. Suppl. 56 *Podargus marmoratus* . . Marbled Frogmouth. **1968** D. Fleay *Nightwatchmen* 150 The sixty-four dollar question, as to whether the Marbled Frogmouth ranges through other parts of eastern Queensland, remains an intriguing possibility. **1985** *Parks & Wildlife News* Summer 19 Four endangered bird species have their home in this park—the . . Marbled Frogmouth [etc.].

marblewood. Any of several trees yielding timber with an attractive mottled grain, esp. the tall rainforest tree *Acacia bakeri* (fam. Mimosaceae) of Qld. and N.S.W.; the wood of these trees.

1889 J.H. Maiden *Useful Native Plants Aust.* 580 *Olea paniculata* . . 'marble-wood'. . . The heart-wood is nicely mottled. It is of a whitish colour, darkening towards the centre, and prettily figured. **1915** *Bulletin* (Sydney) 16 Dec. 24/4 The job of picking out the more classic timber . . marblewood, ash, etc. **1938** C.T. White *Princ. Bot. Qld. Farmers* 181 *Acacia Bakeri*, the Marble Wood, a light-coloured timber with a beautiful grain. **1948** P.J. Hurley *Red Cedar* 143 One can picture this Dorrigo scrub in its primaeval grandeur . . marblewood . . and enormous Stinging Nettle Trees. **1981** Pugh & Ritchie *Guide to Rainforests N.S.W.* 12 Brunswick Heads Nature Reserve. . . Rare tree species occurring here include . . Marblewood.

March fly. [f. the name of the month (see quot. 1948), although the fly is usu. most noticeable in the spring or wet season.] A blood-sucking fly of any of several genera of the widely-distributed fam. Tabanidae.

1852 J. Bonwick *Notes of Gold Digger* 22 The nuisance is the flies, the little fly and the stinging monster March fly. **1855** W. Howitt *Land, Labor & Gold* I. 247 The March fly . . is a great gray-black blundering fly, very like an aged beef-fly. **1867** 'Clergyman' *Aust. as it Is* 35 The March fly, the same as the gad-fly, is very tormenting to horses and cattle. **1876** J.A. Edwards *Gilbert Gogger* 87 Horses . . switched their tails savagely, to drive away the blood-sucking, intolerably annoying March flies. **1889** E. Giles *Aust. twice Traversed* II. 103 We were troubled also with myriads of the large March flies, those horrid pests about twice the size of the blow-fly. **1926** M. Forrest *Hibiscus Heart* 183 Perhaps they would only think a March fly had stung the Colonel. **1948** W.W. Froggatt *Insect Bk.* 96 These thickset active flies are known as March Flies because they usually appear about the end of summer. In England they are better known as Horse or Gad Flies. **1975** *Bronze Swagman Bk. Bush Verse* 82 You'll soon forget our March-flies, the midge and sergeant ants.

marching, *vbl. n.* Used *attrib.* in Special Comb. **marching chain** *hist.*, a connecting chain to which the fetters of each member of a party of travelling convicts are attached to prevent escape.

1837 *Rep. Select Committee Transportation* 14 July (1838) 82 He will apply to the officer of the guard for an adequate escort and will, in all cases, attach the hand cuffs of the prisoners to a marching chain before they quit the stockade. **1899** G.E. Boxall *Story Austral. Bushrangers* 278 The prisoners were seated in the body of the coach, and were connected together by 'a marching chain', to which their handcuffs and leg irons were attached.

marching, *ppl. a.* In the collocation **marching girl,** a girl trained to march in formation.

[N.Z. **1952** *Here & Now* 9 July, Not for a long time have I observed such a symptom of our *malaise* as the business of 'marching girls'.] **1953** *About Turn* Dec. 3 The badge features a Marching Girl in the centre. **1958** *Herald* (Melbourne) 29 July 4/8, I don't want to see the RSL take part in any clown act. Marching girls mean whistling boys. **1964** *Mount Isa Mail* 5 May 3/4 The immaculately clad marching girls performed difficult manoeuvres. **1974** *Herald* (Melbourne) 28 Feb. 21/6, I wanted to become a marching girl but my father said no.

margoo /'magu/. [a. Western Desert language *maku*.] Witchetty 2.

1916 S.A. White *In Far Northwest* 78 These grubs are much sought after by the natives who call them 'margoo'. **1950** V.E. Turner *Ooldea* 110 The children . . could . . pull the succulent margoo or witchetty grub out of its hole in a tree. **1973** V. Serventy *Desert Walkabout* 13 He had dragged out a four-inch long white grub and swallowed it with much satisfaction. 'Margo,' he exclaimed, eyes gleaming with epicurean delight.

marine settler. *Hist.* One who, having served as a marine, remains in an Australian Colony as a settler.

1792 P.G. King Jrnl. Norfolk Island 24 Those Marine Settlers, who brought their Wives & Families from England, were supplied. **1799** D. Collins *Acct. Eng. Colony N.S.W.* May (1802) II. 209 A marine settler (as those were styled who had formerly belonged to the marine detachment). **1804** *HRA* (1915) 1st Ser. V. 28 In your Return I observe Nine old Marine Settlers. **1813** *Ibid.* (1921) 3rd Ser. I. 18 The Marine Settlers are . . to receive one Cow each from the Government Herds.

mark, *n.*[1] [Spec. use of *mark* target, that which may be aimed at: see OED(S *sb.*[1] 7 d. (but see also OED(S *sb.*[1] 21 and 22).] A person who is an object of attention: freq. with qualifying *adj.*, as **good (bad,** etc.) **mark,** having reference esp. to the person's financial probity.

1835 *Cornwall Chron.* (Launceston) 14 Mar. 3, It is currently reported that several *gentlemen*—known amongst the trades-people of Sydney as 'bad marks'—intend embracing the present opportunities of leaving the Colony with a 'flying topsail'. **1845** R. Howitt *Impressions Aust. Felix* 233, I wondered often what was the meaning of this, amongst many other peculiar colonial phrases, 'Is the man a good mark?' Our bullock-driver had it familiarly in his mouth. I heard it casually from the lips of apparently respectable settlers as they rode on the highway. 'Such and such a one is a good mark!'—simply a person who pays his men their wages, without delays or drawbacks; a man to whom you may sell anything safely. **1854** C.A. Corbyn *Sydney Revels* 132 They knows I'm the wrong mark to peach on 'em. **1867** J.R. Houlding *Austral. Capers* 339 My agent can manage to 'raise the wind' as he calls it—at any time. He says I am considered a 'first-rate mark' in Sydney, and he can exchange my bills . . without the least trouble. **1941** S.J. Baker *Pop. Dict. Austral. Slang* 46 *Mark, good (or bad)*, a general term of approval (or disapproval) for a person. **1951** S. Hickey *Travelled Roads* 38 They were usually long-winded and otherwise bad marks, through trying to make one pound do the work of ten.

mark, *n.*[2] *Hist.* [Spec. use of *mark* symbol in respect of conduct: see OED *sb.*[1] 11 g.] A point or unit of credit (or penalty) counting towards a total which may earn the remission or measure the passage of a convict's sentence.

1839 J. Ward Diary of Convict Nov. 118 Marks of approval were kept by the Doctor; and when you got three of these good marks, your irons was taken off. **1845** A. Maconochie *On Managem. Transported Criminals* 2, I propose that a form of *Wages* (marks) be introduced into all our penal Establishments. **1865** 'Special Correspondent' *Transportation* 34 Upon the arrival of a convict in the colony, a calculation is made of the time he would have to serve under ordinary circumstances before becoming entitled to his ticket-of-leave. An account is then opened with him, and he is debited with a certain number of marks, at the rate of three per day, for this period. These marks he has to work off before he receives his liberty. **1877** *Vagabond Ann.* 179 Every sentence will be reduced to a certain number of marks, nine of which marks will represent an ordinary day—*three for labour, three for conduct while at work . . three for conduct beyond labour hours.*

Hence **mark system** *n.*

1862 Backhouse & Tylor *Life & Labour G.W. Walker* 272 The experiments which were made on Norfolk Island and elsewhere, of the Mark System . . were considered by some to be unsuccessful. **1877** *Vagabond Ann.* 178 The remissions of sentences are calculated on the 'mark' system, according to the . . regulations issued by Mr Macpherson, as Chief Secretary, under date 21st March, 1876.

mark, *n.*[3] *Australian National Football.* [Transf. use of *mark* heel-mark made by a Rugby Union player who has made a 'fair catch': see OED(S *sb.*[1] 12 d.]

1. a. (The taking of) a fair catch (see quot. 1931); the catch itself.

1859 C.C. Mullen *Hist. Austral. Rules Football* 11 A mark is made when a player catches the ball before it hits the ground and after it has been clearly kicked by another player. **1885** D.E. McConnell *Austral. Etiquette* 640 Any player catching the ball directly from the foot of another player may call 'mark'. He then has a 'free kick' from any spot behind. **1900** B. Kerr *Silliad* 30 Napoleon Jinks sailed up and took the mark. **1931** J.F. McHale et al. *Austral. Game of Football* 48 A mark may be obtained either from a place, drop, or punt kick, and consists of catching a ball directly from a kick or bounce from below the knee, not less than ten yards distant, the ball being held a reasonable time and not having been touched while in transit from kick to catch. **1960** *N.T. News* (Darwin) 8 Mar. 10/4 Marcellus took a spectacular mark but kicked badly. **1964** B. Wannan *Fair Go, Spinner* 138 Cynical barracker to showy player who goes through flash actions after a mark: 'Orlright, mate, we've got yer photo!' **1966** M. Green *After Boolucburras* 35 Besides an ordinary mark a 'little mark' could be claimed if a player could get hold of the ball, touch the toe of his boot, and then throw it, but one had to be nippy to get away with that. **1973** P. McKenna *My World of Football* 75 The high overhead mark is unique to Australian football and the most spectacular aspect of the game.

b. See quot. 1968.

1894 J.M. MacDonald *Thunderbolt* 87 A burly Bendigonian kicked it into the hands of the Melbourne skipper. He could have had a mark—*i.e.* a free kick behind a mark on the ground. **1968** Eagleson & McKie *Terminol. Austral. Nat. Football* ii. 23 *Mark*, . . the spot at which a player caught the ball ('took a mark') and behind or over which he must make his kick.

c. The kick awarded to a player who has taken a fair catch.

1894 J.M. MacDonald *Thunderbolt* 89 Harrison kicked off along the right lower side to Greaves . . marked the ball, and chose to take his mark . . He coolly went back ten yards, and then kicked a drop-kick on along the lower centre. **1906** *Gadfly* (Adelaide) 30 May 14/1 Mr Gray, whom courtesy titles 'umpire', is a most dramatic person, and his Julius Knight style of awarding a man a mark . . caused great hilarity on the Norwood Oval. **1960** *N.T. News* (Darwin) 5 Jan. 8/4 Saints won the knock and . . a soaring mark was followed by a sixer.

d. A player skilled at taking a fair catch and gaining advantage with the subsequent kick.

1936 E.C.H. Taylor et al. *Our Austral. Game Football* 34 *Centre back* . . a good kick and safe mark, cool and intelligent. **1963** L. Richards *Boots & All!* 105 A terrific mark, he knew how to make position on the half-forward line with perfection.

2. In the collocation **high mark,** a fair catch taken in the course of a high leap; a player who does this.

1936 E.C.H. Taylor et al. *Our Austral. Game Football* 20 It is not necessary to be very tall to become a good high mark. **1963** *Footy Fan* (Melbourne) I. iii. 22 What better satisfaction can a player have than taking a well judged high mark over the top of the pack? **1984** *Bulletin* (Sydney) 2 Oct. 36/3 The high mark provided the drama for Australian football . . but it required time, first so that a pack of players could develop to compete for the ball and second so that one of the players could hitch a ride on the shoulders of another.

mark, *v.*[1] *trans.* To mark the ear of (a lamb), completing at the same time other processes, as the castration of male lambs, docking, etc. Also as *vbl. n.* See also *lamb-marking* Lamb *n.*

1883 E.M. Curr *Recoll. Squatting Vic.* 153 Shortly after taking charge I marked two thousand lambs. **1898** A. Joyce *Homestead Hist.* (1942) 82 It was usual . . to give them a bonus of a shilling a head for all lambs marked over a certain percentage, generally 86 per cent. **1907** C. MacAlister *Old Pioneering Days* 17 One morning just before the marking—or 'docking' as it was then called—Brentnall and his mate found they were six or seven lambs short of their tally. **1946** D. Stivens *Courtship of Uncle Henry* 140 There are a few lambs that want marking. **1959** H. Lamond *Sheep Station* 193 Th' last markin' they had at Barcaldine Downs was a bit better 'an forty-eight thousan' lambs from about sixty thousan' ewes. **1960** D. McLean *Roaring Days* 236 Hugh and Jim are out marking a few hoggets that they missed on the lamb marking. **1965** A.W. Upfield *Lure of Bush* 150 Moving a flock of ten thousand sheep toward the marking camp. **1982** *Sydney Morning Herald* 8 May 13/2 As he signed the last departmental file yesterday . . Killen remembered the blessed relief he felt long ago at the end of a long, hot, morning marking (castrating) a couple of thousand lambs the old way (dragging them out with your teeth).

mark, *v.*[2] *Australian National Football.* [f. Mark *n.*[3]] *trans.* To take (the ball) in a fair catch; to kick (the ball) after taking a fair catch. Freq. *absol.*

1894 J.M. MacDonald *Thunderbolt* 94 The ball sailed long and low . . about four feet above the forest of hands raised to mark it. **1900** B. Kerr *Silliad* 31 He passed it neatly to Adonis Vane Who, driving forward, marked to Green again. **1960** *N.T. News* (Darwin) 5 Jan. 8/5 Twice Marrego marked well over the pack and sent the ball soaring. **1967** *Austral.* (Sydney) 24 Apr. 12/5 Peter Hudson, Hawthorn's star full-forward recruit from Tasmania flies in front of his opposing full-back . . to mark in the VFL game at Princes Park in Melbourne. **1973** J. Dunn *How to play Football* 28 Height . . is the best advantage any player can have for marking. **1981** A.B. Facey *Fortunate Life* 230, I did well at marking (or catching) the ball.

Hence **(high) marking** *vbl. n.* and *ppl. a.*

1936 E.C.H. Taylor et al. *Our Austral. Game Football* 20 Marking is perhaps the most spectacular feature of our game, especially high marking. **1939** P. McGuire *Austral. Journey* 285 The most spectacular feature of the game is its 'high-marking'. If a man catches the ball cleanly from a kick, he is entitled to an unimpeded kick himself, and when one sees three or four young giants soaring into the air together to battle for a ball ten feet above the ground, it is enough to set any crowd roaring. **1960** *N.T. News* (Darwin) 8 Jan. 6/3 Pott, a high-marking rover for the aboriginal team, Wanderers, pleaded not guilty. **1982** G. Atkinson *Everything about Austral. Rules Football* 164 Around the mid-1880s, the development in high marking was extraordinary.

marked, *ppl. a. Obs.* [f. U.S. *mark, v.* to blaze (a tree): see DAE *v.* 1 and OED *marked, ppl. a.* 1.] Of a series of trees: marked with blazes to indicate the line of a track or road. Freq. in the collocation **marked tree line (road, track).**

[**1788** J. White *Jrnl. of Voyage N.S.W.* 22 Apr. (1790) 147 We likewise took with us a small hand hatchet, in order to mark the trees as we went on; those marks (called in America *blazing*) being the only guide to direct us in our return.] **1831** *Acct. Colony Van Diemen's Land* 40 The traveller has now only marked trees to guide him along a thick, scrubby road, which is as yet impassable for carriages. **1832** J. Backhouse *Narr. Visit Austral. Colonies* (1843) 25 There was 'a marked tree road', or a way through 'the bush' . . marked by pieces of bark being chopped off the sides of trees. **1840** H.S. Russell *Genesis Qld.* 2 July (1888) 167 We encamped the drays . . and making my way by our own marked tree line, I met Dalrymple. **1848** T.L. Mitchell *Jrnl. Exped. Tropical Aust.* 14, I rode to look at my old line of marked trees. **1854** H.B. Stoney *Yr. in Tas.* 192 Offering his services to set us on the marked-tree track the next morning. **1857** F. de B. Cooper *Wild Adventures* 55 The only guide being a marked tree-line, formed by taking a chip out of a tree at every three or four hundred paces. **1867** 'Clergyman' *Aust. as it Is* 75 There was, properly speaking, no road, the track being merely a 'marked tree-line'. **1875** Campbell & Wilks *Early Settlement Qld.* 1 The road they came to has since been known as Leslie's marked-tree line. **1893** J. Demarr *Adventures in Aust.* 165 A 'marked tree line' is a track through the bush, seldom used and the marked trees are the only guide. **1913** M.A. McManus *Reminisc. Maranoa District* 10 My father made the first marked tree line from Mount Abundance to Wallumbilla Station in 1859.

market. In the phr. **to go to market,** to lose one's temper, to behave angrily; to behave excitably.

1870 *Austral. Town & Country Jrnl.* (Sydney) 12 Nov. 13/4 He slackens the rein, and saying, 'Go to market now old fellow', sits the wild plunge of the colt like a Mexican vaquero. **1887** W.S.S. Tyrwhitt *New Chum in Qld. Bush* 127 'I say, are you going to ride Customer?' 'Yes.' 'I expect he'll go to market, won't he?' (Euphemism for buck-jumping). **1898** *Bulletin* (Sydney) 17 Dec. (Red Page), To *get narked* is to lose your temper; also expressed by *getting dead wet* or *going to market.* **1908** W.H. Ogilvie *My Life in Open* 83 Playful or vicious, according to their breeding and temperament, almost all of them 'prop' or 'go to market' in some form or other. **1918** *Kia Ora Coo-ee* July 4/2 Later on, in the mess, a brother officer was 'going to market' because he had been rebuked for his failure to name men whose names the General sought. **1948** R. Raven-Hart *Canoe in Aust.* 76 Melbourne and Adelaide get what they call 'dust-storms', and 'go to market about it', grousing to high heaven. **1950** F.J. Hardy *Power without Glory* 35, I have me instructions, so it's no use going to market on me.

marl /mal/. [a. Nyungar *maal.*] The small bandicoot *Perameles bougainville*, light grey-brown above and white below, with a striped rump, now occurring only on Bernier and Dorre Islands, Shark Bay, W.A.

1941 E. Troughton *Furred Animals Aust.* 67 Marl or Western Barred-Bandicoot . . *Perameles myosura.* . . The native's name of 'Marl' has been advocated as the popular name for the western race. **1952** J.F. Haddleton *Katanning Pioneer* 100 The marl or native pig resembled the bandicoot . . as regards food, but was much smaller . . being very light in colour, long thin snout, small thin ears, and a very thin tail and very tender. **1977** H. Butler *In Wild* 104 The little Marl, a beautiful small desert bandicoot, seems to be gone: no trace for seventy years. **1983** R. Strahan *Compl. Bk. Austral. Mammals* 101 Marl appears to be derived from *Mala*, quoted by Gould as the Aboriginal name for the Barred Bandicoot from the Toodyay district of Western Australia. This is actually an Aboriginal name of the Rufous Hare-wallaby in Western Australia and its application to a bandicoot is confusing.

marlock /'malɒk/. [a. Nyungar *marlok.*] Any of several small, mallee-like trees of the genus *Eucalyptus* (fam. Myrtaceae) occurring in s.w. W.A.: see quot. 1971. Also *attrib.*

1894 A.F. CALVERT *Coolgardie Goldfield* 46 The first 14 miles consists of broken sand-plain and marlock country. **1903** *Emu* III. 11 A dwarf eucalyptus called 'marlock' which much resembles mallee scrub. **1944** C. FENNER *Mostly Austral.* 88 In Western Australia we find the name 'marlocks'... Maalock, also maalok, is an old spelling, and means a thicket more or less dense. **1971** C. DEBENHAM *Lang. Bot.* (ed. 2) 131 The marlock is noted for its mallee-like form but poor development of a ligno-tuber.

marloo /ma'lu/. *W.A.* Also **merloo.** Pl. **marloo.** [a. Western Desert language *marlu.*] The kangaroo *Macropus rufus* (see *red kangaroo* (a), RED *a.* 1 b.).

1935 H.H. FINLAYSON *Red Centre* 57 The kangaroo, or merloo as the Luritjas call him, is the familiar red kangaroo (*Macropus rufus*) of the saltbush tablelands farther south. **1967** E. HUXLEY *Their Shining Eldorado* 215 Among the native fauna .. the Red kangaroo—here called the marloo .. is under attack. **1984** W.W. AMMON et al. *Working Lives* 149 The big red roos, the marloo, keep to the plain country.

marmalade. Also **marmelade.** [See quot. 1919.] In Services' speech: a new recruit.

1918 R.H. KNYVETT *Over there with Australs.* 53 New arrivals in camp were always called 'Marmalades', because they were distinguished by their relish for marmalade jam. **1919** *7th Field Artillery Brigade Yandoo* Sept. 160 'Marmelade!' .. The term arose through the frequency of marmelade in the jam ration and was an appellation which would be applied to the new troop until he became familiar with the ways and methods of a soldier. **1943** S.W. KEOUGH *Around Army* 14 When handling raw recruits .. the sar'-major becomes a headache on two legs .. as he tries to lick some 'marmalades' into shape.

marri /'mæri/. [a. Nyungar *marri.*] The tree *Eucalyptus calophylla* (fam. Myrtaceae) of s.w. W.A., having rough grey-brown bark and ornamental flowers; the hard, durable wood of the tree.

1833 *Jrnls. Several Exped. W.A.* 133 The mahogany and red gum, of Perth, (the tyarreil and marré of the natives here) are predominant. **1926** J. POLLARD *Bushland Man* 280 It was the flowering season for the marri, the jarrah .. and many other eucalypts. **1952** A.C.C. LOCK *Travels across Aust.* 230 We saw the first trees that Dave called red gums. In the trade they were called marri (*Eucalyptus calophylla*). **1963** *Times* (London) 12 Mar. (Austral. Suppl.) p. v/7 Marri and gimlet and .. other valuable timbers. **1972** B. FULLER *West of Bight* 123 Marri, the most widely distributed eucalypt in the south-west, is the old red-gum of the early settlers, who used the secretions for tanning. **1985** *West Austral.* (Perth) 6 Nov. 54/4 Very hot fires .. severely reduced the occurrence of fungus in the marri forest.

marron /'mærən/. In the pl. freq. **marron.** [a. Nyungar *marran.*] The large fresh-water crayfish of s.w. W.A. *Cherax tenuimanus.*

1943 *Land Girls Gaz.* (Perth) Apr. 7 Last night we caught twelve marrons in a fishing bag. **1948** H.A. LINDSAY *Bushman's Handbk.* 95 Most people know how to catch the small freshwater crayfish known as .. gilgie, marron .. and other aboriginal names which we have adopted. **1968** *What Migrants need to Know* (W.A. Dept. Immigration) 83 There is also a closed season during which it is an offence to catch marron. **1983** *Austral. Fisheries* Jan. 31/2 The Minister for Fisheries and Wildlife .. said the bag limit was not more than 20 marron in any one day... The only means by which marron could be legally taken were by drop net, pole snares or hand scoop nets.

marsh. Chiefly *Tas. Obs.* [Br. dial. *marsh(-land)* rich alluvial soil: see EDD *marsh, sb.*[1] 1. (5 b) and 4.] A tract of rich alluvial land, suitable for agricultural use after draining. Also **marsh land.**

1833 *Trumpeter* (Hobart) 24 Sept. 178 The convenient distance from town, and the great advantage of water carriage, so essential to convey to market the superabundant crops, which the marsh land affords, are indeed objects of some importance. **1836** *Cornwall Chron.* (Launceston) 1 Oct. 3 The *Forton Estate* .. about one third of which is of the richest possible description of Marsh, and at a very small expense if desirable, may be made secure from floods, about 75 acres is under cultivation. **1841** *Launceston Courier* 22 Feb. 3/3 About 4,000 Acres, might be put into cultivation at a trifling expence, and nearly 2,000 is rich Marsh land. **1852** MRS C. MEREDITH *My Home in Tas.* I. 163 A 'marsh' here is what would in England be called a meadow, with this difference, that in our marshes, until partially drained, a growth of tea-trees .. and rushes in some measure encumbers them.

marshmallow. [Transf. use of *marshmallow, Althaea officinalis*, of marshy country.] Any of several plants of the fam. Malvaceae esp. the naturalized European *Malva parviflora*, widespread in Aust. and generally regarded as a weed, and the tall *Lavatera plebeia* of all mainland States.

1835 J. BATMAN *Settlement Port Phillip* 4 June (1856) 18 We travelled over the richest land I had ever seen in my life; marsh mallows, with leaves as large as those of the cabbage tribe, and as high as my head. **1863** W.J. WILLS *Successful Exploration Interior Aust.* 132 Sheltered from the sun by .. tall marshmallows, and luxuriant salt bushes. **1880** 'OLD HAND' *Experiences of Colonist* (ed. 2) ii. 24 In places the marsh mallow (malva) grew in dense and almost impenetrable masses. **1926** *Bulletin* (Sydney) 11 Nov. 24/1 The symptoms of poisoning are similar to those of the well-known sheep poisons 'marshmallow' and 'stagger-nettle'. **1935** R.B. PLOWMAN *Boundary Rider* 248 Near the river was a small forest of unbelievably big marsh mallows. **1974** S.L. EVERIST *Poisonous Plants Aust.* 364 *Malva parviflora* .. commonly known in Australia as *marshmallow* .. is now widespread as a weed in many parts of the world.

marsh tern. The black-crowned, predom. grey and white bird *Chlidonias hybrida*, of inland swamps, lagoons, and lakes.

1848 J. GOULD *Birds of Aust.* VII. Pl. 31, *Hydrochelidon fluviatilis* .. Marsh Tern. **1903** *Emu* II. 176 A pair of silvery-plumaged Marsh Terns (*Hydrochelidon hybrida*) were daily to be seen. **1964** M. SHARLAND *Territory of Birds* 42 Marsh Terns were dipping into the water for insect food.

marsupial.

1. Used *attrib.* in the names of animals: **marsupial lion,** the extinct, carnivorous marsupial *Thylacoleo carnifex* of Aust. incl. Tas.; **mole,** the small, blind, burrowing marsupial *Notoryctes typhops*, widely distributed in sandy country in arid Aust.; **mouse,** any of many small carnivorous marsupials of the fam. Dasyuridae, esp. of the genera *Sminthopsis* (see DUNNART) and *Antechinus*, some of which are also known as bush mice (see *bush mouse* BUSH C. 3), and pouched mice (see POUCHED MOUSE); **rat,** the small carnivorous marsupial of arid central Aust. *Dasyuroides byrnei* (fam. Dasyuridae); **wolf,** *Tasmanian tiger*, see TASMANIAN *a.* 2.

1867 *Illustr. Sydney News* 16 July 204/2 The fossil remains picked out, yielding a rich harvest of many bones and teeth, among them the left incisor of the much talked about **marsupial lion** (*Thylacoleo carnifex*). **1878** R.B. SMYTH *Aborigines of Vic.* I. 149 The dingo was alive and well when the now extinct marsupial lion .. roamed throught the forests of Australia. **1895** E.T.H. HUTTON *Narr. Tour Inspection N.S.W.* 20 In and around the more elevated lands the now extinct thylacoleo lived, a great marsupial lion. **1985** *Bulletin* (Sydney) 28 May 78/2 The marsupial lions were apparently rather possum-like in appearance but most un-possum-like in behaviour. They were specialised meat-eaters which had long and very powerful front incisors. **1901** C. WRIGHT *Historic Melbourne* 46 In real life the **Marsupial Mole** is unlike any other animal, and very like nothing else... It was first discovered by whites in the neighbourhood of the Finke River. **1917** *Bulletin* (Sydney) 18 Oct. 22/3 The marsupial mole .. is occasionally met with among the sand-hills of Central Australia. **1934** W.A. OSBORNE *Visitor to Aust.* 76 The visitor is not likely to see the .. marsupial mole, except in a zoo or museum. **1952** B. BEATTY *Unique to Aust.* 35 A primitive creature found only in Australia is the golden-haired marsupial mole of the Nullarbor Plain. **1973** V. SERVENTY *Desert Walkabout* 13 We caught a frog and geckoes but our search for the rare marsupial mole was fruitless. **1983** R. STRAHAN *Compl. Bk. Austral. Mammals* 87 The resemblance of the Marsupial Mole to the true (placental) moles .. is a striking example of convergent evolution. **1872** 'RESIDENT' *Glimpses Life Vic.* 18 A tiny **marsupial mouse.** **1941** E. TROUGHTON *Furred Animals Aust.* 36 The marsupial mice are most useful little animals, and havoc by grasshoppers and other insect pests might be considerably reduced if they were not preyed upon by domestic cats. **1956** T.Y. HARRIS *Naturecraft in Aust.* 72 The Insectivorous Marsupial Mice are rarely seen unless brought in by cats or injured during clearing operations... They are .. distinguished from true rats and mice by their sharply tapered snouts, and by the fact that their jaws have a number of small incisor-like teeth instead of the paired chisel-incisors of the rodents. **1977** J. CARTER *All Things Wild* 1 Spotted native cats .. stalking unwary birds or tiny marsupial mice. **1906** J.W. GREGORY *Dead Heart Aust.* 150 On its shores lived .. wallabies, bandicoots, and **marsupial rats.** **1962** I. SOUTHALL *Woomera* 91 Desert marsupial rats and nocturnal snakes sneak out of the earth. **1970** J.V. MARSHALL *Walk to Hills of Dreamtime* 66 It was a marsupial rat which the leader had spotted: a two-foot bandicoot scavenging for food in the mosaic of spinifex and scrub. **1973** V. SERVENTY *Desert Walkabout* 36 Ken had to make do with tinned food, three marsupial rats, two crested pigeons and damper. **1885** *Illustr. Austral. News* (Melbourne) 19 Dec. 218/3 The group of the **marsupial wolf** .. represents the largest, most formidable and, in many respects, the most remarkable of the carnivorous marsupial animals. It is now entirely confined to Tasmania. **1926** A. EDEN *Places in Sun* 77 The 'Tasmanian Tiger' or marsupial wolf, is only found on the island [*sc.* Tasmania]; slightly smaller than a full-grown wolf and greedy for sheep, it is now rare. **1952** B. BEATTY *Unique to Aust.* 34 The Tasmanian Tiger or Marsupial Wolf is .. the rarest of the world's living mammals... It .. resembles a wolf in general shape and carries its ears erect.

2. Special Comb. **Marsupial Board,** a body established in a rural district to control kangaroos, wallabies, etc., and other animals regarded as pests.

1881 *Act* (Qld.) 45 Vict. no. 4 Sect. 2, The following items in inverted commas shall bear the meanings set against them... 'Board.'—The Marsupial Board to be elected or appointed for any district hereinafter defined... 'Marsupial.'—Any kangaroo, wallaroo, wallaby, or paddamelon. **1898** C.L. MORGAN *Rabbit Question in Qld.* 33 The Bulloo Marsupial Board had carried on destruction on 17 stations. **1911** ST. C. GRONDONA *Collar & Cuffs* 63 A bonus of 2s. 6d. is paid for eaglehawks' talons by the marsupial board. **1913** W.K. HARRIS *Outback in Aust.* 90 Each station is represented on the nearest Marsupial Board, usually by the storekeeper. **1930** HIVES & LUMLEY *Jrnl. of Jackeroo* 52 The Government passed an ordinance which declared kangaroos, wallabies, and dingoes to be pests. What were known as Marsupial Boards were formed, and to these the squatters paid certain fees.

martin. [Transf. use of *martin* the bird of the swallow fam. *Chelidon urbica.*] Any of several swallow-like migratory birds, some of which build a mud nest, usu. nesting in colonies, incl. the *fairy martin* (see FAIRY *n.*[1] 1), *tree martin* (see TREE), and *masked wood swallow* (see MASKED). Also *attrib.*

1838 *S. Austral. Rec.* (London) 14 Mar. 45 Two beautiful little martins are building their nests over the porch of the door-way. **1842** J. GOULD *Birds of Aust.* (1848) II. Pl. 14, *Collocalia arborea.* Tree Martin... *Martin* of the Colonists. **1886** W.J. WOODS *Visit to Vic.* 24 There are Swallows, Martins, and Robins, but none of them sing; and, indeed, these English names are most of them as misleading as those given to the native fruits. **1955** H.G. LAMOND *Towser* 269 *Martin*, masked wood swallow (*Artamus personatus*). **1981** A.B. FACEY *Fortunate Life* 89 The martin sparrow went in packs of hundreds; it lived on small insects and made its nest in hollow limbs of large trees... It was .. about the size of a canary, and had a black head, brown feathers along the sides and back, light grey underneath .. and around the neck, and bright brown under its wings.

Martin Place. [The name of a street, now a pedestrian plaza, in central Sydney.] Used allusively to connote urban decadence.

1938 *Bulletin* (Sydney) 28 Dec. 19/3 Martin-place outbackers. **1961** *Ibid.* 1 Mar. 32/3 Wish I was a Martin Place bludger. **1979** S. MORAN *Reminisc. of Rebel* 59 More unusual ones [*sc.* nicknames] were .. Martin Place (full every lunch time) [etc.].

Marvellous Melbourne. See quot. 1966.

1885 *Argus* (Melbourne) 8 Aug. 5/1 *The land of the golden fleece by George Augustus Sala. . . Marvellous Melbourne.* . . It was on the 17th of March in the present year of grace, 1885, that I made my first entrance, shortly before high noon, into Marvellous Melbourne. **1887** *Illustr. Austral. News* (Melbourne) 25 June (Suppl.) 2/1 Marvellous Melbourne . . in half a century has run such a race that she now stands equal with some of the great cities of the old world. **1888** *Ibid.* 1 Aug. (Suppl.) 20/1 Hobart, Adelaide, Sydney, Dunedin or Auckland are attractive and beautiful capitals, but 'marvellous Melbourne' possesses features peculiarly its own. **1896** N. GOULD *Town & Bush* 118 *Marvellous Melbourne* is a term often applied to the Victorian capital, and the city is not unworthy of it. **1966** M. CANNON *Land Boomers* 3 Visitors to the colony of Victoria in the 1880s were awed and dazzled by the astonishing progress of the city. They began to call it 'Marvellous Melbourne'. **1973** J. MURRAY *Larrikins* 15 The larrikins soon to maraud the city of Sydney, its southern counterpart, Marvellous Melbourne, and almost every place where population had grown too fast for control or planning. **1984** *Age* (Melbourne) 10 Apr. 23/6 When the subject of a visitation to our own, to Marvellous Melbourne's underground came up, I leapt on it, or in it, as a subject full of fascination and dread.

Mary. *Austral. pidgin.* [Also in other Pacific pidgins.]

a. An Aboriginal woman.

1830 R. DAWSON *Present State Aust.* 65 Mary come me. Dat husband murry bad man: he waddy (beat) Mary. Mary no like it, so it leabe it. Dat pellow no goot, massa. **1847** *Moreton Bay Courier* 13 Feb. 2/4 He said that . . a Mary, whom I understand to be his daughter, was taken in childbirth—pickaniny tumbled down—and that she herself was very sick. **1913** *Bulletin* (Sydney) 17 Apr. 16/1 In Narrandera . . I saw Binghi swop Black Mary to a white rabbiter for a sheep dog. **1919** *Ibid.* 6 Mar. 24/3 Here in North Queensland if a boy desires to take a gin for his Mary he persecutes her with attentions. **1939** T.E. JONES *These Twenty Yrs.* 66 'Mary' was only a black lubra. **1980** L.G. FOGARTY *Kargun* 28 Are they told that Jacky Jackys and Marys are going to be killed Tell the abo child the true history.

b. Any non-white woman.

1886 P. CLARKE *'New Chum' in Aust.* 294 If you set a kanaka 'Mary' or woman to clean a floor you must expect it to be somewhat dirtier after than before. . . The women . . were all 'Mary' if you didn't know their proper name. **1893** *Antipodean* (Melbourne) 83 The Kanaka and his Mary, if he is fortunate enough to possess one, as a rule dwell happily together. **1899** *Progress* (Brisbane) 13 May 7/3 The Burdekin kanakas . . sport . . a decent suit of clothes on Sunday when driving their Marys and families out. **1918** *Passed by Censor: Souvenir Austral. Naval & Military Exped. Force New Guinea* Christmas 4 A fascinating and beautiful young Mary. **1952** T.A.G. HUNGERFORD *Ridge & River* 172 The kanaka shrugged and walked out of the hut. . . 'What did he say, Alec?' . . 'The coons reckon he's been having a lash at the maries.'

c. A white woman. Freq. as **white Mary.**

1853 H.B. JONES *Adventures in Aust.* 147 He wished to know, pointing to a hut, whether my wife and children lived there. 'You white fellow—Mary—piccaninie—sit down humpy,' pointing to the building. We gave him to understand we were blessed with neither a Mary nor piccaninie. **1870** C.H. ALLEN *Visit to Qld.* 183 With the black people a husband is now called a 'benjamin'. . . All white men are called 'Willy', all white women 'Mary'. **1881** A.C. GRANT *Bush-Life Qld.* II. 121 All white women are termed 'White Marys' by the natives. **1898** *Bulletin* (Sydney) 21 May 14/1 Several dusky Kitties have lately donned a wedding-ring 'allee same white Mary'. **1927** 'S. RUDD' *Romance of Runnibede* 65 Those wild and simple-minded women of the bush . . for years loyally served and loved her as their own 'White Mary'. **1939** J.G. PATTISON *'Battler's' Tales Early Rockhampton* 100 One of them gave the show away about the murder of the White Mary. **1956** T. RONAN *Moleskin Midas* 326 'Harness up the buggy and take this Mary back to town.' Belinda was too bewildered to notice the insult of Mary instead of Missus. **1974** N. CATO *Brown Sugar* 139 They made their usual inquiries, saying they were investigating the death of a 'white Mary' at the coast.

masked, *ppl. a.* Used as a distinguishing epithet in the names of birds: **masked gannet,** the large seabird *Sula dactylatra*, of islands of n.w. and n.e. Aust. and elsewhere in the tropics and subtropics, having white and black plumage with black face-markings; **plover,** the wading bird *Vanellus miles miles* of n. Aust. and nearby parts of the s.w. Pacific, having predom. olive-brown and white plumage, with a black crown and yellow wattles on the face; **wood swallow,** the nomadic, predom. grey bird *Artamus personatus* of mainland Aust. (see quot. 1849); see also *blue martin* b., BLUE *a.*, MARTIN.

1846 J. GOULD *Birds of Aust.* (1848) VII. Pl. 77, *Sula personata* . . **Masked Gannet.** **1890** G.J. BROINOWSKI *Birds of Aust.* I. Pl. 7, The captain and officers of H.M.S. 'Fly' . . surveying the waters of Torres Strait . . found the masked Gannet in greatest abundance on Raine's Island. **1945** C. BARRETT *Austral. Bird Life* 96 The brown gannet . . and the masked gannet (*S[ula] dactylatra*) are tropical birds which nest on islands off the coast. **1978** N. COLEMAN *Look at Wildlife Great Barrier Reef* 37 The masked gannet is a distinctive well known bird which ranges along the length of the Great Barrier Reef. **1890** G.J. BROINOWSKI *Birds of Aust.* II. Pl. 42, This **Masked Plover** . . frequently utters a cry not unlike the name bestowed on it by the natives (Al-ga-ra-ra). **1945** C. BARRETT *Austral. Bird Life* 102 The masked plover (*Lobibyx miles*) . . is closely related to the spurwing. **1964** M. SHARLAND *Territory of Birds* 114 Some lily growths are so substantial that they would support far heavier birds. I have seen Masked Plover . . walking on these floating masses. **1842** J. GOULD *Birds of Aust.* (1848) II. Pl. 31, *Artamus personatus* . . **Masked Wood Swallow.** **1849** C. STURT *Narr. Exped. Central Aust.* II. 20 App. *Masked wood swallow.* So called because of a black mark on the throat and cheek resembling a mask in some measure. **1916** S.A. WHITE *In Far Northwest* 94 A large flight of masked wood swallows. **1934** H.G. LAMOND *Aviary on Plains* 112 It is the blue martin (Masked Wood-swallow). **1956** A.C.C. LOCK *Tropical Tapestry* 139 Masked wood swallows were nesting in some of the gums. **1984** M. BLAKERS et al. *Atlas Austral. Birds* 631 The Masked Wood swallow inhabits open wooded country.

mason wasp. [Transf. use of *mason-wasp* a solitary wasp *Odynerus murarius*.] Any of many stout-bodied, solitary wasps, esp. of the fam. Eumenidae and Sphecidae, building mud cells in which to store food for the larvae; *mud wasp*, see MUD 1. Formerly also **mason fly** (or **hornet**).

1872 MRS E. MILLETT *Austral. Parsonage* 56 Hanging nests of puddled clay, looking somewhat as if they belonged to a colony of swallows. The proprietors, however, were not birds, but of the race of mason-hornet, properly called a sphex. **1894** *Proc. Linnean Soc. N.S.W.* IX. 27 *Alastor eriurgus* . . a very common 'mason wasp' in the neighbourhood of Sydney. **1896** B. SPENCER *Rep. Horn Sci. Exped. Central Aust.* I. 98 A black and white mason fly was making persistent efforts to drag a heavy spider up the smooth trunk of a red gum to its nest. **1922** *Bulletin* (Sydney) 20 Apr. 22/3, I have been interfering with mason-wasps' nests lately, to find out the exact breed of spider immured in the clay cells as food for the wasp grub. **1934** W.A. OSBORNE *Visitor to Aust.* 85 Mason wasps, which build cells of clay to enclose their eggs . . are very common. **1941** *Bulletin* (Sydney) 1 Jan. 16/2 A mason wasp is building on the back wall of my bookcase.

Ma State. A name for New South Wales, the earliest Australian Colony (see quot. 1914). Also abbrev. as **Ma.**

1906 *Bulletin* (Sydney) 18 Jan. 14/4 Strange how the importing mania clings to the Ma State. **1914** H.M. VAUGHAN *Australasian Wander-Yr.* 61 The mother colony of New South Wales is often referred to as 'Ma State'. **1927** *Bulletin* (Sydney) 12 May 24/2 Within certain shires of the Ma State . . the cape-tulip has spread apace. **1934** *Ibid.* 24 Jan. 25/1 The Cabbage Gardeners will have to be licked outright if Ma is to have a hope. **1942** *Ibid.* 18 Feb. 12/2 In various parts of the Ma State. **1954** *Ibid.* 10 Feb. 12/4 South Australia . . missed a great opportunity by not bunging a few million over to the Ma State.

Hence **Ma Stater** *n.*

1933 *Bulletin* (Sydney) 2 Aug. 10/3 In 1923 a warrant was issued for a Ma Stater charged with disobeying a magisterial order.

master. *Hist.* One to whom a convict is assigned: see ASSIGN *v.*

1796 *N.S.W. Instruct. to Watchmen* 11 Gentlemen's Servants will have Passes from their respective Masters. **1802** *Gen. Orders issued by Governor King* 6 Feb. 80 A Convict servant . . is this day ordered to receive 100 lashes and remain in the Gaol gang 1 year, for gross abuse to his master (an officer), and refusing to sleep on his Farm. **1813** *Regulations respecting Assigned Convict Servants* 24 July (1821) 17 If any Female Convict Servant be ill-treated by her Master or Mistress, she is . . to prefer her complaint to a Magistrate. **1828** *Austral. Almanack* 86 Should the Master of any Prisoner, applying for a Ticket of Leave, consider the Applicant undeserving the Indulgence, he should state the Circumstance, in Writing, to the Bench. **1847** J.D. LANG *Phillipsland* 68 The masters of assigned convict-servants in New South Wales were allowed to carry these servants along with them if they removed. **1873** J. BONWICK *M. Howe* 34 Howe found a master, to whom he was assigned as a servant, a few days after landing. **1900** W. DELAFORCE *Life & Experiences Ex-Convict Port Macquarie* 6 If a man had a seven years' sentence, he had to serve four years with a master before he got a 'ticket-of-leave'.

matchbox bean. [See quot. 1933.] The large, shiny, dark brown seed of the vigorous climber *Entada phaseoloides* (fam. Caesalpiniaceae); the long flattened pod of the plant; the plant itself, occurring in Qld., N.T., and elsewhere; *Queensland bean*, see QUEENSLAND 2.

1917 *Bulletin* (Sydney) 7 June 22/4 The bucks went into the surrounding scrubs and gathered matchbox beans . . and clothes-line props. **1933** *Ibid.* 27 Dec. 21/4 A matchbox bean (*Entada scandens*) was washed up on a beach near Eden. . . Bushmen scoop out the kernel and make very fine waterproof matchboxes from these beans. **1948** H.A. LINDSAY *Bushman's Handbk.* 93 The matchbox bean is a vine carrying pods about two feet long, containing large brown seeds. **1969** R. LAWRENCE *Aboriginal Habitat* 166 The preparation of the Matchbox Bean was evidently so arduous . . that it was regarded more as a stand-by than a staple.

mate. [Spec. use of Br. *mate* 'habitual companion, an associate, fellow, comrade; a fellow-worker or partner. Now only in working-class use': see OED(S *sb.*[2] 1.]

1. a. An equal partner in an enterprise: see quots. 1838, 1845, and 1921. Also **working mate.**

1834 N.S.W. Magistrates' Deposition Bk. 19 Nov., Just before I got to my own hut I heard the dogs making a great noise and I asked my mate John Rolfe whose dogs they were. **1838** A. MACONOCHIE *Thoughts on Convict Managem.* 220 These men when they contract to do heavy work, as clearing, fencing, etc. almost always do it in parties of two, or more, being prompted to this in the first place by the hardness of the work, which a man cannot face alone, requiring always the assistance of 'neighbours', or 'mates', or 'partners', as they are severally called, even in the minute details. **1843** *Sydney Morning Herald* 11 July 2/2 The prisoner and witness had been working as mates sawing timber. **1845** C. GRIFFITH *Present State & Prospects Port Phillip* 79 Two generally travel together, who are called mates; they are partners, and divide all their earnings. **1857** *Illustr. Jrnl. Australasia* III. 66, I had gained nothing but a partner, or, as the vernacular of the diggings has it, a mate. **1859** 'EYE WITNESS' *Voyage to Aust.* 18 Two working mates occupy the same tent if working together. **1867** W. MILTON *Victim Nineteenth Century* 17, I consider there was no more imprudence on my part, by allowing the person that I was taking to the diggings as a mate to know that I had money on me, than there is for a broker to exhibit money or valuables on his counter. **1880** J.B. STEVENSON *Seven Yrs. Austral. Bush* 60 My mate and I (every one has a mate on a trip) wandered up the ravine. **1887** MRS D.D. DALY *Digging, Squatting, & Pioneering Life* 152 A 'mate' was a 'mate'—share and share alike, no matter how bad might be the times. ***c* 1907** W.C. CHANDLER *Darkest Adelaide* 5 She (to her mates)—'Gor' blime have I scored?' **1921** W.H. CORFIELD *Reminisc. Qld.* 46, I have alluded several times to 'partners', or 'mates', which was the more popular term. These partnerships were quite common amongst carriers and diggers in bygone days. It was simply chums, owning and sharing everything in common, and without any agreement, written or otherwise. **1939** G. DIGBY *Down Wind* 185 Advertisement in the *Sydney Morning Herald.*

'Wanted', it read, 'mate to go rabbiting.' **1952** *Bulletin* (Sydney) 20 Aug. 16/1 I've been working 'mates' with a very New Australian.

b. In the phr. **to go mates,** to work as an equal partner (with someone, etc.).

[**1842** *S. Austral. Mag.* (Adelaide) 286, I think I went a shepherding. Oh yes, I went mate to Donald ---, to herd sixteen hundred sheep at Glenelg.] **1876** 'Eight Yrs.' Resident' *Queen of Colonies* 119 They [*sc.* the Chinese] appear to have no quarrels among themselves when working in partnerships, or as the digging phrase is, 'going mates'. **1893** G.S. Williams *New Aust.* 8 We do not want anybody who does not feel ready to go 'mates' with everybody else that joins. **1898** *Worker* (Sydney) 22 Jan. 7/1 If you and I go mates on a selection, it will often be desirable that you should go on clearing or ploughing for both, while I mend the roof of the bark humpy for both. **1940** I.L. Idriess *Lightning Ridge* 188 None of us liked going mates with a man unless we could pay our own way.

2. An acquaintance; a person engaged in the same activity.

1841 *Port Phillip Patriot* 23 Dec. 4/3 We told him our mates were gone, and that we had heard two shots fired. **1849** A. Harris *Emigrant Family* (1967) 69 Boasting, among his mates in the bush. **1853** J. Capper *Emigrant's Guide to Aust.* (ed. 2) 235 The outward garb forms no mark of distinction—'all are mates'. **1874** *Adelaide Observer* 26 Dec. (Christmas Suppl.) 12/1 'Syd the swell seems down on his luck heavy,' was the passing comment of his rough mates. **1879** 'Australian' *Adventures Qld.* 7 Kipper Tommy was . . acknowledged by his mates to be the crack driver of the district. **1911** A. Searcy *By Flood & Field* 29 Covered with large green ants . . how they stang! and how my dusky mates laughed! **1919** A. Wright *Game of Chance* 9 The boy had joined his mates in one of the little cemeteries on the Western front. **1934** *Red Star* (Perth) 3 Aug. 2/2 Seventeen of our mates were killed in the mining industry last year. **1963** J. O'Grady *Things they do to You* 121 Not me mate. Me mate's mate. **1967** D. Horne *Educ. Young Donald* 68 As a term used in civilian life 'mate' was simply a slang word and you would lose marks in English composition for using it. **1971** *Bulletin* (Sydney) 8 May 42/3 The old soldiers watch him, look around at their mates and don't listen. **1972** K. Dunstan *Knockers* 52 A mate in Australia is simply that which a bloke must have around him. Mates do not necessarily want to know you. **1978** J. Rowe *Warlords* 23 It was as formalized and meaningless as the Communist *comrade* or the Australian *mate*. **1985** *Canberra Times* 21 June 1/1 High Court judge Mr Justice Murphy denied yesterday that he had ever said to N.S.W. Chief Magistrate Mr Briese anything like, 'And now, what about my little mate?'

3. One with whom the bonds of close friendship are acknowledged, a 'sworn friend'.

1891 'Smiler' *Wanderings Simple Child* (ed. 3) p. iv, Where his mate was his sworn friend through good and evil report, in sickness and health, in poverty and plenty, where his horse was his comrade, and his dog his companion, the bushman lived the life he loved. **1913** H. Lawson *Triangles of Life* 237 The man who hasn't a male mate is a lonely man indeed, or a strange man, though he have a wife and family. **1914** 'B. Cable' *By Blow & Kiss* 186 Stevie's more to me than a man is to a girl—yes, I know you'll grin at that, but you don't rightly know what men are to each other out here. He's my mate—we're mates, and good mates. **1928** A. Wright *Good Recovery* 141 Norma was sobbing in the arms of her old mate, Betty. **1930** *Bulletin* (Sydney) 24 Dec. 21/2 One of the best mates I ever had was a woman, but I didn't know it till we parted. **1945** *Ibid.* 12 Sept. 12/2 You can't kid me that a woman could ever be a *mate* like you an' me know it. **1948** F. Clune *Wild Colonial Boys* 628 You've been a good mate and a man can't say more than that. **1954** J. Cleary *Climate of Courage* 38 G'day, dig. Me ol' mate, me cobber. **1965** F. Hardy *Yarns of Billy Borker* 80 No matter what you do, your Australian mate will defend you—'A mate can do no wrong.' **1977** R. Beilby *Gunner* 177 'He's me mate. I gotta help 'im,' he stated simply and incontrovertibly. . . There was no answer to that, Gunner knew: the outcome of this incident had been predetermined by the peculiar chemistry of compatibility, by social mores and by the almost tribal ties of marriage, all pledged with countless beers. It was personal, traditional, and deeply masculine. **1986** *Bulletin* (Sydney) 21 Jan. 36/1 Silence was the essence of traditional mateship. . . The gaunt man stands at his wife's funeral; his mate comes up, says nothing but rests a gentle hand briefly on his shoulder.

4. A mode of address implying equality and goodwill; freq. used to a casual acquaintance and, esp. in recent use (but see quot. 1855), ironic.

1843 *Trifler* (Launceston) 12 July 2/2 Before Comray fired, he said, 'Where are you, mate?' **1855** R. Carboni *Eureka Stockade* 4 'Your licence, mate', was the peremptory question from a six-foot fellow in blue shirt, thick boots, the face of a ruffian, armed with a carabine and fixed bayonet. **1857** W. Howitt *Tallangetta* I. 308 A woman with a child under her arm . . said, 'Shall you bring him off, think you, sir?' 'Shall we?' said Mr Martin, 'of course we shall, make yourself sure of that, mate.' **1873** W. Thomson-Gregg *Desperate Character* III. 110 'Same for me,' said the girl, 'and what for you, mate?' addressing Hubert. **1892** *Truth* (Sydney) 31 July 1/2 And I often fancy how you, old mate, Must feel when you think of sweet, blue-eyed Kate. **1900** R. Bruce *Benbonuna* 103 The word 'mate' greeted [*sic*] harshly on his sensitive British ear, especially when uttered by such a vulgar-looking fellow as Jack Jones, the horse-driver, with whom . . he was not at all inclined to fraternize. **1944** A.S. Smith *Boys write Home* 194 One of the boys called him 'Dig.' another 'Mate', and the rest of us 'Lord'. When we asked him how we should address him he replied: 'You are all doing fine.' **1953** T.A.G. Hungerford *Riverslake* 50 I'll remember you, mate. You'll keep! **1957** R. Beynon *Shifting Heart* (1960) 69 This is forty-three, mate; you got the wrong house. **1964** *Realist* (Sydney) xv. 6 When Shirl finally said, 'That's the lot, mate!' Joy was able to smile back and reply, 'Thank God for that.' **1967** A. Seymour *One Day of Yr.* 32 England? Bugger England. I'm a bloody Australian, mate. **1977** B. Reed *Cass Butcher Bunting* 38 I've just been sweating on an opportunity to do you a damage, mate. **1983** *Bulletin* (Sydney) 13 Sept. 60/1 When they call you 'mate' in the N.S.W. Labor Party it is like getting a kiss from the Mafia.

mateless, *a.* Companionless; lone.

1896 H. Lawson *While Billy Boils* 170 The everlasting stars . . keep the mateless traveller from going mad as he lies in his lonely camp on the plains. **1926** L.C.E. Gee *Bush Tracks & Gold Fields* 72 'Possum Bill was a 'hatter', that is, a mateless river man, who roamed about by himself.

mateship. [Spec. use of *mateship* the condition of being a mate, companionship: see OED(S.] The bond between equal partners or close friends; comradeship; comradeship as an ideal. Also *attrib.*

1864 J. Rogers *New Rush* 54 As typical of mate-ship ever true, Accept this melody—my last. Adieu. **1894** *Worker* (Sydney) 22 Dec. 3/3 Real mateship! It is what the lowly Nazarene taught. But it will never be learned so long as we are more jealous of our own reputation than anxious for the welfare of our fellows. **1897** *Bulletin* (Sydney) 11 Dec. 29/2 Seven weeks of lurid mateship—ruined soul and four pounds six. **1898** *Worker* (Sydney) 4 June 4/5 Look here, lads, cultivate the spirit of mateship; love one another. **1909** W.G. Spence *Aust.'s Awakening* 78 Unionism came to the Australian bushman as a religion. . . It had in it that feeling of mateship which he understood already, and which always characterised the action of one 'white man' to another. **1913** H. Lawson *For Aust.* 182 River banks were grassy—grassy in the bends, Running through the land where mateship never ends. **1915** T. Skeyhill *Soldier-Songs from Anzac* 16 But nevermore shall I forget, not though I live for ever, The days when we in mateship met along the Moonie River. **1922** A. Wright *Boss o' Yedden* 10 Carl, with angry words and threats, spurned the offer of continued mateship. They would be mates no longer, for friendship was now impossible. **1931** Lawson & Brereton *H. Lawson* 15 So mateship became the lonely poet's watchword, and he made it the watchword of Australia. **1935** J.P. McKinney *Crucible* 63 The one compensating aspect of life as then lived was the element of mateship. Inside the wide family circle of the battalion and the company were the more closely knit platoon groups. **1943** H.W. Malloch *Fellows All* 18 The Bread and Cheese Club had to have a motto, and the admirable one chosen was 'Mateship, Art and Letters'. **1954** J. Waten *Unbending* 95 You've always told me . . that the boss class works the mateship business in this country. **1964** E. Lane *Our Uncle Charlie* 89 He joined the Mateship of Austral Scribes, one of the many literary societies in the Commonwealth whose members tirelessly grubbed over huge slagheaps of unreadable Australian writing in search of a few precious grains of exegetical paydirt. **1968** G. Dutton *Andy* 95 It was part of mateship that on the surface you always abused your mate and rubbished him. **1973** P.Y. Medding *Jews in Austral. Soc.* 6 Much of mateship was exclusive rather than inclusive . . based upon strong solidarity against outsiders, and antipathy and antagonism towards them. **1984** *People Mag.* (Sydney) 7 May 40/1 Shearing to me is the mates I've made. . . There's no greater mateship in any industry in Australia. **1985** *Canberra Times* 4 Mar. 8/3 That such a rift should be developing between Australia and New Zealand on the eve of the 70th anniversary of our forging such a famous mateship is deeply to be regretted.

matey. [f. Mate 4 + -Y.] A mode of address implying friendliness and goodwill.

1854 C.A. Corbyn *Sydney Revels* 93, I say matey . . go and lie down in my bunk. **1861** H. Earle *Ups & Downs* 125 Some rest, matey . . and a little information. **1871** *Emigrant's Wife* I. 284 *Mate*, I may explain, is a term of friendliness; but *matey* is one of endearment itself, quite a word, indeed, following the Italian system of adjectives of love or contempt. **1891** *Bulletin* (Sydney) 19 Dec. 22/1 Put a good face on it, matey. **1910** *Ibid.* 29 Sept. 13/2 Good-day, matey. Wanter buy a buncher flowers fer yer tart? **1930** A.E. Yarra *Vanishing Horsemen* 138 Good on yeh, matey. **1959** B. Jefferis *Half Angel* 53 Don't you worry about that, matey. **1981** C. Wallace-Crabbe *Splinters* 30 Listen, matey, I don't want any fancy academic analyses of the situation.

Matilda. [Transf. but unexplained use of the female name.]

1. A swag. Also *fig.*

1892 *Bulletin* (Sydney) 9 Apr. 18/2 An old stager of a sundowner . . slung 'Matilda' off his back, and leant across the rail. **1895** *Worker* (Sydney) 10 Aug. 1/4 Aye, some people named her 'bluey', and others call her 'swag', Who christened her 'Matilda' was the essence of a wag. **1905** *Truth* (Sydney) 26 Feb. 1/8 A man dressed in clerical garb passed through recently carrying a 'matilda'. **1916** *Ibid.* 21 May 7/4 The full private in Napoleon's army carried a Marshall's baton *in his matilda.* **1920** H.F. Mollard *Humour of Road* 40 He's got 'Matilda' in that pram. When those old blokes get too weak to carry swags they push 'em on bikes or in prams. **1939** *Bulletin* (Sydney) 15 Feb. 20/4 The swaggie dropped Matilda against the wall and put down a sprat on the bar. **1944** M.J. O'Reilly *Bowyangs & Boomerangs* 44 With a little practice 'Matilda' can be put in her place with one swing with the tucker bag balancing the weight in front. **1962** Marshall & Drysdale *Journey among Men* 146 We unrolled our Matildas between the dunes. **1978** R.A.F. Webb *Brothers in Sun* 53 The swagmen, each with his blue blanket tied at either end like a long sausage, his few worldly belongings inside, and carried over his shoulder by a piece of rope, had long lost truck with families and friends. Their 'wives' now were the matildas (i.e. swags) they carried around the bush.

2. In the phr. **to waltz Matilda,** to carry one's swag; to travel the road. Also *fig.*

1893 *Bulletin* (Sydney) 18 Nov. 20/3 No bushman thinks of 'going on the wallaby' or 'walking Matilda', or 'padding the hoof'; he goes on the track—when forced to 't. **1895** A.B. Paterson *Singer of Bush* (1983) 254 Who'll come a-waltzing Matilda, my darling, Who'll come a-waltzing Matilda with me. Waltzing Matilda and leading a water-bag, Who'll come a-waltzing Matilda with me. **1898** *Bulletin* (Sydney) 20 Aug. (Red Page), *Pushing the knot.* . . The variant *Waltzing Matilda* (now rarely heard) was born from a 'tender' swagman's habit of resting his back by carrying the burden in his arms, when he and it are really suggestive of a lydy and gent, embracing in the wrestlers' hug of a 'push' dance-room. **1925** *Smith's Weekly* (Sydney) 14 Mar. 21/3 The turtle is a pretty considerable land-traveller on occasions. When the billabongs dry up in drought time he waltzes Matilda to the river as straight as the crow flies. **1937** Wisberg & Waters *Bushman at Large* 83 Waltzing Matilda is a gay occupation. **1945** J. Devanny *Bird of Paradise* 144 Nowadays they waltz Matilda on bikes. **1956** A.C.C. Lock *Tropical Tapestry* 114 Why, I thought everybody had heard of Waltzing Matilda. That's the name of a swagman's bag; his billy and blankets. **1966** O. Mendelsohn *Waltz with Matilda* 107 'Waltzing matilda' as a saying is arty, precious, smelling of the study. In all my life I have never heard anybody of any social stratum say anywhere at any time that he was going waltzing matilda. **1972** R. BOYD *Great Austral. Dream* 75 'I don't believe in nationalism in the 'Waltzing Matilda' sense,' he added. He wanted an Australian Style without the outback intruding too far.

3. In the phr. **(with) Matilda up,** carrying a swag.

1895 K. MACKAY *Yellow Wave* 58 D' ye mind that day on the Flinders when you met me with Matilda up. **1902** *Bulletin* (Sydney) 8 Nov. 3/2 For thirty odd years Dan has camped Among the Bogan bends, And with Matilda up has tramped A track that never ends. **1912** M.C. DONALD *Real Austral.* 48, I wonder whether Miss Desmond ever . . fell into step with the lean, brown, dusty, travelling worker, 'Matilda up'.

4. Special Comb. **Matilda-bearer (-carrier, -hawker, -lumper, -man, -waltzer),** a swagman.

1910 *Bulletin* (Sydney) 26 May 15/2 The average Matilda-hawker, if he happens on a 'stiff' mate, rushes into the nearest town with the news. **1911** *Ibid.* 19 Jan. 14/4 We were joined by a veteran Matilda-carrier. **1927** *Smith's Weekly* (Sydney) 30 Apr. 19/7 Hence the hearty welcome to any Matilda bearer who . . succeeds in passing the deep crossing. **1933** *Bulletin* (Sydney) 3 May 20/2 Matilda-waltzers with one black (or brown) shoe or boot are an everyday sight. **1936** *Ibid.* 30 Sept. 21/2, I struck a veteran Matilda-man preparing his bed. **1939** *Ibid.* 28 June 20/3 Your modern Matilda-lumper doesn't fool around on a wet day with damp chips.

McGinness, McGinnis, McGuiness, var. MAGINNIS.

meara, var. MEERA.

meat. Used *attrib.* in Special Comb. **meat ant, (a)** any of a small group of related species of ant of the large genus *Iridomyrmex*, esp. the mound-building *I. purpureus* (= *detectus*), having a reddish head and purple body, and capable of inflicting a painful bite; *road ant*, see ROAD 3; **(b)** *fig.*, in the phr. **game as a meat ant,** courageous; **-bag,** a hessian safe used to protect meat from flies; **-billy,** a billy in which meat is cooked; **pie, (a)** *attrib.* in **meat-pie bookie** (or **bookmaker**), a small-time bookmaker; see also PIE; **(b)** in the phr. **as Australian as (a) meat pie,** quintessentially Australian; **-works,** an abattoir; an establishment where meat is processed.

(a) 1900 *Bulletin* (Sydney) 7 Apr. (Red Page), On the nest of a colony of these **meat ants** I placed a large green caterpillar. **1936** *Austral. Writers' Ann.* 33 The red ant, or meat ant . . loves meat, nicely cooked, but attacks other foods as well, and fouls everything he touches. **1963** X. HERBERT *Disturbing Element* 7 Meat ants would run up his legs at table. **1973** J. GREENWAY *Down among Men* 70 The meat ant *Iridomyrmex detectus* . . deals with the human skin the way heated pincers of medieval torture chambers were said to do. **1981** *Ecos* xxviii. 26/2 Meat ants and medium-sized species do compete for food and even attack one another, and the meat ant usually wins. **(b) 1932** J.J. HARDIE *Cattle Camp* (1944) 9 She's like a well-bred filly—**game as a meat-ant. 1933** W. HATFIELD *Desert Saga* 65 The kid's all right . . he only fainted. Game as a meat-ant, ain't he? **1982** *Overlander* Sept. 27 He's as game as a meat ant but if we ride further he will be impaired. **1904** *Bulletin* (Sydney) 4 Feb. 36/2 Flies have got into the **meat-bag** and the meat is only fit to throw to the dogs. **1925** *Makeshifts & Other Home-Made Furniture* (New Settlers League Aust.) 38 For a hanging meat-bag for joints, fit a pole along the side of a large bag and put a hook at either end by which to hang it up. Make a board floor to fit. **1902** *Bulletin* (Sydney) 11 Jan. 32/1 Every traveller has . . one or two billies. Some have three—of varying sizes to fit one in the other. The tea-billy and **meat-billy** are the most common. **1963** M. BRITT *Pardon my Boots* 135 There were no cooking utensils except for three blackened billy-cans and one large meat-billy. **1915** A. WRIGHT *Sport from Hollowlog Flat* 24 Don't bet with these **meat-pie bookies.** Dave Doem'll offer a fair price directly. **1919** C. DREW *Doings of Dave* 89 I've done with all these meatpie bookmakers for good. **1922** A. WRIGHT *Colt from Country* 122 'They're meat-pie bookies all right,' he exclaimed, displaying a bunch of tickets. 'Had to make four bets of it.' **1972** *Sunday Austral.* (Sydney) 16 Apr. 4/6 Apart from his name and his forebears, Barassi with his wide grin and fierce desire to win is **as Australian as a meat pie. 1979** K. DUNSTAN *Ratbags* p. xiv, As Australian as meatpie. **1981** L. KRAMER *Oxford Hist. Austral. Lit.* 420 In some poems he uses a dramatic voice which is as Australian as a meat pie. [**1895 meat-works:** T.A. COGHLAN *Wealth & Progress N.S.W. 1894* 367 All the cattle killed, except 27,891 treated in the meat-processing works, were required for local consumption.] **1936** *Bulletin* (Sydney) 23 Sept. 20/4 The Koolinda called at Wyndham recently to convey 200 returning meatworks employees to Fremantle. **1956** S. GORE *Overlanding with Annabel* 23 We came in sight of the meatworks . . rather a misnomer, actually, for there were no signs of 'meat' or of 'works'. **1960** *N.T. News* (Darwin) 5 Feb. 6/2 They are planning a very large meatworks at Alice Springs. . . The company also plans a smaller abattoirs at Darwin. **1977** C.T. CASSIDY *Random Thoughts* 4 A crocodile filled with real remorse, Because for breakfast it had a horse, Or made its dinner on a Meatworks bull.

medicine man. [Spec. use of orig. U.S. *medicine man.*] KORADJI.

1865 G.S. LANG *Aborigines of Aust.* 8 The second class is that of the sorcerers or medicine men. **1896** B. SPENCER *Rep. Horn Sci. Exped. Central Aust.* IV. 184 He again conceals the *injilla* and returns to camp—the victim being supposed to sicken and die within a month unless he be saved by the skill of the medicine-man. **1923** T. HALL *Short Hist. Downs Blacks* 26 Unless a medicine man sucked the Muddlo out they would die with fear. **1935** H. BASEDOW *Knights of Boomerang* 43 The influence of the medicine-man is great. . . They are the only persons who treat the sick. **1944** J.K. EWERS *Tales from Dead Heart* 75 Ngangan . . became the wisest and most respected medicine-man the tribe had ever known. **1962** D. LOCKWOOD *I, Aboriginal* 9 The Medicine Man, the Doctor Blackfellow.

medifraud. [f. *medi(cal insurance* + *fraud.*] The practice of making fraudulent claims against a medical insurance scheme; an instance of this. Also *attrib.*

1982 *Age* (Melbourne) 6 Aug. 3/7 PS staff rapped on attitude to medifraud. . . Senior officials of the Commonwealth Health Department . . were severely criticised at a Federal inquiry into medifraud yesterday. **1983** *Advertiser* (Adelaide) 22 July 12/5 Federal police . . visit as a result of an alleged medifraud and with a warrant which empowers them to seize documents or records that will provide evidence of an offence. **1984** *Age* (Melbourne) 28 Mar. 4/5 A report released yesterday . . says that the number of Medifraud prosecutions has dropped by half in the past year. **1986** *Canberra Times* 4 Mar. 7/1 A former Department of Health medifraud investigator has failed in his attempt to force the Australian Federal Police to hand over documents concerning a joint medifraud case involving a medical practitioner. **1986** *Nat. Times* (Sydney) 2 May 5/3 *Medifraud*. . . During the taped conversation, Ryan told Thomas the doctor had at his disposal huge sums of money and that he, Ryan, acted for the doctor and would like something done for the doctor to reduce the number of charges he faced.

Mediterranean. Used allusively to refer to behaviour supposedly characteristic of an Australian of Italian or Greek descent: (of an injury, illness, etc.) feigned.

1973 *Bulletin* (Sydney) 24 Feb. 12/1 There was . . the case of the laborer suffering a severe case of 'Mediterranean Back' after an accident at work. **1981** *Austral.* (Sydney) 20 Apr. 7/1 For afflictions such as vertebrate disease—known by many as 'Greek back' or 'Mediterranean back'—Greeks are 15 times more likely to be disabled than Australians. **1982** N. KEESING *Lily on Dustbin* 51 There are racist overtones to the 'Mediterranean syndrome', an over-emotional patient or performance; the 'Mediterranean back', which denotes derisive suspicion about a back-ache and 'Mediterranean gut-ache', usually shortened to 'MGA' which is just as suspect as the back-ache. **1983** *Austral.* (Sydney) 9 Dec. 9/1 A report by the Human Rights Commission published yesterday dwells on complaints which can be an incitement to racial hatred. 'Mediterranean back', 'ethnic jokes' (especially Irish ones) and the use of the word 'Pom' receive special mention.

meera /ˈmirə/. Also **meara, merro, meru.** [a. Nyungar *mira.*] An Aboriginal throwing stick used to launch a spear.

1828 *Austral. Q. Jrnl. Theol., Lit. & Sci.* Jan. 29 The hammers and knives were of singular formation, and the *mearas* ingeniously constructed. **1841** G. GREY *Jrnls. Two Exped. N.-W. & W.A.* I. 304 The old lady . . went up to him . . seizing his merro, or throwing stick. **1878** R.B. SMYTH *Aborigines of Vic.* I. p. xlvi, The lever used to propel the spear—the *Kur-ruk, Gur-reek, Murn-wun, Meera*, or *Womerah*, of the east, west, and south, the *Logorouk* or *Wondouk* of the north—is the same in principle in all parts of Australia. **1901** M. VIVIENNE *Travels in W.A.* 52 There are some fine native shields, spears, knife dabbas, meeras or throwing sticks, kileys or boomerangs, &c. **1935** H.H. FINLAYSON *Red Centre* 80 The *meru* or spear-thrower.

meet. [Spec. use of *meet* a meeting, an appointment.] An assignation with a person of the opposite sex; a 'date'.

1915 C.J. DENNIS *Songs of Sentimental Bloke* 23, I dunno 'ow I 'ad the nerve ter speak, An' make that meet wiv 'er fer Sundee week! **1937** J. McKELLAR *Sheep without Shepherd* 78 'Did you get a meet?' . . To get an assignation with a girl one had met for the first time . . set a seal upon one as a knight to be respected. **1947** N. LINDSAY *Halfway to Anywhere* 83 The group of youths now closed up on the girls with badinage to mark the approach amorous. 'Pull up, Lottie, you haven't got a meet on, have you?' **1951** I.L. IDRIESS *Across Nullarbor* 12 The Super's blandishments make no impression, for the cook has an important 'meet on'. **1974** N. PHILLIPSON *As Other Men* 118 This guy had a meet on with the girl.

melaleuca /mɛləˈlukə/. [The plant genus *Melaleuca* was named by Swedish botanist Carl von Linné (Linnaeus) (in *Syst. Nat.* ed. 12 509; *Mantissa Plant.* I. 14, 105 (1767)) f. Gr. *μέλας* black + *λευκός* white, referring to the fire-blackened white bark of some Asian species.] Any plant of the large, chiefly Austral. genus *Melaleuca* (fam. Myrtaceae) many of which are cultivated as ornamentals; the wood of these plants. See also TEA-TREE. Also *attrib.*

1814 R. BROWN *Gen. Remarks Bot. Terra Australis* 15 The maximum of Melaleuca exists in the principal parallel, but it declines less towards the south than within the tropic. **1829** R. MUDIE *Picture of Aust.* 141 The *tea-tree* of the colonists belongs to the beautiful genus *melaleuca*, of which there are many species in Australia, though only two have been found in other parts of the world. **1831** *W. Austral.* (Fremantle) 10 Feb. 3 The material of which [the spear] is most commonly made is the melaleuca. **1846** C.P. HODGSON *Reminisc. Aust.* 261 A melaleuca scrub, very interesting, but not when pack-bullocks are carrying your provisions. **1861** *Burke & Wills Exploring Exped.* 19 The water flows over sand and pebbles, winding its way between clumps of melaleuca. **1880** *Argus* (Melbourne) 5 Jan. 6/7 A very beautiful species of melaleuca . . is now in flower on the Buffalo lawn; the blossoms are creamy white. **1926** A.S. LE SOUEF et al. *Wild Animals Australasia* 118 The roots of the melaleuca-trees. **1942** E. ANDERSON *Squatter's Luck* 1 Feathery sour-sapped bent-boughed melaleucas. **1966** N. SIDNEY *Beyond Bay* 11 They would . . drive the short steep clay and limestone path and pull up under a sprawling melaleuca. **1982** R. HALL *Just Relations* 111 Granny Collins buys a dark brocade curtain . . and hangs it on a melaleuca rod hammered to the slab-timber wall of her shack.

Melba /ˈmɛlbə/. [f. *Melbourne* and adopted by Helen Mitchell (1861–1931), an operatic soprano.] Used allusively of a person who retires but makes repeated 'farewell' performances or come-backs. Esp. in the phr. **to do a Melba.** See also quot. 1972.

1971 *Austral.* (Sydney) 20 Feb. 22/4 The later years were marked by a seemingly endless round of farewell performances. 'Doing a Melba', they call it. **1972** *Bulletin* (Sydney) 22 Jan. 33/3 *Germaine Greer's* visit to Australia to promote the paperback edition of her book, 'The Female Eunuch', is in the classic, Melba tradition: the expatriate returning to her homeland at the close of her public career. **1974** *Sydney Morning Herald* 1 June 8/7 It has been intensified by talk from Sir Robert that he is under pressure to stay on, thus giving rise to speculation that he is planning to 'do a Melba'. **1982** *Bulletin* (Sydney) 25 May 37/3 Gee! I made so many comebacks they called me 'Tommy Melba Burns'.

Melbourne, Marvellous: see MARVELLOUS MELBOURNE.

melon. [Spec. use of *melon* a gourd: see PADDY-MELON *n.*[2]]

1. Used *attrib.* in Special Comb. **melon blindness,** an illness of horses, characterized by blindness and believed to result from feeding on the paddy-melon; also **melon-blind** *a.*; **hole,** GILGAI b.; *paddy-melon hole*, see PADDYMELON *n.*[2] 2; freq. *attrib.*; **vine,** PADDYMELON *n.*[2] 1.

1932 M.R. WHITE *No Roads go By* 108 Paddy-melons grew in a green riot along the base of this hill, and many horses were afflicted with **melon blindness** that year—a disease caused through eating the vines. **1976** C.D. MILLS *Hobble Chains & Greenhide* 146 Some bullocks are melon-blind like horses. They're menaces. They'll rush your mob every night if you're not careful. **1844** L. LEICHHARDT *Jrnl. Overland Exped. Aust.* 8 Oct. (1847) 9 The soil of the Bricklow scrub is a stiff clay, washed out by the rains into shallow holes, well known by the squatter under the name of **melon-holes.** **1846** *Melbourne Argus* 1 Sept. 4/4 These trees generally indicated a stiff soil, which in the level country was never free from shallow holes, such as are called melon-holes by the squatters, formed, no doubt, by the infiltrating rain and standing water. **1881** A.C. GRANT *Bush-Life Qld.* I. 220 The plain is full of deep melon-holes. **1895** *Bulletin* (Sydney) 23 Nov. 3/2 He was cautious 'mong the melon-holes, but when the plain was sound He led 'em at a gallop with his eyes upon the ground. **1915** *Ibid.* 5 Aug. 24/3, I had to walk far to school over wet melon-hole flats. **1929** H. MACQUARRIE *We & Baby* 75 Melon-hole country—great caverns in the clay surface disguised and hidden by tall grass, where horses broke their legs and collapsed in untidy messes. **1947** ROE & SHAW *Mint Weed* 10 The soils which carry mint weed in these areas are the black 'melon hole' soils which, before clearing, support a closed brigalow . . belah . . scrub formation. **1956** A.C.C. LOCK *Tropical Tapestry* 55 There were bad patches of 'melon hole' country, where the soil was grey and sandy, the timber stunted and the grass scantier. **1984** H.W. DAVIS *Bachelors in Bush* 12 The area to be fallen for the season . . would embrace a few acres of 'melon hole' country. I have never learned how the name 'melon-holes' originated. They appeared to be natural depressions or holes in certain parts of the standing scrub, several yards in circumference. **1911** *Bulletin* (Sydney) 6 Apr. 15/3 Pretty well every noxious weed . . finds a barracker . . **melon-vine**, sweet briar and the rest . . turn up as 'capital fodder for stock in drought time'. **1935** R.B. PLOWMAN *Boundary Rider* 46 In springtime they are covered with luxuriant grasses and wild flowers, as well as melon-vines.

2. *fig.*

a. A head.

1907 *Truth* (Sydney) 12 May 8/5 (*heading*) Woodford wields a waddy *and mangles Monaghan's melon.* **1919** C. DREW *Doings of Dave* 64 What put the Museum into your melon? **1960** R. PULLAN *Hardskins* 29 Human beings are all the same . . they got arms and legs and a melon. **1971** D. IRELAND *Unknown Industr. Prisoner* 98 One of the engineers . . bravely approached the hole, lowering his head to look inside. 'Why don't you shove your melon right in?' roared the Humdinger.

b. A fool. Also **melonhead.**

1937 E. PARTRIDGE *Dict. Slang & Unconventional Eng.* 516 *Melon* . . the Australian and New Zealand sense . . a simpleton, a fool. **1941** S.J. BAKER *Pop. Dict. Austral. Slang* 46 *Melon*, a simpleton or fool. Whence 'melon-head'. **1955** R. LAWLER *Summer of Seventeenth Doll* (1965) 111 Whose fault was it we come a cropper? . . Nobody's fault, yer melon! **1968** S. GORE *Holy Smoke* 27 This poor coot, squattin' on the edge of the pig trough, rolling himself a smoke, and trying to nut something out . . suddenly . . thinks, '*Strewth*—how big a melon can a man be?'

melt, *v.*[1] *Obs.* [Spec. use of *melt* to reduce to a liquid condition by heat.] *trans.* Freq. with **down.** In the preparation of tallow: to render animal fats. Also *absol.*

1840 *Port Phillip Gaz.* 30 Nov. 3 The Proprietors are purchasers of fat Stock or will melt down for the settlers upon reduced terms. **1847** *Port Phillip Herald* 16 Nov. 1/1 The undersigned is prepared to melt stock on the usual terms. **1848** *Ibid.* 16 Mar. 2/4 Tens of thousands of sheep and thousands of cattle *melted down* that their mere tallow may be sent to Europe, their flesh being cast away in the fields.

Hence **melter** *n.*

1844 *Port Phillip Gaz.* 30 Nov. 3 *Important Sale of 150 Head of Cattle without reserve.* To butchers, melters, dairymen, and stockholders.

melt, *v.*[2] *Obs.* [Spec. use of Br. (slang) *melt* to spend, squander (money): see OED *v.*[1] 13 a. Perh. also infl. by MELT *v.*[1]] *trans.* To squander (one's accumulated earnings) on alcoholic drink, esp. in the phr. **to melt (down) a cheque.** Also with the publican as subject (see quot. 1914).

1869 *Bushmen, Publicans, & Politics* 8 Whatever he may want at the bush township he may choose to visit, he has to cash his cheque to obtain it. Its amount is immediately known, and it is no less sad than true that every snare is thereafter employed to induce him to 'melt it down'. **1882** *Bulletin* (Sydney) 17 June 9/2 A played-out shearer was ordered off the premises of a shanty-keeper out west after he had melted his cheque. **1903** *Ibid.* 16 May 3/2 The wages that I'm getting aren't grand; But a fellow can't go picking when his loot is 'melted down'. **1907** *Ibid.* 7 Feb. 15/2 When shearing cheques were as large as the proverbial blanket . . several knights of the blades . . after 'cut-out', used to travel to Japan to melt their cheques there. **1914** *Ibid.* 15 Jan. 22/1 He said he'd made enough money to do without melting down drunks' cheques, so when they got to a certain stage he limited them to a beer an hour. **1930** *Ibid.* 30 July 20/1 I've melted cheques an' found the mornin' after 'ard.

melting, *vbl. n. Obs.* [f. MELT *v.*[1]]

1. In the preparation of tallow: the rendering of animal fats. Also *attrib.*

1843 *Port Phillip Patriot* 10 Aug. 4/2 No process, whether of boiling, roasting, or melting, will ever be found to answer when the *fat* and *lean* portions, or the whole carcass of the sheep is put down together. The juices of the *flesh* will *soften* and *discolour* the tallow, and render it much less valuable in the home market. **1843** *Sydney Morning Herald* 26 Dec. 2/3 Killing, dressing and cutting up the carcases, before being placed in the melting vats. **1845** *Portland Guardian* 15 Mar. 2/5 Mr Barnes has . . been a shipper of tallow from this colony, of his own melting. **1847** *Port Phillip Gaz.* 27 Sept. 3 The undersigned are prepared to purchase stock for melting and salting. **1847** *Port Phillip Herald* 16 Nov. 2/2 The market continues much overstocked with fat cattle, and good quality are selling a shade over melting prices.

2. Comb. **melting(-down) establishment.**

1840 *Port Phillip Gaz.* 30 Nov. 3 Melbourne. Melting Establishment, the first steam establishment formed in the colonies. **1843** *Colonial Observer* (Sydney) 23 Aug. 1257/1 Messrs. Watson and Wright . . made application for a squatting license, to enable them to form a melting-down establishment in the neighbourhood of Melbourne. **1848** J.C. BYRNE *Twelve Yrs.' Wanderings* I. 116 Swine . . are kept in the neighbourhood of dairy-farms or melting establishments, on the offal of which they are fed. **1857** J. BONWICK *Early Days Melbourne* 27 Melting-down establishments were erected.

menura /mɛn'jurə/. *Obs.* [mod. L. *menura* f. Gr. μήνη moon + οὐρά tail: see quot. 1800.] LYRE-BIRD 1.

[**1800** *Trans. Linnean Soc. London* (1802) 207 *Menura superba.* . . The general colour of the under sides of these two [tail] feathers is of a pearly hue, elegantly marked on the inner web with bright rufous colured crescent-shaped spots, which, from the extraordinary construction of the parts, appear wonderfully transparent.] **1823** J. LATHAM *Gen. Hist. Birds* VIII. 161 The Menura inhabits New-Holland. **1843** J. GOULD *Birds of Aust.* (1848) V. Pl. 63, The same kind of conditions that are suited to . . the Menura and the Satin Bower-bird are equally adapted to those of the Wonga-wonga. **1855** J. BONWICK *Geogr. Aust. & N.Z.* (ed. 3) 198 The Menura or Lyre bird of Victoria, has a magnificent tail like a Bird of Paradise. **1874** J.G. WOOD *Nat. Hist.* (1885) 337 (OED) The Menura seldom, if ever, attempts to escape by flight.

merejig, var. MERRYJIG.

meridian ant. *Magnetic termite*, see MAGNETIC.

1896 B. SPENCER *Rep. Horn Sci. Exped. Central Aust.* I. 129 We came across a small patch of the mound nests of what are called the meridian or compass ants. **1927** M. DORNEY *Adventurous Honeymoon* 79 They were flat slab-like structures . . built by a particular kind of termite called the meridian ant.

merino. *Hist.* [Fig. use of *merino* a breed of fine-woolled sheep introduced early in small numbers and valued more highly than coarse-woolled sheep.] One who has chosen to settle in Australia (as opposed to a convict or ex-convict); one who finds in this a basis for social pretension. Esp. as **pure merino.** Also *attrib.*

1826 *Monitor* (Sydney) 24 Nov. 221/2 One of the late petit-jury has this week been committed for compounding felony, and another is expected shortly to be put in the House of Correction, as he is constantly amusing himself with beating his wife and his father. Remember, reader, these are all *pure Merinos*! **1827** *Ibid.* 10 Feb. 306/2 The *pure Merinos* always prick up their fox-like ears on such occasions, in hopes of keeping down the convicts. **1837** *Cornwall Chron.* (Launceston) 5 Aug. 3 Proceedings . . commenced against this Merino paper, whose Editor considers his own writing to be the very quintessence of everything that is good and virtuous. **1844** *Colonial Times* (Hobart) 16 Apr., We think that its principal patrons, the pure Merino colonial aristocracy, will duly appreciate this deference to their refined taste. **1865** S. BENNETT *Hist. Austral. Discovery* 526 Unwarrantable assumptions of the 'pure merinos', as the official or aristocratic class or clique began to be called during Brisbane's time. **1887** *Boomerang* (Brisbane) 24 Dec. 13/3 It is generally accepted in Melbourne that the Earl of Buckinghamshire is engaged to Miss Chirnside. In squatting phraseology, this will be the conjunction of the golden fleece with the pure merino. **1897** *Bulletin* (Sydney) 23 Jan. 7/2 To sum up, the University is at present run in the interest of the professors and the pure merinos. **1907** *Ibid.* 26 Sept. 13/3 The average bishop loves the pure merinos of his flock. **1922** *Daily Mail* (Sydney) 19 Jan. 5/7 (*heading*) Will pure merino progressives invade city fold? **1934** J.C. LEE *Boshstralians* 15 'He *was* a boss. . . ' 'One of the whitest. . . ' 'A true merino.' **1944** R. BEDFORD *Naught to Thirty-Three* 37 Our 'history' became a laudation of the ruffians of the Rum Corps, and their successors, the pure Merinos. **1953** 'CADDIE' *Caddie* 41 She used to boast that her ancestors had come out as free settlers . . and that she was entitled to mix with the Pure Merinos. **1976** K. AMOS *New Guard Movt.* 111 The attempt made by W.C. Wentworth in the 1850s to found an hereditary upper house in the New South Wales parliament based on an 'aristocracy' of the 'pure merino' class.

merloo, var. MARLOO.

mernong, var. MURNONG.

merro, var. MEERO.

merryjig /'mɛrɪdʒɪg/, *a. Austral. pidgin. Obs.* Also **merejig, merrijig, merrygig.** [a. Wathawurung *mirijig.*] Very good.

1839 *Port Phillip Gaz.* 13 Nov. 3 *Constable*: My name Harry Stokes. *Native*: Ah ha! merrygig you. **1843** *Colonial Observer* (Sydney) 1 Feb. 790/3 'Merri jig' means in English 'very good'. **1862** G.T. LLOYD *Thirty-Three Yrs. Tas. & Vic.* 427 The natives . . discovered that the 'piccaniny boulganas merejig cogalla'—the little sheep were very good eating. **1872** 'RESIDENT' *Glimpses Life Vic.* 25 'Merryjig' that fellow!

meru, var. MEERA.

mesembryanthemum. Also **mesembrianthemum.** [Transf. use of *mesembryanthemum* the name of a plant genus.] PIGFACE.

1840 J. FRANKLIN Diary Visit S.A. 31 Dec. 52 (typescript) Covered with mesembrianthemum. **1849** C. STURT *Narr. Exped. Central Aust.* I. 300 There was little, if any grass to be seen; but the mesembryanthemum reappeared upon it, with other salsolaceous plants. **1862** C. WILHELMI *Manners & Customs Austral. Natives* 12 The most important and abundant fruit is that of a mesembrianthemum, to which the Europeans have given the somewhat vulgar name of pig faces, but the natives the more euphonical one of karkalla. **1935** T. RAYMENT *Cluster of Bees* 131, I had searched . . the blossoms of the coast tea-tree . . the Mesembryanthemum, and dozens of other plants . . and there were no plumed bees.

message-stick. A piece of wood carved with symbolic patterns which convey a message from one Aboriginal community to another and which may also indicate the bearer's standing or totem: LETTER-STICK.

1878 R.B. SMYTH *Aborigines of Vic.* I. p. xliv, It is by no means certain that message-sticks were in common use amongst the people of the southern parts of Australia. **1886** E.M. CURR *Austral. Race* I. 150 *Message-sticks* . . are often flat, from four to six inches long, an inch wide and a third of an inch thick; others are round, of the same length, and as thick as one's middle finger. **1897** *Antipodean* (Melbourne) 97 There was a message stick carried by an ambassador who went to other tribes. **1919** *Bulletin* (Sydney) 3 July 20/2 Message sticks . . were familiarly known to Western Queenslanders of the early days as 'blackfellows' letters'. **1928** W. ROBERTSON *Coo-ee Talks* 63 A message-stick is a piece of wood usually from about four to six inches long, but at times much longer, and the one sent to me was of brigalow. **1936** C. CHEWINGS *Back in Stone Age* 43 Messengers are often sent with verbal messages to distant tribes. . . They are given a message-stick—a small stick with burnt-in markings thereon—and that stick is his passport. **1944** M.J. O'REILLY *Bowyangs & Boomerangs* 151 The natives use a message stick which they send to neighbouring tribes when they want them to attend meetings, corroborees, etc. **1963** I.L. IDRIESS *Our Living Stone Age* 186 Without weapons, they held up green bushes and a message-stick, emblems of truce, advanced a little, and then stood still. . . The strangers presented the message-stick, and explained what had happened, urging the Kulkadoons to hurry back to their Council with the message, which was to invite the Elders to come. **1980** T.A. ROY *Vengeance of Dolphin* 135 Clutched in her right hand was the paperbark cover belonging to the message-stick.

messmate. [See quots. 1889 and 1902.] Any of several rough-barked trees of the genus *Eucalyptus* (fam. Myrtaceae), esp. the tall *E. obliqua* of s.e. Aust. incl. Tas., and the Gympie messmate, *E. cloeziana*, of e. Qld.; the wood of these trees. Also *attrib.*

1861 'OLD BUSHMAN' *Bush Wanderings* 223 The 'messmet' as we called it—a species of bastard gum. **1880** J. BONWICK *Resources Qld.* 80 The *Messmate*, of Moreton Bay corner, may reach 300 feet. . . It is the *E. obliqua.* **1889** J.H. MAIDEN *Useful Native Plants Aust.* 429 *Eucalyptus amygdalina* . . has even more vernacular names than botanical synonyms. . . Because it is allied to, or associated with, 'Stringybark', it is also known by the name of 'Messmate'. **1902** *Proc. Linnean Soc. N.S.W.* XXVII. 573 The appellation of Messmate infers that these trees 'messmate' with or partake of the characters of other trees. **1908** J.H. MAIDEN *Forest Flora N.S.W.* III. 17 It is usually known as 'Stringybark' in Tasmania . . and to a less extent in Victoria; in the last State, however, it is usually known as 'Messmate', because it is associated or mess-mates with other Stringybarks and fibrous-barked Eucalypts. **1915** *Bulletin* (Sydney) 23 Sept. 24/4 Messmate or bastard stringy are fair fuel. **1920** *Land of Lyre Bird* (S. Gippsland Pioneers' Assoc.) 35 In the heart of the scrub there was very little messmate—sometimes not a tree to 100 acres—but towards the fringe there was a great deal. It was very good for posts and rails, lasting well in the ground, but not much good for milling purposes. **1939** FRANKLIN & CUSACK *Pioneers on Parade* 154 You townies don't look too sensible to us when you can't tell . . a messmate from a brittle jack. **1943** *Bulletin* (Sydney) 11 Aug. 13/2 Out hunting on the messmate flat my foxies disturbed a kangaroo-rat. **1978** R.F. ZACHARIN *Emigrant Eucalypts* 25 *E[ucalyptus] obliqua* or messmate was the first recognized eucalypt, and the species on which the genus was botanically founded. **1983** K.W. MANNING *In their Own Hands* 204 Messmate (swamp mahogany) could scarcely be coaxed to burn. Its pungent smoke would gum up flues and the wood generally was an invitation to domestic discord.

metallic starling. The bird *Aplonis metallica* of rain-forests of n.e. Qld. and nearby s.w. Pacific, having glossy black plumage with a metallic green and purple sheen; *shining starling*, see SHINING.

1912 *Emu* XII. 25 We do not refer to them as the Metallic Starling . . or *Calornis metallica*, but as 'Tealgon', the accent on the first syllable. **1982** R. ELLIS *Bush Safari* 63 We stopped . . to observe a nesting colony of Metallic Starlings, a native species.

metho, *n.*[1] [f. *meth(ylated spirits* + -O.]

1. Methylated spirits. Also *attrib.*

1933 *Bulletin* (Sydney) 18 Oct. 10/2 A metho. drinker—a regular visitor—came into the pharmacy the other day. **1938** F. CLUNE *Free & Easy Land* 138 'Metho' drinkers of the Domain. **1947** V.C. HALL *Bad Medicine* 261 He's an auld dingo-poisoner . . goes on a jag. Rum. All hard stuff. When he's done his cash in he generally . . sobers up on metho. **1956** A.C.C. LOCK *Tropical Tapestry* 120 After you've had a shot of metho you eat like an elephant. **1968** D. IRELAND *Chantic Bird* 11 He put his real eye in a bottle with some metho before it went bad. **1973** *Overland* lvii. 46 Yuh tried metho yet? It ain't too bad if you have somethin' beforehand. **1984** B. DIXON *Searching for Aboriginal Lang.* 176 Old Jimmy Taylor had gone a bit in the mind, from drinking too much beer and metho.

2. One who is addicted to drinking methylated spirits.

1933 *Bulletin* (Sydney) 1 Nov. 11/1 A John Hop who has helped to deal with many 'methos.' tells me not a few prefer petrol. **1955** M. CORBEN *Not to mention Kangaroos* 223 These wretched souls are referred to as 'methos' because they drink methylated spirits. **1968** J. ALARD *He who shoots Last* 230 The old metho snored on. **1973** *Brisbane City Mission* Sept. 17/2 The methos. . . When a man takes to drinking methylated spirits you know . . that he has no thought for betterment of his lot.

Metho, *n.*[2] Abbrev. of 'Methodist'. Also as adj.

1940 *Rutherford Rumblings* (Tamworth) 17 May 1 Why did the 41st pinch our Metho. Padre? **1961** P. WHITE *Riders in Chariot* 232 Only the civil servants are Roman Catholics here. . . Arch and me are Methoes, except we don't go; life is too short. **1965** J. O'GRADY *Aussie Eng.* 60 Members of the Methodist Church are also known as 'Methos', or 'Metho drinkers', although they don't drink metho.

mial, var. MYALL *n.*[1]

miall, var. MYALL *n.*[1] and *n.*[2]

mia-mia /'maɪə-maɪə/. Formerly with much variety, as **mai-mai, miam, miami, miam-miam, mi-mi, myam-myam, mya-mya.** [a. Wathawurung and Wuywurung *miam miam.*]

1. A temporary shelter of the Aborigines: see quot. 1851. See also GUNYAH 1. (Quot. 1839 may be *transf.*: see sense 2.)

1839 *Port Phillip Gaz.* 2 Nov. 3 Where stood . . two years past the 'myam myam', or hut of the first settler, will tower five years hence the ceiled and painted roof of some gaudy theatre. **1840** P.L. BROWN *Clyde Co. Papers* 9 Dec. (1952) II. 400 They walked in regular order, each carrying his spear, & a cockatoo's feather in his head; the women and children followed, & made thier [*sic*] miam miams close to the house. **1841** *Geelong Advertiser* 27 Dec. 3/1 At their mi-mis we found two double-barrelled guns and one single-barrelled, and a brace of pistols. **1843** *Melbourne Times* 25 Mar. 4/2 Should the arrangements entered into be of a friendly nature they retire and fix up their miams, and a grand corrobery is given in honour of the strange tribes. **1845** *Observer* (Hobart) 18 July 4/5 Three blacks came to Mr Cameron's and made a 'mia-mia' by the garden fence. **1851** H.R. RUSSELL *Short Descr. Austral. Colonies* 11 They are still the same wanderers as at first . . living in the same 'mai mais', consisting of a sheet of bark stripped from a tree, and laid to windward against a forked stick, opposite which they light a fire, and under the shelter of which they rarely sleep two nights in succession. **1857** *Illustr. Jrnl. Australasia* II. 60 That liquid evening star no more Shall gleam his fragile mya-mya o'er. **1863** J. DAVIS *Tracks of McKinlay* 189 Seven or eight dark houris camped close to us by themselves, in a 'mia-mia'. **1872** 'RESIDENT' *Glimpses Life Vic.* 21 The murderer slunk with cat-like steps round the mia-mi, where his victim was sleeping. **1889** E. GILES *Aust. twice Traversed* I. 82 We . . saw dilapidated old yards, where they had formerly yarded emu or wallaby, though we saw none of their wurleys, or mymys, or gunyahs, or whatever name suits best. **1905** J. FURPHY *Rigby's Romance* (1946) 44 'Tabernacles' is Latin for mia-mias, and 'unleavened bread' is damper. **1928** B. SPENCER *Wanderings in Wild Aust.* 208 The Mia-mia (pronounced my-my), or wurley, as it is often called, consists only of two upright forks, perhaps six or eight feet apart, with a horizontal one against which leafy boughs are slanted to protect the occupants from wind. . . It is merely a bush shelter. **1944** M.J. O'REILLY *Bowyangs & Boomerangs* 15 A young abo. boy was passing close to our camp, making in the direction of the Blackfellows' 'Mia Mias'. **1960** J. WALKER *No Sunlight Singing* 11 One home stood humbly erect to claim the title of hut, while a few crouched, well enough clad in bark and brush to warrant the name of mia-mia. **1981** A.B. FACEY *Fortunate Life* 163 He took me to a fairly large mia-mia. Inside there were several older natives.

2. *transf.* A temporary shelter erected by a traveller.

1855 G.H. WATHEN *Golden Colony* 153 We received a volley of shots from a sort of mia-mia on the side of the road. **1861** *Burke & Wills Exploring Exped.* 29 This evening I camped very comfortably in a mia-mia. **1873** W. THOMSON-GREGG *Desperate Character* III. 38 Others busied themselves in erecting a 'mia-mia', or shelter of boughs and bark, after the most approved fashion of the bush. **1883** 'KEIGHLEY' *Who are You* 60 Within our leafy mia-mia then we crept, And ere a man could fifty count, we slept. **1904** *Rec. Castlemaine Pioneers* (1972) 195 Selecting a clear spot we erected a mia-mia and spread our blankets for the night. **1924** A.B. PEIRCE *Knocking About* 13 Here I erected a *mia-mia*, which consists of a pole placed horizontally between two trees with long dried strips of bark from the red gum or eucalyptus tree resting against it. These slabs are shifted from one side of the pole to the other in accordance with the direction from which the wind is blowing. **1984** P. READ *Down there with me on Cowra Mission* 48 The first time I came to this place [*sc.* Erambie, near Cowra] there was only four houses, and there used to be mia mias . . built all around. That'd be about 1918.

mick, *n.*[1] Abbrev. of MICKEY 1.

1894 A.B. BELL *Oscar* 67 Some few of the wildest mickeys broke away through the cordon of stockmen and scoured round the yard, only to be tackled by the cattle dogs. One fierce mick, about eighteen months old, became enraged. **1898** *Western Champion* (Barcaldine) 12 Apr. 9/2 Two of the calves were 'micks' and the other a heifer. **1934** *Bulletin* (Sydney) 1 Aug. 46/3, I lifted nearly two hundred Poolpee micks on my way back. **1954** H.G. LAMOND *Manx Star* 260 *Mick*, an unbranded, fully sexed male animal, adolescent. **1976** C.D. MILLS *Hobble Chains & Greenhide* 145 This bloke's a 'thick-horn'. Evidently been a mick. He is almost a stag—coarse as hell too.

mick, *n.*[2] [Transf. use of U.S. *Mick* an Irishman. Used elsewhere but recorded earliest in Aust.] A Roman Catholic.

1902 *Truth* (Sydney) 20 July 6/4 He's a tyke. He's a Mick. Chuck him out. **1934** 'L. PARKER' *Trooper to Southern Cross* 151 We used to have a song at school: *Catholic dogs, Jump like frogs* which we always yelled at the Micks. **1969** C. BRAY *Blossom* 108 Yer a load of Micks, you eat spaghetti, you act like women, and you talk too much. **1981** C. WALLACE-CRABBE *Splinters* 51 I've been ordered off the road, anyway. Just because I'm a Mick. **1985** *Canberra Times* 1 Sept. 8/4 No wonder we 'Micks' used to have slanging matches . . with the State-school kids.

mick, *n.*[3] *Two-up.* [Of unknown origin.] The reverse side of a coin; the tail.

1918 *Aussie: Austral. Soldiers' Mag.* (Sydney) Dec. 3/1 They were playing the good old game and a big dope they called Snow was spinner. Presently, up went two browns in the air. They came down showing two micks. **1919** *Ibid.* Jan. 2/1 Up went the browns again carrying the Prince's twenty francs. He was backing 'Heads', but 'Micks' turned up. **1924** A.W. BAZLEY et al. Gloss. Slang A.I.F. (typescript), *Micks*, the tails of the pennies used in a game of 'Two-Up'. **1953** T.A.G. HUNGERFORD *Riverslake* 126 'Ten bob he tails 'em!' he intoned. . . 'I got ten bob to say he tails 'em—ten bob the micks!' **1966** S.J. BAKER *Austral. Lang.* (ed. 2) 242 If a spinner throws two 'tails' he is said to *mick them* or throw *two micks.* **1977** [see MICK *v.*].

mick, *v. Two-up.* [f. MICK *n.*[3]] *trans.* To spin (the coins) so that they land tail uppermost.

1918 *Home Trail: Souvenir Issue Voyage H.M.T. 'A. 30'* Dec. 12, I bet a quid he Micks 'em. **1944** E. LOCKE *From Shore to Shore* 27 He's 'eaded 'em or 'micked' 'em. **1977** T.A.G. HUNGERFORD *Wong Chu* 56 Ten bob the mick! I got ten bob says he micks 'em.

mickery /'mɪkəri/. Also **mickeri, mickerie, mickri.** [a. Arabana Waŋgaŋuru *migri.*] SOAK; *spec.*, an excavated and formed soak, esp. in a dry river bed (see quots. 1947 and 1971). Also *attrib.*

1899 *Western Champion* (Barcaldine) 25 July 3/2 Then to a sandal wood break . . and he stuck himself, into the mickerie just where the niggers' brush gunyahs were. **1915** F.R.B. LOVE *Aborigines* 12 At times one finds a 'mickri' or native well, containing water. **1925** M. TERRY *Across Unknown Aust.* 76 A mickery is a shallow hole in the bed of a dry sandy creek where water has been obtained by sinking down a few feet. **1934** *Bulletin* (Sydney) 6 June 20/2 In the days before the artesian bore the mickery man was an institution on most stations in n.-w. Queensland. A mickery was a timbered well-shaft sunk into the sandy bed of a creek; it was worked by means of a pole placed across a forked stick, the pole having a bucket attached to one end and a weight to the other. **1947** A.W. NOAKES *Water for Inland* 6 Stock was watered from mickeries in the Flinders River, that is a chock and log structure about four feet wide, twenty feet long and eight to ten feet high, according to the depth of water from the surface, which was lowered down through the sand to the water. **1956** T. RONAN *Moleskin Midas* 76 The elder lubras dug the postholes squatting on their haunches, breaking the soil with mickeri sticks and scooping it out with their fingers. **1963** I.L. IDRIESS *Our Living Stone Age* 7 There is a little mickerie of sweet water hidden in a clump of mulga over the first hill! **1971** W.A. WINTER-IRVING *Beyond Bitumen* 118 The mickery was two long logs four feet apart sunk in the sand for about thirty feet or more. Between the logs we dug out the dry sand to water level where it stayed to water the cattle.

mickey. Also **micky.** [Spec. use of *Mick(e)y* familiar form of *Michael*, prob. infl. by (orig. U.S.) *Mick* an Irishman.]

1. A bull calf, usu. unbranded and freq. wild.

1876 *Austral. Town & Country Jrnl.* (Sydney) 9 Dec. 942/2 The wary and still more dangerously sudden 'Michie', a two-year-old-bull (so called after an eminent Australian barrister famous for bringing his 'charges' to a successful issue). **1881** A.C. GRANT *Bush-Life Qld.* I. 227 The branding-pen is getting . . lively now. There are three or four Mickies and wild heifers who are determined to have their owner's hearts-blood. **1889** *Illustr. Austral. News* (Melbourne) 2 Sept. 18/1 At branding he causes more profanity even than a pig, and it takes more men to drive one 'mickey' than ninety and nine grown bullocks. **1911** A.L. HAYDON *Trooper Police Aust.* 350 He is an expert at cutting out 'mickies' (unbranded steers). **1926** M. FORREST *Hibiscus Heart* 124 The cattle slayers had gone their way, with their smoking rifles and the mob of 'mickies' they intended . . to brand. **1932** J.J. HARDIE *Cattle Camp* (1944) 90 Intent on roping a big mickey, the last of the bunch, and, as usual, the biggest rogue. **1954** H.G. LAMOND *Manx Star* 143 Mickeys roamed through the camping cattle. **1968** W. GILL *Petermann Journey* 43 Some protesting calves were being drafted from their anxious mothers. I got there in time to see Tum scruff a two months old 'mickey', throw it, then hold it squealing for Johnson to castrate it. **1972** *Bronze Swagman Bk. Bush Verse* 19 We were running scrubber cattle out the Thargomindah way, Wild cows and cleanskin mickeys were the order of the day. **1984** *N.T. News* (Darwin) 22 Dec. 13/1 Mike told us a mickey was a bull that had escaped castration, gone wild and gathered a harem of wild cows.

2. *fig.* In the phr. **to throw** (or **chuck**) **a mickey,** to have a tantrum.

1952 T.A.G. HUNGERFORD *Ridge & River* 22 And he don't chuck a micky every time something goes off behind him! **1960** M. HENRY *Unlucky Dip* 90 Not that it was such a terrible thing really—but the Boss threw a mickey. **1978** L. RANDALL *Austral. Family Plays* 118 Don't throw a micky, Bert, it only cost fourpence.

3. *Noisy miner*, see NOISY.

1911 J.A. LEACH *Austral. Bird Bk.* 173 Noisy Miner, Garrulous Honeyeater, Snake-Bird, Cherry-eater, Soldier, Micky, Squeaker, *Myzantha garrula.* **1927** *Bulletin* (Sydney) 13 Jan. 23/4 A friend living in open forest country runs a small colony of soldier-birds fed regularly on bread soaked in water. . . Strange mickies occasionally make claim to a share of the tucker but are invariably driven away. **1934** H.G. LAMOND *Aviary on Plains* 52 Another mickey (soldier bird), secure in its shelter of bush. **1952** *Bulletin* (Sydney) 19 Mar. 14/3 'Those vines look well, anyhow.' 'Yair, but the mickeys'll get all the grapes.' **1971** *Courier-Mail* (Brisbane) 24 July 12/8 Mickeys, or Soldier Birds, or Noisy Miners, are great little fighters. **1981** M. SHARLAND *Tracks of Morning* 74 A brown goshawk preening itself on a dry branch not far from its nest, with half a dozen 'mickeys' (noisy miners) to whom it is normally Public Enemy No. 1, preening on a branch a few feet below.

4. The vulva.

1969 A. BUZO *Front Room Boys* (1970) 49 Barry Anderson reckons he got her in the locker room the other day. Mucked around, played with mickey, she didn't mind. **1975** D.J. TOWNSHEND *Gland Time* 238 Can't blame her for it, 'cause her mickey was probably throbbin' for it.

mickri, var. MICKERY.

micky, var. MICKEY.

middla, var. MIDLA.

middy. A medium-sized measure of beer; the glass containing this.

1945 S.J. BAKER *Austral. Lang.* 169 The *middy*, a beer glass containing nine ounces, is a measure used only in N.S.W. hotels. **1956** S. HOPE *Diggers' Paradise* 230 In 1950 a 33-year-old weighbridge operator of Balmain, Sydney, who tipped the scales at 15 stone, displayed his prowess to admiring mates by downing sixty middies of beer. (A middy glass contains ten liquid ounces.) **1961** *Bulletin* (Sydney) 1 Feb. 50/2 Nell . . sings beautifully after a few middies. **1969** A. BUZO *Rooted* (1973) 54 Ever had a middy of Bacardi neat? **1972** J. O'GRADY *It's your Shout, Mate!* 15 'A middy is seven ounces. . .' The second man said, 'A middy's a schooner in the bush.' **1981** P. RADLEY *Jack Rivers & Me* 57 The Sulphide where the cement-workers, footballers and small businessmen unwound with middies and schooners, and on festive occasions with pints. **1986** *Age* (Melbourne) 13 Mar. (Green Guide) 8/3 'How much do you drink a day? Six middies?'—'Look, son, I'd spill more than that.'

midla /'mɪdlə/. *Obs.* Also **middla, midlah.** [a. Gaurna *midla.*] An Aboriginal throwing stick: see quot. 1863.

1842 *S. Austral. News* (London) 15 Oct. 46/2 The weapon is thrown by the midla (propelling stick) a distance of sixty or eighty yards with considerable precision. **1847** G.F. ANGAS *Savage Life & Scenes* I. 111 Their weapons are the throwing-stick (*midlah*), which is made of the she-oak wood, [etc.]. **1853** F. GERSTAECKER *Narr. Journey round World* II. 328 They all go armed, using in this part of the country the boomerang, and short spears, sometimes with the midla, or the lever, sometimes without it. **1860** *Trans. & Proc. R. Soc. Vic.* (1861) 169 This kind of spear . . is always thrown with the so-called 'middla'. **1863** J. BONWICK *Wild White Man* 50 The *Wommera, Midla* or *Throwing Stick* is an ingenious contrivance for accelerating and directing the motion of the spear. **1879** *Native Tribes S.A.* 213 Spears are thrown with the wooden lever, known by the name of wommara, but here called midla.

migrant. [Spec. use of *migrant* one who leaves a country to settle in another.]

1. An immigrant to Australia. Now more usual than IMMIGRANT 1. Also *attrib.* See also EMIGRANT *n.* 1.

1922 *Daily Mail* (Sydney) 17 Jan. 1/2 Please don't speak of those arriving in Australia from Britain as immigrants. . . Call them rather migrants, because to go from Britain to Australia is only to pass from one part of Great Britain to another. **1928** R.G. STAPLEDON *Tour in Aust. & N.Z.* 27 The thorough-going 'Aussie' may not appear to offer the heartiest of welcomes to the migrant or settler. **1954** J. WATEN *Unbending* 11 He was the kind of migrant most beloved of fellow migrants, the true believer, forever optimistic about the future, never casting doubts, never questioning any favourable report about Australia, no matter how fantastic. **1961** *Southerly* ii. 26 Aren't you migrant blokes supposed to come out here and build up the country? **1968** G. BAKER *Montgomery & I* 62 Montgomery sternly replied: Surely the native sons should have my autograph before migrants and dagos. **1969** A. BUZO *Front Room Boys* (1970) 84 These migrants, they're all alike. Always on the make. **1976** D. HEWETT *This Old Man* p. xiv, I suspect Redfern has assimilated its migrants. **1980** S. ORR *Roll On* 3 A great deal of nonsense has been written in recent years about the changes in Australian eating habits brought about by the Great Migrant Invasion. **1980** S. THORNE *I've met some Bloody Wags* 66 The funniest incident that comes to mind concerned one of the locals—a migrant.

2. Special Comb. **migrant camp, hostel,** a place in which temporary accommodation is provided for newly-arrived immigrants; **ship,** a vessel carrying (assisted) immigrants to Australia.

1953 T.A.G. HUNGERFORD *Riverslake* 68 It had been worked for him by a Lithuanian girl in the **migrant camp** at Bathurst. **1958** M. WARREN *No Glamour in Gumboots* 29 Rosita and the baby, aged five months, were in a migrant camp two hundred miles from Sydney. **1961** *Bulletin* (Sydney) 11 Nov. 12/1, I approached Bonegilla migrant camp by car. **1969** T.M.A. GRAHAM *Paper Men* 229 How come you're living here, anyway? This is a migrant camp—it's not for Aussies. **1964** *Bulletin* (Sydney) 18 Jan. 12/1 This is Villawood, biggest of Australia's **migrant hostels** (population around 1,425 at last count, capacity 2,750) and temporary home for a steady flow of assisted newcomers, English, Dutch, Italian and other nationalities. **1980** *Southerly* iii. 339 She wrote she had moved out from the migrant hostel, to a flat near the hospital. **1948** *Listening Post* (Perth) July 15 Films depicting various phases of life and conditions in Australia . . shown on **migrant ships.** **1964** *Bulletin* (Sydney) 18 Jan. 13/3 Welfare Officers are present on all migrant ships.

Mike. Shortened form of 'Michael': see quot. 1967 and see also OEDS *angel, sb.* 8.

1954 *Sporting Life* Jan. 31/1 It was suggested that he become a bookmaker's 'Mike' (a man who finances a bookie's bag). **1967** *Kings Cross Whisper* (Sydney) xxxvi. 4/2 *Mike,* a backer. Usually for a promoter. From Michael the Archangel, guardian angel.

Mile. Abbrev. of *golden mile* (see GOLDEN 1).

1938 W. HATFIELD *Buffalo Jim* 34 'That'll see you pretty well to the Mile.' 'The Mile?' 'Kalgoorlie. They call it the Golden Mile.' **1953** *Tobruk to Borneo* (Perth) June 7 He's still working underground on the 'Mile'. **1978** D. STUART *Wedgetail View* 238 She's a town and a half, that Kal[goorlie]. . . Booze enough to flood every stope on the Mile.

military settler. *Hist.* One who, having served as a military officer in an Australian Colony, elects to remain as a settler.

1837 *Perth Gaz.* 11 Feb. 847 It has become necessary to make a . . change in the arrangements which have hitherto been in force with respect to Military Settlers. **1838** *Tegg's N.S.W. Pocket Almanac* 73 Officers on Half-pay, residing in the Colony where they propose to settle, may be admitted to the privileges of Military and Naval Settlers.

milk.

1. Used *attrib.* in the names of plants: **milk-bush,** any of several plants having a milky sap, esp. *Sarcostemma australe* (see *caustic bush* CAUSTIC); **-wood,** *milky pine*, see MILKY; also *attrib.*

1886 *N.T. Times Almanac* 6 The country abounds in edible bushes; those which stock are most partial to are the orangebush and whitewood or **milkbush.** **1897** L. LINDLEY-COWEN *W. Austral. Settler's Guide* 489 There has been published in the *Journal* of the Bureau of Agriculture . . a number of letters from residents of the north-west, descriptive of the indigenous valuable fodder plant, known locally as the 'milk-bush'. **1903** H. BASEDOW *Jrnl. Govt. N.-W. Exped.* 19 July (1914) 181 The so-called 'milk bush' (*Sarcostemma australe*) grows in crevices upon its surfaces. **1956** GARDNER & BENNETTS *Toxic Plants W.A.* 154 Caustic bush is a leafless plant with somewhat succulent stems and abundance of latex, hence one of its common names, 'milkbush'. **1965** *Austral. Encycl.* VI. 84 Milkbush, a popular name for several shrubs and small trees with a milky sap, especially *Wrightia saligna* in the family Apocynaceae. **1880** R. ROSE *Austral. Guide: Qld.* 17 The tulip wood is one greatly admired in cabinet work, so also is the **milk-wood.** **1908** E.J. BANFIELD *Confessions of Beachcomber* 214 The edge of the precipice looks over a tangle of jungle down upon the top of a giant milkwood tree (*Alstonia scholaris*). **1928** B. SPENCER *Wanderings in Wild Aust.* 660 The really old men are allowed to decorate themselves in a most remarkable way that gives them . . a grotesque, not to say fearsome appearance. For this purpose a tree called 'milk-wood' . . is tapped. **1951** C. SIMPSON *Adam in Ochre* 28 We're camped under a big milkwood-tree in a clump of shade near a waterhole.

2. Special Comb. **milk billy,** a billy used as a container for milk; **opal,** white opal, a variety of precious opal (see quot. 1974); **run,** *transf.* [cf. Br. *milk round,* OEDS *milk, sb.* 10], a regular trip with stops at a number of places.

[N.Z. **1912** K. MANSFIELD *Stories* (1984) 113 She trailed over to us with a basket in her hand, the **milk billy** in the other.] **1935** DAVISON & NICHOLLS *Blue Coast Caravan* 154 We were invited across to the farm to have our milk billy filled. **1944** *Bulletin* (Sydney) 25 Oct. 15/1 A woman . . milk-billy in hand, rests arms and chin on the split-rail fence. **1961** F. LEECHMAN *Opal Bk.* 129 **Milk Opal** . . probably owes its colour to white clay in the solutions from which it was made. **1974** B. MYATT *Dict. Austral. Gemstones* 134 Milk opal is the name given to a translucent to opaque milk white, pale bluish-white or greenish-white variety of opal. **1942** *Bulletin* (Sydney) 25 Nov. 13/2 A Winton (Q.) boundary rider . . established his '**milk run**' during the great rat plague. **1959** *Ibid.* 23 Sept. 16/2 We were doing the 'milk run' by DC3 from Cairns, delivering mail, groceries, reels of Sylko, nylons and hi-fi records to cattle-stations in the Gulf Country around Normanton. **1963** *Air Action* (Melbourne) 8 Ten Japanese bombers took off . . on what they fondly expected to be a 'milk-run'. **1971** *Bulletin* (Sydney) 13 Nov. 55/1 Many Australians who've made two or three voyages around the South Pacific 'milk run', Suva, Tonga, and Port Moresby, are now wanting more exotic and remote ports to call at.

milkie. An opaque playing marble.

1908 *Bulletin* (Sydney) 10 Dec. 16/4 Peter signified his willingness to adventure two alleys. 'Commonies or milkies?' demanded Sam. **1936** N. LINDSAY *Saturdee* 50 After consultation with his alley-bag, he selected two peewees, a chalkey and a slatey, which he placed in the ring. Enraged at this proposal to fob off such stuff on honourable milkies, Waldo snatched them up and threw them out of the ring.

milkmaids, *pl.* Any of several plants, usu. of the genus *Burchardia* (fam. Liliaceae), esp. *B. umbellata* of temperate Aust. incl. Tas., bearing an umbel of scented white flowers.

1930 A.J. EWART *Flora of Vic.* 287 *B[urchardia] umbellata* . . Milkmaids . . Flowers white, often tinged with red on the outside, very fragrant. **1941** C. BARRETT *Aust.* 29 Between post-and-rail fence and the water channel, is a wide untamed strip, where . . milkmaids and Early Nancies grow. **1965** *Austral. Encycl.* II. 186 The name 'milkmaids' is popularly applied in allusion to the cluster of white flowers.

milko. Also **milk-oh.** [f. the call 'Milk-O!' (see quot. 1865). Used elsewhere but recorded earliest in Aust.: see -O.]

1. A milkman.

[**1865** J.F. MORTLOCK *Experiences of Convict* 115 He proposed that I should carry his pails round the town and shout out 'Milk O!' at the customers' doors.] **1907** *Truth* (Sydney) 20 Jan. 1/7 A milk-oh . . has been convicted of selling adulterated milk more than once. **1916** *Ibid.* 6 Feb. 10/4 Called him 'A threepenny quart ---', possibly the lowest kind of vituperation one milk-oh could use *towards a rival.* **1932** *Bulletin* (Sydney) 2 Nov. 20/3 A milkman . . found a man strapped tightly to a fence post. . . Milko was unable to release the prisoner. **1953** *Ibid.* 11 Nov. 12/1 Our local milk-oh bought a trim little bay mare. **1968** D. IRELAND *Chantic Bird* 6 The milko chased me all the way home and I wet my pants when he caught me. **1985** *Canberra Chron.* 10 July 19/3 He has spent a fair bit of time in banking and an oil company business, but also doubled as a pretty good milko.

2. A cow-hand.

1946 F. CLUNE *Try Nothing Twice* 111 What with watering the milk and letting calves strip the cows, I was candidly a failure as milk-oh.

milky, *a.* Used as a distinguishing epithet in the names of plants: **milky mangrove,** the mangrove tree of tropical and subtropical Aust. and elsewhere *Excoecaria agallocha* having an irritant milky sap, and known also as BLIND-YOUR-EYE; **pine,** any of several trees or shrubs of the fam. Apocynaceae having a milky sap, esp. the tall rainforest tree *Alstonia scholaris* of n.e. Qld., and its soft whitish wood; *milkwood,* see MILK 1.

1888 *Proc. Linnean Soc. N.S.W.* III. 380 *Excaecaria agallocha* . . '**Milky Mangrove**', 'Blind-your-eyes'. **1920** J.H. MAIDEN *Weeds N.S.W.* 7 In swampy estuaries at the extreme north coast of this State is a formidable tree . . known as 'Milky Mangrove' or 'Blind-your-eyes'. **1934** *Bulletin* (Sydney) 15 Aug. 21/2 Gympie isn't as dangerous as the milky mangrove. . . A drop of sap in the eye will cause blindness. **1948** H.A. LINDSAY *Bushman's Handbk.* 94 The milky mangrove . . when cut . . exudes a milky juice which is intensely irritating should it get into the eyes or on the bare skin. **1981** D. LEVITT *Plants & People* 31 A float . . was made from the wood of the Milky Mangrove. **1934** C. MACKNESS *Young Beachcombers* 128, I thought I never would get up that **milky-pine** you made me tackle. **1948** H.A. LINDSAY *Bushman's Handbk.* 39 In the Queensland rainforests look for fallen logs of the candle-nut, milky pine or similar softwoods. **1962** *Daily Mercury Centenary Story Mackay* 43 The more popular scrub woods include . . Mackay cedar, and milky pine. **1980** H.W. CUMMINGS *Confessions of 'Mud Skipper'* 268, I have noticed in several placed along the inland road to Cooktown, the Milky Pine (Alstonia Scholaris) growing alongside the road.

milli-milli /'mɪli-mɪli/. [Prob. reduplication f. (Eng.) *mail.*] A written message. Also **milli.**

1929 K.S. PRICHARD *Coonardoo* (1961) 16 The milli-millis passed from Wytaliba to Nunniewarra. **1940** J. POLLARD *Out of West* 26 Snowy Barker up at the store . . sent out one of his niggers will [*sic*] a milli-milli for Snakey. **1976** C.D. MILLS *Hobble Chains & Greenhide* 24 Long Jack turned up with a 'milli'—'Start bullock-muster as soon as you can' the letter read.

million. In the phr. **gone a million,** done for, finished; beyond redemption.

1913 *Bulletin* (Sydney) 25 Sept. 22/2 *Inebriated* . . loaded . . gone a million [etc.]. **1918** A. WRIGHT *Breed holds Good* 45 He was . . 'gone a million', meaning that he was in love with Dorrie. **1922** —— *Colt from Country* 142 What hope would you have when that came out? You'd be gone a million. **1942** G.S. CASEY *It's Harder for Girls* 212 No doubt about it, Sim was right. If they drop their bundles they're gone a million. **1953** J.E. MACDONNELL *Wings off Sea* 111 British, Australian or Siamese—she better get here right smart or we're gone a million. **1965** G.H. FEARNSIDE *Golden Ram* 82 One slip-up here, Harry, and we're gone a million. **1976** *Austral.* (Sydney) 1 Mar. 1/2 'Gough's gone. Gone a million. He's had it. I'd give him inside two weeks before we get his resignation . . ' a Federal executive member said.

mi-mi, var. MIA-MIA.

mimi /'mimi/. [a. Gunwinygu *mimi.*] A category of spirit people depicted in rock and bark paintings of western Arnhem Land: see quots. 1956 (2) and 1981. Freq. *attrib.*

1949 *Nat. Geographic Mag.* (Washington) Dec. 780 The art of the Mimi consists largely of single-line drawings, almost exclusively of human beings. . . One design of a man throwing a spear shows remarkable resemblance to figures painted by primitive bushmen of Africa and Stone Age men of Europe. **1951** R.M. & C.H. BERNDT *Sexual Behaviour Western Arnhem Land* 176 The 'Mi:mi spirits . . lived in a rock cave . . east of Oenpelli. **1956** C.P. MOUNTFORD *Rec. American-Austral. Sci. Exped. Arnhem Land* I. 112 The *Mimi* artists had a feeling for composition and movement which the X-ray artists lacked. Their main subject was man in action, running, fighting and throwing spears. All *Mimi* paintings were executed in red which, according to the myth, was made up of blood and red ochre. *Ibid.* 181 The general term of *Mimi* covers a large group of spirit people. Some . . live under similar conditions to the aborigines; that is, they have the same hunting implements, eat the same foods, and know the way to make fire. . . The cave-painting *Mimi,* whose specific name I did not find out, are supposed, by the aborigines, to have been responsible for the single-line rock paintings in the caves of the Arnhem Land plateau, adjacent to Oenpelli, particularly those of human beings. **1964** R.M. & C.H. BERNDT *World First Australs.* 7 The beautifully drawn stick figures called *mimi,* near Oenpelli. **1967** E. HUXLEY *Their Shining Eldorado* 276 The so-called 'Mimi figures', often only three or four inches high, depicting in silhouettes troops of scurrying little humans armed with bows and spears. These paintings are thought to be the work of a race now extinct. **1981** J. MULVANEY et al. *Aboriginal Aust.* 163 Mimi spirits are characterised by their elongated and slender form. They are trickster spirits, sometimes cannibalistic, which inhabit rocky places. Where they disappear into the rock walls of caves and shelters, they sometimes leave their shadows behind, which appear as paintings on the rock surfaces. **1984** *Bulletin* (Sydney) 6 Mar. 50/3 The figures were the work of the Mimi people, the rock spirits.

mimosa. Used *attrib.* in Special Comb. **mimosa bush,** the tangled spiny shrub or small tree *Acacia farnesiana* (fam. Mimosaceae) of n. Aust. and elsewhere in the tropics, having foliage and pods palatable to stock.

1959 H. LAMOND *Sheep Station* 87 A pair of top-knot pigeons had nested in the thorny tangle of a mimosa bush. **1979** B. MARTYN *First Footers S. Gippsland* 14 There were dark green mimosa bushes. **1981** J.A. BAINES *Austral. Plant Genera* 15 *A[cacia] farnesiana,* Mimosa Bush, unique in that it is native in five continents.

mina, minah, var. MINER *n.*[1]

mindi /'mɪndaɪ/. *Obs.* Also **mindai.** [a. Wemba *mirndayi.*] A fabulous serpent: see quots.

1844 H. MCCRAE *Georgiana's Jrnl.* 21 Aug. (1934) 129 The natives north of the Grampians talk about a species of Boa called *Mindi,* which lies in wait by waterholes, and, if an emu comes to drink, makes a meal of the complete bird! **1846** 'COLONIAL MAGISTRATE' *Remarks on Probable Origin* 15 A superstitious horror rather than reverence of a large species of *Serpent,* which they call *Mindyè,* asserted by the Natives to exist in the hitherto unexplored country between Sir Thomas Mitchell's outward boundary and the River Murray. **1848** J.C. BYRNE *Twelve Yrs.' Wanderings* II. 274 The *Mindai* . . is described as a serpent of immense size and length, with a black mane. **1851** *Empire* (Sydney) 17 Feb. 3/4 A shepherd . . discovered an enormous snake lying asleep. . . It was found to measure within two inches of eighteen feet, and was of the species known by the natives as the 'mindi', and by them represented to be oviparous, and without fangs, consequently not poisonous. **1872** 'RESIDENT' *Glimpses Life Vic.* 251 The snakes commonly seen in Victoria rarely exceed six feet in length, but the aborigines used to speak of a far larger kind, known among themselves as the 'Mindi'. **1880** *Papers & Proc. R. Soc. Tas.* (1881) 8 With reference to the 'Mindi', or Mallee Snake, it has often been described to me as a formidable creature, of at least 30 ft. in length, which confined itself to the mallee scrub. No one, however, has ever seen one for the simple reason that to see it is to die, so fierce it is, and so great its powers of destruction. Like the 'Bunyip', I believe the 'Mindi' to be a myth. **1896** F.G. AFLALO *Sketch Nat. Hist. Aust.* 83 Nor did I give any account in the foregoing of the black-maned 'Bunyip' and 'Mindai' of Lake George and elsewhere. These fabulous creatures rank with the sea-serpent.

mindic /'mɪndɪk/, *a. Austral. pidgin.* [a. Nyungar *mindaik.*] Ill; sick.

1845 E.J. EYRE *Jrnls. Exped. Central Aust.* II. 35 He would lie down, and roll and groan, and say he was 'mendyt' (ill). **1929** W.J. RESIDE *Golden Days* 164 She replied, 'Black fella welly mindic,' which meant that one of the tribe was sick. . . Whether the chlorodine cured the 'mindic' native I never learned. **1984** W.W. AMMON et al. *Working Lives* 180, I began to think he must be 'mindic', 'sick fella', or 'gone walkabout' even as far as Lake Way or Wiluna.

miner, *n.*[1] Also **mina, minah, mynah,** the latter two being increasingly reserved for *Acridotheras tristis.* [Spec. use of *miner,* var. of *mina* any of various birds of India and elsewhere.] **a.** Any of the several yellow-billed, Austral. honeyeaters of the genus *Manorina.* **b.** The introduced, starling-like *Acridotheras tristis,* native to India and s. China, an omnivorous, ground-feeding, predom. brown bird with yellow bill, eye patches, and legs, often confused with the *noisy miner* (see NOISY). Also *attrib.*

1832 J. BACKHOUSE *Narr. Visit Austral. Colonies* (1843)

30 Birds of various kinds . . abound . . the Wattle-bird, the Miner. **1832** J. HENDERSON *Observations Colonies N.S.W. & Van Diemen's Land* 41 The restless and noisy minas are disputing. **1844** J. GOULD *Birds of Aust.* (1848) VI. Pl. 76, *Myzantha garrula* . . Miner, Colonists of Van Diemen's Land. **1861** 'OLD BUSHMAN' *Bush Wanderings* 135 By far the commonest and boldest bird in the Australian bush is the *Miner* . . which . . appeared to mind everybody's business but its own. **1880** R. ROWE *Roughing It* 55 The mina is a grey bird about the size of an English thrush, with bright eyes and pointed beak and claws; a very Paul Pry amongst birds, except that it never hopes it does not intrude. It pokes its beak in everywhere. **1903** *Emu* II. 165 Miner . . rare in the forest, common elsewhere. **1914** *Bulletin* (Sydney) 13 Aug. 26/1 Here in Tassy, where it never droughts to any extent, a spell of dry weather will bring the . . minahs hustling to the troughs. **1938** F. BLAKELEY *Hard Liberty* 178, I knew only one type of miner before I came here, but every hundred miles or so we seemed to get a new variety. **1948** M. UREN *Glint of Gold* 210 In Australia there is the Mynah bird, whose call is two long notes and three short quick ones. **1968** *Coast to Coast 1967–68* 130 The movement of a myna-bird, stalking importantly four feet away from him. **1973** V. SERVENTY *Desert Walkabout* 52 Miner is a name given to several rather similar honeyeaters. All have the brush tongue of the group and use this for sopping up pollen and nectar in flowers. . . The name miner is interesting and not to be confused with mynah, an introduced bird from Asia and related to the starlings. It too has the yellow beak and legs and I feel that this coloration led to the name for the Australian birds. **1975** D. MALOUF *Johno* 83 The glossy black mynah birds, picking about between the roots of the Moreton Bay figs.

miner, *n.*[2] In special collocations: **miner's complaint (disease, lung),** a name given to a pulmonary disease, such as silicosis, to which a miner is especially susceptible; **licence,** LICENCE 2 a.; *miner's right*; **right,** a document entitling the holder to search for and remove a mineral (orig. gold); land occupied under such an entitlement.

1896 J. HOLT *Virgin Gold* 48 *Phthisis*, or what is popularly termed The **Miner's Complaint.** **1909** W.G. SPENCE *Aust.'s Awakening* 27 A form of phthisis called 'miner's lung' overtook men after a few years, and led to a more or less lingering death. **1935** *Red Star* (Perth) 18 Oct. 6/1 A worker named Goldsworthy died of miner's complaint a few months back. **1945** G. CASEY *Downhill is Easier* 67, I don't suppose you ever seen a bloke with miners' complaint—not with real miners' complaint. **1948** K.S. PRICHARD *Golden Miles* 118, I reckon there's more accidents on the mines and more men going out to miner's complaint, now, than there was in the old days. **1977** STIRLING & RICHARDSON *Memories of Aberfeldy* 8 Men died young with the dust from mining on their chests that they called Miners' Disease. **1862** H. BROWN *Vic. as I found It* 148 Every person carrying goods into the gold fields ought to have a **miners' license.** **1968** F. ROSE *Aust. Revisited* 25 The Miner's Licence was a tax on labour which struck at the miner's right to follow his chosen occupation. **1855** *Illustr. Sydney News* 14 Apr. 181/3 To exact a registration fee of £1 per annum per head, on miners, the production of which constitutes a '**Miner's Right**', without which, in case of dispute, no claim can lie. **1862** H. BROWN *Vic. as I found It* 151 All those without a miner's right have no permission to mine on Crown Land. Their claim (as the piece of ground they mine on is called) may be jumped, (i.e.) taken possession of by any one holding a miner's right. **1863** F. ALGAR *Handbk. to Colony N.S.W.* 10 The elective franchise is extended to all permanent residents, and all persons holding a 'miner's right' on the gold-fields. **1875** MRS N. WOOD *Waiting for Mail* 26 No sin-born cloud its lustre dim, no vice or folly blight, But Heaven's blessing ever rest upon our 'Miner's Right'. **1884** *Goldfield's Reminisc.* 21 A miner's right at the present day . . is issued at a fee of five shillings, and is a good and sufficient title against all comers for one year for a holding of 60 feet along a quartz lode by 400 feet wide, and, in addition thereto, a residence area of a quarter of an acre anywhere in the district, providing that the mining bye-laws of the district are complied with. **1901** *Handbk. Mining* (S.A. Dept. Mines) 12 A miner's right is obtainable at the Department of Mines, Adelaide . . at a cost of 5s. . . The holder of a miner's right is authorised to prospect on any mineral lands for any metal, mineral, coal, or oil, and to peg out . . claims. **1921** K.S. PRICHARD *Black Opal* 68 They hold their blocks of land by miner's right. **1931** W. BARAGWANATH et al. *Guide for Prospectors in Vic.* 87 *Miner's right*, a Government certificate, obtainable for 2s. 6d., and renewable yearly. It entitles the holder to take possession of an area for mining or for residence. **1936** *Bulletin* (Sydney) 17 June 21/4 Near Laurel Hill, southern N.S.W. tablelands, I was occupying a miner's right. **1948** G. FARWELL *Down Argent Street* 18 Within two days he had located the outcrop, pegged his claim. . . Stockie put the facts before him and together they applied . . for a miner's right. **1979** N. & R. PERRY *Gemstones in Aust.* 17 A 'Miner's Right' must be obtained in order to mine for gemstones in Queensland.

mingil /ˈmɪŋgəl/. Also **mingle, mingul.** [a. Pitjantjatjara dial. of Western Desert *mingul* roll of pituri for communal chewing.] PITURI.

1935 H. BASEDOW *Knights of Boomerang* 67 To 'dope' the emus . . they had employed only the leaves of a plant they called 'mingul' ('Duboisia hopwoodii'), the same as they themselves use for chewing. **1935** H.H. FINLAYSON *Red Centre* 85 The narcotic known variously as mingil or okiri . . a true tobacco . . which grows luxuriantly at the foot of the ranges. **1959** C. & E. CHAUVEL *Walkabout* 62 Bushes called Quondong and Yarran and Mingle.

min-min /ˈmɪn-mɪn/. [Prob. f. a Qld. Aboriginal language.] A will-o'-the-wisp: see quot. 1956. Also **min-min light.**

1956 H. HUDSON *Flynn's Flying Doctors* 115 'We're catching up with the Min-Min.' 'What's that?' I asked. My mates explained that it is an Aboriginal name for a mysterious dancing light or will-o'-the-wisp that moves about on the plains. Some say it is caused by luminous gases or luminous insects, but the Aborigines believe it is an apparition of evil spirits, anyway nobody has ever caught up with a Min-Min. **1964** *N. Austral. Monthly* Aug. 11 That was where the mysterious debbil-debbil glow, known as 'The Min Min Light', used to do its tricks. **1970** *Matilda* (Winton Tourist Promotion Assoc.) 13 Where the stars are pale and the min-min glows. **1977** *Bronze Swagman Bk. Bush Verse* 33 Here the Min Min dances, flickers, flutters, fades away And leaves its victims stranded where the desert shadows sway. **1981** *Austral. Women's Weekly* (Sydney) 2 Dec. 33/2 Boulia is a nice little far-west Queensland town, with the Min-Min Store (named for the famous min-min 'ghost' light of the area). **1982** D. HARRIS *Drovers of Outback* 4 The Min Min light has been seen in various parts of Queensland and the Northern Territory but has never been satisfactorily explained. Min Min, a term of aboriginal origin, means a 'ghost light'. It is similar to a car light but does not throw a beam.

minnerichi /mɪnəˈrɪtʃi/. Also with much variety, as **minnaritchi, minni ritchi.** [Prob. a. Garuwali *minariji*.] The shrub or small tree *Acacia cyperophylla* (fam. Mimosaceae) of arid inland Aust., having typically thin, peeling curls of reddish bark; the wood of the tree; *red mulga*, see RED *a.* 1 a. Also *attrib.*

1929 K.S. PRICHARD *Coonardoo* (1961) 102 If the room got too hot and stuffy with the smoke of mulga, minnerichi, and tobacco, she opened a door. **1944** —— *Potch & Colour* 99 Thorn-bush and minnereechi casting black shadows. **1952** A.M. DUNCAN-KEMP *Where Strange Paths go Down* 227 He built up the paddock corners with fresh-cut, heavy minnareetchie (red mulga)—the toughest wood in the west—rails and ten-foot posts. **1970** *Matilda* (Winton Tourist Promotion Assoc.) 40 Trunks of Minnaritchis smouldering Ruby-red upon the screes. **1973** C. AUSTIN *I left my Hat in Andamooka* 148 There is a saying that 'where the minaritchi grows, there you will find opal.' **1980** J. WOLFE *Crocodile Soup* 57 We stopped . . at a small, dry water-course where the strange 'Minnarichy' trees grew. The trunks of these trees are covered with thousands of little red curls, actually coils of bark. **1983** *Austral. Plants* June 131 It . . resembles the rich red-brown crisped bark of some species of *Acacia* for which the term 'Minni Ritchi' bark is now widely used. **1984** W.W. AMMON et al. *Working Lives* 189 The bark of the minni richi tree is a bright red, and for some reason, horses love it.

minor. *Australian National Football.* BEHIND 1. See also MAJOR.

1903 *Sporting News* (Launceston) 16 May 4/4 Brown from a mark on the magazine wing put up the first minor. **1981** L. MONEY *Footy Fan's Handbk.* 39 'Only a minor', a behind.

mint. Used *attrib.* in the names of plants: **mint bush** (formerly **mint tree**), any shrub of the large genus *Prostanthera* (fam. Lamiaceae) of Aust. incl. Tas., many of which are cultivated as ornamentals for their aromatic leaves and profusion of flowers in spring, incl. *P. lasianthos* (see *Christmas bush* (a) CHRISTMAS); **weed,** the naturalized annual plant *Salvia reflexa* (fam. Lamiaceae) of North America, having aromatic, greyish-green leaves, and being sometimes poisonous to stock.

1887 [**mint bush**] *Proc. Linnean Soc. N.S.W.* II. 9 *Prostanthera lasiantha* . . from the scent of its foliage is sometimes called the 'Mint Tree'. **1903** *Tasmanian Timbers* (Tas. Lands & Survey Dept.) 30 Native laurel . . Mint Tree (*Prosthanthera lasianthes*) . . are small trees, occasionally used for inlaying and turnery. **1942** C. BARRETT *Austral. Wild Flower Bk.* 39 There are more than forty kinds of *Prostanthera*, all popularly known as mint bushes. **1956** E. MITCHELL *Black Cockatoos* 207 The mintbush she trained against the rocks in the garden. **1980** J. WOLFE *End of Pricklystick* 76 Near the house was a little patch of native mint-bush. We called it Christmas Bush because it was covered with flowers at Christmas time. **1984** E. WALLING *On Trail Austral. Wildflowers* 72 The Mint-bush is a dainty little plant with scarlet flowers at the tips of short branches clothed with small and narrow leaves. **1933** *Bulletin* (Sydney) 5 Apr. 21/3 A plant that is rapidly spreading in Queensland is the wild **mint weed** (*Salvia lanceifolia*), the eating of which has resulted in the death by poisoning of hundreds of cattle on the Darling Downs. **1947** ROE & SHAW *Mint Weed* 7 Mint weed, *Salvia reflexa*, is a summer-growing annual plant. . . The earliest reports of its occurrence . . suggest that seeds were introduced from America in fodder during the 1902 drought. **1956** K. TENNANT *Honey Flow* 282 Ken Musselton had some hives he was willing to let us have—good hives that were on mintweed. **1974** S.L. EVERIST *Poisonous Plants Aust.* 272 If animals are forced to traverse stock routes where mintweed is plentiful and grass is scarce, they should be well fed with hay or other roughage.

Mintie. Also **mintie.** [The proprietary name of a peppermint flavoured sweet. The advertising slogan 'It's moments like these you need Minties' is now widely current as a catch-phrase (see quot. 1963).] Used allusively as an emblem of solace.

1926 *Austral. Official Jrnl. Patents* (Canberra) 879 *Minties* 42,344. Confectionary. James Stedman-Henderson's Sweets Ltd. **1932** *Listening Post* (Perth) May 16 Weak moments, when even minties will not put things to rights. **1963** F. HARDY *Legends Benson's Valley* 192 It's moments like these you need Minties! **1983** *Bushdriver* May 60 We lost *everything* for three months of our trip. 'Minties' would not have helped; Kleenex were the only things that consoled me. **1985** *Canberra Times* 7 June 15/2 Our pal, Billy, died the other day. Loved by all, religious and lay . . Gave them a Mintie then wandered away.

mirr'n-yong, var. MURNONG.

mirrnyong /ˈmɜnjɒŋ/. Also **mirnyong.** [Prob. f. a Vic. Aboriginal language.] A mound of ashes, shells, and other debris, accumulated in a place used by Aborigines for cooking; a kitchen midden; *native oven*, see NATIVE *a.* 5. Also **mirrnyong heap.**

1878 R.B. SMYTH *Aborigines of Vic.* II. 232 As we travel through the country, we find but few indications of a previous race having occupied it. Two of these are, the marks cut on trees, which will soon disappear; and the 'native ovens', or mirnyongs. **1890** *Proc. Linnean Soc. N.S.W.* V. 259 Fragments of tomahawks and bone needles have been dug out of *Mirrn-yong* heaps on the seacoast, covered wholly or partially by blown-sand. **1944** S.J. ENDACOTT *Austral. Aboriginal Native Words* (ed. 2) 27 *Mirrnyong*, midden, or ash heap. **1969** D.J. MULVANEY *Prehist. Aust.* 168 Both the Western District and Riverina Plains were dotted with 'mirrnyongs' or 'native ovens'—isolated middens up to 100 feet in diameter and several feet thick, often crammed with burials.

mirror dory. [See quot. 1965.] The marine fish *Zenopsis nebulosus* of s. Aust. incl. Tas., and elsewhere.

1951 T.C. ROUGHLEY *Fish & Fisheries Aust.* 28 The mirror dory . . grows to a length of 14 inches. **1965** *Austral. Encycl.* III. 272 Another rarer but equally palatable species is the mirror dory .. of deep water, whose smooth, scaleless, and circular body is brilliantly silvered like a looking-glass. **1985** *Canberra Times* 1 June 13/5 Mirror dory had become scarce.

miserable, *a.* [Br. dial. *miserable* miserly: see OED *a.* 6.] Parsimonious; stingy.

1903 J. FURPHY *Such is Life* 14 The more swellisher a man is, the more miserabler he is about a bite o' grass for a team, or a feed for a traveller. **1941** S.J. BAKER *Pop. Dict. Austral. Slang* 46 *Miserable*, mean-spirited, miserly. **1958** F. HARDY *Four-Legged Lottery* 183 He's a miserable bastard... Not all bookies are miserable; some of them are happy-go-lucky, generous blokes. **1976** *Austral.* (Sydney) 20 May 6/5 A 'lousy dollar a day!' Could any government be more miserable?

mission. [Spec. use of *mission* missionary post.]

1. Used *attrib.* and in Comb. to denote an establishment administered by a religious community for the spiritual and material welfare of Aborigines, as **mission black, boy, native, station.**

1841 *Geelong Advertiser* 27 Dec. 2/4 Mr Hurst .. I believe, is now at the mission station. **1841** *Port Phillip Patriot* 30 Dec. 2/2 A settler in the neighbourhood of Portland Bay, had called at the Mission Station and informed us, that great numbers of the natives had been shot. **1856** J. BONWICK *W. Buckley* 73 One who had quietly endured a long discourse at a mission station in the hope of a good *tuck out*, was very much disgusted at the small donation he received. **1890** *Braidwood Dispatch* 15 Jan. 2/3 One of the most serious complaints was that whenever they had black girls at the mission station who behaved themselves properly they were seduced by the whites. **1910** *Huon Times* (Franklin) 14 Sept. 4/3 Bowman was speared in the head by mission blacks. **1935** K.L. SMITH *Sky Pilot Arnhem Land* 38 There is a mission boy here .. waiting for the mail. **1936** C. CHEWINGS *Back in Stone Age* p. xi, The road to Glen Helen from the mission station lay through the Finke Gorge. **1937** L.R. MENZIES *Gold Seeker's Odyssey* 202 A Latin inscription on one side and a numeral on the other [of a disc] marked him as a mission boy from New Norcia. **1937** *Bulletin* (Sydney) 8 Sept. 21/1 The mission natives excitedly prepared for David's wedding. **1938** X. HERBERT *Capricornia* 293 The Mission natives .. were always too scared to follow tracks with certainty. **1941** K.S. PRICHARD *Moon of Desire* 44 'Yes, sir,' Gabriel replied. 'I am good man—mission boy.' **1945** J. DEVANNY *Bird of Paradise* 57 The chimes of the Angelus brought all activity on the Mission station to a standstill. **1951** C. SIMPSON *Adam in Ochre* 76 Two of them had shirts and old hats. They looked like 'mission blacks'. **1958** D.S. LESLIE *Green Singers* 203 'Me not desert blackfellow!' shrilled Jack indignantly. 'Me mission boy!'

2. *transf.* Such an establishment or community administered by a government agency or by Aborigines themselves. Also *attrib.*

1948 A. MARSHALL *Ourselves writ Strange* 219 Milingimbi mission did not interfere in 'native trouble', the term used to distinguish disagreements and quarrels of a tribal nature, or those misdemeanours for which the native laws provided a punishment. It concerned itself with 'mission trouble', which covered thieving from the mission .. or the breaking of certain rules and regulations governing the permanent residents. **1958** J. BECKETT Study Mixed Blood Aboriginal Minority (M.A. thesis) 51 No Church Missions have ever been established in the West (although government settlements are generally called Missions). **1975** R.J. MERRITT *Cake Man* (1978) 18 Inside a house on a mission for Aborigines. It is night. The walls are wooden below, fibro on top. **1978** K. GILBERT *People are Legends* 9 Whites didn't pay us wages in those days. Gave us 7s. 6d. mission ration a week. **1980** *N.S.W. Parl. Papers* 3rd Sess. IV. 899, I think the main problem was that they were seen as mission people... They lived on the outskirts of town. **1981** A. WELLER *Day of Dog* 15 The full-blood boy from Mowanjum mission .. teamed up with a city aboriginal. **1984** *Aboriginal Hist.* VIII. 34 Three successive governmental moves institutionalised the Ngiyampa on 'Aboriginal stations', or, as the people themselves called them, 'missions'.

mistletoe. [Transf. use of *mistletoe* the parasitic plant *Viscum album*.]

1. Any of many partly-parasitic plants, usu. dependent from the branches of a tree, and chiefly of the fam. Loranthaceae and Viscaceae of mainland Aust. Also *attrib.*

1862 R. HENNING *Lett.* (1952) 52 We hung over the pictures some Australian mistletoe, a pretty parasite, with bright-yellow drooping branches—like willow in the autumn—which grows in the gum trees here. **1892** M. NORTH *Recoll. Happy Life* II. 153 One plain .. surrounded by the nuytsia or mistletoe trees, in a full blaze of bloom. **1909** A.J. EWART *Weeds Vic.* 1 The following native plants are included under the head of proclaimed weeds: the Mistletoe (*Loranthus pendulus* and *L. celastroides*) [etc.]. **1938** X. HERBERT *Capricornia* 88 Every tree was flowering and most were draped with crimson mistletoe. **1965** *Austral. Encycl.* VI. 105 No Loranthaceae occur in Tasmania, but species of *Cassytha* .. are often called 'mistletoes' there. **1973** V. SERVENTY *Desert Walkabout* 21, I was interested to see a number of mistletoe berries which had dropped on a branch. **1981** D. LEVITT *Plants & People* 21 The hardwood pegs came from .. the Mistletoe Tree (*Exocarpos latifolius*).

2. Special Comb. **mistletoe bird,** the small bird *Dicaeum hirundinaceum*, widespread in mainland Aust. and also occurring on islands to the north, feeding chiefly on mistletoe berries.

1878 R.B. SMYTH *Aborigines of Vic.* II. 38 Mistletoe-bird, *Chirtgang*. **1917** *Bulletin* (Sydney) 5 July 24/1 The mistletoe-bird, or Australian flower-pecker .. is attired in a glossy steel-blue coat with scarlet and white vest. **1945** C. BARRETT *Austral. Bird Life* 180 The brightly coloured, dumpy little mistletoe bird .. belongs to a genus with headquarters in the Indian region. **1953** A. RUSSELL *Murray Walkabout* 134 A sudden glimpse of the mistletoe-bird .. hanging like a living jewel to a pendulous mistletoe spray. **1983** MORLEY & TOELKEN *Flowering Plants Aust.* 235 The mistletoebird .. has a short, simple gut, so that the seeds pass through the bird quickly (3 to 12 minutes).

mistress. *Hist.* A woman to whom a convict is assigned; the wife of a man to whom a convict is assigned: see ASSIGN *v.*

1813 *Regulations respecting Assigned Convict Servants* 24 July (1821) 17 If any Female Convict Servant be ill-treated by her Master or Mistress, she is .. to prefer her Complaint to a Magistrate. **1826** *Tasmanian Almanack* 77 If any Person, keeping a licensed Public-house, shall be proved to have allowed Prisoners of the Crown to drink or gamble, without leave of such Prisoner's Master or Mistress, he shall pay a fine. **1850** *Irish Exile* (Hobart) 16 Mar. 7 The woman stated that she had asked her mistress for a 'pass', and she had refused to give her one. **1856** J. BONWICK *Bushrangers* 9 No female convict was allowed to be in the streets after dusk without her master or mistress.

Mitchell. Abbrev. of MITCHELL GRASS.

1906 G.M. SMITH *Days of Cobb & Co.* 37 On the country there's a blight, There's not a blade of blue, or mitchell on the plain. **1916** T. WARLOW *By Mirage & Mulga* 3 To the south-west nothing but a vast stretch of plain, carpeted with 'Mitchell' and blue grass. **1936** J.C. DOWNIE *Galloping Hoofs* 45 The whole country was heavily grassed with mitchell. **1943** H.G. LAMOND *From Tariaro to Ross Roy* 118 All the natural plains are covered with Mitchell. **1976** C.D. MILLS *Hobble Chains & Greenhide* 136 That's Mitchell, good feed, 'specially when its hayed-off like it is now.

Mitchell grass. [f. the name of the explorer T.L. *Mitchell* (1792–1855): see MAJOR MITCHELL *v.*]

1. a. Any species of the genus *Astrebla* (fam. Poaceae), hardy, tussock-forming perennial grasses of arid and semi-arid Aust. providing valuable fodder; MITCHELL.

1880 J. BONWICK *Resources Qld.* 44 As to native grasses, one has forty varieties growing .. the perennial, fattening, drought-resisting *Mitchell*. **1897** *Antipodean* (Melbourne) 49 A crown of withered Mitchell grass. **1907** *Bulletin* (Sydney) 4 Apr. 14/1 On the great plains the blue and Mitchell grasses at full growth stand as even as a wheat field. **1911** A.G. STEPHENS *Pearl & Octopus* 95 The Mitchell-grass left by the rains had been scorched to dry roots. **1938** C.T. WHITE *Princ. Bot. Qld. Farmers* 200 The Mitchell Grasses are widely spread over the heavy blacksoil plains of Northern Australia, Central Australia, Queensland, and New South Wales, but find their greatest development in Queensland. **1949** G. BERRIE *Morale* 144 The thought of Queensland and waist-high Mitchell grass gave him a catch in the throat. **1962** MARSHALL & DRYSDALE *Journey among Men* 25 The blacksoil is covered with a rich growth of Mitchell grass, named, like the pink- and yellow-crested Major Mitchell cockatoo, after an early explorer. **1983** *Ecos* xxxvi. 30/2 Even during drought, hardy Mitchell grass tussocks usually can be relied upon to provide some fodder for sheep and cattle.

b. Comb. **Mitchell grass(ed) country, plains.**

1890 W.F. BUCHANAN *Aust. to Rescue* 59 We emerged from the timber into an open Mitchell grassed plain. **1927** M.H. ELLIS *Long Lead* 76 It is a series of long, golden, Mitchell grass plains, more coarsely pastured than the Mitchell country of the South. **1947** W.E. HARNEY *Brimming Billabongs* (1963) 135 We crossed over plains of Mitchell grass country and into the basalt hills. **1957** V. PALMER *Rainbow-Bird* 10 The sun spread over the Mitchell-grass plains. **1969** A. GARVE *Boomerang* 56 It's not like the Mitchell grass country up on the Tableland. That's real bonza.

2. With distinguishing epithet, as **bull Mitchell (grass),** *Astrebla squarrosa*; **curly Mitchell (grass),** *A. lappacea*; **wheat-eared Mitchell (grass),** a Mitchell grass, esp. *curly Mitchell*.

[**1937 bull Mitchell:** *Publicist* (Sydney) xvii. 15/1 Mitchell grass has three species, Hoop (Astrebla elymoides), Curly (A. pectinata) and Bull (A. triticoides) of which the two latter are perhaps better than the first.] **1938** C.T. WHITE *Princ. Bot. Qld. Farmers* 200 *Astrebla squarrosa* is the Bull Mitchell... It yields a very large seed-head and correspondingly large grain. **1952** A.M. DUNCAN-KEMP *Where Strange Paths go Down* 135 She flew with whirring wings ten to fifteen feet into the air, then to elude her pursuers dropped like a stone into a clump of bull Mitchell. **1975** E.R. ROTHERHAM et al. *Flowers & Plants N.S.W. & Southern Qld.* 180 Bull Mitchell .. will grow in .. badly drained soils. **1903** E. PALMER *Early Days N. Qld.* 236 **Curly Mitchell** grass; plant forming erect tufts one or two feet high, the leaves narrow and much curved. **1938** C.T. WHITE *Princ. Bot. Qld. Farmers* 200 *Astrebla lappacea*, known as the Wheat-eared or Curly Mitchell .. has a long, wheat-eared seed-head, and is probably the most important species of the genus from an economic standpoint. **1961** A.M. DUNCAN-KEMP *Our Channel Country* 11 Between stretches of natural grasses such as bull Mitchell, wheat-eared and curly-leafed Mitchell. **1981** G.M. CUNNINGHAM et al. *Plants Western N.S.W.* 61 Curly mitchell grass was first collected by Sir Thomas Mitchell on the Bogan River near Bourke in 1835. **1903** E. PALMER *Early Days N. Qld.* 236 'A. triticoides', **wheat-eared Mitchell grass** .. is taller and coarser than [common Mitchell grass], attaining a height of four or five feet. **1938, 1961** [see *curly Mitchell*].

mixed, *n.* [Abbrev. of *mixed train*.] A train which carries both passengers and freight.

1934 T. WOOD *Cobbers* 192 Goods trains and sheep trains and cattle trains run .. but they do not concern the passenger. He has to rely on the Mail and the Mixed. **1945** *Bulletin* (Sydney) 4 July 12/4 As the weekly mixed rounded the bend a figure leaped out of the hop-bush... The driver slammed on the brakes and the train shrieked to a slow, chattering stop. **1951** *Ibid.* 24 Jan. 13/1 The weekly mixed came down through the cutting and round the rather sharp bend where the line is partly hidden by a thick patch of blackberries. **1956** *Ibid.* 22 Aug. 12/2 As the once-a-week 'mixed' started to gain speed the guard noticed a case of eggs which were addressed to our station. **1969** P. ADAM SMITH *Folklore Austral. Railwaymen* 39 My longest trip with the 'mixed' from Alice Springs took me two weeks. It was January 1938. This 'mixed' ran alternate weeks to the Ghan.

mixed, *ppl. a.* In special collocations: **mixed allotment** *W.A., hist.*, see quots.; **business,** see quots. 1904 and 1962; **farmer,** one engaged in more than one kind of farming; **herd** *obs.*, a herd of heterogeneous cattle; **lounge,** a public room in which both men and women may drink.

1841 H.S. CHAPMAN *New Settlement Australind* 126 To each of the lots of 100 rural acres are attached .. four town sections of one quarter of an acre each, which rural acres and town selections (called **mixed allotments**) are offered at £101 each. **1843** *Sketch W.A.* 36 A 'mixed allotment' .. consists of 100 rural acres and four quarter-acre sections in the town. **1903** *Sydney Morning Herald* 6 Nov. 8/6 **Mixed businesses.** I have a Special Selection of Genuine Concerns Suitable for 1 or 2 ladies. **1904** *Ibid.* 16 Jan. 11/8 Mixed bus., Groc.,

Conf., Haberd., Tob., Cigar., Drinks, chp. rent, gd. liv. **1920** *Ibid.* 24 Apr. 21/8 Residentials, Confectionery, and Mixed Businesses of all kinds . . for Sale. **1940** *Ibid.* 9 Apr. 17/2 *Businesses for sale or wanted . . mixed.* Grocery, Smallgoods, Drinks, Tobacco, etc. (no fruit). Conducted by a woman we have known for years. **1962** HUNT & TOAL *Princ. Profitable Retailing* 29 Many hundreds of Australian retailers conduct what is called a 'mixed' business . . centred around a milk bar and/or delicatessen and/or sub-newsagency, with a bit of stationery and confectionery thrown in. **1969** *On Guard* (Broken Hill) Apr. 11 For many years the Robertson brothers conducted a mixed business in Blende Street. **1986** *Canberra Times* 24 May B16/4, 26 km. south of Bateman's Bay, on the beach, mixed business, petrol, groceries, takeaway food. **1909** R. KALESKI *Austral. Settler's Compl. Guide* 12 The . . **mixed farmer** selects too much. **1925** J.A. COLLUM *New Settlers' Handbk.* 89 The occupation of . . sugar-grower, fruit-grower, grazing farmer, and general and mixed farmer. **1843** A. CASWALL *Hints from Jrnl.* 46 A person beginning should buy (besides cows and heifers) three and two-year-old steers and yearlings (called a **mixed herd**). **1845** D. MACKENZIE *Emigrant's Guide* 110 To the emigrant who intends to commence as a cattle-grazier, I would recommend to buy a *mixed* herd. By a mixed herd is meant cattle consisting of cows, heifers, bullocks, steers and calves. **1969** *On Guard* (Broken Hill) Mar. 1 The work entails extending the **mixed lounge.** **1971** *Bulletin* (Sydney) 24 Apr. 55/3 More than a hundred people packed into the 'mixed lounge'. A notice reading 'Gents must be accompanied by a Lady' was not enforced.

mo. Abbrev. of 'moustache'.

1894 *Bulletin* (Sydney) 4 Aug. 2/2 He used to sport a ragged 'mo', my face was then quite bare. **1900** 'CASHAMBA' *Sketchy Characters* 31 He twirled his 'mo' with all the self-assurance of a cavalier. **1914** E. DYSON *Spats' Fact'ry* 94 She could never live with a ginger mo, she said. **1943** S.W. KEOUGH *Around Army* 10 In no time his long, thick walrus mo. was inextricably mixed up with several yards of chewing gum. **1948** *Bulletin* (Sydney) 3 Nov. 29/4 A heavy mo on a miner is a protection against 'dusting'. Fifty years ago stonemasons firmly believed in the efficiency of face draperies as dust-screens. **1981** K. GARVEY *Rhymes of Ratbag* 54 His mo he paused to wipe.

mob, *n.* [Transf. use of *mob* a rabble, a riotous crowd: see OED(S *mob, sb.*[1])]

1. a. *Hist.* A (potentially hostile) party of Aborigines. **b.** An Aboriginal community.

1828 *Hobart Town Courier* 13 Sept. 3 The tribe of natives who murdered the unfortunate man named Samuel Clarke, at the Lakes last week, consisted of what is generally known as the Big river mob and another united. **1835** *True Colonist* (Hobart) 17 Jan. 2/4 The party of natives were brought in. . . The *mob* consists of one man, four women, and three children. **1846** *Bell's Life in Sydney* 19 Dec. 1/4 A skilled Rifleman ought to be with you, his long shots would tell easily . . at a mob of blackies at 500 yards, his ball would hit and kill. **1861** J. DAVIS *Tracks of McKinlay* 22 Nov. (1863) 120 Five or six whites to that mob of natives. **1875** CAMPBELL & WILKS *Early Settlement Qld.* 7 We found them encamped between two scrubs with a mob of blacks about them. **1897** *Papers & Proc. R. Soc. Tas.* (1898) 179 Although Robinson dignifies the tribes with the name of 'nations', they were known to the settlers by the designation of 'mobs'. **1900** *Bulletin* (Sydney) 21 Apr. 14/1 He intended to run in a mob of *30* black lepers, and see what the Govt. would do. **1938** D. BATES *Passing of Aborigines* 167 On the steep hills about the soak, the visiting mobs camped, each in the direction of his own ground. **1948** C.P. MOUNTFORD *Brown Men & Red Sand* 35, I had been admitted as a member of the tribe, therefore one half of the people were *tamaniltjan* to me, or to use a well-worn but expressive outback term, they were 'my mob'. **1951** E. HILL *Territory* 308 Gener'ly a big mob of myalls round there. **1976** K. BROWN *Knock Ten* 67 When you have a mob of them you do think they had it better in the old days when you could use a whip on them. **1978** 'B. WONGAR' *Track to Bralgu* 1 What a pity that my people, the Riratjingu mob, did not understand it. **1984** *Aboriginal Hist.* VIII. 37 The old people . . when talking about the past, do not . . retain these names in their Ngiyampa form. Instead, they use names which link people with parts of the country by reference to pastoral stations. Thus the Nhiiyikiyalu are referred to as the 'Marfield mob'.

2. An assembled body of animals (orig. with some sense of the body being threatening); a flock or herd; a group.

1828 *Hobart Town Courier* 12 July 2 The wild mob [of cattle] . . not content with devouring our grass, walk off with every horn and hoof belonging to us. **1834** G. BENNETT *Wanderings N.S.W.* I. 244 'The mob' of these screaming and destructive birds attack a field of grain. **1838** T. WALKER *Month in Bush Aust.* 8 'Mobs' of cattle scattered over the surface, like flies resting on a billiard table. **1840** A. RUSSELL *Tour through Austral. Colonies* 154 A young colt . . was running with a mob (term applied to a herd) of horses. **1846** G.H. HAYDON *Five Yrs. Experience Aust. Felix* 59 The 'old men' kangaroos are always the largest and strongest in the flock, or in colonial language, 'mob'. **1848** *Adelaide Miscellany* 9 Dec. 303 Stockmen mounted their horses and scoured the Bush, bringing in mob after mob, and in about an hour the whole herd was collected and secured in the yard. **1852** MRS C. MEREDITH *My Home in Tas.* II. 20 A mob of *lambs* . . a rare mob of chickens . . a great mob of quail. **1875** *Observer Miscellany* (Adelaide) 3 July 425/1 When that mob of whiting comes near the bridge stamp your feet. **1889** E. GILES *Aust. twice Traversed* I. 72 The horses wandered all over the country during the night, in mobs of twos and threes. **1895** E.T.H. HUTTON *Narr. Tour Inspection N.S.W.* 6 Dead sheep in mobs of six and seven were seen on every side. **1917** A.B. PATERSON *Saltbush Bill* 7 The eager stockhorse pricks his hears And lifts his head on high In wild excitement when he hears The Brumby mob go by. **1935** *Bulletin* (Sydney) 2 Jan. 20/2, I overtook a drover. . . Most of his mob had pink-eye. **1956** S. HOPE *Diggers' Paradise* 74 A 'mob' of pelicans preening themselves. **1978** D. STUART *Wedgetail View* 56 Four or five thousand wethers in one mob.

3. A number, or class, of people sharing a distinctive characteristic, identity, etc.

1848 *Atlas* (Sydney) IV. 379/1 The Electors of Geelong and Portland have been disfranchised by a Melbourne mob. **1860** *Bell's Life in Sydney* 26 May 3/2, I met a large mob of South Australians returning from Kiandra. **1884** 'R. BOLDREWOOD' *Old Melbourne Memories* 119 The 'Mount Gambier mob', as in colonial parlance described, was at that time composed of men the majority of whom had attained to social distinction. **1918** *Kia Ora Coo-ee* Apr. 2/2 Cooking for a mob of Dinkums is about the most thankless job that I know of. **1929** F. MANNING *Middle Parts of Fortune* I. 10 'They can say what they bloody well like,' he said appreciatively, 'but we're a fuckin' fine mob.' **1950** K.S. PRICHARD *Winged Seeds* 24 The mob on the flat weren't dinkum prospectors. **1955** F. LANE *Patrol to Kimberleys* 84 It took eleven ships to bring the first mob to 'Stralia. **1965** G.H. FEARNSIDE *Golden Ram* 83 The more he drinks, the more he talks. He's one of that mob. **1975** *Bulletin* (Sydney) 29 Nov. 6/2 There is no place in the Liberal Party for this alien philosophy [*sc.* democracy]—invented, I believe, by some mob of Greeks. **1981** P. RADLEY *Jack Rivers & Me* 173 There'd be some bloody good forwards among that mob of sheilas if we could get 'em to play Rugby. **1985** *Bulletin* (Sydney) 18 June 72/2 His crew was 'certainly not a mob of high rollers'.

4. A (large) quantity; a (considerable) number: see quot. 1934 (1). Now esp. in *pl.* and also as quasi-*adv.*: see quot. 1934 (2). See also *big mob* BIG 3 d.

1852 *Wanderer* (Adelaide) (1853) June 53, I took down a mob of quarts and pints, so strung together that for a time I could not disentangle them. **1853** H.B. JONES *Adventures in Aust.* 114 Wool from the interior is brought down, to be placed on board these steamers, and then shipped for Sydney, by schooners from Brisbane. 'There will be a great mob of things going down to-day,' said one to another, which meant, that there would be a heavy cargo in number. **1902** E.B. KENNEDY *Black Police Qld.* 66, I . . brought a mob of nuggets there to begin as an overlander. **1911** *Bulletin* (Sydney) 2 Nov. 14/1 The Abo. Protection officials are doing their best to carry out an unworkable Act . . and the niggers have 'gone walkabout alonga bush' in mobs. **1927** M.H. ELLIS *Long Lead* 81 See 'mobs of scenery'. 'Mobs' is the superlative of everything in the Territory. It is the equivalent of superabundance. **1934** T. WOOD *Cobbers* 175 The supplanting of all collectives by one single upstart—mob. When two or three are gathered together, then you have a mob. Men, birds, animals, fish—all mobs. Mountains and mosquitoes—all mobs. **1934** A. RUSSELL *Tramp-Royal* 91 There'll be mobs of water on the track, we'll get mobs of beef at the runs, the stages'll be mobs shorter, an' there'll be mobs better camping grounds . . and of course we'll be able to take it mobs easier. **1976** N.V. WALLACE *Bush Lawyer* 123 Some interesting words are used in this cattle country. You never say lots of fish or lots of anything but always mobs, even mobs of firewood; mobs of channels ran through the station with mobs of fish in them. **1980** ANSELL & PERCY *To fight Wild* 104 He had to drink mobs of grog and he wasn't good at drinking mobs of grog. **1984** B. DIXON *Searching for Aboriginal Lang.* 122 The policeman said there really weren't any Aborigines in town . . but there were mobs at a cattle station some way to the west.

mob, *v.* [f. MOB *n.* 2.] *trans.* To muster (stock). Also as *vbl. n.*

1856 J. BONWICK *Bushrangers* 45 A long continued course of success in the art of mobbing, branding and slaughtering had made him less cautious. **1913** W.K. HARRIS *Outback in Aust.* 137 Many of my Missionary friends have shorn sheep with them, mobbed and drafted cattle and sheep.

mock. [Transf. use of *mock* a mocking: see OEDS *mock, sb.*[1] 1 b. and *mocker, sb.*[1] 1 d.] A jinx; a stop (to an activity, etc.). Also **mocker.** Esp. in the phr. **to put a mock** (or **mocker**) **on** or **the mock** (or **mockers**) **on.**

1911 E. DYSON *Benno & Push* 33 'All toms is 'erlike t' me,' he said . . 'but, all the same, it's up t' me t' put a mock on that tripester.' **1922** C. DREW *Rogues & Ruses* 115 I've got a mocker hung on me. **1938** X. HERBERT *Capricornia* 523 'He put the mocks on me,' roared Norman. . . 'What's he saying, dear?' 'He—he reckons I told the police on him.' **1942** L. MANN *Go-Getter* 181 'God's truth,' he said, almost aloud, 'there seems to be a mock on me.' **1963** J. DUFFY *Outsville Pub* 26 'Like I said this car goes like a bird.' But as the words came from his mouth, the engine coughed once, and died completely. 'Damn . . put a mocker on it.' **1981** *Sydney Morning Herald* 6 July 33/1 Someone has really put the mockers on the Canterbury-Bankstown Rugby League team. **1983** *Bulletin* (Sydney) 2 Aug. 34/2 The double loss put the mockers on everything. Lake Macquarie is not the place to live without wheels.

mocker. Also **mokker.** [Of unknown origin.] Attire; dress.

[N.Z. **1947** P. NEWTON *Wayleggo* 147 Climbing out of bed and donning clammy, greasy shearing mocker.] **1953** S.J. BAKER *Aust. Speaks* 106 *Mocker*, clothes in general. **1965** K. MCKENNEY *Hide-Away Man* 49 'Yer bin ter a fancy dressed ball?' . . Bluey skipped in a small circle. 'It's me groppy mocker. I bin ter a weddin'.' **1968** *Kings Cross Whisper* (Sydney) li. 7/2 Look your best at this interview . . however, carry a small bag with some shabby mocker in it. **1979** D.R. STUART *Crank back on Roller* 214 'Snow is a hell to all of them if they're not clothed and fed. . . ' 'Well, we're right . . we've got good mocker, good boots, the lot.' **1984** *Austral. Short Stories* viii. 54 Just wear ordinary mokker.

Also **mockered up** *ppl. a.*, dressed up.

[**1938** E. PARTRIDGE *Dict. Slang & Unconventional Eng.* (rev. ed.) 1014 *Mockered up*, dressed in one's best: low: late C. 19–20.] **1943** S.J. BAKER *Pop. Dict. Austral. Slang* (ed. 3) 5 *All laired up*, flashily dressed, dressed up to the nines, also 'All Mockered Up'. **1953** 'CADDIE' *Caddie* 223, I won't be likely to be gettin' mokkered up before Satadey, so I'll pop me clobber termorrer. **1957** D. NILAND *Call me when Cross turns Over* 174 Don't think of the Apostles as silvertails, all mokkered up in the best, and a cheque-book for every pocket. **1977** D. STUART *Drought Foal* 180 Or an Admiral, any of them coves, all mockered up, real bloody desert lairs?

model. *Obs.* Abbrev. of MODEL PRISON. Also *attrib.*

1845 *Cumberland Times* (Parramatta) 27 Dec. 4/3 Forgery is become of common occurrence in Melbourne—the last offender was one of the recently arrived 'model' pets. **1845** *Standard* (Melbourne) 8 Jan. 2/4 *The Pentonvillains.* Some idea may be formed of the worst of the model men, by the sample we have just seen. **1883** 'ONE WHO WAS THERE' *Prison Sketches* 16 At the back of these cells is what is called the 'models', where prisoners are placed for the first month of their confinement, and for that time are only allowed a half-ration dinner, and kept confined to their cells. **1910** L. ESSON *Three Short Plays* (1911) 14 *Constable*: How did he take it? It was his first stretch in the Jug. *Smithy*: Rotten. I done model with him.

model prison. *Hist.* A prison in which the inmates are kept in separate confinement and considerable emphasis is placed upon their reformation.

1846 *Moreton Bay Courier* 24 Oct. 3/1 These convicts are mostly from the model prison, where they have been taught useful trades, and will have the opportunity of making themselves useful men in the new convict colony. **1893** M. JEFFREY *Burglar's Life* 81 He imposed upon me an additional sentence of six months, which I was to undergo in the Model Prison. . . The severity of this punishment will be understood by those who are conversant with the rigid discipline which existed in this institution. **1975** I. BRAND *'Separate Prison' Port Arthur* 7 Of all the buildings at Port Arthur, the one which raises most interest is the 'Model Prison', or, as it was officially known, the 'Separate Prison'.

mogo /'moʊgoʊ/. *Obs.* Also **maga, mago, mogin, moko.** [a. Dharuk *mugu.*] An Aboriginal stone hatchet.

[**1793** W. TENCH *Compl. Acct. Settlement* 68 *Bùlla Mògo Parrabùgò* (two hatchets tomorrow) I repeatedly cried.] **1798** D. COLLINS *Acct. Eng. Colony N.S.W.* I. 586 This is the Mogo, or stone hatchet. **1801** *HRA* (1915) 1st. Ser. III. 178 From what I observed of trees cut down by the natives, which must have been with a much sharper edged tool than what their stone maga is. **1820** J. OXLEY *Jrnls. Two Exped. N.S.W.* 175 They were entirely unarmed, and there was but one mogo, or stone-hatchet, among them. **1830** R. DAWSON *Present State Aust.* 59, I presented to each man a tomahawk (or maga, as they call it). **1838** T.L. MITCHELL *Three Exped. Eastern Aust.* II. 338 The elasticity and lightness of the simple handle of the mogo or stone hatchet . . are well adapted to the weight of the head. **1840** T.J. BUCKTON *W.A.* 99 The *mago* is a stone-hatchet, the handle of which is so light and elastic as greatly to aid the effect of the blow. **1848** *Bell's Life in Sydney* 5 Feb. 1/1 The silence of the woods is startling—you do not hear even the 'moko' of the aborigines, all of whom have been exterminated in the march of civilization, and in accordance with our national system of ethics. **1853** J. SHERER *Gold Finder Aust.* 222 A mountain of serpentine . . famous amongst the natives formerly for producing the best mogos or stone hatchets. **1872** G.E. LOYAU *Colonial Lyrics* 24, I saw the savages, a scattered band, All armed with mogo, boomerang, and spear. **1895** G. RANKEN *Windabyne* 275 He had not a weapon, not even the little stone 'Mogin' that stands for axe, and carpenter's chest in general, with the blacks.

moiety. *Anthropology.* [Spec. use of *moiety* one of two parts into which something is divided. Used earliest in reference to Aborigines: see OED(S 4.] One of two units into which an Aboriginal people is divided, esp. on the basis of lineal descent.

1882 *Jrnl. Anthrop. Inst.* (London) (1883) XII. 510 If we now . . separate the whole into its two constituent moieties, we shall have exactly a representation in each of the assumed forms of the divided commune, in which the two divisions are in fact totems. **1888** A.W. HOWITT *Further Notes Austral. Class Systems* 39 The primary classes have names which convey a meaning as words independently of their signification as class names. They are in fact in such cases totems which each apply to one moiety of the tribe. **1899** SPENCER & GILLEN *Native Tribes Central Aust.* 70 The four [subclasses] are Panunga and Bulthara, Purula and Kumara; the first two forming one moiety of the tribe, and the latter two forming another. **1937** W.L. WARNER *Black Civilization* (1958) 5 The moiety is a still larger unit than the clan, dividing the sixty-odd clans into two groups which intermarry. By the device of the moiety, the whole of the life of the Murngin, as well as nature, is placed in two opposing groups called Yiritja and Dua. **1946** W.E. HARNEY *North of 23°* 46 Divisions, perhaps based on the mother's local group, and moieties are again divided into totems.

moit. Usu. in *pl.* [Br. dial. *moit* particle of wood, stick, etc., caught in the wool of a sheep: see OEDS.] See quot. 1899.

1899 A. SINCLAIR *Clip of Wool* 66 *Moits*, short pieces of stick and scrub, principally found in the neck wool. **1953** R.F. COOPER *Practical Woolclassing* 31 Moits (such as sticks, straw and vegetable matter). **1965** J.S. GUNN *Terminol. Shearing Industry* ii. 4 *Moit(s)*, pieces of stick and rubbish matted in wool, especially the neck wool.

moity, *a.* [Br. dial. *moity*: see prec.] Of wool: containing particles of wood or other foreign substances.

1878 'R. BOLDREWOOD' *Ups & Downs* 83 The 'heavy and moity' parcels were not touched by the cautious operators at any price. **1921** L.G. JONES *Flockmaster's Companion* 77 *Moity* is a term used when referring to a wool carrying foreign matter, such as leaves, small sticks, etc., mostly found in the neck or back. **1928** C.E. COWLEY *Classing Clip* 36 The wool grown on the scragg . . is . . often 'moity', that is, containing pieces of vegetable matter, sticks, pieces of thistles, etc.

mokani /mə'kani/. *Obs.* [a. Yaralde *mokani.*] See quot. 1846.

1846 H.E.A. MEYER *Manners & Customs Aborigines Encounter Bay* 8 The mokani is a black stone, shaped something like the head of an axe, fixed between two sticks bound together, which serve for a handle. The sharp side of the stone is used to enchant males, the other side females. **1879** *Native Tribes S.A.* 195 They fancy that they can charm or enchant by means of two instruments, one called plongge, the other mokani.

moke. [Transf. use of *moke* a donkey.] A horse; sometimes an inferior horse.

1863 *Frank Gardiner, or Bushranging in 1863* 9, I didn't know what had become of the moke. **1873** M. CLARKE *Holiday Peak* 60 Numerous horses, 'mokes', as their owners termed them. **1886** *Bulletin* (Sydney) 13 Mar. 14/1 A bush missionary, riding a very miserable moke, recently appeared at Casino. **1892** J.B. STEPHENS *Fayette* 6 A horse! A mare! My kingdom for a moke! **1900** *Tocsin* (Melbourne) 3 May 1/3 A great many of their mokes are perfect scrubbers, and certainly a bad advt. as Australian bred horses. **1913** *Bulletin* (Sydney) 17 Apr. 16/2 Thousands of valuable mokes are killed every year by these well-named horse-breakers. **1917** A.B. PATERSON in C. Semmler *World of Banjo Paterson* (1967) 35 His horse . . was a ragged, unkempt pony, pitifully poor and very footsore, at first sight, an absolute 'moke'. **1934** 'S. RUDD' *Green Grey Homestead* 145 He was the finest looking animal ever ye clapped eyes on, though before that he was just a sleepy old clothes-peg of a sheep-drover's moke. **1961** *Meanjin* 10 My Pop has a few horses and we had ponies when we were little. Come down some time and we'll put you on a moke. **1968** *Swag* (Sydney) i. 19/2 Screaming his head off at some moke which, needless to say, gets beaten. **1976** C.D. MILLS *Hobble Chains & Greenhide* 29 'How's my horse?' . . 'Your old moke's alright,' laughed the Boss.

mokker, var. MOCKER.

moko, var. MOGO.

molared, var. MOLO.

mole, *n.*[1] *Obs.* [Transf. use of *mole* a small, burrowing mammal.] PLATYPUS.

1825 B. FIELD *Geogr. Mem. N.S.W.* 462 This is New Holland . . where the mole (ornithorhynchus paradoxus) lays eggs, and has a duck's bill. **1837** *Lit. News* (Sydney) 21 Oct. 106 The young moles . . were 'cobbong fat',and in plump condition, whilst the old one was miserably thin.

mole, *n.*[2] [Abbrev. of MOLESKIN.]

a. Used *attrib.* in Comb. **mole pants, trousers.**

1860 *Northern Star* (Kapunka) 26 May 1/3 Men's Mole Trousers at 4s. 6d. **1896** W.H. WILLSHIRE *Land of Dawning* 101 Here you get a rough book, by a rough author, written in the garb of a real bushman, viz., mole pants and a cotton shirt.

b. *pl. Moleskin trousers*, see MOLESKIN.

1879 *Kelly Gang* 125 His dress . . consisted of . . an ordinary flannel singlet, covered by an olive-green Crimean shirt; trousers of a kind known in the slop-shops as 'coloured moles'. **1888** J. POTTS *One Yr. Anti-Chinese Work Qld.* 8 Certainly we did not cut a very aristocratic figure in our moles, flannel, and jam pot of liquid paste, with which to stick up the bills. **1913** H. LAWSON *Triangles of Life* 227 He was a stout, nuggety man, in clean white 'moles', crimson shirt, and red neck-handkerchief. **1929** *Bulletin* (Sydney) 27 Mar. 25/1 White moles were considered by some to be too flash. **1953** A. MARSHALL *Aust.* (1981) 2 Those pants were white moles but they're covered with mud. **1976** C.D. MILLS *Hobble Chains & Greenhide* 60 The only other pair of pants I had were old stagers, and their seat was so delicate it had a sort of gossamer effect. This left only the 'moles', and I treasured them beyond rubies.

mole, *n.*[3] [Prob. var. of *moll* girl or woman.] A girl or woman: see esp. quot. 1983.

1965 W. DICK *Bunch of Ratbags* 270 Just because you've got yourself some rich bloke's mole of a bloody daughter, don't come telling me and the boys what to bloody do. **1979** R.D. JONES *Walking Line* 19 Give us a hand you lazy mole! **1983** *Sun-Herald* (Sydney) 15 May 51/2 'If a girl does it all the time then she's a mole. Moles are scum, worse than dirt.' . . 'I know one girl who goes out with someone for one night and hops into bed with them—I'd call her a mole.'

moleskin. [Spec. use of *moleskin* a strong, cotton cloth: see OED(S 2 and 4. As *moleskin trousers* recorded earliest in Aust.]

1. Used *attrib.* in Special Comb. **moleskin trousers,** trousers made of moleskin, esp. as regarded as part of the customary dress of a rural worker or gold-miner.

1839 *Tasmanian* (Hobart) 15 Feb. 51/1 Moleskin and cord trowsers. **1846** *Citizen* (Sydney) 26 Dec. 139/2 In New England the price charged for a pair of moleskin trousers was 14s. **1855** G.H. WATHEN *Golden Colony* 63 His [*sc.* the digger's] dress is a blue elastic vest, or *jersey*, like that worn by sailors, and thick moleskin trousers. **1882** *Bulletin* (Sydney) 5 Aug. 6/3 The 'Plume' Brand Moleskin Trousers White And Printed, In Stockman's Or Ordinary Cut. **1894** J.K. ARTHUR *Kangaroo & Kauri* 12 Moleskin trousers are much patronized by the colonists who have manual labour or much riding to do.

2. Usu. in *pl.* Abbrev. of *moleskin trousers.* Also *attrib.* and *fig.*

1850 *Monthly Almanac* (Adelaide) 10 The body of the moleskins is napless—the soles of the Bluchers become attenuated—the cabbage-tree hat has acquired a suitable greasiness in the region of the ribbon. **1881** G.C. EVANS *Stories* 235, I divested myself of my civilized attire donned the blue shirt and moleskins and at once started for the diggings. **1892** *Bulletin* (Sydney) 20 Feb. 7/3 The ordinary artisan whose horny-handed mole-skin-lined wages are, in most cases, much greater than the pittance of the servile, yet vain, black-coated quill-driver. **1918** A.M. MOORE *Autumn Grey* 45 His gaunt frame clothed in moleskin and soft Crimean shirt; in the background his hut of galvanised iron. **1921** K.S. PRICHARD *Black Opal* 11 An old man in worn white mole-skins and cotton shirt. **1976** MULLALLY & SEXTON *Stir Possum* 13 There were stockmen in snow-white mole-skins. **1978** F. HOWARD *Moleskin Gentry* 2 In a country that still thought in English terms and judged by English values, they were the gentry—the moleskin gentry.

Hence **moleskinned** *ppl. a.*, clad in moleskin trousers.

1885 N.W. SWAN *Couple of Cups Ago* 122 The public, moleskinned and pipeclayed, looked on. **1930** A.E. YARRA *Vanishing Horsemen* 12 He saw a white mole-skinned trouser-leg.

molled, var. MOLO.

molly. In the phr. **molly the monk,** rhyming slang for 'drunk'.

1966 *Kings Cross Whisper* (Sydney) xxvi. 6/1 Now the basic type of booze . . and that which induces the most popular result (gets you molly the monk) is—wait for it—beer. **1973** *Ibid.* cliv. 2/4 Ophelia was more than a little bit Molly the Monk after Parkinson had been loosening her up a bit with three bottles of Quelltaler hock.

molly-dook. Also **molly-dooker, molly-duke.** [Prob. f. *molly* an effeminate man, a milksop (see OED *sb.*[1] 2) + *dook*, var. *duke* hand.] A left-handed person. Also *attrib.*, and **molly-hander.**

[**1926** 'J. DOONE' *Timely Tips New Australs., Mauldy*, left handed.] **1934** *Bulletin* (Sydney) 21 Mar. 11/3 Hence the trade is taboo to the molly-hander. **1941** S.J. BAKER *Pop. Dict. Austral. Slang* 47 *Mollydooker*, a left-handed person. Whence, *mollydook* (adj.), left-handed. **1943** *Signals* (Melbourne) Christmas 7 Who is the molly duke Lieut. who forgot to endorse her cheque? **1968** *Swag* (Sydney) ii. 23/2 Is your kid a southpaw? . . The last time Sammy got a hiding it was a molly-dooker who did it. **1975** B. Foley *Shearer's Poems* 9 We're shearing here at Kylie And the frost is on the grain The 'molley dooker' is deucin [*sic*] 'em And the Kiwi's draggin' the chain. **1983** *Northern Daily Leader* (Tamworth) 2 Dec. 6/2 Five of the top seven batsmen doing battle for Australia are left-handers. Kepler Wessels, Wayne Phillips [etc.] . . are all molly dookers.

Hence **molly-dooked**. *a.*, left-handed.

1969 *Southerly* xxix. 8 It could be being written by someone else with the same absurdly decorous aim, someone molly-duked, atheist, over-educated. **1982** J. Hibberd *Country Quinella* (1984) 76 Give it another bash, Jock. . . Practice makes perfect. . . See if I can do it molly-dookered.

molo /'moʊloʊ/, *a.* Also **molared, molled, mowlow.** [Of unknown origin, but see OED *molly, sb.*[2] 2., a meeting of ship-captains: the quots. (1874 and 1885) suggest this might also be a drinking party.] Inebriated.

1906 *Truth* (Sydney) 28 Oct. 9/4 She herself told me she was half-molled. What did you understand her to mean by that? That she was half-drunk. **1916** *Rising Sun: On Board 'Themistocles'* 26 Aug. (Suppl.), When you're 'molo' in a crowd. **1926** M. Forrest *Hibiscus Heart* 146 Most people in the township considered him not much more than a fool, who was always 'half molared'. **1939** *Bulletin* (Sydney) 15 Mar. 20/1 He was much too often 'molo', and he mostly travelled solo. **1953** *Ibid.* 25 Nov. 12/4 Nobody *worried* much about it when Curl was sober, but when he was molo he'd recite the dashed thing over and over again. **1972** A. Macdonald *Ukulele Player* 264 'Don't you get molo in your spare time,' he said, glaring at the bottle of red wine he'd ordered. **1978** H.C. Baker *I was Listening* 56 He got mowlow at a dance one night. **1979** D.R. Stuart *Crank back on Roller* 96 By the time he ran us down to the wharf to catch the boat back, we were nicely molo.

moloch. [See quot. 1898.] *Mountain devil* (a), see Mountain. Also **moloch lizard.**

1845 J.E. Gray *Catal. Specimens Lizards Brit. Museum* 263 The Moloch, *Moloch horridus*, Gray. **1855** J. Bonwick *Geogr. Aust. & N.Z.* (ed. 3) 200 The Moloch lizard has horns on its head and spines on its back. **1896** F.G. Aflalo *Sketch Nat. Hist. Aust.* 178 The Moloch (*Moloch horridus*) . . is a most formidable-looking creature, entirely covered with spines. **1898** E.E. Morris *Austral Eng.* 300 Moloch . . an Australian lizard . . the adjective (Lat. *horridus*, bristling) seems to have suggested the noun, the name probably recalling Milton's line ('Paradise Lost', I. 392)—'First Moloch, horrid king, besmeared with blood'. **1933** R.B. Plowman *Camel Pads* 284 Another denizen of the sandhills holds second place in the bush folk's affection—the Moloch lizard or mountain devil. **1945** 'Master-Sarg' *Yank discovers Aust.* 74 The Moloch Lizard . . you can find . . in the desert with some sand and stones and maybe a bit of brush.

monaych /'mɒnaɪtʃ/. Also **monarch.** [a. Nyungar *monayj* white cockatoo; *transf.* a police officer.] A police officer; the police.

1961 N. Gare *Fringe Dwellers* 35 Skippy gets off. An ya know the first thing e says ta them monarch? E turns round on em an yelps, 'An now ya can just gimme back that bottle.' **1975** R. Beilby *Brown Land Crying* 10 Myra was terrified. The coppers! Monaych! The native word contained a history of oppression: the Men with Chains! **1979** N. Braham *Dwarf* 28 When I'm broke I'm just Tommy Caylun, the boong, shuffling down the street, with an eye out for the monaych—coppers. **1981** A. Weller *Day of Dog* 2 'Nuh, gotta go. See Mum.' 'Yeah, well, look out for the monaych, budda.' ' . . 'Ard luck if 'e goes back, first day out.'

mong /mʌŋ/. [Abbrev. of *mongrel* a dog of mixed breed.]

1. A dog (not necessarily of mixed breed).

1903 *Sporting News* (Launceston) 2 May 1/3 Trotting like 'mongs' in the two mile events. **1924** *Bulletin* (Sydney) 6 Mar. 24/3 Ringer was a decidedly unsociable mong. in a Bungendore rabbiter's pack. **1934** *Ibid.* 22 Aug. 21/3, I know of a 12-year-old mong which has spent the last eight years in the company of turkeys, and now his . . bark is a good imitation of a turkey's gobble. **1941** *Ibid.* 16 July 16/1 When you see the mongs as mudfat as they are y' can bet the missus is a rotten cook an' has to throw a lot of stuff to 'em. **1956** E. Lambert *Watermen* 93 'Whose mong?' inquired the Member. 'My boys swiped him from somewhere the other week.' 'He'll never work sheep.' **1970** J. Cleary *Helga's Web* 86, I backed a mong last night that had only three legs . . and it finished up beating the bunny home. **1980** J. Wright *Big Hearts & Gold Dust* 127 Gor'on, ya bloody mong. Git ta buggery. Ya probably lousy with fleas.

2. *transf.* Applied to a person: see Mongrel. Also *attrib.*

1926 *Aussie* (Sydney) Jan. 36/3 'E never gave anybody er chance . . the dirty mong. **1933** *Bulletin* (Sydney) 16 Aug. 39/1 And the mong fired him! **1968** W.N. Scott *Some People* 120 The little bloke said, 'Mong jew!!'

Mongolian. *Obs.* [Transf. use of *Mongolian* a native of Mongolia.] A Chinese immigrant to Australia; Chinese immigrants to Australia in general.

1859 *Colonial Mining Jrnl.* Feb. 94/1 The mongolian . . follows the caucasian as the scavenger succeeds civilization. **1870** *Sydney Morning Herald* 4 July 3/1 In the outer room were seated three ugly Mongolians. **1881** *Bulletin* (Sydney) 7 May 9/1 The Right Worshipful Mayor of Sydney, speaking at the anti-Mongolian meeting, said that we were Anglo-Saxons now, but if the Chinese were allowed to come here in swarms we 'might go back to monkeys again'. **1899** *Austral. Tit-Bits* (Sydney) 18 Feb. 20/1 English representatives . . sell on behalf of the Mongolian the vegetables produced by market gardeners. **1913** J.B. Castieau *Reminisc. Detective-Inspector Christie* 19 He saw a Chinaman, the first he had ever seen. Curiosity caused him to regard the Mongolian attentively.

mongrel. [Survival of Br. use: see OED *sb.* 1 b.] Applied to a person: a term of contempt or abuse (cf. 'cur'). Also *attrib.*, and *transf.*

1919 A. Wright *Game of Chance* 20 A mongrel she'd known before me . . put a tale over on her. **1954** T. Ronan *Vision Splendid* 38 Conversation languished but for the 'get along, you mongrel bastards!' **1956** J.E. Macdonnell *Commander Brady* 248 The ladies of this here mongrel joint are puttin' on a gut-rub for Navy gents ternight. **1974** *Meanjin* 280 A mate of mine was exterminated like that. In a cellar. Some mongrel dropped a niner through a trapdoor.

monkey. [Transf. and fig. use of *monkey*.]

1. See Monkey bear.

2. A sheep. Also *attrib.*

1876 J.A. Edwards *Gilbert Gogger* 109, I don't think that calling a sheep, a jumbuck or a monkey . . is talking pure English. **1880** *Blackwood's Mag.* (Edinburgh) Jan. 73/2 The last lot of 'monkeys', as the shearers usually denominated sheep, leave the head-station. **1892** *Western Champion* (Barcaldine) 26 Jan. 11/2 The monkeys are safe tonight in the brush yards. **1905** A.B. Paterson *Old Bush Songs* 126 You've only to sport your dover and knock a monkey over—There's cheap mutton for the Wallaby Brigade. **1921** *Bulletin* (Sydney) 3 Feb. 22/2 To corn mutton . . soak a couple of thick cornsacks in water and lay them out. . . Then kill and dress . . 'monkey' and divide it longitudinally. **1939** *Ibid.* 22 Feb. 21/4 Are y' blanky well scaldin' the wool off of these monkeys, or are y' pluckin' it out with yer fingers an' thumb? **1944** *Ibid.* 30 Aug. 13/4 This superb drover worked his epic way till he reached a mail-change on the Ayrshire Downs road, whence he collected a few monkey conductors suffering a holiday.

3. *Mining.* A vertical shaft: see quots. 1869 and 1968. Also **monkey shaft.**

1869 R.B. Smyth *Gold Field & Minerals Districts* 616 *Monkey-shaft* is a shaft rising from a lower to a higher level (as a rule perpendicularly) and differs from a blind-shaft only in that the latter is sunk from a higher to a lower level. **1871** *Austral. Town & Country Jrnl.* (Sydney) 8 Apr. 440/4 Grainger in moving about fell down a monkey shaft; a depth of fifty feet. *c* **1880** A.F. Gardner *Flooding of Mine* 3 There are Jump-ups and Monkeys and numerous Levels. **1968** M.T. Clark *Spark of Opal* (1973) 133 Sometimes a miner put down an exploratory hole, known as a 'monkey', to the next level through the floor of the drive instead of working back from the main shaft, and sometimes it rewarded him. **1980** S. Thorne *I've met some Bloody Wags* 74 Luckily the shaft was only a 'monkey'—about 3 metres deep.

4. A looped strap attached to a saddle pommel and used by a (novice) rider as an aid to mounting and when riding a spirited horse. Also **monkey strap.**

1911 E.S. Sorenson *Life in Austral. Backblocks* 207 Novices and others who lack proficiency use . . a monkey (a strap looped between the D's for the right hand to grip). **1915** V. Palmer *World of Men* (1962) 35 He always was a grip rider. . . No broncho-straps, or monkey-straps or top rails for him. **1932** J.J. Hardie *Cattle Camp* (1944) 72 He fitted a toe into the stirrup-iron, right hand feeling for the 'monkey strap' on the pommel. **1945** F. Cork *Tales from Cattle Country* 18 The rough-rider does not scorn the use of the monkey-strap, or the term 'grabbing leather' as is generally supposed. The professional rider of the rodeos scorns these aids for obvious reasons—particularly the loss of points—but the average rider prefers 'hugging-the-monkey' to biting the dust. **1958** J.R. Spicer *Cry of Storm-Bird* 115 To aid mounting, the rider often twisted a short strap on the right side of the pommel, a fixture that came in very useful when dealing with a lively horse. . . The strap in question was known as a 'monkey' or 'jug-handle'.

5. Special Comb. **monkey dodger,** one who musters sheep; **dodging** *vbl. n.*, the mustering of sheep.

1912 R.S. Tait *Scotty Mac* 138 Head **monkey dodger** to . . Hungry Harris. **1913** *Bulletin* (Sydney) 10 Apr. 13/3 He has seen monkey-dodgers mustering sheep in sulkies. **1900** *Western Champion* (Barcaldine) 27 Nov. 9/1 By jove, this game beats **monkey dodging** all to pieces. **1902** *Bulletin* (Sydney) 4 Oct. 16/2 'Monkey-dodging', as slang for mustering sheep, is seldom heard nowadays; it is said to have had its origin in the fact that the aborigines in the early days never called a sheep anything but a monkey—though what the aborigine knew about monkeys is hard to say.

monkey bear. Koala 1. Also **monkey.**

1836 *Saturday Mag.* (London) 31 Dec. 249 They are called by some monkeys, by others bears, but they by no means answer to either species. **1840** *S. Austral. Rec.* (London) 24 Oct. 261 Their provisions during the last eighteen days of their journey consisted only of a very scanty supply of the flesh of the native bear, or monkey. **1845** R. Howitt *Impressions Aust. Felix* 306 In Gippsland has been found a kind of sloth, called by the working people 'the Gippsland Monkey'. **1854** *Illustr. Sydney News* 15 Apr. 12/2 The Koala, commonly called the Native Bear or Monkey by the Colonists, is one of the most singular of our Marsupial animals and bears a considerable resemblance to the Sloth. **1872** A. McFarland *Illawarra & Manaro* 113 Some of the men were roasting opossums and 'monkeys' (Native Bears). **1880** 'Erro' *Squattermania* 219 He fell into a miserable doze for two or three hours, half conscious of the lugubrious cries of a monkey-bear, in a neighbouring tree. **1906** E. Dyson *In Roaring Fifties* 93 A monkey-bear grunted disgustedly, and then all was still again. **1916** 'T.O. Lingo' *Austral. Comic Dict.* 33 *Monkey Bear*, I forbear: ask Norman Lindsay. Thereby hangs no tail. **1928** M.E. Fullerton *Austral. Bush* 114, I have seen the monkey bear under every sort of provocation, 'stuck up' by man or dog, but I have never seen him strike a blow for life. So helpless and so foolish is he with his round, owl-like face, and his thick lumpish body. **1979** B. Martyn *First Footers S. Gippsland* 48 'Monkey bears' were often about the camp, the deep voices of grown bears broke the silence at night. **1980** P. Pepper *You are what you make Yourself* 23 They made the toe-holds to go up after possums and monkey bears (koala).

monotreme. [f. Gr. μονο-, comb. form of μόνος sole + τρῆμη, var. of τρῆμα hole, referring to the single opening for reproductive and excretory organs.] Any of the egg-laying mammals of the order Monotremata, occurring only in Aust., incl. Tas., and New Guinea. See also Echidna, Platypus. Also *attrib.*

1835 W. Kirby *On Power Wisdom & Goodness of God* II. 483 This Sub-class is divided into two Orders, *Monotremes*, and *Marsupians*. **1890** *Century Dict.* IV. 3845 *Monotreme* mammals; a *monotreme* egg. **1928** G.H. Wilkins *Undiscovered Aust.* 11 There are the two unique and extraordinary creatures, the egg-laying mammals or monotremes—the platypus and the echidna. **1943** C. Barrett *Austral. Animal Bk.* 25 A motherless monotreme bairn, discovered in the scrub near Cranbourne, Victoria, was brought . . by the finder, who was puzzled by the little naked creature not unlike an animated rubber toy of nondescript shape. **1983** R. STRAHAN *Compl. Bk. Austral. Mammals* p. xviii, Female monotremes lay soft-shelled eggs and suckle their young on milk secreted through numerous ducts opening onto the abdomen, not via nipples.

monster, *v. trans.* To attack (a person, policy, etc.); to put pressure on.

1967 *Kings Cross Whisper* (Sydney) xxxvi. 4/2 *Monster*, make unwelcome passes at a female. **1983** *Sydney Morning Herald* 5 Mar. 13/6 Ian Macphee was in trouble for saying something good about the prices and incomes policy while the Prime Minister was monstering it, although at times Fraser seemed to have trouble deciding whether it was a monster or a mouse.

monte. Also **monty.** [Transf. use of U.S. *monte* a game of chance played with cards.]

1. *Obs.* A racecourse tipster. Also **monte man.**

1887 K. MACKAY *Stirrup Jingles* 6 In the Leger the 'Monties' are shouting. **1909** A. WRIGHT *Rogue's Luck* 2 The monte man (with his following of buttoners) still works hard to make an honest crust, but the breed of 'mugs' on whom he lives . . has lessened.

2. A certainty.

1894 *Worker* (Sydney) 18 Aug. 2/5 Chaps, I've got a vote for Hughie—but it ain't no monte yet. **1898** *Ibid.* 1 Jan. 7/2 Yes, the signs are undeniable 'montes' when the rain is close at hand, or shortly after it begins coming down. **1901** *Bulletin Reciter* 182 It's the biggest bloomin' monte Dat 'as ever come our way. **1904** L.M.P. ARCHER *Bush Honeymoon* 136 I'm goin' to *peg out*. . . It's a *monte* Sandy; I'll be a stiff 'un by th' mornin'. **1927** K.S. PRICHARD *Brumby Innes* (1974) 65 It'll be him for a monte. **1945** A.W. UPFIELD *Death of Swagman* 73 It's a monty that that poor devil was hanged. **1947** V. PALMER *Cyclone* 7 It's a monty there'll be a few skulls broken before it's settled. **1965** J. WYNNUM *Jiggin' in Riggin'* 128, I was given the drum . . that if I put my name to the dotted line, I'd be a monty to get drafted to the U.S. destroyer. **1976** LLOYD & CLARK *Kerr's King Hit* 7 Kerr was regarded as a 'monte' for school captain but he was pipped at the post.

monterry, montry, var. MUNTRY.

mook-mook owl /ˈmʊk-mʊk aʊl/. [Poss. a. Ngaliwuru *mug mug* owl.] **a.** An owl, perh. *barking owl* (see BARKING). **b.** *transf.* See quot. 1978 (1). Also **mook-mook, muk-muk.**

1946 W.E. HARNEY *North of 23°* 266 The mook mook owl gives its cry. **1961** —— *Grief, Gaiety & Aborigines* 21 We were lulled to sleep by the glass-blower's tunes that blended with a muk-muk's call in the still night's air. **1962** D. LOCKWOOD *I, Aboriginal* 25 A *mook-mook* owl hooted solemnly from its perch in a paperbark overhanging the Alawa camp. **1978** R.D. EAGLESON *Urban Aboriginal Eng.* 61 *Muk-muk*, spirit, ghost. **1978** J. & P. READ View of Past (typescript) 254 Why they rush, those bullocks . . ? Yeah, they gettem fright. Mook-mook (owl) dingo.

mooley apple. /ˈmuli æpəl/. [f. *mooley*, prob. f. a N.S.W. Aboriginal language + *apple*.] *Emu apple* (a), see EMU *n.*[1] 3. Also **mooley plum.**

1888 *Proc. Linnean Soc. N.S.W.* III. 534 'Emu apple.' 'Mooley apple' is a western New South Wales name. **1933** C.W. PECK *Austral. Legends* (ed. 2) 48 The Owenia acidula or 'mooley plums' quickly grew. **1966** A. MORRIS *Plantlife W. Darling* 70 'Mooley Apple.' Handsome tree, fruit a drupe, dark red.

Moomba. /ˈmumbə/. [See quot. 1981.] A carnival, held annually in Melbourne from 1955. Also *attrib.*

1955 *Herald* (Melbourne) 12 Mar. 1/1 All was set for the Governor, Sir Dallas Brooks, to open the Moomba officially. **1958** *Ibid.* 29 July 4/8 We already have marching girls in Moomba. **1966** C. MCGREGOR *Profile Aust.* 69 Melbourne's Moomba (an aboriginal word meaning 'Let's get together and have fun') a yearly event during which floats parade through the city. **1971** *Bulletin* (Sydney) 1 May 11/1 The crowd that turns up for this sort of thing is phenomenal—it beats football, beats Moomba, beats everything. **1981** B.J. BLAKE *Austral. Aboriginal Lang.* 84 Undoubtedly the most unfortunate choice of a proper name from Aboriginal sources was made in Melbourne when the city fathers chose to name the city's annual festival 'Moomba'. The name is supposed to mean 'Let's get together and have fun', though one wonders how anyone could be naive enough to believe that all this can be expressed in two syllables. In fact 'moom' (*mum*) means 'buttocks' or 'anus' in various Victorian languages and '-ba' is a suffix that can mean 'at', 'in' or 'on'. Presumably someone has tried to render the phrase 'up your bum' in the vernacular. **1985** *Age* (Melbourne) 4 Mar. 1/2 *Moomba antics.* Melbourne's annual festival has begun.

moon, *v. trans.* To hunt (a possum) on a moonlit night: see quot. 1893. Freq. as *vbl. n.*

1886 D.M. GANE *N.S.W. & Vic.* 177 It is necessary to 'moon them', as the bushmen say, that is, to get them in a line with the moon. **1893** E.D. CLELAND *White Kangaroos* 66 A 'possum was amongst the branches somewhere but though all three peered into them nothing could be seen. Then they had to go through the process known as 'mooning'. Walking backwards from the tree, each one tried to get the various limbs and branches between him and the moon, and then follow them out to the uttermost bunch of leaves where the 'possum might be feeding. **1906** *Steele Rudd's Mag.* (Brisbane) Mar. 179 He started to re-load under the tree while I mooned the 'possum. **1916** C. VAUDE *Tivoli* 19 While Billy's 'possum mooning, the tracker was a-spooning. **1930** *Bulletin* (Sydney) 27 Aug. 21/3 In the old days there was a bit of sport about shooting 'possums by 'mooning' them. . . With the moon as the only illuminant it requires a good pair of eyes to distinguish between one end and the other of the silhouette . . and to then bring the sights of a rifle to bear faultlessly on the small area of the head. **1965** *Ibid.* 9 Jan. 30/2 You . . had a whale of a time 'mooning' possums and wild cats in the moonlight with a fifteen-shilling pea rifle.

moonlight, *v. trans.* To muster (wild cattle) by night: see quot. 1887. Chiefly as *vbl. n.*

1880 J.B. STEVENSON *Seven Yrs. Austral. Bush* 128 Moonlighting on frosty nights is severe work, particularly when there are not many cattle about. We often worked all through a long winter's night, coaching round scrub after scrub, without coming across a single mob. **1887** W.S.S. TYRWHITT *New Chum in Qld. Bush* 151 Wild cattle . . are commonly called 'scrubbers' because they live in the larger scrubs. . . There is a way of catching them . . called 'moonlighting'. . . A party of men go out at night, or more often in the small hours of the morning, with a mob of quiet cattle, and take their places on the edge of a scrub so as to intercept the scrubbers as they return from watering and feeding outside. They are then driven in amongst the quiet ones, and if possible the whole mob is taken down to a yard or put in a paddock. **1900** J. MAJOR *Leaves from Squatter's Note Bk.* 10, I had now to resort to what is termed moonlighting and gully-raking. **1933** A.J. COTTON *With Big Herds in Aust.* 63 Moonlighting wild cattle . . belongs only to the past. **1951** E. HILL *Territory* 307 The poddy-dodgers were hard-riding, hard-living lads, out in the wet and the dry, 'moonlighting' and 'coaching'. **1962** D. LOCKWOOD *I, Aboriginal* 172 On clear nights we drove quiet decoy cattle we called 'coaches' on to the plains to attract others. This was Moonlighting, the salt of mustering. **1978** TEECE & PIKE *Voice of Wilderness* 112 Bushmen experienced in the ways of handling wild cattle use different methods. 'Moonlighting' is one way. . . I would kill a beast and pour some blood on the back of the quiet 'coachers'. The cattle in the scrubs around would smell it and they would come out.

moonlighter.

1. [f. prec.] One who musters wild cattle by night.

1886 F. COWAN *Aust.* 32 The manor-born Moonlighter: austral Guacho [*sic*]: fearless, skillful, breakneck rider: in the bush and in the open: over stones and through marshes. **1892** 'R. BOLDREWOOD' *Nevermore* 46 Have you had a ride with the moonlighters lately?

2. [Infl. by U.S. *moonshiner* one who makes 'moonshine' or illicitly distilled liquor.] One who distils liquor illicitly.

1913 J.B. CASTIEAU *Reminisc. Detective-Inspector Christie* 113 Public-housekeepers of a certain class were always ready customers of the 'moonlighters', as they could purchase spirit for about 5s. per gallon. **1926** *Bulletin* (Sydney) 7 Jan. 24/2 The bush has made a good many powerful beverages, but the most powerful of the lot was potato spirit. The moonlighter cut up the spuds, skins and all.

3. [See quot. 1974.] The marine fish *Vinculum sexfasciatum*, having a silver head and body with six vertical black bands, occurring near rocky reefs of s. Aust. incl. Tas.

1948 W. HATFIELD *Barrier Reef Days* 20 Bream and 'moonlighters' and 'fingermarks' that took your bait. **1974** T.D. SCOTT et al. *Marine & Freshwater Fishes S.A.* 221 It is said that it takes the hook . . better at night, and the species is often called the Moonlighter by fishermen. The flesh is of a fine texture and well flavoured. **1980** G. DUTTON *Wedge-Tailed Eagle* 36 We anchored off the rocks . . and caught . . zebra-striped moonlighters.

moorhen. [Transf. use of *moorhen* the bird *Gallinula chloropus.*] Any of several waterbirds of the genus *Gallinula*, incl. *G. ventralis* (see *native hen* (a), NATIVE *a.* 6 b.), and the predom. black *G. tenebrosa* of e. and s.w. Aust., New Guinea, and Indonesia.

1820 C. JEFFREYS *Van Dieman's Land* 35 This lake abounds with . . moor-hens. **1845** J. GOULD *Birds of Aust.* (1848) VI. Pl. 72, *Tribonyx ventralis* . . Moor-hen of the Colonists. **1860** G. BENNETT *Gatherings of Naturalist* 169 The Black-tailed Tribonyx, or Moor Hen of the colonists . . when strutting along the bank of a river, has a grotesque appearance, with the tail quite erect like that of a domestic fowl. **1935** DAVISON & NICHOLLS *Blue Coast Caravan* 60 The clear water was speckled with little black moor-hens. **1984** *A.N.U. Reporter* (Canberra) 26 Oct. 5 Moorhens defend territories throughout spring and summer—and the larger the group, the larger the territory.

moosh, var. MUSH.

mopoke /ˈmoʊpoʊk/, *n.* [Imitative of the bird's call, the forms *mope-hawk* and *morepork* being interpretative.]

1. a. BOOBOOK. **b.** TAWNY FROGMOUTH (to which the call has often been erroneously attributed). **c.** Any of several other nocturnal birds. Also **mope-hawk, morepork.**

1825 J.H. WEDGE *Diaries* 31 Aug. (1962) 19 They killed one [possum]—and a More Pork. **1829** *Cornwall Press* (Launceston) 24 Mar. 36/2 The specie of owl peculiar to this Island, vulgarly known by the name of mope hawk, is held in high veneration by the native blacks. **1831** G.A. ROBINSON in N.J.B. Plomley *Friendly Mission* 14 July (1966) 377 The doleful sound of the mopoke. **1834** J. BACKHOUSE *Narr. Visit Austral. Colonies* (1843) 213 The eye of the Morepork or Greater Night Jarr . . is wonderfully adapted for enabling it to see the insects in the dark, on which it feeds. **1852** W.H. HALL *Practical Experience* (ed. 2) 22 The low, melancholy but pleasing cry of the Mope-hawk, broke the unearthly silence. **1872** 'RESIDENT' *Glimpses Life Vic.* 246 The 'mopoke', a kind of owl, is so called from its note, which is said to be in approximation of these two syllables. **1896** B. SPENCER *Rep. Horn Sci. Exped. Central Aust.* I. 124 In the gum trees the 'mopokes' (*Ninox boobook*) were calling to one another. **1900** *Bulletin* (Sydney) 28 July 14/2 Recently saw two magpies trying to drive a mopoke (genuine caprimulgus—not the Boobook owl) out of the fork of a tree near their nest. **1912** J.H.L. ZILLMAN *Austral. Poetry* 9 Prompt as mope-hawk after prey. **1922** *Bulletin* (Sydney) 20 Apr. 22/2 The morepork (frogmouth) is a good mouser. **1934** 'S. RUDD' *Green Grey Homestead* 72 Murphy'll whisper in a way that will make the night seem more haunted than the mopokes behind the sheds. **1941** *Bulletin* (Sydney) 26 Mar. 16/4 A land where 'flying foxes' are not foxes, but bats; where one bird is called 'mopoke' but a different fowl croaks it. **1953** D. STIVENS *Gambling Ghost* 34 The bunyip started groaning like a hundred mopokes in a torture chamber. **1962** T. RONAN *Deep of Sky* 185 The two blackboys had been awakened by a morepork owl which sounded a bit off key. **1968** D. FLEAY *Nightwatchmen* 92 (*caption*) Confusion over call notes has led to the erroneous label of Mopoke for the Frogmouth. The true Mopoke is the Boobook Owl. **1984** B. DIXON *Searching for Aboriginal Lang.* 73 Chloe followed the noise, a low 'mm, m, m', and suddenly saw two big eyes in the grass. . . A mopoke owl was sitting in the grass, staring at her.

2. The call of the mopoke.

1827 J. BISCHOFF *Sketch Hist. Van Diemen's Land* 13 Mar. (1832) 177 The owl's doleful cry of 'more pork', and the screaming of the opossum, were the only disturbances we experienced during the night. **1852** S. MOSSMAN *Gold Regions Aust.* (ed. 2) 64 Hark to the distant Mopauk, with its strange note, which the unromantic settler translates into 'more pork', while the man who prides himself on having a 'soul above buttons', calls it the cuckoo. **1859** W. BURROWS *Adventures Mounted Trooper* 75 The goat-sucker, or, as it is called in the colony, the cuckoo, and also the mopoke; the cadence of its cry resembling that of the cuckoo, while it articulates the word 'mopoke'. **1942** E. ANDERSON *Squatter's Luck* 28 For you the tawny frogmouth, when he spoke Croaked, 'More pork', 'More pork', 'Mopoke'. **1968** D. FLEAY *Nightwatchmen* 4 The sound itself was reminiscent of the 'mopoke' of the Boobook Owl.

3. *fig.* A tedious or stupid person. Also *attrib.*

1845 R. HOWITT *Impressions Aust. Felix* 233 'A more-pork kind of fellow', is a man of cut-and-dry phrases; a person remarkable for nothing new in common conversation. This, by some, is thought very expressive; the more-pork being a kind of Australian owl, notorious for its wearying nightly iteration, 'More pork, more pork'. **1891** *Bohemia* (Melbourne) 4 June 6 The jury .. sat as solemn as mopokes deciding on the issue of a recent welshing case. **1905** J. FURPHY *Rigby's Romance* (1946) 81 'Think I ain't game, you (adj.) morepoke?' says she. **1930** 'BRENT OF BIN BIN' *Ten Creeks Run* (1952) 182 He must know it now or else he's a bigger mopoke than ole Teddy O'Mara. **1963** D. NILAND *Dadda Jumped* 182 You long-nosed morepork, I ought to let you have it good and hard.

mopoke /'moʊpoʊk/, *v.* [f. prec.] *intr.* **a.** Of a mopoke: to call. **b.** To imitate the call of a mopoke.

1915 *Bulletin* (Sydney) 4 Mar. 14/4 The ardent Billjim .. imitates the call of the mopoke to announce that he has arrived... I mopoked under a big peach tree. **1968** D. FLEAY *Nightwatchmen* 87 Trees from which the Boobook Owl has 'mopoked' the prior night.

moral. [Survival of Br slang *moral*, abbrev. of *moral certainty*. Now chiefly Austral.: see OED(S *sb.* 9.] A certainty.

1878 *Austral. Town & Country Jrnl.* (Sydney) 30 Mar. 602/2 It was understood that he was entered on the chance of the two cracks destroying each others chances, in one of the numerous accidents to which such races are liable, in which case Bargo would be a 'moral'. **1890** *Quiz* (Adelaide) 16 May 10/2 The result of the Adelaide and South Adelaide match was—Adelaide, 3 goals 7 behinds; South Adelaide, 6 goals 2 behinds. The finish was a surprise to the Adelaide 'barrackers', who thought it was a 'moral' for their side. **1915** DREW & EVANS *Grafter* 130 It's a moral... You'll do it just as easy as you did the others. **1934** *Bulletin* (Sydney) 17 Oct. 21/2 Earbiters anxious to give you a moral for the lars'. **1945** *Two Bar Four Three Bull.: Austral. Infantry Battalion* Sept. 6 And if Blamey gives haloes as prizes You're a moral to cop the whole lot. **1949** L. GLASSOP *Lucky Palmer* 36 That no-hoper... It's a moral. They're going to give it the sting. They'll hit it with enough dope to win a Melbourne Cup. **1965** R.H. CONQUEST *Horses in Kitchen* 136 Two of them, he reckoned, were 'b— good gallopers, morals to win a race some day.' **1967** D. HEWETT *This Old Man* (1976) 38 So you reckon I'm a moral to go to the bad, Tommy? **1977** W. MOORE *Just to Myself* 99 'Give her a guzzle of cherry cocktail', Merv would say, 'and she's a moral.' **1986** *Canberra Times* 7 May 25/5 The senior puisne judge (who is an absolute moral for the Chief Justiceship come February next year) .. is almost certainly among the ranks of the deeply concerned.

morepork: see MOPOKE *n.*

Moreton Bay. [The name of the bay at the mouth of the Brisbane River, Qld., given by James Cook as *Morton*, after James Douglas (1702–1768), 14th Earl of *Morton* and member of the Royal Society, and subsequently spelt *Moreton*. The name was applied to the penal settlement on the bay (1824–1839) and until 1859, when separation from N.S.W. was effected, to the whole of Queensland.] Used *attrib.* in the names of flora and fauna: **Moreton Bay ash,** the tree of Qld., n. N.S.W., and New Guinea *Eucalyptus tesselaris* (fam. Myrtaceae); the wood of the tree; CARBEEN; also *attrib.*; **bug,** any of several marine crustaceans valued for their edible tail flesh, esp. *Thenus orientalis* of n. Aust.; see also SHOVEL-NOSED LOBSTER; **chestnut,** *black bean* (a), see BLACK *a.*[2] 1 a.; **fig, (a)** any of several large trees of the genus *Ficus* (fam. Moraceae), esp. the massive, spreading *F. macrophylla* of near-coastal n. N.S.W. and s. Qld., widely planted as an ornamental and shade tree; also **Moreton Bay fig-tree** and *ellipt.* as **Moreton Bay; (b)** rhyming slang for FIZGIG, an informer; also *ellipt.*; **oyster,** *Sydney rock*, see SYDNEY 2; **pine,** HOOP PINE; **rosella,** the parrot of Qld., and n. N.S.W. *Platycercus adscitus*, having a blue body, and mottled black and yellow back.

1844 L. LEICHHARDT *Jrnl. Overland Exped. Aust.* 15 Dec. (1847) 75 The **Moreton Bay ash** (a species of Eucalyptus)—which I had met with, throughout the Moreton Bay district, from the sea coast of the Nynga Nynga to Darling Downs—was here also very plentiful. **1856** A.C. & F.T. GREGORY *Jrnls. Austral. Explorations* 13 Nov. (1884) 192 This part of the country is very poor and scrubby, with large Moreton-Bay ash-trees. **1870** E.B. KENNEDY *Four Yrs. in Qld.* 31 The Moreton Bay ash is common about the creek, and in fact almost over the whole of Queensland. **1880** J. BONWICK *Resources Qld.* 80 The Moreton Bay Ash, *E. tesselaris*, has a brownish, tough, but not hard wood. **1908** *Emu* VII. 180 Flew off to the nest on the Moreton Bay ash. **1935** DAVISON & NICHOLLS *Blue Coast Caravan* 156 The Moreton Bay ash. .. The bark, for six or eight feet above the ground, is grey in colour and rough and tesselated like crocodile skin. Above that it is light buff, smooth and of fine texture. **1944** F. CLUNE *Red Heart* 64 Here he saw a Moreton Bay ash tree blazed with the letter L, made on Leichhardt's 1846 expedition. **1965** P. JONES *Johnny Lost* 9 A pile of Moreton Bay ash blocks split ready for the stove. **1978** R.J. BRITTEN *Around Cassowary Rock* 10 The few uprights were made of skinny little Moreton Bay ash saplings that *were* all sap. **1970** HEALY & YALDWYN *Austral. Crustaceans* 58 The 'Balmain bug' of New South Wales and the similar-looking **'Moreton Bay bug'**, *Thenus orientalis*, of Queensland and northern Australia, are both taken with prawn trawls. **1974** J.M. THOMSON *Fish Ocean & Shore* 77 A .. penchant for labelling all jointed creeping things as bugs gave the Moreton Bay bug its name... This crustacean has become more familiar in the fish shops following the growth of the prawn-trawling industry. **1977** *Commercial Fish Aust.* (Dept. Primary Industry) 72 Bay lobsters are found around northern Australia from Moreton Bay in Queensland to Exmouth Gulf in Western Australia. They are also known as Moreton Bay bugs or shovel-nosed lobsters. **1979** GOODE & WILLSON *Orig. Austral. & N.Z. Fish Cookbk.* 47 These flattened crustaceans with their somewhat prehistoric appearance are best known during the summer months where they are sold as Moreton Bay 'bugs'. Similar animals are sold in Sydney as Balmain 'bugs', or more often, just as 'bugs'. **1983** *Canberra Chron.* 14 Dec. 18/3 Apart from the standard range of products they bring in .. Moreton Bay bugs. **1836** J. BACKHOUSE *Extracts from Lett.* (1838) iii. 57 Some of the pods of the **Moreton Bay chesnut** [*sic*], which is a fine tree, with leaves like those of the European walnuts, are ten inches long and eight round. **1851** J. HENDERSON *Excursions & Adventures N.S.W.* II. 221 The Moreton Bay Chestnut is a handsome tree, bearing a beautiful scarlet and yellow flower. **1880** R. ROSE *Austral. Guide: Qld.* 16 The Moreton Bay chestnut is another fine tree producing good wood; it grows from 70 ft. to 100 ft. in height. **1894** *Agric. Gaz. N.S.W.* V. 1 Moreton Bay Chestnut is an old name for the tree, because it was first found in the Moreton Bay district. **1908** E.J. BANFIELD *Confessions of Beachcomber* 259 One of the chief vegetable foods of the blacks is the fruit of 'tinda-burra' (Moreton Bay chestnut). **1935** DAVISON & NICHOLLS *Blue Coast Caravan* 160 Moreton Bay chestnuts, dark and wide-spreading, in the plantation. **1982** K. MCARTHUR *Bush in Bloom* 124 The Moreton Bay Chestnut (*Castanospermum*) is still scattering its red and yellow blossoms over the forest floor. **(a) 1849** J. PATTISON *N.S.W.* 95 The oak, the elm, and those of the mother country, are seen growing along side the **Moreton Bay fig.** **1855** J. BONWICK *Geogr. Aust. & N.Z.* (ed. 3) 205 The Moreton Bay Fig tree is of immense height and size. **1859** F. SINNETT *Acct. 'Rush' Port Curtis* 55 Trees and shrubs, among which from time to time shone out the large glossy laurel green leaves of the Moreton Bay fig. **1888** *Centennial Mag.* (Sydney) 319 Lonely station-houses, and mansions surrounded with pines, araucarias, and the great Moreton Bay fig. **1928** M. FORREST *Reaping Roses* 139 There were scraps of dry wood, nests of dead, resiny leaves lying about in the circle the moreton bay fig so generously sheltered. **1948** A.J. MCLACHLAN *McLachlan* 48 He would not allow a huge Moreton Bay fig to be uprooted, although its roots were interfering with the wall structure of the house. **1953** C. WILLS *Austral. Passport* 15 Moreton Bay fig trees, extraordinary trees, vast and spreading as old oaks, with grey bark like elephant-hide, dark, glossy leaves, and round fruit of the size of chestnuts that ripened to a purplish red and dropped in sticky masses .. with a sweet, lazy smell. **1967** D. HEWETT *This Old Man* (1976) 23 Kisses in Moore Park under the Moreton Bays after the pitchers on Saturdee nights. **1984** B. DIXON *Searching for Aboriginal Lang.* 23 Cattle now grazed among the black bean trees, the Moreton Bay Figs, and the imported oranges and mangoes. **(b) 1953** S.J. BAKER *Aust. Speaks* 134 **Moreton Bay (fig)**, any witness who lays an information, anyone who unwarrantably attends to or meddles in the affairs of others; by rhyme of *gig* .. which may be a contraction of *fiz-gig*, an informer. **1970** *Kings Cross Whisper* (Sydney) lxxxiii. 3/1 On the plant side, conservationists are desperately trying to save the Moreton Bay Fig (gig) and the tea leaf (thief). **1975** *Bulletin* (Sydney) 26 Apr. 46/2 There were Moretons nearby (Moreton Bay Figs; gigs, meaning busybodies). **1984** *Ibid.* 19 June 69/1 Fifty percent of the Drug Squad's arrests are based on information received and woebetide a user, supplier or anyone else who becomes a dog, a gig or, as the police term it, a Moreton Bay. **1870** *Sydney Morning Herald* 6 July 3/3 **Moreton Bay oyster** .. could be made to yield an annual local and export value second to none. **1928** M.E. FULLERTON *Austral. Bush* 224 The most popular, as the most expensive oyster, is the Sydney Rock product... The Moreton Bay oyster comes next to this succulent fellow in popularity. **1826** J. ATKINSON *Acct. Agric. & Grazing N.S.W.* 13 **Moreton Bay Pine**—Found in great abundance at Moreton Bay. **1829** R. MUDIE *Picture of Aust.* 148 Moreton Bay pine (*araucaria Cunninghami*) is a light-coloured timber, fine in the grain, very close and handsome, and by no means weighty. **1856** *Moreton Bay Free Press* 8 Jan. 2/7 The Moreton Bay pine attains a height of from 200 to 300 feet, with a perfectly straight, solid stem, to be procured in inexhaustible quantities. **1882** *Austral. Handbk.* 391 The pine timbers are furnished by the 'Moreton Bay Pine' .. a large tree of very wide range. **1904** J.H. MAIDEN *Notes on Commercial Timbers N.S.W.* 23 Colonial or Moreton Bay pine .. called 'Moreton Bay pine', because at one time it was largely supplied to Sydney from the Moreton Bay (Brisbane) district. **1928** M.E. FULLERTON *Austral. Bush* 106 In Queensland they use the Moreton Bay pine for butter boxes. [**1841 Moreton Bay rosella:** J. GOULD *Birds of Aust.* (1848) V. Pl. 26, *Platycercus palliceps* .. Moreton Bay Rose-hill, Colonists of New South Wales.] **1845** L. LEICHHARDT *Jrnl. Overland Exped. Aust.* 30 Oct. (1847) 460, I observed a Platycercus, of the size of the Moreton Bay Rosella. **1854** *Illustr. Sydney News* 27 Jan. 58/1 One of our beautiful Australian parrots commonly called the Moreton Bay Rosella or Pale-Headed Broad Tail Parrot. **1911** ST. C. GRONDONA *Collar & Cuffs* 63 Parrots are scarce, excepting the Moreton Bay rosella. **1956** A.C.C. LOCK *Tropical Tapestry* 38 Moreton Bay rosellas climbed among the top-most branches for seeds.

morning glory. See quots. Also **morning glory cloud.**

1934 *Bulletin* (Sydney) 12 Sept. 20/4 A 'morning glory' is a frequent occurrence in the Gulf Country... A low bank of clouds lined the horizon early in the morning, and gathered speed at an alarming rate... Soon the sky was completely overcast. A few drops of rain fell; then we had a delightful breeze which lasted for a couple of minutes. Away went the dark cloud as quickly as it had come, and the sun continued to blaze as mercilessly as ever. **1973** P. ADAM SMITH *Barcoo Salute* 173 The ink-indigo purple cloud that rolls across the sky and disappears beneath the horizon beyond the Gulf of Carpentaria is called the 'Morning Glory' by the Gulfites. It is a phenomenon unique to the Gulf. **1984** *Bulletin* (Sydney) 13 Nov. 75/2 Another phenomenon, the solitary wave, is much more common and is beginning to worry meteorologists and pilots. The waves are induced by the flow of air over the Australian land mass. They can be up to 500 km. long... Sometimes the wave is visible because it generates cloud. The classical instance is the 'morning glory' cloud of the Queensland and Northern Territory Gulf Country .. a daily occurrence at this time of year.

morning tea. A mid-morning break; the refreshment taken during that break. See also SMOKO 1 a. Also *attrib.*

1916 V.G. DWYER *Conquering Hal* 139 She had stayed to pull Sandra's hatpins out, and drink morning tea with her. **1933** J. MCCARTER *Love's Lunatic* 51 We have two smokos daily. . . Smoko is morning and afternoon tea. Morning tea at ten, and four o'clock marks the afternoon time. **1942** *Bulletin* (Sydney) 19 Aug. 12/3 At the morning-tea roll up of the Works and Parks gang, tea was scarce and coffee not plentiful. **1944** T.R. ST. GEORGE *C/O Postmaster* 131 The next meal might be dished out about 10 a.m. (which made it 'morning tea'). **1957** *Bulletin* (Sydney) 28 Aug. 18/2 The alarm-clock in her stomach went off and she declared for morning-tea. **1963** A. LUBBOCK *Austral. Roundabout* 6 One of the first things to get straight on arrival in Australia is the meals called 'tea'. There are three; and they are all as indispensable as breakfast or dinner. First you have 'morning tea', which consists of cups of tea and biscuits, or savouries, at eleven o'clock. **1971** J. O'GRADY *Aussie Etiket* 5 Office workers, notably public servants, specialize in morning-tea—coffee-break to you Americans.

morrel /ˈmɒrəl, məˈrɛl/. Also **morrell.** [a. Nyungar *morril.*] Any of several trees of the genus *Eucalyptus* (fam. Myrtaceae) of s.w. Aust., esp. the rough-barked trees *E. longicornis*, yielding a strong, durable, reddish wood, and *E. melanoxylon*, yielding a very hard, strong, blackish wood; the wood of these trees. Also *attrib.*

1837 G.F. MOORE *Evidences Inland Sea* 48 We passed another variety of *Eucalyptus*—a tall, straight stem and scaly bark, called 'Morrail'. **1869** F. ALGAR *Hand-Bk. Qld.* 14 The only other hard wood of the colony is the Moorel, a species of Eucalyptus with a rough bark, which, on account of its elasticity, is found useful for light shafts. **1897** L. LINDLEY-COWEN *W. Austral. Settler's Guide* 47 The morrell gum is . . commonly met with on the eastern agricultural lands, and is indicative of rich country. **1911** E.D. CLELAND *W. Austral. Mining Practice* 43 Sawn hardwood—salmon-gum or morrel. **1954** *Bulletin* (Sydney) 18 Aug. 13/4 Morrell, which grows in the same localities as salmon-gum, is similar to that tree in many ways even to color; but it's not nearly as hard, and it splits far more readily. **1971** B.Y. MAIN *Twice Trodden Ground* 33 The shelter of the old umbrella-topped morrel trees out across the flat was gone. **1973** G.M. CHIPPENDALE *Eucalypts W. Austral. Goldfields* 99 The name 'morrel' is an aboriginal name applied to several species.

morrison. [See quot. 1981.] Any of several shrubs bearing decorative flowers of the genus *Verticordia* (fam. Myrtaceae), chiefly of W.A. Also *attrib.*

1929 I.A. SCOULER *Dowerin Story* 7 The numerous varieties of morrison, and the many shades of leschenaultia are perhaps the more conspicuous. **1935** T. RAYMENT *Cluster of Bees* 191 The larvae . . feast on the sweet blossoms of the tea-tree . . and, in Western Australia, on the Morrison flower, *Verticordia nitens.* **1956** F.B. VICKERS *First Place to Stranger* 254 The morrison was all ready to burst out in blossom and look like golden cauliflowers. **1969** L. HADOW *Full Cycle* 77 The managing editor prefers roses, but while he's campaigning to *save the wildflowers* Mrs Wallis would like smokebush and yellow morrison for the suite. **1981** J.A. BAINES *Austral. Plant Genera* 390 *V[erticordia] nitens*, Morrison Featherflower, Yellow Morrison (after Alexander Morrison, 1849–1913, Govt. botanist W.A. 1897–1906; few botanists have been commemorated in this way as a vernacular name).

morwong /ˈmɔwɒŋ, ˈmoʊwɒŋ/. [Prob. f. a N.S.W. Aboriginal language.] Any of several edible marine fish of the fam. Cheilodactylidae, esp. *Nemadactylus douglasii* of s. Aust. and N.Z., having a distinctive elongated ray of the pectoral fin, and the JACKASS-FISH; MOWIE.

1871 *Industr. Progress N.S.W.* 791 The . . morwong . . may be taken by the line in almost unlimited quantities. **1896** F.G. AFLALO *Sketch Nat. Hist. Aust.* 205 The only fish I found bite in any way like the schnapper was the Morwong. **1906** D.G. STEAD *Fishes of Aust.* 119 The Jackass-fish is generally confounded . . with the Morwong. **1948** F.D. MARSHALL *Let's go Fishing* 114 The morwong is a good table fish which grows to a fair size. **1978** J. ROWE *Warlords* 206 The red bream, snapper and morwong . . were being hauled up from the reef twenty metres below.

moscow, *v.* [Altered form of Br. slang *moskeneer* to pawn an article for more than it is worth.] *trans.* To pawn (an article).

1910 STEPHENS & O'BRIEN Materials Austrazealand Slang Dict. 100 *Moscow*, the pawnshop: to moscow anything is to pawn it. **1917** C. DREW *Reminisc. D. Gilbert* 50 Do you know where a man can 'moscow' a couple of snakes? **1919** —— *Doings of Dave* 20 When I moscow'd it with Hungry. **1941** S.J. BAKER *Pop. Dict. Austral. Slang* 47 *To moscow something*, to pawn it.

moscow, *n.* [f. prec.] A pawnshop. Also **gone to Moscow, in Moscow,** in pawn.

1941 S.J. BAKER *Pop. Dict. Austral. Slang* 47 *Moscow*, a pawnshop. **1953** 'CADDIE' *Caddie* 217 Me clobber's already in Moscow, an' so is me tan shoes. . . There don't seem nuthin' a man can raise a deaner on. **1955** N. PULLIAM *I traveled Lonely Land* 377 *Gone to Moscow*, pawned.

mosh. [Of unknown origin.] An illegal gambling game. Also **mosh game** and *attrib.*

1925 A. WRIGHT *Boy from Bullarah* 14 Sporting clubs, gambling 'schools', mosh, faro, two-up. **1934** F.E. BAUME *Burnt Sugar* 176 All nationalities met at Parks' mosh shop and two-up school. *Ibid.* 194 Throwing the dice became boring to everyone. The mosh game at Speranthos' place was without a minyon.

mosquito fleet. *Australian National Football.* [Transf. use of *mosquito fleet* a fleet of small light vessels adapted for rapid manoeuvring.]

1. *Hist.* See quot. 1931.

1931 J.F. MCHALE et al. *Austral. Game of Football* 66 The Essendon team of 1922–1926 contained a number of very fast, skilful little players, known as the 'mosquito fleet', and by their tactics they worked havoc among the opposing back players. **1954** *Footy—& Clubs that make It* 10 Memories of the early '20s, when it created the famous 'mosquito fleet', will live long in supporters' minds. **1963** *Footy Fan* (Melbourne) I. xii. 18 They developed what has come to be known as the famous 'mosquito' fleet—a naval term of First War origin. And I firmly believe that Essendon's 'mosquito' fleet was the means of whipping up the tempo of our game.

2. *transf.* See quot. 1968.

1968 EAGLESON & MCKIE *Terminol. Austral. Nat. Football* ii. 24 *Mosquito fleet*, small players in a team, especially if the team exploits the fleetness of its small men in attack. **1983** HIBBERD & HUTCHINSON *Barracker's Bible* 132 *Mosquito fleet*, . . a batch of shortish players, sawn-offs, usually rovers, who dominate or distinguish a team.

mosquito peg. One of two or more stakes used to support a mosquito net over a person sleeping in the open.

1908 MRS A. GUNN *We of Never-Never* 27 Our camp was very simple; just camp sleeping mosquito nets . . hanging by cords between stout stakes driven into the ground. 'Mosquito pegs', the bushmen call these stakes. **1935** K.L. SMITH *Sky Pilot Arnhem Land* 28 Each one has his own camping necessities, and as a rule requires little save a couple of 'mosquito pegs' for his net.

mossie /ˈmɒzi/. Also **mozzie.** [f. *mos(quito* + -Y; now used elsewhere but recorded earliest in Aust.: see OEDS *sb.*[2]] A mosquito. Also *attrib.*

1936 C.P. CONIGRAVE *N. Aust.* 146 The net has not yet been made that will prevent some of the North Australian 'mossies' from finding a way into their human prey. **1939** *Bulletin* (Sydney) 29 Mar. 21/2 Mozzies? Ar! people down 'ere don't know wot they are. **1944** A.S. SMITH *Boys write Home* 235 One of the boys says the mozzies up here are so strong that the other night two of them lifted up his net, turned over his identification disc, and, finding the blood group didn't suit them, flew away. **1960** *N.T. News* (Darwin) 12 Feb. 3/3 *(heading)* Council may open anti-mossie drive. **1965** F. HARDY *Yarns of Billy Borker* 28 The mossies are big in the Territory. **1972** *Kings Cross Whisper* (Sydney) cxxxiv. 2/2 Down the pub Clarry has fixed up one of the rooms real nice for the Premier with a mossie net and a clean bedspread. **1982** N. KEESING *Lily on Dustbin* 100 The 'mozzie coil' is just about burned to powdery ash. **1985** *Age* (Melbourne) 20 Feb. 1/3 Scientist develops a soap that offends no one but the mozzie.

mote, *v.* [Prob. abbrev. of *motor* to travel (in a motor car).] *intr.* Of a car, person running, etc.: to move fast.

1937 *Bull. Australasian Eng. Assoc., Sydney Branch* July 3 *To mote* is defined by Mr Partridge as 'to drive or ride in a motor car', but for many years now Australian schoolboys have been using it in the more general sense of 'move quickly', so that often they say in praise of an athlete 'There is no doubt he can mote.' **1938** H. HODGE *Death in Morning* 31 Yes, he'd seen the Packard. Yes, two men in the front seat. . . Yes, they were certainly 'moting'. **1941** S.J. BAKER *Pop. Dict. Austral. Slang* 47 *Mote*, to move quickly (used of a vehicle or athlete). **1949** R. PARK *Poor Man's Orange* 181 The pair of them surely would look tricks moting around together.

mother. Used *attrib.* in Special Comb. **(a) mother country (or -land)** [spec. use of *mother country* (or *mother-land*) a country in relation to its colonies], the British Isles; **(b) mother colony (province, state),** New South Wales. See also PARENT.

(a) 1832 J. HENDERSON *Observations Colonies N.S.W. & Van Diemen's Land* 27 Bathurst is to Sydney, as Sydney is to the **Mother Country. 1840** *Tasmanian Weekly Dispatch* (Hobart) 24 Apr. 3/2 A Colony fit for the free people of the lower classes of the Mother Country to come to. **1856** S.C. BREES *How to farm & settle in Aust.* 9 The prevailing malignant diseases of the mother country are unknown in Australia. **1869** J. MARTINEAU *Lett. from Aust.* 149 The Australian colonies should . . be cast loose from the Mother-country. **1885** MRS C. PRAED *Austral. Life* 1 Fast steam boats and new mail routes have brought the Australian colonies into comparatively intimate relations with the mother-land. **1898** H. MATTHEWS *Chat about Aust.* 33 The system of farming in Australia is somewhat different to that customary in the Mother Country. **1907** F.T. BULLEN *Advance Australasia* 114 What strikes one as being quite touching is the way the Motherland is continually being spoken of affectionately, regretfully as 'Home'. **1912** *Rep. Working of Factories & Shops Act* (N.S.W. Dept. Labour & Industry) 31 Some girls and women from the Mother Country are gradually finding their way into the factories. **1924** F.J. MILLS *Happy Days* 131 They were for the moment, at home—to some a palace in the Motherland . . to many a hut somewhere in the great heart of Australia. **1936** E. SCOTT *Aust. during War* in *Official Hist. Aust. 1914–18* XI. 514 Their supreme function would be to maintain a more or less undisturbed supply of food and other material for the Mother Country. **1948** A.J. MCLACHLAN *McLachlan* 131 Dignitaries from the Dominions, the Motherland and elsewhere graced the proceedings. **1953** *Meanjin* 358 There were some, even in this town, who would deny the government the men promised to the mother country so as to save civilisation. **1972** *Bulletin* (Sydney) 4 Mar. 12/3 No wonder so many Australians turn into yahoos when they reach the mother country. **1986** *Canberra Times* 15 Feb. B4/1 Cut off from the 'Mother Country' by thousands of miles, successive governments have sought security in 'an alien sea'. **(b) 1824** J. LYCETT *Views in Aust.* 12 The native dog of the **mother colony** is, however, unknown here. **1841** *Sydney Herald* 25 Mar. 2/2 When it [*sc.* Port Phillip] shall have discharged its debt to the mother colony [*sc.* New South Wales], and have become a really self-supporting and self-governed province, its claim to the entire proceeds of its own waste lands will be beyond dispute. **1855** J. BONWICK *Geogr. Aust. & N.Z.* (ed. 3) 26 The mother colony of New South Wales has greatly progressed since the gold discoveries. **1873** W. THOMSON-GREGG *Desperate Character* I. 79 Paddy Reilly had been 'sent out' during the early days of the mother-colony of New South Wales. **1892** *Bulletin* (Sydney) 9 July 7/2 To uplift the renown, glory, and credit of the mother-province, the N.S.W. Government is now actively engaged in carrying on the patriotic work of holding up the mirror to convict nature. **1897** J.J. KNIGHT *Brisbane* 25 Petitions to the Queen were got up by the advocates of Separation. The mother colony had to be fought. . . The Separationists desired to include in the new colony the Clarence, Richmond and Tweed River districts. **1898** *Bulletin* (Sydney) 19 Feb. 6/3 N.S.W. has special rights as the 'mother-province' of Australia. **1907** *Truth* (Sydney) 17 Feb. 1/2 See what blessings of peculiar promise Barton's Victoria Policy has in store for this unhappy Mother State. **1914** A. WRIGHT *In Last Stride* 200 The crowd now looked calmly forward to a certain win for the Mother State. **1936** C.P. CONIGRAVE *N. Aust.* 51 The desire to open up the pastures of the unknown interior to the increasing flocks of the Mother Colony. **1938** W. DENNING *Capital City* 19 Differences of opinion between New South Wales and Victoria, the other States . . left the bone of contention to be snarled over by the Mother State and her strong daughter. **1961** M. KIDDLE *Men of Yesterday* 47 Many Vandemonians, having chosen the locations of their mainland stations, or even deputing a superintendent to do so, returned to the well established mother colony.

motherless, *a.* and quasi-*adv.* Used as an intensive, esp. in the phr. **motherless broke,** destitute of money; also *ellipt.* for *motherless broke.*

1898 *Bulletin* (Sydney) 17 Dec. (Red Page), To these are prefixed the adjectives *motherless* and *dead*, thus *dead motherless broke.* **1916** *Bostall Boshter* (Bostall Heath, England) 23 Feb. 1 Wanted some kind person to adopt a poor soldier who is motherless broke. **1920** *Smith's Weekly* (Sydney) 18 Sept. 10/6 He was motherless broke. **1934** F.H. BROWN *Songs of Plains* 44 And motherless stoney was I at the time. **1958** *Bulletin* (Sydney) 11 June 19/2 The worrying starts when he is flat, skinned, motherless, stony hearts-of-oak, or has 'gone bad'. **1948** K.S. PRICHARD *Golden Miles* 67 'But I know what it is to be hard up, don't forget,' he said. 'Stony, motherless broke, like I was in Sydney.' **1976** B. BENNETT *New Country* 34 He let half-a-dozen others out at the same time. The motherless hooer.

motser /'mɒtsə/. Also **motsa, motza, motzer.** [Prob. a. Yiddish *matse* bread.] A large sum of money, esp. as won in gambling; a great amount. Also *transf.*, a certainty.

1936 A.B. PATERSON *Shearer's Colt* 180 It's a motzer. It's a schnitzler. We'll have to pack 'em in on the roof of the grandstand. **1943** S.J. BAKER *Pop. Dict. Austral. Slang* (ed. 3) 51 *Motser, motza*, a large sum of money. **1950** *Austral. Police Jrnl.* Apr. 116 *Motza*, a lot of money. **1955** N. PULLIAM *I traveled Lonely Land* 77 The gentleman with the 'motser' (big hunk of dough to us) has been gone a full 30 minutes. **1967** *Kings Cross Whisper* (Sydney) xxxvi. 4/2 *Motzer*, a lot, a great amount of anything. **1970** R. BEILBY *No Medals for Aphrodite* 214 You better let that bugger get well ahead. . . The Stuka'll be a motsa to have a go at him. **1985** *Bulletin* (Sydney) 17 Sept. 70/1 Canberra might have cost a motza but it's worth every cent.

mound-bird. *Obs. Mound-building bird*: see MOUND-BUILDING.

1886 F. COWAN *Aust.* 19 *The Mound-birds*, Megapods: as yet which have not learned to build a nest and hatch their young themselves, but still, remembering their reptile origin, when they have scratched and scraped together a great mound of sand and herbage mold, depositing their eggs therein, and leaving them to be brought forth by the engendered heat and moisture of the heap fermenting in the sun. **1896** B. SPENCER *Rep. Horn Sci. Exped. Central Aust.* I. 83 Riding through the scrub . . we passed a mound-bird's nest (*Leipoa ocellata*).

mound-building, *ppl. a.* [Used elsewhere but recorded earliest in Aust.] Used to describe the habit of a ground-dwelling bird of the fam. Megapodiidae, having strong legs, feet, and claws, and incubating its eggs in a large mound. Esp. as **mound-building bird.** See also *brush turkey* BRUSH *n.*[1] B. 2, *mallee fowl* MALLEE 6, MOUND-BIRD, *scrub fowl* SCRUB *n.* 5.

[**1842** J. GOULD *Birds of Aust.* (1848) V. Pl. 79, *Megapodius tumulus* . . Mound-raising Megapode.] **1846** J.L. STOKES *Discoveries in Aust.* I. 417 This . . must have been the *Leipoa ocellata* of Gould, one of the mound or tumuli-building birds, first seen in Western Australia. **1853** S. SIDNEY *Three Colonies* (ed. 2) 289 The leipoa, or mound-building bird, improperly named by the colonists the wild turkey, is found in great numbers. **1935** H.H. FINLAYSON *Red Centre* 30 It is in the occasional clearings of these dense patches that the mound-building *Leipoa* has her nest. **1962** H.J. FRITH *Mallee-Fowl* 23 Throughout the whole mound-building process, the rainfall has a great influence on the rate at which the birds work.

mound spring. *Mud spring*, see MUD 2.

1891 *Jrnl. & Proc. R. Soc. N.S.W.* XXV. 290 Natural artesian water rises to the surface in many parts of the east-central portions of Australia from mud or mound springs. **1936** C.T. MADIGAN *Central Aust.* 52 At this south-western rim of the basin, the water-bearing beds come to the surface, and give rise to springs, those interesting 'mound springs'. **1944** C. FENNER *Mostly Austral.* 114 At a few places there are the remarkable features called 'mound springs', which are really natural artesian springs. **1955** *Lake Eyre, S.A.* (R. Geogr. Soc. Australasia) 35 Some water is known to escape upward to form the 'mound springs' (*vide* Madigan) in the lake bed. **1985** *Austral. Nat. Hist.* Spring 432 Some of the mound springs are within the Lake Eyre National Estate Area.

mountain. Used *attrib.* in the names of flora and fauna: **mountain ash,** any of many trees, usu. of the genus *Eucalyptus* (fam. Myrtaceae), and esp. (*Vic.*) *E. regnans* of Vic. and Tas., favouring cool, moist mountain gullies; the wood of these trees; **devil, (a)** the small, spiny lizard *Moloch horridus* of arid and semi-arid central, s., and w. Aust.; HORNED DRAGON; MOLOCH; THORNY DEVIL; **(b)** *honey flower*, see HONEY; **duck** [see quot. 1976], the large duck *Tadorna tadornoides* of w. and s.e. Aust. incl. Tas., having predom. black and brown plumage with a white ring around the neck; *chestnut-breasted shelduck*, see CHESTNUT *a.*; **eagle** *obs.*, *wedge-tailed eagle*, see WEDGE-TAILED; **gum,** any of several trees of the genus *Eucalyptus* (fam. Myrtaceae), esp. the tall *E. dalrympleana* subsp. *dalrympleana* of Vic., N.S.W., and Tas., having a smooth white and grey bark, and *E. cypellocarpa* of Vic. and e. N.S.W., having smooth greyish bark; the wood of these trees; **hickory,** the shrub or small tree *Acacia penninervis*, occurring on rocky hills in N.S.W., Qld., and e. Vic.; the tough, durable, and flexible wood of the tree; **oak,** any of several trees incl. *Allocasuarina verticillata* (fam. Casuarinaceae) of s.e. Aust., having slender drooping branchlets and occurring on stony ridges and rocky soils; **pheasant** *obs.*, LYRE-BIRD 1; **pygmy possum,** the small terrestrial marsupial *Burramys parvus* of alpine and subalpine n.e. Vic. and s.e. N.S.W.; see also *pygmy possum* PYGMY; **shrimp,** the small fresh-water crustacean *Anaspides tasmaniae*, occurring in mountain waters of Tas.; **thrush,** the bird *Zoothera dauma* (see *ground thrush* GROUND *n.*[1]); **trout,** any of several small fresh-water fish of the fam. Galaxiidae, found at higher altitudes in s. Aust.

1837 *Colonist* (Sydney) 350/3 **Mountain ash**, for carriage work. **1880** J. BONWICK *Resources Qld.* 81 The Mountain Ash is an *Alphitonia*, of excellent range, and used for gun-stocks for its hardness, polish, and wear. **1904** J.H. MAIDEN *Notes on Commercial Timbers N.S.W.* 29 Species of *Elaeocarpus*, which variously go under the names of 'blue-berry ash', 'pigeon-berry ash', and sometimes 'mountain ash'. **1915** *Bulletin* (Sydney) 9 Sept. 26/1 What in the Braidwood (N.S.W.) district is called mountain-ash . . is as hard as a Hun's heart. **1934** W.A. OSBORNE *Visitor to Aust.* 65 The great Mountain Ash (*Eucalyptus regnans*) soars to heights that challenge the Californian sequoias. **1968** V. SERVENTY *Southern Walkabout* 35 The mountain ash must be among the most beautiful of the world's trees. Rising from a bed of ferns its grey rough-barked base gradually strips away to show the gleaming white smoothness of the trunk. **1983** *S. Gippsland Sentinel-Times* 24 May 22/4 Mountain ashes . . grow naturally straight, so pruning is almost unnecessary. **(a) 1872** MRS E. MILLETT *Austral. Parsonage* 183 The '**Mountain Devil**' is about five or six inches long. **1899** *Bulletin* (Sydney) 15 July 15/1 Any reader tell me if the 'mountain devil' (common a few years ago in W.A.) is known in any other part of Australia? **1903** A.G. CHARLETON *Gold Mining & Milling W.A.* 13 Lizards, amongst which the Mountain Devil (*Moloch horridus*) is one of the most conspicuous. **1944** C. BARRETT *Austral. Nature Wonders* 54 Though called 'Mountain' Devil, it is a typical desert form, inhabiting arid, sandy areas of Western, Southern and Central Australia. **1963** V.B. CRANLEY *27,000 Miles through Aust.* 39 The mountain devil . . covered with leathery horns and looking like something out of hell . . is quite harmless and feeds on ants. **1981** K. GARVEY *Rhymes of Ratbag* 60 The mountain devil in his spiny regalia Relaxes on rocks around Northern Australia. **(b) 1949** B. O'REILLY *Green Mountains* 91 **Mountain devils** are the joy of Blue Mountain children; following a tulip-shaped flower of flame-red comes the seed pod—a perfect little devil's head with two sharp horns and a sinister-looking pointed beard. **1961** *Bulletin* (Sydney) 1 Mar. 52/2 A path ran . . to Middle Harbor, past bottle-brush and . . the spidery flowers of mountain-devils. **1979** WRIGLEY & FAGG *Austral. Native Plants* 245 (*caption*) Fruits of *Lambertia formosa* (mountain devil) are frequently made into dolls for the tourist trade in the Blue Mountains, New South Wales. **1820** C. JEFFREYS *Van Dieman's Land* 35 This lake abounds with . . teal, **mountain ducks**, coots. **1844** J. GOULD *Birds of Aust.* (1848) VII. Pl. 7, *Casarca tadornoides* . . Mountain Duck, Colonists of Swan River. **1892** 'R. BOLDREWOOD' *Nevermore* II. 162 A magnificent specimen of that finest of all the family—the 'mountain duck'—with his bronzed-fawn and metallic plumage. **1931** N.W. CAYLEY *What Bird is That?* 246 Chestnut-breasted Shelduck . . also called Mountain-duck . . is generally shy and wary and keeps far out on the shallow lakes or swamps. **1955** S. OSBORNE *Duck Shooting Aust.* 12 The Mountain Duck is a general black colour with a chestnut breast. **1976** *Reader's Digest Compl. Bk. Austral. Birds* 100 Contrary to its popular name, most mountain ducks do not live or breed in high places. The main populations live in the lowland areas. **1980** *Ecos* xxiv. 12/2 A female mountain duck chose to lay her eggs in the same hollow. **1800** D. COLLINS *Acct. Eng. Colony N.S.W.* (1802) II. 288 (Pl.) **Mountain Eagle** of New South Wales will kill a large sized Kangaroo. **1842** J. GOULD *Birds of Aust.* (1848) I. Pl. 1, *Aquila fucosa* . . Wedge-tailed Eagle . . Mountain Eagle of New South Wales. **1863** F. ALGAR *Handbk. to Colony S.A.* 6 The mountain eagle is a magnificent creature. **1831** W. BLAND *Journey of Discovery Port Phillip* 16 They are at present among a species of **mountain gum**, of the finest description. **1855** J. BONWICK *Geogr. Aust. & N.Z.* (ed. 3) 201 The chief of these are the blue, red . . and mountain Gum trees. **1891** *Braidwood Dispatch* 14 Jan. 2/1 On our coast ranges are to be found the mountain gum, blackwood [etc.]. **1904** J.H. MAIDEN *Notes on Commercial Timbers N.S.W.* 15 Mountain Gum (*Eucalyptus goniocalyx*) . . is a pale-coloured timber, somewhat intermediate in character between that of a box and a stringybark. **1955** F. LANE *Patrol to Kimberleys* 106 They were in lightly timbered country where Bill pointed out the mountain gum with its chalky-white bark, and the coolibah. **1963** C. BURGESS *Blue Mountain Gums* 24 'Mountain Gum' was named *Eucalyptus dalrympleana* by Maiden in 1920. . . It is a tall, straight tree, with a smooth bark . . common in the high, cold country. **1882** *Illustr. Austral. News* (Melbourne) 24 Jan. 10/3 Here also were found many other woods, equally if not more valuable, myrtle, dogwood, **mountain hickory**, and blackwood. **1891** *Proc. Linnean Soc. N.S.W.* VI. 138 *Acacia penninervis* . . 'Mountain Hickory'. . . An expert in the Bombala district considers it excellent, being very durable and very tough, on which account he prefers it to anything else for axe and tool-handles. **1904** J.H. MAIDEN *Notes on Commercial Timbers N.S.W.* 28 Closely resembling blackwood in appearance and properties is the mountain hickory. **1933** D. MACDONALD *Brooks of Morning* 115 The wattles are the Mountain Hickory (*penninervis*) and the Alpine Wattle (*pravissima*), hardly separable. **1984** E. ROLLS *Celebration of Senses* 151 The pale-flowered acacias, Hickory and Mountain Hickory with small white or lemon balls of flowers. **1900** *Proc. Linnean Soc. N.S.W.* XXV. 713 Another tree now appearing for the first time is *Casuarina quadrivalvis* (She Oak and **Mountain Oak**). **1911** *Bulletin* (Sydney) 20 July 14/2, I do not know the Dago names for the two oaks. . . Locally they are distinguished by the names 'mountain-oak' and 'meadow-oak'. **1926** *Qld. Agric. Jrnl.* XXV. 441 *Lysicarpus ternifolius* Tom Russell's Mahogany, Mountain Oak. **1936** J.E. HAMMOND *Western Pioneers* 86 During the early 'nineties he collected many kinds of West Australian woods . . jam-wood, mountain oak, sandalwood. **1800** Banks Papers 20 Feb. XIX. 124 The **Mountain Pheasant** (as it is called) which I sent by Captain Raven for Lady Banks. **1823** J. LATHAM *Gen. Hist. Birds* VIII. 162 The Menura . . called by the inhabitants the Mountain Pheasant. **1847** *Heads of People* (Sydney) 8 May 38, I hear the mountain pheasant whistle o'er the distant hills. **1851** J. HENDERSON *Excursions & Adventures N.S.W.* II. 177 The . . Mountain Pheasant . . is found in the forests upon high ranges, or hills. **1971** J. CALABY et al. *Mountain Pigmy Possum* (CSIRO Division Wildlife Research Techn. Paper no. 23) 3 The **mountain pigmy possum** . . was unknown as a living animal until August 1966 when a specimen was caught in the kitchen of a ski-lodge at Mt. Hotham in the Victorian alps. **1980** *Ecos* xxvi. 5/3 The mountain pigmy possum was for 70 years known only from fossil remains. **1985** *Austral.* (Sydney) 6 June 1/4 Australia's rare mountain pygmy possums have a problem . . because males and females of the species live strictly segregated lives for most of the year. **1909** G. SMITH *Naturalist in Tas.* 80

The remarkable **Mountain Shrimp** of Tasmania (*Anaspides tasmaniae*) . . is found at a high elevation on Mount Wellington and in the clear tarns upon Mount Field, the Harz [*sic*] Mountains, and on some of the mountains on the west coast. **1941** C. BARRETT *Aust.* 73 Streams that rise in the plateau of Hobart's mountain are famous for their shrimps! Their proper name is Anaspides; but Tasmanians call them mountain-shrimps. **1968** P. ADAM SMITH *Tiger Country* 198 It is the two-inch mountain shrimp *Anaspides tasmanii* that is peculiar to Tasmania. **1985** *Mt. Field Nat. Park* (Tas. Nat. Parks & Wildlife Service), In the highland pools the mountain shrimp (*Anaspides tasmaniae*) is found. This small crustacean is a 'living fossil' as it is almost identical with fossil shrimps 200 million years old. **1848** J. GOULD *Birds of Aust.* IV. Pl. 7, *Oreocincla lunulata* . . **Mountain Thrush**, Colonists of Van Diemen's Land. **1861** 'OLD BUSHMAN' *Bush Wanderings* 138 The *Mountain Thrush* of Australia is identical with 'White's thrush' of Britain. **1929** A.H. CHISHOLM *Birds & Green Places* 28, I think now of the ground-thrush, termed also mountain-thrush and fern-thrush, technically *Oreocincla* (*oreos*, mountain; *cinclos*, bird). **1959** V. PALMER *Big Fellow* 117 Flocks of silver-eyes kept up a lively chirruping in a nearby cedar, and a couple of mountain-thrushes fluttered down. **1882** J.E. TENISON-WOODS *Fish & Fisheries N.S.W.* 108 In the upper and shallower parts of the creeks and rivers rising in the Blue Mountains one or two species of *Galaxias* are found. . . They are known to some as the '**Mountain trout**'. **1906** D.G. STEAD *Fishes of Aust.* 49 *The Australian minnows* (Family: *Galaxiidae*) . . are very prettily marked and spotted, and this . . has given rise to the name of Mountain Trout, which is so often applied to them. **1916** *Bulletin* (Sydney) 21 Sept. 24/2 The only tucker . . to be found in the King at that height was a diminutive and almost transparent fish, which we called mountain 'trout'. **1939** J. GALBRAITH *Garden in Valley* (1985) 77 In a biscuit tin half filled with water . . were two frightened mountain trout, under six inches long, with brown and steel-blue spots on their grey bodies. **1974** L. WEDLICK *Sporting Fish* 30 A small native fish . . which is of sporting value . . one of our species of galaxia (*Galaxias coxii*) . . more frequently known by the name of 'mountain trout'.

mountaineer. *Obs.* A (wild) beast which has strayed from the main herd into high country which is difficult of access.

1849 A. HARRIS *Emigrant Family* (1967) 125 They'd better go into that mob of mountaineers that always runs separate from your quiet cattle in the ranges. **1857** F. DE B. COOPER *Wild Adventures* 58, I went with a party of four to beat up the ranges, and bring in any stray mob of mountaineers.

mounted police. *Hist.* A cavalry force responsible for the maintenance of law and order in (remote) rural districts; orig. (see quot. 1825) such a force engaging in the pursuit and capture of bushrangers.

1825 *HRA* (1919) 1st Ser. XII. 85, I had some time since carefully selected and equipped as light cavalry, 2 Officers, 2 Serjeants, and 22 Rank and File from the Regiment under my Command to act as a Mounted Police, for the express Purpose of pursuing and capturing Bushrangers. **1831** *Sydney Herald* 1 Aug. 4/1 Settlers . . in the neighbourhood of Hunter's River are much obliged for the stationing of the mounted police in that district. **1835** J. HOLMAN *Travels* IV. 481 The natives are very useful in giving information to the mounted Police concerning the bush-rangers. **1844** *Duncan's Weekly Register* (Sydney) 20 July 30/2 Men of the *Mounted* Police are also often employed as Border Police men, though no part of the expense of maintaining them is charged against the squatting districts. **1849** S. & J. SIDNEY *Emigrant's Jrnl.* 63 The Mounted Police.—For the protection of the settlers established, in the remote interior, there is a body of mounted police, the expense of which is defrayed by an annual assessment upon the stock, of 1d. for each sheep, and 6d. for each head of cattle. **1852** W.H. HALL *Practical Experience* (ed. 2) 43 The Mounted Police Force of Victoria is composed principally of expirees and emancipists from Van Diemen's Land. **1854** W. HOWITT *Boy's Adventures* 301 The mounted native police was obliged to be given up. **1884** J.T. HINKINS *Life amongst Native Race* 34 The mounted black police . . had been camping at our station for several days.

Hence **mounted policeman** *n.*

1834 'EMIGRANT' *Party Politics Exposed* 36, I saw the mounted policeman . . fire. **1848** *Portland Gaz.* 18 Aug. 2/5 There were for a time some half dozen mounted policemen here, but we believe that there are at present only the two required for town duty. **1914** C.H.S. MATTHEWS *Bill* 27 You can guess that in those days the mounted policeman's lot was an exciting, if not always a happy, one.

mounter. *Obs.* [f. Br. slang *mount* to give false evidence for money: see OED *v.* 7.] One who gives false evidence in return for payment.

1812 J.H. VAUX *Mem.* (1819) II. 189 *Mounter*, a man who lives by *mounting*, or perjury, who is always ready for a guinea or two to swear whatever is proposed to him. **1847** *Melbourne Argus* 15 Oct. 2/6, I have been in the police in Sydney; I'm not a 'mounter'; I haven't frequently given evidence. **1896** M. HORNSBY *Old Time Echoes Tas.* 38 For ten bob I could find mounters (false swearers) enough to hang a county.

Mount Pitt bird. *Obs.* Also **Mount Pit bird.** [f. the name of *Mount Pitt*, Norfolk Island.] The brown and grey bird *Pterodroma solandri*, now breeding only on Lord Howe Island, but formerly abundant on Norfolk Island; BIRD OF PROVIDENCE.

1790 R. CLARK Jrnl. 18 Apr. 159 The haversack contained 68 of the Mount Pit Birds. **1791** D. COLLINS *Acct. Eng. Colony N.S.W.* (1798) I. 162 The ration at Norfolk Island was . . regulated by the plenty or scarcity of the Mount Pitt birds. **1794** P.G. KING Jrnl. Norfolk Island 145 The Mount Pit Birds are as Numerous as ever, Notwithstanding upwards of Two Hundred thousand have been killed Yearly. **1805** *HRA* (1921) 3rd Ser. I. 327 Kangaroos and Emus affording us as providential a Supply as the Mount Pitt Birds once did.

mouser. *Shearing.* See quot. 1965.

1895 *Bulletin* (Sydney) 13 July 23/2 And there isn't any hurry, as it takes you all the day To get the 'sweet-lips' going, and the boss severely damns The mercenary 'mouser' who opens out on rams. **1965** J.S. GUNN *Terminol. Shearing Industry* ii. 5 *Mouser*, a slang name given to the man who is out to make all the money he can and never 'misses a trick'. Such a person could disturb the peace and good fellowship in a shed, and thus upsets the boss as well as the other shearers.

mouse spider. [See quot. 1976.] Any of several large, black, burrowing spiders of the genus *Missulena*, widespread in mainland Aust., esp. *M. occatoria*.

1965 *Austral. Encycl.* VIII. 233 Two of the species [of *Missulena*] are widely distributed over Australia; they are *M. occatoria*, sometimes termed the 'mouse' spider, and *M. insigne*. **1976** B.Y. MAIN *Spiders* 65 Many years ago *Missulena* was designated the mouse spider apparently as a result of someone finding a spider, probably a male specimen, in a deep sinuous burrow. Presumably the spider had crawled down an old hole of a beetle or perhaps even a mouse. **1986** *Canberra Times* 29 Jan. 21/3 'Mouse' spiders (*Missulena* species) are also black, but the most common local species has a bright red patch about the 'head'.

mouth, *v. trans.* To examine the mouth of (a sheep), in order to estimate its age. Also as *vbl. n.*, and *attrib.*

1870 J.R. GRAHAM *Treatise Austral. Merino* 32 When they were 'mouthed', at the time of delivery, fully 25 per cent. of them were found with teeth worn down to the gums. . . None of these sheep could by any possibility be over six, and many no more than four or five years old. **1896** G. SUTHERLAND *Australasian Live Stock Man.* 174 On large stations where sheep are frequently boxed up for various reasons, it enables the overseer to draft, by the swing gate, all the separate ages without resort to 'mouthing'. **1930** A. HAWKESWORTH *Australasian Sheep & Wool* (ed. 6) 273 If no age mark is used, it is then necessary to 'mouth' every animal, which is not only laborious work, but greatly knocks the sheep about. **1933** *Bulletin* (Sydney) 6 Sept. 24/1 Graziers buy old ewes without troubling to 'mouth' them. **1961** J.W. JORDAN *Practical Sheep Farming* 214 In the days when 'bullocking' was in favour, owners had mouthing races. They used to 'up-end' every sheep, and open its mouth, to find out its age from its teeth.

Movement. *Hist.* Shortened form of 'Catholic Social Studies Movement', a body formed in 1945 to counter the influence and activity of communists in trade unions. See GROUPER 2.

1945 *Catholic Action at Work* 4 Because of this necessity to hide its religious affiliation, the report points out, it was decided to call the organisation '*The Movement*'. **1946** *'Movement' in Railways* (Communist Party Aust., North Rail Branch) 4 In 1942 a small group of supporters of 'The Movement' met on several occasions in a room at the Victorian Railways Institute. . . These meetings were organised very secretly under the name of 'The Railway Glee Club'. **1950** F.J. HARDY *Power without Glory* 634, 'The Movement' . . is the arm of Catholic Action in the Trade Unions. . . In each diocese or suburb we have set about establishing cells of The Movement and in many factories and Trade Unions we have similar groups. **1964** *Sydney Morning Herald* 16 Dec. 2/5 His sanctimonious comments on the 'excesses' of the 'movement' a decade ago are really too much. **1970** R. MURRAY *Split* 14 In the emergency conditions of wartime, stronger anti-communist organisation was soon coming from three main sources. The first, most exotic and best known of these was the Catholic Social Studies Movement, led by B.A. Santamaria and best known simply as 'The Movement'. **1981** B.A. SANTAMARIA *Against Tide* 76 The initial meeting of the organization, later known as 'the Movement', which was held on 14 August 1941, had only four people present. **1982** *Bulletin* (Sydney) 7 Sept. 63/2 Although the Movement rarely had more than 5000 members at any one time, it was a formative influence on the early years of some 100,000 Australian Catholics.

mowie /ˈmoʊi/. [f. MOR(WONG + -Y.] MORWONG.

1973 *Kings Cross Whisper* (Sydney) clv. 16/4 A nice haul of snapper, mowies and even a dozen or so trag. **1984** *Canberra Chron.* 25 July 19/1 At Montague Island . . there have been a few good mowies around the north-western corner.

mowlow, var. MOLO.

mozz, *n.* Also **moz.** [Abbrev. of MOZZLE.] In the phr. **to put the moz on,** to exert a malign influence upon (a person), to jinx.

1924 C.J. DENNIS *Rose of Spadgers* 75 Too much soul-ferritin' might put the moz On this 'ere expedition. **1941** S.J. BAKER *Pop. Dict. Austral. Slang* 47 *Put the moz on someone*, to inconvenience a person. **1956** A. MARSHALL *How's Andy Going?* 200 'Looking ahead like that never does any bloody good to any man,' observed Pat. 'It puts the moz on him.' **1963** H. PORTER *Watcher on Cast-Iron Balcony* 81 Mother is wishing Miss Brewer some female ill, is putting the mozz on her. **1967** D. HEWETT *This Old Man* (1976) 96 E's buried under them newspapers. Don't go puttin' the mozz on 'im. **1985** *Canberra Times* 6 Sept. 1/1 He has put the mozz on runners before. He backed Mr Peacock against Mr Fraser and lost.

mozz, *v.* Also **moz.** *trans.* To jinx; to deter. Also as *vbl. n.*

1941 S.J. BAKER *Pop. Dict. Austral. Slang* 47 *Moz*, to interrupt, to hinder. **1965** F. HARDY *Yarns of Billy Borker* 107 'If I back it, it won't win, I'm too unlucky. It'll get left at the post or fall over if I back it.' 'Don't mozz a man,' I tells him. **1973** J. POWERS *Last of Knucklemen* (1974) 49 Don't let him mozz you, Monk. You've made it through the first week—that's the hard one. **1983** HIBBERD & HUTCHINSON *Barracker's Bible* 132 *Mozz* . . to attempt to distract a player kicking for a goal, or a batsman waiting for the bowler to deliver. . . 'No mozzing' is a schoolkids' rule often adopted in the interest of fair play.

mozzie, var. MOSSIE.

mozzle. [a. Heb. *mazzāl* luck.] Luck; fortune.

1898 *Bulletin* (Sydney) 17 Dec. (Red Page), *Mozzle* is luck . . *Good mozzle* = good luck; *Kronk mozzle* = bad luck. **1901** *Truth* (Sydney) 20 Oct. 5/5 'Down on your luck. . .' 'Yes, you're right, boss, been regular out of mozzle for a fortnight.' **1903** J. FURPHY *Such is Life* 225 How much do you stand to lose if your mozzle is out? **1919** E. DYSON *Hello, Soldier* 32 'Twas rotten mozzle, Neddo. We had blown every clip. **1982** N. KEESING *Lily on Dustbin* 147 'Mozzle' for luck which comes from the Yiddish *mozel* (pronounced to rhyme with nozzle).

Mrs Potts. *Hist.* [Of unknown origin.] The name of a type of smoothing-iron: see quot. 1913.

1907 *Anthony Hordern Catal.* 542 Mrs Potts' Chinese Polishing Irons . . 2s. 6d. each. Extra Handles . . 8d. **1913** *Lassetters' Compl. Gen. Catal.* 333 *'Mrs Potts' Irons.* Nickel-Plated. The great merits of these irons are universally known. They are better made and fine finished, and hold the heat longer than any other iron, and being double pointed will iron either way. The handle is made of walnut, and detachable by a spring, and being circular shape fits the hand naturally, so all straining is avoided. The sets comprise three irons and one handle. **1959** *Bulletin* (Sydney) 25 Nov. 18/2 She . . used Mrs Pott's irons (*not* 'Granny' Potts, and they're not flatirons, but the deep kind with detachable wooden handle). **1978** R. Dobson *Over Frontier* 14 Talking to Mrs Potts, put out to simmer down, on the back veranda. **1980** E. & J. Trantman *Jinkers & Jarrah Jerkers* 28 Other run-of-the-mill laundry facilities were a collection of Mrs Potts', which were flat-irons heated on the wood stove for ironing. **1982** N. Keesing *Lily on Dustbin* 27 They would . . wash personal and domestic linen . . and press it later with a mangle, flat iron or, for the innovative and affluent, a 'Mrs Potts' (a pre-electric heated iron).

mud.

1. Used *attrib.* in the names of fauna: **mud crab,** the large swimming crab *Scylla serrata*, valued as food, occurring along muddy shores in estuaries of n. Aust., and widespread in the Indo-Pacific region; *mangrove crab*, see Mangrove; Muddie; **-eye,** the larva of a dragonfly, used by anglers as bait; **fish,** any of several marine, estuarine, or fresh-water fish living amongst or over mud beds, incl. Lungfish and Mudskipper; **lark,** *magpie lark*, see Magpie *n.* 2; **oyster,** the oyster of s.e. Aust. *Ostrea angasi*; **wasp,** Mason wasp.

1966 T.C. Roughley *Fish & Fisheries Aust.* (ed. 7) 127 **Mud** or Mangrove **Crab**. . . This large crab has a powerful pair of nippers which can easily crush a finger carelessly placed. **1969** J. Pollard *Austral. & N.Z. Fishing* 161 These large meaty claws help make the mud crab Australia's most important commercial variety as the claws contain a fine-flavoured meat considered more succulent than the body meat. **1980** S. Thorne *I've met some Bloody Wags* 31 We'd chuck our sandwiches to the dogs and put our mudcrabs on the hot coals after we had boiled our quarts. **1911** D.A. Macdonald *Bush Boy's Bk.* 95 They live on the yabbie, the shrimp, and the **mud eye**—which is the water form of the dragon-fly. **1951** T.C. Roughley *Fish & Fisheries Aust.* 296 The sluggish dragonfly larvae, popularly known as 'mud-eyes', which are found in the mud of streams, are . . relished by the fish. **1969** *Sporting Globe* (Melbourne) 2 July 23/1 'Mudeye dobbing' still remains the deadliest bait method of catching trout. **1985** *Canberra Chron.* 10 July 19/4 When they cleaned the fish they found it had 26 mudeyes in its stomach. **1829** R. Mudie *Picture of Aust.* 196 A **mud-fish**, found on the north-west coast . . is about nine inches in length, and buries itself under the mud with more rapidity than any other fish that is known. **1864** *Jrnls. & Rep. Two Voyages Glenelg River* 66, I have now captured many specimens of the rare Lepidosiren, a genus placed by some naturalists amongst the fish, by others included in the amphibia, called popularly on our first visit to the Glenelg, 'the walking' or 'mud fish'. **1903** J.T. Reilly *Reminisc. Fifty Yrs. W.A.* 532 We witnessed the gambols of that curious little creature the mud-fish. **1906** J.W. Gregory *Dead Heart Aust.* 151 Crocodiles swarmed in the lake and its estuaries, and preyed on the primitive Queensland mudfish (*Ceratodus*). *Ibid.* 49 Our sportsmen did good practice on the birds—teal . . and **mud-larks**—that swarmed around the pond. **1921** K.S. Prichard *Black Opal* 65 The piping of mud-larks—their thin, silvery notes. **1948** R. Raven-Hart *Canoe in Aust.* 97 The black-and-white 'mudlarks' as Bevan called them. . . It builds a mud nest, a saucer reinforced with grass and hairs and feathers. **1978** D. Stuart *Wedgetail View* 36 Magpie, mudlark and shell parrot spearing in jewelled wave through spinifex. **1770** J. Cook *Jrnls.* 23 Aug. (1955) I. 394 The Shell-fish are Oysters of 3 or 4 sorts, viz. Rock oysters and Mangrove Oysters which are small, Pearl Oysters, and **Mud Oysters,** these last are the best and largest. **1827** P. Cunningham *Two Yrs. in N.S.W.* I. 68 Mud oysters are brought over from Botany Bay. **1855** H. Hume *Brief Statement* 25 The same day we came upon a black-fellow's camp, with the mud-oyster shells lying about it. **1882** *Proc. Linnean Soc. N.S.W.* VII. 124 *Ostrea Angasi* . . our Mud Oyster. **1965** *Austral. Encycl.* VI. 433 On the southern Australian coast the rock oyster is replaced by the larger, coarser mud oyster. 'Mud' is a misnomer, for the oyster does not live in mud, but on a firm bottom, in rock crevices, or actually attached to rocks, below low-tide mark. **1983** *Canberra Chron.* 24 Aug. 22/3 Dave Gill . . had to settle for a bag of mud oysters. **1894** *Proc. Linnean Soc. N.S.W.* IX. 29 *Abispa splendida*. . . Among our 'mason or **mud wasps**' this takes the palm for being one of the largest and handsomest. **1925** *Bulletin* (Sydney) 14 May 22/2 In Queensland mud-wasps build everywhere.

2. Special Comb. **mud-fat** *a.* [Br. dial.] in prime condition; also as *n.*; **map,** a diagram of a district, route, etc., drawn with a stick in earth or dust; so **mud-map** *v. trans.*; **rain,** see quot. 1872; **spring,** see quot. 1901; Mound spring; **tank,** an earth dam.

1880 *Argus* (Melbourne) 17 Feb. 9/3 Bullocks are '**mud-fat**' almost all the year round. **1891** 'R. Boldrewood' *Sydney-Side Saxon* (1925) 114 There's half this fine body of veal mud-fat, and tender as a chicken. **1902** *Bulletin* (Sydney) 4 Oct. 16/2 Sheep in drought country in N.Q. sometimes come in mud-fat, said fatness being a puzzle to everyone on the station. Explanation—quantities of bush hay have been blown into the huge cracks in the ground and the sheep have discovered the fact to their manifest advantage. **1912** J. Bradshaw *Highway Robbery under Arms* (ed. 3) 39 The two constables . . kept my stolen horse . . and when I came back for him he was mud fat. **1932** W. Hatfield *Ginger Murdoch* 18, I got this thing, chunky little creamy, orf a Pong in Cunnamulla, mud-fat he was (the horse). **1941** *Bulletin* (Sydney) 16 July 16/1 When you see the mongs as mud-fat as they are y' can bet the missus is a rotten cook an' has to throw a lot of stuff to 'em. **1919** E.S. Sorenson *Chips & Splinters* 14 Phineas Jones was a native of Wattle Gully, an obscure little place that isn't marked on any map excepting always the **mud maps** that Phineas draws, when directing some unfortunate wanderer to the awful place. **1930** A.E. Yarra *Vanishing Horsemen* 116 While waiting for the trial the two men spent many an hour 'mud-mapping' the scene of their arrest and advancing theories to account for the starting event. **1935** R.B. Plowman *Boundary Rider* 49 With a small stick the owner drew a 'mud map' for the other man's guidance, giving distances and landmarks. **1953** *Bulletin* (Sydney) 7 Oct. 13/2 Lawson . . first made me aware of the tendency old miners had to work old ground over again, complete with mud-maps, fault-lines, cross-courses, etc. **1959** H. Lamond *Sheep Station* 95 They dismounted . . to draw mud maps—as diagrams in the dust were commonly called. **1965** R.H. Conquest *Horses in Kitchen* 30 Anyway, he knew outback Queensland and New South Wales to such an extent that he could draw mud-maps of 'foreign parts' for any drover. **1976** C.D. Mills *Hobble Chains & Greenhide* 105 He started to undo the paper. 'This'll be the 'mud-map' of where the rest of the remains are.' **1872** 'Resident' *Glimpses Life Vic.* 109 Rain has fallen which was impregnated with dust, and the drops of which left deep stains of reddish brown. . . This phenomenon is familiarly known as **mud-rain.** **1881** *Proc. Linnean Soc. N.S.W.* VI. 155 In putting down some tube-bores at the so-called '**Mud Springs**' of Wee Wattah and Mulyeo, at Killarah, Mr David Brown . . struck a strong flow of water. **1895** W.G. Cox *Artesian Wells* 38 This well was sunk in proximity to a mud spring, and at a depth of 140 feet artesian water was tapped that rose 26 feet above the curb. **1901** E.F. Pittman *Mineral Resources N.S.W.* 466 An account of the Artesian basin would be incomplete without a reference to the peculiar occurrences known as Mud Springs. They are the visible evidence of the efforts of the water, stored underground in a state of pressure, to force its way through the Cretaceous shales to the surface; in other words, they are natural Artesian wells. They consist of mounds of yellow clay mixed with water-worn pebbles, and in outward appearance they are not unlike large ant-hills; in the centre of each is a vertical pipe through which water, or rather liquid mud comes to the surface. The mounds have been formed by the very slow over-flowing of the liquid mud, and, as some of them are of very large dimensions, they must have been forming for a very long period. **1912** R.S. Symmonds *Our Artesian Waters* 74 The drying-up of the mud springs on the artesian 'intake' [*sc.* outlet] may be the result of tapping our artesian waters; the lowering of pressure consequent upon escape of gas through bore holes may have reduced the pressure so as to make it difficult for the waters to rise to their natural outlet on the outskirts of the basin. **1935** M. Gilmore *More Recoll.* 36 The mud-spring in the orchard had built its own mound, and spread its own silt. **1898** *Bulletin* (Sydney) 1 Jan. 3/2 The weak are falling back; Closely guarded by the **mud-tank** just abreast the western wing. **1939** Franklin & Cusack *Pioneers on Parade* 7 Her face was . . brown as a half-caste's and criss-crossed with lines like a mud tank in drought.

3. In the phr. **up to mud,** unsatisfactory.

1931 G.C. Bolton *Fine Country to starve In* (1972) 157 We meet by chance in the street. 'Hullo! How's things?' 'Up to mud!' **1933** *Bulletin* (Sydney) 1 Nov. 42/2 Still, men today are mostly up to mud. **1945** S.J. Baker *Austral. Lang.* 128 *Up to putty, up to mud* . . describe things that are bad, disliked or out of order. **1965** J. O'Grady *Aussie Eng.* 60 Anything 'up to mud' is 'not up to much'. It's no good. It's buggered.

4. *fig.* In the sugar industry: see quot. 1966.

1938 F. Clune *Free & Easy Land* 236 The juice from the mills now runs into juice tanks, where it is steam-heated and treated with lime, which precipitates the impurities to the bottom. The precipitate is known as 'mud'. **1966** B. Beatty *Around Aust.* 224 Nothing goes to waste in the North Queensland sugar industry. 'Mud', the residue left after the juices have been filtered from the crushings, makes a rich fertilizer.

muddie. Also **muddy.** [f. *mud(crab* + -Y.] *Mud-crab*, see Mud 1.

1953 S.J. Baker *Aust. Speaks* 104 *Muddy*, a mud crab. **1969** *Telegraph* (Brisbane) 5 June 2/5 We've been getting up to 50 muddies a week—some of them old enough to vote. **1977** *Austral.* (Sydney) 8 Jan. 1/1 Each year the people of N.S.W. eat 200,000 of the prize Queensland muddies, which is all right except that they are eating mud crabs that Queenslanders are not allowed to eat. **1981** *Weekend Austral. Mag.* (Sydney) 26 Dec. 4/3 They don't even know what a mangrove is in America, let alone muddies.

muddlo, var. Mudlo.

Mudgee stone. /mʌdʒi 'stoʊn/. [f. the name of *Mudgee* a town in N.S.W.] A slate found in the Mudgee district and particularly suitable for use as a whetstone; a whetstone of this material. Also **Mudgee.**

1909 R. Kaleski *Austral Settler's Compl. Guide* 24 The oilstones I prefer are the Lily white Washita or the best Mudgee stone. **1913** *Lassetters' Compl. Gen. Catal.* 691 Stones, Turkey and Mudgee, in 14 lb. boxes. **1964** H.P. Tritton *Time means Tucker* (rev. ed.) 47 A good whetstone was a prized possession and 'Mudgee Stones' (a slate found only in that district) were always admired and envied. . . Few shearers would allow anyone to use their 'Mudgee'.

mudhopper: see Mudskipper.

mudlo /'mʌdloʊ/. *Obs.* Also **muddlo.** [a. Jagara *madlo.*] See quot. 1876.

[**1861** J.D. Lang *Qld., Aust.* 342 Daggar mudlo yacca, The stranger has bewitched him.] **1876** 'Eight Yrs.' Resident' *Queen of Colonies* 333 When one of the tribe is sick he is said to have a 'mudlo'. Mudlo is a stone, and their belief is that death is caused by some hostile black placing a stone in that portion of the body which is affected. We have seen blacks with mudlos in their heads, some in their stomachs or breasts, and some in the legs. They will tell you with the greatest composure whether the mudlo will be got out, or whether the patient will 'go bong'. **1923** T. Hall *Short Hist. Downs Blacks* 26 Unless a medicine man sucked the Muddlo out they would die with fear.

mudskipper. [Transf. use of *mudskipper* any fish of the genus *Periophthalmus*: see OED(S *mud, sb.*[1] 4 b.] Any of several small, amphibious marine fish of the fam. Gobiidae of tropical n. Aust. and elsewhere, esp. of the genera *Periophthalmus* and *Periophthalmodon*, having modified pectoral and ventral fins which enable it to move about on mudflats; *climbing fish*, see Climbing; *Johnny jumper*, see Johnny 2; *kangaroo fish* (b), see Kangaroo *n.* 5. See also *mud fish* Mud 1. Also **mudhopper.**

1896 F.G. Aflalo *Sketch Nat. Hist. Aust.* 248 The curious little Mudhoppers (*Perioptthalmus*) of Queensland . . springs [*sic*] in advance of the rising tide and leaps and skips over the wet mud. **1906** D.G. Stead *Fishes of Aust.*

187 The Mud-Skipper 'is an essentially-tropical species'. **1936** T.C. ROUGHLEY *Wonders Great Barrier Reef* 146 It is on the mud and about the stilt-like roots of the mangroves that the mud-skipper loves to bask . . and to forage. **1952** B. BEATTY *Unique to Aust.* 75 Another amphibious fish of Queensland is the Mudskipper or Climbing fish. At low tide these small fish . . about five inches—come ashore . . in hundreds hopping, skipping . . in the mangrove swamps and mud flats. **1965** *Sunday Mail Mag.* (Brisbane) 21 Nov. 14/1 The mud-hopper . . is notable for its strange eyes and for the stiff fins which it seems to be able to use like limbs. **1965** M. PATCHETT *Last Warrior* 19 Mud-skippers with goggle eyes and limb-like fins clambered up the saturated trunks for a foot or more. **1979** B. SCOTT *Tough in Old Days* 151 The boles of the mangrove trees were inhabited by thousands of mudskippers.

mug, *v.* [Used elsewhere but recorded earliest in Aust.: see OEDS *v.*[3] 4 and *vbl. n.* 3.] *intr.* To kiss; to 'neck'. Freq. as *vbl. n.*. Also with **up.**

1890 *Bull-Ant* (Melbourne) 28 Aug. 17/3 B.M. was specially favoured with the mugging and kissing which M.E. (a new arrival) bestowed so freely on certain young ladies. **1893** *Bulletin* (Sydney) 9 Sept. 13/1 A witness in Melb. Divorce Court defined 'mugging' as 'putting his arms round her waist'. What an innocent man—unless putting your arm round a woman's waist means also kissing her. **1911** 'S. RUDD' *Bk. of Dan* 85 'Garn! gerrout with yer!' and Dan ducked her embrace. 'I'll get all th' muggin' I want from his bloomin' old cows.' **1930** 'BRENT OF BIN BIN' *Ten Creeks Run* (1952) 164 Ask Jane Humphreys, she's seen 'em kissin' an' muggin' like a house on fire. **1977** T.A.G. HUNGERFORD *Wong Chu* 82 You been mugging up with the postie.

mugga /'mʌgə/. [a. Wiradhuri *magar.*] The tree *Eucalyptus sideroxylon* (see *red ironbark* RED *a.* 1 a.).

1834 G. BENNETT *Wanderings N.S.W.* I. 253 Different species of *Eucalypti* . . among them . . 'iron bark' ('Mucker' of the natives). **1901** *Proc. Linnean Soc. N.S.W.* XXV. 715 E. sideroxylon . . the aboriginal name is Mugga. **1956** K. TENNANT *Honey Flow* 5 Good bee country . . ironbark mainly, narrow-leaf, a bit of mugga.

mug lair: see LAIR *n.* b.

muk-muk: see MOOK-MOOK OWL.

Mules /mjulz/, *n.* [The name of J.H.W. *Mules* (1876–1946), sheep-raiser.] Used *attrib.* in Special Comb. **Mules operation,** a surgical procedure designed to reduce the incidence of blowfly strike in sheep: see quots. 1945 and 1950. Also **Mules' operation.**

1932 *Jrnl. Dept. Agric. S.A.* Aug. 115 *Blowfly strike in sheep and the 'Mules' operation for reducing the incidence*. . . 'Mr J.H.W. Mules . . carried out some observations which led him to believe that the irritation of the skin by urine in the breech of the Merino ewe, was the chief predisposing factor to blowfly strike. . . Mr Mules' treatments date back from 1929.' **1933** *Council Sci. & Industr. Research Pamphlet* no. 37 9 The surgical removal of the side folds (e.g., Mules' operation). **1945** E.H. PEARSE *Sheep, Farm & Station Managem.* 388 The Mules operation is designed, by cutting away the wrinkles that are causative of this susceptibility, and by stretching the bare skin area below the tail, to deprive the ewe of her attraction for the fly. **1950** H.G. BELSCHNER *Sheep Managem. & Diseases* 157 The modified Mules operation reduces the tendency to crutch strike, partly by removing the wrinkles beside the vulva, but chiefly, it would appear, by stretching and enlarging the area of wool-less skin around the vulva, that is, the so called 'bare area'. **1957** J.F. GUTHRIE *World Hist. Sheep & Wool* 246 The well known Mules operation evolved by the late J.H.W. Mules, of South Australia . . is undoubtedly the greatest advance that has yet been made in lessening the susceptibility of sheep to fly strike.

mules /mjulz/, *v.* [f. prec.] *trans.* To perform a Mules operation. Freq. as *ppl. a.* and *vbl. n.*

1946 *Qld. Country Life* 18 Apr. 3 Mulesed sheep are much easier to crutch. *Ibid.*, We don't say that mulesing will stop the fly altogether. **1975** L.A. POCKLEY *Handbk. for Jackeroos* 109 *Mulesing* . . markedly reduces the amount of stained and dirty wool at shearing and crutching time. **1984** *Sydney Morning Herald* 11 June 8/4 Mulesing . . is a severe surgical procedure which . . involves literally skinning the animal alive (in the crutch area) without any anaesthetic. **1985** *Western Farmer* (Perth) 17 Oct. 29/2, I know my farmers pretty well and I am sure there is no way they are going to inflict pain to get their kicks in life—but they would rather mules than have the following tragedy of fly blown sheep. **1986** *Bulletin* (Sydney) 4 Mar. 19/3 Animal Liberation groups are not alone in their opposition to mulesing.

mulga, var. MALKA.

mulga /'mʌlgə/, *n.*[1] and *attrib.* Formerly also **malga, mulgah, mulgar.** [a. Yuwaalaraay *malga.*]

A. *n.*

1. Any of several plants of the genus *Acacia* (fam. Mimosaceae) of dry inland Aust., esp. the widespread shrub or tree *A. aneura*, having grey-green foliage regarded as useful fodder, and yielding a distinctive brown and yellowish timber; the wood of these trees. Also *attrib.*, esp. as **mulga bush, tree, wood.**

1848 T.L. MITCHELL *Jrnl. Exped. Tropical Aust.* 176 On the summit, grew the Malga tree; which is an acacia of such very hard wood. **1858** J.M. STUART *Explorations in Aust.* 18 June (1865) 6 The hills are very stony with a little salt bush, and destitute of timber, except . . the mulga bushes in the sand hills. **1861** *Ibid.* 11 Apr. (1865) 267 The first four miles was over a beautiful grassy plain with mulga wood. **1862** W. LANDSBOROUGH *Jrnl. Exped. from Carpentaria* 106 The scrub consisted of mulgah with a few other trees. **1875** R. BRUCE *Dingoes* 164 Perch'd on some mulgar bare and dead. **1878** R.B. SMYTH *Aborigines of Vic.* I. 127 (*note*) Giles . . supposed that the natives get water in this arid tract from the roots of the Mulga-tree. **1885** *Once a Month* (Melbourne) May 375 We always used as firewood a species of acacia, known by the blacks' name for it—Mulga. It burns with a great flame, and gives out intense heat. **1890** 'R. BOLDREWOOD' *Colonial Reformer* II. 71 The frown on the face of the mulga-studded lowlands deepened. **1893** E. FAVENC *Last of Six Tales* 16 Noontide found him lying under a mulga-bush, praying for death. **1896** J.M. PRICE *Land of Gold* 173 The mulgar-tree, which is the principal growth of the surrounding bush, is practically useless for mining purposes. **1900** R. BRUCE *Benbonuna* (1904) 361 A nervous hand clutched a long, heavy mulga spear. **1913** H. LAWSON *Triangles of Life* 231 Under the alleged shade of three stunted mulga saplings, we found two green hands, slight young Sydney jackaroos. **1929** K.S. PRICHARD *Coonardoo* (1961) 152 The mulga now and then was hung with pale-yellow tasselled blossom, and long flat seedpods. **1932** J.J. HARDIE *Cattle Camp* (1944) 200 This country's all sand and rabbit-holes, and the mulga's too thick for a dog to bark in. **1956** S. HOPE *Diggers' Paradise* 202, I . . groped for the switch of my bedside lamp. This was on a mulga-wood stand about five feet in height. **1963** R.H. CONQUEST *Spurs are Rusty Now* 30 We flogged mulga-trees with our stockwhips and the cattle ate the leaves as they showered onto the hard ground. **1968** V. SERVENTY *Southern Walkabout* 83 The name mulga is tending to be used for wide variety of wattles of fairly similar habits, but it should be reserved for the true mulga, *Acacia aneura.* **1970** J.V. MARSHALL *Walk to Hills of Dreamtime* 82 The puce wet flowers of the mulgawood turned brittle and dry. **1974** 'E. LINDALL' *Search for Tomorrow* 7 The poor lacklustre mulga of that area was uprooted with a few quick jolts, cut into stove lengths with an axe, and stacked on the tray. **1981** A.B. & J.W. CRIBB *Useful Wild Plants Aust.* 103 More book ends, serviette rings and ink stands must have been made from mulga than from any other Australian timber.

2. a. With **the:** remote, sparsely populated country, as opposed to that which is more closely settled; the outback. Also **Mulgaland.**

1898 *Worker* (Sydney) 28 May 6/3 'That's right,' says the man from the Mulga, 'I think I'll do the rest myself.' **1905** *Steele Rudd's Mag.* (Brisbane) June 568 Mulgaland, with its vast open spaces, impressed them in a way that would be utterly impossible in crowded Surrey. **1922** *Bulletin* (Sydney) 5 Jan. 22/1 Not having heard any tidings of a certain cattleman I asked Long Tom, just in from the Mulga, what had become of him. **1936** *Ibid.* 26 Aug. 20/2 The most luxurious 'nap' I ever struck in the mulga was a feather bed that 'Stuttering' Mick carried with him. **1959** J. CLEARY *Strike me Lucky* 185, I could be out the back of Alice Springs, out on me own in the mulga, and there'd allus be some nosey parker shoving his nose in to complain. **1967** J. WYNNUM *I'm Jack, all Right* 27 Everyone knows everyone out in the mulga. **1969** *Kings Cross Whisper* (Sydney) lxxv. 2/3 'This town will really boom. We'll be the Melbourne of the mulga before long,' said the Mayor. **1978** D. BALL *Great Austral. Snake Exchange* 114 Stranded in the bloody mulga with no transport.

b. An inhabitant of such country.

1904 *Bulletin* (Sydney) 15 Sept. 18/2 The back-'o-beyond Jay Pee is often a tricky bit of mulga. **1908** *Ibid.* 16 Jan. 15/1 The bushy-detection question arouses much difference of opinion. Know how we pick them in Brisbane? If in a mixed party, the mulgas invariably clasp hands before venturing to cross the street—girls inside, older boys at each wing.

B. *attrib.*

1. Characterized by the presence of mulga, as **mulga country, flats, paddocks, scrub.**

1858 J.M. STUART *Explorations in Aust.* 25 July (1865) 27 Our journey has been through a very thick mulga scrub and sand hills. **1875** P.E. WARBURTON *Journey across Western Interior* 90 The course had to be altered repeatedly to avoid the mulga (*Acacia aneura*) scrub. **1889** W.H. TIETKENS *Jrnl. Central Austral. Exploring Exped.* 21 Apr. (1891) 15 These mulga flats are intersected by small gum creeks. **1896** *Bulletin* (Sydney) 15 Feb. 3/2 Where the mulga paddocks are wild and wide, That's where the pick of the stockmen ride. **1898** *Ibid.* 19 Feb. 14/2 Scrub-cutting will soon be a thing of the past in mulga country. **1911** E.S. SORENSON *Life in Austral. Backblocks* 59 Bringing back his mate Rattler across a mulga paddock. **1922** V. PALMER *Boss of Killara* 8 The country around was ridgy, and covered with a tangle of mulga scrub. **1924** *Smith's Weekly* (Sydney) 23 Feb. 23/6 Pioneers of the mulga country, up Gascoyne (W.A.) way, recently formed an aerial ambulance corps. **1938** F. BLAKELEY *Hard Liberty* 179 The cock-a-whizzle is found in all mulga country. **1938** F. RATCLIFFE *Flying Fox & Drifting Sand* 238, I doubt if any of the men who had the job of mustering Mr Coleman's mulga paddocks could persuade the theorist that he was talking tripe. **1950** C.E. GOODE *Yarns of Yilgarn* 13 The old road past the disused soak . . through the gully, where the jam and mulga scrubs were a smother of yellow bloom. **1978** D. STUART *Wedgetail View* 57 Featureless mulga scrub stifling in heat.

2. Rustic; countrified.

1895 *Worker* (Sydney) 23 Feb. 4/1 He forgets his Mulga-verses aren't very high in rank. **1904** *Bulletin* (Sydney) 8 Dec. 19/4 This mulga Orpheus would play 'Abide With Me', and the stock would peacefully settle down. **1906** G.M. SMITH *Days of Cobb & Co.* 13 He was togged in Mulga fashion, His moleskin pants were new. **1929** W.J. RESIDE *Golden Days* 378 With joy to greet old Pat, My mulga cobber. **1937** M. TERRY *Sand & Sun* 211 With a stick of tobacco and some tucker the mulga mailman set off for the home of the cattleman. **1942** F. CLUNE *Last of Austral. Explorers* 104 A mob of mulga miners were ready at Clune's pub.

3. In the names of flora and fauna: **mulga ant,** the ant *Polyrachis macropus* of inland Aust. which builds a mud nest to which mulga leaves are applied; **apple,** a large, edible gall produced by the mulga tree; **grass,** any of several grasses (fam. Poaceae) of mulga country and elsewhere, esp. the common *Thyridolepis mitchelliana*, a tufted perennial regarded as good fodder, and *Aristida contorta*, having tufts which whiten on drying; see also WIND-GRASS; **parrot** (or **parakeet**), the parrot of drier mainland Aust. *Psephotus varius*, a predom. green bird with yellow, blue, and red markings; MANY-COLOURED PARAKEET; **snake,** *king brown*, see KING *n.*[1] 2.

1948 C.P. MOUNTFORD *Brown Men & Red Sand* 58, I saw many homes of the curious **mulga ant**, an insect which builds a mud wall, up to fourteen inches in diameter and five inches in height, round the mouth of its nest, and then thatches the wall with dead mulga leaves. **1973** V. SERVENTY *Desert Walkabout* 88 A more conspicuous ant is the mulga ant which builds a volcano-shaped nest with sides lined with mulga leaves. **1888** *Proc. Linnean Soc. N.S.W.* III. 483 *Acacia aneura*. . . In western New South Wales two kinds of galls are commonly found on these trees; one kind is very plentiful . . but the other is less abundant, larger, succulent and edible. These latter galls are called '**Mulga apples**', and are said to be very welcome to the thirsty traveller. **1889** E. GILES *Aust. twice Traversed* I. 71 The mulga bears a small woody fruit called the mulga apple. It somewhat resembles the taste of apples and is sweet. **1904** A.W. HOWITT *Native Tribes S.-E. Aust.* 791 They travelled farther north, gathering the mulga apples by the way, some of which they roasted. **1924** A.G. Bolam *Trans-Austral. Wonderland* (ed. 3) 94 In the season, he [*sc.* the Aboriginal] eats the native peach (or quondong) and the mulga apple, two of the fruits indigenous to this part of the world. **1938** D. Bates *Passing of Aborigines* 209 Mulga apples, acrid but sustaining. **1967** V. Serventy *Nature Walkabout* 32 The children found a strange 'fruit' which turned out to be one of the galls called mulga apples. . . This swelling, the size of a small apple, was a twig which had reacted to the presence of the egg by growing a kind of cancer. **1981** P. Hay *Meeting of Sighs* 79 There are mulga apples all soft and sweet. **1882** *Austral. Handbk.* 392 The '**Mulga Grass**' . . is valuable as thriving under shade in poor soil. **1889** J.H. Maiden *Useful Native Plants Aust.* 82 *Danthonia racemosa* . . 'Mulga Grass'. . . It derives its vernacular name from being only found where the Mulga-tree (*Acacia aneura* and other species) grows. **1890** A. Mackay *Austral. Agriculturist* (ed. 2) 140 Neurachne Mitchelliania, the 'mulga grass' of stockmen. **1935** H.H. Finlayson *Red Centre* 33 The mulga-grass (*Anthistiria* sp.), one of the best fodder grasses is conspicuous in summer owing to the curious spirally twisted habit assumed by the tussocks during desiccation. **1966** A. Morris *Plantlife W. Darling* 7 Grasses which favour hilly situations are . . Neurachne Mitchelliana . . (Mulga Grass) [etc.]. **1951** [**mulga parrot**] *Bulletin* (Sydney) 3 Jan. 12/1 We rise as mulga-parakeets go whirring through the dawn. **1952** A.M. Duncan-Kemp *Where Strange Paths go Down* 95 The Mulga parrot, one of the most beautiful of the outback species. Because of its rich and varied colouring . . [bushmen] have named it 'Joseph's coat'. Its general colour scheme is green, but the chest and thighs are a bright scarlet. **1973** V. Serventy *Desert Walkabout* 40 We also saw the beautifully-coloured mulga parrots, or at least the brilliant males, since the females are much duller. **1984** M. Blakers et al. *Atlas Austral. Birds* 281 The Mulga Parrot is aptly named because its distribution closely follows that of the mulga. **1941** *Bulletin* (Sydney) 16 Apr. 16/4 For sheer pugnacity I'll put the blue ribbon on the **mulga snake** of the Lower Thompson (W.Q.) as champ. of the ophidian world. **1968** M.T. Clark *Spark of Opal* (1973) 37 A writhing brown, yellow-bellied mulga snake. **1978** O. White *Silent Reach* 120 One of the two ancient yardmen . . identified the still lively corpse as that of a mulga snake. . . 'If that bugger'd took a nip of yer, yer'd be playin' a harp by now!'

4. Special Comb. **Mulga Bill,** see quot. 1972; **black,** an Aboriginal from a remote place; **-bred** *a.*, reared in the country; **madness,** eccentricity attributed to living in the outback; also *attrib.*; **mafia,** a name for the National Country Party; **message,** a message conveyed by Mulga wire; also *fig.*; **rum,** crude or illicitly made alcoholic liquor; **scrubber,** see quot. 1945; **wireless (radio, telegram, telegraph),** Mulga wire.

1905 *Truth* (Sydney) 23 Apr. 7/5 The spieler notes his vacant gaze And quickly he swoops down, The magsman understands the ways Of **Mulga Bills** in town. **1972** A. Chipper *Aussie Swearers Guide* 66 *Mulga Bill*, a simpleton, specifically from the Bush. **1900** J. Bradshaw *20 Yrs.' Experience Prison Life* (*c* 1927) 105 The disgraceful stupidity of a doctor who knew as little about the game as a **Mulga black.** **1910** C.E.W. Bean *On Wool Track* 7 The Mulga blacks from out-back had to come down to the Darling for water. **1899** *Bulletin* (Sydney) 21 Jan. 3/2 I'd forgotten for a moment you are not all **mulga-bred.** **1930** A.E. Yarra *Vanishing Horsemen* 56 Mr Somerville . . was mulga-bred and had never lived in Sydney. **1905** *Bulletin* (Sydney) 13 Apr. 18/2 He said he had had several rums but the **mulga madness** brands never upset his digestion. **1909** *Ibid.* 25 Feb. 14/1 There are many phases and manifestations of mulga madness; but only three distinct stages—(1) wearing corks on the rim of the hat; (2) carving quondongs; (3) carrying puppies in the billy. **1928** R.M. Macdonald *Opals & Gold* 67, I was often near that township with the aborigines when I had the mulga (madness). **1980** S. Thorne *I've met some Bloody Wags* 115 He was a prime example of 'mulga madness'. Given a good drench and put on a small lush block in the 'inside country' he would be a new man. **1978** *Sydney Morning Herald* 24 Feb. 7/2 The National Country Party is . . a rustic clan of tough, like-minded politicians who know what they want and how to get it. Its critics might see the party as a kind of **mulga mafia.** **1985** *Bulletin* (Sydney) 29 Oct. 30/1 In Malcolm Fraser's government he was one of the mulga mafia, with Anthony and Peter Nixon. **1926** *Ibid.* 8 Apr. 22/1 Watching the red coals fashion a picture filming a bar-girl's business smile—Only a sordid **mulga message**, blacking out in a little while! **1943** L. McLennan *Spirit of West* 24 They sent a mulga message through all of cattle-land For Dingo Joe, the trapper, to come and try his hand. **1910** *Bulletin* (Sydney) 21 Apr. 39/2 You . . poured gallons of **Mulga rum** down your throat! **1911** A.G. Stephens *Pearl & Octopus* 97 'And this is mulga rum?' 'Ay; distilled from the sap of the mulga.' **1897** *Bulletin* (Sydney) 20 Mar. 28/1 And he loves the merry rattle of the stockwhip and the tramp Of the cockhorned **mulga scrubbers** when they're breaking in the bush. **1945** S.J. Baker *Austral. Lang.* 67 *Mulga scrubbers*. . , stock that have run wild and deteriorated in condition. **1932** I.L. Idriess *Flynn of Inland* (1965) 138 '**Mulga wireless**' had advertised the coming of those dresses far and wide. **1934** W. Hatfield *River Crossing* 102 You've heard about 'mulga-telegrams'—say something away in the mulga scrub, an' the trees theirselves seems to pass it along. **1939** *Kalgoorlie Digger* Jan. 5 This message received per Mulga wireless. **1948** F. Clune *Wild Colonial Boys* 171 The 'mulga telegraph' was the word-of-mouth link of communication. **1950** G.M. Farwell *Land of Mirage* 98 'We heard the Inspector was on his way up.' For once the mulga radio had proved unreliable. **1960** *N.T. News* (Darwin) 5 Feb. 10/3 According to 'mulga wireless' Hank will put in a period studying Jim's method of chasing and mustering wild scrub cattle.

mulga /ˈmʌlgə/, *n.*[2] Abbrev. of Mulga wire 1; a (false) rumour; a tall story.

1899 *Bulletin* (Sydney) 4 Mar. 15/2 A lie or false report is, in N.S.W., a 'Mulga' or 'Mulga-wire', while in Centralia it's 'gidyea'. **1900** *Western Champion* (Barcaldine) 26 June 12/3, I hear the country is good from Wampah to Broken Hill, there being plenty of grass and water; but I think it's a 'mulga'. **1904** *Shearer* (Sydney) 15 Oct. 8/5 The A.W.U. organisers are having rough rows to hoe at nearly all sheds in Victoria. It's real lovely to hear some of their mulgas. **1912** *Bulletin* (Sydney) 15 Feb. (Red Page), Next day a mulga coaxes him to pack; He hoists his drum, and ambles down the track. **1931** *A.I.M. Frontier News* Aug. 12 *Stop that 'mulga'!* Again and again it has been revived—a false rumour that the A.I.M. had come into a fortune of a quarter-of-a-million. **1936** J. Devanny *Sugar Heaven* 216 'D'ye hear the rumour that they've signed on a few boys in the mill today, Royle?' 'Yes. Might be 'mulga'. We'll have to be sharp about the rumours.' **1942** *Mulga* (Alice Springs) 13 Dec. 1 Mulga has apparently come to stay. **1950** K.S. Prichard *Winged Seeds* 297 The troops've had it all by mulga.

mulgara /ˈmʌlgərə/. [Prob. f. an Aboriginal language.] The small carnivorous marsupial *Dasycercus cristicauda* (fam. Dasyuridae) which inhabits burrows in sandy regions of drier Aust.

1941 E. Troughton *Furred Animals Aust.* 33 A rat which provided a meal for three hungry Mulgaras was skinned as by a skilled taxidermist, no bones being left attached to the skin which was inside-out and almost perfect. **1973** V. Serventy *Desert Walkabout* 35 Some mulgaras he kept as pets. **1977** P. Wrightson *Ice is Coming* 19 A round-eyed mulgara whiffled at his sleeping-bag, then veered off after the scent of a mouse. **1984** *Daily Tel.* (Sydney) 22 Aug. 15/7 The Mulgara has an unusual ability to conserve precious water by producing extremely concentrated urine and surviving only on the moisture gained from its prey.

mulga wire /mʌlgə ˈwaɪə/.

1. Bush telegraph *n.* 2.

1899 *Bulletin* (Sydney) 15 July 31/1 Swaggie . . pulled up . . and hailed the boss. 'Any show of a job, *sir?*' (The 'mulga wires' had posted him as to civilities.) **1917** H. Lawson *Lett.* (1970) 263 The cook . . either knew Jim by sight (and reputation) and recognized me by a portrait—or he'd got a Mulga wire. **1923** J. Armour *Spell of Inland* 114 Charlie was the first outsider to hear about the wedding, but Mulga wires would soon publish the news throughout the neighbourhood. **1928** B. Cronin *Dragonfly* 253 With incredible speed the 'mulga wires' -which is the bush term for the almost telepathic dissemination of news in the outback—had collected for the inquiry. **1948** G. Farwell *Down Argent Street* 108 This radio-telegraphic system . . has brought station people as closely in touch with the outside world as any city dweller. . . It is the old-style mulga wire brought up to date. **1959** A. Upfield *Bony & Mouse* 222 No good going to Kalgoorlie because Constable Harmon he send mulga wire to police fellers there to arrest him. **1977** G.W. Lilley *Lengthening Shadows* 28 Seaton got a 'mulga wire' that there had been good storms about the southern end of the run. **1983** M. Durack *Sons in Saddle* 123 Local gossip flourished through a word-of-mouth medium referred to as 'the bushman's mulga wire'.

2. An Aboriginal smoke signal; the message so conveyed; Bush telegraph *n.* 3.

1927 M. Dorney *Adventurous Honeymoon* 134 The blacks have a wonderful code for signalling by smoke. Messages sent in this way are said by the whites to have been sent by 'mulga wire'. **1935** F. Birtles *Battle Fronts Outback* 174 Long columns of smoke were rising. . . The 'Stone Men of the Hills' were replying. . . They, too, were coming down to the coastal plains. . . 'Mulga wires' had told them of the arrival of 'Motor car Frank' and plenty of tobacco. **1936** J.C. Downie *Galloping Hoofs* 201, I would get news by mulga wire (black's signalling) that there had been storms. **1940** E. Hill *Great Austral. Loneliness* (ed. 2) 230 Warned by the mulga wires of the approach of a white woman . . there were some of them who 'went bush'. **1944** A.W. Upfield *No Footprints in Bush* 65 This morning I found Itcheroo squatted before a little fire and sending or receiving a mulga wire.

mulla mulla /ˈmʌlə mʌlə/. [a. Panyjima *mulumulu.*] Pussy tail.

1967 V. Serventy *Nature Walkabout* 31 Mulla mullas were in flower and tall speargrass rose seven feet into the air. **1978** D. Stuart *Wedgetail View* 127 The scattered clumps of purple mulla-mulla stiffening into skeletons of grey leaves and brittle stalks topped with harsh purple brushes of florets. **1984** *Age Weekender* (Melbourne) 7 Dec. 7/3 Pussy Tails or Mulla Mulla (*Ptilotus exaltatus*) carpet the rocky slopes with pink and grey hairy flowers.

mullenize, *v. Hist.* [Prob. f. the name of Charles *Mullen*, farmer: see quot. 1962.] *trans.* To clear and prepare for cultivation (scrub-covered land): see quots. 1962 and 1979 (1). Chiefly as *vbl. n.*

1892 *Trans. & Proc. R. Soc. S.A.* XV. 196 Wherever that mode of cultivation known as 'mullenizing' has been sufficiently prolonged to ensure the death of the primitive growth by uprooting the underground stem—popularly known as the 'mallee root'—regeneration is almost wholly unknown. **1931** Mrs E.P. Halford *Pioneers of Yesterday* 18 A scrub walloper . . chops down the Mallee trees for mullonizing—a system of cultivating the mallee country without grubbing the stumps first. **1957** *Overland* x. 17 Another, not-so-well-known short cut from scrub to crop is still called Mullenising. The Mullenses lived a few miles north of Gawler (S.A.), and . . did not emulate their hard-working neighbours. No toilsome grubbing of stumps. . . The crop was sown broadcast among the roots. **1962** O. Pryor *Aust.'s Little Cornwall* 180 Many farms were cleared in this way before the job was rendered easier by the introduction, by Charles Mullen, of Wasleys, of the process known as mullenizing. In mullenizing, the larger mallees were cut off at ground level with an axe, and the smaller stuff was left standing, ready to be broken down by a four-horse team, dragging a heavy roller made from the shell of an old Cornish boiler. **1979** J. Birmingham et al. *Austral. Pioneer Technol.* 21 'Mullenising' involved smashing down the mallee using a heavy roller (often an old boiler) drawn by twelve oxen; burning the felled mass of timber; and scratching over the soil with a spiked log to prepare for the first sowing. *Ibid.*, Many variants of this plough were made as the innovation caught on and as more and more mallee was mullenised.

Hence **mullenizer** *n.*, a heavy roller for crushing scrub.

1910 C.H. Spence *Autobiogr.* 44 The stump-jumping plough and the mullenicer, which beats down the scrub or low bush so that it can be burnt, were South Australian inventions, copied elsewhere, which have turned land accounted worthless into prolific wheat fields.

mullet. In the phr. **like a stunned mullet,** dazed; uncomprehending; unconscious.

1953 S.J. Baker *Aust. Speaks* 267 Dullness: (looking) *like a stunned mullet.* **1963** Harney & Lockwood *Shady Tree* 185 We were like stunned mullets, as though awakened in the dead of night by an earthquake to find the walls falling down around us. **1968** S. Gore *Holy*

Smoke 52 And you just layin' around like a stunned mullet! What about gettin' off your spine. **1972** A. CHIPPER *Aussie Swearers Guide* 55 *Guernseyed* . . bodies . . lie there, not like logs, or giants fallen, but like *stunned mullet*. **1980** R. DAVIDSON *Tracks* 62 They turned to me like stunned mullets, Frankie's eyes popping out, Clive's downcast with guilt.

mullock /'mʌlək/, *n.* [Spec. use of Br. dial. *mullock* rubbish, refuse matter.]

1. a. Mining refuse.

1855 R. CARBONI *Eureka Stockade* 13 Crossing the holes, up to the knees in mullock, and loaded like a dromedary. **1869** M. CLARKE *Peripatetic Philosopher* 51 A blazing sun. The white and red heaps of mullock cropping up among the dusty dwarf-gums. **1873** W. THOMSON-GREGG *Desperate Character* I. 167 How is it that our 'mullock' doesn't look like any of the rest? . . Nothing but soft clay. **1881** G. WALCH *Vic.* 146 Great heaps of refuse soil, or 'mullock' somewhat disfigure the immediate neighbourhood. **1896** *Worker* (Sydney) 29 Aug. 4/1 All this was wheeled away as mullock and only the bottom stuff got washed. **1910** *Huon Times* (Franklin) 13 Apr. 4/1 Nothing had been done in the stope for about two years, and it was filled with mullock right up to the solid ground. **1928** R.M. MACDONALD *Opals & Gold* 29 Sufficient space has been dug out and the 'mullock' hauled to the surface. **1948** K.S. PRICHARD *Golden Miles* 73 Your mate fired last night, Ted. Two misses, so keep off the west wall. Y're breakin' too much bloody mullock. **1973** M.T. CLARK *Spark of Opal* (rev. ed.) 211 The mullock, or refuse, he hoists to the surface and discards. **1979** *Ecos* xxii. 22/3 Have you ever heard of mullock? It's waste rock from mining operations.

b. Comb. **mullock dump, heap.**

1925 *Smith's Weekly* (Sydney) 10 Jan. 23/7 Not all the **mullock** and gravel **dumps** marking the deserted mines in Victoria . . have been put to practical use. **1950** A.W. UPFIELD *Bachelors of Broken Hill* 35 Jimmy had imagined Broken Hill to be a mullock dump far beyond a deceitful mirage. **1978** D. STUART *Wedgetail View* 196 They crowded to the windows to see the headframes and the mullock dumps, the sands dumps, the smokestacks of the distant Golden Mile. **1859** *Colonial Mining Jrnl.* Feb. 88/3 It would be well always to prospect its value before it is thrown away in the **mullock heap.** **1892** *Bohemia* (Melbourne) 7 Jan. 10 As Mount Macedon to a mullock heap. **1914** M. HALL *Woman in Antipodes* 162 Ballarat . . roused itself, filled up the worked-out mines, removed the 'mullock-heaps', and generally healed the scars left by the diggers. **1960** E. O'CONNER *Irish Man* 150 What was left of the miners . . scratched about the mullock-heaps under the blazing sun. **1978** M. WALKER *Pioneer Crafts Early Aust.* 108 The heap of slate refuse known as a 'mullock heap'.

2. *fig.*

a. Rubbish; nonsense; 'muck'.

[N.Z. **1866** R. BURGESS Autobiogr. 127 (typescript) No b--y fear. I should know it was a lot of mullock they were telling for you are not like this Jew.] **1878** 'HUMANITY' *Sketches Chinese Character* 7 'A lot of *mullock*' . . is a gold fields phrase, and means, according to my views, anything of no use. **1891** *Bohemia* (Melbourne) 31 Dec. 14 Phillips filled rather more space than Horan, and, in addition, batted flukily but pluckily, and bowled cartloads of 'mullock'. **1908** *Truth* (Sydney) 28 June 1/6 A lot of mullock in the city dailies on 'How to go on the Land' would be more appropriately labelled, 'How to go Broke on the Soil'. **1919** E. DYSON *Hello, Soldier* 30 A bullet in me gizzard where I took it good and hard, A-dealin'-stoush 'n' mullock to the Prussian flamin' Guard. **1936** E. HARRINGTON *Boundary Bend* 40 She would land you in the mullock with a well-directed kick. **1965** H. PORTER *Cats of Venice* 139 What mullock has been unloaded on us this fair morn? **1981** P. RADLEY *Jack Rivers & Me* 172 Most of the men went to the Rugby union field to watch the Chadla Chickens make mullock of the still-pissed Boomeroo Bulls.

b. In the phr. **to poke mullock,** to mock; to deride.

1916 *Bostall Boshter* (Bostall Heath, England) 3 Apr. 1 After photographing . . and poking mullock at it. **1924** E.T. SHORLEY *Poetic Reflections* 17 You laugh at me, and jest and joke, And fun and mullock also poke. **1933** J. TRURAN *Where Plain Begins* 66 Silas . . was . . engaged in what he would have called 'pokin' mullock' at Crispin's daughter. **1957** V. PALMER *Rainbow-Bird* 35 D'you think I'm going to sit in that galley with . . the other blokes all poking mullock at me? **1973** J. MORRISON *Austral. by Choice* 8 Poking mullock at us because we won't go out over an empty hatch. **1981** D. STUART *I think I'll Live* 163 You're no Mister bloody Australia y'self . . so don't poke mullock at anyone for being a bit skinny.

mullock /'mʌlək/, *v.* [f. prec.]

1. *trans.* With **over:** to shear (sheep) in a rough and careless fashion; to perform (a task, etc.) in a slovenly manner.

1893 *Age* (Melbourne) 23 Sept. 14/4 No man could shear 321 sheep in eight hours, although . . he might do what we shearers call 'mullock over' that number. **1941** S.J. BAKER *Pop. Dict. Austral. Slang* 48 *To mullock over*, to work shoddily. **1965** J.S. GUNN *Terminol. Shearing Industry* ii. 5 *Mullock over*, to rush the work quickly and carelessly, thus turning out badly shorn sheep.

2. With **up**: to excavate mullock; to litter or block with mullock.

1940 I.L. IDRIESS *Lightning Ridge* 96 The owners had found their drives mullocked up, broken opal everywhere. **1941** D. O'CALLAGHAN *Long Life Reminisc.* 144, I had a narrow travelling way at each end of the timbers which I was mullocking up on. **1977** J. DOUGHTY *Gold in Blood* 243 In stoping to the surface on both ends we had mullocked up the shaft.

mullocker /'mʌləkə/. One who clears away the refuse in a mine.

1905 *Steele Rudd's Mag.* (Brisbane) Dec. 1073 A young clerk . . had an argument with a mullocker from the Lady Shenton. **1913** A. PRATT *Golden Kangaroo* 5 A crowd of miners, mullockers and truckers. **1950** G. FARWELL *Surf Music* 94 A big-shouldered mullocker stood in front of him. 'Where're you to, mate?' **1982** M. WALKER *Making Do* 84 What was taken out from underground and processed, the residue, had to be put back to fill it up again, and I was one of those that helped in that department, pushing the trucks. I was a mullocker.

mullocky /'mʌləki/, *a.*

1. Rubbishy: see quot. 1886.

1862 'W.T.G.' *Quite Colonial* (*c* 1948) 18 It is bottom, and a preciously mullocky looking one it is, too. **1886** H. FINCH-HATTON *Advance Aust.* (rev. ed.) 168 Having hit on the reef, if it is what is known as 'mullocky'—that is soft and rotten—the next thing is to take out a prospect from between the walls. **1894** W.H. BARKER *Gold Fields W.A.* 28 In the Yilgarn Gold Field . . the Southern Cross . . appears to possess . . three lines of true lodes—one white, one ferruginous, one mullocky. **1934** S.J. CASH *Prospecting for Gold* 50 If the sand be composed of quartz or of a mullocky nature.

2. In the collocation **mullocky leader,** see quot. 1944.

1882 W. SOWDEN *N.T. as it Is* 59 Those mullocky leaders are curious. **1914** *Bull. N.T.* x. 6 The Chinese miners are rather fond of working these mullocky leaders as no explosives are needed. **1944** M.J. O'REILLY *Bowyangs & Boomerangs* 37 Working what was known as a 'Mullocky leader'. That is a quartz leader running through soft, barren country. **1977** B. SCOTT *My Uncle Arch* 9 The stone carrying the gold was in little mullocky leaders . . and you had to shift tons of overburden to get a few hundredweight of stone.

mulloway /'mʌləweɪ/. Formerly also **mullaway.** [a. Yaralde *malowe*.] The large, edible fish *Argyrosomus hololepidotus*, occurring in marine and estuarine waters of Aust. See also BUTTERFISH, JEWFISH, KINGFISH.

1846 H.E.A. MEYER *Manners & Customs Aborigines Encounter Bay* 6 They use the spear at the Murray in catching the large fish, *Mallowe*. **1853** J. ALLEN *Jrnl. River Murray* 82 The mallaway, a species of cod, furnishes useful isinglass and good oil. **1871** *Austral. Town & Country Jrnl.* (Sydney) 22 Apr. 486/4 As much as three tons at a haul, consisting principally of mullaway, bream [etc.]. **1882** A. TOLMER *Reminisc.* I. 187, I accompanied . . Governor Grey . . to the mouth of the Murray, and . . came upon . . natives engaged in fishing for mullaway. **1906** D.G. STEAD *Fishes of Aust.* 114 The Jewfish . . at the mouth of the Murray the fishermen call it 'Mulloway', or 'Butterfish'. **1933** D. MACDONALD *Brooks of Morning* 180 Adelaide has called a particular fish of the Murray mouth, quite large enough for angling romance, a mulloway. If the mulloway . . ranges as far east as Port Phillip it becomes a kingfish. **1948** F.D. MARSHALL *Let's go Fishing* 76 One of the best table fish, the jewfish (. . mulloway) grows up to 120 pounds in weight. **1978** N. COLEMAN *Austral. Fisherman's Fish Guide* 84 A large schooling species, the mulloway may be found in a number of different situations.

mullygrub. [Prob. transf. use of Br. dial. *mullygrub* meal grub: see EDD *mullygrub-gurgin*.] A grub, esp. WITCHETTY 2.

1924 F.J. MILLS *Happy Days* 61 If fruit-trees are not sprayed at the correct time . . leaves will curl up (caused by a mullygrub shaped like a corkscrew). **1959** J. WRIGHT *Generations of Men* 28 A gin had gone over to look for mully-grubs in the bush. **1966** *Courier-Mail* (Brisbane) 26 Nov. 8/8 The woman . . had told him frequently to 'go and eat his mully grubs', and to 'go back to the bush where you came from'.

multy /'mʌlti/, *a. Obs.* [Shortened form of Parlyaree *multicattivo*, a. It. *molto cattivo* very bad: see Partridge *multee kertever*.] Bad; in poor condition; unpleasant; low.

1880 *Bulletin* (Sydney) 11 Sept. 8/1 The Franzini Variety Company, at St. George's Hall, Melbourne, did not fizzle; the houses were 'multy', and the shutters are up. **1903** *Ibid.* 11 Apr. 16/4 There's another cove lookin' a bit multy, so I s'pose he'll kill it. **1908** *Truth* (Sydney) 19 Apr. 10/5 The only fairies as she seen Were a multy kind of set. **1913** *Ibid.* 14 Sept. 9/5 (*heading*) Advertising agent's affair. *Multy doings at Manly.* **1914** *Ibid.* 6 Dec. 12/6 (*heading*) *Multy Morris.* A scurvy scoundrel.

mundic /'mʌndɪk/. Also **mundick.** [A Cornish miners' term: see OED.] Iron pyrites.

1834 C.O. BOOTH *Jrnl.* (1981) 179 Descended the new Shaft—crawled into the 'level'—the Mundick just above the second stratum of Coal lying in a bed of grey or dark Stone bind. **1858** *Colonial Mining Jrnl.* Nov. 40/3 The Old Man vein . . contains a quantity of mundic where cut in the levels, but little gold. **1880** J. BONWICK *Resources Qld.* 111 Quartz pits are often left when the mundic level is reached. **1889** *Braidwood Dispatch* 12 Oct. 2/2 A new mundic reef has been found in the alluvial working of the company. **1926** 'S. WESTLAW' *White Peril* 133 This brighter stuff is mundic, or new chum's gold; but here, and here—where it's dull red—that's all pure gold. **1935** M. & E. DURACK *All-About* (1940) 73 'Old man, we got the gold at last!' 'Mundick,' says the Boss from force of habit.

mundie /'mʌndi/. *Obs.* Also **mundy.** [Prob. a. Awabakal *mandi*.] See quot. 1847. Also **mundie-stone**.

1847 G.F. ANGAS *Savage Life & Scenes* II. 224 Mundie is a crystal, believed by the natives to be an excrement issuing from the Deity, and held sacred. **1851** J. HENDERSON *Excursions & Adventures N.S.W.* II. 157 The natives have charms which they carry about with them. . . These are bits of rock crystal, which they find on the mountains, and are called *mundy-stones*.

mundowie /mʌn'doʊi/. Chiefly *Austral. pidgin.* Also **mundoey, mundoie.** [a. Dharuk *mandawi*.] A foot; a footstep.

1822 A. CUNNINGHAM Table of Lang., *Foot*, mundoe. **1880** 'OLD HAND' *Experiences of Colonist* (ed. 2) i. 36 Uriah commenced . . by saying, 'You make alight jumbuck along here! You no make alight mundowie along with grass!' The only two words that the Australian savage could understand were 'jumbuck' and 'mundowie'—the former meaning sheep, and the latter foot. **1890** A.A. BOSWELL *Recoll. Some Austral. Blacks* 4 'Stockyard in mundowie' was found to mean that she had a splinter of wood in her foot. **1896** *Bulletin* (Sydney) 18 Apr. 27/1 The Botany dialect . . gave us 'mundowie', the word for leg, though widely used for the foot by the whites. **1909** *Ibid.* 16 Dec. 13/3 Chocking one of the wheels of bullock-dray with his big mundoeys. **1928** W. ROBERTSON *Coo-ee Talks* 167 There are also three mundoie (ghost) steps carved in a certain position. **1943** *Bulletin* (Sydney) 22 Dec. 12/3 That boong squatted, hams on heels, the toes of his mundowies gripping the ground. **1976** C.D. MILLS *Hobble Chains & Greenhide* 11 We saw tracks about a mile from the hole, and though the big, splayed 'mundoies' meant nothing to me, Pebble could read them like a printed page.

munga /ˈmʌŋgə/. Also **mungar, munger, mungey.** [Abbrev. of Br. slang *mungaree* food, f. It. *mangiare* to eat: see OEDS *mungaree* and also *munga, n.*[2]] In Services' speech: food.

1918 *Kia Ora Coo-ee* Oct. 14/3 I've enjoyed munger in a 'special' more than six course dinners in Cairo. **1920** *Aussie* (Sydney) Apr. 18/3 'What'll you have, Maisie?' . . 'A meat pie, please, Bob.' It was a little bit of heaven to see her put the mungar away. **1933** E.J. RULE *Jacka's Mob* 206 They had made a present of our 'mungey' to some Digger whom they'd never seen before. **1945** *Chocolate & Green* (Sydney) July 16 Seven say their record attendance is due to the 'Hungry Nine' hogging the 'Munga' and leaving them weak from malnutrition. **1960** L.H. EVERS *Make Way for Tomorrow* 177 Did you ever see him last on the queue when the munga was shared out? **1967** *Kings Cross Whisper* (Sydney) xxxvi. 4/2 *Munga*, food, from the Australian Aboriginal. **1970** R. BEILBY *No Medals for Aphrodite* 37 'Food.' Turk explained the soldier-Arabic 'mungaree', shortened Australian-wise to 'munga'. **1982** *Sydney Morning Herald* 27 Nov. 28/5 There were odd complaints about the food . . from mouths that nonetheless wrapped themselves gleefully around the free munga and booze.

mungite /ˈmʌŋgaɪt/. *W.A.* [a. Nyungar *maŋayj* a sweet substance, esp. the flower of the banksia.] The nectar-rich flowering spike, becoming a woody cone, of the BANKSIA; the plant itself.

1836 H.W. BUNBURY *Early Days W.A.* (1930) 80 At this season food was plentiful—both fish . . and 'Munghites' as they call the flower of the Banksia, from which they extract by suction a delicious juice resembling a mixture of honey and dew. **1841** G. GREY *Jrnls. Two Exped. N.-W. & W.A.* II. 298 If the land of any native is deficient in any particular article of food, such as, *by-yu, mungyte* (Banksia flowers), etc. he makes a point of visiting some neighbour, whose property is productive in this particular article. **1849** J.S. ROE *Rep. Exped. S.-Eastward Perth* 44 We felt another stage had been accomplished in our journey by the appearance of the 'Mūngart', or honey-bearing Banksia, so prized by the natives during its flowering season. **1916** E. & M.S. GREW *Rambles in Aust.* 17 The banksia . . looked as if a fir-cone had suddenly burst into bristling pink flowers; the hard cone of it is called by the natives a 'mungite', and is used to kindle fire. **1948** H.A. LINDSAY *Bushman's Handbk.* 79 It's a simple job if you can get the big banksia cones (mungites). **1979** E. SMITH *Saddle in Kitchen* 26 Grandpa had strange names for some things too—native names many of them. Banksias he called what sounded like 'mungites', though I've never heard the term used by anyone else.

mungo /ˈmʌŋgoʊ/. [Prob. a. Ngiyambaa *maŋgar* bark (canoe).] An Aboriginal bark canoe.

1847 G.F. ANGAS *Savage Life & Scenes* I. 219 The natives, in their canoes of bark (*mungo*). **1853** A. KINLOCH *Murray River* 13 We managed to upset a native canoe or 'mungo', propelled by a black and his 'lubra', or spouse. **1953** A. RUSSELL *Murray Walkabout* 89 The bark canoe, or 'mungo', the only float known to the Murray-Darling aborigines . . simply a sheet of bark stripped in one piece from a gum tree trunk and turned up a few inches at its ends and sides.

munjon /ˈmʌndʒən/. *W.A.* Also **mungus, munjong, murndong.** [a. Yinjibarndi *manjaŋ* stranger.] An Aboriginal who has had little contact with white society. Also *transf.*, an Aboriginal brought up in white society and unfamiliar with the traditional way of life.

1948 M. UREN *Glint of Gold* 250 The Munjons, the wild bush aboriginals. **1955** F. LANE *Patrol to Kimberleys* 13 Once in a while the munjons—they're the wild blacks who live in the bush—will raid a station to get themselves new lubras. **1964** H.M. BARKER *Camels & Outback* 112, I saw a young native man on his knees drinking from the sheep trough. That showed he was a *myall*, or 'munjon' as they say in the west; a more civilized black would have gone to the tank and drawn clean, cool water. **1966** S.J. BAKER *Austral. Lang.* (ed. 2) 325 A *munjong* (from the W.A. goldfields area) is a derogatory expression for any unsophisticated bush-Aboriginal—'He's a proper *munjong*!' **1970** *Matilda* (Winton Tourist Promotion Assoc.) 60 A thousand miles from the West they'd come, from the land where the 'munjons' ride. **1975** R. BEILBY *Brown Land Crying* 107 Ya a bit of a newchum ain'tcha? What we call a murndong. **1975** X. HERBERT *Poor Fellow my Country* 628 Anyone of them who could not ride a horse or was scared of a train or motor vehicle was considered a 'mungus' or a 'myall'. **1976** C.D. MILLS *Hobble Chains & Greenhide* 40, I was coming down from the top end one time . . and as we had a team of 'munjong' boys we were half-nightin' em. **1984** W.W. AMMON et al. *Working Lives* 42 There was nearly always work at the dead-end job of fencing . . waiting for the mugs, the munjongs and the new chums.

muntry /ˈmʌntri/. Now usu. in the pl. form **muntries,** constr. as sing. Formerly also **monterry, montry, muntree** and **muntri.** [a. Yaralde *mandari.*] The edible fruit of the prostrate shrub *Kunzea pomifera* (fam. Myrtaceae) of dry sandy soils and near-coastal w. Vic. and e. S.A.; the plant itself; *native apple* (a), see NATIVE *a.* 6 a. Also *attrib.*.

1847 G.F. ANGAS *Savage Life & Scenes* I. 65 Monterries, or native apples. This fruit is a little berry, the production of a running plant that grows in profusion upon the sand-hills. These berries are precisely like miniature apples, and have an aromatic flavour, which is not unpleasant. When the monterry is ripe, the natives disperse themselves over the sand-hills in search of them. **1893** S. NEWLAND *Paving Way* 137 Before leaving the beach . . he gathered a handful of *montries*, a small indigenous berry with the flavour of a sour apple. **1916** S. CONIGRAVE *Reminisc.* 44 Once a year we used to go over to the Peninsula to gather montrees—a fruit that grew on a creeper that ran across the sand, and really kept the sand from drifting. It was about the size of a blackcurrant, but had the smell of an apple, therefore it was called 'native apple'. 'Montree', I suppose, was the blacks' name for it. **1926** J.M. BLACK *Flora S.A.* iii. 405 The berries, called 'muntries' in Victoria, are used for making tarts. **1937** *Bulletin* (Sydney) 7 July 20/1 On swampy areas inland from the S.A. coast between Robe and Beachport grows a small creeping plant which bears heavy crops of a berry. . . The abos. knew it as 'muntry' berry. **1948** H.A. LINDSAY *Bushman's Handbk.* 54 *Muntrey or muntree*, small creeping ground plant, bearing a fruit exactly like a tiny apple in appearance, smell and flavour. Can be eaten raw but is better stewed. **1955** M. BUNDEY *My Land* 34 There is a berry called the muntri and with this you can make a lovely pie and tasty jam. **1975** A.B. & J.W. CRIBB *Wild Food in Aust.* 37 Muntries is a plant of dry sandy desert areas. **1984** E. WALLING *On Trail Austral. Wildflowers* 69 The grey-green and silvery pink sea-heath combines with Muntries (a creeping Kunzea) in the task of protecting and beautifying the ground.

munyeroo /mʌnjəˈru/. Also **munyeru.** [a. Diyari (and related languages) *manjaru.*] Either of two succulent plants of the fam. Portulacaceae having seeds and leaves used as food, orig. *Calandrinia balonensis* (see PARAKEELIA), and now usu. *pig weed* (see PIG *n.*[1]).

1885 *Trans. & Proc. R. Soc. S.A.* (1886) VIII. 27 *Claytonia Balonnensis*—This showy plant, called 'Munyeroo' by the aboriginals . . has a cluster of thick fleshy leaves, with a flower stem some six or more inches high, crowned with bright deep pink flowers as large as a shilling. **1896** B. SPENCER *Rep. Horn Sci. Exped. Central Aust.* IV. 56 *Claytonia balonnensis*. . . By the blacks of Alice Springs (Arunta) this seed is called 'Ing-witchika', which appears to be the real native name, though the term 'Munyeru', by which it is known to Europeans, is invariably understood. **1922** J. LEWIS *Fought & Won* 69 We found plenty of green feed in the bed of the creek, with munyeroo, which we boiled with meat, and it gave us a good vegetable in the form of spinach. **1936** C. CHEWINGS *Back in Stone Age* 4 The succulent plant, munyeroo . . yields quantities of edible seeds. **1963** O. RUHEN *Flockmaster* 57 He had appreciated the lilies and the parakeelia and the star-garlanded munyeroo as fodder indications. **1976** B. SCOTT *Compl. Bk. Austral. Folk Lore* 376 I've starved on yowah and munyeroo.

murawirrie, var. MURRAWIRRIE.

murlonga /mɜˈlɒŋgə/. Also **murlonger, myrnonga.** [Poss. a. Yolŋu sub-group *munaŋa* a white person.] A white man who sexually exploits Aboriginal women.

1912 *Bulletin* (Sydney) 15 Feb. 13/2 There is the much less widely known aboriginal term 'myrnonga'. The myrnonga is a person of more promiscuous habits [than the combo] who . . prowls with furtiveness when the moon is young. **1949** H.G. LAMOND *White Ears* 9 'Don' you talk 'bout my mother thataway!' Emma screamed. 'You combo-you! You murlonga!'. **1971** K. WILLEY *Boss Drover* 45 Combos, murlongers, or gin burglars.

murndong, var. MUNJON.

murnong /ˈmɜnɒŋ/. Also with much variety, as **mernong, mirr'n-yong, murnung, murrnong, myrnong.** [a. Wathawurung and Wuywurung *mirnaŋ.*] The edible tuber of the perennial herb *Microseris scapigera* (fam. Asteraceae) of temperate Aust.; the plant itself, bearing a yellow, dandelion-like flower-head. See also YAM.

1836 *Bent's News* (Hobart) 3 Sept. 3 Pigs . . feed well on the 'murnung', a root on which the natives here often subsist. **1837** P.L. BROWN *Clyde Co. Papers* 16 Aug. (1952) II. 91 Saw a woman digging murnong, a native root, about five miles from the scrub. **1845** C. GRIFFITH *Present State & Prospects Port Phillip* 148 Their principal food consists of roots, which they dig up, particularly the *murnong*—a plant with a flower like the dandelion. **1851** H. MELVILLE *Present State Aust.* 68 Mr Gellibrand . . almost lived upon the nutritious root, '*Mernong*', or native parsnip. **1859** D. BUNCE *Lang. Aborigines Vic.* p. xi, The whole of the tribes to form one great family, where they may adopt their primitive habits of . . digging for myrnong, burrowing for wombats and porcupines. **1862** G.T. LLOYD *Thirty-Three Yrs. Tas. & Vic.* 42 To revel in . . 'mernong', a saccharine root, baked in a roughly-constructed stone oven. **1878** R.B. SMYTH *Aborigines of Vic.* I. 49 *Mirr-n'yong*, a kind of white radish bearing a yellow flower, is dug up and eaten by the children and adults in all places where it grows. **1883** E.M. CURR *Recoll. Squatting Vic.* 81 The yam generally, and in some cases the myrnong, or native carrot, prevailing. **1922** C. DALEY *Early Squatting Days* 5 *Murnong* . . is about the size of the upper half of a small carrot, a milky juice exudes through the skin, and when roasted in the ashes it is palatable, and no doubt wholesome and nutritious. The Port Phillip tribes bake these roots in a hole in the ground when they half melt down into a sweet dark-coloured juice. **1942** E. ANDERSON *Squatter's Luck* 41 Radish-like 'mynong' root. **1961** M. KIDDLE *Men of Yesterday* 7 Opossums, which with murnong-roots and eels were the staple diet. **1965** *Austral. Encycl.* IX. 524 *Microseris scapigera* . . is called yam throughout Victoria. Its tuberous roots furnished one of the chief vegetable foods of many native tribes, those near Melbourne calling it *murrnong* (literally, 'the fingers of a hand', from the clusters of small finger-like tubers). **1983** J. FLOOD *Archeol. of Dreamtime* 202 The men could have existed on . . the region's one abundant plant food, the daisy yam or mirr'n-yong (*Microseris scapigera*).

murrawirrie /mʌrəˈwɪri/. Also **murawirrie.** [a. Arabana-Waŋgaŋuru *mara* hand + *wirri* throwing club.] A heavy boomerang used for striking at an opponent: see quot. 1879.

1879 *Native Tribes S.A.* 288 Murawirrie . . two-handed boomerang, from 6 to 14 ft. long, and 4 in. broad. **1931** A.W. UPFIELD *Sands of Windee* 108 Moongalliti, attired only in a loincloth, clutched a heavy murrawirrie in his left hand, and three or four wooden spears. **1965** —— *Lure of Bush* 70 The Central Australians employ the last two—the Kirras for throwing and the Murrawirrie for use as a sword.

Murray. [The name of a river in s.e. Aust.]

1. Used *attrib.* in Comb. **Murray scrub.**

1843 *S. Austral. Mag.* Jan. 129 The Murray scrub is well known. **1853** T.F. BRIDE *Lett. Victorian Pioneers* 20 Oct. (1898) 369 The plains are sometimes intersected by a belt of Murray scrub, running down to the very river. **1868** *Pasquin* (London) 11 Apr. 417 Daybreak in the Murray-scrub, with a pot of tea, a solemn pipe, and the discourses of Agamemnon to read undisturbed. **1890** J.I. WATTS *Family Life S.A.* 137 By the time he had got half way through the Murray scrub, he sank down under a bush exhausted, and poor Gog was at the point of death.

2. In the names of flora and fauna: **Murray catfish,** the fresh-water catfish *Tandanus tandanus*, a thickset, robust fish brown to olive-green above and paler below, formerly widespread in the Murray River; **cod,** the large, groper-like *Maccullochella peeli*, a mottled, greenish, fresh-water fish of the Murray-

Darling river system and elsewhere in Aust.; **cray-fish,** the large fresh-water crayfish *Euastacus armatus*; also **Murray River crayfish; grey,** a breed of grey, beef cattle (see quot. 1964); **lily** *obs.*, *Darling lily*, see DARLING; **magpie,** *magpie lark*, see MAGPIE *n.* 2; **perch,** any of several fresh-water fish of the Murray-Darling river system, incl. *golden perch* (see GOLDEN 3), and MACQUARIE PERCH; **pine,** any of several trees of the genus *Callitris* (fam. Cupressaceae), esp. *C. preissii* subsp. *murrayensis* of N.S.W., Vic., and S.A. and *white pine* (see WHITE *a.*[2] 1 a.); the close-grained, resinous wood of these trees; **red gum,** the tree *Eucalyptus camaldulensis* (see RED GUM 1); **smoker,** *yellow rosella*, see YELLOW 1.

1873 F. DE CASTELNAU *Edible Fishes Vic.* 15 The **Murray catfish** (*Copidoglanis Tandanus*) from the Murray river. It is a hideous-looking fish, but fit for the table. **1932** H. PRIEST *Call of Bush* 48 To what family the Murray catfish belongs I do not know. It is a most unappetising creature to find on the end of your line, having a scaleless, mud-brown skin, a most repulsive eye, and rather nasty-looking barbels, from which it derives its name, about its mouth. **1954** *Bulletin* (Sydney) 17 Nov. 12/1 Murray catfish . . is sold cut up and labelled 'Murray cutlets'. **1843** *S. Austral. News* (London) 15 Dec. 166/2 So plentiful are the **Murray cod** that the men at the station merely throw out their lines in the evening and the next morning they find them full. **1866** L. DE BEAUVOIR *Voyage round World* 14 Aug. (1870) I. 161 There soon lay on the banks a dozen fine freshwater cod, the Murray cod, some of them four feet long. **1872** A. MCFARLAND *Illawarra & Manaro* 97 The Manaro portion of the Murrumbidgee used to be well stocked with Murray cod. **1887** A. NICOLS *Wild Life & Adventure* 127 So this was the 'Murray cod' of which he had heard so much! The head closely resembled that of a perch, while the tail and two fins nearest to it were almost exactly those of a pike, and along the back was stretched a low dorsal fin quite out of character with the others. The capacious mouth was armed with formidable rows of teeth. **1898** *Tocsin* (Melbourne) 3 Feb. 3/2 The close season for Murray cod extends from July 1st to October 15th. **1906** D.G. STEAD *Fishes of Aust.* 99 The Murray Cod . . inhabits the whole of the immense Murray River system, from the limits of tidal influence in South Australia right up into Queensland. **1923** *Bulletin* (Sydney) 4 Oct. 24/4 The Murray cod (*Oligorus macquariensis*) is indigenous to Australia and is not found anywhere else. . . A Murray-Darling abo. name for the cod is 'murree', which suggests that the river may have got its name from the fish. **1944** C. BARRETT *Platypus* 59 The Platypus has but one enemy—the Murray cod, which . . is capable of swallowing a duckbill at a gulp. The giant perch (the Murray 'cod' actually is a perch), however, is a minor menace compared with the fish-traps set to catch the fish itself. **1960** E. NORTH *Nobody stops Me* 29, I found a place where they know how to grill Murray cod. **1985** *Sydney Morning Herald* 6 Feb. 6/2 Native fish in the Murray and Murrumbidgee rivers, including the murray cod, are declining drastically in numbers because their breeding cycles have been upset by dams and weirs. **1878** [**Murray crayfish**] R.B. SMYTH *Aborigines of Vic.* I. 205 The cray-fish commonly found in creeks and ponds—the large Murray one (*Astacoides serratus*), and the smaller (*A. quinquecarinatus*) afford excellent food. **1880** 'OLD HAND' *Experiences of Colonist* (ed. 2) i. 79 The antennae of a number of Murray crayfish. **1927** H.M. HALE *Crustaceans S.A.* i. 77 The flesh of the Murray Crayfish is esteemed as food. **1944** A. MARSHALL *These are my People* 28 He brought us a bag of Murray River crayfish. **1971** W.A. WINTER-IRVING *Beyond Bitumen* 123 Murray crayfish . . took hours to prepare but we thought them the best of all food. **1985** *Sydney Morning Herald* 6 Feb. 6/4 He said it was likely that the open season on catching murray crayfish (yabbies) would be closed soon. **1963** *Pastoral Rev. & Graziers' Rec.* 18 Oct. 1135 The unusual feature of this year's beef cattle section was the inclusion for the first time of two breeds, Galloways and **Murray Greys.** **1964** *Ibid.* 19 Oct. 1146 Murray Greys. 'Crossley', writing in *The Pastoral Review* of November 1955 . . is acknowledged to be the first to have placed on record a detailed chronicling of the origins of this interesting breed. On his way to the Melbourne Royal of that year he visited Thologolong, the upper-Murray River property of Mr Keith Sutherland. He also wrote at length about the intriguing new breed of 'Scottish Greys', as they were then known. Having been first recognized by Mr Keith Sutherland's father in 1914, the Murray grey is fast becoming a force to be reckoned with in the rough country in the southern half of Australia. **1975** L.A. POCKLEY *Handbk. for Jackeroos* 50 *Murray Grey*. . . They have a grey colour, are polled and have a very thick and meaty conformation. **1985** *Canberra Times* 13 Oct. 13/3 Murray grey cattle are quiet and easy to look after. . . The breed was begun beside the upper Murray in 1905 with a cross between a shorthorn cow and an Angus bull. **1847** G.F. ANGAS *Savage Life & Scenes* I. 62 We frequently met with that large and beautiful straw-coloured amarryllis, the **Murray lily**; the perfume of its blossoms frequently betraying its locality, at a considerable distance. **1851** G.P.R. JAMES *Convict* 288 They found the bank of a little stream gemmed with the Murray lily. **1896** B. SPENCER *Rep. Horn Sci. Exped. Central Aust.* I. 14 Along by the river flats the clusters of red fruit of the Darling or Murray lily were frequently seen. **1940** L.E. SHEARD *Austral. Youth among Desert Aborigines* (1964) 5 Remarking on the number of '**Murray Magpies**' about, the hotel proprietor told us that these birds have been proved by tagging to migrate to the north of Japan. **1953** A. RUSSELL *Murray Walkabout* 107 The magpie-lark, colloquially called the Murray magpie, or peewit, whose plaintive peewit-like notes are seldom silent on these river banks and backwaters. **1981** B.J. BROCK *Catharsis* 63 Murray magpie piping. **1880** G. WALCH *Vic.* 124 Our noble old 1,400-mile river, the Murray, well christened the Nile of Australia . . produces 'snags' and that finny monster, the Murray cod, together with his less bulky, equally flavourless congener, the **Murray perch.** **1897** 'OLD HOUSEKEEPER' *Austral. Plain Cookery* 46 Murray perch . . is considered a delicious fish by many, and is rather troublesome to clean. **1949** VESEY-FITZGERALD & LAMONTE *Game Fish* 306 The callop, or Murray perch, as it is sometimes called, grows to a length of 23 ins. and weighs up to 9 lbs. **1853** J. SHERER *Gold Finder Aust.* 188 A new tree, a species of pine, with foliage like a Scotch fir, but tapering like a larch or silver fir. Its cones are about the size of marbles. I believe it is the **Murray pine.** **1880** R. ROSE *Vic. Guide* 11 The Murray pine is a handsomely marked useful wood. **1898** A.S. MURRAY *Twelve Hundred Miles* 23 The land, in its original unimproved state, grew . . Murray pine. **1916** S.A. WHITE *In Far Northwest* 44 Among the rocks grew the shapely trees of the Murray pine (Callitris robusta). **1935** T. RAYMENT *Cluster of Bees* 19 The characteristic vegetation of the sand-hills is the altogether delightful Murray pine, and . . the needle-like foliage presents a strong contrast to the two Eucalypts. **1952** A.C.C. LOCK *Travels across Aust.* 174 We had our first glimpse of Murray pines, hardy, ragged-looking trees with olive-coloured foliage. **1972** ANDERSON & BLAKE *J.S. Neilson* 124 The blockies' homes, more than one built of Murray pine logs in cabin style. **1904** J.H. MAIDEN *Notes on Commercial Timbers N.S.W.* 17 **Murray red gum** (*Eucalyptus rostrata*) . . is the red gum *par excellence* of the States of New South Wales, Victoria and South Australia. **1953** A. RUSSELL *Murray Walkabout* 204 The Murray red gum, with its immense bole, trunk-like arms and hardwood character is a most valuable tree to the timber-getter. **1917** *Bulletin* (Sydney) 7 June 24/4 A very rare bird, the yellow parrot, or '**Murray smoker**' (*Platycercus flaveolus*), appears occasionally on the Monaro (N.S.W.) plains. **1954** C. BARRETT *Wild Life Aust. & New Guinea* 134 The yellow rosella, or 'Murray smoker' . . inhabits the interior of New South Wales, Victoria and South Australia. **1967** V.G.C. NORWOOD *Long Haul* 54 Murray Smokers—small, yellow rosella parrakeets—were active in the thickets.

3. Special Comb. **Murray whaler**: see WHALER *n.*[1] b.

4. In the phr. **on the Murray (cod),** rhyming slang for 'on the nod', on credit.

1967 *Kings Cross Whisper* (Sydney) xxxvi. 4/2 *Murray cod*, on the nod, to bet on credit, on the Murray. **1973** *Ibid.* clv. 16/1 There is even talk of changing pubs, and . . that is a very serious step to contemplate, specially as we can get on the murray when we are short. **1977** *Weekend Austral. Mag.* (Sydney) 23 July 1/6 A punter, well known in Sydney, who bets on 'the murray cod' (the nod) walked into City Tattersalls on Monday settling day carrying $240,000 cash in two suitcases.

Murray Valley. [The name of the valley of the *Murray* River (see MURRAY).] Used *attrib.* to designate **(a)** a severe form of encephalitis; **(b)** the mosquito-borne virus that causes it.

1951 *Med. Jrnl. Aust.* I. 526 A severe human encephalitis of virus origin spread diffusely along the Murray Valley during the early months of 1951. This has been provisionally referred to as Murray Valley encephalitis. **1974** *Sydney Morning Herald* 6 Feb. 7/2 Why some people develop encephalitis, or inflammation of the brain, after infection by Murray Valley virus, while the vast majority merely build antibodies to it in the blood, is one of the most puzzling aspects of the enigmatic disease. **1976** *Bulletin* (Sydney) 4 Dec. 85/2 Murray Valley encephalitis (often known as MVE) which caused consternation in wide areas of Australia in 1974, has now officially been termed 'Australian encephalitis'. **1978** *Ecos* xvi. 25 Four years ago an epidemic of Australian (or Murray Valley) encephalitis swept across the continent, covering an unprecedented area. Of the 58 cases reported, 12 died and the remaining 46 became so ill they had to receive treatment in hospital. **1985** *A.N.U. Reporter* (Canberra) 22 Nov. 1 In the last year attention has been focussed on Murray Valley encephalitis virus. Under certain climatic and ecological conditions the virus can break out in epidemics around Australia.

murri /'mʌri/. Also **murrey.** [a. Kamilaroi (and many Qld. languages) *mari* Aboriginal man, men in general.] An Aboriginal person; the Aboriginal people.

1884 J.B. GRIBBLE *Black but Comely* 125 It has been the misfortune of the Murri . . to be found in the way of European colonisation. **1896** *Bulletin* (Sydney) 18 Apr. 27/2 Crossing the range we enter the two great and widespread dialects of Kamilroi and 'Wiradhuri'. . . Here we have the generic word 'murri' (murree) for all blacks. **1918** *Ibid.* 27 June 22/3 The ancient gin was chuckling over reminiscences of Greenvale station . . particularly of a murri who came in from the bush in search of tobacco. **1930** K.G. TAYLOR *Pick & Duffers* 49 'I bet it's someone dressed up to frighten the blacks.' 'No fear; murreys never come to Yeller Cap in the moon.' **1962** *Overland* xxiv. 11 The whites roared and whistled. . . The murris were silent. **1978** M. KAMIEN *Dark People of Bourke* 5 A 'Murrie' (sometimes spelt Murree) is the word for man in the Wiradjuri language. It is now widely used by New South Wales Aborigines as a collective term for all Aborigines. **1978** K. GARVEY *Tales of my Uncle Harry* 19 That little murri was a terror to go on walkabout. **1983** *Sydney Morning Herald* 14 Feb. 7/8 There are two Aboriginal words for the races in Moree. One is 'murri', an Aboriginal word for themselves, which is quite acceptable.

murrillo /mə'rɪloʊ/. *Obs.* Also **murilla.** [Prob. f. a N.S.W. Aboriginal language.] See quot. 1881. Also *attrib.*

1881 *Jrnl. & Proc. R. Soc. N.S.W.* XV. 43 A conglomerate composed chiefly of waterworn quartz pebbles, called on the Barwon and Narran murrillo, but not known by this name in other parts of the country where the conglomerate is found. On making inquiries among the blacks I found that in their language murrillo means ant-hill. . . These ant-hills are nearly always built on the highest ground in that part of the Colony, to avoid floods, and as the highest ground is generally that which is composed of the quartz conglomerate it is easy to understand how the word which first meant ant-hill came also to mean the ridges on which the ant-hills are found. **1915** T. SKEYHILL *Soldier-Songs from Anzac* 13 By yarran clumps and coolabah, and up murilla ridges.

murrnong, var. MURNONG.

Murrumbidgee /mʌrəm'bɪdʒi/, *attrib.* and *n.* [The name of a river in s. N.S.W.]

A. Used *attrib.* in Special Comb. **Murrumbidgee blanket,** see quot. 1926 and WAGGA; **camper,** *Murrumbidgee whaler*, see WHALER *n.*[1] b.; **jam,** see quot. 1901; **pine,** the tree *Callitris glaucophylla* (see *white pine* WHITE *a.*[2] 1 a.), and poss. other trees of the genus *Callitris*; **rug,** see quot. 1924; **whaler, whaling** *vbl. n.*, see WHALER *n.*[1] b.

1906 *Bulletin* (Sydney) 26 July 16/2 *Re* Wagga rugs and **Murrumbidgee blankets** . . the latter is a bare bag, split open. **1926** *Aussie* (Sydney) Aug. 50/1 The 'Murrumbidgee blanket' . . was a wheat bag split down the seams, and used as a quilt. **1936** *Bulletin* (Sydney) 19 Aug. 21/1 You rarely see . . a Murrumbidgee blanket in a swag these days. **1906** *Ibid.* 5 July 17/1 Swears they'll join some push o' rampers or some **Murrumbidgee campers.** **1914** *Ibid.* 12 Mar. 22/1 I'm a Murrumbidgee camper who can knock out beef and damper. **1901** *Ibid.* 14 Sept. 16/4 '**Murrumbidgee jam**' consists of brown sugar muddled up with cold tea. **1920** *Ibid.* 24 June 22/3 'Murrumbidgee jam'—brown sugar made into a thick paste by mixing it with cold tea . . was also well known as Whalers' Delight. **1943** S.J. BAKER *Pop. Dict. Austral. Slang* (ed. 3) 52 *Murrumbidgee jam*, brown sugar moistened with cold tea and spread on damper. **1834** G. BENNETT *Wanderings N.S.W.* I. 263 Large quantities of a species of Callitrys, called the '**Murrumbidgee pine**' by the colonists, from having been seen first on the hills in the vicinity of that river. **1904** *Proc. Linnean Soc. N.S.W.* XXIX. 686 During the first 10 miles the only trees noticed . . were . . *Callitris robusta* . . White or Murrumbidgee Pine. **1948** R. RAVEN-HART *Canoe in Aust.* 69 The Murrumbidgee pine, a cypress-pine. **1924** *Smith's Weekly* (Sydney) 24 May 23/6 The . . **Murrumbidgee rug** . . is . . a split bag . . with an old woollen blanket that has become too thin to keep out the cold, sewn on for lining. **1941** *Bulletin* (Sydney) 7 May 16/1 If blanket prices keep on soaring quite a few Australians will be getting back to the wagga or Murrumbidgee rug.

B. *n.* A game of chance played with dice, resembling craps. Also *attrib.*

1917 *Bk. of Ballarat* 41 Producing a dice-box, he invites all and sundry to 'have a go at the good old game of Murrumbidgee'. **1917** C.L. DREW *Reminisc. D. Gilbert* 34 Cards (mostly 'poker') were a constant source of revenue, while 'Murrumbidgee' helped to fill in the idle hours occasionally. **1941** D. O'CALLAGHAN *Long Life Reminisc.* 5 He experienced . . the sly-grog shops and the two-up and Murrumbidgee rings. **1982** P. ADAM SMITH *Shearers* 280 These men remember the big tin shed on the banks of the Thompson River where they broke down their cut-out cheque playing local variants of Crap called Yankee Grab, Murrumbidgee and Sevens.

murry /ˈmʌri/, *adv. Austral. pidgin. Obs.* [a. Dharuk *mari.*] Very. Also as *adj.*, great.

[**1793** W. TENCH *Compl. Acct. Settlement* 65 They called him *Mùr-ree Mùl-la* (a large strong man).] **1803** J. GRANT *Narr. Voyage N.S.W.* 90 You know me *murrey jarrin*, that is *much afraid*. **1818** J. HOLT *Mem.* (1838) II. 150 They say . . that there is a *murry* devil, of whom they are very much afraid. **1827** P. CUNNINGHAM *Two Yrs. in N.S.W.* II. 19 Murry boodgeree (very good), massa, *'pose he rain.* **1831** *Sydney Monitor* 5 Jan. 3/1 Two Aborigines . . charged with being *murry groggy*, in which state they were consigned to the watchhouse by a *countryman.* **1847** G.F. ANGAS *Savage Life & Scenes* II. 272 To convey an idea of remote antiquity, they . . say 'Murrey-murrey-*murrey*-long time ago'. **1860** G. BENNETT *Gatherings of Naturalist* 132 'Murry budgeree patta' (very good to eat). **1878** R.B. SMYTH *Aborigines of Vic.* I. 161 They merely told me . . that Henry and the other men were 'murry stupid' to act as they did.

mush. Also **moosh.** [Spec. use of U.S. *mush* a kind of porridge: see OED *sb.* 1.] Gaol food, esp. porridge.

1945 S.J. BAKER *Austral. Lang.* 141 Jail food is *moosh.* **1950** *Austral. Police Jrnl.* Apr. 116 *Moosh*, gaol porridge. **1967** B.K. BURTON *Teach them no More* 17, I knew an old lagger once. . . He made little statues out of his mush. Didn't eat breakfast for years. **1967** *Kings Cross Whisper* (Sydney) xxxvi. 4/2 *Mush*, pronounced moosh, prison porridge. **1979** L. NEWCOMBE *Inside Out* 25 'What's mush?' I asked. . . 'Breakfast, kid,' said George. 'A dixie full of lumpy, gluey, weevilled wheat.'

mushy, *a.* [Spec. use of *mushy* soft, pulpy.] Of wool: yielding a high percentage of waste (see quot. 1951).

1901 *Bulletin* (Sydney) 12 Oct. 16/3 'Strong' wool is fashionable now because . . in a hot climate it is not nearly so liable to become 'mushy' or 'wasty' as 'fine'. **1921** L.G. JONES *Flockmaster's Companion* 77 *Mushy* means a wasty wool, a wool that gives a large percentage of noil (waste). . . Such wool is mostly found on the backs, or in wool from a hot, dry, plain country. **1945** S.J. BAKER *Austral. Lang.* 67 *Mushy, open, frizzy, perished* (used of a fleece). **1951** *Concerning Wool* (Austral. Wool Board) 102 *Mushy*, wool which is lacking character, open, badly weathered, and very wasty or noily.

music stick. CLAP STICK.

1944 *Coast to Coast 1943* 1 From his left hung a long bag of banyan-cord containing his big painted dijeridoo and music-sticks. **1962** C. GYE *Cockney & Crocodile* 87 The chant changed from rhythm to rhythm always accompanied by the music sticks and always in perfect time. **1979** A. WELLS *Forests are their Temples* 45 The old man, seated on the ground, began to clap his music-sticks for quietness. Then verse by verse he told the story while the clap-sticks marked each quiet pause between. **1981** D. LEVITT *Plants & People* 21 Boomerangs were clapped together as 'music-sticks' during corroborees.

musk. [Transf. use of *musk* odoriferous glandular secretion of the male musk-deer.]

1. The small tree or tall shrub *Olearia argophylla* (fam. Asteraceae) of Tas., Vic., and s.e. N.S.W., the leaves of which are silvery underneath and have a musky aroma; the wood of the tree. Also **musk tree, muskwood.**

1827 H. HELLYER Diary 5 July, Thickly wooded with . . musk and Dogwood. **1835** *Hobart Town Almanack* 68 *Aster argophyllus.* Musk tree. . . This beautiful shrub, peculiar to Van Diemen's land, is already common in our gardens and shrubberies about Hobart-town, to which it is a great ornament. The light green oval leaves are highly odoriferous in a warm day. **1867** *Colonial Monthly* Dec. 248 The musk, with its rich green leaves lined with downy white. **1880** R. ROWE *Roughing It* 11 He had to cross a lonely ridge, covered with evergreen beeches and musk-trees. **1904** J.H. MAIDEN *Notes on Commercial Timbers N.S.W.* 28 Muskwood (*Olearia argophylla*) . . requires the most careful seasoning, otherwise it warps and twists very much. **1973** D. WOLFE *Brass Kangaroo* 195 A dense under-forest of blackwoods, hazel, musk and other mountain species struggled towards the dim light above. **1985** *Mt. Field Nat. Park* (Tas. Nat. Parks & Wildlife Service), Beneath the towering gums, native musk (*Olearia argophylla*) and the occasional myrtle (*Nothofagus cunninghamii*) grow, forming a 'mixed forest'.

2. Special Comb. **musk duck,** the brown and black duck *Biziura lobata* of s. Aust. incl. Tas., the male of which has a large, pendulous lobe under the bill and a musky odour; **lorikeet** (formerly **parakeet**), the lorikeet *Glossopsitta concinna* of s.e. Aust. incl. Tas., having bright green plumage with a red face stripe.

1805 Banks Papers 7 Jan. XX. 13 Wild Ducks several kinds, a large Bird which I think is new from the very strong smell it has of Musk they have here named it the **Musk Duck.** **1836** J.F. O'CONNELL *Residence Eleven Yrs. New Holland* 92 The *musk duck* is one of the freaks of nature peculiar to New Holland. **1861** 'OLD BUSHMAN' *Bush Wanderings* 84 The *Musk Duck*, so called from the strong musky scent peculiar to the male, especially in the breeding season, is a singularly ugly bird. **1888** 'R. BOLDREWOOD' *Robbery under Arms* (1937) 1 Swim like a musk-duck, and track like a Myall blackfellow. **1940** *Bulletin* (Sydney) 17 Jan. 16/3, I give the bell jointly to the musk duck, the blue-billed duck and the little 'bob-down diver' as the champion feathered submarines. **1968** R. HILL *Bush Quest* 38 Close by the bank a huge old male musk duck wallowed low in the water. **1974** J. BYRNE *Duck Hunting Aust. & N.Z.* 192 The Musk Duck is found in Australia in deep swamps with heavy cover. It makes a queer 'plonking' sound which has caused much speculation. **1843** [**musk lorikeet**] J. GOULD *Birds of Aust.* (1848) V. Pl. 52, In the more southern country of Van Diemen's Land . . it is known by the name of the Musk Parrakeet, from the peculiar odour of the bird. **1889** *Proc. Linnean Soc. N.S.W.* IV. 418 *Trichoglossus concinnus* . . known as 'Green-leek' and 'Musk-paroquet'. **1903** *Emu* II. 166 Musk Lorikeet (*Glossopsittacus concinnus*)—Plentiful enough at times. **1932** H. PRIEST *Call of Bush* 164 The Musk Lorikeet, when not in motion, with his little touches of red and yellow 'matches' his surroundings perfectly. **1969** J.M. FORSHAW *Austral. Parrots* 35 The Musk Lorikeet derives its name from a musky odour that is said to be associated with it.

muskwood.

1. The rainforest tree *Alangium villosum* (fam. Alangiaceae) of e. Qld. and N.S.W.; the wood of the tree. Also **musk tree.**

1880 J. BONWICK *Resources Qld.* 82 The Musk-tree, *Marlea*, though of bright yellow wood, is black at the centre. **1889** J.H. MAIDEN *Useful Native Plants Aust.* 568 'Musk Tree' . . wood . . is close in the grain, has a musk-like scent. **1906** *Proc. Linnean Soc. N.S.W.* XXXI. 374 There is only one genus and species (*Marlea vitiensis* . .) of *Cornaceae* known in Australia, and this . . yields a very good timber, which is known locally as 'Muskwood'. **1932** R.H. ANDERSON *Trees of N.S.W.* 169 Muskwood (*Marlea vitiensis*) occurs as a small to medium-sized tree northwards from the Clarence. **1984** *Flora Aust.* XXII. 11 *Allangium villosum* . . tree to 9 m. . . Muskwood.

2. See MUSK 1.

muso /ˈmjuzoʊ/. [f. *mus(ician* + -O.] A musician.

1967 *Kings Cross Whisper* (Sydney) xxxix. 9/1 *Musos blow cold.* Members of the Sydney symphony orchestra will work to rule. **1969** *Telegraph* (Brisbane) 26 July 5/2 I'm really super anti-narcotics. The musos get carried away. They make mistakes. **1977** K. GILBERT *Living Black* 162, I used to be a muso and a hustler from the city but I'm a tribal man too.

mustard. Used *attrib.* in Special Comb. **mustard gold,** gold in extremely fine particles; **tree** (or **bush**), any of several plants, esp. the almost-leafless shrub or small tree *Apophyllum anomalum* (fam. Capparaceae) of N.S.W. and Qld., and the HORSERADISH TREE.

[N.Z. **1912** N.Z. Geol. Survey Bull. No. 15 New Ser. 110 Some of these small sulphide patches showed '**mustard gold**'.] **1932** I.L. IDRIESS *Prospecting for Gold* 57 Black sands on the sea beach have been very rich with 'mustard gold'. **1939** —— *Cyaniding for Gold* 198 Practically the only gold this cloth fails to collect is 'mustard' gold. **1977** J. DOUGHTY *Gold in Blood* 180 As one loams closer to the point of contact the samples become richer and the gold finer, until it is soft as mustard or flour, and is known as 'mustard gold'. **1898** [**mustard tree**] D.W. CARNEGIE *Spinifex & Sand* 179 Little clumps of what is locally termed 'mustard bush', so named from the strong flavour of the leaf. **1933** *Bulletin* (Sydney) 7 June 25/2 Another hardy northwesterner is the mustard bush. It is of dwarf habit, with a dense growth of leaves relished by sheep. **1956** GARDNER & BENNETTS *Toxic Plants W.A.* 26 The native poplar . . also known as the mustard tree . . contains a mustard oil. **1965** *Austral. Encycl.* II. 263 The mustard-bush or mustard-tree (*Apophyllum anomalum*) . . is an inland species whose young shoots have a somewhat mustard-like flavour.

muster, *n.* [Spec. use of *muster* an assembly of soldiers, etc., for inspection: see OED(S *sb.*[1] 3 and *v.*[1] 2.]

1. *Hist.* **a.** A routine assembling of convicts in order to ascertain that all are present. **b.** An assembly of the population of a district, Colony, etc., or a specified sector thereof, for the purpose of taking a census; a census.

1788 J. WHITE *Jrnl. Voyage N.S.W.* 5 Feb. (1790) 124 On a muster of the convicts this morning, some were found to be missing, and supposed to have gone to Botany Bay. **1804** *HRA* (1915) 1st Ser. V. 9, I have the honour to transmit the result of the free people and convicts' muster. **1807** *Ibid.* (1916) 1st Ser. VI. 147 By the result of the Muster taken in August last . . it will be seen that upwards of Thirteen Thousand Acres were cultivated. **1822** J.T. BIGGE *Rep. State Colony N.S.W.* 14 The muster of 150 convicts . . occupies the secretary from five to seven hours. **1826** *Monitor* (Sydney) 24 Nov. 218/2 We are happy to find the plan of compelling the colonists to appear personally at muster is about to be abandoned. **1831** *Acct. Colony Van Diemen's Land* 221 Persons holding Tickets of Leave are required to attend a monthly muster at the Police office of the district in which they reside. **1831** *HRA* (1923) 1st Ser. XVI. 418 No Muster of them having been received in this Country since the year 1825. **1837** *Colonist* (Sydney) 9 Feb. 45/1 The results of the Census taken last year . . have at length been officially laid before the public; and we now propose to examine them . . and compare them with those of former musters. **1838** *Cornwall Chron.* (Launceston) 29 Sept. 2 Two ticket-of-leave men, were summonsed for not attending church muster. **1840** *Tasmanian Weekly Dispatch* (Hobart) 10 July 7/3 A number of ticket-of-leave men were . . dealt with . . for missing church muster. **1843** C. ROWCROFT *Tales of Colonies* (1858) 220 We knew that if we were not present at muster, the officer would send to look after us. **1871** M. CLARKE *Old Tales of Young Country* 89 The morning after the *Woodman* arrived in Hobart, the usual muster of prisoners took place.

2. *transf.* The gathering together of (freq. widely dispersed) livestock in one place for the purpose of branding, counting, etc.

[N.Z. **1841** S. REVANS Lett. I. 90 (OEDS), I am not yet confident of the mode in which flock and stock musters will be dealt with by the natives.] **1844** Macarthur Papers LXII. 106, I hope this year we shall have a great increase to this muster, as the Ewes will lamb in September next. **1845** *Southern Queen* (Sydney) 69/2 *Cattle 'Muster'.* Once in two or three months, it is necessary to 'muster' the cattle, in order to see what casualties have occurred during the period they have been running wild. **1852** G.C. MUNDY *Our Antipodes* I. 314 The riding after cattle in the bush, for the purpose of driving them in or collecting them for muster, is very hard and sometimes dangerous work. **1854** W. HOWITT *Boy's Adventures* 141 The herds had been for some days gathered from their different beats, for a muster. **1870** C.H. ALLEN *Visit to Qld.* 174 'Mustering' . . consists in driving all the cattle from their particular run to a station and placing them in the immensely strong stockyards . . where they are all inspected and counted. . . A muster is to a squatter what stock-taking is to a merchant. **1888** 'R. BOLDREWOOD' *Robbery under Arms* (1937) 88 The stockmen hardly came out till the autumn musters. **1926** A.A.B. APSLEY *Amateur Settlers* 115 A 'muster' in many ways is like a miniature Rodeo. **1937** *Bulletin* (Sydney) 21 July 21/4 Just when the annual muster had started his best stock boy, 'Apricot', wanted to go on an extended walkabout. **1956** T. RONAN *Moleskin Midas* 74 Yates volunteered to tail right through the muster with Wilmot Lake for offsider.

3. In the collocation **general muster.**

a. *Hist.* MUSTER *n.* 1 b.

***c* 1795** G. BARRINGTON *Voyage to Botany Bay* 51 In the morning a general muster took place. **1801** *HRA* (1915) 1st Ser. III. 257 A general *muster* of all the male prisoners off and on the stores . . will be taken at Hawkesbury, Parramatta and Sydney. **1804** *Sydney Gaz.* 15 July, *A General Muster* of Settlers, and People holding Ground by Grant, Lease or Hire, will be taken by the *Governor*. **1814** *Van Diemen's Land Gaz.* 20 Aug., The Lieut. Governor is pleased to direct, that a General Muster of the whole of the Inhabitants (Civil and Military excepted) shall take place at the several Settlements. **1837** *HRA* (1923) 1st Ser. XIX. 113 The last General Muster taken in N.S. Wales was in Decr. 1828. **1842** *Austral. & N.Z. Monthly Mag.* 109 The agent will have a general muster of the immigrants, and ascertain the name, age, and . . trade of each. **1845** R. COBBOLD *Hist. M. Catchpole* III. 165, I have no government work to do; nor has the officer of government anything to do with me. When there is a general muster of the convicts, then only shall I have to appear. **1850** *Irish Exile* (Hobart) 29 June 6/4 The woman was discharged to the service of Government, her ticket-of-leave being revoked, because she did not attend the last general muster.

b. A muster of all stock on a property.

[N.Z. **1892** W.E. SWANTON *Notes on N.Z.* 97 There is the general muster, which means the rounding up and bringing in of all the sheep, good or bad, on the 'run'.] **1927** A. CROMBIE *After Sixty Yrs.* 41 Arranged for a general muster of their herd. **1931** *Bulletin* (Sydney) 29 July 20/4 On the big cattle stations of western Queensland . . a general muster on such occasions as the sale of the run is necessary.

4. Special Comb. *Hist.* **muster bell,** a bell which is rung to summon convicts (later prisoners) to an assembly; **book,** a register of the population of a Colony; a register of the names, etc., of convicts; **clerk,** a clerk employed in keeping the record of a census; **day,** a day appointed for a census; a day on which livestock are mustered; **ground,** a place at which a muster is held; **master,** an official responsible for keeping a *muster-roll*; **-roll,** a register of convicts (see quot. 1822); **station,** the office in which a *muster-roll* is kept; **yard,** *muster ground*; an enclosure into which livestock are mustered.

1846 L.W. MILLER *Notes of Exile Van Dieman's Land* 263 At six o'clock the **muster bell** rang, and about twelve hundred men answered their names, took their place in their respective gangs, and under the charge of overseers marched out of the barracks to their daily labour. **1973** R. HALL *Poems from Prison* 33 A muster bell hangs from a wrought iron frame where a warder parades on the square. **1826** *Colonial Times* (Hobart) 6 May, To this Officer also the General Muster of the Colony will be entrusted. He will have charge . . of the **Muster Books.** **1849** T. ROGERS *Corresp. relating to Dismissal* 100 He had the muster-book in his hand calling the names. **1830** *Sydney Monitor* 10 Mar. 3/2 Alexander Still, Esq. late principal **muster-clerk.** **1833** *HRA* (1923) 1st Ser. XVII. 18 Some one similar to that called the 'Muster Clerk' in this Colony. **1844** *Colonial Times* (Hobart) 9 Nov., A number of ticket-of-leave men have been variously dealt with for their accustomed jollification on **muster day.** **1849** A. HARRIS *Emigrant Family* (1967) 91 To keep an eye on the gathering in the stockyard when the next muster-day came. **1852** G.B. EARP *Gold Colonies Aust.* 120 His repugnance to muster-days is scarcely to be wondered at. **1848** J. SYME *Nine Yrs. Van Diemen's Land* 277 The whole gang . . hear prayers read on the **muster-ground** morning and evening. **1932** W. RADCLIFFE *Port Arthur Guide* 27 The commandant sentenced the whole of the boys—about 400—to three months on the muster ground. As soon as these boys came from labour—morning, noon, and evening (Sundays excepted)—they were ranked up, two and three deep, and were made to stand erect until their meals were ready. **1827** *HRA* (1922) 3rd Ser. V. 766, I have . . appointed Mr Josiah Spode to be **Muster Master.** **1830** *Ibid.* 1st Ser. XV. 766 A Superintendent of Convicts, an Officer called the 'Muster Master'. **1839** *Tasmanian* (Hobart) 11 Jan. 11/4 Assistant Police Magistrate and Muster Master at Hobart Town. **1883** 'ONE WHO WAS THERE' *Prison Sketches* 8 After dinner is over and they have answered to their names, read by the muster-master, they adjourn to the yard to enjoy a smoke. **1892** 'P. WARUNG' *Tales Convict System* 7 'Damn it!' said the Muster-Master at last, 'we are losing time.' **1802** *N.S.W. Gen. Orders* 22 Oct. (1806) 8 The **Muster Rolls** are to continue the same as when delivered to the *Governor* by Captain Balmain. **1822** J.T. BIGGE *Rep. State Colony N.S.W.* 15 The lieutenant-governor's secretary proceeds on board the convict ships, attended by the lieutenant-governor's clerk, and makes a list or muster roll of the convicts, describing the number, name, time and place of trial, their sentences, age, native place, trade, description of person and character. **1848** C. COZENS *Adventures of Guardsman* 255 When the muster-roll was called at five o'clock, the three absentees were of course not forthcoming, and a general search ensued. **1864** *Sydney Punch* 11 June 17/2 No muster-roll can mark the whole Of those that perish truly, fully. **1820** *Sydney Gaz.* 19 Sept., It is further ordered and directed that the Clerk of the General Muster do furnish to the Principal or Senior Magistrate at each **Muster Station,** a suitable Book and Forms for the taking the said Musters. **1892** 'P. WARUNG' *Tales Convict System* 2 The building is the gaol . . of Oatlands, a small township in the midlands of Van Diemen's Land, which has gradually grown up round a convict 'muster-station', established by Governor Davey. **1845** *Port Phillip Gaz.* 23 July 3 A good . . cottage, with . . stock and **muster yards** for 1500 head of cattle. **1892** *Bulletin* (Sydney) 7 May 21/4 The System sent a masked man into the muster-yard of the ironed men.

5. *fig.* With distinguishing first element: **tarpaulin muster** [spec. use of nautical slang *tarpaulin muster* a collection of money (see OEDS *tarpaulin, sb.* 4)], **(a)** the collecting of a pool of money, to be used either to buy drinks for the contributors or to provide assistance to some other person or cause (see quot. 1960); **(b)** *transf.*, see quot. 1945. Also **blanket, calico, canvas, tambaroora muster.**

1897 *Bulletin* (Sydney) 18 Dec. (Red Page), The essence of a present-day tambaroora is a sweep for the purchase of drinks—frequently on the principle that more liquor can be purchased wholesale for 1s. 6d. than six thirsty people can buy for 3d. each. Hence 'tambaroora muster', when the droughty party musters all the coin it's possessed of, and one individual goes and bargains for the beer. **1904** *Sporting News* (Launceston) 27 Aug. 2/8 Then raked through all our pockets, 'mongst tobacco, string, and grease; Till by tarpaulin muster, we raised just a drink a piece. **1904** E.S. EMERSON *Shanty Entertainment* (1910) 100 There was a loud outcry for Micky the Drover, who either had to subscribe to the tarpaulin muster or shout. **1936** L. FOX *Depression Down Under* (1977) 17 Knowing his plight, friends made a 'tarpaulin muster' and paid the fine for him. **1945** E. GEORGE *Two at Daly Waters* 102 As she had not brought a town outfit Daly Waters had what we call in the bush a tarpaulin muster (the loan of everybody's best clothes). **1960** *Bulletin* (Sydney) 30 Nov. 18/2 A calico-muster . . dates from the time when shearers and other casual bush-workers all had swags usually with calico or tarpaulin covers. At night a swag-cover would be spread on the ground for a table, and the shearers would sit around . . and gamble against their earnings. When cut-out came, a calico-muster or, more commonly, tarpaulin-muster, might be held for the benefit of the hospital . . or any other suitable object of charity; that is, the swag-cover was spread as usual, and contributions were thrown into it. **1964** K. WILLEY *Eaters of Lotus* 45 He leapt off the bunk and broke both his toes. Everyone thought that was very humorous, so they held a blanket muster and sent him off to hospital in an aeroplane. **1965** *Mount Isa Mail* 16 Nov. 2/1 Claimed his department colleagues were to take up a canvas muster to provide him with sufficient money to survive. **1976** *Bronze Swagman Bk. Bush Verse* 67 The cook took 'round the billy can for a tarpaulin muster. **1980** *N.S.W. Parl. Papers* (1981) 3rd Sess. IV. 1883, I did a tarpaulin muster and pulled in a bit of money from certain Aborigines.

muster, *v.* [As prec.]

1. *Hist.*

a. *trans.* To assemble (convicts) for counting, inspecting, etc.; to take a census of (the population, or a sector thereof).

1789 J. HUNTER *Hist. Jrnl. Trans. Port Jackson* (1793) 361, I gave orders for the convicts to be mustered in their huts three times every night. **1803** *Sydney Gaz.* 3 July, Every Prisoner Victualled from the Public Stores at Sydney will be Mustered at Government House on Friday Morning next. **1816** *Hobart Town Gaz.* 16 Nov., The Lieutenant Governor will Muster the Settlers, Prisoners, and other Persons resident in the District of Pitt Water. **1826** *Monitor* (Sydney) 24 Nov. 218/2 After being mustered, the gentlemen of the colony were invited by His Excellency to retire to government-house and take lunch. **1835** *Cornwall Chron.* (Launceston) 20 June 1 Muster the men who justly enjoy tickets-of-leave, every Sunday morning, and march them to church as the chain gangs are marched, and the indulgence will lose its virtue. **1844** *Dispatch* (Sydney) 13 Apr. 2/3 This afternoon, the convict mechanics employed in the various colonial departments will be mustered, and their trades ascertained. **1850** *Irish Exile* (Hobart) 9 Mar. 6/3 Witness . . mustered the gangs at one, and at half-past eight in the evening, when the prisoner was not present. **1883** 'ONE WHO WAS THERE' *Prison Sketches* 12 After breakfast the prisoners are mustered in the yard, their names called, searched, and then marched off in separate gangs to work. **1899** G.E. BOXALL *Story Austral. Bushrangers* 319 He was not missed until evening, when the prisoners employed at this work were mustered.

b. *refl.*

1811 *Sydney Gaz.* 2 Mar., Many Persons have omitted to come forward and muster themselves.

c. *intr.* for *refl.* To assemble (for inspection, a census, etc.). With **for:** to declare at a muster.

1810 *Sydney Gaz.* 7 Jan., Some ill-disposed Person or Persons, with an Intent to injure me most maliciously have falsely propagated a Report, that I had not the Number of Acres of Wheat, Barely, and Corn in Cultivation that I mustered for at the last General Muster. **1814** L. MACQUARIE *Let.* 10 Sept. (1821) 88 Ticket of Leave Men are to muster on the right of Assigned Government Men. **1833** J. BACKHOUSE *Narr. Visit Austral. Colonies* (1843) 158 The hulks, on board of which they sleep . . are moored close alongside of the yard in which the men muster. **1838** *Tegg's N.S.W. Pocket Almanac* 99 Women holding tickets-of-leave are not required to muster in person. **1844** *Colonial Times* (Hobart) 19 Mar., Pass-holders residing in this District are required to muster at the Police Office, Campbell Town.

2. *transf.*

a. *trans.* To gather (livestock) together in one place for the purpose of branding, counting, drafting, etc. Also *absol.*

1813 *HRA* (1916) 1st Ser. VII. 747 You must in Person Muster the whole of the Horned Cattle, Sheep and Horses belonging to the Crown. **1824** *Austral.* (Sydney) 9 Dec. 2, I remember him getting into trouble about a fortnight before his cattle were mustered. **1826** *Monitor* (Sydney) 30 June 51/2 Emigrants, after twelve months' exertions to obtain a footing in that unfortunate island, are obliged to muster up their little stock, and emigrate to New South Wales. **1837** *Lit. News* (Sydney) 9 Sept. 51 The . . Cattle . . are now being mustered, and when collected will be sold in lots to suit purchasers. **1849** J.P. TOWNSEND *Rambles & Observations N.S.W.* 49 The cattle are mustered once a year, and marked with a brand, denoting that they have attended that year's general levee. **1861** J. DAVIS *Tracks of McKinlay* 3 Sept. (1863) 83 Found him and several neighbours mustering cattle. **1886** H. FINCH-HATTON *Advance Aust.* (rev. ed.) 55 Neighbouring stations always . . send up a spare hand or two to help muster and brand. **1902** *Bulletin* (Sydney) 24 May 14/1 It's grand to be a cockie, With wife and kids to keep, To find an all-wise Providence Has mustered all your sheep. **1926** A.A.B. Apsley *Amateur Settlers* 104 Cattle are marked... They all run loose in the Bush, being 'mustered' or collected every now and then. **1946** *Bulletin* (Sydney) 23 Jan. 13/3 While mustering sheep on Kosciusko snow leases on an early winter day we were caught by a premature fall of snow. **1960** *N.T. News* (Darwin) 22 Jan. 6 Arthur has a share in all the cleanskin cattle he musters. **1972** *Bulletin* (Sydney) 29 Apr. 44/3 Farmer-graziers who used to muster sheep with a motor bike or Mini-Moke and a dog, now find they are returning to the saddle to drive cattle.

b. *trans.* To clear (an area specified) of livestock in order to gather them together in one place. Also with **off** and **up.**

1886 P. Clarke *'New Chum' in Aust.* 168 This is the paddock we have, in bush phraseology, to 'clean' or 'muster'. **1909** *Bulletin* (Sydney) 3 June 15/2 They had mustered the paddock adjoining us, and *there wasn't a single jumbuck missing.* **1925** M. Terry *Across Unknown Aust.* 121 No country can be mustered 'clean', i.e. entirely. **1938** F. Ratcliffe *Flying Fox & Drifting Sand* 238 The men .. had the job of mustering Mr Coleman's mulga paddocks. **1960** R.S. Porteous *Cattleman* 20 Parts of the runs were never mustered, the head stockman being too lazy or too indifferent to see that his men scoured the outlying country. **1962** D. Lockwood *I, Aboriginal* 172 We mustered the open country around the billabongs on the river flats.

musterer. One who musters livestock.

[N.Z. **1863** E.R. Chudleigh *Diary* 19 Dec. (1950) 114 All the musterers dogs have come home.] **1889** *Illustr. Austral. News* (Melbourne) 1 May 74/2 The distribution of the musterers under the leadership of one of the stockmen that knows the most likely places to find cattle suitable for the southern market. **1894** *Bulletin* (Sydney) 10 Feb. 20/4 Stir yourselves, you penners-up, and shove the sheep along, The musterers are fetching them a hundred-thousand strong. **1913** W.K. Harris *Outback in Aust.* 154 Musterers are constantly arriving with sheep for the shears. **1935** *Red Star* (Perth) 5 Apr. 3/1 Musterers' conditions were exceptionally bad as no cook was supplied for them. **1953** *Bulletin* (Sydney) 25 Nov. 13/1 The boongs swept across-country at their leisure on a five-mile face lighting spinifex smokes, driving the sheep ahead of them with green bushes, while the mounted musterers rode up and down the cordon. **1963** *N. Austral. Monthly* Nov. 13 The cook got about five bob a week more than a musterer or ordinary station hand. **1980** Ansell & Percy *To fight Wild* 76 Any faint possibility that might have crossed my mind about some musterers turning up, from anywhere .. was dispelled.

mustering, *vbl. n.*

a. The action of gathering together in one place (freq. widely dispersed) livestock. Also *attrib.*

1847 T. Woore *Diary* May (1935) 68 Should 'Pomeroy Run' be leased separately from the Homestead there are stock yards, mustering paddock of 300 acres, [etc.]. **1859** W. Burrows *Adventures Mounted Trooper* 132 It may be desirable to give a sketch of the scene exhibited at mustering time. **1872** C.H. Eden *My Wife & I in Qld.* 69 Here take place the annual musterings. **1899** P.W. McNally *Life & Adventures Wild Scotchman* 5 He was put 'tailing' cattle, that is, minding them at mustering time around the head station. **1917** *11 CAR* 423 At the exceptional times of mustering .. it is the general practice of employers .. to give the men something extra. **1931** F.D. Davison *Man-Shy* (1962) 1 The mustering for drafting and branding was a distressing time for the cattle. **1942** *Bulletin* (Sydney) 22 July 13/1 Every blackfellow in my mustering team carried on his saddle a koondy—a heavy stick. **1978** *Transcript of Proc. Alyawarra Land Claim* 10 Oct. 478 With the helicopter mustering and that, we don't employ quite as many as we used to.

b. Comb. **mustering camp, dog.**

1911 E.S. Sorenson *Life in Austral. Backblocks* 82 This class of cook is frequently met with in **mustering-camps** on the big cattle stations of Western Queensland. **1927** R.S. Browne *Journalist's Memories* 76 In the shearers' huts in the West, on mustering camps and at those little meetings of 'billabong whalers'. **1935** M. & E. Durack *All-About* (1940) 10 The boys, with the exception of 'Old Man Charlie', the gardener, and Tommy, the odd-job man (very odd) are out in the mustering camp. **1977** A. Thomas *Bulls & Boabs* (1980) 89 The days of the mustering camp, with the night watch singing to the cattle, have gone. **1937** *Bulletin* (Sydney) 16 June 20/2 Jack was the finest **mustering dog** I ever saw. **1942** R.B. Kelley *Animal Breeding* 142 In New Zealand the equivalent of the Australian mustering dog is called a 'heading' dog.

c. Special Comb. **mustering plant,** see Plant *n.*[2]

1934 C. Sayce *Comboman* 217 A mustering plant! It was Jim Hindley's plant. He had been out for a fortnight, mustering horses and was taking a mob back to Kendal station for drafting. **1956** T. Ronan *Moleskin Midas* 105 If you have any yard or paddock where stock can be held, the mustering plant will put them there, and my own trackers will mind them. **1962** C. Gye *Cockney & Crocodile* 102 One mustering plant we passed, trying no doubt to save the remaining cattle. **1980** Ansell & Percy *To fight Wild* 123 He had been with the last mustering plant sent in to try and get some of the cattle out of the Fitzmaurice country, about seven years before.

mutting /ˈmʌtɪŋ/. *Obs.* Also **mutach, muton.** [a. Dharuk *mudiŋ.*] An Aboriginal fish spear.

1790 D. Southwell Correspondence & Papers, *Mūding*, fish-gig. **1803** J. Grant *Narr. Voyage N.S.W.* 163 He threw down his *muton*, so they name the fish-gig, and came readily to us. **1851** J. Henderson *Excursions & Adventures N.S.W.* II. 137 They spear fish from a canoe, or from the bank, in which case they use commonly a *mutach*, or smaller spear, having four or five points, and discharged from the hand. **1892** Hill & Thornton *Notes on Aborigines N.S.W.* 2 A blackfellow in his way, as a rule, is very clever .. and with the mutting (four-pronged spear) .. not easily surpassed.

mutton. [Transf. use of *mutton* the flesh of sheep, used as food.]

1. The flesh of goat, used as food. Also **goat mutton.**

1897 J.J. Murif *From Ocean to Ocean* 57 No sheep beyond Oodnadatta either... The goat's flesh is called 'mutton'. **1905** *Bulletin* (Sydney) 30 Nov. 15/3 There really isn't enough difference to make a fuss about between sheep-mutton and goat-mutton. **1922** 'J. Bushman' *In Musgrave Ranges* 23 This was why the mutton they had eaten .. was so tough; for, because sheep cannot thrive in that part of the country, goats are kept and killed for meat. **1925** M. Terry *Across Unknown Aust.* 154 A most excellent dish of mulga mutton—goat. **1927** M. Dorney *Adventurous Honeymoon* 30 We had some 'mutton' which was really goat, but was quite as nice as mutton. **1930** D. Cottrell *Earth Battle* 125 She put .. the damper and cold goat mutton on a newspaper.

2. In the collocation **underground mutton,** the flesh of rabbit, used as food.

1919 *Bulletin* (Sydney) 1 May 22/2 Here where I am (4th A.G.H.) the Diggers call rabbit 'underground mutton'. **1933** J. Truran *Where Plain Begins* 182 A man can trap rabbits for tucker o' course, but 'e wants something else besides 'underground mutton' to keep 'im goin'. **1951** *New Settler in W.A.* (Perth) Mar. 21 You fed [*sic*] underground mutton (rabbit) and slept in the stable with the horses. **1965** E. Lambert *Long White Night* 138, I thought a feed of underground mutton would go all right for my tea, so I shot one. **1977** J. O'Grady *There was Kid* 83 My lasting dislike of rabbit as edible protein dates from my childhood... Tripe .. leaves 'underground mutton' for dead. And dead underground mutton is fit only for crows. **1981** *Bulletin* (Sydney) 22 Dec. 206/1 The rifle was for rabbits: we ate a lot of underground mutton in the 30s.

mutton-bird, *n.* [See quot. 1839 (2).]

1. The brownish-black, migratory bird *Puffinus tenuirostris*, breeding in s.e. Aust., esp. on Bass Strait islands, and harvested for its fat, feathers, and edible flesh; any of several other birds of similar appearance or usefulness. See also *short-tailed shearwater* Short-tailed.

1790 R. Clark Jrnl. 28 Aug. 202 A Box for my beloved woman, Containing .. a Mount Pit Bird, a Mutton Bird. **1833** *Jrnls. Several Exped. W.A.* 149, I took advantage of a boat going to Coffin Island to look for seals, mutton birds (sooty petrel, procellaria fuliginosa), to obtain a conveyance thither. **1839** W.H. Leigh *Reconnoitering Voyages* 109 There is .. a bird called the 'Mutton Bird', which is salted and dried, but it requires a desperate stomach to attack such an oily mess. **1839** W. Mann *Six Yrs.' Residence* 51 They are web-footed, of the puffin species, and are commonly called *mutton birds*, from their flavour and fatness; they are migratory, and arrive in Bass's Straits about the commencement of spring, in such numbers that they darken the air. **1844** *Port Phillip Gaz.* 6 July 3 The islands are infested with many idle and worthless characters, who .. subsist chiefly on the mutton bird, which are prodigiously numerous. **1857** F.R. Nixon *Cruise of Beacon* 6 The hoarse, discordant scream of the mutton-birds, the male of which species come annually to the island to prepare nests for the females. **1874** *Illustr. Sydney News* 28 Feb. 14/2 The slope of the island was one vast mutton-bird burrow... In appearance they are a smallish black seagull with a red beak and a spread of wings about thirty inches. **1881** E. Davies *Story Earnest Life* 110 We found a strange bird... It burrows in the earth like a rabbit; then lays one or two enormous eggs... It is called the Sooty Petrel, better known out at sea as the Sheerwater. Governor Munroe called it the 'Mutton Bird'. **1900** *Tocsin* (Melbourne) 9 Aug. 6/1 For some days lived on an abundance of magpies and black jays; the latter pass in some parts under the title of mutton-birds. **1917** *Bulletin* (Sydney) 5 July 24/1 The pied bell-magpie, erroneously called mutton-bird, is fairly common in open timber on the south-eastern coast of N.S. Wales. **1945** *Aust. Week-End Bk.* 9 If you would eat mutton-bird, you should do so in Tasmania. **1959** *Never kill Dolphin* (Writers' Guild Qld.) 9 The fishermen had beaten up the Japanese seamen for taking mutton birds from their burrows and plucking them alive before cooking. **1968** V. Serventy *Southern Walkabout* 112 The most noticeable of the petrels is the fleshy-footed shearwater. This is an ugly name for a fine-looking bird but the local name, muttonbird, is even more inappropriate. **1978** N. Coleman *Look at Wildlife Great Barrier Reef* 32 During the months from October to April some islands of the Reef are inundated by thousands of mutton birds when they return from their long migratory flights to breed on the islands of their birth. **1986** *Mercury* (Hobart) 26 Mar. 39/2 Mutton birds may only be taken subject to the provisions of the Wildlife Regulations 1971.

2. *fig.* A non-Aboriginal resident of northern Tasmania.

1892 *Truth* (Sydney) 19 June 4/7 North Tasmanians resent being nicknamed Mutton birds. **1941** S.J. Baker *Pop. Dict. Austral. Slang* 48 *Mutton-bird*, a resident of Northern Tasmania. Also, 'mutton-bird eater'.

3. *attrib.* esp. as **mutton-bird feather, oil, pillow, rookery.**

1830 G.A. Robinson in N.J.B. Plomley *Friendly Mission* 18 June (1966) 176 The Stack Island is a small rocky island with herbage, and there is a mutton bird rookery. **1846** *Britannia* (Hobart) 10 Sept. 3/2 A protest against 'the abomination of mutton bird feather beds'. **1846** C.W. Schürmann *Aboriginal Tribes Port Lincoln* 33 An extensive trade in their feathers is .. carried on, but these have generally a strong and unpleasant smell; so that a 'mutton-bird pillow' is spoken of as something proverbially disagreeable. **1852** Mrs C. Meredith *My Home in Tas.* II. 122 The odour of the abominable 'mutton-bird' pillow on which he had lain was most sickening. **1872** M.B. Brownrigg *Cruise of Freak* 55 At the southern end of the island there is a mutton-bird rookery. **1872** *Illustr. Sydney News* 20 Jan. 12/4 At present it [*sc.* Phillip Island, Vic.] is inhabited by a few Chinamen, whose chief avocation is the procuring of mutton bird oil and fishing. **1883** E.M. Curr *Recoll. Squatting Vic.* 27 The unsavoury odour of our mutton-bird feather pillows. **1909** H. Button *Flotsam & Jetsam* 43 A bed deliciously soft and warm, but disgustingly redolent of mutton-bird feathers. **1918** *Huon Times* (Franklin) 28 May 1/1 It is a palatable Emulsion of the Mutton Bird Oil, and is in our opinion superior to Cod Liver Oil.

4. Special Comb. **mutton-bird eater,** Mutton-bird 2; **gales** *pl.* (but see quot. 1980), seasonal gales coinciding with the annual arrival of flocks of mutton-birds to nest on islands in Bass Strait and on the coast of Tasmania; *transf.* the flocks of mutton-birds themselves.

1914 *Bulletin* (Sydney) 28 May 22/3 'Moana' .. has never been in Tassy, or he would include the inhabitants of the Fly Speck in his category as **muttonbird-eaters.** **1941** [see sense 2 above]. **1972** A. Chipper *Aussie Swearers Guide* 66 *Mutton Bird Eater*, a Tasmanian. **1910** F.M. Littler *Handbk. Birds Tas.* 167 The birds commence to come in for laying purposes just a few minutes after sunset. Just at this time of the year heavy gales usually blow, which are known as '**Mutton-bird gales**'. **1956** B. BEATTY *Beyond Aust.'s Cities* 77 When the heavy gales rock the coastline around September, fishermen nod heads wisely and congratulate themselves that the Mutton Bird Gales have started... On and around September 20th, the birds arrive in flocks that crowd the sky. **1957** *Sydney Morning Herald* 10 Nov. 41/1 Down in Bass Strait they are awaiting the Mutton Bird Gales, one of nature's most majestic and mysterious phenomena. Beginning about November 17, millions of mutton birds will come whirling up the strait on the pinions of the gales that bluster up from the Antarctic. **1958** *Papers & Proc. R. Soc. Tas.* 169 This association of boisterous weather with the egg-laying season of the mutton-birds has led to the use of the term 'mutton-bird gales' in Bass Strait. **1971** *Open Road* Dec. 29/1 By the millions they [*sc.* mutton birds] come whirring up the Strait in the so-called Mutton Bird Gales. **1980** H.W. CUMMINGS *Confessions of 'Mud Skipper'* 42 As we ran for Bass Strait it turned into a full 'mutton bird gale'.

mutton-bird, *v.* [f. prec.] *intr.* To catch mutton-birds as food; to catch mutton-birds and prepare their flesh and by-products for the market. Chiefly as *vbl. n.*

1872 M.B. BROWNRIGG *Cruise of Freak* 55 To this place Mr Baudinet and his family annually resort for about two months, for mutton-birding operations. **1881** G. WALCH *Vic.* 49 One of the sports of the neighbourhood is 'mutton-birding'. **1896** *Papers & Proc. R. Soc. Tas.* (1897) p. vi, Mutton-birding, a unique industry, and only carried on in the Furneaux Islands as a regular one... The 'birding' begins on March 20. **1899** *Bulletin* (Sydney) 24 June 16/1 Mutton-birding is a very uncertain game. **1902** *Emu* I. 69 Mutton-birding (according to the species of Petrel).. in Bass Strait (where alone it is reckoned that the number of young birds taken for food amounts annually to about 600,000). **1945** *Aust. Week-End Bk.* 9 I've heard of snake-bite, but never witnessed it while mutton-birding. **1971** *Open Road* Dec. 29/1 Apart from a little farming and fishing their chief pursuit is mutton-birding.

Hence **mutton-birder** *n.*

1881 G. WALCH *Vic.* 49 Armed with a piece of stout curved wire, fastened at the end of a long stick, the mutton-birder fishes in the holes for his prize, and is generally rewarded.. by either the egg or the young bird. **1899** *Bulletin* (Sydney) 24 June 16/1 Mutton-birders.. say snakes are always asleep when in their holes. **1943** *Ibid.* 15 Dec. 13/3 The majority of the mutton-birders are taken to the islands of the Furneaux Group.. at the close of 'birdin''. **1965** *Austral. Encycl.* VI. 234B (*caption*) A mutton-birder's hut, with casks of dressed and salted mutton-bird carcasses. **1986** *Mercury* (Hobart) 26 Mar. 39/2, I hereby issue a general authority to licensed mutton birders to take mutton birds.. March 29 to April 15, 1986.

mutton-fish. Any of several marine gastropods with an edible flesh, esp. *Haliotis ruber*, having a flat, oval shell with a nacreous lining. See quot. 1974.

1830 G.A. ROBINSON in N.J.B. Plomley *Friendly Mission* 16 Feb. (1966) 120 The natives procured some mutton-fish, which the natives of the south call *par.rar.* **1832** J. BACKHOUSE *Narr. Visit Austral. Colonies* (1843) 103 Adhering to the rocks, *Haliotis tuberculata* and *levigata*, called in this country Mutton-fish, are met with abundantly. **1861** 'OLD BUSHMAN' *Bush Wanderings* 254 But the finest shell-fish in this bay was the 'mutton-fish', which in the island of Jersey is called the 'ormer'. **1883** *Examiner* (Launceston) 7 Apr. (Suppl.), Our native companion brought me a bag of mutton fish. **1928** S.E. NAPIER *On Barrier Reef* 141 *Haliotis* is tropically known as the 'mutton-fish'. **1948** J. FAIRFAX *Run o' Waters* 88 The muttonfish is a shellfish found growing on rocks. Taken from the shell, they are scrubbed with a brush, rolled in a cloth, hit with an axe, and then boiled in a pot. **1956** *Bulletin* (Sydney) 22 Feb. 12/1 Few people would know what a muttonfish is, but fewer who have rambled along the rocks on the N.S.W. coast have never seen its shell. It is the one that seems to have been designed by nature as a soap-holder. **1974** J.M. THOMSON *Fish Ocean & Shore* 89 Abalone.. were known as mutton fish in Australia before the American term abalone took over.

muzzlewood. [See quot. 1982.] *Black sallee*, see BLACK *a.*[2] 1 a.

1895 *Proc. Linnean Soc. N.S.W.* X. 597 *Eucalyptus stellulata*... It is called 'Muzzle-wood' in Gippsland, but the meaning of the name is unknown to us. **1898** *Ibid.* XXIII. 798 We stated that we were in doubt as to the meaning of the term Muzzlewood as applied to this species. We have ascertained that on account of its toughness it is often selected for making muzzles for unweaned calves. **1982** K. HUENEKE *Huts of High Country* 189, I passed several stands of black sallies (*Eucalyptus stellulata*) and he told me the origin of their common name—the muzzlewood. It was in the days of shepherds and unfenced holdings that cattle owners hit on the idea of a wooden muzzle to help wean young calves. Without fences they could not be kept away from their mothers so they fashioned a wooden flap suspended from the nostrils. The calves could still eat grass and drink from a dam or a creek but as soon as they lifted their heads to suckle the muzzle flopped down and prevented access... It was discovered that black sally was the most durable and naturally enough it became the muzzlewood tree.

myall /'maɪəl/, *n.*[1] and *attrib.* Formerly also **mial, miall, myal.** [a. Dharuk *mayal* a stranger.]

A. *n.*

1. *Obs.* In Aboriginal use: a stranger.

1798 D. COLLINS *Acct. Eng. Colony N.S.W.* I. 610 *Mi-yal*, a stranger... This word has reference to sight; *Mi*, the eye. **1818** J. HOLT *Mem.* (1838) II. 148 About fifty natives collected round his house. They are very inquisitive, and said to me, 'Name you? You are miel.' That is to say, 'You are a stranger, what is your name?' **1826** Macarthur Papers XII. 4 Feb., This festivity is.. always given to do honor to and entertain strangers, whom they call 'Myall'. **1830** R. DAWSON *Present State Aust.* 41 Called by the natives 'Myall', meaning, in their language, stranger, or place they never frequent.

2. An Aboriginal living in a traditional manner (esp. as distinct from one accustomed to, or living amongst, whites). See also WARRIGAL *n.* 2.

1837 *Colonist* (Sydney) 2 Feb. 40/2 'They are only *myalls*' i.e. *wild* natives. **1848** *Sidney's Austral. Hand-Bk.* 7, I have encountered hundreds of wild blacks, fierce myals, who had never before eaten bread, smoked tobacco, or beheld a white face. **1862** *Bell's Life in Sydney* 27 Dec. 4/1 The wild Myals had grown into the tame, blanket-clothed dependents of the settlers. **1876** J.A. EDWARDS *Gilbert Gogger* 188 There is another thing that I have never yet seen in a myall's camp, the bow and arrow. **1891** A. DE LORENSKI *Austral. & Other Poems* 37 Like half famish'd myalls they snatch at each bite. **1905** H. LAWSON *Elder Son* 201 Round the Myalls creep the trackers—there's a sound like firing crackers And—the blacks are getting scarcer in the Dry Countree. **1910** *Huon Times* (Franklin) 5 Oct. 4/3 It was further stated that the black was not a mission black, but a myall. **1925** M. TERRY *Across Unknown Aust.* 176 Myall is a wild uncivilised black as compared with the ones that hang around stations for work or gleanings. **1944** *Bulletin* (Sydney) 9 Aug. 13/4 The myall's ability to keep warm.. was largely due to his inherited thick hide being toughened by exposure. **1950** A. GROOM *I saw Strange Land* 111 The lad was a myall, unable to speak a word of English. **1964** H.M. BARKER *Camels & Outback* 36, I had a young black boy with me, Sambo. He was a real *myall* when I got him, straight from the desert. **1976** S. WELLER *Bastards I have Met* 98 Charlie's people were Myalls and never saw a white man.

3. *transf.* One who is placed in an unfamiliar environment.

1982 *Yulngu* Aug. 23 Chips lost the *Mimi* Toyota out bush one weekend!!.. He is a bit of a myall in the bush.

B. *attrib.* passing into *adj.*

1. *Obs.* In Aboriginal use: strange.

1827 W.J. DUMARESQ in G. Mackaness *Fourteen Journeys Blue Mountains* (1950) ii. 96 These *mial* or strange blacks have related.. to us, that there exists in the western country, many days off, a vast interior sea. **1830** R. DAWSON *Present State Aust.* 103 The fear of meeting the strange or 'Myall pellows', as they called them. **1844** C. WILKES *Narr. U.S. Exploring Exped.* II. 197 They always betray the greatest fear of falling in with some Myall or stranger blacks. **1845** *Sydney Morning Herald* 10 June 2/5 On my return.. I found that some myall blacks, belonging to the north-west.. had been in.

2. *transf.* Of an Aboriginal. **a.** *Obs.* Hostile. **b.** Living in a traditional manner; unaccustomed to white society. See also WARRIGAL *a.* 1.

1839 T.L. MITCHELL *Three Exped. Eastern Aust.* (rev. ed.) I. 50 He had been unwilling to acknowledge to me, his dread of the 'myall' tribes. **1846** *HRA* (1925) 1st Ser. XXV. 9 These, generally known as 'Myall' or wild Blacks, are joined at certain periods by large parties of Aborigines. **1870** E.B. KENNEDY *Four Yrs. in Qld.* 34 The term Miall denotes Blacks who are perfectly wild. **1892** *Bulletin* (Sydney) 14 May 7/3 King Billy was a Myall black Of very early type, He never used a handkerchief His royal nose to wipe. **1912** *Bull. N.T.* i. 45 Only a short distance from the station is a native settlement consisting of small bark huts, and still further away a 'Myall camp', where the natives from the surrounding parts of the country may stay a few days. **1927** *Bulletin* (Sydney) 5 May 27/1 The myall binghi is ingenious in contriving patterns wherewith to decorate his cobber's body. **1945** E. GEORGE *Two at Daly Waters* 89 Friendly myall natives played an important part. **1954** T. RONAN *Vision Splendid* 111 As soon as a cook arrived all lubras with the slightest vestige of comeliness were taken out of the kitchen and replaced by some weak-eyed, half-myall misfits. **1965** R.H. CONQUEST *Horses in Kitchen* 150 The gold-seeking Chinese was an extra special prize so far as myall blacks were concerned. **1976** N.V. WALLACE *Bush Lawyer* 121 He lived on game and sometimes camped with wild tribesmen known as 'Myall blacks'; not a bad life for a man of seventy. **1984** B. DIXON *Searching for Aboriginal Lang.* 49 Willie was the most myall of all, and if anyone knew any language it would be him.

3. *fig.* Of an animal or plant: wild.

1851 J. HENDERSON *Excursions & Adventures N.S.W.* I. 271 We were unable to feed our dogs, and they had assumed somewhat the appearance of the *Myall Dingo* or wild dog. **1888** 'R. BOLDREWOOD' *Robbery under Arms* (1937) 12 Didn't like the thought of his children growing up like myall cattle. **1890** *Bulletin* (Sydney) 29 Mar. 15/1 A stout old myall bullock p'raps ud learn yer somethin' new. **1902** R.C. PRAED *My Austral. Girlhood* 48 Old Mooney on Seaforth, came a buster yesterday when a *myall* brute of a heifer cleared while he was cutting him out of a mob of scrubbers. **1963** D. ROBERT *Look at me Now* 92, I found a bush of wild lemons or 'myall lemons' as they are called.

myall /'maɪəl/, *n.*[2] Formerly also **miall, myal.** [Transf. use of prec.; applied by speakers of Kamilaroi to the wood they traded with speakers of Dharuk, who were 'strangers'.] Any of several trees of the genus *Acacia* (fam. Mimosaceae), esp. *A. pendula* of inland N.S.W., Qld., and Vic., having silvery foliage sometimes used as fodder, and the similar *A. melvillei*; the wood of these trees. See also BOREE, *weeping myall* WEEPING. Also *attrib.*

1840 J. GOULD *Birds of Aust.* (1848) II. Pl. 22, The only parts where I observed it [*sc.* the Red-backed Halcyon] was the myall-brushes (*Acacia pendula*) of the Lower Namoi. **1845** J.O. BALFOUR *Sketch of N.S.W.* 11 In less than half an hour after the Myall bark is thrown into the pond, the surface of the water is covered with fish apparently dead. **1849** S. & J. SIDNEY *Emigrant's Jrnl.* 44 Cattle or sheep will *fatten* on myals when there is not a *blade* of grass. **1851** *Empire* (Sydney) 30 Jan. 2/2 The sable Australian.. never contrived a defter thing than.. his boomerang of plain-cut miall. **1853** J. ALLEN *Jrnl. River Murray* 29 There is a great deal of myall scrub in this neighbourhood, a species of sandalwood, of which it has a faint smell. **1860** G. BENNETT *Gatherings of Naturalist* 336 The wood of the 'Myall', being handsome in appearance and sweet-scented, is used by stockmen and others for whip-handles. **1874** *Illustr. Sydney News* 30 Jan. 5/1 A beautiful myall-wood casket, mounted by handsome silver figures of Australian scenery. **1881** E. DAVIES *Story Earnest Life* 378 The miall is a beautiful tree, with a delicious scent like that of violets. **1890** 'R. BOLDREWOOD' *Squatter's Dream* 43 Mr Hawkesbury.. stood smoking the small myall pipe. **1896** A. MACKAY *Austral. Agriculturist* (rev. ed.) 301 The wattles and myals of the Australian bush. **1927** 'S. RUDD' *Romance of Runnibede* 27 Calls of the mopokes outside in the myall trees were the only sounds to be heard. **1935** E. COLEMAN *Come back in Wattle Time* 26 The wood of the Myall of the Interior (*A. pendula*), sometimes called Gidgee, is hard, rich in colour and beautifully marked. **1963** R. STOW *Tourmaline* 7 Trees are rare.. some kind of myall with leaves starved to needles that fans out from the root and gives no shade. **1980** G. DUTTON *Wedge-Tailed Eagle* 2 Up he flaps, slow and awkward, to a myall where he sits all bunched-up looking as if he's going to overbalance the little tree.

myall country. An area inhabited by Aborigines living in a traditional manner; an area in which myall (see *n.*[2]) is predominant.

[**1857** F. DE B. COOPER *Wild Adventures* 68, I was well-known to be acquainted with the topography of the 'myal' districts... Myal—(Comeleroi dialect)—Wild; unreclaimed.] *Ibid.* 123 A similar question in the myal country would have been taken as an insult. **1867** 'CLERGYMAN' *Aust. as it Is* 20 Cattle are very fond of eating the leaves, and, as a consequence, 'Myall country' is usually considered first-class. **1896** *Bulletin* (Sydney) 18 Apr. 27/2 The coast blackboys, with pioneer squatters, when they reached myall country, recognised the wood and called it myall. **1911** *Ibid.* 26 Oct. 13/2 Away out on the myall country at the back of the Hodgkinson. **1930** D. COTTRELL *Earth Battle* 39 On dubious errands he had ventured far into 'the Myall Country' of the Blacks.

myam-myam, mya-mya, var. MIA-MIA.

myna(h), var. MINER *n.*[1]

myrnong, var. MURNONG.

myrnonga, var. MURLONGA.

myrtle. [Transf. use of *myrtle, Myrtus.*]

1. The tall tree of Vic. and Tas. *Nothofagus cunninghamii* (fam. Fagaceae) which has small, shiny, dark-green leaves; the wood of the tree; *Tasmanian myrtle,* see TASMANIAN *a.* 2. Also *attrib.*, esp. as **myrtle beech.**

1816 *Hobart Town Gaz.* 15 June, The Mountains on the Northern Shore where the Coal is, are barren, but the rest are generally covered with Myrtle. **1832** J. BACKHOUSE *Narr. Visit Austral. Colonies* (1843) 48 Myrtle, allied to Beech, but with leaves more like Dwarf Birch, is suited for keels. **1842** *Tasmanian Jrnl. Nat. Sci.* I. 151 In the dense myrtle forests of the Colony, the number of food-plants is very limited. **1854** H.B. STONEY *Yr. in Tas.* 284 The Fagus, or native myrtle tree, generally accompanied by the fern tree, is frequently met with in the interior. **1877** *Illustr. Austral. News* (Melbourne) 3 Sept. 138/1 The most luxuriant growth of forest vegetation, such as the myrtle (fagus cunninghamii). **1887** *Papers & Proc. R. Soc. Tas.* (1888) 116 On suddenly entering one of these beautiful woods, ignominiously called 'myrtle scrubs', the traveller is translated in an instant to the cool, shady, and romantic forests of Southern or Central Europe. **1898** E.E. MORRIS *Austral Eng.* 312 In Tasmania, all the *Beeches* are called Myrtles, and there are extensive forests of the Beech *Fagus cunninghamii* .. which is invariably called 'Myrtle' by the colonists of Tasmania. **1920** B. CRONIN *Timber Wolves* 21 It was of polished red myrtle, every grain as smooth and sound as a bell. That comes from Tasmania. **1957** *Forest Trees Aust.* (Cwlth. Forestry & Timber Bur.) 220 Celery top pine occurs in cool temperate rain forest .. with myrtle beech. **1979** B. ROBERTS *Stones in Cephissus* 19 You could be lost forever in this dank forest of King Billy Pine and .. the old, old myrtle-beech. **1985** *Mercury* (Hobart) 30 July 14/5 Myrtle wilt, a fungus, killed myrtle, *Nothofagus cunninghamii,* the predominant species in Tasmanian rainforest, in much the same way as the infamous Dutch elm disease.

2. Any of several other trees or shrubs, sometimes of the myrtle fam. (Myrtaceae); also with distinguishing epithet, as *native myrtle* (see NATIVE *a.* 6 a.).

1825 B. FIELD *Geogr. Mem. N.S.W.* 461 Myrtle trees (myrtaceae) are burnt for fire-wood. **1849** *Adelaide Miscellany* 7 July 361 The handsome myoporum (commonly called the myrtle by the settlers, with which it has no affinity) spread abroad its deep green foliage covered with lovely flowers. **1849** J.P. TOWNSEND *Rambles & Observations N.S.W.* 131 A species of myrtle, *eugenia myrtifolia* .. often six feet in girth, is covered with myrtle flowers, and bears a wax-like fruit. **1887** *Proc. Linnean Soc. N.S.W.* II. 11 *Eugenia Smithii* .. or the 'Myrtle', rises to the height of 40 or 50 feet in the chocolate soil. **1958** *Coast to Coast 1957–58* 138 Leschenaultia made patches as blue as the sky everywhere, with the peach-blossom pink of wild myrtle.

3. Special Comb. **myrtle acacia,** the shrub *Acacia myrtifolia* (fam. Mimosaceae): see quot. 1942; also **myrtle-leaved acacia, mimosa, wattle.**

1793 J.E. SMITH *Specimen Bot. New Holland* 51 Mimosa myrtifolia. Myrtle-leaved Mimosa .. is now not uncommon in our greenhouses, having been raised in plenty from seeds brought from Port Jackson. **1828** R. SWEET *Flora Australasica* Pl. 49, *Myrtle-leaved Acacia* .. a handsome evergreen bushy Shrub, with slender smooth branches. **1835** *Hobart Town Almanack* 63 Myrtle leaved Acacia, a very small shrub. **1856** *Jrnl. Australasia* I. 37 You may now plant .. myrtle-leaved wattle. **1910** L. RODWAY *Some Wild Flowers Tas.* 32 In the pretty little Myrtle-leaved Acacia .. the flowers .. are placed singly or a few together on the branched flower-stalks. **1935** E. COLEMAN *Come back in Wattle Time* 37 Myrtle Acacia (*A. myrtifolia*). Broad green phyllodes (myrtle-like). **1942** C. BARRETT *Austral. Wild Flower Bk.* 35 Myrtle Acacia, a small shrub with pale yellow flower-heads and myrtle-like leaves, which ranges throughout Australia, excepting only the Northern Territory.

myxo /ˈmɪksoʊ/. [Abbrev. of *myxo(matosis* a disease introduced (into several countries) to exterminate rabbits. Now used elsewhere but recorded earliest in Aust.: see OEDS.] Myxomatosis.

1953 *Sydney Morning Herald* 3 Jan. 6/2 'Myxo', an abbreviation of myxomatosis, the rabbit-killing disease. **1958** *Meanjin* 135 The myxo's killed off all the rabbits hereabouts. **1969** *Kings Cross Whisper* (Sydney) lxxv. 3/2 *Myxamatosis injections to combat politicians.* The first myxo injections will be administered by taxation officials over the next few years. **1972** *Bulletin* (Sydney) 19 Aug. 38/3 He describes rabbits as 'quite fantastic' animals, genetically nimble, able to quite quickly develop resistance to myxo. **1982** J. MORRISON *North Wind* 101 The myxo'll look after the rabbits... You could walk right across this property and never see a rabbit.

N

Nabawa /ˈnæbəwɔ/. [The name of the town in W.A.] A variety of wheat: see quots.

1917 *V & P* (W.A.) (1918) II. no. 7 541 At Chapman we have a variety we call Nabawah. I always endeavour to give names taken from the district in which the wheat is grown. This has been grown now for two seasons, and has given us more satisfaction than any other variety. Next year it will be out amongst the farmers in large enough quantities for them to work on. **1937** H. WENHOLZ *Improvement Austral. Wheat* 8 The third generation cross-bred material which was left at Wagga Farm by Sutton was grown on for a few years, and as no promising material appeared to be developing in it, it was discarded in 1915. Material of the same generation was grown on in Western Australia under the direction of Sutton at Chapman Experiment Farm, where a strain was fixed in 1915, and named Nabawa. **1956** CALLAGHAN & MILLINGTON *Wheat Industry Aust.* 277 Amongst the material was the progeny of a cross between Early Gluyas and Bunyip made at Wagga Experiment Farm in 1908, and from it was developed the variety Nabawa. Although it was selected initially because of its resistance to stem rust, Nabawa is also very resistant to flag smut. **1984** W.W. AMMON et al. *Working Lives* 235 'Nabawa', a wheat which became very popular in the 1920s and 1930s.

naga. /ˈnagə/. Also **naga-naga, narga, nargar, narger.** [a. Yulbarija dial. of Western Desert *naka.*] A loin-cloth (as worn by an Aboriginal).

1907 A. SEARCY *In Austral. Tropics* 81, I employed about thirty niggers . . and paid them with tobacco and rice, and Turkey-red for the women for nargers (waist cloths). **1911** —— *By Flood & Field* 55 The hunter, naked save for a nargar (waist-cloth), speeding on the outskirts of the mob. **1930** J.S. LITCHFIELD *Far North Memories* 172 *Naga*, loin-cloth. **1938** X. HERBERT *Capricornia* 29 A young lubra wearing nothing but a naga of paper-bark rose and came forward shyly. **1951** E. HILL *Territory* 93 Two young warriors . . fitted out with nagas of turkey red. **1959** D. LOCKWOOD *Crocodiles & Other People* 82 A dozen natives, men and women, in brief nargas or no clothes at all. **1962** C. GYE *Cockney & Crocodile* 50 There a bush native, tall and thin and proud and black in a tiny red naga-naga (loincloth). **1969** A.A. ABBIE *Original Australs.* 65 In northern Arnhem Land . . where the first observers described the Aborigines as naked, contact with Indonesians over the past two or three centuries had led to adoption of the naga, the common term for both the male breech-cloth and—the female skirt. **1981** A. MARSHALL *Aust.* 52 He had a loose naga (loin cloth) around his loins.

nagoora burr, var. NOOGOORA BURR.

nailcan. [Prob. alteration of *nail-keg (-kag)* a small barrel containing nails; also (U.S.) a hat of similar shape.]

1. A container for nails.

1904 L.M.P. ARCHER *Bush Honeymoon* 39 Cold, soaking rain falling outside, and three scrub-cutters drawn up close to a *nailcan* filled with hot coals. **1956** T. RONAN *Moleskin Midas* 77 With his beefhouse completed, he got himself a killer from the Twin Hills side and picked up a nailcan beef-bucket from Sam Slack's deserted homestead.

2. See quot. 1955. Also **nailcan hat.**

1941 S.J. BAKER *Pop. Dict. Austral. Slang* 48 *Nail-can*, a tall (top) hat. **1955** N. PULLIAM *I traveled Lonely Land* 382 *Nail can*, a top hat. **1971** H. ANDERSON *Larrikin Crook* 2 The clerks sneered at in *Truth* and called suburban snobs 'going to the city every day on a first class ticket in a nail can hat and bum-banger coat'.

nailrod. [Transf. use of *nailrod* a strip or rod of iron from which nails are cut.] Coarse dark tobacco in the form of a thin roll.

[N.Z. **1886** *N.Z. Herald* (Auckland) 8 Nov. 7/3 Nailrod and 1 lb. bars . . with Havana . . Cigars.] **1890** A.J. VOGAN *Black Police* 200 He hands our black friend a piece of 'nailrod' with which to charge his evening pipe. **1896** H. LAWSON *When Billy Boils* 142 Our nose-bags were nice and heavy, and we still had about a pound of nail-rod between us. **1900** R. BRUCE *Benbonuna* (1904) 139 Producing as he spoke some sticks of 'nailrod' from a leather pouch. **1967** J. STUART *Part of Glory* 157, I could smoke or leave it alone, and as the jail weed was 'nail rod' or 'sheep dip' I left it severely alone.

nail-tailed wallaby. a. Any of the three species of wallaby of the genus *Onychogalea*, members of which have a horny nail at the tip of the tail. **b.** With distinguishing epithet: **bridled nail-tailed wallaby,** the wallaby *O. fraenata*, now known only from e. central Qld., with bridle-like white markings on the head and shoulder; also **bridled wallaby; crescent nail-tailed wallaby,** WURRUNG; also **crescent nail-tail wallaby.** Also **nail-tail, nail-tailed kangaroo.**

[**1841** G.R. WATERHOUSE *Nat. Hist. Marsupialia* 201 Nail-bearing kangaroo. *Macropus unguifer.* The tail is whitish . . and the point is provided with a tuft of long black hairs which conceal a nail, with which the tip of the tail is furnished. This nail is of a black colour, thin and hollow beneath, and in fact nearly resembles a finger nail both in texture and form.] **1859** J. GOULD *Mammals of Aust.* (1863) II. 52 *Onychogalea unguifer*, Nail-tailed Kangaroo. **1886** F. COWAN *Aust.* 36 Wallaby being a generic term of native origin for a number of kangaroo-like animals specifically distinguished as the . . nail-tailed-wallaby, and the like. **1894** R. LYDEKKER *Handbk. Marsupialia & Monotremata* 48 The three species of Nail-tailed Wallabies, which are confined to Australia . . form a well-marked group. *Ibid.* 50 Bridled Wallaby. *Onychogale frenata.* **1917** *Bulletin* (Sydney) 10 May 24/3 Westralia possesses the most peculiar example of the marsupial tribe, viz. the nail-tailed kangaroo, sometimes called wallaby. **1926** A.S. LE SOUEF et al. *Wild Animals Australasia* 211 Mr G.S. Shortridge found the crescent nail-tailed wallaby very local, living in low scrubby thickets. **1975** *Ecos* v. 28/1 A few bridled nail-tailed wallabies turned up last year at Dingo, between Emerald and Rockhampton. *Ibid.*, The crescent nail-tailed wallaby also lived in thickets. **1978** M. DOUGLAS *Follow Sun* 199 'It's a nail-tail.' The little macropod lay still, limp and exhausted. **1984** *Age* (Melbourne) 9 Aug. 1/7 Species already extinct in Australia . . crescent nail-tail wallaby.

namma hole, var. GNAMMA HOLE.

nana /ˈnanə/. Prob. f. *banana.*]

1. In the phr. **off one's nana,** mentally deranged; **to do** (or **lose**) **one's nana,** to lose one's temper.

[**1894** A.B. PATERSON in C. Semmler *World of Banjo Paterson* (1967) 29 'Off his nanny again', thought the boss, 'the sooner he goes the better.'] **1966** S.J. BAKER *Austral. Lang.* (ed. 2) 293 *Lose one's nana*, . . an equivalent of *lose* (or *do*) *one's block.* **1968** *Coast to Coast 1967–68* 9 Arright, Mister Mighty Boss. Don't do your nana. **1975** *Austral.* (Sydney) 8 Feb. 13/6 'We've all learned to laugh at ourselves and at our predicament,' Trevor England said. 'If we hadn't we'd all be off our nanas.'

2. [Used elsewhere but recorded earliest in Aust.] A foolish person; a fool. Also *attrib.* as **nana-cut,** a style of hair-cut.

1941 S.J. BAKER *Pop. Dict. Austral. Slang* 48 *Nana (hair) cut*, a utilitarian haircut in which the back of the head is closely shaved. **1965** G. MCINNES *Road to Gundagai* 148 Although he was obviously a gent, he was not a 'tonk' or a 'nana'. **1967** *Coast to Coast 1965–66* 35 If you . . horror of horrors, had a *nana* haircut. **1971** *T.V. Times* (Sydney) 18 Dec. 19/4 It's only the famous ones who get fired. . . They're the ones making statements like 'The management is a nana'.

nangry /ˈnæŋgri/, *v. Austral. pidgin. Obs.* Also **nangerie.** [a. Dharuk *naŋgari.*] *intr.* To sleep; to rest; to reside. Also as *n.*, a sleep.

1790 D. SOUTHWELL Corresp. & Papers, *Nan-gă-ră*, to sleep. **1830** R. DAWSON *Present State Aust.* 73 It was much too far without *nangry* (sleep, rest, or night). **1839** T.L. MITCHELL *Three Exped. Eastern Aust.* (rev. ed.) I. 269 They violently shook their boughs at me, and having set them on fire, dashed them to the ground, calling out 'Nangry' (sit down). **1853** H.B. JONES *Adventures in Aust.* 147 'Where you 'nangerie',' i.e., where do you live? was his next interrogatory.

nankeen. [Transf. use of *nankeen* the colour.] Used *attrib.* in the names of birds having a red-brown back: **nankeen kestrel** (formerly **hawk**), the small falcon *Falco cenchroides* of Aust. and New Guinea, having a characteristic hovering flight; KESTREL; SPARROWHAWK b.; **night heron,** the nocturnal heron *Nycticorax caledonicus*, occurring near water throughout Aust. and widespread in the s.w. Pacific; also **nankeen crane, heron,** and (formerly) **bird.**

1827 [**nankeen kestrel**] *Trans. Linnean Soc. London* XV. 184 This bird . . is called Nankeen Hawk by the settlers. . . On the 3rd of August 1804, I made the following note:- I saw no *Nankeen Hawks* this autumn.— I never observed it attacking the fowls. **1849** C. STURT *Narr. Exped. Central Aust.* II. 14 App. Tinnunculus Cenchroïdes. *Nankeen Kestril.* . . This bird is generally distributed over the continent and is known by the nankeen colour of his back. **1903** *Emu* II. 141 Cerchneis cenchroides (Nankeen Kestrel) . . this graceful bird. **1945** C. BARRETT *Austral. Bird Life* 37 Only one of our hawks, the graceful little nankeen kestrel (Falco cenchroides), enjoys game law protection. **1976** *Reader's Digest Compl. Bk. Austral. Birds* 83 Two other birds named after nankeen in early colonial days have red-brown backs. These were the nankeen hawk, now called the nankeen kestrel [etc.]. **1837** [**nankeen night heron**] J. BACKHOUSE *Narr. Visit Austral. Colonies* 13 Nov. (1843) 500 We also noticed the Nankin-bird, a species of Heron, which is cinnamon-coloured on the back, sulphur-coloured on the breast, and has a long, white feather, pendant from the back of the head. **1846** J. GOULD *Birds of Aust.* (1848) VI. Pl. 63, *Nycticorax caledonicus.* Nankeen Night Heron. **1849** C. STURT *Narr. Exped. Central Aust.* II. 52 App. Nycticorax Caledonicus. *Nankeen Bird.* A Night Heron with nankeen-coloured back and wings. **1886** D.M. GANE *N.S.W. & Vic.* 200 The nankeen crane . . is seldom within gunshot. **1928** B. SPENCER *Wanderings in Wild Aust.* 551 Spoonbills, cranes and Nankeen night-herons were enjoying themselves in and around the pool. **1968** R. HILL *Bush Quest* 16 Three nankeen herons came planing in on russet wings to land amongst the glossy green leaves of a Moreton Bay fig. **1976** *Reader's Digest Compl. Bk. Austral. Birds* 83 In the daytime the nankeen night heron usually roosts in heavily foliaged trees . . in or near water.

nan-nan. *Obs.* [Perh. f. *nancy* effeminate man.] A straw hat (in quot. 1899 used *attrib.*); also *transf.*, a dandy.

1899 *Bulletin* (Sydney) 8 Apr. (Red Page), A boarding-house keeper with two or three grown-up, white-shirted . . straw-hatted, cigarette-smoking sons. . . I'd like to paint her and the children—and the 'nan-nan' sons. **1907** *Truth* (Sydney) 24 Feb. 1/7 Colonel Bell has given politics best while he explains to the University nan-nans the theory of earthquakes. **1910** STEPHENS & O'BRIEN Materials Austrazealand Slang Dict. 104 *Nan-nan*, a straw hat for men's wear: by transference, to the gangs of youths who affect these hats, either for cheapness or for showiness. They are well known in Sydney as the 'Nan-nan or Straw-hat' push. A straw hat a few years ago was known as a donkey's breakfast. The cry to the wearer was 'Ba, ba, who shook/stole the donkey's breakfast?' The genesis, no doubt, of 'Nan-nan'. **1941** S.J. BAKER *Pop. Dict. Austral. Slang* 48 *Nan-nan*, a straw hat for men's wear. Obs.

nannygai /'nænigaɪ/. [Prob. f. a N.S.W. Aboriginal language.] The marine fish of s. Aust. *Centroberyx affinis*, a short-bodied, reddish fish valued as food. See also *red fish* (b), RED *a.* 1 b.

1871 *Industr. Progress N.S.W.* 791 The .. king-fish, 'moorra nennigai' .. and a variety of other less familiar forms, may be taken by the line in almost unlimited quantities. **1874** *N.S.W. Rep. R. Comm. Fisheries* (1880) 11 *Mura gnin a gai*—aboriginal. 'Mother nan a di'—corruption *Nannygey*—abbreviation and accepted name of the red fishes caught off North Head during the months of October and November is of the family *Berycidae* and of the genus *Beryx*. . . The nannygey has a very large eye. **1896** F.G. AFLALO *Sketch Nat. Hist. Aust.* 205 The Nannygai . . is supposed to feed at the same time as the big schnapper. **1944** J. DEVANNY *By Tropic Sea & Jungle* 5 On the two-hundred mile coastline from Townsville to Cairns the name nannygai was applied to several different fish. **1968** G. DUTTON *Andy* 176 Some good fish in Tasmania. Nannygai, now there's an incomparable fish! **1981** *Canberra Chron.* 25 Jan. 19/4 A lot of evening meals along the coast . . are made up of small fillets of nanygai.

nanto /'næntoʊ/. *Obs.* Also **nanta, nantah, nantu.** [a. Gaurna (and neighbouring languages) *nantu* kangaroo, (*transf.*) horse.] A horse.

1839 W. WILLIAMS *Vocab. Aborigines S.A.* 16 *Nan-tah*, horse. **1893** H.J. WHITE *Round Camp Fire* 61 Well the 'nantos' were ready and the tucker-box stowed away snug. **1900** R. BRUCE *Benbonuna* (1904) 55 'Where you bin put 'em Peter? and where your 'nantoo'. . . ' 'He led me a nice dance, and I knocked up my own horse following him,' said Heslop, correctly guessing that 'nantoo' was native for horse. **1907** 'S. PARTRIGE' *Rocky Section* 12 Take old Vagabond and run him on the section, and you'll always have a second nanto if anything happens to the other. **1924** F.J. MILLS *Happy Days* 8 'That ain't much of a lookin' nanto,' said one, indicating a large chestnut horse. **1929** 'A. RUSSELL' *Bungoona* 7 Bungoona .. means 'good', or, rather, the superlative of good. That is to say, if I were to remark that old Blossom was a *bungoona nanta*, I'd really mean to convey to you, in the lingo of the blacks, that Bloss was a jolly good old horse. **1935** H.H. FINLAYSON *Red Centre* 98 The horse-boys knew 'nantos' from A to Z, and were good trackers. **1936** 'L. KAYE' *Black Wilderness* 26 Kombi sit down close up nantos-horses. **1957** W.E. HARNEY *Life among Aborigines* 12 They saw many 'kutebas' come to Mudba with their strange 'nantus' (a word in reference to the distended nose of a horse after it has been ridden hard).

nap, var. KNAP.

nap, *n.*[1] [Prob. f. *knapsack.*] A bed-roll; a swag.

1892 *Bulletin* (Sydney) 2 Apr. 13/1 Drip, drip, drip! and one's 'nap' is far from dry Tis hard to keep the water out—however one may try. **1899** *Ibid.* 5 Aug. 35/1 Often there are no bunks. The naps are spread in the dust, and everyone lies on his bed smoking. **1913** W.K. HARRIS *Outback in Aust.* 144 In Australia the 'swag' (or 'nap') consists of blanket, tent (if one is carried), change of clothing, etc., rolled up in a bundle carried across the shoulders. **1921** *Bulletin* (Sydney) 19 May 20/4 You just blow in, unroll your own nap on a decent bed, boil the 'knock me silly' and grill a chop. **1936** *Ibid.* 26 Aug. 20/2 The most luxurious 'nap' I ever struck in the mulga was a feather bed that 'Stuttering' Mick carried with him. **1950** K.S. PRICHARD *Winged Seeds* 18, I got a wire from Mick Larkin sayin': 'Feelin' crook, shake a leg, bring nap.' **1968** W. GILL *Petermann Journey* 24, I knew where to put my 'nap', the Territory word for a 'swag'.

nap, *n.*[2] [Neg. use of *to go nap* to stake all one can: see OED(S *sb.*[3] 2 b.] In the phr. **not to go nap on,** to have no enthusiasm for (someone or something).

1918 *Kia Ora Coo-ee* Dec. 3/3 Talking of souvenirs, I don't go nap on any of the ordinary kind which lose their interest after they have been looked at once or twice. **1932** W. HATFIELD *Christmastown* 43 Didn't go nap on wine himself. A drop of whisky, now. **1939** FRANKLIN & CUSACK *Pioneers on Parade* 105 She knows I don't go nap on him, and I have to be careful not to seem prejudiced. **1955** P. WHITE *Tree of Man* 80, I never went nap on the priests meself. **1965** R.H. CONQUEST *Horses in Kitchen* 170 He didn't go nap on the idea of young fellows eyeing the shapely one. **1966** D. NILAND *Pairs & Loners* 143, I got a marquee. Don't go nap on this tent-living, but what can a man do?

napunyah /nə'pʌnjə/. YAPUNYAH. Also *attrib.*

1949 H.G. LAMOND *White Ears* 21 A giant napunia-tree had fallen across two rocks. **1968** LINKLATER & TAPP *Gather No Moss* 6 The manager of a sheep station . . set me taking out napunya roots near the homestead to fill in time till the shearing began. **1976** *Bulletin* (Sydney) 25 Sept. 21/2 Away out in the Paroo Channel country, back o' Bourke, there flourishes the Napunyah, a white-flowered eucalypt rich in nectar: bee-keepers rattle for hundreds of kilometres in their trucks to place hives among these trees.

narang /nə'ræŋ/, *a.* Chiefly *Austral. pidgin. Obs.* Also **narrangy, nerangy.** [a. Dharuk *ŋaraŋ.*] Little.

1790 J. HUNTER *Hist. Jrnl. Trans. Port Jackson* (1793) 409 *Narrong*, any thing small. **1827** P. CUNNINGHAM *Two Yrs. in N.S.W.* II. 28 They could not contain their astonishment. . that the '*cobawn* (big) gobernor, had not mout *so* (screwing theirs into the appropriate shape), like the *narang* (little) gobernor'. **1838** T. WALKER *Month in Bush Aust.* 6 The blacks say . . that there are two deep holes in it a 'cabonn' (large and deep) and a 'narang' (small). **1861** *Burke & Wills Exploring Exped.* 8 Sandy said he could only understand 'narrangy word' they said; but I believe that he could not understand them at all. **1870** *Illustr. Sydney News* 24 Dec. 2/2 The latter were occasionally met on the runs by shepherds, who gave them a 'narang' bit of tobacco, and they passed away without molesting anyone. **1879** 'AUSTRALIAN' *Adventures Qld.* 31 That fellow been sit down here *nerangy* while (a little while).

narangy /nə'ræŋgi/. [See NARANG.] See quot. 1967. Formerly also **rangie.**

1891 *Truth* (Sydney) 8 Mar. 7/3 Remember that the jackeroo without perfolio (alias the *rangie* pur et simple) has a chance of promotion to drover, shed-boss, overseer, and manager. *Ibid.* 15 Mar. 7/3 So we bushmen changed the names Colonial experience, pannikin-overseer, rangie-boss, and all that 'push' into Jackeroo. *Ibid.* 19 Apr. 7/3 The reduced rate continues, and the Rangies are afraid to strike. **1903** J. FURPHY *Such is Life* 53 Jack Ward, the senior narangy, made some remark . . the two junior narangies supported Ward. *Ibid.* 204 Being a little too exalted for the men's hut, and a great deal too vile for the boss's house, I was quartered in the narangies' barracks. **1967** G. JENKIN *Two Yrs. Bardunyah Station* 73 *Narangies*, salaried people on the staff of a station, as distinct from the stockmen and others on a weekly wage.

nardoo /na'du/. Formerly also **nardu.** [a. Diyari *ŋardu* or Kamilaroi *nhaaduu.*]

1. The perennial, rhizomatous fern *Marsilea drummondii* (fam. Marsileaceae) of mainland Aust., having clover-like fronds and occurring chiefly in arid areas along stream-beds and near lakes; any of several other ferns of the genus *Marsilea*; the sporocarp of these plants, which is ground into flour and used by Aborigines as a food; *clover fern*, see CLOVER. Also *attrib.*

1860 *Trans. & Proc. R. Soc. Vic.* 203 While the foregoing sheets were going through the press, intelligence having reached Melbourne of the value, as an edible seed, of the *Marsileae hirsuta* (or Nardo), as found so useful in the Victorian Expedition . . it has occurred to me that it would be well to mention that I found the same plant growing in Dumby Bay, Port Lincoln. **1861** *Bell's Life in Sydney* 9 Nov. 2/6 For some time we were employed gathering nardoo, and laying up a supply. **1867** 'S. MCTAVISH' *Chowla* 16 There are a devoted band of Moravian Missionaries bound for Cooper's Creek . . exchanging the sausages and sauer-kraut of the Vaterland for opossum and nardoo. **1892** J. FRASER *Aborigines N.S.W.* 77 From many kinds of seeds, such as the 'nardu' . . the natives make a rough kind of meal which is baked into 'damper'. **1893** *Proc. Linnean Soc. N.S.W.* VIII. 215 Nardoo was first encountered in quantity near Lake Kopperamana on Cooper's Creek. I learnt . . that the plant is a *Marsilea*, as had been originally stated, but doubted by some, who thought it impossible that sufficient involucres (sporocarps) to serve for food could be obtained from a *Marsilea*, the Nardoo of Burke and Wills being regarded by them as the seed of *Sesbania aculeata*. **1896** T. HENEY *Girl at Birrell's* 131 Around its shore grew scrub and bush, no grass or herbage save here and there in marshy pools, where the surface was covered with the larger round disks of the nardoo, split into four leaves, green above, frost-white beneath, or red with decay, stretching out long filaments. **1905** A.B. PATERSON *Old Bush Songs* 121 On the far Barcoo, where they eat nardoo, a thousand miles away. **1934** C. SAYCE *Comboman* 107 A woman, pounding nardoo-seeds in front of her wurley, broke into a quavering corroboree dirge. **1948** H.A. LINDSAY *Bushman's Handbk.* 56 Nardoo 'seeds' . . are really the spore cases of a fern with a leaf like the shamrock which grows in swamps; when the swamp dries these 'seeds' can be swept up by the handful. **1977** J. O'GRADY *There was Kid* 39 Although often short of food on the farm, our father said that he hoped we would never have to 'come at nardoo bread', or porridge.

2. Comb. **nardoo cake, flour, stone.**

1861 *Burke & Wills Exploring Exped.* 30 Next came a supply of **nardoo cake** and water. **1944** J.K. EWERS *Tales from Dead Heart* 7 Ngangan ate his nardoo cakes until he was . . full. **1970** J.V. MARSHALL *Walk to Hills of Dreamtime* 155 *Nardoo cake*, cakes made by grinding up into paste and then baking the hard pea-like fruit of the nardoo or clover-fern (*marsilea quadrifolia*). **1861** *Burke & Wills Exploring Exped.* 30 Fetched a large bowl of the raw **nardoo flour.** **1886** F. COWAN *Aust.* 23 His Nardoo-flour: the crushed seeds of the Clover-fern: the one extreme of his variety of food. **1912** SPENCER & GILLEN *Across Aust.* 16 The natives make a kind of flour out of them by grinding them to powder between their so-called **nardoo stones.** **1919** *Emu* XVIII. 171 Large stones once used for grinding the seeds of the nardoo (Marsilea drummondii) . . plant, which made a valuable sort of flour for these natives. One of these bottom nardoo stones . . had two grinding hollows worked into it. **1933** W. HATFIELD *Desert Saga* 4 The women's *nardoo* stones tap-tap-tapped all day grinding to rude flour the gravelly imperishable *mulga* seeds. **1949** H.E. THONEMANN *Tell White Man* 52 Alice then got out her Nardoo stones and ground the damp seeds to flour between them. **1979** C. STONE *Running Brumbies* 44, I was also to see many nardoo stones throughout my stay at Clifton Hills.

Naretha parrot /nəriθə 'pærət/. [f. the name of a railway station in s.e. W.A.] See quot. 1976.

1922 *Bulletin* (Sydney) 12 Jan. 20/3 From so accessible a place as Naretha, on the East-West line, F. Whitlock lately secured a new species of parrot, the Naretha. **1943** C. BARRETT *Austral. Animal Bk.* 233 The little blue bonnet, or Naretha parrot .. was discovered in the locality after which it is named—a station on the Trans-Australian Railway. **1976** *Reader's Digest Compl. Bk. Austral. Birds* 287 There are four rather distinct forms of the blue bonnet. One, the Naretha parrot *Northiella haematogaster narethae*, lives along the south-western fringe of the Nullarbor Plain, and differs mainly from others in its pure yellow belly, red undertail-coverts, turquoise brow and small size.

narga, nargar, narger, varr. NAGA.

nark, *v. Obs.* [Spec. use of *nark* to exasperate.] *trans.* To thwart (a scheme, etc.).

1891 *Truth* (Sydney) 15 Mar. 2/1 They would surely know that I lied to them, and would crab my pitch, or to speak more plainly . . they would nark my lurk. **1892** *Ibid.* 24 Apr. 1/5 There's nothing in it, as you know, but *Truth*, don't 'nark' our game. **1916** *Ibid.* 19 Mar. 4/3 Assisting to 'nark Andy Fisher's pitch'. **1947** N. LINDSAY *Halfway to Anywhere* 120 Waldo occupied a room with elder brother, Bags, who might nark the whole thing. **1975** R. BEILBY *Brown Land Crying* 200 Ya'd do anything to nark me, anything to put me down, wouldn't ya?

Nar Nar Goon /na na 'gun/. [The name of a small town s.e. of Melbourne.] Used allusively to denote a small and insignificant place.

1918 *Kia Ora Coo-ee* Sept. 18/2 Jimmy was thinking of home, how his mother would be feeling, what his father would say about him, and how things in general were at Nar Nar Goon. Yes, dear, old, sleepy Nar Nar Goon. **1963** L. RICHARDS *Boots & All!* 176 They've had some shockers, too, players who would have struggled for a game with the South Nar Nar Goon fifths! **1981** *Age* (Melbourne) 8 June 2/2 Television football commentaries tend to be about as rewarding as a night game at Nar Nar Goon football ground in a power strike.

narrangy, var. NARANG.

Narrawa burr /nærəwə 'bɜ/. [Perh. f. the name of the small town *Narrawah*, N.S.W.] The small, prickly shrub *Solanum cinereum* (fam. Solanaceae) of s.e. Qld., N.S.W., Vic., and naturalized in the Flinders Ranges, S.A.

1917 *Bulletin* (Sydney) 27 Sept. 22/4 There is but one 'native' in that bunch—the Narrawa burr. **1945** *Queanbeyan Age* 6 Nov. 3/2 Owners of land within the Australian Capital Territory are hereby notified that the undermentioned plants have been declared to be noxious weeds... Narrawa Burr (Solanum cinereum) [etc.]. **1958** J.N. WHITTET *Weeds* 358 Narrawa burr is considered to be responsible for causing mortalities in sheep and horses in New South Wales.

narriwadgee /nærə'wædʒi/. [Prob. f. an Aboriginal language.] *Night well*, see NIGHT.

1923 *Bulletin* (Sydney) 25 Jan. 22/3 The mysterious waterhole . . is no doubt a 'narriwadgee', or night well. **1930** *Ibid.* 16 July 21/2 The night well, known to abos. as narriwadgee.

narrow-billed bronze cuckoo. The cuckoo *Chrysococcyx basalis*, widely distributed in Aust. and occurring elsewhere, having a copper-green back, black bill, and barred underparts.

1903 *Emu* II. 165 Narrow-billed Bronze Cuckoo (*Chalcoccyx basalis*) . . very common on the plains. **1916** S.A. WHITE *In Far Northwest* 152 Three species of cuckoos were seen—the pallid cuckoo . . the black-eared cuckoo, and the narrow-billed bronze cuckoo. **1945** C. BARRETT *Austral. Bird Life* 149 [The egg colour] of . . the narrow-billed bronze cuckoo . . is pinkish, with a uniform sprinkling of tiny reddish spots.

narrow comb: see COMB 2.

narrow-leaved, *a.* Used as a distinguishing epithet in the names of plants: **narrow-leaved ironbark,** a tree of the genus *Eucalyptus* (fam. Myrtaceae), esp. *E. crebra* of N.S.W. and Qld.; also **narrow-leafed ironbark**; **peppermint,** the tree *Eucalyptus radiata* (fam. Myrtaceae) of s.e. mainland Aust., having narrow green to grey-green leaves with a peppermint smell when crushed; **poison,** any of several shrubs of the genus *Gastrolobium* (fam. Fabaceae), esp. *G. stenophyllum* of s.w. W.A., having narrow leaves, and yellow and red flowers; also **narrow-leaf poison.**

1845 L. LEICHHARDT *Jrnl. Overland Exped. Aust.* 18 Jan. (1847) 112 We came across an open forest of **narrow-leaved Ironbark** (E. resinifera). **1904** J.H. MAIDEN *Notes on Commercial Timbers N.S.W.* 9 Narrow-leaved ironbark (*Eucalyptus crebra* . .). So called because of its narrow, slender, graceful foliage. **1976** *Ecos* ix. 29/3 The woodlands include . . narrow-leafed ironbark, and grey box communities. **1896** *Proc. Linnean Soc. N.S.W.* X. 603 *E. amygdalina* . . var. *radiata*. . . We have a fairly distinct tree which goes under the names of 'White Gum', 'River Gum', 'River White Gum', 'Ribbon Gum', and even '**Narrow-leaved Peppermint**'. **1926** A.S. LE SOUEF et al. *Wild Animals Australasia* 260 Other narrow-leaved peppermints. **1963** C. BURGESS *Blue Mountain Gums* 50 'Narrow leaved peppermint' . . was named *Eucalyptus radiata* . . by Sieber . . in 1828. It is easily distinguished from *E. piperita* . . by its narrow, almost willow-like foliage. **1897 [narrow-leaved poison]** L. LINDLEY-COWEN *W. Austral. Settler's Guide* 582 Narrow-leaf and marlock poison bushes. **1926** *Poison Plants W.A.* (W.A. Dept. Agric.) 33 The name 'Narrow-leaved Poison' as here adopted for *Gastrolobium crassifolium* . . in some districts . . is also applied to Champion Bay Poison . . Pituri . . White Gum Poison . . and Rock Poison. **1939** A. GASTON *Coolgardie Gold* 182 They get the leaves of a small shrub known to the whites as 'narrow-leaf poison'. **1956** GARDNER & BENNETTS *Toxic Plants W.A.* 75 Narrow-leaved poison may be distinguished from all other species [of poison] by its crowded narrow leaves. **1965** A.R. BARRETT *Hist. War Service Land Settlement Scheme W.A.* 24 Careful picking and stocking was necessary to eliminate or control the native poison plants—Box poison (*Oxylobium parviflorum*) and Narrow Leaved poison (*Gastrolobium crassifolium*) which came up thickly after burning and cultivation. **1973** R. ERICKSON et al. *Flowers & Plants W.A.* 183 Several toxic species of . . *Gastrolobium* occur in the region. One is endemic, being known only from the Fitzgerald River valley. This is Narrow-leaved Poison, *Gastrolobium stenophyllum*.

nasho. [Abbrev. of *nat(ional* + -O.] Compulsory military training, as introduced under the National Service Act of 1951; one who undergoes this. Also **nasho training.**

1966 B. BEAVER *You can't come Back* 5 Sam, the new one, was just eighteen and due for his Nasho training. **1967** *Kings Cross Whisper* (Sydney) xxxv. 8/4 (*heading*) *Nashos for jungles of Toorak.* South Vietnam will shortly send National servicemen to Australia. **1973** *Bulletin* (Sydney) 27 Jan. 27/1 Some 'nashos' have shown outstanding zeal by signing on with the Regular Army. **1975** W. NAGLE *Odd Angry Shot* 13 'You'll be scouting for one of the battalions. . . ' 'That should make us look nice and obvious with seventy odd bloody nashos wandering around us.' **1980** C. JAMES *Unreliable Mem.* 141 National Service was designed to turn boys into men and make the Yellow Peril think twice about moving south. It was universally known as Nasho. **1981** Q. WILD *Honey Wind* 85 One of the worst things . . was something that happened in nasho . . before there was any fighting or anything.

national game.

1. Two-up.

1930 L.W. LOWER *Here's Luck* 50 He had a small piece of flat wood in his hand, on which were balanced two pennies. The national game was in progress. **1944** S. ARNEIL *One Man's War* 31 July (1980) 188 'Two-up', our national game is severely frowned upon in the camp and all efforts are made to suppress it. **1963** F. HARDY *Legends Benson's Valley* 108 Sunday sessions of Australia's national game. The two-up school operated on the plateau above the valley. **1976** *Bulletin* (Sydney) 10 Jan. 45/2 There's no greater humiliation than being a failure at the national game. **1983** *Sun-Herald* (Sydney) 23 Jan. 35/3 You can't wipe out two-up; it's our national game.

2. Australian National Football.

1936 E.C.H. TAYLOR et al. *Our Austral. Game Football* 9 'The University of Hard Knocks' as Sir Isaac Isaacs so aptly termed our National Game. **1953** *A.N.F.C. Rev.* (Austral. Nat. Football Council) 1 The Council was charged with the responsibility of developing, and extending, the game in the minor States so that it could become established, and recognised, as *the* truly National Game, played throughout the Commonwealth. **1985** *Canberra Times* 11 Aug. 9/4 Failing attendances this year should be sharp enough to jolt the VFL out of the smug complacency and token concern for the future of the national game.

native, *n.*

1. An Aboriginal; AUSTRALIAN *n.* 1.

1770 J. COOK *Jrnls.* 29 Apr. (1955) I. 305 Saw as we came in on both points of the bay Several of the natives and a few hutts. **1787** *HRA* (1914) 1st Ser. I. 13 You are to endeavour by every possible means to open an intercourse with the natives. **1791** S. MACARTHUR ONSLOW *Some Early Rec. Macarthurs* (1914) 33 The natives are certainly not a very gallant set of people, who take pleasure in escorting their ladies. No; they suffer them to follow in Indian file. **1803** G. BOND *Brief Acct. Colony Port Jackson* 3 A gentleman of considerable respectability informed me that a native, whom he kept as a servant for three years, afterwards deserted. **1819** *Sydney Gaz.* 2 Jan., The Natives, or Aborigines of this Territory, assembled together to partake of the kindness and hospitality held out to them by Government. **1829** R. DAWSON *Statement* 90 The natives who were employed by the Company received *no wages in money*. **1836** J.F. O'CONNELL *Residence Eleven Yrs. New Holland* 65 Trusty natives are created 'bush constables'. These are about the only blacks who have guns and ammunition. **1845** L. LEICHHARDT *Jrnl. Overland Exped. Aust.* 2 Dec. (1847) 502 A fine native stepped out of the forest with the ease and grace of an Apollo. **1852** *Awful Execution 17 Convicts* 3 The settlers consider the natives a nuisance that ought to be exterminated. **1854** W. SHAW *Land of Promise* 21 Under the majestic tree where the band now ranged, the native danced his wild '*Corrobery*'. **1876** 'RESIDENT' *Girl Life in Aust.* 137 Grandpapa had a station up bush, and the natives were just like flies—such a plague—and he used to trap them and kill them one by one, but they would not die fast enough, and he got a lot of white stuff and mixed it with their flour—arsenic it was—and they died. **1890** *Braidwood Dispatch* 4 Jan. 2/5 At the Roeburne (W.A.) a native has been sentenced to death for the murder of a native boy at Ashburton. After killing the boy, the murderer proceeded to cook and eat him. **1901** *Bulletin* (Sydney) 7 Sept. 14/2 The native got 15 years; but in consideration of good conduct . . he is now on duty as black tracker under a sort of ticket-of-leave. **1918** G. WHITE *Thirty Yrs. Tropical Aust.* 71, I was informed that the natives see in the Magellan clouds surrounding the Southern Cross the form of an emu. **1935** H. BASEDOW *Knights of Boomerang* 13 The tendency . . is for the natives to drift to the white people's settlement. **1946** C.T. MADIGAN *Crossing Dead Heart* 21 It was most important to take a native, the wilder the better. **1960** *N.T. News* (Darwin) 5 Jan. 1/6 Bush hermit Jack . . Jensen is building holding yards at Munmulary. He is alone on the job except for four natives. **1963** *Bulletin* (Sydney) 23 Nov. 10/3 Most of West Australia's 20,000 'natives', within the meaning of the Act, should be able to have a legal drink soon.

2. A non-Aboriginal person born in Australia; AUSTRALIAN *n.* 2.

1806 *Sydney Gaz.* 20 July, *Thomas Ford* and *William Evans*, Boys; the latter a native of this Colony. **1819** W.C. WENTWORTH *Statistical, Hist., & Pol. Descr. N.S.W.*, W.C. Wentworth Esq. A native of the colony. **1830** T.J. MASLEN *Friend of Aust.* 132 As there are now so many white natives in Australia, the term *native*, as applied to the aborigines should be discontinued. **1851** H. MELVILLE *Present State Aust.* 321 Cricket is a game much played in Van Diemen's Land. . . The grand play is between the natives and all England; and, generally speaking, the natives are the winners. **1859** F. FOWLER *Southern Lights & Shadows* 70 Mr James Martin . . is within a month or two of being a native. He came to the colony in long clothes. **1867** *Sydney Punch* 2 Nov. 185/2 By *natives* I don't mean *the blacks*, dear—*They* are called Aboriginals—these Are fair as yourself—what your brother At Eton would call 'quite the cheese'. **1896** H. LAWSON *In Days when World was Wide* 157 Long to feel the bridle-leather tugging strongly in the hand And to feel once more a little like a native of the land. **1909** *Truth* (Sydney) 11 July 7/4 Sydney has lost one of its oldest natives in the person of Mrs Mary Anne Pickering. . . Her mother was also a native, and was on the staff of Governor Macquarie. **1917** *Huon Times* (Franklin) 16 Feb. 6/1 She was born at Pitt Town, near Windsor, New South Wales, in 1821 . . and was possibly the oldest living native of the Commonwealth. **1964** J.S. MANIFOLD *Who wrote Ballads?* 43 They were a bit of a problem to thoughtful Governors, these local-born among the currency men. Even to give them a collective name was a problem. Some called them 'natives'—unsatisfactorily because it confused them with aboriginals.

3. An animal or plant indigenous to Australia.

1793 J.E. SMITH *Specimen Bot. New Holland* 31 *Flax-leaved Pimelea* . . is a native of the coast of New South Wales, among rocks. **1842** *Sydney Herald* 26 Feb. 2/7 The whole of the flowers exhibited, with the exception of the natives, were made previous to the hot weather. **1916** *Bulletin* (Sydney) 20 Jan. 24/1 Many families . . have . . removed beef from the menu and inserted wallaby. . . Numbers of people eat the native for a change. **1917** *Ibid.* 27 Sept. 24/4 There is but one 'native' in that bunch—the Narrawa burr. **1955** *Ibid.* 11 May 12/3 Don't know another native who, waiting for a tucker handout, indicates impatience as elaborately as a kookaburra. **1969** G. JOHNSTON *Clean Straw for Nothing* (1971) 156 The trees are all what the nurseryman calls 'natives'—acacia and seven different kinds of eucalyptus, bottle brush and grevillea. **1977** *Times Lit. Suppl.* (London) 14 Oct. 1213/3 A notice by the gate will stop the stranger short: 'Australian natives', it says, 'one dollar each.' **1979** V. CRITTENDEN *Front Garden* 38 We thought we were very modern as we had a Sydney Christmas bush in the centre of the bed, an Australian native although we didn't call them that in those days. **1985** *Canberra Times* 23 Aug. 34/6 Old style home nestled among natives and orchard trees.

4. *Obs.* In phr.

a. native of New Holland, an Aboriginal.

1805 J. TURNBULL *Voyage round World* I. 43 The natives of New Holland . . have gained nothing in civilization since their first discovery. **1826** *Monitor* (Sydney) 15 Dec. 247/2 The Portuguese *Jesuit* of the 16th century, did more for the cannibal of Paraguay, than the British Protestant, up to 1826, has done for the native of New Holland! **1842** R.G. JAMESON *NZ., S.A., & N.S.W.* 60 To the natives of New Holland has been ascribed the lowest place on the scale of intellect. **1852** J. SHAW *Tramp to Diggings* 21 Generally, the natives of New Holland have dark brown skins, large eyes, massive foreheads, broad noses, wide mouths, short lower jaws, large white teeth, and long sinewy limbs.

b. native of the colony, a non-Aboriginal person born in an Australian Colony.

1834 *Sydney Herald* 17 Nov. (Suppl.) 1/6 Samuel Leverton, a Native of the Colony, who had shipped himself a few weeks back, as Steward of the *Australia.* **1845** C. CHISHOLM *Emigration & Transportation* (1847) 40, I am a native of the Colony; my father was an Englishman from Kent. **1856** *Moreton Bay Free Press* 28 Apr. 3/5 The Acting General is not a native of the colony, as 'he was born before he arrived'. **1880** 'ERRO' *Squattermania* 36 They were natives of the colony, bred in the Bush.

c. native of Australia, native of New South Wales: (i) an Aboriginal; **(ii)** a non-Aboriginal person born in Australia.

1830 R. DAWSON *Present State Aust.* 132 It is not customary with the **natives of Australia** to shake hands. **1851** J.H. BURTON *Emigrant's Man.* ii. 3 The aborigines or natives of Australia are now very inconsiderable in numbers. **1860** 'LADY' *My Experiences in Aust.* 205 The natives of Australia occupy almost the lowest place among the human race. **1878** R.B. SMYTH *Aborigines of Vic.* I. 1 Very different accounts have been used by voyagers and explorers relative to the color and form of the natives of Australia. . . The greater number regard them simply as 'blacks', with such conformations generally as belong to the African. **1883** R.E.N. TWOPENY *Town Life Aust.* 245 An aboriginal is always a 'black fellow'. A native of Australia would mean a white man born in the colony. **1805** J. TURNBULL *Voyage round World* I. 73 It is one thing to catch, and another to civilize, a **native of New South Wales.** **1817** *First Rep. Auxiliary Bible Soc. N.S.W.* 9 The Natives of New South Wales . . are to this day worshipping dumb idols. **1831** *HRA* (1923) 1st Ser. XVI. 14 The Civilization of the Natives of New South Wales is of so much importance. **1843** C. ROWCROFT *Tales of Colonies* (1858) 117 We were not sufficiently ingenious to construct an extempore canoe from the bark of a tree as the native of New South Wales are accustomed to do. **1867** J. BONWICK *J. Batman* 12 Mr Batman . . is a native of New South Wales.

native, *a.*

1. a. Of or pertaining to the Aborigines; Aboriginal.

1807 Banks Papers 18 Dec. XX. 177, 3 Kangaroo Skins, Two of which are native mantles. **1809** *Sydney Gaz.* 24 Sept., Last Thursday night a native banditti, 15 in number, attacked the house of Joseph Marcus. **1817** Macarthur Papers 8 Mar. XII., The little creatures have been taught to read and write . . and in the hands of Providence let us hope they may be instrumental in civilizing their countrymen. Pray pardon the partiality of a native for native subjects. **1838** *Colonist* (Sydney) 6 Jan. 2/4 Our courts of law should . . be supplied . . with native barristers, and also . . the colonial public should take an interest . . in educating . . them. **1839** *S. Austral. Rec.* (London) 1 Nov. 254 It being now sunset, we formed a native 'breakweather' of boughs, and passed the night in this place. **1852** R. MORGAN *Reminisc. Aboriginal Station Cummeranguna* 101, I put some fire into one of our native buckets. **1853** A. KINLOCH *Murray River* 39 Its course could not be found without native assistance. **1856** J. BONWICK *W. Buckley* 76 They stood before him in usual native undress. **1863** —— *Wild White Man* 78 There is little need now in Victoria to argue the subject of native rights. **1867** —— *J. Batman* 10 Having such severe struggles with famine, bushranging, and native aggression. **1879** *Native Tribes S.A.* p. xxix, A native burial-ground, on the banks of the Torrens. **1896** B. SPENCER *Rep. Horn Sci. Exped. Central Aust.* IV. 125 On the walls of these rock shelters, or on the adjacent rock faces, were occasionally, but not frequently, found native drawings done in red or yellow ochre, charcoal, or some white pigment, or in a combination of these colours. **1908** J. FLOOD *New Norcia* 109 The first season the native cricket team went from home to try their prowess against the outside world they were an object of deep interest. **1939** J.W. COLLINGS *8000 Miles by Air* 3 He had to preside at a Native Court, when a full-blooded aborigine was being tried for the murder of his woman. **1944** J. DEVANNY *By Tropic Sea & Jungle* 65 Days spent yarning with the fishermen, white and native. **1964** F. GALE *Study of Assimilation* p. xx, 'Native' is commonly used in South Australia to describe both Aborigines and Part-Aborigines. . . Many Part-Aborigines consider it a term of disparagement and take exception to being so designated. **1986** *Sydney Morning Herald* 8 Mar. 41/6 The Pope has expressed a desire to visit 'the native people of Australia'. A committee of 15 people—all Aborigines—is being formed to plan the encounter.

b. In collocations: **native black, camp, canoe, children, constable, encampment, grave, guide, hut, inhabitant, man, name, path, savage, shepherd, tongue, track.**

1816 *HRA* (1917) 1st Ser. IX. 53 The **Native Blacks** of this Country, Inhabiting the distant Interior parts. **1827** *Tasmanian* (Hobart) 14 June 4 This native black was an aboriginal native. **1840** *Tegg's N.S.W. Pocket Almanac* 52 In several districts of the Colony the native blacks have been supplied with fire arms and ammunition. **1849** A. HARRIS *Emigrant Family* (1967) 38 It's only the native blacks . . that the cattle are afraid of; and I dare say it's more because they're without clothes, than because of their colour. **1856** *Plea on Behalf Aboriginal Inhabitants Vic.* 9 We have . . taken up our pen . . to urge the claims of the native blacks upon the public. **1874** *Illustr. Sydney News* 28 Feb. 4/4 The telegraph station at Borrow Creek on the line from Adelaide to Port Darwin was attacked by native blacks. **1927** A. CROMBIE *After Sixty Yrs.* 45 At this time the native blacks were fairly numerous. **1842** *Portland Mercury* 31 Aug. 2/5 A double-barrelled gun, which had belonged to the man, was found at the **native camp.** **1852** J. MORGAN *Life & Adventures W. Buckley* 122, I went up to the native camp, and addressed the tribes as to the conduct they should pursue. **1865** G.S. LANG *Aborigines of Aust.* 48 A man is killed by blacks, and eight weeks afterwards a native camp is charged. **1874** J.J. HALCOMBE *Emigrant & Heathen* 164 The native camp was a mile out of the township. **1898** D.W. CARNEGIE *Spinifex & Sand* 39 Numerous old native camps surrounded the water, and many weapons, spears, waddies, and coolimans were lying about. **1853** A. KINLOCH *Murray River* 13 We managed to upset a **native canoe** or 'mungo', propelled by a black and his 'lubra'. **1864** J. MORRILL *Sketch of Residence* 208 The captain found in his rambles a native canoe. **1819** W.C. WENTWORTH *Statistical, Hist., & Pol. Descr. N.S.W.* 18 A school for the education and civilization of the aborigines of the country . . was founded by the present governor three years since, and by the last accounts from the colony, it contained eighteen **native children,** who had been voluntarily placed there by their parents, and were making equal progress in their studies with European children of the same age. **1841** G. GREY *Two Exped. N.-W. & W.A.* I. 145 The native women and children wandered about in the distance, conversing in groups. **1855** J. BONWICK *Geogr. Aust. & N.Z.* (ed. 3) 193 Native children are laughing, happy creatures. **1839** W. MANN *Six Yrs.' Residence* 287 Onkaparinga Jack, Captain Jack, both **native constables.** **1872** MRS E. MILLETT *Austral. Parsonage* 242 In the task of searching for runaway prisoners the police are almost always assisted by native constables, whose keen sight and extraordinary powers of observation are capable of following a track even over the hardest rocks. **1881** W. FEILDING *Austral. Trans-Continental Railway* 51 The native constable and our Kanaka lad . . got drunk. **1841** G. GREY *Jrnls. Two Exped. N.-W. & W.A.* II. 329 When I went to the **native encampment,** I found that the first forms of the marriage ceremony had taken place. **1852** J. MORGAN *Life & Adventures W. Buckley* 137 Falling in with a native encampment . . I endeavoured to obtain some information. **1879** G. TAPLIN *Folklore S. Austral. Aborigines* 119 As we travelled along the Murray we noticed a scarcity of native encampments. **1856** G. WILLMER *Draper in Aust.* 68 Encamped for the night very near a **native grave.** I particularly noticed the care which the relatives had taken to fence it all around with sticks. **1860** J.M. STUART *Explorations in Aust.* 29 Mar. (1865) 144 From the native grave, I am led to conclude that the water there is permanent. **1808** *Sydney Gaz.* 18 Sept., I have frequently occasion to traverse the interior . . and finding the utility of a **native guide**, always made election of such as I found most tractable and obliging. **1831** W. BLAND *Journey of Discovery Port Phillip* 5 The unexpected desertion of a native guide. **1848** T.L. MITCHELL *Jrnl. Exped. Tropical Aust.* 63 Our native guide was very shy. **1851** H. MELVILLE *Present State Aust.* 368 Despatching parties with the native guides, in order to secure . . the chief of the various tribes. **1803** C.M.H. CLARK *Select Documents* (1950) 90 Saw a canoe and two **native huts.** **1831** W. BLAND *Journey of Discovery Port Phillip* 13 They had passed some native huts about half a mile before their arrival. **1844** D.G. BROCK *Jrnl.* 25 Nov. 49 Native huts to the number of 16 I counted. **1855** R. AUSTIN *Jrnl. Interior W.A.* 16 There were three recently constructed native huts of the usual shape, formed of dead logs. **1886** R. HENTY *Australiana* 11 In a mia mia (native hut) in the middle of the camp . . was a perfect living skeleton. **1808** *Sydney Gaz.* 21 Aug. The little attention which we pay to the customs of the **native inhabitants** of this country. **1839** *S. Austral. Register* (Adelaide) 11 July 2 *Vaccination*, as a protection against Small-pox, will be performed for the Native Inhabitants every Wednesday . . at the Native Huts on the Torrens. **1848** J. STEPHENS *Voice from Aust.* 9 The native inhabitants of the country bear no comparison in power or number to those who have so unceremoniously occupied their soil. **1793** J. HUNTER *Hist. Jrnl. Trans. Port Jackson* 132, I observed a **native man** of this country, who was decently cloathed, and seemed to be as much at his ease at the tea-table as any person there. **1832** BACKHOUSE & TYLOR *Life & Labours G.W. Walker* 12 Oct. (1862) 103 Our party consisted of the Commandant, four native men, two of their wives, and ourselves. **1845** L. LEICHHARDT *Jrnl. Overland Exped. Aust.* 11 May (1847) 256, I passed a few native men sitting before their gunyas. **1852** W. HUGHES *Austral. Colonies* 90 The native man of Australia is of a dark, sooty-brown complexion. **1834** G. BENNETT *Wanderings N.S.W.* I. 70 As well as the scientific (or hard names, as the ladies call them), let also the popular, colonial and **native names**, be attached. **1841** *S. Austral. Mag.* Aug. 46 As a general rule, I think it highly undesirable, that the native names either of places or of rivers should be superseded by English ones. **1863** J. DAVIS *Tracks of McKinlay* 210 The native name of this place is 'Appocoldarinnie'. **1959** K.S. PRICHARD *N'Goola* 12 Most of the girls in the settlement would not remember if they ever had a native name. They were all Jeans and Janeys, Kittys and Dulcies, these days. **1981** A.B. FACEY *Fortunate Life* 13 A town named Narrogin (a native name). **1791** S. MACARTHUR ONSLOW *Some Early Rec. Macarthurs* (1914) 33 Nor do I think there is any probability of my seeing much of the inland country until it is cleared, as beyond a certain distance round the Colony there is nothing but **native paths**, very narrow and very incommodious. **1831** W. BLAND *Journey of Discovery Port Phillip* 20 A native path, bearing impressions of the feet of a considerable number of natives. **1841** G. GREY *Jrnls. Two Exped. N.-W. & W.A.* II. 9 For the next three miles we still followed the native path, which continued to run S. by E. **1847** G.F. ANGAS *Savage Life & Scenes* I. 68 We observed narrow native paths in all directions leading towards the water. **1893** S. NEWLAND *Paving Way* 29 A black fellow [was] engaged to show him the native path and accompany him back to the whaling station. **1831** *Independent* (Launceston) 24 Sept. 2/3 The dogs in the possession of the hordes of **native savages.** **1888** A. MCLEAN *Harry Bloomfield* 5 Daily exposed to the attacks of native savages. **1845** E.J. EYRE *Jrnls. Exped. Central Aust.* II. 447 On the Murray River **native shepherds** and stock-keepers have hitherto been employed almost exclusively. **1860** 'LADY' *My Experiences in Aust.* 222 A poor squatter . . has three or four of his flocks in the hands of native shepherds. **1872** MRS E. MILLETT *Austral. Parsonage* 146 Binnahan's father, being a native shepherd, and therefore not without a few shillings in his pocket. **1840** *S. Austral. Rec.* (London) 15 Jan. 11 This proclamation is . . the first that has ever appeared in Australia in the **native tongues.** **1860** 'LADY' *My Experiences in Aust.* 161 The kangaroo, in the native tongue also called *bundarra.* **1837** J. BONWICK *Wild White Man* 6 Feb. (1863) 5 We . . crossed the Yallack by a **native track.** **1864** *Jrnls. & Rep. Two Voyages Glenelg River* 80 The native tracks are well beaten paths, traversing the district. **1897** J.J. KNIGHT *Brisbane* 42 A small tract of 'kopi country' (powdered gypsum). Here were numerous old native tracks, and we could see where mallee roots had been dragged up.

2. a. Of a non-Aboriginal person: born in Australia.

1821 *Austral. Mag.* 217 The Society employs 32 Clergymen . . and Settlers, European and Native. **1838** R. GOUGER *S.A. in 1837* 23 Mr Wade (a native Tasmanian, of considerable property). **1843** *Sydney Morning Herald* 12 Sept. 2/7 Horse stealing—four charges and five prisoners, one free, one native, two freed, and one bond. **1843** J. HOOD *Aust. & East* 89, I have not yet seen what I should call a fine woman among the native ladies of Australia, the currency lasses, as they are termed. **1850** T. McCOMBIE *Colonist in Aust.* 14 A man of the world . . to be slighted by a native '*cornstalk*'. **1859** R.H. HORNE *Austral. Facts & Prospects* 67 A limited number of scions of the old stock of native or long-resident colonial ladies. **1887** W.S.S. TYRWHITT *New Chum in Qld. Bush* 201 England is spoken of as home, even by native colonials, who are never likely to see it.

b. In collocations: **native colonist, lad, settler, white.**

1824 E. CURR *Acct. Colony Van Diemen's Land* 150 The **native colonist** has no recollections to raise discontent; what he never knew, he can never miss. **1838** T. WALKER *Month in Bush Aust.* 13 The caves . . are thought more wonderful by the native colonists, than they would be by travellers. **1845** T. McCOMBIE *Adventures of Colonist* 135 Their influence must effect a radical change in the mental standard of the native colonists. **1863** J. BONWICK *Wild White Man* 64 Of sixty native colonists of Poonindie twenty-four were married. **1828** *Hobart Town Courier* 16 Aug. 2 The leader of the band is a **native lad** called Biffin or Bevin, who made his escape from gaol here sometime ago. **1832** *Colonial Times* (Hobart) 12 June, Some of the Native Lads were for letting the Kentish Men have two 'Innings' to their one. **1852** *Empire* (Sydney) 16 Jan. 579/5 There are tall . . native lads that would do credit to any country under the sun, making their way to the diggings. **1822** J. DIXON *Narr. Voyage N.S.W. & Van Dieman's Land* 67 The **native settlers**, born in this colony . . have been long inured to it. **1839** L.A. MEREDITH in G. Mackaness *Fourteen Journeys Blue Mountains* (1951) iii. 53 A native settler returning from Sydney to Bathurst with his wife & family were in possession of all the accommodation. **1837** *Rep. Select Committee Transportation* 18 Apr. (1838) 28 Is juvenile prostitution among the **native whites** of the lower order common?—I believe it to be so. **1853** J. SHERER *Gold Finder Aust.* 320 The native *white* Australian is warmly attached to his country. **1899** *Progress* (Brisbane) 1 Apr. 9/2 One expects better things from the native white than apologetics or defences for the black and yellow alien.

3. a. Of flora and fauna: indigenous.

1804 S. MACARTHUR ONSLOW *Some Early Rec. Macarthurs* (1914) 81 The Native Woods instead of making the Grass sour are generally so open as not to deteriorate its quality. **1831** *Acct. Colony Van Diemen's Land* 89 Through the vista of this natural arch . . might be seen on one side of the native verdant plain, grazing by a small flock of sheep. **1837** *S. Austral. Rec.* (London) 11 Nov. 14 Fencing I am afraid will be dear, as the native wood is dear, and there is not much of it on any of the town acres. **c 1849** *Aust., Van Diemen's Land, & N.Z.* (rev. ed.) 5 The only species of *native* eatable fruit produced by New Holland is the cranberry. **1843** C. ROWCROFT *Tales of Colonies* (1858) 406 The brown, coarse tufts of the native plains beyond. **1860** 'LADY' *My Experiences in Aust.* 124 Kangaroos or wallabies, the best known among the native quadrupeds. **1880** J. BONWICK *Resources Qld.* 43 Absolutely dependent . . upon the indigenous supply, the native growth. **1893** *Picturesque Tas.* 103 Mobs of cattle . . can be seen grazing for miles around here, and they seem to be if anything wilder than the native game. **1986** *Canberra Times* 16 Feb. 5/5 After nearly two centuries of believing that Australia's rainforests were invading outliers of South-East Asia's rainforests, botanists had finally arrived at the view Australia's rainforests were not 'second-hand' but truly native.

b. In collocations: **native animal, bird, flower, forest, pasturage, pasture, plant, shrub, timber, tree.**

1856 J. BONWICK *Bushrangers* 2 The commissariat was obliged to rely upon **native animals** furnished by hunters. **1860** 'LADY' *My Experiences in Aust.* 53 The few *native* animals among the collection were the only ones that possessed much interest for me. *Ibid.* 54 Of the **native birds**, there was the Emu, with its long legs and curious *fibry* feathers. **1875** G. WALCH *On Cards* 4 Native birds are heard, and in the distance up looms the great red summer sun. **1843** *Teetotal Advocate* (Launceston) 2 Oct. 3/5 Bouquets of **Native Flowers. 1918** *Huon Times* (Franklin) 27 Sept. 2/6 The hall was very prettily decorated with native flowers, shrubs, and patriotic emblems. **1831** TYERMANN & BENNET *Jrnl. Voyages & Travels* II. 149 In travelling through the **native forests** . . we found many ants' nests. **1855** W. HOWITT *Land, Labor & Gold* I. 13, I see your native forest of Eucalyptus. **1967** A. RULE *Forests Aust.* 61 He also did something towards improving the condition of the native hardwood forests. **1833** *Colonist* (Hobart) 13 Aug. 3/3 The benefit of occasionally burning off the **native pasturage. 1835** *Hobart Town Almanack* 10 The **native pasture** on the hills now puts on a verdant appearance. **1848** *Information for Emigrants* ii. 31 The native pastures are indeed exceeding rich. **1975** L.A. POCKLEY *Handbk. for Jackeroos* 142 *Native pastures* consist of grasses and other plants that have been evolved by nature in the particular area by a process of natural selection for survival. **1985** *Canberra Times* 19 Dec. 3/6 Millions of woody shrubs . . have overrun . . native pastures. **1803** *N.S.W. Gen. Orders* 4 Oct. (1806) 69 The Trees and other **Native Plants** had been suffered to remain. **1828** *Tasmanian* (Hobart) 2 May 3 Gentlemen's grounds most tastefully laid out, and ornamented, with **Native**, and other Plants and **Shrubs. 1848** *Emigrant's Friend* 4 The native shrubs are generally harsh, ugly, and dark-coloured—the flowers are many of them very pretty. **1862** BACKHOUSE & TYLOR *Life & Labours G.W. Walker* 115 A natural basin, on the rocky borders of which, are a variety of native shrubs in full flower. **1837** *Perth Gaz.* 4 Feb. 845 No tenders having been received for the supply of **native timber** for the use of His Majesty's Dock-yard at Portsmouth. **1880** R. ROSE *Vic. Guide* 10 Turning . . to the indigenous or native timbers, Victoria has a vast and almost inexhaustible supply of these. **1910** *Huon Times* (Franklin) 19 Oct. 2/6 Even without the belts of native timber still standing on the surrounding rises, the orchard is sheltered from prevailing winds. **1828** *Tasmanian* (Hobart) 22 Aug. 3 The ground is cleared and laid out with English grasses, and ornamented with **Native Trees. 1838** *S. Austral. Rec.* (London) 12 Sept. 94 The native trees which abound here are the gum, the stringy bark . . tea-tree, and mimosa. **1910** *Pastoral Homes Aust.* 5 In many places beautiful native trees have been left for the shelter belts. **1957** *Forest Trees Aust.* (Cwlth. Forestry & Timber Bureau) 7 It is hoped that this book will be of use . . to the many individuals with a natural interest in our native trees.

4. In collocations occurring in both sense 1 and sense 2: **native Australian, boy, girl, population, race, son, woman, youth.**

1832 *Colonist* (Hobart) 28 Sept. 2/4 The new Sydney journal, called 'The Currency Lad' produced . . entirely by **native Australians. 1852** W. HUGHES *Austral. Colonies* 2 Even amidst the crowded streets of the populous and busy city, is seen the scarcely half-clothed form of the native Australian—the 'black fellow'. **1865** G.E. SARGENT *Frank Layton* 263 There were . . native Australians, both aboriginal and white. **1893** D. HEALEY *Cornstalk* 97 The native Australian, i.e. aboriginal, bursts into spontaneous expressions of loyalty, or joyousness—'Good man, de Queen; plenty blankets and bacca'. **1800** *HRA* (1914) 1st Ser. II. 404 Enquiring of them if they knew anything about the two **Native Boys** being murdered. **1811** D.D MANN *Present Picture N.S.W.* 33 The circumstance of several settlers being capitally convicted of the murder of a native boy, in January, 1800, acts as a check. **1827** *Monitor* (Sydney) 22 Nov. 783/1 All our six-feet high native boys and girls, have sprung from these 'reprobates'. **1849** *Bell's Life in Sydney* 29 Dec. 2/1 Engaged in watching a few half drunken men, or noisy native boys, or publicans. **1874** *Illustr. Sydney News* 28 Feb. 4/4 The operator and a native boy, are badly hurt but likely to recover. **1888** 'R. BOLDREWOOD' *Robbery under Arms* (1937) 36 I'm going to show you a trick that none of you native boys are up to, smart as you think yourselves. **1889** W.H. TIETKENS *Jrnl. Central Austral. Exploring Exped.* 14 Mar. (1891) 2 The party consisting of . . a black-tracker (Billy, from the ranks of the native police at Alice Springs), and a small native boy, left the Bond Springs station at 1 p.m. **1965** *N. Austral. Monthly* Jan. 6 There were two young Australian stockmen there with eight native boys. **1826** M. HINDMARSH *Lett.* (1945) 27 The **Native girls** of the Country or Currency Girls are so very pert that I do not think I will ever have one of them for a wife. **1844** E. GEOGHEGAN *Currency Lass* (1976) 25 My good uncle, like many of our countryfolks, is under the impression that 'native' and 'Aboriginal' mean one and the same thing, and when, therefore, in one of my last letters I mentioned my attachment to my dear Susan, and spoke of her as a 'native girl', her image was immediately associated in his mind with ebony visage, flat nose, sausage lips and woolly hair. **1856** J. BONWICK *Bushrangers* 49 He was attended by a faithful native girl called Black Mary. **1881** *Bulletin* (Sydney) 28 May 5/3 Miss Mary Casey . . is the first native (girl) of New South Wales who has passed the Cambridge University matriculation examination. **1890** W.F. BUCHANAN *Aust. to Rescue* 25 Native girls, as a rule, will not go out to service. **1829** E.G. WAKEFIELD *Let. from Sydney* 129 That low-lived Englishman who . . distinguishing the Emigrant and **Native population** of New South Wales, by nicknaming the one Sterling, and the other Currency, was, no doubt, a man of taste. **1843** J.F. BENNETT *Hist. & Descr. Acct. S.A.* 59 The native population of Australia is by no means numerous. Within the settled districts of South Australia, the whole number of aborigines does not exceed 700. **1858** J.B. MARSDEN *Mem. S. Marsden* 253 The one spot on which no cheering ray seemed to fall . . was the native population, the aborigines of New South Wales. **1811** *Sydney Gaz.* 19 Jan., In the center [*sic*] of the ball-room . . the representation of our **Native Race. 1830** *Van Diemen's Land Corresp. Military Operations* 5 Nov. (1831) 56 The extinction of the Native race, could not fail to leave an indelible stain upon the character of the British Government. **1848** S. & J. SIDNEY *Emigrant's Jrnl.* 73 It is a fashion . . of many British colonists to abuse and despise the native race; that is to say, Australians born in the country, of European parents. **1863** J. BONWICK *Wild White Man* 60 The native race would become . . enervated at the missions. **1891** *Braidwood Dispatch* 30 May 2/2 In no country in the world has a native race with such an interest attaching to their lineage, language, habits and customs been so cruelly destroyed as . . in our Fair Australia. **1968** G. BAKER *Montgomery & I* 62 Montgomery sternly replied: Surely the **native sons** should have my autograph before migrants and dagos. **1973** *Bulletin* (Sydney) 20 Jan. 40/1 New South Wales was still guilty about the way it had treated its brilliant native son. **1827** *Monitor* (Sydney) 3 Feb. 299/2 A humane Correspondent describes an outrage upon the person of a **native woman** on Tuesday night near the new Court House. **1854** MRS C. CLACY *Lights & Shadows* I. 282 Beneath a corpse a solitary native woman was sitting. **1857** J. ASKEW *Voyage Aust. & N.Z.* 223 Much has been said and written touching the loveliness of the 'currency lasses', or native women of New South Wales. **1879** G. TAPLIN *Folklore S. Austral. Aborigines* 119 The overland parties have not acted judiciously in allowing the native women to be brought to their encampments. **1880** 'OLD HAND' *Experiences of Colonist* (ed. 2) i. 41 As they approached nearer, they proved to be two native women. **1938** X. HERBERT *Capricornia* 12 He began to take an interest in native women, or Black Velvet as they were called collectively, affairs with whom seemed to be the chief diversion of the common herd. **1804** *Sydney Gaz.* 2 Dec., On Wednesday a **native youth** died at Sydney of a dysentery, who was the first of the savage inhabitants of this colony introduced to civil society. **1826** *Austral.* (Sydney) 19 Jan. 3/1 The name which the Native Youth have acquired for loyalty, steadiness, and sobriety. **1839** T.L. MITCHELL *Three Exped. Eastern Aust.* (rev. ed.) II. 325 It must, indeed, be admitted that the intelligence of the native youth . . is little inferior to that of the aborigines. **1848** J. FOWLES *Sydney* 68 Native youths delight to contend for the laurels of victory in the noble game of cricket. **1867** J.R. HOULDING *Austral. Capers* 15 The native youths—the white ones I mean—are nearly all six feet high. **1877** *Free Trade Papers* ii. 1 The native youths are fine chields [*sic*], bigger than their fathers, and the lasses bonnier than their mothers.

5. In special collocations (freq. *obs.*): **native affairs,** Aboriginal welfare; a name given to a government department responsible for this; also *attrib.*; **chief,** KING *n.*[1] 1 a.; **doctor,** DOCTOR *n.*[1]; **evidence,** evidence given by an Aboriginal as admitted in a court of law; **fire,** a fire lit by an Aboriginal (see quots. and also FIRE *v.*); **honey** *obs., bush honey*, see BUSH C. 2; **industry,** Australian, as distinct from foreign, industry; **Institution,** a publicly-funded establishment for the care and education of Aboriginal children; **interpreter,** one who translates from or into an Aboriginal language; **king,** KING *n.*[1] 1 a.; **language,** an Aboriginal language; **location,** land allocated to an Aboriginal community; **oven (a),** an Aboriginal cooking-place (see quot. 1845); **(b)** MIRRNYONG; **pock,** see quot. 1892; **(mounted) police,** a police force of male Aborigines recruited to serve (esp. in rural districts) under white officers; also *attrib.*; **policeman,** a member of the *native police*; **protector,** PROTECTOR; **reserve,** an area of land set aside for the exclusive use of Aborigines; **school,** a school for the instruction of Aboriginal children; **smoke,** a column of smoke rising from a fire, as indicating the presence of Aborigines; **soak,** a SOAK frequented by Aborigines; **tracker,**

Tracker; **tribe,** Tribe; **trooper,** a member of the *native police*; **village,** a (temporary) Aboriginal settlement; **weir,** *fishing weir*, see Fishing; **well,** a natural source of water used by Aborigines; see also *native soak*, Gnamma hole.

1938 J.F.W. Schulz *Destined to Perish* 10 There could be . . a permanent commission for **native affairs** with a national policy and a continuous programme of development. **1947** V.C. Hall *Bad Medicine* 277 He was a policeman, acting as a Native Affairs Officer. . . He had police powers and he had Native Affairs powers. **1953** *Bulletin* (Sydney) 15 July 13/2 An investigating native-affairs officer has found that several tribes of the eastern goldfields and the Nullarbor Plain are uniting into one tribe. **1960** J. Walker *No Sunlight Singing* 159 This job of yours with Native Affairs would be a fair old bludge, wouldn't it? **1818** *Hobart Town Gaz.* 31 Jan., His Excellency the Governor held his usual annual Meeting of the **Native Chiefs** and their Tribes at Parramatta. **1832** J. Hanson *Let.* 29 The Native Chief, Nakinah, was dressed up in a most splendid uniform. **1852** J. Morgan *Life & Adventures W. Buckley* 119 They had seen several native chiefs, with whom—as they said—they had exchanged all sorts of things for land. **1861** W. Westgarth *Aust.* 20 A native chief . . was detected in the act of purloining some property. **1841** G. Grey *Jrnls. Two Exped. N.-W. & W.A.* I. 215 The cave was frequented by some wise man or **native doctor,** who was resorted to by the inhabitants in cases of disease or witchcraft. **1851** *Athenaeum* (London) 24 May 557 The native doctors are priests and soothsayers also. **1878** R.B. Smyth *Aborigines of Vic.* I. 265 Though this disease (venereal) in the first instance must have been contracted from the whites, the native doctors have prescribed a cure which, though simple, has proved efficacious: they boil the wattle bark until it becomes very strong, and use it as a lotion to the parts affected. **1845** E.J. Eyre *Jrnls. Exped. Central Aust.* II. 497 For the purpose of obtaining redress for a wrong, or of punishing cruelty, or the atrocity of the European, no amount of **native evidence** would be of the least avail. **1848** J. Stephens *Voice from Aust.* 9 Native evidence is now received in our Courts of Justice. **1856** J. Bonwick *W. Buckley* 92 The New South Wales legislature passed a law in 1839 to admit native evidence. **1805** *Sydney Gaz.* 31 Mar., The plaintiff's property was in danger of being destroyed by **native fires** the night before the unfortunate event took place. **1833** *Perth Gaz.* 23 Feb. 31 *The native fires.* The fires kindled by the Natives, in different parts of the country, have spread with alarming rapidity. **1851** H. Melville *Present State Aust.* 346 Native fires were . . easily distinguished from those of bush-rangers or settlers. **1861** J. Davis *Tracks of McKinlay* 22 Nov. (1863) 119 Many native watch fires on the other side of the lake. **1841** *Sydney Herald* 26 Apr. 2/2 **Native honey** is delicious, from the flavour of the wild flowers. **1870** E.B. Kennedy *Four Yrs. in Qld.* 76 Blacks . . are exceedingly fond of native honey. **1881** A.C. Grant *Bush-Life Qld.* I. 236 John, who is faint with hunger, asks his sable friend to procure him some native honey, of which the bush is full. **1861** W. Westgarth *Aust.* p. vii, The miners . . petitioned the authorities for the expulsion of the Chinese, 'protection to **native industry**'. **1877** *Free Trade Papers* ii. 1 Cost or no cost, they will prove that Protection pays over and over again, by setting up 'native industries', and keeping people employed instead of sending money out of the country to pay for imported rubbish. **1880** *Bulletin* (Sydney) 21 Aug. 4/1 Messrs. G.R. Maclean and John Vicars stand for South and West Sydney respectively on the 'Native Industries' and 'No Chinkee' ticket. **1890** J. Haslam *Glimpse Austral. Life* 23 The chief aim of protectionists in New South Wales appears to be . . what they term 'encouragment to native industry'. **1910** *Huon Times* (Franklin) 5 Mar. 4/6 If you go in for native industry in the way of a factory . . you will probably have to get a special Act of Parliament. **1818** *Hobart Town Gaz.* 31 Jan., The Children of the **Native Institution** were conducted by their Tutor to the Meeting, where their interview with their parents became a most interesting spectacle. **1825** B. Field *Geogr. Mem. N.S.W.* 227 An intelligent and experienced member of the committee of our Native Institution . . feels this impediment to their civilization so strongly, that he would compel them not to come into our towns naked. **1837** *Colonist* (Sydney) 3 Aug. 250/1 An establishment has been formed at Port Phillip, called the Native Institution, where the children of the blacks are clothed at the Government expense, and educated by the missionary. **1856** J. Bonwick *W. Buckley* 46 My **native interpreter** told them who I was. **1936** J. Hamilton *Sailortown Shanties* 190 Because of his knowledge of the native tongue, [he] was given the position of the native interpreter for the Law Courts. **1857** W. Westgarth *Vic. & Austral. Gold Mines* 51 These '**native kings**', as the ready colonial nomenclature might have styled them. **1880** *Bulletin* (Sydney) 4 Sept. 3/4 'Jemmy' . . whose right to the title of Native King there was . . none to dispute . . died on Tuesday week. **1831** *HRA* (1923) 1st Ser. XVI. 14 Form an acquaintance with the **Native Languages** of the country. **1838** *S. Austral. Rec.* (London) 13 Jan. 30 S. is now nearly master of the native language, and can make them understand anything. **1852** J. Morgan *Life & Adventures W. Buckley* 107 The native language varies according to the tribe. **1854** W. Howitt *Boy's Adventures* 28, I think these birds must speak the native language, they talk away in so odd and grotesque a style. **1887** A. Nicols *Wild Life & Adventure* 135 The overseer entered into conversation with a white-haired old man, addressing him in the native language. **1839** *Southern Austral.* (Adelaide) 9 Oct. 3/2 The Public Officers of the Colony are invited to attend his funeral, and to meet for this purpose at the Old **Native Location**. **1849** C. Sturt *Narr. Exped. Central Aust.* II. 282 The Adelaide tribe is not numerous; they occupy a portion of the Park lands, called the native location. **1897** H. Hussey *Colonial Life & Christian Experience* 62 Not far from the Gaol, on the opposite side of the river, was what was called the Native Location. **1834** G. Bennett *Wanderings N.S.W.* I. 170 A **native oven** is made in the ground, similar to those in use among the New Zealanders, and throughout the Polynesian Archipelago. **1845** E.J. Eyre *Jrnls. Exped. Central Aust.* II. 289 The native oven is made by digging a circular hole in the ground, of a size corresponding to the quantity of food to be cooked. It is then lined with stones in the bottom, and a strong fire made over them. **1855** W. Howitt *Land, Labor & Gold* II. 95 We saw here what we have seen nowhere else in this colony—heaps of wood ashes, partly overgrown with grass, and resembling the barrows of the ancient Britons. They are called native ovens. **1878** R.B. Smyth *Aborigines of Vic.* I. 371 A very thin axe . . was found in a native oven (*Mim-yong*), on the banks of the River Werribee. **1890** 'R. Boldrewood' *Colonial Reformer* II. 82 Smouldering fires, heaps of mussel-shells and fish-bones lay scattered around, while the stones in the native ovens were not yet cold. **1910** C.E.W. Bean *On Wool Track* 99 Little heaps of hard-baked sand, capped with charred brick . . those are the old beds of the fires at which the natives used to boil their fish and flesh on the sand. Rain and wind swept the other sand away, but this is too hard. There cannot be a doubt that this explanation of the 'native ovens' is the right one. **1946** K.S. Prichard *Roaring Nineties* 149 Scooped a native oven out of the ground. ***c* 1960** C. Mackness *Clump Point & District* 55 He found three white bodies in a native 'oven' on Murdering Point. **1832** *Sydney Monitor* 4 Jan. 3/1 The **native pock** is prevalent in many parts of Sydney, and the effects of the malady are as conspicuous as those of the small pox. **1851** *Empire* (Sydney) 17 Feb. 4/2 The disease known by the name of 'native pock', if not actually a modified form of small-pox, is a disorder of the same class. **1892** Hill & Thornton *Notes on Aborigines N.S.W.* 4 The natives all over the continent, at the time the first white people arrived for the purposes of settlement, were subject to a disease resembling small-pox; the native name of this disease was 'Galgala', and it was known to the early settlers as 'Native Pock'. **1839** *Southern Austral.* (Adelaide) 27 Feb. 4/4 The **native police** . . left this place under Mr De Villiers, in quest of the murderers. **1846** *Melbourne Argus* 7 July 3/1 The Native Police Force do not seem to have been of any great use, and this is said to be caused by the difficulty of keeping the natives to their duty. **1852** W. Hughes *Austral. Colonies* 101 The experiment which has met with most success . . has been that of enrolling a native mounted police . . to act as a border force against bush-rangers and other depredators. **1867** 'Clergyman' *Aust. as it Is* 88 The native police . . are a body of aborigines trained to act as policemen, serving under a white commandant. **1879** *Illustr. Austral. News* (Melbourne) 12 Apr. 58/2 It is said of these Native Police that so keen is their faculty of seeing and pursuing on a given trail . . that they never lose it. **1902** E.B. Kennedy *Black Police Qld.* 2, I served in the more northern parts of the colony in the Native Mounted Police. **1913** M.A. McManus *Reminisc. Maranoa District* 14 About the end of 1859 . . Mr William Morehead formed a Native Police barracks. **1923** T. Hall *Short Hist. Downs Blacks* 10 To a great extent . . the Native Police were recruited from such men, and the latter took every opportunity, under the protection of the uniform, to carry out their villainy with other tribes. **1935** A. Francis *Then & Now* 22 The northern part of Queensland was at that time under the protection of native police, the units of which consisted of a white sub-inspector and native black-boy troopers. ***c* 1960** C. Mackness *Clump Point & District* 43 The majority of blacks from the whole district had been rounded up by the Cardwell native police. **1843** *Arden's Sydney Mag.* Oct. 78 Under this system, the **Native Policemen** have become, in a few months, civilized beings. **1918** G. White *Thirty Yrs. Tropical Aust.* 182 They [*sc.* councillors] are aided by a native policeman. **1984** B. Dixon *Searching for Aboriginal Lang.* 100, I could then talk to him in the courthouse, under the supervision of a native policeman. **1842** *Austral. & N.Z. Monthly Mag.* 26 Habits of decorum, order, and regularity, have gradually been introduced amongst them . . owing principally to the continued watchfulness . . of the two gentlemen who have been appointed **native protectors** for the colony. **1872** 'Resident' *Glimpses Life Vic.* 17 In order to secure the aborigines against injustice from the settlers . . it was early found necessary to appoint an officer to reside with each tribe . . under the title of 'Native Protector'. **1842** *Austral. & N.Z. Monthly Mag.* 171 **Native reserves** . . the whole of the sections reserved for the use of the aborigines are to be let on lease for a term not exceeding seven years. **1875** R. & F. Hill *What we saw in Aust.* 189 Large tracts granted in various localities as Native Reserves. **1947** V.C. Hall *Bad Medicine* 276 He was acting at that time as Patrol Officer and superintendent of Native Reserves. **1959** L. Rose *Country of Dead* 6 The doctor . . visited the native reserve in Fern Valley. **1838** *Aboriginal Claims Discussed* 14 In the formation of **native** and colonial **schools,** it should be a matter for serious consideration, whether there is not a fundamental error in all *general* schools. **1849** S. & J. Sidney *Emigrant's Jrnl.* 211 At Adelaide there is a native school of about 100, where they are clothed, fed, and educated after the English fashion. **1864** N. Shreeve *Short Hist. S.A.* 38 Mrs Taplin . . keeps the native school supported by Government. **1886** J.A. Froude *Oceana* 148 On the way home we turned aside to see a native settlement—a native school, &c.—very hopeless, but the best that could be done for a dying race. **1920** *Huon Times* (Franklin) 9 July 3/4 Some of the pupils, after only a few months at the Native School, could handle the English language much better than many a modern politician. **1831** G.A. Robinson in N.J.B. Plomley *Friendly Mission* 23 Nov. (1966) 528 Ascended to the top of a hill, when the chief descried the **native smoke.** **1860** J.M. Stuart *Explorations in Aust.* 28 Apr. (1865) 170, I saw a native smoke rise up in the creek below. **1898** D.W. Carnegie *Spinifex & Sand* 200 Between us and the hills one or two native smokes were rising. *Ibid.* 80 **Native soaks** dug out with sticks and wooden 'coolimans' . . are by no means uncommon. **1933** F.E. Baume *Tragedy Track* 150 The native soaks are wretched affairs in the subsoil, only containing a few gallons of water. **1949** G. Farwell *Traveller's Tracks* 56 Water from the native soaks is piped up to the vegetable garden. **1878** R.B. Smyth *Aborigines of Vic.* I. 7 The **native trackers** have on many occasions rendered important services to the Government, and when any one is lost in the bush the whites rely with the utmost confidence on the sagacity and skill of the 'black-tracker'. **1891** J.J. Roche *Life J.B. O'Reilly* 75 Hide his trail from the keen scent of the native trackers. **1946** A.W. Noakes *Life of Policeman* 48 There had been a native tracker some years previously. **1931** A.W. Upfield *Sands of Windee* 18, I . . took two native trackers from a small tribe camped near the homestead in an effort to pick up tracks near the car. **1984** B. Dixon *Searching for Aboriginal Lang.* 27 A full-blood Girramay, he had spent years away as native tracker for the police at Bowen. **1805** *Sydney Gaz.* 7 July, She had never been observed to intermingle with the **Native Tribes.** **1833** *Perth Gaz.* 5 Oct. 157 It being considered expedient by the local Government to appropriate that part of the reserves . . to the service of the Native tribes. **1847** *Maitland Mercury* 20 Nov. 2/6 The native tribes are unanimous . . that the seasons are altered to the 'dry way' in comparison of what they were antecedent to [white settlement]. **1907** *Bulletin* (Sydney) 7 Mar. 15/3 The desert-bred native tribes of N.W. Australia practise a quaint method of capturing the common brown kite. **1968** *Coast to Coast 1967–68* 47 On this side, out from Fortitude Valley, we had the native tribes. **1847** *Port Phillip Herald* 20 Apr. 2/7 The **native troopers** are now on the Murray, endeavouring to capture . . the two undetected murderers of Mr Beveridge. **1853** A. Kinloch *Murray River* 29 He has allotted to him a certain force of police—white or native troopers. **1870** C.H. Allen *Visit to Qld.* 186 'Native troopers' . . are half-civilised 'blacks' from another colony, so as to be quite free from all sympathy with the tribes of that district. **1882** A.J. BOYD *Old Colonials* 195, I enjoyed a hearty meal, although . . the beef [was] salted by native troopers. **1884** G. WIGHT *Qld.* 88 It [*sc.* the police force] consisted of five hundred and eighty-six officers and constables, and two hundred native troopers and trackers. **1943** *Jest: Digestion Good Humor* 5 A native-trooper standing by a big pile of government blankets. **1835** T.B. WILSON *Narr. Voyage round World* 210 We suddenly came to a **native village**. **1846** J.L. STOKES *Discoveries in Aust.* II. 69 We came upon a native village. . . It contained thirteen huts of paper bark. **1896** W.H. WILLSHIRE *Land of Dawning* 48 On its fern-carpeted margin was a little native village. **1841** G. GREY *Jrnls. Two Exped. N.-W. & W.A.* II. 85 Across the bed, where we passed it, was a **native weir.** **1863** J. DAVIS *Tracks of McKinlay* 290 There is a native weir here, and the fish are very numerous. **1927** *W. Austral. Hist. Soc. Jrnl. & Proc.* 25 On the Serpentine River is a 'manga', or native weir constructed long ago, but still easily distinguishable by the salmon totem members of that district. **1836** H.W. BUNBURY *Early Days W.A.* (1930) 75 We found some at a low promontory in a small **native well** amongst the Tea trees, but it was exceedingly bad, brackish, and stinking. **1847** E.B. KENNEDY *Extracts Jrnl. Exped. Central Aust.* 238 We discovered a native well at a junction of a creek with the river. **1855** R. AUSTIN *Jrnl. Interior W.A.* 9 We passed Mellingerring, a native well, that fails in dry seasons. **1875** J. FORREST *Explorations in Aust.* 26 We found a native well, and by digging it out seven feet we obtained sufficient water for ourselves and horses. **1886** D. LINDSAY *Exped. across Aust.* 12 Passed a native well, and cleared out four feet to blue clay bed of creek, but found no water. **1889** E. GILES *Aust. twice Traversed* II. 214 He soon found a small native well in a grassy water-channel. **1890** 'R. BOLDREWOOD' *Colonial Reformer* II. 87 At its foot was a native well—a natural tank—scooped out of solid rock, gourd-shaped, with a small man-hole at the top. **1912** SPENCER & GILLEN *Across Aust.* 107 In the middle of the Ti tree we found a curious 'native well'. **1937** L.R. MENZIES *Gold Seeker's Odyssey* 98 Thought they could induce him to lead them to one of the hidden native wells. **1975** G. BLAINEY *Triumph of Nomads* 178 Here and there a native well went down perhaps fifteen or twenty feet.

6. a. Used as a distinguishing epithet in the names of plants: **native apple (a)** *obs.*, MUNTRY; **(b)** any of several trees of the genus *Angophora* (fam. Myrtaceae); see also *apple tree* APPLE 3; **apple tree** *obs.*, *apple tree*, see APPLE 3; **apricot,** the tree *Pittosporum phylliraeoides* (see BUTTERBUSH); **artichoke** *Tas.*, the tufted perennial herb *Astelia alpina* (fam. Liliaceae) of alpine N.S.W., Vic., and Tas., having rosettes of stiff, silvery, pointed leaves; **banana,** any of several species of banana of the genus *Musa* (fam. Musaceae) of n.e. Qld.; *wild banana*, see WILD 1; **bluebell,** BLUEBELL; **box (thorn),** *sweet bursaria*, see BURSARIA b.; **bramble,** *native raspberry*; **bread,** the large, heavy, tuber-like sclerotium of the fungus *Polyporus mylittae* of s. Aust. incl. Tas.; *blackfellow's bread*, see BLACKFELLOW *n.* 2; *black's bread*, see BLACK *n.* 2; **cabbage,** any of several plants used as a vegetable, esp. the succulent shrub *Scaevola frutescens* (fam. Goodeniaceae) of n. Aust. and elsewhere; **carrot,** any of several plants, esp. the annual herb *Daucus glochidiatus* (fam. Apiaceae) of temperate Aust., having carrot-like leaves eaten by stock; the root of these plants; *wild carrot*, see WILD 1; **cedar** CEDAR 1; **cherry, (a)** the small cypress-like tree *Exocarpos cupressiformis* (fam. Santalaceae); **(b)** CHERRY; also **cherry-tree; cotton,** *cotton tree* (a) and (b), see COTTON; also **cotton bush, cotton tree; cranberry,** any of several plants of the fam. Epacridaceae and Ericaceae with edible fruits, esp. the prostrate shrub *Astroloma humifusum* (fam. Epacridaceae) of N.S.W., Vic., Tas., S.A., and W.A., bearing an edible greenish drupe with a sweet viscid pulp; the fruit of these plants; also *ellipt.* as **cranberry; cucumber,** any of several plants bearing a melon-like fruit, esp. the trailing vine *Cucumis melo* (fam. Cucurbitaceae) of n. Aust.; the fruit itself; *native melon*; **cumquat** (or **kumquat**), the tangled, often spiny, shrub or small tree *Eremocitrus glauca* (fam. Rutaceae) having greyish-green foliage and an edible, globular fruit yellow when ripe; *native lime* (a); *wild lime*, see WILD 1; **currant,** any of many plants bearing fruit resembling the currant in appearance or flavour, esp. *Leptomeria aphylla* (fam. Santalaceae) and *Coprosma quadrifida* (fam. Rubiaceae) of s.e. Aust. incl. Tas.; the fruit of these plants; CURRANT; *wild currant*, see WILD 1; **fig,** any of several plants of the genus *Ficus* (fam. Moraceae), esp. the small tree or shrub *F. platypoda* of drier Aust., often growing among rocks, and bearing a globular reddish fig; the fruit of these plants; **flax,** the perennial plant *Linum marginale* (fam. Linaceae) of temperate Aust. which, like the related European flax, yields a strong fibre; FLAX; **fuchsia,** any of several plants bearing flowers reminiscent of those of the *Fuchsia*, esp. the species of the genus *Correa* (see CORREA), *Epacris longiflora* (fam. Epacridaceae) of Vic. and N.S.W., and *Eremophila maculata* (fam. Myoporaceae) of drier mainland Aust.; **grape,** any of several perennial woody climbers of the fam. Vitaceae, esp. *Cissus hypoglauca* (see *water vine* WATER); **grass,** any of many grasses of the fam. Poaceae; **heath,** HEATH; **hibiscus,** any of several Austral. species of *Hibiscus* (fam. Malvaceae), incl. ROSELLA *n.*[2]; also *attrib.*; **honeysuckle,** HONEYSUCKLE 1; **hop** (or **hops**), any of several plants resembling the hop *Humulus* (often in the winged fruit or bitter leaves), incl. HOP-BUSH; *wild hop*, see WILD 1; also *attrib.*; **indigo,** INDIGO a.; **jasmine,** any of several plants bearing fragrant, often pale-coloured, flowers, incl. the desert jasmine *Jasminum didymum* ssp. *lineare* (fam. Oleaceae) of inland Aust.; **laurel** *Tas.*, the tall shrub or small tree *Anopterus glandulosus* (fam. Cunoniaceae) of Tas., having glossy, serrated, dark green leaves and showy, usu. white, flowers; **leek,** any of several plants of the genus *Bulbine* (fam. Liliaceae) of temperate Aust. incl. Tas., and elsewhere, having narrow, succulent, hollow leaves; *native onion*; see also *onion weed* ONION 1; **lilac,** any of several plants incl. FALSE SARSAPARILLA; **lime, (a)** *native cumquat*; **(b)** the thorny shrub or small tree *Microcitrus australis* (fam. Rutaceae) of Qld., bearing a green, rough-skinned, edible fruit; **mahogany** *obs.*, JARRAH 1; **melon,** *native cucumber*; **millet,** any of several grasses (fam. Poaceae), usu. of the genus *Panicum*, esp. the tussock-forming perennial *P. decompositum* of all mainland States; see also COOLY; **mulberry,** the small, soft-wooded tree *Pipturus argenteus* (fam. Urticaceae) of e. Qld., n.e. N.S.W., and elsewhere, bearing a white, mulberry-like fruit; **myrtle,** any of several plants incl. the shrub *Myoporum acuminatum* (fam. Myoporaceae) of all mainland States, having bright green leaves; **oak,** SHE-OAK 1; **onion,** *native leek*; **orange,** any of several shrubs or trees, usu. bearing a rounded, edible fruit, esp. of the genera *Capparis* (see *wild orange* WILD 1) and *Citriobatus* (fam. Pittosporaceae) of n. Aust.; the fruit itself; also **orange-tree; parsley** *obs.*, the herbaceous plant *Apium prostratum* (fam. Apiaceae) of all States and elsewhere, occurring on coastal land and swampy areas inland; **peach,** any of several plants esp. QUANDONG 1 a.; the fruit of the plant; **pear,** the fruit of any of several plants, often of the genus *Xylomelum* (fam. Proteaceae), esp. the shrub or small tree *X. pyriforme* of N.S.W. and Qld., and ALUNQUA; the plant itself; see also WOODEN PEAR; also *attrib.*; **pepper,** any of several plants bearing a pungent fruit, incl. species of the genus *Piper* (fam. Piperaceae), and PEPPER TREE 1; the fruit itself; **pine,** CYPRESS PINE; **plum,** any of several trees or shrubs bearing a plum-like fruit, incl. *Santalum lanceolatum* (fam. Santalaceae) of drier mainland Aust., having greyish foliage and an edible bluish fruit, *Planchonella australis* (see *black apple* BLACK *a.*[2] 1 a.) and (*Tas.*) *Cenarrhenes nitida* (fam. Proteaceae) of Tas.; the fruit itself; PLUM; *wild plum*, see WILD 1; **pomegranate, (a)** *wild orange*, see WILD 1; **(b)** *W.A.* the low shrub *Balaustion pulcherrimum* (fam. Myrtaceae) of s.w. W.A.; **poplar,** any of several trees, esp. HORSERADISH TREE; **potato, (a)** POTATO ORCHID; **(b)** either of the two twining plants *Marsdenia viridiflora* and *M. flavescens* (fam. Asclepiadaceae), having tuberous roots; **raspberry,** any of several prickly shrubs of e. Aust. of the worldwide genus *Rubus* (fam. Rosaceae), bearing an edible, red fruit, as *R. parvifolius* of s.e. Aust. incl. Tas., and elsewhere; the fruit itself; *native bramble*; *wild raspberry*, see WILD 1; **rose,** any of several plants, esp. the shrub *Boronia serrulata* (fam. Rutaceae) of sandstone heaths of e. N.S.W., bearing fragrant bright-pink (or occas. white) flowers; **sarsaparilla,** any of several plants esp. *sweet tea* (see SWEET *a.*[1]); **spinach,** any of several plants used as a green vegetable; **tamarind,** the large tree *Diploglottis australis* (fam. Sapindaceae) of s.e. Qld. and n.e. N.S.W., the fruit of which has an edible, acid pulp; the fruit itself; TAMARIND; **tobacco,** any of several plants resembling, or used as, tobacco, incl. soft-leaved species of the genus *Nicotiana* (fam. Solanaceae) and PITURI; **tulip** *obs.*, the plant *Telopea speciosissima* (see WARATAH 1); **willow,** any of several trees of pendulous habit incl. *Pittosporum phillyraeoides* (see BUTTERBUSH), and esp. *Acacia salicina* (fam. Mimosaceae), usu. occurring near watercourses in drier mainland Aust.; see also COOBA; **yam,** YAM.

1843 J.F. BENNETT *Hist. & Descr. Acct. S.A.* 44 There are some kinds of small berries which have been dignified with the names of the '**native apple**', 'cherry', &c., but most of them are no larger than peas. **1847** G.F. ANGAS *Savage Life & Scenes* I. 65 Monterries, or native apples . . are precisely like miniature apples, and have an aromatic flavour, which is not unpleasant. When the monterry is ripe, the natives disperse themselves over the sand-hills in search of them. **1857** J. ASKEW *Voyage Aust. & N.Z.* 74, I have . . tasted some of the native apples . . but they are very insipid. **1886** W.J. WOODS *Visit to Vic.* 22 Equally unsatisfactory were the Native Grapes, Mulberries, and Apples. **1916** S. CONIGRAVE *Reminisc.* 44 It was about the size of a blackcurrant, but had the smell of an apple, therefore it was called 'native apple'. **1965** *Austral. Encycl.* I. 218 The names native apple and apple-myrtle are used for indigenous trees of the genus *Angophora* . . so conspicuous on Hawkesbury sandstone formations, N.S.W. **1805** *Sydney Gaz.* 3 Feb., The fine foliage of the iron bark and **native apple tree.** **1901** H. LAWSON *Joe Wilson & his Mates* 60 Behind us was a dreary flat covered with those gnarled, grey-barked, dry-rotted 'native apple-trees' (about as much like apple-trees as the native bear is like any other). **1967** B.Y. MAIN *Between Wodjil & Tor* 27 On the pendulous boughs of the *Pittosporum phillyraeoides* or **native apricots** a faint yellow was beginning to tinge the green bivalved fruits. **1984** E. ROLLS *Celebration of Senses* 39 One Native Apricot in its summer season hangs its pendulous branches with bitter, splitting, orange-pink fruit. **1909** G. SMITH *Naturalist in Tas.* 60 Wherever the ground is at all marshy the **native Artichoke**, which is really a Lily (*Astelia alpina*), forms prickly, dense tufts. **1981** M. SHARLAND *Tracks of Morning* 53 Tough, high-land plants like kerosene bush, native artichoke and some others, having dug themselves in among the cavities, have reduced both its size and its stark bareness. **1878** R.B. SMYTH *Aborigines of Vic.* I. 231 *Musa Brownii* . . **Native banana.** **1884** E. PALMER *Notes Austral. Tribes* 45 *Musa Brownii* . . the native banana. Grows in scrubs on the alluvial banks of rivers from Cleveland Bay northward. The fruit is full of black seeds. **1911** A.J. BOYD *Banana in Qld.* 31 In the dense scrubs of North Queensland the Banana is indigenous, and may be seen growing everywhere in great luxuriance, but the fruit . . is quite inedible. . . The three best known of these native bananas are—*Musa Banksii* . . *Musa Fitzalani* . . *Musa Hillii.* **1900** H. LAWSON *Verses Pop. & Humorous* 28 Where groves of wattle flourish And **native bluebells** grow. **1930** *Aussie* (Sydney) Nov. 59/1 The slender native blue bells swing their dear And delicate steeples in the Summer grasses. **1835** *Hobart Town Almanack* 73 *Bursaria spinosa.* **Native Box** . . is easily propagated from the seeds, which are produced very abundantly, and when planted in rows and clipped makes excellent hedges. It has already been introduced into the conservatories in England, to which its elegant odoriferous flowers are a great ornament. **1855** W. HOWITT *Land, Labor & Gold* I. 35 The native box and tea-scrub in flower closed in the drive. **1889** E.E. MORRIS *Cassell's Picturesque Australasia* IV. 692 There are numerous other little shrubs and plants, such as the white-flowering native box. **1916** *Emu* XV. 177 The islet . . is covered in parts with a prickly shrub locally known as 'native box thorn'. **1965** *Austral. Encycl.* II. 81 The native box [is] a *Bursaria.* **1848** T.L. MITCHELL *Jrnl. Exped. Tropical Aust.* 351 On the river bank, we observed this day the **native bramble**, or Australian form of *Rubus parvifolius.* **1890** A. MACKAY *Austral. Agriculturist* (ed. 2) 157 Native Bramble . . is called the wild raspberry here, and is well known to old bushmen, but may not be so well known to new hands. **1973** G.R. COCHRANE et al. *Flowers & Plants Vic.* (rev. ed.) 151 Queensland Bramble . . is distinguishable from other native brambles by the simple coarse leaves. **1831** G.A. ROBINSON in N.J.B. Plomley *Friendly Mission* 23 Oct. (1966) 490 One of the native women, Sall, found a bulbous plant called by the white people '**native bread**'. **1842** *Tasmanian Jrnl. Nat. Sci.* I.

48 *Mylitta Australis.* Native Bread. 'This species of tuber is often found in the colony.' **1846** L.W. MILLER *Notes of Exile Van Dieman's Land* 363 The native bread—a bulbous root weighing from three to seven pounds, growing in the earth from one to three feet below the surface, which when boiled is tasteless, and resembles rice in appearance. **1855** W. HOWITT *Land, Labor & Gold* I. 218 A very rare sort of fungus, growing in the ground, called native bread, which the natives roast and eat. **1880** R. ROWE *Roughing It* 70 The . . native bread, or Tasmanian bread-fruit, a big truffle which grows about the roots of trees, being about the most insipid viand known. **1927** *Bulletin* (Sydney) 28 July 24/4 The largest piece of 'native bread' that has come under my notice was discovered near Burnie (Tas.) recently; it weighed nearly 70 lb. . . *Mylitta australis* is generally found on new ground and adjacent to the roots of stringybark. **1985** *Austral. Nat. Hist.* Spring 410 The 'stones', up to 20 kilos in weight, are storage organs of a curious fungus known as native bread (*Polyporus mylittae*). **1863** *Adelaide Observer* 5 Dec. 6/6 They fish, shoot, hunt up **native** potatoes, carrots, **cabbage,** and a multiplicity of other strange edibles which require a considerable deal of looking after before the seekers can eat. **1872** H. HEAD *Under Cloud* 57 We shot some parrots, And wattle birds as well, Off which, and native cabbage, We made a hearty meal. **1888** *Proc. Linnean Soc. N.S.W.* III. 532 *Nasturtium palustre* . . called 'Native Cabbage' on the banks of the River Nepean (New South Wales). This and other species afford excellent pot-herbs when luxuriant and flaccid. **1908** E.J. BANFIELD *Confessions of Beachcomber* 15 Dome-shaped shrubs of glossy green (native cabbage—*Scaevola Koenigii*). **1928** S.E. NAPIER *On Barrier Reef* 85 The scaevola, a white-flowered bush, called on the mainland, presumably from its appearance, 'Native Cabbage'. **1965** *Austral. Encycl.* VIII. 13 *S[caevola] frutescens* (syn *S. koenigii*), sometimes called 'native cabbage', is a large succulent coastal plant which ranges through the Old World tropics. **1842** *Tasmanian Jrnl. Nat. Sci.* I. 36 *Geranium parviflorum.* Small-flowered Geranium. . . The Aborigines were in the habit of digging up its roots . . and roasting them. It was called about Launceston '**native carrot**'. **1844** L. LEICHHARDT *Jrnl. Overland Exped. Aust.* 8 Dec. (1847) 64 The native carrot, which was so green when we passed Darling Downs, was here withered and in seed. **1873** J. BONWICK *Tasmanian Lily* 126 'What is the native carrot?' 'The root of a pretty geranium. It is fleshy, and when roasted is not objectionable.' **1890** A. MACKAY *Austral. Agriculturist* (ed. 2) 145 The native carrot (Daucus brachiatus) and saltbush are . . well worth encouraging. **1966** A. MORRIS *Plantlife W. Darling* 74 *Daucus glochidiatus* . . 'Native carrot'. Common annual. Spring. **1854** G.E. SARGENT *Frank Layton* (1865) 139 Its furniture was . . manufactured of **native cedar** principally. **1857** J. ASKEW *Voyage Aust. & N.Z.* 101 The native cedar and the she oak . . are beautiful woods. **1887** *Illustr. Austral. News* (Melbourne) 23 July 140/4 Some of the Richmond River (New South Wales) timbers are very attractive, particularly the native beech, pine and cedar. **1965** *Austral. Encycl.* VI. 237 *A[gonis] juniperina* has needle-shaped leaves and is often called native cedar in the west of Australia. **1817** A. CUNNINGHAM in I. Marriott *Early Explorers Aust.* 21 May (1925) 217 The **Native Cherry,** our common eastern coast plant, Exocarpus cupressiformis. **1828** *Tasmanian* (Hobart) 17 Oct. 2 Among the best of Mr Scott's preserves, is the seed of the Native *Cherry Tree*, the most ornamental of our evergreens. **1833** H.W. PARKER *Life, Progress, & Present State Van Dieman's Land* 139 The native cherry grows to the height of sixteen feet, in the form of a cone of a bright green color . . destitute of leaves . . flowers are very minute . . fruit is a small fleshy berry, and has the nut on its exterior. The tree has no resemblance to the cherry tree. **1844** *S. Austral. Odd Fellows' Mag.* Oct. 191 The thick foliage of the native cherry-tree . . studded with small fruit just blushing into ripeness. **1852** J. SHAW *Tramp to Diggings* 221 The native cherry (*Exocarpus cupressiformis*) is another ridiculous and useless appellation, although the tree itself is very beautiful. **1872** 'TASMANIAN LADY' *Treasures, Lost & Found* 108 The native cherry, reminding you of a cypress that has grown stout and left off mourning. **1886** W.J. WOODS *Visit to Vic.* 22 The Native Cherry, whose stone grows outside the fruit, is of the size of a pea, acrid and dry. **1908** W.H. OGILVIE *My Life in Open* 5 A quandong or a native cherry stands like a trim bush in the grounds of some country houses. **1916** *Emu* XV. 166 The white-eye returned to a native cherry tree. **1948** H.A. LINDSAY *Bushman's Handbk.* 58 The native cherry is rare but good; the shrub is practically leafless and has flattened stems. **1968** D. FLEAY *Nightwatchmen* 89, I found this species of owl spending the day in branches of the pretty native cherry trees. **1984** E. WALLING *On Trail Austral. Wildflowers* 12 A Native Cherry, or Cherry Ballart a tree with striking green, velvety cypress-like foliage that gives a wonderful note of contrast in the bush. **1838** *Sydney Herald* 30 July 2/5 A **native cotton** tree, and a small kangaroo, with a nail or hook at the end of its tail, comprise the whole of the curiosities discovered. **1845** L. LEICHHARDT *Jrnl. Overland Exped. Aust.* 27 May (1847) 270 The native cotton tree of Port Essington, whose bright showy yellow blossoms and large capsules full of silky cotton, attracted our attention; its leaves are deciduous, and the trees are entirely leafless. **1878** R.B. SMYTH *Aborigines of Vic.* I. 226 *Mootcha,* native cotton-bush. When the leaves sprout and become quite green, the natives gather and cook them, and at seed-time they pluck and eat the pods. **1903** F. TURNER *Bot. Darling, N.S.W.* 409 One of the most beautiful flowering plants of this family is the 'native cotton', *Gossypium sturtii* . . which I have seen successfully cultivated in a garden at Bourke. **1927** M. TERRY *Through Land of Promise* 25 Yellow flower of the native cotton bush. **1829** R. MUDIE *Picture of Aust.* 151 The Australian **cranberry** (*lissanthe sapida*) is a beautiful fruited shrub. **1834** *Hobart Almanack* 133 *Astroloma humifusa.* The native cranberry has a fruit of green, reddish, or whitish colour. **1840** *Aust., Van Dieman's Land, & N.Z.* 5 The only species of *native* eatable fruit produced by New Holland is the cranberry. **1855** W. HOWITT *Land, Labor & Gold* I. 36 We were shown the Australian cranberry, which produces its berries *under* the creeping plant, and which, though well tasted, have stones in them. **1889** J.H. MAIDEN *Useful Native Plants Aust.* 39 'Native Cranberry.' The fruit is edible. It is something like the Cranberry of Europe both in size and colour, but its flesh is thin, and has been likened . . to that of the Siberian Crab. **1963** W.M. CURTIS *Student's Flora Tas.* ii. 424 *A[stroloma] humifusum* . . Native Cranberry. A small much-branched shrub. **1980** L. ATKINSON *Excursions from Berrima* 6 In January 1865 one of her articles was accompanied by a jar of jam to enable members of the Horticultural Society to appreciate the potential of the Native Cranberry, *Lissanthe sapida.* **1984** M. BLAKERS et al. *Atlas Austral. Birds* 643 The Grey Currawong . . will raid soft fruit and apple orchards. In Tas. the berries of native plants such as the native cranberry are important. **1859** J.M. STUART *Explorations in Aust.* 13 Apr. (1865) 49 The **native cucumber** grows about here. **1878** R.B. SMYTH *Aborigines of Vic.* I. 230 *Cucumis sp.* Native cucumber. **1903** H. BASEDOW *Jrnl. Govt. N.-W. Exped.* 15 Apr. (1914) 67 In the neighbouring sandhills the edible 'native cucumber' . . is common. **1924** HORNE & AISTON *Savage Life Central Aust.* 53 A trailing vine with a small yellow flower creeps over the neighbouring bushes. It is the native cucumber and has a fruit which somewhat resembles that of a gooseberry, with a green and white colouring that goes yellow when ripe. **1984** ELLIOT & JONES *Encycl. Austral. Plants* III. 130 *Cucumis melo* . . ssp. *agrestis* . . Qld., N.S.W., N.T. Native Cucumber, Ulcardo Melon. . . The rind is bitter but the flesh is palatable, and quite refreshing and sweet when ripe. **1880** J. BONWICK *Resources Qld.* 81 The **Native Cumquat,** an *Atalantia*, is a Darling Downs shrub with a close grain, and taking a good polish. **1888** *Proc. Linnean Soc. N.S.W.* III. 489 *Atalantia glauca* . . 'Native Kumquat', 'Desert Lemon.' The fruit is globular, and about half-an-inch in diameter. **1903** F. TURNER *Bot. Darling, N.S.W.* 410 Included under *Rutaceae* is . . the 'native cumquat'. **1981** J. JESSOP *Flora Central Aust.* 194 *E[remocitrus] glauca* . . Native cumquat. Shrub to 5 m. **1826** J. ATKINSON *Acct. Agric. & Grazing N.S.W.* 19 The **native currant** . . resembling the cranberry. **1830** G.A. ROBINSON in N.J.B. Plomley *Friendly Mission* 8 Feb. (1966) 117 Discovered a variety of berries which the natives eat, among which were the native currant, of white colour and pleasant flavour. **1832** J. BACKHOUSE *Narr. Visit Austral. Colonies* (1843) 116 *Coprosma spinosa* . . has small, red and rather insipid berries, that are sometimes preserved, under the name of Native Currants. **1842** *Tasmanian Jrnl. Nat. Sci.* I. 39 *C. microphylla*—one of the many plants called in the Colony by the name of 'native currant'. **1852** J. SHAW *Tramp to Diggings* 221 The native currant, *Leptamenia acida,* bears but little resemblance to the English one, but I have been informed that both jam and wine are made from it. **1890** *Proc. Linnean Soc. N.S.W.* V. 276 *Apophyllum anomalum* . . is still another of our numerous 'Native Currants'. **1903** *Tasmanian Timbers* (Tas. Lands & Survey Dept.) 29 Native currant (*Leptomenia [sic] billardieri*) . . grows little larger than a bush, but produces a very nice yellowish-brown timber. **1939** *Trans. R. Soc. S.A.* LXIII. 26 *Plectronia latifolia* . . Native Currant. . . The very dark-coloured juice of the fruit is squeezed out and drunk. **1958** *Ibid.* (1959) LXXXII. 126 In the gorges grow . . the Native Currant (*Carissa brownii*) . . and many other under-shrubs and herbs. **1829** G.A. ROBINSON in N.J.B. Plomley *Friendly Mission* 19 Sept. (1966) 74 Learnt that the Kangaroo eat the prickly mimosa and likewise the **native fig.** **1841** G. GREY *Jrnls. Two Exped. N.-W. & W.A.* II. 100 He had nothing to eat but a few native figs. **1852** J.D. LANG *Austral. Emigrant's Man.* 50 The native fig-tree, a species of caout-chouc, from the upper branches of which festoons of cane resembling the sugar cane frequently occur. **1889** E. GILES *Aust. twice Traversed* I. 54 On the top was a native fig-tree in full bearing; the fruit was ripe and delicious. **1896** B. SPENCER *Rep. Horn Sci. Exped. Central Aust.* IV. 57 *Ficus platypoda.* 'Native fig' . . fruits, which are dry and full of seeds, are eaten. **1925** M. TERRY *Across Unknown Aust.* 222 Some native figs and plums were found. **1953** *Trans. R. Soc. S.A.* (1954) LXXVII. 82 Native figs (*Ficus platypoda*) growing amongst rocky hills and having fruits like small Moreton Bay figs. **1982** R. HALL *Just Relations* 422 Kitchen on a tilt because of the roots of that damn native fig. **1799** Banks Papers 28 Nov. XIX. 95 There is also some of the **Native Flax** which grows all over the Country but near the [Hawkesbury] River it is much stronger. **1826** *Colonial Times* (Hobart) 15 Apr., The native flax is a plant well worthy the attention of the experimentalist. **1836** *True Colonist* (Hobart) 19 Feb. 6/2 Their [*sc.* Port Philip Aborigines] twine, manufactured from the native flax, is equal to any New Zealand fishing lines. **1841** *S. Austral. Mag.* (Adelaide) Nov. 156 A species of native flax, growing to the height of four feet, has been found in great abundance, at Boston Island, and is now used by the labouring people for filling their beds. **1855** W. HOWITT *Land, Labor & Gold* I. 109 The native flax . . grows all over the country, showing its azure blossoms. **1878** R.B. SMYTH *Aborigines of Vic.* I. 209 The mucilaginous seed of the native flax. **1982** N.C.W. BEADLE et al. *Flora of Sydney Region* (ed. 3) 195 Perennial. . . Grasslands and open forest. . . Native Flax . . *L[inum] marginale.* **1860** G. BENNETT *Gatherings of Naturalist* 372 The *Correa virens,* with its pretty pendulous blossoms (from which it has been named the '**Native Fuchsia**'). **1880** J. BONWICK *Resources Qld.* 47 Among poison plants are . . the native Fuchsia. **1890** 'LYTH' *Golden South* 209 Pillars wreathed with . . epacris longiflora or native fuchsia. **1901** J.H. MAIDEN *Plants reputed to be Poisonous* 27 *Eremophila maculata*—called 'Native Fuchsia' in parts of Queensland. It is often sent to Sydney as a suspected plant. **1909** F.E. BIRTLES *Lonely Lands* 22 The Button-flower, the Native Rose, and the Native Fuchsia. **1981** M. SHARLAND *Tracks of Morning* 71 Our curious little shrub, the native fuchsia, *Correa* . . its dark green leaves in pairs hanging down as though wilted. **1838** *Sydney Herald* 30 July 2/5 A **native grape** of good flavour, was found near the banks of the Fitzroy River. **1861** 'OLD BUSHMAN' *Bush Wanderings* 218 The native grape, of a transparent greenish-yellow hue, as large as a blackcurrant. **1888** *Proc. Linnean Soc. N.S.W.* III. 552 *Vitis hypoglauca* . . 'Native grape'. . . This evergreen climber yields black edible fruits of the size of small cherries. **1965** *Austral. Encycl.* IV. 227 *Cissus hypoglauca,* native grape. . . Tall jungle climber or small tree. . . The small blue-black berries are edible, but have neither much flavour nor pulp. **1981** A.B. & J.W. CRIBB *Useful Wild Plants Aust.* 188 Amongst the climbers of the rainforest, the various species of native grape. **1804** *HRA* (1915) 1st Ser. VI. 491 Dry weather . . has dried up all the **native grasses.** **1840** J.P. JOHNSON *Plain Truths* 17 There is nothing but the native grasses for the cattle to feed upon, which of course are not by any means so nutritious as the English grasses. **1861** J.D. LANG *Qld., Aust.* 162 Of all the natural productions of Australia the native grass is . . the most valuable. **1880** J. BONWICK *Resources Qld.* 46 A cry of failure of native grasses has brought others into notice. **1924** *Bulletin* (Sydney) 9 Oct. 24/2 Two of us were walking across a native-grass plain when the dogs put up a wallaby. **1938** C.T. WHITE *Princ. Bot. Qld. Farmers* 142 The native grasses of Queensland number over 500 different sorts or species and represent very largely the basis of the wealth of the State. **1972** *Bronze Swagman Bk. Bush Verse* (1973) 44 'Ere the floods recede and the cattle feed Knee deep in the native grass. **1860** 'LADY' *My Experiences in Aust.* 45 There is the **native heath,** or *Epacris,* of which there are many varieties. **1889** E.E. MORRIS *Cassell's Picturesque Australasia* IV. 692 Masses of the beautiful epacris or native heath . . growing among the gum-trees and the scrub. **1890** 'MRS A. MACLEOD' *Austral. Girl* (1894) 108 A whole range-side of early epacris. . . Here were acres of this radiant native heath, white, and scarlet, and tender

pink. **1986** *Your Garden* Jan. 61 *Epacris*—Native Heath. . . Propagation by cuttings is recommended. **1935** H. Basedow *Knights of Boomerang* 60 Under the cover of a **native hibiscus**-bush. **1980** L. Fuller *Wollongong's Native Trees* 51 Native hibiscus (*Hibiscus heterophyllus*) with its 100 mm. wide white and red throated flowers is an attractive and easily grown plant. **1831** W. Bland *Journey of Discovery Port Phillip* 6 The plains . . were interspersed with occasional clumps of the **Native Honeysuckle. 1841** *S. Austral. Mag.* (Adelaide) Dec. 198 The native honeysuckle, which, with many other sweet smelling plants sends its delicate perfume on the air. **1856** *Jrnl. Australasia* I. 19 A dwarf species of Banksia, or native honeysuckle. **1880** J. Bonwick *Resources Qld.* 82 The Banksia, or Native Honeysuckle, delighting in sandy wastes. **1903** *Emu* II. 204 Short, thick scrub, consisting of . . *Banksia*, or native honeysuckle. **1924** K. McKell *Old Days & Gold Days Vic.* 78 Near by there was a clump of the native honeysuckle—the name, Banksia was unknown to us then. **1855** W. Howitt *Land, Labor & Gold* I. 109 The **native hop** . . only so called because it is intensely bitter—is a shrub with oval leaves, growing in the bush. . . Instead of a humulus, it is a Daviesia, the latifolia. **1872** Mrs E. Millett *Austral. Parsonage* 258 The native hop is a little groundplant, named by botanists *Erythrea Australis*, with which, on account of its intensely bitter taste, sugar-beer used to be flavoured when English hops could not be procured. **1889** J.H. Maiden *Useful Native Plants Aust.* 23 *Dodonaea spp.* . . 'Native Hops', on account of the capsules bearing some resemblance to hops, both in appearance and taste. **1896** *Proc. Linnean Soc. N.S.W.* XXI. 438 *D[aviesia] latifolia* . . is called 'Native Hops' on account of the bitter principle contained in its leaves. **1905** *Emu* V. 67 Lyre-Birds are fond of . . 'native hop'. **1914** E.E. Pescott *Native Flowers Vic.* 36 The Native Hop, or one of the plants called native hop, is a legume. **1934** M. Gilmore *Old Days* 24 In the thick, unfelled bush above the horse and cattle yards were native hop, 'sarsparilla', the bottle-brush flower. **1967** B.Y. Main *Between Wodjil & Tor* 25 In the undergrowth . . native hop bushes (*Dodonaea attenuata*) were covered with withered papery fruits, pinkish-green in colour. **1974** P. Adam Smith *Desert Railway* 34 The native hop, with its rich, reddish-brown masses of flowers. **1981** J. Jessop *Flora Central Aust.* 32 Much photographed by tourists as 'Native Hops'. This vernacular name is unsuitable because it [*sc. Rumex vesicarius*] is neither native nor a hop. **1826** *Hobart Town Gaz.* 15 Apr., Of all our indigenous plants, none equals in value the **native indigo. 1845** C. Griffith *Present State & Prospects Port Phillip* 124 There is a considerable variety of beautiful flowers at Port Phillip. . . Among these are . . the native indigo [etc.]. **1856** *Jrnl. Australasia* I. 37 Indigofera Australis, native indigo, is a highly ornamental plant, with a profusion of rich lilac-coloured papilionaceous blossoms and pinnatifid leaves. **1891** J. Fenton *Bush Life Tas.* (1964) 127 This summer I have grown in pots and boxes . . the native indigo. **1965** *Austral. Encycl.* V. 81 *I[ndigofera] australis* extends into Victoria and Tasmania and is known as austral or native indigo. **1860** 'Lady' *My Experiences in Aust.* 45 There is also a **native Jasmine,** its flower precisely resembling the white Jasmine we are all familiar with at home, but the plant itself bearing more likeness to the broom. **1930** V. Palmer *Passage* (1957) 217 A sweep of honey-coloured grass . . whitened by patches of native jasmine that looked like the sand showing through. **1965** *Austral. Encycl.* IV. 398 *G[uettarda] speciosa* . . is a coastal shrub or small tree with . . large fragrant and stalkless white flowers. . . In North Queensland the tree is popularly known as native frangipani or native jasmine, common names applied to many plants with strongly scented blooms. **1986** K. Brennan *Wildflowers of Kakadu* 104 Native Jasmine *Jasminium aemulum*. . . On still, balmy evenings . . there is nothing so delightful as the wafting fragrance from its flowers. **1842** D. Burn *Narr. Journey Hobart Town to Macquarie Harbour* 11 Apr. (1955) 25 A singularly beautiful shrub, styled in unlearned phrase, the '**Native Laurel**'. **1903** *Tasmanian Timbers* (Tas. Lands & Survey Dept.) 30 Native laurel (*Anopterus glandulosus*), Mint tree (*Prosthanthera lasianthes*) . . are small trees, occasionally used for inlaying and turnery. **1909** G. Smith *Naturalist in Tas.* 51 The underscrub consisted here chiefly of the native Laurel, really a large tree [etc.]. **1969** King & Burns *Wildflowers Tas.* 34 Native laurel. . . The early settlers saw a resemblance in the flowery stage to the Cherry Laurel. **1985** *Austral. Garden Jrnl.* Dec. 50 Nearby is the Fern House, where many examples of Tasmanian indigenous plants flourish, like Huon Pine, . . Native Laurel [etc.]. **1866** *Australasian* (Melbourne) 25 Aug. 665/2 There are a variety of herbs on which stock are found to thrive exceedingly; amongst which may be enumerated 'salt-bush', '**native leeks**' [etc.]. **1901** J.H. Maiden *Plants reputed to be Poisonous* 30 *Bulbine bulbosa* . . 'Native or Wild Onion', 'Native Leek' . . has several times been sent to me as a poisonous weed. **1974** S.L. Everist *Poisonous Plants Aust.* 353 *Bulbinopsis bulbosa* . . native leek, also known as onion weed or wild onion. The last two common names are also applied to many unrelated plants with narrow, succulent leaves. **1847** G.F. Angas *Savage Life & Scenes* I. 225 The brilliant clusters of the **native lilac. 1852** Mrs C. Meredith *My Home in Tas.* II. 69 A little purple, which is equally common, so vividly recalls to my mind, both by its scent and colour, an Old-World favourite, that I always know it as the native Lilac. **1909** F.M. Bailey *Comprehensive Catal. Qld. Plants* (ed. 2) 11 *H[ardenbergia] ovata*, known as 'Native Lilac' in South Australia. **1911** *Huon Times* (Franklin) 18 Jan. 2/4 Here and there the native lilac in bloom. **1965** *Austral. Encycl.* IV. 428 *H[ardenbergia] violacea* is often called false sarsaparilla, also purple coralpea and native lilac. Its numerous racemes of vivid purple to deep violet flowers contrast delightfully with the gold of various wattles in spring. **1880** J. Bonwick *Resources Qld.* 81 The Native Orange, a *Citrus* of the scrubs, has a hard close-grained wood, like the **Native Lime. 1912** *Emu* XII. 73 Noticed a flock of several of the little white-browed Babblers . . moving amongst the native lime trees (*Atalantia glauca*). **1975** A.B. & J.W. Cribb *Wild Food in Aust.* 42 *Microcitrus australis* Native Lime, Native Orange. . . Found in rainforests, *M. australis* is a taller tree than the finger-lime. **1837** *Perth Gaz.* 7 Jan. 825 His Excellency the Governor . . received authority for the supply of 200 loads . . of **Native Mahogany** for the use of His Majesty's Dock-yard, Portsmouth. **1847** *Bell's Life in Sydney* 16 Jan. 1/2 A splendid sideboard from the jarrah, or native mahogany. **1857** P.J. Murray *Not so Bad* 102 The native mahogany, almost as hard and durable under water as English oak. **1844** L. Leichhardt *Jrnl. Overland Exped. Aust.* 29 Dec. (1847) 87 The **native melon** of the Darling Downs and of the Gwyder. **1845** *Ibid.* 9 July (1847) 325 The plains were . . covered . . with the long trailings of the native melon, the fruit of which tastes very tolerably, after the bitter skin has been removed; but when too ripe, the fruit is either insipid or nauseous. **1855** J. Bonwick *Geogr. Aust. & N.Z.* (ed. 3) 205 The Native Melon, half an inch long on a prickly scrub, is refreshing. **1878** R.B. Smyth *Aborigines of Vic.* II. 303 Various plants, native melons, and some fruits . . are eaten raw. **1888** *Proc. Linnean Soc. N.S.W.* III. 536 '**Native Millet**'. . . The seed used to be called 'Cooly' by western New South Wales aboriginals. . . The grains pounded yield excellent food. . . This plant is not endemic in Australia. **1938** C.T. White *Princ. Bot. Qld. Farmers* 202 Grasses with wide-spreading, much-branched seedheads, such as *Panicum decompositum*, often referred to as Native Millet. **1983** Morley & Toelken *Flowering Plants Aust.* 391 Native millet, the seeds of which were ground to a paste. **1846** *Portland Guardian* 18 Sept. 4/3 A **native mulberry**, with small white fruit of a sweet taste, grew on the fields of lava, at the Burdekin. **1878** R.B. Smyth *Aborigines of Vic.* I. 231 *Pipturus propinquus* . . Native mulberry. **1888** *Proc. Linnean Soc. N.S.W.* III. 538 'Native Mulberry'. . . The white berries are eaten by the aboriginals. **1965** *Austral. Encycl.* VII. 123 *P[ipturus] argenteus* . . extends to Java; it is called native mulberry or Queensland grass-cloth plant. . . The inner bark affords a fibre of fine texture and great strength, but it is not easy to prepare. **1984** K.A.W. Williams *Native Plants Qld.* II. 224 Native Mulberry. . . The small, mulberry-like fruits . . are sweet and juicy. The true fruit is embedded in the soft fleshy structures. **1835** *Hobart Town Almanack* 84 *Dodonaea truncata.* **Native Myrtle.** . . Their beauty consists only in the foliage, the flowers being green and inconspicuous. **1888** *Proc. Linnean Soc. N.S.W.* III. 512 *Eugenia myrtifolia* . . 'Brush cherry' or 'Native myrtle'. The fruit is acid, and makes a good preserve. *Ibid.* 532 *Myoporum serratum* . . 'Native Myrtle'. **1981** J.A. Baines *Austral. Plant Genera* 248 *M[yoporum] montanum*, Waterbush . . called 'Native Myrtle' in S.A. **1831** G.A. Robinson in N.J.B. Plomley *Friendly Mission* (1966) 386 The **native oak** (sheoak). **1841** *Sydney Herald* 26 Apr. 2/2 Dry native oak is the best wood for heating ovens. **1862** H. Kendall *Poems & Songs* 56 A mass of mournful tresses, drooping down the Native Oak. **1887** W.H. Suttor *Austral. Stories Retold* 117 On the low-lying, black, flooded land, the belar, a species of native oak or casuarina, is found, casting so dense a shade as to prevent all other vegetation from showing. **1935** Davison & Nicholls *Blue Coast Caravan* 52 The only forest trees remaining were native oaks—she-oak or bull-oak—growing in the numerous small swamps. **1891** *Proc. Linnean Soc. N.S.W.* VI. 135 *Bulbine bulbosa* . . '**Native Onion**' . . is recorded as poisonous to stock in Queensland and South Australia. **1897** L. Lindley-Cowen *W. Austral. Settler's Guide* 590 *Bulbine semibarbata* . . a 'native onion' or 'native leek'. A strong poison. **1901** J.H. Maiden *Plants reputed to be Poisonous* 7 A dwarf form of *Bulbine bulbosa* . . (not *Bulbine semibarbata*), the 'native onion', abounds in the Paroo district, and is dreaded there as poisonous. **1860** J.M. Stuart *Explorations in Aust.* 24 Apr. (1865) 166 The **native orange**-tree abounds here. **1863** J. Davis *Tracks of McKinlay* 300 We found abundance of the native oranges. Why it should be called 'orange' I don't know, as it is as much like that fruit as a gooseberry is like a pine-apple. **1880** J. Bonwick *Resources Qld.* 81 The Native Orange, a *Citrus* of the scrubs, has a hard close-grained wood . . and is yellow in colour. **1889** E. Giles *Aust. twice Traversed* I. 38 Near our pool of slime a so-called native orange tree (*Capparis*), of a very poor and stunted habit, grew. **1936** C. Chewings *Back in Stone Age* 27 In rocky ground in the ranges the native orange (*Capparis nummularia*) is common enough. **1948** H.A. Lindsay *Bushman's Handbk.* 58 The native orange is a tree up to twenty feet high; its leaves droop and are narrow and yellowish in colour; the fruit is green and marked with a few red flecks when ripe. **1982** Elliot & Jones *Encycl. Austral. Plants* II. 459 *Capparis lasiantha* . . Native Orange. . . Bears hundreds of flowers which are scented and attract butterflies. An ideal ornamental for subtropical regions or in warm inland areas. **1835** *Hobart Town Almanack* 67 *Apium prostratum.* **Native Parsley. 1857** D. Bunce *Australasiatic Reminisc.* 39 Native parsley, was also abundant on the bank of the stream, and forms an excellent ingredient in soup, and otherwise may be used as a pot-herb. **1880** J. Bonwick *Resources Qld.* 44 There are herbaceous plants, of the umbelliferous kind, as native parsley and carrot. **1839** H. Ward Diary 6 Farther in land I soon discovered several sorts of Bryanthemuns in flower and one the purple I found to be of Grate use in plucking of the pericarp or seed vessel and peelling of the outer skin and sucking it there are called heer by some **native peaches** and I have had some trouble to pursuade some to the contrary. **1853** J. Allen *Jrnl. River Murray* 55 The native peach-tree (not dissimilar to the English peach) grows along the bank in profusion, giving the land quite a cultivated appearance. **1892** Mrs F. Hughes *My Childhood in Aust.* 57 There was a pretty fruit called the native peach, but it was so bitter no one could eat it. **1916** *Emu* XV. 153 Fine trees of the quandong or native peach (*Fusanus acuminatus*) were breaking down under burdens of crimson fruit. **1965** D. Martin *Hero of Too* 4 The Quandongs, well-named after a small tree which abounds there and produces a rather bitter fruit, the native peach. **1975** A.B. & J.W. Cribb *Wild Food in Aust.* 57 The pitted stone is probably responsible for the less common name of native peach. **1805** S. Marsden *Some Private Corresp.* 15 Jan. (1942) 36 Mr ··· . . promised to call on you and deliver a letter and small box containing some **native pears. 1827** P. Cunningham *Two Yrs. in N.S.W.* I. 220 Our native pears are tolerably tempting to the look, but defy both mastication and digestion, being the pendulous seed-pods of a tree here. **1853** Mossman & Banister *Aust. Visited & Revisited* 270 A few specimens of what is called the native pear-tree of New Holland, from the exact shape its seed-vessel bears to that fruit. **1886** W.J. Woods *Visit to Vic.* 22 As for the Native Pear, its flavour is not half as definite as that of a raw Swede turnip, nor is it half as succulent. **1901** *Twentieth Century Impressions W.A.* 184 The native pear (*Xylomelum*) grows in the Swan River area, and is of much interest to botanists. **1926** J.M. Black *Flora S.A.* iii. 463 *C[ynanchum] floribundum*. . . The fruit, which is edible and astringent, is called 'native pear' by bushmen. **1948** H.A. Lindsay *Bushman's Handbk.* 58 The native pear is a climber with woody stems and a milky juice; seeds from the green pods are eaten. **1965** *Austral. Encycl.* VII. 42 The term [pear] is applied to various Australian trees and shrubs with pear-shaped fruits or pear-like foliage. So called native pears are *Eugenia* (*Syzygium*) *eucalyptoides* (the fruit of which is used for jam-making) in Queensland and *Hakea sericea* and *Pomaderris apetala* in parts of Tasmania. **1969** A.A. Abbie *Original Australs.* 75 Australia has several wild fruits that the Aborigines eat in season such as . . the 'native pear' or 'langu' [etc.]. **1981** G.M. Cunningham et al. *Plants Western N.S.W.* 554 Although widespread, native pear is seldom common in any situation. **1826** *Colonial Times* (Hobart) 2 Dec., Most interesting of all is the **native pepper**, which grows on a small prickly bush, and is red until ripe, when it has generally attained a black colour. The pepper corns are then stronger than any from the spice islands. **1846** N.L. Kentish *Work in Bush Van Diemen's Land* 22 The *Native Pepper* is an exceedingly pungent aromatic spice, of an agreeable flavour. **1888** *Proc. Linnean Soc. N.S.W.* III. 389 *Piper novae-hollandiae* .. 'Native Pepper'. An excellent stimulant tonic to the mucous membrane. **1968** V. Serventy *Southern Walkabout* 28, I sampled the black berries of the native pepper and found it lived up to its name. **1838** *Southern Austral.* (Adelaide) 29 Sept. 2/4 On sale .. half-inch and inch **native pine.** **1864** E.A. Oppen *Descr. N.T.* 34 Occasionally a few native pines (*frenela*), were seen. **1901** K.L. Parker in M. Muir *My Bush Bk.* (1982) 64 The walls were of native pine, oiled to bring out the grain of the sherry-coloured wood, which defies the white ants. **1912** *Emu* XII. 127 Many of the slopes were covered in the rich dark foliage of the native pine. **1958** *Trans. R. Soc. S.A.* (1959) LXXXII. 126 Native pines (*Callitris glauca*) are uncommon here [*sc.* Haast Bluff, central. Aust.] **1818** A. Cunningham in I. Marriott *Early Explorers Aust.* 6 Oct. (1925) 404 *Podocarpus sp.* (**native Plum**), a low, humifuse, spreading plant, of the habit of Taxus, with a large purple fleshy receptacle. **1835** *Hobart Town Almanack* 76 *Cenarrhenes nitida.* Native Plum... A shrub resembling the Common Laurel, bearing black bitter fruit, about the size of a cherry, at Port Davy and Macquarie harbour. **1847** G.F. Angas *Savage Life & Scenes* I. 56 The native plum is a bushy shrub, growing in sandy places, on the margin of the Murray and the neighbouring lakes... The fruit, when ripe, is about the size of a sloe, growing in clusters at the end of the branches, with a flavour partaking at once of salt, acid, and sugar. **1852** J. Shaw *Tramp to Diggings* 221 There is also a native plum; I think the botanical name is *Cupama Australis.* I believe this is used as a preserve. **1888** *Proc. Linnean Soc. N.S.W.* III. 538 *Podocarpus spinulosa* .. 'Native Plum' or 'Native Damson'. This shrub possesses edible fruit, something like a plum, hence its vernacular names. **1910** J. Mathew *Two Representative Tribes Qld.* 92 A few wild fruits, such as the quandong, the native plum, and the native lime, were the most common. **1953** *Trans. R. Soc. S.A.* (1954) LXXVII. 82 Of the fruits the most important are the .. native plum (the plum-coloured smaller fruit of *Santalum lanceolatum*) [etc.]. **1981** J.A. Baines *Austral. Plant Genera* 85 *C[enarrhenes] nitida*, Native Plum, Tas., a small tree in rainforests .. but in exposed situations a shrub .. has cream flowers, and large purplish-black berries. **1880** J. Bonwick *Resources Qld.* 82 The **Native Pomegranate**, a *Capparis*, has a hard, close-grained scrubwood. **1881** *Proc. Linnean Soc. N.S.W.* VI. 740 *Capparis canescens* and *C. Mitchellii* are common, and *C. Shanesii* is less frequent, and of recent discovery; the fruit of these shrubs is known by the name of 'Native Pomegranates'. **1903** *Austral. Handbk.* 280 Some of the trees which furnish wood suitable for carving or engraving purposes:- 'Native Pomegranate' (*Capparis nobilis* and C. Mitchellii) [etc.]. **1938** C.T. White *Princ. Bot. Qld. Farmers* 45 Species of *Capparis* (Bumbil Tree or Native Pomegranate). **1965** *Austral. Encycl.* I. 394 *B[alaustion] pulcherrimum* is known as the native pomegranate, from the shape of its small, brilliantly scarlet bell-flowers. **1975** A.B. & J.W. Cribb *Wild Food in Aust.* 24 *Capparis* Native Caper .. Native Pomegranate. **1982** Elliot & Jones *Encycl. Austral. Plants* II. 280 Native Pomegranate... A prostrate to low, spreading shrub... An outstanding ornamental species. **1889** E. Giles *Aust. twice Traversed* II. 195 There was nothing but the **native poplar** for the camels to eat, and they devoured the leaves with great apparent relish, though to my human taste it is about the most disgusting of vegetables. **1896** B. Spencer *Rep. Horn Sci. Exped. Central Aust.* I. 47 Now and again .. a Codonocarpus, the 'native poplar' with light green leathery leaves. **1906** *Proc. Linnean Soc. N.S.W.* XXXI. 445 *Carumbium populifolium* .. (Native Poplar). **1979** Wrigley & Fagg *Austral. Native Plants* 194 *Codonocarpus cotinifolius* .. Native poplar. Tall, pyramidal tree. Leaves are poplar-like, grey-green. **(a)** **1833** J. Backhouse *Narr. Visit Austral. Colonies* 2 Jan. (1843) 119, I dug up a *Gastrodium sesamoides*... It grows among decaying vegetable matter, and has a root like a series of kidney potatoes .. and is sometimes called **Native Potato.** **1857** F.R. Nixon *Cruise of Beacon* 27 The native potato, so called by the colonists, though never tasted by them. **1888** *Proc. Linnean Soc. N.S.W.* III. 515 'Native potato' .. tubers were roasted and eaten by the Tasmanian natives. **(b)** **1890** *Ibid.* V. 275 *Marsdenia flavescens* .. and *M. viridiflora* .. the tuberous roots of these species are edible. They are called '**Native Potatoes**', and the blacks were accustomed to eat them after some preparation. **1981** D. Levitt *Plants & People* 34 Native Potato (*Marsdenia viridiflora*)... The green fruit is 5 to 6 cm. long. When ready for eating it is slightly yellow. **1844** L. Leichhardt *Jrnl. Overland Exped. Aust.* 9 Dec. (1847) 67 The **native raspberry**, and *Ficus muntia*, were in fruit. **1921** *Bulletin* (Sydney) 15 Sept. 22/3 The native raspberry, found in Tasmania and N.S. Wales, is probably the best of the native fruits of the southern States. **1878** R.B. Smyth *Aborigines of Vic.* I. 230 *Rubus rosaefolius* .. Native raspberry. **1938** C.T. White *Princ. Bot. Qld. Farmers* 178 Five species of *Rubus* (Native Raspberries or brambles). **1975** A.B. & J.W. Cribb *Wild Food in Aust.* 54 *Rubus hillii* .. is one of the most vigorous of the native raspberries. **1827** R. Sweet *Flora Australasica* Pl. 19, Boronia serrulata... Its beauty and the delightful fragrance of its flowers .. has [*sic*] obtained for it the name of the **native Rose** in New South Wales. **1838** J. Martin *Austral. Sketch Bk.* 22 An armful of the fragrant native rose. **1860** 'Lady' *My Experiences in Aust.* 45 There is the *Native rose* .. which, however, bears no other resemblance than that of colour to the old garden favourite. It is known to botanists, I believe, as the *Borronias serrulata.* **1891** W. Tilley *Wild West of Tas.* 8 Bauera shrub .. is the only one native to Tasmania which bears a double flower. This is very pretty and has been named by Spicer the 'Native Rose'. **1941** C. Barrett *Aust.* 80 We went looking for the 'native rose', really a pink Boronia, with bright green, overlapping leaves nearly hiding the stem. **1968** C.A. Gardner *Wildflowers W.A.* 77 *Diplolaena*—inaptly called the native rose. **1980** B. Roberts *Penalty of Adam* 101 They reached the green wall of bauera, sweet native rose. **1856** *Jrnl. Australasia* I. 38 Glycine monophylla; one-leaved glycine, the rich blue flowering trailer, erroneously known as the **native sarsaparilla.** **1888** *Sydney Morning Herald* 24 Jan. (Centennial Suppl.) 1/6 Another most useful plant is the .. native sarsaparilla. **1896** J.H. Maiden *Flowering Plants & Ferns N.S.W.* 55 The sweet leaves are used in the case of the ordinary native or Colonial Sarsaparilla (*S. glycyphylla*). **1965** *Austral. Encycl.* VIII. 144 Both [*Smilax australis* and *S. glycyphylla*] are called native sarsaparilla, and *S. glycyphylla* was one of the earliest plants to be used medicinally in New South Wales. **1975** A.B. & J.W. Cribb *Wild Food in Aust.* 177 *Smilax glyciphylla* Native sarsaparilla... Perhaps it would be better classed as a medicinal than as an edible plant since its leaves were widely used to produce a bitter-sweet tea which was reputedly a good tonic and effective in the prevention of scurvy. **1846** *Portland Guardian* 18 Sept. 4/2 We boiled the young shoots of **native spinach** (mesembrianthemum) .. as vegetables. **1878** R.B. Smyth *Aborigines of Vic.* II. 303 The green *Portulac*: the native spinach (strongly resembling the New Zealand spinach of our gardens) .. eaten raw. **1927** *Bulletin* (Sydney) 24 Feb. 22/3, I .. added to my menu goanna flesh, wambi-snakes, wood-grubs, 'fat hen' (native spinach). **1854** F. Eldershaw *Aust. as it really Is* 43 The **native** Plum, **Tamarind,** Chestnut .. are .. well-recognized delicacies among the rising Anglo-Australian generation. **1871** *Illustr. Austral. News* (Melbourne) 21 Jan. 114/1 Attention has been called to the native Tamarind, found on the Hunter .. but there is a good deal of difference in the descriptions of the tree, some stating that it is branched, with the bulk of its foliage at the top, others that it is a palm with a soft woody stem. **1880** J. Bonwick *Resources Qld.* 81 The Native Tamarind, whose fruit is preserved, has a wood which will be useful for its compactness. **1919** *Emu* XIX. 7 Feeding on the berries of the .. native tamarind. **1938** C.T. White *Princ. Bot. Qld. Farmers* 29 The first few leaves in seedlings of .. the Native Tamarind (*Dipoglottis*) .. are quite simple and entire. **1975** A.B. & J.W. Cribb *Wild Food in Aust.* 29 Native tamarind is one of the most easily recognized of rainforest trees. **1985** N. & H. Nicholson *Austral. Rainforest Plants* 26 If given a favourable position out of frost and wind, Native Tamarind will grow in sun or shade. **1844** L. Leichhardt *Jrnl. Overland Exped. Aust.* 2 Oct. (1847) 5 **Native tobacco** in blossom. **1848** T.L. Mitchell *Jrnl. Exped. Tropical Aust.* 352 Yuranigh found more of the native tobacco, which the men eagerly asked for some of. This was a variety of the southern *Nicotiana suaveolens* with white flowers, and smoother leaves. **1862** G. Bourne *Jrnl. Landsborough's Exped. from Carpentaria* 36 We got some native tobacco yesterday, it is a poor substitute for negrohead. **1896** B. Spencer *Rep. Horn Sci. Exped. Central Aust.* IV. 61 'Native tobacco' .. growing freely in most places the chewing of its leaves and stems is a general practice amongst both the Arunta and Luritcha tribes. **1903** H. Basedow *Jrnl. Govt. N.-W. Exped.* 29 Apr. (1914) 85 We found .. the dried leaves of the native tobacco, or 'pituri' (*Duboisia hopwoodi*). **1916** S.A. White *In Far Northwest* 76 A round mass of greenish substance between their lips .. proved to be a ball of native tobacco (*Nicotiana*). **1948** C.P. Mountford *Brown Men & Red Sand* 128 He first squirted a stream of chewed native tobacco (*Nicotiana* sp.) on a flat stone. **1975** G. Blainey *Triumph of Nomads* 175 Native tobacco was chewed, not smoked. It was usually known as *pituri*, or by a variation of that name. **1826** J. Atkinson *Acct. Agric. & Grazing N.S.W.* 19 The wood of the warrataw or **native tulip**, the most magnificent flower of New Holland. **1851** *Empire* (Sydney) 3 Nov. 322/7 The magnificent native tulip is strikingly conspicuous. **1881** E. Davies *Story Earnest Life* 379 The most beautiful is the waratah, or native tulip. **1925** I. Marriott *Early Explorers Aust.* 511 The waratah or native tulip (*Telopea speciosa*), its crimson flower, upon its upright stalk. **1861** *Sydney Mail* 6 July 3/3 The graceful *Acacia floribunda*, the sallee, or **'native willow'**, is golden with bloom .. a slender tree, with long lance-shaped leaves. **1875** R.P. Falla *Knocking About* (1976) 29 The well is in close proximity to a few native willows. **1888** *Proc. Linnean Soc. N.S.W.* III. 538 *Pittosporum phillyraeoides* .. called variously 'Butter-bush', 'Native Willow', and 'Poison-berry' tree. **1901** *Ibid.* XXVI. 209 Another tree growing on the river flats is *Acacia salicina* .. (Cooba or Native Willow). **1914** *Bulletin* (Sydney) 26 Feb. 22/4 The most common fish poisons used are the 'goobang' or native willow [etc.]. **1934** W.A. Osborne *Visitor to Aust.* 64 The native willow, known strangely enough to few Australians, gives a furniture timber of beautiful colour and veining. **1975** Holliday & Hill *Field Guide Austral. Trees* 22 'Native Willow' has an extensive range in the dry inland regions of all mainland States... As its common name implies, it is a tree with a drooping, willowy habit. **1827** P. Cunningham *Two Yrs. in N.S.W.* I. 300 They [*sc.* the pigs] feed on the grasses, herbs, wild roots, and **native yams,** on the margins of our rivers or marshy grounds. **1844** *Swan River News* June 47/1 The native yam, of the class Dioeceae, is stated by Mr Drummond to be the finest esculent vegetable the colony produces. **1899** *Proc. Linnean Soc. N.S.W.* XXIV. 387 The plant was referable to *Parsonsia*... The tubers are known locally as 'Native Yams'. **1889** J.H.L. Zillmann *Past & Present Austral. Life* 58 Searching for the wild honey amongst the branches of the trees, eating the roots and native yams. **1913** *Bulletin* (Sydney) 6 Feb. 15/4 The native-yam workings .. resemble an old alluvial gold diggings.

b. In the names of animals: **native bear,** Koala 1; **bee,** any of several small, stingless bees of the genus *Trigona*, producing honey which is stored in a comb, often in the hollow of a tree trunk; also *attrib.*; **canary,** any of several birds having an attractive song or yellowish colour, esp. *white-throated warbler* (see White *a.*[2] 1 b.); **cat,** any of the several carnivorous, long-tailed, spotted marsupials of the genus *Dasyurus* of Aust. incl. Tas., and New Guinea, incl. the *tiger cat* (see Tiger *n.* 6); Quoll; *spotted native cat*, see Spotted; Wild cat *n.*[1]; see also Dasyure; also *ellipt.* as **cat; companion,** Brolga; **devil** *obs.*, *Tasmanian devil*, see Tasmanian *a.* 2; **dingo** *obs.*, **dog,** Dingo *n.* 1; **hedgehog,** Echidna; **hen, (a)** either of two species of moorhen, the *Tasmanian native hen* (see Tasmanian *a.* 2), and the black-tailed native hen *Gallinula ventralis*, a nomadic bird occurring near water in inland mainland Aust.; **(b)** *mallee fowl*, see Mallee 6; **herring** *obs.*, **(a)** Tommy Rough; **(b)** Herring 2; **hyena** *obs.*, **(a)** *Tasmanian tiger*, see Tasmanian *a.* 2; **(b)** *Tasmanian devil*, see Tasmanian *a.* 2; **magpie** *obs.*, Magpie *n.* 1 a.; **pheasant, (a)** Lyre-bird 1; **(b)** *mallee fowl*, see Mallee 6; **porcupine,** Echidna; **salmon,** the fish *Arripis trutta* (see Salmon); **sloth** *obs.*, Koala 1; **tiger** *obs.*, *Tasmanian tiger*, see Tasmanian *a.* 2; **turkey** *obs.*, Turkey *n.*[1] 1.

1827 P. Cunningham *Two Yrs. in N.S.W.* I. 317 Our *coola* (sloth or **native bear**) is about the size of an ordinary poodle dog, with shaggy, dirty coloured fur, no tail, and claws and feet like a bear, of which it forms a tolerable miniature. **1842** *Portland Mercury* 7 Sept. 4/4 Their only means of subsistence was a little wet flour, occasionally eked out with the flesh of the native bear, or monkey, for the capture of which they were generally indebted to their sable companion. **1870** E.B. Kennedy *Four Yrs. in Qld.* 98, I never found the native bear far north: it is common enough about the Brisbane scrubs. **1888** *Sydney Morning Herald* 24 Jan. (Centennial Suppl.) 1/5 The native bear is a small stupid animal, easily caught in the daytime, when it is generally asleep and refuses to awake, and it is easily tamed. **1903** *Truth* (Sydney) 11 Jan. 1/4 There is something funny about a native bear's tail—probably because brevity is the soul of wit. **1926** A.S. Le Souef et al. *Wild Animals Australasia* 291 The quaint koala, or native bear, a creature which, perhaps, holds the affection of Australians more than any other of their wild animals. **1965** N. LINDSAY *Bohemians of Bulletin* 31 He always reminded me of a native bear. **1979** B. MARTYN *First Footers S. Gippsland* 48 The plumber .. professed an aptitude for handling native bears. **1845** L. LEICHHARDT *Jrnl. Overland Exped. Aust.* 12 Feb. (1847) 148 In the scrub Fusanus was observed in fruit .. and the white Vitex in blossom; from the latter the **native bee** extracts a most delicious honey. **1875** P.E. WARBURTON *Journey across Western Interior* 167 We .. worked hard to cut out a native bees' hive, but got no honey. **1912** A. GALE *Austral. Bee Lore* 1 In Australia the only social honey-storing insect in any way resembling the true hive bee is the little so-called native bee, *Trigona carbonaria.* **1935** T. RAYMENT *Cluster of Bees* 8 We have occupied Australia for over 100 years, and no one thought it worth while to write an account of the life-histories of our horde of native-bees. **1960** R.S. PORTEOUS *Cattleman* 28 The native bee honey drained from a crack in an old coolibah while the little black native bees crawled like sticky ants all over their hands and faces. **1981** Q. WILD *Honey Wind* 1 Around the rock pool the small native bees, like tiny flies, their wings soft because they are young, stingless, gather .. in the blossoms of the stringybark tree. **1889** *Proc. Linnean Soc. N.S.W.* IV. 407 *Gerygone albigularis* .. local name '**Native Canary**'. **1900** A.J. CAMPBELL *Nests & Eggs Austral. Birds* 156 *Gerygone albigularis*. . . From its song (not that it resembles the notes of any other bird), and partly on account of its yellow breast, it has gained the local name of 'Native Canary'. **1916** S.A. WHITE *In Far Northwest* 9 The orange-fronted chat, often called the 'Native Canary' by the bushman, is a common bird on the open country. **1929** A.H. CHISHOLM *Birds & Green Places* 113 In Australia the warbling of the flyeaters has won for several of them the name of 'native canary'. **1965** *Austral. Encycl.* IX. 159 Most species [of warbler] are plain-coloured but some few have the underparts yellow, and this, coupled with their sweet songs, has given rise to the term 'native canary'. **1804** *Sydney Gaz.* 11 Mar. 3/3 From the prodigious increase of the brood of wild or **native cats** great quantities of poultry have been destroyed. **1825** *London Mag.* May II. 61 There is the native cat, a very pretty animal, mostly dark brown with white spots all over them as thick as they can well be, they are the sise [*sic*] of our cats. **1834** J. BACKHOUSE *Extracts from Lett.* (1838) ii. 18 He .. has encouraged his men to destroy the native cats by giving them eightpence a skin. **1848** *Maitland Mercury* 19 Apr. 2/2 The native cat domesticated, or in a partially domestic state, is the best and most efficacious extirpater of rats that can be imagined. **1863** F. ALGAR *Handbk. to Colony Tas.* 9 Skins of the tiger and native cats are suitable for muffs. **1872** 'RESIDENT' *Glimpses Life Vic.* 237 The so-called native cat .. partly resembles the ferret, but is marsupial. **1911** *Bulletin* (Sydney) 17 Aug. 13/2 The Monaro P.P. Boards issued a proclamation that the cat was to be protected as a rabbit-destroyer. **1935** F. BIRTLES *Battle Fronts Outback* 99 Dinkum growled at something in a crevice that hissed and growled fiercely back at him—the smell told me that it was a native-cat. **1962** B.W. LEAKE *Eastern Wheatbelt Wildlife* 51 The native cat is still found further south in the jarrah country. **1981** A.B. FACEY *Fortunate Life* 42 A domestic dog usually won't attack a dingo or native cat on account of their viciousness. **1817** J. OXLEY *Jrnls. Two Exped. N.S.W.* 12 May (1820) 33 That large species of bittern, known on the east-coast by the local name of **Native Companions**, I believe from the circumstance of their being always seen in pairs, was observed. **1845** J.O. BALFOUR *Sketch of N.S.W.* 28 The native companion .. stands about three or four feet high, and its feathers are of a beautiful slate colour. **1857** J. D'EWES *China, Aust. & Pacific Islands* 51 A tall and elegantly-feathered bird, something between the flamingo and stork, called the 'Native Companion', from the facility of taming it and inculcating domestic habits. **1859** W. BURROWS *Adventures Mounted Trooper* 76 There is another bird found on the plains, called the 'native companion'. Why it has received that name would be hard to tell, unless it be used in an ironical sense, as it is a bird of remarkably solitary habits. **1864** *Sydney Punch* 3 Sept. 114/1 Lifting his legs like a native companion in long grass. **1887** W.H. SUTTOR *Austral. Stories Retold* 161 Native-companions dance and make love with ridiculous antic awkwardness in the propitious season. **1911** A. SEARCY *By Flood & Field* 60 We often saw Native Companions bowing and scraping to each other, as if dancing a set of quadrilles or a minuet. **1941** C. BARRETT *Aust.* 57 The old Colonial name for Australia's only crane has been displaced by 'brolga', an aboriginal word; but 'native companion' pleases me better. **1955** D. CLARK *Boomer* 40 Only a 'native companion', a tall gray crane with cheeks of apoplectic red, stalked stiffly across her path. **1980** T.A. ROY *Vengeance of Dolphin* 28, I looked up and saw circling against the backdrop of the blue sky two 'Native Companions'—members of the family of Australian cranes. **1833** W.H. BRETON *Excursions* 408 Of the **native devil** (dasyuris ursinus) I saw only one specimen. **1841** G.R. WATERHOUSE *Nat. Hist. Marsupialia* 129 The Ursine Dasyurus inhabits Van Diemen's Land , and is called by the colonists the native Devil, by which name it was known upwards of thirty years back. **1865** G.F. ANGAS *Aust.* 76 The *Thylacinus*, or 'tiger-wolf' and the *Sarcophilus*, or 'native devil', are the two largest and most ferocious of all the Australian carnivorous pouched animals. **1880** J.J. JONES *Openings for Emigrants* 57 In the fastness of this wild and uncultivated country the hyaena, or native tiger, is found, and also the native devil, both of which used formerly to be so destructive of sheep. **1892** J. FRASER *Aborigines N.S.W.* 53 The Tasmanians, for instance, would not eat their native tiger and native devil. **1842** *S.A. News* (London) 15 Jan. 69/1 The **native dingoes**, now spread thinly over the country, skulking in holes and caves, seek to avoid the light of day. **1865** J.M. STUART *Explorations in Aust.* 19 It is commonly supposed that the native dingo or wild dog does not bark. This is an error. **1890** W.F. BUCHANAN *Aust. to Rescue* 21 No wild beasts of any sort to molest flocks and herds, nothing more formidable than the native dingo (wild dog). **1788** *HRA* (1914) 1st Ser. I. 32 Five ewes and a lamb had been killed in the middle of the day, and very near the camp, I apprehend by some of the **native dogs.** **1792** D. COLLINS *Acct. Eng. Colony N.S.W.* (1798) I. 252 Four fine kangaroos, and several native dogs. **1806** *Sydney Gaz.* 7 Dec., On Thursday a native dog made his way into a flock of geese. **1825** *London Mag.* May II. 61, I have known a native dog get into a sheep pen of a night and kill no less than 25 sheep. **1839** H. WATSON Let. to Parents 9 Sept. 3 The native dog is prowling sometimes about in the night but he is like the fox in Scotland; he only attacks the sheep and as there is a price set upon their heads, I believe they will soon be extinct. **1841** *Geelong Advertiser* 11 Oct. 2/3 Two pounds for the destruction of a native dog or tiger. **1848** *Austral. Sportsman* (Sydney) 30 Sept. 1/3 Several hack races, together with a native dog hunt wound up a tolerable day's sport. **1863** J. DAVIS *Tracks of McKinlay* 177 A native dog came into camp last night, and tried to get at a sheep in the fold. **1888** *Sydney Morning Herald* 24 Jan. (Centennial Suppl.) 1/5 The dingo, or native dog .. does not bark but makes a dismal whine. **1913** W.K. HARRIS *Outback in Aust.* 89 No pouch was provided in the make-up of the dingo. He is erroneously called the native dog of Australia, but is merely the descendant of a few domesticated Dutch dogs, which were left, in a diseased state, on the shores of Western Australia by the officers of a Dutch vessel cruising about Cape Leeuwin in 1622. **1945** B. BEATTY *With Shame Remembered* (1962) 39, I have often taken grass, pounded it, and made soup from a native dog. **1970** W.S. RAMSON *Eng. Transported* 42 It is only later that *native dog* has given way to *dingo.* **1848** *Portland Gaz.* 27 Oct. 3/5 **Native hedge-hog. . .** In shape and size it resembles the Hedge-hog of the Mother Country, but is covered with strong, short, and sharp quills or bristles, somewhat different from that well-known animal. **1880** J. BALLANTYNE *Our Colony* 92 Among other animals may be mentioned .. the native hedge-hog. **1965** *Austral. Encycl.* VIII. 241 The alternative popular names for the ant-eater are inappropriate: .. 'native hedgehog' because the true hedgehogs belong to the order Insectivora. **1804** M. HOOKEY *B. Knopwood & his Times* 24 Mar. (1929) 20 Killed a **Native Hen,** which first took the sea. **1829** H. WIDOWSON *Present State Van Diemen's Land* 182 The baldcoot, and a large bird, called the native hen .. frequent the lakes and lagunes. **1848** J. GOULD *Birds of Aust.* VI. Pl. 71, *Tribonyx mortieri* .. Native Hen, of the Colonists. **1852** G.C. MUNDY *Our Antipodes* III. 183 We saw several of that species of water-bird called the Native-hen—quite new to me as a sportsman. It is a rail, nearly as large as a cock pheasant. **1861** 'OLD BUSHMAN' *Bush Wanderings* 63 The *Lowan* or native hen, is peculiar to the country in the vicinity of the 'Mallee Scrub'. **1886** W.J. WOODS *Visit to Vic.* 24 The *Lowan*, or native hen, has a curious practice of heaping up its eggs in the form of a pyramid, and leaving them to get hatched in the sand. **1905** *Emu* V. 19, I did see .. a Native-Hen (*Tribonyx ventralis*) on a claypen flat. **1941** C. BARRETT *Aust.* 59 Black-tailed native hens went pattering to cover. **1962** MARSHALL & DRYSDALE *Journey among Men* 43 A small flock of native hens beside a swampy stream. **1976** *Ecos* viii. 30/1 Native hens need the reeds and undergrowth; remove these and they go elsewhere. **1864** *Colonial Cook Bk.* (1970) 52 **Native herring**, or ruff. A small but delicate fish. **1889** 'MOOSAFIR' *N.-W. Coast Tas.* 30 The River Mersey .. abounds with .. the native herring or cucumber fish as it is called—really the grayling. **1904** R. SLATER *Rod & Line Tas.* 9 Blackfish and native herring are also becoming plentiful. **1831** *Acct. Colony Van Diemen's Land* 53 Considerable numbers of the **native hyena** prowl the mountains near this in quest of prey among the flocks at night. **1857** D. BUNCE *Australasiatic Reminisc.* 25 Mr Davidson submitted to our notice the *Dasyuris*, or native hyena, or devil. **1873** J. BONWICK *M. Howe* 68 No lion raged through the woods, and no wolf entered the folds. But there was the dreaded devil, and the sanginary [*sic*] native tiger or hyena. **1842** *S. Austral. Mag.* (Adelaide) Aug. 469 **Native magpies**—properly, a very beautiful species of the jack-daw tribe—colours, black, white, and grey; their notes about daylight are exceedingly melodious. **1859** R.H. HORNE *Austral. Facts & Prospects* 171 The native magpie on the fence warbles with up-turned eyes. **1869** J. MARTINEAU *Lett. from Aust.* 89 The native magpie fills the air with the music of his delicious dreamy note. **1909** *Papers & Proc. R. Soc. Tas.* 50 A native magpie, which most unmelodiously the zoologists call a 'piping crow'. **1826** J. ATKINSON *Acct. Agric. & Grazing N.S.W.* 26 The **native pheasant** is remarkable for its beautiful tail, but is not fit to eat. **1834** G. BENNETT *Wanderings N.S.W.* I. 277 The 'Native or Wood-pheasant', or 'Lyrebird' of the colonists, the '*Menura superba*' of naturalists. **1840** J. GOULD *Birds of Aust.* (1848) V. Pl. 78, *Leipoa ocellata* .. Native Pheasant, Colonists of Western Australia. **1858** *Illustr. Jrnl. Australasia* IV. 120 The Lyre Bird .. has sometimes been called the native pheasant; this name, however, is not only inappropriate in itself, but is now applicable to another bird of totally different character. **1889** E. GILES *Aust. twice Traversed* I. 153 We saw a native pheasant's nest. . . This bird is known by different names in different parts of Australia. On the eastern half of the continent it is usually called the Lowan, while in Western Australia it is known as the Gnow. **1895** W.H. WILLSHIRE *Thrilling Tale Real Life* 36 During the afternoon I sent the girls out in search of native pheasant's eggs. **1926** L.C.E. GEE *Bush Tracks & Gold Fields* 59 The native pheasant belongs to the .. family Megapodidae. **1834** G. BENNETT *Wanderings N.S.W.* I. 299 The *Echidna*, or '**native porcupine**'. **1856** *Jrnl. Australasia* I. 20 One of them caught a native porcupine. . . When properly cooked it is a dish by no means to be despised. **1886** W.J. WOODS *Visit to Vic.* 37 Those queer creatures the ornithorhynchuses and native porcupines. **1909** G. SMITH *Naturalist in Tas.* 124 The native Porcupine .. is quite distinct in appearance from the *Echidna aculeata* of the mainland, having much fewer quills and more abundant fur, whence its name *E. setosa.* **1943** C. BARRETT *Austral. Animal Bk.* 24 The true porcupines of Europe and America belong to the Order Rodentia, containing the rabbits, squirrels, rats and mice .. whereas the so-called 'native porcupines' are monotremes. **1889** 'MOOSAFIR' *N.-W. Coast Tas.* 22 The river contains plenty of .. mullet, **native salmon,** etc. **1901** *Advocate* (Burnie) 8 Nov. 2/5 Principally native or black back salmon. **1924** LORD & SCOTT *Synopsis Vertebrate Animals Tas.* 60 Australian 'salmon' .. *Arripis trutta*. . . The Arripis is generally known as the Native or Colonial 'Salmon' among fishermen. **1852** W. HUGHES *Austral. Colonies* 79 There is a **native sloth**—a kind of bear, about the size of a poodle dog, with shaggy, dirty-coloured fur. It climbs trees with facility, getting very fat and unwieldy: the flesh is esteemed by the natives. **1906** E. DYSON *In Roaring Fifties* 64 When the Australian diggers were not indulging in the extreme of frenzied exertion .. their inertia surpassed that of their own koala, the native sloth. **1832** *Hobart-Town Almanack* 85 During our stay, a **native tiger** or hyena bounded from its lair beneath the rocks. **1841** *Geelong Advertiser* 11 Oct. 2/3 Two pounds for the destruction of a native dog or tiger. **1892** J. FRASER *Aborigines N.S.W.* 53 The Tasmanians .. would not eat their native tiger and native devil. **1897** *Bulletin* (Sydney) 3 July 28/4 A fine sample of that scarce and rapacious carnivorous marsupial the 'native tiger', which has a beautiful spotted and banded skin, something like the native cat's, was shot at Lilliemir, Wimmera, Vic., the other day. **1909** G. SMITH *Naturalist in Tas.* 95 He told me many stories of the Thylacine or Native Tiger. . . Since this carnivorous Marsupial is regularly hunted and trapped by the shepherds, and since it occurs only in the little island of Tasmania, it will not be very long before it becomes extinct. **1822** B. FIELD *Geogr. Mem. N.S.W.* 12 Oct. (1825) 443 At Bathurst, saw what is called the **native**

turkey. It is the New Holland vulture of Dr Latham, and is one of the most remarkable birds found in Australia, appearing to form a connecting link between the rapacious and gallinaceous orders. **1833** W.H. BRETON *Excursions* 63 There are numerous wild, or native turkies, the Bustard of New Holland. **1835** J. BATMAN *Settlement Port Phillip* 31 May (1856) 15 We travelled this day, in going and returning, at least thirty miles, and . . observed a number of the bustard or native turkey; but they were too shy to allow us to approach within shooting distance. **1842** J. GOULD *Birds of Aust.* (1848) VI. Pl. 4, *Otis australasianus* . . *Turkey*, Colonists of New South Wales. *Native Turkey*, Colonists of Swan River. . . When seen at freedom slowly stalking over its native plains, no Australian bird, except the Emu, is so majestic, or assumes in its carriage so great an air of independence. **1854** J. CAPPER *Aust.* 39 The bustard, or native turkey, weighing from 16 to 18 lbs., is good eating. **1891** *Quiz* (Adelaide) 19 June 6/2 What do the Zoological authorities mean by advertising for kangaroo, native turkeys, 'and other birds'?

native-born, *a.* [Spec. use of *native-born* belonging to a place by birth, applied esp. to persons of immigrant race in a colony.]

1. Of a non-Aboriginal person: born in Australia (as opposed to 'immigrant' or 'naturalized'). Also as quasi-*n.*

1820 *HRA* (1921) 3rd Ser. III. 442 Four out of the Five marriages performed, since I have been here, are between native born people. **1827** *Monitor* (Sydney) 21 June 460/3 It is alleged, that the Colonists who were British-born, are loyal; but the adult native-born in this respect, are but so so. **1845** C. CHISHOLM *Emigration & Transportation* (1847) 39 We have our land on a five years' clearing lease, and our landlord is a native-born gentleman. **1860** 'LADY' *My Experiences in Aust.* 17 My first remark on seeing the younger, and for the most part native-born among the newcomers, was, 'What a set of Yankees!' **1875** J. FORREST *Explorations in Aust.* 329 Mr John Forrest is proud to acknowledge himself as belonging to that colony—indeed native-born. **1894** *Bulletin* (Sydney) 20 Jan. 14/2 The newly-branded Australian ennoblees are nearly all native born. **1915** W.J. WYE *Souvenirs Sunny South* 42 The native-born mustered that day in full force 'Tis well the Australians should worship the horse. **1928** M.E. FULLERTON *Austral. Bush* 61 By 'Australian literature' is meant, of course, simply writing that takes the life actually known and felt by the native-born authors. **1954** *Bulletin* (Sydney) 20 Jan. 12/1 Mac, another New Aussie . . expressed a hope that the fowls on his drills did not eat seed-peas. The native-born owner laughed with confident assurance—his chooks never touched 'em. **1973** *Ibid.* 27 Jan. 9/3 Scratch any native-born West Australian and you will find a secessionist at heart.

2. In collocations: **native-born Australian, colonist, population, white, youth.**

1842 *Colonial Observer* (Sydney) 16 Nov. 612/3 One half of the whole number of the City Councillors, are not **native-born Australians** at all, but free immigrants from the mother-country. **1860** 'LADY' *My Experiences in Aust.* 58, I should not think the native-born Australians, or those who have emigrated in childhood, are likely to be a very long-lived race. **1891** D.E. FALK *Rick* 127 He is a capital specimen of a native-born Australian. Tall, strong, and good-looking, a splendid horseman, a thorough man of business, and as bold as a lion. **1936** C.P. CONIGRAVE *N. Aust.* 249, I write as a native-born Australian. **1971** *Bulletin* (Sydney) 1 May 19/1 Immigrants have fewer dependants than native-born Australians. **1831** *Independent* (Launceston) 22 Oct. 2/2 Recommend it to the attention of a **native born colonist. 1852** *Guardian* (Hobart) 4 Aug. 4/3 Affecting both my rights as a subject and my privileges as a native-born colonist. **1872** *Illustr. Sydney News* 28 Sept. 4/1 Many of our native-born colonists will remember with feelings of pleasure the old Fig-tree, 'where, as boys, we all used to swim'. **1848** H.W. HAYGARTH *Recoll. Bush Life* 123 The **native-born population** (I allude, of course, only to the whites) . . are not, upon the whole, equal in form to the parent stock. **1869** *Bushmen, Publicans, & Politics* 3 Our labour in the bush has been supplied from four sources: the first is most familiarly known as 'old hands'; the next is the young native-born population [etc.]. **1835** BACKHOUSE & TYLOR *Life & Labours G.W. Walker* (1862) 233 The bulk of the population are **native born whites. 1848** H.W. HAYGARTH *Recoll. Bush Life* 96 He was a native-born white. **1928** G.H. WILKINS *Undiscovered Aust.* 44 The healthy-bodied native-born whites. **1827** *Hobart Town Courier* 1 Dec. 1 One of them is Edward Hannigan, a **native born youth. 1849** *Melbourne Argus* 1 Sept. 2/3 The fall of snow was welcomed by our native-born youth, some of whom . . had never seen such a thing during their existence. **1881** J.F.V. FITZGERALD *Aust.* 56 'Currency', a name bestowed upon the native-born youth as contradistinguished from the 'sterling', by which term the immigrant was known.

nature strip. A name applied in some Australian towns to a piece of publicly-owned land between the front boundary of a dwelling or other building and the street, usu. planted with grass; a median strip.

1948 *Architecture in Aust.* Jan. 34, I did not see one allotment where the whole of the ground was cared for and the street nature strip in front attended to. **1952** R. BOYD *Aust.'s Home* 91 The narrow bed of grass outside the fence has long been called the 'nature strip'. **1961** B. HUMPHRIES *Nice Night's Entertainment* (1981) 52, I was round the front, doing a spot of watering. After that summer we had the nature strip was on its last legs. **1964** K. TENNANT *Summer's Tales* 32 There was I pounding along on the grass-plots (surely they weren't nature strips in 1937?). **1973** *Bulletin* (Sydney) 3 Feb. 62/1 If you drive through many country towns these days you see the nature strips in the centres of roads and parks neat and tidy and lots of new kerbing and guttering. **1982** *Ibid.* 4 May 32/1 He described the Left's policy as 'wider nature strips, more trees and let's go back to making wicker baskets in Balmain'. **1985** *Canberra Times* 30 Oct. 1/2 They were sped along polished streets between irrigated nature strips to pink and laughing crowds.

naughty. (An act of) sexual intercourse.

1959 E. LAMBERT *Glory thrown In* 106 Until I met Thelma, I always thought sheilas had to be talked into a bit of a naughty. **1963** D. ROBERT *Look at me Now* 84 The general use of the euphemism 'naughty' or 'a naughty' for sexual intercourse illustrates the excessively puritan attitude which is generally held. **1967** J. HIBBERD *White with Wire Wheels* (1970) 160, I don't even remember the naughty. **1977** R. BEILBY *Gunner* 82 It was also the opinion of the platoon, privately expressed, that Peppie had enjoyed more thoughties than naughties. **1982** N. KEESING *Lily on Dustbin* 40 A widely used Australian term for the sexual act is 'to have a naughty', but one religious lady, circa 1930s, referred to intercourse as 'a naught'. **1985** *Sydney Morning Herald* 20 June 11/6 The Poms are often accused of spending all their time at a party chatting up girls—an offence against Mateship. Not for nothing do Australians call sexual intercourse 'having a naughty'.

Hence **naughty** *v. trans.*, to have sexual intercourse with.

1977 C. KLEIN *Pomegranate Tree* 61 He didn't want to dob the hard word on her, last thing he had on his mind was to try and naughty her.

near enough, *phr.* See quot. 1962.

1939 H.M. MORAN *Viewless Winds* 12 This has begotten the slipshod character of all we make and the spirit of 'near enough will do'. **1954** *Bulletin* (Sydney) 25 Aug. 12/1 If a no-hoper does a rough job he dismisses any qualms with: 'She's near enough!' **1960** *Ibid.* 28 Sept. 16/3 To the old bush sayings recalled here, add 'a shepherd's boil'—that state of simmering but refusing to boil that a quart-pot can keep up for what seems like hours when you're really thirsty; 'near enough for a sheepstation', which is what you say when thirst wins and you wait no longer for a true boil. **1962** *Texas Q.* 62 'Near enough' is the national philosophy: a deliberate cult of antifinesse, of outbackmanship. **1977** E. PARTRIDGE *Dict. Catch Phrases* 152 *Near enough is good enough* has, since c. 1945, been an Australian [catch phrase] applied to a very common attitude.

Nebuchadnezzar. [So called in allusion to Daniel's interpretation of the dream of *Nebuchadnezzar* King of Babylon (d. 562 B.C.): see Daniel iv. 25.] A salad.

1859 F. FOWLER *Southern Lights & Shadows* 53 At some of the taverns they serve bread-and-cheese, salads, and sandwiches for luncheon. The vernacular for these stands thus: . . Salad . . Nebuchadnezzar [etc.]. **1941** S.J. BAKER *Pop. Dict. Austral. Slang* 48 *Nebuchadnezzar*, salad.

neck, *n.*

1. *pl.* The wool shorn from the neck of a sheep.

1928 C.E. COWLEY *Classing Clip* 36 In large sheds it may be advisable to remove the 'necks', that is, the wool grown on the scragg.

2. a. In the phr. **under** (someone's) **neck,** see quot. 1966.

1953 T.A.G. HUNGERFORD *Riverslake* 220 Why jack up? . . You just race in the mob from the office and go under our necks. **1961** M. CALTHORPE *Dyehouse* 120 She knew she was going under Patty What's-her-name's neck. **1966** S.J. BAKER *Austral. Lang.* (ed. 2) 239 Worthy of record is the expression *get under someone's neck*, which is in general use and apparently has horsey antecedents. A person who beats, outwits or anticipates the moves of another is said to *get under his neck*; it means to get in front of him. **1977** *Sunday Tel.* (Sydney) 6 Feb. 128/4 In Queensland Premier Joh Bjelke-Petersen getting under Neville Wran's neck. **1982** *N.T. News* (Darwin) 7 Dec. 7/1 Bob-a-job Boy Scouts in England have got under the neck of the Pommie Post Office by starting a cheap Christmas card delivery service.

b. In the *attrib. phr.* **neck-to-knee(s),** see quot. 1902.

[**1902** *N.S.W. Govt. Gaz.* VI. 8690 All persons bathing in any waters exposed to view from any wharf, street, public place, or dwelling-house in the Municipal District of Manly, before the hour of 7.30 in the morning and after the hour of 8 o'clock in the evening, shall be attired in proper bathing costume covering the body from the neck to the knee. Any person committing a breach of this By-law shall be liable to a penalty not exceeding one pound.] **1910** *Daily Tel.* (Sydney) 20 June 17/8 Neck-to-knee costumes have been for some time past insisted on at all the popular resorts. **1934** *Sydney Morning Herald* 31 Oct. 14/2 Seaside municipalities are perturbed that, with the surfing season in full swing, they are forced to sit in judgement on the costumes worn on the beaches in accordance with a local government ordinance, which was drawn up in 1908, and provides for neck-to-knee costumes. **1961** R.S. HARRIS *Heroes of Surf* 6 Anyone could bathe at any time, provided the person was suitably attired (in neck-to-knee costume). **1965** G. MCINNES *Road to Gundagai* 261 Refusing to wear the regulation 'neck-to-knee' bathing togs.

3. Special Comb. **neck-bag,** a water-bag; **rope,** a rope used to tether an animal by the neck; so, **rope** *v. trans.*

1936 *Bulletin* (Sydney) 12 Aug. 20/2 Another test is with a **neck-bag**. The city cove will put his mouth to the nozzle of the bag; the mulga-trained one will pour the water from the bag to his pint. **1947** E. HILL *Flying Doctor Calling* 19 There are water-bags, veranda-bags, saddle-bags, tucker-bags, neck-bags. **1982** D. HARRIS *Drovers of Outback* 15 Quart pots for tea making and neck bags for water were . . carried. **1849** A. HARRIS *Emigrant Family* (1967) 129 The leg-rope is first cautiously unloosed; next the **neck-rope** is slackened. **1938** A. UPFIELD *Bone is Pointed* (1966) 49 Both animals . . appeared to be neck-roped to their respective trees. *Ibid.* 89 He neck-roped the mare to a shady cabbage-tree.

neck, *v. trans.* To carry (a burden) across the shoulders.

1976 R. THIELE *Ketch Hand* 43 Sometimes even the skipper did an hour 'necking a few bags' to speed up the loading. **1982** LOWENSTEIN & HILLS *Under Hook* 50 With bags you arsed 'em or necked 'em. . . Necking 'em means that you carried them across your shoulders, on your neck.

necking, *vbl. n.* See quot. 1967.

1967 *Kings Cross Whisper* (Sydney) xxxvi. 4/2 *Necking*, the practice of putting one arm around a victim's neck and a free hand into his pocket. **1968** J. ALARD *He who shoots Last* 173 All his boob dreams of performing future neckings (his favourite method of earning a living) were fading.

neddy. [Transf. use of *neddy* a donkey.]

1. A horse.

1887 *Tibbs' Pop. Song Bk.* 9 So they saddled up their Neddys And like loafers sneaked away. **1891** 'SMILER' *Wanderings Simple Child* (ed. 3) 128 He had been pretty wealthy once, but had had a bad time backing the 'neddys', and one morning he woke up and found himself, like Byron, famous, but dead broke. **1912** *Bulletin* (Sydney) 21 Nov. 15/2 The man in the two-horse waggon was nodding on his seat as the neddies jogged lazily. **1922** J. LEWIS *Fought & Won* 18 We were exceptionally pleased when we got our 'neddies'. **1942** T. KELAHER *Digger Hat* 12 I've dropped the slip-rails down and let my neddy free. **1956** *Truth* (Sydney) 8 Jan. 8/3 The neddy, Turonio, did no good but the kid came good later on when he piloted Alahuii to victory in the First Ashbury Stakes. **1967** J. WYNNUM *I'm Jack, all Right* 10 They say he's a sucker for slow neddies. **1981** *Bulletin* (Sydney) 8 Sept. 47/2 Needing extra money for the neddies, he'd let it be known that guests were expected to cough up.

2. *transf.* A swagman's tucker-bag.

1898 *Bulletin* (Sydney) 30 July 32/2 'Neddy' the tucker-bag is of more importance than the 'blue one', and by way of precedence dangles in front, mostly hanging to Matilda's apron-strings.

Ned Kelly, *n.* [f. the name of *Ned Kelly* (1857–1880), bushranger.]

1. Used allusively to designate one who is unscrupulous in seeking personal gain or resistant of authority. See also *Kelly gang* KELLY *n.*[1] 1. Also *attrib.*

1893 F.W.L. ADAMS *Australs.* 66 This Ned Kelly of colonial politics . . may yet jockey himself into a local immortality, as the father of Australian Federation. **1918** *Truth* (Sydney) 17 Nov. 12/5 Would you kindly allow me a small space to expose the Ned Kelly methods of a great majority of Sydney shopkeepers. **1919** J. ANDREWS *Garrison Ginger* 12 They called us Ned Kelly's army, A battalion of awkward squads. **1943** S.W. KEOUGH *Around Army* 28 The private . . dons the clobber that he's either had specially tailored or has got from the Q.M. store—in the latter case, by issue according to King's Regs. or Ned Kelly technique. **1953** A.W. UPFIELD *Murder must Wait* 12 This detective inspector of the Queensland C.I.B., this cross between Sir Galahad and Ned Kelly. **1964** B. SUTTON *Snow & Me* (1966) 36 The Ned Kelly parliamentary pay rise grab. **1965** E. LAMBERT *Long White Night* 85 The Australian with a bit of Ned Kelly in him, the man with the deadly bayonet, teeth bared in a wolfish laugh beneath the shading brim. **1966** *Meanjin* 283 An escaped convict, too, although he was only in for car-stealing or something like that. Anyhow, everybody was a bit in his way. The old Ned Kelly coming out, eh? **1982** *Bulletin* (Sydney) 20 July 41/1 Unfortunately the old Ned Kelly syndrome rears its head. People look up at all the big insurance buildings and reckon they can afford it.

2. In the phr. **(as) game as Ned Kelly,** fearless in the face of odds; foolhardy.

1938 *Point* (Melbourne) I. i. 8 Sleet-smarted face and snow-filled eye, Vigilant in the dark before the dawn Game as Ned Kelly. **1942** C. TURNBULL *Ned Kelly* 3 The phrase, 'Game as Ned Kelly', is part of the national idiom. **1956** S. HOPE *Diggers' Paradise* 89 A common expression on the lips of Aussies of both sexes to describe someone engaged in a risky enterprise is 'he's as game as Ned Kelly'. **1962** *Meanjin* 368 We should say, 'as self-righteous as J.D. Lang', or 'as devious as Henry Parkes', or 'as sanctimonious as Nathaniel Pidgeon', just as we do say, 'as game as Ned Kelly'. **1973** J. MURRAY *Larrikins* 158 There was already a national chip on the shoulder and those who felt it would come out fighting, or admire those who did. To die as 'game as Ned Kelly' would become part of the language. **1979** C. STONE *Running Brumbies* 28 I'd never seen old Squeaky move so fast and he was game as Ned Kelly. **1983** B. DAWE *Over here, Harv!* 102 You know me—game as Ned Kelly—so I said, 'What're you doing after you knock off?'

3. Rhyming slang for 'belly'.

1945 S.J. BAKER *Austral. Lang.* 271 *Ned Kelly*, the belly. **1951** D. STIVENS *Jimmy Brockett* 86, I got his arm and rammed a right into his Ned Kelly. **1971** B. HUMPHRIES *Bazza pulls it Off*, If I don't get a drop of hard stuff up me old Ned Kelly there's a chance I might chunder in the channel.

4. *Fishing.* An unsporting fishing rig: see quots.

1948 F.D. MARSHALL *Let's go Fishing* 45 The 'Ned Kelly' is the answer. It consists of a bamboo pole (Indian Cane) approximately 12 feet long. At the end, whip on a loop of greenhide to which is attached the line . . from 12 to 15 feet of steel wire. **1951** S.H. EDWARDS *Shooting & Bushcraft* 48 A 'Ned Kelly' rig to a fisherman is a rod without a reel and a short line to skull-drag a fish.

Ned Kelly, *v.* [f. prec.] *intr.* To bushrange; also *trans.*, to kill (a bird, etc.) unsportingly.

1906 *Gadfly* (Adelaide) 2 May 9/3 Gipsy Smith was a second-rate bushranger, who Ned-Kellied on a small scale about Bendigo in the days of the Forest Range goldfield. **1951** S.H. EDWARDS *Shooting & Bushcraft* 48 When raising yourself above . . the bank of a dam, go up very, very slowly . . and you will have ample time to plan your shot, whether you intend to 'Ned Kelly' them or take them on the wing.

needlebush: see NEEDLEWOOD.

needle-tail. [See quot. 1968.] *Rainbow bird*, see RAINBOW 2.

1941 *Bulletin* (Sydney) 20 Aug. 16/2 A needle-tail . . is more like Willie Wagtail than a kingfisher, and his favorite insect is the good old working bee. A few of them will clean up a dozen hives in no time. **1968** F. HARDY *Unlucky Australs.* 48 She waged a constant war with her shotgun against the needletails. These are beautiful birds, with red eyes, long savage beaks and two long tail feathers sharp as needles.

needlewood. Any of several shrubs or small trees, chiefly of the genus *Hakea* (see HAKEA), having rigid needle-like leaves, esp. *H. leucoptera* and *H. tephrosperma* of drier inland Aust.; PIN BUSH. See also *water tree* WATER. Also **needlebush,** and *attrib.*

1884 *Once a Month* (Melbourne) Dec. 453 The *hakea stricta*, or needlebush of the colonists, with its roots just under the surface, had them full of water. **1898** W. REDMOND *Shooting Trip* 35 This timber is called needlewood, because the foliage resembles fine needles. **1904** J.H. MAIDEN *Notes on Commercial Timbers N.S.W.* 26 Needlewood (*Hakea leucoptera*) . . has been used for making pipes for very many years by bushmen. **1915** *Bulletin* (Sydney) 4 Feb. 14/1 The needle bush . . grows on the sandhills and red ground in the Darr and Diamantina (Q.) country. **1936** I.L. IDRIESS *Cattle King* 135 Lonely country, sand-ridges and needlewood flats. **1936** C.T. MADIGAN *Central Aust.* 76 The twisty needlewood sticks of the desert. **1962** I. SOUTHALL *Woomera* 2 They thrived where not a drop of water flowed—needle-bush, Desert Finish, mulga. **1973** A. BURNETT *Wilful Murder in Outback* 26 The sap of the needlewood is a life-saving fluid.

neelia, neelya, varr. NELIA.

neg, *a.* [Abbrev. of *negligent.*] In the collocation **neg driving:** see quot. 1984.

1969 A. BUZO *Rooted* (1973) 44 Hammo had a prang in his B and got dobbed in for neg driving. **1984** A. DELBRIDGE *Aussie Talk* 217 *Neg driving, n.*, the offence of negligent driving.

negro. *Obs.* A name applied by colonists to an Aboriginal.

1834 G. BENNETT *Wanderings N.S.W.* I. 171 It is probable that the negroes of New Holland have extended into the Australian continent, by New Guinea and the eastern islands, and that the migration has been made from the coast of Africa. **1838** *Austral. Mag.* (Sydney) 77 The New Hollanders form a distinct race, to which the term *papuas*, or *oriental negroes*, has been assigned. **1859** J.D. MEREWEATHER *Diary Working Clergyman* 107 This district is thinly populated by innumerable small tribes of blacks, whom some call Malays, others Australian negroes. **1878** R.B. SMYTH *Aborigines of Vic.* I. 245 The Jardines, on their overland expedition from Rockhampton to Cape York, found 'at a native fire the fresh remains of a negro roasted'.

negrohead. [Used elsewhere but recorded earliest in Aust.: see quot. 1802.] NIGGERHEAD 1.

1802 M. FLINDERS *Voyage Terra Australis* 5 Oct. (1814) II. 83 The reefs were not dry in any part, with the exception of some small black lumps, which at a distance resembled the round heads of negroes. *Ibid.* 7 Oct. (1814) II. 85 Upon these reefs were more of the dry, black lumps, called negro heads, than had been seen before; but they were so much alike as to be of no use in distinguishing one reef from another; and at high water, nearly the whole were covered. **1859** *Aust. Directory* (London) II. 275 At low tides the edges of the reefs are nearly level with the water, with large masses of black coral rock (those appropriately termed negro heads by Capt. Flinders) strewed over some of them. **1931** J.S GARDINER *Coral Reefs & Atolls* 7 Corals are broken off to be swept perchance on to an island shore behind, and fractured rock masses may be cast on to the reef as giant sentinels or 'negroheads'.

negrohead beech: see BEECH.

nelia /'niliə/. Formerly also **neelia, neelya.** [Ngiyambaa *nhiilyi* the tree *Acacia loderi.*] Any of several small trees or shrubs of inland Aust. of the genus *Acacia* (fam. Mimosaceae), esp. *A. rigens*, having needle-like foliage, and *A. loderi.*

1867 *Illustr. Sydney News* 16 Jan. 104/2 The banks of the Murray . . abound in fancy woods. . . The sweetly scented myall is known, but there is another description, known by the blacks as Nelia. . . Both woods are valuable, from their colour and texture, for cabinet work. **1885** *Once a Month* (Melbourne) June 448 There is a small tree very common along the seventy-mile track. It is an acacia; its leaves are long and very narrow, but are in great masses. The wood . . is what is used by the blacks for making their spears. They call it Neelya. **1910** *Emu* X. 89 The neelia (*Acacia rigens*) just coming into bloom. **1936** I.L. IDRIESS *Cattle King* 326 Where had all the mulga gone . . the black oak and nelia, and bullocky bush. **1981** G.M. CUNNINGHAM et al. *Plants Western N.S.W.* 366 Nelia produces a gum which was eaten by aborigines. **1984** *Aboriginal Hist.* VIII. 24 'Nilyah' spelt 'nelia' in many reference books is the local English name for *Acacia loderi.*

Nelly. Also **nelly.** [Transf. use of *Nelly* a female name.]

1. A cheap wine. Also **Nelly's death.**

1935 K. TENNANT *Tiburon* 128 Staines . . tenaciously kept a bottle of Nellie's Death out of circulation. **1941** S.J. BAKER *Pop. Dict. Austral. Slang* 49 *Nelly*, cheap wine. **1953** D. STIVENS *Gambling Ghost* 57 Clutching the five bottles of nelly's death he was carrying, [he] took to his heels. **1967** A.E. DEBENHAM *All Manner of People* 84 They spent that . . on cheap wine (better known as 'plonk', 'Nellie', or 'fourpenny dark'). **1973** *Kings Cross Whisper* (Sydney) cliii. 16/2 You've got to get up very early in the morning to catch them sober and then you can't always be sure on account of their habit of keeping a flagon of nellie by the bed. **1980** HEPWORTH & HINDLE *Boozing out in Melbourne Pubs* 15 Other affectionate nicknames for the stuff itself were . . nelly [etc.].

2. In the collocation **nervous Nelly,** a timid or cautious person.

1974 *Bulletin* (Sydney) 30 Nov. 15/1 The Nervous Nellies—those people in the Federal Government who take fright at some of the devil-may-care attitudes of Prime Minister Whitlam. **1975** *Ibid.* 19 Apr. 25/1 He was the principal 'Nervous Nellie' lashed by the PM in that famous speech. **1984** *N.T. News* (Darwin) 10 Dec. 7/1 Another architectural masterpiece in the same mould is not required. I am neither a 'flat earther' nor a 'nervous nellie', just a concerned Territorian.

3. As **Nelly Bligh,** rhyming slang for 'pie'; also *ellipt.* as **Nelly.**

1967 *Kings Cross Whisper* (Sydney) xxxvi. 4/2 *Nelly Blighs*, eyes, meat pies. *Ibid.* xxxiv. 5/4 *Nellie at Expo 67.* An Australian meat pie is to be sent to Expo '67. **1968** *Swag* (Sydney) i. 24/3 A pie is called a dog's eye, or perhaps, a Nelly Bligh.

nerangy, var. NARANG.

net, *v. trans.* To surround (an area) with wire-netting in order to protect it from vermin. Also with **in, round.**

1896 *Bulletin* (Sydney) 4 Apr. 22/2 Rabbit-net the country, of course, answers the man who knows all about Eastern and Central squattages. . . This 'net the paddocks' solution of the problem will be seen to have weak features about it. **1900** *Ibid.* 28 Apr. 14/3 A 'remittance' farming drunk . . wired in alarm to his wealthy English father that the rabbits were approaching, and please wire £140 for netting round selection. **1923** J. ARMOUR *Spell of Inland* 13 A vegetable garden was netted in, and, by the aid of plenty of water, the vegetables looked healthy. **1938** J.F.W. SCHULZ *Destined to Perish* 22 Though the station was netted in, the rabbits gradually broke through from the South.

net fence. NETTING FENCE.

1905 *Bulletin* (Sydney) 16 Mar. 16/1 The net fences are banked up by roly-poly and sand.

netted, *ppl. a.* Protected with a wire-netting fence; made of wire-netting.

1936 *Bulletin* (Sydney) 5 Feb. 21/1 In a netted paddock beside the Wollondilly . . we had paused to watch a platypus in the stream. **1938** J.F.W. SCHULZ *Destined to Perish* 22 The rabbits gradually broke through from the South and in a devastating column reached the northern and western netted boundary line. **1940** J.A. BROOK *Jim of Seven Seas* 52 Rabbits in their thousands run along these netted fences, seeking a way through or under. **1943** L. MCLENNAN *Spirit of West* 48 North of the netted border the grassland rolls away. **1949** *Walkabout* May 18/2 It rushed men and materials by rail to Burracoppin . . and constructed the fence which is known as the longest netted fence in the world.

netting fence. [Abbrev. of *wire-netting fence.*] A fence of wire-netting erected as a barrier against vermin.

1900 *Bulletin* (Sydney) 1 Sept. 14/2 Have never *seen* a rabbit climb a netting-fence. **1912** *Stockowner's Guide* 9 Experience . . has proved that in vermin-infested country netting fences are an absolute necessity if the land is to be put to full use. **1924** J. HARPER *Splashes from Narran* 58 The blanky jackeroo . . wasn't game to ride a netting fence. **1935** R.B. PLOWMAN *Boundary Rider* 261 Commonly known as The Netting Fence, its purpose was to prevent the migration of dingoes and rabbits. **1936** W. HATFIELD *Aust. through Windscreen* 244 Netting fences defeated the rabbits, and everything was lovely.

nettle tree. STINGING TREE. Also **nettle.**

1827 P. CUNNINGHAM *Two Yrs. in N.S.W.* I. 201 The nettle-tree will tell you at once by the touch whence comes its designation. **1837** *Colonist* (Sydney) 350/1 The nettle is a lofty tree, and the poplar a dwarfish shrub. **1845** L. LEICHHARDT *Jrnl. Overland Exped. Aust.* 30 Apr. (1847) 230 A large tree, with dark green broad lanceolate stinging leaves, grew on its banks; it resembled the nettle tree, but belonged to neither of the two species growing in the bushes of the east coast. **1849** J.P. TOWNSEND *Rambles & Observations N.S.W.* 35 In the scrubs is found a tree, commonly called 'the nettle tree' (*Urtica gigas*). . . It is appropriately named; and the pain caused by touching the leaf is, I think, worse than that occasioned by the sting of a wasp. **1867** 'CLERGYMAN' *Aust. as it Is* 21 There is a nettle-tree which has been fatal to horses and cattle. **1872** A. MCFARLAND *Illawarra & Manaro* 32 The nettle is usually met with as a large bush. **1882** A.J. BOYD *Old Colonials* 186 A black boy was started on ahead with a cutlass to clear away the nettle-trees. **1916** E. & M.S. GREW *Rambles in Aust.* 257 In the thick undergrowth are . . poisonous 'nettle tree', or 'stinging tree' (*Laportea gigas*). **1933** H.J. CARTER *Gulliver in Bush* 201 A young Victorian tourist couple was badly stung by the nettle-tree.

neutral. *Obs.* A recruit not yet on active service (see quot. 1917); a deserter.

1917 C.E.W. BEAN *Lett. from France* 224 Then the 'Neutrals', 'We know they are not against the Allies', the others said when news came of the latest drafts still training under peace conditions, 'we know they are not against us—we suppose they are just neutral.' **1919** C.H. THORP *Handful of Ausseys* 202 A neutral . . is a bloke who's fed up with soldierin', an' hops it, so's the Jacks can't trace 'im. **1945** S.J. BAKER *Austral. Lang.* 152 Later groups that went abroad were called *War Babies, Chocolate Soldiers, Hard Thinkers* and *Neutrals.*

never.

1. Abbrev. of NEVER-NEVER 1 a. Also *attrib.*

1892 *Bulletin* (Sydney) 29 Oct. 24/1 Harry . . back to old Vic, man, Down from the Never Land? Now, what's yer game? **1903** *Ibid.* 18 Apr. 16/1 They stood beside a 'Never' pub. **1918** W.M. MCDONALD *Soldier Songs Palestine* 36 In the stretches of the Never, where the sand-hills merge together. **1978** G. HALL *River still Flows* 16 We rode in the 'Never' by twos and by threes.

2. [Used elsewhere as *never never, a.* denoting a system of periodic payments (see OEDS *never* 9 c.) but recorded earliest in Aust.] In the phr. **on the never,** at no cost to oneself; in a (financially) exploitative manner. Also **on the never-never.**

1882 *Sydney Slang Dict.* 6 *On the Never*, to take advantage of, to best. **1891** *Truth* (Sydney) 29 Mar. 7/5, I must explain that getting in on the *nod* is the same as on the 'never never', 'Freeman's key', 'the ready'. *Ibid.* 19 Apr. 7/3 You and your boy: had your chuck for two days on the never! **1892** *Ibid.* 1 May 2/7 They both travel on the 'never', For to pay is not their game; And they never purchase tickets, But they get there just the same. **1892** *Bulletin* (Sydney) 29 Oct. 24/1 Not the woman to liquor, or go on the never, But skittish an' queer in her tantrums, yer know. **1893** F.W.L. ADAMS *Australs.* 95 We don't let our theatrical critics go into the theatres on the never-never. . . We pay for their places. **1955** N. PULLIAM *I traveled Lonely Land* 383 *On the never*, making the most of, taking advantage of.

3. In special collocations: **never-sweat** [Br. dial.: see EDD *never, adv.* 12], one who works without exertion, a loafer; **-touch-it,** a teetotaller.

1939 *Menace of Speed Coursing* (Plympton Park Citizen's Committee) 4 Dog racing produces nothing. It simply keeps a number of bookmakers and '**never-sweats**' in their jobs. **1945** S.J. BAKER *Austral. Lang.* 102 The . . *never-sweat, sooner, river-banker* [etc.]. . were other vagabonds who loafed in the outback. **1978** T. DAVIES *More Austral. Nicknames* 72 *Never sweat*, a council worker. **1895** *Worker* (Sydney) 26 Jan. 4/3, I am a **never-touch-it** of some years' standing. **1904** *Bulletin* (Sydney) 21 Jan. 16/3 The clerical calling gathered a rich store of opprobrious appellations from irreverent Australians. Some that I have heard: . . never-touch-it, spirit-merchant [etc.].

never-fail. Any of several plants, usu. of the genus *Eragrostis* (fam. Poaceae), regarded as useful, drought-resistant fodder, esp. the tussocky perennials *E. setifolia* and *E. xerophila* of inland Aust. Also **never-fail grass.**

1923 E. BREAKWELL *Grasses & Fodder Plants N.S.W.* 19 In the dry periods only drought-resistant grasses like *Eragrostis* (Never-fail) . . grow to any extent. **1930** D. COTTRELL *Earth Battle* 204 He was riding over a low open hill shoulder covered with short grey never-fail grass. **1936** F. CLUNE *Roaming round Darling* 114 He has a marvellous collection of native grasses, nardoo, Mitchell, neverfail, and a dozen others. **1946** W.E. HARNEY *North of 23°* 23 Its grass, called 'neverfail', had broom-like, wiry stems, each with a tiny head of food. **1956** A.C.C. LOCK *Tropical Tapestry* 74 'What's the name of that short white grass?' Hobbs pointed. 'Never-fail,' said George. **1976** N.V. WALLACE *Bush Lawyer* 129 On we went through country recently flooded, now a waving mass of grass: Mitchell grass . . never-fail [etc.].

nevergreen. [Punning alteration of *evergreen.*] See quot. 1945.

***c* 1840** ST. HUBERT Foreign & Colonial Stations Brit. Army Van Diemen's Land, Those persons who remain at home in the old country have been led to suppose that the beauty of the scenery must be much enhanced, by the trees described as 'evergreens', with far . . greater propriety would they have been called 'never-greens'. **1945** S.J. BAKER *Austral. Lang.* 215 *Never greens*, a semi-humorous description for our eucalypts.

Never-Never.

1. a. The far interior of Australia; the remote outback. Also *attrib.*

1833 W.H. BRETON *Excursions* 213 The Never-never blacks . . are so called because they have hitherto kept aloof from the whites. **1857** F. DE B. COOPER *Wild Adventures* 68, I had the cattle mustered, and the draft destined for the Nievah vahs ready for the road. . . Nievah vahs, sometimes incorrectly pronounced never nevers, a Comeleroi term signifying unoccupied land. **1882** A.J. BOYD *Old Colonials* 202 *Never-never* is the far outside country beyond the centres of civilization. **1893** F.W.L. ADAMS *Australs.* 11 The outskirts of the great central desert are reached, and we pass into no man's land, or 'the never-never'. **1906** *Bulletin* (Sydney) 11 Jan. 14/1 Go into the Neverest-Never-Never and begin work there. **1919** *Smith's Weekly* (Sydney) 26 July 9/3 The Never Never . . calls men back again. **1931** J. DEVANEY *Earth Kindred* 63 The grey Never-Never in its fastnesses undared. **1945** E. GEORGE *Two at Daly Waters* 101 Once a year in the Never Never we eat fish. We have to go 126 miles for it. **1950** J. MORRISON *Port of Call* 32 We aren't right out in the Never-Never here, you know. The baker calls every day if you want him. **1957** F. CLUNE *Fortune Hunters* 2 I'm going out into the Never-Never, to prospect for uranium. **1977** R. BEILBY *Gunner* 91 It all made that country town seem so far away, lost in the never-never of Australian isolation. **1980** S. THORNE *I've met some Bloody Wags* 23 He was working up there in the never-never to dodge paying his wife maintenance. **1986** *Canberra Times* 19 May 19/2 The Never Never . . is pock-marked with places of interest.

b. Comb. **never-never country, land.**

1877 'CAPRICORNUS' *Land Law of Future* 47 The outside districts have next to be dealt with—the dry, waste, '**never-never country**'. **1886** F. COWAN *Aust.* 10, I see and sing the *never-never country.* Word within itself an Epic of the Austral Continental Isle! **1899** *Austral. Tit-Bits* (Sydney) 16 Sept. 534/1 Mrs Hayseed, on a visit to Sydney from the Never-Never country, entered the shop. ***c* 1926** E. MCKENZIE-HATTON *Moluscut* 30, I believe in God, and it is only because of His help I have been able to stick it out in the never-never country, where I belong. **1942** *A.C.F. News* Aug. 2 The wide-spread organisation of the war has reached to the 'Never-Never' country. **1957** *Ford News* June 33 To the lonely inhabitants of this 'Never Never' country it also brings meat, groceries, vegetables, even furniture. **1974** B. ROLAND *No Ordinary Man* 169 The Never Never country, the remote Australian outback. **1884** A.W. STIRLING *Never Never Land* p. vi, Queensland some day, and above all the '**Never Never Land**'—as the colonists call all that portion of it which lies north or west of Cape Capricorn—will be among the greatest of England's dependencies. ***c* 1887** R.G. GALLOP In Never Never Land 1 The 'Never Never' Land is a piece of nomenclature full of weariness & desolation & suggestion of all sorts of ill defined terrors & possibilities. It is the name popularly applied to that portion of Queensland lying to the North & West of Rockhampton. . . The Blacks called the country 'Niva Niva', & the white man immediately contorted this into a term which has caused so much puzzling reflection & ingeniously evolved suggestion to those who have sought a more rational explanation of its origin. **1905** H. LAWSON *When I was King* 40 A phantom land, a mystic land! The Never-Never Land. **1915** W.J. WYE *Souvenirs Sunny South* 20 Out west of Never Never land, in Oodnadatta town, Where all the social outcasts go who earn Dame Fortune's frown. **1937** L.R. MENZIES *Gold Seeker's Odyssey* 156 On the whole the wide expanse of the desert plain remained the unknown 'Never-Never Land'. **1963** *N. Austral. Monthly* Dec. 7 Royal Flying Doctor Base . . the network is also used for the every-day needs of the stalwart people who live in this Never-Never land. **1977** J. DOUGHTY *Gold in Blood* 106 It was a never-never land then, as it is still; hard, hungry, sun-scorched and lifeless.

2. *fig.* The abode of the dead.

1891 *Truth* (Sydney) 3 May 4/5 Most of these subjects are . . shattered old derelicts who would have a short lease of life anyhow, but the departure of some of them for the Never Never is . . hastened by harsh treatment. **1894** W. CROMPTON *Convict Jim* 36 Till I enter through ther slip-rails of ther never never gate. **1900** H. LAWSON *Verses Pop. & Humorous* 35 Mates who have gone to the great Never-Never. **1911** *Bulletin* (Sydney) 5 Oct. 16/1 His mates . . informed me that Uncle Dick had 'kicked the bucket', . . 'gone to the Never Never' [etc.].

3. In the phr. **on the never-never:** see *on the never* NEVER 2.

new, *n. N.S.W.* [Abbrev. of *new beer.*] A light beer, made by the bottom fermentation method and so-called because it was regarded as a 'new' style when introduced. See OLD *n.*

1935 *First Hundred Yrs.* (Tooth & Co. Ltd.) 71 We make our way across a wide platform on which barrels full of 'Old' and 'New' are being assembled in readiness for despatch. **1967** N. OTTAWAY *Pub & I* 32, I was drowsing in the saloon bar one Saturday morning with a glass of new before me. **1976** *Southerly* i. 89 Two middies of new and a scotch, thanks. **1984** B. DRISCOLL *Great Aussie Beer Bk.* 22 When bottom-fermented lagers were introduced into New South Wales they became the 'new' style of brewed beers. Therefore, the dark top-fermented ale as brewed by, say, Toohey's, was called Toohey's Old, while the lighter, bottom-fermented lager became Toohey's New.

new, *a.*

1. Used with nouns denoting land or an area, region, etc., to mean 'not previously occupied or worked by white people', as **new colony, country** [also U.S. (see OED *a.* 6 e.)], **district, field, ground, land** [also U.S. (see Mathews 2 b.)], **settlement.**

1835 *True Colonist* (Hobart) 21 Feb. 2/2 We continue this day the extracts from the Westminster Review relating to the **New Colony. 1847** *Moreton Bay Courier* 23 Jan. 2/2 His plans respecting the site for the new colony have undergone great alteration. **1896** M. CLARKE *Austral. Tales* 122 He had been squatting in Sydney before that, but hearing much of the 'new colony', came over to better his fortunes. **1821** Macarthur Papers XII. 56 Our son James has lately made a Tour into the **new Country**, as it is called in 'Westmoreland', where we have an Establishment of Cattle. **1832** *Sydney Herald* 6 Feb. 4/4 Mr Langdon . . killed two oxen . . bred by him in the new country. **1844** *Atlas* (Sydney) I. 39/3 Exclude future settlers from the 'new country' (the places where the squatters now are). **1864** N. SHREEVE *Short Hist. S.A.* 41 Much new country has been found out, which is North Australia. **1874** C. DE BOOS *Congewoi Correspondence* 169 It's just like what they useter call the 'new country', when I waser young man. If any chap talked about a place as he didn't care about fixin partiklar, he'd say, 'Oh, it's out in the new country'. What they called the new country them days iser precious old country now, for it ain't more'n thirty year ago as Braidwood was in the new country. **1888** *Bulletin* (Sydney) 10 Mar. 14/1 A young fellow . . was sheep-droving . . away in the 'New Country' north of the alligator line, during the early sixties. **1910** H. LAWSON *Skyline Riders* 35 He's looking for new country, The old folks used to say; Our boy has gone exploring, Fond parents say to-day. **1932** J. TRURAN *Green Mallee* 62 Hoffmeyer's block was not, strictly speaking, 'new country', having been worked over several times with the usual disk implements, but this was the first time that anyone had used an ordinary plough on it. **1956** T. RONAN *Moleskin Midas* 72 The Barcoo and the Thompson were not bad places to steal horses, and at that season of the year any stock thus stolen could be sold anywhere in the Gulf to drovers outward bound with herds for the new country over on the Territory side. **1963** I.L. IDRIESS *Our Living Stone Age* p. x, In my mining days we were ever seeking 'new country', because of the simple practical reason that in country not already prospected . . there was a far greater chance of finding gold or other mineral. **1977** R. EDWARDS *Austral. Yarn* 14 We were dryblowing the tin and the fellows that were there they'd go out and prospect the alluvial to find out what would pay. They would walk out into new country and pick up handfuls of soil. **1811** *Sydney Gaz.* 23 Feb., All those Persons to whom he has promised to give small Grants of Land in the **New District** of Airds, shall attend at Mr Meehan's Farm. **1870** E.B. KENNEDY *Four Yrs. in Qld.* 46 *Low fever* sometimes appears in new districts. **1888** 'R. BOLDREWOOD' *Robbery under Arms* (1937) 96 A lot of farmers and small settlers . . had taken up a new district. **1890** A.J. VOGAN *Black Police* 35 The Warden of the **new field** has only just arrived . . besides being Police Magistrate, Warden, Senior-constable Surveyor, Clerk of Petty Sessions, etc., etc. **1936** W. HATFIELD *Aust. through Windscreen* 118 It was a great source of annoyance to the crowd of gold-seekers itching to be in the first rush to The Granites, a new field which had 'broken out'. **1857** F. DE B. COOPER *Wild Adventures* 140 Working in the old gullies is always a safe speculation, while sinking in **new ground** is never certain. . . In the latter it is mere chance whether gold lies there or not. **1862** *Burrangong Courier* 13 Aug. 2/3 The rush to the Three Mile Diggings . . is . . going ahead . . and a large extent of new ground has lately been taken up. **1868** *Rep. Mining Surveyors & Registrars* (Vic. Dept. Mines) Sept. 36 At Barkly some new ground has been opened south of the main lead. **1944** M.J. O'REILLY *Bowyangs & Boomerangs* 11 A Reward Claim is granted to a prospector for finding new ground carrying payable gold. **1849** A. HARRIS *Emigrant Family* (1967) 12 A farm . . would suit you, in the first instance, rather better than **new land. 1961** M. KIDDLE *Men of Yesterday* 58 All new lands were ploughed during November. Hay-making began again to complete the yearly round. **1792** R. ATKINS Jrnl. 2 June, Walked to the **New Settlement** and shot some beautiful Parraquets. **1805** *N.S.W. Gen. Orders* 12 Oct. (1806) 173 From this destruction occasioned by the Fly Moth to the Wheat in Stacks, and the necessity of supplying the New Settlements, the Full Military Ration is to cease. **1829** *Extracts Lett. Swan River* 7 Sept. (1830) I. 3 The following letter . . is from Captain Stirling, the Governor of the New Settlement at Swan River. **1847** *Moreton Bay Courier* 23 Jan. 2/2 Nearly all the official gentlemen connected with the new settlement of Northern Australia, left Sydney in the *Lord Auckland*. **1945** J. DEVANNY *Bird of Paradise* 42 There's only one way to grow cane on new settlement land.

2. Used with nouns denoting people to mean 'recently arrived (in Australia)', as **new arrival, -comer, settler.**

1842 *Sydney Morning Herald* 1 Aug. 1/7 The great advantage to a **new arrival** especially, of having a station and herd broke in to it all ready formed to hand. **1859** W. BURROWS *Adventures Mounted Trooper* 128 The word 'shout' . . is a quaint specimen of Australian slang. New arrivals for the most part attach a literal meaning to it. . . The new comer literally shouts at the top of his voice the word 'Grog!' **1864** *Illustr. Sydney News* 15 Oct. 13/3 New arrivals . . whose knowledge of the aborigines is limited to seeing a half drunken blackfellow on the streets . . must have a very low opinion of the race. **1890** 'R. BOLDREWOOD' *Colonial Reformer* 34 A 'black hat' in Australian parlance means a new arrival. **1843** *Sydney Morning Herald* 21 Aug. 4/1 To give **new-comers** an idea of the financial state and requirements of the colony. **1859** [see *new arrival*]. **1840** *S. Austral. Rec.* (London) 11 July 18 In consequence of such large and frequent arrival of '**new settlers**', there is always a great demand for all kinds of live stock. **1843** C. ROWCROFT *Tales of Colonies* (1858) 231 Their men were despatched to prepare the rude log-hut which usually forms the first habitation of the new settler. **1925** J.A. COLLUM *New Settlers' Handbk.* 21 The term 'New Settler' is defined as 'any person who desires to make Queensland his or her permanent home'. **1963** R. MCGREGOR-HASTIE *Compleat Migrant* 58 You are a New Settler. You have to begin at the beginning. **1981** A.B. FACEY *Fortunate Life* 49 A new settler took up land adjoining Uncle's.

3. In miscellaneous collocations: **new-come-up** *n. phr.*, see quots.; **New Guard,** a right-wing, paramilitary organization formed in Sydney in 1931; a member of this organization; **hand,** NEW CHUM *n.* 1, 2, and 3; also *attrib.*; **New Protection,** an approach to the protection of Australian industries which was conditional on employers paying reasonable wages (see quot. 1899); **rush,** a fresh movement of people to a newly discovered goldfield; such a goldfield; see also RUSH *n.* 2 a. and c.; **New State,** an additional (proposed) State, to be formed by the division of an existing State; freq. *attrib.*; so **New Stater** *n.*, a proponent of such a proposal.

1913 W.K. HARRIS *Outback in Aust.* 42 The new chum (or the '**New-come-up**' as the new chum is termed Outback) cannot tell the difference. **1968** W. GILL *Petermann Journey* 6 When he spoke, it was in the Territory idiom. For example, I heard him call a recent arrival in the country, 'a new-come-up'. **1932** C. HADE *Ebenezer* 12 The leader of all was a big white card, Said, 'I'm a member of the **New Guard**.' **1965** *Realist* (Sydney) xviii. 27 The New Guard . . was allegedly at full strength to deal with the unemployed. **1976** K. AMOS *New Guard Movt.* 4 When Francis de Groot dramatically 'opened' the Sydney Harbour Bridge in March 1932, the fame of the New Guard spread to all corners of the Empire. **1977** L. FOX *Depression Down Under* 54 Mr Steve Purdy . . was being attacked by three New Guards, one holding his arms while the others rained 'rabbit-killers' on the back of his neck. **1817** *HRA* (1921) 3rd Ser. II. 643, I Have not the least Doubt But you are glad that these **New Hands** joaning [*sic*] Us. **1825** *London Mag.* May II. 52 A man to take a new hand of [*sic*] the stores must be a free man. **1835** G.C INGLETON *True Patriots All* (1952) 160 If an iron-gang man has served any number of years in the country, he must begin again; he is the same as a new hand. **1841** *Port Phillip Patriot* 5 Aug. 4/4 A boat . . was run away with by nine convicts, six new hands and three old ones. **1843** *HRA* (1924) 1st Ser. XXII. 618 A greater degree of sickness and mortality among the 'New Hands' than among the 'Old' or Penal Prisoners. **1844** *Colonial Times* (Hobart) 13 Aug., Being what is termed a 'new hand' in the colony, I am naturally anxious to gain all the information I can. **1857** *Moreton Bay Free Press* 7 Oct. 3/5 What makes this strange story more wondrous strange, is the fact of Mrs Laskett being only a new hand in the colony. **1882** A.J. BOYD *Old Colonials* 13 A new hand in the bush would have despaired of life. **1902** *Bulletin* (Sydney) 8 Feb. 14/3 A couple of new-hand tank-sinkers—Australians, too—on the Rock Station (N.S.W.), once conceived the brilliant idea of undermining the 'face' of the tank. **1921** *Ibid.* 22 Dec. 22/2 The Northern nigger's English has the new-hand puzzled. **1934** *Ibid.* 7 Mar. 20/4 The new hand had been bitten by a black snake. **1899** *Age* (Melbourne) 8 Nov. 6/4 What is called the '**New Protection**' extends beyond the manufacturer's industry to his workers. Protectionists are now claiming that just as the manufacturer shall be adequately protected by tariff duties against the competition of sweater-made goods from abroad, so the domestic worker shall be adequately protected by Factory legislation against any possible sweating of the laborer at home. **1909** H.I. JENSEN *Rising Tide* 113 The 'New Protection' is an Australian ideal which has already endeared itself to the majority of Australians. **1937** W. DENNING *Caucus Crisis* 9 'New protection' with its policy of industrial concession for tariff protection. **1955** G. HEALEY *A.L.P.* 40 The election of 1906 was fought on . . a fresh outlook on the fiscal question. This was known as the New Protection and meant in essence that protection would be afforded only to those industries which paid reasonable wages to their employees. **1855** *Ovens & Murray Advertiser* (Beechworth) 20 Jan. 6/1 We received intelligence of a **new rush** having taken place on Spring Creek. **1858** *Colonial Mining Jrnl.* Dec. 62/2 The Indigo has progressed . . from the position of a 'New Rush' to that of a large and established gold-field. **1865** *Jrnl. Australasia* I. 232 A theatre for the 'new rush', at Hokitika, is being constructed in Sydney. **1886** W.J. WOODS *Visit to Vic.* 33 No phrase is better understood in Victoria than 'The New Rush', which describes the scamper of adventurers into any place where the precious metal is being found in considerable quantity. **1894** A.F. CALVERT *Coolgardie Goldfield* 20 There are new rushes breaking out at short intervals. **1936** J. KIRWAN *My Life's Adventure* 66 Everyone . . talked of nothing but mining, 'new rushes', selling shows. **1891** *Draft Bill to constitute Cwlth. Aust.* (Nat. Australasian Convention) 66 The Parliament of the Commonwealth may from time to time establish and admit to the Commonwealth **new States. 1900** *Act* (G.B.) 63 & 64 Vict. no. 12 Sect. 124, A new State may be formed by separation of territory from a State but only with the consent of the Parliament thereof. **1915** (*title*), A new State: proposed separation of northern New South Wales. **1923** *Austral.* (Sydney) Mar. 40 The idea that the establishment of New States in the North and Riverina will hurt Sydney is puerile. **1948** *QPD* 17 Aug. 3 There has been raised, recently, the question of the formation of a new State in the northern portion of Queensland. **1949** D.H. DRUMMOND *Austral. Constitution & New States* 7 A fourth matter for constitutional amendment is that which has to do with the creation of new States. . . It is significant that since the Imperial Parliament handed over the control of Australia to the Commonwealth, no new State has been created. **1960** *N.T. News* (Darwin) 2 Feb. 2/3 The New State movement had another important victory. **1972** *Bulletin* (Sydney) 26 Feb. 27/3 There is a history of new-State movements fizzling out. **1923** *Austral.* (Sydney) Mar. 34 So many misleading criticisms of the **New Staters'** proposals. **1960** *N.T. News* (Darwin) 2 Feb. 2/3 New Staters have become respectable. Events of quite recent years have certainly moved in favor of the formation of further States within the Commonwealth.

New Aussie: see NEW AUSTRALIAN *n.* 2.

New Australia. *Hist.* The name of a socialist utopian settlement formed in Paraguay in 1893 by members of the New Australia Co-operative Settlement Association under the leadership of William Lane (1861–1917).

1893 *Braidwood Dispatch* 26 Apr. 2/2 The Jesuits taught the world how to manage a 'model colony' in Paraguay long before 'old Australia' was discovered or 'New Australia' thought of. **1894** *Bulletin* (Sydney) 6 Jan. 7/1 In New Australia everything was to be decided by popular vote, but instead the Paraguayan Government made Lane . . the whole system of local government in himself. **1897** *Tocsin* (Melbourne) 2 Oct. 10/3 These men are nearly all of them Australians, and teetotallers without exception. They were formerly members of the now defunct 'New Australia' colony. **1909** W.G. SPENCE *Aust.'s Awakening* 471 New Australia took a large number of our best men and women. **1944** 'S. CAMPION' *Pommy Cow* 285 Why didn't Socialism work in New Australia? **1978** P. WOOLLEY *Art of living Together* 98 In 1893 Lane established the socialist community of New Australia in Paraguay.

New Australian, *n., attrib.* and *a.*

A. *n.*

1. *Hist.* A colonist of NEW AUSTRALIA.

1893 *Braidwood Dispatch* 26 Apr. 2/2 It is said that 500 'New Australians' will leave Sydney early in May. **1899** *Western Champion* (Barcaldine) 7 Feb. 3/1 Murtho .. was established to put to a test the altruistic enthusiasm of the original settlers, who were mostly men who believed in the principles of the New Australians. **1900** *Truth* (Sydney) 21 Jan. 1/2 With your Spanish half-breed allies and your revolver you kept the New Australians under the yoke. **1921** *Bulletin* (Sydney) 9 June 22/1 When the New Australians went to South America they were unconsciously harking back to a very early line of migration. **1931** *Century of Journalism* 339 The people of this Colony will follow the story of this movement to Paraguay... It is unnecessary to recount the disappointments, and the struggles which the 'New Australians' were forced to encounter.

2. An immigrant to Australia, esp. one (from continental Europe) whose first language is not English. Also **New Aussie.**

1905 *Bulletin* (Sydney) 21 Sept. 39/1 For what the new Australian knows as 'shikkar' is just another word for good old 'fou'. **1924** *New Settlers' Handbk. Vic.* 41 Welcoming the New Australian. **1939** *Melbourne Univ. Mag.* 84 Why can we not have decent, humane treatment for such doctors as are here, men and women, so that they may be established as New Australians? **1949** *Sydney Morning Herald* 11 Aug. 3/2 The Minister for Immigration .. to-day appealed to the Australian people not to call migrants 'Balts', 'Displaced Persons', and 'D.P.s' He suggested they should be called 'new Australians', 'newcomers', or 'new settlers'. **1950** *Bulletin* (Sydney) 4 Oct. 13/4 Knud, the New Australian, was picking up English with commendable speed. **1952** *New Settler in W.A.* (Perth) June 35 New Australians must learn to speak English and read English and to talk to one another in English. **1954** *Bulletin* (Sydney) 20 Jan. 12/1 Mac, another New Aussie. **1956** 'A.B.C.' *What is A?* 36 The New Australian is sometimes a pain in the neck for the old Aussies, but keep smiling, they will improve, and old and new will go hand in hand to make Australia great, greater, greatest ever. **1959** C. PEARL *So, you want to be Austral.* 21 The first New Australians came to Australia at the express request of His Majesty King George III. **1961** *Realist* (Sydney) v. 10 It was twenty minutes later when Tess led a flushed and excited Pepita and all the new Aussies out into the rain again. **1965** K. SMITH *OGF* 51 Some of the older New Aussies there to be naturalized had gone off to sleep. **1968** E. PAGRAM *Never had it so Good* 60 In Australia migrants of any nationality—except the English—are referred to as 'New Australians'. While we are always referred to as 'Poms'. **1975** 'N. CULOTTA' *Gone Gougin'* 34, I told him, 'you will in future refrain from referring to me as a New Australian, which is in my opinion a derogatory term'. **1984** *Bulletin* (Sydney) 21 Aug. 54/1 Confronted with post-war prejudices about reffos, Canberra came up with New Australians.

3. *fig.*

1955 *Bulletin* (Sydney) 8 June 13/1 Some once-'new' Australians, who don't figure in the statistics of heavy drinkers, are being exported—some wild camels that are wanted by American zoos and circuses. **1980** S. THORNE *I've met some Bloody Wags* 33 Yarding and drafting Brahman cattle always meant plenty of action. Those lop-eared 'New Australians' could really give you a lift!

B. *attrib.* becoming *adj.* Immigrant; foreign.

1955 N. PULLIAM *I traveled Lonely Land* 313 Almost the entire mining colony there is New Australian. **1958** *Austral. Lett.* (Adelaide) Apr. 46 Soon after we reached Australia I wanted to take my wife, who is French, or as they say around here, New Australian, to visit Gippsland. **1960** *N.T. News* (Darwin) 22 Jan. 3/4 The New Australian couple who spent more than a week by the road south of Daly Waters, stopping cars and asking for food, have annoyed Territorians. **1970** *Coast to Coast 1967–68* 37, I drifted .. bar steward, greenkeeper .. freelance journalist for a New Australian paper. **1973** *Bulletin* (Sydney) 20 Jan. 18/1 'I want to take a look at this new Australian Australia that seems to be emerging,' said the 61-year-old expatriate. **1985** *Canberra Times* 18 Aug. 17/6 A sprinkling of Englishmen and Scotsmen play and watch the game, but it is overwhelmingly and accurately regarded as a 'New Australian' code—to use another archaism.

new chum, *n.* and *a.*

A. *n.*

1. *Hist.* A prisoner newly admitted to a gaol or hulk; a newly arrived convict.

1812 J.H. VAUX *Mem.* (1819) II. 163 *Chum*, a fellow prisoner in a jail, hulk, &c.; so there are *new chums* and *old chums*, as they happen to have been a short or a long time in confinement. **1831** H. SAVERY *Quintus Servinton* III. 59 There's near a thousand chaps here [in the hulk], and many of 'em are real hell-fire devils .. and 'twont do to draw no distinctions like, with new chums. **1841** J. WARD Diary of Convict 1 Nov. 82 We were parted, (I mean the men I came on board with) two in a ward or cell, containing from 12 to 32. All eyes are on you as a new '*chum*'. **1845** J. TUCKER *Ralph Rashleigh* (1952) 73 On their dismissal a host of the older prisoners insinuated themselves among them for the purpose of bargaining for clothes, trinkets or other property, and many a poor *new chum*—the distinctive name bestowed upon them by the old hands—was deprived of his little stock of comforts. **1846** L.W. MILLER *Notes of Exile Van Dieman's Land* 328 We found a convict overseer... His first salutation was 'Now you bloody new chum ---! I have you!' **1865** J.F. MORTLOCK *Experiences of Convict* 110 Rather a clever 'new chum'. Had the attempt failed, he, as a ticket-of-leave 'bolter', would have been sentenced to three years at Port Arthur.

2. *transf.* A newly arrived immigrant. Also *attrib.*

1828 *Tasmanian* (Hobart) 15 Aug. 4, I understood .. that I was called a *new chum*, my English name being Stranger. **1836** J.F. O'CONNELL *Residence Eleven Yrs. New Holland* 51 There, there's a new chum, just come out! **1845** *Atlas* (Sydney) I. 595/2 The new chum is a very important personage in our catalogue of characters. There he is—you can tell him from the exact nicety of his dress—just landed from the last ship—full of notions of the superiority of English manners and customs—prejudiced beforehand against the sharp practice of the colonists—he is cautious, incredulous, distrustful. **1858** C.R. THATCHER *Colonial Songster* (rev. ed.) 18 In the colony I've just arrived, My togs, I know, look rum; And you can see with half an eye, That I'm a green new chum. **1869** M. CLARKE *Peripatetic Philosopher* 3 Every man who .. has not had the good fortune to be born in this favoured land .. must come here as a new chum some time or other. **1876** J.B. STEPHENS *Hundred Pounds* 5 His mate had been born a new chum, and no extent of longevity will prevent him from dying one. **1889** *Centennial Mag.* (Sydney) 541 The new lodger was 'a real lady', and looked like a 'new chum'. **1898** W. DOLLMAN *Bush Fancies* 41 There is as much joy over the advent of a new chum as there is at the appearance of a clown at a circus ring. **1912** *Truth* (Sydney) 25 Feb. 12/4 At a large works recently erected .. a new-chum Scotchman will get preference to a colonial. **1917** *Ibid.* 18 Feb. 1/6 A new chum .. who had only been in the country eighty years, died at Forbes on Monday at the age of 98. **1937** D. GUNN *Links with Past* 10 She was a new chum of a good Bristol family. **1963** J.F. HARLEY *Mantle of Safety* 143 'You get used to the mossies in time,' she said. 'They always go for the new chums.' **1971** *Bulletin* (Sydney) 6 Nov. 42/3 In .. one of the shrewdest observations made by a new chum, Fauchery points out that expatriate peasants are rarely homesick. **1980** P. FREEMAN *Woolshed* 28 New-chums to this golden land, never dream of failure.

3. A novice; one inexperienced in a particular activity, occupation, etc. Also *attrib.*

1851 J. HENDERSON *Excursions & Adventures N.S.W.* I. 182 He seemed to think that his being a beginner, or (as it is termed) 'new chum', had been taken advantage of. **1871** *Illustr. Sydney News* 25 Nov. 197/1 In the year 1852 many a footsore new chum, whom the fame of the Bendigo diggings lured to try his fortune .. was told by returning diggers .. that old Bendigo was worked out. **1880** 'ERRO' *Squattermania* 83 'Ye're no making verra guid warrk.' 'No,' said Sutton, 'I am only a new chum at it.' **1891** J. FENTON *Bush Life Tas.* 153 One or two mishaps more grave than gay happened to the new-chum carriers when they got lost in the bush. **1900** *Truth* (Sydney) 21 Apr. 5/7 Imperial officers would be much struck with the capacity of Australia's new-chum bushmen. **1917** 'D. DELANEY' *White Champion* 92 The lad's a new chum at this game. **1923** 'J. NORTH' *Son of Bush* 8 To a western mining rush there had come, in the late eighties, a quiet, reserved man, who had all the appearance of a newchum miner. **1933** J. MCCARTER *Love's Lunatic* 43 Somehow, he had reckoned she was a new chum to station work from the jump-off. **1948** *Coast to Coast 1947* 224 The Mate, a new chum on the coast, is not satisfied with the Master's position! **1956** A. UPFIELD *Battling Prophet* 19 Ben Wickham had been a new chum, a towny, an outsider lost in a rough man's country. **1973** F. PARSONS *Man called Mo* 128 A sketch in which he played a new-chum dairy farmer who picked up a cow-pad under the impression that it was Field-Marshal Montgomery's beret. **1984** *Canberra Times* 31 July 1/4 The new chums [*sc.* the Chinese Olympic team] leapt to second place on the official medals table by taking out a second gold.

4. *Obs.* Abbrev. of *new-chum hole* (see sense 5).

1869 MRS W.M. HOWELL *Diggings & Bush* 5 'My word, Tom, come up quick,' exclaimed a dirt-begrimed digger, who was looking over a hole resembling a well, 'this must be a new chum'.

5. Special Comb. **new chum gold,** a name given to any of several mineral substances commonly mistaken for gold by an inexperienced miner; also **new chum's gold; hole,** see quot. 1944.

1873 'DEMONAX' *Mysteries & Miseries* 16 He was shown some stone which was streaked with **'new chum' gold**—a sort of coppery, cobwebby, affair, like Dutch metal. **1928** R.H. CROLL *Open Road Vic.* 67 A sparkling stream with its sands aglitter with 'new chum gold'. **1931** W. BARAGWANATH *Guide for Prospectors in Vic.* 65 Some substances are frequently mistaken for gold; for instance .. chalcopyrite (new chum gold). **1948** M. UREN *Glint of Gold* 102 He spat on the shiny mineral. 'That,' he said slowly, 'is pyrites; new chum's gold.' **1956** A.C.C. LOCK *Tropical Tapestry* 189 A man tried to fool me with new-chum gold one day, but I knew the difference. **1963** W.E. HARNEY *To Ayers Rock & Beyond* 186, I look at the specimen he holds out. It is mundic or new-chum's gold. I hand it back to him with a smile but from his face I see he does not believe my judgement. **1984** W.W. AMMON et al. *Working Lives* 75 You would see him disgustedly throw away a specimen and grunt, 'New chum gold!' **1881** J.C.F. JOHNSON *To Mount Browne & Back* 14 Some of them .. were amusing themselves by putting down small '**new chum holes**' in the neighbouring gullies. **1944** M.J. O'REILLY *Bowyangs & Boomerangs* 41 He started a real 'new chum hole', that is a hole in the loose ground without any means of holding the sides or ends.

B. *adj.* Inexpert; raw.

1903 *Bulletin* (Sydney) 28 Feb. 16/2 One is struck by the new-chum methods of conserving water. **1939** A. GASTON *Coolgardie Gold* 41 After blowing off several dishes in a very new-chum style and not seeing colour I was not so sure. **1948** G. FARWELL *Down Argent Street* 150 Whyalla is .. a new-chum sort of place perhaps, with little history. **1956** B. BEATTY *Beyond Aust.'s Cities* 14 He was so tolerant of my new-chum ignorance that I pursued my questions. **1963** O. RUHEN *Flockmaster* 59 The blanket bed that she had slept in. There had been a new-chum attempt to soften the ground beneath it with tufts of straw-like grass.

Hence **new chumism** *n.*, behaviour which is characteristic of a newly arrived, and therefore inexperienced, immigrant; an instance of this; **chumship** *n.*, the condition of being a new chum.

1850 *Australasian Sporting Mag.* 124 The other, needs but the addition of local experience to his preformed habits of life, to exempt him from those retributive pains and penalties, which follow from the ridiculous follies, vices, and conceits, of genuine and unmitigated **new chumism.** **1859** F. FOWLER *Southern Lights & Shadows* 15 The battle of 'old-handism' against 'new-chumism' is not everlasting waging in Victoria as it is New South Wales. **1876** J.B. STEPHENS *Hundred Pounds* 5 A young man whose innate and ineradicable new-chumism had caused him to be despised and rejected of universal diggerdom. **1898** *Bulletin* (Sydney) 8 Jan. 29/2 It is a stupid error to call the Australian tea-tree a 'ti-tree'. More than this, it is a new-chumism, a relic of Gov. Phillip. **1843** *Sydney Morning Herald* 9 Sept. 4/3 Those who, on their first arrival among us .. looked upon the traffic as wicked and discreditable, gradually become familiarised with the aspect of the monster, and yet ere out of their **new chumship** begin to consider the profession of usurer as not only righteous but even honourable. **1888** A.P. MARTIN *Oak-Bough & Wattle-Blossom* 153 How long the poor immigrant caterpillar must remain in the dark chrysalis of new chumship before he can be supposed to have expanded into the full-blown Colonial butterfly is a question upon which a great variety of opinion prevails.

new chummy. NEW CHUM *n.* 2 and 3. Also *attrib.*

1869 'PERAMBULATOR VON VELOCIPEDESTRIAN' *Anecdotes Vic.* 11 The largest of dreaded blackfellows came up, and he and the young farmer exchanged a few guttural sounds which were gibberish to new chummie. **1889** *Bulletin* (Sydney) 15 June 13/4 If in luck, inclined to brag it, 'No up-country' *then* he votes, When he's down he'll gamely swag it, *Then* new chummy *minus* 'notes'. **1926** *Aussie* (Sydney) Jan. 12.1 Near Emudilla I was joined by a young man of fresh and new-chummy appearance.

New Holland. [An anglicization of L. *Nova Hollandia* a name given by Dutch navigators in the seventeenth century to that part of the Australian continent lying west of the meridian which passes through Torres Strait.]

1. *Hist.* A name formerly given to the Australian continent or part thereof, sometimes including Tasmania.

1770 J. HAWKESWORTH *Acct. of Voyages* (1773) III. 237 New Holland, or, as I have now called the eastern coast, New South Wales, is of a larger extent than any other country in the known world that does not bear the name of a continent. **1793** J. HUNTER *Hist. Jrnl. Trans. Port Jackson* 1 The east coast of New Holland is that country, which was discovered and explored by Captain James Cook . . and by him called New South Wales. **1820** C. JEFFREYS *Van Dieman's Land* 1 Van Dieman's Land, or Tasmania, is an island of considerable extent . . divided from New Holland by a strait, about 90 miles wide. **1829** *Hints Emigration New Settlement Swan & Canning Rivers* 3 The following Document . . has been issued by the Colonial Department for the encouragement of a new Settlement on the West Coast of New Holland. **1841** H.S. CHAPMAN *New Settlement Australind* 26 Australia is the name given by modern geographers to . . what was formely known as New South Wales and New Holland. **1842** *Austral. & N.Z. Monthly Mag.* 23 The territory of Western Australia includes all that portion of New Holland situated to the westward of the 129th degree of longitude. **1857** H. TURNBULL *Leichhardt's Second Journey* (1983) 11 My intention is to give you a sort of narrative of my journey with Leichhardt into the interior of New Holland. **1860** 'LADY' *My Experiences in Aust.* 248 The dingo is found in every part of New Holland except the island of Tasmania. **1861** W. WESTGARTH *Aust.* 4 The old term New Holland may now be regarded as supplanted by that happier and fitter one of Australia. New Holland, properly, comprised only the western section, that is now West Australia. **1870** *Illustr. Sydney News* 17 Feb. 343/2 At best New Holland was regarded as a convenient spot to which the overflowings of vice might be exported.

2. In the names of birds: **New Holland cassowary** *obs.*, EMU *n.*[1] 1; **honeyeater,** the honeyeater *Phylidonyris novaehollandiae* of s.w. and s.e. Aust. incl. Tas., having black and white plumage with yellow on the wings and tail; *white-bearded honeyeater*, see WHITE *a.*[2] 1 b.; *yellow-wing*, see YELLOW 1; **vulture** *obs., brush turkey*, see BRUSH B. 2.

1789 A. PHILLIP *Voyage to Botany Bay* 271 **New-Holland Cassowary**. . . This is a species differing in many particulars from that generally known, and is a much larger bird, standing higher on its legs, and having the neck longer than in the common one. **1811** G. PATERSON *Hist. N.S.W.* 424 The New Holland Cassowary stands seven feet high, measuring from the ground to the upper part of his head, and, in every respect is much larger than the common Cassowary of all authors, and differs so much therefrom, in its form, as to clearly prove it a new species. **1865** G.F. ANGAS *Aust.* 97 The largest bird peculiar to Australia is the emeu or New Holland cassowary, of which there are now known to be two distinct kinds. **1860** G. BENNETT *Gatherings of Naturalist* 216 For a long period, and even to the present time, this bird has been called the 'New Holland Cassowary', but we consider the name of 'Emeu' to apply exclusively to the New Holland bird. **1822** J. LATHAM *Gen. Hist. Birds* IV. 171 **New-Holland Honey-eater** . . inhabits New South Wales, chiefly seen in January. **1887** *Illustr. Austral. News* (Melbourne) 21 Dec. 218/1 Only the New Holland and spine bill honey-eaters resemble the Victorian. **1943** C. BARRETT *Austral. Animal Bk.* 290 Coastal heathlands and tea-tree scrub are favoured by the white-bearded or yellow-winged honeyeater . . commonly known as the New Holland honeyeater. **1985** *Newsletter* (Soc. for Growing Austral. Plants, Canberra Region) Sept. 2 As I write I can hear a New Holland honeyeater whistling in the garden. **1822** B. FIELD in G. Mackaness *Fourteen Journeys Blue Mountains* 12 Oct. (1950) 44 At Bathurst, saw what is called the native turkey. It is the **New Holland vulture** of Dr Latham, and is one of the most remarkable birds found in Australia, appearing to form a connecting link between the rapacious and gallinaceous orders. **1841** *S. Austral. Rec.* (London) 2 Jan. 10 The most singular, on account of its habits, is the wattled talegalla, or brush turkey, hitherto known as the New Holland vulture, but which Mr Gould decides to belong to the gallinaceous tribe. **1918** A.J. CAMPBELL *Renaming Austral. Birds* 2 Take, for instance, the Brush-Turkey, which Latham called the 'New Holland Vulture'. He also called the Pallid cuckoo a 'Pigeon'. **1962** H.J. FRITH *Mallee-Fowl* 3 He . . was misled by the bird's bare red head and neck and thought it a kind of bird of prey, and so named it the New Holland vulture.

New Hollander. *Obs.* An Aboriginal.

1699 W. DAMPIER *New Voyage round World* (1703) III. 147 Among the *N[ew] Hollanders* .. there was one who . . seem'd to be the Chief of them. **1770** J. HAWKESWORTH *Acct. of Voyages* (1773) III. 657 They made much the same appearance as the New Hollanders. **1803** J. GRANT *Narr. Voyage N.S.W.* 163 The New Hollander feeds most filthily. **1805** J. TURNBULL *Voyage round World* I. 75 Bennelong . . became again as compleat a New Hollander, as if he had never left his native wilds. **1819** *Sydney Gaz.* 14 Aug., The poor New Hollanders had been neglected, and apparently consigned to perpetual ignoramia and endless wretchedness. **1827** *Monitor* (Sydney) 29 Nov. 798/3 A bodily injury, or . . some mental outrage . . all will allow it is possible might be inflicted upon the body or mind even of an Indian or New Hollander. **1841** H.S. CHAPMAN *New Settlement Australind* 95 The natives of Western Australia . . form a superior class of New Hollanders. **1853** *Visit to Aust. & Gold Regions* (S.P.C.K.) 156 All idea respecting the fabled innocence of the state of nature must vanish on beholding the New Hollander. **1888** R.J. FLANAGAN *Aborigines Aust.* 50 The corroboree appears to be the great festival among the New Hollanders.

newie. [Abbrev. of NEW (CHUM *n.* 2 and 3 + -Y: see also the perh. independently formed *newie* something new (OEDS 1947).]

1. One who has recently arrived in Australia; one who is new to a place or situation.

1917 *Truth* (Sydney) 1 Apr. 6/7 Two newies had a rough-up at Rozelle. **1925** A.A.B. APSLEY *Why & how I went to Aust.* 9 The next 'blue' period the migrant passes through is when he arrives as a 'newy' on the farm where work has been found for him. **1934** C. MACKNESS *Young Beachcombers* 64 The only girls I chummed up with in the least have just left, and there'll be hosts of newies. **1941** *Cobbers* (Brisbane) 31 Jan. 1 'Cobbers' says welcome to the newies. **1951** *Bulletin* (Sydney) 21 July 13/4 Bloke that carries his swag through town is either a newy, a galoot or a sympathy chaser. **1954** *Ibid.* 6 Jan. 12/1 Ted reckoned on his farm-employment problem being finally solved with the New Australian, but each time he told him what to do Newie nodded agreeably and looked vague.

2. *transf.*

1924 H.E. RIEMANN *Nor'-West o' West* 60 I've got a few newies since you were here last. **1944** *Bulletin* (Sydney) 1 Mar. 13/2 When I asked him what brand he usually smoked he replied 'Popeye'. That was a newie on me. **1951** CUSACK & JAMES *Come in Spinner* 413 You haven't heard this one, this is a newy. **1969** A. BUZO *Front Room Boys* (1970) 25 Are these the new type of report, Rabbo? . . Yeah, these are the newies. **1976** D. IRELAND *Glass Canoe* 55 Someone in the government got rid of it [*sc.* a car] and bought a newie.

New South. Abbrev. of 'New South Wales'.

1892 *Bulletin* (Sydney) 17 Dec. 19/1, I took a turn in New South, and tried Tassy and New Zealand. **1901** *Ibid.* 19 Jan. 31/1 In New South, in 'sixty-three, They raised cotton on the eastern slope by river-head and sea. **1922** A. WRIGHT *Colt from Country* 83 We can kiss good-bye to sunny New South for a spell. **1948** R.A. PEPPERALL *Emigrant to Aust.* 25 'New South' is the first and still the best State. **1958** G. COTTERELL *Tea at Shadow Creek* 146 In New South it's better, they've given way on the six o'clock closing there. **1981** B. GREEN *Small Town Rising* 149 He . . set out into New South on his bicycle.

New South Waler. *Obs.* A non-Aboriginal inhabitant of the Colony of New South Wales.

1844 *Sydney Morning Herald* 12 Apr. 3/1 The New South Walers could obtain immigrants at half the Coolie cost. **1850** *Bell's Life in Sydney* 9 Feb. 2/4 The New South Walers are certainly a lathy lot. **1864** *Sydney Punch* 27 May 4/1, I feel rather doggedly dyspeptic myself among these South Sea whalers—New South Walers I mean—beg pardon.

New South Wales Corps. *Hist.* A military force raised in Great Britain for service in the penal colony of New South Wales.

1789 *Hist. Rec. N.S.W.* II. 422 Warrant for Raising New South Wales Corps—George R. .. we have thought proper to direct that a corps of foot shall be forthwith raised, which is intended to be stationed in New South Wales. **1793** J. HUNTER *Hist. Jrnl. Trans. Port Jackson* 214 All the marines and the New South Wales corps, who were off duty, came down and cheered our people. **1805** J. TURNBULL *Voyage round World* III. 131 Seeing the New South Wales corps under arms, they were in the most extravagant raptures. **1821** J. WALLIS *Hist. Acct. Colony N.S.W.* 22 Three transports might be hourly expected, having on board . . detachments of a corps raised for the service of the Colony, and called 'The New South Wales Corps'. **1837** J. MUDIE *Felonry of N.S.W.* 30 The New South Wales corps, a military force specially raised in and sent from England to be the colonial garrison. **1945** J.A. ALLAN *Men & Manners in Aust.* 33 The Rum Corps—officially the 'New South Wales Corps' . . garrisoned the settlement.

New South Welshman. A non-Aboriginal inhabitant of the Colony of New South Wales; one who is native to or resident in the State of New South Wales. Also **New South Welsher.**

1860 *Bell's Life in Sydney* 26 May 3/2 A batch of New South Welshmen. **1887** J.J. RUTTER *Ulladulla to New England* 18 The Yankee seems to have more 'go' than the New South Welshman. **1891** *Bohemia* (Melbourne) 26 Nov. 6 He is a New South Welsher. **1905** *Truth* (Sydney) 5 Mar. 1/6 Other New South Welshers thought our Georgie was only half a Premier with McLean. **1925** *Australasian* (Melbourne) 3 Jan. 29/5 The Victorians were hopeful of winning the rubber outright . . but the New South Welshmen batted vigorously. **1939** *Referee* (Sydney) 9 Feb. 16/7 Every New South Welshman who knows what real cricket was must be proud of Stan McCabe. **1964** *Bulletin* (Sydney) 23 May 37/2 For the first Test he named nine New South Welshmen and only two Victorians. **1977** D. WILLIAMSON *Club* (1978) p. vii, You've either spent the last few years in a Tibetan monastery or you're a New South Welshman.

Newstralian. *Obs.* Shortened form of NEW AUSTRALIAN *n.* 2.

1951 *Bulletin* (Sydney) 12 Dec. 13/4 Some Newstralians are nothing if not thorough. **1952** *Ibid.* 27 Feb. 17/3 His housekeeper is a Newstralian still a bit shaky on our language.

New Zealand flax. [The name perh. became established because of the importance of the flax from N.Z. as a source of fibre in the Austral. colonies.] The perennial, tufted plant *Phormium tenax* (fam. Agavaceae) of New Zealand and Norfolk Is., having long, stiff, pointed leaves yielding a useful fibre, and cultivated as an ornamental.

[**1777** G. FORSTER *Voyage round World* II. 445 The New Zeeland flag (*phormium tenax*), shot stalks eight or nine feet high, having flowers much larger and brighter than we had seen at Queen Charlotte's Sound.] **1789** W. TENCH *Narr. Exped. Botany Bay* 147 The New Zealand flax, plants of which are found growing in every part of the island. **1800** *HRA* (1914) 1st Ser. II. 513 You are also to allot three acres of ground for the purpose of cultivating the European flax . . if found preferable to the New Zealand flax. **1801** G. BARRINGTON *Sequel to Voyage N.S.W.* 31 New Zealand Flax . . is of the same kind as that at Norfolk Island. **1819** *HRA* (1917) 1st Ser. X. 63 A Vegetable substance of the nature and quality of Hemp, commonly called New Zealand Flax, can be raised and procured in this Colony. **1827** *Monitor* (Sydney) 23 Aug. 603/2 The Exports of New Zealand Flax, on their arrival in England were bought up with avidity. **1846** *Cumberland Times* (Parramatta) 21 Feb. 1/3 An outhouse belonging to Mr Sly was discovered to be in flames... Fortunately not a breath of air was stirring.. as a vast quantity of New Zealand flax was upon the premises. **1896** A. MACKAY *Austral. Agriculturist* (rev. ed.) 118 New Zealand flax.. grows freely all over the colonies. **1908** FREEMAN & CHANDLER *World's Commercial Products* 322 Phormium fibre, often incorrectly known as New Zealand Flax or Hemp.. is said to be unrivalled for its yield of fibre, the sword-shaped leaves.. giving upward of fifteen per cent. of their green weight as cleaned fibre. **1950** R.G. EDWARDS *Austral. Garden Bk.* 135 New Zealand flax grows to fifteen feet and has long narrow leaves and numerous dull-red flowers clustered on long stems. **1978** V.H. HEYWOOD *Flowering Plants World* 316 The Agavaceae is a family of considerable economic importance. A number of species are the source of strong, durable fibres... Examples include.. *Phormium tenax* (New Zealand flax).

ngoora burr, var. NOOGOORA BURR.

ngowa, ngowoo, varr. GNOW.

nick, *v.*[1] [Prob. fig. use of Br. dial. or slang *nick* to steal: cf. *steal* to depart, withdraw surreptitiously (OED *v.*[1] 9); but see also OED(S *nick, v.*[2] 13 b.]

1. *intr.* To go on the spur of the moment; to slip (away, out, etc.).

1896 E. TURNER *Little Larrikin* 274 Trying to induce the driver of the motor, for whom he had a friendship, to promise at the end of the journey to 'nick away and come too'. **1928** 'BRENT OF BIN BIN' *Up Country* 120 Bert and I could just nick down to Mungee. **1946** K.S. PRICHARD *Roaring Nineties* 116 I'll nick over to the camp and put on the billy. **1962** V.C. HALL *Dreamtime Justice* 64 If the blasted launch had been in good repair we could have nicked over before the onset of the stinking south-easter. **1969** W. DICK *Naked Prodigal* 227 People were nicking out and having a few grogs, and bringing back bottles. **1978** C. GREEN *Sun is Up* 129 'Y-yes,' said Johnny, pop-eyed and stuttering, 'I saw it n-nickin' down that hole.' **1981** *Sydney Morning Herald* 11 Apr. 13/2 There is no lavatory so the Labor candidate.. and his helpers nick across the road to use Ansett's.

2. With **off**: to depart (often without ceremony or surreptitiously). As an imperative, 'Clear out!'

1901 M. FRANKLIN *My Brilliant Career* 258 If you go to a picnic, just when the fun commences you have to nick off home and milk. **1938** X. HERBERT *Capricornia* 257 You're only humming for a drink. Nick off home. **1941** *Air Force News* (Melbourne) 4 Oct. 12 No more would I 'nick off'. **1955** R. LAWLER *Summer of Seventeenth Doll* (1965) 124 'Is it the boys he's nicking off with on Monday?'.. 'Yeh. Up the Murray for the grapes.' **1969** W. MOXHAM *Apprentice* 20 It was a pity he'd taken the kid along. He could have nicked off with a good job lot. **1977** H. GARNER *Monkey Grip* 40, I got up and got dressed and nicked off. **1979** CAREY & LETTE *Puberty Blues* 1 Things like have sex, smoke cigarettes, nick off from school. **1981** P. BARTON *Bastards I have Known* 96, I was in this spot first.. so nick off.

nick, *v.*[2] [Spec. use of *nick* to make a nick or notch in.] *trans.* In clearing scrub: to cut a 'scarf' or notch in (the trunk of a small tree), esp. to facilitate the progress of a *mallee roller* (see MALLEE 8).

1920 *Land of Lyre Bird* (S. Gippsland Pioneers' Assoc.) 72 As the scrub-cutting progressed, the process known as 'nicking' became popular. This was done by cutting a small notch front and back in each tree; in hazels and small growths, just a few blows front and back would be sufficient, and in gum saplings, blackwoods, or wattles, a 'scarf' say, a third through front and back, and so on.. as it required both skill and judgment to successfully negotiate a good 'fall'. **1939** *Bulletin* (Sydney) 8 Feb. 21/4 Dad and Choom, following a scrub roller 'nicking' the big stuff unearthed a bottle that the tractor-driver had planted. **1982** M. WALKER *Making Do* 136, I was with him over twelve months, swinging the axe, nicking mallee that he was rolling down. **1983** A. CANNON *Bullocks, Bullockies & Other Blokes* 20 If there were any heavy trees—in that country one of four inches diameter was considered heavy—they had to be 'nicked' at the base with an axe, before the scrub could be rolled.

nicked, *past pple.* In the imprecation **get nicked,** 'get lost'; esp. euphemistically.

1968 D. O'GRADY *Bottle of Sandwiches* 179, I yelled, 'Last one in can get nicked' and took off after Boof. **1971** D. IRELAND *Unknown Industr. Prisoner* 249 Did you tell God to get nicked? **1973** D. FOSTER *North South West* 199 Get nicked says Bonchance only semi-audibly as the door closes. **1982** J. HIBBERD *Country Quinella* (1984) 75 Hello, Marmalade. I'm your great aunty Val... Get nicked.

nicki-nicki /'nɪki-nɪki/. *Austral. pidgin.* Also **nikki-nikki,** etc. [Austral. pidgin; formed on *niggerhead.*] Black twist tobacco; *nigger tobacco, twist,* see NIGGER 4.

1938 X. HERBERT *Capricornia* 137 It was a parcel from a Chinese store, containing.. one pound of niki-niki. **1940** W. HATFIELD *Into (Great?) Unfenced* 101 All they get's flour and tea an' sugar, an' a stick of Nickey-nick. **1946** A. GREEN *We were (Riff) R.A.A.F.* 70 The responsibilities earned him an extra ration of 'nicky-nicky' (black twist tobacco). **1960** J. WALKER *No Sunlight Singing* 17 'Here's what you bin wan'um,' he said, laughing and holding out a plug of nicki-nicki. **1964** K. WILLEY *Eaters of Lotus* 87 We smoked nikki-nikki (native twist tobacco). **1985** B. ROSSER *Dreamtime Nightmares* 21 They used to get this tobacco sent out to the outstations, but you couldn't really call it tobacco. We called it *nicki-nicki.* You couldn't smoke it, it was too hard.

nig. Abbrev. of NIGGER 1.

1880 H. KENDALL *Songs from Mountains* 107 I'll give him education; A 'nig' is better when he's tamed, Perhaps, than a Caucasian. **1893** J.A. BARRY *Steve Brown's Bunyip* 58 When the cattle.. moves quietly off afore daybreak, one lot of nigs follers 'em up, an' one lot stops to 'tend on me. **1913** *Bulletin* (Sydney) 13 Mar. 13/1 Brother Binghi of those parts is very fond of baked croc... Every nig. had his equator full to the limit of its capacity. **1925** J.E. LIDDLE *Selected Poems* 110 Many wild 'nigs' were hunted down. **1931** A.W. UPFIELD *Sands of Windee* 80 'Now about the nigs, Morris. Do you known why they are at Range Hut?' 'Oh, just on a walk-about, I think.' **1940** W. HATFIELD *Into (Great?) Unfenced* 190 The courts held it murder to plug a nig. **1973** D. WOLFE *Brass Kangaroo* 56 Never knock a nig back. I always give 'em a ride. **1981** A. WELLER *Day of Dog* 48 Ya want to look out for those wackers. They hate us nigs.

nigger. [Transf. use of *nigger* a Black.]

1. An Aboriginal. Also *attrib.*

1845 G. DE C. LEFROY in C.T. Stannage *New Hist. W.A.* (1981) 95 It is shocking.. to see a fine young fellow cut off by the odious detestable niggers. **1853** *Moreton Bay Free Press* 8 Feb. 3/3 Constable Giles states that when they saw themselves surrounded so suddenly the two niggers turned quite white. **1861** J. DAVIS *Tracks of McKinlay* 17 Nov. (1863) 114 Frank, our nigger, got a story.. that there was only one white man killed. **1875** R. THATCHER *Something to his Advantage* 8 He swears the niggers are like sheep on the billybongs. We may have a pop at some of them. **1890** A.J. VOGAN *Black Police* 201 'Spose you're a runaway nigger? Station or police? **1902** L. BECKE *Breachley* 67 In using the term 'nigger', instead of 'blackfellow' or 'black', I adopt the Queensland expression for aboriginal. **1905** *Bulletin* (Sydney) 22 June 13/1 The nigger-lovers of Australia love the nigger in an impersonal fashion only. **1915** N. DUNCAN *Austral. Byways* 99 'Find a nigger,' said our bushman.. 'and you'll get water.' **1927** M. DORNEY *Adventurous Honeymoon* 43 A gunyah—the unpretentious dwelling of the Australian nigger. **1937** M. TERRY *Sand & Sun* 26 Nigger wells, soaks and rockholes. **1944** F.S. GREENOP *Verses* 46 Her mother was a nigger and her father was a fool—She was born among the grasses by the scintillating pool. **1959** E. WEBB *Mark of Sun* 14 No one else called me a farting nigger; at least, not to my face. **1969** F.B. VICKERS *No Man is Himself* 58 He came back to my bloody nigger camp that same night. **1984** B. DIXON *Searching for Aboriginal Lang.* 20 The policeman came straight to the point, showing that little had changed in Cardwell during the last ninety years: 'There are no niggers in this town.' **1986** *Austral. Geographic* Jan. 76/3 The Duncans represent Moree's small but expanding Aboriginal middle class... The Duncans have enjoyed so much success they have earned the epithet 'uptown niggers' from other Aboriginal people who cannot.. 'break out of the poverty circle'.

2. *Obs.* A Kanaka.

1869 P.A. TAYLOR *Colony of Qld.* 11 One planter.. said, 'What can you supply me a hundred niggers for?' **1892** *Truth* (Sydney) 5 June 4/4 *Truth* has had some experience of the way in which the niggers are trapped and treated and unhesitatingly affirms that 'blackbirding' and slave-trading are so very much alike. **1897** *Western Champion* (Barcaldine) 26 Jan. 3/1 A young planter in the district happened to call his kanaka boys 'niggers', and they at once went into town to see if their agreements could not be broken in consequence. **1903** *Truth* (Sydney) 6 Dec. 1/7 There is no possibility of plutocratic slave-owners in the sugar districts getting supplies of fresh niggers to replace the 'returns'.

3. *transf.* LUDERICK.

1927 A. WRIGHT *Squatter's Secret* 38 The big catch of lively 'niggers' splashing in a rock-bound pool behind him. **1948** F.D. MARSHALL *Let's go Fishing* 65 The 'darkie' or 'nigger'.. is a most worthy opponent. **1962** 'N. CULOTTA' *Gone Fishin'* 76 We were fishing for niggers. The official name for niggers, or blackfish, is 'luderick'. They are listed as luderick on the monthly returns, but fishermen call them niggers. **1983** *Sun* (Sydney) 30 Sept. 28/4 Brisbane Water has been best of the estuaries, with bream, niggers and mullet.

4. Special Comb. **nigger country,** an area inhabited by Aborigines living traditionally; also **nigger's country; farming** *vbl. n.*, the exploitation by a non-Aboriginal of a government subsidy paid to an employer of Aboriginal labour or to fund an Aboriginal welfare project; **hunt,** the organized pursuit of Aborigines (see DISPERSE); so **hunting** *vbl. n.* and *attrib.*; **tobacco, twist,** strong, coarse tobacco of the type issued to an Aboriginal worker on a rural property; NICKI NICKI.

1915 N. DUNCAN *Austral. Byways* 86 Traveling the edge of the '**nigger country**' to the north, he had fallen in with a roving band of gins. **1936** I.L. IDRIESS *Cattle King* 191 Twelve hundred miles as the crow flies... Nearly all 'nigger country' too. **1937** M. TERRY *Sand & Sun* 77 In nigger country one develops the faculty of sleeping soundly. **1942** G. CASEY *It's Harder for Girls* (1944) 57 "Strewth!' said a bloke who was leaning through the window. 'It's nigger's country, ain't it?' **1968** F. HARDY *Unlucky Australs.* 17 A person is said to engage in '**nigger farming**' in the Northern Territory when he relies on income from aboriginal subsidies to keep his station solvent. **1982** *Canberra Times* 8 Nov. 8/7 Authorities are seeing this as an exercise in nigger farming, a process whereby professional people and administrative staff will be employed on a long-term basis without ever achieving eradication of trachoma nor dealing fully with eye health problems. **1882** P. O'FARRELL *Lett. from Irish Aust.* (1984) 68 Crawford apologised to Lillie for the monotony of his letters: 'the only incidents that occur are '**nigger hunts**'.' **1901** *Bulletin* (Sydney) 8 June 31/1 There had been some little talk lately in Perth of.. 'nigger-hunts'. **1917** *Life & Experiences Successful W. Austral.* 76 We started out on our nigger hunting enterprise, and making a wide circle, closed in behind the native camp. **1910** *Bulletin* (Sydney) 22 Dec. 13/4 Each nig. received his wages mostly in '**nigger tobacco**'. **1940** E. HILL *Great Austral. Loneliness* (ed. 2) 108 Beef and a fig of nigger-tobacco are the only hand-outs. **1937** WISBERG & WATERS *Bushman at Large* 21, I filled a pipe with **niggertwist,** a cheap tobacco the very smell of which would knock a white man into a coma. **1945** *Aust. Week-End Bk.* 152 He was cutting sticky verandah-cured tobacco into nigger twist.

niggerhead.

1. [Spec. use of *niggerhead* a rock, stone, etc.: see OED(S 2 and NEGROHEAD.] A large block of coral deposited high on a reef by a storm, frequently blackened and rounded; a submerged isolated coral spire, pinnacle, or head, usu. reaching close to the surface; NEGROHEAD.

1876 J. MORESSY *Discovery New Guinea* 3 A crowd of 'nigger heads', black points of coral rock, peep up in places. **1880** *Proc. Linnean Soc. N.S.W.* V. 194 All along the Barrier Reef.. at the side of the pillars of dead coral which go by the name of 'Nigger Heads'. **1893** W. SAVILLE-KENT *Naturalist in Aust.* 49 It frequently happens, however, more especially on the outer or weather edge of the reef, that the detached storm-stranded blocks are of such dimensions that their crowns are elevated several feet above high-water mark. Under these conditons their upper surfaces become perfectly black and weathered; and, standing up in bold colour, are in contrast with the snow-white line of breakers. They are popularly known as 'nigger heads'. **1928** S.E. NAPIER *On Barrier Reef* 35 Large blocks of coral, all torn and twisted by the seas, and black as the 'nigger-heads' from which they have received their local name. **1934** T. WOOD *Cobbers* 219 You see the blue change to apple green, in patches, on your starboard hand, and the deadly niggerheads emerge, backed by a line of snowy surf. **1936** T.C. ROUGHLEY *Wonders Great Barrier Reef* 45 As these coral boulders weather they usually lose their rounded outline and develop hollows and depressions bordered by jutting edges that in many cases become encrusted with a black lichen, and so have received the name of 'nigger-heads' . . though their resemblance to the woolly heads of negroes is usually far from striking. **1950** W.J. DAKIN *Great Barrier Reef* 53 Near the margin of the reef-flat one should notice the different zones which run parallel to the edge. Not far from the margin, curious rough pillar-like blocks of dead coral may be seen. They are called 'niggerheads'. These have once been coral growths projecting up from the sea-bottom, near the reef margin. They have been torn loose in some more than usually heavy storm and hurled on to the reef-flat. **1972** K. WILLEY *Tales Big Country* 141, I stood on one niggerhead of coral with my head above water. **1979** R. MILLER *Sugarbird Lady* 64 After drifting for three days it was wrecked on a coral 'niggerhead' about a mile from Bernier Island.

2. The small, tufted perennial grass *Enneapogon nigricans* (fam. Poaceae) of all mainland States but not N.T., having dark seed-heads; (occas.) any of several other grasses of the genus *Enneapogon*. Freq. in *pl.*

1923 *Census Plants Vic.* (Field Naturalists' Club Vic.) 9 *Pappophorum nigricans* . . Niggerheads. **1955** *Lake Eyre, S.A.* (R. Geogr. Soc. Australasia) 71 Not possible to identify, but may be one of the *Enneapogon sp.* (Nigger heads). **1975** E.R. ROTHERHAM et al. *Flowers & Plants N.S.W. & Southern Qld.* 180 In the winter . . the flexible silky heads of the Spear Grass bend to the inland wind whilst in summer they are replaced by the stiffer black-green Nigger-Heads (*Enneapogon nigricans*).

niggerhead beech: see BEECH.

night. Used *attrib.* in Special Comb. **night-camp,** the overnight, outdoor rest taken by a traveller, esp. a drover; the resting-place; also as *v. intr.*; **-cart,** *sanitary cart*, see SANITARY a.; so **-cartman; fossicker** *obs.*, one who raids a gold-miner's claim by night; **-horse** [also U.S. (see OEDS *night, sb.* 14)], a horse used at night, esp. one used to round up the animals required for the coming day (see quots. 1923 and 1977); **-horse paddock,** an enclosure in which such horses (or other animals required during the coming day) are kept; also **night paddock; -man,** *sanitary man*, see SANITARY a.; **watch,** a watch kept over (unenclosed) stock at night; the time this occupies; *night watchman*; **watchman,** one who keeps watch over (unenclosed) stock at night; **-well,** see quots. 1906 and 1908.

1882 MRS J.C. STANGER *Journey from Sydney* 12 A smell of burning, which proved to be the drivers' **night-camp. 1927** *Bulletin* (Sydney) 28 July 27/1 The man on the wallaby almost invariably makes his night-camp under a tree. **1943** G. MCIVER *Bunyip & Other Verses* 16 We . . showed the men Where they would find the night camp when We had a bend selected. **1953** *Bulletin* (Sydney) 28 Oct. 13/2 Bringing a mob through Pooncarie . . we night-camped on the Garnpang-No Man's Land boundary. **1957** F. CLUNE *Fortune Hunters* 34 In the cool of the evening we pushed on a few miles . . looking for a spot for a night-camp. **1979** D. LOCKWOOD *My Old Mates & I* 91, I remembered our first night-camp at the Burketown crossing of the McArthur River near Borroloola. **1840** *Tasmanian Weekly Dispatch* (Hobart) 1 May 8/1 **Night Cart!!!** The above is kept in constant readiness. Any orders for the emptying of Cesspools, etc. . . immediately attended to. **1903** *Truth* (Sydney) 4 Jan. 7/3 The . . abominable noise made by the nightcarts on their way to the Tip. **1955** D. NILAND *Shiralee* 90 He'd have a mansion with rugs on the floor and a built-in nightcart. **1965** D. MARTIN *Hero of Too* 9 A nightcartman's professional view of local inhabitants is as valid as anyone else's. **1971** P. HASLUCK *Open Go* 86 The water supply in Perth is much better than wells in the back yard used to be, the deep sewerage better than the night carts. **1978** J. ANDERSON *Tirra Lirra* 18 Never again shall I hide behind a tree . . as the nightcart approaches. **1986** *Austral. Geographic* Apr. 98/2 Len Bates, one of Sydney's few remaining nightcart men, has been collecting and emptying pans from outside dunnies of about 70 unsewered homes for the past five years. **1853** C.R. READ *What I heard, saw, & Did* 149 The man was what they called a **night fossicker**, who slept or did nothing during the day, and then went around at night to where he knew claims to be rich, and stole the stuff by candle light. **1855** G.H. WATHEN *Golden Colony* 80 'Holes' plundered of gold by the 'night fossickers'—miscreants who watched for the richest holes during the day, marked them, and plundered them at night. **1904** *Bulletin* (Sydney) 8 Dec. 19/3 When cattle have 'rushed' . . Wheelbarrow, like every other **night horse**, takes simultaneous action. **1907** *Ibid.* 11 Apr. 15/3, I collared the spare night-horse and lit out to the old man's assistance. **1923** *Ibid.* 1 Nov. 24/4 A practice which hasn't much to recommend it is that of keeping a 'night horse' yarded all night on the far-out stations, so that it can be used to run up the mob in the morning. **1932** J. MCCARTER *Pan's Clan* 145 The station night-horse . . was utilised for running-up the hacks in daily use on Pincha Downs. **1955** J. MORRISON *Black Cargo* 52 My hut was in a corner of the paddock where the night-horse was kept. **1964** *Meanjin* 59 They had in the plant two proved night horses. **1965** R. OTTLEY *By Sandhills* 172 Each night a horse called a night-horse is shut in the yards for a stockman to use in the early morning to bring in the 'work' horses. **1977** *Pastoral Rev. & Graziers' Rec.* Sept. 303 The nighthorse is of no particular breeding and is kept on his own. His singular duty is to run in (muster) the working horses every morning. As his job is generally completed before daylight, it is desirable that he be sure-footed and possess good eyesight. **1922** [**night-horse paddock**] V. PALMER *Boss of Killara* 124 He stole softly over the dewy grass of the night-paddock. **1931** A.W. UPFIELD *Sands of Windee* 20 Two miles . . from a homestead would be within a night- or horse-paddock, where one or more of the hands would be riding almost daily. **1945** —— *Death of Swagman* 188, I am wondering how the horse will get on for water in the night paddock. **1976** J.H. TRAVERS *Bull Dust on Brigalow* 48 The night horse paddock was built of heaped-up stones picked up by the blacks and was about 4 feet high and horse proof. **1977** *Pastoral Rev. & Graziers' Rec.* Sept. 303 Some three hundred yards from the homestead there was . . the night-horse paddock. **1898** *Truth* (Sydney) 27 Nov. 1/3 *Molong*, a sweet town of the west, is in the throes of a municipal crisis—and all about a **night man. 1903** *Ibid.* 27 Dec. 1/7 Some suburban nightmen have left a poetical appeal for Xmas boxes in the back parlors of patrons. **1942** L. MANN *Go-Getter* 27 You can get used to a nasty life, a nasty person, or a nasty smell as a nightman gets used to his job and eats his lunch on the cart. **1965** N. LINDSAY *Bohemians of Bulletin* 111 The suburban privy was still serviced by the night man. **1977** *Ink No. 2* 21, I would make a quick dash for the privy. As if he had been waiting for this very moment, the Night Man would come bounding down the steps balancing the spare pan on his flannel-clad shoulder. **1907** *Bulletin* (Sydney) 10 Oct. 14/1 They were for years most valuable to drovers saving **night watches**, dogs, calico fences, etc. **1934** C. SAYCE *Comboman* 46 Jumbo started to sing a corroboree dirge, for the custom of stockmen is to sing on night-watch in order to let the cattle know they are about. **1946** *Bulletin* (Sydney) 17 July 29/1 Most of the drovers, poking borak at the envious nightwatch, departed for the township. **1954** T. RONAN *Vision Splendid* 163 There's enough of us for the night watches. **1836** J. BACKHOUSE *Extracts from Lett.* (1838) iii. 73 The different flocks are counted into the folds at night, and committed to the charge of a **night-watchman**, and are re-counted to the respective shepherds in the morning. **1841** *Sydney Herald* 27 Sept. 2/4 They are then counted over and left in charge of the night watchman, whose duty it is to take care of the flocks in the folds until the morning. **1849** A. HARRIS *Emigrant Family* (1967) 15 One flock of sheep requires half the labour of a second man as hut-keeper and night watchman. **1906** *Bulletin* (Sydney) 17 May 15/3 Ever hear of a **night-well?** Thirty or forty miles east of Wagin . . W.A., there is a hill, on top of which is a small cavern. Part of the floor of the cavern is water-worn into a basin holding about 50 gallons. A little after sundown a tiny thread of water starts trickling from an inlet in the wall of the cave, and continues till shortly before sunrise. During the day not a drop flows. **1908** *Ibid.* 6 Aug. 14/3 As to 'night-wells', I know one on the Ravensthorpe road, sixty miles east of Broome Hill. It is in the bed of a salt-water river. You can get fresh water from it at any time. . . The strange thing about these 'night wells' is that the water rises every night to the surface and sinks about a foot during the day. **1948** *Ibid.* 5 May 22/3 There used to be a night-well on the way to Jerramungurup (s.-w. W.A.). Originally an abo drinking place it was enlarged by Groper teamsters to a capacity of about 100 gallons.

night parrot. The rare, nocturnal parrot *Geopsittacus occidentalis*, a ground-dwelling, predom. green, yellow, and black bird of arid and semi-arid inland Aust. See also *spinifex parrot* SPINIFEX 4.

1913 *Emu* XIII. 16 The Night-Parrot (*Geopsittacus occidentalis*). **1918** A.J. CAMPBELL *Renaming Austral. Birds* 4 The remarkable *Atrichornis* and the unique Night-Parrot are practically gone. **1929** A.H. CHISHOLM *Birds & Green Places* 98 Then there are the night-parrot and the ground-parrot, both of which make nests after the manner of quail, under or in tussocks of grass. **1951** E. HILL *Territory* 23 The voiceless night-parrot that nests in the ant-hills may not be sighted once in thirty years. **1970** P. SLATER *Eagle for Pidgin* 38 The rediscovery of the night parrot, an insignificant and indeed mislaid bird, was the sergeant's Holy Grail. **1981** *Woman's Day* (Sydney) 9 Sept. 94/2 The night parrot . . an elusive bird of the inland, found by white explorers in 1845 and reasonably common for 50 years . . was last collected in 1912. Since then, many naturalists had searched vainly for this desert will-o'-the-wisp. **1985** *Sydney Morning Herald* 11 Apr. 10/4 The quite fabulous night parrot, said to be near extinction.

nikki-nikki, var. NICKI-NICKI.

nilla-nilla, var. NULLA-NULLA.

nine. A keg containing nine gallons of beer. Also **niner.**

1943 *Bully Tin* (Baronta) 17 Apr. 3 Now, there is *the nine*. This must be of course the nine gallon keg. **1960** R. PULLAN *Hardskins* 135 Those days you got a niner of beer and you got a night. **1963** B. HESLING *Dinkumization & Depommification* 82 Brother Frank had managed to get a 'nine' (and this he did by following a brewery dray in a taxi and biding his time). **1969** A. BUZO *Rooted* (1973) 77 He backed five winners at the picnic races, floored three locals in a brawl, demolished a niner, and torpedoed the minister's daughter. **1974** *Meanjin* 280 A mate of mine was exterminated like that. . . Some mongrel dropped a niner through a trapdoor. Split his skull in two. **1980** H. STEPHENSON *Cattlemen & Huts High Plains* 336 W'jer 'appen to 'ave a niner?

ning nong. [f. Br. dial. *ning-nang* a fool: see EDD and OEDS.] A fool.

1957 'N. CULOTTA' *They're Weird Mob* 15, I 'ave ter get landed with a bloody ning nong who doesn't know where he's bloody goin'. **1968** D. O'GRADY *Bottle of Sandwiches* 179 He had another kind [of bark] which meant 'what sort of a stupid ning-nong of a galah have I got for boss?' **1977** E. MACKIE *Oh to be Aussie* 43 The trainee Aussie must not go to King's Cross—it's only for the tourists, ningnongs and geezers all the way from Woop Woop.

nip, *n.* [See BITE *n.*]

1. a. In the phr. **to put the nips in** (or **into**) (someone), to cadge (from).

[N.Z. **1917** *Chrons. N.Z. Exped. Force* 19 Sept. 63, I put the nips in the other night.] **1919** [see NIP *v.*]. **1937** W. & T.I. MOORE *Best Austral. One-Act Plays* 398 He came along to put the nips in, so I gave him a couple of bob. **1949** L. GLASSOP *Lucky Palmer* 230 You can't put the nips into old Alf. He's got death adders in his pockets. **1955** D. NILAND *Shiralee* 46 Put the nips into me for tea and sugar and tobacco in his usual style. **1977** R. BEILBY *Gunner* 237 'I'm putting the bite on you,' Gunner explained gently, 'Putting the nips in, touching you for a loan.'

b. In the phr. **to get the nips into** (someone), to attempt to gain an advantage, etc., from (a person).

1959 D. NILAND *Gold in Streets* 60 That sheila's got the nips into me. She must have, or she wouldn't have been so easy.

2. One who responds sympathetically to a cadger; a 'soft touch'.

1937 *Bulletin* (Sydney) 4 Aug. 21/2 Most 'bucks' would be good nips for . . a handout from their always loaded tucker-boxes.

nip, *v. trans.* To cadge (something); to cadge from (someone). See BITE *n.* and *v.*

1919 W.H. DOWNING *Digger Dialects* 35 *Nip*, to cadge (or 'Put in the Nips'). **1978** H.C. BAKER *I was Listening* 7 No chance of nippin' the bricky for a smoke—he don't smoke.

nipper, *n.*[1] [Spec. use of *nipper* one who nips.] Any of several small burrowing shrimp-like marine crustaceans, commonly used for bait.

1882 J.E. TENISON-WOODS *Fish & Fisheries N.S.W.* 126 *Alphaeus socialis* . . locally named the 'Nipper', is abundant in Port Jackson, and is a good deal sought for, but not so much for food as for bait for black bream fishing. **1895** C. THACKERAY *Amateur Fisherman's Guide* 82 Raw prawns and nippers are the best baits. **1948** F.D. MARSHALL *Let's go Fishing* 50 Nipper (a saltwater crustacean found in mud—called in coastal areas a 'yabby'). **1952** W.J. DAKIN *Austral. Seashores* 174 Sometimes called nippers or ghost-nippers by fishermen who use them as bait, and they are yabbies to Queenslanders. **1983** *Fishing Information & Services Handbk.* 76 The top baits . . would naturally include . . nippers, harbour prawns.

nipper, *n.*[2] [Spec. use of *nipper* the smallest or youngest of a family.] A youth employed to do odd jobs in a labouring gang, esp. to make tea.

1915 *Bulletin* (Sydney) 9 Dec. 22/1 When the slips were all written out the jobless ganger sent the nipper after the 'head'. **1953** 'CADDIE' *Caddie* 29 A nipper was the name given to a young boy whose job it was to boil the billies and carry the various tools . . to the men when required. **1965** *Tracks we Travel* 40 'What time is it?' we ask the 'nipper' as we see him collecting the billy cans. **1981** A.B. FACEY *Fortunate Life* 12 Eric got a job on the same gang . . of messenger, and bringing tools to the men and so on—they called him a 'nipper'.

Hence **nippering** *pr. pple.*

1938 F. BLAKELEY *Hard Liberty* 22 My job was nippering in a navvy gang for the contractors.

nit. [Prob. var. of *nix* 'a word used as a signal that someone in authority is approaching', also used in the phr. *to keep nix*: see OED(S *nix, sb.*[1] 3 and *nit, sb.*[2])]

1. *Obs.* A word used as a signal to warn an accomplice of the approach of a third party. Also as *v. intr.*, to escape, to flee.

1882 *Sydney Slang Dict.* 10 *Nit*, get away (usually from a foe), make tracks. **1895** *Worker* (Sydney) 15 June 4/2 'Nit, you chaps,' said Bill, 'and wait for me.' **1898** *Bulletin* (Sydney) 29 Oct. 15/1 Nit! . . Stop it. **1899** *Ibid.* 8 Apr. (Red Page), I'd like to paint her and the children—and the 'nan-nan' sons hurrying past in the background. I'd call it 'Nit! there's Mother.' **1905** *Truth* (Sydney) 11 June 3/3 The sleuths said but one word—'twas 'nit!'—and sidled softly and silently towards the apparently unsuspicious pedestrian. **1910** *Ibid.* 28 Aug. 1/8 Bellows of 'Nit! The John Hops.' **1962** D. MCLEAN *World turned upside Down* 197 'Nit! Nit!' the warning from David Dawes sent the youths running before they had done much harm.

2. In the phr. **to keep nit,** to keep watch while an accomplice engages in an (illegal) activity.

1903 *Truth* (Sydney) 19 July 3/5 She was aided in securing patrons by a bludger, who . . stood near the Railway Bridge and *kept 'nit' for the traps* so that Amy could walk freely when she got on her beat. **1913** *Bulletin* (Sydney) 6 Feb. 15/1 Always interesting is the art of signalling, from that of the lighthouse keeper to the methods of the mute, inglorious cobber 'keeping nit' for the coming of John Dunn. **1918** *Euripidean: Troopship Souvenir* 6 When I says workin' I means I keekin [*sic*] nit to see 'as 'ow th' D's don't hop in an' cop the brass. **1936** 'SWEENEY, EX-CROOK' *I Confess* 11 It is often necessary for someone to 'keep nit' whilst the other enters the house. **1950** F.J. HARDY *Power without Glory* 33 Jigger . . in case the police should be deceitful enough to come from that direction . . kept 'nit' on the corner. **1960** N. CATO *Green grows Vine* 63 Mother Mac and Maria went with them to 'keep nit' as they had no bathing-costumes with them. **1968** *Swag* (Sydney) i. 44/1 The Bower Bird, who was sentry for the school of arts group, abandoned his post to have his jug refilled. That was his stipend, a night's free drinking for keeping nit. **1977** B. SCOTT *My Uncle Arch* 3 They'd pick a couple of the mob to keep nit then they'd hoe into the corn.

nit-keeper. One who keeps watch while an accomplice engages in an (illegal) activity.

1935 *Bulletin* (Sydney) 22 May 21/1 That outlaw the sulphur-crested cockatoo is not the only bird to post a 'nit-keeper' when transgressing against society. **1942** *Ibid.* 8 July 13/2 The 'boonch of lambs' was a flock of white cockatoos hoeing into some melons in a shallow depression about half a mile away, and, believe it or not, without a nit-keeper. **1964** B. WANNAN *Fair Go, Spinner* 192 The nit-keepers must have been dozing, for a party of policemen managed to get fairly close to the large ring behind the pub where the devotees were watching the rites of this strange religion of the two coins. **1971** F. HARDY *Outcasts of Foolgarah* 49 Men who worked with their wits . . nit-keepers for two-up schools. **1981** M. GRANT *Inherit Sun* 183 Red knew there would be a nit-keeper, a man keeping watch who could slip out for the police if there was trouble.

Hence **nit-keeping** *vbl. n.*

1978 W. LOWENSTEIN *Weevils in Flour* 139 In Kandos I'd get a day nit-keeping for the SP bookmaker bloke now and again.

no, *a.*

1. *Obs.* Of a cheque: in the phr. **no mercy,** 'the full value is to be spent (on alcoholic drink)'.

1916 *Bulletin* (Sydney) 10 Feb. 22/2 When a drover, fencer or tank-sinker handed a cheque over the bar Pat would ask, 'Is it 'No mercy'?' 'Yes.' Then 'No mercy' would be written across the back, and Pat would take down a bugle . . and blow . . and a general rush would be made for the pub. *Ibid.* 30 Mar. 24/3 He passes his cheque which is seized in a crack, And the landlord takes pen and writes 'No Mercy' on the back.

2. Used in various conventional tags, as **no risk,** without doubt; **worries,** no bother, no trouble; also *attrib.*

1969 G. JOHNSTON *Clean Straw for Nothing* (1971) 285 Everything duty free, you know. You know, you could spend a bloody fortune. **No risk.** **1973** J. POWERS *Last of Knucklemen* (1974) 63 Anyone working in this dump is nuts. Gotta be. No risk. **1979** B. HUMPHRIES *Bazza comes into his Own*, The game was nearly up for Australia, no risk. **1967** J. HIBBERD *White with Wire Wheels* (1970) 159 'Well. How was she?' . . 'Who, Sue? **No worries.**' **1969** T.M.A. GRAHAM *Paper Men* 19 No worries. It's been a bad day. **1974** N. GILLESPIE *Into Hollow Mountains* 61, I took care of him for ya Ruby. No worries. **1978** *Westerly* ii. 11 Thanks very much. No worries, she said, making space for my gear on the seat. **1982** LOWENSTEIN & HILLS *Under Hook* 70 You'd get behind in your rent and do a moonlight flit round the corner, overnight and you'd be in another place—no worries. **1986** *Mercury* (Hobart) 25 Mar. 10/1 'No worries' reaction to Bell pullout.

Noah's Ark.

1. Rhyming slang for 'nark'.

1898 *Bulletin* (Sydney) 17 Dec. (Red Page), An informer or mar-plot is a nark or a Jonah or a Noah's Ark. **1914** E. DYSON *Spats' Fact'ry* 72 'Feathers, don't be a Noah's Ark!' 'A nark—me?' **1943** S.W. KEOUGH *Around Army* 59 'Don't be a Noah's Ark, Corp.,' will go up the cry. 'Pick on someone else, can't y'.' **1968** J. ALARD *He who shoots Last* 97 Ya knows Bill, yer gettin' to be a real Noah's Ark.

2. Rhyming slang for 'shark'. Also **Noah.**

1945 *Dit* (Melbourne) Sept. 129 'Poor blighter, what about the 'Noah's Arks'?' voices exclaimed. **1967** *Kings Cross Whisper* (Sydney) xxxvi. 4/2 *Noah's Ark*, shark. Applied also to moneylenders. **1968** D. O'GRADY *Bottle of Sandwiches* 52 Any water that's swarming with Noah's Arks is water I like to be a long way away from. . . We . . pulled in to a place where the liquid came in glasses and had no Noahs in it. **1979** B. HUMPHRIES *Bazza comes into his Own*, A lotta them beaches in Oz are full of Noahs. **1982** *Bulletin* (Sydney) 13 July 65/1 'I'll tell you what's worse than the Noahs,' said Edgar. 'What about those bloody dragon-flies?'

nob. [Spec. use of Br. slang *nob* head.] A coin having two heads, esp. in the game of two-up. Cf. GREY *n.* Also *attrib.*

1903 *Bulletin* (Sydney) 2 May 17/2 Amongst the peculiar animals evolving in Australia the bush spieler is one of the most interesting. . . His methods are still of the old order . . 'nob-ringing', and double-banking lone-hand simpletons in play. **1906** A.G. LESLEY *Rifle Sketches* 59, I might have suspected the existence of a grey or a nob, which my sons tell me are cant terms for pennies with two heads or tails. **1918** *Aussie: Austral. Soldiers' Mag.* Dec. 3/1 Snow had spun the pennies himself and that was just his way of getting out of paying up when he found that he had failed to ring in the nob. **1941** D. O'CALLAGHAN *Long Life Reminisc.* 59 There was plenty of two-up played there and a fair amount of nob and gray spinning.

nobbler. Also **nobler.** [f. *nobble, v.*, either in the sense 'to drug or lame (a horse)' or 'to strike (esp. on the head or 'nob')': see OED(S *v.* 1 and 3.] A measure of spirits; the glass in which this is served.

1842 *Sydney Herald* 19 May 2/7 A wag enquired whether Mr Tegg . . was endeavouring to escape the licensing act by an admixture of a little salt and at the same time selling 'nobblers' instead of glasses. **1843** *Melbourne Times* 29 Aug. 2/1 What is a 'nobbler'? A small glass of spirits, your Worship. **1849** *Argus* (Melbourne) 12 Nov. 4/1, I always take things in their due moderation, I never exceed thirty *noblers* a day. **1854** J. CAPPER *Aust.* 101 This especial party will not leave their 'nobblers' (which is Australian for brandy and water) till their pockets are at low ebb. **1864** *Bell's Life in Sydney* 21 May 4/4 A person who only takes this very moderate quantity of three nobblers daily, spends a sum that in twenty-five years, with interest and compound interest, amounts to £1923 15s. **1886** D.M. GANE *N.S.W. & Vic.* 51 At the bars of the hotels the customers are allowed to pour out their 'nobblers' from the general bottle. **1902** R.C. PRAED *My Austral. Girlhood* 166 He . . would take the 'nobbler' which was customary, to the edge of the verandah, and propping himself against a post would yarn about over-landing. **1926** M. FORREST *Hibiscus Heart* 145 The tall nobbler of whisky neat. **1946** J.G. EASTWOOD *More about Cairns* 61 Neilson . . could always accommodate a friend . . with a stiff nobbler of over-proof rum. **1960** D. MCLEAN *Roaring Days* 116 He poured the rum himself, as was not customary; other publicans passed over the bottle and only frowned or winced if you poured enough to show above the nobbler mark, which was purposely set a little low to allow for a shaky hand. **1971** *Walkabout* Nov. 73/1 Whisky costs around 300 rupiahs, or some 75 cents, for a generous nobbler.

nobblerize, *v.* [f. prec.] *intr.* To drink nobblers; to drink spirits generally, esp. in company with others. Freq. as *vbl. n.*

1847 *Port Phillip Gaz.* 30 June 2 He was comfortably nobblerizing in the William Tell. **1848** *Sydney Daily Advertiser* 17 Oct. 2/5 *Nobblerizing.*—The Sydney Morning Herald is all astonishment at discovering that the Port Phillip people excel the Sydney folks in their annual potations by half a gallon per head. **1857** J. D'EWES *China, Aust. & Pacific Islands* 64 This gentleman . . was sadly inoculated with the prevailing failing of the colony, 'nobblerizing'. **1868** J. BAIRD *Emigrant's Guide Australasia* 176 She discovered him *nobblerising* at the bar of the hotel at which she was quartered. **1869** 'E. HOWE' *Boy in Bush* 84 Nobody here seems to be doing anything but smoking and nobblerizing. **1885** *Australasian Printers' Keepsake* 142 As soon as 'the cut' was out we used to adjourn to Waldies . . nobblerise for a bit, and then go home with the milk in the morning. **1899** MRS A. HAY *Footprints* 107 It is said that in the early years of the colony there was a terrible habit of 'nobblerizing'.

Hence **nobblerizer** *n.*, one who drinks nobblers.

1858 R. ROWE *Peter 'Possum's Portfolio* 92 She is flirting with an early nobbleriser.

nobby, *n. Opal-mining.* See quot. 1976.

1919 *Huon Times* (Franklin) 21 Nov. 3/3 A little seam-opal is found on the field, but most of the gem occurs in 'nobbies', a species of flat, pebble-shaped stone. To test these (for colour) a small pair of pincers (termed 'snips') is used. **1931** M.S. BUCHANAN *Prospecting for Opal* 6 The hydrated silica or opal crystallised in the opal dirt either in sheets or in nobbies which are rounded drops of silica opal. **1967** R.O. CHALMERS *Austral. Rocks* 309 Almost all the precious opal is found lying in the soft clayey opal horizon as detached masses known as 'nobbies'. **1967** N. FERNANDEZ *Rockhound Walkabout* 20 A flash of blue caught my eye. . . A nobby an inch and a half across! I could hardly believe my luck. Was it a thousand pound specimen? **1975** 'N. CULOTTA' *Gone Gougin'* 56 Would any of us recognize an opal if we found one? They were called 'nobbies' .. and were coated with sandstone. **1976** STONE & BUTT *Guide Austral. Precious Opal* 108 *Nobby*, a nodule of opal coated with sandstone or opal dirt—commonly found at Lightning Ridge, N.S.W. **1979** N. & R. PERRY *Gemstones in Aust.* 71 Most of the opal is won from six to eighteen metres from the surface, and occurs as irregular shaped nodules, locally called 'nobbies'.

nobby, *a.* [Alteration of Br. dial. *knobby* lumpy, as applied to a beast: see EDD.] Of a beast: lean, and therefore having protuberant bones, joints, etc.

1860 *S. Austral. Advertiser* 2 July 4/5 One white nobby steer. **1879** 'AUSTRALIAN' *Adventures Qld.* 93 If a 'nobby' bullock slips his head out of the yoke, it is easy to bow him up a bit shorter. **1891** *Rec. Castlemaine Pioneers* 26 June (1972) 126 He set out on his journey, his equipment being a tilted cabbage-cart, to which was harnessed a nobby bullock. **1977** T. RONAN *Mighty Men on Horseback* 94 He'd eaten all the nobby cattle.

nod, *v.* In the phr. **to nod the nut** (or **head**), to plead guilty.

1950 *Austral. Police Jrnl.* Apr. 116 *Nod the nut*, plead guilty. **1967** *Kings Cross Whisper* (Sydney) xxxvi. 4/2 *Nod the nut*, plead guilty, nod the noodle up and down that you did it. **1968** J. ALARD *He who shoots Last* 140, I sez I ain't gonna nod me head ta dat. Den dey sez 'suit yerself, but we'll make it stick'. **1975** *Bulletin* (Sydney) 26 Apr. 45/1 Gulcher asked the Pig if he had pleaded guilty in court (nodding the nut, or getting your head down to it).

nodding blue lily. The tufted perennial plant *Stypandra glauca* (fam. Liliaceae) of s. and e. Aust. incl. Tas., having starry, usu. bright blue flowers on slender nodding stalks.

1914 E.E. PESCOTT *Native Flowers Vic.* 91 A fine blue lily, with bright green grassy foliage, is Stypandra glauca, or the 'nodding blue lily'. **1942** C. BARRETT *Austral. Wild Flower Bk.* 60 Among the rocks of low hills around Canberra nodding blue lilies, *Stypandra glauca*, display their star-like flowers. **1985** J. GALBRAITH *Garden in Valley* 9 In the silver-lichened granite outcrops, crevices overflowed with heath-myrtle, nodding Blue-lily and small orchids.

nog. [Transf. use of *(nig-)nog* f. *nigger.*] A Vietnamese (soldier).

1969 J.J. COE *Desperate Praise* (1982) 49 During the night the 41 ambush killed 6 nogs. **1975** W. NAGLE *Odd Angry Shot* 15 'We suspect that there are about twenty or thirty nogs dug in. . . ' 'VC or NVA?' asks Harry.

noggy. [f. *(nig-)nog* + -Y. See also NOG.] An Asian, esp. an Asian immigrant to Australia. Also *attrib.*

1954 N. BARTLETT *With Australs. in Korea* 217 This old bloke says there are about a hundred noggies [*sc.* Chinese soldiers] in the village. **1972** R. POLLARD *Cream Machine* 48 Oh these noggies, ha ha ha what a circus. **1975** *Bulletin* (Sydney) 10 May 14/2 The Australian Press has barely given a glimpse of how our rank-and-file infantrymen really felt about Vietnam and its people. . . The word 'noggy' .. that Australian Army slang word, with all its harshness and ugliness, gives a sense of how our bitter troops felt the waste of it all. **1981** C. WALLACE-CRABBE *Splinters* 56 They had led him on a fair treat with questions about Noggy women. **1982** *Canberra Times* 23 Sept. 3/3, I guess you blokes know why I am around .. looking for 'noggies' and 'dapto dogs'.

no-hoper.

a. A racehorse with no chance of winning; a rank outsider.

1943 S.J. BAKER *Pop. Dict. Austral. Slang* (ed. 3) 54 *No-hoper*, an outsider (Racing slang). **1945** T. RONAN *Strangers on Ophir* 121 Overlander was in the field; the Milderi boys willingly agreed to let Monty ride him to set a pace for Queen o' My Heart, and the other three could be classed as no hopers. **1949** L. GLASSOP *Lucky Palmer* 36 That no-hoper. . . It's a moral. They're going to .. hit it with enough dope to win a Melbourne Cup. **1957** J. WATEN *Shares in Murder* 30 I've given the mare away. She's a no-hoper . . I wouldn't put a penny on her again.

b. [Used elsewhere but recorded earliest in Aust.] An incompetent or ineffectual person; a failure. Also *attrib.*

1944 *Atebrin Advocate: Mag. 2/4 Austral. Armoured Regiment* 9 Dec. 1 Probably the greatest little bunch of No-hopers. **1954** *Bulletin* (Sydney) 25 Aug. 12/1 If a no-hoper does a rough job he dismisses any qualms with: 'She's near enough!' **1955** *Khaki Bush & Bigotry* (1968) 185 *None* of my children's going to marry a no-hoper rouseabout. **1956** *Overland* vi. 9 They think I'm a no-hoper. But I've got a house. **1959** J. CLEARY *Strike me Lucky* 228 The Town Drunk, the one we had all despised and written off as the champion no-hoper of all time, the derelict, the bum. **1977** F.B. VICKERS *Stranger no Longer* 101 You're all a lot of bloody no-hopers from what I see of you. **1982** R. HALL *Just Relations* 27 That no-hoper! . . If you turn out like him I shan't go on lettin you buy me a beer.

Hence **no-hoping** *ppl. a.*

1957 *Westerly* i. 6 Save me from a no-hoping whinger.

noisy, *a.* Used as a distinguishing epithet in the names of birds: **noisy friar bird,** the honeyeater *Philemon corniculatus* of e. mainland Aust. and New Guinea; see also FRIAR BIRD; **miner,** the honeyeater of e. Aust. *Manorina melanocephala*, a predom. grey and white bird with black face-markings; MICKEY 3; **pitta,** the bird *Pitta versicolor* of rainforest in n.e. Qld., having a loud, whistling call; ANVIL-BIRD; DRAGOON BIRD; **scrub-bird,** the ground-dwelling, predom. brown bird *Atrichornis clamosus* of s.w. W.A., having a loud, penetrating whistle and inhabiting areas of dense heathy vegetation.

1943 C. BARRETT *Austral. Animal Bk.* 292 The **noisy friar-bird** is nomadic in its habits. An amusing and pugnacious bird .. its head is ink-black and naked, and the friar-bird's long, curved bill bears a knob. **1978** B.P. MOORE *Life on Forty Acres* 96 The positively ugly Noisy Friar-bird (*Philemon corniculatus*). **1984** E. ROLLS *Celebration of Senses* 77 The raucous Noisy Friar-bird chortling 'Scratch your cock'. **1901** *Emu* I. 137 **Noisy Miner** (*Manorhina garrula*). Two of these were shot at Malkuni. **1928** G.H. WILKINS *Undiscovered Aust.* 23 The friendly soldier-birds, or noisy minahs as they are called .. flew from tree to tree. **1945** C. BARRETT *Austral. Bird Life* 160 Inquisitive, 'cheeky' and garrulous, the noisy miner .. has many nicknames. **1964** M. SHARLAND *Territory of Birds* 84 The Noisy Miner .. whose notes at dawn take on the quality of bells. **1973** V. SERVENTY *Desert Walkabout* 52 The noisy miner is well named, pugnacious and active. **1982** *Bulletin* (Sydney) 16 Mar. 11/2 Through the drought we have gained authentic Oz noisy miners. **1942** J. GOULD *Birds of Aust.* (1948) IV. Pl. 1, *Pitta strepitans* .. **Noisy Pitta.** **1908** E.J. BANFIELD *Confessions of Beachcomber* 123 Many of the birds are distinguished and named in accordance with their notes. 'Wung-go-bah' describes the noisy pitta. **1930** *Aussie* (Sydney) May 17/3 Here and there in the dense jungle under the Macpherson Range a heap of broken shells is found, with a fair-sized stone alongside. That is the work of the noisy pitta, or dragoon bird, one of the most beautiful of the scrub denizens. **1945** C. BARRETT *Austral. Bird Life* 130 The noisy pitta or 'dragoon bird' (*Pitta versicolor*), ranges from Cape York to north-eastern New South Wales. **1976** *Reader's Digest Compl. Bk. Austral. Birds* 330 The shy and beautiful noisy pitta is seldom seen. [**1844 noisy scrub-bird:** J. GOULD *Birds of Aust.* (1848) III. Pl. 34, *Atrichia clamosa*. . . Noisy Brush-bird. Few of the novelties received from Australia are more interesting than the species to which I have given the generic name of *Atrichia*.] **1891** G.J. BROINOWSKI *Birds of Aust.* V. Pl. 17, *Atrichia clamosa* .. Noisy scrub-bird. From .. the little that is known of its habits, this species will no doubt prove to be one of the most interesting of all the Australian birds. **1905** *Emu* V. 80 A search was made for that *rara avis*, the Noisy Scrub-Bird. **1933** *Bulletin* (Sydney) 1 Feb. 21/3 One of the rarest and most curious of Australian birds is the 'noisy scrub-bird' (*Atrichornis clamosus*). **1967** E. HUXLEY *Their Shining Eldorado* 204 The Noisy Scrub-bird has powerful friends and managed to secure its little bit of territory beside Two People Bay [W.A.]. **1985** *Age* (Melbourne) 9 Sept. 15/3 He somehow obtained for analysis egg whites of one of Australia's rarest birds, the noisy scrub-bird.

nolla-nolla, var. NULLA-NULLA.

nominated, *ppl. a.* In the collocation **nominated emigrant (immigrant, migrant),** one proposed as an assisted immigrant by an Australian resident (who normally meets some part of the cost and takes some responsibility for the person on arrival).

1873 A. TROLLOPE *Aust. & N.Z.* II. 138 Nominated emigrants would remain—emigrants nominated by friends in the colony. **1896** J.M. PRICE *Land of Gold* 180 The Government grant assisted passages to Western Australia to nominated immigrants, upon the payment of £7 10s. per adult by sailing vessel. **1911** *Huon Times* (Franklin) 18 Feb. 4/2 A declaration of the policy of the State Cabinet in regard to nominated immigrants was made on Monday. **1912** *Truth* (Sydney) 4 Aug. 6/5 'Nominated' immigrants have part of their passage money paid by the State of New South Wales, as do those who are 'assisted'. **1912** *Cwlth. of Aust. for Farmers* (Dept. External Affairs) 94 *Nominated Immigrants.* Residents of Queensland, having at least a six months' permanent residence therein, can pay for passages for their friends and relatives from Great Britain and Europe. **1928** PHILLIPS & WOOD *Peopling of Aust.* 98 Nominated immigrants are those nominated by persons resident in Australia, who undertake to be responsible for them on arrival so that they shall not become a burden on the State. **1949** A.A. CALWELL *Immigration* 21 The categories approved by the Premiers' Conference in order of priority were: 1. Nominated migrants who can be accommodated by their nominators and are classed as essential workers for Australian industry.

nonda /'nɒndə/. [Prob. f. a Qld. Aboriginal language.] The tree *Parinari nonda* (fam. Chrysobalanaceae) of Qld. and N.T., bearing an astringent, edible, yellow fruit; the fruit itself. Also *attrib.*

1845 L. LEICHHARDT *Jrnl. Overland Exped. Aust.* 3 July (1847) 315 A middle sized shady wide spreading tree, resembling the elm in the colour and form of its leaves, attracted our attention, and excited much interest. Its younger branches were rather drooping, its fruit was an oblong yellow plum, an inch long and half an inch in diameter, with a rather rough kernel. When ripe, the pericarp is very mealy and agreeable to eat, and would be wholesome, if it were not so extraordinarily astringent. We called this tree the 'Nonda', from its resemblance to a tree so called by the natives in the Moreton Bay district. **1849** W. CARRON *Narr. Exped. Rockingham Bay & Cape York* 55 We collected a great many nondas today and baked some of them with our bread. **1867** F.J. BYERLEY *Narr. Overland Exped. Northern Qld.* 21 The timber is .. nonda, and acacia. **1888** *Proc. Linnean Soc. N.S.W.* III. 536 *Parinarium nonda* .. The 'Nonda-tree' of N.E. Australia. The aborigines use the esculent drupes as food. When ripe they taste somewhat like a mealy potato. **1922** R.L. JACK *Northmost Aust.* II. 454 It was inferred that the blacks were wont to camp in this region during the season when the nonda fruit was ripe. **1965** *Austral. Encycl.* VI. 483 Nonda timber is yellowish, close-grained and strong, but soft enough to be worked easily.

nong. [Prob. shortened form of NING NONG.] A fool; also as quasi-*adj.* Also **nong-nong.**

1944 *RAF RAAF: Souvenir Crenferry Cruise No. 3* Feb. 9 That we were just collossal [*sic*] nong Was the theme of his daily song. **1953** S.J. BAKER *Aust. Speaks* 171 *Nong*, a simpleton or fool. **1962** *Overland* xxvi. 12 I'm not gunna stand around exchanging words with any long-haired nong. **1967** D. HEWETT *This Old Man* (1976) 17 'Ere comes the Bride, fair, fat and wide, Who's that poor nong-nong she's got by 'er side. **1970** *Coast to Coast 1967–68* 8 Reuben was a bit of a nong, everyone said so. **1978** R. MACKLIN *Newsfront* 54 'What I can't understand is how John the Baptist could eat these bloody things.' Gawd. 'A different sort of locust, you bloody nong.' **1980** K. SHORTT *Echoes of Clarence* 49 Fancy, a 'nong nong' like that having a go at me. **1986** *Bulletin* (Sydney) 18 Feb. 50/3 Rod Cavalier has, in a flash, turned himself into a ridiculous nong.

nonpareil parrot. *Eastern rosella*, see EASTERN 2.

1794 G. SHAW *Zool. New Holland* 1 *Psittacus Eximius.* The Nonpareil Parrot. . . It may indeed be doubted whether any bird can exhibit a plumage more elegant, or colours of a nobler hue. **1822** J. LATHAM *Gen. Hist. Birds* II. 138 Nonpareil Parrot. . . Inhabits New-Holland, and is a common species. **1832** J. BACKHOUSE *Narr. Visit Austral. Colonies* (1843) 30 Nonpareil Parrots .. are very troublesome in corn fields, and pick about on the roads. **1845** C. Hodgkinson *Aust., Port Macquarie to Moreton Bay* 92 The Rosella or Nonpareil parroquet, a bird extremely common throughout the colony generally. **1931** N.W. Cayley *What Bird is That?* 145 Eastern Rosella *Platycerus eximius*... Also called Rosella, Rosehill Parakeet, and Nonpareil Parrot... It spends much of its time on the ground in search of seeds of grasses, which, with wild fruits and berries, constitute its normal food.

noodle, *v.* [Of uncertain origin: perh. transf. use of Br. dial. *noodle, v.* to saunter about aimlessly, to waste time (see EDD); but see also quot. 1948.]

1. *trans.* To search (an opal-mining dump or mullock heap) for opals. Also *intr.* and as *vbl. n.* See also Louse a.

1902 *Geol. Survey No. 177* (Qld. Dept. Mines) 20 (OEDS) Some splendid opal is found.. by turning over and searching the old heaps and mullock—'noodling'. **1919** *Huon Times* (Franklin) 21 Nov. 3/3 'Now, not a word!' says Bogan. 'We'll noodle this on our 'pat' later on.' **1932** I.L. Idriess *Prospecting for Gold* 248 On a 'nobby' field, noodling is a great standby for the man who is broke. **1948** E.F. Murphy *They struck Opal* 129 Small egg-shaped opals in an open cut in a gully. A visiting geologist tabbed these 'nodules', and explained that they had originally formed inside a soft stone (like yowah nuts), which had later decomposed. The miners soon altered the name to 'noodles'—and hence the 'noodling' game. **1963** A. Lubbock *Austral. Roundabout* 79 Anyone can.. 'puddle' or 'noodle' in the gravelly tailings of the mine. **1965** K.J. Buchester *Austral. Gemhunter's Guide* 80 Most of the old heaps have been noodled for opal of all grades, even down to a low grade of 'potch with a bit of colour'. **1973** M.T. Clarke *Spark of Opal* (rev. ed.) 211 But if he overlooks some good stones in the mullock.. he can't protest if someone else finds them while 'noodling' his dump. **1975** 'N. Culotta' *Gone Gougin'* 22 Noodlin' means pickin' over the old mullock. Abos are the best at it. They've got sharp eyes. Palefaces need a bit of rain. **1978** B. St. A. Smith *Spirit beyond Psyche* 101 On this trip Bob was forced to fossick about by himself, half-heartedly noodling the dumps for opal-chips. **1983** *Overlander* June 40 The Aborigines 'noodle' or fossick the mullock heaps.. with infinite patience.

2. a. *trans.* To remove surrounding matter from (an opal). Also *transf.*

1921 K.S. Prichard *Black Opal* 68 The brushwood shelters near the mines in which the men sit at midday to eat their lunches and noodle—go over, snip, and examine—the opal they have taken out of the mines. **1976** *Bulletin* (Sydney) 20 Mar. 40/3 It takes two months for a novel to germinate with me. One fiddles with it, noodles it and then the day comes when I'm ready to go.

b. To obtain (an opal) by searching through mining refuse.

1931 M.S. Buchanan *Prospecting for Opal* 10 Dick Huggard's famous claim on Bald Hill must have produced ten thousand pounds, with what was 'noodled' or picked up from the dumps.

noodler. One who 'noodles'.

1919 *Smith's Weekly* (Sydney) 21 June 17/6 Should he see nothing, nor feel anything with his pick, he is apt to bring the dirt down in lumps—which accounts for the number of stones found on his dump by 'noodlers'. **1932** I.L. Idriess *Prospecting for Gold* 248 Thousands of pounds' worth have been recovered by noodlers. **1967** —— *Opals & Sapphires* 79 You only lose a very occasional stone or two to the noodlers. **1975** 'N. Culotta' *Gone Gougin'* 131 'I'll show them to those noodlers over there. You never know your luck.' The noodlers were two ladies and a man. **1982** *Sun-Herald* (Sydney) 31 Jan. 100/7 Thousands of noodlers will have been there before you, but the chances of digging a cuttable opal from the dumps are good provided you work at it.

nooer /'nuə/. [Repr. pronunc. of abbrev. of *manure.*] In the phr. **in the nooer,** in a difficult situation.

1970 R. Beilby *No Medals for Aphrodite* 88 How come you blokes blew the bridge so soon? .. You really dropped us in the nooer, you did. **1975** B. Foley *Shearers' Poems* 9 Two Kiwis left, their mother sick And took off for Rotorua Two Aussies occupied their pen Now the cockie was in the 'nooer'.

Noogoora burr /nəgurə 'bɜ/. Also **nagoora, ngoora, nugura burr.** [See quot. 1973.] The naturalized annual *Xanthium occidentale* (fam. Asteraceae), a proclaimed noxious weed having rough, lobed leaves and a spiny, woody burr; the burr itself, a nuisance, esp. in the wool of sheep.

1883 F.M. Bailey *Synopsis Qld. Flora* 259 *X[anthium] strumarium*.. known as 'Noogoora Burr', and supposed injurious to stock. **1898** *Western Champion* (Barcaldine) 17 May 3/2 The noogoora burr is a terrible scourge in the Laidley district. **1902** *Bulletin* (Sydney) 7 June 16/4 The Noogoora burr, a recently-introduced weed-pest in N.S.W. is spreading fast in the rich dairying districts of the north coast. **1920** J.H. Maiden *Weeds N.S.W.* 11 The Bathurst Burr (*Xanthium spinosum*), and its close relation the Noogoora Burr (*X. strumarium*) figured in the *Agricultural Gazette* for July, 1917, p. 489, and October, 1899, respectively. **1957** *Westerly* ii. 26 The grey Gulf country stretched away into the hot afternoon... I chopped viciously at an obstreperous bush of ngoora burr. **1973** W.T. Parsons *Noxious Weeds Vic.* 117 Noogoora burr.. was first discovered in Australia in the 1860s at Noogoora Station near Ipswich in Queensland, from where it has now spread to all mainland states. **1976** S. Weller *Bastards I have Met* 8 Jock was the big dark Scotchman.. and he had a burr thicker than the nagoora after a good wet season. **1978** Hanigan & Lindsay *No Tracks on River* 48, I had them nugura burrs all over me. In my hair, in my jeans, in my t-shirt. **1984** *Austral.* (Sydney) 9 May 1 Bathurst and Noogoora burr infestations.. have already overrun thousands of hectares of good pastoral country, choking out the native vegetation and ruining much valuable wool.

noongah, noongar, var. Nyoongah.

Norfolk Island. [The name of an island some 1500 kilometres n.e. of Sydney.]

1. *Hist.* Used *attrib.* in allusion to the penal settlement established on the island (1788–1814 and 1825–1856), and esp. for the detention of recalcitrant convicts.

1843 *Sydney Morning Herald* 16 May 2/5 Terry M'Guiggan, a Norfolk Island expiree, for neglecting to register his place of abode, to be confined in Sydney Gaol for fourteen days. **1848** T.L. Mitchell *Jrnl. Exped. Tropical Aust.* 417 The concentration of convicts in that island (Cockatoo) was intended, I believe, to follow out the Norfolk Island system. **1855** *Illustr. Sydney News* 7 Apr. 155/1 Having proved to be a Norfolk Island expiree he was sentenced to be worked on the roads for ten years. **1855** W. Howitt *Land, Labor & Gold* I. 158 Thieves and murderers from every quarter of the globe; Norfolk Island devils, Sydney and Van Diemen's Land convicts. **1858** N.L. Kentish *Treatise on Penal Discipline* 59 They should be *all* treated severely without the slightest distinction, like slaves, like Norfolk Island 'Lifers', without remission of labor and *without hope*. **1876** H. Parkes *Speeches* p. ix, Their fixed idea of the only political institutions suitable for the mass of their fellow-colonists was what, in one of the speeches, is caustically but truthfully described as a 'Norfolk Island Government'.

2. Special Comb. **Norfolk Island grant** *hist.*, a grant of land made to a settler removed from Norfolk Island, chiefly in Tasmania and without conditions as to use or disposal; **pine,** the tall coniferous tree *Araucaria heterophylla* (fam. Araucariaceae) of Norfolk Island, having a symmetrical, conical shape and widely planted elsewhere; also **Norfolk pine.**

1820 Tas. Colonial Secretary's Office Rec. 1/44 40, The Estate at Pitt Water consists of three separate Grants (unconditional, or what are termed **Norfolk Island Grants**). **1833** *Trumpeter* (Hobart) 10 Dec. 265 This Farm is a Norfolk Island Grant, free from all restrictions. [**1788 Norfolk Island pine:** J. White *Jrnl. Voyage N.S.W.* (1790) 212 It [*sc.* Norfolk Island] promised some advantages; particularly in furnishing us with pine trees, which grow here to a size nearly equal to those of Norway.] **1803** *HRA* (1915) 1st Ser. III. 743 An island upon which grows the Norfolk Island pine. **1804** *Ibid.* (1921) 3rd Ser. I. 620 The Mimosa.. grows here.. not unlike the Norfolk Pine in miniature. **1835** J. Backhouse *Extracts from Lett.* (1838) ii. 69 We measured a Norfolk Island pine twenty-three feet, and another twenty-seven feet in circumference. **1845** C. Hodgkinson *Aust., Port Macquarie to Moreton Bay* 25 Norfolk Island pine.. is grown as an ornamental tree in the Sydney gardens. **1853** *Illustr. Sydney News* 8 Oct. 2/3 The gorgeous and almost geometrical foliage of the Norfolk Island Pines. **1881** E. Davies *Story Earnest Life* 206 A favorite little arbor under the wide-spreading branches of a majestic Norfolk pine. **1900** *Advocate* (Burnie) 6 June 4/6 Norfolk Island Pines, 2s. 6d. ea. **1914** R. Stock *Pyjama Man* 257 The glistening white curve of Manly beach and the dark green grove of Norfolk Island pines. **1948** P.J. Hurley *Red Cedar* 14 There was a grim relic in an old ruin at Wyong.. a quaint building.. said to house convicts... On its site grew a lofty Norfolk Island pine.. called the 'Whipping Tree'. **1963** G. Taylor *Sir* 146 To the south, opposite the scraggy arms of the Norfolk pines, still stood the old building. **1979** H. Oakman *Garden & Landscape Trees Aust.* 152 Because of its ability to grow in sand and resist sea breezes, the Norfolk Island Pine has been extensively planted at coastal resorts in warm regions.

Hence **Norfolk-Islandized** *a.*

1840 D. Burn *Vindication Van Diemen's Land* 34 *Norfolk-islandised*—that is, utterly degraded and hardened in depravity.

Norfolk Islander. *Hist.* One who is, or who has been, a convict sentenced to penal servitude on Norfolk Island.

1842 *Sydney Herald* 21 Apr. 3/2 *Norfolk Islanders.* The Superintendent of Police some time since issued an order that expirees from Norfolk Island shall be visited at their residences once a week at least, by the inspectors of the parishes in which they reside. **1855** *Illustr. Sydney News* 16 June 327/3 Doubly convicted Norfolk Islanders have been, by the wicked policy of our late Governor scattered through the length and breadth of Tasmania. **1855** W. Howitt *Land, Labor & Gold* II. 23 A striking example of the character and doings of escaped Norfolk Islanders in this colony.

nork. [Of uncertain origin: see quot. 1966.] A woman's breast. Freq. in *pl.*

1962 'C. Rohan' *Delinquents* 157 Hello, honey, that sweater—one deep breath and your norks will be in my soup. **1966** S.J. Baker *Austral. Lang.* (ed. 2) 215 *Nork*, a female breast, usually in plural. (Ex Norco Co-operative Ltd., a butter manufacturer in N.S.W.). **1968** *Swag* (Sydney) iii. 41/3, I move in on those two delicious hills of wonderful flesh... Under each nork is a tattoo. **1968** J. Hibberd *Who?* (1970) 132 Marilyn Monroe has had an operation. They've gone and chopped one of her norks off. **1974** *Bulletin* (Sydney) 26 Jan. 16/2 Get big hello from Carol who is taking up a collection... Make largish donation on account of her aggressive norks. **1977** W. Moore *Just to Myself* 98 Never used to know where to stick the norks though, and they always got in the way. **1984** *Austral.* (Sydney) 18 Aug. 14 (*caption*) The minimum requirement is an 'Aw, whacko, cop the norks!' followed by at least a six decibel wolf whistle.

north. Freq. with **the.**

1. The northernmost part of Australia: the northern parts of Queensland, the Northern Territory, and Western Australia. See also Deep north. Also **northland.**

1891 *Truth* (Sydney) 5 Apr. 6/1 His tour—or 'tower', as it is usually called up North—has been a prodigious 'burst'. **1923** J. Armour *Spell of Inland* 7 They tell me that there really is such a thing as the 'Call of the North'. **1925** M. Terry *Across Unknown Aust.* 91 Up till these days, the North has been left almost unattended. **1927** A. Wright *Squatter's Secret* 41 Get back to the great Northland, where he could bury himself in the bush, and forget. **1930** V. Kennedy *By Range & River* 8 The other and oft-repeated phrase, 'Too long in the North', has its own peculiar measure of appeal. **1938** *Listening Post* (Perth) Jan. 3 At long last, something is to be done about the defence of the unguarded North. **1964** *N. Austral. Monthly* Aug. 8 North Queensland, the Northern Territory, and North-West W.A... The North has captured the imagination of the Southern public. **1979** R. Duffield *Rogue Bull* 124 The Great North would be so invaluable to the rest of the world that it would be permanently protected from predators.

2. In the collocation **Empty North,** the northernmost part of Australia as an especially sparsely populated region.

1918 G. White *Thirty Yrs. Tropical Aust.* 261 The empty North and the White Australia ideal. **1920** J.N. MacIntyre *White Aust.* 5 The empty North is so called the Never Never because they who have lived in it and loved it Never-Never voluntarily leave it. **1936** C.P. CONIGRAVE *N. Aust.* 199 The nation has . . to have the prescience to be up and doing something . . rather than merely talk about 'The Empty North' as a great resort for the sportsman. **1936** W. HATFIELD *Aust. through Windscreen* 141 Darwin is the nearest Australian port to London . . and it must be kept clearly in the forefront in all discussions of the problem of the Empty North. **1947** F. CLUNE *Roaming around Aust.* 182 The trouble is, that taxpayers 'Down South' are not interested in developing our 'Empty North'. **1957** —— *Fortune Hunters* 167 To conserve this water during the seven months of the Dry Season, from April to October, is the practical problem which has to be solved, if this part of Australia's Empty North is to be peopled.

northern, *a.* Used as a distinguishing epithet in the names of birds: **northern fantail,** the grey and white bird *Rhipidura rufiventris* of open forest in n. Aust. and elsewhere; **rosella,** the rosella *Platycercus venustus* of n.w. Aust.

1847 J. GOULD *Birds of Aust.* (1848) II. Pl. 85, *Rhipidura isura* . . **Northern Fantail**. **1945** C. BARRETT *Austral. Bird Life* 173 The northern fantail (*R. setosa*) belongs to tropical Northern Australia. **1964** M. SHARLAND *Territory of Birds* 71 The Northern Fantail . . resembles the southern White-shafted Fantail but with bolder and more pleasant patterns. **1945** C. BARRETT *Austral. Bird Life* 80 The **northern rosella** (*P[latycercus] venustus*) is found in the north-west of the state [*sc.* W.A.] and the Northern Territory. **1964** M. SHARLAND *Territory of Birds* 36 The Northern Rosella, with body tones of yellow, blue wing patches, grey-blue tail, and warm-black crown of head, is also attractive. **1975** *Bulletin* (Sydney) 22 Feb. 20/1 A pair of Northern Rosellas . . is worth at least $4000 a pair in Europe.

northerner. A non-Aboriginal inhabitant of any of the northernmost parts of Australia.

1889 F. CRAWFORD *Native Companion Songster* 16 'Neath a ragged banana a Northerner sat, A'twisting the leaf of his cabbage-tree hat. **1930** V. KENNEDY *By Range & River* 14 Farthest North as it is called in Australia, is also called the 'Garden of the Commonwealth' by visitors, and the northerner is proud of the distinction. **1964** *N. Austral. Monthly* Feb. 6 Hardened Northerners go prepared for anything.

northland: see NORTH 1.

nor'-west. Also **north-west.** The northern part of Western Australia. Also *attrib.*

1899 *Bulletin* (Sydney) 19 Aug. 32/1 Battled from the Diamantina to the 'North West Corner' without having so much as got their hands into wool during the whole dreary ten weeks. **1908** *Ibid.* 15 Oct. 14/3 He became fashionable in the blacks' camps along the Nor'-West frontier. **1914** T.C. WOLLASTON *Spirit of Child* 88 The far waters of our Nor-West—that enchanted land of pearling. **1927** M. DORNEY *Adventurous Honeymoon* 166 What they called a 'North-west Cockeye' (really a fierce dry gale) came up. **1929** K.S. PRICHARD *Coonardoo* (1961) 158 His spurs, the ends of his narrow pull-on stockman boots and his big Nor'-West hat were struck against the light behind him. **1962** C. GYE *Cockney & Crocodile* 142 South and West of that is the other large area of stations, mostly sheep and not usually quite a million acres, called the North-West.

Hence **nor'westy** *a.*, characteristic of n. Western Australia.

1977 J. DOUGHTY *Gold in Blood* 158 Here . . the country began to turn definitely Nor-westy. The dirty looking greyness of the south was gone.

nor'-wester. A non-Aboriginal inhabitant of n.w. Australia. Also *attrib.*

1900 *Truth* (Sydney) 28 Jan. 3/5 The beauty of these names is singularly indicative of the poetic temperament of the Nor'Wester. **1937** R. FAIRBRIDGE *Pinjarra* 211 Unfortunately this experienced Nor'-Wester had never before been into the south-west of Western Australia, and the whole aspect of the country was strange to him. **1940** E. HILL *Great Austral. Loneliness* (ed. 2) 90 In far North-west Australia . . the *Koolinda* is the State Government's mail steamer, that hurries up and down 5,000 miles of coastline twelve times a year, the Nor'-wester's lifelong friend. **1954** N. BARTLETT *Pearl Seekers* 167 In Perth, Gribble devoted himself to exposing the attitude of the nor'-westers towards the natives. **1965** L. WALKER *Other Girl* 10 Four men's faces stared out from under dusty nor'-wester ten-bale hats. **1984** W.W. AMMON et al. *Working Lives* 134 Nor'westers don't say a great deal—they act more than they talk.

nose. In the phr. **on the nose,** distasteful, offensive; smelly.

1941 S.J. BAKER *Pop. Dict. Austral. Slang* 49 *Nose, on the*, (said of things) disliked, offensive. **1942** *Wog Jrnl.: Mag. Headquarters 3rd Austral. Infantry Brigade* 25 Dec. 1 *On the nose*, anything that does not meet with general approval. **1957** D. WHITINGTON *Treasure upon Earth* 34 This sentimental mushy business is on the nose. **1968** G. DUTTON *Andy* 308, I don't want no dead shiela as my responsibility. I tell yer, it's on the nose. **1971** B. HUMPHRIES *Bazza pulls it off*, Excuse I not shakin' hands sport but me *mits* are pretty much on the nose. **1974** *Austral.* (Sydney) 12 Dec. 13/4 She renounced her Australian citizenship and swore everlasting loyalty to the Stars and the Stripes. A bit on the nose, we think. **1982** *Bulletin* (Sydney) 5 Jan. 25/1 The swing against us in Bass was about 17 percent. . . We were on the nose, electorally speaking.

nose-bag. [Transf. use of *nose-bag* a horse's feeding-bag.]

1. A bag in which a swagman carries provisions.

1894 *Bulletin* (Sydney) 12 May 2/1 The 'nose-bags' heavy on each chest (God bless one kindly squatter!). **1900** H. LAWSON *Verses Pop. & Humorous* 243 The nose-bag getting cruel light, The traveller getting silly. **1908** C.H.S. MATTHEWS *Parson in Austral. Bush* 155 In addition to his swag, the swagman carries . . a 'nose-bag', or 'tucker-bag', containing such bread, meat, tea, and sugar, as the owner is lucky enough to possess. **1927** A. WRIGHT *Squatter's Secret* 123 He was attired in the orthodox swagman outfit, with swag, billy and nosebag complete.

2. *fig.* A meal; in the phr. **to put on the nose bag,** to have a meal.

1919 C. DREW *Doings of Dave* 28 What's wrong with us putting on our nose-bags? I ain't had a feed all day. **1962** J. DALTON *Walk back with Me* 65 'Got any tucker out there, Pop?' Dasher asked. 'It's about nosebag time for me.' **1966** D. NILAND *Pairs & Loners* 144 'Well,' Goldie said. 'Time to put the nosebag on.' **1968** D. O'GRADY *Bottle of Sandwiches* 66 After the third beer . . Bill's shout . . the first carpenter said, 'Better put the nosebag on.'

nosey bob. [The nickname of R.R. Howard (*c* 1836–1906), public executioner in N.S.W. (*c* 1874–1904), so-called because of a facial disfigurement.] A hangman; an inquisitive person, a 'nosey parker'.

1892 *Truth* (Sydney) 1 May 4/7 He would not risk his own carcase, or do anything likely to put his neck in Nosey Bob's noose. **1909** *Ibid.* 2 May 10/3 Spite of galloes [*sic*], cat o' nine tails, Spite of 40 Nosey Bobs—Why we constantly do see 'em Run in by the Johnny Hobbs. **1930** *Listening Post* (Perth) 24 Jan. 23, I suggest that space be devoted to the 'nosey bobs'.

note. [Spec. use of *note* a bank-note.] A one-pound note; the sum of one pound.

1863 *Frank Gardiner, or Bushranging in 1863* 10 If I had known that the boot was only fifteen notes and a ticker, I wouldn't have started on such a wet night. **1872** M. CLARKE *His Natural Life* 616 Good sort of moke. . . Worth about forty notes. **1888** A.P. MARTIN *Oak-Bough & Wattle-Blossom* 106 We each invested a pound—or, as Paget called it, a 'note'—on her ladyship at six to one. **1899** G.E. BOXALL *Story Austral. Bushrangers* 191 The wideawake traveller could understand that 'Jack the Kid' was the man who planted his horses, and would not return them for less than 'a note', that is £1. **1956** J.T. LANG *I Remember* 115 When he was not in Macquarie Street, he was operating at Randwick. He became a 'big note' man. At one stage he was a book-maker's agent, laying-off bets for one of the leviathans of the day. At other times, he acted as a betting commissioner, placing bets for wealthy patrons. **1963** B. BEAVER *Hot Summer* 14 He'd had more than half their luck already and was still little more than half their age. Nineteen and a chainman drawing thirty-five notes clear a fortnight. **1978** K. GILBERT *People are Legends* 11 I'll sell me moot for half a note And a bottle of wine.

Novocastrian. [Transf. use of *Novocastrian* a native or inhabitant of Newcastle upon Tyne.] A non-Aboriginal native or resident of Newcastle, N.S.W.

1902 *Newcastle Morning Herald* 8 Nov. 7/7 (*heading*) Novocastrians on tour. **1929** *Souvenir Civic Week* (Newcastle City Council), Novocastrians use the term 'The Hill' when referring to that portion of the city lying above King Street. **1948** P.J. HURLEY *Red Cedar* 50, I asked a native-born Novocastrian whether he could say that the causeway to Nobby's Island was built by convicts. **1976** *Bulletin* (Sydney) 11 Sept. 18/3 Novocastrians inundated their newspaper editor with their vociferous protests. **1977** *Sea Notes* Dec. 17/1 Newcastle people, or Novocastrians as they label themselves. **1986** *Sydney Morning Herald* 12 Apr. 11/4, 30,000 Novocastrians crowded on to the main beach.

nuddy /'nʌdi/. Also **nudee.** [f. *nud(e* + *d* + -Y. Used elsewhere but recorded earliest in Aust.] In the phr. **in the nuddy,** in the nude, naked.

1953 *Bulletin* (Sydney) 11 Nov. 12/2 The young matron of the 'blacksoil country' whom the artist depicted in the nuddie killing a snake . . did a good job. **1959** D. HEWETT *Bobbin Up* 139 The sheet slipped down and bared her little pendulous breasts. 'What are you lyin' there in the nuddy for?' **1966** H. PORTER *Paper Chase* 127 That we euphemistically say 'swimming in the nud-ee' indicates our respectability, our tender consciences. **1972** L. IRISH *Time of Dolphins* 127 She bakes, in the nuddy down on the rocks. **1976** S. WELLER *Bastards I have Met* 87 Quick—ring her back—she's in the nuddy—give her a scare. **1980** E. METCALFE *Garden Party* 43 The day I can slip into something of Eleanor's, I'll paint myself bright green all over and walk down the Mall in the nuddy! **1985** B. ROSSER *Dreamtime Nightmares* 132 We either wore them or walked around in the nuddy.

nudge. [Fig. use of *nudge* a slight push.] Esp. in the phr. **to give it (a bit of) a nudge,** to drink (alcoholic liquor) to excess; to over-indulge. Also *transf.*, and as *v. trans.* and *intr.*

[**1959** H. DRAKE-BROCKMAN *West Coast Stories* 139 Last time I saw Wheelbarrow he had been drinking heavy—the bombo again. 'Just to nudge me liver,' he says.] **1966** S.J. BAKER *Austral. Lang.* (ed. 2) 178 *Nudge*, used in reference to drinking, e.g. *give it a nudge, nudge it*, to drink alcoholic liquor. **1977** H. GARNER *Monkey Grip* 15 Today I gave the junk a nudge. **1978** R. MACKLIN *Newsfront* 51 Gave it a bit of a nudge last night, did you? **1979** B. HUMPHRIES *Bazza comes into his Own*, 'I'm on my way to your country for a conference on alcoholism and drug dependency.' 'G'day Doc. You'd have to be the world expert. . . Did you ever nudge the turps!!' **1984** P. JARRATT *Aussie* 21 The high-powered executives of his company all repair to the boardroom on Friday afternoons where they give the chairman's scotch an almighty nudge and sort out the problems of the week's business.

nugget, *n.* [Br. dial. *nugget* a lump of anything; a short, thickset person or animal: see EDD. Used elsewhere in senses 1 a. and b. but recorded earliest in Aust.]

1. a. A lump of native gold. Also *attrib.*

1851 J.H. BURTON *Emigrant's Man.* ii. 116 Small lumps, called 'nuggets', are . . discovered in a remarkably pure state. **1852** F. LANCELOTT *Aust. as it Is* I. 299 Lumps (or, as they are locally termed, nuggets) were found weighing from 1 oz. to 4 lbs. each. **1857** W. HOWITT *Tallangetta* I. 156 Huge nuggets lay about like boulder-stones. **1865** J.F. MORTLOCK *Experiences of Convict* 115, I beg to suggest that the much sought for derivation of the word 'nugget' is the Hindostanee term 'nagut', signifying 'hard cash', or bullion. **1876** J.A. EDWARDS *Gilbert Gogger* 184 There is a cave all full of nuggets of gold lying about the floor, just like English potatoes; I reckon the author has never seen a diggings. **1889** F. CRAWFORD *Native Companion Songster* 7 Says she 'my husband and myself Know of a tidy nugget, It's quite as much as we can do About the place to lug it'. **1941** D. O'CALLAGHAN *Long Life Reminisc.* 5 The prospector's 'nugget-kickers' led out into the shimmering and pitiless Never Never.

b. *transf.* Someone or something precious.

1853 MOSSMAN & BANISTER *Aust. Visited & Revisited* 191 She was delirious with joy, as she clasped Browne in her arms, and called him her 'nugget'. **1869** MRS W.M.

HOWELL *Diggings & Bush* 20 What I'd like would be just to get a girl for my wife, such as I saw this very day, with these very eyes, for by Jove she *was* a nugget. **1887** A. NICOLS *Wild Life & Adventure* 372 It's only a small place, you see, Bertram (under two hundred square miles), but a real 'nugget'. **1897** *Bulletin* (Sydney) 19 June 28/1 He's mastered a method of 'turning' That never was taught in a school. His manners are rugged and vulgar, But he's nuggets of gold in our need.

2. A small stocky animal or person; also, a runt. Hence freq. as a nickname for a small person.

1852 G.C. MUNDY *Our Antipodes* III. 322 The word nugget among farmers signifies a small compact beast—a runt; among gold miners a lump, in contra-distinction to the scale or dust gold. **1906** *Truth* (Sydney) 18 Nov. 9/3 Jimmy Tonner and Charley White are *a pair of nuggets* about 5 ft. 3 in. with corporations in comparison. **1919** W.H. DOWNING *Digger Dialects* 36 *Nugget*, a short soldier. **1941** S.J. BAKER *Pop. Dict. Austral. Slang* 50 *Nugget*, a small, weedy horse or other animal . . a small stocky man. **1944** *Barging About: Organ 43 Austral. Landing Craft Co.* Nov. 11 A measly little sawn-off runt who's known as 'Nugget' Kean. **1955** N. PULLIAM *I traveled Lonely Land* 383 *Nugget*, a no-good horse. **1971** *Sydney Morning Herald* 28 Oct. 7/1 Widely known as 'Nugget' because of his short, stocky build . . he [*sc.* H.G. Coombs] was one of a number of young intellectuals recruited during World War II to work in Canberra.

3. An unbranded calf.

1872 G.S. BADEN-POWELL *New Homes for Old Country* 182 Fresh-born calves as yet unbranded . . go by the name of 'nuggets'. **1892** B. MORANT *Poetry* (1980) 4 And never the 'nugget' was calved that could break Michael's whips. **1902** E.B. KENNEDY *Black Police Qld.* 66, I made up my mind to try a spec., so from Grafton I did wander, And brought a mob of nuggets there to begin as an overlander. **1920** J.N. MACINTYRE *White Aust.* 183, I considered it only right to indulge in my fancies and never missed a 'nugget' (that is a big unbranded calf). **1943** H.G. LAMOND *From Tariaro to Ross Roy* 46 There were . . quite a number of big clean-skins on camp. One estimate put those nuggets at about 800. **1976** J.H. TRAVERS *Bull Dust on Brigalow* 23 We saw quite a few cattle and plenty of nuggets (unbranded cattle).

nugget, *v. Obs.* [f. prec.]

1. *trans.* To search for and prise out from surrounding material (gold in nuggets); also *intr.*, to search for and obtain nuggets of gold. Also with **out,** and as *vbl. n.*

1851 *Empire* (Sydney) 22 Aug. 75/5 One old man, while nuggetting on the hills was fortunate enough to turn out a piece of gold weighing thirteen ounces. **1852** R.A.T.G.C. SALISBURY *Lord Robert Cecil's Gold Fields Diary* 30 Mar. (1945) 24 He . . was snugly 'nuggetting' (picking out nuggets with a penknife or oyster-knife). **1854** *Illustr. Sydney News* 28 Feb. 163/3 The party picked out with their knives alone, nuggets amounting to four hundred and sixty pounds weight. A second party nuggetted out upwards of two hundred pounds weight. **1857** F. DE B. COOPER *Wild Adventures* 103 Nuggetted from the surface-rocks three ounces of the pure metal. **1861** *Bell's Life in Sydney* 16 Nov. 2/3 Nuggetted some fine pieces. **1871** *Austral. Town & Country Jrnl.* (Sydney) 28 Jan. 113/3 The Bishop Brothers obtained a prospect of 22 oz. of gold nuggeted out. **1874** S.W. SILVER *Handbk. Aust. & N.Z.* 148 Nuggeting is a pleasant and profitable occupation. **1881** G.C. EVANS *Stories* 129 My mate and I sunk a hole about 10 feet deep, and nuggeted two ounces off the bottom.

2. *trans.* To steal (unbranded calves). Also *intr.* and freq. as *vbl. n.*

1881 MRS C. PRAED *Policy & Passion* I. 52 My lady breaks in the horses and takes care that the calves are branded. It is said that she has an eye to business, and does not disdain nuggeting. [*Note*] To *nugget*: in Australian slang, to appropriate your neighbours' unbranded calves. **1885** —— *Head Station* III. 100 Nobody would go there except after calves to nugget. **1886** F. COWAN *Aust.* 32 *Nuggeting*, calf stealing. **1905** *Bulletin* (Sydney) 13 Apr. 18/1 They go 'nuggeting', *i.e.*, 'scrub-running' for clean-skins.

nuggetty, *a.* Also **nuggety.** [f. NUGGET *n.* + -Y.]

1. a. Of gold: occurring as nuggets.

1852 F. LANCELOTT *Aust. as it Is* II. 2 The gold is nuggetty, and often found in the schist rocks. **1855** *Ovens & Murray Advertiser* (Beechworth) 24 Feb. 5/3 The gold is of the description usually known as 'nuggetty'. **1862** J.A. PATTERSON *Gold Fields Vic.* 175 The gold . . is coarse, nuggetty, and very bright. **1872** 'QUIRIS' *Port Darwin* 10 Holes Nos. 4 and 8 . . will . . prove payable, considering we obtained half an ounce to two ounces to the load, all rough nuggetty gold. **1889** J.H.L. ZILLMANN *Past & Present Austral. Life* 242 That's gold, rough gold, too—the right sort, nuggetty. **1935** *Vic.: Gold & Minerals* (Vic. Dept. Mines) 26 Nuggety patches of gold were obtained from the quartz veins cutting the Indicators. **1984** I.A. MUMME *Gold Fossicking Aust.* 11 Of the many methods that are now being used to recover gold only a handful merit description as far as the fossicker and the small miner are concerned. These are: locating or chasing nuggetty gold with metal detectors [etc.].

b. Rich in nuggets.

1853 *Austral. Gold Digger's Monthly Mag.* v. 192 Nuggetty Gully has turned out fine golden boulders. **1888** W. EVANS *Diary Welsh Swagman* (1975) 169, I attended her funeral at the nuggetty cemetery. **1931** W. BARAGWANATH et al. *Guide for Prospectors in Vic.* 33 Every nuggetty patch is followed by poor stone or by a blank, but a little fine gold is generally found in the 'floor' or cross vein between the richer portions. **1932** I.L. IDRIESS *Prospecting for Gold* 171 Numbers of mining fields have their 'Nuggetty Gullies'. Perhaps a field has twenty payable gullies and yet only one Nuggetty Gully. **1980** R. SHEARS *Gold* 17, I went out at weekends to areas in Gippsland because my research had shown me there were nuggety gullies there.

2. a. Of a person: compactly built; stocky; tough.

1856 W.W. DOBIE *Recoll. Visit Port-Phillip* 40, I was nuggety-looking, not enough of the digger, bushman, or old leg [*sic*] about me to command the respect of the public. **1879** 'AUSTRALIAN' *Adventures Qld.* 37 'How many niggers did you wipe out, Ford?' 'Let me see—that big fellow behind the tree where the watchman was. That little nuggetty fellow up the tree . . four, all told.' **1900** H. LAWSON *Over Sliprails* 165 Jimmy Nowlett was a nuggety little fellow, hard as cast iron. **1908** *Truth* (Sydney) 11 Oct. 11/5 A nuggety lump of a young fellow, John W. Hoad, a brick carter. **1930** V. PALMER *Passage* (1957) 245 A nuggetty little fossicker. **1942** G.S. CASEY *It's Harder for Girls* 22 He was a nuggety little chap, and he looked a bit dangerous. **1965** H. PORTER *Cats of Venice* 182 She was short, stocky-short—nuggety. **1974** *Southerly* ii. 170 He was the type . . who became more and more unwholesomely noticeable; too nuggety, his hair too grizzled.

b. Of an animal: stocky; small but sturdy.

1893 *Pall Mall Gaz.* (London) 28 Jan. 3/1 The light spring waggon drawn by a pair of sleek, nuggetty cobs. **1899** *Austral. Tit-Bits* (Sydney) 8 Apr. 143/1 'Toby', who was a 'nuggety' bay . . was in Mr Tonkin's service for over sixteen years. **1927** 'S. RUDD' *Romance of Runnibede* 39 The nuggetty grey shook his head violently and cow-kicked under the shaft at his tormentor. **1931** *Bulletin* (Sydney) 29 July 21/3 To hand-throw 300 nuggety calves before breakfast might be considered a good morning's work. **1940** I.L. IDRIESS *Lightning Ridge* 126 All the horses were nuggety little grey ponies.

nugura burr, var. NOOGOORA BURR.

nulla /ˈnʌlə/. Also **nullah.** Shortened form of NULLA-NULLA. Also *attrib.*

1878 R.B. SMYTH *Aborigines of Vic.* I. 85 He saw the gins carrying spears and shields on the march, the men carrying only a nulla or two. **1891** W.H. THOMES *Belle of Aust.* 62 Old Kebblewhite will bang you over the head with a native's *nulla*, and crack your skull. **1912** J.H.L. ZILLMAN *Austral. Poetry* 12 The crash on shield by nullah thrust. **1929** R.D. LANE *Romance Old Coolgardie* 8 Before them lies their neighbour . . with his head bashed in with a black man's nulla (stick). **1935** G. MCIVER *Drover's Odyssey* 12 They . . used wooden nullas or clubs. **1963** I.L. IDRIESS *Our Living Stone Age* 204 This old wretch will get his skull cracked by a waddy—an ironwood nullah, hard and heavy. **1976** C.D. MILLS *Hobble Chains & Greenhide* 22 The boy had hit her with a nullah as she went to get a coolamon of water.

nulla-nulla /ˈnʌlə-nʌlə/. Formerly also with much variety, as **nilla-nilla, nolla-nolla, nullah-nullah.** [a. Dharuk *ŋala ŋala.*] An Aboriginal war club: see quot. 1808.

c **1790** W. DAWES Grammatical Forms Lang. N.S.W., *Gnallangulla* . . a particular club. **1798** D. COLLINS *Acct. Eng. Colony N.S.W.* I. 585 Of clubs they use several sorts. . . They have one, the head of which is flat, with a sharp point in the centre. The flat part is painted with red and white stripes from the centre, and does not look unlike what they term it, Gnal-lung-ul-la, the name given by them to a mushroom. **1808** *Sydney Gaz.* 6 Nov., A perhaps deadly stroke with a *nulla-nulla*. . . [*Note*] This weapon is formed by affixing to the end of a club a circular piece of a very hard wood, 8 or 10 inches in diameter, with a sharp edge, and of a mushroom form. It is frequently carried as a weapon of defence, but the natives seldom exercise it against each other. **1818** J. HOLT *Mem.* (1838) II. 163 They . . take a weapon called a *Nulanula*, which is a kind of battleaxe made of very hard wood. **1833** W.H. BRETON *Excursions* 239 The waddies . . and nullah-nullahs, are clubs. **1849** A. HARRIS *Emigrant Family* (1967) 130 Probably . . the nullah-nullah is of mace or axe form; whilst the waddie is strictly a staff. **1867** A.K. COLLINS *Waddy Mundoee* 22 Plunge your hands into their heart's blood, and scatter their brains abroad with your nulla nullahs. **1885** MRS C. PRAED *Austral. Life* 9 The Blacks crept stealthily down the chimney and battered in his skull with a *nulla-nulla* while he slept. **1895** A.C. BICKNELL *Travel & Adventure Northern Qld.* 44 A weapon the native usually carries is the 'nolla-nolla', or club. **1903** J. FURPHY *Such is Life* 241 A sharp jerk, and the whipstick would snap, supplying a nilla-nilla which would make him an over-match for a dozen Folkestones in rotation. **1924** A.B. PEIRCE *Knocking About* 35 The beating was done with nully-nullys, short sticks with knobs at the end. **1930** HIVES & LUMLEY *Jrnl. of Jackaroo* 75 The man would be carrying a couple of spears, a nullah-nullah, and the indispensable tomahawk. **1934** P. WIRTH *Life* 26 Our black friends provided each of us with a nulla nulla to use in killing the fish. **1949** H.E. THONEMANN *Tell White Man* 64 We women are taught to use nulla nullas . . like the men. **1955** D. CLARK *Boomer* 48 In one hand he held two long spears, in the other a nolla-nolla—a short, heavy club. **1963** V.B. CRANLEY *27,000 Miles through Aust.* 45 Here is the Nulla-Nulla as a souvenir. . . We were handed a thick, black, round stick, weighing about fifteen pounds made of iron-hard wood . . a fearsome weapon used in close-in fighting. **1980** *Canberra Times* 22 July 8/4 The shooting came after an attack on a two-man police patrol by eight men wielding *nulla nullas* (clubs).

Hence as *v. trans.*, to strike (a person) with a nulla-nulla.

1849 A. HARRIS *Emigrant Family* (1967) 239 Three fellows I nullah-nullahed on their way home. **1940** E. HILL *Great Austral. Loneliness* (ed. 2) 306 He and his gang had nulla-nulla-ed a camp of seven. **1986** *Sydney Morning Herald* 9 Aug. 41/3 A man in the hire-car office sneered: 'The boongs will probably throw spears at Peter Garrett's bald head, and nulla-nulla the drummer. Most of them have never heard of Midnight Oil. They like Country and Western music.'

Nullarbor doctor: see DOCTOR *n.*[3]

numbat /ˈnʌmbæt/. [a. Nyungar *numbat.*] The small, termite-eating marsupial *Myrmecobius fasciatus*, now occurring only in s.w. W.A., having red to grey-brown fur with light stripes across the back and rump; ANTEATER 2.

1923 F.W. JONES *Mammals S.A.* i. 123 Banded Ant-eater. Marsupial Ant-eater. White-banded Bandicoot. *Myrmecobius fasciatus*. . . These names are all merely book designations, for the animal appears never to have been sufficiently common or conspicuous to have earned a popular or familiar name. To the aboriginals, however, it is known as the Numbat, and this name will be adopted here. **1952** B. BEATTY *Unique to Aust.* 36 The beautiful numbat, sometimes called the banded ant-eater . . lives on termites and is a good climber. **1955** *Bulletin* (Sydney) 28 Dec. 12/4 The numbat (or banded-anteater) is on the way out, fast, and is only found now around Kojonup in sou'-Westralia. **1975** W. HOWCROFT *Old Working Hat* 45 The Numbat roams the desert waste In search of tit-bits to his taste. **1984** *Age* (Melbourne) 10 Apr. 28/7 The numbat—an attractive marsupial anteater the size of a large rat.

number. [From the practice of declaring the result of a horse-race by posting the numbers of the winners.] In the phr. **the numbers are** (or **go**) **up,** and varr., the result is known.

1890 'TASMA' *In her Earliest Youth* III. 228 'And then

your children, a growing family, you know, you have *two* already,' suggested the agent blandly. 'Yes, we've got two,' said George meditatively; 'and as for the family, it's the same as with everything else—you never can tell till the numbers are up.' **1920** F.A. RUSSELL *Ashes of Achievement* 199 He thinks the chances are in favour... And my guess is as good as his, before the numbers go up. **1969** M. CALTHORPE *Defectors* 181 You can expect a few sharp counter moves... You'll be hard at it until the numbers go up. **1982** J. ANDERSON *Winners can Laugh* 123 The numbers were up and that's what the bookies pay on.

nun. [Spec. use of *nun* a name applied to any of various birds.] *White-fronted chat*, see WHITE *a.*² 1 b.

1918 *Bulletin* (Sydney) 14 Feb. (Red Page), *White-fronted Bush-Chat* (Tang, Nun, Tintac) and other members of the genus *Epthianura.* **1942** E. ANDERSON *Squatter's Luck* 28 'Nun', the white-throated chat. **1965** *Austral. Encycl.* II. 334 The white-fronted chat.. known by a number of local names, the commonest of which are 'nun' (from the white head of the male) and 'tang', an imitation of the note.

nunga, var. NYOONGAH.

nunger. Usu. in *pl.* [Of unknown origin.] A woman's breast.

1966 G. WYATT *Strip Jack Naked* 54 'I see she's got the raffle books stuck down the front of her dress.' 'That's not raffle books,' Evan said. 'That's her. She was born with paper nungers.' **1967** J. HIBBERD *White with Wire Wheels* (1970) 161 I'll never forget those nungers, and their red jelly-bean nipples.

nut-brown. *Obs.* A name applied to a convict. Also **nut-brown face.**

1834 *Sydney Herald* 20 Oct. 2/4 It is a common saying 'spare the rod and you spoil the child'; this nursery proverb is fully verified in the spoiled *innocents* of the Government gangs, y'clept by Humanitas the 'Nut-brown faces'. **1835** *Sydney Times* 13 Jan. 3/1 The learned Editors seem to think that from this authentic account of the 'convict system', the 'nut browns' have not such a pleasant time of it. **1840** *Sydney Herald* 17 Feb. 2/2 Captain Maconochie has applied to the Government to be allowed a band of musicians to accompany him to Norfolk Island to entertain the gentlemen 'nutbrowns' there.

nutmeg. [Transf. use of *nutmeg* the tree *Myristica fragrans.*]

1. Either of two trees, *Myristica muelleri* and *M. insipida* (fam. Myristicaceae), occurring in n.e. Qld. and n. N.T.; the fruit of these trees; *wild nutmeg*, see WILD 1.

1814 M. FLINDERS *Voyage Terra Australis* II. 188 We found upon Chasm Island.. many large bushes covered with nutmegs... It is the *Myristica insipida* of Brown's *Prodrom. Nov. Holl.* p. 400. **1825** B. FIELD *Geogr. Mem. N.S.W.* 291 Two species of nutmeg were found, but they are not fit for use. **1845** *Sydney Morning Herald* 15 Oct. 2/2 The indigenous plants of importance otherwise than as producing timber of various kinds are a true nutmeg (*Myristica lancifolia*) [etc.]. **1886** F.A. HAGENAUER *Rep. Aboriginal Mission Ramahyuck Vic.* 47, I collected many kinds of seeds, from the three feet long Moreton Bay bean to the fragrant nutmeg. **1908** E.J. BANFIELD *Confessions of Beachcomber* 118 All sorts of nuts and seeds, and even fruits are consumed—quandongs, various palm seeds.. nutmeg (*Myristica insipida*, not the nutmeg of commerce, though resembling it). **1983** MORLEY & TOELKEN *Flowering Plants Aust.* 36 The native nutmeg, *Myristica insipida*, has been used as a nutmeg substitute, and its wood used to make Aboriginal canoe paddles and spear-throwers.

2. Special Comb. **nutmeg pigeon,** TORRES STRAIT PIGEON.

[**1841** G. GREY *Jrnls. Two Exped. N.-W. & W.A.* I. 94 The large white pigeons, which feed on the wild nutmegs, cooed loudly to their mates.] **1901** *Emu* I. 130 The Nutmeg Pigeon (*Myristicivora spilorrhoa*).. build substantial nests. **1936** T.C. ROUGHLEY *Wonders Great Barrier Reef* 208 The Torres Strait pigeon, also called the nutmeg pigeon because of its partiality for the fruit of the wild nutmeg. **1945** *Bulletin* (Sydney) 10 Jan. 13/4 Black-and-white nutmeg pigeons were plentiful. ***c* 1960** C. MACKNESS *Clump Point & District* 4 Nutmeg pigeons were then very numerous... They could be pulled off their nests with the bare hands at dusk.

nut tree. [Spec. use of *nut-tree* a tree that bears nuts, esp. the hazel.] A nut-bearing tree, any of several species, perh. incl. NUTWOOD and QUANDONG 1 a.

1834 *Perth Gaz.* 10 May 283/2 In the neighbourhood of York we found the nut tree in flower: it belongs to the same class and order, and agrees in the form of the seed with the sandal wood of India; but the seeds of our plant are about four times as large: they contain a large portion of pure, tasteless oil, and burn with a clear light. **1837** H.W. BUNBURY *Early Days W.A.* (1930) 47 The Nut tree.. is a species of Sandalwood with a very sweet scent. **1864** E.A. OPPEN *Descr. N.T.* 32 The nut trees, a species of *terminalia*, or perhaps, *achras*, are very plentiful near here. **1885** *S.A. Parl. Papers* III. no. 53 2 The only timber being nut tree, similar to the quondong. **1986** K. BRENNAN *Wildflowers of Kakadu* 57 Nut Tree *Terminalia grandiflora*... This tall, slender, narrow-leafed tree is partly deciduous in the Dry Season.

nutwood. The tree *Terminalia arostrata* (fam. Combretaceae), of N.T. and the n.e. Kimberley region (W.A.), the fruit of which has an edible kernel.

1915 *Bull. N.T.* xiv. 7 Then more volcanic downs with bauhinia and nutwood for about six miles. **1931** M. TERRY *Hidden Wealth* 326 At Flora Valley there was.. nutwood, two hakeas and acacia stenophylla. **1964** *N. Austral. Monthly* Nov. 5 We came on Bauhinia arostrata, the Nutwood again. This decorative little tree with its pendant foliage and edible nuts followed us for hundreds of miles. **1983** R.J. PETHERAM *Plants Kimberley Region W.A.* 517 *Terminalia arostrata* Nutwood, Crocodile Tree... A small tree, 4 to 10 m. high, with willow-like drooping branches.

nyoongah /ˈnjʊŋə/. Also **noongah, noongar, nunga.** [a. Nyungar *nyungar* an Aboriginal, man.] A person of Aboriginal, or part-Aboriginal, descent. Also *attrib.*

1845 E.J. EYRE *Jrnls. Exped. Central Aust.* II. 396 Men or people... Yoon-gar. **1954** *Coast to Coast 1953–54* 105 N-Yoongars not black. Most all us N-Yoongars brown. **1961** *Polynesian Soc. Jrnl.* (Wellington, N.Z.) June 202 Adelaide people.. use.. different native words to refer to aborigines... Point Pearce people say *Nunga.* **1969** L. HADOW *Full Cycle* 157 Jimmy Dabchick turned a cartwheel. 'Us all N-Yoongars' [*Note*] Aborigine of south-west Australia. **1975** R. BEILBY *Brown Land Crying* 3 You're as much coloured as white, as much Noong-ah as wadjullah. **1977** K. GILBERT *Living Black* 88 The most effective means of communication.. we call.. the 'noongar grapevine'... It used a sort of communication that can only be understood by Aborigines and it's highly functional. **1980** D. MILERA *Walkabout to Nowhere* 30 The Aboriginal comes from a different environment altogether. There are city nungas, country nungas and outback bush nungas. **1981** A. WELLER *Day of Dog* 58 Every nyoongah gets itchy feet and feels restless, like a cat or a moonstruck dog, sooner or later. **1984** *A.N.U. Reporter* (Canberra) 27 Apr. 3 Archie describes himself as an 'octoroon', being one-eighth Aborigine. But in conversation he uses the Aboriginal word 'Nyoongah', meaning 'people' or 'man', when referring to his mates and himself. **1984** B. DIXON *In Search of Aboriginal Lang.* 74 Nyungas still funny here. All on the nulung you know and still acting the goat. Aboriginal people still behaving badly here.

N.Z., var. ENZED.

O

o-, *suffix.* [Prob. infl. by the use of the *-o* suffix as a final syllable in street cries such as 'milk-o' (see MILKO 1) and in other calls such as RUSH-OH, 'smoke-o' (see SMOKO 1 a., quot. 1872), SPELL-OH; similarly attached to personal names, as 'John-o', and so widespread as elsewhere in informal English, esp. as a mark of familiarity.] Added as a final syllable to **(a)** shortened forms, as **carpo** [f. *car(pet snake)*], **cemo** [f. *cem(etery)*], **delo** [f. *del(egate)*], **euco** [f. *euc(alyptus)*], **evo** [f. *ev(ening)*], **fiftho** [f. *fifth (columnist)*], **houso** [f. *hous(ekeeping)*], **Jappo** [f. *Jap(anese)*]; **(b)** monosyllabic forms, as **Greeko, juggo, kicko, maddo.** See separate entries for the following settled forms: ARVO, BIZZO, BOMBO, BOTTLE-OH, BRONZO, BULLO, COMBO, COMPO, DEMO, DERRO, GALVO, GARBO, IMBO, JACKO (*n.*[1] and *n.*[2]), JOLLO, JOURNO, LESO, METHO *n.*[1], MILKO, MUSO, NASHO, PANNO, PLONKO, PRESBO, PROVO, RABBIT-OH, RABBO, REFFO, REGGO, REO, ROBBO, SALVO, SAMBO, SANO, SARVO, SECKO, SMOKO, SPEARO, SPELL-OH, SUSSO, TOADO, etc.

1907 *Truth* (Sydney) 30 June 9/5 If a forward miss his 'kicko' He's not 'worth his blanky oats'. **1911** *Ibid.* 14 May 11/4 Mary Neary was fined £3, in default a month's juggo. **1914** E. DYSON *Spats' Fact'ry* 90 Here's a maddo offerin' marriage to all ours. **1918** *Truth* (Sydney) 6 Jan. 5/5 Mr Love sentenced defendant to a month's juggo. **1934** *Bulletin* (Sydney) 14 Nov. 41/3 A carpet-snake was thrown into the car by a wheel, landing across the driver's shoulder... In the end carpo called it a day; he was probably as frightened as we were. **1942** *Plane Speaking from R.A.A.F. Amberley* 15 Oct. 8 We'd rather be in Tokio drinking Jappo beer. **1943** H.E. BEROS *Fuzzy Wuzzy Angels* 73 A dirty thieving rotter came, a proper fiftho pest. **1944** L.J. LIND *Escape from Crete* 64, I was awakened by .. two black-bearded Greekos. **1955** N. PULLIAM *I traveled Lonely Land* 114 Tot it all up and then communicate with the headwaiter at the place where the mob's going that evo. **1964** *Bulletin* (Sydney) 22 Aug. 32/1 Merely ran a little way in among the graves and hid... The birds and lizards in the cemo taught us. *Play dead*, they said. **1974** J. GABY *Restless Waterfront* 204 According to the delegate, a dello wasn't only as good as the master .. but he was better. **1975** *Bulletin* (Sydney) 1 Nov. 19/1 My wife's increasing demands for more housekeeping money .. 'Could you give me the houso?' she said. **1982** K. HUENEKE *Huts of High Country* 182 Harry and Plonkey were both avid 'euco cutters' in the 1930s and 1940s. The new term had me stumped... They were humble old gum tree cutters.

oak. [See quot. 1965.]

1. Any of many trees thought to resemble the English oak, generally in the appearance of the timber, esp. those of the fam. Casuarinaceae (see CASUARINA); the wood of these trees. Also *attrib.*

1789 J. HUNTER *Hist. Jrnl. Trans. Port Jackson* (1793) 357 Pines, and oak-trees of the largest size, were blown down every instant. **1820** C. JEFFREYS *Van Dieman's Land* 19 Immense quantities of what is there called the blackwood, a species of oak, very hard, but easily worked. **1829** R. MUDIE *Picture of Aust.* 136 To the *casuarina*, though it has no resemblance whatever to any species of oak, the colonists give the name of oak tree. **1838** *Southern Austral.* (Adelaide) 29 Sept. 1/4 These portable dwellings are constructed of well-seasoned Stringy Bark (the Oak of South Australia). **1846** L.W. MILLER *Notes of Exile Van Dieman's Land* 299 High hills .. partially covered with 'she oak' as it is commonly called. These oak forests were by far the most agreeable to the eye of any thing which I saw of the kind on the island. **1867** 'CLERGYMAN' *Aust. as it Is* 20 The oak resembles a pine-tree, and is never found save where there is water. **1880** J. BONWICK *Resources Qld.* 81 The Oaks—Forest, Swamp, He, She, Fire, and River sorts—are *Casuarinae.* **1889** W.H. TIETKENS *Jrnl. Central Austral. Exploring Exped.* 19 Apr. (1891) 14 Camped at 5 p.m. in oak sandhills and spinifex. **1935** F. CLUNE *Rolling down Lachlan* 192 One gets used to this .. when travelling in the Australian bush... Our iguana isn't a real iguana, our oak isn't an oak. **1965** *Austral. Encycl.* VI. 381 The word 'oak' is usually applied in Australia to various members of the genus *Casuarina* .. because the grain of their timbers resembles that of the English oak, having large conspicuous medullary rays.

2. With distinguishing epithet, as **desert, forest, he, river, she, silky, swamp, Tasmanian,** etc.: see under first element.

3. Special Comb. **oak grub,** the large larva of a variety of insects, usu. beetles or moths, sometimes used as bait.

1900 H. LAWSON *Over Sliprails* 111 We got a rusty pan without a handle, and cooked about a pint of fat yellow oak-grubs... We had broken a new pair of shears digging out those grubs from under the bark of the she-oaks. **1983** *Canberra Chron.* 26 Oct. 19/5 Bob Reid .. has begun his famous summer-bait service again and has good stocks of large oak grubs.

oat grass. Any of several usu. tufted grasses used as fodder, esp. TALL OAT GRASS. Formerly also **oaten grass.**

1825 *Austral.* (Sydney) 21 July 4 A late *danthonia*, or gigantic oatgrass was most remarkable. **1839** *S. Austral. Rec.* (London) 15 Nov. 269 Sandy soil, on which there is abundance of fine feed for cattle, the oat grass growing luxuriantly. **1846** C.P. HODGSON *Reminisc. Aust.* 156 The oat grass (*anthistiria*) is an enormous fellow; growing to the height of seven and eight feet, with stems as yellow as corn. **1846** *Sydney Morning Herald* 26 Mar. 2/5 The oaten grass of the Isaacks, which grew to a considerable height, and the stem of which is very juicy and sweet. **1851** J.H. BURTON *Emigrant's Man.* ii. 2 The coarse scanty grasses are extremely nutritious; those named oat-grass and kangaroo-grass are distinguished for their fattening qualities. **1871** *Austral. Town & Country Jrnl.* (Sydney) 5 Aug. 172/4 *The oat grass* (Bromus Australis) is found abundantly on the great inland plains. **1874** J.J. HALCOMBE *Emigrant & Heathen* 58 Barley grass, kangaroo grass, and oaten grass; and the last, unlike most of the things in the colony which have a popular name, really bears an oat, as it professes to do. **1903** G. SUTHERLAND *Australasian Live Stock Man.* (ed. 2) 390 So far as sheep are concerned, 'Oat grass', or *D. carphoides*, is one of the most valuable of the perennial Danthonias in New South Wales, Victoria, and South Australia. **1938** C.T. WHITE *Princ. Bot. Qld. Farmers* 203 Many other grasses go to make up the mixed native pasture—Love Grasses, Kangaroo Grasses, Oat Grasses. **1984** E. ROLLS *Celebration of Senses* 130 Bunches of Oat Grass in seed, that lovely native with heavy fawn heads borne on purple stems.

oath. In the phr. **my oath,** an emphatic exclamation of agreement or endorsement; an expletive. See also BLOODY *a.* 2, COLONIAL *a.* 5.

1869 *Lictor* (Sydney) 16 Dec. 347 My oath! I'm as right as a first-rate quondong. ***c* 1872** J.C.F. JOHNSON *Over Island* 21 My oath, ain't that duff o' mother Mac's a ring-tailed snorter, jest? **1898** *Critic* (Adelaide) 26 Feb. 5/3 My oath! But I'm 'appy when the sun goes down. **1905** H. LAWSON *When I was King* 22 And he reached for my hand, which I gave, nothing loth, And replied in two words, and those words were 'My Oath!' **1918** *Huon Times* (Franklin) 20 Sept. 3/3 'Didn't get you, did they?' said the tall one. 'My oath, no.' **1936** N. CALDWELL *Fangs of Sea* 180 'You'll beat his fish one day, mum.' 'My oath, I will,' she replied. **1948** G. FARWELL *Down Argent Street* 68 'Ought to shift a few ton this arvo, Butch.' 'My oath!' **1957** R.S. PORTEOUS *Brigalow* 96 A beer? My oath! I'll be in that. **1972** *Bulletin* (Sydney) 12 Aug. 7/3 'Does the Trust hold any classes for the public?' I asked. 'My oath. We conducted a seminar lately.' **1981** H. MILLIGAN *Sprig of Light* 28 'You're not going to ring up now are you?' 'My oath I am, you can't let the grass grow under your feet.'

obsidianite. AUSTRALITE.

1898 *Proc. R. Soc. Vic.* 23 As long as this uncertainty exists, some other name would be more appropriate, and I suggest and will refer to them in this paper as 'obsidianites', a term which will at least not be open to this objection, and will be more convenient for use. **1916** *Geol. Survey Bull. No. 67* (W.A.) 135 Neglecting as of unknown origin the many thousands of 'Australites' or 'Obsidianites' which have been discovered on the surface of the central plateau of the State, only twelve undoubted meteorites have been found. **1933** C. FENNER *Bunyips & Billabongs* 40 Most of us have seen an Australite, either in our own or in a friend's collection, or in a museum. They are also known as 'blackfellows' buttons', obsidianites, emu-stones, and 'trans-line' meteorites.

occupation licence. *Hist.* A permit to graze stock on a specified tract of Crown land for a stipulated period.

1843 *Colonial Observer* (Sydney) 25 Mar. 909/2 Occupation Licenses... The sale of Licenses for the occupation of Crown Lands, within the boundaries of location. **1846** W. WESTGARTH *Rep. on District Port Phillip* 49 A minor grievance .. is the system of 'Occupation Licenses', by which a large area of surveyed country, within the counties of the colony, is declared open to the selection of the public, in sections of one square mile each, for occupation for a period of twelve months. **1869** E.C. BOOTH *Another England* 147 When the 'occupation licenses' were issued, he took up twenty acres at the back of his farm. **1880** J. BONWICK *Resources Qld.* 34 To obtain a *Run* in the first instance, the applicant secures from the Commissioners of the district an *Occupation License* for one year. **1891** *Austral. Handbk.* 100 Occupation licenses .. may be granted to the run-holder on his paying a deposit of £2 per section of 640 acres, on account of the first year's license fee. **1932** B.U. BYLES *Rep. on Reconnaissance Mountainous Part River Murray Catchment N.S.W.* 42 Occupation licences cover very large areas of country of very low grazing value, rentals vary from 6d. to 12d. per acre per annum and the size of the blocks from 14,000 to 20,000 acres.

Ocean Hell. *Hist.* A name given to the penal establishment on Norfolk Island.

1850 *Britannia* (Hobart) 4 Apr. 2/2 We designated it [*sc.* Norfolk Island] for the first time '*the Ocean Hell*'. **1855** G.H. WATHEN *Golden Colony* 143 Dalton was transported at an early age, and had for a time been confined in the 'Ocean Hell' of Norfolk Island, the gaol of the double-damned convict. **1865** J.F. MORTLOCK *Experiences of Convict* 65 The commandants preceding him having ruled with such injudicious severity, as to make the place well deserving its Australian name, 'the Ocean Hell'. **1939** J.G. PATTISON *'Battler's' Tales Early Rockhampton* 42 Haynes left the Albion on her return to Sydney and joined the 'Morayshire', which ship had been hired by Sir William Denison to remove any of the Pitcairn Islanders who wished to go to Norfolk Island, known as 'The Ocean Hell' and 'Earthly Paradise'.

ock. Abbrev. of OCKER *n.* 2.

1976 *Bulletin* (Sydney) 21 Aug. 21/3 Get the average Ock to take a holiday in his own country. **1982** *Ibid.* 6 July 65/1 He had tins of beer zipped into the front of his parka jacket, resting on his fat stomach... 'That's the historical ock.'

ocker /'ɒkə/, *n.* and *attrib.* Also **okker.** [A nickname, esp. for a person named *Oscar*, used as a nickname for a character devised and played by Ron Frazer (1924–1983) in a television series, 'The Mavis

Bramston Show' (1965–1968), and hence applied generically.]

A. *n.*

1. a. Used as a masculine nickname.

1916 R.H. ADAMS Diary 26 Feb., Considerable helio work done on the station owing to fault on line to Bde. called up by Ocker's Co. Heard a voice, could swear it was Jim's. **1927** *Sunday Sun* (Sydney) 1 May (Sunbeams Suppl.) 1 You know what I did to 'Ocker' Stevens at school on Wednesday don't you? **1935** K. TENNANT *Tiburon* 42 Okker Slade's bag shelter had joined those of Dutch and Old Grey in the little circle round the fire. **1943** S.W. KEOUGH *Around Army* 39 Eh, Ocker, if y're passin' near a canteen will you get us a coupla packets of smokes? **1943** *Bulletin* (Sydney) 20 Oct. 13/1 'Ocker' Simpson quoted the legendary 'Crooked' Mick of Speewah Bluff shed and the duffs he cooked for the shearers. **1959** J. CLEARY *Strike me Lucky* 39 Then Ocker Oodskirt gave voice... Ocker is the porter at the railway station. **1972** *Bulletin* (Sydney) 26 Feb. 11/1, I only realised afterwards that I was suspected of being 'Ocker' Campbell, the notorious Australian smash-and-grab man.

b. Used as a derisive nickname for a person who exploits an exaggerated Australian nationalism.

1968 *Kings Cross Whisper* (Sydney) li. 3/3 This was the theme in the winter showing of fashion designer Fred 'Ocker' Smith. **1969** *Ibid.* lxxv. 1/2 Sir Ocker Fairfax, leader of the famous Foot and Mouth Jumping Brigade, received his gong for devising Operation Skippy. **1978** *Ibid.* lxxx. 1/2 'It is in keeping with our image as a fair dinkum all-Australian company,' the general manager, Mr W. (Ocker) Leadhead, said today.

2. *transf.* A rough and uncultivated Australian male, often aggressively Australian in speech and manner.

1971 G. JOHNSTON *Cartload Clay* 71 The big man would be a good player, a vigorous clubman, a hearty participant in the companionship of the club bar. He was .. what the boy called an 'Ocker'. **1973** *Bulletin* (Sydney) 24 Feb. 56/3 He's slicker, more the professional comedian and less the genuine ocker-in-the-street. **1975** *Ibid.* 31 May 13/3 Ocker is a title which should be bestowed only on those with an uncommon likeness to the average suburban garbo. **1977** *Ibid.* 9 Apr. 43/1 And you have the poofter problem. There seem so many poofs in Sydney as might cause serious concern about overcrowding to the housing authorities of Sodom. It is a statistical and biological impossibility for all these poofters to be homosexuals. They are refugees from the other Australian tyrannical myth, the ocker. Any young Australian man with a normal fondness for dressiness, an interest in the arts, a liking for a varied diet, a penchant for European travel, a preference for comfort, even a weakness for after-shave, measures himself against the ocker and instantly assumes himself queer. Once he thinks himself queer, he acts queer. **1979** *Canberra Times* 9 Sept. 2/1 After all, what self-respecting South-East Asian would wish to play host to a sloppy, noisy, ill-clad, boorish, boozy, insensitive ocker? **1980** R. DAVIDSON *Tracks* 137, I went into the bar for a beer, there to be met by a group of typical ockers, all talking, as is their wont, about sex and sheilas. **1981** B. DICKINS *Gift of Gab* 28 Huge mobs of Orange-Fanta ockers queueing up for beach tickets.

3. Australian English.

1979 DOUGLAS & HEATHCOTE *Far Cry* 29 *Talking okker.* Mother used to whip us if we pronounced anything incorrectly. This meant I grew up with a New Zealand accent and I have always felt sorry that I could never sound like a true Aussie.

B. *attrib.* passing into *adj.* Characterized by a discernibly Australian vulgarity.

1972 *Australasian Post* (Melbourne) 30 Nov. 4/1 'I've got a Charger parked out the front and some classy clob-ber on me back,' he said, in an accent only a shade less Strine than his Ocker alter ego. **1975** *Bulletin* (Sydney) 4 Oct. 45/3 It's essential to conquer the ocker attitude... You know, the Australian's use of language is limited; he might know 100 or 300 words. **1979** *Overland* 78/37 Make it ocker, sing a song, show muscles and boobs. **1982** *Canberra Times* 3 Mar. 2/8 Her tight-stretched skivvy carried the legend 'Ocker Knockers'. **1984** *Ibid.* 12 Feb. 2/1 The gallery has nothing of the ocker oeuvre of Rolf Harris.

Hence **ocker** *v. intr.*, to behave as an ocker; **ockerization** *n.*, vulgarization; **ockerized** *a.*, vulgarized.

1976 B. BENNETT *New Country* 42 Winter liked to **ocker** it up occasionally. **1975** *Bulletin* (Sydney) 6 Sept. 21/1 The annual general meeting of the Australian Society of Authors threw up its hands in horror at the idea, many a silver-haired lady and tweedy gentleman getting up to protest at the **ockerisation** of modern society, the well known crassness of marketing people, et cetera. **1978** K. GARVEY *Tales of my Uncle Harry* 8 Both would writhe in their graves if they could see some of the modernized, deodorized, glamorized, Americanized, televisionized, **Ockerized**, social-serviceized, Aussies of the present permissive decadent era.

ockerdom. Ockers collectively; their social impact.

1974 *Gayzette* (Sydney) 19 Sept. 19/3 We are going through an artificial revival, not of the Lawson male ethic, but of a curious and pugnacious Ockerdom. **1978** D. BALL *Great Austral. Snake Exchange* 16 Brooks was 'the pearl of ockerdom', a rascist [*sic*], a crypto-Country Party supporter and a citified yahoo. **1979** K. DUNSTAN *Ratbags* p. xv, Ockerdom and the whole cult of the Ocker is so engaging.

ockerina. A female ocker.

1975 *Sunday Tel.* (Sydney) 27 July 96/6 Ockerina of the week was surely the woman on the Eastern Suburbs bus, studying a race guide while slurping down a meat pie. **1980** B. HORNADGE *Austral. Slanguage* 136 The use of bad language was entirely a male prerogative, but it seems the Ockerinas of the nation are fast catching up.

ockerism.

1. Behaviour characteristic of an ocker: see quot. 1974.

1974 *Austral.* (Sydney) 5 Oct. 13/4 The new Australian boorishness is known as Ockerism, from a slob-like character called Ocker in a television series, the embodiment of oafish, blinkered self-satisfaction. **1977** R. MCKIE *Crushing* (1978) 53 There's plenty in it for them, mate, all the way to the bank mate, and that's the nitty-gritty o' yore ockerism mate. **1979** *Overland* lxxviii. 33 Their politics and public personalities tacitly favour ockerism. **1982** *Bulletin* (Sydney) 5 Jan. 6/1 Nobody wants to be an 'Ocker knocker', for ockerism can have a certain charm, in small doses. **1984** *Canberra Times* 14 Apr. 2/1, I would find it easier to read *The Canberra Times* .. if some members of your team of sports writers were to rein in the ethnocentric machismo, also commonly known as ockerism.

2. AUSTRALIANISM 1; Australian English.

1975 *Daily Mirror* (Sydney) 9 May 5/4 'A few of 'em are adoptin' a few ockerisms that don't come natural to 'em,' says Hogan. **1981** *Bulletin* (Sydney) 15 Dec. 6/2 If on the other hand we choose to invent a new language .. teach our children 'ockerism' instead of English and end confusion.

ocky. [f. *oc(topus* + -Y.] An octopus; octopus flesh.

1968 R. HILL *Bush Quest* 101 There were two buckets of octopus pieces for bait. The 'ocky', as they call it, was bluish white and rather slimy looking. **1976** B. SCOTT *Complete Bk. Austral. Folk Lore* 239 Not that any crayfisherman would refer to an octopus by its right name. An octopus is merely an ocky, more than one are ockies. **1984** *Canberra Chron.* 29 Feb. 19/3 Watch out for the ockies that roam all over the sand flats.

octo. Abbrev. of 'octopus'.

1912 *Bulletin* (Sydney) 24 Oct. 16/2 The octo. let go and sunk [*sic*] hurriedly, and the girl shrieked. **1936** N. CALDWELL *Fangs of Sea* 202, I never went looking for that octo again.

octoroon. [Transf. use of *octoroon* a person of one-eighth Negro descent.] A person of one-eighth Aboriginal descent.

1933 R.S. SAMPSON *Through Central Aust.* 28 The child of a white person and a mulatto is a quadroon; of a white person and a quadroon, an octoroon. **1936** C.P. CONIGRAVE *N. Aust.* 120 Every gradation of skin colour from the veriest pale-faced octoroon to the half-caste who is almost as dark as the full-blood. **1966** D. NILAND *Pairs & Loners* 142 The boy had aboriginal blood in him, but not much. An octoroon, he thought. **1984** *A.N.U. Reporter* (Canberra) 27 Apr. 3 Archie describes himself as an 'octoroon', being one-eighth Aborigine.

offside, *a.*[1] [Spec. use of *offside* the right side of an animal, vehicle, etc.] Of a bullock team: of or pertaining to the right-hand side (as opposed to the near or left-hand side).

1847 *Bell's Life in Sydney* 25 Dec. 3/2 I'd sooner .. be an off-side bullock driver. **1887** W.H. SUTTOR *Austral. Stories Retold* 47 Bob and his 'off-side driver' yoked up the team to start on their long journey. **1934** J.C. LEE *Boshstralians* 12 Marjory ran a critical eye over the horses. 'Your off-side leader looks fresh.' **1979** W.D. JOYNT *Breaking Road for Rest* 39 The off side leader I will call Blackie, and near side leader, Tiger. **1981** E. ROLLS *Million Wild Acres* 28 (*caption*) The offside leader and the offside pinner both shook their heads during the long exposure necessary to the slow film.

offside, *a.*[2] [Transf. use of *offside* away from one's own side (in football, hockey, etc.).]

a. *transf.* Unacceptable; in bad taste.

1910 H. LAWSON *Rising of Court* 90 It seems that Brutus objected to Cassius's or one of his off-side friends' methods of raising the wind. **1939** K. TENNANT *Foveaux* 142 You only had to say something a bit offside to Bramley and he would blush like a girl.

b. In the phr. **offside with,** on the wrong side of; in bad odour with.

[N.Z. **1947** COMBS *Half-Lengths* 8 Harris began to put himself off-side with some of the leading citizens.] **1979** *Southerly* i. 54 It was about this time, by the way, that I got offside with some of the sports writers.

offside, *v.* [Back-formation from OFFSIDER 1 a.] *intr.* To act as an offsider. Also as *vbl. n.*

1883 M. DURACK *Kings in Grass Castles* (1959) 256, I have put up a yard on Galway since Uncle Jerry left—Pumpkin and Kangaroo offsiding. **1910** L. ESSON *Woman Tamer* (1976) 65 You couldn't offside in a fourpenny fish joint. **1936** I.L. IDRIESS *Cattle King* 18 Greasy Jack, the cook, congratulated him... 'I'll get you a job offsidin' for me.' **1946** *Bulletin* (Sydney) 21 Aug. 28/3, I went off-siding to a professional bird-catcher. **1956** T. RONAN *Moleskin Midas* 141 Toby seemed to need the rest of the staff to offside. **1980** M. MCADOO *If only I'd Listened* ('Tom Parker'), My father broke me in with some of the bullocks. I used to 'ave to offside for 'im.

offsider. [f. OFFSIDE *a.*[1]: see quot. 1910.]

1. a. A bullock-driver's assistant; an assistant in an occupation or enterprise.

1879 'AUSTRALIAN' *Adventures Qld.* 108 Mr Brown, George Martin, and the Malcolms, lent him two hands each, who, with his off-sider and himself, made a good strong clearing party. **1890** MRS H.P. MARTIN *Under Gum Tree* 171, I was appointed 'off-sider' to Old Jimmy, the bullock driver. **1910** C.E.W. BEAN *On Wool Track* 168 An 'offsider', by the by, is a gentleman who is learning bullock-driving, and who is allowed to try his apprentice-tongue on the offside of the bullock team. **1919** E.S. SORENSON *Chips & Splinters* 14 He was able to ride after bullocks and act as offsider at pinches for his father. **1928** *Bulletin* (Sydney) 25 Apr. 23/2 Years ago a drover who brought down a mob of cattle to Adelaide had as offsiders a couple of abos. **1939** K. TENNANT *Foveaux* 212 He liked being offsider for 'Headlights', a wizened, bespectacled, racing driver. **1951** E. HILL *Territory* 291 His black offsider, bare feet immune to prickles and burrs, gathers firewood. **1960** *N.T. News* (Darwin) 22 Jan. 6/3 Bella was Clerk and Chief offsider to the late Charles Harvey J.P., storekeeper and owner of the only market garden here. **1983** *Canberra Times* 18 Sept. 7/1 Her common-law husband .. was a bricklayer, and she had often worked as his offsider and gained the reputation of being able to do the work of two men.

b. With occupation specified: **cook's offsider.**

1910 *Bulletin* (Sydney) 28 Apr. 13/1, I can .. smell the buns the cook's offsider is bringing. **1918** R.H. KNYVETT *Over there with Australs.* 154 From the brigadier down to the cook's off-sider. **1944** L. GLASSOP *We were Rats* 69 'You're only the cook's bloody offsider, anyhow.' 'Go and get ---,' said the cook's offsider. **1960** *N.T. News* (Darwin) 5 Jan. 5/5 Sarah .. in my hawking days through the station, was a cook's offsider. **1979** W.D. JOYNT *Breaking Road for Rest* 42, I took over as men dropped out, and handled in turn nearly every one of the vacant jobs, even cook's offsider and butcher.

2. *transf.* and *fig.*

1924 F.J. MILLS *Happy Days* 8 A chap lookin' as if 'e 'ad crawled out of a rabbit's burrow, came up, leadin' a 'orse, what looked like as if 'e was offsider to the missin' link. **1944** *Bulletin* (Sydney) 1 Mar. 12/1 The yarn about the bull-ant and its offsiders raiding the honey . . isn't as far-fetched as it reads. **1946** *Ibid.* 18 Dec. 28/3 The Portuguese man-of-war rates as No. 1 public enemy; his offsider the sea-wasp has been responsible for a number of deaths. **1951** *Ibid.* 15 Aug. 12/1, I spotted the eagle on the dead limb of a gum. . . A shadow across the sun, and the wedgie's offsider arrived on the end of the limb.

oil, *n.* [Fig. use of *oil* as the substance essential to the running of a machine.]

1. Information; news.

1915 DREW & EVANS *Grafter* 56, I can guarantee that he's trying, because I got the right oil about it. **1916** *Anzac Rec. Gaz.* (Alexandria, Egypt) 4 Mar. 14/2 An acquaintance greets you with . . 'What's the oil'. **1919** C. DREW *Doings of Dave* 132, I ain't got the oil yet whether he is or not. **1929** 'F. BLAIR' *Digger Sea-Mates* 54 Tom's got the oil we reach port in the morning. I'll believe him—thousands wouldn't. **1941** K.S. PRICHARD *Moon of Desire* 295 Like to come down to the saddling paddock. . . If there's any oil about for the next race, we may as well have it. **1957** V. PALMER *Seedtime* 38 If it wasn't for you he'd never come inside the gate and we wouldn't get the real oil about what was going to win on Saturday. **1977** F.B. VICKERS *Stranger no Longer* 73 'That's if all goes well, mate,' said the man who was giving me the oil.

2. With qualifying epithet: **dinkum** (or **straight**) **oil**, reliable information; an accurate report; also *fig.* (see quot. 1918); **good oil,** reliable (and therefore welcome) information.

1915 (*title*) The **Dinkum Oil** War News. **1916** R.H. ADAMS Diary 8 Mar., We hear dinkum oil re Turks having thrown in the sponge. **1917** A.C. PANTON *Dinkum Oils*, The 'dinkum oils' come pouring in, Morning noon and night. Startling yarns of every kind. **1918** N. CAMPBELL *Passing Cheer* (1919) 8 You'll give the Hun the 'dinkum oil' The Anzacs gave of old. **1923** *Bulletin* (Sydney) 21 June 24/4 Here's the straight oil for keeping ants out of safes. **1933** H.B. RAINE *Whip-Hand* 43 A friend of mine . . has a half interest in a horse running tomorrow. He'll give you the dinkum oil. **1959** *Bulletin* (Sydney) 25 Mar. 19/1 I'd like the dinkum-oil from someone in the know about the signals left at homestead-gates by itinerants. **1968** *Swag* (Sydney) iv. 54/2 We get the dinkum oil off him. He knows all the jockeys and trainers. **1916** *Astra* (Melbourne) Sept. 2/1 The **Good Oil.** **1933** H.B. RAINE *Whip-Hand* 140 This was the good oil, too. The nice little haul of 'white stuff' proves that. **1945** 'MASTER-SARG' *Yank discovers Aust.* 75 'The good oil', 'the gen', 'the griff'—correct information. **1962** V.C. HALL *Dreamtime Justice* 80 If we could get the 'good oil' from the islanders we might be able to stage a daylight raid. **1974** *Bulletin* (Sydney) 16 Nov. 32/1 It seemed Young had some good oil on the Adelaide races. **1979** *Austral. Rodsports & Drag Racing News* 2 Mar. 11/1 This week's good oil (apart from Valvoline) on what is being built is . . a new Chevy-powered Datsun. **1986** *Nat. Times* (Sydney) 14 Feb. 2/3 Spreading the word, spilling the beans . . having the good oil are all as much part of the female make-up as lipstick and blusher.

oil, *v.*[1] [Fig. use of *oil* to lubricate.] *trans.* To gratify (one's taste for alcoholic liquor). Also with **up** and freq. in *pass.*

1898 *Bulletin* (Sydney) 1 Oct. 14/3 To have a whisky is to 'oil up'. **1919** *All abaht It* (London) Feb. 16 Everybody needs oiling again. **1924** F.J. MILLS *Happy Days* 155 There was three or four Frenchies oilin' their Adam's apples at the counter. **1936** *Bulletin* (Sydney) 22 Apr. 21/1 An' you can gamble that the cove 'oo, when 'e's oiled, looks round fer fight Will, if 'e's challenged when 'e's on the wagon, damn near die of fright. **1971** D. IRELAND *Unknown Industr. Prisoner* 165 In order to have me my venereal Dad and Mum got blind, blotto, lushed . . oiled.

oil, *v.*[2] [f. OIL *n.* 1.] *trans.* With **up**: to provide (a person) with information.

1968 S. GORE *Holy Smoke* 106 *Oil up*, to explain; or to warn someone about something. **1968** D. O'GRADY *Bottle of Sandwiches* 30, I gotta go to Perth tomorrow for a couple o' weeks, so I'll oil you blokes up on what's what. **1955** N. PULLIAM *I traveled Lonely Land* 383 *Oil up, to*, to inform.

okiri /ˈɒkəri/. [a. Yankundjara dial. of Western Desert *okiri.*] A plant of the genus *Nicotiana* (fam. Solanaceae): see *native tobacco* NATIVE *a.* 6 a.

1891 *Trans. & Proc. R. Soc. S.A.* (1896) XVI. 293 The blacks had gathered some native tobacco plants which they call 'okiri'. **1935** H.H. FINLAYSON *Red Centre* 85 The narcotic known variously as mingil or okiri . . a true tobacco . . which grow[s] luxuriantly at the foot of the ranges.

okker, var. OCKER.

old, *n. N.S.W.* [Abbrev. of *old beer.*] An ale, so-called because made by top fermentation in the traditional manner. See NEW *n.*

1935 *First Hundred Yrs.* (Tooth & Co. Ltd.) 71 We make our way across a wide platform on which barrels full of 'Old' and 'New' are being assembled in readiness for despatch. **1945** *Southerly* ii. 37 Oscar walked into the bar, where Jim brought him 'half of old'. **1966** B. BEAVER *You can't come Back* 10 Mike pushed two middies of flat old at us. **1972** J. O'GRADY *It's your Shout, Mate!* 90 The bottom fermentation product, a relatively new process, they called 'old'. . . Old beer I found to be dark in colour, caused by a darker malt used in its making. This also gave it a distinctive malty flavour. **1976** B. HOWARD-SMITH *Adult Gift Bk. Poetry* 20 I'll have a middie of new An old and a squash. **1984** B. DRISCOLL *Great Aussie Beer Bk.* 22 The dark top-fermented ale as brewed by, say, Toohey's, was called Toohey's Old.

old, *a.*

1. Used in collocations denoting the British Isles, esp. England: **old country** [also U.S.: see OED(S *a.* 12 b.]; **Dart** [dial. pronunc. of *dirt*; see also DART and cf. *(old) sod* (OED(S *sb.*[1] 4 b.)]; **land.**

1834 G. BENNETT *Wanderings N.S.W.* I. 142 The barn-doors about the farms (in imitation of a similar custom in the '**old country**') were decorated by the brushes and tails of that shepherds' pest, the Dingo. **1855** G.H. WATHEN *Golden Colony* 171 Happily, however, for the peace of the infant community of Victoria, the spirit of sectarianism is far less rife than in the Old Country. **1873** W. THOMSON-GREGG *Desperate Character* III. 3 Nonsense, my lads; you have not got rid of your old-country notions yet, I see. **1893** F.W.L. ADAMS *Australs.* 41 Ten years ago England was spoken of affectionately as the Old Country or Home. **1917** *Huon Times* (Franklin) 20 Apr. 5/3 He went to Sydney to meet the Prime Minister on his return from the Old Country. **1936** T. HOSE *Austral. Magpie* 99 Our national leaders are sending gifts of primary produce to the Old Country. **1950** F.J. HARDY *Power without Glory* 256 Australia must stand shoulder to shoulder with the old country. **1964** P. ADAM SMITH *Hear Train Blow* 74 Joan Moran came from Ireland with her family. . . They brought their furniture with them from the old country. **1978** B. OAKLEY *Ship's Whistle* (1979) 27 They don't much like us Brits, that's the trouble. . . Forget about the Old Country, your honour. **1981** *New Idea* (Melbourne) 12 Sept. 143/2 Margaret Fulton has just returned from the 'old country' and she has brought you a collection of terrific true blue British recipes. **1892** *Quiz* (Adelaide) 18 Nov. 7/2 He was from England. . . He is one of the sort who return to the **old dart** and say that fruit-growing here is a failure. **1909** *Truth* (Sydney) 24 Jan. 1/8 But the young English tart, like the frigid old Dart, I should think must be nothing but ice. **1918** *Ibid.* 3 Feb. 1/6 One of the Labor papers in the Old Dart unkindly suggests that . . the King would be better employed at the front. **1932** J. MCCARTER *Pan's Clan* 225 The money-bags in the Old Dart are forever squealing about costs of production. **1941** D. O'CALLAGHAN *Long Life Reminisc.* 21 Dad commenced brewing his hop beer from a recipe acquired in the 'Old Dart' from a brewer of Guinness' Stout. **1955** N. PULLIAM *I traveled Lonely Land* 57 Britain is Old Dart, although the only reason anyone could give me for this was that the word 'dart' once indicated something which was alluring or seductive, while concealing some scheme or skulduggery. **1971** F. HARDY *Outcasts of Foolgarah* 23 He's the greatest know-all who ever migrated from the Old Dart for its own good on a tenner. **1980** HEPWORTH & HINDLE *Boozing out in Melbourne Pubs* 34 There are no less than seven Albions listed in the Melbourne phone book—all no doubt named for the perfidious Old Dart. **1986** *Canberra Times* 9 Mar. 9/1 Dick the shepherd has been blowing his nail a lot recently in the old Dart. **1891** E. HULME *Settler's 35 Yrs. Experience Vic.* 1 When living in the '**Old Land**' . . I belonged to a class of which there are many thousands. **1924** MRS H.A. DOUDY *Magic of Dawn* 35 South Australia gave opportunities that the Old Land could never offer to men of our class. **1911** *Huon Times* (Franklin) 27 Sept. 2/5 The growing, storing and packing of fruit, have been noticed with approval by authorities in the Old Land. **1940** *Bulletin* (Sydney) 17 July 17/2 Westralia occasionally boasts that its people are the most English of all Australians; certainly its nomenclature keeps nearer to that of the Old Land than most other parts.

2. *Obs.* In miscellaneous collocations: **old chum,** OLD HAND; also *attrib.*; **colonist,** see COLONIST 3; **colony,** New South Wales; **settler,** see SETTLER 3; **squatter,** a long-established, substantial land owner (see SQUATTER 2 and 3); **thing,** see quots.

1832 *Sydney Monitor* 25 July 2/5 A gold mine, which a fellow-servant, an **old chum**, had gulled him with the belief was in existence. **1847** *Melbourne Argus* 27 Aug. 4/1 *Old chum*: Well, Mr New Chum, how do you like the country now? **1855** R. CALDWELL *Gold Era Vic.* 42 'Old chums' and 'New chums' are the terms used in Victoria to designate old and new comers. Three years were required to make an old chum. . . The old chum then considered himself bound to look upon the new chum with the most supercilious contempt and pity. **1873** A. TROLLOPE *Aust. & N.Z.* I. 285 A bushman of any refinement has the pannikin for drinking; but the rough old chum will dispense with it as a useless luxury, and will drink his tea out of his billy. **1859** W. KELLY *Life in Vic.* I. 34, I should be afraid to repeat the valuation put upon these properties . . by my old chum friend. **1893** 'OLD CHUM' *Chips* 5 This little book is the joint work of an *old chum* and a *new chum*. **1915** A. SAFRONI-MIDDLETON *Sailor & Beachcomber* 276 They were men of all degrees, swagsmen of long experience, and men of no experience, new chums and old chums. **1853** S. SIDNEY *Three Colonies* (ed. 2) 91 The remoteness of Swan River from the **old colony** rendered importations of any kind difficult, expensive, and uncertain. **1856** J. BONWICK *W. Buckley* 73 The old colony had been settled above thirty years. **1849** S. & J. SIDNEY *Emigrant's Jrnl.* 4 Let him buy no land, but go up the country two or three hundred miles, and settle on one of the rivers with some **old squatter.** **1861** C. CAMPBELL *Squatting Question Considered* 23 In many cases old squatters have bought new stations. **1872** 'CAPRICORNUS' *Bush Essays* 24 The old squatters clutched their lands in an iron monopoly. **1848** H.W. HAYGARTH *Recoll. Bush Life* 6 The traveller's entertainment is confined to the '**old thing**' as it is contemptuously called, that is to say, beef and 'damper'. **1865** G.F. ANGAS *Aust.* 279 Eggs and bacon [are] . . generally preferred to the 'old thing', as salt beef and damper is contemptuously called in bush parlance. **1945** S.J. BAKER *Austral. Lang.* 80 It was what W.W. Dobie called the *muttonous* diet of the outback that produced the expression *the Old Thing* for a meal of mutton and damper.

old fellow. The penis. Also **old boy.**

1968 B. HUMPHRIES *Wonderful World Barry McKenzie*, All that ice cold Fosters has gone straight to the old feller. Am I bustin' for a nice long snakes! **1971** F. HARDY *Outcasts of Foolgarah* 114 Florrie opening her legs like the woman in the story. . . Chilla cursing under his breath, having just sunk the old fella. **1980** J. WOLFE *End of Pricklystick* 46 There was this bloke working in Tarra Valley and a leech crawled up the eye in his oldfeller. They had to take him to hospital to get it out. **1972** G. MORLEY *Jockey rides Honest Race* 172 Well what is it, your old boy fall off? **1981** C. GORMAN *Night in Arms Raeleen* (1983) 44 She . . caught me scorin' ten from the usherette up the local pictures. Chock-a-block. Old feller was in there, right up to the maker's name. **1982** *Bulletin* (Sydney) 9 Mar. 96/1 I'll never forget the look on guests' faces in a Manchester hotel one night, when they arrived back to find a well-known Australian player draped on a chaise-longue in the public lounge, having what is commonly referred to as his 'old boy' autographed by a member of the opposite sex.

old hand.

1. *Hist.* A convict with long experience of life in a penal colony (as opposed to one newly arrived); an ex-convict.

1826 *Colonial Times* (Hobart) 14 Jan., We want a

Governor-in-Chief, No dummies to afford relief, No subjects for a Lawyer's brief, And 'old hands' in the Council! **1837** *Elliston's Hobart Town Almanack* 97 Attempts at escape . . are now seldom made, and in the technical phrase the 'old hands declare it is no use to chance it'. **1843** *HRA* (1924) 1st Ser. XXII. 629, I now pass to the consideration of the doubly convicted Prisoners or 'Old Hands' at Norfolk Island. **1848** *Maitland Mercury* 30 Sept. 4/3 We are annoyed by some fierce jealousies and feuds between the Vandiemonians and Pentonvillains, and the two *castes* can never agree. The 'old hands' denounce the others as 'Johnny Newcomes', and believe that the road-gangs of Port Arthur are a far more honourable martyrdom than the cloisters of Pentonville. **1862** J.A. PATTERSON *Gold Fields Vic.* 88 It was supposed to be a favourite resort of 'old hands' . . convicts. **1879** 'RECENT SETTLER' *Emigration to Tas.* 5 The 'old hands' are gradually dying off (for the colony has ceased to be a penal settlement for many years past). **1897** *Bulletin* (Sydney) 28 Aug. 21/1 Yet another of the 'old hands' who connect the convict-days with the present, has gone. Solomon Blay, ex-convict and ex-public executioner, died last week at Hobart. **1910** *Ibid.* 17 Mar. 14/1 The district was spotted with 'birth stain'. The 'old hands' formed almost a community of themselves. **1931** *Ibid.* 31 Dec. 20/1 The fact remains he was a lag—'old hand' the euphemistic phrase.

2. *Hist.* An immigrant with some experience of life in Australia (as opposed to one newly arrived).

1839 W. MANN *Six Yrs.' Residence* 163 Combinations are . . entered into by what are termed the old hands who are long established in the colony. **1843** *Port Phillip Patriot* 2 Jan. 2/4 If that was the case he was quite an old hand. . . 'I have not been here seven years yet—I am only a 'new chum'.' **1848** J. BYRNE *Twelve Yrs.' Wanderings* I. 415 The men were unaccustomed to the work, and progressed much more slowly with it, than 'old hands' in the country would have done. **1850** W. GATES *Recoll. Van Dieman's Land* 133 The old hands, as those are termed who have been there from England a year. **1862** A. POLEHAMPTON *Kangaroo Land* 60 It was . . a constant source of ambition among '*new chums*', especially the younger ones, to be taken for '*old hands*' in the colony. **1870** *Sydney Morning Herald* 1 July 5/2 Those gentlemen of extensive colonial experience, who are popularly known as 'old hands'.

3. One who has had long experience of an activity, occupation, or place.

1846 N.L. KENTISH *Work in Bush Van Diemen's Land* 12 The 'old hands' on the north and western side of the island. **1852** *Moreton Bay Free Press* 9 Nov. 3/4 From what I could see and learn from the old hands at the diggings they seem to be doing very well. **1892** 'MRS A. MACLEOD' *Silent Sea* I. 268 As for the miners, of course they're always shifting about except a few old hands who have their families here. ***c* 1907** C.W. CHANDLER *Darkest Adelaide* 9 He . . thought perhaps that I would have to take on a green hand—one that had just joined the ranks of public women, though, so far as he himself was concerned he didn't care a pink benediction whether they were green or old hands—he'd bally soon break them in. **1922** *Smith's Weekly* (Sydney) 15 July 19/6 My driver was one of the old hands of back o' Bourke, and not prone to conversation. **1935** J.P. MCKINNEY *Crucible* 64 Barclay and Ballan, two 'old hands', who had been in hospital in England after being wounded on the Peninsula. **1945** E. GEORGE *Two at Daly Waters* 32 Mrs Cranston . . was an old hand at Territory housekeeping. **1964** *Bulletin* (Sydney) 8 Feb. 13/1 The real 'old hands', the early originals, will tell you that Palm Beach has been spoilt.

Hence **old-handish** *a.*, **old-handism** *n.*

1873 W. THOMSON-GREGG *Desperate Character* II. 57, I never saw a more **old-handish** looking customer since I've been in the colony. **1859** F. FOWLER *Southern Lights & Shadows* 15 The battle of '**old-handism**' against 'new-chumism' is not everlasting waging in Victoria as it is New South Wales, where the natives are more intolerant and intolerable than the Bowery boys of America.

old man, *n.* and *attrib.*

A. *n.*

1. A fully grown male kangaroo, esp. the *grey kangaroo* (a) (see GREY *a.*). Also **old man kangaroo, 'roo.**

1827 P. CUNNINGHAM *Two Yrs. in N.S.W.* II. 160 One of our backwoodsmen . . relates . . that he has been fortunate enough to kill *an old man*. . . The 'old man' turns out to possess the appendage of *a tail*, and is in fact no other than one of our acquaintances, the kangaroos! **1830** R. DAWSON *Present State Aust.* 139 The male kangaroos were called by my natives, old men, 'woolman'; and the females, young ladies 'young liddy'. **1834** G. BENNETT *Wanderings N.S.W.* I. 286 Many persons when alone are afraid to face a large 'old man' kangaroo. **1843** *Portland Mercury* 23 Aug. 4/2 Betts replied that he wanted to kill some old men kangaroo. **1848** *Atlas* (Sydney) IV. 121/1 It is highly picturesque to behold a large 'old man' (as the blacks call an aged male), hopping along the side of a ridge. **1854** MRS C. CLACY *Lights & Shadows* I. 36 Why, he's a regular 'old man kangaroo', and must have stood pretty nigh six feet. **1859** W. KELLY *Life in Vic.* I. 235 Old man kangaroo is the patriarch of his flock, who, having escaped hurt for years, attains a great size. **1873** 'LADY IN AUST.' *Memories Past* 75 They went after a forester kangaroo, or what we call 'an old man'. **1886** R. HENTY *Australiana* 244 There were very few red kangaroos of the old man species (old man, blackfellow for 'big'). **1911** E.J. BRADY *King's Caravan* 243 A 'boomer' suddenly leapt across the track a few yards ahead, wagon and horses followed the chase at a hard gallop . . until the clever speed caught that 'old man' by the tail. **1927** 'S. RUDD' *Romance of Runnibede* 199 While the half-growns, or 'flyers', were swifter than greyhounds, many of the 'old men' were in difficulties after spurting a few hundred yards. **1935** F. BIRTLES *Battle Fronts Outback* 159 A big old man 'roo rose from his noon-day camp. **1942** H.H. PECK *Mem. of Stockman* 24 His account of running down, with a mate, a big old man kangaroo, dressing him in an overcoat and letting him go to his mob, and of the scare the 'old man' thereby created among all the 'roos for miles around. **1963** HARNEY & LOCKWOOD *Shady Tree* 188 We have only the warm winds of summer which lure me to the eastern side, where I sit each afternoon, following the shade like an Old-Man Kangaroo around a cassia bush in the desert lands. **1977** B. FULLER *Nullarbor Lifelines* 152 On our first crossing we nearly collided with an old man 'roo. **1978** E. HARDING *A. Marshall Talking* 171 Then I saw the kangaroos coming up from the gully . . lots of them, led by a big old man in front. **1979** K. GARVEY *Absolutely Austral.* 24 The old man kangaroo is tough, His wife is fleet and wild, And has a built-in stroller For the transport of their child.

2. An Aboriginal elder (see also quot. 1854).

1848 T.L. MITCHELL *Jrnl. Exped. Tropical Aust.* 269 Each of them carried . . three or four missile clubs. . . They said, by signs, that the whole country belonged to the old man. **1854** W. HOWITT *Boy's Adventures* 306 The Old Man, as they call Pungil their god, not unlike the Hebrew term, Ancient of Days, now held out his hand to 'Gerer', the sun, and made him warm. **1960** *N.T. News* (Darwin) 26 Jan. 1/1 The 'Old Men' of Windi's tribe had tried to take Windi's sick brother Wimmarty and initiate him. **1962** C. GYE *Cockney & Crocodile* 134 She . . had broken a tribal law, become pregnant by one of the wrong 'skin', and stood her trial before the Old Men. **1963** I.L. IDRIESS *Our Living Stone Age* 131 What a wonderful power, deeply ingrained into every tribe, is this power of the Council of the Old Men!

3. In the collocation **old man's beard,** any of several climbing plants of the genus *Clematis* (fam. Ranunculaceae), esp. *C. aristata.*

1914 E.E. PESCOTT *Native Flowers Vic.* 101 We are familiar with the Clematis or 'old man's beard', with white starry flowers. **1942** C. BARRETT *Austral. Wild Flower Bk.* 43 Old English names for Clematis, such as 'traveler's joy' and 'virgin's bower', rarely are used for the Australian species, though the glistening silvery-white bearded fruits have earned for some the nick-name 'old man's beard'. **1984** T. NOTTLE *Cottage Garden Revived* 72 Colonial gardeners in Australia and New Zealand also had some native species of clematis—Old Man's Beard, Traveller's Joy or Virgin's Bower they were called. *Clematis aristata* from Australia is a common bushland climber and it was brought early into settlers' gardens because of its similarities to the Old Man's Beard (*C. vitalba*) of the homelands, and for its perfumed flowers.

B. 1. *attrib.* passing into *adj.* Of exceptional size, duration, intensity, etc.

1845 R. HOWITT *Impressions Aust. Felix* 233, I stared at a man one day for saying that a certain allotment of land was 'an old-man allotment': he meant a large allotment—the old-man kangaroo being the largest kangaroo. **1856** W.W. DOBIE *Recoll. Visit Port-Phillip* 92 He would crunch away at the green stuff with the relish of a cow or a pig, and exclaim every now and then . . 'Mĕrrijig old man cabbage!' **1863** J.B. AUSTIN *Mines S.A.* 47 A blackfellow was the first to discover the Yudanamutana Mine, which he called 'Big one old man Copper'—'old man' being an expression in use among the blacks to denote anything of full size, or maturity. **1869** MRS W.M. HOWELL *Diggings & Bush* 34 'Old man snake,' said the black sententiously. 'What does he mean?' asked Rosalie. 'He means that it was very cunning,' replied Grey. **1888** J.C.F. JOHNSON *Austral Christmas* 56 Mrs Mac was going to get up a whoppin' old man Christmas duff. **1893** E. FAVENC *Last of Six Tales* 134 It had been 'an old man spree'. Duncan had damaged the sergeant of police, who was good-naturedly trying to induce him to leave town. **1912** J. BOWES *Comrades* 183 Wouldn't be surprised if the father of an old-man storm wasn't working up. **1922** *Bulletin* (Sydney) 29 June 22/1, I have by me a piece of wood with one old man bardie's blazed trail running clean through a half-inch railway dog-spike which had been driven into the tree. **1932** I.L. IDRIESS *Flynn of Inland* (1965) 169 The homestead is built on piles, for floods there are of the 'old man' variety. **1942** F. CLUNE *Last of Austral. Explorers* 112 The know-alls . . predicted an old man dust-storm. **1968** D. O'GRADY *Bottle of Sandwiches* 201 Between a large submerged log and an old-man willow.

2. Comb. **old man cod, crocodile, drought, fern, flood, goanna, possum, wombat.**

1902 *Bulletin* (Sydney) 22 Mar. 14/2 *Re* cod fish. . . In '95 one was caught in the Burdekin . . the *head and shoulders* thereof weighing 87 lbs. This **'old man' cod** smelt as rank as a W.A. boom prospectus. **1936** *Ibid.* 29 Jan. 20/4 Murray cod bait . . ? 'The O.D.' omits the two best ones for an old-man cod. **1929** H. MACQUARRIE *We & Baby* 26 A great **'old man' crocodile** emerged. **1978** R.J. BRITTEN *Around Cassowary Rock* 19 It was so deep-throated it could have been nothing less than a really big 'Old Man' crocodile. **1904** *Truth* (Sydney) 25 Sept. 1/6 In many parts of the interior the **'old man' drought** never broke. **1928** *Bulletin* (Sydney) 21 Mar. 23/2 It would be an old-man drought that could starve a wild abo. **1949** G. BERRIE *Morale* 144 The Bushman solemnly rolled in the green grass. He had done that before, after the break of an old-man drought in Australia. **1879** 'RECENT SETTLER' *Emigration to Tas.* 51 One of the most remarkable features of Myrtle Bank is the immense number of tree ferns, commonly called **'old men ferns'**, the stems of which are often from ten to twenty feet high. **1903** *Bulletin* (Sydney) 29 Oct. 16/3 I've seen sticks four inches in diameter in a rest between two huge old-man ferns near Blackwarry, in the South Gippsland ranges. **1916** T. WARLOW *By Mirage & Mulga* 51 At last it rained, and the blacks predicted an **old-man flood.** **1947** *Bulletin* (Sydney) 23 July 28/1 There was an old-man flood on the river. **1900** *Ibid.* 7 July 15/2 Found an **old-man-goanna** with nearly half the arm down his throat. **1958** H.D. WILLIAMSON *Sunlit Plain* 180 That Regan is as cunning as an old-man goanna. **1963** I.L. IDRIESS *Our Living Stone Age* 11 Warmly sheltered from cold and wind and danger—except from a voracious old-man goanna or hungry dingo ready to take a snap and a risk—baby can sleep in comfort. **1847** A. HARRIS *Settlers & Convicts* (1953) 17 In one place we saw a very large opossum (in the language of the country an **old man 'possum**). **1849** *Argus* (Melbourne) 13 Nov. 4/2 If there is in the world any unconquerable dare devil animal, it is the old man Possum. **1909** *Bulletin* (Sydney) 21 Jan. 14/1, I was hailed by an **old-man wombat** who was much the worse for wear. . . His wombatess was not at home at the time. **1964** D. ROWBOTHAM *Man in Jungle* 69 Any dingo would feel that way about an old-man wombat.

3. Special Comb. **old man saltbush,** either of two shrubs of the fam. Chenopodiaceae, *Atriplex nummularia* (also CABBAGE SALTBUSH) of arid and semi-arid Aust., having grey-green foliage used as fodder, and (occas.) *Rhagodia parabolica* of central and e. Aust.; formerly also **old man's saltbush; snapper,** a large SNAPPER (see quots. 1965 and 1974); also **old man schnapper; spinifex** *obs.*, BUCK SPINIFEX.

1885 P.R. MEGGY *From Sydney to Silverton* 13 The plains on either side are fairly covered with this not very pleasant-tasting bush—common salt bush, **old man's salt-bush** [etc.]. **1887** S. NEWLAND *Far North Country* 17 There is plenty of saltbush in parts, the 'old man' kind in particular being very abundant. **1907** F. TURNER *Anderson's Man. Farm* 132 Round-leaved or

Old Man Salt-Bush (*Atriplex nummularia*) . . bears a great resemblance to the true 'Old Man Salt-Bush' (*Rhagodia parabolica*). **1934** *Bulletin* (Sydney) 18 Apr. 28/4 Old-man saltbush, so called from its white appearance. **1938** C.T. WHITE *Princ. Bot. Qld. Farmers* 165 *Atriplex nummalaria* is the Old Man Saltbush, a shrubby species extensively planted both as a fodder plant and as a hedge. **1953** A. RUSSELL *Murray Walkabout* 55 The old man saltbush is . . the father, so far as size is concerned, of the saltbush tribe. . . It occasionally attains the growth almost of a small tree, eight or ten feet high or more. **1984** *West Austral.* (Perth) 10 Dec. 58/2 Plants such as 'old man' saltbush are preferred hosts for the young [sandalwood] plants. **1882** J.E. TENISON-WOODS *Fish & Fisheries N.S.W.* (*caption*), An **'old man schnapper'**. **1911** D.A. MACDONALD *Bush Boy's Bk.* 99 They are called 'old man' schnapper, but they are really old woman schnapper because all these big fish with the enlarged noses are females. **1918** 'J. SCOTT' *How, when and where to catch Fish* 31 As snapper grow after passing the squire stage they develop a knob or bump on their head, which as their age increases grows more pronounced, and one often hears the name, 'Old Man Snapper', applied to one which has a lump in a pronounced form. **1965** *Austral. Encycl.* VIII. 169 Full-grown specimens develop a large bony protuberance on the nape, and a peculiar flabby and fleshy nose, which produces a somewhat human appearance and has earned for them the name of old-man snapper. **1974** J.M. THOMSON *Fish Ocean & Shore* 126 A squire becomes a snapper at about one and a half kilos and thereafter matures to the old man snapper stage which may reach eighteen kilos. **1882** *Illustr. Austral. News* (Melbourne) 25 Jan. 10/3 After travelling some miles through **'old man' spinifex,** it is almost impossible to force horses along. **1897** A.F. CALVERT *My Fourth Tour W.A.* 262 The coarsest species is what is known as 'old man spinifex', which even the native horses turn from in disgust, so tough and prickly is its growth. **1898** D.W. CARNEGIE *Spinifex & Sand* 177 There are two varieties of spinifex known to bushmen—'spinifex' and 'buck' (or 'old man') spinifex. The latter is stronger in the prickle and practically impossible to get through.

old people. Aborigines who live in the traditional manner; Aborigines of an earlier generation, regarded by their descendants as repositories of traditional knowledge.

1938 X. HERBERT *Capricornia* (ed. 6) 324 Let's consider the Old People for a jiffy. . . They're starved and sickened and kicked and stupefied and generally jiggered out of all recognition. **1948** A. MARSHALL *Ourselves writ Strange* 47 There were still a few old men and women there who were once Myall blacks and who could still speak their native tongue. These were 'The Old People'. **1964** K. WILLEY *Eaters of Lotus* 30 He is a half-caste who, years ago, made his decision to go with 'the old people', instead of adopting the white man's way. **1967** G.J. HENRY *Girro Gurrl* 11 The 'Old People', the tribal aborigines who once roamed in the valleys of the Davidson Creek, Tully and Murray Rivers. **1977** B. FULLER *Nullarbor Lifelines* 87 The old people, true myalls, speak no English and are still very superstitious. **1983** *Bulletin* (Sydney) 1 Nov. 80/2 The 'Old People' (as the part-Aborigines called their full-blood progenitors).

old wife. [Spec. use of *old wife* any of various fish of several families.] Formerly any of several marine fish, now usu. *Enoplosus armatus* of s. Aust., a silvery fish with black vertical stripes. See also *zebra fish* ZEBRA.

1699 W. DAMPIER *New Voyage round World* (1703) III. 140 In the night while Calm we fish'd with Hook and Line, and caught good store of Fish, *viz* Snappers, Breams, Old Wives, and Dog-Fish. **1770** J. COOK *Jrnls.* 23 Aug. I. 394 The sea is indifferently well stock'd with Fish of various sorts, such as . . old wives. **1789** A. PHILLIP *Voyage to Botany Bay* 281 Bag-Throated Balistes. . . This fish is found pretty commonly on the coast of New South Wales, and was called by the sailors the Old Wife. **1824** *HRA* (1922) 3rd Ser. V. 778 The fish our seine has produced are Mullet . . that which the seamen call the *Old Wife*. **1880** *Proc. Linnean Soc. N.S.W.* V. (1881) 309 *Enoplosus armatus* . . 'Old Wife' of the Sydney Fishermen. **1906** D.G. STEAD *Fishes of Aust.* 105 The Old Wife . . is purely an Australian fish and is found principally in the waters of New South Wales and Victoria. **1951** *Bulletin* (Sydney) 14 Mar. 12/1 He took small yellowtail and 'old wives' off the hook and flung them contemptuously into his sugarbag. **1978** N. COLEMAN *Austral. Fisherman's Fish Guide* 71 The old wife is edible. **1983** HUTCHINS & THOMPSON *Marine & Estuarine Fishes S.-W. Aust.* 44 Old Wife . . named after its habit of 'grunting like an old wife' when caught. Dorsal fin spines reputed to be venomous.

olive, *a.* Used as a distinguishing epithet in the names of birds: **olive-backed oriole,** the bird *Oriolus sagittatus* of n., e., and s.e. mainland Aust., and s.e. New Guinea, having olive to grey upper parts; **whistler,** the bird *Pachycephala olivacea* of s.e. Aust. incl. Tas., having olive-brown upper parts; formerly also **olive thickhead.**

1945 [**olive-backed oriole**] C. BARRETT *Austral. Bird Life* 137 The yellow oriole . . is restricted to tropical Northern Australia. The olive-backed species (*O. sagittatus*) has a much wider range—Northern, Eastern, and Southern Australia. **1956** A.C.C. LOCK *Tropical Tapestry* 281 The olive-backed orioles were named cedar birds. **1984** *A.N.U. Reporter* (Canberra) 26 Oct. 5 The next few months will be marked . . by the 'ori-ori-ole' calls of the Olive-backed Oriole. **1903** [**olive whistler**] *Emu* II. 207 *Pachycephala olivacea* (olive thickhead)—this large Thickhead with beautiful aesthetic markings. **1911** J.A. LEACH *Austral. Bird Bk.* 152 Olive Whistler, Olivaceous Thickhead . . olive brown; head dark-gray . . liquid, whistling note. **1929** A.H. CHISHOLM *Birds & Green Places* 1 The gloomy, sun-streaked haunts of the rufous scrub-bird and olive whistler. **1949** B. O'REILLY *Green Mountains* 151 From the moss above, the elusive ventriloquial cry of the olive whistler. **1964** M. SHARLAND *Territory of Birds* 73 It is hard to believe that the melodious 'pee-poo' call heard in the Macpherson Range of southern Queensland is made by the Olive Whistler, particularly after hearing the call of the same species in Tasmania. **1984** M. BLAKERS et al. *Atlas Austral. Birds* 384 In northern parts of its range . . the Olive Whistler lives mainly in rainforest and eucalypt forest above 500 m.

ominny, ominy, var. HOMINY.

on, *prep.*

1. [Chiefly Austral.: see OED(S *prep.* 26 b. and quot. 1883.] Denoting 'place where': at; in.

1853 *Bendigo Advertiser* 9 Dec. 1/1 We have . . endeavoured to procure suitable materials for publishing a Newspaper on Bendigo, to be devoted Exclusively to the Mining Interests. **1883** R.E.N. TWOPENY *Town Life Aust.* 245 When speaking of a goldfield a colonists says 'on'. Thus you live 'on Bendigo', but 'in' or 'at' Sandhurst—the latter being the name for the old goldfield town. **1892** *Bohemia* (Melbourne) 4 Feb. 13 We'll get plenty of Warrigal cabbage on the middle camp for supper. **1901** H. LAWSON *Joe Wilson & his Mates* 47 The expression 'on' came from being on the 'diggings' or goldfield—the workings or the goldfield was all underneath, of course, so men lived (or starved) *on* them—not in nor at 'em. **1930** 'BRENT OF BIN BIN' *Ten Creeks Run* (1952) 23 He had dummied for Larry Healey's on Monaro in '61 when the Free Selection Act came in. **1954** T. RONAN *Vision Splendid* 153 They were still on the open country. **1976** C.D. MILLS *Hobble Chains & Greenhide* 162 On dinner camp I saw this dusky imp Pluto approaching Ned with a 'frilly'.

2. In phr.: **on gold,** see GOLD 1; **on opal,** see OPAL 2.

3. [See OED(S *prep.* 1 l.] In the phr. **on it,** drinking (alcoholic liquor) heavily.

1908 *Truth* (Sydney) 19 July 1/7 People who have in the dim religious light of the previous evening, been 'on it', next morning are fined 'five shillings'. **1938** E. LOWE *Salute to Freedom* 38 He knew how drink affected Brand, and he muttered to his wife, 'He's on it proper today mother'. **1951** S. HICKEY *Travelled Roads* 27 If George was 'off it' before, the sight of the gold watch put him 'on it' again. **1978** D. STUART *Wedgetail View* 69 Y' know he got on it once in a while.

4. [See OED(S *prep.* 6 b. and 26 b.] In the phr. **on (the) weekend(s),** at or during (the) weekend(s).

1958 R. ROBINSON *Black-Feller White-Feller* 3 Jack, as usual on week-ends, was drunk. **1973** —— *Drift of Things* 467, I had discovered this drive after I met Rosaleen, on a week-end when she could not come with me. **1977** A. MACKAY *Life Pieces* II. 219 'Are you . . gunna go away, Bob?' . . 'Yeah! For good, not just on weekends.' **1985** *Good Weekend* (Sydney) 25 Aug. 19/2 More urgent . . is a review of the food retailing outlets that appear on the weekends.

on, *adv.* [Br. slang *on* on the way to intoxication: see OED *adv.* 10 c.]

1. Under the influence of alcohol.

1871 *Austral. Town & Country Jrnl.* (Sydney) 18 Feb. 20/1 Perks, poor fellow, was well—yes, a trifle 'on'. **1880** 'ERRO' *Squattermania* 176 This fellow walked right into my tent, in a stupid kind of way, as if he was a little on. **1893** *Bulletin* (Sydney) 29 Apr. 23/1 When the store is closed for dinner, if you feel a trifle 'on', Take a drop of good bulk whisky with your bread and cheese at one. **1921** K.S. PRICHARD *Black Opal* 46 Paul was a bit on. . . I was a bit on meself, too. **1970** K.E.C. GRAVES *Third Chance* 27, I won't serve anyone who's getting a bit on.

2. a. In the phr. **on with,** amorously involved with.

1903 *Truth* (Sydney) 8 Mar. 3/5 Thousands of grande dames will be only too anxious to be 'on with' the man who could win the . . love of a Crown Princess. **1924** F.J. MILLS *Happy Days* 118, I was on with a taxi-driver named Phyllis. . . She was the neatest tart outside of a baker's shop. **1972** *Southerly* iv. 281 Soon after she was on with David Murray, Nina arranged a dinner party.

b. In the phr. **on for,** amorously interested in.

1907 *Truth* (Sydney) 6 Jan. 9/2 You're on for the donah up there. **1936** N. LINDSAY *Saturdee* (ed. 2) 181 'Conkey Mender! Is he on for Trix?' 'He's on any day.'

3. In the phr. **it is (was, etc.) on (for young and old):** a description of a battle, party, argument, etc., characterized by the participants' lack of inhibition or restraint.

1945 'MASTER-SARG' *Yank discovers Aust.* 17 'Its on' means that a battle or something else has started. **1951** E. LAMBERT *Twenty Thousand Thieves* (1952) 258 Peter Dimmock bounded between the tents leaping into the air at every few paces and whooping: 'It's on! It's on for young and old!' **1953** T.A.G. HUNGERFORD *Riverslake* 181 'It's on, all right,' Murdoch said. . . In the centre of the crowd . . two men in their shirt sleeves swung punches at each other. **1956** *Tennant Creek Times* 1 June 4/3 Davies, hitting well, was pretty to watch. Now he has his eye in, it will be 'on' for loose pitchers. **1965** J. WYNNUM *Jiggin' in Riggin'* 36 Things don't start moving much before midnight, but when they do, it's on for young and old. **1971** D. MARTIN *Hughie* (1972) 106 He almost forgot about it until the evening of Sunday when the party was due and when, in Harry's words, it was on for young and old. **1983** HIBBERD & HUTCHINSON *Barracker's Bible* 143 *On! it's*, . . Enthusiastic announcement that there is a blue occurring.

oncer. [Spec. use of *oncer* one who does a particular thing only once.] A person elected as a member of parliament (esp. in a marginal seat), who is considered unlikely to hold the seat for more than one term.

1974 BLAZEY & CAMPBELL *Political Dice Men* 47 When he got to Canberra, with all the other new Liberal members, he found he was treated with sympathy because everyone regarded him as a 'oncer'. **1976** *Bulletin* (Sydney) 25 Sept. 29/1 There are quite a few Liberals in the Federal House who are considered 'oncers'—they got in because of the size of the anti-Whitlam swing, but have only slim hopes of holding their seats next election. **1977** F. DALY *From Curtin to Kerr* 41 There were friends and enemies who said that I had fluked winning the Martin electorate in 1943 and was a 'oncer'. **1983** *Austral.* (Sydney) 4 Feb. 11/4 However, it soon became apparent that Mr Hayden was something more than one of those political irrelevancies, the 'oncer'—the bolter who wins a seat for one term, which he spends gazing wide-eyed at the activities around him before returning to obscurity.

one, *a.*

1. [Cf. *one too many, etc.* OED(S 1 d.] With ellipsis of *glass* or *drink*, not always with the implication 'sole'. Also in the phr. **one for the bitumen,** 'one for the road'.

1945 *Aust. Week-end Bk.* 164 'What the hell are you two doing here, eh? Have one with me!' Presently Bill says, 'You'd better have one with me now. . . ' and a little while later Jack says, 'This one's mine.' **1957** *Overland* x. 8 I'll force one down just to be sociable. **1962** *Texas Q.* 29 A bloke comes in in the middle of the afternoon when there's only you and the blowfly on the window in the bar and . . asks you to have one. **1977** B. SCOTT *My Uncle Arch* 108 Two hours later it's have one for the bitumen. **1984** P. JARRATT *Aussie* 171 'Having the one' is a typically Australian understatement. Aussies rarely have one, or even two.

2. In the phr. **one day of the year,** ANZAC DAY. Also *transf.*

[**1945** C. MANN *River* 149 As you all heard the Padre and Premier both say at the service, it is the one day in the year which we, with very great pride, can call our *own* Day.] **1962** A. SEYMOUR *(title)* The One Day of the Year. **1971** F. HARDY *Outcasts of Foolgarah* 211 A retired officer of high rank . . out late celebrating the One Day of the Year. **1972** *Bulletin* (Sydney) 14 Oct. 44/1 *Melbourne's* one day of the year has passed. The Grand Final is over for 1972. **1974** D. IRELAND *Burn* 115, I never went to a march on Anzac Day. I can always remember the kids that died up there in the slush. . . I don't have to wait for one day of the year. **1985** *Centralian Advocate* (Alice Springs) 6 Sept. 2/2 Aborigines throughout Australia are gearing up to celebrate their 'one day of the year' next week. National Aborigines' Week . . will culminate in a march and speeches on National Aborigines' Day on Friday.

3. In collocations: **one flag (only),** the signal for a BEHIND 1 b.; **-pub** *a.* (of a settlement), small, uninteresting, 'one-horse'; **-teacher school,** see quot. 1973.

1968 EAGLESON & MCKIE *Terminol. Austral. Football* ii. 26 ***One flag*** [***only***], a behind (a goal is signalled by two flags, a behind by one). **1981** L. MONEY *Footy Fan's Handbk.* 39 *Terms for a behind* . . Ahrrrr! One flag only! **1983** HIBBERD & HUTCHINSON *Barracker's Bible* 143 *One flag only*, . . a behind . . a singleton. **1901** H. LAWSON *Joe Wilson & his Mates* 54 Along the bush roads and tracks that branch out fanlike through the scrubs to the **one-pub** towns and sheep and cattle stations out there in the haunting wilderness. **1920** *Aussie* (Sydney) Oct. 36/2 Hotel-keeper in our one-pub township. **1946** F. CLUNE *Try Nothing Twice* 118, I was sent . . to the one-pub village of Wee Wee Rup. **1978** R.H. CONQUEST *Dusty Distances* 156 Ilfracombe, in early 1935, was a hot and dusty, one-pub sheep town. **1931** B. CRONIN *Bracken* 90 Guruwa's only a **one-teacher school** as they call it. **1973** W.G. WALKER *Gloss. Educ. Terms* 84 *One-teacher-school*, a school usually in an isolated area, in which one teacher teaches all grades. **1978** P. ADAM SMITH *Anzacs* 14 Our little bush school in the Koo-Wee-Rup swamplands combined with other equally small one-teacher schools for the annual Anzac Day ceremony. **1981** *Austral. Women's Weekly* (Sydney) 22 July 18/1 A move was made 15 years ago to close the one-room, one teacher school.

ones, *pl. Two-up.* A call indicating that one coin has landed with the head facing upwards and one with the tail facing upwards. In full, **two ones.**

1911 L. STONE *Jonah* 217 He set two pounds of his winnings, and tossed the coins. 'Two ones!' cried the gamblers, with a roar. **1925** A. WRIGHT *Boy from Bullarah* 17 Ronter possessed himself of the kip, and, placing the pennies upon it, spun them high into the air. 'Two ones.' **1965** *Kings Cross Whisper* (Sydney) Nov. 1/2 He must be able to yell 'Come in Spinner' and 'Ones'. **1972** J. O'GRADY *It's your Shout, Mate!* 26 Two more pennies . . came down, one showed a head, and the other rolled around the ring . . and showed its white-crossed tail. 'Ones,' said the keeper. **1979** *Bulletin* (Sydney) 14 Aug. 36/3 If one head and one tail showed, then it was 'ones', meaning that the spinner must continue spinning until two sides showed together.

Hence **one** *v. trans.*, to throw (the coins) so that they land showing a head and a tail.

1949 L. GLASSOP *Lucky Palmer* 168 The pennies hit the canvas. One jumped in the air, landed and lay flat. It was a tail. 'And he's—' began the fat man. The other penny ran a few feet and stopped. It was a head. '—one'd 'em!' finished the fat man. **1966** S.J. BAKER *Austral. Lang.* (ed. 2) 242 If he tosses one 'head' and one 'tail' he *ones them.*

onion.

1. Used *attrib.* in the names of plants: **onion-grass,** any of several species of the introduced genus *Romulea* (fam. Liliaceae), incl. GUILDFORD GRASS; **orchid,** any species of the chiefly Austral. genus of terrestrial orchids *Microtis* (fam. Orchidaceae), having a single, onion-like leaf and flower-spike of small, usu. green flowers; **weed, (a)** the naturalized perennial herb *Asphodelus fistulosus* (fam. Liliaceae), common on disturbed land and along roadsides; **(b)** the S. American perennial *Nothoscordum inodorum* (fam. Liliaceae), having leaves which smell of onions when crushed; **(c)** any of several other similar herbs, esp. of the widespread genus *Bulbine* (fam. Liliaceae); *wild onion*, see WILD 1.

1909 J.M. BLACK *Naturalised Flora S.A.* 147 [*R. Bulbocodium*] . . **Onion-grass** in Victoria. **1928** R.H. CROLL *Open Road Vic.* 21 The capeweed . . battling with that other, equally hardy, alien, the onion grass. **1949** *Bulletin* (Sydney) 12 Oct. 13/4 In Suburbia . . what we used to call 'pudding-grass' or onion-grass is generally called nut-grass. **1969** G. JOHNSTON *Clean Straw for Nothing* (1971) 223 In short pants lying on the ground nibbling at onion-grass. **1961** *Meanjin* 6 Cucumber, potato and even **onion orchids.** **1984** D.T. & C.E. WOOLCOCK *Austral. Terrestrial Orchids* 78 The glabrous terete leaves of the *Microtis* group have given them the popular name of onion orchids. **1985** *Melbourne Winner's Weekly* 2 Sept. 23/2 There are all kinds of greenhoods, sun-orchids . . and the minutely flowered onion-orchids. She recommended a magnifying glass for these last ones. **1909** A.J. EWART *Weeds Vic.* 60 *Asphodelus fistulosus*. . . This plant, known locally as the **Onion Weed,** is a native of Southern Europe. **1917** *Bulletin* (Sydney) 29 Nov. 22/4 Beware the onion weed, which has sprung up in the highways and byways. **1935** T. RAYMENT *Cluster of Bees* 264 The tiny pink funnel-flowers of the onion weed. **1977** J. GALBRAITH *Wild Flowers S.-E. Aust.* 37 Onion Weed . . with greyish onion-like leaves and small bell-flowers that turn miles of the drier sandy country into a lilac-brown sea.

2. *fig.* An occasion upon which a number of males have intercourse one after another with the same female; the female.

1969 *Sydney Morning Herald* 16 July 13/4 When he had passed the circle of men, he knew an 'onion was going on'. . . The court was told on Monday that the expression 'onion' meant a girl was available for sexual intercourse with two or more men. **1976** *Southerly* ii. 136, I would like to win his confidence so that he would admit me to their brotherhood and to rites that I could write about, the inside story of onions, gang-bangs, pack rapes. **1978** *Weekend Austral.* (Sydney) 1 July 3/8 Woodhouse told the man the girl was to be the 'onion' for the night. . . He understood that an 'onion' in bikie jargon meant a girl having repeated intercourse. **1980** B. HORNADGE *Austral. Slanguage* 191 *Onion* is a modern term, not recorded by Sidney Baker, and refers to the practice of bikie gangs in common sexual sharing of one of the girl-followers or of an outsider unwillingly abducted for the occasion. **1984** *Nat. Times* (Sydney) 30 Nov. 17/2 The girl alleges the traditional on-i-on or onion as it is sometimes incorrectly pronounced, by a group of motor bike riders in a disused gravel pit after several hours of riotous drinking.

onka: see ONKAPARINGA 2.

onkaparinga /ɒŋkəpəˈrɪŋɡə/. Also **onkaparinka.**

1. With initial capital. The proprietary name of a blanket; such a blanket.

1926 *Austral. Official Jrnl. Patents* (Canberra) 336 *Onkaparinga* 41,194. Cloths and stuffs of wool, worsted and hair. *South Australian Woollen Co. Ltd.* **1968** *Coast to Coast 1967–68* 121 Bodies were carried out of the crumpled cars, and she remembered a past occasion when she had run with blankets, and Hazel's Onkaparinka, and a pillow from their own beds. **1972** J. HIBBERD *Stretch of Imagination* (1973) 10 I'll fetch you a blanket. . . I did just that. . . Brought out a thick old Onkaparinga . . and laid it gently over his slumbrous limbs.

2. Rhyming slang for 'finger'. Also abbrev. as **onka.**

1967 *Truth* (Sydney) xxxviii. 10/1 *Onkaparingas*, fingers. **1974** *Bulletin* (Sydney) 2 Nov. 57/3 When one gets around to plighting one's troth to a charlie, one claps a frank on her onka . . a Frank Thring on her Onkaparinga . . a ring on her . . aaar, work it out for yourself. **1981** *Nat. Times* (Sydney) 1 Feb. 14/4 Rhyming slang, not in heavy evidence during the formal side of the competition, showed up strongly in last week's entries. There were Onkaparingas (fingers), Warwick Farms (arms) [etc.].

onkus, *a.* [Of unknown origin.] Disagreeable; distasteful; disordered.

1918 G.C. COOPER Diary 17 Nov., Felt pretty 'onkus' in consequence of fall I had on deck the previous night. **1941** S.J. BAKER *Pop. Dict. Austral. Slang* 51 *Onkus*, all wrong, incorrect; (of machinery) out of order. **1941** *Furphy Flyer: Official Organ 2/24 Austral. Infantry Battalion* 15 Oct. 1 The tucker may be onkus. **1947** N. LINDSAY *Halfway to Anywhere* 84 It's booze of a sort . . a bit onkus, but drinkable. **1962** D. MCLEAN *World turned upside Down* 121 All this yabber about Danny is onkus.

oooah, var. YOHI.

Oodnagalahbi /udnəɡəˈlabi/. Also **Oodnagalabie.** [f. *Oodna(datta* the name of a town in n. S.A. + GALAH + *-bi.*] An imaginary place, remote and supposedly backward. See also BULLAMAKANKA, WOOP WOOP 1.

1968 *Kings Cross Whisper* (Sydney) xlviii. 9/3 Secretary of the Oodnagalabie branch of the United Pastoralists Union . . said yesterday politicians had reached plague proportions in many areas of Australia. **1969** *Sydney Morning Herald* 1 Dec. 6/4 Last night the show was firmly bogged down in Oodnagalahbi (may it be eaten by grasshoppers) and Dad and Dave and Mabel wore felt hats pulled down on their foreheads and cracked jokes about carpet snakes in the dunny. **1972** G. MORLEY *Jockey rides Honest Race* 93 Fifty per cent of the Australian population only buy their newspaper to see if Nancy and Sluggo finally get married. The other fifty per cent want to find out who won the third race at Oodnagallabi. **1981** *Canberra Times* 30 July 15/3 Canberra was chosen for the premiere season of 'Centrespread' in an effort to qualify the film for this year's Australian Film Institute awards. It would have been better to have opened it in Oodnagalahbie, where it could have sunk without a trace as it deserves.

oont /ʊnt/. [a. Hindi (and Urdu) *ūnṭ* camel; also in Indian English: see OEDS.] A camel. Also *attrib.*

1918 *Barrack: Official Organ Imperial Camel Corps* 1 Feb. 9/2 *The laws of the oont.* Now these are the Laws of the Camel. **1923** *Smith's Weekly* (Sydney) 21 July 23/3 If the 'oont' is standing up, you generally knock him well off the line. **1936** W. HATFIELD *Big Timber* 172 'Can camels drag a car?' he said. 'Depends,' said the bushman. 'I gotta keep them oonts in nick for the mail, once a fortnight.' **1957** *Bulletin* (Sydney) 16 Oct. 19/1 Any Moslem oont-driver knows that the bull-camel is frustrated and resentful of humans. **1978** D. STUART *Wedgetail View* 120 It's funny about camels, y' know. . . I've seen teams go for miles with miles of water on the ground, and so long as it doesn't get slippery, an' so long as the wheels'll keep rolling without bogging the old oonts'll keep moochin' along.

ooroo, var. HOOROO.

oowa, var. YOHI.

opal.

1. Used *attrib.* in Special Comb. **opal dirt,** the type of earth in which opal occurs; **-gouger,** an opal-miner (see also GOUGER); so, **-gouging** *vbl. n.*

1925 *Ann. Rep.* (N.S.W. Dept. Mines) 85 The **'Opal Dirt'** is picking ground, being simply a layer of clay or sandy clay overlain by sandstone. **1931** M.S. BUCHANAN *Prospecting for Opal* 5 You sink a shaft gradually into the sandstone from the surface, and in 5 feet to 40 or 50 feet you break through into a layer of fine soft fireclay called the '*level*' or 'Opal dirt'. **1962** WHITING & RELPH *Occurrence of Opal* 8 A grey to buff-coloured clay shale is formed. It is soft, free from grit, and it is within this horizon that most of the precious opal is found. It is commonly called 'opal dirt'. **1975** 'N. CULOTTA' *Gone Gougin'* 124 We've got a new dunny . . and Carl spread some opal dirt along the track to it, so you won't get lost on a dark night. **1904** *Bulletin* (Sydney) 17 Mar. 16/3 Came the way of a White Cliffs (N.S.W.) **opal-gouger** lately. **1928** R.M. MACDONALD *Opals & Gold* 32 The cosmopolitan crowd of 'opal gougers' . . are not real opal prospectors. **1943** *Bulletin* (Sydney) 27 Jan. 12/3 Tim . . had had a tough apprenticeship in a shanty pub among the opal gougers. **1964** 'E. LINDALL' *Kind of Justice* 17 He had recognized early that the big man was not the usual type of opal gouger and gold fossicker you met in the odd corners of the Territory. **1965** A.W. UPFIELD *Lure of Bush* 9 He spent twenty years in the bush, working at many kinds of jobs: . . opal gouging [etc.].

2. In the phr. **to be on opal,** to have found or to be mining an opal deposit.

1878 J.H. NICHOLSON *Opal Fever* 4 I'm on opal sure as beans. **1921** K.S. PRICHARD *Black Opal* 8 'We're on opal,' he cried; 'on opal!' **1932** I.L. IDRIESS *Prospecting for Gold* 235 A patch means, generally, hundreds of stones. You may be weeks, months, 'on opal'.

open, *a.*[1] [Spec. use of *open* unobstructed, clear: see OED *a.* 8 and, for U.S. examples, Mathews.]

1. a. Of land bearing scattered trees or stands of trees: without undergrowth or similar obstruction to movement or to use as pasture. See FOREST 1.

1829 [see *open forest land*]. **1840** *S. Austral. Rec.* (London) 27 June 351 North of the Great Bend, the brush almost wholly disappears, and the open brush spreads out into enormous plains. **1844** *Tasmanian Jrnl. Nat. Sci.* III. 19 Open myall scrub was frequent, particularly along the Condamine. **1846** *Portland Mercury* 14 Apr. 4/3 These creeks are accompanied by fine open box and narrow-leaved ironbark flats. **1852** J.E. ERSKINE *Short Acct. Late Discoveries Gold* 74 The *forest* consists of the usual open bush of gum-trees. **1862** G.T. LLOYD *Thirty-Three Yrs. Tas. & Vic.* 64 The fine forest kangaroo, so called from its frequenting the open park grounds. **1875** J. FORREST *Explorations in Aust.* 54 Continuing for six miles over clear, open sand-plains, with spinifex and large white gums. **1880** A. FORREST *N.-W. Exploration* 10 The country was first class; clear open flats in places, with palms, black wattle, and cajeputs studded here and there. **1944** *Bulletin* (Sydney) 29 Nov. 13/3 What has come over the Queensland wild lime? This tree was once found only in widely separated clumps, generally on broken-plain country .. but now the little tree has gone mad, overrunning forests and open-scrub country. **1954** T. RONAN *Vision Splendid* 188 Before them, open bloodwood country stretched towards a range of low hills. **1960** R.S. PORTEOUS *Cattleman* 20 The coolibah gave way to brigalow, in places open brigalow that made excellent grazing country.

b. Also **open forest country, land.**

1834 G. BENNETT *Wanderings N.S.W.* I. 163 We passed an interesting **open forest country**, possessing some good land for cultivation, and abundance of fine herbage. **1848** T.L. MITCHELL *Jrnl. Exped. Tropical Aust.* 97, I returned to the camp through some fine open forest country. **1881** W.E. ABBOTT *Notes Journey on Darling* 41 The massive trees running up some hundreds of feet and shutting out the light of day with their leaves and branches are altogether wanting in what the auctioneers describe as 'open forest country'. **1829** *Hints Emigration New Settlement Swan & Canning Rivers* 41 Mr Frazer did not rate the trees upon an average of more than two to an acre, but *probably* he referred only to large trees or what is termed **open forest land.** **1845** L. LEICHHARDT *Jrnl. Overland Exped. Aust.* (1847) 13 Jan. 107 We travelled .. through open forest land .. skirted on both sides by scrub. **1853** MOSSMAN & BANISTER *Aust. Visited & Revisited* 62 These open forest-lands have very much the appearance of Hyde Park and Kensington Gardens. **1871** J. BAIRD *Emigrant's Guide Australasia* 229 The bush lands—that is, the open forest lands, along the coast for hundreds of miles, and inland for about fifty—are well adapted to the cultivation of the cotton plant, the sugar cane.

2. a. Of land: without any obstruction to movement or use; *spec.*, without (or with very few) trees.

1849 J.S. ROE *Rep. Exped. S.-Eastward Perth* 5 They soon joined a continuous river of brackish water .. flowing E. and S.W. through open scrubby plains. **1852** S. MOSSMAN *Voice from Aust.* 6 We can muster now, on good grassed forest land and open prairie ground, not far short of 18,000,000 sheep. **1876** G.H. REID *Essay on N.S.W.* 169 The badly-watered and open runs .. now carry fully one half more. **1926** A.S. LE SOUEF et al. *Wild Animals Australasia* 333 The crested-tailed phascogale is an inhabitant of the sand-hills and the open salt-bush plains of Central and South-central Australia. **1932** J. MCCARTER *Pan's Clan* 155 The camp was found, sometimes in a fenced stock route, other times in the bend of a river, still again in the open reserves provided. **1934** 'S. RUDD' *Green Grey Homestead* 131 Ahead a clump of grass trees and patches of wallaby bush obscured an open valley coated with feathery grass from view.

b. In collocations: **open downs, paddock, plain** (chiefly in *pl.*).

1848 T.L. MITCHELL *Jrnl. Exped. Tropical Aust.* 158, I travelled steadily .. over the **open downs,** but with scrubs on either side. **1872** A. MCFARLAND *Illawarra & Manaro* 147 The kangaroo or wallaby would have no chance upon the open downs. **1909** *Bulletin* (Sydney) 21 Jan. (Red Page), The worst stage is the Open Downs, one hundred and thirty miles of sun-baked, crab-holed, practically trackless plain. **1954** T. RONAN *Vision Splendid* 140 The big shady fig and Leichardt pine trees were like a refreshing eye-bath after years on the unshaded open downs country. **1929** *Bulletin* (Sydney) 31 July 19/2 A gum-tree .. grew in solitary state in an **open paddock**. **1946** *Ibid.* 10 Apr. 14/2 One day I saw a chap—in an open paddock, mind you—pass a hare in the squat without seeing it. **1971** W.G. HOWCROFT *This Side Rabbit Proof Fence* 73 A woman in our district was walking across an open paddock... Suddenly, the dogs put up a large goanna. With no tree nearby in which it could climb to safety, the goanna clawed its way up the woman's dress. **1841** G. ARDEN *Recent Information Port Phillip* 32 The spur-winged plover, with its plaintive cry, the native companion a gigantic species of crane, and the stately emu, dwell in the **open plains. 1843** *Sydney Morning Herald* 6 May 2/4 The lands we speak of .. are *open plains*, ready at once for either plough or pasturage. **1874** R.P. FALLA *Knocking About* (1976) 10 What few small open plains this station once possessed, have all been taken up by selectors, only quartz ranges being left. **1890** A. MACKAY *Austral. Agriculturist* (ed. 2) 141 Panicum flavidum, 'black soil cow grass' .. is still spreading on the open plains country. **1930** D. COTTRELL *Earth Battle* 275 After the fourth rain the death-white spider-petalled lillies had sprung up even on the open plains: in ones and twos by the corners of the sandy grey-fenced sheep-yards. **1941** C. BARRETT *Aust.* 57 Thousands of budgerigahs rose from the ground as we drove across open plain country. **1942** *Bulletin* (Sydney) 3 June 12/3 Cattle from the open plains are afraid of timber when first introduced to it.

c. In the collocation **open forest**: a tract of such land. See also FOREST 1.

1832 J. BACKHOUSE *Narr. Visit Austral. Colonies* (1843) 26 Much of the country was settled: it consisted of hills, generally covered with open grassy forest, and interspersed with little patches of cultivated ground. **1836** *Tegg's Monthly Mag.* (Sydney) I. 63 On the banks of rivers the bush changes its character very materially, for in these situations, instead of the open forest in which you can trot along briskly among the lofty trees, it becomes a sort of impenetrable jungle, or as the colonists term it, a *thick brush*. **1843** W. PRIDDEN *Aust.* 63 Vast and extensive tracts .. are what is termed 'open forest', that is, are dotted about with fine trees, dispersed in various groups, and resembling the scenery of an English park. **1853** W. WESTGARTH *Vic.* 31 The open forest, free from underwood, with its grassy carpet beneath and its park-like aspect, is common to all latitudes of the country. **1861** J.D. LANG *Qld., Aust.* 162 In those parts of the country where the pasture-land is of the character designated by the term 'open forest', not more than about 800 sheep can be run in a flock. **1888** *Austral. Handbk.* 368 A small palm named Livistonia Humilis is abundant throughout the Territory in the open forest. **1926** J. POLLARD *Bushland Man* 58 A small open forest of York gum and jam appeared. **1934** WARBURTON & ROBERTSON *Buffaloes* 11 There were miles upon miles of open forest with occasional clay-pans.

open, *a.*[2] [f. OPEN *v.*[1]] Of land: available for settlement. Also in the phr. **to throw open,** to make (land) available.

1830 [see OPEN *v.*[1] 1]. **1855** *Ovens & Murray Advertiser* (Beechworth) 24 Feb. (Suppl.) 5/3 The Government has at length seen the necessity for throwing open the lands in the vicinity of the gold fields for farming and agricultural purposes. **1870** C.H. ALLEN *Visit to Qld.* 101 Acres of the finest land are thrown open for selection. **1886** P. FLETCHER 'Hints to Immigrants' in P. Fletcher *Qld.* 8 All Queensland is not open for anyone to go and pick out a piece of land, but from time to time large districts are proclaimed open, and you can take up your block anywhere in those districts. **1899** *Progress* (Brisbane) 1 Apr. 1/2 All pastoral lands, as the pastoral leases fall in, should be thrown open for grazing farm settlement. **1920** B. CRONIN *Timber Wolves* 47 Crown purchase land is open for selection at from 5s. up to £1 per acre. **1944** F. BERKERY *East goes West* 39 The Commonwealth authorities are anxious to have this land thrown open for occupation.

open, *v.*[1] *Hist.* [Spec. use of *open* to render accessible or available for settlement: see OED *v.* 12.]

1. a. *trans.* To release (Crown land) for settlement. Also with **up.**

1798 D. COLLINS *Acct. Eng. Colony N.S.W.* (1798) I. 266 The lieutenant-governor proposing to open and cultivate the ground commonly known by the name of the Kangaroo Ground. **1830** *Extract of Despatch: Progress of Settlement Swan River* 3, I found it necessary to open a district of country for location. In the first instance I selected for that purpose the banks of the Swan River; and, being urged by further applications for land .. I threw open the country .. fifty miles southward from Perth. **1844** *Sydney Morning Herald* 6 Apr. 2/4 Another district .. has been recently opened for settlement. **1900** *Bulletin* (Sydney) 1 Dec. 15/1 Newly 'opened-up' farming district, consequently great preponderance of men. **1924** *Ibid.* 6 Mar. 24/3 The *Argus* declares dogmatically that the term 'cocky' .. originated from the flight of city men to the country, 'in droves strongly reminiscent of the flight of cockatoos', when the Vic. lands were opened up in 1869.

b. *trans.* To occupy (such land) as a settler.

1794 D. COLLINS *Acct. Eng. Colony N.S.W.* (1798) I. 340 Williams and Ruse .. were permitted .. to open ground on the banks of the Hawkesbury... They chose for themselves allotments of grounds conveniently situated for fresh water. **1873** *Yorke's Peninsula Advertiser* (Moonta) 16 May 4/3 A party of practical miners—to open up the country. **1899** *Progress* (Brisbane) 1 Apr. 1/2 The rental obtained is a secondary matter so long as settlement is secured, the prime consideration of land legislation being the settlement on the land of a white population which will open up the land and create traffic. **1929** 'OLD STOCKMAN' *Sensational Cattle-Stealing Case* 7 The backblockers were a hard-riding, hard-swearing lot, but they opened up the country. **1940** G. MORPHETT *Simple Story Rural Dev.* 4 Great-hearted folk, the people who opened up our country lands!

2. *intr.* To become settled.

1794 D. COLLINS *Acct. Eng. Colony N.S.W.* (1798) I. 375 A country gradually opening, and improving every where upon us as it opened.

open, *v.*[2] [Spec. use of *open* to cut or break into.]

1. *Mining. trans.* To break (the surface of the earth) preparatory to a mining operation. Also with **up.**

1845 *S. Austral. Register* (Adelaide) 11 Oct. 2/2 The face of the hill .. had been opened in three separate places. **1850** *Ibid.* 11 July 2/5, I opened and sunk upon Butler's Lode, and in four days took therefrom about eleven tons of ore. **1869** *Wallaroo Times* (Kadina) 4 Sept. 5/2 Levels driven and the ground opened up. **1962** O. PRYOR *Aust.'s Little Cornwall* 92 Some showed considerable promise when the ground was first opened.

2. *Shearing. trans.* To begin the removal of (the fleece) from a sheep. Usu. with **up.**

1882 ARMSTRONG & CAMPBELL *Austral. Sheep Husbandry* 167 The fleece should be opened up the neck, commencing at the brisket. **1886** P. FLETCHER 'Hints to Immigrants' in P. Fletcher *Qld.* 4 You .. may have the chance of getting hold of a sheep which a shearer has already 'opened up', or begun. **1914** H.B. SMITH *Sheep & Wool Industry* 37 The machine is then driven up the front of the neck several times till the neck wool is well opened. **1965** J.S. GUNN *Terminol. Shearing Industry* ii. 6 *Open up*, to shear wool away from a certain area.

open call. An informal Stock Exchange: see quot. 1898. Also **open call Stock Exchange.**

1896 J.M. PRICE *Land of Gold* 74 One of the principal features of Coolgardie, and one which struck me as being quite unique, was the evening 'open call' Stock Exchange. **1898** R. RADCLYFFE *Wealth & Wild Cats* 39 'Open calls' .. are curious. At night, about eight o'clock, all the miners and gamblers stroll into one of the tin-roofed halls... Presently a Jewish gentleman comes in and takes the chair. 'We will call the list,' says he, and with stentorian voice shouts, 'Adelaide Queens—who sells?' .. It is a rough-and-ready Stock Exchange, and thousands of shares change hands. **1933** A. REID *Those were Days* 19 Several Open Calls and auction marts were doing a big business.

open go: see GO *n.*[1] 3.

open slather: see SLATHER.

opossum, *n.* [Transf. use of *opossum* an arboreal marsupial; now largely superseded by POSSUM.]

1. POSSUM 1.

1770 J. BANKS *Jrnl.* 26 July (1896) 291 While botanising to-day I had the good fortune to take an animal of the opossum (*Didelphis*) tribe. **1784** G.W. ANDERSON *New Collection Voyages* 426 The only quadruped we saw distinctly was a species of opossum, about twice the size of a large rat. **1831** *Acct. Colony Van Diemen's Land* 100 A tall fellow overtook us with a bunch of seven fat but strong smelling opossums slung on his back and round his neck. **1848** J. SYME *Nine Yrs. Van Diemen's Land* 63 Opossums are . . harmless and inoffensive, living like squirrels, chiefly in holes of trees, and eating the leaves or branches. **1860** 'LADY' *My Experiences in Aust.* 124 Opossums might be obtained were parties to employ a Black or two to procure them, but these little creatures are rarely eaten by the settler. **1877** *Illustr. Austral. News* (Melbourne) 21 Feb. 23/4 An opossum has been captured at the Loddon station, having pure white fur and pink eyes. **1911** *Huon Times* (Franklin) 7 June 3/1 The Executive Council today passed a regulation protecting opossums all the year round. **1949** H.E. THONEMAN *Tell White Man* 48 One of our greatest pleasures was smoking out opossums . . by burning sticks in a little fire and then heating green branches and putting them into the opossums' holes in the trees. **1963** V.B. CRANLEY *27,000 Miles through Aust.* 135 Now and then they looked at us over their shoulders as if to say: 'Cripes, what a fuss. Can't you blokes even spare a couple of apples for us Opossums? Stingy foreigners.' . . Canberra or no Canberra, wild-life goes on everywhere in Australia. **1973** R.J. DOOLIN *Boy from Bush* 15 The dogs had an o'possum up a tree.

2. Comb.

a. opossum belt, cloak, fur, hair, rug, skin, yarn.

1830 R. DAWSON *Present State Aust.* 226 He stuck one end of it in his **opossum belt. 1845** C. HODGKINSON *Aust., Port Macquarie to Moreton Bay* 232 Afterwards . . they are invested with the opossum belt. **1832** J. HENDERSON *Observations Colonies N.S.W. & Van Diemen's Land* p. xiii, We had carried . . our **oppossum cloaks. 1843** *N.S.W. Monthly Mag.* Feb. 54 The opossum cloaks are less prized than and less commonly worn than formerly. **1849** A. HARRIS *Emigrant Family* (1967) 53 The stockman's own opossum cloak, made a comfortable shakedown. **1878** R.B. SMYTH *Aborigines of Vic.* I. p. xxxix, The opossum cloak, the strips of skin worn around the loins, and the apron of emu feathers, are their clothing. **1892** 'R. BOLDREWOOD' *Nevermore* II. 159 Lance was invited to avail himself of a comfortable shake-down, where opossum cloaks and wallaby rugs protected him from the searching night air. **1833** *Perth Gaz.* 7 Sept. 143 Mr Armstrong has shown us some **oposum** [*sic*] **fur**, worked up into a ball, similar to a ball of worsted, and equally fine. A stocking of this fur is nearly finished. **1847** G.F. ANGAS *Savage Life & Scenes* I. 85 A cloak of opossum-fur, or a piece of kangaroo-skin, is worn by the women of the Mount Barker and Adelaide tribes. **1883** F. BONNEY *On Some Customs Aborigines* 9 A piece of twine, made of opossum fur, is fastened to one end with some black gum (nynia). **1894** A.F. CALVERT *Aborigines W.A.* 24 The equipment of the Blackboy consists of his kiley (boomerang), hatchet, and dow-uk (a short heavy stick), which are stuck in his belt of opossum fur. **1844** *Swan River News* 1 June 40/1 Their sole clothing is a kangaroo skin . . and a girdle round the loins, woven from **opossum hair. 1841** *Port Phillip Patriot* 11 Nov. 2/1 *Thomas Arbuthnot*, ship, for Calcutta . . 1 parcel (**oppossum rug**). **1842** *Colonial Observer* (Sydney) 30 Mar. 202/3 The blacks returned and rifled the store, carrying off with them a quantity of flour, an opossum rug, and a blanket. **1853** J. CAPPER *Emigrant's Guide to Aust.* (ed. 2) 77 Roaming in the wilds of his native forests, the aboriginal man, with his opossum rug hung gracefully over his shoulder, is an object of natural dignity. **1865** G.S. LANG *Aborigines of Aust.* 13 The happy lover threw an opossum rug over the bride. **1881** G.C. EVANS *Stories* 92, I strapped a large opossum rug on my shoulders. **1918** K.L. PARKER *Walkabout Wur-Run-Nah* 28 The men dropped the opossum rugs. **1820** J. OXLEY *Jrnls. Two Exped. N.S.W.* 19 They were covered with cloaks made of **opossum skins. 1833** *Launceston Advertiser* 22 Aug. 3 The gloves are made from leather manufactured in the colony from Opossum or other skins. **1839** T.L. MITCHELL *Three Exped. Eastern Aust.* (rev. ed.) I. 322 A rather short cloak of opossum skins was drawn tightly around his body with one hand, his bommerengs and waddy being grasped fast in the other. **1849** A. HARRIS *Emigrant Family* (1967) 19 A mounted bushman's accoutrements are his horses hobbles . . a good blanket or cloak made of opossum skins sewn together. **1872** MRS E. MILLETT *Austral. Parsonage* 75 An opossum-skin wallet between the shoulders, or under one arm, is an indispensable female appendage, where sits the baby if there is one. **1884** J.T. HINKINS *Life amongst Native Race* 48, I felt ashamed at the appearance of my child in her bush-dress and opossum-skin bonnet. **1891** J. FENTON *Bush Life Tas.* (1964) 30 We went to roost in our opossum-skin rugs. **1830** R. DAWSON *Present State Aust.* 115 His long hair was turned up and bound about the head with **opossum yarn. 1863** J. BONWICK *Wild White Man* 54 A net of opossum yarn. **1878** R.B. SMYTH *Aborigines of Vic.* I. 387 *Mur-ra-mai*, the name of a round ball about the size of a cricket ball, which the Aborigines carry in a small net suspended from their girdles of opossum yarn.

b. opossum hunt, hunter, -hunting, -shooting.

1837 *Perth Gaz.* 18 Mar. 869 We enjoyed a capital **oppossum hunt. 1855** W. HOWITT *Land, Labor & Gold* I. 214 Prim . . is a famous **opossum hunter**, following them often, where a tree slants, right up it. **1879** *Native Tribes S.A.* 194 In this district the Raminjerar are the only opossum hunters. **1840** *S. Austral. Rec.* (London) 24 Oct. 269 At **opossum-hunting**, they observe the marks of the animal's claws on the trunks of trees before they get close up to them. **1868** *Illustr. Sydney News* 3 Oct. 52/1 Opossum hunting is one of the most popular of our sports. **1894** A.F. CALVERT *Aborigines W.A.* 28 In opossum hunting the savage climbs the tree, which he notches into footholds as he proceeds; then either smokes or prods the animal out of his hole, when he seizes it by the tail and dashes it to the ground. **1845** *Star* (Parramatta) 18 Jan. 2/1 He was . . staying away all night **opossum shooting. 1868** C.G.S. FOLJAMBE *Three Yrs. Austral. Station* 269 We used to go opossum-shooting with dogs. **1886** D.M. GANE *N.S.W. & Vic.* 177 Opossum-shooting is as entertaining and lucrative as any Australian sport.

3. Special Comb. **opossum hyena,** HYENA; **mouse,** *pygmy possum*, see PYGMY.

1824 J. LYCETT *Views in Aust.* 12 The kangaroo, the emu . . and the **opossum-hyena,** are all natives of Van Diemen's Land. **1832** H. MARTINEAU *Homes Abroad* 112 Susan is taming an **opossum mouse. 1865** G.F. ANGAS *Aust.* 75 In constrast to this large species is the smallest of the flying opossums, the beautiful little 'opossum mouse' of the colonists. **1886** W.J. WOODS *Visit to Vic.* 38 There is . . a tiny fellow about three inches long, named the Opossum Mouse. **1894** R. LYDEKKER *Hand-Bk. Marsupialia & Monotremata* 118 *Acrobates pygmaeus* . . resembling a Common Mouse in size, and hence known to the colonists as the Flying Mouse, or Opossum-Mouse. **1909** G. SMITH *Naturalist in Tas.* 118 The little Opossum Mice of the genus *Dromicia* are found nesting in holes in the Myrtles. **1921** *Bulletin* (Sydney) 22 Dec. 22/2 *Dromicia nana*, or opossum mouse, makes a nest . . in a hollow limb. **1926** A.S. LE SOUEF et al. *Wild Animals Australasia* 239 *Family Phalangeridae*. . . This group includes many forms, ranging in size from the tiny flying mice (*Acrobates*) and the plump opossum-mice (*Dromicia*) to the graceful flying phalangers.

opossum, *v. intr.* To hunt possums. Also as *vbl. n.*

1847 *Atlas* (Sydney) III. 93/2 The Worrigals went out 'oppossuming'. **1867** F.J. BYERLEY *Narr. Overland Exped. Northern Qld.* 17 They . . had to go 'oppossuming', and succeeded in catching three. **1917** 'H.H. RICHARDSON' *Fortunes of Richard Mahony* 211 There is to be opossuming and a moonlight picnic to-night.

opportunity shop. A shop run by a charitable organization in which donated second-hand goods, esp. clothes, are sold.

1961 B. HUMPHRIES *Nice Night's Entertainment* (1981) 52 It ruined the lining of a lovely raffia bag that Beryl had bought at the opportunity shop. **1978** J. COLBERT *Ranch* 35 Keep it up and people will think I get my clothes from the opportunity shop.

op shop. Also **opp shop.** Shortening of OPPORTUNITY SHOP. Also *ellipt.* for 'op shop clothes'.

1978 P. WOOLLEY *Art of living Together* 91 Be sure to donate your old clothes and old furniture to the opp shop in your neighbourhood. **1979** H. WELLER *Lip Service* 86 Likes toffee apples, live theatre and people who wear Op Shop when Fiurucci [*sic*] would do. **1985** *Austral. Women's Weekly* (Sydney) Jan. 160 Why do I have to have new clothes, there are a lot of much nicer things in the Op shop.

orange, *a.* Used as a distinguishing epithet in the names of animals and birds: **orange-bellied parrot,** the rare, chiefly coastal parrot *Neophema chrysogaster* of w. Tas., s. Vic., and s.e. S.A.; also **orange-breasted parrot,** and formerly **orange-bellied grass-parakeet; chat,** the nomadic bird *Epthianura aurifrons* of arid inland Aust., the mature male having an orange-yellow head and underparts; also **orange-fronted chat; horseshoe bat,** the bat of tropical n. Aust. *Rhinonicteris aurantius*; **-speckled hawk** *obs.*, *brown hawk*, see BROWN *a.* 1; **-winged sittella,** the s.e. Austral. form of the bird *Daphoenositta chrysoptera*, having striped plumage and an orange patch on the wing; formerly also **orange-winged nuthatch, tree-runner.**

1841 [**orange-bellied parrot**] J. GOULD *Birds of Aust.* (1848) V. Pl. 39, *Euphema aurantia* . . Orange-bellied Grass-Parrakeet. **1943** C. BARRETT *Austral. Animal Bk.* 235 Distinguished by a rich orange colour-patch on the undersurface, the orange-breasted parrot (*N*[*eophema*] *chrysogaster*) has grass-green plumage above, and is a brilliant little bird. **1969** J.M. FORSHAW *Austral. Parrots* 261 Orange-bellied Parrots are generally seen singly, in pairs, or in small flocks. . . When alarmed they emit a '*chitter-chitter*', repeated so rapidly as to produce an overall 'buzzing' effect. This strange call is a valuable aid to identification. **1981** *Woman's Day* (Sydney) 9 Sept. 94/3 The numbers of another rare bird, the orange-bellied parrot, have also dropped to about 300 individuals. **1983** *Bulletin* (Sydney) 1 Feb. 38/3 The orange-bellied parrot, a lovely one in grave danger of extinction. Western Tasmania is the only area in which it breeds, although it winters on a few mainland sites in Victoria and South Australia. [**1842 orange chat:** J. GOULD *Birds of Aust.* (1848) III. Pl. 65, *Epthianura aurifrons* . . Orange-fronted Epthianura.] **1916** S.A. WHITE *In Far Northwest* 124 The pretty little orange-fronted chats . . were also plentiful. **1943** C. BARRETT *Austral. Animal Bk.* 274 The orange chat . . which inhabits the interior of Australia . . is nomadic. **1962** MARSHALL & DRYSDALE *Journey among Men* 183 A variety of birds came to water. The most beautiful, perhaps, were two or three pairs of orange chats, lovely little creatures whose black and orange markings flashed in the sunlight. **1984** M. BLAKERS et al. *Atlas Austral. Birds* 570 The Orange Chat lives in acacia scrub, spinifex, tussock grassland and saltbush, specially round salt lakes. **1926** A.S. LE SOUEF et al. *Wild Animals Australasia* 53 **Orange horseshoe bat.** *Rhinonycteris aurantia* . . North and North-west Australia, especially abundant in the Coburg Peninsula. **1965** *Austral. Encycl.* I. 460 The orange horseshoe-bat (*Rhinonicteris aurantius*) of coastal northern Australia is distinguished by its bright orange-yellow fur and the scalloped upper nose-leaf. **1981** *Ecos* xxviii. 29/2 *Macroderma gigas* (the ghost bat) and *Rhinonicteris aurantius* (the orange horseshoe bat) are from genera found only in this country. **1827** *Trans. Linnean Soc. London* XV. 185 It is called by the settlers **Orange-speckled Hawk. 1840** *S. Austral. Rec.* (London) 21 Mar. 124 The cream-bellied falcon, the orange speckled hawk, and the milk white hawk, are common varieties. **1860** G. BENNETT *Gatherings of Naturalist* 176 The Orange-speckled Hawk of the colonists (*Ieracidea Berigora*). **1801** [**orange-winged sittella**] J. LATHAM *Gen. Synopsis Birds* Suppl. II. 146 Orange-winged N[uthatch] . . inhabits *New Holland*. **1844** J. GOULD *Birds of Aust.* (1848) IV. Pl. 101, *Sittella chrysoptera* . . Orange-winged Sittella. **1860** G. BENNETT *Gatherings of Naturalist* 193 That interesting little bird, the Orange-winged Nuthatch, or Moreton Bay Woodpecker of the colonists. **1896** B. SPENCER *Rep. Horn Sci. Exped. Central Aust.* II. 98 The Orange-winged Sittella loves to work head downwards, or hopping along under the limbs of trees inspecting the crevices in the bark in search of spiders or small insects. **1903** *Emu* II. 165 Orange-winged Tree-Runner . . in the Otway. **1943** C. BARRETT *Austral. Animal Bk.* 266 The orange-winged sittella (*N*[*eositella*] *chrysoptera*) ranges from southern Queensland to Victoria. **1965** *Austral. Encycl.* VIII. 137 Six species of sittellas occur in Australia, but none extends to Tasmania. The best-known are the orange-winged sittella [etc.].

orchardist. [App. in more freq. use in Aust. and N.Z. than elsewhere.] A commercial fruit-grower.

1887 *Illustr. Austral. News* (Melbourne) 23 July 126/2

Orchardists also have reason to rejoice, as their trees have been watered to the very lowest roots. **1913** *Truth* (Sydney) 27 Sept. 1/6 A Ryde orchardist advocates the abolition of middlemen. **1933** D. MACDONALD *Brooks of Morning* 25 Can any orchardist explain why the largest pears are almost invariably highest on the tree? **1947** V. PALMER *Cyclone* 93 The land was sour and had ruined every orchardist who had tried to settle on it. **1972** *Bulletin* (Sydney) 6 May 60/3 Most of the farmers were orchardists, but some were vegetable growers. **1980** J. SEAGER *Kangaroo Island Doctor* 20 An orchardist at Young offered a 'fiver' (£5) to anyone who could eat a case of cherries straight off. **1986** *Canberra Times* 15 Mar. 7/3 Jeff Ashmann, part-time teacher and orchardist, Moruya.

order. *Hist.* [Spec. use of *order* an instruction.]

1. Abbrev. of *land order* (see LAND 1).

1836 A. BARCLAY *Life* (1854) 7 Governor Macquarie gave me an order for a grant of 500 acres there, and also for a [*sic*] allotment of building-ground in the town of Launceston. **1841** *Port Phillip Patriot* 11 Mar. 2/5 The arrival of Mr Dendy at Port Phillip with his five-thousand-acre order, has, I presume, opened the eyes of the Government. **1843** *Sydney Morning Herald* 11 May 3/3 He could not obtain from the Governor (his brother-in-law) a confirmation of an order, which he previously had for a town allotment. **1853** S. SIDNEY *Three Colonies* (ed. 2) 215 When any particularly desirable plot of land was brought into the market, a speculation arose to discover and purchase the oldest 'order' in the colony. **1855** H. HUME *Brief Statement* 13 An order to select 1,200 acres of land was given me; that order, however, I was under the necessity of selling.

2. A written direction to a third party to discharge a financial obligation: see quots. 1848 and 1977. Also *attrib.*

1848 H.W. HAYGARTH *Recoll. Bush Life* 86 The 'order' system, which has long been adopted in the interior of the colony, being found desirable as a substitute for payment in cash. It is usual for proprietors of stations 'up the country' to keep an account current with a Sydney merchant or agent, from whom they also purchase their annual supplies, and, when discharging any debt in the interior, they simply draw an 'order' upon him for the amount. **1865** G.F. ANGAS *Aust.* 284 Very little coin passes through the hands of these storekeepers, the 'order' system being found a more convenient method of payment in the more remote districts. **1902** *Bulletin* (Sydney) 4 Oct. 17/1 Jimmy, behind the wool-press, patted a pocketful of silver and 'orders', and smiled beatifically. **1944** *Ibid.* 27 Dec. 12/1 In the early Coolgardie days the usual outback currency was an 'Order on Monger'—Monger's W.A. stores being then the Anthony Hordern's of the West. **1977** T. RONAN *Mighty Men on Horseback* 83 The 'order on Monger & Co.'. I would say that this would have been an order, engraved, or perhaps printed, on heavy parchment much thicker and less durable than what is used for banknotes; it would have been an order on Monger & Co.'s bankers and it would have been signed in ink by the head of the establishment.

ordnance tree. *Obs.* [See quot. 1855.] KURRAJONG 1.

1855 R. AUSTIN *Jrnl. Interior W.A.* 27 The tree resembling the fig tree . . and which we called the Ordnance Tree, as the leaf was formed like a broad arrow. **1875** J. FORREST *Explorations in Aust.* 64 Two natives . . had a great many dulgates and opossums, which they carried in a net bag, made out of the inner bark of the ordnance-tree, which makes a splendid strong cord. **1893** D. LINDSAY *Jrnl. Elder Sci. Exploring Exped.* 38 Numerous kurrajong or ordnance trees.

organ bird. [See quot. 1847.] Either of two birds of the fam. Cracticidae having a melodious song, the *pied butcherbird* (see PIED), and *Gymnorhina tibicen* (see MAGPIE *n.* 1 a.). Also **organ magpie.**

1847 J. GOULD *Birds of Aust.* (1848) II. Pl. 48, When perched on the dead branches of the trees soon after day-break, it pours forth a succession of notes of the strongest description that can be imagined, much resembling the sounds of a hand-organ out of tune, which has obtained for it the colonial name of the Organ-Bird. **1852** G.C. MUNDY *Our Antipodes* II. 287 The organ-magpie, pied crow, or barita, is somewhat larger than the English magpie, with a tail as much shorter as his voice is sweeter. **1872** G.S. BADEN-POWELL *New Homes for Old Country* 343 'Organ-birds' and 'mockers' abound, giving vent to various calls. **1893** *Western Champion* (Barcaldine) 24 Jan. 1/2 A period of protection shall be in certain districts . . for the whole year, in respect of the following birds . . magpies (organ birds) [etc.]. **1985** *Austral. Nat. Hist.* Spring 427 Also known as the Organ Bird, the Pied Butcherbird has an extraordinary variety of flute-like calls.

organ-grinder. [See quot. 1930.] Any of many lizards of the fam. Agamidae having a characteristic waving movement of a forelimb, as members of the genera *Diporiphora* and *Lophognathus.* Also **organ-grinder lizard.**

1930 J.S. LITCHFIELD *Far-North Memories* 172 *Organ-grinder*—Small lizard, with a long, whip-like tail. Has a habit of sitting erect, and 'grinding the organ' with a paw. **1980** N. WATKINS *Kangaroo Connection* 103 An organ-grinder lizard . . paused, stood up on its hind legs, waving its forelegs in a circular motion, as if turning a handle of an old fashioned organ.

oriental pratincole. [f. *oriental*, first applied by English naturalist William Leach in 1820 (*Trans. Linnean Soc. London* (1822) XIII. 132) as the specific epithet *orientalis* eastern or Asian.] The bird *Glareola maldivarum*, breeding in Asia and migrating to n. Aust. in summer, having brownish-grey to olive plumage with a black throat band.

1824 J. LATHAM *Gen. Hist. Birds* IX. 365 *Oriental pratincole*. . . In this the bill is black; gape yellow; plumage above brownish ash-colour, beneath white. . . Inhabits Java, and called Tre; brought by M. Leschenault. **1848** J. GOULD *Birds of Aust.* VI. Pl. 23, *Glareola orientalis* . . Oriental Pratincole. . . The true habitat of the Oriental Pratincole is India and the neighbouring islands; it is most likely, therefore, that its visits to Australia are only occasional. **1945** C. BARRETT *Austral. Bird Life* 108 The Oriental pratincole (*Glareola maldivarum*) breeds in Northern Asia. **1964** M. SHARLAND *Territory of Birds* 114 The Oriental Pratincole also occurs in the North. **1984** M. BLAKERS et al. *Atlas Austral. Birds* 189 The Oriental Pratincole feeds on insects, many taken on the wing.

original, *a. Hist.*

1. ABORIGINAL *a.* 1.

1840 *S. Austral. Miscellany* Mar. 117 This poor fellow, who was the last of the original lords of the soil known to be left at liberty in his native land, died at Pitwater. **1843** W. PRIDDEN *Aust.* 116 How very serious an injury is inflicted upon the original people of a district in Australia, when Europeans *sit down*, as they term it (i.e. *settle*), upon their lands. **1881** A.C. GRANT *Bush-Life Qld.* II. 172 Southern squatters . . in bequeathing to their followers the country they had wrested from the original inhabitants, had, along with it, transmitted to them a complicity and share in any injustice and guilt exercised in its acquisition. **1883** *Bulletin* (Sydney) 7 July 6/3 Near Braidwood are five of the original proprietors of the soil of N.S.W. They have their ancient jins with them.

2. Of a colonist: first, earliest.

1839 *Sydney Standard* 7 Jan. 2/4 The increasing wealth of the original settlers. **1858** T. MCCOMBIE *Hist. Colony Aust.* 240 The majority of the original colonists had some other mode of living. **1863** J. BONWICK *Wild White Man* 88 Our original colonist got the tale of the past from Buckley. **1891** 'ROUSEABOUT' *Jackeroo* 43 Mr Sharp, the owner of Bulletta Station . . was the original holder, or, to speak more plainly . . he was the first and only man who had ever leased the station from the Crown.

3. Of a soldier: belonging to the first Australian contingent to serve in the war of 1914–18. Also as *n.*

1919 C.H. THORP *Handful of Ausseys* 161 Whether he is of an 'original' battalion or a reinforcement company. **1941** *Bulletin* (Sydney) 15 Jan. 16/3 My mate, Kelly, never previously out of Melbourne, got away with the originals in 1914.

ornithorhynchus /ɔnəθə'rɪŋkəs/. Formerly also with unsettled variety. [The animal genus *Ornithorhynchus* (orig. *Platypus*) was named in 1800 by German anatomist J.F. Blumenbach (*Götting. gel. Anz.* 1 609) f. Gr. ὀρνιθο- comb. form of ὄρνις bird + ῥύγκος bill, referring to the duck-like bill of the animal.] PLATYPUS.

1800 *Philos. Trans. R. Soc. London* XC. 432 My opportunities of examining the *Ornithorhynchus* were procured through Sir Joseph Banks. **1827** *Colonial Times* (Hobart) 10 Feb., Ornithornicus or Platapus. Wanted, two specimens of the above Animal. **1837** *Lit. News* (Sydney) 21 Oct. 105 When the Ornithorynchus is captured it makes great efforts to regain its liberty. **1866** L. DE BEAUVOIR *Voyage round World* 16 Aug. (1870) I. 170 We suddenly caught sight of an ornythorynx. . . It is a curious creature, this web-footed quadruped; a kind of flattened otter, a foot and a half long, with the fur of the beaver and the beak of a duck, and the most eccentric thing of all is that it lays eggs and suckles its young. **1886** W.J. WOODS *Visit to Vic.* 37 Those queer creatures the ornithorhynchuses and native porcupines. **1924** L. ST. C. GRONDONA *Kangaroo keeps on Talking* 116 The duck-billed platypus, or ornithorhynchus. **1944** C. BARRETT *Platypus* 11 The Platypus was the greatest zoological puzzle that the learned men of Europe had ever tried to solve. Solve it they did at last—almost a century after the first specimen of Ornithorhynchus reached England.

Orstralia /ɔ'streɪljə, ɔ'straɪlja/. Also **Orstralier.** A representation for comic effect of an exaggerated pronunciation of 'Australia'.

1918 N. CAMPBELL *Dinky-Di Soldier* 29 All the bush in wide Orstralia can't compare with Shepherd's Bush! **1955** STEWART & KEESING *Austral. Bush Ballads* 252 Lord, I don't know wot Orstralier is comin' to. **1962** T. RONAN *Deep of Sky* 135 In the days when this country's name was often spelt 'Orstralia', we did not develop a peon class.

Hence **Orstrylian, Ostrylian,** etc., *n.* and *a.*

1948 J. FAIRFAX *Run o' Waters* 44 That famous cabbage-tree hat . . led to the old cockney jibe 'That's an Orsetrillian, 'e's got on a cabbage-tree 'at'. **1956** S. HOPE *Diggers' Paradise* 121 Why don't you get someone to learn you how to speak Ostrylian? **1965** G. MCINNES *Road to Gundagai* 30 Corcoran lacked the more outrageous diphthongs of what, at that early time, she still called the Orsetrylian Accent. **1981** A.J. BURKE *Pommies & Patriots* 62, I conducted an accountancy practice which did Taxation Returns for emigrant pommies, ethnics or orstraleens.

ort. [Of unknown origin.] The backside; the anus.

1952 P. PINNEY *Road in Wilderness* 62 You're a big bronzed Anzac sitting on your ort drinking free tea. **1962** J. WYNNUM *Tar Dust* 116 Take it from me, there's more ways of killin' a cat than fillin' its ort with sand. **1984** A. DELBRIDGE *Aussie Talk* 227 *Ort n.*, the anus: *In your ort, sport.*

oscar. Abbrev. of OSCAR ASCHE.

1917 *Ca ne fait Rien: 6th Battalion A.I.F.* Oct. 1 So readers may rest assured they will get value for their oscar. **1929** *Bulletin* (Sydney) 2 Jan. 20/1 A bloke should be as easy as 'is oscar will permit. **1943** S.W. KEOUGH *Around Army* 39 Get us a coupla packets of smokes? . . I'll let y' have the Oscar for it payday. **1954** V. KELLY *Shadow* 59 No one's got any oscar to spend. **1959** D. NILAND *Big Smoke* 21 If you'd been fighting all those blokes in the ring you'd have more oscar in your kick now than the Prime Minister. **1971** B. HUMPHRIES *Bazza pulls it Off*, I can do with the oscar, but I don't know if I can draw any more photos.

Oscar Asche. [The name of *Oscar Asche* (1871–1936), an actor.] Rhyming slang for 'cash'.

1905 J. MEREDITH *Learning to talk Old Jack Lang* (1984) 15 Two years ago I was . . spending all my *Oscar Asche* on . . two-up, fighting and brawling, stoushing *John Hops*, hetting run in. **1916** *Battery Herald: Jrnl. 14th Field Artillery* 9 Oct. 6 You can get four, for the same amount of 'Oscar Asche'. **1926** 'DRYBLOWER' *Verses* 50 A bank-roll unto him is 'Oscar Asche'. **1929** *Rising Sun* (Melbourne) Oct. 7 Billee Hughes will pay zee Oscar Asche.

Oss, var. OZ.

Ossie, var. AUSSIE.

ossie. [f. *os(miridum* + -Y.] Osmiridum, a natural alloy. Also *attrib.*

1936 M.J. O'REILLY *Pinnacle Road* 19 When old

Adamsfield is finished and the pioneers are gone, And we ossie diggers all have passed away. **1955** STEWART & KEESING *Austral. Bush Ballads* 74 We joined the Tassie push, Forgetting all the Ossie And the Adams River Rush. **1968** P. ADAM SMITH *Tiger Country* 76 Saviour Simmonds ran a billiard-saloon-cum-sly-grog-shop and he'd buy your 'ossie' when you were hard up.

ostrylian: see ORSTRALIA.

O.T. Abbrev. of OVERLAND TELEGRAPH. Also **O.T. line,** and *attrib.*

1898 *Bulletin* (Sydney) 31 Dec. 31/2 The Overland telegraph ends at Palmerston and employs a large staff, known as the O.T. men. **1915** E.R. MASSON *Untamed Territory* 19 The value of the Overland Telegraph has never diminished. . . A man from out back will tell you that he lives 'three weeks from the O.T.'. **1927** M.H. ELLIS *Long Lead* 201 Illegal for travellers to pass down the 'O.T.' line unless they carried firearms. **1936** C.P. CONIGRAVE *N. Aust.* 61 The O.T., as all northerners call the line. **1955** N. PULLIAM *I traveled Lonely Land* 288 One of man's intrusions on the desert is the Overland or the O.T., as the overland telegraph is sometimes called. **1968** W. GILL *Petermann Journey* 11 The same building [*sc.* the post office] houses the repeater-station on the Overland Telegraph Line, known as the O.T.

other side.

1. Used variously to designate a part of Australia which is removed from the speaker by a natural barrier or border. See also SIDE *n.*[1] 1, TOTHER SIDE *n.*[1] 1.

1827 *Tasmanian* (Hobart) 24 May 2 The districts, at the other Side, require a Pastor like Mr Robinson. **1833** *Perth Gaz.* 28 Sept. 154 Maize, except in particular spots, does not appear to answer so well here as on the other side. **1855** W. HOWITT *Land, Labor & Gold* II. 387 'On the other side', as they call Victoria, and as the Victorians call Van Diemen's Land. **1857** F. DE B. COOPER *Wild Adventures* 104 This person was an 'old hand' and got into some trouble on the other side (*i.e.* the Bathurst side) by using a 'frying-pan brand'. **1884** 'LOCAL LETTER CARRIER' *After Twenty Yrs.* 51 About fully half the population consisted of persons having a peculiar gait, as if accustomed to hobbles, and they were understood, in polite terms, as hailing from the 'other-side' (Van D.L.). **1899** G.E. BOXALL *Story Austral. Bushrangers* 265 He crossed the King River, and set fire to Mr Evans' barns and granary for 'having shot my fingers off', an event which had taken place some time previously, in one of his many encounters on the 'other side'. **1900** R. BRUCE *Benbonuna* (1904) 189 The kettle ('billies' had not then come over from the other side—*i.e.*, Victoria) hung from one of the chain-hooks. **1933** R.B. PLOWMAN *Camel Pads* 80 Jack, a Queenslander, and an exceptionally fine stockman, had been known to the padre on the 'other side'—north-east South Australia and south-west Queensland. **1952** J.R. SKEMP *Memories Myrtle Bank* 221 Quite a number went 'over the other side', as the Australian mainland is rather ambiguously described by Tasmanians.

2. a. A place in the northern hemisphere; *spec.* England.

1892 *Quiz* (Adelaide) 29 Apr. 6/2 When a politician visits England he generally has a job on hand. Dibbs . . is going to float a bank. Most banks on the other side hequire floating. **1937** A.R. GRANT *Memories of Parliament* 1 Five years on the 'other side' had given me a love for Australia.

b. *W.A.* The eastern States; TOTHER SIDE 2.

1893 *Quiz* (Adelaide) 7 Apr. 6/1 The West Australian cricketers underwent a terrible collapse on the other side. Perhaps it was the Melbourne stinks that overcame them. **1917** 'PEGASUS' *So Drover Said* 13 A man Whose life they said was under a ban For a crime on the 'other side'. **1950** G.M. FARWELL *Land of Mirage* 167 The plain fact about rustling—as they call cattle-lifting, poddy-dodging, or gully-raking over the other side—is that after all it is only droving, with an extra note of gambling and suspense.

other-sider. *W.A.* TOTHERSIDER 1.

1883 *Bulletin* (Sydney) 17 Nov. 20/4 To 'other-siders' as they are called some Western Australian experiences have been of a decidedly phenomenal character. **1891** *Quiz* (Adelaide) 9 Oct. 6/3 The influx of 'othersiders' into West Australia . . has made a vast difference in the appearance of the principal towns. **1891** E.H. HALLACK *W.A. & Yilgarn Goldfields* 5 'Othersiders', as they in the west call Adelaidens.

out, *adv.*[1]

1. At a distance from one's place of origin: in or to Australia.

1790 *Extracts Lett. Arthur Phillip* 12 Feb. (1791) 5 If settlers are sent out, and the convicts divided amongst them, this Settlement will very shortly maintain itself. **1799** D. COLLINS *Acct. Eng. Colony N.S.W.* (1802) II. 141 Many convicts having been sent out, who had not more than two years to serve after their arrival. **1826** M. HINDMARSH *Lett.* (1945) 29 There are so many Mechanics come out here as Prisoners. **1839** *S. Austral. Rec.* (London) 15 Nov. 268 There exists a difficulty in getting good land by anyone just come out. **1847** J.B. ATKINSON *Penal Settlements* 18, I was accommodated at a farm-house, where both the heads of the family happened to have been *sent out* by Her Majesty's Government. **1859** 'EYE WITNESS' *Voyage to Aust.* 3 Single females . . should try to get out by the Government Emigration. **1872** MRS E. MILLETT *Austral. Parsonage* 329 To have 'come out' in one of the first ships was a point on which a man might deservedly pride himself. **1889** J.H.L. ZILLMANN *Past & Present Austral. Life* 53 There are still to be found among some of the oldest and wealthiest of our colonists those of whom it may be said 'his father was sent out', or as it is more vulgarly expressed, 'he is the son of a lag'. **1910** H. LAWSON *Rising of Court* 26 An old handy man . . had been 'sent out' in past ages for 'knocking a donkey off a hen-roost'. **1915** N. DUNCAN *Austral. Byways* 95 Came out from Home, you know. **1942** H.H. PECK *Mem. of Stockman* 44 He brought his whole family . . out from the Old Country. **1956** F.B. VICKERS *First Place to Stranger* 130 Pommie in a shearing team, eh? Never seen one before. How long you been out, chum? Two weeks all but a fortnight. **1978** J. ANDERSON *Tirra Lirra* 88, I got out of hospital, weakened and considerably poorer, but there were no more passenger ships out.

2. Absent from a place of confinement; at large.

1792 P.G. KING Jrnl. Norfolk Island 50 A convict who has been some time past, a vagabond in the woods, was seen plundering some maize but could not be taken, this man has been out since the 25th September. **1839** N.M. TAYLOR *Jrnl. Ensign Best* 6 Mar. (1966) 201 Two of the Men who took the Bush a day or two ago were brought in this morning but *Dignum* is still out. **1848** H.W. HAYGARTH *Recoll. Bush Life* 120 Bushrangers are 'out', and mounted police are sent to hunt them down. **1854** G.H. HAYDON *Austral. Emigrant* 142 Baccy's scarce, and I hear the bushrangers are out. **1855** G.H. WATHEN *Golden Colony* 151 We are the two bushrangers that you have heard of being out. **1930** HIVES & LUMLEY *Jrnl. of Jackaroo* 175 If, as I suspected, one of the tribes was 'out', they would certainly loot and burn whatever came in their way. **1946** L. PIRANI *Old Man River* 27, I remember the trembling and hushed voices that spread around the news: 'The Kelly's are out'.

3. In the phr. **to go out (to),** to die (from).

[**1907** A. MACDONALD *In Land of Pearl & Gold* 10 'Out or in', it should be explained, is Queensland vernacular for dead or alive.] **1929** C.E.W. BEAN *Official Hist. Aust. 1914–18* III. 598 He had found it more than he could bear, put his rifle to his head, and 'went out' uncomplaining. **1934** J.S. NEILSON *Autobiogr.* (1978) 74 King Edward had been operated on & unless one had a first-class surgeon there was a big risk of going out under the operation. **1948** K.S. PRICHARD *Golden Miles* 118, I reckon there's more accidents on the mines and more men going out to miner's complaint, now, than there was in the old days.

out, *adv.*[2] Abbrev. of OUTBACK *adv.* Also **out there.**

1897 *Bulletin* (Sydney) 19 June 3/2 And I thought of piny sand-ridges!—and somehow I could swear That this tailor-made young johnnie had at one time been 'out there'! **1911** 'S. RUDD' *Bk. of Dan* 55 I've fattened cattle out there in three weeks. **1917** A.L. BREWER *'Gators' Euchre* 44 On the way out I met many fences, mostly with sheep-wires, while now and then one was rabbit-proof. **1926** *Smith's Weekly* (Sydney) 22 May 19/7 Thirty odd years ago when I was working 'back-o'-Bourke', and in Western Queensland . . those out there always spoke of going 'inside', and when we were 'in' we always spoke of going 'out'. **1950** A. GROOM *I saw Strange Land* 9 He was going 'out' to the Sandover River country, east of the Overland Telegraph Line. . . He intended to take up land somewhere 'out there'.

out, *a.* (or as an adv. combinative element) [Not necessarily excl. Austral. but of historical interest.]

1. *Obs.* Used in collocations in the sense of 'distant from a central establishment or main settlement', as **out-district, -farm, -gang, -settlement, -settler, -squatter.**

1835 *Hobart Town Almanack* 191 The carelessness of persons engaged in the **out-districts**, the remote stock-keepers. **1858** T. MCCOMBIE *Hist. Colony Vic.* 78 Now a very important out-district of the colony. **1805** *Sydney Gaz.* 28 Apr., The impropriety of encouraging any of these people about the **out-farms**. **1809** *Ibid.* 14 May, Numerous petty depredations have been committed about the out-farms. **1805** J. TURNBULL *Voyage round World* I. 113 One of the prisoners belonging to the **out-gangs**, being sent into camp on Saturday . . fell unfortunately into the company of a party of convicts. **1832** J. BACKHOUSE *Extracts from Lett.* (1838) i. 28 Some of the out-gangs are occasionally allowed to fish, when they are industrious and behave well. **1803** *HRA* (1915) 1st Ser. IV. 330 When any person is sent to an **Out-Settlement** as a punishment, the Magistrate or Magistrates before whom they were convicted will inform the Magistrate of the place they are sent to of their crime and term of punishment. **1805** *Sydney Gaz.* 28 Apr., The *Natives* in different parts of the Out-Settlements have . . lately committed the most brutal Murder. **1811** *Proc. Court-Martial Lieut.-Col. G. Johnston* 19 Paterson was . . at one of the out-settlements, at Port Dalrymple. **1827** *Monitor* (Sydney) 2 Mar. 333/1 He had lived many years with his female friend—he had not married her, because he felt he might at any moment be transported to an out-settlement. **1839** *Sydney Herald* 5 July 2/2 How many carcases of murdered white men have been suffered to moulder in various parts of the out-settlements of the Colony. **1861** L.A. MEREDITH *Over Straits* 157 Crowded with diggers and their wives, who had come in from the out-settlements. **1802** *HRA* (1915) 1st. Ser. III. 582 Prevent the **out-settlers** from being robbed and plundered. **1805** *N.S.W. Gen. Orders* 30 Apr. (1806) 162 The Governor has judged it necessary, for the Preservation of the Lives and Properties of the Out Settlers and Stockmen, to distribute Detachments from the New South Wales Corps among the Out Settlements. **1843** W. PRIDDEN *Aust.* 32 In these parts of the bush the small hut of the humble out-settler may often be espied. **1867** F.J. BYERLEY *Narr. Overland Exped. Northern Qld.* p. x, The construction of works on the worst portions of the roads, have largely reduced the difficulties of transport for the out-settlers. **1870** E.B. KENNEDY *Four Yrs. in Qld.* 71 Our Government . . are still reducing the Native Police force, which is the only protection that the out-settlers have from the Blacks. **1847** G.F. ANGAS *Savage Life & Scenes* II. 192 The settler and the **out-squatter**, who, perhaps, have lived like hermits in the bush. **1856** J. BONWICK *Bushrangers* 43 An out squatter in the early days, once an unwilling servant of the Government, and subsequently one of the richest carriage nabobs of the Colony.

2. Used in collocations in the sense of 'situated at some distance from the principal establishment on a rural property', as **out-camp, -hut, -paddock.**

1905 *Bulletin* (Sydney) 7 Dec. 15/2 Every year resolutions are made in **out-camps** and huts to . . go down and see the Melbourne Cup. **1913** *Ibid.* 21 Aug. 18/1 There was an outcamp hut, which, like a lot more bush huts, had the reputation of being haunted. **1927** M. DORNEY *Adventurous Honeymoon* 94 An outcamp of Victoria River Downs was forty miles from the homestead. **1953** *Bulletin* (Sydney) 30 Sept. 12/2 When I was a nipper Top Hut was always known as an out-camp of Arumpo. **1962** C. GYE *Cockney & Crocodile* 78 We're only an out-camp of the big joint. **1981** D. STUART *I think I'll Live* 303 Just let me settle down in a nice quiet job, outcamp man, or horsetailer for a drover. **1873** Tas. Non-State Rec. 103/11 19 July, The two boys and myself left our bedding at the **out hut** three miles from the yards. **1874** R.P. FALLA *Knocking About* (1976) 6 Some of the out huts belonging to this station are from forty to sixty miles away from the home-station. **1886** *Bulletin* (Sydney) 12 June 20/1 And the **out-paddocks**—holy frost! . . They really are immense. **1899** *Ibid.* 9 Dec. 19/1 Hurst ordered him to boundary-ride the fences of the out-paddocks. **1910** *Ibid.* 28 July 14/2 The calf goes on quietly grazing in the out-paddock. **1919**

A. WRIGHT *Game of Chance* 103 Brought him to the out-paddocks of the big Murrubee holding.

out, *v.* [Spec. use of *out* to dismiss.] *trans.* To suspend (a football player) from a team.

1962 *N.T. News* (Darwin) 1 Feb. 1/5 Noted footballer Brien Durrington was 'outed' by the Australian Rules Tribunal for five years last night . . charged with knocking down a goal umpire. **1963** *Footy Fan* (Melbourne) I. vii. 22 Stan Vandersluys was the only player suspended. . . He was 'outed' for four matches. **1984** *N.T. News* (Darwin) 17 Oct. 47/3 This suspension is the first he has received since 1976 when he was outed for two matches for striking.

outback, *adv., a.,* and *n.* Now usu. as one word, but formerly often as two or hyphened. [Ellipt. *out* in(to) the *back* country.]

A. *adv.* Out in or to country which is remote from a major centre of population.

1869 *Wagga Wagga Advertiser* 17 Apr. 3/3 Grass will be abundant out back, and those pleasant and welcome visitors the travelling sheep will have comfortable quarters all the way down the river. **1875** *Austral. Town & Country Jrnl.* (Sydney) 13 Feb. 264/1 The whole party . . rode silently along the indistinct trail which led 'out back'. **1887** K. MACKAY *Stirrup Jingles* 49 We were humping our drums 'out back'. **1898** *Worker* (Sydney) 22 Jan. 5/2 You mustn't leave the city, lad, In search of work out back; You need not wrap your dunnage, As a prelude to the track. **1910** *Huon Times* (Franklin) 21 May 2/3 The land in question is 'out back', and in the Huon that term has a more terrible meaning than, perhaps, in any other part of the state. **1922** *Ross's Monthly* May 14/2 Railway fettlers outback . . Live where some would not keep their flash dogs. **1932** J. TRURAN *Green Mallee* 141 Travel where you will outback, from Gippsland to the Gulf Country, you will find very much the same type of house, sheet iron or thin 'weatherboarding', with a dazzling galvanized roof atop. **1939** G. DIGBY *Down Wind* 225 Australian men and women 'out back' endure unconcernedly hardships which are . . unknown elsewhere. **1951** G. FARWELL *Outside Track* 11 My friend . . was not a bushman, though a year or two outback had infected him with what Lawson calls the 'wanderlight'. **1965** L. WALKER *Other Girl* 12 Do you mean to say you came outback without a *spare?* **1981** A. MARSHALL *Aust.* 24 He talked of his experience outback.

B. *adj.* Of, pertaining to, or characteristic of remote parts of the country.

1893 *Bulletin* (Sydney) 18 Nov. 20/4 We wish to Heaven that Australian writers would leave off trying to make a paradise out of the Out Back Hell. **1896** H. LAWSON *While Billy Boils* 89 Every true Australian bushman must try his best to tell a bigger out-back lie than the last bush-liar. **1911** *Bulletin* (Sydney) 13 July 14/3 In an Outback mining centre in W.A., a man sold his camp *and a woman* for half a crown. **1919** *Smith's Weekly* (Sydney) 5 Apr. 9/5 Well-to-do but countryfied . . out-back settlers . . put themselves on their very best behaviour. **1937** E. FLYNN *Beam Ends* 67 You will never see finer horsemanship than in one of these small Rodeos in an 'out back' North Queensland town. **1953** *Bulletin* (Sydney) 16 Dec. 12/1 Before the war a Queensland firm with a big outback trade used to sell stockman's-cut pants made of a dark-blue material as thin as shirting. **1965** G.H. FEARNSIDE *Golden Ram* 15 The town grew up about them, as so many Australian outback towns had done in the days when the railways were expanding. **1976** J. HIBBERD *Three Pop. Plays* 5 Popular Theatre . . is a theatre of gum without being gumnut, as in the more jejune and sentimental outback literature. **1984** *N.T. News* (Darwin) 26 Sept. 18/4 An outback road could become a new tourist corridor linking two of Australia's greatest attractions, the Great Barrier Reef and Ayers Rock.

C. *n.*

a. Sparsely inhabited country which is remote from a major centre of population.

1893 J.A. BARRY *Steve Brown's Bunyip* 51 'Yes, I'm from out back,' said a dark, wiry little man, as he dismounted from his horse at a Queensland frontier-township hotel. **1901** H. LAWSON *Joe Wilson & his Mates* 105 'Out-Back' is always west of the Bushman, no matter how far out he be. **1907** *Gentleman's Mag.* (London) July 78 Young dwellers in the Out Back have often no educational opportunities. **1911** E.M. CLOWES *On Wallaby through Vic.* 115 The Outback can still breed some true mates. **1923** 'J. NORTH' *Son of Bush* 9 Jack joined up with a teamster . . and journeyed slowly but surely to many parts of the Outback. **1928** M.E. FULLERTON *Austral. Bush* 40 So long as there is an outback. **1936** C.P. CONIGRAVE *N. Aust.* 56 Men who had thrown down the gauntlet to Australia's out-back. **1942** *Welcome to Aust.* 18 Bushmen are white men who are at home in the outback. **1953** D. STIVENS *Gambling Ghost* 1, I was in the back of the outback, two hundred miles from anywhere. **1962** J. MACKENZIE *Austral. Paradox* 42 The vast areas of the Outback where nothing much grows higher than a man's waist. **1968** J. WOODBERRY *Come back Peter* (1974) 55 His mother thought that this was the Outback—the Never-Never—but he knew that despite its 700 miles from the city, the Outback did not start here. **1971** *Bulletin* (Sydney) 13 Nov. 47/1 It's the cinematic season for fresh visions of the Australian outback. **1983** *Weekend Austral.* (Sydney) 8 Oct. 9/1 The Outback—that festering scab of shimmering salt lakes, red sands freckled with wiry spinifex, and once-great mountain chains ground down by time into relic ridges. **1984** *Bulletin* (Sydney) 7 Feb. 6/2 People of the outback still do not have an efficient telephone service.

b. In the collocation **great (Australian) outback,** the outback, esp. as perceived in a romanticized literary depiction of life there.

1936 C.P. CONIGRAVE *N. Aust.* 54 Only one of the many, many lonely graves in the great Australian Outback. **1954** T. RONAN *Vision Splendid* 52 Four closely penned pages of his impressions of the Great Outback. **1957** F. CLUNE *Fortune Hunters* 36 These poets and story-writers of the 'dying stockman' school of thought derive their inspiration from books, or from plonk-saloons in the cities, rather than from the reality of the Great Outback today. **1965** R.H. CONQUEST *Horses in Kitchen*, In no way whatsoever have I tried to depict the great outback as sun-blistered and drought-scorched, with dead cows, horses and sheep cluttering up the bone-dry waterholes. **1972** *Bulletin* (Sydney) 30 Sept. 40/3 He describes the Great Outback or Heart as a place where 'the drover is driven and the shearer is shorn'.

Hence **outbackmanship** *n.*

1962 *Texas Q.* 62 'Near enough' is the national philosophy: a deliberate cult of antifinesse, of outbackmanship.

outbacker, *n.*[1] A non-Aboriginal person native to or resident in the outback.

1900 *Bulletin* (Sydney) 1 Sept. 15/1 Surat (Q.), from a travelled 'out-backer's' view, may be considered an elysium. **1904** *Ibid.* 4 Aug. 16/2 The outbacker's abnormal appetite for patent medicines. **1914** 'B. CABLE' *By Blow & Kiss* 42 You can't be a real out-backer till you've boiled your billy over a camp fire. **1923** 'J. NORTH' *Son of Bush* 23 You should not confound the Australian outbacker with the English labourer. **1927** *Bulletin* (Sydney) 1 Sept. 26/3 Menindie, on the Darling, has been a watering-place for outbackers ever since the first white man went into 'the corner'. **1942** L. & K. HARRIS *Lost hole Bingoola* 81 At any rate he was Outbacker enough always to have a smooth pebble in his pocket when out on the run. **1975** L. WALKER *Runaway Girl* 18 He looked at them from under a broad-brimmed Outbacker's hat. **1981** *Austral. Women's Weekly* (Sydney) 18 Nov. 21/1 Part of the route was along a 'highway'—the Connie-Sue, cleared by legendary outbacker Len Biddell.

out-backer, *n.*[2] *Two-up.* See quot. 1941.

1919 C. DREW *Doings of Dave* 34 The 'out' backers were winning. **1922** —— *Rogues & Ruses* 157 The 'out' backers swore profusely. **1941** E. BAUME *I lived These Yrs.* 122 If they both come down heads the man who is tossing wins; if tails the 'out' backer, or man betting against the tosser, collects the bet.

outbackery. [f. OUTBACKER *n.*[1]] The cultivation of attitudes and values supposedly characteristic of those who live in the outback. Also *attrib.*

1961 *Bulletin* (Sydney) 1 Feb. 32/3 People . . are suspicious of the current outbackery cult. **1974** *Gayzette* (Sydney) 17 Oct. 3/4 A Rigby spokesman said . . 'We seem to have a reputation for Australiana and outbackery and this book is a radical departure for us.' **1979** D. LOCKWOOD *My Old Mates & I* 2 They'll groan about another dose of outbackery while wishing like hell they were here to enjoy it with us. **1986** *Bulletin* (Sydney) 14 Jan. 44/1 On the whole issue of outbackery, the author finds curious contradictions in the Australian psyche.

out beyond. OUTBACK *n.*

1906 *Bulletin* (Sydney) 25 Jan. 14/4 What is this strange fascination to the sundowner, the Out Beyond? **1907** A. SEARCY *In Austral. Tropics* p. v, It is only the man who has lived in the far-removed 'out-beyond' . . who can understand the charm and poetry of the Australian bush.

out bush, *adv.* and *a.*

A. *adv.* Into or in an area of back country.

1908 MRS A. GUNN *We of Never-Never* 220 Out-bush we take the good with the bad as we find it. *Ibid.* 256 Our life was . . peaceful and regular, with an occasional single day 'out-bush'. **1911** A. SEARCY *By Flood & Field* 57 A big crowd of blacks were mustered and instructed to go 'out bush' in parties. **1931** M. TERRY *Hidden Wealth* 4 If you are able to enjoy, as we did, the time out bush. **1932** M.R. WHITE *No Roads go By* 226 The men would go for another two or three weeks 'out bush'. **1935** R.B. PLOWMAN *Boundary Rider* 208 The padre invited him to do the trip to Birdsville; promising that he would have a chance to see life outbush and that he could return to it if he so desired. **1938** J.F.W. SCHULZ *Destined to Perish* 60 He was better able to pursue his work living among the natives out-bush. **1954** H.G. LAMOND *Manx Star* 57 The spell out bush should do him good. **1963** X. HERBERT *Disturbing Element* 94 They called him Bushy . . because he was lately from somewhere out bush.

B. *adj.* Situated in the back country.

1911 A. SEARCY *By Flood & Field* 274 We chanced on a little fellow camped on the track, who some time before had left one of the outbush stations with a mate. **1927** M. TERRY *Through Land of Promise* 230 The man who does the 'bronco-ing' (the local term for this roping of cattle, only found in the most bushy out-Bush stations) rides amongst the mob.

outer.

1. An uncovered area for non-members at a racecourse or sports ground and, as such (at a racecourse), a place where bets can be laid; (*two-up*) the periphery of the ring in which the game is played.

1915 DREW & EVANS *Grafter* 54 'Hello, Grafter!' . . 'What's the strong of this? I thought you were fielding on the Outer?' **1919** C. DREW *Doings of Dave* 19 They were the 'Outer' frequenters, straight from the hill behind the course. **1920** 'J. NORTH' *Harry Dale's Grand National* 167 The crowds on the lawn and the outer and the flat took up the cheering. **1943** *Troppo Tribune* (Mataranka) 4 Oct. 3 On the football field, from information told him by the kid whose old man sells peanuts in the outer. **1944** F. BRUNO *Sa-eeda Wog!* 10 You and I, brother, can pierce the cloak of harmless amusement which hovers about the 'outer' of the two-up school. **1980** B. JEWSON *Stir* 78 Dave would race around the jail getting tobacco so they would have a smoke. . . They would dream of the day they would be on the outer together.

2. *fig.* In the phr. **on** (or **of**) **the outer,** disadvantaged; ill-favoured; excluded.

1902 *Truth* (Sydney) 6 Apr. 7/2 Our statesmen are Of the grimy outer outer. **1919** A. WRIGHT *Game of Chance* 202 I'm standin' Cobber to give me a new start, and if he gets touched off for the Epsom, I'll be right on th' outer again. **1924** *Truth* (Sydney) 27 Apr. 6 *Outer, on the*, to be poor; to be outside. **1940** W. HATFIELD *Into (Great?) Unfenced* 151 People think I'm only frothing at the mouth because *I'm* on the outer meself. I am, of course, and I don't fancy it. **1952** *Coast to Coast 1951–52* 170 It's been a long road for most . . bitter struggles 'on the outer' for all the wretched scraps of jobs. **1975** 'N. CULOTTA' *Gone Gougin'* 41, I was feeling depressed because I did not understand. . . 'Well,' he said, 'that's a relief. I thought I was on the outer.'

outlaw. [Spec. use of *outlaw* a wild, untamed beast.] An intractable horse. Also **outlaw horse.**

1900 *Truth* (Sydney) 28 June 5/6 Several . . of the horses presented to the Bushman are 'outlaws'—that is, horses with whom it has been found impossible to do anything. **1916** *Bulletin* (Sydney) 19 Oct. 22/1 The most untamable outlaw is the renegade thoroughbred horse. **1927** 'S. RUDD' *Romance of Runnibede* 131 Tom called to the merry blacks on the yard-top, as he hitched his pants and approached the outstretched quivering outlaw, 'If he bucks me off some of you fellows will have to get on him'. **1936** J.C. DOWNIE *Galloping Hoofs* 108 Every horse that bucks is not necessarily an outlaw. . . What we call an outlaw is a horse that will not see reason, refuses to be ridden, and bucks worse each time he is saddled and mounted. **1945** *Queanbeyan Age* 28 Sept. 1/6 Come and see champion horsemen ride noted outlaws. **1960** R.S. PORTEOUS *Cattleman* 18 One old hand tried to outdo the other in tales of wild cattle or outlaw horses! **1978** R.H. CONQUEST *Dusty Distances* 20 Australia's outback in 1930 couldn't have functioned without its horses, which were outlaws in rodeos and outback settlements before being broken.

outside, *a.*, *n.*, and *adv.*

A. *adj.*

1. a. Situated at or pertaining to the outer limit of settlement; situated in an area remote from a major centre of population.

1847 E.B. KENNEDY *Extracts Jrnl. Exped. Central Aust.* 233 After travelling 14 miles reached Roach's, the outside station of the settlers. **1864** R. HENNING *Lett.* (1952) 73 When Biddulph first took up Exmoor it was the very outside run northwards. . . Now it is quite an inside station, every bit of country is taken up for several hundred miles round it. **1870** E.B. KENNEDY *Four Yrs. in Qld.* 148 The 'outside squatters', the pioneers of sheep-farming, have a hard time of it . . as anyone will allow who visits . . districts in the 'far west'. **1879** S.W. SILVER *Austral. Grazier's Guide* 9 For a certain number of years the pastoral tenant of an 'outside run' had little to do and nothing to dread. **1891** W.B. DEAN *Notorious Bushrangers* 31 It was invariably his custom to supply the outside station stock-keepers with tobacco, tea, sugar, and, in some cases, grog. **1923** *Bulletin* (Sydney) 4 Jan. 22/2 I've had over 40 years of droving, with both 'inside' and 'outside' stock. **1933** R.B. PLOWMAN *Camel Pads* 12 The outside blacks, that had never been anywhere near civilization before, came in to the stations. **1936** I.L. IDRIESS *Cattle King* 78 'Any 'outside' news?' 'Yes, I hear rumours there's gold being found away out. I don't take much notice of mulga wires.' **1951** E. HILL *Territory* 310 In the early days these 'outside' men . . worked their cattle with lubras, quicker to learn and more to be trusted.

b. In collocations: **outside country, district, track.**

1879 *Queenslander* (Brisbane) 31 May 684/1 A man knows what he has to expect in the **outside country.** **1890** A.J. VOGAN *Black Police* 125 Dr Junelle has travelled through a great deal of the little-known and less populated districts of Australia called generally the 'outside' country. **1914** 'B. CABLE' *By Blow & Kiss* 180 A doctor is a doctor, but in the outside country he is a great deal more—or he is a great deal less. **1944** J.H. PICK *Aust.'s Dying Heart* (rev. ed.) 27 The Outside country, that with a ten-inch rainfall or less. **1965** K. TENNANT *Summer's Tales* 78 There would be good grazing on this 'outside' country and they would stock it with cattle. **1876** 'CAPRICORNUS' *Colonisation* 21 In the **outside districts** there is always hanging about a sprinkling of population which partakes in some degree of the character of the original squatters. **1929** *Bulletin* (Sydney) 4 Sept. 25/2, I was returning from an outside-district run. **1888** 'R. BOLDREWOOD' *Robbery under Arms* (1937) 95 We kept working by all sorts of **outside tracks** on the main line of road. **1900** H. LAWSON *Verses Pop. & Humorous* 106 'Twas We and the World—and the rest go hang—as the Outside tracks we trod. **1913** W.K. HARRIS *Outback in Aust.* 51 They could ride 'outside tracks' with the best.

2. *Fishing.* Off-shore.

1896 F.G. AFLALO *Sketch Nat. Hist. Aust.* 201 The skill employed by the 'outside men', 'groper-men', 'black-brimmers', and others in catching their favorite fish, is such as to astonish . . fishermen all the world over. **1906** D.G. STEAD *Fishes of Aust.* 126 The adults frequent principally the 'outside' grounds in the vicinity of sunken reefs and bomboras. **1947** H. DRAKE-BROCKMAN *On N.-W. Skyline* 34 All the fleet was in, 'laid-up' out of danger in Dampier Creek, the luggers being reconditioned, the crews enjoying themselves in Chinatown after months of 'outside' monotony. **1951** *Manning River Times* (Taree) 6 Oct., A representative . . told of the possibilities of tuna fishing to about 15 outside fishermen. **1962** L. WEDLICK *Fishing in Aust.* 161 Silver trevally can be caught in all Australian States in outside and inside waters. **1982** R. HUNGERFORD *Compl. Bk. Austral. Fishing* (ed. 3) 95 We have no banks or extended shallow continental shelf. Thus, most of our outside fishing is in deep water.

B. *n.* An area remote from a major centre of population.

1869 'E. HOWE' *Boy in Bush* 171 The Kakadua was then 'outside'—as the colonists used to call unsettled districts. **1888** 'R. BOLDREWOOD' *Robbery under Arms* I. 95 Dick Dawson came in from outside, and he said things are shocking bad; all the frontage bare already, and the water drying up. **1909** F.E. BIRTLES *Lonely Lands* 100 Being so far out back this place is a little world in itself. Christmas celebrations were observed in the usual outback fashion. . . Everyone rode in from the outside on horseback. **1913** *Bulletin* (Sydney) 4 Dec. 22/2 To a person who has left the South and put in years on the Outside, there is something tragic about the coming back. **1938** A. UPFIELD *Bone is Pointed* (1966) 46 Bony saw the road to 'outside' winding away to the eastern horizon. **1949** G. FARWELL *Traveller's Tracks* 16 The Darling is something of a frontier. . . It separates the familiar and well settled Inside Country from the far west, the great and mysterious Outside. **1979** D. LOCKWOOD *My Old Mates & I* 157 The Territory was once back-of-Bourke, back-of-beyond, the Outside.

C. *adv.*

1. In a remote area.

1911 C.E.W. BEAN *'Dreadnought' of Darling* 317 Be the 'inside' country never so tame and densely populated, there will always be a huge stretch of country 'outside' which cannot by any known means be closely settled. **1930** J.S. LITCHFIELD *Far-North Memories* 207 Perhaps a young man brings up a bride from the south, and takes up work 'outside', i.e., in the bush.

2. *Fishing.* Out to sea.

1902 *Bulletin* (Sydney) 11 Oct. 33/1 We were 'outside' schnappering. **1908** *Ibid.* 17 Sept. 14/4 Fleets of steamers . . go 'outside' on Saturdays, Sundays, and Wednesdays loaded with citizens, whisky, 'cobber' lines and schnapper-bait. **1913** *Cwlth. Parl. Papers* III. 682 Some are on the boats outside. **1966** W. HARDY *Saltwater Angler* 217 Outside, but still close inshore, there are usually big areas of rocky bottom which are fairly fished. **1982** R. HUNGERFORD *Compl. Bk. Austral. Fishing* (ed. 3) 95, I avoided the wide, blue water—until two friends invited me to 'have a day outside'.

outsider. *Obs.* One who lives in a remote place.

1867 *S.A. Parl. Papers* II. no. 14 40, I believe you have been engaged on runs all your life?—Ever since I was ten years old. Since 1840 I have been an outsider. **1870** E.B. KENNEDY *Four Yrs. in Qld.* 152 The 'outsider' is in a country depending upon nature entirely for a supply of water. **1879** *Queenslander* (Brisbane) 19 Apr. 492/4 Ye gentlemen of Brisbane, who sit at home at ease, How little do ye know of—the sort of life we poor unfortunate 'outsiders' have to pass.

out-station.

1. a. *Obs.* An outpost, esp. a military garrison or convict settlement.

1817 *Hobart Town Gaz.* 9 Aug., At this Muster are to attend all Free Men and Women resident at . . Stony Hut Plains, and all Out-stations and Stock Yards in that Quarter. **1820** *Sydney Gaz.* 17 May, Issue from the King's Stores . . an extra Ration of one Pound of fresh beef to each Non-commissioned Officer and Soldier at Sydney and the Out-stations. **1826** *Hobart Town Gaz.* 6 May, The Commandants of all Out-stations will address their general Communications to the Colonial Secretary. **1827** *HRA* (1920) 1st Ser. XIII. 83 At all the Out Stations, the Troops are attended by the Colonial Surgeons. **1831** *Acct. Colony Van Diemen's Land* 75 The party halted for the night near a stock-keeper's hut. This was at the time an outstation from Westbury for a small party of military. **1837** *HRA* (1914) 1st Ser. XVIII. 676 In reference also to the Out Stations, viz. Bathurst, Moreton Bay, and Norfolk Island. **1842** *Colonial Observer* (Sydney) 16 Nov. 613/3 Constable Watson, of the out-station of the Sydney police. **1844** *HRA* (1914) 1st Ser. XXIV. 155 The cost of the spirit ration . . at the Out Stations of New South Wales is much lower than the average of the whole Colony. **1855** *Melbourne Monthly Mag.* May 58 A circular from the Chief Commissioner of the Gold Fields, 'to furnish the fullest possible report' on the district under his charge—I, being at that time in charge of the large out-stations of Warranga, otherwise known as the 'Goulburn Diggings'. **1859** W. BURROWS *Adventures Mounted Trooper* 24 Eight of the men . . were sent further off to an out-station, that is, a smaller post formed near a head-station, as a means of connexion between the more distant points. **1880** J. BONWICK *Resources Qld.* 10 The so-called *Moreton Bay District* was an out-station of New South Wales.

b. *Obs.* An outpost of settlement; a run or station established at a distance from a settled district. Also *attrib.*

1834 J.D. LANG *Hist. & Statistical Acct. N.S.W.* II. 64 Ticket-of-leave holders, of reputable character, might be advantageously settled in the out-stations of the colony. **1843** J.F. BENNETT *Hist. & Descr. Acct. S.A.* 73 There is a tribe to the north which has yet had but little intercourse with the whites, and the squatters at the out-stations are sometimes liable to inroads from them. **1844** *Swan River News* June 43/1 No matter however remote a settler had chosen to locate himself, he was not long isolated, the interval between the out-stations and the more settled parts being immediately filled up by successive settlers. **1845** *Observer* (Hobart) 18 July 4/1 Collisions between the aborigines and the inhabitants at the out-stations. **1856** D.J. GOLDING *Emigrant's Guide Aust.* (1973) 103 The out-station settlers furnish their dwellings with few articles of domestic convenience. **1864** *Illustr. Sydney News* 16 Dec. 12 To become properly acquainted with the *genus* squatter, we must visit him at home in the wilds of the bush, away from society, and, in a great measure, from civilized life—must rough it with him in his bark hut on some out-station. **1870** J. BONWICK *Last Tasmanians* 67 The cruelty took an indirect turn with some of these out-station people. **1893** S. NEWLAND *Paving Way* 106 It's only three days' ride to the out-stations of South Australia.

2. a. On a grazing property: a subordinate station at some distance from the main establishment (see quot. 1853). See *home station* HOME *attrib.*[2] b.

1829 R. DAWSON *Statement* 50 They visited the principal out-stations, and nearly all the sheep folds. **1840** *S. Austral. Rec.* (London) 13 June 316 A party of aborigines . . came to an out station . . and brandishing their spears, ordered the shepherds and watchmen into the hut. **1848** J.C. BYRNE *Emigrant's Guide* 40 At the head station is grown grain sufficient for all; and from it, weekly or monthly, rations are sent to the out-stations. **1853** MOSSMAN & BANISTER *Aust. Visited & Revisited* 65 An out-station is simply a hut at a convenient distance from the homestead, or from any other out-station on the 'run' or sheep-walk, so as to allow ample feeding-ground for two flocks of sheep. **1867** 'CLERGYMAN' *Aust. as it Is* 1 A shepherd's hut . . formed one of the numerous out-stations of a large grazing establishment. **1889** *Illustr. Austral. News* (Melbourne) 9 Feb. 26/2 Have station troughs cut in logs round either the head or the out station. These are filled with salt, and the cattle eat out of them. **1895** J. KIRBY *Old Times in Bush* 157 The shepherd's huts, or, as they were more frequently called, 'out stations', would not be all built at once, but accordingly as the sheep increased. **1913** M.A. MCMANUS *Reminisc. Maranoa District* 42 The term 'Head' Station is so named to distinguish the owner's residence or headquarters from the out stations, whether cattle or sheep. **1927** A. CROMBIE *After Sixty Yrs.* 73, I passed an out-station, occupied by a cook only. **1947** W.E. HARNEY *Brimming Billabongs* (1963) 98 The station was divided into many stock camps, each called after some waterhole near by, and each of these out-stations had its little group of native families who were ruled by the white head stockman of that section. **1964** T. RONAN *Packhorse & Pearling Boat* 47, I went with Dad to the twelve-mile-distant sheep out-station. **1980** M. DUGAN *Early Dreaming* 18 Many of his borrowers were people who kept windmills and troughs operating on lonely out-stations.

b. Comb. **out-station hut.**

1844 *Port Phillip Gaz.* 18 May 3 On the night of the 23rd March, Peter Stratton came to the out station hut. **1848** *Port Phillip Herald* 27 June 2/7 Many shepherds . . were in a continual state of intoxication for several days after the wreck, from the beer and spirits which washed on to the beach adjoining their runs and out-station huts. **1928** V. PALMER *Man Hamilton* 93 The weekly rides to the out-station hut . . were resumed as the winter drew on. **1950** G. FARWELL *Surf Music* 42 An out-station hut built many years ago by Kidman, the Cattle King . . used to house a couple who looked after his travelling stock. **1978** R.H. CONQUEST *Dusty Distances* 7 The fires come, burning for weeks on end and destroying millions of acres of grazing country, hundreds of miles of fencing and scores of out-station huts.

3. An autonomous Aboriginal community located at some distance from a centre on which it is dependent for services and supplies: see quot. 1981 (1). See also HOMELAND. Also *attrib.*, esp. as **outstation movement.**

1972 DOUGLAS & OLDMEADOW *Across Top* 29 One of Sheppy's deepest interests is in his 'out-stations'; small groups of Aborigines still clinging to their traditional ways in their tribal territories. **1976** *West Austral.* (Perth) 10 July 9/4 The 'outstation movement'—under which family groups moved away from settlements and used them only as service centres—appeared to have achieved some success by returning to tribal patterns of authority. **1979** M. HEPPELL *Black Reality* 90 A prototype house which was introduced into one outstation community twelve months ago has been used fairly regularly for simple storage. **1981** J. MULVANEY et al. *Aboriginal Aust.* 193 *Outstations*, since the early 1970s there has been a growing movement of Aboriginal people out of the Mission Stations, Government Reserves and pastoral properties of central and northern Australia, back to tribal lands where autonomous communities have been established. **1981** Q. WILD *Honey Wind* 148 On the way back to Darwin, they visited Aboriginal out-stations on several locations, and saw how Aborigines were experimenting in developing their own cattle runs. **1982** *Canberra Times* 6 Nov. 9/2 The 'Ngurrantiji mob', whose settlement on a narrow tract of land in their traditional area has often been praised as one of the most successful examples of the 'outstation movement'. **1984** *Age* (Melbourne) 10 Nov. (Saturday Extra) 12/8 The outstation movement is helping the resurgence of traditional art, as families are leaving the old mission settlements and returning to their traditional lands. **1986** *Canberra Times* 15 Mar. 2/4 With some assistance . . outstations can provide for greater self-sufficiency and self management than on the fringe.

out west, *adv., n.,* and *a. Eastern States.*

A. *adv.* In or to the sparsely populated western districts; OUTBACK *adv.*

1895 *Worker* (Sydney) 21 Dec. 1/3 We were tank-sinking out West when the news came that one of our crowd had struck the first in Tattersall's big sweep. **1905** *Truth* (Sydney) 29 Jan. 1/8 Out West the other day a travelling parson attacked a cocky because the sunburnt land-scratcher had neglected to have his youngest baptised. **1920** H.F. MOLLARD *Humour of Road* 21 All right, Tom. Any rain out west? **1976** L. HAYLEN *Tracks we Travel* 2 Parents had a big property 'out west'. **1977** R. MCKIE *Crushing* (1978) 131 It came from a place out west. Mother gave it to me when I passed the Intermediate down south.

B. *n.* The sparsely populated western districts; OUTBACK *n.*

1902 *Blackwood's Mag.* (Edinburgh) May 638/1 On the streets of Sydney or Melbourne the appearance of a copper-skinned back-blocker excites as much comment as might a being from another planet. The man from 'out west' cares little for the opinion of the townsman. **1969** A. GARVE *Boomerang* 39, I was thinking rather of the interior—'out west' I believe you call it—where my Corporation could expect to get in on the ground floor.

C. *adj.* Of or pertaining to, or situated in, the sparsely populated western districts; OUTBACK *a.*

1917 *Bulletin* (Sydney) 22 Nov. 22/3 The most wicked parrot of my acquaintance was the property of Janet O'Brown an Out West licensee. **1923** *Ibid.* 1 Nov. 24/3 At many Out-West peeling establishments goats—always more manageable than the woollies—are regularly used as leaders, and poddied calves are also often pressed into the service.

oval. [Transf. use of the name of Kennington *Oval*, the Surrey County cricket ground in s. London.] A sports ground (not necessarily elliptical in shape).

1822 T. REID *Two Voyages N.S.W. & Van Diemen's Land* 113 The greater part of the fence enclosing the Cricketing Association's oval was levelled to the ground. **1901** A. HASLUCK *A. Tennyson's Vice-Regal Days* 15 July (1978) 168 That afternoon we again went to the Oval where 6000 children took part in a Demonstration. **1917** 'PEGASUS' *So Drover Said* 5 We have spent them on the oval, When we played a dashing game. **1940** *Sentry Go* (Keswick) Nov. 12/2 Drilling . . on the oval of the Soldiers Memorial Park. **1960** *N.T. News* (Darwin) 12 Feb. 6/3 The new school will have a big playing oval. **1974** N. PHILLIPSON *As Other Men* 51 'What's he mean? What'sa oval?' . . 'It's a place where they play football.' **1977** D. WILLIAMSON *Club* (1978) 33 We're going to graze 'em on the oval and save on lawn mowing costs.

oven. Abbrev. of *native oven* (see NATIVE *a.* 5).

1878 R.B. SMYTH *Aborigines of Vic.* II. 232 When a company of natives returns after a day's hunting and foraging, the women take a fresh supply of firewood and stones. These last are sometimes found in the 'ovens' in localities remote from where any stones are known to exist. **1951** A. MARSHALL *Aust.* (1981) 157 In a wind-scooped patch of red sand, lie the remains of a blackfellow's midden—'ovens' the bushmen call them. Mussel shells lie scattered around. There are lumps of baked clay and quite a number of artifacts.

over, *adv.* In the phr. **over there,** on the other side of the world, in Europe (esp. during the war of 1914–18).

1918 R.H. KNYVETT *Over there with Australs.* 5 Only earth that has been blown on by the wind is fresh 'over there'. Don't, if you have a weak stomach, ever turn up any earth; though there may not be rotting flesh, other gases are imprisoned in the soil. **1918** N.P.H. NEAL *Back to Bush* 35 Here's to the boys who are out 'over there', And the skulls of the Huns that they cracked, Sir. **1922** A. WRIGHT *Colt from Country* 13 Young Doug Manon . . had 'done his bit' on the other side . . but many a time 'over there' had he prayed for a 'dinkum blighty' so that he could get away from it all. **1936** N. CALDWELL *Fangs of Sea* 235 He, too, had been 'over there' and had brought home a souvenir he would never lose—a bullet in one lung. **1972** *Bulletin* (Sydney) 21 Oct. 36/3 The ABC . . is still reluctant to promote Australian talent unless it has first found recognition, fame and fortune 'over there'. **1978** G. HALL *River still Flows* 69 Something happening 'over there' while we went on living lives that were almost normal.

overcoat. *transf.* The fleece of a sheep.

1919 *Bulletin* (Sydney) 11 Dec. 20/2 It was widely circulated that a Westralian shearer barbered 321 jumbucks in one day. True, he was paid for 321, but he took the overcoats off only 180. **1941** *Ibid.* 22 Jan. 16/3 The shearing contractor . . had been urging his team on, resulting in their 'skimming the wrinkles' and leaving the sheep with a fair overcoat.

overdrive, *v.* [Spec. use of *overdrive* to drive or work to exhaustion.] *trans.* To drive (cattle) too hard. Freq. as *vbl. n.* and *ppl. a.*

1851 *Empire* (Sydney) 15 Mar. 7/2 Cattle are known to die . . from overdriving. **1923** *Bulletin* (Sydney) 4 Jan. 22/2 If you want cattle to camp you must feed and water them well and not overdrive them. **1936** 'L. KAYE' *Black Wilderness* 59 He was in sight again, driving on his mob of over-driven cattle. **1975** G.A.W. SMITH *Once Green Jackaroo* 81 We were doing our best to hustle them along for otherwise we might be driving until midnight. . . He made us stop the front immediately. . . There we stood for an hour while the cattle recovered from 'over-driving'.

overland, *a.* and *n.* [Spec. use of *overland* proceeding across land.]

A. *adj.*

1. a. *Hist.* Of or pertaining to a journey by land from New South Wales to South Australia. **b.** *transf.* Of or pertaining to a long journey by land, esp. the driving of stock over a long distance.

1838 *S. Austral. Rec.* (London) 11 July 76 An *overland* importation on a great scale, which we hail as the introduction of a system of internal communication and supply between the Colonies. Nearly 2,000 head of cattle, and from 4,000 to 6,000 sheep, were on the route overland from New South Wales to the Province. **1841** *S. Austral. Mag.* (Adelaide) Dec. 206 The only 'lions' are the overland gentlemen; but, being less rare than formerly, they do not create so great a sensation. **1849** G.F. ANGAS *Descr. Barossa Range* 7 The stock of *cattle*, partly by overland supplies from the other colonies. **1859** W. FAIRFAX *Handbk. to Aust.* 6 The trade of the town is chiefly supported by the overland stock traffic. **1864** H. JONES *New Valuations* 24 Large numbers of overland sheep passing over my run. **1909** F.E. BIRTLES *Lonely Lands* 99 There were some hundred and fifty souls waiting anxiously for the arrival of the 'overland ships', as the teams are called. **1914** A.R. RICHARDSON *Early Memories Great Nor-West* 59 Mr John Brockman then took charge of Clarkson's overland mob, taking them on through to Roebourne. **1954** T. RONAN *Vision Splendid* 165 Marty, pack-bags bursting with all available varieties of rations, was excelling himself as an overland chef.

2. In collocations: **overland herd, party.**

1839 *S. Austral. Rec.* (London) (1840) 27 June 358 Three **overland herds** of cattle have just arrived, consisting in all of about 1,800 head. **1847** *Port Phillip Gaz.* 24 Mar. 3 Mr Henry Kingston Jarvis, of Yass, New South Wales . . reached Adelaide on Friday, and reports that the whole of his overland herd . . reached Moorundee on the 19th instant. **1840** *S. Austral. Register* (Adelaide) 30 Apr. 4 The peace . . has been sometimes interrupted between the **overland parties** and the aborigines. **1840** *S. Austral. Rec.* (London) 1 Aug. 70 The overland party which has just arrived consists of 800 head of cattle. **1844** *Duncan's Weekly Register* (Sydney) 19 Oct. 199/2 The overland party was headed . . by a tall, slight man who had come overland before when he lost all his sheep. **1847** T. MCCOMBIE *Austral. Sketches* 66 However wild and dissipated the Overlander may be in the towns, such a thing as grog is never heard of in an Overland party. **1879** G. TAPLIN *Folklore S. Austral. Aborigines* 119 The overland parties have not acted judiciously in allowing the native women to be brought to their encampments. **1899** J.C. HAWKER *Early Experiences S.A.* 78 We blazed some trees near the crossing and marked on them, 'Beware of the blacks', to notify overland parties.

3. In the collocation **overland fish** (or **trout**), a lizard or snake, esp. when used as food.

1881 J.C.F. JOHNSON *To Mount Browne & Back* 13 The Jew lizard is known as 'overland fish'. **1940** *Bulletin* (Sydney) 6 Mar. 17/4 Jack's oft-expressed desire for a feed of 'overland trout' induced a couple of us to take a bush walk. The tally was half a dozen. . . Jack . . managed to . . build a fire and cook his lizard abo. style. **1974** B. KIDMAN *On Wallaby* 62, I come from the far west. . . Only fish out there are . . 'overland trout'—and I can't bring myself to tackle snake.

B. *n.*

1. Ellipt. for 'overland stock route'.

1894 *Bulletin* (Sydney) 10 Feb. 20/3 From South and East the shearers come across the Overland. **1897** J.J. MURIF *From Ocean to Ocean* 118 There is no need to apologise on the Overland. **1927** M.H. ELLIS *Long Lead* 74 'Where might you be bound?' he asked 'Darwin,' we said, 'and back to Sydney down the Overland.'

2. Ellipt. for 'overland journey (driving stock)'.

1936 J.C. DOWNIE *Galloping Hoofs* 111 The 'fats' are culled out for the overland to the freezing works. **1955** STEWART & KEESING *Austral. Bush Ballads* 160 Now this is the law of the Overland that all in the West obey—A man must cover with travelling sheep a six-mile stage a day. **1974** *Austral. Folksongs* (Folk Lore Council Aust.) 36 We rolled our swags and packed our bags, and, taking our lives in hand, We started away with a thousand goats on a Billygoat Overland.

overland, *v.*

1. a. *trans.* To drive (stock) overland, esp. for a great distance.

1882 A.J. BOYD *Old Colonials* 9 As to droving, I have overlanded sheep and cattle. **1902** E.B. KENNEDY *Black Police Qld.* 37, I helped to 'overland' cattle. **1910** *Huon Times* (Franklin) 19 Oct. 4/3 Mrs Bates and her son overlanded cattle from Broome to Peak Hill (N.S.W.), a journey of 3,000 miles. **1912** J. BOWES *Comrades* 91 A drover's 'outfit' was expected at the station during the course of a few days to 'overland' the bullocks to Adelaide. This meant driving the cattle right across the continent, a big undertaking, often occupying twelve months. **1936** J.C. DOWNIE *Galloping Hoofs* 111 Stockmen drive their own company's fat stock back over the boundaries of their runs, and they are overlanded in their turn. **1954** J. CLEARY *Climate of Courage* 109 Right now they're overlanding all the cattle they can move out of the Kimberleys across to western Queensland. **1961** *Bulletin* (Sydney) 11 Nov. 30/2 Ten years ago 100,000 cattle were overlanded out of the Territory annually. **1979** D. LOCKWOOD *My Old Mates & I* 81 The annual droving schedule of cattle being overlanded from Halls Creek to Thargomindah.

b. To convey (a cargo) by land.

1948 B. CRONIN *How runs Road* 39 Joseph Hawdon . . agreed to overland the mails for £1,200 a year.

2. *intr.* To travel by land. Also *trans.*

1885 *Australasian Printers' Keepsake* 126 Jerry proposed to 'overland' the distance. **1925** *Bulletin* (Sydney) 8 Oct. 22/4 The eel he saw overlanding between the McLaughlin and Snowy may not have come directly from either river. **1943** *Ibid.* 18 Aug. 13/2 Even in the 'fifties goldseekers overlanding from S.A. to Ballarat found game so scarce that they had to shoot crows to survive. **1948** M. Uren *Glint of Gold* 154 They left the ship and overlanded to Coolgardie. **1956** S. Gore (*title*), Overlanding with Annabel.

overland, *adv. Hist.* [Spec. use of *overland* over or across land.] From New South Wales to South Australia by land.

1837 *S. Austral. Gaz.* (Adelaide) 8 July 4 During the period that . . Messrs Barnard and Fisher were at Sydney as Commissioners from this Government to purchase supplies for the use of the Colony, they made some enquiries on the important subject of transporting cattle, horses, and sheep, *over land.* **1838** *S. Austral. Rec.* (London) 12 Dec. 125 Capt. Sturt . . may be expected overland in about ten days, with a herd of fine cattle. **1847** T. McCombie *Austral. Sketches* 68 At first the name was 'overland gentlemen', or 'gentlemen who came overland'. **1849** J.P. Townsend *Rambles & Observations N.S.W.* 69 The father . . was a squatter, and annually sent overland many fat cattle (from his stations in the district called Maneroo) to Adelaide in South Australia. **1871** M. Clarke *Old Tales of Young Country* 163 Young men . . purchased cattle and sheep in New South Wales and drove them 'overland'. **1882** [see Overlander 1].

overlander.

1. Orig. one who drove stock from New South Wales to the new Colony of South Australia; one who drives stock over a long distance.

1841 G. Grey *Jrnls. Two Exped. N.-W. & W.A.* II. 195 The first step taken by the Overlanders was the connexion of Port Phillip with Sydney. . . At this period they did not, however, bear the name of Overlanders, which was only given to them after Adelaide had been reached in 1838. **1853** *Bell's Life in Sydney* 31 Dec. 1/2, I accepted the offer of a rough diamond of an overlander, who had come across from the old colony with a lot of cattle and horses to sell to the Adelaidens. **1868** C.W. Browne *Overlanding in Aust.* 1 The men . . employed in the transmission of stock are called overlanders, or, by another term, drovers. **1882** J. Allen *Hist. Aust. 1787 to 1882* 180 Ever since the gentlemen known as 'Overlanders' began first to drive cattle, and then sheep, overland from the New South Wales side, South Australia has paid great attention to pastoral pursuits. **1900** *Pastoral Times* (Deniliquin) 5 May 3/3 Look here, with three good overlanders, an' a couple of smart dogs like Two Up, there, I'd take a mob of cattle up the bloomin' pyramids. **1916** *Bulletin* (Sydney) 18 May 24/2 The cattle-man and overlander of the Gulf and the Territory stand right out on their own in the stock-handling business. **1935** G. McIver *Drover's Odyssey* 217 A man who had ventured into the interior at least as far as the remote areas of South Australia or into the Northern Territory from the south was looked upon as a hero, and his feat won him the appellation of 'Overlander'—a coveted title which carried much weight in the drover's camp. **1951** E. Hill *Territory* 293 In the days of the overlanders, from Wave Hill to Wodonga, from Ord River to Bourke, it might be two years. **1972** Anderson & Blake *J.S. Neilson* 40 From here one only had to journey nine miles by way of Haycroft's to Nhill—the place the overlanders first called Melbourne Swamps. **1979** D. Lockwood *My Old Mates & I* 81 When I was an overlander I hated bull trains. I could see they were going to take my living from me.

2. One who travels overland: see quots.

1847 T. McCombie *Austral. Sketches* 68 The term Overland is not . . confined to such alone as brought over stock; as, whoever arrives at a new settlement overland, is designated an Overlander. **1866** *Adventures ashore & Afloat* (1887) 157 He was one of the very few amongst the 'overlanders' (as the parties first coming from the older settlements were termed) who refrained from shooting down the aborigines for slight causes. **1898** E.E. Morris *Austral Eng.* 333 *Overlander*, . . a slang name for a *sundowner.* **1905** A.B. Paterson *Old Bush Songs* 120 Crying, 'Mother, quick! take in the clothes, Here comes an overlander.' **1927** M. Terry *Through Land of Promise* 34 This well-known Overlander, with his famous car. **1941** S.J. Baker *Pop. Dict. Austral. Slang* 52 *Overlander*, a traveller. . . (3) A settler from another State. (4) A drover. (5) A sundowner. **1957** F. Clune *Fortune Hunters* 147 Beer bottles and lolly-water bottles, empty memorials to the thirsts of overlanders.

3. *transf.*

a. A motor vehicle equipped for rugged conditions.

1957 F. Clune *Fortune Hunters* 35 We pushed on another few miles and found an overlander with a trailer sand-bogged in another creek. **1965** L. Walker *Other Girl* 10 The car, a great fawn-coloured overlander thickly red with the desert dust, thundered round the curve.

b. See quots.

***c* 1887** K.G. Gallop In Never Never Land, Huge mosquitoes known here as 'Scotch Greys' or 'Overlanders' added their quota of misery. **1934** *Bulletin* (Sydney) 14 Nov. 24/1 Take a sugar-bag, sew together the sides of the open end, and split down the centre of the bag as one does with a split bag—the old time drover's 'overlander'. . . The stuffed split bag will keep the saddle well off the sore.

overlanding, *vbl. n.*

1. The driving of stock over a long distance. Also *attrib.*, and as *ppl. a.*

1847 *Port Phillip Herald* 5 Jan. 3/2 *Wanted.*—the situation of Overseer upon a Sheep and Cattle Station, by a party who can give the most unexceptionable references. N.B.—The above would be glad to engage in the overlanding of stock, &c. **1850** Tas. Non-State Rec. 103/6 1 Dec., The overlanding of your wethers to Hobart Town. **1868** C.W. Browne *Overlanding in Aust.* 1 The sending down large droves of sheep or cattle, overland, for sale at any of the colonial markets . . is termed overlanding. **1871** M. Clarke *Old Tales of Young Country* 163 'Overlanding' was a profitable and withal, romantic occupation. Young men . . purchased cattle and sheep in New South Wales and drove them 'overland'. ***c* 1891** Mrs P. Martin *Coo-ee* 272 When you are sitting over a camp fire brewing quart-pot tea and smoking store tobacco . . ask one of the overlanding hands to tell you what he knows about the Bunyip. **1915** W.J. Wye *Souvenirs Sunny South* 21 And I gazed in admiration on this truly perfect horse—I had done some overlanding, and had learnt a bit, of course. **1936** J.C. Downie *Galloping Hoofs* 50 Crocs . . have often caused stampedes among cattle during overlandings. **1956** S. Hope *Diggers' Paradise* 59 They shift beef carcasses by air freight to save the overland trek on the hoof—not that overlanding is a thing of the past. **1977** T.L. McKnight *Long Paddock* 9 Purists may say that these terms are not synonymous; that 'overlanding' should be applied only to the moving of large mobs of stock over long distances to open up new areas of settlement, whereas 'droving' involves any other kind of shepherd livestock movement that is more than casual.

2. *transf.*

1937 *Bulletin* (Sydney) 25 Aug. 20/3 In other countries besides Australia overlanding crocodiles . . are a commonplace.

3. Special Comb. **overlanding camp,** a drover's overnight camp; a resting place for stock being overlanded.

1868 C.W. Browne *Overlanding in Aust.* 61 These opinions are all very well when kept in his own bosom, but they will not do in any overlanding camp. **1954** *Bulletin* (Sydney) 15 Sept. 12/2 All overlanding camps are dry in W.Q. **1979** D. Lockwood *My Old Mates & I* 4, I was frequently in stock camps and overlanding camps without . . being present at even the smallest stampede.

overland mail. [Also U.S.: see Mathews.]

a. An inter-colonial postal service operating by land (as opposed to 'by sea'); the mail so conveyed.

1838 *Melbourne Advertiser* 15 Jan. 4 The overland mail for Sydney closes this day at 6 oclock. **1843** *Sydney Morning Herald* 22 May 2/2 We cannot but remark upon the regularity with which the overland mail is conveyed. **1852** *Moreton Bay Courier* 24 June 3/2 It has been arranged to dispatch the overland mail from Brisbane at two p.m. on Tuesdays. **1880** R. Rose *Austral. Guide: S.A.* 20 There are overland mails thrice a week, and regular intercolonial steam communication by sea. **1931** *N.T. Times* (Darwin) 13 Jan. 2/2 An overland mail will be sent away by the train on Wednesday 28th. inst.

b. A vehicle used for the conveyance of mail.

1954 T. Ronan *Vision Splendid* 119 He just missed the connection to the Port by sea and his shortest road home was to go to Big Knob by the overland mail.

Overland Telegraph. The telegraph line between Port Augusta in South Australia and Darwin in the Northern Territory, completed in 1872 and linking by submarine cable to Java with the telegraphic networks of Asia and Europe. Also **Overland Telegraph line.**

1870 *Illustr. Austral. News* (Melbourne) 5 Dec. 208/1 (*heading*) Planting first post of the Overland Telegraph at Port Darwin. **1889** *Ibid.* 2 Dec. 18 The Australian portion of the English and Australian telegraph lines commences at Port Darwin, the most northern portion of South Australia, and runs through the entire centre of that colony to Adelaide, a distance of close upon 2000 miles. . . The overland telegraph line was originally planned, and afterwards carried out, by Mr Tedd, C.M.G., the present P.M.G. and astronomer of South Australia, assisted by Mr Geo. Goyder, the Surveyor-General. **1915** E.R. Masson *Untamed Territory* 19 The value of the Overland Telegraph has never diminished. **1942** H.H. Peck *Mem. of Stockman* 85 The country beyond, until they struck the overland telegraph line about Newcastle Waters, was unknown. **1954** T. Ronan *Vision Splendid* 119 The bridge over the river was the biggest construction job undertaken in the north since the Overland Telegraph back in the 'seventies. **1983** *Canberra Times* 26 Oct. 23/2 Radiating out from Alice are two major highways, a railway line and the great Overland Telegraph.

overseer. [Spec. use of *overseer* one who superintends.]

1. *Hist.* One appointed, freq. from the convict body, to superintend the work of a party of convicts; *convict overseer* Convict B. 3.

1788 D. Collins *Acct. Eng. Colony N.S.W.* (1798) I. 33 Had a few persons been sent out who were not of the description of convicts, to have acted as overseers, or superintendents [etc.]. **1789** J. Hunter *Hist. Jrnl. Trans. Port Jackson* (1793) 363 A convict, was punished with sixty lashes, for refusing to work, on being ordered by the overseer. **1813** *Van Diemen's Land Govt. & Gen. Orders* 14 Apr. (1814) 11 The Prisoners being now distributed into Gangs under Superintendants and Overseers, who are accountable for their Labour, they are not upon any occasion whatever to be taken from those Gangs. **1829** *Launceston Advertiser* 6 July 2 We opine, that whenever an Overseer is to be made . . if the Government wishes these men to cause any work to be done, they must invariably give them a salary sufficient to support life, with a promise of a pardon or emancipation. **1835** J. Backhouse *Narr. Visit Austral. Colonies* (1843) 263 Volunteer-overseers, are prisoners, of New South Wales, holding tickets-of-leave, who have volunteered to become overseers on Norfolk Island, for salaries of from 1s. to 2s. 3d. a day. **1842** *Tasmanian Jrnl. Nat. Sci.* I. 270 They were drawn up in three lines, each gang forming a separate division—the overseers (convicts) taking their stations in the rear. **1843** C. Rowcroft *Tales of Colonies* (1858) 219 You must know that the different gangs that work in chains are watched by overseers, who have their eyes constantly on them. **1848** C. Cozens *Adventures of Guardsman* 118 An overseer (generally speaking, one of themselves) is appointed to each gang, who marches his men by twos to their respective scenes of operation.

2. One who manages a rural property or who supervises a part of the work on such a property.

1806 *Sydney Gaz.* 15 June, *Wanted*—A Free man as an Overseer on a large Farm. **1822** J.T. Bigge *Rep. State Colony N.S.W.* 25 Cultivation is extended under the direction of an overseer, who was a convict, and has received his emancipation. **1833** W.H. Breton *Excursions* 64 Proprietors do not generally reside upon their farms, but leave them in charge of overseers. **1839** *Port Phillip Gaz.* 21 Dec. 3 A *gentleman* aged 28, of active habits, would be happy to treat with any party requiring an Overseer or Manager on his Estate or large Stock Property. **1856** D.J. Golding *Emigrant's Guide Aust.* (1973) 100 A careful selection of stock, with a steady keeper or two and a trusty overseer, will generally ensure a return of twenty to twenty-five per cent. **1868** J.K. Tucker *Aborigines & Chinese Question* 7 There are now on the station a clergyman, an overseer of the run, and a school-master. **1890** E.T. Towner *Selectors' Guide to Barcoo* 21 At present a station of two hundred thousand sheep keeps a manager at £200 to £300 a year, about two overseers at £80 to £100, and about ten boundary riders. **1913** W.K. Harris *Outback in Aust.* 154 Care is exercised by the overseer to prevent 'scamping' and careless shearing. **1925** M. Terry *Across Unknown Aust.* 118 The overseer (under-manager) from Wangenu. **1946** *Bulletin* (Sydney) 11 Dec. 21/1 'You'll be on shed-hand rates,' said the overseer. 'So don't go for tallies; take your time and don't rough 'em.' **1955** F. Lane *Patrol to Kimberleys* 145 Both station owners and their overseers are out mustering.

3. In the collocation **overseer's hut,** a (temporary) dwelling occupied by the overseer of a convict gang or an employee on a rural property: see also Hut *n.* 2 and 3.

1835 *Colonist* (Sydney) 23 July 237/2 A road party stationed near, called after the name of their overseer, Thorpe's gang, and the escort . . proceeded to the overseer's hut. **1840** *Port Phillip Gaz.* 1 Jan. 2 Good overseer's and men's Huts. **1848** *Ibid.* 4 Jan. 3/7 Upon the station there is a well-watered paddock, consisting of several hundred acres, besides a wheat paddock, stock yards, and a good overseer's hut, with all the usual implements, &c. of a well-found cattle station. **1856** W.W. Dobie *Recoll. Visit Port-Phillip* 94 His lubra was generally about the overseer's hut during the day.

Hence **overseer** *v. trans.*

1841 *Morning Advertiser* (Hobart) 15 Oct. 4/2 We . . abhorred his system of keeping the prisoner gangs overseered by prisoners. **1900** *Advocate* (Burnie) 4 Dec. 4/2 Catlin . . was employed to overseer the crushing. **1903** *Bulletin* (Sydney) 1 Oct. 16/2 Coffee-planter in Big Scrub, overseeing trench digging. **1931** A.W. Upfield *Sands of Windee* 24 You go out to Stewart's Well and overseer that engine.

overstock, *v.* [Spec. use of *overstock* to stock to excess; also U.S. (see DAE).] *trans.* To stock (an area of land) with more animals than can be supported. Also *absol.*

1825 J.H. Wedge *Diaries* (1962) 12 It is only adapted for a cattle and sheep run and it may easily be overstocked. **1851** *Bell's Life in Sydney* 1 Mar. 1/4 Overstocked with cattle. **1888** 'R. Boldrewood' *Robbery under Arms* (1937) 197 It would never have paid to have overstocked the Hollow. **1893** D. Lindsay *Jrnl. Elder Sci. Exploring Exped.* 146 These flats . . appear to have been overstocked some few years ago. **1945** *Bulletin* (Sydney) 26 Sept. 13/2 Joe had overstocked and was one of the first to be hit by the drought. Soon he was looking for agistment country.

Hence **overstocked** *ppl. a.*

1848 J.S. Roe *Rep. Exped. S.-Eastward Perth* 20 Nov. (1849) 59 Render available a tract of pasturage sufficiently extensive to relieve the present overstocked districts. **1879** S.W. Silver *Austral. Grazier's Guide* 14 He has heard the station hands and the under-overseer . . talk . . of those weaklings who have . . bought overstocked runs. **1910** *Emu* X. 26 The rabbits and drought on an overstocked run brought about this result.

overstocking, *vbl. n.* The stocking of an area of land with more animals than it can support.

1867 'Clergyman' *Aust. as it Is* 204 Experience comes so much to the aid of the Australian settler, in the making of 'dams', and guarding against the great danger of 'overstocking'. **1880** J. Bonwick *Resources Qld.* 44 This grass . . does not suffer so much from overstocking. **1884** G. Ranken *Dry Country* i. 1 The herbage has not been trampled out by previous overstocking. **1893** F.W.L. Adams *Australs.* 136 Man has exterminated the kangaroo and the emu, and even the dingo, as much with over-stocking as with lead and strychnine. **1936** E.W. Cox *Evol. Austral. Merino* 135 Rabbits, overstocking, and wanton destruction of timber, bringing about soil erosion, have sadly depleted the land of many of its most valuable grasses.

over there: see Over.

Owen. [From the name of E.E. *Owen* (1915–1949), the Australian inventor of a sub-machine-gun.] A type of sub-machine-gun. Also **Owen gun.**

1941 *Sydney Morning Herald* 30 Sept. 5/6 When all three guns were subjected to the test of being buried in a heap of sand the Owen gun was the only one to continue firing automatically. **1948** *Listening Post* (Perth) Oct. 27 Facing them, with owens at the ready, stood four big men. **1961** D. Dexter *New Guinea Offensives* 51 All sections testing the Owen preferred it to the Tommy-gun. **1966** 'E. Lindall' *Northward Coast* 149 He jerked around as Owens ripped out from the far end of the column. **1970** M. Kelly *Spinifex* 132 The Owen, your best and only friend from now on. **1977** R.E. Gregory *Orig. Austral. Inventions* 39 Evelyn Owen of Wollongong . . had invented a submachine-gun. . . Late in 1942 the first Owen guns were issued to Diggers in New Guinea replacing the heavy Thompsons.

owlet nightjar. The small nocturnal bird *Aegotheles cristatus*, predom. grey or brown with barred wing and tail feathers, widespread in Aust. incl. Tas., and also occurring in s. New Guinea.

1840 J. Gould *Birds of Aust.* (1848) II. Pl. 1, *Aegetholes novae-hollandiae* . . Owlet Nightjar. **1849** C. Sturt *Narr. Exped. Central Aust.* II. 17 App. *Owlet night Jar.* This small bird, although a night bird, is very frequently seen in the day time, sleeping on the branch of a Casuarina. **1896** B. Spencer *Rep. Horn Sci. Exped. Central Aust.* II. 67 Owlet Nightjar . . nocturnal in their habits. **1933** F.E. Baume *Tragedy Track* 103 Rogers, who explored the district in 1911, gives the following list of native birds which should concern everyone interested in the native birds of the Commonwealth:- Owlet night jar; red-backed kingfisher [etc.]. **1968** D. Fleay *Nightwatchmen* 150 The nocturnal midget, smallest of all our night birds and not even the size of a Noisy Miner, is named Owlet Nightjar (*Aegotheles cristatus*). **1982** *Ecos* xxxiii. 15/2 Specimens of stone curlews and owlet nightjars have also been found.

ox. Used *attrib.* in facetious Special Comb. as: **ox conductor,** a bullock driver; **persuader,** a bullock driver; a bullock whip (see Persuader); see also Bullock *n.* 1.

1902 *Truth* (Sydney) 3 Aug. 7/3 The **ox-conductor**, we're often told, Can make the air turn blue. **1913** *Bulletin* (Sydney) 15 May 15/3 A young ox-conductor left Charleville with his team. **1934** J.C. Lee *Bosh-stralians* 204 Bullock-dray . . drawn by sixteen bullocks and driven by Nosey Hawkins . . the best swearer, therefore the best 'Oxen conductor' on the Maxwell selection. **1980** [see *ox persuader*]. **1899** W.T. Goodge *Hits! Skits! & Jingles* 170 Jack McCamley, Lank and long, **Ox-persuader**, Billabong. **1911** *Bulletin* (Sydney) 7 Dec. 44/2 The worn-out ox persuader feels the need of a reviver in the shape of a glass of whisky. **1926** *Ibid.* 1 July 22/3 Black myrtle when procurable is the only whip-stick the bullocky will use for his ox-persuader. **1945** *Ibid.* 31 Jan. 14/4 A hard-bitten teamster pulled in with his team one morning. After several hours of steady guzzling, Bullocky became pretty cranky, so Bung, an ex-trooper, threw him out. Back came the oxen-persuader with a demand for more. **1980** O. Ruhen *Bullock Teams* 164 The terms 'ox' and 'oxen' haven't had much currency in Australia, except perhaps as persiflage: 'ox-persuader' for the bullock whip and 'oxen-conductor' for the teamster.

oxy-weld, *v.* [Abbrev. of *oxy(-acetylene + weld.)* *trans.* To weld (metal), using a mixture of oxygen and acetylene. Also as *vbl. n.*

1945 J. Devanny *Bird of Paradise* 31, I went into Atherton to get some oxy-welding done. **1956** K. Tennant *Honey Flow* 54 What looked like the spine of a dinosaur was a set of caterpillar tractor-treads waiting to be oxy-welded.

oyster, *a.* [Abbrev. of *oyster-like* uncommunicative.] Unforthcoming; secret.

1910 L. Esson *Woman Tamer* (1976) 63 You might tell us, Chopsey. Don't be oyster. I won't word nobody, not me. **1916** J.B. Cooper *Coo-oo-ee!* 171 One stipulation I must make . . what takes place in my hut tonight, is oyster. **1971** H. Anderson *Larrikin Crook* 3 The boy was dragged off to the police station where he remained 'oyster'.

Oyster Bay pine. *Tas.* [f. the name of *Oyster Bay*, on the e. coast of Tas.] The pyramidal tree or tall shrub *Callitris rhomboidea* (fam. Cupressaceae) of s.e. Aust. incl. Tas.

1832 J. Backhouse *Narr. Visit Austral. Colonies* (1843) 73 On the hills, are the Blue Gum, the Oyster Bay Pine. **1833** *Ibid.* 102 The Oyster Bay Pine, *Callitris pyramidalis*, a Cypress-like tree, attaining to seventy feet in height, and affording narrow plank and small timber useful in building, but not easy to work, being liable to splinter. **1849** *Tasmanian Jrnl. Nat. Sci.* III. 279 The *Oyster-Bay Pine*, a species of the widely distributed Australian genus, Callitris, is the only other coniferous plant commonly known amongst the colonists of Tasmania. **1861** L.A. Meredith *Over Straits* 16 Scraggy gum-trees . . here and there relieved by groups of our beautiful Oyster Bay Pine (*Frenela Australis*). **1903** *Tasmanian Timbers* (Tas. Lands & Survey Dept.) 25 Oyster Bay Pine (*Frenela rhomboidea*) . . a tree on the East Coast, deriving its name from the locality in which it is chiefly found. **1956** W.M. Curtis *Student's Flora Tas.* 5 *C[allitris] tasmanica* . . Oyster Bay Pine. . . Locally abundant on the east coast from Prosser River to Elephant Pass.

oyster blenny. [See quot. 1974] The small marine fish *Cyneichthys anolius* of e. Aust.

1906 D.G. Stead *Fishes of Aust.* 211 The Oyster Blenny . . is very often to be found amongst dead and empty oyster-shells, along the coast of New South Wales. **1935** *Bulletin* (Sydney) 31 July 20/4 The oyster blenny is a rival to the lung-fish when it comes to living out of its element. . . If left in a heap of oysters, with no moisture other than that originally contained in the mass, the blenny will live more than a week. **1974** T.D. Scott et al. *Marine & Freshwater Fishes S.A.* 277 Oyster Blenny. *Cyneichthys anolius*. . . This unusual little fish shelters in the empty shells of oysters, and deposits its eggs therein, guarding them till they hatch.

Oz /ɒz/, *n.* and *a.* Also **Aus, Oss.** [Repr. pronunc. of abbrev. of 'Australia' or 'Australian'.]

A. *n.* Abbrev. of 'Australia'.

1908 *Bulletin* (Sydney) 2 July 15/3 My home is near Kingston, which is in the S.E. of South Oss. **1944** *Barging About: Organ of 43rd Austral. Landing Craft Co.* 1 Sept. 6 All the tribes of Oz did gather together. **1971** B. Humphries *Bazza pulls it Off*, If they guess I'm from Oz the shit will really hit the fan! **1972** A. Chipper *Aussie Swearers Guide* 20 Oz, Australia, a big dry place in the Pacific Ocean, where people swear like nowhere else on earth. **1981** C. Wallace-Crabbe *Splinters* 162 Foreign countries sound so horrid nowadays. Dad was right to always stay home in the old Aus. **1983** *Down to Earth News* Apr. 2 I've been to quite a few festivals all over Oz, bar W.A. and the Territory, and I reckon this site has got it over all the other ones. **1986** *Bulletin* (Sydney) 28 Jan. 11/3 A weapon of defence against the voice of the yahoo which is now the voice of Oz.

B. *adj.* Abbrev. of 'Australian'. Also as **Ozman.**

1971 *Bulletin* (Sydney) 18 Dec. 30/2 Then I got back to England and found myself facing the 'Oz' educational attitudes. **1972** *Ibid.* 10 June 9/1 The Oz habit of shaking hands while looking away at an angle of ninety degrees. **1979** R. Macklin *Journalist* 59 A rough gesture. Very Oz. **1985** *Bulletin* (Sydney) 15 Oct. 10/3 Modern Ozman is the direct descendant of the first white boat people. **1986** *Canberra Times* 13 June 11/3 (*heading*) Reservations on 'Buy Oz'.

Ozzie, var. Aussie.

P

Pacific, *a.* Used as a distinguishing epithet in the names of birds occurring on the Pacific coast: **Pacific gull,** the large gull *Larus pacificus* of coastal s. Aust. incl. Tas., having white and black plumage and a heavy yellow beak; **heron,** the predom. grey-black waterbird *Ardea pacifica*, chiefly of mainland Aust., having a white head and neck; *white-necked heron*, see WHITE *a.*[2] 1 b.

1801 J. LATHAM *Gen. Synopsis Birds* Suppl. II. 332 **Pacific G[ull]** inhabits *New South Wales.* **1847** J. GOULD *Birds of Aust.* (1848) VII. Pl. 19, *Larus pacificus* . . Pacific Gull. **1887** *Illustr. Sydney News* 21 Dec. 218/2 On Wednesday some of the party went on to the Ettrick River, and on the way found the eggs of the Pacific gull. **1945** C. BARRETT *Austral. Bird Life* 94 The Pacific gull (*Gabianus pacificus*) neglects no opportunity to steal an egg or seize an unprotected nestling. **1968** R. HILL *Bush Quest* 40 Further out from the pier, the great black and white shapes of Pacific gulls rode on the water amongst the swimming prions. **1984** M. BLAKERS et al. *Atlas Austral. Birds* 195 The Pacific Gull lives on ocean beaches and offshore islands, only exceptionally appearing far inland. **1801** J. LATHAM *Gen. Synopsis Birds* Suppl. II. 305 **Pacific H[eron]** . . inhabits the sea-shores in various parts of *New Holland* . . but is not a common species. **1847** J. GOULD *Birds of Aust.* (1848) VI. Pl. 52, *Ardea pacifica* . . Pacific Heron. . . *White-necked Heron* of the Colonists. **1890** G.J. BROINOWSKI *Birds of Aust.* II. Pl. 21, The Pacific Heron is a summer visitant to the southern coasts of Australia. **1931** M. TERRY *Hidden Wealth* 325 Birds included . . Pacific heron. **1984** M. BLAKERS et al. *Atlas Austral. Birds* 49 The Pacific Heron forages in water or wet paddocks, often alone.

pack, *a.*

1. Used *attrib.* in Special Comb. not necessarily peculiar to Aust. but of local historical significance: **pack bullock, camel,** a bullock or camel used for carrying a pack; **(horse)bike,** a second bicycle, attached alongside the one being ridden and used to carry a pack.

1832 *Sydney Monitor* 19 Dec. 3/6 Pack-saddles constructed on this tree will . . save the back of many a poor **pack-bullock** from writhing sores. **1843** *Sydney Morning Herald* 31 Oct. 4/1, I found the five drays I had formerly the cause of much delay on my former expeditions, and should therefore prefer a greater number of light carts or pack bullocks. **1848** H.W. HAYGARTH *Recoll. Bush Life* 16 When the roads are so bad as to be impassable for drays, pack-bullocks are used, which will carry about two hundredweight each. **1879** *Native Tribes S.A.* 68 Another tribe regarded the first pack-bullocks they saw as the white fellows' wives, because they carried the luggage. **1888** 'R. BOLDREWOOD' *Robbery under Arms* (1937) 46 They had an old pack bullock. **1919** G.W. HANDSLEY *Two-&-Half Yrs. P.O.W. in Turkey* 16 Not the ordinary camel, but old scraggy, bony beasts, who had been used formerly for **pack camels**. **1925** M. TERRY *Across Unknown Aust.* 179 Get supplies . . by pack-camel. **1937** L.R. MENZIES *Gold Seeker's Odyssey* 147 There is as much difference between a pack camel and racing camel, as between a draught-horse and a race-horse. **1903** *Bulletin* (Sydney) 6 Aug. 16/2, I saw a **pack-horse bike**. . . The biker had a huge swag strapped on, over, under, and round his second jigger, which was attached to the riding bike by a curious outrigger contrivance. **1912** *Ibid.* 10 Oct. 15/2, I have often met a party of shearers, camped for tucker-time, with their bikes all set up in a mulga garage. . . Even in the time of my sunset sojourn, the pack-bike was not uncommon.

2. a. In the phr. **to send** (someone or something) **to the pack,** to discard; to dismiss.

1915 C.J. DENNIS *Songs of Sentimental Bloke* 94 I've sent the leery bloke that bore me name Clean to the pack wivout one pearly tear. **1926** *Bulletin* (Sydney) 18 Feb. 22/2 The local vet. says I may as well send her to the pack any time, as a horse with founder never completely recovers.

b. In the phr. **to go to the pack,** to decline or deteriorate to a lower state; to 'go to pieces'; to 'go to the dogs'.

1919 W.H. DOWNING *Digger Dialects* 26 *Go to the pack*, deteriorate. **1922** A. WRIGHT *Colt from Country* 83 Came over from W.A. with a fat roll. . . Expects to win the Cup with Western Chief. If he don't he's gone to the pack sure. **1934** T. WOOD *Cobbers* 200 The country was going to the pack. The Government was a cow. **1958** G. CASEY *Snowball* 118 You wait till he gets a bit older. Them abos always go t' the pack. **1978** HANIGAN & LINDSAY *No Tracks on River* 22 He lost his job when the steamers folded up. Mum says it was real sad how he went to the pack. **1980** F. MOORHOUSE *Days of Wine & Rage* 357 All the places overseas where the British have pulled out are going to the pack.

pack, *v.* In the phr. **to pack them,** to be frightened, to have lost one's nerve (see quot. 1970). Also with explicit objs.

1945 *Atebrin Advocate: Mag. 2/4 Austral. Armoured Regiment* 31 Mar. 1, I don't mind admitting I was packing them. **1952** T.A.G. HUNGERFORD *Ridge & River* 46, I suppose the poor cow *would* pack 'em a bit. He's on'y a kid, by the look of him. **1963** J. CANTWELL *No Stranger to Flame* 79 'You're really packing them. Maybe you're troppo, happens to a lot of blokes.' 'My nerves went long before I came here.' **1970** J.S. GUNN in W.S. Ramson *Eng. Transported* 52 It is some time since I heard anyone talk of *packing the tweeds* for being scared. **1979** CAREY & LETTE *Puberty Blues* 10 I'm so nervous. I didn't do *any* study. I'm packin' shit. **1982** *Sydney Morning Herald* 10 July 12/3 Of course, girls would be 'packin' it', going down an aisle in front of about thirteen hundred people, including photographers and TV cameras, which would be a very nerve-wracking experience for any 17-year-old-girl.

pack-rape. The rape of a woman by a number of men in turn. Also *attrib.* and as *v. trans.*, and *fig.*

1965 *Bulletin* (Sydney) 17 Apr. 27/2 I've had letters from girls who have been pack-raped. **1970** *Ibid.* 16 May 22/2 Organisers of the Moratorium are political bikies pack-raping democracy. **1976** *Southerly* ii. 136 The bikie has just been acquitted on a pack rape charge. **1986** *Canberra Times* 26 May 2/3 It does not take a war to engender rape—pack or otherwise.

pad. [Spec. use of *pad* a path.]

1. A track made by animals: see also *cattle pad* CATTLE 2.

1893 D. LINDSAY *Jrnl. Elder Sci. Exploring Exped.* 23 He must have been on one of the pads close to the camp instead of on the main track. *Ibid.* 25 Numerous kangaroo pads leading to the ranges. **1903** J. FURPHY *Such is Life* 191 We could all see the marks of the little bare feet. . . But in sixty or eighty yards this pad run [*sic*] into another, covered with fresh sheep-tracks since the little girl had passed. Nothing for it but to spread out, and examine the network of pads scattered over the country. **1920** *Bulletin* (Sydney) 8 Apr. 22/1 'Yarrum' is unnecessarily alarmed about the wombat. . . Let him . . sink pit-traps . . preferably at a hole in the fence where a pad exists. **1935** F. BIRTLES *Battle Fronts Outback* 193 The route to the far north was at that time just a camel-pad and overlanding cattle-track. **1949** H. LAMOND *White Ears* 59 An old-man 'roo came hopping along the pad. **1968** V.C. HALL *Sister Ruth* 28 They had wandered into a beautiful grassed valley . . deeply imprinted . . by dingo and kangaroo trails. . . or 'pads' as bushmen term them. **1981** *Overland* lxxxvi. 58 The 'pads' (camel- and man-made) were so important to the travel of local cyclists that 'the Goldfields Bicycle Pad Protection League' was formed in mid-1897.

2. *transf.* A journey on foot, esp. as made by a swagman.

1897 A.F. CALVERT *My Fourth Tour W.A.* 84 A camel that has done a dry 'pad' for the last few days will scream with impatience while his drink is being run out of the tap for him. **1902** *Bulletin* (Sydney) 5 Apr. 14/3 During my first 'pad' in N.S.W. it was usual, when I met a swaggie, for him to ask if I had any Deadwood-Dicks to swop. **1911** W.H. ELSUM *Aust.* 110 And we humped the lonely road to Sydney city 'on our pad'. **1913** *Bulletin* (Sydney) 30 Jan. 15/2 From Wagga they tramped . . to Yanco, 70-odd miles, doing the pad in three days.

3. Special Comb. **pad-flogger,** a swagman.

1938 *Bulletin* (Sydney) 29 June 20/1 Various pad-floggers . . nominated their entries for the worst walking in the outback. **1939** *Ibid.* 7 June 20/3 Show me the padflogger who wouldn't swap a sod, as big as a cartwheel for just one loaf of baker's bread. **1940** *Ibid.* 21 Feb. 16/4 The tricks used by pad-floggers to grab free transport . . are pretty clever.

paddock, *n.* [Spec. use of *paddock* small field or enclosure.]

1. a. A piece of land, fenced, defined by natural boundaries, or otherwise considered distinct; usu. a section of a rural property and, on a sheep or cattle station, often of considerable size. Also *attrib.*

1808 *HRA* (1916) 1st Ser. VI. 370 A six railed Fence forming different Paddocks or enclosures for stock. **1809** *Sydney Gaz.* 5 Feb., A Capital *Fifty-Acre farm* at *Prospect* . . containing two fine paddocks of 20 acres inclosed. **1819** *Ibid.* 4 Sept., Also, a Paddock adjoining, containing 530 Acres, fenced in with a 5-rail Fence. **1824** *Austral.* (Sydney) 16 Dec. 4 To be *let*, that highly eligible and most desirable Villa . . in Parramatta. . . The paddock consists of about three acres of rich clover, in which is a large pond of water. **1831** *Acct. Colony Van Diemen's Land* 83 This road . . passes over the very fine enclosure or paddock of 400 acres of grazing land. **1833** *Currency Lad* (Sydney) 23 Feb. 1 There is . . a paddock of wheat, containing from six to eight acres nearly ready for reaping. **1835** *Cornwall Chron.* (Launceston) 14 Feb. 1 A good Paddock, containing 100 Acres . . well fenced-in with a four-rail fence. **1849** N.L. KENTISH *Proposals* 90 In one instance I have surveyed a bend of the Murray, (or series of bends) of six miles, enclosing for my fortunate employer, a paddock of many thousand acres, (for no enclosed tract of land is too large to be designated 'a paddock' in these colonies) by a fence of a few rods. **1864** H. JONES *New Valuations* 12 The Cadgee paddock contains 28,800 acres. **1879** S.W. SILVER *Austral. Grazier's Guide* 40 When ewes are shepherded, and the paddock system is not in operation, additional help and extraordinary measures are necessary to ensure the highest average of increase. **1888** A.P. MARTIN *Oak-Bough & Wattle-Blossom* 132 The sheep were well in sight . . their usual run was almost like a paddock, fenced in as it was by the river and scrub. **1890** E.T. TOWNER *Selectors' Guide to Barcoo* 20 As a rule there is only one or two waterholes in a 40,000-acre paddock. **1897** R. NEWTON *Work & Wealth Qld.* 18 Sheep are now run in paddocks, enclosed by wire fences, in flocks of from 10,000 upwards. **1906** *Bulletin* (Sydney) 15 Feb. 39/3 'Rouse up. The Paddock weaners—they're amongst us.' The paddock sheep must have come up during my watch. **1917** *Ibid.* 2 Aug. 24/2 The 'manna' . . is found under gum-trees. . . This manna is not the manna of the paddock in which Moses and the tribes lost their way. **1936** I.L. IDRIESS *Cattle King* 223 'The cattle will be poor by the time they reach Fremantle.' 'Yes, Dick. But the Emmanuels will have paddock country near Perth. We will fatten them.' **1957** J. HAWKE *Follow my Dust* 108 Each had two paddocks to ride every week, each paddock something like forty miles around the fences. **1975** L.A. POCKLEY *Handbk. for Jackeroos* 64 There are two types of droving—'paddock' droving of mustered sheep through paddocks, or 'road' droving of travelling mobs. **1977** C. MCCULLOUGH *Thorn Birds* 258 The great fields of cane (one couldn't call them paddocks, since they were small enough to encompass with the eyes) plumed lushly in the wind. **1981** A.B. FACEY *Fortunate Life* 57 They had a five acre pig paddock.

b. *transf.* A playing field.

1839 *Tasmanian* (Hobart) 8 Feb. 43/1 The Match . . will take place, in the Paddock. **1856** H.B. STONEY *Vic.* 31 The Melbourne Cricket Club hold their meetings in the Paddock, and have erected a spacious club-house. **1978** *Austral.* (Sydney) 3 July 17/2 'The general opinion is to get him off the paddock and the game will be all right,' Glossop said. **1981** *Bulletin* (Sydney) 9 June 98/3 Though rugby union is no longer the old-school-tie game it once was . . it continues to be Australia's most 'pukka' football code. Being Aboriginal boys from such working-class origins, have the brothers encountered any resistance . . ? 'Not off the field,' grins Glen, 'but we copped a few racist comments out on the paddock.' **1984** *Daily Mirror* (Sydney) 6 Apr. 85/3 Young set the example for the team where it mattered most in the centre of the paddock.

c. *transf.* and *fig.* [In some cases prob. influenced by ACCOMMODATION PADDOCK.]

1876 *Argus* (Melbourne) 1 July 4/5 We have as yet only seen the doings of the *demi-monde* in the stalls, vestibules and paddock of the Theatre Royal. ***c* 1905** *Tourists' Guide Geelong* 48 There are two 'paddocks' for the gentlemen's baths—a deeper and a shallower one. **1910** H. LAWSON *Rising of Court* 5 We are bailed or removed to the 'paddock' (the big drunks' dormitory and dining cell at the Central). **1939** H.W. DINNING *Austral. Scene* 178 He had noticed that the General's occupation was given in *Who's Who* as 'grazing', which was similar to Nebuchadnezzar's. It was a coincidence that both had captured Jerusalem. He hoped that Australia had a nice paddock ready for the departing guest. **1951** R.H. WHITECROSS *Slaves* 126 That night I slept well. At last we had found a good paddock. **1960** *N.T. News* (Darwin) 5 Feb. 18/3 Merv Hunt must have been in a very good paddock. He put on three stone while on holidays in the City of Churches.

2. *Mining.*

a. In shallow alluvial mining, an area marked out and systematically excavated for wash-dirt.

1855 W. HOWITT *Land, Labor & Gold* II. 161 We have since tried to reach the bottom of the river, and see what gold there was there, by making what they call a paddock; that is, enclosing a square piece of the river with a strong bank of earth between two walls of stones. **1862** J.A. PATTERSON *Gold Fields Vic.* 319 The 'paddocker' is another class of the alluvial diggers. The system was introduced by the Chinese, and is followed by them almost exclusively. . . It consists simply of removing the whole of the superincumbent soil, digging out the wash-dirt down to the bed-rock . . and then carrying back the earth and refilling the paddock. **1883** *Rec. Castlemaine Pioneers* 28 Sept. (1972) 81 We soon commenced our digging operations and sank numerous holes and paddocks in different parts of Bendigo, but did not meet with any wonderful finds. **1888** *Tasmanian* (Launceston) 1 Sept. 22/2 The wash shows fair tin, and if it continues the same all over the paddock, it will be the best . . we have had for some time. **1932** I.L. IDRIESS *Prospecting for Gold* 46 Bring in another light race, followed by a series of such races, about three feet apart, so as to 'grid-iron' the first 'paddock' you intend sluicing out. **1944** M.J. O'REILLY *Bowyangs & Boomerangs* 9 The procedure is to strip a paddock of the overburden, until one comes to the wash-dirt. A paddock may be any size, say from six feet square upwards. **1980** R. SHEARS *Gold* 58 If you do want to find . . areas of gold you will have to do a bit of farming—digging portions of the river bed in designated sections. These divisions . . are known as 'paddocks'.

b. A storage place for wash-dirt or uncrushed quartz.

1858 *Colonial Mining Jrnl.* Sept. 3/2 The new shaft is being sunk . . and a close and substantially constructed paddock has been erected. **1873** W. THOMSON-GREGG *Desperate Character* II. 96 The working progressed beautifully after that: they made a 'paddock' for their washing-stuff beside their tent, and lined it throughout with calico, so that not a speck of the precious metal should be lost. **1896** J.W. ROBERTS *Mining Industry N.S.W.* 57 After these men had got out 'paddocks' of wash-dirt and were preparing for washing up, they were informed that their licenses did not include water rights. **1915** J.P. BOURKE *Off Bluebush* 66 Hello, on top! Hello! Ease off, and have a blow! We've a crushin' in the paddock, and there's more below! **1974** B. MYATT *Dict. Austral. Gemstones* 32 Old alluvial workings in which all the unwanted material ended on the 'paddock'.

3. On a racecourse: an enclosure for spectators adjacent to the saddling paddock.

1892 *Truth* (Sydney) 27 May 1/6, I was punting in the paddock at Swindle Park one day When the gaffer of some ponies comes up and says 'I say'. **1898** *Western Champion* (Barcaldine) 11 Jan 9/1 The A.J.C. are about to make an effort to put down the 'runners' engaged by some of the bookmakers who do business in the paddock at Randwick. **1940** *Age* (Melbourne) 18 Nov. 4/6 A bookmaker in the paddock at Flemington on Saturday was the victim of the 'duplicate ticket' fraud. **1960** *Ibid.* 9 Nov. 27/10 Increased admittance charges will operate during the carnival. They are: Paddock, 13s. for men and 11s. for women, and Ledger, 6s. 6d. **1981** *Austral.* (Sydney) 3 Nov. (Cup Suppl.) B/7 Television coverage in more recent years, when we have had more than 100,000 congregated in the paddock area.

4. Comb. **paddock fence**.

1808 *HRA* (1916) 1st Ser. VI. 363 A Paddock Fence with Posts and Railing. **1855** W. HOWITT *Land, Labor & Gold* I. 76 They advised us to take a rail out of the paddock fence. **1879** 'AUSTRALIAN' *Adventures Qld.* 106 They put up about half a mile of rough paddock fence, of split posts and round rails, across an angle of the lagoon, which made a capital paddock for the horses. **1887** A. NICOLS *Wild Life & Adventure* 112 Several posts of the paddock-fence had been attacked by white ants.

paddock, *v.*

1. *trans.*

a. To confine (livestock) within a paddock; to provide pasture for (livestock), as in agistment.

1847 *Bell's Life in Sydney* 11 Dec. 3/1 The horses were paddocked for the night. **1860** J. PARKINSON *Essay on Husbandry* 13 The Adelaide Park Lands, where the police horses are paddocked. **1882** *Three L's* 183 Will you allow me to paddock my horse without any charge? **1892** *Western Champion* (Barcaldine) 7 June 12/1 After a week's spell, a move was made towards Muswellbrook, where the 'Boss' intended paddocking the sheep for a week or so before trucking them to further south. **1901** *Illawarra Mercury* (Wollongong) 5 Jan. 2/6 It has occurred to the Organising Committee that those breeders through whose farms the railway passes might so paddock their cattle that they should be easily visible from the windows of the trains. **1915** *Bulletin* (Sydney) 14 Jan. 22/4 Feed has come on rapidly, and now . . the usually dry northern parts of S. Aus. are offering to paddock the suffering stock from the usually moist southern region. **1931** 'L. KAYE' *Tybal Men* 166 You bought a few sheep . . you shepherded them by day and paddocked them by night. **1946** A. THURIAN *Bush Tea & Overlanders* 16 Fifteen hundred Gulf-bred bullocks paddocked on Rutland Plains. **1971** J. HETHERINGTON *Morning was Shining* 34 The horses paddocked, I took Dad's hand and covered the remaining few yards homeward on my feet.

b. *fig.*

1849 *Bell's Life in Sydney* 10 Mar. 3/4 These suspicions were subsequently made certainties, which rendered it necessary for the Ministers of Justice to *paddock* Thomas instead of allowing him free *run* of the country without paying the *licence-fee*. **1937** *Bulletin* (Sydney) 17 Feb. 21/1 Net-fishers yarded up about five tons of Westralian kingfish. . . They gathered about half for the Perth market, leaving the rest paddocked.

c. To fence or enclose (an area) in a paddock.

1873 A. TROLLOPE *Aust. & N.Z.* I. 302 When a run is 'paddocked', shepherds are not required;—but boundary-riders are employed, each of whom is supplied with two horses, and these men are responsible not only for the sheep but for the fences. **1967** E. HUXLEY *Their Shining Eldorado* 247 Less than half the property is paddocked, and beyond the fences cattle live and breed free.

d. *intr.* Of livestock: to enter into, and accept the confinement of a paddock.

1959 E. WEBB *Mark of Sun* 49 The cattle were tired and paddocked easily for the night.

2. *Mining.* **a.** *trans.* To excavate (a PADDOCK *n.* 2 a.); also *absol.* or *intr.* **b.** To store in a PADDOCK *n.* 2 b.

1855 G.H. WATHEN *Golden Colony* 56 In Eagle-Hawke Gully parties were 'paddocking' the old workings. . . That is, marking out and working large areas of ground already once wrought. **1871** *Austral. Town & Country Jrnl.* (Sydney) 1 Apr. 399/4 There is about a foot of blue slate with small quartz leaders running through it which also carries gold, and which is being taken and paddocked. **1880** 'ERRO' *Squattermania* 28, I looked over the heap they've got paddocked, and couldn't find a speck. **1896** J.W. ROBERTS *Mining Industry N.S.W.* 64 These gullies . . were potholed by jackaroos, paddocked by Chinese, and afterwards ground-sluiced by Europeans! **1901** O. OSBORNE *Golden Jubilee* 14 In depth John paddocked thirty feet, And picked two feet of bottom up. **1906** *Bulletin* (Sydney) 15 Feb. 15/2 We've sunk and we've driven and paddocked and gouged for scarcely a color a week. **1932** I.L. IDRIESS *Prospecting for Gold* 12 To prove such ground after having located it with the dish, the one method is to 'paddock' it. Strip a square of the surface. . . Next day take up the bottom and dish it. The resulting gold won will tell you what you have made on the labour expended.

Hence **paddocked** *ppl. a.*, **paddocker** *n.*, **paddocking** *vbl. n.*

1871 *Austral. Town & Country Jrnl.* (Sydney) 4 Feb. 138/3 Ours are shepherded sheep running on black soil, and are therefore not so easily washed as **paddocked** sheep. **1882** ARMSTRONG & CAMPBELL *Austral. Sheep Husbandry* 146 Previous to the great gold rush of 1852 the system of shepherding was in general use, and the existence of paddocked sheep at that time was quite as rare as is that of shepherded ones now. **1907** *Bulletin* (Sydney) 12 Sept. 14/4 With paddocked sheep, if tucker-bags Runs low, when on the tramp. You 'aven't Buckley's show to strike A (lurid) lambin' camp. **1862** J.A. PATTERSON *Gold Fields Vic.* 319 The '**paddocker**' is another class of the alluvial diggers. **1871** *Austral. Town & Country Jrnl.* (Sydney) 8 July 42/4 The splendid herds . . are the result of a gradual but sure process of improvement by selection, special importation, and **paddocking.** **1872** W.M. HUGO *Hist. First Bushmen's Club* 22 A little land would be required . . to afford paddocking for horses. **1887** 'OLD GOLD DIGGER' *Gold Digger's Guide* 9 The size of the paddocking ought not to be less than 8 feet by 8 feet, leaving sufficient room for two or three men to work. **1903** *Advocate* (Burnie) 10 Jan. 4/3 Not having the means, in many cases, to pay for paddocking. **1910** *Bulletin* (Sydney) 27 Oct. 13/4 In the early days of Stanthorpe . . when tin was to be had for the 'paddocking', and was worth selling, the Chows flocked there in droves. **1931** W. BARAGWANATH *Guide for Prospectors in Vic.* 24 Paddocking, that is, excavating all material at a face. **1980** D. STONE et al. *Metal Detecting for Gold* 152 The Chinese appear to have . . introduced the technique of 'paddocking'.

Paddy. In collocations: **Paddy's lucerne,** the perennial shrub *Sida rhombifolia* (fam. Malvaceae) of n. Aust. and widespread in the tropics, having mucilaginous leaves and fibrous stems; JELLY LEAF; *Queensland hemp*, see QUEENSLAND 2; also **Paddy lucerne; Paddy's Market,** a name applied to any of various markets; also **Paddy market,** and *fig.*

1888 *Proc. Linnean Soc. N.S.W.* III. 391 *Sida rhombifolia* . . called '**Paddy Lucerne**' on the Richmond and Clarence Rivers, New South Wales, and 'Lucerne' in other parts of the colony (cows being very fond of it). **1896** A. MACKAY *Austral. Agriculturalist* (rev. ed.) 120 The 'paddy's lucerne' of colonial farming populations, is one of the best known fibre-yielders. **1920** *Bulletin* (Sydney) 19 Aug. 22/1, I saw an old carpet-snake in ambush in a prolific growth of 'paddy's lucerne'. **1944** J.H. PICK *Aust.'s Dying Heart* (rev. ed.) 90 Such weeds as . . 'Paddy's Lucerne' have recently been hailed as potential saviours of the eroded country. **1958** J.N. WHITTET *Weeds* (1968) 319 In India, paddy lucerne was one of the so-called 'hemps' which were grown and sent to Europe. . . By reason of its invasion of paddy (rice) fields, the name paddy lucerne was applied to the weed. **1964** P. WHITE *Burnt Ones* 236 This machine will cut closer, wear better than any other on the market. It will demolish the worst growth of Paddy's lucerne. **1875** R. THATCHER *Something to his Advantage* 120 **Paddy's market**, as it is popularly called, is a kind of bazaar, or poor man's fair, which is held every Saturday in the three, long narrow, stable-like buildings in the Haymarket Square. **1891** H. NISBET *Colonial Tramp* I. 103 Paddy's Market is one of the institutions of Melbourne. **1915** E. BELLAMY Diary 18 Dec., Got leave in the afternoon and went into Cairo and wandered around the bazaars. They are weird and strange and you can buy all sorts of things, produce, curios and a regular paddy markets sort of a place. **1930** *Listening Post* (Perth) July 30 Included in the branch's activities . . were . . Paddy's markets. **1950** J. MORRISON *Port of Call* 210 Ships have been scarce for days, and every division is packed with work-hungry men. . . It's impossible to be shy in this Paddy's Market of human flesh and blood, because everybody else is pushing. **1978** T. Davies *More Austral. Nicknames* 77 Paddy's Market, named after Sydney's famed market, was in this case a large area where troops sold illegally manufactured goods in a certain overseas area of combat during the second World War. **1985** N. Medcalf *Rifleman* 55 Paddy's Market, the illegal gambling casino and bazaar, flourished.

paddymelon /'pædimɛlən/, *n.*[1] [Poss. a. Dharuk *badimalion.*] Also **pademelon** (esp. in modern scientific literature) and formerly with much variety, as **pademella, paddymalla, paddymellon.**

1. Any of several small, compact-bodied wallabies of the genus *Thylogale*, inhabiting dense vegetation in moist forests of e. Aust. incl. Tas., and New Guinea; (occas.) any of several other, usu. small, macropods; the flesh of the animal. Also *attrib.*

1802 Banks Papers 1 June VIII. 103 Patty mellon. It is of reddish colour and much inferior in size to the forest one. **1827** P. Cunningham *Two Yrs. in N.S.W.* I. 310 The *wallabee* and *paddymalla* grow to about sixty pounds each, and inhabit the brushes and broken hilly country. **1830** R. Dawson *Present State Aust.* 212 The natives however had shot several guanas, and had hunted down a paddymelon (a very small species of kangaroo, which is found in the long grass and thick brushes). **1836** J. Backhouse *Extracts from Lett.* (1838) iii. 79 A small species of kangaroo, called in this part of the colony a paddy-melon: making allowance for difference of form, it may be said to be about the size of the hare of England, which it is said to resemble when roasted. **1844** *Sydney Morning Herald* 20 Apr. 2/5 Mr Strange found in its stomach a paddymellon, a species of wallaby. **1845** C. Hodgkinson *Aust., Port Macquarie to Moreton Bay* 33 This tribe left us to go on a pademella hunt. **1846** C.P. Hodgson *Reminisc. Aust.* 301 Two excellent paddy melons, a species of kangaroo, the victims of Bobby's gun. **1857** W.S. Bradshaw *Voyages* 85 The wallabee and paddymalla are the next species. **1861** E.P. Ramsay-Laye *Social Life & Manners* 188 The kangaroo-dog . . gave chase to a Paddy melon or kangaroo rat. **1879** J.B. Stephens *Marsupial Bill* 13 The stricken paddamelon moaned Its ineffectual prayer. **1888** *Sydney Morning Herald* 24 Jan. 1/5 The most representative is the kangaroo class. . . Amongst the smaller kinds are the wallaby, the pademelon, and the bandicoot. **1891** *Truth* (Sydney) 3 May 3/4 So-called experts . . know no more about mining than a pademelon does about astronomy. **1904** *Bulletin* (Sydney) 11 Aug. 16/4 *Re* 'Paddymelon' . . the probable derivation of the name of this queer little marsupial is from the native name, 'parrimalla'. That is the name by which it was known by the Lake Victoria and Lake Bonney tribes (Murray River). **1924** J. Harper *Splashes from Narran* 35 Porcupine and paddy melon Stuffed with Darling pea. **1925** M. Gilmore *Tilted Cart* 33 There the timid paddymelon Made his nest so soft and round. **1944** C. Fenner *Mostly Austral.* 102 The little paddymelon, whose colloquial name is spelt in as many ways as there are letters in it, is a wallaby (*Macropus thetedis*) . . corruption of 'patta malla'. **1958** E.O. Schlunke *Village Hampden* 68 The paddymelons . . come out of the scrub and eat my pastures. **1963** I.L. Idriess *Our Living Stone Age* 209 Round her upper leg a leg-band of pademelon or bandicoot fur. **1965** *Austral. Encycl.* V. 159 The term 'pademelon' is a corruption of the name applied by aborigines about Sydney to the red-necked species (*Thylogale thetis*) that still inhabits parts of north-coastal New South Wales and south-eastern Queensland. **1965** *Tracks we Travel* 104 Paddy melons and bandicoots, the makers of the tracks, abounded on the mountain. **1977** W.A. Winter-Irving *Bush Stories* 91 What we called the pademelons, small kangaroo rats . . were numerous and . . would explode from a scrubby bush, hopping in panic to escape a passing rider and sometimes collide with the horses. **1981** H. Hannah *Together in Jungle Scrub* 73 The Paddymelon or Red Legged Wallaby . . inhabits the brush and is very common. **1983** R. Strahan *Compl. Bk. Austral. Mammals* 224 Pademelons . . are grazers upon rather succulent grasses and also browse on shrubs.

2. Special Comb. **paddymelon stick** *obs.*, an Aboriginal weapon used as a missile in hunting small game.

1851 J. Henderson *Excursions & Adventures N.S.W.* II. 129 These are hunted in the brushes, and killed with paddy mellon sticks, with which they are knocked down. These sticks are about two feet long, and an inch or less in diameter. *Ibid.* 136 The emu and brush turkey are both hunted by the natives, the former being speared, and the latter killed with the boomerang, or paddy-mellon sticks. *Ibid.* 150 The *paddy-mellon* sticks . . I have seen thrown with such force and precision as to stick in the bark of a gum-tree. **1865** G.S. Lang *Aborigines of Aust.* 41 A black fellow, with some eight or ten spears in his hand and some paddy-melon sticks, will throw them all while a white man is reloading after firing two shots. **1881** A.C. Grant *Bush-Life Qld.* I. 66 Nullah-nullahs, paddy-melon sticks, boomerangs [etc.] . . lay about in every direction.

paddymelon /'pædimɛlən/, *n.*[2] Also **pademelon.** [Prob. from an erroneous assoc. with Paddymelon *n.*[1] 1.]

1. Any of several plants of the fam. Cucurbitaceae, esp. the trailing or climbing annual plant *Cucumis myriocarpus* of Africa, naturalized in inland Aust., bearing a small, bristly, melon-like fruit, and widely regarded as a weed; the fruit itself; *melon vine*, see Melon 1. Also *attrib.*

1891 *Bulletin* (Sydney) 19 Dec. 19/4 They stole my pears—my native pears—Those thrice convicted felons, And ravished from me unawares My crop of paddy-melons. **1907** *Ibid.* 19 Sept. 14/2 The pademelon vine . . is a prolific plant, which bears spiky little melons about the size of gooseberries. There are hundreds of acres of them Outback, and countless patches of them Inback. **1951** J. Devanny *Travels N. Qld.* 156 All along the line lay heaps of paddy-melons, iron-skinned fruits the size and colour of an orange. **1972** R. Ericksen *West of Centre* 165 Across wide acres . . through long, tangled runners of paddymelon. **1964** E. Lane *Our Uncle Charlie* 53 Every now and again I'd lift one foot from the sheeptrack to stamp on the soft, sour-smelling little round paddymelons just to feel them burst with a pop under my feet.

2. Special Comb. **paddymelon hole,** Gilgai b; *melon hole*, see Melon 1; also ellipt., as **paddymelon country,** and *attrib.*

1910 C.E.W. Bean *On Wool Track* 79 Up in the north, whirling along a hilltop amongst paddymelon holes—which, whether the paddymelon really makes them or not, are uncomfortable little pitfalls, nearly a yard deep. **1925** M. Terry *Across Unknown Aust.* 159 The ground became honeycombed with 'paddy melon' holes, or as they are sometimes called 'crab' holes. These are formed by the inrush of rain. **1943** *Bulletin* (Sydney) 8 Dec. 12/4 Viewed from surrounding hills or the sand dunes which separate it from the sea, southern Queensland's 'paddymelon-hole country' appears as a fine series of flats level enough for a landing ground. **1957** V. Palmer *Seedtime* 159 She had gone out early in search of wild-flowers in the paddymelon country behind the settlement losing herself in the tall grass, falling into swampy gutters.

pademella, var. Paddymelon *n.*[1]

pademelon, var. Paddymelon *n.*[1] and *n.*[2]

pai-alla, var. Pialla.

paint, *v.* [Ironic use of *paint* to colour.] *trans.* To bruise (a person or part of the body).

1841 *Port Phillip Gaz.* 29 Oct. 3/2 Connell said he was certainly drunk, but the constables had 'walloped' him sober; to which Constable Waller, who appeared to be suffering under the effects of a severe thrashing, replied that if he had 'painted' Connell's face, the defendants had returned the compliment by 'painting' his ribs. **1896** M. Hornsby *Old Time Echoes Tas.* 145 Even after the handcuffs were on him he painted Sam a trifle.

painted, *ppl. a.* Used as a distinguishing epithet in the names of animals: **painted burrowing frog,** the frog *Neobatrachus pictus* of s.e. mainland Aust., grey, light brown, or green above with dark brown to olive patches; **crayfish,** any of several colourful tropical rock lobsters, esp. *Panulirus ornatus* and *P. versicolor*; also **painted cray, (spiny) lobster; dragon,** the lizard *Amphibolurus pictus* of drier s. and central Aust., blue-grey to reddish-brown above, usu. with black markings; **finch,** the bird *Emblema pictum* of arid Aust., esp. in the n.w., inhabiting rocky hills and gorges near permanent water; (occas.) any of several other colourful finches; **honeyeater,** the honeyeater *Grantiella picta* of e. mainland Aust., having black, white, and yellow plumage; **pigeon,** Wompoo pigeon; **quail,** the mottled chestnut-coloured bird *Turnix varia* of s.w., s., and e. Aust. incl. Tas.; see also Partridge.

1969 D. Clyne *Austral. Frogs* 104 **Painted Burrowing Frog** . . is found near temporary pools and marshes after rain. **1978** B.P. Moore *Life on Forty Acres* 115 The . . blunt-nosed Painted Burrowing Frog (*Neobatrachus pictus*) is . . closely adapted to temporary habitats and spends much of its time aestivating . . in a sealed burrow. **1928 [painted crayfish]** S.E. Napier *On Barrier Reef* 129 Deserves his name of Painted Spiny Lobster. **1955** V. Serventy *Austral.'s Great Barrier Reef* 37 Similar to the less colourful crayfish of southern waters, at least where structure is concerned, the painted crayfish is a thing of beauty. **1962** N. Monkman *Quest Curly-Tailed Horses* 185 Out came a gorgeous crayfish, the painted lobster, as it is called by the fishermen of the reef. What a pity that they are such a delicacy! It is as if one cooked and ate a Picasso. **1978** N. Coleman *Look at Wildlife Great Barrier Reef* 90 Painted crays do not readily enter traps or pots and in the past this has led fisherman [*sic*] to believe they are vegetarian. **1948** *Bulletin* (Sydney) 17 Nov. 29/2 A minute or two of digging will disclose half a dozen inches of lizard—the little '**painted dragon**' (*Amphibolurus pictus*) of the sandhills. **1955** *Lake Eyre, S.A.* (R. Geogr. Soc. Australasia) 74 *Lizards* from lake bed, S.-E. corner of Madigan Gulf . . *Amphibolurus pictus* . . Painted Dragon [etc.]. **1842** J. Gould *Birds of Aust.* (1848) III. Pl. 97, *Emblema picta* . . **Painted Finch.** **1855** J. Bonwick *Geogr. Aust. & N.Z.* (ed. 3) 198 The Painted finch of North Australia has plain upper part [*sic*], but black and red underneath. **1901** *Emu* I. 26 Painted Finches (*Emblema pictata*) have been quite common lately (June). **1916** S.A. White *In Far Northwest* 49 Another beautiful bird was found in the deep silent gorges of the mountains, the painted finch. **1936** C.T. Madigan *Central Aust.* 103 There is quite a business in the . . sale of the various finches of the Northern Territory . . notably the painted finch, which looks as if it had been brushed with broad splashes of bright paint. **1964** M. Sharland *Territory of Birds* 137 The Painted Finch, with red head and face, red lower back, and white spotted black vest, seems curiously able to do without water. **1972** J. Jones *Memories Golden Gate* (rev. ed.) 8 The birds we trapped and hoped to trap, particularly the tiny beautiful creatures called as a group, painted finches, but the varieties were called 'black Throats', 'double bars', 'zebras', etc. **1843** J. Gould *Birds of Aust.* (1848) IV. Pl. 50, I had been led to suspect that the actions and economy of the **Painted Honey-eater** would be found to differ materially from those of the other members of its family, and such proved to be the case. **1945** C. Barrett *Austral. Bird Life* 156 The painted honeyeater (*Grantiella picta*) has much yellow in its plumage. **1965** *Austral. Encycl.* IV. 528 A very distinctive member of the [honeyeater] family is one which is known, for lack of a better name, as the painted honeyeater. Actually its taste for honey (if it ever had such a taste) has long since been subordinated to a fondness for mistletoe berries. **1984** M. Blakers et al. *Atlas Austral. Birds* 550 The endemic Painted Honeyeater is migratory, breeding in southern Australia . . and moving north in winter. **1870** E.B. Kennedy *Four Yrs. in Qld.* 111 One may find a large one with green back and purple and yellow breast, called the Whompoa, or **painted pigeon.** **1876** 'Eight Yrs.' Resident' *Queen of Colonies* 240 The painted pigeon is of gorgeous plumage and large size, equal to a small chicken. **1897** R. Newton *Work & Wealth Qld.* 70 There are many varieties of pigeons, the wonga and the gorgeous painted pigeon being the most prized. **1845** J. Gould *Birds of Aust.* (1848) V. Pl. 82, *Hemipodius varius* . . **Painted Quail**, Colonists of Van Diemen's Land and Swan River. **1848** H.W. Haygarth *Recoll. Bush Life* 118 The painted quail, which is found among the long grass in 'open forest' land, flies not unlike a woodcock. **1859** H. Kingsley *Recoll. Geoffrey Hamlyn* III. 4 The painted quail, and the brush quail . . whirred away from beneath their horses' feet. **1902** *Emu* II. 17 In the ironbark scrub about Chiltern the Painted Quail (*Turnix varia*) has curiously enough taken up its abode. **1966** Slater & Lindgren *Wildlife W.A.* 8 A bird of the open woodland, the Painted Quail favours Wandoo forest.

paint-gold. See quot. 1869.

1869 R.B. Smyth *Gold Fields & Mineral Districts* 616 *Paint-gold*, gold found in cement, of such remarkable fineness as to resemble paint or gilding. **1896**

B.S. JAMES *Westralian Goldfields* 37 Paint gold is often produced on the surfaces of quartz along its cleavage planes.

pair. *Hist.* Also **pare.** [Br. dial. *pair*, used chiefly in Cornwall: see OED *sb.*[1] 7.] A party of miners working together.

1848 *S. Austral. Register* (Adelaide) 22 Nov. 3/5 The vast heaps .. are now being let to 'pairs' or parties of workmen (a 'pair' of miners generally consisting of some half dozen). **1850** *Ibid.* 19 Apr. 2/3 From one pitch 'the pair' (takers) broke out last month one hundred and fifty tons of ore. ***c* 1860** 'AURIFERA' *Victorian Miners' Man.* 104 *Pair* or *Pare*, a gang or party of men, 'The shaft was 'set' to a 'pair' of eight men.' **1867** *Wallaroo Times* (Kadina) 27 Nov. 5/1 Several pares of men working on tribute. **1889** *Yorke's Peninsula Advertiser* (Moonta) 1 Mar. 3/6 If a pare finished a contract .. the names of the .. pares should be given on tendering. **1962** O. PRYOR *Aust.'s Little Cornwall* 15 It was usual for a party—known as a *pare*—of tributers to form themselves together to work a *pitch*, or portion of a lode, sharing equally between them the money they earned.

pakapoo. Also **pakapu** and with some variety. [a. Chinese *pai ko p'iao* white pigeon ticket; used elsewhere but recorded earliest in Aust.: see OEDS.]

1. A Chinese gambling game played with slips of paper marked with columns of characters. Freq. *attrib.*

1886 F.J. STEEL *Miscarriage of Justice* 13 There is no pretence to any sort of trade except in pak-ah-pu tickets. These are sold by a blank little Pagan... His customers plank a 'lokoloey' (sixpence, or any multiple of it) and mark off 10 characters out of the 80 printed upon the rice-paper voucher handed them by the blank heathen, who, thereupon, proceeds to take a duplicate for the use of the 'bank'. **1903** *Truth* (Sydney) 22 Feb. 6/2 A gambling den at 48 Campbell-street, Haymarket .. one of the most important pak-a-pu banks of the celestial sub-city. **1911** *Ibid.* 21 May 5/4 The pakapu case at the Water Police Court on Monday tends to show that ye ancient game is not dead in Sydney. **1911** A. WRIGHT *Gamblers' Gold* (1923) 66 Foong Lee's establishment was well patronised. The front shop .. walls .. were covered with pak-a-pu tickets. **1938** F. BLAKELEY *Hard Liberty* 254 We .. made our first survey of Chinatown... We soon grew interested in the Pakapoo house, where .. one might win seventy-five pounds with one sixpenny investment, and, if not legal, the business was carried on openly enough. **1958** F.B. VICKERS *Mirage* (ed. 2) 78 The silk turns out to be an old pair of Mrs Gordon's knickers, which the old man has won from Tugara when playing pac-a-poo. **1974** J. GABY *Restless Waterfront* 235 They wanted multiple marks on the bales, 'more marks than on a pak-a-poo ticket', as the wool foreman said, and he was pretty right.

2. *fig.*, and in fig. contexts, as **pakapoo ticket,** something which is difficult to decipher.

1951 E. LAMBERT *Twenty Thousand Thieves* (1952) 89 Henry opened Dooley's pay-book, the pages of which showed liberal sprinklings of the red ink with which fines and convictions were entered. 'What a pay-book!' he sighed. Dooley grinned. 'Like a pak-a-poo ticket,' he agreed. **1975** *Bulletin* (Sydney) 29 Nov. 17/1 Senate elections, because of the complexity of the system .. are more in the nature of a pack-a-poo ticket. **1976** B. BENNETT *New Country* 39 I'm a bit of a pakapoo-ticket. I was born in Lithuania. Then we were shunted off to Germany. The war, you know. When it was finished we were in France.

paling, *vbl. n.*

1. Used *attrib.* in Special Comb. **paling knife,** a cutting tool used to split palings, shingles, etc., from the block; a froe; **splitter,** one whose occupation is the cutting of palings, etc.; also **splitting** *vbl. n.*

1881 *Australasian Sketcher* (Melbourne) 8 Oct. 327 The **paling knife** is made to work by leverage, but in this beautiful free-splitting timber, little leverage is required, and the knife almost divides the clean, smooth shingles by merely driving it with the mallet into one end. **1901** *Advocate* (Burnie) 28 Nov. 2/3 The old pioneers can tell stories galore of wonderful performances with the paling knife in the golden fifties. **1978** M. WALKER *Pioneer Crafts Early Aust.* 39 The froe was the forged-iron, broad-ended wedge that cleaved the billets. Later, the colonists called the froe the 'paling knife'. **1837** *S. Austral. Rec.* (London) 27 Nov. 24 We have .. men come .. as labourers .. that is to say, stock keepers, shepherds, and **paling** and shingle **splitters.** **1900** *Bulletin* (Sydney) 28 Apr. 14/2 Paling-splitters had a superstitious dislike to [*sic*] 'left hand twists', though trees winding to the right were in great favor for palings. **1902** *Axeman's Jrnl.* (Ulverstone) Mar. 168/2 Thirty years ago paling splitting was probably the leading industry of the North-West Coast of Tasmania. **1960** *Bulletin* (Sydney) 16 Mar. 19/2 The paling-splitter worked and lived in noble solitude, and because only one stick in a hundred was a 'splitter' he ranged widely and vetted a lot of trees.

2. Used *attrib.* with nouns designating a construction in the sense 'made from palings'.

1849 A. HARRIS *Emigrant Family* (1967) 89 The construction of paling-yards, or hurdle enclosures, being a job of some time. **1855** 'RUSTICUS' *How to settle in Vic.* 20 *Paling huts* may be erected with more speed .. but are not .. so desirable, as they are much colder in winter, and communicate the heat much more readily in summer. **1861** L.A. MEREDITH *Over Straits* 135 Substantial buildings are surrounded by the heterogeneous crowd of weather-board, slab, paling, and calico tenements always found in digging locations. **1865** *Wallaroo Times* (Kadina) 20 May 3/2 It was a paling house. **1901** *Advocate* (Burnie) 13 Apr. 2/7 He was born in a paling shanty. **1910** *Emu* X. 128 Wherever a settler .. erects his slab or paling hut.

pallid cuckoo. [f. *pallid*, first applied as the specific name *pallida* by the English ornithologist J. Latham (*Index Ornithol.* (1801) lx.).] The cuckoo *Cuculus pallidus* occurring throughout Aust., incl. Tas.; BRAIN-FEVER BIRD.

1883 A.J. CAMPBELL *Nests & Eggs Austral. Birds* p. iii, The egg of the Pallid Cuckoo, being about half the size of the foster-bird's eggs and of a uniform pinkish tint—a beautiful specimen. **1911** A. MACK *Bush Days* 64 The rollicking note of the pallid cuckoo. **1931** J. DEVANEY *Earth Kindred* 55 Rang out the first-heard pallid cuckoo's clear Triumphant call. **1937** *Bulletin* (Sydney) 7 July 21/4 The pallid cuckoo is a sad-looking individual only half the size of his stormbird cousin. **1980** J. WOLFE *End of Pricklystick* 30 The dreary, sleepy call of the pallid-cuckoo announced that the time of frosts was over. **1984** E. ROLLS *Celebration of Senses* 76 The Pallid Cuckoo arrives in the spring with a lovely rising five-note song.

palm cockatoo. [See quot. 1943.] The large, slaty black cockatoo *Probosciger aterrimus* of Cape York Peninsula (n. Qld.) and northwards to New Guinea. See also MACAW.

1898 E.E. MORRIS *Austral Eng.* 92 Palm C[ockatoo]—*Microglossus aterrimus.* **1943** C. BARRETT *Austral. Animal Bk.* 220 Few naturalists have observed the palm cockatoo in a wild state... A shy bird in its native haunts, it usually associates in pairs, frequenting the palm scrubs. **1964** M. SHARLAND *Territory of Birds* 117 On Cape York where it is confined, there lives the steely black Palm Cockatoo. It has a red face that suggests a perpetual blush, and long, untidy head plumes, slightly grey and very elongated, that made me think it was well overdue for a hair-cut. **1982** R. ELLIS *Bush Safari* 66 A small flock of Palm Cockatoos provided the highlight... They are black cockatoos with a head one-third the size of their large body, and an enormous bill that is said to be able to bend a five-cent piece double.

palmer. [Of unknown origin.] The fish *Lates calcarifer*: see BARRAMUNDI a. Also **palmer perch.**

1896 F.G. AFLALO *Sketch Nat. Hist. Aust.* 211 The Fitzroy perch, allied to the 'palmer' of the Mackay. **1901** K.W. MANNING *In their Own Hands* (1983) 14 The Palmer, the gigantic perch which has been found in north and north-east coast rivers; a big scaled fish with a ruby eye .. and christened .. 'the Palmer' because he was caught in a pool beneath some palm trees. **1971** P. BODEKER *Sandgropers' Trail* 231 *Lates calcarifer* (palmer perch, giant perch). Biggest freshwater fish of the North.

pandanny /pæn'dæni/. Also **pandani, pandanni.** [See quot. 1965.] The palm-like tree or shrub *Richea pandanifolia* (fam. Epacridaceae) of Tas. See also GRASS-TREE 2. Also *attrib.*, and **pandanus palm.**

1944 C. BARRETT *Isle of Mountains* 33 There were tall 'pandanny' Richeas—a whole colony of them in a swampy glade. **1963** W.M. CURTIS *Student's Flora Tas.* ii. 460 *R[ichea] pandanifolia* .. Giant Grass Tree, Pandani. **1965** *Austral. Encycl.* VI. 443 Pandanus, the generic name (often used as a vernacular) for palm-like tropical plants better known as screw pines .. in the family Pandanaceae. A corruption of this name is 'pandanny', by which the tall mountain heath *Richea pandanifolia* .. is commonly known in Tasmania. **1968** V. SERVENTY *Southern Walkabout* 54 There is the giant grass tree or 'pandanni'... Richea is the scientific name, and it is called pandanni because of the resemblance of the leaves to the pandanus of the mainland. **1979** B. ROBERTS *Stones in Cephissus* 19 You could be lost forever in this dank forest of King Billy Pine and Richea (the tall pandanus palm). **1984** *Austral. Plants* Sept. 372 *Richea pandanifolia*... Known locally as .. 'Pandani', it can be a large shrub or even a tree to 15 m.

panel van. [Cf. U.S. *panel truck.*] A motor vehicle similar in size and shape to a station wagon, having a single row of seats and a flat tray in the rear.

1955 *Wheels* July 10 Station wagons .. aren't yet as popular for private owners as cars, or as favored as panel vans for light commercial work. **1963** *Bulletin* (Sydney) 6 July 15/3 Moveable brothels, each of a couple of girls in a panel van, are still doing well in the district, a taxi-driver told me. **1979** *Westerly* ii. 10 He should trade in his two-wheeler on a panel van. **1980** *Southerly* iii. 294 The panel van had been chock-a-block with their worldly belongings. **1981** A. WELLER *Day of Dog* 158 They pile into the panel van; Doug in the back, with the thick, rich, purple carpet. **1986** *Mercury* (Hobart) 27 Mar. 1/4 A girl gets pregnant .. from smoking a cigarette injected with hashish oil and then climbing into the back of a panel van to have nookie-nookie.

pan jam. *Obs.* See quot. 1864.

1864 *Colonial Cook Bk.* 72 Pan Jam. This dish used to be made from kangaroo tails. Roast them in the ashes with the skin on. When nearly done, scrape them well, and divide at the joints. Then put them into a pan, with a few slices of fat bacon, to which add a few mushrooms, pepper, etc. Fry gently, and serve. **1970** J.S. GUNN in W.S. Ramson *Eng. Transported* 63 Such food references as *saddle pouch tucker, salt junk, slippery bob* and *pan jam* are well left to history.

pannikin. Formerly also **pannican, pannakin, panniken.** [Br. dial. *pannikin* small (earthenware) pan or jar: see EDD and OED(S.]

1. a. A metal drinking vessel; the contents of such a vessel.

1830 R. DAWSON *Present State Aust.* 101 Several tin pannicans .. served us for tea and drinking-cups. **1835** BACKHOUSE & TYLOR *Life & Labours G.W. Walker* 17 Sept. (1862) 223 A pannakin of tea however restored me. **1837** *S. Austral. Gaz.* (Adelaide) 8 July 3 We picked up several pints of periwinkles, filled our bottles with salt water, returned to some sand-hills at the side of the creek, lighted a fire, cooked them in a panniken we fortunately had with us, and made a hearty supper. **1848** *Adelaide Miscellany* 16 Sept. 104 On the pommel of his saddle was strapped his blanket, over which were the hobbles for his horse, a quart pot, and a pannican. **1857** J. BONWICK *Early Days Melbourne* 24 Shepherds and bullock-drivers were seen drinking champagne out of buckets with pannikins. **1862** H. BROWN *Vic. as I found It* 73 With our tin vessels, or as they are called in Australia, pannikins, we dipped into the billy, and partook of the fragrant effusion. **1881** G.C. EVANS *Stories* 92 We had been lucky enough to obtain from our claim nearly three pannikins full of gold. **1899** *Bulletin* (Sydney) 15 July 31/2 ''Ere, you dunno how to dip up flour. Lemme show yer,' and, grabbing the pannikin, he had dipped about 30 lb. into his bag in half-a-minute. **1906** *Gadfly* (Adelaide) 13 June 21/3 While I was there they arranged a real bush picnic... We got a billycan all right, but upon enquiring for pannicans were told everywhere 'we don't keep 'em'... They were known in America as 'tin-cups'. **1923** J. ARMOUR *Spell of Inland* 99 'Hold hard a minute,' said the old cook, who appeared in the kitchen door with a bucket of steaming tea, a bundle of pannikins, and a tray of scones and cakes. **1945** S.J. BAKER *Austral. Lang.* 169 *A friendly pannikin*, a drink with a companion. **1960** E. O'CONNER *Irish Man* 153 As the boy walked in she was pouring tea into an enamel pannikin. **1982** R. HALL *Just Relations* 208 The men leaving the dressing station, one by one, dipped biscuits into their pannikins of hot cocoa.

b. With distinguishing epithet, as **pint pannikin,** a pannikin holding one pint.

1842 *Legends of Aust.* Mar. 48 A three-legged stool, formed the table, on which were placed two pint pannikins, and half a 10 lb. damper. ***c* 1852** A. MANN *Goldfields Aust.* 27 What a pint pannikin of gold weighs I do not know. **1865** G.E. SARGENT *Frank Layton* 111 The slab-formed table was removed, the fire was replenished, the quart pots and pint pannikins were replenished with tea also.

c. *fig.*

1866 *Austral. Monthly Mag.* (Melbourne) II. 14 Jack . . swore . . 'a pannikin full' at Mr Graham.

2. Abbrev. of *pannikin boss.*

[N.Z. ***c* 1926** 'MIXER' *Transport Workers' Songbk.* 7 My power is such to make or break—I'm a Pannikin, get me?] **1951** *Bulletin* (Sydney) 21 Feb. 12/2 By 'smoke-oh' he'd thawed out enough to say that his hand was crook. . . When, at blow-up, the 'pannikin' succeeded in bringing him back to life he crawled back to work like a blue-tongued lizard.

3. *Obs.* The head; in the phr. **off one's pannikin,** 'off one's head'.

1894 'H. GOLDSMITH' *Our Alma* 128 He's a bit off his pannikin to-night and I can't do nothin' with him. **1904** *Truth* (Sydney) 6 Nov. 4/4 The horsey section of the community goes off its pannikin at Cup time. ***c* 1918** D.H. MEIKLE *Humorous Verses* 3 A yearning in your wifey's brain to join the Tango Teas, Presuming that she did it (there's nothing to forbid it) You'd go clean off your pannikin and baggy at the knees. **1934** B. PENTON *Landtakers* 383 He's gone off his pannikin in Sydney.

4. Special Comb. **pannikin boss, overseer,** one who has only a small degree of authority; **snob,** a small-time snob; **squatter,** a small-time landholder; **wash,** see quot.

1898 E.E. MORRIS *Austral Eng.* 339 **Pannikin-boss** . . applied colloquially to a man on a station, whose position is above that of the ordinary station-hand, but who is only a 'boss' . . in a small way. **1916** *Truth* (Sydney) 5 Nov. 3/4 The Coal Kings employ as 'pannican bosses' men who know enough about the 'common' pitmen (being in most cases 'jumped ups' from the ranks). **1929** *Bulletin* (Sydney) 27 Mar. 23/4 The prayers and profanity of the pannikin boss. **1937** J. MCKELLAR *Sheep without Shepherd* 39 The sub-foreman appeared, the 'pannican boss', he was called. **1947** V. PALMER *Cyclone* 82 Every manjack of us who's swung a bit of wood to defend himself, will have to answer charges as long as a scrubber's tail, with, maybe, months in quod and the chance of being blacklisted by every pannikin boss between here and Brisbane. **1959** D. HEWETT *Bobbin Up* 72 'Yeah, Dick's pretty easy goin' but . . ' And in that 'but' was expressed all their unshakable distrust of the pannikin boss, the boss's man. **1968** F. ROSE *Aust. Revisited* 92 The men seeking work congregated at the wharf gates and the foreman or 'panot' (pannikin boss) selected what labour he wanted. **1983** A. CANNON *Bullocks, Bullockies & other Blokes* 100 We came upon a station homestead near the road. The owner was away and a foreman, or 'pannikin-boss', was in charge. **1891** *Truth* (Sydney) 15 Mar. 7/3 So we bushmen changed the names Colonial experience, **pannikin-overseer**, rangie-boss, and all that 'push' into Jackeroo. **1898** W. DOLLMAN *Bush Fancies* 41 The new chum, *alias* the Jackeroo, *alias* the Pannican Overseer! **1906** *Bulletin* (Sydney) 13 Sept. 16/1 Boundary-riders or at least 'pannikin overseers' (who are a size larger and a shilling cheaper than the genuine article), are now supplied with strychnine, to destroy dingoes in their spare time. **1912** J. BRADSHAW *Highway Robbery under Arms* (ed. 3) 33 These two men were pannikin overseers, who had got a bit tangled with rum, and were trying the speed of their mokes. **1953** 'CADDIE' *Caddie* 41 My mother-in-law was a **pannikin snob** as my father would have said. **1919** *Smith's Weekly* (Sydney) 10 May 14/2 A certain N.S.W. **pannikin squatter** once stuck up notices all over his shed. **1974** B. KIDMAN *On Wallaby* 29, I had to be content with a '**pannikin wash**'. This consisted of putting some water from the bag into the mug which formed the lid of my quartpot, holding the handle between the teeth and tipping a little into my cupped hands. A lather was then rubbed up . . another trickle . . washed it off and the remainder . . rubbed over my face and neck.

panno. [f. *pann(ikin boss* + -O.] *Pannikin boss,* see PANNIKIN 4.

1957 T. NELSON *Hungry Mile* 50 So we decided to follow the 'panno' and tracked her to the Australian Stevedoring Industry Board. **1961** *Realist* (Sydney) vii. 4/1 The worst pannos (pannikin bosses, otherwise foremen) on the waterfront. **1978** W. LOWENSTEIN *Weevils in Flour* 243 There was six men below and the pannikin boss was working with us. He got threepence an hour more. This panno had me loading eighteen bags.

pants man. A womanizer.

1968 *Swag* (Sydney) i. 19 You remember he was Sydney's greatest pants man. He's doing even better now, knocking off daughters of barons and earls, etc. **1979** B. HUMPHRIES *Bazza comes into his Own,* Dad was always a bit of a pants man before he dropped off the twig. They dunno what killed him: booze or stalk-fever.

paper. *Austral. pidgin.* Used *attrib.* in Special Comb. **paper talk, yabber,** a written message; a letter; also *transf.*

[**1849** C. STURT *Narr. Exped. Central Aust.* I. 139 'Papung,' he exclaimed, meaning paper or letters.] **1857** W.S. BRADSHAW *Voyages* 106 The natives have a superstitious belief respecting letters, or as they term them **paper talk.** **1872** MRS E. MILLETT *Austral. Parsonage* 81 They were always ready to act as messengers and carriers of letters or 'paper-talk', as such missives are styled by the natives. **1887** 'OVERLANDER' *Austral. Sketches* 24, I determined to send him off first with a **paper yabber** to the other stockman telling him where we had gone. **1901** F.J. GILLEN *Diary* 22 Oct. (1968) 303 The letter is carried securely tied in a cleft stick which is the usual method of conveying paper yabbers. **1928** B. SPENCER *Wanderings in Wild Aust.* 546 We saw two blackfellows coming up, one of them carrying what is called in these parts a 'paper yabber'. **1937** C. WARBURTON *White Poppies* 150 Carthew sat down and wrote a note to Warren. . . A black took the 'paper-yabber' and, placing it in a cleft stick, mounted a stock-horse and ambled off. **1958** *Coast to Coast 1957–58* 34 Even the songmakers of the white people had made a 'paper-yabba' of the story. **1968** LINKLATER & TAPP *Gather no Moss* 76 They carried paper yabbas (letters, usually held in a cleft stick) in accident and sickness, sometimes covering up to eighty miles on foot in twenty-four hours in extreme emergency.

paper-bark. [See quot. 1955.]

1. Any of several trees of the genus *Melaleuca* (fam. Myrtaceae) having a papery, often peeling, bark, as *M. leucadendra* of n. Aust. and elsewhere. Also **paper-bark(ed) tree (tea-tree,** etc.), **paper-tree,** and *attrib.*

1827 *HRA* (1923) 3rd Ser. VI. 267 'Tea Tree' of which there are two or three varieties, the 'paper Barked' with white wood affecting moist situations. **1837** G.F. MOORE *Evidences Inland Sea* 9 Each family had its separate hut soon completed from the ready materials of blackboy spears and paper-tree bark. **1841** G. GREY *Jrnls. Two Exped. N.-W. & W.A.* I. 93 Lofty paper-bark trees grew here and there. **1863** J. DAVIS *Tracks of McKinlay* 352 This river . . is the 'Flinders'. It has lots of paper-barked trees on it. **1869** *Illustr. Sydney News* 13 May 184/3 The paper bark and corkscrew palm frequently are seen together. **1878** R.B. SMYTH *Aborigines of Vic.* II. 250 Their only mode of cooking was to put their food into the hot ashes, sometimes wrapping small fish and frogs in paper-tree bark. **1893** A.F. CALVERT *W.A. & its Gold Fields* 19 The Paper Bark tree (*Melaleuca leucadendron*) must not be omitted from our survey. The bark is used by the natives in building their huts, and it is extremely durable. **1926** *Bulletin* (Sydney) 21 Oct. 22/3, I personally conducted experiments on timber ranging from saplings to the giant paper-barked 'ti-tree'. **1935** K.L. SMITH *Sky Pilot Arnhem Land* 49 The paper-bark is to the aboriginal in Arnhem Land what the stringy-bark is to the white settler in the outback. **1955** F. LANE *Patrol to Kimberleys* 216 Paperbarks belong to the Melaleuca family, trees of the lowlands, following the water courses. . . The bark resembles several sheets of thin, pale-brown papers laid together, and appears as thin and flimsy as tissue. Yet it provides a finer water-proof, grease-proof wrapping than any manufactured product which can be bought. **1959** *Westerly* ii. 8 The shade of the big paperbarked kadjibuts was welcome. **1979** D. MAITLAND *Breaking Out* 22 His black, tightly curled hair poking up through a thicket of crew-cuts . . with the majesty of a young fir in a stand of scraggy paper-barks.

2. The bark of these trees.

1836 H.W. BUNBURY *Early Days W.A.* (1930) 75 Many deserted huts, some of them made with some care of the paper bark, i.e. the bark of the tea tree. **1841** G. GREY *Jrnls. Two Exped. N.-W. & W.A.* II. 276 A piece of thick and tender paper bark is selected, and torn into an oblong form; the fish is laid in this, and the bark wrapt round it. **1855** J. BONWICK *Geogr. Aust. & N.Z.* (ed. 3) 195 Some in North Australia place the corpse in the paper bark of the Tea tree. **1917** *Emu* XVI. 121 A large bundle of natives' spears wrapped in paper-bark was found. **1938** X. HERBERT *Capricornia* 29 A young lubra wearing nothing but a naga of paper-bark rose and came forward shyly. **1962** V.C. HALL *Dreamtime Justice* 21 He dug the little hole in the ground, dropped in a few live coals from the fire, laid a plug of tobacco on the coals, and covered the hole with a piece of paperbark. **1978** B. SCOTT *Boori* 6 He gently straightened the wasted body, and rolled it in great sheets of paper-bark brought from the level country at the foot of the mountain.

3. Comb. **paper-bark** (or **-tree**) **swamp, torch.**

1869 *Illustr. Sydney News* 23 Dec. 310/3 Large **paper-bark swamps** existing between the west bank of the river and the highest lands flanking the plain. **1897** L. LINDLEY-COWEN *W. Austral. Settler's Guide* 7 Our best spots . . are in paper bark swamps. **1918** B. CRONIN *Coastlanders* 9 Over yonder, in the paper-tree swamp. **1965** *Overland* xxxii. 6 It was a big paperbark swamp and the ducks were quacking all over it. **1974** N. CATO *Brown Sugar* 51 The first settlers had carved the place out of paperbark swamp and vine-forest. **1935** K.L. SMITH *Sky Pilot Arnhem Land* 45 We lit great **paper-bark torches**, and waved them to an fro during the crossing, in order to keep any venturesome crocodiles at bay. **1979** D. LOCKWOOD *My Old Mates & I* 156 Sticks and spears and paperbark torches.

paper daisy. Any of many plants of the genera *Helipterum* and *Helichrysum* (fam. Asteraceae) bearing a daisy flower-head with stiff, papery, petal-like bracts.

1921 K.S. PRICHARD *Black Opal* 5 The faint, dry fragrance of paper daisies was in the air. **1932** J. TRURAN *Green Mallee* 129 Myriads of 'paper-daisies', the yellow-and-white everlasting flowers of the outback, raised their horny petals and grey leaves. **1957** M. PAICE *Valley in North* 31, I do wish it would rain. . . Even the paper-daisies are hanging their heads. **1981** G.M. CUNNINGHAM et al. *Plants Western N.S.W.* 692 Common white sunray is the most widespread and common of the paper-daisies in the region.

paper man. *Hist.* A convict holding a ticket-of-leave.

1848 *Guardian* (Hobart) 25 Mar. 6/4 As to punishment (being a 'paper man') he was ordered 3 months road-making. **1851** *Britannia* (Hobart) 10 Mar. 2/4 He made the statement of being a 'paper man', but he . . was not misled by it. **1851** *Guardian* (Hobart) 26 Apr. 2/3 Recommended the unlucky wight of a 'paper' man, to have his indulgence revoked.

paper-tree: see PAPER-BARK 1.

Papua. *Hist.* A name formerly applied to an Aboriginal. Also **Papuan,** *n.* and *a.*

1833 *N.S.W. Mag.* (Sydney) 181 Our *Papuas* (the aborigines) generally know nothing but to starve and to die. **1835** 'IMPARTIAL OBSERVER' *Illustr. Present State N.S.W.* 39, I begin to write names and words of our Aborigines ('the Papuas'). **1841** *Port Phillip Patriot* 9 Aug. 4/1 Mr Gould took the opportunity of visiting Flinders Island, where the scanty remnants of the Papuan Indigines of Van Diemen's Land still exist. **1852** *Four Colonies* 26 *The aborigines* or natives of Australia, though in several tribes, are all of one common stock—the Papuas—considered to be the most degraded and unimprovable race upon earth. **1853** *Visit to Aust. & Gold Regions* (S.P.C.K.) 156 The aboriginal inhabitants of Australia belong to the class of Papuans, or oriental negroes. **1861** J.D. LANG *Qld., Aust.* 378 The absence of everything like a religion among the Papuan aborigines of Australia is a strong presumptive evidence of the extreme antiquity of the race. **1899** J. MATHEW *Eaglehawk & Crow* 1 When the Australian continent was known as New Holland, its inhabitants were loosely designated Papuans. In an old ethnological atlas in my possession they are classed among the Malays.

paradise honeysucker: see PARADISE RIFLE-BIRD.

paradise parrot. [See quot. 1976.] The parrot *Psephotus pulcherrimus*, a predom. brown, red, and turquoise bird now poss. extinct, formerly known from central e. Aust. See also ANTHILL PARROT.

1929 A.H. CHISHOLM *Birds & Green Places* 98 The paradise-parrot, of central and southern Queensland and the north of New South Wales. **1964** M. SHARLAND *Territory of Birds* 205 Three species of parrots use termites' mounds for nesting—the Hooded Parrot of the Northern Territory, the Golden-shouldered Parrot of north Queensland, and the rare Paradise Parrot of southern areas in Queensland. **1976** *Reader's Digest Compl. Bk. Austral. Birds* 286 The name paradise parrot was conceived by bird-keepers in England when live specimens began to arrive there. **1986** *Sydney Morning Herald* 15 Jan. 13/1 There was a time when multicoloured parrots gouged nesting chambers out of termite-mounds scattered across the woodland plains of northern N.S.W., before Europeans came to graze cattle there. The paradise parrot, a jewel in the crown of Australia's avifauna, was last seen in N.S.W. more than a century ago and disappeared soon after in Queensland. It is no more.

paradise rifle-bird. [*Paradise*, first applied as the specific name *paradiseus* by English naturalist William Swainson: see quot. 1825.] The rainforest bird *Ptiloris paradiseus* of e. Qld. and e. N.S.W., the mature male having velvety black plumage with iridescent blue-green markings. Formerly also **paradise honeysucker.**

[**1825** *Zool. Jrnl.* (London) I. 481 *Ptiloris paradiseus*... It is impossible for any written description, or coloured representation, to convey an adequate idea of the rich and varied tints of this superb creature. Its *size* is about that of the six shafted Paradise bird.] **1860** G. BENNETT *Gatherings of Naturalist* 215 The Paradise Honeysucker, the Rifleman or Rifle-bird of the colonists (*Ptiloris paradiseus*). **1941** C. BARRETT *Aust.* 85 Paradise rifle-birds frequent the palm brush. **1975** *Ecos* vi. 7/1 The paradise rifle-bird, rufous scrub-bird, and Albert's lyrebird live only in subtropical rainforests.

paradox. *Obs.* [f. the specific epithet *paradoxus* of paradoxical character, applied by the German anatomist J.F. Blumenback (*Voigt's Mag. Naturk.* (1800) II. 205, *Götting. gel. Anz.* (1800) I. 609).] PLATYPUS.

1815 *HRA* (1916) 1st Ser. VIII. 573 In the reaches or pools of the Campbell River, the very curious animal called the Paradox, or Watermole is seen.

parakeelia /pærəˈkiljə/. Also with much variety, as **parakeelya, parakelia, parakylia, parrakeelya.** [Poss. a. Adnyamadhanha *baragilya*.] Any of several herbs of the fam. Portulacaceae, having thick succulent leaves and occurring in arid inland Aust., usu. of the genus *Calandrinia*, esp. *C. balonensis* and *C. polyandra*; JUNGA. See also MUNYEROO. Also *attrib.*

1885 *Adelaide Observer* 22 Aug. 10 Pigface and parakylia abound. **1896** B. SPENCER *Rep. Horn Sci. Exped. Central Aust.* IV. 56 *Claytonia*, spp. 'Parakylia' of the settlers and, probably, of some native tribes ['Pericula' (Stuart)] .. is eaten raw or baked in the ashes. **1898** D.W. CARNEGIE *Spinifex & Sand* 215 'Parakeelia' .. is a local, presumably native, name in Central Australia for a most wonderful and useful plant. A specimen brought back by me from this locality was identified at Kew as *Calandrinia balonensis*. **1920** C.H. SAYCE *Golden Buckles* 114 There were plenty of cattle tracks about, but it was parakelia country, and .. the beggars can go for weeks without a drink if that stuff is at all green. **1936** C. CHEWINGS *Back in Stone Age* 10 The principal food of the emaciated beings .. dwelling in .. the interior are snakes .. parakeelia-seeds [etc.]. **1945** T. RONAN *Strangers on Ophir* 10 The parakilya on the sandhills will last for months. **1951** *Bulletin* (Sydney) 3 Jan. 12/1 The parakeelia's purple blooms are crushed in the dry, red sand. **1967** M. & M. LEYLAND *Where Dead Men Lie* 122 He came upon the green jelly-like Parakeelya plant with its juicy water-filled leaves. **1973** R. ROBINSON *Drift of Things* 418 We were in parakelia country. **1978** K. WILLEY *Joe Brown's Dog* 6 A drink of water at considerable intervals and a feed of parrakeelya or some of the other desert herbages, and a camel would go anywhere.

paralytic, *a.* [Used elsewhere but recorded earliest in Aust.] Extremely intoxicated, 'dead drunk'. Also **paralytic drunk.**

1891 *Truth* (Sydney) 10 May 3/3 This friend was paralytic drunk. **1918** H. DINNING *Byways on Service* 107 'If I could get drunk,' said a man wearing his equipment, 'I would—blue-blind paralytic. I never felt so like it in my life.' **1962** A. SEYMOUR *One Day of Yr.* 10 You'd stick up for him if he was paralytic.

Paramatta, var. PARRAMATTA.

parcel. [Spec. use of *parcel* a quantity or amount. Used elsewhere but recorded earliest in Aust. and prob. of Br. dial. origin: see OED(S 4 b.] A quantity of a mineral, esp. as prepared for sale.

1848 *S. Austral. Register* (Adelaide) 25 Oct. 3/5 A parcel of Burra Burra ore. **1852** D. MACKENZIE *Gold Digger* 37 Another parcel, weighing 14 ½ oz., consisting chiefly of small pieces and dust, was procured by a butcher. **1856** H.B. STONEY *Vic.* 168 A parcel of Steiglitz gold has not turned out quite as well as some former assays made by us. **1890** H.Y.L. BROWN *Rec. of Mines S.A.* (ed. 2) 9 Parcels of ore yielding 18 per cent of metallic copper. **1928** R.M. MACDONALD *Opals & Gold* 13 At length we decided we had enough first-class ore to make a good 'parcel'. **1944** M.J. O'REILLY *Bowyangs & Boomerangs* 132 There is a lot in classifying a parcel of opal, as there may be twenty classes in the one packet. **1973** M.T. CLARK *Spark of Opal* (rev. ed.) 210 A good 'parcel', or find, of opal has been made. **1980** S. THORNE *I've met some Bloody Wags* 74, I was told he had just sold a 'parcel' (meaning a quantity of opal) to the opal dealer sitting behind us.

parcel post. [Joc. use of *parcel post* branch of a postal service.] **a.** Used *attrib.* to designate the inexperience or recent arrival of a station hand. **b.** Used allusively with reference to such a person's acquisition of a job.

1931 W. HATFIELD *Sheepmates* 118 Hallett took charge of the three 'parcel post' men and showed them a bunk where they could deposit their belongings. **1946** W.E. HARNEY *North of 23°* 23 'Parcel post men' they called them; that is, they were labelled and addressed to a certain place, and travelled as a parcel does in the mail. **1951** E. HILL *Territory* 431 'Parcel post' was influence—a station manager, or a jackeroo from the cities, who might be the boss's nephew, or going to marry his daughter... 'He come up by parcel post,' they still say. 'He don't know nothin'.' **1974** *Austral.* (Sydney) 28 Dec. 14/2 In the old days, no fences at all. You just went from one place to another mustering. But everyone got lazy. All parcel post boys, new chums from the city.

Hence **parcel poster** *n.*

1935 R.B. PLOWMAN *Boundary Rider* 151 'He's a parcel-poster, that bloke,' the padre heard a bushman say, referring to the English-man... 'Up one mail an' down the next... A few sticks it out; but most of 'em don't.'

parchment. *Hist.* [Spec. use of *parchment* a document on parchment.] A certificate issued to a pardoned convict.

1848 R. MARSH *Seven Yrs. of my Life* 175 We are now in Hobart Town and at the office receiving our parchments or pardon. **1853** *Guardian* (Hobart) 8 June 3/1 On presenting his 'parchment', to the Captain, it was found illegible, and the Captain, refused to take him.

pardalote /ˈpadəloʊt/. [The bird genus *Pardalotus* was named by the French ornithologist L.J.P. Vieillot (*Analyse d'une nouvelle Ornithologie* (1816) 31), a. Gr. παρδαλωτός spotted like a pard.] Any bird of the genus *Pardalotus*, of all States. See also *diamond bird* DIAMOND *n.*[1] Often with distinguishing epithet, as **red-browed, red-tipped, spotted, striated** (see under first element).

[**1826** J.F. STEPHENS in G. Shaw *Gen. Zool.* XIII. ii. 252 Olive-green Pardalotus, with the back spotted with fulvous.] **1841** *S. Austral. Rec.* (London) 2 Jan. 10 The pardalotes, beautiful little birds, of which .. two species are figured. **1918** *Bulletin* (Sydney) 14 Feb. (Red Page), *Pardalotes* (Chip-chips, Ground-Diamonds). **1948** P.J. HURLEY *Red Cedar* 33 Tits, pardalotes and other small fry often used these ironbarks as a hiding place. **1970** J.V. MARSHALL *Walk to Hills of Dreamtime* 15 The long sad wail of the pardalote. **1984** SIMPSON & DAY *Birds of Aust.* 332 Pardalotes are distinctive in appearance—small and colourful with short tails and short blunt beaks.

pardon. *Hist.* [Spec. use of *pardon* remission of the legal consequences of a crime.] A remission of (a convict's) sentence; a document certifying this. See also ABSOLUTE PARDON, *conditional pardon*, CONDITIONAL.

1793 J. HUNTER *Hist. Jrnl. Trans. Port Jackson* 563 A general pardon was therefore promised to all those who came back within a certain time. **1794** D. COLLINS *Acct. Eng. Colony N.S.W.* (1798) I. 342 Samuel Burt, was deemed to have merited the pardon... He was declared absolutely free. **1811** *Sydney Gaz.* 19 Jan., Those who have received Emancipations or Pardons will be required to produce them. **1822** *Australasian Pocket Almanack* 77 Sixpence on the free and conditional pardons, and twopence on certificates and tickets of leave, are to be paid to the Government Printer, as a remuneration for the paper and printing. **1838** W. BLAND *N.S.W.* 12 Convicts .. became free, either by ticket, emancipation, pardon, or expiration of their respective sentences. **1850** W. GATES *Recoll. Van Dieman's Land* 191, I saw my name gazetted for a free pardon... We called at the police office for our 'Pardons'.

Also **pardoned** *ppl. a.*

1818 T.E. WELLS *M. Howe* (1945) 31 Howe .. being in fact considered a *pardoned offender* .. was afforded a last chance of atoning in some degree for his past crimes by an amended life. **1837** *Rep. Select Committee Transportation* 13 The pardoned convict or the free convict enjoys all the political rights of the free emigrants .. from the date of the governor's pardon. **1848** R. MARSH *Seven Yrs. of my Life* 76 The principal overseer was a pardoned felon.

pare, var. PAIR.

parent. Used *attrib.* in Special Comb. **(a) parent country, land, state,** the British Isles; **(b) colony,** New South Wales. See also MOTHER.

(a) 1789 W. TENCH *Narr. Exped. Botany Bay* 5 Some have been sanguine enough to fore-see the most beneficial effects to the Parent State, from the Colony we are endeavouring to establish. **1808** *To Viscount Castlereagh* 3 Indebted originally to the parent country. **1828** *Austral. Q. Jrnl. Theol., Lit., & Sci.* Jan. p. viii, Her Settlers have brought with them, and have retained that active perseverance and energy, peculiar to the British character, which entitles them to the sympathy and good opinion of the Parent State. **1839** W. BLAND *N.S.W.* 3 The late inundation of hypotheses and misrepresentations respecting this Colony .. have proceeded from the press, both here and in the parent country. **1842** *Colonial Observer* (Sydney) 20 Jan. 122 It was not the policy of Great Britain to permit the formation of one great and united community at so immense a distance from the Territory of the Parent State. **1853** J. CAPPER *Emigrant's Guide to Aust.* (ed. 2) 15 There will no longer be a convicted criminal from the parent land within its [*sc.* New South Wales] limits. **1854** H.B. STONEY *Yr. in Tas.* 22 Rising from the thick jungle of crime which has for many years been sent amongst them from the Parent Country. **1858** J.B. MARSDEN *Mem. S. Marsden* 59 The wool of the government flocks and the flesh of the wild cattle was already sufficient to provide both food and raiment for the convicts without any expense to the parent state. **1861** N.W. POLLARD *Homes in Vic.* 5 Liberty .. which has taken so many centuries to come to maturity in the mother country, was imported here by our first settlers... The people of Victoria have even out-run the parent country. **1863** F. ALGAR *Handbk. to Colony Vic.* 4 The land fund .. failed in 1841 .. and affected the inflocking of immigrants from the parent land. **(b) 1821** J. WALLIS *Hist. Acct. Colony N.S.W.* 10 The population of Norfolk Island would be very considerably increased by this detachment from the parent Colony. **1841** *Sydney Herald* 30 Mar. 2/2 The one great cause of all this alarm and excitement in the counties, is the proposal to separate *Port Phillip* from the parent Colony. **1851** J.H. BURTON *Emigrant's Man.* ii. 11 New South Wales .. is the parent colony of Australia. **1873** A. TROLLOPE *Aust. & N.Z.* II. 95 The parent colony, New South Wales, could not have been founded without convicts. **1904** G.A. BROWN *Austral. Merino Studs* 92

Pure Merino sheep were introduced into the parent colony of Australia towards the end of the last century.

parentie, parinti, varr. PERENTIE.

Parkhurst. *Hist.* [f. the name of *Parkhurst* Prison on the Isle of Wight.] Used *attrib.* of a juvenile who, having served part of a sentence in Parkhurst Prison, was sent to Australia or New Zealand between 1842 and 1852.

1844 *Parramatta Chron.* 22 June 3/2 *Swan River.*—John Gavin, one of the Parkhurst boys, has been tried and found guilty at the Supreme Court of this colony for the murder of a youth named George Pollard. **1848** *Sydney Daily Advertiser* 13 July 2/7 Seventy three Pentonville and Parkhurst boys had arrived at Swan River. **1852** G.C. MUNDY *Our Antipodes* III. 226 The worst class of men .. were separated from a more juvenile class, the Parkhurst lads.

parkinsonia tree. [The plant genus *Parkinsonia* was named by Swedish botanist Carl von Linné (Linnaeus) (*Species Plantarum* (1753) 375), after English apothecary John *Parkinson* (1569–1629).] The introduced tree or shrub *Parkinsonia aculeata* (fam. Caesalpiniaceae), naturalized and cultivated in n. Aust., having fragrant yellow flowers.

1953 J.K. EWERS *With Sun on my Back* 90 Clusters of date palms, and Parkinsonia-trees bright with yellow blossom. **1963** O. RUHEN *Flockmaster* 177 There was an aborigine camp .. and dotted all about were planted stands of parkinsonia trees, white cedars, athel pines and pepperinas.

park lands, *pl. S.A.* A green belt along the Torrens River, and surrounding the centres of Adelaide and North Adelaide, as planned by Colonel William Light (1786–1839) in 1837.

1838 T.H. JAMES *Six Months S.A.* 32 Most of the new comers settle down on what is called the Park Lands, where they are handy to the little rivulet. **1843** J.F. BENNETT *Hist. & Descr. Acct. S.A.* 122 A considerable space on each side of the river, and a belt all round the town, was reserved on the original plan as park lands, or pleasure grounds for the citizens. **1853** S. SIDNEY *Three Colonies* (ed. 2) 291 In the park lands surrounding and intersecting the straggling streets .. Colonel Gawler encouraged the blacks to camp by frequent feasts of flour and mutton. **1860** *S. Austral. Advertiser* (Adelaide) 2 July 3/3 *Football.* The match between the clubs was continued on the South Park Lands on Saturday afternoon. **1897** H. HUSSEY *Colonial Life & Christian Experience* 61 Mr Ind, on his arrival in the Colony, became one of the 'squatters' on the Park Lands. **1924** MRS H.A. DOUDY *Magic of Dawn* 27 The reserve of park lands .. surrounded the city. **1936** M.E.P. SHARP et al. *Early Days St. Peter's College* 16 In May the aborigines camped in the parklands near the Frome (now Albert) bridge, and held corroborees. **1965** *Kings Cross Whisper* (Sydney) Mar. (ed. 3) 12/3 Victoria Park race-course and the surrounding parklands of Adelaide were raged [*sic*] by a bush-fire. **1979** K. BONYTHON *Ladies' Legs & Lemonade* 224 We lived with his oft-repeated catchcry of 'Hands off the parklands! Restore Adelaide to Colonel Light's Vision!'

Hence **Park Lander** *n.*

1838 *Southern Austral.* (Adelaide) 17 Nov. 3/3 In December next all Park Landers would be compelled to quit.

parma wallaby /pamə 'wɒləbi/. [The specific name *Parma*, prob. f. a N.S.W. Aboriginal language, was applied by the English naturalist G.R. Waterhouse (*Nat. Hist. Mamm.* I. (1845) 149).] The greyish-brown wallaby *Macropus parma* of N.S.W., and introduced to Kawau Is., New Zealand, having a white throat and white cheek stripe. Formerly also **parma (kangaroo).**

1843 J.E. GRAY *List of Specimens Mammalia Brit. Museum* 91 The Parma. *Halmaturus Parma*, Gould, P.Z.S. *a.* Male. New South Wales.—From Mr Gould's Collection. *b.* Female. **1845** G.R. WATERHOUSE *Nat. Hist. Mammalia* I. 149 *Macropus* (Halmaturus) Parma. Parma Kangaroo. *Halmaturus Parma...* Fur moderate; general colour rich rufous brown, pencilled with whitish. **1894** R. LYDEKKER *Handbk. Marsupialia & Monotremata* 40 Parma Wallaby... This species seems to be very rare and locally distributed. **1926** A.S. LE SOUEF et al. *Wild Animals Australasia* 200 Parma wallaby. *Macropus parma* .. south-eastern New South Wales. **1980** C. ALLISON *Hunter's Man. Aust. & N.Z.* 48 Some animals, such as the Parma wallaby, are greatly endangered if not quite yet extinct. **1986** *Sydney Morning Herald* 15 Jan. 13/4 All of the parma wallabies in the scrubs of the Central Coast were thought to have been shot last century until a healthy population was found on an island off New Zealand, introduced there by an enterprising gamekeeper. Since then they have been found again in some of their old haunts.

parrakeelya, var. PARAKEELIA.

Parramatta. /pærə'mætə/. *Hist.* Also **Paramatta.** [f. the name of the second settlement in New South Wales, now a city in the Sydney metropolitan area.]

a. Used *attrib.* in Special Comb. **Parramatta cloth,** a coarse woollen cloth, orig. manufactured by the inmates of the Female Factory at Parramatta: see quot. 1946.

1826 J. ATKINSON *Acct. Agric. & Grazing N.S.W.* 131 The coarse woollens are known in the Colony by the appellation of Parramatta cloth, having been first made there. **1834** J.D. LANG *Hist. & Statistical Acct. N.S.W.* II. 52 The inmates of the Factory are employed .. chiefly in the processes connected with the manufacture of a coarse woollen-cloth, called *Parramatta cloth*, of which blankets and slop-clothing are made for the convict-servants of settlers. **1845** J.O. BALFOUR *Sketch of N.S.W.* 61 Too much praise cannot be given to the Paramatta cloth. It has quite superseded the use of west of England cloths in the bush. **1855** H. HUME *Brief Statement* 12 The government .. furnished us with .. one tent of Parramatta cloth. **1860** J. NORTON *Condition Colony N.S.W.* 15 An article was and still is manufactured in England, and sold under the designation of Parramatta cloth. **1905** D. REID *Reminisc.* 6 This Parramatta cloth was made at the female factory at Parramatta. **1946** *Concerning Wool* (Austral. Wool Board) 91 Simeon Lord who had established a mill on the swamps at Botany in 1816 entered into an agreement with Governor Macquarie to burl, mill, dye and dress the cloth from the Parramatta factory. Known as 'Parramatta cloth', this was well spoken of in the wool trade for many years. Other mills followed and in 1852 the output had reached 235,000 yards a year, and Parramatta tweed exported to England gained such a favourable reputation that Bradford manufacturers began production of a tweed which they called Parramatta cloth.

b. Abbrev. of *Parramatta cloth.* Freq. *attrib.*

1827 P. CUNNINGHAM *Two Yrs. in N.S.W.* I. 46 The government gangs of convicts .. with their white woollen Paramatta frocks and trowsers .. tell a tale too plain to be misunderstood. **1836** J.F. O'CONNELL *Residence Eleven Yrs. New Holland* 84 The government distribute [*sic*] Paramatta frocks and blankets to each native man and woman. **1846** *Melbourne Argus* 3 July 2/6 About two years ago a new era commenced, the .. homely Parramatta gave place to the refined and expensive broad cloth. **1849** *Belfast Gaz.* (Port Phillip) 14 Sept. 2/5 He obtained a white Parramatta coat with satin vest and black hat before he left. **1884** J.B. MARTIN *Reminisc.* 41 The great tailor artist, Hayes, used to boast that he served the swell and the bullock driver from the same roll of 'Parramatta', but that the refinements of his art preserved their identities.

c. A blanket made from *Parramatta cloth.*

1883 'ONE WHO WAS THERE' *Prison Sketches* 11 Touching the bedding, I may remark that it consists of a sort of a flock and a kind of flax bed, two single blankets and a rug in summer, and in winter an extra rug, called a 'parramatta'.

Parramatta grass. The naturalized African grass *Sporobolus africanus* (fam. Poaceae), an erect, tussocky perennial; the similar, closely-related native grass *S. elongatus.*

1895 F. TURNER *Austral. Grasses* I. 52 *Sporobolus indicus* .. 'Parramatta' or 'Tussock Grass'... An erect-growing, tussocky grass, sometimes attaining a height of 2½ feet, and found in all the Australian Colonies. **1938** C.T. WHITE *Princ. Bot. Qld. Farmers* 41 Panicle .. may be narrow and spike-like, as in some grasses—e.g. Parramatta or Rat's Tail grass. **1976** D. IRELAND *Glass Canoe* 20 The smell of it. Some sweet, some dry and hard, and some, like the clumps of Parramatta grass, didn't care if humans lived or died... Hard as nails. **1983** G.G. ROBINSON *Native Grasses Northern Tablelands* 10 Parramatta grass [*sc. Sporobolus elongatus*] is generally more frequent on the lighter soil types where it is very persistent even under intense grazing... It is one of the poorer of the common native grasses.

parrot. The flesh of a parrot, used as food. Freq. *attrib.*, esp. as **parrot pie.**

1837 *S. Austral. Rec.* (London) 11 Nov. 14 Strange as it may appear to you, a stewed cockatoo, a parrot pudding, a steak off the leg of an emu, or a tureen of kangaroo soup, is a dish that you would relish even in London. **1839** *Ibid.* 13 Mar. 160 While you crowd round the fire and read this, we shall be eating the leg of a kangaroo or a parrot-pie in the open air. **1854** W. HOWITT *Boy's Adventures* 34 We used to hear that parrot and damper was a favourite breakfast in this country. **1861** E.P. RAMSAY-LAYE *Social Life & Manners* 46 We .. could not make up our minds to eat *parrot-soup*, so much the fashion amongst the diggers. **1907** A. MACDONALD *In Land of Pearl & Gold* 91, I reckon a spell down south, where we can get something different from tinned dog and parrot pie to eat, would be a darned good thing just now. **1930** J.S. LITCHFIELD *Far-North Memories* 107 Lunch: Parrot soup, prawn fritters, bread and butter pudding made with turtle eggs, tea. **1944** K.S. PRICHARD *Potch & Colour* 24 You can't beat the missus's parrot-pie when she's made up her mind it's to be a good one, with bacon, port wine and all to bring up the flavour. **1956** S. HOPE *Diggers' Paradise* 225 On one such occasion, not only was kangaroo tail and goanna on the menu, but also parrot and bacon stew. **1977** *Westerly* iv. 16 Geoff promised you parrot pie for dinner and slunk off behind the bulkhead.

parrot fish. [Transf. use of *parrot-fish* a fish having a brilliant colour or beak-like mouth.] **a.** Any fish, usu. brightly coloured, of the fam. Scaridae, having fused teeth resembling a parrot's beak. **b.** Any of many brightly coloured marine fish of the fam. Labridae.

1827 *HRA* (1923) 3rd Ser. VI. 271 The Fish we caught were 'Parrot Fish'. **1843** *Sketch W.A.* 15 The parrot fish, the rock cod, and the diamond fish, or yellow tare, answer in appearance in every respect to fish of the same name in the West Indies. **1849** J.P. TOWNSEND *Rambles & Observations N.S.W.* 10 In Port Jackson is found the parrot-fish, whose varied colours have given it that name. **1876** F. NAPIER *Notes Voyage N.S.W. to N. Coast* 71 The parrot fish is very plentiful here [*sc.* N.T.]. **1889** *Lord Howe Island* 66 *Labrichthys inscripta...* This 'Parrot Fish' (all the members of the family go by the same name) is abundant. **1911** D.A. MACDONALD *Bush Boy's Bk.* 94 The gorgeous primrose and purple parrot fish. **1934** T. WOOD *Cobbers* 223 Parrot fish, which had two blue front teeth, a blue star radiating from the eyes, and blue bones. **1974** J.M. THOMSON *Fish Ocean & Shore* 140 The purple tusk-fish (*Chaerodon cephalotus*) .. is the 'parrot-fish' most frequently caught in Moreton Bay in southern Queensland. **1978** N. COLEMAN *Austral. Fisherman's Fish Guide* 74 For many years .. many .. wrasses have been termed 'parrot fish', even by people who know better... A parrot fish, like a toad, has fused teeth, while wrasses have separated teeth.

Parry's wallaby. [First applied as the specific name *Parryi* by E.T. Bennett, secretary of the Zool. Soc. London (*Proc. Zool. Soc. London* (1834) 151) after the English naval officer and Arctic explorer Sir William Edward *Parry* (1790–1855), who took the type specimen to England.] WHIPTAIL WALLABY.

[**1834** *Proc. Zool. Soc. London* 151 A specimen was exhibited of a *Kangaroo*, recently brought from New Holland, by Capt. Sir W. Edward Parry, R.N., and presented by him to the Society. Mr Bennett .. stated it to be his intention to describe it in detail under the name of *Macropus Parryi.* **1852** J. GOULD *Mammals of Aust.* (1863) II. Pl. 13, Parry's Wallaroo. The known range of this fine species extends along the east coast from Port Stephens to Wide Bay.] **1894** R. LYDEKKER *Hand-Bk. Marsupialia & Monotremata* 30 Parry's Wallaby. *Macropus parryi...* Size medium; form slender and graceful... General colour of upper-parts clear grey, with a bluish tinge. **1926** A.S. LE SOUEF et al. *Wild Animals Australasia* 189 Parry's wallaby is a very beautiful species. It can be readily distinguished .. by its long slender tail, which gives it another local name, the 'whip-tail'. **1954** C. BARRETT *Wild Life Aust. & New Guinea* 6 Parry's wallaby, with a slender body and very long tail, and white and grey markings.

parson's bands, *pl.* [See quot. 1911.] The terrestrial orchid *Eriochilus cucullatus* (fam. Orchidaceae), of all States exc. W.A. and N.T.

1911 R.S. ROGERS *Introd. S. Austral. Orchids* (rev. ed.) 11 The 'parson's bands', so called from the two little white sepals which stick out in front. **1942** C. BARRETT *Austral. Wild Flower Bk.* 137 Flowering in the autumn, *Eriochilus cucullatus* often is called 'autumn wings', but usually 'Parson's bands'. **1978** B.P. MOORE *Life on Forty Acres* 51 Parson's Bands . . a pale pink and very delicate orchid that blooms in late summer.

part, *adv.* [Spec. use of *part* in part, partly.] Of an Aboriginal: partly descended from another race.

1959 E. WEBB *Mark of Sun* 133 It's going to look good, him having a part-aborigine boy working for him. **1961** *Bulletin* (Sydney) 1 Feb. 32/2 He was married to a part-aboriginal girl. **1962** *N.T. News* (Darwin) 26 Apr. 1/5 A nation-wide talent quest for new native and part-colored artists. **1973** P. BISKUP *Not Slaves not Citizens* 5 Most aborigines, and even most part-aborigines, are not assimilated. **1977** K. GILBERT *Living Black* 8 It's an interesting thing that in Darwin you hear a lot about 'part-Aboriginal'. It's a big thing here, whether you're part- or full-blood. **1981** A.B. FACEY *Fortunate Life* 39 He was a part-blood Aboriginal. *Ibid.* 140 Six part-blooded Aboriginals and two full-bloods.

partridge. *Obs.* [See quot. 1847.] Either of two birds, the *painted quail* (see PAINTED) and the *brown quail* (see BROWN *a.* 1). Also **partridge quail.**

1803 J. GRANT *Narr. Voyage N.S.W.* 110 We sprung some coveys of quails, or more properly the partridges of New Holland. **1847** J. GOULD *Birds of Aust.* (1848) V. Pl. 90, They are distinguished as the greater and lesser Brown Quail, and sometimes the name of Partridge was given to the bird here figured [*sc.* the 'Van Diemen's Land Partridge']; doubtless from its going in coveys and resembling the Common Partridge of Europe in many of its actions. **1849** C. STURT *Narr. Exped. Central Aust.* II. 47 App. Synoïcus Australis—*Swamp Quail, or Partridge* . . is generally found in marshes, or marshy ground, and frequently in bevies. **1861** 'OLD BUSHMAN' *Bush Wanderings* 107 The *Scrub Quail*, or as we called it in the bush, the partridge quail, is the largest of all the species. **1878** R.B. SMYTH *Aborigines of Vic.* II. 159 Partridge quail—Choo-irrp.

partridge pigeon. [See quot. 1976.] The bird of tropical woodlands of the Kimberley Ranges (W.A.) and Arnhem Land (N.T.) *Geophaps smithii*; occas. *G. scripta* (see *squatter pigeon* SQUATTER 5).

1842 J. GOULD *Birds of Aust.* (1848) V. Pl. 68, *Geophaps smithii* . . Partridge Pigeon, Residents at Port Essington. **1844** L. LEICHHARDT *Jrnl. Overland Exped. Aust.* 5 Oct. (1847) 8 The partridge pigeon (Geophaps scripta) abounded in the Acacia groves. **1956** A.C.C. LOCK *Tropical Tapestry* 115 We flushed a magnificent partridge pigeon whose habits are similar to that of the squatter pigeon. **1964** M. SHARLAND *Territory of Birds* 181 The northern Partridge Pigeon, with handsome dark brown plumage, white face, slightly spangled breast, and large red eye-patch. **1976** *Reader's Digest Compl. Bk. Austral. Birds* 246 Partridge pigeons fly like partridges, in short, swift bursts close to the ground.

part up, *v.* [f. *part* to give or pay money, prob. infl. by *to pay up.*] *intr.* To pay money. Also *trans.*

1889 *Bulletin* (Sydney) 21 Sept. 20/1 An' then they reckoned I'd been usin' 'em all the time, and they made me part up. ***c* 1907** W.C. CHANDLER *Darkest Adelaide* 84 If Christ came down again He would have to part up the full traybit, or sleep out in the park, no matter how cold and frosty the night might be. **1912** *Bulletin* (Sydney) 25 Apr. 43 Employees at the adjacent boot factory, having received their 'tin' at mid-day, have parted up like gentlemen. **1923** J. ARMOUR *Spell of Inland* 149 When they had all 'parted up', as he put it, he brought back the plate and handed it solemnly to the padre. It proved to be a record collection. **1953** K. TENNANT *Joyful Condemned* 39, I guess Rene might part up to know who her mum was.

pass. *Hist.* [Spec. use of *pass* a written permission.]

1. A document authorizing and regulating the movement of a convict.

1796 *Instruct. for Constables Country Districts* 13 They are to apprehend all Persons passing to and from the different Settlements who are not furnished with proper Passes signed by any of the Acting Magistrates, the Governor's Aid de Camp or the Commanding Officer at the Hawkesbury. **1809** *HRA* (1916) 1st Ser. VII. 147 Our Property plundered by Bands of lawless Ruffians wandering about with impunity for months at a time, protected by a Pass granted by a Convict Overseer. **1822** J.T. BIGGE *Rep. State Colony N.S.W.* 79 A pass, signed by the master of a convict, is requisite to enable him to travel to any part of his own district on his master's business. **1828** *Austral. Almanack* 87 *The Benches* are authorised to grant Passes for any Period not exceeding One Month, to any Man holding a Ticket of Leave, to proceed from one District to another. **1833** *Colonist* (Hobart) 15 Oct. 3/2 This self-same convict received what is termed a General Pass, a higher indulgence than a Ticket-of-Leave, the latter confining locomotion to a particular district, but the former being quite unlimited. **1837** *Rep. Select Committee Transportation* 81 Has every settler the power of granting passes?—To his own servants; there is a printed form. **1850** *Irish Exile* (Hobart) 16 Mar. 7 The woman stated that she had asked her mistress for a 'pass', and she had refused to give her one, when she immediately took French leave, and absconded. **1865** J.F. MORTLOCK *Experiences of Convict* 87 Foot-travellers must exhibit their 'pass' and satisfy enquiries on pain of apprehension.

2. Special Comb. **pass-holder,** a convict to whom a pass has been issued.

1845 *Sydney Morning Herald* 13 Mar. 2/6 The remainder, ticket-of-leave men and pass-holders, remain in this colony. **1847** Z.P. POCOCK *Transportation & Convict Discipline* 4 The average number of passholders, male and female, in service in Van Diemen's Land is 9,294. **1848** J.A. JACKSON *Regeneration Van Diemen's Land* 6 The passholder is still subject to the summary control of convict law, but he may hire himself out to private service, in any capacity to which he may feel suited. **1853** *Austral. Gold Diggers Monthly Mag.* vii. 251 Within there were two shepherds, two kangaroo hunters . . and a couple of passholders sent to enclose a paddock for sheep. **1854** *Guardian* (Hobart) 22 Feb. 3/5 A female passholder . . was charged . . with refusing to work.

Also **passed** *ppl. a.*, issued with a pass.

1827 *Monitor* (Sydney) 20 Sept. 655/2 Some of the vigilant Constables were not to be deprived of their prey . . and Buler Hewson . . seized upon the '*passed*' fugitives, and lodged them in custody.

passport. *Hist.* [Transf. use of *passport.*] PASS 1. Also **passport of leave.**

1796 *N.S.W. Instruct. to Watchmen* 11 If they are People travelling from Parramatta, the Hawkesbury or any other distant place to Sydney, they are to produce their Passports of Leave from the persons authorised to give them. **1810** *Sydney Gaz.* 18 Aug., No Person whatever (excepting the Officers Civil and Military, Gentlemen, and Settlers or Tradesmen who came out free from England) shall be permitted to Travel or Pass from one Settlement to another in this Colony without being furnished with a regular written Passport from a magistrate, or his master if an Indented Servant. **1840** A. RUSSELL *Tour through Austral. Colonies* 184 The unicorn in the royal arms of the passport, which every convict on leave carries. **1843** *Sydney Morning Herald* 23 Aug. 3/5 All passports or passes for more than fourteen days, enabling ticket of leave holders or assigned servants to visit Sydney shall cease to be in force.

pastoral, *a.* [Spec. use of *pastoral* 'relating to, or occupied in, the care of flocks or herds'; (of land) used for pasture: see OED(S *a.* In Austral. use there is a firm distinction between AGRICULTURAL (q.v.) and PASTORAL and the latter is substantially without literary connotations.]

1. Of, pertaining to, or engaged in, stock-raising as distinct from crop-raising.

1839 *S. Austral. Rec.* (London) 15 Nov. 271 Does not every quality and inclination they have shown prove their fitness for *pastoral* occupations? **1843** *Port Phillip Mag.* 84 The agricultural (as well as pastoral) resources of this colony are now rapidly developing themselves. **1845** *Sydney Morning Herald* 16 Aug. 2/2 The great, the dominant interest of the colony—the Pastoral—was perhaps never in so good a state. **1853** W. WESTGARTH *Vic.* 103 The circumstance that was eventually attended by the most important effects was the formation of 'The Pastoral Association'. **1870** W.B. WITHERS *Hist. Ballarat* p. v, The pastoral pioneers are still with us. **1881** *Bulletin* (Sydney) 21 May 1/2 He spent fifteen years in the Murrumbidgee district; and (as might be expected) the pastoral princes of that region were not likely to allow a man of his culture 'to live at home at ease'. **1888** A.P. MARTIN *Oak-Bough & Wattle-Blossom* 38 The whole colony was suffering under the distress; pastoral and agricultural interests were dead. **1896** T. HENEY *Girl at Birrell's* 85 Early in the pastoral 'boom' of Riverine runs it had been bought by a wealthy firm of squatters. **1916** *Truth* (Sydney) 5 Nov. 12/1 The organisation . . to-day covers the pastoral industry workers. **1936** E.W. COX *Evol. Austral. Merino* 31 Hume . . was greatly struck with the pastoral prospects of the country. **1942** H.H. PECK *Mem. of Stockman* 245 Scion of an old South Australian pastoral family. **1961** *Bulletin* (Sydney) 8 Feb. 15/1 The most vocal members of the Federal house are apt to come from pastoral stock. **1965** G.H. FEARNSIDE *Golden Ram* 160 It has been estimated that present agricultural and pastoral production in Australia is being achieved with 250,000 fewer rural workers than was required under pre-war methods.

2. Of a tract of land: used for, or suitable to be used for, stock-raising.

1839 S. BUTLER *Hand-Bk. Austral. Emigrants* 115 Both colonies must necessarily be pastoral settlements for a long time to come. **1843** *Sydney Morning Herald* 23 Nov. 4/6 Queanbeyan is the centre of a vast district, the main line of communication to the great pastoral prairies of Maneroo. **1859** W. FAIRFAX *Handbk. to Australasia* 115 The Waste Land of the Crown is divided into three classes. . . The third division comprises Pastoral Lands. **1887** W. BANNOW *Emigrant's Hand-Bk.* 105 An extent of 8,300,000 acres is to be set apart for pastoral purposes, and is to be divided into 'pastoral allotments', each capable of carrying from 1000 to 4000 sheep, or from 150 to 500 head of cattle. **1908** L.S. CURTIS *Hist. Broken Hill* 33 Charles Rasp . . a boundary rider on the Mount Gipps pastoral holding. **1927** A. CROMBIE *After Sixty Yrs.* 95 Over most of pastoral Australia. **1939** *Austral-Asiatic Bull.* Apr. 11 The pastoral stations employ a number of natives. **1950** G. CASEY *City of Men* 290 Up in the pastoral outback, where one sheep can gain a fat living from five acres of land, things are slow. **1960** R.S. PORTEOUS *Cattleman* 20 This was the big pastoral holding of Wavering Downs, rich grazing country with its heavily grassed downs broken by clumps of brigalow and bauhinia. **1973** *Agriscene Aust.* Jan. 44/1 For the better part of three years now the crisis in the wool industry, especially in the Pastoral Zone, has been widely heralded.

3. Special Comb. **pastoral company,** a commercial enterprise engaged in large-scale stock-raising; **country,** a territory, or tract of land within a territory, devoted principally to stock-raising; **district,** an area in which the principal industry is stock-raising; an area officially designated for this purpose; **lease,** an agreement under which an area of land is held on condition that it is used for stock-raising; the land so held; **lessee,** one who holds a *pastoral lease*; **property, run,** a stock-raising establishment (see also PROPERTY, RUN *n.*[2] 2); **settlement,** the occupation of land for stock-raising; **settler,** one who takes up land for the purpose of stock-raising; **station,** a stock-raising establishment (see also STATION 3); **town,** a town which depends for its existence upon the stock-raising industry in the surrounding district.

1852 J. WEST *Hist. of Tas.* I. 110 Captain Dixon . . came to Van Diemen's Land in 1820. . . He suggested the formation of a **pastoral company**, with a capital divided into £100 shares, as a profitable scheme. **1887** 'OVERLANDER' *Austral. Sketches* 71 Forming a pastoral company. **1898** G. GARNET *Barrier Bride* 48 One of those immense tracts of the south-western part of New South Wales which . . was now probably in the hands of a bank or a big pastoral company. **1957** J. HAWKE *Follow my Dust* 46 The call for boundary riders emanated from Elder Smith & Co., who controlled subsidiary pastoral companies. **1981** *Bulletin* (Sydney) 7 Apr. 98/1 The company which is most likely to feel the effects of the drought is Dalgety Australia Ltd., which is the dominant pastoral company in N.S.W. and Queensland. **1840** *S. Austral. Rec.* (London) 15 Jan. 11 Concentration can never exist in a **pastoral country** like Australia. **1851** J. HENDERSON *Excursions & Adventures N.S.W.* II. 265 New South Wales is emphatically a pastoral country; and so it must continue. But a very small portion of its soil is fit for culture. **1892** 'R. BOLDREWOOD' *Nevermore* II. 97 A stretch of thinly-inhabited pastoral country. **1955** H.G. LAMOND *Towser* 23 The kite hawks and crows . . were part of the feature of any camp or habitation in the pastoral country. **1831** *Acct. Colony Van Diemen's Land* 27 The road . . passes through a **pastoral district** of fine thinly wooded downs, principally adapted for sheep grazing. **1876** *Austral. Handbk.* 104 The colony of New South Wales is divided into thirteen Pastoral Districts. **1905** E.C. BULEY *Austral. Life* 11 The importance to the new colony of the wool they produced . . was recognised by the introduction of a system dividing the back country into 'pastoral districts', which might be occupied on the payment of a reasonable yearly rental. **1972** W.K. HANCOCK *Discovering Monaro* 6 Let us look quickly at successive maps of Monaro, starting with the map of the Squattage District (called later the Pastoral District) as it was in 1840. **1850** *Illustr. Austral. Mag.* (Melbourne) July 78 There appears to be no power over the Crown lands except for **pastoral leases**, and these confined to one year. **1869** *Bushmen, Publicans, & Politics* 18 The remaining quarter million of acres held under pastoral lease. **1905** *Truth* (Sydney) 8 Jan. 1/7 The list of rents fixed by the Western Lands Board for pastoral leases is an interesting document. It shows that the great bulk of the land is held by banks and trading companies. **1938** W. HATFIELD *Buffalo Jim* 233 It's *not* a shooting lease. There's no such thing in the North. It's a pastoral lease. I'm only interested in shooting to try and *clear* it of buffalo. **1960** *N.T. News* (Darwin) 5 Feb. 14/5 Applications are being invited for three pastoral homestead leases north-east of Alice Springs. . . Picton is 940 square miles, Jinka 787 and Jervois 1101. **1985** *Bulletin* (Sydney) 4 June 32/3 There are about 230 pastoral leases in the territory, running about one to one and a quarter million cattle. **1880** *Argus* (Melbourne) 6 Jan. 5/5 It would be a great help . . if every **pastoral lessee** were to report to the Government all particulars relating to every well sunk. **1892** 'E. KINGLAKE' *Austral. at Home* 116 In official returns . . the name 'squatter' is not used, there he is called grazier or pastoral lessee. **1927** A. CROMBIE *After Sixty Yrs.* 23 Satisfactory compact with the pastoral lessees. **1946** A.J. HOLT *Wheat Farms Vic.* 9 A temporary device, allowing Mallee pastoral lessees to select 320 acres out of their grazing allotments for purposes of cultivation was instituted in 1889. **1883** *Illustr. Austral. News* (Melbourne) 28 Nov. 194/3 Shearing time on **pastoral properties** and stations is the busiest and most important time of the whole year. **1964** *Mount Isa Mail* 2 Jan. 1/1 Two established pastoral properties in the Territory are to be thrown open for leasing. **1965** R.H. CONQUEST *Horses in Kitchen* 13 Chinese shepherds . . employed on the huge pastoral properties in the middle of the last century. **1868** J.K. TUCKER *Aborigines & Chinese Question* 6 A **pastoral run** was leased from the Government with a view of establishing an industrial farm and self-sustaining mission. **1897** L. LINDLEY-COWEN *W. Austral. Settler's Guide* 79 It has been pointed out that there is no lack of pastoral runs which do not offer great inducement to turn them into arable lands. **1841** *S. Austral. Almanack* 3 The quantity of stock stated as in the possession of those colonists only *commencing* their **pastoral settlement**, gives no fair criterion to judge of the extent of their intended operations. **1875** J. FORREST *Explorations in Aust.* 263 The whole of the country . . is admirably suited for pastoral settlement, and in a very short time will be taken up and stocked. **1839** *Port Phillip Patriot* 24 Apr. 3 A clause in the **Pastoral Settlers** Act. **1852** W. HUGHES *Austral. Colonies* 69 These periodical droughts . . are productive . . of the most serious injury to the great pastoral settlers, or *squatters*, of the interior. **1870** W.B. WITHERS *Hist. Ballarat* p. vi, Besides the pastoral settlers . . there are yet with us some of the first discoverers. **1928** H.C. PERRY *Son of Aust.* p. xi, The early pastoral settler. **1848** W. WESTGARTH *Aust. Felix* 109 It is common practice to have an aboriginal boy at the **pastoral stations** for assisting in tracking stray cattle. **1869** *Colonial Soc.* 18 Feb. 10 He resided on a pastoral station known as Rotinhoofs. **1957** F. CLUNE *Fortune Hunters* 62 His plan was to visit the twelve pastoral stations to the south of the MacDonnell Ranges. **1901** H. LAWSON *Joe Wilson & his Mates* 47 The place was only a dusty little **pastoral town** in the scrubs. **1938** W. DENNING *Capital City* 24 About 37 miles north-west of Canberra is the wealthy pastoral town of Yass. **1978** R.H. CONQUEST *Dusty Distances* 15 It was a pastoral town—still is in fact. . . The bulk of the male population, excluding railway employees, worked on the surrounding stations, or in the shearing and droving industries.

pastoral, *n. Obs.* PASTORALIST.

1890 'R. BOLDREWOOD' *Colonial Reformer* 20 One of the pastorals looked at the other in astonishment.

pastoralist. [Spec. use of *pastoralist* 'one who lives by keeping flocks of sheep and cattle': see OED(S.] The owner of a substantial stock-raising establishment or of a number of such establishments. See also GRAZIER.

1880 *Gentleman's Mag.* (London) CCXLVI. 62 The outside districts, occupied only by pastoralists. **1885** *Illustr. Austral. Mag.* (Melbourne) Nov. 175/2 The low price of wool is discouraging to both pastoralists and selectors. **1897** *Tocsin* (Melbourne) 16 Dec. 5/2 The Australian pastoralist has got a whole-souled abhorrence of the Shearers' Union and a land tax. **1907** *Emu* VI. 97 The inestimable value of insectivorous birds to the farmer, pastoralist, and fruit-grower. **1919** *Smith's Weekly* (Sydney) 15 Mar. 15/3 Old-time selectors used to complain bitterly of how the eyes were picked out of the country by obliging surveyors in the interests of the big pastoralist. **1931** M.M. BANKS *Memories Pioneer Days Qld.* 17 My father, David Cannon McConnel, was a 'pastoralist'. In the family record he compiled and published for private circulation in 1861 he describes himself as a 'sheep and cattle farmer and landed proprietor in Moreton Bay, Queensland, Australia'. **1939** FRANKLIN & CUSACK *Pioneers on Parade* 11 They had risen above themselves as squatters. . . They had reverted to being pastoralists. **1955** G. HEALEY *A.L.P.* 16 In 1890 the Pastoralists' Union became a federation and affiliated with the Employers' Union. **1965** N. LINDSAY *Bohemians of Bulletin* 87 A politician lobbied for the Canberra pastoralists so successfully that he was able to retire from politics. **1985** *Bulletin* (Sydney) 28 May 66/3 An outback pastoralist who fitted in a war between incredibly varied and tough days on the land in Queensland.

pat. Abbrev. of PAT MALONE.

1908 *Austral. Mag.* (Sydney) 1 Nov. 1251 'On my own' (by myself) became 'on my Pat Malone', and subsequently the tendency to abbreviation . . soon had the effect of rendering this 'on my Pat' a very general expression nowadays. **1910** L. ESSON *Three Short Plays* (1911) 20 It's lonely on yer pat. **1919** *Huon Times* (Franklin) 21 Nov. 3/3 'Now, not a word!' says Bogan. 'We'll noodle this on our 'pat' later on.' **1943** *Troppo Tribune* (Mataranka) 20 Sept. 4 The truck is gorn. I'm on me flamin' pat. **1955** D. NILAND *Shiralee* 136 'On your pat?' 'I had a mate, but he got himself pinched.' **1963** X. HERBERT *Larger than Life* 26 It ain't good for a man to spend all the time you do here on your Pat. **1978** R.H. CONQUEST *Dusty Distances* 10 He rode, on his pat, close on 800 miles.

patch. [Spec. use of *patch* an area, body of material, etc., different from its surrounds.] A (profitable) mining claim; an isolated body of mineral.

1857 A. FAUCHERY *Lettres d'un Mineur en Australie* 197 Une simple plaque souterraine,—ce qu'un nomme, en langage de mines, une *tache* (patch) ou une *poche* (pocket). **1869** *Wallaroo Times* (Kadina) 8 May 4/4 Sinking on the poorer lode of the two . . they have come upon some nice patches of payable ore. **1885** N.W. SWAN *Couple of Cups Ago* 18 He'd a bin marking off of his patch. **1881** G.C. EVANS *Stories* 88 Hearing so much about the Thames gold fields, I went to Grahams Town, and was fortunate enough to find a rich patch, almost in one of the streets. **1892** *Bulletin* (Sydney) 17 Dec. 19/1 Now I had no thought of patches, but I needed tucker badly, And this job, I think, jest saved me being lumbered on the vag. **1929** W.J. RESIDE *Golden Days* 336, I once came upon a deserted alluvial patch nearly decayed with age. **1940** I.L. IDRIESS *Lightning Ridge* 77 The 'Big Four' had 'struck it', had 'bottomed on large nobbies' (black opal) and looked like developing into a big patch! **1944** M.J. O'REILLY *Bowyangs & Boomerangs* 11 Sometimes the finders of a rich patch will keep it quiet. **1962** O. PRYOR *Aust.'s Little Cornwall* 52 If a party struck a rich patch they worked to the limit of their strength to break as much ore as possible during the two month time limit.

Paterson's curse. Also **Patterson's curse.** [Prob. f. the name of Richard Eyre *Patterson* (1844–1918), a grazier occupying various stations near Albury from *c* 1874.] Any of several naturalized European herbs of the genus *Echium* (fam. Boraginaceae), esp. the common *E. plantagineum*, having usu. bluish-purple flowers, variously regarded as a noxious weed, useful drought fodder, or valuable honey plant; *the curse*, see CURSE 2; RIVERINA BLUEBELL; SALVATION JANE.

1904 J.H. MAIDEN *Weeds N.S.W.* (1920) 67 Mr P. Hore, of Mugwee Estate, kept a number of sheep in a small paddock last spring that was covered with 'Paterson's Curse', and the sheep completely ate it out, and appeared to do well on it. **1905** *Agric. Gaz. N.S.W.* XVI. 268 That 'Paterson's Curse' produces some feed is undoubted, but it is a smothering, rough, coarse plant, whose room is far better than its company. **1907** *Bulletin* (Sydney) 12 Sept. 14/1 Around southern Riverina the cocky dilates on the general cussedness of a disrespectful person named Patterson, who, with a bag and forethought, introduced the seed of the purple weed now known as Patterson's Curse. **1930** A.J. EWART *Flora Vic.* 971 *E[chium] plantagineum* . . Paterson's Curse. . . A weed, proclaimed for the whole State, native to Southern Europe, widely spread in N. Victoria, and recorded as naturalized in 1869. The bluish-purple flowers are occasionally white. **1942** H.H. PECK *Mem. of Stockman* 279 Rotherfield, part of Bowna, was held early by Richard Patterson. . . From Rotherfield that free-flowering purple weed known as Patterson's Curse originated, but (though detested by all cattle-men on the Upper Murray) in the north of South Australia from Port Augusta to up around Lake Torrens, where the rainfall is only about 10 inches, the same weed is considered a valued herbage, relished by all stock and called 'Salvation Jane'—an instance of climate and environment changing economic value. **1956** K. TENNANT *Honey Flow* 342 The bees rubbed themselves all shiny, burrowing down into the great bells, and it frayed their wings working the Paterson's Curse, but it was certainly beautiful, pale clear honey and wonderful pollen. **1973** W.T. PARSONS *Noxious Weeds Vic.* 32 The origin of the name 'Paterson's curse' can be traced back to a Victorian stock inspector who in 1888 asked the name of the purple plant he could see on the other side of the Murray River, growing on a stock reserve near Albury. He was told it was 'Patterson's curse' as the Patterson family owned the property adjoining the reserve. The name has stuck but the spelling has been modified over the years. There are two versions of how the plant first came to the stock reserve near Albury. One is that a Mrs Patterson, in travelling to Albury in the early 1860s, brought with her a garden plant which eventually became established on her property and the adjoining reserve. The other version is that the plant first appeared about 1888 after sheep from South Australia had been held on the reserve. **1982** R. HALL *Just Relations* 476 Onward past paddocks stifled in a purple blanket of Paterson's curse. **1982** K. HUENEKE *Huts of High Country* 181 Dilapidated dairies and weatherboard homesteads contrasted against less sympathetic modern brick veneer farm houses, many hectares of Patterson's curse and big fat black cattle. Here and there are miniature clusters of beehive villages, no doubt moved elsewhere when the rich deep blue carpet has wilted.

Pat Malone. Rhyming slang for 'own'; esp. in the phr. **on one's Pat Malone,** on one's own; alone. Also **Pat Maloney**.

1908 MRS A. GUNN *We of Never-Never* 146 A thousand miles on horseback, 'on me Pat Malone', into the Australian interior and out again. **1910** *Truth* (Sydney) 3 July 11/4 The photograph for which you have sat on your Pat Malone. **1945** *Atebrin Advocate: Mag. 2/4 Austral. Armoured Regiment* Jan. 6 The gunner too to disappear, leaving me on my Pat Malone. **1950** J. MORRISON *Port of Call* 174 'All on your Pat Maloney?' . . 'I guess.' **1955** A. GROOM *Wealth in Wilderness* 89 I'm all on me Pat Malone. It's good to talk to somebody white, like. **1966** *Overland* xxxv. 37 Wheel him in here and grill him on his pat malone? **1981** *Austral.* (Sydney) 7 Oct. 18/6 And was John Snow the most ferocious bowler he faced?. . . 'I had probably had as much trouble as anyone against him when we lost the Ashes in 1970–71, but I was not on my Pat Malone,' he said.

patter /ˈpætə/, *v. Austral. pidgin. Obs.* Also **patta.** [a. Dharuk *bada* to eat.] *trans.* To eat (food). Also *absol.*

1790 D. SOUTHWELL Corresp. & Papers, *Pāt-ta*, to eat. **1803** J. GRANT *Narr. Voyage N.S.W.* 109 These natives would kill and *patter*, that is, *eat him*. **1833** C. STURT *Two Exped. Interior S.A.* II. 223 He himself did not *patter* (eat) any of it. **1838** T. WALKER *Month in Bush Aust.* 31 The watchful creature's nose is at the ground 'pattering' (*nibbling grass*). **1847** *Maitland Mercury* 27 Oct. 4/4 White fellow too much sick, patter too much jumbuck.

1851 J. HENDERSON *Excursions & Adventures N.S.W.* II. 114 When a gin has had intercourse with a European, and produces a half-caste child, they say, 'That been *patter* (eaten) white bread'. **1854** R.E. MALONE *Three Yrs.' Cruise Australasian Colonies* 196 We'll form a precious crew, That digs the gold at Wellington, and patters Kangaroo. **1881** A.C. GRANT *Bush-Life Qld.* I. 236 You patter (eat) potchum?

patter /'pætə/, *n. Austral. pidgin. Obs.* Also **pattor.** [f. prec.] Food.

1824 Methodist Missionary Soc. Rec. 26 Jan., 'Boodjerry patta! murry boodjerry!—fat as jimbuck!!' i.e. good food, very good, fat as mutton. **1845** D. MACKENZIE *Emigrant's Guide* 206 Patter, food. **1847** A. MARJORIBANKS *Travels N.S.W.* 91 Old Paddy, licking his lips, added it was 'Cabon budgery patter like it Emu'. **1853** H.B. JONES *Adventures in Aust.* 170 At these large stations there are generally hanging about some of the natives, who are looking out for 'patter' (food); the scraps which are left. **1880** J.B. STEVENSON *Seven Yrs. Austral. Bush* 147 Billy .. made his appearance, holding a large carpet-snake aloft in triumph, 'Buddgery Pattor this fellow'. **1884** A.W. STIRLING *Never Never Land* 174 White men never eat these birds; the blacks, however, are not so particular, and even where food is plentiful say kites make good 'patter'. **1904** *Shearer* (Sydney) 17 Dec. 2/2 Almost anyone from a 'slushy' to a spieler .. can become a parrot and 'patter' organiser .. as most of the members of the A.W.U. are cooks and 'cockies'.

Patterson's curse, var. PATERSON'S CURSE.

pav. Abbrev. of PAVLOVA.

1966 G.W. TURNER *Eng. Lang. Aust. & N.Z.* 173 *Pavlova cake* .. sometimes shortened to *pav.* **1973** *Woman's Day* (Sydney) 27 Aug. 10 For those readers who haven't sampled or seen a 'pav', its a crusty meringue-like sweet-cake topped with whipped cream and (usually) passionfruit. **1977** E. MACKIE *Oh to be Aussie* 54 Nice to 'ave a pav after a baked dinner. Created in Melbourne in 1926 to honour the greatest pav of them all, Anna Pavlova, it's a grand finish to an Aussie meal. **1977** W. MOORE *Just to Myself* 104 I've got some drop scones and a pav ready for you. **1981** *Bulletin* (Sydney) 13 Jan. 74/1 The Pav, a kind of meringue the size and shape of a truck wheel, is the country's national dish.

pavlova. [f. the name of Anna *Pavlova* (1885–1931), Russian ballerina: see quot. 1971.]

1. A dessert; a large, soft-centred meringue topped with whipped cream and fruit.

[N.Z. **1927** *Davis Dainty Dishes* (Davis Gelatine N.Z., Ltd.) (ed. 6) 11 Pavlova. . . Dissolve all but a teaspoonful of Gelatine in the hot water, and all the sugar [etc.]. **1929** K. MCKAY *Practical Home Cookery* 155/1 *Pavlova cakes*. . . Cook like meringues. . . They are delightful and simple to make besides being a novelty.] **1940** WESTACOTT & LOWENSTERN *275 Choice Recipes* 40 *Pavlova Cake.* Four eggs, 8 ozs. castor sugar, 1 dessertspoon vinegar, 1 dessertspoon cornflour, 1 pinch cream of tartar. Beat whites stiff, fold in sugar, beat till dissolved, add other ingredients, lastly vinegar. Line a 9-inch tin with grease-proof paper slightly moistened; allow sides to stand up 4 inches as it rises very much, bake 1½ hours in slow oven. Turn out and leave upside down to cool. Turn over and put whipped cream and passion fruit on top. **1967** M. HORNER *Austral. One-Act Plays: Bk. 3* 76 The Pavlova was a terrible flop. . . My Pavlovas never go like that as a rule. **1969** A. CLARK *Austral. Adventure* 47 The Australians' favorite dessert is a 'Pavlova'. It is like a meringue with fruit and whipped cream. **1971** *Bulletin* (Sydney) 11 Dec. 13/1 Harrods is still London's most classy department store .. so I felt a touch of satisfaction when I saw in their cake department a sign saying 'Pavlova Cake—20 p. a slice' (that is, A43 cents). The Pavlova, a distinctive Australian contribution to cuisine, had been officially recognised as posh. But I was shocked to read the rest of the notice. It said: 'Pavlova Cake was created in New Zealand as a tribute to the dancer Anna Pavlova'. Furthermore, the specimen on display was not authentic. Instead of the traditional passionfruit on top of the cream it had strawberries. And the base did not seem to be the proper meringue; it was some brown crusty stuff. **1976** B. HUMPHRIES *Dame Edna's Coffee Table Bk.* 35 Many young lasses couldn't run up .. a decent Pavlova these days. **1980** E. METCALFE *Garden Party* 87 He pretends to be a connoisseur of everything, that man—but I notice he eats his wife's pavlova. **1985** *Bulletin* (Sydney) 28 May 8/2 New Zealand's No. 1 indigenous dessert, the 'Pavlova' was created there after a visit by Pavlova in 1926. **1986** P. GOLDSWORTHY *Zooing* 114 *Pavlova* n. (comm. abbrev. pav), a famous Australian dessert, named due to its mouth-watering properties, in honour of the distinguished Russian physiologist Ivan Pavlov (1849–1936).

2. Used allusively as an emblem of insubstantiality. Also *attrib.*

1972 BERMAN & CHILDS *Why isn't she Dead!* 63 As a graduate of the pavlova belt he was too inhibited to try anything novel or unfamiliar. **1972** *Bulletin* (Sydney) 30 Dec. 15/1 What it most sadly didn't seem to merit was the recent final softening of TDT into television's equivalent of the pavlova, a nightly pudding of feeble comedy and stingless comment.

pay, *v. Mining.* [Spec. use of *pay* to yield an adequate return; to be profitable.] *intr.* Of a mine, mineral-bearing deposit, etc.: to be profitable to work. Also *trans.*, to yield (a return).

1852 *Murray's Guide to Gold Diggings* 24 The rock was too deep for them to reach, or to pay well even if there was gold when they did. **1858** *Colonial Mining Jrnl.* Sept. 2/2 The mine has been deepened . . and certainly would pay well, if washed in a skilled and mining-like manner. **1871** *Austral. Town & Country Jrnl.* (Sydney) 11 Mar. 303/4 Notwithstanding the bad name that has been given to the reef . . it will now pay splendidly to work. **1902** *Bulletin* (Sydney) 22 Mar. 3/2 Two ounces to the dish she pays. **1977** R. EDWARDS *Austral. Yarn* 14 The fellows . . go out and prospect the alluvial to find out what would pay.

payable, *a.* [Spec. use of *payable* capable of yielding an adequate return: see OED *a.* 3.]

a. In collocations: **payable gold, goldfield, ground, ore.**

1859 *Colonial Mining Jrnl.* May 145/1 A claim at the end of Wilson's lead has struck **payable gold.** **1870** C.H. ALLEN *Visit to Qld.* 156, I had satisfied myself payable gold was to be found. **1889** *Braidwood Dispatch* 25 Sept. 2/5 A discovery of rich payable gold is reported from the Mitchell River, Queensland. **1907** *Bulletin* (Sydney) 17 Oct. 14/4 The most difficult man to find in this country is the miner who is actually on payable gold. **1931** C.B. SMITH *Austral. Gold Prospectors Handbk.* 63 'Payable gold' means gold sufficient to pay current wages to the men employed. **1939** J.W. COLLINSON *Early Days Cairns* 31 Mulligan . . reported payable gold on a tributary of the Mitchell River. **1863** F. ALGAR *Handbk. to Colony Tas.* 10 By a **payable gold-field** is meant one capable of yielding five thousand ounces a week for a period of twelve months. **1882** J. ALLEN *Hist. Aust.* 303 There may be more payable goldfields in Western Australia than in some of the other colonies if diligent search were made for them. **1941** D. O'CALLAGHAN *Long Life Reminisc.* 239 He and Ford received £1,000 reward from the Government . . for finding a payable goldfield. That reward is always on offer. **1859** *Colonial Mining Jrnl.* May 145/2 The company found a small patch of **payable ground** of some 50 feet square. **1864** *Illustr. Sydney News* 16 July 6/1 He reports the existence of payable ground along the Onga-paringa. **1896** J.W. ROBERTS *Mining Industry N.S.W.* 32 That represents the length of what is considered payable ground, and consequently constitutes the mine. **1868** *Wallaroo Times* (Kadina) 1 Apr. 5/3 The lode . . is yielding good **payable ore.** **1941** D. O'CALLAGHAN *Lone Life Reminisc.* 239 My block was only a position block and no payable ore to break. **1962** O. PRYOR *Aust.'s Little Cornwall* 122 Big blocks of payable ore were found in the Wallaroo mines.

b. In the collocation **payable dirt,** pay-dirt.

1859 *Colonial Mining Jrnl.* June 162/2 The party has driven across two or three wide runs of payable dirt. **1870** *Sydney Morning Herald* 5 July 2/4 The Big Engine claim is the only fresh one that has started washing. . . They have . . come on to some payable dirt. **1911** A. WRIGHT *Gamblers Gold* (1923) 143 Men were bottoming on payable dirt. **1946** K. TENNANT *Lost Haven* 352 Mr Cassell's party was the only one that approached anything like payable dirt.

pay-back. *Austral. pidgin.* An act of revenge, as sanctioned by traditional Aboriginal practice; the code governing this. Also *attrib.*, and *transf.*

[**1930** *Amer. Anthrop.* (Menasha, Wisconsin) 214 Warlumbopo wailed for his dead brother. He refused to allow the wives of the dead man to bury him. 'I'll cry no more for you. I'll not show my sorrow now. I'll buy you back first.' He went down to the country where the brother had been mortally wounded; through cunning and skill he killed the slayer of his wawa and escaped.] **1935** D. THOMSON *In Arnhem Land* (1983) 67 Many remembered feuds of long standing—for blood feuds among these people are carried on for many generations. The 'pay back' as they call it, may be delayed for years in order to catch a man, or a group, off guard. **1962** D. LOCKWOOD *I, Aboriginal* 22 Aborigines never forget. All wrongs must be set right by a system known as *Pay-Back.* **1963** F. FLYNN *Northern Gateway* 117 The primitive native code of ethics which amounts, in matters of 'pay-back', or revenge, to a simple conviction that it doesn't matter how you get your man, so long as you kill him. **1970** M. KELLY *Spinifex* 63 'I can remember him taking part in a big pay-back raid a few years later.' 'Pay-back?' 'Pidgen [*sic*] for vendetta.' **1980** *Sun-Herald* (Sydney) 26 Oct. 1/2 Someone rang the police and the mob thinks it was me. The bricks—and the rest—are a payback. **1984** *Age* (Melbourne) 19 Sept. 11/3 It is simply asking too much of human nature for people not to see Mr Wran's advertising switch as pay-back to Fairfax. **1985** *Canberra Times* 15 Nov. 10/5 The payback system still appeared to prevail among full-blood Aboriginals.

Paymaster. *Hist.* Used with reference to a paymaster of the New South Wales Corps in the collocations **Paymaster's bill, note,** a note recording payment due to a member of the Corps, which was consolidated into a bill on a regimental agent in London.

1803 *Sydney Gaz.* 24 Apr., Paymaster's Bills and Copper Coin received in payment of any of the above Articles. **1804** *Ibid.* 26 Feb., Payment required on delivery in Cash, Government or Paymasters' Bills. **1808** *Ibid.* 18 Dec., Payment to be made in Paymasters' [*sic*] or Government Bills. **1811** *Ibid.* 9 Feb., Payment to be made on delivery, in Government or Paymaster's Notes. *Ibid.* 13 Apr., Prompt payment to be made in Government or Paymaster's Bills or Dollars.

pay note. *Obs.* Shortened form of *Paymaster's note* (see PAYMASTER).

1804 *Sydney Gaz.* 25 Nov., New South Wales Corps . . the Committee of Paymastership of the said Corps will consolidate their Pay Notes for this and the preceding months. **1809** *Ibid.* 26 Mar., The Pay Notes issued for the subsistence of the Corps . . will be consolidated in Cash or Bills on the 30th instant, at the Paymaster's Office.

pea, *n.*[1] [Shortened form of *Darling pea* (a) (see DARLING).] Used *attrib.* in Special Comb. **pea-eater,** an animal which has been poisoned as a result of eating Darling pea; **-struck** *ppl. a.*, afflicted by this poisoning; also **-stricken.**

1901 J.H. MAIDEN *Plants reputed to be Poisonous* 16 'Darling Pea'. . . It's effect on sheep is well-known; they separate from the flock, wander about listlessly, and are known to the shepherds as '**pea-eaters**', or 'indigo eaters'. **1916** *Bulletin* (Sydney) 5 Oct. 24/2 Can any . . scientist put a name to the toxic principle in the Darling pea . . ? When a cow develops a wild glare . . and doesn't appear to have any real desire for tucker . . it is safe to assume in pea country that she has become a 'pea-eater'. **1935** *Ibid.* 2 Jan. 20/2, I overtook a drover. . . Most of his mob had pink-eye, a few were pea eaters, and his dogs were too sore-footed to walk. **1902** [**pea-struck**] *Ibid.* 17 May 14/3 Concerning a certain pea-stricken horse: 'D.H.R.' . . recommends hand-feeding as a possible remedy for the effects of Darling pea. **1934** A. MELROSE *Song & Slapstick* 96 A pea-struck steer. **1966** J.F. MACADAM *Some Poisonous Plants N.-W.* 74 Stock poisoned by Darling peas are said to be 'pea struck'. **1974** S.L. EVERIST *Poisonous Plants Aust.* 341 Many [*Swainsona*] species can produce a peculiar form of locomotory disturbance known as 'pea-struck' in sheep, cattle and horses.

pea, *n.*[2] [Fig. use of *pea*, as in the (swindler's) game of *thimblerig*, in which one of three inverted thimbles allegedly conceals a pea; *obs.* except in Aust.: see OEDS *n.*[1] 1 e.]

1. In horse-racing: a favourite; a likely winner (see

quot. 1953). Also *transf.*, one in a favoured or favourable position.

1911 E. Dyson *Benno & Push* 206 Mr Dickson . . ran his eye down the card and chanced it. 'Dandy's the P,' he said. 'Put yer whole week's wash on Dandy, 'n hold me responsible if the goods ain't delivered.' **1953** S.J. Baker *Aust. Speaks* 118 Other expressions used by racing fans include: *pea*, a horse that is being ridden to win, especially when there is doubt about the genuineness of other runners. **1958** F. Hardy *Four-Legged Lottery* 190 I've got the tip about it. . . Swordsman is the pea. **1969** M. Calthorpe *Defectors* 17 'For the time being, I'm satisfied.' 'You're the pea,' Mick said. **1969** A. Buzo *Rooted* (1973) 92 He's had his eye on her for some time, you know, but I'm the pea, she said. **1980** B. Hornadge *Austral. Slanguage* 248 A *pea* or a *goer* is a horse that is being ridden to win whilst one that is not trying is *dead*.

2. In the *attrib.* phr. **pea and thimble,** engaged in swindling.

1918 *Euripidean: Troopship Souvenir* 6 An me arunnin' messages for th' barmaid at th' 'Spreading Sun' and workin' in conjunction with a pea an' thimble joint. **1966** J. Waten *Season of Youth* 32, I started to walk, hardly taking any notice of the horses pounding round the course. . . There were pea and thimble men displaying their skill and fleecing the half-shrewd mugs.

pea-bush. Any of several shrubs of the genus *Sesbania* (fam. Fabaceae) occurring in n. Aust., as *S. benthamiana* of N.S.W., Qld., and N.T.

1881 T. Archer *Some Remarks on Proposed Qld. Trans-Continental Railway* 18 The pea-bush, a species of *sesbania*, also found abundantly on the flooded flats of the Gilbert, growing in patches, or more open scrubs, to a height of from ten to fifteen feet, is eagerly devoured by stock when green. **1883** E. Palmer *Plants N. Qld.* 18 *Sesbania aegyptiaca* . . called peabush; grows in the beds of creeks and plains. **1906** *Emu* VI. 41 They invariably frequent the pea-bush (*Sesbania aculeata*) flats. **1972** R. Magoffin *Chops & Gravy* 107 *Peabush*, a tall spindly legume which grows in abundance in good seasons. **1981** A.B. & J.W. Cribb *Useful Wild Plants Aust.* 207 *Sesbania benthamiana* (*S. aculeata*) Sesbania Pea, Pea-bush. . . The dried stems were used by the Aborigines as drills for making fire.

peaceful dove. The dove *Geopelia placida* of e. and n. mainland Aust. and elsewhere, a predom. grey to brown bird with black bars.

1845 J. Gould *Birds of Aust.* (1848) V. Pl. 73, *Geopelia tranquilla* . . Peaceful Dove. **1945** C. Barrett *Austral. Bird Life* 66 Popularly known as 'doodoo' from its call notes, the peaceful dove (*Geopelia placida*) is distributed generally over the continent, the South-western region excepted. **1956** A.C.C. Lock *Tropical Tapestry* 38 Peaceful doves . . and green fruit pigeons settled on the bank. **1984** Simpson & Day *Birds of Aust.* 310 Many pigeons, including this Peaceful Dove, drink by sucking.

peacock, *v. Hist.* [In punning allusion to the eye-like markings on the tail feathers of a peacock: see Eye.] *trans.* To obtain (the choicest parts of a tract of land, esp. those controlling access to water), in order to render the surrounding land of little or no value to others. Also *intr.*

1892 *Truth* (Sydney) 17 Apr. 2/1 'Peacocked' in the most scientific manner all over the vast holding, literally 'picking the eyes out' of this fine country. **1894** *Bulletin* (Sydney) 27 Oct. 23/1 The staunch souls who had 'peacocked', to the gnashing of squatters' teeth, and who declined to be bought out, were by no means rare. **1928** 'Brent Of Bin Bin' *Up Country* 347 They had been able to 'peacock' their runs and safeguard their holdings. **1945** H.S. Roberton *Now blame Farmer* 16 They 'peacocked' the land and held the squatter up for ransom. They selected where it would do the squatter the greatest harm, and then they offered to sell. They were our first land-jobbers. **1953** A. Morris *Rich River* 84 Squatters . . 'peacocked' by having dummies take possession of land round waterholes. **1972** Anderson & Blake *J.S. Neilson* 12 As early as 1872 he had successfully peacocked the land north-east and north-west of the lake in Minimey parish.

Hence **peacocker** *n.*

1892 *Truth* (Sydney) 17 Apr. 4/3 These princes among 'peacockers'. **1936** P. Staal *Foreigner looks at Aust.* 136 He began by putting dummy selectors on the most valuable parts of his run to forestall the undesirable practices of the peacockers.

peacocking, *vbl. n.* [f. prec.] See quot. 1945.

1892 *Truth* (Sydney) 17 Apr. 2/1 This 'peacocking' was commenced . . under Sir John Robertson's new Land Act of 1861. **1919** C.A. Bernays *Qld. Politics during Sixty Yrs.* 316 It was in these days [*sc.* after 1868] that the term 'peacocking' first came into vogue—a term of reproach applied to the act of picking the eyes out of the country. **1945** H.S. Roberton *Now blame Farmer* 15 The squatters had exercised their right of pre-emption. When their licences had been converted to leases they were given the right to buy at the unimproved capital value, and they bought. But they did not buy the whole of their runs. They bought small and strategically situated areas all over their runs, in the pious hope that it would discourage intrusion. The device came to be known as 'peacocking'. **1968** F. Rose *Aust. Revisited* 29 'Peacocking' or 'picking the eyes out of the run' was another way of getting round the law. The squatter or his dummy would select the water-holes or creeks on the run so that the rest of the land was useless for farming.

peacock sole. [See quot. 1969.] The marine fish *Pardachirus pavoninus* of n. Qld., having the typically flattened body of a sole, and the similar *P. hedleyi* of N.S.W. and Qld.

1906 D.G. Stead *Fishes of Aust.* 183 Amongst other species of our Flat-Fishes might be mentioned . . the Peacock Sole (*Achirus pavoninus*). **1945** *Marketable Fish Cairns Area* (N. Qld. Naturalists' Club) 8 Peacock Sole. *Parachirus* [*sic*] *pavoninus*. **1965** *Austral. Encycl.* VIII. 197 The . . peacock soles (*Pardachirus*), and banded soles . . are highly ornate, with striking colours and variegated patterns, but are too small to be of economic importance. **1969** J. Pollard *Austral. & N.Z. Fishing* 200 Peacock Sole. . . This is a prettily-marked sole, with an array of dots or spots that are paler than the rest of the fish scattered across a reddish-brown background. **1978** N. Coleman *Austral. Fisherman's Fish Guide* 57 The peacock sole is rarely found out of its sandy habitat and is usually caught in relatively shallow waters.

pea-dodger. *Obs.* A bowler hat.

1933 *Bulletin* (Sydney) 5 Apr. 12/3 'Elizabeth Owen': . . the different terms applied to 'bowler' hats—I have also heard them called 'egg-boiler' and 'pea-dodgers'. **1945** S.J. Baker *Austral. Lang.* 181 Among . . the Australia equivalents of what the Englishman calls a *bowler* . . peadodger.

pear.

1. *Obs.* Any of several plants, esp those of the genus *Xylomelum* (see Wooden pear); the fruit of the plant. Also **pear-tree.**

1804 *Sydney Gaz.* 7 Oct., The timber consisted chiefly of cedar, pear and tea tree. **1805** J.H. Tuckey *Acct. Voyage to establish Colony Port Phillip* 228 The pear-tree is so called from its bearing a fruit resembling a pear in shape, but of the hardness of wood. **1829** R. Mudie *Picture of Aust.* 150 The pear (*xylomelum pyriforme*) is something in the shape of a pear, but instead of being esculent, is of a more rigid structure than most timber, and can hardly be cut with a knife. **1837** *Colonist* (Sydney) 350/1 The pears are of wood . . with stalks at the broad end. **1852** G.C. Mundy *Our Antipodes* II. 26 The pear-tree is, I believe, an eucalyptus, and bears a pear of solid wood, hard as heart of oak. **1965** *Austral. Encycl.* VII. 42 As a substantive, the term [pear] is applied to various Australian trees and shrubs with pear-shaped fruits or pear-like foliage. . . *Terminalia platyphylla* is called pear-tree in tropical north-western Australia.

2. a. Shortened form of 'prickly pear'. Also *attrib.*

1908 *Bulletin* (Sydney) 9 July 15/3 Runs have been given up as hopeless for stock owing to the prickly anathema. Right down the line from Roma to Dalby pear is seen all the way. **1917** W. Lees *Coaching in Aust.* 57 The land, freed from pear, is wonderfully productive. **1936** W. Hatfield *Aust. through Windscreen* 34 Mentally backward settlers . . maintained that the 'pear' was an asset, drought-proof, an inexhaustible fodder-supply. **1959** *Overland* xiv. 17 His eyes classified us with drought, fire, the pear, flood and Noogoora burr. **1973** H. Lewis *Crow on Barbed Wire Fence* 29 You seen pear? It's cactus. Put a piece on that barbed wire fence and it'll grow.

b. *attrib.*, esp. as **pear country.**

1914 H.M. Vaughan *Australasian Wander-Yr.* 231 The sole method of destruction that has so far proved serviceable is the injection of some poisonous fluid . . which is squirted into each leaf of the plant by means of a 'pear-gun'. **1917** W. Lees *Coaching in Aust.* 57 Some 12 miles through open pear country we pass through a cypress pine scrub. **1929** A.H. Chisholm *Birds & Green Places* 55 Repeatedly halted by bushmen—sheep-musterers, pear-cutters, general labourers. **1957** D. Whitington *Treasure upon Earth* 90, I reckon we'll go across to Goondiwindi. Might get some pear poisoning there. **1977** *Pastoral Rev. & Graziers' Rec.* Sept. 302 The pear country was alive with the dreaded death adder.

pearl. Used *attrib.* in Special Comb. **pearl-cleaner, -doctor, -faker,** one who prepares pearls for sale (see quots.).

1937 J.M. Harcourt *It never Fails* 130 The **pearl-cleaner** sat at a table working on a blister with a file. **1940** E. Hill *Great Austral. Loneliness* (ed. 2) 70 Four hours' concentration . . secured the pearl-cleaner £200. **1937** I.L. Idriess *Forty Fathoms Deep* 158 Layers of nacre are the coats or skins of the pearl. Some skins may be slightly discoloured, dinted, or spotted. To find this perfect skin is the job of the '**pearl doctor**'. **1941** K.S. Prichard *Moon of Desire* 73 Broome pearls were the most beautiful . . and he was considered the best pearl doctor in the world. **1903** H. Taunton *Australind* 226 Defective and blotchy pearls are often rendered valuable by the art of the '**pearl-faker**'. **1972** P.L. Brown *Coast of Coral & Pearl* 121 The pearls . . were 'skinned' to lighten their colour, to remove any blemishes and reveal their hidden lustre. In the old days the man who performed this task was called the 'pearl-faker'.

pearler, var. Purler.

pearl perch. [See quot. 1974.] The greenish to silvery-grey marine fish *Glaucosoma scapulare* of offshore reefs in n. N.S.W. and s. Qld.

1884 *Proc. Linnean Soc. N.S.W.* IX. (1885) 7 *Glaucosoma scapulare* . . is known to some of the fishermen as the 'Pearl Perch', and is said to be a most excellent food fish. **1906** D.G. Stead *Fishes of Aust.* 104 The Pearl Perch . . is another of our tropical or semi-tropical forms. . . In Queensland it is known usually as 'Epaulette-Fish'. **1936** T.C. Roughley *Wonders Great Barrier Reef* 246 The pearl perch or epaulette fish which grows to a weight of about ten pounds and is one of the finest edible fish found in Australian waters. **1974** J.M. Thomson *Fish Ocean & Shore* 135 The name pearl perch is derived from a bony protuberance behind the head which in life is covered by a thin black skin. But this is often ruptured during handling so that the pearly white bone beneath is revealed. **1985** *Austral. Gourmet* Aug. 47 Just sauteed the pearl perch for one and a half minutes precisely.

peasouper. *Obs.* [In allusion to the 'pea-soup fog', long associated with London.] A recently arrived British immigrant.

1862 C. Stretton *Mem.* II. 40 Twig that new chum; he's a real pea-souper. **1906** E. Dyson *In Roaring Fifties* 66 'Pea-souper!' trumpeted a horseman through his hands. There were sarcastic references to 'lime-juice', and Jim was asked by several strangers . . if his mother knew he was out. *Ibid.* 68 They've been hazing you properly, mate. Pea-soupers and lime-juicers are strangers off shipboard.

peb. *Obs.* [Abbrev. of Pebble 1.] A larrikin.

1903 R. Bedford *True Eyes & Whirlwind* 129 The session broke up—pebs and donahs wandered off in couples. **1907** *Bulletin* (Sydney) 2 May 14/2 A lovely glove-fight between rivals in Melbourne 'peb' circles came off in a patch of suburban bush. . . The trouble was a donah. **1912** L. Esson *Red Gums* 37 'E's the bloke to fite, 'E's the peb, gorblime. **1916** C.J. Dennis *Moods Ginger Mick* 102 They wus pebs, they wus narks, they wus reel naughty boys. **1959** S.J. Baker *Drum* 133 *Peb*, a larrikin.

pebble. [Br. slang, but chiefly Austral.: see OED(S *sb.* 1 c.]

1. A person, esp. a convict or (later) a prisoner in

a gaol, whose behaviour is incorrigible; a reprobate.

1848 *Port Phillip Herald* 29 June 2/4 A few days ago, a carpenter showed a note in one of the public houses in town which circumstance having been observed by three 'pebbles', who were watching him outside, they followed him till he got opposite the Church, when they attacked and attempted to rob him, but having a handsaw with him he resisted and eventually put them to flight. . . The Pentonvillains are becoming a complete pest to Corio. **1854** *Guardian* (Hobart) 22 Feb. 3/5 A Lady 'Pebble', a female passholder . . was charged . . with refusing to work. **1886** *Tasmanian* (Launceston) 27 Feb. 24 The boasted 'pebble' of his brother convicts for many years. **1896** M. HORNSBY *Old Time Echoes Tas.* 22 A 'pebble', one of Major D'Gellon's men, 'here for always' i.e. a lifer . . regaled the select party. **1903** *Bulletin* (Sydney) 2 July 36/2 They sent him . . to Berrima, and there opinion was divided as to whether he was more of a 'pebble' or a 'crank'. **1921** D. GRANT *Through Six Gaols* 93 In this shop were the men who are known in gaol as 'Pebbles', that is, the hard doers. **1962** D. MCLEAN *World turned upside Down* 10 You're new round here and I think I ought to warn you that those two pebbles you was talkin' to would oozle the eyes out of y'r head.

2. *transf.* and *fig.* A stayer, esp. in the phr. **(as) game as a pebble.**

***c* 1863** T. TAYLOR *Ticket-of-Leave Man* 11 Doctor? Nay; I'm as game as a pebble and as stell as a tree! **1888** 'R. BOLDREWOOD' *Robbery under Arms* III. 123 The Turon favourite—a real game pebble of a little horse—began to show up. **1893** K. MACKAY *Out Back* 188 Cabbage Tree Ned is as game as a pebble, and may try to dash through in spite of us. **1918** C. FETHERSTONHAUGH *After Many Days* 277 Traveller was game as a pebble, and he just passed Quadrant on the post and no more. **1945** M. RAYMOND *Smiley* 13 Got your marbles? . . Look at my new tor. It's a real pebble. **1959** S.J. BAKER *Drum* 133 *Pebble*, a person (occasionally a horse) hard to control. Whence, *game as a pebble*, extremely courageous. **1974** D. STUART *Prince of my Country* 166 He was as hard as nails and as game as a pebble.

pedal. *Hist.*

1. Used *attrib.* with various nouns, as **pedal radio, set, transceiver, wireless,** etc., to designate a small radio transceiver with a generator powered by a foot-pedal, invented by A.H. Traeger (1895–1980) to provide a means of communication in remote inland areas.

1930 *A.I.M. Frontier News* Aug. 3 (*caption*) A 'Woman of the West', busy at her work of shattering isolation with the aid of an A.I.M. 'Pedal' Radio Transmitter. **1932** *Ibid.* Mar. 35 The installation of a pedal wireless set at the Wimmera Home at Victoria River Downs is recommended for consideration by the Executive. **1939** J.W. COLLINGS *8000 Miles by Air* 1 Mr A.H. Traeger, well-known to all in the Outback as the manufacturer of the Pedal Transceiver (wireless receiving and transmitting set). *Ibid.* 3 That evening, Dr Vickers had arranged for me to address the pedal set outposts. **1946** E.A. FELDT *Coast Watchers* 5 The invention of the pedal radio gave them a link with the outside world. **1947** F. CLUNE *Roaming around Aust.* 236, I wanted to go on to Darwin, so I sent a message by pedal wireless to the Hon. Drakeford, Minister for Air, a couple of thousand miles away across the continent in Melbourne. **1950** *New Settler in W.A.* (Perth) July 11 At last Mr Alf Traeger produced the 'pedal transceiver'—a wireless set powered by an ingenious contraption similar to bicycle pedals and capable of transmitting as well as receiving. **1961** *N. Austral. Monthly* Dec. 9 It was from here that Flynn and Alfred Traeger experimented with the first pedal wireless sets. **1973** M. STEEL *Red Rover* 156 Messages were transmitted from Beltana on Alf Traeger's 'pedal wireless' and successfully picked up at Cordillo. **1976** J.H. TRAVERS *Bull Dust on Brigalow* 34 By the use of the pedal wireless . . everybody knew of our whereabouts.

2. In the phr. **on the pedal,** through the medium of the *pedal transceiver.*

1962 C. GYE *Cockney & Crocodile* 71 Mr and Mrs Arnold welcomed us with tea and scones at Ivanhoe, having heard us 'on the pedal' (the radio telephone, or Traeger transceiver, so called as it used to be worked by pedalling on a thing like a bicycle while speaking).

Hence **pedal** *v. trans.*, to transmit (a message) in this way.

1940 *Frontier News* Apr. 2/3 He called us periodically and we pedalled back news to him.

peel, *v.* [Joc. use of *peel* to strip.] *trans.* To shear (a sheep). Also as *ppl. a.*

1912 *Bulletin* (Sydney) 28 Nov. 16/4 One of the fraternity confided to me on the board . . that he 'had peeled 88, and was dragging the chain behind Nugget Smith', but had bet him a bottle of sheep dip 'that he'd 'wheel him next day'. **1915** *Ibid.* 14 Oct. 24/2 The unfortunate quadrupeds he gets his 'bit of dough' for 'peeling' are 'the woolies' [*sic*]. **1923** *Ibid.* 1 Nov. 24/3 At many Out-West peeling establishments goats—always more manageable than the woollies—are regularly used as leaders.

peewee /'piwi/. [Transf. use of *peewee*, var. of imitative *pe(e)wit* lapwing.]

1. *Magpie lark*, see MAGPIE *n.* 2. Also **peeweet, peewit.**

[**1827** P. CUNNINGHAM *Two Yrs. in N.S.W.* I. 232 In the morning . . the dull monotonous double note of the *whee-whee* (so named from the sound of its calls), chiming in at as regular intervals as the tick of a clock.] **1904** *Emu* IV. 72 Peewees (*Grallina*) with young in the nest. **1922** M. GILMORE *Hound of Road* 141 A peeweet clashed his wings as he called with plangent cries to his mate. **1948** J. FAIRFAX *Run o' Waters* 115 The sacred kingfisher, chasing a worried pee-wit from his private hunting ground. **1952** *Coast to Coast 1951–52* 165 A gum-tree in which a pee-wee had built its neat mud nest. **1981** A.B. FACEY *Fortunate Life* 90 The peewit was a light brown bird with some black streakings on its back and wings, and a white breast marked with a U-shaped black half circle.

2. A bowler hat. Also **peewee hat.**

1910 *Truth* (Sydney) 13 Mar. 11/6, I bought some bran' noo clobber, an' a little peewee hat. **1926** G. BLACK *Hist. N.S.W. Political Labor Party* ii. 10 In Sydney, most city men wore either tall hats, or straw boaters (stiff and hard), or 'pee-wees' (now known as 'bowlers') [etc.]. **1966** A.R. CHISHOLM *Familiar Presence* 80 A hat was a 'cady', and consequently a boater became a 'straw cady'; and what is now called a 'bowler' used to be a 'hard-hitter' or a 'pee-wee'. **1975** G.A.W. SMITH *Once Green Jackaroo* 54 Sydney was raucous over my bowler hat: it was called a 'bloody peewee 'at', presumably after the little pee-wee bird that flaps rather than flies, is black and white, and swings its bottom fantastically while standing still.

peg, *n.*[1] *Obs.* [Scot. dial. *peg* a shilling.] One shilling (but see quot. 1950).

1882 *Sydney Slang Dict.* 3 *Deaner*, a shilling. Also, Peg, Twelver, &c. **1895** *Bulletin* (Sydney) 16 Feb. 21/2 'Peg', larrikinese for shilling. **1904** L.M.P. ARCHER *Bush Honeymoon* 213 I'm old an' lonely an' poor—ten peg per week, an' lucky to get it. ***c* 1907** W.C. CHANDLER *Darkest Adelaide* 58 Dig up another sprat so that I will have a couple of peg for myself. **1950** *Austral. Police Jrnl.* Apr. 117 *Peg*, 2s.

peg, *n.*[2] *Obs.* [Of unknown origin.] In the phr. **to put in the peg,** to desist from an activity, esp. the consumption of alcoholic liquor.

1896 *Bulletin* (Sydney) 22 Feb. 27/2 Mr Murphy . . had been 'on a fair bend' for a week. The grog had got on to his nerves, and there was a hand of iron gripping the back of his neck. The doctor said that it was 'cerebral congestion', and that if Mr Murphy didn't put the peg in there would be trouble. ***c* 1907** W.C. CHANDLER *Darkest Adelaide* 4 Little kids whose parents takes them Out upon the streets to beg, Ain't supposed to grow up honest, Never can't put in no peg. **1919** *Bulletin* (Sydney) 14 July 20/2 This is the record for 'putting in the peg'. . . A local identity was one of the best customers that the only pub in the place had. One day he . . called for a long sleever. 'Wait a minute, Joe,' said the beer-hoister. . . 'No, I'll be blanked if I wait. I'll go out to the pump, and I'll never take another blanky drop of your or anybody else's beer.' And he never did. **1921** K.S. PRICHARD *Black Opal* 59 Michael says he works like a chow . . has to make him put in the peg. **1929** W.J. RESIDE *Golden Days* 334 For several weeks he had 'put in the peg'.

peggy. [Transf. use of *peggy* a ship's mess-steward.] An unskilled worker responsible for tea-making, etc.

1971 J.P. GILDERS *Man Alone* 44 'Who'd work on the railways for a lousy $36 a week. Only a poor bastard like me.' 'You've got it easy,' Paul laughed. 'You're only the 'peggy' aren't you?' **1971** J. O'GRADY *Aussie Etiket* 5 On the Peggy's call of 'Smoko' all tools are dropped, and work ceases for an official ten minutes. **1986** *Bulletin* (Sydney) 8 Apr. 36/1 There are refrigerated water fountains . . a subsidised canteen and a 'peggy', a man paid by the contractors to make the tea and organise the lunches in each of the crib huts.

peg-leg. Chiefly *N.T.* [See quot. 1985.] A disease of cattle attributed to phosphorus deficiency. Also *attrib.*

1953 T.G. HUNGERFORD *Diseases of Livestock* (ed. 3) 469 *Phosphorus deficiency disease in cattle.* Other names . . peg-leg disease (Northern Territory). **1954** W.A. BEATTIE *Beef Cattle Breeding* 361 Peg-leg is a nutritional disease of cattle common in certain parts of Queensland. **1962** *N. Austral. Monthly* Mar. 30 In the well-known 'peg-leg' country around Charters Towers and in the Cloncurry-Barkly Tableland area, phosphorus deficiency is severe. **1985** P.J. SCHMIDT *Beef Cattle Production* (ed. 2) 48 *Hypophosphorosis* or phosphorus deficiency is very widespread in Australia. . . The classical symptoms are increasing porosity and fragility of the bones, painful stiff-legged gait (hence the alternative name of 'peg-leg'), depraved appetite and bone chewing.

pen. [Spec. use of *pen* a small enclosure for domestic animals.]

1. A division in a shearing shed.

1879 'AUSTRALIAN' *Adventures Qld.* 113 There was a pen in front of the shearing-floor, holding from thirty to sixty sheep, according to the number of shearers. **1891** *Conference Amalgam. Shearers' Union & Pastoralists' Fed. Council* 8 Before commencing work the shearer shall draw lots for his pen. **1893** 'OLD CHUM' *Chips* 42 Down each side [of a woolshed] is a clear space about ten feet wide called the 'board'. Here the shearing is done by a long row of men on each side. In the middle is a large enclosure, or 'pen', into which the sheep are driven from outside, and there are smaller pens, called 'catching pens', on each side, which are fed from this large one. **1895** *Worker* (Sydney) 21 Sept. 4/4 On Mena Murtra the other day the boss, after imbibing a little too freely, 'pounded' a man's sheep and up to the present time has refused to count them to him. What about getting back to the good old days of 'raddling' and opening the gate of a man's pen? **1908** W.H. OGILVIE *My Life in Open* 36 In a 'centre-board' shed the pens containing the sheep are around the outside of this board; in a 'double board' shed the pens are in the middle. **1912** J. BRADSHAW *Highway Robbery under Arms* (ed. 3) 37 You could not leave the shed without the permission of the man over the board, or you would be fined the ensuing pen of sheep.

2. *transf.* A job as a shearer.

1897 *Worker* (Sydney) 11 Sept. 1/1 Now when by chance he gets a 'pen' he buys a pair of 'tongs'. **1904** *Shearer* (Sydney) 6 Aug. 3/5 To Shearers. Your Applications for Pens will be promptly acknowledged. Can give Runs of Three and Four Sheds. **1912** R.S. TAIT *Scotty Mac* 25 You are almost sure to get a pen there. **1924** H.E. RIEMANN *Nor'-West o' West* 112 Every shearer hankered after a 'pen' at this station, many even went to the expense of 'buying in', in order to be with the chosen few. **1957** D. WHITINGTON *Treasure upon Earth* 12 Anxious to help organise the pastoral industry workers, he 'took a pen' in a shearing shed several years in succession. **1975** B. FOLEY *Shearers' Poems* 9 Two Kiwis left, their mother sick And took off for Rotorua. Two Aussies occupied their pen. **1984** P. READ *Down there with me on Cowra Mission* 43 'Yes, I want to ring up about a pen.' That's what they call the shearing, see, a pen.

3. Special Comb. **pen-mate,** a shearer who takes sheep from the same pen as another shearer.

1895 *Worker* (Sydney) 28 Sept. 4/1 And when I asked my pen-mate's name Off one of the chaps I know, 'Why old son,' says he 'that's Billy McGee, 'Big dog' of the old Barcoo.' **1912** R.S. TAIT *Scotty Mac* 9 Men from the Western plain Are greeting from the Eastern hills old pen-mates once again. **1956** F.B. VICKERS *First Place to Stranger* 236, I was shearing on number three stand, and working pen-mates—as we call it—with Curly the

Union rep. **1980** J. WRIGHT *Big Hearts & Gold Dust* 83 Just tell him ya was pen-mates with Barney Walsh.

penal, *a. Hist.* [Spec. use of *penal* of, pertaining to, or relating to punishment. Used elsewhere but esp. with reference to Aust.] In special collocations: **penal colony, establishment, settlement, station,** *convict colony, establishment, settlement, station,* see CONVICT B. 3; **gang,** GANG; **servitude,** see SERVITUDE.

1827 P. CUNNINGHAM *Two Yrs. in N.S.W.* I. 212 A **penal colony**, however, to prove fully beneficial to the mother country, must be regulated so as efficiently to *punish* the crime committed, before the *reform* of the criminal is thought of; and in this particular has hitherto consisted the great defect of our New South Wales system. **1838** *S. Austral. Rec.* (London) 14 Nov. 116 There is nothing which so strongly recommends the new colony of South Australia as its entire freedom from convicts and *convictism*. Perhaps it might be called the most distinguishing feature in the whole picture, and the very one which gives it so vast a superiority over the old penal colonies of New South Wales and Van Diemen's Land. **1840** *Port Phillip Patriot* 11 June 2/3 The inhabitants of Australia Felix are residents of a Free Province now forming an integral part of a penal colony. **1843** *Sydney Morning Herald* 4 Sept. 2/8 We have been living here under the blackness of the shadow of being a penal colony. **1848** *Maitland Mercury* 2 Aug. 1/6 We regret to state that the arrival of the *Bangalore* places beyond doubt the intention of the home government to still inflict upon this island the lasting stigma of a penal colony. **1861** W. WESTGARTH *Aust.* 90 Criminals, after expiating some part of their sentence in the penal colony, received a pardon conditional on their not returning to England. **1837** W.B. ULLATHORNE *Catholic Mission Australasia* 8 From 1803 . . to 1821, it continued to be a mere **penal establishment.** **1840** *HRA* (1924) 1st Ser. XX. 529 Norfolk Island may not be . . a fit place for an extensive Penal Establishment. **1858** N.L. KENTISH *Treatise Penal Discipline* 5 There are attached to the Penal establishment of this colony of Victoria, in Australia, and were in November, 1856 . . four floating hulks. **1827** P. CUNNINGHAM *Two Yrs. in N.S.W.* II. 297 The police magistrate . . should . . sentence him to work a certain period, in single or double irons, in a **penal gang** employed in the distant interior of the colony upon road and bridge making. **1841** *Port Phillip Patriot* 22 Nov. 4/2 He has never yet been assigned, or had one single chance of doing good extended to him, but has now been kept three years in a penal gang. **1847** J.B. ATKINSON *Penal Settlements* 15 We find that old form of gregarious punishment, penal gangs, still retained, but under the new name of probation gangs. **1820** H.G. BENNET *Let. to Earl Bathurst* 20 It has now risen from the degraded state of a **penal settlement,** to the station of a colony, peopled by many thousand free Englishmen. **1824** *HRA* (1921) 3rd Ser. IV. 143 A penal Settlement like Macquarie Harbour . . can only be effectual with those whose habits of life require very strong measures to change them. **1829** *Sydney Monitor* 16 Feb. 1500/4 Does the King allow his servants at penal settlements the luxury of mangles, emu-egg stands, work-boxes, bush-canteens, etc. etc.? **1836** J.F. O'CONNELL *Residence Eleven Yrs. New Holland* 72 'Penal settlements' . . are the places to which criminals are sent after conviction, before a colonial court, of offences which degrade them even below the Botany Bay standard. **1839** *Port Phillip Patriot* 20 Mar. 3 Australia Felix . . is as *free* from being a *penal* settlement as the most Antipenal Adelaidian can wish. **1845** G. COMBE *Penal Colonies* 13 Penal settlements . . should be separated from free colonies altogether. **1857** M.B. HALE *Transportation Question* 17 The progress of the two free colonies has been more rapid than that of the two penal settlements. **1869** F. ALGAR *Hand-Bk. Qld.* 3 Whatever benefit Western Australia may have gained from the labour of convicts, it has suffered far more injury from the unpopularity which is attached to it as a penal settlement. **1885** MRS C. PRAED *Austral. Life* 3 Queensland, then Moreton Bay, was a small penal settlement, when convicts and bushrangers abounded. **1825** Tas. Colonial Secretary's Office Rec. 1/2 154, The privations he must necessarily be subject to at that **Penal Station.** **1837** *Colonist* (Sydney) 9 Feb. 47/1 There are now five penal stations or jails about Sydney. **1845** J. FRANKLIN *Narr. Hist. Van Diemen's Land* 40 The object of this expedition was to visit the abandoned penal settlement of Macquarie Harbour . . to re-establish a penal station there for the reception of the doubly-convicted felons . . sent . . from New South Wales and Norfolk Island. **1852** J. MORGAN *Life & Adventures W. Buckley* 14 The particular locality had been chosen as the site of a penal station, it being six hundred miles from the nearest settlement, Sydney. **1878** R.B. SMYTH *Aborigines of Vic.* I. 174 Port Macquarie and Moreton Bay are both occupied at present as penal stations.

penalty rate. A 'penalty' imposed on an employer: an additional payment prescribed in an award for work required of employees outside normal hours or under abnormal conditions: see quots. 1950 and 1981.

1948 *Industr. Information Bull.* Feb. 89 The Commissioner made orders increasing the penalty rate applicable to work performed on a holiday. **1950** *Ibid.* July 599 The insulation board concerned . . was not loose insulation material, for which the award prescribed a penalty rate. **1956** S. HOPE *Diggers' Paradise* 98 All workers when they 'work back'—do overtime—come on to 'penalty rates' as they are called. **1973** *Bulletin* (Sydney) 25 Aug. 3/3 We will expect to be dealt with on exactly the same basis as any other Commonwealth public servant, i.e. a 36¾-hour-week, penalty rates for overtime [etc.]. **1981** SHEEHAN & WORLAND *Gloss. Industr. Relations Terms* (ed. 2) 56 Penalty rates are special payments prescribed in awards for work outside the normal spread of hours, e.g. overtime, work on weekends, and public holidays. **1985** *Austral.* (Sydney) 18 Aug. 1/2 N.S.W. shop assistants have had their penalty rate for working Saturday afternoon reduced from time-and-a-half to time-and-a-quarter.

pen and ink. Rhyming slang for 'drink'.

[N.Z. **1963** *N.Z. Truth* (Wellington) 21 May 19 We wander over to the bar for a pen and ink.] **1967** *Kings Cross Whisper* (Sydney) xxxviii. 10/1 *Pen and ink*, drink. **1968** J. ALARD *He who shoots Last* 106 Are ya gonna have a pen an' ink?

pencil, *n.* Used *attrib.* in the names of plants: **pencil cedar,** any of several trees of various fam., yielding a useful timber, as *Glochidion ferdinandi* (fam. Euphorbiaceae) of n. and n.e. Aust.; the wood of these trees; **orchid,** either of two epiphytic orchids (fam. Orchidaceae) of Qld. and N.S.W., *Dendrobium teretifolium*, having long pendulous leaves, and *D. beckleri*, having thick, erect leaves; **pine** *Tas.*, a coniferous tree, usu. *Athrotaxis cupressoides* (fam. Taxodiaceae) of wet sites in Tas.

1820 *HRA* (1921) 3rd Ser. III. 18 An inferior kind called **pencil Cedar** is abundant and useful as a Common Wood. **1848** J. SYME *Nine Yrs. Van Diemen's Land* 60 The woods that are most esteemed for the fitting up of houses . . are Huon pine, black and silver mimosa, pencil cedar, and sassafras. **1871** *Austral. Town & Country Jrnl.* (Sydney) 3 June 683/1 This small tree, regularly scored up and down, is a pencil cedar, with sap like blood. **1882** *Austral. Handbk.* 391 Several species of *Dysoxylon* produce valuable timber, which is sometimes called 'Pencil-cedar'. **1903** *Tasmanian Timbers* (Tas. Lands & Survey Dept.) 25 King William pine (*Athrotaxus selaginoides* and *Athrotaxis cupressoides*—Cypress-like) . . is extremely light and has a scent like cedar, from which it is called 'Pencil Cedar' locally. **1944** J. DEVANNY *By Tropic Sea & Jungle* 128 The cedars, with the exception of the pencil cedar which is pinkish cream, are all shades of red. **1981** *Access* Dec. 6/1 The handsome palm-like *Tieghemopanax murrayi* (Pencil Cedar) is restricted to East Gippsland, occurring in isolated pockets in the Howe Ranges. **1909** F.M. BAILEY *Comprehensive Catal. Qld. Plants* (ed. 2) 526 *Dendrobium teretifolium* . . **Pencil Orchid.** **1935** DAVISON & NICHOLLS *Blue Coast Caravan* 239 The green-leafed and delicate-hued blooms of the pencil orchid and golden orchid. **1966** B. BEATTY *Around Aust.* 248 Other beautiful and unusual orchids found in Cape York Peninsula are the Pencil orchid [etc.]. . . The Pencil is a very sweetly-scented variety and when in bloom the whole plant has the appearance of an exquisite wedding bouquet. **1979** K.A.W. WILLIAMS *Native Plants Qld.* I. 88 *Dendrobium teretifolium* . . Pencil Orchid. . . The long pencil-like leaves grow from the rhizome. **1846** N.L. KENTISH *Work in Bush Van Diemen's Land* 22 The Celery-topped Pine is met with in the ranges of the upper part of the River Forth. [*Note*] This wood, also called the '**Pencil Pine**', is a handsome specimen of the Fir species. **1891** J. FENTON *Bush Life Tas.* (1964) 168 He also discovered at that period the beautiful pencil pine which grows in the southern and still unsettled parts of the district. **1964** D.J. BOLAND et al. *Forest Trees Aust.* 57 Pencil pine (*Athrotaxis cupressoides*) growing alongside Pine Creek near Cradle Mountain, central Tasmania. This species is usually a small tree occurring near the tree-line on cold wet sites in Tasmania. **1985** *Mt. Field Nat. Park* (Tas. Nat. Parks & Wildlife Service), Thickets of fagus . . grow with . . Pencil pines (*Athrotaxis cupressoides*) by the roadside near Lake Fenton.

pencil, *v. Horse-racing.* [Extended use of *pencil* to enter (a horse's name) in a betting book (apparently rare in Br.): see OED *v.* 2 b.] *intr.* To act as a bookmaker's clerk. Also as *vbl. n.*

1919 C. DREW *Doings of Dave* 84 The first thing to be done was to find a clerk, as Thimble could not pencil. **1949** L. GLASSOP *Lucky Palmer* 30 We did all right nine years ago when we took the punters on. What about me pencilling for you? **1950** 'B. JAMES' *Advancement Spencer Button* 61 Mr Jennings . . 'pencilled for a bookie' on Saturdays. **1978** N. EVERS *Tas. Paradise & Beyond* 40 She recalled doing some 'pencilling' for Gunboat Smith who was S.P. Bookie.

penciller. [Survival of Br. slang *penciller* bookmaker's clerk: see OED 2 a.] A bookmaker or bookmaker's clerk.

1891 *Truth* (Sydney) 11 Jan. 55 The recognised professional 'pencillers'. **1913** A. PRATT *Wolaroi's Cup* 62 This horse 'pulled' at the secret instance of the 'pencillers'. **1933** H.B. RAINE *Whip-Hand* 271 The notes were splendid imitations, and in the bustle of the betting-ring there was hardly a chance that the busy pencillers would detect them. **1949** L. GLASSOP *Lucky Palmer* 240 A good penciller is a bookmaker's first essential to success. At any time the penciller can tell them their potential liability on every horse and often warns them it would be dangerous to lay any more. **1965** *Tracks we Travel* 178 Andy was 'Arry's clerk at the dogs! One of the best pencillers in the country. **1978** H.C. BAKER *I was Listening* 187 This fellow should make a fair bricklayer, but his real vocation would be as a bookmaker's penciller.

penda /'pɛndə/. [Prob. f. a Qld. Aboriginal language.] Any of several trees of the genera *Xanthostemon* and *Ristantia* (both fam. Myrtaceae), esp. (and orig.) the large *X. oppositifolius* of s.e. Qld., having very hard, brown wood; the wood of the tree. Also **penda tree.**

1890 F.M. BAILEY *Catal. Indigenous & Naturalized Plants Qld.* (ed. 2) 101 Penda-tree—Xanthostemon oppositifolius. **1903** *Austral. Handbk.* 279 Large trees . . which furnish hard durable timber are . . 'Peebeen' . . 'Penda' (*Xanthostemon oppositifolius*). **1938** C.T. WHITE *Princ. Bot. Qld. Farmers* 190 *Xanthostemon* is a genus of few species scattered throughout the Malay Archipelago, New Guinea, and Australia. Several are found in Queensland, and most of them are known as Penda. **1944** J. DEVANNY *By Tropic Sea & Jungle* 130 The penda, startlingly heavy, weighing like iron in the hand, has the rosy glow of the sky after sunset. **1956** A.C.C. LOCK *Tropical Tapestry* 227 We proceeded farther along this superb road, lined with black penda trees.

Penguin award. [From the supposed resemblance between the award, a stylized sculpture of the human ear surrounded by a television screen, and a penguin.] One of the annual awards for excellence in the industry made by the Television Society of Australia.

1966 *Age* (Melbourne) 7 Nov. 11/4 Two Penguin awards were given for documentary films after 13 entries had been considered. **1973** *Sun News-Pictorial* (Melbourne) 3 Dec. 13/3 The ABC serial 'Seven Little Australians' made a virtual clean sweep in this year's Penguin awards. **1985** *Age* (Melbourne) 26 Jan. 13/4 The society held its annual Penguin Award presentation last night.

penner-up. In a shearing shed: one who pens sheep preparatory to their being shorn. Also **penner.**

1887 K. MACKAY *Stirrup Jingles* 46 It was during last shearing that the boss gave a penner the go. **1894** *Bulletin* (Sydney) 10 Feb. 20/4 Stir yourselves, you penners-up, and shove the sheep along. **1908** C.H.S. MATTHEWS *Parson in Austral. Bush* 136 There are the 'penners-up', who had the difficult job of driving the sheep into the pens in the sheds. **1922** *Bulletin* (Sydney)

6 Apr. 20/4 Every shearer seems to think the penner-up shoves all the hard sheep on to him. **1927** J. MATHIEU *Backblock Ballads* 6 And the penners yell and quiver As they jam the jumbucks down. **1934** E. STOREY *Eve's Affairs* 59 The 'penner-up' .. deals out sheep to the shearers and is kept really busy. **1963** D. NILAND *Dadda Jumped* 58 Maybe I had a yarn with the presser, or the penner-up, or one of the shearers. **1979** HARMSWORTH & DAY *Wool & Mohair* 150 The *penner-up* is responsible for the sheep in the shed. He keeps the catching pens full and helps to put the woolly sheep in the sweating pens.

pensioner. *Hist.* [Spec. use of *pensioner.*]

1. A person in receipt of a pension for military service, as a Chelsea pensioner, who has commuted the pension for a passage and emigrated to Australia. Also *attrib.*

1832 *Colonist* (Hobart) 28 Sept. 3/2 Useless free people, such as the poor pensioners, who have in fact been defrauded by the British Government. **1834** J.D. LANG *Hist. & Statistical Acct. N.S.W.* II. 217 Most of the pensioner-emigrants .. had been induced to commute their pensions for a passage to the Australian colonies. **1847** *Hobart Town Herald* 23 Jan. 3/1 Some poor old commuted pensioners who stand most grievous in need of relief. **1852** *Guardian* (Hobart) 10 Jan. 3/3 Four Pensioners, who were employed as police constables, have preferred to forsake all their claims on Government. **1865** 'SPECIAL CORRESPONDENT' *Transportation* 9 Even in the towns, the only peculiarity he will observe is the presence of the pensioners, who do military duty here, and who are attired in the quaintly ugly uniforms familiar to all frequenters of Chatham or Chelsea. **1872** MRS E. MILLETT *Austral. Parsonage* 237 A mixed party of pensioners and convicts to act as road-makers and well-sinkers. **1933** J.L. GLASCOCK *Jarrah Leaves* 32 Her own father had been one of the pensioner guards.

2. See quot. 1812.

1812 J.H. VAUX *Mem.* (1819) II. 195 *Pensioner*, a mean-spirited fellow who lives with a woman of the town, and suffers her to maintain him in idleness in the character of her *fancy-man*. **1903** *Truth* (Sydney) 20 Dec. 5/3 *Pragmatical police* .. permit pensioners on prostitutes to pollute the pavements.

Penton. *Obs.* Abbrev. of PENTONVILLE. Also *attrib.*

1847 *Port Phillip Herald* 29 July 2/5 At the trial of Dr Barker's 'Penton' pets, at the Supreme Court on Tuesday, it oozed out that the five stolen books specified in the indictment were of a rather heterogeneous nature. **1848** *Ibid.* 6 Jan. (Suppl.), The other fellow that escaped is a noted robber, and turns out to be a Van Diemonian; the present prisoner is a Penton.

Pentonvillain. *Obs.* Also **Pentonvillian.** [Blend of PENTONVILLE and *villain.*] An opprobrious term for a PENTONVILLE. Also *attrib.*

1844 *Melbourne Weekly Courier* 21 Dec. 2/3 The degrading of our free and untainted immigrants to a level with the crime-stained Pentonvillains, of whom the first sample came by the *Royal George.* **1847** *Port Phillip Herald* 16 Mar. 2/5 A Pentonvillain named George Rolfe, was fully committed for uttering a forged order. **1848** *Ibid.* 25 May 2/7 If our Downing-street rulers will insist upon our receiving their Pentonvillain and other prison 'pets', they, or the Colonial Government must very soon be prepared to defray the expense of another gaol. **1855** W. HOWITT *Land, Labor & Gold* I. 22 Several of these escaped Van Demonians, or Pentonvillians. **1859** J.D. MEREWEATHER *Diary Working Clergyman* 59 The style of convicts most universally disliked by the gentry, and thoroughly hated by the other prisoners, are those from Pentonville, called 'Penton-Villians'. **1899** G.E. BOXALL *Story Austral. Bushrangers* 176 These contained some prisoners who were supposed to be reformed characters, and were known in Australia as 'Pentonvillains', from the name of the Reformatory in London through which they had passed.

Hence **Pentonvillainy** *n.*, the Pentonvilles collectively; the scheme under which they were sent to the Port Phillip District.

1847 *Port Phillip Herald* 12 Oct. 2/3 With respect to the question of *Pentonvillainy*, it would appear .. that Port Phillip is to be converted into a vast *reportiorum* [*sic*] of sublimated felony. **1848** *Ibid.* 25 Apr. 2/4 It is no harm to say that this province is now enjoying the fruits of *Pentonvillainy.* **1848** *Maitland Mercury* 13 May 4/3 Our gallant delegate .. boasts of .. directing the current of Pentonvillainy to this fair province.

Pentonville. [f. the name of *Pentonville* Prison, London.] One sentenced in Britain to transportation, but required first to serve eighteen months in Pentonville (or another reformatory prison) receiving moral and religious instruction and learning a trade, before being sent to Australia, esp. to the Port Phillip District, on a conditional pardon. Also **Pentonville exile** (see EXILE), **man, prisoner,** etc.

1845 *Portland Gaz.* 22 Jan. 3/1 Pentonville Exiles .. are not so dangerous as colonial convicts. **1845** BACKHOUSE & TYLOR *Life & Labours G.W. Walker* 10 Apr. (1862) 521 The Pentonville men are decidedly the most hopeful set I have seen land here. **1846** W. WESTGARTH *Commercial, Statistical & Gen. Rep. Port Phillip* 21 Some opposition was displayed as to the meeting being committed to an entire approval of an influx of criminal population, even under the mitigated aspect of the Pentonville prisoners. **1847** *Port Phillip Herald* 16 Sept. (Suppl.), The Colonial Government has determined upon defraying one-half the expense of conveying to this colony the families of all Pentonvilles who may have arrived at Port Phillip. **1848** *Maitland Mercury* 19 Feb. 4/4 *Pentonvilles.*—Not a few of these young gentlemen, after having been hired by the settlers to proceed up the country, have refused to enter into their engagements. **1850** J.B. CLUTTERBUCK *Port Phillip* 103 The class known as the 'Pentonville Exiles' (*Pentonvillains*, as they are usually styled) have, with very few exceptions, proved themselves to be sunk in the lowest depths of vice. **1851** *Illustr. Austral. Mag.* (Melbourne) 319 At shearing time .. he had a gang of Pentonville washers and some very bad shearers.

Hence **Pentonville system** *n.*

1847 *Hobart Town Herald* 6 Mar. 2/1 Either by the Probation or Pentonville system. **1847** *Port Phillip Herald* 25 Mar. 2/4 We hear it vauntingly mentioned, that the Pentonville system is giving every satisfaction. Now, after it has had some time to work, experience is beginning to demonstrate the advantages resulting from the importation of half-caste convicts. We are credibly informed that amongst the greatest ruffians in Melbourne a large proportion are Pentonvillains.

pepper, *v. Obs.* [Spec. use of *pepper* to sprinkle like pepper, to scatter in small particles.] *trans.* To make (a mine) appear to be profitable by fraudulently introducing samples of the mineral sought. Also as *vbl. n.*

1851 *Empire* (Sydney) 1 Dec. 418/7 The fraudulent practice of 'peppering', as it is termed—disposing of a barren hole, in which grains of gold are judiciously interspersed to deceive the unwary purchaser. **1853** H.B. JONES *Adventures in Aust.* 288 Advices had previously come out that spurious nuggets and gold dust had been extensively manufactured in Birmingham, either to be sold to gold buyers or else for the purpose of 'peppering' or 'salting' claims, for fraudulent sale on the diggings. **1858** C.R. THATCHER *Colonial Songster* (rev. ed.) 19 Of course you know they'd peppered it, The gold was all a hum; They'd sold it me because they saw I was a green new chum.

peppercorn tree. PEPPER TREE 2. Also **peppercorn.**

1954 *Coast to Coast 1953–54* 76 Who do you think we see sittin' under a pepper-corn tree but this old sundowner. **1965** R. OTTLEY *By Sandhills* 11 Under the peppercorn trees surrounding the homestead, it was already dark. **1984** *Sun* (Sydney) 2 Oct. 18/2 If the meat has a scented taste, most probably the lambs were eating peppercorns, which are grown as shade trees on many western properties.

pepper grass. [Perh. transf. use of *pepper-grass* a plant of the genus *Lepidium* having a pungent taste.] The leafy annual or short-lived perennial grass *Panicum whitei* (fam. Poaceae), of drier parts of all mainland States exc. Vic.

1927 M. TERRY *Through Land of Promise* 265 Spinifex, nardoo, box or pepper grass. **1947** *Proc. R. Soc. Qld.* 158 Panicum Whitei .. sometimes forming a prominent part of the pasture of the 'channel country'. .. It is commonly known as 'pepper grass'. **1976** E.H. MCFARLANE *Land of Contrasts* 43 Another seed .. called 'pepper-grass' seed was ground in a slightly different manner. **1981** G.M. CUNNINGHAM et al. *Plants Western N.S.W.* 122 Pepper grass should be grazed early to retard maturity and encourage new growth.

pepperina. PEPPER TREE 2. Also **pepperina tree.**

1930 V. PALMER *Men are Human* 166 Nothing grew save the drooping pepperina that trailed its sheeny leaves over the kitchen roof. **1944** *Bulletin* (Sydney) 5 July 12/3 Pepperina-trees .. in s.-w. Queensland can easily be kept in check with the ringbarker's axe or poison. **1959** M. RAYMOND *Smiley roams Road* 11 He came to the Greevins' house beneath the lacy, drooping fronds of a tall and beautiful pepperina tree. **1978** D. STUART *Wedgetail View* 102 Two buildings, roofless, with window spaces gaping, walls leaning, and a few pepperina trees.

peppermint. [Transf. use of *peppermint*: see quot. 1790.]

1. Any of many small to large trees of s.e. Aust. incl. Tas., of the genus *Eucalyptus* (fam. Myrtaceae), the leaves of which yield aromatic, peppermint-like essential oils, the trunk often having a fine, fibrous bark; the wood of these trees. Also *attrib.*

1790 J. WHITE *Jrnl. Voyage N.S.W.* 227 App. The name of Peppermint Tree has been given to this plant by Mr White on account of the very great resemblance between the essential oil drawn from its leaves and that obtained from the Peppermint (*Mentha piperita*) which grows in England. **1824** *Hobart Town Gaz.* 1 Oct., Colonial Timber may at any time be purchased of an inhabitant of this town... Peppermint for shingles. **1839** *S. Austral. Rec.* (London) 11 Sept. 232 The trees are mostly of the gum species, as the blue, red, the peppermint or swamp gum, and the gum wattle; the first three are large forest trees. **1853** J. ALLEN *Jrnl. River Murray* 28 We find the wood we shipped at the Darling (peppermint wood) very inferior, and from the small power of steam it generates, we are making but little way. **1861** 'OLD BUSHMAN' *Bush Wanderings* 40 Wherever the gum or peppermint trees grow to any age or size, there you will always find the large opossum. **1874** G. WALCH *Adamanta* 75 Well, mate, it's snug here by the logs—That's peppermint—burns like a match. **1885** *Australasian Printers' Keepsake* 15 Dwarf peppermint-gums, blue-leaved and aromatic, sticky to touch but grateful to smell. **1898** *Proc. Linnean Soc. N.S.W.* XXIII. 796 *E. Sieberiana*, var. *Oxleyensis*, var nov. .. has been called Peppermint with reference to the appearance of the bark alone. **1905** *Emu* IV. 110 The peppermint gum (*E. amygdalina*) .. help to make up the scrub. **1948** F. CLUNE *Wild Colonial Boys* 612 It was wild country, the rugged ranges covered with stringybark and peppermint-gum scrubs. **1955** J. MORRISON *Black Cargo* 201 A flock of magpies flapped noisily upwards out of the peppermints. **1978** *Ecos* xv. 15/2 Nine eucalypt species grow in the forest, the most widespread being .. a peppermint (*E. radiata*), and manna gum. **1984** D.J. BOLAND et al. *Forest Trees Aust.* (rev. ed.) 332 Most peppermint species are notable for their 'peppermint' bark which is persistent, rather short-fibred .. at first brownish weathering to grey. **1985** *Trees & Natural Resources* Dec. 26 The remnant vegetation in the area is *Eucalyptus odorata* (peppermint box) woodland.

2. Any of several other plants, esp. (*W.A.*) the tree or shrub *Agonis flexuosa* (fam. Myrtaceae) of s.w. W.A., having pendulous, peppermint-scented foliage and widely cultivated as an ornamental. See also *willow myrtle* WILLOW 2. Also **peppermint tree.**

1838 *Swan River Guardian* (Perth) 15 Feb. 4 Our peppermint tree is a fine species of *Metrosideros.* **1893** A.F. CALVERT *W.A. & its Gold Fields* 18 For boat crooks, *Agonis flexuosa*, known as the peppermint tree from its odour, is much esteemed by local boat-builders. **1935** E. COLEMAN *Come back in Wattle Time* 40 Cedar wattle (*A*[*cacia*] *elata*). Often called Peppermint. A tall, graceful tree, with large bi-pinnate leaves. **1977** H. BUTLER *In Wild* 79 Peppermint's not a eucalypt—it's a plant called *Agonis.*

pepper-pot, *v. intr.* See quot.

1980 *N.S.W. Parl. Papers* (1981) 3rd Sess. IV. 1749 What is the policy of the Housing Commission—does it pepperpot? A. We are pepperpotting, which is one of the recommendations of the previous select committee, that we should put them [*sc.* Aborigines] into towns and spread them round various streets. What we are doing in non-black towns . . is trying to keep it at two or three to a street. . . Our policy is one of scatteration.

pepper tree. [Transf. use of *pepper-tree* a name given to various trees.]

1. Any of several small trees or shrubs of the genus *Tasmannia* (fam. Winteraceae) having a pungent fruit (but see also quots. 1839 and 1979), esp. *T. lanceolata* of e. N.S.W., e. Vic., and Tas., having reddish stems and a purplish-black fruit. See also *native pepper* NATIVE *a.* 6 a. Also **pepper bush, pepper shrub.**

1827 *HRA* (1926) 3rd Ser. VI. 267 'Pepper Shrub' . . found in Land [*sic*], good soil. **1830** *Hobart Town Almanack* 65 The traveller enters a thick grove of the pepper shrub, Tasmania fragrans of Smith. **1839** T.L. MITCHELL *Three Exped. Eastern Aust.* (rev. ed.) II. 280 We also found the aromatic tea, *Tasmania aromatica*. . . The leaves and bark of this tree have a hot biting cinnamon-like taste, on which account it is vulgarly called the pepper-tree. **1845** *Standard* (Melbourne) 30 Apr. 2/5 The medicinal yielding sassafras, the brilliant myrtle, the pungent pepper tree, the damson like plum, and the coffee tree abound. **1867** *Colonial Monthly* Dec. 245 The tall brake and the graceful crown-fern, and the black-berried pepper-tree with crimson stems, grow in the cool shade of those massive-foliaged lightwoods. **1888** *Proc. Linnean Soc. N.S.W.* III. 506 *Drimys aromatica* . . 'Pepper' tree. **1979** WRIGLEY & FAGG *Austral. Native Plants* 292 *Tasmannia* spp. vary from medium-sized shrubs to trees and most bear the common name of pepper or pepper bush, because of the hot flavour of fruit, seeds or sometimes foliage.

2. [U.S. *pepper tree* the tree *Schinus molle*.] The introduced S. American tree *Schinus molle* var. *areira* (fam. Anacardiaceae), bearing a small, red, aromatic fruit, widely planted as an ornamental and shade tree, esp. near homesteads in inland Aust.; PEPPERCORN TREE; PEPPERINA.

1892 'MRS A. MACLEOD' *Silent Sea* I. 241 There was also an avenue of blue gums and pepper-trees round the house. **1907** *Jrnl. Dept. Agric. Vic.* V. 29 That place where you see the rows of pines and pepper trees. **1923** J. ARMOUR *Spell of Inland* 13 The shearing shed and men's quarters could be seen from the house verandah. . . Around the house there were a few palm and pepper trees. **1941** *Coast to Coast* 2 There was a dogleg fence around it and a pepper-tree drooping over the wood-heap. **1967** M. HORNER *Austral. One-Act Plays: Bk. 3* 87, I used to stand and . . crush the berries from the pepper-trees in my fingers. They had papery shells and hard, sticky seeds. **1981** *Woman's Day* (Sydney) 16 Sept. 6/1 Pink and grey galahs wheeled over the shining tin roof of the infants' school and fluttered through the pepper trees and the blue gums.

per boot, *adv. phr.* [f. *per* by means of + *boot*.] On foot.

1895 K. MACKAY *Yellow Wave* 58 'When you were on the wallaby, you mean?' said Dick, with a laugh. 'Yes, per boot.' **1900** *Bulletin* (Sydney) 8 Dec. 29/3 Johnson and his mate came to the cattle-station 'per boot', and camped beside the garden. **1917** *Ibid.* 4 Jan. 22/2 The worst pastime I know of is travelling per boot. **1922** *Daily Mail* (Sydney) 9 Jan. 7/6 The traveller per boot has now completed the 'first side' of Australia. **1927** *Smith's Weekly* (Sydney) 30 Apr. 19/7 Swagmen, travelling 'per boot', are a rarity on the track. **1941** *Bulletin* (Sydney) 3 Dec. 14/1 Touring Gippsland per boot, Mat was hailed . . by a dog-tired cocky.

perch. [Transf. use of *perch* the fresh-water fish *Perca fluviatilis* and other fish of the fam. Percidae.]

1. Any of many fresh-water or marine fish of various fam., usu. of the order Perciformes and esp. those of the fam. Teraponidae.

1825 B. FIELD *Geogr. Mem. N.S.W.* 48 We were fortunate enough to . . catch a good dish of perch. **1827** P. CUNNINGHAM *Two Yrs. in N.S.W.* I. 328 A vast variety of fish teem in our rivers, but the *perch* is the species oftenest put into requisition by the settler on this side of the Blue mountains. **1840** *S. Austral. Rec.* (London) 21 Mar. 127 The cod is found in the rivers, and the perch in the sea. **1842** *Tasmanian Jrnl. Nat. Sci.* I. 63 *Cheilodactylus carponemus* . . known locally as the Perch. **1870** E.B. KENNEDY *Four Yrs. in Qld.* 123 There are plenty of fish in all the lagoons and rivers . . a fish called perch, which is not at all like one. **1888** *Austral. Handbk.* 368 Most of the fresh-water rivers abound in fish, such as . . perch (therapon). **1906** D.G. STEAD *Fishes of Aust.* 120 The Jackass-Fish (*Dactylosparus macropterus*) . . is generally confounded . . with the Morwong. . . In Tasmania it is fairly common, and is known both as 'Perch' and 'Silver Perch'. **1940** W. HATFIELD *Into (Great?) Unfenced* 16 Naida set a line and caught the delicious inland perch or 'yellow-belly'. **1965** *Austral. Encycl.* VII. 54 *Perch*, a name applied in Australia to many very different species of native fish. There are no indigenous members of the family Percidae, but the English perch or redfin (*Perca fluviatilis*) . . was introduced . . and has become a pest in several rivers. **1978** D. VAWR *Ratbag Mind* 21 The 'perch' (bass) . . would never take anything except, rarely a live prawn in the darker creeks.

2. With distinguishing epithet, as **giant, golden, Macquarie, Murray, pearl, sea, silver,** etc.: see under first element.

perentie /pə'rɛnti/. Also with much variety, as **parentie, parinti, perenty, prenti, printhy, printy.** [Prob. a. Diyari *pirindi*.] The large monitor lizard *Varanus giganteus* of rocky country in arid central and w. Aust. Also *attrib.*

1905 *Observer* (Adelaide) 30 Sept. 48/2 But this is not the Territory you read of—might as well call a printhee an alligator. **1925** H. BASEDOW *Austral. Aboriginal* 127 Of the Lizards, the most favoured are the species of *Varanus*, popularly known as the printhy and the goanna. **1929** E.R. WAITE *Reptiles & Amphibians S.A.* 125 The Perentie is . . the largest Australian species. **1931** *Bulletin* (Sydney) 9 Sept. 21/4 While prospecting east of Charlotte Waters I caught a prenty alive and partly tamed it. **1944** M.J. O'REILLY *Bowyangs & Boomerangs* 120 Circling around and around as far as the sapling would allow was a six-foot prenti caught across the loins with the steel-wire snare. **1946** W.E. HARNEY *North of 23°* 30, I listened wide-eyed to his tales of 'parintis', giant monitor lizards, that would attack a man. **1952** B. BEATTY *Unique to Aust.* 62 The Prenty whose correct name is Perentie often attains a length of seven feet. On its back are round yellow spots. **1957** F. CLUNE *Fortune Hunters* 56 A man could . . live happily . . on a diet of parentie lizards, grubs, berries, roots, honey-ants and grilled euro. **1958** M.D. BERRINGTON *Stones of Fire* 56 'Sounds to me like a printy,' he said. . . He told us about printies as we went. The creature he described . . was a very good word-picture of a dragon. It looked, he said, like a cross between a lizard and an alligator. **1962** D. LOCKWOOD *I, Aboriginal* 12 Fat dripped from the cooking perentie, its tail alone more than a yard long. **1978** O. WHITE *Silent Reach* 203 Carrying her riding boots in one hand and dragging a dead perenty lizard with the other.

perform. [Transf. use of *perform* to act in a play.] *intr.* To display anger or bad-temper; to make a fuss.

1891 *Truth* (Sydney) 3 May 4/5 The 'doing' they get in the padded cells, and often in the associated cells, is explained to the doctor by the allegation that they 'performed'. **1895** *Worker* (Sydney) 3 Aug. 2/4 He cooks for rouseabouts for 3s. per man, and demands 4s. of the shearers, or at least 'performs' when he doesn't get 4s. per man. **1911** L. STONE *Jonah* 45 Ow'l Chook perform, if 'e ain't at Ada's? **1941** S.J. BAKER *Pop. Dict. Austral. Slang* 53 *Perform*, to swear luridly, to give way to temper. **1967** *Kings Cross Whisper* (Sydney) xxxviii. 10/1 *Perform*, make a nuisance of oneself. Bung on an act.

perish, *n.* [f. *perish, v.* to come to a violent, sudden, or untimely end.]

1. a. A period of extreme privation, esp. as caused by lack of water.

1884 A.V. PURVIS Heroes Unsung, I am nearly perished I have left two mates behind both nearly perished. . . I found the three men none the worse for their bit of a perish. **1914** *Bulletin* (Sydney) 18 June 16/4 The sheep were still alive, and even had sufficient strength to make a frenzied dash for the boredrain. . . Their six-day perish, with not one succumbing, must go close to a record. **1922** 'J. BUSHMAN' *In Musgrave Ranges* 148 It would be some time before even their strong young bodies recovered from the 'perish'. **1936** J. KIRWAN *My Life's Adventure* 73 Thirsty men suffer agonies in the bush. . . Bill told us of a 'perish' he had endured. **1941** D. O'CALLAGHAN *Long Life Reminisc.* 56, I would willingly go through it again, except for the three dreadful perishes I underwent. **1955** STEWART & KEESING *Austral. Bush Ballads* p. xix, What seems to be the story of an actual 'perish' from thirst in the desert becomes, if half a lament, half a joke. **1964** D. LOCKWOOD *Up Track* 52 Not that they ever stopped laughing, even at the height of the 'perish'.

b. PERISHER 3.

1968 LINKLATER & TAPP *Gather No Moss* 95 According to bush ethics the dying 'perish' must free his animals to give them a chance of survival.

2. In the phr. **to do a perish. a.** To suffer a period of extreme privation; to be without sustenance (esp. water). See also PERISHER 2.

1897 P. O'FARRELL *Lett. from Irish Aust.* (1984) 94 We were lucky enough to get water and only did a perish twice and then only for the horses. **1911** D.A. MACDONALD *Bush Boy's Bk.* 188 'Doing a perish' is the expressive way bushmen have of describing the sufferings of a lost man who may be at the last extremity for the want of food and water. **1919** *Smith's Weekly* (Sydney) 15 Mar. 2/3 Two dryblowers have done a 'perish' into town from away beyond 'Dead Finish'. **1938** *Bulletin* (Sydney) 23 Mar. 20/2 Have never done a perish . . but have starved once or twice. **1948** M. UREN *Glint of Gold* 29 Bayley fed and tended McPherson, who was suffering from a perish he had done coming in from south of Lake Lefroy. **1952** *Meanjin* 201 There's a chance that Janey, at least, may be still alive. I just can't endure the thought of her doing a perish, out there, in the sand-hills. **1969** A. GARVE *Boomerang* 71 His intention was to enjoy this trip as a well-organised adventure—not to 'do a perish' in the Never Never. **1984** *Overlander* Apr. 29 It must have been mighty reassuring for him to know he had that water to fall back on . . even though he might have to do a 'perish' while covering the intervening distance.

b. To die, esp. of thirst.

1897 A.F. CALVERT *My Fourth Tour W.A.* 141 The party had, indeed, very narrowly escaped 'doing a perish', as the expressive phrase goes out West to describe the fate of a gold-seeker, whose skeleton, picked clean by carrion birds, is found by those who chance upon his tracks. **1908** E. DYSON *Missing Link* 70 Be quiet . . and do a perish here from thirst? **1933** F.E. BAUME *Tragedy Track* 166 When they reached the soak, they found what many a nomad tribe has found in this country: it was empty, having been drained to its last muddy drop by a previous desert party. They were too exhausted to go on. In short, they were on the fringe of what the bushman calls 'doing a perish'. **1944** 'S. CAMPION' *Pommy Cow* 259 Called by Civilisation 'passing out', 'over', or 'on', called quite simply by uncivilised Australians 'slipping your wind' or 'doing a perish'. **1958** F.B. VICKERS *Mirage* (ed. 2) 149 Like a good bushman he conserved the water in his waterbag. He remembered a saying of Mick's: 'Don't drink her dry till you're doin' a perish.' **1973** C.E. GOODE *Stories Strange Places* 142 In one place we pulled up and George stumped over to the grave of a mate of his who had done a perish in the old days. **1980** ANSELL & PERCY *To fight Wild* 31 Something was saying 'maybe you've made a boo-boo, that you'll die, do a perish, which is a pity, a bit of a shame really'.

c. *transf.* To suffer hardship or privation of any kind, not always of an extreme nature (see quot. 1907).

1899 H. LAWSON *Lett.* (1970) 91 Did a three-months' unemployed 'perish', and then went with a mate to a sawmill. **1900** *Pastoral Times* (Deniliquin) 16 June 2/7, I expected to be relieved in the morning, but it was not until 4 p.m., so all hands did a perish on biscuits and very little water. **1907** *Bulletin* (Sydney) 11 July 14/2 At Milparinka did a 'perish' several times at one pub—no whisky, no nothing, except flies and goat. **1925** A. WRIGHT *Boy from Bullarah* 176 I'm doing a perish here at the police station, barefooted and hatless. **1928** —— *Good Recovery* 9 'Over in the Domain, Ada,' he mused, 'there's scores of fellows doin' a perish, while we're living on the best that money can buy.' **1951** CUSACK & JAMES *Come in Spinner* 307 I'm not the bloke to see an old pal what pulled me out of the mud at Passchendaele do a perish for the want of a drink. **1975** X. HERBERT *Poor Fellow my Country* 173 What about opening the joint and getting me a drink. I'm doing a perish.

perish, *v.* [f. prec.]

1. *intr.* To suffer (extreme) thirst. Also *fig.*

1909 *Truth* (Sydney) 25 July 1/6 Many a big skulking fellow in this city reports himself as perishing if he be only two hours without beer and counter lunch! **1917** C. DALEY *Poems* 40 I've sought for gold in East and West,

I've 'perished' on the Bar. **1934** C. SAYCE *Comboman* 60 The country was perishing for rain. **1936** A.W. UPFIELD *Wings above Diamantina* 38 'Pardon me, Nettlefold,' said Knowles, 'for helping myself to your whisky. Ah . . but I was perishing.' **1944** K.S. PRICHARD *Potch & Colour* 56 'There we were,' said Bill, 'the three of us, perishin' for water, eighty miles from anywhere.'

2. [Apparently independent of the obs. Br. use: see OED *v.* 3 a.] *trans.* To kill (a person, etc.).

1934 T. WOOD *Cobbers* 202 'Longreach, the Glory of the West.' Masts & Yards [*sc.* travelling salesmen] . . said it would perish the crows. **1975** B. FULLER *Ghan* 75 'I'll perish you,' he threatened. 'I'll put a half-moon in your belly.'

Hence **perished** *ppl. a.*, **perishing** *vbl. n.* and *ppl. a.*

1876 *Queenslander* (Brisbane) 22 Apr. 11/4 It's a fools' errand we're on, and it would be better to give in and turn back before we get **perished** for want of water. **1879** *Ibid.* 12 Apr. 461/2 The greatest **perishings** I have ever had were in country which I knew, and occurred because I didn't take the simplest precaution. **1922** 'J. BUSHMAN' *In Musgrave Ranges* 128 Down-country, it is quite pleasant to be thirsty, for it makes a drink taste so nice; but desert thirst—or 'perishing' as it is called—is caused by the drying up of the moisture of the body till the organs inside actually cease to work, and the blood clogs in the arteries because it is not liquid enough. **1957** F. CLUNE *Fortune Hunters* 49 I've had to put up with a lot of tough going to bring in perishing blokes who got off the beaten track, and a few who were on the beaten track!

perisher.

1. In the phr. **to go in a perisher,** to pursue (a course of action) with dedication or vigour.

1864 *Sydney Punch* 23 June 40/1 Like a second Quintus Curtius, 'go in a perisher' against that quagmire of slush and corruption known as the Circular Quay. **1867** W.M. AKHERST *Tom Tom, Piper's Son* 12 *Mary* (aside): Spooney he's growin'; I know the signs. *Tom* (aside): A perisher I'll go in. **1868** *Sydney Punch* 25 July 72/1 Henceforth he would 'go in a perisher' for the prosperity of this great country. **1879** 'AUSTRALIAN' *Adventures Qld.* 8 You went in a perisher that there spree. We all thought you was a going to croak. **1888** 'R. BOLDREWOOD' *Robbery under Arms* III. 87 He . . went in an awful perisher—took a month to it, and was never sober day or night the whole time.

2. PERISH *n.* 2 a. and c. Esp. in the phr. **to do** (or **perform**) **a perisher.**

1892 *Bohemia* (Melbourne) 3 Mar. 15 Many thirsty travellers arrived and were languishing for a 'reviver'. Doing, in bush parlance, a 'perisher' for a 'nip'. **1905** J. FURPHY *Rigby's Romance* (1946) 43 'Have it so, then,' says the Lord, 'but they got to go back into the Wilderness of Sin an' do another perisher.' **1911** *Bulletin* (Sydney) 19 Oct. 43/2 The stinging tree and the lawyer vine are unpleasant . . but they keep out of the way in dark scrubs, and, when your business takes you there, and they get hold of you, though you perform a perisher for a minute, you see the 'joke' immediately afterwards. **1936** A. RUSSELL *Gone Nomad* 44 Where one flood will leave behind a well-filled waterhole . . the next, probably, will fill the hole with sand. And that is precisely what had happened here. . . It looked as if we were in for what the Inlander calls a 'perisher'.

3. One who suffers a period of privation; PERISH *n.* 1 b.

1956 H. HUDSON *Flynn's Flying Doctors* 187 Before the days of Flying Doctors, he rescued many a perisher lost in the lonely regions, going out on the track with his camels and blackboys. **1957** F. CLUNE *Fortune Hunters* 49 Australia's Number One Salvager of Desert Perishers squatted on his haunches, tilted his hat, scratched his ear, and grinned.

perk, *n.*[1] *Obs.* [Abbrev. of Br. slang *perkin* beer, 'dandy or affected shortening of the widely-known firm, Barclay and Perkins' (Hotten 1864). Partridge also records *purko.*] Beer.

1913 *Truth* (Sydney) 6 July 3/1 *A battalion of bobbies* put in an appearance, and proceeded to search the house for perk. Their search revealed two demijohns, one of which was about half-full.

perk, *n.*[2] [f. PERK, *v.*] A vomit.

1965 J. O'GRADY *Aussie Eng.* 67 'Perks' are the little extras. . . There is, however, another kind of 'perk'. . . You'll know when you're going to do it.

perk, *v.* [Poss. f. PERK *n.*[1]] *intr.* To vomit, esp. after excessive drinking.

1941 S.J. BAKER *Pop. Dict. Austral. Slang* 53 *Perk, to,* to vomit. **1960** K. SMITH *Word from Children* 93, I perked over my brother's boot. **1965** J. O'GRADY *Aussie Eng.* 67 Never, never, never, perk into the wind. **1967** *Kings Cross Whisper* (Sydney) xxxviii. 10/2 *Perk,* to vomit, usually after large quantities of grog. **1972** A. CHIPPER *Aussie Swearers Guide* 33 An alternative to *chundering* is *perking*. . . Down Under, *perk up* often means *chunder.*

permanent, *a.*

1. Used as a qualifying element with nouns designating a watercourse or other natural source of water, to signify the security of the source in all seasons: **permanent creek, water, waterhole.**

1890 'R. BOLDREWOOD' *Colonial Reformer* III. 117 By degrees it began to be asserted that 'back country' . . paid the speculative pastoral occupier better than the 'frontage', or land in the neighbourhood of **permanent creeks.** **1894** *Bulletin* (Sydney) 6 Jan. 2/1 Every farmer shall have a frontage to the main road and another to a permanent creek. **1963** X. HERBERT *Disturbing Element* 74 An extensive government reserve . . was watered by a permanent creek. **1843** *Sydney Morning Herald* 31 Oct. 4/1 When once known . . the **permanent waters** could be followed, and journeys made accordingly. **1848** T.L. MITCHELL *Jrnl. Exped. Tropical Aust.* 36 Piper was told that the nearest permanent water was 'Niminè'. **1861** *Burke & Wills Exploring Exped.* 2 Spend two or three days at Torowoto . . to find permanent water. **1890** 'R. BOLDREWOOD' *Colonial Reformer* III. 118 He still haunted, cormorant-like, the rivers and creeks—the 'permanent water' of the colonist. **1920** C.H. SAYCE *Golden Buckles* 116, I found water there, too: good, permanent water. **1938** F. BLAKELEY *Hard Liberty* 75 Mount Brown Goldfield . . lacked permanent water. **1966** *Meanjin* 36 When the rest of the north dried out this valley remained because of its permanent water. **1981** A.B. FACEY *Fortunate Life* 70 Many settlers had trouble getting permanent water on their properties and had to cart water from Government wells miles away. **1845** L. LEICHHARDT *Jrnl. Overland Exped. Aust.* 13 June (1847) 289 It . . was the almost constant companion of the **permanent waterholes.** **1858** J.M. STUART *Explorations in Aust.* 21 June (1865) 7 Halted at a large permanent water hole (Andamoka). **1875** J. FORREST *Explorations in Aust.* 36 He found a fine permanent water-hole. **1912** J. BOWES *Comrades* 75 The lagoon, as luck would have it, was a permanent water-hole.

2. In the collocation **permanent head**, the senior executive officer of a department in the public service; the Secretary of such a department.

1915 *Sydney Morning Herald* 14 July 9/3 He said Mr Edwards was recalled on the recommendation of the permanent head of the department. **1922** *Act* (Cwlth. of Aust.) no. 21 Sect. 25 (2), The Permanent Head of a Department shall be responsible for its general working, and for all business thereof, and shall advise the Minister in all matters relating to the Department. **1945** *Cwlth. Parl. Papers* (1945–46) IV. 994 Permanent Heads had reported that officers were listed for consideration for promotion in seniority order. **1957** H.A. SCARROW *Higher Public Service Cwlth. Aust.* 77 The office of permanent head has been the highest to which public servants could aspire. **1978** SMITH & WELLER *Public Service Inquiries* 171 Reasonable security makes it easier for a permanent head to give objective advice to a minister, especially new ministers. **1986** *Canberra Times* 1 Jan. 1/3 Many a minister has been saved from himself by timely advice from his permanent head.

permit. In the collocation **permit to travel**, see quot. 1878.

1878 *Act* (N.S.W.) 41 Vict. no. 19 Sect. 14, Every owner intending to travel three hundred or more sheep from any run shall before leaving the Sheep district in which such run is situated forward to the Inspector of the district a statement in writing of the number description brands and marks of the said sheep and of their intended route and destination and shall obtain from the Inspector a permit containing the particulars set forth in the Second Schedule hereto to travel the said sheep. And every owner introducing sheep from any of the adjoining Colonies shall in like manner obtain a permit to travel as aforesaid from the Inspector for the district into which such sheep shall first pass on crossing the Border. **1882** ARMSTRONG & CAMPBELL *Austral. Sheep Husbandry* 161 Every person travelling with sheep requires a 'Permit to Travel', and must also have a 'Travelling Statement'. The permit is obtained from the inspector of sheep for the district, and the statement from the owner or superintendent of the station from which the sheep start. **1932** J. MCCARTER *Pan's Clan* 155 I've th' travellin' statement in my pocket, with brands and ear marks shown, also the permit to travel . . so we are O.K. with the travelling sheep laws. **1957** *Law Bk. Company's N.S.W. Land Laws Service* Mar. 307 The defendant made an application . . for a permit to travel one hundred and twenty sheep from Dalrye Station to Wagga Wagga.

persuader. [Spec. use of *persuader* something used to compel obedience.] A whip, esp. that used by a bullock driver.

1890 *Observer* (Adelaide) 15 Mar. 41/5, I soon dismounted and from a bush cut a nice pliant 'persuader' for my camel. **1916** *Bulletin* (Sydney) 16 Mar. 22/3 In what remote part does 'Barcoo' find the bullocky with the diminutive leather thong. . . The only pilots I met navigating overland ships used the long-handled persuader, the historic vocabulary and the long teams. **1919** *Ibid.* 13 Nov. 20/4 The bullock-dray was well bogged, and the conductor seemed at the end of his resources. Knowing something of the game I offered to 'give 'em a go', and he handed me the persuader. **1936** *Ibid.* 4 Mar. 21/1 A 'persuader' (stock-whip). **1956** *Truth* (Sydney) 29 Jan. 16/4 George appeared to be in all sorts of trouble trying to locate the persuader. . . Then Mulley parted company with the whip. **1976** C.D. MILLS *Hobble Chains & Greenhide* 123 The twelve or fourteen-foot 'death adder', 'persuader', or 'badge of authority' (whip), is the be-all and end-all of driving the 'serpents'. A good driver seldom hits his bullocks with it. **1984** A. DELBRIDGE *Aussie Talk* 235 *Persuader,* . . a jockey's whip.

Perth doctor: see DOCTOR *n.*[3]

perv, *n.* and *a.* Also **perve.** [Abbrev. of (sexual) *perversion, pervert.*]

A. *n.*

1. *Obs.* Pornographic literature (*attrib.* in quot.).

1942 *'Havildar' Havalook: Mag. H.M.A.T. 'Havildar'* 14 Mar. 1 'Logical Love' . . by that well-known perv-merchant, John . . Hunt.

2. A sexual pervert.

1949 R. PARK *Poor Man's Orange* 38 That dirty old cow, always making up to kids. . . Merv, Merv, the rotten old perv. **1959** E. LAMBERT *Glory thrown In* 18 We used to call him Mud Guts. He was a perv. Special attention given to small boys. **1963** B. HESLING *Dinkumization & Depommification* 116 Two cops, according to the inquiry, booked nearly two hundred 'pervs' a year from this one dunny. **1971** *Bulletin* (Sydney) 6 Feb. 50/2 Get this flaming book even if you have to go through all the indignities of a dirty old perve in a raincoat and shades to buy it. **1978** L. HORSPHOL *Turn down Empty Glass* 125, I don't want your dirty old perv, you lying slut! Why, I wouldn't touch the bastard with a fifty foot pole!

3. One who observes another (or others) with erotic or sexual interest; the act of so observing.

1963 J. CANTWELL *No Stranger to Flame* 15 'Never even saw him. Might have been a spook.' She did up the top button on the green blouse. 'Even spooks like a bit of a perv.' **1968** B. HUMPHRIES *Wonderful World Barry McKenzie,* I feel a bit of a *perve* standing here like this, but I can't help getting an earful of them two lovebirds. **1969** A. BUZO *Front Room Boys* (1970) 38 Like your short dress. . . Ar, get out of it, y'old perv. **1971** J. BARLOW *In All Good Faith* 15 'Let's go have a perve,' suggested Harback. The dance hall was two hundred yards away at the village cross-roads. **1978** D. BALL *Great Austral. Snake Exchange* 49 Come out here for a perve.

B. *adj. Obs.* Pornographic.

1944 L. GLASSOP *We were Rats* 177 Bluey brought a perv book back from Cairo with him.

perve, *v.* [As prec.] *intr.*

a. To act in a sexually perverted manner. Now usu. in weakened sense: to observe with erotic or sexual interest. Freq. with **on,** and as *vbl. n.*

1941 S.J. BAKER *Pop. Dict. Austral. Slang* 53 *Perve, to,* to act as a sexual pervert. **1944** L. GLASSOP *We were Rats*

183 'Doing a bit of perving again?' I asked, looking at the gallery of nudes he had gathered from all sorts of magazines. **1960** *Westerly* iii. 30 He saw our naked bodies and we couldn't tell if he 'perved' on us or was just dreary of watching the same scenery. **1963** B. HESLING *Dinkumization & Depommification* 116 What did they get you for, perving? **1968** D. IRELAND *Chantic Bird* 59 She only took half an hour over that bath, with me up there perving like mad. **1978** R.H. CONQUEST *Dusty Distances* 150 They were pretty enough, I suppose, if you perved on them from a distance. **1981** *Canberra Times* 24 May 8/5 Perve on a naked Brigitte Bardot or Romy Schneider.

b. *transf.* To observe with interest.

1984 *Sydney Morning Herald* 12 July (Life & Home Suppl.) 4/3 More than a million people a year set out on sea trips from the east and west coasts of the United States with the sole purpose of perving on whales.

per.-way. Shortened form of 'permanent way', a railway track. Freq. *attrib.*

1919 *Smith's Weekly* (Sydney) 19 Apr. 10/6 Several gangs of per.-way workers belonging to the Railway Workers' Branch of the A.W.U. are .. denouncing the Commissioners, who refuse to pay award rates. **1953** *Bulletin* (Sydney) 7 Oct. 13/4 One of the per.-way men got hold of an ancient recipe for honeymead. **1969** P. ADAM SMITH *Folklore Austral. Railwaymen* 21, I hired a coach to bring men from camps working on the pipeline that the railways were laying out to the desert and some of the per-way gang came too but not many of them because most of those had their wives living out beside the line with them and they couldn't get away.

peter. [Transf. use of Br. slang *peter* a box or safe.]

1. A prison cell; a prison. See also *black peter* BLACK *a.*[2] 2.

1890 BARRÈRE & LELAND *Dict. Slang* II. 125 *Peter* .. (Australian prison), punishment cell. **1894** *Bulletin* (Sydney) 16 June 20/1 'No. 5 Yard,' said a warder to me .. on the morning after my night's rest in 'the peter'. **1919** C. DREW *Doings of Dave* 68 It's a bit cold in the Peter these times. Hadn't you better let him bail himself? **1941** A.E. CLARKE *Man nobody Understood* 5 He was the one man the prison officials were constantly on their guard against .. whose 'peter' was invariably searched both by day and by night for evidence of some newly-planned villainy. **1950** G.M. FARWELL *Land of Mirage* 122 The snap of handcuffs put an end to the first event. .. Dolly spent the rest of the day, howling for revenge, in the 'peter' at the back of the town. **1962** P.A. KNUDSEN *Bloodwood Tree* 116 Just 'cause the bloody demons had to come out and spill their guts about me spending a night in the peter! .. Why the hell the bloody cop didn't keep *his* mouth shut I don't know. **1971** J. MCNEIL *Chocolate Frog* (1973) 34 Every time a nit lobs in this can, they shove 'im in my peter! **1979** L. NEWCOMBE *Inside Out* 26 Gotta see the doc this morning. Probably get a couple of days in the 'peter'.

2. A witness box.

1895 C. CROWE *Austral. Slang Dict.* 56 *Peater*, the witness box. **1958** V. KELLY *Greedy Ones* 14 Mounting the peter. Going into the witness box.

3. *Obs.* A pack-saddle.

1897 *Worker* (Sydney) 11 Sept. 1/2 Now when the shed at last 'cuts out' he gets his 'little bit' And straps his 'peter' on his 'croc' and quickly does a get. **1898** *Bulletin* (Sydney) 17 Dec. 15/2 The pack-saddle is called the *peter*.

Peter Peter. [Imitative.] *Jacky Winter*, see JACKY *n.*[2]

1917 *Bulletin* (Sydney) 23 Aug. 22/2 Some appropriate names bestowed by the white pfella are .. four-o'clock (the friar-bird or leatherhead) and Peter Peter (the brown fly-catcher). **1954** C. BARRETT *Wild Life Aust. & New Guinea* 157 'Post-boy' and 'Peter Peter' (the call note) are other names for 'Jacky Winter', who ranges throughout Australia.

petrol bowser.

1. See BOWSER 1.

2. *pl.* Rhyming slang for 'trousers'. Also **petrols.**

1971 B. HUMPHRIES *Bazza pulls it Off*, This *randy* Australian bastard passed out cold even before I could get him out of his petrols. **1974** *Bulletin* (Sydney) 2 Nov. 57/2 Trousers are petrols—petrol bowsers.

phascogale /ˈfæskəgeɪl, fæskəˈgali/. [The animal genus *Phascogale* was named by Dutch naturalist C.J. Temminck (*Monographies de Mammalogie* (1824) I. 56), f. Gr. φάσκωλος pouch + γαλῆ weasel, with reference to the long-bodied appearance of the marsupial. The genus formerly included many of the smaller carnivorous Austral. marsupials.]

1. a. Either of the two species of largely arboreal, carnivorous marsupials of the genus *Phascogale* (fam. Dasyuridae); TUAN a.; WAMBENGER. **b.** (Formerly) any of several other marsupials of the fam. Dasyuridae. Formerly also **phascologale.**

1852 J. WEST *Hist. of Tas.* I. 324 The Phascogales are small insectivorous animals, found on the mountains and in the dense forest parts of the island. **1896** B. SPENCER *Rep. Horn Sci. Exped. Central Aust.* II. 19 *Phascologale cristicauda* .. the crest-tailed Phascologale. **1926** A.S. LE SOUEF et al. *Wild Animals Australasia* 332 *Genus Dasycercus* .. and *Phascogale*. .. Small rat-like carnivorous animals. **1970** W.D.L. RIDE *Guide Native Mammals Aust.* 110 Tuans or wambengers are brushy-tailed carnivorous marsupials. .. They are sometimes called phascogales, a name which is an anglicized version of the scientific name *Phascogale*. **1976** *Ecos* vii. 10/1 It took the phascogale only 2 years to regain its former abundance.

2. With distinguishing epithet, as **brush-tailed, Swainson's:** see under first element.

pheasant. [Transf. use of *pheasant.*]

1. a. LYRE-BIRD 1. **b.** *Pheasant coucal.*

1798 D. COLLINS *Acct. Eng. Colony N.S.W.* (1802) II. 88 A few birds which, from the length of the tail feathers, they denominated pheasants. **1804** G. CALEY in A.E.J. Andrews *Devil's Wilderness* (1984) 88, I shot a hen Pheasant as we came along Fern tree Hill. **1825** *Austral.* (Sydney) 10 Mar. 3 The serjeant after travelling all night returned without him, having left him a large kangaroo dog, two pheasants, and a hatchet. **1846** G.W. EARL *Enterprise, Discoveries & Adventures* 80 Another gallinaceous bird, the pheasant, a scraggy creature, rather a libel upon its English namesake, feeds in the swamps, and is a sluggish, stupid groveller. **1859** F. SINNETT *Acct. 'Rush' Port Curtis* 63 Contrary to what a general knowledge of Australian nomenclature would lead one to expect, Pheasant Creek is not so called because destitute of pheasants, but because they exist here in considerable numbers. **1909** LINDSAY & HOLTZE *Territoria* 24 Pheasants (small birds with lovely fantails). **1928** B. SPENCER *Wanderings in Wild Aust.* 551 We came across the Coucal, which is really a cuckoo, but quite unlike most of these in appearance. It is commonly called a 'pheasant' because the male bird has a long, black, arching tail. **1951** D. COLLINS *Vic.'s my Home Ground* 136 He had a bushman's turn for a phrase, and lyre-birds were pheasants to him. **1970** W.S. RAMSON *Eng. Transported* 42 In the case of the *lyrebird*, described also as a *pheasant* or *bird of paradise*, it was the bird's arresting appearance that gave rise to the name.

2. Used *attrib.* in the names of birds: **pheasant coucal,** the long-tailed nest-building cuckoo *Centropus phasianinus* of n. and e. Aust., New Guinea, and nearby islands; COUCAL: *swamp pheasant*, see SWAMP *n.*; also ellipt. as PHEASANT 1 B., and formerly **pheasant cuckoo**; **parrot,** ADELAIDE ROSELLA; **-tailed pigeon,** *brown pigeon*, see BROWN *a.* 1; also **pheasant pigeon.**

[**1801 pheasant coucal:** J. LATHAM *Gen. Synopsis Birds* Suppl. II. 137 Pheasant C. This is a beautiful species .. the whole of the back and wings varied with rufous, yellow, brown, and black, somewhat similar to a *Pheasant* or *Woodcock*. .. Inhabits *New South Wales*, known there by the name of *Pheasant*.] **1827** P.P. KING *Narr. Survey Intertropical & Western Coasts* II. 8 Several black cockatoos and the pheasant cuckoo were seen. **1846** J.L. STOKES *Discoveries in Aust.* II. 24, I shot over [Valentine] island, and enjoyed some very fair sport; especially the pheasant-cuckoo. [*Note*] Centropus Phasianellus—Gould. **1908** E.J. BANFIELD *Confessions of Beachcomber* 103 The swamp pheasant, or pheasant coucal (*Centropus phasianus*) is also an early bird. **1935** DAVISON & NICHOLLS *Blue Coast Caravan* 100 Close by the bracken was a pheasant coucal; a large brownish-coloured bird with a head like a hawk and a long pheasant tail. **1964** M. SHARLAND *Territory of Birds* 180 Coming from the scrub I surprised a clumsy Pheasant-coucal that was feeding by the creek. **1981** A. WILKINSON *Up Country* 69 In the undergrowth creep families of quail and .. the occasional skulking pheasant coucal. **1841** J. GOULD *Birds of Aust.* (1848) V. Pl. 22, *Platycercus adelaidiae* .. Adelaide Parrot .. **Pheasant Parrot,** Colonists of South Australia. **1900** A.J. CAMPBELL *Nests & Eggs Austral. Birds* 631 The Adelaide Rosella or Pheasant Parrakeet is a beautiful species in radiant colouring. .. The South Australians have an equally good vernacular name—Pheasant Parrot. **1969** J.M. FORSHAW *Austral. Parrots* 189 Adelaide Rosella .. other names: Adelaide Parakeet, Pheasant Parrot. **1844** J. GOULD *Birds of Aust.* (1848) V. Pl. 75, From what I could personally observe during my residence in New South Wales, the **Pheasant-tailed Pigeon** resorts entirely to the brushes, as in no instance did I meet with it in the open parts of the country. **1852** J. MACGILLIVRAY *Narr. Voyage H.M.S. Rattlesnake* I. 62 Pheasant-tailed pigeon and the brush-turkey. **1909** *Emu* VIII. 254, I discovered a nest and egg of the Pheasant-tailed Pigeon (*Macropygia phasianella*). **1929** A.H. CHISHOLM *Birds & Green Places* 156 The 'Whoop-a-whoop' of the brownie or pheasant-pigeon. **1943** C. BARRETT *Austral. Animal Bk.* 157 The white-headed pigeon .. and the 'brownie', or pheasant-tailed pigeon .. belong to the wood-pigeon family. .. The brown pigeon with a long tail is native to the Northern Territory, Queensland and New South Wales.

Phillip Island parrot. *Hist.* [f. the name of an island s. of Norfolk Island.] The extinct parrot *Nestor productus* formerly found on Norfolk and Phillip Islands.

1841 J. GOULD *Birds of Aust.* (1848) V. Pl. 6, *Nestor productus* .. Phillip Island Parrot. **1860** G. BENNETT *Gatherings of Naturalist* 214 There was a species of Parrot, now extinct, the Phillip Island Parrot (*Nestor productus*). **1886** F. COWAN *Aust.* 20 The extinct Phillip Island Parrot: cousin-german to the honey-sucking, sheep-destroying and -devouring kea of Zealandia.

phizgig, var. FIZGIG.

phizzer, var. FIZZER *n.*[2]

pialla /paɪˈælə/ *v. Austral. pidgin. Obs.* Also with much variety, as **pai-alla, pialler, pile, piola, pyalla.** [a. Dharuk *bayala.*] *trans.* To tell (news, etc.). Also *intr.*, to talk.

1790 D. SOUTHWELL Corresp. & Papers, *Pī-ă-la*, to speak or talk. **1828** *Sydney Gaz.* 2 Jan., 'All gammon white fellow pai-alla cabon gunyah, me tumble down white fellow.' It was all false that the white fellows said in the Court house, that I killed the white fellow. **1830** R. DAWSON *Present State Aust.* 162 What for piola (talk to) me dat. **1834** G. BENNETT *Wanderings N.S.W.* I. 210 The following is a definition of a clergyman, as once given by one of the aborigines: 'He, white feller, belonging to Sunday, get up top o' waddy, pile long corrobera all about debbil debbil, and wear shirt over trowsel.' **1845** C. HODGKINSON *Aust., Port Macquarie to Moreton Bay* 52, I .. sent Wongarini Paddy, and Billy, to pialla (tell the news) to them. **1845** *Parramatta Chron.* 23 Aug. 4/3 The sable murderers 'pialled news' to a black boy who is attached to the party of Border Police, that they would spear cattle whenever they please, in spite of the Settlers or Police. **1846** *Cumberland Times* (Parramatta) 25 Apr. 4/1 Hearing some alarm was felt in Sydney respecting them, they at once dispatched one of the tribe to Sydney, as a special Courier, to *pialler* news, as to their whereabouts. **1849** A. HARRIS *Emigrant Family* (1967) 213 Stock-keeper pialla (tell). *c* **1891** MRS P. MARTIN *Coo-ee* 274 Debil-debil must be 'piall-ed' (entreated) by the sick person to unbury the hair. **1896** *Bulletin* (Sydney) 18 Apr. 27/1 From Botany came the once familiar words, 'paialla' to tell [etc.].

pic. Abbrev. of PICCANINNY *n.* 1.

1906 *Bulletin* (Sydney) 25 Jan. 14/2 A black gin died .. leaving .. a 'pic' of eight months. **1942** Austral. Archives CRS F1 44/172, He has 8 wives & a number of Pics—the Pics are always fed. **1969** J. DINGWELL *One String* 27 'The schoolteacher aims to have the pics join in,' Brother Seb said. 'Why haven't they joined in all along?' 'Because all along', Brother Seb reminded her, 'they didn't know how to speak our lingo.' **1976** C.D. MILLS *Hobble Chains & Greenhide* 12, I waited behind an anthill, and the 'pics' worked them up close.

picaninna, picaninny, varr. PICCANINNY.

piccabeen /ˈpɪkəbin/. Chiefly *Qld.* [a. Jagara (and neighbouring languages) *bigi* or *bigibin*.] The palm *Archontophoenix cunninghamiana* (see BANGALOW). Also **piccabeen palm.**

1926 M. FORREST *Hibiscus Heart* 118 All along the banks were piccabeen and full-skirted tree fern. **1935** DAVISON & NICHOLLS *Blue Coast Caravan* 165 They ate also the green heart of the piccabeen palm. **1967** E. HUXLEY *Their Shining Eldorado* 367 The piccabean, one of the country's few native palms. **1984** D. JONES *Palms in Aust.* 101 The name of 'Pikki' was used by the Aborigines of Moreton Bay. This ostensibly referred to the expanded leaf base which was used as a water carrier. The name was later extended to 'Piccabeen'.

piccaninny, *n.* and *a.* Chiefly *Austral. pidgin.* Also with much variety, as **picaninna, picaninny, piccanin, pickaninny,** etc. [Transf. use of West Indian *piccaninny* a little one, a child: see OED(S for use elsewhere.]

A. 1. *n.* An Aboriginal child; any child.

1817 *Sydney Gaz.* 4 Jan., Governor, that will make good Settler—that's my Pickaninny! **1826** *Monitor* (Sydney) 18 Aug. 106/3 He had seen the white woman often with her daughter and younger '*picaninna*'. **1832** *Hill's Life N.S.W.* 27 July 2 *Margaret Shannon*, a very *dacent* sort of a body from the Isle of Isles, with a *picaninny* slung gracefully across her shoulders, was accused by her spouse Michael of being too *obstropolus*. **1845** *Port Phillip Gaz.* 13 Sept. 4 A most important looking fellow, with an unusual number of lubras and piccaninnies at his heels. **1854** W. SHAW *Land of Promise* 228 The shrivelled picaninny might have been taken for a log of mahogany. **1864** *Bell's Life in Sydney* 2 Apr. 3/1 Why should Lucas go through the almost superhuman fatigue of getting government situations for his 'piccaninnies' at the rate of three per day. **1875** CAMPBELL & WILKS *Early Settlement Qld.* 5 The blacks . . gathered . . to see us off. Many of the gins and piccaninnies had a regular crying match over it. **1887** 'COMMERCIAL TRAVELLER' *Diary Three Months Trip Qld.* 10 One fine looking blackfellow was seated on a log with his piccaninni in his lap. **1914** R. KALESKI *Austral. Barkers & Biters* 30 An old gin often thinks more of her pup than her piccaninny—not that there is anything to choose between them. **1921** *Bulletin* (Sydney) 6 Jan. 20/3 An old mammie ran to our hut and called us—'Piccaninny tumble down,' she whispered. **1938** X. HERBERT *Capricornia* 48 'These his piccanins?' She nodded to Nawnim and muttered, 'Dat one belong Mark.' **1948** A. MARSHALL *Ourselves writ Strange* 211 A piccaninny clothed in the smooth, lustrous skin of Babyhood, crawled across the floor towards the woman. **1962** *N. Austral. Monthly* Jan. 29 A truck full of lubras in neat print dresses, hair sleekly combed, picaninnies in their arms shining with soapy cleanliness. **1983** K.W. MANNING *In their Own Hands* 188 As a lad . . he was referred to by the Islanders as 'white fella piccaninny b'long Boss'.

2. *transf.* A young animal.

1824 Methodist Missionary Soc. Rec. 14 Sept., Young—shot her down: and he thought she had something in her belly, so he took his knife and cut her open, and a little *pickerninny* tumbled out. **1850** *Bell's Life in Sydney* 22 June 3/2 About twenty kangaroos of all sizes, from the old man down to the picananny. **1965** R. OTTLEY *By Sandhills* 132, I show you kangaroo. Big fella one, an' mary gottim piccanin. Piccanin along belly.

B. *adj.*

a. Little; tiny.

1842 J. HAYTER *Landsman's Log-Bk.* 126 They are afraid of . . pistols, which they call '*pickaninny muckett*'. **1847** G.F. ANGAS *Savage Life & Scenes* I. 131 The girls paid us a visit, asking for 'piccaninny damper', but they had lost their red cheeks owing to the rain. **1852** *Austral. Gold Digger's Monthly Mag.* ii. 46 Their good-humored mates of Ballarat denominated them the 'Picanniny Escort'. **1859** *Colonial Mining Jrnl.* Jan. 75/3 The township here . . is of rather piccaninni dimensions. **1872** 'RESIDENT' *Glimpses Life Vic.* 16 When me piccaninny fellow. **1885** *Adelaide Observer* 29 Aug. 10 Euro is only a piccaninnie run, but its 178 square miles of country carry 17,000 sheep. **1893** *Bulletin* (Sydney) 18 Feb. 15/2 'Old-man' is used to denote anything large. . . The adopted corruption 'picanniny', to denote anything small and insignificant, such as the church-collection currency. **1900** R. BRUCE *Benbonuna* (1904) 58 'How far is it to the station . . ?' . . 'Only pickaninny way; but you see me plenty tired.' **1911** A. SEARCY *By Flood & Field* 23 A trepang camp . . only a 'piccaninny' way off. **1951** E. HILL *Territory* 322 Somewhere there he had heard of a native well or soak—picaninny water, he showed them with his hand. **1968** S. GORE *Holy Smoke* 17 Bimebye plenty piccaninny, tree longa that one seed.

b. Special Comb. **piccaninny dawn, daylight, light, sun,** the approach of dawn, first light; **twilight,** the last glow of the setting sun.

1936 M. FRANKLIN *All that Swagger* 125 At **piccaninny dawn**, the billy with the lid off was found rolling on the floor. **1955** F. LANE *Patrol to Kimberleys* 91 The sky was tinged with the gray pallor of false daylight which Dave and his father called 'picaninny dawn'. **1958** G. CASEY *Snowball* 125 He was up before the piccaninny dawn, and in the first gentle glow of it he slid out of the house. **1969** C. BRAY *Blossom* 71 The earth cools a little under the stars and in the morning, at the piccaninny dawn, the first light wind is cool and refreshing. **1975** L. WALKER *Runaway Girl* 116 The piccaninny dawn was growing up fast. First in its strange otherworld way it had become temporarily darker, then quite suddenly, the sky, and all the world, became grey. Next pale grey. Then there was light. It was daybreak. **1982** *Bulletin* (Sydney) 19 Oct. 35/1 Just on piccaninny dawn on Batavia Downs, high up Cape York Peninsula, grey light filtered through a canopy of eucalypts. **1866** *Adventures ashore & Afloat* (1887) 172 He . . refused, on the plea that it was '**picaninny daylight**'—*i.e.*, that the day was short, and we had no time to lose. **1905** E.C. BULEY *Austral. Life* 34 The day's work on the selection begins at 'piccaninny daylight', when the stars are still shining in the grey sky. **1922** 'J. BUSHMAN' *In Musgrave Ranges* 73 Piccaninny daylight . . is the bush term for the rising of the morning star. **1938** C.P. CONIGRAVE *Walk-About* 171 'Piccaninny daylight' saw us travelling over a dusty track . . and at sun-up we were at Iron Knob. **1956** H. HUDSON *Flynn's Flying Doctors* 116 Piccaninny daylight revealed the railway line alongside the Highway, with a kangaroo hopping lazily along the sleepers. **1970** R. BEILBY *No Medals for Aphrodite* 219 It was almost dawn, the 'piccaninny daylight' of the Big Country back home. **1980** J. WOLFE *End of Pricklystick* 167 It was piccaninny-daylight now, and kookaburras were laughing. . . 'What time is it ever?' 'About an hour to sun-up,' I said. **1962** J. MARSHALL *Journey among Men* 107 We were up at **piccaninny light**. After breakfast we loaded the dinghy with guns and cameras and sailed up the gorge. **1846** *Port Phillip Patriot* 23 Nov. 2/5 You no sleep to-night—plenty thousand Murray black fellow come **piccannini sun** (daylight) take him other one black fellow all same quamby hut and plenty Gilbert (kill) white fellow. **1856** W.W. DOBIE *Recoll. Visit Port-Phillip* 91 Sometimes 'picaninny sun' came long before Syntax had completed his self-allotted daily task. **1965** L. HAYLEN *Big Red* 180 The **piccaninny twilight** shimmered and died.

Hence **piccaninnyhood** *n.*, childhood.

1920 *Smith's Weekly* (Sydney) 22 May 17/5 The late John Nevell . . reared a blackfellow from piccaninnyhood.

pick, *n.* Abbrev. of PICKING *vbl. n.*

1960 *N.T. News* (Darwin) 11 Mar. 7/4 On the Goyder there is a good feed from No. 7 to Mallee Bore with a fair pick from there to Finke. **1977** V. PRIDDLE *Larry & Jack* 102 'It's surprising the way the country has changed colour in such a short time,' said George. 'Why in another few days the cattle will be able to get hold of that pick.'

pick, *v.*[1] *Shearing. trans.* With **up**: to gather up (a shorn fleece), preparatory to placing it on a table for skirting, classing, etc. Freq. *absol.*, and as *vbl. n.*

[N.Z. **1862** J.G. WALKER Jrnl. 10 Nov. 24 (typescript) My job at first was picking up fleeces.] **1897** *Bulletin* (Sydney) 30 Oct. 14/1 During the late shearing, black gins were employed 'picking-up'. **1900** H. LAWSON *Verses Pop. & Humorous* 146 I'm just in from west the Darling, 'picking-up' and 'rolling wool'. **1910** *Bulletin* (Sydney) 22 Dec. 13/4 The board comprised 24 black shearers; picking was done by gins and sweeping by piccaninnies. **1919** A. WRIGHT *Game of Chance* 135 See me at the shed. . . Bring the boy; he can go on picking up, I suppose. **1928** C.E. COWLEY *Classing Clip* 32 'Picking-up' is sometimes looked upon as a very simple task, and, consequently, does not always receive the consideration it is entitled to. **1957** D. WHITINGTON *Treasure upon Earth* 115, I was pickin' up when I first bumped him. 'Tar boy,' he'd yell and I'd rush up with the tar stick. **1974** J. HORNER *Vote Ferguson* 4 In July 1896, when he was legally entitled to leave school at fourteen, young Ferguson went to the shearing sheds, 'picking up' the shorn wool. **1982** J. MORRISON *North Wind* 125 He'd been away picking-up in the shearing sheds.

pick, *v.*[2] *intr.* To pick fruit. Freq. as *vbl. n.*

1913 W.K. HARRIS *Outback in Aust.* 70 Even overlanders from Queensland, have been in evidence during the picking season. **1941** K. TENNANT *Battlers* 211 Anyway, we might get a married couple's job in Orion, if we don't get on picking. **1946** A.M. LAPTHORNE *Mildura Calling* 48 The grapes are almost ready for harvesting and the 'picking', is the topic uppermost in the minds of all. **1955** J. MORRISON *Black Cargo* 155 We've been picking here for four weeks, and the A.W.U. is the wealthiest trade union in Australia. **1963** X. HERBERT *Disturbing Element* 95 The Picking Sheds were where fruit brought by boat from the Eastern States and from the northern Asiatic islands . . were sorted.

pick, *v.*[3] [Shortening of *to pick on*.] *trans.* To pick on (a person), to victimize.

1953 T.A.G. HUNGERFORD *Riverslake* 212 'If you're picking me,' he said at length, 'don't go off half-cocked.' **1976** *Bulletin* (Sydney) 3 July 28/2 The usual roughie, with enough drink in him to make him nasty, was misled by Mat's mild manner into picking him. **1978** H.C. BAKER *I was Listening* 51 One night three lairs picked him. **1981** *Bulletin* (Sydney) 10 Nov. 46/3 'Chicks fight heaps round here,' said Cheryl, 14, 'Ya get picked if ya look at someone too long, if there's somethin' about cha someone doesn't like, if ya dob, or wear the wrong clothes.'

pickaninny, var. PICCANINNY.

picker.

1. Abbrev. of PICKER-UP.

1895 *Bulletin* (Sydney) 13 July 23/3 There's the flying hurry-scurry up and down the greasy floors Of the pickers and the broomies; there's the banging of the doors, And the rattle of the wool-press.

2. Shortened form of 'fruit picker'.

1913 W.K. HARRIS *Outback in Aust.* 70 The pickers earn from 6s. to 8s. a day of eight hours. **1926** C.B. FLETCHER *Murray Valley* 76 Pickers . . have to be paid overtime. **1942** E. LANGLEY *Pea Pickers* 117, I began to pick peas. One row apiece is allotted to the picker. **1948** *Bulletin* (Sydney) 18 Feb. 23/3 We were in the pickers' camp at Pinkie Bend, Mildura, one grape season and there was a lot of skiting going on. **1955** J. MORRISON *Black Cargo* 154 They're his grapes. He's a good employer, even as employers go these days, but I'd be interested to see his form if pickers were easier to get. **1969** L. HADOW *Full Cycle* 21 Next season wouldn't see her feeding the pickers on the verandah. **1980** *Southerly* iii. 335 The return rail voucher that employment officers issued to pickers, had to be endorsed by the employer before a free return rail pass was issued. But as long as a picker stuck out the season, the blockie couldn't refuse to sign.

picker-up. *Shearing.* A shed-hand who gathers up the shorn fleeces: see quot. 1899. Also **picker-upper.**

1870 *Austral. Town & Country Jrnl.* (Sydney) 12 Nov. 13/4 The woolpress-men—the fleece-rollers—the pickers-up—the yarders—the washers' cooks—the hut cooks—the spare shepherds . . all . . paid off. **1874** M. WALKER *Pioneer Crafts Early Aust.* (1978) 153 As the shearing proceeds, 'pickers up', who are generally natives, take the fleeces from the shearers, and throw them on the wool table at the end of the shed. **1889** H. EGBERT *Pretty Cockey* 45 Some of the rouseabouts did duty as wool-rollers, some as picker-ups of the fleeces, as they were shorn off the sheep, some as separators of the trimmings into scourings and wastes. **1890** *Bulletin* (Sydney) 20 Sept. 11/4 The 'picker-up' and the 'penner', with the rest of the shearers' horde. **1899** G. JEFFREY *Princ. Australasian Woolclassing* 39 As soon as the fleece is off the sheep's back, the pickers-up take it by the breeches and place it on the rollers' tables, then sweep the floor clean of trimmings or locks as they are called. **1918** R.H. KNYVETT *Over there with Australs.* 29 At shearing-time the 'gaffers' (grandfathers) and young boys get employment as 'pickers-up' and 'rollers'. **1936** *Bulletin* (Sydney) 8 Jan. 19/1 The best picker-up I ever saw was Barefooted Joe. Any shearing contractor would find a job for him; he always managed to keep the board clean and the wool away from any six of the fastest 'guns'. One day strict unionists among the shedhands spread tacks along Joe's track. **1948** R. RAVEN-HART *Canoe in Aust.* 56 The 'pickers-up' (the aristocrats of the boys, who handle the fleeces only). **1962** *Bulletin* (Sydney) 3 Feb. 43/3 The young picker-uppers got frisky after a couple of ponies. **1980** P. FREEMAN *Woolshed* 20 The 'fleece' itself . . is immediately removed from the board by the 'pickers-up', and cleverly thrown over a 'wool' table where the 'skirtings' or rough flanks are removed, and the fleece prepared for classing by the wool classer.

picking, *vbl. n.* [Spec. use of *picking* that which may be picked up; *pl.* gleanings.] Sparse pasture; FEED; PICK *n.* See also *green pick* GREEN 2.

1901 F.J. GILLEN *Diary* 16 Oct. (1968) 290 There is good green picking here for the horses. **1933** W. HATFIELD *Desert Saga* 130 The strongest of the cattle are managing to get the barest of rough picking to keep them alive. **1934** C. SAYCE *Comboman* 60 They put the cattle on Stony Water Hole and shepherded them there for a week to get them used to the place and to spell their horses also, for there was still some dry picking on Stony Plains. **1938** J. MATHESON *Day Dreams*, There's picking upon those flats below and shade.

picking-up, *vbl. n.*

1. The process of clearing land of fallen timber, branches, etc., after burning off: see quot. 1952.

1879 'RECENT SETTLER' *Emigration to Tas.* 73 The picking up should be done as soon as possible after the fire, and consists in collecting in piles, and burning whatever timber and rubbish the fire may have spared, hoeing up and adding to the heaps, fern heads, roots, etc., so as to leave the land ready for chipping in the first grain crop. **1914** *Bulletin* (Sydney) 10 Dec. 22/2 The old lady . . gazed at the fire-tortured timber. . . 'There's a bit of picking-up to be done over there this summer, and there's the gully to be 'brushed' again. It takes a lot of keeping down.' **1920** *Land of Lyre Bird* (S. Gippsland Pioneers' Assoc.) 81 The term 'picking up' in itself does not explain the work it is expected to describe. After the burning of the Scrub, as described, all the operations of stacking the fallen timber that remains after the 'burn' is included under the term 'picking up'. **1941** *Bulletin* (Sydney) 2 Apr. 16/3 On a Westralian wheat farm we were 'picking up' after the burn. **1952** J.R. SKEMP *Memories Myrtle Bank* 67 The next job of the settler was 'picking up', the pieces not consumed by the fire being carried into heaps or piled against a fallen tree, and there burnt. **1972** K. SILLCOCK *Three Lifetimes* 32 After the burn came 'picking up'. Small unburned sticks and branches were collected and heaped, usually against a log too large to be moved, ready for further burning.

2. See PICK *v.*[1]

pickle and pork. Rhyming slang for 'walk'. Also **pickled pork.**

1940 *Sixer* (Mornington) 22 May 9 Pickle and pork . . a walk. **1944** *Biscuit Bomber Weekly: Mag. 1st Austral. Air Maintenance* 4 Nov. 2 Going for a Pickle-and-Pork down the Frog-and-Toad I saw a beautiful Twist-and-Twirl, so I put my Warwick-Farm around her bushel-and-peck and kissed her on the North-and-South. **1957** D. WHITINGTON *Treasure upon Earth* 87 What about coming bush with me? . . We'll go for a pickled pork into Queensland, pick up some work harvesting.

pick up. The act of engaging casual employees; the time and place at which this is done.

1940 E.A. MCCOMBE *Whales & Whalers* 30 Of the thirty-five signed on at Hobart . . seventy-five per cent . . were . . Tasmanians, while the remainder had travelled from the mainland to be present at the 'pick up'. **1946** F. CLUNE *Try Nothing Twice* 85 There was an army . . of shearers and rouseabouts waiting for the 'pick-up' at Yanco shed. **1954** *Meanjin* 57 The wharfies coming away from the pick-up are crowding the trams. **1957** D. WHITINGTON *Treasure upon Earth* 78 There was a deeper reason behind this strike than the announced issue of whether there should be one pick-up a day or two. **1966** *Realist* (Sydney) xxii. 20 For months Tommy Brand had been among the 'seagulls' who hung around the pick-up each day waiting for the crumbs of work that fell when the employers wanted more labour than the registered port quota. **1974** J. GABY *Restless Waterfront* 38, I can't think of a more frightening pick-up in all my days as a foreman. **1978** W.F. MANDLE *Going it Alone* 49 Curiously enough for one ostensibly concerned to reduce idle standing about, he also restored the system of two 'pick-ups', that is times when men could be engaged for work. **1982** LOWENSTEIN & HILLS *Under Hook* 15 They'd go to a pick-up from eight to ten in the morning.

picnic.

1. [Ironic use of *picnic* a pleasurable excursion.] An awkward or disordered occasion or experience; an unpleasant situation. Also *attrib.*

1896 E.E. MORRIS *Austral Eng.* (1898) 351 If a man's horse is awkward and gives him trouble, he will say, 'I had a picnic with that horse', and so of any misadventure or disagreeable experience when travelling. **1903** *Sporting News* (Launceston) 12 Sept. 3/4 As heavy showers of rain fall during the engagement, enthusiasts in the pastime can easily realise the 'picnic' time the teams had. **1911** A. SEARCY *By Flood & Field* 275 A fine picnic was before us what with outlaws and blacks. **1938** *Kalgoorlie Digger* Apr. 7, I intend to review a book dealing with the Palestine picnic. **1945** *Atebrin Advocate: Mag. 2/4 Austral. Armoured Regiment* 12 May 2, I shan't forget The picnic that we had here [in wartime New Guinea]. **1955** D. NILAND *Shiralee* 38 All I know is I'm going to have one helluva picnic if she doesn't find it. **1959** S.J. BAKER *Drum* 68 We call a wild confusion or a particularly difficult task a picnic.

2. a. Special Comb. **picnic (race) meeting, races** (*pl.*), a race meeting which is primarily an informal social occasion, usu. in a rural district. Also **picnic race** *attrib.*, see quot. 1985.

1896 N. GOULD *Town & Bush* 224 Picnic race-meetings are got up in various parts of the country. These meetings are for amateur riders only, and as a rule they are well managed. **1911** *Bulletin* (Sydney) 23 Mar. 40/2 It was the first meeting of the Sandy Creek Amateur Turf Club Picnic Races. **1923** T. HALL *Short Hist. Downs Blacks* 19 The joy or excitement [of a kangaroo hunt] to the blacks was on a par with that of the picnic races to the white people at the present time in the same district. **1936** I.L. IDRIESS *Cattle King* 350 Gone were nearly all the station and bush 'picnic meetings'. **1948** *Bulletin* (Sydney) 25 Feb. 28/1 Harry Barr told me that he had certainties for the first three at Bogolah's picnic races. **1958** F. HARDY *Four-Legged Lottery* 76 Tests of skill for horse and rider were organised and soon developed into picnic race meetings on crude courses carved out of the bush. **1967** D. HORNE *Educ. Young Donald* 21 The most serious events of the year were the two-day Picnic Race Meeting and the Picnic Races Ball. **1985** *Bulletin* (Sydney) 2 July 12/2 His view of the country is obviously obtained by mixing with the picnic race set. These people who grace the social pages do rural Australia a great disservice by perpetuating the myth of the wealthy farmer.

b. A *picnic meeting*; also *attrib.* as **picnic horse.**

1904 *Sporting News* (Launceston) 30 Apr. 1/2 Recently one of those New South Wales 'picnic' horses took up quarters in J.H. Davis's stables at Caulfield. *Ibid.* 13 Feb. 1/2 Probably on the strength of the good form he has been showing lately on the flat and over obstacles the 'picnic' horse Speculation . . received a little better attention. **1942** T. KELAHER *Digger Hat* 36, I miss the chestnut filly, I thought she'd have some pace, And when the 'Picnics' came again be fit to win a race.

Hence **picnicker** *n.*, a horse which runs at a picnic race meeting.

1921 G.A. BELL *Under Brigalow* 89 None of them were really trained racehorses, only what bushmen call 'good picnickers'.

picture-show. *Obs.* [Transf. use of *picture-show* a film showing.] A cinema. Also **picture theatre.**

1915 *St. Kilda Ann.* 137 Seven years ago there was but one important picture theatre in Melbourne. **1918** A. WRIGHT *Over Odds* 51 It was hard indeed to have to daily play the clown outside a picture-show to amuse a frivolous crowd. **1919** *Smith's Weekly* (Sydney) 1 Mar. 6/4 We never knew what a boon picture shows were until they were closed. **1930** *Bulletin* (Sydney) 16 Apr. 57/1 Moses Brodziel was proud because he was a picture-show proprietor. **1930** L.W. LOWER *Here's Luck* 211 George . . sneaked off whenever he could to the local picture-show. He had a passion for pictures, especially the highly emotional kind. **1935** K. TENNANT *Tiburon* 139 One of his worst memories was that of arresting Bill for drunk and disorderly conduct outside the picture-show. **1947** H. DRAKE-BROCKMAN *On N.-W. Skyline* 36 No picture-theatre where the whole town, white, black and brindle, once met twice weekly. **1949** R. PARK *Poor Man's Orange* 8 It was as much part of Surry Hills life as the picture-show or the police station, the ham and beef or the sly-grog shop.

pie. [Shortened form of *meat pie.*]

1. Used *attrib.* in Comb., as **pie-biter, -eater, -eating** *ppl. a.*, to connote 'second rate', 'small-time'. See also *meat pie bookmaker* MEAT.

1911 E. DYSON *Benno & Push* 144 He was that angry with the South pie-biters, he didn't care what happened to them. **1949** L. GLASSOP *Lucky Palmer* 96 The trouble is, Mr Hughes, you're too good for the pie-eating bookmakers round these parts. You bet too well for them Mr Hughes. **1953** K. TENNANT *Joyful Condemned* 166 He's one of those big he-men that go sneaking round the park waiting to snitch some chromo's handbag. Just a pie-eater. **1966** *Sunday Tel.* (Sydney) 22 May 25/2 The Australian appetite for pies has even added to our slang with the term 'pie-eater'. Once meaning a small time crook, it is now used as a derogatory expression, close in meaning to 'a dill'. **1972** A. CHIPPER *Aussie Swearers Guide* 9 'Ya pie-eating drongo!' . . I liked being among a nation that could turn pastry-munching into a heavy vilification. **1978** H.C. BAKER *I was Listening* 180 Did you know 'pie-eater' is an insulting expression? **1980** L.G. FOGARTY *Kargun* 33 The half caste says you Queensland banana benders you pie eaters and the full blood says, where is our identity going down or up. **1980** B. HORNADGE *Austral. Slanguage* 209 *Pie eater* was for a long time a derogatory term for a South Australian. The term is now obsolete and its origin is puzzling since statistics clearly reveal that Victorians have always been the major consumers of pies on a per head of population basis. **1984** A. DELBRIDGE *Aussie Talk* 237 *Pie eater n. (sometimes offensive)*, an Australian.

2. *transf.* and *fig.* An informal grouping of wool buyers who do not bid against one another at a wool sale, and divide the wool purchased amongst their number. Also *attrib.*

1959 *N.S.W. Parl. Papers* 2nd Sess. IV. 1310 The facts that pies are formed, generally speaking, between buyers interested in the same types of wool, and that their admitted purpose is to avoid the competition of members *inter se* show clearly the distinct advantages to pie members. **1960** *Pastoral Rev. & Graziers' Rec.* 18 Mar. 218 Mr McMillan then made reference to such controversial subjects as wool buying 'pies', lot splitting, forward selling, wool futures and bulk classing. **1962** A. BARNARD *Simple Fleece* 493 A pie is essentially an informal unwritten agreement between two or more buyers not to bid against each other. **1966** S.J. BAKER *Austral. Lang.* (ed. 2) 58 The Australian public became aware in 1958 that wool-buying was not always a straightforward operation. . . Some buyers were combining into pies (also called rings) to bid and then share purchases, so that competition was reduced.

piebald, *a.* and *n.*

A. *adj.*

1. Half-caste; of part white and part non-white descent.

1899 *Progress* (Brisbane) 13 May 7/3 Even in Mount Morgan we see the piebald population increasing—mixing in our public schools with our children. **1901** *Tocsin* (Melbourne) 31 Oct. 1/1 Cook, of Brunswick, has 'cooked' his political hash by voting for a 'Piebald Australia'. **1906** *Truth* (Sydney) 20 May 6/2 How many residents of Bananaland ever saw a respectable married kanaka with a loving white wife and fragrant piebald family? **1910** *Bulletin* (Sydney) 15 Sept. 13/1 There are not many selectors in No Man's Land, but those that there are think a bough shed or grass humpy is good enough. I shall never forget camping with one selector in the Far North. He lived alone except for his six dusky wives and 17 piebald children. **1911** R.J. CASSIDY *Land of Starry Cross* 200 This is the song of a piebald love—of a love that is White and Brown.

2. Applied as a derogatory epithet to: **(a)** one who favours admitting non-whites, esp. Kanakas, to Australia, and **(b)** the resultant society.

1901 *Tocsin* (Melbourne) 3 Oct. 1/2 Victoria has 23 members in the Federal House of Representatives, 19 of whom are 'Piebald Austr-Aliens'. **1902** *Bulletin* (Sydney) 22 Feb. 14/1 Will Queensland record a piebald vote? **1903** *Truth* (Sydney) 15 Mar. 1/8 Here's something for the advocates of a piebald Australia to chew before they encourage the immigration of smellful and cruel aliens. **1904** *Ibid.* 24 Jan. 3/4 Surely Australians will cease now to turn their eyes to this piebald paradise!

B. *n.* One who is of mixed race.

1903 'BOONDI' *Boondi's Bk.* 35 So few full-blooded blacks and so many 'piebalds'. **1908** *Truth* (Sydney) 5 Apr. 7/3 Are you an Englishman?—No, *I am an Australian.* 'No,' retorted Mr Levien, 'by God you are not! (Laughter) You are a piebald!'

Hence **piebaldism** *n.*

1901 *Bulletin* (Sydney) 20 July 15/2 Piebaldism in North Queensland. A sugar-planter has a half-caste illegitimate son, whose mother is an aboriginal gin. This young man recently married his half-caste *cousin*, whose mother is a Kanaka woman who is now 'kept' indiscriminately by Chows and other aliens.

piece. [Spec. use of *piece* (small) portion.]

1. *pl. Shearing.* Oddments of wool detached from the skirtings of a fleece; the skirtings.

[N.Z. **1881** A. BATHGATE *Waitaruna* 173 The 'pickers up' were . . carrying [the fleeces] to the sorting table, where they were stripped of the 'pieces', which were thrown aside.] **1891** R. WALLACE *Rural Econ. & Agric.* 384 The washing of wool, either before or after shearing, is, with the exception of locks and pieces, which are generally scoured, almost entirely given up. **1897** L. LINDLEY-COWEN *W. Austral. Settler's Guide* 653 *Pieces.*—These are the parts of the fleece not sufficiently coarse, stained or seedy as to go with the locks, and yet not good enough to go with the fleece. **1928** C.E. COWLEY *Classing Clip* 45 *Pieces,* wool shorter in staple and more irregular, heavier in condition, and more uneven in every respect than *a* and *b* grades. **1971** J.S. GUNN *Distrib. Shearing Terms N.S.W.* 20 The south was the only area where . . there was a preference for *pieces* rather than *skirtings*. **1979** E. SMITH *Saddle in Kitchen* 80 There'd be catching pens to fill and wool to be pressed, with us jumping and tramping on 'pieces' and 'bellies' in two bales held upright from the shed rafters by wire.

2. Special Comb. **piece picker,** one who gathers up and sorts the pieces; so **piece picking** *vbl. n.*

1899 G. JEFFREY *Princ. Australasian Woolclassing* 51 The skirtings are thrown on the floor until the 'Piece Pickers' gather them up and sort them. **1905** *Shearer* (Sydney) 20 May 6/2, I was on the Liverpool Plains . . last year piece-picking in a shed. **1914** H.B. SMITH *Sheep & Wool Industry* 184 *Piece-pickers,* men employed on stations at shearing time to pick or sort the pieces into the sorts. **1928** C.E. COWLEY *Classing Clip* 41 To carry out the duties of 'piece-picking' with the fullest measure of success, a certain degree of skill and dexterity is required. *Ibid.* 44 Increases the quantity of wool to be handled by the piece-pickers. **1949** D. WALKER *We went to Aust.* 97 The piece-pickers . . separate the neck and leg fleece from the main body of wool. **1962** *Bulletin* (Sydney) 3 Feb. 44/1 The old piece-picker went on: 'I picked for ten guns on me own and not a frib in the broken.' **1979** HARMSWORTH & DAY *Wool & Mohair* 150 The *piece-pickers* takes [*sic*] the pieces of wool removed from the fleece by the wool rollers and sort them into such lines as the classer may direct.

3. In the phr. **to have** (or **take**) **a piece (out) of** (someone), to rebuke, to take to task.

1958 *Coast to Coast 1957* 125 I'd made up my mind to 'have a piece of him', as the good Australian phrase goes, and had, therefore, confined my activities to a few minor jobs which could be cleared up at a minute's notice. **1966** S.J. BAKER *Austral. Lang.* (ed. 2) 125 A man who attacks another successfully is said *to . . take a piece out of him. Ibid.* 427 *Reprove (v.)* . . take a piece out of someone. **1972** A. CHIPPER *Aussie Swearers Guide* 77 *Have a piece of you:* . . (Compare Brit.: *Have your guts for garters*). **1984** A. DELBRIDGE *Aussie Talk* 237 *Take a piece out of,* to reprimand severely.

pied, *a.* Used as a distinguishing epithet in the names of black and white birds: **pied butcherbird,** the bird *Cracticus nigrogularis* of mainland Aust., except parts of the south; see also ORGAN **bird**; **cormorant,** the large bird *Phalacrocorax varius* occurring near coastal and inland waters of Aust. and N.Z., having a black back, white front, and orange-yellow face patch; **currawong (crow-shrike, bell magpie),** the bird *Strepera graculina* of e. Aust. exc. Tas.; *black magpie* (b), see BLACK *a.*[2] 1 b.; **goose,** *magpie goose,* see MAGPIE *n.* 2; **grallina** *obs., magpie lark,* see MAGPIE *n.* 2; **heron** (or **egret**), the predom. blue-black and white bird *Ardea picata* of coastal and near-coastal n. Aust. and elsewhere; **honeyeater,** the bird *Certhionyx variegatus* of arid mainland Aust., the male of which has black and white plumage; **oyster-catcher,** the bird *Haematopus longirostris* of coastal Aust. and elsewhere; see also *red bill* RED *a.* 1 b.; **robin,** *hooded robin,* see HOODED.

1902 *Emu* II. 90 **Pied Butcher Bird**. . . These birds generally go in pairs. **1945** C. BARRETT *Austral. Bird Life* 217 The grey or collared species (*C[racticus] torquatus*) . . rivals the whistlers. . . The pied or black-throated butcher bird (*C. nigrogularis*) perhaps is the grey bird's peer. **1962** B.W. LEAKE *Eastern Wheatbelt Wildlife* 84 The pied butcher bird has a beautiful song and to hear this is something to remember. **1985** *Austral. Nat. Hist.* Spring 427 The Pied Butcherbird is a bold fellow with a wicked-looking hooked bill, which it sometimes uses to wedge small birds, insects and reptiles between branches or onto thorns. The common name of butcherbird is derived from this habit. **1843** J. GOULD *Birds of Aust.* (1848) VII. Pl. 68, The **Pied Cormorant** may be regarded as a gregarious species. **1903** *Emu* II. 167 Pied Cormorant (*Phalacrocorax hypoleucus*) . . on the plains. **1968** R. HILL *Bush Quest* 74 A shimmer of black and white caught my eye; across the lake were a late flock of Pied Cormorants. They sat in a long row on a concrete promontory, 170 birds, almost all with their wings hanging open. **1976** *Reader's Digest Compl. Bk. Austral. Birds* 70 In early colonial times and during both World Wars, the pied cormorant formed the basis of a small guano industry at Shark Bay, W.A. **1844** [**pied currawong**] J. GOULD *Birds of Aust.* (1848) II. Pl. 42, *Strepera graculina.* Pied Crow-Shrike. **1896** *Bulletin* (Sydney) 18 Apr. 27/3 The word 'jackeroo', a station new-chum, comes also from the old Brisbane blacks, who called the pied crow shrike . . 'tchaceroo', a gabbling and garrulous bird. **1928** C.G. LANE *Adventures in Big Bush* 114 Great grey Crow-shrikes, and their smaller relative the Pied Crow-shrike, called, at intervals, to their mates. **1945** C. BARRETT *Austral. Bird Life* 216 Currawongs . . feed chiefly upon native fruits and berries, and insects. Perhaps the best known species are the pied currawong and the grey bird. **1965** *Austral. Encycl.* III. 149 Currawong, a name based on one of the calls of the pied currawong and applied to the genus *Strepera.* **1984** E. ROLLS *Celebration of Senses* 77 In winter the cling-clang of Pied Currawongs wakes us fittingly after the sun is well up. **1884** 'R. BOLDREWOOD' *Old Melbourne Memories* 22 The **pied goose**, here in large flocks, with . . an occasional wild turkey, were our chief support and sustenance. **1903** *Emu* II. 159 *Anseranas semipalmata* (Pied Goose). . . These birds are plentiful in the Northern Territory. **1964** M. SHARLAND *Territory of Birds* 56 Although the Territory has other geese, of the pygmy variety, the Pied Goose is the chief one, and most prominent in its pattern of long black neck, white face, and peculiar knob at the upper base of the beak, white body, black wings, and stout greenish-yellow legs. **1979** D. LOCKWOOD *My Old Mates & I* 11 Here were pied geese in thousands, the magpie-honkers that fly by night, guzzling aquatic food by day and nesting beyond the reach of man. **1843** J. GOULD *Birds of Aust.* (1848) II. Pl. 54, *Grallina australis* . . **Pied Grallina.** **1849** C. STURT *Narr. Exped. Central Aust.* II. 22 App. *Pied Grallina.* This harmless bird, somewhat larger than a fieldfare, is found near water, where the banks are muddy. **1896** B. SPENCER *Rep. Horn Sci. Exped. Central Aust.* II. 71 Pied Grallina . . was found near all permanent waters. **1909** *Emu* VIII. 266 He gave us the notes of the Pied Grallina. **1846** [**pied heron**] J. GOULD *Birds of Aust.* (1848) VI. Pl. 62, *Herodias picata* . . Pied Egret. **1890** G.J. BROINOWSKI *Birds of Aust.* II. Pl. 17, One or two explorers to the northern parts of Australia have succeeded in procuring specimens of the Pied Egret. **1913** *Emu* XII. Suppl. 40 Pied Egret . . range: N.W. Australia, Northern Territory, N. Queensland (New Guinea, Aru Id., Celebes). **1963** D. ATTENBOROUGH *Quest under Capricorn* 30 Pied herons standing in tightly packed ranks on the shores. **1981** C. THIELE *Little Tom Little* 23 The pied heron put on his mating plumage and danced and nodded to his love. **1844** J. GOULD *Birds of Aust.* (1848) IV. Pl. 49, *Melicophila picata* . . **Pied Honey-eater.** **1901** *Emu* I. 102 *Entomophila leucomelas* . . Pied Honey-eater . . will rise to a great height in the air, and then fall suddenly into another tree. **1922** A.H. CHISHOLM *Mateship with Birds* 159 It is the more retiring of the bi-coloured species, such as . . the rare Pied Honeyeater-birds without any assertive system or means of protection that are restricted to certain favourable areas. **1945** C. BARRETT *Austral. Bird Life* 156 The pied honey eater (*Certhionyx variegatus*) . . ranks among the rarer species. **1984** SIMPSON & DAY *Birds of Aust.* 328 Mobile species, such as . . Pied and Painted Honeyeaters, are irregular visitors to southern parts of their range. **1785** J. LATHAM III. 219 **pied Oister-catcher.** . . The *Oister-catcher* is pretty common in England. **1888** *Centennial Mag.* (Sydney) 14 On the shore, the beautiful little hooded dotterel, and the sooty and pied oyster-catcher. **1903** *Emu* II. 166 Pied Oyster-catcher (*Haematopus longirostris*) . . noted at the River Aire. **1955** V. SERVENTY *Aust.'s Great Barrier Reef* 55 Commonly known as Red-bills, the correct names are Pied Oystercatcher and Sooty Oystercatcher. As yet, I have still to see either catching oysters. Both these waders are home lovers, and . . nest on the Barrier Reef Islands. **1968** R. HILL *Bush Quest* 39 Also on the bar, waiting for the receding water to lay bare their feeding ground, were scattered groups of pied oyster-catchers. **1984** M. BLAKERS et al. *Atlas Austral. Birds* 147 The Pied Oystercatcher is continuously distributed round Australia except where cliffs replace beaches such as on the Nullarbor coast. **1842** J. GOULD *Birds of Aust.* (1848) III. Pl. 7, *Petroica bicolor* . . **Pied Robin.** **1933** F.E. BAUME *Tragedy Track* 103 Rogers, who explored the district first in 1911, gives the following list of native birds . . pale flycatcher, pied robin [etc.].

pie-dish beetle. [See quot. 1935.] Any of many beetles, usu. of the genus *Helaeus* of drier Aust.

1896 F.G. AFLALO *Sketch Nat. Hist. Aust.* 271 The nocturnal *Tenebrionidae* . . include the grotesque Pie Dish Beetle (*Helaeus princeps*). **1935** K.C. MCKEOWN *Insect Wonders Aust.* 5 The so-called 'Pie-Dish' Beetles are typical of the drier areas. They are queer creatures, flattened in shape, and with a wide flange running round the outer edge of the elytra or wing-covers, a feature which gives them their popular name. **1978** B.P. MOORE *Life on Forty Acres* 136 There is only one true Pie-dish beetle in this district—a small coal-black species (*Helaeus ovatus*), just over a half an inch long, its elytra studded with shining bosses, arranged in irregular rows.

pie-melon. [Poss. transf. use of U.S. *pie-melon* a melon used for pies.] Any of several plants bearing a melon-like fruit, esp. a cultivated variety of the watermelon *Citrullus lanatus* (fam. Cucurbitaceae). See also *wild melon* WILD 1.

1907 *Truth* (Sydney) 24 Feb. 12/5 The scallywags who would rob a chinkie's pie melon patch deserve nothing better than a seat on an ounce of shot. **1916** *Emu* XV. 155 Birds . . were feeding on the seeds of a wild pie-melon which had grown plentifully since the last rain. **1959** H. DRAKE-BROCKMAN *West Coast Stories* 185 He . . took a large mouthful of a particularly nauseous vegetable which was a cross between a pie-melon and a marrow. **1975** L. BEADELL *Still in Bush* 140, I had found a wild pie-melon . . so for tea I had my first sample of a melon boiled in claypan water. . . It could easily have resembled stewed apples.

pig, *n.*[1] In the names of flora and fauna: **pig fish,** any of several marine fish, esp. those of the fam. Congiopodidae, and some of the fam. Labridae, as *Bodianus oxycephalus* of n. and e. Aust. and elsewhere; **-footed bandicoot,** the bandicoot *Chaeropus ecaudatus* of drier southern and central Aust., having only two well-developed toes on the forefoot, prob. now extinct; **melon,** see quot. 1872; **weed** [transf. use of *pigweed* a plant used as animal fodder or as a pot-herb], the spreading, prostrate plant *Portulaca oleracea* (fam. Portulacaceae) of Aust. and elsewhere, having thick, succulent stems and leaves, and often regarded as a weed of cultivation; PORTULAC; see also MUNYEROO.

1842 *Tasmanian Jrnl. Nat. Sci.* I. 104 *Ostracion* . . known at Port Arthur by the name of **Pig-fish.** **1878** *Proc. Linnean Soc. N.S.W.* III. 390 *Cossyphus unimaculatus* . . often called 'Pig Fish' on account of its elongated snout. **1895** C. THACKERAY *Amateur Fisherman's Guide* 80 At La Perouse . . hauls of . . pigfish . . are got. **1906** D.G. STEAD *Fishes of Aust.* 142 The Pigfish (*Diastodon unimaculatus*) . . is well-known on the New South Wales coast. **1933** D. MACDONALD *Brooks of Morning* 181 The pig fish and the boar fish were inspirationally named, because neither of them grunted. As soon as Australians met with a fish which really did grunt they had to dip down abruptly from the pinnacles of metaphor to the plains of plain fact, and call it a grunter. **1978** N. COLEMAN *Austral. Fisherman's Fish Guide* 76 A southern species entering into the state of Queensland, the pigfish inhabits broken rocky reef in depths of 15 to 40 metres. [**1836 pig-footed bandicoot:** T.L. MITCHELL *Three Exped. Eastern Aust.* II. 131 This animal was of the size of a young wild rabbit, and of nearly the same colour... The feet, and especially the forelegs were singularly formed, the latter resembling those of a hog.] **1838** *Proc. Zool. Soc. London* 26 Mr Ogilby exhibited a drawing, made by Major Mitchell, of a Marsupial animal found by that officer on the banks of the river Murray... It would appear that there were only two toes on the fore-feet, which were described as having been so perfectly similar to those of a pig, as to have procured for the animal the name of the pig-footed bandicoot, among the persons of the expedition. **1896** B. SPENCER *Rep. Horn Sci. Exped. Central Aust.* II. 17 *Chaeropus castanotis*.. the pig-footed bandicoot.. is one of the most difficult of the smaller marsupials to secure. **1926** A.S. LE SOUEF et al. *Wild Animals Australasia* 305 The curious little pig-footed bandicoot is an inhabitant of the drier inland parts of Australia. **1962** B.W. LEAKE *Eastern Wheatbelt Wildlife* 46 The Bertie was about half the size of the Boodie with very long ears.. its colour.. varying from dark grey to light brown.. called the Pig footed bandicoot. **1975** *Ecos* v. 28/2 The desert and the pig-footed bandicoots lived in squats dug under grass tussocks. **1872** MRS E. MILLETT *Austral. Parsonage* 103 A large field-melon, called the **pig** or cattle **melon**, which, in spite of its natural insipidity, produced, when largely helped out with vinegar and sugar and baked under a crust, an imitation by no means despicable of apple-pie. **1959** D. STUART *Yandy* 88 He ate stewed pigmelon at Moogareenya. **1985** T. WINTON *Scission* 32, I used to do that as a boy; skidding half pig-melons under car wheels until nothing was left but a greenish, wet pulp. **1862** G. BOURNE *Jrnl. Landsborough's Exped. from Carpentaria* 30 **Pigweed**, or portulac, is plentiful here. **1864** R. HENNING *Lett.* (1952) 67 'Pig-weed', rather a nasty wild plant, but supposed to be exceedingly wholesome, either chopped up with vinegar or boiled. **1879** 'AUSTRALIAN' *Adventures Qld.* 10 Cold salt-beef and pig-weed salad. **1890** A. MACKAY *Austral. Agriculturist* (ed. 2) 15 Life is rendered well nigh a burden by the encroachments of the persistent 'pig-weed'. **1937** W. HATFIELD *I find Aust.* 122 It was pigweed and saltbush.. with a bit of tufty *never-fail* grass in the sandhills as a luxury. **1978** HANIGAN & LINDSAY *No Tracks on River* 57, I know you can eat pigweed and that grows all along the river.

pig, *n.*[2]

1. [f. U.S. *in a pig's eye, ear, arse*: see OEDS *sb.*[1] 10 g.]

a. In the possessive, as an abbrev. of 'pig's eye', etc.: used as a derisive retort. Also with **to**.

1906 E. DYSON *Fact'ry 'Ands* 5 'Pigs to you!' said Benno, with incredible scorn. **1933** N. LINDSAY *Saturdee* 165 Peter had to cover his confusion by saying 'Pigs to you' as he went out kicking the door. **1953** T.A.G. HUNGERFORD *Riverslake* 102 'Kerry's all right.' 'Pigs, is he! He's tailing round with Mister bloody Randolph an' that flamin' Balt!' **1968** S. GORE *Holy Smoke* 8 '*Pigs*', calmly retorted old Bill. 'I say pigs to that sayin'.' **1975** L. RYAN *Shearers* 119 'Ar, pigs to you!' 'In your dinger, too!'

b. As a possessive with various anatomical nouns: used as a derisive retort; freq. as a strong negative.

1919 W.H. DOWNING *Digger Dialects* 38 *Pig's ear*, a contemptuous ejaculation. [**1924** A.W. BAZLEY et al. Gloss. Slang A.I.F. 21 (typescript) *Pig arse*, a contemptuous ejaculation.] **1951** E. LAMBERT *Twenty Thousand Thieves* 322 'Pig's arse to that!' another voice cried. 'A jack-up—that's the shot.' **1966** D. NILAND *Pairs & Loners* 13 'You know my reputation then,' I said. He snapped his fingers. 'Pig's bum to your reputation!' **1974** D. WAUGH *Master White Grass* 23 'The pidgin for bully beef is bullamacow.' 'Pig's tit!' **1978** HANIGAN & LINDSAY *No Tracks on River* 60 'Pigs foot,' said Mike. 'They just put up signs like that to scare you.' **1981** J. SAXTON *Something will Come* 163 'Pig's arse' could mean almost anything... 'I won ten thousand pounds...' P.A.—disbelief. 'Me crop caught fire...' P.A.—sympathy. 'Western Australia should secede...' P.A.—one hundred per cent agreement. 'Me wife ran off...' P.A.—half your luck.

2. Abbrev. of PIG-ROOT *n.*

1911 A. SEARCY *By Flood & Field* 251 He contented himself with a couple of 'pigs', and then walked quietly away.

pig-dog. A dog bred to hunt the wild pig.

[N.Z. **1845** E.J. WAKEFIELD *Adventure in N.Z.* II. 6 It soon became a fashion for travelling settlers like myself to have a pack of pig-dogs, known for their strength, skill, and courage.] **1925** *Bulletin* (Sydney) 19 Nov. 24/4 To bail up a pig in its jungle without trained dogs is almost impossible and certainly unsafe. This explains why.. a good 'pig-dog' is prized. **1978** D. LAVERS *Vet in Clouds* 55 Most hunters breed pig-hunting dogs (colloquially known as 'pig-dogs') by mating a bull terrier with another breed like a staghound or boxer.

pigeon-berry ash. [Prob. transf. use of U.S. *pigeon-berry* any of several plants having fruit attractive to birds.] Any of several, usu. large, rainforest trees of e. Aust., esp. *Cryptocarya erythroxylon* (fam. Lauraceae), having a fragrant, pinkish-brown wood and *Elaeocarpus obovatus* (fam. Elaeocarpaceae), having a pale, tough wood; the wood of these trees. Also **pigeon-berry tree.**

1884 A. NILSON *Timber Trees N.S.W.* 55 *E[laeocarpus] obovatus*—Ash; Pigeon-berry Tree. A noble tree, attaining sometimes a height of 130 feet and a diameter of 5 feet. **1889** J.H. MAIDEN *Useful Native Plants Aust.* 423 *Elaeocarpus obovatus*.. 'Pigeon-berry Ash'... This wood is white, hard, tough, and used for oars, etc. **1945** J. DEVANNY *Bird of Paradise* 19 Pigeonberry ash and watergum don't pop... They've got a water crack right up through the heart. **1965** *Austral. Encycl.* III. 137 The rose maple or rose walnut (*C[ryptocarya] erythroxylon*), found in the hill rain-forests of south-east Queensland and northern New South Wales, where it is most generally known to timber-getters as pigeon-berry ash.

pigface. [See quot. 1965.] Any of several succulent, prostrate, perennial plants of the genera *Disphyma* and *Carpobrotus* (fam. Aizoaceae) of coastal and dry inland Aust., esp *D. crassifolium* which also occurs in N.Z. and S. Africa; CANAGONG; MESEMBRYANTHEMUM. See also KARKALLA. Also **pig's face,** and *attrib.*

1830 G.A. ROBINSON in N.J.B. Plomley *Friendly Mission* 1 Feb. (1966) 113 The natives gathered a marine plant called pigface which they eat and of which they appear very fond. **1838** J. HAWDON *Jrnl. of Journey N.S.W. to Adelaide* (1952) 2 The plains.. are for the most part covered with the salsuginous plant vulgarly called 'Pig's face'. **1855** W. HOWITT *Land, Labor & Gold* 22 The beautiful crimson mesembryanthemum which we grow at home in pots grows wild here... They call this pretty flower 'pig's-faces'. **1880** 'OLD HAND' *Experiences of Colonist* (ed. 2) i. 61 After supper, which constituted of some excellent young kangaroo steak, damper, and pickled mesembrianthem (or pig's face).. conversation commenced. **1902** L. BECKE *Breachley* 13 A ridge of soft white sand, covered with a thick-leaved saline plant locally called 'pig-face'. **1926** *Bulletin* (Sydney) 15 July 24/3 Abos. have more uses for pigface-weed than curing jellyfish sting. **1947** F. CLUNE *Roaming around Aust.* 16 'Pig's Face'—that's an ugly name for a pretty little flower. **1965** *Austral. Encycl.* VII. 112 *Pigface*, a name widely applied in Australia to fleshy-fruited succulent plants of the genus *Carpobrotus*.. because the ripe, reddish fruiting structure is subtended by two ear-like floral leaves and the whole bears a fanciful resemblance to a pig's head. **1972** R. ERICKSEN *West of Centre* 177 The velvet-smooth petals of the flowers are in shocking contrast to the thick, watery oedema of the stems and leaves; like angelic Botticelli heads on monsters' bodies. And we call them Pig-face! **1986** *Herald* (Melbourne) 22 Jan. 7/6 You found so few words for the beach.. its dunes bearded with marram, tea tree, pigsface.

pig-iron polisher: see quot. 1982.

1968 J. O'GRADY *Gone Troppo* 85 'Pig-iron polishers go last.' he said. The Engineer put money on the bar. **1982** LOWENSTEIN & HILLS *Under Hook* 175, I remember the only time I was sorry for a ship's engineer—pig iron polishers you'd call them if you wanted to annoy them.

pig-jump, *v. intr.* Of a horse: to jump as a pig does, from all four legs but without bringing them together (as in a buckjump). Freq. as *vbl. n.*

1884 A.W. STIRLING *Never Never Land* 190 She habitually rode a skittish pony of about fourteen hands, who used to buck, or, as she called it, pig jump for about five minutes after its mistress got seated. **1895** K. MACKAY *Yellow Wave* 58 D'ye mind that day on the Flinders when you met me with Matilda up, pig-jumping over them blooming sand-hills, leading my blooming water-bag? **1916** J.M. CREED *Recoll. Aust.* 88 The prairie horses rarely do more than buck straight ahead, which in Australia is looked on with contempt and called 'pig-jumping'. **1924** J. HARPER *Splashes from Narran* 21 So kicking, striking, pig jumping and snorting the horses were forced into line. **1938** D. BATES *Passing of Aborigines* 54 My mount began to 'pig-jump' and threw me.

Hence **pig-jumper** *n.*

1920 *Bulletin* (Sydney) 24 June 20/2 In far-western Queensland, where you *do* get brumbies and rough horses, they are considered soft snaps unless they can 'spin' and 'buck back'. The straight-ahead prad, no matter with how great a jar he hits the ground, is a mere 'rooter' or 'pig-jumper'. **1937** W. HATFIELD *I find Aust.* 213 We'll see what you can do on this pig-jumper of ours.

pig-jump, *n.* [f. prec.] The act of pig-jumping.

1924 FUNK & WAGNALLS *New Standard Dict.* 1873 *Pig-jump, vi.* [Austral.] To buck, as a horse.—*pig-jump, n.*—*pig-jumper, n.* **1937** W. HATFIELD *I find Aust.* 52 Sending it [*sc.* a mule] away in a series of flying pig-jumps while Tim felt for his off-stirrup. **1946** *Bulletin* (Sydney) 28 Aug. 29/2 'C'n y' ride?' asked the boss. 'Aw,' mumbled Skinny, 'I c'n ride a quiet hack.' 'S'pose you're good for a few pigjumps?'

pigmeater. *Obs.* A beast which is unfit for human consumption: see quot. 1890.

1879 S.W. SILVER *Austral. Grazier's Guide* 14 He has learned to comprehend what.. 'scrubbers', 'pig-meaters', and 'stags' mean as disparaging terms when applied to live stock. **1884** 'R. BOLDREWOOD' *Old Melbourne Memories* 105 The original cattle had been neglected... Among them was a large proportion of bullocks, which declined with fiendish obstinacy to fatten... They were what are known by the stock-riders as 'ragers' or 'pig-meaters'. **1890** —— *Colonial Reformer* II. 100 'Pigmeaters!' exclaimed Ernest; 'what kind of cattle do you call those? Do bullocks eat pigs in this country?' 'No, but pigs eat them, and horses, too,' affirmed Jack Windsor; 'and a very good way of getting rid of rubbish.' **1900** *Bulletin* (Sydney) 16 June 15/1 On many cattle-stations on the Clarence and Richmond Rivers all lumpy, cancerous, and other diseased cattle are—or were a few years ago—known as pig-meaters.

pig-root, *v.*

1. *intr.* Of a horse or other animal: to kick upwards with the hind legs, head down and forelegs firmly planted. Also as *vbl. n.*

1900 *Bulletin* (Sydney) 14 July 15/1, I saw a colt after much buck jumping and pig-rooting, get rid of rider, saddle and girth. **1912** J. BOWES *Comrades* 93 The protesting animal was 'pig-rooting' all over the stockyard... Holding on to the crupper with a frantic clutch, the rider managed to stick to the horse's back. **1923** *Bulletin* (Sydney) 18 Oct. 24/2 He apparently didn't know the ABC of pig-rooting, let alone bucking. **1924** L. ST. C. GRONDONA *Kangaroo keeps on Talking* 96 In 'pigrooting' the horse kicks up his hind heels with great vigour and in an apparent effort to stand on his forefeet. **1931** W. HATFIELD *Sheepmates* 161 Hallet gave Atherton an old rogue mule that always pigrooted a little whenever he was saddled up. **1951** *Bulletin* (Sydney) 1 Aug. 14/2 Hey, that horse y' sold me pig-roots too much. **1969** W. MOXHAM *Apprentice* 162 Wouldn't surprise me he'd pigroot, make a show of himself in the middle of a race. **1980** A. HOPGOOD *And here comes Bucknuckle* 48 He fell out of the stall, pig-rooted and the jockey went sailing into the air.

2. a. *Joc. intr.* To ride.

1919 E. DYSON *Hello, Soldier* 17 'N' Privit Artie Rowe along with others in the force Goes pig-rootin' inter battle, holdin' converse with his horse.

b. *trans.* (in *pass.*). To be thrown by a pig-rooting horse.

1965 *Coast to Coast 1963–64* 158, I was pig-rooted off a horse, and broke my wrist.

c. *intr. fig.*

1925 M. TERRY *Across Unknown Aust.* 48 He announced laconically that his car was pig-rooting!

Hence **pig-rooting** *ppl. a.*

1913 *Bulletin* (Sydney) 20 Mar. 16/4 I've seen a monkey in a circus remain on a pig-rooting Australian outlaw, but was it a horseman? **1946** *Ibid.* 30 Oct. 29/2 The Mopoke's opening bowler is a long, lean cove with the action of a pigrooting brumby.

pig-root, *n.* [f. prec.] The act of pig-rooting.

1917 A.L. BREWER *'Gator's Euchre* 30 Starlight snorted frequently, and delivered a few violent pig-roots; though these did not perturb Walsh, who had sat the horse on more than one occasion when it was fresh after a long spell. **1920** *Bulletin* (Sydney) 25 Mar. 22/3 Some stock-horses get so accustomed to having a few 'pig-roots' on being mounted that it becomes a sort of sacred rite with them. **1935** A. CROCKER *Aust. hops In* 53 The pig-root is mostly the effort of the amateur buck-jumper. **1953** *Bulletin* (Sydney) 7 Oct. 13/1 Soon as the barrier goes up Ginger gives a dozen flyin' pig-roots, nearly plants me, then tears off like he's jet-propelled. **1960** R.S. PORTEOUS *Cattleman* 194 Ken was moderately fond of riding. He had his own pony and could even stick its playful winter-morning pigroot, but he showed none of Dan's reckless horsemanship.

pig-rooter. An animal that 'pig-roots'.

1933 J. MCCARTER *Love's Lunatic* 123 I've fallen as heavy as a mug rider from a pig-rooter. **1936** J.C. DOWNIE *Galloping Hoofs* 36 A lot of people in town call a pig-rooter a buckjumper, which is wrong. A true broncho leaves the ground with all four feet at once while a pig-rooter only lifts his hind legs. **1977** H. TOWSON *Black & White* 69 This is Old Charlie's pig-rooter. He's never been ridden for years.

pigsty. [Transf. use of *pigsty* a pen for pigs.] A (temporary) structure of logs built as a support on a mine, for a section of railway track, etc.

1911 E.D. CLELAND *W. Austral. Mining Practice* 145 In wide stopes it is sometimes found necessary to support the ore at points where it threatens to come away... The support given usually takes the form of 'pig-stys'. These are constructed of round logs, built up in the form of a hollow square, and forming a support of great strength. **1929** W.J. RESIDE *Golden Days* 24 Owing to washaways on the line we often had to alight and build up 'pig-sties' underneath the rails. **1950** C.E. GOODE *Yarns of Yilgarn* 82 We made a 'pigsty' of bull-oak logs around the mouth of the show and hoisted the windlass-bole into a set of crossed and bolted saplings. **1969** P. ADAM SMITH *Folklore Austral. Railwaymen* 15 In 1929 we put in pig-sties at the washaways for nearly a hundred miles down as far as Bundoomah.

pigtail. *Obs.* [Transf. use of *pigtail*: used elsewhere but recorded earliest in Aust.] A Chinese immigrant to Australia.

1858 A. PENDRAGON *Queen of South* 169 There's no good to be done by a whitefellow where those thundering pig-tails are. **1871** *Illustr. Sydney News* 30 Sept. 165/4 The respectable looking pigtail seated in the chair at the table is the presiding genius who .. gathers in the winnings of the bank and pays out its losses without a muscle on his celestial countenance becoming disarranged. **1887** 'WANDERER' *Down on their Luck* 28 The Mayor has asked you to sign a petition to get rid of the pigtails. The Chinkies must go. **1895** *Worker* (Sydney) 19 Jan. 2/5 A pigtail is an antiquated prejudice, rooted in ignorance and superstition. **1907** C. MACALISTER *Old Pioneering Days* 207 The fall broke the poor 'pigtail's' neck.

Hence **pigtailed** *a.*, Chinese.

1871 *Austral. Town & Country Jrnl.* (Sydney) 10 June 720/2 A solid stare and 'No savee' being the extent of news to be elicited from the pig-tailed geologists. **1896** *Bulletin* (Sydney) 17 Oct. 10/4 As the immigrating Chows did not report themselves to the police, the Government and its officials took no cognisance of this increase in the pig-tailed population.

pike. [Transf. use of *pike* a large, voracious, freshwater fish of the fam. Esocidae.] Any of several voracious marine fish, esp. of the fam. Sphyraenidae, having an elongated head and sharp teeth, as *Sphyraena novaehollandiae* and *S. obtusata*.

1847 *Port Phillip Herald* 25 Mar. 2/4 The banks of the Yarra may be daily seen lined with anglers... The bream is the principal sport, although occasionally a pike of large size rewards the angler's perseverance and tact. **1873** F. DE CASTELNAU *Edible Fishes Vic.* 11 The pike .. attains a large size, and is considered by many as the most delicate of the Victorian fishes. **1881** *Proc. Linnean Soc. N.S.W.* VI. 34 *Sphyraena obtusata*... This is the '*Pike*' of the Sydney Fishermen. **1906** D.G. STEAD *Fishes of Aust.* 82 The Pike family is well represented in Australian waters. The most important species is the Short-finned Pike (*Sphyraena novaehollandiae*). [*Note*] Called 'Short-finned' to differentiate it from the 'Long-finned' Pike, a fish of another family .. and with which it is often roughly classified by fishermen and others as simply 'Pike'. **1965** *Austral. Encycl.* VII. 116 *Pike*, a name used for several distinct marine fishes in Australia, where the Old World freshwater pikes (Esocidae) do not occur. All the Australian fishes have a pointed head and huge teeth, but their fins and scales are very different. **1983** *Age* (Melbourne) 19 Sept. 11 Fifteen years ago 38 per cent of Westernport Bay was covered with seagrass. Rock flathead and pike grazed in the grass.

piker. [Transf. use of *piker* a vagrant: see OED(S *piker, n.*^{3} 2.] A bullock living in the wild.

1887 K. MACKAY *Stirrup Jingles* 16 Gone is the rush and rattle Of pikers on the rails, When wings were full of cattle, And thongs came down like flails. **1897** *Bulletin* (Sydney) 11 Dec. 22/4 Are the 'pikers' as wild, and the scrubs just as dense .. ? **1920** L. ESSON *Dead Timber* 40 That baldy-faced piker gets slewing out on the left wing. **1936** I.L. IDRIESS *Cattle King* 62 The boy bought a teamster's cast-off bullock for two pounds. It was an old piker, worked to the very bone. **1951** E. HILL *Territory* 298 They were driving old pikers through thick scrub, a troublesome mob with double watch. **1963** M. BRITT *Pardon my Boots* 81 One old bullock—a piker—stood for a long time gazing dolefully at the big mob he had come from, listening to the shouts and thundering hooves. **1980** S. THORNE *I've met some Bloody Wags* 9 Back to Queensland—back to where the scrubs are deep and dense, to God's own land where the pikers roam, across the border fence.

pile, var. PIALLA.

pile. *Mining. Obs.* [Transf. use of *pile* a heap of money.] A very rich claim. Also **pile claim, pile hole.**

1854 *Illustr. Sydney News* 28 Oct. 324/2 The writer states (with all the enthusiasm of a fortunate digger who has at length discovered his pile) that himself and his party had been successful in striking the gutter. **1871** *Austral. Town & Country Jrnl.* (Sydney) 4 Feb. 143/3 There is little fear but their labours will be soon rewarded with what they deserve—a pile hole. *Ibid.* 17 June 751/3 There is doubtless a large area of payable ground in it; but we think no 'pile' claims. **1885** G. DARRELL *Sunny South* 23, I have to go back and prospect for a pile once more. **1896** *Worker* (Sydney) 26 Dec. 1/2 As success does not always reward merit, our friends had never yet come across their 'pile'.

pilot bird. [Transf. use of *pilot bird* a name applied to a number of birds.] The reddish-brown, chiefly terrestrial bird *Pycnoptilus floccosus* of s.e. mainland Aust., having a penetrating whistle.

1893 *Argus* (Melbourne) 25 Mar. 4/6 Here, close together, are eggs of the lyre bird and the pilot bird—the last very rare, and only found quite lately in the Dandenong Ranges, where the lyre bird, too, has its home. **1901** *Emu* I. 60 Live in the densest scrub, on the ground, as does the Pilot Bird (*Pycnoptilus*). **1944** L. WELSH *Kookaburra* 9 An inhabitant of the timber and scrub, the Pilot Bird is more often heard than seen. **1976** *Reader's Digest Compl. Bk. Austral. Birds* 423 The pilot bird is so named because it is usually seen with the lyrebird. **1984** M. BLAKERS et al. *Atlas Austral. Birds* 456 The range of the Pilotbird is completely within that of the Superb Lyrebird but they are rarely seen together.

pimelea /pɪˈmiljə, paɪˈmiljə/. [The plant genus *Pimelea* was named by naturalists Daniel Solander and Joseph Banks (in Gaertner, J. (1788) *De Fructibus et Seminibus Plantarum* I. 186) from Gr. πιμελή fat, perh. referring to the oily seeds of the plant.] Any plant of the genus *Pimelea* (fam. Thymelaeaceae), shrubs and herbs of the Australasian region, many of which are cultivated as ornamentals. See also *rice-flower* RICE.

1793 J.E. SMITH *Specimen Bot. New Holland* 32 The name of *Pimelea* .. is derived from πιμελή, fat, but is rather a pleasantly sounding than a very apt denomination, unless there may be any thing oily in the recent fruit. **1810** W. AITON *Hortus Kewensis* (ed. 2) I. 25 Flax-leaved Pimelea. Nat[ive] of New South Wales. **1842** W. COLENSO *Let.* 1 Sept. in *Lond. Jrnl. Bot.* (1844) III. 8, I found a handsome *Pimelea* in flower, a shrub of 2–3 feet in height. **1856** *Jrnl. Australasia* I. 38 Pimelia gracilis; P. lygustrina, privet-like pimelia .. called native privet, after English shrub of same name, which it resembles in fruit, foliage, and habits. **1914** F. SULMAN *Pop. Guide Wild Flowers N.S.W.* II. 159 The Pimeleas are the most abundant Australian representatives of this widespread family [Thymelaeaceae]. **1942** C. BARRETT *Austral. Wild Flower Bk.* 178 The Pimeleas or rice-flowers belong to the same family as sweet-scented Daphne... There are between seventy and eighty species, but only a few may be seen in Australian gardens, including species that are cherished under glass in England. **1963** *N. Austral. Monthly* Dec. 11 The only 'wild flowers' I saw were a few lovely pimeleas which would grace any garden. These are small shrubby plants with narrow two-inch long leaves and red stems. The tall flower heads form a dense spike, two to four inches long with blood-red flowers. **1986** *Canberra Times* 30 Jan. (Suppl.) 11/5 Depending on the time of year, even the less knowledgeable gardener will find the 'familiar' growing in the park as nature intended—grevilleas in many forms, mint bushes, pimelea, kunzea.

pimlico. *Obs.* [Imitative, prob. assimilating to the name of a London suburb.] FRIAR BIRD.

1841 J. GOULD *Birds of Aust.* (1848) IV. Pl. 58, The Friar Bird .. has obtained from the Colonists the various names of 'Poor Soldier', 'Pimlico', 'Four O'Clock', etc. **1918** *Bulletin* (Sydney) 2 May 24/3 The bobala has probably more *aliases* than any other Australian bird, being variously known as friar bird, monk, pimlico, four o'clock, poor soldier and leatherhead. **1944** L. WELSH *Kookaburra* 12 Noisy friar birds .. have many names—Leatherhead, Monk, Four O'Clock, Pimlico, and Poor Soldier.

pimp, *n.* [Transf. use of *pimp* a pander.] An informer; a tell-tale.

1899 J. BRADSHAW *Highway Robbery under Arms* (1912) 8 Yes, savagely they murdered him, The cowardly Blue Coat imps, Who were led on to where he slept By informing Peeler's pimps. **1914** M. CANNON *That Damned Democrat* (1981) 142 A willing tool to help any police grafter or criminal pimp to secure stripes. **1919** V. MARSHALL *World of Living Dead* 62 Some pimp puts the pot on, and they starts awashin' out yer mouth be noo reg'lations. **1938** X. HERBERT *Capricornia* 567 'I'm not a pimp.' 'What you mean pimp?' 'I'm not a police informer.' **1942** G. CASEY *It's Harder for Girls* 51 'I just say I'm not a pimp,' Brownie insisted, beginning to blubber. **1969** D. NILAND *Dead Men Running* 290 'There's a pimp at work'... 'The same pimp is it, that potted Shannessy and Halloran?' **1974** *Age* (Melbourne) 12 Oct. 12/1 You fat pimp! The standard response to 'I'm going to tell on you'.

pimp, *v.* [f. prec.] *intr.* To tell tales; to inform. Usu. with **on.**

1938 X. HERBERT *Capricornia* 524 He reckons I pimped on him—and that's how the johns went out and grabbed 'em both. **1941** S.J. BAKER *Pop. Dict. Austral. Slang* 54 *Pimp*, .. to inform on. **1945** G. CASEY *Downhill is Easier* 109 This dago bastard pimped on him to Hayes, an' lost him his job. **1957** J. WATEN *Shares in Murder* 155 You made up to me so you could get me to pimp on Charlie for you.

pin-bullock. [Transf. use of *pin* the middle place in a tandem team of three horses + BULLOCK.] One of the two (or four) bullocks in a team harnessed to the end of the pole: see quot. 1959; CLAMPER; POINTER *n.*^{3} 1.

1898 *Bulletin* (Sydney) 13 Aug. 3/2 From pin-bullocks to the leaders, every beast was wearied out. **1959** H.P. TRITTON *Time means Tucker* 36 A bullock-team is made up in four parts: polers, pin, body and leaders... The pin-bullocks take the pull. **1980** O. RUHEN *Bullock Teams* 172 Pin-bullocks were often referred to as 'the clampers'.

pin bush. [See quot. 1902.] NEEDLEWOOD.

1888 *Proc. Linnean Soc. N.S.W.* III. 518 *Hakea leucoptera* .. 'Needle bush', 'Pin bush'. Good drinking water is got from the fleshy-roots of this bush in the arid districts in which it grows. **1902** *Ibid.* XXVII. 580 Various shrubs and trees passed between Cowra and Grenfell were: . . *Acacia diffusa* (sometimes called Pin Bush from the shape of the rigid pointed leaves) [etc.]. **1933** *Bulletin* (Sydney) 7 June 25/2 Pin bush . . will grow in poor soils.

pinch. [Br. dial. *pinch* short, steep hill; recorded earliest in U.S.: see OED(S.)] A steep or difficult part of a road; a steep hill. Also *fig.*

1846 *Bell's Life in Sydney* 25 July 3/3 The passage through the gap is not very difficult until you begin to descend on the eastern side, when the pinches are real bursters. **1852** S. Mossman *Gold Regions Aust.* (ed. 2) 40 Here are what the colonists name 'pinches'—ascents in the mountains that would puzzle a London drayman. **1871** *Austral. Town & Country Jrnl.* (Sydney) 7 Jan. 17/1 Turning his horse northward, the driver must not be troubled with the heart disease, the incline, upon two 'pinches', as they are called, being rather steep. **1885** 'W.G.C.' *Some Acct. Mount Morgan Gold Mine* 10 Some five miles further is the Razor-back Range, a sharp 'pinch' on the road leading up to a tableland. **1913** C.J. Dennis *Backblock Ballads* 19 So we punched 'em on by inches, liftin' 'em across the pinches, Till we struck the final section of the worst part of the road. **1923** J. Moses *Beyond City Gates* 37 I'm trottin' along the road of life . . and I feel the uphill pinches. **1924** J. Nisbet *Scraps* 6 Half-way up the hill were the drivers with two teams all of a string on one dray, 'double banking' over the stiff pinch. **1931** Lawson & Brereton *H. Lawson* 18 We were near Soldier's Pinch, a mile on the Sydney side of Mount Victoria. **1958** F.B. Vickers *Though Poppies Grow* 15 He charged up the last pinch and stood on the peak within the shade of a small thicket of banksia trees. **1985** P. Carey *Illywhacker* 31 When he met someone on the track, bogged to the axles under ten tons of wool, or in trouble on a pinch, he would see that . . they had not stopped long enough to think.

pindan /'pɪndæn/. [a. Bardi *bindan.*]

1. A tract of arid, sandy country characteristic of the s.w. Kimberley region, in n. W.A.; the low, scrubby vegetation occurring on the sandy soils of such country; any of several plants typifying such vegetation, as *Acacia tumida* (fam. Mimosaceae). Also *attrib.*

1888 *Proc. Linnean Soc. N.S.W.* II. 1018 The coast on the east side of King's sound is low and swampy, bounded eastwards by 'Pindan' sands and gravels, a pliocene formation which extends inwards for upwards of 60 miles. **1926** K. Dahl *In Savage Aust.* 273 Further inland one met the peculiar stunted forest called 'pindan' by the Colonists. **1927** M. Dorney *Adventurous Honeymoon* 147 It is very similar to what is called 'desert country' in the Northern Territory, only that the sandy soil of the 'pindan' is loose and makes travelling very difficult, which is not the case with the hard red sandy soil of the 'desert' in the Territory. **1937** M. Terry *Sand & Sun* 269 Pindan black. [*Note*] West Australian for desert black. **1948** H.A. Lindsay *Bushman's Handbk.* 59 The areas of good country in the Kimberley are separated by arid plains of red sand known as Pindans. **1951** E. Hill *Territory* 294 The mob goes drifting down, through the pindan, light scrub in red sand, 'Bay o' Biscay' country. **1955** F. Lane *Patrol to Kimberleys* 216 *Pindan*, a kind of wattle which thrives in the red sandhill areas where the grass is thin. Seldom exceeding twenty-five feet in height, pindan gives a harsh, monotonous aspect to the country. **1962** C. Gye *Cockney & Crocodile* 111 We drove the eighty four miles along the straight red road through the pindan, that low scrub of spindly fire-blackened trees and tall grass which looks hopeless but with a bore or two will support sheep and cattle well. **1983** R.J. Petheram *Plants Kimberley Region W.A.* 363 In the North Kimberley region periodic burning is considered necessary to prevent Pindan Wattle invasion of improved pastures.

2. Comb. **pindan country, scrub.**

1910 *Emu* IX. 148 The country immediately around Broome is covered with fairly dense scrub, and is known locally as **Pindan country.** **1948** H.A. Lindsay *Bushman's Handbk.* 59 In the pindan country it is almost useless to seek food. **1964** T. Ronan *Packhorse & Pearling Boat* 38 It was typical pindan country: heavy red soil, stunted trees, sour, branch-high spear grass, and with no features other than the ant-beds, and no watercourses of any description. **1978** O. White *Silent Reach* 22 Until I was forty years old all I owned was the leasehold of half a million acres of pindan country that carried two thousand head of merino sheep in a good season. **1952** I.L. Idriess *Outlaws of Leopolds* 18 A darkness before them darker than the night was the dense edge of the **pindan scrub**—small trees densely growing together, interlaced by creeper and vine. **1970** P. Slater *Eagle for Pidgin* 76 The grey-green of the pindan scrub with its patches of red earth stopped abruptly at highwater mark and bright green mangroves took over. **1978** D. Stuart *Wedgetail View* 58 Barren waterless pindan scrubs and points of stunted kadjibuts that faced one way the coastal plain, one way the age-old d esert.

pindaner. Chiefly *W.A.* Also **pindana.** [f. prec.] An Aboriginal from the inland. Also *attrib.*

1938 D. Bates *Passing of Aborigines* 20 Big pindana (inland) mob blackfellows come up. **1954** I.L. Idriess *Nor'-Westers* 220 At Lulugui station a skinny pindaner came in from the bush. . . Dick the stockman christened him Spider.

pine. [Transf. use of *pine* a tree of the genus *Pinus* or various allied coniferous species.]

1. Any of several, usu. large, coniferous trees generally yielding a useful timber, now usu. with distinguishing epithet, as **celery-top, Huon, Norfolk Island** (see under first element); the wood of the tree. Also *attrib.*

1788 *HRA* (1914) 1st Ser. I. 21 The pine-trees [on Norfolk Island] rise fifty and sixty feet before they shoot out any branches. **1791** *Extracts Lett. Arthur Phillip* 16 The pine trees are of a great size, many of which are from 180 to 220 feet in height, and from six to nine feet in diameter. **1793** J. Hunter *Hist. Jrnl. Trans. Port Jackson* 121 Here the banks of the river are low, and covered with what we call the pine-trees of this country; which indeed have received that name merely from the leaf, which is a good deal like the pine, but the wood is very different. **1801** G. Barrington *Sequel to Voyage N.S.W.* 33 Several Pine Trees from one hundred and eighty, to two hundred feet in length, and from twenty to thirty in the girt [*sic*], were blown down. **1826** Tas. Colonial Secretary's Office Rec. 1/9 73, The pine required at Launceston has been ordered from Macquarie Harbour—it is impossible to supply what is required from here. **1848** C. Cozens *Adventures of Guardsman* 173 The most esteemed and most valuable are mahogany, cedar and pine woods, which in many parts are very abundant, and grow to an enormous size. **1861** J.D. Lang *Qld., Aust.* 43 Close to the water's edge rises a complete wall of luxuriant foliage; fig-trees, bean-trees, pines. **1903** *Advocate* (Burnie) 11 June 3/2 Some of the upper reaches of the Gordon River still contain treasures in the way of Huon pine . . notwithstanding the fact that the pine beds there have been worked for almost half a century. **1965** *Austral. Encycl.* VII. 119 The name 'pine' is popularly given to a number of different indigenous conifers.

2. Cypress pine. Also *attrib.*

1805 J.H. Tuckey *Acct. Voyage to establish Colony Port Philip* 161 Timber trees are very thinly scattered. . . They are . . box, and a kind of pine. **1837** J. Backhouse *Extracts from Lett.* (1839) V. 17 Among the trees is one called here pine, belonging to the genus callitris, of pyramidal figure, and distinct from any we have before met with. **1846** *Sydney Morning Herald* 8 Dec. 3/2, I saw no callitris (*pine* of the colonists) in all that country. **1849** C. Sturt *Narr. Exped. Central Aust.* I. 183 We crossed a ridge of sand, on which numerous Pine-trees were growing. **1867** A.K. Collins *Waddy Mundoee* 7 Where the myall flourishes, and the white box, and sandal-wood, and pine, spring into glorious life. **1890** 'R. Boldrewood' *Squatter's Dream* 32 A sand-ridge picturesquely wooded with . . pine (*callitris*). **1902** *Emu* II. 17 Sand ridges, clothed with pine & bull-oak. **1938** C.T. White *Princ. Bot. Qld. Farmers* 142 The inner bark . . contains an oleo-resin which, when the bark is injured, exudes in tears, the resin being variously known as 'Pine Resin', 'Cypress Pine Resin', [etc.]. **1981** E. Rolls *Million Wild Acres* p. v, The fragrant yellow pine . . was milled.

3. Used *attrib.* in both senses in Comb. **pine brush, scrub.**

1839 *S. Austral. Register* (Adelaide) 11 July 4 Belts of scrub and **pine brush.** **1852** J.D. Lang *Austral. Emigrant's Man.* 50, I . . found . . some of the nooks presenting pine brushes. **1888** H.S. Russell *Genesis Qld.* 296, I have . . watched in the moonlight by the edge of a pine-brush, dense enough to exclude light almost in some places. **1827** *Monitor* (Sydney) 20 Aug. 599/2 Towards evening my route eastward was completely terminated, by mountains covered with **pine scrubs,** to the summit. **1847** *Portland Guardian* 18 Jan. 3/3 After travelling for about an hour, we reached the outskirts of an extensive pine scrub, an obstacle always to be avoided if possible. **1898** W. Redmond *Shooting Trip* 21 The monotony of the gum-tree was relieved from time to time by scrub—'pine scrub' it is called. **1904** *Bulletin* (Sydney) 25 Aug. 36/2, I went an' cut a lot uv posts an' rails in some pine-scrub. **1923** J. Bowes *Jackaroos* 154, I was in a pine scrub once . . boxed up . . among the cyprus[*sic*]-pines. **1935** F. Clune *Rolling down Lachlan* 167 The broad trail was followed for a long time, till the party entered a dense pine-scrub. **1948** —— *Wild Colonial Boys* 165 He returned to the Weddin Mountains with two racehorses, and camped with them in a pine scrub.

pineapple.

1. Used *attrib.* in Special Comb. **pineapple grass-tree** *obs.* [see quot. 1842], the plant *Richea pandanifolia* (see Grass-tree 2); also **pine-apple tree.**

1842 D. Burn *Narr. Journey Hobart Town to Macquarie Harbour* (1955) 25 The pathway is everywhere skirted by . . a very remarkable and exceedingly graceful plant, which, from its striking similitude to the lordly fruit, is styled the 'Pine-Apple Tree'. **1877** *Illustr. Austral. News* (Melbourne) 3 Sept. 138/1 The pine-apple tree (richea pandanifolia) may also be frequently met with.

2. [See quot. 1974.] An opal cluster, formed where glauberite crystals are replaced by opal.

1928 M.E. Fullerton *Austral. Bush* 212 Bunches of crystal, belonging to a remote geological period, and called by the miners 'pineapples'. **1940** E. Hill *Great Austral. Loneliness* (ed. 2) 269 At White Cliffs . . were unearthed . . 'pineapples' of aggregated crystals. **1961** F. Leechman *Opal Bk.* 148 The opalised pseudomorphs—one can hardly include them with organic fossils—known as 'pineapples', which were found at White Cliffs, do not seem to occur in the South Australian fields. **1974** *Austral. Gem & Minerals Fossicker* I. 74/3 The types of opal to be found in the rock at White Cliffs are fascinating in themselves. The favorite, and most valuable form is a 'pineapple'. Although it may look nothing like a pineapple, it gets its name from the way it is formed from many small pieces apparently glued together by nature.

3. In the phr. **the rough** (or **wrong**) **end of the pineapple,** a raw deal; inequitable treatment.

1961 R. Lawler *Piccadilly Bushman* 37 He'll know what I mean when I talk of getting the wrong end of the pineapple. **1976** *Sydney Morning Herald* 23 Oct. 9/1 Waffling witnesses, even those of lofty social standing, were given short shrift, if not the rough end of the pineapple. **1980** B. Hornadge *Austral. Slanguage* 69 One amusing expression of Australian origin is 'To get the rough end of the pineapple'—meaning to get a raw deal or unfair treatment. **1981** P. Barton *Bastards I have Known* 114 There was no way that I was going to get the 'rough end of the pineapple' from Wally so I kept out of his way.

piner.

a. *Tas.* One employed in felling Huon pine trees and getting the logs to market.

1871 *Mercury* (Hobart) 5 Apr. 2 The piners have to go some 15 or 20 miles up the Davey River to the timber beds. **1875** *Papers & Proc. R. Soc. Tas.* (1876) 94, I hope that a few personal observations on the locality, its pine industry and forests . . will be interesting, even to those who fully know and appreciate the details and hardships of the occupation of a piner. **1901** *Axeman's Jrnl.* (Ulverstone) Oct. 77/1 A . . sore grievance with our hardy piners, now that the pine forests are becoming thinned of big timber. **1917** *Bulletin* (Sydney) 4 Jan. 22/4 A few timber-getting families are . . the only dwellers. . . The piners formerly went nearly 100 miles up the Gordon, disregarding its rapids. **1949** W. Lawson *Blue Gum Clippers* 76 Her crew were rescued by the chief officer of the *Flying Childers* and two piners, Heather and Smith, of Port Davey. **1968** P. Adam Smith *Tiger Country* 4 A Sydney editor told me to 'pick up a story about the piners. They float logs down a river'. **1983** P. Dombrovskis *Wild Rivers* 26 He often passed beneath the Angel and grew to believe that anyone who destroyed it would meet with ill-fortune. For the piners it was a unique, sacred presence in the heart of the rivers region.

b. *transf.* An artefact made of pine.

1895 *Bulletin* (Sydney) 26 Jan. 15/1 A Melbourne

undertaker complains that the local cadaver is now almost invariably content with a stained 'piner'.

pining, *vbl. n. Tas.* The occupation of a piner.

1919 *Huon Times* (Franklin) 28 Sept. 3/3 This gentleman has for many years engaged in pining at the Craycroft, Picton, and Huon rivers. **1968** P. ADAM SMITH *Tiger Country* 6 Pining, the collecting of Huon pine logs, began in convict times. **1984** J. & K. HEPPER *Gordon River Cruise Bk.* 11 Pining was . . taking place to the south at Port Davey.

pink, *a.* Used as a distinguishing epithet in the names of flora and fauna: **pink bells** *pl.*, see PINK-EYE *n.*[1] 2; **-breasted robin,** the small bird *Petroica rodinogaster* of Vic. and Tas., the mature male having predom. grey-brown plumage with a deep pink breast and belly; also **pink robin,** and formerly **pink-breasted wood-robin; cockatoo,** MAJOR MITCHELL COCKATOO; **-eared duck,** the nomadic duck *Malacorhynchus membranaceus*, having a pink patch behind the eye, white underparts with brown bars, and a shovel-shaped bill; PINK-EYE *n.*[1] 1; *whistling duck*, (b) see WHISTLING; *zebra duck*, see ZEBRA; see also WIDGEON; also **pink-ear; wood,** any of several trees or tall shrubs, esp. of the genus *Eucryphia* (fam. Eucryphiaceae), as *E. moorei* (see PLUMWOOD) of s.e. N.S.W. and e. Vic., having dark-green, pinnate leaves and large, white, showy flowers, *E. lucida* (see LEATHERWOOD), and (*Tas.*) *Beyeria viscosa* (fam. Euphorbiaceae) of s. Aust.; the wood of these trees.

1842 J. GOULD *Birds of Aust.* (1848) III. Pl. 1, *Erythrodryas rhodinogaster.* **Pink-breasted** Wood-**Robin**. . . The food of the Pink-breasted Wood-Robin consists solely of insects. **1903** *Emu* II. 163 Pink-breasted robin (*Petroeca rhodinogastra*) abundant in parts of the Otways, as on the Upper Erskine. On the plains it is not to be seen except in the scrub near the coast, where it is plentiful. **1909** G. SMITH *Naturalist in Tas.* 65 In another of the Tasmanian Robins, known as the Pink-breasted Robin, the male has the breast of a most beautiful claret colour. **1945** C. BARRETT *Austral. Bird Life* 175 The pink robin (*P[etroica] rodinogaster*) and the rose robin . . keep to the mountain gullies. **1965** *Austral. Encycl.* VII. 470 The pink-breasted robin, an inhabitant of heavy forests in Tasmania and Victoria. **1976** *Reader's Digest Compl. Bk. Austral. Birds* 357 The nest of the pink robin . . is a beautiful compact cup of soft green moss, deftly bound with spiderweb and camouflaged outside with pale green or grey lichen. **1843** J. GOULD *Birds of Aust.* (1848) V. Pl. 2, *Cacatua leadbeateri* . . **Pink Cockatoo**, Colonists of Swan River. **1865** G.F. ANGAS *Aust.* 94 The pink cockatoo is a very handsome bird, with a large crest of yellow and scarlet feathers. **1884** A.W. STIRLING *Never Never Land* 170 'Leadbetter's' or the pink cockatoo, resembles the 'corilla' in almost every point. **1912** *Emu* XII. 117 Pink Cockatoo . . getting exceedingly scarce. **1932** H. PRIEST *Call of Bush* 210 Here the rather rare Pink Cockatoos . . also came in small flocks to drink. **1945** C. BARRETT *Austral. Bird Life* 74 The name of a famous early explorer, Sir Thomas Mitchell, long ago was given to the pink cockatoo. **1984** M. BLAKERS et al. *Atlas Austral. Birds* 248 The Pink Cockatoo inhabits a variety of country in the inland providing there is fresh surface water and large hollow trees for nesting. **1898** E.E. MORRIS *Austral Eng.* 127 **Pink-eared D[uck]**, or Widgeon . . *Malacorhynchus membranaceus*. **1964** M. SHARLAND *Territory of Birds* 106 The delightful little Pink-ear, with broad bill, zebra stripes, and white-rimmed eye, is well distributed. **1982** R. ELLIS *Bush Safari* 124 Hundreds of tiny Pink-eared Duck were taking advantage of the flood conditions. **1824** *Hobart Town Gaz.* 1 Oct., Colonial Timber may at any time be purchased of an inhabitant of this town. . . Cherry Tree and **Pink Wood**, for furniture and gun stocks. **1832** J. BACKHOUSE *Extracts from Lett.* (1838) i. 28 Celery-topped pine . . pink wood, and some other trees also afford fine and useful timber. **1877** *Illustr. Austral. News* (Melbourne) 3 Sept. 138/1 The bases of the mountains are clad with the most luxuriant growth of forest vegetation, such as . . the beautiful pinkwood (eucryphia billardieri). **1903** *Tasmanian Timbers* (Tas. Lands & Survey Dept.) 29 Pinkwood or Rosewood (*Beyera viscosa*) . . a small tree with a reddish wood. **1942** C. BARRETT *Austral. Wild Flower Bk.* 41 The pink wood, *Eucryphia Billardieri* . . with its glistening winter buds and large snow-white flowers. **1967** N.A. WAKEFIELD *Naturalist's Diary* 20 The Pinkwood (*Eucryphia moorei*), a large jungle tree resembling a beech but with foliage like that of an ash.

pink, *v. trans.* To shear (a sheep) so closely that the colour of the skin is visible. Also *absol.*

1897 *Worker* (Sydney) 11 Sept. 1/1 He 'shaves' his sheep, or 'pinks 'em', when he shears them nice and clean. **1904** L.M.P. ARCHER *Bush Honeymoon* 61 Every shearer *pinks* his sheep as the manager passes. **1911** A.G. STEPHENS *Pearl & Octopus* 105 He had finished that big wether in five minutes . . and had pinked as if the boss was at his hip. **1930** *Bulletin* (Sydney) 8 Oct. 21/4 The jumbuck these days has to be 'pinked' without being butchered. **1944** *Ibid.* 19 Apr. 12/1 McFowler 'pinked' every sheep and never drew blood. **1975** G.A.W. SMITH *Once Green Jackaroo* 151 If you see any ridges of wool left on the sheep, give the man one warning but not two. I want my sheep pinked. I pay for that.

Hence **pinker** *n.*, one who shears carefully (and therefore slowly).

1939 J. SORENSEN *Lost Shanty* 22 Now 'Billy the Pinker' and 'Quality Jack', With 'Jimmy the Moulder', were shearing out back.

pink-eye, *n.*[1]

1. *Pink-eared duck*, see PINK a. Also **pink-eyed duck.**

1845 J. GOULD *Birds of Aust.* (1848) VI. Pl. 13, *Malacorhynchus membranaceus* . . Pink-eyed Duck, Colonists of Swan River. **1861** 'OLD BUSHMAN' *Bush Wanderings* 82 The *Whistle-wing*, or Pink-eye . . is a pretty little duck, of a light silvery mottle, with a faint pink mark over each eye. **1896** F.G. AFLALO *Sketch Nat. Hist. Aust.* 100 The Pink-Eyed Duck . . is found only in Australia, where it keeps to the southern districts. **1941** C. BARRETT *Aust.* 53 A few pairs of pink-eyes rose from the creek.

2. *pl.* Any of many small shrubs of the genus *Tetratheca* (fam. Tremandraceae) of s.w. and s.e. Aust. incl. Tas., having often pendant, usu. purplish-pink to red flowers with a dark centre. Also **pink-bells.**

1914 E.E. PESCOTT *Native Flowers Vic.* 31 Tetratheca ciliata and Tetratheca ericfolia [*sic*] . . are low-growing plants, known as 'pink-eyes', sending out long sprays of magenta bells in spring and early summer. **1942** C. BARRETT *Austral. Wild Flower Bk.* 83 There are about twenty-five species in the exclusively Australian family to which *Tetratheca* belongs, all but a few being pink-eyes. **1967** N.A. WAKEFIELD *Naturalist's Diary* 26 The ground shrubbery included the best patches of Pink-bells (*Tetratheca*) that I have ever seen. **1984** E. WALLING *On Trail Austral. Wildflowers* 24 Heathy Tetratheca or Pink-bells, a low slender plant with open mauve flowers at the tips of the wiry stems.

pink-eye /'pɪŋkaɪ, 'pɪŋki/, *n.*[2] Chiefly *W.A. Austral. pidgin.* Also **pink-hi, pinki.** [a. Yinjibarndi *piŋkayi* f. *piŋka* hunting.] WALKABOUT 3 a. and 4 a.

1899 [see PINK-EYE *v.*]. **1901** *Bulletin* (Sydney) 22 June 32/3 A common practice at these stations is . . 'Pinki' (native holiday)—a picnic where the tucker is flying in the air, or crawling the earth, the natives having first to catch before they can satisfy their hunger. This 'pinki' takes place when the kind 'master' has no immediate work for his 'indentured' black goods. **1902** *Ibid.* 29 Mar. 14/2 A squatter . . sends the blacks (signed-on) whom he does not want, out on what is termed pinki (or holiday)—that is to say, he stops their rations and turns them out where there is no food till he wants them again. **1919** *Ibid.* 22 May 22/4 Yandying lead is the chief industry of the tribes, who make a good thing out of it, pretty nearly every buck having some sort of sulky for his frequent 'pinkeye' outing. **1927** K.S. PRICHARD *Brumby Innes* (1974) 85 The rest of the camp's gone pink-eye, till Brumby gets back. **1935** I.L. IDRIESS *Man Tracks* 66 Soon Tommy would return . . would seize his spears and go laughing with Clabby on *pinki* (walkabout). **1948** M. UREN *Glint of Gold* 219 The natives had gone 'pink-hi', as they often do, quite suddenly. **1962** MARSHALL & DRYSDALE *Journey among Men* 89 We talked with a party of aborigines. . . They had quit their station jobs, as they are prone to do, and had gone on a hunting walkabout and a 'pink-eye'. This is aboriginal slang for holiday, derived from their condition at the end of it. **1972** P.L. BROWN *Coast of Coral & Pearl* 173 The Aboriginal obsession with walkabout or 'pink hi' has a contagious effect on white Australians. **1984** W.W. AMMON et al. *Working Lives* 21 Dido and me are in for a bit of pink-eye and to do some business as well.

pink-eye, *n.*[3] [Of unknown origin.] A labourer who is given preferential treatment when work is allocated. See BULL *n.*[4]

1915 *Bulletin* (Sydney) 9 Dec. 22/1, I was wielding the pick and banjo in a gang on a big channel job once when the ganger got his 'slip' for giving his 'pink-eye' (pet) an easy job. **1955** J. MORRISON *Black Cargo* 218 Go for your pink-eyes, Hills! **1966** S.J. BAKER *Austral. Lang.* (ed. 2) 215 *Pink-eye*, a sycophant. **1975** V. WILLIAMS *Yrs. of Big Jim* 71 They selected their own labour in what was known as the open pick-up or bull system. Every day thousands of men were herded into the compound like slaves in a slave market. When work was scarce the pickup boss only picked up his pink-eyes or bulls. **1978** W. LOWENSTEIN *Weevils in Flour* 241 I've seen them there in Sydney, picking-up [*sic*] labour on the Hungry Mile. The foreman would pick up all his pink-eyes, all his plums. **1982** LOWENSTEIN & HILLS *Under Hook* 81 As soon as the deck cargo was off, you'd be finished. Now you might get that once a week, but the regular gangs, the bloody pink-eyes, they'd be kept on till the ship was finished.

pink-eye, *n.*[4] [Prob. altered form of PINKY *n.*[2]]

a. Cheap alcoholic liquor; alcoholic liquor in general. See also quot. 1945. Also *attrib.*

1922 *Bulletin* (Sydney) 6 July 22/2 The Speck's early settlers learned from the blacks how pink-eye can be got from the cider-tree. **1941** *Coast to Coast* 23 Somebody'll be getting into trouble for setting Charley pink-eye again. Where does he get the money to buy drink, anyhow? **1945** S.J. BAKER *Austral. Lang.* 166 Recipes as published by an outback newspaper in 1936. . . Methylated spirits and Condy's crystals (*Pinky*). . . Addicts of these noxious drinks are known as *meths* . . and *pinkeyes*. **1956** A. UPFIELD *Battling Prophet* 84 I'm game to bet there was fifty empty Pink-Eye brandy bottles. He hadn't been dead long. . . Lying on the floor, and the place stinking of Pink Eye. **1966** B. HESLING *Stir up Stew* 217, I mentioned the grapevine. . . You cut it back—or the chap next door does so in exchange for fruit which he makes into pink-eye.

b. A drinking bout.

1958 F.B. VICKERS *Mirage* (ed. 2) 247 He reckoned we'd been havin' a pink-eye—layin' up on the grog. **1982** M. WATTONE *Winning Gold in W.A.* 51 Jim Clarke was often having a go at these three men and named them the roadside prospectors because he believed they just went out having a pink eye (boozing).

pink-eye, *v.* [See PINK-EYE *n.*[2] 1.] *intr.* To go on a walkabout; to holiday. Also as *vbl. n.* and *ppl. a.*, and **pink-eyer** *n.*, a holiday-maker.

1899 *Truth* (Sydney) 9 Apr. 5/4 The diabolical and dastardly doing of the 'Pinkeyeing' Squattocracy of the nor-west. **1919** *Smith's Weekly* (Sydney) 10 May 11/2 Pearlers crowd away for a holiday—known as a 'pink-eye' in nor-west slang—in the off-season, when the boats cannot operate. One such party happened to 'pink-eye' on a small island off the N.W. coast. . . The island soon disappeared, all but a rock or two, from which derisive crabs watched the shivering 'pink-eyers' steer for the mainland. **1929** K.S. PRICHARD *Coonardoo* (1961) 24 I'll be glad when all this pink-eyeing is over.

pinko, var. PINKY *n.*[1]

pinky /'pɪŋki/, *n.*[1] *S.A.* Also **pinkie,** and formerly [a. Gaurna *piŋki*.] BILBY.

1840 TEICHELMANN & SCHÜRMANN *Outlines of Grammar* 39 Pingko, *s.* a small animal with a white tail that burrows in the earth. **1844** D.G. BROCK *To Desert with Sturt* (1975) 54 The white fur of an animal they call the 'Pinkoe'. **1885** N. ROBINSON *Stagg of Tarcowie* 17 July (1977) 36, I caught one of them curious things the night before last. . . Willie Cubby says they call them pinkies over at Warrabar [*sc.* Wirrabara] where there is plenty of them. **1898** *Bulletin* (Sydney) 23 July 15/3 Something apparently new in zoology has been taken into Kalgoorlie from way-out—something between the 'bilbee' (of N.S.W. and Q.) and the 'pinkie' (of S.A.). **1926** A.S. LE SOUEF et al. *Wild Animals Australasia* 299 White men in the bush usually refer to the species as the 'pinkie', or 'bielby'. **1943** C. BARRETT *Austral. Animal*

Bk. 55 Little more than a generation ago . . it was usual for rabbit trappers to take more 'pinkies' than rabbits in their traps. **1969** E.C. Rolls *They All ran Wild* 49 'Pinky' referred to the bare skin on the nose and 'pinto' probably to the black and white tail.

pinky, *n.*[2] Also **pinkie.** [Orig. Br. slang but chiefly Austral.: see OEDS *sb.*[3]]

1. Cheap or home-made (fortified) wine. Also *attrib.*

1904 *Worker* (Sydney) 10 Sept. 2/2 One vile decoction, known locally as 'Pinky', is so full of ether and raw spirit that it sends drinkers stark, staring mad. **1913** *Bulletin* (Sydney) 9 Oct. 24/3 'Pinky' drinking is physically undermining a large number of otherwise good Australians. **1920** *Smith's Weekly* (Sydney) 13 Nov. 9/4 The queerest sly-grogger I know was one, an Italian, who owned a vineyard and manufactured 'pinky'. **1932** J. McCarter *Pan's Clan* 138 Who th' hell said I wiz drinkin' *cheap* pinkie? **1944** *Bulletin* (Sydney) 19 Jan. 12/2 They soused the stonkered one in the river till he came to. 'Take much pinkie t' knock y'?' Charlie inquired thoughtfully. **1952** C.J. Dennis *Random Verse* 90 Then let the purple pinkie flow! One last wild wassail ere we go! **1963** X. Herbert *Disturbing Element* 164 Everybody who had a backyard in W.A. grew grapes, and . . would brew a drop of what was called Pinky. **1970** N.A. Beagley *Up & Down Under* 80 Port was called 'Pinkie', and those who preferred port were Pinkie drinkers. **1980** Hepworth & Hindle *Boozing out in Melbourne Pubs* 15 Other affectionate nicknames for the stuff itself were: scarlet runner, ink, paint, bombo, nelly, pinky, plonk and plink.

2. Comb. **pinky joint, shop.**

1958 M.D. Berrington *Stones of Fire* 7 'That's the store and the wine saloon,' Roger told me. 'The bush name for them is '**pinky joint**'—don't ask me why.' **1920** *Bulletin* (Sydney) 5 Aug. 24/2 Jacky had just recovered from the horrors which he had contracted at the local **pinky shop. 1942** *Ibid.* 1 July 13/4 It was near to closing time when the town's chief vag. entered my favourite pinky shop with a quart wine bottle that he had salvaged somewhere around the parks.

Hence **pinkyite** *n.*

1904 *Worker* (Sydney) 10 Sept. 2/2 The following day the wine . . was sold to the pinkyites.

pinnaroo /pɪnə'ru/. [a. Diyari *pinaru* an elder.] An Aboriginal elder (in quot. 1938 *attrib.*, and *fig.*).

1938 R. Ingamells *Sun-Freedom* 17 Dark pinnaroo gums go straggling over the plain. **1966** K. Walker *Dawn at Hand* 42, I look at you and am back in the long ago, Old pinnaroo lonely and lost here, Last of your clan.

pint pannikin: see Pannikin 1 b.

piola, var. Pialla.

pioneer. [U.S. *pioneer* one who goes into new country to settle: see Mathews.]

1. One of the first or early settlers in a district. Also *attrib.*, esp. as **pioneer settler.**

1842 *Austral. & N.Z. Monthly Mag.* 23 Considerable augmentation . . has been received by the arrival . . of the pioneers of the new settlement of Austral-Ind. **1852** S. Mossman *Gold Regions Aust.* 76 Wool . . became a golden fleece to those pioneer settlers. **1860** 'Lady' *My Experiences in Aust.* 126 The early settlers of the colony—the 'pioneers of civilisation', as they have well been called. **1861** N.W. Pollard *Homes in Vic.* 4 To place before our countrymen in the old country, a picture of the homes which we already enjoy, and to which their pioneer relatives . . are ready to assist them to share. **1870** W.B. Withers *Hist. Ballarat* 6 George Cabb, George Coleman, and others were the pioneers in the Buninyoung settlement. **1881** W. Allen *Immigration & Co-op. Settlement* 1 The pioneers of settlement came, and gradually spread o'er the land with their flocks and herds. **1901** *Advocate* (Burnie) 18 Jan. 2/3 If we take the settler for example, he is without question spoken of as the pioneer of the country. . . We are afraid the title of 'pioneer' is about the only crumb he can command. **1910** *Huon Times* (Franklin) 31 Dec. 3/3 About that period the grand old pioneer settlers of the district entered upon the work of opening up this part of the country. **1922** J. Lewis *Fought & Won* 1 My parents were pioneers and landed in South Australia in 1836. **1936** G.C. Morphett *Life & Lett. Sir J. Morphett* 119, 1845, the year fixed by the Old Colonists' Association as the limit of 'Pioneers'. **1956** *Bulletin* (Sydney) 23 May 12/4 The farm on which I was born carried the whole range of fences marking the progress of the pioneer-settlers, with wire unknown. **1961** *Ibid.* 8 Feb. 15/3 Representatives . . of the pioneer pastoral families . . do pretty well. **1979** D. Lockwood *My Old Mates & I* 122 Years ago, in Arnhem Land, I was with an old mate, a pioneer bushman who is now dead.

2. Comb. **pioneer colonist, squatter.**

1871 *Great Northern Run Case* 111 An enterprising **pioneer colonist** embarked capital, and risked both life and health in occupying the runs Ludwig, Dura, and Kilmore, situated in the pastoral district of Leichhardt. **1897** T.W. Beilley *Australasia's Goldfields* 7 The author . . a pioneer colonist of Victoria of nearly fifty-six years' standing. **1899** Mrs A. Hay *Footprints* 30 We must look for the moral stamina that made such pioneer colonists as Alexander Hay. **1841** G. Arden *Recent Information Port Phillip* 75 The first faint bush track of the **pioneer squatter. 1861** F. Algar *Handbk. Colony Qld.* 10 Encouragement is given to the pioneer squatter, by permitting him to hold his run on a fourteen years' lease, at a gradually increasing rental. **1879** 'Australian' *Adventures Qld.* 1 The pioneer squatters had to work and rough it with the meanest of their men. **1898** A.P. Martin *Beginnings Austral. Lit.* 20 As he had spent a couple of years on an 'up-country' station, he should write another novel dealing with what I have called the 'Pastoral Epoch'—the period of the pioneer squatters.

pioneering, *vbl. n.* [f. U.S. *pioneer* to go into new country as a settler.]

1. The opening up of new country by settlers.

1867 'Clergyman' *Aust. as it Is* 49 The work of pioneering, and 'taking up country', still continue to be prosecuted with as great vigour as ever. **1876** 'Capricornus' *Colonisation* 21 Of unstocked country there is plenty yet in Australia. . . Pioneering is always going on more or less. **1896** *Bulletin* (Sydney) 18 Apr. 3/2, I don't want no pioneerin'—I am off to Collingwood! **1939** Franklin & Cusack *Pioneers on Parade* 11 Pioneering had become a cult among the cliques; it had class nowadays. **1940** G. Morphett *Simple Story Rural Dev.* 1 Pioneering on the West Coast was a grim affair.

2. Comb. **pioneering days.**

1902 *Bulletin* (Sydney) 21 June 17/1 J.D. Moore, who writes as an old-chum . . I take to belong to a class which is over-fond of blowing about its 'pioneering days'. **1930** *Ibid.* 27 Aug. 21/3 A bush tipple that has gone the way of most features of the pioneering days was honey-beer. **1948** E.H. Collis *Lost Yrs.* 1 The pioneering days emphasized personality and lasted into the early years of this century. **1964** P. Adam Smith *Hear Train Blow* 85 We had only one thing in common: we admired the pioneering spirit. She would tell me stories by the hour of the pioneering days. **1965** R.H. Conquest *Horses in Kitchen* 131 The pioneering days when cattle stampedes and kangaroo drives were the order of the day in northern parts.

Hence **pioneerage** *n.*

1939 Franklin & Cusack *Pioneers on Parade* 12 Felonry, of whatever virtue, was taboo in the pioneerage, but descendants of free settlers, however humble or undesirable, were recognized.

piosphere /'paɪəsfɪə/. [f. the stem *πι-* of Gr. *πίνειν* to drink + combining *-o-* + *sphere.*] An ecological system defined as the area around a watering point, in an arid zone, in which grazing animals interact: see quot. 1969. Also *attrib.*

1969 R.T. Lange in *Jrnl. Range Managem.* (Baltimore) vi. 396 In an arid zone, the animals forage outwards from a watering-point, to which they are obliged to return frequently for drink. . . This leads to the development of a distinct ecological system. . . For convenience, the system is called in this paper the *piosphere* (from the Greek word 'pios' = to drink). It may be envisaged as a zone, but it is defined by the interactions, not by any spatial limits of area. **1979** Graetz & Howes *Chenopod Shrublands* 83 The more or less radial vegetation pattern generated by the dependence of stock on a particular water point in a paddock (Lange's 'piosphere' effect). **1980** J. Douglas *S.A. from Space* 51 Sheep only graze 3 or 4 km. from water and the *piospheres* created by them are isolated and 6–8 km. in diameter. **1981** V. Squires *Livestock Managem.* 34 The ability of the animals to forage away from the water point . . creates a series of concentric zones of use. The technical term for this phenomenon is the 'piosphere' effect.

pipe.

1. *Hist.* A lampoon against a prominent person, written on a piece of paper rolled into a tube and left in a public place; a pasquinade. Also *attrib.*

1816 W.C. Wentworth Miscellanea 1816–45 6 Mar., By the Pipe Maker on seeing the advertisement in the Gazette offering on the part of the Officers of the 46th a reward of two Hundred Pounds for the detection of him. **1816** *Sydney Gaz.* 9 Mar. 1/1 Copies of a *paper*, usually called a *pipe*, were circulated in the Town of Sydney . . containing a false, malicious, and scurrilous Attack upon the Character of His Honour the Lieutenant Governor. **1827** P. Cunningham *Two Yrs. in N.S.W.* (rev. ed.) II. 16 Among the 'distinguished characters' who have visited our shores, none afforded greater conversational amusement, or had more *pipes* blown about in his ironic praise than Beau V--. [*Note*] *Pipes*, a colonial term for pasquinades and squibs, personal and political, now no longer necessary since the institution of a free press. **1836** *Hobart Town Almanack* 106 These were the days of 'pipes'. Certain supposed home truths or lively descriptions were indicted in clear and legible letters on a piece of paper which was then rolled up in the form of a pipe, and being held together by twisting at one end was found at the door of the person intended to be instructed on its first opening in the morning. **1852** J. West *Hist. of Tas.* I. 107 Malice or humour, in the early days, expressed itself in what were called *pipes*—a ditty, either taught by repetition or circulated on scraps of paper.

2. A long, tubular cavity in the centre of a tree trunk or log of wood.

1882 A.J. Boyd *Old Colonials* 20 Logs with a bit of a pipe in suits me best. They ain't so hard to burst. **1887** A. Nicols *Wild Life & Adventure* 377 A substantial log, one end of which . . showed a 'pipe' or hollow. **1892** W.H. Warren *Austral. Timbers* 3 Dry rot appeared soon after its [*sc.* a timber viaduct's] erection, being most conspicuous in the piles. This decay, together with the cavity or pipe which occurred in many of the piles, has since necessitated considerable renewals. **1908** *Bulletin* (Sydney) 27 Feb. 15/1 From a perfectly-solid log a few more sleepers could certainly be sawn than may be chopped; but where there is a pipe in the log, the difference isn't worth arguing about.

Hence **piped** *ppl. a.*, **pipy** *a.*

1898 R. Radclyffe *Wealth & Wild Cats* 20 Poor Coolgardie has only its bush—and what bush! Wretched, miserable gum trees, half-grown, most of them '**piped**'. **1879** *Queenslander* (Brisbane) 12 July 58/3 The bigger the tree the better for shingle-splitting. . . If it is '**pipey**', that is, hollow all up the centre, it does not matter. **1882** A.J. Boyd *Old Colonials* 20 Them as gets timber for saw-mills doesn't want no pipy logs.

pipe-clay. [Spec. use of *pipe-clay* fine white clay used for making tobacco-pipes.]

1. A fine white clay which forms a paste when mixed with water and is used as body paint by Aborigines. Also *attrib.*

1832 *Sydney Monitor* 21 Mar. 3/3 The widow went into the usual mourning for her gallant husband, by streaking her face, breast, and arms with pipe clay. **1848** H.W. Haygarth *Recoll. Bush Life* 105 Her cheeks were besmeared with pipeclay, a mark of mourning. **1854** W. Shaw *Land of Promise* 73 Pipe-clay hieroglyphics adorn her countenance; her main article of covering is an opossum-skin cloak. **1857** J. Bonwick *Early Days Melbourne* 37 The women shaved off their hair, and covered their head with lumps of moistened pipeclay. **1879** *Native Tribes S.A.* 212 The white paint is a soft kind of chalk or pipeclay, and is only applied on particular occasions, such as dancing or mourning. **1896** *Amer. Anthrop.* (Menasha, Wisconsin) 342 These pieces of bark are painted with lines and dots of pipe-clay to make them ornamental. **1906** *Trans. R. Soc. S.A.* (1907) XXXI. 16 At ordinary corrobborees . . a tall conical headgear is made with grass, bound round with fur-string, the outside being smeared with pipeclay. **1932** *Mankind* Aug. 104 For white outlined figures pipe-clay was employed. **1954** A.P. Elkin *Austral. Aborigines* (ed. 3) 223 (*caption*) Painting-up in pipe-clay: initiation ritual. Southern Arnhem Land. **1982** B. Spencer *Aboriginal Photographs* 54 She adds parrot and cockatoo feathers to her hair and covers herself with white pipe-clay to make her more conspicuous to her husband's spirit.

2. *transf. Gold-mining.* A layer of soft clay lying immediately below an auriferous stratum: see quot. 1869.

1852 J. Bonwick *Notes of Gold Digger* 9 Some greasy substance with streaks of yellow sand, is at once concluded by you to be the pipe clay bottom. **1853** W. Westgarth *Vic.* 139 The 'pipe clay', a formation apparently always subjacent to the auriferous gravel. **1860** W.B. Clarke *Researches Southern Gold Fields N.S.W.* 84 Much of what the gold diggers call 'pipe clay'. **1869** R.B. Smyth *Gold Fields & Mineral Districts* 617 *Pipe-clay*, a soft white clay, which is often found lying between the bed-rock and the wash-dirt. Its thickness varies from a mere trace to many feet. **1931** C.B. Smith *Austral. Gold Prospectors' Handbk.* 20 You will soon learn to recognize bedrock when you come to it. It is usually soft and decomposed just where the alluvial deposit rests on it, and in that condition is often known as 'pipe-clay' on account of its whiteness.

Hence **pipe-clay** *v. trans.*, to paint (part of the body) with a paste made from pipe-clay.

1852 J. Morgan *Life & Adventures W. Buckley* 43 They all pipe-clayed themselves, and had another corrobberree.

pipi /'pɪpi/. Also **pippie.** [Transf. use of N.Z. *pipi*, usu. referring to the edible bivalve *Amphidesma australe*.] The edible marine bivalve *Plebidonax deltoides* of coasts from s. Qld. to s. W.A., incl. Tas., often used as bait; Ugari.

1895 C. Thackeray *Amateur Fisherman's Guide* 70 The absolutely best baits are the lug or sea worm, and the pippie, a species of mussel. **1904** *Shearer* (Sydney) 22 Oct. 6/3 'Living ought to be cheap there?' 'Yes, if you are content to live on fish, oysters, pippies, praties, and peaches.' **1926** *Austral. Encycl.* II. 135 The Pipi (*Donax deltoides*) is a smooth, wedge-shaped, purple bivalve... The aborigines consumed it largely; modern fishermen use it for bait. 'Pipi', the name in use in New South Wales, has been adopted from the Maori. **1941** H.D.A. Joske *Life to Live* 29, I did learn the art of collecting pippies, which I found later were called in Queensland by their native name of eugaries. **1977** R. Edwards *Austral. Yarn* 140 He was going to live on nothing else but pipis (*a small shellfish*), seaweed and coconuts. **1985** I. & T. Donaldson *Seeing First Australs.* 150 (*caption*) Gathering pipis (*Plebidonax deltoides*), ocean beach shellfish species, on Tacking Point Beach.

piping crow. Magpie *n.* 1 a. Also **piping crow-shrike, piping shrike.**

[**1827** *Trans. Linnean Soc. London* XV. 260 Cracticus.. Tibicen.. Piping Roller.. 'The birds of this species,' Mr Caley informs us, 'are gregarious... In the morning they make a loud whistling noise high up in the trees.'] **1832** J. Backhouse *Narr. Visit Austral. Colonies* 31 Numbers of Piping Crows called also White Magpies, were hopping about. **1844** J. Gould *Birds of Aust.* (1848) II. Pl. 46, *Gymnorhina tibicen.* Piping Crow-Shrike.. Piping Roller. **1854** W. Howitt *Boy's Adventures* 26 The piping crows, or, as they will call them here, the whistling magpies, though to my eye they have nothing of the magpie but their pied feathers about them. **1880** 'Old Hand' *Experiences of Colonist* (ed. 2) i. 29 The handsome black-and-white magpie, or piping crow, as ornithologists now call him, flitted about singing his peculiar song. **1914** H.M. Vaughan *Australasian Wander-Yr.* 271 The whole of the Bush remains for the rest of the day marvellously silent, save for the melodious call of the piping crow. **1933** C. Fenner *Bunyips & Billabongs* 188 A beautiful songster, the Australian magpie or piping crow-shrike. **1981** *Bulletin* (Sydney) 13 Jan. 93/3 Now South Australia has its State emblem—the piping shrike... The symbol depicts a piping shrike with wings spreading in the shape of a Union Jack.

pippie, var. Pipi.

pippy. [Prob. independently f. *pip* ill-humour, poor health, but see OEDS 2 b. for an 1886 instance.] Depressed; irritable.

1941 S.J. Baker *Pop. Dict. Austral. Slang* 54 *Pipped, pippy*, irritated, angry, out of sorts. **1965** L. Rowlands *Bird in Hand* 105 'Well, naturally,' Glory said. She was a bit pippy today. **1978** Mullally & Sexton *Libra & Leprechaun* 115 I'll admit I get a bit pippy at times.

pirate, *n.*

1. One who seeks a casual acquaintance with the intention of having a sexual relationship.

1916 *Truth* (Sydney) 23 Jan. 9/3, I have not for many years past been a 'Pirate', one of those men who molests young women in the streets.

2. The act of seeking such an acquaintance; esp. in the phr. **on the pirate.**

1943 *Gabber: Qld. Lines of Communication Army Trade Training Depot* Oct. 4 She sees them and laughs when a pirate is attempted. **1946** A. Marshall *Tell us about Turkey, Jo* 61, I leaves this piece—she isn't much—and gets in with 'em. They are on the pirate... We drives along the beach and, near Hampton, sees four beauts. **1964** G. Gelbin *Australs. have Word for It* 99 They are on the pirate. We goes round St. Kilda and tries a few but we want three together.

pirate, *v.* [f. prec.] *trans.* To seek a casual acquaintance with (a person) with the intention of having a sexual relationship. Also as *vbl. n.*

1927 F.C. Biggers *Bat-Eye* 26 An' me an' Skin—we pirates two young tarts. **1939** K. Tennant *Foveaux* 362 A beautiful green limousine cruising past slowed down and the driver tried to attract their attention. This struck Mabel as richly humorous. 'He's trying to pirate us,' she giggled. **1981** L. McLean *Pumpkin Pie* 53 They were supposed to be shopping, but most of the time was spent in 'Pirating', or looking for suitable members of the opposite sex. **1982** N. Keesing *Lily on Dustbin* 40 Who but a woman would complain that a man is a 'linen lifter', or is 'trying to pirate me' or 'put on the hard word' or 'get me into the bushes/scrub/mulga'?

pirri /'pɪri/. Also **pirrie.** [a. Arabana-Waŋgaŋuru *birri.*] An Aboriginal engraving tool made of stone: see quot. 1961.

1924 Horne & Aiston *Savage Life Central Aust.* 90 The last stone of the ideal type to be described is the *pirrie*; this is a small pear-shaped tool running to a fine point. It is used as a graving tool to make decorative marks on wooden weapons, and occasionally it is used as a drill for light boring work, such as making the hole to take the string of an *inchitcha* (bull-roarer). **1930** C.C. Towle *Certain Stone Implements* 10 They did not possess an implement like the 'pirrie' and other symmetrical 'points', such as those which may be found in the far west of New South Wales and in parts of South Australia. **1948** *Bulletin* (Sydney) 14 Jan. 22/1 Very rarely one finds what Lake Eyre tribes called a *pirrie.* This tool has a rounded back end, two long, straight sides that meet as a needle-point, and a very shallow triangular section that is the result of many hours of precision chipping. Mounted with resin on the end of a stick, the *pirrie* was used as a graver for etching the designs on a boomerang. **1961** *Proc. Prehist. Soc.* (Cambridge) XXVII. 75 A pirri is a symmetrical, leaf-shaped, uniface point, retouched over all or part of its upper surface, apparently by pressure flaking... Specimens vary in length from about 1 to 7 centimetres, and even the smallest are made sometimes from intractable quartz. This combination of superb craftsmanship with the production of aesthetically pleasing artefacts.. makes the pirri one of the most distinctive items of prehistoric culture. **1976** *West of Peesey* (Warooka Hist. Committee) 2 The pirrie itself was a leaf shaped point, with some exceptionally fine specimens found on the 'bottom end'. It has been said that the aboriginal pirrie compares more than favourably with any stone artefact in the world! **1981** J. Mulvaney et al. *Aboriginal Aust.* 26 The favoured practice was to trim only one face of the point (*pirris*).

pisonia /pɪ'zoʊniə/. [The plant genus *Pisonia* was named by Swedish botanist Carl von Linné (*Species Plantarum* (1753) II. 1026, *Genera Plantarum* (1754) ed. 5 451) in honour of the Dutch physician Willem Piso (*fl.* 1648), author of a work on medicinal plants of Brazil.] Either of two trees or shrubs of the widespread tropical and subtropical genus *Pisonia* (fam. Nyctaginaceae), occurring in n. and e. Aust., and elsewhere, *P. grandis* and *P. umbellifera.*

1928 S.E. Napier *On Barrier Reef* 86 The trunks and limbs of the pisonia are gnarled and twisted. **1936** T.C. Roughley *Wonders Great Barrier Reef* 17 The principal trees are Pisonias, which grow to a height of about sixty feet, with mottled grey trunks that may be several feet in diameter at the base. Their timber is soft and brittle... The foliage is a.. soft green. **1948** W. Hatfield *Barrier Reef Days* 19 They could sit out.. on the little rustic tables Father made from the easily worked pisonia branches. **1978** N. Coleman *Look at Wildlife Great Barrier Reef* 25 Pisonias are large, easily recognised trees which dominate inner forest areas of most vegetated coral cays.

piss, *v.* In the phr. **to piss in** (someone's) **pocket,** to ingratiate oneself with (someone).

1967 K. Tennant *Tell Morning This* 283 Soon's they knew you was in with Numismata, they all want to piss in your pocket. **1971** F. Hardy *Outcasts of Foolgarah* 77, I appeared before him many a time when I worked for the Union. If we piss in his pocket, he's just as apt to come our way. **1978** R.H. Conquest *Dusty Distances* 35 He's kiddin' us. When a Queenslander starts pissin' in your pocket, watch the bastard! **1980** E. Barcs *Backyard of Mars* 52 'It's just that we Australians don't piss in one another's pockets.' The colloquialism mystified me with my struggling English.

pissant, *n.* In the phr. **game as a pissant,** brave; foolhardy.

1944 J. Hetherington *Austral. Soldier* 13 'The Trump'll do us,' his men said. 'He's as game as piss-ant!' **1962** R. Tullipan *March into Morning* 59 The old white lady makes you as game as a pissant. **1965** J. O'Grady *Aussie Eng.* 68 Courageous little men, or small dogs with lots of fight in them, are 'game as pissants'.

pissant, *v. intr.* With **around:** see quot. 1945.

1945 S.J. Baker *Austral. Lang.* 87 Someone is pissanting around when he is messing about. **1951** Cusack & James *Come in Spinner* 307, I been pissantin' around the Northern Territory most of the time. **1959** G. Hamilton *Summer Glare* 138 Struth, you pissant around like a rooster that's too old.

piss pot. [Fig. use of *piss-pot* a chamber-pot.] A heavy drinker.

1974 *Bulletin* (Sydney) 2 Nov. 65/3 Eventually every house in the area will have a bottle collection crate and we'll be collecting more than Mosman. As the Mayor told me, they're much bigger pisspots over here. **1981** C. Wallace-Crabbe *Splinters* 53 Me poor dad used to say that God never speaks to a drunk man. Dear old dad was never a pisspot.

pitch. *Mining. Obs.* [Cornish dial.: see OED *sb.*[2] 12.] A specific portion of a mine allotted to a particular workman, esp. a tributer (one who receives a proportion of the ore raised). Also *transf.*, a productive claim.

1846 *S. Austral. Register* (Adelaide) 9 Dec. 2/5 The present pitch at the Burra Burra Mines ends on the 23rd inst., and the next will not be made till the 11th January, that the men may have time, if they wish it, to enjoy the Christmas holidays. **1853** J. Capper *Emigrant's Guide to Aust.* (ed. 2) 253 The men remaining are working the pitches in the dry levels. **1855** G.H. Wathen *Golden Colony* 65 Thus a likely 'pitch' we seek, Such is life on the Forest Creek! **c 1860** 'Aurifera' *Victorian Miners' Man.* 104 *Pitch*, limits of the piece of ground set to tributors. **1869** R.B. Smyth *Gold Fields & Mineral Districts* 617 *Pitch*, a portion of a mine let to a number of miners to work on terms.

pitcheri, pitcherie, var. Pituri.

pitcher plant. [Spec. use of *pitcher-plant* any of several plants having leaves modified as pitchers.] The insectivorous, perennial herb *Cephalotus follicularis* (fam. Cephalotaceae) of s.w. W.A. Also **Albany pitcher plant.**

1818 A. Cunningham in I. Marriott *Early Explorers Aust.* 31 Jan. (1925) 323, I made a diligent search for the curious Pitcher Plant, *Cephalotus follicularis.* **1829** R. Mudie *Picture of Aust.* 156 The pitcher plant.. is.. a very singular one. The pitchers are not at the end of the leaves, as in the common pitcher plant, but upon separate stalks. **1933** J.S. Glascock *Jarrah Leaves* 68 Our unique Pitcher Plant.. is especially noteworthy. 'No flower of its kindred', no other representative of its family, exists anywhere on earth. **1985** *Age* (Melbourne) 29 July 15/3 One Australian insect-eating species that has been declared endangered from collection is the Albany pitcher plant *Cephalotus follicularis.* The W.A. Government has banned all commercial exploitation of the plant in the wild but according to Mr Cheers 'backyarders are still digging up the plants'.

pitchery, var. PITURI.

pitchi /'pɪtʃi/. Also **pitchie, pittji.** [a. Aranda *pityi.*] COOLAMON 1.

1896 B. SPENCER *Rep. Horn Sci. Exped. Central Aust.* IV. 56 'Munyeru' . . is collected in large quantities by the females on their 'Pitchis' or wooden boat-shaped receptacles. **1903** H. BASEDOW *Jrnl. Govt. N.-W. Exped.* (1914) 64 An unusual form of shallow bark food carrier, called 'kuleman' by the Aluridjas and 'pitchi' by the 'Arunndtas', was also observed. **1928** B. SPENCER *Wanderings in Wild Aust.* 187 The young child is carried about in a wooden trough or *pitchi.* **1934** C. SAYCE *Comboman* 107 It was Koomilya with a pitchie of food. **1936** C. CHEWINGS *Back in Stone Age* 1 All the women and most of the young girls carried wooden trays, or *pittjis*, mostly . . shallow . . and twice as long as they were broad. **1943** *Bulletin* (Sydney) 7 July 12/1 The coolamon—it was known elsewhere as the pitchi or yandi—was the abo.'s one universal utensil. **1955** DEAN & CARELL *Dust for Dancers* 125 A pitchi, or barada in the Wailbri language, is the women's more shallow carrying dish. **1964** D. LOCKWOOD *Lizard Eaters* 21 The equipment of the Pintubi consisted of hardwood spears, woomeras, throwing sticks . . , coolamons for carrying babies and pitchis for carrying water. **1970** 'E. LINDALL' *Gathering of Eagles* 119 In her hands . . was a wooden pitchi full of water.

Pitt Street. Also **Pitt-street.** [The name of a principal business street in Sydney.] Used allusively with reference to urban incomprehension of rural matters; freq. *attrib.* in Comb. with nouns designating a rural occupation, as *bushman, farmer*, etc., in (usu.) derogatory reference to a person whose principal interests are in the city but who invests in rural property: see quot. 1972. See also COLLINS STREET, QUEEN STREET.

1842 *Colonial Observer* (Sydney) 23 Feb. 161/1 The Pitt-Street Corrobbory! We were in no way disappointed at the result of the late meeting in the Victoria Theatre, to petition the Queen and Parliament for a Representative Government for this Colony. **1911** *Truth* (Sydney) 7 May 5/8 *(heading)* Prodigious production of Pitt-street porkers. **1922** *Bulletin* (Sydney) 19 Oct. 20/3 These Pitt-street stockmen who periodically name Australia's best horseman, make me tired. **1923** *Ibid.* 25 Jan. 22/2 As for lighted lanterns encircling the camp, no-one but a Pitt-street pen-drover would mention such a ridiculous thing. **1932** *Ibid.* 10 Feb. 21/4 What do they know of jumbucks that only Pitt-street know? **1936** *Ibid.* 16 June 21/2 As for the military waterbottle, only Pitt-street bushmen would use one. **1962** V.C. HALL *Dreamtime Justice* 82 'You got bushed,' I pointed out. 'Came down the wrong river. That's the worst of you Pitt Street bushmen.' **1971** *Bulletin* (Sydney) 21 Aug. 9/2 He boldly agrees that Section 75 (1) B, which allows Pitt Street farmers to clear indigenous timber and then get the Taxation Department (read 'taxpayers') to foot a large part of the bill, is an amazing taxation provision. **1972** K. WILLEY *Tales Big Country* 28 Communities where the same families had cultivated their land for 150 years are having their own quiet revolutions as 'Pitt Street farmers'—doctors, lawyers, businessmen, and so on—buy up the properties for a combined weekend retreat and tax dodge. **1977** J. CARTER *All Things Wild* 5 They reckon around here a white gate puts a couple of thousand dollars on to the price of a Pitt Street farm. **1982** *Canberra Times* 5 Dec. 1/3 Many of the people who have come out on to the land recently have been the Pitt-Street-farmer types. **1985** *Bulletin* (Sydney) 2 July 41/2 Pitt and Collins Street farmers are people with incomes earned in cities by stockbrokers—doctors, dentists, businessmen and lawyers—who buy farms. They operate these enterprises at losses, ensuring that the funds expended on the land and written off against taxable non-farm income go to enhance its capital value.

pituri /'pɪtʃəri/. Also with much variety, esp. as **pitcheri, pitcherie, pitchery.** [a. Pitta Pitta *pijiri.*] The shrub *Duboisia hopwoodii* (fam. Solanaceae), widespread in arid, sandy, central Aust., the leaves being traditionally used as an animal poison and a narcotic; any of several other plants of the fam. Solanaceae, used as a drug. See also *emu bush* (b), EMU *n.*[1] 3, *native tobacco* NATIVE *a.* 6 a. Also *attrib.*

1861 *Burke & Wills Exploring Exped.* 13, I distributed the few remaining presents, and they gave in return some chewed pitchery and nardoo balls. *Ibid.* 28 They gave us some stuff they call bedgery, or pedgery. It has a highly intoxicating effect when chewed even in small quantities. It appears to be the dried stems and leaves of some shrub. **1872** *Austral. Med. Jrnl.* (1876) Nov. XXI. 368, I obtained . . a quantity of dried leaves . . of a plant used by the natives as a stimulating narcotic. These leaves, called 'pituri', were obtained in the neighbourhood of the water-hole Kulloo, eight miles beyond Eyre's Creek. **1878** *Queenslander* (Brisbane) 1 June 262/1, I have seen pitcherie growing only five miles to the west. **1887** 'COMMERCIAL TRAVELLER' *Diary Three Months Trip Qld.* 44 Pituri is a bush which the natives chop up into small pieces and then chew. They then take a small green bush, called 'gee gee', and after burning it to ashes, which are placed in a hollowed out piece of wood, the pituri is removed from the mouth and rolled in these ashes. This disgusting compound is then rolled into the shape of a cigar. **1889** R.B. ANDERSON tr. Lumholtz's *Among Cannibals* 49 The pituri pouch obtained by me was secured from natives about 200 miles west of Diamantina river, and was knitted with great skill in about two hours. **1915** *Bulletin* (Sydney) 4 Feb. 13/3 Amongst the S. Australian and West Queensland aboriginals 'pitchery', whether to chew or smoke, is a big-fella luxury. **1928** B. SPENCER *Wanderings in Wild Aust.* 158 The Pitcheri, or Pituri, plant, which is presumably its native name in some part of Australia. The natives use it both as a narcotic and as a means of catching emus. **1935** H.H. FINLAYSON *Red Centre* 85 The word 'pituri' . . used by the settlers to designate this [true tobacco] . . has no currency among the blacks of the area. . . It has evidently been derived from western Queensland, where, however, it is rightly applied to another plant *Duboisia Hopwoodi.* **1946** W.E. HARNEY *North of 23°* 55 Nothing like the Wolaria or Pitjari, a true species of the wild tobacco plant of the McDonald Ranges and the northern tribes of the Northern Territory. **1951** G. FARWELL *Outside Track* 142 There were spear wounds in his thighs, and he preferred to chew pituri rather than smoke the white man's tobacco. **1978** M. NIXON *Rivers of Home* 75 They did have a plant which they used for chewing just as they used European tobacco. The one I have seen, pitchuri, is from a low plant which grows in sandstone ridges, and has the most horrible smell imaginable. **1980** B. SCOTT *Darkness under Hills* 84 'Chew on these until you are ready to leave your body,' he instructed. 'They are the pituri plant from the far-off fringe of the desert, and they will help you.' **1985** *Canberra Times* 8 Nov. (Royal Visit Souvenir), A problem once arose because of the inclusion on the trail of an Aboriginal narcotic 'Pituri'. Staff at the botanic gardens found that the plant was being progressively pruned. It was eventually removed from the . . trail route.

piturine. An alkaloid derived from PITURI: see quot. 1979.

1880 *Jrnl. & Proc. R. Soc. N.S.W.* (1881) XIV. 127 Piturine mixes with every proportion of water, alcohol, and ether. . . The yield was about 1 per cent. of alkaloid from the dried plant. **1890** *Pall Mall Gaz.* (London) 13 Sept. 7/1 The actions of nicotine and piturine are in every respect identical. **1895** POWER & SEDGWICK *Lexicon Med. & Allied Sci.* (OED), *Piturine*, a volatile alkaloid prepared from the leaves and branches of the Australian plant *Pituri.* **1965** *Austral. Encycl.* VII. 127 Early workers established the nicotine-like nature of the plant's alkaloid, at first known as piturine, but which in 1935 was shown to be nor-nicotine, previously found in tobacco. **1979** J.G. HAWKES et al. *Biol. & Taxon. Solanaceae* 42 The active alkaloid in *D[uboisia] hopwoodii* was variously identified as pituria, piturine, duboisine and nicotine. . . Eventually in 1934, Hicks and Le Messurier established that it was not nicotine, but d-nor-nicotine. . . However . . chemical properties of the plant vary not only with seasons and state of maturity, but apparently by region.

Pivot City. *Obs.* A name given to the city of Geelong, Victoria: see quot.

1859 W. KELLY *Life in Vic.* I. 160 The Pivot City is a sobriquet invented by the citizens of Geelong to symbolise it as the point on which the fortunes of the colony would culminate and revolve.

Hence **Pivotite** *n.*

1884 *Austral. Tit-Bits* (Sydney) 26 June 14/2 The Pivotites won a very easy victory from the Melbournites on Saturday.

pizzle. [Br. dial., now apparently more freq. in Aust. than elsewhere: see OED(S and quot. 1965.]

1. The penis of an animal, esp. of a bull or ram. Also *attrib.*

1891 *Conference Amalgam. Shearers' Union & Pastoralists' Fed. Council* 8 The shearer shall not . . cut the teat of any ewe or pizzle of any wether or ram. **1965** J.S. GUNN *Terminol. Shearing Industry* ii. 8 *Pizzle*, a sheep's penis. This word has no taboo and is the formal word in written articles. **1967** G. JENKIN *Two Yrs. Bardunyah Station* 66 A 'pizzle cap' is an ingenious mythical device with which the shearer is supposed to protect that certain most important part of the ram's anatomy. . . It is made of a piece of broom handle 5⅞ inches long with a bottle top nailed on one end. **1969** *Coast to Coast 1967–68* 7 Ruben had caught the farmer's bull one night and tied a length of plastic cord around its pizzle. **1973** H. LEWIS *Crow on Barbed Wire Fence* 172 The machine clipper was steered through the yellow pizzle wool. **1982** P. ADAM SMITH *Shearers* 302 'Pizzle guards' are one of the tricks played on young new chums. 'Hop down to the expert and ask for a pizzle guard!' A common reply . . will be 'I've only got a left-handed one,' or, 'Will the cap of a pen do?'

2. *transf.*

1969 F.B. VICKERS *No Man is Himself* 153 'He cut me pizzle off with a bit o' broke bottle.' He felt at his penis through the cloth of his trousers. 'He never made much of a job of it. It's got a head on it now like a bloody frilly lizard.'

placer. See quot. 1945.

[N.Z. **1921** H. GUTHRIE-SMITH *Tutira* 383 'Placer' is a term used to denote a gold digger who remains year after year on the one spot, on the one place.] **1940** *Bulletin* (Sydney) 31 Jan. 41/2 *(title)* The placer sheep. **1945** S.J. BAKER *Austral. Lang.* 66 *Placer*, a sheep which becomes attached to a spot and refuses to budge.

plain. [Spec. use of *plain* a tract of country of which the general surface is comparatively flat.]

1. a. An extensive tract of land which is open and generally suitable for pasture, freq. undulating and lightly treed.

1814 M. FLINDERS *Voyage Terra Australis* II. 66 Towards Double Mount and Shoal-water Bay, the country consisted of gently-rising hills and extensive plains, well covered with wood and apparently fertile. **1820** J. OXLEY *Jrnls. Two Exped. N.S.W.* 83 The immediate vicinity of the river was free from timber or brush in various places; and these tracts have hitherto received the particular denomination of *plains*, which might with equal propriety be extended to the whole country. **1825** B. FIELD *Geogr. Mem. N.S.W.* 16 The country . . had much the appearance of an extended plain, formed of low undulating hills and vales, well, but not heavily, wooded. **1839** T.P. BESNARD *Voice from Bush* 13 Goulburn plains . . are not *flat* level ground, but an undulating country; the word *plain* here means *open*, either partially or wholly free from *bush.* **1850** *Illustr. Austral. Mag.* (Melbourne) July 13 Soon after starting they entered upon some beautiful grassed plains, the rises and undulations of which forcibly reminded them of the thyme and camomile scented downs on which they had disported in their fatherland. **1852** J.B. JUKES et al. *Lectures on Gold* 20 'Plains' in Australia are open, park-like districts, with merely clumps of trees standing at intervals, the undulating ground being covered with fine grass. **1861** J.D. LANG *Qld., Aust.* 103 The plains, or rather I should say downs, for they were nowhere levels, but everywhere gently undulating, were first seen in white streaks. **1867** 'CLERGYMAN' *Aust. as it Is* 20 There may be plains, and of very considerable extent, without trees . . but they bear no proportion to the country described as *plains* which have trees growing upon them. **1899** *North-Western Advocate* (Devonport) 18 Jan. 3/5 The country all along the coast is open heathy plain, with rising ground at intervals. **1948** F. CLUNE *Wild Colonial Boys* 21 Ben wondered why timbered land should be called 'plains', but realized that the trees were more sparse here than on the lower regions of the stream, and that the country was level—in parts swampy.

b. A flat expanse of arid, or semi-arid, land, freq. covered with low scrub.

1847 E.W. LANDOR *Bushman* 291 The cracked, baked, clay-plains in the interior. **1848** T.L. MITCHELL *Jrnl. Exped. Tropical Aust.* 116, I crossed a small plain, bounded by a casuarina scrub. **1855** *Moreton Bay Free Press* 2 Jan. 3/2 He crossed, when there, a stony plain, on which there was no vegetation, and another plain covered with sand. **1862** W.R.H. JESSOP *Travels & Adventures* II. 279 The plain looks hard and stony, and abounds in small low bushes, like clumps of spinifex or porcupine-grass. **1867** A.K. COLLINS *Waddy Mundoee* 7 On the Condamine, away to the North, the country of plains and salt bush; where the myall flourishes. **1893** *Southerly* (1964) iv. 204 A plain is not necessarily a wide, open space covered with waving grass or green sward. . . It is either a desert or a stretch of level country covered with wretched scrub. **1909** *Bulletin* (Sydney) 21 Jan. (Red Page), The worst stage is the Open Downs, one hundred and thirty miles of sun-baked, crab-holed, practically trackless plain. **1951** G. FARWELL *Outside Track* 135 A stony plain lifted towards us, so that we could see there was grass upon its surface, stiff clumps of canegrass, although yet no habitation. **1962** J. MACKENZIE *Austral. Paradox* 42 The dry plains of the dead heart.

2. Used *attrib.* in the names of animals: **plain turkey, (a)** *wild turkey*, see WILD 1; also **plains turkey; (b)** *transf.*, see quot. 1978; **wanderer,** the terrestrial bird *Pedionomus torquatus* of s.e. mainland Aust., having mottled brown plumage with a black and white spotted collar in the female; also **plains wanderer.**

(a) 1872 C.H. EDEN *My Wife & I in Qld.* 122 The bird that repaid the sportsman best was the **plain turkey.** **1887** W.S.S. TYRWHITT *New Chum in Qld. Bush* 158 There is a magnificent bird to be found on the great plains of the Darling Downs and Western Queensland, usually called the plain turkey. **1899** R. SEMON *In Austral. Bush* 272 The Australian bustard, *Choriotis australis* . . chooses wide plains for its home, and is therefore called 'plain turkey' by the colonists. **1914** H.M. VAUGHAN *Australasian Wander-Yr.* 241 Now and again a 'Plains turkey', or great grey bustard . . would be seen. **1916** *Bulletin* (Sydney) 28 Sept. 22/2 Plain-turkey . . is not as toothsome as the wood-duck. **1932** J. MCCARTER *Pan's Clan* 157 The three men . . sat with heads raised like scared plain turkeys. **1958** J.R. SPICER *Cry of Storm-Bird* 41 A plain-turkey walked sedately in the middle of the road. **1976** J.H. TRAVERS *Bull Dust on Brigalow* 40 We had just had a late tea and I had my plain turkey on cooking. **1980** ANSELL & PERCY *To fight Wild* 96 There are quite a few plain turkeys around there, tall fawn and grey birds with black 'caps' on their heads, fairly slow moving. **1986** *Sydney Morning Herald* 15 Jan. 13/4 The stately bustard, or plains turkey, reappeared last year in far western N.S.W. after an absence of decades. **(b) 1955** D. NILAND *Shiralee* 27 An old bundle of a man came down the road from the west. Macauley watched him approaching and recognized him at once for what he was, a flat-country bagman, a type on his own. . . In his time he had met plenty of these **plain-turkeys**, as they were known. **1964** H.P. TRITTON *Time means Tucker* (rev. ed.) 15 Many of these men never left the Plains, but between burr cutting and work in the shearing sheds managed to exist. The regulars were known as 'Plain Turkeys'. **1972** J. BOOTH *Only Tracks Remain* 36 There was a rattling of loose iron sheets in the early hours of morning. A couple of Plain Turkeys were up and around. **1978** T. DAVIES *More Austral. Nicknames* 80 *Plain Turkey*, a generic nickname for any swaggie who plodded the Central Queensland plains. Such men were usually loners, like the game bird from which they took their name. **1849** C. STURT *Narr. Exped. Central Aust.* II. 45 App. Pedionomus Torquatus . . the **plain Wanderer** . . was first discovered on the plains of Adelaide by Mr Gould. **1901** *Emu* I. 26 Dr Charles Ryan, when out quail-shooting, near Melbourne . . captured a number of Plain Wanderers. **1965** *Austral. Encycl.* VII. 136 Plain-wanderer, a quail-like terrestrial bird . . about 6 inches in length, peculiar to south-eastern Australia. **1984** *Age* (Melbourne) 27 Mar. 26/8 Declining are the thick-billed grass-wren and that odd quail, the Plains Wanderer (of which the latest reports are that new populations have been discovered).

plant, *n.*[1] [Extended use of Br. slang *plant* hidden stolen goods, their hiding-place: see OED(S *sb.*[1] 7.]

1. a. Something hidden, esp. a quantity of stolen goods; the hiding-place.

1812 J.H. VAUX *Mem.* (1819) II. 196 Any thing hid is called, *the plant*, when alluded to in conversation; such article is said to be *in plant*; the place of concealment is sometimes called *the plant*, as, I know of a fine *plant*; that is, a secure hiding-place. To *spring a plant*, is to find any thing that has been concealed by another. **1827** *Hobart Town Courier* 29 Dec. 1 We remember a little while ago, giving our readers a short description of a remarkable lake in South America, which the people there were draining for the sake of a large quantity of jewels, cash and plate, that had been thrown into it some centuries before; and that treasure is what we here would call a valuable plant. It is the nature of this particular sort of plant, when set in the earth, to grow down. **1838** D.L. WAUGH *Three Yrs. Practical Experience N.S.W.* 36 There is an immense deal of slang in the language of the country—'cove', 'gammon', 'plant', are as familiar as household words. **1842** *Geelong Advertiser* 9 May 2/4 Fogarty is expected to turn Queen's evidence. On Monday he accompanied Mr Wright to the house of a man named Cam, where a plant was discovered. **1847** *Maitland Mercury* 16 Oct. 2/6 Smith, the ex-constable, seems to have been if not the contriver of the 'plant', very deeply concerned as the recipient of its contents. **1861** A. JACKSON *R.O. Burke* 16 May (1862) 133 Finding our loads rather too heavy, we made a small plant here of such articles as could best be spared. **1867** F.J. BYERLEY *Narr. Overland Exped. Northern Qld.* 3 Large flocks of cockatoo parrots (*Nymphicus Nov. Holl.*) were seen during the day and a 'plant' of native spears was found. **1874** *Adelaide Observer* 26 Dec. (Christmas Suppl.) 15/2 It revealed a large 'plant' of stolen goods. **1896** *Worker* (Sydney) 26 Dec. 1/3 Tom and Jan find the door-key in the usual 'plant' and enter. **1929** W.J. RESIDE *Golden Days* 19 Went to my 'plant'—a secret place where I kept my chamois. **1956** T. RONAN *Moleskin Midas* 19 By the time he was twelve he had as many pounds in silver and coppers hidden in various limestone crevices around the shanty. He could have found any of these plants, so carefully disguised that even the blacks never located them. **1967** S. LLOYD *Lightning Ridge Bk.* 8 Gibson never located this plant of opal again.

b. In the phr. **to spring a** (or **the**) **plant,** to discover that which has been hidden. See also SPRING.

1812 [see sense 1 a.]. **1828** *Tasmanian* (Hobart) 4 Jan. 3 After some search . . a *plant* of two casks were *sprung* one containing rum and the other wine. **1840** *S. Austral. Miscellany* June 178 The animals were what in colonial slang is termed 'planted' (i.e. concealed), and, the only way 'to *spring* the plant' was, by offering a reward to those that would produce the errant cattle. **1854** W. SHAW *Land of Promise* 100 He informed him that he had a 'plant', which he would, make over to him, as it might be 'sprung' whilst he was in gaol. **1872** C.H. EDEN *My Wife & I in Qld.* 45 They got a great deal of credit from their friends at having 'sprung the new chums plant'. **1888** 'R. BOLDREWOOD' *Robbery under Arms* (1937) 46 If the police are on his tracks they'll spring the plant here and the whole thing'll be blown. **1893** *Braidwood Dispatch* 27 May 2/4 There's a couple thousand sovereigns . . up there somewhere; I vote . . we spring the plant, and whack the boodle. **1918** C. FETHERSTONHAUGH *After Many Days* 250 The Scotchmen had by some means 'sprung' the bushrangers' plant, and got away to Scotland with it.

c. In the phr. **in** (or **out of**) **plant,** in (or out of) a hiding-place.

1841 *Sydney Gaz.* 4 Sept., Mr Dogherty . . while riding over the run in the vicinity of Mookia, discovered 'in plant', a large number of calves . . variously branded, which he laid down at once as having been stolen. **1847** A. HARRIS *Settlers & Convicts* (1953) 113 He had come to the corner of the fence . . the night before, and was now 'in plant' (hiding) in the creek till night again. **1854** G.H. HAYDON *Austral. Emigrant* 100 Happening to have a half bottle of rum in store, I took it out of plant. **1856** *Moreton Bay Free Press* 18 Aug. 2/7 It was believed that a large amount of gold was being kept 'in plant' at the diggings, the owners not liking to risk the journey in the absence of an efficient guard.

2. *Obs.* A salted claim; a quantity of the mineral sought placed in a claim: see PLANT *v.* 3.

1859 W. KELLY *Life in Vic.* I. 189 It was a regular plant—a salted hole. . . Salting a hole is sprinkling it artificially, with the view of perpetrating a cheat. **1871** 'IOTA' *Kooroona* 139 The surface copper was what, among miners, is called a plant, which, translated into modern English, means that it was not deposited in the place where it was found.

plant, *n.*[2] [Spec. use of *plant* equipment, implements, etc., used in an (industrial) operation: see OED(S *sb.*[1] 6.] The working animals, equipment, vehicles, and sometimes personnel employed by a drover, stockman, etc., on the move.

1867 *S.A. Parl. Papers* no. 14 86 One pound per head for the sheep, with plant and all included. **1894** *Western Champion* (Barcaldine) 2 Jan. 14/3 He had been a cattle-horse attached to the plant of a drover. **1913** W.K. HARRIS *Outback in Aust.* 27 The droving party of which I was a member, had several playful pack-horses in its 'plant'. **1923** 'J. NORTH' *Son of Bush* 12 He made enough . . to purchase a teamster's plant. **1934** C. SAYCE *Comboman* 33 Lately there had been added to the 'plant' another white man, one of the best cattle men in the North, Dan Sharpe. Between them, these two managed the run. **1946** W.E. HARNEY *North of 23°* 190 The buffalo-shooters of old required a large plant of horses to carry on their trade. **1956** T. RONAN *Moleskin Midas* 244 All the station plants were too busy shifting cattle. **1965** L. WALKER *Other Girl* 17 'So you know the plant?' he said. 'Nobody ever mistakes a shearer for a stockman or vice versa. You know the outback, young lady.' **1976** S. WELLER *Bastards I have Met* 86 He was riding one horse and leading one and I said facetiously, 'That's a pretty big plant for one horse-tailer, mate.' **1982** D. HARRIS *Drovers of Outback* 13 In my day most of the big back country plants were about forty to fifty horses and an open wagonette (often an old Cobb & Co. coach cut down) pulled by four or five horses.

plant, *v.* [Br. slang *plant* to hide (stolen goods): see OED *v.* 8.]

1. *trans.* To hide (articles, animals, etc.); freq. (esp. formerly) used of stolen goods.

1793 J. HUNTER *Hist. Jrnl. Trans. Port Jackson* 373 Some villains dug up every one of the potatoes . . a very strict search was made, in order to find out the offender, but to no purpose, as the potatoes were (in the cant phrase) *all planted*; viz. buried in the ground, so as to be taken out as they were wanted. **1799** R. JOHNSON *Some Lett.* 26 Aug. (1954) ii. 37 Suspecting something was there *planted*: (i.e.) some property that had been stolen was concealed, he put in his hoe and removed the boughs. **1820** L. MACQUARIE *Let.* 31 Jan. (1821) 61 *Planting* (as the slang phrase is here) their stolen goods. **1825** *Hobart Town Gaz.* 4 Feb., When the sheep was killed, Fielding said '*we must plant the skin or it will sell us!*' **1833** J. BACKHOUSE *Narr. Visit Austral. Colonies* (1843) 169 The prisoners have adopted the expression, 'to plant' a thing, to signify, to hide or conceal it, especially in regard to things stolen. **1845** D. MACKENZIE *Emigrant's Guide* 193 To plant travellers' horses and settlers' working bullocks is a common trick played by Botany Bay convicts, who will afterwards offer to find them for a specified reward. **1861** *Burke & Wills Exploring Exped.* 3 We cured the meat, and planted it. **1879** 'AUSTRALIAN' *Adventures Qld.* 79, I once stayed at M'Phail's, at Coorang, and lost my horses for a week. I know the rascal planted them. It is a regular dodge of these bush publicans, just to keep a fellow running up a score at the house. **1892** *Western Champion* (Barcaldine) 26 Jan. 12/3 Just you tell me where that 270 oz. of gold's planted and I'll let you out. **1917** C. DREW *Reminisc. D. Gilbert* 21 Shaw could easily reach over and grab my money. I think I'll plant it in my boots. **1922** J. LEWIS *Fought & Won* 63 Several horses got away from Gum Creek. . . They were found by a man living in the neighbourhood, and I had a great suspicion that they had been 'planted'. **1947** N. LINDSAY *Halfway to Anywhere* 75 Bill having planted his half-bottle of sherry in the back paddock, came lounging innocuously back. **1978** H.C. BAKER *I was Listening* 69 He'd lift anything. Tom's yarn went that Jack had whizzed off an electric drill and planted it.

2. *trans.* Of an animal: to settle (another animal, esp. its offspring) in a safe place.

1849 *Argus* (Melbourne) 13 Nov. 4/1 When the calf is too young to follow the cow, she conceals it, colonially, *plants* it, when she goes to feed. **1880** 'ERRO' *Squattermania* 76 He could not find the calf. . . 'No doubt it's planted somewhere in the timber at the bottom of the paddock.' **1901** *Bulletin* (Sydney) 7 Dec. 30/2 A quiet milking-cow will 'plant' a young calf with such skill that 10 stockmen cannot find him in a one-mile paddock. **1929** *Ibid.* 2 Jan. 19/4 The dog had planted the mob in the shade of a big coolabah and was giving them a smoke-oh. **1936** J.C. DOWNIE *Galloping Hoofs* 148 Bushbred or wild cattle always 'plant' their calves for safety when they have to go a distance to water, the young animals being too weak to undertake the long journey.

3. *trans. Obs.* To salt (a claim); to place (a quantity of the mineral sought) in a mining claim in order to give a false impression of its productivity. Also as *vbl. n.*

1853 C. READE *Gold* 17 *Levi*: This dust is from Birmingham, and neither Australian or natural. *Rob*: The man planted it for you. **1853** H.B. JONES *Adventures in Aust.* 287 The Bishop of Sydney, in laying the foundation stone of a church at Sofala, at each turn of the trowel brought to light a nugget of some value, which however it appeared had been placed there with a view of enhancing the value of the neighbouring land. This in technical gold-digging phraseology, is called '*planting*'. **1886** P. CLARKE *'New Chum' in Aust.* 72 A 'salted claim', a 'pit' sold for a £10 note in which a nugget worth a few shillings had before been 'planted'.

4. *intr.* and *refl.*

a. To conceal oneself.

1846 C.P. HODGSON *Reminisc. Aust.* 347 The ladies however more provident of their offspring, 'planted' in the rushes or creeks, till we had passed. **1847** *Bell's Life in Sydney* 8 May 3/1 The other man we got *planted* in a gerenium [*sic*] bush. **1866** *Sydney Punch* 22 Dec. 35/1 Wishing to know what the two would beat, Just quietly plants at the back of the urn To see, if she could, which way matters would turn. **1870** J. BONWICK *Last Tasmanians* 223 Sending forward some Native decoys, he and the rest *planted*, or hid, themselves in a thick scrub. **1880** R. ROWE *Roughing It* 22 I'll plant somewhere about here; I can see what goes on down there without their seeing me. **1888** 'R. BOLDREWOOD' *Robbery under Arms* (1937) 122 Don't go planting in the gully or someone'll think you're wanted, and let on to the police. **1894** A.B. BELL *Austral. Camp Fire Tales* 105 Now tell me where the blazes you planted all this time that I couldn't find you. **1983** G. SAVAGE *Tournament* 9, I nicked around the house and planted myself behind the mile-high pile of fruit cases standing there.

b. *transf.* Of an animal: to conceal itself.

1890 MRS H.P. MARTIN *Under Gum Tree* 173 A dense scrub, in the edges of which horses would often 'plant', and remain concealed for hours. **1946** *Coast to Coast 1945* 146 It was Peter's job as horse-tailer to be mounted and away in the dark each morning... He had to find the horses where they had planted themselves in the gullies. **1951** S.H. EDWARDS *Shooting & Bushcraft* 49 If only wounded he may 'plant', so, look round a bit... He is probably quite handy.

planter. [f. PLANT *v.*] One who steals and hides stock.

1890 'R. BOLDREWOOD' *Colonial Reformer* III. 54 What's a little money .. if .. your children grow up duffers and planters. **1955** N. PULLIAM *I traveled Lonely Land* 384 *Plant*, to hide sheep or cattle which have been stolen. *Planter*, one who does so.

planter's friend. A plant of the genus *Sorghum* (fam. Poaceae), cultivated as a crop.

1870 'JACKAROO' *Immigration Question* 10 The 'Planter's Friend' bids fair to be tested this year, and I shall look forward with interest to the result. **1871** *Austral. Town & Country Jrnl.* (Sydney) 15 Apr. 462/2 He believes that he could make twenty-four hundredweight of sugar from an acre of planter's friend. **1902** *Bulletin* (Sydney) 7 June 16/2 The frequent poisoning of cows by young sorghum and 'planters' friend' begins to alarm South Coast (N.S.W.) dairymen.

planting, *vbl. n.* The hiding of stolen goods; esp. the practice of hiding stolen horses and 'discovering' them when a reward is offered.

1799 *HRA* (1914) 1st. II. 288 The witness discovered the tobacco, but did not remove it in order that from the *planting* of a constable over ye same some discovery might be made by someone coming for it. **1840** *Port Phillip Patriot* 8 Feb. 3 The *planting* of horses has been carried on to a great extent in the neighbourhood of the town. **1851** *Empire* (Sydney) 16 Dec. 471/1 Horse-stealing, or rather 'planting', prevails to a fearful extent. A gang of scoundrels infests the town, who seize every opportunity of driving off straggling nags and securing them in some inaccessible mountain gully. They wait till a reward is offered and bring back the beast to its owners. **1895** G. RANKEN *Windabyne* 92 They opened a business for the 'planting' of horses and the sale of adulterated rum at the solitary water-hole. **1955** N. PULLIAM *I traveled Lonely Land* 318 Riding the boundary fences, looking out for poddy dodging and guarding against planting, moonlighting and droving—all these the abo does quite well.

plate. [Also N.Z.: see OEDS *sb.* 18 h.] A plate of food contributed by a participant towards the catering at a social gathering; BASKET *n.*

1961 *Gumsuckers' Gaz.* (Melbourne) Aug. 2 Visitors will be welcome. Ladies bring a 'plate', and gentlemen make a donation. **1972** R. ERICKSEN *West of Centre* 69 As jealous of his reputation as a suburban housewife baking a 'plate' for a matron's tea party. **1976** L.R.M. HUNTER *Woodline* 35 It did not take long to educate everyone into the Australian custom of 'bringing a plate', necessary if you are going to have supper. **1985** *Canberra Times* 27 Sept. 2/1 It is a tradition in Australia that when friends and neighbours come together for a party or celebration everyone 'brings a plate' in a spirit of co-operation. **1986** *Sydney Morning Herald* 14 June 41/7 At the Australian Opera .. Veitch announces a new Australian production of Patrick White's Kerr, to be performed on alternate Tuesdays by the Police Choir and Pipe Band: BYO; ladies, a plate please.

platibus, var. PLATYPUS.

platman. *Mining.* One who works on a plat; the person responsible for loading a cage for despatch to the surface.

1934 *Red Star* (Perth) 14 Dec. 1/3 One skipman went on, and a platman was transferred to be his mate and another platman was sent for. **1957** F. CLUNE *Fortune Hunters* 165 At 530 feet the cage jolted to a halt, and we emerged into a drive where a 'platman' was loading trucks of ore into the cage. **1962** *Gumsuckers' Gaz.* (Melbourne) Sept. 5 The 'plat-man' .. was to see that the men were safely loaded in the cage, then he would signal the engine-driver by a system of knocks. **1978** D. STUART *Wedgetail View* 19 Machine miners, boggers, platmen, timbermen, and the men on the surface jobs, all known to him.

platypus /ˈplætəpʊs/. Pl. **platypuses.** Formerly with much variety, as **platibus, platybus,** etc. [mod. L. *platypus*, a. Gr. *πλατύπους*, given as the name of the genus by English naturalist G. Shaw (see quots. 1799 and 1809) but changed in 1800 to *Ornithorynchus*.]

1. The amphibious, burrowing, egg-laying mammal *Ornithorhynchus anatinus* of fresh-water lakes and watercourses of e. Aust. incl. Tas., having thick brown fur, a bill with leathery skin, webbed feet, and a broad, flattened tail; DUCK-BILL; DUCK-MOLE; MOLE *n.*[1]; ORNITHORHYNCHUS; PARADOX, *water mole*, see WATER. See also DUCK-BILLED. Also *attrib.*

1799 G. SHAW *Naturalist's Miscellany* X. Pl. 386, The Platypus is a native of Australia or New Holland, and is at present in the possession of Mr Dobson, so much distinguished by his exquisite manner of preparing specimens of vegetable anatomy. **1809** —— *Zool. Lectures* I. 78 This genus, which at present consists but of a single species and its supposed varieties, is distinguished by the title *Platypus* or *Ornithorhynchus*; the former name having been given it on account of the very expanded webs of its fore-feet, and the latter from the appearance of the snout, which has the resemblance of the bill of a bird. **1821** *Austral. Mag.* 72 The Duck-Billed Platypus, A Native of New Holland. Of all the mammalia yet known, it seems the most extraordinary in its conformation; exhibiting the perfect resemblance of the beak of a duck engrafted on the head of a quadruped. **1828** *Hobart Town Courier* 28 June 4 Have we not our platy-pusses, with their long straight ducks bills, and their long crooked ornithorincus name. **1833** A. PRINSEP *Jrnl. Voyage Van Diemen's Land* 100 An extraordinary animal is common on the banks of rivers and in lagoons, of which you may have heard, combining the species of quadrupeds and birds; it is called the Platibas, or Platibus. **1850** W. GATES *Recoll. Van Dieman's Land* 212 It has a mouth very greatly resembling a duck's bill, and is sometimes known by that name, but more generally by that of platipus. **1854** G.H. HAYDON *Austral. Emigrant* 87 A pouch made from the skin of a platybus. **1858** K. CORNWALLIS *Yarra Yarra* 16 The long croak of the lone platypaus. **1860** 'LADY' *My Experiences in Aust.* 251 The 'Platypus' is .. an awkward-looking creature, but its fur is beautifully fine and soft, a mixture of silvery gray and black. **1862** A. POLEHAMPTON *Kangaroo Land* 259, I used to fish .. sometimes by moonlight when numbers of platypi, *i.e.* duck-billed moles with webbed feet, might be seen disporting themselves on the water. **1876** J.A. EDWARDS *Gilbert Gogger* 190 Hume shot a platypus to-day and showed it to me; it is like a puppy in the body, with four webbed duck's feet, two wings, a beaver's tail, and a goose's head and bill; now a country that can produce such a monstrosity as this can produce anything. **1887** A. NICOLS *Wild Life & Adventure* 349 Being very curious to know how platypus tasted, he baked the fore-quarters on the embers. **1893** *Scribner's Mag.* (N.Y.) June 794 Platypus shopping-bags and purses are not disdained by the fair who crowd the marts .. in Melbourne, or .. in Sydney. **1915** W.J. WYE *Souvenirs Sunny South* 34 Her velvety coat, that had never known brands, shone soft as the platypus fur. **1928** B. SPENCER *Wanderings in Wild Aust.* I. 152 The Platypus does not live in the interior of Australia because it must have permanent water. In fact it is only found in Tasmania and on the well-watered coastal country of Victoria, New South Wales and Southern Queensland, and has just as restricted a distribution as the hardy Echidna has a wide one. **1936** *Publicist* (Sydney) I. 3/1 The patriot in Australia may be a dwindling species, like the koala, the lyrebird, the platypus, and the Aborigines themselves. **1945** M. HODGES *Veil of Time* 41 The headlines were .. big and .. black about a couple of platypusses producing a young one. **1952** B. BEATTY *Unique to Aust.* 38 Platypuses inhabit fresh water rivers and lagoons from Tasmania to North Queensland. **1976** E. WORRELL *Things that Sting* 22 It is not generally known that such a delightful animal as a Platypus is venomous. In the summer months the male Platypus carries venom in the hollow curved spur of each hind foot... Platypuses are very shy and rarely seen. **1980** W. MAYNE *Salt River Times* 132 She had to say how rare is the Platypus. She did not care about the Platypus, that looked like a worn slipper.

2. Special Comb. **platypus frog,** GASTRIC BROODING FROG (esp. *Rheobatrachus silus*).

1983 *Courier Mail* (Brisbane) 21 Nov. 13/2 A search for the rare platypus frog in the Sunshine Coast's Conondale and Blackall ranges at the weekend was unsuccessful. **1984** *Age* (Melbourne) 18 Jan. 7/1 The first species, located around the Conondale Ranges, north of Brisbane, and known as the platypus frog was endangered by logging of rain forests and drought. It had not been seen in its natural environment since 1979.

platypusary. Also **platypusery, platypussery.** [f. prec.] An enclosure in which the natural conditions preferred by the platypus are simulated.

1942 A.L. HASKELL *Waltzing Matilda* 95 It was necessary to create an artificial burrow on the banks of an artificial river, which in itself created a new word—platypusery. **1958** *Bulletin* (Sydney) 16 Apr. 18/3 'A platypussery is to be made in a plane to take platypusses to New York'... The late Harry Burrell .. built (and christened) a platypusary—not 'platypussery'—at his home in the Sydney suburb of Kensington. **1968** V. SERVENTY *Southern Walkabout* 37 The platypusary was in full swing... It was an excellent idea to have a tape recording which concisely explained all the average visitor would want to know about the platypus, then a polite request to keep moving so that the people waiting could come and see the show.

play, *v. Australian National Football. intr.* With **on:** to keep the ball in play without stopping to take a mark or penalty. Freq. as *imp.*

1885 D.E. MCCONNELL *Austral. Etiquette* 641 The Field Umpire, on being appealed to, may either award a 'free kick', call 'play on', or stop the play and throw the ball in the air. **1931** J.F. MCHALE et al. *Austral. Game of Football* 52 The field umpire shall call 'Play on', and the ball shall immediately be, or remain in play. **1969** A. HOPGOOD *And Big Men Fly* 36 A beautiful stabpass, right down the throat of team-mate Morris .. and Morris is playing on. **1973** P. MCKENNA *My World of Football* 88 He signalled 'play-on' and old Sergio Silvagni grabbed it, booted it to Jesaulenko who dribbled it through for a goal.

play-about, *n.* and *a. Austral. pidgin.*

A. *n.* A corroboree the main purpose of which is to provide entertainment.

1914 *Bulletin* (Sydney) 11 June 24/2 Charlie found himself 'disqualified' from ever again taking part in a 'play-about'. **1927** M. DORNEY *Adventurous Honeymoon* 99 We asked her if we could see the corroboree or 'play-about' as the half civilized ones call it. **1933** C.H. HOLMES *We find Aust.* 20 In their 'play about' the Pitjintaras still mimic the episode of 'old-man' goanna. *Ibid.* 79 At night they have their 'play about' at which they mimic anything unusual that has happened during the day. **1959** E. WEBB *Mark of Sun* 116 The stock-boys and their lubras . . were preparing to stage a small-fella corroboree or 'playabout' for the visitors on Christmas night.

B. *adj.* Of an artefact, activity, etc.: for entertainment or recreation.

1914 *Bulletin* (Sydney) 11 June 24/1 Port Darwin residents used to enjoy going out at sundown towards the Junction to see the 'play-about' spear fights between different Northern Territory Tribes. **1914** *School Paper* (Melbourne) 1 Sept. 134, I can throw my play-about boomerang. **1928** B. SPENCER *Wanderings in Wild Aust.* 64 The curious thing is that one and the same design will be 'play-about' in one place and *Churinga*, or sacred, in another. **1930** HIVES & LUMLEY *Jrnl. of Jackaroo* 83 Boomerangs were of three kinds, the 'play-about' one, the hunting one and the fighting one. **1937** G.H. SUNTER *Adventures Trepang Fisher* 280 The blackfellows stood out, two armed with half a dozen 'play-about' spears each and a wommera. **1955** M. DURACK *Keep him my Country* 36 'Was she fighting?' 'Playabout,' Liddy said shortly.

play-boomerang. A boomerang designed for entertainment or recreation. See also PLAY-ABOUT *a.*

1851 J. HENDERSON *Excursions & Adventures N.S.W.* II. 147 Some are made and used for amusement, and are called play-boomerangs. With these, the boys practice a great deal. **1878** R.B. SMYTH *Aborigines of Vic.* I. 329 The boomerangs . . from the north-east coast in my collection are not 'come-back' or 'play' boomerangs.

play-lunch. A snack taken by children to school to eat during the mid-morning break; the break itself.

1963 E. SPENCE *Green Laurel* 109 She was not hungry enough to go back for her play-lunch, and to stay close to the classroom appeared to be the safest thing to do. **1974** *Age* (Melbourne) 12 Oct. 12/5 *Play lunch*, emergency rations for morning recess, usually being a piece of fruit, cake or some chocolate crackles. **1982** N. KEESING *Lily on Dustbin* 120 The Queensland coal mining town of Blair Athol gave the world 'elevenses'—the morning break, or recess in a school day or 'playlunch' as it might be called further south.

plenty, *a. Austral. pidgin.* Many; much. Also as quasi-*adv.*

1834 *Perth Gaz.* 10 May 283, I told *Weeip* to put down their spears, when they all threw them down, and ran towards us, calling out '*babbin babbin* (friend) plenty'. **1847** A. HARRIS *Settlers & Convicts* (1953) 131 Plenty water before white man come, plenty pish (fish), plenty kangaroo, plenty 'possum, plenty everything. **1852** J. BONWICK *Notes of Gold Digger* 19 Me plenty rich black-fellow. **1856** —— *W. Buckley* 66 Never mind, plenty lubra one day. **1856** W.W. DOBIE *Recoll. Visit Port-Phillip* 91 White fellow was not *big one* stoopid to *plenty* work like it that along o' garden. **1870** J. BONWICK *Last Tasmanians* 211 There he gave them 'plenty tucker', as they called it. **1880** J.B. STEVENSON *Seven Yrs. Austral. Bush* 144 Plenty Possum sit down up there. **1951** I.L. IDRIESS *Across Nullarbor* 53 We were 'plenty feller' hungry.

pleuro /ˈpluroʊ/. Also **pleura, ploorer.** [Chiefly Austral.: see OED(S.]

1. Abbrev. of 'contagious bovine pleuro-pneumonia'.

[N.Z. **1863** E.R. CHUDLEIGH *Diary* 13 Aug. (1950) 98 A horse that was showing signs of pleura. **1864** C.R. THATCHER *Songs of War* 13 We are by this Pleuro haunted.] **1871** *Austral. Town & Country Jrnl.* (Sydney) 25 Feb. 230/3 There were some indications of pleuro in several herds during the very wet season. **1881** A.C. GRANT *Bush-Life Qld.* I. 190 It is a two-year-old steer. . . As we ride past he shows the white of his eye, and gathering up his strength, he gives a deep hollow cough. . . 'Pleura,' said Fitzgerald, reading West's enquiring glance. 'We always have it more or less on the run.' **1896** H. LAWSON *While Billy Boils* 10 The cows contracted a disease which was known in those parts as 'plooro permoanyer', but generally referred to as 'th' ploorer'. **1903** R.J. CLOW *Pillar of Salt* 93, I knew as every poor 'swagie' knows that pleura bullocks or flukey sheep may have drunk from the same hole. **1919** R.J. CASSIDY *Gipsy Road* 65 The smut gets in the wheat crop, or, failing that, the rust. . . The cattle get the pleuro. **1929** S.C. SMITH *Original Ideas* 12 The pleuro comes and carries off cattle, They die as fast as men fall in battle. **1949** I.L. IDRIESS *One Wet Season* 57 'Not too good at present, Jack,' he frowned. 'The blasted pleuro has broken out.' **1960** M. HENRY *Unlucky Dip* 41 'What is this pleuro I keep hearing about?' asked Hilary hastily. 'Is it a sort of pleurisy they get?' 'Partly, Hilary; partly an extremely contagious form of pneumonia. Pleuro-pneumonia it is really, and it's one of our worst cattle epidemic diseases.' **1968** F. FLYNN *Northern Frontiers* 62 Perhaps the greatest achievement in the cattle industry is the virtual conquest of pleuro-pneumonia. In 1967, for the first time in a century, not one case of pleuro was reported anywhere in the Territory. **1973** J. WILLIAMS *Tom Collins* 21 When he bought the bullock team to haul wool to the coast and bring back provisions for the farmers around, she would wait patiently for his homecoming: or even go with him, camping on the river banks or in the scrub, until they were beggared by the pleuro.

2. Special Comb. **pleuro line,** see quot. 1978.

1960 *N.T. News* (Darwin) 26 Feb. 3/2 The Central Australian area is now officially recognised as a 'pleuro free zone' because of the A.I.B. pleuro line separating the south from the north. **1978** D. STUART *Wedgetail View* 5 The Government drew a line on the map . . and declared the country north of the line an area infected with bovine pleuro-pneumonia. Pleuro. Contagious. . . It meant the end of all their plans, that pleuro line.

plink. [Joc. var. of PLONK.] Wine of very poor quality: see quot. 1943.

[**1919** W.H. DOWNING *Digger Dialects* 52 *Von blink*, a humorous corruption of vin blanc. **1924** A.W. BAZLEY et al. Gloss. Slang A.I.F. 31 (typescript) *Von blinked*, drunk.] **1943** S.J. BAKER *Pop. Dict. Austral. Slang* (ed. 3) 60 *Plink*, described as 'a cheap form of plonk'. **1950** *Southerly* iii. 145 A Gargantuan zest for that common horror of the dipsodes: plink. **1971** J. CARTER *Wild Country* 5 Two decidedly scruffy, heavyweight gents visited me after sundown, bringing with them a bottle of plink (a poor substitute for plonk). **1980** HEPWORTH & HINDLE *Boozing out in Melbourne Pubs* 16 Plink is defined as being cheap plonk.

plod. [Cornish dial. *plod* 'a short or dull story; a lying tale': see OEDS *sb.*[2]]

1. A tale; a 'line'; a piece of information.

1928 *Bulletin* (Sydney) 5 Sept. 27/1, I 'ad to grin When 'e starts pitchin' that plod to me. **1943** *Double Gee* (Kalgoorlie) Christmas 4 A private applied to R.Q.M.S. for a paliasse. He put up a good plod. **1948** G. FARWELL *Down Argent Street* 70 Outside the lamp-room they meet their opposites on the incoming shift, discuss problems, hand on information and tips—or, in miner's parlance, pass the plod. **1954** T.A.G. HUNGERFORD *Sowers of Wind* 241 That's the plod he put up any-way. **1975** X. HERBERT *Poor Fellow my Country* 1126 Put in a plod for me, mate.

2. *transf.* Chiefly *W.A.* A work-sheet recording details of an employee's day's work; the day's work. Also **plod card.**

1935 *Red Star* (Perth) 20 Sept. 2/1 As the day's plods had not been signed the men decided to get them at the timekeeper's office. **1948** K.S. PRICHARD *Golden Miles* 72 He had to go to the office for his plod—the card on which he filled in particulars of the work he was doing, its position in the mine, and the hours he was working. *Ibid.* 74 Most of the boggers rushed their plod before crib sweating and cursing as they pushed the truckloads of from fourteen to twenty hundredweights. **1974** N. PHILLIPSON *As Other Men* 103 He . . showed them how they were supposed to fill out their plod cards, listing the number of holes drilled [etc.] **1984** S. MACINTYRE *Militant* 76 The foreman issues each man with a 'plod', a record of hours he has worked and the rate of pay.

plongge /ˈplɒŋgi/. *Obs.* [a. Yaralde *plonge.*] A club used in Aboriginal ritual: see quot. 1846.

1846 H.E.A. MEYER *Manners & Customs Aborigines Encounter Bay* 8 The plongge is a stick about two feet long, with a large knob at the end. They believe that if a person is tapped gently upon the breast with this instrument he will become ill and die, or if he should shortly afterwards receive a wound that it will be mortal. **1879** *Native Tribes S.A.* 195 They fancy that they can charm or enchant by means of two instruments, one called plongge, the other mokani.

plonk. [Prob. altered form of Fr. *blanc* in *vin blanc* white wine: see early quots. and cf. PLINK. Now also used elsewhere.]

1. Wine, or fortified wine, of poor quality. Also *attrib.*

[**1919** W.H. DOWNING *Digger Dialects* 52 *Vin blank*, white wine. **1924** A.W. BAZLEY et al. Gloss. Slang A.I.F. 22 (typescript) *Point blank*, the white wine commonly used in France.] **1933** *Bulletin* (Sydney) 11 Jan. 12/3 The man who drinks illicit brews or 'plonk' (otherwise known as 'madman soup') by the quart does it in quiet spots or at home. **1938** H. DRAKE-BROCKMAN *Men without Wives* (1951) 77 What cow'd be such a dope as t' waste a perishin' thirst like we got, on plonk? It's beer we want. **1944** J.F. DETTMAN *Here was Glory* 63, I knew 'e liked th' bombo—even then I got a shock 'e Not merely smelt uv plonk, 'e simply stunk! **1955** D. NILAND *Shiralee* 76 Getting blown about like an old moll at a plonk party. **1964** K. WILLEY *Eaters of Lotus* 65 A bottle of beer will do if you have no plonk. **1969** A. GARVE *Boomerang* 86 'Plonk', Dawes called it derisively, unimpressed by Talbot's assurance that it was a sound Gewurztraminer. **1974** *Bulletin* (Sydney) 27 Apr. 24/3 The Australian word 'plonk' is now well established in the English of England. The word is not used disparagingly but with a kind of self-conscious affection to describe bulk table wines imported from the Continent and bottled in Britain. **1984** B. DIXON *Searching for Aboriginal Lang.* 15 'Well, the question is, are you going to be having any plonk?' We had absolutely no idea what plonk was, but from his tone of voice it was obviously a good thing, so I said: 'Yes, of course we are going to have plonk.' We drove off with a tin-opener that had a corkscrew attached.

2. Comb. **plonk bar, shop.**

1965 E. LAMBERT *Long White Night* 187 Prim . . rented a room above the **plonk bar.** **1970** N.A. BEAGLEY *Up & Down Under* 80 The wine saloons were called 'Plonk Bars' by the fraternity who frequented them. **1980** HEPWORTH & HINDLE *Boozing out in Melbourne Pubs* 17 The buggers tore all the old plonk bars down, didn't they? **1965** D. MARTIN *Hero of Too* 58 'We will give them wine to make it special.' 'They'll call it a **plonk shop.**' **1980** HEPWORTH & HINDLE *Boozing out in Melbourne Pubs* 16 The plonk shops . . seem to have been in direct line of descent from the grog shanties and shebeens of our colonial beginnings.

Hence **plonk-up** *n.*, a party; **plonked-up** *ppl. a.*, intoxicated.

1966 *Kings Cross Whisper* (Sydney) xxv. 5/2 Entertained the four and a half Persians to a **plonk-up** on the shores of Lake Hurley-Burley. **1972** J. DE HOOG *Skid Row Dossier* 6 You get **plonked up** and the bouncer chucks you out.

plonker. *Obs.* In the war of 1914–18: a shell.

1918 *Aussie: Austral. Soldiers' Mag.* Jan. 3 Fritz was putting over some big stuff. Every time a plonker landed near them, one of the officers energetically fired his revolver into the air. **1920** *Aussie* (Sydney) Dec. 36/3, I had helped him out when he had got chucked into a shell-hole by a plonker. **1941** S.J. BAKER *Pop. Dict. Austral. Slang* 55 *Plonker*, a shell. Digger's slang.

plonko. [f. PLONK + -O.] One who is addicted to 'plonk'. Also **plonky.**

1963 A. MARSHALL *In mine Own Heart* 187 You end up a plonko with bells ringing in your head. **1964** *Realist* (Sydney) xvii. 24 'Look! A plonky!' 'Probably been on the metho.' **1972** *Bulletin* (Sydney) 10 June 9/1 An old plonko taught me . . how to walk down the street picking up butts without the crowds noticing and despising me. **1978** K. GILBERT *People are Legends* 21 I'm Joe. Tired Joe. The 'plonky' the wino you see on the street I piss at the public corner, I'm a drunk, I'm never discreet. **1981** B. GREEN *Small Town Rising* 9 Mayor Frank knew the bloke was a plonko come down to the river bank to avoid the authorities.

ploorer, var. PLEURO.

ploughed, *ppl. a.* In special collocations: **ploughed field** *Tas.*, see quot. 1896; **land** *obs.*, terrain characterized by ridges resembling the furrows made by a plough.

1885 *Once a Month* (Melbourne) June 457 On the summit there is a singular assemblage of boulders, which have not been inappropriately designated the '**Ploughed Field**'. **1896** J.B. WALKER Corresp., Ploughed field. In Southern Tasmania applied to extensive fields of large stones, usually basaltic, which occur on mountain sides. The name had its origin in a noticeable area of this kind near the summit of Mount Wellington, which seen from Hobart has the colour and appearance of a ploughed field. **1909** G.W. SMITH *Naturalist in Tas.* 61 Another feature is the presence upon the plateau of Wellington and Ben Lomond of extensive level fields of large rounded boulders of diabase, known locally as 'potato' or 'ploughed' fields. **1981** M. SHARLAND *Tracks of Morning* 51 Tasmania isn't unique in having what most of us know as 'ploughed fields' on the slopes of our mountains... They have some resemblance to newly ploughed fields angled on hillsides, and the name commonly given them may be distinctly Tasmanian in character. **1831** [**ploughed land**] T.L. MITCHELL *Three Exped. Eastern Aust.* 28 Nov. (1838) I. 14 Portions of the surface . . bore that peculiar, undulating character which appears in the southern districts, where it closely resembles furrows, and is termed 'ploughed ground'. **1833** W.H. BRETON *Excursions* 97 The land rises in ridges exactly as though it had once been in a state of cultivation. . . This 'ploughed land', as it has been termed, was observed only where the soil was a rich black mould. **1844** L. LEICHHARDT *Jrnl. Overland Exped. Aust.* 6 Nov. (1847) 32 Rich black soil, which appeared several times in the form of ploughed land, well known, in other parts of the colony, either under that name, or under that of 'Devil-devil land'. **1855** W. HOWITT *Land, Labor & Gold* II. 92 The ground was thrown up in hummocks, as in all the volcanic plains of this country; and, in places, ran in ridges as if ploughed up, and hence denominated here ploughed lands.

pluck, *v.* In the phr. **to pluck a brand:** see quot. 1945.

1911 A.L. HAYDON *Trooper Police Aust.* 352 One popular form of 'faking' that has been introduced with success is that of 'plucking a brand'. This is done by pulling out hairs from a colt. . . Such a mark only lasts a comparatively short time. **1945** S.J. BAKER *Austral. Lang.* 50 *To pluck a brand*, to fake a new brand on stolen cattle or horses by pulling out the hairs round the existing brand.

plugger. [f. *plug* to keep on persistently.] One who runs, rides, etc., doggedly.

1896 *Bulletin* (Sydney) 14 Mar. 17/3 Wallace, after all, is only a great 'plugger'. The chestnut can't come with a rush at the finish. **1898** *Worker* (Sydney) 20 Aug. 3/3 Plugger Bill Martin, who raked in most of the Australian dollars on his bike, has succeeded in beating a Yankee champion over 50 miles. **1900** *Western Champion* (Barcaldine) 24 Apr. 13/1 The two bicycle races fell to Hoskins, who is a genuine 'plugger'.

plug hat. *Obs.* [U.S. *plug hat* hat with a tall cylindrical crown: see Mathews.] A top hat (quot. 1941 appears erroneous).

1883 G.E. LOYAU *Personal Adventures* 78 Frank . . disguises himself in a 'plug hat' and great coat, and carries a banjo. **1885** *Austral. Tit-Bits* (Sydney) 5 Feb. 4/2 A smooth-faced young man, attired in a plug hat, a bright green bobtail frieze coat and tight check pants. **1908** *Bulletin* (Sydney) 4 June 14/2, I would not . . risk a new chimney-pot or plug or bell-topper or top or 'lum' hat that wombats never undermine a tail race. **1941** S.J. BAKER *Pop. Dict. Austral. Slang* 55 *Plug hat*, a bowler hat.

Hence **plug-hatted** *ppl. a.*

1903 *Truth* (Sydney) 4 Jan. 7/3 Alexander is . . entitled to as much protection . . as is the most bloated, plug-hatted plutocrat in the State.

plum. [Transf. use of *plum* the fruit of *Prunus domestica*; the tree itself.] *Native plum*, see NATIVE *a.* 6 a.; the wood of a native plum. Also *attrib.*

1770 J. BANKS *Jrnl.* 26 Aug. (1896) 299 A fruit we called plums—like them in colour, but flat like a little cheese. **1824** *Hobart Town Gaz.* 1 Oct., Colonial Timber may at any time be purchased of an Inhabitant of this town. . . Plum Tree, for furniture. **1825** B. FIELD *Geogr. Mem. N.S.W.* 463 Excepting . . the plum (cargillia australis) . . the wood-cutters had no names for the many trees of gigantic growth which cover this mountain. **1845** *Melbourne Standard* 30 Apr. 2/5 The damson like plum, and the coffee tree abound. **1880** J. BONWICK *Resources Qld.* 81 The Plums belong to the *Owenia*, running sixty feet, with a fine rose-coloured wood, of great strength and first-class polishing properties. **1916** *Emu* XV. 155 A quantity of wild fuchsia bushes, often called 'plum-bush' (*Eremophila*) were growing. **1926** *Bulletin* (Sydney) 13 May 22/3, I have used wild plum-tree or other edible bush gums. **1935** H.H. FINLAYSON *Red Centre* 31 On the fringes of the mulga colonies . . a score or more of large shrubs or small trees . . quondong, plum-bush [etc.]. **1953** H.G. LAMOND *Big Red* 283 *Plum*, edible tree (*Santalum lanceolatum*).

plumed, *a.* Used as a distinguishing epithet in the names of birds: **plumed egret,** the waterbird *Egretta intermedia* of n. and e. Aust. incl. Tas., and elsewhere (see quot. 1976); **pigeon,** *spinifex pigeon*, see SPINIFEX 4; **tree duck,** the duck *Dendrocygna eytoni* (see *whistling duck* (a), WHISTLING).

1848 J. GOULD *Birds of Aust.* VI. Pl. 57, *Herodias plumiferus* . . **Plumed Egret.** **1912** *Emu* XII. 120 Plumed Egret . . owing to the cruel craze for 'osprey' plumes, this is a bird with a 'past' and but little future. **1945** C. BARRETT *Austral. Bird Life* 54 Of egrets we have three species: the white egret . . the plumed egret (*E*[*gretta*] *intermedia*), and the little egret. **1976** *Reader's Digest Compl. Bk. Austral. Birds* 80 Long, lacy, filamentous nuptial plumes have given the plumed egret its name. As with its relatives . . only breeding birds have these plumes. **1945** C. BARRETT *Austral. Bird Life* 66 The **plumed pigeon** (*Lophophaps plumifera*) frequents stony areas in the interior of Southern Australia. **1948** H.A. LINDSAY *Bushman's Handbk.* 21 The little plumed pigeon, with a cockatoo-like crest. **1976** *Reader's Digest Compl. Bk. Austral. Birds* 247 Many types of birds are found in the arid spinifex grasslands of central and northern Australia, but few are permanent residents. The plumed pigeons are included in these few. [**1945 plumed tree duck**: C. BARRETT *Austral. Bird Life* 48 Those curious birds called tree-ducks are better known in Northern Australia than in the south. However, the plumed species (*Dendrocygna eytoni*) ranges into South Australia, and is an occasional visitor to Victoria.] **1955** S. OSBORNE *Duck Shooting Aust.* 16 Plumed tree duck. . . These have the same general appearance as the Whistling Tree Duck, but they are a paler greyish colour and have no chestnut on the shoulders. **1964** M. SHARLAND *Territory of Birds* 105 Here also was a pair of unusual perching ducks, the handsome *Dendrocygna*, commonly called 'Whistler', and in ornithological vernacular 'Plumed Tree Duck'.

plume grass. [Transf. use of *plume-grass* a grass of the genus *Erianthus* having a plume-like inflorescence.] Any of several perennial grasses (fam. Poaceae) having a plume-like flower-head, esp. those of the genus *Dichelachne* of all States.

1847 G.F. ANGAS *Savage Life & Scenes* I. 152 Tufts of a gigantic species of plume grass, with sharp-edged leaves, grew in vast quantities upon several of the flats. **1897** L. LINDLEY-COWEN *W. Austral. Settler's Guide* 402 *Dichelachne* ('plume' grass). **1935** C.W. WINDERS *Managem. Sown Pastures* 713 The native pasture . . contains a large proportion of winter-growing species, such as . . plume grass. **1966** N.T. BURBIDGE *Austral. Grasses* I. 78 Plume Grass is very common in dry forest and woodland areas and is also found in the mountains.

plum pine. [See quot. 1985.] *She pine*, see SHE 2.

1904 J.H. MAIDEN *Notes on Commercial Timbers N.S.W.* 24 We have another timber allied to 'colonial pine', but much harder and more durable, namely, that one which is variously known as . . 'plum pine', and 'berry pine'. **1956** E. MITCHELL *Black Cockatoos* 83 Aromatic shrubs grew close to the water's edge, and the alpine plum pine. **1985** N. & H. NICHOLSON *Austral. Rainforest Plants* 55 *Podocarpus elatus* Plum Pine. Although the swollen stalks of the fruit are sweetish and quite edible, they are hardly as delectable as a plum.

plumpton. [The name of a village in Sussex, England, where the first enclosed greyhound racing took place in 1877.] A kind of enclosed racecourse for greyhounds; a race held on such a course (as opposed to one held in the open). Also *attrib.*

1884 *Australasian Coursing Calendar* 30/1 We much question whether any enclosed ground in the old country can hold a candle to the colonial Plumpton. *Ibid.* 35/1 The opening day of the important produce meeting at the Oval was anything but favourable or inviting to coursers who affect the Plumpton system. **1942** H.H. PECK *Mem. of Stockman* 9 They took part together also in many private coursing matches in the open, but gave coursing up when fenced plumptons came into vogue. **1966** J. ALDRIDGE *My Brother Tom* 73 Lockie had once promoted Sunday football just over the bridge, and Sunday plumpton (greyhound coursing with five hares).

plumwood. The tree *Eucryphia moorei* (see *pinkwood* PINK *a.*). Also **plum.**

1889 J.H. MAIDEN *Useful Native Plants Aust.* 530 *Eucryphia moorei* . . 'Plum' of the Southern districts of New South Wales . . is a beautifully clear, moderately hard wood, of a warm, light brown colour. **1965** *Austral. Encycl.* III. 411 *E*[*ucryphia*] *moorei* . . is sometimes called plumwood or stinkwood—an unfortunate name for such a handsome tree. **1984** *Bogong* V. iii. 4 Only one tree, the Plumwood or Pinkwood, *Eucryphia moorei*, is present in many high altitude forests. This species is particularly interesting in that it occurs only in southern N.S.W. and just over the border in East Gippsland.

plurry, *a.* [Joc. representation of a Maori pronunc. of BLOODY.] An intensive: BLOODY. Also as *adv.*

1900 H. LAWSON *Verses Pop. & Humorous* 227 Their language that day, I am sorry to say, Mostly consisted of 'plurry'. **1904** *Bulletin* (Sydney) 18 Aug. 16/2 I'll take away your plurry license. **1918** *7th Field Artillery Brigade Yandoo* Jan. 93 They might induce old Fritz to confess that it was he who started this plurry war! **1927** W. BLACKET *May it please your Honour* 238 Knowing but two words of the Kamilaroi dialect, I could only advise them to 'make plenty of plurry yabber longa plurry big fella plurry jury'. **1943** *Troppo Tribune* (Mataranka) 30 Aug. 3 Have sworn an oath, a plurry oath. **1968** S. GORE *Holy Smoke* 18 You eat that one, you gett'im plurry sick longa your 'ead. Longa your binjy, too! **1984** *Bulletin* (Sydney) 3 Apr. 106/3 When Ginger was asked whether he preferred the infantry or the cavalry, he thought for a while and then voted for the infantry. Asked why, he replied, 'One day, retreat will be sounded and then I don't want to be hindered by no plurry horse!'

plute. *Obs.* [Used elsewhere but recorded earliest in Aust.: see OEDS.] Abbrev. of *plutocrat*. Also *attrib.*

1894 *Vagabonds* 2 It is by this monopolisation of currency as well as of the land and other means of production that the Plutes are enabled to levy their weighty taxes on human industry. **1903** *Truth* (Sydney) 27 Dec. 1/3 No wonder the defeated and dismayed 'plute' push cry aloud in real alarm, 'Where the devil is Labor driving us?' **1906** M. CANNON *That Damned Democrat* (1981) 88 *Plute against people.* Squatterdom scores. **1918** *Ross's Monthly* July 1/2 *Agree*—What the Plutes want the Mutes not to.

Hence **plutish** *a.*, plutocratic.

1907 *Truth* (Sydney) 25 Aug. 4/7 They 'sool' their plutish prints on to proclaim him a cocktail, a renegade, a coward.

poached, *ppl. a.*

1. In special collocations: **poached egg,** see quot. 1941; **egg daisy,** the annual herbaceous plant *Myriocephalus stuartii* (fam. Asteraceae); also **poached eggs daisy.**

1941 S.J. BAKER *Pop. Dict. Austral. Slang* 55 **Poached egg,** a yellow-coloured 'silent cop' placed in the centre of intersections as a guide to traffic. **1948** R. RAVEN-HART *Canoe in Aust.* 187 Motorists often ignore 'Silent cops' at corners, yellow iron domes with white surrounds, 'poached eggs', typically Australian neat slang. **1965** *Austral. Encycl.* II. 494 The so-called 'ham-and-eggs' or '**poached-egg daisy**' (*Myriocephalus stuartii*) grows prolifically on mallee sandhills across Australia; its hairy viscid stems are up to 2 feet high, with rather large yellow compound heads surrounded by a common involucre of white bracts, the whole reminiscent of a poached egg. **1973** V. SERVENTY *Desert Walkabout* 102 Mulla mullas, poached egg daisies were only some of the wildflower species. **1981** J. BURT *Shutterbug in Bush* 74 Sandy plains carpeted with poached egg daisies. **1986** *Trees & Natural Resources* Mar. 2 Wild Turnip . . and Poached Eggs Daisy (*Myriocephalus stuartii*), became the dominant plants in the dune grasslands.

pobblebonk. [Prob. f. Br. dial. *pobble* the noise made by water bubbling as it starts to boil (see EDD *sb.*[2]) + imitative *bonk*.] Either of two frogs of the genus *Limnodynastes* having a loud, single note call, *L. dorsalis* of s.w. W.A. and *L. dumerilii* of s.e. Aust. incl. Tas.

1967 B.Y. MAIN *Between Wodjil & Tor* 84 The resonant twangs of the 'banjo' or pobble-bonk frogs. **1978** B.P. MOORE *Life on Forty Acres* 113 The most distinctive call . . is that of the local Pobblebonk (*Limnodynastes dumerili*). Each male utters but a single 'bonk' at a time but others immediately follow.

pocket. *Australian National Football.* A side position, esp. in the forward and back rows; a player occupying such a position. Freq. as **back pocket, forward pocket.** Also *attrib.*

1931 J.F. MCHALE et al. *Austral. Game of Football* 66 The back pocket players always kept slightly in front of their opponents. **1936** E.C.H. TAYLOR et al. *Our Austral. Game Football* 56 The extra man will most probably be taken from one of the full forward 'pockets'. **1959** PARNELL & ANDREW *Austral. Football* 40 Back pocket players should always kick to their respective wings and never across goals. **1963** *Footy Fan* (Melbourne) I. xv. 5 The Hawks . . managed to 'bottle up' the game in a forward pocket . . on the wide M.C.G. **1973** P. MCKENNA *My World of Football* 90 The pocket specialists are a new idea in League football. **1982** J. WARREN *Austral. Football Fundamentals* 32 Back pocket players seldom need to take high marks but should practise their body skills, their tackling and smothering and, above all else, be two-sided in both kicking and handball.

podargus /pəˈdagəs/. [The bird genus *Podargus* was named by the French ornithologist L.J.P. Vieillot (*Nouveau Dict. Hist. Nat.* (ed. 2, 1818) XXVII. 151) f. Gr. *πόδαργος* swift-footed.] A nocturnal, grey to brown frogmouth of the genus *Podargus* of all States, New Guinea, and adjacent islands, esp. the TAWNY FROGMOUTH.

[**1837** *Proc. Zool. Soc. London* 67 The sclerotic ring of the great *Podargus* does not present the slightest appearance of distinct plates.] **1841** *S. Austral. Rec.* (London) 2 Jan. 10 Besides the owlet night-jar . . there is the podargus, another night-bird, that sleeps so soundly during the day as only to be disturbed by being knocked off its perch, when it flies lazily to another tree, and resumes its slumbers. **1865** G.F. ANGAS *Aust.* 88 The podargus, or goatsucker, is a stupid-looking creature, with very large eyes, and an enormous mouth, fitted for capturing moths and other large insects. **1890** *Act* (Vic.) 54 Vict. no. 1095 3rd Sched., Podargus or Mopokes . . the whole year. **1933** *Bulletin* (Sydney) 19 Apr. 21/4 My choice for the quietest bush bird is the tawny frogmouth, or podargus. **1961** *Coast to Coast 1959–60* 66 'You know the podargus?' 'It's a bird. The tawny-shouldered frogmouth.'

poddied, *ppl. a.* [f. PODDY *v.*]

1. Of an animal: hand-fed.

1921 *Bulletin* (Sydney) 17 Feb. 20/2 The reason the poddied sheep-pups . . turned out duffers was more likely psychological than physiological. **1923** *Ibid.* 1 Nov. 24/3 At many Out-West peeling establishments goats—always more manageable than the woollies—are regularly used as leaders, and poddied calves are also often pressed into service. **1952** *Meanjin* 19 There were three poddied calves frisking in the overgrown grass.

2. *Obs.* Intoxicated.

1905 *Shearer* (Sydney) 4 Mar. 4/2 Personal effort, self-abnegation, libertarian ideas, and ethical standards are, however, very distressing and distasteful to the 'poddied' State socialist or befooled A.W.U. member. **1909** J.S. RYAN *Splinters on Wall* 8, I long to be 'poddied' with beer; Have brandy on every shelf.

poddy: see PODDY MULLET.

poddy, *n.* and *a.* [Spec. use of Br. dial. *poddy* corpulent, f. *pod* large protuberant stomach: see OED *pod, sb.*[2] 3 and OED(S *poddy*.]

A. *n.*

1. a. A calf; orig. one old enough to wean and fatten, later (esp.) one as yet unbranded. Also *attrib.*

1872 A. MCFARLAND *Illawarra & Manaro* 76 Three or four 'selections', good for wheat, 'poddies', and snipe. **1893** K. MACKAY *Out Back* 75, I did occasionally put my brand by mistake on one of Massey's 'poddies'. **1900** *Truth* (Sydney) 6 May 4/6 Now we don't feed pigs and poddies, 'Cos we're full-blown British swaddies. **1915** G. SARGANT *Sweet Heart of Bush* 148 The cattle they were after were a mob made up of a bull, two stags, and a few stores and poddies. **1918** *Kia Ora Coo-ee* Oct. 8/3 He counts his deferred pay in poddies and has a supreme contempt for 'townies' and their inability to do anything in proper Australian bush style. **1944** *Coast to Coast 1943* 229 A mob of twenty-four skinny little milkers' poddies, about as big as sheep. **1951** E. HILL *Territory* 307 Mustering cows and cleanskin calves just old enough to wean—the 'poddies'—they headed them up into the ranges. **1956** T. RONAN *Moleskin Midas* 149 For every poddy that's up in the Coronet breakaways there's a dozen blokes trying to dodge it off. **1960** *Khaki Bush & Bigotry* (1968) 209 Their poddies was through again this mornin'. I put the dog on 'em. **1963** HARNEY & LOCKWOOD *Shady Tree* 84 A poddy is a calf, and a poddy-dodger is a man who spirits them away from their owners before they've been branded, and quickly gets his own brand on them.

b. A calf (less freq. a lamb or foal) which is hand-fed.

1898 *Bulletin* (Sydney) 8 Jan. (Red Page), Prof. Morris defines 'Poddy' as 'a Vic. name for sand-mullet', but leaves out its meaning of motherless calf or foal (common in the bush). A poddy calf or a poddy foal is heard all over Australia. **1913** W.K. HARRIS *Outback in Aust.* 43 Besides their other stock, the Kennedys have some half-dozen 'poddies' (hand-fed calves), all in splendid condition. **1941** *Coast to Coast* 21 Molly was very useful, helping with the milking and feeding the poddies. **1956** 'B. JAMES' *Bunyip of Barney's Elbow* 154 Taking the milk in and bringing back the skim for pigs and poddies. **1965** M. PATCHETT *Last Warrior* 107 'Ow about feedin' the poddy and the fowls? **1974** J. DINGWELL *Cattleman* 63 I'm bringing him in for your special care because his mother isn't up to it. . . You call a lamb like that a poddy. **1983** M. HAYES *Prickle Farm* 80 A little one-eyed ewe, who'd obviously been someone's poddy and considered herself a little above the common throng of paddock sheep.

c. *transf.* See quots.

1958 J. BECKETT Study Mixed Blood Aboriginal Minority (M.A. thesis) 145 In fact, young men, or 'poddies' as they are called, find single life very pleasurable. **1982** G.B. EGGLETON *Last of Lantern Swingers* 13 Occasionally, a pair of rabbits may be overlooked in the 'gutting' operation, and on reaching the freezing room would be found to be bloated and unfit for use. These were known as 'poddies'.

2. A bottle containing an alcoholic beverage.

1891 *Truth* (Sydney) 5 Apr. 7/3 Formerly the riding men did not drink much, but as there is now a pub. on every run they frequently come home rolling from side to side and with a poddy in their kick. **1953** H.M. EASTMAN *Mem. of Sheepman* 58 For anaesthetic he would use a couple of 'poddies' (lemonade bottle of whisky) obtained from Coree pub.

B. *adj.* Hand-fed; most freq. in the collocation **poddy calf.**

1899 *Bulletin* (Sydney) 18 Mar. 14/2 She . . talked a lot about pigs and 'poddy' calves. **1911** E.S. SORENSON *Life in Austral. Backblocks* 40 They are tethered like poddy-calves near by the residence to keep them from rambling. **1919** *Bulletin* (Sydney) 1 Mar. 6/3 Many a small selector, buying a few poddy calves here and there, or a few store beasts and fattening them, has blossomed in a few years into a rich grazier. **1930** *Ibid.* 5 Nov. 20/4 Poddy sheep are useful as decoys. **1934** *Ibid.* 17 Jan. 20/2 The bookmaker's best friend . . has come in contact with plenty of 'poddy' horses. **1934** *Ibid.* 28 Mar. 20/3 'H.C.M.' . . *must* be a newchum never to have seen a poddy leader at the woolshed before. Here on Cambalong station there is a crossbred wether that has been doing duty for some years. **1944** *Land Army Gaz.* (Brisbane) 3 July, Mothering baby lambs and feeding poddy calves have kept Land Girls busy. **1954** T. RONAN *Vision Splendid* 150 He noticed a milker's poddy bullock which had always been on the tail when he had been looking after the mob, and was surprised that such a docile, lazy beast should be so near the lead. **1956** —— *Moleskin Midas* 223 Mrs Dolman was now bottle-feeding a poddy foal. **1961** X. HERBERT *Soldiers' Women* 52 The home of her dreams was a white-roofed homestead on a wide red plain with a lily-coated billabong and a winding windmill: with a flock of galahs and kids galore and poddy lambs and a bright bit of garden blooming in the wilderness. **1978** G. HALL *River still Flows* 15 Farmers along the river might leave their poddy calves unfed while they hastened to the river-bank. **1983** M. HAYES *Prickle Farm* 11 Six poddy calves some enterprising cattle baron has grazing on the reserve behind the War Memorial.

poddy, *v.* [f. prec.] *trans.*

a. To feed (a young animal) by hand. Also **poddy-feed.**

1896 *Worker* (Sydney) 21 Mar. 1/3 He carried the slop-buckets to the pig sty for her, and helped to 'poddy' (hand-feed) a young calf. **1902** *Bulletin* (Sydney) 29 Mar. 14/4 When calves are being reared, he has to poddy-feed his share daily. **1915** K.S. PRICHARD *Pioneers* 276 Mrs Ross talked of her milking, and the calves she had poddied during the wet weather. **1920** *Bulletin* (Sydney) 2 Sept. 24/3 There is nothing out of the ordinary about a 14-year-old merino wether. . . A grazier near Cooma (N.S.W.) has one which he poddied in 1901. **1956** *Ibid.* 8 Feb. 12/4 Our old maiden ewe, poddied over 11 years ago, doesn't consider herself a sheep at all. **1964** K. TENNANT *Summer's Tales* 95 Lots of blokes gave him calves to poddy, when a cow they were taking on the road dropped one.

b. *transf.*

1924 *Bulletin* (Sydney) 17 Jan. 24/2 Mrs Cocky came in carrying an infant about a month old. I offered my congratulations. 'Oh, it's not ours,' exclaimed Cocky; 'it belongs to the missus's sister. But she's too crook to rear it, so the missus is poddying it for her.'

Hence **poddying** *vbl. n.*

1913 *Bulletin* (Sydney) 29 May 48/3 The cows had been milked, buckets washed and 'poddying' completed, all in record time. **1926** *Ibid.* 14 Jan. 22/3 The monotony of churning and poddying is unknown.

poddy-dodge, *v.* [f. PODDY *n.* 1 + DODGE *v.* 2.] *trans.* To steal (unbranded cattle). Also *absol.*, and freq. as *vbl. n.*

1919 *Bulletin* (Sydney) 25 Sept. 22/3 Owing to the rise in price of cattle and the difficulty stations have in branding-up, 'poddy-dodging' has become an established trade about Cloncurry (Q.). **1925** M. TERRY *Across Unknown Aust.* 125 Whites may be poddy-dodging. **1947** W.E. HARNEY *Brimming Billabongs* 152 At times Bob would pack up his horses, and he and I would go to distant cattle stations and pick up some cattle from their herds and drive them to our station in the wet lands. 'Poddy dodging' this was called, for it is against the law. **1958** *Bulletin* (Sydney) 17 Sept. 18/1 In parts where tourists were unknown, runs unfenced and poddy-dodging (within limits) a recognised practice, few owners begrudged the occasional traveller a bit of fresh meat. **1967** F. HARDY *Billy Borker yarns Again* 120 He bought a few cattle and poddy-dodged a few more. **1977** W.A. WINTER-IRVING *Bush Stories* 96, I don't think anybody will . . poddy-dodge our calves.

poddy-dodger. [See prec.] One who steals unbranded cattle.

1919 *Smith's Weekly* (Sydney) 26 Apr. 19/4 The luck of the poddy-dodgers in these parts is right out just now. They expend time and cunning in mustering clean-skins, and . . a station manager or policeman comes nosing around. **1923** *Bulletin* (Sydney) 18 Oct. 22/2, I would like the cattle-duffers and poddy dodgers of the Council to give their views on the merits of twisted and plaited green-hide ropes. **1939** J.G. PATTISON *'Battler's' Tales Early Rockhampton* 113 Some of the Queensland poddy dodgers . . were not satisfied with pinching a man's cattle, but they would pinch his gins as well. **1950** G.M. FARWELL *Land of Mirage* 171 Harry Power, the poddy-dodger who trained Ned Kelly, brought an artist's hand to the work. **1964** K. TENNANT *Summer's Tales* 99 He's been top-off man for the cattle thieves ever since he could walk. . . The sergeant told me he'd never catch any of those poddy dodgers out while the kid's in the district. **1972** D. SHEAHAN *Songs from Canefields* 37 They took him to court but old Bill had them tricked—A wise poddy dodger is hard to convict.

poddy-feed: see PODDY *v.* a.

poddy mullet. [f. **poddy,** poss. alteration of Jagara *punba* (see PUDDING-BALL) + (Eng.) *mullet*.] Any of several fish, esp. the young of *Mugil cephalus* (see *sea mullet* SEA). Also **poddy.**

1890 *Act* (Vic.) 54 Vict. no. 1093 2nd Sched., Sand-mullet or poddies. **1941** *Bulletin* (Sydney) 29 Oct. 14/1 We caught two pickle-jar full o' poddy mullet, shoved 'em in the fire an' ate them. **1977** *Commercial Fish Aust.* (Dept. Primary Industry) 50 Sea mullet, also known as poddy or grey mullet, are distributed worldwide. **1982** *Sun-Herald* (Sydney) 7 Mar. 141/6 The use of poddy mullet is illegal in N.S.W. because they are less than legal size.

poddy-rear, *v.* [f. PODDY *n.* 1 b.] *trans.* To hand-feed (a young animal). Also as *vbl. n.* and *ppl. a.*

1901 M. FRANKLIN *My Brilliant Career* 17 They do all the milkin', and pig-feedin' and poddy-rarin'. **1934** *Bulletin* (Sydney) 28 Mar. 20/3 This year a merino wether, poddy-reared, is to be broken in. **1976** C.D. MILLS *Hobble Chains & Greenhide* 82 A pet camel that has been 'poddy-reared' is a menace about a homestead. It will reach out and eat anything available. *Ibid.* 150 A peculiar thing with buck-jumpers is that they are often 'bread-eaters'—poddy-reared round a drover's cart.

pogie /'poʊgi/. *Hist.* Also **pogey, poggy, poogie.** [Of unknown origin.] Used *attrib.* in the Special Comb. **pogie pot** (or **tub**), a vat in which oysters are left to decompose before being boiled down, pearls being removed from the residue: see quot. 1979.

1903 H. TAUNTON *Australind* 145 He cheerfully replied, 'Oh! it's only some one stirring his poogie tub', and then went on to explain the process of obtaining pearls from the oysters. **1933** *Bulletin* (Sydney) 27 Sept. 20/4 It's time to look out at Denham Camp, Shark's Bay (W.A.), when the pogey pots are stirred up. The smell of a flying-fox rookery is as violets compared with a whiff from one of the pots, into which are placed the live Shark's Bay pearlshells. **1940** E. HILL *Great Austral. Loneliness* (ed. 2) 26 To obtain the pearls, the oysters are placed in 'pogey-pots', boilers and barrels that line the seashore. **1947** H. DRAKE-BROCKMAN *On N.-W. Skyline* 13 The small oysters are scooped out of the Bay and scraped into pots where they decompose and any pearls drop to the bottom—I was glad to be far above smells. Last time I had been landed from a lighter, right amongst the 'pogie pots' on the beach. **1955** A.C.V. BLIGH *Golden Quest* 31 The waters of the bay are leased . . to . . pearlers and . . they gather the shell by dredging. . . After gathering the shell it is filled into large iron pots called 'poggy pots'. **1960** H.H. WILSON *Where Wind's Feet Shine* 34 There were several heaps of pearl shell on the sand, four or five days old. Three coloured women were engaged in opening these and extracting the fish, which they threw into a kerosene tin. When the tin was full, it was emptied into a pogie pot. Sometimes pearls were embedded in the oyster itself, instead of the shell, and when the decomposed fish was boiled down and became liquid, the pearls sank to the bottom and were easily recovered. **1979** *Pearling Industry W.A.* 8 Recovery of the pearl was by an extremely primitive and offensive method. The shucked oysters were put into large drums called 'pogie pots', allowed to rot, and the pearls then recovered from the residue in the bottom.

pogo. Rhyming slang for *pogo stick*, 'prick', as a term of abuse.

1972 R. POLLARD *Cream Machine* 2 Be men, not mouths . . men, not Pogos and 'support' turd-burglars who spin war yarns and bullshit in the bars and R.S.L.s. **1975** W. NAGLE *Odd Angry Shot* 1 'Ready to emplane. . . Ready to emplane. . . ' 'Jesus, does he think a man's deaf, bloody RAAF pogo.' **1982** J.J. COE *Desperate Praise* 24 'We're on road clearing again. . . ' 'What about bloody 7 section doing it . . ?' 'Yeah, bloody pogos.'

point, *n.*[1] *Shearing.* Usu. in *pl.* See quot. 1899.

1871 *Austral. Town & Country Jrnl.* (Sydney) 18 Mar. 331/2 Sheep that strip at the points, and lose the belly-wool, having a clean head without topknot. **1897** *Worker* (Sydney) 11 Sept. 1/2 Though at a 'clean point' 'bare belly' he'd hardly ever scoff. **1899** A. SINCLAIR *Clip of Wool* 66 *Points*, the points or extremities of the fleece, i.e., the flanks, shanks, neck and head pieces. **1920** J.B. CRAMSIE *Managem. & Diseases Sheep* 57 In skinning a sheep a knife should be used to open up the skin at the points. **1944** E.H. PEARSE *Sheep, Farm & Station Managem.* (ed. 5) 199 With regard to covering, the main fleece is concentrated on, and a certain lightness about the head and points may be forgiven. **1950** H.G. BELSCHNER *Sheep Managem. & Diseases* 47 The Polworth may be described as resembling a plain-bodied, extra-long-stapled wool Merino with less wool on the points. **1970** HARMSWORTH & PAGE-SHARP *Sheep & Wool Classing* 56 Only coarse portions, heavy fribby points, and stained or discoloured pieces should be removed and placed in a basket for the piece pickers to collect and sort.

point, *n.*[2] *Hist.* A unit in measuring rainfall, the hundredth part (.01) of an inch.

1889 *Australasian* (Melbourne) 20 Apr. 816/2, 92 points were registered at Wilcannia, and more rain has already fallen this year than during the whole of 1888. **1895** *Queenslander* (Brisbane) 7 Dec. 1061 Rain set in early this morning, ninety-eight points having fallen up to 2.30 p.m. **1914** 'B. CABLE' *By Blow & Kiss* 244 You'll think me an awful new-chum, but I've a confession to make. I don't know what a point of rain means. **1937** A.W. UPFIELD *Mr Jelly's Business* 6 If only it hadn't rained thirty points the black tracker . . would have picked out Loftus's tracks. **1968** R. MAGOFFIN *We Bushies* 75 It was the wettest year we've had, Our score was sixty points!

point, *v.*[1] *Obs.* [f. the phr. *to get points* to gain an advantage.] *intr.* To take unfair advantage of a person, situation, etc. Freq. as *vbl. n.*

1853 H.B. JONES *Adventures in Aust.* 216 Doubtless, as the colony advances, this spirit of 'pointing' will disappear, and a fair legitimate system of trading and commerce will be introduced. **1886** J.F. STEEL *Miscarriage of Justice* 14 There is the glaring swindling of the tan-dealer and the frequent 'pointing' of the cashier. **1896** J.B. WALKER Corresp., *Point, pointing,* to scheme, to manoeuvre with the object of avoiding work. A man is 'pointing' when he is adopting various manoeuvres to avoid doing his proper amount of work. **1903** *Sporting News* (Launceston) 14 Mar. 4/3 A great number hooted . . at what they ignorantly termed 'Taylor's pointing' in forcing Morgan into the lead.

point, *v.*[2] *Point the bone*, see BONE *n.* 1. Also as *vbl. n.*

1927 SPENCER & GILLEN *Arunta* 402 Take part in the 'pointing'. **1933** C.W. PECK *Austral. Legends* (ed. 2) 159 (*note*) Some people who have been on most intimate terms with the blacks aver that 'boning' is more than simply pointing. They say that the expression 'to point' is the only one the natives had when they wished to convey something like 'to shoot'. They did not mean that the bone was only 'pointed'. They actually pierced. **1977** J. CARTER *All Things Wild* 58 My informants claimed another Aranda artist had been 'pointed', about the time of Joshua Ebatarinja's death. (Since then I've heard on the mulga wire that this man was repeatedly 'sick', and died in 1975.)

pointer, *n.*[1] *pl.* [Transf. use of *pointers, pl.* the two bright stars in the Great Bear.] The two stars Alpha and Beta *Centauri* in the Southern Cross, a line drawn through which passes almost through the head of the Cross.

1864 J. BONWICK *Astronomy for Young Australs.* 63 Look at the two bright ones pointing toward the Cross. . . They are the Pointers to the Cross. **1872** MRS E. MILLETT *Austral. Parsonage* 173 Without its 'pointers', as the two splendid stars are called that accompany it, the Cross would lose much of its attraction. **1885** *Australasian Printers' Keepsake* 126 The Cross and Pointers were high in the zenith. **1914** A.C. DE LA C. CROMMELIN *Star World* 19 Two of the stars in the body are known as the Pointers (marked with an arrow in the map since they point to the Pole Star, Polaris). **1926** *Austral. Encycl.* II. 488 Two much more conspicuous neighbouring stars—Alpha and Beta *Centauri*—are known as 'the pointers' because a line drawn through them passes through the northern limb of the Cross, and so makes it easily found. **1950** W.A. MCNAIR *Starland of South* 13 They are sometimes called the Pointers, because they point to the Southern Cross. But their usual names are Alpha Centauri and Beta Centauri.

pointer, *n.*[2] *Obs.* [f. POINT *v.*[1]] A sharper; an idler.

1853 H.B. JONES *Adventures in Aust.* 301 For safety the well disposed camp together, for the 'pointers' go in gangs and large bodies. **1896** J.B. WALKER Corresp., A 'pointer' is synonymous with a scheming idler. **1904** L.M.P. ARCHER *Bush Honeymoon* 85 She'll want *shepherding* at her work. Give her a bit o' bacca, after she's 'ad her tucker, and make her *run up to the bit*, mum. She's a rare *pointer* at her work. *Ibid.* 346 *Pointer*, shirker. **1954** T. RONAN *Vision Splendid* 164 There was no nark or pointer in the camp, they rode good horses by day and champions at night.

pointer, *n.*[3] [Spec. use of *pointer* that which points out.]

1. PIN-BULLOCK.

1872 C.H. EDEN *My Wife & I in Qld.* 36 Twelve bullocks is the usual number in a team, the two polers and the leaders being steady old stagers; the pair next to the pole are called the 'pointers'. **1941** S.J. BAKER *Pop. Dict. Austral. Slang* 55 *Pointers*, two of the bullocks in a team, placed next to the 'polers'.

2. *Pointing-bone*, see POINTING.

1899 *Proc. Linnean Soc. N.S.W.* XXIV. 330, I discovered the curious bone ornament or implement now to be described. It is made from the fibular of a kangaroo, is 9¾ inches in length, well polished. . . Three uses have been suggested for it, viz., netting needle, 'death bone' or 'pointer', and 'nose bone'.

pointing, *ppl. a.* In special collocations: **pointing bone, stick,** BONE *n.*[1]

1904 SPENCER & GILLEN *Northern Tribes Central Aust.* 459 The pointing apparatus . . consists of a long strand of human hair-string, to one end of which five small **pointing-bones** are affixed. **1928** W. ROBERTSON *Cooee Talks* 78 The pointing-bones differed in type, but they were always taken from a woman's body. The most common was that taken from the arm. It was ground to a fine point at one end—the grinding as a rule was done at Yarkamata's stone—while at the other a small hollow was made to receive the victim's blood. **1931** A.W. UPFIELD *Sands of Windee* 148 Ludbi told Moogalliti who killed Marks and how, and Moongalliti threatens the pointing-bone to any one of his tribe who says a word about it. **1938** F.J. HAYTER *Deadly Magic* 13 The Pointing Bone . . is usually made use of in cases of tribal reprisal for wrong doing, included in the native term Kurdaitcha. **1901** F.J. GILLEN *Diary* 21 Aug. (1968) 235 The Puntudia crept up and 'boned' him with their **pointing sticks**. . . He became very ill and finally died. **1928** B. SPENCER *Wanderings in Wild Aust.* 251 Pointing sticks and bones . . are used by all Australian tribes. . . There are various forms, but the essential feature of them all is that, in some way or another, usually by being what is called 'sung', they are charged, so to speak, with evil magic, or *Arung-quilta* as the natives call it. **1938** F.J. HAYTER *Deadly Magic* 13 The Pointing Stick is an accessory of bad, very bad magic which is made use of by the aborigines in some parts of Australia to cause the death of another human being without leaving any evidence of the means employed in so doing.

poison. Any of several plants poisonous to stock, esp. shrubs of the genus *Gastrolobium* (fam. Fabaceae) occurring mainly in s.w. W.A. Also *attrib.*, esp. as **poison bush, plant,** and with distinguishing epithet, as **heart-leaf, York road** (see under first element).

1843 *Port Phillip Gaz.* 18 Apr. 4 A tolerable sheep country badly watered, but a fair average feed and plenty of poison. **1872** MRS E. MILLETT *Austral. Parsonage* 108 Feeding upon the 'poison', the term always used in the colony to express the existence of any or all of these deleterious plants. **1884** A.W. STIRLING *Never Never Land* 137 The poison bush . . grows as a low spreading bush not more than about two feet high, bearing a reddish flower of the pea kind. . . This poison plant is not only fatal to sheep, but to horses and cattle also. **1891** W.A. HALLACK *W.A. & Yilgarn Goldfields* 9 In the cultivated districts, such as that of York, the poison plant, like the blacks, disappears. **1898** *Bulletin* (Sydney) 19 Mar. 3/2 The poison-weed's a-growing, and the 'norther' is a-blowing. **1906** *Ibid.* 6 Dec. 16/3 'Poison punchers' . . chiefly inhabit the south-eastern portion of the State, where they obtain a living grubbing poison plant on the large estates. **1931** M. TERRY *Hidden Wealth* 326 Gastrolobium grandiflorum, the deadly poison bush, was collected on the bank of a creek. **1948** C.P. MOUNTFORD *Brown Men & Red Sand* 71 Camels . . which have lived in 'poison bush' country for any length of time seem to learn that the plant is dangerous. **1968** C.A. GARDNER *Wildflowers W.A.* 58 The pea-flowered poisons (*Gastrolobium* and *Oxylobium*). **1985** *W. Austral.* (Perth) 6 Nov. 54/2 The regrowth of marri and the poison plant Gastrolobium biloba.

poison-cart. A vehicle designed to lay poison for the destruction of vermin, esp. the rabbit: see quots. 1910 and 1931.

1898 'R. BOLDREWOOD' *Romance Canvas Town* 61 All this time the poison-cart was kept going. **1898** C.L. MORGAN *Rabbit Question in Qld.* 87 Four poison carts . . are not nearly enough to keep the rabbits in check. **1910** C.E.W. BEAN *On Wool Track* 113 A poison-cart is a cart which lays poison for rabbits. It has a knife underneath it which scratches a furrow in the surface of the ground, into which the poison falls and is covered up. Rabbits will grub for poison but sheep do not. **1913** W.K. HARRIS *Outback in Aust.* 98, I believe the poison cart more than anything else accounts for the rapid diminution of our Australian birds. **1931** A.W. UPFIELD *Sands of Windee* 26 The poison-carts . . were light two-wheeled affairs, carrying an iron cylinder in which was placed the poisoned pollard when it was churned up into small pills and carried by a pipe down to a position behind a disk-wheel and dropped into the furrow the wheel made. **1940** I.L. IDRIESS *Lightning Ridge* 74, I was driving a poison cart on Woorawadian station. **1948** J.K. EWERS *For Heroes to live In* 79 The other farmers had to make shift with poison-carts. They had to poison every so often because there was a government inspector on the look-out to catch those who didn't.

poisoner. A cook, esp. one catering for a party of shearers, etc.

1905 E.C. BULEY *Austral. Life* 23 The shearer's cook is always a competent man, and supplies his clients with the best fare obtainable, utterly 'belying' the name of 'poisoner', usually bestowed upon him. **1913** *Bulletin* (Sydney) 30 Oct. 22/2 The ganger of a party of canecutters . . received . . application from a cook anxious for the billet of 'poisoner' to the gang. **1926** *Smith's Weekly* (Sydney) 24 July 16/3 Female 'Poisoner'. At Bolgelly . . last shearing season . . male cooks being unobtainable, we voted a woman in. **1936** *Bulletin* (Sydney) 23 Dec. 20/2 The new poisoner could *chef* all right. **1955** *Ibid.* 9 Mar. 12/1 He went as a piece-picker, but, like all bushmen, commented on the quality of the cooking, whereupon the reigning poisoner asked how Dad would go cooking for 88 greasies. **1963** *N.T. News* (Darwin) 3 Jan. 2/5 In the Territory at least, Bill's fame rested as much on his abilities as a 'poisoner', or bush cook, as on his writing. **1969** L. HADOW *Full Cycle* 208 'I'm not much good at cooking but I'll try.' 'Never you mind about that. Up north we've got the best poisoners in the country.'

Hence **poison** *v. intr.*, to serve as cook.

1934 C. SAYCE *Comboman* 138 He engaged Mick as station cook, a grizzled old man who boasted that he had 'poisoned'—as he described his occupation—on every station in Queensland.

poke, *v.* [Shortened form of *to poke borak* (see BORAK *n.* 2).] In the phr. **to poke it at** (a person), to ridicule or deride. Also **to poke crap, to poke mud.**

1890 *Bull-Ant* (Melbourne) 28 Aug. 15/1 There was a big crowd drawd up about th' worfs watchin' th' toffs, an' pokin' mud at them. **1902** *Truth* (Sydney) 2 Nov.4/7 He had imbibed more 'inspiration' than he was licensed to carry, and got 'poking it' at the 'boys', who 'dealt out stoush'. **1905** J.H.M. ABBOTT *Outlander in England* 268 Perhaps some opulent fellow has come over from the other side, with a cheque to 'knock down', and has offered to pay for the water he uses, and so now they make a point of 'poking it' at all Australians. **1906** *Truth* (Sydney) 11 Feb. 1/6 Up at Narrandera a lad was poking it at a Chow by singing 'Under the Bamboo Tree' on his doorstep. **1908** *Ibid.* 19 Jan. 1/8 The police are 'poking it at us' when they say there is a decrease in crime. **1919** C.H. THORP *Handful of Ausseys* 203 When the train pulls out, they leans out uv the carriage and 'pokes it' at the Jacks. 'Struth! they seem ter like jeerin' an' pokin' borax at those blokes. **1932** W. HATFIELD *Ginger Murdoch* 203 To go and tell a cove you don't brand your own calves on your own country looks like you're deliberately poking it at 'em. **1960** D. IRELAND *Image in Clay* (1964) 61, I don't hear her slinging off at you; why poke crap at her?

poker machine. A coin-operated gaming machine which pays out according to the combination of symbols (often representations of playing-cards) appearing on the edges of the wheels spun by the operation of a lever.

1903 *Advocate* (Burnie) 6 Jan. 2/6 It was considered that the use of the poker machine was too much in the publican's favor; it was a one-sided game of chance. **1904** *Ibid.* 14 Sept. 3/5 It was not a 'poker machine' but a 'crack a jack'. **1934** C. SAYCE *Comboman* 222 A poker machine, and a small spinning-jinny, were at one end of the bar. **1957** *Meanjin* 229 The calculated disgorgement of the poker machines was miraculous as manna from heaven. **1969** *Kings Cross Whisper* (Sydney) lxxviii. 7/2 The Martian landed in Sydney and walked into a Leagues Club. He passed a poker machine that suddenly whirred noisily. **1977** E. JONES *Barlow Down Under* 22 Spent time developing their muscles at one-arm bandits of which the club had only some four dozen. To call them poker machines is an insult to a great game of skill.

pokie. Also **pokey.** [f. POK(ER MACHINE + -Y.] POKER MACHINE. Also *attrib.* and freq. in *pl.*

1965 I. HAMILTON *Persecutor* 87, I always know how much I lose on the pokies. **1970** *Kings Cross Whisper* (Sydney) lxxxii. 2/3 Jackpots on pokey bandits. **1971** *Bulletin* (Sydney) 1 May 16/3 A meeting of representatives of 24 of the 36 licensed clubs in the A.C.T. recently voted 20–4 in favor of pressing for the pokies. **1972** *Ibid.* 26 Feb. 41/1 Idling away the time by marvelling at the block of 40 pokies at the back of the hall. **1977** E. MACKIE *Oh to be Aussie* 34 He must check that he has brought . . change for the pokies. **1979** R. ENGLISH *Toxic Kisses* 20 The rest of suburbia would flee to the clubs for a cheap meal and the pokies, or stay home for a fight. **1983** *Canberra Standard* 9 Feb. 22/4 (*heading*) Clubs call for draw pokie ban.

pole, *n.* [Spec. use of *pole* a shaft fitted to the fore-carriage of a vehicle and attached to the yokes or collars of the draught-animals.] Used *attrib.* in Special Comb. **pole bullock,** POLER 1; **cart, dray,** a vehicle fitted with a central pole rather than a pair of shafts.

1844 *Sydney Morning Herald* 29 July 2/7 He was kicked by one of the **pole bullocks**, and the wheel passed over his chest. **1851** J. HENDERSON *Excursions & Adventures N.S.W.* 303 The pole-bullocks (that is, the hindmost) and the leaders are the steadiest and most valuable. **1874** J.J. HALCOMBE *Emigrant & Heathen* 35 Bullock-drays . . have a strong pole, to which the yokes of the pole-bullocks, and the chain of the leaders, are fastened. **1891** D. FERGUSON *Vicissitudes Bush Life* 101 At length the pole bullocks . . with a most prodigious effort seemed to lift the dray. **1824** E. CURR *Acct. Colony Van Diemen's Land* 97 It may also be advisable to take with him a pair or two of strong broad wheels and iron axles for a **pole cart.** **1843** A. CASWALL *Hints from Jrnl.* 33 A two-wheeled dray with a pole, is certainly better than with shafts, as if it upsets it turns in the ring-bolt of the pole yoke, and the bullocks sustain no injury; whereas when one with shafts is capsized, the shafter is frequently killed; besides, the shafter should be a large heavy animal, and therefore more valuable, but two indifferent ones suffice for a **pole dray.** **1848** H.W. HAYGARTH *Recoll. Bush Life* 49 In some districts, chiefly in the vicinity of Bathurst, shaft-drays are used; but pole-drays are found to be more suitable to the nature of the country. **1915** *Bulletin* (Sydney) 4 Nov. 26/4 Before pole-drays appeared many families navigated themselves in drays drawn by a bullock.

pole, *v.*

1. *intr.* [See quot. 1924.] To take advantage of someone; to contribute less than one's share to a group enterprise. Freq. with **on.**

1906 E. DYSON *Fact'ry 'Ands* 66 'What rot, girls; why don't yer get er shift on?' cried Feathers virtuously. . . "Taint ther mealy pertater, polin' on the firm like this.' **1919** W.H. DOWNING *Digger Dialects* 38 *Poll*, to take advantage of another's good nature. **1924** A.W. BAZLEY et al. Gloss. Slang A.I.F. 22 (typescript) *Poling*, to do less than one's share thereby rendering the other fellows more difficult. This term was also borrowed from Australian Bullock driving parlance. The 'Polers' the pair of bullocks nearest to the pole of the wagon, are generally regarded as being not only the strongest, but next to the leaders the cutest pair in the team, and therefore more inclined to take things easy and let the other bullocks do the pulling, if the driver is not observant. **1938** X. HERBERT *Capricornia* 451 You—why, you're poling on Jesus Christ! **1950** G. FARWELL *Surf Music* 17 'Long as there's breath in my body,' the old man said. . . 'I'm poling on no government.' **1950** N. LINDSAY *Dust or Polish* 12 This room is cheap and I may need to pole on her for my share of the rent if I'm out of a job. **1956** B. BEATTY *Beyond Aust.'s Cities* 129 Much of the bullocky's slang became part of the Australian language. For example, 'poling'. That word was originally applied by the old-time Australian bullocky to the lazy, low-down bullock who would not pull his weight, and allowed the bulk of the work to be done by the rest of the team. **1963** 'C. ROHAN' *Down by Dockside* 14 He was too little to be a wharfie, and he never poled and he never bellyached and many a time he paid my Union money when I didn't have it.

2. *trans.* POLE-FISH. Also *intr.*

1965 *Canberra Times* 9 Jan. 9/1 The Australians take only the smaller bluefin, poling nearer the shoreline. **1980** *Ecos* xxiv. 24/2 (*caption*) Poling for southern bluefin tuna off Australia. **1983** *Canberra Chron.* 7 Dec. 19/1 Ken Stevenson, on the Carmela T, is reported to have spotted a massive school of bluefin tuna offshore. . . He poled seven to have a look at them. **1984** *Bulletin* (Sydney) 23 Oct. 62/1 Poling, the backbreaking task of hooking on to 20 kg. or more of vibrating tuna muscle and hoisting it on to the deck of a boat. Puglisi, like other tuna fishermen, has damaged discs in his back—a legacy of younger days as a poler. At 47 years of age, he poles no more.

pole-fish, *v. intr.* To fish (esp. for tuna), using a pole, a short line, and a barbless lure. Chiefly as *vbl. n.*

1951 *Daily Tel.* (Sydney) 4 Jan. 7/1 Australian tuna can be caught by live bait pole fishing. **1951** *Mercury* (Hobart) 10 Apr. 3/1 If pole-fishing methods were successful, the foundation probably would be laid for a sound tuna fishing industry in the State. **1956** *News* (Adelaide) 23 Jan. 9/2 They would demonstrate the method of pole fishing for tuna using live bait. **1962** W.G. SAMPSON *Tuna Fishing in Aust.* 2 So far, only pole-fishing has been developed in Australia. **1981** *Encycl. Austral. Fishing* XII. 1856 Four-fifths of the Australian catch . . are taken chiefly by means of pole fishing with feather jigs or live baits.

poler.

1. One of the pair of bullocks harnessed to the pole of a vehicle; *pole bullock*, see POLE *n.*

1860 'LITTLE JACOB' *Colonial Pen-Scratchings* 85 There was a bullock dray going lazily down the road—one of the bullocks, a poler (see colonial dictionary), fell from sheer exhaustion. **1872** M. CLARKE *His Natural Life* 617 The wild wilderness, the huge waggons, the white body of a camping 'poler', and three ragged figures round the glowing logs. **1886** H. FINCH-HATTON *Advance Aust.* (rev. ed.) 214 In order to save the necks of his 'polers', he tried to get the wagon as near to the edge of the paddock as possible. **1904** *Bulletin* (Sydney) 15 Dec. 40/1 Eighteen to twenty constitute a team, which includes polers—those nearest the waggon—clampers, body bullocks and leaders. **1915** G. SARGANT *Sweet Heart of Bush* 11 The leading bullocks had swerved off, pulling the polers and the fore carriage of the wagon on to the bridge railing. **1943** H.G. LAMOND *From Tariaro to Ross Roy* 25 A 7-ton load going up a hill might incline to lift the poler bullocks from the ground. **1956** C.D. MILLS *Stockwhip & Spur* 31 I've heard the off-side poler snort Across the mountain stream. **1959** H.P. TRITTON *Time means Tucker* 3 A bullock-team is made up in four parts: polers, pin, body and leaders: The polers have to be good . . for they have the job of steadying the dray or wagon while the pin-bullocks take the pull.

2. [f. POLE *v.* 1.] A loafer; a shirker.

1938 X. HERBERT *Capricornia* 528 'You long-jawed poler,' Norman roared. 'Living on the fat of the land, while your poor damn flock feeds on soup and coconuts and what they root out of the bush.' **1945** *Bulletin* (Sydney) 7 Feb. 13/3 'Even the most honest worker in the world might stand in the shade for a minute as he rolls a cigarette!' 'Of course he could,' heartily agreed her spouse, 'but a poler wouldn't—he'd have his eyes on the track as he was loafing and be grafting like a slave when the boss arrived.' **1953** C. WILLS *Austral. Passport* 43 When an' 'orse . . when he's loafin', he leans agin the pole, an' let's the other one carry 'im. So we call 'im a poler. . . And when a man loafs . . we call him a poler, too.

3. [See POLE-FISH.] One who hoists tuna fish on board with the aid of a pole.

1969 C. THIELE *Blue Fin* 2 With four polers they

would really tumble the fish aboard if each man could work by himself; but when they had to team into pairs or even threes it slowed everything down. **1975** *West Austral.* (Perth) 10 Feb. 16/6 The boats were manned by some of the most experienced tuna polers in Australia. **1984** [see POLE *v.* 2].

poley, *a.* and *n.* Also **poly.** [Br. dial. *poley*, etc. f. *poll* a hornless cow or ox: see EDD *poll, sb.*[2]]

A. *adj.*

1. Hornless.

1843 *Port Phillip Patriot* 9 Jan. 3/4 One yellow-sided poly cow. **1843** *Port Phillip Gaz.* 15 Mar. 3 *Impounded* . . a brindle poley cow, both ears notched. **1853** F. TRELOAR *Extracts from Diary* 4 July 16 While I was away the Poly cow had a calf. **1871** *Austral. Town & Country Jrnl.* (Sydney) 18 Mar. 331/2 Almost every one seems to have an objection to poley or snail-horned rams. **1880** H. KENDALL *Songs from Mountains* 71 Far better to be turned to grass To feed the poley cow, Than be the half boiled bream, alas, That I am really now! **1897** *Bulletin* (Sydney) 7 Aug. 31/1 Nehemiah . . had a fixed conviction that the polar star and a poley cow had something in common. **1923** *Ibid.* 29 Mar. 22/2, I was helping . . one of Australia's crack scrub dashers, to put a poly bullock into a small pen. **1933** J.L. GLASCOCK *Jarrah Leaves* 15 Red, white, spotted, and roan; long horn, short horn, and poley; baby 'fats' of three short summers. **1976** B. SCOTT *Complete Bk. Austral. Folk Lore* 294 Old poley cow ran off the track.

2. *transf.* and *fig.*

a. *Obs.* Of a domestic utensil: having a broken handle.

1848 *Bell's Life in Sydney* 4 Mar. 1/1 A poley-quart-pot is simmering at the fire. **1901** M. FRANKLIN *My Brilliant Career* 233 A couple of dirty knives and forks, a pair of cracked plates, two poley cups and chipped saucers. **1902** *Bulletin* (Sydney) 13 Dec. 21/4 He was useful, too; he put tin handles on the 'poley' cups and jugs, and mended a hole in the kitchen-floor.

b. *Obs.* [Perh. in punning allusion to CROPPY.] Of a person: at large; wanted by the police. Also as *n.*

1854 C.A. CORBYN *Sydney Revels* 43 A wild looking man . . who responded to the name of Henry Bull, and who only lacked the horns of his patronymic (being a poley), was summoned. **1884** J.B. MARTIN *Reminisc.* 14 These men [*sc.* police] . . zigzagged about . . in search of what they called their 'poley cattle' [*sc.* bushrangers].

c. Of a rifle: see quot. 1918.

1918 *Bulletin* (Sydney) 25 July 22/2 The breech-loader was then a rarity on Monaro, and the 'poly'—hammerless—gun had hardly been evolved, much less perfected. **1954** *Coast to Coast 1953–54* 14 Home made cartridges? There they go again! No. Poley chokes on their guns. That American idea for greater range.

B. *n.*

1. Abbrev. of 'poley bullock', 'poley cow,' etc.

1843 *Sydney Morning Herald* 16 Aug. 3/4, I think another motion is imperatively called for, namely, a return of all the sheep, horned cattle (not forgetting the *poleys*) horses, and pigs in the colony. **1848** *Adelaide Miscellany* 2 Dec. 280 My bucolic knowledge . . left me in total ignorance of the nice distinction between yearlings, steers, heifers, stags, poleys. **1871** *Austral. Town & Country Jrnl.* (Sydney) 18 Mar. 331/2, I would prefer a poley to a snail-horn. **1905** *Bulletin* (Sydney) 12 Oct. 14/4 She sent Brown to a cow-spanking friend on the South Coast to purchase a milker... He chose a paunchy poley old enough to have a vote. **1909** *Ibid.* 28 Oct. 13/3 There's not a poley in the mob. Two thousand horns glisten. **1914** *Ibid.* 24 Dec. 13/2 And bullicks—they invariably had a bald-face poley that once shifted two ton. **1976** C.D. MILLS *Hobble Chains & Greenhide* 138 'That slab-sided poly,' indicating a poor-quality beast moving almost under Laddies' nose, 'Spoil the look of any mob.'

2. *transf.* A type of saddle which does not have knee-pads. Also **poley saddle.**

1930 A.E. YARRA *Vanishing Horsemen* 16 Maggie gets the blue-roan, and I'll throw in the old poley saddle for her—and a bridle! **1957** R.S. PORTEOUS *Brigalow* 31 'I'd clout on that king poley if I was you... The boss uses the light poley...' The king poley was a nice deep-seated saddle in good condition. **1973** R. ROBINSON *Drift of Things* 93 The station-hand whom Ivor was to ride against rode long in the stirrups and used a light 'Poley' saddle. **1975** *Sunday Mail Mag.* (Brisbane) 26 Jan. 15/1 My own poley had had its day... Good second-hand saddles were not easy to come by. **1981** G. MITCHELL *Bush Horseman* 25 Daily I hear young riders referring to all stock saddles as poleys. This is incorrect. The difference between the two types of stock saddles is in the shape of the pads. You can't go wrong if you use the term 'stock' saddle, but call a knee pad a poley and every bushman around will know the limits of your experience.

police. Used *attrib.* in Special Comb. **police boy,** an adult Aboriginal male employed in the police force, esp. as a *police tracker*; **paddock,** an enclosure for the confinement of impounded animals or animals used by the police; **tracker,** TRACKER; **trooper,** TROOPER.

1937 M. TERRY *Sand & Sun* 269 'Then there's all the sorts of 'em,' Stan added. 'Stock boy, . . camp boy, mission boy, **police boy,** camel boy.' **1938** X. HERBERT *Capricornia* 372 A sneakin' coot of a police-boy stationed at the Compound got to hear of it and told the jonnops. **1949** D. WALKER *We went to Aust.* 237 Without the 'police boys', or native trackers, white men would be helpless. **1977** A. THOMAS *Bulls & Boabs* (1980) 97 Jack was a man of great dignity, respected as a tribal elder, and not a common Aboriginal his superiors would dismiss as a 'police boy'. **1840** *Port Phillip Gaz.* 21 Mar. 4 The Public are hereby cautioned against putting Cattle, or any other description of Stock, in the Paddock . . which is situated immediately beyond the **Police Paddock**, and enclosed by a four railed fence. **1864** W. WALKER *Acct. Great Flood Hawkesbury* 7 The court house, gaol, and Mr Edgerton's residence, are now on a peninsula, there being only a narrow track of land in the police paddock, to connect them with the town. **1882** A. TOLMER *Reminisc.* I. 282 A hostile meeting was to have taken place . . in the police paddock near the company's bridge, Adelaide. **1910** *Bulletin* (Sydney) 28 Apr. 13/3 Outback . . there are no police horse-paddocks from which remounts may be obtained. **1936** W. HATFIELD *Aust. through Windscreen* 50 One suspected cattle-thief . . rode into the police paddock where seventeen head of alleged cross-branded cattle were being held as exhibits. **1960** R.S. PORTEOUS *Cattleman* 29 Within an hour the Wavering Downs bullocks were on their way to Baranda police paddock. **1910** *Huon Times* (Franklin) 18 May 4/2 Normanton . . had been a **police tracker**, and was running away because he wanted to go to the Baranibah mission. **1931** A.W. UPFIELD *Sands of Windee* 133, I remember Bony now. He was a police-tracker at Cunnamulla. **1947** W.E. HARNEY *Brimming Billabongs* 62 One of your troopers married a young girl to one of his police trackers—a man of the same totem, which is taboo. **1962** V.C. HALL *Dreamtime Justice* 14 He thought of his renegade cousin, Jarat, the Police Tracker. **1839** *Tasmanian* (Hobart) 17 May 159/4 Two mounted **police troopers**. **1863** W.J. WILLS *Successful Exploration Interior Aust.* 261 A police trooper in the north had sent down information. **1887** MRS D.D. DALY *Digging, Squatting, & Pioneering Life* 52 Sentimental ballads . . were generally sung by a police trooper. **1927** A. CROMBIE *After Sixty Yrs.* 41 Overtook a police trooper, a stockman, a black tracker, and a long, lean Sydney native.

policeman. Used *attrib.* in the names of animals: **policeman bird,** JABIRU; **fly,** any of many small wasps, esp. of the subfamily Nyssonidae, hunting flies as food for the larvae.

1928 C.G. LANE *Adventures in Big Bush* 131 Wallabies were numerous, also . . Australian storks (commonly called '**Policeman-birds**'). **1963** *N. Austral. Monthly* Nov. 34 For two seasons now we have watched this 'Policeman Bird' nest in the same tall scrub-tree at the edge of the swamp. **1965** *Austral. Encycl.* V. 114 Sometimes the jabiru is quite solitary, hence perhaps the term 'policeman-bird', by which it is known in North Queensland. **1970** J.V. MARSHALL *Walk to Hills of Dreamtime* 152 *Jabiru.* The black-necked stork or policeman bird (*Xenorhynchus asiaticus*). A four-foot black-and-white bird with red legs, becoming rare. **1905** *Bulletin* (Sydney) 23 Mar. 16/2 The '**policeman fly**' . . is a black fly... When 'the force' arrives at a camp, the common fly has to clear out. I have seen a camp swarming with common flies, and a few days after the 'policemen' appeared it was hard to find one... Consequently the 'policeman fly' is very popular in a camp. **1918** *Ibid.* 28 Mar. 24/4 The 'policeman fly' is a wasp, and there are several species in Australia. **1948** W.W. FROGGATT *Insect Bk.* 50 Policeman Flies are . . small, black, shining wasps, not much bigger than a housefly. **1965** *Austral. Encycl.* IX. 168 Mention must be made of the well-known 'policemen-flies'. These small wasps, of the families Nyssonidae, Arpactidae, and Stizidae, are fly-hunters, swooping down on small bush-flies (*Musca sorbens*) and carrying them off to their nests.

pollutionist. *Hist.* One who advocates the continuation of transportation.

1847 *Abolitionists & Transportationists* 32 From you Pollutionist I sickening turn, To feel my soul's indignant feelings burn. **1847** *Hobart Town Courier* 24 Apr. 4/1 The first of the five acknowledges the broad fact upon which the pro-convict party, or, as the *Argus* happily styles them, the 'Pollutionists', base the whole superstructure of their rickety cause,—'the scarcity of labour, and the injury to property resulting therefrom'. **1847** *Guardian* (Hobart) 26 June 2/5 The emigrant will allow himself to be lured from his home, and remain amongst us, for the convenience of anti-pollutionists. **1852** *Ibid.* 7 Feb. 3/4 That holy place is not considered defiled by the polutionists who enter there—aye, and practice their depravities too.

polly. [Orig. U.S.: see OEDS.] Abbrev. of 'politician'.

1967 *Kings Cross Whisper* (Sydney) xxxviii. 10/2 *Polly*, politician. **1968** *Swag* (Sydney) ii. 46/2 Half-stewed pollies are a race apart. **1971** *Bulletin* (Sydney) 20 Nov. 20/1 Since then we have at various times and for varying periods . . stopped having Poms, pollies or old wharfies [as Governors General]. **1973** H. WILLIAMS *My Love* 63 Our pollies are too busy putting the money we pay in taxes into their own pay packets to do anything for the motorist. **1975** *Bulletin* (Sydney) 1 Nov. 48/3 Canberra citizens treat the goings on in the parliament—variously known as the zoo because of its inmates and the wedding cake because of its appearance—with the right amount of disdain. The populace is used to weathering the crises of its pollies. **1978** *Truckin' Life* II. xiii. 85 The best way to get some attention from the pollies, is to stop all road freight into Canberra. **1986** *Sydney Morning Herald* 1 May 13/1 Pollies don't matter much any more.

Polwarth /ˈpɒlwəθ/. [The name of a county in s.w. Vic.] A breed of sheep (see quot. 1965); a sheep of this breed. Also as **Polwarth sheep.**

1919 *Pastoral Rev.* 16 Oct. 965 The standard type of Polwarth sheep is a sheep of fairly level top, with well-sprung ribs and generally robust frame. **1935** *Ibid.* 16 Feb. 145 Many runs in western Victoria are now stocked with Polwarths instead of Merinos. **1950** H.G. BELSCHNER *Sheep Managem. & Diseases* 46 The Polwarth, which originated about 1880 at Tarndwarncoort in Victoria, is another breed of sheep to meet the environmental conditions of certain parts of Australia. **1965** *Austral. Encycl.* VII. 184 The name comes from the district in which the sheep were evolved and was officially given to the breed in 1919. The Polwarth was evolved by Richard and Alexander Dennis by mating first-cross Lincoln x Merino ewes with Carr's Plains Merino rams (Ercildoune blood). **1975** L.A. POCKLEY *Handbk. for Jackeroos* 55 *Polwarth*, developed in Australia to suit light cold country and agricultural areas... The Lincoln Merino cross matched back to the Merino is the basis.

poly, var. POLEY.

polygonum /pəˈlɪgənəm/. *Obs.* [Spec. use of *polygonum* a herb of the genus *Polygonum*, formerly incl. members of the genus *Muehlenbeckia*.]

1. LIGNUM 1.

1819 *HRA* (1917) 1st Ser. X. 28 A barren marsh, overrun with a species of polygonum. **1841** J.C. HAWKER Diary 9 May 137 The river flats are very uninteresting being covered with long reeds and the Polyginum scrub, a kind of matted bramble without thorns. **1855** J. BONWICK *Geogr. Aust. & N.Z.* (ed. 3) 203 The Polygonum is a small Tea tree, but very harsh and compact. **1901** K.L. PARKER in M. Muir *My Bush Bk.* (1982) 62 The next day seemed more monotonous; all coolabah and polygonum—the 'leafless bramble' of Sturt.

2. Used *attrib.* in Comb. **polygonum bush, scrub, swamp.**

1849 *Adelaide Miscellany* 11 Oct. 50 It was not long before two pretty little crested pigeons fluttered out of a **polygonum-bush.** **1861** *Burke & Wills Exploring Exped.* 30 Camped for the night under some polygonum bushes. **1893** S. NEWLAND *Paving Way* 60 They continued on through a gum and box covered flat interspersed with polygonum bushes. **1851** *Bell's Life in Sydney* 15 Mar. 7/2 A high condition is so easily sustained by the abundance of salt Bush (Rhagodia) and **Polygonum scrub.** **1879** *Queenslander* (Brisbane) 26 Apr. 531/3 We came to a coolibah forest . . from this into a vile **polygonum swamp,** the worst I was ever in. [*Note*] That is, a swamp after a wet season—the driest of dry country during a dry season. **1900** R. BRUCE *Benbonuna* (1904) 15 The great polignum [*sic*] swamps of the sand-ridged plains bordering the waterless Lake Torrens. **1965** G. MCINNES *Road to Gundagai* 125 Polygonum swamps over which the long legged jabiroo flew creaking on its way.

pom. Abbrev. of POMEGRANATE, and subsequently of POMMY. Also *attrib.*, and as *adj.*

1912 *Truth* (Sydney) 10 Nov. 1/8 The immigrant ('desirable') Will p'r'aps amuse you most—The comic British citizen, That leans against a post; They used to say colonials did, But I'm very much afraid, Upon the 'Poms' I'd put my quid, At the gay 'Chateau de Wade'. **1913** *Ibid.* 11 May 1/6 'There are a lot of bad characters about Pott's Point', said a Pomegranate at the Central, 'and I fired off my revolver to frighten them.' It did not take that Pom. long to discover the reputations of the Pott's Point Plutes. **1923** *Bulletin* (Sydney) 12 July 23/1 It was a Pommy bloke wot put me wise. I was in Snotty Padger's bar one day 'Avin' a quiet couple wiv the flies When Pom. lobs in. **1944** L. GLASSOP *We Were Rats* 26, I seen ya score that century against the Poms that time. Crikey, ya didden half get stuck inter them Poms! **1962** A. SEYMOUR *One Day of Yr.* 8 The place is full of . . Poms and I-ties. **1963** B. HESLING *Dinkumization & Depommification* 16 He was in the Northern Territory droving cattle. They weren't keen on the 'poms' up there. That's why they put those horses under him. Of course, when he managed not to break his neck, it proved that he wasn't a 'pom' at all but a dinki-di Aussie. **1970** C. NOLAN *Bride for St. Thomas* 45 You'll never fit into the Pom way of life. **1971** B. HUMPHRIES *Bazza pulls it Off*, I've never been overseas before—youse wouldn't count Pom-land. **1973** *Bulletin* (Sydney) 6 Jan. 36/2 Fat Welsh Poms aren't all bad. **1978** D. BALL *Great Austral. Snake Exchange* 36 Brooks had always thought of New Zealand as the southernmost county of England. Poms in sheep's clothing. **1978** W.F. MANDLE *Going it Alone* 15 The story of when and how attitudes to the 'Pom', ranging from dislike to a mere sense of difference, arose is a topic no historian has yet had the bad taste, bloody mindedness or courage to tackle. **1978** WARD & SMITH *Vanishing Village* 8 As the saying goes, if you get a good Pom, you shoot the bastard before he goes bad. **1981** C. WALLACE-CRABBE *Splinters* 63 'I don't think you can call Gilbert and Sullivan opera,' said Bob. 'Not even the Poms would go that far.' **1982** *Bulletin* (Sydney) 9 Nov. 126/1 Ticket sales moving as briskly as a Pom when you shake a cake of Palmolive at him.

pomegranate. *Obs.* Also **pommygranate, pommygrant.** [Formed by word-play: see quot. 1920.] An immigrant from the British Isles (now superseded by POM and POMMY *n.*).

1912 *Bulletin* (Sydney) 14 Nov. 16/4 The other day a Pummy Grant (assisted immigrant) was handed a bridle and told to catch a horse. **1912** *Truth* (Sydney) 22 Dec. 1/3 Now they call 'em 'Pomegranates' and the Jimmygrants don't like it. *Ibid.* 22 Dec. 1/7 In the country, it seems, the people entertain a poor opinion of the 'pomegranates'. An inland exchange, telling of a groom who harnessed up a horse without putting the bit in its mouth, says, 'He is an immigrant, so some allowance should be made for him.' **1913** *Ibid.* 23 Feb. 9/8 *Pomegranate Plucked*. . . Another newly-arrived jimmygrant from Dear Old England . . was presented before Magistrate Smithers. *Ibid.* 1 June 5/7 In course of time the Pomegranates could themselves *go on the land*, and make enormous fortunes out of growing beef, wool, swedes or spuds. The Poms, however, have not found Australia to be a Tom Tiddlers' Ground. **1916** W.C. WATSON *Mem. Ship's Fireman* 61 As I hailed from the Old Dart, I of course, in their estimation, was an immigrant, hence the curl up of the lip. But 'pommygrant' or 'jimmygrant', they always had a helping hand for me. **1916** *Truth* (Sydney) 1 Oct. 12/4 As for the conceit of the average Pommygranite it is hard to beat. **1920** H.J. RUMSEY *Pommies* Introd., The colonial boys and girls . . ready to find a nickname were fond of rhyming 'Immigrant', 'Jimmygrant', 'Pommegrant', and called it out after the new-chum children. **1924** LAWRENCE & SKINNER *Boy in Bush* 120 'Here you, young Pommy Grant,' he said to Jack. **1963** X. HERBERT *Disturbing Element* 91 He still wore the heavy clumsy British type of clothing of the day. When we kids saw people on the street dressed like that we would yell at them: 'Jimmygrants, Pommygranates, Pommies!'

pommy, *n.* and *attrib.* Also **pommie.** [f. POMEGRANATE + -Y.]

A. *n.* An equivocal term for an immigrant from the British Isles; applied also, more recently, to an inhabitant of the British Isles (esp. of England). Also *transf.* (see quots. 1922 and 1953). See also POM, WHINGEING POM.

1912 *Bulletin* (Sydney) 14 Nov. 16/4 The other day a Pummy Grant (assisted immigrant) was handed a bridle and told to catch a horse. . . Pummy sneaked up behind the quadruped. **1913** *Truth* (Sydney) 8 June 1/8 *The plaint of the 'Pommie'* 'Orrible country, there isn't no doubt of it, Nothing but sunshine and flowers and sport, Tell me, oh tell me a way to get out of it, Back to old Lambeth, for 'ere yer gits nought. *Ibid.* 29 June 1/7 Britishers get a cheap trip to Australia by shipping as 'pommies'. **1913** *Sun* (Sydney) 17 Aug. 22/2 The term 'new chum' invariably conjures up visions of a fresh arrival, ignorant of the customs and ways of the country of his adoption, who is consequently made the butt—good humouredly of course—of sundry thoughtless Australians. . . The old phrase 'new chum' is, however fast giving way to the newer and clippier appellation of 'pommy', but he is still the same good-hearted, mirth-provoking individual. **1913** *Theatre Mag.* Oct. 14 For this firm he is writing—and producing—what will be known as the 'Pommy' series. . . The first of the series is already being screened under the title 'Pommy Arrives in Sydney'. **1914** *Truth* (Sydney) 22 Mar. 3/5 A man . . asked for work. The boss, a 'pommy', told him there was nothing doing. Later the same day a 'jimmygrant' comes along . . and is put on just because he is a 'pommy' and nothing else. **1916** 'MEN OF ANZAC' *Anzac Bk.* 31 We don't call the like of 'im 'Pommies' because we dislike 'em, but as a matter of description. Of course, sometimes one of 'em gets 'is back up and calls us sons of convicts for chuckin' off at 'im and then he's told lots of things—sometimes true and very often untrue; but Australia's all right mate. You need not be ashamed to be called a 'Pommy' out there. *Ibid.*, *Pommy*, short for pomegranate, and used as a nickname for immigrants. **1916** *Truth* (Sydney) 10 Sept. 5/5 Australians have nothing to learn from Pommies unless it is how to crawl, and until the Creator endows them with a pliable backbone they will ever remain duff-heads in the only art of which the Pommy is a past master. **1918** *Ibid.* 10 Mar. 6/8 No matter how Australia favors the pommy, he always remains at heart . . a barracker for the cold country and a 'Wales, Scotia, or Cockney for ever bester.' *Ibid.* 9 June 11/7 The Pommy who is anxious and willing to stand shoulder to shoulder with the Australian worker—and I keep meeting him everywhere—is my cobber. *Ibid.* 29 Dec. 7/5 The mention of 'Pommy' renders it timely to describe the *origin of the term.* It is generally assumed that the term is a contraction of 'pomegranate' to denote the red cheeks of the new arrival, really a term flattering to those to whom it is applied. The term was originated in 'Truth' some years back when immigration was in full swing. There was an outcry that the new arrivals had been selected by certain sectarian cliques, and that intending Irish emigrants were discriminated against. A clamor arose locally, and some of the would-be wits wrote letters to the papers ridiculing the claims of the 'Murphies'. A 'Truth' writer banteringly derided the writers of the letters, and suggested that the daily papers editors should substitute a more euphonious term than 'Murphies' and instanced 'Pommes-de-terre' as apt to fit the bill. The term caught on at the time, but was soon shortened to *'Pommy'.* **1920** H.J. RUMSEY *Pommies* (*Introd.*), The title that I have selected for the book: 'The Pommies' is now a common name for recent arrivals from Britain. During the last few weeks, I have scores of times heard the Prince of Wales affectionately described as a 'dear little pommy'. **1922** *Bulletin* 23 Feb. 20/2 One pommy who is rapidly becoming a good Aussie is that wonderful songster, the blackbird. **1923** D.H. LAWRENCE *Kangaroo* 142 Pommy, is supposed to be short for pomegranate. Pomegranate, pronounced invariably pommygranate, is a near enough rhyme to immigrant, in a naturally rhyming country. Furthermore, immigrants are known in the first months, before their blood 'thins down', by their round and ruddy cheeks. So we are told. Hence again, pomegranate, and hence Pommy. Let etymologists be appeased: it is the authorised derivation. **1925** S. HICKS *Hullo Australs.* 190 Pommie is a term of contempt, sir. The Australian calls British immigrants Pommies who have received Government assistance to come out. They ain't by any means popular neither, sir. **1927** J. POLLARD *Rose of Bushlands* 81 Nestor . . does not like newcomers more especially when they're Englishmen—pommies. Your uncle isn't an Englishman, I know—he's Irish; but he's a pommy, all the same. **1929** D.J. HOPKINS *Hop of 'Bulletin'* 104 Thinking people find it difficult to persuade the Briton that the form 'pommy' as applied to the immigrant, is not unkind and provocative. **1932** J. TRURAN *Green Mallee* 121 He found himself face to face with a weedy youth who might have been taken as a model by any artist wishing to make a drawing of a 'pommy' according to the accepted style. **1937** J.M. HARCOURT *It never Fails* 70 Being a pommy doesn't matter. . . A shell-opener needs to be honest. It doesn't matter if he isn't very bright. **1944** J. HETHERINGTON *Austral. Soldier* 32 Their discussion drifted round to the British units who were fighting with the Australians in the desert. 'You know, Bill,' said Australian Number One, 'these 'Pommies' a man meets here are good blokes.' 'My oath!' said Australian Number Two. 'As a matter of fact, Bill, after what I've seen of 'Pommies' out here, I'm never going to sling off at a 'Pommy' again.' 'No, Harry, neither will I.' 'In fact, Bill,' said Australian Number One, warming to his subject, 'I'll go so far as to say this. They're as good as us.' 'Cripes, Harry,' said Australian Number Two, 'you can't say that. But they're bloody wonderful fellers just the same.' **1946** *Coast to Coast 1945* 63 He was an Englishman, not a 'pommy', mind you. It seemed he hadn't even reached to that dignity. **1953** D. STIVENS *Gambling Ghost* 28 You and I are Australians but the rabbits ain't—they're pommies. **1959** *Bulletin* (Sydney) 11 Nov. 16/2 Mention of 'Pommy' . . brings to mind that my grandfather, of Breton origin, born Braidwood, N.S.W., 1850, died 1913, used the term during the whole of his life when referring to a particularly tough citizen. *Pommé*, he said, pronounced 'pommy', as distinct from *pomme*, pronounced 'pom' (apple), was current in France for centuries when referring to hard traders, and was applied to the English in particular. Napoleon, in one of his speeches classed the British as *'Boutiquiers pommés'* (hard-headed shopkeepers). **1960** D. MCLEAN *Roaring Days* 127 That pommy turned out to be one of the best Australians I ever met. He became a rich station-owner and married a squatter's daughter. **1967** R. DONALDSON et al. *Cane!* 12 Four years ago last month he had stepped off a boat from England and become a Pommy. **1975** X. HERBERT *Poor Fellow my Country* 119 They had baited her for a Pommy, a term she'd later learnt was applied only to English of lower class. **1977** F.B. VICKERS *Stranger no Longer* 177 'It's not much of a place,' he answered. 'There's a few Abos there, a few dogs and a few Pommies like yourself, but not many white men.' **1984** B. DIXON *Searching for Aboriginal Lang.* 53 The weatherbeaten, red faces of the cattlemen sitting on stools around the bar all slowly swivelled and surveyed me. 'Pommy!' ejaculated one of them. I was made to feel that no one had ever asked for a gin and tonic in that pub before.

B. *attrib.* or as *adj.*

1. Of or pertaining to a 'pommy'; British, English. Esp. (often as a term of affectionate abuse) as **pommy bastard.**

1915 *Bulletin* (Sydney) 18 Mar. 14/4 The river was 'a swim', and the pommy rouseabout who had been cut off couldn't cross. **1916** *Truth* (Sydney) 10 Sept. 10/1 Two young women possessed of *strong 'pommy' accents.* **1917** R.W. JONES *With 'Roos* 27 But some are good at chucking dirt, And there are fellers who assert That Pommy tarts are prettier. **1918** *Truth* (Sydney) 24 Mar. 9/3 Native-born Australian leaders are good enough for us in this State, and we will make a present of all Pommies to the Pommy State (Western Australia). *Ibid.* 24 Mar. 9/4 Cut out the blasted pommy. This is a democratic country, this is. Sure, cut out *all pommy literature*, Dickens, Burns, Shakespeare—the whole damn family of 'em were born in pommy land. Any true Australian that isn't satisfied with Nat Gould deserves to be turned into a Scotch cuss of a lecturer. **1922** *Bulletin* (Sydney) 9 Mar. 20/2 And help with sunwarmed Pommie blood to keep Australia white. **1927** T.S. GROSER *Lure of Golden West* 122 No wish to be caught napping again in the dark by 'Pommy' fences (those of immigrants, or new settlers). **1936** J. HAMILTON *Sailortown Shanties*, With a Pommy bride, a crook inside, an' a Service Home as a gift. **1951** D. STIVENS *Jimmy Brockett* 80 The brawls we used to have with the pommy kids in our street, and how they reckoned a colonial would never do anything right. **1954** T. RONAN *Vision Splendid* 89 He would refer to him to his face as the 'Pommy', once going so far as to call him a 'Pommy bastard'. **1957** R. OLLIS *101 Nights* 154 When I call *you* a Pommy bastard, sir, that's meant to be friendly. But a Pommy bloody officer is different. **1958** J.R. SPICER *Cry of Storm-Bird* 8 Why Rob Saunders, you old pommy bastard. Jeez, it's good to see you, mate! **1958** G. COTTERELL *Tea at Shadow Creek* 51 'What's your first name, dearie?' she asked me. 'Charles.' 'That's a real pommy name, too.' **1959** E. WEBB *Mark of Sun* 10 You stubborn pommy bastard.. take your bloody blackgin and get out of it! **1967** R. DONALDSON et al. *Cane!* 113 You're a jumped-up Pommy bastard, a stupid sod, a flamin' dingo, a dirty arse-licker and you oughta piss off back where yuh came from. **1968** K. DENTON *Walk around my Cluttered Mind* 30 Typical bloody silly Pommy bastard stunt. **1969** A. GARVE *Boomerang* 143 You know, Birdie, for a Pommie bastard you're quite a bright cove. **1972** *Bulletin* (Sydney) 5 Feb. 31/3 The English actress playing Bazza's first Pommy sheila is muttering darkly about ringing her agent. **1973** *Ibid.* 6 Jan. 24/2 Our next Pommie migrant will be Robert Morley who opens here in How the Other Half Loves also on January 16. **1977** R. BEILBY *Gunner* 12 I'd know the sound of those big Pommy feet anywhere. **1977** F.B. VICKERS *Stranger no Longer* 100 He shouted after me: 'Stupid Pommie bastard!' **1980** G. DUTTON *Wedge-Tailed Eagle* 23 'I was at school in England, my father took me over there with him.' 'At least you haven't got a Pommie accent.' **1981** A.B. FACEY *Fortunate Life* 245 He then told me.. to get the hell out of there before he threw me in the guard-house... I replied, 'All right, you just do that. I'm not scared of you pommy upstarts.'

2. Special Comb. **pommy jackeroo,** an English jackeroo (see JACKEROO *n.* 2); *transf.* an inept or inexperienced person; **land,** the British Isles; England.

1915 B. GAMMAGE *Broken Yrs.* (1974) 240 They're only a b-- lot of **Pommie Jackeroos** and just as hopeless. **1964** J.S. MANIFOLD *Who wrote Ballads?* 86 The jackaroos.. were usually educated young men studying the art and mystery of station management; sometimes they included a 'colonial-experiencer' or 'pommy jackaroo'. **1916** *Truth* (Sydney) 1 Oct. 12/1 It amuses me to hear the way the Pommies run the Australian girls down. They are forgetting that they come out here for their bread and butter, and also good money in hand, more than they got in **Pommyland.** **1917** R.W. JONES *With 'Roos* 26 And I, fer one, can't understand How quick the tarts in Pommy land In Cupid's chains can bind 'em. **1918** *Truth* (Sydney) 24 Mar. 9/3 The average Briton has a tender place in his heart for the land that gave him birth.. it does not matter whether he was born in Pommy Land or any other place. **1950** J. MCLAREN *New Love for Old* 73 Aw, shut up, you blasted Pommie. If you're so proud of it why don't you go back to your Pommie-land? **1967** F. HARDY *Billy Borker yarns Again* 61 Some kind of wharfie over in Pommy Land. **1979** B. HUMPHRIES *Bazza comes into his Own*, When they crawl back to Pommyland and see what a shithouse it is, they come back for another cheap trip! **1984** *Weekend Austral. Mag.* (Sydney) 21 Apr. 20/3 Pommieland has just been hit by a new magazine called the *Royal Magazine* which informs a breathlessly waiting public that 'Princess Anne's favorite ploy at parties is to dress up as a charlady and go around dusting chairs and tables'.

Hence **pommified** *a.*, affecting an English manner; influenced by an English model.

1936 *Publicist* (Sydney) iv. 10/1 The West is not yet yankified and pommified to the same extent as is Sydney. **1978** J. ANDERSON *Tirra Lirra* 84 If you stay more than five years you become a pommified Aussie, than which there is no more pitiful creature on God's earth.

pommygranate, pommygrant, varr. POMEGRANATE.

Pompey. *Obs.* [Poss. f. Br. dial. *pompey*, a name for a house of correction or reformatory: see EDD *sb.* 3.] In the phr. **to dodge Pompey,** to evade detection (while engaged in an illegal activity); to avoid carrying out one's responsibilities, esp. to malinger, out of the sight of one's supervisor.

1868 C.W. BROWNE *Overlanding in Aust.* 53 He is necessitated to do a little trespassing on the quiet, which he calls 'dodging Pompey', thereby getting his sheep better feed. **1891** *Truth* (Sydney) 5 Apr. 7/3 The footmen are divided into two lots, *old hands and strangers.* The latter work whilst the former loaf, smoke, *dodge Pompey*, tell lies and spit. **1904** *Ibid.* 18 Dec. 2/2 Attempts to 'dodge Pompey' are futile. **1908** 'G. SEAGRAM' *Bushmen All* 234 Yer don't s'pose that Dick the Devil an' Black Jim are just dodgin' Pompey at Bullabullina waiting for the traps to come and fetch 'em. **1920** C.W. BRYDE *Chart House to Bush Hut* 67 Didn't like to palm myself off as an expert mill hand. I thought even the 'rat-gangers' had to be skilled men. Afterwards I was one of a rat-gang myself for awhile, and found one only had to be expert at 'dodging Pompey'. **1943** *Jest: Digestion Good Humor* 44 *Dodging Pompey* was another accomplishment of mine... I had no superior at this scientific pastime of dodging the boss and keeping out of the range of vision of the bloke in control.

Hence **Pompey dodger** *n.*

1905 *Shearer* (Sydney) 2 Dec. 3/5 State payment to 'Pompey dodgers', when taken advantage of for a lifetime, only benefits the few at the cost of the many.

pond. [In Br. use applied mainly to an artificially-formed body of water, in U.S. to a small naturally-formed lake: see OED(S *sb.* 1 a. and b.] A pool in a watercourse; such a body of water remaining after the watercourse has ceased flowing, esp. in the collocation **chain of ponds** (see CHAIN *n.*[2]). Freq. in placenames.

1835 *Trans. Zool. Soc. London* I. 234 A tranquil part of the river, such as the colonists call a 'pond'. **1837** *Lit. News* (Sydney) 21 Oct. 105 It was at a tranquil part of the Yas river, which the colonists call 'ponds', on the surface of which numerous aquatic plants grew, that I first beheld these animals. **1844** L. LEICHHARDT *Jrnl. Overland Exped. Aust.* 10 Dec. (1847) 70 This water-hole was found to be one of a chain of ponds... On following it farther down, we came to a fine pool of water... Next morning, finding several other ponds well supplied with water, we returned. **1860** G. BENNETT *Gatherings of Naturalist* 104 At a tranquil part of the river, called by the colonists a 'pond'. **1886** D.M. GANE *N.S.W. & Vic.* 197 It abounds, as do most Australian rivers, in 'ponds' or occasional basins, which are distinguishable by their dark and placid surfaces.

Pong. [Joc. formation in resemblance to a Chinese name.] A Chinese. Also as *adj.* and *transf.* (quot. 1985 refers to a Japanese).

1906 *Truth* (Sydney) 28 Oct. 11/1 To-day there are 20 whites to 150 *Ah Pongs.* **1910** *Bulletin* (Sydney) 1 Sept. 13/4 A fat, full-blooded Pong got into the compartment. 'Welly nice day,' he said. **1913** *Ibid.* 4 Sept. 8/3 Of the Chinese characters Arthur Bertram can take three cheers to himself. No other 'Pong' is in the same province. **1929** P.R. STEPHENSEN *Bushwhackers* 43 We youngsters thought.. that it was more legitimate to steal the peanuts of Willy Ah Foo, because they were the peanuts of a Pong. **1938** X. HERBERT *Capricornia* 309 You slant-eyed yeller-bellied pong, you. **1951** *Southerly* iv. 208 It didn't sound like English to us but more like Pong yabber or Eyetoe or Dago gibberish. **1962** T. RONAN *Deep of Sky* 38 You'll tell yourself that it's only fair for you to have better horses than an old pig-tailed Pong. **1971** *Bulletin* (Sydney) 18 Sept. 46/3 Australian attitudes towards the almond-eyed celestials, the chinks, chows, pongs [etc.]. **1985** N. MEDCALF *Rifleman* 18 Me and that Pong... I got him.

pongello /pɒŋ'gɛloʊ/. *Obs.* [Transf. use of *pongelo* beer: see OEDS.] A game in which the throw of a die determines which of the participants pays for a round of drinks.

1898 *Bulletin* (Sydney) 1 Oct. 14/3 To shake for drinks is a 'pongello'. **1920** *Ibid.* 15 Jan. 20/2 Some Western Queensland slang of my day:.. to get drunk was to get 'inked'. To shake for drinks 'pongello'.

Pongo /'pɒŋgoʊ/. [Transf. use of *pongo* a soldier, a marine.] An Englishman. Also as *adj.*

[N.Z. **1942** *2nd N.Z. Exped. Force Times* 7 Sept. 5 A big bronzed Pongo came in.] **1944** *RAAF Saga* 65 Amazing blokes, the Pongos. **1946** *Slipstream: No. 81 (Fighter) Wing Brit. Cwlth. Occupation Force Japan* 29 June 2 *'Pongos' too strong.* The English lads.. proved far too superior against our boys.. in soccer. **1957** J.M. HOSKING *Aust. first & Last* 123 We call them New Australians now; once we called some Dagoes, Others Balts and Squareheads, Pongoes, Grills and Rice and Sagoes. **1957** R. OLLIS *101 Nights* 154 What I'd call a typical bloody Pommy officer. I can't stand these pongo bastards. **1964** *Courier-Mail* (Brisbane) 19 Nov. 12 Mr Arthur Bryan.. dislikes what he calls the 'pongo' Englishman. 'This is the bloke who is so bound by tradition and the old establishment that he can think of nothing else.' **1982** *Weekend Austral. Mag.* (Sydney) 30 Jan. 6/5 It came from somebody in the British Legion (the pongo equivalent of the RSL).

pony. *Shearing.* [Transf. use of *pony* small (working-) horse.] See quot. 1915.

1911 *Bulletin* (Sydney) 2 Mar. 14/2 At one of the biggest sheds in the land of the Prickly Pear.. a.. meeting was held, and it was decided to approach a shearer who was known to be a 'rousies' man'. The result of the vote.. was a majority of one for 'wet sheep'... But on the Monday our man deserted us, and the verdict was 'dry sheep'... Result: 'Classers' pony' instructed to become ill. I happened to be the 'pony', and by first smoko I had a very bad cough. **1915** *Ibid.* 28 Oct. 22/4 A 'pony' is a rouseabout who carries the fleeces from the classer to the wool-bins. **1966** S.J. BAKER *Austral. Lang.* (ed. 2) 56 The shearer.. has had many workers behind him—the *carrier away* or *pony* [etc.]. **1982** P. ADAM SMITH *Shearers* 405 *Pony*, assisted woolclasser in days of big shearing sheds. Responsible for placing individual fleeces in bin line for classer as in a big shed the classer would not have time to walk to the bins.

poofter /'pʊftə/. Also **poofta, poufter.** [Formed on *poof* homosexual: see OEDS *sb.*[1]]

1. A male homosexual; a man whose manner or behaviour does not conform with that conventionally regarded as masculine. Also used (of a man) as a general term of abuse. Also *attrib.*

1903 *Truth* (Sydney) 5 Apr. 5/6 It was the sort of talk that put the political 'poofter's' nose out of joint. **1910** O'BRIEN & STEPHENS *Materials Dict. Austral. Slang (typescript), Pouf or poufter*, a sodomite or effeminate man. **1941** S.J. BAKER *Pop. Dict. Austral. Slang* 56 *Poofter*, a homosexual. **1953** T.A.G. HUNGERFORD *Riverslake* 49 They want men in the unions, not poofters! **1955** D. NILAND *Shiralee* 228 They'd give him his medicine, some medicine, not half enough. They'd play around like poofters, with the kid gloves and the soft soap. **1957** *Westerly* iii. 13 Boyd is a poufter. **1967** C. RUHEN *Wild Beat* 67 A poofter? What'd he do? Make a grab for you in the park? **1967** J. HIBBERD *White with Wire Wheels* (1970) 154, I wish I'd puked all over his poofta pants. **1971** *Bulletin* (Sydney) 14 Aug. 50/3 He supports the Vietnam War on the ground that it makes men, convicts or corpses out of a lot of draft-dodging poofters. **1972** *Ibid.* 21 Oct. 45/1 If it was raining sheilas.. I'd be washed down the drain with a poofter. **1982** P. RADLEY *My Blue-Checker Corker* 96 Sixth Class never did get to the end of the ballet, because the schoolboy diggers got sick of the poofter dancing and started to tickle the fairies. **1985** *Sydney Morning Herald* 20 June 11/6 'Banks was a pooftah.' 'Have you got any proof of that?' 'He was a botanist and a Pommy—what more proof do you want?'

2. Special Comb. **poofter basher,** a male who engages in physical violence against, or verbal denigration of, homosexuals; so **bashing** *vbl. n.*; **rorter,** see quots.

1974 N. PHILLIPSON *As Other Men* 143 The sergeant had that sort of look about him. The look of a confirmed **poofter-basher.** **1978** *Weekend Austral. Mag.* (Sydney) 4 Mar. 5/6 Poofter-bashing in Australia is an ancient and honourable sport, and quite a few men have died of it. **1978** D. BALL *Great Austral. Snake Exchange* 46 It was unconscious, the stare of the latent poofter-basher. **1981** *Canberra Times* 12 Nov. 3/4 Existing homosexual laws made 'poofter bashing' a safe sport, the NSW Parliament was told yesterday. **1983** G. LEWIS *Real Men like Violence* 51 Anti-homosexual violence is nothing new in Australia. The practice of 'poofter bashing' was one of the marks of manhood for tough young men. **1984** *Southern Cross* 5 Dec. 2/5 If AIDS is to be arrested it will not be poofter bashing—the Australian colloquialism for written and spoken denigration of homosexuals—that will stop it. **1945** S.J. BAKER *Austral. Lang.* 123 A procurer for homosexuals is known as a **poofter rorter.** **1967** *Kings Cross Whisper* (Sydney) xxxviii. 10/2 *Poofter rorter*, one who preys on homosexuals.

Hence **poofterish** *a.*, **poofterism** *n.*

1969 W. DICK *Naked Prodigal* 89 'Oh, yes,' he said in a **poofterish** voice. **1982** N. KEESING *Lily on Dustbin* 62

Customers .. would once have thought it impossibly juvenile or 'poofterish' to order anything lighter than beer. **1978** L. HORSPHOL *Turn down Empty Glass* 29 The only rules that we're strict about are the ones governing rowdiness, drunkenness and **poofterism.**

poogie, var. POGIE.

pooh. In the phr. **in the pooh,** a euphemism for 'in the shit', in trouble.

1961 'J. DANVERS' *Living come First* 177 You're rather in the pooh with the Adelaide police. **1970** R. BEILBY *No Medals for Aphrodite* 229 And if they catch you with her, then you're really in the pooh. **1972** *Bulletin* (Sydney) 3 June 27/1 We're going to wash out our hangups on the Sunbury line, Cos we think that things are really in the pooh. **1975** X. HERBERT *Poor Fellow my Country* 873 She'll put you in the poo if she writes anything 'bout you.

pool, *v.* [Spec. use of *pool* to share.] *trans.* To implicate (a person); to inform on. Also as *ppl. a.*

1907 M. CANNON *That Damned Democrat* (1981) 92 The Poor, Pooled Public. Buncoed, Boomed and Busted. **1919** A. WRIGHT *Game of Chance* 202 I'm a witness for the prosecution, and the police have a statement from me, so I'm pooled. **1923** C.E. SAYERS *Jumping Double* 98 For the sake of your skin, you'll keep good with me for a while, or I'll pool you quick. **1961** X. HERBERT *Soldier's Union* 351 He was eyeing her shrewdly. 'What, you scared if you say you knew her you'll get pooled in somepin'?' **1967** I. TURNER *Sydney's Burning* 120 Davis .. mentioned something about 'pooling' Pauling and two other detectives. **1981** K. GARVEY *Rhymes of Ratbag* 141 It doesn't do to shake some beef. The police narks always pool yer.

pool, *n.* [See prec.] In the phr. **in** (or **out of**) **the pool,** in (or out of) trouble.

1923 C.E. SAYERS *Jumping Double* 97 You're not the only one who has a cover at headquarters. You don't think I've kept out of the pool so long without feeding the D's, do you? **1928** A. WRIGHT *Good Recovery* 145 'They're gone to the pack now,' put in Ric. 'Punting put them in the pool properly.' **1967** *Kings Cross Whisper* (Sydney) xxxv. 6/2 *In the pool*, to be in trouble.

poon, *n.* [Of unknown origin.] A simpleton or fool. See also quot. 1941. Also *attrib.*

1941 S.J. BAKER *Pop. Dict. Austral. Slang* 56 *Poon*, a lonely, somewhat crazy dweller in the Outer Beyond... A simpleton or fool. **1955** *Overland* iv. 10 I'd give a fiver To see you smash snakeheaded through Palings, poons, illywhack and guyver. **1972** G. MORLEY *Jockey rides Honest Race* 73 Then they can get up and shoot their mouths off and everybody else nods wisely and tries to pick up the mistakes of the poon that's just said his piece. **1972** D. WILLIAMSON *Jugglers Three* (1974) 69 What possessed Keren to shack up with a poon like you? **1982** T. WINTER *Mountain Verse* 51 'Golden Triangle is a euphemism for 'poon-patch' also known as antigravity land' i.e. the area between Perisher Range and Perisher Creek.

poon, *v.* [Of unknown origin.] *intr.* With **up**: to dress in order to impress. Also as *ppl. a.*

1943 S.J. BAKER *Pop. Dict. Austral. Slang* (ed. 3) 61 *Poon up*, to dress up, especially in flashy fashion. **1945** —— *Austral. Lang.* 206 School slang .. *poon up*, to dress up, especially with considerable care. **1962** *Southerly* ii. 79 It was not often Ironbark got himself pooned up like this but he was heading off to Sydney to bust his roll. **1972** A. CHIPPER *Aussie Swearers Guide* 48 *Pooned up*, dressed to impress, often with sexual success in view.

poonce /pʊns/. Formerly also **punce.** [Var. of *ponce* one who lives off the earnings of a prostitute, perh. infl. by POON *v.*] An ineffectual male; a homosexual; a general term of abuse for a man.

1941 S.J. BAKER *Pop. Dict. Austral. Slang* 57 Punce (pronounced with a short vowel as in 'book'), an effeminate man, a homosexual. **1945** —— *Austral. Lang.* 26 *Ponce*, 'a degraded man who lives on a woman', which we have converted into *punce* (or *poonce*) and given a different meaning. **1966** G. WYATT *Strip Jack Naked* 52 'Snake,' she hissed, 'Worm, Seducer, Bludger, Hoon, Poonce!' **1967** —— *Bit of Canter* 9 Waddya doin ya great poonce? **1969** A. BUZO *Front Room Boys* (1970) 103 Ar shut your big gob, you pie-faced poonce. **1982** T. WINTON *Open Swimmer* 28 'Bit of fight for a small fish,' said Jerra... 'That's 'cause they swim sideways coming up.' 'Smart fish, skippy.' 'Trevally.' 'Not this side of the border.' Jerra cast again. He spread some pollard onto the water. 'What are you, a Sydney poonce?'

Hence **pooncy** *a.*, affectedly refined; 'precious'.

1982 T. WINTON *Open Swimmer* 76 Sean's pissed off to his pooncy townhouse in South Perth.

poor black. *Hist.* Used with intense irony of an Aboriginal miscreant.

1837 *Colonist* (Sydney) 20 Apr. 130/4 An assigned servant of Lieutenant Wood's, at West Maitland was speared and killed a few days since by a *poor black.* **1838** *Sydney Herald* 19 Apr. 2/7 The 'poor blacks' are again at work... A labourer named Pegler was inhumanely murdered by some of these savages. **1840** *Colonist* (Sydney) 28 Nov. 2/4 The poor blacks .. are represented as 'poor' indeed, ragged beggars all of them, some making *bull* and drinking most bestially. **1843** *Sydney Morning Herald* 12 June 2/7 We are sorry to state that the 'poor blacks' have been committing great depredations in the McLeay district. *Ibid.* 4 Nov. 4/4 When discovered in the scrub every preparation had been made by 'the poor blacks' for a glorious feed. **1845** *Sydney Morning Herald* 19 Aug. 2/7 Speaking to you some time since about the doings of our 'poor' dark brethren in this quarter. I send you a list of unfortunate white beings murdered by these 'poor blacks'.

poor man. *Gold-mining.* [Also U.S.] Used in the collocation **poor man's digging(s), (gold)field, rush,** etc., (alluvial) terrain from which gold may be mined without substantial capital investment.

1855 W. HOWITT *Land, Labor & Gold* II. 226 You now hear Bendigo called the Poor Man's Digging. **1870** E.B. KENNEDY *Four Yrs. in Qld.* 215 What are known as 'a poor man's diggings' are *alluvial*, while *reefs* require capital to work them. **1894** A.F. CALVERT *Coolgardie Goldfield* 81 There are several rich patches of alluvial gold, which seldom last long enough or deep enough to count for much as 'poor men's diggings'. **1901** H. LAWSON *Joe Wilson & his Mates* 158 She went with the rush to Gulgong (about the last of the great alluvial or 'poor-man's' goldfields). **1907** M. CANNON *That Damned Democrat* (1981) 93 The ground was ridiculously easy to work. It was eminently a poor man's field. **1949** G. FARWELL *Traveller's Tracks* 33 The 'poor man's rushes' of Gulgong and Pipeclay. **1980** D. STONE et al. *Metal Detecting for Gold* 154 There were still some of the so called 'poor man's rushes' (where little skill or capital was needed) occurring in the 1860s and 70s in Victoria, Queensland and New South Wales.

Hence **poor man's gold** *n.*, gold obtained from such terrain.

1946 K.S. PRICHARD *Roaring Nineties* 360 You know as well as I do alluvial's been recognized as poor man's gold on every field in the colonies.

poor soldier. *Obs.* [See quot. 1841.] FRIAR BIRD; (occas.) any bird having a similar call.

1841 J. GOULD *Birds of Aust.* (1848) IV. Pl. 56, The Friar Bird .. from the fancied resemblance of its notes to those words .. has obtained from the Colonists the various names of 'Poor Soldier', 'Pimlico', 'Four O'Clock', etc. **1860** G. BENNETT *Gatherings of Naturalist* 233 The Mocking-bird, or Poor Soldier of the colonists (*Anthochaera mellivora*). **1896** F.G. AFLALO *Sketch Nat. Hist. Aust.* 119 There are five Friar Birds... Of these, the Poor Soldier (*Tropidorhynchus corniculatus*) occurs only in New South Wales and Queensland. **1945** S.J. BAKER *Austral. Lang.* 212 *Poor soldier*, noisy friar-bird.

pop, *v. Obs.* In the phr. **how are you popping (up)?**, 'how are you getting on?'

1894 H. LAWSON *Short Stories* 89 'How are yer?' 'Oh! I'm alright!' he says. 'How are ye poppin' up!' **1907** N.F. SPIELVOGEL *Cocky Farmer* 16 Whatto, Joe. How are you popping up? **1933** N. LINDSAY *Saturdee* 10 Whatoh Stinker, how you poppin' up? **1942** 'S. CAMPION' *Bonanza* 207 Howya poppin', cobber?

pop, *adv.* In the phr. **to go off pop,** to explode into angry speech.

1904 *Shearer* (Sydney) 17 Sept. 4/5 McManus is having a hot time at sheds in the Cobar district; and how he does go off, pop! when the boys corner him. **1929** W.J. RESIDE *Golden Days* 397 Then he cut no caper nor went off 'pop', But closed the shutters of Cupid's shop. **1972** F. BLAKELEY *Dream Millions* 101 When he made this statement I went off pop at him, and told him that it was very unlikely that the West Australian Government was paying for dingo scalps in those days.

poplar gum. [See quot. 1846.] The partly deciduous tree *Eucalyptus alba* (fam. Myrtaceae) of n. Aust., New Guinea, Timor, and nearby islands, having a pale, smooth bark and broad juvenile foliage.

1846 *Sydney Morning Herald* 26 Mar. 2/5 A new species of gum, which we called poplar gum, as its leaf and its foliage resembles very much in form and verdure the trembling poplar of Europe. **1867** F.J. BYERLEY *Narr. Overland Exped. Northern Qld.* 12 The river banks .. were .. lightly timbered with .. poplar-gum. **1938** F. CLUNE *Free & Easy Land* 171 A forest of tall blue gums, white poplar gums, and Moreton Bay ash. **1963** *N. Austral. Monthly* Dec. 11 The white-trunked poplar gums are always beautiful especially in the spring with their new pale-green leaves. The leaves are broad and vary in shape; the creamy flowers and gumnuts are small.

poppy. [See OED *poppy* 1 b. and *poppy-head* 1 for 17th century examples of a similarly allusive use.] In the collocation **tall poppy,** a person who is conspicuously successful; freq. one whose distinction, rank, or wealth attracts envious notice or hostility.

1902 H.L. NIELSEN *Voice of People* 8 The 'tall poppies' were the ones it was desired to retrench, but fear was expressed that, as usual, retrenchment might begin at the bottom of the ladder, and hardly touch those at the top at all. **1931** *NSWPD* 2nd Ser. no. 128 4840 The Premier cannot truthfully say that a measure which deals with a certain section of the community which he refers to as the privileged class and as the 'tall poppies' is in accord with the Melbourne agreement. **1956** A.C.C. LOCK *Tropical Tapestry* 119 Marcus Oliphant, Professor of Physics at the National University .. told an eminent audience of tall poppies, 'that sheep are eating the guts out of Australia'. **1957** W.F. CONNELL *Growing up in Austral. City* 85 One frustrated citizen has picturesquely described Sydneysiders as 'a race of knockers', alluding to the tendency to knock down not merely the tall poppies, but even to knock back the aspirations of the smaller ones. **1970** J.T. LANG *Turbulent Yrs.* 147 Next was the introduction of the bill to reduce all government salaries to a maximum of £10 a week. I referred to those being paid more than that amount as the 'tall poppies'. **1972** *Bulletin* (Sydney) 4 Nov. 46/3 Dunstan says evidence is growing that Australians at last are beginning to accept a few tall poppies, and to applaud local talent before it has been measured abroad. **1973** *Ibid.* 27 Jan. 38/1 (*heading*) Some tallish poppies in the mediocre corn. **1977** P. TENNISON *Heyday or Doomsday?* 15 'Mateship' .. produced a society in which the cutting down of 'tall poppies' became an automatic reflex. **1981** *Overland* lxxxv. 9 It used to be said of Australia that it was a country that cut down its tall poppies. **1986** *Canberra Times* 26 Jan. 1/5 Our national immaturity led us to cut down tall poppies and denigrate achievements.

populate or perish. A slogan coined by W.M. Hughes (1864–1952) when, as Minister for Repatriation and Health, he drew attention to Australia's falling birth-rate: see quot. 1937.

1937 *Sydney Morning Herald* 2 Feb. 10/4 'Australia must advance and populate, or perish,' said the Federal Minister for Health (Mr Hughes) to-day. **1943** J.H. GAFFNEY (*title*) Populate or perish. **1945** A.A. CALWELL *How Many Australs. Tomorrow* 1 'Populate or Perish' .. has become part of the small talk to be used jokingly whenever we talk of population problems. **1956** S. HOPE *Diggers' Paradise* 112 The late William Morris Hughes said that Australia 'must populate or perish'. **1986** *Sydney Morning Herald* 1 May 13/7 Calwell would no doubt be pleased to hear his call 'populate or perish' resurrected decades later.

porcupine. [Transf. use of *porcupine* a rodent of the fam. Hystricidae.] ECHIDNA. Also **porcupine anteater.**

1799 D. COLLINS *Acct. Eng. Colony N.S.W.* (1802) II. 145 The dogs found a porcupine ant-eater but could make no impression on him; he escaped from them by burrowing in the loose sand, not head foremost, but sinking himself directly downwards, and presenting his prickly back opposed to his adversaries. **1803** Banks Papers 7 Aug. XX. 101 As I have to go to the Blue Mountains . . I am in great expectation of meeting with the Porcupine there. **1826** J. ATKINSON *Acct. Agric. & Grazing N.S.W.* 25 The porcupine of New South Wales is a small kind, in nothing differing from the same animal in other places. **1832** J. BACKHOUSE *Narr. Visit Austral. Colonies* (1843) 89 The Porcupine of this land, *Echnida Hystrix*, is a squat species of ant-eater with short quills among its hair; it conceals itself in the day-time among dead timber in the hilly forests. **1855** W. HOWITT *Land, Labor & Gold* II. 113 To-day we have killed a porcupine, the first that we have caught. It is, in appearance, between the English hedgehog and the porcupine. **1878** R.B. SMYTH *Aborigines of Vic.* I. 350 The lancet used by the natives . . is a spine taken from the hinder part of the porcupine (*Echidna hystrix*). **1891** H. NISBET *Colonial Tramp* I. 123 A porcupine ant-eater near a camp is a sign of death. **1918** K.L. PARKER *Walkabouts Wur-Run-Nah* 14 Next he saw a Porcupine running towards him. **1949** E. NAPIER *Winter is in July* 102 Once I saw a black-and-white ant-eating porcupine, which is rare to find in daylight. **1960** R.S. PORTEOUS *Cattleman* 27 Ben could recall the delicious flavour of porcupine roasted on the coals. **1970** W.D.L. RIDE *Guide Native Mammals Aust.* 191 The most widespread Australian monotreme is the Echidna or Spiny-anteater which is called 'The Porcupine' by many country people and Aborigines. **1981** K. GARVEY *Rhymes of Ratbag* 170 The spiny echidna, or porcupine Is considered by murries a meal divine.

porcupine grass.

1. SPINIFEX 1 a. Also **porcupine bush** and (*ellipt.*) **porcupine.**

1842 G.C. HAWKER Diary Station Life Bungaree 15 June, Passed through a few patches of scrub & some very bad country covered with porcupine grass. **1861** *Burke & Wills Exploring Exped.* 16 We met with porcupine grass (*Triodia pungens* . .) and only two sand ridges. **1885** P.R. MEGGY *From Sydney to Silverton* 21 The porcupine grass, so named from the porcupine like bristles springing from a mound resembling a porcupine's back. **1916** *Emu* XV. 157 Some of the more rounded hills were covered in porcupine-bush (*Triodia*). This prickly plant is more often and incorrectly, called 'spinifex'. **1934** *Bulletin* (Sydney) 14 Nov. 21/1 There appear to be two breeds of spinifex . . the small variety, which grows about a foot high, and the porcupine-grass, which flourishes in huge spiny clumps often as tall as a horse and impenetrable to anything bar tractors or war-tanks. **1950** A. GROOM *I saw Strange Land* 58 It was hard going . . with the stabbing needles of the spinifex 'porcupine'-bush. **1962** *N. Austral. Monthly* Mar. 16 One of the strangest of Australian grasses is the spinifex or porcupine grass which thrives on sun and sand. **1984** E. WALLING *On Trail Austral. Wildflowers* 76 Grasses, poa and porcupine that mulch and hold the dry inland.

2. Special Comb. **porcupine grass resin** (or **gum**), *spinifex gum*, see SPINIFEX 3.

1927 SPENCER & GILLEN *Arunta* 24 Small lump of porcupine-grass resin. **1938** A. UPFIELD *Bone is Pointed* (1966) 145 Nero from his dilly-bag took a ball of porcupine-grass gum and proceeded to knead it into the form of a plate.

pork and bean. Rhyming slang for 'queen', a male homosexual.

1967 *Kings Cross Whisper* (Sydney) xxxviii. 10/2 *Pork and bean*, queen. Also a feminine homosexual. **1969** W. DICK *Naked Prodigal* 13 Listen mate, I don't like yuh either, so I might hit yuh yet, specially if yuh a pork and bean 'cause I don't like pork and beans, mate. **1970** *Kings Cross Whisper* (Sydney) lxxxii. 1/3 Revelations that Captain Cook was a pork and bean. . . Captain Cook only discovered Australia by accident while looking for Camp Cove, Sydney. **1972** L. IRISH *Time of Dolphins* 114 If a pork-and-bean as much as comes near me I want to vomit. Can't help it. **1977** J. RAMSAY *Cop it Sweet* 72 *Pork and bean*, rhym. *quean*, female homosexual.

pork fritz: see FRITZ.

port. [Abbrev. of *portmanteau.*] A suitcase; any (travelling) bag; hence (in *pl.*) baggage. Also locally with distinguishing epithet, as quots. 1968 and 1982.

1898 *Western Champion* (Barcaldine) 3 May 7/1 Various styles of traps laden with swags, ports, and refreshments. **1904** C.W. JOHNSTON *Out-Back Homestead* 73 '*Pack* your 'port' and come up to the Hall for a week's shooting,' said my friend. **1912** *Truth* (Sydney) 22 Dec. 8/3 He placed his portmanteau . . on the floor beside him; but, presto! when he turned round to pick up his port and depart, it was conspicuous by its absence. **1913** *Bulletin* (Sydney) 23 Oct. 22/3 He carried a relic 'port' of huge dimensions and a cumbrous hessian bundle. **1934** T. WOOD *Cobbers* 236 A dignitary . . opened the door and asked me if I had any more ports. . . He found them, four blue suitcases. **1944** J.J. HARDIE *Cattle Camp* 204 We're staying at the Metropole! Landed there like a couple of hay-seeds—we didn't have a port, between us—only our swags! **1954** *Coast to Coast 1953–54* 149 The foreman laughed. He had lived twenty years in the Northern Territory. 'Well grab your ports, and I'll take you out to the huts,' he called out. The men picked up kitbags and a few suit-cases. **1964** G. JOHNSTON *My Brother Jack* 75 Flannery carries in his baggage—his 'ports', as he calls them—a full swagman's outfit complete with blanket-roll, billy, and cork-hung sundowner's hat which he brings out for shipboard fancy-dress occasions. **1965** P. TODHUNTER *Aust. under Scalpel* 94 With my little attache case (called my 'port' by my new abbreviation-crazy friends) I made a sortie on all the magazine and newspaper offices. **1968** P. ADAM SMITH *Tiger Country* 10 He brought his 'Gordon River port' (a chaff bag carried on the back and supported by hessian strips across the chest) to the camp. **1977** V. PRIDDLE *Larry & Jack* 149, I wouldn't blame her if she packed her ports and walked out. **1980** *Austral.* (Sydney) 11 Aug. 4/5 He would carry my port home from school in the afternoon. **1982** N. KEESING *Lily on Dustbin* 107 In Queensland a Millaquin port was a sugar bag, the term deriving from the Millaquin Sugar Mill.

portable soup. *Hist.* Dehydrated meat which may be reconstituted in liquid form: see quot. 1846.

1843 *Colonial Observer* (Sydney) 16 Aug. 1235/4 Gelatine, or German Portable Soup . . from its extreme convenience as a provision for travelling in the bush we feel little doubt that it will soon become an article of considerable consumption. One ounce of the cake will make a quart and two thirds of a pint of excellent soup. **1844** *Sydney Morning Herald* 26 July 4/1, With reference to the exertions now being made to manufacture a portable soup, erroneously called gelatine, at the boiling down establishments, Mr Hogg . . assures us that he is confident large quantities of it would be purchased by the Indian Government for hospital use. **1846** *Ibid.* 27 May 2/7 We are glad to perceive that the portable soup made at the boiling-down establishments, is beginning to attract notice in England. . . In a London paper of December, the following paragraph appeared:– Recent arrivals of ships from Australia have introduced a new article of food into the London market. It is a kind of concentrated gravy, the result of the boiling down of sheep and cattle for the supply of the English tallow market, and which has hitherto been of little or no value. It is imported in a good state of preservation, and, on the addition of a few condiments, makes a very palatable soup. **1930** BILLIS & KENYON *Pastures New* 94 Even 'soup' made from colonial meat, was exported to England. This was in the form of dried or powdered meat, packed in tins. The idea came from Sydney, where the product was called 'portable soup', and in England it was termed 'concentrated gravy'.

port cart. *Hist.* A light cart used to convey passengers between Adelaide and Port Adelaide: see quot. 1848.

1848 *Adelaide Miscellany* 9 Sept. 90 Looking about for some conveyance to take me to the City of Adelaide, I discovered that a man . . was the driver of what is here called a *Port cart*, which is a Colonial imitation of our English short stages. **1851** *Illustr. Austral. Mag.* (Melbourne) Mar. 175, I soon learned that I was looking at one of the 'port carts', that the passenger traffic was carried on almost exclusively through their agency, at a charge of one shilling per head, and that there was nothing for me, if I wished to go to Adelaide, but to mount without a murmur. **1857** 'OLD YET YOUNG COLONIST' *One Mode* 25 We are able to do without being compelled to bear the miseries of an omnibus, or what is ten times worse, a Port cart. **1867** 'COLONIST' *Life's Work* 17 At Port Adelaide . . numbers of men were earning a good living by driving port carts. **1881** T. BASTARD *Autobiogr. 'Cockney Tom'* 23, I . . went down to the Port in the first cart, for there were no railways in those days, nor was it anything unusual for the Port cart to be upset. **1915** *Lone Hand* June 52 The journey from Port Adelaide to the capital was accomplished in a 'Port cart'.

Hence **port-cart** *v. intr.*, to travel by port cart.

1850 *Monthly Almanac* (Adelaide) 43 We went ashore, and an hour or two afterwards, port-carted it to Adelaide.

porter-gaff. [f. *porter* a dark beer + *shandy)gaff.*] A drink made by mixing stout with lemonade.

1891 *Truth* (Sydney) 8 Mar. 5/1 He brought her a porter-gaff, but she refused to drink it. **1979** P. PAVY *Bush Surgeon* 8, I was afraid to drink too many beers, so I spent several hours consuming glasses of 'Portergaff', a mixture of stout and lemonade.

port-hole. In the wall of a shearing-shed: a small doorway, adjacent to a shearer's stand, through which a shorn sheep is pushed into a counting-out pen.

1882 ARMSTRONG & CAMPBELL *Austral. Sheep Husbandry* 175 'Port-holes', or small doorways are made (one for each shearer), through which the sheep are turned when shorn. **1965** J.S. GUNN *Terminol. Shearing Industry* i. 14 The 'porthole' . . is a low opening and ramp through which the shorn sheep are passed down to the counting-out pen.

Port Jackson. [The name of the port of Sydney, N.S.W.] Used *attrib.* in the names of flora and fauna: **Port Jackson fig,** the shrub to large tree *Ficus rubiginosa* (fam. Moraceae) of e. N.S.W.; **shark,** any shark of the fam. Heterodontidae, esp. *Heterodontus portusjacksoni* of s. Aust.

1889 J.H. MAIDEN *Useful Native Plants Aust.* 225 *Ficus rubiginosa* . . '**Port Jackson Fig**' . . like other figs, exudes a juice when the bark is wounded. **1935** DAVISON & NICHOLLS *Blue Coast Caravan* 55 The road . . was planted . . with planes and Port Jackson flags [*sic*]. The former were in yellow leaf and made a strong contrast with the black-green density of the latter. **1954** *Coast to Coast 1953–54* 133 Today Ellen planted the Port Jackson Fig. **1965** *Austral. Encycl.* IV. 58 The Port Jackson . . fig . . is confined in its native state to New South Wales but is extensively planted as a shade and ornamental tree throughout Australia. **1985** M. STEWART *Autobiogr. of my Mother* 167 Towards the end of Pitt Street near the harbour was a spreading fig tree, not a Moreton Bay but a smaller branching Port Jackson. **1789** A. PHILLIP *Voyage to Botany Bay* 283 **Port Jackson Shark.** . . At first sight the above might be taken for the *Prickly Hound-fish*, or *Squalus Spinax* of *Linnaeus*. **1860** G. BENNETT *Gatherings of Naturalist* 27 The singular species of Shark, known by the name of the Port Jackson Shark (Cestracion Philippii). **1874** *N.S.W. Rep. R. Comm. Fisheries* (1880) 19 The Port Jackson shark is of the family *Cestraciontidae*. . . It was supposed that Port Jackson alone had this shark. . . It has since been found in many of the coast bays of Australia. **1896** F.G. AFLALO *Sketch Nat. Hist. Aust.* 215 Of greatest interest to the scientific world, excepting perhaps the Port Jackson Shark . . is the group of Lung Fishes. **1936** N. CALDWELL *Fangs of Sea* 19 We made huge hauls of large stingrays, Port Jackson sharks . . and other inedible fish. **1975** X. HERBERT *Poor Fellow my Country* 1191 Sharks? But the Port Jackson Shark was not a man-eater.

Port Lincoln parrot. [f. the name of a town in S.A.] The parrot of central and w. Aust. *Barnardius zonarius*, a predom. green bird with a black head, and yellow collar and belly. See also TWENTY-EIGHT. Formerly also **Port Lincoln parakeet.**

1896 B. SPENCER *Rep. Horn Sci. Exped. Central Aust.* II. 63 Port Lincoln Parrakeet . . were afterwards found throughout the trip wherever water existed. **1916** S.A. WHITE *In Far Northwest* 74 This bird is closely allied to what is known as the Port Lincoln parrot (Barnardius zonarius). **1937** R.H. CROLL *Wide Horizons* 12 The Ulbujas, better known as the Port Lincoln Parrots, display their sleek dark heads and golden collars as they feed in the higher branches. **1976** *Reader's Digest Compl. Bk. Austral. Birds* 282 The Port Lincoln parrot is much more widely distributed than its name suggests.

Port Phillip. *Hist.* [Named after *Port Phillip* Bay, a large inlet on the south coast of Victoria, near which the city of Melbourne now stands.] The name given to that part of the Colony of New South Wales which in 1851 became the Colony of Victoria. Also *attrib.*, esp. as **Port Phillip District.**

1836 G. MERCER *Copy Lett.* 2 If Port Phillip be constituted a subordinate colony . . the proximity . . to Van Dieman's Land might be taken to render Hobart Town a more eligible station for controls than Sidney. **1841** *Port Phillip Patriot* 1 Mar. 2/2 There are private individuals in the Middle District who have more convicts assigned them than are accorded to the whole public service of Port Phillip. **1845** C.J. BAKER *Sydney & Melbourne* p. vi, The title of 'Port Phillip' has been in common use extended from the harbour of that name to the whole province of Australia Felix. **1850** *Illustr. Austral. Mag.* (Melbourne) Aug. 118 Her father, like many of the Port Phillip Settlers, was a gentleman by birth and education; and had, from his first location in the Bush, carefully abstained from contracting any of those vulgar or *flash* habits. **1853** W. WESTGARTH *Vic.* 73 The mania of locomotion had for some time been recognised in Van Diemen's Land under the title of the Port Phillip fever. **1858** T. MCCOMBIE *Hist. Colony Vic.* 62 This formed what was afterwards known as the southern or Port Phillip district of the colony of New South Wales until separation. **1859** W. FAIRFAX *Handbk. to Australasia* p. xxiii, The Port Phillip mania was . . strongly felt in Van Diemen's Land. **1862** G.T. LLOYD *Thirty-Three Yrs. Tas. & Vic.* 325 An old Port Phillip native was discovered hunting in a secluded valley. **1878** 'R. BOLDREWOOD' *Ups & Downs* 61 Don't ye lay a finger on me, ye hungry, grinding Port Phillip Yankee slave driver.

Port Phillipian. A resident of the Port Phillip District. Also as *adj.*

1836 *Cornwall Chron.* (Launceston) 17 Dec. 2 We have statements before us of the extreme dissatisfaction caused to the Port Phillipians generally, by the troublesome interference of Captain Lonsdale in matters, in which, as Commandant, he supposes himself justified—but in which the Phillipians think that he is not. **1841** *Port Phillip Patriot* 8 Feb. 2 Our Sydney friends wonder at the presumption of the Port Phillippians in asking or expecting a government of their own. **1850** *Irish Exile* (Hobart) 28 Dec. 7/2 The Port Phillipians—we beg their pardon, the Victorians—have displayed their loyalty. **1867** J. BONWICK *J. Batman* 35 How much the Port Phillipians owe him. **1888** E. FINN *Chron. Early Melbourne* I. 371 A big feast of 'bubble-bubble'—a mess of flour and water to which the Port Phillipian Aborigines were even more partial than to the squatters' rum or beef. **1906** S. GRIFFITHS *Turf & Heath* 16 To the disappointment of the Port Phillipians, this crack failed to make an appearance. **1930** BILLIS & KENYON *Pastures New* 179 If the broad Australian rather than the Port Phillipian view be taken.

portulac. *Obs.* [Var. of *portulack* the common purslane, *Portulaca oleracea.*] *Pigweed*, see PIG *n.*[1]

1861 *Burke & Wills Exploring Exped.* 18 There had been a considerable fall of rain in some places, which had raised a fine crop of grass and portulac. **1863** W.J. WILLS *Successful Exploration Interior Aust.* 228 Fine salt bush and portulac being abundant in the vicinity, we camped here at 4.30 a.m. **1883** E. PALMER *Plants N. Qld.* 11 *Portulaca oleracea* . . the common pigweed or portulac; grows after the wet season on the banks of rivers and on sand ridges in great quantities. **1911** C.E.W. BEAN *'Dreadnought' of Darling* 234 They helped their provisions by eating a good deal of a shrub known as portulac.

possie /'pɒzi/. Also **possy** and less freq. **pozzie, pozzy.** [f. *pos(ition* + -Y.] A position of supposed advantage to the occupant; a place; a job. Orig., in trench warfare, an individual soldier's place of shelter or firing position.

1915 I.L. IDRIESS Diary 29 Aug. i. 25 His possy is in a good position and he had already got 105 Turks, which is the record for a single man on the Peninsula. **1915** R.H. ADAMS Diary 7 Sept., This morning we moved from our possy in the support trenches. **1915** T. SKEYHILL *Soldier-Songs from Anzac* 16 'E climbs up stunted pine-trees, An' snipes away at us. But 'e never shows 'is pozzy. **1916** 'MEN OF ANZAC' *Anzac Bk* 125 'Possie!' exclaimed the inquiring General. 'What is a 'Possie'?' 'That, sir,' said the C.O., 'is Australian for recess, either firing or sleeping. It's a contraction of 'position'.' 'Now that's where you're wrong,' said the Chief Staff Officer, in a tone which admitted no argument. 'Posse! -p-o-double s-e. Posse—a small force. Your firing recess is manned by a small force—what?' And the C.O. was overcome by very great emotion. **1916** O. HOGUE *Trooper Bluegum at Dardanelles* 188 The enemy scored next time. One of their snipers, over-bold, crept up in the scrub to within twenty yards of the trenches . . and started blazing away. Our fellows could not get him from the trenches, so Sergeant Ducker, and three others volunteered to rush the Turk's 'posey' and bring him in, dead or alive. **1917** P. AUSTEN *Bill-Jim* 5 Well, I'm back again in Aussie, An' I got me ticket, too, An' each week I draws out thirty o' the best; Say, it ain't too bad a possie. **1918** *Two Blues: Mag. 13th Battalion A.I.F.* Oct. 3 Here lies Fritz—he met an Aussie We don't know his name but this is his possie. **1923** F.E. TROTTER *Tales of Billzac* 46 Bluey, our company cook, had established his cook house in a bonzer possie. **1924** C.E.W. BEAN *Official Hist. Aust. 1914–18* II. 376 They lay packed on the floor of communication saps, or in 'pozzies' in the trench-wall inhabited by other men before them. **1928** 'C. DENISON' *Glimpses* 82 The moment hammocks were obtainable from the bins, he was there to claim his; and after a night or two his position was recognised. One soldier never jumps another's 'possie'. **1935** P. LAWLOR *Confessions of Journalist* 27 If he was not in the dock Chittle was present in the public enclosure . . When, however, he contrived to be arrested . . he would take his place in the dock . . and look down at his old 'possie' with the greatest of contempt. **1945** G. CASEY *Downhill is Easier* 12 He's taking damn good care nobody works their way up from the bottom while he's got the possy at the top. **1946** F. CLUNE *Try Nothing Twice* 5 Peering from a possie on the stairs, I saw Mum open the door. **1948** K.S. PRICHARD *Golden Miles* 72 Been boggin' seven years on this mine, and these bastards of foreigners, just started, get all the best pozies! **1954** *Bulletin* (Sydney) 17 Feb. 12/4, I left them parked in what I reckoned was a first-class possie along the Royal Procession-route. **1955** D. NILAND *Shiralee* 81 Up here, mate, there's a possy, if you can work yourself in. **1969** L. HADOW *Full Cycle* 250 Only the odd, dead-end jobs until they were eighteen . . all dead-end possies that led, inevitably, to the mines. **1977** H. GARNER *Monkey Grip* 12, I smoked a couple of joints and took a cup of brandy to a little pozzy I found. **1984** *Palmerston & Northern Suburbs Herald* (Darwin) 16 Nov. 5/1 The bridge will not only link south western areas with Palmerston, locals say it could provide a good fishing possie.

Hence **possie** *v. trans.*, to position (*refl.* in quot.).

1963 *Sunday Mirror* (Sydney) 20 Jan. 43/2 Gilli, with Mulley apparently 'curling the mo' was possied behind them for his challenge.

possum, *n.* [Transf. use of *possum*, aphetic form of *opossum*; now the preferred form in Aust.]

1. Any of many chiefly herbivorous, long-tailed, arboreal marsupials of the fam. Phalangeridae, Petauridae and Burramyidae, some of which are gliding animals; OPOSSUM *n.* 1. Often with distinguishing epithet, as **brush-tailed, dormouse, flying, honey, mountain pygmy, pygmy, ringtail** (see under first element). See also LEADBEATER'S POSSUM. Also *attrib.*

1770 J. COOK *Jrnls.* 4 Aug. (1955) I. 367 Here are . . Possums. **1842** *Legends of Aust.* Mar. 56 He was constantly . . laying traps for 'possums' and native cats. **1847** A. HARRIS *Settlers & Convicts* (1953) 131 Before white man come . . plenty 'possum, plenty everything. **1860** 'LADY' *My Experiences in Aust.* 209 The hunter selects some tree which he imagines likely to be 'possum's' abiding place, and examines the bark carefully to see if there are any fresh marks of claws. **1880** J.B. STEVENSON *Seven Yrs. Austral. Bush* 69 We . . saw . . a blackfellow busily engaged cutting a possum out of a tree with his stone tomahawk. **1903** *Emu* II. 173 Poisoned food laid out as bait for 'possums. **1925** *Bulletin* (Sydney) 8 Jan. 22/3 Stewed 'possum can be good tucker. **1952** 'N. SHUTE' *Far Country* 139 A black and silver animal about the size of a large cat, with a bushy tail like a silver fox fur . . she learned that this was a possum. **1979** K. GARVEY *Absolutely Austral.* 72 We used to find a possum once in every hollow spout On all the river-gums before the myxo thinned them out.

2. *transf.*

a. Used as a mildly derogatory term for a person: a 'creature'. Also as an (affectionate) mode of address.

1894 A.B. BELL *Austral. Camp Fire Tales* 104 Bob Fogarty, as I'm a living sinner, delighted to meet you, old possum. **1921** W.H. PHIPPS *Bush Yarns* 55 He was a pretty useless possum was Tom, and a bit starchy when he had his fancy clothes on. **1965** K. SMITH *OGF* 250 The cheeky possum! Walking into our house like that without even an invite! **1982** R. HALL *Just Relations* 88 Goodness what an ugly little possum you've turned into.

b. A fraudulent substitution, RING-IN *n.* 1; the practice of this.

1903 *Sporting News* (Launceston) 17 Jan. 1/2 Although the field was a painfully weak one, the game of ' 'possum' appeared in more than one instance to have been well rehearsed. **1943** S.J. BAKER *Pop. Dict. Austral. Slang* (ed. 3) 61 *Possum*, a 'ring-in'. **1955** *Bulletin* (Sydney) 27 July 12/3 Whence do we get the colloquialisms 'playing possum' and 'a possum' (meaning a racetrack ring-in)?

3. [Prob. as the obverse of *to play possum.*] In the phr. **to stir** (or **rouse**) **the possum,** to excite interest or controversy; to liven things up.

1900 *Truth* (Sydney) 29 Apr. 5/7 Why, old George Reid would be comparatively forgotten if he didn't keep stirring the possum. **1906** *Ibid.* 30 Dec. 6/6, I only wanted to stir the possum! **1907** C. MACALISTER *Old Pioneering Days* 51 An ambitious carrier or drover would 'rouse the 'possum' by giving some long-winded ditty of the time. **1949** R. PARK *Poor Man's Orange* 9 A mission was like a tonic. It stirred the 'possum in the people, and for months afterwards they could still feel the enthusiasm. **1968** *Kings Cross Whisper* (Sydney) xxxxviii. 3/4 A drunken office boy in the Commonwealth Electoral office in Canberra has admitted shuffling the ballot papers 'to stir the 'possum a bit'. **1973** L. OAKES *Whitlam PM* 169 In December, Calwell decided to 'stir the possum' on the Vietnam issue. **1981** *Age* (Melbourne) 18 July 15/2 Treasury secretary John Stone has a grand way of stirring the possum.

4. In the phr. **possum up a gum tree,** used allusively as an expression of approbation.

1885 R. CANNON *Savage Scenes Aust.* 16 The Australian delights in 'possum up a gum tree'. **1894** A.B. BELL *Oscar* 37, I scooted up that wall like a 'possum up a gum-tree. **1898** *Bulletin* (Sydney) 17 Dec. (Red Page), 'Like a possum up a gum tree' is not bad to express quickness or cleverness in doing anything. **1928** B. SPENCER *Wanderings in Wild Aust.* 151 The expression ' 'possum up a gum tree' was really brought over to Australia in early days by miners of the celebrated 'forty-niner' period, who left California to try their luck on the goldfields. **1955** N. PULLIAM *I traveled Lonely Land* 381 *Like a possum up a gum tree*, completely happy.

5. Comb. **possum cloak, hunt, hunting, rug, shooting, skin, snarer, snaring trapper.**

1848 H.W. HAYGARTH *Recoll. Bush Life* 21 He rolls himself for the night in the blanket or **''possum cloak'**, which by day is strapped on before him. **1864** *Illustr. Sydney News* 16 Dec. 11/1 The Lubras . . now commenced a tum-tumming kind of music on their 'possum cloaks. **1878** R.B. SMYTH *Aborigines of Vic.* I. 64 The *Jerryale* go up with their 'possum cloaks over their heads, and eat the kangaroo flesh. **1888** 'R. BOLDREWOOD' *Robbery under Arms* (1937) 165 One tallish gin, darker than the others, and with her hair tucked under an old bonnet, wrapped her 'possum cloak closely round her shoulders. **1857** W. DENISON *Varieties Vice-Regal Life* 20 July (1870) I. 249 On coming down the hill we had a **'possum' hunt**: a shepherd had set fire to a hollow tree, and smoked the opossum out of his hole; he was sitting disconsolately at the end of a branch, watching a dog that was barking below, and bobbing his head occasionally to get out of the way of the sticks and stones which flew about his ears; he was often hit, but kept his post to the last, and in fact tired us out. **1898** R. RADCLYFFE *Wealth & Wild Cats* 13 There is the beach at Cottesloe for picnics, or the bush for 'possum hunts by midnight. **1849** A. HARRIS *Emigrant Family* (1967) 258 There is actually good **'possum hunting** now, within a day's stage of Sydney. **1899** *Austral. Tit-Bits* (Sydney) 25 Feb. 42/2 There was no time to spare for 'possum hunting today. **1840** *S. Austral. Rec.* (London) 26 Dec. 410 The natives are a harmless race of people . . a blanket, or **possem rug,** completes their dress. **1845** *Portland Guardian* 6 May 3/2, I have no bed of luxurious down, My apartments are not very snug, But still my light cares I can drown, When rolled up in a warm 'possum rug. **1878** R.B. SMYTH *Aborigines of Vic.* I. 247 One woman had a fine little boy at her back, in her 'possum rug. **1896** J.M. PRICE *Land of Gold* 4 A good possum rug can . . be had for about four or five pounds.

1930 'BRENT OF BIN BIN' *Ten Creeks Run* (1952) 63 You should have been curled up in your possum-rug hours ago. **1860** 'LITTLE JACOB' *Colonial Pen-Scratchings* 94 The two young men were very thick, and cattle-hunted and went **possum-shooting** together. **1901** H. LAWSON *Joe Wilson & his Mates* 24 Next evening the Jackaroo and one or two other chaps and the girls went out 'possum-shooting. **1854** *Illustr. Sydney News* 7 Jan. 108/3 The invaluable qualities of the cloak made from the rich grey and buff fur of the animal and which is vulgarly called a **'possum skin'**. **1864** J. MORRILL *Sketch of Residence* 219, I was .. making a possum skin rug. **1878** S. TANDY *Children in Scrub* 63 That's where the natives have cut the bark out to dry the 'possum skins on. **1921** G.A. BELL *Under Brigalows* 74 A number of gins squatted under a tree, in their laps were possum skin rugs folded up in square packets, with the hide outside. These were the drums. **1962** E. LANE *Mad as Rabbits* 12 Then he'd roll his possum-skin swag and be off again. **1981** A.B. FACEY *Fortunate Life* 29 Albert bought them out of his possum skin money. **1908** *Bulletin* (Sydney) 16 Jan. 14/2 The **'possum-snarer** is no longer known in the land; his place has been taken by the rabbit-snapper. **1922** *Ibid.* 31 Aug. 20/3 How's this for a 'possum-snarer's cheque? *Ibid.*, He thought he'd try his hand at **'possum-snaring. 1981** A.B. FACEY *Fortunate Life* 45 Help with the clearing and possum snaring. **1899** *Bulletin* (Sydney) 7 Oct. 14/3, I know a **'possum-trapper's** horse that will eat raw 'possum. **1928** M.E. FULLERTON *Austral. Bush* 36 A 'possum-trapper maybe, or a 'bullocky'.

6. Special Comb. **possum eater,** a parsimonious person; a country bumpkin; **-eating** *ppl. a.*, countrified; **guts,** a coward; **-gutted** *ppl. a.*, cowardly; **(pumpkin) pie,** see quot. 1960.

1942 H.H. PECK *Mem. of Stockman* 72 That .. was characteristic of James Tyson as a young man, when he denied himself many a necessity in order to save money, and no doubt was the origin of his reputation as a ''**possum eater'**, of which he was not ashamed. **1959** D. NILAND *Gold in Streets* 144 Silly looking sonk. Head like a melon, big feet, shovel hands. King of the cow-bails, possum eater, the pride of Woop-Woop. **1878** 'R. BOLDREWOOD' *Ups & Downs* 67 Do I look like a slouchin' **'possum-eating**, billy-carrying crawler of a shepherd? **1962** D. MCLEAN *World turned upside Down* 10 The big bloke's Danny Fenton, one of the Rocks push, and his mate's Skinny Harford, a proper **possum-guts. 1959** D. NILAND *Gold in Streets* 194, I ought to push your bloody teeth down your throat, you **possum-gutted** halfwit. **1871** 'OLD BOOMER' *Story of Mathinna* 10 Her full and restless coal-black eye Turned sometimes to the passer-by And sometimes to the **'possum pie. 1960** B. HARNEY *Cook Bk.* 35 *Possum pumpkin pie.* In the early days, possums were caught, cleaned and cut up, put into a hollowed-out pumpkin which was then roasted until the meat was cooked.

possum, *v.* [Also U.S.] *intr.* To hunt possums. Freq. as *pres. pple.* and *vbl. n.*

1852 J. BONWICK *Notes of Gold Digger* 22 Some amuse themselves with going out 'possuming. **1857** 'RETURNED DIGGER' *Six Yrs. in Aust.* 13 If it is clear to-night we are going 'possoming', by moonlight. **1884** *Austral. Tit-Bits* (Sydney) 25 Dec. 14/1 He had dropped in expecting to find Jack alone, and ask him to come out for an hour's 'possuming. **1892** A. CAMERON *Aust. Felix* 12 The lady's been a-'possumin'. **1915** K.S. PRICHARD *Pioneers* 156 She was always more eager to be 'possuming and chasing calves with Davey. **1926** L.C.E. GEE *Bush Tracks & Gold Fields* 70 Fishing, 'possuming, rabbiting. **1931** B. CRONIN *Bracken* 133 They would .. take the dogs 'possuming in the moonlight. **1957** R.S. PORTEOUS *Brigalow* 88 Mick and Wonga .. knew, from their possuming experiences, every gully, every water-hole, and every patch of open plain. **1951** A. MARSHALL *Aust.* (1981) 64 We used to go possuming a lot. We'd walk miles through the bush looking for them on moonlight nights.

possumer. One who hunts possums.

1905 J. FURPHY *Rigby's Romance* (1946) 47 'Allowed to be the best (adj.) possumer on the track,' he resumed. **1922** E. MERYON *At Holland's Tank* 12 No man went out there—not even the kangarooers and 'possumers. **1943** *Bulletin* (Sydney) 1 Sept. 12/4 The population included whalers .. illicit possumers, doggers. **1979** J. LINDEMAN *Red Rumps & White Faces* 42 By that time the semi-professional 'possumers had just about finished the cream. New chums arriving on the opening day of the season .. reported that the 'possums were almost extinct.

possy, var. POSSIE.

post, *v. trans.* To leave (someone) in the lurch. Freq. as *ppl. a.*

1967 *Kings Cross Whisper* (Sydney) xxxviii. 10/2 *Posted*, to be left waiting. **1973** *Ibid.* cxlvii. 3/1 Soon as his back's turned, Stalky does a bunk with the wife and leaves her old man posted. **1975** *Bulletin* (Sydney) 26 Apr. 45/3 The guy's willin' and there's no way he'll post you on the job. **1979** *Sydney Morning Herald* 30 Apr. 24/1 Not once was Beetson left 'posted' with no one to get the ball to. **1977** J. RAMSAY *Cop it Sweet* 73 *Posted*, be left waiting.

postal note. An order issued by a post office for any required sum of money, payable at any other post office.

1885 *Victorian Yr.-Bk. 1884–85* 481 Postal notes were first issued on the 1st January, 1885. **1907** *Truth* (Sydney) 26 May 1/4 It has been decided to issue sixpenny postal notes. **1939** M. MORRIS *Dark Tumult* 132 Walking into the Post-Office store and buying a five-shilling postal note to pay for his licence. **1949** J. CLEARY *Long Shadow* 72 'How's the postal racket?' 'Fine, fine. Making a mint of money from dud postal notes.' **1964** *Surfabout* (Sydney) I. vi. 3 A postal note for £1 7s. (6 issues) sent to us will get you that subscription. **1973** *Bulletin* (Sydney) 25 Aug. 3 Enclosed please find my cheque/postal note.

post and rail. [Used elsewhere (esp. U.S.) but of considerable local significance: see OEDS.]

1. a. *pl.* The component parts of a *post and rail fence* (see sense 1 b.).

1802 D. COLLINS *Acct. Eng. Colony N.S.W.* II. 313 A stock-yard, consisting of about 30 acres, was inclosed [*sic*] with posts and rails. **1832** J. BACKHOUSE *Narr. Visit Austral. Colonies* (1843) 25 A prisoner was at work splitting the wood of the Peppermint-tree, a species of *Eucalyptus*, into posts and rails. **1845** C. GRIFFITH *Present State & Prospects Port Phillip* 11 The stringy-bark .. is peculiarly valuable to the settler, who thus obtains his slabs (rough planks) for building, and his posts and rails for fencing. **1852** MRS C. MEREDITH *My Home in Tas.* I. 159 'Split stuff', by which is meant timber .. which is *split* into 'posts and rails', slabs or palings. **1857** W. WESTGARTH *Vic. & Austral. Gold Mines* 79 The prevailing feature of improvement throughout the colony .. is the post-and-rail fencing. Posts and rails, well-known articles of colonial trade, are freely supplied throughout the country. **1859** J.D. MEREWEATHER *Diary Working Clergyman* 55 The land is inclosed by a strong fence of posts and rails, which have more utility than grace. **1870** J. BONWICK *Last Tasmanians* 198 Three were servants sent to cut posts and rails for fencing. **1872** MRS E. MILLETT *Austral. Parsonage* 54 Its own glebe field of nine acres, surrounded by straight rows of split posts and rails, after the hedgeless fashion of Australia. **1880** J.B. STEVENSON *Seven Yrs. Austral. Bush* 115 A cattle yard capable of working a moderate herd of cattle usually covers about two acres, and is constructed of posts and rails. **1899** *Austral. Tit-Bits* (Sydney) 25 Mar. 111/2 A wood-splitter was at work, getting posts and rails, and he was engaged on a big log. **1948** F. CLUNE *Wild Colonial Boys* 171 The stockyards were built of heavy posts and rails, seven feet high.

b. In the phr. **post and rail fence,** a strongly constructed wooden fence, consisting of two or more horizontal rails morticed into upright posts. Also **post and rail fencing.**

1820 *Sydney Gaz.* 20 May, Supposed to have a cross-cut saw, and other implements for putting up post and rail fence. **1830** *Hobart Town Almanack* 187 Upwards of 600 miles of substantial post-and-rail fencing have been erected during the year. **1849** *Portland Gaz.* 9 Feb. 3/1 By the original plan of the township no street is shown in front of the Court House, or along either side of the post-and-rail fence which surrounds it. **1868** *Mr Newcome in Search of Cattle Station* 7 Dotted here and there with the homesteads of some rich old farmers, the holdings of whom are all enclosed by post and rail fencing, and divided into convenient paddocks. **1878** E. BRADDON *Lett. to India from N.W. Tas.* (1980) 63, I was put on to a post and rail fence and told to hug it all the way. **1891** J. FENTON *Bush Life Tas.* (1964) 56 Russell Street was not even visible, for it was enclosed in a grass paddock by a rough post and rail fence. **1914** 'B. CABLE' *By Blow & Kiss* 6 The cattle wi' as much flesh on 'em as a post an' rail fence. **1942** E. LANGLEY *Pea Pickers* 37 There were post-and-rail fences on either side of the road, thick with lichen, and every mile or so there was an enamel placard on them, advertising soap. One of the saddest sights you could see. **1971** *Bulletin* (Sydney) 3 July 13/1 Ansett has the Jackaroo Bar, which features a typical Wild West corral with hide and cow horns on the walls, post-and-rail fences to lean on, wall-to-wall carpets and air-conditioning. **1978** M. WALKER *Pioneer Crafts Early Aust.* 32 Station owners found the costs of maintaining shepherds and the outposts with their temporary fencing too large a cost to bear and enclosed and subdivided their large holdings with post and rail fencing.

c. Used *attrib.* and *ellipt.* for *post and rail fence.*

1829 R. DAWSON *Statement* 127 Above *fifteen miles* of permanent Post And Rail inclosures had been finished. **1836** *Cornwall Chron.* (Launceston) 27 Feb. 4 A farm of 2,560 acres .. the whole fenced in, part post and rail and partly log. **1843** R.D. MURRAY *Summer at Port Phillip* 124 The fence most in use is that called 'post and rail', stout and durable in its nature, usually about five feet high. **1852** F. LANCELOTT *Aust. as it Is* I. 137 The three rail 'post and rail' is the most usual. **1861** 'OLD BUSHMAN' *Bush Wanderings* 238 It is little wonder that steeple-chasing should be a favourite amusement in this land of 'posts and rails'. **1887** A. NICOLS *Wild Life & Adventure* 101 The sheep-yard at Mike's consisted of the usual circular post-and-rail enclosure, four feet high. **1902** F. RENAR *Bushman & Buccaneer* 52 The Honourable Dorothy Brand has earned quite a reputation in the post-and-rail country over which hounds run in N.S.W. **1909** *Bulletin* (Sydney) 18 Feb. 14/1 Bill Williams and Dad were holding up the post-and-rail at the south-west corner of the rape paddock. **1929** C.H. WINTER *Story of 'Bidgee Queen* 17 And by his side a pony swings A mile along the post-and-rail. **1940** E. HILL *Great Austral. Loneliness* (ed. 2) 339 The loneliness that they have valued .. takes them to itself, leaving a few nameless post-and-rail graves in the rank grasses. **1947** J.W. GORDON *Under Wide Skies* 20 And my thoughts drift back to childhood with a sentimental yearning For the old-time dog-leg fences and the sturdy post-and-rail. **1973** R. ROBINSON *Drift of Things* 123 Two piglets .. were put into a post and rail sty and fed with all the scraps and slops from the kitchen.

2. a. In the phr. **post and rail tea,** a coarse tea of inferior quality, so-called because particles of stalk, etc., float on its surface (but see also quot. 1907, sense 2 b.).

1843 *Sydney Morning Herald* 5 Oct. 4/3 Awful accounts related of cruel masters, boney meat, post-and-rail tea, black flour, etc. **1852** G.C. MUNDY *Our Antipodes* I. 329 A hot beverage of 'post and rail' tea; it might well have been a decoction of 'split stuff' or 'iron bark shingles' for any resemblance it bore to the Chinese plant. **1855** W. HOWITT *Land, Labor & Gold* I. 256 Post-and-rail tea, that is, a collection of sticks, rather than of tea-leaves. **1873** J.C.F. JOHNSON *Christmas on Carringa* 1 Good 'post and rail' tea in abundant quantity. **1896** *Bulletin* (Sydney) 25 Jan. 27/1 If I'd strained some of the post-and-rail tea I've seen there wouldn't be much left to drink. **1901** H. LAWSON *Joe Wilson & his Mates* 72, I didn't feel inclined for corned beef and damper, and post-and-rail tea. **1946** A. THURIAN *Bush Tea & Overlanders* 18 Time doesn't count, one's job comes first, always fresh the dampers, With fresh-cut beef, post and rail tea, johnny cake that pampers. **1956** T. RONAN *Moleskin Midas* 16 He .. robbed a few stores which carried no goods more precious than post-and-rail tea and moleskin trousers. **1975** R.O. MOORE *Sunlit Plains Extended* 17 The 'post and rail' tea cost about 1s. 6d. per lb.

b. *Ellipt.* for *post and rail tea.* Also **post(s) and rails.**

1858 'A. PENDRAGON' *Queen of South* 19 'Good tea this,' asserted Jack... 'Rather full of stems,' ventured Frank, dubiously. 'Stems be hanged,' replied Jack; 'you should have tried the 'posts and rails' at Currumbumbula.' **1871** *Illustr. Sydney News* 18 Mar. 154/1 Many a pannikin of tea has been dipped up from the posts and rails in the billy. **1884** *Austral. Tit-Bits* (Sydney) 10 July 8/3 The beverage being that delicious one known as post and rails. **1907** C. MACALISTER *Old Pioneering Days* 12 The tea for which we paid 6s. per lb. was known as 'posts and rails', because it was generally retailed mixed with small chips or shavings to add to the grocer's weight. **1916** 'T.O. LINGO' *Austral. Comic Dict.* 28 *Post and rail*, in Australia a frequent fence; in bush tea a frequent offence. **1948** F. CLUNE *Wild Colonial Boys* 128 'Sit down, Bill, and have a bit of fish and some post-and-rails'. . . This was the bushman's name for bulk tea. The tea merchants added wooden chips for make-weight. **1976** C.D. MILLS *Hobble Chains & Greenhide* 105 Give us another mug of that 'post and rail' and don't be so damn curious.

post and wire. *Obs.* In the phr. **post and wire fence,** a fence of vertical uprights and wire horizontals. Also *ellipt.*

1891 'ROUSEABOUT' *Jackeroo* 50 Brand's next move was to let a contract to grub and burn off one hundred acres of land for cultivation. This he enclosed with a post-and-wire fence, known as a cattle fence. **1897** *Bulletin* (Sydney) 11 Dec. 30/1 We heard them lift the post and wire and fling the cap-rails down. **1913** W.K. HARRIS *Outback in Aust.* 150 It is now sub-divided into sixty-eight sheep-proof paddocks, by well-constructed fences, mostly of the 'post and six-wire' style.

post-boy. *Jacky Winter*, see JACKY *n.*[2] Also **post-sitter.**

1911 J.A. LEACH *Austral. Bird Bk.* 121 Australian Brown Flycatcher . . Post-Boy. **1919** *Bulletin* (Sydney) 16 Jan. 24/4 'Post-sitter' (brown fly-catcher). **1931** N.W. CAYLEY *What Bird is That?* 64 Brown Flycatcher . . also called . . Post-boy. **1954** C. BARRETT *Wild Life Aust. & New Guinea* 157 'Post sitter', 'post-boy' . . are other names for 'Jacky Winter'.

pot, *n.* [Spec. use of *pot* vessel for cooking, boiling or (sense 2) for holding liquor.]

1. *Obs. Boiling establishment*, see BOILING 3.

1847 J.D. LANG *Cooksland* 135 They are 'sent to pot', as it is termed, or boiled down for their tallow. **1848** *Maitland Mercury* 31 May 2/4 The cattle are every day gathering tallow, and qualifying themselves to go to *pot* in the plenitude of fatness. **1879** *Queenslander* (Brisbane) 19 Apr. 495/2 Stockowners will to the last hope for a change in their favor whereby they may escape the prospect of the relief afforded them by 'the pots'. . . A few weeks dry weather, and materials for devastating fires will be far too abundant for safety. . . It will then be to 'the pots', or 'to pot' as an alternative. **1888** A.P. MARTIN *Oak-Bough & Wattle-Blossom* 126 A good time had arrived for the squatters of the Heaton district, an actual buyer having suddenly come amongst them, and for the time, at any rate, they were independent of 'the Pots', as the boiling-down establishments were called.

2. A medium-sized measure of beer.

1915 A.T.M. JOHNSON *Austral. Life* 55 'Oh! Colonial Beer. Well give me a glass.' . . 'Ain't got no glasses; sell it by the pot.' **1917** *Huon Times* (Franklin) 19 Jan. 2/5 It was resolved that an ultimatum be presented to local publicans informing them that unless 'pots' and 'long glasses' were not [*sic*] reduced by Wednesday a strike would ensue. **1938** *Bulletin* (Sydney) 16 Mar. 21/2 The cost of living down there is the same as in Sydney—'sixpence a pot'! **1945** G. CASEY *Downhill is Easier* 9 They were working-men's pubs, and they didn't have any bars where pots weren't served. **1955** *Overland* v. 5 I've just had a chicken counter lunch and a couple of pots up at the pub. **1974** R. ROBINSON *Give it Bloody Go, Mate!* 85 When you got to the big stuff a ten ounce 'pot' followed at twenty-five cents and measured up roughly to the Pommie half pint. **1978** B. ST. A. SMITH *Spirit beyond Psyche* 20 He swallowed the rest of his beer in a gulp and raised his fingers in a Vee-sign. 'Make that two pots, barman,' he shouted. **1984** *Canberra Times* 6 July 1/6 'In my youth I used to drink up to 30 pots a day,' he said. 'My body doesn't need it any more. I still have a few grogs, but now I like to get to bed at about half past seven.'

3. *fig.* In the phr. **to put the** (or someone's) **pot on,** to inform on, to thwart the prospects of.

1864 *Bell's Life in Sydney* 4 June 2/6 The police are, of course, severely censured by everybody for 'neglect of duty', and they, in turn, 'put the pot on' magistrates for the mischievous leniency they show. **1899** *Truth* (Sydney) 24 Sept. 7/1 P.M. Caswell 'Puts the Pot on' the In Camera Process. **1907** *Ibid.* 30 June 10/8 *Alleged blackmail.* A threat to put Potts's pot on. **1916** *Ibid.* 26 Mar. 4/2 This 'severely reprimanded' gentleman Hummer Hosie is presumably still a policeman zealously engaged in 'putting the pot on' spielers. **1934** W. HATFIELD *River Crossing* 211 He's pretty near put his own pot on, by tearin' out here so's he'll be back when he's called at ten in the mornin'. **1949** R. PARK *Poor Man's Orange* 190 By God, if she opens her big mouth I'll tell the world she was right in there with the rest of them. I'll put her pot on, the bitch, thinking she's so holy. **1957** V. PALMER *Seedtime* 119 There's an election coming on, and there's a chance I'll be dumped. . . This afternoon's work has probably put my pot on. **1977** J. O'GRADY *There was Kid* 127 Our parents, however, had a saying for every occasion. . . 'Somebody put his pot on.'

pot, *v.* [f. prec., perh. infl. by *pot* to outdo, outwit.] *trans.* To inform on (a person); to secure the conviction of.

1911 A. WRIGHT *Gamblers' Gold* (1923) 100 You can't come that tale. Why should I pot th' bloke? **1911** W.G. SPENCE *Hist. A.W.U.* 40 Mr Head was arrested in court and run into the dock without being given a chance to instruct a lawyer or give up the keys of his office. Judge Windeyer did his best to 'pot' him with the rest, but the jury did not accept his urgent appeal to them. **1916** J.B. COOPER *Coo-oo-ee!* 108 They've got to try to hang some cove or else they'd lose their job. The more men they pot the better they're fixed in their jobs. **1945** S.J. BAKER *Austral. Lang.* 207 A few general expressions connected with school life . . *to pot someone* or *to put someone's pot on*, to inform on. **1953** 'CADDIE' *Caddie* 230 What dirty swine has potted me?

potato.

1. [Prob. Br. dial.: see OED(S 5 c. and EDD 2. Used elsewhere but chiefly Austral.] In the collocation **clean potato,** a person whose character is beyond reproach; a plan, activity, etc., which is 'above board'. Freq. in the negative.

1853 H.B. JONES *Adventures in Aust.* 119 You do not know whether the man who addresses you is or has been a convict; and it is not very complimentary to ask one who speaks to you, 'Are you', in the idiomatic phraseology of the bush, 'a clean potato?' **1867** *Sydney Punch* 29 June 42/1 A strategem which was anything but the 'clean potato'. **1892** *Truth* (Sydney) 7 Feb. 3/2 Some time ago *Truth* ventured to gently insinuate that the smiling and large-mouthed Rosa was not exactly the clean potato. **1917** R.D. BARTON *Reminisc. Austral. Pioneer* 57 The gentleman who had purchased my father's station was not what we call 'the clean potato'. **1921** K.S. PRICHARD *Black Opal* 148, I ain't always been what you might call the clean potato. **1931** 'BRENT OF BIN BIN' *Back to Bool Bool* 233 She was only the great-granddaughter of old Larry Healey of Little River, none so clean a potato, if rumour was correct. **1941** S.J. BAKER *Pop. Dict. Austral. Slang* 56 *A clean potato*, a free or unconvicted person, one with unblemished character. **1962** T. RONAN *Deep of Sky* 42 Some of the grand old pioneers and land-takers of history were not quite the clean potato.

2. Used *attrib.* in Special Comb. **potato field** *Tas. obs.*, *ploughed field*, see PLOUGHED; **land,** fertile land; land esp. suitable for growing potatoes.

1909 G. SMITH *Naturalist in Tas.* 61 Another feature is the presence upon the plateau of Wellington and Ben Lomond of extensive level fields of large rounded boulders of diabase, known locally as '**potato**' or 'ploughed' **fields**, which do not support any soil or vegetation owing to the gaps between the rocks, through which the rain washes all the detritus away. **1886** J.A. FROUDE *Oceana* 92 Behind the crags the land was green and undulating, and extremely rich. They call it the **Potato Land**; all the Australian sea-towns are supplied from it. **1903** *Sporting News* (Launceston) 31 Jan. 3/6 But what sort of a time of it will my relative have when he returns to 'potatoland'. **1920** B. CRONIN *Timber Wolves* 163 Nature's about the most inconsistent cuss that ever was. . . She'll cover potato land with a mess of sage, sword-grass and gum sticks that you'd swear wouldn't grow nowhere but on the edge of the plains.

3. Shortening of 'potato peeler', rhyming slang for SHEILA.

1959 D. NILAND *Gold in Streets* 54 'He got hold of a potater. He'll see us later.' 'Any good?' Danno whispered. 'Who?' 'The sheila.' **1966** —— *Pairs & Loners* 99 Even the potater, I'd given her a fiver for herself, and I didn't even want her garters for it. **1971** B. HUMPHRIES *Bazza pulls it Off*, If I don't make it with a nice broad-minded potato tonight I'll give that quack a knuckle sandwich!!!

potato orchid. The saprophytic terrestrial orchid *Gastrodia sesamoides* (fam. Orchidaceae) of s. and e. Aust., incl. Tas., and N.Z., having large, thick rhizomes; *native potato* (a), see NATIVE *a.* 6 a.

1914 F. SULMAN *Pop. Guide Wild Flowers N.S.W.* II. 179 *Gastrodia sesamoides.* 'Potato Orchid'. . . The potato-like tubers of this species were roasted and eaten by the natives of Tasmania. **1930** C. BARRETT *Sherbrooke* 37 The Potato-orchid is a Sherbrooke Gully plant more curious than beautiful. **1961** *Meanjin* 6 Cucumber, potato and even onion orchids. **1984** D.T. & C.E. WOOLCOCK *Austral. Terrestrial Orchids* 74 The cinnamon-brown colouring of the flower has given it one common name of Potato Orchid.

potch. Also **potsh.** [Of unknown origin; now used elsewhere but recorded earliest in Aust.] Opal that has little or no play of colour and is of no value; opaliferous material found in association with precious opal. Also in the phr. **potch and** (or **with**) **colour** and as **potch opal.**

[**1857** A. FAUCHERY *Lettres d'un Mineur en Australie* 197 Une simple plaque souterraine,—ce qu'on nomme, en langage de mines, une *tache* (patch) ou une *poche* (pocket).] **1896** *Jrnl. & Proc. R. Soc. N.S.W.* XXX. 256 The dull, milky, and opaque stones are called 'potsh' by the miners. **1900** J.S. GUNN *Opal Terminol.* (1971) 35 Demand for potch with color . . active. **1907** A. MACDONALD *In Land of Pearl & Gold* 119 Potch is simply opal without the living fire, or, as the miners say, 'opal a million years too young'. **1912** *Empire Mag.* (London) Nov. 282/1 A pocketful of 'potch-and-colour'—that is 'potch' with a slight 'colour' of opal. **1921** K.S. PRICHARD *Black Opal* 16 They had not seen anything but bony potch for a while. **1937** R.H. CROLL *Wide Horizons* 28 'Potch' . . suggests opal in the course of formation—'unripe opal', as someone called it. It is often charged with fire and shot with lovely blues and greens, but these do not gleam in shadow as true opal does. **1944** K.S. PRICHARD *Potch & Colour* Foreword, The chips opal-miners put in a small bottle and call 'potch and colour'—poor and fiery opal, that is. **1956** B.J. RAYMENT *My Towri* 36 Opals were almost always dotted through the band, but a great number were valueless, being what is usually called 'potch' opal. **1965** C. JOHNSON *Wild Cat Falling* 125 His eyes are faded like potch opal. **1981** A. WILKINSON *Up Country* 6 How to follow a trace of opal from its first tentative flicker until it . . peters out in a sea of muddy 'potch' (colourless worthless opal).

pot-hole. *Mining.* [Transf. use of *pot-hole* a naturally-worn hole.] A shallow excavation made in prospecting for gold or opal.

1890 'R. BOLDREWOOD' *Miner's Right* 55 All the gold in the locality appeared to have been shovelled by malignant gnomes into one crevice, in the familiar phrase of the miners, 'a pot hole'. **1940** I.L. IDRIESS *Lightning Ridge* 90 For a time I sank pot-holes alone then went mates with little Archie Campbell. **1967** —— *Opals & Sapphires* 112 Keep the find quiet until you have sunk more potholes to prove that it is worth while pegging out.

Hence **pothole** *v. trans.*, to search (an area) for gold or opal by digging such holes. Also as *vbl. n.*

1885 H. FINCH-HATTON *Advance Aust.* 185 In Queensland the run of gold is very irregular, and never of any great extent. Seldom at any depth, it is generally confined to 'pot-holing' and 'crevicing' in the banks and bed of the creeks. **1896** J.W. ROBERTS *Mining Industry N.S.W.* 64 These gullies . . were potholed by jackaroos, paddocked by Chinese, and afterwards ground-sluiced by Europeans!

potoroo /pɒtə'ru/. [Prob. a. Dharuk *badaru*.] A small, long-nosed, nocturnal macropodoid of the genus *Potorous* inhabiting areas of dense ground vegetation of s.e. (and formerly s.w.) Aust. See also *kangaroo rat* KANGAROO *n.* 5.

1789 J. WHITE *Jrnl. Voyage N.S.W.* (1790) 286 (*caption*) A Poto Roo. **1840** T.J. BUCKTON *W.A.* 77 The Potoroo is . . only of one species . . a diminutive kangaroo, commonly called the kangaroo rat. **1907** FOUNTAIN & WARD *Rambles Austral. Naturalist* 38 There are several local varieties of the potoroo. **1943** C. BARRETT *Austral. Animal Bk.* 100 The dark rat-kangaroo, known to the natives of Port Jackson as the potoroo . . is now a rare animal. **1970** W.D.L. RIDE *Guide Native Mammals Aust.* 64 Potoroos apparently require the dense natural vegetation of their habitat for protection. **1981** *Bulletin* (Sydney) 17 Mar. 35/1 Scientists in Tasmania have been given nearly $150,000 to study baby potoroos.

potsh, var. POTCH.

potstick. [Transf. use of *potstick* a stick for stirring food or washing in a pot.] A pole used to agitate a fleece immersed in a cleansing liquid. Also *attrib.*, and as *v. trans.*

1899 G. JEFFREY *Princ. Australasian Woolclassing* 89 When wool is scoured by the pot-stick system it is first soaked in one or two tanks of scouring liquid, and then lifted out and drained before being finally washed off. **1904** *Worker* (Sydney) 16 Oct. 8/1 Potsticking looks easy—and so simple. You just work the wool to and fro in the crate with a stick for a few minutes then lift it out, also with the stick, and dump it on a hand barrow. **1977** G.W. LILLEY *Lengthening Shadows* 73 They did not overload the boxes with wool but what they did put in was pot-sticked from one end to the other until it was clean.

pouched mouse. [f. *pouched* marsupial + *mouse*, from the mouse-like appearance and size of the animal.] Any of several small carnivorous marsupials, esp. DUNNART and PHASCOGALE 1. See also *marsupial mouse* MARSUPIAL 1.

1888 O. THOMAS *Catal. Marsupialia & Monotremata* 287 Little Pouched Mouse. Size rather small, general form murine. **1894** R. LYDEKKER *Hand-Bk. Marsupialia & Monotremata* 166 Although . . the name of Pouched Mice is far from being free from objection, yet since the scientific names of neither this nor the following genus lend themselves readily to conversion into English, we are compelled to use the colonial designation. **1899** R. SEMON *In Austral. Bush* 37 *Sminthopsis crassicaudata*, the 'pouched mouse' of the settler. **1926** A.S. LE SOUEF et al. *Wild Animals Australasia* 354 The *Sminthopsis* are the smallest of the pouched mice, and may be distinguished by their small, slender feet. **1935** H.H. FINLAYSON *Red Centre* 61 Several species of pouched-mice which are at least occasional flesh eaters. **1974** *Bulletin* (Sydney) 30 Nov. 27/3 The pouched mouse has caused quite a stir of excitement in the Wildlife Service.

poufter, var. POOFTER.

poultice, *n.* [Fig. use of *poultice* a medicament.]

a. *Obs.* A large wager.

1902 *Sporting News* (Launceston) 22 Nov. 3/1 The connections of the stable which shelters the son of Tostig followed the nag, and put a good 'poultice' on him. **1903** *Ibid.* 20 June 3/1 The party connected with her will gather in more than shekels, for they are just the company to have a good 'poultice' on. **1915** A. WRIGHT *Sport from Hollowlog Flat* 3 We're going to put a poultice on a cert.

b. *transf.* A (large) sum of money.

1904 *Truth* (Sydney) 28 Aug. 1/8 Well, it would take a pretty big 'poultice' to enable a girl to stand being cuddled by coal-black Merzouk! **1918** A. WRIGHT *Over Odds* 26 It turns out that yer noble's heir to all her dough—an' it's er tidy poultice I don't mind tellin' yer, a fortune in fact. **1951** E. LAMBERT *Twenty Thousand Thieves* 235 It's only two days to pay day and I've got a poultice in that pay-book of mine. **1956** —— *Watermen* 47 Used to have a couple of service stations at Albury. Suddenly sold 'em, bought a boat, and became a fisherman. Mad the bastard! Reckons he likes it! Making a poultice with his garages. **1979** *Sun-Herald* (Sydney) 24 June 143 A bloke . . made a poultice in recent weeks when he sold Rupert a quarter of a million Channel Ten shares.

c. *spec.* A mortgage.

1932 K.S. PRICHARD *Kiss on Lips* 184 Mick Mallane . . sayin' if the bank wanted his farm, poultice or no poultice, it'd have to go out and take it from him. **1934** T. WOOD *Cobbers* 134 Men talked about their blister, or their poultice, which means a mortgage, with complacency. **1959** K.S. PRICHARD *N'Goola* 38 When the farm was free of its 'poultice', her father had promised to hand over to Sam . . but droughts, and a fall in the price of wheat, kept him battling to pay even interest on the mortgage. **1980** B. HORNADGE *Austral. Slanguage* 267 A mortgage, often is referred to as a *poultice*, probably because it is something which, when applied, is difficult to lift off the object (i.e. house or farm).

poultice, *v. Obs.* [f. prec.] *trans.* To back (a horse) heavily; to exact money from.

1904 *Sporting News* (Launceston) 2 Jan. 3/1 The figures would have been larger had there been no other channel available for punters to 'poultice' their fancies. *Ibid.* 9 Jan. 3/1 Stebbings made no secret that his neddy was after the honor, and he was poulticed a warm favorite. **1907** *Truth* (Sydney) 26 May 10/7 *(heading) A common cabby* has the haw-don't-cher-know-dacity to *poultice patrician Egan, of Parramatta*, for a 'arf jim cab fare.

pound. [Prob. transf. use of *pound* enclosure.]

1. See quot. 1953.

1937 M. TERRY *Sand & Sun* 247 Issuing from a low gap, where it drained a 'pound', a sandy creek linked up with an attenuated arm of Lake White. **1950** A. GROOM *I saw Strange Land* 18 The Waterhouse Range . . contains an excellent example of a 'pound'—the term given to these larger hollowed centres surrounded by the remaining outer walls of a mountain that was once high and massive. **1953** C.F. LASERON *Face of Aust.* 93 In the Flinders Range [S.A.] . . pressure came from north and south also, resulting in the formation of large domes and basins. In the final erosion the hills retained their dome-shaped forms; the harder layers stand out in series of concentric steps, the outward slopes gradual but the inward slopes steep. The basins remain as huge natural amphitheatres encircled by tier above tier of rocky ledges. These basins are known locally as pounds. **1986** *Canberra Times* 26 Oct. 12/6 Wilpena Pound . . is a massive basin preserved by jagged quartzite peaks around its edge. . . The pound and the ranges are ideal for hiking, bushwalking . . and camping.

2. A punishment cell in a prison; solitary confinement.

1967 *Kings Cross Whisper* (Sydney) xxxviii. 10/2 *Pound*, punishment cells in boob. **1974** J. MCNEIL *How does your Garden Grow* 54 Yer know it's a *pinch*, I suppose? Get sprung with it and yer off tap, yer know that? . . Three days pound its likely to get yer.

poverty bush. [Spec. use of *poverty*, as in the names of plants growing in poor soil: see OED 8.] Any of many shrubs of drier Aust., usu. of the genera *Eremophila* (see *emu bush* (a), EMU *n.*[1] 3) and *Sclerolaena* (fam. Chenopodiaceae).

1931 M. TERRY *Hidden Wealth* 41 Poverty bush, fresh young spinifex . . scrub of a hundred kinds and shapes hide the red sand of this land. **1958** F.B. VICKERS *Mirage* (ed. 2) 55 They went down to a wash where there were a few sparse clumps of poverty bush. **1977** D. STUART *Drought Foal* 182 Poverty bush stretching from the grey green salt grass coastal flats to the pitiless sands and pindan scrub.

poverty pot. A (small) container in which an alluvial miner accumulates particles of gold.

1948 M. UREN *Glint of Gold* 40 Dryblowing is a term used for the process of obtaining gold from the surface material without the use of water. . . The gold won is put in a receptacle called by the miners the 'poverty pot'. **1966** E. WALLER *And there's Gold out There!* 21 Alluvial produced a small pill-bottle—his own empty 'poverty-pot'. **1975** H.K. GARLAND *Panning & Prospecting* 35 If you only intend to wash each dish down to the point where you can roughly assess its value, then you need a larger container which is usually called a 'poverty-pot'. A tin billycan makes a good poverty-pot. **1980** N. KING *Colourful Tales* 75 Father taught us how to pan off correctly and to save the specks of gold in 'poverty pots', which in our case were glass jars.

powerful owl. The large owl *Ninox strenua* of e. and s.e. mainland Aust., having predom. brown and cream plumage and a deep, resonant, two-note hoot.

1844 J. GOULD *Birds of Aust.* (1848) I. Pl. 35, *Athene strenua* . . Powerful Owl. **1909** *Emu* VIII. 247 Among them could be heard . . the screech of the Powerful owl (*Ninox strenua*). **1942** *Bulletin* (Sydney) 29 July 13/2 The powerful owl is a monument of strength and stoush. **1953** A. RUSSELL *Murray Walkabout* 49 The powerful owl is the largest of the Australian owls, and one of the largest in the world. **1984** M. BLAKERS et al. *Atlas Austral. Birds* 306 The Powerful Owl . . lives alone or in pairs and occupies a permanent territory containing a number of roost sites.

pozzie, pozzy, varr. POSSIE.

P-plate. One of a pair of plates bearing the letter P which must be displayed on the front and rear of a vehicle being driven by the holder of a provisional licence. Also *attrib.*

1969 *Statutory Rules* (Vic.) 94 These Regulations may be cited as the Motor Car ('P' Plates) Regulations 1969. **1971** J. O'GRADY *Aussie Etiket* 55 With four surf boards on top, and a P-plate on the stern, they will overtake you. **1978** L. RANDALL *Austral. Family Plays* 86 He's just got himself a new red sports car. You wouldn't believe it, but he's still a 'P. Plate' driver.

prad. [Br. slang *prad* a horse, by metathesis from Du. *paard*. Not attested in Br. use after *c* 1900: see OED(S.] A horse.

1812 J.H. VAUX *Mem.* (1819) II. 198 *Prad*, a horse. **1841** *Sydney Herald* 21 Sept. 3/1, I really think their crack prads are fed on old butter firkins. **1860** *Bell's Life in Sydney* 19 May 3/1 Gallant policemen on proud prancing prads, Gracefully danced. **1875** R. BRUCE *Dingoes* 106 And 'tis the stockman's place to shoe What he calls his own prads. **1894** A.B. BELL *Austral. Camp Fire Tales* 88, I rolled on to me ole prad arter a partin' glass with me mates, and continued my journey. **1918** *Truth* (Sydney) 13 Jan. 1/6 Racing prads are like women's tempers—very uncertain. **1930** A.E. YARRA *Vanishing Horsemen* 57 'Where's those prads o' yours Mister?' . . 'I'll lay you an even hundred my mare beats yours.' **1943** *Bulletin* (Sydney) 22 Dec. 12/3 Horses have a love for an early-morning camp, but old bushmen hold it as infallible the rule that a prad which lies down at sunset is ailing. **1967** G. JENKIN *Two Yrs. Bardunyah Station* 40 We've got a dozen prads out there that make old Curio look like a broken-down brewer's horse. **1977** *Courier-Mail* (Brisbane) 31 Mar. 4/5 It would surely be more appropriate for the riding [for democracy] to be done on some business man rather than on a prad.

prat, *v.* [Perh. f. *prat* the backside: see OED(S *sb.*[2] Prob. not excl. Austral.: see Partridge.] In the phr. **to prat** (oneself, one's frame) **in,** to butt in, to push oneself forward. Also *intr.*

1903 *Truth* (Sydney) 1 Feb. 5/4 When speaking about the safe at Auburn Woolford said, 'You ought to 'prat' yourself in with the two men,' and witness replied, 'No, I am too weak.' **1918** *Kia Ora Coo-ee* Mar. 11/3 And when the war came, I prats in my frame. **1927** F.C. BIGGERS *Bat-Eye* 10 These dancin' stunts was jakeloo—a bloke Jist prats 'is frame in, an' selects a girl. **1956** T. RONAN *Moleskin Midas* 97 If you hadn't pratted in, I could'a got clean away to the Territory before Devlin got back. **1964** G. JOHNSTON *My Brother Jack* 111, I didn't know you were going to have a bit of a rort here. . . I had no intention of pratting in.

prawn.

1. *fig.* [In sense 1 a. used elsewhere but chiefly Austral.]

a. A fool; also as a generalized term of contempt.

1893 D. HEALEY *Cornstalk* 50 Well, boys, the 'Worker' is a prawn—A fool for all his pains; He has the muscle and the brawn, The 'Fat Man' has the brains. **1914** C. MACKANESS *Gem of Flat* 49 'He's a gentleman.' 'A conceited prawn, I suppose.' **1942** A.J. MCINTYRE *Putting over Burst* 16 The flamin' silly prawn! **1944** L. GLASSOP *We were Rats* 27 What an odious prawn this Anderson is, I thought. **1969** A. O'TOOLE *Racing Game* 153 The prawn has talked this little sheila into wanting to sell our horse. **1977** C. MCCULLOUGH *Thorn Birds* 385 'Jussy, this is Cardinal de Bricassart! . . Kiss his ring, quickly.' The blind-looking eyes flashed scorn. 'You're a real prawn about religion. . . Kissing a ring is unhygienic.'

b. (i) In the collocation **raw prawn,** an act of deception; a 'swiftie'; an unfair action or circumstance, a 'raw deal'; something which is 'difficult to swallow'. Also *attrib.*

1940 *Any Complaints* (Newcastle) 4 Apr. 2 Voice . . is invariably heard muttering something about a raw prawn. **1946** R.D. RIVETT *Behind Bamboo* 398 *Raw prawn*, something far-fetched, difficult to swallow, absurd. **1954** *Qld. Guardian* (Brisbane) 20 Jan. 2/5 Snow says he thinks that this is the raw prawn. We do all the work, the mob behind Menzies gets all the dough. **1948** *Khaki Bush & Bigotry* (1968) 103 Andy: I wasn't sitting on your hat. Mac: Think I'm blind, do you? Andy: You big fat loafer. . . Don't come back here trying any of your raw prawn stuff. **1965** E. LAMBERT *Long White Night* 117 Looking like a reprimanded schoolboy, he flushed and apologised: 'Sorry, Johnny. That was a bit like the raw prawn. Seriously, what's she like?' **1972** *Bulletin* (Sydney) 21 Oct. 45/3 It's that kind of inventive grossness that's going to sell the film to those who've got the taste for raw prawn culture.

(ii) In the phr. **to come the raw prawn (on, over, with,** etc.), to attempt to deceive (a person); to misrepresent a situation.

1942 A.J. MCINTYRE *Putting over Burst* 9 They argue there for hours—They start at early morn; Till a loud disgusted voice drawls out, 'Don't come the old raw prawn'. **1951** CUSACK & JAMES *Come in Spinner* 306 Coupla bastards come the raw prawn over me on the last lap up from Melbourne and I done me last bob at Swy. **1963** J. WYNNUM *No Boats to Burn* 38 'Don't come the raw prawn stunt with me,' the girl cried. 'That feller wouldn't shout his old woman a glass of water if she was dying of thirst out in the middle of the Nullabor!' **1948** *Khaki Bush & Bigotry* (1968) 36 The filthy rotten Crab, he'd better not come the raw prawn on us. **1961** L. GLASSOP *We were Rats* (ed. 3) 183 'Hey, just a minute, Mick,' he said. 'Don't come the raw prawn.' **1973** *Woman's Day* (Sydney) 26 Mar. 4/3 'Don't come the raw prawn with me, mate,' he said. 'I can get it back home at Woollies for that price.' **1983** *Canberra Times* 17 Nov. 14/5 Sceptical groans which were, if I translate them correctly, requests for Mr Hawke to stop coming the raw prawn.

2. Special Comb. **prawn (and beer) night,** a social function, chiefly for the male members of a club, at which prawns and beer are served and entertainment offered.

1976 *Bulletin* (Sydney) 19 June 17/1 The RSL was in the ambivalent position of seeming to foster, through its various clubs . . a State network of 'prawn nights' complete with seedy strippers and 'blue movies'. **1977** E. MACKIE *Oh to be Aussie* 55 The men get together and gorge themselves on grog and prawns—they keep their own sheilas out but invite others in—everyone loses their inhibitions. An orgy, Aussie style! . . Quite often after prawn nights, people have prangs with their motor cars. **1980** S. ORR *Roll On* 84, I wouldn't have invited the wives to an RSL prawn and beer night. **1984** *Bulletin* (Sydney) 21 Aug. 53/1 The agency . . will line up . . a top-notch speaker for conventions. . . Some . . draw the line at prawn nights.

preference.

1. [Used elsewhere but important in Aust. where a preferential voting system is commonly employed.] In a system of preferential voting:

a. The numerical ranking given to a candidate on a ballot paper.

1900 E.J. NANSON *Real Value of Vote* 7 All the elector has to do is to number the names on his voting paper in accordance with the order of his preferences for the candidates so far as he has any preferences. **1938** D. WILSON *Preferential Voting System Explained* 8 No candidate having yet received over 50 votes, Davis is declared defeated, and his 18 ballot-papers . . were allotted to the next preferences. **1951** *Official Yearbk. Cwlth.* 83 The candidate with the lowest votes is excluded, and the whole of his ballot papers are transferred to the continuing candidates according to preferences. **1961** D.W. RAWSON *Aust. Votes* 218 The exact size of the government's majority in both Houses depended on the allocation of preferences. **1984** *Sydney Morning Herald* 16 Mar. 4/7 The Liberals admit that even a 10 per cent leakage of preferences would be disastrous.

b. In the collocation **first preference (vote),** the first choice, as expressed by a voter on a ballot paper.

1911 E.E. STENBERG *Principal Electoral Systems* 24 If, for argument's sake, the candidate whom a certain elector has marked on his Ballot Paper as his No. 1 choice, is found to have the *lowest number of 'First Preference' votes*, such candidate is declared 'defeated', and the Returning Officer then proceeds to re-examine and transfer such candidate's Ballot Papers, according to the preferences shown thereon. **1922** *Age* (Melbourne) 19 Dec. 10/2 When the whole of the ballot papers have been counted the first time the candidate with the least first preference votes will be excluded. **1954** MAYER & RYDON *Gwydir By-Election* 157 The swing to the Government was . . greater on the first preference votes than on the final results. **1961** D.W. RAWSON *Aust. Votes* 218 This could not begin until all the first preference votes had been counted. **1972** M. MACKERRAS *Austral. Gen. Elections* 245 Even when the final first preferences are counted, there remains a most important element to consider—the distribution of preferences. **1977** H.R. PENIMAN *Aust. at Polls* 338 Any candidate who has then received a number of first preference votes equal to or greater than the quota is deemed to be elected.

2. With reference to the employment of waterside workers. In the collocation **first** (or **second**) **preference:** see quot. 1934. Freq. *attrib.* as **first** (or **second**) **preference man.** See also BLANK.

1934 *Statutory Rules* (Cwlth. of Aust.) 335 After the expiry of a period of one month from the date of the appointment of a [Waterside Employment] Committee in respect of a port to which Part III. of the Act applies, engagement of waterside workers at that port shall be made in the following order of priority: (a) Waterside workers who are available for employment and are holders of current licences bearing the endorsement 'First Preference'; and (b) Waterside workers who are available for employment and are holders of current licences bearing the endorsement 'Second Preference'; and (c) Waterside workers to whom neither of the last two preceding paragraphs applies who are holders of current licences. **1936** *Argus* (Melbourne) 11 June 9/7 Shipowners and wharf labourers have been asked to nominate representatives for an employment committee which will decide which licences may be endorsed 'First Preference'. Holders of these licences will receive preference in employment. **1950** J. MORRISON *Port of Call* 208 Second Preference defines men entitled . . to second preference for work. **1952** *Coast to Coast 1951* 169 Three hundred Second Preference men all agog at the prospect of becoming Federation men in the next few blessed hours . . with the magical little blue button in our lapels. . . Of getting good ships and being in on the big money. **1955** J. MORRISON *Black Cargo* 24 It is divided into four parts; one for members of the Permanent and Casual Waterside Workers' Union . . one for Second Preference men, and one for Blank Licence men. **1982** LOWENSTEIN & HILLS *Under Hook* 78 About 1933 I went in for a licence. The First Preference was P and C and Federation men, the Second Preference was men that used to follow the wharf as much as they could and the Third Preference was the blanks.

preggo, *a.* [f. *preg(nant* + -O.] Pregnant. Also as *n.*, a pregnant woman.

1951 CUSACK & JAMES *Come in Spinner* 226 Guinea's face lighted with unholy glee. 'A Parker prego? Did I hear right?' **1962** P. WHITE *Four Plays* (1965) 94 'Can't resist the bananas.' 'Yeah. They say you go for them like one thing when you're preggo.' **1975** V. ELLISTON *Tides of Spring* 198 'I can't very well leave you if I'm preggo, can I?' Josie said. **1984** P. ADAM SMITH *Austral. Women at War* 288 We were very down to earth in the WAAF. . . To us, preggos were preggos. Contraceptives were available to the RAAF.

preliminary, *a. S.A. Hist.* Used with reference to the sale of lots of land prior to settlement: see quot. 1859. Freq. as **preliminary land order, section.**

1837 *S. Austral. Rec.* (London) 11 Nov. 13 The situation being one of the best next to the 437 selected by the preliminary holders, there was great competition. **1838** *Ibid.* 13 June 66, I am surprised to see land orders for preliminary sections selling at the price you quote. *Country* sections alone are here considered worth more. **1838** *Southern Austral.* (Adelaide) 23 June 1/4 The Owners and Representatives of Owners of Preliminary or other Land Orders . . are requested to meet at My Office. . . J.H. Fisher, Colonial Commissioner. *Ibid.* 2/1 The Property comprises *two preliminary country sections*, selected with great care and judgment on the admired *banks of the Torrens*, that beautiful river running through, and dividing the land into two sections, forming Nos. *284 and 479* of the Preliminary Survey. **1839** *S. Austral. Rec.* (London) 10 Apr. 176 After the holders of preliminary sections had chosen their land in that district, the purchasers of 80 acre sections were allowed to select their land. *Ibid.* 14 Aug. 228 To be Sold two Preliminary Acres in the City of Adelaide. **1839** *Southern Austral.* (Adelaide) 15 Dec. 3/2 The Commissioner has waived all idea of granting any leases which may have a tendency to defer the right of prior choice, to which the holders of Preliminary Land Orders are undoubtedly entitled. **1840** *S. Austral. Rec.* (London) 1 Jan. 3 The districts near Adelaide . . have been 'gutted' as it were by the preliminary land orders. **1840** *S. Austral. Register* (Adelaide) 23 July 7 The great question at issue in the present correspondence—whether the aboriginal inhabitants or the European preliminary purchasers have the first right of selection from the waste lands of the province—is one of bare justice. **1843** J.F. BENNETT *Hist. & Descr. Acct. S.A.* 14 The price was reduced from *one pound* to *twelve shillings* per acre—one hundred and thirty-four acres of Country, and one acre of Town Land, being given for £81. Hence the 'Preliminary Sections', as those originally purchased were termed, consisted of 134 acres instead of 80 acres as at present. **1859** W. FAIRFAX *Handbk. to Australasia* 145 The first purchasers of land, to whom the colony was indebted for its very existence . . were called 'preliminary' land holders. And, as they had purchased in London, of course, before the first settlers had landed, or surveys had commenced, it became necessary to hit upon some expedient for determining the priority of choice of the land, or 'preliminary section', as it was termed.

premier.

1. With initial capital. The chief minister of the government of an Australian Colony or State. Also used as a title prefixed to the surname of a premier.

1858 N.L. KENTISH *Valedictory ('P.P.C.') Let.* 5 John O'Shanassy, Esq. . . presented my petition to the Legislature . . being himself ex-Premier. **1873** A. TROLLOPE *Aust. & N.Z.* I. 232 Mr Parkes . . was premier and colonial secretary. **1886** F.A. HAGENAUER *Rep. Aboriginal Mission Ramahyuck, Vic.* 3 Report to the Premier the Hon. S. Griffith, at Brisbane. **1891** E.H. HALLACK *W.A. & Yilgarn Goldfields* 6 Now, as first Premier of the colony, his clothes were more suitable for those of a Prime Minister, in the matter of size. **1892** *Bulletin* (Sydney) 7 May 8/1 For the farewell dinner to Premier Dibbs . . tickets were sold. **1903** *Truth* (Sydney) 19 Apr. 1/2 You, no more than any other Premier, can maintain your position. **1909** W.G. SPENCE *Aust.'s Awakening* 267 One Premier after another retired to a good fat billet. **1921** C. CROWE *Policemen & Politicians* 10 The Premier has supplemented this endorsement in Parliament by becoming a member of the I.O.F. **1931** *Age* (Melbourne) 5 June 9/7 The Premiers yesterday devoted most of their time to consideration of the question whether tax-free loan securities should be taxed if they are not converted into the proposed conversion loan. **1943** R. DIXON *Story J.T. Lang* 8 In May-June of 1931, there took place a Premiers' Conference, where . . the 'Premiers' Plan', was devised . . to reduce Government expenditure, including wages, salaries and pensions, by 20%. **1966** *Sun-Herald* (Sydney) 18 41/1 Lang, twice Premier of New South Wales . . will be 90 on Wednesday. **1978** *Age* (Melbourne) 2 Aug. 9/2 Mr Batt . . quickly bowed out of the race for Premier. **1986** *Sydney Morning Herald* 8 Mar. 3/2 The headquarters has now officially joined the Premier, Mr Wran . . in criticism of the Prime Minister.

2. *pl.* A team which wins a PREMIERSHIP.

1891 *Bohemia* (Melbourne) 18 June 20 'I know I'm an awful barracker', admitted the elder frankly, 'but I do so hope the South Melbourne Club will be premiers this year.' **1915** E.M. WEETWOOD *Lure of Land* 114 'Would you like to be put on to a sure thing, straight dinkum?' he asked Mary. 'It's rather early, isn't it, to say who are going to be premiers?' Mary asked, thinking of football. **1930** *Australasian* (Melbourne) 4 Oct. 26/5 *Baseball. Carlton premiers.* Carlton last Saturday annexed its first A grade premiership. **1946** *Sun* (Melbourne) 7 Oct. 23/1, 1945 Bowls Premiers open well. The premiers—Murrumbeena—won its second match on Saturday. **1960** *N.T. News* (Darwin) 12 Feb. 16/8 Saints are minor premiers with Works as runners-up. **1968** K. DENTON *Walk around my Cluttered Mind* 106 Whaddya mean, who's gonna go Premiers, Kev? Sa Kilda, a course. **1973** *Sunday Tel.* (Sydney) 24 June 54/2 Walgett must start favorites to beat last year's premiers Cobar on their home ground.

premiership. [Spec. use of *premiership* the state of being first.] Any organized sporting competition, esp. for team games; the winning of this. Also *attrib.*

1891 *Bohemia* (Melbourne) 11 June 10 Don't go off your heads and back Geelong for premiership. They won't be higher than third, if so high. **1894** C.P. MOODY *Austral. Cricket* 1 Forty years ago cricket in Australia was played by its votaries simply and solely as a means of healthful recreation. There were then none of those incentives to that keen rivalry which has since been created by the establishment of contests for 'Premierships' and 'Pennants'. **1914** *Truth* (Sydney) 7 June 1/4 *Middleweight championship.* Two greatest Americans battle in Sydney for world's premiership. ***c* 1920** 'HAMER' *Search for Bonzer Tart* 75 What? And us lose the chance of getting the premiership? **1930** *Australasian* (Melbourne) 20 Sept. 28/2 A B grade challenge match in connection with the premiership contests of the Victorian Women's Hockey Association was played on September 13. **1939** H.W. DINNING *Austral. Scene* 189 Games . . are all organized into 'fixtures', in which the chief motive to play is to climb through grades to trophies and premierships. **1944** C.S. WATTS *Selected Verse* 38 And game by game the 'Tigers' Slowly tightened their grip On the prize they worked and played for, And they won the Premiership. **1962** *Meanjin* 325 The local footballers won the premiership and decided to hold a private party. **1977** D. WILLIAMSON *Club* (1978) 14 We might have the proudest tradition in the League but we haven't won a premiership in nineteen years. **1986** *Examiner* (Launceston) 21 Mar. 50/2 Devonport . . is after its fourth premiership in 10 years.

prenti, var. PERENTIE.

Presbo. [f. *Presb(yterian* + -O.] A Presbyterian.

1965 L. HAYLEN *Big Red* 78 Catholics were Catholics, Methos were Methodist, Presbos were Presbyterian and the other Protestants were Protestant. **1978** *Bulletin* (Sydney) 28 Nov. 35/3 My sympathies are with the 'continuing' Presbos, who decided they weren't going to have any truck with the Methos, and the Congros and so on. **1982** *Ibid.* 14 Dec. 60/3 These very active Presbos have outlaid nearly a million on erecting buildings at a variety of centres ranging from Bega in the south to Forster to the north of Sydney.

preselection. [Spec. use of *preselection* selection in advance. Used elsewhere but recorded earliest in Aust.] The process by which a political party selects a candidate to stand in an election; the ballot which decides this. Freq. *attrib.*

1930 W.K. HANCOCK *Aust.* 207 Members of branches join with the unionists who live in the same area to choose by a preselection ballot the local party candidate and to elect delegates to attend the State conference of the party. **1941** E. BAUME *I lived These Yrs.* 124 Vital were the Labour [*sic*] leagues, whose preselection ballots decided which candidate would be allowed to stand in the official Labour interest at any election. **1943** J.J. CUSACK *Cusack Plan* 13 This is Jack Cusack, pre-selection candidate for Eden-Monaro. **1957** D. WHITINGTON *Treasure upon Earth* 101 One of these moves was to win The Rocks seat, either by taking the pre-selection from McCann . . or by some other means. **1983** *N.T. News* (Darwin) 27 Sept. 2/4 The blame for bad blood over preselection must go to Pam O'Neil.

press, *n. Shearing.* Shortened form of *wool press* (see WOOL 2).

1848 H.W. HAYGARTH *Recoll. Bush Life* 48 The fleece is . . set aside to be ready for the press, which is in full operation throughout the day. **1851** *Empire* (Sydney) 8 Aug. 27/3 It was the deceased's duty to sew up the wool bales, as they came out of the press. **1874** *Illustr. Sydney News* 19 Dec. 15/1 Mr Fisher had a shed erected at his own expense, floored with deal, fitted up with pens for sheep, bench for rolling fleece and press for packing. **1926** *Bulletin* (Sydney) 11 Feb. 24/1 The pressmen swear that the cross-eyed bum who fed at the shearers' mess Stalked through the shed to dodge the boss and looked at the blasted press.

press, *v. Shearing.* [Spec. use of *press* to compress.] *trans.* To compress (wool) into bales; also with shed as obj.

1840 *Port Phillip Gaz.* 15 Jan. 5 Having engaged a very experienced sorter . . it is their intention to Store, Sort, and Press Wool. **1889** H. EGBERT *Pretty Cockey* 44 The first four classes were pressed into the wool-packs, and duly branded as such, together with the name of the Station. **1965** *Tracks we Travel* 97, I had a shed to press at Stagmount, for ten shearers. **1965** L. WALKER *Other Girl* 110 They had nothing to do but shear sheep, pass fleeces and press wool.

Hence **pressed** *ppl. a.*

1889 H. EGBERT *Pretty Cockey* 45 Some of the rouseabouts did duty as . . sewer-ups of the pressed bales.

presser. *Shearing.* Shortened form of *wool presser* (see WOOL 2).

1872 G.S. BADEN-POWELL *New Homes for Old Country* 176 'Pressers' fill bales out of one of these bins, sew them up, and brand them. **1883** *Illustr. Austral. News* (Melbourne) 28 Nov. 194/3 From these places the 'pressers' are constantly engaged in filling the press with 320 lb. to 400 lb. weight of the various kinds. **1894** *Bulletin* (Sydney) 10 Feb. 20/3 The pressers standing in their box are waiting for the wool. **1911** ST. C. GRONDONA *Collar & Cuffs* 83 One glance at each fleece, as it is thrown to him by one of his subordinates, is sufficient to indicate which truck it has to be put into. It has then to be bundled over to the pressers, where it is baled by steam power. **1953** *Bulletin* (Sydney) 4 Mar. 12/3 We'd just kicked off on the first run of the day when the presser (an ex-pug), his mate and a shearer showed up, each full and highly belligerent. **1965** L. WALKER *Other Girl* 44 Neither of the girls could be shed-hand, presser or shearer, that was clear. **1979** HARMSWORTH & DAY *Wool & Mohair* 150 The *presser's* duty is to press the wool into neat bales at the direction of the classer and brand them with the station brand, description of the wool and number, and enter those details in the wool book.

pretty face. [See quot. 1943.] WHIPTAIL WALLABY. Also **pretty-face wallaby.**

1887 W.S.S. TYRWHITT *New Chum in Qld. Bush* 145 The smaller kind, known as pretty faces or whip tails . . are rather smaller and of a grey colour, with black and white on the face. **1943** C. BARRETT *Austral. Animal Bk.* 93 'Pretty face' (*Wallabia elegans*), is among the most beautiful of all marsupials, with its slender, graceful body, its very long and slender tail, and white-and-grey face markings. **1956** T.Y. HARRIS *Naturecraft in Aust.* 77 The Pretty-face Wallaby . . grazes quietly in open country, usually in the cooler parts of the day, and is not easily disturbed.

prezzie. [f. *pres(ent* + -Y.] A present.

1961 J. ROSE *At Cross* 141 Bella said, 'I brought you quite a lot of prezzies.' **1974** *Bulletin* (Sydney) 30 Apr. 6/1 Was this article a prezzie for Chrissie to your readers in Australia? **1977** P. WHITE *Big Toys* (1978) 18 Darling, I brought you a prezzie from the Other City. **1986** *Nat. Times* (Sydney) 14 Feb. 2/2 Last year's his-and-hers prezzies, matching yellow diamonds.

pricker.

1. A device studded with sharp points, attached to the side of the snaffle against which a horse with a one-sided mouth leans.

1871 *Austral. Town & Country Jrnl.* (Sydney) 13 May 601/3 The followers of The Pearl accounted satisfactorily for his Saturday performance, by his having been ridden in 'prickers', which cut him so much about the mouth as to completely cow him. **1898** *Western Champion* (Barcaldine) 15 Feb. 12/1 The charge arose out of the use of a 'pricker', which was affixed to Passion Fruit's bridle to prevent his habit of 'hanging out'.

2. In the phr. **to have** (or **get**) **the pricker,** to be angry.

1945 S.J. BAKER *Austral. Lang.* 121 A man in a temper is said . . *to have the dingbats, the pricker* or *the stirks.* **1955** D. NILAND *Shiralee* 102 You've got the pricker properly, eh? You'll knock him into next week, will ya? **1965** K. McKENNEY *Hide-Away Man* 103 Trevor said, easily, hiding his interest in a cloak of colloquialism, 'What you got the pricker about?'

prickly, *a.* Used as a distinguishing epithet in the names of plants: **prickly acacia (mimosa, wattle),** any of several prickly shrubs of the genus *Acacia* (fam. Mimosaceae), esp. *A. paradoxa* (see *kangaroo thorn* KANGAROO *n.* 5), and *A. verticillata* of e. Aust., which is also known as *prickly Moses*; **box,** *sweet bursaria*, see BURSARIA; **jack,** DOUBLE-GEE; **Moses** [see quot. 1953], any of several prickly shrubs of the genus *Acacia* (fam. Mimosaceae), esp. *A. verticillata* and *A. ulicifolia* of e. Aust., and *A. pulchella* of w. Aust.; **poison,** the spiny shrub *Gastrolobium spinosum* (fam. Fabaceae) of W.A.

1827 P. CUNNINGHAM *Two Yrs. in N.S.W.* II. 176 The attention of the colony is beginning to be directed toward the **prickly acacia** for hedges. **1829** G.A. ROBINSON in N.J.B. Plomley *Friendly Mission* 19 Sept. (1966) 74 Learnt . . that the kangaroo eat the prickly mimosa. **1835** *Hobart Town Almanack* 63 *Acacia verticillata*. . . Prickly Mimosa, so called from its sharp pointed leaves standing out in whirls round the stem like the spokes of a wheel. **1842** *Tasmanian Jrnl. Nat. Sci.* I. 37 The seeds of *A. verticillata* (prickly Acacia) . . might doubtless be eaten. **1856** *Jrnl. Australasia* I. 37 You may now plant . . acacia virticulata [*sic*] . . commonly known as the prickly wattle. **1868** *Adelaide Punch* 19 Dec. 9/1 The children of the district, bearing beautiful bouquets of prickly acacia (*fencium kangarooium*). **1886** *Once a Month* (Melbourne) Apr. 333 A wide tract of country, with reefs of quartz, and all openly covered with forest trees and much prickly acacia (*acacia armata*) as an undergrowth. **1909** A.J. EWART *Weeds Vic.* 1 The following native plants are included under the head of proclaimed weeds . . the Chinese scrub . . and the Prickly Acacia (*Acacia armata*). **1920** G. SARGANT *Winding Track* 16 The prickly mimosa, being rain-laden, bent with its weight. **1921** A.J. CAMPBELL *Golden Wattle* 42 The Prickly Wattle (*Acacia armata*), or so-called 'Kangaroo Thorn' . . is perhaps the oldest known of Australian Wattles. **1956** F.B. VICKERS *First Place to Stranger* 197 On each side of the track was scrub, prickly wattle and woolly-bush. **1981** G.M. CUNNINGHAM et al. *Plants Western N.S.W.* 375 Prickly Wattle . . can withstand clipping, hence can be used as a hedge plant or for windbreaks. **1984** *N. Qld. Register* (Townsville) 5 Apr. 9/3 Prickly Acacia has been present on properties in this area for more than 30 years and was originally introduced to provide shade for sheep in an attempt to boost lambing percentages. **1904** *Emu* III. 216 Found a Fire-tailed Finch's . . nest just begun in a **prickly box.** **1935** T. RAYMENT *Cluster of Bees* 170 (*note*), I have captured bees . . while they were loaded with bright yellow pollen collected from the 'prickly box' (*Bursaria spinosa*). **1949** *Bulletin* (Sydney) 2 Mar. 14/1, I was chopping at a patch of prickly-box. **1903** H. BASEDOW *Jrnl. Govt. N.-W. Exped.* 23 June (1914) 150 The **prickly Jacks** and burrs are more than a tax on a fox terrier's patience. **1909** J.M. BLACK *Naturalised Flora S.A.* 134 *Emex australis*. . . The fruit forms a larger and fiercer *Prickly-jack* than the *Tribulus terrestris* of the Far North. **1980** J. FITZPATRICK *Bicycle & Bush* 138 *E[mex] australis* is still commonly referred to as 'doublegee' in Western Australia, although eastern states immigrants during the 1890s goldrush introduced their terms, such as . . 'prickly jack'. **1887** *Austral.* (Melbourne) Apr. 9/3 (OEDS) An expedition was now made into the scrub for fishing rods. . . I cannot recommend . . that awful thing which our philosopher called '**prickly moses**'. **1914** N.F. SPIELVOGEL *Gumsucker at Home* 13 A brambly bush locally known as 'Prickly Moses'. **1920** B. CRONIN *Timber Wolves* 130 Thorns on it like a bundle of prickly-moses bush. **1935** T. RAYMENT *Cluster of Bees* 256 At lower depths the dense tea-tree and the 'Prickly Moses' effectively stopped all progress. **1953** T.Y. HARRIS *Austral. Plants* 212 *Acacia juniperina*. . . This species has been known in many localities as 'Prickly Moses', a modification no doubt, both of the now obsolete older generic name 'Mimosa', and of the descriptive title for the foliage. **1963** *N. Austral. Monthly* Dec. 11 Prickly Moses, sometimes called camel bush, is a straggly prickly wattle with small yellow ball flowers. **1968** C.A. GARDNER *Wildflowers W.A.* 55 The common prickly Moses (*A[cacia] pulchella*) . . is a spiny shrub with small feathery leaves. **1980** O. RUHEN *Bullock Teams* 187 In more settled districts Prickly Moses caused some damage. **1897** L. LINDLEY-COWEN *W. Austral. Settler's Guide* 580 **Prickly Poison.** *Gastrolobium spinosum.* A shrub of two to four feet. **1901** J.H. MAIDEN *Plants reputed to be Poisonous* 12 'Prickly Poison' . . Victoria Desert, Western Australia, is poisonous to camels. **1926** *Poison Plants W.A.* (W.A. Dept. Agric.) 46 Prickly Poison is sometimes known as Grover Poison being named after a stock owner who suffered considerable losses from it. **1968** C.A. GARDNER *Wildflowers W.A.* 58 Prickly poison can be destroyed by cutting at the level of the ground. It does not produce root suckers. **1981** J. JESSOP *Flora Central Aust.* 145 Prickly poison . . very poisonous to stock.

priest. *Obs.* KORADJI.

1845 *Sentinel* (Sydney) 29 Jan. 2/6 About half an hour after the body has lain, the Doctor or Priest provides each of the inner class of mourners with a short stick about 6 inches long. **1846** 'COLONIAL MAGISTRATE' *Remarks on Probable Origin* 10 Although the word *Priest* does not appear in the vocabulary of the Natives—the words *Doctor* or *Conjuror* is [*sic*] applied to those old men who assume the guidance in *Coroborees.* **1851** *Athenaeum* (London) 24 May 557 The native doctors are priests and soothsayers also. **1878** R.B. SMYTH *Aborigines of Vic.* I. 28 With them was an old man of an odd and striking appearance, supposed to be a coradje or priest.

prill. *S.A. Mining. Hist.* [Br. dial. (Cornwall) *prill*: see OED *sb.*[4] 1.] Rich copper ore. Freq. as **prill ore.**

1871 *Austral. Town & Country Jrnl.* (Sydney) 4 Mar. 270/3, I was informed that, although only 'prill ore', it would yield from 25 to 35 per cent. pure copper. **1914** *Wallaroo & Moonta Mines* 15 The better class of ore (locally known as 'prill'). **1919** *Guide Bk. Prospectors N.S.W.* (ed. 2) 41 The Carpathia alone has produced many tons of 'prill' ore. **1962** O. PRYOR *Aust.'s Little Cornwall* 85 The pickey-boys .. picked out the prill or high-grade ore and dropped it into boxes.

primary. *First preference,* see PREFERENCE 1 b. In full **primary vote.**

1902 G.A. WOOD *Electoral Reform* 4 He knew he had a chance of just getting through on his primaries only. **1946** E.D. SENIOR *Austral. Systems Voting* 25 The preference votes to the number of the vacancies to be filled shall be termed the 'primary' votes, and shall have equal value in the first count. **1961** C. BURNS *Parties & People* 67 The A.L.P. candidate's marginal lead on the primary votes was nothing like enough to give him a chance of winning the seat. **1962** *Meanjin* 355 There was rather an extraordinary situation in your electorate, was there not? You refer no doubt to the remarkable parity of primary votes between all candidates, including myself? **1970** K.N. GRIGG *How Representative is House of Representatives?* 3 For reasons stated earlier, it is likely that .. the D.L.P. primaries may well fall. **1974** *Mercury* (Hobart) 23 July 5/2 He was third on primaries behind Mr Davies. **1985** *Sydney Morning Herald* 29 Apr. 6/2 An academic has branded coming changes to Queensland electoral system as 'the world's worst zonal gerrymander'. The 'Bjelkemander', as it is known locally, is partly responsible for allowing the National Party to rule Queensland with 38.9 per cent of the primary vote.

Prince Alberts, *pl. Hist.* [Ironic use of the name of *Prince Albert* (1819–1861), Consort of Queen Victoria: see quot. 1945.] Strips of cloth wound round the toes or feet and worn, esp. by a swagman, in place of socks (see esp. quot. 1974); TOE-RAG 1. Also **Royal Alberts.**

1893 K. MACKAY *Out Back* 191 They 'mouched' along .. showing glimpses of brown, unwashed skin above the frayed edges of their 'Prince Alberts', the toes of their bluchers gaping wide. **1900** *Truth* (Sydney) 29 Jan. 7/4 It was a dreary, dirty man, With furtive, foxy leer, And royal-alberts round his toes. **1903** J. FURPHY *Such is Life* 31 Unlapping from his feet the inexpensive substitute for socks known as 'prince-alberts', he artistically spread the redolent swaths across his boots to receive the needed benefit of the night air. **1905** E.C. BULEY *Austral. Life* 54 The rags that serve him for socks are 'Prince Alberts'; he lodges each night in the Moon and Stars Hotel, ground floor. **1912** 'IRONBARK' *Ironbark Splinters* 44 'Prince-Alberts' ain't the fashion now, The shearers all wear socks. **1930** *Bulletin* (Sydney) 29 Jan. 23/3 One of the hallmarks of the genuine swagman used to be the wearing of foot-rags instead of socks. These rags were cut like bandages and were rolled on round toes and foot, finishing just above the ankle. .. Today there are few who know what 'Prince Alberts' are. **1945** S.J. BAKER *Austral. Lang.* 105 Prince Alfreds or Prince Alberts. .. These terms developed from the malign suggestion that the Prince Consort was so poor when he came to England to marry Queen Victoria that he wore toe-rags instead of socks. **1948** M. UREN *Glint of Gold* 107 Most of the entrants in the pedestrian events ran barefooted. Two wore Prince Alberts, which was the rakishly aristocratic name for the primitive practice of tying bits of rag around the toes. **1958** T. QUILTY *Drover's Cook* 5 A chap that takes the time off, Creating such a fuss, I'll wager my Prince-Alberts, Is not as good as us. **1974** B. KIDMAN *On Wallaby* 58, I was introduced to 'Prince Alberts' as a substitute for socks .. long strips of calico, rubbed with a little suet to minimise chafing and wrapped around the foot after the style of puttees.

Prince Alfreds, *pl. Hist.* [The name of *Prince Alfred* (1844–1900), second son of Queen Victoria.] PRINCE ALBERTS.

1896 H. LAWSON *While Billy Boils* (1975) 53 Occasionally someone gets some water in an old kerosene-tin and washes a shirt or pair of trousers, and a pair or two of socks—or foot-rags—(Prince Alfreds they call them). **1945** [see prec.].

Prince of Wales feather. [Amplified and transf. use of *prince's feather* a garden plant of the genus *Amaranthus.*] Any of several plants of the genera *Amaranthus* and *Ptilotis* (both fam. Amaranthaceae). Also **Prince of Wales's feather,** and in *pl.*

1945 J. DEVANNY *Bird of Paradise* 36 The leaves of the Prince of Wales Feather weed which abounded among the grass in the grazing paddocks was used by the farmers as a substitute for cabbage. **1948** H.A. LINDSAY *Bushman's Handbk.* 59 There are many patches of Prince-of-Wales's Feather plant (Amaranthus) whose young leaves make good greens. **1973** H. HOLTHOUSE *S'pose I Die* 37 There was a weed they called Prince of Wales Feathers growing down by the fence along the river. It was a sort of wild spinach.

Princess parrot. [f. the title of Alexandra (1844–1925), Princess of Wales and later Queen-Consort of King Edward VII: see quot. 1863.] The delicately-coloured parrot *Polytelis alexandrae* of arid inland central and w. Aust.; ALEXANDRA PARAKEET. See also *spinifex parrot* SPINIFEX 4. Also **Princess Alexandra('s) parakeet** (or **parrot**), **Princess of Wales(')s) parakeet.**

[**1863** *Proc. Zool. Soc. London* 232 It will enable me to make known .. a new and very beautiful species of Parrakeet pertaining to the genus *Polyteles.* .. The specific appellation I would propose for this novelty is *alexandrae,* in honour of that Princess who .. is destined at some future time to be the queen of these realms and their dependencies.] **1867** J. GOULD *Birds of Aust.* Suppl. (1869) Pl. 62, *Polytelis Alexandrae,* Gould. The Princess of Wales's Parrakeet. **1890** *S. Austral. Register* (Adelaide) 23 Aug. 7/2 Princess of Wales's Parrakeet. .. I yesterday saw two caged specimens of this almost unknown bird. So far as I can learn no other living ones have been brought to Adelaide. **1896** B. SPENCER *Rep. Horn Sci. Exped. Central Aust.* I. 100 It was during this part of the journey that the only specimens seen of the rare Princess Alexandra Parrakeet (*Spathopterus* (*Polytelis*) *alexandrae*) were secured. **1903** H. BASEDOW *Jrnl. Govt. N.-W. Exped.* 20 Sept. (1914) 236 Several Princess of Wales parrakeet (*Spathopterus alexandrae*) were found breeding in the hollows of the gums. **1937** M. TERRY *Sand & Sun* 171 On the Finke River .. at least one hundred Princess Alexandra parrots made life worth while. **1945** C. BARRETT *Austral. Bird Life* 78 Long-tailed birds are the regent parrot or 'smoker' (*Polytelis anthopeplus*) .. the 'green leek' or superb parrot (*P. swainsonii*) .. and the exquisitely coloured Princess parrot (*P. alexandrae*). **1964** M. SHARLAND *Territory of Birds* 37 The first known specimen of the lovely Princess Parrot, whose range extends into the north-western part of the Territory, was taken at Howells Pond near Newcastle Waters. **1976** *Reader's Digest Compl. Bk. Austral. Birds* 270 The princess parrot was named in honour of Queen Alexandra when she was still Princess of Wales. **1982** R. ELLIS *Bush Safari* 79 He thought he had seen a pair of rare Princess Alexandra's Parrots. .. I had seen them in the Gibson Desert some years before. .. One of our party .. recorded them as a possible sighting on her Australian bird-atlassing sheets.

printhy, printy, varr. PERENTIE.

prisoner. *Hist.*

1. CONVICT *n.* 1. Also *attrib.,* and **prisoner of the Crown.**

1800 *Gen. Orders issued by Governor King* 6 Sept. (1802) 11 No Prisoner or Free-man (who is not a Settler) is to leave the place where he is stationed or resides, without a Pass from the nearest Magistrate. **1804** *Sydney Gaz.* 29 July, All Prisoners whatever, either Male or Female, having the *Governor's* permission to be off the Stores, and holding Tickets of Leave, are to appear at the respective Settlements near where they are situated and employed. **1822** *Hobart Town Gaz.* 10 Aug., All Prisoners of the Crown (except those employed on Government Duty), are forbidden to enter the Domain at any Time. **1826** *Monitor* (Sydney) 19 May 2/3 The decent term of *Prisoner* had been substituted by Macquarie, for the degrading one of *Convict,* as the latter designation had in its turn taken place of the old British appellation of *Felon.* **1833** A. OSBORNE *Notes Present State & Prospects N.S.W.* 15 It may be gratifying to learn that there are now no convicts in New South Wales, and also that it is no longer a penal colony. The name appropriated to the convicts is now 'Prisoners of the Crown' as more in accordance with the refined sentiments of humanity. **1839** *Sydney Standard* 7 Jan. 2/3 A very considerable portion of the wealth of this colony is in the hands of persons, who have been, and still are prisoners of the Crown. **1847** *Port Phillip Herald* 28 Sept. 2/3 Instead of having now, as formerly, prisoner shepherds and stock-keepers for nothing, they are compelled to employ men as uncontaminated as themselves at .. more than remunerative wages. **1854** S. SIDNEY *Gallops & Gossips* 58 Big Jem was a convict, or, speaking colonially, 'a prisoner'. **1865** 'SPECIAL CORRESPONDENT' *Transportation* 11 Add to the classes already mentioned the prisoners of the Crown, and the community is complete.

2. Comb. **prisoner labour, labourer, population.** See also CONVICT B. 2.

1828 *Tasmanian* (Hobart) 18 July 2 **Prisoner Labour** cannot be obtained without considerable difficulty. **1835** J. BACKHOUSE *Narr. Visit Austral. Colonies* (1843) 345 The road .. is formed by prisoner labour. **1828** *Tasmanian* (Hobart) 15 Aug. 3 We cannot help congratulating the Colony on the arrival of so many **prisoner labourers.** **1827** *Ibid.* 18 Oct. 2 His uneasy mind seems not to be at rest, till he shall see the **prisoner population** bound down as slaves to their several masters. **1836** *Bent's News* (Hobart) 11 June 4 That part of the prisoner population, being Catholics, who attended to hear Mr Connolly, should in future attend to hear Rev. Mr Ullathorne and Cotham. **1851** H. MELVILLE *Present State Aust.* 51 The British Government .. have lately forwarded some portion of the prisoner population to Western Australia. **1862** BACKHOUSE & TYLOR *Life & Labours G.W. Walker* 265 They published two christian addresses; one to the free, the other to the prisoner population of the Colony.

3. Special Comb. **prisoner constable, overseer, police, servant, settler**: see *convict constable,* etc. CONVICT B. 3.

1834 J. BACKHOUSE *Narr. Visit Austral. Colonies* (1843) 227 Attended by a **prisoner constable,** we returned to Norfolk Bay. **1847** T. ROGERS *Corresp. relating to Dismissal* 25 Jan. (1849) 28, I was attended by a turnkey and a sentry, and sometimes by a prisoner constable. **1829** *Sydney Monitor* 16 Feb. 1500/3 On what ground of propriety did Capt. Crotty employ **prisoner-overseer** Chrawn .. to shoot him birds. **1834** J. BACKHOUSE *Narr. Visit Austral. Colonies* (1843) App. lxi, The employment of prisoner overseers in the Chain-gangs and Road-parties, is liable to many objections. **1838** A. MACONOCHIE *Thoughts on Convict Managem.* 47 Provoked by an unreasonable overseer (such as prisoner overseers often prove). **1839** *Extracts Papers & Proc. Aborigines Protection Soc.* Aug. 110 Field Police .. would also be more steadily well-behaved than a **Prisoner Police,** otherwise so common in the Australian colonies. **1840** *Tasmanian Weekly Dispatch* (Hobart) 24 Apr. 3/2 On the subject of the present order of Prisoner Police. **1807** *HRA* (1916) 1st Ser. VI. 147 **Prisoner Servants** of the Crown are allotted to Settlers. **1827** *Monitor* (Sydney) 20 Apr. 388/2 The late capture of certain run-a-way cut-throats, by some of the prisoner-servants of the settlers on the South Creek. **1840** *Colonial Mag.* (London) II. 73 The free master was greatly in the trammels of his prisoner-servant. **1848** J. SYME *Nine Yrs. Van Diemen's Land* 175 The members of the society engaged not to suffer their prisoner-servants to become possessed of stock. **1832** *HRA* (1923) 1st Ser. XVI. 713, I collected the **prisoner Settlers** and these men .. and performed Divine Service to them.

prison population. *Hist.* [See also *prisoner population* PRISONER 2.] The convict population (of an Australian Colony).

1827 *Monitor* (Sydney) 1 Oct. 679/2 Malicious and libellous comments were dangerous in a colony like this, where the prison population was so great as compared with the free population. **1834** J.D. LANG *Hist. & Statistical Acct. N.S.W.* II. 2 Incite the convict or prison-population to good conduct. **1840** *S. Austral. Rec.* (London) 3 Oct. 211 Not only the prison population is confounded in these libels, but the whole community is represented as demoralized and depraved. **1845** J. DREDGE *Brief Notices* 20 In the older portion of the colony .. the native tribes had long been in pernicious contact with the prison population.

probation, *n.* and *attrib. Hist.* [Transf. use of *probation* 'testing or trial of a person's conduct' (see OED 2); this precedes the U.S. and Br. use of the term in criminal jurisdiction (see OED 3).]

A. *n.*

1. A system for the management of convicts, introduced in Tasmania after the abolition of assignment in 1839: under the system a convict whose conduct continued satisfactory progressed through stages, as confinement, supervised public labour, paid employment, etc., to a pardon. Usu. as **probation system.**

1840 *True Colonist* (Hobart) 24 Jan. 4/1 The Colony is already beginning to feel the effects of the new 'probation system'. **1843** *Portland Mercury* 4 Jan. 1/3 The recent reversion from the Probation to the Assignment System, in Van Dieman's Land, a country previously enjoying abundant and cheap labour, has rendered nearly two thousand prisoners eligible for private service. **1848** J.C. Byrne *Twelve Yrs.' Wanderings* II. 25 Public works are almost at a stand-still for want of money to pay the convicts employed, as it is the policy of the probation system not to exact labour without remuneration. **1851** H. Melville *Present State Aust.* 140 The present probation system is attributed to the late Captain Foster. **1852** J. Bonwick *Notes of Gold Digger* 162 The old Assignment system of convictism was changed for that of Probation in 1840.

2. The condition of one serving a sentence under the probation system; the period of probation; a stage in this.

1840 *True Colonist* (Hobart) 24 Jan. 4/2 Under the new system . . they must work out their advanced probation in the Government gangs, and when they become free, they will be turned loose upon society. **1846** L.W. Miller *Notes of Exile Van Dieman's Land* 268 You whose sentences are for life, will be required to do two years probation on the roads. **1846** C. Rowcroft *Bushranger Van Diemen's Land* I. 35 Nearly a hundred and fifty government servants working on their probation. **1848** J.C. Byrne *Twelve Yrs.' Wanderings* II. 56 The pass-holder is in a lower stage of probation than the ticket-of-leave-holder. The former is retained in a gang or depôt, until he is employed; whereas, the latter is at liberty to go whither he pleases within a certain district. **1865** J.F. Mortlock *Experiences of Convict* 84 My first three years of 'probation' in Australia being at an end, I received a pass making me eligible for employment upon my own account.

B. 1. *attrib.*

1841 *Van Diemen's Land Papers Legis. Council* no. 26 46 The present ticket-of-leave man has served an apprenticeship; the Probation man has learned nothing but to work with pick and shovel. **1844** *Colonial Times* (Hobart) 13 Feb., Four probation lads, the very personification of impudence. **1847** *Hobart Town Herald* 20 Feb. 2/4 The man replied he was the *probation servant* of Mr Parker. **1847** *Launceston Examiner* 12 May 302/4 There was no comparison between probation labour and that under the assignment system. *Ibid.* 303/1 He knew a ticket-of-leave man who formerly received 10s. a-week, who now hired himself out at probation wages of £9 a-year. **1848** *Britannia* (Hobart) 2 Nov. 2/3 Four magistrates in favour of the probation police. **1850** *Ibid.* 28 Feb. 2/3 Doing the dirty work of the Home Government, in trying probationmen already under sentences for life.

2. Special Comb. **probation department,** the government department responsible for the administration of *probation gangs*; **gang, party,** a detachment of prisoners required to complete a term of supervised labour on public works; also *attrib.*; **pass,** a document issued to a prisoner who has served a term of probation, authorizing the holder to obtain private employment; also **pass-holder; station,** an establishment for the accommodation of prisoners serving in probation gangs.

1844 *Colonial Times* (Hobart) 6 Feb., Salaries for the superintendents and overseers in the **Probation Department**, two thousand pounds, and contingent expenses eight hundred and three pounds eight shillings. **1845** J. Franklin *Narr. Hist. Van Diemen's Land* 42, I had . . formed the superintendence of the government gangs into a new department, under the name of the 'Probation Department'. **1841** *Van Diemen's Land Papers Legis. Council* no. 26 39 Would you think a large Immigration so desirable, if you knew that any considerable number of men from the **Probation gangs** would soon be available, when holding tickets-of-leave? **1843** *HRA* (1924) 1st Ser. XXII. 518 Probation Gangs . . will be assembled in Van Diemen's Land. They will be composed first of Convicts who have passed through the period of detention at Norfolk Island, and secondly of Convicts sentenced to transportation for a less term than life, who may be indicated by the Secretary of State for the Home Department as proper to be placed in this class. **1847** *Moreton Bay Courier* 8 May 4/3 All the convicts in probation gangs in Van Diemen's Land will have passed into the state of pass-holders in the course of the next four years. **1856** J. Bonwick *Bushrangers* 10 Despite the festering corruption of probation gangs, there were men of noble generosity. **1841** *Morning Advertiser* (Hobart) 1 Oct. 4/2 We hear so much said against the **probation party** system. **1843** *Colonial Observer* (Sydney) 17 June 1103/1 An officer, entitled Comptroller of Convicts, to be appointed to the charge of the probation parties. **1865** 'Special Correspondent' *Transportation* 32 The others are . . formed into road-gangs—'probation parties' should rather be said, for the convicts are treated with no little deference, and so coarse a word as 'gang' is never used in connection with them. **1843** *HRA* (1924) 1st Ser. XXII. 519 After a Convict shall have passed through the Probation Gang, he will next proceed to the third stage of punishment and become the Holder of a **Probation Pass.** **1843** *Sydney Morning Herald* 15 Sept. 2/4 The holder of a probation pass may, with the consent of the Government, engage in any private service for wages. **1844** *Colonial Times* (Hobart) 9 Jan., In order to afford every facility to the hiring of probation pass-holders, two principal hiring depôts will be formed. **1845** *HRA* (1925) 1st Ser. XXIV. 382 A portion of them will only receive Tickets of Leave or Probation Passes. **1846** *Cumberland Times* (Parramatta) 18 Apr. 3/3 It seems that the bushrangers in their hurry had overlooked a small hut, or outhouse, serving as the dormitory of a probation passholder in the service of Dr Browne. **1842** *Tasmanian Jrnl. Nat. Sci.* I. 283 *Complete* **probation station** is governed by a superintendent, three assistant-superintendents, a competent number of overseers (all free men) a surgeon, a catechist, and a military detachment. **1844** *Portland Mercury* 19 June 4/3 Sundry tons of potatoes, with some turnip and carrot seed, from the 'probation station at Maria Island'. **1851** H. Melville *Present State Aust.* 137 The probation stations being . . placed out of sight, no longer afford amusement to the inhabitants, and the 'jolly probationers' as the colonists term them, are now cooped up on the island. **1861** L.A. Meredith *Over Straits* 7 At Maria Island, the rocky hills, and other so-called 'probation-stations' . . the prisoners were used in tens and twenties, attached to ploughs, harrows, and light carts, with *two* or *three* to each common wheelbarrow, for the purpose of cultivating land.

probationary, *a. Hist.* [f. Probation *n.* 2.] (That consists of) undergoing probation.

1840 *Tasmanian Weekly Dispatch* (Hobart) 21 Aug. 4/3 The immediate effects of the establishment of Probationary Gangs, and the consequent non-assignment of the Convicts on arrival, are already seriously felt. **1841** *Morning Advertiser* (Hobart) 5 Aug. 1/3 To induce the local government to break up the probationary gangs of convicts. **1848** J.A. Jackson *Regeneration Van Diemen's Land* 5 Having passed through this period of rigid discipline . . the convict, if considered eligible for 'transition to a less severe stage of punishment', is introduced into the 'probationary gang'. **1851** *Illustr. Austral. Mag.* (Melbourne) Mar. 159 Among the convict gangs of Tasmania, there prevails an extent of vice and infamy, not exceeded, perhaps never equalled, in the worst ages of pagan darkness. And these gangs too, after their 'probationary' ordeal, are finally scattered over Australasia.

probationer. *Hist.* [f. Probation *n.* 1.] One who is serving a sentence under the probation system.

1840 *S. Austral. Rec.* (London) 29 Aug. 133 By the introduction of the probationers, after a sojourn at Norfolk Island . . more vice will be introduced than by the present system. **1844** *Colonial Times* (Hobart) 2 Jan., We trust the Government will see the urgent necessity of adopting a more stringent system of discipline towards the probationers. *Ibid.* 3 Sept., The lady probationers are 'going a-head' too, in consequence of the delightful manner in which they are indulged in the Branch Factory in the Brickfields. **1845** *Melbourne Standard* 26 Feb. 2/4 In Port Fairy whole acres of grain are lying uncut, from the difficulty in procuring labour; this state of things . . has a speedy prospect of termination from the arrival of immense bodies of probationers from Van Diemen's Land. **1851** H. Melville *Present State Aust.* 135 The probationers were at first worked on the roads and the public works. **1858** T. McCombie *Hist. Colony Vic.* 227 Two thousand probationers, and the like number of free emigrants.

probationism. *Hist.* [f. Probation *n.* 1.] The probation system.

1844 *Colonial Times* (Hobart) 27 Feb., He offered them wages at £9 a year, with rations, etc., for a further period: but the men, feeling the high importance of Probationism, declined so paltry an offer. **1847** *Hobart Town Herald* 30 Jan. 2/2 That ruinous, delusive, and destructive system to the colony 'probationism'. **1847** *Britannia* (Hobart) 16 Dec. 2/3 The power of probationism is fast forcing out of the colony all those who can leave. **1856** J. Bonwick *Bushrangers* 7 Convictism, according to most old settlers, was attended with fewer evils when in the early days, and before the hated period of Probationism.

processional caterpillar. [See quot. 1926.] The caterpillar *Ochrogaster lunifer*, having slender hairs which can cause severe skin irritation. See also Itchy grub. Also **processionary caterpillar, procession caterpillar.**

1918 *Emu* XVIII. 75 The heads waved in exactly the threatening manner of the tails of processional caterpillars. **1926** J. Pollard *Bushland Man* 231 When they migrate, or when seeking a place to pupate, they trek along the ground in single line. . . 'Processional caterpillars' they are called. **1935** K.C. McKeown *Insect Wonders Aust.* 110 This is the Bag-Shelter Moth, the parent of the well-known Processionary Caterpillar. . . When the caterpillars are full fed, they emerge from their shelter, and wander about the countryside in long chains or processions. **1950** *Bulletin* (Sydney) 4 Oct. 12/4 The 'itchy grub' (processional caterpillar) left behind a powerful irritant where 'er he walked. **1980** F.D. Hockings *Friends & Foes Austral. Gardens* 42 (*caption*) Procession Caterpillar. These destructive, hairy caterpillars appear in large numbers. . . Unless removed, they will soon defoliate plants.

Progress Association. An association of residents, usu. in a suburb or small town, concerned primarily with the improvement of local amenities.

1907 *Truth* (Sydney) 9 June 1/7 The Sefton Park Progress Association take themselves seriously. . . The principal result of their efforts last year was the establishment of a telephone bureau at the local post-office. **1944** A.J. & J.J. McIntyre *Country Towns Vic.* 118 The actual work necessary for, say, gardens, is sometimes carried out by the men of the town and district, in a 'working bee' led by the Progress Association. **1947** M. Morris *Township* 63 At the next meeting of the Progress Association, held in the murky end of the little public hall, Mr Vagg spoke. **1960** *N.T. News* (Darwin) 2 Feb. 6/6 Katherine Progress Association will hold its annual general meeting. **1982** *Canberra Times* 14 Nov. 6/4 The chairman of Broulee Progress Association . . said last week that it would be a disaster if the road was built. **1985** *Bombala Times* 18 July 20/2 The Delegate Progress Association has once again achieved a successful public service for our community.

prop, *v.* [Prob. f. Br. dial. or slang *prop* 'the leg; also, the arm extended in boxing; hence, a straight hit': see OED *sb.*[1] 1 e.]

1. a. *intr.* Of a horse: to stop abruptly when moving at speed. Also *transf.*

1844 H. McCrae *Georgiana's Jrnl.* 15 Feb. (1934) 110 Suddenly my pony propped, and I had just time to disengage my limb from the pommel before he started to roll himself on the beach. **1870** E.B. Kennedy *Four Yrs. in Qld.* 194 When almost against it, the animal would stop in his stride (or prop), when the rider vaulted lightly over his head on to the verandah. **1875** R. Bruce *Dingoes* 138 By rushing under a low bough, Or what is here called pigging Or propping . . They send him flying like the fowls, To lay among the boulders. **1890** 'R. Boldrewood' *Colonial Reformer* I. 12, I didn't think he'd ha' propped like that. **1908** W.H. Ogilvie *My Life in Open* 83 Playful or vicious, according to their breeding and temperament, almost all of them 'prop' or 'go to market' in some form or other. **1928** 'Brent Of Bin Bin' *Up Country* 171 How they raced and propped and wheeled on desperate courses bristling with pitfalls. **1944** M.J. O'Reilly *Bowyangs & Boomerangs* 139 Have you ever seen a camel buck? . . His long suit is propping. **1962** MARSHALL & DRYSDALE *Journey among Men* 30 We saw the big red 'roos pause and prop. In turn they watched us curiously and with caution as we passed. **1970** P. WHITE *Vivisector* 602 The present mob might have trampled Rhoda underfoot if it hadn't suddenly realized she was something beyond its experience, so it propped, and divided. **1984** *Courier-Mail* (Brisbane) 30 June 26/2 A joey wallaby . . hopped and propped not three metres away.

b. *trans.* Of a horse: to throw (a rider) as a consequence of stopping abruptly.

1887 A. NICOLS *Wild Life & Adventure* 83 If he should happen to prop you off when turning a beast, he'll stand by till you get on again.

2. *intr.* Of a person: to stop (often with the intention of establishing a presence). Also *trans.*, to accost.

1950 *Austral. Police Jrnl.* Apr. 117 *Prop*, stop; stop and question. **1965** E. LAMBERT *Long White Night* 65 She gave him a motherly, unoffended smile and kept walking. 'I think I'll prop here,' mused Clancy, looking after her. **1965** *Kings Cross Whisper* (Sydney) Nov. 6/3 Walk through the door and prop. Stand there with your arms folded, legs slightly apart and slowly look from face to face. **1976** B. BENNETT *New Country* 34 He leapt out of the driver's seat . . and propped in the doorway.

prop, *n.* [f. PROP *v.* 1.] A sudden stop made by a horse moving at speed.

1881 A.C. GRANT *Bush-Life Qld.* I. 201 A sudden fierce prop, and Roaney has shot behind Sam's horse. **1884** 'R. BOLDREWOOD' *Old Melbourne Memories* 115 The 'touchy' mare gave so sudden a 'prop', accompanied by a desperate plunge, that he was thrown. **1895** G. RANKEN *Windabyne* 47 Once or twice, when Stumpy tried to double on us, an electric-like 'prop' by the grey mare showed me the quickness and mettle of the true stock-horse.

property. [Spec. use of *property* 'a piece of land owned, a landed estate': see OED *sb.* 2 b.] A rural landholding which is used for stock-raising or crop-growing.

1825 *Hobart Town Gaz.* 18 Mar., Every Property on which the Proprietor is not actually resident, as well absolute Grants, as Reserves, distant Farms, Stock runs or Grazing Grounds. **1838** A. MACONOCHIE *Thoughts on Convict Managem.* 46, I have two ticket-of-leave men on my property. **1847** J.D. LANG *Phillipsland* 334 Dairy and draught-cattle . . to stock a property . . are much cheaper than in the mother-country. **1872** 'RESIDENT' *Glimpses Life Vic.* 305 The owner has left his property in charge of an overseer, and has gone to swell the list of absentees who yearly return to the old country. **1890** 'R. BOLDREWOOD' *Colonial Reformer* III. 150 The idea of consolidating into one magnificent property the two crack cattle runs of Rainbar and Mildool. **1927** A.W. PEARSE *Windjammer 'Prentice* 126 Retire to a small orange property I owned in New South Wales, on the Blue Mountains. **1934** 'E.N. SPEER' *Destiny* 249 My property covers forty thousand acres and carries about twenty thousand sheep. **1950** 'N. SHUTE' *Town like Alice* 81 'Wollara's two thousand seven hundred square miles.' . . 'But is that all one place—one farm, I mean?' 'It's one station,' he replied. 'One property.' **1960** R.S. PORTEOUS *Cattleman* 141 'What size is this property?' 'Near enough to thirty thousand acres.' **1971** *Bulletin* (Sydney) 6 Feb. 56/3 A property carrying fewer than 5000 sheep is unlikely to be an economic proposition. **1981** *Woman's Day* (Sydney) 16 Sept. 7/3, 12-year-old Shane Egan leads an isolated life doing school by correspondence on a property 75 km. away from Bourke. **1985** A. HILL *Bunburyists* 77 Suburban householders may own property. Graziers, however, have Properties. And they do not farm. Small people do that.

proppy, *a.* [See PROP *v.* 1.]

1. Of a horse: disposed to be restive when being ridden.

1866 *Australasian* (Melbourne) 10 Nov. 1002/4 We listened in wrapt attention to the horsey crowd as they severally gave their opinion of the quadrupeds. No. 1 says she is every inch a racer. No. 2 is of the opinion that she is 'proppy'. **1877** *Illustr. Austral. News* (Melbourne) 31 Oct. 170/2 How quickly it is ascertained that . . the Derby crack goes short in his work and is 'proppy'! **1916** T. WARLOW *By Mirage & Mulga* 17 There was . . a long inshore swell that made the steamer bob about and us to feel as if we were riding a proppy horse. **1940** W. HATFIELD *Into (Great?) Unfenced* 89 He had the horse into a stiff, tight canter. . . Still a bit 'proppy', though. **1945** S.J. BAKER *Austral. Lang.* 70 The adjectival use of *proppy* for a horse that jibs and plays up when ridden or driven. **1969** *Austral.* (Sydney) 24 May 35/5 King's Delight had a bruised sole on the near fore, and Clare said the horse was proppy in its action.

2. *transf.* Unsteady.

1904 L.M.P. ARCHER *Bush Honeymoon* 134 Old cove's gettin' a bit *proppy*, too, since last shearin'.

Hence **proppily** *adv.*

1951 MURDOCH & DRAKE-BROCKMAN *Austral. Short Stories* 213 Both [dogs] walked proppily on tiptoes. **1957** H.G. LAMOND *Dingo* 173 White Ears moved forward proppily. The hair along his back stood an erect hedge of bristles; his eyes shot flashes of flame when the moon struck them.

proprietary company. A private company.

1890 *Act* (Vic.) 54 Vict. no. 1074 Sect. 354, Every proprietary company shall provide a book to be called the 'Shareholder's Address Book'. **1896** *Ibid.* 60 Vict. no. 1482 Sect. 2, 'Proprietary company' means a company . . which fulfils all the following requirements, namely:- (a) has not more than twenty-five members or share-holders; (b) does not receive deposits, except from its members or share-holders. . . Does not use its title without the additon thereto immediately before the word 'limited' of the word 'proprietary'. **1921** J.L. DONALDSON *Proprietary Company Vic.* 7 Victoria is the home of the Proprietary Company. **1947** J.J. BURKE *Company Law Accountancy Students* 49 Joint holders of a share (or shares) in a Proprietary Company shall, under Section 37, be treated as a single member. **1955** E.N. DAWES *Austral. Proprietary & Private Companies* 6 By forming a proprietary company when commencing business or by forming such a company to take over or acquire their existing business . . any two or more persons (not exceeding the permissible limit) may now limit their liability to the amount (if any) unpaid on their shares in the company. **1969** MASON & O'HAIR *Austral. Company Law* 5 The policy of the Act is to recognise that certain persons . . do not wish to enter the public company field but wish to carry on business with limited liability. Proprietary companies were introduced for this purpose and these companies do not have to make public their profit and loss accounts and balance sheets. **1986** P. LATIMER *Austral. Business Law* 570 A proprietary company need have only two members, whereas a public company must have five.

protection area. *Gold-mining. Obs.* See quot. 1895.

1871 *Austral. Town & Country Jrnl.* (Sydney) 18 Feb. 207/4 We hear of several protection areas being taken up, some of which look well. *c* **1882** T.F. de C. Browne *Miners' Handy Bk.* (ed. 2) 32 The 'protection area' allowed to any miner seeking for any new and unworked reef or vein shall be double the length of the prospecting claim to which he would be entitled under Regulation 55. **1895** G.C. ADDISON *Miners' Man.* 7 Any miner shall be entitled to mark off a protection area double the length by four times the width of the prospecting claim . . and shall be protected in holding and occupying such area until payable gold shall have been discovered therein, or until it shall have been abandoned. **1898** R. RADCLYFFE *Wealth & Wild Cats* 51 The fields had not been proclaimed a goldfield then, the men having merely pegged out 'protection areas'.

Protector. *Hist.* [Spec. use of *protector* one who protects from injury or harm.] An official responsible for the welfare of the Aboriginal population of a particular district: see quot. 1845 (where the reference is to South Australia); *black protector*, see BLACK *a.*[1] 7; *native protector*, see NATIVE *a.* 5. In full **Protector of (the) Aborigines.**

1835 *Colonist* (Sydney) 25 June 201/3 It is the intention . . to recommend the appointment of a Protector of the Aborigines of this territory. **1837** H. CAPPER *S.A.* 55 Lord Glenelg has appointed an officer, whose especial duty is indicated by his title, the *Protector of the Aborigines.* **1839** *Tasmanian* (Hobart) 26 Apr. 132/3 On Thursday last, the chief Protector, aided by the four assistant Protectors, gave a feast. **1845** M. COLLISSON *S.A.* 46 An officer entitled the 'Protector of Aborigines' . . whose duty it is to secure to the natives 'the due observance of justice and the preservation of their rights, and in particular to protect them from personal violence; to secure for them permanent subsistence, shelter, and lodging, and to afford them moral and religious instruction'. **1846** G.H. HAYDON *Five Yrs. Experience Aust. Felix* 89 Each of these districts has a protector, who has formed a homestead intended to serve as a centre of operation in his district, and as an asylum for such of the aboriginal inhabitants as are disposed to settle. **1848** T.L. MITCHELL *Jrnl. Exped. Tropical Aust.* 414 Protectors of aborigines have been most active; and in Van Dieman's Land, the race has been extirpated. **1857** J. BONWICK *Early Days Melbourne* 31 *Protectors* were appointed by the British Government to watch over the rights of the natives. **1911** *Cwlth. Parl. Papers* III. 518 The extent and prevalence of venereal diseases is regrettable. This is one of the most serious questions that the Protector of Aborigines and his officers will have to deal with. **1927** K.S. PRICHARD *Brumby Innes* (1974) 64 With this damned Morrison chap about—Protector of Aborigines, they call him—it'll go hard with yer. **1938** X. HERBERT *Capricornia* 66 The Protector of Aborigines might discover that he was the father of the child and charge him with the cost of his maintenance. **1947** V.C. HALL *Bad Medicine* 277 He made a special report to the Chief Protector of Aborigines. **1950** G.M. FARWELL *Land of Mirage* 164 No black may now be engaged for station work in Queensland without a legal agreement, which must be signed by the manager and the local policeman, who represents the Queensland Protector. **1964** D. LOCKWOOD *Up Track* 146, I objected, because I thought that if a man was drawing a salary as a protector he should not be doing this sort of thing.

Protectorate. *Hist.* [Spec. use of *protectorate*: see prec.]

1. The office or function of a Protector of (the) Aborigines; the body of Protectors collectively. Also **protectorate of (the) Aborigines.**

1841 *Herald* (Melbourne) 5 Jan. 2/1 It was devised by somebody strongly imbued with the prevailing Whig ideas . . that what is called a Protectorate of the Aborigines should be established in Australia. **1841** *Geelong Advertiser* 8 May 2/3 The Protectorate is a job which originated in the ignorance, cupidity, and Pharisaical cant of the Home Government, and our chances of redress are distant and doubtful. **1845** P.E. DE STRZELECKI *Physical Descr. N.S.W.* 349 Since the time that the fate of the Australasian awoke the sympathies of the public, neither the efforts of the missionary, nor the enactments of the Government, and still less the protectorate of the 'Protectors', have effected any good. **1847** A. HARRIS *Settlers & Convicts* (1953) 213 The final mischief, and indeed infinitely the worst was done by the 'Protectorate of Aborigines', as it was called. **1856** J. BONWICK *W. Buckley* 91 The Squatters in their meetings condemned the Protectorate, and recommended the establishment of Land Reserves and Provision Depots for the Blacks.

2. Special Comb. **Protectorate station,** an area of land reserved for Aborigines under a *protectorate system*; **system,** the practice of delegating responsibility for Aboriginal welfare to Protectors of (the) Aborigines.

1840 *Port Phillip Herald* in *S. Austral. Rec.* (London) (1841) 2 Jan. 4 In future each protector shall have under his superintendence a reserve of ten square miles, one square mile of which will be kept in cultivation for the purpose of affording subsistence for such blacks as may rendezvous at the **Protectorate station. 1843** *Portland Mercury* 11 Jan. 2/4 A gentleman who arrived in town from the Goulburn . . has informed us that the blacks at the Protectorate station there, were in a state of insubordination. **1845** *Standard* (Melbourne) 14 June 2/3 It is a well established fact, that in the neighbourhood of every Protectorate station in the province, the adults prefer resorting to the settlers stations, where they are universally treated with kindness, plentifully fed, and rarely asked to carry even a bucket of water, whereas on the Protectorate runs, they are required to work, than which they prefer almost starvation. **1842** *Geelong Advertiser* 29 Aug. 2/2 This absurd conduct of the Government is harmless, compared to the evils which they intend again to inflict upon both *settlers and blacks* by the re-institution of the **Protectorate system. 1845** *Standard* (Melbourne) 14 June 2/3 It appears to us that the progress of civilization among the blacks, if the present Protectorate system be continued, will not be perceptible for many years, and then, not through its instrumentality.

pro-transportationist: see TRANSPORTATIONIST.

province. *Hist.* Before Federation: used as an alternative to 'colony'; also used of the Port Phillip District to designate its relationship to New South Wales.

1829 D. Burn *Bushrangers* (1971) 15 Let official Proclamations forthwith be circulated throughout the Province, offering—let me see—yes—one hundred sovereigns for each of those miscreants, dead or alive. **1837** *S. Austral. Rec.* (London) 11 Nov. 16 The British Province of South Australia is that part of New Holland, or Australia, as it is now called, lying between Swan River and New South Wales. **1840** *Port Phillip Gaz.* 18 Jan. 4 The land we live in, the province of Australia Felix, the youngest, but most promising of Her Majesty's Colonies. **1845** C.J. Baker *Sydney & Melbourne* 16 Australia Felix is a province of New South Wales, and is governed by a 'superintendent', resident at Melbourne, and acting under the immediate orders of the Governor of the Colony. **1851** J.H. Burton *Emigrant's Man.* i. 1 Attached solely to the provinces of New South Wales and Victoria, there are three hundred millions of acres in the hands of the crown. **1861** A. Kinloch *Lett. from S.A.* 7 The following letters were in great part written before the change in the Constitution of the Province of South Australia. **1880** R. Rose *Austral. Guide: S.A.* 20 A uniform rate of twopence per ½ oz. is charged upon letters carried to places within the Province, and a like rate upon those posted to the sister colonies of Australia. **1898** M. Davitt *Life & Progress* 6 'W.A.' (as the colonists familiarly call their province) was a Crown colony. **1898** A.P. Martin *Beginnings Austral. Lit.* 23 'Rolf Boldrewood' here describes the 'up-country' social life among the delightful sheep and cattle stations of the Western District of what is now the colony of Victoria, but which was then the Port Phillip province of the mother-colony—New South Wales.

provisional school. *Obs.* A private school established in a district too sparsely populated to support a public school, receiving government support and subject to inspection.

1873 H. Parkes *Speeches* 7 Aug. (1876) 379 The provisional school is a school established where there are not 25 children, the number legally required to found a public school. **1881** A.C. Cruttwell *Sketches of Aust.* 68 All schools are erected by the Government except provisional schools; these . . are built by the inhabitants, and then rented by the Government. **1896** *Bulletin* (Sydney) 9 May 27/2 This hut was called a 'provisional' school, and we connected the word vaguely with tucker. **1905** *Nineteenth Century* (London) Nov. 824 Wherever twelve children can be gathered together a 'provisional' school may be opened. **1910** H. Lawson *Rising of Court* 15 Jack Denver and Big Ben Duggen were boys together on the old selections, and at the new provisional bark school at Pipeclay. **1916** E. & M.S. Grew *Rambles in Aust.* 178 'Bush' children have 'Provisional' . . schools, provided for them.

provo /ˈproʊvoʊ/. [f. *prov(ost-marshal*, an army officer acting as head of the military police in a camp, etc. + -O.] A military policeman.

1943 *Gabber: Qld. Lines of Communication Army Trade Training Depot* May 6 Those provos seek him everywhere! **1972** R. Pollard *Cream Machine* 9 Well, Victorian, the provos have brought in deserters from the tip of Western Australia to the bottom of your home state. **1972** J. McNeil *Old Familiar Juice* (1973) 82 Our favourite provo, a bastard named Hunter.

prunella. *Obs.* [Transf. use of *prunella* material used for the uppers of women's shoes.] A shoe; a boot. Usu. in *pl.*

1908 E.G. Murphy *Jarrahland Jingles* 151 From her down-at-heel prunellas peeped her corn-encrusted toes. **1912** *Truth* (Sydney) 28 Jan. 1/5 Fined three quid for shaking a pair of workmen's prunellas from a Salvation Army building.

pubbery. [f. *pub* + *-ery* suffix designating place or establishment.] A public house.

1910 *Bulletin* (Sydney) 2 June 15/3 Five miles from Fred Daylight's wayside pubbery you meet your old friend Bill. . . After a chat you say: 'I'll leave a drink for you at Fred's.' **1920** *Aussie* (Sydney) Oct. 36/2 He . . broke the fire-alarm directly opposite the pubbery. **1929** 'Old Stockman' *Sensational Cattle-Stealing Case* 43 The racecourse was just in front of the hotel, marked out with poles, the pubbery forming the grandstand judge's box, etc. **1939** *Bulletin* (Sydney) 11 Jan. 18/1 Bung and myself were the only occupants of the bar of his pubbery in a one-dog s.w. Q. township.

public, *a. Hist.* [Spec. use of *public* provided at public expense, under public control: see OED(S 4.]

1. Provided, maintained, or employed by the government (of a penal colony) for the benefit of the community.

1788 J. Hunter *Hist. Jrnl. Trans. Port Jackson* (1793) 340 If they wish to remain as settlers . . you may give them such part of the public stock to breed from as you may judge proper. **1790** *HRA* (1914) 1st Ser. I. 195 The public farm at Rose Hill goes on well. **1791** D. Collins *Acct. Eng. Colony N.S.W.* (1798) I. 166 Some rain had fallen which had encouraged the sowing of the public grounds. **1792** *Ibid.* 199 James Collington . . had broken into the public bakehouse. *Ibid.* 200 A person . . was detected in giving corn to a selector from the public granary. **1793** *Ibid.* 260 These, together with some other seamen . . were . . employed in the public boats belonging to the colony. **1793** J. Hunter *Hist. Jrnl. Trans. Port Jackson* 456 Their being indulged with having their own gardens is a spur to industry, which they would not have, if employed in a public garden. **1800** *HRA* (1914) 1st Ser. II. 443 Government to open a public warehouse, from which the settlers might be supplied with every necessary article. **1803** *Sydney Gaz.* 24 July, Some daring Villains, at present Unknown, Broke into the . . Public Brewery at Parramatta . . and Stole thereout the Iron Bars made up in the Mason Work for the Malt Kiln. **1803** *HRA* (1915) 1st Ser. IV. 74 The cleared ground on the new public agricultural settlement at Castle Hill, is about 300 acres. **1804** *Ibid.* 468 The flour being made into bread, baked at public ovens. *Ibid.* 480 The average was 350 to 400 convicts employed at public cultivation. **1808** *Ibid.* (1916) 1st Ser. VI. 36 Seventy or Eighty Sheep on his Farm, originally drawn from the Public Flocks. **1809** *Sydney Gaz.* 14 May, A return of the Stock of every description disposed of from the Public Herds. **1810** *Ibid.* 19 May, *Samuel Briton*, for robbing the Public Factory at Parramatta. **1812** *HRA* (1916) 1st Ser. VII. 535 Quantities of the Public Cattle were slaughtered to supply the place of Salted meat. **1817** *Hobart Town Gaz.* 7 June, All Cattle for His Majesty's Stores will be Slaughtered . . by the Public Butchers, and under an Inspector of Stock. **1843** *HRA* (1924) 1st Ser. XXII. 509 A large portion of the produce of the public Farm in Norfolk Island.

2. In special collocations: **public gang,** a party of convicts detailed to perform *public labour*; **labour,** forced labour on a project or construction which benefits the community; **store,** the stock of provisions, clothing, etc., maintained by the government; the building which houses this; Store 1 a.; **work** (usu. in *pl.*), *public labour*; a project or construction so undertaken.

1796 D. Collins *Acct. Eng. Colony N.S.W.* (1798) I. 485 Two men from each officer were ordered to join the **public gangs.** **1813** *HRA* (1916) 1st Ser. VIII. 45 Several Convicts having absconded and deserted from the Public Govt. Gangs. **1792** *Ibid.* (1914) 1st Ser. I. 372 The colony, having been almost constantly on a reduced ration, is a great check on the **public labour.** **1802** *N.S.W. Gen. Orders* 28 Oct. (1806) 15 The Hours for Public Labour until further Orders, are as follows . . from sunrise to 8 in the Morning . . from 9 till 3 in the Afternoon . . Saturdays from Sunrise to 8 in the Morning. **1813** *HRA* (1916) 1st Ser. VII. 779 Tickets of Leave give no further Advantage or Privilege to the Holders of them, than that of Exemption from Public Labor. **1827** *Tasmanian* (Hobart) 5 Apr. 4, I am not insensible of the efforts which the *Colonial Times* has repeatedly made in directing the right application of Public labour. **1832** *Colonist* (Hobart) 5 Oct. 3/3 How comes it that you have taken no notice of this projected application of the Public labour, when so many parts of the Colony are without roads. **1790** *Extracts Lett. Arthur Phillip* 12 Feb. (1791) 5 He has returned the quantity of corn . . into the **public store.** *Ibid.* 13 Feb. (1791) 10 It will be necessary to give . . convicts to those settlers who come out, and to support them for two years from the public stores. **1802** *HRA* (1915) 1st Ser. III. 520 To all males victualled from the public stores—Wheat, 9 lb.; maize, 3 lb. shelled, or 4½ lb. in cob. **1813** *Van Diemen's Land Govt. & Gen. Orders* 6 Mar. (1814) 4 No person whatever his Situation may be, shall be hereafter allowed to draw Provisions from the Public Store beyond his weekly allowance in advance. **1829** *Tasmanian Almanack* 70 When a prisoner is in future to be assigned to a Settler, he will receive a complete suit of slop clothing from the Public Stores, for which his master must pay, on delivery. **1849** A. Harris *Emigrant Family* (1967) 28 Twelve or eighteen months' ration from the public store. **1789** J. Hunter *Hist. Jrnl. Trans. Port Jackson* (1793) 345 The convicts would have an opportunity of saving time to themselves; and, as that time was to be employed in clearing gardens and ground to cultivate for their own use, what was thus saved from the **public work** would not be lost to society. **1791** P.G. King Jrnl. Norfolk Island 12 Nov. 2 The Women they married, were to cease receiving any support from the Public Stores at the end of Twelve Months from the time they quitted public Work. **1801** G. Barrington *Sequel to Voyage N.S.W.* 27 Will be found to amount to an enormous sum when the expences of the public works erected in this colony come to be calculated. **1816** *Hobart Town Gaz.* 13 July, The Weather has put a partial stop to all out door Public Works. **1822** J.T. Bigge *Rep. State Colony N.S.W.* 16 Those who are not so allotted, are distributed amongst the public works at or near Hobart Town, and are afterwards assigned, as they are applied for, by the settlers. **1827** *Tasmanian* (Hobart) 18 Oct. 3 John M'Carty, from the Public Works, was sentenced to Macquarie Harbour for absconding, this being the third offence. **1834** *Colonist* (Hobart) 21 Jan. 3/3 We have been given to understand that the Government have refused to lend the men from the Public Works to assist in getting in the harvest. **1835** *Hobart Town Almanack* 229 The number of convicts in the public works amount to upwards of 2000. **1850** W. Gates *Recoll. Van Dieman's Land* 157 Ticket-of-leave men . . have their rations, which are generally but a little more in quantity, and sometimes not much better in quality, than on the public works.

public, *n.* Abbrev. of Public school 1; a pupil of such a school.

1956 'B. James' *Bunyip of Barney's Elbow* 140 People spoke of keeping their children at home, or . . 'putting them to the convent', or 'the public', as the case might be. **1959** D. Hewett *Bobbin Up* 56 Frank was a Forbes boy, youngest son of a local cockie. He and Beryl had gone to the 'public' together, partnered each other at the local 'hop'. **1972** P. Kenna *Slaughter St. Teresa's Day* 7 They were even further isolated by the Roman Catholicism into which they were born. The world was divided into Catholics and 'Publics'. **1984** *Nat. Times* (Sydney) 20 Apr. 13/1 These were known as the Publics. They went to public school, they ran about in the streets, they didn't believe in the Pope, and they went to something called Sunday school instead of Mass. The Publics never seemed to have to go to boarding school.

public school. [Used elsewhere in both senses: see OED(S 1 and 3.]

1. A school established and maintained at public expense as part of a system of public (and usually free) education. Also *attrib.*

1813 *N.S.W. Pocket Almanack* 30 Masters of the Public Day Schools throughout the Territory. **1828** *Austral. Q. Jrnl. Theol., Lit. & Sci.* Jan. 110 In this Colony . . there are now 30 Public Schools, entirely supported by Royal Bounty. **1842** *HRA* (1924) 1st. Ser. XXII. 426 The public Schools for Children of the poorer classes are for the most part under the management of the Clergy. **1859** W. Fairfax *Handbk. to Australasia* p. xliii, The feeling prevailing in the house was in favour of the National Education system. But as the 'Denominational' was in the ascendant, and dissatisfaction with both were expressed by the parties examined by the committee, they concluded to recommend assistance to be given to 'public schools'. **1875** R. & F. Hill *What we saw in Aust.* 327 A public school may be established in any district where it can be shown that there are twenty-five children who will attend it regularly. **1895** *Bulletin* (Sydney) 28 Dec. 16/3 A Bill to abolish public-school fees and make education absolutely free in N.S.W. was pushed half-way through the Assembly by Griffith. **1917** *Truth* (Sydney) 29 Apr. 4/1 The fat 'uni', and starved public schools. **1953** T.G. Tucker *Aust. as Home* 16 Elementary (or 'primary') education—which we may call the first grade—is mainly supplied gratis by the schools of the State, and hence they are sometimes called 'state' schools, sometimes 'public' schools. **1965** P. Todhunter *Aust. under Scalpel* 88 How should I know that a Public School in Australia means a council school in England. **1983** *Canberra Times* 30 Mar. 6/1 The expression 'government schools' or 'State schools' should be resisted, and the expression 'public school' insisted upon, the chairman of the Australian Law Reform Commission, Mr Justice Kirby, said in Melbourne last night. . . 'Let not the private or religious schools presume upon the adjective 'public',' Mr Justice Kirby said. 'That is the preserve of the school system of the overwhelming majority of Australians. It is a proud adjective and it should be jealously guarded.'

2. A private, fee-paying school on the English model. Also *attrib.*, and **great public school.**

1848 J. FOWLES *Sydney* 7 Those considered as *public*, are—the Sydney and Australian Colleges (each a School under the control of a Committee), the Anglican College at Lyndhurst, the St. James' Grammar School, the Archiepiscopal Seminary at St. Mary's, and the Normal Institution. **1859** *V & P* (N.S.W. L.A.) IV. 138 Perhaps you think those things are almost unavoidable in a large school? I believe in all public schools of the kind it is unavoidable. **1876** J. CLEVERLEY *Half Million Children* (1978) 253 The amount of public school feeling in this colony as compared with that borne by boys in England is very small. **1883** R.E.N. TWOPENY *Town Life Aust.* 143 The public schools of Australia may not be all that could be wished. **1919** *Argus* (Melbourne) 24 May 21/1 That public school rowing has an extraordinary hold on the public was demonstrated yesterday, when the heats of the Head of the River boat race attracted a crowd of 20,000 people to the River Yarra. **1929** C.E.W. BEAN *Official Hist. Aust. 1914–18* III. 53 The break was no different from that which happens between school-mates at a great public school when one of them becomes a prefect. **1936** E.C.H. TAYLOR et al. *Our Austral. Game Football* 69 School football, especially public school football, has reached a very high standard. . . Jack Elder . . once said that a Wesley-Grammar match . . was the fastest game that he had ever refereed. **1948** K.S. PRICHARD *Golden Miles* 14 Sally wondered whether she had been right to send Dick to a public school in Adelaide where the mine managers sent their sons, while Tom and Lal had grown up on the fields with nothing but a state school education. **1955** M. CORBEN *Not to mention Kangaroos* 89 When Australians . . say it is a 'public school' they mean it is a strictly private school with a limited clientele. **1961** *Bulletin* (Sydney) 7 Oct. 51/3 *The Armidale school N.S.W.* The only *great public school* situated in the Country. **1976** *Ibid.* 17 Apr. 20/2 No, no. Public actually means private. In Sydney they call it GPS—Great Public School. Grammar . . well, any grammar, really, is a public . . that is, private.

public servant.

a. *Obs.* A convict assigned to public labour.

1797 *HRA* (1914) 1st Ser. II. 18 Thus you will discover, my Lord, how impossible it was for me to do anything on Government account for want of public servants. **1799** D. COLLINS *Acct. Eng. Colony N.S.W.* (1802) II. 266 Such of the . . public servants as might have taken to concealments on shore for the purpose of avoiding their work, or making their escape from the colony. **1820** *HRA* (1917) 1st. Ser. X. 221 Whose Conduct, as a Public Servant of the Crown, Since his Arrival . . has been irreproachable.

b. A member of the PUBLIC SERVICE, a civil servant.

1812 *HRA* (1916) 1st Ser. VII. 477 Institute Judicial Proceedings against one of the Public Servants who is accused of the grossest acts of Fraud and Peculation. **1832** *Colonial Times* (Hobart) 25 Apr., Mr Henry Melville certainly cannot boast of being in receipt of a handsome salary, as a public servant. **1841** *HRA* (1924) 1st Ser. XXI. 206 There is scarcely a Public Servant from the Governor downwards. **1860** 'LADY' *My Experiences in Aust.* 86 In the Australian colonies . . the number of legislators and public servants is so large in proportion to that of the middle classes, that any person of moderate means and ability . . can . . enter into political life. **1899** *Bulletin* (Sydney) 18 Nov. 15/2 The N.S.W. public servant . . does get a rise of salary now and then. **1924** C.E.W. BEAN *Official Hist. Aust. 1914–18* II. 113 Lieut. L.G. Casey; 15th Bn. Public servant. **1935** J. HAMLET *Salmagundi* 24 Our so-called 'public servants', instead of listening to obey our behests, spent months manufacturing excuses for disregarding their duty. **1947** F.C. BROWNE *Public be Damned!* 97 Did you ever plead for sympathy with a public servant? **1965** G.E. CAIDEN *Career Service* 55 Public servants were warned that the economies of centralization would lose them their jobs. **1979** R. BATH *Jamaica* 7 You don't look like a Public Servant. . . No insult—I meant it as a compliment. **1986** *Sydney Morning Herald* 8 Mar. 11/2 The time had come to make it pretty clear that public servants had a clear professional responsibility to act professionally.

public service. Service to the community as provided under the direction of the government; now the preferred term (cf. Br. and U.S. 'civil service') for the administrative departments of each State and Territory Government, and the non-military administrative departments of the Commonwealth of Australia; the body of people so employed. Also *attrib.*

1793 W. TENCH *Compl. Acct. Settlement* 176 Many a night have I toiled . . on the public service . . hauling the seine in every part of the harbour of Port Jackson. **1814** *HRA* (1916) 1st Ser. VIII. 209 At all times ready to proceed on any Public Service, which they may respectively be Ordered to perform. **1819** *Ibid.* (1917) 1st Ser. X. 44 The Town of Newcastle exhibits various Strong Substantial Buildings for the Furtherance of the Public Service. **1834** J.D. LANG *Hist. & Statistical Acct. N.S.W.* II. 10 When a convict-ship arrives in Sydney harbour, it is the practice of Government to reserve as many of the convicts . . as are required for the public service. **1839** *Sydney Herald* 6 Nov. 2/1 The enormous amount of expenditure for what is called the 'public service' in a colony containing so trifling an amount of free persons, is, we believe, unprecedented. **1850** *Bell's Life in Sydney* 26 Jan. (Suppl.) 2/2 Addressed to the Departments and Officers of Government on the Public Service. **1858** T. MCCOMBIE *Hist. Colony Vic.* 69 Many large landowners on the Sydney side had more prisoners of the Crown assigned to them than was awarded to the whole public service of Port Phillip. **1876** *VPD* XXIII. 2311/2 He believed a considerable saving might be effected in the cost of the public service without impairing the efficiency of the service. **1889** *Ibid.* LX. 90/2 He had had several complaints from men who were thoroughly able to give efficient service to the State that the public service of the colony was barred against them. **1902** A. COCHRANE *Granite Rocks & Ozone* 5 Miss Braddock only smiled, for well she knew that gentlemen holding responsible positions in the Public Service would not transgress the proprieties in a railway station. **1922** *CPD* CI. 2840 The Public Service now really partakes of the nature of a profession. **1934** F.A. BLAND *Planning Modern State* 110 After 1901, the breaking down of the principle of unitary management of the public service gained new momentum. **1957** H.A. SCARROW *Higher Public Service* 66 The system of public service arbitration has . . helped to keep the general wage level of public employment in line with the going wage of the community. **1964** K. WILLEY *Eaters of Lotus* 5 The public service majority of the population pay no direct council or swimming-pool rates. The government puts in the money for them. **1979** R. BATH *Jamaica* 7, I start in February, so I'm getting in early—check the lie of the land, dirty up my trendy little Public Service flat.

puddenba, puddinba, var. PUDDING-BALL.

pudding. The fruit of any of several plants, popular with children for chewing.

1903 *Bulletin* (Sydney) 31 Jan. 36/2 We knew all about five-corners, ground berries, 'puddings'. **1953** *Ibid.* 4 Nov. 13/4 Along with wattle-gum as a free bush sweet went 'puddins' . . the green, embryo seeds of the lawngrower's nightmare, onion-grass. **1978** E. SIMON *Through my Eyes* 126 The apple berries which we called 'puddings' and which we chewed because they were supposed to be good for general health.

pudding-ball /'pʊdɪŋ-bɔl/. Also **puddenba, puddinba.** [a. Jagara *punba.*] An edible marine fish resembling a mullet, perh. *Mugil cephalus* (see *sea mullet* SEA).

1847 J.D. LANG *Cooksland* 96 The species of fish that are commonest in the Bay are mullet, bream, puddinba (a native name, corrupted by the colonists into pudding-ball). . . The puddinba is like a mullet in shape, but larger, and very fat; it is esteemed a great delicacy. **1896** *Australasian* (Melbourne) 29 Aug. 407/4 'Pudding-ball' is the name of a fish. It has nothing to do with pudding, nothing with any of the various meanings of ball. The fish is not specially round. The aboriginal name was 'pudden-ba'. **1932** N. PALMER *Talking it Over* 46 There arose names like *pudding-ball* for the fish in Moreton Bay called by the natives *puddenba.* **1945** S.J. BAKER *Austral. Lang.* 214 Popular fish names . . include . . *puddingball*, corrupted by the law of Hobson-Jobson from the aboriginal *puddinba.* **1952** *Austral. Museum Mag.* June 315 The Puddinba (corrupted to Puddingball) is a mullet-like fish of Queensland. Any reader catching one . . is invited to present his . . puddingball . . to the Australian Museum, so that the scientific name can be associated with the ordinary one.

puddle, *v.* [Spec. use of *puddle* to stir (wet clay, etc.) into a puddle; used elsewhere but recorded earliest and used chiefly in Aust.] *trans.* To work (clayey auriferous or opal-bearing material) with water in a tub so as to separate out the mineral sought. Also *intr.*

1852 J. BONWICK *Notes of Gold Digger* 13 The dirtied water is gently poured off every now and then, and, with a fresh supply from the stream, you puddle away. **1853** A. MACKAY *Great Gold Field* 13 The washing stuff at Tambaroora is very stiff, and must be puddled before it can be passed through the cradle. This is done by putting it into troughs slightly inclined, into which the water is continuously poured, and the mass is worked with shovels until the clay is dissolved and run off. **1881** G.C. EVANS *Stories* 22 We dug a hole about two feet deep in hard ground and puddled our stuff in it, instead of a tub. **1895** *Worker* (Sydney) 7 Sept. 4/1 The creek was sluiced, and several of the points puddled; and finally the reefs were discovered. **1921** W.H. CORFIELD *Reminisc. Qld.* 32 As I puddled the wash-dirt he cradled it. **1932** I.L. IDRIESS *Lasseter's Last Ride* 9 When your dish is full, carry it to the nearest water, immerse it, and 'puddle' the dirt with your fingers. **1963** *Pix* (Sydney) 13 July 21 Machines are used to 'puddle' (separate and sieve) opal dirt. **1967** S. LLOYD *Lightning Ridge Bk.* (1968) 1 Opal-dirt can be brought to the surface and examined or puddled.

puddler. [f. PUDDLE.]

1. One engaged in puddling for gold or opal.

1855 *Ovens & Murray Advertiser* (Beechworth) 14 Apr. 5/1 The rejected tailings of the ordinary miner are eagerly sought after by the puddlers. **1862** J.A. PATTERSON *Gold Fields Vic.* 53 A puddler's dam now occupies the ground they worked; but the puddler continues to pick up fine specimens. **1871** *Austral. Town & Country Jrnl.* (Sydney) 10 June 710/1 The price charged by the puddlers is 4s. a load. **1890** 'R. BOLDREWOOD' *Colonial Reformer* II. 210 He was not a miner, a speculator, a reefer, nor an engine-driver, a clerk, or puddler. **1967** S. LLOYD *Lightning Ridge Bk.* (1968) 99 Puddlers have ruined the whole Lightning Ridge Field.

2. A puddling machine.

1888 F. HUME *Madame Midas* 44 The wash was carried along in the trucks from the top of the shaft to the puddlers, which were large circular vats into which water was constantly gushing. **1893** J.A. BARRY *Steve Brown's Bunyip* 79 Surfiss is my dart—roun' about the old tailin's and puddlers. Down below's too risky. **1967** A. KALOKERINOS *In Search of Opal* 19 Modern miners remove the . . 'pay dirt', in bulk . . and spin it in a machine that sifts the dirt out and leaves the nobbies behind. . . These machines are called 'puddlers' and their variety is almost endless. **1969** B. GARLAND *Pitt Street Prospector* 135 He . . welcomed the idea of seeing Rabbo's puddler at work. **1971** J.S. GUNN *Opal Terminol.* 37 There are two dams . . at which miners rent sites . . where they operate power-driven wet puddlers capable of handling several tons of dirt in one operation.

puddling, *vbl. n.* [f. PUDDLE.]

1. The working (of clayey auriferous or opal-bearing material) with water so as to separate out the mineral sought. Also *attrib.*

1852 J. BONWICK *Notes of Gold Digger* 13 Good puddling makes easy and profitable cradling. **1853** J. SHERER *Gold Finder Aust.* 218 *Puddling* . . is performed by means of a spade being worked to and fro in a tub filled with auriferous earth and water. **1861** T. MCCOMBIE *Austral. Sketches* 133 There are four methods of obtaining the auriferous metal—surface washing, deep sinking, puddling and quartz crushing. **1895** J.W. ANDERSON *Prospector's Handbk.* (ed. 6) 164 *Puddling* (Australia and America), mixing gold-bearing clays with water. **1931** C.B. SMITH *Austral. Gold Prospectors' Handbk.* 19 Should the wash dirt be mixed with clay, it will require 'puddling' before washing in either the prospecting dish or the cradle. **1956** R.G. EDWARDS *Overlander Songbk.* 67 'Tis puddling not quartz reefing now keeps up Bendigo. **1974** B. MYATT *Dict. Austral. Gemstones* 25 Any clay in the gravels must be washed out before panning is commenced. This is done by submerging the gold pan and rubbing the washdirt between the hands or stirring it with a flat stick. This operation is known as puddling. **1971** J.S. GUNN *Opal. Terminol.* 37 *Puddling tank*, large dam at which wet puddling takes place.

2. Special Comb. **puddling claim,** see quot. 1890; **machine,** an apparatus in which puddling is done mechanically; **tub,** a container in which puddling is done by hand.

1862 J.A. PATTERSON *Gold Fields Vic.* 59 A **puddling-claim** . . had given an average of three pounds per week after paying expenses. **1890** *N.T. Times Almanac* 123 A puddling claim may be taken up on alluvial ground which has been previously worked and abandoned, or on ground which has been tested, and found to be too poor to pay for the ordinary method of working, such ground to be worked in connection with a puddling machine, and must be registered. **1931** W. BARAGWANATH et al. *Guide for Prospectors in Vic.* 75 *Puddling claim*, a puddling claim of not more than 1 acre may be taken possession of in old or partially worked ground, or in new ground where the average depth from the surface does not exceed 10 feet, and where steam, horse, or water power shall be used in puddling. **1855** *Illustr. Sydney News* 13 Jan. 19/2 They intend to construct a large drain sufficient to contain water for three or four months and also to erect a **puddling machine** on the Bendigo principle. **1856** S.C. BREES *How to farm & settle in Aust.* 62 Conspicuous . . are the puddling-machines, by which, with the aid of horse power and apparatus on a large scale, the washing is far more effectively conducted than by the old mode of hand-cradling. **1871** J. BALLANTYNE *Homes & Homesteads* 41 By-and-by came the puddling machine wrought by horse-power, doing the work of many tubs wholesale. **1931** W. BARAGWANATH et al. *Guide for Prospectors in Vic.* 11 The simplest form of puddling machine is a trough cut in somewhat raised ground in the form of a ring, and closely lined with well-fitting slabs. **1851** R. TESTER *Wombat Wallaby* 61 (OEDS), I spurred my little mare off, and in doing so she made a plunge, and very nearly bundled me and my mutton into the **puddling tub.** **1853** J. SHERER *Gold Finder Aust.* 189 There is the creek . . and rows of puddling tubs standing by it, and men busy washing their earth in tins and cradles. **1855** G.H. WATHEN *Golden Country* 71 The diggers now commonly use the 'puddling-tub'. This is merely one-half of a porter cask. The tub is half filled with the 'washing-stuff'; water is baled in from the creek, and the whole worked about with the spade. **1859** W. KELLY *Life in Vic.* I. 200 The externals of a digging store are for the most part pillars of washing pans, nests of buckets and Yankee tubs, cradles, and puddling-tubs.

puffs, *pl.* With **the:** a disease of stock, esp. horses, in hot climates, characterized by absence of sweating.

1898 D.W. CARNEGIE *Spinifex & Sand* 366 Another horse-sickness common in the North is called the 'Puffs'. **1911** *Cwlth. Parl. Papers* III. 519 There are three diseases, however, that seem to constitute drawbacks to horse breeding in this part of the country. These are commonly known as (1) the 'Walk-about' disease, which is generally fatal; (2) the 'Puffs', and (3) the so-called 'Swamp-cancer'.

puftaloon /pʌftəˈlun/. Also with some variety, as **puff de loon, puff de looney, pufftaloon, pufftalooner,** etc. [Of unknown origin; perh. f. *puff* light pastry, light porous cake.] A small fried cake, usu. spread with jam, sugar, or honey.

[**1853** MOSSMAN & BANISTER *Aust. Visited & Revisited* 126 Leather-jackets—an Australian bush term for a thin cake made of dough, and put into a pan to bake with some fat. . . The Americans indulge in this kind of bread, giving them the name of 'Puff ballooners'.] **1871** *Austral. Jrnl.* July 602/2 'Have a puffterlooner, Master Dick,' suggests Derwent Jack, 'or a bit o' sweet-cake.' **1887** W.H. SUTTOR *Austral. Stories Retold* 121 Mrs Maybud prepares some pufftalooners and eggs and tea. **1908** MRS A. GUNN *We of Never-Never* 189 The cooking lessons proceeded until the fine art of making 'puff de looneys', sinkers, and doughboys had been mastered. **1921** G.A. BELL *Under Brigalows* 121 Golden brown crisp 'puff-de-loons', very good if somewhat greasy. **1933** W.L. OWEN *Cossack Gold* 124 The puftaloon . . is a member of the immense fritter family, a sort of unsweetened doughnut. **1948** A. MARSHALL *Ourselves writ Strange* 249 To compensate for the absence of bread and butter, she sometimes attempted to make a damper-like scone that I had known in my childhood as a 'puftaloon'. **1959** H. LAMOND *Sheep Station* 34 He fried some pufftaloonas. Those fried scones did not rise in the frying-pan and offer the delicacy of taste they had done when other and more expert hands had cooked them. **1967** M. SELLARS *Carramar* 69 Puftaloons, dipped in golden syrup. **1977** J. O'GRADY *There was Kid* 33 Wondering today—an elderly delinquent writing this—about the origin of the word 'puftaloon', I consulted my dictionaries. According to them the word does not exist. **1979** DOUGLAS & HEATHCOTE *Far Cry* 6 We'll have puftaloons . . for dinner.

pug, *n.*[1] [Transf. use of *pug* clay used as a building material.] An auriferous clay. Also *attrib.*

1896 E. DYSON *Rhymes from Mines* 66 To puddle off the pug and clay And pan the gleaming prospect bare. **1900** 'CAS-HAMBA' *Sketchy Characters* 8 For hundreds of miles there is a belt of auriferous country; the very slimes that exude and forms itself [*sic*] into what is known as 'pug' and alluvial, is both extensive and deep. **1928** R.M. MACDONALD *Opals & Gold* 135 The auriferous old pug grounds are again waiting re-discovery. **1932** I.L. IDRIESS *Prospecting for Gold* 24 A tiptop idea for 'dissolving' thick clay or 'pug' is to throw a few shovelfuls of coarse sand or gravel into the trough, then stir. **1941** D. O'CALLAGHAN *Long Life Reminisc.* 107 The valley was more like a Kaline pug lead. The gold was mostly in the pug and was very fine. **1972** N. KING *Nickel Country* 4 A peculiar feature of mining in the Kanowna district was a 'clayey' deposit, known as 'pug'. Although richly impregnated with gold it formed a difficult extraction problem.

Hence **puggy** *a.*

[N.Z. **1907** *N.Z. Geol. Survey Bull. No. 3* New Ser. 98 Quartz and puggy material.] **1932** I.L. IDRIESS *Prospecting for Gold* 41 Puggy clay is unusual. 'Puggy' ground often breaks up under the pick to form into sticky clay balls exceptionally awkward to disintegrate. **1941** D. O'CALLAGHAN *Long Life Reminisc.* 113 The puggy wash, after soaking in water, would easily wash off the gold.

pug, *n.*[2] *Obs.* [Of unknown origin.] A lift on a horse ridden by another. Also as *v. trans.*

1934 *Bulletin* (Sydney) 5 Sept. 20/1 Victorian philologists are becoming alarmed over an outbreak in the State schools of a new form of slang. Two words in particular have gained great popularity—'dink' and 'pug'. These are, apparently, both used to express a request for a double-bank ride. The fortunate Melbourne schoolkid with a bike, when time comes to go home, is asked by his cobbers for a 'dink'. In the country the other word seems more popular, horses being largely used there. When a cobber wants a lift home behind the kid in the saddle he asks for a 'pug'. *Ibid.* 26 Sept. 20/2 In 1915 I was riding to my first job in Mildura when another boy asked me to 'pug' him to Fourteenth-street.

pull, *v.*

1. *trans. Timber-getting.* To pull out (a tree) by the roots; to haul (felled timber).

1920 *Bull.* (W.A. Dept. Forests) xii. 4 All persons pulling, cleaning and carting sandalwood must be registered at the Forests Department, Perth, in accordance with forest regulations, and may only operate on Crown lands after obtaining an order from one of the firms who hold a license to pull and remove a stipulated quantity of sandalwood per month from Crown lands. **1923** *W.A. Govt. Gaz.* 30 Oct. 2096/1 All sandalwood trees removed under this license shall be pulled up by the roots. The main trunk of the tree shall not be severed until the tree is pulled. **1975** G.A.W. SMITH *Once Green Jackaroo* 115, I had me own team pullin' timber outa them bloody gorges and mountains in the Northern Rivers. **1982** M. WALKER *Making Do* 144 At that time I used to pull about five spotted gum logs, and they were cut before nine o'clock. **1982** *Bulletin* (Sydney) 23 Nov. 44/3 Supplying the temples of Asia are 24 West Australian contractors licensed to 'pull' sandalwood.

2. *Opal-mining.* In the phr. **to pull dirt,** to haul the material excavated by a miner to the surface.

1931 M.S. BUCHANAN *Prospecting for Opal* 12 You can use your motor car instead of pulling the dirt by hand. **1940** E. HILL *Great Austral. Loneliness* (ed. 2) 261 She . . accompanied her brother to the shaft, 'pulling dirt' in buckets while he excavated down below. **1950** C.E. GOODE *Yarns of Yilgarn* 88 We all took turns to work below or pull dirt. **1963** D. NILAND *Dadda Jumped* 129 He was pulling dirt for his mate at Lightning Ridge when the windlass rope broke. **1973** C. AUSTIN *I left my Hat in Andamooka* 19 Maybe I should meet a lone miner who would be glad to have, even for a short period, an extra pair of hands to 'pull dirt' or scratch at the promising clay and sandstone.

3. In the imperative phr. **pull your head** (or **skull) in,** 'shut up', 'mind your own business'.

1942 *Whizz* (Perth) Aug. 1 Pull your skull in, sport. **1953** T.A.G. HUNGERFORD *Riverslake* 199 'Pull your flaming heads in!' he cried in answer to their unspoken criticism. **1955** *Overland* iii. 18 In good plain 'Australian', I think that Mr Hatfield ought to 'pull his head in'. **1968** G. DUTTON *Andy* 200 Pull yer head in, sport. I got plenty of cash. **1972** *Bulletin* (Sydney) 12 Aug. 7/3 He got as mad as a cut snake and told her to pull her head in. **1982** *Ibid.* 5 Oct. 12/1 Pull yer head in, Germaine—your inferiority complex is showing again.

4. To play (a didgeridoo).

1949 W.E. HARNEY *Songs of Songmen* 7, I heard . . the didjeridoo player 'pulling' (blowing) his instrument.

pull-away hand. *Obs.* On a whaling-boat: an oarsman.

1845 *Inquirer* (Perth) 7 May 2/1 Wanted, For the Fremantle Whaling Company, a few stout pull-away hands. **1878** R.B. SMYTH *Aborigines of Vic.* II. 244 Wherever whaling stations have been established, the natives have proved themselves to be very valuable assistants. . . They enter heartily into the sport, and make excellent 'pull-away hands' in the whale-boats.

puller.

1. *Timber-getting.* One who pulls sandalwood from the ground.

1920 *Bull.* (W.A. Dept. Forests) xii. 4 In order that the sandalwood getter may be protected, payment to the puller for sandalwood of fair average quality is fixed. **1942** *Walkabout* Nov. 33/3 Martin, who was the 'puller' . . would then back his dray to within fifteen feet of the tree. Attached to the axle of the dray was a stout chain, at one end of which was a large hook that was fastened around the butt of the tree. At a command from Martin the horse would move forward, and the tree would be pulled right out of the ground, brandishing many roots, which were then cut away and discarded. **1970** B. FULLER *Nullarbor Story* 28 'Pullers', as sandalwood gatherers are known. **1972** —— *West of Bight* 26 Sandalwood pullers were important among track-makers. **1982** *Bulletin* (Sydney) 23 Nov. 44/2 One group of sandalwood 'pullers' has been practising its trade on a Murchison sheep station 500 km. north of Perth. **1983** P. ADAM SMITH *When we rode Rails* 68 The line opened on 1 June 1889 and it was claimed . . that it followed . . the tracks of sandalwood pullers. These gatherers of the fragrant scrubby timber that was pulled out, rather than cut, for sale to the Chinese for use in the manufacture of incense had driven their horse and camel teams into uninhabited areas.

2. One who plays the didgeridoo.

1943 W.E. HARNEY *Taboo* 80 From the river bank came the droning of the didgeredoo. The player—or puller as he is called—was playing a walika. **1947** —— *Brimming Billabongs* 65 The puller of the didgeridoo waved it about as he beat out the dance. **1951** C. SIMPSON *Adam in Ochre* 67 Marawana was a good didjeridoo player or 'puller', as the native usually says when he speaks our language. **1953** J.K. EWERS *With Sun on my Back* 25 Each group had its own 'puller', as they call the didjerdoo player.

pumpkin beetle. A beetle of the genus *Aulacophora*, esp. *A. hilaris*, commonly feeding on pumpkins and other plants of the fam. Cucurbitaceae.

1915 *Bull. N.T.* xiii. 3 Pumpkin beetles. *Aulacophora hilaris . . Aulacophora palmerstoni . .* are common pests of cucurbitaceous plants in the northern part of the Territory. **1938** *Bulletin* (Sydney) 2 Feb. 21/1 Where pumpkin-beetles are active a sharp rise in the mortality of working bees follows. **1948** W.W. FROGGATT *Insect Bk.* 69 The Pumpkin Beetle, ¼-inch long, is reddish yellow, with four black blotches on the elytra. **1982** F. HUTCHINSON *What Pest is That?* 42 *Pumpkin beetle*, Australian native insect that is a serious pest of pumpkins.

pumpkin-squatter. *Obs.* A small farmer.

1898 *Bulletin* (Sydney) 15 Jan. 14/2 *Pumpkin-squatter*, a little cocky with a swelled head. **1902** *Ibid.* 29 Mar. 14/1 At sundown, struck the humpy of a 'pumpkin-squatter', and put up a yarn about losing a horse. **1903** *Truth* (Sydney) 18 Jan. 1/6 'I believe you had a pretty tough time in Sydney,' said the pumpkin squatter to his friend who had just returned from a trip to the big smoke.

punce, var. POONCE.

punch, *n. Obs.* [Fig. use of *punch* a blow.] In the phr. **to make a punch,** to make a killing.

1902 *Bulletin* (Sydney) 8 Feb. 32/3 If the mounted man does make a 'punch' in the tucker line he can carry it, whilst the swaggie has either to sit down and eat it or else leave it behind. **1903** J. MARSHALL *Battling for Gold* 108 The hardship endured by the pioneers on the Westralian goldfields would have been well nigh intolerable had it not been for the hope that 'ere long, perhaps, they would make a 'punch'. **1914** M. CANNON *That Damned Democrat* (1981) 98 The only chance a punter in shares has of making a punch is an unforeseen heavy rise.

punch, *v.* [Spec. use of *punch* to poke or prod; also U.S. but recorded earliest in Aust.: see OED(S *v.*[1] 2 a.]

1. *trans.* To drive (a beast) forward by poking or prodding (see quot. 1859); to drive (cattle). Also *intr.*, and as *vbl. n.* See also BULLOCK PUNCHING.

1859 W. KELLY *Life in Vic.* I. 172 The teamster, whose whip-shaft is always armed with a spike to punch an over-obdurate animal. **1886** H. KENDALL *Poems* 207 At punching oxen, you may guess There's nothing out can 'camp' him. **1898** E. DYSON *Below & on Top* 322, I must drop fooling or go and punch cattle for my tucker for the rest of my days. **1907** *Bulletin* (Sydney) 11 Apr. 15/3 For 20 years I've punched cattle with the roughest of 'em. **1911** E.S. SORENSON *Life in Austral. Backblocks* 58 Punching is the mainspring of Bullocky Bill's existence, and he could hardly be happy if released from the thraldom of the yoke. **1918** *Kia Ora Coo-ee* Mar. 15/1 Once I was punching with a team of bullocks up in North Queensland. **1943** *Bulletin* (Sydney) 1 Sept. 12/3 He strikes a job in the unfenced top-end of S.A., punching cattle.

2. *transf.*

1933 R.B. PLOWMAN *Camel Pads* 67 Loading half a ton of gear on to his camels nearly every morning required plenty of brute strength, and 'punching' them over an almost roadless area .. was no weakling's job. **1967** F.T. MACARTNEY *Proof against Failure* 49 The job was punching weaners, which means mustering ewes with lambs to separate the latter when weaned. **1984** W.W. AMMON et al. *Working Lives* 157 We covered twenty-seven kilometres that day—a bit different to punching the sheep on the stock routes at thirteen kilometres a day.

punch pass. *Australian National Football.* HANDPASS *n.* Also as *v. intr.*

1936 E.C.H. TAYLOR et al. *Our Austral. Game Football* 23 *Punch pass*, stand still, and hold the ball in one hand, and punch it with the other with the fist clenched. Then try it on the run. **1963** *Footy Fan* (Melbourne) I. v. 12 If you can only do a flick pass as a youngster it would be very hard to learn to punch pass properly with speed and accuracy if you want to play senior football later. **1964** *Ibid.* II. viii. 27 Players must practise, and master, the two methods of hand passing. The 'punch pass'—hitting the ball with the clenched fist—and the 'open hand pass'—hitting the ball with the front of the four fingers of the hand.

puncture, *v.* [Fig. use of *puncture*: see quot. 1980.] *intr.* To tire. Also as *ppl. a.*

1903 *Sporting News* (Launceston) 13 June 2/4 Both men were 'punctured' but finally, amid cheers, the Forth veteran got his block down. **1911** C.E.W. BEAN *'Dreadnought' of Darling* 16 The tank may have dried up, and indeed the hut may be in the next paddock, or you may walk along the fences and give out ('puncture' as they say out there) before you reach it. **1980** J. FITZPATRICK *Bicycle & Bush* 231 The pneumatic tyre made its own contribution to Australian English. The word 'puncture', with the meaning extended through the concept of deflation to mean giving out, or tiring, was in use by early this century at least. **1982** P. ADAM SMITH *Shearers* 171 A new word entered the shearers' language from the coming of the bicycle: punctured. To be exhausted, done in, beaten, was to be punctured. 'I tell you, by the end of the day I was punctured.'

punishment gang. *Hist.* A detachment of convicts subject to severe disciplinary measures as a punishment.

1832 *Sydney Monitor* 12 Dec. 2/5 If it be a punishment gang, we think that it would form a very proper part of their punishment to withhold their tobacco. **1838** *HRA* (1923) 1st Ser. XIX. 469 These Gangs to be kept separate from what are now considered the 'punishment Gangs' consisting of Criminals twice convicted. **1846** *Observer* (Hobart) 6 Mar. 3/3 Acting as overseer over a punishment gang at Swan Port.

punk. [Spec. use of *punk* rotten wood or a fungus growing on wood, used when dry as tinder: see OED(S *sb.*[3]] The fruiting body of any of many fungi, sometimes used as tinder when dry, esp. *white punk* (see WHITE *a.*[2] 1 a.).

1798 D. COLLINS *Acct. Eng. Colony N.S.W.* I. 561 She made use of the small bone of the leg of the kangooroo, round the point of which Bennilong had rolled some punk, so that it looked not unlike the button of a foie. **1833** J. BACKHOUSE *Narr. Visit Austral. Colonies* 1 Jan. (1843) 119 On a Myrtle, we met with a large fungus, such as is eaten by the natives in cases of extremity. It is known in the colony by the name of Punk, and is white and spongy; when dried it is commonly used instead of timber. **1857** F.R. NIXON *Cruise of Beacon* 26 Various epiphytic fungi, of which one of the most important is that which grows on the Eucalypti, and is known, when dry, under the name of Punk. **1880** *Proc. Linnean Soc. N.S.W.* V. 52 Some of the larger *Polypori* are known to bushmen by the name of 'Punk'. **1914** *Observer* (Adelaide) 4 July 47/4 The dried plants of *Polyporus portentosus*, called by the settlers 'punk', was of use to both whites and blacks for carrying fire. **1941** J.H. WILLIS *Victorian Fungi* 62 Hard bracket-fungi have been known collectively as 'punks'; they have the power of smouldering for many hours when once ignited, and it is interesting to recall that a certain 'punk' was employed by the Tasmanian aborigines in carrying fire. **1948** H.A. LINDSAY *Bushman's Handbk.* 70 That large, white, bread-like fungus ('punk') found growing on dead trees and rotting logs. **1977** M. TUCKER *If everyone Cared* 38 There was a fungus that grew on the gum trees, sometimes weighing six pounds, all shapes and sizes. We called it *punk*. When it was dry, we would soak it with white man's kerosene and light it at night.

punkari /'pʌŋkəri/. Also **punkary.** [a. Yaralde *paŋgari.*] *White-eyed duck*, see WHITE *a.*[2] 1 b.

1879 *Native Tribes S.A.* 42 Dense flocks of widgeon (native, punkeri) .. abound on the lakes. **1955** S. OSBORNE *Duck Shooting Aust.* 11 Punkary are generally fat and well rounded in the body; the flesh is very dark, and they are good eating. **1974** J. BYRNE *Duck Hunting Aust. & N.Z.* 189 The Hardhead, White-eyed Duck or Punkari (Aythya australis). The Hardhead is the sole Australian representative of the Pochards, of which several species are found in the Northern Hemisphere.

punt. [f. *punt, v.* to bet upon a horse, etc.] A gamble, usu. in the phr. **to take a punt.**

1965 J. O'GRADY *Aussie Eng.* 71 To 'take a punt at' anything is the equivalent of to 'have a go'. **1969** *Sydney Morning Herald* 7 June 25/9 Melbourne .. selectors have 'taken a punt' in naming 20-year-old Russell Collingwood as centre half-forward. **1978** O. WHITE *Silent Reach* 253 Blackness and silence. So take a punt. . . He eased .. the pencil torch out of his bag.

punty /'pʌnti/. [a. Western Desert *panti.*] Any of several shrubs of the genus *Cassia* (fam. Caesalpiniaceae), incl. *C. nemophila* var. *nemophila* of all mainland States; *kangaroo bush* (a), see KANGAROO *n.* 5. Also **punty bush.**

1892 G. PARKER *Round Compass in Aust.* 43 The sheep have gone from grass to salt-bush .. and from salt-bush to the puntie .. for their food. **1921** K.S. PRICHARD *Black Opal* 154 Once, in the springtime, he had caught a glimpse of a spray of punti—the yellow boronia. **1975** R.O. MOORE *Sunlit Plains Extended* 34 Puntee, a bush of golden buttercup-shaped flowers. **1977** *Ecos* xiii. 17/3 At first they neglected the woody weeds, desert cassia (*Cassia eremophila*) and its close relative punty. **1981** G.M. CUNNINGHAM et al. *Plants Western N.S.W.* 379 Numerous paddocks adjacent to homesteads and once cleared and ploughed for the growing of oats .. now support dense pure stands of punty bush.

pup. In the phr. **the night's (only) a pup,** 'the night is young'. Also **the day's (only) a pup,** and in other contexts.

1915 *Bulletin* (Sydney) 11 Dec. 32/2 The night was not even a pup yet; it was broad daylight, being Northern summer. **1921** K.S. PRICHARD *Black Opal* 104 You're not taking her away yet, Michael? The night's a pup! **1928** 'BRENT OF BIN BIN' *Up Country* 167 The night is only a pup yet. **1934** T. WOOD *Cobbers* 138 'What's the worry?' they say; 'the day's a pup.' **1949** L. GLASSOP *Lucky Palmer* 73 We'll get him in. The day's only a pup yet. **1968** G. DUTTON *Andy* 198 'Are you thinking of driving out to Hangingstone to-night?' 'It's only forty miles and the night is a pup.' **1983** *Newcastle Herald* 26 Apr. 2/7 So far the national shearers' strike is only a pup. Four weeks may be a long time without work in most industries, but in shearers' terms it is nothing.

pure merino: see MERINO.

purge. *Obs.* [Joc. use of *purge* an aperient medicine.] Alcoholic liquor.

1891 *Truth* (Sydney) 17 May 3/4 We had no credit for purge at the nearest shop. **1898** *Ibid.* 21 Aug. 7/1 Those grosser, but more satisfying, liquids, known as 'purge' and 'tanglefoot'. **1910** *Ibid.* 25 Dec. 6/4 If he went for inspiration to the 'purge' he praises, he would be, if it were possible, a much worse poet. **1929** *Bulletin* (Sydney) 13 Mar. 23/3 That's larrikin jargon of a 50-year-old vintage. . . We used to call food 'scran' and beer 'purge'.

purler. Also, and now more commonly, **pearler.** [Transf. use of *purler* 'a throw or blow that hurls anyone head-foremost; a knock-down blow': see OED(S.] Something surpassingly good, or otherwise remarkable (of its kind).

1935 R.B. PLOWMAN *Boundary Rider* 149 My face was covered in blood and I had a pearla of a headache. **1941** S.J. BAKER *Pop. Dict. Austral. Slang* 57 *Purl, purler*, something excellent, outstandingly good. **1948** R. RAVEN-HART *Canoe in Aust.* 66 'A purler' meant something super-excellent and not a bad fall, usually from a horse. **1951** W. HATFIELD *Wild Dog Frontier* 32 Hit him fair astern. . . A pearler! But what a shot I am, eh? Two chances .. and two clean misses! **1953** D. STIVENS *Gambling Ghost* 99 Afterwards he heard the owner and the trainer telling each other what a beauty, a pearler and a trimmer the other racehorse was. **1961** X. HERBERT *Soldiers' Women* 302 You must be a pearler cook, Jackie! **1980** *Weekend Austral.* (Sydney) 16 Aug. 13 Flo's 35-minute speech was a pearler. **1984** *Age* (Melbourne) 12 June 40/8 Michael Egan played a pearler in the back pocket for Footscray.

purple, *a.* Used as a distinguishing epithet in the names of flora and fauna: **purple apple berry,** the twining shrub *Billardiera longiflora* (fam. Pittosporaceae) of N.S.W., Vic., and Tas., bearing a shiny, usu. purple, berry; **-backed wren,** the bird *Malurus lamberti assimilis* of arid Aust., the male having a purplish mantle; **coral pea,** see *coral pea* (b), CORAL; **-crowned lorikeet,** the brightly-coloured lorikeet *Glossopsitta porphyrocephala* of s.w. and s.e. mainland Aust.; **-crowned wren,** the predom. brown and white, blue-tailed bird *Malurus coronatus*, occurring near water in parts of n. Aust., the breeding male having a purple and black crown; **-top,** any of several plants bearing purple flowers, esp. the naturalized S. American perennial *Verbena bonariensis* (fam. Verbenaceae).

1835 *Hobart Town Almanack* 71 **Purple** fruited **Apple berry**. . . The purple berries, full of seed, hang in elegant festoons for several months in the latter part of the season. **1930** A.J. EWART *Flora Vic.* 559 Purple Apple-berry .. found in S., N.E., and E. Victoria, usually along mountain streams and gullies. **1984** E. WALLING *On Trail Austral. Wildflowers* 69 The climbing Purple Apple-berry that elbows its way to the light through dwarf tea-tree. **1985** *Canberra Times* 20 June (Suppl.) 1/5 *Billardiera longiflora* (purple apple berry) occurs in the A.C.T., N.S.W., Victoria and Tasmania. This very attractive creeper is suitable for training against a shady fence. **1903** *Emu* III. 36 *Malurus assimilis* (**Purple-backed Wren**) . . not uncommon on coast and inland. **1945** C. BARRETT *Austral. Bird Life* 193 The purple-backed wren . . is a northern and western species. **1964** M. SHARLAND *Territory of Birds* 140 The Purple-backed Wren . . is reported to occur around Larrimah. **1902** *Emu* I. 124 *Glossopsittacus porphyrocephalus*, **Purple-crowned Lorikeet**. . . The distinctive porphyry-coloured patch on the crown of the head showed itself. **1929** A.H. CHISHOLM *Birds & Green Places* 209 The purple-crowned lorikeet, the only one of Australia's nectar-loving parrots not recorded in Queensland. **1962** B.W. LEAKE *Eastern Wheatbelt Wildlife* 76 Practically gone are the vast flocks of purple crowned lorikeets. **1984** M. BLAKERS et al. *Atlas Austral. Birds* 257 The Purple-crowned Lorikeet inhabits mallee, eucalypt woodland and forest. **1898** E.E. MORRIS *Austral Eng.* 519 **Purple-crowned W[ren]**—*M[alurus] coronatus*. **1945** C. BARRETT *Austral. Bird Life* 191 The lovely purple-crowned wren (*Rosina coronata*), forms a genus of its own. **1964** M. SHARLAND *Territory of Birds* 139 On the far western side of the Territory along the edge of the mighty Victoria River the elusive Purple-crowned Wren . . was found living in clumps of rank canegrass. **1984** *Age* (Melbourne) 10 Apr. 28/8 The beautiful Purple-crowned Wren . . lives in pandanus thickets along northern rivers, where grazing cattle threaten their habitat. **1890** A. MACKAY *Austral. Agriculturist* (ed. 2) 148 Malignant weeds . . are taking the place of so many valuable grasses . . cobblers' pegs . . **purple top** (*Vitadenia Australis*), and several other pests. **1920** J.H. MAIDEN *Weeds N.S.W.* 70 'Wild Verbena or Vervain', 'Purple-Top or Weed' . . is a very old Australian colonist, and now it is found practically over the settled parts of Australia. **1965** *Austral. Encycl.* IX. 104 South American *V[erbena] bonariensis* (purple-top) and *V. rigida* . . are violet-flowered and have become annoying weeds in many parts of the Commonwealth. **1981** G.M. CUNNINGHAM et al. *Plants Western N.S.W.* 569 Purple-top is rarely abundant. . . Its tall erect habit, characteristic bundled purple flowers and squarish stems make it quite conspicuous.

push. [Spec. use of *push* a 'press' of people, a crowd: see OED(S *sb.*[1] 8 and 9.]

a. A group of people having a common interest or background; a coterie.

[**1812** J.H. VAUX *Mem.* (1819) II. 199 *Push*, a crowd or concourse of people, either in the streets, or at any public place of amusement, &c., when any particular scene of crowding is alluded to, they say, *the push*, as *the push*, at the *spell* doors; *the push* at the *stooping-match*, &c.] **1884** *Bulletin* (Sydney) 30 Aug. 10/1 We wished we were in the 'push' to go with them overland to Sydney. **1890** *Quiz* (Adelaide) 10 Oct. 8/1 No one would be any the worse, except perhaps the North Adelaide 'push'. (*Quiz* notices that this classic word of the larrikins is now being used by our polite society.) They—the 'push'—might never reconcile themselves to a locally chosen Governor, but then the honest, simple section of the community would. **1892** *Bulletin* (Sydney) 20 Feb. 7/4 The artificial hole-and-corner 'push' known as the Victorian 'country party'. **1895** W. MCMILLAN *Austral. Gossip & Story* 32 If you took Australia and scattered our little push all over the land, we'd have about one person to each square mile. **1905** *Truth* (Sydney) 14 May 4/6 There is a big push of sanctimonious saints in Wanganui. **1916** *Ibid.* 11 June 8/1 Along comes the Federal push and makes me close at six, then at eight. **1937** A.W. UPFIELD *Mr Jelly's Business* 13 The farm push are short-handed, and there's a chaff order to be sent away. **1943** C. SHAW *Warrumbungle Mare* 13 They'll strum their 'arps, an' 'owl their songs, an' gaze in 'ouris eyes, Or join th' 'erald-angel push an' romp aroun' the skies. **1971** *Bulletin* (Sydney) 13 Nov. 13/1 Would you also believe that at this freezing Melburnian hour the South Yarra push was still dressed for the occasion . . gorgeous shirts, dashing cravats and girls in hot pants. **1976** *Ibid.* 21 Aug. 31/3 Its new 'Adelaide Push', under station manager Paul Thompson, 33 . . is implementing a . . model designed exclusively for Sydney radio audiences. **1986** *Sydney Morning Herald* 8 Mar. 3/6 The piece was produced by a New York push which appears so far to be dominating the festival.

b. *Hist.* A gang of larrikins; *larrikin push*, see LARRIKIN 1 c. Also *attrib.*

1890 *Truth* (Sydney) 19 Oct. 3/6 Suppose a live policeman is on the ground while the gay and festive members of a 'push' are 'giving him Bondi'. **1892** *Bulletin* (Sydney) 20 Feb. 15/4 The Sydney 'pushes' are becoming as formidable as the Italian secret societies. **1893** D. HEALEY *Cornstalk* 66 The remaining larrikins are all members of organized gangs, called 'pushes' or 'talents'. . . As these . . gangs, the members of which range in age from 15 to 30 years, have feudal quarrels raging between them, a war of extermination is being continuously waged. **1896** N. GOULD *Town & Bush* 100 They band together in 'pushes', and are known by the names of the localities in which they reside—such as the 'Rocks Push', the 'Gipp Street Push', or the 'Woolloomooloo Push', as the case may be. **1901** *Brisbane Courier* 24 Aug. 4/4 Each push has its own elected king—generally a pawnbroker, publican, or small storekeeper—to whom tribute must be paid by all his subjects. **1912** T.E. SPENCER *Bindawalla* 92 Come out to the camp, an' be men, you wall-eyed scrapings of the Rocks' Push. **1922** *Daily Mail* (Sydney) 6 Jan. 1/6 Sydney can get along without a revival of the pushes who ruled the roost in less ordered times. **1932** K.S. PRICHARD *Kiss on Lips* 45 Deceased, who was an associate of thieves and criminals, has probably paid the penalty of a push vendetta. **1951** D. STIVENS *Jimmy Brockett* 80, I told her about Glebe, and being out of work, and the old days with the push. **1963** *Bulletin* (Sydney) 6 July 15/1 The Fitzroy murderers were one of the bad pushes at the end of the last century, say 1870 to 1890. **1980** C. JAMES *Unreliable Mem.* 139 The world of crime started just where the Push finished, and often the edges overlapped.

c. *Hist.* A libertarian group in Sydney: see quot. 1963.

1963 *Sunday Tel.* (Sydney) 20 Jan. 2/2 The Royal George Hotel, at the corner of King and Sussex Streets . . has for some years been the headquarters of members and ex-members of the Sydney University Libertarian Society—known simply as 'The Push'. **1964** *Oz* (Sydney) June 13/1 In response to his article in the 'Libertarian Broadsheet' (which attacked the 'gutlessness' of Sydney's Push), Frank Morehouse was asked to speak at a recent meeting of the Humanist Society. **1967** *Kings Cross Whisper* (Sydney) xxxviii. 10/3 *Push*, a group of bohemian type characters to evolve since the war. **1971** *Bulletin* (Sydney) 28 Aug. 6/3 The Push to my knowledge consists of a strange pack of academic bores, bar-room intellectuals of various persuasions, homo-sexuals, crooks and alcoholics, with some reasonable, human and charming people in all sections. **1972** *Ibid.* 1 Jan. 39/1 On the street side are students and academics, remnants of Sydney's Push, old anarchists, advertising people and miscellaneous aged drunks. **1973** *Ibid.* 17 Feb. 40/3 He knew Germaine from the old days of the Push.

d. *transf.*

1903 H. TAUNTON *Australind* 92 We suddenly darted from our hiding-places with loud yells and cracking of stock-whips to gallop round between the wild mob and the edge of the thicket to force them to take refuge in the midst of our tame 'Push'. **1913** *Bulletin* (Sydney) 25 Sept. 22/2 It was a common, barnyard fowl that squared the deal between me and the scorpion push.

Hence **pushism** *n.*, the practice of forming street gangs; **pushite** *n.*, a member of a push, esp. in sense b; **pushy** *a.*, having the characteristics of a *pushite*.

1892 *Truth* (Sydney) 15 May 3/7 'Larrikinism' and '**pushism**' are growing, and it is time to take steps. **1901** *Tocsin* (Melbourne) 10 Oct. 2/3 The extent to which 'pushism' has any relation to slums is simply this, that where homes are not such as afford proper accommodation the children necessarily pass a great deal of time in the streets. **1899** *Worker* (Sydney) 11 Feb. 2/2 Strike the fear of the law deep down into the hearts of the '**pushites**'. **1901** *Truth* (Sydney) 11 Aug. 1/3 Every sane man who has taken the trouble to observe the manners of the 'pushite' must at once admit that there is no greater cur on earth than the Australian larrikin. **1915** *Bulletin* (Sydney) 3 June 22/4 The olden time bullock-driver, like the Woolloomooloo pushite, is degenerating out of sight almost. **1929** *Ibid.* 13 Mar. 23/3, I remember—yes, I was a pushite. **1946** A.H. CHISHOLM *Making of Sentimental Bloke* 76 It was a simple thing, perhaps, for an imaginative writer to take one of these 'pushites' . . subject him to romantic treatment, and show him . . in process of mellowing under the influence of a wholesome girl. **1902** *Bulletin* (Sydney) 12 July 16/3 Hard faces, shaven upper lips, straw and Mount Rennie hats, shoddy suits and bludger's neckerchiefs—all of the 'Push', **Pushy**!

pusher. Alteration of 'push-chair'.

1953 A.W. UPFIELD *Murder must Wait* 60 Several prams and pushers parked in an alcove. **1965** D. MARTIN *Hero of Too* 311 Lacy was standing there, too, looking proud, with Charlie in his pusher. **1983** *Austral. Women's Weekly* (Sydney) Aug. 21/1 Pushers (push-chairs to the Poms), the collapsible chair on wheels for conveying small children, is a stroller in N.S.W. and Queensland.

push the knot, to: see KNOT 1.

pussy, *v. intr.* To move (in) quietly or unobtrusively.

1919 E. DYSON *Hello, Soldier* 31 We held that stinkin' cellar, though, 'n' when the day was done Son pussied on his bingie where a Maxie trim 'n' neat Had spit out loaded lightnin'. **1975** *Bulletin* (Sydney) 26 Apr. 45/3 Ratty Jack was stallin' for me to pussy in as soon as Limp slews the tart.

pussy tail. Any of many herbs or shrubs of the large genus *Ptilotus* (fam. Amaranthaceae), chiefly of arid Aust., bearing a soft, fluffy flower-head; MULLA MULLA. Also **pussy tails**.

1916 *Emu* XV. 154 Many acres were covered in the fluffy purple plumes of *Trichinium exaltum*, commonly called 'pussy tails'. **1937** M. TERRY *Sand & Sun* 67 Salvation Jane, buck-bush, and pussy-tail predominated. **1965** *N. Austral. Monthly* Jan. 5 The small headed Pussy Tail with sweet scent re-appeared. **1981** J. BURT *Shutterbug in Bush* 197 The mulla mullas (*ptilotus*) in particular thrilled us as these specimens, popularly known as pussy tails in central Australia, were the finest I'd seen . . their plum mauve blooms swaying gracefully in the breeze.

put, *v.*

1. [See OED(S *v.*[1] 44 l. *put in*.] In the phr. **to put in,** to inform on; to 'frame'; to secure the conviction of (a person); to send to prison. Also *transf.*

[**1888** G. ROCK *Colonists* 55 Ye'll put me in the logs too? There's not a crusher on the diggin's as can do it.] **1911** A. WRIGHT *Gambler's Ghost* (1923) 82, I ain't wantin' anythin' ter do with th' police. . . They put me in fer six weeks after your affair. **1922** —— *Colt from Country* 153 'I might have a chance with the girl again.' 'After what you did to put her in?' laughed the detective. 'I like your hide.' **1951** 'S. MACKENZIE' *Dead Men Rising* 52 Nothing would give me greater pleasure than to put you in, only that's about the one thing I've never done in my life. **1957** D. NILAND *Call me when Cross turns Over* 174 Don't put me in. Don't try to hang anything on me. **1966** P. COWAN *Seed* 106, I suppose when they make you a prefect you'll put us in. **1975** *Sydney Morning Herald* 3 July 11/1 A lagger is someone who puts people in to the police.

2. [See OED(S *v.*[1] 53 *put up*.] In the phr. **to put up a drink,** etc., to buy (an alcoholic drink) on credit.

1896 H. LAWSON *While Billy Boils* (1975) 13 We walked right into the bar, handed over our swags, put up four drinks, and tried to look as if we'd just drawn our cheques and didn't care a curse for any man. **1902** —— *Children of Bush* 282 'Put up a drink'—i.e., 'Give me a drink on credit,' or 'Chalk it up.' **1936** *Bulletin* (Sydney) 4 Mar. 21/1 Murlonga . . can 'put up' a beer in my name anywhere.

3. [See OED(S *v.*[1] 50 b. *put through*.] In the phr. **to put through,** to shear (sheep).

1908 C.H.S. MATTHEWS *Parson in Austral. Bush* 137 At one station last shearing season 110,000 sheep were 'put through', as the shearers say, in about 7 weeks. **1917** T.J. BRIGGS *Life & Experience Successful W. Austral.* 101 The tallies were not so high. However, I made a decent cheque as I put through about 100 jumbucks per day. **1921** G.A. BELL *Under Brigalows* 143 The 'Nindarra' sheep had been 'put through'. **1937** E. HILL *Great Austral. Loneliness* 266 Mrs Giles was wool-classing. . . She has a little flock that she 'puts through' herself for pin money.

4. [See OED(S *v.*[1] 46 *put on*.] In the phr. **to put it on** (a person), to exert strong pressure (upon someone), esp. to secure a favour. See also *to put the acid* ACID and *to put the hard word on* HARD.

1943 *Austral. New Writing* 44 Put it on the boys yet, Sid? . . Pull 'em all out, eh, Sid? **1944** A.E. MINNIS *And*

All Trees are Green 68 He told me it wasn't a bagman's camp when I put it on him this afternoon—me, that was a gun shearer years before he was dropped. **1946** *Bulletin* (Sydney) 7 Aug. 28/4 The boss asks what I want, so I put it on him for a hand-out an' he tells the other bloke t' get it for me. **1961** L. GLASSOP *We were Rats* (ed. 3) 19 'O.K., Spike. Only I gotta have the blonde, see? You take the chance on her cobber.' 'Suits me, Mick... I'll have a pint at the Royal tomorrer and put it on the blonde. She'll be jake.' **1977** B. SCOTT *My Uncle Arch* 135 He came good, when we put it on him for a job without any argument.

put the acid: see ACID.

Putt's pine. [f. the name of the settler Edward A. *Putt* (1865–1951) of Barron River, n. Qld.: see quot. 1945.] The rainforest tree *Flindersia acuminata* (fam. Rutaceae) of the Atherton Tablelands, n. Qld.; the soft, silvery wood of the tree, having an unpleasant smell when green.

1926 *Qld. Agric. Jrnl.* XXV. 435 Flindersia acuminata. Putts Pine (Atherton). **1945** J. DEVANNY *Bird of Paradise* 37 A chap named Putt came to my father in the mill and offered to sell him some pine... When it reached the yard he found it was timber he had never seen before... A timber man.. asked him what sort of wood it was... Dad answered: 'That's Putt's pine.' **1965** *Austral. Encycl.* IV. 112 *F[lindersia] acuminata* .. is restricted as far as is known to the Atherton Tableland, where it is most commonly known as Putt's pine... It has soft wood, suitable for cabinet work and general indoor purposes.

putty. [Perh. fig. use of *putty* a powder, in contradistinction to *snuff* in the phr. *up to snuff* 'up to scratch' (see OED(S *snuff, sb.*[3] 3 a.).] In the phr. **up to putty,** worthless; ineffectual; 'in a mess'.

1916 'MEN OF ANZAC' *Anzac Bk.* 32 A man's got a chance to hit back there, but down 'ere it's up to putty. **1918** *Kia Ora Coo-ee* May 5/2 She took it, with the remark, that issue fags were up to putty. **1920** 'RETURNED SOLDIER' *Anzac Mem.*, 'What do you think of it? ..' 'Up to putty, sir... It's the dirtiest regiment I ever inspected.' **1936** *Bulletin* (Sydney) 18 Nov. 20/4 The camp greasy.. always.. knows what is going on at the other end of the run; that the improvements are up to putty; when the manager will get the sack; when the station will go broke. **1951** S. HICKEY *Travelled Roads* 47 In politics all are for the party, whether up to snuff or up to putty. **1973** *Bronze Swagman Bk. Bush Verse* (1974) 14 Can't ya see her tail was broken... And her breeding's up to putty.

pyalla, var. PIALLA.

pycnantha wattle /pɪknænθə 'wɒtl/. [The specific epithet *pycnantha* was applied by the English botanist George Bentham (Hooker in *Lond. J. Bot.* (1842) I. 351); a. Gr. πυκνός dense + ἄνθος a flower, referring to the dense flowering of the plant.] *Golden wattle*, see GOLDEN 3.

[**1842** *London Jrnl. Bot.* I. 351 *A. pycnantha* (sp. n.) glaberrima, nitida, ramulis teretibus, phyllodiis elongatofalcatis obtusis [etc.].] **1938** C.T. WHITE *Princ. Bot. Qld. Farmers* 181 The wattle yielding bark richest in tannin is the Golden Wattle of South Australia (*Acacia pycnantha*), commonly known in commerce as 'pycnantha wattle'. **1979** C. KLEIN *Women of Certain Age* 60 The gold of the last pycnantha wattles shone strident.

pygmy. Used *attrib.* in the names of birds and animals: **pygmy goose,** either of the two short-billed waterbirds of the genus *Nettapus* occurring on deep lagoons in Aust. and elsewhere, *N. pulchellus* of n. and n.e. Aust. and *N. coromandelianus* of e. Aust.; see also *white-quilled goose* WHITE *a.*[2] 1 b.; **possum** (formerly **opossum, phalanger**), any of the small, mainly nocturnal, marsupials of the fam. Burramyidae of n.e., e., and s. Aust. incl. Tas., and New Guinea; DORMOUSE POSSUM; see also *mountain pygmy possum* MOUNTAIN.

1842 J. GOULD *Birds of Aust.* (1848) VII. Pl. 5, *Nettapus coromandelianus.* **Pygmy Goose.** **1910** *Bulletin* (Sydney) 29 Sept. 14/3 Pigmy geese are not found solely in the Northern Territory. **1934** WARBURTON & ROBERTSON *Buffaloes* 40 Pygmy geese—the exact replica in miniature of the goose we know in civilization. **1946** D. BARR *Warrigal Joe* 100 You could travel all over Australia without seeing a prettier sight than pygmy geese among blue water-lilies on an inland lagoon. **1964** M. SHARLAND *Territory of Birds* 104 Here, too, were Pigmy Geese, the quaintest and most delightful of geese... Who would imagine a goose to be no more than thirteen inches in length, smaller even than our smallest teal! **1980** C. ALLISON *Hunter's Man. Aust. & N.Z.* 115 A number of other birds are rare enough to be fully protected, including the Green pygmy goose, the White pygmy goose and the Burdekin Duck. **1794** [**pygmy possum**] G. SHAW *Zool. New Holland* 5 *Didelphis Pygmaea.* The Pygmy Opossum .. (exclusive of its diminutive size, not exceeding that of a common domestic mouse) forms as it were a kind of connecting link between the genera of Didelphis and Sciurus, or Opossum and Squirrel. **1829** Tas. Colonial Secretary's Office Rec. 1/44 241, Among some dead wood near the stream Mr Frankland caught a pigmy oppossum. **1855** *Illustr. Sydney News* 7 Apr. 156/1 The Pigmy Phalanger .. much resembles the common dormouse of Europe. It inhabits the southern portions of Australia especially the Swan River district. Its habits are strictly nocturnal, it secretes itself during the day in the hollows of trees, and at night leaves its retreat for the flowering branches of low shrubs. **1927** *Bulletin* (Sydney) 23 June 27/3, I wonder if 'WO3' .. ever 'witnessed the birth' of a pygmy 'possum? **1932** *Victorian Naturalist* XLIX. 169 'Erastus', the Pigmy Possum .. was sent by post from the Murray River in a match-box. **1955** N. PULLIAM *I traveled Lonely Land* 150 The engaging sugar glider and the pygmy possum. **1968** R. HILL *Bush Quest* 131 Now a pigmy possum has also been found. Hitherto known only from skeletal remains, this small and pretty animal was discovered sheltering in a hut on Mt Hotham. **1985** *New Idea* (Melbourne) 20 Aug. 3 Rob rears all varieties of possums, from pygmy possums .. to the big fellows cursed by orchardists and householders.

pyjama cricket. Cricket as played under the rules governing one-day international matches: see quot. 1983.

1982 *Sun-Herald* (Sydney) 31 Jan. 35/3 He feels indulgent towards 'pyjama' cricket, the name he gives to the one-day variety, but prefers the challenge that Test cricket poses. **1983** *Ibid.* 9 Jan. 4/2 The very mention of 'pyjama' cricket—a name born of the players' multi-coloured uniforms—makes veteran observers like former Test bowler, Bill O'Reilly, cringe.

python. [Fig. use of *python* a snake.] In the phr. **to syphon the python**: (of a male) to urinate.

1968 B. HUMPHRIES *Wonderful World Barry McKenzie*, I'm flamin' urgently desirous to syphon the python! **1978** D. BALL *Great Austral. Snake Exchange* 16 Brooks was struck with an overpowering urge to piss. Syphon the python, he thought.

Q

q, var. CUE *n.* and *v.*

Q fever. [See quot. 1964.] An acute infectious disease caused by the rickettsial organism *Coxiella burneti.*

1937 *Med. Jrnl. Aust.* II. Aug. 282 The suspicion arose and gradually grew into a conviction that we were here dealing with a type of fever which had not been previously described. It became necessary to give it a name, and 'Q' fever was chosen to denote it until fuller knowledge should allow a better name. **1964** *Qld.'s Health* Dec. 11/2 'X' is a recognised term for an unknown quantity. But Australia already had an 'X disease', now known as Murray valley encephalitis. However, the rest of the alphabet was open. Query also signified the unknown. 'Q (for query) fever' it became. . . Many have wrongly assumed that the 'Q' stands for Queensland. **1982** P. ADAM SMITH *Shearers* 230 Since 1970 small numbers of men in central and western Queensland have suffered from what they call 'Q' fever. A dengue-type heat and delirium builds up until the man must be hospitalised. Some take months to recover. Shearers believe doctors are mystified . . but other observers believe it to be just another manifestation of the Barcoo Rot. **1985** *Age* (Melbourne) 1 Apr. 15/2 Bairnsdale ulcers is one of the few diseases—Q fever is another—to be described first and fully identified in Australia.

quack. [Joc. use of *quack* (medical) charlatan; used elsewhere but recorded earliest in Aust.] A medical practitioner; an army medical officer.

1919 W.H. DOWNING *Digger Dialects* 40 *Quack,* a medical officer. **1922** C. DREW *Rogues & Ruses* 8 A man can't talk in front of the quack here. **1943** *Coast to Coast 1942* 29 Might be he lose his leg if we don't get him across right away to the quack. **1957** V. PALMER *Rainbow-Bird* 84 Looks as if he might peg out before they get him to the quack. **1968** J. ALARD *He who shoots Last* 145 Ya didn't eat yer grub and ya looks like ya gonna conk out. Ya better see da quack. **1976** D. IRELAND *Glass Canoe* 136, I go along to this quack and he says Get back to the surf and get some green vegetables into you.

quadroon. [Transf. use of *quadroon* one who has a quarter of Negro blood.] A person of one quarter Aboriginal descent; also (loosely) one of part Aboriginal descent. Also as *adj.*

1901 *Truth* (Sydney) 17 Mar. 4/6 The common method of procuring a wife (gin, quadroon, or white) is to buy her. **1915** J.R.B. LOVE *Aborigines* 32 The quadroon child is white, and should be treated as such. **1933** R.B. PLOWMAN *Man from Oodnadatta* 26 The son's full-blooded black wife; the bride's quadroon sister. **1955** J. CLEARY *Justin Bayard* 38 'That's the trouble! They've been here too long. Blanche was born here.' Julie came to the foot of the bed, grasping the rail with both hands. 'She's a quadroon!' **1965** C. JOHNSON *Wild Cat Falling* 70 He has a right to challenge me to produce my exemption ticket. As a quadroon I would be eligible for this.

quagga, var. QUOKKA.

quail. [Transf. use of *quail* a migratory bird allied to the partridge, esp. *Coturnix coturnix.*]

1. a. Any of several small, ground-dwelling birds of the fam. Phasianidae, as STUBBLE QUAIL. **b.** Any of several similar birds of the genus *Turnix* (fam. Turnicidae). **c.** *Plain wanderer,* see PLAIN 2.

1770 J. BANKS *Endeavour Jrnl.* (1962) II. 59, I made a small excursion in order to shoot anything I could meet with and found a large quantity of Quails, much resembling our English ones. **1788** *HRA* (1914) 1st Ser. I. 32 Here are wild ducks, teal and quails. **1821** T. GODWIN *Descr. Acct. Van Diemen's Island* 9 The birds are . . snipes, quails and a variety of other birds not known in Europe. **1847** J. GOULD *Birds of Aust.* (1848) V. Pl. 90, During my visit to Van Diemen's Land I was frequently informed that there were two kinds of Quail besides the stubble and painted Quails, the former of which is a true *Coturnix* and the latter a *Hemipodius.* **1853** S. SIDNEY *Three Colonies* (ed. 2) 245 As they rode along, ground pigeons, grass parroquets, and quails rose up in thousands. **1945** C. BARRETT *Austral. Bird Life* 67 While all the quails are engaging birds, some are useful too, since they eat the seeds of noxious plants. **1976** *Reader's Digest Compl. Bk. Austral. Birds* 141 Quails are small, plump birds with rounded wings and tails so short as to seem absent. They are separated as a group from the button quails as they have a small hind toe.

2. With distinguishing epithet, as **brown, king, little, painted, stubble, swamp:** see under first element.

quail-thrush. Any bird of the genus *Cinclosoma*: see *ground thrush* GROUND *n.* 1

1926 *Official Checklist Birds Aust.* (R. Australasian Ornith. Union) p. iv, Vernacular names have also been closely examined. Some indefinite names like Ground-bird have been replaced by more appropriate names, such as Quail-thrush. **1962** J. MARSHALL *Journey among Men* 172 Next day Tom Moriarty took us to a part of his property where he said we could obtain the quail-thrush. **1984** SIMPSON & DAY *Birds of Aust.* 324 Genus *Cinclosoma,* the quail-thrushes, includes four endemics. Shy, elusive, ground-dwellers, they usually flush away with a quail-like 'whirr'.

Qualup bell /ˈkweɪləp bɛl/. Also **Quailup.** [f. the name of *Qualup* in s.w. W.A.: see quot. 1933 and 1977.] The shrub *Pimelea physodes* (fam. Thymelaeaceae) of s.w. W.A.: see quot. 1981.

1916 *Bulletin* (Sydney) 9 Mar. 22/2 Almost every bush and tree has its blossom. The two most beautiful are the hibiscus . . and the Quailup bell. **1921** E.H. PELLOE *Wildflowers W.A.* 50 'Qualup Bell' . . an erect shrub of about 3 ft., glabrous except the flowers. **1933** *W. Austral. Hist. Soc. Jrnl. & Proc.* II. xiii. 25 Riding along Wellstead's bullock dray track, which rises from the Qualup Valley . . the writer, in the spring of 1878 suddenly found himself surrounded by a galaxy of beautiful blooms. . . The 'Qualup Bell', as it is now called, has great bell-shaped flowers of a delicate greenish-yellow colour, splashed and flushed with crimson. **1949** D. WALKER *We went to Aust.* 184 Another gravel plant is the qualup bell with almost the colour of a ripe Cox's orange pippin. **1977** M. BIGNELL *Fruit of Country* 4 Among the unending variety of plants . . is to be found the exquisite Qualup bell (*Pimelea physodes*). . . Originally the area of the West Mount Barren was known as 'Queelup' and a derivation of this word was given to a small outpost that was eventually made in the locality by an early settler. **1979** *Ecos* xxii. 12/3 The Qualup bell . . is a rare Western Australian plant extensively traded, locally and overseas. **1981** J.A. BAINES *Austral. Plant Genera* 286 The magnificent . . Qualup Bell, the only sp. in this genus with a large bell-like inflorescence, which consists of reddish-green bracts enclosing greenish-yellow flowers, extending from Gairdner River to Ravensthorpe but named from Quallup [*sic*] . . near the mouth of that river.

quamby /ˈkwɒmbi/, *n.* [f. next.] A camp; a temporary shelter.

[**1833** H.W. PARKER *Rise, Progress, & Present State Van Dieman's Land* 77 Quamby's Bluff.] **1841** *Geelong Advertiser* 9 Jan. 3/5 The name of the town was originally the same as that of the district in Geelong. . . We defy the English gazetteer to produce a prettier name for a prettier township, than the one given by the ignorant aboriginal blacks, to this white man's *quamby.* **1846** G.H. HAYDON *Five Yrs. Experience Aust. Felix* 128 We . . erected our shelters or quambys as they are generally called after the native name. **1848** *Britannia* (Hobart) 27 July 4/5 Then came total darkness, while 'starry night' spread her canopy over their cheerless *quamby.* **1851** *Empire* (Sydney) 13 Dec. 464/5 There have been a number of robberies here lately, and in almost every instance the quamby has been entered at night, when the dog was asleep, and the bag taken away. **1911** J. MOORE-ROBINSON *Rec. Tasmanian Nomenclature* 79 *Quamby Bluff*—said to have been named from the aboriginal word, which means 'mercy', from the fact that a pursued native fell on his knees on the spot, and exclaimed 'Quamby! Quamby!'

quamby /ˈkwɒmbi/, *v.* Also **quambi, quambie, quomby.** [a. Wuywurung and Wathawurung *guwambi* to sleep; a sleeping place.] *intr.* To lie down; to camp. Also, as an imp., 'stop' (see quot. 1830).

1830 *Hobart Town Almanack* 53 This native . . is said to have fallen on his knees, calling out Quamby! quamby! that is, in the native language, mercy, mercy, spare me, spare me. **1839** *Port Phillip Gaz.* 3 Native—Where that white fellows 'quambi' (lie down)? **1845** T. McCOMBIE *Adventures of Colonist* 75 Even the aborigines say the 'Dible, Dible quambies there,' and avoid it. **1848** *Britannia* (Hobart) 13 Jan. 4/5 The spots where they [*sc.* sheep] camped every night were easily discovered, and it appeared that they had returned every evening to the place where they quambied the previous night. **1846** *Melbourne Argus* 1 Sept. 2/5 The advance party caught sight of the Cape Otway tribe, quambying on the opposite side of the river. **1859** W. BURROWS *Adventures Mounted Trooper* 112 'Black fellow quomby dead, by and by jump up white fellow . . ,' meaning, that if a black should 'quomby' i.e. lie down, and die, they would rise again white.

quandong /ˈkwɒndɒŋ/. Also **quondong,** and formerly **quandang, quantong.** [a. Wiradhuri *guwandhaŋ.*]

1. a. The shrub or small tree *Santalum acuminatum* (fam. Santalaceae) of dry country in s. Aust., bearing a globular, usu. bright red fruit with a deeply wrinkled stone containing an edible kernel; the edible fruit of the plant; see also *native peach* NATIVE *a.* 6 a. **b.** With distinguishing epithet, as **bitter quandong,** *S. murrayanum* (see quot. 1975, 2). **c.** The large rainforest tree *Elaeocarpus grandis* (fam. Elaeocarpaceae) of e. Qld. and e. N.S.W., bearing a globular blue edible fruit with a deeply wrinkled stone, and yielding a useful timber (see quot. 1937); *blue fig,* see BLUE *a.* **d.** Any of several other plants, usu. of the genera *Santalum* and *Elaeocarpus.* Also *attrib.*

1836 T.L. MITCHELL *Three Exped. Eastern Aust.* 9 May (1838) II. 69 The plain we traversed this day exactly resembled the best of the ground on the Darling, and in some places I observed the Quandang bushes having their branches covered with a parasitical plant, whose bright crimson flowers were very ornamental. *Ibid.* 19 June (1838) II. 135 In all these scrubs on the Murray, the *Fusanus acuminatus* is common, and produces the 'quandang' nut (or kernel). **1845** *Sydney Morning Herald* 19 Feb. 4/4 The roots of a shrub, called by the natives 'Quondong', are good food after having been roasted for some time under the ashes. **1850** J.B. CLUTTERBUCK *Port Phillip* 30 The indigenous *Quandang* (*Fusanus acuminatus*) is the only really palatable fruit that grows in the wilds of Port Phillip. **1859** H. KINGSLEY *Recoll. Geoffry Hamlyn* II. 249 There's plenty of quantongs over there, eh, mother, and raspberries? **1865** G.F. ANGAS *Aust.* 123 Amongst the few barely edible fruits indigenous to Australia may be mentioned . . the 'quondong' or wild peach (having a large round stone, covered with a bright scarlet pulpy skin). **1878** R.B. SMYTH *Aborigines of Vic.* II. 172 Bitter quandong-tree—Gutchu. Quandong-tree—Bitchigal. **1881** E. DAVIES *Story Earnest Life* 156 The quandong, a tree that grows only in the sandy plains of the interior. **1902** *Bulletin* (Sydney) 5 Apr. 14/3 Travellers had usually quondong buttons in their waistcoats and sometimes corks on their hats. **1911**

'ROSE BOLDREWOOD' *Complications at Collaroi* 34 One old gin . . gave me a quandong necklace and a gunny-bag for some old clothes. **1928** M.E. FULLERTON *Austral. Bush* 107 For ornamental work these states have a remarkable variety from which to draw; such as . . white quandong, coachwood. **1933** D. MACDONALD *Brooks of Morning* 46 The trained eye of a Mallee bushman picks out from a distance the 'ming' or bitter quandong, growing as a rule upon the lighter soils. **1937** *Bulletin* (Sydney) 15 Sept. 20/1 The quandong, known in some parts as the 'blue-fig', mills into a light, strong, hard timber. **1948** H.A. LINDSAY *Bushman's Handbk.* 55 *Quandong* (*wild peach*). Small tree bearing a red fruit with a large, hard, wrinkled nut inside. Eat raw, stewed or made into jam. **1959** C.V. LAWLOR *All This Humbug* 98 Don't be surprised if I go rabbiting, or gathering quandong stones at 2s. per bag. **1967** R. DONALDSON et al. *Cane!* 221 An old quandong tree stood guarding the exit, eighty feet of straight-barrelled trunk rising to pale green bell flowers and red leaves, then forty more to the sky. **1975** X. HERBERT *Poor Fellow my Country* 467 He . . made up a little fire . . nibbling the thin rosy flesh of quondongs and spitting out their great pitted seeds. **1975** A.B. & J.W. CRIBB *Wild Food in Aust.* 140 Bitter quandong, as the name suggests, has bitter and inedible fruit. **1981** B.J. BROCK *Catharsis* 56 Out on the salt crust looking at emu shit with its bitter quandong seeds.

2. *transf.*

a. In the phr. **to have (the) quandongs,** to be stupid.

1899 *Bulletin* (Sydney) 4 Mar. 15/2 F'rinstance . . the man with wheels in his head . . in the Cobar and Lachlan country . . has 'quandongs' or 'rabbits' ('Rabbits' means very severe quandongness). **1945** S.J. BAKER *Austral. Lang.* 130 The state of being stupid is described variously as . . having any one or more of . . *the quandongs* [etc.].

b. One who exploits or imposes upon another.

1939 K. TENNANT *Foveaux* 311 In this crowd of low heels, quandongs and ripperty men, she looked at her ease and yet not one of them. **1967** *Kings Cross Whisper* (Sydney) xxxviii. 10/3 *Quandong*, a girl who makes a practice of remaining virtuous after being wined and dined. **1973** F. HUELIN *Keep Moving* 178 *Quandong*, hobo who bludges or imposes on another. **1980** B. HORNADGE *Austral. Slanguage* 197 A woman who refuses to have sex after being wined and dined is called a *quandong*; the origin of the term is unknown. **1985** P. CAREY *Illywhacker* 246 'What's an illywhacker?' . . 'A spieler . . a trickster. A quandong. A ripperty man. A con-man.'

c. A country bumpkin.

1978 T. DAVIES *More Austral. Nicknames* 84 *Quandong*, was born and bred in the bush.

quanger /'kwæŋə/. [Prob. f. Fr. *coing* quince.] A quince. Also *attrib.*

1966 S.J. BAKER *Austral. Lang.* (ed. 2) 344 *Quanger*, a quince (reported from Gippsland). **1977** *Sydney Morning Herald* 5 Mar. 11/4 We had an abandoned quince orchard where we used to wage the most fantastic quanger wars.

quantong, var. QUANDONG.

quarrion /'kwɒriən/. Also **quarien, quarrian, quarrien.** [a. Ngiyampaa *guwarrayiŋ*.] COCKATIEL.

1900 A.J. CAMPBELL *Nests & Eggs Austral. Birds* 622 The Grey and Yellow Top-knotted Parrot ('Quarrion', native name among bushmen) flies round about waterholes. **1925** *Bulletin* (Sydney) 1 Oct. 24/2 Quarrians . . are now eagerly searching for nesting-places. **1926** M. FORREST *Hibiscus Heart* 92 Two quarrions sulked in a small galvanized wire cage: the bright rose and orange ear-patches contrasting with their neutral-tinted plumage and brown-barred tails. **1944** *Bulletin* (Sydney) 23 Aug. 12/3 Galahs, budgerigars and quarriens were plentiful in the early days on the eastern Darling Downs (Q.). **1945** C. BARRETT *Austral. Bird Life* 75 The quarrion . . has long been familiar as an aviary bird, overseas as well as in Australia. **1958** O. RUHEN *Naked under Capricorn* 20 All the noisy parrot world was momentarily silent—the budgerigars, the galahs . . and the quariens. **1976** N.V. WALLACE *Bush Lawyer* 129 There were flocks of green budgerigars and grey and white parrots, or quarrions.

quart. Abbrev. of QUART-POT.

1857 W. HOWITT *Tallangetta* I. 146 Cooling it by pouring it repeatedly from the quart to the pannikin and back. **1870** E.B. KENNEDY *Four Yrs. in Qld.* 36, I had to dip the pint pot in carefully to fill the *quart*, for fear of disturbing the mud. **1881** A.C. GRANT *Bush-Life Qld.* I. 44 They had almost finished their meal before the new quart 'corroborreed', as the stockmen phrased it. **1902** *Bulletin* (Sydney) 11 Jan. 32/2 The boundary-rider, musterer and such men, invariably carry a quart, which is strapped to the side of the saddle. The favorite style is the double-handled quart—one handle at the side and one over the top—with a pannikin-lid, which fits tightly into the quart. **1926** *Ibid.* 6 May 24/2 We put our 'quarts' on the edge of the fire, and in lieu of a lid . . we laid a stick across the top of the quart. **1943** G. MCIVER *Bunyip & Other Verses* 9 We camped to boil our quarts and rest 'Till the heat of the day went by. **1954** T. RONAN *Vision Splendid* 35 He's one of the old school: boiled his quart under every tree between Brewarrina and Broome. **1968** W. GILL *Petermann Journey* 24 Fifteen minutes after we arrived, the animals had been turned ahead of us to graze, the fires were lit, and the 'quarts' were on for supper. **1972** R. MAGOFFIN *Chops & Gravy* 107 *Quarts*, quartpots, a combination mug and billy-can, carried on the saddle, not necessarily always one quart capacity. **1980** S. THORNE *I've met some Bloody Wags* 31 We'd chuck our sandwiches to the dogs, and put our mudcrabs on the hot coals after we had boiled our quarts.

quart-pot. [Spec. use of *quart-pot* vessel capable of containing a quart: see OED(S.)]

1. A tin vessel, orig. of a quart capacity, used for boiling water, etc.

1806 *Sydney Gaz.* 11 May, Iron Kettles, quart pots, frying pans. **1834** J.D. LANG *Hist. & Statistical Acct. N.S.W.* II. 104 My fellow-traveller . . kindled a fire, on which he placed the tin-jug or quart-pot, which he had strapped for the purpose to his saddle-bow. **1845** D. MACKENZIE *Emigrant's Guide* 108 Every shepherd is expected to provide himself with a blanket, tin quart-pot and pint-pot; in the quart-pot he makes, and out of the pint-pot he drinks his tea. A quart-pot is often used at sheep-stations as a measure for dealing out the wheat rations to the men, 8 qts. being 1 peck. **1859** F. SINNETT *Acct. 'Rush' Port Curtis* 58 An old nail-can serving for a fire grate, wherein quart pots were placed and water boiled for tea. **1875** R. & F. HILL *What we saw in Aust.* 109 A 'quart pot' . . is a strong tin mug, with two handles of wire fixed on the same side, through which a stick can be conveniently passed, to remove the pot from the fire when too hot for the hand to approach. **1881** A.C. GRANT *Bush-Life Qld.* I. 43 'Look out there', he continued, 'quart-pot corroboree,' springing up and removing with one hand from the fire one of the quart-pots, which was boiling madly. **1902** *Bulletin* (Sydney) 11 Jan. 32/1 Billy is famous. . . He is probably an evolution of 'Old Quart-pot'—or is Quart-pot an overlander's improvement on Billy? **1922** 'J. BUSHMAN' *In Musgrave Ranges* 63 The three whites were sitting near an open pack-bag, eating damper and salt meat, and drinking tea from the drover's quart-pot. **1938** A. UPFIELD *Bone is Pointed* (1966) 102 At the lunch camp . . I discovered proof that Anderson had boiled his quart-pot there. **1956** *Bulletin* (Sydney) 24 Oct. 12/3 The jackeroos were sitting by a coolibah-shaded waterhole, waiting for their quartpots to boil. **1977** W.A. WINTER-IRVING *Bush Stories* 85 In preparation for our trip we packed corned beef, blankets, and quart pots.

2. *fig.* Used *attrib.* in various contexts: see quots.

1880 *Bulletin* (Sydney) 13 Mar. 6/2 New Chum 'Quart Pot Overseer' (*who has missed his way*): 'Haw, my abowiginal fwiend. Pway infawm me the diwection to the homestead.' **1917** W. LEES *Coaching in Aust.* 9 But oh! they were good days; rough days, quart-pot days, damper days, perhaps. **1944** *Bulletin* (Sydney) 2 Feb. 13/2 A fortnight's quartpot droving. **1973** D. STUART *Morning Star, Evening Star* 9 Tom went off horsedealing, or droving, or working at anything . . to get money for his run. 'A pair of quart pot squatters' they called themselves.

3. Special Comb. **quart-pot tea,** tea made in a quart-pot.

1854 W. HOWITT *Boy's Adventures* 112 Made our quart-pot tea. **1862** R. HENNING *Lett.* (1952) 46 You must travel in the bush to know how good quart-pot tea is. **1878** MRS H. JONES *Broad Outlines* 87 Ralph . . taking a long draught of the quart-pot tea, pronounced that nothing was ever like it made in teapots. **1894** A.B. BELL *Austral. Camp Fire Tales* 88 We gathered round our cosy camp fire, and did full justice to the hot johnny-cakes and quart-pot tea. **1903** *Bulletin* (Sydney) 31 Jan. 16/1 When I was a kiddy, quart-pot tea was as much cracked up as billy-tea is now. **1920** C.H. SAYCE *Golden Buckles* 164, I can't stand black quart-pot tea.

queeai /'kwiaɪ/. Also **kwee-ai, quee-eye, qui-ai.** [a. Aranda *kwiya*.] An Aboriginal girl; but see also quot. 1965.

1886 D. LINDSAY *Exped. across Aust.* (1889) 11 While I was after the Quus (girls) a native crossed the creek in sight of the camp. **1933** R.B. PLOWMAN *Man from Oodnadatta* 168 Ordered the blackfellow to return Maggie's qui-ai (little girl). **1945** S.J. BAKER *Austral. Lang.* 197 *Kwee-ai*, a young lubra. **1957** F. CLUNE *Fortune Hunters* 55 Mick told me how Lasseter was found by the tribe, south of Lake Amadeus. . . Then he continued: 'There was a *nungoo* (big mob) of *waddies* (men), *koonga* (married women), *quee-eyes* (girls), *nuringa* (boys) and *chidgee* (babies). **1965** F.G.G. ROSE *Wind of Change* 137 He had a wife in the Petermann Ranges . . and as he expressed it, [she] . . is a 'proper Queeai' and not a young girl. **1968** W. GILL *Petermann Journey* 83 Th' door of the meat-house opened, and in comes two nigs draggin' two young 'qui'ais' (young native girls). **1971** K. WILLEY *Boss Drover* 12, I had been told that the queeais, native girls, up that way were mighty willing. **1976** C.D. MILLS *Hobble Chains & Greenhide* 12, I would look at one of the 'queeais', who, like little girls the world over, would turn her head away, suddenly overcome with the giggles.

queen. *Hist.* A title occas. given by colonists to the consort of an Aboriginal leader: see KING *n.*[1] 1.

1830 G.C. INGLETON *True Patriots All* 27 Nov. (1952) 112 His Aboriginal Majesty . . will be interred at Rose Bay, beside the remains of his late Queen Gooseberry. **1840** *S. Austral. Rec.* (London) 18 Apr. 191 We have the chief or king (Wagamy), and his two black queens, or *jins*, always with us, who have their camp just beside us. *Ibid.* 31 Oct. 279 Every [Aboriginal] man may have as many wives as he can maintain; there are kings and queens amongst them.

queenfish. [See quot. 1965.] Any of several marine fish, esp. of the genera *Scomberoides* and *Chorinemus* (fam. Carangidae), valued as game in n. Aust., and *Nemadactylus valenciennesi* (fam. Cheilodactylidae) of s. Aust.

1906 D.G. STEAD *Fishes of Aust.* 264 Queen-Fish. *Scomberoides sancti-petri*. Found principally in Q[ueensland]. **1948** A. MARSHALL *Ourselves writ Strange* 49 Dragged from the cool sea, their irridescent scales soon faded. . . David called the queen fish, 'Barretree'. **1965** *Austral. Encycl.* VII. 317 *Queenfish*, a name applied in southern and western Australia to *Nemadactylus valenciennesi* . . is also loosely applied by fishermen to a number of other fishes, the implication being that they are the consorts of 'kingfish' of various species. **1978** M. DOUGLAS *Follow Sun* 48 The queenfish is not accepted as a good eating fish, because the flesh is dry. **1985** *Canberra Times* 24 June 16/5 Over the week this safari captured . . 50 skinnies (queenfish) [etc.].

Queensland. [The name of the British Colony established in n.e. Aust. in 1859 and previously part of New South Wales (see MORETON BAY); one of the federated States of the Commonwealth of Australia.]

1. Used *attrib.* in Special Comb. **Queensland billy,** a semi-circular billy; **cattle,** goat meat; **gate,** an improvised gate (see quot. 1928); **hitch,** see quot. 1979; **lamb,** goat meat; **rum,** (illicitly distilled) rum; also *attrib.*; **salute,** see quot.; **sore,** *Barcoo sore*, see BARCOO A. 2; **stock saddle,** see quot. 1972.

1902 *Bulletin* (Sydney) 11 Jan. 32/2 The **Queensland billy** is the handiest for mounted men. It is flat on one side, and has a D in the centre of the round side for a strap. **1924** *Smith's Weekly* (Sydney) 9 Aug. 17/7 A common utensil on Queensland roads was a half-round billycan, one side being flat so as to make it convenient for strapping on top of a pack. . . It was known as the Queensland billy. **1915** *Truth* (Sydney) 19 Sept. 12/6 Although Western Queensland is largely sheep country, quite a quantity of **Queensland cattle** (goats) are consumed, instead of the orthodox beef and mutton. **1928** *Bulletin* (Sydney) 25 July 25/2 The stick-

and-wire gate . . is merely a number of wires, spaced apart by stakes or droppers, and attached at each end to a stake, over which the catch, usually a piece of fencing-wire is slipped. . . Victorian settlers refer to these as '**Queensland gates**', while the Bananalanders blame the Victorians for introducing them. **1957** *Ibid.* 14 Aug. 18/2 Driving . . from one outback Queensland town to another, we came to a 'Queensland gate'—two sticks joined by three strands of wire. The 'gate' is latched by a wire loop to the fence-post and collapses when 'opened'. **1979** R. EDWARDS *Skills Austral. Bushman* 23 A **Queensland hitch** . . requires no skill to tie; a length of fencing wire is doubled and then put around whatever is to be tied. A piece of metal . . is put into the loop and turned around until the hitch is tight. **1981** G. MITCHELL *Bush Horseman* 45 The usual rein fastening is a Queensland hitch, which is both decorative and strong. **1936** N. CALDWELL *Fangs of Sea* 39, I had my first helping of **Queensland lamb!** Tender and sweet, I would never have known it was goat flesh. **1892** 'E. KINGLAKE' *Austral. at Home* 132 These men . . get gloriously drunk on spirits or wine with a little cognac flavouring in it, or a fearful decoction called **Queensland rum.** **1908** *Bulletin* (Sydney) 6 Aug. 15/1 Queensland rum . . isn't altogether a myth even now. The sugar mills up north sent 520,000 gallons of molasses to the distilleries last year, and 223,573 gallons of rum resulted. Not, of course, that bush rum necessarily has any connection with molasses. **1913** *Ibid.* 13 Mar. 14/3 In the N. Queensland forest and scrub country you can see more snakes when you're sober than you can in most places after you've started a bad attack of Queensland rum-fever. **1958** J.R. SPICER *Cry of Storm-Bird* 76 As they ate, the men kept their hands waving continuously before their faces and over their food. It had become an almost unconscious gesture, born of habit, and was generally known as 'the **Queensland salute**'. **1892** G.L. JAMES *Shall I try Aust.?* 242 '**Queensland Sores**' . . are, I believe, generally attributed to excessive thinness and poverty of the blood, caused by the great heat and an absence of vegetable diet. **1945** S.J. BAKER *Austral. Lang.* 65 *Barcoo rot, Kennedy rot* or *Queensland sore*, a festering sore difficult to cure under inland conditions. **1901** *Australasian Saddler* Dec. 77/2 No. 2 shows the main features of a popular **Queensland stock saddle.** **1916** *J.J. Weekes Catal.* 12 Queensland Stock Saddles. **1972** J. BYRNE *Horse Riding Austral. Way* 21 Australia is unique in its styles of saddle. . . (1) Queensland Stock Saddle with its 6 inch kneepad set high on the pommel, so the front of the rider's thigh lies comfortably on it, with a small 3 inch back thigh pad and a 4½ inch to 5 inch dip in the centre to give our boundary rider . . the comfort necessary for arduous work.

2. In the names of flora and fauna: **Queensland bean,** MATCHBOX BEAN; **blue (heeler),** *Queensland heeler*; **blue (pumpkin),** a variety of pumpkin having a deep blue-grey skin, cultivated in Qld. and elsewhere; **blue grass,** the tufted perennial grass *Dichanthium sericeum* (fam. Poaceae), widespread in e. and central mainland Aust.; **bottle tree,** the tree *Brachychiton rupestris* (fam. Sterculiaceae) of Qld., having a swollen, bottle-like trunk; see also BOTTLE TREE; **cane toad,** *cane toad*, see CANE 2; **fruit fly,** a small fly of the genus *Dacus*, esp. *D. tryoni* of Qld. and elsewhere, a pest of cultivated fruits; **groper,** GROPER *n.*[1]; **heeler,** *blue heeler*, see BLUE *a.*; **hemp,** *Paddy's lucerne*, see PADDY; **Johnstone River hardwood,** see JOHNSTONE RIVER HARDWOOD; **maple,** the wood of either of two rainforest trees of the genus *Flindersia* (fam. Rutaceae), *F. brayleyana* of n.e. Qld. and New Guinea, and (occas.) *F. pimenteliana* (see SILKWOOD); the trees themselves; see also MAPLE; **nut,** MACADAMIA; **stinging tree,** STINGING TREE; **tick,** the introduced cattle tick *Boophilus microplus* of n. Aust. and elsewhere; also **Queensland cattle-tick; walnut,** the tall, rainforest tree *Endiandra palmerstonii* (fam. Lauraceae) of n.e. Qld.; the wood of the tree.

1882 *Proc. Linnean Soc. N.S.W.* VII. 139 *Entada scandens* . . is the well known '**Queensland Bean**', the large seeds of which are made into match boxes. **1905** A. SEARCY *In Northern Seas* 29 On the beach I found a Queensland bean just sprouting. **1956** *Coast to Coast 1955–56* 80 It was a noble animal, a true **Queensland-blue**, with jaws like an alligator, sagacity in its eye, and limbs like a well-muscled leopard. **1977** *Bronze Swagman Bk. Bush Verse* 66 Bert's dogs were the best and the game he knew And he swore by the breed of the Queensland Blue! **1980** M. GRANT *Barrier Reef* 210 There was a Queensland Blue Heeler dog on the verandah. **1966** H. COX *Are Pigs People* 20 'How are your pumpkins?' . . 'Not coming away,' said Sam. 'How much have you got in?' 'Three acres. All **Queensland Blues.**' **1979** E. SMITH *Saddle in Kitchen* 82 She came in the direction of home with her arms full of Queensland Blues and Ironbarks. **1986** *Canberra Times* 22 Apr. 5/2 Hot soup of Queensland blue pumpkin. **1901** *Advocate* (Burnie) 6 June 2/7 Supply seed of the **Queensland blue grass.** **1947** ROE & SHAW *Mint Weed* 10 The country, Queensland blue grass (*Dichanthium sericeum*) downs, and Mitchell grass downs, is grazed mainly by sheep. **1965** *Austral. Encycl.* IV. 366 *Dichanthium sericeum* (Queensland blue-grass) . . is a particularly valuable fodder grass; it dominates large areas in Queensland and New South Wales, on heavy black soils with an average annual rainfall of between 25 and 35 inches (blue-grass country). **1902** *Proc. Linnean Soc. N.S.W.* XXVII. 579 The soft wood of the **Queensland Bottle Tree,** *Sterculia rupestris* . . after being sawn and put through a chaff cutter, is useful as a fodder. **1948** H.A. LINDSAY *Bushman's Handbk.* 14 The best results are obtained from the Queensland bottle-tree by cutting a V-shaped gash through the bark and into the sapwood, and catching the water in a billy as it drains from the bottom of the V. **1981** *Bulletin* (Sydney) 6 Oct. 18/3 The baobab sheds its leaves in the dry season. It is not related to the Queensland bottle tree of the Kurrajong family. **1966** *Kings Cross Whisper* (Sydney) xxvii. 2/4 The frogs will be the large, **Queensland cane-toads** which will be guaranteed to frighten hell out of anyone. **1979** D. MAITLAND *Breaking Out* 274 He puffed up like a Queensland cane toad at mating time and unleashed a vitriolic wind at Murphy's head. **1899** *North-Western Advocate* (Devonport) 13 Feb. 3/1 The discovery of the dreaded **Queensland fruit fly** in Hobart. **1907** *Jrnl. Dept. Agric. Vic.* V. 305 Queensland Fruit Fly. . . This fly is the common species all over the fruit-growing districts of Queensland, the northern rivers and the New England districts of New South Wales. **1929** VEITCH & SIMMONDS *Pests & Diseases Qld.* 59 With two notable exceptions—namely, the Queensland fruit fly and the Rutherglen bug—all the important enemies of deciduous fruits in this State have been introduced from overseas. **1948** W.W. FROGGATT *Insect Bk.* 101 The Queensland Fruit Fly . . was first recorded from Queensland; but it breeds in many of our wild fruits in our coastal forests. **1969** E.C. ROLLS *They all ran Wild* Pref., The list of pests is not exhaustive . . the Queensland fruit fly. **1906** D.G. STEAD *Fishes of Aust.* 103 The **Queensland Groper** . . frequents the coast of Queensland and the northern portions of that of New South Wales. **1936** T.C. ROUGHLEY *Wonders Great Barrier Reef* 246 That veritable giant, the Queensland groper, a fish that is badly named for it is in no way related to the gropers of the other States but is a member of the family of perches. **1963** B. CROPP *Handbk. for Skindivers* 116 The Queensland groper is a tropical fish, common off the Queensland coast and Western Australia and even as far south as central New South Wales. It grows to a length of over 9 ft. and a weight of 800 lb. **1971** P. BODEKER *Sandgropers' Trail* 232 *Promicrops lanceolatus* (. . Queensland groper) the biggest known Australian fish. **1984** *Canberra Chron.* 2 May 19/1 Anglers . . have trouble in differentiating black cod from estuary cod and Queensland groper, which already are on the banned list. **1943** *Bulletin* (Sydney) 8 Dec. 13/3 Boozer, the **Queensland heeler**, came idly along, stopped, nipped in with his inimitable, silent, sidelong rush and chopped her heels. **1959** A. UPFIELD *Bony & Black Virgin* 11 A Queensland heeler appeared from the kennel and opened his jaws to bark a greeting. **1978** E. HARDING *A. Marshall Talking* 146 This old man had a dog with one wall-eye, a real Queensland heeler. **1985** P. CAREY *Illywhacker* 589 The hostess . . accompanies him, circling her missing passenger like a Queensland heeler driving home a recalcitrant bullock. **1888** *Proc. Linnean Soc. N.S.W.* III. 391 *Sida rhombifolia* . . '**Queensland hemp.**' **1896** A. MACKAY *Austral. Agriculturist* (rev. ed.) 120 Queensland Hemp . . is one of the best known fibre-yielders. **1920** J.H. MAIDEN *Weeds N.S.W.* 58 Paddy's Lucerne or Queensland Hemp . . is of course not a hemp nor is it confined to Queensland, but let that pass. **1919** R.T. BAKER *Hardwoods of Aust.* 33 The soft woods . . such as Red Cedar, Red Bean, **Queensland Maple** [etc.]. **1926** *Qld. Agric. Jrnl.* XXV. 433 A timber resembling Queensland Maple, which is not a Maple . . but was originally called Red Beech (because it is somewhat like White Beech). **1934** W.A. OSBORNE *Visitor to Aust.* 67 The Queensland maple, really allied to mahogany, gives a wood in much demand for panelling and furniture. **1950** 'B. JAMES' *Advancement Spencer Button* 171 The Shaw-Wilsons had a suite in Queensland maple (not Pacific maple). **1965** G. MCINNES *Road to Gundagai* 103 Bill himself clambered up into the pulpit above which was a large sounding board of Queensland maple. **1981** A.B. & J.W. CRIBB *Useful Wild Plants Aust.* 135 Queensland maple is one of the most highly regarded and widely used cabinet timbers in Australia. **1870** *Illustr. Sydney News* 6 June 3/1 The Government have proclaimed that the cutting and removal of certain timber, named the 'Bunya Bunya' and the '**Queensland nut**' is now absolutely prohibited. **1882** *Austral. Handbk.* 392 The 'Queensland Nut' (*Macadamia ternifolia* . .) is equal in flavour to the filbert. **1938** C.T. WHITE *Princ. Bot. Qld. Farmers* 162 The best-known species is *M. ternifolia*, the common Macadamia Nut, Queensland Nut . . unquestionably one of the finest flavoured nuts in cultivation. **1950** E.M. ENGLAND *Where Turtles Dance* 81 Two brass bowls, one piled with sugar-bananas, one with Queensland nuts. **1981** T. SHAPCOTT *Stump & Grape & Bopple-Nut* 11 Bopplenuts Y'can call them Queensland Nuts. **1930** HIVES & LUMLEY *Jrnl. of Jackaroo* 212 **Queensland 'stinging' trees,** with their large heart-shaped leaves and fruit resembling mulberries, were seen and given a wide berth; for a touch of the leaves meant days of agony, swollen glands and disablement. **1958** E. WORRELL *Song of Snake* 137 The Queensland stinging-tree grows in python country. A passing encounter may result in months of pain. **1897** L. LINDLEY-COWEN *W. Austral. Settler's Guide* 56 The introduction into the herds of the colony of the destructive **Queensland tick.** **1909** *Bulletin* (Sydney) 29 Apr. 13/1 The Queensland tick . . has passed over the Tweed River and has put in an appearance on the upper reaches of the Richmond River. **1935** DAVISON & NICHOLLS *Blue Coast Caravan* 103 One of us suggested that the purpose of the fence and gate was to keep Queensland cattle-ticks out of New South Wales. **1919** R.T. BAKER *Hardwoods of Aust.* 339 *Cryptocarya Palmerstoni* . . '**Queensland Walnut**' . . is fairly heavy, of a chocolate colour, approaching English and American Walnut . . takes a good polish, and possesses a fine figure. **1929** W.D. FRANCIS *Austral. Rain-Forest Trees* 22 The principal cabinet woods of Australia are from rain-forest trees. Included among them are . . Queensland Walnut (*Endiandra Palmerstoni*) [etc.]. **1955** *New Settler in W.A.* (Perth) July 11 Queensland has the Queensland maple and walnut trees. **1981** A.B. & J.W. CRIBB *Useful Wild Plants Aust.* 120 Some of the panelling in the once well-known passenger liners *Strathmore* and *Queen Mary* was of Queensland walnut.

Queenslander. One who is native to or resident in Queensland. Also *transf.*

1860 *Moreton Bay Courier* 6 Mar. 2/5 In your issue of Thursday last appeared a letter signed a 'Queenslander'. **1865** *Sydney Punch* 19 Aug. 514/2 Am I not a Queenslander and a Brisbaneite? **1878** J.H. NICHOLSON *Opal Fever* 89 No violence! Let us remember we are gentlemen and Queenslanders. **1888** *Plea for Separation* 9 We . . with the exception of the stalwart Queenslanders, accept without a murmur taxation without representation. **1911** I.A. ROSENBLUM *Stella Sothern* 9 Your business was the sale of some Queenslanders—cattle, you know. **1932** R.W. THOMPSON *Down Under* 219 Of all Australians, Queenslanders and Western Australians were the best, he said—really good-hearted, honest fellows. **1959** *Jrnl. R. Hist. Soc. Qld.* 273 A Queenslander has won the mile championship of Australia on only one occasion. **1974** *Daily Mirror* (Sydney) 10 Sept. 4/5 While Senator Field did not actually advocate the Bomb, he was starting to sound more like a Queenslander by the minute. **1979** *Meanjin* 41 On a number of important counts Queenslanders are different, although no one has yet suggested that, like Tasmanians, we all have pointed ears. **1984** H. LUNN *Queenslanders* 137/2 The Sydney down-and-out can immediately elevate himself by making some disparaging remark about Queenslanders.

Queen Street. [The name of a principal business street in Brisbane.] Used *attrib.* in Comb. as a Queensland equivalent of PITT STREET.

1898 'OLD COLONIST' *How Constitutional Govt. was Won* 30 The planting of a race of sturdy yeomen on the soil by the Queen Street (Brisbane) politicians of the period, as well as in later times, was regarded as an infringement of the rights of the class who have controlled the destinies of Australia so long. **1948** *Khaki Bush & Bigotry* (1968) 73 Goin' South . . going to be a couple of Queen Street Commandoes. **1983** P. KILVINGTON *P. Kilvington* 88 The Queen Street cockie who publicly said my friend was a 'lucky dog' is probably still wondering why he got a thump.

Queen Victoria rifle-bird: see VICTORIA RIFLE-BIRD.

Queen Victoria's lyre-bird. *Obs.* [f. the name and title of *Queen Victoria* (1837–1901), first applied as the specific name *victoriae* by English naturalist John Gould (see quots. 1862 and 1865) + LYRE-BIRD 1.] The southern form of *Menura novaehollandiae* (see LYRE-BIRD 1), formerly regarded as a distinct species.

[**1862** *Proc. Zool. Soc. London* 23 Mr Gould exhibited a specimen of a Lyre-bird (*Menura*) from Port Philip [*sic*], and pointed out the characters in which it differed from the closely allied *Menura superba* of New South Wales. Mr Gould proposed the name *Menura victoriae* for this new species.] **1865** J. GOULD *Handbk. Birds Aust.* I. 302 Queen Victoria's Lyre-bird. *Menura victoriae.* **1883** A.J. CAMPBELL *Nests & Eggs Austral. Birds* p. xvi, There are three species of Lyre-bird in Australia, of which the Gippsland Queen Victorias [*sic*] (*Menura Victoriae*) is the most handsome. **1956** A. CHISHOLM *Bird Wonders of Aust.* 22 About forty years after the initial discovery, John Gould, the English birdman, examined a Lyrebird from Victoria which appeared to differ slightly from the Sydney form, and he called this Queen Victoria's Lyre-bird.

qui-ai, var. QUEEAI.

quick smart, *adv. phr.* Very quickly.

1966 S.J. BAKER *Austral. Lang.* (ed. 2) 215 *Quick smart*, rapidly. **1967** *Coast to Coast 1965–66* 165 Skipper had quick-smart put her out to sea. **1970** *Kings Cross Whisper* (Sydney) xcv. 5/2, I got out of the place quick smart, I can tell you. **1973** C. EAGLE *Who could love Nightingale?* 162 He hunted us off quicksmart.

quid. [Fig. use of *quid* the sum of one pound.] In the phr. **the full quid,** (in) full possession of one's faculties.

1944 *Austral. New Writing* 36 He'll back down; I said he wasn't the full quid, just a skite. **1968** G. DUTTON *Andy* 93 'Yer mad. I don't think yer got a full quid,' commented the sailor. **1973** D. FOSTER *North South West* 173 The general view . . was that he was not the full quid. **1978** H.C. BAKER *I was Listening* 128 Decimal currency has made an archaism of an old and valuable Australian colloquialism, 'Not quite the full quid'. It's a pity, because the expression was more kind than cruel. It established to a fine degree the extent of a person's mental handicap. **1983** *Weekend Austral. Mag.* 27 Aug. 20/7 Hayden's the full quid when it gets around to slang. **1984** J. HIBBERD *Country Quinella* 101 Though not the full quid, a bit sawn-off, impossible to live with.

quietly, *adv.* [Also N.Z.: see OEDS *quietly, adv.* b.] In the phr. **just quietly,** confidentially, between ourselves.

1938 X. HERBERT *Capricornia* 145 He'd love to see you 'fore you goes. Thinks a lot of you, you know, just quietly. **1941** S.J. BAKER *Pop. Dict. Austral. Slang* 40 *Just quietly*, between you and I. **1951** E. LAMBERT *Twenty Thousand Thieves* (1952) 123 That Chips Prentice is a soldier and a half. Just quietly, he's up for a decoration. **1966** G.W. TURNER *Eng. Lang. in Aust. & N.Z.* 177 Much New Zealand colloquialism is shared with Australia, e.g. *just quietly* 'between you and me', [etc.]. **1979** *N.T. News* (Darwin) 17 Oct. 6/6 Apparently the team has nothing to do with houses and just quietly, doesn't agree with the present policy.

quilt, *v.* [Br. dial. *quilt* 'to beat, thrash, flog': see OED(S *v.*[3]) *trans.* To punch (a person), to beat soundly. Also as *vbl. n.*

1895 *Bulletin* (Sydney) 23 Nov. 19/2, I quilted Jim. Jim, senr., quilted me; nine stone seven cannot argue against 13 odd. **1945** S.J. BAKER *Austral. Lang.* 120 An extensive vocabulary of fighting terms. Here are some of the best . . *roll into, vacuum, quilt* and *stoush* a person. **1973** D. STUART *Morning Star, Evening Star* 111 More than one bloke I've seen Joe quilt good and proper for trying to make a joke of it. **1980** G. BEER *Dust, Sweat & Tears* 28, I was promptly set upon by the school's bully and given a proper workover. I sure got a quilting.

quince. [Fig. use of *quince*, the fruit.] In the phr. **to get on** (one's) **quince,** to irritate or exasperate.

1941 S.J. BAKER *Pop. Dict. Austral. Slang* 58 *Get on one's quince*, to annoy or aggravate deeply. **1948** *Sydney Morning Herald* 3 July 9/1 Aw, can it boss! You're gettin' on me quince. **1959** *Overland* xvi. 16 It's starting to get on my quince already. **1974** D. O'GRADY *Deschooling Kevin Carew* 95 In an unguarded moment, he told Bill Moynihan 'This joint is getting on my quince.'

quinine tree. [Spec. use of *quinine*, referring to the bitterness of part or parts of the plant, formerly attributed to the presence of quinine.] **a.** Any of several bushes or small trees esp. of the genus *Petalostigma* (fam. Euphorbiaceae), bearing bitter orange fruits. **b.** BITTER BARK. Also **quinine bush** and, as **quinine berry,** the fruit of the tree.

1886 F.A. HAGENAUER *Rep. Aboriginal Mission Ramahyuck, Vic.* 47 You can see the . . quinine tree. **1894** G. BOOTHBY *On Wallaby* 215 The only vegetation being Quinine bushes (a tall slender tree, with a rough dark bark and glossy leaves). **1912** *Emu* xii. 80 Noticed that the native quinine trees (*Alstonia constricta* . .) grew to a good size. **1936** F. CLUNE *Roaming round Darling* 161 The quinine-tree grows about fifteen feet high, is tall and thin, and the sheep like it. **1944** J. DEVANNY *By Tropic Sea & Jungle* 173 A few yards from my camp door a big quinine-tree was literally loaded with hard yellow berries. **1954** B. MILES *Stars my Blanket* 139 The quinine tree, so called because of the bitter taste of the tiny leaves. **1973** H. HOLTHOUSE *S'pose I Die* 67, I knew it was going to be a dry trip and as a precaution I brought with me a supply of 'quinine berries', a native berry about the size of a cherry. **1986** K. BRENNAN *Wildflowers of Kakadu* 46 Common, widespread shrubs are the Quinine Bush *Petalostigma quadriloculare*, the Turkey Bush [etc.].

quinkan /'kwɪŋkən/. Also **quinkin.** [a. Kuku-Yalanji *kuwinkan* ghost, spirit.] A category of spirit people depicted in rock paintings of n. Qld.: see quots. Also *attrib.*

1969 BAGLIN & MULLINS *Aborigines Aust.* 22 Aborigines will make a Quinkan trap by placing dry leaves—or nowadays a sheet of newspaper—between two twigs . . so they will hear his movements. *Ibid.*, Many of these galleries feature Quinkans, a phenomenon of northern Queensland. According to the Aborigines, these strange creatures live in rock crevices and emerge at night, waiting just outside the light of the campfire to grab the unwary. **1979** *Cwlth. Parl. Papers* VIII. 2 The Quinkan galleries, which were discovered in 1960 and are located in the Laura region of the Cape York Peninsula, contain several hundred Aboriginal rock art galleries which have been described as one of the largest and most exciting bodies of prehistoric art in the world. **1982** R.M. BERNDT et al. *Aboriginal Austral. Art* 149 Galleries of rock abound near Laura, north-west of Cairns. . . In the one noted here, the paintings belong to what has been called the 'Quinkin' tradition because many concern spirits known by this general term.

quoit. Also **coit.** [Fig. use of *quoit* rope ring.]

1. The backside.

1941 S.J. BAKER *Pop. Dict. Austral. Slang* 58 *Quoit*, the buttocks. **1951** E. LAMBERT *Twenty Thousand Thieves* 165 See those jokers sitting on their quoits over there? **1954** T.A.G. HUNGERFORD *Sowers of Wind* 176 Gawd, he blew the tripes outa me for nothing at all, and then he kicks a Nip in the coit. **1967** *Kings Cross Whisper* (Sydney) xxxviii. 10/3 *Quoit*, backside. **1972** J. BAILEY *Wire Classroom* 82 'I think he needs a good kick up the coit,' says Cromwell.

2. In the phr. **to go for one's quoit,** to hurry.

1941 S.J. BAKER *Pop. Dict. Austral. Slang* 58 *Go for one's quoits*, to travel quickly, go for one's life. **1952** J. CLEARY *Sundowners* 42 Going for the lick of his coit up the street. **1968** S. GORE *Holy Smoke* 107 *Quoit, to go for one's*, to exert all possible effort; or to run.

quokka /'kwɒkə/. Also **quagga.** [a. Nyungar *kwaka.*] The small, short-tailed wallaby *Setonix brachyurus* of s.w. W.A., incl. Rottnest and Bald Islands, having long, greyish-brown fur; *short-tailed wallaby*, see SHORT-TAILED. Also *attrib.*

1855 J. GOULD *Mammals of Aust.* (1863) II. Pl. 38, At Augusta . . its [*sc.* the short-tailed wallaby's] native name, Quäk-a, is the same as at King George's Sound. **1928** J. POLLARD *Bushland Vagabonds* 225 A shadow skippin' among them rocks looked to me like a quagga or some other wallaby. **1943** C. BARRETT *Austral. Animal Bk.* 96 The quokka or short-tailed pademelon . . is distinguished by its small size and certain dental features. **1968** V. SERVENTY *Southern Walkabout* 150 It is the famous quokka, one of the pademelon wallabies, which creates most interest. It was this wallaby, mistaken by Dutch visitor Vlaming for a large rodent, which led to the island's name, Rottnest or 'Rat's Nest'. **1970** W.D.L. RIDE *Guide Native Mammals Aust.* 50 Until the mid-1930s the Quokka was a very common animal in the South West where it occurred in swampy thickets; Quokka-shooting was even a familiar sport. **1985** *Canberra Times* 7 July 2/1 Rottnest's 'rats' are in fact quokkas, small marsupials about the size of stunted corgis.

quoll /kwɒl/. [a. Guugu Yimidhirr *digwol.*] *Native cat*, see NATIVE *a.* 6 b.

1770 J. BANKS *Endeavour Jrnl.* (1962) II. 117 Another [quadruped] was calld [*sic*] by the natives *Je-Quoll.* **1770** J. HAWKESWORTH *Acct. of Voyages Southern Hemisphere* (1773) III. 626, I can add only one more [quadruped], resembling a polecat, which the natives call *Quoll*; the back is brown, spotted with white and the belly white unmixed. **1968** D. FLEAY *Nightwatchmen* 14 In those early days . . we domesticated quolls ('native cats'). **1983** R. STRAHAN *Compl. Bk. Austral. Mammals* 16 The similarity of quolls to European carnivores was noted by early settlers.

quomby, var. QUAMBY *v.*

quondong, var. QUANDONG.

R

rabbit, *attrib.* and *n.*

A. Used *attrib.* in Special Comb.

1. In the names of animals having a supposed resemblance to the rabbit: **rabbit bandicoot,** BILBY; also **rabbit-eared bandicoot; rat, (a)** any of the rodents of the chiefly n. Austral. genera *Mesembriomys* and *Conilurus,* having long ears and a long, somewhat brushy tail, incl. the prob. now extinct *C. albipes* of inland s.e. mainland Aust.; **(b)** any of several other animals, incl. BILBY and STICK-NEST RAT.

1832 J. BISCHOFF *Sketch Hist. Van Diemen's Land* 28 The bandicoot is as large as a rabbit. There are two kinds, the rat and the **rabbit bandicoot. 1896** B. SPENCER *Rep. Horn Sci. Exped. Central Aust.* I. 34 A 'fig-leaf', often made of the white tips of the tails of the rabbit-bandicoot .. is worn as an ornament. **1903** H. BASEDOW *Jrnl. Govt. N.-W. Exped.* 15 May (1914) 102 The dogs caught a small rabbit bandicoot (*Peragale lagotis*), which Annie is preparing for her tea. **1923** A.G. BOLAM *Trans-Austral. Wonderland* 27 The Ooldea sandhills and the Nullarbor Plain abound in various species of the Bandicoot family, the principal varieties being .. the Rabbit-eared Bandicoot (Thalacomys lagotis), otherwise known as the Bilby, Pinkie, Dalgoo, etc. **1926** A.S. LE SOUEF et al. *Wild Animals Australasia* 299 The rabbit-bandicoots, so called because their long ears resemble somewhat those of a rabbit, have a wide range over inland Australia. **1953** A. RUSSELL *Murray Walkabout* 175 The rabbit bandicoot—or 'bilbee', as the bushmen call it—is not an animal commonly seen. **1974** *Bulletin* (Sydney) 16 Mar. 32/3 The preservation of the really endangered species... But who has heard of the numbat or the dibbler or the rabbit-eared bandicoot? **1982** M. WATTONE *Winning Gold in W.A.* 29 Nullagine is 110 km. from Marble Bar... While staying there a photograph .. of a rabbit-eared bandicoot was given me. **1837** G. BENNETT *Catal. Specimens Nat. Hist. Austral. Museum* 6 (OEDS) The **Rabbit Rat** of the Colonists. Habitat, Interior of Australia. **1855** J. BONWICK *Geogr. Aust. & N.Z.* (ed. 3) 199 The Rabbit rat, of New South Wales, likes sugar. **1864** 'E.S.H.' *Narr. Trip Sydney to Peak Downs* 18 He had no rest from the fleas and the hosts of rabbit rats (Hapolotis allcipes [*sic*]). **1882** *Proc. Linnean Soc. N.S.W.* VII. 49 The lining is of hair or fur of the 'Rabbit-rat' *Lagorchestes.* **1885** A.W. HOWITT *Jeraeil* 316 The novice may not eat the female of any animal, nor the emu, nor the porcupine; but he may eat .. the rabbit-rat. [*Note*] *Perameles lagotis.* **1900** *Bulletin* (Sydney) 10 Mar. 14/3 The bilby .. is common in Western Queensland .. where .. it is called the 'rabbit-rat'. **1924** *Austral. Museum Mag.* Jan. 18 Known as the 'Native Rabbit' or 'Rabbit-Rat', by the colonists of the long ago, these building rats are remarkable for their proportionately very long ears, which give them the appearance of small rabbits with rat-like tails. **1941** E. TROUGHTON *Furred Animals Aust.* 305 Genera *Mesembriomys* .. and *Conilurus*... The size of the body .. is considerably larger than the average full-sized rat... It is almost impossible to find distinctive popular names for the various species, which are sometimes called 'rabbit-rats' in reference to the rather large ears. **1970** W.D.L. RIDE *Guide Native Mammals Aust.* 142 Little is known of the habits of the White-footed Tree-rat of eastern Australia; early settlers called this the Rabbit Rat because of its rounded form and long ears. It has not been seen alive this century.

2. With reference to the control and extermination of rabbits, esp. on rural properties: **rabbit board,** a (local) body responsible for the control of rabbits; **fence,** *rabbit-proof fence,* see RABBIT-PROOF *a.* 1; also *attrib.*; **inspector,** an officer appointed to enforce rabbit-control regulations; **netting,** rabbit-proof netting; **poisoner,** one employed to poison rabbits; **scalper,** one who kills rabbits, retaining the scalps in order to obtain a bounty.

1898 C.L. MORGAN *Rabbit Question Qld.* 5 Netting fencing in use by the **Rabbit Boards** and others. **1915** *Bulletin* (Sydney) 28 Jan. 22/2, I was in charge of a string belonging to the Mitchell Rabbit Board. **1917** W. LEES *Coaching in Aust.* 61 It is the meeting place for the Balonne Shire Council, Maronoa Rabbit Board and the Marsupial Board. **1896** *Bulletin* (Sydney) 19 Sept. 10/3 Queensland boasts altogether 4719 miles of **rabbit fence,** inside which the rabbits are gaily breeding in millions. **1913** *Ibid.* 28 Aug. 22/2 He said an ordinary rabbit-fence was sufficient to hold a dingo back. **1930** E. ANTONY *Hungry Mile* 35 The men whose dreary job is to repair the rabbit fence. **1956** A.C.C. LOCK *Tropical Tapestry* 115 We came upon another wire-netting fence. 'This', said Alan, 'is the rabbit fence. It goes for hundreds of miles.' **1980** J. FITZPATRICK *Bicycle & Bush* 204 Harry Jordan, a 'lengthrunner' along the Kalgoorlie pipeline, met a rabbit fence rider still using a bicycle sometime between 1912 and 1916. **1896** *Western Champion* (Barcaldine) 22 Sept. 3/2 The **rabbit inspector** at Broken Hill recently reported that very few of the land owners are taking any steps to destroy the rabbits, which are increasing at an alarming rate. **1908** C.H.S. MATTHEWS *Parson in Austral. Bush* 106 Outside the cultivation paddock he will have to poison with jam and strychnine, or phosphorized pollard, or he will be dropped on by the rabbit inspector and mulcted in a more or less heavy fine. **1927** J. POLLARD *Rose of Bushlands* 42 He .. repaired the fence .. the district rabbit-inspector had discovered broken. **1941** *Bulletin* (Sydney) 12 Feb. 16/1 Old Mac's daughter married the rabbit inspector. **1925** *Makeshifts & Other Home-Made Furniture* (New Settlers League Aust.) 29 Make a strainer .. of fencing wire and **rabbit netting** of small mesh. **1930** D. COTTRELL *Earth Battle* 94 In five years' time he must have the whole of Tharlane enclosed with rabbit netting. **1953** H.G. LAMOND *Big Red* 231 It .. swept .. everything ahead of it on to a rabbit-netting fence. **1981** A.B. FACEY *Fortunate Life* 214 There was rabbit-netting, pipes, troughs, pumps and fittings. **1982** *Elders Weekly* (Perth) 21 Oct. 108/1 Fencing being ringlock, rabbit netting and plain. **1913** W.K. HARRIS *Outback in Aust.* 90 Sometimes the 'dogger' is independent, but in most cases he is the **rabbit-poisoner** employed by the station. **1919** E.S. SORENSON *Chips & Splinters* 34 It had been newly patched at Johnny Rogan's pub at Warri Warri, and given to a rabbit-poisoner. **1906** *Bulletin* (Sydney) 22 Mar. 15/2 The Victorian and Grampian Ranges (Vic.) .. are well stocked with emus, wallaby, and a few 'great reds' in spite of the exertions of the **rabbit scalper** and station hand to exterminate them. **1935** DAVISON & NICHOLLS *Blue Coast Caravan* 42 The rabbit scalper and his family very rarely ate rabbits.

3. *fig.* As **rabbit-killer:** a 'rabbit punch', a sharp, chopping blow to the back of the neck delivered with the side of the hand. Also *attrib.*

1942 G. CASEY *It's Harder for Girls* 23, I took a rush and gave him a rabbit-killer that must have nearly broken his neck. **1951** D. STIVENS *Jimmy Brockett* 99 'He told me he was going to use a rabbit-killer punch on Hill.' 'If he does, I'll disqualify him,' Bob said. **1965** G. MCINNES *Road to Gundagai* 257 It lay panting and bewildered on the ground easily despatched by a 'rabbit killer' with the heel of the hand on the back of the neck. **1966** B. BEAVER *You can't come Back* 53 Alice's laugh followed us out the door, a pat on the back compared to Norma's rabbit killer. **1973** K. DUNSTAN *Sports* 242 Combined with every tackle was a rabbit killer, a punch or a forearm jolt. **1977** L. FOX *Depression Down Under* 54 Mr Steve Purdy .. who was being attacked by three New Guards, one holding his arms while the others rained 'rabbit-killers' on the back of his neck.

B. *n.*

a. *fig.* Alcoholic liquor, usu. beer. In the phr. **to run the rabbit,** to procure this, sometimes illegally.

1895 E. GIBB *Thrilling Incidents Convict System* 46 'Ike-ing the rabbit for a fake for his Bingy' .. convict slang. .. It may be freely translated as having surreptitiously concealed some liquor under the excuse that one was ill and it was required for medicine. **1910** *Bulletin* (Sydney) 21 Apr. 15/2 At my hash-house the other evening the recent arrival from 'Ome consented to join in a Carbine... It was agreed that he who drew 'Carbine' should run the rabbit. The new-chum, drawing first, yanked the famous moke out by the tail. The liquid having materialised, it was proposed that we should try again. **1911** *Ibid.* 1 June 13/1 When you see three or four scandal-agents foregather at the house of one of them in certain Melbourne suburbs, you will presently see one emerge—or a small girl may be despatched—with a handbag, basket, or other vehicle. In that article will be a bottle, for the seemly conveyance of liquid refreshment. The woman, or girl or damsel may go thus once, twice, or half a dozen times .. and if a mate asks her what she is doing, she will reply, 'Runnin' th' rabbit.' **1914** *St. Kilda Ann.* 143 He .. rose to the level of respectability of 'running the rabbit'. **1941** S.J. BAKER *Pop. Dict. Austral. Slang* 58 *Rabbit,* a bottle of beer. **1955** N. PULLIAM *I traveled Lonely Land* 386 *Run the rabbit,* to buy liquor illegally after closing hours or in some zone supposed to be closed.

b. *transf.* See quot.

1956 *Bulletin* (Sydney) 15 Feb. 13/4 My apprenticeship started in the railway-workshops... First you had to 'run the rabbit'; pulling a hand-cart loaded with rivets and coke to the lines of butty gangs, and returning with clinker and scrap as back-loading.

rabbit, *v.*

1. *intr. Australian National Football.* To duck down in the path of an opposing player, so causing the player to trip or fall. Also *trans.*, to trip (a player) in this way, and as *vbl. n.*

1885 D.E. MCCONNELL *Austral. Etiquette* 641 Tripping, hacking, rabbiting, slinging, or catching hold of a player below the knee are prohibited. **1918** J.A. PHILP *Jingles that Jangle* 28 In the game Ginger Mick was a tricky galoot, He might 'trip', he might 'rabbit'—or 'put in the boot'. **1925** *Laws of Football* (Australasian Football Council) 14 Rabbiting is one player stooping down so as to cause another to fall by placing his body below the other's hips. **1975** R.O. MOORE *Sunlit Plains Extended* 59 The constable had almost caught him when Luke dropped down on all fours and 'rabbited' him. **1980** B. HORNADGE *Austral. Slanguage* 240 One Australian slang invention common to all football codes is to *rabbit* meaning to (illegally) trip an opposing player. **1983** HIBBERD & HUTCHINSON *Barracker's Bible* 165 A player 'rabbits' another when he ducks down as the other is about to use his back to take a mark... Regarded as poor form.

2. *trans.* To borrow; to steal.

1943 S.J. BAKER *Pop. Dict. Austral. Slang* (ed. 3) 63 *To rabbit,* to borrow, 'scrounge'. (R.A.N. slang.) **1953** K. TENNANT *Joyful Condemned* 198 Why were Australian Navy men better at 'rabbiting' little valuable articles than Americans? **1955** N. PULLIAM *I traveled Lonely Land* 385 *Rabbit* .. to borrow.

rabbit-eared bandicoot: see *rabbit bandicoot* RABBIT A. 1.

rabbit-ears, *pl.* The terrestrial orchid *Thelymitra antennifera* (fam. Orchidaceae) of s. Aust. incl. Tas., occurring on coastal heaths and inland.

1923 *Census Plants Vic.* (Field Naturalists' Club Vic.) 19 *Thelymitra antennifera* .. Rabbit-ears. **1942** C. BARRETT *Austral. Wild Flower Bk.* 131 Sandy areas suit the needs of 'rabbit-ears', a very abundant little sun orchid whose flowers are yellow inside and striped with red-brown externally. **1961** *Meanjin* 6 There were rusty-hoods, rabbit-ears, parson-bands and running-postmen. **1985** *Austral. Plants* Dec. 223 *Thelymitra antennifera* (Rabbit Ears). Bears 1–3 large scented yellow flowers which open freely on warm days in spring. It has brown 'ears' on top of the column.

rabbit-oh. Also **rabbit-o.** [f. *rabbit* + -O.]

a. One who sells rabbits as food (usu. an itinerant but see quot. 1946). Also *attrib.*

1902 *Truth* (Sydney) 11 May 5/7 The poor animal finishes its slavery in the shafts of the 'bottle-oh' van, or amidst the floggings of the 'rabbit-oh' push. **1905** *Bulletin* (Sydney) 3 Aug. 36/2 'Wish ter Gawd a cyclone wud strike the big vat?' wailed a rabbit-oh. **1912** *Ibid.* 25 Jan. 14/4, I have a voice like an oyster-vendor or 'rabbit-O'. **1919** *Smith's Weekly* (Sydney) 7 June 1/2 The Government is proposing to sell cheap rabbits to the public. There will be some really wild 'rabbit-ohs'! **1931** *Bulletin* (Sydney) 16 Sept. 26/3, I happen to know that the rabbit-oh buys his wares at the markets. **1946** F. CLUNE *Try Nothing Twice* 21, I made for the haven of Paddy's Markets, seeking a refuge among the rabbit-ohs. **1954** *Bulletin* (Sydney) 10 Nov. 12/1 He was a rabbit-oh; the drought had knocked him down to leg—very few bunnies coming down. **1977** D. STUART *Drought Foal* 68 There is the rabbit-o, with a horse pulling a two-wheeler flat-top, with boxes of rabbits.

b. *transf.* A rabbit sold as food; also a rabbiter.

1920 J.N. MACINTYRE *White Aust.* 196 Gathering old bottles and rags or selling 'rabbitohs' in the cities. **1937** A.W. UPFIELD *Mr Jelly's Business* 16 'The men employed along the pipe-line are called Water Rats because often they have to work deep in water when a pipe bursts.' 'Thank you. And what are the Snake Charmers?' 'They are the permanent-way men. Now that you are a Rabbit Department employee you are a Rabbitoh.' **1982** K. HUENEKE *Huts of High Country* 101 The rusty rabbit traps and skin stretchers are still there waiting for another depression and a 'Rabbito'.

rabbit-proof, *a.* and *n.* [Not necessarily excl. Austral. but of local significance.]

A. *adj.* Secure against rabbits.

1. In the collocation **rabbit-proof fence.**

a. A fence erected to exclude rabbits, esp. on the border of a State.

1883 J.E. PARTINGTON *Random Rot* 270 The rabbits here [*sc.* S.A.] are so numerous that they have had to adopt rabbit-proof fences. **1888** *Brisbane Courier* 15 Aug. 3/1 A sum of £75,000 has already been expended in erecting a rabbit-proof fence on the border separating Queensland from New South Wales and South Australia. **1896** H. LAWSON *While Billy Boils* (1975) 26 The town is right on the Queensland border, and an interprovincial rabbit-proof fence—with rabbits on both sides of it—runs across the main street. This fence is a standing joke with Australian rabbits. **1911** *Bulletin* (Sydney) 26 Oct. 14/2 The rabbit-proof wire-netted fence . . has proven a complete baulk to the inroads of the Nunnick warrigals which, in the old days, attended mutton banquets on the sheep-runs. **1926** *Ibid.* 15 Apr. 24/1 One of the greatest farces out back is the rabbit-proof fence on the N.S.W.-Queensland border. **1942** M.L. MACPHERSON *I heard Anzacs Singing* 160 Western Australia has the longest rabbit-proof fence in the world. **1962** *N. Austral. Monthly* Feb. 26 The rabbit scare was at its top then; the government offered extension of leases to owners erecting rabbit-proof fences. **1981** A.B. FACEY *Fortunate Life* 148 This was the first rabbit-proof fence built across Western Australia to prevent rabbits from migrating into the stock and wheat portions of the State. This fence was a failure and two more fences were built further south. . . They were shorter and only fenced in special sections. There were gates all along at intervals for travellers to pass through. The Government built these fences and employed boundary riders to take care of them and to see that the gates were properly shut.

b. Such a fence as marking the border of a State.

1927 T.S. GROSER *Lure of Golden West* 221 Beyond the Rabbit-Proof Fence. **1946** *Bulletin* (Sydney) 25 Dec. 29/2 Dummy was . . the . . most silent man west of the rabbit-proof fence. **1965** *Tracks we Travel* 75 A little, bow-legged, gappy-toothed ex-shearer from the other side of the rabbit-proof fence, chipped in. **1971** J. O'GRADY *Aussie Etiket* 30 You would be the greatest bloody galah this side of the rabbit-proof fence.

2. In collocations: **rabbit-proof fencing, gate, netting, wire (netting).**

1886 *Bulletin* (Sydney) 4 Sept. 13/1 **Rabbit-proof fencing** . . is nothing to the intruder-proof phalanx which surrounds Lady Carrington. **1898** C.L. MORGAN *Rabbit Question in Qld.* 12 To facilitate and encourage the erection of rabbit-proof fencing. **1934** W.A. OSBORNE *Visitor to Aust.* 155 A curious feature of West Australia is the double line of rabbit-proof fencing. **1965** *N. Austral. Monthly* Dec. 7 Hundreds of miles of 'rabbit-proof' fencing erected by the Government. **1898** C.L. MORGAN *Rabbit Question in Qld.* 123 **Rabbit-proof gates** can be left [in the fence] for the purpose of enabling stock to water during the day. **1930** A.E. YARRA *Vanishing Horsemen* 231 She pointed to the great rabbit-proof gates in the fence that divided the two states. **1956** B. BEATTY *Beyond Aust.'s Cities* 111 The following terse inscription . . appears on the gate of a property on the south coast of New South Wales: 'This is a rabbit-proof gate. Only dingoes will leave it open.' **1900** *Bulletin* (Sydney) 28 Apr. 14/3 **Rabbit-proof netting** is *not* any good. If the rabbits don't climb over, crawl under, or break through, the swaggie who wants work heaves them over. **1925** M. TERRY *Across Unknown Aust.* 87 Wire fence with rabbit-proof netting. **1956** B.J. RAYMENT *My Towri* 28 In 1896, Dad contracted to attach 137 miles of rabbit-proof netting to the Wellshot boundary fence. **1909** R. KALESKI *Austral. Settler's Compl. Guide* 94 Five No. 8 galvanised wires, posts 40 feet apart, four cyclone-droppers in between, **rabbit-proof wire netting** on the bottom. **1980** S. ORR *Roll On* 88 We have managed to rescue about 80 metres of tolerable rabbit-proof wire.

B. *n. ellipt. Rabbit-proof fence.*

1894 *Bulletin* (Sydney) (1895) 20 July 27/3 Beyond the furthest rabbit-proof, barbed wire and common wire. **1895** *Ibid.* 5 Jan. 23/4 When once we're through the 'rabbit-proof'—its certain since the rain—There's whips o' grass and water. So its West by North again! **1907** *Ibid.* 25 July 40/2 Ties, snips and pliers, pick and shovel he Begins to scatter 'rabbit-proofs' about. **1927** M.H. ELLIS *Long Lead* 75 Second last gate in the 'rabbit proof', the barrier of small-meshed wire netting which Queenslanders believe to be the longest fence in the world. For three thousand miles it runs down into the corner of South Australia from the Gulf of Carpentaria and along the boundary between N.S. Wales and Queensland to the sea. **1972** D. HEWETT *Bon-Bons & Roses* (1976) 28 Best little ticket this side of the rabbit-proof.

Hence **rabbit-proof** *v. trans.*, to make secure against rabbits. Also *absol.*

1949 J. MORRISON *Creeping City* 141 Clavering came upon Smith while the latter was rabbit-proofing his fence on the frontage. **1981** A.B. FACEY *Fortunate Life* 200 The Western Australian Water Supply wanted men to go into the country fencing-in Government dams, rabbit-proofing, and fixing dam pumps.

rabbo. [f. *rabb(it* + -O, a street-cry.] A rabbit, or rabbit meat, sold as food.

1911 I.A. ROSENBLUM *Stella Sothern* 121 The bawling of hawkers with vegetables and 'Wild rabbo, wild rabbo,' and 'Fish, O!' almost distracted her. **1911** *Bulletin* (Sydney) 19 Jan. 14/4 'Pick' may be an authority on the keeping qualities of 'rabbo' on a hand-cart in a disembowelled and negotiable condition.

race, *n.*[1] [Transf. use of *race* artificial channel (of water): see OED(S *sb.*[1] 8 c. and f.] A narrow passage-way in a stock yard; esp. one through which animals pass singly, for branding, loading, washing, etc.

1862 A. POLEHAMPTON *Kangaroo Land* 216 When the sheep had undergone a preparatory cleansing in the first pen, they were passed . . under the dividing beam, into the next pen, and so on from one pen to another; till . . they were passed into the last division, called the 'Race'. **1879** S.W. SILVER *Austral. Grazier's Guide* 66 A succession of small yards guided the sheep to the 'race'—another Australian invention—by which the sheep followed one another rapidly through a passage too narrow to permit of their turning round; and finally they slid down a slide which terminated the race. **1897** R. NEWTON *Work & Wealth Qld.* 75 He stands all day working a swing gate in a race, till the two living streams have flowed into separate yards. **1912** R.S. TAIT *Scotty Mac* 10 Still the bleating woolly sheep are coming up the race. **1928** C.E. COWLEY *Classing Clip* 159 The quickest, safest and most reliable means of drafting sheep is through the 'race'. **1934** T. WOOD *Cobbers* 41 'This is a race,' and he pointed to narrow gangways, railed in on both sides, which sloped from the main deck down to the catch deck, branched right and left, and went on to the deck below. **1950** *Bulletin* (Sydney) 30 Aug. 12/4 Barney was on the drafting-gate . . and the jummies weren't running very well. They fought the dogs, balked in the race, and charged out of the forcing-yard. **1960** *Ibid.* 6 July 16/3 It was an old-time shed, holding a couple of thousand sheep or more, 50 stands (meaning 25 pens, races and other inconveniences), all of which had to be filled. **1978** M. WALKER *Pioneer Crafts Early Aust.* 153 In the morning the sheep are driven into a 'race' running along the middle of the shed, and from that find their way into the 'shearer's pens', on each side of the race.

race, *n.*[2] [Fig. use of *race* contest of speed.] In the phr. **to be in the race,** to have an opportunity of succeeding (used in negative contexts).

1904 *Worker* (Sydney) 6 Aug. 3/3 'What snout!' said Din; 'it's emu dung, and not too bad in place Of 'bacca when you're stony broke And graft's not in the race.' **1945** M. TRIST *Now that we're Laughing* 73 'With you and Daffy dressed up, none of us others will be in the race,' said Maureen. **1953** T.A.G. HUNGERFORD *Riverslake* 227 'See that bloke?' He pointed down the road after the vanished car. 'A few years ago he wouldn't have been in the race to own a car like that.' **1972** A. CHIPPER *Aussie Swearers Guide* 78 *You're not in the race*, this old Aussie racecourse phrase signifies no chance of success. **1984** *Sydney Morning Herald* 10 May 18/5 'How could three men fight so? They were not in the race,' he said.

race, *v.* In the phr. **to race** (a person) **off,** to seduce; to hurry (a person) off with the intention of seduction.

1965 W. DICK *Bunch of Ratbags* 185 Three of Knuckles's boys had raced Sharon off to the park to see if they could do any good for themselves. **1966** *Kings Cross Whisper* (Sydney) July 8/3 If she even looks sideways she'll be raced off. **1967** *Coast to Coast 1965–66* 250 Peter thought he would try to race her . . off. He relished the phrase, *race off*. He had not heard it in England. **1967** J. HIBBERD *White with Wire Wheels* (1970) 224 By Christ, if he races her off, it'll be the last fat he cracks. **1977** H. GARNER *Monkey Grip* 137 What do you reckon my chances are of—you know—racing him off?

racehorse. [Spec. use of *racehorse* anything sleek or racy: see OEDS 3.]

1. Used *attrib.* in the names of swift, usu. sleek, lizards: **racehorse goanna,** any of several goannas, esp. the large *Varanus tristis* of central and n. Aust.; **lizard,** any of several lizards, esp. the small *Amphibolurus caudicinctus* of central and n. Aust.; also *ellipt.* **racehorse.**

1962 B.W. LEAKE *Eastern Wheatbelt Wildlife* 100 The lace goanna . . generally called **racehorse goanna** is well distributed through the Eastern Wheatbelt . . growing up to four feet long. **1967** B.Y. MAIN *Between Wodjil & Tor* 35 From the hollowed, termite-eaten trunk of a standing salmon gum tree, appeared the long, pointed head of a race-horse goanna (*Varanus tristis*). **1984** W.W. AMMON et al. *Working Lives* 250 A two-metre long bungarra had made his home under our cottage. . . With a slim, metre-long body, long snout and tapered metre-long tail, this giant lizard (or race-horse goanna in popular parlance) was quite harmless. **1923** A.G. BOLAM *Trans-Austral. Wonderland* 36 The **racehorse** or bicycle **lizard** . . runs at an incredible speed (hence it receives the name of 'the Racehorse'). **1924** *Smith's Weekly* (Sydney) 17 May 17/7 One of the fastest things in the Australian reptile world is the race-horse lizard. . . They are found on the Nullabor Plains. **1937** *Discovery* (London) May 137/1 Place a Racehorse Lizard on a pink handkerchief and it will quickly assume that colour.

2. A thinly-rolled cigarette, swag, etc. Also *attrib.*

1953 K. TENNANT *Joyful Condemned* 164 He sat rolling a very thin cigarette, known as a 'racehorse'. **1965** R.H. CONQUEST *Horses in Kitchen* 46 A hobo's swag was known as a 'racehorse' swag—long and lean. **1967** *Kings Cross Whisper* (Sydney) xxxviii. 10/3 *Racehorse*, a very thin cigarette. More the rule than the exception in nick.

rack, *v.* [Of uncertain origin; perh. transf. use of *rack* (of a horse) to move with the gait called a rack: see

OED(S *rack, v.*[4]] In the imp. phr. **rack off,** 'clear out', 'get lost'.

1975 *Sun-Herald* (Sydney) 29 June 83/2 (*title of record*) Rak off Normie. **1979** CAREY & LETTE *Puberty Blues* 66 'K'niver cig Jacko?' I asked, under the strain of the game. 'Rack off.' **1980** *Courier-Mail* (Brisbane) 18 Aug. 26/3 An altercation with the waiter, whom Bruce has told to rack off, ends with Joan physically attacking him. **1984** R. & P. THYER *Streetlight* 21 'Rack off mate, or you are going to cop it,' he bellowed.

raddle, *v. Shearing.* [Spec. use of *raddle* to mark with raddle.]

1. *trans.* To mark (an imperfectly shorn sheep) with raddle: see quots. 1891 and 1980. Also as *vbl. n.*

1879 S.W. SILVER *Austral. Grazier's Guide* 57 He .. 'raddles', or marks, for non-payment any specially discreditable sheep. **1886** *Austral. Town & Country Jrnl.* (Sydney) 17 July 127/1 No shearer shall suffer his sheep to be raddled. **1891** *Braidwood Dispatch* 6 May 2/4 Freedom of contract .. proposed by pastoralists .. said that 'any sheep not shorn to the satisfaction of the employers or their managers would be raddled or not paid for'. **1909** W.G. SPENCE *Aust.'s Awakening* 63 Another scheme was known as 'raddling'. This means that a whole penful of sheep would be marked and not paid for because the last one or any other one was not done to please the boss. **1926** G. BLACK *Hist. N.S.W. Political Labor Party* I. 31 One manager boasted that he raddled 8000 sheep in each of five successive years. **1965** *Tracks we Travel* 90 The sheep started to go down to the counting-out pens, a bit wet with their own blood, and tufts of wool sticking up on some of them. I blinked and thought they must be raddled. **1980** P. FREEMAN *Woolshed* 124 The raddle stick was the pencil used for putting a mark on the sheep's wool to indicate that the sheep was improperly shorn and should not be counted. In some cases, the board manager might even condemn a whole penful of sheep when only a few had been actually 'raddled'.

2. *Obs.*

a. *transf.* To swindle (a person).

1897 *Worker* (Sydney) 11 Sept. 1/2 But when he puts the 'stopper' on, because he finds he's broke, He swears that he was 'raddled' by that shanty-keeper 'bloke'.

b. *fig.* In the phr. **to raddle** (someone's) **toe,** to call on (a person) to buy a round of drinks.

1899 *Truth* (Sydney) 3 Apr. 8/3 According to custom, her Ladyship's toe was 'raddled'. I suppose everybody ought to know what that means, but for those who don't, I will explain. To 'raddle' the toe of a visitor to a shearing shed, means that the visitor shouts for the crowd.

radjah shieldrake, var. RAJAH SHIELDRAKE.

Rafferty. [Joc. use of the Irish surname *Rafferty*, in punning allusion to Br. dial. *raffety* irregular, f. *raff* confused heap, medley: see EDD but also OEDS for the suggestion that the word is a var. of *raffatory* or *reffatory*, a Br. dial. form of *refractory*.]

a. Used *attrib.* or in the possessive, as **Rafferty('s) rules,** no rules at all. Also **the rules of Rafferty.**

1918 *Port Hacking Cough* (Sydney) 14 Dec. 8 *Rafferty's rules*... A dog is kept to do all the barking on the premises. **1930** E. ANTONY *Hungry Mile* 38 There's two thousand scrapping with you 'neath the rules of 'Rafferty'. **1935** *Sydney Morning Herald* 28 Dec. 11/7 Rafferty rules may suit .. the Communist party, but they are repugnant to the trade union movement. **1941** *Base Blather: Unofficial Organ H.Q. A.I.F. Base Area* 1 May 3 A judicious application of Rafferty's rules. **1945** A.W. UPFIELD *Death of Swagman* 124 Not according to Queensberry... Pretty good under Rafferty's rules, though. **1959** H. LAMOND *Sheep Station* 66 'I'll go up myself and get the rams.' 'And where y' goin' to run 'em?' Harry offered a glad objection. 'Goin' t' give 'em Rafferty's Rules an' let 'em run with th' ewes?' **1971** *Bulletin* (Sydney) 11 Dec. 14/2 The minister for Labor and Industry in Victoria has the incomparably charming name of Mr Rafferty, and for nigh on five months now he has tried to apply Rafferty's Rules to Melbourne's shopping hours. **1973** L. OAKES *Whitlam PM* 57 The pre-selection campaign was a rough one, fought according to Rafferty's rules.

b. *ellipt.* for **Rafferty's rules.**

1948 H.W. CRITTENDEN *Rogues' Paradise* 8 Who could imagine any Rafferty Labor Prime Minister repeating.. 'We are with you to the last man and the last shilling'?

rager. *Obs.* An (old) untamed and aggressive bullock or cow: see quot. 1876.

1876 *Austral. Town & Country Jrnl.* (Sydney) 16 Dec. 982/1 The resources in attack or defence, developed in the confirmed 'rager', are only to be learned by experience. He is the grizzly bear of Australia. **1894** A.B. BELL *Oscar* 66 The cows were real old ragers, rag-eaters. **1901** *Western Champion* (Barcaldine) 26 Feb. 9/1 These 'ragers', mulga fed, and reared with as little knowledge of humanity, black or white, as a sixteen or twenty years sojourn in the dense mulga scrubs of the back country of the Warrego, Paroo, and Bulloo could render them, were .. things of beauty and joy for ever.

Rag Fair. *Obs.* [Transf. use of *rag-fair* a market in London for the sale of used clothing.] A market in Melbourne at which newly arrived immigrants sold clothing, etc.: see quot. 1856.

1853 J. ROCHFORT *Adventures Surveyor* 62 Emigrants who arrive with a large outfit and little money stand in a spot called 'Rag Fair', in the midst of their pile of clothes, etc., selling them to passers-by at an *awful sacrifice*. **1856** W.H.G. KINGSTON *Emigrant's Home* 169 At Melbourne, the beach is called Rag Fair, because there the poor creatures who have just landed turn out the contents of their boxes and sell them at ruinous prices, to enable them to go to the diggings. **1858** T. MCCOMBIE *Hist. Colony Vic.* 234 A mart for a peculiar kind of traffic; it was held daily on the line of Flinders street .. and was designated 'Rag Fair'. **1862** A. POLEHAMPTON *Kangaroo Land* 122 New arrivals in the colony .. were wont to dispose of their outfits on a spot near the wharf known as 'Rag Fair'.

rahzoo, var. RAZOO.

rail-splitter: see SPLITTER.

rain. Used *attrib.* in Special Comb. with reference to Aboriginal rain-making ritual: **rain-maker** (or **-doctor**), one competent to perform such a ritual; so **-making** *ppl. a.*; **(-making) stone,** a stone used in such a ritual (see quot. 1883).

1847 G.F. ANGAS *Savage Life & Scenes* I. 59 The green bough being symbolical of his situation, according to the **'rain-makers'** or wise old men. **1879** *Native Tribes S.A.* 65 The blacks also have their rainmakers. **1898** *Bulletin* (Sydney) 26 Mar. 14/4 These rev. gentlemen led a rain-making corroboree which lasted five nights. **1898** D.W. CARNEGIE *Spinifex & Sand* 348 The implement .. is used by the 'Mopongullera', or Rain-doctor, at their ceremony which they hold annually when they are making the rain. **1930** A.E. YARRA *Vanishing Horsemen* 15 He had spent a year in the Northern Territory, and he knew all about the rainmakers... He had seldom known those medicine men to fail to forecast rain. **1950** G.M. FARWELL *Land of Mirage* 52 The repertoire of rainmakers in this country is marvellously varied. Having taken their magic stones out of hiding—usually striated fragments of gypsum or *kopi* as the blacks call it—they will sing their secret incantations over them, working themselves up for days until a cloud allegedly appears in the sky. **1883** *Proc. Linnean Soc. N.S.W.* VIII. 436 Gypsum occurs abundantly in the soil, but the fibrous variety known as *Satin Spar* .. is highly prized by the natives, and is called by them **'rain-stone'**, for they believe that the Great Spirit uses it in making rain. **1916** *Bulletin* (Sydney) 16 Nov. 24/1 Who has seen our dusky brother produce moisture by the manipulation of 'rain-stones'? **1930** A.E. YARRA *Vanishing Horsemen* 16 Instead of following the white men's method .. the rainmakers undertook to 'make' the heavens give down their store, in return for great gifts from the tribe. The rainstone was the visible medium used and the process was accompanied by weird rites and much feasting and high carnival. **1949** G. FARWELL *Traveller's Tracks* 89 Minchuli, the gnarled and aged rainmaker, carefully wrapping up his rain-stones beside the Diamantina. **1959** A. UPFIELD *Bony & Black Virgin* 98 The abos never start 'singing' to their rainstones unless they are pretty sure rain isn't far away. They're cunnin' enough for that. **1964** *N. Austral. Monthly* Nov. 4 Spider, our pathfinder, had mentioned earlier that the stone was his tribe's 'rainmaking' stone... He had better bring some back and throw it in the river to break the drought.

rain bird. [Transf. use of *rain-bird*, orig. the green woodpecker *Picus viridis*.] Any of several birds, esp. cuckoos, whose call is believed to presage rain, as the CHANNEL-BILLED CUCKOO, *grey currawong* (see GREY *a.*), and PALLID CUCKOO.

1827 *Trans. Linnean Soc. London* XV. 213 Vanga .. Destructor .. Mr Caley thus observes on this species. '*Butcher-bird.*—This bird used frequently to come into some *green wattle-trees* near my house, and in wet weather was very noisy; from which circumstance it obtained the name of *Rain-bird.*' **1860** G. BENNETT *Gatherings of Naturalist* 283 A nest of full-fledged birds of the Australian Shrike or Butcher-bird, also called Rain-bird by the colonists. **1902** *Emu* II. 72 *Psophodes nigrogularis* (Black-throated Coachwhip-Bird) .. is locally known as the 'Rain-Bird' by reason of the fact that immediately preceding rain it .. utters a series of beautiful, clear, liquid, penetrating notes. **1916** E. & M.S. GREW *Rambles in Aust.* 27 She came from up-country, and was able to tell us that two handsome large grey and black birds with a singularly limpid note were 'rain birds'. **1947** W.E. HARNEY *Brimming Billabongs* (1963) 54 The cry of the rain bird was a welcome one to us children. **1949** B. O'REILLY *Green Mountains* 249 Cuckoos are our most renowned harbingers of rain, and any species of the large family may be known in some corner or other of Australia by the vernacular of 'rain bird' or 'storm bird'. **1965** *Austral. Encycl.* VII. 381 Rain-bird, a name casually applied to various birds whose calls in special circumstances are supposed to presage rain. Australia's chief 'rain-birds' are cuckoos and black cockatoos.

rainbow.

1. In Services' speech: a late reinforcement (see quots.). Also *attrib.*, as **rainbow soldier,** and *transf.*

1919 W.H. DOWNING *Digger Dialects* 40 *Rainbow*, a reinforcement, or member of non-combatant corps, who joined a fighting unit after the Armistice. **1920** *Our Empire* (Melbourne) 19 Jan. 17 'Rainbows' .. is the nickname of the last reinforcements to arrive 'After the storm they cometh'. **1943** A. DAWES *Soldier Superb* 86 Doubtless it will be a glossary of obsolete terms which will explain 'Chocko', 'Rainbow'—the men who came after the storm. **1944** T.R. ST. GEORGE *C/O Postmaster* 104 Even we Selective Service men could more or less look down on the A.M.F. and refer to them as 'Rainbow Soldiers'. **1947** V. PALMER *Cyclone* 181 Rainbow, eh? Mighty good, Clive always was, at showing up after the storm was over! **1949** G. BERRIE *Morale* 252 *Rainbows*, reinforcements who came 'after the storm'.

2. Used *attrib.* in the names of flora and fauna: **rainbow bird,** the bee-eater *Merops ornatus*, a largely migratory, insectivorous bird of mainland Aust. and islands to the north; NEEDLE-TAIL; **fish,** any of several fish, esp. the marine *Odax acroptilus* of s. Aust., the MAORI, and fresh-water fish of the fam. Melanotaeniidae, esp. *Melanotaenia splendida*; **lorikeet,** the very brightly-coloured lorikeet *Trichoglossus haematodus* of e. Aust., and introduced to the Perth (W.A.) area; *blue mountain parrot*, see BLUE *a.*; **pitta,** the predom. black and green bird *Pitta iris* of Arnhem Land (N.T.) and the Kimberley region (W.A.); **plant** (chiefly *W.A.*), any of several insectivorous plants, esp. those of the genus *Drosera* (fam. Droseraceae), and *Byblis gigantea* (fam. Byblidaceae) of s.w. W.A.; also *ellipt.* as **rainbow.**

1911 J.A. LEACH *Austral. Bird Bk.* 107 **Rainbow-bird,** Aust. bee-eater .. *Merops ornatus*. **1930** V. PALMER *Passage* (1957) 50 He found himself watching the way a rainbow-bird poised at the top of its curve in the air. **1950** *Coast to Coast 1949–50* 12 Rainbow-birds flashing from their nests in the sandy banks. **1956** A.C.C. LOCK *Tropical Tapestry* 258 Pin-tailed bee-eaters, or rainbow birds, uttered their cries which always reminded Hobbs of sleigh bells. **1980** ANSELL & PERCY *To fight Wild* 75 Swooping over the plain, bee-eaters or rainbow-birds: very pretty little birds, green, pale blue and golden bronze, with a distinctive call, a sort of descending purring whistle. **1895** C. THACKERAY *Amateur Fisherman's Guide* 57 *Tumble-down* is the .. habitat of the beautiful **rainbow** and parrot **fish.** **1906** D.G. STEAD *Fishes of Aust.* 142 The Maori or Rainbow-Fish (*Coris lineolatus*). **1928** G.H. WILKINS *Undiscovered Aust.* 45 A beautiful 'rainbow' fish was captured and examined. **1967**

M. SELLARS *Carramar* 15 The parrot fish and the rainbow fish, the latter with its long trailing fins and tail, are particularly beautiful. **1974** T.D. SCOTT et al. *Marine & Freshwater Fishes S.A.* 148 The Rainbow Fish . . is quite common in our larger rivers, particularly the Murray River. It makes an excellent aquarium fish. [**1911 rainbow lorikeet:** J.A. LEACH *Austral. Bird Bk.* 88 Blue Mountain Lorikeet . . Rainbow Lory . . *Trichoglossus novae-hollandiae*.] **1929** A.H. CHISHOLM *Birds & Green Places* 209 Just a sprinkling of the larger 'blueys' (rainbow lorikeets). **1945** C. BARRETT *Austral. Bird Life* 75 The rainbow lorikeet or Blue Mountain parrot . . a beautiful, noisy bird of the eastern states, South Australia and Tasmania, is the best known of our brush-tongued parrots. **1965** *Austral. Encycl.* VII. 25 The largest member of the group [*sc.* of lorikeets] is notably beautiful, its head and breast being vivid in blue, red and yellow; hence it is known as the rainbow lorikeet. **1984** *Tourist: Ansett Airlines Mag.* Jan. 1, Kindly hosts Fred & Elaine . . give free meals to over one thousand visitors a day . . Rainbow lorikeets of course. **1842** J. GOULD *Birds of Aust.* (1848) IV. Pl. 3, *Pitta iris* . . **Rainbow Pitta.** **1928** W. ROBERTSON *Coo-ee Talks* 36 The Rainbow Pitta . . inhabits the dense bamboo-jungles near the coast, and builds its nest of the sheaths and strips of the plant. **1945** C. BARRETT *Austral. Bird Life* 131 The rainbow pitta . . inhabits North-western Australia and the Northern Territory. **1964** M. SHARLAND *Territory of Birds* 72 A patch of scrub which produced my first sighting of the Rainbow Pitta, an 'ant-thrush', flamboyant in its multicoloured dress. **1984** SIMPSON & DAY *Birds of Aust.* 318 (*caption*) A Rainbow Pitta feeds its nestling. **1901** [**rainbow plant**] M. VIVIENNE *Travels in W.A.* 322 The desert octopus or tiger-plant is most remarkable . . and is also known as 'Rainbow' or 'Fly-trap'. **1917** *Bulletin* (Sydney) 15 Feb. 22/2 The Darling Ranges of Westralia produce a great number and variety of carnivorous plants. Commonest among these is one called by children rainbow-plant. It is a creeper which grows to a length of about 18 inches and has tiny sundew cups on short stems at irregular intervals. **1928** J. POLLARD *Bushland Vagabonds* 151 Here was the 'rainbow' plant with tiny pink and white stars, and hairy leaves and stems that caught insects and sucked their body juices. **1965** *Austral. Encycl.* II. 230 They [*sc.* spp. of *Byblis*] are often called rainbow plants because of the innumerable sticky glands that glisten like raindrops on the narrow slender leaves, stems and sepals. **1967** B.Y. MAIN *Between Wodjil & Tor* 76 Ladders of *Drosera* (sundews or rainbow plants) climbed amongst the cord rushes and up the stems of jam trees.

3. Special Comb. **rainbow serpent,** a widely venerated spirit of Aboriginal mythology: see e.g. quot. 1970. Also **rainbow snake, spirit.**

[**1906** N.W. THOMAS *Natives of Aust.* 43 The rainbow is a great fish, or a snake, taking away the rain which enemies have sent. **1910** J. MATHEW *Two Representative Tribes Qld.* 171 Dhakkan, or Takkan, was the most distinctly imaged supernatural being. This was the name for the rainbow, with which the spirit was identified. In form, he was a combination of fish and snake.] **1926** *Jrnl. R. Anthrop. Inst. London* LXI. 24 The rainbow-serpent is not confined in Australia to any particular ethnological province. **1928** W. ROBERTSON *Coo-ee Talks* 38 There was a time when stinging-nettles grew so thickly round the lake that the aborigines regarded them as having been placed there by the rainbow-spirit to keep away intruders. **1948** C.P. MOUNTFORD *Brown Men & Red Sand* 135 The legend of the Wonambi, known to the scientific world as the rainbow-serpent, belongs in one form or another to all living Australian tribes. **1963** E. WORRELL *Reptiles of Aust.* p. x, In most North Australian aboriginal tribes the seed of a child is said to enter the womb of the mother when she bathes in a pool inhabited by the Rainbow Snake, creator of all life. **1970** J.V. MARSHALL *Walk to Hills of Dreamtime* 156 *Rainbow serpent* . . (*Yurlunggur* to the Bindubi) moves through the myths of all the tribes of Australia . . nearer to godhead than any other creature. The great snake is said to have appeared in Dreamtime, the time of creation, to have fashioned the earth and then gone to ground east of the Kimberleys at a place where the rainbow plunges from earth to sky. Rain, according to some tribes, is the serpent spitting; and when the rainbow appears they say *Kaio Kuriaio* (no more rain). **1980** ANSELL & PERCY *To fight Wild* 135 According to Aboriginal legends, the Rainbow Snake lives in rivers and estuaries, and sometimes turns boats and things over; doesn't attack anyone, just gets them dumped in the water. **1984** B. DIXON *Searching for Aboriginal Lang.* 4 So the original forest still grew around the pool at the base of Murray Falls where the rainbow serpent is said to live. **1986** *Canberra Times* 22 Apr. 15/1 The spring was where the Rainbow Snake, or Wagyl, had come out of the river and gone underground. It had laid an egg . . and is now near the start of Perth's Narrow Bridge.

rajah shieldrake. Also **radjah shieldrake.** [Spec. use of *rajah* Indian title, first applied as the specific epithet *radjah* by French physician and naturalist Prosper Garnot (in L.I. Duperry *Voy. la Coquille* (1828) I. 303 Pl. 49).] *Burdekin duck* (a), see BURDEKIN. Also **radjah shelduck.**

1844 J. GOULD *Birds of Aust.* (1848) VII. Pl. 8, *Tadorna radjah* . . Radjah Shieldrake. **1845** C. HODGKINSON *Aust., Port Macquarie to Moreton Bay* 204 There are several varieties of ducks in New South Wales, such as . . the white-headed or Rajah shieldrake, the Australian shoveller, etc. **1900** A.J. CAMPBELL *Nests & Eggs Austral. Birds* 1030 The fine Rajah Shieldrake inhabits the northern half of Australia. **1976** *Reader's Digest Compl. Bk. Austral. Birds* 101 Burdekin duck *Tadorna radjah.* Other names Radjah shelduck, white-headed shelduck. . . Nowadays seldom found on east coast except in small numbers in some places in northern Queensland.

ram, *n.*

1. Used *attrib.* in Special Comb. **ram paddock,** an enclosure in which rams are kept segregated from ewes; **stag,** a ram castrated after reaching maturity; also *attrib.*

1882 ARMSTRONG & CAMPBELL *Austral. Sheep Husbandry* 147 By having the **ram paddock** enclosed by a good chock and log fence the evil effects of constant lambing will be avoided. **1905** *Bulletin* (Sydney) 11 May 16/3 Crossing a ram-paddock t'other day, I witnessed something extra in the way of ram fights. **1939** FRANKLIN & CUSACK *Pioneers on Parade* 122 He crossed the orchard, vaulted the rabbit fence and made for the ram-paddock. **1897** L. LINDLEY-COWEN *W. Austral. Settler's Guide* 642 *Stags* (or **ram stags**). Rams that are no longer wanted for use in the flock . . are a trouble if kept as rams, and it seems a waste to destroy them. The usual plan is to castrate them, and use them for food next season. . . Ram stags when fattened make excellent mutton, though some people have a prejudice against it. **1902** R. BRUCE *Reminisc. Old Squatter* 19 You had better cut it mate, that is if you can eat ram stag, cos, you see, that's what we lives on here. **1917** *11 CAR* 428 'Ram Stags' mean rams who have been castrated after they have attained eighteen months. **1956** R.G. EDWARDS *Overlander Songbk.* 96 You'll forget the ram-stag mutton on the Banks of the Condamine.

2. *fig.* See quot. 1941 and RAM *v.*

1941 S.J. BAKER *Pop. Dict. Austral. Slang* 59 *Ram*, a trickster's confederate. **1966** —— *Austral. Lang.* (ed. 2) 246 The ram would say, 'Give the old boy a fair go; he's nearly too old to spin them!'

ram, *v.* [f. prec.] *intr.* To act as a swindler's accomplice.

1952 *Coast to Coast 1951–52* 199 Siddy might have been ramming for you, but what you didn't know, my lad, was that he was helping me to hook you. You were a goner from the start. **1964** H.P. TRITTON *Time means Tucker* (rev. ed.) 33 A gentleman with an umbrella, three thimbles and a pea was demonstrating how 'the quickness of the hand deceives the eye' and was raking in the money at a great rate. When business slackened, another gentleman would pick the pea with surprising regularity. This would bring the crowd back to try their luck again. No one seemed to wake up to the fact that the second gentleman was 'ramming' for the first gentleman.

rammies, *pl.* Altered form of 'round me (or the) houses', rhyming slang for 'trousers'.

[**1905** J. MEREDITH *Learn to talk Old Jack Lang* (1984) 12, I reckoned I'd have a *lemon squash* and liven up a bit. So I threw off my *barrel of fat, dicky dirt, rammy rousers.*] **1906** *Bulletin* (Sydney) 20 Dec. 15/3 Philological research has . . enabled me to discover how a pair of pants was transmogrified into rammies. Rhyming slang transmuted trousers . . into 'round my houses'—cockney pronunciation, 'rahand me 'ouses'. **1919** W.H. DOWNING *Digger Dialects* 41 *Rammies*, breeches. **1936** *Bulletin* (Sydney) 25 Mar. 20/1 When fossickers go mooching round for gold to fill their 'shammies', A cove can dress to suit himself an' save his precious 'rammies'. **1946** *Ibid.* 7 Aug. 28/2, I pulls on me rammies, jus' walks straight up to him, says 'sniff this bunch o' fives'. **1953** T.A.G. HUNGERFORD *Riverslake* 42 Elastic for the old girl's rammies. **1982** *Bulletin* (Sydney) 25 May 50/2, I well remember my father describing trousers as *rammies.*

ramp, *n.*[1] [Spec. use of *ramp* swindle: see OED(S *sb.*[5]] A search made in a gaol of a prisoner's person or cell.

1919 V. MARSHALL *World of Living Dead* 85 Toe the arrer for the ev'nin' ramp. *Ibid.* 87 *Crabs*, boots; *ramp*, search; *toeraggers*, short timers. **1968** L.H. EVERS *Fall among Thieves* 47 Once, a warder carrying out a 'ramp' (cell-search) reported hearing a race-broadcast. **1980** B. JEWSON *Stir* 34 China stood looking at the door. . . He must have missed Tony telling him there would be a ramp—a search.

ramp, *n.*[2] GRID *n.*[2]

1948 R. RAVEN-HART *Canoe in Aust.* 82 The road had grating across it at every gate. . . (The gratings are locally 'ramps', a curious misnomer). **1955** 'M. HILL' *Land nearest Stars* 107 We were coming at last to the great sheep stations and the instructions in the Itinerary now consisted of several pages of monotonous repetition of a single word: *ramp.* This was sometimes expanded to *ramp and gate*, or *ramp and shed.*

ramp, *v.* [f. RAMP *n.*[1]] *trans.* To search (a prisoner or cell) in gaol.

1919 V. MARSHALL *World of Living Dead* 12 It would take minutes to make him secure, for he must deliver up his braces, his boots, his books, and be ramped to the skin. **1950** *Austral. Police Jrnl.* Apr. 117 *Ramp*, search a prisoner in gaol, as distinct from a search anywhere else. **1979** *Courier-Mail* (Brisbane) 2 Aug. 9/3 He heard noises from Gage's cell, but presumed the cell was being 'ramped' (searched). **1982** R. DENNING *Diary* 177 The screws ramped every cell in the jail this morning looking for Xmas brews.

ranch. Chiefly *n. Qld.* [Joc. use of *ranch(-house).*] A canteen (or boarding-house) for employees.

1937 W. HATFIELD *I find Aust.* 198 There were eighty-four men eating at the 'ranch' as they called it. **1944** J. DEVANNY *By Tropic Sea & Jungle* 21 We hiked a few miles to a sawmill, where we ate at the mill ranch—'ranch' in North Queensland means cookhouse.

Hence **rancher** *n.*

1967 F. HARDY *Billy Borker yarns Again* 70 Ah, not real ranchers. In North Queensland a rancher is a bloke who runs a sort of boarding house out in the bush, near some big job.

range, *n.* [Spec. use of *range* line or series of mountains: see OED(S *sb.*[1] 2 c.]

1. Chiefly in *pl.* Hilly or mountainous country, not necessarily forming a single divide. Also *attrib.* in sing.

1805 *HRA* (1915) 1st Ser. V. 580 Those Cow tracks sometimes branch off to the most inaccessible parts of the Hills. The Range and Summits of which appear to be the general Resort of the Cattle. **1839** *S. Austral. Register* (Adelaide) 24 Oct. 3 These ranges were devoid of timber, of a barren appearance. **1843** *Sydney Morning Herald* 19 Sept. 2/6 On the 4th of that month a parcel of blackfellows came down the range towards my hut. **1843** D.G. BROCK *Recoll.* 13 Sept. (1981) 23, I made one of Mr Perer's stations, stopped an hour, then struck off in a N. West direction across some ranges. **1848** *Adelaide Miscellany* 23 Sept. 121/1 To the eastward cultivated fields reached the foot of the ranges; these rose up in beautiful variety: the openly wooded hills, . . gradually merged into the densely-clothed forest; and hill rose above hill, until Mount Lofty towered over all. **1850** *Britannia* (Hobart) 7 Mar. 4/6 Camp in high sheltered spots, if you can get on the tops of the ranges so much the better. **1854** S. SIDNEY *Gallops & Gossips* 99 Steep hills (colonially, *ranges*), covered with Australian pine. **1880** 'OLD HAND' *Experiences of Colonist* (ed. 2) i. 30 Our trackers were now among the ranges. The general tendency of these elevated lands was in a north and south direction. These hills or ranges were covered with the Eucalypti. **1881** R. CRAWFORD *Echoes from Bushland* 23 After a few hours puzzling through trackless solitudes of range and scrub, we dropped down, by a leading spur. **1890** 'MRS A. MACLEOD' *Austral. Girl* 108 One day . . she discovered a whole range-side of early epacris. **1925** *Smith's Weekly* (Sydney) 21 Feb. 20/5 The Australian abo .. gave the show away by leading the inspector to a secluded spot in the ranges. **1934** 'S. RUDD' *Green Grey Homestead* 127 The 'big house' of English architecture, built of red cedar from the ranges, stood in the centre of a glorious garden. **1978** D. STUART *Wedgetail View* 8 No one would know if he had died or had survived to live out his life in the ranges back from the river country.

2. a. In the phr. **over the range(s),** on the other side of a tract of mountainous country.

1864 'E.S.H.' *Narr. Trip Sydney to Peak Downs* 8 We proceeded to what is called 'over the ranges', on a good sound road. **1940** E. HILL *Great Austral. Loneliness* (ed. 2) 88 Kimberley is a country of wanderers, stockmen and 'ringers', swaggies .. men 'out dogging' in the wilderness. 'Over the ranges', the rugged King Leopolds to the north, lies a magnificent coast.

b. [U.S.: see Mathews *n.* 4 b.] In the phr. **to go over the range,** to die.

1936 J.C. DOWNIE *Galloping Hoofs* 72 Of course a lot of them do go 'over the range', and are laid to rest in the great outback. **1942** *Frontier News* (Sydney) Sept. 4/2 The only set item is the reading of the list of those Old-timers who, since we last met, have gone on 'Over the Range'.

range, *v. Obs.* [Spec. use of *range* to rove.]

a. *intr.* To live in the bush in the manner of an outlaw: see BUSHRANGER 1.

1805 *Sydney Gaz.* 24 Nov., *Desmond* .. is again a fugitive from the settlement of King's Town and ranges about the skirts of these settlements. **1815** *HRA* (1916) 1st Ser. VIII. 472 The Bushrangers have at length become so outrageous and alarming .. that I have accordingly sent armed parties into the Woods with Orders to Apprehend all Persons, illegally ranging therein. **1818** T.E. WELLS *M. Howe* (1945) 6 Howe may not unaptly be compared to Three-fingered Jack, who was so long the terror of the peaceable settlers in the plantations of Jamaica; and who, notwithstanding every exertion to take him, long ranged the woods of that Island. **1829** *Sydney Monitor* 1 Aug., Several bushrangers are reported as ranging about Botany Bay.

b. *trans.* In the phr. **to range the bush** (or **woods**).

1834 J. MUDIE *Vindication* p. vii, He was, for absconding and ranging the bush several weeks without means of subsistence (except by pilfering or robbing on the road to Sydney ..) sent twelve months to an ironed-gang. **1846** *Bell's Life in Sydney* 12 Sept. 1/3 Some miscreants by way of raising the wind without pawning, have been deriving a profit by ranging the bush. **1858** A. HARRIS *Secrets* (1961) 138 The outlaw now speaks of his purpose. Once a month he will see his angel; the rest of the time range the bush. **1964** J.S. MANIFOLD *Who wrote Ballads?* 25 Bushrangers existed before Donahue. A convict who escaped could only 'range the bush'.

ranger. BUSHRANGER 1.

1817 *HRA* (1921) 3rd Ser. II. 194 The party under Ensign Mahon of the 46 had just before killed two and wounded a third of the Rangers. **1829** *Launceston Advertiser* 21 Sept. 4 No ranger is so dangerous as one who is aware that his life is already forfeited to the offended laws of his country. **1846** S. SNOW *Exile's Return* 20 These desperadoes, when they are driven to the necessity of *bolting*, or breaking loose from the restraints of slavery, and joining the standard of the Rangers, are ripe for any deeds of daring that may offer. **1851** MRS R. LEE *Adventures in Aust.* 319 'Perhaps, sir, you have also seen Harry Blunt, the famous bushranger'... 'We had long heard that rangers were about.' **1891** 'OLD TIME' *Convict Hulk 'Success'* 9 Daring bushrangers made it dangerous to travel... Every 'ranger' was mounted; and the number of horses stolen was almost incredible. **1900** *Truth* (Sydney) 17 June 6/4 The poor woman was dreadfully frightened that the rangers would kill her husband. **1917** W. LEES *Coaching in Aust.* 26 One of the 'rangers pointed the muzzle of the gun at my head. **1980** O. RUHEN *Bullock Teams* 86 A few experiences with bushrangers had taught him to be careful of the way he carried money... Usually, however, the 'rangers did not rib the teamsters.

rangie: see NARANGY.

rangy, *a.* [f. RANGE *n.* 1 + *-y*.] Hilly, mountainous.

1861 *Burke & Wills Exploring Exped.* 2 Between the tropics and Carpentaria a considerable portion is rangy. **1888** 'R. BOLDREWOOD' *Robbery under Arms* (1937) I. 10 Our farm was on a good little flat, with .. a scrubby, rangy country at the back for miles. **1909** E. WALTHAM *Life & Labour in Aust.* 64 We were now rapidly approaching the 'Rangy' or hilly district. **1945** S.J. BAKER *Austral. Lang.* 243 *Rangy* (meaning mountainous).

rank duffer. *Obs.* A complete failure (orig. of a gold mine): see DUFFER *n.* 2.

1873 W. THOMSON-GREGG *Desperate Character* II. 177 Their neighbours, outside, bottomed a rank 'duffer' at sixty-four feet. **1876** J.A. EDWARDS *Gilbert Gogger* 129 Emphatically pronounced Ballarat in particular, and gold diggings in general, rank duffers. Rank duffers: thorough cheats. **1900** *Truth* (Sydney) 10 June 3/1 Instructors become strict disciplinarians by reason of their office; they often have some rank duffers to lick into shape. **1906** S. GRIFFITHS *Turf & Heath* 60 All Nightlight's dark brown progeny were 'clinkers', while the light-coloured ones were 'rank duffers'. **1913** W.K. HARRIS *Outback in Aust.* 167 The wild rush to Port Curtis, in Queensland, took place in 1857, and proved a rank duffer.

rap, *n.* Also **wrap.** [See next.] A boost; a commendation. Also **rap up.**

1939 K. TENNANT *Foveaux* 176 Everyone wants to be seen with a high-up feller. When I pass the time of day to a cove he feels that's a rap for him, see? **1959** *R.A.N. News* (Sydney) 20 Mar. 4 'Wagga' [the ship] got a 'rap up' from 'Voyager'... 'Congratulations.' **1973** K. DUNSTAN *Sports* 229 If someone does something good, take a good mark, give him a rap. Tell him. You're a team, remember. You got to *love* each other. **1978** H.C. BAKER *I was Listening* 170 One verse gave the nursing sisters from Baggot a good rap-up. **1980** A. HOPGOOD *And here comes Bucknuckle* 58 You had to put your money where your mouth was. I've never heard anybody give a horse a wrap like the one you gave Bucknuckle after that first race at Manangatang. **1982** *Sun-Herald* (Sydney) 1 Aug. 77/4 'Give Tony a rap. He was so cool under pressure,' said Gordon coach.

rap, *v.* Also **wrap.** [Prob. transf. use of Br. dial. *rap* to boast: see EDD *v.*[1] 11.] *trans.* To praise (exaggeratedly). Freq. with **up.**

1957 D. NILAND *Call me when Cross turns Over* 138 'You dream and feel hopeless, I don't.' 'Rapping yourself up a bit, aren't you?' **1967** *Kings Cross Whisper* (Sydney) xliii. 11/3 To praise a person is to give him a wrap. If you can't wrap a bloke don't roast him. **1973** *Sun* (Sydney) 1 May 78/3 Last week I wrapped him over his display of whistle blowing in the Easts-Manly game and this was virtually the 'kiss of death'. Anytime referees get a wrap they seem to get banished to the suburbs. **1975** X. HERBERT *Poor Fellow my Country* 875 Pat guffawed, 'Does she wrap you up! Look... 'This sweet and lovely creature.'

rapt: see WRAPPED.

raspberry jam. [See quot. 1872.] The shrub or small tree of s.w. W.A. *Acacia acuminata* (fam. Mimosaceae), yielding a fragrant, durable timber; the wood of the plant; JAM *n.*[1] Also **raspberry jam tree** (or **wood**).

1833 *Perth Gaz.* 10 May 283 The acacia, called from the smell of the wood, raspberry-jam tree. **1837** *Ibid.* 11 Nov. 1004, 4 logs (5 cwt.) raspberry-jam wood. **1845** L. LEICHHARDT *Jrnl. Overland Exped. Aust.* 23 July (1847) 341 The plains along the right side of the river were occupied by a scanty vegetation consisting of Phyllanthis shrubs, scattered box, and the raspberry jam trees .. growing densely along the creek .. which smelt like raspberry jam. **1872** MRS E. MILLETT *Austral. Parsonage* 49 An acacia of that kind familiarly named the 'raspberry jam', because the perfume of the wood when freshly cut resembles that of the preserve. **1893** D. LINDSAY *Jrnl. Elder Sci. Exploring Exped.* 125 Camped at Little Jam Hill, so called because on the hill a quantity of stunted raspberry jam wood is growing. **1935** E. COLEMAN *Come back in Wattle Time* 26 From the Raspberry Jam Wattle .. many ornamental articles are made. **1979** J. BIRMINGHAM et al. *Austral. Pioneer Technol.* 33 Wandoo and an acacia known as 'raspberry jam' were good fencing timbers in Western Australia.

rat, *n.*

1. a. In the phr. **to get** (or **have**) **a rat** (or **rats**), to be eccentric, disturbed, or deranged; also **to give** (someone) **a rat,** to cause derangement.

[**1890** BARRÈRE & LELAND *Dict. Slang* II. 171 (American), 'to have *rats*', to have wild or eccentric fancies. **1894** H. LAWSON *Short Stories* 2 He was scowling malignantly at a stout, dumpy swag which lay in the middle of the track. 'Well, old Rats, what's the trouble?' asked Sunlight. 'Oh, nothing, nothing,' answered the old man, without looking round. 'I fell out with my swag, that's all. He knocked me down, but I've settled him.'] **1898** G.T. BELL *Coolgardie* 51 They get fat fees for their reports, but oft times they get rats, When the ten-ounce reef a duffer proves and the mines are called 'wild cats'. **1899** *Truth* (Sydney) 23 July 3/5 The solitude of the bush is giving him rats. **1911** V. DESMOND *Awful Austral.* 75 The Australian bushman has, what is generally known as a 'rat'; in fact, the lunacy of Australia is most alarming. **1913** H. LAWSON *Triangles of Life* 165 The old shepherd had died, or got drunk, or got rats. **1918** L.J. VILLIERS *Changing Yr.* 12 She didn't kid yer long—er bloomin' dart Ud git yer goin' till yer 'ad a rat. **1924** A.W. BAZLEY et al. Gloss. Slang A.I.F. 23 (typescript) *Rat* (to have a), to be crazy. **1955** STEWART & KEESING *Austral. Bush Ballads* 240 The Boss has got a rat today: he's buckin' everywhere.

b. In the phr. **in the rats,** in a state of derangement, esp. as a result of excessive consumption of alcoholic liquor.

[N.Z. **1921** LORD 'Stunology' in *Ballads of Bung* (1976), We say a man is .. A 'ribald reveller', 'on the rag', or mayhap 'in the rats'.] **1937** W. HATFIELD *I find Aust.* 138 A brumby-runner .. was 'in the rats' after a prolonged boozing spell. **1957** D. NILAND *Call me when Cross turns Over* 116 Your own brother is half in the rats with worry and anxiety. Unless something's done he'll end up in the giggle-house. **1967** *Kings Cross Whisper* (Sydney) xxxix. 4/4 *Rats*, delerium tremens, in the rats, in the horrors.

2. RATTER.

1921 K.S. PRICHARD *Black Opal* 34 Rats, the men who sneaked into other men's mines when they were on good stuff, and took out their opal during the night, were never Ridge men.

3. In the phr. **like a rat up a drain(pipe),** very quickly, 'quick as a flash'.

[**1959** E. LAMBERT *Glory thrown In* 104 First time we spoke she turned it on—I was like a rat up a rope!] **1962** C. ROHAN *Delinquents* 76 He'd be up you like a rat up a drainpipe, given the chance. **1968** B. HUMPHRIES *Wonderful World Barry McKenzie*, Up her like a rat up a drainpipe. **1978** R. MCKIE *Bitter Bread* 158, I figured that when I told the demons about 'em they'd be down 'ere like rats up a drain diggin' like mad. **1981** P. BARTON *Bastards I have Known* 4 Old Bert lived just up the road and I took to him like a 'rat up a drainpipe'.

4. Special Comb. **rat-house,** a psychiatric hospital.

1900 J. BRADSHAW *Highway Robbery under Arms* (*c* 1927) 120 The doctor certified him to be a madman. Bertrand then got packed off to the rat-house. **1922** A. WRIGHT *Colt from Country* 83 He'll be the long-lost boy, instead of the guy that's missed and landed in the rat-house. **1931** O. WALTERS *Shrapnel Green* 33 But a man 'ud be right for the rat-house if he could remember. **1953** T.A.G. HUNGERFORD *Riverslake* 190 You want to make up your mind and dice whatever you don't want. Otherwise you'll end up in the rat-house. **1965** J. WYNNUM *Jiggin' in Riggin'* 38 Ugh! A man would finish up in the rathouse after an evening with her. **1978** M.J. BURTON *Bush Pub* 94 He'll reverse you into the clink and into the rathouse before you know what's hit you.

rat, *v. trans.* To loot; to rob (a person, claim, etc.); to steal (money, etc.). Also as *vbl. n.* and *ppl. a.*

1898 *Bulletin* (Sydney) 17 Dec. 15/2 *Ratted* or robbed is meant by *raddled*. **1918** *Twenty-Second's Echo: Mag. 22nd Battalion A.I.F.*, From the pocket of a Fritz who was ratted in No Man's Land. **1921** K.S. PRICHARD *Black Opal* 47 There had been ratting epidemics on the Ridge before; but robbery of a mate by a mate had never occurred before. **1932** —— *Kiss on Lips* 246 Blacks .. ratted Beck's camp, and Mrs Jinny's shroud was missing. **1946** —— *Roaring Nineties* 20 Tommy Talbot and his mates tried rattin' the reward claim, but Ford pulled his gun on them. **1954** T. RONAN *Vision Splendid* 92 If you like to rat another man's pack-bag for grog . . it isn't my place to interfere. **1973** F. PARSONS *Man called Mo* 46 'And where do you think she got the gelt from, pal?' Roy chuckled. 'She ratted Mumma's handbag.' **1980** S. THORNE *I've met some Bloody Wags* 73 Occasionally a specker is lucky, but a lot of stones sold as 'specked' opal are in reality 'ratted' opal.

ratbag. A trouble-maker, a rogue; an eccentric; a person to whom some opprobrium attaches. Also *attrib.*

1890 *Quiz* (Adelaide) 1 Aug. 2/2 The Imperial ratbag amongst us brings these insults upon us. **1937** W. HATFIELD *I find Aust.* 138 'You brought one rat-bag *in*', said Ewens to me, 'so now do me a favour by taking one off my hands.' **1944** A.J. & J.J. MCINTYRE *Country Towns Vic.* 160 In some towns anti-intellectualism is more positively expressed. . . 'A lot of rat-bags.' **1948** V. PALMER *Golconda* 107 Why the hell, Donovan, are you backing that old ratbag, Christy Baughan? **1964** K. WILLEY *Eaters of Lotus* 10 The next ten years will show if Darwin is to be in fact, as well as in name, a frontier to the North and the gateway to Australia—or whether it will remain, as it is now, a ratbag fringe. **1965** *Overland* xxxii. 40 University students! They're a pack of ratbags! **1969** *Bulletin* (Sydney) 8 Mar. 10/3 Teachers are all ratbags. **1976** *Overland* lxiii. 45, I jovially agreed with him that radicals were poofs and ratbags. **1986** *Canberra Times* 15 Feb. 2/4 A self-opinionated mediocrity . . this guru of the ratbag right.

Hence **ratbaggery** *n.*

1943 S.J. BAKER *Pop. Dict. Austral. Slang* (ed. 3) 64 *Ratbag*, an unpleasantly disposed or vicious person: a term of contempt, though not always offensive. Whence, 'ratbaggery'. **1965** R.H. CONQUEST *Horses in Kitchen* 131 It is a moral to spread to other Queensland towns, as ratbaggery can't be confined to any fixed boundary. **1980** F. MOORHOUSE *Days of Wine & Rage* 423 The sensibility trained to conform can only benefit when the culture shifts and one's basic assumptions turn into the stuff of ratbaggery.

ration, *n.* Freq. in *pl.* [Transf. use of *ration* the daily amount of certain articles of food allotted to military personnel: see OED(S 3 a.]

1. a. An allowance of provisions made to a hand on a rural property as a condition of employment. Also *attrib.*

1843 *Sydney Morning Herald* 6 Oct. 3/7 Wanted some shepherds. Wages, £15, and a good ration. **1852** D. MACKENZIE *Gold Digger* 73 When living at a grazing establishment, or on large farms, your weekly rations consisting of 10 lbs. flour, from 10 lbs. to 14 lbs. butchers' meat . . 2 lbs. sugar, and 1/4 lb. tea for each adult, are weighed and given to you every Saturday evening. **1854** W. HOWITT *Boy's Adventures* 9 The shepherds and herdsmen of this country are called Stockmen. They often live far away up in the woods, or the bush as it is called here . . and frequently see nobody but the man who brings their weekly rations, that is, their week's allowance of provisions. **1869** *Bushmen, Publicans & Politics* 4 They have been accustomed to receive their rations and their cheque for their spree, giving the smallest possible amount of labour in return. **1887** W.H. SUTTOR *Austral. Stories Retold* 118 Of the skillions, one is a store for the rations, and the other is the older children's room. **1902** R.C. PRAED *My Austral. Girlhood* 94 Altogether ration, blanket, tobacco, everything belong to blackfellow. **1913** H. LAWSON *Triangles of Life* 166 Take some tucker along to the Mile Hut, and give it to the new shepherd. . . Go to the storekeeper, and he'll give you a bag of rations. **1936** *Bulletin* (Sydney) 20 Nov. 21/2 Droving out on the Mulligan (W.Q.) I was about to kill a sheep for rations. **1948** *Ibid.* 14 Jan. 23/3 Mum was passing the killing-tree when she stopped to stare in consternation at the carcass Dad was dressing for rations. **1949** H.E. THONEMANN *Tell White Man* 11 As it was, the station supplemented their native foods with white men's rations. **1959** *Bulletin* (Sydney) 1 July 18/2 Station ration-scales, as authorised by the Central Queensland Pastoral Employers' Association in 1893 . . included: Flour 8 lb.; tea, 6 oz.; sugar, 3lb.; meat, 20 lb.; salt, ½ lb.; soda, 2 oz. **1960** *N.T. News* (Darwin) 22 Jan. 6/4 Visitors to Borroloola recently were old-timer Jack Shadforth and Arthur Alpin, both of whom were in for rations.

b. A gift of food made to an itinerant.

1879 S.W. SILVER *Austral. Graziers' Guide* 41 The labourer generally arrives at the station store about sundown, with a request for 'a little ration' (always supplied gratis) and a rather languid inquiry as to whether 'there's any work goin'". **1889** *Centennial Mag.* (Sydney) 537 Swagsmen too, genuine, or only sun-downers—men who loaf about till sunset and then come in with the demand for the unrefusable 'rations'. **1899** *Bulletin* (Sydney) 30 Dec. 14/3 No outback station refuses to sell rations; very few refuse to *give* when coin is not forthcoming. . . Stop the rations . . and only 'financial' travellers will venture out, and these . . can refuse work until offered suitable wages. **1918** *Ibid.* 31 Oct. 22/2 'Fact is', said the boss, grudgingly handing out some rations to the traveller, 'if the number of you blokes keeps up I'll have to start out with Matilda myself.' **1920** *Ibid.* 11 Mar. 20/3 It was said to be a common thing for men who had been refused rations to drop scabby wool on a 'pinchgut' run. **1924** H.E. RIEMANN *Nor'-West o' West* 143 W'en he wants rations, he catches the teams going up-river loaded with stores, an' takes his supply of flour an' tea an' sugar. An' its unnerstood that the teamies let him. **1974** W.G. HOWCROFT *Sand in Stew* 2 Some sundowners acquired a sinister reputation for allegedly using veiled threats of 'letting the red steer loose' to station owners who refused them rations.

c. An allowance of provisions (but see also quot. 1913) made to a member of an Aboriginal community or group by a government or religious body.

1884 *V & P* (N.S.W. L.A.) XI. 943 Gresford—Clothing and rations supplied to old and infirm aborigines. **1913** W.K. HARRIS *Outback in Aust.* 115 A patronising Government doles out rations and blankets to those who have been in the settlement the longest. **1948** *N.S.W. Parl. Papers* 2nd Sess. II. 1073 Every aged, infirm and indigent aborigine received a full-scale ration.

d. With distinguishing epithet, as **dry, government, station, track, travelling,** etc.: see under first element.

2. Special Comb. **ration bag,** a bag used by the recipient of a ration; **carrier,** one employed on a rural property to deliver rations to out-stations; **cart,** a cart used for the conveyance of rations; **day,** the day appointed for the issue of rations to employees on a rural property; **dray,** *ration cart*; **hut,** the provision-store on a rural property; **man,** *ration carrier*; **sheep,** a sheep killed for immediate consumption, esp. as part of an allowance; **sugar,** an inferior grade of sugar issued as rations; **tea,** an inferior grade of tea issued as rations.

1849 A. HARRIS *Emigrant Family* (1967) 198 Carrying up their **ration bags** to the farm-store. **1862** R. HENNING *Lett.* (1952) 46 The 'ration bags' contained flour, sugar, tea, sardines, bacon. **1891** *Bulletin* (Sydney) 9 May 18/1, I bring thee here my ration-bags, And, lo, they are but small; I prithee now, good overseer, Pray fill them one and all. **1910** C.E.W. BEAN *On Wool Track* 222 'Can you give me some tea and sugar and a bit of flour?' 'Yes', I said; 'where are your ration bags?' **1868** C.W. BROWNE *Overlanding in Aust.* 59 Such is his daily routine varied by the visit of the **ration-carrier** once a week. **1882** A.J. BOYD *Old Colonials* 7, I never see any one but the ration-carrier once a week. **1890** 'R. BOLDREWOOD' *Squatter's Dream* 122 The boundary-riders come in for their rations, so a ration-carrier is unnecessary. **1904** L.M.P. ARCHER *Bush Honeymoon* 76 Poor beggars, not much wonder they did—living all alone, and only seeing the ration carrier once a fortnight. **1925** *Bulletin* (Sydney) 8 Oct. 24/3, I once pulled up at an old shepherd's camp . . and . . he had fresh chops in the pan a fortnight after his ration-carrier had called. **1937** D. GUNN *Links with Past* 139 Bill . . was the ration carrier. **1849** A. HARRIS *Emigrant Family* (1967) 41 Willoughby . . was seen conveying three ladies in the little green **ration-cart** towards the Rocky Springs. **1860** 'LADY' *My Experiences in Aust.* 207 They prefer trusting for their subsistence to the precarious gains of a hunter, rather than to the weekly 'ration cart' of an employer. **1918** C. FETHERSTONHAUGH *After Many Days* 367 The story goes that the ration cart had just left the store. **1929** K.S. PRICHARD *Coonardoo* (1961) 37 Ted'd drive the ration cart and she'd drive the bullocks. **1849** A. HARRIS *Emigrant Family* (1967) 198 The hands found **ration-day** again come round, and no supply. **1937** D. GUNN *Links with Past* 139 Ration day was Thursday. **1976** S. WELLER *Bastards I have Met* 5 He walked in with a big newspaper parcel of beef ends two days before ration day and said 'Fill the billies, boys. Stew for tea.' **1859** H. KINGSLEY *Recoll. Geoffrey Hamlyn* II. 163 Send him down on the **ration dray.** *c* **1891** J. GARDINER *Twenty-Five Yrs. on Stage* 123, I thought you wanted to put your wife with mine on the 'ration dray'. **1896** *Bulletin* (Sydney) 11 Jan. 18/1 Mrs Mitchins and the kids amid the general fray Got access to the **ration-hut** and took the 'junk' away. **1952** *Ibid.* 2 Apr. 17/1 Several of the young bucks . . by collusion with a gin . . were able to squeeze nightly down the chimney of the ration-hut and take toll of the stores. **1900** *Ibid.* 29 Dec. 14/1 Old Andy, a boundary-rider, was much-valued by the boss, who, whenever the drink-crave attacked the old chap, would send him by the **ration-man** a couple of bottles of brandy. **1924** C. BLOXSOME *How Wonder won Cup* 7 We were now in need of a ration man, For the boss last week had sacked young Dan. **1976** B. SCOTT *Complete Bk. Austral. Folk Lore* 376 Another economy practised by station storekeepers was the supply of what the ration men called 'post and rail' tea, mainly consisting of the stalks and roughest leaves. **1872** G.S. BADEN-POWELL *New Homes for Old Country* 156 Meat has to go out twice a week, unless the system of '**ration sheep**' be in vogue. Then each shepherd will have in his flock, sheep which he is allowed to kill. **1899** *Bulletin* (Sydney) 29 Apr. 14/2 Two of us rode out to get ration-sheep. **1914** H.B. SMITH *Sheep & Wool Industry* 34 On the station the first sheep that are usually shorn are the ration sheep. These are the sheep that are killed for household and shearers' use. **1938** *Bulletin* (Sydney) 13 Apr. 21/2 Wet weather, and we needed a ration sheep; so one of the pets, a four-toothed wether, had his death warrant issued. **1967** G. JENKIN *Two Yrs. Bardunyah Station* 3 Dingo, will you pick up a couple of ration sheep and drop them off at Kurlina. **1873** J.C.F. JOHNSON *Christmas on Carringa* 1 Jam ingeniously concocted of brown **ration sugar** and water. **1887** H.A. LONG *Austral. Lett.* 38 At Yenyarie they make what is called 'ration sugar'—namely, brown sugar of a coarse type. **1892** *Missing Friends: Adventures Danish Emigrant Qld.* 54 The most inferior goods which are in the market are called *ration-tea* and *ration-sugar.* **1878** E. BRADDON *Lett. to India from Tas.* (1980) 88, I quite wonder why anybody goes through the farce of buying **ration tea** for these sons of toil. It would answer just as well to go into the bush and pick a teapotful from the bushes there. **1903** *Bulletin* (Sydney) 31 Jan. 16/1 At times when the drays have been late, I have 'rung' the ration tea into 'the house', and no one was any wiser. **1943** H.G. LAMOND *From Tariaro to Ross Roy* 20 The staple rations in those days . . were: Flour (Californian), tea (probably China, known as 'ration' tea, and commonly referred to as 'post and rails') [etc.].

ration, *v.* [Used elsewhere but recorded earliest in Aust.: see OED *v.* 1.] *trans.* To supply (a person) with an allowance of provisions. Also as *ppl. a.*

1834 BURNS & SKEMP *Van Dieman's Land Correspondents* 10 May (1961) 33 Assist me by the loan of three labourers for about two months rationed by the Government. **1835** G.C. INGLETON *True Patriots All* 18 June (1952) 163 It is reported, but it cannot be true, that the Sydney blacks are still rationed by the Government of Van Dieman's Land. **1840** *S. Austral. Rec.* (London) 14 Mar. 110 The arrangement for receiving and rationing government immigrants at the public cost until they obtain situations. **1843** *Sydney Morning Herald* 29 Sept. 4/3 Our agents have hired men in Sydney, paid their passage in the steamers, and got them rationed in Maitland to enable them to come up here. **1929** K.S. PRICHARD *Coonardoo* (1961) 88 There he made a great noise about tucker bags which had not been washed or could not be found; rationed the blacks. **1950** V.F. TURNER *Ooldea* 8 The Aborigines' Board received the proposal to open the Station with sympathy, and eventually removed the ration depot from Tarcoola to Ooldea, Miss Lock becoming the rationing officer.

rat-kangaroo. *Kangaroo-rat* (a), see KANGAROO *n.* 5.

1896 B. SPENCER *Rep. Horn Sci. Exped. Central Aust.* I. 28 On the Porcupine sandhills the Rat-kangaroos (*Bettongia lesueuri*) are constantly dodging in and out amongst the tussocks. **1905** *Bulletin* (Sydney) 13 July 18/2 The animal is a common scrub wallaby . . quite distinct from the rat-kangaroos, or jerboaroos. **1925** *Ibid.* 3 Sept. 22/2 One of the prettiest little animals of the Tassie bush is the bettong, known to bushmen as the rat-kangaroo. **1948** R. RAVEN-HART *Canoe in Aust.* 146 They're not kangaroo-rats, they're rat-kangaroos. . . They keep hidden all day: carry grass in their tails they do, and make a nest of it and hide in it as long as there's any daylight. **1983** R. STRAHAN *Compl. Bk. Austral. Mammals* 177 Referred to in the past simply as 'rat-kangaroos', the Potoroidae is now seen to comprise three subgroups; potoroos, bettongs and the Musky Rat-kangaroo.

ratshit. Used allusively to denote insignificance, the lowest point or level; also as *adj.*, 'rock-bottom', and as a general term of opprobrium.

1970 *Kings Cross Whisper* (Sydney) lxxxiv. 5/4 Look at Ample's plan to drill the Barrier Reef to rat-shit in our greed to get our grubby hands on more oil. **1971** D. WILLIAMSON *Don's Party* (1973) 59 'We saw these two magnificent waitresses. . . ' 'Absolute ratshit. The bottom of the barrel.' **1977** D. FOSTER *Escape to Reality* 11 He looks ratshit. **1979** CAREY & LETTE *Puberty Blues* 98 Then Jacko come up, you know Jack? . . and he says to me, 'Your eyes look ratshit.' That was the biggest compliment. **1980** F. MOORHOUSE *Days of Wine & Rage* 421 In 1970 I thought that various things would happen, that, spectacularly, didn't, but now I have a much better idea of why they should and a much improved estimation of their chances (ratshit).

ratter. [f. RAT *v.*] One who steals, esp. opal from another's mine.

1932 I.L. IDRIESS *Prospecting for Gold* 239 Ratters are men, a gang as a rule, who work your opal out for you while you sleep. **1973** D. WOLFE *Brass Kangaroo* 24 Big Mervyn was afraid of the 'ratters' . . men who studied progress on new shafts then when the opal level was reached, came in at night and got away with as much of the 'concrete' as they could. **1977** J. CARTER *All Things Wild* 115 True or false, the tale has almost certainly deterred some would-be opal mine 'ratters', as they are called. **1980** S. THORNE *I've met some Bloody Wags* 73 The miners usually deal with ratters (people who steal opals from someone else's claim) themselves.

rattlepod. [U.S.: see Mathews *rattle, n.* 5.] Any of many herbs or shrubs of the genus *Crotalaria* (fam. Fabaceae) of central and n. Aust. and elsewhere.

1935 DAVISON & NICHOLLS *Blue Coast Caravan* 268 Rattle-pod, a shrub that lived up to its name . . when its branches were shaken. **1955** J. CLEARY *Justin Bayard* 170 'Rattlepod,' he said. 'Is there much of it around here?' 'We're always troubled by it. We lost four horses during the Wet from it.' **1967** E. HUXLEY *Their Shining Eldorado* 236 A condition known as 'walkabout', caused by a poisonous plant which acts on the liver. One of the plant's popular names is rattle-pod, its scientific one *Crotolaria* [*sic*] *retusa*. **1981** J.A. BAINES *Austral. Plant Genera* 108 *Crotalaria* . . Gk. krotalon, a rattle or clapper; because the seeds rattle in the inflated pods, hence the common name rattlepods.

ratty, *a.* [f. RAT *n.* 1 + *-y.*]

a. Mad, deranged.

1895 *Worker* (Sydney) 5 Jan. 1/5, I suppose its the heat that makes all of us a bit ratty at times. *Ibid.* 14 Dec. 3/3 Further, that persons like myself are 'ratty' who think otherwise. **1898** *Bulletin* (Sydney) 26 Feb. 14/3 Struck an old-established Darling whaler, and asked him what he thought about the alleged 'rattiness' of himself and co. 'Ratty?' he asked. 'Who says we're ratty?' **1903** J. MARSHALL *Battling for Gold* 138 These fellows are ratty! They must have been having a big spree. **1908** *Truth* (Sydney) 27 Dec. 1/4 A few months ago Australia went ratty over the American Fleet; for the past few weeks it has gone rattier trying to decide which of the Americans is the fleetest. **1911** *Ibid.* 23 July 7/5 The people are going ratty over the Coronation, and paying all sorts of prices for a look at the peep-show. **1927** J. MATHIEU *Backblock Ballads* 10 He started to go ratty, and began to fancy that he Was an Injun on the warpath. **1942** G.S. CASEY *It's Harder for Girls* (1944) 18 He was ratty, and he was drunk, but he was fierce and strong. **1973** C.E. GOODE *Stories Strange Places* 80 The bush life may have been making him a bit 'ratty' like several others in the neighbourhood. The incendiarist patiently waited for the next harvest.

b. In the phr. **to be ratty over (on, about)**, to be infatuated with.

1900 *Western Champion* (Barcaldine) 24 Apr. 11/1 The girls are real 'ratty' on anyone in dungarees. You cannot shake them off. **1909** *Truth* (Sydney) 24 Jan. 1/4 The Male Train: Wimmin who go ratty on a matinee hero. **1923** *Aussie* (Sydney) July 20/3 He can't sleep for lovin' you. . . It's the truth. He's fair ratty over you. **1932** *Listening Post* (Perth) Aug. 4 But you needn't have kept on praising [the girl] you are ratty about.

raven. [Transf. use of *raven* the large black bird *Corvus corax.*] Any of three large, glossy black birds of the genus *Corvus, C. coronoides* of e. and s.w. mainland Aust., *C. mellori* of s.e. mainland Aust., and *C. tasmanicus* of Tas., southernmost Aust., and n.e. N.S.W. See also CROW *n.*[1] 1.

1805 J.H. TUCKEY *Acct. Voyage to establish Colony Port Phillip* 163 The land birds are eagles, crows, ravens. **1822** J. LATHAM *Gen. Hist. Birds* III. 7 South-Sea Raven . . inhabits the Friendly Isles, in the South Seas; found also at New-Holland; not uncommon in Van Diemen's Land: is probably a further Variety of the Common Raven. **1903** *Emu* II. 205 *Corone australis* (Raven)—Parties of these birds frequently cross the Strait to and from Tasmania. **1945** C. BARRETT *Austral. Bird Life* 221 Though omnivorous, the raven . . does much good by including insects in its dietary. **1976** *Ecos* viii. 30/1 Most of us would be quite content to label the large black birds of the genus *Corvus* as crows or ravens. . . They all look very much alike. Crow body feathers have white bases, while those of ravens are grey. The crows tend to live in the northern half of the continent and the ravens in the south. **1978** B.P. MOORE *Life on Forty Acres* 98 'Crows' to the layman, or more correctly ravens, are . . ready to accept any titbit.

raw prawn: see PRAWN 1 b.

razoo /ra'zu/. Also **rahzoo.** [Of unknown origin.] A (non-existent) coin of trivial value, a 'jot' or 'tittle'. Also in the phr. **brass razoo.** Used in negative contexts only.

1919 C. DREW *Doings of Dave* 28 'Did you have any bank to kick off with?' 'Not a razoo,' returned his companion. **1932** W. HATFIELD *Ginger Murdoch* 35 The town shrieked money, yet Ginger had not a 'rahzoo' to his name. **1942** L. MANN *Go-Getter* 39 'I thought you might allow a little more under the circumstances, Joe!' 'Not a razoo.' **1955** D. NILAND *Shiralee* 69 There's not one amongst them worth a razoo. **1965** R.H. CONQUEST *Horses in Kitchen* 61 My main worry was that when I did leave hospital. . . I wouldn't have a razoo to my name. **1968** G. DUTTON *Andy* 92 But I reckoned you'd never get a brass razoo out of the Commos. **1973** F. MOORHOUSE *Austral. Stories* 30 They didn't get any rain for three years, and the lousy government never gave them a brass razoo. **1977** J. CARTER *All Things Wild* 132 We won't get a razoo of tax until 1980 at the earliest! **1982** R. HALL *Just Relations* 487 For all their pestering they never got a brass razoo, she shrieks triumphantly. **1986** A. BUSHELL *Yesterday's Daughers* 101 Two children knocked on the door . . with some cornflakes and milk and bread and butter. . . The constable . . thought we didn't have a 'razoo' between us.

razor-back. [The name of a steep ridge south of Sydney; now also used elsewhere.] A narrow, steep-sided ridge of land. Also as *adj.*

[**1831** *HRA* (1923) 1st Ser. I. 34, I might instance here his Road to the Southward . . the Banks of the 'Cataract River' over which it must pass are very steep and difficult; the 'Razor Back' was therefore undertaken as more consistent with our means. **1838** T.L. MITCHELL *Three Exped. Eastern Aust.* II. 322 The Razor-back range is a very remarkable feature in this part of the country . . being, very level on some parts of the summit, and so very narrow in others, while the sides are also so steep, that the name it has obtained is descriptive enough.] **1901** F.J. GILLEN *Diary* 19 Apr. (1968) 41 Had a pleasant drive for 14 miles over undulating country with razor back hills of desert sandstone scattered here and there. **1916** 'MEN OF ANZAC' *Anzac Bk.* 83 Old No. 3 Post connected with Table Top by a razor back. **1921** N. TRITTON *Poems* 30 For we did not wish to look back till we'd crossed the 'razor-back', And reached the highest point above outlined. **1944** G. HAMLYN-HARRIS *Through Mud & Blood* 29, I shall never forget that day's march along razorbacks, down sudden dips. **1957** P. WHITE *Voss* 153 Presently the path, which had reached a razorback . . wound suddenly . . and plunged down. **1979** J. WILLIAMS *White River* 40 You didn't know the half of it till you were cornered in these barren razor-backs, working for nothing till you paid off your air-fare.

razor gang. [Transf. use of Br. Railway slang *razor gang* 'economy men from Headquarters': see OEDS *razor* 3 c.] A parliamentary committee established to examine ways of reducing public expenditure: see quot. 1981. Also *attrib.*

1981 *Bulletin* (Sydney) 5 May 20/1 Canberra reports said that Sir Phillip Lynch's 'Razor Gang' had recommended an overall staff cut in the Federal public service of 2 percent. **1982** *Western Farmer* (Perth) 16 Dec. 19/2 In its report last week, the Senate committee called on the government to go back on a 1981 Razor Gang decision to scrap the Commonwealth Council for Rural Research and Extension. **1983** *Austral.* (Sydney) 18 Mar. 1/2 Labor has established its own 'razor gang'—the Expenditure Review Committee. **1983** *Bulletin* (Sydney) 22 Mar. 24/1 As Labor discovered with its Coombs task force and Malcolm Fraser found with his Razor Gang it is difficult to eliminate a tax lurk or cut down a government program without incurring the wrath of those affected. **1985** *Good Weekend* (Sydney) 5 Oct. 5/3 The Government, in the midst of the infamous razor-gang cost cuts, agreed to fund and complete the building's shell.

Hence **razor ganging** *vbl. n.*

1986 *Canberra Times* 9 Feb. 2/4 A long season of razor-ganging has made the problem much worse. The Canberra bus fleet is getting old and . . has not been replaced at anything like the rate it needs.

razor-grinder. [Transf. use of *razor-grinder* one who grinds or sharpens razors.] RESTLESS FLYCATCHER.

1822 B. FIELD in G. Mackaness *Fourteen Journeys Blue Mountains* 9 Oct. (1950) ii. 42 The notes of the birds of New Holland are rather cries than songs. . . Some are harsh and vulgar, like those of the . . razor grinder. **1827** P. CUNNINGHAM *Two Yrs. in N.S.W.* II. 159 Neither must you be astonished on hearing the *razor-grinder* ply his vocation in the very depths of our solitudes; for here he is a *flying* instead of a *walking* animal. **1834** M. DOYLE *Extracts Lett. & Jrnls. G.F. Moore* 127 The indefatigable little warbler, or razor-grinder, is singing its sweet notes at nine o'clock P.M. **1845** R. HOWITT *Impressions Aust. Felix* 332 The razor-grinder, fitly so called from making a grinding noise as it wavers in one position a foot or two from the ground. **1865** MRS A. CAMPBELL *Rough & Smooth* 65 We saw . . a swallow called 'razor-grinder', from the ugly noise he makes. **1898** E.E. MORRIS *Austral Eng.* 383 Razor-grinder . . a bird-name, *Seisura inquieta*. **1911** A. MACK *Bush Days* 13 A razor-grinder stopped a few minutes on the fence, and, instead of his usual harsh scold, uttered a few, soft tender notes. **1976** *Reader's Digest Compl. Bk. Austral. Birds* 386 Restless flycatcher *Myiagra inquieta*. Other names . . razor grinder [etc.].

read, *v.* In the phr. **you wouldn't read about it (in Pix)**: an exclamation used to express incredulity and chagrin.

1950 J. CLEARY *Just let me Be* 135 Everything I backed ran like a no-hoper. Four certs I had, and the bludgers were so far back the ambulance nearly had to bring 'em home. You wouldn't read about it. **1962** D. CUSACK *Picnic Races* 249 He drew a deep breath. 'You wouldn't read about it.' **1972** *Bulletin* (Sydney) 26 Feb. 11/2 Some local London criminals practise Australian speech in order to throw Scotland Yard off the scent. I was told of a successful English robber who spent his spare time reading the works of John O'Grady, Sidney J. Baker and Afferbeck Lauder. He allegedly rehearsed sentences like 'Ow yer goin' mate?' and 'You wouldn't read about it in Pix' until his accent was perfect. **1979** B. HUMPHRIES *Bazza comes into his Own*, 'When they crawl back to Pommyland and see what a shithouse it is, they come back to us for another cheap trip!' 'Poor old Poms—you wouldn't read about it!' 'My oath, you wouldn't neither!' **1981** P. BARTON *Bastards I have Known* 127 Mathematical genii, or is it genius's? I dunno; you wouldn't read about this language of ours.

reap-hook. *Obs.* (except in place-names). Used *attrib.* to describe a hill resembling a reap-hook in shape: see quot. 1863.

1860 J.M. STUART *Explorations in Aust.* 17 Apr. (1865) 160 There are three reap-hook hills about three miles west. **1863** J.B. AUSTIN *Mines S.A.* 43, I must not omit to mention the remarkable form assumed by many of the hills in the North, and hence called 'reap-hook ranges'; one side rises abruptly and culminates, generally, in a knob of rocks, while the other side slopes away gradually in a graceful concave form, very much the shape of a sickle. **1889** E. GILES *Aust. twice Traversed* I. 109 We had to follow the trend of a valley formed by what are sometimes called reap-hook hills.

receiving yard. The enclosure in a stock yard into which mustered sheep or cattle are first driven.

1848 H.W. HAYGARTH *Recoll. Bush Life* 68 A cattle enclosure is usually subdivided into five yards: two of them facing the entrance are large, the three others are smaller; the former are known as 'receiving', and the latter as 'draughting' yards, all of which communicate with one another. **1871** *Austral. Town & Country Jrnl.* (Sydney) 22 Apr. 491/3 On proceeding to load up the sheep, they would be divided into two lots in the receiving yard, and one-half put into the forcing yard. **1888** 'R. BOLDREWOOD' *Robbery under Arms* (1937) 209 Muster them twice a week, run 'em into the big receiving yard. **1934** C. SAYCE *Comboman* 154 At last the big receiving-yard was empty and the drafting over. **1944** *Bulletin* (Sydney) 17 May 12/2 The neatest bit of work I have seen among cattle was in the receiving-yard of an Upper Dawson (Q.) run. **1960** M. HENRY *Unlucky Dip* 25 They all looked across the receiving-yard to the iron side, roof and supports of the dip.

recovery. In the phr. **to suffer a recovery,** to be afflicted with a hangover.

1885 *Australasian Printers' Keepsake* 72 He had indeed the appearance of one 'suffering a recovery'. **1892** *Braidwood Dispatch* 31 Dec. 2/3 Chain-lightening rum .. particularly soothing to the bush-man after knocking down his cheque and doing penance in what is known as suffering a recovery. **1895** *Worker* (Sydney) 30 Mar. 4/2 Some of the men are 'suffering recov'ry' and are only too glad to get away at any price. **1941** S.J. BAKER *Pop. Dict. Austral. Slang* 74 *Suffer a recovery*, to recover from a drinking bout.

recruiting, *vbl. n. Obs.* [Transf. use of *recruiting* the raising of an army.] BLACKBIRDING. Also *attrib.*

1892 *Truth* (Sydney) 5 June 4/4 There is every reason to believe the 'recruiting' for Queensland plantations will develop into simple slave-trading. **1901** W.T. REAY *White Aust.* 10 In those days it was that atrocious outrages incidental to 'recruiting', as the term is in the South Seas, called for intervention of the Imperial Government. **1904** L. HOPKINS *On the Hop* 41 When the Kanaka labour system was in full swing, life in the South Sea Island was insupportable. The natives spent all their time at the seashore scouring the horizon for incoming recruiting ships. **1911** E.J. BRADY *King's Caravan* 275 He had been in the recruiting trade. As he whisked me from one place of refreshment to another, he poured out stories of blackbirding in the South Seas.

red, *n. Red kangaroo* (a), see RED *a.* 1 b.

1896 *Western Champion* (Barcaldine) 25 Aug. 3/4 Starting now to cross the long-furred reds with the blue flyers. You should see the joeys—big and strong as young lions. **1926** A.S. LE SOUEF et al. *Wild Animals Australasia* 169 Kangaroos usually lie up during the day in some sheltered spot. The 'reds' favour the lee-side of a shady tree; the 'greys' prefer a dry, sheltered spot. **1964** D. LOCKWOOD *Up Track* 62 A favourite grass of the big reds is woollybutt. **1973** V. SERVENTY *Desert Walkabout* 60 The 'red' is the kangaroo of the inland plains, being found everywhere in Australia or in every Australian mainland State.

red, *a.*

1. a. Used as a distinguishing epithet in the names of plants: **red almond,** either of the trees *Alphitonia excelsa* and *A. petriei* (see *red ash*); **ash,** any of several trees, esp. *Alphitonia excelsa* (fam. Rhamnaceae) of N.S.W., Qld., W.A., and N.T., and the related *A. petriei* of N.S.W. and Qld.; the wood of the tree; see also *red almond,* SOAP TREE; **bean,** any of several trees, esp. the large *Dysoxylum muelleri* (fam. Meliaceae) of n.e. N.S.W. and e. Qld., yielding a deep red timber; the wood of the tree; see also TURNIPWOOD; **bloodwood,** the tree *Eucalyptus gummifera* (fam. Myrtaceae)of s.e. mainland Aust., yielding a durable red timber; the similar *E. intermedia* of n.e. mainland Aust.; the wood of the tree; **box,** any of several trees yielding a reddish timber, esp. *Eucalyptus polyanthemos* (fam. Myrtaceae) of s.e. mainland Aust.; the wood of the tree; also *attrib.*; **cedar,** the tree *Toona australis* (see CEDAR 1); the wood of the tree; *native cedar,* see NATIVE *a.* 6 a.; **-flowering gum,** see FLOWERING GUM; **grass,** any of several grasses, esp. *red leg grass*; **heart,** either of two trees, the rainforest tree *Dissiliaria baloghioides* (fam. Euphorbiaceae) of Qld., having a hard, durable timber, and *Eucalyptus decipiens* (fam. Myrtaceae) of s.w. W.A.; the wood of the tree; **honeysuckle,** the tree or shrub *Banksia serrata* (fam. Proteaceae) of near-coastal s. Qld., N.S.W., Vic., and n.w. Tas.; the wood of the tree; **ironbark,** any of several IRONBARK trees, esp. *Eucalyptus sideroxylon* (also known as MUGGA) of Vic., N.S.W., and s. Qld., having a deeply furrowed dark bark which is red under the surface, and yielding a tough, durable, red timber; **leg grass,** any of several grasses of the genus *Bothriochloa* (fam. Poaceae) esp. *B. macra* of e. mainland Aust., usu. having red to purple stems; *red grass*; **mahogany,** any of several trees of the genus *Eucalyptus* (fam. Myrtaceae) yielding a red timber, esp. the rough-barked *E. resinifera* and *E. pellita* occurring on sandy near-coastal soils in N.S.W. and Qld.; the durable wood of the tree; see also JIMMY LOW; **mallee,** any of several mallee eucalypts of drier s. Aust. having red branchlets or other parts, as *Eucalyptus oleosa* and *E. calycogona* (fam. Myrtaceae); **mangrove,** any of several trees, chiefly of the fam. Rhizophoraceae, as *Rhizophora stylosa* of n. Aust. and elsewhere in the tropics; **mulga,** MINNERICHI; **myrtle,** any of several trees, esp. *Syzgium australe* (see *brush cherry* BRUSH *n.*[1] B. 2); the wood of the tree; **pine,** a tree having a reddish wood, esp. *Callitris endlicheri* (fam. Cupressaceae) of e. mainland Aust.; the wood of this tree; **river gum,** the tree *Eucalyptus camaldulensis* (see RED GUM 1); the wood of this tree; **stringybark,** any of several rough-barked trees of the genus *Eucalyptus* (fam. Myrtaceae), esp. *E. macrorhyncha* of s.e. mainland Aust.; the wood of the tree; also **red stringy.**

1948 P.J. Hurley *Red Cedar* 158 In the Forestry Offices some of our treasures in timber are displayed. .. Polished **red almond** (*Alphitonia*) adorned the walls. **1965** *Austral. Encycl.* I. 165 *A[lphitonia] excelsa*, the red almond .. is a smooth-barked tree, up to 60 or even 80 feet in the drier portions of eastern brush forests... The rather tough durable timber .. darkens on exposure to a rich red colour. **1889** J.H. MAIDEN *Useful Native Plants Aust.* 373 *Alphitonia excelsa* .. variously called 'Mountain Ash', '**Red Ash**', [etc.]... Wood near the outside somewhat pinkish, the inner wood dark-brown, or parti-coloured. *Ibid.* 581 *Orites excelsa* .. 'Red Ash'... Timber hard, durable, nicely marked. **1909** F.M. BAILEY *Comprehensive Catal. Qld. Plants* 100 *Alphitonia excelsa* .. Red Ash. The leaves, with water, rubbed on the hands by school-children to remove ink-stains. **1948** H.A. LINDSAY *Bushman's Handbk.* 94 The red ash has leaves which are silvery white on the under side and when crushed they smell like flytox. **1981** A.B. & J.W. CRIBB *Useful Wild Plants Aust.* 106 Red ash is a common tree in both rainforests and eucalypt forests. **1895** *Agric. Gaz. N.S.W.* V. 1 Because of the dark colour of the wood, and partly by way of distinction from the **red bean,** it is usually known by timber merchants as black bean. **1903** *Bulletin* (Sydney) 26 Nov. 17/1 Red bean .. and sassafras grow in the same neighborhood. **1930** V. KENNEDY *By Range & River* 73 A full list of Atherton timbers would include such building timber as .. black bean, red bean [etc.]. **1981** J.A. BAINES *Austral. Plant Genera* 137 Red Bean, Onionwood .. a large rain-forest tree, the sapwood and bark of which has a strong onion-like odour. **1907** J.H. MAIDEN *Forest Flora N.S.W.* II. 28 The wood loses considerably more weight than the **Red Bloodwood** as it seasons. **1926** *Qld. Agric. Jrnl.* XXV. 439 *Eucalyptus corymbosa* Red Bloodwood. **1963** C. BURGESS *Blue Mountain Gums* 18 'Red Bloodwood' is distributed throughout coastal areas from Gippsland in Victoria to Fraser Island in Queensland. **1984** D.J. BOLAND *Forest Trees Aust.* (rev. ed.) 222 Red bloodwood occurs largely in coastal areas. **1878** R.B. SMYTH *Aborigines of Vic.* II. 160 **Red-box**—Tee-ring. **1889** J.H. MAIDEN *Useful Native Plants Aust.* 505 'Red Box', of a brownish-red colour, fine in the grain, and very tough. **1900** *Proc. Linnean Soc. N.S.W.* XXV. 597 A new Eucalypt with pale leaves appears, *E. intertexta*... It is known variously as 'Red Box', 'Bastard Box', and is one of the largest trees in the west. **1928** M.E. FULLERTON *Austral. Bush* 108 Red-box and yellow-box honey are among the best. **1942** R.T. PATTON *Know your Own Trees* 43 Red Box... The term 'red' refers to the timber, not to the bark. **1952** E. WALLING *Austral. Roadside* p. xii (*caption*) An old Red Box .. on a typical stretch of the Hume Highway not far from Benalla Victoria. **1969** S. KELLY *Eucalypts* 66 The juvenile leaves of red box .. are blue-grey or silver .. and this species is cultivated both in the United States of America and in Europe, for the cut flower trade. **1985** *Trees & Natural Resources* Sept. 32 Wastelands such as railway sidings have local species among the weeds. Species include .. *Eucalyptus polyanthemos* (Red Box) [etc.]. **1818** J. OXLEY *Jrnls. Two Exped. N.S.W.* 29 Sept. (1820) 317 In this brush was a quantity of fine **red cedar** trees. **1855** W. HOWITT *Land, Labor & Gold* II. 354 The *Cedrela Australis*, the red cedar of New South Wales, more resembling a walnut tree than an ordinary cedar. **1869** F. ALGAR *Handbk. Qld.* 13 The Red Cedar of the rivers is one of the best and most beautiful woods for manufacturing purposes in the colony. **1876** 'EIGHT YRS.' RESIDENT' *Queen of Colonies* 40 The huge red cedars with their vine-trellissed boles and branches are here and there encountered. **1888** *Sydney Morning Herald* 24 Jan. (Centennial Suppl.) 1/6 Growing generally within the coast is the far-famed red cedar, now, unfortunately, getting very scarce. **1904** J.H. MAIDEN *Notes on Commercial Timbers N.S.W.* 21 Red cedar .. resembles the mahogany of commerce a good deal, with the advantage of possessing only half its weight. **1948** F. CLUNE *Wild Colonial Boys* 17 The port had an extensive timber trade, exporting the giant red cedars which grew in the dense forests of the lower Hunter Valley. **1956** A.C.C. LOCK *Tropical Tapestry* 305 The Bloomfield produced some of the finest red cedar in Australia. There were timber-getters there as early as the 1870s. **1980** B. SCOTT *Darkness under Hills* 45 Downstream was a tall stand of black bean trees, red cedar and lemon gums. **1886** *N.T. Times Almanac* 6 Flinders or **red grass.** **1934** *Bulletin* (Sydney) 9 May 28/3 The menace of red grass on the Upper Murray and in Riverina has developed this year, probably because of an abnormal summer rainfall. **1983** G.G. ROBINSON *Native Grasses Northern Tablelands* 9 Redgrass is very similar to Queensland blue grass but is much more common on the tablelands and is very widely distributed. Redgrass is distinguished from blue grass by its red coloured stems. **1911** *Bulletin* (Sydney) 28 Sept. 13/4 Nobody has nominated **red-heart,** a timber which frequents the coastal scrubs of Queensland, for the hardest wood championship. **1935** DAVISON & NICHOLLS *Blue Coast Caravan* 124 We learnt to know new trees: brown bean, red heart, gap axe. **1973** G.M. CHIPPENDALE *Eucalypts W. Austral. Goldfields* 93 Redheart is a spreading, twisted, gnarled tree up to 30 ft. (9 m.), or a mallee up to 15 ft. (4.5 m.) high. **1824** *Austral.* (Sydney) 21 Oct. 2 **Red** and white **honey-suckle** for boat timbers. **1826** J. ATKINSON *Acct. Agric. & Grazing N.S.W.* 16 *Red honeysuckle*, a low tree, found about the sea coast. **1895** J.H. MAIDEN *Flowering Plants & Ferns N.S.W.* 31 The red honeysuckle. *Banksia serrata*... The prefix 'red' is in allusion to the intensely red colour of the wood, and to distinguish it from the White Honeysuckle. **1935** *Honey Flora Vic.* (Vic. Dept. Agric.) (rev. ed.) 91 It [*sc. Banksia integrifolia*] is also called White Honeysuckle to distinguish it from Red Honeysuckle (*Banksia serrata*), the timber of which is far redder. **1880** *Proc. Linnean Soc.N.S.W.* V. 505 *E. crebra*, which is commonly known as the narrow-leaved or **Red Ironbark,** is a tree of considerable size, rising to 100 or 120 feet in height. **1900** *Ibid.* XXV. 715 *E. sideroxylon* .. by some .. is called Black and by others Red Ironbark owing to the colour of the bark and wood respectively. **1908** J. MANN *Suitability Australasian Timber* 2 Generally, the red, or shades of red, represent the most durable timber, e.g., Red Gum, Jarrah, Red Ironbark. **1969** S. KELLY *Eucalypts* 64 Mugga, or red ironbark as it is often called, is a typical ironbark, with perhaps the hardest, most deeply furrowed and blackest bark of the group. **1985** *Parkwatch* (Vic. Nat. Parks Assoc.) Sept. 29 The corrugated, dark red bark of the Red ironbark has been retained on the upright posts. **1923** E. BREAKWELL *Grasses & Fodder Plants N.S.W.* 202 **Red Leg grass** is fairly easily eradicated by cultivation. It is very sensitive to frosts, and is therefore best ploughed in the winter months. **1981** E. ROLLS *Million Wild Acres* 28 The excellent Forest Blue Grass (*Bothriochloa intermedia*) was replaced by the unpalatable Red Leg Grasses. **1817** A. CUNNINGHAM in I. Marriott *Early Explorers Aust.* (1925) 176 *E. resinifera*; (**red mahogany**). **1882** *Proc. Linnean Soc. N.S.W.* VII. 625 The Red or Forest Mahogany. **1893** D.J. FROST *Crown Lands N.S.W.* 19 Among the timbers which these northern river forests contain are .. red mahogany. **1904** J.H. MAIDEN *Notes on Commercial Timbers N.S.W.* 16 Red mahogany (*Eucalyptus resinifera*, m.) .. is the timber called mahogany, because it reminded the early settlers of the Central American wood. **1911** *Bulletin* (Sydney) 27 July 14/2 Ordinary 'stringy' takes fire easily enough, though red 'stringy' (also known as red mahogany) . . does not. **1926** *Qld. Agric. Jrnl.* XXV. 433 There is a Red Mahogany in New South Wales, called so by the early settlers because of its superficial resemblance to Honduras Mahogany. **1962** *Daily Mercury Centenary Story Mackay* 43 The best known forest hardwoods are . . red and white mahogany. **1983** *Victorian Timber News* Apr. 8/2 Red Mahogany . . is distinguished by dark red heartwood with distinctly marked sapwood. **1855** J. Bonwick *Geogr. Aust. & N.Z.* (ed. 3) 202 The **red** or water **mallee,** from the cut rootlets of which water may be procured. **1900** *Proc. Linnean Soc. N.S.W.* XXV. 600 On the left are about a dozen acres of Mallee, *Eucalyptus oleosa* . . often called Red Mallee from the colour of the wood. *Ibid.* 318 *Eucalyptus viridis*, sp. nov. . . 'Red Mallee' and 'Brown Mallee', both names referring to the colour of the bark. **1935** *Honey Flora Vic.* (Vic. Dept. Agric.) (rev. ed.) 83 The Red Mallee [*sc. Eucalyptus calycogona*] is a tall shrub or small tree . . with smooth silvery grey bark. **1981** G.M. Cunningham et al. *Plants Western N.S.W.* 530 Red mallee [*sc. Eucalyptus oleosa*] receives its common name from its reddish-coloured branchlets. **1880** J. Bonwick *Resources Qld.* 81 The **Red Mangrove** is proof against ant attack. **1888** *Proc. R. Soc. Qld.* (1889) V. 10 Rhizophora mucronata . . the red mangrove. The honey which the native bees collect from the blossoms of this tree is reputed to be of a poisonous nature. **1908** E.J. Banfield *Confessions of Beachcomber* 243 The haft of the harpoon is probably red or orange mangrove (*Bruguiera rheedi*). **1915** *Bulletin* (Sydney) 4 Mar. 14/4 The red mangrove makes an excellent tannin. On stations kangaroo skins have been tanned with it and made up into stockwhips. **1936** T.C. Roughley *Wonders Great Barrier Reef* 173 The red mangrove . . gives the impression that it has been pulled well out of the mud for the trunk may begin some feet above it. **1984** K.A.W. Williams *Native Plants Qld.* II. 158 *Rhizophora stylosa* . . Red Mangrove . . is a tree which attains a height of . . 5 m. **1896** B. Spencer *Rep. Horn Sci. Exped. Central Aust.* I. 13 The lines of the water-courses are marked by belts of gum trees and acacias . . *Acacia cyperophylla*, the **red mulga**, a very local tree. **1922** 'J. Bushman' *In Musgrave Ranges* 229 The head of the spear was broad and flat, and was made of red mulga, a hard, tough, poisonous wood. **1951** G. Farwell *Outside Track* 137 A single red-barked minnaritchi tree—red mulga as they call it in the Centre. **1889** J.H. Maiden *Useful Native Plants Aust.* 531 *Eugenia myrtifolia* . . called '**Red Myrtle**' in Southern New South Wales. **1917** *Advocate* (Burnie) 11 Aug. 4/2 The red myrtle or beech, encumbered by the botanists with the name of Fagus Cunninghami . . resembles the hardest and heaviest English beech. **1926** *Qld. Agric. Jrnl.* XXV. 437 *Eugenia helimampra* [*sic*] . . Red Myrtle (Fraser Island). **1803** *Sydney Gaz.* 9 Oct., And 72 **red pine** spars, from 28 to 33 feet in length. **1884** A. Nilson *Timber Trees N.S.W.* 81 *F*[*renela*] *Endlicheri*.—Red Pine; Black Pine. **1891** J. Fenton *Bush Life Tas.* (1964) 168 It appears that there are three sorts of pine belonging to West Devon—the red pine, pencil pine, and celery top. The two former are similar in appearance. **1910** Baker & Smith *Research on Pines Aust.* 192 *Callitris calcarata* . . 'Black', 'Red', or 'Mountain Pine'. . . The name 'Black Pine' alludes to the colour of the bark . . whilst it is called 'Red' owing to some of the trees having a red-tinted timber. **1926** *Qld. Agric. Jrnl.* XXV. 437 *Callitris calcarata* . . Black Pine and Red Pine (N.S.W.). **1899** *Proc. Linnean Soc. N.S.W.* XXIV. 469 'Forest Red Gum' (*E*[*ucalyptus*] *tereticornis*) as compared with '**Red River Gum**' (*E. rostrata*). **1981** A. Wilkinson *Up Country* 166 Supper bubbles away in our two blackened billies over a small fire of aromatic red river and scribbly gum. **1896** *Proc. Linnean Soc. N.S.W.* XXI. 447 *E. macrorrhyncha* . . '**Red Stringybark**'. This is considered the best stringybark in regard to durability of timber, and is highly prized. *Ibid.* 799 *Eucalyptus capitellata* . . 'Red Stringybark' is a name generally applied to this species in this colony in allusion to the darker colour of the wood as compared with that of *E. eugenioides*, White Stringybark. **1911** *Bulletin* (Sydney) 27 July 14/2 Ordinary 'stringy' takes fire easily enough, though red 'stringy' . . does not. **1935** *Honey Flora Vic.* (Vic. Dept. Agric.) (rev. ed.) 51 The Red Stringybark is more subject to periodical ravages by the caterpillar of the cup moth than any other Eucalypt. **1952** E. Walling *Austral. Roadside* 84 (*caption*) One of the best hardwood building timbers Red Stringybark (*Eucalyptus macrorrhyncha*). **1986** *Age* (Melbourne) 7 Feb. 2/4 A few weeks ago . . the red stringybarks in north-eastern Victoria burst into bloom. . . Bee-keepers from all over Australia . . are now flocking to the north-east.

b. In the names of animals: **red ant,** see *red meat ant*; **-bellied black (snake),** the snake *Pseudechis porphyriacus* (see *black snake* Black *a.*[2] 1 b.); **bill,** any of several birds having a red bill, esp. *swamp hen* (see Swamp *n.*), *pied oystercatcher* (see Pied), and formerly *red-browed finch*; **bream,** a young Snapper (see quot. 1906); **breast** *obs.*, Robin redbreast 1; also **red-breast(ed) robin** (or **warbler**); **-breasted babbler,** the bird *Pomatostomus temporalis rubeculus* of central and w. mainland Aust., the reddish-breasted form of the *grey-crowned babbler* (see Grey *a.*); formerly also **red-breasted pomatorhinus** (or **pomatostomus**); **-breasted cockatoo** *obs.*, Galah 1; **-browed finch** (or **firetail**), the small bird *Neochmia temporalis* of e. Aust. and naturalized elsewhere, having predom. olive-green and grey plumage with scarlet rump, eyebrow, and sides of the bill; see also *red-head*; **-browed pardalote,** the small bird *Pardalotus rubricatus* of n. and central Aust., nesting in a tunnel which it excavates in sandy banks; formerly also *red-lored pardalote*; **-capped dotterel** (or **dottrel**), the wading bird *Charadrius ruficapillus* of all States and elsewhere, having predom. grey-brown and white plumage with a rufous crown; *sand lark*, see Sand; also **red-capped plover; -capped parrot** (or **parakeet**), the red-crowned parrot of s.w. W.A. *Purpureicephalus spurius*, having green, blue, yellow, and red plumage, and occurring in eucalypt forests, where it feeds on marri; **-capped robin,** the small bird *Petroica goodenovii* of s. and central mainland Aust., esp. the drier inland; **-collared lorikeet** (or **parrot**), the brightly-coloured lorikeet *Trichoglossus rubritorquis* of forested country in n. W.A. and N.T., having a yellowish-orange collar on the nape; *blue bonnet* (b), see Blue *a.*; **-crowned pigeon** (or **fruit-pigeon**), the predom. green and grey bird *Ptilinopus regina* of n. and n.e. Aust. and elsewhere, having a reddish crown; **-eared finch** (or **firetail**), a red-eared bird, usu. the small bird *Stagonopleura oculata* of s.w. W.A., having a scarlet bill and earpatch; **emperor,** the red and white marine fish *Lutjanus sebae* of n. Aust.; *government bream*, see Government B. 4; see also Emperor; **fish, (a)** any of several holothurians, esp. *Actinopyga echinitis* and *A. mauritiana* of n. Aust. and elsewhere; **(b)** (usu. as **redfish**) any of several fish, esp. Nannygai; **-footed booby** (or **gannet**), the brown or black and white,oceanic bird *Sula sula* of islands in n. Aust., and elsewhere in the tropics; formerly also **red-legged gannet; fruit bat,** the reddish, nomadic bat *Pteropus scapulatus* of e., n., and n.w. Aust.; **gurnard** (or **gurnet**), any of several fish, esp. the usu. reddish, marine *Chelidonichthys kumu* of all States and elsewhere; **-head,** a bird having red head markings, esp. *red-browed finch*; **-headed honeyeater,** the honeyeater *Myzomela erythrocephala* of n. Aust. and elsewhere, the mature male having a glossy red head; see also *blood-bird* Blood; also *ellipt.* as **red head; kangaroo, (a)** the large kangaroo *Macropus rufus*, widely distributed in drier inland Aust., having red to blue-grey fur above and white below; Marloo; Red *n.*; also **red plain kangaroo** (or **'roo**), **red 'roo; (b)** any of several other rufous macropods, esp. (*N.T.*) the wallaroo *Macropus antilopinus*; **-kneed dotterel** (or **dottrel**), the widespread *Erythrogonys cinctus* of Aust. and s. New Guinea, a black, brown, and white bird having greyish legs with red around the knees; **-lored pardalote** *obs.*, *red-browed pardalote*; **lory (lowrie, lowry),** *crimson rosella*, see Crimson; **meat ant,** *meat ant* (a) (see Meat), esp. the red *Iridomyrmex sanguineus* of n. Aust.; **morwong,** the marine fish *Cheilodactylus fuscus* of N.S.W. and s. Qld.; **-necked avocet,** the bird *Recurvirostra novaehollandiae* of mainland Aust., having a bright chestnut head and neck, and black and white body; **-necked stint,** the migratory wading bird *Calidris ruficollis*, occurring in all States from spring to autumn; **-necked wallaby,** the wallaby *Macropus rufogriseus* of e. and s.e. Aust. incl. Tas.; see also Bennett's wallaby; **rock cod, (a)** the reddish marine fish *Scorpaena ergastulorum* (fam. Scorpaenidae) of e. Aust. incl. Tas.; **(b)** any of several other, usu. related, fish; **-rump(ed) parrot (parakeet, paroquet),** the predom. green parrot *Psephotus haematonotus* of s.e. mainland Aust.; *red-backed parrot*, see Red-backed; **-shouldered parakeet** (or **paroquet**) *obs.*, Swift parrot; **soldier (ant)** *obs.*, *soldier ant*, see Soldier *n.* 1; **-tailed black cockatoo,** the predom. black cockatoo *Calyptorhynchus banksii* of mainland Aust., the mature male having a bright red band on the tail; *western black cockatoo*, see Western; see also Banksian cockatoo; also **red-tailed cockatoo; throat,** the small, predom. grey-ish-brown bird *Sericornis brunneus* of drier s. and central mainland Aust., the mature male having a rufous throat patch; **-tipped pardalote,** the small bird *Pardalotus striatus ornatus*, a form of the Striated pardalote; **wattle bird,** the large, common honeyeater *Anthochaera carunculata* of s. mainland Aust., a brown and white streaked bird having reddish facial wattles; **-winged parrot (or lory),** the predom. green parrot *Aprosmictus erythropterus* of n. and n.e. Aust., the mature male having a crimson patch on the wing; *crimson-winged parrot*, see Crimson; **-winged wren,** the small bird *Malurus elegans* of s.w. W.A.

1936 *Bulletin* (Sydney) 1 Apr. 20/2 While snake yarns grow taller and fewer laborers use the wrigglers as bowyangs, there *are* a few genuine close shaves. A **red-bellied black** went up with the last sheaf of hay aboard the dray. **1956** A.C.C. Lock *Tropical Tapestry* 103 Next morning we study the dead reptile, a red-bellied black snake, *Pseudechis porphyriacus*; venomous, but not as deadly as the Queensland brown snake. **1978** B.P. Moore *Life on Forty Acres* 110 The Red-bellied Black Snake . . is common enough in the mountains. Rather large (up to five feet) and venomous but timid and retiring, it seldom bites unless cornered and severely provoked. **1985** P. Carey *Illywhacker* 301 A jut-jawed child in short pants, playing with a red-bellied black snake, cooing to it on the floor. **1799** D. Collins *Acct. Eng. Colony N.S.W.* (1802) II. 146 There were a few ducks, teal . . and a bird named from its bill the **Red-bill**, upon the lagoons. **1803** J.G. Grant *Narr. Voyage N.S.W.* 124 They saw plenty of black swans, and red bills, an aquatic bird so called, whose back is black, the breast white, beak red, and feet not full webbed. **1824** J. Latham *Gen. Hist. Birds* IX. 359 *New-Holland oyster-catcher* . . inhabits New-Holland: is a solitary bird, being only found in pairs at any time . . called by the English the Red Bill. **1827** *Trans. Linnean Soc. London* XV. 259 'This bird', says Mr Caley, 'which the settlers call *Red-bill*, is gregarious, and appears at times in very large flocks. I have killed above forty at a shot. They frequently visited my garden in the winter to feed on a species of grass-seed.' **1842** J. Gould *Birds of Aust.* (1848) III Pl. 82, *Estrelda temporalis* . . Red-Bill of the Colonists. **1854** H.B. Stoney *Yr. in Tas.* 92 On this beach is sometimes seen the redbill or great oyster catcher, which is often shot by the sportsman, and is not unlike the wild duck in flavour. **1860** G. Bennett *Gatherings of Naturalist* 187 The Black-backed Porphyrio (*Porphyrio melanotus*), named Red-bill or Australian Moor-hen by the colonists, has a wide range. **1955** V. Serventy *Aust.'s Great Barrier Reef* 55 Two larger waders may also attract attention. Both have scarlet beaks and legs. One has an all black plumage, while the other is black and white. Commonly known as Redbills, the correct names are Pied Oystercatcher and Sooty Oystercatcher. As yet, I have still to see either catching oysters. **1965** *Austral. Encycl.* VII. 357 The largest Australian rails are the swamp-hens or bald coots (*Porphyrio*). . . They are handsome birds, with blue and black plumage and bright red beaks, hence they are often called red-bills. **1982** N. Keesing *Lily on Dustbin* 99 It was commonly said of him that 'he fed his family on cracked corn and redbill soup', the redbill being a native swamp hen, common in that region but regarded as virtually useless tucker. **1857** J. Askew *Voyage Aust. & N.Z.* 228 The harbour abounds with fish, of which the . . black and **red bream** and the yellow-tail, are used for food. **1882** J.E. Tenison-Woods *Fish & Fisheries N.S.W.* 40 The time of the appearance of the 'school schnapper' is the early part of summer; it is then believed to be at least three years old, the previous stages of its existence being well known under the names of 'red bream' at the age of one year, and of 'squire' at two. **1906** D.G. Stead *Fishes of Aust.* 126 Beyond the 'Cockney' stage and up to a weight of about a pound and a half, the Snapper is known as Red Bream. **1944** J. Devanny *By Tropic Sea & Jungle* 17 Just waiting for a red bream to heave in sight. **1978** J. Rowe *Warlords* 206 Red bream, snapper and morwong . . were being hauled up from the reef twenty metres below. **1804** G. Caley in A.E.J. Andrews *Devil's Wilderness* (1984) 66 Saw . . 2 small **red breasts**, with black and white heads. **1813** J.W. Lewin *Birds N.S.W.* 5 Red Breast Warbler . . inhabits Forests Frequents low trees. **1838** *Cornwall Chron.* (Launceston) 15 Sept. 1 The red-breast all drooping, sits upon the sill, beseeching with its sad look and tuneless note a morsel from some feeling heart within. **1842** J. GOULD *Birds of Aust.* (1848) III. Pl. 3, *Petroica multicolor* .. Red-breasted Warbler. **1878** R.B. SMYTH *Aborigines of Vic.* I. 225 The animal and vegetable food of the people of the Dieyerie tribe (Cooper's Creek) is, according to Mr Samuel Gason, as follows .. *Choonda*—Red-breasted robin. **1844 [red-breasted babbler]** J. GOULD *Birds of Aust.* (1848) IV. Pl. 21, *Pomatorhinus rubeculus* .. Red-breasted Pomatorhinus. **1896** B. SPENCER *Rep. Horn Sci. Exped. Central Aust.* II. 91 Red-breasted pomatostomus .. are extremely sociable... Their habit of mewing like a cat has gained for them the local cognomen of 'cat-birds'. **1900** A.J. CAMPBELL *Nests & Eggs Austral. Birds* 274 Red-Breasted Babbler... This bird is numerously dispersed over the northern parts of Australia. **1945** C. BARRETT *Austral. Bird Life* 199 The red-breasted babbler (*P[omatostomus] rubeculus*) is found in North-western Australia .. and the central region. **1964** M. SHARLAND *Territory of Birds* 42 As we sat and made a billy of tea, Red-breasted Babblers scolded from the scrub. **1975** X. HERBERT *Poor Fellow my Country* 465 The red-breasted babblers only wanted to talk about him, flying from bush to bush ahead and hanging upside down to get a different aspect of him to babble about. **1845** L. LEICHHARDT *Jrnl. Overland Exped. Aust.* 29 Aug. (1847) 380 We .. came to a plentiful supply of water, which was indicated .. by the call of the **red-breasted cockatoos**, noticed a few days since; but which was probably only a variety of the common species. **1861** *Burke & Wills Exploring Exped.* 15 Our attention had been attracted by some red-breasted cockatoos. **1878** R.B. SMYTH *Aborigines of Vic.* I. 225 *Killunkilla* .. Red-breasted cockatoo. **1889** R.B. ANDERSON tr. Lumholtz's *Among Cannibals* 35 No sooner is the range passed than we meet with the red-breasted cockatoo (*Cacatua roseicapilla*), which is never found on the eastern side. **1898** E.E. MORRIS *Austral Eng.* 145 **Red-browed F[inch]**—*Aegintha temporalis*. **1903** *Emu* II. 164 Red-browed Finch .. in immense numbers on all the creeks in the Otway. **1925** *Bulletin* (Sydney) 19 Mar. 22/4, I had always looked upon the wax-bill, or red-browed finch (vulgarly 'red-head'), as a harmless but rather useless little fowl. **1945** C. BARRETT *Austral. Bird Life* 206 While the beautiful firetail is a rare bird around Sydney and Melbourne, the red-browed firetail .. is fairly common in the neighbourhood of those cities. **1981** A. WILKINSON *Up Country* 144 It was a red-browed finch, beautiful as a little red and green jewel. **1898** E.E. MORRIS *Austral Eng.* 340 **Red-browed P[ardalote]**—*P[ardalotus] rubricatus*. **1913** *Emu* XII. (Suppl.) 85 Red-browed Pardalote .. Range: Australia generally (except Victoria). **1964** M. SHARLAND *Territory of Birds* 144 Around Darwin it is principally the Red-browed Pardalote which is heard, whether the season is the Wet or the Dry. **1976** *Reader's Digest Compl. Bk. Austral. Birds* 517 Red-browed pardalotes easily pass unnoticed unless their distinctive call is recognised... The name 'red browed' is something of a misnomer. The colour is no more than a deep orange, and it is only an elongated spot on the otherwise pale fawn eyebrow. **1984** M. BLAKERS et al. *Atlas Austral. Birds* 579 The Red-browed Pardalote lives .. in eucalypt and paperbark woodland. **1846** J. GOULD *Birds of Aust.* (1848) VI. Pl. 17, The **Red-capped Dottrel** is universally dispersed over every part of the sea-shores of Australia that I have visited. **1903** *Emu* II. 212 Red-capped Dottrel... Only once .. have I come across this little Dottrel. **1945** C. BARRETT *Austral. Bird Life* 102 The red-capped dotterel (*Charadrius ruficapillus*) .. is among the most engaging of all the small plovers. **1976** *Reader's Digest Compl. Bk. Austral. Birds* 176 A friendly and attractive small wader, the red-capped dotterel is common over much of its range. **1984** M. BLAKERS et al. *Atlas Austral. Birds* 159 The Red-capped Plover lives on sand or shingle beaches along the coast or inland waters. **1845 [red-capped parrot]** J. GOULD *Birds of Aust.* (1848) V. Pl. 32, *Platycercus pileatus*. .. The Red-capped parrakeet is an inhabitant of Western Australia. **1943** C. BARRETT *Austral. Animal Bk.* 233 The red-capped parrot .. is generally known as the 'king parrot'... It raids orchards and wheatfields. **1972** B. FULLER *West of Bight* 5 'What about birds? Any unique to the south-west?' .. 'Yeah. We've got some. Like the Red-capped Parrot.' **1842** J. GOULD *Birds of Aust.* (1848) III. Pl. 5, *Petroica goodenovii* .. **Red-capped Robin** of the Colonists. **1849** C. STURT *Narr. Exped. Central Aust.* II. 24 App. *Red-capped Robin* .. the feathers over the nostril in this bird are a fine deep red, as well as its breast. **1896** B. SPENCER *Rep. Horn Sci. Exped. Central Aust.* II. 76 Red-capped Robin .. were met with wherever scrub of any description afforded them shelter from the numerous Hawks. **1948** R. RAVEN-HART *Canoe in Aust.* 194 A Red-capped Robin .. with a 'song' like someone nervously tapping a pencil on a desk. **1962** B.W. LEAKE *Eastern Wheatbelt Wildlife* 90 Red capped robins, the males of which with their crimson caps and breasts are the gems of the Eastern Wheatbelt. **1981** B.J. BROCK *Catharsis* 56 Where red-capped robin sat in mulga grey Above scorpion holes. **1842** J. GOULD *Birds of Aust.* (1848) V. Pl. 49, *Trichoglossus rubritorquis* .. **Red-collared lorikeet.** **1945** C. BARRETT *Austral. Bird Life* 75 The red-collared lorikeet .. inhabits the North-west, the Northern Territory and the Gulf country of North Queensland. **1964** M. SHARLAND *Territory of Birds* 36 The gaudy Red-collared Parrots, usually referred to around Darwin as 'blue bonnets', have, as the name suggests, heads of rich blue, fringed with a scarlet collar, and with vermilion beneath the wings. **1984** M. BLAKERS et al. *Atlas Austral. Birds* 253 The Red-collared is one of the commonest parrots in the Top End. **1898 [red-crowned pigeon]** E.E. MORRIS *Austral Eng.* 156 Red-crowned F[ruit]- P[igeon]—*P[tilinopus] swainsonii*. **1945** C. BARRETT *Austral. Bird Life* 61 The smaller fruit-pigeons are charmingly coloured. The red-crowned species .. is a migratory bird. **1965** *Austral. Encycl.* VII. 112 Particularly striking are the .. king pigeon .. and its smaller associates the .. red-crowned, and purple-crowned pigeons. **1981** PUGH & RITCHIE *Guide to Rainforests N.S.W.* 15 A good area for fruit pigeons with many Red-crowned Pigeons coming here to feed. **1845** J. GOULD *Birds of Aust.* (1848) III. Pl. 79, *Estrelda oculea*. **Red-eared Finch.** **1913** *Emu* XII. Suppl. 94 *Zonaeginthus oculatus* .. Red-eared Finch .. *Range*: W. Australia. **1937** R.H. CROLL *Wide Horizons* 12 Red-eared Finches wheeze in their funny asthmatic way. **1976** *Reader's Digest Compl. Bk. Austral. Birds* 530 The shy and beautiful red-eared firetail is the most solitary of all Australian grass finches. **1936** T.C. ROUGHLEY *Wonders Great Barrier Reef* 9 Some fish from the reef .. **red emperor** and coral trout. We like the name 'red emperor' and .. find ourselves repeating our order for its white, flaky flesh is delicious. **1965** *Austral. Encycl.* IX. 41 The red emperor—an excellent food fish, caught by line fishing. **1975** N. COLEMAN *Look at Wildlife Great Barrier Reef* 96 Because of its good edible qualities, the red emperor is a well known Reef fish; it reaches a weight of a little over 20 kilograms. **(a) 1880** *Proc. Linnean Soc. N.S.W.* V. 128 He enumerates four, viz. *Trepang edulis, T. ananas, T. impatiens*, and *T. peruviana*. The first of these is certainly found on the reefs, and is called by the fishermen '**red fish**'. It is an elongated oval, somewhat shapeless mass of dull, reddish-brown color. **1893** W. SAVILLE-KENT *Great Barrier Reef of Aust.* 236 Deep-water Red-fish, *Actinopyga echinites*—Closely resembling ordinary Red-fish [*sc. A. obesa*]... Of high commercial value. **1936** T.C. ROUGHLEY *Wonders Great Barrier Reef* 242 The different kinds of bêche-de-mer are known in the trade under curious but long-established names... For instance, we have .. red fish .. and deepwater black fish. **(b) 1944** J. DEVANNY *By Tropic Sea & Jungle* 5 The weedfish—other names for him are **red-fish** .. and pigfish—likes deep water and bites mostly at night. **1951** T.C. ROUGHLEY *Fish & Fisheries Aust.* 26 The nannygai, or redfish .. occurs round the southern half of Australia. **1974** J.M. THOMSON *Fish Ocean & Shore* 119 Of the .. main trawled species the redfish lives up to its name, being a bright red on the back, paling somewhat on the sides and having a large glistening eye. **1846 [red-footed booby]** J. GOULD *Birds of Aust.* (1848) VII. Pl. 79, The Red-legged Gannet is very abundant along the northern shores of the Australian continent. **1890** G.J. BROINOWSKI *Birds of Aust.* I. Pl. 5, In its habits generally and in its mode of procuring its food, the Red-legged Gannet resembles the other members of the tribe. **1945** C. BARRETT *Austral. Bird Life* 96 The red footed species (*S[ula] sula*), and the masked gannet .. are tropical birds which nest on islands off the coast. **1965** *Austral. Encycl.* IV. 239 The smallest species [of gannet] is the red-footed booby, which is the only gannet that nests off the ground. **1985** *Bulletin* (Sydney) 24 Sept. 137/2 There are birds at Lizard I had never heard of before—the black-naped tern, red-footed booby [etc.]. **1965** *Austral. Encycl.* I. 458 Another much smaller species, which also migrates south to the Victorian border, is the little **red fruit-bat** (*P[teropus] scapulatus*). It is more exclusively a blossom feeder. **1985** *New Idea* (Melbourne) 7 Dec. 25/1 A variety of grey-haired and red fruit bats. **1873 [red gurnard]** F. DE CASTELNAU *Edible Fishes Vic.* 9 The red gurnet (*Upeneichthys porosus*) .. is highly considered as a table fish, and is also remarkable for its beautiful carmine hues, and the pretty blue stripes of its head. **1906** D.G. STEAD *Fishes of Aust.* 200 The Red or Kumu Gurnard (*Chelidonichthys kumu*) .. is found along the whole of the eastern coast of Australia as well as in Tasmania, and has been recorded from Western Australia. **1978** N. COLEMAN *Austral. Fisherman's Fish Guide* 20 A brilliantly coloured fish when landed on the deck, the red gurnard is, like many other sea floor dwellers, able to change its colours to suit its surroundings. **1889** *Proc. Linnean Soc. N.S.W.* IV. 411 *Estrilda temporalis* .. called '**Red-head**'. **1911** A. MACK *Bush Days* 52 Redheads went squeaking across the track with a protest at our intrusion. **1925** *Bulletin* (Sydney) 19 Mar. 22/4, I had always looked upon the wax-bill, or red-browed finch (vulgarly 'red-head'), as a harmless but rather useless little fowl. **1965** *Austral. Encycl.* VI. 64 The spotted-sided finch .. and the red-browed finch or 'red-head' (*Aegintha temporalis*) are confined to eastern Australia. **1843** J. GOULD *Birds of Aust.* (1848) IV. Pl. 64, The **Red-headed Honey-eater** is so distinctly marked as almost to preclude the possibility of its being confounded with any known species of the genus. **1913** *Emu* XII. Suppl. 87 *Myzomela erythrocephala* .. Red-headed Honey-eater .. *Range*: N.W. Australia, Northern Territory, N. Queensland (New Guinea). **1943** C. BARRETT *Austral. Animal Bk.* 286 The red-headed honeyeater .. comes as far south as Brisbane. **1964** M. SHARLAND *Territory of Birds* 137 The Scarlet Honeyeater .. doesn't trespass on the territory of the Red-head. **1973** R. ROBINSON *Drift of Things* 32 In spite of belonging to the school's 'Gould League of Bird Lovers', many of the boys had shanghais with which they were expert in knocking 'Red 'eads' out of the branches as they fed on the flowers. **1982** *Reader's Digest Compl. Bk. Austral. Birds* (rev. ed.) 508 Red-headed honeyeaters, especially the colourful males, can be seen flitting through the upper and middle foliage of the mangroves in northern Australia. **1793** W. TENCH *Compl. Acct. Settlement* 269 One of them we called the **red kangaroo**, from the colour of its fur, which is like that of a hare, and sometimes is mingled with a large portion of black; the natives call it Bàg-a-ray. **1820** J. OXLEY *Jrnls. Two Exped. N.S.W.* 116 We killed this day a red kangaroo, and three emus. **1865** G.F. ANGAS *Aust.* 71 The red kangaroo .. measures eight feet from the nose to the end of the tail. **1895** *Bulletin* (Sydney) 2 Feb. 3/2, I always considered the kangaroo and horse the most graceful animals I have seen, especially the red kangaroo. They are certainly a long way before either the aborigine or Chinaman, both in point of good looks and cleanliness. **1928** B. SPENCER *Wanderings in Wild Aust.* 91 Amongst the marsupials, the large red kangaroo (*Macropus rufus*) is constantly seen during good seasons on the open flats. **1952** R. ROBINSON *Legend & Dreaming* 38 When Koopoo, the red plain-kangaroo, was travelling from Arnhem Land. **1959** L. ROSE *Country of Dead* 65 He saw the tracks of myriads of small animals: .. the soft, rounded pad of the red kangaroo, and the thin line where its tail had dragged over the ground. **1962** MARSHALL & DRYSDALE *Journey among Men* 30 We saw the big red 'roos pause and prop. In turn they watched us curiously and with caution as we passed. **1974** D. STUART *Prince of my Country* 44 There are the red plain 'roos, bigger than the dark brown hill 'roos. **1980** C. ALLISON *Hunter's Man. Aust. & N.Z.* 34 The red kangaroo is the traditional marsupial of the Australian inland. The 'old man 'roo', the 'boomer', and other colloquial titles are applied to him. **1903** *Emu* II. 212 **Red-kneed Dottrel** (*Erythrogonys cinctus*)—This smart-looking Dottrel is fairly common from December to May. **1945** C. BARRETT *Austral. Bird Life* 102 The red-kneed dotterel .. really is a wattled plover without the wattle. **1962** MARSHALL & DRYSDALE *Journey among Men* 172 Stumpy little red-kneed dotterels were using the piles of debris as island nest-sites that protected them from dingos, imported European foxes and feral cats. **1984** M. BLAKERS et al. *Atlas Austral. Birds* 153 The Red-kneed Dotterel feeds both in water and on muddy shores. **1846** J. GOULD *Birds of Aust.* (1848) II. Pl. 36, *Pardalotus rubricatus* .. **Red-lored Pardalote.** **1896** B. SPENCER *Rep. Horn Sci. Exped. Central Aust.* II. 69 Red-lored Pardalote .. in the eucalypts along Petermann Creek .. were numerous. **1861 [red lory]** 'OLD BUSHMAN' *Bush Wanderings* 161 In certain places they are as common as the red lowry. **1902** *Emu* II. 17 The Red Lory (*Platycercus elegans*) are only found visiting the hills to the south. **1952** A.C.C. LOCK *Travels across Aust.* 174 A gorgeous red lowrie, or a crimson rosella, flashed its geranium-like plumage. **1834 [red meat ant]** G. BENNETT *Wanderings N.S.W.* I. 114 Avoid making their dormitory upon the nest of the red ant, which cannot endure intrusion. **1865** MRS A. CAMPBELL *Rough & Smooth* 103 Red ants were .. a nuisance, and frightfully numerous. **1914** *Pastoral Rev.* 16 Mar. 242 Insect enemies of flies [such as] the red meat ant. **1930** E.R. GRIBBLE *Forty Yrs. with Aborigines* 179 The red ant gathers the seed and places it in little piles. **1981** *Ecos* xxviii. 26/1 The nest of a colony of red meat ants looks a careless affair, resembling a spill of gravel from a passing truck. **1882** J.E. TENISON-WOODS *Fish & Fisheries N.S.W.* 46 The **red Morwong** or Carp, *C[hilodactylus] fuscus* . . is of a uniform reddish colour. **1906** D.G. STEAD *Fishes of Aust.* 119 The Sea-Carp or Red Morwong (*Cheilodactylus fuscus*) . . is restricted to the waters of New South Wales. **1963** B. CROPP *Handbk. for Skindivers* 121 The red morwong is found wherever there is a reef—deep or shallow. **1978** N. COLEMAN *Austral. Fisherman's Fish Guide* 29 Occasionally taken by line fishermen on prawn bait, the red morwong is a delicious eating fish. **1824** J. LATHAM *Gen. Hist. Birds* X. 40 **Red-necked avoset** [*sic*] . . inhabits the shores of the south of Asia, and is to be met with in various ornithological collections. **1842** J. GOULD *Birds of Aust.* (1848) VI. Pl. 27, The Red-necked Avocet frequents the shallow parts of lakes, inlets of the sea, and the muddy banks of rivers. **1854** *Illustr. Sydney News* 1 July 136/1 The Red-necked Avocet . . both . . its beak and its feet together with its graceful and elegant appearance is one of those remarkable forms of birds so beautifully adapted by nature to its mode of living and procuring its food. **1901** *Emu* I. 137 Red-necked Avocet (*Recurvirostra novae-hollandiae*) . . seen on all the large holes of the two rivers. **1926** K. DAHL *In Savage Aust.* 286 Here and there would be seen . . a red-necked avocet. **1963** *N. Austral. Monthly* Dec. 23 It was a red necked avocet. . . How many Inanders know that little water bird of the lakes and tidal bays? **1984** SIMPSON & DAY *Birds of Aust.* 302 The Banded Stilt and Red-necked Avocet are endemic Australians. **1934** H.G. LAMOND *Aviary on Plains* 141 They are sandpipers (**Red-necked stint**). **1945** C. BARRETT *Austral. Bird Life* 107 Among other waders . . are the red-necked stint (*Erolia ruficollis*) [etc.]. **1976** *Reader's Digest Compl. Bk. Austral. Birds* 197 The red-necked stint's breeding plumage gives it the popular name; it takes on a deep salmon-pink on its face, neck and breast, and its upper parts become suffused with pink. **1985** *Bulletin* (Sydney) 24 Sept. 137/2 There are birds at Lizard I had never heard of before . . grey-tailed tattler, and red-necked stint. **1894** R. LYDEKKER *Hand-Bk. Marsupialia & Monotremata* 26 **Red-necked Wallaby.** *Macropus ruficollis*. . general colour of upper parts greyish-fawn, with the back of the neck and rump bright rufous. **1926** A.S. LE SOUEF et al. *Wild Animals Australasia* 189 The red-necked wallaby, commonly known as the scrub and in places as the brush wallaby, is found in the drier forest country of Eastern Australia. **1968** V. SERVENTY *Southern Walkabout* 28 At about 4.30 p.m. most afternoons red necked wallabies came out of the forest country. **1986** *Canberra Times* 29 Jan. 21/5 The Red-necked Wallaby *Macropus rufogriseus* is also in the ACT but is not common. **1880** *Proc. Linnean Soc. N.S.W.* V. 430 *Scorpaena cruenta* . . the '**Red Rock Cod**' . . Tasmania, Port Phillip, Port Jackson. **1896** F.G. AFLALO *Sketch Nat. Hist. Aust.* 228 Red rock-cod . . is a thickset crimson and orange fish armed with many spikes. **1906** D.G. STEAD *Fishes of Aust.* 193 The Red Rock-Cod is found along the greater part—if not the whole—of the eastern coast of Australia, abounding also in Tasmania. **1951** T.C. ROUGHLEY *Fish & Fisheries Aust.* 129 Owing to the rocky nature of the localities frequented by the red rock cod very few are taken in nets, and it is therefore not often seen in the markets. **1975** *Bulletin* (Sydney) 9 Aug. 17/2 The *ling* (long, pinkish) and the *sea perch* (bright red, plump, sometimes called red rock cod) were magnificent in both taste and texture. **1976** E. WORRELL *Things that Sting* 51 Stinging fish which are well known to fishermen are the Red Rock Cod, Fortescues and Bullrouts, found along most coastlines and estuaries. **1983** HUTCHINS & THOMPSON *Marine & Estuarine Fishes S.-W. Aust.* 26 Western Red Scorpioncod. Common on offshore reefs. Deepwater coloration normally bright red. . . Also known as the Red Rockcod. [**1837 red-rumped parrot:** *Proc. Zool. Soc. London* V. 88 Mr Gould exhibited from his Australian collection of Birds two species of the genus *Platycercus* . . for one of these he proposed the specific name of *haematonotus*, from the red spot upon its rump.] **1849** C. STURT *Narr. Exped. Central Aust.* II. 39 App. *Red-rumped Parroquet* . . is a bird of the interior, and was found on the most distant creeks, amongst the gum-trees. **1896** B. SPENCER *Rep. Horn Sci. Exped. Central Aust.* II. 64 They were always in pairs, and were never seen in flocks like the Red-rumped Parrakeet (P. haematonotus). **1952** A.C.C. LOCK *Travels across Aust.* 161 A bevy of red-rump parrakeets on the ground were having a feast from seeds. **1969** J.M. FORSHAW *Austral. Parrots* 214 Seeds of grasses and herbaceous plants are the food of the Red-rumped Parrot. **1973** S. & K. BREEDON *Wildlife Eastern Aust.* 168 Scattered amongst the slim and elegant Red-rumped Parrots are pairs of a larger, more robust parrot, the Eastern Rosella. **1984** M. BLAKERS et al. *Atlas Austral. Birds* 280 The Red-Rumped Parrot has expanded its range towards the coast in the South-East Region. **1789** A. PHILLIP *Voyage to Botany Bay* 269 **Red-Shouldered Parrakeet.** . . This species inhabits New South Wales; and we believe it to be hitherto non-descript. **1790** J. WHITE *Jrnl. Voyage N.S.W.* 263 Red shouldered paroquet. *Psittacus discolor.* Long tailed Green Parrot, with the tail feathers ferruginous towards the base, the shoulders blood-red beneath. **1801** J. LATHAM *Gen. Synopsis Birds* Suppl. II. 90 Red-shouldered Parakeet . . length ten inches and a half: general colour of the plumage green, paler beneath: the whole face and throat are crimson, mixed with yellow around the eye. **1811** G. PATERSON *Hist. N.S.W.* 426 The Red Shouldered Paroquet, is a species, which appears to be generally new. **1840** J. GOULD *Birds of Aust.* (1848) V. Pl. 47, *Lathamus discolor* . . Red-shouldered Parrakeet . . Swift Parrakeet, Colonists of Van Diemen's Land. **1872** G.S. BADEN-POWELL *New Homes for Old Country* 272 In Australia, there are vast numbers of ants: one, a large red variety, nearly an inch in length . . goes by the name of the '**red soldier**'. **1889** G.T. BLAKERS *Useless Young Man?* (1986) 62 There are in Australia a great variety of ants. . . Another kind . . reach fully three-quarters of an inch in length; and . . from their colour and viciousness, are popularly called red soldier ants. . . They make a hill only a few inches high. **1836** J. BACKHOUSE *Narr. Visit Austral. Colonies* (1843) 434 **Red-tailed Black Cockatoos,** numerous Aborigines, and many plants of truly Australian features, prove we are still at the antipodes. **1847** J. GOULD *Birds of Aust.* (1848) V. Pl. 9, *Calyptorhynchus naso* . . Red-tailed Black Cockatoo of the Colonists. **1917** *Bulletin* (Sydney) 5 July 22/2 There is a similarity in several of the cockatoo names, as karrak (the western black or redtailed cockatoo) and larawak (the great-billed black cockatoo). **1934** A.H. CHISHOLM *Bird Wonders Aust.* 88 The Red-tailed . . and Glossy Black Cockatoos range through an extensive portion of eastern Australia. **1962** B.W. LEAKE *Eastern Wheatbelt Wildlife* 90 The red tailed black cockatoos . . generally prefer the most northerly parts. **1969** J.M. FORSHAW *Austral. Parrots* 64 Red-tailed Cockatoos are impressive in captivity and will thrive if housed in spacious flight aviaries. **1980** *Ecos* xxiv. 12/1 An even stranger episode involved a red-tailed black cockatoo, *Calyptorhynchus magnificus*. When the nestling was about 25 days old, a female mountain duck chose to lay her eggs in the same hollow. **1896** B. SPENCER *Rep. Horn Sci. Exped. Central Aust.* II. 84 *Pyrrholaemus brunnea* . . **Red-throat** . . was first found amongst the scrub at Hermannburg [*sic*]. **1907** *Emu* VI. 141 An interesting field note regarding the Redthroat. **1916** S.A. WHITE *In Far Northwest* 27 Among these bushes that glorious little songster, the red throat . . and the white-winged wren . . had made their home. **1945** C. BARRETT *Austral. Bird Life* 194 The red-throat . . a gifted songster, ranges from the Victorian Mallee country to Western Australia. **1976** L.R.M. HUNTER *Woodline* 43 It took us . . three visits before we were able to identify the bird as a redthroat. And that didn't happen until we saw the male bird perched on a bush singing. The rusty red patch on the throat was then very clear. **1984** M. BLAKERS et al. *Atlas Austral. Birds* 467 The Redthroat lives in acacia scrub and saltbush, specially along watercourses, generally where rainfall is less than 250 mm. per year. **1898** E.E. MORRIS *Austral Eng.* 340 **Red-tipped P[ardalote]**—*P[ardalotus] ornatus.* **1903** *Emu* III. 11 The Red-tipped Pardalotes . . were found in good alluvial country only. **1942** C. BARRETT *From Bush Hut* 79 We see the diamond birds of Wattle Creek. There are two kinds in our district: 'Spotty', of the subterranean nursery, and the red-tipped pardalote. **1964** M. SHARLAND *Territory of Birds* 144 The Red-tipped Pardalote . . has come into the Northern Territory from Western Australia. **1976** *Reader's Digest Compl. Bk. Austral. Birds* 521 A red spot can be seen at the base of the white wing stripe on this striated pardalote, so it is sometimes called the red-tipped pardalote. **1913** *Emu* XII. Suppl. 92 *Anthochaera carunculata* . . **Red Wattle-Bird** . . Range: S. Queensland, New South Wales, Victoria, S. and W. Australia. **1928** R.H. CROLL *Open Road in Vic.* 103 A red-wattle bird sat on its nest. **1948** R. RAVEN-HART *Canoe in Aust.* 56 The Red Wattlebird, someone told me later—'and some folks call it 'Muttonbird', and it's mighty good eating'. **1986** *Canberra Times* 29 Jan. 21/6 The Red Wattle Bird *Anthochaera carunculata*, at about 35 cms long, is the largest of the mainland honey-eaters and, in the vigour of its assaults, can shake a quite substantial shrub as though a gust of wind had hit it. **1842** [**red-winged parrot**] J. GOULD *Birds of Aust.* (1848) V. Pl. 18, *Aprosmictus erythropterus*. Red-winged Lory . . Crimson-winged Parrot. **1909** *Emu* VIII. 278 Red-winged Lories . . very plentiful, and feeding . . on the introduced ink-weed. **1929** A.H. CHISHOLM *Birds & Green Places* 48 The radiance of the red-winged parrots. **1945** C. BARRETT *Austral. Bird Life* 75 The red-winged lory . . and the red-sided parrot . . both rival the king parrot in colour beauty. **1962** MARSHALL & DRYSDALE *Journey among Men* 90 Nearby we saw our first northern bird, a glorious red-winged parrot that had been allowed this far south by a tongue of timber that speared into the yellow of the grass-lands. **1984** M. BLAKERS et al. *Atlas Austral. Birds* 261 In northern Australia the Red-winged Parrot lives in eucalypt woodland and mangroves. **1898** E.E. MORRIS *Austral Eng.* 519 **Red-winged W[ren]**—*Malurus elegans.* **1902** *Emu* II. 71 *Malurus elegans* (Red-winged Wren)—On my first visit secured one specimen. **1945** C. BARRETT *Austral. Bird Life* 193 The red-winged wren . . is restricted to coastal districts in the South-west. **1976** *Reader's Digest Compl. Bk. Austral. Birds* 414 Most of the areas near Perth where the red-winged wren used to live have been cleared and drained.

2. In special collocations: **red blanket,** see quot. 1926; **centre,** CENTRE 1 (so called because of the reddish colour of iron oxide in the soil and rocks); **country,** country with reddish soil; **hand,** an impression of a human hand made with red ochre, a freq. motif in Aboriginal rock-painting; **heart,** *red centre*; **ned,** red wine of inferior quality; **steer,** a destructive fire, esp. a bushfire; **terrors,** a dust storm.

1926 A. GILES *Exploring in 'Seventies* 127 Tinned meat in six-pound tins ('**red blanket**' we called it). The tins were painted red, without labels or description of contents. **1951** E. HILL *Territory* 106 Nicknamed 'red blanket' because of its red label . . it was breakfast, dinner and tea for five hundred men. **1935** H.H. FINLAYSON *Red Centre* 22 The Luritja Country—the south-west portion of Central Australia and contiguous tracts in the adjoining States . . might well be known as the **Red Centre**. Sand, soil, and most of the rocks are a fiery cinnabar. **1955** N. PULLIAM *I traveled Lonely Land* 349 The Alice sits here at 2,000 feet above sea level in the midst of the Red Center of the continent, where you meet again your old friend the Tropic of Capricorn. **1967** H. SAINT-THOMAS *Night of Long Shadows* 162 A three-week, seven thousand mile journey through the Red Centre to Darwin. **1979** *Jrnl. R. Soc. Arts* (London) Apr. 293 Farther south is the Centre. Nearly a decade of good rains have turned the famous Red Centre into something approaching a Green Centre. **1984** *N.T. News* (Darwin) 22 Sept. 3/2 After spending a week wallowing in bogs with camels and beating off the bities in the swamps around Buffalo Creek . . are heading for the Red Centre. **1910** C.E.W. BEAN *On Wool Track* 117 Almost every possible plant—grows when irrigated in the **red country** along the Darling. **1935** D.G. STEAD *Rabbit in Aust.* 28 Areas in which the red ridges (particularly the sandy ridge type) are isolated from the main 'red country' . . by great stretches of low-lying black soil plains. **1980** S. THORNE *I've met some Bloody Wags* 13 Found 'im out in the red country near the northern boundary. [**1803 red hand:** M. FLINDERS *Voyage to Terra Australis* 14 Jan. (1814) II. 188 In the steep sides of the chasms were deep holes or caverns, undermining the cliffs; upon the walls of which I found rude drawings, made with charcoal and something like red paint upon the white ground of the rock. These drawings represented porpoises, turtle, kanguroos, and a human hand.] **1852** W. HUGHES *Austral. Colonies* 100 Some strange and mysterious belief is associated with this figure of the 'red hand', and the natives are reluctant to communicate any information regarding it, except that it was made 'before white fellow came'. **1856** J. BONWICK *W. Buckley* 87 At Ryalstone, New South Wales . . is a cave with the bottom paved. Among other impressions are those of a number of red hands; some with the fore finger cut off, others crossing one another. **1899** J. MATHEW *Eaglehawk & Crow* 137 From the occurrence of these 'red hands' in places very far apart and from the peculiar position and arrangement of groups of them, I cannot help concluding that they are in the first instance sacred symbols. **1928** W. ROBERTSON *Cooee Talks* 177 *White red and black stencilled hands.* Among the cave-drawings in central and northern Australia the representations of human hands are very common. The method of producing these is usually by pressing some one's hand against the previously moistened rock. **1931** *Mankind* Mar. 21/2 Red hands, which are fairly common in this country, have their similarities in other parts of the world. **1964** *Rec. Austral. Museum* 5 June 231 The superimpositions are as follows: . . white hand over two well preserved dark red hands and shield. **1931** 'Brent Of Bin Bin' *Back to Bool Bool* 45 The dawn was murky. Particles of the **red heart** of Australia had reached the pampered city, staining the arum lilies and irritating the housewives. **1932** I.L. Idriess *Flynn of Inland* (1965) 184 He sleeps now in the harsh Red Heart of Australia. **1952** Miller & Rutter *Child Artists* 74 Albert Namatjira and his more outstanding followers . . had encouraged a deal of tourist traffic to the 'Red Heart'. **1957** F. Clune *Fortune Hunters* 56, I came into communion with the mystery of the Red Heart of Australia and worshipped there. **1963** S. Mussen *Beating about Bush* 94 We came to the gibber country, like an ocean of small red pebbles. Not a tree, not a bush, not a blade of grass. This was the country described by tourist brochures as the 'red heart', by others as the 'dead heart', of Australia. **1984** *Austral.* (Sydney) 8 Oct. 3/3 It starts in Waltzing Matilda country where the song was written and Qantas was born. It ends in the red heart. The proposed Outback Highway is now a corrugated track. **1941** S.J. Baker *Pop. Dict. Austral. Slang* 59 **Red Ned**, cheap red wine. **1953** T.A.G. Hungerford *Riverslake* 35 There's a bottle of Red Ned in my room—slip down and hit it. You need a kick! **1965** *Kings Cross Whisper* (Sydney) 1 Jan. 7/3 Your main fault is not leaving that flagon of Red Ned at home when you go out on Christmas Day. **1974** *Southerly* iii. 306 The old red ned, bitter as shit, poured down his throat, spilling over his already filthy shirt. **1983** *Canberra Times* 18 Nov. 2/7 I'll join Mr Jeffery for a glass of red ned any day. [**1930 red steer:** *Bulletin* (Sydney) 21 May 20/3 There had been a number of grass fires in the district, and suspicion falling on 'Monkey' Brown . . he was accused of loosing the 'red bull' on the community.] **1936** J. Devanny *Sugar Heaven* 100, I put 'red steer' in cane. That'll fix the bloody bosses. **1940** J.W. Gordon *Call of Bush* 43 The wild Red Steer roams free to-night. **1973** C.E. Goode *Stories Strange Places* 20 Look out or we'll put the red steer through your place too. **1977** *Bronze Swagman Bk. Bush Verse* 19 The sky turned dark, the dust clouds rolled, One hot, dry summer's morn. 'Long before this day is through, I think, We'll see the 'Red Steer' born.' **1985** *Land* (Sydney) 24 Jan. 6/2 While most fire activity last week was confined to the southern half of the State, scarcely a region escaped the attention of the 'red steer'. **1956** H. Hudson *Flynn's Flying Doctor* 211 Broken Hill is a fine modern city, but until recently was subject to violent dust storms, known as **Red Terrors**, due to soil erosion caused by denuding the surrounding country. **1959** C.& E. Chauvel *Walkabout* 45 Broken Hill . . is often proudly alluded to as the Silver City. . . Drought and the dust storms called 'The Red Terrors' dogged the town that was . . making millions.

red-back. [From the distinctive red to orange-red stripe on the upper abdomen of the female spider.] The small, venomous, black and red spider *Latrodectus hasselti* of Aust., the female having a pea-sized body and toxic bite; Jockey spider. Also **red-backed spider,** and *attrib.*

1898 *Bulletin* (Sydney) 8 Jan. 13/4 Are insects—red-back spiders and the like—more venomous some seasons than others? **1911** *Ibid.* 10 Aug. 14/4 Now want to know what amount of covering . . would stop the sting of these 'red-backs'. **1912** *Emu* XII. 72 Saw many of the poisonous red-backed spiders (*Latrodectus hasselti*) when getting firewood. **1930** K.G. Taylor *Pick & Duffers* 11 Red-backs by the billion. . . This veranda isn't safe to walk on. **1946** *Service Publication No. 6* (School Public Health & Tropical Med.) 243 Destruction of spiders in wood heaps, gas meter boxes, etc., will do much to decrease the red back danger. **1947** E. Hill *Flying Doctor Calling* 77 A woman bitten by a red-backed spider. **1955** F. Lane *Patrol to Kimberleys* 52 That was a Red-back, Glen. Keep a sharp eye out for these black, skinny-legged spiders with a body about the size of a pea and a bright red stripe on the belly. Their bite causes intense pain and, sometimes, it proves to be fatal. **1958** P. Cowan *Unploughed Land* 94 Look, there's a red-back in it. They won't hurt you unless you interfere with them. **1976** E. Worrell *Things that Sting* 31 Redback spiders are found throughout Australia. Only the female Redback is dangerous. **1981** C. James *Charles Charming's Challenges* 40 Just be careful in the dunny. A red-back up your arsehole isn't funny. **1984** *Canberra Times* 9 Apr. 10/4 Before the discovery of an anti-venene in 1956, the health of bite victims would fail gradually over several days. There had been no fatalities from red-back bites since the treatment was introduced.

red-backed, *a.* Used as a distinguishing epithet in the names of birds: **red-backed kingfisher** (formerly **halcyon**), the predom. blue-green and white kingfisher *Halcyon pyrrhopygia*, widespread in mainland Aust.; **parrot** (formerly **parakeet**), *red-rumped parrot*, see Red *a.* 1 b.; **sea eagle,** the white and chestnut-brown bird of prey *Haliastur indus*, the Brahminy kite, of coastal n. Aust. and elsewhere; *white-headed sea eagle*, see White *a.*[2] 1 b.; see also *white-headed fishing-eagle* White *a.*[2] 1 b.; **wren** (or **fairy wren**), the small bird *Malurus melanocephalus* of n. and n.e. Aust.

1840 [**red-backed kingfisher**] J. Gould *Birds of Aust.* (1848) II. Pl. 22, *Halcyon pyrrhopygia* . . Red-backed Halcyon. **1849** C. Sturt *Narr. Exped. Central Aust.* II. 20 App. *Red-backed Halcyon* . . having dull red feathers over the rump. **1896** F.G. Aflalo *Sketch Nat. Hist. Aust.* 117 The Red-backed and Sordid kingfishers are allied species. **1902** *Emu* I. 136 Red-backed kingfisher (*Halcyon pyrrhopygius*)—Shot near the rain-water hole. **1945** C. Barrett *Austral. Bird Life* 144 The red-backed kingfisher . . inhabits open timbered country and is widely distributed over the interior of the continent. **1964** M. Sharland *Territory of Birds* 202 The Red-backed Kingfisher . . catches dragonflies and grasshoppers in the Darwin streets, using overhead wires as watching stations. **1984** M. Blakers et al. *Atlas Austral. Birds* 328 Inland, the Red-backed Kingfisher is often present far from water but always where there are trees. **1845** [**red-backed parrot**] J. Gould *Birds of Aust.* (1848) V. Pl. 36, *Psephotus haematonotus* . . Red-backed Parrakeet. **1901** *Emu* I. 74 A pair of Red-backed Parrakeets . . has been for months frequenting the vacant piece of ground. **1912** *Ibid.* XII. 118 Red-backed Parrakeet . . very common. **1948** R. Raven-Hart *Canoe in Aust.* 27 Elegant Grass Parrots with green backs and blue wings and yellow fronts, and Red-backed Parrots, with splotches of red in addition. **1968** R. Hill *Bush Quest* 29 Red-backed parrots tore down wind, shrilling as they came, to land in the tossing branches of the wattles and red gum. **1945** C. Barrett *Austral. Bird Life* 33 The Brahminy kite of India and Ceylon is identical with the **red-backed sea eagle** (*Haliastur indus*). **1964** M. Sharland *Territory of Birds* 98 Above the twisting trio was poised the figure of a Red-backed Sea Eagle, for all the world like an umpire at a fight. **1982** R. Ellis *Bush Safari* 105 Vin thought that he saw a Brahminy Kite (Red-backed Sea Eagle) in the distance. **1901** *Emu* I. 89 *Malurus dorsalis* . . **Red-backed wren**. . . Fifteen skins have been received. **1949** B. O'Reilly *Green Mountains* 133 Redbacked wrens fluttered like living rubies from the high kangaroo grass. **1964** M. Sharland *Territory of Birds* 139 The Red-backed Wren . . proved to be fairly common in the grass country and Katherine and Pine Creek. **1984** Simpson & Day *Birds of Aust.* 325 The fairy-wrens are well-known for the beauty of the male's plumage, usually consisting of blues (red and black in Red-backed Fairy-wren).

Redfern. [The name of a suburban railway station in Sydney which immediately precedes the terminus of the line.] In the phr. **to get off** (or **out**) **at Redfern,** to employ the practice of *coitus interruptus*.

1970 *Times Lit. Suppl.* (London) 4 Dec. 1422/5 *To get off at Redfern* . . is dull and unoriginal. Since the nineteenth century, natives of Newcastle upon Tyne have described the procedure alliteratively as *getting out at Gateshead*. **1980** B. Hornadge *Austral. Slanguage* 190 The term *getting off at Redfern* has been used as a euphemism for the practice of coitus interruptus, Redfern being the suburban station immediately prior to Sydney Central. **1984** P. Jarratt *Aussie* 179 Cheryl and Troy . . concluded their lovemaking in the fashion Troy knew as 'getting out at Redfern'—one stop short of the final destination.

redfin. The European fresh-water fish *Perca fluviatilis*, naturalized in streams of s. Aust. incl. Tas., having a deep, banded body and orange to bright red pectoral, ventral, and anal fins. Also **redfin perch.**

1946 A.D. Butcher *Freshwater Fish Vic.* 9 Non-indigenous or introduced species . . English perch or redfin. **1951** T.C. Roughley *Fish & Fisheries Aust.* 152 English perch (Redfin—*Perca fluviatilis*). **1969** *Southerly* ii. 127 Twice, in the dusk, he caught a red-fin. **1974** T.D. Scott et al. *Marine & Freshwater Fishes S.A.* 206 The Redfin Perch, a freshwater species . . was introduced into Australia many years ago. It is believed that the species was liberated first in Tasmania in 1862. **1985** *Benalla Ensign* 5 Dec. 1/1 Juvenile redfin perch are extremely susceptible to the virus.

red gum. [Orig. referring to trees yielding a reddish gum-like kino, and later applied also to trees having a smooth bark and yielding a hard red wood.]

1. Any of many trees, often considered a group, of the genus *Eucalyptus* (fam. Myrtaceae), esp. the widespread *E. camaldulensis* (formerly *E. rostrata*), typically a large spreading tree with smooth mottled bark, and (*W.A.*) Marri; the wood of the tree. See also *creek gum* Creek 3, *flooded gum* Flooded, *Murray red gum* Murray 2, *red river gum* Red *a.* 1 a., *river gum, river red gum* River 2. Also *attrib.*

1788 J. White *Jrnl. Voyage N.S.W.* (1790) 201 We picked up . . plants and shrubs of different genera and species, specimens of which I have transmitted to Mr *Wilson*, particularly the Red Gum Tree. **1801** *HRA* (1915) 1st Ser. III. 414 The timber blue and red gum, apple tree and iron-barked trees. **1829** R. Mudie *Picture of Aust.* 147 Red gum (*eucalyptus robusta*). Very hard, and apparently tough in the individual fibres; but of a bad colour; rough, splintery, full of decayed portions here and there. **1838** J. Backhouse *Extracts from Lett.* (1839) v. 30 A eucalyptus, called here red-gum, has capsules the size of crab-apples. **1857** W. Westgarth *Vic. & Austral. Gold Mines* 32 They are called, in common speech, gum trees, because gum is exuded from some of the species. But the red gum, with his fine glossy and massive stem, is not one of these. **1880** R. Rose *Austral. Guide* 11 The red gum (*Eucalyptus Rostrata*) is a dense hard wood, with handsome curly grain. **1890** 'R. Boldrewood' *Colonial Reformer* I. 46 That's the worst of Australia—there's nothing a hundred years old in it except a red-gum tree. **1920** *Bulletin* (Sydney) 16 Dec. 20/2 Gippsland red gum (*E. tereticornis*) is not the red gum of S. Aus. (*E. rostrata*) nor of W.A. (*E. calophylla*) but it *is* the blue-gum of Queensland. **1952** A.W. Upfield *New Shoe* 21 Red-gum she is. . . They come from ring-barked trees on the Murray River flats. **1964** P. Adam Smith *Hear Train Blow* 183 Cutting up condemned red-gum sleepers for firewood. **1973** R. Erickson et al. *Flowers & Plants W.A.* 16 When burnt . . the Marri usually exudes a dark red resin, hence the alternative common name Red Gum. **1984** *Canberra Times* 10 Sept. 12/5 Red gum, a hard, close-grained timber with a dark ruby-red colouring, is water-resistant and virtually immune from attack by termites, which makes it ideal for use in bridge and wharf constructions and for fencing and stumps.

2. The astringent kino of any of several trees of the genera *Eucalyptus* and *Angophora*, used for medicinal purposes and tanning.

1788 J. White *Jrnl. Voyage N.S.W.* (1790) 178 The trees of this country are immensely large. . . At the heart they are full of veins, through which an amazing quantity of an astringent red gum issues. This gum I have found very serviceable in an obstinate dysentery that raged at our first landing. **1796** P.G. King Jrnl. Norfolk Island 15 Mar. 255 A woman died this day of dysentery . . which she imprudently concealed from the Surgeon; having been advised to make use of the Red Gum from Port Jackson, which removed it out of the Surgeons Power to afford her the least relief. **1805** J.H. Tuckey *Acct. Voyage to establish Colony Port Philip* 179 Their war-spears are barbed with pieces of white spar, or shark's teeth, fastened on with red gum. **1821** J. Wallis *Hist. Acct. Colony N.S.W.* 5 In the dysentery . . the red gum of the tree which now goes by that name . . was found a very powerful and efficient remedy. **1946** *Bulletin* (Sydney) 25 Sept. 28/1 In Westralia there is nothing better than redgum or kino for the tanning of fishing nets or lines.

red hot, *a.* and *n.*

A. *adj.* As **red-hot,** unfair; unreasonable.

1896 H. Lawson *While Billy Boils* 281 When . . she paused for breath, he drew a long one, gave a short whistle, and said: 'Well, it's red-hot!' **1907** A. Wright *Keane of Kalgoorlie* 107 'It's red 'ot,' put in Dave, 'th' way these 'ere owners makes er pore man give 'em a lump in th' sweep.' **1910** L. Esson *Three Short Plays* (1911) 15

That's red 'ot—yer carn't book me fer ther vag. **1941** S.J. Baker *Pop. Dict. Austral. Slang* 59 Unreasonable, unfair, e.g., 'a red hot price'. **1980** *Sun* (Sydney) 22 Feb. 21/4 (*heading*) Tomato prices are red hot.

B. *n. pl.* Rhyming slang for 'trots'. Also *attrib.*

1979 *Herald* (Melbourne) 24 Feb. 35/6 It's not often I'd consider giving the red hots a miss on Saturday night—especially when I've got a couple of certainties. **1983** *Sydney Morning Herald* 22 Apr. 27/6 The reason for the press conference, was to defend trotting and lay to rest the 'red hots' stigma. It is an unjustified tag which has remained with the industry since the late 1920s and early 1930s when, Judge Goran pointed out, someone with a penchant for rhyming slang coined the term.

Red Indian fish. [See quot. 1965.] The scarlet marine fish *Pataecus fronto* of Qld., N.S.W., S.A., and W.A. Also **Red Indian.**

1906 D.G. Stead *Fishes of Aust.* 212 The Red-Indian Fish . . lives in weedy, rocky localities, along parts of the coast of New South Wales. **1934** *Bulletin* (Sydney) 16 May 20/3 Someone identified the thing as *Pataecus fronto*, better known as the 'Red Indian' in N.S.W., where it is sometimes caught on the reefs. **1965** *Austral. Encycl.* VII. 395 Red Indian fish . . of the southern Australian rocky shore-lines. Its high dorsal fin forms a crest like the feathers of a Red Indian's head-dress. **1983** Hutchins & Thompson *Marine & Estuarine Fishes S.-W. Aust.* 28 Whiskered Prowfish . . easily distinguished from the Red Indian Fish . . by the prominent gap between dorsal and caudal fins.

red light. *Obs.* [Fig. use of *red light* a sign of danger.] A supervisor; a manager.

1915 *Bulletin* (Sydney) 9 Dec. 22/1, I was wielding the pick and banjo in a gang on a big channel job once when the ganger got his 'slip' for giving his 'pink eye' (pet) an easy job. The riding 'redlight' then unknowingly picked out another 'spur' in the horde, gave him the book and rode away. **1916** *Ibid.* 6 July 24/1 Here are a few of the pet names given by the wielder of the pick and banjo to the ganger: 'The red light', 'the big bloke', 'the gun', 'the nark' [etc.]. **1925** *Ibid.* 9 Apr. 24/1 The shed overseer or boss of the board is the 'red light'. **1929** *Aussie* (Sydney) Apr. 17/2 'Come, come, my man,' said the red light. 'This kind of shearing won't do me.' . . The 'red light' was the boss, dissatisfied with the work. **1933** L.A. Sigsworth *Verse* 7 'The redlight' strolls with an easy gait, but his lamps are everywhere; His time book peeps from 'is side coat 'kick', like a signboard says 'beware!'

red-ragger. [In allusion to the *red flag* as a symbol of revolution, socialism, or communism.] A communist; a socialist.

1916 *Ross's Monthly* June 13/2 Dear Editor . . I can honestly say I have read a lot of Labor papers, also socialist literature, but I never saw any that would come within coo-ee of 'Ross's' for straightforwardness and sincerity. '*A red ragger.*' **1923** *Aussie* (Sydney) Apr. 16/2 It is easiest . . for the employer to forget that the men he reviles as red-raggers and 'go slow' gospellers are mainly the same men that kept his capital and profits secure eight years ago. **1930** *Listening Post* (Perth) 21 Mar. 15 The left wing (polite phrase for red-raggers). **1950** F.J. Hardy *Power without Glory* 396, I don't trust these Communists. . . I don't want too much of my good money going into the pocket of a red-ragger. **1954** T. Ronan *Vision Splendid* 179 'There's only the cook here, and I'm afraid he's a bit of a red-ragger.' 'Too bloody right he is!' snarled a voice behind them. 'And if you blokes aren't coming down for your smoko I'll throw it away.' **1970** P. Amos *Silver Kings* 102 None of the buggers had ever heard of the word till some red-ragger flung it at 'em with a lot of other socialist jabber. **1972** G.C. Bolton *Fine Country to starve In* 17 He was known during the Depression to notify employers if they inadvertently gave work to a man with a reputation as a 'red ragger'. **1974** D. Ireland *Burn* 114 You don't have to be a bit of a red-ragger to know that first our people have to be given some things. Like houses with electric light. **1985** N. Medcalf *Rifleman* 78 Bluey was considered a bit of a red-ragger.

reed-bird: see Reed-warbler.

reed spear. *Obs.* An Aboriginal spear: see quots. 1859 and 1884.

1847 G.F. Angas *Savage Life & Scenes* I. 93 The reed spear . . is like an arrow, and pointed with wood hardened by fire. **1859** W. Burrows *Adventures Mounted Trooper* 97 The reed spear is made, as its name implies, of reeds, joined together by the fibres of the bark of trees, and kangaroo sinews, terminating in a point of hard, heavy wood. They can throw this spear a distance of eighty or a hundred yards with surprising accuracy. It is used for killing small game. **1879** *Native Tribes S.A.* 37 They showed great dexterity in the use of the reed spear, or kaikye. . . It is thrown with a taralye or throwing stick. **1884** E. Palmer *Notes Austral. Tribes* 12 All the northern tribes of blacks use the reed-spear, generally barbed, which is thrown by the aid of the *wommera.*

reed-warbler. [Transf. use of *reed-warbler* the British bird *Acrocephalus streperus.*] The predom. brown bird *Acrocephalus stentoreus australis* of reedy wetlands. Also **reed-bird.**

1808 J.W. Lewin *Birds New Holland* 22 (*caption*) Reed Warbler. . . These birds frequent the banks of rivers, and the sides of ponds in the Summer months; they harbour among the reeds, where they also breed and sing both night and day. **1847** J. Gould *Birds of Aust.* (1848) III. Pl. 37, *Acrocephalus australis* . . Reed Warbler. **1889** *Proc. Linnean Soc. N.S.W.* IV. 410 *Calamoherpe australis* . . known as 'Reed-bird'. **1892** 'Mrs A. Macleod' *Silent Sea* I. 151 The trills of the reed-warblers among the tall sedges still went on. **1903** *Emu* II. 164 Empty Reed-Birds' nests in great numbers in the reeds. **1929** A.H. Chisholm *Birds & Green Places* 113 The voice of our reed warbler, for instance, neglects each of . . Fowler's requirements in a warbler. **1953** A. Russell *Murray Walkabout* 135 Hidden among a little bed of green rushes, was a reed-warbler singing its wild melodious song. **1984** M. Blakers et al. *Atlas Austral. Birds* 427 The Reed-Warbler lives singly or in pairs usually in wetlands where reeds grow.

reef, *n. Gold-mining.* [Transf. use of *reef* a narrow ridge or chain of rocks. Used elsewhere but recorded earliest in Aust.] A lode or vein of auriferous quartz (but see also quots. 1869 and 1895). Also *attrib.*

1854 *Illustr. Sydney News* 28 Oct. 324/3 A new reeff has been lately opened in Lang Gulley . . and several new claims have been taken up . . in the quartz reeff. **1859** *Colonial Mining Jrnl.* Feb. 93/2 Intelligent Cornish miners inform me that our 'reefs' and 'leaders' are exactly similar to the 'lodes' and 'branches' in the tin mines in England. **1869** R.B. Smyth *Gold Fields & Mineral Districts* 619 *Reef*, the term is applied to the upturned edges of the palaeozoic rocks. The reef is composed of slate, sandstone, or mudstone. The bed-rock anywhere is usually called the reef. **1877** *Free Trade Papers* xi. 4 Tell you what, mate, lets up swag and make to-night for the Reefs. **1895** G.C. Addison *Miners' Man.* 31 The terms 'vein' and 'reef' shall mean any substance, other than alluvial, containing gold. **1916** A. Wilson *Lays & Tales of Mines* 65 They had followed the 'reef' down from the 'cap', and they were . . working on ounce-and-half stone. **1935** F. Clune *Rolling down Lachlan* 122 An old-timer told me that reef-mining started on the Mount in 1891. **1946** K.S. Prichard *Roaring Nineties* 374 Under the old Act the lessee acquired the reef gold: alluvial remained for the man with a miner's right. **1978** D. Stuart *Wedgetail View* 83 Above them the quartz reef, the full width of the drive, shone dripping wet in the light of the softly hissing lamps.

reef, *v. Gold-mining.* [f. prec.] *intr.* To mine auriferous quartz. Freq. as *vbl. n.*

1859 *Colonial Mining Jrnl.* May 143/1 Reefing bids fair to be the main feature, but alluvial workings are also likely to turn out satisfactorily. **1862** J.A. Patterson *Gold Fields Vic.* 320 'Reefing', as it is called is followed both by small parties of miners, and by large companies. If the vein is a surface one, it is opened up much as a quarry is opened. **1871** *Austral. Town & Country Jrnl.* (Sydney) 28 Jan. 102/4 Reefing, which was entirely unknown a couple of years back, is rapidly assuming gigantic proportions, threatening to throw the alluvial entirely into the shade. **1876** 'Eight Yrs.' Resident' *Queen of Colonies* 149 There have been large fortunes made on Gympie, in the reefing line more especially. **1890** *Truth* (Sydney) 3 Aug. 7/1 He started 'reefing', and for a time he did pretty well. **1901** *Handbk. Mining* (S.A. Dept. Mines) 7 Valuable reefing fields have been discovered in the Echunga district. **1944** M.J. O'Reilly *Bowyangs & Boomerangs* 40 'Reefing' is part of the education which every prospector must acquire. . . As most of the reefs outcrop they are easily discovered. The method is to knap off part of the reef, powder it in a 'Dolly pot', and wash in a gold dish, where values, if any, will show up.

reefer. *Gold-mining.*

a. *Obs.* A mining claim in a reef.

1854 *Illustr. Sydney News* 28 Oct. 234/3 Few claims have been bottomed on the gravel pits for some considerable time and such as have been lately bottomed are reefers, by which however we do not mean blanks as many of these same reefers are paying as much as eight ounces to the tub.

b. One who mines such a claim.

1859 *Colonial Mining Jrnl.* Mar. 108/3 The Reefers have objected to mining leases, and I do not think they are far wrong as far as the reefs are concerned. **1871** *Emigrant's Wife* I. 272 Three of his company were 'reefers', or substantial men, who worked a quartz-reef by machinery. **1864** E.A. Murray *Ella Norman* III. 64 The 'reefers' think themselves the aristocracy of the mining population and with reason. **1898** D.W. Carnegie *Spinifex & Sand* 23 We are not the only successful reefers since you left. **1904** *Worker* (Sydney) 27 Aug. 2/5 The reefers strive for the hidden wealth and live in a golden dream. **1964** H.P. Tritton *Time means Tucker* (rev. ed.) 58 We found we were 'diggers', not miners, mining being the work of the 'reefers', or hard rock men.

reef heron. The bird *Egretta sacra* of coastal mainland Aust. and elsewhere, having either white or bluish-grey plumage.

1848 J. Gould *Birds of Aust.* VI. Pl. 60, *Herodias jugularis* . . the Blue Reef Heron is universally distributed over the whole of the coasts of the great continent of Australia. *Ibid.* Pl. 61, *Herodias greyi* . . White Reef Heron. . . This species of Heron is abundantly dispersed over the whole of the northern and eastern coasts of Australia wherever low islands and reefs of coral running parallel to those coasts are found to exist. It presents so many points of similarity in size and in form to the *H. jugularis*, that I have long been of opinion that it is merely an albino variety of that species. **1898** E.E. Morris *Austral Eng.* 195 Reef H[eron]—*Demiegretta sacra.* **1904** *Emu* III. 210 *Demiegretta sacra* (Reef-Heron . .)—Common on the beach and reefs. **1928** S.E. Napier *On Barrier Reef* 61 The Reef Herons are . . the most graceful. **1936** T.C. Roughley *Wonders Great Barrier Reef* 213 Reef herons are . . common on most . . islands; when the tide is out they are . . seen wading over the reef searching for the various forms of marine life on which they feed. **1964** M. Sharland *Territory of Birds* 94, I had discovered a rare and novel combination of black and white—two Reef Herons, one the white phase, the other the dark, and in such close company as to infer they had mated. **1976** *Reader's Digest Compl. Bk. Austral. Birds* 81 Reef herons occur in two forms—white, which is the more common in tropical areas, and dark or slate-blue, which is the more numerous in temperate regions.

reffo. Also **refo.** [f. *ref(ugee* + -O.] Orig. a refugee from Europe; any migrant other than from the British Isles. Also *attrib.*

1941 S.J. Baker *Pop. Dict. Austral. Slang* 59 *Reffo*, a refugee from Europe. **1951** *New Settler in W.A.* (Perth) May 37 While we have that small-minded attitude that they are 'Pommies' or 'D.P.s' or 'Reffos', we won't get them as migrants. **1963** B. Hesling *Dinkumization & Depommification* 162 People didn't want to be mistaken for 'reffos', for Australia was no more tolerant of foreigners then than Yorkshire was tolerant of those homeless Belgians who allegedly ate our cats and dogs in 1914. **1965** K. Smith *OGF* 52 Now, this is only one instance of how important it is for reffos—er—new citizens—to learn to speak English properly. **1967** A. Seymour *One Day of Yr.* 119 Rotten reffos overrunnin' the joint, bloody Hitler had the right idea. **1970** J. Cleary *Helga's Web* 37 Bloody reffo women. . . You get 'em all da time down this a way, you know? **1971** *Bulletin* (Sydney) 1 May 18/2 Highly skilled reffos were let in only if they worked as navvies for three years. **1977** E. Mackie *Oh to be Aussie* 58 There's a new breed of refos. These are, of course, the ethnos. Nowadays one in three births is an 'ethnic' birth. **1984** *Canberra Times* 10 May 9/7 Bloody refos, I hate them.

regent. Used *attrib.* in the names of birds.

1. regent bird. [Named in compliment to the Prince Regent, later King George IV.] The bower bird *Sericulus chrysocephalus* of dense forests in near-coastal Qld. and N.S.W., the adult male having brilliant golden-yellow and black plumage. Also **regent bower bird,** and *ellipt.* as **regent.**

1813 T. Skottowe Select Specimens Birds & Animals N.S.W., *Regent.* This charming Bird is given as large as Life... I am I believe the first possessor of any of its Kind, and having procured the specimen from which the Drawing here given is taken on the same day that I receiv'd in this distant part of the World the news of the Regency Restrictions on His Royal Highness, the Prince Regent, having been taken off, as a small tribute from the Esteem I bear that exalted Character, I have named it as above. **1827** P. Cunningham *Two Yrs. in N.S.W.* I. 325 The *regent* and *rifle-bird* outvie all I have seen from any part of the world, in the chaste splendour of their plumage. **1845** L. Leichhardt *Jrnl. Overland Exped. Aust.* 24 Feb. (1847) 161 Mr Gilbert observed the female of the Regent-bird. **1861** J.D. Lang *Qld., Aust.* 371 *Beegy-beegy* is the name of an object possessing the peculiar quality of the sun, a bright yellow colour in a high degree—the Regent Bird. **1887** H. Gullet *Tropical N.S.W.* 12 There is the rifle bird .. the regent, brilliant in black and orange yellow. **1929** A.H. Chisholm *Birds & Green Places* 168 Regent bower-bird... Distribution: throughout approximately a thousand miles of coastal jungle from central Queensland to central New South Wales. **1959** *Meanjin* 135 He .. follows the flight of a black-and-orange regent-bird.

2. *transf.* [Prob. from the similarity in colouration.] **regent honeyeater,** the predom. black and yellow honeyeater *Xanthomyza phrygia* of s.e mainland Aust.; Warty-faced honeyeater; **parrot,** Smoker.

1913 G.M. Mathews *List Birds Aust.* 270 *Zanthomiza phrygia phrygia.* **Regent Honey-eater.** **1934** A.H. Chisholm *Bird Wonders of Aust.* 192 The Sun-bird .. and the Regent Honeyeater (yellow and black), are perhaps the loveliest among the large band of blossom-birds. **1967** A. Rutgers *Birds Aust.* 262 Regent Honey-eaters make a lot of noise and have a loud laughing call. **1983** *Goulburn Post* 16 Nov. 14/2 At a recent meeting of Goulburn Field Naturalist Society, a letter was received from the Bendigo club, asking the society to take part in a Regent Honeyeater survey, as this bird is becoming extremely rare. **1945** C. Barrett *Austral. Bird Life* 77 Long-tailed birds are the **regent parrot** or 'smoker' (*Polytelis anthopeplus*) [etc.]. **1962** B.W. Leake *Eastern Wheatbelt Wildlife* 85 The regent parrot or smoker is different in many ways to the twenty eight, and the body when plucked of feathers is a trifle larger. **1984** M. Blakers et al. *Atlas Austral. Birds* 263 The Regent Parrot eats seeds, berries, buds, blossom and rarely insects.

reggo /ˈrɛdʒoʊ/. Also **rego.** [f. *reg(istration* + -O.] (Motor vehicle) registration. Also *attrib.*

1967 J. Wynnum *I'm Jack, all Right* 39 Everything is sweet except for the bloody silly reggo sticker. **1973** H. Williams *My Love* 12 There's a bit of bull and form-filling about reggo and comprehensive insurance and number plates. **1982** R. Hall *Just Relations* 130 If the cops catch us they'll have us cold: no rego, one headlamp, baldy tyres. **1984** *N.T. News* (Darwin) 15 Sept. 42/3 Nissan MQ 4X4 S/Wagon Diesel Air-con tow/bar Air shocks, Bullbar, Driving lights, F.W.H. long rego.

Hence **reggo** *v. trans.*

1967 J. Wynnum *I'm Jack, all Right* 35 A car doesn't have to be reggoed in Queensland to have an accident up there.

rehab /ˈrihæb/. Abbrev. of 'rehabilitation': see quot. 1966.

1945 *Weekend: 15th Austral. Infantry Brigade* 14 Nov. 1 The stands were packed to hear Mr Mash .. on demob and rehab respectively. **1946** *Strictly Personal* (Ministry Post-War Reconstruction) 12 He went to the Rehabilitation Section of the Commonwealth Employment Service. 'Rehab' had a little trouble in finding him a suitable job. **1966** G.W. Turner *Eng. Lang. Aust. & N.Z.* 172 *Rehab*, pronounced with stress on the first syllable, was a common word in the years following the Second World War for 'rehabilitation', referring to loans, bursaries and other help given to returned soldiers.

reinstoushment. *Obs.* [Insertion of Stoush *n.* 2 in *rein(force)ment.*] One of a number of soldiers, etc., sent as reinforcements.

1918 *Aussie: Austral. Soldiers' Mag.* Aug. 11/2 A dopy re-instoushment recently lobbed into our wagon lines. **1920** *Ibid.* July 33/2 My Battalion owned a reinstoushment who, although several years late in arriving at the war, was an enthusiastic soldier. **1931** O. Walters *Shrapnel Green* 19 These reinstoushments .. have got us beat .. and it's us for the Front again. **1943** S.W. Keough *Around Army* 17 It is a common sight to see one of the hard-heads, tough in the ways of war, taking one of the 'green' reinstoushments under his wing.

relief country. An area having pasture available for stock from drought-affected areas.

1905 *Shearer* (Sydney) 18 Mar. 8/5 Probably 40,000 sheep will leave this station for relief country. **1923** J. Bowes *Jackaroos* 184 The region through which they were passing was unoccupied, and would make good relief country. **1942** W. Glasson *Our Shepherds* 11 It was decided to send on agistment nineteen thousand sheep to Hall's property .. where relief country was available.

remittance man. [Spec. use of *remittance man* an emigrant supported by remittances from home. Used elsewhere but recorded earliest in Aust.: see OED(S *remittance* 2.] A male immigrant to Australia financially supported by his family: see quot. 1984. Also ellipt. as **remittance,** and formerly **remittance immigrant.**

[**1854** W. Shaw *Land of Promise* 304 A colony is very uncongenial without money, and, should 'the governor' suspend the 'remittances', the *bad shilling*, as he is technically called, will very frequently return to those who uttered him.] **1873** *Austral. Handbk.* 51 The Commissioner for Railways is authorized to grant a free railway ticket to any assisted, free, or remittance immigrant, being a steerage passenger, who may be desirous of proceeding into the country within fourteen days after arrival in the colony. **1888** *Bulletin* (Sydney) 10 Mar. 14/1 Having brought discredit upon the judicial wig of his father (a Scotch law lord) he found himself a remittance-man in the back-blocks. **1899** H. Furniss *Austral. Sketches* 68 Here come the 'new chum' .. the feckless 'remittance man' to see if that letter 'with enclosure' has arrived. **1918** A.M. Moore *Autumn Grey* 50 Perhaps your father was a remittance man... There used to be a lot of 'em... I remember Nick'less O'Brien... His people in auld Ireland paid him a pretty penny to keep away from them. **1934** T. Wood *Cobbers* 46 'What's he like? Remittance man?' 'No fear. He's a good sort.' **1952** J. Cleary *Sundowners* 50 'A bloody Pommy remittance man!' Paddy leapt to his feet as if the kelpie had suddenly attacked him. **1967** K. Lloyd *Black Opal* 56 I'm what used to be known as a 'remittance man'—plenty of money to keep me away from home, and no need to work. **1975** 'E. Lindall' *Day for Angels* 20 He was the last of the old-time remittance men—his cheque came from London every quarter. **1984** *Midweek Territorian* (Darwin) 24 Oct. 5/2 A remittance man, for the benefit of those who don't know of them .. was generally an Englishman unwanted by his family for one or another reason. He was paid to live as far away as possible .. definitely in another country. They were generally unwanted because they drank too much, or had been caught in compromising circumstances with the maid .. or worse still with the butler, or had committed some other dreadful social sin.

rendezvous. *Obs.* [Transf. use of *rendezvous* a meeting place.] The habitual resting place of a mob of cattle.

1848 H.W. Haygarth *Recoll. Bush Life* 59 A spot on which cattle are thus in the habit of assembling and basking during the day is called a 'rendezvous', and is easily known, for, from the constant pressure of innumerable vast bodies, the surface of the ground becomes smooth and hard, resembling a blighted ring in the midst of verdure. **1865** G.F. Angas *Aust.* 282 From the main body of the herd, dimly seen through a dense cloud of dust, a succession of furious animals break off on all sides, some making back to their 'rendezvous' (as the spot where the herd is in the habit of resting is called).

reo. [f. *re(inforcement* + -O.] In Services' speech: one of a party of reinforcements. Usu. in *pl.*

1931 O. Walters *Shrapnel Green* 19 For the 'reos' were talking of Passchendaele. **1942** *Action Front: Jrnl. 2/2 Field Regiment* Dec. 9 'Welcome' to our new bunch of 'Reos'. **1951** E. Lambert *Twenty Thousand Thieves* 225 One day the ex-men's platoon and two platoons of 'reos', as the ex-men called the reinforcements, were being drilled. **1958** R. Graves *On Gallipoli* 12 The re-o looked at us—we saw a child. **1972** R. Pollard *Cream Machine* 42 We 'reos' .. had our initial dose of good advice. **1982** J.J. Coe *Desperate Praise* 83 We were Reo's. We'd been in the infantry reinforcement unit since we'd arrived, no weapons and very green.

rep. [Spec. use of *rep.*, abbrev. of *representative.*] The elected representative of a party of employees, esp. shearers (see quot. 1919); *shearer's rep* Shearer b. Also **rep shearer.**

1899 *Bulletin* (Sydney) 19 Aug. 32/1 Sheedy asked to see the 'Rep.' The latter .. was ringer as well as union representative. **1907** C. MacAlister *Old Pioneering Days* 357 While fortunes are made from wool .. so long will the shearer be worthy of his hire; and so long, we believe, will the A.W.U. and the shed 'Rep.' be absolute necessities of the shearer's 'plan of campaign' for his just rights. **1919** A.B. Paterson *Song of Pen* (1983) 411 The shearers then drew apart and held a ballot for a 'rep', i.e. shearers' representative, whose duty it would be to bring forward any grievances, see that union rules were observed, and union dues collected from all hands in the shed. **1924** *Bulletin* (Sydney) 24 Apr. 22/2 When Stumpy was ringer at Burnima, a back country 'gun', Wild Rorty, got a pen there. The speed of this rep. was broadcasted around, mostly by himself. **1949** D. Walker *We went to Aust.* 98 Each team is not composed of shearers only... The leader of the team is known as the 'Rep.' and it is he who represents the men in all arguments with the station owner. **1962** *Bulletin* (Sydney) 3 Feb. 43/3 Old Big Ted, the rep .. clapped his hands for silence... 'Gentlemen and shearers, we want to thank the boss for the beaut big shout up.' **1973** J. Morrison *Austral. by Choice* 127 It lasted six weeks, and when it cut out the rep shearer, with whom I'd palled up took me with him as a fully blown presser to Mingowallah Station. **1977** J. Doughty *Gold in Blood* 37 And I, the elected roustabouts' 'rep', seemed to be bearing the brunt of everything.

Repat /ˈripæt/. [Abbrev. of *repatriation.*] The Repatriation Commission. Also used *attrib.* of benefits made available to former Service personnel through the agency of the Commission.

1920 *Smith's Weekly* (Sydney) 24 Apr. 23/2 The Repat. will give him £10 worth of instruments as tools of trade. **1946** *Strictly Personal* (Ministry Post-War Reconstruction) 10 She was so appreciative of the friendly help given her by the officers of the Repatriation Commission... We shouldn't wonder, if she has a baby, if its middle name isn't 'Repat'. **1948** J.K. Ewers *For Heroes to live In* 156 He ought to go down to Perth and have a thorough examination in the Repat Ward. His right lung's just red-raw. **1952** J.R. Skemp *Memories Myrtle Bank* 229 The paddock was actually 'repat' property under the administration of the Repatriation Commission set up after the war to settle soldiers on the land. **1960** *Bulletin* (Sydney) 14 Sept. 18/3 Five a.m. in the Repat. Hospital. **1972** *Ibid.* 7 Oct. 15/1 Department officers were ordered to cease the common practice which previously prevailed of touring RSL clubs virtually browbeating ex-servicemen into applying for 'repat benefits'. **1978** B. St. A. Smith *Spirit beyond Psyche* 208, I told him once t' try the Repat. for warnerves. I told 'im what a terrible good lurk it was.

reporter. *Obs.* A member of a droving team who goes ahead of a mob to give notice of its approach.

1890 'R. Boldrewood' *Colonial Reformer* II. 267 The usual 'reporter' of travelling sheep. **1914** C.H.S. Matthews *Bill* 97 With a mob of 1000 bullocks there will be about ten drovers, a cook, and a man, who is known as a Reporter... The reporter has charge of the spare saddle-horses. **1927** J. Mathieu *Backblock Ballads* 39 Luck sped us on with no mishap, Till our 'reporter' left one day, And Bill took on another chap.

Also **reporting** *vbl. n.*

1904 L.M.P. Archer *Bush Honeymoon* 281 What game are you at—*reportin'*?

rep shearer: see Rep.

reserve. [Spec. use of *reserve* a district or place set apart for some particular use, or assigned to certain persons: see OED(S *sb.* 5 b.]

1. a. [Also U.S.: see Mathews *n.* 6.] A piece of land

set aside for a specific public use. See also *government reserve* GOVERNMENT B. 3, *town reserve*, TOWN 3, *township reserve* TOWNSHIP 1, *village reserve* VILLAGE 3.

1815 *HRA* (1916) 1st Ser. VIII. 638, I have no information upon the Nature of the large Reserves above alluded to, which are marked E on the Charts of the Colony. **1827** P. CUNNINGHAM *Two Yrs. in N.S.W.* I. 133 It would be presumption in us to hint to His Excellency Governor Darling .. the necessary caution in bestowing such grants to settlers as may not interfere with future townships or other public reserves. **1829** H. WIDOWSON *Present State Van Diemen's Land* 21 The first store next to the sea is Mr W.A. Bethume's, government having what is termed a reserve, to erect a battery in case of need upon a rock that runs into the water. **1838** R. GOUGER *S.A. in 1837* 3 In South Australia no reserves can be made, excepting for roads and footpaths. **1844** *Duncan's Weekly Register* (Sydney) 20 July 35/1 The water reserve, he contended, belonged to the whole city. **1858** T. MCCOMBIE *Hist. Colony Vic.* 233 The Corporation—not behind in cupidity—leased out the two market reserves for similar purposes; and there were, therefore, two small 'Canvas Towns' in the centre of the city. **1864** H. JONES *New Valuations* 26 Nearly all the waters in which, except the reserve for travelling stock, are in my freehold. **1870** C.H. ALLEN *Visit to Qld.* 230 At Warnambool there is a most useful and ornamental property, called the 'Reserve'. It consists of nearly two thousand acres of splendid grazing land, lying close to the town... Householders are allowed to keep a certain number of cows and horses on this Reserve. **1877** 'CAPRICORNUS' *Land Law of Future* 6 Reserves from purchase shall be cancelled; gold-fields and mineral reserves shall be maintained. **1892** *Truth* (Sydney) 17 Apr. 2/2 *These reserves are very numerous*, and have, from time to time, been made and declared at the request of, and through backstairs influence exercised by the squatters in Parliament, and over the Lands Department. **1919** *Bulletin* (Sydney) 8 May 20/1 An interesting find has been made in some newly-trenched ground in the Maryborough (Q.) municipal reserve. **1944** *Ibid.* 26 Jan. 12/2 Pulling on to the small unfenced reserve beside the Government tank he unyoked. **1953** T.G. TUCKER *Aust. as Home* 29 In numerous picturesque or convenient quarters there have been set apart 'public reserves' and 'national parks' of hundreds, and sometimes of many thousands, of acres. **1978** B. KENNEDY *Silver, Sin, & Sixpenny Ale* 8 The town's planners optimistically set apart reserves for a school, hospital, several public buildings, and parklands.

b. A public park.

1851 H. MELVILLE *Present State Aust.* 60 On either side of the Torrens is a reserve or Government domain of two hundred acres. **1864** *Bell's Life in Sydney* 21 May 2/6 *Wanted to Know immediately*, whether the *public reserve*, commonly known as *Hyde Park*, and always supposed to be *inalienable* has been either sold, leased or lent to any person whatever. **1888** M.M. BALLOU *Under Southern Cross* 129 There are besides the Botanical Gardens three other 'reserves', as they are universally denominated in Australia; namely, Queen's Park, Victoria Park, and Bowen Park. **1908** L.S. CURTIS *Hist. Broken Hill* 105 There are five Parks or Reserves .. each being well fenced in and planted with trees, shrubs, flowers, and grass. **1924** MRS H.A. DOUDY *Magic of Dawn* 27 The reserve of park lands .. surrounded the city. **1950** J. CLEARY *Just let me Be* 104 Joe walked across the short-grassed reserve to the promenade. **1960** *N.T. News* (Darwin) 12 Jan. 7/3 The need to declare the Katherine River low-level bridge camping area a reserve is becoming more urgent. Judging by the number of 'dead marines' it is the site of regular drinking orgies.

2. *Obs.* [Also U.S.: see Mathews *n.* 2.] A piece of land reserved for the future use or occupancy of an individual.

1822 *HRA* (1822) 3rd Ser. IV. 55 Mr Meredith .. proposed then to waive his Claim to the reserve adjoining his Grant. **1826** *Hobart Town Gaz.* 17 June, A gentleman who has obtained a reserve of Betsy Island in the Derwent, is bringing out a large importation of rabbits. **1827** *Tasmanian* (Hobart) 28 June 3 One of those whose rank does not *yet* entitle him to embrace the advantages held forth, has, nevertheless, made an application for a reserve of 2000 acres of land!!! **1828** H. DANGAR *Index & Directory River Hunter* 27 These locations were ordered by Sir Thomas Brisbane, K.C.B. to the choice of the individuals named, and called 'Reserves of Land', being a liberality evinced to those whose intention it was to become settlers, but whose avocations would not immediately allow of their doing so... These are now converted into grants. **1835** J. HOLMAN *Travels* IV. 419, I think it much more advantageous to purchase a farm that has been partly cleared, than to receive a grant of land, unless it was a part of some choice 'reserve'. **1843** *HRA* (1925) 1st Ser. XXIII. 267 Let him receive authority to select four square miles as a Reserve, on condition of its being Stocked and improved.

3. A piece of land set aside for the exclusive use of Aborigines; *Aboriginal reserve*, see ABORIGINAL *a.* 2; *native reserve*, see NATIVE *a.* 5. Also *attrib.*

1839 *Extracts Papers & Proc. Aborigines Protection Soc.* Oct. 133 The reserves for the Aborigines .. will be enclosed and cultivated. **1846** *HRA* (1925) 1st Ser. XXV. 12 A reserve for the Aboriginal Natives should be formed .. at the junction of the Murray and Murrumbidgee rivers. **1880** 'ERRO' *Squattermania* 97 A benevolent Government had enclosed a large extent of ground for the special benefit of the aborigines .. which was generally known as the Blacks' Reserve. In one portion of this reserve was a small paddock. **1904** *Bulletin* (Sydney) 31 Mar. 17/2 On the Castlereagh (N.S.W.) .. near each town is a 'black's reserve', and here the darkie must reside, under penalty of losing the State ration and blanket. **1930** A.E. YARRA *Vanishing Horsemen* 18 Tamporina, the official king of the Government blacks' reserve, was committing sorcery—making rain. **1937** C. WARBURTON *White Poppies* 194 The 'gubment' had sent word to the Arnhem Land tribes that certain country was to be set aside for their use only—'reserve, you call 'im,' added T'Kala. **1955** M. DURACK *Keep him my Country* (1966) 47 This was the reserve country—idealist's illusion of aboriginal freedom. **1959** L. ROSE *Country of Dead* 6 Sometimes when he was away longer than usual, the boy went looking for him in the shanties on the town reserve. **1978** HANIGAN & LINDSAY *No Tracks on River* 2 Where I live is across the river from the town, with my auntie. She has one of a line of houses that was put up on the reserve. **1984** P. CORRIS *Winning Side* 14, I was going to wipe the fact that I was a reserve Aborigine off the slate, that was essential, especially for the union ticket. **1986** *Sydney Morning Herald* 8 Mar. 28/6 It is not sufficient that Aborigines will have tenure over existing reserves.

Reserve Bank. A central bank; that bank which is responsible for the administration of the monetary policy of a government.

1959 *CPD* (H. of R.) XXII. 377 The Reserve Bank will be a worthy successor to the Commonwealth Bank as Australia's central bank. **1969** *Austral.* (Sydney) 10 June 1/8 The Reserve Bank has foreshadowed government moves to lift interest rates. **1978** *Austral. Financial Rev.* (Sydney) 15 June 1/6 The Reserve Bank is moving towards the establishment of a foreign exchange market in Australia. **1985** *Nat. Times* (Sydney) 22 Nov. 17/1 The Reserve Bank no longer collects exchange control data.

reserved, *ppl. a.* [Also U.S.: see Mathews b.] Of land: retained unsold for some public use.

1823 *Hobart Town Gaz.* 26 July, As a sporting farm, or farm for profit, is perhaps equal to any on the island... A reserved road to this estate, from the brook .. gives it the advantage of communication by land with Hobart Town. **1838** *Southern Austral.* (Adelaide) 15 Dec. 3/4 His Excellency .. pledged himself to the survey of the reserved districts at as early a period as possible. **1839** T.L. MITCHELL *Three Exped. Eastern Aust.* (rev. ed.) I. 161 Part of the reserved land of the township, has been given to small farmers. **1861** J.D. LANG *Qld., Aust.* 142 The bidding very spirited especially for the lots that front the reserved quay which runs along the river edge. **1873** A. TROLLOPE *Aust. & N.Z.* II. 179 All round the city there are reserved lands, of which I may best explain the nature to English readers by calling them parks for the people. **1876** 'CAPRICORNUS' *Colonisation* 37 In the case of villages and homesteads, water should be always permanently reserved. **1911** ST. C. GRONDONA *Collar & Cuffs* 11 After the fire on 'Macara' station the sheep had to get a 'wriggle on' pretty quickly, as nearly the the whole reserved paddocks suffered from the fire. **1934** 'S. RUDD' *Green Grey Homestead* 151 'The Mount' consisted of waste country reserved by a Government of squatters for 'closer settlement' and bordering this reserved area were mighty stations .. lying there within their cheap, pointed sheep fences, like living land sharks.

respite gang. *Hist.* A detachment of convicts whose capital sentences have been commuted to sentences of penal servitude for life.

1834 *N.S.W. Mag.* (Sydney) 220 Proceeded towards the goal [*sic*], headed by the man in the apparel of the doctor's mate, and were taken by the guard as the respite gang. ***c* 1844** T. COOK *Exile's Lamentations* (1978) 47 Another Wild and desperate undertaking was put into execution at the Boat Harbour by Eight of the Respite Gang, who had been respited from Death in Sydney to be worked here for Life in chains.

rest. Imprisonment for one year.

1882 *Sydney Slang Dict.* 9 He's gone in the country for a rest... He's gone to jail for one year. **1945** S.J. BAKER *Austral. Lang.* 141 Here is a brief glossary of jail sentences: *lag*, three months .. *rest*, twelve months [etc.].

restless flycatcher. The black and white bird *Myiagra inquieta* of mainland Aust. and s. New Guinea; RAZOR-GRINDER; SCISSORS-GRINDER. Formerly also **restless thrush.**

1801 J. LATHAM *Gen. Synopsis Birds* Suppl. II. 181 Restless Thr[ush] .. inhabits *New Holland*, said to be a restless species. **1848** J. GOULD *Birds of Aust.* VI. Pl. 40, *Seïsura inquieta.* Restless Flycatcher .. Restless Thrush. **1902** *Emu* II. 12 The Restless Flycatcher .. lives and breeds on the red gum and box flats. **1917** *Bulletin* (Sydney) 17 May 22/2 The scissors-grinder, or restless flycatcher, closely resembles willy wagtail in appearance. **1945** C. BARRETT *Austral. Bird Life* 172 There is no mistaking the notes of the restless flycatcher .. uttered while the bird is hovering. **1962** B.W. LEAKE *Eastern Wheatbelt Wildlife* 90 The black and white fantail or Willie Wagtail and Restless Flycatcher .. have exactly the same colours—jet black and white. The restless flycatcher has practically disappeared. **1984** E. ROLLS *Celebration of Senses* 76 Another busy black and white bird, the Restless Flycatcher, stops grating out his daytime scissors-grinder notes and instead calls musically 'Jury. Jury. Jury.'

retention money. *Cane-cutting.* A sum withheld from earnings: see quots.

1936 J. DEVANNY *Sugar Heaven* 20 The cockies keep sixpence a ton out of our cheque as a guarantee that we'll stay the season... The cockies are supposed to pay this retention money into the bank and we are supposed to draw interest on it but normally they don't pay it in. **1965** J. BECKETT *New-Chum looks at Qld.* 39 Sixpence per ton is retained by the farmer. This is called retention money. It is part of the contract to induce the men to stay on until all the crop is cut... At the finish of 'crushing' the retention money is paid and the men are often engaged on day labour chipping the young cane to keep it free of weeds.

retransport, *v. Hist. trans.* To commit (a convict guilty of a further offence) to a penal settlement, esp. one at which a more severe form of punishment is imposed. Usu. *pass.*

1799 *HRA* (1914) 1st Ser. II. 352 They are well aware of the consequences of detection in their robberys [*sic*], many having been retransported, a sentence they dread more than death. **1819** W.C. WENTWORTH *Statistical, Hist., & Pol. Descr. N.S.W.* 55 These .. are all incorrigible offenders, who have been convicted either before a bench of magistrates, or the Court of Criminal Judicature, and afterwards re-transported to this place. **1831** *Rep. Select Committee Secondary Punishments* (Great Brit. Parl.) 139 Four convicts .. escaped from the colony and were re-transported by the 'Mary'. **1834** 'EMIGRANT' *Party Politics Exposed* 8 Prisoners .. retransported to an Iron Gang .. or to a Penal Settlement. **1837** J. MUDIE *Felonry of N.S.W.* 224 One of his own convicts is re-transported from Sydney to a subsidiary penal settlement. **1839** J. DIXON *Condition & Capabilities Van Diemen's Land* 47 The incorrigible offenders are re-transported to a penal settlement, away from the settled districts, named Port Arthur. **1847** A. MARJORIBANKS *Travels N.S.W.* 109 Norfolk Island contained in 1837 about 1200 convicts, most of whom had been re-transported from New South Wales or Van Diemen's Land. **1862** BACKHOUSE & TYLOR *Life & Labours G.W.*

Walker 53 They were punished . . lastly, by being re-transported, as it were, to a penal settlement.

Hence **retransportation** *n.*

1845 *HRA* (1925) 1st Ser. XXIV. 603 The position of these men essentially differs from that of Expirees from a Settlement for re-transportation, such as Norfolk Island. **1851** H. MELVILLE *Present State Aust.* 158 Convicts, when their probations have terminated, have been returned to the settled districts, there to commit fresh crimes, and to suffer re-transportation.

retread. [Used elsewhere but recorded earliest in Aust.] A retired person (orig. a discharged soldier) who is re-engaged.

1941 *Salt* (Melbourne) 22 Dec. 36 Characteristically the Australians call . . a 1914–1918 soldier enlisted a second time a 'retread'. **1942** *Southerly* i. 15 *Retread (Australian)*, a returned soldier of the Great War who enlists a second time. **1950** 'B. JAMES' *Advancement Spencer Button* 267 There were three 'retreads' among the men. One of these was Mr Shanks, one time Headmaster of a country High School. **1984** *Sydney Morning Herald* 9 July 3/5 During his long service Mr Culgin did work with some retired teachers for brief periods and they were referred to as 'retreads'.

return boomerang: see RETURNING BOOMERANG.

returned, *ppl. a.*

a. *Obs.* Designating a miner who has returned from the goldfields, as **returned digger.**

1852 *Guardian* (Hobart) 24 July 2/2 A Returned Digger. **1853** *Austral. Gold Digger's Monthly Mag.* v. 170 The returned digger wants no town allotment, no suburban acre. **1864** *Sydney Punch* 22 Oct. 176/1 A returned digger named Wilson, from the Southern Gold Fields, began the quarrel. **1904** *Rec. Castlemaine Pioneers* (1972) 193 The soldiers were carousing with returned diggers, who 'shouted' freely.

b. [Used elsewhere but recorded earliest in Aust.: see OEDS 2 b.] Designating a person discharged from the armed services who has returned home from a war.

1902 *Truth* (Sydney) 6 July 5/8 In the present state of Australia, with a dearth of employment owing to the drought, these returned soldiers, who were offered good opportunities in South Africa, are no welcome addition to the country's population. **1903** *Ibid.* 1 Feb. 1/6 A returned New South Wales swaddy of high degree has a tame tiger following him about. **1916** *Ibid.* 16 Apr. 5/2 Returned soldiers who are in the country are to be given free railway passes. **1919** *Smith's Weekly* (Sydney) 15 Mar. 1/3 The wonderful things the Repatriation Department was going to do for returned men. **1920** *Bulletin* (Sydney) 6 May 22/3 The returned Digger was perspiring on a job for the local Road Board in front of the pub, and Bung was standing on the verandah gazing on the exertions of Billjim. **1932** J. TRURAN *Green Mallee* 84 He's a returned soldier, battlin' for a livin' like a whole lot more of 'em. **1946** *Victorian Naturalist* LXII. 219 Many of our students are returned men and we want to give them the best we can. **1956** T. RONAN *Moleskin Midas* 268 His two nephews had drawn the Ambush Creek block in a returned soldiers' ballot. **1967** D. HORNE *Educ. Young Donald* 58 On Anzac Day Dad would put on his three medals and join the other 'returned men'. **1977** F.B. VICKERS *Stranger no Longer* 27 It's an abandoned block. Another returned bloke had it before me. **1981** A.B. FACEY *Fortunate Life* 289 He said that if I wasn't a returned soldier he would have had to fail me but they could not reject a returned man on war injuries.

returning boomerang. See BOOMERANG *n.* 1. Also **return boomerang, returner.**

1901 *Bulletin* (Sydney) 2 Mar. 15/1, I am a pretty fair boomerang-thrower, except with the 'returner'. **1905** *Ibid.* 8 June 16/2 The 'return' boomerang. . . According to authentic records, the earliest European visitors to Australia found the coastal aborigines provided with this weapon. **1928** W. ROBERTSON *Coo-ee Talks* 8 Another toy was the 'returning boomerang'. It was a rather weighty toy-weapon, one arm of which was a little longer and heavier than the other. **1960** D. McLEAN *Roaring Days* 93 There are two types: returning boomerangs and killing boomerangs. The returning boomerang, properly thrown, will fly two or three hundred feet from the thrower, and then, spinning flat like a helicopter plane, will return in a wide arc to the hand of the thrower.

reward claim. *Mining.* A mining claim granted to a miner who discovers payable gold in a new district: see quot. 1944. Also *ellipt.* as **reward.**

1894 W.H. BARKER *Gold Fields W.A.* 32 The White Feather Claim . . is a 'reward' claim, and is about forty miles from Coolgardie. **1896** J.M. PRICE *Land of Gold* 69 The nearest mine is that called after its finder 'Bayley', and is situated on the plot of ground which, in accordance with a custom in these parts, is always given by the Government free to the lucky discoverer of the first lode of the precious metal in a new district. These 'Reward Claims' are quite a feature in all the various mining areas round here. **1931** C.B. SMITH *Austral. Gold Prospectors' Handbk.* 63 A 'reward claim' is the additional area granted as a reward to the discoverer of payable gold. **1944** M.J. O'REILLY *Bowyangs & Boomerangs* 11 A Reward Claim is granted to a prospector for finding new ground carrying payable gold, outside a specified distance from an existent goldfield. **1946** K.S. PRICHARD *Roaring Nineties* 136 We never seen colours on that trek, got wind of Paddy Hannan's reward on our way back, and Gord, did we whip the cat!

ribbed-up, *ppl. a.* Having ample money (for a purpose), 'flush'.

1918 *Home Trail: Souvenir Issue Voyage H.M.T. 'A. 30'* Dec. 5 The others were well 'ribbed-up' too. **1919** C. DREW *Doings of Dave* 99 Here I am ribbed up, with a certainty for the first race. **1933** *Bulletin* (Sydney) 6 Sept. 40/3 And we would have run out of tucker, too, if I hadn't been well ribbed up with coin.

ribbon gum. [See quot. 1902.] Any of several trees of the genus *Eucalyptus* (fam. Myrtaceae) having bark which tends to hang in ribbons as it is shed, esp. *E. viminalis* (see *manna gum* a., MANNA 2). Also **ribbony gum.**

1889 *Proc. Linnean Soc. N.S.W.* IV. 609 *E[ucalyptus] amygdalina* var. *radiata*. 'Ribbon Gum.' Nelligen, Clyde River, N.S.W. **1902** *Ibid.* XXVII. 574 *E[ucalyptus] radiata* . . is known sometimes as Peppermint but often as Ribbony Gum from the appearance of the streamers of decorticating bark as they hang from the upper parts of the trees. **1917** *Bulletin* (Sydney) 6 Sept. 22/1 The ribbon-gums are better known by the name 'manna trees'. **1927** *Ibid.* 21 July 27/3 Old but erroneous is the theory that the sweet exudation of the Monaro (N.S.W.) ribbony-gum is the excreta of locusts. **1963** C. BURGESS *Blue Mountain Gums* 27 Ribbon gum is frequently tall and straight in the damp, cool, mountainous country, but in more open forest and grassland its habit is shorter and spreading.

ribuck, var. RYEBUCK.

Rice: see JACK RICE.

rice. Used *attrib.* in the names of plants having some resemblance to cultivated rice (*Oryza sativa*): **rice flower,** any of many species of the genus *Pimelea* (see PIMELEA); **grass,** any of several plants, esp. *Leersia hexandra* (fam. Poaceae), occurring in or near water in N.S.W. and Qld.

1898 E.E. MORRIS *Austral Eng.* 355 A gardener's name for some of the species [of Pimelea] is **Rice-flower.** **1914** E.E. PESCOTT *Native Flowers Vic.* 107 The Pimeleas . . commonly known by the name of 'rice flowers'. **1956** E. MITCHELL *Black Cockatoos* 207 The alpine rice flowers were pretty, and the mintbush she trained against the rocks in the garden. **1965** *Austral. Encycl.* VII. 118 *Pimelea*, a genus of about 100 species of slender shrubs or under-shrubs. . . They are commonly called 'rice-flowers'—from the granular appearance of the dense white flowerheads in many species. **1849** C. STURT *Narr. Exped. Central Aust.* I. 274 At that time they [*sc.* pigeons] were feeding upon the seed of the **rice grass,** and were scattered about. **1889** J.H. MAIDEN *Useful Native Plants Aust.* 93 *Leersia hexandra* . . 'Rice Grass'. A rough-leaved species, common along the watercourses of Queensland. Stock are remarkably fond of it. **1909** F.M. BAILEY *Comprehensive Catal. Qld. Plants* 612 Rice Grass; often found in shallow, scant water. **1938** C.T. WHITE *Princ. Bot. Qld. Farmers* 206 A distinct type of pasture in coastal Queensland are freshwater swamp pastures of a high grazing value. In these the following grasses are the most important . . Rice Grass [etc.]. **1961** A.M. DUNCAN-KEMP *Our Channel Country* 10 Wild sorghum, rice-grass, and barley grasses thrive there. **1965** *Austral. Encycl.* IV. 370 *Oryza australiensis* (rice-grass) is a perennial rice of the swamps of northern Australia.

richard. [Ellipt. form of *Richard the Third*, rhyming slang for 'bird'; f. theatrical slang *to get the bird* (or *goose*), to be hissed, to be given a bad reception.] In the phr. **to have had the Richard,** to be finished, to be irreparably damaged. See also DICK.

1967 *Kings Cross Whisper* (Sydney) xxxv. 6/1 *Had the Richard*, tired, weary, same as frigged. **1974** *Smoke Signal* (Palm Island) May 2 The D.L.P. were almost put out of business. . . They've had the richard. **1978** M.J. BURTON *Bush Pub* 126 These wishy-washy, ignorant bloody imbeciles wouldn't realise that it's them that's bein' chased; it's not them doin' the chasin' at all. Then when they gits cornered they've had the Richard. **1980** HEPWORTH & HINDLE *Boozing out in Melbourne Pubs* 44 What he didn't know . . was that actually she had shot through to London with another feller. . . He was going to discover at the end of the three months that he'd had the richard.

richea /ˈrɪtʃiə/. [The plant genus *Richea* was named by British botanist Robert Brown (*Prodr. Fl. Nov. Holl.* (1810) 555) after French naturalist Claude *Riche* (1762–1797) of the Bruny D'Entrecasteaux expedition.] A shrub or tree of the chiefly Tas. genus *Richea* (fam. Epacridaceae).

1850 *Papers & Proc. R. Soc. Van Diemen's Land* (1851) 278 The graceful palm-like Richea (*Richea pandanifolia*), found in the dense forests between Lake St. Clair and Macquarie Harbour, where it attains the height of 40 to 50 feet in sheltered positions. **1892** M. NORTH *Recoll. Happy Life* II. 171 The pretty, pandanus-looking plant they call grass-trees or richea, really a sort of heath. **1933** C.W. PECK *Austral. Legends* (ed. 2) 228 The jet-black king had chosen a burnt patch on the side of a Richea . . his colour and that of the grass-tree making him almost invisible. **1942** C. BARRETT *Austral. Wild Flower Bk.* 158 Richeas, decorative plants belonging to the Australian heath family (*Epacridaceae*), grow in the sub-alpine zone, and are popularly known as 'grass-trees'. **1980** G.R. COCHRANE *Flowers & Plants Vic. & Tas.* (rev. ed.) 160 A number of the smaller Richeas . . favour a damp windy site.

ride, *v. trans.* To traverse (the line of a boundary, an area occupied by stock, etc.) on horseback in order to make an inspection or carry out maintenance.

1914 'B. CABLE' *By Blow & Kiss* 173 Up to the Ridge from the back paddocks, where now there were no sheep to ride boundary on. **1923** J. BOWES *Jackaroos* 110 Smith and Billy were to remain and ride boundary on the lower part of the water-course. **1935** R.B. PLOWMAN *Boundary Rider* 188 Part of Joe's duties was to 'ride the fences' each week. Each boundary-rider has so many paddocks to look after. **1938** A. UPFIELD *Bone is Pointed* (1966) 26 Left to ride the fences yesterday morning. **1959** W.E. HARNEY *Tales from Aborigines* 92 His job as a cattleman was to leave the station homestead each day and 'ride the tracks'—a bush term that meant he would saddle his horse each morning and ride in a wide arc of many miles around the open range country to see that no cattle-tracks led away from the main herd. **1962** T. RONAN *Deep of Sky* 176 His first job was to ride the run, no easy task, as it was in the wet and there were ten thousand square miles of it to inspect. **1967** R. HAWKER *Emu in Fowl Pen* 52 'You'll have to do your bit of work. . . We don't keep horses to play with here.' 'She can fetch the mail.' . . 'And ride paddocks.'

riders, *pl.* [Transf. use of *riders* additional set of timbers used to strengthen the frame of a ship.] Wooden poles used to hold a bark roof in place: see quot. 1945.

1872 G.S. BADEN-POWELL *New Homes for Old Country* 162 The hut is of oblong shape, slab walls, and bark roof, with heavy wooden framework of 'riders', to keep the bark from being blown away. **1905** *Bulletin* (Sydney) 2 Mar. 17/1 The logs which 'anchor' the roof—known as 'riders' and 'jockeys'. The first-named are perpendicular, in pairs; and the ends overlapping the ridge are loosely held together with wooden pins, to allow their spread to conform to the roof-angle and lie close to the bark when the weight of the jockey comes on their loose ends—those nearest the eaves. **1911** E.S. SORENSON *Life in Austral. Backblocks* 26 It was roofed with stringybark, the latter being hung with greenhide and held down with poles ('riders' and 'jockeys') pegged together. **1945** S.J. BAKER *Austral. Lang.* 78 *Riders* are slabs or logs running from the ridge of the roof to the eaves.

ridge, *a.* [Fig. use of *ridge* gold, gold coin: see OED(S *sb.*[2]] All right; genuine; 'dinkum' (see DINKUM *a.* 1.).

1938 E. PARTRIDGE *Dict. Slang & Unconventional Eng.* (ed. 2) 1026 *Ridge*, adj., good; valuable: Australian. **1953** K. TENNANT *Joyful Condemned* 4 'It's ridge, Hec,' she assured him. 'He won't come here again.' **1966** D. NILAND *Pairs & Loners* 133 That hare swerves and doubles... I inspected the animal to see if it had a key and clockwork bowels, but it was ridge all right. **1971** D. IRELAND *Unknown Industr. Prisoner* 130, I convinced her the whole thing was ridge! **1978** D. STUART *Wedgetail View* 166 It seems we're off to Matta any day now. It's ridge; he reckons it's an open secret. **1978** H.C. BAKER *I was Listening* 166 Within seventy miles we heard (and that was supposed to be 'ridge'—direct from the ship's officers).

ridgey-dite. [After RIDGY-DIDGE.] Rhyming slang for 'all right'.

1953 K. TENNANT *Joyful Condemned* 295 He'd tell you himself I'm ridgey-dite. I worked for him.

ridgy-didge, *a.* Also **ridgey-(the-)didge, ridgie-didge, ridgy-dig.** [Elaboration of 'ridgy', f. RIDGE + *-y.*] RIDGE.

1953 S.J. BAKER *Aust. Speaks* 102 *Ridgy-didge* or *ridgy-dig* . . , honest, genuine, okay. **1963** L. GLASSOP *Rats in New Guinea* 153 'It's ridgie-didge,' said Eddie. 'Spit me death.' **1965** E. LAMBERT *Long White Night* 64 'You've got an address here? Square dinks?' 'Ridgy didge.' **1967** *Kings Cross Whisper* (Sydney) xxxii. 6/3 The ridgey didge Australian dictionary. **1968** S. GORE *Holy Smoke* 65 'Yes. Ridgey-the-didge, mate,' says Jesus. **1977** W. MOORE *Just to Myself* 115 Ridgy-didge. You wouldn't either. **1983** B. DAWE *Over here, Harv!* 101 'Ridgie-didge!' I said. 'We went to two-up school together.' **1986** *Sydney Morning Herald* 1 Feb. 43/2 The old-timers insist that Kalgoorlie two-up is 'the real game' and that ridgie-didge players will skirt the casino ring.

rifle-bird. [See quot. 1898.] Any of three species of bird of the genus *Ptiloris* of e. Aust., the mature male having velvety black plumage with metallic patches. Also with distinguishing epithet, as **paradise, Victoria** (see under first element). Formerly also **rifleman.**

1827 P. CUNNINGHAM *Two Yrs. in N.S.W.* I. 325 The *regent* and *rifle-bird* outvie all I have seen from any part of the world, in the chaste splendour of their plumage. **1833** *N.S.W. Mag.* (Sydney) 12 In the long recesses of their thick and trackless scrubs . . the call of the 'khagghak', or rifleman, would be most likely heard. **1837** *Colonist* (Sydney) 350/4 The Rifle Bird (*Ptiloris paradiseus*) is nearly the size of a jay, its bill long and sickle shaped, and colour of a rich dark greenlike velvet. **1852** J. MACGILLIVRAY *Narr. Voyage H.M.S. Rattlesnake* I. 90 A new and splendid rifle-bird, which Mr Gould has since . . named *Ptiloris Victoriae.* **1873** 'LADY IN AUST.' *Memories Past* 20 There are also some other very rare birds to be found in that region [*sc.* Port Macquarie, N.S.W.]; the 'regent bird', and the 'rifleman'. **1881** E. DAVIES *Story Earnest Life* 380 The rifle bird is the most gorgeous of all the birds of Australia. **1898** E.E. MORRIS *Austral Eng.* 387 Rifle-bird... The male is of a general velvety black, something like the uniform of the Rifle Brigade. This peculiarity, no doubt, gave the bird its name, but, on the other hand, settlers and local naturalists sometimes ascribe the name to the resemblance they hear in the bird's cry to the noise of a rifle being fired and its bullet striking the target. **1915** *Bulletin* (Sydney) 4 Mar. 14/4 There is also the voice of the wit-e-chu and the sharp, bursting noise of the whipbird . . the creaky whistle of the drongo . . and the soft, cheery hail of the rifle bird. **1941** C. BARRETT *Aust.* 85 One morning . . they took me to a rifle-bird's territory. **1956** A.C.C. LOCK *Tropical Tapestry* 234 We did see something worth while, a magnificent rifle bird, cousin of the New Guinea bird of paradise. It flashed from out of the jungle, just in front of us, and for two or three seconds we were witness to its brilliantly coloured plumage in flight.

rifle-fish. [See quot. 1926.] A fish of the fam. Toxotidae, occurring in fresh water and estuaries of n. Aust. and elsewhere in the tropics.

1906 D.G. STEAD *Fishes of Aust.* 95 One species of this family is found on the coast of Queensland, where it is known by the name of Rifle-Fish (*Toxotes jaculator*). **1926** J. MCLAREN *My Crowded Solitude* 45 On the shore-reef he showed me a rifle-fish—so called because of its habit of shooting with a drop of water insects which flew close to the water. **1935** F. BIRTLES *Battle Fronts Outback* 89 Rifle-fish . . were about ten inches long, brown on the back, with strips in black and silver underneath. **1973** V. SERVENTY *Desert Walkabout* 81 These archer or rifle fish have a central hole left when the mouth closes. The gills can be compressed and this sends a jet of water along a groove in the palate out of the hole, into the air to distances of four or five feet.

right, *n.* Abbrev. of *miner's right*, see MINER *n.*[2]

1870 J.O. TUCKER *Mute* 42 But who are these to whom the digger yields Obedience prompt, when questioned for his 'right'?

right, *a.*

1. In the phr. **all right.** [Spec. use of *all right* satisfactory, acceptable: see OED(S *right, a.* 15 c. and 8 e.]

a. *Obs.* In morally dubious contexts: (of a person) trustworthy, safe, 'on side'; (of a situation) 'all clear'.

1841 Register of Flash Men 11 This man was apprehended . . by Inspector Ryan... A person known to Ryan came up at the time saying, This man is all right, he has two horses at stables. **1843** *Sydney Morning Herald* 21 Nov. 2/4 Wright told Tracey that he knew the animals well, that they were his master's . . property, and were all *right.* **1847** A. HARRIS *Settlers & Convicts* (1953) 28 On my mate telling them, with reference to me, that it was 'all right', the cards were brought to light again, and the game went on. **1854** C.A. CORBYN *Sydney Revels* 47 Fancying that it was 'all right', he picked up half a chest of tea from the door and wheeled it off. **1858** C.R. THATCHER *Colonial Songster* (rev. ed.) 30 Your attention I beg to invite, And I'll prove it quite plain by my song, That when folks exclaim, 'It's all right', Nine times out of ten it's all wrong. **1873** W. THOMSON-GREGG *Desperate Character* II. 57 'What did he mean by asking if it was 'all right'?' demanded Charley of his companion, as they walked along. 'Mean? just a façon de parler, Master Woodward, what else? He's some new chum or other, and thinks to pass himself off for an old hand by using a few colonial slang expressions, out of their ordinary connection.' **1875** A. PYNE *Reminisc. Colonial Life* 287 Seeing (to use a colonial phrase) I was 'all right', he cried out.

b. In neutral contexts, often with deliberate understatement: up to standard.

1898 *Bulletin* (Sydney) 4 June (Red Page), On the N.S.W. plains, say from Liverpool to Bourke, the word 'alright' is used by bushmen as an adjective; and it means a lot, too. **1908** C.H.S. MATTHEWS *Parson in Austral. Bush* 85 The miners are, most of them, full of energy and grit, ready to do anything for the parson, if once they believe him to be, in their own phrase, 'all right' or 'a white man'. **1917** A.B. PATERSON *Saltbush Bill* 34 An all-right tart with ginger 'air, and freckles on 'er nose. **1918** *Kia Ora Coo-ee* Oct. 5/2 Later I was informed that I had missed a bit of 'all right duff'.

2. [Spec. use of *right* in good health and spirits: see OED(S 13 b. Now chiefly Austral. and N.Z.] Of a person: in good shape, 'all right'.

1864 *Bell's Life in Sydney* 28 May 3/2 So people imagined, and well they might, That, like Croesus of old, our hero was 'right' In the matter of 'tin'; for money still sends, To those who possess it, a number of friends. **1869** *Lictor* (Sydney) 16 Dec. 347 My oath! I'm as right as a first-rate quondong. **1898** *Bulletin* (Sydney) 21 May 32/4 And the men who fight in the Dry Country grim battles by day, by night, Will believe in me, and will stand by me, and will say to the world, 'He's right.' **1922** A. WRIGHT *Colt from Country* 114 But I'm right mate. I ain't shikkered, only on the verge, that's all. Another pint, as you say, and it'd be me f'r th' deadhouse. **1928** —— *Good Recovery* 137 'You're havin' er trot of 'outs', all right', agreed Doods cheerfully, 'but you'll be right when you marry th' bookmaker's daughter, won't y'?' **1944** *Coast to Coast 1943* 166 'Think you'll be all right? Anything you want?' 'I'll be right,' Mac said. **1957** D. NILAND *Call me when Cross turns Over* 67 'You had a bite?' 'I'm right, thanks.' **1970** J.M. COUPER *Thundering Good Today* 56 You'll be right, young un. Right as Bob Menzies, you will, an' it's far too right for me. **1974** *Bulletin* (Sydney) 14 Dec. 27/2 'You right?' It is—for the benefit of new settlers—an abbreviation of 'Are you all right?' which, in turn, is a shorter way of asking: 'Are you, in the matter of looking for, selecting and purchasing something . . or could I do something to help you . . ? Could I . . even sell you something?' **1985** *Ibid.* 16 July 61/3 Cedric Felspar . . was lost in thought in . . David Jones . . when a salesgirl crept upon him from behind and whined: 'You right?'

3. [Used elsewhere but recorded earliest in Aust.: see OEDS *right, a.* 14 c. and *too, adv.* 5 h.] In the phr. **too right,** an expression of agreement or approval.

1919 W.H. DOWNING *Digger Dialects* 51 *Two eyes right* or *too right*, certainly. **1921** F. GROSE *Rough Y.M. Bloke* 30 Princess Patricia asked them if they were Australians. 'Too right!' they replied, still sitting, and the Princess standing meekly in front of them. **1928** A. WRIGHT *Good Recovery* 36 'You thrashed him?' queried Trilet. 'Too right, I did.' **1942** *Bulletin* (Sydney) 21 Jan. 12/3 'You must've made a welter of it', his parent observed, 'the way she sang out.' 'Too right,' replied Jim. 'That's because I kept the two deeners.' **1947** M. RAYMOND *Smiley gets Gun* 19 'Smiley, did you pinch Jean?' 'Too right, teacher. I pinched 'er bum.' **1957** R.S. PORTEOUS *Brigalow* 96 'That's the lot... What about a beer?' Mick and Steve said, 'Too right!' and licked their lips in anticipation. **1972** *Bulletin* (Sydney) 12 Aug. 7/2 'Does your organisation oppose the discarding of fine old idioms like these?' 'Too right we do,' Dr Bottler replied. **1980** *Westerly* i. 8 'Jacky is it?' 'Too right, and a mate,' said Jacky.

4. a. In the phr. **she'll be right,** 'all will be well': see quots. 1962 and 1967. Also as *adj. phr.*, designating an attitude of unreasoning optimism (see quot. 1971).

1947 G. CASEY *Wits are Out* 154 'I only hope Kitty'll be willing to forget it, too.' 'She'll be right,' Jerry promised. 'I'll square her off, don't you worry.' **1954** *Bulletin* (Sydney) 25 Aug. 12/2 An independent man will call on the feminine pronoun in politely refusing proffered assistance: 'She'll be right, thanks, mate.' **1962** J. MACKENZIE *Austral. Paradox* 154 So long as individuals are not obviously adversely affected, Australians show little concern about matters of principle. 'She'll be right' is a well used and familiar phrase revealing an attitude which implies: 'Why bother, why fuss; it will all turn out right in the end.' **1967** D. HORNE *Southern Exposure* 22 *'She'll be right.'* Their combination of high hope and deep doubt can make Australians devastatingly cool-headed and wry-witted. **1971** *Bulletin* (Sydney) 10 July 21/1 With social consciences progressively insulated by more and more creature comforts and with a sense of 'she'll be right' isolationism, the yarn and the shrug were seeming to become national characteristics. **1973** H. WILLIAMS *My Love* 104 With some blokes the old she'll-be-right-mate idea gets the upper hand and they throw the sandpaper away and start slapping the paint on. **1976** *Bulletin* (Sydney) 7 Aug. 63/2 Well, Dad, that's the last hundred acres. Reckon a good shower of rain and some decent weather and she'll be right. **1977** W. MOORE *Just to Myself* 85 She'll be right. I'll just prop it up again with a couple of four-by-twos. No sweat. **1981** D. STUART *I think I'll Live* 196 She'll be right, mate. I can see smoke ahead, an' a bit of open country. Might be a camp, an' maybe we'll get a feed; maybe. **1983** *Austral.* (Sydney) 9 Aug. 9 The 'she'll be right' attitude is about to get its worst-yet jolt.

b. In the phr. **she's right,** 'all is in order'.

1958 F.B. VICKERS *Though Poppies Grow* 76 'You're free until we take a firm order. But bring the permit with you.' 'She's right mate. Thanks a lot.' **1959** D. NILAND *Gold in Streets* 208 'Chris, can you lend me a tenner?' Chris said: 'Sure, Danno; she's right.' **1963** R. STOW *Tourmaline* 83 'Stay the night with us?' 'Ah, she's right,' Dave said. 'Thanks all the same.' **1977** B. SCOTT *My Uncle Arch* 80 'Need a hand, 'Arry?' Good bloke, Mick. 'She's right, Mick!' **1978** D. STUART *Wedgetail View* 21 'What d' y' reckon, should I drop back a bit an' put up a smoke, let them know where we are?' 'No, she's right, Col. Davey's got one going.'

righteous, *a.* Jocular alteration of 'riotous (behaviour)'.

1891 *Truth* (Sydney) 8 Feb. 6/5 Abe Willis was lumbered and fined 10s. and costs for being 'righteous' in Auckland Street. **1919** V. MARSHALL *World of Living*

Dead 71 The grisly 'toe-ragger', who is doing a 'sleep' of three months for 'righteous' . . will tell him of the best road to take if it comes to 'hoofin' it'.

ring, *n.*[1] [Abbrev. of (orig.) U.S. *ringer* an exact counterpart: see OEDS *ringer, sb.*[2] 5 and *ring, sb.*[2] 3 d.] In the phr. **the dead ring for** (or **of**), the exact likeness of, the 'spitting image' of.

1899 J. Bradshaw *Quirindi Bank Robbery* 37 You are the dead ring for the veiled prophet himself. **1917** T.J. Briggs *Life & Experiences Successful W. Austral.* 91 He was, according to reports, the dead ring for the notorious outlaw. **1924** H.E. Riemann *Nor'-West o' West* 56 A man the dead-ring of this lucky embezzler was here a month ago. **1945** I.L. Idriess *Horrie Wog-Dog* 50 It appeared that the mascot they had smuggled aboard was the 'dead ring' of Horrie, apparently the same breed. **1951** E. Hill *Territory* 318 Now you're the dead ring o' that girl, and you speak the same.

ring, *n.*[2] *Two-up.* [Spec. use of *ring* (enclosed) circular space within which a sport or performance takes place.]

1. The site of a two-up game; the area within which the coins are tossed and must fall; the assembly of players; the game itself. Also **two-up ring.**

1896 [see *ring-keeper*]. **1913** *Bulletin* (Sydney) 30 Jan. 15/2 Their joint capital ran to a blanket apiece and two spins in the two-up ring. **1919** R.T. Wyatt *Digger on 'Durham'* 43 Notice the 'two-up' ring in the centre of the queue. Where two or three diggers are gathered together there you will find a 'two-up' school. **1920** *Huon Times* (Franklin) 21 May 5/2 The gamblers had left but little money on the ground as they took to their heels, but near the 'ring' the constable found a lunch bag. **1925** A. Wright *Boy from Bullarah* 18 From all around the ring head backers rose to gather in their winnings, and stake again on the next spin. **1941** D. O'Callaghan *Long Life Reminisc.* 5 He experiences . . the sly-grog shops and the two-up and Murrumbidgee rings. **1946** *Austral. New Writing* 36 The ring or gutz now needs a pound, for the original ten bob is doubled. **1950** K.S. Prichard *Winged Seeds* 63 What set the whole town agog . . was their attempt to visit the 'swy': the famous two-up ring on a sand hill near the old Rising Sun Inn. **1964** B. Wannan *Fair Go, Spinner* 192 The nit-keepers must have been dozing, for a party of policemen managed to get fairly close to the large ring behind the pub where the devotees were watching the rites of this strange religion of the two coins. **1967** F. Hardy *Billy Borker yarns Again* 3 The gamblers sit around the square (which is called a ring).

2. Special Comb. **ring-keeper,** (formerly **-master**), the person in charge of a two-up game.

1896 *Worker* (Sydney) 4 July 4/1 Well, Charlie is 'ring-master' (I believe that's the correct title, the 'two-up' ain't a pet vice of mine) of the Boulder 'school'. **1911** A. Wright *Gambler's Gold* (1923) 57 Heaps of silver and gold at the ringkeeper's feet. **1931** O. Walters *Shrapnel Green* 26, I was bettin' a dollar he'd tail them. . . Proved I was showin' good judgement when the ring-keeper said, 'Nicks are right!' **1941** D. O'Callaghan *Long Life Reminisc.* 51 The ringkeeper was set for all the money he wanted. **1946** *Austral. New Writing* 36 The ring-keeper inspects the pennies on the kip. **1953** T.A.G. Hungerford *Riverslake* 129 The ring-keeper began to have trouble in getting the stake covered. The tail-betters had folded. **1967** F. Hardy *Billy Borker yarns Again* 3 A ringkeeper is the bloke who stands in the square with a torch. He puts the two pennies on their kip and checks that they are turned tail upward, then calls the result after the spinner has thrown the pennies up: heads, tails or two ones. **1977** R. Beilby *Gunner* 180 A two-up game proceeded intermittently, the ring-keeper's calls pealing faintly. . . 'Set in the centre! Up 'n' do 'm, spinner!'

ring, *n.*[3] [f. Ring *v.*[2]] A milling mob of restless cattle.

1890 'R. Boldrewood' *Colonial Reformer* II. 111 If the 'ring' crowds too near the fence, the men on that side would walk along the middle rail. **1922** 'J. Bushman' *In Musgrave Ranges* 55 Others followed till the cattle were going round and round like water in a whirlpool. What cattlemen most fear had happened: a ring. **1934** J. Kirwan *Empty Land* 202 Others will follow, forming a ring of cattle swimming round and round. . . In 1904 no fewer than 300 cattle were drowned in crossing the Georgina, the result of their 'ringing' in midstream whilst crossing.

ring, *v.*[1] [Spec. use of *ring* to deprive (a tree) of a ring of bark: see OED *v.*[1] 9 b.] *trans.* Ring-bark *v.* 1. Also *absol.*

1846 J.L. Stokes *Discoveries in Aust.* I. 315 Ringing the trees; that is to say, they cut off a large circular band of bark, which destroying the trees, renders them easier to be felled. **1852** Mrs C. Meredith *My Home in Tas.* II. 3 Several very large dead gum-trees, which had been 'ringed' and left to perish. **1859** W. Burrows *Adventures Mounted Trooper* 42 The next thing is to 'ring it', as it is technically called; that is, to cut off a strip of bark all round the tree for about a foot in depth. **1892** E.H. Hallack *Our Townships, Farms, & Homesteads* 16 The gumtrees have been cleared or rung. **1905** *Steele Rudd's Mag.* (Brisbane) July 695 Gangs of Chinamen ring for sixpence in parts of West Queensland. **1912** *Bulletin* (Sydney) 18 Jan. 14/2, I took up a selection (1280 acres), fenced it myself, and 'rung' 200 acres. **1935** *Ibid.* 30 Oct. 21/3 Chinese ringbarkers . . rang most of the box flats along the Murray (N.S.W.). **1942** *Ibid.* 21 Jan. 12/2, I gave old Moonji the job of ringbarking the stallion paddock. Returning late one afternoon, I could see from the homestead verandah with the glasses that the trees were well rung. **1979** K. Garvey *Absolutely Austral.* 72 In ridgy country farther out, where timber had been rung, In every stump and log you'd find big heaps of possum dung.

ring, *v.*[2]

a. *intr.* Of livestock, esp. cattle: to keep moving restlessly round and round in a mass, to mill. Also *fig.*

1868 [see Ringing 2]. **1876** *Austral. Town & Country Jrnl.* (Sydney) 16 Dec. 982/2 A desultory entry into the receiving yard then takes place. . . The 'ragers' observing this moment keep wildly and excitedly 'ringing', like a first-class Maëlstrom. **1878** 'Ironbark' *Southerly Busters* 60 The cattle 'ring' and strive again To force a passage to the plain. **1884** 'R. Boldrewood' *Old Melbourne Memories* 20 The cattle were uneasy, and 'ringed' all night. **1895** G. Ranken *Windabyne* 85 Terror seemed to affect all the cattle in the same way. As the fire approached on different sides, they began ringing, and as they pressed and crushed each other, the outside beasts were pushed from these mounds. **1902** *Bulletin* (Sydney) 22 Mar. 14/4 The sheep 'rung' round and round past the closed gate. **1921** G.A. Bell *Under Brigalows* 53 The cattle started 'ringing', and could not be persuaded to enter the rails for some time. **1934** C. Sayce *Comboman* 73 If the beggars start to ring in the creek, there'll be hell to pay. **1938** F. Blakeley *Hard Liberty* 65 Although we were getting opal we soon found ourselves 'ringing', as miners term it when restlessness begins. **1942** H.H. Peck *Mem. of Stockman* 167 Simpson mistook the crossing and, putting the cattle in, they started to ring badly. He forced his horse in to break the ring, and failing, was drowned. **1960** R.S. Porteous *Cattleman* 17 Head them off and turn them back until you had the mob ringing, churning round and round in a bewildered, bellowing mass. **1975** L.A. Pockley *Handbk. for Jackeroos* 65 Use may be made of the natural tendency of sheep particularly young sheep, to 'ring' or circle around the mob.

b. *trans.* To turn (a mob, esp. of cattle) back on itself; to cause (a mob) to mill.

1907 *Bulletin* (Sydney) 11 Apr. 15/3, I collared the spare night-horse and lit out to the old man's assistance. He had the lead blocked on the edge of the scrub when I came up, and was ringing 'em finely. **1909** *Ibid.* 28 Oct. 13/3 It's not always easy to steady a big mob and make them feed again. . . Of course, they *can* be stopped. They can be 'rung' and worried into a confused mass; but that's bad droving. **1914** C.H.S. Matthews *Bill* 99 When the mob begins to break it is his work to get near the leaders and turn them, or, as we call it, 'ring' them. **1930** A.E. Yarra *Vanishing Horsemen* 169 The cattle . . never really got a good gallop and he had been able to 'ring' them in the first mile or two. **1935** A. Francis *Then & Now* 68 All the men . . had been . . 'ringing' the cattle—that is, making the outside beasts move slowly round and round, keeping the bull as nearly as possible in the centre so as not to arouse his suspicions. **1949** *Bulletin* (Sydney) 26 Jan. 15/3 'Rings' the cattle (*i.e.*, turns the leaders back into the mob) when he is mustering. **1957** R.S. Porteous *Brigalow* 38 Albert . . quite often turning the entire mob about-face. At other times he achieved the highly undesirable effect of ringing them and we would find ourselves with a milling, bewildered herd.

c. *intr.* To work with cattle as a drover, musterer, etc. Also *trans.*, to drive (a mob), and as *vbl. n.*

1949 *Bulletin* (Sydney) 26 Jan. 15/3 Now, especially in North Queensland and the Territory . . 'How do you like 'ringing' for a job?' 'I was yarning with a mob of 'ringers' from the Gulf', are common expressions. **1958** *Ibid.* 26 Mar. 19/1 Jacky, tired of ringing in the Territory, pulled-out and went into Cloncurry and took a job on a station. **1961** *Ibid.* 7 Oct. 29/1 Our ringer had come up from Pandy Pandy, over the South Australian border, after breaking down a cheque. But for a tube of tooth paste, he'd be ringing the ghost herds in the sky. **1976** C.D. Mills *Hobble Chains & Greenhide* 26 When I was ringing on the road, we were up at about four o'clock, set off with the bullocks at daylight, and fed them as we tailed them along the outside of the track.

ring, *v.*[3] [Back-formation f. Ringer *n.*[1] 2 a.] *trans.* To beat (one's fellow shearers) by shearing the most sheep in a given period. Also *transf.* (see quots. 1926 and 1967). Usu. with 'shed' as obj.

1894 *Bulletin* (Sydney) 13 Jan. 7/3 Legge got the run, Fogg cleared, Bell 'rung' the shed, and Warte turned out to be a 'scab'. **1894** *Ibid.* 10 Feb. 20/3 The man that rang the Tubbo shed is not the ringer here. That stripling from the Cooma side can teach him how to shear. **1895** A.B. Paterson *Man from Snowy River* 88 They had rung the sheds of the east and west, Had beaten the cracks of the Walgett side. **1899** *Western Champion* (Barcaldine) 15 Aug. 5/1 George Eyre 'rung' the shed, with an average tally of 175 sheep. **1904** *Shearer* (Sydney) 19 Nov. 4/2, I would advise . . old H.J.G. to have a cut at my tally of 194 wethers in seven hours and fifteen minutes, before he 'skites' about 'ringing' sheds. **1914** C.H.S. Matthews *Bill* 247, I have been trying to ring the shed (i.e. shear a larger number of sheep than any other shearer). **1926** *Bulletin* (Sydney) 11 Feb. 24/1 What cares the cook if it don't fine up? It's he who'll ring the shed. **1930** *Ibid.* 8 Oct. 20/4 The bloke who rings the board ain't always the fastest shearer in the shed. **1940** *Digger Yarns: Cream of 'Aussiosities'*, One boaster was describing how he 'rung' the shed in Nor' Westralia. **1964** E. Lane *Our Uncle Charlie* 186 When he was well into his seventies he still tried to ring each shed, with the result that . . he became so rough and ready that the sheep suffered. **1967** *Telegraph* (Brisbane) 25 Mar. 2/5 To 'ring the shed' a shearer's cook has to earn more money than the top shearer. **1978** J. Dingwall *Sunday too far Away* 37 He's an impossible bugger that Teddy. First shed he's ever rung in his life and now he's walking around like his shit don't stink.

ring, *v.*[4] In the phr. **to ring the tin (on),** to summon a meeting (of workers) to consider a specific (industrial) matter; to refuse to communicate with a foreman, etc. Also as **ring the tin ruling.**

1958 M.D. Berrington *Stones of Fire* 93, I had often heard the expression used jokingly, 'we ought to ring the tin on him', and, on inquiry, had heard all about this outback custom so seldom practised nowadays—a custom that was common in remote places when transport was slow and it took days to contact the police. Except in major offences, the residents administered their own law and order. The entire population was called together to decide what course of action must be taken. They were summoned by 'ringing the tin'. **1972** *Sydney Morning Herald* 24 Feb. 12/1 A recent meeting of about 70 men who work under the foreman, decided to 'ring the tin' because they had no confidence in him. According to union officials 'ring the tin' ruling means that the foreman will not be spoken to by WIU men who work under him. **1977** B. Fuller *Nullarbor Lifelines* 73 It was no soothing bell, but a kerosene tin. . . If any officer or ganger had fallen from grace in Union eyes he knew that that evening the tin would be 'rung on him'. **1978** B. Kennedy *Silver, Sin, & Sixpenny Ale* 146 The unions could declare a shop or business out of bounds to unionists and their families or under a 'black-ban'. An individual, usually a 'scab', was 'blackballed' or ostracized. To inflict a similar fate on a shift boss was to 'ring the tin'.

ring-bark, *v.* [f. Ring *v.*[1]]

1. *trans.* To kill (a tree) by cutting a ring of bark

from around the trunk; to prepare (land, scrub, etc.) for clearing in this way. Also *absol.*, and as *vbl. n.* and *ppl. a.*

1866 *Australasian* (Melbourne) 30 June 409/5 Will you, or some of your practical readers, kindly inform me if what is called 'ring-barking', or the cutting and removal of a piece of bark from the indigenous trees, can be carried on successfully throughout the year, with a view to kill the trees? **1874** *Illustr. Sydney News* 19 Dec. 14/3 The prisoners account for the marks upon their clothes and the axe-handle by saying that the stains are the juice of the apple-tree .. and that they were obtained when ringbarking some trees. **1885** P.R. MEGGY *From Sydney to Silverton* 55 The box scrub along the river frontage is ringbarked for miles, in order to clear the land. **1886** D.M. GANE *N.S.W. & Vic.* 192 The Government has sanctioned the practice of ring-barking to such an extent that the country for miles round appears nothing but a barren waste. **1886** *Proc. Linnean Soc. N.S.W.* I. 530 Many of the large Eucalypts on the farm have been 'ringbarked' for some years. **1892** *Truth* (Sydney) 1 May 1/7 It is well known that no white man can take a job ring-barking: the Chinese have a monopoly. . . A 'boss' Chinaman takes a contract to ring-bark at sixpence an acre. **1912** *Cwlth. of Aust. for Farmers* (Dept. External Affairs) 30 Land that has been ringbarked for many years can be cleared for £1 or less per acre in the wheat belt. **1929** P.R. STEPHENSEN *Bushwhackers* 12 Hundreds of thousands of great trees were ring-barked, the sap cut off in its channel from the roots to the lofty tops. **1942** E. ANDERSON *Squatter's Luck* 12 Ring-barked belars and brigalows stood three dry years at attention. **1957** R.S. PORTEOUS *Brigalow* 20 Even the ring-barking had been carried out with discretion. . . Odd patches of green timber had been left to form shady camps for cattle. **1965** R.H. CONQUEST *Horses in Kitchen* 87 The local doctor had to go ring-barking in the brigalow belts to make ends meet. **1982** R. HALL *Just Relations* 111 The hillsides of forest trees are ringbarked to clear the land for pasture, tree by tree the ringbarking work goes forward.

2. *transf.* and *fig.*

1899 *Western Champion* (Barcaldine) 1 Mar. 3/3 'Oh no, dash it all, don't go and spoil a cove for riding,' protested the lively young man from outback; 'just you ringbark it.' **1903** *Advocate* (Burnie) 13 Nov. 3/4 He [*sc.* King O'Malley] denied ever having made use of the words 'ring-barking the cockies'. **1940** 'K. BRUCE' *Digger Tourists* 113 Insect powder! . . Of course I tried it, and all it did was to make 'em so angry that they tried to ring-bark me round the legs. **1960** J. WALKER *No Sunlight Singing* 25 He hit so hard we both come down and that damned chain ringbarked my leg. **1967** C.W. WILLIAMS *Yellow, Green & Red* 215 We propounded at the time the previous Tory Government of Queensland, the notorious Moore Government, had 'ringbarked' the Court that had been established by a Labor Government. **1974** W.G. HOWCROFT *Sand in Stew* 7 He went on to declare that while the operation in itself had been more or less successful, it had left him with a permanent headache, acute dizziness and had brought about his early baldness. 'How could an operation on your knees do all that?' I ventured. 'Well', he explained, wiping his nose on his shirt-sleeve, 'that there operation, d' ya see, it kinda ringbarked me!' **1974** *Forum* vii. 37 Actually the ring-barking was the first part of a ceremonial. . . They would circumcise him roughly with a sharpened stone. **1981** Q. WILD *Honey Wind* 107 All that pioneering has been cordoned off in suburbia, ringbarked with picket fences.

Hence **ring-bark** *n.*, a tree which has been ringbarked.

1951 G. FARWELL *Outside Track* 52 Reckless early settlement, particularly in western New South Wales, bequeathed us a landscape whose ghostly ringbarks symbolize not only erosion and declining land values but poverty of the imagination.

ring-barker. One engaged in ring-barking trees.

1886 D.M. GANE *N.S.W. & Vic.* 191 The country has been devastated far and wide by the ring-barker, a person who cuts off a circle of bark round the tree, the consequence being that in a very short time the leaves fall, and the tree, lacking sustenance, rots and tumbles to the ground. **1901** *Bulletin* (Sydney) 12 Jan. 14/1 Was camped in the bush on Queensland border lately, cooking for ring-barkers. **1911** 'S. RUDD' *Bk. of Dan* 42, I sent one in advising ringbarkers to soak their axes in bluestone. **1928** *Bulletin* (Sydney) 26 Dec. 20/2 While working in a ring-barkers' camp Yabbering Billy was accused of stealing half a bottle of rum. **1944** *Ibid.* 5 July 12/3 Pepperina-trees .. in s.-w. Queensland can easily be kept in check with the ringbarker's axe or poison. **1965** D. MARTIN *Hero of Too* 6 Deer in the wooded patches which the ring-barker's axe has not yet transformed into timber cemeteries. **1972** *Bulletin* (Sydney) 11 Nov. 61/2 One job that gave me great pride, if only from an etymological point of view, was that of ring-barker, sucker-basher.

ring-coachman. THUNDER-BIRD.

1931 J. DEVANEY *Earth Kindred* 14 The little ring-coachman crackt his whip. **1944** L. WELSH *Kookaburra* 10 One of the earliest of dawn-singers is the Rufous-breasted Whistler, alias the Ring Coachman.

ring dollar. Chiefly *Tas. Hist.* HOLEY DOLLAR.

1828 *Tasmanian* (Hobart) 29 Aug. 3 George Jones, charged with fraudulently obtaining a ring dollar from J. Hardy, was found *Guilty*. **1855** J. BONWICK *Geogr. Aust. & N.Z.* (ed. 3) 161 One fourth part punched out of the centre was a substitute for a shilling, and was called a Dump; the other part was known as the Ring dollar. **1880** R. ROWE *Roughing It* 16 Coin at one time was so scarce in Van Diemen's Land that the middles of dollars were punched out and circulated as 'dumps', the silver circles left passing from hand to hand as 'ring-dollars'. **1927** A. CROMBIE *After Sixty Yrs.* 15 The original currency was in dollars, and as smaller coins were urgently needed for the purpose of change, relief was afforded by the 'ring dollar', i.e., a circular coin was punched out of the centre of a regulation dollar, which was then worth so much less, while the piece which resulted from the punch may have been worth a shilling.

ringed snake: see RING SNAKE.

ringer, *n.*[1] [Spec. use of Br. dial. *ringer* anything superlatively good: see EDD *sb.*[2]]

1. a. One who excels (at an activity, etc.).

1848 *Port Phillip Herald* 20 June 2/7 Another Melbourne 'Ringer' named Edwards has proceeded to Sydney, resolved to defeat his man there as well as Sinclair. **1900** *Western Champion* (Barcaldine) 1 May 3/2 All lovers of cricket, and admirers of the 'ringers' at the game, will be pleased. **1903** *Sporting News* (Launceston) 14 Feb. 3/5 Mention of good foals reminds me that Mr . . is said to have 'a regular ringer' by Leeholme from the Jacinth mare. **1904** *Bulletin* (Sydney) 19 May 16/3 The A.W.U. is still the 'ringer' among N.S. Wales' labor unions, though its tally isn't what it was by a long way. **1908** *Austral. Mag.* (Sydney) Nov. 1251/1 'Ringer', another term of approbation and excellence, is said to have . . come from quoits, but there are those who hold it to have first signified a man so fast that while his competitors ran in a straight line he was able to 'run rings around them'. **1917** *Byron Bay Rec.* 2 June 4 On every hand the young men seek her and pronounce her 'a peach' or a 'ringer'. **1921** *Bulletin* (Sydney) 25 Aug. 20/2 The top scorer at a hare- or wallaby-drive still earns his three cheers for being the 'ringer' when the day's slaughtering is done; the best dog in a rabbiter's pack is always his 'ringer', and there is a 'ringer' in every bullock-team. **1927** *Ibid.* 7 July 24/1 A 'ringer' among Northern Territory buffalo-hunters is Harry Hardy.

b. Something surpassingly good of its kind.

1891 *Truth* (Sydney) 1 Feb. 6/5 I'd like to see the mill, for it will be a ringer if the officials let them fight to a fair decision. **1892** *Ibid.* 31 July 7/3 He soaked the left on the mouth and the right on the ribs, a ringer. **1904** *Ibid.* 2 Oct. 1/7 The sugar season is a ringer; 11,000 or 12,000 tons of sugar are being shipped weekly.

2. a. The shearer with the highest tally of sheep shorn in a given period.

1871 *Cornhill Mag.* (London) Jan. 85 Billy May stood for the fashion and 'talent', being the 'Ringer', or fastest shearer of the whole assembly, and as such truly admirable and distinguished. ***c* 1872** J.C.F. JOHNSON *Over Island* 7 He would get an early shed for the shearing, and manage to knock out a tidy cheque—for, mind you, he was a regular ringer when he went at it in earnest, and could turn out his hundred-and-fifty a day as easy as roll off a log. **1883** *Illustr. Austral. News* (Melbourne) 28 Nov. 194/2 Those who do 100 or more per day are running each other close like racehorses to . . secure the proud position of boss shearer, or, in the language of the shed, 'ringer'. **1897** *Worker* (Sydney) 11 Sept. 1/1 'The ringer' is the 'cove' who takes the biggest cheque away. **1911** *Huon Times* (Franklin) 4 Nov. 6/3 The ringer of the shed received a cheque for £35 8s. 11d. for 2954 sheep in 19 days. **1925** *Bulletin* (Sydney) 12 Feb. 22/2 Forty years ago one of the main attractions at most bush social gatherings was a shooting gallery with the 'shilleny pools' in connection therewith. A consistent winner was spoken of as 'ringing the bell' nearly every time (*i.e.* getting bull's-eyes). The expression spread to ordinary occupations, in which any element of contest was possible; and as there was always a contest among the fastest men to shear the largest number of sheep during a shearing, the winner was at first said to ring the bell at a certain shed. Of course he soon became simply 'the ringer'. **1934** T. WOOD *Cobbers* 196 He can shear . . even three hundred and twenty . . if he is a Ringer—that is the quickest of the team. **1952** J. CLEARY *Sundowners* 150 Paddy had established himself as the ringer of the shed: each day he shore ten or twelve sheep more than anyone else. **1965** R.H. CONQUEST *Horses in Kitchen* 191 In his prime he was ringer in so many sheds, and for such a long period, that he was considered unbeatable. **1984** *People Mag.* (Sydney) 7 May 40/2 (*caption*) Des Bourke . . the ringer with a small comb, is out of work, out of hope and 3300 km. from home.

b. *transf.*

1890 *Braidwood Dispatch* 26 Nov. 2/2 *Wallaby drive*. . . The country . . was thoroughly scoured with the result that no less than 250 of the marsupial pests were destroyed. Mr John Gumel was 'ringer' with 26, Mr McWilliams being close up with 23. **1949** B. O'REILLY *Green Mountains* 245 The guns fell silent; the wallabies which had not fallen had escaped through the line. A count was made and the man with the biggest bag was proclaimed 'ringer'.

ringer, *n.*[2] [Prob. f. RING *v.*[2] b and c.] A stockman, esp. as employed in droving: see quot. 1977.

1909 J. CAMERON *Spell of Bush* (1910) 48 Dam-sinkers, fencers, scrub-cutters, ringers, and other men doing contract work in the vicinity. **1918** *Aussie: Austral. Soldiers' Mag.* Oct. 5/1 A ringer from Wollondilly reckoned that it was the best water that he had ever tasted. **1943** *Bulletin* (Sydney) 14 July 12/3, I can imagine the reception 'H.D.' or any other ringer would get if he rode up to a cattle station in Queensland or the Territory . . and asked for a job. **1950** 'N. SHUTE' *Town like Alice* 80 'What's a ringer?' 'A stockman.' **1957** D. WHITINGTON *Treasure upon Earth* 155 'Always been a ringer till the war—up round Cloncurry and them parts.' 'A shearer?' 'No. Cattle. Stockman.' **1960** *Meanjin* 16, I drank a lot of beer that night. Matter of fact, I got full with some ringers. **1967** M. SELLARS *Carramar* 37 'A ringer', Gary explained, 'is the drover's man who musters the cattle, and keeps them ringing in a circle. Care has to be taken to prevent them rushing, as it is called in Australia—in other words stampeding.' **1977** T.L. McKNIGHT *Long Paddock* 12 The ordinary members of the droving team are usually referred to simply as *ringers*. Their job is primarily to ride along with the stock, keeping the mob out of trouble, mustering strays etc. In cattle droving night riding around the perimeter of the resting stock is normally also required. **1980** N. WATKINS *Kangaroo Connection* 6 A half-caste 'ringer', who had come back from weeks of stock droving. **1986** *Bulletin* (Sydney) 28 Jan. 67/2 Ringers on the seven stations branded 30,057 calves in 1985.

ringer, *n.*[3] *Two-up.* [f. RING *n.*[2] 1.] *Ring-keeper*, see RING *n.*[2] 2.

1943 H.M. MURPHY *Strictly for Soldiers* 17 And you throw the caser yonder to the boxer's waiting hand; Then the ringer loudly bellows: 'Spread the ring—now fair go, fellows!'

ringie. *Two-up.* [f. RING *n.*[2] 2 + -Y.] *Ring-keeper*, see RING *n.*[2] 2.

[N.Z. **1917** *Chrons. N.Z. Exped. Force* 16 May 137 The 'ringies' they were bending low And yelled for 'centre hoot!'] **1941** S.J. BAKER *Pop. Dict. Austral. Slang* 54 *Ringie*, the keeper of a two-up school. **1950** F.J. HARDY *Power without Glory* 323 Red Ted was 'Ringie'. He supervised the game in the ring itself, seeing that the pennies were spun fairly, and calling the results. **1952** P. PINNEY *Road in Wilderness* 97 The games were crooked, but the 'ringies' were clever. **1977** R. BEILBY

Gunner 298 'Right! Up 'n do 'em, spinner,' the ringie sang.

ring-in, *v.* [Spec. use of *ring in* to substitute fraudulently: see OED *ring, v.*[2] 13 b.]

a. *trans. Horse-racing.* To substitute fraudulently (a horse) for another entered in a race. Also as *vbl. n.*

1898 *Western Champion* (Barcaldine) 18 Jan. 10/1 The disgraceful practices now going on, such as 'ringing-in' horses, pulling, foul riding. **1903** *Sporting News* (Launceston) 14 Mar. 3/3 Three months' imprisonment for 'ringing-in' the trotter Major Robin under the name of Fancy Free. **1919** *Smith's Weekly* (Sydney) 5 July 5/1 Two years ago an attempt was made to ring-in a pony which had come from Queensland... Subsequently the case of ringing-in was proved, and the operators were disqualified for life. **1933** S. GRIFFITHS *Rolling Stone on Turf* 50 'Lady' was proved .. a first-class performer in New Zealand, where also, it was said, she had been 'rung in'. **1984** *Austral.* (Sydney) 23 Aug. 7/5 Endeavour to frustrate those who would attempt to ring in horses.

b. *Two-up.* To substitute (a double-headed or double-tailed coin) for a genuine coin.

1898 *Western Champion* (Barcaldine) 11 Jan. 4/5 He had been playing 'two-up' on the racecourse, and took a man down for 23s. by 'ringing-in a grey' (a two-tailed penny) on him. **1899** *Bulletin* (Sydney) 6 May 14/2 A simple, good-natured old publican .. used to be a good deal victimised by cadgers and bogus shearers at two-up and so forth. One of these 'mongers' once rang-in a bad half-sov. on 'Old George'. **1918** *Aussie: Austral. Soldiers' Mag.* Dec. 3/1 Snow had spun the pennies himself and that was just his way of getting out of paying up when he found that he had failed to ring in the nob. **1946** K.S. PRICHARD *Roaring Nineties* 152 Some of them had been fleeced by spielers 'ringing in the nob', a two-headed penny, or 'the grey', a penny with two tails. **1948** V. PALMER *Golconda* 26 'Dirty work. That dago, Joe Comino, trying to ring in a freak.' 'What?' 'A double header.' **1964** E. LANE *Our Uncle Charlie* 87 Even with his double-headed penny being occasionally 'rung into' the game of two-up he usually came home from a shearing trip not much better off.

ring-in, *n.* [f. prec.]

1. A fraudulent substitution, esp. of one horse for another in a race; the act of making such a substitution.

1918 A. WRIGHT *Breed holds Good* 79 Wiseacres would declare that it was another of Maff's 'hot 'uns', a 'ring-in' probably. **1930** A.E. YARRA *Vanishing Horsemen* 58 'It's a flamin' racehorse,' said Rusty. 'A damned cornfed, ring-in, off the track.' **1954** *Bulletin* (Sydney) 17 Nov. 12/1 Undetected ring-ins I've known in country pubs include roasting a couple of young rabbits in the same pan as a fowl or turkey. Each person gets a slice or two of bunny .. with the poultry. **1957** J.M. HOSKING *Aust. first & Last* 19 We'll see the best of bloodstock round about, Hear talk of ring-ins from the city. If that's so it's a pity. **1965** J. O'GRADY *Aussie Eng.* 74 A good racehorse disguised as a poor one is a 'ring in'. **1971** G. MORGAN *We are borne On* 354 It was not often a horse that had been racing as a ring-in got away with it. **1985** *Canberra Times* 29 Nov. 10/2 The alleged mastermind in the Fine Cotton racehorse ring-in .. was jailed. Two charges arising from the ring-in of Bold Personality for Fine Cotton.

2. One who, or that which, is not of a kind with others in a set: see quots. 1967 and 1975.

1945 *Mud & Blood* 18 Every starter has four legs, even those few 'ring-ins' that were picked up for a song after being boarded out of the Labor Corps because of flat feet. **1965** *Meanjin* 293 She had expended all her energies acquiring, and then projecting, the approved antipodean attitudes. Somehow it had not worked. They always saw she was a 'ring-in'. **1967** E. HUXLEY *Their Shining Eldorado* 82 'I'm a ring-tail, or ring-in.' That means an outsider, one not born in Broken Hill. **1975** *Bulletin* (Sydney) 3 May 42/1 The entrance to his establishment is a 20-foot high glass tower made entirely of stubbies... He has used only standard South Australian stubbies, no ring-ins. **1984** *Austral. Short Stories* viii. 52 But tell me, are you a fair dinkum pom or a ring-in?

ringing, *vbl. n.*

1. [f. RING *v.*[1]] The removal of a ring of bark (from around the trunk of a tree) in order to kill it.

1860 *T.H.A.J.* no. 84 3 The system of 'scrubbing' by which the underwood alone is removed, and of 'ringing' whereby the larger trees are simply killed (by cutting through the bark and sapwood all round). **1873** A. TROLLOPE *Aust. & N.Z.* I. 312 The ringing of trees consists of cutting the bark through all round, so that the tree shall die, and cease to suck up the strength of the earth for its nutrition. **1896** W. BANNOW *Colony of Vic.* 205 The ringing of trees on land for either cultivation or grazing purposes should receive early attention. **1908** *Emu* VII. 143 The thinning out of the plains timber, consequent on settlement, with the usual procedure of ringing and burning out. **1934** 'S. RUDD' *Green Grey Homestead* 56 You'll have a notion of 'doing a bit of ringing in one of the gorges where the grass always seems to be sour'.

2. [f. RING *v.*[2] a.] Of livestock: the action of milling (see quot. 1868).

1868 C.W. BROWNE *Overlanding in Aust.* 77 Sometimes two or three commence butting each other, and then start running round the mob; this is taken up by all the rest, and away they go round and round like a whirlpool, kicking up their legs and buckjumping like horses. They then suddenly turn and go the other way, blowing and puffing the whole time, and kicking up an awful dust... After an hour's amusement of this sort, they stop of their own accord. This evolution is termed 'ringing'. It is a good sign rather than otherwise, and proves the sheep are in good pluck. **1908** K. MACKAY *Songs Sunlit Land* 3 The swift, uneasy stamp of 'ringing' cattle. **1934** C. SAYCE *Comboman* 73 There's one thing that'll make a mess of the mob more than anything else and that's ringing. **1941** S.J. BAKER *Pop. Dict. Austral. Slang* 60 *Ringing*, the milling of cattle.

ringneck. Any of several predom. green parrots of the genus *Barnardius*, having a narrow yellow collar on the darker plumage of the neck. Also **ringneck** (or **ringnecked**) **parrot.**

1888 W.H. WILLSHIRE *Aborigines of Central Aust.* 6 Parrots of many kinds—ring-necks, blue bonnets, and goolahs, furnish the natives with many a meal. **1897** J.J. MURIF *From Ocean to Ocean* 60 Now and again .. one catches sight of the gaudier galah or the gay ring-necked parrot. **1907** *Bulletin* (Sydney) 15 Aug. 13/4 Can any consistent borrower of *The Bulletin* tell me why the outback parrots (galah, ring-neck .. etc.) take so kindly to cooked and uncooked meat when in a state of captivity? **1945** C. BARRETT *Austral. Bird Life* 80 The ringneck parrot (*Barnardius barnardi*) inhabits the interior of southern Queensland, New South Wales, Victoria (north-western areas), and South Australia. **1962** *Texas Q.* 162 Flocks of ringnecks were settling in the mallees. **1972** ANDERSON & BLAKE *J.S. Neilson* 41 The birds that young Neilson loved, delighted him in Little Desert... Ringnecks, and rosellas flashed past.

ring snake. Any of several banded snakes, esp. BANDY-BANDY. Also **ringed snake.**

1844 *Duncan's Weekly Register* 16 Nov. 246/1 The Water or Ring snake is usually found in wells, water holes, or stagnant pools. **1865** G.F. ANGAS *Aust.* 106 The ringed snake, a small species beautifully banded with black and white, is also poisonous. **1918** *Bulletin* (Sydney) 3 Oct. 24/1 *Re* bunda bunda, bandy bandy, or ring-snake. I have been hunting snakes for the last 50 years, and have come across a few of the above. **1944** J. DEVANNY *By Tropic Sea & Jungle* 165 Specially the little ring-snakes, about fifteen inches long and banded black and white. **1956** T.Y. HARRIS *Naturecraft in Aust.* 51 The Bandy Bandy or Ringed Snake, which is also venomous but not dangerous, grows from 1 foot 8 inches to 2 feet 6 inches long.

ringtail.

1. [See quots. 1854 and 1941.] Any of several possums of the genera *Pseudocheirus* and *Hemibelideus* of e. Aust. incl. Tas., s.w. W.A., and New Guinea, esp. the common *P. peregrinus.* In full **ring-tail** (or **ring-tailed**) **possum.** Also *attrib.*

1820 J. OXLEY *Jrnls. Two Exped. N.S.W.* 171 He threw down to us the game he had procured (a ring-tailed opossum). **1825** *London Mag.* May 61 There is the ring-tail possom [*sic*], a very harmless creature, the colour of a rat. **1831** G.A. ROBINSON in N.J.B. Plomley *Friendly Mission* 23 July (1966) 385 It was a young ringtail opossum. **1854** W. HOWITT *Boy's Adventures* 185 There is a smaller kind, called the ring-tailed opossum, because the tail curls itself up into the shape of a ring, not upwards, but downwards. **1861** 'OLD BUSHMAN' *Bush Wanderings* 41 The flesh of the little ring-tail is much more white and palatable. **1883** E.M. CURR *Recoll. Squatting Vic.* 279 The spinning of yarn out of the fur of the ring-tailed opossum .. was done with a sort of spindle. **1886** A.W. HOWITT *On Austral. Medicine Men* 52, I used to keep it in a bag of ringtail 'possum skin. **1909** E. ASH *Austral. Oracle* 15 The dogs had scented a ringtail to a gum tree. **1941** E. TROUGHTON *Furred Animals Aust.* 104 In its broadest scope, this genus [*Pseudocheirus*] embraces all the familiar little ring-tailed possums which derive their popular name from the long and tapered tail, the prehensile end of which is usually curled into a ring owing to its constant use in gripping branches when climbing. **1952** J.F. HADDLETON *Katanning Pioneer* 99 The ringtail opossum, a trifle smaller than the grey, very dark brown with a very long tail with short hair on the tail and about three inches of white on the end. **1970** W.D.L. RIDE *Guide Native Mammals Aust.* 74 Ringtails are not as large as the larger possums; they are mostly about two feet in length and smaller than domestic cats. **1982** R. HALL *Just Relations* 37 The next child I have will be a ringtailed possum! She clapped her hands over her ears. **1985** C. PALLIN *Bat came to Stay* 2 A ring-tail possum curled tighter in its corner.

2. RING-IN *n.* 1; also *transf.*, RING-IN *n.* 2.

1908 *Truth* (Sydney) 19 Jan. 9/5 Then you'll follow our example, and you'll never run a bye—When you've got a good old 'ringtail' on the job. **1919** *Smith's Weekly* (Sydney) 5 July 5/1 Ringing-in has become a lost art. Racing officials, and followers of the sport are too keen to permit of its success nowadays; the ringtail is quickly recognised, and the plans of the schemers fall through. **1967** [see RING-IN *n.* 2].

3. A coward. Also as *v. intr.*, to act in a cowardly manner; to desert.

[**1924** A.W. BAZLEY et al. Gloss. Slang A.I.F. 24 (typescript) *Ring it* or *ring his tail*, play the coward.] **1941** S.J. BAKER *Pop. Dict. Austral. Slang* 60 *Ringtail*, a coward. **1955** N. PULLIAM *I traveled Lonely Land* 385 *Ring-tail*, a coward. **1959** E. LAMBERT *Glory thrown In* 212 'Private Watford back?' asked Christy. 'Yair. Why?' .. 'Reckon he might ringtail?' 'Anyone of us might.'

Hence **ringtailer** *n.*, one who hunts possums.

1919 *Bulletin* (Sydney) 18 Sept. 20/2 Up in the north-east of Tasmania there has been a dreadful slaughter of 'possums. Some 'ringtailers' have raked in as much as £200 for skins this winter.

ring the tin ruling: see RING *v.*[4]

ringy, *a.* Of cattle: inclined to mill.

1976 C.D. MILLS *Hobble Chains & Greenhide* 40 'I was coming down from the top end one time', he related, 'with eighteen hundred ringy six and seven year olds.'

rip, *v.*

1. In the phr. **to rip (it) into** (someone), 'to tear a strip off' (someone).

1940 *Cobbers* (Brisbane) 20 Dec. 1 Many .. watched Sgt. Gordon Owens .. drilling the two culprits and ripping it into them. **1970** D. WILLIAMSON *Coming of Stork* (1974) 5 They've been ripping into me about punctuality. I can't afford to be late. **1978** HANIGAN & LINDSAY *No Tracks on River* 101 He got his belt off, but I ripped it into him for being so hard on all the kids.

2. [Prob. as a euphemism for ROOT *v.*[2] 2.]

a. In the phr. **wouldn't it rip you**: see WOULD. **b.** In the imp. phr. **get ripped,** 'shut up!' 'get lost!'

1948 *Khaki Bush & Bigotry* (1968) 96 'Aw, get ripped.' .. 'You big galah .. get a great big woolly pup.' **1966** D. NILAND *Pairs & Loners* 16 'So I pity you.' 'Get ripped,' he said. 'What's more', I said, 'you're unintelligent.' **1977** S. LOCKE ELLIOTT *Water under Bridge* 234 Oh get ripped.

ripper. [Br. slang and dial. *ripper* something especially good; now chiefly Austral. (see OED(S *sb.* 3 a.).] Something (or someone) which excites admiration. Also *attrib.* and as *exclam.*

1858 C.R. THATCHER *Colonial Songster* (rev. ed.) 87 One of them had a frying-pan, And 'twas a regular ripper; And another laid about him With an old tin dipper.

1875 R. BRUCE *Dingoes* 134 He is lucky who obtains One sheepskin for a hipper; And when he gets it will exclaim—'By George, this is a ripper.' **1911** *Anthony Hordern Catal.* 769 Sorts of saddles. Rippers every one of them. Comfortable, sound and durable. **1943** *Troppo Tribune* (Mataranka) 20 Dec. 2 What a ripper my son Jack has turned out to be. **1969** A. O'TOOLE *Racing Game* 60 I've got another lad at home, who'll be a ripper too in a year or so. Not as fast as Lenny, but he's a better kick and a lovely mark. **1976** *Bulletin* (Sydney) 12 June 32/2 The woman .. will be Cynthia Morisey, a little ripper from Perth... Miss Morisey, from every aspect, is almost derangingly beautiful. **1977** W. MOORE *Just to Myself* 82 'Hang on!' yells Tip, trying to get back to the steering wheel. 'Watch this for a skid!' and next thing you know we go into this almighty skid, do a beaut figure eight, and finish up the way we came. 'Bloody ripper, eh?' bawls out Tip. **1977** E. MACKIE *Oh to be Aussie* 58 Everyone had a ripper time on rum at the Rocks. **1981** *Sydney Morning Herald* 3 Oct. 44/5, I finish up by saying that this new dictionary is a ripper (not a ring ripper, since that expression fails to appear in it). **1985** *Bulletin* (Sydney) 25 June 68/1 The formula is a ripper. You need to be a tax expert to work it all out.

rise. [f. U.S. *to make a rise* to win or make money: see Mathews *rise, n.* 2 b.] A substantial profit or gain, esp. from gold-mining. Freq. in the phr. **to make a rise.**

1876 'EIGHT YRS.' RESIDENT' *Queen of Colonies* 165 Hundreds who had before been in great poverty, 'made a rise' on Jimna. **1888** 'R. BOLDREWOOD' *Robbery under Arms* (1937) 92 What a paltry thing working for a pound a week seemed when a rise like this was to be made. **1898** *Bulletin* (Sydney) 2 July 15/1 A Gippslander tells of the origin of his 'rise'... I picked up a stone to throw at my dog .. but saw gold glistening... It was a half ounce specimen, an' set me hunting for the reef. **1918** A. WRIGHT *Breed holds Good* 167, I suggested making a rise by robbing the homestead, thinking no one was there. **1929** W.J. RESIDE *Golden Days* 256 Many of the prospectors in the early days made their 'rises' by the merest flukes. **1944** M.J. O'REILLY *Bowyangs & Boomerangs* 49 A likely place to make a rise. **1978** D. STUART *Wedgetail View* 111 He made this great rise on the Melbourne races, practically backed the card, and practically all-upped all the way, so you can guess he'd made a killing.

rising. Short for 'the rising of the court' (see quot. 1908).

1907 *Truth* (Sydney) 9 June 9/6 Some people after 'doing' their sentence find themselves in a queer position. At the Water Police Court .. a woman .. was fined 5s. or 'the rising'. Not having the 5s., she did the latter, and then, when discharged, found herself without even the fare back to Manly. **1908** *Ibid.* 19 July 1/7 People who have in the dim religious light of the previous evening, been 'on it', next morning are fined 'five shillings, or the rising'... Those that choose the alternative are escorted back to the cells, and again placed under lock and key, where they are kept until 'checked'. It is quite a common occurrence, however, for those so incarcerated to be liberated long after the rising of the court.

rising sun. A badge, originally a half-circle of swords and bayonets radiating from a crown, esp. as worn by a member of the Australian Imperial Force in the war of 1914–18. Also *transf.* (see quot. 1919).

[**1916** *Rising Sun: On Board 'Themistocles'* 9 Aug. 1 Hence the great need of a newspaper... The 'Rising Sun' has come to fill that gap... As the Australian military badge it is associated with all the glory achieved .. on the Gallipoli Isthmus.] ***c* 1919** J.A. GAULT *Padre Gault's Stunt Bk.* 125 A surprise for this Hun was the 'Old Rising Sun', That smashed up his Hindenberg Line. **1929** 'F. BLAIR' *Digger Sea-Mates* 112 Whose boots were not bright as a mirror, 'Kiwied' to the highest perfection? Whose 'rising suns' were not as resplendent as their shining prototype above? ***c* 1937** *We of A.I.F.: Souvenir*, When, at the beginning of 1902, the 1st Battalion Australian Commonwealth Horse (the first Commonwealth contingent) was raised for service in South Africa, General Sir Edward Hutton, who was then in command of the Australian Military Forces, decided it should have a special badge... General Hutton .. wanted something martial. 'Something like that,' he said, pointing to a trophy of arms hanging on the wall of his office. This consisted of a semi-circular board, red in colour, on which was placed a large brass crown, surmounted by a half-circle of swords and bayonets. Such was the origin of the Commonwealth badge, which, in a later form, became popularly known as the Rising Sun. **1949** G. BERRIE *Morale* 67 'Got any badges to give away, mate?' he asked. The Bushman promptly took a 'rising sun' from his tunic. **1958** *Sabretache* (Melbourne) June 7 When was the badge first called the Rising Sun? .. Officially it has always been and still is, known as the 'Badge, Commonwealth, large, for hat' or 'small, for collar'. **1964** *Ibid.* Apr. 77 Upon the outbreak of war in 1914 the official issue to all units of the 1st AIF was the Commonwealth badge. This was and is known as the 'Rising Sun' badge... The 'Rising Sun' badge was still used about 1931 when regimental badges were issued to all units of the Citizen Military Forces and the Permanent Forces. They were worn until 1942 when the 'Rising Sun' once again become the universal badge for all units of the Australian Military Forces. This was issued to the members of the 2nd A.I.F. in 1939. **1964** *Austral. Army Jrnl.* Nov. 21 The origin of the 'Rising Sun' title given to the badge .. is connected with a brand of jam. Until about 1906, the only building near Victoria Barracks, Melbourne, was Hoadley's jam factory which produced the well-known and universally advertised 'Rising Sun Jam'... Large quantities of Hoadley's jam were issued to Australian troops in South Africa and the similarity of the badge of the Australian Commonwealth Light Horse to Hoadley's trademark caused the returned servicemen, at least in Melbourne, to be given the satirical nickname, of 'Hoadley's Horse'.

rissole, *v. trans.* Euphem. var. of ARSEHOLE.

1971 *Bulletin* (Sydney) 3 July 40/3 When today's footie heroes look like yesterday's poofters there's not much spice in rissoling short-hairs. **1979** *Age* (Melbourne) 2 July 9/1 He was West Australian, he reminded his team-mates. Over there pitches played truly, and if you picked the right ball you could *'safely tug four bits off the deck at the WACA without fear of getting rissoled for a gozzer by a guzunder'*.

river.

1. Used *attrib.* in Special Comb. **river claim** [also U.S., see Mathews 2], a mining claim that extends into a watercourse; **flat,** FLAT *n.*[1]; **frontage,** FRONTAGE 1.

1859 *Colonial Mining Jrnl.* June 79/1 Claims are divided into three sorts—alluvial claims, **river claims,** and quartz claims. **1886** *N.T. Times Almanac* 84 Any holder of a river or creek claim may construct dams within his claim for the purpose of turning water into his flood-race. **1838** *Southern Austral.* (Adelaide) 8 Sept. 3/1 Lagoons and creeks intersected the **river flats.** **1862** E. STRICKLAND *Austral. Pastor* 77 Ever since I came to Albury, I have seen more than 100 blacks present at the corrobberies they used to hold on the river flat. **1896** B. SPENCER *Rep. Horn Sci. Exped. Central Aust.* I. 14 Along by the river flats the clusters of red fruit of the Darling or Murray lily were frequently seen. **1935** T. RAYMENT *Cluster of Bees* 463 These .. were collected on a river-flat, which was not swampy, but covered with grass and a thick growth of 'swamp mahogany'. **1951** G. FARWELL *Outside Track* 50 Unlike American projects such as the Boulder Dam, the Hume is not concentrated in a deep gorge, but spread over inundated river flats. **1965** A.W. UPFIELD *Lure of Bush* 49 Over the grey river flats. **1839** R. TORRENS *Emigration Ireland to S.A.* 28 The Surveyor-General, sold some rural land having **river frontage,** and containing brick earth, for £90 per acre. **1844** Macarthur Papers LXII. 111 The land is unoccupied, and will be so, as you monopolize the river frontage. **1870** C.H. ALLEN *Visit to Qld.* 94 Running along a considerable length of the river frontage, extend the very beautiful Botanical Gardens. **1893** S. NEWLAND *Paving Way* 239 The whole of the long river-frontage was already being quickly taken up and occupied. **1921** *Smith's Weekly* (Sydney) 1 Jan. 17/4 It was the cutting up of the river frontages of Tomki run, 36 years ago, that started the farming and dairying rush to Richmond River (N.S.W.). **1947** W. LAWSON *Paddle-Wheels Away* 157 He reckoned you was selectors, taking a river frontage out of his run.

2. In the names of flora and fauna: **river blackfish,** the fish *Gadopsis marmoratus* (see BLACKFISH); **garfish,** any of several fish of the fam. Hemirhamphidae, esp. *Hyporhamphus ardelio* of all mainland States but not N.T.; see also BEAKIE, GARFISH; **gum,** any of several trees of the genus *Eucalyptus* (fam. Myrtaceae) occurring near watercourses, esp. *E. camaldulensis* (see RED GUM 1); **oak,** any of several trees of the fam. Casuarinaceae, esp. the usu. large *Casuarina cunninghamiana*, occurring along rivers and fresh-water streams in N.S.W., Qld., and N.T.; *creek oak*, see CREEK 3; **red gum,** the tree *Eucalyptus camaldulensis* (see RED GUM 1).

1906 D.G. STEAD *Fishes of Aust.* 210 The so-called 'Slippery' or **River Blackfish** (*Gadopsis marmoratus*), also known occasionally as the 'Marbled River-Cod'. **1969** J. POLLARD *Austral. & N.Z. Fishing* 83 River blackfish are believed to have evolved thousands of years ago when Tasmania was part of the Australian mainland. **1984** E. ROLLS *Celebration of Senses* 135 Once we went by night into the Warrumbungle mountains and fished a mountain creek for the sweet, scaleless, slimy River Blackfish we had never tasted. They are plentiful there but they are becoming rare in most New South Wales streams. **1881** *Proc. Linnean Soc. N.S.W.* VI. 245 *Hemirhamphus regularis* .. '**River Gar Fish**' of Sydney Fishermen. **1882** J.E. TENISON-WOODS *Fish & Fisheries N.S.W.* 83 *Hemirhamphus melanochir*, or 'river garfish', is a still better fish [than *H. regularis*], but has become very scarce. **1906** D.G. STEAD *Fishes of Aust.* 67 The River Garfish... Large numbers of this delicious little fish are to be seen daily in the various fish-markets in Sydney. **1951** T.C. ROUGHLEY *Fish & Fisheries Aust.* 21 River garfish are caught in seine nets of fine mesh .. and because they are not used for any other purpose they are known to fishermen as garfish or beakie nets. **1969** J. POLLARD *Austral. & N.Z. Fishing* 273 River garfish grow to 14 inches and are pale green above, with narrow dark streaks running along the back. **1974** J.M. THOMSON *Fish Ocean & Shore* 131 In contrast to .. primarily marine garfish, the river garfish (*Hemirhamphus ardelio*) is very common in estuaries and the young penetrate even into fresh water. **1881** W.E. ABBOTT *Notes Journey on Darling* 42 After crossing the Darling on the western side, except along the edge, I saw nothing deserving the name of a tree. The coolabar .. and the **river gums,** which grow only within about 100 yards of the water, are the only trees to be found. **1903** F. TURNER *Bot. Darling, N.S.W.* 411 The 'River' or 'Red Gum', *Eucalyptus rostrata* .. grows fairly plentifully on the margins of the watercourses. **1918** *Bulletin* (Sydney) 5 Sept. 22/1 In its single river-gum Sang the shepherd-bird no more. **1933** J. TRURAN *Where Plain Begins* 3 The white-boled river-gums lifted their sombre plumes above dense, clinging swathes of fog. **1963** *N. Austral. Monthly* Dec. 11 The river gums grow into lovely old trees with tall thick trunks and mottled loose bark. **1979** K. GARVEY *Absolutely Austral.* 72 We used to find a possum once in every hollow spout On all the river-gums before the myxo thinned them out. **1817** A. CUNNINGHAM in I. Marriott *Early Explorers Aust.* 9 Apr. (1925) 176 *Casuarina torulosa* (**River Oak**) .. with another species of Eucalyptus called by the colonists 'Stringy Bark'. **1835** J. BACKHOUSE *Narr. Visit Austral. Colonies* (1843) 307 There are some fine specimens of the species of *Casuarina*, called River-oak. **1845** J.O. BALFOUR *Sketch of N.S.W.* 38 The river oak (*casuarina*) grows on the banks of rivers... It is very hard and will not split. **1882** *Proc. Linnean Soc. N.S.W.* VII. (1883) 548 This river and most of its tributaries .. are fringed throughout by River Oaks (*Casuarina suberosa*) of very rich and umbrageous foliage. **1918** H.H. CORBIN et al. *Federal Capital Territory* 7 In the bed of the Cotter and Murrumbidgee, and also other rivers, one finds a very excellent growth of the 'river oak', *Cas. cunninghamii.* **1948** R. RAVEN-HART *Canoe in Aust.* 69 There were casuarinas again, but now I think 'River Oak' rather than 'She-oak'. **1971** W.A. WINTER-IRVING *Beyond Bitumen* 92 On the banks the River Oaks were full of the gorgeous multi-coloured lorikeets. **1984** E. ROLLS *Celebration of Senses* 118 Water swirled over the roots of our own River Oaks. **1900** *Proc. Linnean Soc. N.S.W.* XXV. 712 Forest Red Gum, in some situations, is scarcely distinguishable from *E*[*ucalyptus*] *rostrata* (**River Red Gum**) except by the fruits. **1916** *Emu* XV. 153 Fine river red gums .. in many instances grow in the sandy beds of the creeks. **1935** D.G. STEAD *Rabbit in Aust.* 86 A few dwarf River Red Gums. **1956** N.K. WALLIS *Austral. Timber Handbk.* 5 River red gum is one of the most widespread of the native trees, but grows in true forest formation only on alluvial flats which are subject to occasional flooding. **1973** V. SERVENTY *Desert Walkabout* 51 Hans Heysen painted more river red-gums than any other Australian painter. **1986** *Age* (Melbourne) 7 Feb. 2/4 The river red gums, black box and yellow box trees had all failed to flower, leaving many professional apiarists scraping the bottom of the jar.

Riverina bluebell. [f. the name of a district in s. N.S.W.] PATERSON'S CURSE.

1976 W.A. BAYLEY *Border City* (rev. ed.) 84 Patterson's curse . . has been sold as Riverina Bluebell on the flower stalls in Martin Place, Sydney and as Riverina Heath in Melbourne. Its beauty blooming in paddocks remains undisputed. **1980** *Canberra Times* 23 July 1/2 Paterson's curse, sometimes known as Salvation Jane or Riverina bluebells, is a purple-flowered plant which grows extensively throughout southern Australia.

road.

1. *pl. Obs.*

a. [Orig. Br. but not attested after 1771: see OED *sb.* 5 b.] In the phr. **to take to the roads**: see quot 1835.

1835 *Colonist* (Sydney) 330 July 243/2 Punishments of runaways have not been sufficiently felt to discourage a repetition of the crime of absconding. 'Taking to the bush', or roads, as usually termed, must in general be considered as taking to robbery. **1889** J.H.L. ZILLMANN *Past & Present Austral. Life* 77 Scoundrels from every part of the world . . infested the gold-fields to 'take to the roads', as it was called, and make themselves the possessors of immense wealth by one daring onslaught upon the gold escort.

b. Of a convict (later a convicted person): in the phr. **(up)on** (or **to**) **the roads,** *ellipt.* for 'forced labour on the roads'.

1837 *Rep. Select Committee Transportation* 283 The principal superintendent holds in his hand the assignment list . . stating to what service he is assigned, whether he is to go to any individual, or whether to be sent upon the roads. **1840** *Tasmanian Weekly Dispatch* (Hobart) 7 Feb. 7 Indulgence suspended, and three months to the roads. **1843** *Sydney Morning Herald* 10 July 2/5 The Court sentenced the prisoner to be kept at hard labour on the roads for twelve calendar months. **1847** Z.P. POCOCK *Transportation & Convict Discipline* 11 Now convicts, though they do not mind a few months on the roads, are decidedly averse to Port Arthur. **1871** *Austral. Town & Country Jrnl.* (Sydney) 29 Apr. 516/1 At the circuit court today, Jacob Donovan was convicted of cattle stealing, and sentenced to five years on the roads. **1888** 'R. BOLDREWOOD' *Robbery under Arms* (1937) 42 A very smart crowd to be on the roads inside of five years, and drag us in with 'em.

2. Used allusively with reference to droving, esp. in the phr. **on the road.** See also TRACK *n.* 2 a. Also *attrib.*

[N.Z. **1874** KENNAWAY *Crusts* 48 One of our evening camps 'on the road'.] **1901** *Bulletin* (Sydney) 7 Dec. 30/2 Cattle 'on the road' are unaccountable animals. **1904** *Ibid.* 8 Dec. 19/2 One does not use pyjamas 'on the roads'. **1919** *Smith's Weekly* (Sydney) 1 Mar. 6/3 He managed to go on the road with a mob of 50 head of cattle. **1922** 'J. BUSHMAN' *In Musgrave Ranges* 80 One day, when the routine of 'the road' had gone on for more than a fortnight, they were crossing a broad expanse of hard stony country. **1929** *Bulletin* (Sydney) 14 Aug. 23/3, I wanted a cook on a road camp. . . A dapper chap blew along with Matilda and said: 'You want a cook?' **1937** W. HATFIELD *I find Aust.* 81 You could get three pounds a week on the road with cattle.

3. Special Comb. **road ant,** *meat ant* (a), see MEAT; **board** [used elsewhere but recorded earliest in Aust. (see OEDS *road, sb.* 10 a.)], a local body having responsibility for the maintenance of roads (but see also quot. 1927); also **roads board; gang** *hist.*, a detachment of convicts (later prisoners) detailed to work at road construction; **hut** *obs.*, a dwelling provided for the accommodation of convicts working on the roads; **paddock,** a paddock adjacent to a road; **party** *obs.*, *road gang*; also *transf.* and *attrib.*, as **road party boots; station** *obs.*, an outpost at which a road gang is based; **train,** see quot. 1968; LAND TRAIN.

1925 *Bulletin* (Sydney) 25 June 24/4 If they are '**road**' or 'meat' **ants,** let him run a circle of coal tar around the nests. **1945** *Coast to Coast 1944* 140 Davie always had a pickle bottle for staging heroic contests between red-joes and black-joes—or either of these against twice their number of road ants. **1856** W.H.G. KINGSTON *Emigrant's Home* 170 A letter to the **Road Board,** offering to construct the bridges at £60 each. **1872** MRS E. MILLETT *Austral. Parsonage* 162 A 'road board' is now formed in each district, consisting of the principal inhabitants; a certain amount of convict labour is placed at its disposal by the Government, and the control over the highways lodged in its hands. **1904** *Bulletin* (Sydney) 4 Aug. 16/3 This particular native can read and write, and his conversation is better than that of the ordinary roads-board member. **1927** J. POLLARD *Rose of Bushlands* 174 'The Culgoa Roads Board', he explained, 'allows us three months in which to fumigate and poison. . . It means that a farmer is frequently done with it before his neighbour begins, and naturally rabbits come from his neighbour's farm to his.' **1958** G. CASEY *Snowball* 12 The chief stock-and-station agent, and the head officials of the local Road Board were often linked up with some of the boss-cockies from round about to form a clique. **1978** D. STUART *Wedge-tail View* 30 State Battery, bush work, Road Board, anything. Not a bludger, old Bill. **1819** *Sydney Gaz.* 23 Jan., Four Men who had eloped from the Sydney **Road Gang.** **1827** *Colonial Times* (Hobart) 20 Jan., *John Bully*, of the road gang at Glenarchy, was ordered to work in irons. **1834** J. MUDIE *Vindication* p. xviii, In the road-gangs it has . . become a common practice to let the men *hire themselves out to the settlers.* **1839** *Sydney Standard* 21 Jan. 3/2 It is shameful to expose prisoners of the crown working in road gangs to the meridian sun. **1844** *Colonial Times* (Hobart) 20 Feb., Our city prison is crowded with some desperate offenders, chiefly runaways from the several road-gangs. **1865** 'SPECIAL CORRESPONDENT' *Transportation* 32 The others are . . formed into road-gangs—'probation parties' should rather be said, for the convicts are treated with no little deference, and so coarse a word as 'gang' is never used in connection with them. **1891** J.J. ROCHE *Life J.B. O'Reilly* 70 The political prisoners who had not been soldiers were sent to Perth, twelve miles away, to work in the road-gangs or quarries. **1825** *Hobart Town Gaz.* 8 Oct., If it is thought requisite to inspect all cattle and sheep brought into Hobart Town, it is surely no less necessary to have those intended for the road parties examined before slaughtering them; yet those supplying are allowed to kill, either at their own houses, or at the **road huts.** **1827** *Tasmanian* (Hobart) 26 Apr. 2 McLanaghan . . then proceeded to the road-huts for assistance. **1902** *Bulletin* (Sydney) 8 Nov. 16/4 My mate and I were stripping wattle in the **road-paddock.** **1943** *Ibid.* 14 July 12/3 Mooney, chipping burrs up on the road paddock, pricked up his ears as he caught the sound of protesting bellowings coming from Minnie, one of his best milkers. **1822** J.T. BIGGE *Rep. State Colony N.S.W.* 38 The labour of the **road parties,** and the shell gangs, exposes the convicts to the evil effects of slight control and great temptation. **1835** J. LHOTSKY *Journey from Sydney* 12 Road Parties are formed by probationary Convict Servants, returned to Government by their masters, where they must remain six months, before they are again assignable to private service. They do not work in irons. **1843** *Teetotal Advocate* (Launceston) 24 Apr. 2/5 An assigned servant to Mr Keene, charged with indecency and being drunk was ordered two months to a road party, and to be returned to Government. **1850** *Bell's Life in Sydney* 28 Sept. 1/1 Road parties were formed, and marched about in public to break stones on the highways. **1882** A.J. BOYD *Old Colonials* 186 No road party had been at work here for over a couple of years. **1900** W. DELAFORCE *Life & Experiences Ex-Convict Port Macquarie* 35 When a man had finished his sentence in the chain gang, he was sentenced to a road party, and it was Heaven to the chain gang. **1945** S.J. BAKER *Austral. Lang.* 182 Leggings worn by outback travellers and workers are known as *dog stiffeners*. . . Heavy boots were called road party boots. **1831** *Sydney Herald* 8 Aug. 3/1 Masters are to pay twenty shillings for every assigned servant they may receive from the ship or **road stations,** as a remuneration to Government for slops. **1841** *Morning Advertiser* (Hobart) 3 Sept. 3/3 The appointment of prison medical attendants at road stations. **1849** *Britannia* (Hobart) 20 Dec. 3/4 The obnoxious . . plant . . is spreading destruction over the best lands of the colony, but especially near the old road-stations. **1940** *Aust.: Nat. Jrnl.* Sept. 17 Recent developments in the use of **road trains** carrying over 20 tons of goods. **1956** *Tennant Creek Times* 22 June 1/5 A typical Territory 'road train' taking live cattle on the first stage of its journey. **1964** *N. Austral. Monthly* Oct. 3 The cafe . . was chock-a-block with road train drivers and their mates. **1968** D. O'GRADY *Bottle of Sandwiches* 159 In case you don't know what a road-train is, it's a prime-mover pulling anything up to half a dozen big trailers loaded up with live cattle, or all sorts of everything. **1977** *Truckin' Life* I. v. 11 It should be noted that because of the length of these Road Trains, once they have begun to travel a road it is almost always impossible to turn them around. **1986** *Canberra Times* 19 May 20/6 Road trains are something you have to contend with when driving in the Northern Territory.

roany. [f. *roan* + -Y.] A roan-coloured animal.

1891 *Truth* (Sydney) 17 May 1/5 He was cremating the dead 'Roany' or 'Strawberry'. **1929** W.J. RESIDE *Golden Days* 381 Castieau's raking roanies Could show their dust to most.

roar, *v.* [Chiefly Austral.: see OEDS *roar, v.* 4 c.] *trans.* With **up:** to reprimand; to berate. Also as *vbl. n.*

1917 *Advocate* (Burnie) 13 July 3/6 Mag will roar me up if I get back without a settlement. **1919** W.A. CULL *At all Costs* 24 Leave was Johnson's folly. He would 'roar up' the whole camp on his return. **1925** *Smith's Weekly* (Sydney) 25 Apr. 19/5 The householder was 'roaring up' the agent over the smallness of the vest-pocket house she had rented. **1933** 'TRAMWAY WORKERS' *Shock Brigader* 5 'You were tryin' to scale me, you young varmint,' said Mick with an angry scowl, and didn't he give that young varmint a 'roaring up'? **1947** M. RAYMOND *Smiley gets Gun* 170 I'd like to give you a knockdown to 'er—fair dinkum I would. But she'd only roar us up a treat and you wouldn't git nothin' outer ole Granny. **1979** R. DUFFIELD *Rogue Bull* 194, I generally don't roar people up who are working for me.

roarer. Abbrev. of BULLROARER.

1928 B. SPENCER *Wanderings in Wild Aust.* 274 When whirled round the little slab rotates in the air, tightening the string, which then vibrates and gives out a sound, the quality of which depends upon the size of the 'roarer'. **1963** I.L. IDRIESS *Our Living Stone Age* 113 Hidden somewhere where the formation of rock and earth would cause sound to reverberate with increasing volume, there would be forty or more practised men whirling those roarers round their heads.

roaring, *ppl. a.* [Spec. use of *roaring*, characterized by riotous or noisy behaviour.] In special collocations: **roaring days,** the time of the gold rushes; **fifties,** the 1850s, the time of the gold rushes in Victoria.

1896 H. LAWSON *In Days when World was Wide* 33 And you and I were faithful mates All through the **roaring days!** **1907** M. CANNON *That Damned Democrat* (1981) 93 The rush had some of the characteristics of the 'roaring days'. **1936** I.L. IDRIESS *Cattle King* 127 The famous Cobb and Co. line of coaches, originally started by Freeman Cobb in the roaring days of the Victorian gold-diggings. **1949** G. FARWELL *Traveller's Tracks* 30 There is little to remind you now of those 'roaring days', for men mainly lived in tents and shanties. **1966** G.W. BROUGHTON *Men of Murray* 126 In the 'roaring days' between 1853 and late 1920s. **1896** *Worker* (Sydney) 26 Dec. 1/1 One . . has been privileged to listen to the yarns of the 'old timers', the diggers of the '**roaring fifties**'. **1899** G.E. BOXALL *Story Austral. Bushrangers* 139 It was the custom here in the 'roaring fifties', for the diggers to fire off their guns and pistols every night after dark. **1927** 'VIATOR' *From up along Down Under* 260 Ballarat . . during 'the Roaring Fifties'. **1930** T.S. MARSHALL *Mem. Victorian Fire Service* 4 The old 'digging days' in Victoria, the roaring '50s, was an era of money-making and mad excitement. **1931** *Century of Journalism* 235 Mark the sudden jump when the 'roaring 'fifties' came along, with their excitement and consequent reckless abandonment of the common round!

roart, var. RORT *n.*

robbery under arms. BUSHRANGING 1.

1864 *Illustr. Sydney News* 16 Nov. 2/3 Three troopers . . have arrested a man . . suspected of . . several charges of robbery under arms. **1864** *Act* (Vic.) 27 Vict. no. 233 Sect. 111, Whosoever shall being armed with any offensive weapon or instrument rob or assault with intent to rob any person . . shall be guilty of felony . . [*Note*] Robbery under arms. **1882** 'R. BOLDREWOOD' in *Sydney Mail* 1 July 6/2 (*title*) Robbery under arms. **1912** J. BRADSHAW *Highway Robbery under Arms* (ed. 3) 41 Bushranging, for instance—or robbery under arms.

robbo. *Obs.* [f. *Rob(inson* (see quots. 1897) + -O.]

Orig. in the derisive call **four-bob robbo**: see quot. 1897 (2). Used *transf.* of something in a deteriorated or unsatisfactory condition, esp. a (horse and) light conveyance. Also *attrib.*

1897 *Bulletin* (Sydney) 2 Jan. 13/4 Sydney's wild-rabbit and bottle-merchants now take their 'donahs' out driving on Sundays in a 'four-bob robbo', *i.e.*, sulky. Now what is the derivation of 'robbo'? **1897** *Ibid.* 23 Jan. 11/3 'Four Bob Robbo'—four shillings Robinson, who lived in the classic suburb of Waterloo, Sydney . . came into a bit of money and bought a horse and trap. The money was spent, and Robinson tired of the horse, which got poor; so he then sometimes let out the horse and trap (both somewhat worse for wear) for 4s. per half-day. There was a run on the cheap hire, and Rob. bought two other horses and traps, which he let out at the same price. A neighbouring livery-stable keeper and his employés resented Rob's cutting-down prices; and, when any of the rival's equipages passed, used to cry out, in derision, 'Four Bob Robbo!' The cry was taken up by the kids, and has now become a Waterloo classic. *Ibid.*, Robbo has in an extensive Sydney circle come to mean anything unsatisfactory. For instance, a girl enters a jeweller's shop with: 'Watcher been givin' us? Look at the clasp of this 'ere bracelet I bought . . last week. It's gone bung already. It's a fair robbo.' *Ibid.*, Also 'robbo' has come to mean amateur. **1907** *Truth* (Sydney) 11 Aug. 3/2 These ex-Castlereagh-street women and their 'honey's and 'hubbys'—the robbo and bottle-oh men—hold forth almost daily. **1909** R. Kaleski *Austral. Settler's Compl. Guide* 20 Carefully avoid delivery vans, 'robbo' fruit carts and such like, they are too wide and heavy. **1939** K. Tennant *Foveaux* 430 There was old Bert Robinson. . . 'E kept a livery stable down at the Foot. I s'pose you've 'eard of the Four-bob Robbos, then? The chaps used to go an' hire a cart for four bob and take it round loaded with vegetables. The kids used to call after 'em 'Four Bob Robbo, Four Bob Robbo'. Old Bob Noblett, 'e's an old man now, but I can remember when Bob Noblett was a four-bob robbo.

robin. [Transf. use of *robin* the robin redbreast: see next.] Any of many small, active birds, some having a brightly coloured breast, of the fam. Pachycephalidae. Also with distinguishing epithet, as **dusky, flame, pink-breasted, red-capped, rose, scarlet, scrub, white-breasted, yellow** (see under first element).

1823 J. Latham *Gen. Hist. Birds* VI. 211 [Scarlet-bellied Flycatcher] . . called the Robin of New South Wales, and Norfolk Island, where it is most numerous. **1834** M. Doyle *Extracts Lett. & Jrnls. G.F. Moore* 47 There is a bird called here the robin, like our own in its habits of familiarity. **1838** *Cornwall Chron.* (Launceston) 15 Sept. 1 The robin of this country—unlike that in England—is devoid of all melody, a shrill whistle being its only accent. **1860** 'Little Jacob' *Colonial Pen-Scratchings* 89 Robins twittering all about, robins with such vermilion breasts, and such black velvet feathers that one never sees in England. **1886** W.J. Woods *Visit to Vic.* 24 There are Swallows, Martins, and Robins, but none of them sing; and, indeed, these English names are most of them as misleading as those given to the native fruits. **1932** A.H. Chisholm *Nature Fantasy in Aust.* 130, I sometimes wonder what would have developed in the 'christening' of Australian birds had not such crisp, old-world terms as *robin* and *wren* been available. For . . at least twenty species, some of them only dubiously related, grace the ancient name of *robin*. **1985** *Age* (Melbourne) 9 Sept. 15/5 The Australian wrens, warblers and robins are quite unrelated to their namesakes in the Northern Hemisphere.

robin redbreast. [Transf. use of *robin redbreast* the European bird *Erithacus rubecula*.]

1. A red-breasted robin, esp. *scarlet robin* (see Scarlet); *red breast*, see Red *a.* 1 b.

1845 C. Griffith *Present State & Prospects Port Phillip* 127 The robin-redbreast is worthy of particular mention. It is a beautiful little bird, with black and grey body, and bright scarlet breast. **1872** 'Resident' *Glimpses Life Vic.* 242 The robin red-breast of the antipodes is an exquisite little creature. **1878** R.B. Smyth *Aborigines of Vic.* II. 186 *Tolorim* . . robin redbreast. **1892** Mrs F. Hughes *My Childhood in Aust.* 91 The robin redbreast is a very lovely little bird. **1909** Lindsay & Holtze *Territoria* 24 Among others, there are the . . robin redbreasts, skylarks [etc.]. **1948** P.J. Hurley *Red Cedar* 160 They are robin red breast, rose and hooded robins. Few birds are more loved.

2. *fig. Obs.*

1886 *Once a Month* (Melbourne) IV. 33 My attention was attracted by a bullock-driver taking his team along the bank. . . He was one of the old stamp known as 'Robin Red-breasts'. His open serge shirt exposing his chest to the sun and weather had made it as red as an Aberdeen moon.

rock, *n.*

1. *Gold-mining. Obs.* Bedrock: see quot. 1856.

1856 S.C. Brees *How to farm & settle in Aust.* 57 This lowest bottom, 'the rock', as it is emphatically termed, in reference to its character as a bar to further digging for gold, is often the depository upon its irregular surface of considerable gold deposits. **1857** W. Westgarth *Vic. & Austral. Gold Mines* 248 They reached 'the rock' without finding any auriferous drifts.

2. In the names of flora and fauna: **rock cod,** any of several marine fish inhabiting reefs and rocky waters, incl. *Pseudophycis barbata* of s. Aust.; also with distinguishing epithet, as **black, red** (see under first element); **fern,** any of several ferns of the genus *Cheilanthes* (fam. Adiantaceae), esp. *C. austrotenuifolia* of all States and elsewhere; **flathead,** any of several marine fish of the fam. Platycephalidae, living among weed-covered rocks or reefs, esp. *Platycephalus laevigatus* of s. Aust. and *Thysanophrys cirronasus* of W.A., S.A., and N.S.W.; **kangaroo,** any of several macropods, esp. Wallaroo; **lily** (or **orchid**), an epiphytic or lithophytic orchid of the genus *Dendrobium* (fam. Orchidaceae), esp. *D. speciosum* of e. mainland Aust., cultivated as an ornamental; **lobster,** any of several marine crayfish, some of which are fished commercially for the tail-meat, the most important being the western rock lobster *Panulirus cygnus*; **melon** [also U.S.], the fragrant edible fruit of the cultivated melon *Cucumis melo* ssp. *agrestis* (fam. Cucurbitaceae); the plant itself; any of several other similar plants; **oyster,** any of several oysters occurring on the rocky substrate of estuaries and bays, esp. *Saccostrea commercialis* (see *Sydney rock* Sydney 2); **parrot** (or **parakeet**), the predom. olive to yellow-olive parrot *Neophema petrophila* of rocky islands and coastal s. and s.w. Aust.; **pebbler** (**pebblar, peplar**), Smoker; also *attrib.*; **pigeon,** either of two brown pigeons of the genus *Petrophassa* inhabiting rocky parts of n. Aust., the *white-quilled rock pigeon* (see White *a.*[2] 1 b.) and the chestnut-quilled rock pigeon *P. rufipennis*; any of several other pigeons of similar habitat; **poison,** the poisonous shrub *Gastrolobium callistachys* (fam. Fabaceae) of s.w. W.A.; **python,** any of several snakes of the fam. Boidae, esp. *Morelia amethistina* of n.e. Qld. and elsewhere, the largest Austral. python, and the olive python, *Bothrochilus olivaceus* (syn. *Liasis olivaceus*) of n. Aust.; **ringtail,** the possum *Pseudocheirus dahli* of n.e. W.A. and n. N.T.; Wogoit; also **rock possum, rock-haunting ringtail; wallaby,** any small wallaby of the genera *Petrogale* and *Peradorcas*, inhabiting rocky ranges and rock-strewn outcrops of mainland Aust.; Wirrang; also with distinguishing epithet, as **brush-tailed, yellow-footed** (see under first element); **warbler,** the predom. dark brown and rufous bird *Origma solitaria* of rocky sandstone gullies and caves in e. N.S.W.; **whiting,** any of several marine fish of the fam. Odacidae, esp. *Haletta semifasciata* of s. Aust.; Stranger 2.

1790 R. Clark Jrnl. 19 Apr. 159, 16 fishes consisting of Snappers Blue fish and one **Rock Cod. 1810** E. Bent Lett. 4 Mar. 95 The Rock Cod . . is very different from the fish so called which is caught on the Coast of Ireland. **1826** J. Atkinson *Acct. Agric. & Grazing N.S.W.* 25 The coasts of New South Wales abound with fish. . . The best kinds are snappers, king fish, rock cod. **1843** *Sketch W.A.* 15 The parrot fish, the rock cod, and the diamond fish . . answer in appearance in every respect to fish of the same name in the West Indies. **1851** H. Melville *Present State Aust.* 315 Rock cods are very plentiful. **1873** J. Bonwick *Tasmanian Lily* 25 There were a dozen Flatheads, and quite as many Rockcods. The latter, not bigger than their mates, being less than a foot long, were thought much nicer. Their flesh was firmer and the bones were more complacent. **1873** F. De Castelnau *Edible Fishes Vic.* 15 *Rock cod* . . is much esteemed for food . . the chin bears a short barbel. **1890** 'R. Boldrewood' *Colonial Reformer* II. 22 A rock-cod or two, with their brilliant colouring, added to his wondering observation. **1911** D.A. Macdonald *Bush Boy's Bk.* 106 Some people regard rock cod as a rather poor fish, being soft and flabby. **1933** —— *Brooks of Morning* 181 The rock cod, which is the solace of winter fishermen about Black Rock, is transformed to a ling in Botany Bay. **1965** *Austral. Encycl.* VII. 473 Rock cod, a vernacular name applied to several fishes that have little or no affinity with the true cod (*Gadus*) and differ widely from one another. **1978** N. Coleman *Austral. Fisherman's Fish Guide* 33 Red scorpion fish *Scorpaena cardinalis.* This fish has been referred to for many years as a rock cod, but this term is inaccurate. **1923** *Census Plants Vic.* (Field Naturalists' Club Vic.) 3 *Cheilanthes tenuifolia* . . **Rock Fern. 1955** N.A. Wakefield *Ferns of Vic. & Tas.* 17 The Rock Fern grows well in a fernery as a pot plant, or in cool pockets of soil in a rockery. **1975** E.R. Rotherham et al. *Flowers & Plants N.S.W. & Southern Qld.* 155 *Cheilanthes lasiophylla*, a rock fern. A small, tufted fern, up to 15 cm. high . . chiefly on rock outcrops and arid mountain ranges. **1984** E. Rolls *Celebration of Senses* 38, I took out buckets of water . . and poured them over a Rock Fern. These plants are known as resurrection plants. Their recovery after drought is phenomenal. **1873** F. De Castelnau *Edible Fishes Vic.* 11 They [*sc.* the flat-heads, or *Platycephalus*] form several sorts, of which the two most common are the *Bassensis* and the *Laevigatus*; the latter is called **rock flat-head. 1911** D.A. Macdonald *Bush Boy's Bk.* 108 A fine fish known as rock flathead, is less often caught. **1965** *Austral. Encycl.* IV. 98 The rock flathead (*Thysanophrys cirronasus*) . . harmonizes with weed-covered rocks among which it lives. **1983** *Age* (Melbourne) 19 Sept. 11 Fifteen years ago 38 per cent of Westernport Bay was covered in seagrass. Rock flathead and pike grazed in the grass. **1826** J. Atkinson *Acct. Agric. & Grazing N.S.W.* 23 The wayrang or **rock kangaroo. 1827** P. Cunningham *Two Yrs. in N.S.W.* I. 310 The *rock kangaroo* is very small, living among the rockiest portions of the mountains. **1854** S. Sidney *Gallops & Gossips* 54, I remember now seeing two huge rock kangaroos go bounding down the mountain side. **1875** J. Forrest *Explorations in Aust.* 48 Jemmy shot four rock kangaroos today. **1898** W. Redmond *Shooting Trip* 30 The wallaroo or rock kangaroo is a splendid fellow much darker in colour than the ordinary one. **1943** C. Barrett *Austral. Animal Bk.* 90 Of wallaroos or rock-kangaroos there are at least half a dozen species. **1833** W.H. Breton *Excursions* 89 **Rock lillies** . . are uncommonly beautiful. **1847** G.F. Angas *Savage Life & Scenes* II. 238 The rock-lily is a superb plant, generally growing on the edge of some rocky precipice. **1849** *Narr. Exped. Rockingham Bay & Cape York* 5 At the edge of the rocks . . one beautiful specimen of *dendrobium* (rock lily). **1860** G. Bennett *Gatherings of Naturalist* 282 The Rock Lily of the colonists—a species of *Orchis* (*Dendrobium speciosum*)—with its masses of yellow waxy blossoms. **1888** *Sydney Morning Herald* 24 Jan. (Centennial Suppl.) 2/1 The well known rock lily (Dendrobium speciosium), so abundant on the rocks and trees about Sydney and along the coast. **1923** *Census Plants Vic.* (Field Naturalists' Club Vic.) 18 *Dendrobium speciosum* . . Rock Orchid. **1925** *Bulletin* (Sydney) 6 Aug. 22/4 The coastal area of Eastern Australia is the habitat of a flower known popularly as the 'rock-lily', though actually one of the finest varieties of the true orchid. **1967** N.A. Wakefield *Naturalist's Diary* 20 Masses . . of Australia's largest orchid, the 'rock-lily' (*Dendrobium speciosum*). **1979** Wrigley & Fagg *Austral. Native Plants* 107 The common name of rock lily is incorrect, but unfortunately well established. Rock orchid would be preferable. **1986** *Your Garden* Jan. 10 (*caption*) A massive clump of Rocklily (*Dendrobium hillii*) flourishes with palms and staghorn. **1909** G. Smith *Naturalist in Tas.* 108 In Tasmania the term crayfish is applied to the marine **Rock Lobster** (*Panulirus*). **1976** *Ecos* ix. 7/2 Adult rock lobsters are caught in pots on reefs at depths of between 30 and 90 metres. **1841** *Sydney Herald* 6 Mar. 2/6 The **rock** and water **melons** are even superior to what you see in Sydney. **1858** A.C. & F.T. Gregory *Jrnls. Austral. Explorations* 29 Apr. (1884) 39 A small species of rock-melon was . . found in great abundance. **1880** R. Richardson *Beneath Southern Cross* 5 Brings out the flavour of rock-melon, I assure you. **1895** G. Ranken *Windabyne* 74 And lastly a basketful of rock-melons (pump-irrigated). **1969** *Jrnl. Agric. S.A.* LXXII. 241 The most common variety of rock melon grown in South Australia is Hale's Best Powdery Mildew Resistant No. 45. **1770** J. Cook *Jrnls.* 23 Aug. (1955) I. 394 The Shell-fish are Oysters of 3 or 4 sorts, viz **Rock oysters** and Mangrove Oysters which are small, Pearl Oysters, and Mud Oysters, these last are the best and largest. **1827** P. CUNNINGHAM *Two Yrs. in N.S.W.* I. 68 Rock oysters .. are .. sold shelled at a shilling a quart. **1850** *Illustr. Austral. Mag.* (Melbourne) July 60 The extraordinary abundance of rock oysters in George's River and the Weronora, was particularly noticed. **1851** H. MELVILLE *Present State Aust.* 45 At Sydney there are abundance of oysters, some like those of England; these are called the 'mud' oyster: there are others, the 'rock', which receive their name from adhering to the rocks. **1882** *Proc. Linnean Soc. N.S.W.* VII. 130 *Ostrea mordax* .. is a Rock Oyster found adhering very firmly to the rocks by the whole of the lower valve from Brisbane in Queensland to far North beyond Port Denison. **1949** C. BENHAM *Diver's Luck* 207 On the rocks were oysters nearly as good as the famous rock oysters of Sydney. **1985** *Sydney Morning Herald* 13 Sept. 4/7 The Pacific oyster grows so rapidly that it will most certainly interfere with the conventional stick culture in Port Stephens by dislodging and overgrowing the native rock oysters. **1844** [**rock parrot**] J. GOULD *Birds of Aust.* (1848) V. Pl. 40, *Euphema petrophila* .. Rock Parrakeet, Colonists of Swan River. **1867** 'COLONIST' *Life's Work* 118 Many of the parrots are most gorgeous in plumage .. blue mountain parrots, rock parrots, ground parrots. **1905** *Emu* IV. 131 *Neophema petrophila* (Rock-Parrakeet). .. For a nesting site it takes advantage of any natural hollow in the limestone rock. **1929** A.H. CHISHOLM *Birds & Green Places* 98 The rock-parrot, a small bird confined to the coast of south-west Australia, breeds in cavities in rocks and earth. **1945** C. BARRETT *Austral. Bird Life* 82 When the island [*sc.* Goat Island, S.A.] .. was approached in a boat, many rock parrots came flying over. **1976** *Reader's Digest Compl. Bk. Austral. Birds* 291 Rock parrots,stocky birds that live on the coast and offshore islands, are rarely seen even as far as 10 km. inland. **1890** 'MRS A. MACLEOD' *Austral. Girl* (1894) 231 'And parrots scream rather loudly, too; don't they?' 'Yes; but there are times when they warble most musically; not only the smaller kinds .. but also larger ones, like the **rock-pebblers.** **1903** *Emu* III. 79 The Black-tailed Parrakeet (*Polytelis melanura*), commonly known in Australia as the 'Rock-Pebbler'. **1952** A.C.C. LOCK *Travels across Aust.* 173 At Wood Wood the river was close, and among the gums here we caught glimpses of rock pebblar parrakeets. **1965** *Austral. Encycl.* VII. 474 Rock pebbler .. rock-peplar. .. It may be that 'pebbler', or 'peplar', was corrupted by dealers from the specific name, *anthopeplus*, meaning 'robed in flowers'. **1845** L. LEICHHARDT *Jrnl. Overland Exped. Aust.* (1847) 11 Nov. 476 A new species of **rock pigeon** (Petrophassa ..) with a dark brown body, primaries light brown without any white. **1896** B. SPENCER *Rep. Horn Sci. Exped. Central Aust.* II. 99 *Lophophaps leucogaster* .. White-bellied Bronze-wing[s] .. on several occasions made a welcome addition to our table. .. Their love of rocky country has gained for them the appellation of 'Rock Pigeons'. **1898** D.W. CARNEGIE *Spinifex & Sand* 303 The prettiest of all the birds is a little plump, quail-like rock- or spinifex-pigeon, a dear little shiny, brown fellow with a tuft on his head. **1904** *Emu* IV. 42 Being this time alone, I had an opportunity of seeing the rare Rock-Pigeon (*Petrophassa albipennis*) in numbers. **1948** *Austral. Bushcraft* (Austral. Army Educ. Service) 18 The rock pigeon, found in very rocky, broken country or among craggy hills. **1954** I.L. IDRIESS *Nor'-Westers* 126 Out on the hills live scattered flocks of dainty little rock pigeons, feathered darlings of the sun. With their tufted topknots, quaintly turned-down tails and liquid brown eyes. **1964** M. SHARLAND *Territory of Birds* 172 Did you see the Chestnut-quilled Rock Pigeons? They were sitting on the rocks on the right hand side of the creek just at its exit from a cleft in the range. **1984** SIMPSON & DAY *Birds of Aust.* 310 (*caption*) The nest site and eggs of a Rock-Pigeon. [**1865 rock poison:** 'SPECIAL CORRESPONDENT' *Transportation* 14 Whole districts are overrun with strong quick-growing bushes, the juices of which are fatal to animal life. There are no less than fourteen known varieties of these plants, but only four are commonly pointed out. These are the York-road, the heart-leaf, the rock, and the box-scrub.] **1875** J. FORREST *Explorations in Aust.* 61 Country studded here and there with granite rocks, with good feed around them—in some places rock poison. **1897** L. LINDLEY-COWEN *W. Austral. Settler's Guide* 577 *Rock poison* .. an erect shrub of 2 or 3 feet, with twiggy branches. **1926** *Poison Plants W.A.* (W.A. Dept. Agric.) 30 Rock Poison. .. The range of this plant is a wide one, extending from the Murchison district through the Victoria and Avon districts to the Mount Barker and Ravensthorpe districts. **1956** GARDNER & BENNETTS *Toxic Plants W.A.* 76 Rock poison .. flowers between September and November, and is highly toxic at all stages of its growth. **1974** S.L. EVERIST *Poisonous Plants Aust.* 301 *Gastrolobium callistachys* .. Rock Poison. .. It grows on granitic soils, usually on granite outcrops. **1934** A. RUSSELL *Tramp-Royal* 251 We rode almost on top of a **rock python** one day. .. He was ten feet long. **1955** J. CLEARY *Justin Bayard* 91 Started rustling cattle just to get my own back on those men who wouldn't know a poddy from a rock python. **1967** H.G. COGGER *Austral. Reptiles & Amphibians* (rev. ed.) 78 The largest of all Australian snakes, indeed one of the largest in the world, is the Amethystine or Rock Python of northern Queensland. **1983** M. DURACK *Sons in Saddle* 195 The thirty-foot rock pythons that made wide, curving swathes through the long grass and were held in awe, and sometimes even regarded as sacred, by the blacks, were .. falling prey to the white man's bullets. [**1895 rock ringtail:** *Zoologischer Anzeiger* (Leipzig) XVIII. 464 *Pseudochirus dahlii* n. sp. The Rock Phalanger. .. 7 Specimens (1 male, 6 females) collected by a Norwegian traveller, Dr Knut Dahl, May 1895.] **1941** E. TROUGHTON *Furred Animals Aust.* 115 It seems therefore that the rock ring-tail has somewhat lowered the arboreal standard of its near relatives in adapting its habits to the unusual surroundings, at the north-west extremity of its mainland range. **1942** C. BARRETT *From Bush Hut* 37 'Got it from a lubra for half a stick o' 'bacca,' he informed me, holding up the spitted *wogoit* (that's a blackfellow name for the rock-possum). **1943** —— *Austral. Animal Bk.* 71 The rock-haunting ringtail (*Petropseudo dahli*) .. lives among granite formations in the Northern Territory, and was discovered by Dr Knut Dahl, after whom it was named, in the Mary River country. **1972** *Bulletin* (Sydney) 18 Mar. 17/3 The banded pigeon, the rock possum and a rock wallaby are found only in this area. **1983** R. STRAHAN *Compl. Bk. Austral. Mammals* 124 The Rock Ringtail from arid northern Australia is essentially terrestrial and has a tail which is so short that it can be of little use as a prehensile organ. **1844** L. LEICHHARDT *Jrnl. Overland Exped. Aust.* 25 Nov. (1847) 49 According to Mr Gilbert, **rock wallabies** were very numerous. **1845** *Ibid.* 5 Nov. (1847) 470 Charley shot a rock wallabi of a different species from any we had previously seen: it was of a light grey colour; the tail was smooth, and its black tip was more bushy than in other species; there were two white spots on the shoulder. **1850** *Australasian Sporting Mag.* 92 The Woorang or Wirring, as it is there called, is the Rock Wallaby. They average about twenty five pounds weight, and would bother a chamois with their pace over a country all but impracticable to human beings. **1864** E.A. OPPEN *Descr. N.T.* 31 The common rock wallaby was found throughout in rocky ranges. **1886** D.M. GANE *N.S.W. & Vic.* 183 Rock-wallaby shooting is a good pastime. **1894** R. LYDEKKER *Hand-Bk. Marsupialia & Monotremata* 43 The Rock-Wallabies are confined to the mainland of Australia, on which they are generally distributed, but are unknown in Tasmania. Although closely allied to the true Wallabies, their habits are markedly distinct, the Rock-Wallabies frequenting rugged rocky districts instead of the open plains. **1896** B. SPENCER *Rep. Horn Sci. Exped. Central Aust.* I. 77 The gorge led away back into the range, and climbing over the rocks we made our way, disturbing several rock wallabies (*Petrogale lateralis*) as we did so. **1914** *Emu* XIII. 211 My supper consisted of Johnnie-cake and roast rock wallaby. **1935** F. BIRTLES *Battle Fronts Outback* 141 Rock wallabies, in frantic haste, bounded up the hillsides. **1963** D. ATTENBOROUGH *Quest under Capricorn* 58 We sometimes caught sight of little black rock wallabies, miniature kangaroos the size of terriers, that scampered away from us, often leaping up sheer rock faces with the most astonishing agility. **1985** P. CAREY *Illywhacker* 493, I am more taken by the little rock-wallabies which hop to and fro across this pretty scene and one of them, in particular, eating an apple, holding it daintily between its two front paws. **1813** J.W. LEWIN *Birds N.S.W.* 3 **Rock Warbler** .. frequents caverns inaccessible to Mankind, and deep rocky Gullies, creeping in the Cavities and Chasms. **1846** J. GOULD *Birds of Aust.* (1848) III. Pl. 69, *Origma rubricata.* Rock-Warbler. **1929** A.H. CHISHOLM *Birds & Green Places* 113 The grass-warbler and the rock-warbler, no less contemptuous of the nomenclatural gropings of man, are content chiefly to pipe and whistle in their sound. **1945** C. BARRETT *Austral. Bird Life* 195 With headquarters in the neighbourhood of Sydney, the rock-warbler (*Origma rubricata*) is confined to the Hawkesbury sandstone area, with its innumerable caverns, ravines and gullies. **1968** V. SERVENTY *Southern Walkabout* 11 The rock warbler .. flits along the ground, and under rock ledges looking for food. **1986** *Sydney Morning Herald* 15 Jan. 13/3 The rock warbler, a diminutive reddish-brown bird with a golden voice. **1878** *Proc. Linnean Soc. N.S.W.* III. 390 *Odax semifasciatus* .. is called '**rock whiting**' at Sydney, and is fourteen inches long; obtained in May. **1896** F.G. AFLALO *Sketch Nat. Hist. Aust.* 238 The little Rock Whitings, so-called (*Odax*), allied to the Melbourne 'Stranger' and the Kelp-fish of Hobart. **1906** D.G. STEAD *Fishes of Aust.* 146 The Rock-Whiting is quite common along the shores of New South Wales, Victoria and Tasmania, while in South Australia and Western Australia it is also known to abound. **1924** LORD & SCOTT *Synopsis Vertebrate Animals Tas.* 76 The Rock 'whiting' is generally known to Tasmanian fishermen as the 'Stranger', a vernacular designation which is also applied to it in Victoria. **1951** T.C. ROUGHLEY *Fish & Fisheries Aust.* 105 As a food-fish the rock whiting cannot be regarded as of prime quality, for its flesh is rather soft. **1974** T.D. SCOTT et al. *Marine & Freshwater Fishes S.A.* 313 This species [*sc. Haletta semifasciata*] is our most abundant Rock Whiting in South Australia. It is usually found in weedy and rock areas in shallow to moderately deep-water.

3. Special Comb. **rock ape,** a derogatory term for a (black) person; **-chopper,** a navvy; also *transf.*, a Roman Catholic; so **-chopping** *vbl. n.*; **-hole,** GNAMMA HOLE; also **rock water-hole; -hopper,** one who fishes from coastal rocks; **shelter,** an Aboriginal cave-dwelling (see also GIBBER-GUNYAH); also *attrib.*

1972 *Bulletin* (Sydney) 17 June 4/3 The good relationships which these expatriates develop is too often counteracted by the Territorian who refers to his workers as '**rock apes**' .. or 'kanakas' and treats them as 'idle, useless blacks'. **1974** *Ibid.* 13 July 20/3 To them the Aborigines and Islanders who make up some 10 percent of the town are the 'coloreds' (polite) .. or 'rock apes' (impolite for any shade of black). **1984** M. ELDRIDGE *Walking Dog* 217 Who's walking you home, not those rockapes, I trust? **1985** *Nat. Times* (Sydney) 25 Jan. 22/1 To be a Territorian, you've got to talk about rock apes and black bastards, things like that. **1908** *Truth* (Sydney) 22 Mar. 4/7 Ninety per cent. of the **rock-choppers** do not follow the vocation more than about three or four years before they are in an advanced stage of consumption, victims to what is known among them as the 'sewer disease'. This is caused by the stone-dust continually inhaled by the men. **1909** A. GRIFFITH *Griffith-Moroney Debate* 34, I say too, that the Labour party was responsible for the gaoling of the rockchoppers. **1912** *Bulletin* (Sydney) 4 Jan. 14/2 If these ants could only be trained to make tracks in the right direction, the Sydney rock-choppers could knock off work. **1918** *Huon Times* (Franklin) 20 Dec. 3/2 Mrs Bill Smith, whose old man has got a job rock-chopping at Cremorne. **1982** E. CAMPION *Rockchoppers* 2 A symbol of such unfriendliness was the nickname 'rockchoppers'. Unknown to most Catholics, the word was used privately by ascendant Protestants to express their dislike of the Irish-Australians whose proletarian roots went back to the convict rockchoppers. 'Rock-choppers' remained an underground word, outside the reference books, until last year, when the *Macquarie Dictionary* gave it an entry, guessing (wrongly, in my view) that its origins lay in the initials RC. **1982** *Nat. Times* (Sydney) 5 Sept. 19/2 *Goatriders and Rockchoppers.* Richard Hall reports on sectarianism in Australia. **1985** *Bulletin* (Sydney) 23 July 78/3 Our first census showed a heavy concentration of Catholics among the stonemasons—the first Rockchoppers! **1875** J. FORREST *Explorations in Aust.* 111 Camped on a grassy rise, close to a small **rock** water-**hole.** **1889** E. GILES *Aust. twice Traversed* II. 192, I been pray to my God to give you a rock-hole to-morrow. **1903** *Emu* III. 95, I have frequently been indebted to them for finding rock-holes containing water. **1923** *Bulletin* (Sydney) 4 Jan. 24/4 The natives said the rockholes there 'never died', but scarcity of water depopulated the field more than once during the days of the first alluvial finds. **1933** M. TERRY *Untold Miles* 186 The term 'rockhole' does not correctly describe these supplies, as it indicates, in the usual Bush parlance, a trap in a gully or rocky creek where concentrated drainage has filled up some natural receptacle or hole for storage. **1948** C.P. MOUNTFORD *Brown Men & Red Sand* 163 Moanya suggested we should visit Kuna rock-hole, for it was a very 'big' water, and never went dry. **1967** E. KETTLE *Gone Bush* 30 Our aboriginal guides showed us their waterholes, or rather 'rock-holes', as they are best known; sources of water which could have saved lives. .. These rockholes are hidden away, usually in fissures between rocks. **1973** V. SERVENTY *Desert Walkabout* 24 Bunjil rockhole was unusual in that a vertical tunnel went down about twenty-four feet into the rock. **1917** C. THACKERAY *Goliath Joe* 74

Several **rock-hoppers**—users of long rods and landing nets—were clustered round the corner. **1949** *Bulletin* (Sydney) 28 Sept. 10/4 The 'wirrah', also known among rockhoppers as 'old boots' . . is tough. . . I dropped a four pounder into the basket. **1953** *Sydney Morning Herald* 3 Jan. 6/3 'Rock-hopper', a person who fishes from a rocky coast. **1978** T. DAVIES *More Austral. Nicknames* 86 *Rock spider*, a weekend rockhopper (fisherman) at Bondi. **1892** *N.S.W. Geol. Survey Rec.* 34 The aboriginal name for these **Rock-shelters** appears to have been that of 'Gibber-gunyas', literally, 'houses of rock', at any rate, in the Port Jackson and Hawkesbury Districts. **1899** J. MATHEW *Eaglehawk & Crow* 138 Caves and rock-shelters . . are found to be covered with much ruder sketches of men, animals, weapons, and symbols. **1925** H. BASEDOW *Austral. Aboriginal* 322 We have before us a rock shelter or *abris* on the Forrest River in the north of Western Australia, a more or less vertical wall at the base, overhung at the top by a solid ledge or 'roof' of quartzite. For the better part of the day this spot is protected from the intense heat of a tropical sun; and during the 'wet season', also, it provides a shelter from the prolific rains. **1954** A.P. ELKIN *Austral. Aborigines* 191 The ritual means of increasing man and natural species . . is associated with cave and rock-shelter paintings. **1965** A. MARSHALL *These were my Tribesman* 193 The entire ceiling of the rock-shelter was flat and covered in paintings.

rock, *v. Gold-mining.* [Orig. U.S.: see OED *v.*[1] 4 b.] *trans.* To wash auriferous material (in a CRADLE *n.* 1). Also *absol.*

1851 *Empire* (Sydney) 20 May 2/2 Many a hand which had been trained to kid gloves . . became nervous to clutch the pick and crow-bar or 'rock the cradle' at our infant mines. *Ibid.* 18 June 2/3 A son of Mr Neals and another person have been working with a cradle yesterday and today . . and the small quantity they have obtained, after two days hard rocking, will prove that it could not be worked profitably. **1852** D. MACKENZIE *Gold Dipper* 45 One washes (that is, rocks the cradle) while another is employed in pouring water on the earth, or slaty rubbish in the cradle. **1852** J. BONWICK *Notes of Gold Digger* 13 You fill the hoppers of your cradle with the stuff, keep on pouring water with the dipper, and rock carefully and evenly. **1884** 'R. BOLDREWOOD' *Old Melbourne Memories* 168 Each man dug, or rocked, or bore, As if salvation with the ore Of the mine monarch lay. **1941** D. O'CALLAGHAN *Long Life Reminisc.* 22 After being through the puddling tubes and rocking cradles, a certain amount of gold is often lost.

rocker. *Gold-mining. Obs.* [Orig. U.S.: see OED(S *n.*[1] 4 c.]

a. CRADLE *n.* 1.

1851 *Bell's Life in Sydney* 31 May 1/4 The rocker or cradle may be made of half inch soft stuff—and consists essentially of first, a trough say 10 inches deep, 18 inches broad, and 4 feet long. . . This trough, placed on rockers like a cradle . . forms the rocker. **1852** *Murray's Guide to Gold Diggings* 27 The inclination of the rocker, when set to work, should not exceed half an inch in a foot. . . The gold will traverse gradually over the first inclined plane (the slide) and drop on to the second (the rocker bottom). **1853** J. SHERER *Gold Finder Aust.* 190 A great crowd gathered round a little green rocker, as they called it—a little green-painted cradle. . . The party belonging to that rocker had washed 7 lb. of gold. **1855** G.H. WATHEN *Golden Colony* 71 The method of washing the earth has been also much modified by time and experience. At first, all was done by the *cradle* or *rocker*, and the tin dish.

b. Abbrev. of *cradle-rocker* (see CRADLE *n.* 2).

1853 J. SHERER *Gold Finder Aust.* 60 When all the earth is washed away, the rocker and washer cast their longing eyes into the sieve to see if there be a 'nugget' too large to get through the holes.

rocking horse. Used allusively of something not readily obtainable, esp. in the phr. **as rare as rocking-horse manure.**

1944 G.H. FEARNSIDE *Sojourn in Tobruk* 33 Australian cigarettes were as rare as rocking-horse manure hereabouts. **1954** T. RONAN *Vision Splendid* 41 Tailor-made smokes are as rare as rocking-horse manure around here. **1967** *Kings Cross Whisper* (Sydney) xxxix. 4/4 *Rocking horse manure*, a very scarce commodity. **1968** D. O'GRADY *Bottle of Sandwiches* 96 Vehicles were scarcer than rocking-horse dung around those parts. **1981** *Bulletin* (Sydney) 16 June 81/2 The price in Australia, allowing freight and costs, is nearly par with the sterling price. And that, these days, is as rare as rocking horse manure.

rogaine /'roʊgeɪn/. [See quot. 1986.] A rogaining event.

1982 N. & R. PHILLIPS *Rogaining* 1 Although rogaines are defined as being 12 hours or longer, the classic rogaine is the 24 hour event. *Ibid.* 10 This latter rogaine attracted 170 starters. **1984** *Vic. Rogaining Assoc. Newsletter* 19 May, *Novice* (all team members on first rogaine). **1986** *ACT Orienteering News* Mar. 7 According to the book 'Rogaining—cross-country navigation' by Neil and Rod Phillips, the term was introduced in 1976 to coordinate and promote a rapidly developing sport which had originated as the Melbourne Uni. Mountaineering Club 24 hour walk (a line event) . . and, later, the Surrey Thomas Rover Crew annual hike. The contribution of Neil, Rod and also Gail Phillips in promotion of the sport initially in Victoria and later in W.A. and Tas. is understated in the book, and no explanation is offered for the term which *they* introduced. However, it is altogether too much of a coincidence that '*rogaine*' is a compound word of the first letters of each of their names: *Rod, Gail* and *Neil.*

rogaining /roʊ'geɪnɪŋ/, *vbl. n.* [f. prec.] A sport similar to 'orienteering', in which teams compete over a course which requires at least twelve hours to complete: see quot. 1982.

1982 N. & R. PHILLIPS *Rogaining* 1 Rogaining is the sport of long distance cross-country navigation in which teams of two to five members visit as many checkpoints as possible in an allocated period. Teams travel entirely on foot, navigating by map and compass in terrain that varies from open farmland to thick, hilly forest. A central base camp provides hot meals throughout the event and teams may return there at any time to eat, rest or sleep. **1984** *5th Austral. Rogaining Championships* (Advt.), Rogaining is a relatively new sport which may be described as competitive bushwalking or marathon orienteering. **1986** [see ROGAINE].

Hence **rogainer** *n.*, one who engages in rogaining.

1982 N. & R. PHILLIPS *Rogaining* 8 The easy terrain of Kimbolton Forest suited the many beginners and was a new experience for the seasoned rogainers. **1985** *Canberra Times* 25 Sept. 42/7 The absence of leading ACT rogainers has left the men's open class wide open.

roley-poley, var. ROLY-POLY.

roll, *v.*[1] *Hist.* [Spec. use of *roll* to travel or move about (see OED(S *v.*[2] 12 a. and b.); the sense 'to arrive, to appear on the scene' is later and used elsewhere.] *intr.* With **up**: to assemble for a meeting (see ROLL UP 1). Freq. *imp.*

1861 *Miner & General Advertiser* (Lambing Flat) 20 Feb. 3/2 *'Roll up! Roll up!'* is the general watchword of the miners on the diggings. **1861** *Goulburn Herald* 18 Sept. 2/2 It is not by accident that flags are unfurled with mottoes upon them, as 'roll up', 'no Chinese'. **1872** C.H. EDEN *My Wife & I in Qld.* 266 Should any unfortunate Celestials show their flat faces and squinting eyes on a gold field, a cry of 'roll up' passes from hole to hole [and] up come the occupants. **1887** J. FARRELL *How he Died* 26 The miners all rolled up to see the fun. **1889** *Bulletin* (Sydney) 2 Mar. 12/3 A digger murdered in the camp! his murderer at large! Roll up! Roll up! the pregnant cry awakes the evening air. **1892** 'R. BOLDREWOOD' *Nevermore* III. 16 We heard as the Ballarat men was talking of 'rolling up' if the licenses wasn't lowered. **1902** E.B. KENNEDY *Black Police Qld.* 56 'Roll up, roll up,' we heard roared all through the camp, and at once celestials were flying helter-skelter, taking flying leaps over claims, sometimes into them, when they would be dragged out by their pigtails and cuffed on again.

roll, *v.*[2] [Spec. use of *roll* to form into a roll or ball: see OED(S *v.*[2] 8.]

1. *trans.* To pack (one's belongings, swag, etc.) prior to departure. Freq. *absol.* with **up.**

1872 G.S. BADEN-POWELL *New Homes for Old Country* 124 In the morning one of them starts the flock, leaving his mates to 'roll up' and follow. **1892** *Truth* (Sydney) 15 May 6/5 So, yer want me to tell yer a yarn, lads, Before I roll Bluey and go? **1892** *Bulletin* (Sydney) 20 Aug. 21/2 He 'rolled-up', very gladly, for he had bush-fever badly When he left the smoke 'to wander where the wattle-blossoms wave'. **1897** *Worker* (Sydney) 18 Sept. 3/3 These latter . . had to roll up their swags and make tracks, as the cook, H. Williams (to whom I raise my hat) positively refused to cook for any of their sort. **1899** *Western Champion* (Barcaldine) 9 May 14/1 Great guns and ringers, smart shed hands and steady labourers . . have rolled up and started for the scene of action. **1904** L.M.P. ARCHER *Bush Honeymoon* 9 My *father*'d tell him to *roll-up* and take his cheque. **1913** H. LAWSON *Triangles of Life* 247 Cooney . . had rolled his swag at daylight. **1968** S. GORE *Holy Smoke* 27 Why, what's wrong with rolling me bluey, making tracks for home per boot, and just telling the old man I'm sorry? **1978** R.H. CONQUEST *Dusty Distances* 37 We rolled our swags, the two New South Welshmen giving me hints about balance, tightness of binding straps, and so on.

2. *Shearing. trans.* To roll (a newly-shorn fleece): see quot. 1979.

[N.Z. **1863** E.R. CHUDLEIGH *Diary* (1950) 75, I was picking up and rowling [*sic*] the fleeces.] **1874** *Illustr. Sydney News* 19 Dec. 15/1 Mr Fisher had a shed erected at his own expense, floored with deal, fitted up with pens for sheep, bench for rolling fleece and press for packing. **1897** *Bulletin* (Sydney) 11 Dec. 29/1 I'm just in from west the Darling, 'picking-up' and 'rolling wool'. **1928** C.E. COWLEY *Classing Clip* 38 The objects of rolling fleeces are, to give an attractive appearance and, to reduce the fleece to a more convenient form or compass. **1979** HARMSWORTH & DAY *Wool & Mohair* 159 The reason for rolling the fleece is to keep each fleece separate so that it can be handled readily for classing and pressing, to command the attention of the buyer by presenting it in an attractive manner, and so that it can be readily opened when being sorted for the manufacturer.

Hence **rolling-table** *n.*, a bench upon which a fleece is rolled.

1899 G. JEFFREY *Princ. Australasian Woolclassing* 39 Second cuts . . fall beneath the spokes of the rolling tables and are called locks, and do not bring one-third of the price of fleece wool. **1928** C.E. COWLEY *Classing Clip* 32 The fleece should be thrown upon the rolling-table.

roll, *v.*[3] [Spec. use of *roll* to flatten with a roller: see OED *v.*[2] 10.] *trans.* To crush and flatten (mallee scrub). Also with **down.**

1910 'YARRAN' *Mallee* 5 In some districts the Government, by means of a traction engine, rolls down the scrub, charging the settler 3s. per acre. **1941** C. BARRETT *Aust.* 105 We were standing near a great pile of Mallee roots. 'Great stuff for fires,' I ventured. 'We burn tons of it down home in winter.' 'Yes; but it's a devil's job grubbing them out after the scrub's rolled down.' **1946** A.J. HOLT *Wheat Farms Vic.* 1 Australia has made some notable contributions to the world pool of agricultural technology. These include the stripper and the header, the technique of rolling Mallee scrub [etc.]. **1981** J. SAXTON *Something will Come* 160 Ken had 'rolled' some of the lighter scrub, burnt if off and put in his first crop. **1983** A. CANNON *Bullocks, Bullockies & Other Blokes* 19 Rolling scrub, which was necessary to clear the land before farming could commence, was too rough and risky for horses, and, as few settlers owned bullock teams, they let out these jobs to contractors.

roll-call. *Shearing. Obs.* The reading out of names of shearers who have booked a stand in a shed in advance.

1899 *Bulletin* (Sydney) 19 Aug. 32/1 They never seemed to strike a union shed until at least a week after roll-call. **1904** *Shearer* (Sydney) 13 Aug. 7/3 If unsuccessful in securing a pen at roll-call, they at once push on to other sheds where there may be a chance of obtaining employment. **1908** *Bulletin* (Sydney) 15 Oct. 15/2 The bike . . is a boon to the 'big gun' and 'ringer'—who always aspire to catch a distant roll call. **1909** W.G. SPENCE *Aust.'s Awakening* 82 Organisers were kept very busy, often knocking up several horses during the season in rapid riding to get from one shed to another in time to be at roll-call.

roller. *Shearing.* [f. ROLL *v.*[2] 2.] One who rolls a newly-shorn fleece. Also **roller-man.**

[N.Z. **1892** W.E. SWANTON *Notes on N.Z.* 96 The wool-classer with his assistant rollers.] **1899** G. JEFFREY *Princ. Australasian Woolclassing* 39 As soon as the fleece is off the sheep's back, the pickers-up take it by the breeches and place it on the rollers' tables. **1910** *Bulletin* (Sydney) 28 Apr. 13/1, I can see . . the boys racing up the board, the piece-pickers and rollers getting the wool away. **1918** R.H. KNYVETT *Over there with Australs.* 29 At shearing-time the 'gaffers' (grandfathers) and young boys get employment as 'pickers-up' and 'rollers'. **1927** J. MATHIEU *Backblock Ballads* 7 And the pickers-up are streaking To the tables all a-grin, But the roller-men ain't peaking Though they've nearly built them in. **1955** N. PULLIAM *I traveled Lonely Land* 217 There are many others involved in the business of running the sheep station .. the penners-up, the rollers [etc.].

roll up. [f. ROLL *v.*[1]]

1. *Hist.* A mass meeting of gold-miners called to consider an individual grievance or an issue of common concern; a summons to attend such a meeting: see quots. 1861 (2) and 1896. Also *attrib.*

1861 *Sydney Morning Herald* 28 Jan. 8/1 On the 18th instant there was a small roll up against the unfortunate Chinese. **1861** *Miner & General Advertiser* (Lambing Flat) 3 July 2/2 *Monster roll up.* The words which head our article have a peculiar meaning and significance; they remind us at once of those movements which had for their object the removal from amongst us of the Chinese, and which a few months ago caused the most profound sensation from the remotest interior to the metropolis. **1864** J. SNODGRASS *N.S.W. as it Is* 46 They actually caused them to assemble at .. a 'Roll up' for the purpose of driving these unfortunate creatures off the diggings. **1878** *Squatter's Plum* 12 Some years have now elapsed since the Roll-up took place at Lambing Flat (Young). **1896** J.M. PRICE *Land of Gold* 103 Immediately a man is caught stealing, the 'roll up' is sounded, that is to say, a tin pannikin is beaten vigorously drumwise, and, on hearing this ominous sound, all the miners in the camp hurry up to the place. The case is roughly explained to them, an impromptu court is immediately formed, a president elected, and there and then the culprit is tried. If he is found guilty, and when he has been caught *in flagrante delicto*, there is of course no doubt about it, he is ordered to leave the camp .. and never return to it again under the risk of being tarred and feathered. **1914** *Bulletin* (Sydney) 29 Oct. 13/2 The 'roll-up' of the prospectors at gold-rushes, or the 'muck-heap trial' of the opal-gougers, gives an accused a fair run for his money... The most extraordinary 'roll-up' I ever ran across was at Korrumburra (Vic.)... Thirty women laid hold of and court-martialled three non-unionists. **1929** R.D. LANE *Romance Old Coolgardie* 59 He had been reading in his tent (not playing at the two-up school) when, in response to the roll-up call he ventured forth. **1935** F. CLUNE *Rolling down Lachlan* 95 A roll-up was .. called, and .. the diggers marched to the camp jail. **1946** K.S. PRICHARD *Roaring Nineties* 51 Now and then, there was a roll-up, a muster of all the miners and prospectors on the field, to settle some dispute about a claim or row between mates. **1948** M. UREN *Glint of Gold* 125 A roll-up was called by the rattling of two prospecting dishes. Three diggers were chosen to act as judges, and the assembly was to act as a communal jury.

2. *transf.* An assembly.

1889 *Bulletin* (Sydney) 2 Mar. 12/4 And of such men there'll many be, and of such leaders some, In the roll-up of Australians on some dark day yet to come. **1913** *Ibid.* 25 Dec. 22/3 Arrived in a cow locality a fortnight prior to the annual meeting of subscribers to the School of Arts. The roll-up filled the hall... Only 17 persons were eligible to vote. Others were unfinancial. **1942** *Ibid.* 19 Aug. 12/3 At the morning-tea roll up of the Works and Parks gang, tea was scarce and coffee not plentiful. **1962** *N.T. News* (Darwin) 11 Jan. 6/4 He hoped for a big roll-up at next Thursday's meeting. **1965** K. SMITH *OGF* 186 'We should get a big roll-up, Darce.' 'Yeah. It should be a great show. We'll keep the poker machines locked up and turn on the sherry.'

rolly-poley, rolly-polly, varr. ROLY-POLY.

roly. Abbrev. of ROLY-POLY.

1911 *Bulletin* (Sydney) 30 Mar. 44/2 A hundred rolies racing across a plain in the moonlight is a weird sight. **1973** R. ROBINSON *Drift of Things* 129 On a property near the Pilliga Scrub I landed a job cutting galvanized roly.

roly-poly. Also **roley-poley, rolly-poley** (or **-polly**). [See quot. 1907.] Any of several plants, usu. of arid and semi-arid Aust., which break off at ground level and roll along in the wind, esp. the rounded shrubs *Salsola kali* (fam. Chenopodiaceae), also known as BUCKBUSH, and *Sclerolaena muricata.* Also *attrib.*

1857 D. BUNCE *Australiasiatic Reminisc.* 168 Very common to these plains, was a large-growing *salsolaceous* plant, belonging to the *Chenopodeaceae*... These weeds grow in the form of a large ball... No sooner were a few of these balls (or, as we were in the habit of calling them, 'rolly-poleys') taken up with the current of air, than the mules began to kick and buck. **1862** G. BOURNE *Jrnl. Landsborough's Exped. from Carpentaria* 33 Far as the eye can reach these Downs extend, seldom relieved by timber, and covered with the eternal 'roley poley'. **1881** *Proc. Linnean Soc. N.S.W.* VI. 742 We saw .. *Salsola Kali* 'Salt-wort' or 'Rolly polly'. **1885** P.R. MEGGY *From Sydney to Silverton* 121 Much of the country was spoiled by the roly poly, which .. is utterly valueless for food except when just shooting above the ground. **1898** *Bulletin* (Sydney) 12 Mar. 14/3 Around a station near Breeza, the plains for miles were covered with what are known as 'rolly-poleys', and the crows were in swarms. **1907** *Ibid.* 13 June 15/1 The strange 'roly-poly'.. This plant is one of Nature's marvels. Growing to a height of about 20 in., it looks like the back of a porcupine. It overturns sideways when a strong wind arrives, and rolls along and so scatters its seeds over the soil. **1912** SPENCER & GILLEN *Across Aust.* 42 One of the most characteristic plants of this part of the country is the so-called roly-poly (*Salsola kali*). **1930** D. COTTRELL *Earth Battle* 298 Dried grass and roly-polies had been blown over the tracks of the ploughs. **1935** *Know your Weeds* (N.S.W. Dept. Agric.) 18 *Bassia quinquecuspis* ('roley poley') .. being .. brittle and prone to form balls. **1946** W.E. HARNEY *North of 23°* 61 The rolypoly grass bounding past, jumping and leaping in the wind. **1955** D. NILAND *Shiralee* 26 The wind whuddered across the waste, scattering the roly-poly not unlike a lot of sheep making a stupid run for it. **1959** M. RAYMOND *Smiley roams Road* 40 The huge, dead round plants, snapped off by the wind, came tumbling across the plain. 'Aw, they're only ole rolly-pollies.' **1976** K. BROWN *Knock Ten* 54 He went stumbling through the high clumps of roly-poly and prickly bush thick in the gullies. **1978** L. HORSPHOL *Turn down Empty Glass* 158 The balls of tumble-weed (or rolly-polly), as many Australians call them .. were catherine-wheeling past my car on their endless journeys across the stony desert. **1982** P. ADAM SMITH *Shearers* 232 Roly-poly .. the big, dried-out pieces of stick matting the wool together—sometimes binding the sheep's legs together—rip into the shearers' flesh.

Rome Beauty. [Of unknown origin.] A variety of eating apple; the tree bearing such apples.

1893 D.A. CRICHTON *Australasian Fruit Culturist* I. 179 *Rome Beauty* (*Gillett's Seedling*)—An excellent American variety .. a first-class dessert Apple, and an excellent variety for a local market and export. **1905** *Jrnl. Dept. Agric. Vic.* III. 388 Rome Beauty .. is an American variety, which originated in Southern Ohio, U.S.A. It was first introduced to Victoria by the Royal Horticultural Society, and distributed under the name of Grimes' Golden, and it was only after the trees came into bearing that it was found to be Rome Beauty, Grimes' Golden being an entirely distinct apple... The Rome Beauty is a good bearer, and is also a good variety for export. **1936** *Austral. Writer's Ann.* 77 Ruddy Democrats, Golden Pippins and gaily striped Rome Beauties. **1966** E.C. WHITTAKER *Apple Growing* (ed. 4) 26 Rome Beauty is a coloured dessert apple, usually large in size, with a good appearance and of good quality. **1972** *Mercury* (Hobart) 18 Nov. 1/2 Rome Beauty is probably the only variety which escaped serious damage, being much later to bloom.

roo, *n.*[1] Also **'roo.** Shortened form of JACKEROO *n.* 2.

1891 *Truth* (Sydney) 19 Apr. 73 They .. will allow the dealers to feed in the hut, or even alongside of the *Roos.* **1973** *Bronze Swagman Bk. Bush Verse* (1974) 17 The Roo has been to the best of schools And considers he knows the rule. **1976** *Bulletin* (Sydney) 3 Apr. 20/2 There soon became a certain fascination about jackarooing for the Minister for War, as one 'roo put it.

roo, *n.*[2] Also **'roo.**

a. Shortened form of KANGAROO *n.* 1. Also *attrib.*

1898 *Bulletin* (Sydney) 12 Nov. 14/4 There is a brisk demand for 'roos tails among London epicures. **1904** M. WHITE *Shanty Entertainment* 4 As shy as an old man 'roo. **1920** *Huon Times* (Franklin) 18 June 3/1 'Kanga' was a small-sized 'roo. **1935** H.H. FINLAYSON *Red Centre* 53 The 'roos 'sit down like a mob of waxbills'. **1946** *Bulletin* (Sydney) 24 July 29/1, I was runnin' the herd in the paddick with the 'roo-proof fence at night. **1955** *Ibid.* 16 Feb. 12/2 The 'roo-barbecue was organised by visiting American scientist. **1963** *Ibid.* 14 Sept. 30/1 This would be most important in areas which would always, inevitably, carry a lot of 'roos, i.e. marginal land. **1971** *Ibid.* 30 Oct. 24/1 Delegates will be able to pose with 'roos and koalas for their friends' cameras. **1983** *Daily News* (Perth) 11 Aug. 10/7, I used to shoot roos.

b. Used *attrib.* in Comb., as **roo dog, hunter, -hunting, -killing, meat, scalper, shooter, -shooting, skin, tail soup.**

1900 *Bulletin* (Sydney) 7 July 32/1 'I've seen the same thing ..,' said the 'roo-hunter. **1900** *Ibid.* 28 July 14/4 The dingo and 'roo-scalper can shoot. **1917** T.J. BRIGGS *Life & Experiences Successful W. Austral.* 120, I was there for a certain purpose .. namely to obtain 'roo skins. *Ibid.* 122, I put in another winter at 'roo hunting. **1932** I.L. IDRIESS *Lasseter's Last Ride* 17 'Roo-tail soup was a welcome addition to the bill of fare. **1932** K.S. PRICHARD *Kiss on Lips* 83 She was as good a 'roo dog as I've seen and no mistake. **1945** *Bulletin* (Sydney) 30 May 13/2 Doughy .. was .. responsible for some big 'roo-skin tallies from n.-w. Queensland. **1946** *Ibid.* 27 Feb. 15/3 Why do so many outback Australians shy off 'roo meat? **1946** J.J. FAHEY *Slim Sullivan hits Wallaby* 14 His decision to become a roo shooter. **1953** H.G. LAMOND *Big Red* 36 'Roo skins were best during the winter months. **1960** *Bulletin* (Sydney) 14 Sept. 19/1 Kang, the old 'roo-dog, failed to return from one of his usual sorties. **1967** W. WATKINS *Shadow of Whip* 52 Took Jake's ute and went roo shooting. **1968** E.M. NOBLET *Winds that Blew* 34 'Roo tail soup and mutton shank soup and toast and toast and toast. **1968** D. O'GRADY *Bottle of Sandwiches* 142 A hunk of roo meat skewered onto the biggest fork we had. **1975** X. HERBERT *Poor Fellow my Country* 1027 The publican .. brought the drovers, fencers, shearers, doggers, 'roo-shooters, ringers, well-sinkers, and all the rest of rural workers and loafers, to take a spell there. **1979** D. MAITLAND *Breaking Out* 127 We fell in with this bloke from out West who'd done a lot of roo-shooting for the dog-food factories. **1981** D. STUART *I think I'll Live* 223 Saw him once, open a tin o' salmon, put it out on an enamel plate, put three or four big spoonfuls o' marmalade on it an' hog it into him like a 'roo dog gutsin sausages. **1986** *Canberra Times* 30 Aug. 6/2 (*heading*) Qld. 'threatening' mass roo-killing.

c. Special Comb. **roo bar, guard,** BULLBAR.

1973 J. GREENWAY *Down among Wild Men* 135 Unbendable '**roo bar**' to shunt kangaroos as the cowcatchers on our old locomotives. **1975** L. WALKER *Runaway Girl* 29 By the notable absence of dents in your 'roo bars you didn't hit any kangaroos. **1979** J. WILLIAMS *White River* 79 'Everything's already been written about Kalgoorlie', I'd retorted, 'even the one about the underground miner who drove off to Port Hedland with a solid gold 'roo bar'. **1982** *Bulletin* (Sydney) 24 Aug. 57/1 Vehicles are fitted with roo bars, which keep the big animal from coming through the windscreen. **1972** *Southerly* iii. 216, I rinsed my mouth and drank sparingly from the waterbag on the **'roo guard.**

roo, *v. intr.* Shortened form of KANGAROO *v.* 1.

1907 *Bulletin* (Sydney) 17 Oct. 14/1 Meeting the boss 'rooing .. Midnight was invited to join the hunt. **1923** *Ibid.* 22 Nov. 22/3, I have 'rooed on some of the largest holdings in N.S.W. **1932** K. PRICHARD *Kiss on Lips* 82 'Rooin' this week, Colonel? **1964** E. LANE *Our Uncle Charlie* 134 It always amazed anyone going rooing with Uncle how he could ride into the scrub.

roof. *Opal-mining.* [Transf. use of *roof* the stratum lying immediately over a bed of coal.] The stratum lying immediately above opal-bearing material.

1931 M.S. BUCHANAN *Prospecting for Opal* 8 Almost all the sheet of potch containing opal lies within two ft. from the roof. **1932** I.L. IDRIESS *Prospecting for Gold* 232 Thousands of pounds' worth of valuable opals have been won in this thin, flinty hard band. Far more have been got *under* the band, which is the 'roof'. **1960** *People Mag.* (Sydney) 27 Apr. 51 Pipe opal .. is mostly found in soft white clay between one and six inches below the over-lying sandstone 'roof'.

Rooshan, Rooshian, varr. RUSSIAN.

root, *n.*[1] Shortened form of PIGROOT *n.*

1930 'BRENT OF BIN BIN' *Ten Creeks Run* (1952) 7 'He can't ride! The colt's only pig-rootin'!' 'Pooh! He's hangin' on by his spurs!' 'The next root will bring him a buster.'

root, *n.*[2] [See ROOT *v.*[2]]

a. An act of sexual intercourse.

1959 R. CHAMBERLAIN *Stuart Affair* (1973) 111 Did you have a root? **1969** E.D. PRICHARD *Bachelor's Guide Sydney* 99 'Root' and 'stuff' mean sexual intercourse here. **1969** A. BUZO *Rooted* (1973) 43 Hey, do you remember the time he got pissed out of his mind and fronted up to this old duck and asked her for a root? **1971** B. HUMPHRIES *Bazza pulls it Off*, I hear tell these *artists* in London don't exactly have to chase the odd root. **1971** D. WILLIAMSON *Removalists* (1972) 77 My private life may not be spotless, Sergeant, but I want you to know that I'm very fond of my husband... If roots were hamburgers, you could feed a bloody army. **1979** CAREY & LETTE *Puberty Blues* 24 At South Cronulla we'd let the boys 'tit-us-off' and occasionally get a hand down our pants. At North Cronulla we'd progressed to dry roots. **1985** *Canberra Times* 6 Dec. 12/2 Which one of you girls is going to take your clothes off and give me a root?

b. A (female) sexual partner.

1961 F. HARDY *Hard Way* 77 The conversation led inevitably to women. Our shabby criminal struck a match revealing .. a sign scrawled on the wall: 'Best American root—ring such and such a number.' **1969** A. BUZO *Front Room Boys* (1970) 89 All she wants is a bit of fun on the side... She's a good root, too. **1979** CAREY & LETTE *Puberty Blues* 5 She walked everywhere in her bikini. That meant she was showing off her body and was an easy root. **1982** *Bulletin* (Sydney) 9 Nov. 34/1 Globe trotting Australians certainly have become noted for their high sex drive... At their mother's knee, little Australians learn that 'good root' is the highest term of approval.

root, *v.*[1] *intr.* Shortened form of PIGROOT *v.* 1.

1929 K.S. PRICHARD *Coonardoo* (1961) 49 He'd begin with a flying root and a couple of high bucks .. and go on buckin' and rootin' in a circle. **1934** *Bulletin* (Sydney) 31 Jan. 32/2 Give the horse that can root a bit to the horse-breaker or the head stockman is the general rule, or, better still, to the blacks. **1938** C.P. CONIGRAVE *Walk-About* 36 'Can you put us on to a few good nags for our trip, Billy?' I inquired. He told me that he had some good sorts... The 'cows' might 'root' for a start, he thought, but they'd soon steady down. **1955** H.G. LAMOND *Towser* 269 A horse 'roots' when not bucking hard.

root, *v.*[2] [Of unknown origin: it is likely that sense 2 is older and sense 1 a fig. use of sense 2.]

1. *trans.* To ruin; to exhaust; to frustrate. Freq. in pass. and as *ppl. a.*

1944 J. HETHERINGTON *Austral. Soldier* 28 'Listen', the dying man said, 'I'm rooted.' **1957** D. WHITINGTON *Treasure upon Earth* 89 A general strike had been ordered... 'Roots our plans a bit,' Mick said ruefully. 'We're a bloody long way from home, but the walk won't hurt us.' **1962** R. TULLIPAN *March into Morning* 34 The country is rooted for the want of an Irish King and a Yankee pope. **1968** D. O'GRADY *Bottle of Sandwiches* 52 Starter motors rooted, engines rooted, batteries rooted, tyres rooted. **1974** *Smoke Signal* (Palm Island) June 6, I think Bjelke-Petersen has got you rooted! **1976** K. CLIFT *Soldier who never grew Up* 145 'God, Ken, where have you been?' .. I was too rooted to explain. I ate some iron rations .. then I fell asleep. **1982** J. HIBBERD *Country Quinella* (1984) 66 Er, why don't you grab a pew, Valhalla. You must be rooted.

2. *trans.* To have sexual intercourse with (a person); also *intr.*, to engage in sexual intercourse.

1958 R. CHAMBERLAIN *Stuart Affair* (1973) 12, I took her bathers off. Then I raped her. She was hard to root. **1966** P. WHITE *Solid Mandala* 185 We'll root together so good you'll shoot out the other side of Christmas. **1970** D. WILLIAMSON *Coming of Stork* (1970) 14 Country tarts would root a wombat if they thought he was going to be a doctor one day. **1974** *Southerly* 271 'She's obviously a convent girl,' Singleton said, with the aplomb of a connoisseur. 'They root like rabbits.' **1977** C. MCGREGOR *See-Through Revolver* 80 The media think women aren't good for anything else. Except rooting. **1981** P. RADLEY *Jack Rivers & Me* 161 Brake .. caught Duxie Tremayne jacking-off during a dance-break and was presently rooting him under the building.

3. In phrases.

a. wouldn't it root you: see WOULD **b.**

b. root (someone's) **boot,** an expression of exasperation.

1967 J. HIBBERD *White with Wire Wheels* (1970) 153 Root my boot. What a night. **1981** B. DICKINS *Gift of Gab* 5 'Gawd, it's flamin' rainin'?' says Old Baldy... 'Wouldn't it root your boot?'

c. get rooted, 'get lost', 'get fucked'.

1961 M. CALTHORPE *Dyehouse* 186 'He can get rooted, for all I care,' Collins said bitterly. **1974** D. IRELAND *Burn* 29, I can tell anyone in the world to go and get rooted. **1979** J. SUMMONS *Lamb of God* 30 Get rooted. I can't write in the bus. I'll lend you mine to copy—you'll get it right for a change.

rootable, *adj.* Sexually attractive.

1973 D. WILLIAMSON *What if you died Tomorrow* (1974) 156, I had a gorgeous young dancer lined up. Quite stupid—apologies to you two feminists—but very rootable.

rooter, *n.*[1] Shortened form of PIG-ROOTER.

1920 *Bulletin* (Sydney) 24 June 20/2 In far-western Queensland, where you *do* get brumbies and rough horses, they are considered soft snaps unless they can 'spin' and 'buck back'. The straight-ahead prad, no matter with how great a jar he hits the ground, is a mere 'rooter'. **1930** *Ibid.* 11 June 20/4 They were talking about buckjumpers when Sam, the cook, chipped in. 'Ever see a rooter chuck the saddle an' not the rider?' he asked. **1933** *Ibid.* 13 Dec. 25/2 The only rooter that got the better of Jack was a sullen brute that threw himself down and rolled.

rooter, *n.*[2] One who is sexually promiscuous.

1965 J. BEEDE *They hosed them Out* 149 It was at one of these unscheduled bludging periods that the Rooters' Club was born. Its function was for a closer and more intimate relationship with all females. **1984** B. REED *Crooks* 159 Club Finese is still for the higher class naughty little rooter.

ropable, var. ROPEABLE.

rope, *v.* [Also U.S.] *trans.* To catch (an animal) with a noosed rope; to lasso.

1827 P. CUNNINGHAM *Two Yrs. in N.S.W.* I. 291 The young heifers in their first calf, too, ought to be broken in to milk, as, if that period is passed over, they are afterwards most untractable milkers:—by *roping* two or three times, they are soon taught to walk quietly up to the milking pail. **1849** A. HARRIS *Emigrant Family* (1967) 38 He roped a young bullock, that he wanted yoked. **1852** MRS C. MEREDITH *My Home in Tas.* II. 19 'Rope' them (*i.e.*, catch them by flinging a noose over their heads). **1884** 'R. BOLDREWOOD' *Old Melbourne Memories* 150 You could 'rope' .. any Clifton colt or filly, back them in three days, and within a week ride a journey. **1893** R. BRUCE *Echoes from Coondambo* 156 I'll rope that steer before long! **1912** *Bulletin* (Sydney) 11 July 14/2, I saw women and girls toiling in the branding yard. They used to rope and help to throw a colt. **1960** E. O'CONNER *Irish Man* 210 He and Paula and Dalgliesh mustered near the homestead, and worked cattle in the yards close to the house. He learned to rope a calf, and to have the hot brand ready to be placed quickly in Dalgliesh's outstretched hand.

Hence **roper** *n.*

1849 A. HARRIS *Emigrant Family* (1967) 129 The pole drops clear, leaving the rope only in the roper's hands.

ropeable, *a. fig.* Also **ropable.** Requiring to be restrained; angry; bad-tempered.

1874 C. DE BOOS *Congewoi Correspondence* 195, I don't know a nastier smell than the smeller new togs just fresh from the tailor's goose, and the thoughter that amost made me ropable. **1891** *Argus* (Melbourne) 10 Oct. 13/4 The service has shown itself so 'ropeable' heretofore that one experiences .. satisfaction in seeing it roped. **1903** *Truth* (Sydney) 14 June 1/4 A rope-able man: Nosey Bob. **1912** T.E. SPENCER *Bindawalla* 71 He'll be ropable. He's a snorter when he starts. **1922** *Bulletin* (Sydney) 12 Jan. 22/1, I don't mind calling a Chow a thief and even a liar (which makes him still more ropeable), but when it comes to addressing him as Paddy someone else can have it on his own. **1934** E. STOREY *Eve's Affairs* 121 Robert had already drifted away to put up three new telephone poles. Imagine it, someone went off with the others for firewood. Robert, I believe, was ropeable. **1947** N. LINDSAY *Halfway to Anywhere* 167 Cripes, the idea of a bloke going with rough tarts gets my old man absolutely ropeable. **1959** D. HEWETT *Bobbin Up* 185 The agent never bothered to tell us about this little technicality .. no water. There was another bloke there. He was ropable. **1973** J. POWERS *Last of Knuckleman* (1974) 60, I kept tellin' meself I wasn't gonna get upset. But it don't work—'cause I am upset! Fuckin' ropeable! **1983** HIBBERD & HUTCHINSON *Barracker's Bible* 172 Barrassi is ropeable out there after that lamentable quarter by the Kangas.

roping, *vbl. n.* [f. ROPE.]

1. The action of catching (an animal) with a rope.

1890 'R. BOLDREWOOD' *Colonial Reformer* (1891) 119 The drafting, the roping, the branding .. were novelties of a very high order.

2. Special Comb. **roping pole, stick,** a long pole used to drop a noosed rope over the head of an animal.

1890 'R. BOLDREWOOD' *Colonial Reformer* I. 192 Jack Windsor being a first-class stockman, and handy with the **roping-pole**, was always invited to join the party. **1916** T. WARLOW *By Mirage & Mulga* 52 You are a fright! I never thought you would let a few toads put you in that state. Why, any one of your hairs would do for a roping-pole. **1927** K.S. PRICHARD *Brumby Innes* (1974) 74 I'm handy with the roping pole, I'm handy with the brand. **1981** G. MITCHELL *Bush Horseman* 70 When catching unbroken horses in yards, many of the old bushmen used a roping pole. While more cumbersome than the thrown lasso, less skill was required, and a good throwing rope was not necessary. **1846** C.P. HODGSON *Reminisc. Aust.* 115 A **roping-stick** about ten feet long, to which is attached a noose for throwing round the calf's neck. **1849** A. HARRIS *Emigrant Family* (1967) 129 This roping-stick or catching-pole, as it is indiscriminately called, is a thin sapling .. twelve or fifteen feet in length, just large enough at one end to be handily managed by both hands, and having a small fork at the other. Over the forked extremity the slip-noose of the catching-rope is hung, the rope itself being brought loosely down along the pole toward the person using it, with the far end trailing on the ground. **1888** 'R. BOLDREWOOD' *Robbery under Arms* III. 201 He stuck to his roping-stick—a good, heavy-ended gum sapling, six or seven feet long.

rort, *n.* Also **roart, wrought.** [f. *rorty* boisterous, rowdy; of dubious propriety.]

1. An act of fraud or sharp practice; a 'lurk'.

1926 'DRYBLOWER' *Verses* 50 A bank-roll unto him is 'Oscar Asche', A swindle is to him a 'joke', a 'wrought'. **1936** J. DEVANNY *Sugar Heaven* 20 The cockies are supposed to pay this retention money into the bank and we are supposed to draw interest on it but normally they don't pay it in. They keep the use of it through the season and we draw the bare amount at the end of the cut. It's the greatest rort ever. **1941** *Men may Smoke* (Sydney) May 7, I think this is a rort. **1945** *Atebrin Advocate: Mag. 2/4 Austral. Armoured Regiment* 10 Feb. 4 Insurance was his civil 'roart'. **1962** R. TULLIPAN *March into Morning* 49 'I'll be getting the award wage on this road job, but you've got to sling a quid to the foreman every week. He splits it with the Main Roads engineer.' 'Great old rort,' Dixon growled. 'It's done everywhere.' **1965** R.H. CONQUEST *Horses in Kitchen* 107 Willie, although an honest man, had what is known today as a gimmick. The word was unknown to us then. We referred to it as 'Willie's rort'. **1977** R. BEILBY *Gunner* 279 So this was the big secret. A wrought, a put-up job. **1985** *Canberra Times* 28 May 1 (*heading*) Tax rorts hit collections.

2. A wild party; an escapade.

[**1941** S.J. BAKER *Pop. Dict. Austral. Slang* 61 *Rort*, .. a crowd .. (something) particularly good.] **1952** T.A.G. HUNGERFORD *Ridge & River* 81 Out we go on another bloody rort, so what's the use of saving a day? **1964**

G. Johnston *My Brother Jack* 111, I didn't know you were going to have a bit of a rort here. I mean, I had no intention of pratting in, if you follow what I mean. **1972** *Bulletin* (Sydney) 12 Aug. 7/3 Our committee bunged on a rort for some of them, with plenty of snags and red Ned. **1974** *Ibid.* 19 Jan. 13/1 Every night when he comes home after knockin' back the curried prawns . . at some posh Canberra rort or Press piss-up, you can bet yer life he's straight into the ensuite dunnee. **1985** *Canberra Times* 6 Mar. 23/1 (*heading*) Big annual rort a blunt peace push.

rort, *v.* [As prec.]

1. a. *intr.* To engage in sharp practice. Freq. as *vbl. n.*

1919 C. Drew *Doings of Dave* 142 'Melbourne . . I've been down there doin' a bit of rortin'.' . . 'What line are you on?' 'Clocks', answered Tiger, 'They're the best line of clocks you ever slung your eyes on.' **1980** *Sunday Mail* (Brisbane) 15 June 6 (*heading*) Overseas tax havens and 'rorting' claimed. $3,000 m. a year in tax dodges.

b. *trans.* To manipulate (a ballot, records, etc.) fraudulently, to rig: see quot. 1981. Freq. as *vbl. n.*

1980 *Sydney Morning Herald* 21 July 1/2 He felt the ALP should urgently close several inner city branches, including one whose real membership was only a tenth of its fraudulently manipulated membership records. 'This rorting is all about control over public office preselections and particularly in local government and the avenues for graft which it provides.' **1980** *Nat. Times* (Sydney) 27 July 3/1 The 'rorting', as it is called, of branch books to influence the selection of local, State and Federal . . candidates. **1981** *Sydney Morning Herald* 10 June 6/1 Both sides blamed the other for massive 'rorting' in party branches. Rorting, in Labor jargon, is a charmingly flexible term to cover such practices as stacking branch membership, rigging elections, cooking branch records and, as a last resort, losing all branch records to frustrate a head office inquiry. Rorting, in short, means working hot in the Labor Party. **1985** *Bulletin* (Sydney) 19 Nov. 47/2 About 1500 of the union's 22,000 N.S.W. members were rendered with false addresses on the union's roll. . . A plan to rort the roll could involve isolating the names of members who are listed under out-of-date addresses and substituting . . 'letterbox'. That is a false address which could be used as a pick-up point for ballot papers. The members whose names are used never receive their ballot papers, which are filled in by whoever picks them up at the letterbox.

2. *intr.* To go 'on the town'. Also with **up**, and as *vbl. n.*

1956 J.E. Macdonnell *Commander Brady* 249 Now don't forget. Nobody grogged-up. Nobody rortin' it up with them Yanks. Behave yerselves. **1981** D. Stuart *I think I'll Live* 179, I got to be mates with him, out dancing, shielah rortin' together.

Hence **rorted** *ppl. a.*, rigged.

1981 *Austral.* (Sydney) 1 Apr. 8/6 Mr Wright said the fund involved a 'rorted system' of adjusting rates in the party's newspaper.

rorter. Also **wroughter.** [f. Rort *n.* 1.]

1. One who engages in sharp practice: see quot. 1941.

1926 'Dryblower' *Verses* 93 He'd been a race course wroughter In the years that yester dwell. **1941** S.J. Baker *Pop. Dict. Austral. Slang* 61 *Rorter*, a professional sharper: a hawker of worthless goods: one who practises sly dodges to obtain money. **1962** A. Marshall *This is Grass* 159 Rorters like Flogger prepared to fleece any man who stood staring around him. **1975** *Bulletin* (Sydney) 31 May 23/2 Even criminals have their little snobberies and professional rivalries; and so the big-money rorter insists on being known as a confidence trickster. None of that low-class, street-rorter bit for him.

2. One who engages in rorting (see Rort *v.* 1 b.).

1981 *Nat. Times* (Sydney) 6 Dec. 18/3 On balance the Right—because they have much more experience and also happen to run the party's head office—are more accomplished rorters.

3. With distinguishing element, as **poofter rorter**: see Poofter 2.

rose, *a.* Used as a distinguishing epithet in the names of flora and fauna: **rose apple,** any of several plants, incl. *Burdekin plum* (see Burdekin), trees of the genus *Owenia* (fam. Meliaceae), and esp. the rainforest tree *Syzygium moorei* (fam. Myrtaceae) of n.e. N.S.W. and s.e. Qld.; **-breasted cockatoo,** Galah 1; formerly also **rose(-coloured) cockatoo; -crowned (fruit) pigeon,** the bird *Ptilinopus regina ewingii* of Arnhem Land (N.T.) and the Kimberley region (W.A.); **gum,** the tree *Eucalyptus grandis* (see *flooded gum* Flooded); **robin,** the small, predom. grey bird *Petroica rosea* of s.e. mainland Aust., the mature male having a rose-coloured breast; also **rose-breasted robin.**

1846 *Portland Guardian* 18 Sept. 4/3 We collected three species of **rose-apple** (eugenia), one was a large scarlet fruit, with longitudinal ribs of a coarse and strong aromatic taste; another was of a delicate rose colour, and extremely pleasant. **1855** J. Bonwick *Geogr. Aust. & N.Z.* (ed. 3) 205 The . . Rose apple, and the Crimson lily flourish in North Australia. **1888** *Proc. Linnean Soc. N.S.W.* III. 534 *Owenia cerasifera* . . 'Sweet plum', 'Rose apple'. . . This plant bears a fine juicy red fruit with a large stone. **1926** *Qld. Agric. Jrnl.* XXV. 440 *Owenia venosa*. Rose Apple . . (Yarraman). **1932** R.H. Anderson *Trees of N.S.W.* 153 The Rose Apple (*Eugenia Moorei*) has . . large pink flowers borne on the old wood. **1965** *Austral. Encycl.* III. 412 *S[yzygium] moorei* . . has dense masses of large rosy-red flowers springing from the older branchwood, and is sometimes called 'rose apple'. **1985** N. & H. Nicholson *Austral. Rainforest Plants* 62 Rose Apple is one of the most impressive of the tall rainforest trees, with its thick trunk and dense crown of large glossy leaves. **1838** [**rose-breasted cockatoo**] *S. Austral. Gaz.* (Adelaide) 21 July 4/1 Those very beautiful birds the rose cockatoo and the crested pigeon of the marshes. **1841** *Port Phillip Patriot* 9 Aug. 4/2 Flocks of . . rose-breasted cockatoos, were seen in every direction, restless and busy. **1845** J. Gould *Birds of Aust.* (1848) V. Pl. 4, *Cacatua eos* . . Rose-coloured Cockatoo. **1845** L. Leichhardt *Jrnl. Overland Exped. Aust.* 30 July (1847) 350 Six rose-breasted cockatoos . . were shot on the plains. **1849** C. Sturt *Narr. Exped. Central Aust.* II. 36 App. *Rose Cockatoo* . . seen in the depressed interior in such great numbers, has a slate coloured back, wings and tail, whilst its breast and neck are of a beautiful rose-pink colour. **1860** J.H. Lewis *Stuart's Journey Interior Aust.* 16 Stuart . . came upon a large gum creek, divided into numerous channels, in one of which he found a native well. . . The rose-colored cockatoo was seen here. **1867** F.J. Byerley *Narr. Overland Exped. Northern Qld.* 3 The creek received the name of Galaa Creek, in allusion to the galaa or rose cockatoo (*Cacatua Rosea*). **1882** *Proc. Linnean Soc. N.S.W.* VII. 53 The Rose Cockatoo nests in the hollow branches of large trees. **1896** B. Spencer *Rep. Horn Sci. Exped. Central Aust.* II. 111 In cages were young Warbling Parrakeets . . and rose-breasted cockatoos. **1926** *Official Checklist Birds Aust.* (R. Australasian Ornith. Union) p. v, Some long formal names such as Great Brown Kingfisher . . and Rose-breasted Cockatoo, have been replaced by Laughing Kookaburra . . and Galah respectively. **1959** H. Lamond *Sheep Station* 178 Galahs, we call 'em. Those more learned refer to the things as Rose-breasted Cockatoos. **1986** *Canberra Times* 5 Mar. 18/5 It is hard to imagine that Canberra's most common bird was once something of a rarity on the Southern Tablelands. Canberra's first birdwatcher, the head teacher at the Duntroon Public School, saw the galah or rose-breasted cockatoo as he called it, on only one occasion between 1913 and 1928. **1903** *Emu* II. 153 *Ptilopus ewingi* (**Rose-crowned Fruit-Pigeon**). . . This bird was found breeding in the mangroves. **1945** C. Barrett *Austral. Bird Life* 61 The rose-crowned pigeon . . is a form of the red-crowned species. **1982** H.J. Frith *Pigeons & Doves Aust.* 107 For the north-western form [of the Red-crowned Pigeon], 'Rose-crowned Pigeon' is a common name. **1945** J. Devanny *Bird of Paradise* 20 The tractor had deposited two scrub gum—or **rose-gum**-logs. **1956** N.K. Wallis *Austral. Timber Handbk.* 4 On the local market Sydney blue gum and rose gum are used for shipbuilding . . and construction work. **1962** *Daily Mercury Centenary Story Mackay* 43 The best known forest hardwoods are rose gum, blue gum [etc.]. **1968** D. Fleay *Nightwatchmen* 62 The tall flooded or rose gum (*E. grandis*). **1887** [**rose robin**] *Illustr. Austral. News* (Melbourne) 21 Dec. 218/1 Three kinds of robins were found—the dusky, the flame-breasted and the rose-breasted, all fairly numerous. **1903** *Emu* II. 163 Rose-breasted Robin (*Petroeca rosea*)—in the forest only. **1922** L.G. Chandler *Bush Charms* 85 Those [nests] that I have seen of the Rose-breasted Robin have been gems of nest-architecture. **1929** A.H. Chisholm *Birds & Green Places* 36 The rose robin wandering far afield. **1945** C. Barrett *Austral. Bird Life* 175 The pink robin . . and the rose robin (*P[etroica] rosea*) keep to the mountain gullies. **1965** *Austral. Encycl.* VII. 470 The dainty rose-breasted robin, a denizen of eastern Australia. **1984** Simpson & Day *Birds of Aust.* 321 Rose Robin, the most arboreal and acrobatic [of *Petroica* spp.], catches flies in outer canopies of trees.

Rose Hill parrot. *Obs.* [f. *Rose Hill*, the original name for Parramatta, w. of Sydney.] Rosella *n.*[1] 1. Also **Rose Hill (parakeet).**

[**1789** A. Phillip *Voyage to Botany Bay* 130 This spot is very pleasant, and has been named by the Governor, *Rose-Hill*.] **1810** E. Bent Lett. 27 July 187, I have now . . two Rose Hill Parrots. **1817** J. Oxley *Jrnls. Two Exped. N.S.W.* 7 Aug. (1820) 157 A rose-hill parrot was seen for the first time for many months. **1827** *Trans. Linnean Soc. London* XV. 281 [Platycercus Eximius] . . In Mr Caley's MSS. are the following observations on this bird. '*Rosehill Parrot*—So called from the name of the settlement afterwards known by the name of Paramatta.' **1827** P. Cunningham *Two Yrs. in N.S.W.* I. 323 Our parrot-tribes are of infinite variety. . . The little *rosehill* with his red head, yellow breast, and tastefully mottled plumage, the *blue mountain* decked out in all the colours of the rainbow. **1833** H.W. Parker *Rise, Progress, & Present State Van Dieman's Land* 187 The parrot tribe is very abundant, and the plumage of most of them, especially the Rose-hill, is extremely beautiful. **1845** J. Gould *Birds of Aust.* (1848) V. Pl. 29, *Platycercus icterotis*. . . *Moy-a-duk*, Aborigines of the mountain districts of Western Australia. *Rose-hill* of the Colonists. **1846** *Ibid.* Pl. 27, *Platycercus eximius* . . Rose-hill Parrakeet, Colonists of New South Wales. **1852** J. West *Hist. of Tas.* I. 330 Many of the parrots have beautiful plumage, and the white cockatoo and rose-hill parrot have occasionally been taught to speak. **1860** *Sydney Mail* 22 Sept. 6/5 The Rosehill parrot, erroneously called rosella, is nesting. The bird received its designation from having been first seen at Rosehill, a property on the Windsor road, some miles from Parramatta. **1965** *Austral. Encycl.* VII. 491 Rosella, a derivation of 'Rose Hill parrot', the name given by early settlers in Australia to a beautiful and common bird, *Platycercus eximius*, frequently seen in the district of Parramatta, then known as Rose Hill (sometimes spelt Rosehill) in honour of George Rose, a secretary of the British Treasury. From 'Rose Hill parrot' to 'Rosehiller' and then 'rosella' were easy transitions, and in time the last-mentioned term became widely familiar.

rosella /roʊˈzɛlə/, *n.*[1] Formerly also **roselle.** [Altered form of the place-name *Rose Hill*: see Rose hill parrot.]

1. Any of the brightly-coloured parrots of the genus *Platycercus* of all States, originally and still esp. the *eastern rosella* (see Eastern 2). Also with distinguishing epithet, as **Adelaide, crimson, eastern, Moreton Bay, northern, red-headed, western, yellow** (see under first element), and *attrib.*, esp. as **rosella parrot.**

1829 *Sydney Gaz.* 21 July, The doleful dying quails, And roselles golden. **1836** J. Backhouse *Narr. Visit Austral. Colonies* (1843) 438 Some of the birds of V.D. Land abound. . . The Rosella, Rosehill, or Nonpareil Parrot, *Platycercus eximius*. **1836** T.L. Mitchell *Three Exped. Eastern Aust.* 21 Apr. (1838) II. 46 On the bank of the river a new species of roselle appeared amongst the birds, and several were shot as specimens. **1838** J. Hawdon *Jrnl. of Journey N.S.W. to Adelaide* 15 Mar. (1952) 51 Parrots now appeared more numerous, Rosellas and others, similar to those on the Eastern coast. **1845** C. Hodgkinson *Aust., Port Macquarie to Moreton Bay* 92 The Rosella or Nonpareil parroquet, a bird extremely common throughout the colony generally. **1851** J. Henderson *Excursions & Adventures N.S.W.* I. 78 Some of the parrots, including the Rosella, I succeeded in shooting and skinning. The last-named species is extremely beautiful, and is said to derive its name from Rosehill (very properly now bearing the native name Parramatta), where it was first found, and abounded. **1855** F.H. Cockburn *Lett.* (1856) 86 The lovely Rosella parrots are not at all bad eating when roasted and accompanied by a good sauce. **1860** *Sydney Mail* 22 Sept. 6/5 The Rosehill parrot, erroneously called rosella, is nesting. **1869** J. Martineau *Lett. from Aust.*

89 The blue, red, and green Rosella parrot is the commonest bird of any in the bush. **1872** MRS E. MILLETT *Austral. Parsonage* 217 A pomegranate-tree with half-a-dozen Rosellas perched amongst its shining leaves, and ripening fruit, looks like an illuminated initial vignette in an old missal. **1886** W.J. WOODS *Visit to Vic.* 25 And then the Parrots—King-parrots with breasts of fire, rosellas green and golden, scarlet lowries. **1909** G. SMITH *Naturalist in Tas.* 45 Another very beautiful bird which haunts lightly timbered sandstone country and is even common in orchards . . is the Rosella Parakeet. **1926** M. FORREST *Hibiscus Heart* 97 A flight of rosellas, scarlet, green, and blue, crossed the paler blue overhead just as the billy came to the boil. **1951** *Bulletin* (Sydney) 28 Nov. 13/3 I'm settled amongst some tea-tree near a scribbly gum in which my camera is trained on the nesting hollow of a rosella. **1969** J.M. FORSHAW *Austral. Parrots* 177 Parrots belonging to this genus [*sc. Platycercus*] are known collectively as rosellas. They may be readily identified by two obvious plumage characteristics—well defined cheek-patches and pronounced 'mottling' on the back. **1977** J. CARTER *All Things Wild* 20 We had a rosella parrot (injured by a car) recuperating in a cage on the front verandah. **1981** A.B. FACEY *Fortunate Life* 90 The ring-neck parrot . . was most destructive on cereal crops and fruit. Another parrot, smaller and of different markings, was the rosella. This bird was also destructive on cereal crops and fruit.

2. *transf.* A sheep which is losing its wool, and is therefore easy to shear.

1849 *Stephen's Adelaide Miscellany* 8 Nov. 81 If at shearing he chooses to pick all the 'Rosellas' (clean-bellied sheep), no one grumbles. **1897** *Worker* (Sydney) 11 Sept. 1/2 'Rosellas' he likes best of all, for half their fleece is off. **1903** *Bulletin* (Sydney) 10 Jan. 17/1 In Q. and N.S.W. out-back districts . . the sheep grow tufts of belly-wool and so little on any other portion of their bodies that they are termed 'rosellas', after a parrot that fights so viciously as to be generally devoid of neck and back feathers. **1918** *Huon Times* (Franklin) 29 Nov. 3/5 All big-framed animals, with wrinkles, and body covered with beautiful wool from nose to toe—not a 'rosella' amongst them. **1937** D. GUNN *Links with Past* 246 Then each man picked a sheep and caught And took him to the floor, Though some awhile rosellas sought And searched a little more. **1952** J. CLEARY *Sundowners* 212 He had grabbed an old ewe, a 'rosella', with most of the wool along her belly worn off. **1963** O. RUHEN *Flockmaster* 47 Oh, we lost a ewe yesterday. The eagles got it. . . It was that little Roman-nosed one, the rosella, the one that's always going. **1972** G.W. TURNER *Good Austral. Eng.* 60 Few shearers recognised *flyer, cop, gunbarrel* . . as terms for what is usually called a *barebelly* or *rosella.*

3. *Military.* A staff officer.

1919 *Aussie: Austral. Soldiers' Mag.* Jan. 11/1 A certain Rosella in the Aussie Army is known as Old Bloodlust. **1924** A.W. BAZLEY et al. Gloss. Slang A.I.F. 24 (typescript) *Rosella*, a Staff Officer, who with his gold lace, scarlet cap, medal ribbon etc. was supposed to resemble the Rosella. **1940** *Puckapunyal: Offical Jrnl. 17th Austral. Infantry Brigade* Nov. 8 *Rosellas*, staff officers with red tabs on shoulders. **1943** *Troppo Tribune* (Mataranka) 5 July 1 This accounts for the success he has attained with the big birds of the Army in later years; rosellas also hold a prominent position.

rosella /roʊˈzɛlə/, *n.*[2] Also **rozella.** [Transf. use of *rosella, roselle* the red sorrel *Hibiscus sabdariffa.*] The shrub or small tree of n. Aust. *Hibiscus heterophyllus* (fam. Malvaceae), used as a food plant and an ornamental; the flower bud of the plant. See also *native hibiscus* NATIVE *a.* 6 a. Also *attrib.* as **rosella jam.**

1854 *Moreton Bay Free Press* 10 Jan. 3/5 This is the plant from the fruit of which Rosella jam is made. **1871** *Austral. Town & Country Jrnl.* (Sydney) 20 May 619/1 The Rosella, or Hibiscus sorbifolia, of Queensland, bearing an orange-coloured flower, the capsule of which, after flowering, makes such excellent jam. **1890** G.J. BROINOWSKI *Birds of Aust.* III. Pl. 3, Of its food . . the rosella (var. Hibiscus) and the cabbage palm (Corypha Australis) berries would appear to form the staple. **1928** W. ROBERTSON *Coo-ee Talks* 7 Central Queensland is the home of the rozella-bush, and the women of that day made large quantities of rozella jam. **1953** *Bulletin* (Sydney) 22 July 13/4 'It's rosella jam—it's made out of rosellas,' insisted Stan. 'Gaw starve the crows,' breathed his best mate. 'I always knew you were a bit weak in the skull. Now I suppose you'll tell me them Bananalanders make pickles out of peewees and tomato-sauce out of galahs?' 'You blasted idiot', yelled Stan, 'a rosella is a *flower* in Queensland; it's a big red blossom that grows on a bush and people make jam out of it.' **1973** H. HOLTHOUSE *S'pose I Die* 71 A very good effervescent drink from the wild rosella plant.

rosener, var. ROSINER.

rosewood. Any of several trees or shrubs having a fragrant or reddish timber, esp. the tall rainforest tree *Dysoxylum fraserianum* of n.e. N.S.W. and s.e. Qld., *Synoum glandulosum* of e. N.S.W. and e. Qld. (both fam. Meliaceae), and the small tree *Heterodendrum oleifolium* (fam. Sapindaceae) of drier mainland Aust.; the wood of these trees, esp. that of *D. fraserianum.* See also BOONAREE, *bullock bush* BULLOCK *n.* 2. Also *attrib.*

1819 *Sydney Gaz.* 26 June, To the Productions of the Country as then reported, may now be added great Quantities of Rose Wood, the Flooded Gum and Coal. **1821** *HRA* (1917) 1st Ser. X. 490 Covered with Vines and Timber, among which are considerable numbers of Cedar and Rosewood Trees. **1825** B. FIELD *Geogr. Mem. N.S.W.* 320 The rose-wood (of the meliaceae—trichilia glandulosa?) grows in forests with the cedar at Newcastle. *Ibid.* 463 The rosewood, so called from its scent, not colour. **1839** T.L. MITCHELL *Three Exped. Eastern Aust.* (rev. ed.) I. 205 The warmer green of one or two trees of Australian 'rose-wood', relieved the sober greyish green of the pendent acacia. **1844** *Sydney Morning Herald* 12 Dec. 4/4 We were stopped by an impenetrable rosewood scrub, running north and south. **1861** J.D. LANG *Qld., Aust.* 175 *Rose or Violet-Wood* . . is . . similar to our lance-wood at home. **1889** J.H. MAIDEN *Useful Native Plants Aust.* 603 *Synoum glandulosum* . . Rosewood . . Timber firm, and easily worked. When fresh it is of a deep red colour, and emits a scent like that of the common rose. **1890** F.M. BAILEY *Catal. Indigenous & Naturalised Plants Qld.* 102 Rosewood—Acacia fasciculifera and A. glaucescens. **1898** *Proc. Linnean Soc. N.S.W.* XXIII. 124 *Dysoxylon fraseranum* . . is of course the same as the 'Rosewood' of the mainland, which is a valuable timber. **1915** *Forestry Question in N.S.W.* (Austral. Forest League) 4 The Rosewood, which still exists in large quantities in our northern brush forests, rivals the West Indian Mahogany. **1923** J. BOWES *Jackaroos* 83 Open plain country perfectly treeless with the exception of clumps of rosewood and sandalwood at intervals, with patches of casuarina along dry creek-beds. **1948** P.J. HURLEY *Red Cedar* 115 Rosewood is the most beautifully coloured wood, and it lasts forever. Borers will not touch it. **1959** C.V. LAWLOR *All This Humbug* 14 The timber consisted of beautiful wilga and rosewood trees, and heavy clumps of belah. **1984** E. ROLLS *Celebration of Senses* 153, I sit to write on a chair of leather and Australian rosewood made by a craftsman. . . One sits among a soft perfume, a suggestion of distant roses.

rosiner /ˈrɒzənə/. Also **rosener, rozener, roziner.** [f. *rosin* (var. of *resin*), alcoholic drink. Also Irish slang: see OEDS.] A (generous) measure of spirits.

1933 *Bulletin* (Sydney) 10 May 20/1 Fill up the cup, a rozener, a hummer! **1947** H. DRAKE-BROCKMAN *Fatal Days* 114 I've not had a solitary spot since four. I need a rosiner. **1954** T. RONAN *Vision Splendid* 345 They were rozeners I'll admit, but still the three I've had out of this second bottle haven't exactly been small ones. **1976** S. WELLER *Bastards I have Met* 25 Dad had a regular who came in twice a day for a scotch and if you gave him a bloody bucket he'd fill it. He was a dead loss. One day he poured himself a rosener. Dad took his shilling and gave him three-pence change. He said, 'Mr Weller—haven't you made a mistake?' Dad said, 'No—that's right. It's cheaper when you buy it in bulk.' **1978** D. STUART *Wedgetail View* 33 He got him to get outside a bit o' breakfast, an' a good roziner of whisky.

Ross River virus. [f. the name of a river near Townsville, Qld.] A mosquito-borne virus causing a non-fatal disease characterized by a rash, and joint and muscle pain; the disease itself, also known as **Ross River fever.** Also *attrib.*

1966 *Austral. Jrnl. Exper. Biol. & Med. Sci.* 365 Infections of man with Ross River virus or a closely related agent were shown to have occurred on at least 4 occasions between 1957 and 1964 at Mitchell River Mission near the Gulf of Carpentaria. **1972** *Med. Jrnl. Aust.* May I. 1083 Ross River Virus was first isolated from mosquitos of the species *Aëdes vigilax* collected at Townsville in 1959. **1977** *Austral. Encycl.* II. 384 Ross River virus, which is considered to be the cause of this disease [*sc.* epidemic polyarthritis], has been recovered from the mosquitoes *Aedes vigilax* and *Culex annulirostris,* the former from Townsville and Nelson Bay, the latter from Nelson Bay. **1984** *Daily Tel.* (Sydney) 10 Jan. 8/2 Forty-five cases of the crippling Ross River virus have been reported in the past week in south-western N.S.W. **1984** *Area News* (Griffith) 21 Nov. 3/2 If the Ross River Fever mosquito is to be beaten the CSIRO will need to become involved in research to destroy its larvae.

rotate, *v.* In the phr. **wouldn't it rotate you**: see WOULD **b.**

rotten, *a.*

1. In the phr. **to knock rotten,** to kill or stun. Also *fig.*

1919 W.H. DOWNING *Digger Dialects* 31 *Knocked rotten*, killed or stunned. **1941** *Coast to Coast* 179 'He pulled it down on top of him,' continued Joe. . . 'It knocked him rotten.' **1968** S. GORE *Holy Smoke* 47 I'd say he was knocked rotten.

2. Drunk. Also in the phr. **to get rotten.**

1864 *Drinkamania* 8 In 'lush' we are not merely ripe, But only—nearly rotten. **1941** S.J. BAKER *Pop. Dict. Austral. Slang* 61 *Rotten, to get*, to become exceedingly drunk. **1953** T.A.G. HUNGERFORD *Riverslake* 135 Monday to-morrow—blasted work again. God I could get rotten! **1966** R. MORLEY *Cool Change* 13 Something the late Ezra Norton designed himself when he got rotten after a clean-up at the races. **1977** R. HEWISON *Slocum* 10 The corporal was a bit rotten from cans of airline beer.

3. In the collocation **rotten egg,** a children's game: see quot. 1957.

1957 A. MARSHALL *Aust.* (1981) 73 Do you remember 'Rotten Egg' in which a row of our caps lay against the school wall and turns were taken to throw a ball into one of them? I forget exactly how the game developed but there came a stage when, at the shout of Rotten Egg there was a scatter and the ball was thrown at those fleeing. **1979** B. MARTYN *First Footers S. Gippsland* 125 He held a little girl by each hand. He had been out by the barn playing 'rotten egg' with them.

rough, *a.*

1. In the names of plants: **rough-bark(ed) apple,** a rough-barked tree of the genus *Angophora* (fam. Myrtaceae), esp. *A. floribunda* of e. mainland Aust.; **(-leaved) fig,** SANDPAPER FIG.

1919 R.T. BAKER *Hardwoods of Aust.* 7 Pale [timber colour].—*Angophora intermedia* **Rough-barked,** or Narrow-leaved **Apple.** *Ibid.* 130 *Angophora subvelutina* . . 'Rough-bark' or 'Broad-leaved Apple Tree'. . . A tree attaining a considerable size with a rough, persistent, deeply-furrowed bark. **1956** T.Y. HARRIS *Naturecraft in Aust.* 131 Common Angophoras of the bush are: . . Rough-bark Apple—*Angophora intermedia* [etc.]. **1963** C. BURGESS *Blue Mountain Gums* 63 'Rough-barked apple' . . *Angophora floribunda* ('floribunda' from the Latin, referring to the abundance of flowers produced by this species in summer). **1985** D. FOSTER *Dog Rock* 123 Derry works the non-commercial species like river peppermint and rough-barked apple most bee men don't bother with. **1845** L. LEICHHARDT *Jrnl. Overland Exped. Aust.* 4 Aug. (1847) 359 The **rough-leaved fig** tree . . grew on its sandy banks. **1884** A. NILSON *Timber Trees N.S.W.* 78 *F[icus] aspera.*—Rough-leaved Fig.—A large tree, attaining sometimes a height of 100 feet. **1917** EWART & DAVIES *Flora N.T.* 80 *F[icus] scabra* . . (*F. aspera*)—Roper River, Gilruth and Spencer, July-August, 1911. Rough or Purple Fig.

2. In special collocations: **rough cut** *obs.*, a careless style of shearing; **sheep,** a sheep which is difficult to shear; also *ellipt.* as **rough; shop** *obs.*, a place which presents difficulties of some kind (cf. ROUGH-UP c); **spin,** see SPIN *n.*[1] 2; **trot,** a period of misfortune.

1898 *Bulletin* (Sydney) 17 Dec. 15/1 *Cut* stands for shed-job. There are *fine cuts* and **rough cuts.** In the former the boss is particular. In a *rough-cut* he is lenient, and shearers can shear anyhow. **1914** *Ibid.* 12 Nov. 14/2 Big tallies are generally an indication of a rough cut, which accounts for so many records being put up out in Western sheds. **1904** *Shearer* (Sydney) 10 Sept. 4/4 Amongst the noted **rough sheep** at Nowranie, a board of 25 has shorn 2,600 in a day of seven hours.

1915 *Bulletin* (Sydney) 28 Oct. 22/3 As the pen cuts out there is keen rivalry among . . pen-mates, each trying to force the other to take the roughs. **1892** 'R. BOLDREWOOD' *Nevermore* 199 Well you know Growlers' always was a **rough shop.** **1908** 'FIFTY THREE YRS. MINER' *So Long* 210 The gully was a 'rough shop', being full of 'lawyer' and 'wait-a-while' vines. **1909** E. ASH *Austral. Oracle* 13 Connewarre Lake and the district around was then a very rough shop. **1917** T.J. BRIGGS *Life & Experiences Successful W. Austral.* 101 As a rough shop, Kendenup not only took the bun among shearing sheds, but the entire bakery. **1944** *H.M.A.S. Westralia* Dec. 8 Hell, wouldn't that be a **rough trot.** **1968** G. DUTTON *Andy* 223 They give you a rough trot sometimes, but at least you know where you are with them. **1969** *Kings Cross Whisper* (Sydney) lxvi. 5/4 We've had a rough trot lately. All the once empty spaces are already taken up with beer bottles, fag packets and newspapers.

3. *Obs.* [See quot. 1885.] In the phr. **rough on rats,** bad luck.

[**1885** *Australasian* (Melbourne) 11 July 91/2 (Advt.) '*Rough on rats*' clears out rats, mice, roaches, flies, ants, bed-bugs, beetles, insects, skunks, jack-rabbits, gophers. At druggists.] **1888** J. POTTS *One Yr. Anti-Chinese Work Qld.* 16 The foregoing may appear 'rough on rats'; but Northerners speak their minds and do not take shelter behind flowery terms. **1889** *Bulletin* (Sydney) 15 June 13/4 Tho' his last and he have parted (Meaning 'rough on rats' for some): Still more game than chicken hearted Is the 'broke' new chum.

rough, *v.*

1. *trans.* To shear (a sheep) carelessly and unevenly.

1878 'IRONBARK' *Southerly Busters* 180, I allus roughs 'em when the boss Ain't on the shearin' floor. **1896** *Bulletin* (Sydney) 14 Nov. 11/2 A Darling-shed shearer was roughing his sheep. Next morning he found a note over his pen: 'Sheep rough; please improve.' He sheared cleaner next day and the following morning found this note: 'Improved. Thanks.' **1899** *Ibid.* 3 June 14/1 Out-back shearer (just discharged for 'roughing 'em') to mate on board, who enquires 'What's up?' 'Nuthin.' **1946** *Ibid.* 11 Dec. 21/1 'You'll be on shed-hand rates,' said the overseer. 'So don't go for tallies; take your time and don't rough 'em.'

2. See quot.

1945 F. CORK *Tales from Cattle Country* 37 Some riders prefer to 'rough' a horse. This consists in blindfolding, saddling, and 'riding the buck'.

rough and tumble. [Spec. use of *rough and tumble* roughly improvised: see OED(S 4.] A fence made from untreated saplings and branches: see quot. 1956. Also **rough and tumble fence.**

1956 *Bulletin* (Sydney) 23 May 12/4 The bush-paddock was still enclosed by the original 'rough-and-tumble'; just saplings and heavier branches piled in line to resist big stock. **1980** HOLTH & BARNABY *Cattlemen of High Country* 37 We'd cut the snow-gums off so high up and built what they call a brush fence, a 'rough and tumble' fence.

roughie. Also **roughey, roughy** [f. *rough* + -Y.]

1. A cheat; a deception; a 'swiftie'; esp. in the phr. **to put a roughie over.**

1914 *Kan-Karoo Kronikle: Mag. H.M.T.S. 'Karroo'* 24 Oct. 20 Ginger springs a roughy: 'Though we are not aboard a P & O we have a PI-AN-O aboard. **1924** A.W. BAZLEY et al. Gloss. Slang A.I.F. 24 (typescript) *Roughey*, a statement difficult to believe. **1936** *Red Star* (Perth) 3 Apr. 3/4 A Low Trick. How is this for a 'roughy' put over by the Lake View and Star. **1939** K. TENNANT *Foveaux* 122 Kelly put a roughie over Charlie to-day. **1953** D. STIVENS *Gambling Ghost* 103 He heard them shouting, 'Swindler! Thief! Diddler! Roughie! Cheat! Rub them out!' and many other things besides. **1965** W. MOXHAM *Follow That Horse* 78 You never know, with some of the roughies they put over, what might happen. **1970** R. BEILBY *No Medals for Aphrodite* 269, I bluffed him, put a roughie over him.

2. In dog- and horse-racing: an outsider.

1922 C. DREW *Rogues & Ruses* 11 Dig into them roughies. **1934** 'S. RUDD' *Green Grey Homestead* 155 Those who had lost a wager or two will turn to Bell and say: 'You knew something about the roughie!' **1958** F. HARDY *Four-Legged Lottery* 14, I might just have a shilling on a roughie. I'm just trying to pick a long-pop. Just invest a bob or two, maybe, and win enough to pull up the rent. **1979** *Sporting Globe* (Melbourne) 8 Aug. 42 Another former captain, Bruce Comben, did Chitty the inestimable favor of tipping him heavily a 33-to-1 roughie, which ran like a 33-to-1 roughie, and Chitty was last seen practising freestyle for his return home. **1985** *Bulletin* (Sydney) 29 Oct. 48/1 Picking a winner is difficult. . . Alan Jones must be considered a roughie.

3. An unbroken horse.

1929 K.S. PRICHARD *Coonardoo* (1961) 124 Hugh was there to see that the roughie, as they called him, got more riding and handling before he went out of the yards again. **1938** C.P. CONIGRAVE *Walk-About* 36 Billy . . had been rough-riding champion of Queensland. . . 'Ah, go on,' said Billy, 'that was a few years ago when I wasn't so big in the gut. I never try a roughie now. I always let a damned nigger have a go first and risk his neck.' **1978** R.H. CONQUEST *Dusty Distances* 16 Ready to ride a real roughie?

rough-up. [Spec. use of *rough-up* an informal encounter: see OED(S.]

a. A fight; a brawl. Also *fig.*

1891 *Truth* (Sydney) 1 Feb. 6/5 Mr Sydney Broomfield is one of the hardest sort of men in a rough-up of his inches in the city, and he absolutely loves a turn up now and then. **1914** *Bulletin* (Sydney) 19 Mar. 22/2 For an all-out 'go' give me a rough-up between two camels. **1927** A. WRIGHT *Squatter's Secret* 182 Oh, there was a rough-up there right enough. **1928** E. FOREMAN *Hist. & Adventures Qld. Pioneer* 130, I have seen rough-ups that have happened in America. **1933** *Bulletin* (Sydney) 6 Dec. 24/4 The council . . wants to make it clear that in future all inter-State rough-ups will be *its* pigeon. **1950** K.S. PRICHARD *Winged Seeds* 26 There'd 've been a rough-up in no time, and only half a dozen of us with Paddy against forty or fifty men. **1976** C.D. MILLS *Hobble Chains & Greenhide* 140, I have all the time in the world to break him. No rough-up, mouth and ride this chap. He is going to be a camp-horse.

b. A thug.

1911 *Bulletin* (Sydney) 23 Nov. 13/4 Micko, from Collingwood, may be a 'tug' or a 'crook' or a 'rough-up' or a 'hotty', but if you called him a larrikin he'd look at you and wonder. **1919** V. MARSHALL *World of Living Dead* 69 The 'donkey-dipper' is another kind of pick-pocket. He works alone, and his methods are to grip, to rip, and to run. 'A dead rough-up'—thus the more scientific of the fraternity designate him. **1920** G. SARGANT *Winding Track* 43 He had no time for me, anyway; he thought me too much of a rough-up.

c. *transf.* A difficult stretch of terrain: cf. *rough shop* ROUGH *a.* 2. Also *attrib.*

1938 C.P. CONIGRAVE *Walk-About* 79 We took the risk of descending a 'rough-up', in the hope of getting water at the bottom of it. *Ibid.* 120 Looking behind we saw range after range that we had crossed on our 'rough-up' journey from Mount Casuarina.

roughy, var. ROUGHIE.

roughy. [f. TOMMY) ROUGH + -Y.] **a.** TOMMY ROUGH. **b.** *transf.* The small, reef-dwelling fish *Trachichthys australis.*

1864 *Colonial Cook Bk.* (1970) 49 Ruffy—Small. Exquisitely delicate. **1873** F. DE CASTELNAU *Edible Fishes Vic.* 8 The genus *Arripis* is entirely Australian, and is represented by the *roughy* (*arripis Georgianus*). **1906** D.G. STEAD *Fishes of Aust.* 89 The curious little fish known as the Roughy (*Trachichthys australis*) . . inhabits very similar situations to those in which the Nannygai is found. **1965** *Austral. Encycl.* VII. 540 *A*[*rripis*] *georgianus* is common in the southern markets, and is known as 'roughy' in Melbourne, 'tommy rough' in Adelaide and 'herring' in Perth. **1980** N. COLEMAN *Austral. Sea Fishes* 70 The roughy is a small reef-dwelling fish which during the day is mostly confined to its particular hole or ledge. **1980** J. WOLFE *Crocodile Soup* 52 Small fish should not be cleaned at all. . . I had enjoyed 'roughies' at Port Germein which by local custom were grilled whole.

round, *v.* [The Austral. use precedes and is apparently independent of U.S. *round up, v.*: see OED(S *round, v.*[1] 5 e. and Mathews *round up, v.* 1.] *trans.* To gather (scattered livestock) together by riding round a paddock, etc., to muster. Freq. with **up.** Also *transf.*

1847 C. STURT *Narr. Exped. Central Aust.* (1849) I. 228 We rounded up cattle till the moon should rise. **1865** J.O. TUCKER *Golden Spring* 108 Rounding some cattle for the purpose of yarding them. **1881** A.C. GRANT *Bush-Life Qld.* II. 198 The eager stock-horse rounded up the panting mob. **1885** MRS C. PRAED *Head Station* 54 A stockman and a brace of black boys rounded the mob. **1891** E. HULME *Settler's 35 Yrs. Experience Vic.* 22, I often took my blankets and slept outside by the large fires, where the large logs were being burned off; these, also, required 'rounding-up' during the night. **1893** F.W.L. ADAMS *Australs.* 150 A wild ride through the scrub after 'brumbies' (wild horse), 'rounding-up' a refractory steer, swimming a swollen creek that runs a banker. **1899** G.E. BOXALL *Story Austral. Bushrangers* 85 One of the stories told of the Jewboy was that he 'rounded up' the chief constable of the district with a party of constables and volunteers who had gone out to seek for him, and after having 'yarded them like a mob of cattle', took their horses, arms, and whatever money they had, and rode away laughing. **1929** C.E.W. BEAN *Official Hist. Aust. 1914–18* III. 73 Several hundreds from one ship streamed into the town, and were partly 'rounded up' the same night by an armed party from the nearest Australian camp. **1960** *N.T. News* (Darwin) 5 Jan. 4/2 Bolmarr had been employed rounding up buffaloes for taming before he came to Darwin. **1982** H. KNORR *Private Viewing* 104 Don't get y' knickers in a knot sport! We'll be right back when we've rounded 'em up.

rouse, *n. Obs.* Abbrev. of ROUSEABOUT *n.* a.

1898 *Worker* (Sydney) 26 Feb. 7/2 As rouses we may not be of electric breed, but for all that we are quick and lively, especially on 'Duff Days'.

rouse /raʊs/, *v.*[1] [f. Scot. dial. *roust* to roar, to bellow: see EDD *roust, v.*[2] and OED(S *roust, v.*[1] and *v.*[3]] *intr.* To scold. Freq. with **at, on:** to berate (someone).

1896 *Worker* (Sydney) 29 Aug. 3/3 Some very thin-skinned individuals have been 'rousing' on me for what they term my 'strong language'. **1899** *Ibid.* 18 Feb. 5/1 Called them crawlers and robbers; that they robbed the men who were Unionists, and altogether roused on them properly. . . Since then I have gone on rousing. I find it acts well. **1908** *Truth* (Sydney) 6 Sept. 1/6 A Parramatta boy roused on the military authorities because they wouldn't provide proper guns for the cadets. **1922** *Aussie* (Sydney) Sept. 10, 7.30 oklok: Mum rouses and bangs me hed becos the blarsted wood won't burn. **1932** J. TRURAN *Green Mallee* 233 'Ain't yer goin' to rouse on me, then? I been askin' for it these many months, ain't I?' 'Rouse me foot. I ain't in the mood for findin' fault with any cove, barrin' meself.' **1949** *Austral. Women's Weekly* (Sydney) 16 July 23/3 Mum rouses if I don't come to tea with clean hands. **1962** G. CASEY *Amid Plenty* 79 'You don't think she done wrong?' the boy said, anxiously. 'You and Mrs Mayhew, you're not rousing at her.' **1984** H.W. DAVIS *Bachelors in Bush* 82, I called out loudly. Tommy heard me and he had to stop the team and take me back home. Naturally I was roused at for that.

Hence **rousing** *vbl. n.*

1923 M.J. PETERSEN *Jewelled Nights* 164 He told me to give you a good rousing for not looking him up. **1948** C.B. MAXWELL *Cold Nose of Law* 22 A rousing-on when he's done wrong is good enough.

rouse /raʊs/, *v.*[2] *Obs. intr.* Abbrev. of ROUSEABOUT *v.*

1919 *Bulletin* (Sydney) 9 Oct. 20/2, I was coming in for a spell after 'rousin'' at a run of sheds in the West.

rouseabout, *n.* [Spec. use of Br. dial. *rouseabout* a rough, bustling person: see EDD and OED(S.]

a. A general hand on a rural property, esp. in a shearing shed.

[N.Z. **1861** *Lett. from N.Z.* 20 July (1914) 54 Shearing, it happens, is in full swing, so there are a number of extra men, besides the shepherds of the station, shearers, fleece-pickers, wool-sorters, and 'rouse-abouts'.] **1881** *Austral.: Monthly Mag.* (Sydney) V. 147 At Warrena my billet was that of 'rouseabout', or in more civilized terms generally useful. **1892** E. MITCHELL *Labour Question in Aust.* 6 No rouseabout was permitted to advance from his humbler position into the jealously guarded circle of the shearers. **1908** W.H. OGILVIE *My Life in Open* 33 The 'rouseabout' is the unskilled labourer, the assistant and concomitant of the shearer, who gathers up the fleeces, winds and ties them, sweeps the floor, yards the sheep, tars the wounds and helps in the yards. **1919** *Smith's Weekly* (Sydney) 22 Mar. 5/3 A rouseabout on Gilgandra station rose to rank of commander of Royal Flying Corps, and is to marry a station heiress with £100,000. **1933** J. TRURAN *Where Plain Begins* 148 A functionary known as a 'rouseabout' whips away the discarded fleece, and hurries off to fling it over the wool-classer's table. **1950** J. MORRISON *Port of Call* 56 'What kind of a job?' 'Rouseabout. Milk the cows, cut the wood, sweep the verandahs, clean the shoes.' **1964** D. LOCKWOOD *Up Track* 83 Lawson would have called him a rouseabout—an odd-jobs man. **1974** J. DINGWELL *Cattleman* 31 Wattie, their aged rouseabout, had his hands filled with the several cows and pigs. **1978** R.H. CONQUEST *Dusty Distances* 13 My job was mainly rouseabout's work. I looked after the station horses, milked the three house cows, chopped wood for the homestead kitchen, and did mustering and yard work whenever the pressure was on. **1984** *People Mag.* (Sydney) 7 May 40/2 My father was a wool-presser and I was a rouseabout at 15... If my son wanted to be a shearer now I'd steer him away from it.

b. *transf.*

1906 E. DYSON *Fact'ry 'Ands* 15 Billy the Boy, the juvenile rouseabout from the printer's flat. **1907** *Truth* (Sydney) 26 May 1/5 A red-headed boss of rouseabouts in a Pitt-street rag emporium is a puzzle to the men over whom he lords it. **1917** *Bulletin* (Sydney) 4 Oct. 24/1 Ann was a sort of confidential domestic rouseabout in Baker's house. **1923** *Ibid.* 7 June 24/4 The shelled maize cob is a good rouseabout on the farm. The small end makes a cork... It is also a quick and ready stopper for mouse-holes... A 3 in. or 4 in. length makes a good file handle... Two cobs held together are a brush and curry comb .. and a handful, dry, are the quickest fire-kindlers out. **1938** *Ibid.* 20 July 20/2, I wus rouseabout with a circus once what had a troupe of 'strong men'. **1946** *Ibid.* 23 Jan. 13/2 The pub rouseabout had taken a message for me, so I invited him to have a drink. **1965** R.H. CONQUEST *Horses in Kitchen* 170 During the depression I acted as a rouseabout for a few weeks in a travelling carnival. **1974** C. THIELE *Albatross Two* 67 'He's been offered a job on the oil rig'... 'A kitchen rouseabout,' Aunt Jessica said scornfully. 'A pot-walloper; a slushy.' **1978** R.H. CONQUEST *Dusty Distances* 154 A rouseabout looking after the caravan horses, helping to put up the big tent and pull it down and so on.

c. *attrib.* Also *fig.*

1884 *Bulletin* (Sydney) 28 June 18/3 What Granny would call an 'embarrassing predicament', happened recently in the gay rouseabout city of Paris. **1887** J. FARRELL *How he Died* 19 It may be that the rouseabout swiper who rode for the doctor that night Is in Heaven with the Hosts of the Blest, robed and sceptred, and splendid with light. **1946** A.J. HOLT *Wheat Farms Vic.* 92 Pensioners were mostly referred to as 'rouseabouts'. The 'rouseabout' pensioner is actually a very useful acquisition on the farm. **1974** D. IRELAND *Burn* 49, I stayed with him for a bit and did some rouseabout stuff and got my tucker and a sleep in the feed shed.

rouseabout, *v.* [f. prec.] *intr.* To work as a rouseabout. Freq. as *vbl. n.*

1897 *Tocsin* (Melbourne) 23 Dec. 6/1 It was grand fun most of the time—rabbit trapping, emu hunting, rouseabouting first and then to the mastership of shearing. **1905** *Shearer* (Sydney) 14 Jan. 8/4 Up-to-date shearing, 'rouseabouting', bush and station life. **1908** *Truth* (Sydney) 12 Apr. 11/3, I was talking to an old rouseabout the other day, who had been in Queensland 30 years, mostly rouseabouting. **1911** E.S. SORENSON *Life in Austral. Backblocks* 41 It falls to her lot also, in dry times when the men are on the roads with teams, shearing, or rouseabouting on stations, to cut scrub for the stock. **1914** *Bulletin* (Sydney) 17 Dec. 44/2, I never done no shearin'; but I rouseabouted one year in a shed near Muttaburra. **1926** *Tasmanian Mail* (Hobart) 3 Feb. 6/3 Used to do rouseabouting in the sheepyards. **1979** B. HARDY *World owes me Nothing* 167 He'd left school to go rouseabouting in the sheds.

rouser. Shortened form of ROUSEABOUT *n.* a.

1896 H. LAWSON *While Billy Boils* (1975) 52 They are all shearers, or at least they say they are. Some might be only 'rousers'. **1897** *Bulletin* (Sydney) 20 Feb. 3/2 The 'rouser' has no soul to save. Condemn the rouseabout! **1908** *Ibid.* 26 Mar. 14/1 He called the new chum rouser, imported the previous day from the Immigration Depôt. **1917** H. LAWSON *Lett.* (1970) 326 The picker-up can be Barcoo's and Moonlight's picker-up (each picked up for four or five) and we can call him a rouser (rouse-about) which was a general term for all save the Boss-over-the-Board, shearers, and cooks. **1967** G. JENKIN *Two Yrs. Bardunyah Station* 66 The aim of the rouser is eventually to become a shearer.

rousie. Also **rousy.** [f. ROUSE(ABOUT *n.* + -Y.] ROUSEABOUT *n.*

1906 *Bulletin* (Sydney) 22 Feb. 14/3 The local 'rousies' are gluttons .. after living for a month or two in a shearers' hut. **1912** *Ibid.* 14 Nov. 16/2 This is the plain, unvarnished lie about Danny, the rousey at The Fair Cow, Woolangrabbit. **1928** L.A. SIGSWORTH *Various Verse* 2 And old-time guns in the rousies mess may brag of their deeds with pride. **1938** *Bulletin* (Sydney) 12 Jan. 20/4 One of the young rousies came dashing in one day .. and blurted out that a snake's head was after him. **1952** *Ibid.* 19 Mar. 14/3 We station-hands joined the greasies and rousies for brownie and tea and yarns. **1972** W. WATKINS *Suddenly of Age* 7 'Are you a shearer?' 'No, just a rousy.' **1984** S. MACINTYRE *Militant* 14 When the men heard Paddy's story, they declared that henceforth the rousies would do no more general work and that if the owner caused further trouble, there would be no sheep shorn.

Hence **rousy** *v. intr.*, to work as a rouseabout.

1979 J. DAVIES *Souvenir Kangaroo Island*, As a neighbour, and rousying for a change of tucker Good days, good country.

roust, *v. intr.* ROUSE *v.*[1] Also with quasi-obj. in the phr. **to roust hell out of** and as *vbl. n.*

1904 L.M.P. ARCHER *Bush Honeymoon* 113, I was to *go lightly* on it, and bring it back in good repair, if I didn't wanted to be *rousted* on about it. **1910** *Bulletin* (Sydney) 30 June 39/2 'Me mother's the one,' said Peter. 'How does she roust.' The small girls old Aunt Johnson, it appeared, also rousted. **1938** X. HERBERT *Capricornia* 314 He rousted hell out of the surveyor fellers for keepin' lubras in their camp. **1950** N. LINDSAY *Dust or Polish* 116 If you don't stop rousting on me I'll do for meself with a chisel. **1960** N. CATO *Green grows Vine* 17 Mike .. never goes crook at yer if your tins is a bit light-on. Only thing he hates to see good fruit left behind on the vine. He wouldn't roust at *you*, anyways: he likes the girls. **1978** M.J. BURTON *Bush Pub* 11 There was scarcely enough food in the kitchen to feed the guests, but Mother solved that problem by rousting out a nearby butcher to provide her with steak and chops.

rousy, var. ROUSIE.

rover. *Australian National Football.* One of three players making up the ruck, usually small, fast, and adept at securing possession of the ball. See RUCK *n.* 1 a.

1894 M. SHEARMAN *Athletics & Football* (ed. 4) II. 422 The rover is an individual chosen for his quickness and readiness to go wherever he is wanted. **1906** *Gadfly* (Adelaide) 16 May 15/1 'Tis a long time since the Norwoods showed such form as they displayed against North Adelaide at football on Saturday... Gibbons, the clever little Norwood rover .. was in particularly good form. **1931** J.F. MCHALE et al. *Austral. Game of Football* 64 The position of the ruck and rover when the umpire bounces the ball in the centre should not be a stereotyped one. **1936** E.C.H. TAYLOR et al. *Our Austral. Game Football* 63 The rover in general play should always mind his opposing rover in defence. **1960** *N.T. News* (Darwin) 8 Jan. 6/3 Pott, a high-marking rover for the aboriginal team, Wanderers, pleaded not guilty. **1973** J. DUNN *How to play Football* 6 No matter how many rabbits a rover can pull out of his top hat he is no good unless he can kick accurately, and even more importantly, with both feet. **1983** HIBBERD & HUTCHINSON *Barracker's Bible* 170 A rover not playing 'on the ball' is said to be resting when he takes up a position in the forward pocket.

Hence **rove** *v. intr.*, and as *vbl. n.*

1936 E.C.H. TAYLOR et al. *Our Austral. Game Football* 75 The full forward centre has a roving commission within kicking distance and must always be trying to make position. **1963** L. RICHARDS *Boots & All!* 78 He went to Fitzroy as a rover, but had to be content with a place on the wing because Bunton was roving. **1983** HIBBERD & HUTCHINSON *Barracker's Bible* 172 Generally small and nippy players, expert at ground play, whose job it is to accept the ball palmed or knocked in their direction by the ruckman, dive at the bottom of packs, ferret out the ball, scout, scavenge, pick up crumbs, snap goals, scrounge kicks. Thus 'to rove' a pack, forward line. To have a 'roving commission' is to have been given permission to wander the ground at will in search of kicks.

roving party. *Tas. Hist.* A detachment of men engaged in the pursuit and detention of Aborigines.

1831 *Van Diemen's Land Corresp. Military Operations* 23 Feb. 82 The Council advised the Lieutenant-Governor to discontinue the roving parties, as the measure appeared to have a bad effect upon the Natives. **1833** *Van Diemen's Land Almanack* 97 Defects in the system of the roving parties which have hitherto been employed. **1838** *Hobart Town Almanack* 112 The present roving parties will be augmented to the greatest possible extent; for which purpose, all the prisoners, holding tickets-of-leave, who are capable of bearing arms, are required to report themselves to the police magistrate of the district in which they reside, in order that they may be enrolled, either in the regular roving parties, or otherwise employed in the public service, under the instructions of their respective employers. **1870** J. BONWICK *Last Tasmanians* 132 After much discussion, it was determined to depend no longer upon the feeble operations of the Roving Parties—the *Five Pounds' Catchers* as they were called.

rowdy, *a.* [Transf. use of *rowdy* rough and disorderly.] Of animals: resistant of control.

1872 C.H. EDEN *My Wife & I in Qld.* 69 [It] consists of several yards for drafting... A lane and a crush .. useful for branding or securing a troublesome or colonially a 'rowdy' bullock. **1887** A. NICOLS *Wild Life & Adventure* 278 The range of hills .. became a refuge for all the 'rowdy' cattle in the neighbourhood. **1895** A.B. PATERSON *Man from Snowy River* 125, I can ride a rowdy colt. **1897** R. NEWTON *Work & Wealth Qld.* 39 Gardens cover the ridges that in his day were dense with iron-bark, bloodwood, and sweet-smelling wattle, and in place of the 'rowdy mob' who grazed in these ravines are troups of children returning from school.

Hence **rowdiness** *n.*

1887 A. NICOLS *Wild Life & Adventure* 203 The cattle .. showed frequent signs of rowdiness.

Roy. *Obs.* [Transf. use of the proper name *Roy.*] A derogatory name for the type of the consciously fashionable Australian. See also ALF.

1960 *Encounter* (London) May 29 A Roy .. would patronise *Art Nouveau* every pay-day .. for arty knick-knacks for his lovely Wahroongah home. **1965** *Nation* (Sydney) 27 Nov. 21/3 Dartmoor is invaded by Melbourne camps, middle class 'Roys' in sports cars and yachting jackets. **1971** C. MCGREGOR *Don't talk to me about Love* 130 It's like those signs hung out by London landladies: *Sorry, no Roys.*

royal, *n. Hist.* [Also Br.: see OEDS *sb.* 2 e.] A name proposed, but not adopted, for a unit of decimal currency.

1963 *Daily Tel.* (Sydney) 6 June 1/1 Federal Cabinet decided tonight to call the major new decimal currency unit a royal. **1963** *Sun* (Melbourne) 6 June 1/1 *'Royal': our new note...* The major unit in the new Australian decimal currency will be called the royal, equal to 10s. **1963** *Sun* (Sydney) 6 June 3/2 The Prime Minister, Sir Robert Menzies, swung the scales in favour of the name royal for the new major unit of the decimal currency. **1963** *Daily Mirror* (Sydney) 6 Aug. 29/1 The Federal Government will decide next week whether to change the name royal as the major unit of decimal currency. .. Dollar is the most favoured name for the unit.

royal, *a.* In the names of flora and fauna: **royal bluebell,** the small perennial herb *Wahlenbergia gloriosa* (fam. Campanulaceae) of higher altitudes in s.e. mainland Aust., the floral emblem of the Australian Capital Territory; **spoonbill,** the large wading bird *Platalea regia*, having white plumage and black face, bill, and legs.

[**1914 royal bluebell:** F. SULMAN *Pop. Guide Wild Flowers N.S.W.* II. 124 *Wahlenbergia gracilis.* 'Australian Blue Bell.'] **1950** J. GALBRAITH *Wildflowers Vic.* 143 *W[ahlenbergia] gloriosa*, Royal Bluebell... Flowers large, rich dark blue or blue purple. **1979** A.B. COSTIN et al. *Kosciusko Alpine Flora* 227 'Royal bluebell' .. mainly in subalpine woodland in the Australian Alps and adjacent ranges as far north as the Brindabella Range, A.C.T. **1985** A. BODEN *Floral Emblems Aust.* 22 The royal bluebell, *Wahlenbergia gloriosa* . . was announced as the floral emblem of the Australian Capital Territory on 26 May 1982. **1842** J. GOULD *Birds of Aust.* (1848) VI. Pl. 50, The **Royal Spoonbill** is tolerably common on the eastern and northern coast of Australia. **1872** 'RESIDENT' *Glimpses Life Vic.* 54 One of the two Australian spoonbills, the royal species (*Platalea regia*) has a black bill. **1984** M. BLAKERS et al. *Atlas Austral. Birds* 66 The Royal Spoonbill ranges through Indonesia, New Guinea and New Zealand to Australia.

royal alberts: see PRINCE ALBERTS.

Royal Alfred. *Obs.* [f. the name of Prince *Alfred* (1844–1900), second son of Queen Victoria, who visited Australia in 1867–68.] A heavy swag: see quot. 1902.

1896 H. LAWSON *While Billy Boils* (1975) 62 A little farther on we saw the first sundowner. He carried a Royal Alfred, and had a billy in one hand and a stick in the other. **1902** —— *Children of Bush* 139 The weight of the swag varies from the light rouseabout's swag, containing one blanket and a clean shirt, to the 'royal Alfred', with tent and all complete, and weighing part of a ton.

Royal George. *Obs.* [f. the name of King *George* IV (1762–1830).] See quot. 1827.

1827 *Monitor* (Sydney) 12 July 507/2 The 'Royal George', (an iron pot holding four gallons of water) was then placed on the fire; tea and sugar were thrown in it by the handful. **1846** *Cumberland Times* (Parramatta) 10 Jan. 4/4 A fire was soon made, a Royal George slung to boil the beef, some flour rubbed up, and leather jackets made, and we made a night of it, having been joined in the course of the evening by two or three down country teams.

rozella, var. ROSELLA *n.*[2]

rozener, roziner, varr. ROSINER.

rub, *v.* [Transf. use of *rub out* to wipe out, to kill.] In the phr. **to rub out,** to disqualify (a competitor).

1902 *Advocate* (Burnie) 29 Jan. 2/5 When men are proved to be non-tryers they will be 'rubbed out'. **1903** *Sporting News* (Launceston) 12 Sept. 1/3 They yelled with a loud voice, 'rub him out for life'. **1904** *Ibid.* 12 Mar. 1/3 There is much diversity of opinion as to whether Lord Harold should have been rubbed out. **1928** L.A. SIGSWORTH *Various Verse* 27, I am the man who owns the quadruped That sundry racing scribblers write about. It's me who takes the blame when he is 'dead'; When punters urge the stipes to 'rub him out'. **1955** N. PULLIAM *I traveled Lonely Land* 386 *Rub out*, to disqualify a horse from a race for some illegal action. **1983** HIBBERD & HUTCHINSON *Barracker's Bible* 173 Players, jockeys and reinsman get 'rubbed out' when they are disqualified from participation by a tribunal or stewards. 'The Derwent Dobber's been rubbed out for a fortnight.'

rub-a-dub-dub. Altered form of RUBBITY-DUB.

[N.Z. **c 1926** 'MIXER' *Transport Workers' Song Bk.* 81, I gazed upon the motley crowd Within this 'rub-a-dub'.] **1941** S.J. BAKER *Pop. Dict. Austral. Slang* 62 *Rubberdy* . . , a public house. Rhyming slang on 'rub-a-dub-dub' for 'pub'. **1966** C. MCGREGOR *Profile Aust.* 36 *Rub a dub dub*, pub. **1971** *Nat. Times* (Sydney) 13 Dec. 20 Let's grab some Kate and Sidney and a pint of apple fritter at the rub-a-dub-dub.

rubbedy, rubberdy, varr. RUBBITY.

rubbie, var. RUBBY.

rubbish, *v.*

1. [Used elsewhere but recorded earliest in Aust.] *trans.* To denigrate (a person); to disparage. Also as *vbl. n.*

1953 T.A.G. HUNGERFORD *Riverslake* 20 'If Verity was going to tramp you for burning the tucker, Slim', one of the cooks . . observed . . 'he would have rubbished you long before this.' **1961** *Bulletin* (Sydney) 1 Feb. 32/4 In his conversation no one is ever 'rubbished'. **1967** A. SEYMOUR *One Day of Yr.* 112 Communists openly making speeches rubbishing all the things Alf believed in. **1971** B. HUMPHRIES *Bazza pulls it Off*, Am I to take it you want to know the secret of my romantic prowess? Look, I can't ask any of me mates or they'd give me a flamin' rubbishing. **1977** F.B. VICKERS *Stranger no Longer* 173 The schools, the Primary more so than the High, were pleasurable experiences. That is not said to rubbish the High Schools. **1985** *Bulletin* (Sydney) 8 Oct. 68/3 The workaphile, with his passion for work, is rubbished by people who couldn't possibly imagine feeling like that.

2. *Surfing.* (Chiefly in *pass.*) To tip (a surfer) off a wave.

1962 *Austral. Women's Weekly* (Sydney) 24 Oct. (Suppl.) 3/3 *Rubbished*, to be thrown off wave and dumped on shore. **1963** *Sun-Herald* (Sydney) 22 Sept. 84/5 The fate the board rider dreads is the 'wipe out'. This is when he is 'rubbished' or tipped violently off a wave. **1966** *Surfabout* (Sydney) III. v. 11 Bob McTavish gets rubbished.

Hence **rubbisher** *n.*

1969 D.S. WILKINS *Diary* 1 June 44 The entertainers expose themselves to the roughest audience of rubbishers in existence.

rubbish, *a. Austral. pidgin.* Inferior in quality.

1959 W.E. HARNEY *Tales from Aborigines* p. xvi, In the early days the native girls travelled around with their white companions, and being excellent cattle and horse-women they became the ones who helped the early settlers to open up the land. They were classed as 'Rubbish-one-whites', 'Comboes', 'clay-pan squatters'. **1970** J.V. MARSHALL *Walk to Hills of Dreamtime* 10 'Your father: he a rubbish-one white?' 'My father', she said between her teeth, 'was a Japanese pearl diver.' **1969** J. DINGWELL *One String* 46 Don't be offended if all they can address you by is 'Missus', and don't be offended, either, if they reject what you offer as 'rubbish tucker'.

rubbity. Also with much variety, as **rubbedy, rubberdy, rupperty.** Abbrev. of RUBBITY-DUB.

1898 *Bulletin* (Sydney) 17 Dec. (Red Page), *Drum*, derived from the kettle-drums (evening parties) of the days of the Georges—was a high-class word, but it fell. The cockney turned it into *rub-a-dum-dum*; the Australian now calls the same thing a *rubadey*. **1944** *Action Front: Jrnl 2/2 Field Regiment* May 15 Overheard in a Melbourne rupperty. **1957** D. NILAND *Call me when Cross turns Over* 101 Gord, I can hardly talk, I'm that dry. How about a gargle? Down to the rubberdy, come on. **1963** J. DUFFY *Outsville Pub* 69 He's going up to the Rubbity for a drink. **1965** M. PATCHETT *Last Warrior* 156 For Albert, the vista of unending beer narrowed down to a prospect of a week or two's 'shivoo at the rubbety' at Wilson's Bend. **1970** *Kings Cross Whisper* (Sydney) lxxxi. 8/3 'Low class, working class rubbities must be abolished,' he said, wiping his nose with a bar towel. **1974** W. HOWCROFT *Sand in Stew* 68 They would usually blow their wages on a three or four day spree at the nearest bush rubbedy. **1977** *Southerly* ii. 202 I'll take it up to the rubbity after breakfast and show it to the mates. **1980** HEPWORTH & HINDLE *Boozing out in Melbourne Pubs* 8 Back in the dear departed heydays of last century, the rubbity used to open at four in the morning and might stay open till midnight.

rubbity-dub. Also with much variety, as **rubbitty-dub, rubby dub.** Rhyming slang for 'pub'.

1898 *Bulletin* (Sydney) 29 Oct. 15/1 His home is 'the rubby dub', his occupation 'the joint'. **1905** J. MEREDITH *Learn to talk Old Jack Lang* (1984) 12, I rambled over to the *rubbity dub* and had a pint of *oh my dear*. In fact I had several and finished up in the dead house, broke to the wide. **1940** *Sixer* (Mornington) 22 May 9 *Rudey-dub*, pub. **1941** *D.O.M.F. Weekly Lyre* (Alice Springs) 31 Aug. 1 Caught in the Alice Springs Rubby de Dubb between 2200 hrs. and 0800 hrs. **1945** A. THURIAN *Bidgeroo & Jumbucks* 12 We'd mooch or ride, To muster at the rubbity-dub. **1969** B. GARLAND *Pitt Street Prospector* 32 'Ow about we ducks into the rubbitty-dub fer a quick 'un? **1976** *Bronze Swagman Bk. Bush Verse* 95 With a song in our hearts and our tongues hanging out we made for the rubbity-dub.

rubby. *Obs.* Also **rubbie.** Abbrev. of RUBBITY-DUB.

1897 *Worker* (Sydney) 11 Sept. 1/2 And I will lay an oil-rag to a pound of 'Darling Pea' He gallops straight away towards a 'rubbie' for a 'spree'. **1911** E.S. SORENSON *Life in Austral. Backblocks* 81 Others swamp their earnings at the wayside rubby, and then have themselves to blame that they are every year humping bluey. **1914** *Bulletin* (Sydney) 16 Apr. 24/1 The saltbush sages . . called all the Outback inns '*rubbies*'. **1926** 'DRYBLOWER' *Verses* 34 So down at a rubby along the road, We lunched on steak and eggs.

ruck, *n. Australian National Football.* [Transf. use of *ruck* scrimmage.]

1. a. A group of three players (two FOLLOWERS and a ROVER) who do not have fixed positions but follow the play.

1900 B. KERR *Silliad* 21 No peer had he for keeping on the ball And in the ruck he marked above them all. **1906** *Gadfly* (Adelaide) 6 June 14/1 At Norwood the West Adelaides paid a good dividend. . . Godby's work in the ruck was specially good. **1963** *Footy Fan* (Melbourne) I. vii. 21 In his first League match against St Kilda in 1946 he was spelled from the ruck at full forward. **1967** *Austral.* (Sydney) 17 Apr. 12/9 Terry Waters, who was moved into the ruck in the third quarter, had two separate chances in the last quarter to win the game from Collingwood. **1983** HIBBERD & HUTCHINSON *Barracker's Bible* 173 Players without fixed positions, who follow the ball, are in the ruck.

b. Abbrev. of *ruckman.*

1931 J.F. MCHALE et al. *Austral. Game of Football* 64 The position of the ruck and rover when the umpire bounces the ball in the centre should not be a stereotyped one. **1936** E.C.H. TAYLOR et al. *Our Austral. Game Football* 35 *Rucks*, two big men with the ability to mark and kick well, but they must not be too slow. **1963** *Footy Fan* (Melbourne) I. i. 18 It is no coincidence that a majority of players who can perform most football tasks (all-round players) finish either in the centre as a ruck or a rover because it is here that they have to be able to perform almost any football feat. **1973** P. MCKENNA *My World of Football* 111 *Rucks*, it is the ruckmen who actually start the game and from first bounce to final siren his is a game of continued physical contact.

2. Special Comb. **ruckman,** FOLLOWER; **play,** play following no set pattern; **rover,** a tall ruckman selected for an ability in loose play; so, **roving** *vbl. n.*

1900 B. KERR *Silliad* 25 The sweeping **ruck-men** on the ball descend. **1959** PARNELL & ANDREW *Austral. Football* 37 Every ruckman is a 'forward' when his own side has the ball, and is a 'backman' when the opposing side has the ball. **1963** L. RICHARDS *Boots & All!* 36 Jack looked as much a half-forward as I do a ruckman, but he kicked four goals. **1973** J. DUNN *How to play Football* 46 Ruckmen usually are the tallest players in a side and, appropriately, they have the tallest job. **1986** *Mercury* (Hobart) 27 Mar. 40/2 Hudson . . made the 198 cm. ruckman an offer he just couldn't refuse. **1936** E.C.H. TAYLOR et al. *Our Austral. Game Football* 62 The Australian Football Council has . . eliminated a great deal of **ruck play.** **1963** *Footy Fan* (Melbourne) I. vii. 21 It was not until 1951 that Wright showed such vast improvement in his ruck play that he won a regular place in the side. . . He rose to the occasion magnificently . . and became one of the most effective ruckmen of the League. **1963** L. RICHARDS *Boots & All!* 73 His ruck-play improved year after year. *Ibid.* 90 By far the greater part of his success has been at centre half-back or centre half-forward and in later years as a **ruck-rover** changing in the forward pocket. **1963** *Footy Fan* (Melbourne) I. ii. 24 Kevin Rose turned in a terrific ruck-roving performance against Richmond on opening day. **1964** J. POLLARD *High Mark* 77 The ruck comprises two followers, a follower who is called ruck-rover, and a cover. **1965** D. MARTIN *Hero of Too* 195 His love-making was of the variety of the ruck-rover, the straight-kicking man who never hesitates in front of goal. **1984** *N.T. News* (Darwin) 9 Nov. 40/4 Smith moves to ruck rover for the clash, despite having played his best games at centre.

ruck, *v.* [f. prec.] *intr.* To play as one of the ruck. Also as *ppl. a.*

1963 *Footy Fan* (Melbourne) I. vii. 21 When he rucked with Bill Morris, he always feared he might spoil Morris' leaps for the ball and more or less played the role of understudy. **1963** L. RICHARDS *Boots & All!* 79 A cagey left-footer, he used big Bert Clay's rucking ability to full advantage. **1965** *Sydney Morning Herald* 2 Aug. 15/5

Powerful rucking . . kept their team within striking distance for the first three quarters.

rufous, *a.* In the names of birds and animals: **rufous bristlebird,** the brown bird *Dasyornis broadbenti* of coastal scrub in w. Vic. and s.e. S.A., and formerly s.w. W.A.; formerly also **rufous-headed bristlebird; -crowned emu wren,** the small brown and blue bird *Stipiturus ruficeps* of parts of drier mainland Aust.; **fantail,** the bird *Rhipidura rufifrons* of n. and e. mainland Aust. and the s.w. Pacific; formerly also **rufous-fronted fantail; owl,** the owl *Ninox rufa* of n. Aust. and New Guinea, having barred rufous plumage; **rat-kangaroo (kangaroo-rat, bettong),** the small marsupial *Aepyprymnus rufescens* of e. mainland Aust.; **scrub-bird,** the predom. rufous-brown ground-dwelling bird *Atrichornis rufescens*, inhabiting areas of dense ground cover in s.e. Qld. and n.e. N.S.W.; **song-lark,** the migratory bird *Cinclorhamphus mathewsi* of mainland Aust., having brown and whitish plumage with a rufous rump; see also SONG-LARK; **treecreeper,** the bird *Climacteris rufa* of s. W.A. and S.A.; **whistler,** the bird *Pachycephala rufiventris*, widespread in mainland Aust. and occurring elsewhere, the mature male having a rufous breast and belly; WIREE; see also THUNDER-BIRD, WHISTLER; also **rufous-breasted whistler** (and formerly **thickhead**).

1897 [**rufous bristlebird**] *Proc. Linnean Soc. N.S.W.* XXII. 58 *Sphenura broadbenti* . . Rufous-headed Bristle-bird. **1903** *Emu* II. 163 Rufous Bristle-Bird . . very common throughout the Otways. **1943** C. BARRETT *Austral. Animal Bk.* 283 The author, after hours of patient waiting, photographed a rufous bristle-bird at the nest, in thick tea-tree scrub near Point Addis, to the west of Geelong. **1984** *Age* (Melbourne) 27 Mar. 24/8 Possibly extinct are the paradise parrot . . and rufous bristle-bird. **1901** *Emu* I. 56, I saw a family party of **Rufous-crowned Emu Wrens** (*Stipiturus ruficeps*). One of the young birds . . had no trace of the bright rufous crown of the adult bird. **1945** C. BARRETT *Austral. Bird Life* 190 The Mallee emu-wren (*S*[*tipiturus*] *mallee*) inhabits north-western Victoria. . . The rufous-crowned bird (*S. ruficeps*) ranges from the Central region to mid-Western Australia. **1984** SIMPSON & DAY *Birds of Aust.* 325 The inland Rufous-crowned Emu-wren which prefers spinifex, and the heath-dwelling Southern Emu-wren. **1846** [**rufous fantail**] J. GOULD *Birds of Aust.* (1848) II. Pl. 84, The Rufous-fronted Fantail is one of the most beautiful and one of the oldest known members of the group to which it belongs. **1903** *Emu* II. 163 Rufous Fantail (*Rhipidura rufifrons*)—common in the Otways. **1945** C. BARRETT *Austral. Bird Life* 173 Shy and rare, compared with the grey species, the rufous fantail (*R*[*hipidura*] *rufifrons*) is a migrant and ranges from the Celebes to New Guinea, thence to Northern and Eastern Australia. **1976** *Reader's Digest Compl. Bk. Austral. Birds* 390 With its black and white throat markings and rufous rump and upper tail, the Australian rufous fantail is unmistakable. **1846** J. GOULD *Birds of Aust.* (1848) I. Pl. 36, *Athene rufa* . . **Rufous Owl.** **1913** *Emu* XII. Suppl. 48 *Ninox rufa* . . Rufous Owl . . N.W. Australia, Northern Territory, N. Queensland. **1964** M. SHARLAND *Territory of Birds* 180, I looked in some of the scrubby patches along the base of the tier hoping I might make acquaintance with the Rufous Owl. **1984** M. BLAKERS et al. *Atlas Austral. Birds* 305 The diet of the Rufous Owl varies according to what is available. It preys on birds as large as the Australian Brush Turkey. **1894** R. LYDEKKER *Hand-Bk. Marsupialia & Monotremata* 71 **Rufous Rat-Kangaroo.** *Aepyprymnus rufescens* . . the largest of the Rat-Kangaroos. **1898** E.E. MORRIS *Austral Eng.* 239 A fourth genus (*Aepyprymnus* . .) includes the Rufous Kangaroo-Rat. . . It is . . distinguished by its ruddy colour, black-backed ears, and hairy nose. **1926** A.S. LE SOUEF et al. *Wild Animals Australasia* 234 Rufous Rat-kangaroo. . . General colour above coarsely grizzled rufescent grey. **1972** *Sunday Mail Mag.* (Brisbane) 3 Sept. 4 The rufous rat-kangaroo . . occurs in many parts of central and south Queensland, particularly in open forest. **1983** R. STRAHAN *Compl. Bk. Austral. Mammals* 190 At night the Rufous Bettong feeds on grasses and herbs and forages for roots and tubers, dug from the ground with its strongly clawed forelegs. [**1869 rufous scrub-bird:** J. GOULD *Birds of Aust.* Suppl. Pl. 26, *Atrichia rufescens.* Rufescent Scrub-bird.] **1898** E.E. MORRIS *Austral Eng.* 406 The Noisy Scrub-bird . . and the Rufous S[crub]-b[ird]. **1929** A.H. CHISHOLM *Birds & Green Places* 1 The gloomy, sun-streaked haunts of the rufous scrub-bird and olive whistler. **1952** *Bulletin* (Sydney) 4 June 17/1 P'raps I've been privileged to hear him, for the Lamington Plateau (Q.) is his last retreat, but I'll back the rufous scrub-bird against all-comers for the most far-reaching bird-call. **1986** *Sydney Morning Herald* 15 Jan. 13/3 Many animals today are confined to the rainforests left in the mountains of north-east N.S.W., among them the rufous scrub-bird, whose song is considered one of the loudest in the world for a bird of its size. **1900** A.J. CAMPBELL *Nests & Eggs Austral. Birds* 276 *Cinclorhamphus rufescens* . . **rufous song lark.** . . While the Black-breasted or Brown Song Lark appears partial to grassy plains, the Rufous loves the grassy glades of the forest or lightly timbered country. **1943** C. BARRETT *Austral. Animal Bk.* 275 The brown song-lark . . and the rufous song-lark (*C*[*inclorhamphus*] *Mathewsi*), which are distributed over Australia generally, rival the bush-larks as songsters. **1984** E. ROLLS *Celebration of Senses* 77 At the first suggestion of daylight . . the Rufous Songlark throbs a succession of notes. Then for half an hour . . he chirrs and whistles and sings as though he is several birds. **1841** J. GOULD *Birds of Aust.* (1848) IV. Pl. 94, *Climacteris rufa* . . **Rufous Tree Creeper.** **1902** *Emu* II. 73 *Climacteris rufa* (Rufous Tree-Creeper) . . the colour of the plumage harmonizes . . with the rufous-coloured bark of the jarrah tree. **1945** C. BARRETT *Austral. Bird Life* 170 The rufous tree-creeper . . is restricted to South-western Australia and portion[s] of South Australia. **1976** *Reader's Digest Compl. Bk. Austral. Birds* 457 The most brightly coloured treecreeper, the rufous treecreeper of south-western Australia, lives in open woodland, mallee and humid jarrah forests. **1896** [**rufous whistler**] B. SPENCER *Rep. Horn Sci. Exped. Central Aust.* II. 72 *Pachycephala rufiventris* . . Rufous-breasted Thickhead . . were always found near water and in the scrub along the Finke River. **1918** *Bulletin* (Sydney) 14 Feb. (Red Page), *Rufous-breasted Whistler* . . and other members of the musical genus *Pachycephala*. **1929** A.H. CHISHOLM *Birds & Green Places* 212 The golden-breasted and rufous whistlers. **1944** L. WELSH *Kookaburra* 10 One of the earliest of dawn-singers is the Rufous-breasted Whistler. **1956** E. MITCHELL *Black Cockatoos* 27 Once Michael heard a rufous whistler in the weeping willows. **1984** E. ROLLS *Celebration of Senses* 77 The Rufous Whistler makes a few musical calls, then cracks like a whip, a good alarm.

rugged billy: see BILLY *n.*[1] 4.

Rules. Shortened form of AUSTRALIAN RULES. Also *attrib.*

1946 D. STIVENS *Courtship of Uncle Henry* 18 In those days in the Mallee before they got the latest city ideas, they played Rules in long pants. **1960** *N.T. News* (Darwin) 11 Mar. 16/6 (*heading*) Big rules game could be close. **1968** K. DENTON *Walk around my Cluttered Mind* 104 What Jerusalem is to Judaism, so the Melbourne Cricket Ground is to Rules. **1980** A.S. VEITCH *Run from Morning* 116 'Short back and sides, I see. . . I bet you never played Rugby, down at Woop Woop.' 'Riverina. . . We played Rules down there, Sarg.'

rum. *Hist.* Used *attrib.* in Special Comb. reflecting the importance of spirits as a medium of exchange during the early days of the Colony of New South Wales: **Rum (Puncheon) Corps,** NEW SOUTH WALES CORPS; **currency,** see quot. 1870; **Hospital,** a hospital in Sydney the building of which was undertaken in return for the granting of a monopoly on the import of spirits from 1810 to 1814; **rebellion,** the rebellion against William Bligh, Governor of New South Wales, by officers of the New South Wales Corps in 1808.

1897 M. CLARKE *Stories Aust.* 31 The New South Wales Veteran Corps (a regiment of pensioners tempted by promise of privilege to emigrate) was called the '**Rum-Puncheon Corps**'. **1944** R. BEDFORD *Naught to Thirty-Three* 37 Our 'history' became a laudation of the ruffians of the Rum Corps, and their successors, the pure Merinos. **1945** J.A. ALLAN *Men & Manners* 33 The Rum Corps—officially the 'New South Wales Corps' . . garrisoned the settlement. **1955** N. PULLIAM *I traveled Lonely Land* 33 There developed the nefarious Rum Corps, which plunged the Colony into the most noisome era of its history. **1962** B. BEATTY *With Shame Remembered* 99 The notorious New South Wales Corps, better known still as the 'Rum Corps', was largely the ruling body of the Colony. **1870** J. BONWICK *Curious Facts* 124 In the primitive period the **rum currency** prevailed. In purchase, the worth was estimated in quarts or gallons of rum. One Serjeant-major Whittle sold a house to Governor Macquarie for two hundred gallons of rum. **1946** O.A. MENDELSOHN *Earnest Drinker's Digest* 217 *Rum currency*, in the earliest days of Australian history, owing to the scarcity of coin or suitable commodities, rum was actually used as a medium of exchange in commercial transactions. **1962** J.T. LANG *Great Bust* 8 The Bank of New South Wales had been the first to issue its own bank notes, having done so since 1817 when a group of Sydney merchants had organized the bank to get over the problems of the rum currency and Spanish 'holey' dollars, which had formed the first currency. **1834** J.D. LANG *Hist. & Statistical Acct. N.S.W.* II. 138 Governor Macquarie . . made an agreement on the part of the Colonial Government with Messrs D'Arcy Wentworth, Blaxcell, and Riley, by which these gentlemen stipulated to erect a building agreeably to the plan proposed, on condition of receiving a certain quantity of rum from the King's Store and having the sole right to purchase, or to land free of duty, all the ardent spirits that should be imported into the colony for a term of years. The **Rum Hospital**, as it was called at the time, was accordingly erected on these conditions. *Ibid.* 139 In the year 1824, the Rum Hospital was calculated to be worth £20,000. **1853** S. SIDNEY *Three Colonies* (ed. 2) 71 The Rum Hospital was a specimen of the tone of morality during the early years of New South Wales. **1855** W. HOWITT *Land, Labor & Gold* II. 125 From the date of this '**rum-rebellion**', and the forcible deposition of poor Bligh, in 1809 up to 1823, the system of political grants went on swimmingly. **1942** C.H. GRATTAN *Introducing Aust.* 39 The clash of wills between Macarthur and Bligh produced, in 1808, the so-called 'Rum Rebellion'. **1971** A. BUZO *Macquarie* (1973) 12 Governor Bligh, lately of the Bounty, had inspired the Rum Rebellion, whereby liquor replaced the pound sterling as the legal currency, and squalid colonial anarchy prevailed.

rumper. [Prob. transf. use of Br. dial. *rumper* a large sheep.]

1. SCRUBBER 1 a.

1899 *Worker* (Sydney) 14 Jan. 3/4 Sometimes I thought it hard When I struck a stranger's yard, And a 'rumper' worked with malice in his eye. **1936** I.L. IDRIESS *Cattle King* 190 A mob of rumpers like these.

2. See quot. 1970.

1970 J.S. GUNN in W.S. Ramson *Eng. Transported* 65 A *rumper* in the poultry trade is now a domestic fowl with a peculiar feather growth from lack of a tail-bone, but it was earlier a possum or koala whose backside fur had been worn away, thus damaging the pelt.

run, *n.*[1] *Obs.* [Chiefly Br. dial. and U.S.: see OED *run, sb.*[1] 9 a.] A small watercourse.

1793 J. HUNTER *Hist. Jrnl. Trans. Port Jackson* 458 They came to a run of water, which they supposed to be the head of the Nepean river. **1805** J.H. TUCKEY *Acct. Voyage to establish Colony Port Phillip* 199 In the vallies or rather chasms between the mountains, small runs of water trickle through an almost impenetrable jungle of prickly shrubs. **1820** *Sydney Gaz.* 11 Mar., A desirable *farm* . . has the Benefit of a fresh water Run through the Farm. **1833** *Launceston Advertiser* 10 Jan. 427 There is . . an excellent run of spring water by the kitchen. **1838** *S. Austral. Rec.* (London) 13 Jan. 30 Stephen has been after the government cattle nearly to the head of the gulph, and found every few miles a fine run of water and beautiful plains. **1877** M. CLARKE *Aust. & Tas.* 24 This interesting exploration discovered several 'runs' of fresh water around the bays. **1878** R.B. SMYTH *Aborigines of Vic.* II. 303 Other food includes fish of three or four kinds, which are caught in nets, or in grass weirs placed across runs of water when the floods subside.

run, *n.*[2] [Prob. Br. dial. in origin, superseding *walk* both in the sense of an enclosure for poultry, etc., and a tract of land used for pasture. There is an isolated North American example (1658) but the earliest sustained evidence of use is Austral.: see OED(S *run, sb.*[1] 21 b. and 22, and *walk, sb.*[1] 11 a. and 12.]

1. a. A tract of land used as pasture; *spec.* a tract of Crown land situated adjacent to a holding and leased or occupied as pasture (see quot. 1849); such a tract situated at some distance from the user's dwelling or holding (see quot. 1828). See also STATION 2 a.

1804 *Sydney Gaz.* 12 Feb., A commodious dwelling-house [with] an extensive Run for Stock. *Ibid.* 24 June, The premises are pleasantly situate in Sydney, being a corner house, and an excellent run for stock. **1805** S. MACARTHUR ONSLOW *Some Early Rec. Macarthurs* (1914) 120, I have got but one Run for Sheep at present. **1821** *Sydney Gaz.* 20 Jan., At the back of the Land is an extensive range of hills unlocated, capable of maintaining a numerous herd of cattle, exclusive of the run on the Farm. **1825** *Austral.* (Sydney) 15 Sept. 1 *To be let...* That beautiful and very valuable farm called 'King's Grove', situate in the district of Botany Bay, and distant from Sydney about 12 miles, containing 500 acres of land, about fifty of which are cleared... Contiguous to this farm is an extensive run for cattle, on unlocated lands. **1826** J. ATKINSON *Acct. Agric. & Grazing N.S.W.* 66 Cattle once accustomed to a run .. seldom or never stray from it. **1828** *Blossom* (Sydney) i. 82 Numerous herds of cattle are moving for pasture to Bathurst and Argyle to have the benefit of more extensive 'runs'. **1834** H. CARMICHAEL *Hints relating to Emigrants* 17 For the purpose of having the command of an unlimited run, it will be necessary for him to rent only one or two sections: as, in this case, he may reckon on being undisturbed for years in the use of the boundless territory outward from his purchased-station. **1836** *Cornwall Chron.* (Launceston) 3 Dec. 4 *To let*, for a Summer Run, 1,000 acres of rich Grazing *land* .. having a double frontage on the river. **1839** *Tasmanian* (Hobart) 8 Feb. 42/4 Has the advantage of a run of 200 acres of government land, not available to any other farm. **1840** *Port Phillip Gaz.* 21 Mar. 4 The home station is situated close to a beautiful fresh water Lake... The other runs are only distant about three miles from the Home Station. **1844** Macarthur Papers LXII. 134 He and I are not very good friends at present, on account of his doing all he can to get the Government lands near Carleroy as a Sheep run, and I am determined he shall not get it, as I consider it your run. **1845** *Portland Guardian* 15 Mar. 4/1 The Commissioner bet me a pony—I won, So he cut off exactly two thirds of my run. **1846** C.P. HODGSON *Reminisc. Aust.* 367 'Runs', land claimed by the Squatter as sheepwalks, open, as nature left them, without any improvement from the Squatter. **1847** A. HARRIS *Settlers & Convicts* (1953) 129 Stockmen are very shy of telling of runs even when they know of them; they of course for their own cattle's sake like to keep unallotted as much land as they can. **1849** S. & J. SIDNEY *Emigrant's Jrnl.* 11 A *run* is a tract of wild land on which cattle or sheep are depastured on a poll-tax, and license or lease from the Crown. **1854** J. CAPPER *Aust.* 60 They will have become thoroughly accustomed to each other, and to the 'run', as the allotment rented for grazing is termed in the colonies. **1865** *Cassell's Emigrant's Guide Vic.* 13 The pasture lands or 'runs' are let under an annual licence, and they vary in extent from about 2,000 acres to 200 square miles. **1875** CAMPBELL & WILKS *Early Settlement Qld.* 1, I immediately removed my cattle from the Gwydir, where my run was disputed. **1878** Tas. Non-State Rec. 103/5 10 Dec., There is so much grass on the runs this season. **1887** W.H. SUTTOR *Austral. Stories Retold* 105 At this time very few, if any, of the leaseholders on the Lachlan resided on their stations. The properties were managed by servants, and the whole of the country was occupied as cattle runs. **1888** A.P. MARTIN *Oak-Bough & Wattle-Blossom* 132 The sheep were well in sight, in fact, they hardly required any shepherding now; their usual run was almost like a paddock, fenced in as it was by the river and scrub. **1896** H. LAWSON *While Billy Boils* (1975) 7 He selected on a run at Dry Hole Creek, and for months awaited the arrival of the government surveyors to fix his boundaries; but they didn't come, and as he had no reason to believe they would come within the next ten years, he grubbed and fenced at a venture, and started farming operations. **1905** E.C. BULEY *Austral. Life* 5 The grazing areas, called 'runs' in Australia, vary in size, some of those in the more remote districts equalling the extent of one of the smaller English counties. **1920** A.G. HALES *McGlusky Gold-Seeker* 8 The big station-owners through whose 'runs' the track wound its way. **1935** M.W. PEACOCK *Black Valleys* 24 'Mr Stewart know yer coming?' 'Mr Stewart?' Ludlow was puzzled. 'Your block's part of 'is run, you know.' **1947** W. LAWSON *Paddle-Wheels Away* 157 He reckoned you was selectors, taking a river frontage out of his run. **1973** D. STUART *Morning Star, Evening Star* 18 There's nothing quite so dismal as a station with every one out on the run. **1977** J. WALLACE *Memories Country Childhood* 11 The black dirt road that led to the woolshed and the stockmen's huts, known as 'Up the Run'.

b. *Obs.* Pasturage.

1820 *Sydney Gaz.* 23 Sept. (Suppl.), A Farm .. well adapted for a Person having Stock, being adjacent to one of the greatest Outlets in the Colony for the Run of Cattle. **1828** *Hobart Town Courier* 8 Mar. 2 A settler in the interior having ample run for 500 or 600 *ewes* on the thirds, will be happy to treat with any Gentleman for the same. **1835** *Cornwall Chron.* (Launceston) 30 May 4 The unlimited run for stock upon unlocated lands, must necessarily produce plenty.

c. *Hist.* In the phr. **right of run,** legal entitlement to the use of a tract of grazing land; such a tract of land. See also STATION 2 b.

1840 *Port Phillip Gaz.* 1 Jan. 2 If desired, the whole or portion of the herd will be sold with the Right of one of the finest Runs in Port Phillip. **1841** *Geelong Advertiser* 14 Aug. 1/4 *For sale. By private contract.* From Ten to Fifteen Hundred *young sheep*, with which will be given a right of Run, fronting on the Barwon River, within twenty miles of Corio, on which are enclosed paddocks, huts, &c., and from 10 to 15 acres of crop. **1846** W. WESTGARTH *Commercial, Statistical, & Gen. Rep. Port Phillip* 31 Sprot .. became a purchaser .. of the live stock and right of run possessed by Osbrey. **1847** *Port Phillip Herald* 2 Mar. 3/7 A valuable Farm of twenty acres .. adjoining the Springs, with the right of run upon three purchased sections, with the additional advantage of two Government runs at the back. **1961** M. KIDDLE *Men of Yesterday* 48 He intended to buy the 'right of run' rather than take up a station.

2. A tract of land used for the raising of stock, together with the requisite improvements such as dwellings, yards, etc. Also with distinguishing epithet, as **cattle, grazing, sheep, squatting, stock** (see under first element). See also STATION 3.

1810 *Sydney Gaz.* 24 Feb., A capital Forty Acre Farm, at the Nepean, well watered, and one of the best runs for Stock in the Country. **1841** *Port Phillip Patriot* 8 Nov. 1/2 An extensive and excellently watered run, with substantial huts and stock-yards, grass and grain paddocks, gardens, &c. **1845** *Port Phillip Gaz.* 4 June 2 A Settler generally fixes upon a locality near a creek, or, if that is not to be found, in close proximity to a water-hole or pond. His hut stands here, as well as his stock-yard or hurdles; if an extensive Stock-owner, he may have various out-Stations upon the same creek, or, scattered about according to the nature of the land: this is termed his Run. **1845** *Sydney Morning Herald* 8 Aug. 4/3 Men's Huts, built of flint stone (those on the other stations belonging to the run, being of wood). **1846** *Cumberland Times* (Parramatta) 17 Jan. 3/4 The run is well adapted for a dairy. **1847** E.W. LANDOR *Bushman* 249 The sheep and cattle runs are excellent, but they are now fully stocked, and new settlers must direct their steps to the southward. **1853** J. SHERER *Gold Finder Aust.* 361 The run is limited indeed that does not possess its out-stations. These are solitary huts, tenanted by a shepherd in charge of a flock, and are separated by considerable distances, sometimes by miles, from the principal one at which the master resides. **1863** R. THERRY *Reminisc. Thirty Yrs. N.S.W. & Vic.* (ed. 2) 241 A *run*, or *station*, may be described as the land the squatter occupies, but with this difference, that a *run* popularly signifies land which often comprises several stations... In Government notices and licences, the word 'station' signifies the land to which their licences and leases refer; and may therefore be regarded as the more appropriate term for designating the entire land, subdivided into runs or stations, as they are often termed indifferently. **1872** G.S. BADEN-POWELL *New Homes for Old Country* 150 The nature of some runs necessitates an almost equal proportion of flocks and herds, and here we have the breeding both of 'store' and 'fat' cattle. **1880** J.B. STEVENSON *Seven Yrs. Austral. Bush* 92 The stockmen were all blacks born on the run. **1887** A. NICOLS *Wild Life & Adventure* 4 Three such 'runs', as they call sheep farms, would just about cover the county of Rutland. **1890** 'R. BOLDREWOOD' *Colonial Reformer* II. 9 Do you happen to want a crack run, my dear Neuchamp? I've got Brigalow Park and Mallee Meadows for sale. **1898** C.G. DUFFY *My Life* 158 It is a .. common practice to squat in the Melbourne Club and leave the run to be managed by a 'super'. **1908** *Bulletin* (Sydney) 30 Jan. 15/1 'Twas the daughter of a squatter with a million-acre run. **1919** *Smith's Weekly* (Sydney) 1 Mar. 6/3 He was a teamster when he took up the small block, afterwards known as the Mount Stuart squattage. He put down a couple of good tanks, and stocked the run with sheep. **1930** BILLIS & KENYON *Pastures New* 22 A run .. consisted of the home station, where the owner or the superintendent resided, and several huts placed at convenient spots for feed and water; but also to command as much land as possible, leaving no room for a newcomer to intrude between. **1955** J. CLEARY *Justin Bayard* 243, I helped him double his stock. I built more than half the yards on the run. **1963** X. HERBERT *Disturbing Element* 48 Magoffin was a grazier, owner of Banyan Station, one of the richest cattle runs of the district. **1982** R. ELLIS *Bush Safari* 96 The ruins of Annandale Station, one of Sir Sidney Kidman's early runs, and the most remote station he ever owned.

3. *transf.* The territory traditionally occupied by an Aboriginal community.

1838 *Port Phillip Gaz.* 22 Dec. 4/3 These poor creatures [*sc.* Aborigines], aware of the penalty that await [*sic*] them when trespassing on the ground of another tribe .. dare not leave their own runs. **1845** L. LEICHHARDT *Jrnl. Overland Exped. Aust.* 2 Aug. (1847) 355 The natives seemed to have burned the grass systematically along every watercourse, and round every water-hole... It is no doubt connected with a systematic management of their runs, to attract game to particular spots, in the same way that stockholders burn parts of theirs in proper seasons. **1856** *Plea on Behalf Aboriginal Inhabitants Vic.* 6 How loudly a Squatter can call out for 'compensation' when there is any danger of his boundaries being curtailed! Did he ever think of compensating the man, whose title to his run is as clear as the right of kings is divine? **1909** W.G. SPENCE *Aust.'s Awakening* 11 When the white man came to Australia he found in possession the aboriginal squatter, whose runs were tribal and whose stock were kangaroos and opossums.

4. Special Comb. **run-holder,** the owner of a stock-raising establishment; one who has a legal entitlement to the use of a tract of grazing land; so, **-holding** *vbl. n.*; **hunter** *obs.*, one who seeks unoccupied grazing land; so, **-hunting** *vbl. n.*; **-jobbing** *vbl. n., obs.*, see quot. 1861.

1863 B.A. HEYWOOD *Vacation Tour Antipodes* 112 Several **run-holders** have jointly subscribed towards the support of a clergyman. **1872** *Causes Ruinous Condition Coal Trade N.S.W.* 15 He may .. invest one portion of his means in a coal-mine, another portion, say £30,000, in a copper-mine, whilst these two may be supplemented by run-holding and stock and station agency. **1879** S.W. SILVER *Austral. Grazier's Guide* 1 The Australian stock-farmer, settler, squatter, station-owner, or run-holder, as he is indifferently termed. **1881** W. FEILDING *Austral. Trans-Continental Railway* 23 Mr Turnbull says that the opinion generally held before my arrival here was that the Railway Company would turn out the present run-holders, and cutting up their runs, offer them for sale or lease to small sheep or cattle farmers. **1891** *Bulletin* (Sydney) 28 Mar. 23/1 The candidates were two—Highlow, the big run-holder; and Davis, a sporting Jew. **1912** *Emu* XII. 66 They never fail to frequent the orchard of the run-holder when the fruit is ripe. **1930** BILLIS & KENYON *Pastures New* 127 So serious was the position with many run-holders. **1848** *Maitland Mercury* 8 Jan. (Suppl.) 1/2 A gentleman recently arrived in town from .. the interior .. met several **runhunters**, who were resorting to the most extraordinary and even fraudulent means to secure right of possession by pre-occupation. **1890** 'R. BOLDREWOOD' *Squatter's Dream* 238 What do you say if I go run-hunting with you? You're just the sort of mate I should like, and I believe there is some grand country to the north-west. **1895** *Aust. Boys & Girls* 3 The party were in an unexplored portion of Central Australia, run-hunting. **1913** M.A. MCMANUS *Reminisc. Maranoa District* 76 Squatters and run hunters were too busy to spare the time to seek sweethearts and wives. **1916** H.L. ROTH *Sketches & Reminisc. Qld.* 9 He found himself stockdriving and run hunting (i.e., looking for new country) in the Central and Northern lands of the then young Colony of Queensland. **1861** F. ALGAR *Handbk. to Colony Qld.* 10 The 'Tenders for Crown Lands Act' was passed with the view of putting an end to the system of **'run-jobbing'**... Parties were fitted out for the object of travelling into the unsettled country, observing what portions of it were fit for occupation, and then tendering for it .. for the purpose of selling the untenanted blocks at enormous prices, to those about to engage in squatting. **1871** *Great Northern Run Case* 97 When Commissioners of Crown Lands, Surveyors and Surveyor-Generals, had a money interest in runs .. run-jobbing became their first consideration. **1884** G. RANKEN *Dry Country* i. 4 At an earlier period .. the practice of run-jobbing stood in the way of any legitimate use of the pasture.

run, *n.*[3] [Spec. use of *run* regular track made by an animal.] The bower made by a bower bird.

1840 *Proc. Zool. Soc. London* (1841) 94 Mr Gould then called the attention of the Members to an extraordinary piece of Bird-architecture, which he had ascertained to be constructed by the Satin Bird, *Ptilonorhynchus holosericeus*, and another of similar structure, but still larger, by the *Chlamydera maculata*. These constructions, Mr Gould states, are perfectly anomalous in the architecture of birds, and consist in a collection of pieces of stick and grass, formed into a bower. . . They are used by the birds as a playing-house, or 'run', as it is termed, and are used by the males to attract the females. **1841** J. Gould *Birds of Aust.* (1848) IV. Pl. 10, The propensity of these birds to pick up and fly off with any attractive object, is so well-known to the natives, that they always search the runs for any small missing article as the bowl of a pipe, &c., that may have been accidentally dropped in the brush. **1913** *Emu* XII. 173 The birds like a dry run, not too stony, and within call of several of the different berries which they eat. I know of about ten different runs now.

run, *n.*[4] [Spec. use of *run* a period of allowing a liquid, machinery, etc. to run: see OED(S *sb.*[1] 19.]

a. *Shearing.* An uninterrupted period worked during a day; a period of employment as a shearer.

1904 *Shearer* (Sydney) 6 Aug. 3/5 To Shearers. . . Can give Runs of Three and Four Sheds. **1916** *Bulletin* (Sydney) 6 July 22/3 After an eight hour run the winner had put through 5850 lambs. **1930** D. Cottrell *Earth Battle* 33, I undressed fifty-one . . wethers at Sunda's Plain last month in a two-hour run! **1949** *Bulletin* (Sydney) 23 Feb. 14/4 The ringer in a shearing-shed . . may have once been the man who shore the most sheep for a run; nowadays the shearer who has shorn the most sheep at the end of the shed is always regarded as the ringer. **1955** E. Barnes *Easier Shearing* 10 The order of the day was: a run of shearing of from one and a half hours upwards according to the amount of daylight. **1963** D. Niland *Dadda Jumped* 150 I'm a shearer. I come in today from Moombala. We cut-out there first run this morning. **1979** M. Rutherford *Departmental* 42 Shearing was okay. Dad took me everywhere to get me learner's pen but I could never get a run of me own.

b. *transf.* A period of employment.

1979 B. Scott *Tough in Old Days* 112 We entered the hall to face the Cane Inspectors from the mill to sign on for our 'run'. **1984** *N.T. News* (Darwin) 22 Sept. 40/2 Bricklayer wanted, good money, long run. . . Solid plasterers required, long run of work.

run, *n.*[5] [Spec. use of *run* the act of running.] In the phr. **to get the run,** to be dismissed from one's employment.

1889 Barrère & Leland *Dict. Slang* I. 403 *Get the run, to*, (English and Australian), to be discharged. **1892** 'J. Miller' *Workingman's Paradise* 2 'You didn't hear that my Tom got the run yesterday, did you?' 'Did he? What a pity! I'm very sorry,' said Nellie. 'Everybody'll be out of work and then what'll we all do?' **1894** *Bulletin* (Sydney) 13 Jan. 7/3 Legge got the run, Fogg cleared, Bell 'rung' the shed, and Warte turned out to be a 'scab'. **1959** S.J. Baker *Drum* 141 *Run, get the*, to be dismissed from employment.

run, *v.*[1] [Used elsewhere but recorded earliest in Aust. and apparently chiefly Austral.: see OED(S *v.* 43 c.]

1. *trans.* To provide pasture for (sheep, cattle, etc.); to raise (livestock). Also *absol.*

1795 R. Atkins *Jrnl.* 15 Feb., By the sale of the late farms it appears many people run upon the Hawkesbury. The land is certainly very fine. **1828** *Tasmanian* (Hobart) 4 Jan. 4 *J.C. Macdougall* hereby cautions all persons from running any Sheep, or Cattle, on his Farm of 1200 acres. **1834** H. Melville *Two Lett. Van Diemen's Land* 8 Mr Bryan . . was induced to receive Arnold into his service, and to permit him to run some cattle on his (Mr Bryan's) land. **1847** *Emigrant's Lett.* 11 Aug. (1850) 17 The wages we are now giving are very high; so high that we should not be able to afford them were we not able to run our sheep in very large flocks. **1862** W. Landsborough *Jrnl. Exped. from Carpentaria* 88 It is not necessary at times to run sheep in large flocks. **1867** J. Bonwick *J. Batman* 38 One of the so-called party of anti-squatters, Mr Evans, assured me that he went with the avowed intention to run sheep. **1890** 'R. Boldrewood' *Colonial Reformer* II. 32 For mysterious reasons he had apparently decided that he, Ernest, was not fit to run alone, in a pastoral sense, for another year at least. **1902** *Advocate* (Burnie) 3 Jan. 2/6 Running about 30,000 sheep. **1940** *Bulletin* (Sydney) 10 July 17/1 'What y' goin' t' do, Paddy?' Sam wanted to know. 'Run poultry?' 'You'll see,' said Paddy mysteriously. After the netted fence was up he began digging. . . 'I was right,' said Sam gloomily. 'He *is* running poultry.' **1944** *Ibid.* 17 May 13/1 Sandy, who ran a couple of thousand sheep on his leasehold . . owned a very intelligent young lead-dog. **1955** A.C.V. Bligh *Golden Quest* 35 Many of the pearlers also owned blocks of country on which they usually ran sheep and cattle. **1963** X. Herbert *Disturbing Element* 8 We ran horses. Dad's sideline, hobby, and delight was horses. He broke them, trained them, traded them.

2. *intr.* Of livestock: to graze.

1810 *Sydney Gaz.* 21 Apr., All Persons having Horses or Stock . . running at Castle Hill are requested to take them away. **1827** *Tasmanian* (Hobart) 19 July 2 A stock hut . . in which was a man, the assigned servant of an individual . . whose stock runs in that neighbourhood. **1833** *Trumpeter* (Hobart) 3 Sept. 154 A flock of about 500 Sheep, now running on the estate of Capt. Moriarty. **1842** *Sydney Morning Herald* 2 Aug. 2/4, I have a goat and a kid running in the bush which I have not put in my schedule. **1851** H. Melville *Present State Aust.* 24 Squatters pay rentals of £10 per annum for depasturing licences, which comprehend a sufficient track of land whereon four thousand sheep may run, or an equivalent number of cattle or horses. **1873** J.C.F. Johnson *Christmas on Carringa* 2 Ned Ballington, a smart, rather well-informed American—a decent mate and a good hand amongst the cattle (for we had both sheep and cattle running). **1890** 'R. Boldrewood' *Colonial Reformer* II. 174 He . . would attend, with Mr Banks, at the Station, some hundreds of miles off, where the cattle were running. **1901** *Advocate* (Burnie) 22 June 4/1 He left Windsor's survey camp on Monday morning to get a horse running on Game's block in order to shift camp. **1927** 'S. Rudd' *Romance of Runnibede* 78 Did you see the mob that those roan poley cows run with, in that wattle gorge?

3. a. *trans. Obs.* Of land: to provide sustenance for (animals).

1840 *Port Phillip Gaz.* 24 Oct. 1 *For sale*, about one hundred head of Cattle, with a splendid Cattle Station, watered by three rivers, and capable of running at least six hundred head of cattle and two thousand sheep. **1841** *Port Phillip Patriot* 11 Mar. 3/3 A Gentleman is desirous of purchasing a good Cattle Station, it must be well watered and capable of running 700 to 1000 head. **1847** *Port Phillip Gaz.* 8 May 3 A Station capable of running 6,000 sheep and 500 cattle. **1849** *Belfast Gaz.* (Port Phillip) 3/1 Those possessed of runs capable of running more than 100,000 sheep, ought to have sold a few head and 'given in' the remainder of their runs to those who wanted them badly and would have paid for them liberally.

b. *transf.* To cover the expense of; to 'run to'.

1905 *Bulletin* (Sydney) 20 July 3/2 He was rabbiting, he told me, and the job would 'run a mate'. **1917** *Flotilla Echo: On Board H.M.A.S. No. 79* Nov. 12 If Tiddly has enough money to 'run' 'Steak and Onions' he can easily afford . . to have his boots cleaned. **1946** A.J. Holt *Wheat Farms Vic.* 112 This Mallee country won't run holidays.

run, *v.*[2] [Transf. use of *run* to pursue, follow up (a scent): see OED *v.* 34 b.] *trans.* To follow (the trail of a person, animal, etc.). Esp. in the phr. **to run the track.**

1841 *Sydney Herald* 21 Jan. 2/6 Lieutenant Christie and his party, who had been running his track with an aboriginal native for three days, came up the next morning and escorted him to Queanbeyan. **1851** *Bell's Life in Sydney* 1 Apr. 3/2 It is impossible to run his track. I tried with three black fellows, but never could even pick it up. **1871** *Austral. Town & Country Jrnl.* (Sydney) 15 Apr. 463/4 Two of the troopers . . saw a blackfellow running our horse-tracks. **1882** A.J. Boyd *Old Colonials* 140, I ran some gins' tracks and found they were spying me. **1895** *Bulletin* (Sydney) 23 Nov. 3/2 They brought a boy from Tallaran to run Mick Dooley's tracks; They yarded him the fastest blood among the station cracks. **1904** L.M.P. Archer *Bush Honeymoon* 350 First we'll set the nigger to track 'bout the place; then *runnin' the track's* simple. **1913** W.K. Harris *Outback in Aust.* 141 We struck out through the trackless Bush, and coming to a fence, 'ran it up' until we found a gateway. **1936** W. Hatfield *Aust. through Windscreen* 59 Very little practice is needed to tell the difference between free-running and driven cattle tracks. I had just cut their track and begun to run it along. **1962** T. Ronan *Deep of Sky* 103 It was a long trip out to the Limmen. They ran the Lanken up to where, some years before, Dad and Mat Wilson and a mob of sheep had just managed to survive a flood.

run, *v.*[3] *Obs.* [U.S. *run* to tease, nag: see OED(S *v.* 52 c.] *trans.* To harass (a person).

1846 L.W. Miller *Notes of Exile Van Dieman's Land* 330 Every new load of prisoners from town [for Port Arthur] always brought some money with them. This was strictly prohibited, and many ingenious plans were devised to smuggle it, one of which was, swallowing pieces of gold. Every person in the gang was of course liable to be suspected of possessing these hidden treasures, and in order to discover the real *Simon pures*, and compel them to '*fork over*', the whole were continually '*run*', as it was termed, for months. Loads which it was impossible to carry were heaped upon them, until some excuse was found to take them to the office. **1891** 'Rouseabout' *Jackeroo* 3 No one else can buy any at those sales. There's a Squatter's League of sixty members to run any objectionable buyer, and they have always been pretty successful in running any person who has been rash enough to compete with them. **1892** 'R. Boldrewood' *Nevermore* II. 132 'Well, I knocked over the head warder at Ballarat.' 'Good boy! What for?' 'He had been 'running' me—wanted to make me break out, I suppose.'

run, *v.*[4] [Transf. use of *run* to chase or hunt: see OED(S 42 a.]

1. To round up (wild cattle, horses, etc.). Also as *vbl. n.* and *ppl. a.*

1871 *Austral. Town & Country Jrnl.* (Sydney) 22 Apr. 490/2 In fact the running of wild horses is the initiation of many of our youths into the vile habit of duffing, which next to drinking is the most demoralizing evil in the country districts. **1889** *Illustr. Austral. News* (Melbourne) 1 May 74/2 On stations where there are any scrub cattle, running coachers, or quiet cattle, are used as decoy for the purpose of running the wild cattle into the yards. **1893** J.A. Barry *Steve Brown's Bunyip* 61 Will readin' an' writin' run brombees, or drive a team o' bullocks, or 'elp to plough or 'arrer? **1912** *Bulletin* (Sydney) 22 Feb. 14/2, I shore wrinklies for Bobby Rand . . drove horses for Sam McCaughey, ran scrubbers for Jack McDonald. **1927** A. Crombie *After Sixty Yrs.* 84 A fresh man and horse would take the running in turn. **1943** H.G. Lamond *From Tariaro to Ross Roy* 37 A stockman broke his leg. . . Six months later he was running wild cattle. **1951** E. Hill *Territory* 305 'Running wild cattle', who was to care if they did chase a few tame ones. **1979** C. Stone *Running Brumbies* 46 Running brumbies like branding is an exciting experience.

2. In phrases.

a. To run in, to pursue and confine (cattle). Also *transf.* (see quots. 1900 and 1907).

1885 Mrs Campbell-Praed *Head Station* I. 124 No end of sport . . in shooting wild horses and running in scrubbers. **1887** A. Nicols *Wild Life & Adventure* 115 With a final rush the beasts were run in, and the rails put smartly up. **1900** *Bulletin* (Sydney) 21 Apr. 14/1, I heard a man from the backblocks say the other day that he intended to run in a mob of *30* black lepers, and see what the Govt. would do then. **1907** *Truth* (Sydney) 7 Apr. 9/7 'But they use them on the stations?' 'Oh, yes, they use them, gins and bucks. Soon as they get tame enough, both squatters and missionaries run 'em in, and the one lot can use the stockwhip just as well as another.' **1917** A.L. Brewer *'Gators' Euchre* 34 'How did you know I was leaving the station, Sheila?' 'I saw you running in your horses.' **1935** R.B. Plowman *Boundary Rider* 158 The sheep had been run in so that they could be gone over for wool blindness, and for blowfly damage. **1960** R.S. Porteous *Cattleman* 35 Instead of running in the saddle horses each morning, he and Biddy put up a small holding paddock and improved the yards. **1977** *Pastoral Rev.* Sept. 303/3 His singular duty is to run in (muster) the working horses every morning.

Hence **run-in** *ppl. a.*

1934 J.C. LEE *Boshstralians* 226 Owen, astride a 'run-in' brumby, cantered briskly up to his own slip-rails.

b. To run into, to drive (an animal) into (a yard, etc.).

1849 A. HARRIS *Emigrant Family* (1967) 138 The mingled flocks must be run into the stockyard. **1904** *Truth* (Sydney) 7 Aug. 5/1 *Went after the sheep*, and ran them into a corner. **1946** F. CLUNE *Try Nothing Twice* 100 Run that creamy heifer into the bail . . then leg-rope her and milk her—it's easy.

c. To run off, to separate (animals) from a mob.

1861 H. EARLE *Ups & Downs* 43 When you can run off any stock from the station, leave two stones on the table in the hut, and one of the party will carry them off into the mountains. **1965** J.S. GUNN *Terminol. Shearing Industry* 15 *Run-off*, to take a group of sheep from the flock without necessarily 'cutting-out' all of this group or 'drafting' them into special lots, for example 'I'll run off some fats'.

d. To run up, to bring (a horse, etc.) in from pasture.

1876 J.A. EDWARDS *Gilbert Gogger* 163 After breakfast, the several guests retired to their rooms to don riding apparel; the stockmen ran up the horses, side-saddles were fastened to the backs of the steeds destined to carry the fair equestrians. . . Dear reader, this phrase is colonial, and not *ours*; we certainly never saw a stockman running *up* a horse. **1888** 'R. BOLDREWOOD' *Robbery under Arms* (1890) 350 Run up the horses. . . They're in the little horse paddock. **1923** *Bulletin* (Sydney) 1 Nov. 24/4 A practice which hasn't much to recommend it is that of keeping a 'night horse' yarded all night on the far-out stations, so that it can be used to run up the mob in the morning.

run, *v.*[5] [Spec. use of *run* to cause to move.] *trans.* With **out:** to split (a plank, post, slab, etc.) from a log of wood. Also *absol.*

1873 C.H. EDEN *Fortunes of Fletchers* 72 Posts and rails are 'run out', as it is technically expressed, from an iron bark, or some other hardwood tree. **1874** C. DE BOOS *Congewoi Correspondence* 119 He 'ud take a big chip outer the sap wood, and he 'ud split it up runnin out ways and grain ways, and he 'ud say, lookin at me, 'Why, it 'ud run out like matches, Johnny!' **1876** 'EIGHT YRS.' RESIDENT' *Queen of Colonies* 217 If he finds a good tree or two the slabs for his house will be 'run out' in a couple or three days.

runaway. *Hist.* A convict who has escaped from official custody or from assigned service. Also **runaway convict, prisoner, transport.**

1790 R. CLARK Jrnl. 4 Sept. 204 Thos. Streets one of the convicts . . has . . gone into the wood to live with Gray and Jones the other Runaway convicts. **1791** D. COLLINS *Acct. Eng. Colony N.S.W.* (1798) I. 190 A boat . . had been taken off by some runaways to get on board one of the ships then about to sail. **1801** *HRA* (1915) 1st Ser. III. 26, I have the honour to enclose a copy of the certificate given to such persons as have been convicts, and who are allowed to quit this colony. Any of that description that may hereafter be found without that certificate are runaways. **1808** *Sydney Gaz.* 18 Dec., Mrs Cox's Government man, has run from her employ since the 12th instant. This is therefore to caution Settlers and others from harbouring or employing the said Runaway. **1818** *HRA* (1917) 1st Ser. IX. 793 It is hardly possible to find these Runaways when the Sailors are in league with them and Connive at their Concealment on board. **1828** *Tasmanian* (Hobart) 18 July 3 A Mr McKevett was fined this week by the Police Magistrate, in the sum of 50 dollars, for harbouring Mary Ann Heagan, a runaway prisoner. **1830** *HRA* (1917) 1st Ser. XV. 767 A Runaway is Gazetted but thrice in the Gazette and is then withdrawn. **1833** *Ibid.* (1923) 1st Ser. XVII. 337 The Shortness of their hair will not only contribute to cleanliness but to the discovery and apprehension of Runaways. **1837** *S. Austral. Rec.* (London) 11 Nov. 12 We allude more particularly to the runaway convicts, a few of whom are suspected to be in the settlement. They are in custody, and if the suspicions of the government are justified, they will be shipped off immediately. **1847** *Maitland Mercury* 14 July 2/5 Coyne was sentenced to three years in irons, to commence after his present sentence was completed, Coyne being now a runaway from Newcastle stockade. **1850** J. PLATT *Horrors of Transportation* 6, I was described as a run-away transport from my master. **1858** T. MCCOMBIE *Hist. Colony Vic.* 127 Runaway prisoners of the Crown, and expiree convicts . . erected huts, and became 'sly grog' sellers, cattle stealers, and receivers of stolen property. **1862** BACKHOUSE & TYLOR *Life & Labours G.W. Walker* 278 They were said to be exceedingly useful in suppressing disturbances between their own countrymen and the Whites, and in capturing runaways. **1872** MRS E. MILLETT *Austral. Parsonage* 242 Confirmed runaways . . were punished by being placed in the chain-gang at the 'Establishment'.

runaway hole. A hole in the soil through which surface water drains away.

1878 MRS H. JONES *Broad Outlines* 177 There is water, but I am inclined to think it comes from those curious runaway holes we have on most of the runs. . . They partially drain the country, and are supposed to empty themselves into the Blue Lake at Mount Gambier. **1893** *Adelaide Observer* 26 Aug. 43/1 The plain is open and well grassed, the soil a stiff, clayey loam, with a dry subsoil and numerous 'crab' or 'runaway holes', through which the surface waters find their way in times of rain. **1906** *Bulletin* (Sydney) 23 Aug. 16/3 The creek . . is fed from the Wimmera, and empties into swamps and 'runaway' holes. . . Curious things are these same 'runaway' holes—the smaller, when dry, are like rabbit burrows leading down to some great subterranean river; when water is running the vortex may be plainly seen. **1913** *Ibid.* 2 Jan. 15/2 The Mundalla Swamp covers about 100 acres and holds 10 ft. of water all over it. At one end is a 'runaway hole', which seems to open and close in spasms. One night the swamp will be full; next day the hole opens up; three days later the swamp is as dry as a churchwarden's meeting.

rung, *ppl. a.* [f. RING *v.*[1]] Of a tree: ring-barked. Of an area: having ring-barked trees still standing. See RING-BARK *v.* 1.

1885 MRS C. PRAED *Austral. Life* 35 They were only pressed into service when shepherds were scarce, or 'rung' trees (that is, gums which had been barked and allowed to wither) required felling. **1894** J.K. ARTHUR *Kangaroo & Kauri* 24 'Rung' trees soon turn sickly and wither away. **1906** *Emu* VI. 61 The giant 'rung' trees are left, 8 or 10 per acre, standing dead and gaunt in the fields and pastures. **1916** J.B. COOPER *Coo-oo-ee!* 2 Cleared patches, fringed with belts of 'rung' timber. **1937** R. FAIRBRIDGE *Pinjarra* 51 Though oppressed by the desolate stretches of 'rung' country, we were delighted with the living bush. **1943** H.G. LAMOND *From Tariaro to Ross Roy* 51 The rankness disappeared from the rung pastures. **1952** J.R. SKEMP *Memories Myrtle Bank* 67 The first act in clearing was to go through the bush and ringbark the larger trees—anything over a foot in diameter; trees so treated were said to be 'rung'.

runner.

1. One who rounds up (wild cattle, horses, etc.). See RUN *v.*[4]

1917 C. DREW *Reminisc. D. Gilbert* 34 The manager of Calendoon Station gave the runners permission to clear the brumbies from off the Calendoon run. **1927** A. CROMBIE *After Sixty Yrs.* 84 The horse runners would leave horsemen dismounted five or six miles apart. **1968** W. GILL *Petermann Journey* 46 Cattle duffers; cattle killing natives, and their cum'-uppance; horse thieves who became station owners; the iniquities of brumby 'runners'. Once he was convinced of my interest, he talked on and on.

2. A proprietor of a stock-raising establishment. See RUN *v.*[1] 1.

1963 X. HERBERT *Disturbing Element* 57 As runners of stock ourselves . . we had to share grazing and water with them.

running postman. [See quot. 1981.] The wide-spread, prostrate, perennial plant *Kennedia prostrata* (fam. Fabaceae), having trifoliolate leaves and scarlet pea flowers. See also *coral pea* (a), CORAL.

1898 E.E. MORRIS *Austral Eng.* 247 *K[ennedya] prostrata* is called the *Coral Pea* . . or *Running Postman*. **1917** 'H.H. RICHARDSON' *Fortunes Richard Mahony* I. 87 The short-lived grass was picked out into patterns by the scarlet of the Running Postman. **1942** C. BARRETT *From Bush Hut* 60 'Running postman', with sealing-wax red flowers, 'ran', over a low ant hill. **1973** J. MORRISON *Austral. by Choice* 74 The whole hillside was speckled with colour. . . The scarlet blobs of running-postman and the pale stars of early nancy. **1981** J.A. BAINES *Austral. Plant Genera* 203 Running Postman (so named from red flowers and prostrate habit of growth, in allusion to the scarlet uniforms of postmen in former times).

run-through.

1. See quot. 1956.

1956 S. GORE *Overlanding with Annabel* 74 Sometimes, to the great joy of the traveller, there is no gate at all! In its place is a 'run-through', which is a deep pit roofed over with equally-spaced iron bars. Animals cannot walk over these but a car can be driven. **1978** D. STUART *Wedgetail View* 101 Hard rough road. . . Rattling grids or twisting run-throughs where fences crossed the road every five or six miles.

2. *Australian National Football.* A screen made of crepe paper or some similar material and in the colours of a team, through which the players run on to the field.

1973 P. MCKENNA *My World of Football* 90 The carnival atmosphere, the tier after tier of packed stands encircling the MCG, the cheer squads with their long club banners and until recently the highly colourful floggers and run-throughs. **1979** *Age* (Melbourne) 1 Oct. 1/5 The giant run-throughs were raised and the Carlton and Collingwood teams battered their way through them on to the ground.

rupee. *Hist.* An Indian coin which circulated in New South Wales during the earlier part of the nineteenth century: see esp. quot. 1835.

1825 *Austral.* (Sydney) 22 Dec. 3/2 Rupees . . might properly pass as half-dollars. **1829** *Sydney Monitor* 28 Nov. 2/1 Rupees imported . . and sold . . at 2s. 6d. now passing for 1s. 9d. **1835** *True Colonist* (Hobart) 4 Sept. 2/3 The *Rupee* Bill has passed, fixing the value of that coin at two shillings, as a legal tender between the Inhabitants. . . Let [the People] resolve not to buy a Treasury Bill, until the Commissary will receive the '*Rupee*' at the legalized Colonial value. **1842** *Sydney Herald* 30 May 2/6 There are at present a great number of rupees in circulation under the name of half-crowns; it has been discovered that the parties principally concerned in carrying on this species of imposition, are the members of the Sydney swell mob.

rupperty, var. RUBBITY.

rural school. A name given to any of several kinds of educational institution: see quots. 1926, 1927, and 1974.

1875 *Act* (Qld.) 39 Vict. no. 11 Sect. 14, It shall be lawful for the Minister from time to time to make provision for the establishment of training schools rural schools night schools and such other State schools as may be authorised by the regulations and deemed expedient. **1917** *Qld. Parl. Papers* II. 138 A rural school, the first of its kind in Queensland, was opened at Nambour, on the 29th January, 1917. In addition to subjects required in an ordinary primary school, instruction of a utilitarian nature is now provided suited to the industries followed by the community which the school is intended to serve, viz., farming, fruit-growing and dairying. **1926** J.W. ELIJAH *Rural School* 1 The Victorian Education Department defines a rural school as one 'the allotment of which does not exceed 150 pupils'. **1927** G.S. BROWNE *Educ. in Aust.* 41 In New South Wales it has a technical significance, a Rural School being a special type of Superior School which has recently been discriminated from the others. *Ibid.* 274 One of the most important developments in Queensland education was the inauguration of a system of rural schools in 1917. . . The Rural School is part of a carefully organized scheme of agricultural education for all grades of students from those in the primary school to University students in the proposed University Faculty of Agriculture. **1930** V. PALMER *Passage* (1957) 81 Sew for the Wiegerts? She hadn't put in two years at the rural school for that! **1940** *Educ. Studies & Investigations* (Austral. Council Educ. Research) 205 The rural schools of Queensland represent real progress toward the solution of the 12 to 15 years problem in country districts. **1974** J. MCLAREN *Dict. Austral. Educ.* 167 *Rural School*, a school with only one teacher and with all the students combined in a single class. Each grade of students is given its own program, but the whole school will combine for excursions, singing or school broadcasts... More than half the schools in Australia are still of this kind.

rush, *n.*

1. *Hist.* The sudden escape of a number of prisoners.

[**1812** J.H. VAUX *Mem.* (1819) II. 202 A sudden and violent effort to get into any place, or *vice versa* to effect your exit, as from a place of confinement, *&c.*, is called *rushing them*, or *giving it to 'em upon the rush.*] **1816** *Hobart Town Gaz.* 13 Sept., On Thursday morning .. a most daring Rush was committed by some of the Prisoners in the Prison Room at Hobart Town, by taking out of the window an Iron Bar. **1890** H.A. WHITE *Crime & Criminals* 67 When at Pentridge he was implicated in planning several rushes. **1964** J.V. BARRY *Life & Death J. Price* 79 When a body of prisoners banded together to effect an escape it was called a 'rush'.

2. a. [Used elsewhere but recorded earliest in Aust.: see OED(S *sb.*[2] 4 a.] A sudden movement of numbers of people to a particular place, esp. to a newly discovered goldfield; the people who take part in such a movement. See also *new rush* NEW *a.* 3.

1841 *Omnibus & Sydney Spectator* 27 Nov. 68/4 Parties who now want runs go over the range to the Moreton Bay side... I understand there is a fine river about one hundred miles to the northward of Moreton Bay called White Bay River which is navigable for a considerable way upwards for large vessels, so that this will no doubt be the next rush. **1849** *Bell's Life in Sydney* 13 Oct. 4/2 A rush—a rush—a general rush From city and hamlet, and station and bush, Leaping, like kangaroos, *pushety push.* **1852** *Argus* (Melbourne) 8 Mar. 2/7 The 'rush' has left little elbow-room for those who are lucky enough in finding places for their tubs and cradles. **1853** E. SAUNDERS *Our Austral. Colonies* 12 At present, it is useless to quote the prices of labour, the market being in a very unsettled state, in consequence of the rush to the Gold-Fields. **1855** *Ovens & Murray Advertiser* (Beechworth) 14 Apr. 5/1 There has been a slight rush this week to a place called Little Bendigo. **1858** L. PEARSON *Emigrants' Guide* (Port Curtis) 17 All ordinary business is interrupted by the rush for Port Curtis—people are madly disposing of their effects, or sacrificing their property to be off to Port Curtis. **1864** J. ARMOUR *Diggings, Bush & Melbourne* 8 In one .. rush we joined, but arrived too late for anything better than an uphill claim .. we bottomed at about one third of the depth that gold might be expected at. **1873** A. TROLLOPE *Aust. & N.Z.* I. 29 There have been gold rushes in various parts of the colony, and new rushes are still made from time to time. **1886** *Bulletin* (Sydney) 5 June 10/1 We advise them to pray Against every temptation to 'prospect' for sin Lest a clerical rush to Bundarra sets in! **1893** 'OLD CHUM' *Chips* 65 We came upon a 'rush' of diggers marking out new claims. **1921** *Smith's Weekly* (Sydney) 1 Jan. 17/4 It was the cutting up of the river frontages of Tomki run, 36 years ago, that started the farming and dairying rush to Richmond River (N.S.W.). **1936** C. CHEWINGS *Back in Stone Age* p. xi, A mild 'rush' to secure suitable land for pastoral pursuits was on. **1938** C.P. CONIGRAVE *Walk-About* 11 One gold-mad hero essayed the rush on a single loaf of bread and a bottle of brandy. **1962** O. PRYOR *Aust.'s Little Cornwall* 91 At Wallaroo, as in all cases where a deposit of a valuable mineral is discovered, there was a rush to peg claims on all the surrounding ground.

b. In the phr. **a rush set in,** 'a sudden movement of people began'.

1866 *Colony of Qld. as Field for Emigration* 17 Rockhampton .. was precipitated into importance some seven years since by a 'rush' which set in from the southern colonies to the Canoona diggings, about forty miles from the town. **1871** *Austral. Town & Country Jrnl.* (Sydney) 21 Jan. 79/4 A rush set in and claims were immediately pegged off in the supposed direction of the reef. **1873** J.C.F. JOHNSON *Christmas on Carringa* 3 A big rush set in to the Pick-a-back in '57. **1898** D.W. CARNEGIE *Spinifex & Sand* 58 We .. arrived at the Red Flag, an alluvial rush that had 'set in' during our sojourn in the sand. **1901** *Brisbane Courier* 5 July 4/8 Shortly after Westcott's prospecting party had met with success, what is known as a 'rush' set in. Within a few weeks from 2000 to 3000 Europeans arrived with horses, stores, mining batteries, &c.

c. *transf.* A goldfield to which a sudden movement of numbers of people has taken place. Also of opal-mining. See also *new rush* NEW *a.* 3.

1855 W. HOWITT *Land, Labor & Gold* II. 249 They are bound for .. distant rushes. **1862** C. ASPINALL *Three Yrs. Melbourne* 176, I was taken to see a little 'diggings" canvas town, called Lamplough... The unhealthiness of the air, arising from the lack of drainage, is fearful at some of these populous 'rushes'. **1873** A. TROLLOPE *Aust. & N.Z.* I. 286 The population at a rush is very precarious, falling as quickly as it rises. **1880** *Bulletin* (Sydney) 8 May 2/1 Six months after marriage the husband bolted to a New South Wales rush. **1888** *Illustr. Austral. News* (Melbourne) 26 May (Suppl.) 106/1 'All sorts and conditions' of men flocked to the 'rushes', as the newly discovered gold fields were called in the fifties. **1898** D.W. CARNEGIE *Spinifex & Sand* 351 She came overland from Queensland, accompanying her husband who, in the early days of the rush, sought to turn an honest penny by the sale of 'sly grog'. **1914** C.H.S. MATTHEWS *Bill* 170 We made off together to an opal rush called the Little Wonder, in Queensland. **1921** *Bulletin* (Sydney) 17 Nov. 20/2 My dad who 'followed the diggings' tells me that to call a man 'Joe' on the Vic. rushes was the surest way of buying a fight. **1944** K.S. PRICHARD *Potch & Colour* 1 When Mick Ryan built a bough shed and started handing out stores on the Far-away, he pegged the best claim on the rush. **1966** H. GYE *Father clears Out* 52 Why is he so poor now, after finding all the rich reefs and rushes.

d. A newly-discovered deposit of gold on a goldfield.

1871 *Austral. Town & Country Jrnl.* (Sydney) 3 June 687/4 This rush is an important addition to the workings of the gold-field. **1872** J.M. CONROY *False* 32 Even diggings have official terms. The original spot of the discovery is speedily christened as a township, and so jumps into the realms of proper names. A mile or two away another less great discovery is made. This is called the Rush. The next is the New Rush. But when the next comes the other two are successively styled the Old Rush, and the Last Rush, and so on. *c* **1872** J.C.F. JOHNSON *Over Island* 17 It was situated between three small rushes, upon which a certain number of men who had got 'on the gutter' as it was termed were getting very good returns. **1887** 'OLD GOLD DIGGER' *Gold Digger's Guide* 3, I .. know of two quartz reefs containing gold, a few miles from the present rush at Teetulpa.

3. A stampede, esp. of cattle.

1881 A.C. GRANT *Bush-Life Qld.* II. 132 A sudden rush—a whirr—a tearing, crashing, roaring, thundering noise was heard; a confused whirl of dark forms swept before him, and the camp, so full of life a minute ago, is desolate. It was 'a rush', stampede. **1921** *Ross's Monthly* May 21/1 A drover is mortally injured in a 'rush' during the night watch; as he lies dying he gives his cheque to his mates, who at once reckon up before him what they are going to buy. **1933** A.J. COTTON *With Big Herds in Aust.* 84, I have seen some funny things happen in a 'rush' at night with bullocks. **1942** *Bulletin* (Sydney) 1 July 12/3 Myself a greenhider of old, I agree .. that a rush off a camp is unaccompanied by vocal efforts. **1951** E. HILL *Territory* 294 The rush is real trouble. **1967** M. SELLARS *Carramar* 37 A rush is a terrifying thing and woe betide anyone caught in its path. **1981** G. PIKE *Campfire Tales* 4 Robbie often spoke of a long droving trip he made in 1894... He told of many 'rushes' and wild rides in the darkness.

rush, *v.*

1. *trans.* To cause (cattle, etc.) to stampede.

1834 N.S.W. Magistrates' Depostion Bk. 6 Nov., He [*sc.* the shepherd] came home and reported to Mr Wightman that his Sheep had been rushed by a native dog. **1836** *Colonist* (Sydney) 25 Feb. 58/1 Sheep are frequently lost, and 'rushed' by native dogs. **1847** G.F. ANGAS *Savage Life & Scenes* I. 141 The wild-dogs howled so dreadfully during the night, coming in packs close to our tents, and *rushing* the sheep. **1849** J.P. TOWNSEND *Rambles & Observations N.S.W.* 113 These wild men .. 'rush' or disperse the cattle. **1920** L. ESSON *Dead Timber* 34 Fancy the Jackeroo firing his revolver and rushing the mob like that—it's the dead finish.

2. [Transf. use of *rush* to attack (in a military context): used elsewhere but recorded earliest in Aust. (see OED(S *v.*[2] 5 b.] *trans.* To assail (a person, etc.) by means of a sudden rush.

1840 *S. Austral. Miscellany* June 181 They would then, in the emphatic phrase of colonial description, *rush him*—the issue of such a conflict being all but certain. **1844** *Parramatta Chron.* 16 Nov. 2/3 From the conversation that was overheard, it appeared that they intended to 'rush' the lock-up keeper, and 'settle' John Downey, the approver against them. **1853** C.R. READ *What I heard, saw & Did* 23 To protect the party .. for fear of having their tents *rushed* by Van Demonian gentry? **1861** T. M'COMBIE *Austral. Sketches* 122 Even if those [cattle] .. run at him or 'rush' as it is termed, few will really toss or gore. **1879** 'AUSTRALIAN' *Adventures Qld.* 37 Whenever he had an opportunity of 'rushing' a station, and murdering the men, he had no scruple in taking the rations that the poor fellows had evidently been using themselves. **1882** J. SCHLEMAN *Life in Melbourne* 40 Men .. live upon a system of 'rushing', picking up some innocent shepherd down for his holiday, or waylaying a new chum and relieving him of his surplus cash. **1927** A. CROMBIE *After Sixty Yrs.* 39 Roach's camp was rushed by wild blacks. **1981** *Bulletin* (Sydney) 15 Dec. 82/1 The long war of attrition between the races, when 'rushing the gins' was a euphemism for rape and 'dispersing the natives' or 'snipe-shooting' meant murder.

3. a. [Used elsewhere but recorded earliest in Aust.: see OED(S *v.*[2] 5 d.] *trans.* To occupy by a rush (esp. of gold-miners).

1852 *Bell's Life in Sydney* 19 June 2/3 Campbell's Hill, has been 'rushed' after the fashion of Rose Hill. **1855** *Ovens & Murray Advertiser* (Beechworth) 24 Feb. (Suppl.) 5/4 Yesterday they were washing out an ounce to seven buckets of dirt. I have no doubt but the ground will be re-rushed and torn up next week. **1862** J.A. PATTERSON *Gold Fields Vic.* 94 If ever the old diggings are re-rushed, there cannot be a doubt that stores of gold will be unearthed. **1871** *Austral. Town & Country Jrnl.* (Sydney) 17 June 751/3 Rapp's Gully, about a mile beyond the three-mile, has been again rushed, a payable prospect being reported. **1882** A.J. BOYD *Old Colonials* 69 The Palmer diggings was just rushed. **1907** *Bulletin* (Sydney) 8 Aug. 14/2, I brought in an 8 oz. slug from country never tried; but, if I showed the gold, I didn't dare to disclose the locality, for I knew a swarm of Chinese were just waiting to rush it. **1922** R.L. JACK *Northmost Aust.* II. 616 Since the date of our visit to these rivers .. the South Coen has been 'rushed' by Chinese. **1939** J.W. COLLINSON *Early Days Cairns* 115 They brought in 2 ozs. of gold... The Mulgrave find was 'rushed'. **1942** H.H. PECK *Mem. of Stockman* 163 The island was thrown open to selection and was rushed, but the Government of the day made the mistake of making the blocks too small. **1973** *Nation Rev.* (Melbourne) 31 Aug. (Suppl.) 1/1 It was first explored by Hume and Hovell, then opened up by cattlemen, rushed by gold seekers, and finally developed as a prosperous agricultural area.

b. *trans.* To exhibit enthusiasm for (something or someone).

1858 L. PEARSON *Emigrants' Guide Port Curtis* 25 The shipping passenger trade has been—to speak colonially—tolerably well *rushed* in the prevailing excitement. **1877** H. TAYLOR *Emigration S.A.* 4, I am bound to confess that they have good cause for complaint in the past in having the immigration business 'rushed' too much, so as materially to affect the price of labour. **1894** *Bulletin* (Sydney) 10 Mar. 6/4 The Alexandra was rushed again on Saturday by an audience that followed the dark intricacies of 'Right's Right' with hungry eyes. **1907** *Truth* (Sydney) 5 May 1/5 There are some noble intellects on Sydney trams since the bush-boys began to rush the job. **1922** *Daily Mail* (Sydney) 6 Jan. 2/4 Although the public rush Albert Wood's mounts, he is not treated with the same amount of confidence by the majority of trainers. **1930** M.B. PETERSEN *Monsoon Music* 17 'In Australia we are more sensible, our people don't rush stars as a rule.' 'They'll rush him all right,' the big fair man asserted.

4. *intr.* Of animals: to stampede.

1838 G.C. INGLETON *True Patriots All* 19 Nov. (1952) 198 With respect to 'rushing' of cattle, our readers lately arrived in the Colony will please to understand, that Cattle when much left to themselves, 'rush', that is, make off at full gallop to a great distance and into the glens. **1892** 'R. BOLDREWOOD' *Nevermore* 178 It's a nice treat on a wet night, sitting on your horse soaking wet through .. afraid to give the bullocks a chance for fear they'd rush. **1900** *Truth* (Sydney) 11 Feb. 8/1 Many a night when the cattle have 'rushed', or a 'scrubber' has set him a go down a mountain. **1919** *Bulletin* (Sydney) 9 Jan. 22/3 Sheep are quiet things on the track; but they rush sometimes. **1932** J.J. HARDIE *Cattle Camp* (1944) 38 The bullocks were quiet all the way—never rushed once! **1965** M. PATCHETT *Last Warrior* 185 Drovers say that grey horses . . have a peculiar smell that can start the cattle rushing. **1976** C.D. Mills *Hobble Chains & Greenhide* 25 It was a moment before our stunned senses grasped that they had 'rushed'. We all raced for the spare night-horses and away in the dark for the lead. **1977** R. Edwards *Austral. Yarn* 32 The cattle rushed every night and Snuffler used to be out risking his life while the boss and the jackeroos and all the silvertails were back in camp.

Hence **rushing** *vbl. n.* and *ppl. a.*

1919 *Bulletin* (Sydney) 17 July 22/3 A stockman on the lead of rushing cattle or horses always turns his mount's tail to the herd. **1938** J.F.W. Schulz *Destined to Perish* 22, I listened to the head stockman recounting experiences with 'rushing' cattle. **1978** Teece & Pike *Voice of Wilderness* 36 The cattle were wild and known for 'rushing', the bushman's term for stampede.

rusher.

1. [Used elsewhere but recorded earliest in Aust.: see OED 2.] One who takes part in a rush to a new goldfield.

1853 *Austral. Gold Diggers Monthly Mag.* iv. 141 The dishes of the first rushers up refused to show the golden sediment. **1894** *Bulletin* (Sydney) 11 Aug. 20/3 It all ended in sulphurous language, the great bulk of the 'rushers' coming back to the town as hungry as hunters. **1946** K.S. Prichard *Roaring Nineties* 388 There must 've been six or seven thousand rushers, most of 'em footsore and shaggy.

2. One who escapes from confinement in a rush (see Rush *n.* 1).

1891 'Old Time' *Convict Hulk 'Success'* 39 The year 1856 was a very important one in the penal records of Victoria. There had been a rush of prisoners in the month of March of that year, and one of the 'rushers' . . had been shot.

3. A stampeding animal.

[N.Z. **1889** Hay *Brighter Britain* I. 158 Occasionally we find it necessary to slaughter some unmanageable rusher, a cow, or bullock.] **1892** *Truth* (Sydney) 31 July 1/2 Could you hang to a buckjumper with your knees, Or rattle a rusher through the trees.

rush-oh. *Obs.* An exclamatory call, announcing the discovery of a new goldfield.

1864 J. Rogers *New Rush* 29 The cry 'Rush oh!' reverberating wide, Attracts the claimless to the rushing tide. **1869** E.C. Booth *Another England* 51 'Rush oh!' rang down Golden Gully and along Bendigo Flat one fine morning. **1887** *Rec. Castlemaine Pioneers* 30 Sept. (1972) 3 Early in 1854 there were constant rumors of fresh discoveries. The cry of 'Rush, Oh!' to Bryant's Ranges was raised.

Russian. *Obs.* Also **Rooshan, Rooshian.** [Prob. a pun on Rush *n.* 3 and *v.* 4.] Esp. of cattle: a beast which is wild or difficult to handle.

1838 J.C. Crawford *Diary* 15 Dec. in *S. Australiana* (1964) Mar. 56 The bullocks . . were not so easily managed as we expected, perhaps from being imperfectly broke at first, or else from having been long turned out to grass they proved to be as wild as Rooshians (to use an Australian phrase). **1843** A. Caswall *Hints from Jrnl.* 35 If you are purchasing a team of bullocks (*said* to be broken-in) make your *own* driver unyoke and yoke them up before you conclude the bargain, or you may find you have got a set of *Rooshans* (so denominated) who have only been put in for sale. **1845** D. Mackenzie *Emigrant's Guide* 118 With wild cattle you can do nothing. . . These wild *Russians*, as they are called, will . . clear at the first leap a stock-yard six feet in height. **1847** A. Harris *Settlers & Convicts* (1953) 197 When a real 'Russian' happens to be among the mob, circumspection must positively be practised as well as bravery. **1849** —— *Emigrant Family* (1967) 53 Are there any 'Rooshans' in the mountains? **1874** C. De Boos *Congewoi Correspondence* 124 We come right atop of er camper reglar out-an-out roosians . . two or three great big black bulls. **1880** 'Old Hand' *Experiences of Colonist* (ed. 2) ii. 64 Only about twenty bullocks now remained to cross, but they were regular 'Russians', and were continually breaking away. **1945** S.J. Baker *Austral. Lang.* 68 An old term worth noting, since it has been obsolete for half a century or more, is *Russians* for wild stock.

rustbucket. [Transf. use of (orig. U.S.) *rustbucket* an old and rusty ship. Used elsewhere but recorded earliest in Aust.] A rusty and dilapidated motor vehicle.

1965 *Daily Tel.* (Sydney) 23 Apr. 20/1 A motor mechanic yesterday described a car which broke in two as a 'rust bucket'. **1969** *Sunday Mail* (Brisbane) 9 Nov. 15/4 *(heading)* Car trade-ins fit for scrap. Dealers stuck with 'rust-buckets'. **1972** I. Moffitt *U-Jack Soc.* 121 They look beautiful, but underneath they're rust-buckets. **1984** *Truck & Bus Transportation* Jan. 12/1 The oldest Volvos . . are far from being rust buckets.

rusty gum. [See quot. 1963.] Any of several trees, esp. *Angophora costata* (fam. Myrtaceae) of N.S.W. and Qld., having a smooth bark and twisted branches.

1845 L. Leichhardt *Jrnl. Overland Exped. Aust.* 6 Feb. (1847) 139 A rather stunted rusty gum grew plentifully on the sandstone ridges. **1862** J. McKinlay *Jrnl. Exploration Interior* 11 May 92 Lagoons wooded round generally with rusty gum. **1909** F.M. Bailey *Comprehensive Cat. Qld. Plants* 188 *Angophora lanceolata* . . Rusty Gum, Sugar Gum, and Cabbage Gum, in different localities. **1963** C. Burgess *Blue Mountain Gums* 60 'Rusty Gum'. . . The smooth *bark* is rich, rusty orange-red in midsummer, changing to salmon-pink and sometimes leaden-grey in autumn and winter.

Rutherglen bug. [f. the name of a town in n.e. Vic.: see quot. 1948.] The small bug *Nysius vinitor*, large aggregations of which cause damage to cultivated food plants.

1900 *Proc. Linnean Soc. N.S.W.* XXV. 760 Mr Froggatt exhibited specimens of cherries from the Armidale district showing the effect of the depredations of the Rutherglen Bug (*Nysius venator*). **1902** *Bulletin* (Sydney) 30 Aug. 14/3 The pear is being killed off in large patches by the Rutherglen bug (*Nysius vinitor*). **1929** Veitch & Simmonds *Pests & Diseases Qld.* 59 With two notable exceptions—namely, the Queensland fruit fly and the Rutherglen bug—all the important enemies of deciduous fruits in this State have been introduced from overseas. **1948** W.W. Froggatt *Insect Bk.* 106 The Rutherglen bug, 1/6th of an inch long, gets its name from a town in Victoria, where it was first discovered as a pest among the vines. **1969** *Victorian Yr. Bk.* LXXXIII. 9 The small grey Rutherglen bug . . occurs in plague numbers on rare occasions, damaging stone fruits and crops. **1983** *Advertiser* (Adelaide) 12 Dec. 17/1 Insects are bugging rural Queenslanders following widespread early summer rains. Earwigs, Rutherglen bugs and flying ants are only part of the problem on the Central Highlands.

ryebuck /ˈraɪbʌk/, *int.*, *a.*, and *n.* Also **ribuck, rybuck.** [Br. slang *ryebuck*, perh. a. G. *reibach*, var. of *rebbach* profit, and orig. Yiddish: see OED *rybek* and OEDS *ryebuck*.]

A. *int.* An expression of agreement or assent, 'all right'.

1890 *Truth* (Sydney) 7 Dec. 4/7 But the boy by his gods he swore, 'Ri-buck, old man, true dinkum,' he said. 'The betting was ten to four.' **1900** *Tocsin* (Melbourne) 4 Jan. 3/1 The general hesitancy was soon dispelled, however, by a hoary-headed old tramp exclaiming: 'Rye buck, matey, wire in.' **1916** J.F. Nugent *Lorblimey* 5 'Eyes front!' 'Quick march!' Sez Bill, 'Rybuck.' **1933** *Bulletin* (Sydney) 27 Sept. 42/2 'We'll meet you at the yards.' 'Ryebuck, Boss,' said the Gov'nor, civilly. **1945** *Ibid.* 5 Dec. 13/1 'Look,' he says, 'eliminate the lintels, will y'?' 'Ribuck,' says me. **1952** C.J. Dennis *Random Verse* 13 Breast up, blokes. Name yer gargle. Rybuck, boss; mine's a pot. **1968** S. Gore *Holy Smoke* 79 Ribuck, mate!

B. *adj.* Good; excellent.

1892 *Truth* (Sydney) 31 July 4/2 He is, as he gracefully would express it, 'rybuck', quite at home. **1895** *Worker* (Sydney) 9 Feb. 3/3 We have had a look at your claim, and, finding it rybuck, we have pegged out six men's ground. **1904** *Truth* (Sydney) 11 Sept. 1/6 George Reid is making frantic efforts to prove that he is the 'ribuck pea' for the Premiership. **1906** *Ibid.* 5 Aug. 1/6 The pious man should bring in a bill to regulate Sunday-school kissing. One in the corner of the choir is rybuck. **1918** R.H. Knyvett *Over there with Australs.* 82 They even knew our slang, for here was 'The 'Fair Dinkum' Store', and across the way 'Ribuck Goods'. **c 1927** J. Bradshaw *Highway Robbery under Arms* 31 Red Lance decided that after sticking up the bank to ride to a well-known lonely cave, and camp like Capuchins until things got rye buck. **1967** Meredith & Anderson *Folk Songs Aust.* 23 The first song Luscombe recorded for John Meredith concerned a man's ambition to become a ryebuck shearer. (Ryebuck means expert; the term 'gun shearer' is used in the same sense).

C. *n.* The 'genuine article'.

1896 H. Lawson *While Billy Boils* 329 There were cakes of tobacco, and books, and papers, and several flasks of 'rye-buck'. **1899** J. Bradshaw *Quirindi Bank Robbery* 30 Let me know if she is acting the ryebuck to me. **1913** *Bulletin* (Sydney) 14 Aug. 15/3 Bill had let fall our beautiful bottle of ryebuck on the hardest boulder along the track. **1942** *Action Front: Jrnl. 2/2 Field Regiment* July 9 A Ryebuck is not a wheat cake.

S

sable, *a. Obs.* [Spec. use of *sable* as applied to a black-skinned person.]

a. A literary epithet for an Aboriginal, with a rhetorical range extending from romantic elevation to ironic denigration. Cf. BLACK *a.*[1] 4 and 5.

1823 W.C. WENTWORTH *Australasia* 5 To you, ye sable hunters, sweeter too To spy the track of bounding kangaroo. **1830** R. DAWSON *Present State Aust.* 66 When a poor gin offends her sable lord, he taps her over the head. **1839** *S. Austral. Rec.* (London) 1 Nov. 257 We found the women and children, and many of the men, lamenting in a most piteous manner, their sable faces bathed in tears, the deaths of the two men. **1843** *Sydney Morning Herald* 11 Aug. 3/3 The folds of the Australian Agricultural Company have been visited by those sable delinquents and several sheep taken away. **1850** *Representative* (Sydney) 25 July 3/2 The sable child of the wild Australian bush. **1862** G.T. LLOYD *Thirty-Three Yrs. Tas. & Vic.* 427 Those sable robbers were detected. **1880** *Bulletin* (Sydney) 15 May 1/1 The Executive in its wisdom decided to execute the blackfellow who a little while ago shot one of his sable countrymen at Dubbo. **1889** J.H.L. ZILLMANN *Past & Present Austral. Life* 57 He preferred to live on with the blacks, and remain with his sable wives, and half-caste children.

b. In collocations: **sable brethren, companion, friend, gentleman, majesty, tribe, warrior.**

1839 *S. Austral. Rec.* (London) 1 Nov. 254 Many a right-hearted colonist will join me in ascribing equal forbearance to our **sable brethren.** **1850** J.B. CLUTTERBUCK *Port Phillip* 48 Our sable brethren are extremely dirty in their persons. **1851** H. MELVILLE *Present State Aust.* 360 Tom .. went frequently with parties that were despatched into the bush to capture his sable brethren. **1845** L. LEICHHARDT *Jrnl. Overland Exped. Aust.* (1847) 11 Oct. 430 To shew my **sable companions** that their secret manoeuvres only tended to increase their own labour, I ordered the bullocks to be loaded immediately. **1909** *Bulletin* (Sydney) 6 May 13/2 'Combo-ism' is the order of the day. Everyone (more or less) has a sable 'companion'. **1833** BACKHOUSE & TYLOR *Life & Labours G.W. Walker* 3 Dec. (1862) 170 W.J. Darling appeared much pleased to see us, and hardly less so, our **sable friends.** **1852** J. MORGAN *Life & Adventures W. Buckley* 128 My sable friends were not at all pleased at our leaving. **1883** E.M. CURR *Recoll. Squatting Vic.* 127 The arrival of a pair of our sable friends from up the river. **1843** *Sydney Morning Herald* 6 July 2/7 It is to be hoped the lately appointed Commissioner of Crown Lands for the Upper District here will, with his border police force, teach these **sable gentlemen** that their recent outrages will not escape unpunished. **1845** L. LEICHHARDT *Jrnl. Overland Exped. Aust.* (1847) 12 Feb. 145 My companions were highly alarmed at the behaviour of the sable gentlemen. **1848** *Adelaide Miscellany* 16 Sept. 107, I left these sable gentlemen in the height of their enjoyment. **1831** *Sydney Herald* 14 Nov. 4/1 Before the party broke up, his **sable Majesty** became done up with *bull*; and .. was floored by a waddie. **1881** *Bulletin* (Sydney) 2 July 9/1 As the niggers numbered 100 and the blankets only reached 52, the majority of the haricot-snake devourers—his sable Majesty among the rest—were literally left out in the cold. **1819** *Sydney Gaz.* 24 July, Nothing of this kind is done for the **sable tribes** of New Holland. **1844** *Colonial Observer* (Sydney) 31 Oct. 1/1 There was a public meeting held last Friday evening, if not of the sable tribes of Sydney and its vicinity, at least of the *men in sables* who support Bishop Broughton. **1852** *Awful Execution 17 Convicts* 3 Thousands of pounds have been expended .. in endeavouring to convert .. the sable tribes of the west. **1843** *Sydney Morning Herald* 24 May 4/6 We have had the pleasure of seeing some of these **sable warriors.** **1845** C.J. BAKER *Sydney & Melbourne* 41 Instead of tents the sable warriors had wigwams, after the manner of their ancestors.

sac, var. ZAC.

sacred kingfisher. The predom. blue, green, and buff kingfisher *Halcyon sancta* of Aust. and elsewhere. Formerly also **sacred kingsfisher.**

1782 J. LATHAM *Gen. Synopsis Birds* I. 621 Sacred K[ingsfisher]. .. This species is common to many parts of the *South Seas.* **1788** J. WHITE *Jrnl. Voyage N.S.W.* (1790) 193 We this day shot the *Sacred Kings-Fisher.* **1840** J. GOULD *Birds of Aust.* (1848) II. Pl. 21, *Halcyon sanctus* .. Sacred Kingsfisher. **1861** 'OLD BUSHMAN' *Bush Wanderings* 129 There is a smaller species, the *Sacred Kingfisher.* .. This bird was sparingly dispersed about the bush. **1902** *Emu* II. 16 The Sacred Kingfisher .. is a summer visitor. **1933** H.J. CARTER *Gulliver in Bush* 73 The unusual sight of a sacred kingfisher .. drilling his nesthole in the nest of a termite. **1948** R. RAVEN-HART *Canoe in Aust.* 24 One sudden kingfisher, with the true darting flight of the English bird but blue-green on wings and tail only, the Sacred Kingfisher, I think. **1968** R. HILL *Bush Quest* 18 As I sat astride the wide old limb of a red gum, a sacred kingfisher appeared with a flash of green wings. **1984** SIMPSON & DAY *Birds of Aust.* 317 Sacred Kingfishers nest in Australia, including the south, then migrate to northern Australia, New Guinea, Timor and the Solomon Islands in winter.

sacred site. A place venerated by Aborigines because of its spiritual significance to them: see quot. 1979. See also DREAMING 1. Also *attrib.*

1933 *Oceania* III. 266 Their sons will preserve the myths, ceremonies and sacred sites, if there be such. **1938** A.P. ELKIN *Austral. Aborigines* 136 The portion of mythology and ritual and the sacred sites entrusted to such a cult group is defined by mythological history. **1952** *Oceania* XXIII. 126 The .. cave just mentioned was the only sacred site I was able to visit. **1959** *Ibid.* XXX. 96 There is .. a desire that a child should be born at or near a particular sacred site. **1974** *Cwlth. Parl. Papers* I. no. 69 102 An official, legally-recognized register should be compiled of all sacred sites which their custodians are willing to declare. **1977** *Nat. Times* (Sydney) 2 May 47 A young English anthropologist .. some years ago got the job of surveying Aboriginal sacred sites in the State. **1979** *N.S.W. Parl. Papers* (1980–81) IV. 735 A sacred site should be understood to mean any object or location whether a natural phenomenon or man-made .. that is sacred to Aborigines or is otherwise of significance according to Aboriginal tradition. **1983** D. BELL *Daughters of Dreaming* 38 The opportunity of returning .. to work alongside Aboriginal women in the *realpolitik* of land claims, law reform and sacred site registration. **1984** *Bulletin* (Sydney) 6 Mar. 26 It is understood that interim sacred sites legislation will be introduced into parliament in April.

saddle, *v. fig.* In the phr. **to saddle up,** to prepare oneself (for something).

1922 C. DREW *Rogues & Ruses* 38 That night .. Finger's saddlin' up for bed. **1967** *Kings Cross Whisper* (Sydney) xxxix. 4/4 *Saddle up,* prepare for work, get into harness.

saddle-my-nag. A game resembling leap-frog. Also **saddle-my-nagger,** one who plays this game.

1953 G.H. FEARNSIDE *Bayonets Abroad* 311 Later events went to prove how badly built were these mess-hut structures. .. The end fell out of one building, followed by some half-a-score of eager 'saddle-me-naggers' who had been leaning a little too heavily on its delicate structure. **1966** A.R. CHISHOLM *Familiar Presence* 78, I don't think the name 'Saddle-my-nag' was ever applied to the complicated, difficult and sometimes painful form of leap-frog that we played in Sydney. .. I believe that in Victoria 'Saddle-my-nag' was the stock term, afterwards transformed by popular etymology into 'Solomon Egg'.

saddling, *vbl. n. Horse-racing.* Used *attrib.* in Special Comb. **saddling enclosure,** *saddling paddock* a.; **paddock, (a)** an enclosure in which the horses are saddled before a race; **(b)** a nickname for a bar in the Theatre Royal, Melbourne, frequented by prostitutes in the late nineteenth century; a similar bar elsewhere; hence, a known place of assignation.

1969 *Sun-Herald* (Sydney) 13 July 33/1 Mr Swales told us he could not get through to the stewards on the phone and gave us permission to return to the **saddling enclosure** to put our case to the stewards. **1982** *Austral.* (Sydney) 3 Nov. 25/5 Harris was greeted with a hostile reception from punters interspersed in the crowd encircling the saddling enclosure. **(a) 1861** *Argus* (Melbourne) 8 Nov. 5/5 His Excellency visited the **saddling paddock** during the half-hour preceding the Cup Race. **1867** *Sydney Punch* 18 May 198/2 The gates of the saddling paddock flew open at his approach. **1880** *Argus* (Melbourne) 30 Jan. 7/5 A protest was entered against Columbus for interfering with Zambesi. This proceeding did not seem to please a number of those in the saddling paddock, and they gave vent to their feeling in a series of most unmusical groans. **1897** *Western Champion* (Barcaldine) 21 Dec. 7/3 The saddling paddock has been increased to double the size. **1933** H.B. RAINE *Whip-Hand* 272 He wandered about the saddling paddock examining the horses for the first race with an expert eye, he gloated over the parade in the bird cage. **1940** *Age* (Melbourne) 6 Nov. 5/2 The appearance of Beau Vite heading the procession of the customary parade from the saddling paddock was greeted with cheers. **1983** *Canberra Times* 2 Nov. 38/1 Gala Supreme led the field into the saddling paddock and on to the track. **(b) 1876** *Argus* (Melbourne) 1 July 4/4 The stranger sees that the women, possibly picking up a male companion, all enter the apartment which was previously closed, and which is now guarded by swing doors. Curiosity will doubtless prompt him to enter, and he will find himself in the far-famed '**saddling paddock**' of the Royal. **1882** J. SCHLEMAN *Life in Melbourne* 43 Between seven in the evening and the hour of closing, the by-parlours and 'saddling paddocks' of the theatres are pretty well filled with these characters, who drink, smoke, and talk in a manner simply disgusting. **1912** M. CANNON *That Damned Democrat* (1981) 138 It is more than a quarter of a century since the days of .. the 'saddling paddock' at the Theatre Royal vestibule bars, when harlotry was openly practised in Melbourne. **1958** G. CASEY *Snowball* 28 The Government Dam was the inland town's beach and playground, its courting-place and secret rendezvous. .. The ribald, popular name of the enclosure round the Government Dam was 'the saddling paddock'. **1972** *Bulletin* (Sydney) 1 Jan. 39/3 In the gay nineties (and a bit before and after) Australians would meet and drink at the 'saddling paddocks' in hotel and theatre bars. But they declined and for about 30 years there was a great shortage of facilities offering the sort of ambience that sexual questing demands.

saffron thistle. [Transf. use of *saffron-thistle* the dye-yielding plant *Carthamus tinctorius.*] The introduced Mediterranean annual *Carthamus lanatus* (fam. Asteraceae), naturalized, and proclaimed a noxious weed, in all States.

1909 A.J. EWART *Weeds Vic.* 37 The Saffron Thistle is widely spread over the whole State, and in many districts is reported to be the worst of all the thistles. **1936** *Council Sci. & Industr. Research Pamphlet* no. 60 22 The saffron thistle .. is a nuisance in wheat fields, where it competes with the growing crop, and the seeds are hard to eliminate from the grain after harvesting. **1945** *Queanbeyan Age* 6 Nov. 3/2 Owners of land within the Australian Capital Territory are hereby notified that the undermentioned plants have been declared to be noxious weeds. .. Saffron Thistle (Kentrophyllum lanatum) [etc.]. **1958** J.N. WHITTET *Weeds* 233 Saffron Thistle. .. One of the most prevalent annual thistles in the wheat-growing and grazing areas of New South Wales and other States. **1986** *West Austral.* (Perth) 25 Jan. (Country ed.) 60/1 Saffron thistle is a widespread and troublesome weed in W.A. About 200,000 ha. of land in the Geraldton region is infested by the weed.

sagg. *Tas.* [Br. dial. *sag* a sedge: see OED *sb.*[1]] A tufted perennial, esp. *Lomandra longifolia* (fam. Xanthorrhoeaceae) of e. Aust.

1898 E.E. Morris *Austral Eng.* 399 Sagg . . the name given in Tasmania to the plant *Xerotes longifolia* . . and also to the White Iris, *Diplarhena moraea.* **1908** *Emu* VII. 150 This little frequenter of rushes, saggs (*Xerotes longifolia*) and patchy undergrowth in the open.

Hence **saggy** *a.*

1908 *Emu* VII. 151 In some soils saggy growth is still provokingly persistent.

Saint Andrew's Cross spider. The orb-weaving spider *Argiope aetherea*, which aligns its legs in pairs along the arms of the cross in the centre of its web.

1936 K.C. McKeown *Spider Wonders Aust.* 44 The St. Andrew's Cross Spider . . is of fair size, and is arrayed in remarkably gaily coloured attire. Its general colour is brown . . while the abdomen is striped crossways with alternate bands of brown, silver, and yellow. **1952** B. Beatty *Unique to Aust.* 63 The St. Andrew's Cross spider superimposes upon the web proper after it has been completed, a broad St. Andrew's Cross. **1976** B.Y. Main *Spiders* 201 The Saint Andrew's cross spider is of medium size with body length of about twenty millimetres.

saleyard. An enclosure in which livestock is sold; a set of such enclosures.

1839 *Tasmanian Weekly Dispatch* (Hobart) 29 Nov. 2/3 Mr Davis' newly erected and well constructed Sale Yards. **1862** C. Stretton *Mem.* III. 224 The distance from the sale-yards to Richmond was about two miles and a half. **1879** 'Recent Settler' *Emigration to Tas.* 83 Have as little to do with buying and selling as possible, particularly at sale-yards. **1897** J.J. Knight *Brisbane* 88 The creek . . ran through Warby's sale-yards to the present Town Hall Reserve. **1910** *Emu* X. 30 Two large mobs of Queensland horses were approaching on their way to a southern sale-yard. **1920** *Pastoral Rev.* 16 Feb. 169 During January four sales were held at the Brisbane Fat Stock Sale Yards. **1940** *Pastoral Rev. & Grazier's Rec.* 16 Feb. 101 At Newmarket saleyards this week the following prices were realised. **1960** *Ibid.* 17 Aug. 853 Fat cattle from the Copmanhurst area can now be moved direct to Grafton abattoir or to Grafton Saleyards for sale for immediate slaughter. **1974** *Pastoral Rev.* Mar. 160/3 Females sold to $12,000 and bulls to $9,000 in a sale grossing $221,850 at the Dandenong, Vic., saleyards. **1982** *Elders Weekly* (Perth) 14 Oct. 40/3 The cattle to be offered will be available for inspection at the saleyards from midday. **1985** *Bombala Times* 18 July 6/3 Telecom is not prepared to install, at its own cost, a telephone in the saleyards.

sally. Also **sallee.** [Transf. use of Br. dial. *sally*, var. of *sallow* a willow.]

1. Any of several trees of the genera *Eucalyptus* (fam. Myrtaceae) and *Acacia* (fam. Mimosaceae), resembling the willow in habitat, habit, or foliage. Formerly also **sallow.**

1826 J. Atkinson *Acct. Agric. & Grazing N.S.W.* 19 A species of sallow, growing about the sides of rivers, furnishes good materials for basket-making. **1837** *Colonist* (Sydney) 350/3 The trees used in the colony for domestic purposes are . . *sallow*, for gig shafts [etc.]. **1875** Campbell & Wilks *Early Settlement Qld.* 17 My greatest difficulty . . was to get suitable casks. . . I finally fixed upon the timber known as silky oak and sally, both of which I found to answer admirably. **1896** *Proc. Linnean Soc. N.S.W.* X. 597 *Eucalyptus stellulata*. . . The name 'Sally', without a qualifying adjective, is in use at Bombala, Boro, Braidwood and Yass. The name is in allusion to the species being often found on the banks of streams, like a sally (sallow or willow). **1897** *Worker* (Sydney) 18 Sept. 1/1 The hand that trimmed its greenhide fall Is hidden underground—There, in the patch of sallee shade Beneath that grassy mound. **1920** *Bulletin* (Sydney) 18 Nov. 22/1 Several bush trees are wrongly named 'sally'. **1955** Stewart & Keesing *Austral. Bush Ballads* 189 They reached the low sally before he could wheel the warrigal mob.

2. Special Comb. **sally wattle,** any of several plants of the genus *Acacia* (fam. Mimosaceae), esp. the shrub or small tree *A. longifolia* of s.e. Aust. incl. Tas., having narrow, elongated phyllodes; also **sallow wattle.**

1935 E. Coleman *Come back in Wattle-Time* 38 Sallow Acacia (*A. longifolia*) . . a hardy, useful shrub. **1943** *Bulletin* (Sydney) 20 Oct. 13/2 For . . Australian trees, graceful and able to weather the worst winds, I'll nominate the shapely 'Sally Wattles' that dot the rolling hilly landscapes near Robertson (N.S.W.). **1955** P. White *Tree of Man* 205 Divide the herd between the sally wattle and the square paddock. **1965** *Austral. Encycl.* VII. 539 *A[cacia] longifolia, A. mucronata* and several related species with long flower-spikes are known as sallow wattles in Victoria. **1981** H. Hannah *Together in Jungle Scrub* 20, I can remember climbing up sally wattle trees and making birds nests.

salmon. [See quot. 1974.] Any of several marine and fresh-water fish, esp. the marine *Arripis trutta* and *A. esper*, abundant in s. and e. Aust. See also *native salmon* Native *a.* 6 b., Salmon trout.

1790 D. Collins *Acct. Eng. Colony N.S.W.* (1798) I. 136 Near four thousand of a fish, named by us, from its shape only, the salmon. **1803** *Sydney Gaz.* 28 Aug., A few days ago a seine was spread near the Mouth of the Cove, and 100 salmon taken in the haul. **1827** P. Cunningham *Two Yrs. in N.S.W.* I. 136 Some of the mullet and salmon when smoke-dried are nothing inferior to the haddock of East Scotland. **1839** *S. Austral. Rec.* (London) (1840) 11 Apr. 179 About a fortnight ago the fishermen of Glenelg had the good fortune to enclose and draw to the land a draught of fine fish dignified here by the name of *salmon.* **1873** J. Bonwick *Tasmanian Lily* 25 Names have been imported, but are absurdly applied. The cod is not a cod, nor the salmon a salmon. **1873** F. De Castelnau *Edible Fishes Vic.* 8 The genus *Arripis* is entirely Australian, and is represented by the *roughy* (*arripis Georgianus*), and the *salmon trout* (*arrip. truttaceus*); the full-grown specimens of the latter are called *salmon* by the fishermen. **1896** F.G. Aflalo *Sketch Nat. Hist. Aust.* 216 The Ceratodus, or Lung Fish, is now caught in only two Queensland rivers, the Mary and Burnett, at Christmas-time. . . The colonials call it salmon. **1948** F.D. Marshall *Let's go Fishing* 93 The salmon which frequents the Australian coast is an entirely different species from the quinnat salmon . . in the northern hemisphere. **1960** A. Upfield *Mystery Swordfish Reef* 68 We've got enough salmon for now, and there's yesterday's bonito in the box. **1974** T.D. Scott et al. *Marine & Freshwater Fishes S.A.* 239 It is thought that the name 'Salmon' was first used in the early days . . possibly from a confusion of the young Australian Salmon with its trout-like spots, with the Salmon-trout of Europe. **1986** *Canberra Chron.* 29 Jan. 19/2 There are a few salmon around the Bermagui beaches and headlands, but local netters pounce on them fairly quickly.

salmon gum. The tree *Eucalyptus salmonophloia* (fam. Myrtaceae) of the drier parts of s.w. W.A., having smooth salmon-red bark when freshly exposed; the durable red to red-brown wood of the tree. Also *attrib.*, and *ellipt.* as **salmon.**

[**1883** F. von Mueller *Eucalyptographia* ix (OEDS), *Eucalyptus salmonophloia* . . a tree, when aged, attaining to fully 100 feet in height, known vernacularly as the 'Salmon-colored Gumtree', in allusion to the smooth grey and somewhat purplish bark of an oily lustre.] **1894** A.F. Calvert *Coolgardie Goldfield* 49 This was another high rock, surrounded by salmon gum. **1897** L. Lindley-Cowen *W. Austral. Settler's Guide* 47 The salmon gum is . . largely found in the country lying between York and Southern Cross. . . The name . . refers to the color of the bark, which is of a reddish, burnt appearance, fairly smooth and somewhat persistent. **1904** *Emu* III. 218 The salmon gums (*E. salmonophloia*) . . held sway. **1908** E.G. Murphy *Jarrahland Jingles* 114 Or underneath the salmons, where on sultry nights we sit. **1911** E.D. Cleland *W. Austral. Mining Practice* 43 Sawn hardwood—salmon-gum or morrel. **1934** *Bulletin* (Sydney) 24 Oct. 20/3 At Ismailia (Egypt) a Digger mate and myself saw three salmon gums, trees of the Westralian wheatbelt and eastern goldfields—and you don't see them anywhere else in Australia. **1952** *Ibid.* 9 Jan. 17/2 Salmon-gum country, hard enough itself to kill any but the experienced bushman, is Garden of Eden stuff compared with the Great Victoria Desert. **1964** D. Lockwood *Up Track* 78 Ah, the salmon gums! The sexiest trees on earth. After they have shed their bark in the dry season the smooth salmon-coloured trunks look like stockinged female legs. **1979** W.K. Beckingham *Red Acres* 47 On the 'Datjoin' block grew Salmon gums and Gimlet trees and this was indicative of soil of a close texture and a heavy clay.

salmon trout. [Transf. use of *salmon-trout* a fish of the rivers of n. Europe, *Salmo trutta.*] The young of either of two fish, *Arripis trutta* and *A. esper* (see Salmon), having brown trout-like markings on the upper surface.

1848 J. Syme *Nine Yrs. Van Diemen's Land* 14 Fish are plentiful and reasonable. You have . . gurnett, a description of salmon trout . . and a variety of others. **1873** F. De Castelnau *Edible Fishes Vic.* 8 The genus *Arripis* is entirely Australian, and is represented by . . the *salmon trout* (*arrip. truttaceus*); the full-grown specimens of the latter are called *salmon* by the fishermen. **1906** D.G. Stead *Fishes of Aust.* 116 The Salmon occurs in abundance along the whole of the New South Wales coastline. . . The young or half-grown forms of this species have the Salmon or Trout-like markings still more pronounced, and they are consequently termed Salmon-Trout. **1934** W.A. Osborne *Visitor to Aust.* 84 Some are coarse in flesh but nutritious and cheap, such as 'salmon trout' (not even resembling the true salmon trout). **1940** *Bulletin* (Sydney) 3 Jan. 16/2 Down on the Hopkins . . a shoal of what we Cabbage Gardeners call salmon trout had come in. **1986** *Age* (Melbourne) 6 May 41/2 Fillets of fresh salmon trout with a light lemon cream sauce.

salt, *a. Obs.* Used in collocations as an abbrev. of Salt water 1, as **salt creek** [also U.S. (see Mathews *n.* 1)], **lagoon.**

1770 J. Cook *Jrnls.* 23 Aug. (1955) I. 395 In the Rivers and **salt Creeks** are some Aligators. **1840** *S. Austral. Register* (Adelaide) 22 Oct. 2 The report of a fine country to the north-east of the salt creek. **1835** *True Colonist* (Hobart) 23 Feb. 2/4 Another [river] . . disappointed expectation by ending in a **salt lagoon**, within a few miles of the sea. **1842** R.G. Jameson *N.Z., S.A., & N.S.W.* 86 The occurrence of numerous salt lagoons which have no communication with the sea, in all the southern regions of New Holland, constitutes one of the many physical peculiarities which distinguish this remarkable continent. **1847** J.D. Lang *Phillipsland* 177 Two respectable Scotchmen . . have squatted near a small salt lagoon. **1858** J.M. Stuart *Explorations in Aust.* 21 June (1865) 8 We came upon a salt lagoon (Wealaroo) two miles long by one broad. **1894** J.D. Woods *Province of S.A.* 125 They travelled along this for a couple of days, when the creek ended in a salt lagoon. **1909** W. Howchin *Geography of S.A.* 227 The so-called salt 'lagoons' of Yorke Peninsula are saucer-shaped depressions varying in size up to ten miles in circumference.

saltbush. [See quot. 1965.]

1. Any of many shrubs or herbs of the fam. Chenopodiaceae, esp. those of the large genus *Atriplex* and the smaller genus *Rhagodia*, typically dominating tracts of saline and alkaline land in drier Aust.

1846 *Sydney Morning Herald* 8 Dec. 3/2 The myall tree and salt bush (*Acacia pendula*, and *salsoloe*), so essential to a good run are also there. **1848** T.L. Mitchell *Jrnl. Exped. Tropical Aust.* 54 The colour of the leaves of such bushes is usually a very light bluish green, and there are many species. That with the largest leaves, called salt bush by stockmen, and by Dr Brown *Rhagodia parabolica*, was very useful as a vegetable after extracting the salt sufficiently from it. **1858** J.M. Stuart *Diary* 9 Aug. in *S. Australiana* (1963) Sept. 59 Plenty of salt bush and green grass, first rate for the horses. **1881** *Proc. Linnean Soc. N.S.W.* VI. 766 One of the most important orders of this division is that of the *Chenopodiaceae*, called '*Salt-bushes*', including species of *Rhagodia, Atriplex, Kochia*, &c. **1885** P.R. Meggy *From Sydney to Silverton* 13 This is the country of salt-bush, of which there are many varieties in the district, some edible and some inedible. **1892** 'Mrs A. Macleod' *Silent Sea* I. 214 In many parts the sole vegetation consists of the salt-bush, a sad-coloured, low-creeping bush, more gray than green, which breaks when trodden on, with a brittle snap like dry stubble. **1903** F. Turner *Bot. Darling, N.S.W.* 413 The order *Chenopodiaceae* includes all those plants popularly known as 'saltbush', which are amongst the most valuable in Australia for feeding stock. **1912** 'IRONBARK' *Ironbark Splinters* 122 Sing a song of saltbush, Sandyblight an' drought, Forty thousand weaners Slowly pegging out. **1952** A.C.C. LOCK *Travels across Aust.* 187 Salt bush, *Atriplex vesicaria*, which is to South Australian graziers what the Flinders and Mitchell grass is to Queensland pastoralists. **1965** *Austral. Encycl.* VII. 541 Saltbush . . alludes both to the salty character and habitat of these plants, which often grow naturally within the influence of salt water—near the seashore, in saline marshes or associated with salt-pans in the arid interior. **1980** BRENNAN & WHITE *Keep Billy Boiling* 82 Saltbush to the north, saltbush to the east, west and south. Everlasting, sombre-hued saltbush. **1982** BARKER & GREENSLADE *Evol. Flora & Fauna* 291 The major *Atriplex* shrubland communities are in the southern arid and semi-arid regions of Australia. . . As the name 'saltbush' implies, most species can occupy saline conditions, and salt excretory mechanisms are clearly established.

2. Comb. **saltbush country, flat, plain.**

1859 J.M. STUART *Explorations in Aust.* 14 Apr. (1865) 49 The country travelled over was fine **salt-bush country.** **1876** G.H. REID *Essay on N.S.W.* 5 The salt bush country succeeds, stretching to our western and north-western boundaries. **1890** W.F. BUCHANAN *Aust. to Rescue* p. xxvii, Wells we did not try in the salt bush country. **1921** L.G. JONES *Flockmaster's Companion* 22 There are some classes of country in which they do not look for salt apart from 'saltbush' country. **1957** F. CLUNE *Fortune Hunters* 19 In the late 1860s graziers began occupying the 'saltbush' country west of the Darling. **1855** R. AUSTIN *Jrnl. Interior W.A.* 24 We struck a small samphire and **salt bush flat** about half a mile from the base of the hills we were steering for. **1875** J. FORREST *Explorations in Aust.* 63 We entered samphire and saltbush flats for four miles. **1920** H.S. TAYLOR *Pioneer Irrigationists' Man.* xxxvi. 4 Salt trouble was not experienced on these saltbush flats for the simple reason that they were alluvial and there was little salt in the soil before irrigation commenced. **1936** J.E. HAMMOND *Western Pioneers* 101 It was a saltbush flat and, pointing in a northerly direction, one of our natives said he could see some cattle. **1848** T.L. MITCHELL *Jrnl. Exped. Tropical Aust.* 66 We encamped on the edge of a **salt-bush plain.** **1874** *Illustr. Sydney News* 22 Aug. 15/1 The best preventive is the removal of diseased sheep in the early stages of the malady to healthy saline pastures, and none are better than our saltbush plains. **1890** 'R. BOLDREWOOD' *Colonial Reformer* II. 54 Swept away over a splendid salt-bush plain, level as a bowling green, though slightly differing in colour. **1927** R.S. BROWNE *Journalist's Memories* 315 It has been shown that in 'high latitudes' and on 'the great salt-bush plains'—which are sometimes there and sometimes not—we grow some of the finest wool in the world. **1949** G. FARWELL *Traveller's Tracks* 24 The most striking feature of Port Augusta . . coming upon it over dry saltbush plains from the west, is the stilling grandeur of the Flinders Range. **1980** BRENNAN & WHITE *Keep Billy Boiling* 82 Times being bad I had to take a billet of boundary rider and live in a pine stubb hut on the edge of an extinct box-swamp, the one oasis of shade in a vast saltbush plain.

3. Special Comb. **saltbush snake** [see quot. 1943], the lizard of s. mainland Aust. *Pygopus lepidopodus*, having rudimentary, scaly hind limbs.

1932 M.R. WHITE *No Roads go By* 32 A saltbush snake (whose bite it was said meant death in twenty minutes) ran across the back of her hand. **1940** A.W. UPFIELD *Bushranger of Skies* 232 He saw the saltbush snake fall from Bony's right foot. **1943** C. BARRETT *Austral. Animal Bk.* 319 The scaly-foot (*Pygopus lepidopodus*), whose tail is more than twice the length of head and body combined, frequents salt-bush country. Rapid in its movements, often it is called the 'salt-bush snake'.

4. With distinguishing epithet: **creeping saltbush,** any of several plants, esp. the spreading *Atriplex semibaccata* (fam. Chenopodiaceae) of all mainland States; **old man saltbush,** see OLD MAN B. 3.

1903 G. SUTHERLAND *Australasian Live Stock Man.* (ed. 2) 384 Saltbush proper is the principal feed in the back country, and good feed it is. Then there is Mallee Salt Bush, and also Creeping Salt Bush—both good. **1938** C.T. WHITE *Princ. Bot. Qld. Farmers* 165 Widely spread in different parts of the State [*sc.* Qld.] . . is the Creeping Saltbush, *A. semibaccata*. **1984** *Flora Aust.* IV. 110 *Atriplex semibaccata* . . prostrate or decumbent perennial herb with slender spreading branches . . Creeping Saltbush.

saltie. [f. SALT (WATER 3 + -Y.] *Salt-water crocodile*, see SALT WATER 3.

1951 J. DEVANNY *Travels N. Qld.* 203 Mr Walker had shot a medium-sized 'saltie' as the man-eating crocodile of the coastal plains was called. **1978** M. DOUGLAS *Follow Sun* 86 There are few natural thrills greater than actually seeing a six-metre 'saltie', perhaps a hundred years old, slide off a mud bank and thunder into the water. **1985** *Age* (Melbourne) 3 Aug. (Saturday Extra) 15/1 It's the 'salties', the saltwater crocs that are really dangerous.

salt water.

1. Used *attrib.* in Comb. to distinguish an expanse of water which is salt, as **salt-water creek, lagoon.**

1837 *S. Austral. Gaz.* (Adelaide) 8 July 3 A **salt water creek**, running into Vivonne Bay. **1843** *Sydney Morning Herald* 17 Aug. 2/1 Extensive salt water creeks run up for many miles; we saw one for twenty miles, but the water was salt for ten miles and the shore all fringed with mangroves. **1864** J. MORRILL *Sketch of Residence* 236 There are a great many alligators in both the fresh and salt water creeks, and particularly in one large freshwater lagoon. **1893** E. FAVENC *Last of Six Tales* 5 The two men would take their boat and pull up one of the salt-water creeks to the open country. **1930** V. PALMER *Passage* (1957) 33 There was the rambling, unpainted house with its garden running down to the saltwater creek. **1938** X. HERBERT *Capricornia* (ed. 6) 4 They found his lugger drifting up the salt-water creek. **1843** *S. Austral. Odd Fellows' Mag.* Oct. 44 There are numerous **salt-water lagoons**, around which may be traced several ancient reaches, far above the present water level, indicating different elevations of the land.

2. Used *attrib.* of an Aboriginal who lives near the sea, as distinct from one who lives inland.

1900 R. BRUCE *Benbonuna* (1904) 347 He also knew perfectly well that the old lubra would attribute their disappearance to the visit of a 'salt-water black'. **1911** A. SEARCY *By Flood & Field* 285 A strange Myall native reported (through the Settlement blacks) that a number of saltwater blacks had a big mob of cattle yarded. **1928** B. SPENCER *Wanderings in Wild Aust.* 565 Of the two main camps near Borraloola, one was situated close to the river where the 'salt-water' natives as they are called—that is, the Anula and Mora, together with a few visitors from the Karawa tribe—built their Miamias. **1935** DAVISON & NICHOLLS *Blue Coast Caravan* 165 The island blacks were real 'salt-water niggers'. They liked especially to get out on the ocean beach and feast on . . a shell fish they dug out of the sand. **1936** C.P. CONIGRAVE *N. Aust.* 217 Every island lying offshore is an open book for the dusky salt-water blackfellow. **1957** W.E. HARNEY *Life among Aborigines* 162 Following her along the bank were the 'salt-water' aborigines heralding her in with the roaring cry of 'Boat come up—boat come up'. **1981** NGABIDJ & SHAW *My Country of Pelican Dreaming* 1 The Gadjerong were not solely 'saltwater people' like those further north.

3. Special Comb. **salt-water crocodile,** the large crocodile *Crocodylus porosus* of coastal and near-coastal n. and n.e. Aust. and elsewhere, inhabiting estuarine, sea, and fresh water; SALTIE.

1943 C. BARRETT *Austral. Animal Bk.* 314 The salt-water crocodile (*Crocodilus porosus*) also frequents estuaries and coastal waters. **1947** F. CLUNE *Roaming around Aust.* 215 There are two kinds of 'croc' in the Northern waters—the freshwater croc and the salt-water croc. **1955** V. SERVENTY *Aust.'s Great Barrier Reef* 64 Further to the north and not likely to be met is the Saltwater Crocodile. **1986** *Courier-Mail* (Brisbane) 6 Jan. 4, Male saltwater crocodiles take 16 years to become sexually mature and by that time they are 3 m. to 4 m. long. Females are 2 m. to 3 m. long when they mature at about 10 years of age.

salute: see *Australian salute* AUSTRALIAN *a.* 4; *Queensland salute* QUEENSLAND 1.

salvage, *v. Obs.* [Also U.S.: see OEDS *v.* 2.] *trans.* To steal; SALVE; SOUVENIR.

1918 *Aussie: Austral. Soldiers' Mag.* Jan. 11/1 *Salvage*, to rescue unused property and make use of it. The word is also used of the property rescued. Property salvaged in the presence of the owner leads to trouble and is not done by an expert. **1941** S.J. BAKER *Pop. Dict. Austral. Slang* 63 *Salvage, to*, to steal, purloin.

Salvarmy. Shortened form of 'Salvation Army'. Freq. *attrib.*

1899 *Bulletin* (Sydney) 10 June 14/1 A Brisbane Salvarmy captain lately held an audience . . entranced. **1905** *Truth* (Sydney) 12 Mar. 2/5 One of Booth's local tray trappers, a lovely Salvarmy lassie, has skipped by the light of the moon. **1914** E. DYSON *Spats' Fact'ry* 93 Baptist, Salv'army, Beardie, old-style kneegrinders, knuckle grinders. **1915** *Bulletin* (Sydney) 18 Mar. 44/3 The Salv. Army band blew the palate out of its trombone in welcome. **1942** *Ibid.* 3 June 13/1 The next time I noticed him he was in the Salvarmy ring.

Salvation Jane. Chiefly *S.A.* [See quot. 1973.] PATERSON'S CURSE.

1910 *Jrnl. Dept. Agric. S.A.* Dec. 524 It was also decided to ask other Branches to co-operate with the object of preventing the blue weed (Salvation Jane, Paterson's Curse, &c.) from being declared a noxious weed north of Petersburg. It was good fodder for sheep, especially in times of drought, and if it was desired to eradicate it the sheep would quickly do it. **1926** A. EDEN *Places in Sun* 96 A bright mass of violet, fresh and smiling, 'Salvation Jane'—a weed, it is said, of South African origin. **1935** F. BIRTLES *Battle Fronts Outback* 211 Every waterhole, creek, and billabong . . was fringed with the bright heliotrope of Salvation Jane—a desert wildflower. **1954** *Bulletin* (Sydney) 29 Dec. 13/1 Summer is come, with Salvation Jane Shouting her purple on the plain. **1955** N. PULLIAM *I traveled Lonely Land* 283, I was introduced on this trip to an insignificant little plant, new to me, called Salvation Jane. It looks much like a wild, purple sweetpea, and it did a lot to save the country from total ruin. **1973** W.T. PARSONS *Noxious Weeds Vic.* 32 In South Australia the plant is known as 'salvation Jane', presumably because it can provide valuable fodder especially in the drier northern areas. It has been suggested, however, that the flower resembles the shape of the bonnets worn by Salvation Army lasses and that the plant was named accordingly. **1980** *Canberra Times* 23 July 1/3 Apiarists regard Paterson's curse as a valuable source of nectar for their bees and in times of drought graziers nickname it Salvation Jane.

salve, *v. Obs. trans.* Abbrev. of SALVAGE. Also as *ppl. a.*

1918 M. ABSON Diary 1 Feb. 29 (typescript) My batman 'salved' a couple of bags of cake. **1918** *Aussie: Austral. Soldiers' Mag.* Dec. 9/1 The brazier . . did . . duty . . for a jumped-up dish of Maconochie, bully beef, and salved spuds.

Salvo. [Abbrev. of *Salv(ation Army* + -O.] A member of the Salvation Army; the Salvation Army. Also *attrib.*

1891 *Truth* (Sydney) 12 Apr. 7/3 Some of them ran behind the huts, some under the wood heap, and one poor devil got stuck in a hollow log, and had to be chopped out. But Salvo prayed. **1904** *Bulletin* (Sydney) 4 Aug. 16/1, I don't believe a Salvo would do it. **1924** A.W. BAZLEY et al. Gloss. Slang A.I.F. 25 (typescript) *Salvoes*, Salvation Army. **1940** *Listening Post* (Perth) Feb. 4 The boys everywhere say the 'Salvo' was his . . friend. **1956** D. ROWBOTHAM *Town & City* 64 The 'Salvoes' had been near to salvaging one or two since they made the Corner a Sunday night rendezvous. **1967** F. HARDY *Billy Borker yarns Again* 3 He lived on cheap wine and hand-outs from the Salvoes. **1977** K. COLE *Winds of Fury* 142 Many were heard to say 'Thank God for the Salvos', and all agreed that this was the finest piece of social work by a voluntary agency that we experienced. **1983** *Serviceman* (Canberra) Apr. 24 The diggers soon got to know the 'Salvo bloke' in the various units. **1985** *Nat. Times* (Sydney) 2 Aug. 12/1 Some are too embarrassed to use the Salvo food vouchers they are given and welfare workers have to do the shopping for them.

sambo. [f. alteration of *sand(wich* + -O.] A sandwich. Also **sambie.**

1976 B. HUMPHRIES *Dame Edna's Coffee Table Bk.* 71 Some exciting sambies . . an increasingly popular diminutive for 'sandwiches'. **1984** *Sydney Morning Herald* 2 Nov. 35/5 The last sprig of parsley disappeared from the final platter of sambos.

Sammy. [See quot. 1976 (1).] An award presented for excellence in the television industry by the Variety Club of Australia. Also **Sammy award.**

1976 *TV Times* (Sydney) 25 Sept. 13/1 The new awards have been christened the Sammys, following a Variety Club custom of nearly 50 years of giving circus names to club officials, such as Chief Barker for Paul Hogan. The Sammys are designed like a circus seal. **1976** *Ibid.* 2 Oct. 10/1 *Here come the Sammys . .* the presentation of the first Australian TV and Film Awards. **1977** *Mercury* (Hobart) 11 Oct. 19/2 Butler's 'In the Wild' series also won a Sammy for the best documentary series. **1980** *Sydney Morning Herald* 18 Oct. 5/1 Last night in Sydney the fifth annual Sammy Awards were handed out. . . Bert Newton, Australia's best known second banana, was awarded the male Golden Sammy Award for consistent excellence.

samson fish. [See quot. 1882.] Any of several marine fish, esp. the large *Seriola hippos* of s. Aust., valued as a game fish.

1871 *Industr. Progress N.S.W.* 791 Flat-head, samson-fish, and a variety of other less familiar forms, may be taken by the line in almost unlimited quantities. **1882** J.E. Tenison-Woods *Fish & Fisheries N.S.W.* 60 The great strength of these fishes is remarkable, and which probably is the cause that gave it the name of Samson-fish, as sailors or shipwrights give to the name of a strong post resting on the keelson of a ship, and supporting the upper beam, and bearing all the weight of the deck cargo near the hold, *Samson post.* **1898** E.E. Morris *Austral Eng.* 401 Samson-fish . . name given in Sydney to *Seriola hippos* . . and in Melbourne to the young of *Arripis salar.* **1906** D.G. Stead *Fishes of Aust.* 153 The Samson-Fish . . is a beautiful fish, the sides being of a fine golden-yellow; with irregular, wide, vertical bars of a darker colour. **1952** *Austral. Museum Mag.* June 310 Originally Hebrew were the names we use for Samson Fish, Jewfish, and Moses Perch. **1971** T.C. Roughley *Fish & Fisheries Aust.* 46 The fish marketed in Queensland as 'samson-fish', although closely related to the samson-fish of New South Wales, is a different species (*Seriola purpurescens*). **1974** T.D. Scott et al. *Marine & Freshwater Fishes S.A.* 203 Samson Fish. *Seriola hippos* . . colour bluish-green above, sides golden, white below.

sand. Used *attrib.* in Special Comb. **sand flathead,** any of several fish of the fam. Platycephalidae inhabiting sandy seabeds, esp. *Platycephalus bassensis* of s. Aust. and *P. arenarius* of e. and n. Aust.; **goanna,** Bungarra; **lark,** *red-capped dotterel*, see Red *a.* 1 b.; **monkey,** see quot. 1981; **mullet,** the small marine and estuarine fish *Myxus elongatus* of s. Aust. exc. Tas.; Tallegalane; (occas.) any of several other similar fish; **palm,** the small, fan-leaved palm *Livistona humilis* (fam. Arecaceae) of n. N.T., usu. occurring on sandy soils; also *attrib.*; **soak,** a sandy Soak from which water can be obtained by digging; **whiting,** the marine fish *Sillago ciliata* of e. Aust., valued as food; (occas.) a similar, related fish.

1885 *Proc. Linnean Soc. N.S.W.* X. 578 *Platycephalus arenarius* . . **Sand Flathead** of Sydney. **1911** D.A. Macdonald *Bush Boy's Bk.* 108 The smaller grey flathead, sometimes called sand flathead, have the same fault as barracouta in occasionally getting thin and milky. **1948** F.D. Marshall *Let's go Fishing* 83 There are three varieties of flathead; the dusky . . the sand flathead . . and the deep sea flathead. **1978** N. Coleman *Austral. Fisherman's Fish Guide* 132 The sand flathead has spots on the top of the tail and the lower half is dark in colour. The body also has brown or red spots along the side. **1907** W.R.O. Hill *Forty Five Yrs. Experience N. Qld.* 75 The bites had come from small **sand 'goannas'**! **1920** *Bulletin* (Sydney) 9 Sept. 22/3 The yellow sand-gohanna is the one that yields the real goanna oil. **1957** M. Paice *Valley in North* 16 A sand-goanna scuttled across the road to rear up on its hind legs in the grass. **1984** B. Dixon *Searching for Aboriginal Lang.* 36 What do you think you are, a sand goanna, wanting to dig up scrub-hen eggs? **1802** M. Flinders *Voyage Terra Australis* (1814) II. 145 On the shores were pelicans . . and **sand-larks.** **1805** J.H. Tuckey *Acct. Voyage to establish Colony Port Phillip* 163 Aquatic birds are found in abundance . . and are . . curlews, and sand larks. **1839** W.H. Leigh *Reconnoitering Voyages* 109 There are sea-gulls of various kinds, sand-larks. **1867** W. Richardson *Tasmanian Poems* p. xi, The nimble sand-lark learns his pretty note. **1976** *Reader's Digest Compl. Bk. Austral. Birds* 176 Red-capped dotterel *Charadrius ruficapillus*. . . Other names . . sand lark. **1958** H.D. Williamson *Sunlit Plain* 59, I was over on a bit of a **sand-monkey** about a mile off, setting a string of traps, so I didn't see you come in. It's marvellous how you can miss a man in this flat country. **1981** E. Rolls *Million Wild Acres* 260 The belts of white sand where the best pine grew were raised about half a metre above the rest of the country and were known as sand monkeys. **1844** *Sydney Morning Herald* 3 May 3/2 The **sand** or sea-**mullet** are just coming in. **1873** F. De Castelnau *Edible Fishes Vic.* 14 The Sand mullet (*Mugil Waigiensis*) . . is . . much esteemed, not only on account of its esculent qualities but also of its large size. **1897** 'Old Housekeeper' *Austral. Plain Cookery* 46 The sand mullet is by many considered one of our most delicate fish, either baked or boiled. **1906** D.G. Stead *Fishes of Aust.* 75 The Sea Mullet is the largest . . of all our Mullets. . . In Victoria it is known as 'Sand Mullet', a name which we, in New South Wales, more judiciously apply to the Mullet which is also known as Tallegallane or Lano (*Myxus elongatus*). **1951** T.C. Roughley *Fish & Fisheries Aust.* 36 As a food-fish the sand mullet is of very good quality, less oily than the sea mullet, but it is not greatly appreciated on account of its small size. **1969** J. Pollard *Austral. & N.Z. Fishing* 377 Sand mullet . . are mainly caught over the shallow sandy flats near the river mouths and along the ocean beaches. **1983** Hutchins & Thompson *Marine & Estuarine Fishes S.-W. Aust.* 50 Sand Mullet. . . A dark blotch usually in upper corner of pectoral fin base. **1935** F. Birtles *Battle Fronts Outback* 157, I lived on young **sand palm** tops and black bream from the creek. **1984** D. Jones *Palms in Aust.* 134 *Livistona humilis* . . Sand Palm. . . This species is very common in open forest frequently growing in scattered colonies and sometimes in pure stands. **1936** C. Chewings *Back in Stone Age* 36 The water . . is ordinary ground water, from . . **sand-soaks.** **1959** D. Stuart *Yandy* 108 They were rough camps; plenty of water, some places had a Government well, some places just a sandsoak. **1962** B.W. Leake *Eastern Wheatbelt Wildlife* 17 The two previous seasons (1863 and 64) had been years of heavy rainfall and dingoes would drink at a number of sand soaks. **1882** J.E. Tenison-Woods *Fish & Fisheries N.S.W.* 65 The 'whitings' are not like those of Europe. There are in all four Australian species—the common **sand whiting** (*Silligo maculata*) [etc.]. **1906** D.G. Stead *Fishes of Aust.* 109 The Sand Whiting . . is plentifully distributed over the whole of the New South Wales coastline, the greater part of that of Queensland and to a lesser extent along a portion of the Victorian coast. **1918** 'J. Scott' *How, when & where to catch Fish* 27 Trumpeter whiting . . are not nearly as plentiful as the sand whiting. **1951** T.C. Roughley *Fish & Fisheries Aust.* 47 The sand whiting enjoys wide popularity as a food-fish; its flesh is very white; it is tender; and it has a most delicate and rather distinctive flavour. **1978** N. Coleman *Austral. Fisherman's Fish Guide* 89 A common wide-ranging species, the sand whiting frequents estuary sandflats, coral reef lagoons, rubble banks and beaches in large schools.

sandalwood, *n.*[1] [Spec. use of *sandalwood* the scented wood of several species of *Santalum*.]

1. Used *attrib.* with reference to the sandalwood industry.

1849 J.S. Roe *Rep. Exped. S.-Eastward Perth* 53 Mr Maxwell had a sandal-wood cutting station, at a good spring. **1903** *Westminster Gaz.* (London) 28 Jan. 9/2 Fierce jealousies arose between the gold-hunters and the sandalwood gropers, as the new people contemptuously termed the old, because the sandalwood trade was one of the most important industries of the old brigade. **1941** D. O'Callaghan *Long Life Reminisc.* 109 Part of his duty in that district was looking for sandalwood cutters. **1948** I.L. Idriess *Opium Smugglers* 2 A sandalwood team was lumbering into town, the pack-horses heavy-laden with the rich yellow wood from the wild west coast away up the Peninsula. **1981** *Austral. Women's Weekly* (Sydney) 18 Nov. 21/1 Most sandalwood camps are deep in remote country, hundreds of kilometres north and east of the gold-mining town of Kalgoorlie, Western Australia.

2. Comb. **sandalwood carter, getter.**

1865 'Special Correspondent' *Transportation* 22 It is the great rendezvous . . of the **sandal-wood carters.** **1981** A.B. Facey *Fortunate Life* 207 It had been put down years ago by sandalwood carters. **1913** *Bulletin* (Sydney) 17 Apr. 16/3 A hardy group of men are the **sandalwood-getters.** **1917** *Emu* xvii. 63 A Parrot that prospectors, sandalwood-getters, and others had spoken to him about as frequenting the scrubs. **1924** Lawrence & Skinner *Boy in Bush* 235 The others last night were mostly sandal-wood getters.

3. Special Comb. **sandalwood track,** a track made by sandalwood cutters.

1849 J.S. Roe *Rep. Exped. S.-Eastward Perth* 53 We proceeded along the beaten sandal-wood track on the eastern side of the Stirling Range. **1894** A.F. Calvert *Coolgardie Goldfield* 46 The whole of this 138 miles is through country intersected by old sandal wood tracks.

sandalwood, *n.*[2] [Transf. use of Sandalwood *n.*[1]] Any of several trees or shrubs of drier Aust. yielding wood with a fragrant aroma (esp. when burnt), esp. *Eremophila mitchellii* (see Budda), and *Myoporum platycarpum* (both fam. Myoporaceae); the wood of these plants.

1852 J. Macgillivray *Narr. Voyage H.M.S. Rattlesnake* I. 98 An inferior kind of sandal wood, the produce of *Exocarpos latifolia* (but which afterwards turned out to be useless) was met with. **1882** *Proc. Linnean Soc. N.S.W.* VII. 349 *Myoporum platycarpum*. . . This tree known to Bushmen by the name of Sandalwood is widely distributed over the Western portions of New South Wales. *Ibid.* 574 *Eremophila mitchelli* . . also goes by the name of Sandal Wood from the pleasant odour given off by the wood. **1932** *Victorian Naturalist* XLIX. 189 The Budda or Sandalwood (*Stenochilus Mitchellii*) is common in the scrub, and arrests attention by its masses of creamy blossom and its neatly-tesselated bark. **1954** H.G. Lamond *Manx Star* 260 *Sandal wood*, shrub with brittle leaves (*Eremophila Mitchelii*).

sandalwood, *v.* In the phr. **to go sandalwooding,** to seek out and cut sandalwood. See Sandalwood *n.*[1]

1894 J.K. Arthur *Kangaroo & Kauri* 23 The high price it once attained induced many of the colonists to go 'sandal-wooding', travelling with their teams in search of this odorous wood. **1973** W.G. Walker *Gloss. Educ. Terms* 9 Pioneer farmers after putting in their crop might go sandalwooding, to return in time for the harvest.

sandalwooder. One engaged in the cutting of sandalwood. See Sandalwood *n.*[1]

1932 C.E. Goode *Grower of Golden Grain* 18, I saw a sandal-wooder with his camel team arrive. **1944** *Bulletin* (Sydney) 20 Sept. 12/3, I came on an old French sandalwooder who through the day had collected a whole panful of these witchetty grubs. **1956** *Ibid.* 11 Apr. 13/2, I camped with a sandalwooder on the Westralian goldfields in my early youth. **1974** N. Cato *Brown Sugar* 9 Of course they were not the first white men the villagers had seen. Before that there had been the sandalwooders.

sand-grope, *v. Obs.* [See Sand-groper.]

a. *intr.* To walk in soft sand.

1924 Lawrence & Skinner *Boy in Bush* 21 They walked off the timber platform into the sand, and Jack had his first experience of 'sand-groping'. The sand was thick and fine and soft, so he was glad to reach the oyster-shell path running up Wellington Street.

b. *fig.* To bungle. (In quot. as *ppl. a.*)

1898 *Bulletin* (Sydney) 15 Jan. 20/1 The W.A. sand-groping Forrest Govt. has a great penchant for importing second-hand English clerks.

Sand-groper. A non-Aboriginal person, native to or resident in Western Australia. (The statement made in quot. 1899 is erroneous). Also *attrib.*

1896 H. Lawson *Lett.* 3 Sept. (1970) 62 The old Sand-gropers are the best to work for. . . The Tothersiders are cutting each others' throats. **1899** *Austral. Tit-Bits* (Sydney) 2 Dec. 6/1 'Sand-groper' is the name given to the aboriginals of West Australia. **1916** E. & M.S. Grew *Rambles in Aust.* 206 In reference to the vast amount of sand in West Australia, the West Australians are called 'Sand-gropers'. **1922** *Daily Mail* (Sydney) 19 Jan. 5/8 *Little Sandgropers are busy.* The 'boys from the west' will be sure to see all there is to be seen in N.S.W.; they are even to see something that isn't. A party is to go down to the Bush Capital at Canberra. **1940** *Artilleryman: Official Newspaper 2/1 Field Regiment* 6 May 7 Was born in Kalgoorlie, W.A. . . and is thus a proper 'Sand groper'. **1950** K.S. Prichard *Winged Seeds* 146 'Nothing doing,' Bill grinned. 'I'll stick to an Aussie-show.' 'There's a sandgroper for you!' **1963** X. HERBERT *Disturbing Element* 2, I doubt if born West Australians have got over the Sand Groper Complex even yet. **1978** D. STUART *Wedgetail View* 140 He's so much the old original Sandgroper; he's never been outside the State . . never been drunk in his life, never been to the races. **1985** *Bulletin* (Sydney) 22 Oct. 72/1 I'm *glad* I was born in Western Australia. . . As a matter of fact there are five Sandgropers on this magazine who feel the same way.

Sandgroperland. A nickname for Western Australia.

1908 *Truth* (Sydney) 12 July 1/3 They do things differently over in Sandgroperland. **1920** *Referee* (Sydney) 11 Feb. 13/5 How the swimmers of Sandgroperland attained the standard they reached under such conditions surpasses my understanding.

sandhill wattle. The tall shrub or small tree *Acacia burkittii* (fam. Mimosaceae), usu. of sandy plains in N.S.W., S.A., and W.A., having long, needle-like phyllodes; *kangaroo bush* (b), see KANGAROO *n.* 5.

1946 C.T. MADIGAN *Crossing Dead Heart* 68 There was green sandhill wattle. **1949** G. FARWELL *Traveller's Tracks* 59 From the homestead you can see 360 degrees of flat horizon . . a few sandhill wattles. **1975** E.R. ROTHERHAM et al. *Flowers & Plants N.S.W. & Southern Qld.* 150 *Acacia burkittii* sandhill wattle . . is scattered throughout the Plains of N.S.W. and in northern S.A.

sand map. A makeshift diagram of an area, route, etc., drawn in sand.

1932 I.L. IDRIESS *Lasseter's Last Ride* 58 'Sand maps' were drawn . . eloquent with . . fingernail in making depressions along the proposed route where soakages were found. **1957** J. HAWKE *Follow my Dust* 73 Ellis glanced up from a sand-map at the toughened new chum. **1959** A. UPFIELD *Bony & Mouse* 221 Bony smoothed the ground, and with a finger rapidly drew a map of the mulga forest. . . About this sand map, white men and black elders squatted on heels.

sandpaper fig. [See quot. 1965.] Any of several trees of the genus *Ficus* (fam. Moraceae) having rough leaves, as *F. coronata*, *F. opposita*, and *F. fraseri*; *rough fig*, see ROUGH *a.* 1. Also *attrib.*

c **1910** W.R. GUILFOYLE *Austral. Plants* 177 *Ficus aspera* . . 'Sand- paper Fig Tree' . . (evergreen tree, 80 to 100 ft.) . . Vic., N.S.W., and Q'land. **1932** R.H. ANDERSON *Trees of N.S.W.* 124 Two Sandpaper Figs are found in the Division, viz., *Ficus stephanocarpa* and *Ficus stenocarpa*. These are distinguished by the harsh, rough feel of the leaves. **1965** *Austral. Encycl.* IV. 59 A number of figs are noted for the roughness of the leaves to the touch and are popularly known as sandpaper figs. **1981** D. LEVITT *Plants & People* 66 Leaves of the Sandpaper Fig were heated on hot stones and applied to the groin to reduce swelling after ceremonies. The rough surface of the leaf held the heat well.

sandy blight. [See quot. 1892.] An acute conjunctivitis, usu. infectious and trachomatous, characterized by granular follicles and common in arid areas; BLIGHT. Also **sand blight.**

1846 H. MCCRAE *Georgiana's Jrnl.* 19 July (1934) 197 Cuts, splinter-wounds, boils, and sand-blight, have been successfully treated. **1852** *Empire* (Sydney) 23 Jan. 602/4 A great many people have lately been troubled with what is called the sandy blight, an affection of the eyes, extremely painful and difficult to get over. **1852** G.C. MUNDY *Our Antipodes* I. 85 These storms sometimes cause the eye-blight or sand-blight as the malady is indifferently called. **1859** W. BURROWS *Adventures Mounted Trooper* 149 The dust frequently causes them to be affected by what is called 'blight'. . . There are . . two kinds of this complaint, commonly known as 'sandy' and 'swelling' blight. **1871** *Great Northern Run Case* 31 An almost intolerable existence, made up of toil and privation, fever and ague, sand flies and sandy blight. **1892** G.L. JAMES *Shall I try Aust.?* 242 One pest of the bush and plains is 'Sandy Blight', or inflammation of the eyes—it is, I believe, called 'sandy' owing to the pain being exactly similar to that which grains of sand upon the eyeball would cause. **1906** *Gentleman's Mag.* (London) Sept. 273 'Sandy blight' . . causes temporary blindness accompanied by intense pain. **1914** C.H.S. MATTHEWS *Bill* 38 Poor Dad got that dreadful complaint, 'sandy-blight'. The doctors call it some name as long as your arm—I forget what. **1933** *Bulletin* (Sydney) 13 Sept. 23/2 The term 'sandy blight' is used for two conditions: trachoma, a chronic eyelid inflammation, and epidemic ophthalmia (or 'pink eye' or 'bung eye') an acute inflammation of the eyelids lasting only a few weeks. **1948** M. UREN *Glint of Gold* 59 Sandy-blight . . is caused by flies which persistently make for the eyes of human beings and infect them with the poison picked up from decayed animal flesh. **1968** D. O'GRADY *Bottle of Sandwiches* 149 'Haven't seen any gentlemen around for years,' Jack said. 'You must be sufferin' from sandy blight—there's two in the truck.' **1969** A.A. ABBIE *Original Australs.* 87 Trachoma is a disease found practically throughout the world. . . The disease is mainly fly-borne and, since bush Aborigines tolerate flies crawling around their eyes, it is still a common but not universal complaint among them. And so it spreads to whites who call the condition 'sandy blight'. **1980** *Nat. Trachoma & Eye Health Program* (R. Austral. College Opthalm.) 1 Among the early settlers, however, trachoma called 'Sandy Blight' was endemic and frequently led to serious visual loss. **1982** R. HALL *Just Relations* 106 First the people are half-blinded by sandy-blight and then they fall victim to dysentery.

sanger. Alteration of 'sandwich'. Also **sango.**

1943 *O-Pip: 'P' Battery Austral. Field Artillery* Aug. 3 We beheld an outsize in double-decker sangos clamped in Irvine's jaw. **1968** D. O'GRADY *Bottle of Sandwiches* 160 Meals consisted of piles of sangers, made by the pub cook, and brought out at odd intervals. **1974** J. MCNEIL *How does your Garden Grow* 26 Nothing like the old cheese sanger for a man on the go. **1980** *Sunday Mail* (Brisbane) 24 Aug. 3/8 A colleague went to order a chicken 'sanger' and decided to ask the serving lady why they seemed 'a little thin of late'.

sanguineous honeyeater: see *scarlet honeyeater* SCARLET.

sanitary, *a.*

a. Used in collocations with reference to the collection of excrement from unsewered areas, as **sanitary cart (truck, van),** a vehicle used for this purpose; *dunny cart*, see DUNNY 2; *night-cart*, see NIGHT; also *ellipt.*; **man,** one who operates such a vehicle; *dunny man*, see DUNNY 2; *night-cart man*, *night-man*, see NIGHT.

1894 [sanitary cart] A.B. BELL *Austral. Camp Fire Tales* 95 The cabby . . set that horse going full sail, and no mistake: as we dashed through the city, everyone stared aghast, while the Jehu remarked as he coughed and spit: 'Oh! Lor, Oh! Lor, they'll take us for a sanitary van.' **1958** F.B. VICKERS *Though Poppies Grow* 202, I was the half-caste bastard working on the sanitary-cart. **1964** B. WANNAN *Fair Go, Spinner* 4 'Where would you have been today if you *had* had an education!' 'Back in Boulia driving the sanitary cart, I reckon.' **1968** *Kings Cross Whisper* (Sydney) li. 2/1 The speed limit for sanitary trucks—better known as night carts and dunny carts—is to be raised. **1973** *Ibid.* clvi. 4/1 Donno's never been a sanitary cart offsider. **1984** P. READ *Down there with me on Cowra Mission* 26 They never had the sewerage. . . We had the sanitary coming once a week. **1903** *Truth* (Sydney) 31 May 1/4 Crapp is the euphonious name of the **sanitary man** in a New South Wales town. **1904** *Ibid.* 16 Oct. 1/8 A small place with about 100 inhabitants and a sanitary man. **1907** *Ibid.* 6 Jan. 11/4 (*heading*) The pilgrim of the night humming humors at Hurstville. A sanitary man 'stoushed'.

b. In the phr. **on the sanitary,** working on a sanitary cart.

1963 P. WHITE *Four Plays* (1965) 113 I've got me run, Digger. I told you I was on the sanitary. I've gotta make meself scarce. Late already. We're short of personnel. The night-soil's not everybody's cuppa tea.

sano. Also **sanno.** [f. *san(itary* + -O.] A sanitary inspector; *sanitary man*, see SANITARY a. Freq. *attrib.* as **sano man.**

1959 S.J. BAKER *Drum* 142 *Sanno*, a sanitary inspector. **1969** *Kings Cross Whisper* (Sydney) lxvi. 5/5 Fifty Sydney dunny carts, manned by sano men carrying dozens of cut lunches, will leave Sydney next week on a survey of the marathon route. **1970** *Ibid.* lxxxiv. 1/4 A spokesman for the dunny men said the sanno men had taken this drastic action to try to win some social standing for their trade. **1971** F. HARDY *Outcasts of Foolgarah* 49 Sanitary carters . . known not too favourably locally as Sanos, or more precisely, shitties. **1977** L. FOX *Depression Down Under* 87 Mother sympathised with the Sanno man's job; she always greeted him.

sap, *v. trans.* To cut a ring round (the trunk of a tree) of sufficient depth to penetrate the sap wood. Also **sap-ring (bark)** *v.*, and as *vbl. n.*

1826 J. ATKINSON *Acct. Agric. & Grazing N.S.W.* 85 Another plan is to stump-fall the trees, and then to open out the stump all round, so as to expose as many of the roots to the air as possible, at the same time *sapping* the stump, as it is termed, that is, cutting off about a hand's breadth of the bark all round, as low down as possible. **1827** *Monitor* (Sydney) 5 July 495/1 There were many of these worthies, who had never handled an axe or a handspike, and to whom, 'felling' and 'lopping', 'sapping', and 'cutting-out', would be almost as strange and irksome, as it would be for a ship's carpenter to attempt the making of a chronometer. **1832** *Colonial Times* (Hobart) 21 Mar., The dry and hardened state of the wood made the execution by means of axes so laborious and tedious in barking and sapping the stumps. **1897** L. LINDLEY-COWEN *W. Austral. Settler's Guide* 220 My experience is that trees that have been sap-ringed do not generally throw out so many suckers. **1902** H. LAWSON *Children of Bush* 312 The tall gum-trees had been ring-barked (a ring of bark taken out round the butts), or rather 'sapped'—that is, a ring cut in through the sap—in order to kill them. **1967** *W. Austral. Selector's Guide* (W.A. Lands Dept.) 6 York Gum is apt to throw out suckers, particularly if sap-ringed. **1947** *Bulletin* (Sydney) 24 Sept. 29/3, I have found that trees 'sap'-ringbarked decay much more rapidly than trees 'collar'-ringbarked.

saratoga. [Of unknown origin.] The fish *Scleropages leichardti* (see BARRAMUNDI c.).

1969 J. POLLARD *Austral. & N.Z. Fishing* 661 *Scleropages leichardti*. . . The species is known as saratoga or saratota in all North Australia, with local exceptions on the Jardine and Dawson River. **1973** V. SERVENTY *Desert Walkabout* 70 In the pool were giant perch, known commonly as barramundi, though the true barramundi is called a saratogo. Perhaps we should accept the inevitable, since saratogo is a corruption of the scientific name *Scleropages*, a fish of ancient lineage. **1984** MERRICK & SCHMIDA *Austral. Freshwater Fishes* 71 This immature saratoga (*Scleropages leichardti*) is 300 mm. long.

sardine. [Used elsewhere but recorded earliest in Aust.] Used *attrib.* in Special Comb. **sardine box, tin,** an extremely small dwelling or other building.

1899 G.E. BOXALL *Story Austral. Bushrangers* 136 Later some boxes, made of corrugated iron, were put up as cells and these were known as 'the Dutch ovens' or 'the **sardine boxes**' and prisoners confined to them on hot summer nights suffered tortures and begged to be put 'on the chain' as a relief. **1976** N. CATO *Mister Maloga* 65 The 'huts' he erected on them were also dummies, known as 'sardine boxes'. **1888** 'SPECIAL CORRESPONDENT' *Barrier Silver & Tin Fields* 6 The '**sardine-tin**', 'rag houses', and 'bandbox' buildings were in ill contrast. **1891** 'SMILER' *Wanderings Simple Child* (ed. 3) 47 Most of the buildings were little tin shanties, commonly and appropriately called 'sardine tins'.

sarsaparilla. [Transf. use of *sarsaparilla*, orig. applied to *Smilax*.]

a. FALSE SARSAPARILLA. **b.** *Sweet tea*, see SWEET *a.*[1] Also *attrib.*

1830 R. DAWSON *Present State Aust.* 199 Sarsaparilla . . grew wild on the banks. **1843** *Portland Mercury* 8 Nov. 3/2 Mr Hull has shipped on board the Dublin, sarsaparilla, both in extract and root. The sarsaparilla shrub has recently been discovered in the Portland Bay district. **1860** *Sydney Mail* 27 Oct. 3/3 The cluster may be tied with the *Hardenbergia monophylla*, erroneously called sarsaparilla, from the resemblance of its leaf to that plant. **1866** *Austral. Monthly Mag.* (Melbourne) I. 357 'What is it?' . . 'A root of sarsaparilla!' **1869** *Illustr. Sydney News* 23 Dec. 318/2 From the ceiling hung a graceful mass of the purple sarsaparilla vine, placed there to do duty for the time honoured mistle-toe. **1887** *Proc. Linnean Soc. N.S.W.* II. 274 *Kennedya* . . *monophylla* . . everywhere . . usually called 'Sarsaparilla' and used in the same way as a bitter, *Smilax* the true Sarsaparilla not extending to this district. **1920** B. Cronin *Timber Wolves* 227 A big clump of purple sarsaparilla that's hanging from a tree. **1934** M. Gilmore *Old Days* 25 The 'sarsaparilla' made naughty little boys good by clearing their 'over-crowded' blood. **1942** E. Langley *Pea Pickers* 220 You are like the rich purple sarsaparilla plant that breaks out of the clay in the heat of the summer. **1957** V. Palmer *Seedtime* 199 She came back trailing a length of purple sarsaparilla. **1981** E. Potter *Scone I Remember* 24 Over the years we watched a small sarsaparilla vine slowly climb to the top of the fence, grow into a luxuriant purple mass and spill over the far side.

sarvo. [f. *thi)s* + Arvo.] 'This afternoon'.

1942 *Welcome to Aust.* 7 *Sarvo*, this afternoon. **1978** D. Stuart *Wedgetail View* 244 An' after the Company parade, 'sarvo, what'll it be, Eddie?

sassafras. [Transf. use of *sassafras* an American tree of the genus *Sassafras*.] Any of several trees, usu. of the fam. Monimiaceae, having an aromatic bark, esp. the rainforest trees *Atherosperma moschatum* of s.e. Aust. incl. Tas. and *Doryphora sassafras* of e. N.S.W. and s.e. Qld.; the bark, leaves, or wood of these trees. Also *attrib.*

1802 *HRA* (1915) 1st Ser. III. 571 The Sassafras wood grows in great abundance. **1820** C. Jeffreys *Van Dieman's Land* 133 For tea, they drink a decoction of the sassafras and other shrubs. **1826** J. Atkinson *Acct. Agric. & Grazing N.S.W.* 3 Here are found the elegant sassafras or kalang; the bark of this tree has a spicy aromatic taste, and is much esteemed in the Colony as a stomachic and purifier of the blood. **1835** *Cornwall Chron.* (Launceston) 28 Feb. 2 Cargo . . 4 logs sassafras wood, 1 bag sassafras bark. **1840** *True Colonist* (Hobart) 13 Nov. 5/4 The walls wainscoted with sassafras deal, which is highly polished and varnished. **1845** *Melbourne Standard* 28 May 3/3 At the latter part of the journey, sassafras tea without sugar, pellucid spring water. 4 ozs. of bread each, per diem. **1855** J. Bonwick *Geogr. Aust. & N.Z.* (ed. 3) 203 The Sassafras or Atherospermum is a tall pyramidal tree, whose bark is medicinal. **1871** *Austral. Town & Country Jrnl.* (Sydney) 3 June 682/3 Descending through a grove of stately sassafras trees. **1888** *Proc. Linnean Soc. N.S.W.* III. 367 *Doryphora sassafras* . . the well-known 'Sassafras', peculiar to New South Wales. **1892** M. North *Recoll. Happy Life* II. 171 We also saw fine specimens of sassafras (which yields an oil rivalling the real American sassafras in value). **1900** C.H. Chomley *True Story Kelly Gang* 7 Wattle and sassafras scrub clothed the banks of the creek. **1935** T. Rayment *Cluster of Bees* 257 The homely teas brewed from curious plants such as the bark of the sassafras. **1956** N.K. Wallis *Austral. Timber Handbk.* 8 Other timbers produced are . . sassafras (turnery, veneers, clothes pegs). **1965** G. McInnes *Road to Gundagai* 16 The tiny cabin smelled of sand and sassafras, of boronia and the flowering gum, and of the great grey continent beyond. **1981** A.B. & J.W. Cribb *Wild Medicine in Aust.* 58 *Atherosperma moschatum* is given the common name of sassafras because of the spicy scent, rather like nutmeg, in the leaves and bark.

satin, *a.* Used as a distinguishing epithet in the names of flora and fauna: **satin bird,** *satin bower-bird*; (occas.) *shining flycatcher*, see Shining; **bower-bird,** the bird *Ptilonorhynchus violaceus* of e. mainland Aust., the mature male having glossy black plumage with a blue sheen; **flycatcher,** the bird *Myiagra cyanoleuca* of e. Aust. incl. Tas., and elsewhere, the mature male having glossy bluish-black upperparts and chest, and white belly; **oak,** a tall rainforest tree of the genus *Oreocallis* (fam. Proteaceae), esp. *O. wickhamii* of n.e. Qld.; also **satin silky oak; top,** any of several grasses (fam. Poaceae), esp. the tufted perennial *Bothriochloa erianthoides* of N.S.W. and Qld., valued as fodder; also **satin top(ped) grass.**

1827 *Trans. Linnean Soc. London* XV. 264 Mr Caley says that 'the male of this species is reckoned a very scarce bird, and is highly valued. The natives call it *Cowry*, the colonists **Satin Bird**'. **1834** G. Bennett *Wanderings N.S.W.* I. 307 The elegant 'satin-bird', (*Ptilinorynchus of Temminck*) . . leaves the Murrumbidgee country during summer. **1849** A. Harris *Guide Port Stephens* 88 There is a bird called by bushmen the 'satin bird', jet black and perfectly satin-like in the appearance of its plumage. **1860** *Sydney Mail* 21 July 6/2 The satin birds seek in the gardens and shrubberies for seeds. **1881** E. Davies *Story Earnest Life* 379 The lovely satin bird, with beautiful eyes. When young they are dark green. **1903** *Emu* II. 164 Satin-Bird (*Ptilonorhynchus violaceus*)—common in parts of the Otways. **1949** B. O'Reilly *Green Mountains* 137 The Satin bird, which gets its name from the handsome purple satin coat which the male bird dons when seven years old, is mainly famous for his bower or playground. **1841** J. Gould *Birds of Aust.* (1848) IV. Pl. 10, *Ptilonorhynchus holosericeus* . . **Satin Bower-bird** . . Satin Bird, of the Colonists of New South Wales. **1851** J. Henderson *Excursions & Adventures N.S.W.* 183 The Satin bower-bird is very beautiful, and is of a rich deep blue satiny colour. It forms strange bowers, or arbours, in which to disport in the cool evenings, and has the magpie-like propensity to collect all shining and pretty nic-nacks on which it can stumble. **1901** *Emu* I. 60 The Satin Bower Bird (*Ptilonorhynchus violaceus*), where the hen is of a mottled green colour. **1926** *Bulletin* (Sydney) 21 Jan. 24/3 The satin bower-bird is fast disappearing from the remnants of our Queensland coastal scrubs. **1955** N. Pulliam *I traveled Lonely Land* 244 You can . . hunt for other fascinating Australian birds—perhaps the surprising satin bowerbird, who loves to collect blue things to decorate his nest. **1985** D. Foster *Dog Rock* 87 Galahs eat wheat. . . Satin bowerbirds eat French beans. **1898** E.E. Morris *Austral Eng.* 404 Satin-Robin . . a Tasmanian name for the **Satin Fly-catcher,** *Myiagra nitida*. **1903** *Emu* II. 163 Have seen a few Satin Flycatchers near home. **1945** C. Barrett *Austral. Bird Life* 171 The satin flycatcher ranges from Queensland to Victoria and Tasmania. **1976** *Reader's Digest Compl. Bk. Austral. Birds* 388 The sheeny black and pure white of the male satin flycatcher distinguishes it from the similarly patterned leaden flycatcher. **1919 [satin oak]** R.T. Baker *Hardwoods of Aust.* 5 Timber Colours . . Pink . . *Embothrium Wickhami* . . Satin Silky Oak. **1926** *Qld. Agric. Jrnl.* XXV. 436 Embothrium Wickhamii . . Satin Oak. **1965** *Austral. Encycl.* VII. 299 A most attractive tree is *Embothrium wickhamii* of brush forests in northern New South Wales and Queensland. . . Satin oak is . . the name that has been standardized in the timber trade for this tree. **1982** K. McArthur *Bush in Bloom* 140 The brilliant North Queensland *Oreocallis wickhamii*—the Satin Oak. **1882 [satin top]** *Austral. Handbk.* 392 There are nearly 200 indigenous grasses, amongst which are . . the 'Satin-topped grass' (*Andropogon erianthoides*) [etc.]. **1917** *Bulletin* (Sydney) 1 Feb. 22/2 The king Blue grasses are . . *Andro[pogon] erianthoides*, or satin-topped; and *Androp. bombycinus*, or silky heads. **1923** E. Breakwell *Grasses & Fodder Plants N.S.W.* 17 *Andropogon bombycinus* (Satin Top grass) . . very rare everywhere; found in protected areas in the north-west. **1933** *Bulletin* (Sydney) 29 Mar. 25/1 Some of the potential plants of these pastures are rib grass, coolah grass, blue, Flinders, Mitchell, sugar or brown top, satin top and native wheat grass. **1965** *Austral. Encycl.* VI. 366 *Bothriochloa erianthoides* (satin-top) is a valuable fodder grass usually found in blue-grass country.

satinwood. [Transf. use of *satin-wood* the satiny, yellowish wood of various trees.] Any of several trees of e. Aust. yielding a glossy, usu. yellowish timber, esp. *Zanthoxylum brachyacanthum* and *Phebalium squameum* subsp. *squameum* (both fam. Rutaceae), and *Daphnandra micrantha* (fam. Monimiaceae); the wood of these trees.

1853 J. Capper *Emigrant's Guide to Aust.* (ed. 2) 9 Cedar and satin-wood are also found in the western and southern sides of the island. **1861** J.D. Lang *Qld., Aust.* 175, I have already mentioned the cypress-pine as an ornamental timber. . . Satin-wood and yellow-wood are the names of two other species that are used in the same way. **1888** *Proc. Linnean Soc. N.S.W.* III. 367 *Daphnandra micrantha* . . 'Satin-wood'. The bark of this tree is intensely bitter. **1906** *Ibid.* XXXI. 370 *Zanthoxylum brachyacanthum* . . yields a beautiful glossy timber, known locally [*sc.* n.e. N.S.W.] as 'Satinwood'. **1968** G.R. Cochrane et al. *Flowers & Plants Vic.* 131 Victorian occurrences are confined to the southern Otways; but Satinwood is frequent on King Island and in many parts of Tas. **1981** J.A. Baines *Austral. Plant Genera* 403 Satinwood, so-called from the glossy yellow timber.

saucy, *a. Austral. pidgin.* See quot. 1860.

1860 G. Bennett *Gatherings of Naturalist* 108 The aborigines saying (alluding to the spur), 'It is very saucy', such being their English expression when they wish to imply that anything is hurtful or poisonous. **1914** J. Mathew *Ballads Bush Life* 9 Their saucy-fellow dillies And sugarbag and billies, Their shells and reeds and rugs and other store.

sausage.

1. *fig.* The penis. Also *attrib.*

1944 *Action* (Toowoomba) July 11 'Sausage Brigade' . . to live up to this term, then, a soldier must have his wife in the area. **1971** B. Humphries *Bazza pulls it Off*, Yeah, you old sausage grappler!!! *Ibid.*, All a bloke wants is some nice little sheilah with a decent pair of top bollocks to take out to the flicks and a swift game of hide the sausage in the back stalls. **1977** D. Williamson *Club* (1978) 25 Raylene's a hell of a nice girl but the word is she's not a great one for hiding the sausage.

2. Special Comb. **sausage wrapper,** a newspaper.

1891 'Smiler' *Wanderings Simple Child* (ed. 3) 6 I'd write a better leader than your old one-horse show has ever had in its columns since it first started on its wild career as a sausage wrapper. **1915** *First Aid Post: Official Organ 2nd Field Ambulance* 14 July 1/1 Heralded its sausage wrapper's arrival with a feeble attack. No doubt our readers are acquainted with this rag.

savage. *Obs.* Used freq. during the nineteenth century, not necessarily pejoratively, of an Aboriginal.

1792 R. Johnson *Address to Colonies N.S.W. & Norfolk Island* 67, I would farther plead with you for the sake of the poor unenlightened savages, who daily visit us, or who reside amongst us. **1808** *Sydney Gaz.* 15 May, The savages immediately took . . the boat. **1830** *Launceston Advertiser* 15 Feb. 3 Much has been said about the Savages, whom by the mere right of *power* we have bereaved of their dominion, and against whose defenceless wretchedness we have waged a war directly tending to extermination. **1846** *Moreton Bay Courier* 25 July 3/1 At no other times have the aborigines exhibited so much ferocity as on this occasion. In their stand-up fights between tribe and tribe a great deal of caution is usually exercised, but in the contest yesterday, the savage exhibited himself in all his native deformity. **1867** G. Walch *Fireflash* 26 As yet I had seen no savages. **1887** A. Nicols *Wild Life & Adventure* 145 The figure of the old savage was not wanting in a certain impressiveness and dignity. **1898** D.W. Carnegie *Spinifex & Sand* 296 Fifteen naked savages came bounding down the sandhill towards us. **1937** M. Terry *Sand & Sun* 269 We've got plenty of names for 'em. . . There's nigger, boong, coon, blackfellow, myall . . savage.

saver. *Horse-racing.* [Used elsewhere but recorded earliest in Aust.: see OED(S 5.] A hedging bet, a bet laid to insure against loss on another bet.

[**1882** *Sydney Slang Dict.* 7 *Save*, to give part of one bet for part of another. A. and B. have backed different horses, and they agree that in the event of either one winning he shall give the other, say, £5. This is called 'saving a fiver', and generally is done when scratchings and knockings-out have left the field so that one of the two speculators must be a winner. Form of hedging.] **1891** N. Gould *Double Event* 123 Wells says Perfection will win . . but I've put a saver on Caloola. **1904** L.M.P. Archer *Bush Honeymoon* 145 Blackbird's the only *saver* they've got in the next race. **1912** S. Locke *Dawsons' Uncle George* 94 They . . arranged a bet on 'Whirligig', and a saver on 'Greenhide'. **1919** A. Wright *Game of Chance* 79 'Isn't it a waste of money to back Chanter if that is the case?' . . 'Just a saver, you know.' **1925** —— *Boy from Bullarah* 144 Terry . . ventured to speak to Punter. 'Have a saver on mine!' **1958** G. Casey *Snowball* 168 A lot of people who had bet on Benny—and made sure of a saver on the Negro—put on a few shillings more at the ringside. **1983** *Sydney Morning Herald* 12 Mar. 13/8 The electorate clearly has had 'a saver' on the Democrats and the Senate. While giving the Labor Party a clear mandate to govern in the House of Representatives, voters have left 'the minders' in control in the Senate, just in case the Government should get out of line.

sawn. Abbrev. of 'sawney' a simpleton.

1953 K. Tennant *Joyful Condemned* 145 Get back, or I'll bung a rock at you. I'm always getting into trouble through sawns. **1961** *Bulletin* (Sydney) 15 Mar. 6/1 During the war, when overcrowding at Parramatta became a scandal . . younger, meeker girls who were there as a result of wretched home and living conditions were contemptuously termed 'sawns'.

saw shark. [See quot. 1974.] A shark of the fam. Pristiophoridae of s. Aust. and elsewhere.

1882 J.E. TENISON-WOODS *Fish & Fisheries N.S.W.* 98 The saw-shark must not be confounded with saw-fish, as their gill-openings are lateral not underneath. **1906** D.G. STEAD *Fishes of Aust.* 236 The Little Saw-Shark . . is a small species, having a somewhat flattened body, and attaining a length of about 4 feet. **1936** N. CALDWELL *Fangs of Sea* 210 A large saw-like object popped out of the water. . . 'Phew! . . The b-- is a saw shark.' **1944** J. DEVANNY *By Tropic Sea & Jungle* 7 The biggest saw shark he had taken had been sixteen feet. **1961** E.S. HERALD *Living Fishes of World* 49 (OEDS) The four known species of saw sharks have small pectoral fins with the gill openings just ahead of these fins. **1974** T.D. SCOTT et al. *Marine & Freshwater Fishes S.A.* 42 The Saw Sharks form an unusual group of fishes which are not uncommon in southern Australian waters. . . They are recognized readily by the long produced and flattened snout, armed with a row of teeth on each side. This formidable weapon is used in defence, or when in search of prey.

scabbery. The betrayal of one's fellow workers; scab workers collectively.

1918 B. KENNEDY *Silver, Sin, & Sixpenny Ale* 160 One militant denounced the local Trades and Labor Council as . . 'born in Scabbery'. **1935** *Red Star* (Perth) 21 June 3/3 The Goldfields Communists will go on maintaining their indifference to one who adds scabbery on the police force to his other 'charming' habits. **1939** E.H. LANE *Dawn to Dusk* 25 Scabbery was exalted by the blatant capitalist press as the sacred duty of every freedom-loving Australian worker. **1963** X. HERBERT *Disturbing Element* 195 Remindful of that shameful era of scabbery.

scabby, *a.* Non-union.

1892 *Bulletin* (Sydney) 24 Dec. 22/1 There were eight or ten dashed Chinamen a-shearin' in a row. . . And I left his scabby station at the old jig-jog. **1935** *Red Star* (Perth) 29 Mar. 2/3 The two men . . were more than justified in refusing to pick burr at the scabby rates offered. **1950** K.S. PRICHARD *Winged Seeds* 234 If you put on any scabs, we'll see how many unionists will drink in your scabby pub, Mr Doherty! **1985** J. SCHULTZ *Steel City Blues* 25 In the Combined Mining Unions, the Burragorang Valley is also known as 'scabby valley', the miners not being noted for their industrial militancy.

scalded, *ppl. a.* Of land: bare of vegetation, often because of soil erosion or salination.

1920 J.N. MACINTYRE *White Aust.* 74 It meant that when I opened it up and had the stumps grubbed out, that it would have been a remarkably fast motor track, as miles and miles of it ran over scalded country. **1935** F. BIRTLES *Battle Fronts Outback* 50, I pursued my way over miles of scalded plain—called scalded because the hot sun scalds up all sign of vegetable life. **1939** P. MCGUIRE *Austral. Journey* 335 The saltbush is gone, tracts of scalded earth, stripped down to the clay. **1949** *Bulletin* (Sydney) 2 Feb. 15/3 After grasshopper swarms had laid their eggs on areas of 'scalded plain' great companys of cockatoos were to be seen busily feeding. **1977** *Weekly Times* (Melbourne) 19 Jan. 17/2 Deep gullies and scalded country are evidence of the worst abuses of valuable farming country.

scale, *n. Gold-mining. Obs.* [U.S.: see Mathews *n.*[2] 2.] A flake of gold. Chiefly as **scale gold,** gold found in flakes.

1851 *Empire* (Sydney) 18 Aug. 59/4 The other specimen consisted of scale gold of a deep yellow colour, nearly orange. **1852** *Moreton Bay Free Press* 24 June 3/5 The greater part of the gold was of a nuggety character, but there was also a great number of scales; there were no large nuggets amongst the lot; the colour principally dark, and the gold evidently water-worn. **1852** D. MACKENZIE *Gold Digger* 42 The earth, or bank, on each side of the creek, contains only *scale* gold, that is, small and flattened fragments of it. **1852** J. BONWICK *Notes of Gold Digger* 41 Who does not love to view them, whether in the form of fibres, scales, or nuggets! **1853** J. SHERER *Gold Finder Aust.* 119 We got very small pieces of scale-gold.

scale, *v.* [Perh. transf. use of *scale* to weigh (a jockey): see OED(S *v.*[1] 3 b. but also *v.*[2] 2 c.]

1. *intr.* To avoid paying what is due; *spec.* to avoid paying one's fare. Also *trans.*, to defraud (a person); to ride (a tram, truck, etc.) without paying; to take (a ride) in this way.

1904 *Truth* (Sydney) 7 Aug. 9/5 'Scaling' consists in the bilking of the woman that has agreed to behave unchastely in return for a pecuniary consideration. **1917** C. THACKERAY *Goliath Joe* 87 Wen 'e tried to scale on the tram for a section he bumped a rough guard who knew 'im by name an' repitation an' 'ad 'im prosecuted. **1933** 'TRAMWAY WORKERS' *Shock Brigader* 5 'Phwere's your ticket?' Mick's suspicions were confirmed. The boy opened his hand and exposed sixpence. 'So you were tryin' to scale me, you young varmint.' **1946** F. CLUNE *Try Nothing Twice* 12 The greatest trick was 'scaling' on trams, as there would be no profit if a newsboy had to pay fares. **1953** 'CADDIE' *Caddie* 132 Getting about the streets with snotty noses, and scaling trams. **1968** S. GORE *Holy Smoke* 56 Its no good whipping the cat if a man's such a dill as to come the double on anyone—like tryin' to scale the trammie for your fare—and then gets the mockers put on him. **1972** *Bronze Swagman Bk. Bush Verse* (1973) 38 We poor old sods Scaling trucks on a northbound train. **1984** *Sydney Morning Herald* 7 Jan. 31/4 The tram guards . . were generally much admired by little boys, even though we did our best to outwit them by 'scaling' a ride, crouching unseen on the footboard on the other side of the tram.

2. To depart stealthily or speedily; also with advs. and *trans.*, to absent oneself from.

1917 G.C. COOPER Diary 30 Sept., Scaled Church Parade—got hand dressed. *Ibid.* 30 July, Went to a concert at night (scaled out and nearly got caught) by the Magpies. **1919** C.H. THORP *Handful of Ausseys* 218 A bloke snatches the little 'and-bag uv the madameaselle in front, an' 'e's scalin' off like 'ell down another alley. **1929** *Aussie* (Sydney) Aug. 52/3 When the dressing gong woke me a couple of hours later, Dad had scaled—carpet-bag and all.

scaler. [f. SCALE *v.* 1.] One who 'scales', a cheat.

1915 *Honk* ix. 5 If you wear a sling, people put their arms around you and weep, but if you have a couple of bullets in your liver and nothing to show them you must be a scaler. **1955** N. PULLIAM *I traveled Lonely Land* 386 *Scale*, to cheat. *Scale a rattler*, to go on board a train without paying. *Scaler*, a person who does those things. **1981** G. CROSS *George & Widda-Woman* 50 The Tramway is very down on scalers, and brings a court action whenever possible . . against people who try to swindle His Majesty's government.

scalie. Also **scaly.** [f. *scale* a weighing machine + -Y.] An official who checks the weight of the load carried by a road transport vehicle. Also **scalie man.**

1976 *Truckin' Life* I. iii. 47 His parting words to Harry left no doubt that the scalies would be waiting for him at the end of the tough road. **1977** *Lights on Hill* 13 Dodge the weights and measure boys, yeah, dodge those scaly men. **1978** *Truckin' Life* II. vii. 32 Did you ever slug it out with a Scalie, Or bleech your logbook up to make times fit? **1984** *Bulletin* (Sydney) 7 Aug. 68/1 The long run up the Newell Highway would . . take no more than 24 hours non-stop—even allowing for detours through the back roads to avoid the 'scalies' who man the highway truck-weight checking stations.

scalp. [U.S.: see OEDS *sb.*[1] 2 c.] Used *attrib.* to designate the scalp of an animal retained as evidence of its death, usu. in order to obtain a bounty.

1891 H.W. HARRIS *Shearers or Shorn* 26 One young Queenslander who has lived the greater portion of his life in the bush, has worked as a shearer, drover, brumby hunter, and scalp collector. **1918** *Bulletin* (Sydney) 10 Oct. 24/1 To fight the dingo Queensland Government is raising the scalp bonus from 5s. to £1. **1930** *Ibid.* 14 May 21/4 Dalby (Q.) used to have a periodical 'scalp day'. Animals regarded by farmers as pests were being slaughtered in great numbers, and the officials found it convenient to set apart a day to receive the scalps. **1935** W. GRAY *Days & Nights in Bush* 33 Took the scalp up to the Police Station for the certificate for the Government scalp money for wild dogs. **1950** G.M. FARWELL *Land of Mirage* 43 No one has ever reckoned the cost of rabbit fencing, nor of bounties, bonuses, scalp money paid to rabbit trappers.

Hence **scalper** *n.*

1897 *Western Champion* (Barcaldine) 12 Oct. 3/3 There is a great commotion amongst the scalpers owing to the reduction in price for kangaroo scalps. **1898** *Ibid.* 25 Jan. 7/4 Richard Eades, a scalper. **1906** *Bulletin* (Sydney) 21 June 17/2 Two scalpers entered a liquor house in Springsure (C.Q.), ordered two pints, and passed a dingo scalp over the bar in payment. Mrs Public-house . . handed over as change three wallaby scalps. **1919** *Smith's Weekly* (Sydney) 26 July 4/3, I was a fortnight in a Maranoa scalper's camp.

scaly, var. SCALIE.

scaly-breasted lorikeet. The lorikeet of e. Aust. *Trichoglossus chlorolepidotus*, having green plumage (see quot. 1976) with bright orange-red underwings, and often occurring in flocks with the *rainbow lorikeet* (see RAINBOW 2). Also **scaly-breasted parrot,** and *abbrev.* as **scaly-breast.**

1843 J. GOULD *Birds of Aust.* (1848) V. Pl. 50, The Scaly-breasted Lorikeet breeds in all the large *Eucalypti* near Maitland on the Hunter. **1929** A.H. CHISHOLM *Birds & Green Places* 209 Just a sprinkling of the larger 'blueys' (rainbow lorikeets) and 'greenies' (scaly-breasts). **1945** C. BARRETT *Austral. Bird Life* 76 The scaly-breasted parrot (*T[richoglossus] chlorolepidotus*) bears a bad name among orchardists. **1976** *Reader's Digest Compl. Bk. Austral. Birds* 261 'Scaly-breasted' aptly describes this bird, which has yellow breast feathers broadly edged with green that look like scales. . . Scaly-breasted lorikeets can be identified in flight by their conspicuous orange-red underwing-coverts and green head. **1986** *Your Garden* May 59 (*caption*) These two Scaly-breasted Lorikeets seem a contented pair while partaking of a snack.

scarf, *v.* [Prob. var. of CARF, infl. by *scarf* to cut a scarf-joint, but see OED(S *scarf, sb.*[5] and *v.*[3]] *trans.* To cut a scarf in (a tree trunk). Also as *vbl. n.*

[N.Z. **1899** J. BELL *Shadow of Bush* 83 The smaller trees . . had been 'scarfed', or cut partly through in readiness, and skilfully, so that each, when struck, might again in its turn strike and bring down another.] **1909** *Bulletin* (Sydney) 26 Aug. 15/2 The judgment is required, in the first place to sufficiently kerf (why do bushmen use the carpenter's term 'scarf'?) the front tree or trees. **1916** *Ibid.* 4 May 22/3 Tassy bushmen of 30 years ago always spoke of 'carfing' a tree, the cut being called front or back carf. The majority of bushmen . . on the mainland . . used the word 'scarf', which . . I took to be correct and smiled at the Speck splitters' corruption of the term. But . . I found 'kerf' to be the English word for cut by axe or saw. . . 'Scarf' is correct when applied to carpenters' cutting for *joining* timber. **1938** F. RATCLIFFE *Flying Fox & Drifting Sand* 102 The two fallers then took up their positions . . and the process of 'scarfing' began. . . The 'scarf' penetrated about half-way to the centre.

scarlet, *a.* Used as a distinguishing epithet in the names of flora and fauna: **scarlet-chested** (or **-breasted) parrot,** the parrot *Neophema splendida* of drier s. Aust.; formerly also **scarlet-chested grass parakeet** (or **grass parrot**); **gum,** either of two small to medium trees of the genus *Eucalyptus* (fam. Myrtaceae), *E. phoenicea* of n. Aust. and *E. ficifolia* (see FLOWERING GUM), cultivated for their showy clusters of red to orange flowers; also **scarlet flowering gum; honeyeater,** the honeyeater *Myzomela sanguinolenta* of e. Aust. and elsewhere, the mature male having predom. scarlet plumage; see also *blood-bird* BLOOD; formerly also **sanguineous honeyeater; robin,** the small bird *Petroica multicolor* of s. Aust. incl. Tas., the mature male having black and white plumage with a scarlet breast; see also ROBIN, ROBIN REDBREAST 1; also, esp. formerly, **scarlet-breasted robin.**

1822 [**scarlet-chested parrot**] J. LATHAM *Gen. Hist. Birds* II. 121 *Scarlet-breasted parrot.* Length fifteen inches. Bill red . . chin and throat yellow, the latter bounded on the breast by a broad scarlet band. . . Inhabits New-Holland. **1900** A.J. CAMPBELL *Nests & Eggs Austral. Birds* 654 (*heading*) Scarlet-chested Grass Parrakeet. **1913** *Emu* XII. Suppl. 54 *Euphema splendida* . . Scarlet-chested Grass-Parrot. . . *Range*: New South Wales, Victoria, S.

and W. Australia. **1931** N.W. CAYLEY *What Bird is That?* 152 Scarlet-chested Parrot... Rarely recorded, then only as isolated pairs. **1976** *Reader's Digest Compl. Bk. Austral. Birds* 283 Only the male scarlet-breasted parrot has a scarlet breast; the female's breast is green. **1982** R. ELLIS *Bush Safari* 27 A small bright green parrot with a brilliant scarlet front suddenly fluttered into our camp under the gums... I realised I had seen my first Scarlet-chested Parrot, a species considered rare. **1880** [**scarlet gum**] *Argus* (Melbourne) 21 Jan. 7/1 The flame tree of Illawarra and northern New South Wales—Brachychiton acerifolium—is very beautiful when in flower; but it is not equal to the splendour of the scarlet flowering gum. **1912** *Bulletin* (Sydney) 25 Jan. 14/3 The sugar gums are now between 18 in. and 2 ft. above the ground, and the scarlet gums and wattles more than half as high. **1947** W.A.W. DE BEUZEVILLE *Austral. Trees for Austral. Planting* 166 Scarlet Gum (*Euc. ficifolia*). This is an extremely ornamental plant when in bloom, producing freely bunches of very striking scarlet to flame coloured blossoms, very attractive in appearance. **1981** Q. WILD *Honey Wind* 2 She admired the Scarlet Gum, Europeans had named after the mythical Phoenix bird, with its floral balls of orange red, the yellowish-brown rough bark of the trunk and the smooth reddish branches. **1985** *Austral. Women's Weekly* (Sydney) Jan. 154 Like the W.A. Scarlet Gum (*E. ficifolia*), the sought-after colour is red, but pink or white forms are also possible from seed. [**1801 scarlet honeyeater:** J. LATHAM *Gen. Synopsis Birds* Suppl. II. 167 *Sanguineous creeper*... All the upper parts of the bird crimson.. with a few irregular large black spots.] **1822** —— *Gen. Hist. Birds* IV. 201 *Sanguineous honey-eater*.. inhabits New South Wales; common in the neighbourhood of the River Nepean, among bushes and thick woods. **1843** J. GOULD *Birds of Aust.* (1848) IV. Pl. 63, In size it [*sc.* the Red-headed Honey-eater] rather exceeds the common Sanguineous Honey-eater. **1904** *Emu* III. 235 In an orchard close by.. the small Sanguineous Honey-eaters (*Myzomela sanguinolenta*) waged ceaseless war on the ripe figs. **1917** *Bulletin* (Sydney) 5 July 24/1 The rare blood-bird, which science clumsily names sanguineous honeyeater. **1929** A.H. CHISHOLM *Birds & Green Places* 159 The bright plumage and bright voice of.. the scarlet honeyeater or 'blood-bird'. **1964** M. SHARLAND *Territory of Birds* 137 The Scarlet Honeyeater.. is well known among shrubs in suburban gardens and along coastal rivers. **1984** M. BLAKERS et al. *Atlas Austral. Birds* 568 The Scarlet Honeyeater lives in Sulawesi, New Caledonia and in Australia. **1842** [**scarlet robin**] J. GOULD *Birds of Aust.* (1848) III. Pl. 3, *Petroica multicolor*.. Scarlet-breasted Robin. **1903** *Emu* II. 163 Scarlet-breasted Robin.. occur in the forest. **1922** L.G. CHANDLER *Bush Charms* 109 Its [*sc.* the Hooded Robin's] cup-shaped nest is similar in many ways to that of the Scarlet-breasted Robin. **1945** C. BARRETT *Austral. Bird Life* 174 The scarlet robin (*Petroica multicolor*) is distributed over the southern parts of Australia, and occurs in Tasmania too. **1978** B.P. MOORE *Life on Forty Acres* 95 Scarlet Robins.. with bright red breasts in true robin fashion, are at best locally in early spring.

scarp, *v. intr.* Abbrev. of 'scarper', to depart hastily.

1910 L. ESSON *Woman Tamer* (1976) 82 *Katie*:.. Get! *Chopsey*: Gaud struth Katie... *Katie*:.. Scarp off! **1941** *Ack Ack News* (Melbourne) Nov. 4 A semi-nude figure, draped only in a towel.. was seen scarping in the direction of the predictor pit at terrific speed. **1970** J.S. GUNN in W.S. Ramson *Eng. Transported* 53 *Scarp*, 'run'.

scarver, *v. Obs.* [Alteration of *scarper* to depart hastily.] *intr.* See quot. 1905.

1905 *Bulletin* (Sydney) 24 Oct. 14/3 *Scarver*, to flit from town secretly, leaving sorrowing creditors behind... 'Leaving a dog tied up' refers to the debts left by the 'scarverer'.

scatter. [Spec. use of *scatter* a dispersion.] In the phr. **to get a scatter on,** to lose touch with someone.

1949 I.L. IDRIESS *One Wet Season* 269 We'd got a scatter on and.. didn't hear of the wedding until too late to send a present. **1978** D. STUART *Wedgetail View* 29 Never seen ole John again. Heard of him once in a while, but y' know how it is; a bloke gets an awful scatter on across the face o' the country over the years.

scheme. *W.A.* Used *attrib.* to designate water supplied to arid inland areas by pipeline from Mundaring Weir, on the Helena River near Perth. Also *absol.*

1915 J.P. BOURKE *Off Bluebush* 81 And thoughts tramp back where I lost the track Of a 'leader' of five-ounce dirt, Before I knelt with a 'Scheme'-cleansed pelt At the shrine of a laundried [*sic*] shirt! **1938** C.P. CONIGRAVE *Walk-About* 180 Before 1938 Norseman was to be on 'scheme' water which fact will be further evidence of the wonder of the scheme whereby water is pumped from the Darling Ranges. **1950** G.S. CASEY *City of Men* 151 She interrupted Joseph and dragged her children off to the bathroom, but they were no longer enthusiastic about it. After all, she thought unhappily, it was only a Scheme-water shower she had to offer.

scheisser, var. SHICER.

schleinter, schlenter, var. SLANTER.

schnapper, var. SNAPPER.

school.

1. In the phr. **School of Arts,** an institution founded in many centres during the nineteenth century which provided a library and arranged lectures, etc., for the local public.

1834 J.D. LANG *Hist. & Statistical Acct. N.S.W.* I. 178 We may hail the present establishment of a 'Mechanics' School of Arts' in Sydney as opening altogether a new era in the history of the colony. **1844** *Colonial Lit. Jrnl.* 4 July 26/1 The existence of such a society as the School of Arts was not anticipated. ***c* 1877** W. ARCHER in R. Stanley *Tourist to Antipodes* (1977) 24 This 'School of Arts' is an unfailing institution in colonial towns. Why it is called a School of Arts I cannot tell, unless it be on the *lucus a non lucendo* principle, for it is not a school and it has no discernible connection with any form of art. It is in short a reading room, with a small library attached, supported partly by Government, I understand, and partly by the subscriptions of its members. **1904** *Bulletin* (Sydney) 7 July 16/4 In some places where most of the dwellings are, at least, respectable, the 'school of arts' is a tumble-down hovel. **1913** *Ibid.* 25 Dec. 22/3 Arrived in a cow locality a fortnight prior to the annual meeting of subscribers to the School of Arts. **1935** MUNN & PITT *Austral. Libraries* 31 In Newcastle and Sydney.. the schools of art own business sites and derive substantial rental from their buildings. **1948** R. RAVEN-HART *Canoe in Aust.* 13 The oddly-named 'Mechanics Institute' or 'School of Arts', used mainly for dances and meetings though perhaps containing also a library. **1957** R.S. PORTEOUS *Brigalow* 17 Why these barren halls were termed 'School of Arts' was a mystery I had never been able to solve, for they rarely contained either a book or a picture of any sort. **1983** C. BINGHAM *Beckoning Horizon* 55 A town in rural Queensland was prouder of its status when it had a 'School of Arts', but in most places this was a vainglorious description of the local hall for meetings concerts and dancing, with perhaps a room or annexe containing a few shelves of books, disordered and ancient.

2. School of the Air, a government-funded educational program which uses a two-way radio communication system to enable children in remote areas to participate in 'classroom' activities for part of each day.

1950 *Centralian Advocate* (Alice Springs) 8 Sept. 1/1 It has been learned that the scheme envisages a broadcast direct from Alice Springs in the form of a 'School of the Air' catering for a normal curriculum. **1953** *S.-W. Pacific* (Dept. of Information) xxx. 16/1 The School of the Air doesn't supplant correspondence lessons. It augments them. **1960** *Bulletin* (Sydney) 17 Feb. 19/1 Queensland's first School of the Air, operating one hour daily from the Cloncurry flying-doctor base, got away to a bad start. **1967** M. SELLARS *Carramar* 49 Now the outback children go to school 'on the air'... They send their homework for checking in to the Correspondence School, which works in conjunction with the school of the air. **1968** G. FULLBROOK *House called Kangaroo* 11 The Headquarters of the School of the Air is here in Adelaide... They broadcast lessons to the children living on the cattle and sheep stations or any other isolated area. **1983** *Bicentenary '88* (Austral. Bicentennial Authority) Nov. 11/1 With the help of the Katherine School of the Air, the radio signal 'Calling all Penguins' broke the air-waves on 17 May this year.

3. *transf.* A group of people assembled for the purpose of playing a gambling game, esp. TWO-UP *n.*; the place where such an assembly takes place; *gaffing school*, see GAFF *v.*

1812 J.H. VAUX *Mem.* (1819) II. 203 *School*, a party of persons met together for the purpose of gambling. **1891** 'SMILER' *Wanderings Simple Child* (ed. 3) 10 As I pushed my way through the throng, I at once perceived that 'school' was in. **1896** *Worker* (Sydney) 4 July 4/1 Charlie is 'ringmaster' (I believe that's the correct title, the 'two-up' ain't a pet vice of mine) of the Boulder 'School'. **1915** A. WRIGHT *Sport from Hollowlog Flat* 13 He tried his fortune at the sordid game of 'two-up', and with success, for he came forth from the 'school' richer to the extent of a tenner. **1930** HIVES & LUMLEY *Jrnl. of Jackaroo* 8 On Sunday mornings there would be a 'school' in the back yard of the hotel, when the game of 'heading them' would be indulged in for high stakes, the punters backing their favourites for large sums. **1950** H.C. WELLS *Earth cries Out* 80 'Had a good win at the 'school' last Sunday.'.. 'I've never played two-up in my life.' **1973** J. POWERS *Last of Knucklemen* (1974) 64 (Waving his winnings with disgust) I'm gonna throw up! In a city school I'd be rakin' in thousands.

schoolie, *n.*[1] Also **schooley.** [f. *school(teacher* + -Y.] A schoolteacher.

1889 H. EGBERT *Pretty Cockey* 57 The rest addressed him sometimes as 'Schoolmaster', sometimes as 'Schooley'. **1895** *Western Champion* (Barcaldine) 5 Nov. 13/1 There is so much.. even in this advanced and excellent curriculum of ours—that has to be 'crammed in', and there is the *bête noir* of the 'schooley's' life. **1914** C. MACKNESS *Gem of Flat* 20 The cracked old schoolie we used to have. **1918** *Truth* (Sydney) 6 Oct. 7/7 Your correspondent seems to think that because Schoolie gets a rise in screw and the village John Hop does not also get a rise, that Schoolie's rise must be unpatriotic. **1944** *Bulletin* (Sydney) 20 Dec. 13/4 The few local kids grew up until, except for the schoolie's tribe, there was on'y my youngest at the school. **1957** D.D. LADDS *We have our Dreams* 14 'What old Masters? Schoolies?'.. 'Don't be h'ignorant, Joe. Old Masters were the fellers who used to paint pitchers costing a thousand pounds!' **1967** D. HORNE *Educ. Young Donald* 22 In the West.. the schoolies *are* invited to the Picnic Races. **1976** *Bronze Swagman Bk. Bush Verse* 32 The schoolie is the one To go to for your paper-work. **1982** R. HALL *Just Relations* 86 She was the last schoolie of Whitey's Fall.

schoolie, *n.*[2] [f. *school* a flock, company (of animals) + -Y.] **a.** SCHOOL SHARK. **b.** A school prawn.

1980 S. SALISBURY et al. *Fishermen's Views* E71 All the sharks and catfish all get into this lukewarm water. Because its [*sic*] only a shark about that long, a schoolie. They won't bite you. **1980** B. SHACKLETON *Karagi* 26 Daylight prawns are light shelled 'schoolies' that run spasmodically soon after sunup.

school shark. [See quot. 1980.] The medium-sized shark *Galeorhinus australis*, abundant in s. Aust., and occurring in New Zealand, an important commercial species.

1852 G.C. MUNDY *Our Antipodes* I. 390 The 'school shark' is dealt with as above. But if the 'grey nurse' or old solitary shark be hooked, the cable is cut. **1881** *Proc. Linnean Soc. N.S.W.* VI. 355 *Galeus australis*.. the '*School Shark*' of the Port Jackson Fishermen. **1936** N. CALDWELL *Fangs of Sea* 160 A small school shark set out after the bait. **1951** T.C. ROUGHLEY *Fish & Fisheries Aust.* 263 The gummy shark was marketed initially for consumption as food in Victoria under the name of 'flake', and this term came later to include the school shark. **1980** ANSELL & PERCY *To fight Wild* 57 The school sharks are genuine sharks, and go around in packs.

schooner. [U.S. *schooner* a tall beer glass: see OED(S *sb.*[2]] A large beer-glass of locally variable capacity; the (measure of) beer contained in such a glass.

1892 *Truth* (Sydney) 8 May 3/6 Maybe you'd like a good schooner, now, wouldn't you? A nice long sleever, hay? **1910** *Ibid.* 25 Dec. 1/4 Whiskies and 'schooners' are to be preferred to Colonial Wine, as sold to Colonial patriots by Dagoes, which is about the only sort of 'Austral Wine' the average Australian has ever known. **1914** A.H. WORTHINGTON *Our Island Captures* 15 Aug. (1919) 6 We were then dismissed for dinner. This proved the proverbial naval midday spread, 'A schooner on the rocks'. **1939** A. GASTON *Coolgardie Gold* 131, I ordered a schooner but.. beer was off.

1948 R. Raven-Hart *Canoe in Aust.* 43, I think it was a 'half-handle' I drank here: in Wagga the size of the glass wanted was a 'schooner'. **1959** D. Hewett *Bobbin Up* 43 There'll be booze tricklin' down the hall, broken schooners and smashed noses. **1962** *N.T. News* (Darwin) 4 Jan. 9/6 Gruiza admitted drinking about a dozen schooners, but said he was not drunk. **1973** F. Moorhouse *Austral. Stories* 19 He's the kind of guy you meet at clubs . . at twelve o'clock slumped over the bar swilling his fifteenth schooner. **1985** *Bulletin* (Sydney) 24 Dec. 62/2 We thought that heroic drinkers drank from the largest glasses—schooners (15 ounces) or pints.

Hence **schoonerful** *n.*

1981 K. Garvey *Rhymes of Ratbag* 76 We start makin' tracks To the village and a schoonerful of two-mile ale.

scissors-grinder. [See quot. 1985.] Restless flycatcher.

1917 [see Restless flycatcher]. **1934** S. King *Molly's Yr. in Camp* 34 Scissors-grinders seemed to be trying over their parts. **1941** *Bulletin* (Sydney) 23 Apr. 16/4 The stormbird . . came winging across the paddock; but his speed was no match for that of the scissors-grinder. **1985** *Austral. Nat. Hist.* Spring 429 The Restless Flycatcher with its whirring, rasping call, which sounds like scissors being sharpened on a grind stone, is often referred to as the Scissors-grinder.

scone /skɒn/, *n.* [Fig. use of *scone* cake: see OEDS *sb.* 3 a. and b.]

1. The head.

[N.Z. **1942** *2nd N.Z. Exped. Force Times* 19 Oct. 5 Don't do your plurry scone, Dig!] **1945** *Atebrin Advocate: Mag. 2/4 Austral. Armoured Regiment* 12 May 3 Pull yer scone in. **1957** D. Whitington *Treasure upon Earth* 79 Neither of you want a crack on the scone. **1962** P.A. Knudsen *Bloodwood Tree* 116 I've had a gutsful. A man'd go off his scone if he stayed with the ol' man. **1968** S. Gore *Holy Smoke* 14 Down he goes, with a lump on his scone like a rockmelon. **1975** 'N. Culotta' *Gone Gougin'* 62 He's not right in the skull. Musta got concussion in that blue he started last night. He's gone in the scone.

2. In the phr. **to go** (someone) **scone-hot,** to attack (someone) with vigour, esp. verbally; to become angry with.

1927 F.C. Biggers *Bat-Eye* 15 Ter see a dinkum parson go a bloke scone 'ot, An' chuck 'im out . . Gawd spare me days! **1938** X. Herbert *Capricornia* 530 Half-caste Shillingsworth goes Copra Co scone-hot! **1944** *Coast to Coast 1943* 116, I don't want Reg going me scone hot because his wife's not capable of looking after herself. **1967** K. Tennant *Tell Morning This* 139 When my big brother Jim come home from work, he went Dad scone hot. **1973** *Bulletin* (Sydney) 6 Jan. 8/2 Instead of the disc jockey patios now adored by the young we could return to 'bonzer, dinkum, cobber, scone hot, [etc.]'. **1981** H. Hannah *Together in Jungle Scrub* 20 One time old Jones sold the last tin of strawberry—his wife went him scone hot!

scone, *v.* [f. Br. dial. *scon* to beat with the flat of the hand: see EDD.] *trans.* To hit.

1948 *Coast to Coast 1947* 187 The bottle broke. Damn! he hadn't meant to scone the bottle first go-off. **1953** T.A.G. Hungerford *Riverslake* 26 He'll scone that galah. **1957** D. Whitington *Treasure upon Earth* 79 'I'd like to see the mug that could scone me,' Mick said belligerently.

scoot. Also **skoot.** [Transf. use of *scoot* to go suddenly.] In the phr. **(up)on the scoot,** engaged in a drinking bout or spree.

1916 *Truth* (Sydney) 29 Oct. 12/2 Elsie Long, a puffeck Lydie, Got upon the scoot one Friday. **1927** K.S. Prichard *Brumby Innes* (1974) 73, I can be a bit of use here, John. . . Look after things when Brum's out musterin' . . or on the skoot. **1940** *Sentry Go* (Keswick) Aug. 8/1 One of the batmen got on the scoot and became thoroughly plastered. **1950** G. Farwell *Surf Music* 49 We'll shout 'em instead. We'll get on the scoot . . and knock smoke out of some poor old coot before the night's out . . and sing and maybe . . we'll wake up sick. **1970** B. Fuller *Nullarbor Story* 12 'Still keen to go off on the scoot?' He climbed out heavily. 'Well, a drink,' he said, and led the way. **1977** F. Daly *From Curtin to Kerr* 94 If a member is going on the scoot for the night he won't tell Annabelle whilst he wouldn't mind if a man knew. **1983** A.F. Howells *Against Stream* 1, I could still afford to lair up a bit, get on the scoot occasionally with my mates, and still have a bob or two.

score, *v.* [Used elsewhere but recorded earliest in Aust.: see OEDS *v.* 16 f.] *intr.* To achieve sexual intercourse with another.

c **1907** W.C. Chandler *Darkest Adelaide* 5 In Flinders street the other night several [prostitutes] were congregated together when one of them was called on one side. . . The following dialogue ensued: He—'Come on. Sling!' She (to her mates)—'Gor' blime have I scored?' Chorus of Shes—'She's never scored to-night, and won't while you keep hanging round.' **1918** C.J. Dennis *Digger Smith* 68 Jim mightn't come back 'ome, yeh know. You 'ave a fly; yeh're sure to score; Besides, all's fair in love an' war. **1971** *Bulletin* (Sydney) 27 Nov. 48/3 Mick Hunter's obsession is to 'score' with a woman. **1978** *Southerly* iii. 268 'You can't seduce that young man. He doesn't know anything about life,' he said. 'You're just jealous because I'm scoring better than you are,' she goaded.

Scotch, *a.* [Spec. use of *Scotch* (supposedly) characteristic of Scotland or its people.] In special collocations: **Scotch coffee,** ersatz coffee (see quots.); **navigation,** see quot. 1907; so, **navigator.**

1836 J.F. O'Connell *Residence Eleven Yrs. New Holland* 47 At dinner they have animal food and vegetables, and at supper '**Scotch coffee**', i.e. burned corn. **1865** J.F. Mortlock *Experiences of Convict* 72 By burning some meal in a shovel, we made 'Scotch coffee', a capital substitute for real Mocha. **1898** G. Dunderdale *Bk. of Bush* 3 The seamen's food on board these transports was bad and scanty, consisting of live biscuit, salt horse, Yankee pork, and Scotch coffee. The Scotch coffee was made by steeping burnt biscuit in boiling water to make it strong. **1903** E. Palmer *Early Days N. Qld.* 178 Very fair coffee was made from the scrapings of the burnt edges of dampers, and was called Scotch coffee. **1904** *Bulletin* (Sydney) 7 Apr. 16/4 In the heart of the Outback, when the tucker-bag gets low . . tea is replaced by 'Scotch coffee', *i.e.*, flour roasted in an oven. **1934** *Ibid.* 14 Feb. 21/2 Scotch coffee . . is flour roasted in the pan—a substitute when the tea bag is empty. **1907** C. MacAlister *Old Pioneering Days* 32 Mr Siggs, also bound to Sydney with a cargo of wool, showed us a better way of running our team than by '**Scotch navigation**' (i.e. brute strength and stupidity). **1903** J. Furphy *Such is Life* 215 Some carriers never learn the great lesson, that to everything there is a time and a season. . . Moreover, the same rule holds fairly well throughout the whole region of industry. But the **Scotch-navigator** can't see it. He is too furiously busy. *Ibid.* 236 Straight into the lion's mouth! Heaven help—but does heaven help the Scotch-navigator?

scotch grey. [Fig. use of the sing. of *Scotch* (for *Scots*) Greys, a cavalry regiment. Cf. the obs. Br. slang use for *louse*.] Hexham grey. Also **Scots grey.**

c **1887** R.G. Gallop In Never Never Land, Huge mosquitoes known here as 'Scotch Greys' or 'Overlanders' added their quota of misery. **1895** A.C. Bicknell *Travel & Adventure Northern Qld.* 39 A large fly known as 'Scots Grey' bit us badly. **1905** J. Furphy *Rigby's Romance* (1946) 41 The Lord He backed up Moses, and sent locusts, an' pleuro, an' Scotch greys, an' all manner o' curses on the country. **1914** H.M. Vaughan *Australasian Wander-Yr.* 270 The horrible Bush Mosquitoes, grey insects of exceptional size and ferocity known as 'Scots Greys'. **1934** Warburton & Robertson *Buffaloes* 29 The mosquitoes acquainted us of their presence. They were mostly the famous Scots Greys; they literally stood on their heads and bored in. **1959** M. Raymond *Smiley roams Road* 165 Scotch Greys—that's what they are. . . This is goin' to be a terrageous night for mozzies.

scotty, *a.* [Fig. use of *scotty* having the temperament of a Scot; used elsewhere but recorded earliest and chiefly in Aust.: see OED(S *a.* b.] Irritable; bad-tempered.

[**1812** J.H. Vaux *Mem.* (1819) II. 203 *Scot*, a person of an irritable temper, who is easily put in a passion.] **1872** 'Demonax' *Mysteries & Miseries* 10 My 'scotty' friend tore his hair and threw his belltopper at the pier-glass. **1896** *Worker* (Sydney) 18 Jan. 1/3 'Don't get scotty, my boy.' . . 'Me, get scotty. I am as cool as a cucumber.' **1903** *Bulletin* (Sydney) 6 June 36/2 Fellows often say things to me they should not say. Don't get 'scotty' with them—the fault is mine. **1912** *Huon Times* (Franklin) 13 Apr. 6/3 He did not always agree with them, and sometimes they got scotty with each other. **1936** M. Franklin *All that Swagger* 334 Uncle William is as scotty as a French hen with her feathers the wrong way. **1948** R.A. Pepperall *Emigrant to Aust.* 96 In Australia people never 'grumble', 'get annoyed', or 'angry'; they 'growl', 'go up in the air', 'fly off the handle' or possibly 'get Scottie'. **1981** P. Radley *Jack Rivers & Me* 169 'I got a pretty scottie teacher, Dad.' 'You're lucky.' 'He means his teacher is a grumpy old bat.' **1982** N. Keesing *Lily on Dustbin* 164 Getting a bit wild was called getting 'scotty'. . . 'Be good now. I'm a bit scotty with you.'

scour. A shed in which wool is scoured. Also *attrib.*

1896 *Worker* (Sydney) 5 Sept. 3/2 The men's only offence was that they welcomed the scour hands, who are standing out against the day wage sought to be introduced by their board. **1898** *Western Champion* (Barcaldine) 11 Jan. 7/5 A mob of 22,000 wethers is to be shorn this week at McLaughlin's scour. **1915** *Pastoral Rev.* 16 Jan. 93 He shore at . . Camoola Park, and also at the West Longreach scour, there being no shearing at Ilfracombe. **1930** E.R. Gribble *Forty Yrs. with Aborigines* 38 At shearing-time forty shearers were employed, besides rouseabouts and scour-men. **1946** J.C. Eastwood *More about Cairns* 31 Accompanied by a young Frenchman, a fellow-worker at the scour, I travelled via Hughenden. **1959** H. Lamond *Sheep Station* 43 Shearing was no trouble; there were scours with shearing sheds at Longreach, Ilfracombe, Barcaldine, Winton, almost any western town which aspired to be a Queen City.

scoured. [Used elsewhere but recorded earliest in Aust.: see OED *scoured, ppl. a.* 2 b.] Abbrev. of 'scoured wool'.

1851 *Empire* (Sydney) 21 Aug. 72/1 *Wool.* A few lots of scoured have been offered during the week. **1874** *Illustr. Sydney News* 22 Aug. 15/3 The object with them has been to solely grow wool for export. . . There was scoured, fleece-washed and in the grease. **1889** *Braidwood Dispatch* 24 Aug. 3/2 *Wool.* I held a most satisfactory sale today offering a good catalogue of both scoured and greasy lots. **1901** *Dalgety's Rev.* 1 Feb. 45 In regard to scoureds the decline [in price] is still greater. **1904** *Shearer* (Sydney) 5 Nov. 4/4 The attendance of buyers was satisfactory, and competition for greasies was keen, but for scoureds the demand was dull. **1920** *Pastoral Rev.* Sept. 687 A few good lines of scoureds have . . been catalogued. **1935** *Ibid.* 16 Jan. 31 The two obvious points taken into consideration by valuers, and which can be more easily assessed from scoureds than from greasies, are those of colour and freedom from vegetable matter. **1960** *Pastoral Rev. & Graziers' Rec.* 18 Mar. 273 Nine bales of scoured sold account Wanora Downs Co. **1977** *Pastoral Rev.* July 212 The market indicator recovered from the end of May low of 297 to 300 cents per kg. clean scoured.

scrammy, *a.* Also **skrammy.** [f. *scram* withered: see OED.] Being or afflicted with a defective hand or arm. Also *absol.* as *n.*

[**1822** *HRA* (1917) 1st Ser. X. 776 He was a little Man, and has a dun or withered Arm. . . A Man, who goes by the name of Scrummy Jack.] **1841** *Port Phillip Patriot* 28 Oct. 2/5 Should the bantling have a 'scrammy' hand, he is the property of the contracted gentleman. **1895** G. Ranken *Windabyne* 8 One was 'Skrammy', or one-armed; another was 'Bothered' or deaf. **1898** *Bulletin* (Sydney) 21 May 14/1 At a woolshed, near Condoblin . . a traveller who 'chucked a scrammy' (pretended to have paralysed arms) . . 'had' the sympathising shearers to the extent of £8.

scrape, *v. intr.* To engage in sexual intercourse. Also *trans.*, to have intercourse with (someone), and as *n.*

1955 *Meanjin* 169 Larrian was ready to scrape with the whitefellers. **1969** O. White *Under Iron Rainbow* 64 She said she didn't mind lying down for white men at three dollars a time. . . All the girls got scraped by someone. . . She'd give the old sergeant a scrape for free and he'd make things easy for her while she was in the lock-up. **1975** R. Macklin *Queenslander* 43 It was fascinating the number of sexy words in the language, words people used every day without thinking about it.

. . Sometimes in a bus he would tune in to other people's conversations. . . Two men: ' . . we rolled her over on the beach and started scraping.'

scratch, *v.*

1. *Obs.* In the phr. **to scratch** (someone's) **back,** to flog (someone).

1858 A. HARRIS *Secrets* (1961) 109 None of the other magistrates dared say no when D'arcy Wentworth said yes. 'Ha!' says the old doctor . . 'not a word out of your head sir. I'll have your back scratched sir, three times a week. . . Two hundred lashes!' **1882** *Austral. Stories* 88 If a cove does get his back scratched now and then, it's easier to stand it with a full belly not an empty one.

2. *trans.* To mine (an area) for gold. Also *intr.* See also *tin-scratching* TIN *n.*[1] 2 a.

1881 W. FEILDING *Austral. Trans-Continental Railway* 45 This mine is about 10 miles from the township, and there are two other reefs which have been 'scratched' close by. **1941** D. O'CALLAGHAN *Long Life Reminisc.* 55 After gully scratching around Coolgardie . . I decided to try around Kalgoorlie. **1971** *Island Authors* 76 He was always rootin' around the other blokes' gear while they were out scratching, trying to find out where they hid their bottles of gold.

3. [Also Br. dial. and U.S.: see EDD *v.* 3 and OEDS *v.* 5 c.] To move; to travel, esp. in the phr. **to scratch (the) gravel.**

1888 'R. BOLDREWOOD' *Robbery under Arms* (1937) 192, I runs his horses up into a yard nigh the angle of his outside paddock and collars this little 'oss, and lets old Johnny go in hobbles. My word, this cove can scratch! **1902** *Bulletin* (Sydney) 6 Dec. 16/3 Some of the far-back pastoralists—who have sheep agisting at several widely-separated places—have to 'scratch gravel' now-a-days to inspect their flocks. One man in the Gulf country coached 950 miles . . and rode 550 . . to see how his much-divided herd was getting on. **1912** 'IRONBARK' *Ironbark Splinters* 18 And assisted in the chase When they had to 'scratch the gravel' for their grub. **1913** G. HERVEY *Australs. Yet* 28 Dig your claws in, scratch grim gravel—make the chips and splinters travel. **1940** W. HATFIELD *Into (Great?) Unfenced* 67 Gawd, but she can scratch gravel! I thought *I* could move a bit!

4. To accept (someone's) resignation. Usu. with **off.**

1915 *Bulletin* (Sydney) 9 Dec. 22/1 Hopping out of the 'gutter' the coot snapped out at him, 'Write it out'. . . The coot's mate . . drawled, 'Scratch me off, too.' **1916** *Ibid.* 6 July 24/1 Here's how they fling him their resignations: 'Write mine out', 'Scratch me off' [etc.]. **1958** *Ibid.* 11 June 19/1 He may demand that the said boss give him his time. Scratch him off, or do various things with the job. **1982** LOWENSTEIN & HILLS *Under Hook* 130 So the Federation bloke says, 'Who's me mate?' I said, 'Him.' The Federation bloke said, 'No, scratch me,' and the other bloke said, 'Scratch me too,' so they both went. They just wouldn't work with each other.

scratcher. One who cultivates the land or engages in surface mining. See also *tin scratcher* TIN *n.*[1] 2 a.

1905 *Truth* (Sydney) 19 Mar. 1/8 The outback ground scratcher is a sadly irreligious person. **1910** *Bulletin* (Sydney) 28 Apr. 14/1 He was living under a bark roof with two Chows who worked his claim. One night the . . tin scratchers asked the Baron to sing. He did. . . The scratchers applauded. **1914** *Register* (Adelaide) 30 July 8/7 Sometimes the gleaning tots up to £100, which is spent in the acquisition of horses, sulkies, spring-carts, rifles, and bikes, to the envy of a lot of old 'scratchers'. **1944** J. DEVANNY *By Tropic Sea & Jungle* 212 The gouger or scratcher goes into gullies or deposits that have been found by the prospector and looks for new patches of ore that have been overlooked. **1978** D. LAVERS *Vet in Clouds* 244 Bill, an agate and topas 'scratcher', had spent years picking over the arid, but mineral-rich wastes of the outback.

screamer. In the collocation **two pot (middy, pint, schooner) screamer,** one who has a very low tolerance of alcohol.

1959 D. HEWETT *Bobbin Up* 21 Look at Lou. She's a two-pot screamer, always 'as been. **1967** *Kings Cross Whisper* (Sydney) xli. 4/5 *Two schooner screamer*, a pest who cannot hold liquor. **1967** F.R. POWER *Stranger at Door* 99 The notorious 'two-pot screamers'—those who show abnormal reactions to small quantities of liquor—regardless of actual tolerance. **1967** J. WYNNUM *I'm Jack, all Right* 25 Our Cocky is a two pint screamer. **1972** *Bulletin* (Sydney) 3 June 67/1 Sefton said she'd become a two middy screamer. He said when she had a few drinks she began to shout and tried to dominate the conversation. **1977** R. MACKLIN *Paper Castle* 67 It wasn't even as though he was a good drinker. . . Duncan was becoming the original two-pot screamer. **1981** G. HUTCHINSON *No Room for Dreamers* 10 And there's no room for poofters or two-pot screamers And there's no room for bludgers—and no room for dreamers.

screaming-woman bird. [See quot. 1958.] *Barking owl*, see BARKING; (occas.) any of several other nocturnal birds to which a screaming call has been attributed.

1958 N.W. CAYLEY *What Bird is That?* (rev. ed.) 40 Barking Owl. . . It is believed to utter appalling nocturnal screams—calls that have caused their author to be termed Screaming-woman Bird and Murder-bird; these cries were formerly ascribed to the Powerful Owl. **1961** *Bulletin* (Sydney) 19 Apr. 28/3 Hearing what I swore was the call of the Screaming-woman Bird (tawny frogmouth), I went out into the orchard to investigate. For frogmouths never scream in the daytime. **1965** *Austral. Encycl.* VIII. 45 Screaming-woman bird. . . It has latterly been established that the author of the screams is . . the winking or barking owl.

screen door. A door fitted with a *fly screen* (see FLY *n.*[1] 1).

1969 *Meanjin* 234, I had raised the venetians, and left the screen door open. **1984** O. MASTERS *Loving Daughters* 96 The kitchen had a screen door to keep out the flies.

screw, *n.*

1. *Obs.* Abbrev. of SCREW-PRESS.

1893 *Bulletin* (Sydney) 29 July 17/1 An' they never ask you whether There is room enough to stand in, or a blessed breath o' air When your layin' on the screw When your haulin' on the screw.

2. [Used elsewhere but recorded earliest in Aust.: see OEDS *sb.*[1] 16.] A look; esp. in the phr. **to have a screw.**

***c* 1907** W.C. CHANDLER *Darkest Adelaide* 20 My heart did not pit-a-pat extra much after I got a screw of her phizog. If the back view was attractive, the face was absolutely repulsive, for the whilom charmer turned out to be one of the ugliest old battlers I ever struck. **1917** C. DREW *Reminisc. D. Gilbert* 52 I've just been down having a screw at that snake. **1929** *Bulletin* (Sydney) 2 Jan. 20/1 Did the blankers see you comin'? Was there anyone about? 'Ave a screw around the corner while I get a bottle out. **1943** *Ibid.* 8 Dec. 12/2 A tall bloke in a striped sweater comes up, takes a screw at the bottle an' starts goin' lemons because he was wantin' gin. **1951** R.H. WHITECROSS *Slaves* 232 You're the smallest bird around here. Come over to me and I'll hoist you up to the ventilator to have a screw around.

screw, *v.*

1. *Obs. trans. Shearing.* To compress (bales of wool) in a SCREW-PRESS.

1851 *Guardian* (Hobart) 15 Oct. 3/2 The Captain of the *Marmion* had to come from Launceston to Hobart Town to employ men to screw his wool. **1892** *Bulletin* (Sydney) 19 Nov. 19/1 Fact, there ain't no mortal man can beat a stevedore to swear, But its screwing wool in summer or its stowing frozen meat An' the stevedore must yacker for the bit he gets to eat.

2. [As for SCREW *n.* 2: see OEDS *v.* 13.] *intr.* To look. Also *trans.*

1917 A.L. BREWER *'Gators' Euchre* 42 'E stood in me blanky cowyard, Surrounded be cows untold. 'E screwed at me blanky milker—Poor cow!—an' 'is feet froze cold. **1922** 'J. NORTH' *Black Opal* 132 From the way he was screwin' her phiz. **1938** *Bulletin* (Sydney) 19 Jan. 20/1 I've bin babblin' for fifty-four years, Cookin' all sorts o' scran—yairs, from wombats to steers; A slush-lamp did *me* when I wanted to screw in th' oven.

screwed, *ppl. a.* [Prob. spec. use of *screwed* awry, contorted: see OED *ppl. a.* 4 but also *screw* a nag (OED *sb.*[1] 17).] Of a horse: irrevocably worn out.

1872 G.S. BADEN-POWELL *New Homes for Old Country* 202 The greater proportion of . . wild horses are worthless; a large number of them being more or less 'screwed'. **1888** *Centennial Mag.* (Sydney) 68 When he was broken down with hard work, 'screwed', as you boys would say. **1891** *Bulletin* (Sydney) 20 June 24/1, I cast one look at the poor old gray; Weary and battered and screwed, of course.

screw pine. Any of several trees of the genus *Pandanus* (fam. Pandanaceae), of W.A., N.T., Qld., N.S.W., and the Old World tropics, yielding edible pulp and nuts. Also **screw palm.**

1829 R. MUDIE *Picture of Aust.* 128 The farinaceous seeds of the screw-pine (*pandanus spiralis, Br.*) and of several cone-bearing trees, are occasionally bruised and eaten by the natives. **1855** J. BONWICK *Geogr. Aust. & N.Z.* (ed. 3) 202 The Pandanus or Screw-palm grows near the sea, and has clusters of red pulpy fruit. **1865** G.F. ANGAS *Aust.* 59 To the north, the pulpy rind of the *pandanus*, or screw-pine . . used as food by these wandering people. **1882** W. SOWDEN *N.T. as it Is* 34 On the creeks' banks grow, besides bright hibiscus, numerous screw-palm and a thick grove of tall bamboo. **1907** A. MACDONALD *In Land of Pearl & Gold* 64 We soon rounded them into a clump of screw pines. **1928** G.H. WILKINS *Undiscovered Aust.* 58 There could be seen some tall 'cabbage-tree' palms and considerable numbers of screw palms or pandanus. **1946** D. BARR *Warrigal Joe* 18 The country was rocky and dodging screw-pines and gum trees no easy job. **1951** E. HILL *Territory* 18 By July . . undergrowth has withered . . leaving the screwy screw-palms burnt black, like warriors on a walkabout in the Scrub. **1967** V.G.C. NORWOOD *Long Haul* 77 Bushy pandanus palms, sometimes called 'screw' palms because of the spiral arrangement of the leaves. **1970** J.V. MARSHALL *Walk to Hills of Dreamtime* 155 *Pandanus*, tropical palm-like tree, also known as the *Screw Pine* from the likeness of its fruit cones to a thin pineapple; it has stilt roots and angular branches carrying tufts of long narrow leaves.

screw-press. *Shearing. Obs.* A machine in which pressure is applied (to a bale of wool) by means of a screw.

1843 *Colonial Observer* (Sydney) 3 May 993/1 The mortgages it held should be foreclosed and the Directors subjected, like their own woolpacks, to the screw-press. **1853** MOSSMAN & BANISTER *Aust. Visited & Re-visited* 77 A powerful screw-press for packing the wool into bales. **1980** P. FREEMAN *Woolshed* 40 The screw press required two men to push a lever around the wool box 150 times, taking 30 minutes.

scribbly gum. [f. *scribbly* (see quot. 1963) + GUM *n.* 1.] Any of several smooth-barked trees of the genus *Eucalyptus* (fam. Myrtaceae) having characteristic scribbles on the bark, formed by the burrowing larvae of the scribbly gum moth, *Ogmograptus scribula*, incl. *E. haemastoma, E. racemosa, E. rossii, E. sclerophylla*, and *E. signata*, some of which are also known as SNAPPY GUM; the wood of the tree.

1902 *Proc. Linnean Soc. N.S.W.* XXVII. 568 *E. coriacea* . . shares with some other trees the names of White Gum, Cabbage Gum, and Scribbly Gum. **1926** *Qld. Agric. Jrnl.* XXV. 434 The lighter, softer gum tree woods such as Flooded and Scribbly Gums. **1935** DAVISON & NICHOLLS *Blue Coast Caravan* 176 The blackbutt accompanied our way . . then scribbly-gum took its place. **1951** *Bulletin* (Sydney) 28 Nov. 13/3 I'm settled amongst some tea-tree near a scribbly gum in which my camera is trained on the nesting hollow of a rosella. **1963** C. BURGESS *Blue Mountain Gums* 54 *'Scribbly gum'*. . . The trunk is invariably marked with the 'scribbles' of an insect which burrows between the layers of bark, the scribbles appearing on the new bark as the old flakes off. **1981** A. WILKINSON *Up Country* 166 Supper bubbles away in our two blackened billies over a small fire of aromatic red river and scribbly gum.

scroucher /ˈskraʊtʃə/. Also **scrousher, scrowcher.** [Perh. altered form of Br. dial. *scringer* 'a person who pries about, looking out for trifles', *skreenger* 'a person of energetic character; esp. used in a bad sense': see EDD *scringe, v.*[1] and cf. *scrounger* (see OEDS *scrounge, v.*[1]).] A derogatory term for a person. Cf. BLUDGER 2 a. Also *attrib.*

1901 *Truth* (Sydney) 22 Sept. 1/3 Some of the scroucher toffs of Sydney, both male and female, treat decent tramguards in a dirty, snobbish manner. **1902**

Ibid. 11 May 5/1 If Australian girls have the slightest respect for themselves, or any thought for the future, they will shun the unclean, brutal, khaki-clad scrouchers as they would the plague. **1903** *Ibid.* 20 Dec. 5/3 *(heading)* Black, white and coffee-colored scrouchers . . should be gaoled. **1905** *Shearer* (Sydney) 4 Mar. 3/3 Men for merely displaying sufficient independence of spirit to stand up against the most contemptible of all tyrannies, have been designated 'scrouchers' and 'blacklegs'. **1916** *Truth* (Sydney) 3 Sept. 1/7 Marvellous how it is that good-natured countrymen are so easily imposed upon by scrouchers who ought to be picking oakum. **1921** *Bulletin* (Sydney) 6 Oct. 20/1 In a neighbourhood exclusive, with no scrouchers near to snub. **1966** D. NILAND *Pairs & Loners* 111 Ah, I could puke. That scrousher, that rough-house annie, what's she got to get uppety about? **1982** N. KEESING *Lily on Dustbin* 89 Where is she off to? To a disco. . . Chorus: Don't mix with scrowchers; Remember what the girl did.

scrub, *n.* [Used elsewhere but chiefly Austral. and N.Z.: see OED(S *sb.*[1])]

1. A name given to any of a wide range of generally low and apparently stunted forms of vegetation, often thick, impenetrable, and freq. growing in poor soil; a constituent of such vegetation; its wood.

1805 *HRA* (1915) 1st Ser. V. 586 In general rocky Scrub and Brush may with propriety be called the Underwood of the Forest. **1831** *Acct. Colony Van Diemen's Land* 60 The soil is exceedingly barren, stony and in places covered with a low scrub resembling heath. **1840** A. RUSSELL *Tour through Austral. Colonies* 86 Amongst the natural productions are the gum tree, the stringybark, the beef-wood tree, and scrub or brush wood. **1848** H.W. HAYGARTH *Recoll. Bush Life* 98 Low, thick bushes, known in Australia as 'scrub'. **1860** J.M. STUART *Explorations in Aust.* 16 Apr. (1865) 160 For five miles the plain was open and well grassed: afterwards it became thick, with mulga bushes and other scrubs. **1874** J.J. HALCOMBE *Emigrant & Heathen* 30 Tall gum and iron-bark trees, growing thickly together, with but little underwood or scrub. **1882** ARMSTRONG & CAMPBELL *Austral. Sheep Husbandry* 196 Bush Drop Fence . . is commenced . . by placing posts, of any description, about 1 foot apart, with panels suitable to the length of the scrub to be used. **1886** P. CLARKE *'New Chum' in Aust.* 232 Of scrub, that is small trees not more than twenty or thirty feet high, there are hundreds of species. **1897** L. LINDLEY-COWEN *W. Austral. Settler's Guide* 135 If the 'thick sticks' are excepted from the contracts for grubbing, £2 per acre is paid for taking out York gums, manna, and saplings, as well as scrub and undergrowth. **1903** G. SUTHERLAND *Australasian Live Stock Man.* (ed. 2) 384 The stockmen's names for some other useful scrubs are Quandong scrub, Leopardswood Scrub, Borea Scrub, Myall Scrub, and Yarran Scrub—which last present a close resemblance to the Myall. **1911** ST. C. GRONDONA *Collar & Cuffs* 69 Bendi, as a very thick scrub is called, is almost impenetrable, certainly so for a horseman. I have never seen any of it alive. . . I have encountered a good deal of dead stuff, however, and it is most awkward if the stock you are after take it into their heads to investigate the interior of a patch of bendi. **1919** *Bulletin* (Sydney) 25 Sept. 22/3 For handles there is nothing better in any bush than the scrub known as 'prickly moses'. **1936** W. HATFIELD *Aust. through Windscreen* 40 Mulga is definitely a dry-country scrub. **1959** H.G. LAMOND *Sheep Station* 65 If those sheep had been on scrub, as most of them had been, then broken teeth would be common. **1976** C.D. MILLS *Hobble Chains & Greenhide* 122 Let's think of how they suffered On the tracks to Further Out, With a scrub-and-water ration, Through the months of blazing drought.

2. a. A tract of land covered in such vegetation: see esp. quots 1805 and 1882.

1805 *HRA* (1915) 1st Ser. V. 586 A Scrub—Consists of Shrubs of low growth, Soil of a bad quality with small Iron gravelly Stones. . . It is not infrequent on the Sea Coast for Scrubs to be void of Trees. **1820** J. OXLEY *Jrnls. Two Exped. N.S.W.* 40 The trees were chiefly cypresses . . together with scrubs of the acacia pendula. **1824** E. CURR *Acct. Colony Van Diemen's Land* 47 The greater part of what is unlocated is a thick scrub of heavy timber closely matted together with underwood. **1833** *Launceston Examiner* 7 Nov. 3 The cattle and sheep are in the scrubs and look well, generally fat. **1838** *S. Austral. Rec.* (London) 12 Sept. 90 When I first saw Kangaroo Island I said I was disappointed. I saw the scrubs—I saw the great expense which would be entailed on the emigrants, and I confess my spirit fell. **1843** *Port Phillip Patriot* 8 June 2/7 The tea-tree scrub is close in some parts, in some thin; horses could gallop about betwixt the two scrubs. **1847** *Atlas* (Sydney) III. 2/3 We reached the skirts of an extensive pine scrub, an obstacle always to be avoided if possible. **1851** E.M. YELLAND *Colonists, Copper & Corn in S.A.* (1970) 81 We ascended the bank of the Hindmarsh into a scrub, but not a dense one, of wattles, she-oaks, and stunted gum-trees. **1855** *Moreton Bay Free Press* 2 Jan. 2/6 The scrubs produce a great abundance of pine and cedar. **1861** J.D. LANG *Qld., Aust.* 122 The principal timber is Kauri, of large growth, and it stands thicker on the ground than in any scrubs I have seen on the Mary. **1873** A. TROLLOPE *Aust. & N.Z.* I. 78 Woods which are open, and passable—passable at any rate for men on horse-back—are called bush. When the undergrowth becomes thick and matted so as to be impregnable without an axe, it is scrub. **1882** *Proc. Linnean Soc. N.S.W.* VII. 565 The vast plains of the interior are . . covered with trees, and when these grow in thickets they go by the colonial name of 'scrubs'. The term is of very varied application. Just as the trees in different localities are of different kinds and different heights, so are the scrubs. There is the greatest possible diversity between what is called a 'scrub' in New South Wales, in Victoria, and in Queensland. The trees are different and the whole aspect is different. To describe the distinctive features of each would be a kind of descriptive botany for each colony. A scrub is usually a dense thicket of the trees which happen to be most common in the locality. **1887** H. GULLET *Tropical N.S.W.* 9 The scrub . . is a peculiar kind of forest or jungle containing forms of vegetation differing in every respect from the ordinary forest of Australia. . . The trees we see here are seen nowhere else. They are the teak, the cedar, the ironwood, the tallow tree, the beech, the bean, the rosewood, and many others. **1902** *Emu* II. 106 The banksia scrubs in and around the Perth district. **1924** *Bulletin* (Sydney) 25 Sept. 22/3 *Flindersia oxleyana* . . attains an enormous girth on the North Coast of Bananaland, the tree being the monarch of the jungles or patches of dense scrubs which botanists generally term 'rain forest'. **1951** G. FARWELL *Outside Track* 23 During a lifetime spent in the big scrubs of the New England Ranges old Charlie had only once been bushed, and that was on the way from Martin Place to Bondi. **1980** S. THORNE *I've met some Bloody Wags* 9 At the ripe old age of nineteen I decided that I was sick of Australia, and would go back to Queensland—back to where the scrubs are deep and dense, to God's own land where the pikers roam, across the border fence.

b. As **underscrub,** undergrowth.

1861 L.A. MEREDITH *Over Straits* 35 The underscrub is rich in lovely plants. **1916** A.I. MACLEOD *Hack's Brat* (1920) 35 He saw her come leaping through the underscrub, her little bare feet impervious to the stones and twigs. **1933** C.W. PECK *Austral. Legends* (ed. 2) 71 There was no underscrub.

3. Usu. with **the.** Country which remains in its natural and generally inhospitable state; the country as opposed to the town. Cf. BUSH *n.* 2 and 3. Also *attrib.*, and as quasi-*adv.*

1827 *Monitor* (Sydney) 13 Jan. 274/1 A district of 20,000 acres, where nine-tenths are *scrub* (to use a colonial term for land perfectly barren). **1840** *Port Lincoln Herald* 7 Mar. 4 All these parties have travelled within the district, that Mr Eyre, has immortalized himself by pronouncing all scrub! **1845** *Standard* (Melbourne) 4 June 3/2 He told them he'd write a Newspaper For 'Squatters' that live in the 'Scrub'. **1862** *Bell's Life in Sydney* 3 May 2/1 We read of a party of these 'sons of the scrub' inviting themselves to spend an evening with a surprised squatter. **1871** 'IOTA' *Kooroona* 102 When you leave Toorak, and enter the scrub, look at your directions. **1878** R.B. SMYTH *Aborigines of Vic.* II. 75 A few months ago an elderly woman and two lads were met with on the upper part of the ana branch, who had come in from the 'scrub', and had never before seen a white man. **1899** K. O'MALLEY *Second Message to Sovereign Electors Encounter Bay* 17 They must either starve in the scrub or return to the city as paupers. **1900** H. LAWSON *Over Sliprails* 39 The banker, the storekeeper, one of the publicans, the butcher . . the postmaster, and his toady, the lightning squirter, were the scrub-aristocracy. The rest were crawlers, mostly pub-spielers and bush larrikins. **1910** *Bulletin* (Sydney) 8 Dec. 13/3 What battalions of bushmen have perished in the howling scrub with winning tickets for Tatt.'s in their swags! **1948** P.J. HURLEY *Red Cedar* 121 'Farther out' on the scrub fringe was the station of one McCaughey. **1955** J. MORRISON *Black Cargo* 93 'We had a bloke in the last gang told his wife he had to work a year's probation before he got full money.' 'He must have lived out in the scrub.' **1965** R.H. CONQUEST *Horses in Kitchen* 3 Mulga said, 'I like the cut of you. You're a good man in the scrub.' **1980** S. THORNE *I've met some Bloody Wags* 114 Harry was completely scrub-happy and rarely left his block for more than a day at a time. **1985** J. SCHULTZ *Steel City Blues* 108 We won't be able to afford to stay there. I'll just have to go over the mountain, go scrub and look for work.

4. Comb. in senses of 1 and 2: **scrub country, land, plain, timber, wood.**

1847 G.F. ANGAS *Savage Life & Scenes* I. 99 The vast **scrub country** to the north west of this part of the Murray. **1880** C. PROUD *S.-E. District S.A.* 7 An area of over 100 square miles of good scrub country to the east of the hundred has been dedicated to their use for grazing purposes. **1895** *Bulletin* (Sydney) 16 Mar. 3/2 No man who disappears mysteriously in Australia can be safely set down as dead until the scrub-country has been raked for him. **1928** M.E. FULLERTON *Austral. Bush* 32 'The bush' . . still comprises a great part of the continent—that is when it is used to mean the actual timber and scrub country. **1965** R.H. CONQUEST *Horses in Kitchen* 151 Chinese also excelled as scrub workers—in the clearing and fencing of virgin scrub country. **1978** R.J. BRITTEN *Around Cassowary Rock* 51 We put up a small tent where the long guinea grass bordered with the scrub country at Cassowary Rock. **1833** W.H. BRETON *Excursions* 130 Maize . . grows very luxuriantly on what is termed '**Scrub Land**'. **1871** J. BAIRD *Emigrant's Guide Australasia* 230 The scrublands, that is, those numerous low, level patches by the margins of rivers and creeks, above high-water mark, clothed with the most luxuriant and beautiful vegetation, composed of black unctuous clay and vegetable mould, will grow anything. **1886** J.F. CONIGRAVE *S.A.* 75 Of late years . . a large area of what are called 'scrub lands' have been brought into requisition by the invention of appliances which efficiently and economically clear the ground of the light timber upon it. **1897** MRS L. RAWSON *Austral. Cook & Laundry Bk.* 80 Every one is acquainted with the little bushes covered with glossy blackberries that come up all over the scrub land when it is first cleared. **1915** W.J. WYE *Souvenirs Sunny South* 39, I left Goondiwindi and rode to the West; through scrublands made joyous with blossoms and birds. **1928** W. ROBERTSON *Coo-ee Talks* 181 He had spent two solitary years in the then dense scrub-lands round Cairns. **1947** M. MORRIS *Township* 5 He thought of . . the patch of yellowish scrub-land by the house. **1980** B. HORNADGE *Austral. Slanguage* 103 In Australia, rough, untamed country with trees of stunted growth is referred to as the *scrub* or *scrub-land.* **1844** L. LEICHHARDT *Jrnl. Overland Exped. Aust.* (1847) 10 Nov. 35 The **scrub plains** were thickly covered with grasses and vervain. **1905** *Rep. W.A. R. Comm. Immigration* 217, I have cultivated scrub plains—tamma scrub and blackboy country. **1932** C.E. GOODE *Grower of Golden Grain* 14 Where the taller trees and the scrub-plain merge. **1952** *New Settler in W.A.* (Perth) July 55 Third class land included the sandy and gravelly scrub plain areas with a variety of scrubby vegetation and small mallees. **1981** A.B. FACEY *Fortunate Life* 201 The hired man looked up and noticed thick smoke. . . It was coming from . . a scrub plain behind the house. **1876** 'EIGHT YRS.' RESIDENT' *Queen of Colonies* 41 Many beautiful scrub woods known by the generic name of '**scrub timber**' are capable of receiving a high polish and are very beautiful. **1886** J.F. CONIGRAVE *S.A.* 75 Where the scrub timber is small . . the scrub is rolled down by a heavy roller and then burned, instead of being cut down by axes and destroyed by fire or sold for firewood. **1934** WARBURTON & ROBERTSON *Buffaloes* 156 Dense scrub timber lined the banks of the Munganilida Creek. **1975** 'N. CULOTTA' *Gone Gougin'* 82 Good camp . . scrub timber, unbarked. **1841** J.D. LANG *Austral. Emigrant's Man.* 5 Dec. (1852) 53 The timber consists chiefly of oak . . with a great many species of **scrub wood.** **1847** *Port Phillip Herald* 28 Oct. (Suppl.), The district constables resolved to scour the river's bank, under a belief that the runaway might remain until nightfall in some scrub wood. **1880** J. BONWICK *Resources Qld.* 82 The Native Pomegranate, a *Capparis*, has a hard, close-grained scrubwood. **1956** N.K. WALLIS *Austral. Timber Handbk.* 2 In addition to the hardwood forests and the cypress pine belt, the coastal strip in Queensland and northern New South Wales provides 'rain' or 'brush' (scrubwood) forests. **1962** *Daily Mercury Centenary Story Mackay* 43 Mackay district abounds in good quality . . scrub woods . . which have proved ideal for building purposes.

5. In the names of flora and fauna: **scrub bloodwood,** the tree *Baloghia lucida* (fam. Euphorbiaceae) of coastal N.S.W. and Qld.; **box,** any of several trees incl. *Lophostemon confertus* (see *brush box* BRUSH *n.*[1] B. 2); **fowl,** the mound-building *Megapodius reinwardt*, a uniformly grey-brown bird of forested coastal n. and n.e. Aust., s.e. New Guinea, and nearby islands; JUNGLE-FOWL; *scrub hen*; **gum,** any of several trees of the genus *Eucalyptus* (fam. Myrtaceae); also *attrib.*; **hen,** *scrub-fowl*; also *attrib.*; **ironwood,** any of several plants, esp. the large rainforest tree *Choricarpia subargentea* of Qld., and some species of the genus *Austromyrtus* (both fam. Myrtaceae) of e. Qld. and e. N.S.W.; **itch,** a skin irritation caused by the parasitic larvae of mites of the fam. Trombiculidae, affecting humans in tropical n. Aust., New Guinea, Asia, and the Pacific; the (larval) mites themselves; also *attrib.*; **kangaroo,** any of several kangaroos incl. *Macropus giganteus* (see *grey kangaroo* (a), GREY *a.*) and *M. rufus* (see *red kangaroo* (a), RED *a.* 1 b.); **leech,** a terrestrial leech, perh. esp. the common *Chtonobdella limbata* of forested coastal and near-coastal e. Aust.; **oak,** any of several trees, esp. some species of the fam. Casuarinaceae; **robin,** either of two small, long-tailed birds of the genus *Drymodes, D. superciliaris* of Cape York Peninsula (n. Qld.) and New Guinea, and the more widespread *D. brunneopygia* of s. Aust.; **tick,** any of several ticks that attack humans, esp. *Ixodes holocyclus* or the introduced *Haemaphysalis longicornis*; BOTTLE TICK; *bush tick*, see BUSH C. 3; **tit,** the small bird *Sericornis magnus* of temperate rainforest in Tas.; **turkey, (a)** *brush turkey*, see BRUSH *n.*[1] B. 2; also *attrib.*; **(b)** *transf.*, a swagman (see quots.); **wallaby,** any of several macropodids of various sizes inhabiting rainforest, brigalow or other densely vegetated country, esp. *Macropus dorsalis* of e. Qld. and e. N.S.W., having a brown back with a dark mid-dorsal stripe; **wattle,** a shrub or tree of the genus *Acacia* occurring in scrub country, as *A. leprosa* of e. Vic. and N.S.W.; **wren,** any of several small, ground-feeding birds of the genus *Sericornis*, usu. inhabiting dense undergrowth and rainforest; also with distinguishing epithet, as **white-browed, yellow-throated** (see under first element).

1889 J.H. MAIDEN *Forest Flora N.S.W.* 382 *Baloghia lucida* . . '**Scrub**', or 'Brush **Bloodwood**'. . . Wood fine and close-grained. It is impregnated with a resinous substance, and burns readily in a green state. **1903** *Austral. Handbk.* 280 The following . . furnish extremely handsome cabinet woods . . 'Scrub Bloodwood' (*Baloghia lucida*) [etc.]. **1965** *Austral. Encycl.* I. 406 On the northern rivers of New South Wales it [*sc. Baloghia lucida*] is known as scrub or brush bloodwood. . . The sap . . makes an indelible paint. **1985** N. & H. NICHOLSON *Austral. Rainforest Plants* 15 When cut, the bark of this tree exudes a pale sap which soon changes to bright red, hence the common name of Scrub Bloodwood. **1840** J. FRANKLIN Diary Visit S.A. 31 Dec. 52 (typescript) **Scrub box** & salsolaceous plants. **1878** R.B. SMYTH *Aborigines of Vic.* I. 230 *Maba sp.* Scrub box, or ebony. **1893** D.J. FROST *Crown Lands N.S.W.* 19 Among the timbers which these northern river forests contain are . . scrub box . . coach-wood [etc.]. **1900** *Proc. Linnean Soc. N.S.W.* XXIV. 621 *E[ucalyptus] largiflorens* . . a box tree attaining a large size. . . In poorer or drier soils it forms a small tree sometimes called 'Scrub Box' or 'Dwarf Box'. **1926** *Qld. Agric. Jrnl.* XXV. 440 Tristania conferta . . Scrub Box. **1965** *Austral. Encycl.* VII. 142 *Tristania conferta* (scrub box, brush box . .) is a giant tree in the wet sclerophyll forests. **1903** *Emu* II. 155 *Megapodius duperreyi* (**Scrub Fowl**) . . is found right across Northern Australia. **1936** T.C. ROUGHLEY *Wonders Great Barrier Reef* 213 The scrub fowl is an omnivorous feeder, mixing insects, centipedes, and spiders with berries, fruits, and seeds, which it obtains by an incessant raking and scratching of the leaves covering the surface of the ground. **1952** B. BEATTY *Unique to Aust.* 54 An exclusive and primitive family are the Megapodidiae, including . . the scrub fowl and the brush turkey of the tropics. **1965** *Austral. Encycl.* VI. 183 The scrub-fowl is the smallest of the three Australian megapodes . . but it forms the largest mounds. **1976** *Reader's Digest Compl. Bk. Austral. Birds* 138 Two and sometimes three pairs of scrub fowl commonly share a mound. **1889** J.H. MAIDEN *Useful Native Plants Aust.* 640 *Eucalyptus cosmophylla* . . a '**Scrub Gum**'. . . Baron Mueller has suggested this gum as highly suitable for decorative purposes. **1902** *Proc. Linnean Soc. N.S.W.* XXVII. 539 *E. morrisii* . . occurs as far west as Mt. Drysdale . . and is known as 'Scrub Gum'. **1923** F.A.C. BISHOP *Rep. on Inspection Barkly Tablelands* 3 The country pased over between the Katharine and Mataranka contains very inferior coarse grasses, and much inferior open country. The timber is mostly scrub gum. **1945** J. DEVANNY *Bird of Paradise* 20 The tractor had deposited two scrub gum—or rose-gum—logs. **1984** D.J. BOLAND et al. *Forest Trees Aust.* (rev. ed.) 514 Queensland Western White Gum . . Scrub gum (*Eucalyptus argophloia*). **1890** A.J. VOGAN *Black Police* 210 The **scrub hen** (Megapodius tumulus), saves herself from the monotonous duty of sitting on her eggs by depositing them in a capital natural incubator, formed of rotting and heated leaves. **1934** C. MACKNESS *Young Beachcombers* 69 The gin smiled and went back to plucking the scrub-hen. **1940** *Bulletin* (Sydney) 14 Aug. 17/3 Though the scrub turkey is most famed as a mound-builder, the scrub hen of N.Q. has it all over his larger uncle for neatness, size, better construction and finish. **1978** R.J. BRITTEN *Around Cassowary Rock* 94 A slight shuffling or chortling disclosed the whereabouts of a couple of wild scrub hens . . nearly always far up in the topmost branches of a big Johnstone River hardwood tree. **1984** B. DIXON *Searching for Aboriginal Lang.* 35 Paddy also described some of the traditional foodstuffs, like black bean nuts, and scrub-hen eggs. **1880** J. BONWICK *Resources Qld.* 82 The Lily Pillies . . of close wood, like the **Scrub Ironwood**, a myrtle. **1882** *Austral. Handbk.* 391 *Myrtus Hillii* . . the 'Scrub Ironwood' . . is perhaps the hardest wood of the Colony. **1926** *Qld. Agric. Jrnl.* XXV. 440 *Syncarpia subargentea* . . Scrub Ironwood (Imbil). **1965** *Austral. Encycl.* VI. 238 *A[ustromyrtus] hillii* . . a small glabrous tree up to 60 feet in height, is called 'scrub-ironwood', but its timber is prone to warp and is not much used. **1984** K.A.W. WILLIAMS *Native Plants Qld.* II. 82 *Choricarpia subargentea* . . Scrub Ironwood. . . This tree . . is now an uncommon species as most of its habitat has been cleared. **1890** A.J. VOGAN *Black Police* 210 The two travellers . . pick the bush-ticks and **scrub-itch** insects from their flesh with the point of the long scrub-knife the old digger carries. **1909** *Emu* VIII. 252 The scrub-itch mites, tiny red parasites hardly visible to the eye, punished me severely again today. **1929** A.H. CHISHOLM *Birds & Green Places* 44 The vicious communistic mite known as the 'scrub-itch'. **1945** J. DEVANNY *Bird of Paradise* 20 The scrub itch is bad. . . A small tick is the cause. **1968** L. BRADEN *Bullockies* 85 Then there was Scrub Itch. A wicked thing—scratch, scratch. **1984** B. DIXON *Searching for Aboriginal Lang.* 15 This turned out to be scrub-itch, a parasitic red mite a bit like ring-worm. **1903** H. BASEDOW *Jrnl. Govt. N.-W. Exped.* 25 Apr. (1914) 79 Large **scrub-kangaroo** (*Macropus rufus*) plentiful. **1900** R. BRUCE *Benbonuna* (1904) 17 Dozens of marsupials, from the little active bush wallaby to the big sorrel-coloured scrub kangaroo. **1983** R. STRAHAN *Compl. Bk. Austral. Mammals* 244 Eastern Grey Kangaroo *Macropus giganteus*. . . Other common names . . Scrub Kangaroo [etc.]. **1880** J.B. STEVENSON *Seven Yrs. Austral. Bush* 87 We were greatly tormented by **scrub leeches. 1905** *Emu* V. 3 Birds were extremely shy, but not so the scrub leeches, which were very bloodthirsty, and kept one on the move. **1934** C. MACKNESS *Young Beachcombers* 122 Did anyone pause to admire a graceful kingfern, or gather a handful of blue quandong berries from the ground, or pull a gorged scrub-leech off a gory leg. **1948** H.A. LINDSAY *Bushman's Handbk.* 139 The tiny scrub leech can make its way through the laceholes of boots or the weave of a sock; its bite causes nasty sores. **1881** *Proc. Linnean Soc. N.S.W.* VI. 742 *Casuarina glauca* or '**Scrub oak**'. **1959** L. ROSE *Country of Dead* 154 The mulga and the scrub-oak gave them shade and food. **1968** D. O'GRADY *Bottle of Sandwiches* 30 Lying under the shade of a scrub-oak. **1982** E.R. ROTHERHAM et al. *Flowers & Plants N.S.W. & Southern Qld.* (ed. 2) 27 *Casuarina distyla* Scrub Oak . . widespread on the N.S.W. Coast and Tablelands but most common on rocky sandstone ridges and plateaus of the Central Coast. **1842** J. GOULD *Birds of Aust.* (1848) III. Pl. 10, *Drymodes brunneopygia* . . **Scrub Robin. 1849** C. STURT *Narr. Exped. Central Aust.* II. 25 (App.) *Scrub Robin.* This bird is . . an inhabitant of scrubs. **1895** *Rep. Sixth Meeting Australasian Assoc. Advancement of Science, Brisbane* 447 By retaining the term 'Robin' for the best known member of the group (*Petroica*), and applying a qualifying noun to the allied genera, such titles as . . Scrub-robin . . were easily evolved. **1933** *Bulletin* (Sydney) 6 Dec. 34/3 Of scrub-robins (*Drymodes*) there are three species, two occurring in Australia and the third in New Guinea and the Aru Islands. **1945** C. BARRETT *Austral. Bird Life* 203 Scrub-robins easily escape observation, being small, light-brown birds in a grey-brown environment. **1962** H.J. FRITH *Mallee-Fowl* 53 If you sit still, the scrub-robins pipe around you and come bouncing up to look. **1984** SIMPSON & DAY *Birds of Aust.* 322 Current thought places *all* Australian flycatchers *and* the scrub-robins *Drymodes*, in an Australo-Papuan complex, taxonomically distinct from 'typical' Old World flycatchers. **1886** P. CLARKE *'New Chum' in Aust.* 272 In the scrub of Queensland it is well to guard by reasonable caution and occasional attention to the state of one's garments from the unpleasant adherence of the **scrub-tick. 1915** *Bulletin* (Sydney) 23 Sept. 24/4 The scrub tick . . is responsible for some awful Australian slanguage. **1926** M. FORREST *Hibiscus Heart* 116 Something burrowing in his neck felt suspiciously like a scrub tick. **1937** *Publicist* (Sydney) xvii. 14/2 The scrub tick seems certainly to be a native, and appears to have caused no inconvenience to its original native hosts, the marsupials. **1959** *Never kill Dolphin* (Writers' Guild Qld.) 50 The dog . . picked-up a scrub tick and died of it. **1968** L. BRADEN *Bullockies* 84 The bullocky had to contend with the Scrub Tick. In the main season, September to March, they would nearly drive you mad. **1983** *Gold Coast Bull.* 15 July 5/1 The CSIRO said it is trying to develop a vaccine that will protect dogs and livestock against paralysis and death caused by the scrub tick ixodes holocyclus. **1898** E.E. MORRIS *Austral Eng.* 470 **Scrub T[it]**—*Sericornis magna.* **1904** *Emu* III. 162 The Scrub-Tit (*Acanthornis magna*) . . was much sought after. **1941** C. BARRETT *Aust.* 74 In the bush on Mount Wellington's lower slopes, I made acquaintance with the scrub-tit. **1985** *Mt. Field Nat. Park* (Tas. Nat. Parks & Wildlife Service), Over 50 species of bird have been identified at Mt. Field. Some of the more common ones include: green rosella, scrub tit [etc.]. **(a) 1846** C.P. HODGSON *Reminisc. Aust.* 166 The **Scrub Turkey** is very plentiful, and a magnificent dish. **1876** 'EIGHT YRS.' RESIDENT' *Queen of Colonies* 243 The scrub turkey is larger than a domestic hen. **1897** R. NEWTON *Work & Wealth Qld.* 70 The scrub turkey . . constructs this great mound in which to deposit its eggs, which are hatched by the sun. **1934** WARBURTON & ROBERTSON *Buffaloes* 106 His hands came out . . and in them were white eggs, larger than ordinary hen eggs. He had found the nest of a scrub turkey. **1939** *Bulletin* (Sydney) 3 May 21/1 Two bad pests in the canefields in N.Q. are the bald coot . . and the scrub turkey. **1958** R. ROBINSON *Black-Feller White-Feller* 5 All the tucker you want, pygmy geese, scrub-turkey, barramundi in the river. **1964** M. SHARLAND *Territory of Birds* 64 The Scrub Turkey . . lives in rain forest jungle along the eastern coast of the continent. **1980** B. SCOTT *Darkness under Hills* 43 He built his fire . . and roasted a swamp-pheasant and some scrub turkey eggs. **(b) 1955** A. MARSHALL *I can jump Puddles* 152 Father . . was familiar with the ways of swagmen. . . The bearded men who kept to the bush he called '**Scrub Turkeys**'. **1973** F. HUELIN *Keep Moving* 178 *Scrub Turkey*, bagman who has gone Bush. Usually slightly mental or eccentric. **1845** L. LEICHHARDT *Jrnl. Overland Exped. Aust.* 14 Feb. (1847) 151 All hands were now employed in shooting crows; which, with . . a small **scrub wallabi,** gave us several good messes. **1887** W.S.S. TYRWHITT *New Chum in Qld. Bush* 65 The quiet is once more broken by . . a muffled patter of feet on the ground from a 'mob' of scrub wallabies. **1918** *Bulletin* (Sydney) 30 May 24/3 The animal with the bristly-haired tail . . was probably the 'brusher' or scrub-wallaby. **1925** *Aussie* (Sydney) Apr. 27/1 Recently I struck a freak pet scrub-wallaby at Goulburn. He was a whale on meat, cooked or raw, and chocolates. **1984** B. DIXON *Searching for Aboriginal Lang.* 134 The cassowary was afflicted with head lice and the scrub-wallaby called out to him: 'Come over here, and we'll pick the lice from your hair.' **1921** A.J. CAMPBELL *Golden Wattle* 40 In the east, notably in Gippsland, there is the **Scrub Wattle** (*Acacia leprosa* of the botanist), of pendulous habit, which illuminates the forested hills with its bunches of blossom of rich lemon chrome. **1958** *Coast to Coast 1957–58* 138 The prickly acacia and scrub-wattle burst into golden bloom. **1978** D. STUART *Wedgetail View* 1 A blind rocky gully choked with buck spinifex and dead scrub wattle. **1898** E.E. MORRIS *Austral Eng.* 407 **Scrub-Wren.** . . Any little bird of the Australian genus *Sericornis*. The species are—Brown Scrub-Wren—*Sericornis humilis* [etc.]. **1921** S.A. WHITE *Bunya* 80 The next most plentiful bird to be found in this low bush is the 'scrub wren'. **1949** B. O'REILLY *Green Mountains* 154 Scrub wrens hung their green moss nests on low branches over creeks. **1964** D. ROWBOTHAM *Man in Jungle* 53 A scrub wren flitted up, white browed, with a harsh scolding note. **1980** M. GRANT *Barrier Reef*

161 The scrub wren, found in the darkest parts of the forest.

6. Special Comb. **scrub block,** a rural landholding which in its natural state is scrub-covered; **bull,** a bull which was bred in, or has escaped into, the wild; also *transf.*, and **scrub bullock, cattle; -chopper,** *scrub-cutter*; **-clearing** *vbl. n.*, the action of clearing land of scrub; **-cutter,** one employed to cut scrub, either to clear land or to provide fodder; so **-cutting** *vbl. n.*; **-faller,** one employed in *scrub-felling*; **-falling** *vbl. n.*; *scrub-felling*; **farm,** a small farm on poor, originally scrub-covered, land; so **farmer; -felling** *vbl. n.*, the felling of some types of scrub, esp. those marketable as timber; **fire,** a bushfire which burns mainly scrub and undergrowth (see quot. 1956); **-hook,** an implement with a hooked blade used for cutting small scrub; **horse,** BRUMBY 1; **-knife** *obs.*, see quot. 1882; **lease,** an agreement under which Crown land classified as scrub land may be held (see quots. 1885 and 1906); **mob** *obs.*, a mob of wild cattle; **native,** an Aboriginal living in an area remote from white settlement; **paddock,** an uncleared paddock; **rider,** one who rounds up strayed or wild livestock; so **-riding** *vbl. n.*; **roller,** *mallee roller*, see MALLEE 8; so **scrub-roll** *v.*; **run,** a tract of inferior grazing land; **-running** *vbl. n.* and *pr. pple.*, the rounding up of wild livestock; **selection** *Qld.*, *scrub lease*; a tract of land so held; **soil,** fertile soil in an area of cultivable land cleared of scrub; **(trap) yard,** a makeshift stock yard constructed of pieces of scrub.

1927 *Murray Pioneer* (Renmark) 27 May 3/3 They purchased a square red iron tank from Chaffeys for £2 10s., which tank the Chaffeys were good enough to cart out to their **scrub block** for them. **1976** *West of Peesey* (Warooka Hist. Committee) 65 As the heavy tea-tree country had been taken up first, it was not until later years after the discovery of deficiencies that so called 'scrub' blocks were taken over by the farmer. **1881** A.C. GRANT *Bush-Life Qld.* 226 Dexterously lassoes a yearling **scrub bull.** **1891** W.H. HARRIS *Shearers or Shorn* 26 My friend . . would face a charge of mounted infantry as fearlessly and smilingly, as he would that of a scrub bull. **1903** *Truth* (Sydney) 18 Jan. 1/6 His gizzard must be as large as a scrub bull's heart. **1923** F.A.C. BISHOP *Rep. on Inspection Barkly Tableland* 17 Very few cattle were seen during the journey, and those seen were mostly clean-skins, among which were several scrub bulls. **1935** A. FRANCIS *Then & Now* 67 We had collected a large mob of cattle, and it was discovered that among them was a 'scrub-bull'. . . Scrub-bulls rarely come out into the open during the day, and are . . enemies of the squatters. . . In addition to eating a certain amount of grass, they entice station cows to join them, and so increase the outlaw herd. **1950** 'N. SHUTE' *Town like Alice* 159 All we do is go out and shoot the scrub bulls when you see them so you keep the best ones breeding. **1959** V. PALMER *Big Fellow* 268 What she had roused in him then had kept him from being quite the tough scrub-bull that he might have been. **1963** X. HERBERT *Disturbing Element* 21 Lone prospectors, for all their propensity for living in solitude, are not usually of the retiring type, as witness the lavish goodfellowship they invariably show when they make a strike, and that truculent misanthropy of their disappointed age which earns them such names as 'mad-hatter', 'death-adder', 'scrub bull'. **1967** B. OAKLEY *Wild Ass of Man* 68 I'm different from the herd, and at that school they don't like the wanderers, the scrub bulls who forage for their nourishment in their own way, alone. **1977** X. HERBERT *Dream Road* p. x, A man like Jeremy Delacy, the 'scrub bull'. **1980** M. DUGAN *Early Dreaming* 33 There were stories of scrub bulls fighting for supremacy on the sandy bars that ran down to the river. **1890** W.F. BUCHANAN *Aust. to Rescue* p. xvi, The principal topics were the various adventures in the bush of celebrated **scrub bullocks** . . and the turf. **1943** *Bulletin* (Sydney) 4 Aug. 13/4 An old scrub-bullock that had escaped time and again from 'bull-tossers' broke twice from the 'coachers'. **1880** J.B. STEVENSON *Seven Yrs. Austral. Bush* 109 A small mob of quiet cattle . . indispensable in working for **scrub cattle.** **1890** 'R. BOLDREWOOD' *Colonial Reformer* I. 195 The sharp gallops, 'when they wheeled the wild scrub cattle at the yard', were exciting and novel. **1932** J. TRURAN *Green Mallee* 92 Bluey the 'milker' squelched through the mud to join the little group of scrub-cattle that placidly awaited her. **1963** M. BRITT *Pardon my Boots* 142 A small mob of quiet cattle . . were used to get in the wild cattle. The scrub cattle were driven into the quiet ones and, in theory, they should steady up and settle with them. **1909** R. KALESKI *Austral. Settler's Compl. Guide* 97 Employ two good **scrub choppers.** **1930** A.E. YARRA *Vanishing Horsemen* 17 The boss was a big feller medicine man, able to smell out the sleeping-places of lazy scrub choppers. **1916** *Truth* (Sydney) 16 Jan. 8/5 There are plenty of men in this country who earn their bread by **scrub-clearing.** **1965** *Coast to Coast 1963–64* 15 Mackay's two big tractors—that they were going to use for the scrub clearing. **1845** *Standard* (Melbourne) 28 May 3/3 *Mr Hoddle at the public expense.* With an equipment of six **scrub cutters,** a groom and butler, drays, bullocks and horses, a spacious tent, containing an elegant brass bedstead and *requisite accompaniments.* **1887** J.H. WRIGHT *Our Victorian Goldfields* 20 In 1884 . . a party of scrub-cutters . . found some small blocks of coal in the bed of Berry's Creek. **1891** *Truth* (Sydney) 26 Apr. 7/3 Fencing, ringbarking, dam-sinking and scrub-cutting are rarely done by wages men on a station. **1905** *Bulletin* (Sydney) 14 Sept. 40/1 We are mainly scrub-cutters . . called sheep-caterers, because the scrub is to keep alive the flocks and herds. **1920** *Land of Lyre Bird* (S. Gippsland Pioneers' Assoc.) 67 The term 'scrub-cutting' has been used in South Gippsland for the last 40 years to describe the felling of forest timber. It is applied in other parts of Australia to the cutting of the smaller growths of timber. **1930** A.E. YARRA *Vanishing Horsemen* 20, I had to borrow money to pay scrub-cutters to fall mulga on the back part of the run. **1946** *Bulletin* (Sydney) 16 Jan. 13/2 Look, missus, I'm a scrub-cutter, not a flamin' snake-charmer. **1959** H. LAMOND *Sheep Station* 18 Preparations were made on the station for several scrub-cutters' camps. Two of these camps, of about 6,000 sheep each, were to be shepherded on felled scrub—the ratio being about 700 sheep to one axeman. **1969** R. OTTLEY *Brumbie Dust* 9 The owner of the property, in return for the scrub-cutting, gave rations for the big family. **1977** G.W. LILLEY *Lengthening Shadows* 15 The scrub-cutters were disbanded as a team and placed in individual camps. **1980** *Sydney Morning Herald* 13 Oct. 3/2 Mr Keith Cochrane, of Calgary station between Walgett and Collarenebri, sold 1,800 sheep in March, and has kept between 1,500 and 2,000 others alive by scrub-cutting. **1927** *Bulletin* (Sydney) 17 Mar. 24/2 Contract **scrubfallers** usually stipulate that all jhitu may be left standing. **1937** *Ibid.* 3 Mar. 20/2 Our abo. scrubfallers were on walkabout when a strange blackboy arrived. **1905** *Ibid.* 15 June 35/2 He would escort me home from **scrub-falling** every night . . on the off-chance of my getting bushed. **1916** *Ibid.* 11 May 24/1 When you're scrub-falling you'll meet them in scores, coiled up in the wilga bushes. **1876** 'EIGHT YRS.' RESIDENT' *Queen of Colonies* 188 In Canada and the States farmers . . can to a large extent rely on a harvest at a certain time and to a certain amount. This the Queenslander can hardly do; there may be a drought and nothing grows, or, if he is on a **scrub-farm,** a flood may come just as his crop is ripe, and destroy the whole. **1887** H. GULLET *Tropical N.S.W.* 13 The proprietor had begun work as a dairy-farmer, and had so well known his way as to make his scrub farm pay from the first. **1893** *Adelaide Observer* 26 Aug. 43/3 'Concert Camp', as the place was duly named after a jolly evening round the camp fire with songs, recitations, and tall yarns, wherein the 'squatter' vied with the 'scrub farmer'. **1926** *Bulletin* (Sydney) 28 Jan. 22/1 These times . . bring back memories of my boyhood days on a Richmond River scrub-farm. **1903** *Sporting News* (Launceston) 20 June 2/4 The annual **scrub felling** period has arrived. **1937** *Bulletin* (Sydney) 1 Sept. 20/4 Scrub-felling from spring-boards may be thrilling . . but 'topping' as practised in the W.A. karri country beats it easily. **1945** *Ibid.* 30 May 12/3, I was scrub-felling out of Mt. Larcom (Q.) and the pests nearly drove us mad. **1939** M. MORRIS *Dark Tumult* 185 A blaze that, beginning as a mere **scrub fire,** easy to handle and curb, could develop into that implacable horror, a crown-fire, which leaping along the tops of trees, sending its sparks and flying embers a mile in advance, was impossible to check. **1949** B. O'REILLY *Green Mountains* 108 Only a volcano in full eruption can depict a scene as fiercely splendid as a big 'scrub fire'. **1956** A. MARSHALL *How's Andy Going?* 164 There's three kinds of bushfires. One just creeps along in a calm. It burns leaves and that on the floor of the bush. It's easy to belt out. This one behind Barret's is a scrub fire. It can travel at a fair bat, but it stops below the heads of the trees. But say it comes out hellishun hot and a north wind comes up. The scrub fire gets going then. It climbs up the messmate bark and sets off on its own. It travels in the tops of the trees. **1909** *Bulletin* (Sydney) 26 Aug. 15/2 You cut all the small undergrowth, vines, etc., with a slasher (or **scrub-hook**); this is 'vining' in N.S.W., 'brushing' in Queensland. **1946** *Ibid.* 16 Jan. 13/2 We grab our scrubhooks and tear down the hill, Mat drawing away in the lead. **1897** J.D. HENNESSY *New-Chum Farmer* 38 A **scrub horse** does not know much for a horse; neither can he learn. **1902** R.C. PRAED *My Austral. Girlhood* 174 He got his name because of brumbies, and brumbies are, as bush people know, scrub horses. **1882** *Proc. Linnean Soc. N.S.W.* VII. 568 Without a **scrub-knife,** an instrument which is a combination of a thin sword-blade and a bill-hook, such forests are absolutely impenetrable. **1892** *Missing Friends: Adventures Danish Emigrant Qld.* 141 Often while I was on the Herbert, I would see them [*sc.* native police] coming past, like regular bloodhounds, quite naked, with their rifle in their hand and a belt round their waist containing ammunition and the large scrub knife. **1885** *Australasian Farmer* 322 **Scrub leases** for areas not exceeding 10,240 or less than 640 acres, for terms not exceeding 15 years, and at rentals not less than 2s. 6d. per section for the first five years, 5s. for the second five years, and 20s. for the last five years, may be granted on prescribed conditions as to the clearing of scrub. **1891** *Austral. Handbk.* 100 The Minister may . . declare any Crown Lands wholly or partly covered by scrub or noxious undergrowth to be scrub-lands; and may grant leases for such lands. . . The term of a scrub-lease may be divided into such periods as the Minister shall fix. **1899** *North-Western Advocate* (Devonport) 8 Mar. 4/1 A great deal of land has been taken up under what are known as the West Bogan scrub leases. **1900** *Albury Banner* 16 Feb. 37/3 As the pastoral lease was to be surrendered a scrub lease should be granted over the Forest Reserve alluded to. **1906** *N.S.W. Yearbk. 1904–5* 66 The holder of a scrub lease must take such steps as the Land Board may direct for the purpose of destroying such scrub as may be specified in his lease, and must commence to destroy the same within three months from the beginning of the lease, and when destroyed to keep the land free from the same. **1847** *Bell's Life in Sydney* 20 Mar. 3/1 Have you tried near the water-holes t' other end of the flats . . for the **scrub mob.** **1881** A.C. GRANT *Bush-Life Qld.* I. 212 When this old feed was young, it was also a favourite feeding-ground of the scrub mobs. **1847** G.F. ANGAS *Savage Life & Scenes* I. 99 The **scrub natives** who are called Wirramayo . . occupy the vast scrub country to the north-west of this part of the Murray. **1922** 'J. BUSHMAN' *In Musgrave Ranges* 134 That wonderful power of imitation known only to the scrub natives of Australia. **1955** E.O. SCHLUNKE *Man in Silo* 212 The teamster's guess was that he was 'in the dead centre of your father's big **scrub paddock**'. **1959** B. JEFFERIS *Half Angel* 86 Down by the waterhole in the scrub paddock. **1962** E. LANE *Mad as Rabbits* 184 She would go out with me for the cows, making sure that they had been turned into the long scrub-paddock that morning. **1881** A.C. GRANT *Bush-Life Qld.* I. 207 It is . . a favourite plan amongst the bold **scrub-riders** to take advantage of the bright moonlight nights, when, shrouded in the misty light, and undistinguishable from the surrounding shadows, they burst on the unsuspecting mob. **1883** E.M. CURR *Recoll. Squatting Vic.* 291 Come to the front in scrub-riding. **1906** L. BECKE *Settlers Karossa Creek* 94 Every Friday the two, accompanied by two blacks, who were good scrub riders, would start off. **1957** R.S. PORTEOUS *Brigalow* 61 He was a good all-round stockman, a good scrub rider, and fond of his work. **1914** *Pastoral Rev.* 16 Dec. 1143 In the first place we roll the Mallee with a **scrub roller.** **1927** T.S. GROSER *Lure of Golden West* 226 The clearing of the Mallee at first presented difficulties, but these were overcome by the advent of the 'scrub-roller'. **1939** *Bulletin* (Sydney) 8 Feb. 21/4 Dad and Choom, following a scrub roller 'nicking' the big stuff unearthed a bottle that the tractor-driver had planted. **1948** J.K. EWERS *For Heroes to live In* 71 He borrowed Tommy's old roller and scrub-rolled a hundred acres of gravelly sand plain in the south-western corner of his block. **1950** C.E. GOODE *Yarns of Yilgarn* 11 Harry . . was getting all the contracting he could—seeding, fallowing, and then scrub-rolling. **1971** B.Y. MAIN *Twice Trodden Ground* 17 In the areas being opened up now . . they were scrub-rolling and bulldozing and making new farms. **1978** A.E. COSH *Jumping Kangaroos* 3 First the mallee scrub was rolled down with a home-made, horse-drawn scrub roller. This was made from a large forked tree with a big wheel fixed at the trunk and a smaller wheel on each of the forks. A heavy log roller was swung between the forks, with a strong rail projecting on one side. This implement was then drawn by a team of 10 horses around and around a patch of mallee scrub. **1880** C. PROUD *S.E. District S.A.* 17 On entering the Bangham property we found it to be a **scrub run,** consisting of 114 square miles of inferior land, and carrying only about 10,000 sheep and lambs. **1905** *Bulletin* (Sydney) 13 Apr. 18/1 Throwing and tying is the ordinary daily occupation of scores of stockmen on part of the Dawson River country (Q.), especially in winter, when they go .. '**scrub-running**' for clean-skins. **1980** ANSELL & PERCY *To fight Wild* 81 They'd have twenty or thirty dogs on the place, even when they're not doing much scrub running. **1900** *Austral. Handbk.* 97 The applicant .. becomes entitled to receive a license to occupy the land in the case of an Agricultural Selection or a Grazing Selection, or a lease in the case of a **Scrub Selection** or Unconditional Selection. **1905** *Ibid.* 100 Except in the case of Scrub Selections, no person who is not a British subject .. will be allowed to select. **1919** C.A. BERNAYS *Qld. Politics during Sixty Yrs.* 331 The tenure was known as 'scrub selection', and was divided into four classes according to the proportion of land overgrown with 'scrub'. **1880** J. BONWICK *Resources Qld.* 65 The best **scrub soil** of Albert River gives 10.623 of organic matters. **1887** J.H. WRIGHT *Our Victorian Coalfields* 34 The soil is what is termed a grey scrub-soil. **1911** A.J. BOYD *Banana in Qld.* 3 The composition of our scrub soils is such that not one banana-grower in a thousand has yet had to apply manure to secure a crop. **1897** *Bulletin* (Sydney) 11 Dec. 7/2 **Scrub-yards** and new bark shanties. **1946** *Ibid.* 13 Mar. 15/4 They sighted the ringers racing to hold and head them into the wings of a scrub trap-yard.

scrub, *v.* [f. prec.]

1. *intr. Obs.* To travel through scrub.

1847 *Sydney Morning Herald* 11 Oct. 2/3 We entered into bricklow scrub, which became so dense, that after five miles scrubbing we were glad to follow a very winding watercourse to the S.E.

2. *trans.* To clear (land) of scrub; to clear (scrub) from land. Freq. as *vbl. n.*

1860 *T.H.A.J.* no. 84 3 The system of 'scrubbing' by which the underwood alone is removed, and of 'ringing' whereby the larger trees are simply killed. **1871** *Austral. Handbk.* 44 Scrubbing, *i.e.*, felling all trees not over a foot through and 'ringing' all large standing ones. **1879** 'RECENT SETTLER' *Emigration to Tas.* 73 Scrubbing requires considerable experience, for if the trees are not felled and cut up so as to be close to the ground, the burning off will prove a failure. **1899** *North-Western Advocate* (Devonport) 11 Jan. 2/5 He was engaged scrubbing myrtle, when a chip turned the blade of his axe. **1910** *Huon Times* (Franklin) 4 June 2/6 The Government will .. scrub and clear the land. **1918** *Ibid.* 13 Dec. 2/6 Cr. Batt seconded the motion that £2 be spent in scrubbing the ground. **1931** B. CRONIN *Bracken* 61 When first scrubbed and burned off it was remarkably free from fern or fireweed. **1945** J. DEVANNY *Bird of Paradise* 28 Mrs Brown alternated these activities with 'scrubbing' timber and driving a bullock team. **1965** A.W. UPFIELD *Lure of Bush* 53 Everyone knew that Daly's Yards was well scrubbed, and that there was a very fine surface claim in the west, and a good well in the east.

3. *Obs. trans.* To feed (cattle, etc.) on scrub. Also as *ppl. a.*

1880 *Blackwood's Mag.* (Edinburgh) Jan. 62/1 They .. maintain a precarious existence by .. breeding a few scrubbing horses and cattle. **1902** *Bulletin* (Sydney) 20 Dec. 17/1 Experience in 'scrubbing' cattle and sheep has taught me that mulga and kurrajong are the only scrubs that cattle will thrive on.

scrub-bash, *v.*

1. *intr.* SCRUB-DASH.

1963 *Gumsucker's Gaz.* Nov. 14 Scrub-bash (chase strays through the bush, throw them by the tail and knife-brand them). **1977** W.A. WINTER-IRVING *Bush Stories* 112 When Big John was seventy-three and galloping the hell out of his horse, scrub-bashing to round up a cow or a wild bull, his horse hit a tree and came down.

2. *intr.* To make a track through the scrub; to travel cross-country. Also as *vbl. n.*

1964 D. LOCKWOOD *Up Track* 13 More often than not we will be off the Track, hundreds of miles from it, scrub-bashing in out-of-the-way spots where it's a good idea to have either double-reduction gears or stout walking shoes. **1966** 'E. LINDALL' *Northward Coast* 134 You can see how thick the scrub is. We'd likely have miles of scrub-bashing, which 'd be harder on him than crossing the lagoon. **1975** —— *Day for Angels* 119 Scrub-bashing in the full fury of a monsoon was above and beyond the normal call of duty. **1981** P.B. CRESWELL *Granite Peak* 1 Herbert's vehicle was a 4 cylinder Dodge, with everything except the bare essentials removed, mostly forcibly as a result of scrub-bashing.

3. *intr.* To clear land of scrub. Also as *vbl. n.*

1966 S.J. BAKER *Austral. Lang.* (ed. 2) 77 *Scrub bashing*, the clearing of scrub-covered land. **1970** N.A. BEAGLEY *Up & Down Under* 58 Well, I got a job scrub-bashing, which means that one contracts to knock off the suckers on the trees that had previously been ring-barked.

scrubbed, *a. Obs.* Scrub-covered.

[N.Z. **1870** R.P. WHITWORTH *Martin's Bay Settlement* 13 The land was densely scrubbed with undergrowth.] **1899** *North-Western Advocate* (Devonport) 10 Mar. 3/2 The country .. was a succession of undulating, heavily-scrubbed land. **1910** *Huon Times* (Franklin) 5 Nov. 2/5 It was necessary for a gate to be erected owing to the property being densely scrubbed and heavily timbered.

scrubber. [f. SCRUB *n.*]

1. a. As applied to cattle: a beast which has been bred in, or has strayed and established itself in, the wild; RUMPER 1.

1848 *Adelaide Miscellany* 2 Dec. 280 My bucolical knowledge .. left me in total ignorance of the nice distinction between yearlings, steers, heifers, stags, poleys, workers, rooshians, and scrubbers. **1859** H. KINGSLEY *Recoll. Geoffry Hamlyn* II. 125 'The half of them are off the ranges.' 'Scrubbers, eh?' **1874** C. DE BOOS *Congewoi Correspondence* 65 What did they do when they found the scrubbers comin down, but fence in the water-holes, with a rough felled tree fence, so as not to frighten the cattle. **1887** W.S.S. TYRWHITT *New Chum in Qld. Bush* 151 Wild cattle .. are commonly called 'scrubbers' because they live in the larger scrubs. **1897** J.D. HENNESSEY *New-Chum Farmer* 34 Better start with five well bred cows 'as kind as kittens' than with fifty scrubbers. **1920** J.N. MACINTYRE *White Aust.* 78 Our stock stray away and get to be scrubbers. **1924** *Aust.* (Sydney) Jan. 1 Scrubbers, in case you are not acquainted with Queensland cattle lingo, are stock that have abandoned the semi-domesticated habits of the ordinary station cattle, and established themselves in little groups in the dense scrub country. **1932** J.J. HARDIE *Cattle Camp* (1944) 16 He had ramped about the team as if he were yarding a mob of scrubbers. **1952** A.M. DUNCAN-KEMP *Where Strange Paths go Down* 136 A scrubber can slip out of a mob of cattle and conceal itself with the aid of a scraggy needlebush. **1969** R. OTTLEY *Brumbie Dust* 32 Scrubbers are more greyhound than bull. Big-chested, lean-gutted, they do great damage to breeding herds and have to be destroyed. **1976** J.H. TRAVERS *Bull Dust on Brigalow* 56 All the scrubbers were unbranded and automatically belonged to the owners of the country they were running on. **1982** G.B. EGGLETON *Last of Lantern Swingers* 67 The scrubbers remained far out west .. managing to obtain sufficient moisture for their needs from native shrubs and grasses.

b. *transf.* and *fig.* A 'wild' person, one only partially assimilated into a society; a person of rough and unkempt appearance.

1858 R. ROWE *Peter 'Possum's Portfolio* 99 A third juridical grandee .. who walketh up and down, driving his thumb into the ribs, and his toe against the shin of any acquaintance less wealthy than himself, exclaiming therewithall, 'Scrubber, Sir, scrubber—show us your bank-book.' **1868** *Colonial Monthly* Apr. 140 'And do you mean .. that those poor children are heathens?' 'I can answer for it, that they are scrubbers—to use a bush phrase—have never been brought within the pale of any church.' .. 'Scrubbers, sir—never been branded.' **1880** J.B. STEVENSON *Seven Yrs. Austral. Bush* 140 A gruff remark from the ostler that 'He's none of yer loafing scrubbers, but knows how to treat the ladies'. **1904** *Bulletin* (Sydney) 16 June 16/2 Truly, Chinamen and other scrubbers are strong in this White Australia of ours! **1911** *Truth* (Sydney) 22 Oct. 1/6 The Sydney charwomen are all right, the real scrubbers are to be found among Sydney chairmen. **1946** K.S. PRICHARD *Roaring Nineties* 27 He was a prospector like the rest of us. After a few days, looked as much of a scrubber as any man on the track. **1965** R.H. CONQUEST *Horses in Kitchen* 7 Reddel on a horse was a shaggy scrubber.

c. An inferior horse.

1874 *Illustr. Sydney News* 28 Mar. 4/1 Horses sell very well, any sort of scrubber will bring from £25 to £30. **1899** P.W. MCNALLY *Life & Adventures* 3 The horses which were used in the mail service .. were of the worst class—'scrubbers', in fact. **1900** *Tocsin* (Melbourne) 3 May 1/3 Many of the so-called bushmen would not know an opossum from a goat. A great many of their mokes are perfect scrubbers, and certainly a bad advt. as Australian bred horses. **1914** J.H.L. ZILLMAN *Career of Cornstalk* 28 When I had purchased one of these animals, I felt like proposing to go back on my bargain, for, as I said at the time, 'he looks a regular scrubber'.

2. One who dwells in the bush: see SCRUB *n.* 3.

1867 *Pasquin* (London) 31 Aug. 194 Taken altogether, the Scrub Lands Act is a very amusing piece of business. What with District Councils, rights of commonage, and migratory mallees, the 'scrubbers' seem destined to come to grief. **1870** 'JACKAROO' *Immigration Question* 16 The Queensland squatters .. have dubbed me a 'jackaroo', the rising generation of New South Wales term me a 'scrubber'. **1890** 'R. BOLDREWOOD' *Colonial Reformer* III. 149 Don't you stick at home all your life, like a mallee scrubber, that has only one dart, on the plain and back to his scrub. **1927** *Murray Pioneer* (Renmark) 11 Nov. 8/3 *Bushed on Lake Victoria.* Mr Watson went rabbitting, and while crossing Lake Victoria station nearly perished from thirst. His story is a bush epic of rare determination and grip. .. Let the old scrubber speak.

3. Special Comb. **scrubber runner,** one who rounds up scrubbers (sense 1 a.); so, **-running** *vbl. n.*

1917 C. DREW *Reminisc. D. Gilbert* 33 Gilbert threw in his lot with some scrubber runners. *Ibid.*, Gilbert soon became a fair hand at scrubber running, often throwing three or four 'nuggets' in a dash. **1943** *Bulletin* (Sydney) 4 Aug. 13/4, I was one of three who did a spot of scrubber-running on a neighbor's place. **1980** ANSELL & PERCY *To fight Wild* 48 My father in his early days was a scrubber-runner and horse-breaker.

scrubby, *a.* [Spec. use of *scrubby* covered with scrub: see OED(S *a.*[1] 2 and SCRUB *n.*] Covered with scrub; consisting of or in the form of scrub; barren, infertile.

1802 J. FLEMMING in J.J. Shillinglaw *Hist. Rec. Port Phillip* 18 Dec. (1879) 17 The land appeared barren, a scrubby brush. **1804** *HRA* (1921) 3rd Ser. I. 296 Thickly covered with .. Scrubby Brush. **1824** *Hobart Town Gaz.* 3 Sept., The banditti escaped into an immense scrubby wood. **1835** *Perth Gaz.* 16 May 495 The Colony will be supplied from Flocks bred in the fine districts .. and the necessity of keeping them on low scrubby lands near the coast will be avoided. **1837** *Ibid.* 23 Dec. 1029 The land on the opposite bank is poor, and intermixed with ironstone pebbles, with scrubby vegetation, chiefly ground blackboys. **1839** *Southern Austral.* (Adelaide) 19 June 4/2 A most scrubby country destitute of wood, water, and grass. **1844** L. LEICHHARDT *Jrnl. Overland Exped. Aust.* 10 Dec. (1847) 68 The principal range .. is well grassed and openly timbered; but to the northward it becomes scrubby. **1848** H.W. HAYGARTH *Recoll. Bush Life* 44 In 'scrubby' or forest 'runs' the shepherds would be unable to prevent a numerous flock from separating, and this, by exposing them to the ravages of the native dog, would entail certain loss. **1859** R.H. HORNE *Austral. Facts & Prospects* 171 On the brow of the hill, so recently the forest or scrubby haunt of the dull and diminutive native bear. **1875** R. BRUCE *Dingoes* 24 The sheep can nothing else obtain On scrubby hill or saltbush plain. **1893** 'PIONEER' *Reminisc. Austral. Early Life* 35 Very thick and scrubby, and difficult to shepherd a flock of sheep to advantage in, being composed of stringybark and box ranges. **1902** *Rep. W.A. R. Comm. Immigration* 33 The country in the immediate neighbourhood is very scrubby sand plain, with a sort of bastard jam locally known as ironbark jam. **1923** R. ROBERTS *Life & Opinions* 479 It was wild scrubby country, but there was a good bush track. **1952** *New Settler in W.A.* (Perth) July 55 Third class land included the sandy and gravelly scrub plain areas with a variety of scrubby vegetation and small mallees. **1964** 'E. LINDALL' *Kind of Justice* 185 The flat scrubby wilderness .. was Pittamooka's barrier with the outer world. **1971** B.Y. MAIN *Twice Trodden Ground* 7 Coming suddenly out of the scrubby thicket to the high-up clearing there is always the same surprise. An old track, much overgrown now, leads through the thicket of acacias and sheokes, hakeas, grevilleas and straggly Burracoppin mallees to the half-wild meadow.

scrub-dash, *v. intr.* To ride at speed through thick scrub, esp. in pursuit of wild or straying livestock. Also as *vbl. n.*

1904 L.M.P. ARCHER *Bush Honeymoon* 144, I pick out some assorted timber which I have acquired in my back hair during our *scrub-dashing*. **1911** *Bulletin* (Sydney) 22 June 14/3 Up here (Moonie Scrub, Q.) 'scrub-dashing' is not a lost art, and it is worth watching—the gallop after the escaped steer, the throw from the tail, the strapping of the hind legs, all in about 1½ minutes. The 'coachers' (quiet cattle) are then brought up, and an attempt made to drive the captured scrubber along with them. **1916** V.G. DWYER *Conquering Hal* 242 We'd come to a thick bit of timber, and have a good gallop through it, for the fun and practice of scrub-dashing. **1924** L. ST. C. GRONDONA *Kangaroo keeps on Talking* 82 Mustering soon follows. The animals are very timid and take a considerable amount of holding when first disturbed. The wildest of them dash into the scrubs and if they are not driven on to the open country, the rest follow, and that herd is soon lost. That is when one shows his prowess at 'scrub dashing'. **1926** *Bulletin* (Sydney) 15 Apr. 22/2 A neighbour .. has spent a few years in the cattle-country and done a bit of scrub-dashing in his day. **1965** R.H. CONQUEST *Horses in Kitchen* 6 It was all scrub-dashing, hurdling over logs and jumping dry gullies. **1977** G.W. LILLEY *Lengthening Shadows* 7 It was in this paddock that I ran my second dingo. . . It was possible to scrub-dash up to a point, after that it was too risky for man and horse.

Hence **scrub dasher** *n.*

1911 ST. C. GRONDONA *Collar & Cuffs* 33 The professional scrub dasher, on a horse that knows his business, just drops the reins and trusts to Providence to bring him through with a whole carcase. **1923** *Bulletin* (Sydney) 29 Mar. 22/2, I was helping .. one of Australia's crack scrub dashers, to put a poly bullock into a small pen. **1965** R.H. CONQUEST *Horses in Kitchen* 6 Mulga had won his spurs in an age when the scrub-dasher was still the most important man in the south-western cattle country.

scruff, *v.* [f. *scruff* the nape of the neck.]

1. *trans. Obs.* To seize (a person) by the nape of the neck; to manhandle. Also *fig.*

1837 *Sydney Herald* 16 Oct. 2/7 The luckless wight was, what is technically called 'scruffed' to the watch-house, and the next morning was fined five shillings for being drunk. **1864** *Bell's Life in Sydney* 9 Apr. 3/2 Once on a time a peeler bold, From Parramatta he—Came for to 'scruff' the bushrangers All, in this wild countree. **1886** H. FINCH-HATTON *Advance Aust.* (rev. ed.) 90 In crossing the Fitzroy River at Yaamba, I once had a narrow escape of being 'scruffed' by an alligator. **1890** *Truth* (Sydney) 16 Nov. 4/5 The 'gentlemen' M.'s P. must do the fighting in Parliament now that Crick's 'scruffed' and kept out for more than a month. **1918** *Ibid.* 6 Jan. 5/5 Muss and Doolan scruff her to the nick. **1941** S.J. BAKER *Pop. Dict. Austral. Slang* 64 *Scruff, to*, to attack, manhandle a person.

2. *transf.* To seize and hold (a calf) for branding, castrating, etc., without the use of a rope: see quot. 1887. Also *absol.*, and as *vbl. n.*

1881 A.C. GRANT *Bush-Life Qld.* I. 228 The smaller calves are scruffed, and soon finished. **1887** W.S.S. TYRWHITT *New Chum in Qld. Bush* 137 Jim and the Boss run after them, and 'scruff' them, seizing them by the hind leg and the scruff of the neck, and in another ten minutes they are all branded and let out with the cows. **1905** *Bulletin* (Sydney) 28 May 17/3 Now for 'scruffing'—throwing a calf by twisting the head. **1922** 'J. BUSHMAN' *In Musgrave Ranges* 160 Most of them .. could be scruffed, which means that one or another of the black-fellows would .. catch the calf, and throw it on the ground with a dexterous twist. . . He would hook one of its front legs behind its horns and hold it there till the brand was applied. **1931** *Bulletin* (Sydney) 29 July 21/3 Townsend scruffed 107 calves. . . Besides the knife operation on male calves and searing with the station brand each calf was year-numbered and ear-marked. **1956** T. RONAN *Moleskin Midas* 99 On the seventh day they scruffed every calf big enough to wear a brand. **1976** C.D. MILLS *Hobble Chains & Greenhide* 17 We do 'scruff' in the yards on light stuff, but I'm sure most ringers will agree that in good hands ropes are the better in the long run.

Hence **scruffer** *n.*, one who so seizes and holds a calf.

1905 *Bulletin* (Sydney) 25 May 17/3 The scruffer's mate—we work in pairs—meanwhile puts a swing-over on to the tail. **1957** R.S. PORTEOUS *Brigalow* 229 Most people would regard scruffing as hard, dirty, and, if the calves are really big, dangerous work. . . Performed by two expert scruffers the job is swift.

scrum. *Obs.* [Rhyming slang for 'thrum', three pence: see OEDS *thrums.*] A threepenny piece; THRUMMER.

1891 *Truth* (Sydney) 10 May 3/5 The slim audience were mighty slow with their money, and it was fun to watch the plates seized by the end man of the seat, sent careening along and returned to the collector without the addition of a solitary 'scrum'. **1898** *Bulletin* (Sydney) 4 Jan. (Red Page), And his naming of the coinage Is a mystery to some, With his 'quid' and 'half-a-caser' And his 'deener' and his 'scrum'. **1902** *Truth* (Sydney) 16 Mar. 4/4 The popular 'tray-bit', 'thrum', 'scrum', or 'boozer's life-saver'. **1915** *Byron Bay Rec.* 25 Dec. 8 Thursday—usual wash, scrums again. **1941** S.J. BAKER *Pop. Dict. Austral. Slang* 64 *Scrum*, a 3d. piece.

scrummy. *Obs.* [f. SCRUM + -Y.] SCRUM.

1894 A.B. BELL *Austral. Camp Fire Tales* 108 Well that's mean, dirt mean, only a scrummy and the valuable information I gave him was worth a quid. **1915** *Byron Bay Rec.* 25 Dec. 8 Notify the public that they must bring along their scrummies (the fee for using the dressing-sheds is reported 3d. for adults, 1d. children).

scuff, *v.* SCRUFF 2. Hence **scuffer** *n.* (see quot. 1945).

1945 F. CORK *Tales from Cattle Country* 29 Scuffing .. calls for expert rope work and perfect co-ordination between the scuffers. A stockman selects a calf and skilfully casts a rope over its head, the strain being taken by passing the rope around a rail of the fence. While the calf bucks and plunges in an effort to free itself, smaller ropes are cleverly thrown over a front and a hind leg, and a quick jerk brings the calf to the ground where it lies, practically helpless, while the iron is applied. **1977** W.A. WINTER-IRVING *Bush Stories* 7 Scuffed by the men at the branding panel.

scungy /'skʌndʒi/, *a.* and *n.* Also **skungey, skungy.** [f. Ir. and Scot. dial. *scunge, n.* a sly or vicious person, a sponger, a vague term of abuse; also as *v.* to sponge: see OEDS.]

A. *adj.* Disagreeable; sordid.

[N.Z. **1964** *Salient* (Vic. Univ. Wellington) 1 *Pitch-hacking* has been in the news. . . Scungy anonymous louts tore up the sacred turf for the first cricket test.] **1965** *Kings Cross Whisper* (Sydney) Dec. 11/2 This is a week for good relations. Unfortunately you don't have any, because they are all a bunch of scungie cruds. **1966** J. SPENCER *Cross Section* 18, I always dislike the scungy feel when you don't show. **1969** W. MOXHAM *Apprentice* 11 He'd grinned because he'd been comparing that lot with skungy old Butch, the baker's horse. **1975** *Bulletin* (Sydney) 12 Apr. 14/3 In Ultimo, N.S.W., one of Sydney's scungiest and most depressing inner city suburbs. **1983** R. WILLIAMS *Best of Science Show* 72 This skungy sediment which accumulates in the settling tanks of the carwash.

B. *n. pl.* Sporting briefs.

1979 CAREY & LETTE *Puberty Blues* 3 Changing in and out of boardshorts at the beach was always done behind a towel or when your girlfriend was at the shop. The ultimate disgrace for a surfie was to be seen in his scungies. They were too much like underpants.

scurvy grass. [Transf. use of *scurvy-grass* a cruciferous plant believed to be an antiscorbutic: see quot. 1951.] Any of several species of the genus *Commelina* (fam. Commelinaceae), erect or spreading annual or perennial herbs commonly with blue flowers, esp. *C. cyanea* of n.e. Aust., often regarded as a garden weed. See also BOGGABRI.

1805 J.H. TUCKEY *Acct. Voyage to establish Colony Port Phillip* 162 Of potable vegetables, wild celery, wild parsnip, scurvy-grass .. were found in great abundance. **1871** *Austral. Town & Country Jrnl.* (Sydney) 20 May 612/2 Scurvy-grass, parsley, mustard, thyme, and all other sorts of pot-herbs are good for the prevention of it. **1887** MRS D.D. DALY *Digging, Squatting, & Pioneering Life* 341 Our sundry experiences of fish-hawks, cockatoos, pig-weed, and scurvy grass. **1951** J. DEVANNY *Travels N. Qld.* 13 Comelina .. commonly called scurvy grass, because formerly mariners threatened with scurvy came ashore and gathered it for food. **1961** *Bulletin* (Sydney) 10 May 28/1 Perhaps the best vegetable of the lot is scurvy grass, sometimes called Boggybri, and perhaps known to botanists as *Commelina cyanea*. . . It grows from Queensland's coast, out past the western border. It's a creeping vine with a purple flower, and it comes prolifically after the wet seasons.

sea. Used *attrib.* in the names of fish: **sea garfish,** any of several fish of the fam. Hemirhamphidae, esp. *Hyporhamphus melanochir* of s. Aust. and *H. australis* of coastal Qld. and N.S.W.; see also BEAKIE, GARFISH; **mullet,** the marine, estuarine, and fresh-water fish *Mugil cephalus* of s. Aust., and widely distributed elsewhere; (occas.) any of several other similar fish; see also HARD-GUT MULLET, *mangrove mullet* MANGROVE, PODDY MULLET; **perch,** any of several marine fish incl. those of the chiefly tropical fam. Lutjanidae, and *Helicolenus papillosus* of s. Aust. and New Zealand.

1906 D.G. STEAD *Fishes of Aust.* 66 The **Sea Garfish** is found in abundance along the greater part of the Australian coastline (including Tasmania); as well as in New Zealand, the Seas of China, Japan, the Malay Archipelago and other waters. **1951** T.C. ROUGHLEY *Fish & Fisheries Aust.* 22 As a food-fish the sea garfish has the same characteristics as the river garfish; its flesh is equally delicate and by some it is actually preferred. **1974** J.M. THOMSON *Fish Ocean & Shore* 131 The single biggest garfishery is that for the sea garfish (*Hemirhamphus melanochir*) in South Australia. The sea garfish of the eastern States is another species (*Hemirhamphus australis*) which enters only the lower estuaries, preferring the gutters along sea beaches. **1844** *Sydney Morning Herald* 3 May 3/2 The sand or **sea-mullet** are just coming in. **1879** *Proc. Linnean Soc. N.S.W.* IV. 412 *Mugil grandis* .. is the well-known '*Sea Mullet*' of the fishermen. **1906** D.G. STEAD *Fishes of Aust.* 80 The Yellow-eye Mullet .. is distributed right round the southern half of Australia. . . In Victoria, this Mullet is known as 'Sea Mullet'. **1965** *Austral. Encycl.* VI. 194 The sea mullet (*Mugil dobula*) .. is known by various names in the several Australian States, being called sand mullet in Victoria and Tasmania and mangrove mullet in Queensland. **1974** J.M. THOMSON *Fish Ocean & Shore* 101 There are about seventeen species of mullet around Australian shores, but the sea mullet .. constitutes more than 90 per cent of the catch. **1873** F. DE CASTELNAU *Edible Fishes Vic.* 8 Some [members of the Perch family] inhabit the sea, such as the **sea perch** (*Lates Antarcticus*). **1898** E.E. MORRIS *Austral Eng.* 409 Sea-Perch .. a name applied to different fishes—in Sydney, to the *Morwong* .. and *Bull's-eye* .. in Melbourne, to *Red-Gurnard*. **1951** T.C. ROUGHLEY *Fish & Fisheries Aust.* 45 Other sea perches in the family Serranidae, most of them fairly common off the Queensland coast and along the Great Barrier Reef, are the narrow-banded rock cod (*Epinephelus undulatostriatus* [etc.]. . . Most of them are beautifully coloured or patterned, and are excellent eating. **1975** *Bulletin* (Sydney) 9 Aug. 17/2 The *Ling* (long, pinkish) and the *Sea perch* (bright red, plump, sometimes called red rock cod) were magnificent in both taste and texture.

sea-gull. [See quot. 1983.]

1. A casual, non-union, waterside worker.

[N.Z. *c* **1926** 'MIXER' *Transport Workers' Songbk.* 46 What a study! Let us paint it As the sea-gulls fly about, While the stringer birds are anxious for the meeting to come out.] **1965** F. HARDY *Yarns of Billy Borker* 115 He was a casual wharfie at the time I'm telling you about, during the Second World War it was, and they call casuals 'seagulls'. **1966** *Realist* (Sydney) xxii. 20 For months Tommy Brand had been among the 'seagulls' who hung around the pick-up each day waiting for the crumbs of work that fall when the employers wanted more labour than the registered port quota. **1974** *Bulletin* (Sydney) 12 Oct. 48/3 'Seagull' the city stiff who combed the waterfront for free feeds off ships. **1983** H.M. MILLER *My Story* 45, I would become a 'seagull'; a casual labourer loading and unloading ships. . . A 'seagull' was a scavenger who hung around the pick-up points, waiting for whatever jobs were going after union members had snapped up the plums.

2. *transf.* A tourist.

1977 A. THOMAS *Bulls & Boabs* (1980) 92 Tourists, known by the wonderfully descriptive word, seagulls. . . 'They fly in, do what they have to do, and fly off again.'

sealed, *ppl. a.* [Spec. use of *sealed*, f. *seal, v.* to render (a surface) impervious: see OEDS *seal, v.*[1] 8 c. and *sealed, ppl. a.* 2 h.] Of a road: surfaced with tar macadam, etc.

[N.Z. **1928** R.G. STAPLEDON *Tour in Aust. & N.Z.* i. 12 Practically every mile of the road so traversed is 'tar sealed'.] **1938** *Ann. Rep. 1937* (N.S.W. Dept. Main Roads) 4 (OEDS) Generally for country roads in New South Wales the sealed gravelled pavement has proved to be quite adequate. **1951** R. DORIEN *Venturing to Aust.* 36 One appreciated the importance to a tourist resort of the road being 'sealed'. That macadam process prevented dust and mud and ruts and was very expensive. **1979** K.A.W. WILLIAMS *Native Plants Qld.* I. 46 A new town where roads are sealed. **1983** *Open Road* Aug. 19/2 From Warren you can make a 220 km. round trip by taking a sealed road north to Willan.

sealing, *vbl. n. Hist.* [Used elsewhere but of local significance: see OED(S *vbl. sb.*[2]]

1. The action or occupation of hunting the seal.

1804 *Sydney Gaz.* 28 Oct., *Wanted*, Four or Five Seamen, or other able Men who are accustomed to the work of a boat; if acquainted with the business of sealing they will find a preference. **1826** *Monitor* (Sydney) 25 Aug. 116/2 Ploughing, sealing, building craft, and cedar-cutting. **1834** *Perth Gaz.* 8 Nov. 386 Their capital [*sc.* that of settlers at Albany] can be applied to much greater advantage to themselves and the community, in the Fisheries or Sealing.

2. Comb. **sealing gang, ground, party.**

1804 *Sydney Gaz.* 29 July, A charge was brought by the master of a vessel trading to the straits against a person going to join a **sealing-gang**, of having embezzled the vessel's provisions. **1809** *Ibid.* 24 Sept., John Stewart, who entered into Articles of Agreement . . to take charge of a Sealing Gang sent out in the Sloop Unity, has absconded from the said Gang. **1808** *Ibid.* 14 Aug., On Monday last sailed the Albion whaler for the fishery, and the colonial vessel Perseverence for the **sealing grounds.** **1828** *Tasmanian* (Hobart) 12 Dec. 2 On Thursday, Dec. 4, the *Henry* sailed from Launceston for the Sealing Grounds. *Ibid.* 26 Dec. 3 *Seal Fishery*—We regret to learn that the **sealing party** on the White Rock, and another party somewhat farther down the river, have as yet not been successful. **1845** *Portland Gaz.* 22 Jan. 3/5 We regret to say that the boat, reported in this journal of the 8th inst. as having proceeded to the Julians to remove certain articles belonging to the sealing party lately there, has not yet returned.

secko. Also **secco, sekko.** [Shortened form of *sex* + -O.] A sexual pervert; a sex offender.

1949 R. PARK *Poor Man's Orange* 38 'Just look at that dirty ole secko, will you?' he said disgustedly. **1961** F. HARDY *Hard Way* 75 'The woman copper picked me up—having a piss, I was. The bitch charged me with indecent exposure.' 'A secco,' the bush lawyer whispered, 'Been flashing it.' **1967** *Kings Cross Whisper* (Sydney) xxxix. 4/5 *Sexos or seckos*, prisoners sentenced for sex crimes against young persons. The most despised of all prisoners. **1969** W. DICK *Naked Prodigal* 13 You look like you'd be the sort a bloke who'd take little kids down a lane and give 'em two bob, yuh bloody secko. **1984** *Bulletin* (Sydney) 20 Mar. 47/1 It was a risk to talk with a bloke who was 'suss'—a risk of being identified with a 'sekko' (sex offender).

second, *a.* In special collocations: **second bottom,** a second stratum of gold-bearing material: see BOTTOM *n.*[1]; so **-bottoming** *vbl. n.*; **-convicted** *ppl. a. hist.*, *double-convicted*, see DOUBLE *a.* 1; **cut,** (the mark of) a blow made to remove poorly-cut fleece; a piece of short or inferior wool resulting from this; so **-cutter** *n.*; **fleet,** see quot. 1851; **-fleeter** *n.*, one who came to Australia aboard one of the ships of the second fleet; **preference,** see PREFERENCE 2; **-sentence(d)** *a. hist.*, *double-convicted*, see DOUBLE *a.* 1; **shed,** the second shearing shed in which a shearer is employed during a particular season.

1855 G.H. WATHEN *Golden Colony* 230 The diggers have sunk shafts through the pipeclay to a great depth in search of 'a **second bottom**', but without success. **1856** S.C. BREES *How to farm & settle in Aust.* 56 Hence arose the terms first and second bottoms: the first, relating to drift resting upon a soft shaly bed of various light hues, called the pipeclay; the second to another driftmass, arrived at in boring through the pipe clay, and beyond which it is supposed there are no further auriferous drifts. *Ibid.* 57 The deep-sinking and second-bottoming have been chiefly exemplified at Ballaarat, where gold digging has . . become even more precarious than elsewhere. **1857** W. WESTGARTH *Vic. & Austral. Gold Mines* 205 The surface of this formation . . was commonly recognized as the 'first bottom', to distinguish it from the second bottom afterwards encountered by the diggers. **1864** J.G. MOON *Tarrangower, Past & Present* 3 They were sinking and slabbing a hole, and not finding payable stuff on the first bottom, were sinking for a second. **1955** H. ANDERSON *Colonial Ballads* 64 The cry was that the goldfield was 'worked out', and as far as alluvial gold was concerned, this was almost so. The quartz reefs, or second bottoms, only a few hundred feet below, were known to exist but, as yet, were unexplored. **1840** *Corresp. on Secondary Punishment* (Great Brit. Parl.) 26 Dec. (1841) 65, I observe that no more **second-convicted** men are to be sent here; but are those now with me to be removed? **1843** *Melbourne Times* 1 Apr. 2/3 On Sunday morning he inspected the colonial or second convicted prisoners. **1849** T. ROGERS *Corresp. relating to Dismissal* 49 Sending me a verbal order by a second convicted prisoner, he acted in defiance of all that was courteous. **1882** ARMSTRONG & CAMPBELL *Austral. Sheep Husbandry* 168 In shearing the first side of the sheep, each blow should be continued round until the back-bone is passed; this avoids the **second cut** caused by the blow up the back which should not be allowed, as the cutting through which results considerably depreciates the value of the wool. **1894** M. ROBERTS *Red Earth* 106 And there he'd be at you all day long, and if you dared to shear more than fifty in a day he'd swear the wool was full of second cut, and want to dock you every time. **1899** G. JEFFREY *Princ. Australasian Woolclassing* 39 Second cuts . . fall beneath the spokes of the rolling tables and are called locks, and do not bring one-third of the price of fleece wool. **1905** *Shearer* (Sydney) 23 Dec. 7/5 They can 'sling out' thirty to fifty sheep per day without giving the wool too many 'second cuts' (any other cuts the sheep gets). **1929** H.B. SMITH *Sheep & Wool Industry Aust. & N.Z.* (ed. 3) 209 Pieces of wool such as second cuts and small black yolky locks from crutch and under forelegs of sheep. **1975** G.A.W. SMITH *Once Green Jackaroo* 151 A man shearing a sheep for the second time . . trying to get rid of the ridges he had left . . was what is known as a first-class 'second-cutter'. **1985** *Canberra Times* 29 June 8/4 A fleece removed in this way is comparable to one removed by shearing and could be superior because of the lack of 'second cuts' where the shearer has made more than one pass to remove the wool. **1791** D. COLLINS *Acct. Eng. Colony N.S.W.* (1798) I. 156 Came in the **second fleet.** **1792** P.G. KING Jrnl. Norfolk Island 28 Jan. 18 Half-starved convicts from the 2nd Fleet. **1851** H. MELVILLE *Present State Aust.* 19 In September 1791 His Majesty's ship Gorgon, with ten transports . . reached Sydney, and this convoy is designated in the colony the *second fleet.* **1831** *Sydney Herald* 18 Apr. 3/1 His Excellency . . gave permission to the **second-fleeter** to occupy his land. **1849** A. HARRIS *Emigrant Family* (1967) 339 The legends of 'first or second Fleeters'. **1827** P. CUNNINGHAM *Two Yrs. in N.S.W.* II. 3 The Newcastle mine has been hitherto worked by the **second-sentence** men, sent down for punishment. **1848** J. SYME *Nine Yrs. Van Diemen's Land* 189 The second or local sentenced men . . are all sent to such labour stations with the view first of undergoing '*hard labour*'. **1904** *Shearer* (Sydney) 17 Sept. 4/3 Bringagee should be out about last week of month. **Second sheds** now being allotted. **1910** *Bulletin* (Sydney) 22 Dec. 44/2 Many cocky flocks are shorn, one after the other, at squatter sheds immediately after the station clip, thus providing the equivalent of a good second shed for the shearers.

secondary, *a.*[1] *Hist.* [Spec. use of *secondary*, pertaining to a second period or condition.] Pertaining to a criminal offence committed by a convict after arrival in Australia and to the punishment inflicted for such an offence, esp. in the collocation **secondary punishment.** See also *double convict*, etc., DOUBLE *a.* 1, *second-convicted, second-sentence* SECOND.

1824 E. CURR *Acct. Colony Van Diemen's Land* 47 George's Town . . is a place of secondary banishment, and possesses a factory for women, the people are for the most part of the worst description of convicts. **1832** *Hill's Life N.S.W.* (Sydney) 14 Sept. 2 The *Australian* has published the examinations of several Gentlemen, late of this Colony . . before a Committee of the House of Commons, appointed to report to the House on 'Secondary Punishments'. **1833** *Sydney Herald* 5 Sept. 2/2 (*heading*) On convict discipline and the laws which regulate secondary punishments in New South Wales. **1835** *Colonist* (Sydney) 30 July 243/2 No. III should be designated the Black Gang, to wear the heavy criminal irons now in use for secondary punishments in the gangs. **1836** *True Colonist* (Hobart) 15 Jan. 4/4 Many men are sent there who did not require the discipline of a secondary penal settlement. **1837** W.B. ULLATHORNE *Catholic Mission Australasia* 25 In the chain-gangs, great numbers of prisoners are brought together for colonial delinquencies of a secondary class. **1842** *Tasmanian Jrnl. Nat. Sci.* I. 289 The Probation System has now put an end to that, and it is used only as a place of secondary punishment for re-convicted offenders. **1851** H. MELVILLE *Present State Aust.* 180 It is only *secondary convictions*, or offences committed in the colony, that entail any kind of punishment.

secondary, *a.*[2] *S.A. Hist.* [Spec. use of *secondary* of minor importance, subsidiary.] Used in special collocations **secondary town, township,** to designate a settlement, or proposed settlement, other than Adelaide.

1838 *Southern Austral.* (Adelaide) 23 June 1/4 The lands . . except such parts as shall be reserved for **Secondary Towns** . . will from and after the 7th day of July next be open to purchase. **1838** *S. Austral. Rec.* (London) 12 Dec. 131 The sites of secondary towns at present are, Glenelg, Yankalillah, Rapid Bay, Encounter Bay, and Nepean Bay, Kangaroo Island. **1839** *Southern Austral.* (Adelaide) 27 Feb. 3/3 Only 150 acres of land are proposed to be reserved for what Mr Fisher is pleased to denominate a *secondary* town at Encounter Bay! **1842** *Austral. & N.Z. Monthly Mag.* 53 *Township of Wellington.* The following notice has been issued at Adelaide respecting this township, which is one of the selections belonging to the Secondary Towns Association. **1843** *Arden's Sydney Mag.* Oct. 119 Mr Boyd endeavoured to obtain special secondary town surveys at Indented Head—Port Phillip, and at Twofold Bay, but succeeded only in the latter. **1839** *S. Austral. Rec.* (London) 13 Feb. 149/1, It is fair, therefore, to expect that land in **secondary townships**, if well selected, will command the attention of the capitalist, and may even prove more valuable than that in Adelaide.

section. *Hist.* [Spec. use of *section* one of the portions into which a thing is divided. Orig. U.S. and in Aust. generally superseded by BLOCK *n.*[1]]

a. Orig. a tract of Crown land, one square mile in area, made available for development; a tract of such land of variable size; such a tract of land after development.

1830 *Sydney Monitor* 16 June 2/1 A respectable settler having an order for two sections of land (1,240 acres). **1830** *Extracts Lett. Swan River* III. 17 The territory is to be progressively divided into counties, hundreds, townships and sections. Each section to contain one square mile of 640 acres, each township 25 sections, each hundred 4 townships, and each county 16 hundreds. **1838** *Southern Austral.* (Adelaide) 23 June 4/2 The locations are to be divided into what are termed 'Country Sections', of 50 acres each—not including the roads, which occur at every second station, and are previously defined. *Ibid.* 3 Nov. 2/2 Country Section 289 . . will be immediately surveyed to form a Village, and divided into 114 allotments of one acre each, leaving 20 acres to be divided into Streets, &c. **1840** *S. Austral. Miscellany* Feb. 83 The suburban sections of Hindmarsh Town and Walkerville—each of 137 acres . . are not now to be purchased but at prices varying from £45 to £100 per acre. **1844** *Colonial Observer* (Sydney) 23 May 57/2 To oblige the Squatters to purchase half a section of Crown Land each at one pound an acre at the close of five years is nothing less than a tax of £128,000 per annum; there being material altogether for about 2,000 squatting stations. **1846** S. DAVENPORT *Lett.* 29 Apr. in *S. Australiana* (1977) Sept. 131, I have let about eight acres of the thirty-two acre section claimed by you of Mr Luck's. **1847** J.D. LANG *Cooksland* 228 The settler of this class would purchase either 80, 160, 320, or 640 acres—that is, either the eighth part of a section, a quarter section, half-a-section, or a whole section or square mile, of land, according to his means. **1848** J.C. BYRNE *Twelve Yrs.' Wanderings* I. 323 The country sections are not at present set up in sufficiently small lots: six hundred and forty acres is the size. **1853** J. ALLEN *Jrnl. River Murray* 17 A poor settler may purchase an eighty-acre section. **1861** *Number One* (Adelaide) Apr. 12 A few yards brought us to the slip-panel, and we struck off for the homestead, situate about half way up the section. **1878** G. WALCH *Australasia* 39 In the midst of an uncleared section, isolated from all surroundings save the noisome waters, stood a wretched wooden shanty. **1886** *N.T. Times Almanac* 61 Any person holding land upon credit of a less area than 1,280 acres, may select a portion of any unselected section to complete the area of 1,280 acres. **1893** S. NEWLAND *Paving Way* 65 Some sections of land have been surveyed . . you had better take them up, and we will help to form your station.

b. A plot of Crown land made available for urban development; such a plot of land after development.

1836 *S. Austral. Gaz.* (London) 18 June 4/2 Surveyed land shall be divided, as nearly as may be, into sections of eighty acres each, with the exception of the site of the first town, which shall be divided into acre sections. **1837** J. MORPHETT *Let.* 198 The whole of the Town Sections ought to be staked off. **1838** *Southern Austral.* (Adelaide) 23 June 1/2 To Let, Acre Section No. 800, delightfully situate in North Adelaide, with a House thereon, consisting of three apartments, as now occupied by Mr Hibernia Smyth. **1839** *S. Austral. Rec.* (London) 10 Apr. 176 A town section, in South Adelaide, with eight houses on it, producing a rental of £256 per annum, was offered for sale. **1841** H.S. CHAPMAN *New Settlement Australind* 126 To each of the lots of 100 rural acres are attached . . four town sections of one quarter of an acre each, which rural acres and town sections (called mixed allotments) are offered at £101 each. **1843** *Sketch W.A.* 36 The choice of rural allotments and town sections is determined by lot, drawn at the Company's office. **1857** J. ASKEW *Voyage Aust. & N.Z.* 289, I was present at one Government sale. The lots comprised small sections in the best business part of the city. **1919** *Smith's Weekly* (Sydney) 19 Apr. 11/2 Naturally the number of sections affects the prices. Cheap selections are available at Double Bay.

sekko, var. SECKO.

select, *v.* [Spec. use of *select* to choose or pick out in preference to another or others.]

1. a. *trans.* To choose (a tract of Crown land), esp. with a view to farming it. **b.** *spec.* FREE-SELECT.

1826 *Monitor* (Sydney) 29 Dec. 258/2 The authority given to *select* land shall not be considered sufficient to possess it. **1832** J. HENDERSON *Observations Colonies N.S.W. & Van Diemen's Land* 38 The settler must . . receive an order to select a grant of land. . . He must then procure an order to take possession of it, or in colonial phrase, to 'Locate'. **1838** *S. Austral. Rec.* (London) 11 July 81 The *purchaser of land* . . will . . after selecting his locations, be obliged to repair to Sydney, 500 miles off, to purchase at the public sales. **1839** R. TORRENS *Emigration Ireland to S.A.* 18 On arriving in the colony he may select his land in any part of the surveyed districts, not already appropriated. **1841** *Port Phillip Gaz.* 3 Feb. 2 Persons wishing to select land must previously pay to the Sub-Treasurer at Melbourne any number of pounds sterling, not less than the number of acres which they intend to select, for which they will obtain receipts from the Sub-Treasurer. Such receipts . . will entitle the holder to priority in the selection of land. **1855** 'RUSTICUS' *How to settle in Vic.* 15 There is no reason why he should not select a station fifteen or twenty miles from town. **1865** 'SPECIAL CORRESPONDENT' *Transportation* 12 A man selects an allotment of not less than forty acres of land, anywhere, pays for it at the rate of 10s. per acre, and obtains large grazing rights. **1887** H. GULLETT *Tropical N.S.W.* 26 It is good second-class land, all more or less available for settlement, and certain to be selected were access to it afforded by the construction of a railway. **1913** *Emu* XIII. 33 All this country has been selected, and a portion of it is under wheat. **1937** C. WARBURTON *White Poppies* 106, I thought to come and tell you I was thinkin' of selecting this block. **1964** E. LANE *Our Uncle Charlie* 127, I can't say whether, in selecting our sandy, scrubby block of land, he'd harboured any ideas of becoming a gentleman-farmer. **1982** J. MORRISON *North Wind* 103 'This used to be one of the best farms in this district.' 'Did you select it?' 'Yes, I did. I suppose I'm what you'd call a pioneer. I broke it in myself.'

2. *absol.* To obtain land under a free-selection scheme; to occupy such land.

1880 J. BONWICK *Resources Qld.* 75 No minor or unmarried woman can select. **1884** A.W. STIRLING *Never Never Land* 52 As the country became developed and thrown open to selection the sheep-farmer found himself obliged to purchase and 'select' in self-defence. **1894** H. LAWSON *Short Stories* 40 The squatter saw his pastures wide Decrease as one by one The farmers moving to the west Selected on his run. **1896** —— *While Billy Boils* 7 He selected on a run at Dry Hole Creek, and for months awaited the arrival of the government surveyors to fix his boundaries; but they didn't come. **1897** L. LINDLEY-COWEN *W. Austral. Settler's Guide* 35 Ringbarking is recommended as the first step after selecting. **1938** *Bulletin* (Sydney) 16 Mar. 20/1 Dan selected on the Yarriambic Creek . . and built a home. **1941** OUTHWAITE & CHOMLEY *Wisdom of Esau* 2 If there's anything left for us it will be away back in the stringy bark country that Harlin doesn't think worth paying for. Will you select there if you have the chance? **1974** *Austral. Folksongs* (Folk Lore Council Aust.) 85 So you rode from the range where your brothers 'select', Through the ghostly grey bush in the dawn.

selection.

1. a. The formal choosing of a tract of Crown land by one who has an entitlement to a specified area of unidentified land or by one who intends to purchase. **b.** FREE SELECTION.

1826 *Monitor* (Sydney) 29 Dec. 258/2 The Public Notice that the authority given to *select* land shall not be considered sufficient to possess it, ought to have been made *at the time*, for it requires settlers to be lexicographers, to understand the difference between selection and possession. **1832** *HRA* (1923) 1st Ser. XVI. 695 No regular Selection has been made of the 400 Acres. **1838** *Tegg's N.S.W. Pocket Almanac* 70 All the lands open for selection, are within the limits of the Colony. **1844** *HRA* (1925) 1st Ser. XXIII. 781 She made selection of the Station in question called Cryan Creek. **1854** *Illustr. Sydney News* 18 Mar. 190/3 As a population increases to occupy the lands in a more profitable manner, the grazing districts may be expected to become agriculturists, and to be open for selection and sale. **1866** *Colony of Qld. as Field for Emigration* 12 A vast number of acres of fertile agricultural soil . . as population increases, will be gradually thrown open to the farmer for selection. **1876** 'EIGHT YRS.' RESIDENT' *Queen of Colonies* 104 On Lake Coorybah many selections have recently been made. **1891** 'ROUSEABOUT' *Jackeroo* 3 'What about the Crown land sales?' said a young man named Monty Galard, who had just arrived. 'Did they not sell 5000 acres to the squatter on Bulleta last week to stop selection?' **1901** *Brisbane Courier* 1 July 6/5 Had more publicity been given to the opening of the land to selection, probably very much more of it would have been taken up. **1941** OUTHWAITE & CHOMLEY *Wisdom of Esau* 4 Men gathered together by Mallock . . to dummy for Harlin, whose run, held now as leasehold, was to be thrown open for selection under the Act. **1957** J. HAWKE *Follow my Dust* 52 My, that used to be a great station at one time. Three shearing sheds, and one year they broke all records by shearing a million sheep. The Gov'ment took bits and pieces off it for selection and now there's only a million acres left.

2. a. Land acquired by selection; a small to medium sized rural property however acquired. Also *attrib.*

1830 *Austral. Almanack* 145 If the selection do not adjoin land already granted, it will be necessary for the applicant to state the exact bearing and distance from some surveyed boundaries. **1842** *Sydney Morning Herald* 1 Aug. 2/5 On the north and north-west the land takes on the character of forest, finely studded with abundance of timber, so much sought after as a distinguished selection. **1871** *Austral. Town & Country Jrnl.* (Sydney) 13 May 598/1 Plaintiff, it appeared, soon after his application, went to reside upon his selection—at first in a temporary bark gunyah. **1876** 'CAPRICORNUS' *Colonisation* 8 The unbridged chasm . . divides our two classes of holdings—the station and the selection. **1886** W.J. WOODS *Visit to Vic.* 25 My brother's place at Porcupine Ridge is a Selection, as distinguished from a Station, and he is a Selector, as distinct from a Squatter. **1890** E.T. TOWNER *Selectors' Guide to Barcoo* 19 A selection of 20,000 acres on the Barcoo. **1897** J.D. HENNESSEY *New-Chum Farmer* 2 We weren't exactly fit to rough it on a selection, but would lease a farm. **1909** *Bulletin* (Sydney) 14 Oct. 39/1 Paradise Valley . . was an island . . in an ocean of big squatters, and out of the seventy 80-acre selections composing it not more than half a dozen were good enough in the pre-dairying days to support the selectors. **1927** T.S. GROSER *Lure of Golden West* 154 A mere pocket-handkerchief block of 25,000 or 50,000 acres would be a 'small man's' block, and be called a grazing farm or selection. **1930** D. COTTRELL *Earth Battle* 123 The actual man-handling of her sheep was the one form of selection work that she dreaded. **1944** E.H. BURGMANN *Educ. Austral.* 1, I had grown up on a selection on the Landsdowne, Manning River, N.S.W. It was a forty-acre block in the dense coastal scrub. **1951** CUSACK & JAMES *Come in Spinner* 93, I couldn't take up one of those wretched soldiers' selections they doled out . . after the last war. **1963** A. UPFIELD *Madman's Bend* 13 'Many sheep?' 'About three thousand. Not a big selection when the poor country is taken out.' **1977** J. CARTER *All Things Wild* 8, I spent every school holiday on Uncle Norm's selection over a period of years. At first he cleared a few hectares in the tall forest and built a slab and bark hut.

b. *transf.* A mining claim.

1878 J.H. NICHOLSON *Opal Fever* 26 If you convince me that you have opal in payable quantities, I advance you money to take up the selection jointly between us, and I also find money to set the whole thing going. **1881** W. FEILDING *Austral. Trans-Continental Railway* 55 On our way we visited some copper selections where the ore appeared to be rich and plentiful.

selector.

1. *Hist.* One who selects a tract of Crown land: see SELECTION 1.

1840 *S. Austral. Rec.* (London) 29 Feb. 83 This person is a 'land shark', who has acquired large means by regularly attending sales and buying up land which he knows to be coveted by another; his object in opposing the original selector being, either to commute his threatened opposition by a high bribe, or to buy with the intention of compelling him to repurchase at an exorbitant profit. *Ibid.* 20 June 334 Whilst the present good feeling exists (it probably arises from no great want of land being experienced) restraining settlers from bidding against the selector, he can almost always calculate on purchasing the number of square miles equal to the 5,000 acres.

2. *spec.* Shortened form of FREE SELECTOR; also *transf.*, a small farmer (see SELECTION 2).

1866 'J.W.T.' *Land Question in Qld.* 23 The Minister for Land and Works shall appoint some duly qualified person or persons to point out to immigrants or intending selectors . . the several farms on the Agricultural Reserves in each district. **1872** 'CAPRICORNUS' *Bush Essays* 41 Whatever the Australian selector may profess to be—whether called selector, farmer, or agriculturist—he is nearly always more a grazier than anything else. **1885** *Illustr. Austral. News* (Melbourne) 7 Nov. 175/2 The low price of wool is discouraging to both pastoralists and selectors. **1887** W. BANNOW *Emigrant's Hand-Bk.* 84 The selector marks the lot he wants, and pays 2s. per acre on application; if not claimed by any prior applicant, a certificate is issued to the applicant. Within three months after issue of certificate the selector enters on the land and resides there continuously for five years. **1892** *Truth* (Sydney) 5 June 6/4 What was his definition of the working class? Shearers, shopmen, carriers, farmers, selectors, and general laborers of all description. **1902** *Bulletin* (Sydney) 25 Jan. 32/2 O'Flaherty was . . working out his perdition as a 'sthruggler', or 80-acre selector. **1919** C.A. BERNAYS *Qld. Politics during Sixty Yrs.* 16 Bell was a squatter pure and simple, with all the high regard which a squatter of those times had for his own importance—living in a day when the squatter claimed the whole earth and the fullness thereof, and when the selector was regarded as being more or less of an impertinent interloper. **1931** A.W. UPFIELD *Sands of Windee* 33 Stanton had bought out a selector holding a Government lease of a hundred thousand acres. **1942** H.H. PECK *Mem. of Stockman* 132 After the Duffy Land Act some of the original squatters lost a large proportion of their best country to selectors. **1964** J.S. MANIFOLD *Who wrote Ballads* 100 No squatter is mentioned so contemptuously in bush songs as the selector, the 'cockatoo' or 'cocky' as he became. **1972**

ANDERSON & BLAKE *J.S. Neilson* 12 If after six years the land had been fenced and rents duly paid, the selector could ask for a Crown lease. **1978** M. WALKER *Pioneer Crafts Early Aust.* 125 Semi-skilled or skilled swagmen were a useful, mobile labour force for selectors and graziers.

semaphore crab. [See quot. 1969.] The burrowing estuarine crab *Heloecius cordiformis* of e. Aust. incl. Tas.

1952 W.J. DAKIN *Austral. Seashores* 194 *Heloecius cordiformis*, the semaphore-crab... When the tide recedes even a little on the mud-flats .. myriads of crabs appear. .. One of the most common is *Heloecius*. **1969** *Crabs Sydney Foreshores* (Austral. Museum Leaflet no. 62) 7 The Semaphore Crab .. has received its popular name from the quaint habit of holding the claw-bearing limbs outstretched while the body is being raised and lowered in a manner simulating signalling.

semi, *n.* [U.S.: see OEDS *semi, prefix*[2] 5.]

1. Abbrev. of 'semi-trailer'. Also *attrib.*

1956 H. FRAUCA *In New Country* 46 The driver and co-driver .. told us that they had been travelling from Meekatharra to Port Hedland together with another 'semi' when one of the axles of their vehicle had broken. **1965** R. FIELD *All over Down Under* 45 You know some of those 'semi' drivers are a bit rough. **1971** *Bulletin* (Sydney) 9 Jan. 31/1 'Want a lift, mate?' comes down from the high cabin of a semi. **1976** *Overland* lxiii. 45 When we were coming down the range again a semi almost ran us off the road. **1986** *Sydney Morning Herald* 12 Apr. 45/1 Solicitors and their clients begin to gather outside the court as the occasional semi rattles by.

2. A semi-detached house.

1959 D. HEWETT *Bobbin Up* 5 Always fighting a losing battle with life in the grey, warped weatherboard semi in Maddox Lane. **1980** N. SCOTT *Wherever we step Land is Mined* 22 Semi, comprising two-and-a-half bedrooms, kitchen, bath, inside W.C., rear access, very handy position.

semi-, *prefix. Obs.*

1. As **semi-civilized, -myall, -wild** *adjs.*, used to designate an Aboriginal still living in part in a traditional manner.

1853 *Austral. Gold Digger's Monthly Mag.* v. 163 A semi-civilized native .. was tending sheep. **1858** T. MCCOMBIE *Hist. Colony Aust.* 86 The semi-civilized tribes are far more deserving of pity than the wild free aborigines of the interior. ***c* 1879** A. MACPHERSON *Mount Abundance* 27 Charley and I started by ourselves, taking with us a semi-wild Balonne black (mounted). **1898** D.W. CARNEGIE *Spinifex & Sand* 60 Semi-civilised natives were prowling about. **1900** T. MAJOR *Leaves from Squatter's Note Bk.* 107 A large number of semi-civilized blacks had camped on a plain, skirted by a brigalow scrub. ***c* 1947** *Home Building Inland* (Flying Doctor Service Aust.) 17 Patient was a semi-myall native with two broken legs.

2. With nouns designating a non-white person, as **semi-native,** (one) of part-Aboriginal and part-white descent.

1901 *Bulletin* (Sydney) 15 June 7/2 What about the rising population of semi-Kanakas that pass as Europeans? **1914** *Ibid.* 2 Apr. 24/3 Decided by the legal advisers of S.A. Government, that 'aboriginal' does not include half-caste, for the purposes of the Birds' Protection Act. Binghi is allowed, if hunting for food, to murder the nesting swan when other people are forbidden to, but semi-Binghi will in future have to rank as one of the other people. **1926** L.C.E. GEE *Bush Tracks & Gold Fields* 69 There was some sort of semi-native names applied by those early, bold navigators.

semipalmated goose. [See quot. 1964.] *Magpie goose*, see MAGPIE *n.* 2.

1824 J. LATHAM *Gen. Hist. Birds* X. 295 *Semipalmated goose*... Inhabits New-Holland: found in flocks near Hawkesbury River, and called New South Wales Goose; its note said to be tuneful, and melodious. **1848** J. GOULD *Birds of Aust.* VII. Pl. 2, *Anseranas melanoleuca*. Semipalmated Goose. **1935** H. BASEDOW *Knights of Boomerang* 71 The semi-palmated magpie goose .. makes a habit of flying from feeding-ground to roost by exactly the same route every night. **1964** M. SHARLAND *Territory of Birds* 56 Although the Territory has other geese .. the Pied Goose is the chief one... Alternative names for it are 'magpie' and 'semipalmated' goose. The 'semipalmate' refers to the feet being only partly webbed.

senate. [Transf. use of *senate* the upper branch of the U.S. legislature.] The upper house of the Federal Parliament. Also *attrib.*

1898 *Austral. Handbk.* 122 The Legislative powers of the Commonwealth shall be vested in a Federal Parliament, which shall consist of the Queen, a Senate, and a House of Representatives. **1901** *Advocate* (Burnie) 9 Jan. 4/3 The Senate may degenerate into a House composed of wealthy old gentlemen partly drawn there by the advantage of railway passes by means of which to visit their sheep stations. **1919** A.P. CANAWAY *Misfit Constitution* 28 Sydney, Adelaide and Melbourne virtually control between them the elections of half the members of the Senate. **1931** *Century of Journalism* 386 As we have seen, practically all the problems that had worried the *Herald* in 1891 had been those represented by 'States' rights' and 'Senate representation'. **1946** W. DENNING *Inside Parliament* 51 The Senate, with power to amend most bills, has no power to amend a money bill. **1966** H. MAYER *Austral. Politics* 394 For Liberal party leaders, on the other hand, the Senate can be an embarrassment. **1982** J.R. NETHERCOTE *Parliament & Bureaucracy* 128 How really effective is the Senate as a 'house of review'?

senator. A member of the SENATE.

1898 A.B. PIDDINGTON *Pop. Govt. & Federation* 16 To a Senator 'public opinion' will mean .. the opinion of the public of his own particular province. **1900** *Act* (G.B.) 63 & 64 Vict. no. 12 Sect. 18, Before or during any absence of the President, the Senate may choose a senator to perform his duties in his absence. **1925** D. KERR *Law Austral. Constitution* 101 The Senate is composed of six senators for each State. **1933** G.V. PORTUS *Studies in Austral. Constitution* 30 In theory the senator is elected, as a representative of the State-as-such. **1956** G. SAWER *Austral. Fed. Politics & Law* 7 The number of members must be as nearly as possible twice the number of senators. **1984** *Canberra Times* 5 Jan. 1/2 Bob Menzies tried to pull a swifty in the 1953 half-Senate election that would have resulted in the Liberals obtaining two more senators.

send, *v.*

1. In the imp. phr. **send it** (or **her**) **down Hughie**: see HUGHIE.

2. In the phr. **to send** (something) **off,** to steal.

1951 *Barbed Wire & Bamboo* (Sydney) June 13 Everyone chose his own method of 'sending off' (that being the transitive form of the intransitive verb 'to go off') petrol. **1968** G. MILL *Nobody dies but Me* 21 So much stuff is sent off that I wouldn't be surprised if someone tries to send home a complete hut through the post, and no one seems to worry about getting caught. Except the pigs, of course, but amongst the men it's mostly always spoken of as simply *sending something off*. It's very common to hear someone say, 'So and so's sent off an Aldis lamp', or 'I wouldn't mind sending off that hammer.'

sensitive plant. [Transf. use of *sensitive-plant* the shrub *Mimosa pudica*, having sensitive leaflets which fold when touched.] Any of several plants of the fam. Mimosaceae, the leaflets of which fold when touched, esp. *Neptunia gracilis* of mainland Aust. (and the naturalized *Mimosa pudica*).

1822 G.W. EVANS *Geogr., Hist., & Topogr. Descr. Van Diemen's Land* 54 Our naturalist observed .. the *sensitive plant*. **1845** L. LEICHHARDT *Jrnl. Overland Exped. Aust.* 6 Feb. (1847) 136 Mimosa terminalis (the sensitive plant) was very plentiful and more erect than usual. **1890** F.M. BAILEY *Catal. Indigenous & Naturalised Plants Qld.* 102 Sensitive-plant—*Mimosa pudica*; native, *Neptunia gracilis*. **1916** *Bulletin* (Sydney) 6 July 24/4 This is one thing that immigrants who go on the land ought to know—the sensitive plant. It has seized on hundreds of acres in the Bloomfield district. **1935** DAVISON & NICHOLLS *Blue Coast Caravan* 219 The sensitive plant grows by the roadside and in open paddocks. It is, in appearance, very like a young wattle... If you touch a frond .. it closes up and droops, and if you give .. a smart tap on the trunk .. every part .. wilts. **1959** M. RAYMOND *Smiley roams Road* 111 It was a slender, dark-green plant about a foot high, and its leaves were narrow and delicate. 'That's my sensitive plant,' he said proudly. **1965** *Austral. Encycl.* VI. 90 No *Mimosa* is indigenous to Australia, but the common sensitive plant (*M. pudica*) from the American tropics has been a widespread prickly weed in North Queensland for many years.

separate, *a.* and *n.* [Used elsewhere but apparently chiefly Austral.: see OED *separate, a.* 1 b. and *sb.* 5.]

A. *adj.* Used with reference to the prison system to designate solitary (confinement), esp. in the collocation **separate treatment.**

1839 A. MACONOCHIE *Gen. Views Convict Managem.* 32 With the philosophy of the Separate system .. social management concurs, *so far as it goes*. **1845** BACKHOUSE & TYLOR *Life & Labours G.W. Walker* 10 Apr. (1862) 522 Those interested in the experiment of the Separate System, as carried into effect at the Pentonville Prison and consumated here, must not be disappointed. **1847** *Guardian* (Hobart) 17 July 2/3 The vast improvements .. in respect to the Separate Treatment System. **1850** *Irish Exile* (Hobart) 9 Feb. 7/4 Mary Brown .. was sentenced to four months imprisonment with hard labor, half of it in the separate working class. **1850** *Ibid.* 6 July 7/4 The sentence .. was six months to the female house of correction, and half the period in the separate working cells. **1852** G.C. MUNDY *Our Antipodes* III. 215 There are long galleries of 'separate apartments', as they are delicately termed; courtyards where the prisoners are brought out one by one to take their exercise under the eye of a constable. **1881** *Bulletin* (Sydney) 8 Oct. 9/3, I will first deal with what are termed long-sentenced prisoners. Anyone who gets a sentence of three years and upwards is sent to Berrima for nine months' 'separate treatment'. This .. consists in being absolutely secluded for that period—or nearly so. **1907** *Ibid.* 17 Jan. 40/1 Ha! 'separate treatment' beckons—nine months of silent doom! Try hominy and water; lift up a 'kit' of soup. **1913** *Ibid.* 26 June 15/2 Old Berrima Gaol, at one time the dread of N.S.W. criminals, because of its awful 'silent' system is now a rabbit-freezery... It was the 'silent' gaol, where offenders of three years and upwards did nine months 'separate' treatment. **1955** N. PULLIAM *I traveled Lonely Land* 271 The highest pride of the authorities at Port Arthur .. was the Dumb cells. These were a very important part of the Model, or Separate Treatment, Prison.

B. *n.* Solitary confinement; a solitary confinement cell.

1866 *Cornhill Mag.* (London) Apr. 512 It is absurd to talk about reforming criminals when you ruthlessly corrupt those with whom lies your only chance. For charity's sake these men, at least, should be kept 'in separates', or only associate with each other. **1881** *Bulletin* (Sydney) 5 Nov. 5/3 While in Berrima in 'separate' he modelled a small altar. **1891** *Truth* (Sydney) 1 Feb. 3/3, I knew one fellow who 'come it very strong' though. He was doing three years .. and used to try all sort of cringing dodges with the doctor to get taken out of 'separate', all to no purpose. **1891** *Ibid.* 17 May 2/1 He had got 'put away' for forgery; and he escaped separate (which, for the benefit of the innocent, I may say, once for all, means nine months solitary confinement on starvation regimen) on the plea that he was subject to epilepsy. **1918** *Ross's Monthly* Sept. 6/1 It was a joy to escape from the eternal murk of the sunless cell and the incessant tinware polishing of 'separate', and so, with a heart almost glad, I one morning found myself lined up for labor out on the prison farm.

separation. [Spec. use of *separation* the action of separating or parting.]

1. a. *Hist.* The division from the Colony of New South Wales, and subsequent establishment in 1851, of the Colony of Victoria. Also *attrib.*

1839 *Port Phillip Patriot* 29 Apr. 3 The 'Sydney Herald' falsely states, that we deprecate the idea of becoming a separate or independent Colony... One short statement will show that we have nothing to lose, but every thing to gain by *separation*. **1841** *Ibid.* 19 Jan. 2/2 (*heading*) Separation of this province from New South Wales, and erection of Australia Felix into an independent colony. **1843** *Port Phillip Gaz.* 10 June 4 Sir Thomas Mitchell, gentlemen, is a most decided promoter of separation. **1845** *Portland Guardian* 20 Sept. 3/1 Mr Wentworth's .. reasoning about separation is as much at variance with truth, as his temper is unsuitable for a statesman and a man of business. **1849** *Belfast Gaz.* (Port Phillip) 13 Apr. 4/5 *Separation* was the watchword in Port Phillip. **1851** *Illustr. Austral. Mag.*

(Melbourne) Aug. 101 Separation has been finally effected. . . His Honor the Superintendent of the District of Port Phillip has become His Excellency the Governor of the Colony of Victoria. **1852** G.C. MUNDY *Our Antipodes* III. 283 One of the *five* newspapers of this little town contains an advertisement for the sale, at a music-shop, of a new air, 'the Separation Polka'—inapplicable title for a dance of which personal proximity in the dancers is a leading feature.

b. Special Comb. **Separation Day,** 1 July, the anniversary of the proclamation of the independent Colony of Victoria; **tree,** see quot. 1977.

1855 *Vic. Govt. Gaz.* (Index) 10 **Separation day** falling on Sunday, holiday to be kept on Monday. **1872** 'RESIDENT' *Glimpses Life Vic.* 394 The 1st of July, the anniversary of Victoria's existence as a distinct colony, known as Separation Day. **1883** J.E. PARTINGTON *Random Rot* 29 It is a most unfortunate day to have arrived in Melbourne, it being 'Separation Day', and a general holiday to celebrate its separation from New South Wales as a distinct colony. **1884** J.B. GRIBBLE *Black but Comely* 17 On the great *separation* day, when Victoria became a separate colony. **1939** *Bulletin* (Sydney) 2 Aug. 20/1 The **Separation Tree** in Melbourne was an old-man red-gum more than 100 years ago. **1977** *Austral. Encycl.* VI. 148 The Separation Tree. A eucalypt in the Botanic Gardens, Melbourne, bears an inscription commemorating the separation of the colony of Victoria from New South Wales on 1 July 1851.

2. *transf.* Used of similar movements in other parts of Australia: see quots. Also *attrib.*

1860 *S. Austral. Advertiser* 2 July 3/1 In New South Wales I went up to the north as far as Brisbane and Ipswich. The people were then (June, 1858) full of the idea of becoming independent. The question of 'separation' was constantly coming up. **1873** A. TROLLOPE *Aust. & N.Z.* I. 46, I . . was initiated into the great question of 'Separation'. Rockhampton . . has been seized with the ambition to become a capital, and therefore hates Brisbane. **1900** *Advocate* (Burnie) 2 May 3/4 Mr W. Griffiths, the Westralian M.P. . . in England on behalf of the separation movement . . will at the interview bring forward the claims of the goldfields to separation. **1919** C.A. BERNAYS *Qld. during Sixty Yrs.* 521 At this period (1890) the two movements in favouring Northern and Central Separation were running, as it were, neck and neck. **1980** P. FREEMAN *Woolshed* 10 The call for the creation of a 'Riverine' state continued well into this century, and was perhaps strongest in the depression of the early 1930s when Charles Hardy junior of Wagga Wagga, gained a seat in the New South Wales Parliament on a 'Separation' ticket.

separationist. *Hist.* One who advocates the political independence of a part of an existing Colony, esp. that of the Port Phillip District from New South Wales.

1843 *Colonial Observer* (Sydney) 22 Mar. 898/2 Curr expounded his political views. He is a thorough separationist, and is sure to be triumphantly returned. **1844** *Sydney Morning Herald* 15 Apr. 2/2 Mr Young has declared himself a Separationist. . . 'Had I entertained any doubt as to the propriety of separating Port Phillip from the Middle District.' **1845** *Portland Guardian* 4 Jan. 2/2 In conclusion we assure our readers that we are *separationists* to the back-bone. **1897** J.J. KNIGHT *Brisbane* 25 Petitions to the Queen were got up by the advocates of Separation. The mother colony had to be fought. . . The Separationists desired to include in the new colony the Clarence, Richmond and Tweed River districts.

septic.

1. a. Abbrev. of 'septic tank'.

1939 M.I. ROSS *Dawn Hill Brand* 14 'It says here 'septics'. Have we got any?' Sidge asked. 'It means septic tanks,' Gene explained. **1961** P. WHITE *Riders in Chariot* 231 Rosetrees lived . . in a texture-brick home—city water, no sewerage, but their own septic. **1977** *Weekly Times* (Melbourne) 19 Jan. 65/2 (Advt.), Lovely new home . . 2 bathrooms, 2 septics and large living area.

b. A 'Yank': see sense 2.

1976 *Cleo* Aug. 33 Even before R and R, Americans were septics (septic tanks—yanks). Septic is now general usage. **1981** D. STUART *I think I'll Live* 31 Jesus, lover of my soul, if it isn't the Goddams, the Septics themselves! . . Stick around long enough, I told myself, and . . you'll see some real live Yanks.

2. In the collocation **septic tank,** rhyming slang for 'Yank', an American.

1967 *Kings Cross Whisper* (Sydney) xxxix. 4/4 *Septic tank*, yank or bank. **1971** J. O'GRADY *Aussie Etiket* 7 Septic Tanks don't get VCs. They get purple hearts. **1972** *Australasian Post* (Melbourne) 30 Nov. 4/4 We've got too many poms and septic tanks floodin' the box, and it's about time we had our own accent heard for a change. **1978** D. BALL *Great Austral. Snake Exchange* 26 Bloody Charles. Bloody septic tank.

serang. Also **sherang.** [Transf. use of Anglo-Indian *serang* a native boatswain, or captain of a Lascar crew: see OED.] A person in authority. Freq. as **head serang.**

1911 *Bulletin* (Sydney) 19 Jan. 14/4, I hereby threaten to produce affidavits from several boundary-riders and one serang that my facts are right. **1918** *Our Empire* (Melbourne) 18 July 6 Miss Butler is the head serang. **1931** *Whiz-Bang* (Brisbane) 1 Oct. 21 Head Serang. Federal President of the League. **1955** D. NILAND *Shiralee* 138 'I'll go down and see the head serang,' he said. 'I'll put it on him to let me bunk up in one of the huts like you.' **1968** *Kings Cross Whisper* (Sydney) lv. 10/3 It's a real happy farm. The head sherang and the boys are still calling me Wally. **1977** B. SCOTT *My Uncle Arch* 66 He saw the head serang for a start.

sergeant baker. [Of unknown origin: see quot. 1965.] The crimson, purple, and white marine fish *Aulopus purpurissatus* of all States.

1871 *Official Rec. Intercolonial Exhib. Australasia* 791 The beautiful 'aulopus' (serjeant baker) . . and a variety of other less familiar forms, may be taken by the line in almost unlimited quantities. **1873** F. DE CASTELNAU *Edible Fishes Vic.* 15 A large and most beautiful fish, very rare on the Victorian coast, but much more common towards Sydney, where it is known as *Serjeant Baker*; its colours are truly magnificent, being a mixture of grey, scarlet, and orange. **1874** *N.S.W. Rep. R. Comm. Fisheries* (1880) 14 The Sergeant Baker in all probability got its local appellation in the early history of the Colony (New South Wales), as it was called after a serjeant of that name in one of the first detachments of a regiment. **1896** F.G. AFLALO *Sketch Nat. Hist. Aust.* 228 The epithet 'Sergeant Baker' may possibly have reference to the brilliant uniform of that fish. **1906** D.G. STEAD *Fishes of Aust.* 53 The so-called Sergeant Baker (*Aulopus purpurissatus*) . . attains a length of over 2 feet, and as a table fish is very fine. **1945** C. MANN *River* 6 The dilettanti who . . wouldn't know a sergeant baker from a morwong. **1951** T.C. ROUGHLEY *Fish & Fisheries Aust.* 12 The flesh of the sergeant baker is white, firm and of good flavour. The name . . is believed to have been derived from a sergeant of that name who was the first to catch one in the early days of settlement in New South Wales. **1965** *Austral. Encycl.* VIII. 74 Sergeant baker (*Latropiscus purpurissatus*), a red, variegated marine fish named after an early colonial sergeant who was probably florid of complexion; possibly it was William P. Baker, one-time sergeant of marines at Norfolk Island, where this fish is common. **1984** *Canberra Chron.* 25 Jan. 19/4 A lot of evening meals along the coast . . are made up of small fillets of nanygai, coral cod, spiky flathead, Sergeant Baker [etc.].

serrated tussock. [See quot. 1973.] The introduced South American grass *Nassella trichotoma* (fam. Poaceae), naturalized as a weed of pasture in much of s.e. Aust.; TUSSOCK GRASS b.

1958 J.N. WHITTET *Weeds* 294 In New South Wales serrated tussock mainly infests the central and southern tablelands. Its general growth, excepting seed heads, is somewhat similar to the native tussocky poa grasses (*Poa caespitosa*). **1973** W.T. PARSONS *Noxious Weeds Vic.* 151 'Serrated tussock' is an obvious name describing the serrated leaves and the tussock type of growth. **1984** *Austral.* (Sydney) 9 May 2/8 The worst weeds in N.S.W. are serrated tussock and blackberries.

servant. *Hist.* [Shortened form of *assigned servant* (see ASSIGNED 2).]

1. A convict assigned to be the servant of a private person.

1802 *Gen. Orders issued by Governor King* 6 Feb. 81 If any person should beat or use their servants ill, they will be taken from them to Government labour, and the offenders dealt with according to their situations in the Colony. **1819** J.H. VAUX *Mem.* I. 178 The Governor . . allotted me . . a government-man, victualled from the King's-stores, as a servant. **1828** *Blossom* (Sydney) i. 62 It was in the power of the Superintendent . . to assign women from the Factory as servants. **1832** J. BACKHOUSE *Narr. Visit Austral. Colonies* (1843) 18 The convicts are assigned as servants to the colonists, and the vacancies occasioned by any others having obtained tickets of leave are first supplied. **1835** *Tegg's N.S.W. Pocket Almanac* (1838) 95 Should the master of any servant applying for a ticket, consider the applicant undeserving the indulgence, he is required to state his opinion in writing to the Bench, stating the grounds of it. **1873** J. BONWICK *M. Howe* 34 Howe found a master, to whom he was assigned as a servant, a few days after landing. **1900** W. DELAFORCE *Life & Experiences Ex-Convict Port Macquarie* 6 If he happened to prove himself a success at any particular vocation, he would never get his 'ticket', as the master for whom he was working would arrange with one of the other servants to quarrel with the handy man, and he would be sent to the lockup to be flogged, and get an addition to his sentence.

2. In the phr. **servant of the crown,** a euphemism for CONVICT *n.* 1, whether in private or official custody.

1788 *HRA* (1914) 1st Ser. I. 34 The convicts being the servants of the Crown till the time for which they are sentenced is expired, their labour is to be for the public. **1809** *Ibid.* (1916) 1st Ser. VII. 3 Amongst other works executed by the Servants of the Crown, the walls and roof of the New Stone Granary at Parramatta, and brick barrack at Sydney . . were completed. **1834** J. ROBERTS *Two Yrs. at Sea* 125 It is said they never forgive a person who accidentally calls them 'convicts'; they denominate themselves 'servants of the crown', and settlers invariably do the same. **1843** C. ROWCROFT *Tales of Colonies* (1858) 266, I am a servant of the Crown. I am assigned to Mr Kale.

serve. In the phr. **to give** (someone) **a serve,** to criticize adversely, to reprimand sharply. See also quot. 1967.

1967 *Kings Cross Whisper* (Sydney) xxxix. 4/5 *Serve*, to give a person a thrashing. 'Give the mug a serve.' **1974** STACKPOLE & TRENGOVE *Not just for Openers* 104, I continued to give Snow a bit of a serve. **1977** *Austral.* (Sydney) 1 June 3/4 He was glad to be leaving and he would be giving the country a serve in an unnamed English newspaper if it was willing to pay enough for his views. **1983** *Woman's Day* (Sydney) 27 June 18/1 'Yeah', he said, 'Oges is set to give the Poms a serve.'

service. *Hist.*

1. Shortened form of *assigned service* (see ASSIGNED 2).

1832 *Hill's Life N.S.W.* 21 Dec. 3, I am assigned to Colonel Damaresq. Two years ago, I was in Mr John M'Intyre's service, lent to him by Mr Potter M'Queen. **1833** *Launceston Advertiser* 31 Oct. 2 The Convicts by the Stakesby who have not been taken off according to their assignments published in the Gazette, September 13, 1833, have been this day ordered to the service of other applicants.

2. In the phr. **service of government,** official custody (of a convict) as opposed to private assignment.

1848 C. COZENS *Adventures of Guardsman* 113 Two young men, prisoners . . happened to be returned from their master's private assignment to the service of Government. **1850** *Irish Exile* (Hobart) 29 June 6/4 The woman was discharged to the service of Government, her ticket-of-leave being revoked, because she did not attend the last general muster.

servitude. *Hist.* [Spec. use of *servitude* absence of personal freedom; for *penal servitude* see OED *penal, a.*[1] 1 c.] The compulsory labour to which a convict (later, a prisoner) is sentenced. Also as **penal servitude** (occas. *attrib.*).

1787 *Hist. Rec. N.S.W.* 25 Apr. (1892) I. ii. 90 Full power and authority to emancipate and discharge from their servitude any of the convicts . . who shall, from their good conduct and a disposition to industry be deserving of favour. **1811** *Sydney Gaz.* 8 June 1/1 No Convict, under Sentence of Transportation for Life . . need apply for a Free Pardon . . until after a Lapse of several Years of Servitude. **1812** *HRA* (1916) 1st Ser. VII. 598 The best Description of Settlers for this Country are Emancipated Convicts, or Persons become free by Servitude, who have been Convicts. **1827** G. Holford *Let.* 9 Means may be devised to facilitate the return of such women as have passed their time of servitude, and are unwilling to remain in the colony. **1848** C. Cozens *Adventures of Guardsman* 159 An assigned servant . . a lifer (that is, one sentenced for life) . . had become eligible, from good conduct and servitude, for the indulgence of a ticket of leave. **1857** P.J. Murray *Not so Bad* 17 The principle of giving a Ticket-of-Leave to the Transport and refusing it to the Penal Servitude man. **1858** J.B. Marsden *Mem. S. Marsden* 31 Most of the convicts after a short servitude, obtained tickets-of-leave, and settled upon the parcels of land allotted to them by government. **1864** *Illustr. Sydney News* 16 Nov. 3/1 Peter Fegan and Daniel Webster were sentenced to twenty years' penal servitude for bushranging and robbery under arms. **1878** G. Walch *Australasia* 32 The defaulter whose non-appearance led to Mr Talfourd's sudden act of folly, was undergoing a term of penal servitude. **1890** *Braidwood Dispatch* 23 Aug. 2/5 Samuel Charles who was in Sydney on Tuesday sentenced to 10 years' penal servitude for breaking and entering a dwelling-house, had, since 1865, served no less than 15½ years in gaol.

session. A period spent drinking; Grog-up.

1949 L. Glassop *Lucky Palmer* 215 I'll join you in a beer later, but I don't want to get into a session. **1955** D. Niland *Shiralee* 58, I don't want to make a session of it. I had a helluva night; I feel bloody half-dead. I'd just like a drink to pick me up. **1962** K. Simons *Not with Kiss* 26 'What's the drum on the party tomorrow night?' 'Oh, just a bit of a session for the boys. For Ava. Thirty years service an' all that.' **1967** *Kings Cross Whisper* (Sydney) xxxix. 4/4 *Session*, the time spent in consuming alcoholic liquor. **1981** C. Williams *Open Cut* 148 She has to go longer hours. . . Bloke'll shoot off for a session. She has to make up her own entertainment.

set, var. Sett.

set, *n.*[1] [Spec. use of *set* 'dead set': see OED(S *sb.*[1] 7.] A hostile attitude; esp. in the phr. **to get (make, take) a set on** (a person), to exhibit a hostile attitude towards.

1866 *Austral. Monthly Mag.* (Melbourne) II. 144 Rather angrily; for he considered we were all making a set on him. **1875** *Illustr. Sydney News* 19 Jan. 14/3 The goat-scented three-card man pursuing his swindling avocation under the very nose of legal authority or hurriedly decamping with his traps when a 'set' is made against him by some more than usually officious policeman. **1885** *Australasian Printers' Keepsake* 24 The Boss had 'got a set on him' to *set* The mullock of the whole establishment. 'You'd better far believe it!' So he said. **1903** J. Furphy *Such is Life* (1937) 36 'Hasn't Warrigal Alf got a set on you, too?' asked Thompson coldly. **1946** K. Tennant *Lost Haven* (1947) 228 If the Old Man hadn't tried to give Mark Thorne such particular hell when he was starting his shop, perhaps Thorne wouldn't have taken a set on all the Sudermans. **1955** R. Lawler *Summer of Seventeenth Doll* (1965) 54 It takes a special sort of woman to understand a bloke like me. Most of them hear a thing or two and then get a set on yer, treat you as if you was poison. **1956** *Tennant Creek Times* 15 June 7/3, I did notice . . a set against Territorian officialdom.

set, *n.*[2]

1. *Surfing.* [Spec. use of *set* a number or group: see OED *sb.*[2]] A series of waves followed by a lull.

1963 J. Pollard *Austral. Surfrider* 20 A group of waves is called a 'set'. **1979** Carey & Lette *Puberty Blues* 47 Yet that's all the boys *did* talk about, way out on the flat sea, sitting on their boards, in between sets.

2. *transf.* A pair of female breasts.

1967 J. Hibberd *White with Wire Wheels* (1970) 155 Jesus. Get on to these for a set. . . This bird. Just have a look at those knockers. **1979** B. Humphries *Bazza comes into his Own*, Cripes! I wish they only gave seven days for rape! This sheilah's got a set on her like a pair of Mudgee mailbags! I bet she goes off like a tin of bad fish!

set, *v.*[1] [Spec. use of *set* to fix on as a victim: see OED(S *v.* 125.] In the phr. **to have** (or **get**) (a person) **set,** to be ill-disposed towards, to 'have it in for' (a person).

1899 *Truth* (Sydney) 5 Nov. 1/3 In bush parlance Speaker Abbott evidently has John Norton set. What's in Reid's mouth but a playful word, is in Norton's rank disorder. **1919** V. Marshall *World of Living Dead* 33 He'd been 'set' for the last three year—ever since he got the four years coomyerlative fer dishin' a screw, an' made a break for it at Bathurst. **1929** 'A. Russell' *Bungoona* 7 It ain't too bad, but when the Jacks get er man set, like they did me over in Melbourne, its got ter slump. **1959** S.J. Baker *Drum* 112 *Get someone set*, to have a grudge against a person; to prepare to pay someone out.

set, *v.*[2] [Spec. use of *set* to wager: see OED *v.* 14.]

a. *trans.* To wager (a sum).

1911 A. Wright *Gamblers' Gold* 56 Taking the 'kip' and pennies. . . Yer set 'arf-a-dollar. **1925** —— *Boy from Bullarah* 17 Fair go! Set a quid. **1946** K.S. Prichard *Roaring Nineties* 152 The spinner backed himself to head 'em. The ring-keeper started the betting; got his bet set.

b. *trans.* (in *pass.*) and *intr.* To arrange (a wager), esp. in the game of two-up. Freq. in the phr. **to get set.**

1915 Drew & Evans *Grafter* 62, I had forty pounds to put on it. Twenty of my mate's, and twenty of my own, and I wanted to get it 'set' all in one lump. I didn't want to draw attention to myself by dribbling it on a fiver at a time. **1919** C.H. Thorp *Handful of Ausseys* 247 All set 'n away she goes—a fair spin an' a good 'un; an' it's—'eads. **1946** *Austral. New Writing* 36 Again the side bettors 'get set' between themselves. **1949** L. Glassop *Lucky Palmer* 4 If any of the six horses the boys had taken won the second race he would have to pay ten shillings and he only had two. How could a man make dough when he couldn't get set, he asked himself. **1960** *Centralian Advocate* (Alice Springs) 22 Jan. 3/3 The betting shop, noted throughout Australia as the place where you could get set on any leading race meeting in Australia. **1971** G. Morgan *We are borne On* 333, I was able to get set for my money at ten to one. **1976** S. Weller *Bastards I have Met* 105 They called one bloke 'Jelly' because if you wanted to get on for more than two quid he'd say, 'You're not set.' **1986** *Canberra Times* 9 Mar. 1/1 Whether you want a $1 flutter on your fancy or whether you are a big punter, you will have no trouble getting set with a bookmaker.

c. *trans.* To arrange a wager with (a person).

1915 Drew & Evans *Grafter* 126 'How much do you want?' 'Six pounds to four. . . ' Brummy 'set' him.

d. *Two-up.* In the phr. **to set the centre,** to ensure that the sum waged by the spinner is covered by the players.

1930 L.W. Lower *Here's Luck* (1955) 50 He had a small piece of flat wood in his hand, on which were balanced two pennies. The national game was in progress. . . 'I spin for the lot,' he called. 'Seven and eightpence. Set the centre! Set the centre!' **1931** O. Walters *Shrapnel Green* 26 The centre was set, the side-bets on, and Mick was ready to toss. **1970** R. Beilby *No Medals for Aphrodite* 278 Turk . . heard the ring-keeper's wheedling chant: 'Right-oh, who'll set the centre?' **1977** —— *Gunner* 297 'Wanna quid inna guts,' the ringie chanted. 'Wanna quid. Come on, who'll set the centre?'

sett. *S.A. Obs.* Also **set.** [Used chiefly in Cornwall: see OED *set, sb.*[1] 3 b.] A mining lease.

1846 F. Dutton *S.A. & its Mines* 300 Two brothers . . obtained the first set, for the space of twelve months, at Kapunda . . whose tribute for that period amounted to above £500. **1849** *S. Austral. Register* (Adelaide) 28 July 3/3 The sett is understood to be one of great promise and lies at a considerable distance north of the Provincial mine. **1850** *Ibid.* 18 Mar. 2/1 The mine is leased from the proprietors. . . The set is on block no. 7 of the property. **1867** *Wallaroo Times* (Kadina) 23 Jan. 5/3 Some parties have formed together for the purpose of working a sett known as 'United Prospecting Party's claims'. **1890** H.Y.L. Brown *Rec. of Mines S.A.* (ed. 2) 6 The operations of the company were confined to leasing setts of its land for mining purposes.

settle, *v.* [Used as elsewhere but of local significance: see OED *v.* 4 and 11 b.]

1. a. *trans. Hist.* To settle (a place) with non-Aboriginal inhabitants.

1788 J. Hunter *Hist. Jrnl. Trans. Port Jackson* (1793) 293 Governor Phillip signified his intention of sending me to Norfolk-Island, with a few people, and stock to settle it. **1794** G. Thompson *Slavery & Famine* i. 39 Concerning the policy of settling a new Colony with convicts, I shall say but little. **1821** J. Wallis *Hist. Acct. Colony N.S.W.* 32 To Major Grose . . belongs the credit of having first settled a district, which has ever since been considered . . the granary of the Colony. **1832** J. Backhouse *Narr. Visit Austral. Colonies* (1843) 26 Much of the country was settled: it consisted of hills, generally covered with open grassy forest, and interspersed with little patches of cultivated ground. **1839** J. Stephens *Land of Promise* 52 Australia has been settled by Englishmen. **1851** *Britannia* (Hobart) 23 June 3/4 A serious impediment will . . be thrown in the way of 'settling' a district. **1875** Campbell & Wilks *Early Settlement Qld.* 6 The late John Kent, Esq. . . was . . of great assistance in settling the country. **1924** *Smith's Weekly* (Sydney) 11 Oct. 22/3 The big cattle runs in the north-east corner of N.S.W. are gradually disappearing. Much of that country was close-settled many years ago.

b. *trans.* To establish (a person or body of persons) in a place. Also with **down.**

1812 *HRA* (1916) 1st Ser. VII. 595 The Tract of Country now Occupied by the Wild Cattle will be required in a few Years more for the purpose of Agriculture and Settling People on. **1857** M.B. Hale *Transportation Question* 29 Reasons . . may be put forward . . for settling down the convict population in Western Australia. **1860** W. Henty *On Improvements in Cottage Husbandry* 21 At Norfolk Plains . . Archdeacon Davies has settled several families of free emigrants. **1862** J.A. Patterson *Gold Fields Vic.* 6 The great plains on which we are now settling a race of farming freeholders under the new Land Act. **1918** *Truth* (Sydney) 10 Nov. 1/6 Sufficient land available to settle 4000 soldiers. **1919** C.A. Bernays *Qld. Politics during Sixty Yrs.* 348 More and still more suitable land is being set apart for the exclusive purpose of settling soldiers and accustoming them once more to the conditions of civil life. **1946** A.J. Holt *Wheat Farms Vic.* 53 Four of the five had been settled under Government land-settlement schemes. **1981** A.B. Facey *Fortunate Life* 296 The Government was settling returned soldiers on the land.

2. *intr.* To establish oneself, esp. as a farmer, on land not previously occupied by non-Aboriginal inhabitants.

1788 J. Hunter *Hist. Jrnl. Trans. Port Jackson* (1793) 341 You will make the report to me . . of such who are not convicts, and who are desirous of settling on the island. **1789** *Ibid.* 301 This man had said that the time for which he had been sentenced was expired, and he wished to settle. **1797** *HRA* (1914) 1st Ser. II. 18 Many who were here for life settled without any conditional emancipation or deed. **1820** C. Jeffreys *Van Dieman's Land* 167 An idea has gone abroad that the permission of Government is necessary to settle in the colony. **1827** *Monitor* (Sydney) 24 Feb. 324/3 Many ticket-men . . would marry and settle, if they could settle where they liked. And what is wanted in this colony so much as a married peasantry? **1838** *Tegg's N.S.W. Pocket Almanac* 73 Officers on Half-pay, residing in the Colony where they propose to settle, may be admitted to the privileges of Military and Naval Settlers. **1843** C. Rowcroft *Tales of Colonies* (1858) 26 'Don't call me a settler,' said Crab. 'I arn't going to settle, as you call it; the bushrangers and the convicts and the thieves of people have settled me.' **1848** T.L. Mitchell *Jrnl. Exped. Tropical Aust.* 12 Under this unfavourable aspect the white man first comes before the aboriginal native; were the intruders accompanied by women and children, they could not be half so unwelcome. One of the most striking differences between squatting and settling in Australia consists of this. **1849** A. Harris *Emigrant Family* (1967) 158 Its fifty to one he would go away and live on his pay, and cut settling, if his cattle got such another drilling as the sheep have got. **1859** W. Kelly *Life in Vic.* I. 4 They constrained him to emigrate to South Australia, where he first settled down in the capacity of a squatter. **1890** 'R. Boldrewood' *Colonial Reformer* III. 244 He settled down, under the conditional purchase clause, section 13, upon the very best part of the run. **1927** *R. Comm. on Wireless* 1556 Induce people to settle on the land. **1981** A.B. Facey *Fortunate Life* 49 A settler could take up land and settle on it without much or any money.

settled, *ppl. a.* [Used as elsewhere: see OED 10 and Mathews.]

1. a. Of land (*spec.* that available for alienation): peopled with settlers. See also Unsettled.

1816 *Hobart Town Gaz.* 15 June, Lime can be obtained for erecting buildings on the newly settled Farms.

1827 *HRA* (1923) 3rd Ser. VI. 15 To bring them in contact with the settled parts of the Island. **1839** *Ibid.* (1924) 1st Ser. XX. 6 The Flocks and Herds of the Colonists, depastured beyond the Settled Limits of the Colony. **1843** *Sydney Morning Herald* 31 Oct. 4/5 The settled parts of New Holland, that is to say Eastern Australia, Australia Felix, and Adelaide. **1848** *Sydney Daily Advertiser* 9 June 2/5, I perceive that the lands of the colony of New South Wales are classed into three divisions, and denominated the settled, the intermediate, and the unsettled. **1879** E. Trenerry *Descr. Plan Austral. Trans-Continental Railway* 26 New South Wales . . the oldest and most settled Colony of the Australian group. **1960** *N.T. News* (Darwin) 19 Feb. 9/2 Darwin . . is the closest settled community in Australia to the East.

b. In collocations: **settled country, district, land.**

1861 W. Landsborough *Jrnl. Exped. from Carpentaria* (1862) 7 We saw large quantities of the small white cockatoos, and the rose-coloured ones, which are to be found only in the inland **settled country** of New South Wales and Queensland. **1897** L. Lindley-Cowen *W. Austral. Settler's Guide* 630 In settled country it is the custom to run ploughed furrows round the fences and burn between, but this plan is not practicable in back country. **1944** *Bulletin* (Sydney) 9 Aug. 13/1 The wild cattle seldom mixed with animals from the settled country. **1822** J.T. Bigge *Rep. State Colony N.S.W.* 165 The retirement of the useless or unemployed convicts from the **settled districts** to those that are more remote. **1839** W. Mann *Six Yrs.' Residence* 55 The Aborigines now at large in this island are (if any) very few, and are never met with in the settled districts. **1843** J.F. Bennett *Hist. & Descr. Acct. S.A.* 72 Even within the settled districts, several instances have occurred of murders having been committed by the blacks while endeavouring to possess themselves of the property of the Settlers. **1847** *Port Phillip Herald* 9 Sept. 2/4 The settled district of Geelong is equal to an average-sized English county, and is sufficient for the support of a population of 200,000 souls, or more than the whole present population of Australia, which has been accumulating for sixty years. **1852** W. Hughes *Austral. Colonies* 181 The eastern portion of New South Wales has been divided into forty-six counties. . . These . . extend to a distance of about 150 miles inland. . . These 'settled' districts (as they are termed) comprise about 35,500 square miles. **1866** 'J.W.T.' *Land Question in Qld.* 13 To lock up our lands in the settled districts for fourteen years would be a disgrace to the science of colonisation. **1896** H. Lawson *While Billy Boils* (1975) 100 If we were down among the settled districts we'd be called tramps and beggars; and what's the difference? **1911** *Huon Times* (Franklin) 24 June 5/3 People living in settled districts in Australia in these days have little conception of the extent to which the Australian wild dog has still to be reckoned with. **1820** *HRA* (1921) 3rd Ser. II. 252 The Mountainous Districts adjoining the **Settled Lands.** **1847** *Ibid.* (1925) 1st Ser. XXVI. 121 Considerable portions of their Runs . . have been brought within the class of Settled lands. **1847** *Port Phillip Gaz.* 14 Aug. 1 Within the boundaries of the settled lands, it shall be competent for the Governor . . to grant leases of lands exclusively for pastoral purposes. **1848** W. Westgarth *Aust. Felix* 233 *The division of all the crown lands into three classes*, namely, the settled, intermediate, and unsettled. The settled lands comprehend the nineteen old counties of the colony. . . The intermediate lands comprehend all the remainder of the counties not already included in the settled territory. . . The unsettled lands comprise the rest of the territory. **1853** S. Sidney *Three Colonies* (ed. 2) 188 The settled lands are to be sold by auction at £1 an acre, upset price. . . In the unsettled lands, every holder of a licence is entitled to *demand* a lease for fourteen years. . . In the intermediate districts the lease is to be for eight years only, and the land is liable to be sold at the end of every year. **1854** *Moreton Bay Free Press* 7 Feb. 2/5 Three of these counties, viz: Clinton, Deas Thomson, and Livingstone, are to be classed as *settled lands.* They are *not*, therefore, open to any extent whatever *to pastoral occupation* or squatting.

2. Of a non-Aboriginal: established in Australia.

1839 *Port Phillip Patriot* 10 June 3 This vile hankering after the filthy lucre, is it not picking the pockets of the newly settled Emigrant. **1964** *Bulletin* (Sydney) 18 Jan. 13/3 A British woman who was a settled migrant . . gave regular talks on board.

settlement. [Spec. use of *settlement*: see esp. OED 6, 14, and 15.]

1. a. *Hist.* The British community established in Australia in 1788 and as subsequently enlarged; the land so occupied.

1788 J. Hunter *Hist. Jrnl. Trans. Port Jackson* (1793) 301 Drank the healths of his Majesty, the Queen, the Prince of Wales and success to the settlement. **1793** *Ibid.* 89 He also directed that I should leave the ship's long-boat behind for the use of the settlement. **1796** 'Society Of Gentlemen' *New & Correct Hist. New Holland* 45 When the plan of the settlement was first projected, it was apprehended, that the stores sent from England, together with the produce of the country would be sufficient for the support of the people. **1802** *HRA* (1915) 1st Ser. III. 586 By the general state of the settlement of this date, your Lordship will observe how little our numbers supported by the Crown are encreased since the last return. **1816** *Hobart Town Gaz.* 1 June, The Anniversary of His Majesty's Birth-day . . will be observed as a Holiday throughout the Settlement. **1820** H.G. Bennet *Let. to Earl Bathurst* 62 The settlement in New South Wales is composed of four principal towns or townships. **1827** *Tasmanian* (Hobart) 14 Dec. 2 Establishing a regular market at Richmond . . will be attended with lasting benefit to the Settlement as well as the community. **1833** *Sydney Herald* 4 Mar. 2/1 To make a fortune in a new Settlement is out of the question; it is more difficult to secure it there, than in an old and well peopled country. **1835** R. Torrens *Colonization of S.A.* 12 You will be perfectly free to remove to the neighbouring settlements of New South Wales and Van Dieman's Land. **1841** H.S. Chapman *New Settlement Australind* 27 These settlements are . . New South Wales, sometimes called Eastern Australia, on the eastern coast; Australia Felix, better known from the name of its harbour Port Phillip. **1842** *Austral. & N.Z. Monthly Mag.* 23 Considerable augmentation . . has been received by the arrival . . of the pioneers of the new settlement of Austral-Ind. **1849** C. Sturt *Narr. Exped. Central Aust.* I. 13 The superfluous stock of an old colony was poured down its banks into the new settlement . . and England . . possessed not . . a fairer or a more promising dependency than the province of South Australia. **1863** T. Foster *Rev. Several Explorers Aust.* 3, I propose to follow the white man from his small village on Port Jackson to his rich settlement along the borders of the great Interior. **1865** 'Special Correspondent' *Transportation* 7 The settlement was hapless from the first. Old colonists give lively descriptions of how ladies, blood horses, pianos, and carriages, were landed on a desolate coast . . and no one knew where his particular allotment lay.

b. A place where non-Aboriginal inhabitants of Australia have established themselves, esp. a small town. See also Back settlement.

1792 *Hist. Rec. N.S.W.* (1893) II. 794 Sydney is the spot where the first settlement was formed. **1792** R. Johnson *Address to Colonies N.S.W. & Norfolk Island* p. iv, The colony already begins to spread, and will probably spread more and more every year, both by new settlements formed in different places under the crown, and by a number of individuals continually becoming settlers. **1803** G. Bond *Brief Acct. Colony Port Jackson* 4, I was . . about forty miles from Sydney Cove, on the road leading to a settlement, called Hawkesbury. **1820** C. Jeffreys *Van Dieman's Land* 97 Government having thought it advisable to form another settlement, or town, called George Town . . Launceston has been suffered to go considerably to decay. **1822** J.T. Bigge *Rep. State Colony N.S.W.* 49 At none of the settlements, except Newcastle, or at least in none of the towns, has it been practicable to prevent the sale of spirituous liquors to the convicts. **1843** *HRA* (1924) 1st Ser. XXII. 631 Now they are allowed to walk about the Settlement (or Village). **1845** J.O. Balfour *Sketch of N.S.W.* 61 There are many small towns, called by the colonists settlements, throughout New South Wales. **1852** J. Morgan *Life & Adventures W. Buckley* 14 The particular locality had been chosen as the site of a penal station, it being six hundred miles from the nearest settlement, Sydney. **1885** N.W. Swan *Couple of Cups Ago* 64 A woman who was a stranger, and utterly unknown to every person in the little settlement. **1900** *Tocsin* (Melbourne) 18 Oct. 6/2 A place called the Yellow Water Hole, which quite deserved its name. The name is not that of a settlement, but simply that of a waterhole resorted to by passing teams. **1954** J. Waten *Unbending* 218 He drove down the main street towards a settlement on the other side of the river. **1972** Anderson & Blake *J.S. Neilson* 2 The children watched bullock teams moving slowly out of the settlement, hauling lumbering drays, loaded with supplies, to up-country stations in the hinter-land.

2. The act of settling in Australia: see Settle 2.

1828 J.D. Lang *Narr. Settlement Scots Church* 5 A very great number of free Scottish emigrants have arrived in the Colony . . and effected settlements in all parts of the territory. **1833** *HRA* (1923) 1st Ser. XVII. 67 The Emigration of Females to Australia and their final Settlement there. **1843** J.F. Bennett *Hist. & Descr. Acct. S.A.* 74 When he has once surmounted the difficulties of a first settlement, he usually finds himself well repaid. **1855** 'Rusticus' *How to settle in Vic.* 100 Before we can expect to realise as a fact, the complete and adequate settlement of the Colony. **1881** W. Allen *Immigration & Co-op. Settlement* 1 Fellow Colonists—During the last six months the question of 'Immigration and Settlement' has been before you in the newspapers of the colony. **1890** *Braidwood Dispatch* 5 Feb. 2/5, I saw plenty of excellent wheat land between Perth and Beverly, but a great deal of it has been shut off from settlement, being in the hands of a large freeholder, to whom it has been granted in the early days. **1899** *Progress* (Brisbane) 1 Apr. 1/2 The rental obtained is a secondary matter so long as settlement is secured, the prime consideration of land legislation being the settlement on the land of a white population which will open up the land and create traffic. **1927** M.H. Ellis *Long Lead* 77 A speech about settlement.

3. a. *Obs.* A tract of rural land held by a settler.

1834 H. Carmichael *Hints relating to Emigrants* 6 The substantial advantages of obtaining a settlement in New South Wales are . . questionless.

b. Special Comb. **settlement lease,** a form of agreement governing the tenure of some rural landholdings; the landholding itself (see quot 1912); **scheme,** a plan to bring about rural development by encouraging the establishment of farmers in underdeveloped areas.

1896 *Austral. Handbk.* 99 Small settlement is provided for by conditional purchase, homestead, **settlement** and improvement **leases.** **1908** *Truth* (Sydney) 11 Oct. 1/8 For eight settlement leases in the Moree district, there were 249 applicants. **1912** *Cwlth. of Aust. for Farmers* (Dept. External Affairs) 99 *Settlement Lease*—Areas up to 1,280 acres for agricultural purposes, and 10,240 acres for grazing, may be obtained as settlement leases. Such leases have a term of forty years, and provision is made for the reappraisement of the rent every ten years. **1921** J.P. Osborne *Nine Crowded Yrs.* 19 In 1895 J.H. (now Sir Joseph) Carruthers had passed a Bill creating new forms of land tenure called Settlement Leases. **1935** B.E. Phelps *Austral. tells England* 167 Austin & Percy Sampson were among the first to obtain Settlement Leases. **1965** *N. Austral. Monthly* Feb. 21 The Daly flows through good agricultural land . . and it would seem that a **settlement scheme** there could be a wonderful thing for the Territory. **1981** A.B. Facey *Fortunate Life* 16 The McCalls were one of the first families to settle in the wheat-belt of Western Australia under the Government land settlement schemes.

4. An Aboriginal community administered by a public authority. Also *attrib.*

1911 A. Searcy *By Flood & Field* 285 A strange Myall native reported (through the Settlement blacks) . . a big mob of cattle. **1961** *Bulletin* (Sydney) 15 Feb. 32/1 The aborigines at the Settlement said that if you were an aboriginal you did not have to do anything. **1964** *N. Austral. Monthly* July 25 He has only had mission and settlement schooling, but is now earning eighteen pounds a week. **1978** *Nungalinya Occasional Bull.* (Darwin) iii. 12 The development of Aboriginal art . . is a facet of settlement life over which Aborigines have considerable pride and control.

settler. [Spec. use of *settler* one who settles in a new country: see OED(S 2.]

1. One who settles in Australia: see Settle 2; a (small) farmer; an immigrant. See also Back settler. Also *attrib.*

1788 J. Hunter *Hist. Jrnl. Trans. Port Jackson* (1793) 340 After the time for which they are sentenced may expire, lands will be granted them, if they wish to remain as settlers. **1788** *HRA* (1914) 1st Ser. I. 95 It must . . be settlers, with the assistance of the convicts, that will put this country in a situation for supporting its inhabitants. **1791** *Ibid.* 243 Such of the convicts, whose term of transportation may be expired, and who have been permitted to live on the above farms, are during the time they stay on the island to consider themselves as servants to the public, except in such cases where they may be allowed to become settlers. **1792** D. COLLINS *Acct. Eng. Colony N.S.W.* (1798) I. 243 Three warrants of emancipation passed the seal of the territory: one to John Trace, a convict who came out in the first fleet; having but three months of his term of transportation remaining, that portion of it was given up to him, that he might become a settler. **1808** 'GENTLEMAN JUST RETURNED FROM SETTLEMENT' *Acct. Eng. Colony Botany Bay* 10 The first settler in this country who declared himself able to live on the produce of his farm, without any assistance from the stores, was James Ruse. **1811** *Sydney Gaz.* 2 Mar., All the Settlers have by this time thrashed out and prepared their Wheat for delivery. **1824** E. CURR *Acct. Colony Van Diemen's Land* p. iv, Frequent excursions through most parts of the country afforded me abundant opportunity of observing . . that class of persons usually called 'settlers'. **1827** *Monitor* (Sydney) 30 Mar. 362/1 More settlers i.e. labourers, not settlers of capital, are wanted. **1829** J. ATKINSON *Distilling & Brewing N.S.W.* 5 The settlers who were establishing themselves in the neighbourhood, and the graziers who were forming new stations . . have hitherto created a temporary and local demand for wheat. **1833** *Launceston Advertiser* 15 Aug. 2 Let us take an individual case. Take a settler—the true colonist. **1838** T. WALKER *Month in Bush Aust.* 53 It was frequently a subject of remark to me, how much leisure the New South Wales settler (farmer) seemed possessed of, compared with the business classes in towns. **1843** *Duncan's Weekly Register* (Sydney) 16 Sept. 106/2 Why should the squatter have a distinct privilege that the settler or citizen does not possess? **1861** C. CAMPBELL *Squatting Question Considered* 4 Settlers arrived . . from New South Wales and Van Diemen's Land and from Home. **1872** W.M. HUGO *Hist. First Bushmen's Club* 93 There should be six trustees in all—viz., two settlers, two citizens and two bush people appointed. **1881** T. ARCHER *Hist., Resources, & Future Prospects Qld.* 3 In the interior the squatter or pastoralist must precede the settler or agriculturist. **1898** M. DAVITT *Life & Progress* 90 The population of the village was 350 at the start, when the number of settlers was ninety. Women do not rank as 'settlers'. **1903** *Truth* (Sydney) 11 Jan. 1/3 Settlers were scuttling off the soil into the towns and cities. **1917** *Huon Times* (Franklin) 18 May 5/3 We can take it for granted that the settler class will nominate someone for the position and we may look forward to having to pay for an election. **1922** *Daily Mail* (Sydney) 20 Jan. 5/2 He will actively support the move to induce the graziers and farmers and settlers to form a new party with a new name. **1945** E.W. CAMPBELL *Hist. Austral. Labour Movt.* 96 The Hon. A.K. Trethowan, President of the Farmers' and Settlers' Association . . Colonel Alfred Spain, of the Graziers' Association. **1945** A.A. CALWELL *How Many Australs. Tomorrow* 51 From 1929 to 1937 . . more British settlers left this country than entered it. **1950** C.E. GOODE *Yarns of Yilgarn* 23 Quite a number of settlers (who now like to be called farmers) were married, and their smart motors could be seen. **1971** *Bulletin* (Sydney) 8 May 24/1 Settlers in professional occupations are, this year, 6.4 percent of the total compared with 5.8 percent last year. **1985** *Ibid.* 24 Dec. 66/1 Settlers come as strangers to select the land, go through times of suspicion and competitiveness but come together in hardship.

2. *Hist.* In the phr. **settler of the first class**: see quot. 1815.

1811 *Sydney Gaz.* 27 Apr., To Gentlemen Settlers, or Settlers of the first Class and the Wives of absent Civil and Military Officers. **1815** *HRA* (1916) 1st Ser. VIII. 559 Settlers of the first Class (that is Gentlemen who are Supposed to be possessed of Sufficient Property to maintain themselves). **1829** *Ibid.* (1922) 1st Ser. XIV. 725 The Equalization of my original Grant to the Extent of *that* allotted to a Settler of the first Class. **1830** *Sydney Monitor* 23 June 3/3 Mr Sharp is a settler of the first class—he has three sections of land at Hunter's River.

3. a. [Also U.S.] In the collocation **old settler,** one of the earliest settlers in Australia or in a particular district. Also *attrib.*

1827 P. CUNNINGHAM *Two Yrs. in N.S.W.* I. 195 An old settler can always readily tell whether it is to be a dewy night or not, by the appearance of the sky and state of the air. **1849** J. PATTISON *N.S.W.* 18 The stoppage of assignment . . was far from palatable to the old settlers. **1859** J.D. MEREWEATHER *Diary Working Clergyman* 50 Some of these were old settlers, who had been induced by the cheapness of land and labour to choose Van Diemen's Land. **1873** A. TROLLOPE *Aust. & N.Z.* I. 321 Windsor . . a quaint little place, inhabited by old settlers. **1888** 'R. BOLDREWOOD' *Robbery under Arms* (1937) 25 Only doing what people said half the old settlers had made their money by. **1944** R. BEDFORD *Naught to Thirty-Three* 193 The old settlers' objections to giving immediate political power to the Easterners was based on sound premises. If the fields failed the invasion would ebb leaving the bill to be paid by the Westerners. **1979** S.W. DUTHIE *Fiddlers Creek* 129, I suppose that there's lots of old settler families around the place besides the Kinnears but I bet not many of them like to look too far back in their family history.

b. In special collocations: **settler's cake** *obs.*, see quot.; **clock,** the kookaburra *Dacelo novaeguineae*; *bushman's clock*, see BUSHMAN 8; SHEPHERD'S CLOCK; **friend** *obs.*, *settler's matches* (and see quot.); **man** *obs.*, a convict assigned to a settler; **matches,** strips of bark useful as kindling.

1843 C. ROWCROFT *Tales of Colonies* (1858) 325 There's a real **settler's cake** for you, gentlemen, made nice and light, like a pancake, only it wants eggs and milk. **1827** P. CUNNINGHAM *Two Yrs. in N.S.W.* I. 232 The loud and discordant noise of the *laughing jackass* (or **settler's clock**, as he is called), as he takes up his roost on the withered bough of one of our tallest trees acquaints us that the sun has just dipped behind the hills. **1845** L. LEICHHARDT *Jrnl. Overland Exped. Aust.* (1847) 234, I usually rise when I hear the merry laugh of the laughing-jackass (Dacelo gigantea), which, from its regularity, has not been unaptly named the settler's clock. **1846** G.H. HAYDON *Five Yrs.' Experience Aust. Felix* 71 The laughing jackass, or settler's clock, is an uncouth looking creature of an ashen brown colour. **1863** B.A. HEYWOOD *Vacation Tour Antipodes* 128 Early in the morning I was aroused by the laughing jackass. This bird is called the Settler's Clock, and commences his mingled laugh and bray at sunset and sunrise. **1876** J.A. EDWARDS *Gilbert Gogger* 80 Scarcely were they at their posts, than the cry of the settler's clock was heard. **1907** *Bulletin* (Sydney) 31 Oct. 15/3 The goburra has been called the 'settler's clock', but he should be altogether an unreliable one. Jacko is apt to go off at any time. **1916** A.I. MACLEOD *Hack's Brat* (1920) 61 She had been up with the Settler's Clocks, and had followed their flight from place to place. **1932** C.M. GRAY *Western Vic. in Forties* 5 We all slept soundly until awakened by the 'Settler's Clock' . . and the sweet note of the magpie. **1943** C. BARRETT *Swagman's Note-Bk.* 14 'Settler's clock' . . has long been obsolete as a name for our laughing cavalier in feathers. **1856** G. WILLMER *Draper in Aust.* 217 It is no uncommon thing still to hear men in the bush speak of this bark and the green hide (the latter is used for halters) as the **settler's friend.** **1804** *Sydney Gaz.* 11 Mar., The Prisoners at Public Labour at Castle Hill, and the **Settlers** [*sic*] **men,** were in a state of Insurrection. **1838** *Rep. Select Committee Transportation* 22 Mar. 122 Do you think some of the settlers treat their convicts harshly?—Yes. Is there a great deal of punishment inflicted?—Not a great deal, on the settlers' men, generally. **1842** *Sydney Herald* 16 July 2/5 The following is an outline of the present state of Cockatoo Island: Iron Gang men, 165 . . Settlers' men under colonial sentence, 74. **1891** *Bulletin* (Sydney) 19 Dec. 21/2 And we walked so very silent—being lost in reverie—That we heard the **'settler's matches'** gently rustle on the tree. **1948** R. RAVEN-HART *Canoe in Aust.* 35 Bits of last-year bark and dry leaves make better fire-lighters than any sold in the shops—they are 'settler's matches' in Australian slang. **1955** M. CORBEN *Not to mention Kangaroos* 204 Sid stripped some stringy bark from a eucalyptus tree and explained, 'We call these 'settler's matches'.'

settling, *vbl. n. Hist.*

1. The action of SETTLE 1.

1789 *HRA* (1914) 1st Ser. I. 127 It has been found by experience that the settling plantees in townships hath very much redounded to their advantage. **1799** D. COLLINS *Acct. Eng. Colony N.S.W.* (1802) II. 200 The government store-house . . had been erected at the first settling of this part of the country. **1816** *Hobart Town Gaz.* 20 July, There has only been one season since the settling of the Colony . . so inclement **1839** *S. Austral. Rec.* (London) (1840) 22 Feb. 63 An hour and a quarter's drive of nine miles brought us to the station of Mr Henty, distant from Portland bay about forty miles. . . The Messrs Henty have the merit of discovery and first settling this fine country, and, in my opinion, have displayed singular judgment in their selection.

2. The action of SETTLE 2.

1789 A. PHILLIP *Voyage to Botany Bay* 174 Having been so short a time in this country, cannot determine whether he would wish to remain or not, as to settling can say nothing. **1804** *HRA* (1921) 3rd Ser. I. 244 With respect to his Settling at King's Island. **1833** *Launceston Advertiser* 29 Aug. 2 Hobart Town, and 'the bush', and practical 'settling' . . effectually dissipated my daydreams. **1841** *S. Austral. Mag.* Dec. 205 Settling has made me very utilitarian in my notions, and housewifery appears to me as no mean science.

seven.

1. *Hist.* In the *attrib. phr.* **seven year(s'),** used to designate a convict sentenced to seven years of penal servitude. See also SEVENER.

1827 P. CUNNINGHAM *Two Yrs. in N.S.W.* II. 269 The youngster I speak of was therefore the second son induced to entitle himself to a seven years' trip to Botany. **1829** H. WIDOWSON *Present State Van Diemen's Land* 63 A seven years' convict . . is . . the best prisoner that can be sent out. **1833** T. BANNISTER *Let. on Colonial Labour* 12 Seven years men, if sent at all, three years in the Gangs. **1837** G. LOVELESS *Victims of Whiggery* 16 No seven years' man is to obtain a ticket-of-leave till he has been four years in the colony. **1849** J. PATTISON *N.S.W.* 16 Seven-years men received their tickets at the expiry of four years. **1869** T. ATKINS *Reminisc.* 76 Two convict servants, one of them a *seven*, the other a *fourteen* years' prisoner of the crown. **1948** F. CLUNE *Wild Colonial Boys* 7 Only three classes of convicts were transported to New South Wales. . . Lifers and fourteeners were destined for hard labour on the roads and public buildings of the colony, while the seven-year men . . were . . assigned as unpaid servants to private employers and landowners in the colony.

2. In the phr. **to chuck (do, throw) a** (or **the**) **seven,** to die; to faint, vomit, or otherwise lose one's composure.

1894 *Worker* (Sydney) 18 Aug. 2/5, I am pretty cronk and shaky—too far gone for hell or heaven, An' the chances are I'm goin'—that I'm goin' to 'do the seven'. **1908** *Truth* (Sydney) 3 May 1/7 We miss him in the morn, We miss him in the noon, We did not think our darling brother Would chuck a seven so soon. **1915** *Bulletin* (Sydney) 28 Jan. 22/2 The Birdsville horse disease is peculiar to the lower Diamantina country. . . A horse may . . be fit and well in the morning, and by midday may suddenly collapse, struggle in agony for perhaps half an hour, and then pass out. The victims may go through several fits before finally throwing a seven. **1927** J. MATHIEU *Backblock Ballads* 2 But that poor old Billy Bevan—All of you remember Bill—Monday morning chucked the seven, And his wife is very ill. **1935** R.B. PLOWMAN *Boundary Rider* 151 'Can't kill you bushmen with a meataxe. . . ' 'All the same, I don't want to come so near chucking a seven as I did that time, not if I live to be a hundred.' **1936** *Bulletin* (Sydney) 1 Apr. 21/1 Any Aboliar know how much electricity it takes to make a snake throw a seven? **1949** C. BENHAM *Diver's Luck* 59 She'll be goin' in with her flag half-mast. Well that's another Japanese what's chucked a seven. **1958** V. KELLY *Greedy Ones* 73 'The padre had gone out to it—thrown a seven.' 'Mr Mathieson had fainted,' said Murrill. **1978** HANIGAN & LINDSAY *No Tracks on River* 96 Of course, his Mum straight away chucked a seven and squealed, 'Careful, Deryck, careful. Oh, do be careful!' **1982** *Bulletin* (Sydney) 25 May 50/3 If you drink enough you'll get *shickered* . . or even *chuck a seven* (which means succumb, in whole or in part).

3. A measure of beer. Also **seven-ounce.**

1962 *Meanjin* 323 He stood erect in the far corner and drank a seven-ounce. **1975** 'N. CULOTTA' *Gone Gougin'* 28 The old Australian sun was hot on my face, and making me sleepy. The three middies and two sevens consumed in Walgett were assisting it. **1972** J. O'GRADY *It's your Shout, Mate!* 66 'Could you make that a beer?' . . Putting it in front of me, she said, 'There you are. Eight ounces. Mind you, in the bush you'll only get seven ounces. They call it a seven.' 'Do you know the reason for that?' 'They reckon it's the freight,' she said. **1984** P. CORRIS *Winning Side* 69 'Get you a seven,' he said. It came, along with his fresh schooner, and he emptied it into my half-full glass.

4. *pl.* See quot. 1982.

1965 K. SMITH *OGF* 106 Bernard Borker . . condemned all lotteries, games of chance . . cards (including fish, sevens and grab) and the T.A.B. **1982** P. ADAM SMITH *Shearers* 280 These men remember the big tin shed on the banks of the Thompson River where they broke down their cut-out cheque playing local variants of Crap called Yankee Grab, Murrumbidgee and Sevens.

sevener. *Hist.* A convict sentenced to seven years of penal servitude: see also SEVEN 1.

1847 *Port Phillip Herald* 3 Aug. 3/1 The Pentonville convict . . exclaimed to a fellow 'exile', 'halloo! there's an old bloke of a 'seven'ner' for you!' **1948** F. CLUNE *Wild Colonial Boys* 7 The lifers and long-sentence men lorded it over the seveners . . for the lifers and long-termers had abandoned hope.

shade. Used *attrib.* and *absol.* to designate a shelter made to afford protection from the sun, esp. for plants.

1886 J.F. CONIGRAVE *S.A.* 87 It is hardly possible to grow camellias, ericas, and similar plants that can be affected by hot drying winds, except under what are termed 'shade houses', which are structures made with lath roofs, having a space of about an inch between each lath. **1890** A. MACKAY *Austral. Agriculturist* (ed. 2) 224 The Shade or Bush Frame . . is one of the handiest and most effective contrivances in our Australian practice. What we require is protection from drying winds and heavy rains, and this we get by making up a seed bed in the ordinary way. . . Then to furnish shade and shelter, stakes are fitted at the corners, and a cover of bushes, calico, or old sacking, is made to fit over the bed in such a manner as allows of its being fitted close to the soil, say six inches above it, or it can be fixed two feet above it. **1929** K.S. PRICHARD *Coonardoo* (1961) 29 She watched Coonardoo swinging down to the uloo one evening when she had left her gina gina in the shade miah. *Ibid.* 53 There was no scrap of green, no tree about it. Only a shade shed of rusty leaves at one side. **1952** *Meanjin* 197 Mary packed her three children and belongings into the mailman's truck at Kakarra, and went out to live with Jim in his tent and the brushwood shade he had made for her. **1962** D. LOCKWOOD *I, Aboriginal* 35 My Uncle Stanley carried me away to a shadehouse and stayed with me there for five days while I recuperated.

shaft. *Obs.* [Spec. use of *shaft* one of the long bars between a pair of which a draught animal is harnessed to a vehicle.] Used *attrib.* in Special Comb. **shaft bullock,** a bullock harnessed between the shafts of a vehicle; **dray,** a two-wheeled cart having a pair of shafts rather than a central pole.

1827 P. CUNNINGHAM *Two Yrs. in N.S.W.* I. 294 Harness, however, is absolutely necessary for the **shaft-bullock,** when setting your carts to work. **1847** A. HARRIS *Settlers & Convicts* (1953) 125 We dismounted and helped to release the shaft bullock. **1849** —— *Emigrant Family* (1967) 176 Mr Hurley . . fetch my shaft-bullock. **1848** H.W. HAYGARTH *Recoll. Bush Life* 49 In some districts, chiefly in the vicinity of Bathurst, **shaft-drays** are used; but pole-drays are found to be more suitable to the nature of the country. **1849** 'BUSHMAN' *Sidney's Austral. Handbk.* 70 There are two sorts of drays, the pole and the shaft. I prefer the pole, because if it capsizes the bullocks are never hurt, whereas with a shaft dray you are liable to kill your shafter.

shafter. [Transf. use of *shafter* a shaft-horse.] *Shaft bullock*, see SHAFT; also (loosely) POLER 1.

1843 A. CASWALL *Hints from Jrnl.* 33 A two-wheeled dray with a pole, is certainly better than with shafts, as if it upsets it turns in the ring-bolt of the pole yoke, and the bullocks sustain no injury; whereas when one with shafts is capsized, the shafter is frequently killed. **1849** A. HARRIS *Emigrant Family* (1967) 30 There is a team of seven bullocks . . a shafter, and three pair of yoke oxen. **1882** MRS J.C. STANGER *Journey from Sydney* 29 The bullock drays were larger and stronger than the horse drays, with single shafts; the heaviest animals were chosen for the 'shafters', which were harnessed the same as horses to the shafts. **1907** C. MACALISTER *Old Pioneering Days* 146 His performance reminded us of the 'shafters' (bullocks) down in the Hawkesbury country, many years agone. **1939** J. SORENSEN *Lost Shanty* 16 The shafters prop, the leaders pull, The wheels creak dismally.

shag, *n.*[1] Used esp. in the phr. **a shag on a rock** (or **stick**) as an emblem of isolation, deprivation, or exposure.

1845 R. HOWITT *Impressions Aust. Felix* 233 The common people are not destitute of what Wordsworth calls 'the poetry of common speech'. . . 'Poor as a bandicoot', 'Miserable as a shag on a rock', &c.; these and others I very frequently heard. **1929** W.J. RESIDE *Golden Days* 16 The flood waters did not subside, and we were there like three shags on a rock. **1951** I.L. IDRIESS *Across Nullarbor* 7 Left us sitting there like shags on a stick! **1957** D. WHITINGTON *Treasure upon Earth* 123 If I moved from here I'd be like a shag on a rock. I wouldn't know a soul in a new suburb. **1965** K. SMITH *OGF* 192 It was the voice of Godley, in high gear, raised to compete with the noise around him, but suddenly left by itself like a shag on a rock, when everybody else quietened down in response to the gong. **1982** *Sydney Morning Herald* 28 Jan. 28/3 Perhaps it was a sympathetic reaction to one who was made to look like an old shag sitting on his proverbial rock that rallied my friends about me.

shag, *n.*[2] [Spec. use of *shag* an act of sexual intercourse.] Used *attrib.* in Special Comb. **shag-bag,** a derogatory term for a woman; **-wagon,** a panel van (or station wagon), appointed as a convenient place in which to engage in sexual intercourse; also **shaggin' wagon.**

1944 *Troppo Tribune* (Mataranka) 21 Feb. 2 Old '**Shag-bag**' is very fond of snakes. **1956** E. LAMBERT *Watermen* 46 'Is that fat shag-bag of mine in there? I feel like playing tonight.' 'She is', said Finnigan, 'and chalking all her beer up to you.' **1975** S. FRENCH *Hey Phantom Singlet* 56 'Didja see Hustler posing off in his **shag wagon** this morning?' . . 'It's not so old—69 Holden.' **1978** J. COLBERT *Ranch* 38 The money he spent on that stupid bike he could have got an old shag-waggon and played the field. **1978** L. O'CHARLEY *Anatomy of Strike* 25 The spectre of surfing bums and shaggin' waggons had faded from the scene. **1979** B. HUMPHRIES *Bazza comes into his Own*, I need wheels. Reckon you can lend me your shag wagon tomorra? **1982** R. HALL *Just Relations* 287 Wasn't he ready to get into her bed . . in as strong a position as any young hoodlum with a shag-wagon.

shake, *v.*[1] [Survival of Br. slang *shake* to steal: see OED *v.* 16 b.] *trans.* To steal (something); to rob (someone). Also as *vbl. n.*

1812 J.H. VAUX *Mem.* (1819) II. 204 *Shake*, to steal, to rob; as, I *shook* a chest of *slop*, I stole a chest of tea. **1845** *Parramatta Chron.* 10 May 1/4 *Till robbing*, a man named Richard Ford, was on Friday committed to take his trial for *titilating* or 'shaking' the cash-box of his employer, Mr Graham of 'The Labor in Vain' in Sussex-street. **1847** *Melbourne Argus* 10 Sept. 2/4 He heard the prisoner boast of having given the flour bag a 'shaking', and it was then discovered that a considerable quantity of flour had also been stolen. **1855** *Ovens & Murray Advertiser* (Beechworth) 3 Feb. 6/2 *Horse-stealing.* John McCarthy attempted to 'shake' a horse on the 27th ult. **1862** H. BROWN *Vic. as I found It* 89 Shake your horses! why you didn't think I wanted to steal them, did you? **1874** A. TROLLOPE *Harry Heathcote* 145 Jerry had unblushingly declared that he himself had 'shaken' the horse (Anglice, had stolen him twelve months since on Darnley Downs). **1892** *Bulletin* (Sydney) 5 Nov. 17/2 And so he went to Brickfield Hill, and from a draper there He 'shook' the proper kind of togs to fetch a 'square affair'. **1903** W. CRAIG *My Adventures* 191 They had been sitting on the side of their bed for some time, smoking and conversing, when the man lowered his voice to a whisper, and wondered if 'he' was worth 'shaking' (*i.e.* robbing). **1914** C.H.S. MATTHEWS *Bill* 132 He was far from being honest, and would think no more of 'shaking' a horse, if he happened to want one, than of having his breakfast. **1925** J.E. LIDDLE *Selected Poems* 127 Theives [*sic*] durst not raid them, none so bold As 'shake' another's gold alone. **1933** J. TRURAN *Where Plain Begins* 13 That'll pay for some o' the fish you've shook from me. **1950** G.M. FARWELL *Land of Mirage* 112 Men 'shook' their neighbours' calves and then diced with them. **1962** MARSHALL & DRYSDALE *Journey among Men* 56 Beside the opener was a notice that requested the rare customer to replace in the refrigerator fresh bottles from the cases for any cold ones that he cared to use, to leave his payment in the meat tin, and above all not to 'for Christ's sake, shake (steal) the bloody opener'. **1981** K. GARVEY *Rhymes of Ratbag* 141 It doesn't do to shake some beef. The police narks always pool yer.

shake, *v.*[2] [Spec. use of *shake* to cause to quiver: see OED(S 11 d.] In the phr. **to be shook on** (or **after**), to be enamoured of; to be well-disposed towards.

1868 *Sydney Punch* 11 July 58/1 And thither I'll quickly repair With the maiden on whom I am shook. **1889** H. EGBERT *Pretty Cockey* 76 The fool seems to think I am 'shook' on him. **1892** *Bulletin* (Sydney) 20 Feb. 14/2 Still 'shook' on some beautiful, blushing she? Girl in the Bogan side, Paddy Magee? **1901** H. LAWSON *Joe Wilson & his Mates* 26 He was supposed to be shook after Mary too. **1922** V. PALMER *Telling Mrs Baker* (1924) 66 I'm not too shook on the whole scheme now we're here. I believe it would have been better for her if we'd settled to tell her the whole truth. **1940** *Bulletin* (Sydney) 15 May 16/1 Old Baldy wasn't too shook on the pair of Uni. undergrads. who pitched their natty tent close to his own humpy on the Murray. **1955** R. LAWLER *Summer of Seventeenth Doll* (1965) 29 She's not too shook on the whole thing. Doesn't understand it, for one thing. **1963** D. NILAND *Dadda Jumped* 39 Norah was shook on a big cane-cutter with more hair on his chest than a goat. **1977** B. SCOTT *My Uncle Arch* 63 Those stories you read about in books where two blokes get shook on the same sheila.

shaker. *Gold-mining.*

a. A machine in which auriferous gravel, sand, etc., is agitated to separate out alluvial gold without the use of water.

1901 *Twentieth Century Impressions W.A.* 202 The gold is being found, not on the surface of the earth, but a thousand feet beneath it, and the rattle of the 'shaker' has long been changed to the 'growl of the sluicing stamphead'. **1903** A.G. CHARLETON *Gold Mining & Milling W.A.* 33 This slow and laborious process is frequently superseded by a 'machine' for sizing the material, operated on the same general principles, which, in its simplest form, is known as a 'shaker', owing to the shaking motion imparted to it. **1915** J.P. BOURKE *Off Bluebush* 103 Does the nebulous fossicker's star ever shed On your shaker, one flickering ray? **1928** R.M. MACDONALD *Opals & Gold* 120 After wheeling their 'shaker', as the dry-blowing machine is commonly termed. **1944** M.J. O'REILLY *Bowyangs & Boomerangs* 9 On account of the scarcity of water . . the 'cradle' could not be employed. We were compelled to adopt new methods to save the gold, so dry panning, the shaker, and the blower were used. **1972** N. KING *Nickel Country* 3 This is the most primitive form of extracting alluvial gold. The men who owned 'shakers', or dry-blowers, shovelled the earth in and began shaking the dirt away.

b. Special Comb. **shaker dryblower** (or **blower**), a machine which combines the properties of a shaker and a DRYBLOWER b.

1939 A. GASTON *Coolgardie Gold* 76 Several different kinds of dryblowing machines were at work, but the shaker and Steve Lordern's patent dryblower were the most popular. The shaker dryblower came in some time later. It is the most perfect dryblowing goldsaver ever invented. **1941** D. O'CALLAGHAN *Long Life Reminisc.* 135, I specked the gold a mile from Shannons' Patch, and gave it a go for a day or two with their shaker dryblowers. **1977** J. DOUGHTY *Gold in Blood* 91 Only it wasn't a shaker now. It was a shaker-blower that I had built myself in Coolgardie under the guidance of Tom Collings. My first dryblower.

Shaky Isles. Also **Shakey Isles.** New Zealand (from the frequency there of earthquakes). Cf. SHIVERY ISLES.

1933 *Bulletin* (Sydney) 2 Aug. 20/2 The widespread notion that they're peculiar to the Shaky Isles. **1943** *Bully Tin* (Baronta) 21 Aug. 1 A team of husky Aussies . . sailed to the Shakey Isles. **1970** N.A. BEAGLEY *Up & Down Under* 111 A kind word for one from the 'Shaky Isles', as New Zealand is called by the Aussies. **1985** *Bulletin* (Sydney) 29 Oct. 21/3 Will you *please* stop referring to New Zealand as the Shaky Isles?

shaler, var. SHEILA.

shallow, *a. Gold-mining. Obs.* Used in collocations with reference to the mining of gold occurring close to the surface, as **shallow (-ground) rush,** (the working of) a goldfield having deposits of gold close to the surface (see RUSH *n.* 2 c.); **sinker,** a miner who works deposits of gold close to the surface; **sinking** *vbl. n.*, see quot. 1871.

1859 *Colonial Mining Jrnl.* Feb. 90/2 One or two **shallow rushes** have taken place on the ground between the Norfolk head and the Catholic Chapel. **1870** B. WITHERS *Hist. Ballarat* 138 To an old goldfields man . . the sight of a little shallow-ground 'rush' now, is like a sweet vision of childhood. **1868** J. BAIRD *Emigrant's Guide* 171 The diggers were of diverse kinds—surfacers, **shallow-sinkers**, deep-sinkers, and quartz crushers—some being all these in turn. **1870** 'COLONIST TWENTY YRS. STANDING' *Vic., Brit. 'El Dorado'* 108 Here and there the 'shallow sinker'—the surface digger—has dug and dug. **1854** *Bell's Life in Sydney* 2 Sept. 1/1 It took its rise at the base of the Black Hill in **shallow sinking**, and has all along been remarkable for the depth and richness of its washing-stuff and the steadiness of its yield. **1868** J. BAIRD *Emigrant's Guide Australasia* 171 By shallow-sinking and surfacing whatever of the precious metal lay within easy reach was got at. **1871** J. BALLANTYNE *Homes & Homesteads* 40 *Shallow sinking*—digging holes in the creeks and low grounds, and getting the gold-impregnated soil from the surface of clay stones, sandstones, and slates.

shammy. *Gold-mining.* A bag of chamois leather in which a miner keeps the gold he finds. Also **shammy bag.**

1874 G. WALCH *Head over Heels* 83 Here it is—in this old Shammy bag. **1898** D.W. CARNEGIE *Spinifex & Sand* 325 When . . a fossicker comes in with a 'shammy' full of gold . . then indeed the hotel-keeper's harvest is a rich one. **1929** W.J. RESIDE *Golden Days* 386 Peep not into digger's larder—Index of his 'shammy', that. **1936** *Bulletin* (Sydney) 25 Mar. 20/1 Fossickers go mooching round for gold to fill their 'shammies'. **1946** K.S. PRICHARD *Roaring Nineties* 63 The pace was fast and furious while the gold in a man's shammy lasted. **1950** J. MCLAREN *New Love for Old* 129 He saw himself putting the gold into the chamois leather bags which prospectors used. They were about the size of a man's pocket and the diggers called them 'shammys'. **1960** I.L. IDRIESS *Wild North* 179 On the grass outside, spilt carelessly on chaff-bags, were shammies of 'shotty' gold.

shandygaff. *Obs.* [Fig. use of *shandygaff* a drink composed of a mixture of beer and ginger-beer.] A compromise which pleases neither side. Also **shandygaffer.** Freq. *attrib.*

1897 *Worker* (Sydney) 11 Sept. 1/1 But when its only second-class (it often makes me laugh) He calls the blessed document a blanky 'shandy-gaff'. **1901** *Tocsin* (Melbourne) 10 Oct. 6/2 Contact with Labourites in the Kanaka State impresses one with their determination, sincerity, ability, and courage. The 'Shandygaff Party', as they term those of the moderate Labour tendency, are not wanted here. **1904** *Shearer* (Sydney) 26 Nov. 3/1 Mount Bute cut out on Nov. 11th. A shandygaff lot, thirteen shearers, five shed hands, and two cooks took tickets out of sixty odd hands. A pity we cannot get the preference clause and bar a lot of the half-breeds. **1908** *Official Rep. Austral. Labour Conference* 27 If alliances and immunity were allowed, it would have a serious disintegrating effect on the Movement in Victoria—and he believed in Australia—and they would get in return nothing but political 'shandy-gaffers'. **1937** *Publicist* (Sydney) xv. 6/1 These are the half-and-halfs, the shandy-gaff Australians, who don't know yet what they are.

Hence **shandygaffy** *a.*, prone to compromise.

1895 *Worker* (Sydney) 10 Aug. 1/4, I want to growl. Your Newcastle contributor 'Shandy Gaff' is true to name—he's very *shandy-gaffy* in politics, judging from his 'Notes' in your issue of August 3.

shanghai /'ʃæŋhaɪ/, *n.*[1] [Prob. altered form of *shangie*, var. of Scot. dial. *shangan* a stick cleft at one end: see OED.] A catapult.

1863 *Leader* (Melbourne) 24 Oct. 17/1 Turn, turn thy shanghay dread aside, Nor touch that little bird. **1875** *Spectator & Methodist Chron.* (Melbourne) 15 May 22/1 (OED) The lads had with them a couple of pistols, powder, shot, bullets, and a shanghai. **1902** *Bulletin* (Sydney) 13 Dec. 19/2 'Jack says you have a shanghai. Is it true!' 'Ye-e-e-s,' faltered Willie. 'Fetch it here.' When Willie brought the catapult Cockie Anderson threw it into the fire. **1907** *Truth* (Sydney) 8 Sept. 1/7 A lad named John Riddle for shooting stones from a shanghai in the street at Artarmon . . was fined 10s. **1918** N. CAMPBELL *Dinky-Di Soldier* 7 I'd like to see *you* try to fire a gun, A kiddie's shanghai suits you best, old son. **1943** *Bulletin* (Sydney) 4 Aug. 13/3 My nipper has already got over the rubber shortage by using two worms as springs on his shanghai. **1954** J.E. MACDONNELL *Jim Brady* 11 A shanghai with rubber bands cut from an old bicycle tube. **1968** S. GORE *Holy Smoke* 13 All I needeth is me shanghai here, and a few of these big coonies that's layin' around, and I'll get stuck into it. **1982** *Yulngu* Dec. 36 When we got up Gary and Simon were making some shanghais.

shanghai /'ʃæŋhaɪ/, *n.*[2] *Obs.* [Prob. altered form of *shandrydan* a rickety old-fashioned vehicle.] A ramshackle old vehicle.

1906 *Bulletin* (Sydney) 3 May 14/2 Waiting . . once for the ramshackle shanghai at Port Pooncarie, I noticed a local blackfellow . . walloping his gin. **1907** *Ibid.* 7 Feb. 14/2, I was taking my first shanghai trip Out-back-o'- Beyond-Bourke. **1914** T.C. WOLLASTON *Spirit of Child* 30 A station shanghai with two mules in it.

shanghai /'ʃæŋhaɪ, ʃæŋ'haɪ/, *v.* [f. SHANGHAI *n.*[1]] *trans.* To catapult. Also *fig.*

1938 C.P. CONIGRAVE *Walk-About* 97 An animal would get irritated at being baulked, would rush ahead, and then the springy, resilient saplings would 'shanghai' him backwards. **1938** F. CLUNE *Free & Easy Land* 41 Shanghai the sugar down this way, Danny Boy. **1942** *Bulletin* (Sydney) 16 Dec. 13/1 In spite of his shanghaiing all the cats within a radius of 20 miles the rodents were still on top.

shanty, *n.*[1] [Spec. use of *shanty* small, mean dwelling: see OED(S *sb.*[1])]

a. A small public house, usu. in a rural area and freq. unlicensed. See also *grog shanty* GROG *n.* 3, *sly-grog shanty* SLY GROG 2.

[N.Z. **1848** W.T. POWER *Sketches N.Z.* 168 A 'pakeha' had built a shanty on the opposite side of the river for the purpose of entertaining travellers.] **1863** *Bell's Life in Sydney* 7 Feb. 2/4, I told him there was a shanty at the crossing-place. **1869** MRS W.M. HOWELL *Diggings & Bush* 32 'What is the meaning, papa, of shanty?' 'A low public house', my dear, 'and now I think you have learnt enough of the colonial vocabulary for one morning.' **1880** 'ERRO' *Squattermania* 222 He . . suddenly found himself before a shanty yclept an hotel. **1892** 'MRS A. MACLEOD' *Silent Sea* II. 23 Wednesday I went to the little shanty at Starvation Creek, where they sell grog on the sly. **1905** *Worker* (Sydney) 30 Sept. 1/3 The bushman has a journey of a mile to go to the nearest store or shanty (man-trap). **1921** W.H. PHIPPS *Bush Yarns* 89 It's only a shanty wherein you sell cheap drinks at fancy prices. **1982** R. HALL *Just Relations* 104 Such is Main Ridge settlement with its shanties selling rum.

b. Comb. **shanty-keeper, -keeping.**

1862 *Bell's Life in Sydney* 22 Mar. 3/1 Burly **shanty keepers** from the gold fields. **1878** *Squatters' Plum* 42 When men have made a few pounds, they are frequently obliged to spend them while travelling in search of more work, or else the foul shanty-keeper drugs and robs them. **1895** *Bulletin* (Sydney) 28 Sept. 3/2 The shanty-keeper *he* was just as steady as a rock, And me as paralytic as a fool. **1921** W.H. PHIPPS *Bush Yarns* 89 Fagan, the shanty keeper. **1934** C. SAYCE *Comboman* 230 It was not only the presence of death that made the shanty-keeper so uneasy. **1962** T. RONAN *Deep of Sky* 7 The boys laughed at him. They had come to give the new shanty keepers a decent pipe-opener for the business race. **1977** W.A. WINTER-IRVING *Bush Stories* 19 The occasional bottle of beer or rum swapped . . with the shanty keeper who maintained a permanent source of beer and rum for the business that he carried on after dark, when the mailman had left for his return journey. **1894** *Western Champion* (Barcaldine) 12 June 12/2 Nell had followed her father, an old reprobate, from diggings to diggings, where he usually followed the occupation of **shanty-keeping**, otherwise sly grog selling.

shanty, *n.*[2] [U.S. *shanty* a bruised eye.] In the phr. **to hang a shanty on** (someone's) **eye,** to give (someone) a black eye.

1943 S.W. KEOUGH *Around Army* 31 When, not unjustifiably narked, she wrote and told him off, and why the sapper thought that to hang a decent shanty on the censor's eye worth ninety days' No. 2 f.p. **1944** *Bulletin* (Sydney) 12 Apr. 12/2 Whenever he appeared with a shanty hung on his eye—and that was not seldom. Never did he attribute it to an upflung bit of firewood or a slipped fence-strainer.

shanty, *v. Obs.* [f. SHANTY *n.*[1]] *intr.* To frequent a shanty; to drink habitually.

1888 'R. BOLDREWOOD' *Robbery under Arms* I. 34, I was put out at his laying it down so about the Dalys and us shantying and gaffing. **1980** B. HORNADGE *Austral. Slanguage* 223 In the outback the illegal seller of spirits was the bush shanty, and this did give rise to the verb *to shanty* (to drink habitually) and *shanty-keeper*. These terms were short-lived.

share. Used *attrib.* in Special Comb. to designate an arrangement under which two or more persons participate in the risks and profits of an undertaking, as **share-cocky,** *share-farmer*; so **-cockying** *pr. pple.*; **-farm** [also U.S.], a rural property the profits from which are shared in an agreed proportion between the owner and the person who farms it; **-farmer,** one who farms such a property; **-farming** *vbl. n.*, the activity of so doing.

1929 *Bulletin* (Sydney) 28 Aug. 25/4 Working for a **share-cocky** on the lower Murray I noticed . . that . . the meat was always slightly 'high'. **1937** *Ibid.* 9 June 21/2 My neighbour, a share-cockie, put in an application for a block. **1961** *Ibid.* 19 Apr. 28/1 They drive the dour and casual Australian alike mad with their wants, share-cockyin' the land, shame him with their industry and return to Italy rich men before they've time to learn the language. **1982** W.G. HOWCROFT *Bushman who Laughed* 64 He obtained a job with a share-cocky in the Wimmera. **1909** *N.S.W. for Settler* (N.S.W. Immigration & Tourist Bureau) 40 Throughout the whole of New South Wales . . the owners of large estates, which have been hitherto given over solely to sheep-raising, are recognising that greater profits are to be made from agriculture, and are cutting up their properties and making blocks available as '**share farms**'. **1928** R.G. STAPLEDON *Tour in Aust. & N.Z.* 28 Many successful men have started as **share-farmers**. **1930** *Bulletin* (Sydney) 22 Jan. 21/1 Share-farmers' sons . . used to go . . rabbiting or felling bee trees. **1942** W. GLASSON *Our Shepherds* 9, I missed each week a sheep from the flock under the care of my trusted share-farmer. **1946** A.J. HOLT *Wheat Farms Vic.* 57 Men with no farming background are very liable to stay as sharefarmers. **1965** D. MARTIN *Hero of Too* 14 Bollman was financing half a dozen share farmers in this way. **1924** *New Settlers' Handbk. Vic.* 129 Four model **share-farming** agreements. **1935** F. CLUNE *Rolling down Lachlan* 111 Green, the owner, decided to subdivide and start farming. He succeeded, and, extending his activities, originated a scheme of share-farming. **1978** A.E. COSH *Jumping Kangaroos* 58 Early in 1937 I went off to Croppa Creek in search of some land for share-farming, and secured 600 acres on Buckie Station three miles from the railway.

shark. Used *attrib.* in Special Comb. **shark bait** (or **baiter**), one who swims alone or well out from the shore; so **-baiting** *vbl. n.*; **bell,** see quot. 1945; **-meshing** *vbl. n.*, the netting of sharks; **patrol,** a patrol of surfing beaches, by boat or aircraft, to give warning of the presence of sharks; **-proof** *a.*, secure against sharks; **spotter,** one who watches for sharks; so **-spotting** *vbl. n.*

1912 [**shark bait**] A. WRIGHT *Rung In* (1921) 29 It might be only some foolhardy 'shark baiter', as he heard the more venturesome of the bathers termed. **1920** A.H. ADAMS *Australs.* 177 Farther out in the deep water swam the venturous line of experts, technically known as 'shark-bait'. **1936** N. CALDWELL *Fangs of Sea* 21 The 'shark baits' as the surfers are called who venture hundreds of yards out. **1940** P. KERRY *Cobbers A.I.F.* 12 Now the Sarg. wus known as Shark Bait, an' 'e raced fer the front line, Whilst Johnny battled thru' the surf an' swallowed lots uv brine. But at last 'e reached the S.M., about 'alf a mile from shore, Where 'e was loafin' on the greenies, an' lookin' out fer more. **1941** K.S. PRICHARD *Moon of Desire* 69 My kids know all about sharks. They'll take jolly good care not to be shark bait. **1951** CUSACK & JAMES *Come in Spinner* 221 I've given up shark-baiting. Mug's game. **1965** *Austral. Encycl.* VIII. 82 Solitary bathers are more often attacked than groups, but the 'shark-baiter' farthest off shore is not necessarily the victim. **1967** K.S. PRICHARD *Subtle Flame* 99 I'm no good at shark baiting! **1940** P. KERRY *Cobbers A.I.F.* 14 An' 'e didn't pause fer breath till 'e wus ringin' the **shark bell.** **1945** J.A. ALLAN *Men & Manners*

138 All beaches of note have their watch-towers and 'shark-bells'—the latter rung in warning whenever a black fin appears inshore. **1936** *Sydney Morning Herald* 24 Nov. 12/5 The State Government has accepted a tender .. for **shark meshing** off the metropolitan beaches from Broken Bay to Port Jackson. **1958** V.M. COPPLESTON *Shark Attack* 211 Although shark meshing was attacked originally as 'a futile waste of money', records show its effectiveness. **1982** *Age* (Melbourne) 6 Mar. 13/4 Between 1962 and 1978 the number of sharks captured through shark meshing off the coast of Queensland beaches amounted to more than 15,000. **1951** *Ann. Rep.* (Surf Life Saving Assoc. Aust., Qld. State Centre) 8 Once again the Courier-Mail provided an aerial **shark patrol** over the waters of the South Coast during the Xmas holidays. **1968** *Herald* (Melbourne) 20 Jan. 10/8 Told of the surf boats which surf life saving clubs use for shark patrols off Australian beaches, he said: 'There is no reason why they couldn't be equipped with electrodes to drive off sharks.' **1986** *Canberra Times* 15 Jan. 8/4 Aria Simmons has flown South Coast shark patrols since the beginning of summer. **1857** J. ASKEW *Voyage Aust. & N.Z.* 259 A neat little bathing-house, with .. a space in front entirely surrounded with a **sharkproof** netting of wattles. **1941** C. BARRETT *Aust.* 125 Darwin has its shark-proof bathing place. **1953** *New Settler in W.A.* (Perth) Mar. 33 Within the harbour itself are many excellent stillwater beaches, but the ubiquitous shark forces the protection of shark-proof nets. **1956** S. HOPE *Diggers' Paradise* 187 Round the harbours and rivers of Sydney are numerous swimming-baths, all protected with shark-proof steel netting. **1965** G. MCINNES *Road to Gundagai* 71 What d' ya mean sharks? Why we've shark proof nets at Bondi and Coogee. **1968** E.M. NOBLET *Winds that Blew* 104 In the afternoon the shark-proof pool was full. **1958** V.M. COPPLESTON *Shark Attack* 207 For some time great faith was placed in the air shark patrol which comprised a Dragon DH4 carrying a **shark spotter.** **1978** *Herald* (Melbourne) 14 Jan. 6/10 Shark spotting is only one of our functions,' Mr Stewart said. **1986** *Canberra Times* 15 Jan. 8/4 Simmons .. and an assistant shark-spotter sweep the beaches scanning the water for the black shapes cruising in the shallows.

shark, *v. Australian National Football. trans.* See quot. 1969. Also *absol.*

1960 *N.T. News* (Darwin) 5 Jan. 8/4 Then Bruno Wilson sharked cleverly and brought up Wanderers' second major. **1964** *Footy Fan* (Melbourne) II. xv. 3 If he did not get the hit-outs from his own followers, he certainly 'sharked' plenty from the opposition. **1969** EAGLESON & MCKIE *Terminol. Austral. Nat. Football* iii. 15 *Sharking*, in bounces, throw-ins and knock-outs, intercepting the ball as it passes between an opposing ruckman, who won the knock, and his rover.

sharp. *Obs.* [Spec. use of *sharp* a cheat, a swindler, a rogue.] One who exploits the simple or inexperienced, orig. an ex-convict as opposed to a newly arrived immigrant. See also FLAT *n.*[2]

1812 J.H. VAUX *Mem.* (1819) II. 205 *Sharp*, a gambler, or person, professed in all the arts of play; a cheat, or swindler; any *cross-cove*, in general, is called *a sharp*, in opposition to *a flat*, or *square-cove*; but this is only in a comparative sense in the course of conversation. **1832** *Hill's Life N.S.W.* (Sydney) 16 Nov. 4 O! what a mob of *flats* and *sharps* Was crowded on the ground. **1849** A. HARRIS *Emigrant Family* (1967) 32 There are some who are emigrants, and some who are freed-men: the emigrants are flats, and the others are sharps. **1890** *Truth* (Sydney) 7 Dec. 2/2 If Carrington, when he arrives among the gilded tophs, substitutes sharps and flats for the broad arrow branded gentry, he will hit the nail fair on the head. **1900** *Ibid.* 25 Feb. 4/8 All the Sydney aristocrats, Guns and mugs and sharps and flats. **1909** A. WRIGHT *Rogue's Luck* 196 As the breed of 'flats' grows less in the cities, the 'sharps' who prey on them are forced to travel far afield in search of plunder.

sharpie. [f. *sharp*, stylish, fashionable, smart + -Y.] A young person who affects certain extreme or provocative styles of hair, dress, etc.: see quot. 1975. Also *attrib.*

1965 *Kings Cross Whisper* (Sydney) Feb. 11/2 Although you might think you're a bit of a sharpie, everyone else reckons you're a cockroach. **1967** C. RUHEN *Wild Beat* 66 Your two gangs have always been at each others' throats. Mods and sharpies. Big deal. **1974** M. GILLESPIE *Into Hollow Mountains* 15 We didn't recognise each other until we'd almost passed, because he'd had a sharpie haircut. **1975** *Sun-Herald* (Sydney) 13 Apr. 7 A sharpie is usually aged between 14 and 19 years. The boys wear their hair cropped short on the top and sides and longer at the back. The girls often wear 'dolly' makeup and have their ears pierced. Tattoos are often worn by both sexes. The sharpies wear blue jeans or high-waisted slacks supported by old-fashioned braces, matched with a tee shirt and sometimes a woollen cardigan. **1977** *Sunday Mail* (Brisbane) 21 Aug. 37/3 Carmel says her mother accepted her being a sharpie—even a punk—till she shaved her hair off.

shave, *v. Shearing. trans.* To shear (a sheep), esp. closely.

1895 *Worker* (Sydney) 14 Sept. 4/2 Fleecing, scraping, shaving, skinning, fit for show or exhibition. **1897** *Ibid.* 11 Sept. 1/1 He 'shaves' his sheep, or 'pinks' 'em, when he shears them nice and clean, But mostly 'roughs' and 'tomahawks', with 'second cuts' between. **1910** *Bulletin* (Sydney) 22 Dec. 13/4 An extra stick of tobacco was awarded each barber who shaved over 50 jumbucks a day.

she, *pers. pron.*

1. [Chiefly Austral. and N.Z.: see OEDS 2 e.] Applied to things (both material and immaterial) to which the female sex is not conventionally attributed: see quots. See also APPLE 4, RIGHT *a.* 4, SWEET *a.*[2] 2 a.

1863 J.B. AUSTIN *Mines S.A.* 96 The miners say the Moonta will be a mine when the Burra is forgotten—*because she* has lodes and the Burra has none. **1881** G. WALCH *Vic.* 73 Placed in a suitable spot by the incendiary, the bush burning-glass remains intact .. until there comes a day of fervid sunshine, and then .. 'off she goes, and the run is in a blaze in less than no time'. **1897** *Bulletin* (Sydney) 8 May 28/1 He tapped the roof. 'Oh she'll do,' he said. **1912** *Mercury* (Hobart) 17 Oct. 5/3 She was a pretty tough affair down there. **1924** C. BLOXSOME *How Wonder won Cup* 21 'How do you light her?' father shouted. 'Just with a taper dipped in methylated spirits; 'old 'er there for a few minutes till she sizzles, then turn 'er on and she blazes up.' **1935** N. HUNT *House of David* 156 The men .. sprinkled along the fences, which were likely to take fire... 'She's euchred, boss! She's hemmed in on all sides! She can't pass them there breaks, nohow.' **1945** *Two Bar Four Three Bull.. Austral. Infantry Battalion* Feb. 5 There was our kids beltin' hell outa the kids next door. Gee! she was a ding-dong stink. **1958** F.B. VICKERS *Mirage* (ed. 2) 216 She stripped better than I thought. I got five bags to the acre of seven hundred I put in. **1962** *Meanjin* 53 Reckon it's an old groper, lying in that hole, there. Had him well hooked, too, coupla times, but—*whi-i-s-sh*! and she's gone. **1969** B. GARLAND *Pitt Street Prospector* 30 Cripes, she's a beaut drain, best I ever saw. **1978** D. STUART *Wedgetail View* 68 We'll push off .. anywhere. She's a big country. **1979** T. ASTLEY *Hunting Wild Pineapple* 25 A sonnet's got fourteen lines... Well, that's half of it. There's a few bits need fixing up but I've only got six lines to go and she's jake. **1980** J. WRIGHT *Big Hearts & Gold Dust* 2 Good-night, mate. Come on over and warm your toes, she's startin' to get a bit chilly.

2. [As used *attrib.* in the names of plants: see OED 10 e. and also SHE-OAK.] **she beech,** any of several rainforest trees of e. Qld. and e. N.S.W., of the genera *Cryptocarya* and *Litsea* (both fam. Lauraceae), esp. *L. reticulata*; the wood of the tree; **pine,** any of several plants of the genus *Podocarpus* (fam. Podocarpaceae), esp. the rainforest tree *P. elatus* of e. N.S.W. and e. Qld., having a small seed at the head of a short, egg-shaped, edible receptacle similar in appearance to a bluish-black plum; the wood of the tree; PLUM PINE.

1894 *Proc. Linnean Soc. N.S.W.* IX. 583 Mr Maiden exhibited specimens of *Litsaea* (*Tetranthera*) *reticulata* .. a plant new for the Colony, from Lismore, Richmond River, where it is known as '**She Beech**'. **1898** E.E. MORRIS *Austral Eng.* 413 The prefix *she* is used in Australia to indicate an inferiority of timber in respect of texture, colour, or other character; e.g. *She-beech, she-pine*. **1909** R. KALESKI *Austral. Settler's Compl. Guide* 32 In the *coastal district* we find: *Softwoods* .. white and she beech. **1926** *Qld. Agric. Jrnl.* XXV. 437 Cryptocarya obovata .. She Beech (N.S.W.). **1962** N.C.W. BEADLE et al. *Handbk. Vascular Plants Sydney & Blue Mountains* 132 *Litsea* .. Coast. Rainforest. *Bolly Gum* or *She Beech.* **1880** J. BONWICK *Resources Qld.* 81 The **She Pine** of the colonists is a Podocarpus, living in the sea-side scrubs, and much admired by the cabinet-makers. **1899** R. SEMON *In Austral. Bush* 15 The colonist calls every conifer a pine. He distinguishes between Kauri pines (dammara) .. 'She pines' (podocarpus), and others. **1930** V. KENNEDY *By Range & River* 73 A full list of Atherton timbers would include such building timbers as .. she pine. **1981** A.B. & J.W. CRIBB *Useful Wild Plants Aust.* 143 *Podocarpus elatus* Brown Pine, She-Pine... The timber is browner than that of hoop pine, a little heavier and not quite so strong, hence the appellation 'she', as in she-oak, as a derogatory prefix.

sheaf tossing, *vbl. n.* The sport of throwing a sheaf: see quot. 1986.

[**1930** *Sydney Morning Herald* 10 Jan. 19/2 At the Lagoon sports, P. Thirlow .. won the sheaf pitching event by throwing a half-lb. over a bar 24 ft. high, a local record.] **1961** *Advertiser* (Adelaide) 9 Sept. 1/2 The Governor was cheered by the crowd at the sheaf tossing arena when he tried his hand. **1977** *Ibid.* 21 June 3/6 S.A., it seems, has the distinction of being the country's leading sheaf-tossing State. **1986** *Canberra Times* 27 Jan. 3/4 The aim of sheaf tossing is to toss, with a pitchfork, a 3.6 kg. bag of straw as high as possible, simulating the old country skill of tossing sheaves of hay on to a hay cart.

Also **sheaf-tosser** *n.*

1947 *Hoofs & Horns* May 25 We cannot close without mention of the sheaf-tossers... A.J. Thiel, who hails from Pinnaroo, clearing the rail at 50 feet as though he were tossing pancakes.

shea oak, var. SHE-OAK.

shear, *v.* [Spec. use of *shear* to cut the fleece from (a sheep).]

1. *intr.* To be employed as a shearer.

1892 *Bulletin* (Sydney) 5 Nov. 20/1 At the last station where he shore he gave the super a sheol of a hiding. **1895** *Ibid.* 22 June 3/2, I had 'shore' on many stations, and had eaten of the "slag'; But so help me Larry Foley! I had never 'struck a snag'. **1917** *Truth* (Sydney) 21 Jan. 11/7 I've shorn at Terramongamine, and on the Talbragar, I ran McDermott for the cobbler when we shore at Buckingbar. **c 1918** R. MCJANNETT *Saltbush Jim V.C.* 3 He'd shorn way back to the far Paroo Then he trekked to the Condamine.

2. In the phr. **to shear (non-)union,** to employ shearers in accordance (or not) with conditions laid down by their trade union.

1891 *Conference Amalgam. Shearers' Union & Pastoralists' Fed. Council* 22, I don't think they ever sheared Union in that shed. **1892** *Bulletin* (Sydney) 24 Dec. 22/1 'We shear non-union, here,' says he. 'I call it scab,' says I. **1892** 'J. MILLER' *Workingman's Paradise* 88 There's a shed starts the next week, and I said I'd be up there to see that it shore union. **1945** E.W. CAMPBELL *Hist. Austral. Labour Movt.* 25 In the 1890 season 90% of the sheds 'shore union'.

shearer. [Spec. use of *shearer* one who removes the fleece from a sheep.]

a. An itinerant worker hired seasonally to shear sheep.

1826 J. ATKINSON *Acct. Agric. & Grazing N.S.W.* 77 Considerable difficulty is sometimes experienced in obtaining good shearers. **1842** *Geelong Advertiser* 28 Nov. 2/2 At this season of the year there is a class of abandoned indolent vagabonds who lounge about town, sponging upon the industrious but improvident shearers who come down the country with their wages. These two classes become boon companions for a time; until the bush labourer gets tipsy, when the hanger-on eases him of the remainder of his 'swag'. **1859** W. BURROWS *Adventures Mounted Trooper* 123 The shearers are men who travel the country for the purpose of obtaining work in various sheds, some of them going from station to station as the season progresses. **1867** A.K. COLLINS *Waddy Mundoee* 9 Nearer the river are the huts occupied by the shearers and others, periodically employed upon the station. **1884** A.W. STIRLING *Never Never Land* 180 The bulk of the population was ever shifting and made up of drovers, shearers, fencers and the like; here one day, gone the next. **1905** *Act* (Qld.) no. 9 Sect. 2, *Shearer*, a shearer or labourer employed in or about a shearing shed. **1919** *Bulletin* (Sydney) 20 Feb. 22/2 Does anyone know a sure remedy for 'shearer's backache'? I've tried the 'hanging to it' cure but after a week seven devils were still probing my kidneys with hot needles. I haven't robbed jumbuck since then. **1943** H.G. LAMOND *From Tariaro to Ross Roy* 27 Shearers then were bushmen, all round men, who did all classes of station work. **1965** L. WALKER *Other Girl* 17 'So you know the plant?' he said. 'Nobody ever mistakes a shearer for a stockman or vice versa. You know the outback, young lady.' **1984** *People Mag.* (Sydney) 7 May 39/2 No man labours as hard or lives as rough as the 40-hour-a-week shearer, whether he's wide-combing, narrow-combing or biting the wool off.

b. In special collocations: **shearers' ball,** an annual dance marking the end of shearing at a particular place; **cook,** one seasonally employed on a rural property to cook for the shearers; **hut, quarters,** accommodation provided for shearers during their period of employment on a rural property; **rep,** REP.

1899 J. BRADSHAW *Quirindi Bank Robbery* 23 Murphy and I went up to Louth, where at Matthew's pub we thoroughly enjoyed ourselves at the **shearers' ball.** **1910** *Bulletin* (Sydney) 1 Sept. 14/4 On a station I know they make a feature of the annual 'Shearers' Ball'. **1953** H.G. LAMOND *Big Red* 96 He was dressed up for Th' Shearers' Ball. **1976** B. SCOTT *Complete Bk. Austral. Folk Lore* 398 'A Shearer's Ball'—The decorations were green boughs tied to the posts in the woolshed... One of the shearers would play a concertina, one a fiddle, sometimes singing would suddenly swell up from the dancers. **1872** W.M. HUGO *Hist. First Bushmen's Club* 216 Mr Peter Campbell, **shearer's cook,** seconded the motion. **1901** *Bulletin* (Sydney) 25 May 14/2 Shearers' cooks on the Darling are mostly fair pugs, and after their first spread often invite any dissatisfied partakers to 'come outside'. **1920** *Huon Times* (Franklin) 30 July 2/7 When the new Shearers' award was announced in Queensland the shearers' cook immediately demanded increased pay per man per week. **1965** L. WALKER *Other Girl* 23 We got one shearers' cook with us—and that's all. **1873** A. TROLLOPE *Aust. & N.Z.* I. 301 About a quarter of a mile from the wool-shed was the **shearer's hut,** in which the men slept, and ate, and smoked their pipes. **1889** H. EGBERT *Pretty Cockey* 44 About a quarter mile off was the Shearers' Hut. It was much larger than the Men's Hut, built and furnished on the same plan, but of coarser material. It was constructed of rough green slabs, that soon shrank and left wide openings between, to admit cold, wet, heat, &c. The bark roof was far from being either sun, moon, wind, fire, native cat, or 'possum proof. **1900** T. MAJOR *Leaves from Squatter's Note Bk.* 133 Rowdyism rose triumphant, turning the shearers' hut into a veritable pandemonium of blackguardism. **1927** R.S. BROWNE *Journalist's Memories* 76 His identity eventually leaked out, and in the shearers' huts in the West, on mustering camps and at those little meetings of 'billabong whalers' where two or three were gathered together the name of 'Billy' Lane was reverenced. **1968** S. GORE *Holy Smoke* 50 It swept the verandah of the shearer's hut like hail. ***c* 1892** J. CAMERON *Fire Stick* 46 While these simple arrangements were making in the **shearers' quarters,** they were not idle up at.. Wycomb's residence. **1965** R.H. CONQUEST *Horses in Kitchen* 16 The men's quarters, of course, should not be confused with the shearers' quarters, which are only in business, one might say, during the shearing season. **1903** *Bulletin* (Sydney) 31 Jan. 17/1 A **shearers' rep.**, in sending an order to a local store, asked the storekeeper to send out 5s. worth of newspapers. **1910** C.E.W. BEAN *On Wool Track* 172 The shearers, being a republic, elect a representative—'the shearers' rep.'—who is their go-between in every dealing with station officials while shearing lasts. **1977** F.B. VICKERS *Stranger no Longer* 82 He was voted in as shearers' 'rep', for his whole heart was in the union.

shearing, *vbl. n.* and *attrib.* [Spec. use of *shearing* the action of cutting the fleece from a sheep; not necessarily excl. Austral.]

A. *vbl. n.*

1. The period during which sheep are shorn at a particular establishment.

1834 N.S.W. Magistrates' Deposition Bk. 24 Dec., Daniel Hogan and Thomas Miller came to me on the 25th Nov[r] with their shears and refused to shear any longer for me being under an engagement to remain during the shearing. **1856** G. WILLMER *Draper in Aust.* 214 The shearing is an exciting time both for master and man. **1865** J.J. WESTWOOD *Jrnl.* 418 At a previous year's shearing, Morgan, the bushranger, rode up to the woolshed, and.. made him sign cheques for thirty pounds to each of his shearers. **1889** H. EGBERT *Pretty Cockey* 79 The ladies have not paid the Wool Shed a visit this shearing. **1891** 'R. BOLDREWOOD' *Sydney-Side Saxon* (1925) 137 He's been a sheep-washer and knock-about man at Wallanbah these three or four shearings. **1908** W.H. OGILVIE *My Life in Open* 32 So-and-so was here two shearings ago. **1933** J. TRURAN *Where Plain Begins* 150 Old Bill.. noted, for the hundredth time that shearing, the inroads made by his little friends the blow-flies.

2. The occupation or activity of the shearer.

1852 G.B. EARP *Gold Colonies Aust.* 112 Shearing is a separate occupation, men travelling from station to station for the purpose. **1874** *Illustr. Sydney News* 19 Sept. 19/3 Shearing is now in full operation in most of the sheep-farming districts... In Riverina, the demand for shearers is so great that at least 800 clippers must have crossed the Murray Border from Victoria to take work during the season. **1888** 'R. BOLDREWOOD' *Robbery under Arms* (1937) 114 We might go in for the shearing till Christmas. **1926** A. EDEN *Places in Sun* 50 Shearing is itself.. a skilled trade. The number of sheep shorn by each man varies with his skill. **1965** *Tracks we Travel* 103 Out where the sheep is king and where the two old 'guns' were crown princes still in the rough camaraderie of the 'shearin''. **1978** N. EVERS *Tas. Paradise & Beyond* 34 A few more old wethers, the last to be brought down from the bush run, and the shearing was finished.

B. *attrib.*

1. Of or pertaining to the occupation of shearing.

1829 R. DAWSON *Statement* 86, I visited the shearing Station no less than *ten* times during the period alluded to. **1844** *Atlas* (Sydney) I. 11/2 The Settlers in the District of Maneroo are informed, that they can be furnished with all necessary shearing supplies at the Store, Boyd Town. **1859** W. BURROWS *Adventures Mounted Trooper* 122 The shearing months are generally the three last of the year. **1893** 'TIMES SPECIAL CORRESPONDENT' *Lett. from Qld.* 84 The shearing camp is usually in the heart of a station isolated by, perhaps, twenty or thirty miles of bush on every side. **1911** *Bulletin* (Sydney) 27 July 14/1 My first acquaintance with Whitely King was in the big shearing strike, when as the P.U. secretary, he was anathema in the union camps. **1943** *Ibid.* 15 Dec. 13/2 'My worst trouble when I joined a shearin' gang', explained Sleepy, 'was wakin' up in the mornin's.' **1959** *Ibid.* 23 Dec. 16/1 A clause in most shearing-agreements signed between boss and shearer still provides for a £50 fine for 'bringing alcohol onto the property'. **1964** P. ADAM SMITH *Hear Train Blow* 160 He had worked his way from Numurkah up the shearing route to Queensland. **1977** F.B. VICKERS *Stranger no Longer* 113 We were .. to develop the poultry farm so that I might unroll my swag and say goodbye to the shearing tracks forever.

2. Comb. **shearing season, team, time.**

1833 *Van Diemen's Land Almanack* 53 When the **shearing season** arrives, a place should be assigned wherein the sheep may be driven. **1843** J.F. BENNETT *Hist. & Descr. Acct. S.A.* 98 The shearing season is, for old sheep in November and December, and for lambs in February. **1872** W.M. HUGO *Hist. First Bushmen's Club* 82 The coming shearing season will demonstrate whether there is to be Bushmen's Home in South Australia or not. **1910** *Bulletin* (Sydney) 8 Sept. 13/2 One shearing season.. a chap that I knew to be among the best and fastest sheep-shearers in Australia invited me to watch him and some mates 'go through' a shed of Angoras. **1965** R.H. CONQUEST *Horses in Kitchen* 16 The shearers' quarters.. are only in business, one might say, during the shearing season. **1926** *Bulletin* (Sydney) 11 Feb. 24/1 None of the swanky **shearing team** have cut their exes. yet. **1956** F.B. VICKERS *First Place to Stranger* 233 The accommodation he provided for the shearing team to live in was up to the standard laid down by the Hut Accommodation Act. **1977** —— *Stranger no Longer* 72 In case I ever made it to the .. shearing team, I enrolled for a course in bookeeping [*sic*]. **1842** *Sketch of Shepherd's Duties N.S.W.* 49 At **shearing time,** the flocks are brought in rotation to the home station. **1854** W. HOWITT *Boy's Adventures* 213 It was now the busy part of the squatter's year—washing and shearing time. There were some dozens of men now about the place, some of them sheep-washers, some shearers. **1873** A. TROLLOPE *Aust. & N.Z.* I. 130 On sheep-stations, at shearing time, to drink is not only to sin—but to commit the one sin that cannot be forgiven. **1886** 'THIRTY-FIVE YRS. COLONIST' *Hard Times* 24 This last shearing time I had it from a credible person that he had travelled over a distance equal to the length and breadth of Britain.. (he was not a shearer) and all the work he had obtained collectively was under a fortnight. **1914** C.H.S. MATTHEWS *Bill* 68 When shearing-time came round both Tom and I got jobs as tar-boys in the shed. **1959** *Bulletin* (Sydney) 23 Dec. 16/1 Publicans too often regard shearing-time as an open-season for charging way over their zoned prices.

3. Special Comb. **shearing board,** see BOARD; **cheque,** the gross earnings of a shearer at the end of a period of employment at a particular place; **contractor,** one who employs a gang of shearers, etc., and who enters into a contract with an owner to shear sheep; **floor,** the part of the floor in a shearing shed on which the sheep are actually shorn; BOARD 1; **machine,** a mechanized device for shearing sheep; **shed,** a building in which sheep are shorn and fleeces processed and packed; *wool shed,* see WOOL 2; also *attrib.*, and *transf.* a job as a shearer.

1882 ARMSTRONG & CAMPBELL *Austral. Sheep Husbandry* 174 There are many descriptions of sheds that find favour with our squatters; some consisting of **shearing boards** on either side, with the sheep in the middle of the shed; others, with the board in the centre and the sheep on each side. **1890** 'R. BOLDREWOOD' *Colonial Reformer* II. 73 It was no unusual occurrence to have the full complement of men in the morning, and in the afternoon, upon the unexpected arrival of an inspector of police, the shearing board would be deserted. **1908** W.H. OGILVIE *My Life in Open* 39 The shearing-board is supervised by an overseer. **1928** C.E. COWLEY *Classing Clip* 149 *Shearing board.* This should be roomy. A narrow board not only impedes the work of both shearers and shed-hands, but introduces an element of danger. **1980** P. FREEMAN *Woolshed* 18 Before shearing starts, the 'rouseabout', or general hand, drives some sheep into each of the 'catching' pens. The shearer 'catches' the sheep from these pens, and drags them out to the shearing 'board'. **1905** *Bulletin* (Sydney) 16 Mar. 3/2 My cheque was not the size of **shearing-cheques** of long ago. **1924** *Ibid.* 21 Feb. 22/1 When the shearing cheque is finished and the publican goes crook, All the friends we had diminished, till the last one takes his hook. **1945** *Ibid.* 7 Feb. 13/2 Sandy sez y' gave a bloke all your shearing cheque an' had to hoof it to the next shed? **1965** R.H. CONQUEST *Horses in Kitchen* 117 He.. had never met one who boozed away his shearing cheque. **1978** J. DINGWALL *Sunday too far Away* 111 He has the biggest pile of money in front of him—his entire shearing cheque. **1936** *Bulletin* (Sydney) 8 Jan. 19/1 The best picker-up I ever saw was Barefooted Joe. Any **shearing contractor** would find a job for him. **1955** P. WHITE *Tree of Man* 190 Some years before, his wife had left with a shearing contractor and not come back. **1965** L. WALKER *Other Girl* 45 I'm the shearing contractor. My team belongs to me and I bring it on to his station to do his shearing. **1984** *People Mag.* (Sydney) 7 May 39/2 Narrow-combers also claim shearing contractors unfairly favour the use of wide-comb gangs. **1850** W. GATES *Recoll. Van Dieman's Land* 162 The sheep to be sheared are driven at night under a long shed... From this shed a door opens to the **shearing floor,** which is sufficiently large for ten or fifteen men to work upon. **1879** S.W. SILVER *Austral. Grazier's Guide* 53 So much of the end of the shed opposite to the sheep entrance as is not required for the shearing-floor is railed off. **1899** J. BRADSHAW *Quirindi Bank Robbery* 3 Put me on a shearing floor and it's there I'm game to bet That I'd give to any ringer ten sheep start. **1927** K.S. PRICHARD *Brumby Innes* (1974) 75, I looked along the shearin' floor before I turned to go, There was eight or ten, damned Chinamen, a-shearin' in a row. **1852** *Guardian* (Hobart) 20 Oct. 3/4 **Shearing Machine.** A gentleman has invented a machine for shearing sheep, which can be employed by hand or steam. **1878** 'R. BOLDREWOOD' *Ups & Downs* 91 Has no more idea of a swing-gate than a shearing-machine. **1897** L. LINDLEY-COWEN *W. Austral. Settler's Guide* 634, I am a great believer in the shearing machine patented by Mr Wolseley, but few sheds on small sheepwalks are strong enough to stand the strain of their use. **1943** H.G. LAMOND *From Tariaro to Ross Roy* 108 Though they had been invented and perfected some time previously, it was during that decade the shearing machine became universal. **1965** R.H. CONQUEST *Horses in Kitchen* 188 There's the engine-driver, the gent who puts the hum into the shearing machines. **1829** R. DAWSON *Statement* 83 He complains.. that the **shearing-shed** was not erected until the season was *close at hand.* **1853**

MOSSMAN & BANISTER *Aust. Visited & Revisited* 22 The shearing-sheds were threatened with desertion, and the boiling-pots were standing empty and fireless. **1880** 'ERRO' *Squattermania* 243 They are generally an awful lot of grumblers in the shearing-shed. **1893** 'TIMES SPECIAL CORRESPONDENT' *Lett. from Qld.* 81 A shearing shed in full swing is a striking sight. **1905** *Act* (Qld.) no. 9 Sect. 2, *Shearing-shed*, any building or structure used for the purpose of shearing sheep, or for the scouring, sorting, or pressing of wool, or in any operation connected with such shearing, scouring, sorting or pressing. **1923** J. ARMOUR *Spell of Inland* 13 Government House stood on a hill. . . The shearing shed and men's quarters could be seen from the house verandah. **1948** V. PALMER *Golconda* 51 Macy the Battler, they had called him at his last shearing-shed after he had tackled a nagging boss-of-the-board. **1955** H.G. LAMOND *Towser* 25 A mile or more away a shimmer of iron roofs showed the shearing shed with its accommodation for men, yards for stock, other equipment. **1976** B. SCOTT *Complete Bk. Austral. Folk Lore* 398 An account of life on the McConnell's station in Queensland in the 1860s in *Tales of Australian Pioneer Women*, by F.M. Johnson, says 'Shearing was followed by the Shearing Shed Dance, opened with a quadrille, followed by sets of lancers, polkas and country dances, with a caller to instruct us when to set partners and swing. **1977** V. PRIDDLE *Larry & Jack* 6 He'd hump his swag further west to the big sheep stations and follow the shearing sheds.

shears, *n. pl.* In the phr. **off (the) shears**: (of sheep) newly shorn. Also as quasi-*n.* and *attrib.*

[N.Z. **1888** J. BRADSHAW *N.Z. of Today* 110 The hoggett . . in 1882 could be readily sold 'off the shears' at twelve shillings.] **1896** T. HENEY *Girl at Birrell's* 69 Now and again a buyer visited the stations to get cheap sheep 'off shears'. **1905** *Shearer* (Sydney) 18 Mar. 8/5 Drover Wood goes out to-morrow to lift 12,000 off the shears, bound for the Darling Downs. **1923** *Bulletin* (Sydney) 25 Jan. 22/2 A mob of about 1500 off-shears was working eastwards, when it was joined . . by another mob of 1000 or so from an intersecting street. **1935** N. HUNT *House of David* 205 'Two thousand prime wether 'off-shears' 'dipped'! Thirty-five shillings in the paddock,' Rowel said. **1946** A.J. HOLT *Wheat Farms Vic.* 82 After shearing, ewes may be graded and culled for impending off-shears sales. **1965** L. HAYLEN *Big Red* 199 We credit the proceeds from the 'off shears' sheep disposed of to No. 2 account. **1975** L.A. POCKLEY *Handbk. for Jackeroos* 67 Drenching and branding races are used for branding sheep 'off-shears' (i.e. after shearing), drenching. **1982** P. ADAM SMITH *Shearers* 218, I took delivery of 6000 old ewes, very poor, right off the shears. And run into a cold snap—it killed nearly 70 of them.

shed, *n. Shearing.* [Abbrev. of *shearing shed* (see SHEARING B. 3) or *wool shed* (see WOOL 2).]

1\. **a.** *Shearing shed*, see SHEARING B. 3.

1853 J. SHERER *Gold Finder Aust.* 233 Thousands of bales of wool were lying in the settlers' sheds. **1857** F. DE B. COOPER *Wild Adventures* 105 He was bound for the shearing through New England. By this time, most likely, he has set in at some of the sheds on the Namoi. **1882** ARMSTRONG & CAMPBELL *Austral. Sheep Husbandry* 174 There are many descriptions of sheds that find favour with our squatters. **1893** B. MORANT *Poetry* (1980) 10 Young Merino bought the station, fenced the run and built a 'shed', Sacked the stockmen, sold the cattle, and put on sheep instead. **1907** *Native Companion* Sept. 45 Likely you'll be makin' for the western sheds? **1921** K.S. PRICHARD *Black Opal* 313 Shearers from Darrawingee sheds who, a few weeks before had been on the Warria board. **1941** *Bulletin* (Sydney) 10 Dec. 15/3 In a S.A. shed a classer came across a well-grown fleece with stripes in it. **1951** *Ibid.* 18 July 14/4 Our shed was simply a very long building with skillion on one side and the other open. The shearers were placed at the posts. **1960** *Ibid.* 6 July 16/3 It was an old-time shed, holding a couple of thousand sheep or more, 50 stands (meaning 25 pens, races and other inconveniences), all of which had to be filled. **1971** W.G. HOWCROFT *This Side Rabbit Proof Fence* 42 Once, after a cut out, I remember humpin' me bluey for three days and nights without water before reaching the next shed. **1978** J. DINGWALL *Sunday too far Away* 6 I'm on my way to a shed.

b. The gang of shearers working in a particular shed. Also *attrib.*

1891 *Truth* (Sydney) 15 Feb. 7/2 He makes his sons . . manager of out-station, boss drover, over the shed, chief of burr-cutters—anything, in fact that draws pay *chargeable to the company*. **1895** J. KIRBY *Old Times in Bush* 147 If allowed by the person 'over the shed', plenty of shearers would do their hundred. **1909** W.G. SPENCE *Aust.'s Awakening* 88 The shed was declared on strike, and the men camped in the town. **1953** *Bulletin* (Sydney) 4 Mar. 12/3 We'd just kicked off on the first run of the day when the presser (an ex-pug), his mate and a shearer showed up, each full and highly belligerent. Declaring shearing 'off' for the day, they stopped the engine, assaulted the 'expert', menaced the boss of the board and remained in undisputed command of an idle shed. **1965** R.H. CONQUEST *Horses in Kitchen* 188 Then there's the engine-driver, the gent who puts the hum into the shearing machines, not forgetting his associate, the expert, one of the most important men in any shed. **1982** *Sydney Morning Herald* 23 Oct. 29/4 The man who tops the shed tally is the ringer.

c. A job in a shearing gang; a contract to shear (an owner's) sheep.

1893 *Southerly* (1964) iii. 204 Men tramping in search of a 'shed' are not called 'sundowners' or 'swaggies'; they are 'trav'lers'. **1897** *Bulletin* (Sydney) 28 Aug. 14/3 New-chum boss to shearer, wanting shed: 'Did you she-ah he-ah last ye-ah?' **1918** R.H. KNYVETT *Over there with Australs.* 30 They wanted to finish the shed so as to get a 'stand' at the commencement of shearing near by. **1949** *Bulletin* (Sydney) 23 Feb. 14/4 The ringer in a shearing-shed . . may have once been the man who shore the most sheep for a run; nowadays the shearer who has shorn the most sheep at the end of the shed is always regarded as the ringer. **1957** *Overland* ix. 9 They were mates of long standing and had followed the sheds all the way down through Queensland. **1963** C.H. SMITH *How y' going Mate?* 7 Sproggins my name—shearing contractor. Eight in the team. Starting a shed near Hobart tomorrow. **1978** N. EVERS *Tas. Paradise & Beyond* 34 It was a big property just west of Oatlands and the shed was nearly cut out.

2\. Comb. **shed boss, manager, overseer.**

1887 *Bungendore Mirror* 12 Nov. 2 The highest tally we have heard of this season comes from the Narrowmine Shed. . . The work was not scamped either, but executed to the full satisfaction of the **shed 'boss'.** **1902** *Bulletin* (Sydney) 8 Feb. 14/4 An amateur shearer gets into the good graces of the shed-boss by 'proving himself a steady worker, and no ringer'! **1905** *Steele Rudd's Mag.* (Brisbane) June 547 If the brand was a bit worn Hughes, the shed boss, said, regardless of breed—'Not your sheep', and it was passed on. **1955** STEWART & KEESING *Austral. Bush Ballads* 233 It was a Western manager, and a language-man was he, Thus spoke he to the shed-boss: 'Send 'The Rager' round to me. **1879** S.W. SILVER *Austral. Grazier's Guide* 50 The object of the overseer or **shed manager** . . is . . to get his sheep into the shed the moment they are dry. **1896** T. HENEY *Girl at Birrell's* 109 The **shed overseer**, the 'man over the board', was present to see that the shearing was properly done. **1916** *Truth* (Sydney) 11 June 11/1 He was employed on the station as shed overseer. **1959** H. LAMOND *Sheep Station* 123 He was the shed overseer, commonly referred to as th' boss o' the board.

3\. Special Comb. **shed hand,** a labourer employed to do the unskilled work in a shearing shed; **representative,** REP; **work,** unskilled work in a shearing shed; **worker,** *shed hand.*

1898 *Bulletin* (Sydney) 21 May 14/1 At a woolshed, near Condoblin . . a traveller . . 'had' the sympathising shearers to the extent of £8. . . After thanking the **shed-hands** . . he set out for the nearest township. **1909** W.G. SPENCE *Aust.'s Awakening* 166 In a camp of Union shearers and shed hands there would not be two per cent. who have arms. **1926** G. BLACK *Hist. N.S.W. Political Labor Party* i. 32 In those days, shedhands usually 'padded the hoof' from station to station; shearers often rode an old screw and led a pack horse. **1936** *Bulletin* (Sydney) 8 Jan. 19/1 The best picker-up I ever saw was Barefooted Joe. Any shearing contractor would find a job for him; he always managed to keep the board clean and the wool away from any six of the fastest 'guns'. One day strict unionists among the shed-hands spread tacks along Joe's track. **1946** *Ibid.* 11 Dec. 21/1 'I'm walkin' orf the board,' he yelled. 'I won't work with scabs who shear for shed-hand's wages.' **1965** R.H. CONQUEST *Horses in Kitchen* 49 Aged about thirty, he was a shedhand by occupation (when working). **1977** D. WHITINGTON *Strive to be Fair* 29 The shed hands had to scrub down the board on Saturdays after shearing finished. **1909** W.G. SPENCE *Aust.'s Awakening* 181 The Union agent, Mr Arthur Rae, at Hay. As agent, he gave a letter to the **shed representative** at Mungadel. **1914** *Pastoral Rev.* 15 Jan. 96 Miller was the shed representative [of the A.W.U.] at Lake Dismal Station. **1902** *Bulletin* (Sydney) 12 July 16/3 Looking for **shedwork** . . I one evening struck a shed that was to start shearing. **1899** *Western Champion* (Barcaldine) 18 July 7/4 On the night of Wednesday, the 12th . . the shed was visited by Mr P. Langston, who addressed a somewhat meagre meeting of the **shed workers** under the verandah of the rouseabouts hut. **1904** *Shearer* (Sydney) 27 Aug. 8/2 We have no time for the 'claptrap' ladled out to the workers by blatherskites of the Cocky Mac type. Being practical shearers and shed-workers ourselves, we know the requirements of the shearer and shed-worker.

sheelah, var. SHEILA.

sheep.

1\. Used *attrib.* in Comb. **sheep bridge, country, downs** *obs.*, **establishment** *obs.*, **fence, -grazing,** *obs.*, **-grower, -growing, -herder, hill** *obs.*, **-holder** *obs.*, **-holding, land** *obs.*, **master, -net, -netting, overseer, owner, paddock, -proof** *a.*, **property, proprietor** *obs.*, **watchman** *obs.*, **-work, -yard.**

1940 G.W. LOVEJOY *In Journeyings Often* 101, I had perforce to travel twenty miles up the creek to cross by the Narrawin **sheep bridge.** **1952** *Bulletin* (Sydney) 3 Sept. 16/3 Talking about the old four-wheeled horse-wagon one used to see rotting on the outskirts of western towns, in the last few years they have mostly been bought up and towed to outlying creeks to make sheep-bridges. **1822** W. BEARD *Old Ironbark* (1967) 11 Delightful country . . best **sheep country** in the world. **1835** J. BONWICK *J. Batman* (1867) 16 Beautiful land, and all good sheep country. **1849** A. HARRIS *Emigrant Family* (1967) 82 This is no sheep country. **1881** W. FEILDING *Austral. Trans-Continental Railway* 18 The country appeared good—myall plains, plenty of saltbush, occasional patches of mulga scrub. If this land were properly fenced in and not overstocked, I believe that it would make excellent sheep country. **1911** *Huon Times* (Franklin) 14 Oct. 2/6 Two years in New South Wales and Queensland, gaining experience in the sheep country. **1934** T. WOOD *Cobbers* 199 We crossed the Alice River . . then opened up sheep country, where a gate marked every ten miles. **1946** *Bulletin* (Sydney) 28 Aug. 29/2 Skinny Smith, the horse-breaker, had wandered down into the sheep country and asked for a job on a mutton run. **1965** G.H. FEARNSIDE *Golden Ram* 59 He thought, inconsequentially, that one would always find blowflies in sheep country. **1831** *Acct. Colony Van Diemen's Land* 79 About 6 miles above New Norfolk the country becomes more open, consisting of fine **sheep downs.** **1841** *Launceston Courier* 31 May 4/1 In its upward course, the valley contracts to a glen, through which the road ascends to the noble sheep-downs called Springhill Plains. **1847** J.D. LANG *Phillipsland* 95 A considerable portion of the road to Mount Macedon traverses what are called Sheep Downs, a comparatively level tract of country, but gently undulating. **1833** *Sydney Morning Herald* 19 Sept. 2/3 Mr C.F. Koelz . . has been for some years employed at the extensive **Sheep Establishments**, at Camden, pointing out to the flock masters in this colony the advantages to be derived from a judicious classification of their sheep. **1837** *Perth Gaz.* 22 July 942 The risks of a sheep establishment are such as to render it hazardous for small capitalists attempting the growth of wool. **1849** *Aust. Felix Monthly Mag.* 83 Sheep establishments are now scattered all over this tract, though it is not by any means fully occupied. **1851** *Empire* (Sydney) 17 Sept. 163/5 Perhaps there are not more than three or four per cent here who can shear, or have been accustomed to the other operations of a sheep establishment at shearing season. **1909** R. KALESKI *Austral. Settler's Compl. Guide* 94 Ran a **sheep-fence** around it (six wires). **1934** 'S. RUDD' *Green Grey Homestead* 152 Bordering this reserved area were mighty stations . . lying there within their cheap, pointed sheep fences, like living land sharks. **1949** H.G. LAMOND *White Ears* 69 White Ears came to his first sheep fence. This was of six wires, with posts only twelve feet apart, and the bottom wire a short four inches from the ground. **1926** *Illustr. Tas. Mail* (Hobart) 14 Apr. 1/2 Sheep Farming v. **Sheep Grazing** . . the advantages of intensive sheep farming as compared with ordinary grazing. **1929** I.A. SCOULER *Dowerin Story* 5 Discovered the value of sandplain for sheep-grazing. **1840** *Port Phillip Gaz.* 8 Jan. 4 Portland Bay at present forms a great scene of attraction to all

sheep growers in Van Diemen's Land. **1899** G. JEFFREY *Princ. Australasian Woolclassing* 32 The Merino sheep in Australia has been, is, and always will be, the most important type from a sheepgrower's standpoint. **1967** W. BEARD *Old Ironbark* 16 He became a most successful pioneer sheep and wool grower. **1923** 'J. NORTH' *Son of Bush* 26 The most picturesque part of the great Wooroodil run was . . utterly unlike the portion of the estate used for **sheep-growing.** **1937** H.E. GRAVES *Who Rides?* 160 It was a rough single-room structure of boards, used by stockmen and **sheep-herders** when on duty. **1978** WARD & SMITH *Vanishing Village* 35 Grandad was a sheep-herder and that was the job he worked at in Roma. **1834** J. BACKHOUSE *Narr. Visit Austral. Colonies* (1843) 188 We proceeded over some fine **sheep-hills.** **1836** T.F. BRIDE *Lett. Victorian Pioneers* 19 Feb. (1898) 23 We observed a Tier of Sheep hills to the right. **1840** *Sydney Herald* 29 July (Suppl.) 1/1 The hills constituting the northerly subdivision of these ridges—that is, from the 'sheep hills' . . nearly to 'Northside Hill' . . are extensively covered with good grass. **1819** W.C. WENTWORTH *Statistical, Hist., & Pol. Descr. N.S.W.* 112 The majority of the **sheep-holders** are actively employed in crossing their flocks with tups of the best Merino breed. **1832** J. BUSBY *Authentic Information N.S.W. & N.Z.* 13 It would not, perhaps, be advantageous for the sheepholder to pay a larger wage. **1845** D. MACKENZIE *Emigrant's Guide* 84 The sheepholder should see that his hut-keeper shifts, that is removes to a new place *daily*, these hurdles. **1855** G.H. WATHEN *Golden Colony* 91 One of the oldest settlers in the colony, now a large sheep-holder. **1928** C.E. COWLEY *Classing Clip* 157 On any **sheep-holding** serviceable drafting-yards are necessary. **1935** F. CLUNE *Rolling down Lachlan* 199 Burrawong station, once the largest sheep-holding. **1832** *Colonial Times* (Hobart) 3 July, For Sale, a Fine Sheep Farm . . 2,560 acres of fine **Sheep Land,** well watered at all seasons. **1841** *Launceston Courier* 15 Feb. 4/2 *On a long lease.* 5,000 Acres of good sound sheep land. **1850** *Britannia* (Hobart) 4 July 4/2, 1,000 acres of ordinary sheep land are worth from £40 to £50 a-year. **1835** *Sydney Herald* 2 Feb. 2/2 Our **sheep-masters** should therefore prepare for a change. **1870** J. BONWICK *Last Tasmanians* 112 Two shepherds were in charge of one flock; thus adding to the expense as well as the anxiety of the unhappy sheep-master. **1936** E.W. COX *Evol. Austral. Merino* 100 Undoubtedly they were great sheepmasters, possessing in no mean degree the flair for breeding. **1849** C. STURT *Narr. Exped. Central Aust.* I. 318 He mistook the **sheep net** for a fishing net, and gave them to understand that there were fish in those waters so large that they would not get through the meshes. **1837** H. CAPPER *S.A.* 70 The materials for large cattle and sheep enclosures, which will require little time to erect, have been obtained; and the **sheep-netting** and chains, to render them more complete for the purposes designated, have been sent out with them. **1946** *Bulletin* (Sydney) 24 July 28/4 I've worked for cockies who propped their fences up with sticks, and even for one who sent me out to mend sheep-netting with binder twine. **1834** N.S.W. Magistrates' Deposition Bk. 6 Nov., I am **Sheep Overseer** to Mr McIntyre and the prisoner himself is employed as a Shepherd and Taylor as Watchman at the same Station. **1844** *Sydney Morning Herald* 3 Jan. 4/6 Assistant Sheep Overseer. Wanted, a person thoroughly acquainted with the management of sheep. **1880** J.B. STEVENSON *Seven Yrs. Austral. Bush* 156 One of the sheep overseers . . asked me to exchange posts with him. **1900** T. MAJOR *Leaves from Squatter's Note Bk.* 84 The sheep overseer or myself often rode round to see that the flocks were properly shepherded. **1920** *Smith's Weekly* (Sydney) 11 Sept. 18/4 McTubb, sheep overseer . . returned from one of his periodical visits to the township. **1839** *Southern Austral.* (Adelaide) 16 Oct. 4/2 Our **sheepowners** should be constantly on the watch to prevent the disorder [*sc.* foot rot] from gaining ground. **1855** J. CAPPER *Philips' Emigrants' Guide* 100 A large sheep-owner told me that he would sooner take a sailor who hardly knew the head from the stern of a sheep, or a clerk who had been in an office all his life, than an English-bred shepherd. **1865** 'OMEGA' *Sheep Vic., Tas., & N.Z.* 31 The efforts of sheep-owners . . should be directed towards preventive measures. **1898** *Bulletin* (Sydney) 28 May 31/1 The sheep-owners . . decided to give £5 for every full-grown dingo-skin stripped in the district. **1929** *Ibid.* 16 Oct. 25/2 The 'long paddock' is not the only place in which sheep-owners have had . . cheap feed. **1965** K. TENNANT *Summer's Tales* 216 What the hell are the three sheepowners' changeling virgins also quaking and trilling with merriment for? **1883** W.A. BRODRIBB *Recoll. Austral. Squatter* 123 This timely assistance enabled me to . . fence a portion of the station into **sheep paddocks.** **1914** A.R. RICHARDSON *Early Memories Great Nor-West* 18 Our brother settlers . . as sheep paddocks were then unknown in Western Australia, took up sheep all their lives used to being shepherded and camping in the open at night. **1930** E.R. GRIBBLE *Forty Yrs. with Aborigines* 33 Two fine young colts had been lost in a large sheep-paddock. **1976** *Bulletin* (Sydney) 2 Oct. 37/2 We race into the past through stone-studded sheep-paddocks—so many stones that it seems the sky has rained them. **1872** G.S. BADEN-POWELL *New Homes for Old Country* 169 A run is cut up into several portions, or 'paddocks', by **sheep-proof** fences. **1882** ARMSTRONG & CAMPBELL *Austral. Sheep Husbandry* 9 The sandy districts of the Darling (where we have seen a sheep-proof yard, that has been built in the morning, rendered almost useless before night, from the quantities of fine sand that have been blowing in clouds all day). **1929** J.L. MOORE *Canine King* 134 Up against the sheep-proof fence the mob was forced. **1946** A.J. HOLT *Wheat Farms Victoria* 37 Grazing rights for sheep are conceded to the share-farmer only in return for some payment or service, e.g., by construction of a portion of sheep-proof fencing, or by leaving so many acres of 'well-worked' fallow over and above that customarily expected. **1957** *Bulletin* (Sydney) 30 Jan. 13/1 They'd been on that particular **sheep-property** doing contract post-cutting. **1965** R.H. CONQUEST *Horses in Kitchen* 16 Not only station hands or stockmen (station hands are employed on sheep properties, stockmen on cattle runs) occupy the quarters. **1972** *Bulletin* (Sydney) 26 Feb. 57/3 Recently assembled data suggests that the number of beef cattle on sheep properties has almost doubled in three years. **1835** F.C. IRWIN *State & Position W.A.* 65 He . . has, for some time, been a **sheep proprietor.** **1845** D. MACKENZIE *Emigrant's Guide* 84 The sheep proprietor should allow none of them to stand on his run while he can buy, beg, or borrow hurdles. **1848** J.C. BYRNE *Emigrant's Guide* 40 One sheep proprietor often possesses numerous stations contiguous to each other, or in different parts of the country. **1822** B. FIELD in G. Mackaness *Fourteen Journeys Blue Mountains* 15 Oct. (1950) ii. 45 The settlers' convict-servants (stockmen and **sheep watchmen**) do little but drone. **1837** *Cornwall Chron.* (Launceston) 23 Sept. 1, I . . went to Port Phillip as a sheep watchman. **1843** *Melbourne Times* 25 July 2/4 On Sunday last one of the Australian Agricultural Company's sheep watchmen was stopped on the road near the washpool by an armed bushranger, and stripped of nearly all his clothes. **1849** 'BUSHMAN' *Sidney's Austral. Handbk.* 66 Sheep watchmen £25 to £17; hutkeepers £25 to £15. **1931** A.W. UPFIELD *Sands of Windee* 85 The men are late to meals having been delayed by **sheep-work** in a paddock. **1937** W. HATFIELD *I find Aust.* 81, I got a little tired of sheep-work. Moore was always saying how much faster and harder cattle-work was, so I was itching to get amongst it, though he told me I would be terribly green, still, at really fast horse-work in open country. **1809** *Sydney Gaz.* 22 Jan., Farm . . with capital cow houses, **sheep yards,** and all other conveniences. **1829** H. WIDOWSON *Present State Van Diemen's Land* 78 The size of the sheep yard will depend upon the numbers you can purchase. **1843** J.F. BENNETT *Hist. & Descr. Acct. S.A.* 96 The hurdles for the sheep yards are moveable. **1860** 'LADY' *My Experiences in Aust.* 171 Brings them home to the sheep-yards (with which each out-station is provided) at night. **1886** R. HENTY *Australiana* 160 Sheep-yards were made . . shaped like a pear. From the narrow end a lane was added, about twelve feet in length, and just wide enough for one sheep to walk down at a time. **1930** D. COTTRELL *Earth Battle* 275 After the fourth rain the death-white spider-petalled lillies had sprung up even on the open plains: in ones and twos by the corners of the sandy grey-fenced sheep-yards. **1955** *Meanjin* 166 From one end stretched the sheepyards, a crisscross maze of heavy-netted fences, with the killing gallows the only vertical line. **1959** D. STUART *Yandy* 18 The camp at the mickery would be an occasional camp for musterers, a good central place for a sheepyard.

2. Special Comb. **sheep barber,** BARBER *n.*; **boiler** *obs.*, one who engages in *sheep-boiling*; **-boiling** *vbl. n., hist.*, BOILING 1; also *attrib.*; **cocky,** a sheep-farmer on a small scale (see COCKY *n.*[2]); **district, (a)** a district suitable for grazing sheep; **(b)** see quot. 1878; **dressing** *obs.*, see DRESS; **-drove** *v. intr.*, see DROVE *v.*; also as *vbl. n.*; so **-drover,** see DROVER 1; **-feed,** vegetation suitable for sheep to graze (see FEED); **feeder** *obs.*, a sheep-farmer; **-feeding** *vbl. n.*, the pasturing of sheep; **grazier** *obs.*, see GRAZIER; **king,** a large-scale sheep-farmer; **-man,** a sheep-farmer; one employed to tend sheep; **race,** see RACE *n.*[1]; **run,** see RUN *n.*[2] 1 a. and 2; **selection,** see SELECTION 2 a.; **shed,** *shearing shed*, see SHEARING B. 3; **-sick** *a.*, see quot. 1979; **slut,** a female sheep-dog; **squatter** *obs.*, see SQUATTER 2 and 3; **station,** see STATION 2 a. and 3; **tank,** see TANK *n.*[1] 1; **tobacco** *obs., sheepwash tobacco*; **town,** a town which serves a sheep-farming district; **-wash** *obs.*, adulterated or inferior alcoholic liquor; **-wash tobacco,** inferior tobacco.

1912 *Bulletin* (Sydney) 14 Nov. 15/2 The shearers . . the **sheep barbers.** **1944** *Ibid.* 19 July 13/3 By noon 300-a-day sheep-barbers were only pickers-up, while brickies who couldn't put away their thousand in eight and three-quarters were only billy-boys. **1959** *Ibid.* 23 Dec. 16/1 Most sheep-barbers either drink one or two bottles of beer between knocking-off and going in to tea or slap a brace of rums down. **1843** *Sydney Morning Herald* 18 July 3/3 Surely such a line of procedure is as necessary to be observed by the editor of a paper as by a **sheep-boiler.** **1843** *Colonial Observer* (Sydney) 26 July 1199/1 Mr Wentworth has commenced **sheep boiling** on his estate. . . Such settlers as may choose to take advantage of the opportunity, may have their surplus stock rendered down. **1844** *Sydney Morning Herald* 8 Jan. 2/3 The flockowners of the southern district . . are about to call a meeting for the purpose of forming a sheep boiling establishment. **1844** *Dispatch* (Sydney) 10 Feb. 3/1 *Sheep boiling*, the process of boiling down sheep and cattle, for the purpose of rendering the fat into tallow. **1897** *Worker* (Sydney) 7 Aug. 3/3 Now, Mr Editor, I wish all our lads to be warned against those **sheep cockeys** who are going to cut down the price. **1932** *Bulletin* (Sydney) 18 May 20/2 A hardened old sheep cocky in W.A. . . discovered that a dingo had invaded the sanctity of his paddocks. **1948** V. PALMER *Golconda* 130 He came upon a German sheep-cocky's horse and sulky. **1977** C. McCULLOUGH *Thorn Birds* 227 Some of the sheep cockies must have given you the glad eye. **1843** *Arden's Sydney Mag.* Oct. 119 His surveyors are at work opening up a direct line of communication with the Maneroo **sheep district.** **1847** *Maitland Mercury* 10 Nov. 3/1 *Wimera* . . is the best sheep district in all Port Phillip. **1847** *Transportation Question Considered* 8 No supply of labor that the adjacent Colonies are likely to receive will overstock the demand of their constantly extending sheep districts. **1878** *Act* (N.S.W.) 41 Vict. no. 19 Sect. 14, Every owner intending to travel three hundred or more sheep from any run shall before leaving the Sheep district in which such run is situated forward to the Inspector of the district a statement in writing of the number description brands and marks of the said sheep and of their intended route and destination and shall obtain from the Inspector a permit containing the particulars set forth in the Second Schedule hereto to travel the said sheep. And every owner introducing sheep from any of the adjoining Colonies shall in like manner obtain a permit to travel as aforesaid from the Inspector for the district into which such sheep shall first pass on crossing the Border. **1977** T.L. McKNIGHT *Long Paddock* 43 The old scab districts were maintained as physical entities, but their names evolved from 'Scab District' to 'Sheep District' to 'Pastures and Stock Board'. **1841** G. ARDEN *Recent Information Port Phillip* 27 Tobacco . . has been cultivated by squatters . . in quantities sufficient to supply their ordinary demands for **sheep dressing.** **1842** *Geelong Advertiser* 26 Sept. 2/3 One fourth of the whole labour and expense on an establishment where there are scabby sheep is expended in sheep dressing. **1874** C. DE BOOS *Congewoi Correspondence* 55 Sheep-dressing or scabbing wasn't done so scientifically then as it is now. **1888** *Bulletin* (Sydney) 10 Mar. 14/1 A young fellow . . was **sheep-droving** with the writer away in the 'New Country' north of the alligator line, during the early sixties. **1889** *Illustr. Austral. News* (Melbourne) 1 Aug. 18/2 Our sketches this month include several illustrative of the daily life of persons engaged in sheep droving. **1925** M. TERRY *Across Unknown Aust.* 24, I went sheep-droving and he went south, far away to a distant cattle station. **1841** *Port Phillip Patriot* 4 Oct. 3/3 A cattle-jobber or a **sheep-drover.** **1851** *Empire* (Sydney) 12 Aug. 39/5 He, however, came out into the room where prisoner, his wife, the sheep drover, and the black man were. **1934** 'S. RUDD' *Green Grey Homestead* 145 He was the finest looking animal ever ye clapped eyes on, though before that he was just a sleepy old clothes-peg of a sheep-drover's moke. **1965** R.H. CONQUEST *Horses in Kitchen* 123 He offered men like me employment as sheep drovers. **1903** *Bulletin* (Sydney)

25 Feb. 16/2 Though splendid rains have fallen .. the prospect for **sheep-feed** even is very remote. **1933** J. TRURAN *Where Plain Begins* 7 The gravelly soil .. will scarce grow enough sheep-feed to repay the cost of clearing. **1934** E. STOREY *Eve's Affairs* 84 There's not much sheep feed owing to a rain shortage. **1840** *Port Lincoln Herald* 7 Mar. 4 A small water hole is valued by an Australian **Sheep feeder** as much as one of Niobe's tears preserved in spirits would be by an English Antiquarian. **1838** *S. Austral. Rec.* (London) 11 July 76/2 **Sheep-feeding** has made the fortune of Australia. **1840** J.P. JOHNSON *Plain Truths* 11 Sheep-feeding on the western side of the Darling Range has proved a complete failure. **1936** G.C. MORPHETT *Life & Lett. Sir J. Morphett* 56 There are hundreds of thousands of acres of land better adapted to sheep-feeding than any he ever saw. **1833** *Colonist* (Hobart) 18 June 1/4 This Estate is admirably adapted for an extensive **Sheep Grazier.** **1844** *Colonial Times* (Hobart) 23 Apr., The same apathy pervades over the sheep-grazier as the agriculturist. **1848** *Maitland Mercury* 26 Aug. 2/3 With regard to shifting, it is my opinion that every sheep-grazier ought, if possible, to have twice the number of stations that he requires in occupation at any one time. **1899** *Bulletin* (Sydney) 14 Oct. 14/3 The chum .. was bidden to drive to the station for the expected **sheep-king.** **1919** *Smith's Weekly* (Sydney) 5 Apr. 2/4 Sheep-king Tyson once lunched at the Brisbane Union Club... 'What have you got?' enquired the man of many jumbucks. **1932** J. MCCARTER *Pan's Clan* 229 I'd sooner be a sheep king like J.M. Niall. **1945** S.D. RAILTON *Southern Cross* 9 One would surely have taken him for the station rouseabout, rather than the first lieutenant of a shrewd old sheep king. **1979** R. DUFFIELD *Rogue Bull* 88 Today Lang Hancock could well be 'sheep king' of the Pilbara rather than the 'iron king'. **1901** *Bulletin* (Sydney) 7 Dec. 30/2 The **sheepman** and his satellites came out; all riding stable-fed horses. **1909** *Ibid.* 28 Oct. 13/3 Only newchums and woolly-stockmen (i.e., sheep-men) use the whip as a plaything. **1917** A.L. BREWER *'Gators' Euchre* 43 The sheep-man who held up his end in the Territory couldn't be reckoned small potatoes. There'll be no room for small potatoes in the N.T. this century. **1937** E. FLYNN *Beam Ends* 66 Tall, bearded sheepmen from the Western districts, in wide brimmed hats and elastic side boots. **1968** *Meanjin* 18 Sheepmen drive their flocks up from the valleys during the Summer months. **1980** J. WOLFE *End of Pricklystick* 39 An old man was driving a mob of sheep through the Strzelecki Ranges .. then slowly he collapsed on the hot road... Luckily for the sheepman, his progress was being watched. **1956** *Bulletin* (Sydney) 4 Jan. 13/1 The boss says for you to pick-up in No. 2 road, kick two down the **sheep-race** and clear the shed-road. **1969** G. JOHNSTON *Clean Straw for Nothing* (1971) 162 We were all filing through the sheep-race, rushing away from one oblivion towards another. **1823** *Hobart Town Gaz.* 4 Oct., A Farm of 200 acres .. with a good but small **sheep run.** **1829** R. DAWSON *Statement* 17 This farm is any thing but a good sheep run. **1832** *Colonist* (Hobart) 16 Nov. 1/5 The Salt-Pan Plains .. is well known to be the finest sheep run in the Island. **1834** *N.S.W. Mag.* (Sydney) 207 It is the interest of those already settled in the territory, to deter Newcomers from fixing their abode in the immediate vicinity; because every such fixation tends to narrow their sheep-run. **1844** *Colonial Times* (Hobart) 24 Sept., The Auctioneer begs to state that it is one of the *very best sheep runs in the district of the Salt Pan Plains.* **1859** J.D. MEREWEATHER *Diary Working Clergyman* 27 He told me that he was one of the early settlers in that part of the country, and that he had several sheep-runs. **1875** *Illustr. Sydney News* 19 Jan. 11/2 These ranges are occupied as sheep runs and are indeed very excellent sheep country. **1888** *Sydney Morning Herald* 24 Jan. (Centennial Suppl.) 1/6 Where cities, towns, and villages now stand, or where well-fenced sheep-runs exist, there was 100 years ago little else than bush. **1906** *Gadfly* (Adelaide) 14 Mar. 19/2 Between an Armytage Queensland sheeprun and its wealthy owner's Melbourne mansion. **1936** G.C. MORPHETT *Life & Lett. Sir J. Morphett* 34 Most of the sheep-runs are obliged to be rented at a high rate. **1948** G. FARWELL *Down Argent Street* 15 Sheep runs near the Darling-Murray junction and Mount Murchison upriver, with Menindee grown to a rough-neck township about a grog shanty. **1965** G. MCINNES *Road to Gundagai* 147 Bourchier had a sheep run—it was too modest to be called a station—of about three hundred acres. **1943** *Bulletin* (Sydney) 22 Sept. 13/2 There is near Adavale (s.w. Q.) a **sheep selection** without a horse on the place. **1956** A.C.C. LOCK *Tropical Tapestry* 141 Hobbs .. rang D. Lynch, whose sheep selection, Lady Wallace, was ten miles or so away. **1829** R. DAWSON *Statement* 83 Mr J. McArthur is compelled to admit .. that the **sheep-shed** .. was a 'well-adapted building'. **1843** *Sydney Morning Herald* 6 Oct. 1/5 Men's huts, sheep-shed, an excellent stock-yard, and milking-bale complete. **1908** *Emu* VII. 145, I have found them flying into the sheep-shed to pick at the sheepskins while shearing was going on with doors opening into the shed. **1895** *Leader* (Melbourne) 3 Aug. 6/1 Certain country in which severe losses have occurred in recent years has been too long carrying sheep, and .. the land has become what is termed **'sheep sick'**. **1920** *Land of Lyre Bird* (S. Gippsland Pioneers' Assoc.) 320 Before the pastures became to some extent 'sheep sick' by stocking continuously with sheep. **1979** J. LINDEMAN *Red Rumps & White Faces* 111 Due to poor seasons and heavy stocking, the country became 'sheep sick'. The majority of the good grasses .. gradually died out and were replaced by natural causes with both black and white spear grasses, both lethal to sheep. **1925** *Bulletin* (Sydney) 9 Apr. 24/4 A well-bred **sheep-slut** of ours in Western Queensland has developed the atrocious habit of devouring her litter. **1933** J. MCCARTER *Love's Lunatic* 102 There's no flamin' scandal-mongers on th' job—no panic-time for *them* if, say, a cattle dog and a sheep slut have pups. **1956** B.J. RAYMENT *My Towri* 140, I would suggest that non-castrated sheep dogs or sheep sluts be registered at £1 each. **1844** *Parramatta Chron.* 9 Nov. 3/1 The lordly **sheep squatter** and over-grown stock holder that comes in and out. **1886** D.E. BANDMANN *Actor's Tour* 88 The Cup of last year (1883) was won by a Mr White, a sheep squatter. **1897** L. LINDLEY-COWEN *W. Austral. Settler's Guide* 120 The old *regime* of the sheep squatters gave place to mixed farming and a large output of produce. **1825** *HRA* (1919) 1st Ser. XII. 69 Their Shepherds' Huts and **Sheep Stations** are established on different parts of it. **1838** *Cornwall Chron.* (Launceston) 4 Sept. 2 According to the accounts we have recently received from Port Phillip, we find, that there are 400 sheep stations, which average five persons; thus there is a population amongst the stations of 2000. **1848** H.W. HAYGARTH *Recoll. Bush Life* 14 The head station, at which the owner or superintendent resides, is generally so situated as to be as nearly as possible equidistant from the several sheep stations, to which frequent visits are necessary. **1855** W. CAMPBELL *Crown Lands Aust.* 57 The youth of his children, if they exceed two or three in number, prevents him from being employed far up the country on sheep stations. **1872** G.S. BADEN-POWELL *New Homes for Old Country* 161 About the run are dotted 'sheep-stations', or 'out-stations', consisting of a hut with sheep-yards attached. **1886** J.F. CONIGRAVE *S.A.* 103 The country was opened up by pioneer squatters; and what were, only a few years ago, vast tracts of waste lands are now converted into thriving sheep and cattle stations. **1912** T.E. SPENCER *Bindawalla* 1 He was the only son of James Raymond, proprietor of 'Bindawalla', the largest sheep station in the district. **1943** J. BINNING *Target Area* 58 Arthur .. has a sheep station the size of Palestine. **1961** X. HERBERT *Soldiers' Women* 67 She's a spinster. Runs her own sheep-station. **1978** R.A.F. WEBB *Brothers in Sun* 25 The large sheep stations in the Burnett district, some of them 1 million acres in extent, began to be cut up into smaller stations, and little townships began to spring up. **1982** R. HALL *Just Relations* 56 Could have made a fortune and bought hisself a sheep station by now. **1890** G.J. BROINOWSKI *Birds of Aust.* II. Pl. 35, The present specimens were found among the herbage usually growing about the **sheep tanks.** **1912** *Emu* XII. 66 This tree stood close to a sheep-tank or dam. **1843** *Portland Mercury* 4 Jan. 1/4 **Sheep tobacco.** **1847** E.W. LANDOR *Bushman* 259 Smoked sheep-tobacco... Coarse pig-tail, used as a decoction for dressing the diseased sheep. **1948** F. CLUNE *Wild Colonial Boys* p. xix, My peregrinations .. brought me as a commercial traveller to .. Binalong, near the old **sheep-town** of Yass. **1965** R.H. CONQUEST *Horses in Kitchen* 192 He was a quietly spoken man, never did his block, and was considered a good 'bite' by down-and-outs in the sheep towns. **1891** M. ROBERTS *Land-Travel & Sea-Faring* 177 In the hotel we did not flourish, for both of us had something there described as brandy, but known to colonials as **'sheepwash'**. It is said that in order to make the vile concoction take quicker effect on the unwary tobacco is put in the cask. **1945** S.J. BAKER *Austral. Lang.* 167 Additional terms for beer include: *sheep wash* [etc.]. **1860** *S. Austral. Advertiser* (Adelaide) 2 July 2/5 *Proposed Amended South Australian Tariff.* Cigars, per lb., 4s. Snuff, per lb., 2s. **Sheepwash Tobacco,** per lb., 3d. **1881** *Bulletin* (Sydney) 26 Mar. 8/3 The villainous sheep-wash tobacco she smoked In the gunyah down there by the lake. **1887** 'OVERLANDER' *Austral. Sketches* 67 A pipe of very suspicious looking sheep-wash tobacco. **1900** *Bulletin* (Sydney) 29 Sept. 14/4 He .. found .. a publican in the act of nailing a quarter twist of 'sheepwash' tobacco inside of a 10-gal rum-keg. **1918** J.A. PHILP *Jingles that Jangle* 38 I'm in for hard yakker and sheep-wash terbaccer.

3. In the phr. **on** (or **off**) **the sheep's back,** used in allusion to wool as the source of national prosperity.

[**1849** S. & J. SIDNEY *Emigrant's Jrnl.* 162 As for capital, it is always growing on the sheep's backs without let or hindrance, except the want of shepherds.] **1932** R.W. THOMPSON *Down Under* 65 The phrase 'riding on the sheeps' [*sic*] back' was heard in a small and quickly hushed voice from certain wiser quarters. **1933** C.H. HOLMES *We find Aust.* 152 Australia is 'carried on the sheep's back', as the saying is. **1949** *Bulletin* (Sydney) 28 Dec. 7/1 Every economist in the land knows that we are still well on the sheep's back, partly held there by the wheatgrower. **1959** A. UPFIELD *Bony & Mouse* 28 It is said that Australia rides on the sheep's back. All tosh, of course, because it floats on beer. **1965** G. MCINNES *Road to Gundagai* 117 We were reminded by politicians and editors, and of course at school, ad nauseum, that Australia 'lives off the sheep's back'. **1970** *Bulletin* (Sydney) 14 Feb. 17/1 Off the sheep's back, into the iron age. **1983** *Bicentenary '88* (Austral. Bicentennial Authority) Nov. 4/1 On the sheep's back to the Bicentenary .. Public Relations Manager for the Australian Wool Corporation.

sheep bush. [See quot. 1885.] WILGA. Also *attrib.*

1885 *Trans. & Proc. R. Soc. S.A.* (1886) 20 *Geijera parvifolia*—The Sheep Bush. Sheep only are particularly fond of this bush, which grows on hard limestone soils, and seems quite unaffected by droughts. **1903** G. SUTHERLAND *Australasian Live Stock Man.* (ed. 2) 385 The 'Sheep-bush willow' is the *Geijera parvifolia* belonging to a peculiarly Australian genus of trees. **1933** *Bulletin* (Sydney) 7 June 25/2 Sheep bush .. is tall and ornamental. It has long narrow leaves. **1965** *Austral. Encycl.* IX. 310 *Geijera parviflora* .. is .. a valuable source of stock fodder in times of scarcity. The smaller related *G. linearifolia* .. is called sheep-bush for a similar reason.

sheep-ho, *int.* and *n.* Also **sheep-o, sheep-oh.**

A. *int.* A shearer's call for a sheep to shear.

1900 *Bulletin* (Sydney) 13 Jan. 32/2 'Go it, you—tigers!' yells a tar-boy. 'Wool away!' 'Tar!' 'Sheep Ho!' **1963** C.H. SMITH *How y' going Mate?* 53 Sometimes, when the shearers called 'Sheep-oh!' Sam would be at the back. **1982** *Sydney Morning Herald* 23 Oct. 29/4 There are cries of Sheep-O! when more sheep are needed in the pen.

B. *n. Obs.* PENNER-UP.

1900 *On Track* 131 Others, the sheep-ho's or the engine drivers at the shed or wool-wash, call him.

sheep-wash, *v. Hist.* [Used elsewhere but recorded earliest in Aust.] *intr.* To wash sheep before shearing. Chiefly as *vbl. n.*

1834 'EMIGRANT' *Party Politics Exposed* 41, I was sheep-washing at Castle Forbes. **1837** *Cornwall Chron.* (Launceston) 18 Nov. 1 A resolution was passed at one of the meetings to discourage the use of ardent spirits at sheep washings. **1843** *Sydney Morning Herald* 8 May 3/5 The station is first-rate, being situated on the banks of the never-failing stream, Murrumbidgee, where all the natural conveniences for sheep-washing it is well known cannot be surpassed. **1847** *Maitland Mercury* 29 Sept. 2/5 As the time for the general sheep washing throughout the country will shortly commence, it will not perhaps be considered unreasonable to offer a few remarks, founded on information we have been favoured with, respecting the treatment of sheep at the wash-pool. **1852** G.C. MUNDY *Our Antipodes* III. 236 Mr K—did not forget to display to us his perhaps unique method of sheep-washing—by the agency of hot water. **1855** 'RUSTICUS' *How to settle in Vic.* 57 Sheep washing and shearing are now proceeded with in some parts of the Colony. **1872** MRS E. MILLETT *Austral. Parsonage* 168 Shortly before the season for sheepwashing, in October .. the bush was green with grass, and water was lying in the still deep pools in the rocky beds of the gullies. **1886** R. HENTY *Australiana* 229, I was in the midst of sheepwashing and shearing—always a critical time for the wool-grower. **1927** A. CROMBIE *After Sixty Yrs.* 115 As fine a man as ever Riverina possessed, discussing the sheep washing question with me. **1943** H.G. LAMOND *From Tariaro to Ross Roy* 35 Sheep washing ended during the early '70s. **1980** P. FREEMAN *Woolshed* 18 Sheep washing has long since been discontinued and the brush pens of Henry King's time have given way in modern woolsheds to well-designed drafting-yards that allow the proper storage, movement and handling of the sheep destined to be shorn.

sheep-washer. *Hist.* [See prec.] One who is employed to wash sheep before they are shorn.

1841 *Geelong Advertiser* 11 Oct. 2/3 The Governor himself dare not offer a glass of wine to a friend, nor a settler give a pannikin of grog to his sheep-washers, without subjecting himself to a penalty of £30. **1854** W. HOWITT *Boy's Adventures* 213 It was now the busy part of the squatter's year—washing and shearing time. There were some dozens of men now about the place, some of them sheep-washers, some shearers. **1862** A. POLEHAMPTON *Kangaroo Land* 213 In the men's hut there were about twenty intending sheep-washers at supper. **1888** *Bulletin* (Sydney) 10 Mar. 14/1 The 'Stockman's Grave' . . I first heard at a sheep-washers' camp in 1865. **1943** H.G. LAMOND *From Tariaro to Ross Roy* 27 The boss of the board would appeal for sheep washers from among the shearers.

sheepy. *Austral. pidgin. Obs.* Mutton; sheep.

1839 *S. Austral. Rec.* (London) (1840) 1 Feb. 22 They [*sc.* aborigines] call mutton *sheepy*, and pork *piggy*, and bread *bready*. **1841** *Port Phillip Patriot* 4/5 The villains laughed at and mocked us, roaring out 'plenty sheepy', 'plenty jumbuck', (another name of theirs for sheep). **1842** *Tasmanian Jrnl. Nat. Sci.* I. 118 *Sheepi-kan-gallan-galla* (sheep-mother) is the name of a shepherd.

sheevo, var. SHIVOO.

sheila. Formerly also **shaler, sheelah, sheilah, shelah.** [Prob. from the generic use of the (orig. Irish) proper name *Sheila*: see quot. 1828. Now Austral. and N.Z. but previously also Br. slang: see OEDS.] A girl or (young) woman.

[**1828** *Monitor* (Sydney) 22 Mar. 1053/2 Many a piteous Shela stood wiping the gory locks of her Paddy, until released from that duty by the officious interference of the knight of the baton.] **1832** *Hill's Life N.S.W.* (Sydney) 17 Aug. 2 *Daniel Delaney*, from Donoghadee, was charged with making love to a Shelah in the Domain, at the unseasonable hour of eleven p.m. **1839** *Tasmanian Weekly Dispatch* (Hobart) 1 Nov. 6/4 Two real spitfire shelahs . . came . . to complain of each other. Betty Allsop said that Polly Hagan had come to her. **1895** C. CROWE *Austral. Slang Dict.* 72 *Shaler*, a girl. **1916** C. VAUDE *Tivoli* 2 The sheiler wot I owns. **1919** C.H. THORP *Handful of Ausseys* 130 Fellows would ride in from anywhere up to twenty miles around to have a hop and see all the sheilas. **1920** *Aussie* (Sydney) Apr. 21/1 For the sheelahs know the Aussie hat, from France to Scapa Flow. **1926** *Bulletin* (Sydney) 11 Feb. 24/1 A sheila robbed him the first night out in a bug-house. **1930** L.W. LOWER *Here's Luck* (1955) 201 'Sheilas!' gasped Woggo as the girls clambered out of the car. **1943** *Bulletin* (Sydney) 27 Oct. 12/1 'I wouldn't have cared if he'd been a good-lookin' feller', lamented Bill, 'but an ugly-looking cow like that beatin' a man to a sheilah.' **1953** T.A.G. HUNGERFORD *Riverslake* 23 That's what my old sheila used to call me, sometimes! **1965** K. SMITH *OGF* 185 As for *Medea*, I thought it was disgusting. The way that old sheila did away with her two kids. **1973** *Bronze Swagman Bk. Bush Verse* (1974) 59 Mother Nature? She's a sheila, but a bloody tough old boss! **1979** J. SUMMONS *Lamb of God* 36 He's one of the only kids in the world who still calls girls sheilas. **1984** *Sydney Morning Herald* 4 May 8/7 My other vote for the most bannable word in the Australian vocabulary would be 'sheila', admittedly not much used by the young, but still surprisingly persistent among the adult male population and encapsulating perfectly and regrettably the speaker's attitude to women. **1985** H. GARNER *Postcards from Surfers* 68 If I was to fight over every sheila I'd ever fucked there'd be fights from here to bloody Darwin.

shelf, *n.* [Prob. in allusion to the phr. *on the shelf* out of the way.] An informer. Also **shelfer.**

1916 *Bulletin* (Sydney) 6 July 24/1 Here are a few of the pet names given by the wielder of the pick and banjo to the ganger: 'The red light', 'the big bloke', 'the gun', 'the nark', 'the spur', 'the shelfer', and 'the nit'. **c 1920** *Breakers of Men* (I.W.W. Prisoners Release Committee) 16 Unless a man is a 'shelf', that is an informer on his fellow prisoners, and prepared to fawn at the feet of officials, the chief warder in particular, he has a hard lot to contend against. **1922** *Daily Mail* (Sydney) 16 Jan. 5/5 The man who can get any evidence to help them in this case will take it to them unasked and seeking no reward. And his brothers of the criminal class, for once, won't call him a 'shelf' for so doing. **1950** F.J. HARDY *Power without Glory* 80 'How do you know he's a nark?' 'Piggy recognised him. . . Says he's been a 'shelf' for years.' **1965** K. SMITH *OGF* 38 'Anyway, I haven't got a screwdriver. I loaned all my tools to Gadley, last week.' 'Well, go over and get them back.' 'I wouldn't trust myself,' I said. 'Bloody shelfer.' **1969** W. MOXHAM *Apprentice* 18 'Who's going to split? His word wouldn't carry much weight.' 'I'm no shelf.' Rufe took a notch in the collar.

shelf, *v.* [f. prec.] *trans.* To inform upon. Also as *vbl. n.*

1936 'SWEENEY, EX-CROOK' *I Confess* 123 No crime is so heinous as that called 'shelfing'—betrayal. **1941** E.A. CLARKE *Man nobody Understood* 72 Prison administrators say that a thief with a 'hungry stomach' would 'shelf' his own mother. But they also know the men who are 'stone cold' and never 'cough up'. **1959** *Overland* xv. 32 The Mong had been known to 'shelf' a fellow-traveller on a goods train by barking, scratching or whining. **1969** W. MOXHAM *Apprentice* 163 Rufe said, 'You mean you're going to shelf Howie?' 'I'm no stoolie!' **1973** F. PARSONS *Man called Mo* 1 He would shelf a stagehand to the management, then defend the same man against the same employers. **1975** V. KELLY *Shark Arm Case* (rev. ed.) 47 'Is he all right?' . . 'Of course he's all right. Pat never shelfed a man in his life. The court records show that.' **1984** *Sun-Herald* (Sydney) 9 Sept. 63/3 For all the pre-planning and agreements not to 'shelf' one another by being seen to start a rush to back Fine Cotton, several of those in the know could not contain their greed.

shell. Shortened form of 'pearl-shell'. Also *attrib.*

1913 *Cwlth. Parl. Papers* III. 747 They have not yet proved themselves as shell-getters. There is no doubt about their being divers. But, at the same time, getting the shell is called the scavenging of the bottom of the sea. **1918** G. WHITE *Thirty Yrs. Tropical Aust.* 52 The white-tipped shell is the natural shell without the gold-lip colouring. . . Gold-lip shell is some pounds sterling per ton of less value than silver-lipped. **1933** J.M. HARCOURT *Pearlers* 19 In three years Gale's three boats had fished just enough shell to pay expenses. **1936** N. CALDWELL *Fangs of Sea* 250 'There it is, lad, that's shell.' He pointed to the dirty looking disks. **1940** E. HILL *Great Austral. Loneliness* (ed. 2) 69 Brian's wife was a lubra with a dash of bitters. He was an expert shell-packer. **1955** A.C.V. BLIGH *Golden Quest* 160 Divers were mostly local men and were usually engaged on their reputations as shell-getters. **1959** D. STUART *Yandy* 97 Down in the white-wood thickets where the De Grey spilled out in floodtime the shell gang went when the tides were against them and hunted wild pigs.

Also **sheller** *n.*, one who fishes for pearl-shell; **shelling** *ppl. a.*, of or pertaining to this.

1902 *Cwlth. Parl. Papers* II. 1009 From this outward the '**shellers**' became divided into two parties. **1905** *Bulletin* (Sydney) 7 Dec. 39/2 The Japanese sheller is not a great drinker. **1913** *Cwlth. Parl. Papers* III. 582 Shellers (as the boat-owners describe themselves). **1918** G. WHITE *Thirty Yrs. Tropical Aust.* 63 Many politicians of to-day advocate a white-worked shelling industry, and a few declare it should be made a white man's industry solely. Shellers contend this cannot be done. **1900** *Qld. Geogr. Jrnl.* XV. 32 The population of the island is about 1,500, and the population working in the **shelling** boats a little over 2,000. **1936** N. CALDWELL *Fangs of Sea* 246 In those days there were many shelling-grounds.

shell-open *v. intr.* To open pearl-shells. Also as *vbl. n.*

1933 J.M. HARCOURT *Pearlers* 111, I know shell-opening isn't a pleasant occupation. **1937** —— *It never Fails* 132, I wouldn't shell-open for another week for another pearl like that one. **1940** E. HILL *Great Austral. Loneliness* (ed. 2) 101 Shell-opening in 1911, he had discovered the biggest single stone ever found in Broome waters.

Also **shell-opener** *n.*

1925 *Bulletin* (Sydney) 14 May 22/4 In the bad old days of Broome there was one shell-opener who realised that there is luck even in dishonesty. **1937** I.L. IDRIESS *Forty Fathoms Deep* 230 A mate of his stabbed a shell-opener on the seas. **1954** T. RONAN *Vision Splendid* 131 He'd gone over west to the pearling grounds and taken a temporary job as shell-opener.

shell parrot. [Perh. in allusion to the colour patterns of the plumage.] BUDGERIGAR. Also **shell parakeet.**

1845 J.H. BROWNE *Jrnl. Sturt Exped.* 12 Mar. in *S. Australiana* (1962) Mar. 43 The Crested Parrot and Shell Parrakeet . . came to this part of the country in November in flights, they immediately paired off and commenced breeding. **1852** F. LANCELOTT *Aust. as it Is* I. 40 The little shell parrot, may be mentioned as exquisitely beautiful both in shape and plumage. **1861** 'OLD BUSHMAN' *Bush Wanderings* 167 Occasionally, but very rarely, a flock of the *Budgere Gar*, a *Shell Paroqueet*, would pay us a visit. **1878** R.B. SMYTH *Aborigines of Vic.* II. 303, I remember seeing a blackfellow with his girdle full of unfledged *Budgerygars* (shell parrakeets), which he had stuffed under by the heads. **1892** 'MRS A. MACLEOD' *Silent Sea* I. 96 She knew when the first broods of the shell parrots would flit through the pale honey-coloured blossoms of the gum-trees. **1925** J.E. LIDDLE *Selected Poems* 84 Shell-parrots flock from bush to bush, All beautiful, bright, black and green. [*Note*] Boodgirrigars. **1951** G. FARWELL *Outside Track* 137 A single red-barked minnaritchi tree. . . Hundreds of shell parrots rose from its foliage in a cloud of emerald wings.

shelter-shed. A roofed structure, usu. partly enclosed, affording protection from inclement weather.

1856 *Plea on Behalf Aboriginal Inhabitants Vic.* 6 When 'Shelter Sheds' were talked of, no one ever thought of suggesting an extra one or two . . for them. **1897** *Bulletin* (Sydney) 9 Oct. 32/3 Convenient enough as a 'shelter-shed', the room was absolutely minus wash-stands, chest of drawers, dressing-tables, and clothes-pegs. **1905** *Truth* (Sydney) 16 July 1/8 Alderman McIvor is agitating for a shelter-shed for tram passengers. **1911** *Huon Times* (Franklin) 2 Aug. 4/1 They favour the erection of pavilions and shelter-sheds in school grounds which can be used as open-air class-rooms when desired. **1920** *Pastoral Rev.* 16 Jan. 17/2 The shelter shed erected by the river is capable of holding 2000 sheep. **1935** K. TENNANT *Tiburon* 8 The shelter-shed on the travellers' reserve, unlike most of the structures erected by charitable town councils, actually did shelter . . and . . during the long rainy spells had saved many a bagman from lying stiff with rheumatism under a bridge. **1937** *Bulletin* (Sydney) 8 Dec. 20/3 Camped in a N.Q. shelter-shed with about a hundred other wanderers, I soon found out that . . it was safe to leave tucker and other gear unattended. **1956** E. LAMBERT *Watermen* 139 We've borrowed the wharfies' shelter-shed down near the dry-dock. **1961** *Realist* (Sydney) xii. 13 Her eyes swept distastefully the ageing yellow weatherboard portables, the rotting fence, the ancient shelter shed, the pot holed playground. **1975** J. ROMERIL *Floating World* 70 Be like that time we did it in the shelter-shed at the North School. **1977** K. GILBERT *Living Black* 47 When I went to school, I remember that the teachers used to make the black kids go out and clean up the shelter shed because they felt we wouldn't learn anything anyway.

she-oak /'ʃi-oʊk/. Also **sheoke** and formerly **shea oak, shiac.** [f. SHE 2 + OAK, the pronoun prob. being indicative of the perceived inferiority of the timber. See also HE-OAK.]

1. Any of many trees or shrubs of the fam. Casuarinaceae, incl. *Casuarina cunninghamiana* (see *river oak* RIVER 2), the rough-barked small tree *Allocasuarina verticillata* of s.e. Aust. incl. Tas., and (*W.A.*) *A. fraseriana* of s.w. W.A.; any plant of this fam. (see CASUARINA); the wood of the tree, the grain of which resembles that of the English oak; *native oak*, see NATIVE *a.* 6 a. Also with distinguishing epithet, as *coast she-oak* (see COAST), and *attrib.*

1792 *Hist. Rec. N.S.W.* (1893) II. 799 There are two kinds of oak, called the he and the she oak, but not to be compared with English oak. **1803** *Sydney Gaz.* 12 June,

A quantity of she-oak for the English market... This wood is allowed to rank in Europe with the mahogany of Jamaica. **1820** J. OXLEY *Jrnls. Two Exped. N.S.W.* 292 That species of casuarina called the beef wood (or she oak), was also seen to-day for the first time. **1829** R. MUDIE *Picture of Aust.* 137 There are three principal species [of *casuarinae*] to which the colonists have given names. These three species are, the she oak (*casuarina stricta*) remarkable for its upright growth; the forest oak (*casuarina torulosa*) .. and the swamp oak (*casuarina paludosa*). **1833** *Perth Gaz.* 27 July 119 The Shea Oak, or Casuarina of this Colony, admitted to be of a superior description to that of either our Eastern or Southern neighbours, is likely to become an article of more extensive export to the Cape than our Mahoganies. **1835** *Hobart Town Almanack* 75 *Casuarina torulosa?* She-oak. *C. stricta?* He-oak. *C. tenuissima?* Marsh oak. The name of the first of these is said to be a corruption of Sheac the name of an American tree, producing the beef wood, like our She-oak. The second species has obtained the name of He-oak in contradistinction of She-oak, as if they constituted one dioecious plant, the one male and the other female, whereas they are perfectly distinct species. **1845** R. HOWITT *Impressions Aust. Felix* 231 Shiac-trees are waving their tresses in the wind. [*Note*] Shiac is the native name—vulgarised to she-oak. **1854** W. SHAW *Land of Promise* 200 The Australian she-oak being one of the weaker sex is of stunted growth, without the durable qualities of the English male one. **1872** C.H. EDEN *My Wife & I in Qld.* 134 The house, in place of the usual slabs, was built of she-oak trees. **1890** 'R. BOLDREWOOD' *Squatter's Dream* 1 Many a ton of she-oak and box had burned away in the great stone chimney. **1904** J.H. MAIDEN *Notes on Commercial Timbers N.S.W.* 26 She-oaks (*Casuarina* of various species)... Various species of she-oak go under the names of 'forest oak', 'river oak', 'swamp oak', 'bull oak', 'belar', 'beefwood', 'black oak'. These are the principal names but there are a number of others. In the English market the darker kinds are known under the name of 'Botany oak'. **1912** B. O'DOWD *Bush* 40 Dodona whispers from the she-oak groves. **1931** *Bulletin* (Sydney) 4 Feb. 20/3 'Sheoke' and 'buloke' are the names that have been adopted for two kinds of casuarinas. It was considered that 'she-oak' and 'bull-oak', the previous names would suggest a relationship with the oak of Europe which the casuarinas cannot claim. **1951** D. CUSACK *Say no to Death* (1959) 44 Bart tied the boat to a sheoke which leaned over the water. **1972** C.D. BOOMSMA *Native Trees S.A.* 70 Drooping Sheoak *Casuarina stricta*... The common name refers to the well-developed drooping habit of the branchlets. **1973** V. SERVENTY *Desert Walkabout* 41 Sheoaks are just as typically Australian as gum-trees, banksias and wattles. **1982** *Canberra Times* 26 Sept. 3/2 One area of the language that has yet to be adjusted by the feminists is forestry. The she-oak, so the tale goes, is so named because early timber-getters in Australia gave the name to a casuarina that resembled English oak but was of poorer quality.

2. *transf.* Beer brewed in Australia.

1848 *Guardian* (Hobart) 5 Apr. 5/1 She had only taken two glasses of 'she-oak', and for so doing was sentenced. **1851** *Britannia* (Hobart) 2 June 3/1 There is a Colonial beer manufactured at New Norfolk, by Mr Mann, which as a table beverage is far superior to the Hobart Town beer, more familiarly denominated 'she-oak'. **1868** *Mope-Hawk* 52 As you're so very pressing I think I'll take a pint of she-oak. **1880** 'ERRO' *Squattermani* 37 'I'm going to shout, boys.' And three sheoaks and a bottle of lemonade caused the transfer of two shillings .. to the till of the landlord. **1897** *Bulletin* (Sydney) 4 Sept. (Red Page), The term she oak as applied in Australia to 'colonial beer' dates back to 1820. About that time a brewery was established on what was then known as She Oak Hill, opposite old Government House, Hobart. The owner, when asked how he made such good beer, replied, 'I put she oak in it.' **1914** T.C. WOLLASTON *Spirit of Child* 154 Each would take a pull from the jug of 'sheoak' between them. **1948** R. RAVEN-HART *Canoe in Aust.* 21 What Jack called 'she-oak' (or you may spell it shea-oak, or she-oke or shea-oke—it is also slang for beer in Australia).

3. Special Comb. **she-oak net,** a safety net slung under the gangway of a ship (see quots).

1886 D.M. GANE *N.S.W. & Vic.* 51 It is called by sailors 'she-oak', whence the term 'she-oak nets' is given to the life-preservers which the Victorian authorities have thought it wise to have slung under the gangways of every ship which is moored to the Melbourne wharves. **1934** T. WOOD *Cobbers* 163 The 'She-oak Net' .. is to catch a man if he slips when going aboard; and the name .. is in memory of She-oak beer, which used to be, and may be still, a powerful agent in making him slip.

shepherd, *v.* [Transf. use of *shepherd* to tend.]

1. *trans. Obs.* To effect token occupation of (a gold-mining claim) in order to comply with the regulations governing possession: see quot. 1869. Freq. as *vbl. n.*

1852 *V & P* (Vic. L.C.) (1852–53) II. 327 There is now a practice of 'shepherding claims'... The way in which this is done is as follows: whenever a new gully is opened, one of the party goes there and marks out a claim, taking out two spits of earth to shew that he has 'taken it up and worked at it'. He repeats this daily until some other party has gone down the full depth, and has discovered whether the locality is worth working or not, and acts accordingly. This being done by the same party in perhaps eight or ten different places at once, men who would really 'set in' to work steadily are driven about from place to place. **1854** *Guardian* (Hobart) 25 Mar. 3/4 The Commissioner having, rather unwisely, I think, set himself against shepherding in any form, considering the depth, water, slabbing etc., decided in favour of the jumpers. **1856** S.C. BREES *How to farm & settle in Aust.* 60 If the lead was detected, every one in expectancy went promptly to work; if not the immediate vicinity was probably abandoned for a trial elsewhere. Hence arose the practice of 'shepherding' claims .. by simply watching, or shepherding, in person on the ground, and effecting some daily but very facile manoeuvring with his spade. **1859** W. KELLY *Life in Vic.* I. 184 This hole, after being first opened for a few feet, was shepherded by three different parties, each going through the form of taking out a few shovelfuls of soil in fulfilment of the digging code... Shepherding means keeping passive possession of a hole, and keeping watch around for the run of the gutter. **1869** R.B. SMYTH *Gold Fields & Mineral Districts* 621 *Shepherding*, the holding possession of claims by doing the minimum amount of labour enforced by the mining by-laws. A system whereby auriferous lands are monopolized by speculators and idlers, often to the injury of the industrious miner. **1871** *Emigrant's Wife* II. 51 You could see well enough that I knew nothing about claiming and pegging, and shepherding. That fellow there is shepherding, I suppose. **1888** 'SPECIAL CORRESPONDENT' *Barrier Silver & Tin Fields* 60 One claim in particular has been shepherded by the same people for four years. **1902** E.B. KENNEDY *Black Police Qld.* 54 The law in this case is, that a digger must 'shepherd' his claim up to twelve o'clock every day—he *must* be on it, whether working it or not—if he fails to do this any one can 'jump' it. **1909** W.G. SPENCE *Aust.'s Awakening* 47 One of the drawbacks to mining development is the evil of 'shepherding'. Mining leases are granted subject to certain labor covenants... Syndicates and companies evade this by securing suspension of labor covenants. **1955** H. ANDERSON *Colonial Ballads* 46 The subject of 'Shepherding' claims. As long as a legal minimum of work was carried out these unscrupulous miners could hold the claim while their neighbours proved whether the ground was payable.

2. *transf.* [Used elsewhere but recorded earliest in Aust.: see OED *v.* 4.] To keep under close surveillance.

1853 H.B. JONES *Adventures in Aust.* 299 A digger who was known to have about forty pounds weight of gold, was 'shepherded' for a considerable time, i.e. watched till a favourable opportunity presented itself to attack him. **1882** *Sydney Slang Dict.* 7 *Shepherd*, to look after carefully; surveillance. **1891** *Truth* (Sydney) 8 Mar. 73 Cooks are souring their bread because they are shepherding the store-door. **1892** *Ibid.* 7 Feb. 3/1 The gang pass the day playing cards or 'shepherding' the girls while they sleep. **1896** *Western Champion* (Barcaldine) 11 Aug. 12/4 The digger who gave him a few shillings a week for shepherding his share didn't know him. **1896** J. BEAR *Impressions Victorian Abroad* 65, I was left with injunctions to 'shepherd the bobby', and to signal if .. his movements became dangerous. **1902** *Bulletin* (Sydney) 13 Sept. 35/1 Half way on a 'dry stretch' of 17 miles. There is a big tank full of good water through the scrub to the right, but it is a private tank and a boundary-rider is shepherding it. **1904** L.M.P. ARCHER *Bush Honeymoon* 85 She'll want *shepherding* at her work. **1907** *Clipper* (Hobart) 28 Dec. 4/2 Potheen wuz a top-notcher and .. when Mother Blarney wuz on the job she never missed. So I shepherds 'em both. **1948** K.S. PRICHARD *Golden Miles* 98 He .. gave his instructions for the bags to be counted and shepherded to the treatment plant.

shepherd, *n. Obs.* [f. SHEPHERD *v.* 1.] One who effects token occupation of a gold-mining claim (see esp. quots. 1862 and 1909); one employed to do this.

1855 R. CARBONI *Eureka Stockade* 71 The shepherds' holes inside the lower part of the stockade had been turned into rifle-pits. **1856** S.C. BREES *How to farm & settle in Aust.* 60 Claims were .. in every promising spot taken up by individuals or co-partneries, who were able to keep on a shepherd, at a cost, usually, of twenty shillings a day. **1859** W. KELLY *Life in Vic.* I. 213 Shepherds are well and deservedly mulcted for their slothfulness by diggers who, after exhausting the gutter within the limits of their own claims continue following it into the shepherd's territory. **1862** J.A. PATTERSON *Gold Fields Vic.* 318 The 'shepherd' is one who marks off a claim on the supposed site of a lead or reef, and watches it while another party are 'bottoming', doing only the minimum of work requisite to secure his right to the ground .. abandoning his claim without trial if those near him should prove 'duffers'—that is to say, unfurnished with gold. **1870** *Sydney Morning Herald* 2 July 5/4 Every morning some 250 'gentle shepherds', may be seen complying with the law, by taking a couple of hours' airing, shepherding the respective claims marked out on the deep lead. **1909** W.G. SPENCE *Aust.'s Awakening* 47 They opposed the 'shepherd'—the man or company who took up a lease and did nothing but merely await a chance to sell.

shepherd's clock. *Settler's clock*, see SETTLER 3 b.

1879 'OLD HAND' *Experiences of Colonist* 24 The first sound heard in the wood was the peculiar note of the laughing jackass (dacelo gigantea), a bird so celebrated in New South Wales for his particular virtue of punctuality, that the colonists gave it the name of the 'shepherd's clock'. **1955** N. PULLIAM *I traveled Lonely Land* 381 *Laughing jackass*—one nickname for the kookaburra, the lovable mischievous and favorite bird of Australia. Other names are .. alarm bird, bushman's clock, clock-bird, settler's clock or shepherd's clock [etc.].

shepherd's companion. WILLY WAGTAIL. Also **shepherd's friend.**

1844 L. LEICHHARDT *Jrnl. Overland Exped. Aust.* 20 Dec. (1847) 80 We also observed .. the shepherd's companion, or fan-tailed fly-catcher (Rhipidura). **1861** 'OLD BUSHMAN' *Bush Wanderings* 151 The Stock-whip Bird, or shepherd's companion, had rather the appearance of the pied wagtail at home. **1901** *Emu* I. 74 A little Shepherd's Companion (*Rhipidura tricolor*) has built in the vine right in front of my window. **1903** *Bulletin* (Sydney) 2 May 16/3 Just before the western Q. heavy rains arrived a 'willie-wagtail', 'shepherds' friend' .. or whatever other alias the vivacious little black and white bird is known by. **1914** H.M. VAUGHAN *Australasian Wander-Yr.* 302 The native 'Willie Wagtail', or shepherd's companion, which is in reality a fly-catcher (*Motacilloides tricolor*) is also a popular favourite. **1948** R. RAVEN-HART *Canoe in Aust.* 39 The ubiquitous 'willie wagtails' .. earning here the title of 'Shepherd's Companion' by this tameness. **1953** A. RUSSELL *Murray Walkabout* 104 As a bush friend the willy wagtail, or shepherd's companion, as the bush folk affectionately call it, excells all other birds I know.

sherang, var. SERANG.

sherbet. Also **sherbert.** [Joc. use of *sherbet* a cooling drink.] Alcoholic liquor, esp. beer.

1904 *Truth* (Sydney) 14 Feb. 1/4 The fellow that frequents a pub draws corks—the chap that drinks sherbert draws cheques. **1915** N. LINDSAY *N. Lindsay's Bk. II.* 28 Here! I've done enough work ter day. Yer can watch me make a break for th' long sherbert. **1916** *Truth* (Sydney) 25 June 11/2 The start for six o'clock sherbert sets in. **1943** S.W. KEOUGH *Around Army* 27 He .. can even be induced in time to take quite an interest in the sermons, except perhaps on the morning after a night 'on the sherbet'. **1962** B. SUTTON *Snow & Me* (1966) 17, I am thinking Snow must be on the sherbert or maybe he is a bit dazed. **1965** J. WYNNUM *Jiggin' in Riggin'* 36 How about .. organising after dinner entertainment before we get stuck into the sherbet. **1968** D. O'GRADY *Bottle of Sandwiches* 93 We skedaddled about eight o'clock, had a few sherbets and a feed, and then flaked out. **1974** F. ARCHER *Treasure House* 18 He had a strident voice and with a few sherbets under his belt you knew he was about. **1981** *Bulletin* (Sydney) 5 May 52/2 Hayden's only chance of hanging on to the leadership would be for Hawke to slip back on to the sherbert.

sherrocker. *Obs.* [Of unknown origin: perh. f. Br. dial. *sherry* to scurry, run away.] In the phr. **to take sherrocker:** see quot. 1912.

1908 *Truth* (Sydney) 6 Sept. 1/5 After the Fleet had taken sherrocker, some of the Sydney business establishments which had a coat of paint .. hurriedly slopped over them, are now leisurely being properly decorated. **1912** *Ibid.* 17 Mar. 7/7 Why, in a remarkably short space of time they (small blame to them) took 'sherrocker', i.e. French leave.

shiac, var. SHE-OAK.

shicer /'ʃaɪsə/. Also **scheisser, shiser, shycer.** [Transf. use of Br. slang *shicer* a worthless person: see OED(S.] An unproductive claim, mine, or goldfield.

1853 F.J. COCKBURN *Lett.* (1856) 23 When a hole is found to be contain [*sic*] no gold it is called a 'shicer'. **1854** *Illustr. Sydney News* 5 Aug. 186/1 Hundreds of shicers (a name given to unproductive shafts) have been put down. **1855** R. CARBONI *Eureka Stockade* 10 One fine morning, a hole was bottomed down the gully, and proved a scheisser. **1861** H. EARLE *Ups & Downs* 330 How great the disappointment, when .. they discovered their hole to be a 'shycer', or a goldless one. **1870** *Sydney Morning Herald* 5 July 2/4 The miners .. have unanimously pronounced it a failure, and the diggings have quietly incarcerated themselves in the limbo of 'shicers'. **1880** 'ERRO' *Squattermania* 53 'That reef they were blowing about so much only went five pennyweights to the ton when they crushed...' 'I always said it would turn out a shiser.' **1881** J.C.F. JOHNSON *To Mount Browne & Back* 3 Our party was turned back .. by the information that the rush had proved a 'shicer'. **1883** R.E.N. TWOPENY *Town Life Aust.* 245 A 'shicer' is first a mining claim which turns out to be useless, and then anything that does so. **1906** E. DYSON *In Roaring Fifties* 99 'We don't want to waste time bottoming shicers—sinking duffers,' he added in explanation... Putting down shafts where there isn't a colour. **1946** F. CLUNE *Try Nothing Twice* 41 Many of the claims were 'jeweller's shops', but many more were 'stringers' or 'duffers'—also named 'shicers'. **1976** B. SCOTT *Complete Bk. Austral. Folk Lore* 286 Remember, when you first came up, Like Shicers, innocent of gold, Quite proud to get the bit and sup The digger's friendly tent foretold.

Hence as quasi-*adv.*, unproductively.

1887 *Illustr. Austral. News* (Melbourne) 25 June (Suppl.) 7/2 God pity the poor solitary wretch .. who had bottomed hole after hole a 'schicer', i.e., without finding gold in it.

shick, *a.* and *n.* [Abbrev. of SHICKER *a.* and *n.*]

A. *adj.* Drunk.

1907 *Bulletin* (Sydney) 21 Feb. (Red Page), Ah, Joy don't *all* consist in Getting Shick! **1910** *Ibid.* 18 Aug. 14/1 One of the unwritten laws of the Bush is: see your mate home when he is 'shick'. **1912** *Ibid.* 7 Jan. 4/5 Sweet Sixteen and Never Been Shick. **1930** *Ibid.* 2 Apr. 57/1 Men getting 'shick' and coming home and raising hell's delight. **1966** J. WATEN *Season of Youth* 3 'I'm sick,' was his everlasting plea. 'Shick you mean,' she screamed.

B. *n.*

1. Alcoholic liquor.

1907 *Bulletin* (Sydney) 7 Mar. 14/2 Went on the shick and stoushed a trap wot tried to snare 'im. **1908** E.G. MURPHY *Jarrahland Jingles* 78 When shanties ran with shick. **1914** *Truth* (Sydney) 8 Nov. 1/3 At some of Sydney's flash shypoo pubs the shick should be called sick—in fact, Inn-valid. **1920** A. L'HOTELLIER *Green Fields of Paraguay* 8 But if they cut the hours for selling shick much shorter, We'll scarce have time to fill-'em-up-agen. **1925** A. WRIGHT *Boy from Bullarah* 44 A nice job I'll have with you soon. What with th' shick, and now goin' crazy over a woman.

2. A drunkard.

1907 *Bulletin* (Sydney) 5 May 1/5 Not a soul behind the barrier at the Water on Wednesday, only one woman in the cowpen (a wretched beggar), and only a few shicks in the men's stockyard.

shicker, *a.*, *n.* and *exclam.* Also **shiker, shikker.** [a. Yiddish *shiker* drunk: see OEDS *shicker* and also *shickery* (EDD *shiggry*). See also SHICKERED, quot. 1843.]

A. *adj.* Drunk.

[**1878** *Austral. Town & Country Jrnl.* (Sydney) 26 Jan. 170/1 I'm always that fresh after a good night's sleep, when I've had a spree, that I could begin again quite flippant. Old Tom had a goodish cheque this time, and was at it a week afore I came in. He *was* rayther shickerry.] **1898** *Bulletin* (Sydney) 17 Dec. (Red Page), *Shiker*, drunk. **1908** *Truth* (Sydney) 27 Sept. 1/8 And Caldecott doth now relate That he and every bowling mate, Were never in that beastly state Termed 'shikker'. **1910** *Ibid.* 15 May 7/5 When you're in that state of liquor Known colloquially as 'shikker'. **1918** F. KNOWLES *With Dinkums* 12 *Parson*: Poor man!—shell shock? *Billjim*: No, Sir—shicker! **1949** J. MORRISON *Creeping City* 111 A decent hard-working cocky that goes down town for a blow, and gets a bit shikker, is liable to be told to get out and walk. **1955** —— *Black Cargo* 173 Have you ever seen me shicker? **1965** H. PORTER *Cats of Venice* 189 She was now immortally shicker. **1977** D. STUART *Drought Foal* 57 She goes crook when he lands home shicker. **1982** N. KEESING *Lily on Dustbin* 147 'Shiker' or 'shickered' for drunk is a direct borrowing from the Yiddish *shikker*.

B. *n.*

1. Alcoholic liquor; a drink of this. Esp. in the phr. **on the shicker.**

1901 *Truth* (Sydney) 31 Mar. 2/5 Toby was taking on the gold-top 'shikker' and the chicken. **1915** J.P. BOURKE *Off Bluebush* 182 He reaches for a bottle of Glen Shicker on the shelf. **1919** A. WRIGHT *Game of Chance* 40 I've had a few shikkers, I can't deny it, but it ain't every day a man has a fortune sprung on him. **1926** M. FORREST *Hibiscus Heart* 182 Men who lived for nothing but the 'going on the shicker'. **1933** A. REID *Those were Days* 74 Ye comrades in shicker, and cobbers in sin. **1952** C. SIMPSON *Come away, Pearler* 187 He knows more about King Sound than any man living .. when he's off the shicker. **1953** G. BROWN *My Descent* 25 Mac loved his beer... Like many a good tradesman before him, he would go on the 'shikker' for days at a time. **1966** *Kings Cross Whisper* (Sydney) Mar. 7 Surfers Paradise beer garden, where everyone got on the shicker.

2. A drunkard.

1906 E. DYSON *Fact'ry 'Ands* 180 It's these cheap 'n' easy shickers rollin' round on their ear what brings discredit on beer. **1916** C.J. DENNIS *Moods Ginger Mick* 71 In some back crib, a shicker's loud 'owled verse Stops sudden, wiv a crash, an' then a curse. **1938** X. HERBERT *Capricornia* 257 He's the biggest shikker in Town. Now nick off, you old sponge.

C. *exclam.* As a mild oath.

1914 E. DYSON *Spats' Fact'ry* 16 S'elp me shicker, Twenty, you was the on'y pebble. **1943** *Austral. New Writing* 18 See that pup? Shicker me grandmother, she's a great bitch!

shicker, *v.* Also **shikker.** [f. prec.] *intr.* To take alcoholic liquor (to excess).

1908 *Truth* (Sydney) 19 July 9/3 But here in Australia! Well, this is a sell, We thought they all shickered, The parsons as well. **1913** *Bulletin* (Sydney) 6 Mar. 48/3 Her Old 'Un 'shickered' till he got 'mucked' every pay day. **1916** J.F. NUGENT *Lorblimey* 13 W'en first I see's Lizzie, lorblimey, I swore I'd chuck up th' mob 'n' I'd shicker no more. **1937** WISBERG & WATERS *Bushman at Large* 279 'You haven't been shikkering have you, Nugget?' 'Shikkering and business don't mix,' declared Nugget. **1951** CUSACK & JAMES *Come in Spinner* 33 He'd gamble his shirt off .. but he doesn't shicker.

Hence **shikkering** *ppl. a.*

1919 *Bulletin* (Sydney) 18 Sept. 22/4 As a God-fearing, non-shikkering Abo. let me discourse freely.

shickered, *ppl. a.* Also **shikkered.** Drunk.

[**1843** *Satirist & Sporting Chron.* (Sydney) 11 Mar. 3/3 A certain Teetotal Gent, accompanied by a companion *Just-it*, entered a public-house the other night, quite 'shuck'.] **1898** *Bulletin* (Sydney) 29 Oct. 15/1 A glass of beer is 'a pot of wollop', and the previous night he was 'on his pink', 'juiced', 'wined', or 'shikkered'. **1900** *Truth* (Sydney) 28 Jan. 1/5 A shanty only shikkered shearers patronize. **1911** *Bulletin* (Sydney) 16 Nov. 14/2 Another aged pub has gone where the shickered cease from troubling and the beery are at rest. **1918** A. WRIGHT *Over Odds* 7 'Am I shikkered?' he asked himself, 'or am I fancying things?' Convincing himself that he was really conscious and sober, he re-read the words. **1922** *Aussie* (Sydney) 15 Feb. 43 'E's passed another exam, so he's dead certain to come 'ome shickered. **1930** D. COTTRELL *Earth Battle* 224 He had not been drunk at all, not even 'shickered'. **1944** *Bulletin* (Sydney) 8 Mar. 13/3 The ganger's .. always harping on blokes getting shickered and being the cause of trains jumping the rails. **1956** *Tennant Creek Times* 1 June 1/5 They'll lock yer up if yer naughty. They'll send yer home if yer shickered. **1966** *Kings Cross Whisper* (Sydney) xxv. 5/2 In Broken Hill the population remains cheerful and shickered. **1977** R. CLOSE *Of Salt & Earth* 86 Thank Christ the bastard's made it—there's always the chance he would be too shickered. **1979** D. STIVENS *Demon Bowler* 77 By five o'clock Metho Bill wasn't the only one shickered.

shield. *Obs.* HIELEMAN.

1787 *Descr. Botany Bay, on East Side New Holland* 7 They use a shield or target of an oblong form, of about three feet long and about half that width, made of the bark of a tree. **1793** J. HUNTER *Hist. Jrnl. Trans. Port Jackson* 55 A party of natives .. all armed with a lance and throwing-stick, and many with the addition of a shield, made of the bark of a tree; some were in shape an oblong square, and others of these shields were oval; these were the first shields we had seen in the country. **1805** J.H. TUCKEY *Acct. Voyage to establish Colony Port Philip* 179 Their arms are spears, used with a throwing stick, like those of Port Jackson; their shields are made of a hard wood and neatly carved. **1825** B. FIELD *Geogr. Mem. N.S.W.* 80 The other .. succeeded in warding it off with a kind of wooden shield called an *elemong*. **1844** C. WILKES *Narr. U.S. Exploring Exped.* II. 203 They use a shield made of the thick bark of the gum tree; this they call *hiclemara*. **1862** BACKHOUSE & TYLOR *Life & Labours G.W. Walker* 242 The shield .. is here of an oval form, and made of wood. **1887** A. NICOLS *Wild Life & Adventure* 143 The shields used by the natives were made of an extremely light kind of wood, such as hibiscus. **1923** T. HALL *Short Hist. Downs Blacks* 17 *Helimon or shield* .. was used for precisely the same purpose as that of our ancient European warriors. It was made out of stinging tree wood, which was very light and soft, but tough.

shiker, shikker, varr. SHICKER *a.* (etc.) and *v.*

shikkered, var. SHICKERED.

shilling.

1. *Hist.* In the phr. **shilling-a-month-man**, see quot. 1898.

1898 G. DUNDERDALE *Bk. of Bush* 3 On the ships conveying women there were no soldiers, but an extra half-crew was engaged. These men were called 'Shilling-a-month' men, because they had agreed to work for one shilling a month for the privilege of being allowed to remain in Sydney. **1933** A.J. COTTON *With Big Herds in Aust.* 52 Most of the crew were 'shilling a month' men; that is, men who used to ship out to Australia for a shilling a month and their passage.

2. A game in which each participant contributes a shilling, the winner buying a round of drinks; a collection, esp. for the purpose of buying a round of drinks; BOB-IN.

[N.Z. **1880** *Evening Post* (Wellington) 7 Jan. 17 A man had paid his shilling in a game of 'shilling in and the winner shout'.] **1900** *Advocate* (Burnie) 29 May 4/1 They were having 'a shilling in and the winner shouts' when he arrived. **1920** *Bulletin* (Sydney) 15 Jan. 20/2 Some Western Queensland slang of my day: .. a shilling-in was 'tambaroora'. **1942** G. CASEY *It's Harder for Girls* 83 We had another shilling in, and bought some bottles to take to the restaurant.

shin cracker. *Opal-mining.* Very hard, brittle, splintery rock. See also ANGEL STONE.

1919 *Huon Times* (Franklin) 21 Nov. 3/3 In a hole of that depth you would first sink through about 10 or 12 feet of 'shincracker', a hard, white substance, very brittle and somewhat resembling limestone. **1921** K.S. PRICHARD *Black Opal* 59 He was carefully working round a brilliantly fired seam through black potch in the shin cracker he had been breaking through two or three days before. **1932** I.L. IDRIESS *Prospecting for Gold* 251 An occasional shaft may go through 'shincracker', very hard stone, and may require hammer, drills and gelignite. **1962** WHITING & RELPH *Occurrence of Opal* 7 A fine-grained white to cream claystone is associated with sandstone throughout the area. Where it is exposed at the surface it has been hardened by the concentration of secondary chalcedony and opaline silica and is known locally as 'shin-cracker'. **1971** J.S. GUNN *Opal Terminol.* 42 *Shin cracker.* Also *shincracker*, common name for the fine-grained Coocoran claystone which on exposure at the surface becomes a hard, brittle, siliceous rock that usually has to be dug through to get to the opal ground. Its name is appropriate because, when worked with a sinking pick or jack hammer, pieces shatter or fly off to strike the digger's shins, hence the injury called 'shin-cracker shin'.

shindykit. *Obs.* [Alteration of *syndicate*.] A derogatory name for a business consortium.

1890 *Truth* (Sydney) 16 Nov. 1/7 When shindykits get on a job That makes their hearts with rapture throb, And I have helped them hook their fish, Do I refuse a small commish? **1916** *Ibid.* 3 Dec. 4/4 (*heading*) The tricky tote. What's Holman giving us? Will the state or a shindykit snavel the siller?

shingle. [Spec. use of *shingle* a thin piece of wood used as a house-tile.]

1. *Hist.* Used in Comb. with reference to the occupation of preparing shingles for use as a building material, as **shingle cutter, getter, splitter**.

1828 *Tasmanian* (Hobart) 3 Oct. 2 A Coroner's Inquest was lately held at Bothwell, on the body of Samuel Cok *alias* Clarke, a shingle splitter in the employ of Mr Kemp. **1829** R. DAWSON *Statement* p. xi, Mr Dawson said that he was very usefully occupied breaking in shingle-splitters and sawyers amongst the prisoners. **1839** J. STEPHENS *Land of Promise* 17 We passed the range at the point where the shingle-splitters have their settlement. **1842** R.G. JAMESON *N.Z., S.A., & N.S.W.* 46 Mr Cock carried his operations into the Stringy Bark Forest, where he employed a number of sawyers, splitters, and shingle cutters. **1849** S. & J. SIDNEY *Emigrant's Jrnl.* 6 He employed a number of sawyers, splitters, and shingle cutters. **1882** A.J. BOYD *Old Colonials* 20 If I am working close alongside a shingle-getter . . we swops [*sic*] logs. *Ibid.* 26 When sickness comes, please God, some one will look after the old shingle-splitter.

2. *fig.* A mental faculty, esp. in the phr. **to be a shingle short** and varr.

1844 D.G. BROCK *To Desert with Sturt* (1975) 64 Strolled among the hills with Kirby; poor fellow is certainly 'wanting a shingle'. **1846** *Cumberland Times* (Parramatta) 3 Jan. 3/2 This direction is applicable to Splitters, Fencers, and Shinglers, but the latter must not have a 'shingle off' when they practise it. **1852** G.C. MUNDY *Our Antipodes* III. 17 Let no man having, in colonial phrase, 'a shingle short' try this country. He will pass his days in Tarban Creek Asylum! **1854** C.A. CORBYN *Sydney Revels* 24 She said if old Bob was not actually crankey, he had at least 'lost a shingle'. **1868** *Sydney Punch* 8 Feb. 79/1 It was bad enough to send a maniac to the ball (although there is a grim humour in entrusting the description of the pavilion, which was roofed three times, to a fellow with a 'shingle short'). **1872** MRS E. MILLETT *Austral. Parsonage* 382 To be 'a shingle short' is a colonial phrase indicative of the same state of mind which is described in Scotland by the expression of 'a bee in the bonnet'. **1895** *Worker* (Sydney) 20 July 1/4 The Fat Man's son was an Anarchist, a couple of shingles short. **1915** J.P. BOURKE *Off Bluebush* 186 Do you know, if a chap could write and write, As editors pay and pay, There'd be whips of sport For the 'shingle short' On the rhymer's inky way. **1923** *Aussie* (Sydney) Dec. 55/1 It is generally conceded that Tim is a shingle short, but he's a harmless old chap. **1930** K.S. PRICHARD *Haxby's Circus* 85 Lord Freddie may be a shingle short—but there's many shorter who think they're all there! **1960** S. WOODFIELD *A for Artemis* 169 The lady minding her is O.K. She thinks she's a shingle short. **1968** *Southerly* i. 3, I reckon we're a shingle short to 'uv ended up on the Parramatta Road. **1983** *Weekend Austral. Mag.* 27 Aug. 20/8 I'd better stop, or you'll begin to think I've got a shingle off the roof, too.

shingleback. [See quot. 1978.] BOBTAIL. Also *attrib.*

1898 *Bulletin* (Sydney) 24 Dec. 15/1 Nack's legged-snake was probably a 'shingleback'. Oily-looking reptile, either jet-black or yellow-and-brown, and never much more than 18 in. long; body thick, comparatively. **1934** *Ibid.* 8 Aug. 21/3 'Lanus's' 'goanna' . . was the rare pine-cone lizard, sometimes called the shingle-back. **1962** H.J. FRITH *Mallee-Fowl* 53 The scrub is silent and breathless; nothing moves: the only signs of life are a few shingle-back lizards lying in the sun. **1968** V. SERVENTY *Southern Walkabout* 115 Lizards proved far more numerous than snakes, and we discovered ten species in all. The most familiar were the bobtail, shingleback, stumpytail or sleepy lizard, according to the name given by local usage. **1978** B.P. MOORE *Life on Forty Acres* 107 The skink family includes an amazing variety of lizards. . . The slowest, roughest and perhaps, most interesting is the Shingleback (*Trachydosaurus rugosus*), a thick-set species with coarse, overlapping scales so large as to give it the appearance of an animated pine-cone.

shining, *a.* Used as a distinguishing epithet in the names of flora and fauna: **shining flycatcher,** the bird *Myiagra alecto* of n. Aust., New Guinea, and adjacent islands, the mature male having glossy black plumage with a blue sheen; see also *satin bird* SATIN; **gum,** the tall tree *Eucalyptus nitens* (fam. Myrtaceae) of e. Vic. and e. N.S.W.; also *attrib.*; **starling,** METALLIC STARLING.

1844 J. GOULD *Birds of Aust.* (1848) II. Pl. 88, *Piezorhynchus nitidus* . . **Shining Flycatcher** . . *Uńg-bur-ka*, Aborigines of Port Essington. **1903** *Emu* II. 144 *Piezorhynchus nitidus* (Shining Flycatcher). . . The large majority of their open nests were found in January. **1945** C. BARRETT *Austral. Bird Life* 171 The shining flycatcher . . lives among mangroves and in paperbark (*Melaleuca*) scrub around swamps. **1964** M. SHARLAND *Territory of Birds* 71, I realized then that I had seen the male and female of the Shining Flycatcher, birds that I'd never seen before! It is a marvellous combination—the red of the hen bird and the contrasting loveliness of her blue mate, each with a pattern so different that they could be totally unrelated. **1986** *Woman's Day* (Sydney) 24 Feb. 6/3 As I sat beside a pool, a pair of shining flycatchers were building a nest a few feet from my head. **1923** *Census Plants Vic.* (Field Naturalists' Club Vic.) 47 *Eucalyptus nitens* . . **Shining Gum.** **1935** *Honey Flora Vic.* (Vic. Dept. Agric.) (rev. ed.) 41 The Shining Gum . . is known by local names, such as White Gum . . in reference to the smooth and shining bark of the upper part of the trunk. **1986** *Parkwatch* (Vic. Nat. Parks Assoc.) Mar. 17 An understorey to a long-undisturbed shining gum forest. **1909** *Emu* VIII. 256 (*caption*) Native climbing Kauri Pine in quest of nests of **Shining Starling** (*Calornis metallica*). **1951** *Bulletin* (Sydney) 31 Jan. 13/2 Is there any land-bird anywhere so thoroughly social, so given to 'apartment' life as the tropical Australian bird known as the shining starling. **1968** V. SERVENTY *Wildlife of Aust.* 100 The shining starling . . like the introduced common starling . . has a metallic look.

shin-plaster. *Hist.* [U.S. *shin-plaster* a piece of privately issued paper money, esp. one of a low denomination, depreciated in value, or not sufficiently secured.] A promissory note: see quot. 1920.

1900 *Truth* (Sydney) 24 June 2/6 Buchanan used to pay his men in orders on his Sydney agents, and the Coonamble storekeeper or publican could never cash these orders except by giving 'shin-plasters', as they were termed, or orders of his own. **1903** H. TAUNTON *Australind* 153 The main medium of exchange in the North-West was what was known as 'shin plasters'. These were promises to pay, printed—sometimes only written—on a thin rubbishy paper, yellow up to a certain limit, then white or red as the face value increased. **1920** *Smith's Weekly* (Sydney) 28 Feb. 9/1 Shinplasters, issued by local business men, were simply promises to pay—flimsy notes of the face value of 10s. and 20s., not drawn on any bank, and with no real guarantee behind them. **1938** F. BLAKELEY *Hard Liberty* 167 Before leaving Alice Springs we cashed our 'shin plasters', of which we carried quite a wad. **1948** B. WANNAN *Treasury Austral. Frontier Tales* (1961) 105 Mining companies in those days did not pay in cash but in 'shinplasters' . . orders for varying amounts issued to Perth merchants. **1965** K. MCKENNEY *Hide-Away Man* 150 Well, yer see, they didn't give yer no change in th' pub. If yer give 'em a fiver they give yer change in shinplasters. They was cheques they wrote themselves. **1977** T. RONAN *Mighty Men on Horseback* 83 It would have been an order on Monger & Co.'s bankers and it would have been signed in ink by the head of the establishment. It would in fact have been a 'shinplaster'.

shiny, *n.* Abbrev. of *shiny arse* (see SHINY *a.* 2).

1971 D. IRELAND *Unknown Industr. Prisoner* 287 Five days later, a shiny in the pay office was rushing about trying to find out why . . number 1208 had not clocked off. **1980** H. LUNN *Behind Banana Curtain* 191 'Don't worry, I will take you fellas,' the driver said. 'All the other cabs are taking the calls for the shiny arses but I won't be in it for the shinies.'

shiny, *a.*

1. In the phr. **just the shiny (shilling** or **bob)**, an expression of approbation.

1901 *Western Champion* (Barcaldine) 26 Feb. 9/2 'Just the shiny bob', remarked the loquacious Bardy. . . 'We'll get the horses in alright.' **1904** *Worker* (Sydney) 6 Aug. 3/3 An it's just the shiny shilling when you larn to cure it right. **1920** *Aussie* (Sydney) Nov. 23/2 The real and compleat Cobber is very rare, like most good things, but he is 'just the shiny' when you've got him.

2. *fig.* In the collocation **shiny arse (bum, seat),** an office worker. Also **shiny-arsed** *a.*

1945 *Atebrin Advocate: Mag. 2/4 Austral. Armoured Regiment* 28 Apr. 3 He liked being a sailor. He didn't like being a 'shiny-bum'. **1945** *Fore & Aft: 42 Austral. Landing Craft Co. A.I.F.* 26 Feb. 3 The North must . . give the 'shiny-seats' . . an idea of the work that is really being done. **1971** D. IRELAND *Unknown Industr. Prisoner* 36 The little bosses protested as reasonably as they could to the office staff—the shiny arses. **1978** B. ROSSER *This is Palm Island* 51 Some shiny arsed chair jockey down in the city . . is administering and enforcing the Queensland Aboriginal Act. **1980** [see SHINY *n.*].

shipoo, var. SHYPOO.

shiralee /ʃɪrəˈli/. Also **shirallee.** [Of unknown origin.] A swag.

1892 G. PARKER *Round Compass in Aust.* 49 Let him down easy and slow. . . Drop in his shirallee and water-bag by him. . . That's right. **1945** S.J. BAKER *Austral. Lang.* 102 A drum . . is the equivalent of *swag* . . *shiralee* . . or bluey as the tramps rolled blanket is variously called. **1955** D. NILAND (*title*) The Shiralee. **1974** *Sunday Sun* (Brisbane) 5 May 4/2 The fences, the barns, the houses—they're all gone and I'm out on the road with my shiralee.

shire, *n.*

1. A rural administrative district in some Australian States. Also *attrib.*

1863 *Act* (Vic.) 27 Vict. no. 176 Sect. 279, If at any time in any district whether single or united which shall contain an area of not less than one hundred square miles the total amount actually paid in respect of the general rate then last made shall have amounted to one thousand pounds it shall be lawful for the Governor in Council to proclaim if it seem fit such district by such name as in and by such Order in Council may be assigned thereto to be a shire within the meaning of this Act. **1870** W.B. WITHERS *Hist. Ballarat* 181 The term 'shire' does not mean here what it does in England, but merely indicates the particular rural territory administered by a given rural local body. **1880** *Argus* (Melbourne) 1 Jan. 3/4 The Government have lately sent up two engineers to report upon the best means of supplying the shire of Echuca with water. **1890** *Braidwood Dispatch* 11 Jan. 2/4 In upwards of one hundred shires in the northern and western districts of Victoria, simultaneous action will be taken early in February for the destruction of rabbits. **1912** *Huon Times* (Franklin) 17 Apr. 4/1 Albert was pumping water from the shire dam into a 1,000-gallon tank. **1927** *Bulletin* (Sydney) 12 May 24/2 Within certain shires of the Ma State . . the cape-tulip has spread apace, and in some localities has been causing much upturning of toes amongst dairy cows. **1948** R. RAVEN-HART *Canoe in Aust.* 16 The 'Shire Clerk'—the secretary of the Shire Council, the local governing body. **1974** *Ecos* i. 27/3 A study of present and possible uses of land in a shire in the south coast region of New South Wales, Eurobodalla. **1985** *Bombala Times* 18 July 6/3 The Shire engineer . . said that instructions had been issued to gas and destroy the rabbit burrows at the cemetery.

2. Comb. **shire council, councillor.**

1880 *Argus* (Melbourne) 7 Jan. 6/7 The council expressed itself in favour of tolls, as advocated by the South Barwon **Shire Council.** **1917** W. LEES *Coaching in Aust.* 61 It is the meeting place for the Ballonne Shire Council, Maronoa Rabbit Board and the Marsupial Board. **1955** V. PALMER *Let Birds Fly* 162 'It's the shire council,' she was told. 'They want the land.' **1971** *Bulletin* (Sydney) 30 Jan. 19 Graziers are joining their sacked station staff, working on drought relief work for their local shire councils. **1985** *Bombala Times* 18 July 1/3 Ideas for road funding policy have been prepared by the Bombala Shire Council. **1935** F. CLUNE *Rolling down Lachlan* 105 We admired the forethought of **shire-councillors**, who had set aside this beautiful spot for the travelling public. **1965** K. TENNANT *Summer's Tales* 217 These filthy-rich peasants and horse-idolaters and toss-pots and shire-councillors' wives.

shirker. *Obs.* [Spec. use of *shirker* one who evades responsibility.] SLACKER.

1918 A. WRIGHT *Breed holds Good* 33 They are not all stay-at-homes, or shirkers if you will, like me. **1918** *Kia Ora Coo-ee* Apr. 7/1 We'll make those same shirkers sit up when we get you all back again. **1929** C.E.W. BEAN *Official Hist. Aust. 1914–18* III. 865 In Australia, too, a large section of the people felt bitterly that the voluntary system was not merely inadequate, but illogical and unfair, and that the time had come when the 'slacker' and the 'shirker' should be compelled to enlist. **1936** E. SCOTT *Aust. during War* in *Official Hist. Aust. 1914–18* XI. 317 The indiscriminate labelling of apparently eligible but unenlisted men as 'shirkers'.

shirt. Used *attrib.* in Special Comb. **shirt-front** *Australian National Football.*, see quot. 1983; also *attrib.* and as *v. trans.*; **-lifter,** a male homosexual.

1964 J. POLLARD *High Mark* 75 There is a vast difference between a deliberate charge and a **shirtfront.** *Ibid.* 36 The rules permit a push in the chest. Misunderstanding of this often leads to boos and hoots when a player bursts strongly through the ruck and is shirt-fronted right down the centre of his body. It is quite legitimate to shirt-front. **1965** J. DYER *Captain Blood* 87 He collected me with the perfect shirt-front, the knee coming up, the shoulder driving into my chest and the punch to the jaw on the follow-through. **1980** *Age* (Melbourne) 21 July 26/4 His full-back .. had gone down in football's fiercest tackle—the shirt-front. **1983** HIBBERD & HUTCHINSON *Barracker's Bible* 182 *Shirt-front*, a rib rattling tackle; a fiercely delivered shoulder to the chest of an opponent who is 'open', i.e. not ready. **1984** *Sunday Independent* (Perth) 9 Sept. 86/1 The Sharks overwhelmed hot favourites Swan Districts using non-stop, tear-through, shirt-front tactics in the first quarter. *Ibid.*, They were not going to tolerate being shirt-fronted all day. **1966** S.J. BAKER *Austral. Lang.* (ed. 2) 216 **Shirt lifter,** a sodomite. **1967** *Kings Cross Whisper* (Sydney) xl. 4/4 Shirt lifter, a homosexual. **1974** *Bulletin* (Sydney) 19 Jan. 12/2 When I first seen them photos of him in his 'Riverina Rig' I took him for an out-of-work ballet dancer or some kind of shirtlifter. **1979** B. HUMPHRIES *Bazza comes into his Own*, 'You'll adore Leo! .. Now he's a top Bondi hairdresser. . .' 'Leo sounds like a flamin' shirt-lifter to me!'

shiser, var. SHICER.

shit.

1. Used *attrib.* in Special Comb. **shit catchers** *pl.*, knickerbockers (see also quot. 1981); **kicker,** an unskilled worker; a person of little consequence; **ringer,** a stockman.

1967 D. HORNE *Educ. Young Donald* 96 Knickerbockers, known among boys as 'poop catchers' or '**shit catchers**'. **1980** G. ROBINSON *Decades of Duntroon Bastard* 33 'Shit-catchers' was the colloquial name for knickerbocker trousers, then commonly worn by teenage boys in Sydney. **1981** P. RADLEY *Jack Rivers & Me* 90 We're wearin' bowyangs. . . That's like when you tie a rope round the legs of your pants to stop snakes from crawling up. The boys call them shit-catchers. **1969** C. BRAY *Blossom* 35 'What's yer job?' asked Brody, grinning. 'What's yer line of country?' .. '**Shitkicker,**' he said. 'What's yours?' **1971** D. WILLIAMSON *Removalists* (1972) 111 It takes an awful lot of bruises for the S.M. to take the word of a shitkicker like you against two members of the force. **1973** J. POWERS *Last of Knucklemen* (1974) 23 Thing is, you see, Pansy's not just an ordinary shitkicker like the rest of us. Pansy's had money. **1940** W. HATFIELD *Into (Great?) Unfenced* 61 How d' you mean—a job?—Here? I'm not a **shit ringer.** Don't know which end of a bull 'd bite me! No, I'm a shearer. **1975** X. HERBERT *Poor Fellow my Country* 403 Looks like I won't be makin' a shit-ringer out o' you after all.

2. In the phr. **shit on the** (or **one's**) **liver** and varr., used in allusion to a supposed cause of ill-temper; S.O.L.

1935 H.R. WILLIAMS *Comrades of Great Adventure* 147 What's up with you, you big stiff. Got hobnails on your liver? **1944** L. GLASSOP *We were Rats* 197 'Them Jerries oughta hunk a few lumps of — off their livers,' said Eddie. **1951** 'S. MACKENZIE' *Dead Men Rising* 14 And how is Captain Hyacinth? I trust the Captain has no more 'n 'is usual amount of s-t on the liver this morning? **1965** K. MCKENNEY *Hide-Away Man* 17 Do yer good ter come along, Benny boy. Get th' shit orf yer liver. **1981** A. WELLER *Day of Dog* 81 Judge must of 'ad shit on 'is liver that day, unna?

shitters, *pl.* Cattle.

1940 W. HATFIELD *Into (Great?) Unfenced* 75, I don't have to frowst out here in these sand-hills chasin' shitters for a livin'.

shitty, *a.* and *n.*

A. *adj.* Bad-tempered.

1971 D. IRELAND *Unknown Industr. Prisoner* 188 'Why doesn't someone tell me?' 'Why don't you keep your ear to the ground?' 'What are you shitty about?' 'I'm not shitty.' **1971** D. WILLIAMSON *Removalists* (1972) 52 She won't be as shitty if she knows I'm getting paid.

B. *n.* A fit of bad temper.

1982 LOWENSTEIN & HILLS *Under Hook* 76 They'd say: 'Go up and tell him that it's too dirty to work today. How about letting us go home?' We wouldn't work, we'd be sitting there for two hours and if he had a shitty, old McKinnon, he wouldn't let us go home.

shiveau, var. SHIVOO *n.*

shivery grass. [Altered form of *shivering grass* a name for the quaking-grass *Briza media.*] The naturalized annual Mediterranean grass *Briza minor* (fam. Poaceae), common throughout s. Aust. incl. Tas.; the similar *B. maxima.*

1935 F. CLUNE *Rolling down Lachlan* 18 Plenty of shivery grass, shivering in the shade of stunted she-oaks. **1969** J. O'GRADY *O'Grady Sez* 7 A pickle bottle full of 'shivery grass' on the old cedar sideboard. **1978** L. WHITE *Memories of Childhood* 1 Prickly bacon-and-egg bushes, shivery grass, blackboys.

Shivery Isles. New Zealand. Cf. SHAKY ISLES.

1933 *Bulletin* (Sydney) 30 Aug. 14/1 He .. lived in the Shivery Isles only a few years. **1945** *Ibid.* 11 July 12/4 'Had a job t' go to in the Shivery Isles once,' said Sam. 'Near Auckland it was.' **1951** *Ibid.* 18 July 14/1 Maorilanders inform me that the shellfish is regarded as a luxury in the Shivery Isles; and .. the pippi lives and feeds in a much cleaner environment than many oysters.

shivoo, *n.* Also **sheevo, shiveau.** [a. Fr. *chez vous* 'at your place', used erroneously to mean 'a party or celebration' and variously Anglicized: see OEDS *chez* (quot. 1804), *shiveau* (where Br. dial. forms are cited), and *shivoo.*] A party or celebration; a revel; a 'shindig'.

1844 J. TUCKER *Ralph Rashleigh* (1952) 165 The notes of a fiddle and tambourine, the staple music of a colonial *sheevo*, or merrymaking. **1849** A. HARRIS *Emigrant Family* (1967) 62 A 'Shiveau' at the Hut. **1882** *Bulletin* (Sydney) 3 June 9/2 At a recent Good Templar shivoo in England, Sir 'Enry .. said his new Licensing Act 'was working well out here and giving universal satisfaction'. **1891** *Truth* (Sydney) 17 May 2/2 'Shivoo' is a frequently-used word, but few understand its meaning, which is Hebrew for seven days' mourning. **1901** *Ibid.* 27 Oct. 2/5 At a recent swagger Sydney shivoo the women swopped cigarettes, lies, blokes' heads and trousers. **1912** *Huon Times* (Franklin) 23 Mar. 2/7 They were returning from a 'shivoo' and were singing 'Home, boys, home', and 'We won't go home till morning', but they did not intend to disturb the peace. **1924** *Aussie* (Sydney) Mar. 10/1 All breasted th' free-lunch counter, jus' like a push of politicians an' their missuses at a Guv'ment 'Ouse shivoo. **1935** C. STEAD *Seven Poor Men* 43 'She's collecting flowers for a Labour Party bazaar and fête: we are going to take them in by car. Come along, you'll meet some new people.' 'No thanks; no Labour party shivoos.' **1947** *Bulletin* (Sydney) 22 Jan. 28/1 Old Mac was a trifle grumpy and refused to go to the New Year sports. . . '*Everybody* can't be goin' spendin' up big at shivoos.' **1957** *Ibid.* 20 Feb. 13/2 For 17 years they have held a reunion and dance every Easter at Marrickville (Sydney) Town Hall. . . This Easter, Sydney Town Hall (April 23) has been booked for the shivoo. **1973** A. BURNETT *Wilful Murder in Outback* 15 Kathleen was driving all the customers to distraction by asking them incessantly for advice about what she could wear to a shivoo that was to be held the next weekend. **1985** *Bulletin* (Sydney) 15 Oct. 68/3 Tell your wife to stop scaling the mullet and .. buy a nice hat for a shivoo at Government House.

shivoo, *v. Obs.* [f. prec.] *intr.* To celebrate. Also *trans.*, to entertain, and as *vbl. n.*

1906 *Gadfly* (Adelaide) 18 Apr. 18/2 Last night the Semaphore shivoo'd at the Ward Street Hall to farewell popular Canon Swan. **1908** *Truth* (Sydney) 28 June 1/6 The shivooing now going on in the Big Smoke. **1908** *Ibid.* 11 Oct. 1/4 Australia, judging by the manner in which it pelted its good splosh away, shivooing the Yankee Fleet .. will shortly be known as 'The Golden Calf'.

shlanter, shlinter, varr. SLANTER.

shoddy dropper. [f. *shoddy* woollen yarn + *dropper* one who delivers goods: see OEDS *shoddy, n.* 5 and *dropper* 1 d.] One who peddles cheap or falsely-described clothing; a hawker.

[**1937** E. PARTRIDGE *Dict. Slang & Unconventional Eng.* 759 *Shoddy-dropper*, a seller of cheap serge: New Zealand c. (–1932).] **1950** *Austral. Police Jrnl.* Apr. 118 *Shoddy droppers*, a hawker [*sic*] of inferior or shoddy clothing which is not true to label. **1964** *Australasian Post* (Melbourne) 28 May 38/3 The 'shoddy droppers' (Indian hawkers) always carried a supply .. of patent medicines with them. **1972** *Telegraph* (Brisbane) 30 Aug. 24/6 The operators were known as dudders and professional shoddy-droppers. **1973** A. BURNETT *Wilful Murder in Outback* 42 Cotadabeen was a shoddy dropper—a travelling draper.

shoe. *Timber-getting.* See quot. 1983.

1901 *Bulletin* (Sydney) 12 Jan. 15/2 Scaffolding of big timber by means of the 'shoe' .. is an every-day occurrence with the splitters in Tasmanian gum forests. The 'shoe' is a piece of timber roughly shaped with the axe, unshod, and driven into a narrow hole previously cut into the tree about 7 in. **1903** *Advocate* (Burnie) 2 July 3/5 It appeared that the deceased had fallen the tree from off a shoe; the stump was about 7 ft. high. **1903** *Sporting News* (Launceston) 22 Aug. 2/5 The tree topped 108 ft. from where the shoe was put in. **1968** P. ADAM SMITH *Tiger Country* 65 Fellers in the timber country climb to a clean part of the trunk above the rubble around the base by means of 'shoes' which are long, narrow boards, tipped with iron. **1983** R. BECKETT *Axemen* 53 A jigger board was a relatively simple thing. . . It narrowed at one end and at this end it had an iron tip or shoe. In Australia, because the boards were made of hardwood, the iron shoe was not often seen in the early days. . . The axemen would cut a small wedge-shaped hole for the tip of the board, insert it, iron tip first, and then balancing on the first board cut his next stand, until he had levered himself up to the required height.

shonky, *a.* and *n.* Also **shonkie.** [Prob. f. *shonk* an offensive name for a Jew: see OEDS.]

A. *adj.* Unreliable; unsound; dishonest; out of sorts.

1970 R. BEILBY *No Medals for Aphrodite* 98 'You shonkie sod!' Harry drove his fist into that vulnerable belly. **1972** N. MILES *Opal Fever* 175 'Turn it up, you still look pretty shonky to me, mate,' replied Bill. 'Why not rest another couple of days.' **1975** *Bulletin* (Sydney) 10 May 32/1 'Shop displays give no indication of the real quality of the sets. The colour you see in a shop is not the colour you can expect in your home.' This is not just the shonky tuning of the shop assistants or the bright lights the sets are displayed under. **1976** P. KELLY *Unmaking of Gough* 246 The letter mentioned the possibility that early appropriation might be needed to cover. . Medibank. . . Fraser maintained . . it showed the Hayden budget was shonky. **1977** *Bulletin* (Sydney) 25 June 27/3 Willis argues that Wran's aim is to control the Upper House to enable him to implement a shonky Legislative Assembly redistribution. **1980** N. HASLUCK *Blue Guitar* 53 After the concrete pour, the shonky one, I mean, he had a lot more on his mind than job cards. **1981** *Austral.* (Sydney) 2 Feb. 7/7 The woman .. was forthright about the cut-price air fares... 'We call these tickets shonky,' she said. **1985** *Canberra Times* 29 Sept. 2/5 (*heading*) Rajneeshees, like Liberals, a 'shonky sect'.

B. *n.*. One who engages in sharp practice.

1979 *Austral. Financial Rev.* (Sydney) 25 July 11/6 Mr Groom is right when he refers to the building industry as being characterized by initiative and drive, but unless something is done to eliminate these shonkies quickly, then such qualities will be characteristic of the past.

shoofty /'ʃʊfti/, *n.* Also **shoofti.** [Var. of Br. slang *shufti* a look, orig. Arabic: see OEDS *shufti, shufty, n.* and *shufty, v.*] A look.

1959 *R.A.N. News* (Sydney) 9 Jan. 2 No, you may *not* have a shoofty through me look-stick. **1972** N. MILES *Opal Fever* 81 Take a shoofty at this. Hit's starting to make colour. **1977** R. BEILBY *Gunner* 14 'What have they got? Fuck all! No planes, buggerall transport... ' 'I'll take a shoofti,' he muttered tautly. **1980** HEPWORTH & HINDLE *Boozing out in Melbourne Pubs* 19 In England, one can tell more about the worth of a strange pub from a quick shoofty at the walls of the dunny than one can from a close inspection of the public bar.

shoofty, *a.* Also **shooftey.** [Alteration of *shifty* not straightforward.] Dishonest; deceitful; 'slippery'.

1962 J. WYNNUM *Tar Dust* 15 Trouble with you is you've been working too many shoofty moves during your long period of shore time. **1963** F. HARDY *Legends Benson's Valley* 207 Years of unemployment had given them the ability to work more shooftey points than any share jobber on the stock exchange. **1967** —— *Billy Borker yarns Again* 100 The shoofties solicitor Sydney ever saw in all its legal history. **1967** T.A.G. HUNGERFORD *Wong Chu* 85 She got that shoofty look they get when they think they're on to something. **1981** P. RADLEY *Jack Rivers & Me* 22 We love burnt toast. .. It does sometimes strike me and Jack that Mum might say she burnt it for us when she did it accidentally. But that would be shoofty, wouldn't it? And Mum's more sugary than shoofty. **1985** *Bulletin* (Sydney) 3 Sept. 34/2 Radley .. is a 'shoofty' Scrabble player—shoofty being a Newcastle word for shifty or tricky.

shook, on (or **after**): see SHAKE *v.*[2]

shoot, *n.* Also **chute.**

1. *Shearing.* An inclined passage down which shorn sheep pass into a counting-out pen.

1900 H. LAWSON *On Track* 134 A great-horned ram, in poor condition, but shorn of a heavy fleece, picks himself up at the foot of the 'shoot', and hesitates, as if ashamed to go down to the other end where the ewes are. **1908** W.H. OGILVIE *My Life in Open* 29 Every sheep put down the shoot represents a few pence more towards the building of the coveted 'cheque'. **1910** *Bulletin* (Sydney) 28 Apr. 13/1, I can see the shearers putting them down the shoots. **1912** R.S. TAIT *Scotty Mac* 11 Guided gently down the shoot To join his comrades there. **1955** STEWART & KEESING *Austral. Bush Ballads* 239 The shearers squint along the pens, they squint along the shoots. **1965** J.S. GUNN *Terminol. Shearing Industry* i. 14 *Chute*, also called the 'porthole', this is a low opening and ramp through which the shorn sheep are passed down to the counting-out pen.

2. *Surfing.* A breaking wave which carries a surfer towards the beach; the act of riding such a wave.

1914 M. GROVER *Minus Quantity* 14 Try a shoot... The great thing is to catch them at the right time. **1930** *Surf: All about It* 10 The gentle art of scraping your nose, after a shoot, on the sand of the beach itself, is in both senses of the word, the high-water mark of surfing. **1940** P. KERRY *Cobbers A.I.F.* 10 An' the surf wus runnin' 'owlers—an' the shoots were good 'uns, too When yeh cracked one on the front line, yeh could see right ter the zoo. **1953** D. CUSACK *Southern Steel* 170 A good shoot was coming in .. then the wave curled and he came shooting in, right up on to the sand. **1956** S. HOPE *Diggers' Paradise* 186 Not seeing another suitable 'shoot', Max began swimming in, when suddenly his leg was seized. **1966** G. BARRY *Bed & Bored* 78 Did you see me handle that shoot. All the way to the beach, you know. **1978** B. ST. A. SMITH *Spirit beyond Psyche* 99 Days of sun, laughter and vigour in the Surf Life-saving Club; long, tough swims across the pull of the sweep, the cross-currents; coming in *on the body* on a *shoot* in the company of whooping friends.

shoot, *v.*

1. *Obs. trans.* [f. *shoot* dismissal, sack: see OEDS *sb.*[1] 3 f.] To dismiss (someone) from employment.

1892 G. PARKER *Round Compass in Aust.* 447 *Shot me dead*, discharged me. **1897** *Worker* (Sydney) 11 Sept. 1/1 Poor Billy Mayne has got 'the spear', and Dick his mate is 'shot'! **1899** *Bulletin* (Sydney) 19 Aug. 32/2 The boss hinted that he could make room for Sheedy and his mate by 'shooting' two less competent hands.

2. *trans. Surfing.* To ride (a wave); also *absol.*

1912 *Truth* (Sydney) 18 Feb. 8/3, I think respectable people may go surf-bathing and, still remain respectable, but people who aren't moral and respectable do not become so by shooting the breakers and airing their figures on the beaches. **1913** *Newcastle Morning Herald* 31 Dec. 5/4 The more timid and cautious .. gain equally thrilling excitement from 'shooting' the smaller rollers. **1914** R. STOCK *Pyjama Man* 100 'You've been everywhere', she said, 'and done everything, and can't shoot the breakers?' **1918** A. WRIGHT *Breed holds Good* 32 They could all swim well, and 'shoot' the breakers with the ease and grace of South Sea Islanders. **1930** *Surf: All about It* 4 You can become a surf-ace as soon as you like—shoot the breakers, if you want to. **1932** *Austral. Ring* II. xxv. 5 Surfing has now become his favorite pastime. He spends all his spare time down at Bondi learning to 'shoot' the breakers. **1949** C.B. MAXWELL *Surf* 12 We'd hang around .. to watch Freddie go for his swim, and at last plucked up enough courage to ask him to teach us to shoot. **1953** *Sydney Morning Herald* 3 Jan. 6/3 'Body shooting', a surfing term for catching a wave without the use of a surf board or surf ski, hence, 'shooting on the body'. **1956** T.I. THOMPSON *Pop. Handbk. Swimming* 42 With a knowledge of the technique of surfing and what to avoid, these people can derive a great deal of enjoyment from 'shooting' the breakers. **1963** J. POLLARD *Austral. Surfrider* 20 Here's a good wave for 'shooting the curl', riding through the hollowest part.

3. In the phr. **to shoot through,** to escape; to disappear; to leave. See also BONDI *n.*[2]

1947 *Pix* (Sydney) 20 Sept. 15 *Shoot through*, escape, abscond. **1955** *Overland* v. 5, I wanted to shoot through early this afternoon, too. **1960** D. IRELAND *Image in Clay* (1964) 95 Well, we were only coming back for a day or two, then we were going to shoot through. **1963** J. O'GRADY *Things they do to You* 111 He could always extricate himself by 'shooting through'. **1968** B. HUMPHRIES *Wonderful World Barry McKenzie*, What a dump for the Queen to live in. No wonder old Phil's always shooting through. **1974** N. PHILLIPSON *As Other Men* 118 The boyfriend panics and shoots through. **1978** L. HORSPHOL *Turn down Empty Glass* 43 O'Malley and some truckie carried you in here, then they shot through. **1985** *Bulletin* (Sydney) 26 Nov. 80/1 Me wife's shot through... Can't get a bird... Can't pay the rent.

4. In the phr. **to be shot in,** to be thrown in (to gaol).

[N.Z. **1947** P. NEWTON *Wayleggo* 38 How we saw that day out without getting 'shot in' is a mystery to me yet.] **1968** S. GORE *Holy Smoke* 108 *Shot in, to be*, thrown in. **1972** J. BOOTH *Only Tracks Remain* 31 Your mate has been 'shot in'; I saw the police take him.

shooter. *Surfing.* [f. SHOOT *v.* 2.] One who shoots a wave.

1949 C.B. MAXWELL *Surf* 8 Bathers hitherto content to find unadventurous pleasure in the swirl round their knees became unhappily aware of the new-style human torpedoes powered by the sea. Early on there came to be a sharp .. cleavage between 'shooters' and 'non-shooters' in the South Steyne surf.

Shop. [Spec. use of Br. slang *shop* a place of business: see OED(S *sb.* 4.] With **the:** a nickname for the University of Melbourne.

[**1833** *Launceston Advertiser* 5 Dec. 3 The people, greatly to their credit, have set up two noble *shops* [*sc.* the Sydney College].] **1889** *Centennial Mag.* 218 It related how 'a medical student came up to the Shop' as a freshman, and 'thought through exams. he would speedily pop'. **1918** A.G.N. WALL *Lett. Airman* 81 After a year at 'the Shop'—well, I can't help thinking sometimes that half a dozen of my Australian friends could clear the ante-room from end to end in five minutes. **1943** *Troppo Tribune* (Mataranka) 25 Jan. 1 He schooled at St. Pat's East Melbourne then to 'the Shop' to swot Pharmacy. **1952** *Farrago* (Melbourne) 5 Aug. 1 A busy weekend for the shop. **1964** *Sydney Morning Herald* 28 Aug. 2/9 Melbourne University is known as 'The Shop'. **1968** G. BAKER *Montgomery & I* 53 *Melbourne University.* The first University in the province of Victoria. Sometimes referred to in ancient documents as 'The Shop'.

shore station. *Pearling.* See quot. 1913. Also *attrib.*

1902 *Cwlth. Parl. Papers* II. 1009 The 'shellers' became divided into two parties, one called the 'shore station party', from their working from the shore, the other called the 'floating station party', from their working from their schooners. **1913** *Ibid.* III. 747 What do you mean by a shore station? In Thursday Island they send the luggers out, and have the schooner coming in periodically. They get all their supplies on shore, instead of on the boats. That is what is known as a shore station? **1954** N. BARTLETT *Pearl Seekers* 176 In the Torres Straits, where dress diving had been commonplace for some time, the early pearlers had set up shore stations on one or other of the tempting coral islands from which they operated with small boats or luggers.

shornie. *Shearing.* [f. *shorn* + -Y.] A newly-shorn sheep.

1965 R.H. CONQUEST *Horses in Kitchen* 187 The shearer, be he a 'gun' or just an average man, could not maintain a steady output of shornies unless he enjoyed the loyal co-operation of the rouseabouts, to wit, the shedhands. **1975** B. FOLEY *Shearer's Poems* 2 The wool appeared much dimmer Than it had ten years before And 'counting out' was difficult With 'shornies' jaw to jaw. **1982** *Bulletin* (Sydney) 13 Apr. 97/2 Instead of a penful of hard-won shornies, there was only one sheep left in the pen.

short-nosed bandicoot. [See quot. 1941.] Any of several marsupials of the genus *Isoodon* of all States, esp. *I. obesulus* of s.w., n.e., and s.e. Aust. incl. Tas.

1894 R. LYDEKKER *Hand-Bk. Marsupialia & Monotremata* 144 Short-nosed Bandicoot. *Perameles obesula.* **1926** A.S. LE SOUEF et al. *Wild Animals Australasia* 307 Short-nosed bandicoot *Isoodon obesulus...* Australia, except north and centre, Tasmania. **1928** *Bulletin* (Sydney) 29 Feb. 19/2 How many different sorts of bandicoot does Australia possess? I have met the pig-footed 'coot, the striped 'coot, the long-nosed, the short-nosed, the golden, the spiny-furred and the grizzled-yellow. **1941** E. TROUGHTON *Furred Animals Aust.* 60 Though an elongated snout is characteristic of all marsupial bandicoots, the head appears to be stouter and the muzzle correspondingly somewhat shorter or more obtuse in this genus [*sc. Isoodon*], which is given the popular title of Short-nosed Bandicoot. **1970** V. SERVENTY *Dryandra* 31 Scattered in large numbers through the forest country are quendas or short-nosed bandicoots. **1984** B. DIXON *Searching for Aboriginal Lang.* 32 Gujila, the short-nose bandicoot, tried following him, and then Midin, the ring-tail possum, took a turn.

short-sentenced, *ppl. a. Obs.* Of a convict: sentenced to seven years of penal servitude.

1835 *Sydney Herald* 27 July 2/3 The Wollombi, comprising its own thickly-settled valley, the small farms on Ettalong, the cattle stations in the mountain ranges, and the retreats of squatters .. themselves short-sentenced expirees .. forms a district of itself. **1840** *Tasmanian Weekly Dispatch* (Hobart) 5 June 4/2 Aided by other long, or short sentenced men. **1851** H. MELVILLE *Present State Aust.* 51 Only a sufficient number of short sentenced men should be sent there.

short-tailed, *a.* Used as a distinguishing epithet in the names of animals: **shearwater,** the bird *Puffinus tenuirostris* (see MUTTON BIRD *n.* 1); formerly also **short-tailed petrel; wallaby,** QUOKKA; also **short-tailed pademelon.**

1847 [**short-tailed shearwater**] J. GOULD *Birds of Aust.* (1848) VII. Pl. 56, *Puffinus brevicaudus*.. Short-tailed Petrel. **1903** *Emu* II. 209 *Puffinus tenuirostris* (Short-tailed Petrel). When on shipboard about the latitude of Wilson's Promontory .. thousands of Mutton-Birds were seen. **1930** C.M. YONGE *Yr. on Great Barrier Reef* 204 Honeycombed with the burrows of the mutton bird. This bird, also known as the short-tailed shearwater, builds long burrows, often only a few inches beneath the surface. **1977** *Ecos* xi. 19/1 In Australia, bands were first used in 1912, when members of the Melbourne Bird Observers' Club .. placed them on Tasmanian mutton-birds (short-tailed shearwater). **1898** E.E. MORRIS *Austral Eng.* 494 **Short-tailed W[allaby]**—*M[acropus] brachyurus*. **1905** *Emu* VI. 129 *Macropus brachyurus*, or short-tailed wallaby, is very common in the acacia scrubs. **1926** A.S. LE SOUEF et al. *Wild Animals Australasia* 200 Short-tailed wallaby .. south-western Australia. **1941** E. TROUGHTON *Furred Animals Aust.* 197 The reference occurs in a brief account published in 1658 by .. Samuel Volckersen, concerning Rottnest Island and the presence of 'two seals and a wild cat...' The 'wild cat' was actually the short-tailed pademelon.

shot, *n.*

1. *Obs.* Dismissal from employment: see SHOOT *v.* 1.

1897 *Worker* (Sydney) 11 Sept. 1/1 'Percentage' is the thing he says the shearer-man has got Who shears his sheep just as he likes but doesn't get the 'shot'. **1898** *Bulletin* (Sydney) 17 Dec. 15/1 *Discharge*, sack, shot, or spear.

2. An attempt to provoke or 'get at' a person, esp. in the phr. **to have a shot at.**

1903 J. FURPHY *Such is Life* 125 'By heaven! I'd like to have a shot at you for a thousand!' I continued, eyeing him greedily. **1915** K.S. PRICHARD *Pioneers* 150 He was working for a shot at Donald Cameron through Young Davey. **1947** J. MORRISON *Sailors belong Ships* 38 Mick, standing in the square, can't resist a shot at Beck. 'You were a long time making up your mind about this!' he yells. **1952** T.A.G. HUNGERFORD *Ridge & River* 31 He was a sour bastard at times, and closed like a clam if he suspected that a man was having a shot at him. **1971** K. WILLEY *Boss Drover* 28 We all knew him as Alec. If you called him 'Sir Alexander' he would reckon you were having a shot at him. **1972** J. O'GRADY *It's your Shout, Mate!* 20 Aussies take great delight in what they call 'having a shot' at people. **1982** R. HALL *Just Relations* 52 The two branches of Swans having a shot at one another, somebody forever getting stoushed.

3. *Obs.* See quot.

1913 W.K. HARRIS *Outback in Aust.* 146 All the greatest .. celebrities of the day, were 'on the wallaby', 'humping bluey', and had called at his particular station for the proverbial free pannikin of 'dust' (flour), pinch of 'shot' (baking powder).

4. An expedient course of action; esp. as an expression of approbation in the phr. **that's the shot.**

1953 T.A.G. HUNGERFORD *Riverslake* 30 Ready to go, eh? That's the shot. **1962** V.C. HALL *Dreamtime Justice* 80 He reckoned that the shot was to go out to the offshore islands to collect information about Wonggo and his mob. **1968** S. GORE *Holy Smoke* 14 *Faith*, mate. That's the shot. I'm drumming yer! **1971** *Kings Cross Whisper* (Sydney) cii. 4/5 It's funny, but sawn-off ALP pollies were all over Tom like a rash until he made that statement about being the shot for short MPs. **1981** C. WALLACE-CRABBE *Splinters* 56 'Beer, Bob?' Sandstone asked... 'Just the shot, thanks.' Bob was thirsty now.

shot, *ppl. a.* [U.S.: see OEDS *ppl. a.* 4 b.] Drunk.

1913 *Bulletin* (Sydney) 25 Sept. 22/2 *Inebriated* .. shot. **1926** M. FORREST *Hibiscus Heart* 276 They were giving a send-off to Carrol Erle at the Stockman's Arms... We .. I .. *all* of us got more or less 'shot'. **1936** *Bulletin* (Sydney) 22 Apr. 21/1 The usually-silent bloke, when he gets shot, 's the first to roar. **1946** L. ESSON *Southern Cross* 76 You're shot. Come on. Supper will sober you up. **1965** L. HAYLEN *Big Red* 132 Everybody got 'shot' in Cooee. **1968** D. IRELAND *Chantic Bird* 29 You don't want to get drunk near them. They'd bottle you for two bob if they thought you were half shot. **1979** D.R. STUART *Crank back on Roller* 218 Ah well, I got shot, real staggery .. but that arrack, hell, it's great stuff.

shotty, *a. Gold-mining.* [Spec. use of *shotty* resembling shot or pellets of lead. Chiefly Austral.: see OED(S.] Of a particle of gold: small and round, resembling gunshot. Freq. in the collocation **shotty gold.**

1860 *Rep. Mining Surveyors* (Vic. Dept. Mines) Aug. 236 There were also some very good patches of shotty gold and small nuggets found in the vicinity of this nugget. **1862** J.A. PATTERSON *Gold Fields Vic.* 157 The Dunolly lead gave masses of gold in considerable abundance, with large quantities of the precious metal in the form known as 'shotty'. **1871** *Austral. Town & Country Jrnl.* (Sydney) 22 Apr. 495/2 The gold is coarse and shotty. **1885** 'W.G.C.' *Some Acct. Mount Morgan Gold Mine* 22 Those who can remember the early days of Bendigo .. when pans full of shotty gold were to be seen in every broker's window in Collins-street. **1893** *Braidwood Dispatch* 27 May 6/2 The gold being coarse, shotty and showing no trace whatever of water action. **1903** J. FURPHY *Such is Life* 158 Rough, shotty, water-worn gold. **1922** R.L. JACK *Northmost Aust.* II. 430 All hands prospected the neighbourhood for *alluvial gold*. 'Colours' and 'shotty specks' were the only reward for their labour. **1931** W. BARAGWANATH et al. *Guide for Prospectors in Vic.* 6 'Shotty gold' is chiefly derived from spurs. **1946** K.S. PRICHARD *Roaring Nineties* 59 Dinny .. knapped a rock that showed fine shotty gold. **1960** I.L. IDRIESS *Wild North* 179 Shammies of 'shotty' gold.

shoulder, *v.* In the phr. **to shoulder** (one's) **drum (knot, Matilda, swag,** etc.), to take to the road.

1894 *Bulletin* (Sydney) 14 Apr. 24/3 With a strong right arm and a willing hand, He shouldered his 'drum' to the Thirsty Land. **1896** H. LAWSON *While Billy Boils* (1975) 41 Macquarie afterwards shouldered his swag and staggered and struggled along the track ten miles to the Union Town hospital. **1911** A. WRIGHT *Gambler's Gold* (1923) 81 Tomorrow the pay-cart would come along; he would draw his time, and shoulder his swag again. **1914** *Bulletin* (Sydney) 21 May 24/1 We took the rattler to Echuca, but .. shouldered our knots from there. **1940** I.L. IDRIESS *Lightning Ridge* 125 Nearly broke, it was a case of again shouldering Matilda and looking for a job.

shouse. Also **shoush, sh'touse.** [Syncopated form of *shit-house*.] A lavatory. Also *fig.* and *attrib.*

1941 S.J. BAKER *Pop. Dict. Austral. Slang* 66 *Shouse*, a privy. **1952** P. PINNEY *Road in Wilderness* 213 Remember that day at Sorele? That Jap sitting in the shouse? **1963** J. O'GRADY *Things they do to You* 107 You should have been a shouse mechanic... You seem to know a bit about dykes. **1965** J. WYNNUM *Jiggin' in Riggin'* 53 Tell me, what happened after the lightning hit the shouse? **1968** J. O'GRADY *Bottle of Sandwiches* 64 Bill reckoned he wasn't cut out to be a shouse mechanic. **1970** *Kings Cross Whisper* (Sydney) lxxxi. 8/5 *Shouses* must be referred to as retirement recesses. **1975** L. RYAN *Shearers* 98 Dewlap, who had been standing at the back of the ring, all alone like a country s'house, now sidled up. **1978** B. ROSSER *This is Palm Island* 39 Instantly a black head .. appeared above the door of the next cubicle... He bounded out of that shoush like a rocket. **1981** B. GREEN *Small Town Rising* 119 That's a pretty sh'touse deal and you know it. **1984** *Austral. Short Stories* viii. 54 This Harvey sounds like a bloke we got at work... He cleans the shoushes out.

shout, *n.* [f. SHOUT *v.* Used elsewhere but recorded earliest in Aust.]

1. a. The purchase of a round of drinks for an assembled company; the round of drinks itself.

1854 T.F. BRIDE *Lett. Victorian Pioneers* (1898) 127 Do you forget the shout you stood—the shout for all hands? **1858** C.R. THATCHER *Colonial Songster* (rev. ed.) 103 In surprise I had my nobbler, And I was going out, When one of the lads came up and said 'I'll toss you for a shout!' **1859** W. KELLY *Life in Vic.* I. 131 There was sure to be 'a champagne shout' for the company. **1862** C. MUNRO *Fern Vale* I. 49 The mere relation of deeds was speedily brought to a stand, by the challenge of Smith to bet 'a shout' to the party all round, or accept the same himself from anyone there, that would ride his own horse into the room. **1869** E.C. BOOTH *Another Eng.* 30 A 'shout all round', that is, a drink at sixpence, or perhaps a shilling each, for every one in the house, is the orthodox method of commencing to 'knock down a cheque'. **1885** *Australasian Printers' Keepsake* 38 A languishing eye when copy or the punchbowl were out; but when .. a shout for the crowd announced, a luminous optic indeed. **1901** *Bulletin* (Sydney) 23 Nov. 14/2 The record 'shout' for Australia probably occurred when .. £240 was planked down on the bar for the first round of drinks. **1911** E.J. BRADY *King's Caravan* 275 At our approach four miserable derelicts left the stool on the verandah and slouched into the bar on the prospect of a 'shout'. **1921** *Bulletin* (Sydney) 31 Mar. 22/2 'J.G.'s' bloke .. squares the four sides of a 5 ft. 3 in. gauge sleeper in 21 clouts—but 'J.G.' omitted to say how many shouts it takes to square the man who passed it. **1955** A.C.V. BLIGH *Golden Quest* 153 Pearlers called for drinks for all hands .. such 'shouts' usually costing £50. **1965** *Oz* (Sydney) Oct. 8/2 No worry .. it's amazing what a few schooners of jolly does for a bloke .. and after gettin' ourselves on the outside of four or five shouts we were just settlin' down to a nice low roar. **1979** K. GARVEY *Absolutely Austral.* 73 So I'll put down my ignorant pen, and stand you all a shout. **1981** Q. WILD *Honey Wind* 15 'First shout's on old Lendy,' said the driver .. patting the note down on the bar. 'He asked me to buy it for him.'

b. *transf.* and *fig.* Also **shout-out,** a helping hand.

1916 H. LAWSON *Lett.* (1970) 238 The receipt for boots represents one 'shout' for the children, two pairs each. **1952** J.R. TYRRELL *Old Bks.* 98 Heading across the road to the pub Fred presently returned with a generous 'shout' for the horse—half a bucket of water and a bottle of whisky. **1975** D. MIDDLEBROOK *Our Trespasses* 5 It's Saturday, and I was wondering if you'd like to have dinner there. It'll be my shout... It goes on the expense account. **1980** O. RUHEN *Bullock Teams* 232, I offered to give him a 'shout-out' and he accepted gladly. I remarked what big sturdy stock he had in the pole and pin. 'No good trying to stir those bastards,' he said... 'When I start your load moving call the bullocks in front.'

2. One's turn to buy a round of drinks for an assembled company.

1882 *Sydney Slang Dict.* 8 *Shout*, to pay for drinks. 'It's my 'shout'!' **1918** *Kia Ora Coo-ee* May 7/3 It was Old Bill's 'shout', and he said as he raised his 'pot', 'Here's to the good old days.' **1949** S. RUDD *Auburn by Night* 21 Should a stranger enter the bar .. it would fly on to his shoulder, and shout in his ear, 'It's your shout, it's your shout!' And you simply had to shout drinks for all hands. **1954** T. RONAN *Vision Splendid* 204 Your shout, Block! **1967** A.E. DEBENHAM *All Manner of People* 95 'Have you three been in the hotel together?' 'Yes... We've been having shout for shout.' **1973** J. POWERS *Last of Knucklemen* (1974) 22 I'll drink to that. Whose shout? **1978** M. PAICE *Shadow of Wings* 194 Just had to finish me drink. You wouldn't expect a man to leave before his shout would you Ben? **1982** R. HALL *Just Relations* 56 My shout, he said, slapping the money down beside the hand.

shout, *v.* [Transf. use of *shout* to call (for drinks).]

1. a. *intr.* To pay for a round of drinks, esp. one given freely to an assembled company.

1850 *Monthly Almanac* (Adelaide) 7 Well, he gets out, and is immediately enjoined to 'shout' on the spot... A moderate request which he, in his innocence, is about complying with literally .. but being naturally apt, ultimately discovers that 'shouting' signifies paying for nine nobblers, four spiders, various glasses, and an indefinite quantity of blunted stunted things, called by courtesy cigars. **1859** W. BURROWS *Adventures Mounted Trooper* 126 Nearly every one drinks, and the first question on meeting generally is, 'Are you going to shout?' *i.e.*, stand treat. **1865** *Adventures Captain Achilles von Humboldt Blowhard* 18 To heighten the discomfiture of poor *Blowhard*, his conductor positively refuses to show him the way back unless he 'shouts' handsomely. **1873** 'DEMONAX' *Mysteries & Miseries* 41 It is drink, drink, all day, and swim in it at night. Everyone you meet will 'shout', and you have to 'shout' in return. **1881** A.C. GRANT *Bush-Life Qld.* II. 51 'Come along, Mr West', another shouted; 'I'm a-goin' to shout; what's yours?' **1894** *Western Champion* (Barcaldine) 2 Jan. 2/1 Most peculiar thing to me as the night wore on, and yarn after yarn went round, the old bloke always shouted, and for all hands each time. **1906** *Gadfly* (Adelaide) 14 Mar. 13/3 Shout, and the world drinks with you; Thirst, and you thirst alone! **1918** C. FETHERSTONHAUGH *After Many Days* 371 On these occasions we always shout for all hands. Let us have some liquor. **1937** W. HATFIELD *I find Aust.* 95 Twelve western cattlemen with money in their pockets can make a two-pub town look quite lively... 'Last man to Dingo Charlie's has to shout for the house!' **1952** A.W. UPFIELD *New Shoe* 40 They drank. Bony would have 'shouted' again but for the quiet air of independence of these men. **1963** D.H.

CRICK *Martin Place* 154 'Oh, hang the expense. I'll shout.' 'Break it down, Paula.' She slapped him playfully. 'Stop arguing.' **1977** V. PRIDDLE *Larry & Jack* 34 George got out a parcel and said to Frank: 'I'd like you to shout for the boys tonight on my behalf.' **1986** *Bulletin* (Sydney) 28 Jan. 46/3 Anyone shooting a hole in one must shout for all players present on the course at that time.

b. *transf.* and *fig.*

1861 H. EARLE *Ups & Downs* 223 The governor shouted heavy, and gave us all a excellent feed. **1908** F. FOX *From Old Dog* 76 He can 'shout' his way to a Premiership, and a title, taking 'shout', in its broadest sense, of providing for this man whisky, for this man flattery, for this man nepotic concessions, for this man afternoon tea. **1925** *Bulletin* (Sydney) 26 Mar. 24/3, I flatly deny the statement . . that when swifts circle high up in a desultory fashion the clouds are about to 'shout' for the thirsty earth.

2. a. *trans.* To buy (a drink or round of drinks); to buy a drink for (a person); also with indirect obj.

1854 *Illustr. Sydney News* 14 Oct. 292/3 The fortunate owners when they bottom on the gutter generally 'shout' champagne for all hands in the immediate neighbourhood. **1855** R. CARBONI *Eureka Stockade* 68 You shouted nobblers round for all hands—that's all right; it's no more than fair and square now for the boys to shout you. **1859** W. BURROWS *Adventures Mounted Trooper* 128 One on being asked to 'shout', naturally inquired, 'What shall I shout?' 'Grog,' is sure to be the reply; and to the amusement and surprise of the bar-keeper, the new comer literally shouts at the top of his voice the word 'Grog!' **1862** H. BROWN *Vic. as I found It* 138 As it was my first appearance on the gold fields, it was my duty to shout noblers all round. **1887** *Illustr. Austral. News* (Melbourne) 25 June (Suppl.) 7/3 Instead of the poet laureate's 'Hands all round', the happy bridegroom always 'shouted drinks all round', *ad lib.* **1898** R. RADCLYFFE *Wealth & Wild Cats* 26 The Captain and Macdonald 'shouted' whiskies at Lees. **1916** J.M. CREED *Recoll. Aust.* 73, I did not think it necessary to insult any elector by supposing it was necessary to shout grog for him in order to secure his vote. **1925** C. LE LIEVRE *Memories Old Police Officer* 12 Boys, I am going to shout any of you who want a drink. **1941** D. O'CALLAGHAN *Long Life Reminisc.* 52 He shouted a case of champagne for all hands. **1956** S. HOPE *Diggers' Paradise* 80 He was also of that species of good Aussie mixers who, if someone 'shouted' a round, would forthwith plank down a handful of silver to indicate payment for the next round before anyone could raise the first glass. **1969** A. GARVE *Boomerang* 54 Come into the bar—I'll shout you a beer. **1977** W. MOORE *Just to Myself* 102 All Merv's mates shouted him at the pub for a week.

b. *transf.* To make (a present), to give (a treat), etc.; to make a present to (someone); also with indirect obj.

1896 *Bulletin* (Sydney) 9 May 3/2 In a Melb. restaurant, the other night, a certain flash young jock condescended to chaff his two middle-aged companions, one of whom had 'shouted' the dinner. **1912** *Ibid.* 26 Dec. 15/4 I'll shout a trip (first-class) for him from Sydney to Narrandera. **1920** *Aussie* (Sydney) Apr. 18/3 Take it from me, it's wiser to wink the glad eye than to shout any bint a meat pie. **1927** *R. Comm. Moving Picture Industry* 841 Once or twice a year I 'shout' the boys of an orphanage to the pictures. **1947** M. MACLEAN *Drummond of Far West* 162 A most hilarious picnic-outing was 'shouted' for all children well enough to go out, by the local taxi-drivers. **1949** R. PARK *Poor Man's Orange* 210 Next year I'm on to a better job down at the factory and I could shout you to a course in typewriting and shorthand. **1959** E. LAMBERT *Glory thrown In* 124 Get some clothes on and I'll shout you some breakfast. **1981** P. RADLEY *Jack Rivers & Me* 137 'I pay my way!' 'You wouldn't shout a moll a packet of Condy's Crystals.'

shouter. One who 'shouts': see SHOUT *v.* 1 a.

1862 C. MUNRO *Fern Vale* I. 50 'A shout', in the parlance of the Australian bush, is an authority or request to the party in waiting in a public-house to supply the bibulous wants of the companions of the shouter, who of course bears the expense. **1864** *Bell's Life in Sydney* 9 Jan. 4/5 Nine times out of ten the individual invited to drink . . has not the slightest wish to do so, but dare not refuse, for he will certainly offend the landlord for 'taking a shingle off his house' and will probably offend the 'shouter'. **1909** *Bulletin* (Sydney) 30 Dec. 14/2 In the Westralian mining towns . . man's class is decided by the number he shouts for, and the J. Woodser is unknown. To shout for the room is common; to shout for the 'house' nothing extraordinary, and if the shouter is 'brassed up' at all, he says: 'Call in them chaps outside.' **1919** A. WRIGHT *Game of Chance* 113 Expressing admiration for the 'shouter'.

shouting, *vbl. n.* The practice of 'shouting': see SHOUT *v.* 1 a. Also *attrib.*

1850 [SEE SHOUT *v.* 1 a.]. **1855** R. CARBONI *Eureka Stockade* 67 Their glory is to stand oceans of grog, joined to their benevolence of 'shouting', for all hands. **1859** F. SINNETT *Acct. 'Rush' Port Curtis* 66 If all the drinkers had been concentrated in one or two crowded places . . the pernicious bibulous rivalry that the practice of 'shouting' engenders would have obtained its full force. **1864** *Bell's Life in Sydney* 9 Jan. 4/5 Of all the folly that has ever beset a community, that of shouting has held the ground the longest, and is the most absurd. **1880** A. SKETCHLEY *Mrs Brown in Sydney* 8 Whoever would think as they was that hignorant as to call standing treat shouting, as if a thing as is mostly done on the quiet without no noise, but of course every think is done the reverse of natur in a place where everyone is upside down. **1892** *Bulletin* (Sydney) 7 May 17/3 He viewed this 'shouting' mania with disgust, As being generosity perverted. **1910** *Huon Times* (Franklin) 9 Mar. 4/3 'If there were less 'shouting' there would be considerably less drinking,' remarked the Premier. **1919** A. WRIGHT *Game of Chance* 69 Showed no inclination to lose sight of him while he held some shouting silver. **1935** J. HAMLET *Salmagundi* 69 The Australian custom of 'treating' or 'shouting' is about due for a right royal roast. **1956** J.T. LANG *I Remember* 195 He would go into the city and collect a few shillings at the *Bulletin* or get an advance from Angus and Robertson against future royalties. He would then forget all about writing, and start shouting for anyone who happened to come along. **1977** H.O. TESHER *Eleven Days* 43 Neither did he know what '*shouting in a school*' meant. The unbreakable custom that if four or five mates grouped together one started to buy all the drinks, but in the circle everyone had to have his turn.

shoveller. Also **shoveler.** [Transf. use of *shoveller* the Northern Hemisphere duck *Anas clypeata*, having a broad shovel-like beak, and recorded as a rare visitor to Aust.] The duck *Anas rhynchotis rhynchotis* of s.w. and e. Aust. incl. Tas.

1845 J. GOULD *Birds of Aust.* (1848) VII. Pl. 13 [The 'Membranaceous Duck'] passes through the air with great quickness, like the Green-necked Duck and Shoveller, with both of which species it is frequently found in company. **1861** 'OLD BUSHMAN' *Bush Wanderings* 82 The *Shoveller* is something like the shoveller at home in size, shape and general appearance. **1898** E.E. MORRIS *Austral Eng.* 417 Shoveller . . the English name for the duck *Spatula clypeata* . . a species also present in Australia. The other Australian species is *Spatula rhynchotis.* **1945** C. BARRETT *Austral. Bird Life* 50 The Australian shoveller, or blue-winged duck (*Spatula rhynchotis*), distinguished by its spoon-shaped beak, sometimes is called the 'stinker'. . . It frequents inland waters—lagoons, swamps, and lakes. **1976** *Reader's Digest Compl. Bk. Austral. Birds* 106 A small bird with a distinctive, big, olive-brown bill, the shoveller has greatly declined in numbers over the last 50 years. **1984** M. BLAKERS et al. *Atlas Austral. Birds* 80 The Shoveler feeds by filtering surface water through its bill, sometimes upending and dredging on the bottom.

shovel-nosed lobster. Any of several marine crustaceans having a flattened appearance and characteristic shovel-shaped ends of the main feelers, incl. the *Moreton Bay bug* (see MORETON BAY) and BALMAIN BUG.

1966 T.C. ROUGHLEY *Fish & Fisheries Aust.* 315 Lobster, shovel-nosed [minimal legal length in inches] 3. **1979** L. MORRISSY *Austral. Crustacean Cookery* 9 The 'northern shovel-nosed lobster' or 'Moreton Bay bug', *Thenus orientalis* . . is considered to have more flavour than the 'southern shovel-nosed lobster' or 'Balmain bug'. **1983** J. JONES *Macquarie Dict. Cookery* 200 *Balmain bug.* An edible crustacean, *Ibacus incisus*, known also as shovel-nosed lobster, and related to the Moreton Bay Bugs of Queensland.

shovel-spear. An Aboriginal weapon: see quot. 1962. Also **shovel-head(ed spear), shovel-nose(d) spear.**

1930 J.S. LITCHFIELD *Far-North Memories* 122 Another kind of blade was made of one flat piece of iron about an inch and a half broad, with its sides and point as sharp as a blackfellow could make them. These were known as 'shovel' spears, and were mostly used for slaying enemies. **1930** E.R. GRIBBLE *Forty Yrs. with Aborigines* 207 One white cow had a broad metal spear-point, called a 'shovel-spear', protruding straight out from her forehead. **1946** W.E. HARNEY *North of 23°* 84 He promptly ordered a ton of shovels to build dams to hold water. These the blackmen used to make shovel-nosed spears to kill the cattle. I believe that is where the name of these things came from. **1955** F. LANE *Patrol to Kimberleys* 132 If some of the blacks take it into their heads to resist arrest, shovel-nosed spears and boomerangs will start flying. **1956** T. RONAN *Moleskin Midas* 209 Cattle which had not fallen to shovel-spear, crocodile, or virulent stock diseases dormant in the Territory buffalo herds . . were being brought back to Queensland. **1960** *N.T. News* (Darwin) 8 Jan. 1/6 However the razor-edged shovel-nose spear sliced the femoral artery and Talkalyiri fell, mortally wounded and bleeding to death. **1962** D. LOCKWOOD *I, Aboriginal* 96 The shovel-nose spear, as its name implies, has a killing-head made of iron. This may be an old horseshoe, a piece of galvanized pipe, or a flat section cut from an abandoned water-tank. In my grandfather's day iron was scarce on the Roper and was highly prized. In his grandfather's day it was unknown. Spears were than made entirely of wood, or with a stone killing-head. **1976** C.D. MILLS *Hobble Chains & Greenhide* 20 I'd got to about fifty yards and I reckoned I would draw a bead on him when a big buck raced up the ant-bed from the back and downed him with a shovel-head (shovel-headed spear).

show, *n.*[1] [U.S.: see OED(S *sb.*[1] 3 c.]

a. An opportunity for doing something; a chance.

1876 *Austral. Town & Country Jrnl.* (Sydney) Nov. 11 782/2 As he's a gentleman, he's bound to give you a show. **1884** *Austral. Tit-Bits* (Sydney) 17 July 5/2 The perambulator had no show, but it died game. When I came out, the ram had a portion of the body against a wall, and was butting it to flinders. **1891** *Braidwood Dispatch* 20 June 4/6 Trust a Chinky for not making himself at home wherever he is. Why darn me, if these fellows got a show they'd have us out o' the colony bag and baggage. Look at their own rabbit warren. **1910** *Huon Times* (Franklin) 28 Dec. 4/4 McLean said he had no money and added, 'Give us a show; my wife is ill and I am anxious about her.' **1950** J. MORRISON *Port of Call* 204 'I thought work was scarce. . . ' 'But I got the drum there'll be a fair bit in tomorrow. You'd have a show for a few days, anyhow.' **1959** D. NILAND *Gold in Streets* 181 Goo' fight, Johnny. I didn't have a show.

b. In the collocation **fair show:** see FAIR *a.*[1] 1.

show, *n.*[2] [Transf. use of *show* an indication of the presence of the mineral sought: see OED(S *sb.*[1] 5 c.] A mine.

1898 E. DYSON *Below & on Top* 130 Jump *this* show, Humpy! Why there is not gold enough in a mile of it to buy a peanut. **1900** *North-Western Advocate* (Devonport) 2 May 3/4 The applicants for tin ground at the 50-Mile are sanguine of getting their show floated at an early date. **1915** N. DUNCAN *Austral. Byways* 60 The Golden Mile and its lesser neighbors of Kalgoorlie—the big shows, as distinguished from the individual enterprises scattered broadcast over the country, which are called little shows. **1928** R.M. MACDONALD *Opals & Gold* 55 Went north to work some gold 'show' he knew. **1940** E. HILL *Great Austral. Loneliness* (ed. 2) 258 They came from . . little 'shows' across the Queensland border, men who knew all about opal and men who had never seen it. **1950** G.S. CASEY *City of Men* 278 Half the shows couldn't exist in spite of high prices if they had to rely on horses. **1962** *N.T. News* (Darwin) 28 Apr. 3/1 He had reached a stage on 'a tin show' near Hayes Creek where some Government assistance would mean real development. **1973** C.E. GOODE *Stories Strange Places* 142 George said we'd run in and have a look at an old show he had worked on. It was the famous Westralia Mine. **1978** D. STUART *Wedgetail View* 42 'Yes, you'll get a job in the Bar, no trouble now that a company's taken over the Comet.' 'She's a good show, is she? A goer?'

shower. [Used elsewhere but recorded earliest in Aust.] In the phr. **I (he, they,** etc.) **didn't come**

down in the last shower, an indication that one is not without experience.

[**1906** J. FURPHY *Rigby's Romance* (1946) 256 *He* didn't come down with the las' rain. Pity that sort o' bloke ever dies.] **1944** L. GLASSOP *We were Rats* 51 'Listen, Mr Wilkerson', I says, 'I'm awake-up, I am. Ya doan need ter come that stuff with me. I didden come down in the last shower.' **1950** F.J. HARDY *Power without Glory* 259 'It's no use lying to me, Arty,' John West said. 'I didn't come down in the last shower.' **1971** B. VERNON *Big Day at Bellbird* 135, I didn't come down in the last shower, and neither did you. **1984** *Weekend Austral. Mag.* (Sydney) 30 June 12/6 An irate theatregoer says its about time they stopped treating patrons as though they had come down in the last shower, especially when they are being charged $25 for the privilege. This week he went to hear Shirley Bassey and had to spend the first hour listening to a ventriloquist.

show pony. One who gives more attention to appearances than to performance.

1964 J. POLLARD *High Mark* 19 Don't become one of those football 'show ponies' who wear more bandages than some of those race horses we see. **1970** R. BEILBY *No Medals for Aphrodite* 15 Turk was a show-pony, one of those men whose every action and attitude had an unconscious grace. **1977** —— *Gunner* 160 He was a good bloke, a bit of a show pony but he was always willing. **1982** *Austral.* (Sydney) 7 Aug. 44/3 Admirers of Carlton's jack-in-the-box half-forward flanker, Peter Bosustow, call him 'Mr Magic' and 'Mr Wonderful'. His detractors call him a mug lair and a show pony. **1985** *Bulletin* (Sydney) 10 Dec. 25/3 He may be an extrovert but he's not a show pony.

shrewdie. Also **shrewdy.** [f. *shrewd* + -Y; used elsewhere but recorded earliest in Aust.]

1. A shrewd or cunning person.

1904 *Truth* (Sydney) 17 July 10/7 He was regarded as what the Sydney boys of the present would call a 'shrewdie'. **1917** C. DREW *Reminisc. D. Gilbert* 34 Hazards and 'two-up' were the usual forms of gambling in between race meetings, and the shrewdies had brought these games down to a science. **1929** 'F. BLAIR' *Digger Sea-Mates* 254 'You're one of the 'shrewdies', Lockie, ain't you?' 'You'll need to know a lot', spoke up Robertson, 'before you'll be a 'shrewdy' in old London yonder.' **1935** H.H. PARRY *Girl of West* 12 The night . . that he took the shrewdies down. **1944** A. MARSHALL *These are my People* 169 A shrewdie, this bloke, eh! **1958** G. CASEY *Snowball* 19 The young shrewdies sometimes seemed to have an uncanny knack of summing certain things up. **1968** W.N. SCOTT *Some People* 118 There was a mob of shrewdies living up Nerang Way. **1985** *Bulletin* (Sydney) 23 July 92/3 The shrewdies in the market recognised the potential significance of the news and smartly marked up the values of the two listed companies involved.

2. A crafty scheme.

1960 J. WYNNUM *Sailor Blushed* (1962) 120 I'll have a gander at that as soon as I'm free, and if I think you're trying to pull a shrewdie, you'll finish up doing jankers.

shrike. [Transf. use of *shrike* a bird of the fam. Laniidae.] Used *attrib.* in the names of birds: **shrike-robin,** any of several greyish or grey and yellow robins of the genera *Eopsaltria* and *Tregellasia* of mainland Aust. (see *white-breasted robin* WHITE *a.*[2] 1 b., *yellow robin* YELLOW 1); **-thrush,** any of the several birds of the genus *Colluricincla* of all States and the New Guinea region, having a melodious song, esp. the widespread *grey thrush* (see GREY *a.*); see also THRUSH; **- tit,** the bird *Falcunculus frontatus* of e., s.w., and n. mainland Aust., having a black and white striped head and a heavy, hooked bill; *yellow-bellied shrike-tit*, see YELLOW 1.

1895 *Rep. Sixth Meeting Australasian Assoc. Advancement of Science, Brisbane* 447 By retaining the term 'Robin' for the best known member of the group (*Petroica*), and applying a qualifying noun to the allied genera, such titles as . . **Shrike-robin** were easily evolved. **1929** A.H. CHISHOLM *Birds & Green Places* 37 The lichen-decked cups of the spectacled flycatcher and the shrike-robins. **1942** C. BARRETT *From Bush Hut* 74 Three kinds of robins frequent the garden: the scarlet-breasted species, the flame robin, and 'Yellow Bob', the shrike-robin. **1896** *Melburnian* 28 Aug. 54 The spotted thrush of England gives forth . . his full and varied notes; notes which no Australian bird can challenge, not even the **shrike-thrush** on the hill side, piping hard to rival his song every bright spring morning. **1907** *Emu* VII. 97 A fine Shrike-Thrush (*Collyriocincla rectirostris*) flew from almost under our feet. **1929** A.H. CHISHOLM *Birds & Green Places* 32 But when thinking of jungle choristers generally I think chiefly of scrub-wrens, shrike-thrushes [etc.]. **1945** C. BARRETT *Austral. Bird Life* 179 Several of the shrike-thrushes are found in the tropical north. **1965** *Austral. Encycl.* VIII. 494 Other Australian birds known as thrushes, but more correctly shrike-thrushes, are members of the genus *Colluricincla*. These comprise seven species of thrush-like insectivorous birds which are in general grey or brown. **1984** SIMPSON & DAY *Birds of Aust.* 323 Whistlers differ most obviously from shrike-thrushes in their often striking sexual dimorphism. **1890** *Act* (Vic.) 54 Vict. no. 1095 3rd Sched., **Shrike-tit** . . from the first day of August to the twentieth day of December next following in each year. **1911** A. MACK *Bush Days* 13 A shrike-tit came, dressed in his party clothes, and . . his bright yellow vest and black and white-striped head lent quite an air to the scene. **1929** A.H. CHISHOLM *Birds & Green Places* 209 A note which sounded very like the monotone of the pretty shrike-tit. **1945** C. BARRETT *Austral. Bird Life* 176 The large-headed, strong-billed shrike-tits are sprightly birds, peculiar to Australia. **1980** L. FULLER *Wollongong's Native Trees* 48 Shrike-tits have a powerful short beak with which they prise off pieces of bark to reveal the insects underneath.

sh'touse, var. SHOUSE.

shycer, var. SHICER.

shypoo, /ʃaɪ'pu/, *n.* and *a.* Chiefly *W.A.* Also **shipoo.** [Of unknown origin; but see sense 2, quot. 1962.]

A. *n.*

1. Inferior alcoholic liquor, esp. beer.

1897 *Bulletin* (Sydney) 25 Sept. 3/2 And he paid for the shypoo With the crispy notes and new. **1902** *Truth* (Sydney) 13 Apr. 1/3 Some of the Sydney shy-poo, or tangle, is painted water. **1908** *Ibid.* 22 Mar. 1/3 Western Australian liquor is called 'Shypoo', and is shy, poo stuff at best. **1916** *Ibid.* 29 Oct. 5/1 (*heading*) Selling of sly shypoo. **1933** W.L. OWEN *Cossack Gold* 32 Colonial ale was not on the market then; although some brews of very poor quality were being made in Perth. The stuff was called 'shypoo'. **1954** N. BARTLETT *Pearl Seekers* 109 You could get drunk, at Cossack's other pub, on Colonial ale or 'shypoo' at sixpence the quart. **1962** MARSHALL & DRYSDALE *Journey among Men* 160 Men in cotton shirts and corduroys met there to buy provisions and to 'blue' their cheques on fiery spirits or *shypoo*, as Colonial beer was called.

2. An (unlicensed) establishment which sells such liquor. Usu. in Comb. as **shypoo house, joint, shop,** etc.

1903 MARSHALL & DRYSDALE *Battling for Gold* 25 Despite the fact that all drinks were 1s. each, all the hotels, as well as the 'shypoo' shops (unlicensed groggeries) were doing splendid business. **1914** *Truth* (Sydney) 8 Nov. 1/3 Some of Sydney's flash shypoo pubs. **1936** H. DRAKE-BROCKMAN *Sheba Lane* 237 How about managing that shipoo for me? **1946** K.S. PRICHARD *Roaring Nineties* 43 They flocked to the shypoo shops and shanties to slake their thirst with the beer that cost no more than water. **1947** F. CLUNE *Roaming around Aust.* 115 Along the beach were sly-grog shops—which are called 'shypoo joints' in the West. **1962** T. RONAN *Deep of Sky* 218 It ran to two pubs and a hostelry named the Bull and Bush Inn, the licensee of which was restricted to the sale of beer and wine. Locally this was known as the 'Shypoo Shop'. I'm not sure of the derivation of 'Shypoo'. I think it is bastard Chinese for soft drink. To the sturdy second wave of pioneers of West Kimberley, beer and wine were soft drinks. **1964** *N. Austral. Monthly* Aug. 22 Derby. . . There was also a 'shypoo' shop there (soft drinks). **1981** H.C. MILLS *No Regrets* 59 There were quite a number of 'sly grog' shops or 'shypoo' shops as they were known locally.

B. *adj.* Inferior.

1902 *Truth* (Sydney) 3 Aug. 7/1 He was a solicitor of the 'shypoo' sort—that is, a lawyer who had few, if any, clients, and who lived 'on his wits'. **1907** M. CANNON *That Damned Democrat* (1981) 91 Now another attempt is to be made to still further gull the public, and get them into what is known, by mining men, at any rate, to be 'shypoo shows'. **1952** C. SIMPSON *Come away, Pearler* 230 There's half a dozen . . decided the beer at the Dampo wasn't such shypoo stuff after all, the week after she arrived.

shyster. Alteration of SHICER. Also **shyster mine.**

1910 L. ESSON *Woman Tamer* (1976) 71 We're all thieves. . . One bloke, he says, does the trick with a silk hat on the Stock Exchange, and a shyster mine. We do it with a jemmy. **1941** S.J. BAKER *Pop. Dict. Austral. Slang* 66 *Shyster*, a worthless mine.

sickie. [f. *sick(-leave* + -Y.]

1. A day's sick leave; esp. as taken without sufficient medical reason. Also *attrib.*

1953 T.A.G. HUNGERFORD *Riverslake* 197 Why don't you go back to bed and have a sickie? **1961** *Bulletin* (Sydney) 7 Oct. 20/2 They allow new restrictive practices to grow up and curry favor . . by extending meal-hours or smoko-breaks, by tolerating absenteeism and actively encouraging 'sickies' and overtime rackets. **1962** *Ibid.* 3 Mar. 13 (*caption*), I don't feel a bit like work today. . . I think I'll take a sickie. **1966** *Kings Cross Whisper* (Sydney) May 2/3 Will prescribe 'sickie' certificates at the usual rates of reward. **1971** J. O'GRADY *Aussie Etiket* 37 The next day, hungover because of Dave's funeral, everybody 'takes a sickie'. **1981** *Woman's Day* (Sydney) 19 Aug. 45/1 'The great Australian sickie'—that casual absence taken by so many employees as unauthorised, irregular, paid extra holidays—is growing at an alarming rate and proving far more devastating and costly to industry than strikes. **1982** *Bulletin* (Sydney) 24 Aug. 40/1 The elimination of another racket involving 'sickies' at Williamstown naval dockyard alone will save $200,000 a year. **1984** *N.T. News* (Darwin) 9 Nov. 7/1 A first-come first-served basis . . excludes working people being present. I considered a 'sickie' but a friend volunteered to take an extended smoko—something my position prohibited. **1985** *Canberra Times* 6 Dec. 1/5 It's probably an Australian disease to take sickies. . . Some people treat it like an entitlement.

2. *transf.* A sick person or animal.

1968 G. MILL *Nobody dies but Me* 138 There were two sickies in the waiting room when I barged in. **1977** C. MCCULLOUGH *Thorn Birds* 400 The bunnies have died in millions. . . You'll sometimes see a few sickies around with huge lumps all over their faces.

side, *n.*[1]

1. Used as an abbrev. for (a specified) side of a natural barrier or border; orig. of New South Wales from a South Australian perspective. See also OTHER SIDE, *Sydney-side* SYDNEY 1, TOTHER SIDE.

1846 [see *Sydney-side* SYDNEY 1]. **1847** G.F. ANGAS *Savage Life & Scenes* I. 167 This was one of the sheep stations of Messrs. Arthur, who had penetrated into this charming country from the New South Wales side, and had brought several of their flocks for the purpose of squatting upon these new pastures. **1861** 'OLD BUSHMAN' *Bush Wanderings* 109 A rare and uncertain visitant to our district . . is . . the common quail on the Adelaide side. **1881** T. BASTARD *Autobiogr. 'Cockney Tom'* 24 Try my luck at gold-digging on the Melbourne side. **1895** J. KIRBY *Old Times in Bush* 220 They did not start bushranging in this colony, but deferred operations until they reached the New South Wales side. **1908** *Bulletin* (Sydney) 27 Feb. 14/3 A youngster on the Soustralian side . . was caught in a barbed-wire fence. **1915** W.J. WYE *Souvenirs Sunny South* 61 We learn that Andy Brady wandered to the Queensland side. **1977** D. WHITINGTON *Strive to be Fair* 28 He'd rung some sheds of larger size out on the Queensland side.

2. *transf.* [Prob. an independent development from sense 1, but see OED *sb.*[1] 15 b.] A (specified) district or region.

1892 N. BARTLEY *Opals & Agates* 105, I soon met Matthew Goggs (also well heard of on the Murrumbidgee side). **1898** *Bulletin* (Sydney) 17 Dec. 14/3 Never heard of 'Jack the Axeman', Over on the Lachlan-side? **1900** *Ibid.* 28 July 26/1 The losses on the Barcoo side have not been so great. **1903** *Ibid.* 4 Apr. 3/2 For I have camped by Goulburn side, Right through the summer season. **1903** J. FURPHY *Such is Life* 188 Daughter of old Walsh, storekeeper at Moogoojinna, on the Deniliquin side. **1906** *Bulletin* (Sydney) 29 Nov. 14/1 On Kurnel side the land is more exposed. **1917** *Truth* (Sydney) 21 Jan. 11/7 I've been shearing on the Goulburn side, I've shorn at Douglas Park. *c* **1918** R. MCJANNETT *Saltbush Jim*

V.C. 3 He lived far out on the Western Plain on the Never-Never side. **1956** T. RONAN *Moleskin Midas* 77 With his beefhouse completed, he got himself a killer from the Twin Hills side. **1954** —— *Vision Splendid* 271, I ain't even a Queenslander. . . I come from the Murray side.

Hence **sider** *n.*, an inhabitant of a (specified) district.

1865 [see *Sydney sider* SYDNEY 1]. **1904** *Bulletin* (Sydney) 15 Dec. 18/2 The Murray-siders are then giving up the ghost. **1907** *Truth* (Sydney) 21 Apr. 11/6 A fellow Lachlan sider . . accompanied him to Sydney. **1941** *Bulletin* (Sydney) 15 Oct. 15/3 An Oodnadatta-sider, Whacker came down to Marree (S.A.).

side, *n.*[2] *Two-up.*

1. The body of players as distinct from the SPINNER and *ring-keeper* (see RING *n.*[2] 2). Esp. in the phr. **on the side**: see *side bet* below.

1918 C.E.W. BEAN Diary 8 May 45 Franc wanted . . Heads one Any on the side Heads ten. Heads forty, forty on the nut. **1946** *Austral. New Writing* 36 We're right. Set 'em between yourselves. Get set on the side. **1953** T.A.G. HUNGERFORD *Riverslake* 129 'All right, gents', he called out, 'there's one hundred and forty quid in the guts—get it set before you bet on the side.'

2. Special Comb. **side bet,** a wager laid by a player with another player rather than with the spinner; so **side bettor.**

1931 O. WALTERS *Shrapnel Green* 26 The centre was set, the side-bets on, and Mick was ready to toss. **1946** *Austral. New Writing* 36 Tail bettors toss in their money and soon the pound is covered. Again the side bettors 'get set'. **1977** R. BEILBY *Gunner* 299 With the centre set the ringie called for the side bets. **1983** HIBBERD & HUTCHINSON *Barracker's Bible* 185 *Side bet*, a wager between spectators in two up, not the main bet. . . A bet between two punters who have already got set with a bookie. 'Like a sidey on what'll come last?'

side board. A shearing shed in which the shearing is done along the two long sides rather than in the centre. Also **side board shed.** See BOARD 1.

1893 'TIMES SPECIAL CORRESPONDENT' *Lett. from Qld.* 81 A shearing shed in full swing is a striking sight. There are two kinds, known respectively as 'central boards' and 'side boards'. In the one the shearing is done in the middle and the sheep penned all round. In the other the sheep are penned in the middle and the shearing is done upon the sides. **1979** HARMSWORTH & DAY *Wool & Mohair* 141 Side board sheds are unsatisfactory because, when sheep are shorn, they must either be dragged cross the board or allowed to walk across at a time when the fleece may still be on the board.

side verandah: see VERANDAH.

siding. Alteration of 'sideling', a slope or declivity.

1852 *Hobarton Guardian* 26 May 4/1 No *culverts* on the 'sidings' of the hills along which the roads passed. **1893** *Bulletin* (Sydney) 9 Sept. 19/2 He cleared another piece of ground on the 'siding' and sowed more wheat. **1896** *Ibid.* 9 May 27/3 Seen along the 'siding', the humpy seemed to be leaning well into the hillside. **1900** H. LAWSON *Verses Pop. & Humorous* 42 Swift scramble up the siding where teams climb inch by inch; Pause, bird-like, on the summit—then breakneck down the pinch. **1913** —— *Triangles of Life* 179 There were three huts on the siding of a spur of the ridge. **1931** F.D. DAVISON *Man-Shy* (1962) 126 On a certain morning . . the scrubbers were grazing along an ironbark siding.

sight. *Mining.* In the phr. **in sight**: (of a mineral) potentially able to be mined.

1845 *S. Austral. Register* (Adelaide) 19 Nov. 2/5 A gentleman who paid a visit to the Burra Burra Mines found 300 tons lying at the mine ready for sending away—and large masses of ore 'in sight' equal to the production of 3000 tons more. **1850** *Ibid.* 23 Nov. 2/2 John Lambs' pitch is looking very kindly in sight. **1911** E.D. CLELAND *W. Austral. Mining Practice* 15 Lessen the apparent amount of ore 'in sight' between any two levels.

silent cop. See quot. 1934.

1934 T. WOOD *Cobbers* 122 A circle in the middle of cross-roads . . round which all traffic changing direction must swing; a round yellow blob, known here as the Silent Cop, or the Poached Egg. **1944** *Soldier* (Julia Creek) Jan. 4 Slow down at Postoffice (mind the silent-cop). **1948** R. RAVEN-HART *Canoe in Aust.* 187 Motorists often ignore 'Silent cops' at corners, yellow iron domes with white surrounds, 'poached eggs', typically Australian neat slang. **1969** E. WALLER *And there's Opal* 41 Look, if you find a hill higher than a 'silent cop', you'll have the Shire people out and naming it Mount Everest.

silkwood. Any of several trees, esp. the rainforest tree *Flindersia pimenteliana* (fam. Rutaceae) of n.e. Qld. and New Guinea; the wood of these trees.

1909 F.M. BAILEY *Comprehensive Catal. Qld. Plants* (ed. 2) 91 Flindersia Chatawaiana . . has . . been called 'Silkwood'. **1938** F. CLUNE *Free & Easy Land* 33 The principal timber is silk-wood, up to a hundred feet high, with foliage only near top. **1944** J. DEVANNY *By Tropic Sea & Jungle* 128 Silkwood . . is marked and shines like watered ribbon. **1986** *Herald* (Melbourne) 2 May (Suppl.) 5/1 Despite the use of timbers such as silkwood . . the cost of each dinghy is around $350 in materials.

silky heads. A tussocky perennial grass of the genus *Cymbopogon* (fam. Poaceae), esp. the aromatic *C. obtectus* of inland mainland Aust.

1895 F. TURNER *Austral. Grasses* I. 4 *Andropogon bombycinus* . . (Referring to the inflorescence resembling masses of silk.) 'Silky Heads'. **1917** *Bulletin* (Sydney) 1 Feb. 22/2 The king Blue grasses are *Andropogon sericeus*, considered by some as the boss indigenous tucker of Queensland . . and *Androp. bombycinus*, or silky heads. **1966** A. MORRIS *Plantlife W. Darling* 7 Grasses which favour hilly situations are Andropogon bombysinus [*sic*] . . (Silky Heads). **1981** J.A. BAINES *Austral. Plant Genera* 113 C[*ymbopogon*] *obtectus*, silky-heads, all mainland States, but extremely rare in V[ictoria].

silky oak. Any of many trees of the fam. Proteaceae, usu. rainforest species of n. and e. Aust. yielding an oak-like timber of silky texture; esp. the tall, commonly cultivated *Grevillea robusta* of n.e. N.S.W. and s.e. Qld., having feathery foliage and golden orange flowers, and *Cardwellia sublimis* of n.e. Qld., having pinnate leaves and a large, woody fruit; the wood of these trees. Formerly also **silk oak.**

1836 J. BACKHOUSE *Narr. Visit Austral. Colonies* (1843) 365 The Silk Oak, *Grevillea robusta*, also forms a large tree. **1861** J.D. LANG *Qld., Aust.* 175 *Silk-Oak* . . is well adapted for the sheathing of vessels. **1875** CAMPBELL & WILKS *Early Settlement Qld.* 17 My greatest difficulty . . was to get suitable casks. . . I finally fixed upon the timber known as silky oak and sally, both of which I found to answer admirably. **1882** A.J. BOYD *Old Colonials* 25 The scrubs were full of hickory, while silky oak was getting scarce. **1904** J.H. MAIDEN *Notes on Commercial Timbers N.S.W.* 25 Silky oak (*Grevillea robusta* . . and *Orites excelsa*) . . is light in colour. **1938** C.T. WHITE *Princ. Bot. Qld. Farmers* 158 To the Queenslander, the main interest in *Proteaceae* arises in the beauty and value of the timbers, several of which are cut and sold indiscriminately under the name of Silky Oak. In previous years the familiar *Grevillea robusta* provided all the Silky Oak of the trade, but now practically all comes from various North Queensland trees—mostly *Cardwellia sublimis.* **1952** A.W. UPFIELD *New Shoe* 47, I made a Mary a glory box outa silky oak from Queensland. **1968** L. BRADEN *Bullockies* 79 In my days silky oak was felled and burnt, or split up for palings. **1981** E. POTTER *Scone I Remember* 52 Fine specimens of the giant silky oak, carrying in October each year a magnificent display of richly-coloured flowers, shaped as all grevillea flowers are, but graded from red through dark brown to brilliant orange, filled with honey.

silver, *a.*

1. Used as a distinguishing epithet in the names of flora and fauna: **silver ash,** any of several rainforest trees of the genus *Flindersia* (fam. Rutaceae) yielding a silvery, ash-like wood, incl. *F. bourjotiana* of n.e. Qld.; the wood of the tree; **banksia,** the shrub or tree *Banksia marginata* (fam. Proteaceae) of s.e. Aust. incl. Tas., having leaves which are silvery-white underneath; **belly,** any of many small marine fish, esp. those of the fam. Gerreidae (also *silver biddy*), incl. the common *Gerres ovatus*; **biddy,** a small fish of the fam. Gerreidae (see *silver belly*); **bream,** any of several fish, esp. *Acanthopagrus butcheri* (see *black bream* BLACK *a.*[2] 1 b.); **dory,** the marine fish *Cyttus australis* of s. Aust.; **eel,** any of several silvery eels incl. *Muraenesox cinereus* and *Anguilla australis*; **-eye,** a small bird of the genus *Zosterops* of Aust. and elsewhere, having a conspicuous white eye-ring, esp. the common widespread *Z. lateralis*; *white-eye*, see WHITE *a.*[2] 1 b.; **fish,** any of several silvery fish, esp. of the fam. Atherinidae, having a silvery band along the sides; **grass,** any of several annual or perennial grasses (fam. Poaceae) incl. the native *Aristida contorta* (see *mulga grass* MULGA *n.*[1] 3), and the introduced European *Vulpia bromoides*; **gull,** the predom. white and grey gull *Larus novaehollandiae* of coastal and inland waters of all States, and elsewhere; **-leaf** (or **-leaved**) **box,** the small tree *Eucalyptus pruinosa* (fam. Myrtaceae) of n. Aust.; **-leaved (-leaf, -leafed) ironbark,** the small to medium tree *Eucalyptus melanophloia* (fam. Myrtaceae) of Qld. and n. N.S.W., having bluish-grey foliage; **perch,** any of several fish, esp. the fresh-water *Bidyanus bidyanus*; see also GRUNTER; **wattle,** any of several shrubs or trees of the genus *Acacia* (fam. Mimosaceae), esp. *A. dealbata* of N.S.W., Vic., and Tas., and naturalized in S.A., usu. having silvery foliage; the wood of the tree.

1927 *Bulletin* (Sydney) 3 Nov. 27/4 Bumpy ash is . . known also as cudgerie, mountain ash and **silver ash. 1956** A.C.C. LOCK *Tropical Tapestry* 45 Different species of fern leaves waved against the background of silver ash. **1970** W.D. FRANCIS *Austral. Rain-Forest Trees* (ed. 3) 429 *Flindersia pubescens* . . Northern Silver Ash. . . Swain includes this species with *F. schottiana* and *F. bourjotiana* under the common name of Silver Ash on account of the similar qualities and applications of the timbers of the three species. The timbers are described by him as firm, tough, strong and usually lustrous white, straight and open grained. **1984** B. DIXON *Searching for Aboriginal Lang.* 75, I was able to make out the names of individual trees, after a few repetitions . . *girruwun* 'silver ash' [etc.]. **1986** *Age* (Melbourne) 29 Apr. 25/4 The chest is made from black bean with silver ash drawers and fragrant Lebanon cedar drawer bottoms. **1923** *Census Plants Vic.* (Field Naturalists' Club Vic.) 24 *Banksia marginata* . . **Silver Banksia. 1935** *Honey Flora Vic.* (Vic. Dept. Agric.) (rev. ed.) 93 In many localities where the Silver Banksia was formerly plentiful, it is now almost extinct. The former trees have died of old age, or have been cut down in drought seasons. **1986** *Canberra Times* 19 Mar. 26/4 B[*anksia*] *canei* somewhat resembles the silver banksia, *B. marginata*. **1882** J.E. TENISON-WOODS *Fish & Fisheries N.S.W.* 44 It is necessary to cook the **silver-belly,** as it is often called, perfectly fresh . . otherwise . . it is flavourless, flabby, and soft. **1906** D.G. STEAD *Fishes of Aust.* 117 A number of species of the Silverbelly family are found in Australian waters and they are chiefly of small size. The principal one is the pretty little common Silverbelly (*Xystaema ovatum*). **1924** LORD & SCOTT *Synopsis Vertebrate Animals Tas.* 49 Family Atherinidae (Silver Fish or Hardyheads). These small fish, known to the Tasmanian fishermen as Silver Bellies, are plentiful in certain localities. **1974** T.D. SCOTT et al. *Marine & Freshwater Fishes S.A.* 222 Family Gerridae. The fishes of this family are known generally as Silverbellies. **1906** D.G. STEAD *Fishes of Aust.* 118 Other names by which it [*sc.* the common Silverbelly] is sometimes known are: 'Silver Bream' and '**Silver-Biddy**'. **1978** K. MCARTHUR *Pumicestone Passage* 82 The large quantities of apparent bream which are periodically reported as seen drifting away dead from professionals' nets are in fact silver biddies (*Gerres ovatus*), which may be useful for bait, but otherwise of no interest to fishermen. **1870** E.B. KENNEDY *Four Yrs. in Qld.* 123 There are plenty of fish in all the lagoons and rivers; black bream, **silver bream. 1906** D.G. STEAD *Fishes of Aust.* 123 The Silver Perch [*sc. Terapon ellipticus*] . . is familiarly-known as 'Grunter'. . . It is also known as . . 'Silver Bream'. **1944** J. DEVANNY *By Tropic Sea & Jungle* 5 Among the summer season fish there are four varieties of bream—silver, black, red and thick-lip. **1965** *Austral. Encycl.* II. 105 Silver bream that [name] given in South Australia and Victoria to *Usacaranx georgianus*, one of the trevallies. **1983** *Nat. Times* (Sydney) 25 Mar. 27/2 Twenty-five boxes of silver bream are unloaded within minutes. **1906** D.G. STEAD *Fishes of Aust.* 176 The **Silver Dory** (*Cyttus australis*) . . is of a beautiful uniform silvery appearance (though more roseate when first captured). **1951** T.C. ROUGHLEY *Fish & Fisheries Aust.* 28 There are two other dories occasionally taken by trawlers on the New South Wales coast—

the silver dory (*Cyttus australis*), which grows to a length of about 16 inches, and the mirror dory. **1974** T.D. Scott et al. *Marine & Freshwater Fishes S.A.* 113 The Silver Dory is the commonest of the South Australian Dories. . . The flesh is excellent eating. **1871** *Austral. Town & Country Jrnl.* (Sydney) 21 June 88/3 A small yellow-backed variety with a shining white belly forming what are denominated '**silver-eels**' abound in waterholes. **1882** J.E. Tenison-Woods *Fish & Fisheries N.S.W.* 88 The 'sea eel', or 'silver eel' (*Muraenesox bagio*), a very fine fish, and never common. . . The silver eel is not uncommon in the Hunter River and is caught by night-lines just in the same manner as the ordinary freshwater kinds. **1906** D.G. Stead *Fishes of Aust.* 48 The Silver Eel . . reaches a length of at least 5 feet. It is really a most beautiful-looking fish. **1980** R.M. McDowall *Freshwater Fishes S.-E. Aust.* 46 Shortfinned eel. . . Other names: Common: Silver eel. **1862** E. Ward *Vineyards & Orchards S.A.* 40 A border of trees of various kinds which had been planted on the east of one vineyard were grubbed up two years ago, because they afforded a shelter to the '**Silver-eye**', a bird very destructive to vines. **1891** E.H. Hallack *W.A. & Yilgarn Goldfields* 12 'Sparrows?' I asked, and he said, 'No; silver-eyes.' **1919** C.A. Bernays *Qld. Politics during Sixty Yrs.* 167 As a boy a very favourite and fascinating Saturday occupation was the trapping of 'silver-eyes'. **1927** J. Pollard *Rose of Bushlands* 76 She saw several silver-eyes, tiny green birds with pale yellow breasts and eyes ringed with whitish down. **1958** *Bulletin* (Sydney) 15 Jan. 18/1 The two types of silvereye in W.A.—the western or greenie, and the yellow—provide a striking example of the way some birds will stick to certain habitats. **1984** *Winestate* Mar. 58/3 Parrots and Silver Eyes destroyed about two-thirds of the Traminer crop. **1832** F. Moore *Diary Ten Yrs. W.A.* 14 Sept. (1884) 136 The **silver fish** (perch), and the guard fish, sometimes come up the river. **1839** J. Stephens *Land of Promise* 61 The silver fish, so called from its colour and glistening appearance, is about eighteen inches long, and without scales. **1885** *Adelaide Observer* 18 Apr. 29/2 The fish known to Port Adelaide fishermen as the 'silver fish', and sometimes as the trumpeter. **1951** T.C. Roughley *Fish & Fisheries Aust.* 57 Silver Trevally (White trevally . . silver fish [etc.]). **1974** T.D. Scott et al. *Marine & Freshwater Fishes S.A.* 155 Silver Fish. *Taeniomembras tamarensis*. . . Colour greenish above, white below. . . A broad silvery longitudinal band along the middle of the sides. **1848** W. Archer Diary 18 Feb., Preparing for burning off the **silver grass** &c. on lower Stony Pt. **1897** L. Lindley-Cowen *W. Austral. Settler's Guide* 79 The chief pasture plants are corkscrew and silver grass, which are very fattening. **1914** Austral. Archives CRS A3 14/2576, It is country that would impress me of being very bare in a dry time where the silver grass grows on the stony country. **1923** E. Breakwell *Grasses & Fodder Plants N.S.W.* 153 Rat's Tail or Silver Grass (*Festuca bromoides*) . . is an extremely common grass on the tablelands, slopes and semi-arid interior of New South Wales during the spring months. It is an introduced, slender, tufted annual. **1948** C.P. Mountford *Brown Men & Red Sand* 11 The country was flatter, with more open valleys, covered thickly with silver, or mulga grass (*Anthistiria* sp.), which at that time of year was dead and bleached a silvery white. **1953** K.E.C. Graves *Tasmanian Pastoral* 78 Native silver-grass (*Danthonia*), like fine hair, meagre of growth but nutritious, keeping the sheep active and healthy enough when subsisting on it to produce the best wool in the world. **1980** G.R. Cochrane et al. *Flowers & Plants Vic. & Tas.* (rev. ed.) 65 (*caption*) Hairy Spinifex or Silver Grass. **1848** J. Gould *Birds of Aust.* VII. Pl. 20, *Xema jamesonii* . . **Silver Gull.** **1887** *Illustr. Austral. News* (Melbourne) 21 Dec. 218/2 Some of the party went on to the Ettrick River, and on the way found the eggs of the . . silver gull and hooded dottrell. **1901** *Emu* I. 135 Silver Gulls (*Larus novae-hollandiae*)—These were fairly plentiful along all the rivers. **1936** T.C. Roughley *Wonders Great Barrier Reef* 213 On every island silver gulls are seen flying over or resting on the water. This handsome bird feeds on small fish and is an effective scavenger along the shore-line. **1978** *Ecos* xvii. 15/1 Silver gulls on their way to and from the dump used to fly through the runway approaches. **1985** *Mercury* (Hobart) 24 Aug. 16/2 By far the most prominent gull in Australia is the Silver Gull. And it's not uncommon or strange for the Silver Gull to live and breed inland as long as there is a water environment. **1884** [**silver-leaf box**] E. Palmer *Notes Austral. Tribes* 47 *Eucalyptus pruinosa*. . . Native name on Cloncurry *Kullingal*. Silver-leaved box, 20 feet high, stunted and crooked growth. **1920** J.N. MacIntyre *White Aust.* 77 Level country covered with stunted ti-tree scrub, stunted wattle and silver-leaf box. **1956** A.C.C. Lock *Tropical Tapestry* 139 The timber dotting the countryside had been silver-leaf box. **1983** R.J. Petheram *Plants Kimberley Region W.A.* 445 *Eucalyptus pruinosa* Silver Box, Silver-leaf Box. . . A small straggly tree with blue-grey foliage. **1844** L. Leichhardt *Jrnl. Overland Exped. Aust.* 5 Nov. (1847) 30 Extensive flooded gum-flats and ridges, clothed with a forest of **silver-leaved Ironbark.** **1849** *N.S.W. Sporting Mag.* (Sydney) 1 Jan. 162 It consisted of alternate downs and open forest, the latter silver-leafed iron bark. **1870** E.B. Kennedy *Four Yrs. in Qld.* 32 Small *broad*-leaved ironbark . . as a rule denotes poor country; while silver-leafed ironbark on the contrary shows good country. **1902** *Proc. Linnean Soc. N.S.W.* XXVII. 226 E[*ucalyptus*] *melanophloia* at Narrabri, the 'Silver-leaf Ironbark'. **1934** 'S. Rudd' *Green Grey Homestead* 82 You'll turn your thoughts to the bee's nest in the gully near your cultivation paddock. It's been there in that silver-leaf ironbark for three years. **1944** J. Devanny *By Tropic Sea & Jungle* 209 On barren stretches of the same range characteristic orchard-like patches of the silver-leaf ironbark occurred. **1956** K. Tennant *Honey Flow* 2 The silver-leaved ironbark is promising. **1963** *N. Austral. Monthly* Dec. 11 The silverleaf ironbarks . . are small spreading trees with peculiar crooked trunks and branches, but with . . black furrowed bark. The leaves are roundish and a silvery-green which make the trees quite distinctive. **1861** *Burke & Wills Exploring Exped.* 9 Caught five **silver perch,** weighing from 1½ lb. to 3 lb. **1880** *Proc. Linnean Soc. N.S.W.* V. 364 *Therapon Richardsonii* . . '*Silver Perch*' of the Colonists. **1906** [see *silver bream*]. **1974** L. Wedlick *Sporting Fish* 11 Silver perch are one of our most important native freshwater fish. **1984** E. Rolls *Celebration of Senses* 136 We can no longer cast light lines baited with small wriggling worms on small hooks into running water to take the active Silver Perch. **1824** *Austral.* (Sydney) 21 Oct. 2 Black and **silver wattle** . . for house work and furniture. **1832** J. Backhouse *Extracts from Lett.* (1838) i. 47 The bush . . is now becoming very gay with the flowers of the silver wattle. **1846** N.L. Kentish *Work in Bush Van Diemen's Land* 21 Silver Wattle . . is a gigantic species of *Mimosa* (*Acacia Mollis*); the bark of which affords the strongest tan known, and has long been an article of export. **1878** R.B. Smyth *Aborigines of Vic.* I. 378 The wood of the silver wattle (*Acacia dealbata*) was used for making the handles of tomahawks. **1903** *Tasmanian Timbers* (Tas. Lands & Survey Dept.) 23 Silver wattle (*Acacia dealbatā*) . . so called from its blue-green silvery foliage . . is a tree that grows up to fifty or sixty feet in height. **1915** *Bulletin* (Sydney) 2 Sept. 26/2 The silver wattle (Cootamundra or baileyana) . . is beautiful when the greenish-blue tops are sprouting. **1928** R.H. Croll *Open Road* 19 Healthy-looking silver wattles. **1980** D.J.E. Whibley *Acacias S.A.* 102 Silver wattle . . was of commercial value for a number of years in the early 1900s for the 'Silver Wattle' gum which was a small and little-known industry.

2. In miscellaneous special collocations: **silver cheque,** a (shearer's) wage-cheque for less than £2; **city,** the silver-mining town of Broken Hill, N.S.W.

1897 *Worker* (Sydney) 13 Nov. 3/4 They not only go in for 'freedom of contract', but likewise, endeavour to apply that principle to 'free drinks' and, when they receive their '**silver cheques**' at the cut-out, *Fold their tents like the Arabs And as silently steal away.* **1904** *Bulletin* (Sydney) 31 Mar. 16/2 On account of the small number of sheep shorn on most of the western (N.S.W.) stations last season, 'silver cheques' were quite common. . . Any cheque under two pounds is a 'silver'. **1956** T. Ronan *Moleskin Midas* 225 He didn't like crowds, particularly when they were made up of station hands with silver cheques. **1891** *Quiz* (Adelaide) 1 May 7/1 The **Silver City** is the scene of the following story. **1913** W.K. Harris *Outback in Aust.* 16 Broken Hill (the famous silver-field in New South Wales) is a great centre for camels, and in paddocks on the outskirts . . of the Silver City the teams may be seen starting off on a long journey. **1956** I.L. Idriess *Silver City* 152 Many who would never even see the Silver City . . were feverishly buying 'silver shares'. **1983** G.A. Grosvenor *Long Way from 'Tipperary'* 73 We travelled from Renmark to Broken Hill back in 1942, by the mail utility to Wentworth and by a rough old service car to the 'Silver City'.

silvertail, *a.* and *n.* [Prob. orig. with reference to the wearing of dress uniforms.]

A. *adj.* Socially prominent; having social aspirations; privileged.

1887 *Bulletin* (Sydney) 12 Nov. 4/1 In their thoughts and expressions they betray the . . 'silver-tail' era. **1894** *Ibid.* 17 Mar. 9/3 And when they're playing billiards in their flannel tennis suits, We feel like heaving something at these 'silver-tail' galoots. **1911** *Truth* (Sydney) 26 Mar. 5/3 (*heading*) Labor leaders' ladies scintillate more strikingly than silver-tail shes. **1930** *Bulletin* (Sydney) 5 Mar. 25/1 Among the allegedly 'silvertail' jobs of Outback is that of station book-keeper. Its lucky possessor lives 'inside'. **1954** T. Ronan *Vision Splendid* 292 Some of the stockmen supported him in this, but what Bob Cressy called the 'silvertail mob', outvoted them. **1977** —— *Mighty Men on Horseback* 166 Just so their bloody silvertail visitors won't get a bad opinion of the place. **1986** *Canberra Times* 31 Mar. 19 (*heading*) Rundown Roos first hurdle for silvertail Swans.

B. *n.* One who is socially prominent or who displays social aspirations; a privileged person.

1891 *Truth* (Sydney) 12 Apr. 1/3 Sir Henry always was a 'silvertail', and his love for a lord is as great to-day as ever. **1902** *Ibid.* 28 Sept. 1/8 Visiting every tinpot function where local silvertails can strut for a few minutes in the Vice-regal presence. **1915** N. Duncan *Austral. Byways* 218 In the Australian bush a Silver-Tail is an incongruously feathered individual of an incongruously aristocratic habit of behaviour and utterance—a human individual, of course. **1929** K.S. Prichard *Coonardoo* (1961) 36 Mrs Bessie knew what she was doin' when she asked that damned young silver-tail to spend a winter on Wytaliba. **1942** *'Havildar' Havalook: Mag. H.M.A.T. 'Havildar'* 25 Mar. 2 Potts Point, the home of the 'silvertails'. **1959** *Bulletin* (Sydney) 30 Dec. 16/1 Not for Jim to coddle any pernickety fellows such as well-nurtured G.P.s, jackeroos or visiting silvertails from overseas. **1974** *New Press* (Perth) I. ii. 5/2 Unlike the Federal Labor silvertails, Gough Whitlam and Bob Hawke, he has the great strength of having had a blue-collar dad. **1985** *Canberra Times* 18 Dec. 28/5 Mr Justice Barry Maddern, who has been described as a silvertail and lives in Toorak, Melbourne, once tried to gain Liberal preselection for the Federal seat of Gellibrand.

silvertail, *v.* [f. prec.] *trans.* See quot.

1922 H. Lawson *Lett.* (1970) 266 When they pointedly gave him the cold shoulder, he wanted to know what they were 'silver-tailin'' *him* for?

silvertailed, *ppl. a.* Silvertail *a.*

1890 A.J. Vogan *Black Police* 116 A select circle of long-limbed members of those upper circles who belong to the genus termed in Australian parlance 'silver-tailed', in distinction to the 'copper-tailed' democratic classes. **1907** *Bulletin* (Sydney) 13 Jan. 9/4 He was . . a companion of Colonel Kelly, Dr Sheehan, of Brunswick, and other luminaries, who as a rule don't too easily bestow their patronage on anything but the real silver-tailed article. **1984** *Nat. Times* (Sydney) 9 Mar. 18/1 Last month in Parliament he spat out a string of acidic references to her as 'this whited sepulchre', 'this scion of society' and as a member of the 'silvertailed aristocracy'.

silvertop.

1. Any of several trees of the genus *Eucalyptus* (fam. Myrtaceae) having smooth-barked, silvery-white upper branches, esp. *E. sieberi* of N.S.W., Vic., and Tas., the trunk of which has a dark, deeply-furrowed bark. Also *attrib.*, and (esp. outside Vic.) **silvertop ash.**

1896 *Proc. Linnean Soc. N.S.W.* XXI. 800 The most westerly locality . . is Mudgee, where it [*sc. Eucalyptus capitellata*] is called 'Silvertop'. **1908** J. Mann *Suitability Australasian Timber* 14 E[ucalyptus] Sieberiana, which is usually named 'silver top'. **1919** R.T. Baker *Hardwoods of Aust.* 219 [Eucalyptus nitens] Known as . . 'Silver-top' or 'Silver-top Gum', in reference to the smooth and shining bark on the upper part of the trunk. **1933** C.W. Peck *Austral. Legends* (ed. 2) 71 Eucalypts (. . even E. Sieberiana, the Silver-top) shut out the daylight. **1939** *Nomenclature Austral. Timbers* (Standards Assoc. Aust.) 59 Silvertop (Vic.), Silvertop ash . . Eucalyptus sieberiana. **1969** S. Kelly *Eucalypts* 51 Silvertop ash . . grows on sandy soils. **1980** M. Williams *Dingo!* 201 A giant goanna hauling itself up a silvertop ash. **1985** J. Galbraith *Garden in Valley* 9 On the drier slopes . . Silvertop forests were more open.

2. [Also U.S.: see Mathews *silver* 1.] An expensive drink: cf. *gold top* GOLD 4.

1855 *Ovens & Murray Advertiser* (Beechworth) 17 Feb. 5/2 This is the first time that we have witnessed a storm of 'sherry cobblers' and 'silver tops'. **1940** *Sentry Go* (Keswick) July 29 Hardly expect a Silver Top for a tray a mile.

silver-topped gimlet: see GIMLET b.

silvery, *a.* Ostentatiously expensive: see SILVER-TAIL.

1979 M. RUTHERFORD *Departmental* 37 Big executive houses just out of town but near the beach. Pool, couple of garages, a few big trees—private you know... Yeah. You don't live in one yourself, I hope?.. No, that would look a bit silvery.

sin-bin, *n. Rugby League.* [Transf. use of N. Amer. *sin-bin* penalty box (in ice hockey): see OEDS *sin, sb.* 6.]

1. A penalty box; the place where a player sent off the field for an infringement of the rules spends a specified period of time.

1981 T. RAUDONIKIS *Rugby League Stories* 11 As we start the 1981 season, we have more changes to get used to, such as differential penalties and the 'sin bin'. **1984** *Austral.* (Sydney) 21 June 17/2 The sin bin is not an International Rugby board law, but is applied to matches in New Zealand and in Fiji. **1985** *Sydney Morning Herald* 22 June 2/6 They started to head-butt each other like a couple of randy Rocky Mountain goats while on their respective ways to the sin bin.

2. *transf. Shag-wagon*, see SHAG *n.*[2]

1980 *Age* (Melbourne) 5 Sept. 1/2 One group of locales that escaped the name of brothel .. was cars, panel vans, and other sin-bins.

sin-bin, *v.* [f. SIN-BIN *n.* 1.] *trans.* To send (a player) from the field as a penalty. Also *fig.* and as *vbl. n.*

1983 *Nat. Times* (Sydney) 1 July 14/3 While Wran is 'sin-binned' the party should be loyal to acting Premier Ferguson. **1984** *Austral.* (Sydney) 21 June 17/2 McInerney was sin-binned for 10 minutes in the second half along with Counties' lock and captain Alan Dawson after a dust-up between the pair. **1986** *Canberra Times* 1 May 30/1 Sin-binning will be introduced in ACT rugby from Saturday.

sing, *v.*

1. *trans.* Of an Aboriginal: to impart supernatural powers to (an object) by incantation; to bring a (freq. malign) supernatural influence to bear on (a person or thing) by incantation.

1896 B. SPENCER *Rep. Horn Sci. Exped. Central Aust.* IV. 130 The man, on being told that the spear which had caused the injury had been 'sung', that is, had undergone an incantation which bewitched it, proceeded to pine away, and he eventually died without the supervention of any surgical complications which could be detected. **1925** M. TERRY *Across Unknown Aust.* 147 There is a custom, common to all Australian natives, whereby an enemy can be killed without violence. It is called 'boning', or 'singing'. **1935** F. BIRTLES *Battle Fronts Outback* 104 Out at sea the Kunalby family was seeking a dugong supper. I could hear faintly their chanting refrain 'singing' this sea-cow. **1949** I.L. IDRIESS *One Wet Season* 133 Mick, Constable Kirk's tracker, was 'sung' and died. **1959** D. LOCKWOOD *Crocodiles & Other People* 16 Then followed two nights of terror during which he was subjected to bone-pointing: he was 'sung' by the blacks. **1964** *N. Austral. Monthly* Aug. 25 A 64-year-old aborigine has regained his sight after being convinced for two years that he had been 'sung' blind by an enemy. **1974** DRYSDALE & DURACK *End of Dreaming* 127 His friends told us that some enemy had stolen his shirt and used it to 'sing' his death. **1980** T.A. ROY *Vengeance of Dolphin* 153 Being 'sung' to death can be the supreme penalty that the elders decide a tribal offender must face. **1984** *N.T. News* (Darwin) 20 Sept. 6/5 'I like to think the black man sang them,' he says. 'They did a lot of singing the white man. They're sort of having their revenge.'

2. *transf.* In the phr. **to sing the cattle,** to soothe resting cattle: see quot. 1971.

1969 J. DINGWELL *One String* 47 Brother Seb rode her once again up the hill to listen to the stockmen 'singing the cattle'. **1971** P. ADAM SMITH *No Tribesman* 9 And then it began. Gently, softly at first, the stockmen began to 'sing' the cattle, make them aware and content in the presence of men... So, they sing the cattle.

Singapore ant. [See quot. 1930.] The small ant *Monomorium destructor*, introduced into tropical Aust. Also *attrib.*

1930 *Northern Standard* (Darwin) 7 Oct. 3/4 Singapore Ants. It is said that these ants came from Singapore secreted in cargo landed at Darwin from India... Anything smellful will draw them to concentrate upon it in straight lines from their nookeries... Townships and bushlands are in a state of Singapore ant saturation. **1935** F. BIRTLES *Battle Fronts Outback* 99 Singapore ants—a minute variety—crawled over me in thousands. **1965** *Austral. Encycl.* I. 212 The few species [of *Monomorium*, etc.] that have been introduced are collectively known (according to locality) as house ants, ship ants and Singapore ants. These pests cause most trouble in Western Australia and Queensland, but are bad enough elsewhere at times.

singing, *ppl. a.* Used as a distinguishing epithet in the names of birds: **singing honeyeater,** the predom. grey-brown honeyeater *Lichenostomus virescens* of mainland Aust.; **lark,** SONG-LARK.

1845 J. GOULD *Birds of Aust.* (1848) IV. Pl. 33, *Ptilotis sonorus* .. **Singing Honey-eater.** **1890** G.J. BROINOWSKI *Birds of Aust.* IV. Pl. 20, The Singing Honey-eater .. is generally found on the she-oak or honeysuckle trees. **1916** S.A. WHITE *In Far Northwest* 64 It answered the description of our common singing honey-eaters (*Meliphaga sonora*). **1945** C. BARRETT *Austral. Bird Life* 157 The singing honeyeater .. hardly deserves its descriptive name, for its loud clear notes do not make a song. **1970** D. STIVENS *Horse of Air* 137 Singing honeyeaters (*Meliphaga virescens*) were feeding among the isolated flowering bloodwoods. **1976** *Reader's Digest Compl. Bk. Austral. Birds* 479 The name singing honeyeater may be suggestive of sweet and musical song, but many who have heard the bird are in agreement that its varied calls are mostly best described as creaking or chattering. Some, however, have a whistling or trilling quality. **1847** J. GOULD *Birds of Aust.* (1848) III. Pl. 76, *Cincloramphus rufescens* .. **Singing Lark** of the Colonists. **1849** C. STURT *Narr. Exped. Central Aust.* II. 31 App. *Singing Lark.* This is .. a good songster. **1865** J. GOULD *Handbk. Birds Aust.* I. 397 *Singing Lark* of the Colonists .. a very sweet songster .. whose note somewhat resembles, but is much inferior to that of our own Skylark. **1889** *Proc. Linnean Soc. N.S.W.* IV. 410 *Cincloramphus rufescens* .. known as 'Singing-lark'. **1943** C. BARRETT *Austral. Animal Bk.* 275 The brown song-lark .. and the rufous song-lark .. rival the bush-larks as songsters. Among their popular names are .. 'singing lark', 'skylark' [etc.].

singing string. OVERLAND TELEGRAPH.

1957 F. CLUNE *Fortune Hunters* 41 The Aborigines called the O.T. line the 'Singing String'. **1962** D. LOCKWOOD *I, Aboriginal* 44 The Singing String—the Overland Telegraph Line—was thrown across the country in my grandfather's day.

single, *n. Australian National Football.* BEHIND 1.

1960 *N.T. News* (Darwin) 5 Jan. 7/5 Three successive kicks .. got singles that should have been goals. **1960** *Ibid.* 8 Mar. 10/4 Marcellus took a spectacular mark but kicked badly, and a charity free to Saturninus got a single. **1969** EAGLESON & MCKIE *Terminol. Austral. Nat. Football* iii. 16 *Single*, a behind... It is difficult to determine whether this variant for *behind* has been derived from the fact that only one flag is raised by the goal umpire when a behind is scored, or from the fact that a behind is worth only one point.

single, *a. Hist.* In special collocations: **single cat,** a whip of nine knotted cords; a cat-o'-nine-tails; cf. *double cat-o'-nine-tails* DOUBLE *a.* 1; **iron,** one fetter, also **single-ironed** *ppl. a.*

1838 *Rep. Select Committee Transportation* 12 Feb. 38 Was the cat with which the floggings were inflicted at Macquarie Harbour of the same description as the ordinary cat-o'-nine-tails?—No, it was a much heavier instrument, and larger; the cat which is generally used in the colony for the punishment of convicts is what is called a **single cat,** such as is generally employed for the punishment of soldiers and sailors. **1802** [**single iron**] *HRA* (1915) 1st Ser. III. 546 Q.2.—Was he in Irons? A.—He was single-Ironed. **1804** *Sydney Gaz.* 23 Dec. 3/2 To labour in a single iron every evening until dusk. **1819** *Rep. Select Committee State of Gaols* (Great Brit. Parl.) 110 For the more atrocious crimes double irons were used, and for the milder offences, single irons. **1832** *Sydney Herald* 23 Apr. 3/1 When he decamped, he was in single irons.

singlet. A woven or knitted undergarment covering the body from the shoulders to the hips; also worn as an outer garment. See also JACKY HOWE.

1882 W. SOWDEN *N.T. as it Is* 27 The Minister in a slashed slouch-hat with a veil—*a la* bushranger—light tweed trousers, with singlet, black umbrella, and long white oil leggings. **1888** *Bulletin* (Sydney) 10 Mar. 14/3 Melbourne society was agitated to its inner singlet last week by the marriage of a certain Dr Hooper to the Governor's governess. **1908** *Truth* (Sydney) 5 Apr. 7/1 Florrie mixed her drinks and ran about in her singlet. **1919** A. SEAGER *Men* 43 In singlets, shorts and bandoliers We rode into the fight. **1946** 'A. SPENCE' *Mystery of Red Gum* 22 A knot of men working in the bush, clad only in singlets and trousers, their muscular brown arms shining with perspiration. **1959** *Overland* xv. 38 Gentlemen are requested to wear their singlets in this bar. **1969** *On Guard* (Broken Hill) Feb. 10 Persons wearing a singlet only will be asked to leave. **1984** *Bulletin* (Sydney) 3 July 110/3 On the Darling Downs, people have erected a monument to gun-shearer Jackie Howe, the man credited with inventing the truckies' navy blue singlet.

sink, *v.*[1] [Spec. use of *sink* to excavate (a shaft, etc.) by digging downwards: see OED *v.* 18.]

1. *intr.* To dig downwards in search of gold.

1851 *Empire* (Sydney) 30 Sept. 207/3 The kind of gold the men of Tarshish are obtaining, is similar to the very fine dust found on the surface of the soil at the Turon. In no case that I saw, have the men sunk deeper than four feet, and the greater number are rooting on the very top; not deeper than a foot or two. **1852** Tas. Non-State Rec. 56/1 1 Aug., A number of us went to sink in a new Gulley today. **1871** *Austral. Town & Country Jrnl.* (Sydney) 7 Jan. 15/4 These men commenced to sink through the cement, and on bottoming were rewarded. **1890** 'R. BOLDREWOOD' *Miner's Right* 37 We .. were soon 'sinking for the reef'. **1899** K. O'MALLEY *Second Message to Sovereign Electors Encounter Bay* 16 He is .. still sinking, but when the gold will begin to rise I am unable to say. **1932** I.L. IDRIESS *Prospecting for Gold* 51 Remember to apply your 'water knowledge' whenever possible, if you happen to work at other forms of alluvial—sinking or tunnelling for an old river-bed. **1939** —— *Cyaniding for Gold* 184 You may locate such an outcrop. Sink on it, for gossan often 'makes' values at shallow depth.

2. *trans.* To dig (a hole, etc.) in the ground in search of gold. Also *fig.*

1852 A. ADAMSON *Lett.* 9 May (1901) 25 On Tuesday Adam and Joseph bottomed the hole they were sinking last week, and again found nothing. **1862** H. BROWN *Vic. as I found It* 244 Those who took the chance of sinking a hole on the outside of what had appeared to be the gutter were rewarded by finding that .. their hole brought them exactly on the run of gold. **1881** G.C. EVANS *Stories* 147, I went straight to Bendigo and sunk a hole. **1887** *Rec. Castlemaine Pioneers* (1972) 4 We threw up our claim in disgust, proclaiming it a 'duffer', having had the honor, in common digging parlance, of sinking another 'for the Queen'. **1896** *Bulletin* (Sydney) 18 Jan. 3/2 Allus sinkin' duffers, allus bottomin' on 'tish'. **1908** *Ibid.* 23 Jan. 15/2 The black cockatoo knows exactly where to bite through the bark to find his breakfast... I have never known him to sink a duffer hole in the bark. **1926** *Ibid.* 3 June 22/3 On Chillagoe (N.Q.) field in the golden long ago a miner died on Saturday night. Sunday morning early a party of diggers left to 'sink the shaft', with the corpse to follow.

sink, *v.*[2] [Spec. use of *sink* to cause (a thing) to descend: see OED(S *v.* 17 e. Used elsewhere but recorded earliest in Aust.] *trans.* To consume (an alcoholic drink); to quaff.

1911 *Bulletin* (Sydney) 31 Aug. 14/2 Poison-Cart Bill had been 'sinking' the proceeds of months of driving the rabbit 'bus, and he was loaded to the nines by the time he .. subsided gloriously on a garbage heap. **1912** *Ibid.* 16 May 15/2 The push sunk the amber swiftly and tumbled into the street .. to where the Army was dispensing blood and fire. **1918** *Kia Ora Coo-ee* Apr. 17 After we had sunk a few boozes we saw the A.P.M.

1923 *Aussie* (Sydney) Oct. 23/1 He goes away an' comes back again with two long mugs o' red wine. We sunk it in quick time. **1945** G. CASEY *Downhill is Easier* 24, I sank my pot, and wondered what it was all about. **1965** I. HAMILTON *Persecutor* 23 Sink six schooners of beer. **1977** K. COOK *Man Underground* 86 Come on Bill . . set up ten stubbies. Ivan's gonna sink a hundred. **1986** *Canberra Times* 27 Jan. 1/2 The typically Australian activity of sinking a cold can on a hot day.

sinking, *vbl. n. Gold-mining.* The process of digging downwards in search of gold; the cavity so formed.

1851 J.H. BURTON *Emigrant's Man.* ii. 121 Several parties have commenced sinking about a mile from Sofala. **1864** J. ARMOUR *Diggings, Bush & Melbourne* 8 We tried surface washing, but got only sore backs by it, and returned to the sinking. **1871** *Austral. Town & Country Jrnl.* (Sydney) 18 Feb. 207/4 The sinking is deep and wet, and all the holes have to be slabbed throughout. **1896** M. CLARKE *Austral. Tales* 51 The place is underlined with 'sinkings', and the inhabitants burrow like moles beneath the surface of the earth.

sirocco. *Obs.* [Transf. use of *sirocco* a hot wind blowing from the north coast of Africa over the Mediterranean.] HOT WIND 1.

1842 *S. Austral. News* (London) 15 May 99/2 We are occasionally afflicted with irregular, or extraordinary visitations of heat, in the shape of hot winds, or siroccos, blowing from the centre of the continent. **1849** *Sydney Guardian* 155/2 He had seen—he had entered the furnace, whence the Australian Sirocco inhales its breath of flame, and had returned alive to describe his perilous adventure. **1852** S. MOSSMAN *Gold Regions Aust.* (ed. 2) 79 As the province of Victoria enjoys the coldest climate of the three colonies, so does it experience the hottest blast of this sirocco. **1881** H.W. NESFIELD *Chequered Career* 211 Adelaide has its hot winds, so has Sydney its 'brick-fielders', but they are becoming rarer there year by year. The farther one travels north, the less you are troubled with these siroccos; and in Queensland they are comparatively unknown. **1891** W.H. THOMES *Belle of Aust.* 73, I am as thirsty as though I had passed through a sirocco, or dust storm. **1897** *Bulletin* (Sydney) 6 Mar. 3/2 With the bush-fires raging round us, and the only breeze that blows A sirocco from the north-west hot enough to singe your clothes. **1903** *Ibid.* 16 May 16/3 A sirocco could bury a good slice of B.H. beneath thousands of tons of tailings.

sis. Also **siss.** Abbrev. of 'sissy', an effeminate person.

1944 A. MARSHALL *These are my People* 59 Jim . . I understood, was regarded as a siss. **1977** W. MOORE *Just to Myself* 10 We all reckoned he was a sis because his mother wouldn't let him get his clothes dirty.

sister. [Spec. use of *sister* in the sense of 'fellow': see OED *sb.* 10.] Used *attrib.* to designate an equality of status between Colonies (occas. States), esp. in the Comb. **sister colony.** Cf. BROTHER COLONIST.

1820 C. JEFFREYS *Van Dieman's Land* 118 They are certainly a superior race to those of the sister colony of Port Jackson. **1832** J. HANSON *Let.* 16 The sister colony of Van Diemen's Land. **1835** H. MELVILLE *Hist. Van Diemen's Land* 159 Had the land about Perth and Norfolk Plains been granted in small lots . . that part of the country alone could grow more wheat than would serve this Colony, as well as the whole of the Sister Settlement. **1839** *S. Austral. Rec.* (London) 12 June 201/2 South Australia and the Sister Colonies. **1841** G. ARDEN *Recent Information Port Phillip* 118 Even this argument on the side of the Sister Province fails in its strength. **1861** N.W. POLLARD *Homes in Vic.* 15 There is no reason why facility of conveyance should not work as well as it has done in the sister Australian Colony of South Australia. **1875** P.E. WARBURTON *Journey across Western Interior* 1 Western Australia occupies a larger space upon the map than any of its sister colonies. **1891** E.H. HALLACK *W.A. & Yilgarn Goldfields* 6, I couldn't see his feet, but I think in the way of boot accommodation he would lose himself in those of the Prime Minister of the sister colony. **1903** *Truth* (Sydney) 18 Jan. 1/6 Ben . . has celebrated his 64th year of residence in Victoria. When Ben arrived in the sister State he could have bought half Port Phillip for a bottle of rum. **1909** *Ibid.* 6 June 1/6 Sydney and suburbs are woefully behind the sister States in the matter of newspaper pillars. Letter boxes . . are plentiful enough, but . . one often has to walk a mile or so to post a paper.

sit, *v.* With **down.** [Spec. use of *sit down* 'to establish oneself in some position or place; to settle, take up one's abode': see OED *v.* 21 c.]

1. [Survival of the Br. and U.S. sense, strengthened by the development of sense 2.] *intr.* Of non-Aborigines: to settle, take up residence, esp. to SQUAT 1. See also quot. 1871.

1798 D. COLLINS *Acct. Eng. Colony N.S.W.* I. 489 There was indeed a woman, one Ann Smith, who ran away a few days after our sitting down in this place, and whose fate was not exactly ascertained. **1830** *Sydney Monitor* 13 Nov. 2/6 The six men who were captured at Hunter's River with a very large number of cattle and horses . . intended to *sit down* as the Blacks say 'far from the busy haunts of men'. **1832** *Sydney Herald* 16 Jan. 3/1 Major-General Stewart, formerly Lieutenant-Governor of this Colony, arrived from Hobart Town on Tuesday evening. . . It is said to be the General's intention of 'sitting down' upon his fine estate at Bathurst. **1835** *Colonist* (Sydney) 3 Sept. 281/2 No sensible man . . would like to *sit down* upon a small allotment of uncleared land. **1846** *Bell's Life in Sydney* 25 July 3/3 These bushmen start off scantily provided with food, and . . at last, quietly sit down on a track of country, even though it may be twice or thrice as large as a German Principality. **1849** J.P. TOWNSEND *Rambles & Observations N.S.W.* 70 Labouring men sometimes 'sit down' on waste land in the bush, paying no rent whatever. **1863** J. BONWICK *Wild White Man* 80 They have no idea of the time of settlement, merely saying, 'plenty long while ago—always sit down here'. **1871** *Great Northern Run Case* 3 Their agent had requested permission to 'sit down' for a time with his sheep, owing to the scarcity of water elsewhere. **1890** 'R. BOLDREWOOD' *Colonial Reformer* III. 245 If all stories were true, they hadn't been very particular themselves, but had sat down on the cove's run that first helped 'em when they were bull-punchers without credit for a bag of flour. **1909** *Bulletin* (Sydney) 26 Aug. 15/2 Two men on the Victoria 'sat down' on a billabong with a bullock-waggon. In two years they had 600 cattle. **1937** D. GUNN *Links with Past* 94 The first people to sit down on these runs had no intentions of stocking them. They went ahead of settlement and had no right to the land, and were glad to sell out cheaply to anyone wanting a place. **1963** *N.T. News* (Darwin) 3 Jan. 4/6 After many years of knocking around the North Billarney 'sat down' at a camp on Two-Fella Creek, around the harbour from Darwin.

2. *intr.* Freq. in Austral. pidgin. Of Aborigines: to be (in a place); to settle (somewhere) permanently. Also *transf.* (see quots. 1880 and 1944), and *absol.*

1805 *Sydney Gaz.* 7 May, A Number of Natives . . are *sit down* at the Brush between Prospect and George's River, they are not to be molested in that situation. **1826** *Monitor* (Sydney) 18 Aug. 106/3 The native . . belongs to a tribe that '*sit down*' near Liverpool Plains. **1832** *Ibid.* 14 Jan. 3/1 Some of the chiefs expressed their willingness to leave off their wandering habits, and 'sit down like white fellow'. **1839** T.L. MITCHELL *Three Exped. Eastern Aust.* (rev. ed.) II. 289 A party of natives were following our track. . . I hastened to meet them, that they might not 'sit down' too close to our camp. **1848** H.W. HAYGARTH *Recoll. Bush Life* 108 In talking to a black . . to be, or exist, is to 'sit down'. **1861** J.D. LANG *Qld., Aust.* 392 You are not to 'sit down' or 'walk all about' over it, to hunt the kangaroo and opossum, or to gather *bangwall* any more. **1880** J.B. STEVENSON *Seven Yrs. Austral. Bush* 144 Plenty Possum sit down up there. **1900** R. BRUCE *Benbonuna* (1904) 65 'Why she sit down long a creek?' inquired Mrs Mac, using the aboriginal 'pigeon' English, as most bush people do in their intercourse with the natives. **1938** D. BATES *Passing of Aborigines* 69 Had no affinity with the poor depraved and drink-sodden old men and women who 'sat down' at Maamba. **1944** M.J. O'REILLY *Bowyangs & Boomerangs* 88, I told one of the old men, who could jabber fairly good English, about the incident. This is what he told me: 'That fellow bean tree is one place where big fellow 'Kaditcha' all the time sit down; no whitefellow, no blackfellow allowed camp alonga that place.' **1962** V.C. HALL *Dreamtime Justice* 160 There was no pension. Rationed and clothed and given tobacco, he 'sat down' in the camp by the Station he had served so well and at such cost. **1965** L. HAYLEN *Big Red* 67 The gins, piccaninnies and the old men 'sat down' a few hundred yards from the house. **1978** H.C. COOMBS *Kulinma* 228 In some communities work on the projects continued while materials were available but increasingly Aborigines became content to 'sit-down'.

Hence **sitting-down** *vbl. n.* (used *attrib.* in the examples).

1959 *Bulletin* (Sydney) 6 May 16/2 The latest for N.T. abos. is three weeks walkabout on full pay, as they are now holding their jobs long enough to get paid annual holidays at native resorts such as Snake Bay, Shoal Bay, and various islands. . . For the less energetic, the most attractive resort is a shady banyan-tree for three weeks 'sitting-down walkabout' at the boss's expense. **1978** H.C. COOMBS *Kulinma* 228 Aborigines found that they would receive in unemployment benefit ('sitting-down money' it was called in some communities) more than it had been possible for them previously to earn for work on their community projects.

sit down, *n. Austral. pidgin.* [f. prec.]

1. A rest; a stay. Also *attrib.*

1931 I.L. IDRIESS *Lasseter's Last Ride* 137 Warts said it was only a little way—'one sit down'. **1952** *Bulletin* (Sydney) 3 Sept. 17/4 It had been her first 'sit-down' in the whiteman's hospital and she was star of the camp for some days. **1981** *Central Austral. Land Rights News* Dec. 13 They say they're very worried that cattle stations won't be used as cattle stations and become sitdown places.

2. Special Comb. **sit-down money,** unemployment or welfare benefits. Also *transf.*

1978 H.C. COOMBS *Kulinma* 202 Community advisers became active in some communities in assisting Aborigines to apply for unemployment benefit. . . Generally Aborigines have been content to accept the 'sit-down' money without working. **1981** *Weekend Austral. Mag.* (Sydney) 31 Oct. 19/1 Mr Tuxworth said these companies should pay the out-of-work miners sit-down money to keep them in the territory for when the uranium boom begins. **1984** *Bulletin* (Sydney) 10 July 77/1 On every second Wednesday when the social security cheques—'sit-down money'—are collected, the queues are much longer. Money as well as moselle flows.

sittella /sɪˈtɛlə/. Also **sitella.** [The bird genus *Sitella* was named by English naturalist William Swainson (*On Nat. Hist. Classif. Birds* (1837) II. 317), f. mod. L. *sitta*, a. Gr. σίττη nuthatch + dimin. suffix *-ella*.] The small, arboreal bird *Daphoenositta chrysoptera* of mainland Aust., usu. grey or brown and white streaked, and having several distinctive forms sometimes regarded as separate species, as **black-capped sittella, orange-winged sittella** (see under first element). See also WOODPECKER 1.

1844 J. GOULD *Birds of Aust.* (1848) IV. Pl. 103, *Sittella leucoptera* . . White-winged Sittella. **1901** *Emu* I. 62 The Sittellas or Treerunners construct a most wonderful nest. **1943** C. BARRETT *Austral. Animal Bk.* 266 Nuthatches, sittellas, or tree-runners, as they are variously termed, are small, short-tailed birds which help to clear the bark of insects and spiders. **1982** J. MORRISON *North Wind* 212 Some pardalotes and sitellas were fluttering about the drooping branch of [a] pepper tree.

six, *a.*

1. In *attrib.* collocations designating the number of horizontal barriers in a fence, as **six-rail (-strand, -wire) fence.**

1897 *Bulletin* (Sydney) 11 Dec. 30 Great curly horned Brewarras bred among the back belars To a scorn of six-wire fences and a dread of twelve-foot bars. **1903** *Ibid.* 27 June 17/1 A man offered for a wager to shear a sheep while on the top strand of a six-wire fence. **1908** *Ibid.* 22 Oct. 14/3 Was once accelerated over a six-rail fence by a masculine cow, and landed fair in the middle of a clump of the Queensland curse. **1925** *Ibid.* 11 June 48/2 Then through a tightly-strained six-wire fence, and so on to Robert's property. **1953** H.G. LAMOND *Big Red* 17 She came to a six-wire sheep fence which was the boundary of a paddock. **1958** F.B. VICKERS *Mirage* (ed. 2) 165 He came out into a clearing around which was a six-wire fence, taut between white-painted posts. **1960** E. O'CONNER *Irish Man* 209 They came to a six-strand fence and after following it for a mile or so saw a few freshly branded calves.

2. In the collocation **six-by-eight,** a tent measuring 6 feet by 8 feet.

1898 *Worker* (Sydney) 21 May 1/2 He'd pitched his

little 6 x 8; and when he saw me there He promptly bade me enter, with a spirit cheering swear. **1929** *Bulletin* (Sydney) 6 May 25/1 Were I king of Ruritania I would quickly abdicate, For I'd miss the homely comforts of my little six-by-eight. **1929** W.J. RESIDE *Golden Days* 364 Where are they who with me camped Within the six by eights.

3. In the phr. **six bob a day,** used with reference to the daily rate of pay to designate an Australian soldier serving in the war of 1914–18, esp. *attrib.* as **six bob a day tourist.**

1915 T. SKEYHILL *Soldier-Songs from Anzac* 22 But 'e called me a chocolate soldier, A six bob a day tourist, too. 'E says, 'You'll not reach the trenches; Nor even get a view.' **1916** Tas. Non-State Rec. 103/11 Apr., They (the tommies) call our men the 'six bob a day tourists'. **1917** C.E.W. BEAN *Lett. from France* 224 The sort of Australian who used to talk about our 'tinpot navy' labelled the Australians who rushed at the chance of adventure the moment the recruiting lists were opened 'the six bob a day tourists'. Well—the 'Tourists' made a name for Australia such as no other Australians can ever have the privilege of making. **1940** T. NELSON *Towards Socialism* 29 The manner in which the I.W.W. approached the public did not assist their cause. It addressed all and sundry as 'boneheads' while the soldiers were hailed as 'six-bob-a-day murderers'. **1942** *Gabber: Qld. Lines of Communication Army Trade Training Depot* July 2 *Handsome soldier*, 'six bob a day man'. **1948** H.W. CRITTENDEN *Rogues' Paradise* 36 It will appease his Irish sectarian soul .. to learn that .. the 'saviors' marched as part of the valiant mob who called the Diggers, among even less complimentary epithets, 'six-bob-a-day-murderers'. **1979** P. PAVY *Bush Surgeon* 3 Australians thought at first that the fighting would be over in weeks. The first contingent of the Australian Infantry Forces was called 'the six bob a day tourists'.

sixer. *Australian National Football.* A scoring kick worth six points; a goal.

1908 *Clipper* (Hobart) 19 Sept. 2/2 Molross took a bonza mark on the wing, and from a pass Rait scored a sixer against great applause. **1910** *Huon Times* (Franklin) 20 July 4/4 The home team were the first to score through the efforts of Johnston who scored a sixer. **1960** *N.T. News* (Darwin) 5 Jan. 8/6 The pass found its mark and Lew Falt got the sixer. **1969** EAGLESON & MCKIE *Terminol. Austral. Nat. Football* iii. 16 *Sixer*, a variant for *goal*.

sixes, *n. pl.* [Spec. use of *six* the number used to grade the uniform.] In naval use: white (summer) dress uniform.

1944 *Quickmatch: Souvenir Mag. H.M.A.S. 'Quickmatch'* 87 Admirably dressed in spanking sixes. **1959** *R.A.N. News* (Sydney) 20 Mar. 5 Sunday divisions are on the programme Clean sixes are due or we'll all be in a jam. **1983** *Canberra Times* 22 May 10/1 The top brass, dressed in 'sixes' (which were very smart uniforms indeed).

six o'clock swill: see SWILL b.

sixpence. *Austral. pidgin. Obs.* Money; TICKPENS.

1851 *Athenaeum* (London) 24 May 557 Never mind, I jump up white fellow—plenty of sixpence. **1859** W. BURROWS *Adventures Mounted Trooper* 112 'Black fellow quomby dead, by and by jump up white fellow, plenty tixpence', meaning, that if a black should 'quomby' *i.e.* lie down, and die, they would rise again white, and have plenty of money, sixpence being their name for money.

sked. [Orig. U.S. abbrev. of *schedule*] An appointed time for a radio call: see quots.

1946 E.A. FELDT *Coast Watchers* 10 Previously the small stations in the area had communicated with key points at fixed times, 'skeds' as they were called. **1950** A. GROOM *I saw Strange Land* 121 Mrs de Brenni .. arranged a 'sked' to enable me to talk over the air with Hermannsburg, Station XH, at 7 o'clock that night. **1957** M. GARTRELL *Dear Primitive* 29 Women hundreds of miles from friends arrange 'skeds' (call times) just for the pleasure of a friendly chat. **1983** *Yulngu* Mar. 6 The radio 'skeds' are so easy to do these days as all communities .. shut up when Katherine Base is talking.

skee. Shortened form of 'whisky'.

[N.Z. **1959** G. SLATTER *Gun in my Hand* 145 In this country a bulged pocket would not mean a gun. More likely a flask of skee or mother's ruin.] **1962** P.A. KNUDSEN *Bloodwood Tree* 122 'Any skee?' Happy squeaked hopefully. 'Yair, git a coupla bottles. Not Scotch—Australian stuff 'll do us peasants.' **1967** G. JENKIN *Two Yrs. Bardunyah Station* 16 And for this here quid and a bottle of skee I'm betting at ten to one.

skeleton weed. [Also U.S.] The naturalized perennial herb *Chondrilla juncea* (fam. Asteraceae), orig. of central Asia, generally regarded as a weed, esp. of wheat and other cereals.

1935 *Agric. Gaz. N.S.W.* XLVI. 16 Skeleton weed is well liked by sheep, especially when it is in the young stages. **1945** *Queanbeyan Age* 6 Nov. 3/2 Owners of land within the Australian Capital Territory are hereby notified that the undermentioned plants have been declared to be noxious weeds .. Skeleton Weed (*Chondrilla juncea* . .) [etc.]. **1963** B. HESLING *Dinkumization & Depommification* 223 Dr Macindae .. entered the floral lecture to find our Japanese friend filling all the spare crockery in Goondiwindi with choice samples of skeleton weed, Bathurst burr and Paterson's curse! **1981** *Bulletin* (Sydney) 9 June 36/3 Take the case of skeleton weed. Wheat farmers regard it as a pest, but some sheep men call it 'the poor man's lucerne' because in a drought it can provide sheep with much needed high-protein feed.

skelly. *Obs.* Alteration of 'skilly', a thin, watery porridge or gruel. Also *attrib.*

1846 *Britannia* (Hobart) 8 Oct. 2/5 He had not been poking his nose into flour bags, and skelly-tubs as part of his duty. **1853** I. CHAMBERLAYNE *Austral. Captive* 82 A pint of *skelly*—a very thin gruel, without salt.

skerrick. [Br. dial. *skerrick* a small amount: see OEDS.] The smallest amount, a 'scrap'. Usu. in negative contexts.

1854 S. SIDNEY *Gallops & Gossips* 88, I have plenty of tobacco, but not a skerrick of tea or sugar. **1914** T.C. WOLLASTON *Spirit of Child* 65 'Had any luck, so far?' I asked. 'Not a skerrick,' he answered, 'not a colour.' **1915** DREW & EVANS *Grafter* 85 He stuck to the paper, and never let up until he read every skerrik there was to read. **1930** 'BRENT OF BIN BIN' *Ten Creeks Run* (1952) 17 She won't have a skerrick on her, and that's all there is about it.' **1946** *Bulletin* (Sydney) 17 July 29/4 Cripes, the soot's that thick I couldn't see even a skerrick o' daylight! **1955** R. LAWLER *Summer of Seventeenth Doll* (1965) 27 'Who's been at my vinegar?' .. 'I took a tiny little skerrick to put in a salad.' **1964** *Overland* xxx. 23 There wasn't a skerrick of grass in the paddocks. **1973** C. EAGLE *Who could love Nightingale?* 5 For the first time Edward had a skerrick of attraction for me. **1985** J. CLANCHY *Lie of Land* 201 'Eighty-seven? For that skerrick of ...?' Couldn't be more than ten squares.

skilling. Also **skillen.** [Spec. use of *skilling* a shed or outhouse: see EDD *skeeling* and OED(S *skilling*, *sb.*[1])

1. A lean-to attached to a dwelling and providing additional accommodation (freq. a kitchen); a small dwelling built in the style of a lean-to (see quot. 1840).

1799 *Lett. to London Missionary Soc. Murder S. Clode* 300 Jones went into the skilling, and coming out a second time took up a large knife. **1804** *Sydney Gaz.* 22 July, Kept in a Skilling or Pantry at the back of the Premises. **1808** *Ibid.* 14 Aug., A capital brick-nogged Dwelling house, with two good rooms unfinished, a skilling with two apartments. **1817** *Hobart Town Gaz.* 25 Oct., No Skillings are permitted; and those which have been Built, being in Breach of a former Order, if they be not added to .. will be Removed. **1833** *N.S.W. Mag.* (Sydney) 317 There are two rooms in the skilling, one for a kitchen, the other for a store-room. **1840** *Port Phillip Gaz.* 5 Sept. 6 *A weather-boarded skilling*, with a piece of Garden ground attached; well adapted for a Mechanic .. situated in the suburbs. Price £100. **1849** *Tasmanian Jrnl. Nat. Sci.* III. 452 Substitutions of good solid houses of brick and stone for wooden huts and unsightly skillings. **1853** E. SAUNDERS *Our Austral. Colonies* 19 They had one room 10 feet by 15, with a fireplace in it, and a skilling, or in the colonial phrase 'a lay to', 10 feet by 6. **1874** J.J. HALCOMBE *Emigrant & Heathen* 34 Sometimes there is a skillen at the back of the hut. **1883** W.A. BRODRIBB *Recoll. Austral. Squatter* 55 We added two rooms to the cottage (skillings). **1890** 'R. BOLDREWOOD' *Colonial Reformer* III. 51 At the back a skilling, a lower roofed portion of the building, contained several smaller rooms. **1936** M. FRANKLIN *All that Swagger* 46 He and Dunn made a hut of logs with a lean-to called a 'skilling' and a roof of stringy-bark.

2. *Skillion roof*, see SKILLION B. 2. Also as **skilling roof.**

1861 L.A. MEREDITH *Over Straits* 94 Stray little bits of dwellings, with perhaps one window and a door to the street, and a slant roof or 'shilling' [*sic*] behind. **1891** J. FENTON *Bush Life Tas.* (1964) 42 With tea-tree rafters nailed on the plate for a skilling roof.

skillion, *n.* and *attrib.* [Alteration of SKILLING.]

A. *n.*

1. SKILLING 1.

1808 *Sydney Gaz.* 13 Nov., A house in Pitt's Row, a skillion of which was tenanted by a person with whom the prisoner was in habits of intimacy. **1818** *Hobart Town Gaz.* 10 Jan., To be Sold .. a remarkable strong Frame of a House, with a Skillion thereto attached. **1827** *Tasmanian* (Hobart) 26 July 4 *David Else*, an assigned servant, is placed under the superintendence of the Chief District Constable, and resides in a skillion near to the Gaol with Constable Little (free). **1840** *Port Phillip Gaz.* 8 Jan. 3 Every mansion, every House, every Skillion would pour out its inmates. **1843** C. ROWCROFT *Tales of Colonies* (1858) 56 At the back of the long room of twenty feet, a skillion, to serve as a kitchen, &c. **1869** 'E. HOWE' *Boy in Bush* 183 Fred .. lugged him back to our hut, an' kicked him into the skillion ahind. **1885** *Australasian Printers' Keepsake* 75 He rushed off at once to a selector's skillion, and returned with half a loaf of bread. **1896** *Bulletin* (Sydney) 9 May 27/3 There was but one room, about 24 x 16 feet, and a little 'skillion' below the surface at the back for the accommodation of the master. **1914** *Ibid.* 30 July 22/1 The scene is the interior of a two-roomed skillion at Egg Hill (Vic.). **1921** *Ibid.* 28 Apr. 22/3 Bryan had a small hardwood, weatherboard skillion on the Charley Napier lease, and by virtue of an old miner's right could not be ejected. **1933** J. TRURAN *Where Plain Begins* 9 A skillion or lean-to room had been added as the family outgrew its lodgings. **1949** *Coast to Coast 1948* 48 Nim .. put skillions on the northern, the eastern, and the southern sides of the original building he had constructed for his wife and the children, so that there was no longer any overcrowding, even if the house appeared to ramble somewhat. **1973** J. WILLIAMS *Tom Collins* 30 After two years he was 'still making the three skillions habitable'. (Skillions were a type of dwelling that could be added to.)

2. Such a structure attached to a shearing shed and accommodating the sheep.

1846 C.P. HODGSON *Reminisc. Aust.* 39 Skillions formed by a sloping verandah to receive the sheep in from the fold as required. **1897** L. LINDLEY-COWEN *W. Austral. Settler's Guide* 637 The main building is 20 ft. wide by 40 ft. long, and there are two skillions 10 ft. broad along two sides. **1951** *Bulletin* (Sydney) 18 July 14/4 Our shed was simply a very long building with skillion on one side and the other open. The shearers were placed at the posts.

3. *Skillion roof.*

1879 S.W. SILVER *Austral. Grazier's Guide* 53 Sloping roofs, after the fashion of a 'lean-to', are called in the colonies 'skillions'. **1953** *Bulletin* (Sydney) 3 June 12/4, I recall one silver-grey who went too far—too far down the skillion of the sleep-out veranda.

B. *attrib.*

1. Lean-to.

1857 *Vic. Parl. Papers* (1856–57) III. no. 48 21 At Pentridge .. a den in the shape of a skillion-building was used as an exempt-ward. **1890** MRS H.P. MARTIN *Under Gum Tree* 169 We each occupied a skillion room. **1900** H. LAWSON *Over Sliprails* 45 Jack Drew camped in a skillion room behind his printing office. **1921** *Bulletin* (Sydney) 31 Mar. 20/1 There are queens in skillion-houses, robed in cotton skirts an' blouses Reignin' grandly o'er selections of pure brumby-scrub an' sand. **1933** J. TRURAN *Where Plain Begins* 236 He arrived home, to find Allan Garland sitting among the fowls in the hot little skillion kitchen. **1943** *Bulletin* (Sydney) 25 Aug. 13/2 The two land girls were given quarters in the skillion bedroom behind the Jupp kitchen. **1963** X. HERBERT *Disturbing Element* 7 It was only a three-room shack, for all the bits and pieces added in the way of verandahs and skillion kitchen.

2. Special Comb. **skillion roof,** the sloping roof characteristic of a lean-to building; also **skillion-roofed** *ppl. a.*; SKILLING 2.

1901 *Bulletin* (Sydney) 7 Dec. 28/1 In a four-roomed, skillion-roofed, red-brick dwelling, upon a 'donkey' sofa, sat a woman. **1907** *Truth* (Sydney) 3 Mar. 1/7 There are 2447 houses—not skillion-roofed humpies—within its borders. **1930** H. REDCLIFFE *Yellow Cygnet* 12 Their home was little better than a shed, containing three rooms, with a skillion roof. **1933** R.D. TATE *Doughman* 32 The office was merely an afterthought; a jerry-built addition to the premises, as its unpainted iron-covered skillion-roof plainly told. **1960** L.H. EVERS *Make Way for Tomorrow* 51 Directly outside the door and sheltered by a skillion roof was a small area of concrete paving. **1965** G.H. FEARNSIDE *Golden Ram* 105 He led Sam to the room adjoining the printery. It sheltered beneath a skillion roof appended to the main building—an architectural afterthought that was realised at minimum expense.

skimps, *pl.* [Abbrev. of *skimpings* mining waste (chiefly in Cornwall): see OED.] Mining refuse. Also **skimpy** *n.* (see quot. 1982).

1978 B. KENNEDY *Silver, Sin, & Sixpenny Ale* 35 Slag Street, aptly named since it ran parallel to the slag tailings or skimps and mullock at the foot of the hill. **1982** M. WALKER *Making Do* 84 What was taken out from underground and processed, the residue, had to be put back to fill it up again, and I was one of those that helped in that department, pushing the trucks. I was a mullocker or a skimpy, because the mullock was nicknamed 'skimps'.

skin, *n.*[1] MOIETY. Also *attrib.*

1926 *V & P* (W.A.) (1927) I. no. 3 83 The hurt, or the injury that I might do to one A, a native, is a hurt done not primarily to him, but done to the ··· group or skin, as they call it, of which he is a member. **1933** *Oceania* III. 401 The common pidgin term for sub-section is 'skin'... Individual Nangiomeri were told .. that their 'skins' were so-and-so, and that such-and-such a natural species, or object, 'belonged' to them. **1949** H.E. THONEMANN *Tell White Man* 61 As well as dividing the tribes into eight sub-sections which we call 'skins' (social groups), we also have 'dreamings', which are the names of animals or other things, such as lilies or whirlwinds, to which our spirit belongs. The 'skin' groups are what you call 'social', the 'dreamings' are cult totemic (spiritual) groups. **1958** R. ROBINSON *Black-Feller White Feller* 25 Clara's real husband worked at their hotel. He was the same 'skin' as Clara, and he said that Clara had been promised to him when she was born. **1972** M. CASSIDY *Dispossessed* 54 Djimidja was horrified at the suggestion. She was wrong-skin. **1980** B. SCOTT *Darkness under Hills* 176 *Skin*, Aboriginal tribes were divided into either four or eight 'skins'. Each 'skin' was associated with an animal, bird or insect, as a totemic division. **1981** NGABIDJ & SHAW *My Country of Pelican Dreaming* 40 It did not matter under that skin Law who looked after you, whether sister, daddy or uncle. **1986** *Canberra Times* 2 Apr. 7/2 The 'skin' name was the way of identifying an Aboriginal as part of a group.

skin, *n.*[2] In the phr. (one's) **skin is cracking** and varr., used allusively of a craving for alcoholic liquor.

[**1930** L.W. LOWER *Here's Luck* (1955) 267 I'm so dry I'm beginning to break out in little cracks.] **1955** H.G. LAMOND *Towser* 48 In the language of the bush, 'Jack's skin was crackin''. He craved a drunken spree. **1957** R.S. PORTEOUS *Brigalow* 96 'Get off yer rump. You know bloody well yer skin's crackin'.' We drank quite a few beers that afternoon. **1959** H.P. TRITTON *Time means Tucker* 67 The hardest thing I've ever done was pouring the good whisky on the ground. Don't think I'll ever forget it. I'm so flaming dry my skin is cracking. **1963** S. MUSSEN *Beating about Bush* 63 'His skin's fair cracking.' 'Fair cracking?' I asked. 'He can't wait to start a drinking spree,' translated Tim.

skinless barley. *Obs.* A variety of barley (see quots.).

1828 *Tasmanian* (Hobart) 12 Dec. 2 On Wednesday last a field of what is called *skinless barley*, was cut on the farm of Mr Mather, at Muddy Plains. **1832** *Sydney Monitor* 14 Nov. 2/5 Skinless barley. (This grain was introduced into this Colony in Macquarie's time.) **1849** W.S. CHAUNCY *Guide to S.A.* 38 There is another kind which is in much esteem, it is termed by the colonists, *skinless barley*, from its resemblance to wheat; it is highly valuable, yielding a large crop and weighing as much as 70 lbs. to the bushel. **1852** F. LANCELOTT *Aust. as it Is* I. 117 The kinds [of barley] cultivated are the English .. the Cape or four-rowed, and the skinless barley.

skinner. [Spec. use of Br. slang *skinner* one who strips another of money: see OED(S 4 b.] A horse that wins a race at very long odds; a betting coup.

1891 *Truth* (Sydney) 1 Feb. 6/2 Then came a complete skinner, in the doubles, straight out and post betting. **1902** *Sporting News* (Launceston) 25 Oct. 3/3 At last got the much-longed for 'skinner' on a big race. **1910** *Truth* (Sydney) 11 Dec. 7/5 Gilbert .. continued to lay against certain horses .. on the 'off-chance' of 'something coming out of the clouds' and giving him a 'skinner'. **1922** C. DREW *Rogues & Ruses* 110 A long succession of 'skinners' had put him in the game. **1934** T. WOOD *Cobbers* 96 He would lay two to one port-wine jelly, five to two apple-pie... We had college pudding... Charles.. said it was a skinner for the books. **1944** J. HOLMES *Punter*, The race being over, and the 'books' get a 'skinner'. **1963** D.H. CRICK *Martin Place* 168 He was holding seven quid of the office money this week, and if he got a skinner, it would put him a hundred in front. **1980** A. HOPGOOD *And here comes Bucknuckle* 20 The bookies are cheering of course. That was a fair dinkum skinner. Not one punter left standing after that.

skinny. Any of several fish of the fam. Carangidae, incl. *Scomberoides lysan* of n. Aust. and elsewhere, having a notably compressed body: see quot. 1971. Also **skinnyfish.**

1962 *N.T. News* (Darwin) 10 Apr. 1/1 The trawling was good. Skinnies averaging 10 lbs. were coming in fast. **1971** P. BODEKER *Sandgropers' Trail* 25, I had never heard of queenies coming so far south... Side-on, it looked as if it had been run through a mangle—the reason they call them shinnies [*sic*] up around Darwin. **1980** G.P. WHITLEY *Handbk. Austral. Fishes* 134 Leatherskin .. also called .. skinnyfish .. are mainly tropical with strongly compressed bodies covered with a shiny, leathery skin. **1985** *Canberra Times* 24 June 16/5 Over the week this safari captured .. 50 skinnies (queenfish) [etc.].

skippy. Chiefly *W.A.* and *Tas.* The silvery marine fish *Pseudocaranx dentex* of s. Aust.

1982 T. WINTON *Open Swimmer* 27 'Smart fish, skippy.' 'Trevally.' 'Not this side of the border.' Jerra cast again. He spread some pollard onto the water. 'What are you, a Sydney poonce?' **1984** *Overlander* Oct. 61 His one great ambition was to get among the big skippy for which Esperance is famed. 'Skippy' are silver trevally.

skirt, *v. Shearing.* [Br. dial.: see EDD *skirt, sb.* 8 and *skirting* 5.] *trans.* To trim the skirtings from (a fleece).

1833 H.W. PARKER *Rise, Progress, & Present State Van Dieman's Land* 167 The fleeces should next be *skirted*, that is, unfolded .. and the coarser extremities taken off. **1874** *Australasian Sketcher* 31 Oct. 119/3 Some hands then 'skirt' the wool—that is, remove the outside pieces—and the 'classer' decides on the classification. **1897** L. LINDLEY-COWEN *W. Austral. Settler's Guide* 654 After separating the stained pieces and locks, the fleeces should be skirted well (especially if the bellies are burry) and then rolled tightly and pressed into bales. **1908** W.H. OGILVIE *My Life in Open* 38 In front of the tables stand the 'wool-rollers', men whose business it is to 'skirt' the fleeces. **1979** HARMSWORTH & DAY *Wool & Mohair* 158 The object of skirting a fleece is to remove all faulty portions and to leave it uniform in quality and style. **1981** A.B. FACEY *Fortunate Life* 299 He gave my wife a lesson in wool-classing... He went to a lot of trouble making my wife understand how to class wool and how to skirt a fleece.

skirter. *Shearing.* One who trims the skirtings from a fleece.

1883 *Leisure Hour* (London) 244 A barefooted boy .. gathers up the fleece and carries it to the skirters' table. **1946** *Bulletin* (Sydney) 28 Aug. 28/4 'Black,' called the classer, as the picker-up flicked out a fleece with a black patch on the rump... 'Aw, cripes, it's only got a tinge on one shoulder,' pointed out an emergency skirter.

skirting, *vbl. n. Shearing.* [f. SKIRT.]

1. *pl.* The trimmings or inferior parts of a fleece.

1881 A.C. GRANT *Bush-Life Qld.* I. 85 The roller-up, with a rapidity which is the result of long practice, separates the skirtings. **1899** G. JEFFREY *Princ. Australasian Woolclassing* 51 The skirtings are thrown on the floor until the 'Piece Pickers' gather them up and sort them. **1905** *Shearer* (Sydney) 2 Dec. 3/3 Very faulty parcels, including skirtings which are affected by burr, are still somewhat neglected. **1933** J. TRURAN *Where Plain Begins* 148 A functionary known as a 'rouseabout' whips away the discarded fleece, and hurries off to fling it over the wool-classer's table, where another scantily-clad tradesman regards it appraisingly, tears off the soiled 'skirtings' or belly-parts which form the edges of the fleece, rolls the rest up, and tosses it into one or other of the bins. **1980** P. FREEMAN *Woolshed* 20 The 'fleece' itself.. is immediately removed from the board by the 'pickers-up', and cleverly thrown over a 'wool' table where the 'skirtings' or rough flanks are removed.

2. Special Comb. **skirting table,** the table at which the skirtings are removed.

1890 *Argus* (Melbourne) 20 Sept. 13/7 At the 'skirting table' we will.. watch while the fleece .. is opened out by the 'roller' and the inferior portions removed. **1899** G. JEFFREY *Princ. Australasian Woolclassing* 49 As soon as the fleece is thrown on the skirting table the two wool-rollers, standing one on each side, begin to skirt it. **1979** HARMSWORTH & DAY *Wool & Mohair* 138 On the skirting table, the fleece is trimmed to remove any ragged, dirty or inferior portions of wool and then rolled into a compact bundle for the classer to inspect.

skirty, *a. Shearing.* Of a fleece: roughly trimmed.

1928 C.E. COWLEY *Classing Clip* 35 If the fleeces are not properly trimmed, or, in other words, are 'skirty', the value of the fleece-wool is lessened.

skite, *n.* [Spec. use of Br. dial. *skite* 'an opprobrious epithet for an unpleasant or conceited person': see EDD *sb.*[1] 3 and OED(S.]

1. A boast; boasting; ostentation.

1860 C.R. THATCHER *Vic. Songster* v. 160 You don't often see a chap given to 'skite, Can do very much when it comes to a fight. **1896** *Worker* (Sydney) 11 Apr. 1/3 Briefly, there's more skite and less gold than on any other goldfield I have ever known. **1901** *Advocate* (Burnie) 7 Jan. 1/8, I think it was young Adams who was doing a 'skite' about me. He really gave me credit. **1918** A.G.N. WALL *Lett. Airman* 85 We have to dress for dinner... This notepaper is a part of it, quite unnecessary skite. **1932** R.W. THOMPSON *Down Under* 99 This was a new phase of 'skite'; he really thought that Sydney was the finest city in the world. **1948** P.J. HURLEY *Red Cedar* 70 Anything which savours of 'skite' soon rebounds on to the braggart's head. **1955** D. NILAND *Shiralee* 213 I've had women. I've had 'em from one end of the country to the other. And that's not the skite of a eunuch, or some poor simpleton that can't get it any more. **1968** S. GORE *Holy Smoke* 12 'Y' could give anyone a shade of odds on the skite,' says the King.

2. A braggart, a boaster; a conceited person. Also *transf.*

1897 *Bulletin* (Sydney) 11 Dec. 14/1, I banged a pewter pot And cried, 'Who is this drunken skite That talks this tommy rot?' **1899** *Austral. Tit-Bits* (Sydney) 1 Apr. 121/3 When the Australian brags about his country in the presence of men belonging to older nationalities .. they dub him a 'skite'. **1906** *Bulletin* (Sydney) 1 Nov. 16/2 Mr Mag is .. the skite of the feathered tribe. **1934** J.S. NEILSON *Autobiogr.* (1978) 103, I found sailors great skites and often very unscrupulous. **1944** E.M. ANDERSON *Typist Tales* 113 He's just the ordinary skite and big-mouth. **1956** B.J. RAYMENT *My Towri* 59 Today, I know many younger fencers would say I am an old skite and a liar. **1965** G. MCINNES *Road to Gundagai* 30, I was .. not exactly a favourite with Sergeant Corcoran who, as he was fond of telling us, had no time for 'skites', that is, boastful know-it-alls. **1973** *Southerly* 309 'She was a skite that one—no doubt about that.' 'What on earth is a skite?' 'A loud mouth—a boaster.' **1981** A.B. FACEY *Fortunate*

Life 82 Charlie was a terrific skite and he told everyone about the incident.

skite, *v.* [See prec.] *intr.* To boast; to brag. Also as *vbl. n.*

1857 C.R. THATCHER *Colonial Songster* 18 If you ever get into a fight, Of course you'll not forget to skite. **1881** A.C. GRANT *Bush-Life Qld.* II. 78 Bosh!—you're always skyting about what you'll do. **1890** *Truth* (Sydney) 23 Nov. 1/7 At Jamberoo on Thursday night (The men up there are truly blue) The Fuller man got up to 'skite, And soap the men of Jamberoo. **1902** *Blackwood's Mag.* (Edinburgh) May 642/1, I knows ye is honest now, an' don't skite when ye doesn't know. **1919** E. DYSON *Hello, Soldier* 87 Cantin' up me bloomin' cady, toyin' with a cig., Blowin' out me pout a little, chattin' wide 'n' big When there's skirt around to skite to. **1925** *Bulletin* (Sydney) 21 May 24/4 He's for ever skiting of ancient times. **1941** *Ibid.* 1 Oct. 14/1 'These blokes', said Dusty, 'who skite about the dry tracks they've struck mostly talk through their hats.' **1965** C. JOHNSON *Wild Cat Falling* 40 'What do you do in there?' she asks. 'Besides crack stones and skite about your jobs?' **1971** G. MORGAN *We are borne On* 344, I bet that little girl will have something to skite about in the years to come, having been carried by the Duke of Edinburgh. **1982** R. HALL *Just Relations* 130 That's skiting if you want to hear me skite. We'd beat the lot of youse, him and me.

skiter. One who boasts; SKITE *n.* 2.

1898 *Bulletin* (Sydney) 17 Dec. (Red Page), An incessant talker is a skiter. **1899** *Austral. Tit-Bits* (Sydney) 1 Apr. 121/3 The Australian is not alone in being a 'bragger', or 'skiter'. **1901** *Truth* (Sydney) 12 May 1/4 King O'Malley will be the champion skiter of the Federal show. **1916** *Ibid.* 24 Sept. 11/3 All Australians are skiters. **1918** *Aussie: Austral. Soldiers' Mag.* Feb. 2/1 Someone took up a bomb, removed the pin and aimed carefully in the direction of the Teuton skiter. **1936** F. CLUNE *Roaming round Darling* 77 A fellow, fed up with city skiters, came out west. **1955** STEWART & KEESING *Austral. Bush Ballads* 234 'You're a (bleeding gory) skiter,' said Billy straight and blunt; 'When the (blessed) rams were finished you weren't in the hunt.' **1966** D. NILAND *Pairs & Loners* 12 All you can do is skite. You're the biggest skiter in this town. **1976** M. POWELL *Down Under* 130 What an independent lot they were, not like the skiters in New South Wales and Victoria.

skol. [Transf. use of *skoal* to drink a health.] *trans.* To drink (a glass, etc. of alcoholic liquor) in a single draught.

1976 J. JOHNSON *Low Breed* 244 Octavia picked up a loose glass of claret and skolled it. **1981** *Bulletin* (Sydney) 10 Nov. 46/2 Older guys staggered back and forth across the car park, with a steady supply of schooners. The 5th year boys 'skolled' them in rapid succession. **1982** *Ozbike* (Sydney) July 44/3 She picked up her drink, skolled it and said, 'How about another?'

skoot, var. SCOOT.

skrammy, var. SCRAMMY.

skull-drag, *v. trans.* To haul (someone or something) along by force. Also *fig.*

1872 'DEMONAX' *Mysteries & Miseries* 11/2 A barrister of note . . was gloriously tight. The barrister had a wife. In the morning that lady drove up in a stylish affair, and 'skull-dragged' her better half from the scene of his excesses. **1891** *Great Qld. Strike* (United Pastoralists Assoc. Qld.) 26, 50 unionists threaten to 'skull drag' men . . if they would not join the union. **1917** C. THACKERAY *Goliath Joe* 27 One of 'em got it by the gills with a shark 'ook on a chain, an' we skull-dragged it over the edge. **1947** E. HILL *Flying Doctor Calling* 48 You had to get a head-rope round a stockman and skull-drag him in to the sisters with a broken thigh. **1948** F.D. MARSHALL *Let's go Fishing* 6 If you 'skull-drag' your fish instead of playing them, some day you will deservedly lose a good one. **1953** *Sydney Morning Herald* 3 Jan. 6/4 'Skulldrag', to haul along by force, as a horse drags calves to branding. **1977** W.A. WINTER-IRVING *Bush Stories* 7 They mustered calves and skull-dragged them behind bronco horses. **1978** B. KENNEDY *Silver, Sin, & Sixpenny Ale* 53 George Dale . . remembered how certain recalcitrant individuals were 'skull-dragged' into the union. **1982** LOWENSTEIN & HILLS *Under Hook* 51 If he doesn't put them in properly you have to pull them out yourself with your hook. Had to skull-drag them.

skull-driving, *vbl. n.* School-teaching.

1899 *Bulletin* (Sydney) 7 Oct. 14/1 The champion cool hand was a man with whom I boarded when skull-driving 'out-back'. **1925** *Ibid.* 9 Apr. 22/3 The best damper ever I had was made by a woman in whose house I lodged when skulldriving handy to Gundagai (N.S.W.).

skungey, skungy, var. SCUNGY.

slab, *n.* and *attrib.* [Spec. use of *slab* flat, broad, thick piece of wood, etc.: see OED(S *sb.*[1] 2 b. and 4 a.]

A. *n.* A thick, rough-hewn plank of wood used for building purposes.

1829 H. WIDOWSON *Present State Van Diemen's Land* 86 Logs, or as they are more commonly called, slabs, for erecting barns or small buildings. **1839** T.P. BESNARD *Voice from Bush* 15 My bush hut . . measures 24 feet by 13, and is built of slabs (literally '*wooden walls*') covered with bark, having unglazed apertures in lieu of windows. **1845** C. GRIFFITH *Present State & Prospects Port Phillip* 11 The stringy bark . . is peculiarly valuable to the settler, who thus obtains his slabs (rough planks) for building. **1857** F. DE B. COOPER *Wild Adventures* 76 Slabs are rough pieces of timber, three or four inches thick, split by wedges from a log from eight to ten feet long. **1871** *Austral. Town & Country Jrnl.* (Sydney) 15 Apr. 462/4 Most of the buildings are slab or bark, with weather-board fronts. **1880** J.B. STEVENSON *Seven Yrs. Austral. Bush* 30 Near the fireplace stood a large rough table made of slabs. **1889** H. EGBERT *Pretty Cockey* 44 The Shearers' Hut . . was constructed of rough green slabs, that soon shrank and left wide openings between, to admit cold, wet, heat, &c. **1912** T.E. SPENCER *Bindawalla* 13 The man was splitting slabs with the evident intention of building a house. **1922** E. MERYON *At Holland's Tank* 27 The hut was built of white gum slabs. **1934** *Red Star* (Perth) 22 June 4/1 We were offered two hours to cut slabs of green jarrah bark for ourselves but no green is standing for at least two miles around, all the country having been ringbarked.

B. *attrib.*

1. Constructed from slabs.

1847 *Port Phillip Herald* 16 Nov. 3/6 Slab verandah cottage and garden, wool-shed, men's and out-station huts and hurdles, will be given in. **1855** *Illustr. Sydney News* 13 Jan. 19/3 The constables' office being a perfect sinecure and the old slab lockup . . requiring no bars or bolts. **1861** L.A. MEREDITH *Over Straits* 135 Substantial buildings are surrounded by the heterogeneous crowd of weather-board, slab, paling, and calico tenements always found in digging locations. **1876** *Illustr. Austral. News* (Melbourne) 27 Dec. 2/3 It boasted a slab chimney and stone fireplace. **1896** H. LAWSON *While Billy Boils* (1975) 36 A used-up looking woman comes from the slab-and-bark house. **1917** A.L. BREWER *'Gators' Euchre* 48 The audience are variously seated on hastily-improvised slab forms, also on bullock-dray poles. **1937** C. WARBURTON *White Poppies* 123 As in all these old fields, a slab joss-house stands. **1979** J. WILLIAMS *White River* 11 My charges, Sheila, Curly and Baldy, were the meekest and stood for me calmly by the slab fence.

2. Comb. **slab building, -built** *ppl. a.*, **cottage, house, humpy, hut, road, shanty, table, wall.**

1836 J. BACKHOUSE *Narr. Visit Austral. Colonies* (1843) 395 We walked about two miles, to the school-house, which we found a miserable **slab-building,** in a ruinous condition. **1874** *Illustr. Sydney News* 18/1 The inn is a long low slab building with a bark roof. **1854** G.H. HAYDON *Austral. Emigrant* 147 The largest was a long **slab built** and bark roofed hut. **1865** *Glenorchy Murders* 10 The hut itself . . is a two-roomed slab built edifice. **1928** M.E. FULLERTON *Austral. Bush* 44 In the slab-built zinc-roofed homestead of some lately broken 'run'. **1856** W.H.G. KINGSTON *Emigrant's Home* 125 We found the family living in a comfortable **slab cottage.** **1895** J.T. RYAN *Reminisc. Aust.* 67 He called at a neat little slab cottage. **1918** W. FREAME *Old Memoirs of Hawkesbury, Nepean & Hunter River Districts* 3 Alongside one of those long, winding roads that connect Windsor (N.S.W.) with the Lower Hawkesbury districts, there stood, until recent years, a picturesque old slab cottage, reputed to be one of the oldest habitations in the state. **1839** D. MACKELLAR *Austral. Emigrant's Guide* 9 One **slab-house** for overseer. **1853** *Illustr. Sydney News* 19 Nov. 51/2 A number of new slab houses are in the course of erection in Oakenville intended . . for public houses. **1861** J.D. LANG *Qld., Aust.* 278 A slab-house . . will afford sufficiently comfortable accommodation for any family. **1892** *Missing Friends: Adventures Danish Emigrant Qld.* 155, I, during the twelve months . . learned . . how to build slab-houses, as they are called—that is, to go into the bush, and with the help of a few tools, single-handed, to make a good house out of the growing trees. **1912** *Bulletin* (Sydney) 18 July 15/1 Lived in a one-roomed slab house. **1951** D. COLLINS *Vic.'s my Home Ground* 25 She had been born away back in the bush on Mt. Delusion, and afterwards had lived by herself in a slab-house in a remote gulley. **1951** R. DORIEN *Venturing to Aust.* 15 He built the weatherproof little slab house in which his family lived for many years. **1865** *Colony of Qld. as Field for Emigration* 14 The **slab 'umpie'** or hut of the small farmer or gardener . . situated here and there along the wide sweeping banks of verdure. **1876** 'EIGHT YRS.' RESIDENT' *Queen of Colonies* 109 After pitching their tent or 'knocking up' a slab humpie on the ridge beyond the water-hole and beyond the reach of floods, the ploughshare is at once put into the virgin soil. **1905** *Bulletin* (Sydney) 28 Dec. 14/3 We found the selector sulking in the middle of his slab humpy. **1836** J. BACKHOUSE *Narr. Visit Austral. Colonies* (1843) 418 The married soldiers have built themselves very small, **slab-huts,** covered with sheets of bark, and white-washed. **1848** W. WESTGARTH *Aust. Felix* 84 Several natives had been induced . . to erect slab huts for their own residence. **1862** C. MUNRO *Fern Vale* I. 36 The next habitation will be a slab hut, roofed with sheets of bark. **1890** 'R. BOLDREWOOD' *Colonial Reformer* II. 35 Even the verandah here is considerably better of a hot evening than those rascally slab huts. **1910** *Huon Times* (Franklin) 2 Nov. 2/5 He could remember the time when slab huts were more in evidence than any other class of building. **1931** *Bulletin* (Sydney) 8 July 21/4 An old chap named August Stibbe hopped the last hurdle the other day . . and under the floor of his tumbling slab hut two hundredweight of coins was discovered. **1956** A.C.C. LOCK *Tropical Tapestry* 238 Her home, originally a slab hut of the pioneer days, is now one of the show places of tropical Queensland. **1982** R. HALL *Just Relations* 175 It was a slab hut with some of the roof still on and most of the walls. **1877** 'ANGLO-INDIAN' *Visit Tas.* 22 The **slab road** is 9 miles long from the coast. **1891** J. FENTON *Bush Life Tas.* (1964) 148 The latter work was part of a Parliamentary vote procured by Mr Meredith for . . a slab road up the Gawler. **1896** J.B. WALKER *Corresp., Slabroad,* road made of slabs of timber, an improvet on corduroy wh[ich] is made of round logs. **1897** *Bulletin* (Sydney) 6 Mar. 3/2 It crowds some forty youngsters (sometimes less and sometimes more) In an iron-roofed **slab shanty** fifteen feet by twenty-four. **1933** J. TRURAN *Where Plain Begins* 211 The dingoes barked at night around the slab shanties. **1948** F. CLUNE *Wild Colonial Boys* 23 The foot-weary lags reached a slab shanty with bark roof . . near a ford of the Hunter River. **1880** 'ERRO' *Squattermania* 108 On the **slab table** beside them stood a half-emptied bottle. **1896** H. LAWSON *While Billy Boils* (1975) 19 He found the tin plate, pint-pot, and things set ready for him on the rough slab table under the bush shed. **1922** V. PALMER *Boss of Killara* 113 Half-a-dozen men were sitting round the slab table playing banker. **1853** *Austral. Gold Digger's Monthly Mag.* vii. 251 Two rude bush bedsteads were rigged against the **slab-wall.** **1872** G.S. BADEN-POWELL *New Homes for Old Country* 151 In Australia the buildings of the head station are usually constructed of 'slab' walls. . . Slabs are rough planks, split out of trees, cut to about ten feet in length and one in breadth. **1897** L. LINDLEY-COWEN *W. Austral. Settler's Guide* 298 Inside the slab walls I commenced to put up 18 inches of pug. **1948** *Bulletin* (Sydney) 16 June 23/1 The whiskered old hatter was sitting in the sun, his back against the slab walls of his entirely roofless hut.

slab, *v. Mining.* [f. prec.] *trans.* To support (the sides of a shaft) with slabs. Also as *vbl. n.*, and *absol.*

1854 *Guardian* (Hobart) 25 Mar. 3/4 The Commissioner . . considering the depth, water, slabbing etc., decided in favour of the jumpers. **1856** S.C. BREES *How to farm & settle in Aust.* 58 Shafts are regularly 'slabbed' down the sides with small split boards of the stringy-bark tree. **1857** W. WESTGARTH *Vic. & Austral. Gold Mines* 205 These long shafts became very expensive, as it was necessary also to 'slab' them, or build up their sides with split slabs so as to prevent water and material from pouring down the pit. **1859** W. KELLY *Life in Vic.* I. 216 As they could not be well or securely slabbed downwards from the surface, the digger first sinks nine feet and slabs upwards, and so continues proceeding in spells of nine feet all the way down. **1869** MRS W.M. HOWELL *Diggings & Bush* 92 It was hard work, for the earth was so light they were obliged to slab it. . . 'Fix boards all the way down.' **1870** *Sydney Morning Herald* 4 July 2/4 The gullies, where our alluvial workings are situated, are in such a miry and swampy state that it is dangerous to work underground, and shafts in spite of slabbing are insecure. **1880** 'ERRO' *Squattermania* 341 We have commenced to slab, in order to be safe, though I think the ground would stand without it. **1927** *Rec. Castlemaine Pioneers* 30 Mar. (1972) 228 With a mate I sank a shaft near the spot, but the drift sand made us desist, and as we knew nothing about 'slabbing' or 'timbering' we abandoned the claim.

slabbed, *ppl. a. Obs.*

a. Constructed from slabs; faced with slabs.

1835 *Commercial Jrnl. & Advertiser* (Sydney) 17 Aug. 3/4 There are twenty acres cleared and stumped, with a good Well of Water, and two slabbed and shingled Huts. **1850** *Bell's Life in Sydney* 5 Jan. 1/5 At the slabbed portal of Bombala's gaol. **1853** *Guardian* (Hobart) 3 Sept. 2/1 Offering to build a slabbed tent. **1883** G.E. LOYAU *Personal Adventures* 23 When you go to a bush inn out North . . the landlord usually takes you into a large-sized slabbed room.

b. *Mining.* Supported by slabs.

1859 W. KELLY *Life in Vic.* I. 216 Slabbed holes are generally four feet by two feet ten inches.

slacker. *Hist.* [Spec. use of *slacker* one who shirks work.] One who has failed to volunteer for military service, esp. during the war of 1914–18; SHIRKER.

1917 *Huon Times* (Franklin) 19 Jan. 5/1 This should make the slackers feel their position and go and help those poor wounded heroes who are war-worn and weary. **1918** *Kia Ora Coo-ee* Apr. 7/1 Your blood boils with rage and hate against the slackers who will not go and release the war-weary ones. **1919** *Ross's Monthly* May 4/1 You remember, eh? How you scorned the 'slacker', And became a fervent 'Waac-ker' Of a day? **1929** F. MANNING *Middle Parts of Fortune* II. 276 I'm not fighting for them bloody slackers an' conchies at 'ome. **1930** *Listening Post* (Perth) Apr. 14 The slacker's wife . . said to the soldier's widow. **1956** V. COURTNEY *All I may Tell* 48 There was a deep resentment against those who would not enlist. The term 'slacker' came into common use. **1963** X. HERBERT *Disturbing Element* 141 She had been sending white feathers round to what she now called Slackers ever since Phil's enlistment.

slag, *v.* [Br. dial. *slag* to besmear: see EDD *sb.*[2] and *v.*[2]] *intr.* To spit.

1965 W. DICK *Bunch of Ratbags* 238 He cleared his throat and spat on the car grille, 'Hell', muttered Ritchie, 'he's slaggin' on me car!' **1985** *Bulletin* (Sydney) 8 Oct. 148/4 'Where do I stick it in?' asked the former minister for the Yartz, wielding the knife. 'Jesus', he laughed, 'I've slagged all over it!'

slanguage. Also **slangwidge.** [Spec. use of *slanguage* a slang expression.] A distinctively Australian expression, esp. of the more colourful variety; colloquial Australian speech. Freq. **Australian slanguage.**

1899 W.T. GOODGE *Hits! Skits! & Jingles* 151 And our undiluted English Is a fad to which we cling, But the great Australian slanguage Is a truly awful thing! **1903** *Bulletin* (Sydney) 27 June 17/2 Our great Australian s'language. . . 'A blanky cops pinched a bloke for nippin' tommy off a pie-stall. There 'e gows in the flounder'; and he pointed to where a hansom was disappearing down the street. **1916** O. HOGUE *Trooper Bluegum at Dardanelles* 168 If a bomb exploded right in the trench or on the parapet the real Australian 'Slanguage' was sure to be heard. **1918** *Aussie: Austral. Soldiers' Mag.* Jan. 2/1 He vomited three mouthfuls of the great Australian slanguage over the figure on the road. **1929** 'F. BLAIR' *Digger Sea-Mates* 149 'They're round in the barracks now . . the pair of blasted hobos.' 'Hush-h-h,' said Kiley, inclining his head in the direction of a lady not far away. 'No slanguage here.' **1939** W. HATFIELD *Sheepmates* (ed. 11) 164 I'm going to learn to say 'My bloody oath!' and 'Dinkum, Bonzer' and all the rest of it. . . You'll have to teach me yourself, Whitbread. You have a good command of slanguage. **1967** M. SELLARS *Carramar* 69 'The Orstralian slangwidge as it is spoke,' he drily commented. **1983** *Weekend Austral.* (Sydney) 27 Aug. 20/8 Actually, Australian slanguage is well stocked with words and phrases to describe those who are a bit slow off the mental mark.

slant. *Obs.* [Spec. use of Br. slang *slant* a chance: see OED(S *sb.*[1] 6 and 7.] An opportunity to go somewhere procured as the result of a stratagem.

1835 *Cornwall Chron.* (Launceston) 2 May 3 This was a prosecution at the instance of Constable Thomas Perkins, who is stationed at Birch's Bay and Long Bay, and has detained him in town from his situation as constable for a week. No prosecutor appeared, and there was not the slightest evidence adduced of a felony. This charge appeared to have been trumped up for no other purpose than but for him to get a *slant* to Hobart Town. **1837** *Ibid.* 25 Nov. 2 David Adams, assigned to Mr Barclay, was charged with feigning sickness, by which getting a 'slant' to go to the doctor, he went to a public house instead. **1851** H. MELVILLE *Present State Aust.* 171 He was sent up to Hobart Town on the '*slant*' for trial. **1897** 'P. WARUNG' *Tales Old Regime* 217 Pedder had got tired of things in general, and had organized that movement which was popularly known in Norfolk Island and Port Arthur as a 'slant', that is, he had planned a murder or a mutiny on purpose to obtain a trial in Hobart or Sydney.

slanter /'slantə/, *n.* and *a.* Also **schleinter, schlenter, shlanter, shlinter, slinter.** [a. Du. *slenter* knavery, trick, perh. through S. African English: see OEDS *schlenter.*]

A. *n.* A trick; a fraudulent stratagem.

1864 C.R. THATCHER *Invercargill Minstrel* 15 'Twas a 'shlinter' for the tenant one morning departed Without paying his rent. ***c* 1919** W. LAWLESS *Darcy Story* 41 Les had, on that occasion clearly answered the wiseacres who stated that the first contest was a schlenter. **1919** A. WRIGHT *Game of Chance* 116 'It was a slanter,' cried Mason. 'The dice were loaded; I saw that man next the thrower helping to ring the changes.' **1925** —— *Boy from Bullarah* 133 'A shlanter!' he bellowed, 'Acted for the pictures, an' me layin' two hundred. . . Robbery.' **1941** *Furphy Flyer: Official Organ 2/24 Austral. Infantry Battalion* 19 Aug. 1 Did you think I was running a bloody slanter Bill? **1950** F.J. HARDY *Power without Glory* 134 One rider was prepared to make a sworn statement that the race had been rigged. . . Cycling enthusiasts became convinced that the Austral had been 'a slanter'. **1963** *Qld. Guardian* (Brisbane) 31 July 6/4 How the silvertails work this kind of business. . . He can become a real expert on these slanters. **1966** D. NILAND *Pairs & Loners* 118 'Mistaken, nothing!' roared Tiny. 'You're crazy, Sergeant—can't you see it's a slinter? They've cooked this up between them.'

B. *adj.* Dishonest; crooked.

[N.Z. **1889** WILLIAMS & REEVES *Colonial Couplets* 51 Broke! Broke! Broke! At the will of the C.J.C. For the slenter race with the favourite dead Will never come back to me.] **1895** *Bulletin* (Sydney) 5 Jan. 3/2 The long-beerians, rabbiters, spielers, fat-heads, slanter-bookies, etc., were all there. **1899** J. BRADSHAW *Highway Robbery under Arms* (1912) 39 There they were, six of them, with guns, squirts, tomahawks, shear blades, ironbark waddies, to give me a slanter-go knockabout if I did not hold my hands up. **1901** *Truth* (Sydney) 20 Oct. 4/8 They are usually about Bourke-street, near the 'schleinter' betting clubs. **1918** L.J. VILLIERS *Changing Yr.* 14 'Ooever put the cow outer my name Is square dink fer a cert ter stop a clout. Them shlanter goes gi' me the pip straight out. ***c* 1919** W. LAWLESS *Darcy Story* 26 If he was attempting any schlenter work would it not have been detected.

slather /'slæðə/. [f. Br. dial. and U.S. *slather* to use in large quantities, to squander: see OED(S *v.* and *sb.*] In the collocation **open slather:** freedom to operate without impediment, a 'free rein'; a free-for-all.

1919 V. MARSHALL *World of Living Dead* 71 Try the races up Dingo Creek way. . . They say she's an open slather up there. Not a demon in the burg. **1951** E. HILL *Territory* 326 Out there in the ranges the Diamond Eighty-eight had 'open slather'. **1953** *Meanjin* 18 Women in . . Williamstown know the wage rates as well as we do. A bloke living in Heidelberg or Murrumbeena's got an open slather. His missus never meets other wharfies' wives down the street to check up with. **1960** L.H. EVERS *Make Way for Tomorrow* 158, I told you—you've got an open slather here, lad. Go where you like, do what you like. **1977** B. SCOTT *My Uncle Arch* 63 The bloke who finished first was to have open slather with Maria. **1983** *Canberra Standard* 9 Feb. 1/4 Introduction of draw poker machines and similar machines for gambling purposes was a step towards 'open slather' gambling in the A.C.T.

slaty gum. [See quots. 1889 and 1969.] Any of several trees of the genus *Eucalyptus* (fam. Myrtaceae) having a smooth, greyish bark, esp. *E. dawsonii* of N.S.W.; the wood of these trees.

1889 J.H. MAIDEN *Useful Native Plants Aust.* 470 *Eucalyptus largiflorens* . . is also called 'Slaty Gum', from the grey and white patches on the bark. **1913** *Bulletin* (Sydney) 2 Oct. 24/1 With regard to the 'faking' of timber . . I assert that slaty gum is passed as grey gum, and grey gum goes as ironbark. **1969** S. KELLY *Eucalypts* 66 Slaty gum is a eucalypt of relatively restricted natural distribution. . . The common name refers to the branchlets, leaves and buds which are covered with a waxy bloom and give a greyish appearance to the tree from a distance.

sledge, *v. Cricket.* [See quot. 1982 (2).] *trans.* Of a fielder: to attempt to break the concentration of (a person batting) by the offering of abuse, needling, etc. Freq. as *vbl. n.*

1975 *Sun-Herald* (Sydney) 21 Dec. 49/4 'Sledging' . . or the gentle art of talking a player out . . has no place in women's cricket. **1977** *Austral.* (Sydney) 1 Dec. 18/4 'I haven't heard any sledging or deliberate baiting of batsmen this season,' he said. **1979** *Age* (Melbourne) 2 July 9/6 A year or so earlier the Australian team coined 'sledging' for needling or gamesmanship. Mr Andrews says Frank Tyson has defined it as 'riding downhill to success on the backs of the opposition'. **1980** *Sydney Morning Herald* 16 Oct. 6/2 Crude language is forbidden. This edict should put an end to the disgraceful practice of 'sledging' opponents, an abomination that has become rampant in the game over the last few years. **1982** *Canberra Times* 2 Nov. 8/7 N.S.W.'s fast-bowling hero Len Pascoe, involved in one of Sheffield Shield's ugliest days at the SCG yesterday, was fired up by a barrage of racist 'sledging'. **1982** *Sydney Morning Herald* 4 Nov. 10/2 The court has been told by Ian Chappell that the expression 'sledging' first came into vogue among cricketers in 1963–64. It came from the expression 'subtle as a sledgehammer' at a time when a man called Percy Sledge had a song on the English hit parade. It meant using words to exploit an opponent's weaknesses and put him off his game. **1985** *Good Weekend* (Sydney) 5 Oct. 6/2 Greg was sledged by several young Kiwis and called them 'cheeky brats' and 'prima donnas' in his newspaper column.

sleeper. Used *attrib.* in Comb. designating the activity of procuring and preparing timber for use as railway sleepers, as **sleeper chopper, cutter, getter, -getting** *vbl. n.*, **hewer, -hewing** *vbl. n.*, **squarer, -squaring** *vbl. n.*

1903 *Bulletin* (Sydney) 24 Dec. 36/3 Gum rings in the trees are a frequent and especial trouble. No good **sleeper-chopper** will work a 'ringy' tree, for the sleepers will split along the gum rings. **1908** *Ibid.* 27 Feb. 15/1 The sawn sleeper is inferior because it is cut across the grain, while the sleeper-chopper 'backs' his off with the grain. **1913** *Ibid.* 2 Oct. 24/1 The sleeper-chopper and girder-squarer make chips instead of sawdust. **1899** *Worker* (Sydney) 14 Jan. 4/4 The **sleeper-cutters** on the Moree-Inverell railway complain of the rate of wages received. **1914** *School Paper* (Melbourne) 1 Apr. 55 His father was a sleeper-cutter . . working in . . the forest. **1935** *Red Star* (Perth) 15 Feb. 4/1 More trouble has occurred at the sleeper-cutters' camp at the 53-mile peg on the Albany Road. **1946** *Service Publication No. 6* (School Public Health & Tropical Med.) 243 The victim, a strong healthy sleeper cutter at Wauchope, N.S.W., was treated by Dr W. Begg. **1981** E. ROLLS *Million Wild Acres* 2 'Have you been there?' a sleeper cutter asked me in a Wee Waa hotel. **1900** *Bulletin* (Sydney) 18 Aug. 15/1, I . . was always sure of having at least four yarns in the week—two to the mailman and two to a couple of **sleeper-getters.** **1903** *Ibid.* 24 Dec. 36/4 In addition to being an expert sleeper-getter, he worked from 'jackass to jackass', going to the bush at daylight and coming back when he could no longer see to work. **1918** B. REYNOLDS *Dawn Asper* 113 The sleeper-getters had made up their minds to try the same dodge. **1903** *Bulletin* (Sydney) 17 Jan. 16/4, I was camped out last Dec. **sleeper-getting** for Narrabri-Walgett railway. **1914** *Ibid.* 11 June 22/3 The bush is no good. It doesn't matter whether it's sleepergetting, or ringbarking, or fencing, or anything else you're at. **1927** T.S. GROSER

Lure of Golden West 104 See the **sleeper-hewer** at work. **1933** C.E.W. Bean *Official Hist. Aust. 1914–18* IV. 460 L/Cpl. R.T. Pettifer, M.M. . . sleeper-hewer, of Bailieston, Vic. **1927** T.S. Groser *Lure of Golden West* 104 **Sleeper-hewing**, in itself, is an important branch of the timber industry. **1885** *Evening News* (Sydney) 3 Mar. 1/5 Goulburn and Cooma railway. . . **Sleeper squarers** . . wanted. . . Apply Fishburn and Co., Young. **1921** *Bulletin* (Sydney) 31 Mar. 22/2 N.S.W. North Coast sleeper-squarers are not a bit surprised at 'J.G.'s' bloke . . who squares the four sides of a 5 ft. 3 in. gauge sleeper in 21 clouts—but 'J.G.' omitted to say how many shouts it takes to square the man who passed it. **1942** *Ibid.* 11 Mar. 12/4 There was no better sleeper-squarer in the district than little Micky. **1903** *Sporting News* (Launceston) 5 Sept. 2/5 With sundry sawing contests, **sleeper-squaring** matches, and other events.

sleeping lizard. [See quot. 1899.] Any of several lizards, incl. Bobtail and some species of the genus *Tiliqua* (see *blue-tongue lizard* Blue *a.*); Boggi 1. Also **sleepy lizard.**

1844 L. Leichhardt *Jrnl. Overland Exped. Aust.* 27 Dec. (1847) 85 Mr Gilbert found a new species of sleeping lizard, with four lighter stripes on the dark brown ground along the back, and with dark spots on the sides. **1846** G.H. Haydon *Five Yrs. Experience Aust. Felix* 74 The sleeping lizard, (*cycladas gigas*) was long considered venomous, but I have reason to think it is not so. **1861** 'Old Bushman' *Bush Wanderings* 206 The *Sleeping* or *Stump-lizard* is another repulsive-looking but inoffensive reptile. ***c* 1872** J.C.F. Johnson *Over Island* 10 As soon as I entered I tripped over a great ugly 'sleeping lizard'. **1882** F. McCoy *Prodromus Zool. Vic.* (1885) I. viii. 15 These Lizards are very sluggish, so that the popular name 'Sleepy Lizard' as well as 'Blue-tongue' comes to be applied to both. **1899** R. Semon *In Austral. Bush* 183 The lazy torpid 'sleeping lizards' (*Tiliqua scincoides*). **1924** Lord & Scott *Synopsis Vertebrate Animals Tas.* 115 *Blue tongued lizard* . . is sometimes referred to as . . the 'Sleepy' or 'Jew Lizard'. **1933** C.W. Peck *Austral. Legends* (ed. 2) 57 A family which claimed the sleeping lizard as its totem was camped in a scrub of Murray Pine. **1956** A.C.C. Lock *Tropical Tapestry* 107 Alan swerved to avoid running over a sleepy lizard. **1970** R. Bustard *Austral. Lizards* 116 The sleepy lizard (*Trachydosaurus rugosus*), more commonly known outside Australia as the stump-tailed skink, is widely distributed on the mainland occurring in inland areas of all States.

sleep-out.

1. A place to sleep outdoors.

1919 *Bulletin* (Sydney) 4 Dec. 20/2 While enjoying a casual after-tea walk in search of a suitable 'sleep-out' an unsympathetic policeman put an end to the great adventure.

2. A verandah, porch, or outbuilding providing sleeping accommodation. Also *attrib.*

1927 *Link* (Melbourne) 1 Oct. 8 The jobs that can be done . . building sleep-outs. **1929** A. Smith *Austral. Home Carpenter* 126 A sleep-out room for the children. An open-air bedroom that is easily and cheaply constructed. **1931** B. Cronin *Bracken* 244 The flat contained three rooms, a bathroom, a kitchenette, and a small balcony sleep-out. **1936** *Bulletin* (Sydney) 28 Oct. 20/1 We retired to the shakedown on the back verandah after some hours yarning. Our host shared the sleep-out with us. **1946** A.J. Holt *Wheat Farms Vic.* 73 About two-thirds of these sleep-outs are used all the year around. In eight houses, including six in the Mallee, the whole family sleeps out. **1959** L. Rose *Country of Dead* 114 He looked up through the gauze wire serving as the outer wall of the sleep-out, across the dry river flat. **1965** G. McInnes *Road to Gundagai* 62 We stirred in our sleep, naked under a thin cotton sheet on the back porch, or 'sleep-out'. **1986** *Good Weekend* (Sydney) 19 Apr. 11/1 He . . bought some land and built a sleep-out with his own hands before extending it into a house.

sleepy lizard: see Sleeping lizard.

sleever. *Obs.* Abbrev. of *long-sleever* (see Long 1).

1901 *Bulletin* (Sydney) 28 Dec. 32/4 Striking a pub . . I unyoked, thinking that a 'sleever' would be welcome.

slew, *v.* Also **sleu.** [Prob. f. *slewed* drunk: see OED.]

1. In the phr. **to get** (or **be**) **slewed,** to be(come) lost, esp. in the bush.

1879 *Truth* (Sydney) 30 Oct. 3/1, I guess you thought that I was high up the river with the Inspector and his black trackers close on my heels, but it is not the first time they have been slewed. **1898** *Western Champion* (Barcaldine) 20 Sept. 5/5, I got to within four miles of the station when I became 'slewed' among a number of dry creeks and gullies. **1904** *Advocate* (Burnie) 7 Mar. 4/5 Mr Frank Thow . . got 'slewed' in the bush between St. Valentine's Peak and the Leven River. **1927** M. Terry *Through Land of Promise* 222 No wonder Wallaby had got 'slewed', as they say locally, before reaching the well and had taken us over half a mile to the sou' east before realising his error. **1935** A. Francis *Then & Now* 76 After walking for a long time in what I thought was the right direction, I happened to look up, and found that I was again opposite to Broad Street station. . . In Queensland I should have been told that I had been properly 'slewed'. **1935** H.H. Finlayson *Red Centre* 129 My faith in Hector as a guide received a shock. When questioned closely he admitted rather sheepishly that he was 'sleued'. **1953** G. Pike *Campfire Tales* (1981) 44 One had to walk wherever one went—no roads and no horses at first. Many a time I got 'slewed' in the virgin scrub. **1978** Teece & Pike *Voice of Wilderness* 179 That is where I must have got 'slewed' for . . the sun came out and I could see we were heading into the sun instead of having sundown at our backs.

2. *trans.* To defeat (a person), to 'settle'.

1890 H.A. White *Crime & Criminals* 152 The fellow, placing his thumb to his nose, said in a jeering manner, 'That slues you mate.' **1903** J. Furphy *Such is Life* 230 Admiral Cry-ton. That slews you! Didn't I tell you you'd be cutting yourself? **1941** S.J. Baker *Pop. Dict. Austral. Slang* 67 *Slew, to*, to beat, outwit a person. **1975** *Bulletin* (Sydney) 26 Apr. 45/3 Ratty Jack was stallin' for me to pussy in as soon as Limp slews the tart.

slice. A one-pound note.

1946 A. Green *We were (Riff) R.A.A.F.* 54 He played the national game until he had lifted a few 'slices' (N.T. slang for pound notes). **1950** *Austral. Police Jrnl.* Apr. 118 *Slice*, £1. **1966** S.J. Baker *Austral. Lang.* (ed. 2) 115 £1, . . slice.

sling, *n.* [f. Sling *v.* 2.] A gift; a bribe. Also **sling-back.**

1948 K.S. Prichard *Golden Miles* 74 'There's some hungry bastards', the men said, 'makin' big money on their ore, and never give the poor bugger boggin' for 'em a sling back.' The sling back might be ten bob on pay-day, or no more than a few pots of beer, but was always appreciated. **1953** K. Tennant *Joyful Condemned* 232 Say I take twenty per cent of the cop for myself. . . All the rest goes in slings. **1967** *Kings Cross Whisper* (Sydney) xl. 4/5 *Sling*, a bribe. The fare home given to losing punters at the two-up. **1977** R. Beilby *Gunner* 296 The ring-keeper was desperate, prowling around the ring at intervals, beseeching . . 'Come on, ya've had a good run. What about a sling?' **1982** *Canberra Times* 29 Apr. 1/4 To have a house, in effect, given to you is, to put it colloquially, a sling of major proportions.

sling, *v.*

1. In the phr. **to sling the billy (kettle, pot):** see Billy *n.*[1] 6.

2. *intr.* To make a gift; to pay a bribe. Also *trans.*

[**1875** *Austral. Town & Country Jrnl.* (Sydney) 4 Sept. 383/4, I dare say he'll sling me a tenner, if it turns out all right.] ***c* 1907** W.C. Chandler *Darkest Adelaide* 5 'Come on. Sling. . . If you don't dub up I'll punch you on the blanky jaw.' This seemed to have the desired effect, for she freely parted with two bob out of the four she had. **1915** Drew & Evans *Grafter* 54 'How does he sling?' 'Fair, but I don't know how he'd sling if he had a good winning day.' **1939** K. Tennant *Foveaux* 172 'I'm slinging it to Hamp,' Bardy said sullenly. **1949** L. Glassop *Lucky Palmer* 21 'Here's a fiver for you,' said Fred, handing Max five crumpled one pound notes. 'That's your chop. Don't say I didn't sling.' **1959** *Bulletin* (Sydney) 16/3 Annual sports-meeting at a Victorian town, and Bung slung a bottle of whisky for the married ladies' race. **1968** J. Alard *He who shoots Last* 292 He once told me dat da hoods dese days sling ta da coppers and shoot deir mates. **1971** F. Hardy *Outcasts of Foolgarah* 56 On first name terms with every shire President so long as they didn't forget to sling when backhanders came in.

3. In the phr. **to sling off,** *throw off*, see Throw *v.* 2.

1900 *Tocsin* (Melbourne) 18 Jan. 8/1 If the Tocsin had for a moment supposed that Brassey's bike and boat idea was inspired by a desire to be unostentatious, it would not have 'slung off' at it. ***c* 1907** W.C. Chandler *Darkest Adelaide* 32 A young fellow . . will come mooching along on a bike. Two or three young chickens sling off at him, he slings off in reply and dismounting from his bike, enters into conversation with the girls. **1916** *Truth* (Sydney) 1 Oct. 12/3 'One of the Bulldog Breed' is also doing some 'slinging off' about food. **1929** K.S. Prichard *Coonardoo* (1961) 92 We sling off at the man who makes his abos 'sir' or 'boss' him. **1942** *Aust.: Nat. Jrnl.* 1 Feb. 12 Through everything we never cease slinging off about the Singapore situation. **1960** D. Ireland *Image in Clay* (1964) 61, I don't hear her slinging off at you; why poke crap at her? **1968** D. O'Grady *Bottle of Sandwiches* 7 You could sling off at him as much as you liked, and it never worried him. **1977** R. Beilby *Gunner* 90, I wasn't slinging off at your religion.

slinging, *vbl. n. Australian National Football.* See quot. 1973.

1885 D.E. McConnell *Austral. Etiquette* 641 Tripping, hacking, rabbiting, slinging, or catching hold of a player below the knee are prohibited. **1903** *Sporting News* (Launceston) 16 May 3/7 The Victorian League has altered the rule, whereby the field umpire is now empowered to award free kicks for 'slinging' or 'attempting to sling'. **1931** J.F. McHale et al. *Austral. Game of Football* 7 Rule 8 now reads: 'Tripping, hacking, rabbiting, and slinging are prohibited.' **1973** B. Hogan *Follow Game* (rev. ed.) 73 Slinging is the act of catching a player by or around the neck and throwing or attempting to throw him on to the ground.

Hence **slinger** *n.*

1931 J.F. McHale et al. *Austral. Game of Football* 58 A sling round the neck . . is always penalised by a free kick given against the 'slinger'.

slinter, var. Slanter.

slip, *n. S.A. Hist.* Abbrev. of Green slip.

1838 *Southern Austral.* (Adelaide) 6 Oct. 3/2 These slips, or residues of preliminary sections, have been tendered for by parties claiming a legal right. **1839** *S. Austral. Rec.* (London) 10 Apr. 176 After the holders of preliminary sections had chosen their land in that district, the purchasers of 80 acre sections were allowed to select their land out of the remaining unselected 134 acre sections, thus leaving unappropriated about 54 acres on each preliminary section. These portions or *slips* were regularly marked on the Surveyor-General's maps and coloured green; some of these *slips* have been tendered for in the usual manner. *Ibid.* 8 May 187 At all events . . his Excellency would be able to resort to the auction, in order to dispose of the troublesome *slips.*

slip, *v.*

1. *trans.* With **up**: to defraud or swindle (a person); to disappoint.

1874 'Special Reporter' *Agric. in S.A.* 35 Mr Hughes has obtained notoriety as a gentleman who has been 'slipped up' by his dummies. This phrase is the one commonly used to describe the breaking of faith with the squatter by the dummy, and the conversion of the land by appropriation or commercial transfer to his own benefit. **1882** *Three L's* 329 To tell you the truth, Mr Brag, I have been awfully 'slipped up' lately by a scoundrel that I had worked hard for. **1891** N. Gould *Double Event* 92 It's deuced hard lines . . to be slipped up like this. **1904** *Rep. R. Comm. Non-British Labour* (W.A.) 75 Whereas the storekeeper had been 'slipped up' by scores of other miners, the Italians had never treated him like that yet. **1904** L.M.P. Archer *Bush Honeymoon* 117 When he came back, he found the girl had slipped him up and married a boundary rider.

2. *intr.* [Survival of Br. slang: see OED *v.*[1] 2 c.] With **into**: to give a beating to (a person). Also *fig.*

1972 J. McNeil *Old Familiar Juice* (1973) 66 Yer forgot ter bring 'em up. . . Yer must be slipping. . . I'll slip inter you inner minute! **1974** Stackpole & Trengove *Not just for Openers* 83 When the crowd reacted by giving Bill a bit of hurry-up, he turned to the grandstand and expressed his feelings. The Press slipped into him over that.

slip-panel. SLIP-RAIL a.

1844 *Parramatta Chron.* 21 Sept. 2/2 John Star, the plaintiff's servant, was in his master's paddock when the defendants and another man pulled down the slip pannel, and insisted on riding through the paddock. **1861** *Number One* (Adelaide) Apr. 12 A few yards brought us to the slip-panel, and we struck off for the homestead, situate about half way up the section. **1873** J.C.F. JOHNSON *Christmas on Carringa* 11 He . . was fumbling at the top rail—slip-panels being to him a novelty. **1891** 'SMILER' *Wanderings Simple Child* (ed. 3) 69 After shaking me until my nose bled, the beast gently carried me to the slip-panel and deposited me on the other side. **1911** *Huon Times* (Franklin) 4 Mar. 6/3 It was resolved that the council had no power to grant permission to erect slip panels across public roads. **1934** J.C. LEE *Boshstralians* 187 Spikey . . was in the act of swinging himself on to the top rail of the slip-panel.

slippery. [f. the heavy coating of slime on the skin of the fish.] The fish *Gadopsis marmoratus* (see BLACKFISH).

1906 D.G. STEAD *Fishes of Aust.* 210 Amongst the Australian Blennies, there is one of considerable economic importance. This is the so-called 'Slippery' or River Blackfish. **1941** *Bulletin* (Sydney) 26 Mar. 16/4 My blackfish was the southern freshwater kind (*Gadopsis marmoratus*). Once plentiful in any Gippsland creek, the 'Slipperies' are vanishing before the sustained attack of trout. **1984** MERRICK & SCHMIDA *Austral. Freshwater Fishes* 269 River Blackfish or Slippery. . . This furtive species . . is usually less than 300 mm. long and 220 to 450 g.

slippery bob. *Obs.* See quot. 1864.

1864 *Colonial Cook Bk.* (1970) 72 Slippery Bob. Take kangaroo brains, and mix with flour and water, and make into batter; well season with pepper, salt, etc.; then pour a table-spoonful at a time into an iron pot containing emeu fat, and take them out when done. **1970** J.S. GUNN in W.S. Ramson *Eng. Transported* 63 Such food references as . . *slippery bob* and *pan jam* are well left to history.

slip-rail.

a. A fence-rail, forming one of a set which can be slipped out so as to leave an opening; the opening so formed: see quot. 1844. Also *attrib.*

1827 P. CUNNINGHAM *Two Yrs. in N.S.W.* I. 206 Some of the young saplings do contract most amazingly, and most quickly. Twice were the slip-rails of a gate reported to me as too short, and tumbling out. **1844** MRS C. MEREDITH *Notes & Sketches N.S.W.* 130 You never see a *gate*. . . 'Slip-rails' are the substitute; five or six heavy long poles loosely inserted in sockets made in two upright posts. **1845** M.T. VIDAL *Tales for Bush* 55 She . . walked on a few steps, and stood leaning over the slip-rail leading into the bush. **1865** *Austral. Monthly Mag.* I. 234 The rider desired them to pull down the slip-rails, which they did, and away went man and beast at a tremendous pace across the plain. **1872** MRS E. MILLETT *Austral. Parsonage* 54 We found our way in by taking a couple of movable rails out of the notches made in two of the posts to facilitate their removal. This awkward contrivance is called a 'slip rail', and is universally resorted to in all cases where the absence of carpenters of sufficient skill to manufacture proper gates renders some such substitute necessary. **1882** A.J. BOYD *Old Colonials* 192 Passing through a sliprail, I dismount at the verandah of a very comfortable-looking slab-and-bark house. **1900** *Bulletin* (Sydney) 21 Apr. 3/2 The lovers standing at the sliprail gate. **1920** *Huon Times* (Franklin) 30 Apr. 3/6 You see, the old bloke has been looking after the goanna farm, but he's getting old and forgetful like. He left the sliprails down one night, and all me blinkin' goannas got out. **1944** 'S. CAMPION' *Pommy Cow* 278 She let the slip-rail down for him . . reaching up for a last kiss as any bush girl would do . . farewelling her lover. **1962** E. LANE *Mad as Rabbits* 123 She could grow almost anything, and Uncle used to say that if she rubbed her big, heavy hands over a slip-rail, and then put grass on it, the grass would grow. **1981** A. MARSHALL *Aust.* p. vii, The Australian countryman's habit of sitting beside a mate on the top of the sliprails while they yarned about the problems common to them both.

b. *fig.*

1892 *Bulletin* (Sydney) 7 May 24/1 He soon must mount his bluey for The last long tramp of all; I trust that when in bush an' town, He's lived and learnt his fill, They'll let the golden slip-rails down For poor old Corny Bill. **1894** W. CROMPTON *Convict Jim* 36 Till I enter through ther slip-rails of ther never never gate.

slop, *n.*[1] *Obs.* [Transf. use of *slops* ready-made clothing and other furnishings supplied to seamen from a ship's stores: see OEDS *sb.*[1] 5. The word is used elsewhere during the 19th century but has a strong local significance.]

A. *n. pl.* Clothing issued by a colonial administration; clothing in general, usu. ready-made, but see quot. 1892.

1791 *HRA* (1914) 1st Ser. I. 239 A supply of provisions we have had, but cloathing not a rag, notwithstanding a great part of the slops sent in the Sirius for the use of the convicts were never put into store. **1801** *Gen. Orders issued by Governor King* 4 Sept. (1802) 60 A proportion of Slops will be issued to the Prisoners and Freemen victualled from the public stores, on Friday the 11th, and Saturday the 12th Inst. when those who do not attend will be excluded. **1816** *HRA* (1921) 3rd Ser. II. 156 A ship will arrive here from England in the course of a month with all kinds of Stores and Slops for the use of the Colony. **1825** *Ibid.* (1917) 1st Ser. XI. 659 A suit of slops, comprising one Jacket or frock, one shirt, one pair Trowsers, and one pair of shoes issued to every man on his completing 6 months in the employ of Government. **1831** *Sydney Herald* 8 Aug. 3/1 Masters are to pay twenty shillings for every assigned servant they may receive from the ship or road stations, as a remuneration to Government for slops. **1842** *Sydney Morning Herald* 5 Aug. 1/2 A general assortment of slops, blankets, rugs, &c., for settlers. **1846** *Moreton Bay Courier* 24 Oct. 1/4 David Jones and Co. beg to apprise their numerous friends and the public generally in the district of Moreton Bay, that . . their stock of Slops and General Clothing . . is at present replete with every article required, both for the bush and private families. **1852** G.C. MUNDY *Our Antipodes* I. 66 Slops are nearly always cheap, for they are mostly the work of the wretched sisterhood of London needlewomen! **1876** G.H. REID *Essay on N.S.W.* 88 He was able to supply Sydney made clothing . . to the country storekeepers cheaper than the importer of English slops. **1880** *Argus* (Melbourne) 16 Feb. 6/7 Slops—i.e., coats, shirts &c.—could be sent to other colonies and sold at prices which enabled them to compete with the imported article. **1892** 'MRS A. MACLEOD' *Silent Sea* III. 293 'Mother, the greatest happiness of your life is having slops made for people,' Rachel says to me sometimes, laughing, and perhaps it is true in a way. **1902** E.B. KENNEDY *Black Police Qld.* 33 We were both free agents, and packing . . consisted of throwing sundry 'slops', as ready-made clothing was called, into a couple of leather bags. **1911** L. STONE *Jonah* 207 Chinamen stand on guard . . clothed in the cheap slops of Sydney. **1917** *Truth* (Sydney) 13 May 1/8 The Dominion soldiers look so much nicer than the Sydneysiders . . because they have their uniforms made to order, while the Australians wear slops.

B. *attrib.*

1. a. Of or pertaining to clothing issued by a colonial administration or to ready-made clothing in general.

1789 [see *slop clothing* below]. **1800** *HRA* 1st Ser. II. 634 A clothing and slop-expence book, for those supported by the Crown. **1839** J. STEPHENS *Land of Promise* 80 Our store-keeper supplied him with slop-trousers and a military jacket. **1841** *Sydney Herald* 26 Apr. 2/3 Slop shoes and boots could be made by male prisoners of the Crown, which would encourage colonial leather. **1848** *Sydney Guardian* 101/1 Edmund Perryon . . I met the other day in a slop suit of clothes. ***c* 1852** A. MANN *Goldfields Aust.* 31 Provisions &c., are at a high rate here . . oats, 18s. per bushel; slop boots, 24s. per pair. **1856** D.J. GOLDING *Emigrant's Guide Aust.* (1973) 103 The usual male attire is a pair of common slop trousers, a blue guernsey, with a leathern belt to keep the trousers up and the guernsey down [etc.]. **1864** J. ARMOUR *Diggings, Bush & Melbourne* 15 These having been made debtors for 'slop' goods . . felt themselves to be on the wrong side of the law. **1882** *Bulletin* (Sydney) 13 May 16/1 Edward Hordern And Sons . . have this week Opened their New Hat And Slop Departments. **1896** H. LAWSON *While Billy Boils* (1975) 61 Slop sac suits, red faces, and old-fashioned, flat-brimmed hats, with wire round the brims. **1907** *Bulletin* (Sydney) 14 Nov. 14/2 Bill Bush doesn't wear slop clothes any more. He gets them tailor-made. **1919** C. DREW *Doings of Dave* 156 His coat slop made. **1978** M. WALKER *Pioneer Crafts Early Aust.* 74 People could buy apparel 'off the hook' from the town retailer but this cheap, standardised costume was anathema to many country women, who referred to it as 'slop clothes'.

b. *transf.* Supported by the government.

1832 *Hill's Life N.S.W.* (Sydney) 27 Aug. 2 The *beaks* . . sent the two victorines among others to the slop shop. *Seven days imprisonment.* **1836** *Bent's News* (Hobart) 3 Sept. 3 *The Courier.* We were much amused this morning with the leading article in the Slop Journal. *Ibid.* 22 Oct. 2 Poor Bent had worked hard, and he also had a large family, when the bread was taken out of their mouths, to pay for the silly drivellings of the Slop Editor.

2. Comb. **slop clothing, made** *a.*, **seller, shop.**

1789 J. HUNTER *Hist. Jrnl. Trans. Port Jackson* (1793) 371 Every free person or convict is strictly forbid buying or selling any article of **slop cloathing.** **1811** *Sydney Gaz.* 5 Jan., Constables will be victualled from His Majesty's Stores from the 1st of January next, inclusive, and receive one Watch-Coat and the usual quantity of Slop Cloathing annually. **1822** J.T. BIGGE *Rep. State Colony N.S.W.* 38 Considerable loss has also been sustained by government, in the quantities of slop clothing and bedding that the convicts in the road parties were perpetually detected in selling to the lower classes of settlers. **1832** J. BUSBY *Authentic Information N.S.W. & N.Z.* 8 The consumption of slop clothing of English manufacture is now almost altogether replaced by that of a coarse woollen cloth. **1849** A. HARRIS *Guide Port Stephens* 129 Tailors are not much in request up the country, as slop-clothing imported is chiefly worn. **1880** 'OLD HAND' *Experiences of Colonist* (ed. 2) i. 61 His annual supply of necessaries sent to the nearest township consisted of some flour, tea, sugar, vinegar, and salt, and occasionally some slop clothing. **1898** *Western Champion* (Barcaldine) 11 Oct. 3/4 No wonder slop clothing is so cheap. **1856** G. WILLMER *Draper in Aust.* 232 There is abundance of **slop-made** goods at present in Australia. **1896** *Bulletin* (Sydney) 11 Apr. 7/3 The amount paid by Sydney clothing-factories for 'slop-made' trousers ranges from 10d. to as low as 5d. per pair. **1925** A. WRIGHT *Boy from Bullarah* 9 In his recently purchased ill-fitting, slop-made suit. **1934** J.C. LEE *Boshstralians* 82 Clad in his 'best Sunday go-to-meeting clobber'—which, being interpreted was a cheap 'slop-made' suit of indefinite texture and cut. **1956** T. RONAN *Moleskin Midas* 265 Yates in his own words, was 'done up to the bitchin' nines' in new slop-made moleskin trousers. **1843** *Dispatch* (Sydney) 11 Nov. 3/4 Draper, hosier, haberdasher, and **slopseller.** **1844** *Duncan's Weekly Register* (Sydney) 7 Sept. 125/3 Country gentlemen who are desirous of obtaining the 'most complete cut' should purchase 'a suit for £3 3s.' of any advertising slopseller. **1845** C. GRIFFITH *Present State & Prospects Port Phillip* 72 Grocers and slopsellers seem to do the most business: the latter branch, as in many other places, being nearly altogether in the hands of the Jews. **1841** *Bell's Life in Sydney* 6 Sept. 1/1 Nearly every tailor in Sydney charges such high prices that it has driven a great portion of the middle and lower classes of society to obtain their clothes from Drapers and **Slop Shops.** **1879** *Kelly Gang* 125 His dress . . consisted of . . an ordinary flannel singlet, covered by an olive-green Crimean shirt; trousers of a kind known in the slop-shops as 'coloured moles'. **1911** L. STONE *Jonah* 156 The crude fashions of the slop-shop . . jarred on her nerves. **1928** B. CRONIN *Dragonfly* 189 'There's that young cub of a Cardew, got up like a slop-shop dummy,' the manager said.

slop, *n.*[2] *pl.* [Orig. U.S.: see OEDS *sb.*[2] 3 c.] Beer; alcoholic liquor generally.

1944 L. GLASSOP *We were Rats* 120 If I ever get ter Germany I'll have a go at their slops. In one er them big beer gardens. **1953** T.A.G. HUNGERFORD *Riverslake* 197 His wife and both of his kids got burned to death when his house went up. . . They reckon that's what sent him on to the slops in the first place. **1968** D. O'GRADY *Bottle of Sandwiches* 14 We did think . . that it would be a good idea to get a dozen of each kind of grog we'd sampled along the way so we'd have a variety in places where no slops were available. **1969** O. WHITE *Under Iron Rainbow* 33 What else is there to do in this godforsaken country except work and go on the slops? **1982** R. HALL *Just Relations* 31 You and my grandson here on the slops, is that it?

sloper. [Spec. use of Br. dial. *sloper* trickster, defrauder: see EDD *slope, v.*[1]] One who leaves a place without discharging a debt.

1896 *Bulletin* (Sydney) 18 Jan. 3/2 You strike the stores for credit. They've all 'heard that yarn before'—They've 'had enough of slopers', an' they 'don't take any more!' **1915** A. WRIGHT *Sport from Hollowlog Flat* 108 As is always the case on large camps, there was a number of 'slopers', men who collected their wages and left their creditors to mourn their loss. **1981** H.C. MILLS *No Regrets* 78 The 'sloper'—the man who decamped without paying his debts, the worst of criminals.

slot. A prison cell; also, a prison.

1947 *Pix* (Sydney) 20 Sept. 15 *Peter* or *slot*, cell. **1950** *Austral. Police Jrnl.* Apr. 118 *Slot*, gaol cell. **1968** J. ALARD *He who shoots Last* 196 Siddy was in the next slot to Taggy. **1975** *Bulletin* (Sydney) 26 Apr. 46/2 A cell is called a peter, slot or tank. **1976** *Cleo* Aug. 33 Some of the old heads are in the slot, he says. The slot is jail.

sloth. *Obs.* [Transf. use of *sloth* an arboreal mammal.] KOALA 1.

1811 G. PATERSON *Hist. N.S.W.* 417 The Koolah, or Sloth, a singular animal of the Opossum species, having a false belly, was found by the natives. **1829** R. MUDIE *Picture of Aust.* 170 The *Koala*, to which the colonists give the name of the sloth. **1845** E.J. EYRE *Jrnls. Exped. Central Aust.* II. 282 The sloth .. is .. caught among the branches of the larger scrub-trees. **1862** J.G. WOOD *Illustr. Nat. Hist.* I. 468 (OED) The name of Australian sloth .. has been applied to it [*sc.* the Koala, *Phascolarctos cinereus*] because it is able to cling with its feet to the branches after the manner of the sloths. **1886** F. COWAN *Aust.* 21 A makeshift Monkey, Bear, and Sloth.

slouch hat. [Fig. use of *slouch hat* the hat worn by an Australian soldier.] Used allusively as an emblem of patriotism and courage.

1927 K. BURKE *With Horse & Morse* 67 The 'butterfly' badges on their slouch hats had faded to a leaden grey. **1941** *Ack Ack News* (Melbourne) May 7 Proud of the old slouch hat. **1944** I. SABEY *Noel Nocturne* 6 The old slouch hat is seldom seen: We lost 'em on the shores of Greece. **1965** D. MARTIN *Hero of Too* 30 Lads who had been too young to don the slouch hat put on cabbage-tree hats with dangling corks, got into shearers' garb and intoned shearers' songs. **1978** B. ST. A. SMITH *Spirit beyond Psyche* 48 As an ex-Dig., I'm ashamed of the disgrace this government of ours has brought to the old slouch-hat. **1985** M. WALSH *May Gibbs* 126 Calendars featuring all the bush creatures, the favourite being a kookaburra depicted as a world war veteran wearing the Australian slouch hat.

Slowbart. *Obs.* Alteration of 'Hobart', the name of the capital city of Tasmania.

1895 *Bulletin* (Sydney) 10 Aug. 15/3 At Slowbart recently, a defending solicitor was questioning a publican, witness for the prosecution. **1905** *Truth* (Sydney) 24 Sept. 1/7 Parramatta has always been regarded as a Sleepy Hollow—sleepier than Slowbart, Tasmania. **1908** *Ibid.* 16 Aug. 9/8 Sinful Slowbart.

slow strike. *Obs.* GO-SLOW a.

1917 *Award for Shearing, Crutching, & Wool-Scouring* (Cwlth. Court Conciliation & Arbitration) 42 A 'slow strike' has been held to be a breach of Clause 1 in that men deliberately shearing slowly are not shearing 'with all reasonable despatch'. **1918** J.H.C. SLEEMAN *Queer Qld.* 32 At the Ross River meatworks, the employees on contract hit upon a 'slow strike' as a means to harass the employers.

slow-worm. [Transf. use of *slow-worm* a small, harmless lizard.] Any of the small, worm-like, burrowing snakes of the genus *Ramphotyphlops* of mainland Aust. and elsewhere; any of many lizards of the fam. Pygopodidae of mainland Aust.

1824 J. LYCETT *Views in Aust.* 4 Of poisonous reptiles, the .. slow-worm and snake, are the most hurtful. **1847** *Moreton Bay Courier* 29 May 4/2 The slow-worms are from three to twelve inches long, and a dirty brown colour. **1943** C. BARRETT *Austral. Animal Bk.* 319 Our legless lizards, generally called slow-worms, belong to a family that is typically Australian. **1970** R. BUSTARD *Austral. Lizards* 81 In Australia they [*sc.* the Pygopodidae] are sometimes called 'slow-worms' perhaps because the early European settlers were familiar with the slow-worm (*Anguis fragilis*) of their original homeland.

slug. [U.S. *slug* a piece of crude metal; a nugget (of gold): see OED(S *sb.*[2] 3 a.]

a. A large piece of crude metal found on or just below the surface; a nugget of gold. Also **slug gold,** and *attrib.*

1888 [see sense b. below]. **1891** 'SMILER' *Wanderings Simple Child* (ed. 3) 34 Silver was found lying round on the surface in lumps, or, as they were called, 'slugs'. **1895** *Worker* (Sydney) 2 Feb. 2/4 A slug of gold weighing 104 oz. has been picked up at Coolgardie. **1903** *Bulletin* (Sydney) 7 Feb. 16/3 Lake Way was a great 'specking patch', and the gins .. were great speckers, and brought in a lot of slug gold. **1913** 'D. DELANEY' *Captain of Gang* 64 He has at least twenty ounces of nuggets and slugs in his leather bag. **1921** W.H. PHIPPS *Bush Yarns* 92 Sailor Bill started a collection with a 5 oz. slug. .. Other delighted men dropped nuggety gold. **1934** T. WOOD *Cobbers* 107 In the early days men grew rich simply by picking up 'slugs'—that is nuggets—which lay on the ground or just below its surface. **1946** K.S. PRICHARD *Roaring Nineties* 33 Tom Risley picked up the first 'slug' on the spot and located the reef. **1977** J. DOUGHTY *Gold in Blood* 49 For weeks they failed to raise a 'colour'. It was slug-or-nothing ground they were told. 'If you get a colour you'll get a slug.'

b. In the phr. **to travel on the slug:** see quot. 1888.

1888 'SPECIAL CORRESPONDENT' *Barrier Silver & Tin Fields* 11 It was a common thing for miners to travel 'on the slug'. A man would walk into a mining township, produce to the storekeeper a slug of very rich silver, and on the strength of having discovered a good claim get anything he wanted in the way of stores for himself and camp for weeks. Travelling 'on the slug' does not obtain now. **1890** *Truth* (Sydney) 14 Sept. 4/4 He has caught all the varying lights and shades of the shifting panorama of mining life, and the managers, the experts, the promoters, the gamblers, the travellers on the slug, the barmaids, the flats, the swindlers and the loafers stand before us as they lived and moved. **1891** 'SMILER' *Wanderings Simple Child* (ed. 3) 35 It would be worse than useless for an enterprising loafer to try to travel on the slug in the present day.

Hence **sluggy** *a.*, (of gold) in the form of a slug.

1881 J.C.F. JOHNSON *To Mount Browne & Back* 25 The gold, which for the most part is heavy and, to use of digger's term, 'sluggy' rather than nuggety, is found in these gullies.

sluicer. *Gold-mining.* An alluvial miner who uses a sluice to separate the particles of gold from the auriferous earth.

1855 W. HOWITT *Land, Labor & Gold* II. 193 It will not pay the cradler or the tommer to put through much rough earth. But the sluicer will come after him, and even out of the earth that he has cast aside as containing little, or nothing, will obtain in the aggregate large quantities. **1862** J.A. PATTERSON *Gold Fields Vic.* 318 The 'sluicer' is only to be found in the Ovens district, and in the valleys of the Dividing Range stretching eastwards along the northern boundary of Gipps Land. It is his business to cut long races for water-supply from the rivers, and them to wash down before him the auriferous hills. **1871** *Austral. Town & Country Jrnl.* (Sydney) 22 July 111/2 Owing to the protracted dry season .. our sluicers have been doing next to nothing. **1908** *Bulletin* (Sydney) 9 July 15/2 *Re* wombat as a cursed nuisance to ground-sluicers .. he is a bosker curse, and I live among dozens of old sluicers who can verify my statement. **1932** I.L. IDRIESS *Prospecting for Gold* 30 The sluicers mainly rely on lining the bottom of the box with a blanket, 'paving' the last two feet of the box with stones, and on the bottom ripple, to save their gold.

slum, *v.* [Prob. spec. use of Br. slang *slum* to cheat: see OED(S.]

a. *trans.* To perform (a task) carelessly, lazily, or incompetently. Also *intr.*, to work carelessly, etc., and as *vbl. n.*

1847 *Hobart Town Courier* 7 Apr. 2/2 The 'Government step' and 'slumming' are fundamental articles of the convict creed, in which willing belief, established by constant habit, is maintained with marvellous tenacity. **1886** P. FLETCHER 'Hints to Immigrants' in P. Fletcher *Qld.* 29 If *well* put up it will last you for many years, but if 'slummed' it will soon get shaky and lean askew. **1891** *Truth* (Sydney) 8 Mar. 7/3 Of course he slums a lot, and makes the work as easy as possible. **1892** *Bulletin* (Sydney) 28 May 21/2 He has a heated argument with his mother, who—judging from the quantity of milk—has reason to believe that he has 'slummed' some of the milkers. **1898** J.J. KNIGHT *In Early Days* (ed. 2) 38 'Wigging'—or, to use a more modern word, 'slumming'—work involved a penalty of either a whipping of twenty-five lashes or a position in the 'lumber gang', whose duty it was to give the necessary motion to the corn mill in what is now the Observatory by means of the treads. **1900** *Tocsin* (Melbourne) 4 Jan. 7/1 The parson's slumming the service, because he wants to get home to his dinner .. and Sam's in the cellar because he forgot to salute the Senior Chief. **1983** K.W. MANNING *In their Own Hands* 79 Ploughmen boosted their earnings by 'slumming', that is by leaving loose soil on unploughed runs in such a way as to give the appearance of a fully ploughed strip.

b. *spec. Shearing.* To shear (a sheep or a number of sheep) carelessly, lazily, or incompetently.

1878 *Squatters' Plum* 42 At one time, shearers might 'slum' their work, and cut the sheep about, so long as the wool came off somehow, but, now, it requires a practised hand to shear 85 sheep a day, so as to please the overseer. **1882** ARMSTRONG & CAMPBELL *Austral. Sheep Husbandry* 176 The double-boarded shed .. gives no man .. a chance to 'slum' his work without being observed by the manager of the shed. **1891** *Truth* (Sydney) 26 Apr. 7/3 There is a terrible difference between contract work and station work. The former is up to the mark, and the men earn their money. The latter is slummed, or done at a snail's pace. **1905** A.B. PATERSON *Old Bush Songs* 27 But I never slummed my pen, my lads, whate'er it might contain. **1914** *Bulletin* (Sydney) 22 Oct. 13/4 The cove who runs the shed is rather a particular sort and doesn't allow slumming, so you may take it that the sheep were well shorn. **1966** J. CARTER *People of Inland* (1967) 165 At shearing time, these same 'guns' can slum pen after pen of fine, clean sheep, because the opportunity to set a new record has presented itself.

slush, *v. Obs.* [f. SLUSHY *n.*[1]] *intr.* To work as a cook's assistant.

1891 *Truth* (Sydney) 22 Mar. 7/1 His brother, a union shearer, was slushing for the lamb-markers.

slush lamp. [Spec. use of *slush* waste fat, etc., aboard a ship: see OED *sb.*[1] 2.] An improvised light made from a container holding fat and fitted with a wick (see quot. 1893); SLUSHY *n.*[2]. Also **slush light,** and *ellipt.* as **slush.**

1862 E.R. CHUDLEIGH *Diary* (1950) 40 Turned into our blankets and read by the light of some slush lamps which is a pot full of fat with a bit of lighted rag in the middle and soon fell asleep, the dogs at our feet, the cats at our head .. and rats everywhere. ***c* 1872** J.C.F. JOHNSON *Over Island* 4 Putting the piece of wood on the slush lamp, he extinguished it. **1893** R. BRUCE *Echoes from Coondambo* 113 A pannican, in which some clay Was kneaded down in such a way As to uphold a piece of stick, Round which was roll'd a moleskin wick, Queer refuse fat was added, and That 'slush lamp' makes, you understand. **1904** M. WHITE *Shanty Entertainment* 14 When the other fellows had dowsed their slushes or blown out their candle-lights. **1922** J.N. MACINTYRE *High Explosive* 61 It leaves them to subsist on yams and bandicoots, or whatever else they can subsist on; to rise to toil in the morning and go to bed at night by the light of a 'slush lamp' (fat lamp)—kerosene is not to be thought of. **1930** HIVES & LUMLEY *Jrnl. of Jackaroo* 61 It was a tiring job after a hard day's work, and it had to be done by the light of a 'slush' lamp, and to the accompaniment of the smoke and stench from that primitive contraption. **1943** H.G. LAMOND *From Tariaro to Ross Roy* 20 Candles were the only illuminant then—candles in the house; slush lamps in the hut. **1951** E. HILL *Territory* 341 Jim sitting in his tent mending saddles by slush light. **1957** J. HAWKE *Follow my Dust* 81 When the first stars appeared, there rose from the ground the Bardee moths, having a wing span as large as your hand, and beautifully marked. They put out the slush-lamps. **1964** K. WILLEY *Eaters of Lotus* 54 Out in the camps he used to read by 'slush-light'—a piece of moleskin trousers shoved into a tin of fat like a wick, which used to give off 'a horrible light'. **1980** BRENNAN & WHITE *Keep Billy Boiling* 82 Mine is decorated with drops from a 40 candle-power slush lamp.

slushy, *n.*[1] [Transf. use of *slushy* a ship's cook: see OED(S.]

1. An assistant to a cook, esp. for a shearing gang.

1880 'OLD HAND' *Experiences of Colonist* (ed. 2) ii. 7 He was cook for the men, and bore the usual title of 'Slushey'. **1891** *Truth* (Sydney) 8 Mar. 7/3 You awake to the clanging of a cracked bell, rung by a relentless cook, or his slushy. **1895** *Worker* (Sydney) 3 Aug. 2/4 He earns from £6 to £8 per week and pays his mate ('slushie') at the sweating rate of 25s. per week. **1904** *Bulletin* (Sydney) 15 Sept. 39/2 The slushy was in the hut, laying out the things for dinner. **1913** *Ibid.* 2 Jan. 47/1 The 'slushy' in the third-class of the Australian liner, straightened his back. **1922** V. PALMER *Boss of Killara* 138 She thinks too much of herself to act as slushy in the kitchen. **1930** 'BRENT OF BIN BIN' *Ten Creeks Run* (1952) 54 They were in danger of the avid observation of boundary-riders or horse-breakers or hotel slushies. **1947** W. LAWSON *Paddle-Wheels Away* 167 Cook's mate—slushy I suppose you'd call it. Worth a pound a week and tucker. **1963** W.E. HARNEY *To Ayers Rock & Beyond* 46 Government house men and women 'slavies' and 'slushies' (the first so-called because they got little pay for hard work; the latter term meant a kitchen-hand, because during early shearing days the men 'slushies' were the ones who kept the fat up to the 'slush-lamps'). **1974** C. THIELE *Albatross Two* 67 'He's been offered a job on the oil rig.' .. 'A kitchen rouseabout,' Aunt Jessica said scornfully. 'A pot-walloper; a slushy.'

2. *transf.* An unskilled assistant.

1900 *Truth* (Sydney) 11 Mar. 1/7 Tommy Atkins in Boerland does the real graft, the contingenters are genteel slushies or offsiders. **1932** W. HATFIELD *Ginger Murdoch* 35 Ginger was now a common rouseabout, a 'slushy'. **1943** H.E. BEROS *Fuzzy Wuzzy Angels* 37 I'd be better down in Sydney as a slushy in a pub. **1953** 'CADDIE' *Caddie* 25 Slushie was the name given to anyone who worked at a camp boarding-house. No one minded being called that.

Hence **slushy** *v. intr.*, to work as a cook's assistant.

1942 *'Havildar' Havalook: Mag. H.M.A.T. 'Havildar'* 16 Mar. 1 It must be rather hard to have to slushie one's way to Australia. **1970** *Coast to Coast 1967–68* 5 That didn't explain why she'd accepted him. Better than slushying at the pub where he'd met her, probably.

slushy, *n.*[2] [f. SLUSH (LAMP + -Y.] SLUSH LAMP.

1928 *Bulletin* (Sydney) 16 May 21/1 The venerable fat lamp, alias 'slushy' and 'greasy', is still used in hundreds of N.S.W. farmers' barns. **1931** J.R. FIDDIAN *R. Mitchell of Inland* 20 They made acquaintance with the primitive bush illuminant, the 'slushie', a piece of rag acting as wick for the melted fat which in burning gave light and smoke, more or less, to all that were in the house.

slutzkin /'slʊtskən/. See quot.

1982 *Age* (Melbourne) 14 Oct. 9/5 Slutzkins go back to February 1977 and a majority judgment by Sir Garfield Barwick, Sir Keith Aickin and Sir Ninian Stephen. In this case, litigants by the name of Slutzkin won court approval for the taxpayer to convert company income, on which tax has been paid, into a capital gain. Thus the shareholder's income is in the form of a capital gain, which is tax free.

sly, *a.* and *n.*

A. *adj.* [Spec. use of *sly* secretive: see OED(S *a.* 5 b. Chiefly Austral.]

1. Illicit, illegal; esp. of the retailing of alcoholic liquor. See SLY GROG.

1828 *Tasmanian* (Hobart) 15 Feb. 3 An application is sent in for a grant of land, and .. there is little difficulty in obtaining it. A house is immediately built, and a license applied for; but—if that cannot be obtained—it then becomes a *'sly house'*, and grog is sold without it. **1840** *S. Austral. Rec.* (London) 26 Sept. 194 The less evil, sly grog shops, has merged, as it were, into a greater, that of sly gambling shops. **1843** C. ROWCROFT *Tales of Colonies* (1858) 325 Sanders had enjoined the sly-shop. **1853** J. SHERER *Gold Finder Aust.* 174 A settlement consisting of three public-houses, a stable, and sundry coffee, *alias* sly tippling tents. **1880** *Bulletin* (Sydney) 3/2 Mrs Brand may be branded for sly brandy selling. **1908** *Truth* (Sydney) 12 Jan. 11/7 Pimps and purge. Sunday sly shicker selling. **1927** T.S. GROSER *Lure of Golden West* 92 Confiscated from .. the sly dealers. **1973** *Bulletin* (Sydney) 27 Jan. 33/2 The Board of Works has actually asked people to dob in their neighbours for sly watering.

2. *Obs.* In the collocation **sly digging** *vbl. n.*, unlicensed gold-mining; the site of this.

1851 *Empire* (Sydney) 8 Aug. 27/4 One of the uninitiated, who had been doing a little sly digging, came to town a few days ago with a sample of something which he believed to be gold. **1852** G.C. MUNDY *Our Antipodes* III. 338 They are watched and followed by others who have been less successful, and the 'sly' diggings .. become known to the Commissioner. **1853** A. MACKAY *Great Gold Field* 59 *Sly gold digging.* It seems clear to me .. that in many a retired creek and gully the gold digger carries on his operations and makes good round sums, without the Commissioner or anyone else being a bit the wiser.

B. *n.* [Spec. use of *on the sly* in a secret manner: OED(S *sb.* 2.] In the phr. **(up)on the sly**: (of the retailing of alcoholic liquor) without a licence.

[1812 J.H. VAUX *Mem.* (1819) II. 206 *Sly*, any business transacted, or intimation given, privately, or under the rose, is said to be *done upon the sly*.] **1830** T. BETTS *Acct. Colony Van Diemen's Land* 49 These small settlements would become the resort of run-a-ways; and .. many of them would turn vendors of grog, on what is called 'the sly'. **1835** BACKHOUSE & TYLOR *Life & Labours G.W. Walker* 13 Dec. (1862) 231 There is hardly a single house or hut belonging to the lower description of settlers from the Nepean River to Bathurst, where grog may not be obtained 'upon the sly'. **1837** J.D. LANG *Transportation & Colonization* 87 By corrupting the convict and emancipated convict population—selling ardent spirits *on the sly*, as it is called. **1851** *Empire* (Sydney) 13 Oct. 251/1 Tea and sugar, firm, yet plentiful—ale and porter in draught 8s. per gallon, i.e. colonial stuff. Rum, on the sly 6d. a nobbler, water, poison, tobacco juice, &c., &c., &c., given in. **1892** 'MRS A. MACLEOD' *Silent Sea* II. 23 Wednesday I went to the little shanty at Starvation Creek, where they sell grog on the sly.

sly grog.

1. a. Alcoholic liquor as sold by an unlicensed vendor. Freq. *attrib.*

1825 *Hobart Town Gaz.* 18 Mar., We therefore felt convinced that in the sequel they would altogether decline applying for licenses, whilst many of them would become sly grog-men to the manifest injury of Government. **1828** *Tasmanian* (Hobart) 16 May 4 Care should be taken, that now when the sly grog system is broken up in the interior, no other schemes of imposition should be permitted. **1844** E.T. HAMILTON *Second Let.* 13 The labouring classes are, with few exceptions, drunkards and sly grog-buyers. **1851** *Empire* (Sydney) 18 Nov. 374/5 Yesterday a sly grog seizure was made by Mr King on Sofala Hill, in the tent of a man named Trebble, who deliberately told the Commissioner that he intended the spirits for sale at Oakey Creek; the seizure consisted of three casks of rum and a case of gin. **1872** 'RESIDENT' *Glimpses Life Vic.* 14 Most of them were sly grog-vendors. **1898** D.W. CARNEGIE *Spinifex & Sand* 351 She came overland from Queensland, accompanying her husband who, in the early days of the rush, sought to turn an honest penny by the sale of 'sly grog'. **1913** *Truth* (Sydney) 30 Nov. 5/5 Sly-grog means bad liquor. **1920** *N.T. Times* (Darwin) 10 Jan. 3/2 Mr Weiwkut referred to the sly grog at Katherine which he described as most disgraceful. Spirit was sold at 30s. a bottle, and it was green, red, white or blue and ladled out of a kerosene tin. It was carted there by a Chinaman. **1933** *Bulletin* (Sydney) 4 Oct. 21/4 The money was promptly invested in 'brandied peaches', the trade name for hawkers' sly grog in those days. **1948** V. PALMER *Golconda* 27 Joe carts sly-grog for those molls that came here a month ago and set up by the boarding-house. **1959** E. WEBB *Mark of Sun* 171 Let these half-bloods buy their booze in pubs like white men, and do away with dirty little sly-grog dumps like Andy's. **1965** K. SMITH *OGF* 177 It was only a matter of negotiating with Ted .. regarding the sale of sly grog by the glass. **1976** T. SHEPHERD *Children of Blindness* 119 Surely selling sly grog and metho to the boongs finds a place in his litany of sins. **1984** *Nat. Times* (Sydney) 21 Dec. 7/1 The family was suspected of being sly grog dealers during the Second World War.

b. Abbrev. of *sly-grog shop* (see sense 2 below).

1955 R. LAWLER *Summer of Seventeenth Doll* (1965) 42 Keepin' nit for the S.P. bookies, eh—drummin' up trade for the sly grogs. **1957** J. WATEN *Shares in Murder* 76 You running a sly grog now too? **1975** LATCH & HITCHINGS *Mr X* 224 I'll tell you where the brothels are and who's running them, the sly grogs, the bookies.

2. Comb. **sly-grog seller, selling** *vbl. n.*, **shanty, shop, tent.**

1826 *Hobart Town Gaz.* 11 Nov., **Sly Grog Sellers.** These avaricious panders to the vices of the worst part of this population have adopted a new method to evade the penalties of the late Act. **1841** *Port Phillip Patriot* 18 Oct. 3/3 On Saturday last no fewer than six sly-grog sellers were summoned to appear at the Police Office. **1847** A. HARRIS *Settlers & Convicts* (1953) 48 A sly grog seller could always afford to pay the fine, heavy as it was, out of his profits for three months. **1848** J.C. BYRNE *Twelve Yrs.' Wanderings* II. 113 Sly grog-sellers and receivers have, in most instances, been convicts. **1855** R. CARBONI *Eureka Stockade* 3 The source of pauperism will be settled in Victoria by any quill-driver, who has the pluck to write the history of public-houses in the towns, and sly-grog sellers on the gold-fields. **1875** P.E. WARBURTON *Journey across Western Interior* 142, I have often .. prosecuted sly grog-sellers. **1900** 'WOOMERA' *Life & Experiences Ex-Convict* 21 Many a wool-grower lost his sheep through the sly-grog sellers. **1916** *Truth* (Sydney) 2 Apr. 1/6 The next thing will be sly-grog sellers .. advertising their businesses for sale. **1976** J.H. TRAVERS *Bull Dust on Brigalow* 39 An old Model T Ford, the driver of which was a sly-grog seller. **1827** *Tasmanian* (Hobart) 6 Sept. 4 The abominable system of **sly-grog selling.** **1839** *Port Phillip Patriot* 3 Apr. 5 James Blake was fined £50, for sly grog selling, second offence. **1859** W. KELLY *Life in Vic.* I. 177 A pair of brothers .. commenced their career in Ballarat by sly grog-selling. **1880** *Argus* (Melbourne) 27 Jan. 7/2 This model citizen was recently fined £25 by the Bacchus Marsh Bench for sly-grog selling. ***c* 1930** 'N. GHURKA' *Graft* 27 He was again picked up during 1928 on counts of sly grog selling and convicted. **1956** A.C.C. LOCK *Tropical Tapestry* 85 In such an assembly of humanity, sly-grog selling became as lucrative as mining. **1882** A.J. BOYD *Old Colonials* 104 As soon as farmers are settled the *bona fide* publican settles amongst them, and the **sly grog shanty**, as it is familiarly called, cannot stand. **1894** 'MRS A. MACLEOD' *Austral. Girl* 226 Jack was a digger, and we had a little general store and a sly-grog shanty. **1911** *Bulletin* (Sydney) 13 July 14/3 W.A. sly-grog shanties, by the way, are known nowadays as 'State hotels'. **1936** F. CLUNE *Roaming round Darling* 109 Although ostensibly looking for a sly-grog shanty, they were really searching for horse-thieves. **1953** D. STIVENS *Gambling Ghost* 63 You pegged out soon after leaving that sly-grog shanty. **1826** *Monitor* (Sydney) 4 Aug. 90/3 We see our sister Colony is cursed .. with heavy licences on public-houses and its consequence, **'sly grog shops'**, i.e. back places where grog is drank [*sic*] in stealth, and coupled with gambling and lewdness. **1827** *Tasmanian* (Hobart) 12 Apr. 2 The plaintiff's wife kept a sly grog-shop in Hobart Town, to which various persons were in the habit of resorting for the purpose of drinking, gambling, &c. **1828** *Murray's Austral-Asiatic Rev.* i. 23 Great evils arise from .. the 'sly grog shops'. **1829** *Sydney Monitor* 2 Mar. 1514/3 One hundred sly grog shops will be in illicit trade in Sydney. **1838** *Hobart Town Almanac* 79 The sly grog-shops, particularly in the interior, were nests for convicts of every description. **1848** *Austral. Sportsman* (Sydney) 23 Sept. 3/2 Over the posts outside of various huts was to be seen *a ginger beer bottle, with a pipe stuck in it*, a colonial sign well understood as implying 'This is a sly grog shop'. **1854** W. HOWITT *Boy's Adventures* 248 The worst places at the diggings are the sly grog-shops. **1870** *Sydney Morning Herald* 1 July 5/3 Liquids of a more potent sort were sold to customers who were familiar with the establishment, and who were not likely to put the police on the scent of a sly grog shop. **1893** *Braidwood Dispatch* 8 Mar. 2/4 Last year in Mildura (Vic.), a drinking-prohibited township (where there are said to be at least thirty sly-grog shops), the fines for 28 cases of proved sly-grog selling totalled £305 with £52 costs. The fine is even cheaper than the license, and the 'shanty' grog needn't be of the best kind. **1920** *Huon Times* (Franklin) 20 Feb. 2/6 Sly-grog shops are known to exist in unusual places, but it rarely happens that a stable is utilised for the illicit sale of spirits and beer. **1944** J. DEVANNY *By Tropic Sea & Jungle* 26, I remember the Springboard Hotel, a sly grog shop. **1970** *Kings Cross Whisper* (Sydney) lxxxiii. 3/1 Conservationists .. were particularly dismayed at the disappearance of Australian sly grog shops. **1976** K. BROWN *Knock Ten* 73 Butch had repaired to one of the new sly grog shops far along the ridges. . . A foreign fellow was vending 'plonk' there . . to the various racials who always preferred wine to Australian beer. **1855** G.H. WATHEN *Golden Colony* 184 At the Diggings every gully and flat was infested with '**sly grog-tents**'. **1859** W. KELLY *Life in Vic.* I. 283, I have seen magistrates . . go into a sly grog-tent . . to eat oysters and drink brandy-and-water. **1862** *Meliora* (London) V. 74 Sly grog tents became the institution of the diggings. **1888** 'R. BOLDREWOOD' *Robbery under Arms* (1937) 230 When the police found a sly grog tent they made short work of it.

sly-grogger. One who sells alcoholic liquor without a licence. Also **sly-grogster.**

1897 *Bulletin* (Sydney) 10 Apr. 10/2 A couple of shanty-keepers were trapped by an excise-officer who gained the confidence of the sly-grogsters by making himself known to them as a brother Mason. **1916** *Truth* (Sydney) 19 Mar. 1/8 Sly groggers take no end of risk, For now they money-making are galore. **1920** *Smith's Weekly* (Sydney) 13 Nov. 9/4 The queerest sly-grogger I know was one, an Italian, who owned a vineyard and manufactured 'pinky'. **1943** H.G. LAMOND *From Tariaro to Ross Roy* 47 A certain notorious sly-grogger had left a case of whisky at the homestead. **1949** H.E. LAFFER *Wine Industry* 112 Prohibition is no remedy, rather the reverse, as it opens the door wide to the bootlegger, or slygrogger, as this type of individual is usually termed in Australia. **1962** *Texas Q.* 163 The dance had been rowdy: a sly-grogger was hawking wine in the scrub at the back of the little hall. **1978** F. HOWARD *Moleskin Gentry* 97 Major Bowler, in his time as magistrate at Carcoar, had imposed a £30 fine on Dick Niten, the sly-grogger. **1980** W.H. O'ROURKE *My Way* 67 Although there was no hotel nearer than Manjimup, a 'sly grogger' attended the local dances and provided the thirst quenchers.

sly-groggery. An establishment at which alcoholic liquor is sold illegally.

1907 *Truth* (Sydney) 9 June 7/8 *Sly groggery.* A 'rum' case at the Central. **1916** *Ibid.* 9 July 8/6 Slygroggeries are as plentiful in Redfern as figleaves in Hyde Park. **1954** H.G. LAMOND *Manx Star* 215 Your boundary is the first pub: Boulia to the south; Urandangie to the north; the first sly-groggery to the east. **1957** J. WATEN *Shares in Murder* 76 What if you were running a sly groggery? It's nothing to us. We're not the licensing squad.

sly-grogging, *vbl. n.* Illegal dealing in alcoholic liquor.

1952 *Bulletin* (Sydney) 3 Dec. 13/1 The local publican went in for a bit of sly-grogging—at a price. **1967** A. WATKINS *Andamooka* 114 Sly grogging, disturbing the peace, resisting arrest. **1981** P. CORRIS *White Meat* 89 Ted's instincts, bred in the SP game and sly grogging, were to avoid the police.

sly-grogster: see SLY GROGGER.

smallgoods, *pl.* Cooked meats and meat products. Freq. *attrib.* as **smallgoods shop.**

[N.Z. **1879** W.J. BARRY *Up & Down* 181, I had also tradesmen at work making up 'small goods' which I sold to retail butchers.] **1905** *Truth* (Sydney) 25 Apr. 1/7 The small goods in a Leichhardt ham and beef shop. **1917** *Ibid.* 2 Sept. 4/7 *The meat muddle.* Smallgoods held up. **1924** F.J. MILLS *Happy Days* 52 Polonious . . was not, as his name suggests, the owner of a smallgoods-shop. **1948** R. RAVEN-HART *Canoe in Aust.* 134 There were better assortments of sausages and the like down here, in the delicatessen shops. . . They are 'Small Goods' shops in Australia. **1955** *Bulletin* (Sydney) 7 Dec. 12/1 A kitten . . was abandoned in a suburban smallgoods shop. **1973** *Ibid.* 25 Aug. 30/3 What are the smallgoods manufacturers putting in their sausages now that mutton, the backbone of their industry, has ceased to be cheap and plentiful?

small grass-tree: see GRASS-TREE 1 b.

smalls, *pl. Mining.* [Spec. use of Br. dial. *smalls* 'thinly powdered tin-stuff': see EDD *small, sb.* 7.] Pieces of ore graded as small: see quot. 1914.

1847 *S. Austral. Register* (Adelaide) 21 Apr. 2/5 The ores . . sent from Glen Osmond mine we beg to inform them that the intended shipment was pretended to be what the miners call 'smalls' and consequently bags were necessary. **1863** J.B. AUSTIN *Mines S.A.* 18 A large quantity of the ore consists of what is called 'smalls'. **1914** *Wallaroo & Moonta Mines* 26 The ores received from the Company's mines comprise, 'roughs' (2½ in.), 'toppings' (¾ in.), 'smalls' (½ in.) [etc.].

small-scaled snake. The highly venomous large snake *Parademansia microlepidota* of e. central Aust., formerly confused with the related TAIPAN.

1980 *Ecos* xxiv. 32/1 The small-scaled snake, *Parademansia microlepidota,* was first found in 1879 by a naturalist named Frederick McCoy. **1983** *Age* (Melbourne) 22 Nov. 3/2 The small-scaled snake which, fortunately, occupies only a small part of central Australia, has the most powerful snake venom in the world, with enough in each bite to kill 250,000 mice.

Smellbourne. Also **Smellbun, Smellburn.** Alteration of 'Melbourne', the name of the capital city of Victoria: see quot. 1898.

1890 A.J. VOGAN *Black Police* 380 My trip to Melbourne—Smelbourne the *Bulletin* calls it, and rightly. **1894** *Bulletin* (Sydney) 10 Mar. 5/4 The doddering old lie that Smellbourne's rottenness was due to the big strike was trotted out. **1898** H. MATTHEWS *Chat about Aust.* 44 Melbourne, situated as it is on the banks of the Yarra, which, coupled with a very faulty system of drainage, has often caused that wonderful city to be called 'Smellbourne'. **1907** *Truth* (Sydney) 27 Oct. 1/4 There has been a rumpus lately in the good old Sydney town, All the 'Holy Joes' of Smellbourne wear the mourning garb and gown. **1911** *Ibid.* 14 May 1/8 Oh, the dear old Smellbun matron Is a model in her house. **1955** N. PULLIAM *I traveled Lonely Land* 225 Beaches? *Beaches?* In Smellburn?

smelt. [Transf. use of *smelt* the small European fish *Osmerus eperlanus* and other species of the fam. Osmeridae.] Any of several small fish, esp. those of the fam. Retropinnidae, as *Retropinna semoni* of s.e. Aust. and *R. tasmanica* of Tas.

1821 T. GODWIN *Descr. Acct. Van Diemen's Island* 9 Fish are caught in abundance. . . Those most known are . . smelt, John Dory, oysters. **1824** J. LYCETT *Views in Aust.* 4 The rivers and seas of New South Wales abound with excellent fish . . peculiar to that part of the globe; besides the eel, smelt, mullet . . so well known in England. **1873** F. DE CASTELNAU *Edible Fishes Vic.* 16 *Meletta Novae Hollandiae,* the *Smelt,* a pretty little fish of a very light green, with a silvery streak on each side; it is commonly brought to the market. **1951** T.C. ROUGHLEY *Fish & Fisheries Aust.* 156 One or two other species of *Galaxias,* and the smelt (*Retropinna tasmanica*). **1974** T.D. SCOTT et al. *Marine & Freshwater Fishes S.A.* 74 Although the smelt is a freshwater species, it is often seen near the mouth of coastal streams, and is able to enter salt water. **1984** MERRICK & SCHMIDA *Austral. Freshwater Fishes* 109 This smelt . . is most frequently found in lakes and slowly flowing water.

smoke, *n.*

1. [Also U.S.] A column of smoke serving as a signal or as a sign of an encampment, etc.

1770 J. HAWKESWORTH *Acct. of Voyages* (1773) III. 490 Seeing a smoke on the shore, we directed our glasses to the spot, and soon discovered ten people, who, upon our nearer approach left their fire. **1833** G.A. ROBINSON in N.J.B. Plomley *Friendly Mission* 7 June (1966) 734 Saw smokes of the natives on the beach. **1846** C.P. HODGSON *Reminisc. Aust.* 292 Having seen smokes yesterday, we were prepared to meet the natives. **1889** E. GILES *Aust. twice Traversed* I. 80 Natives' smokes were seen mostly round the base of some other ridges to the south-east. **1891** *Adelaide Observer* 30 May 6 There was nothing to be done but halt and on the highest eminence 'make a smoke'—a practice generally adopted by bushmen under such circumstances. **1921** S.A. WHITE *Bunya* 87 An effort was made to get clear, but without success, so a 'smoke' was made, but there was no response. Evening coming on, I took a waterbag and walked back to Trevorah's. **1948** C.P. MOUNTFORD *Brown Men & Red Sand* 60 'The abos saw your smokes yesterday.' (We had been lighting spinifex to herald our arrival.) **1968** W. GILL *Petermann Journey* 91 When the wind dropped at sunset, the natives sent up a 'smoke' from a fire they made in the bed of the creek.

2. Abbrev. of *big smoke* (see BIG 2).

1892 *Bulletin* (Sydney) 20 Aug. 21/2 He left 'the smoke' to wander where the wattle-blossoms wave. **1919** A. WRIGHT *Game of Chance* 124 It was back to the 'smoke' for him. **1955** D. NILAND *Shiralee* 15 This dump is the first I've ever been to outside the Smoke. **1966** B. BEAVER *You can't come Back* 12, I wasn't struck on working for the railways up in the bush or down in the smoke but so far it was the only job I'd held down.

3. *Obs.* Abbrev. of *smoke concert* (see sense 5 below). Also *attrib.*

1904 *Truth* (Sydney) 28 Aug. 7/2 The National Sporting Club has decided to entertain the English Football Team at a farewell smoke concert. . . Something extra special in the way of a programme for the smoke. **1906** *Gadfly* (Adelaide) 16 May 8/2 At a farewell 'smoke' to an Adelaide man recently a genial Scot took the chair, and . . declared pathetically that the departing guest left the firm 'respected by all'.

4. In the phr. **in(to) smoke,** in(to) hiding.

1908 *Lone Hand* Dec. 166 When not 'in smoke' (i.e. in hiding), the cheerful Smithy sometimes 'fights in the 'alls'. **1910** L. ESSON *Three Short Plays* (1911) 14, I aint in smoke. Yer'll see me at 4 o'clock any mornin'. **1919** C. DREW *Doings of Dave* 24 She's been in 'smoke' a long time. **1938** W. HATFIELD *Buffalo Jim* 35 You'd better go into smoke now till old Jerry routs you out and says you're Oke. **1951** E. HILL *Territory* 334 Glad to see you, Alf. I'm in smoke. **1962** *N.T. News* (Darwin) 9 Jan. 1/5 Gone into hiding. He remained 'in smoke' until late this morning. **1967** K.S. PRICHARD *Subtle Flame* 252 Meanwhile Tony's got to be kept in smoke? **1968** F. ROSE *Aust. Revisited* 269 *Smoke (in smoke),* to disappear from surveillance, usually from police surveillance.

5. Special Comb. **smoke concert, night, social,** an informal social occasion at which guests smoke and chat, and at which light entertainment is freq. provided. Also *attrib.*

[N.Z. **1888** J.D. WICKHAM *Casual Ramblings* 42 They had a **smoke concert** with a Salvation Army accompaniment.] **1891** *Bird o' Freedom* (Sydney) 25 Apr. 8/3 The Pyrmont Rangers Football Club open their season by a smoke concert, to be held in Pyrmont on May 8. **1899** *Western Champion* (Barcaldine) 29 Aug. 11/2 An impromptu smoke concert was held last night in the shearers' hut at Rockwood Station. **1905** D. REID *Reminisc.* 74 About the year 1902 a smoke concert and an address was given to Mr Reid at Burrumbuttock as an acknowledgment for his services. **1923** J. MOSES *Beyond City Gates* 72 Although it was called a Smoke Concert, the Wattle Flat function took the form of a miniature banquet. **1933** *Limbless Soldier* June 13 Many members attended . . a patriotic smoke concert. **1983** I. WYNER *With Banner Unfurled* 12 Fred Whitton . . would organise a moonlight or weekend excursion, or perhaps a band recital or a 'smoke concert', to raise some little financial assistance. **1906** *Gadfly* (Adelaide) 18 July 20/1 The Sydney Pressman's **smoke-night.** **1910** *Bulletin* (Sydney) 8 Dec. 14/4 Close observation of old tarantula's whiskers satisfied me that he was . . as dry as any Wowser's smoke-night. **1929** *Rising Sun* (Melbourne) Oct. 6 On Monday, October 21, the signalling section of 37th Battalion, A.I.F. held a Smoke Night. **1957** *Bulletin* (Sydney) 20 Mar. 13/1 Our smoke-night pianist, also a magnetic baritone, draws harmony from the timid and boisterous alike. **1965** K. TENNANT *Summer's Tales* 226 I'm coming, wind, I'm nearing the door with the C.W.A. and Smoke Night notices drawing-pinned on. **1901** *Advocate* (Burnie) 31 Aug. 2/7 A well-attended '**smoke social**' was tendered. **1910** *Huon Times* (Franklin) 10 Dec. 2/1 A Smoke Social was held in the Upper Mountain River Hall on Wednesday night as a 'wind-up'. **1926** *Canberra Community News* 12 July 2 A smoke social has been arranged for 5th August, at Acton Hall. **1942** F. CLUNE *Last of Austral. Explorers* 166 A smoke social was given in the cyclists' honour. **1972** C. DUGUID *Doctor & Aborigines* 84, I attended a soldiers' smoke social where we were regaled with a speech by General Sir John Monash.

smoke, *v.*

1. a. *intr.* To make a hasty departure. Also with **off.**

1893 *Sydney Morning Herald* 26 June 8/8 'Let us 'smoke'.' Smoke, it may be explained, is the slang for the 'push' to get away as fast as possible. **1896**

H. LAWSON *While Billy Boils* 144 He saw Tom, and Tom saw him, and smoked through a hole in the palings into the scrub. **1919** C. DREW *Doings of Dave* 89 Some of these bookies are liable to 'smoke'! **1961** P. WHITE *Riders in Chariot* 415 Dubbo had gone all right. Had taken his tin box, it seemed, and smoked off.

b. *trans.* To effect the departure of (a person). Also *reflex.*

1917 C. DREW *Reminisc. D. Gilbert* 51 They always smoke themselves away like that. They're under them leaves. **1919** *Smith's Weekly* (Sydney) 5 July 5/1 He had let the mare out on lease, and the attempt had been made to steal her from him by 'smoking' her away out of the State. ***c* 1930** 'N. GHURKA' *Graft* 5, I got the 'whisper' (information) that Lillian Philby had been 'smoked', and that a police officer had stage-managed her departure for a substantial consideration from Clark.

2. To signal (a message, etc.) by means of smoke from a fire. Also **smoke-talk** *intr.*

1931 I.L. IDRIESS *Lasseter's Last Ride* 140 He bargained with them to . . 'smoke-talk' to distant myalls. **1976** C.D. MILLS *Hobble Chains & Greenhide* 5 Next morning Pebble and Mollampi rode off to 'smoke' the news that we were on to him and would be ready for the run first thing on Thursday morning.

smoke bush. [See quot. 1933.] Any of several shrubs or trees of the genus *Conospermum* (fam. Proteaceae), chiefly of s.w. W.A., having white woolly flowers.

1888 *Centennial Mag.* (Sydney) 15 The whitey-blue green of the smoke bush. **1933** H.J. CARTER *Gulliver in Bush* 232 We journeyed over plains dotted with smoke bush (of which the popular name comes from the woolly white flower showing like smoke in the distance). **1959** *New Settler in W.A.* (Perth) Aug. 7 In a colourful carpet are woven the greys of the smoke-bush, the purples of the hovea. **1984** E. WALLING *On Trail Austral. Wildflowers* 23 Amongst the massive outcrops of sandstone . . there are smoke bushes, impressive plants with umbels of tiny white blue-backed flowers held well above long shining leaves.

smoke-ho, smoke-o, smoke-oh, varr. SMOKO.

smoker. The long-tailed parrot *Polytelis anthopeplus* of s.w. and s.e. Aust., the adult male of which has mustard-yellow plumage and a dark tail; *regent parrot*, see REGENT 2; *rock pebbler*, see ROCK *n.* 2.

1933 D. MACDONALD *Brooks of Morning* 49 The Black-tailed Parrakeet—the 'smoker' of the Mallee—is heard, and seen often in gleams of golden green, amongst the gums. **1948** J.K. EWERS *For Heroes to Live In* 6 A flock of smoker-parrots winged quickly past. They uttered no cry. Only their wings made a shush through the air. **1962** B.W. LEAKE *Eastern Wheatbelt Wildlife* 76 When smokers came back they were very timid, and always ducked low at the slightest unusual sound. **1984** E. WALLING *On Trail Austral. Wildflowers* 48 We had seen . . Smoker Parrots, smoke black and sulphur yellow.

smoke talk: see SMOKE *v.* 2.

smoko. Also **smoke-ho, smoke-o, smoke-oh.** [f. *smoke* a spell of smoking tobacco + -O.]

1. a. A tea-break; a rest from work; the food and drink provided for this period (see also quot. 1969). Also *attrib.*

1865 *Austral. Monthly Mag.* (Melbourne) I. 234 They in a 'smoke oh!' time, commenced to recount feats that they had seen done. **1872** G.S. BADEN-POWELL *New Homes for Old Country* 175 At stated times throughout the day there comes a general spell, commenced as soon as the phrase 'smoke-oh!' is heard. **1885** *Australasian Printers' Keepsake* 17 'Smoke oh!' and a four-handed game of cribbage. **1896** W.E. MURPHY *Hist. Eight Hours' Movt.* 59 A custom prevailed under the long ten-hour system of providing a 'spell', or cessation of work for a quarter of an hour, at 11 o'clock in the forenoon, and again at three in the afternoon, which was called 'smoko'. **1911** ST. C. GRONDONA *Collar & Cuffs* 82 At the 30-minute 'smoko' the shearers have coffee, cocoa and chocolate or tea, with ham or cheese sandwiches, cakes, scones, and pastry. **1914** *Bulletin* (Sydney) 30 July 24/1 Fifty-two shearers were employed, exclusive of rouse-abouts, pickers, classers, cooks, slushies and whalers . . and to save time the cook's off-sider took the 'smoke-ho' around on roller skates. **1927** M. DORNEY *Adventurous Honeymoon* 32 We arrived at Brunette Downs just in time for 'smoko', as morning and afternoon tea are called in the bush. **1933** F.L. STRUTT *Song of Outback Bloke* 30 We'd like a 'smoko' every hour And in between a nice hot shower. **1936** F. CLUNE *Roaming round Darling* 115 At smoke-o a visitor 'got the bird' for taking out his teeth, in order to drink more comfortably. **1949** *Bulletin* (Sydney) 19 Jan. 29/3 Our hopes for a second smoke-oh were futile against the determination of Anderson, the ganger, to get out another 60 cases before knock-off. **1960** M. HENRY *Unlucky Dip* 30 Then the two policemen had eaten a hearty smoko on the homestead veranda. **1969** J. PACKER *Leopard in Fold* 55 Their smokos—the packed lunches prepared by Mrs Wale—were beside their plates. **1977** S. LOCKE ELLIOTT *Water under Bridge* 232 So what you did to get back at them was to catch them having a 'smoko' on duty or spine bashing over at the canteen and put them on an emu parade. **1986** *Sydney Morning Herald* 29 Aug. 17/1 Restrictive work practices—from heavily subsidised housing to the provision of pink salmon and oysters for workers' 'smoko' breaks.

b. *transf.*

1915 *Bulletin* (Sydney) 28 Jan. 22/3 A gentle breeze zephyred from Monday to Friday, not even knocking off for smoko, and taking no notice of Wages Boards' awards respecting holidays. **1923** J. ARMOUR *Spell of Inland* 78 When the men started to speak to the boy, the goats took the opportunity to have a spell. The boy tried to keep them going by freely using his whip, but the men called to him to give the poor brutes a 'smoko', so at length they were allowed to stop, and stood with their sides heaving as they got their breath. **1929** *Bulletin* (Sydney) 2 Jan. 19/4 The dog had planted the mob in the shade of a big coolabah and was giving them a smoke-oh. **1946** F. CLUNE *Try Nothing Twice* 108 My heart went out to the calves, so I let them do the stripping, by opening up the calf pen, so they could have ten minutes smoke-oh with their mothers in the cow-yard.

2. *Smoke concert*, see SMOKE *n.* 5. Also *attrib.*

1918 G.A. TAYLOR *Those were Days* 30 It was a rare incident for that distinguished party to grace an Art Society 'Smoko'. **1923** J. MOSES *Beyond City Gates* 72 Have you got your ticket for the Smoko tonight? **1940** *Any Complaints* (Newcastle) 4 Apr. 8 No. 12 Platoon . . held a smoko evening last week. **1945** *Queanbeyan Age* 24 Apr. 1/6 A 'smoko' has been arranged by the local returned soldier organisations and will be held in the Parish Hall supper room at 8 p.m. tomorrow (Anzac) night. In addition to community singing, songs will be rendered. **1947** *Listening Post* (Perth) Mar. 13 It is proposed to hold the anniversary smoko on May 20. **1973** *Kings Cross Whisper* (Sydney) clvii. 16/1 We held the annual presentation night and smoko last night and everybody . . is feeling terrible crook this morning. **1976** *Austral.* (Sydney) 24 Apr. 18 The Leader of the Opposition, Mr Whitlam, worked in his Sydney office and attended a 'smoko' at Wentworth RSL club last night.

smoodge, *v.* Also **smooge.** [Br. dial. *smudge* to kiss, to sidle up to: see EDD *v.*[1] 2. Cf. OED *smouch, v.*[1] and OEDS *smooch, v.*[3]]

1. *intr.* To behave in an ingratiating manner; to 'make up to' a person.

1898 *Worker* (Sydney) 6 Aug. 4/3 The principal industries and businesses are owned by Japs, Kanakas, Chows and other colored citizens to whom the 'white trash' must smoodge if they are not to be starved out. **1903** *Bulletin* (Sydney) 22 Oct. 35/2 He classes cooks into two species—those who require that all hands shall smooge, and those who smooge to all hands. **1915** C.J. DENNIS *Songs of Sentimental Bloke* 41 They smooge some more at that. Ar, strike me blue! It gimme Joes to sit an' watch them two! **1918** —— *Digger Smith* 45, I ain't the man to smooge with God To get to 'Eaven on the nod. **1927** F.C. BIGGERS *Bat-Eye* 15 An' Bat-Eye looked a mug—an' smooged jist like a dawg. That done it . . there an' then they 'as a little chat, An' soon is good as cobbers. **1934** J.C. LEE *Boshstralians* 236 'I was put on the list when old Fatty Simpson was member.' 'That's because you used to smoodge to Fatty.' **1959** E. WEBB *Mark of Sun* 173 Barney here used to hang around, smooging to mum for the kind of favours she wasn't the kind for giving, see? **1973** P. WHITE *Eye of Storm* 480 She came smoodging up at her father, and he . . kissed her.

2. *transf. trans.* To smooth; to smooth the passage (of something).

1910 W. MOORE *Tea-Room Girl* 18 Watching the wavelets smoodge the glistening sand. **1934** C. STEAD *Seven Poor Men* 66 Marion had little difficulty when she went down to smoodge Fulke's interdicted books in French and German through the customs.

Hence **smoodging** *vbl. n.* and *ppl. a.*

1904 *Shearer* (Sydney) 17 Sept. 3/3 All his . . 'smoogoing' failed to score him any wins. **1915** T. SKEYHILL *Soldier-Songs from Anzac* 39 'E's a sneakin' smoogin' blighter an' 'e'll never make a fighter, Unless it's 'gainst a wounded chap like me. **1916** *Yandoo* Dec. 35 By little bits of smooging which no-one ever knows The Sergeant kindly put him Among the 'R.M.O.s'. **1942** G.S. CASEY *It's Harder for Girls* (1944) 8 A rug was reckoned to provide privacy enough for a bit of smoodging. **1949** J. MORRISON *Creeping City* 8 You pay sixpence to go in and have a gig at his . . fishponds and smoodging nooks.

smoodge, *n.* Also **smooge.** [f. SMOODGE *v.*] Flattery; an act of ingratiation; a display of amorous affection. In the phr. **to do a smoodge, to come the smoodge,** to behave in such a way.

1909 *Truth* (Sydney) 2 May 1/8 It is certainly better to speak In support of your honest beliefs Than in attitude humble and meek Do a smooge for a few paltry briefs. **1911** R.J. CASSIDY *Land of Starry Cross* 122, I bend, and creep, and toady in a Land of Smoodge and Crawl! **1915** J.P. BOURKE *Off Bluebush* 77 Got no time to do a smoodge! Got no time to wed! **1919** *Worker* (Brisbane) 25 Sept. 6/4 'Work! Work! Work! The Great Smoodge to Labor.' (Headline to article about promises of employment.) **1927** A. WRIGHT *Squatter's Secret* 19 Cut out the smoodge and let me have a snack before I get a move on. **1927** 'S. RUDD' *Romance of Runnibede* 39 Seeing his mistake, old Harry resorted to coaxing. But, being a horse with principle and pride, Tommy wasn't to be degraded with smooge. **1955** D. NILAND *Shiralee* 136 If there was no blokes about, he'd come the smoodge to the women for a bit of a love-up. **1980** D. HEWETT *Susannah's Dreaming* (1981) 21 What's wrong with a bit of a smooge between friends? You didn't useta be so choosy. What is it? Got annuver lover or somethin'?

smoodger. Also **smooger.** A flatterer; a sycophant. Also *transf.*

1897 *Worker* (Sydney) 11 Sept. 1/1 While he who 'crawls' and 'runs the cut' and lacks a bushman's pluck, Is known by men as 'smoodger', while the tarboys call him 'suck'. **1899** *Truth* (Sydney) 21 May 1/1 They are, for the most part, Society 'smoodgers', who would sell their servile souls for a smile from Society. **1902** *Ibid.* 19 Jan. 4/3 The opening lines of your letter mark you a 'smoodger', the closing lines brand you a cadger. **1910** *Ibid.* 9 Jan. 5/8 Who meets you with an oily smile, Pretends that he is free from guile, Agrees with all you say, the while, Within his heart he hates your style? The Smoodger. **1928** *Bulletin* (Sydney) 12 Dec. 25/2 A wily old smooger was Jimmy Harrin, who kept a tanglefoot house in Mulgatown. **1958** R. STOW *To Islands* 19 'Sister,' she sighed lovingly, hiding her face against Helen's neck, 'You old smoodger,' Helen said. **1976** C.D. MILLS *Hobble Chains & Greenhide* 116 Gentle, affectionate and a real 'smoodger', with plenty of life though very quiet to ride.

smooge, var. SMOODGE *v.* and *n.*

smooger, var. SMOODGER.

smoogy /ˈsmudʒi/, *a.* Also **smoogey.** Ingratiating; affectionate. Also as quasi-*adv.*

1900 *Truth* (Sydney) 4 Feb. 1/4 You have brass enough for a whole park of artillery, with all your nice, smoogy ways. **1936** E.E. TOURNAY-HINDE *Minds Unmoored* 20 What makes you so smoogy to-day, eh? How's that young family of yours, puss? **1940** *Bulletin* (Sydney) 3 July 16/1 An' jest watch yer step with him; he's a smoogy coot and tries ter talk yer over. **1959** A. UPFIELD *Bony & Mouse* 208 Harmon called me into the office, all smoogey-like.

smooy /ˈsmui/. Also **smooie.** [Abbrev. of SMOO(DGE *n.* + -Y.] See quot. 1967.

1967 *Kings Cross Whisper* (Sydney) xl. 4/4 *Smooy*, 'a bit of smooy' to make love. **1970** R. BEILBY *No Medals for Aphrodite* 279 'We should be able to take it easy, have a swim, bit of grog, perhaps a few sheilas. . . ' 'You tell me what's better than grog and smooie, sarn,' he challenged.

smother.

1. *Obs.* An undercover enterprise; a strategem.

1902 *Truth* (Sydney) 3 Aug. 8/4 We could name several other 'smothers' where the proprietor combines the business of prostitution with that of criminal coddling. **1903** *Sporting News* (Launceston) 23 May 2/6 He has a 'smother' which has saved him from many a well-directed blow, using this in preference to his feet.

2. In the phr. **to put the smother on,** to suppress.

1963 B. SUTTON *Snow & Me* (1966) 18 They are to put the smother on how much dough the toilers are getting done for.

smoush /smuʃ/. [Var. of *smooch*: see OEDS *sb.*[2]] A kiss.

1963 D. NILAND *Dadda Jumped* 182 He clutched the girl and gave her a smoush like the smack of a rubber glove. **1967** *Kings Cross Whisper* (Sydney) xl. 4/4 *Smoush*, kiss. **1971** D. IRELAND *Unknown Industr. Prisoner* 173 Reminds me of a widow I knew at Richmond. Whenever I visited her and a plane went over she'd drop whatever she was doing and rush over for a smoush.

snack. Something easy to accomplish, a 'pushover'.

1941 S.J. BAKER *Pop. Dict. Austral. Slang* 68 *Snack*, a certainty. **1952** T.A.G. HUNGERFORD *Ridge & River* 138 There was nothing to it... It was a snack. **1961** M. CALTHORPE *Dyehouse* 150 In Hughie's day he'd make this a snack. **1970** R. BEILBY *No Medals for Aphrodite* 274 'How could I do that, Harry?' 'Easy. It'll be a snack.'

snag, *n.*[1] [Fig. use of *snag* an obstacle.] An adversary to be reckoned with.

1905 J. FURPHY *Rigby's Romance* (1946) 78 Grand thing to be a (adj.) snag like him. **1906** *Bulletin* (Sydney) 8 Feb. 14/2 Sore-teated or vicious cows are generally called 'snags'. **1910** L. ESSON *Three Short Plays* 13 Bongo's a tough snag. He can fight a bit. **1911** E.S. SORENSON *Life in Austral. Backblocks* 91 Concerning fighting cooks the tales are legion. I remember one snag in a north-western (New South Wales) shed, who cooked abominably, but rendered his position tenable by punching the ringer, spreading out the shed pug, and knocking pieces off the wool-presser. **1954** *Tobruk to Borneo* (Perth) June 7 One for none and the 'snag' out. **1961** C. THIELE *Sun on Stubble* 23 She was sure to be unco-operative, being a teacher. Real snags they usually were. Snags. **1968** LINKLATER & TAPP *Gather no Moss* 179 A splendid type of man physically, standing well over six feet.. a hard living man, master bushman, defiant, cruel on occasion .. he was a snag to arrest. **1978** D. STUART *Wedgetail View* 50 I'm not too bloody sure Sandy wouldn't be a snag himself... He's rangy, he's strong, an' he's certainly not awkward. I think he'd be a surprise packet if anyone put him out too much. An' he's not a bloody flyweight, y'know.

snag, *n.*[2] [Prob. spec. use of Br. dial. *snag* a morsel, a light repast: see EDD *v.*[2] and *sb.*[3] and cf. *snack* (see OED *sb.*[2] 4 b.).] A sausage.

1941 S.J. BAKER *Pop. Dict. Austral. Slang* 68 *Snags*, sausages. **1943** *Bulletin* (Sydney) 15 Dec. 13/4 Waiting only to bolt a couple of cold 'snags' Ted got out his bike. **1953** T.A.G. HUNGERFORD *Riverslake* 198 'Oh God!' Charlesworth cried suddenly. 'The snags!' .. He had put a tray of breakfast sausages into the oven and had forgotten them. **1972** *Bulletin* (Sydney) 12 Aug. 7/3 As an experiment our committee bunged on a rort for some of them, with plenty of snags and red Ned. **1980** *Ibid.* 6 May 112/3, I make my own snags, my own pies and pasties. The Yanks love them after you've twisted their arms to try them.

snag, *v.*[1] *Obs.* [f. *snag* short stump.] *intr.* To clear away stumps, etc., before cultivation. Also *trans.*

1904 *Bulletin* (Sydney) 22 Dec. 16/4 After rolling, the right thing is to 'snag' level with the ground. Feverish haste of cocky to 'get crop in', however, leaves him no time for this. **1910** 'YARRAN' *Mallee* 7 As early as possible after the first year, the beginner should 'snag' a portion of his original clearing, so as to render it fit for a binder to work. **1934** J.S. NEILSON *Autobiogr.* (1978) 47 I knew that by waiting another month I could get clearing and burning off on Tyrell Downs. In this clearing there would be a lot of snagging to do, and there did not seem to be any prospect of my thumb being fit for it.

snag, *v.*[2] *intr.* To shear: see SNAGGER.

1927 J. MATHIEU *Backblock Ballards* 1 And I reckon I'll be snagging Too, this season, when it starts.

snagger. *Shearing.* [Transf. use of *snagger* a billhook.] A slow, inexpert, or inept shearer.

1887 *Tibbs' Pop. Song Bk.* 11, I found a lot of snaggers Not a shearer in the mob. **1897** *Worker* (Sydney) 11 Sept. 1/1 Poor 'snaggers' (50 sheep a day) that's what they mostly are! **1906** J. BARBOUR *Pencillings on Wallaby* 24 The snagger of to-day Next year may beat the champions around The Castlereagh. **1911** *Bulletin* (Sydney) 17 Aug. 14/3 If any snagger boasted of having shorn 32 sheep in the breakfast 'run', there was always someone present to mention that 'Crooked Mick', at Speewah, had done 33 in the same time. **1934** *Austral. Ring* IX. cvii. 4 The 'drummer' and 'snagger' chip-chopping away, The 'ringer' close-pinking ten twenties per day. **1956** F.B. VICKERS *First Place to Stranger* 240 It's all right for you, Paddy you've had the run of the good sheep up North. But I'm just a snagger, I don't get the long runs. **1963** *Gumsuckers' Gaz.* (Melbourne) Aug. 10 A snagger is a shearer who is learning the trade and is handling less than fifty sheep a day. **1975** *Sunday Mail* (Brisbane) 14 Sept. 6/6 The younger men who have taken the old 'snaggers' places, stand up on 'the board' .. and shear along with the best of them. **1985** J. HARRISON *Bit of Dag* 7 One old snagger now retired, having shorn for forty years .. is living on $15,000 a year.

snail. *Obs.* See quot. 1898.

1897 *Worker* (Sydney) 11 Sept. 1/1 Musterers, sometimes he calls .. 'snails'. **1898** *Bulletin* (Sydney) 17 Dec. 15/1 Musterers are snails (originally applied to slow musterers who couldn't keep up with the sheep and stopped the shearing. Now a general term).

snaily, *a.* and *n.* Also **snailey.** [Cf. Br. dial. *snail-horn(ed* (see OED).]

A. *adj.* Of an animal's horn: curled like a snail-shell. Of cattle: having horns of this description.

1884 'R. BOLDREWOOD' *Old Melbourne Memories* 123 That black bullock .. him with the snaily horn. **1891** —— *Sydney-Side Saxon* 133 There's a snailey Wallanbah bullock I haven't seen this two years. **1894** A.B. BELL *Austral. Camp Fire Tales* 32 He swears never again to trust a snailey-horned cow. **1943** *Coast to Coast 1942* 15 He couldn't do any harm with snaily horns like that, and, anyway, the shorthorn had youth on its side.

B. *n.* A beast having snaily horns.

1884 'R. BOLDREWOOD' *Old Melbourne Memories* 68 Snaileys and poleys, old and young, coarse and fine, they were a mixed herd in every sense. **1894** A.B. BELL *Oscar* 9 The big, red baldy's in the lead as usual, so is the magpie, the fat roan, the old razorback, and the white snailey.

snake.

1. Used *attrib.* in Special Comb. **snake charmer** *W.A.*, a railway maintenance worker; **Gully,** an imaginary place, perceived as remote and backward; **-headed** *a.*, angry; vituperative; **juice,** alcoholic liquor, esp. of an inferior sort; a drink of this; also *attrib.*; **yarn,** a tall story.

1937 A.W. UPFIELD *Mr Jelly's Business* 16 'What are the **Snake Charmers**?' 'They are the permanent-way men.' **1948** R. RAVEN-HART *Canoe in Aust.* 174 Platelayers are 'snake-charmers', I learned but could not find the reason. **1983** P. ADAM SMITH *When we rode Rails* 155 Permanent-way men have been given more names than any other occupational group in railways... Unofficially they are known as Snake Charmers (W.A.), Hairy Legs (N.S.W.), Woolly Noses (S.A.). **1945** *Tropic Spread: Mag. 18th Austral. Advanced Ordnance Depot* July 7 Report from our **Snake-Gully** correspondent. **1966** *Kings Cross Whisper* (Sydney) viii. 2 It was called a gas party, probably because so many of them were 'on the bugle', as we say back in Snake Gully. **1976** *Nation Rev.* (Melbourne) 16 Jan. 338/2 South Australia is the quintessential utopia of enlightenment compared with which Valhalla would be thought to resemble Snake Gully. **1980** B. HORNADGE *Austral. Slanguage* 101 The *outback* has an identical geographical twin in the *never never*, and to reinforce the myth of the actual existence of such places the old timers invented equally mythical place names such as *Bullabakanka* (there are several alternate spellings), *Snake Gully* and *Woop Woop*. **1900** *Bulletin* (Sydney) 28 Apr. 32/2 He owed Milligan a big score in bar and store and Pat was turning '**snake-headed**'. **1905** *Shearer* (Sydney) 23 Dec. 7/5 He was a 'snake-headed' and 'ropable' A.W.U. man. **1920** B. CRONIN *Timber Wolves* 63 She got snake-headed about anything. **1946** M. FRANKLIN *My Career goes Bung* 60 Everybody is snake-headed about your blooming old book. **1948** K.S. PRICHARD *Golden Miles* 148 Others thought she had just gone snake-headed for a moment, like aborigines do when they lose their temper; and that she would cool off and realise she had better keep her mouth shut. **1890** *Pall Mall Gaz.* (London) 3 Sept. 3/2 This whisky, or **snake-juice**, as bushmen often call the hell-broth prepared for them. **1894** *Western Champion* (Barcaldine) 20 Feb. 12/1 'Tis the land where the snake-juice flows frantic and free. **1900** *Bulletin* (Sydney) 4 Aug. 15/1 'R.H.' .. must have had snakejuice aboard when he saw the piebald rats. **1904** M. WHITE *Shanty Entertainment* 67 When the sheds are cut out, and the snake-juice boils in one's blood and simmers over into that riotous fancy commonly known as the Joe Morgans, or the D.T.s. **1914** *Bulletin* (Sydney) 27 Aug. 24/4, I would like to know the ingredients of a particular brand of snake-juice that the Japs have popularised in the pearling industry at Broome (W.A.) .. known as 'corpse reviver'. **1920** *Ibid.* 24 June 22/4 The boss was afraid we would break away to the nearest snake-juice factory before the job was done. **1930** A.E. YARRA *Vanishing Horsemen* 55 'Two snakejuices,' he said to the man behind the bar. **1935** 'D. LAURIER' *Two Men from Northern Rivers* 45 The bottle was passed along, but Clive refused it, stating that he did not drink 'snake juice'. **1949** G. FARWELL *Traveller's Tracks* 135 The purveyors of sly grog ('snake juice', as they called it in the back country) mingled with the more respectable crowd. **1962** *Southerly* ii. 79 Ironbark .. went into the poison shop. Old Nick handed him a glass of snake juice. **1903** *Advocate* (Burnie) 27 May 2/6, I believe the crop is near 30 tons per acre... This is no '**snake yarn**'. **1908** 'FIFTY-THREE YRS.' MINER' *So Long* 115 They are all facts which have come under my own observation, not merely 'snake' yarns! **1947** M. RAYMOND *Smiley gets Gun* 26 'We ain't allowed to give anyone a lend of our guns,' said Mick. 'That's a snake yarn!' 'It ain't. My father says a cove's gotter be responsible to use a gun, and you ain't responsible.' **1959** —— *Smiley roams Road* 11 If you haven't told me a snake yarn, then I'm glad. **1968** S. GORE *Holy Smoke* 50, I see in the paper here .. how a couple of dolphins, down around Woy Woy or some place, swum all the way to shore with a bloke to keep the sharks off him. She seems a bit of a snake yarn to me.

2. In Services' speech: a sergeant. Freq. *attrib.* as **snake pen, pit,** the sergeants' mess.

1941 *Action Front: Jrnl. 2/2 Field Regiment* Aug. 3 Have increased our contribution to the Snake Pit. **1943** *Troppo Tribune* (Mataranka) 14 June 2 Following certain events at the Snake Pit (Sergeants Mess to you). **1945** *Tropic Spread: Mag. 18th Austral. Advanced Ordnance Depot* Aug. 22 The snakes helped the MAC boys with the building of a new Sergeants' Mess. **1951** E. LAMBERT *Twenty Thousand Thieves* 314 Baxter reckons the officers and snakes are pinching our beer.

snake flower. See quot. 1916.

1916 *Bulletin* (Sydney) 11 May 24/1 Any flower of a certain unattractive shade of purple is 'snake-flower'. **1934** S. KING *Molly's Yr. in Camp* 21 A deep purple flower has just blown against my foot as if to remind me that its name should go to you as *Ajuga Australis*, and not the easy Snake Flower I prefer to remember. **1981** G. CROSS *George & Widda-Woman* 9 We gathered small bunches of flowers for Mum .. snake flowers, flannel flowers, Christmas bush.

snakewood. A tree having twisted branches, as *Acacia grasbyi* (fam. Mimosaceae) of W.A.

1817 A. CUNNINGHAM in I. Marriott *Early Explorers Aust.* 23 May (1925) 218 We saw some fine specimens of a tree which our people termed Snakewood. **1909** *Emu* VIII. 193 A favourite position was the fork of a snake-wood bush. **1924** H.E. RIEMANN *Nor'-West o' West* 87 And as wiry as the snakewood of their environment. **1953** L. & C. REES *Spinifex Walkabout* 37 Snakewood, possibly a mulga, the boughs of which, rough-barked and dark, writhed about near the ground. **1982** *Bulletin* (Sydney) 23 Nov. 45/1 A kilometre-long belt of bowgada bean and snakewood—wattles known to botanists as *Acacia linophylla* and *Acacia grasbyi.* **1984** W.W. AMMON et al. *Working Lives* 133 The tough and durable snakewood. Snakewood grows most erratically, almost horizontal to the ground, with bends and curves and twists all over.

snaky, *a.* Also **snakey.** Savage; angry. Also *fig.*

1894 *Bulletin* (Sydney) 28 Apr. 23/1 That night I started drinking at the shanty on the Flat Where the o.p. grog is snaky. **1915** *First Aid Post: Official Organ 2nd Field Ambulance* 4 Aug. 1/2 Why 'Feathers' turns snaky. **1918** *Cacolet: Jrnl. Austral. Camel Field Ambulance* June 25/2 If it had been B-- or M-- or K-- they wouldn't have half gone snaky. **1935** P. LAWLOR *Confessions of Journalist* 29 'Crikey,' whispered the 'Truth' man sitting next to me. 'Look at the Beak. He looks so snakey. I think he's going to put on the black cap.' **1943** 'MRS E.F. BOSWORICK' *Amateur* 18 Yer don't think I'm goin' snaky about me bloody coat, do yer? **1970** D. WILLIAMSON *Coming of Stork* (1974) 34 What are you snaky about this time? **1981** *Courier-Mail* (Brisbane) 28 Nov. 23/1 They remain very snaky indeed about allegedly non-impartial treatment from players and umpires in Perth.

snap, *n. Australian National Football.* A quickly taken and opportune kick at goal. Also *attrib.* as **snap drop.**

1894 J.M. MACDONALD *Thunderbolt* 93 Hanks took a snap-drop at the goal, and through it went, score No. 2 for Bendigo. **1960** *N.T. News* (Darwin) 19 Jan. 10/2 Joe Bonson grabbed the ball from a throw-in and shot a major with a neat snap. *Ibid.* 9 Feb. 11/4 Cooper sent to Peter Marrego who raised both flags with a good snap.

snap, *v. Australian National Football. trans.* See quot. 1969.

1960 *N.T. News* (Darwin) 12 Jan. 8/3 Vierk snapped a goal which was disallowed for a free to Wanderers. **1969** EAGLESON & MCKIE *Terminol. Austral. Nat. Football* iii. 17 *Snap a goal (or behind)*, score a goal (or behind) with a sudden opportune kick.

snap and rattle. Also **snappin' rattle.** [See quot. 1935.] Any of several trees, incl. *Eucalyptus gracilis* (fam. Myrtaceae) of s. mainland Aust.

1935 L.J. GOMM *Blazing Western Trails* 171 A tree they call 'snap and rattle' was quite new to me. It grows big like other trees, but just at this time of the year the bark peels off in great long strips... The wind blows these streamers about... They snap and rattle in the wind, hence the name. **1944** K.S. PRICHARD *Potch & Colour* 5 The horse-team swung out from the dark scrub of snap-and-rattle with its crests of golden-green young leaves. **1950** C.E. GOODE *Yarns of Yilgarn* 85 Shingly rises begrudgingly supporting snappin' rattle or thorny-oak or mulga.

snap drop: see SNAP.

snapper. Also **schnapper.** [Spec. use of *snapper* used widely as a name for a fish.] Any of several marine fish of the fam. Sparidae, esp. the pinkish-silver *Chrysophrys unicolor* of w. Aust., *C. auratus* of s. Aust. and elsewhere, and *C. guttulatus* of e. Aust., valued as food. See also COCKNEY, *old man snapper* OLD MAN B. 3, *red bream* RED *a.* 1 b., SQUIRE. Also *attrib.*

1699 W. DAMPIER *New Voyage round World* (1703) III. 140 In the night while Calm we fish'd with Hook and Line and caught good store of Fish, *viz* Snappers, Breams, Old Wives, and Dog-Fish. **1770** 'Endeavour' Log 25 May, Fine clear wea[r]—caught some fish of the snapper kind. **1789** A. PHILLIP *Voyage to Botany Bay* 180 Quantities of fish may be procured... Those they got on board the Supply were of the snapper kind. **1826** *HRA* (1922) 3rd Ser. V. 834 Fish are not abundant... The sorts generally caught are.. swordfish, and, in one instance, a large Snapper. **1840** *S. Austral. Rec.* (London) 18 Apr. 191 The bay and coast abound with fish of every delicacy and variety—oysters, both rock and mud, schnapper.. and a thousand other varieties. **1859** W. KELLY *Life in Vic.* I. 85 Two or three snappers, an uncouth scaly monster. **1867** J.R. HOULDING *Austral. Capers* 216 Sank groaning into the bottom of the boat, upon the slimy schnappers and flatheads. **1897** 'OLD HOUSEKEEPER' *Austral. Plain Cooking* 46 Trevalla and schnapper.. must be cut across, in pieces about half an inch in thickness, or may be filleted. **1914** W. COLLIN *Life & Adventures* 117, I arranged to embark in schnapper fishing for the Sydney market. **1941** *Coast to Coast* 37 It was a huge snapper, so big that the fin on its back jutted out of water like a sail. **1960** *Bulletin* (Sydney) 27 July 18/1 What Queensland calls snapper isn't what we used to get in South Australia. **1969** J. POLLARD *Austral. & N.Z. Fishing* 707 Various other fish may be called snapper. Those most commonly confused are the various members of the emperor or sweetlips family, *Lutjanidae*, and the quite unrelated fish of the red snapper family *Berycidae*. **1986** *Canberra Times* 7 Apr. 5/2 (Advt.) *Whole baby schnapper* with Tangy Seafood sauce.. $9.50.

snappin' rattle, var. SNAP AND RATTLE.

snappy gum. [See quot. 1897.] Any of several tree species of the genus *Eucalyptus* (fam. Myrtaceae) yielding a brittle timber, incl. *E. brevifolia, E. haemastoma,* and *E. rossii.* See also BRITTLE GUM, SCRIBBLY GUM.

1897 *Proc. Linnean Soc. N.S.W.* XXII. 706 *E[ucalyptus] haemastoma* var. *micrantha*.. in one or other of the many districts in which it occurs, usually goes under some name referring to the softness or brittleness of its timber, *e.g.*, 'Cabbage Gum', 'Snappy Gum', 'Brittle Gum'. **1931** M. TERRY *Hidden Wealth* 326 Bloodwood, snappy gum and limewood.. were the most common trees. **1956** A.C.C. LOCK *Tropical Tapestry* 139 Mountain gum became plentiful. In other areas it is known as snappy gum, because of its peculiar brittleness. **1972** *Southerly* iii. 219 Barren rocks with a few centipedes, a few scorpions and in the snappy gums, spiders and nameless small insects. **1978** K. WILLEY *Joe Brown's Dog* 99 Bluey found the next man, Wunduk, in a clump of little snappy gums where he must have tried to hide.

snarler. [Quasi-acronym, f. the initial letters of '*s*ervices *n*o *l*onger *r*equired'.] In Services' speech: see quot. 1943.

1943 S.J. BAKER *Pop. Dict. Austral. Slang* (ed. 3) 74 *Snarler*, a soldier or flier sent back home from overseas service because of some misdemeanour. **1952** T.A.G. HUNGERFORD *Ridge & River* 49 If he just couldn't make the grade, then Lovatt would bundle him back south for a Snarler. **1976** K. CLIFT *Soldier who never grew Up* 53 'Yes, Corporal?' 'I only wanted to add, Sir, that you deeply reconsider sending any of 'J' section home as a 'snarler'.' **1983** *Sun-Herald* (Sydney) 17 July 57/3 In the Navy's Weekly Postings he receives an official 'snarler' which is nautical for a 'services no longer required' notification.

snatch, *v.* In the phr. **to snatch it,** or (one's, the, etc.,) **bit, rent, time,** to resign; to take the wages due and leave a job.

1911 *Bulletin* (Sydney) 13 July 14/3 Will someone on the mainland tell me whether the slang phrase, 'Snatch it', is used there by miners when they announce their intention of 'drawing their time'? It is common on the mining fields of Tassy. **1915** *Ibid.* 28 Oct. 22/4 A shearer.. never gets 'sacked'. He always 'pelts it in' or 'snatches his bit'. **1916** *Ibid.* 6 July 24/1 Here's how they fling him their resignations.. 'I'm snatchin' me time'. **1948** K.S. PRICHARD *Golden Miles* 90 At the graveside, there were some who like Dally thought of 'snatching it': turning down their job in a mine where creepy ground had been responsible for several falls and fatal accidents recently. **1952** *Bulletin* (Sydney) 16 Jan. 17/2 That night, after carefully putting the rag to bed, the comp. snatched his time. He was 20 miles away next morning. **1953** L. & C. REES *Spinifex Walkabout* 76 The cook had a bit of a row with the overseer and had 'snatched his rent'—given notice. **1961** *Bulletin* (Sydney) 21 Oct. 30/3 The woolpresser snaps: 'I'm snatching it as soon as I take this one out of the press. Write it out for me.' **1975** B. FOLEY *Shearers' Poems* 11 Then there was the day He said he'd 'snatch his rent' And when asked why he wanted to go 'I'm a failure as a 'cordon Bleu' it's time I really went'. **1977** *Pastoral Rev.* Oct. 334/3 Very early next morning. The Boss packed his swag and rode into the station, where he said he was snatching his time. **1979** J. WILLIAMS *White River* 40 Once they got you here, you felt the power of the company... To hell with the civil liberties you once thought you possessed. Snatching your time didn't pay.

snavel, *v.* Also **snavvel.** [Br. dial. but now chiefly Austral.: see EDD *v.*[2] and OEDS.] *trans.* To steal; to appropriate; to grab. Also *absol.*

1892 *Truth* (Sydney) 15 May 1/6 He has only managed to 'snavel' £4000 this year. **1902** *Ibid.* 13 July 4/3 Finding that he can neither finger nor filch, snavel nor sneak. **1909** M. CANNON *That Damned Democrat* (1981) 74 To succeed in 'snavelling' the place occupied and just vacated. **1917** A.B. PATERSON *Saltbush Bill* 52 Get all you can borrow, beg, snavel or snare. **1929** K.S. PRICHARD *Coonardoo* 21 He never doubted that it was she, and not Ted, who had snavelled Wytaliba under his nose. **1934** *Austral. Ring* VIII. xcv. 6 Lurich snavvled first fall in the third round. **1948** V. PALMER *Golconda* 100 They're booming the notion o' a new township and snavelling all the land within a mile o' it.

sneezeweed. [See quot. 1965.] Any of the several aromatic herbs of the genus *Centipeda* (fam. Asteraceae) of Aust. and elsewhere.

1877 F. VON MUELLER *Introd. Bot. Teachings* 58 The Sneeze-weed (*Cotula* or *Centipeda Cunninghamii*). A dwarf, erect.. odorous herb... Can be converted into snuff. **1887** *Proc. Linnean Soc. N.S.W.* II. 175 *Myriogyne minuta*.. known in the Southern Districts as 'Sneezeweed'. **1889** *Centennial Mag.* (Sydney) I. xi. 799/2 The sneeze-weed fills the atmosphere in the first summer-months, with a pollen that is frequently blamed for more serious complaints than mere sneezing. **1901** J.H. MAIDEN *Plants reputed to be Poisonous* 24 *Centipeda orbicularis*.. (Syn. *Myriogyne minuta*..) 'Sneeze-weed'.. was believed by the late Baron von Mueller to be injurious to stock; but my own experience does not support this view. **1965** *Austral. Encycl.* VIII. 169 Sneezeweed, the vernacular name for low aromatic herbs in the genus *Centipeda*.. which, when crushed, are strongly irritant to the mucous membranes; the vapour causes sneezing. **1981** G.M. CUNNINGHAM et al. *Plants Western N.S.W.* 671 The powdered leaves apparently act like snuff, hence the name 'sneezeweed', and where it is abundant this species [*sc. Centipeda minima* var. *minima*] produces a piercing aroma which pervades the air.

snide. *Pearling.* [Transf. use of *snide* counterfeit.] A stolen pearl. Also *attrib.*, and as **snide pearl.**

1933 J.M. HARCOURT *Pearlers* 116 As if every mother's son of them wouldn't buy snides from his own brother's boat! **1934** J. KIRWAN *Empty Land* 117 The police say it is not difficult to get rid of pearls that have been stolen—'snide' pearls. **1936** C.P. CONIGRAVE *N. Aust.* 244 What is 'snide'? Just a stolen pearl that never comes to the rightful owner's possession but is passed by an unscrupulous diver to the harpies of the industry. **1937** J.M. HARCOURT *It never Fails* 110 Snides, Julius gathered, were stolen pearls, and snide-buying an industry that yielded precedence in importance only to pearling itself. **1941** K.S. PRICHARD *Moon of Desire* 120 He had been buying snide pearl, as well as the best stuff in the town, for years. **1954** N. BARTLETT *Pearl Seekers* 180 A commercial traveller who dealt in snide, or stolen pearls. **1981** D. STUART *I think I'll Live* 100 Look, they're too smooth for my liking... These three are snides, I tell y'.

snig, *v. Timber-getting.* Past tense **snigged, snug, snugged.** [Br. dial.: see EDD *v.*[1] and OEDS *v.*[2]]

1. *trans.* To haul (a log) by means of ropes and chains. Also with **out** and **up.**

[N.Z. **1866** B. HARPER *Kettle on Fuchsia* (1967) 69 Snigging firewood out.] **1897** L. LINDLEY-COWEN *W. Austral. Settler's Guide* 229 There is a fourth method [of clearing forests], which is certainly the most expeditious, but it requires a large amount of capital and would only pay where a large area of country had to be cleared. I refer to the use of traction engines fitted with long wire ropes by means of which the trees can be pulled down as they stand, without any preliminary preparation, and then 'snigged' up into rows eight or ten chains apart. **1910** C.E.W. BEAN *On Wool Track* 244 He was loading tree trunks—'snigging' them into position (that is, dragging them along by their ends yoked up to some bullocks as if the trunk were a wagon). **1917** *Bk. of Ballarat* 32 When he had the job of cleaning up the Green Swamp.. it was David who fastened the chains and snugged them in on the slippery boulders. **1920** *Land of Lyre Bird* (S. Gippsland Pioneers' Assoc.) 83 The construction of the hundreds of miles of chock and log fencing, the materials for which had to be 'snigged' up hill and down dale through a veritable labyrinth of stumps and logs and holes. **1945** J. DEVANNY *Bird of Paradise* 19 After a log is snug the heart pops out still further and finishes up about a quarter of an inch beyond the rest of the log. **1948** P.J. Hurley *Red Cedar* 65 There's plenty of cedar over those hills. . . We could get it out with hawsers and tractors. "Snig' it out,' he maintained. **1961** *Gumsuckers' Gaz.* (Melbourne) Aug. 2 Mr Suters . . still uses his team for snigging out logs on his property. **1975** G.A.W. Smith *Once Green Jackaroo* 115 Bitchey had taken his teams up those coastal mountains and 'snigged' two and sometimes three logs at a time and loaded them on his wagon. **1982** M. Walker *Making Do* 144, I went out and cut me load of logs, and done 'em up ready for the mill, and then snug 'em (snigged) in the bush, and then got to the mill. **1983** *Overlander* Jan. 84 Diesels . . no more stalling when you stop halfway up a steep hill to . . snig out a log.

2. *transf.*

[N.Z. **1966** P. Newton *Boss's Story* 97 Saw one of the chaps snigging a dog away by its tail.] **1976** J.H. Travers *Bull Dust on Brigalow* 54 Sometimes a brumby horse would be shot and snigged near the house by a couple of draught horses. **1978** Teece & Pike *Voice of Wilderness* 93, I snigged that heavily-loaded old truck across the creek with two horses with greenhide ropes tied to their tails. **1981** H. Hannah *Together in Jungle Scrub* 42 There were big fireplaces, where you'd open a door and snig a big log in.

Hence **snigging** *vbl. n.* and *attrib.*, esp. as **snigging track,** a track along which timber is hauled.

1910 *Emu* X. 209 Some 'snigging' track, cut for the purpose of timber hauling. **1938** F. Ratcliffe *Flying Fox & Drifting Sand* 105 We found the snigging track ('snigging' a log is dragging it over the ground). **1944** J. Devanny *By Tropic Sea & Jungle* 118 The grappling and snigging of the logs. **1945** —— *Bird of Paradise* 14 An old bushman . . spent every hour of daylight . . cutting out snigging tracks from each tree to the haulage way. **1982** *Bulletin* (Sydney) 6 Apr. 79/1 Cutting 4000 super feet of cypress pine . . with three horses snigging them on to a ramp (those snigging horses were bloody good horses).

snig-track. *Timber-getting. Snigging track*, see Snig.

[N.Z. **1953** N.Z. Forest Gloss. (N.Z. Forest Service) (typescript), *Snig track*, a path constructed for snigging.] **1979** *Sydney Morning Herald* 5 Sept. 6 In order to extract logs from the buffer zone, roads and 'snig' tracks will have to be cut through the virgin rainforest. **1980** J. Wolfe *End of Pricklystick* 9 On the ridges snaked the snig-tracks, winding and wearing along the spurs until they reached the screaming circular saws at Balook. **1985** *Age* (Melbourne) 31 Oct. 11/3 The two foresters were proud that guidelines for logging are now being enforced, including . . routes that roads and snig tracks must follow.

snipe, *n.* [Spec. use of U.S. *snipe* an outdoor advertising poster.] See quot. 1966.

1966 S.J. Baker *Austral. Lang.* (ed. 2) 355 *Snipe*, a political election poster, the size of which is limited to 10 in. by 6 in. **1977** F. Daly *From Curtin to Kerr* 75 He went to the same printer as me, got the same kind of snipes printed in blue and white with his photograph and pasted them up all over the electorate on every post: *Vote No. 1* Clark. . . He pasted snipes on nearly every post and on the day had his booths well manned.

sniper. See quot. 1945. Also **sniping** *vbl. n.*

1945 S.J. Baker *Austral. Lang.* 248 A waterfront term of fairly recent origin is *sniper*, a non-union labourer. **1950** J. Morrison *Port of Call* 222 Don't you know what sniping is? Taking work outside the 'Pound or outside pick-up hours. **1955** —— *Black Cargo* 14 It will need only one shout of 'Sniper!' and Lamond will be lucky to get out without being knocked down. **1957** T. Nelson *Hungry Mile* 72 The W.W.F. had preference of work, wharf by wharf. The outsiders (snipers) would stand back at the gate until the W.W.F. men were all used.

snob, *n.*[1] *S.A. Obs.* In *pl.*: see quot. 1863.

1852 *Four Colonies Aust.* 39 The retailers, and all not within a certain indescribable line, were dubbed the 'snobs'; the officials and self-elected aristocracy, the 'nobs'. **1852** D. Mackenzie *Ten Yrs. Aust.* 12 As soon as they had secured the special survey, they agreed to divide it; the officials and gentlemen, or nobs, taking one ten thousand acres, and the tradesmen, or snobs, the other. **1852** F. Lancelott *Aust. as it Is* II. 295 Two associations were formed, one by the wealthy called the *nobs*, the other known as the *snobs*. **1852** J. Fairfax *Colonies Aust.* 15 Two parties, formed respectively of the principal men of Adelaide, sometimes called the 'nobs', and of the tradesmen and other less nobby individuals in Adelaide, more commonly designated 'the snobs'. **1863** J.B. Austin *Mines S.A.* 19 The Princess Royal Mining, and . . the South Australian Mining Association . . were called the 'nobs' and the 'snobs', the former representing the 'aristocracy' of the colony, and the latter the merchants and tradespeople.

snob, *n.*[2] [Punning use of *snob* a shoemaker or cobbler.] Cobbler *n.*[2]

1915 *Bulletin* (Sydney) 28 Oct. 22/3 The last sheep left in the pen is always a very rough one, and is termed the 'cobbler' or the 'snob'. **1945** C.E.W. Bean *On Wool Track* (ed. 3) 135 The sheep most difficult to shear, which naturally is left last in the pen, is also called the 'snob'. Mr Boyer points out that as early as in Elizabethan times 'snob' was slang for cobbler (Shakespeare has 'snip and snob' for tailor and cobbler). The terms have persisted in old fashioned English, and 'snob' has added to its several meanings this peculiarly Australian one. **1971** J.S. Gunn *Distrib. Shearing Terms N.S.W.* 9 As it is the practice to leave rough sheep until last it is only to be expected that *snob* and *cobbler* for both 'rough' and 'last' will occur. . . *Snob* and *cobbler* meant 'last' before specialising to 'rough'. **1975** L. Ryan *Shearers* 49 'Get on to this wrinkled bludger!' he said. It was the last sheep in the pen. . . 'Real snob ain't it?'

snodger, *a.* [Of unknown origin. Cf. Br. dial. *snod* sleek, neat, in good order: see OED *a.* and EDD *a.*] Excellent, very good, first-class. Also as *n.* and *adv.*

1917 *O.P.: Lit. Chron. 10th Battery A.F.A.* 35 An' at that he hits me a snodger in the neck. **1917** G.C. Cooper Diary 6 Sept., Quiet day—good concert at night at Y.M.C.A. 'real snodger'. **1921** F. Grose *Rough Y.M. Bloke* 26 We went through a lot of gardens right up to a 'snodger' 'ouse. **1946** J. Holmes *Is it Dinkum?* 22 As a foal he was a 'snodger', with a silver mane and tail, A neat and compact body, tho' his legs looked long and frail. **1946** *Sun* (Sydney) 11 Aug. (Suppl.) 15 There they find the con-ships fitted up snodger with bulkheads studded with nails. **1976** Boomer & Spender *Spitting Image* 145, I took some to Wallaroo and it was, it was a real snodger. There's nothing like fillet steak.

snodgollion: see Snottygobble.

snooker, *n.* [f. Snooker *v.*] A hiding-place.

1967 *Kings Cross Whisper* (Sydney) xxxv. 6/2 *In smoke*, to hide out. Similar to being in snooker. **1979** L. Newcombe *Inside Out* 84 'It's O.K. they won't find us here.' 'We've still gotta find a better snooker than this.'

snooker, *v.* [Transf. use of *snooker* to prevent (someone) from reaching an object.] *trans.* To hide.

1968 J. Alard *He who shoots Last* 224 We'll have to snooker da dough some place. **1975** Latch & Hitchings *Mr X* 224 The dumps where the bust men snooker their stuff. **1979** L. Newcombe *Inside Out* 80, I suggested to Kevin that . . we could 'snooker' ourselves for a while in the boot of one of the cars parked outside.

snoot. [f. *snooty, a.* supercilious, snobbish.] A supercilious person.

1955 N. Pulliam *I traveled Lonely Land* 388 *Snoot*, a very disagreeable person. **1977** S. Locke Elliott *Water under Bridge* 15 Those Melbourne snoots . . look down their noses at us Sydneyites.

Hence **snoot** *v. trans.*, to snub.

1977 S. Locke Elliott *Water under Bridge* 19 Better than being snooted by those plutos.

snore, *n.*

1. As **snore-off:** a sleep or nap, esp. after drinking.

[N.Z. **1950** *Landfall* (Christchurch) 127, I notice Little Spike's legs sticking out from . . where he is having a snore-off.] **1952** C. Simpson *Come away, Pearler* 185, I go into me room for a bit of a snore-orf, only it turns out to be *'er* room. . . She's only 'alf-'arnessed. **1968** D. O'Grady *Bottle of Sandwiches* 49 He surfaced from his plonk-induced snore-off.

2. A sleeping place, esp. as provided for transients.

1967 *Kings Cross Whisper* (Sydney) xl. 4/4 *Snore*, a place to rest the bod. **1975** *Bulletin* (Sydney) 24 May 26/3 The alternative is a night shelter—one of the eight round Surry Hills and Woolloomooloo run by the Salvation Army, St Vincent de Paul and the Methodists. For skid row derelicts they have about 700 beds. The deros don't choose much between what they call 'snores'—many have lice, they say, except the Catholics—and everyone involved with them is a 'bastard', tough and unfriendly.

snore, *v. intr.* In the phr. **to snore off,** to fall asleep.

1925 S. Hicks *Hullo Australs.* 145 'Good-night, I hope you'll snore off.' 'Snore what,' said Green. 'Snore off, sir—It's Australian. Means go to sleep.' **1962** P.A. Knudsen *Bloodwood Tree* 150 'Well,' Art said, 'you fellas can do what y' like—I'm goin' to snore-off.' . . Presently all the men in the camp were stretched out dozing.

snork. [Transf. use of *snork* a young pig.]

1. A baby.

1941 S.J. Baker *Pop. Dict. Austral. Slang* 68 *Snork*, a baby. **1944** L. Glassop *We were Rats* 273 Got a scar on his hand, but probably he's had it since he was a little snork. **1967** *Kings Cross Whisper* (Sydney) xl. 4/4 *Snorks*, small children. Short for suckers of norks.

2. A sausage.

1941 S.J. Baker *Pop. Dict. Austral. Slang* 68 *Snork*, . . a sausage. **1948** R. Raven-Hart *Canoe in Aust.* 14 Sausages are also 'snags' in Australia, or 'snorks'.

snottygobble. [Transf. use of Br. dial. *snotty-gobble*, var. of *snotergob* the fruit of the yew-tree: see EDD.] Any of several plants incl. (chiefly *W.A.*) trees or shrubs of the genus *Persoonia* (fam. Proteaceae); the fruit of these plants. Also **snodgollion, snotgoblin.**

1854 F. Eldershaw *Aust. as it really Is* 43 Snodgollions, etc., are . . well-recognized delicacies among the rising Anglo-Australian generation. **1906** *Bulletin* (Sydney) 4 Oct. 17/2 The toothsome 'snot-goblin', a pink delicacy growing in the ti-tree mistletoe, whose slimy pulp taxed the powers of the toughest stomach among us. **1957** *Overland* x. 9 'That's a mistletoe isn't it—that creeper with the red berries? Is that what you call it?' 'No, snottygobble.' **1973** R. Erickson et al. *Flowers & Plants W.A.* 169 Two other members of the *Proteaceae*, common as understorey trees in the forest, are the Snottygobbles, so called because of their succulent fruits. **1981** J.P. Gabbedy *Forgotten Pioneers* 73 The 'snotty-gobble' (*Persoonia longifolia* . .) had another . . application. . . The Muir ladies . . used to steep the red-coloured inner bark of the tree and dye their straw hats a vivid and lasting red.

snout, *n.* [Fig. use of *snout* nose.] In the phr. **to have a snout on** or **against** (someone or something), to be ill-disposed towards (someone); to have an aversion to (something).

[N.Z. **1905** *N.Z. Truth* (Wellington) 12 Aug. 1 The Grey candidate has a snout on the law courts. 'I got fourteen days,' he said.] **1919** V. Marshall *World of Living Dead* 33 It was all part of the 'snout' they had ag'in him. **1919** C. Drew *Doings of Dave* 139 He seems to have a dead snout on the boat. **1949** L. Glassop *Lucky Palmer* 212 He's got a snout on the kid for something. **1952** P. Gladwin *Desert in Heart* 87, I never said anything like that. Inspector Ferguson knows I didn't. He's got a snout on me. **1955** R. Lawler *Summer of Seventeenth Doll* (1965) 48 You got a snout on that kid the first day you saw him working. **1962** A. Seymour *One Day of Yr.* 14 Why's she got a snout on Hughie? What's he done? **1977** V. Priddle *Larry & Jack* 13 He . . would often say the police had a snout on him and had him before the bench many times.

snout, *v.* [See prec.] *trans.* To harass; to rebuff; to bear ill-will towards. Freq. as *pa. pple.* and *ppl. a.*

1913 *Bulletin* (Sydney) 25 Sept. 24/1 I'll . . work the other sheds down to Yanco. . . That's where some blokes settle themselves. . . They hang around the town, an' the Johns and pubs get 'em snouted. **1915** C.J. Dennis *Songs of Sentimental Bloke* 13 The world 'as got me snouted jist a treat. **1919** E. Dyson *Hello, Soldier* 18 Little Abdul's quite a fighter, 'n' he mixes it with skill: But the Anzacs have him snouted, 'n', oh ma, he's feelin' ill. **1944** A. MARSHALL *These are my People* 155, I was sore as a snouted sheila for weeks. **1970** R. BEILBY *No Medals for Aphrodite* 149 That officer happened to have me snouted because I got you across the river, against his orders. **1981** D. STUART *I think I'll Live* 150 'On church parade he talks like he's got an egg in his mouth an' don't want to break it.' 'I dunno why you've got the padre snouted. . . He's never been anything but a hanger-on.'

snow.

1. Used *attrib.* in the names of plants: **snow daisy,** any of several perennial herbs, usu. of the genus *Celmisia* (fam. Asteraceae) and esp. *C. asteliifolia* of high country in s.e. Aust. incl. Tas., and New Zealand; **grass,** any of many grasses (fam. Poaceae) of high country in s.e. Aust. incl. Tas., esp. some densely tufted perennials of the genus *Poa*; also *attrib.*; **gum,** any of several trees of the genus *Eucalyptus* (fam. Myrtaceae), esp. *E. pauciflora* (fam. Myrtaceae), of s.e. Aust. incl. Tas., occurring both above and below the snow-line, and having a smooth, usu. whitish bark and thick leathery leaves, and (*Tas.*) *E. coccifera*; the wood of the tree; see also CABBAGE GUM, *weeping gum* WEEPING, *white sally* WHITE *a.*[2] 1 a.

1941 C. BARRETT *Aust.* 90 Millions of **snow-daisies** were out below the drifts. **1948** E.H. COLLIS *Lost Yrs.* 102 The countless snow-daisies on the slopes of Mount Kosciusko. **1968** V. SERVENTY *Southern Walkabout* 34 The silver snow daisies, huge drifts of white flowers with orange centres, almost seemed to bring back the winter snow, so blinding white were they. **1979** *Ecos* xxii. 31/2 Plants like the snow daisy seem to need plentiful spring rain to wash a coating of slimy fungus off their stems before they can grow. **1898** E.E. MORRIS *Austral Eng.* 425 **Snow-Grass** . . *Poa caespitosa*. **1926** A.S. LE SOUEF et al. *Wild Animals Australasia* 294 A large patch of snow-grass. **1945** E. MITCHELL *Speak to Earth* 55 Sleek young Herefords come in from Groggin with older steers that have ranged the snow-grass tops. **1977** *Ecos* xi. 14/3 (*caption*) The leguminous shrubs prevent soil erosion between the snow grass tussocks. **1984** E. WALLING *On Trail Austral. Wildflowers* 2 Lovely clumps of Snow Grass. **1905** *Emu* V. 66, I saw between 20 and 30 male and female Lyre-Birds on the stunted **snow gums** (*E. pauciflora*) on the high ridge running from Feathertop. **1946** *Bulletin* (Sydney) 23 Jan. 13/3 The prospect of midday billy seemed rather bleak, the only timber available being some wet snow-gum. **1952** J. CLEARY *Sundowners* 262 Snow gums posed in frozen corroboree along the ridges. **1980** HOLTH & BARNABY *Cattlemen of High Country* 13 Straight in sheltered positions, snow-gums are gnarled and contorted into strange shapes by severe winds and sub-freezing temperatures and become increasingly stunted on higher levels. **1985** *Mt. Field Nat. Park* (Tas. Nat. Parks & Wildlife Service), Here the dominant trees are yellow gums (*E[ucalyptus] subcrenulata*), with the snow gums (*E. coccifera*) higher up among the lakes.

2. Special Comb. **snow country,** those areas of s.e. New South Wales and n.e. Victoria which are snow-covered for all or part of the winter; **lease,** a contract governing the tenure of an area of Crown land in the snow country; the land so held; also *attrib.*

1906 *Bulletin* (Sydney) 19 July 16/1 Got into the **snow country** of Vic. recently to bring cattle to a warmer situation. **1935** T. RAYMENT *Cluster of Bees* 99 The bees have quite different ecological conditions . . in 'snow country'. **1968** *Swag* (Sydney) iii. 13 Renowned in the Australian snow country. **1983** *Open Road* June 18/3 The Numeralla Bridge on the Monaro Highway—the main sealed road to the NSW snow country—is threatening to sink without trace. **1905** *Austral. Handbk.* 95 **Snow Leases**—Vacant Crown lands or lands held under Annual Lease or Occupation License, which for a part of each year are usually covered with snow, and in consequence unfit for continuous use or occupation, are offered by lease for auction. **1910** C.E.W. BEAN *On Wool Track* 74 Down in the wild valleys in the Snow Leases there still wander plenty of dingoes, and the sheep up here are still shepherded. **1914** *Bulletin* (Sydney) 2 Apr. 22/4, I helped to drive a mob of cattle from near Twofold Bay to a snow lease near Kiandra. **1934** 'E.N. SPEER' *Destiny* 301 Drovers, moving their large travelling mobs of sheep up to the snow leases for the coming summer, would stop and talk to Neville. **1946** *Bulletin* (Sydney) 23 Jan. 13/3 While mustering sheep on Kosciusko snow leases on an early winter day we were caught by a premature fall of snow. **1953** E. MITCHELL *Flow River, blow Wind* 7 Two mobs were starting on their way to the mountain snowlease country. **1968** *Meanjin* 18 On the crown lands above the timber where the tussocky grass grows thick and gentian flowers come in the Spring, sheepmen drive their flocks up from the valleys during the Summer months and leave them to graze on areas they have leased from the government—Snow Leases, they are marked on the maps that define them.

snuffle-buster. *Obs.* A puritanical person.

1890 *Bull-Ant* (Melbourne) 28 Aug. 4/3 This is a fearful blow to the cause of the snuffle-busters and the Pharisees, whose horror of a free and genial Sunday is only equalled by their sycophantic adulation towards their gracious Queen. ***c* 1907** W.C. CHANDLER *Darkest Adelaide* 57 The matter was passed over by the sanctimonious snufflebusters, whose pharisaical plea was that the evil could not be a very alarming one, otherwise the Advertiser and Register would have written it up.

snuffle-busting, *ppl. a. Obs.* Puritanical.

1895 *Worker* (Sydney) 9 Feb. 4/2 Painted by him I am a narrow, bigoted, snuffle-busting son of a gun whose grog blossomed 'conk' gives the lie to his watery protestations. **1905** M. CANNON *That Damned Democrat* (1981) 153 The eminently respectable firm of Beath, Schiess and Co. . . have done more to make a hell upon earth in Melbourne than any other gang of snuffle-busting sweaters we wot of. **1910** *Ibid.* 124 Some years ago . . John Norton branded the snufflebusting, hypocritical crowd in politics as 'a gang of wire-whiskered wowsers'.

snug, snugged: see SNIG.

soak. [Br. dial. *soak* a percolation of water; water which has oozed through or out of the ground: see OED *sb.*[2]] A hollow in (often sandy) soil where water collects, on or below the surface of the ground; a water-hole. Also *attrib.*

1838 T.W. WALKER *Month in Bush Aust.* 44 It appeared . . well watered, for we frequently met with springs or land-soaks. **1865** *Illustr. Melbourne Post* Jan. 14/1 In the whole area of the island all the water that can be found is simply what is known by the term of 'land-soaks', at or near the coast sand-hills. **1894** *Western Champion* (Barcaldine) 13 Feb. 3/4 A day's stage usually varies from 12 to 15 miles, and the waterholes or 'soaks' as they are locally called, seem almost of artificial construction. **1908** J.A. BARRY *Luck of Native-Born* 44 Midway between there [*sc.* Gnarlbine] and Coolgardie, in a clump of wattles at the foot of a granite rise, they came to a 'soak', with water oozing up in several places from the decomposed rocks. **1925** M. TERRY *Across Unknown Aust.* 260 Two galahs came to the soak for a drink. **1932** I.L. IDRIESS *Lasseter's Last Ride* 16 Numbers of dry creeks contain 'soak' water just a few feet below the surface. **1936** 'L. KAYE' *Black Wilderness* 131 That soak don't go down no matter how much we draw, as it must be fed from 'way below. **1948** C.P. MOUNTFORD *Brown Men & Red Sand* 62 'Snowy' had been doubtful whether the soaks at Mt Connor would yield enough water to carry us across the desert to Ayers Rock. **1955** D. CLARK *Boomer* 87 The mob had assembled around a 'soak', a place where, by strenuous digging, they had unearthed seeping fresh water. **1972** W.F. BLAKELEY *Dream Millions* 24 When these waterways or creeks are in the making, big holes are washed out, and in nearly all soaks there is a bar of rock at the lower end that impounds the water. **1977** *Ink No. 2* 16 The soak in the creek bed had started to sink as soon as the rain stopped. **1983** *Bulletin* (Sydney) 27 Dec. 209/3 'It's a soak,' said Tommy. . . Just an imperceptible oozing of water out of the bank to form no more than the suggestion of a puddle, less than a metre long, a few centimetres wide, but it would be enough for the birds and for the animals.

soakage. SOAK. Also *attrib.*

1892 A.F. CALVERT *Narr. Exped. N.-W. Aust.* 14 To detect the basins or natural rock bed, catchments, or using the local term 'soakages' fell to my lot. **1900** *Bulletin* (Sydney) 20 Jan. 32/1 At times, Mac. would dismount and try for a soakage, but the sand was too deep for him. **1920** C.H. SAYCE *Golden Buckles* 149 Who'd have thought there was a soakage in this creek! **1927** *Smith's Weekly* (Sydney) 7 May 22/4 Binghi makes soakage tapping a quick and simple operation. **1934** W. HATFIELD *River Crossing* 147, I found him . . in that gidgee flat. . . It's usually a good spot for a few 'roos, above where that granite outcrop makes a catchment, and the kangaroos dig in the sand for soakages. **1959** D. STUART *Yandy* 88 He sank the well in the creekbed for soakage water. **1973** A. BURNETT *Wilful Murder in Outback* 42 A freshwater soakage provided water for us.

soap. In the phr. **not to know** (someone) **from a bar of soap,** not to have the remotest acquaintance with.

1918 C. PEARL *Morrison of Peking* (1967) 367 No respect except among very restricted class for Gov.-General or Lieut. Gov. 'Don't know 'im from a bar of soap' would be the comment. **1938** *Smith's Weekly* (Sydney) 26 Nov. 23 (*caption*), I don't know you from a bar of soap. **1943** K. TENNANT *Ride on Stranger* 277 'Why doesn't she marry the child's father?' . . 'It's my belief she doesn't know him from a bar of soap.' **1947** G. CASEY *Wits are Out* 184 We can't do that, when we don't know them from a bar of soap. **1970** J. CLEARY *Helga's Web* 145 I've never met any of his—interests. Certainly not this girl. I dunno her from a bar of soap.

soapie. [See quot. 1983.] A young fish, esp. a jewfish. Also *attrib.*

1978 *Sydney Morning Herald* 27 Oct. 23/8 Small 'soapie' jewfish are plentiful but most anglers are not rigging heavily enough to land big jewfish. **1983** *Sun-Herald* (Sydney) 20 Nov. 74/1 Mulloway grow to a weight of more than 50 kg., but . . fishermen are happy when their scales register 5 kg. or 10 kg., while the smaller 'soapie' of 2 kg. or 3 kg. is the norm. The term 'soapie' is used to describe the flavour of the smaller mulloway's flesh. It's unwarranted because such a fish is quite good eating if properly prepared.

soap tree. [Spec. use of *soap-tree* any of several plants the leaves (etc.) of which yield a substitute for soap.] The tree *Alphitonia excelsa* (see *red ash* RED *a.* 1 a.).

1923 *Bulletin* (Sydney) 8 Feb. 22/2 Queensland possesses what we called 'the soap-tree'. It is not unlike the silver-gum, having long tapering leaves and rough bark. **1964** D. LOCKWOOD *Up Track* 128 (*caption*) If you run out of soap, use the leaves of the soap tree, as do these Djouan tribal women at Mataranka. **1979** K.A.W. WILLIAMS *Native Plants Qld.* I. 14 *Alphitonia excelsa* . . Soap Tree. . . The underside of the leaf is silvery and when rubbed in the hand in the presence of water they form a 'soapy' froth.

Socceroo /sɒkə'ru/. [f. *soccer* + KANGAR)OO *n.* 3.] In the *pl.*: the name of the Australian international soccer team; in *sing.*, a member of such a team. Cf. KANGAROO *n.* 3 b. and WALLABY *n.* 4.

1973 *Sydney Morning Herald* 15 Nov. 1/10 Now that the Australian Soccer team is basking in honour and glory after its World Cup victory over South Korea it can surely do without the name 'Socceroos' which is being increasingly applied to it. **1974** W.F. MANDLE *Going it Alone* (1978) 45 Fancy picking on the gallant Socceroos, who didn't do such a bad job against East and West Germany. **1979** L. SCHWAB *Socceroos & their Opponents* 4 Australia's national team, which was dubbed 'the Socceroos' during the 1973–74 World Cup mission, has comprised many extraordinary players. **1983** *Advertiser* (Adelaide) 12 Dec. 33/6 Socceroos through to semi-finals. **1985** *Border Morning Mail* (Albury-Wodonga) 30 Nov. 75/1 Scotland's soccer team manager had high praise for the Socceroos' secret weapon, Jim Patikas.

social system. *Hist.* A method of convict management formulated by Alexander Maconochie (1787–1860), penal reformer: see quot. 1839.

1839 A. MACONOCHIE *Gen. Views Convict Managem.* 23 Prisoners under the Social System would be exactly as free men labouring for wages, and be just as easily managed—or rather, they would be more so, for both their dependance and stake would be greater. **1840** *True Colonist* (Hobart) 3 Jan. 7/3 Sir George Gipps fully enters into all Captain Maconochie's views of the Social System. **1841** *Morning Advertiser* (Hobart) 19 Aug. 2/2

The Hulks, the Penitentiary .. the Silent, and as it termed, the Social or Maconochie systems.

sock, *v.* [Fig use of *sock* to drive or strike into something.] *trans.* To drink (alcoholic liquor) quickly. Also with **away, down.**

1915 *Euripides Ensign: on Board 'Euripides'* 2 June 1 Is a soldier less a soldier 'Cause he socks a pint of beer? **1967** J. HIBBERD *White with Wire Wheels* (1970) 217 Think I'll dash down to the milk bar and sock away a pint or so before I head off to the office. **1969** —— *Dimboola* (1974) 23 Cheer up Reen, it'll seem beaut tomorrow. Sock another one down.

sod. [f. *sod, ppl. a.* (of bread) sodden, poorly risen: see OED *pa. pple., ppl. a.,* and *sb.*[2] 2 a.]

a. A damper which has failed to rise: see also quot. 1980. Also **sod damper** and **soddy damper.**

1852 *Austral. Gold Digger's Monthly Mag.* iii. 86 Beware of bad water and sod damper. **1887** 'OVERLANDER' *Austral. Sketches* 15 Showing us .. how to make a damper—which, I am sorry to say, was a regular sod. **1894** A.B. BELL *Austral. Camp Fire Tales* 115 It was no joke cookin' in the wet weather, and if the damper come out a sod, Montmorency didn't furget to let me know of it. **1951** I.L. IDRIESS *Across Nullarbor* 119 He baked a damper—an awful sod—stuck to their insides like glue. **1954** T. RONAN *Vision Splendid* 42 And Mart the cook the shovel took And swung the damper to and fro. 'Another sod, so help me God, That's fourteen in a flamin' row.' **1957** R.S. PORTEOUS *Brigalow* 206 His dampers were leaden sods. **1980** R. BROPHO *Fringedweller* 19 You'd have .. soddy damper and tea. Soddy damper is plain flour with no self-raising flour or baking powder in it.

b. Hence, loosely, any damper.

1918 *Jackass: First Austral. Gen. Hospital* Christmas 20 He is consolingly informed that everyone buries his first 'Sod', as a Damper is called. **1938** *Woman's Mirror Cookery Bk.* (ed. 2) 393 The art of 'turning out the sod' (Australian for making the perfect damper) is unknown to those thousands of 'Mirror' housewives who are well serviced by town or country bakers. **1939** *Bulletin* (Sydney) 7 June 20/2, I agree .. *re* the general awfulness of damper. Still some sod-punchers are worse than others... Most sodmakers get .. the dough too wet... Show me the padflogger who wouldn't swap a sod as big as a cartwheel for just one loaf of baker's bread. **1947** *Ibid.* 15 Oct. 28/2, I have heard it claimed that the name for the 'sods' munched by bachelor outbackers derived from William Dampier. **1949** *Ibid.* 9 Mar. 15/3 The musterers' cook, stuck a stick in the sod to see if it was cooked and then shoved it up in the fork of a tree.

Hence **sod** *v. trans.*, to spoil (a damper) by failing to make it rise.

1946 F. CLUNE *Try Nothing Twice* 86, I had my first lesson in damper-making, and I've been an expert in charring them and sodding them ever since.

soda. [Prob. transf. use of *soda* deal card in Faro: see OEDS 4.] Any easy victim; a simple task; a 'pushover'.

1917 *All abaht It* (London) Feb. (1919) 10 He is a 'Soda' for anyone who has had any service. **1930** V. PALMER *Passage* 22 'Just one more guess.' .. 'Umph, that's a soda! Must be the old doctor.' **1943** *Bully Tin* (Baronta) 1 May 3 The Job's a soda. **1948** V. PALMER *Golconda* 208 If old Andy had lived he'd have been turfed out at the next elections, anyhow. As soon as this field opened, the seat became a soda for Labour. **1952** A. MARSHALL *Aust.* (1981) 37 Men who ostentatiously prepare to take up a challenge are sodas for the king-hit merchant. A well-known Brunswick street fighter explained it to me thus: 'Never be frightened of the man who takes off his coat and shapes up to you like a praying mantis. He's trying to convince you, as well as himself, that he can fight.' **1966** H. PORTER *Paper Chase* 74 The job, for which I have no really specialized training, is nevertheless a soda.

sod hut. *Obs.* [Used elsewhere but recorded earliest in Aust.] A dwelling built with sods of turf.

1827 Tas. Colonial Secretary's Office Rec. 1/47 238, I would also propose to construct forthwith a *Sod Hut* for the Detachment of 1 Serjent and G of the 40th Reg[t]. **1829** H. WIDOWSON *Present State Van Diemen's Land* 93 You suddenly come in contact with a few weather-boarded and sod huts. **1838** *Southern Austral.* (Adelaide) 23 June 4/3 At present it is little more than a straggling assemblage of tents, sod huts .. and other temporary buildings. **1843** C. ROWCROFT *Tales of Colonies* (1858) 50 The men busied themselves in erecting a sod hut for themselves. **1867** J. BONWICK *J. Batman* 51 We left three white men .. with instructions to build a sod-hut. **1884** 'R. BOLDREWOOD' *Old Melbourne Memories* 37 The walls of a sod hut were indeed already up.

S.O.L. /ɛs oʊ 'ɛl/. *Shit on the liver*, see SHIT 2.

1951 D. STIVENS *Jimmy Brockett* 137 'I don't care what you write about my wrestling matches, brother,' I told him. 'I had a bit of S.O.L. the other day, but I hope you'll lay off my wife.' **1954** J. CLEARY *Climate of Courage* 222 Sorry, chum. I've got a touch of S.O.L., I think. **1978** R. MCKIE *Bitter Bread* 119 This was the first human sign for hours. Blue must be improving, getting rid of his s.o.l.

soldier, *n.* **1.** Used *attrib.* (and *ellipt.*) in the names of animals: **soldier ant,** a BULLDOG ANT, esp. one which is red, and perh. esp. *Myrmecia gulosa*; **bird,** any of several birds, esp. the *noisy miner* (see NOISY); **crab,** a small crab of the genus *Mictyris* occurring in large numbers on sandy tidal flats, esp. the bluish *M. longicarpus*.

1844 L. LEICHHARDT *Jrnl. Overland Exped. Aust.* 20 Nov. (1847) 47 The **soldier ant,** and the whole host of the others, were everywhere. **1853** C.R. READ *What I heard, saw, & Did* 221 Some bushrangers in former days catching a policeman .. binding him hand and foot, then throwing him on to a soldier-ants nest. **1867** J.R. HOULDING *Austral. Capers* 382 The bush is full of snakes, soldier ants, hornets, and horribly naked black gins. **1899** G.E. BOXALL *Story Austral. Bushrangers* 18 In these were placed a number of the great red ants, commonly known in Australia as 'bull-dog' or 'soldier' ants (*Myrmecia gulosa*). These ants are an inch and a quarter long, and of most ferocious appearance. **1936** *Austral. Writers' Ann.* 32 The soldier, or red jumper, is another interesting chap. **1950** C.E. GOODE *Yarns of Yilgarn* 80 A regiment of big red soldier ants, by a series of strategic jumps, routed us. **1845** R. HOWITT *Impressions Aust. Felix* 142 The **soldier-bird** .. is the very sentinel of the woods. **1856** H.B. STONEY *Vic.* 214 Not less than sixty-four honeysuckers are found in Australia. These vary in size from the well-known guild bird and leather-head down to the diminutive little soldier. **1874** C. DE BOOS *Congewoi Correspondence* 6 We have up, in our parts, a nasty, quarrelsome, chattering, noisy, cantankerous, varmint of a bird, as we call a 'soldier'. I don't know what the learned name of it is... Got its name because of its quarrelsome fightable disposition. **1911** *Bulletin* (Sydney) 5 Jan. 13/4 My entry for the friendly bush-bird prize is the soldier .. common in certain parts of Monaro and the South Coast (N.S.W.) districts, and owing his name to his pugnacity. He will fight anything from a cockroach to a Tantanoola tiger. **1934** H.G. LAMOND *Aviary on Plains* 48 A busy soldier bird (Noisy Miner), taking to himself the guardianship of the avian world. **1948** R. RAVEN-HART *Canoe in Aust.* 207 Soldier-birds (Noisy Miners) chasing a kookaburra, speckly grey birds with yellow facings, keeping up a stream of insulting 'Nyah-nyahs'. **1861** 'OLD BUSHMAN' *Bush Wanderings* 254 One, which we called the **soldier-crab,** was handsome and curious. **1924** *Bulletin* (Sydney) 3 Apr. 24/4 The soldier crab is useless as bait. **1928** *Ibid.* 8 Nov. 23/2 The soldier crabs, common on the beaches of N. Q'land, are well named, for in their parades across the sand they resemble a body of troops. **1969** *Crabs Sydney Foreshores* (Austral. Museum Leaflet n. 62) 6 Low tide is feeding time for perhaps the most spectacular of Sydney's foreshore crabs—the Soldier Crab (*Mictyris longicarpus*). **1977** A. THOMAS *Bulls & Boabs* (1980) 6 As I trudged across the sand, dozens of soldier crabs, fully five centimetres high, reared upright with their backs to the sun in protest against the clumsy goliath.

2. *Obs.* An animal used without its owner's knowledge.

1918 [see SOLDIER *v.*]

3. *Hist.* As a shortening of SOLDIER-SETTLEMENT and SOLDIER-SETTLER. Freq. *attrib.*

1919 C.A. BERNAYS *Qld. Politics during Sixty Yrs.* 349 The aggregate area of the soldier leases already taken up (they are all leaseholds). **1939** *Bulletin* (Sydney) 27 Sept. 16/2 When Mac, one of the hard-doers of the old A.I.F., took over his soldier's block in the mallee .. only two things clouded his horizon. **1940** *Aust.: Nat. Jrnl.* Sept. 57 At Berri and Barmera .. kindred soldier towns have repeated [others] encouraging history. **1948** *Bulletin* (Sydney) 17 Nov. 29/4 Dick's soldier block in the foothills showed brown and bare.

soldier, *v. Obs. trans.* To use (another's animal) without the owner's knowledge.

1879 'AUSTRALIAN' *Adventures Qld.* 93 If a 'nobby' bullock .. makes off .. so artfully as to evade all attempts to find him within a reasonable time .. when the runaway is caught, it may be he is in someone else's team, and the poor brute is worked down as poor as a crow... Of course, the poor man who 'soldiered' him was quite innocent! **1918** C. FETHERSTONHAUGH *After many Days* 211 These I recovered next day, and let my two 'soldiers' go... It was the first time I had ever 'soldiered' a horse. Soldiering means using a horse without the owner's leave or knowledge. Two of our lost horses were never found. Probably someone was soldiering them!

soldier-settlement. *Hist.* A scheme under which ex-service personnel are allocated grants of land, usu. land not previously cultivated; the land so acquired. Also **soldier's settlement** and *attrib.*

1919 C.A. BERNAYS *Qld. Politics during Sixty Yrs.* 347 We have a different class of soldier settlement in the fruit-growing Stanthorpe district. *Ibid.* 350 Those in control of soldier settlement recognised with an admirable foresight the futility of putting neophytes on the land and expecting them forthwith to make a living. **1920** *Huon Times* (Franklin) 24 Aug. 3/2 Last week Mr C.T. Hassie, the Secretary of the South Australian branch of the O.B.U. visited the soldiers' settlement at Glossop. **1922** *Daily Mail* (Sydney) 7 Jan. 5/6 The Toole's Creek soldiers' settlement has been devastated. **1936** E. SCOTT *Aust. during War* in *Official Hist. Aust. 1914–18* XI. 845 The states, indeed, at the conference held in 1918 amid the great outburst of enthusiasm occasioned by the Armistice, pushed their advantage; and the Commonwealth Government now agreed to provide money for advances to soldier settlers to the extent of £625 each; also to finance the States in the resumption of private estates for soldier settlement. **1948** *Bulletin* (Sydney) 1 Sept. 22/4 A fellow .. came up to the Tweed to grow bananas on a soldier-settlement. **1963** D. ROBERT *Look at me Now* 60 The government of the time requisitioned some of the land for soldier-settlement. **1972** *Kings Cross Whisper* (Sydney) cxl. 2/3 It was back in 1921 when they was having all that fuss about the soldier settlement blocks.

soldier-settler. *Hist.*

1. An ex-serviceman who acquires land under the soldier-settlement scheme.

1917 *Huon Times* (Franklin) 2 Nov. 5/1 The services of such advisory committee to be available in connection with the valuation of stock, implements, etc., which returned soldier settlers wish to obtain. **1925** *Smith's Weekly* (Sydney) 18 July 15/7 A soldier settler on the Murray has a fine fox skin. **1937** E. HILL *Water into Gold* 234 Soldier settlers and 'closer' settlers were not to be merely orphans in the storm. **1956** F.B. VICKERS *First Place to Stranger* 22 He was a soldier-settler and was developing his farm on money loaned to him by a bank. I think it worked this way. Rob did so much work and then the bank sent an inspector out to assess the value of the work done. This amount was then placed to Rob's credit in the bank and allowed him to go on with more development. **1974** *Southerly* ii. 148 What was left of an old orchard was said to be haunted; a discouraged soldier-settler had killed himself there in the twenties. **1979** C. THIELE *Chadwick's Chimney* 28 When he had been discharged from the Navy he had applied for a Government loan to become what was called 'a soldier settler'.

2. Comb. **soldier-settler block.**

1933 *Bulletin* (Sydney) 13 Dec. 24/1 A young Englishmen took up one of the soldier-settler blocks on Kongbool, Balmoral (Vic.), in 1920. **1978** R.A.F. WEBB *Brothers in Sun* 154 He was posted to Brewarrina with its 20,000 square miles of scrub and sheep farms, many broken up from million-acre properties to smaller soldier-settler blocks of 10,000 to 14,000 acres each. **1984** E. ROLLS *Celebration of Senses* 117 The river farm was our first farm, a soldier settler's block.

sole. [Transf. use of *sole* the European fish *Solea solea* and other fish of the fam. Soleidae esteemed as food.] Any of many flatfish, incl. those of the fam. Soleidae and Cynoglossidae.

1786 *Hist. Narr. Discovery New Holland & N.S.W.* 50 Among a variety of fish, we caught some .. bream, soles, flounders. **1821** T. GODWIN *Descr. Acct. Van Diemen's Island* 9 Fish are caught in abundance... Those most known are .. sole, mackerel, whiting. **1873** F. DE CASTELNAU *Edible Fishes Vic.* 15, I have described under the names of *Rhombosolea Bassensis* and *Pleuronectes Victoriae*, the common *Sole* and *Flounder* of the Melbourne market. **1880** *Proc. Linnean Soc. N.S.W.* V. 49 *Synaptura nigra*... This is the best of our Flat Fish. It is generally called the 'Sole' (though that name is often given to other species of the *Pleuronectidae*). **1882** *Ibid.* VII. 13 *Pseudorhombus Russellii* .. is found in all seas from India to Port Jackson, and is generally called 'The Flounder' by the Fishermen, and not infrequently 'The Sole' by the Fishmonger, who thereby effects a ready sale. **1951** T.C. ROUGHLEY *Fish & Fisheries Aust.* 29 Twenty or thirty years ago considerable numbers of soles and flounders were marketed in Sydney, but today few are seen there. **1969** J. POLLARD *Austral. & N.Z. Fishing* 213 *Ammotretis rostratus*... One of the commonest of the flatfishes, sometimes incorrectly labelled sole in both Tasmania and Victoria.

solid, *a.* [See OED(S *a.* 18.] Severe; difficult; unsparing.

1916 C.J. DENNIS *Moods Ginger Mick* 155 *Solid*, severe, severely. **1948** R. PARK *Harp in South* 62 After all, Auntie Josie's got all them kids to look after. It must be pretty well solid for her with Grandma as well. **1959** E. LAMBERT *Glory thrown In* 66 They'll be solid on him for that, won't they? **1966** P. COWAN *Seed* 53 'Beer's run out,' he said. Walter laughed. 'You were too solid on it.'

sollicker. Also **soliker.** [Prob. of Br. dial. origin: see EDD *sollock* impetus, force.] Something very big, a 'whopper'.

1898 R. GRAEME *From England to Back Blocks* 82 Who was it I heard that in cutting-out some cattle on one of the Methvin plains, did come down a soliker and broke his horse's knees? **1899** 'S. RUDD' *On our Selection* 64 He kicked Farmer what he afterwards called 'a sollicker on the tail'. **1903** L. HENSLOWE *Ann.* 34 We wanted choppers, as the tree was a sollicker, an' pretty solid. **1909** M. FRANKLIN *Some Everyday Folk* 31 If he was a bloke I felt fit to wallop, I'd give him a nice sollicker under the ear. **1939** FRANKLIN & CUSACK *Pioneers on Parade* 168 She gave me a sollicker of a dose out of a blue bottle. **1955** P. WHITE *Tree of Man* 91 'You can jump down, can't you? You're quite big, you know.' 'Of course he can', said the man .. 'he's a sollicker.'

Hence **sollicking** *a.*

1917 C. DREW *Reminisc. D. Gilbert* 54 He gives a bit of a lecture about snakes, first; then he let's a sollickin' cove, as big as a new-chum's swag, bite him. **1946** K. TENNANT *Lost Haven* (1947) 155 It was a great big sollicking stitch if ever there was one.

song-lark. Either of the two birds of the genus *Cincloramphus, C. cruralis* (see *brown song-lark* BROWN *a.* 1) and *C. mathewsi* (see *rufous song-lark* RUFOUS); *singing lark*, see SINGING.

1898 [see *brown song-lark* BROWN *a.* 1]. **1932** A.H. CHISHOLM *Nature Fantasy in Aust.* 62 The fire had returned and completely destroyed the song-lark's home. **1965** *Austral. Encycl.* V. 242 The two song-larks, which belong to the genus *Cinclorhamphus*, are peculiar to Australia and are widely distributed throughout the continent.

songman. An Aboriginal who memorizes and performs the traditional songs of a community.

1943 W.E. HARNEY *Taboo* 19 He is considered a great 'song man' in the tribe. **1947** —— *Brimming Billabongs* 65 In the lead were the song men, chanting away as they beat the beating sticks together. **1949** —— *Songs of Songmen* 7, I heard the Songman chanting and tapping his 'time-sticks'. **1959** D. LOCKWOOD *Crocodiles & Other People* 186 The deep bass of the didgeredoo already filled the air with rhythmic beat and a songman was chanting the overture to the Wonga. **1962** V.C. HALL *Dreamtime Justice* 18 After the meal, groups deserted their family fires to hear the songmen intoning the Kudgingas, the chanted story of the Old Woman, maker of all totems and therefore of all life. **1969** A.A. ABBIE *Original Australs.* 125 Jolly, a talented Njalkpon songman in south-western Arnhem Land, exercised considerable individual judgement in staging publicly dances the old men considered sacred and secret. **1980** M. DUGAN *Early Dreaming* 34 There was the night in Arnhem Land by the banks of the Koolatong river when I talked to a songman who told me how he explained to his people why rivers ran.

sonk. [Back-formation f. SONKY.] A figure of fun; a foolish or ungainly person.

1959 D. NILAND *Gold in Streets* 144 Silly looking sonk. Head like a melon, big feet, shovel hands. King of the cow-bails, possum eater, the pride of Woop-Woop. **1966** H. PORTER *Paper Chase* 131 Her husband .. upsets the good-clean-fun pattern of an open-air drinking bout at Eagle Point Park by accusing his wife and a sonk of a bank clerk of unchaste designs on each other.

sonky, *a.* [f. Br. dial. *sonkie* 'a man like a sack of straw': see EDD *sonk, sb.* 2.] Foolish; gawky. Also as *n.*

1917 C.J. DENNIS *Doreen* 5 Aw, I ain't no silk-sock sonkie 'oo ab'ors the rood an' rough. **1941** S.J. BAKER *Pop. Dict. Austral. Slang* 69 *Sonky*, stupid, idiotic. **1958** F. HARDY *Four-Legged Lottery* 93 Jim and his father began to tease Meg about her handsome lover. 'That sonky thing,' she replied with all the scornful pride of a beautiful young woman. 'When I'm courted it will be by a real man with real prospects in life.'

soogee /ˈsudʒi/. Also **soojee, souge, sougee, sugee, sujee.** [Transf. use of *soojee* a flour obtained by grinding Indian wheat.] Used *attrib.* of a bag in which Indian flour was sold, esp. with reference to the inferiority of the material. Hence used allusively as an emblem of poverty or deprivation.

1836 'W.R.--s' *Fell Tyrant* 46 There are four sorts of settlers, the Swell settler, that is the rich, the Dungaree, the Souge, and the last and poorest of all is the Stringy-bark settler. **1847** *Launceston Examiner* 12 May 301/4 The old prisoners they called 'corn stalks', the present were know [*sic*] as 'sougee bags'; every farmer knew the difference between a good striped Dundee corn sack and a sougee bag, and there was just that difference in the comparison of the two classes of labour. **1862** G.T. LLOYD *Thirty-Three Yrs. Tas. & Vic.* 262 A host of ticket-of-leave men, who flourished under the significant cognomen of 'sugee settlers' .. were evidently guided by the doctrine, that a ticket-of-leave awarded the positive right of appropriating other men's goods and chattels. **1870** *Illustr. Sydney News* 11 May 395/1 That talented individual who was just leaving the dressing-room (a small space partitioned off with soo-gee bags). **1891** D. FERGUSON *Vicissitudes Bush Life* 48 You will let the traveller see, be he common swagger, or 'sujee swell', that you are glad to make him welcome. **1896** M. HORNSBY *Old Time Echoes Tas.* 27 It was well known that the bush hereabout contained no inhabitant, neither cockatoo, soogee-settler, sawyer, splitter, nor charcoal-burner. **1905** J. FURPHY *Rigby's Romance* (1946) 43 I'll jist wipe out these (adj.) soojee (cravens), an' make a great nation out o' you an' yer own piccaninnies. **1935** M. GILMORE *More Recollections* 67 The inexperienced .. unable to get a wheat-bag, would take a soojee-bag, and come home torn... The soojee was often all that could be had. Wheat and flour-bags cost money. **1942** *Bulletin* (Sydney) 11 Nov. 13/4 The man with the soogee swag and makeshift sandals was discoursing on hardship. **1951** *Ibid.* 10 Jan. 12/3 'All this talk about a plague o' fleas invadin' Noo South', remarked the man with the soogee swag, 'reminds me o' the dawg I useter own w'en I wus out on the Paroo.'

sook /sʊk/. [Transf. use of Br. dial. *suck* a 'duffer', stupid fellow: see OEDS *sb.*[1]]

1. A coward, a sissy.

[N.Z. **1933** N. SCANLAN *Tides of Youth* 155 He looked a big sookie and wouldn't say a word.] **1941** S.J. BAKER *Pop. Dict. Austral. Slang* 69 *Sook*, a coward, a timid person. **1950** 'B. JAMES' *Advancement Spencer Button* 9 If he nervously declares he can't fight, and shows that he doesn't want to fight, then he is a 'sook' or a 'sissy'. **1956** K. TENNANT *Honey Flow* 214 She doesn't want a man, she wants a little boy—somebody like Joe who needs mothering. That Joe—he's a big sook—always be the baby of the family. **1975** R.J. MERRITT *Cake Man* (1978) 36 (He goes to her and holds her gently... She sobs a little, but then forces a laugh and leaves him.) *Ruby*: Well! You'll think I'm a sook. **1977** R. MCKIE *Crushing* (1978) 131 He put the ring back on Emily's finger. 'I love good stones. I did a course in them once .. in Canada.' Terry threw sand at him. 'You're a sook... Except on a motor bike.' **1983** *Bulletin* (Sydney) 5 July 86/3 The girl applied a hefty hip .. and flattened him. Sprawled on the bitumen, he began to howl. 'Bloody sook!' said the girl, disgustedly.

2. A timid (race)horse.

1980 *Sydney Morning Herald* 2 Aug. 59/7 White, answering charges that Panamint is unsound, described the horse as a 'big sook'... Invariably when he is taken in and out of the box he is timid. **1983** *West Austral.* (Perth) 17 Dec. 184/2 He is a real sook unless there is another horse with him... If there is not another horse alongside him, he starts to weave and get a bit uptight. **1984** *Age* (Melbourne) 16 Apr. 28/1 According to Smith, the horse lost his confidence and became a dreadful 'sook'. **1986** *Ibid.* 3 July 30/3 The three-year-old is a 'big sook'. 'If anything went wrong in a race, he just used to turn it up.'

sooky /ˈsʊki/, *a.* [See prec.] Babyish; stupid.

1901 *Bulletin* (Sydney) 2 Nov. (Red Page), Big, sooky-looking fellow he was, with ears like little turn-over tarts. **1953** D. CUSACK *Southern Steel* 238 Get along with you: you're getting real sookey. **1985** *Austral. Short Stories* xii. 89 Rosa never failed her sums... Annie felt sick with fear. 'Sookie sook, I'm going to tell on you,' chanted Rosa.

sool /sul/, *v.* Formerly also **sowl.** [Transf. use of Br. dial. *sowl* (of a dog), to seize (a pig) by the ears: see OED *sowl, v.*^{3} 1 and OEDS *sool, v.*]

1. *trans.* Of a dog: to worry; freq. *transf.* to harass. Freq. as imperative.

1849 A. HARRIS *Emigrant Family* (1967) 135 'Hey! hey! sowl her, boys!' roared Morgan: and on went the whole pack, seizing the poor beast by the ears, nose, and even eyelids. **1889** MRS C. PRAED *Romance of Station* 53 S'ool him, Bleuey! **1896** K.L. PARKER *Austral. Legendary Tales* 90 She went quickly towards her camp, calling softly, 'Birree gougou', which meant 'Sool 'em, sool 'em', and was the signal for the dogs to come out. **1897** J.J. MURIF *From Ocean to Ocean* 173 On hearing sticks and things rattle among the spokes I used only to laugh, say 'Sool it, Diamond!' and let them fight the battle out. **1903** *Truth* (Sydney) 15 Nov. 1/6 Dave Wiley, the Newtown State School dominie, has been teaching his pupils to model from Nature. Sool him, ye gimlet brigaders. **1912** T.E. SPENCER *Bindawalla* 4 Sool 'em! Sool 'em! Home, Home! Fetch 'em Brusher. **1935** *Bulletin* (Sydney) 6 Feb. 21/2 The hawk .. is popularly known as the swamp hawk... A pair of these birds will sometimes 'sool' a hare. **1946** A. MARSHALL *Tell us about Turkey, Jo* 13 Urged the dog: 'Sool 'im, Bluey! Get hold of him!' **1974** *Austral. Folksongs* (Folk Lore Council Aust.) 95 With a hool-em-up and a sool-em-up and the fool-em-up decoys. The men who scalp the rabbiters, are the Sydney Market boys. **1981** K. GARVEY *Rhymes of Ratbag* 141 The ringers all are drunk and mad With savage dogs they sool yer.

2. *trans.* To urge or goad; to importune. Freq. with adv., esp. **on.**

1889 *Bulletin* (Sydney) 10 Aug. 8/1 He wakens with a shock, And 'sools' his dog around a score Of 'crawlers' from his flock. **1898** *Truth* (Sydney) 6 Nov. 5/6 'Sooled' on by a pack of psalm-singing nobodies. **1911** *Ibid.* 8 Oct. 1/4 Mahommedans in Calcutta are trying to 'sool' Great Britain on to Italy. **1922** *Ross's Monthly* Apr. 8/1 The English capitalists raised the cry of 'self-government and free rights for all citizens' when they sooled on the British workers against the Boer farmers. **1936** *Publicist* (Sydney) iii. 3/2 Women instinctively sool on the soldiery as soon as a war begins. **1944** 'S. CAMPION' *Pommy Cow* 256 'You're always tryin' to put thoughts into me head an' sool me into thinkin' this or that.' 'Anyone can sool *you* without much trying.' **1959** D. NILAND *Gold in Streets* 155 Who sooled that priest on to me? **1971** K. WILLEY *Boss Drover* 11 Each time she broke away I would sool her into the mob again. **1981** P. BARTON *Bastards I have Known* 45 The cooking teacher, sooled on by a half a dozen or so by-now-tearful girls, took to me with a large wooden spoon. **1985** *Sun-Herald* (Sydney) 28 July 19/2 He had sooled their pet doberman on to her, saying 'Kill, Blitzen, kill'.

Hence **sooling** *ppl. a.*, insistently importunate; also with **on.**

1916 *Truth* (Sydney) 29 Oct. 4/7 God help Australia if

it had to depend for soldiers on the shrieking, sooling, 'race suicide' shemales of snobbish suburbia. **1936** N. LINDSAY *Saturdee* (ed. 2) 249 When willing hands thrust him again to action, he hung back, and Ponkey employed the sooling-on tactics without effect. **1944** 'S. CAMPION' *Pommy Cow* 135 'What about you? You came too.' 'Only because you bungfoodled me into it, you soolin' sod.'

3. *intr.* To run; to travel.

1945 M. RAYMOND *Smiley* 77 The man pulled two half-crowns and handed them to the boy. 'There y' are. Now sool.' Smiley sooled off at top speed. **1947** —— *Smiley gets Gun* 55 Smiley turned and bolted, followed by a wail of disappointment. He ran blindly but instinctively for home, not daring to look behind in case Granny was chasing him down the road. He had never sooled so fast in his life. **1951** J. DEVANNY *Travels N. Qld.* 137 He 'sools' along quietly for a time, as though he does not mean business.

sooler /'sulə/. One who exerts pressure upon another, esp. one who supported the campaign to introduce conscription during the war of 1914–18. Also **sooler-on.**

1916 *Truth* (Sydney) 6 Aug. 6/3 Never before was there so much delight among the sweaters, extortioners, forestallers, 'soolers', sycophants, proxy 'patriots', and bawlers for blood as there is now at the return of 'Billee'. **1916** *Ibid.* 29 Oct. 4/7 The shemale soolers have been very busy of late trying to round up the women voters into the Conscription corral. **1919** *Worker* (Brisbane) 9 Oct. 16/2 Why, almost every parson became a 'sooler-on' of men to kill and be killed. **1934** *Manifesto* (Austral. Labor Party Qld.) 13/2 Now let us consider the attitude of Lang in regard to the Premiers' Plan, which he endorsed and adopted, but upon which his claquers and soolers contend that he broke with the Labor Party. **1936** *Publicist* (Sydney) i. 6/1 The great urgers and soolers-on of the soldiery in that war were the women. **1941** *Listening Post* (Perth) Sept. 19 When that objective was attained he showed he was no 'sooler' by enlisting again himself. **1963** X. HERBERT *Disturbing Element* 141 She had been sending white feathers round to what she now called Slackers ever since Phil's enlistment. She had become what her former comrades of the I.W.W. called a Sooler. **1983** G.G. ROPER *Labor's Titan* 37 The Barrier Empire Loyalists, or 'soolers-on', as George Dale called them, were not slow to attack these 'traitors to King and Country'.

sooner. [See quot. 1945.] An idler, a shirker; applied as a term of abuse to an unco-operative person, or obstructive object, etc. Also *attrib.* as **sooner dog.**

1892 K. LENTZNER *Dict. Slang-Eng. Aust.* 117 *Sooner*, a weak idler, a lazy good-for-nothing. **1919** E. DYSON *Hello, Soldier* 31 He slugged a tubby Hun, Then choked a Fritzie with his dukes, 'n' pinched the sooner's gun! **1929** *Bulletin* (Sydney) 20 Mar. 55/4 The dirty sooners—they've done me down! They made up their minds to beat me for that timber from the start. **1936** F. CLUNE *Roaming round Darling* 270 Tongue-tied Joe, a sooner-dog, a Scotch dog, a dog of all nations, a hungry goat. **1944** *Dit* (Melbourne) Sept. 4 The dirty sooners. **1945** S.J. BAKER *Austral. Lang.* 73 Outback slang terms for dogs include: *sooner* (i.e. one that would sooner rest than work), etc. **1948** V. PALMER *Golconda* 159 'The dirty sooners!' he burst out. 'They don't know a man when they find one, those heads down south.' **1969** P. ADAM SMITH *Folklore Austral. Railwaymen* 117 This was an old sooner of an engine. She'd had it.

sooty, *a.* Used as a distinguishing epithet in the names of birds: **sooty owl,** either of two brownish-grey owls of the genus *Tyto, T. tenebricosa* of s.e Aust. and montane New Guinea, and *T. multipunctata* of the Atherton region, n.e. Qld; **oystercatcher,** the sooty-black bird *Haematopus fuliginosus* of rocky coasts around Aust. incl. Tas.

1848 J. GOULD *Birds of Aust.* I. Pl. 30, *Strix tenebricosus* .. **Sooty Owl.** **1909** *Emu* VIII. 276 We flushed several Sooty Owls (*Strix tenebricosa*). **1943** C. BARRETT *Austral. Animal Bk.* 215 The sooty owl .. is even more rare [than the masked owl], and lives chiefly in dense brushes. **1968** D. FLEAY *Nightwatchmen* 135 Time and again the weird whistle of the Sooty Owl plus the high-pitched chattering that goes with conversation and courting were broadcast. **1984** M. BLAKERS et al. *Atlas Austral. Birds* 312 The Sooty Owl lives in New Guinea and in Australia. **1845** J. GOULD *Birds of Aust.* (1848) VI. Pl. 8, *Haemotopus fuliginosus* .. **Sooty Oyster-catcher.** **1888** *Centennial Mag.* (Sydney) 14 On the shore, the beautiful little hooded dotterel, and the sooty and pied oyster-catcher. **1945** C. BARRETT *Austral. Bird Life* 100 The sooty oyster-catcher .. occurs only in Australia, Tasmania, and New Zealand, and favours rocky shores. **1955** V. SERVENTY *Aust.'s Great Barrier Reef* 56 Two larger waders may also attract attention. Both have scarlet beaks and legs. One has an all black plumage, while the other is black and white. Commonly known as Redbills, the correct names are Pied Oystercatcher and Sooty Oystercatcher. As yet, I have still to see either catching oysters. **1968** R. HILL *Bush Quest* 39 A solitary sooty oyster-catcher sulked out at the end of the spit, with his back turned on the other birds. **1985** *Age* (Melbourne) 13 Sept. 6/3 The sea birds are always fascinating .. sooty oystercatchers, dainty hooded dotterels and crested terns.

sorcerer. KORADJI.

1843 W. PRIDDEN *Aust.* 141 A profound respect, almost amounting to veneration, is paid in many districts of Australia to shining stones or pieces of crystal, which they call '*Teyl*'. These are carried in the girdles of men, especially of the sorcerers or *corad-jes*. **1847** G.F. ANGAS *Savage Life & Scenes* 86 The sick are .. entrusted to the care of sorcerers, or 'wise-men'. **1856** J. BONWICK *W. Buckley* 55 The sorcerers of the land of Toolcoon .. set the bush on fire. **1865** G.S. LANG *Aborigines of Aust.* 8 The second class is that of the sorcerers or medicine men. **1878** R.B. SMYTH *Aborigines of Vic.* I. 261 The *Kuldukke*, men-priests, sorcerers, or doctors—are impostors, and rob the poor natives of their food, in order that they may live in idleness. **1908** G.W. RUSDEN *Hist. of Aust.* 99 In Western Australia the sorcerer (or boyla) watched the fumes arising .. and was deemed capable of seeing .. the way in which the aroused evil spirit would wing its flight. **1928** B. SPENCER *Wanderings in Wild Aust.* 247 The power to perform magic .. is possessed by only a few members of the tribe, who are commonly spoken of by white men as sorcerers, wizards or medicine men. **1947** D. BATES *Passing of Aborigines* (ed. 2) 235 This disease shamed them and no native sorcerer could cure them. **1961** J.W. BLEAKLEY *Aborigines of Aust.* 61 The sorcerers, known as Kadaitcha, seem to work as though members of a secret society. **1985** I. WHITE et al. *Fighters & Singers* 137 Travelling alone I was liable to attack by a sorcerer who had reputedly been seen... I was supposed to know about the dangers of sorcery.

sore, *a.* In the phr. **done** (or **dressed**) **up like a sore finger** (or **toe**), dressed with unusual care; overdressed.

1918 *7th Field Artillery Brigade Yandoo* Jan. 92 Hullo Digger, you're done up like a sore finger—where to? **1939** K. TENNANT *Foveaux* 430 You ought to a seen us in the ole days when we 'ad a procession every year—done up like a sore toe with banners and floats. **1945** M. TRIST *Now that we're Laughing* 125 Done up like a sore toe, she was, too. Looks real nice dressed, does Joycie. **1958** H.D. WILLIAMSON *Sunlit Plain* 10 Get an eyeful of him! Done up like a sore toe. **1963** H. PORTER *Watcher on Cast-Iron Balcony* 81 Dressed up like a sore toe, but hasn't had a bath for weeks. **1962** P. WHITE *Four Plays* (1974) 168 I'm gunna get out of this suit. Dressed up like a sore finger.

sort. [Used elsewhere but recorded earliest in Aust.] A female; esp. one who is young and attractive; a girl-friend.

1933 F. CLUNE *Try Anything Once* 93 Lend me a suit of civvies. I've got to meet a great little sort, and her father has a dead nark on soldiers. **1940** P. KERRY *Cobbers A.I.F.* 14 Then the sorts chiacked 'im loudly, called 'im 'Tarzan uv the Apes', An' they got so darned excited that they nearly burst their tapes. **1957** J.M. HOSKING *Aust. first & Last* 133, I did not wear a uniform and parade about with 'sorts'. The only bit of fun I had was in the foreign ports. Aussie sheilas did not want me, though I had lots of money. **1959** D. HEWETT *Bobbin Up* 157 You shoulda seen the performance when the last Yank ship went out. All the little sorts climbin' on the fence and weepin' buckets. **1965** *Kings Cross Whisper* (Sydney) May 7/5 Laughter inside, half a doz. under the wing, a fair looking sort beside you and the door opens. **1971** *Ibid.* xcviii. 12/1 Well, there's no reason Susie Gibbs should be Sportsgirl of the Week except she's such a good looking sort. **1977** C. KLEIN *Pomegranate Tree* 55 We'd grab the good looking sorts. **1985** N. MEDCALF *Rifleman* 172 This sheila .. is a drack sort.

sosh. *Hist.* Shortened form of 'socialism'; usu. as ANTI-SOSH.

1912 *Bulletin* (Sydney) 22 Feb. 43/1 The Unionist tiger, full brother to 'Sosh'!

souge, sougee, varr. SOOGEE.

soul-case. [Orig. U.S.: see OEDS *soul, sb.* 25.] In the phr. **to worry (belt, sweat) the soul-case out (of),** to vex, to drive, to punish. Also **to work the soul-case off.**

1901 F.J. GILLEN *Diary* 15 Apr. (1968) 34 Flies were celebrating some festival all night and worried the very soul cases out of us. **1937** K.S. PRICHARD *Intimate Strangers* 288 Eviction was what I got after clearing two thousand acres of virgin land: sweating my soul case out to grow wheat. **1943** *Coast to Coast 1942* 61 Where the 'ell you been? I been worryin' me soulcase out. **1945** G. CASEY *Downhill is Easier* 146 He used t' belt the soulcase out o' her till I come along. **1951** CUSACK & JAMES *Come in Spinner* 152 If you've been going in for any of them beach girl competitions, Peggy my girl, I'll belt the soul case out of you. **1962** R. TULLIPAN *March into Morning* 13 Then he got this bright idea of bringin' in orphan kids and working the soulcase off them until they turn eighteen and have to be paid more money.

sounding stick. *Obs.* See quot. 1856.

1856 *Jrnl. Australasia* I. 21 In this locality, too, there is plenty of a light, white wood .. also called 'sounding stick', because a solid, ringing sound can be produced by two round billets being beaten together. **1863** J. BONWICK *Wild White Man* 36 The aborigine procured fire from friction of two pieces of wood, called by some 'Thaal Kalk', or sounding sticks.

sour, *a.* Used as a distinguishing epithet in the names of plants: **sour apple** *obs.*, *emu apple* (a), see EMU *n.*[1] 3; **plum,** any of several plants, esp. *emu apple* (a) and *Owenia venosa* of Qld.

1888 L. BAYER *Muutchaka* 1 To black peller say: get away you kunk Go and die under **sour apple** tree. **1874** LINDLEY & MOORE *Treasury of Bot.* (rev. ed.) 1324 *Owenia venosa* is known by the name of the **Sour Plum** among the colonists. **1888** *Proc. Linnean Soc. N.S.W.* III. 534 *Owenia acidula* .. 'Sour plum'. *Ibid.* 535 *Owenia venosa* .. 'Sour Plum'... A beverage is produced by boiling the fruit, which .. is denominated wine, and forms an agreeable beverage. **1903** *Austral. Handbk.* 279 Other orders .. furnish .. large-sized timber, particularly the following: 'Sour Plum' (*Owenia venosa*) [etc.]. **1926** *Qld. Agric. Jrnl.* XXV. 440 *Pleigynium Solandri* .. Sour Plum. **1965** *Austral. Encycl.* VI. 227 *Owenia acidula* .. sour plum .. the red drupes, about 1 inch in diameter, are sub-acidic and are reputed to relieve thirst. **1983** LASSAK & MCCARTHY *Austral. Med. Plants* 66 *Owenia acidula* .. 'Emu apple' .. less commonly 'sour plum'... The red and hard flesh surrounding the stone is intensely sour.

soursob. Also **soursobs, sowsops.** [Transf. use of Br. dial. *soursops, Rumex acetosa*: see EDD *sour* 2.] Any of several perennial herbs of the genus *Oxalis* (fam. Oxalidaceae), esp. the S. African *O. pes-caprae*, naturalized in all States, a proclaimed noxious weed in Qld., Vic., Tas., and parts of S.A.

1885 *Garden & Field* Sept. 41 Now there's a fellow who wants £500 to tell farmers how to kill the Soursops or oxalis. **1909** J.M. BLACK *Naturalised Flora S.A.* 41 *Oxalis cernua* .. Soursob .. introduced as an ornamental plant in early colonial days, and now very common. **1936** *Bulletin* (Sydney) 15 Apr. 21/4 The Adelaide weed known locally as the soursop is *Oxalis acetosella*, the English wood sorrel, introduced as a pot-plant and gone wild... The soursop of Queensland, on the other hand, is a fruit tree, *Anona muricata*, native of the West Indies. **1949** *S.A. Dept. Agric. Bull.* no. 406 18 As regards *O. cernua*, the names most commonly applied to the plant are 'Soursob', Soursobs', or 'Soursops', in this country, and 'Bermuda Buttercups' in America. **1957** *Bulletin* (Sydney) 16 Oct. 18/2 The oxalis .. soursob in its South Australian habitat is known in Victoria as soursops. **1981** G.M. CUNNINGHAM et al. *Plants Western N.S.W.* 436 Soursob has a high oxalic acid content—the cause of the sour taste—and is not usually eaten by stock. **1984** *Bulletin* (Sydney) 17 July 36/1 Green grass speckled with the gold of the soursops that add color to winter on the Adelaide plain.

Soustralian. *Obs.* Alteration of 'South Australian'. Also as *adj.* Similarly **Soustralia.**

1900 *Truth* (Sydney) 28 Jan. 1/4 Patriotic Soustralians who sent away a cargo of flour to Kruger and Co. **1908** *Bulletin* (Sydney) 27 Feb. 14/3 A youngster on the Soustralian side .. was caught in a barbed-wire fence. **1916** *Truth* (Sydney) 22 Oct. 1/6 Mr Crawford Vaughan, Soustralian Premier .. is endeavouring to kid Sydneysiders to vote as he believes the Croweaters will. *Ibid.* 10 Dec. 6/6 *(heading)* A spookist from Soustralia.

south. Freq. with **the.** The southern parts of Australia: cf. NORTH 1.

[**1897** A.F. CALVERT *My Fourth Tour W.A.* 148 There is no doubt that a great many miners have 'gone South'—as leaving the West is called—after giving the Northern and Eastern goldfields a trial.] **1905** *Bulletin* (Sydney) 13 July 18/3 Some sugar-growers and their barrackers are telling the South that, if they can't have Kanaka, they will have Chow. **1920** J.N. MACINTYRE *White Aust.* 38 The ignoramuses of the South advocate the remedy of the empty North to be black labour. **1965** *N. Austral. Monthly* Jan. 21 It must seem stupid to you folks in the South to think of boys and men up here playing football when the thermometer stands at ninety-odd. **1980** *Sunday Mail* (Brisbane) 28 Sept. 2/5 People are coming up from the south in droves to settle here. Not for the beauty of the City of Brisbane, but for the superbness of the quality of life that surrounds it.

southerly. SOUTHERLY BUSTER.

[**1843** *Sydney Morning Herald* 27 Nov. 2/5 The late heat has not been attended by hot winds, nor has it been followed by any violent southerly squalls.] **1896** *Bulletin* (Sydney) 4 July 28/1 Let her rip till a 'southerly' comes and rocks her out. **1905** *Ibid.* 3 Aug. 36/2 There was a spike in the southerly; it cut one's knees and turned the feet to ice. **1909** *Call* (Sydney) Feb. 22 The bathroom door slamming in the southerly. **1927** A. WRIGHT *Squatter's Secret* 12, I wouldn't mind betting you'll run into a southerly by the time you set out. **1960** S. WOODFIELD *A for Artemis* 51, I wouldn't be surprised if she whipped round into a southerly later. **1964** *Surfabout* (Sydney) I. vi. 39 When the surf has had it, there is no better way to spend the time than freeboarding. When the surf is blown out with the southerly, Rose Bay is ideal. **1965** G. MCINNES *Road to Gundagai* 63 On the heels of the Southerly came driving sheets of rain. **1984** *Overlander* June 52 Governments .. are so bloody jellygutted they'd be hard pressed to stand up to a southerly.

southerly burster. *Obs.* [f. *southerly, a.* + *burster* that which bursts.] SOUTHERLY BUSTER. See also BURSTER *n.*[2]

1850 *Bell's Life in Sydney* 5 Oct. 2/2 The whistlings of old Eolus in the shape of a southerly burster. **1851** *Empire* (Sydney) 8 Feb. 6/4 Row against a strong southerly 'burster' which unluckily sprang up. **1857** J. ASKEW *Voyage Aust. & N.Z.* 234 During summer, the southerly wind, or Brickfielder, as the Sydney people used to term it, is .. most annoying. It is now commonly styled the Southerly Burster. **1867** J.R. HOULDING *Austral. Capers* 137 As much discomposed as an over-dressed dandy who had just slipped down in a muddy roadway, or a fashionable belle who had lost her bonnet in a 'southerly burster'. **1871** *Austral. Town & Country Jrnl.* (Sydney) 4 Feb. 134/2 On the Anniversary Day last year, about 2 o'clock in the evening, a southerly burster and rain set in. **1881** J.F.V. FITZGERALD *Aust.* 28 'Hot winds' .. are almost always terminated by a 'southerly burster', which brings a rapid and severe change of temperature, usually accompanied by a storm of rain. **1888** *Sydney Morning Herald* 24 Jan. 2/3 'Southerly bursters' and thunderstorms are of frequent occurrence in the summer, and are not unwelcome as they help to clear the atmosphere. *c* **1906** L. BECKE *Settlers Karossa Creek* 39 There was every indication that within a few hours one of those short, but violent, storms known as 'southerly bursters' would sweep along the coast.

southerly buster. [f. *southerly, a.* + *buster*, prob. Br. dial. form of *burster*: see SOUTHERLY BURSTER.]

1. A sudden, strong, cool wind from the south, affecting the south-eastern coast: see esp. quot. 1852.

1850 B.C. PECK *Recoll. Sydney* 132 The evening of a hot-wind day brings up a 'southerly buster', as we have heard the vulgar call it, very chill indeed, not only by contrast, but in reality, as this wind comes from the southerly region of the Australian Alps, which always have snow on them. **1852** W. HUGHES *Austral. Colonies* 63 The wind by which the hot blast of the interior is followed is popularly known at Sydney as a 'brickfielder', or *'southerly buster'*—(the good people of the colonies are not remarkable for the refinement of their vernacular phraseology). **1862** C. ASPINALL *Three Yrs. Melbourne* 96 The hot winds .. are always succeeded by one from the opposite direction—colonially called 'a *southerly buster'*—and the air then becomes filled with dense clouds of dust. **1869** 'E. HOWE' *Boy in Bush* 80 When the 'southerly buster' comes after the hot wind, rushing with the chill still on from the South Pole, I have seen people ripping open their shirts to let the cold breeze blow right round them. **1882** J. SCHLEMAN *Life in Melbourne* 83 In the month of January I experienced in Melbourne a 'southerly buster', which increased to a perfect hurricane. **1886** D.M. GANE *N.S.W. & Vic.* 194 The southerly buster, the wind which sweeps over the shore towns, and invigorates those worn out by the heat of the day, does not reach Dubbo. **1899** *Truth* (Sydney) 19 Mar. 4/5 The new century dawned and titles were scattered like the dust on Brickfield Hill in a southerly buster. **1911** A. MARSHALL *Sunny Aust.* 18 Our expedition was of the nature of a paper-chase, and a violent 'southerly-buster' coming up while it was in progress and blowing down trees here and there across the track added to its excitement. **1917** *Truth* (Sydney) 30 Sept. 1/7 The southerly buster last week lifted the roof of a Marrickville washhouse. **1931** LAWSON & BRERETON *H. Lawson* 152 As refreshing to us as a southerly buster. **1949** R. PARK *Poor Man's Orange* 146 The southerly buster, the genie of Sydney, flapped its coarse blusterous wing over the city, a hearty male wind with a cool and spirited breath. **1965** G. MCINNES *Road to Gundagai* 63 The Southerly Buster had blown into town, whooshing up from the high latitudes near Antarctica and covering the suffocating city with a blanket of blessed cool. **1982** P. RADLEY *My Blue-Checker Corker* 90 Granfarver Jones once saw a Southerly Buster turn a chook inside out. **1986** *Nat. Times* (Sydney) 10 Jan. 10/3 Regular southerly busters sent us scattering to cling on to a pole while the tent billowed ominously.

2. *fig.*

1874 C. DE BOOS *Congewoi Correspondence* 19 If it hadn't been for Jack Robertson getting up the southerly buster as he did, and blowing the dust of Free Selection into their eyes.

Southerly doctor: see DOCTOR *n.*[3]

southern, *a.* Used as a distinguishing epithet in the names of flora and fauna: **southern bluefin (tuna),** the large marine fish *Thunnus maccoyii*, bluish above and silvery below; **blue gum,** any of several trees of the genus *Eucalyptus* (fam. Myrtaceae), esp. *E. globulus* ssp. *bicostata* of N.S.W. and Vic.; **stone plover** (or **curlew**), the bird *Burhinus grallarius* (see CURLEW).

1951 T.C. ROUGHLEY *Fish & Fisheries Aust.* 115 There has long been speculation whether the Australian **southern bluefin** tuna is identical with the tunny of Europe and the bluefin tuna *(Thunnus thynnus)* of the Pacific and Atlantic coasts of America. . . However .. the Australian species is entirely distinct. **1969** C. THIELE *Blue Fin* 2 They were southern blue-fins, the most perfectly shaped fish in the sea. . . They were thirty pounders, small as far as tuna went. **1980** *Ecos* xxiv. 24/2 *(caption)* Poling for southern bluefin tuna off Australia. **1984** *Austral. Mag.* (Sydney) 23 Oct. 64/3 The beleaguered southern bluefin is hunted for most of its migratory life. Spawning north-west of Australia in the Java Sea, the tuna swim south along the West Australian coastline and then follow the coast across the Bight, go around the bottom of Tasmania and up the N.S.W. coast. **1919** R.T. BAKER *Hardwoods of Aust.* 8 *E[ucalyptus] Maideni* .. **Southern Blue Gum,** A Spotted Gum. **1948** P.J. HURLEY *Red Cedar* 21 Seeds of Southern Bluegums (*E. bicostata*) were sent to Italy to soak up surplus water in the malaria-infested Pontine. **1977** *Ecos* xiv. 29/1 Plantations of southern blue gum (*Eucalyptus globulus*) .. yielded 4 tonnes of dry stemwood per hectare each year. **1845** J. GOULD *Birds of Aust.* (1848) VI. Pl. 5, *Oedicnemus grallarius.* **Southern Stone Plover.** **1896** B. SPENCER *Rep. Horn Sci. Exped. Central Aust.* II. 109 Southern Stone-Plover .. could not be found, although their tracks were frequently seen in sandhills. **1901** *Emu* 138 Southern Stone Plover (*Burhinus grallarius*)—These were occasionally seen. **1945** C. BARRETT *Austral. Bird Life* 108 The beach stone-curlew .. and the southern form (*Burhinus magnirostris*), which ranges throughout the island-continent, occasionally visiting Tasmania.

Southern Cross.

1. The constellation of *Crux Australis*, four stars of which form a cross.

1842 H. PARKES *Stolen Moments* 98 I've wandered where the Southern Cross Glows o'er th' Antipodes. **1857** J. ASKEW *Voyage Aust. & N.Z.* 51 The Southern cross and the Magellan clouds, were far up in the heavens. **1872** MRS E. MILLETT *Austral. Parsonage* 173 Most persons on first seeing the Southern Cross feel a degree of disappointment, arising probably from the name having led them to expect to see a constellation completely cruciform. **1897** Z.W. PEASE *Catalpa Exped.* 164 O'er our pathway, in the sunshine, flies the wide-winged albatross, O'er our topmast, in the moonlight, hangs the starry Southern Cross. **1914** H.M. VAUGHAN *Australasian Wander-Yr.* 246 You have in the southern horizon that splendid constellation of the Southern Cross, which is the glory of the austral hemisphere. **1927** T.S. GROSER *Lure of Golden West* 145 The stars—perhaps the 'Southern Cross' would be his guide. **1965** G. MCINNES *Road to Gundagai* 32 During the nights that followed he showed us .. the Southern Cross, always a puzzle to us with its fifth star, and the Pointers that led to the faint south polar star. **1975** C. MATTINGLEY *Great Ballagundi Damper Bake* 42 The moon had risen and set. The Southern Cross had paled. **1986** *Canberra Times* 16 Mar. 2/8 The proposed flag, representing the Southern Cross in a velvet night sky over a red desert is pure poetry.

2. a. *Eureka flag*, see EUREKA 2.

1855 R. CARBONI *Eureka Stockade* 50 There is no flag in old Europe half so beautiful as the 'Southern Cross' of the Ballaarat miners, first hoisted on the old spot, Bakery Hill. The flag is silk, blue ground, with a large silver cross, similar to the one in our southern firmament; no device or arms, but all exceedingly chaste and natural. **1917** 'H.H. RICHARDSON' *Fortunes Richard Mahony* 96 The 'Southern Cross' hoisted—a blue bunting that bore the silver stars of the constellation after which it was named. **1984** G. BLAINEY *Our Side of Country* 134 Even the miners at Eureka .. were negative nationalists. . . They hoisted a republican flag, the Southern Cross, but they were not yet Victorians or Australians in their loyalties and affections. **1984** S. MACINTYRE *Militant* 179 On one occasion when the union was under attack it was in keeping that Paddy should repeat the Eureka oath: 'We swear by the Southern Cross to stand by each other and fight to defend our rights and liberties.'

b. The Australian flag.

1965 G. MCINNES *Road to Gundagai* 169 The Southern Cross, neatly balled, sailed up the halyard of the newly erected post, and .. broke out and flew bravely over the new campsite of the First Toorak Troop: five stars and the great seven pointed star in the fly, and in one corner the small Union Jack with: 'The broad white diagonal stripe Nearest the pole at the top.'

3. Used allusively, esp. in the phr. **land of the Southern Cross,** to designate Australia.

1873 J. BONWICK *Tasmanian Lily* 86 However common the plague of drink may be in Australia and Tasmania, the infirmity is witnessed in those trained amidst the supposed superior moral and intellectual advantages of Great Britain and Ireland, and not with those born under the Southern Cross. **1898** H. MATTHEWS *Chat about Aust.* 2 The young man .. will find in this little book facts for information and guidance, in regard to the land of the Southern Cross, most useful and helpful. **1902** *Sporting News* (Launceston) 1 Nov. 2/2 In the land of the Southern Cross. **1903** *Westminster Gaz.* (London) 28 Jan. 9/2 The world could show no finer body of working men than those who lived under the Southern Cross. **1910** *Huon Times* (Franklin) 17 Aug. 4/6 This [*sc.* Hobart's harbour] is the only place .. under the Southern Cross where they can be accommodated with facility and absolute safety. **1919** W.J. DENNY *Diggers* 147 The Hun was soon to learn, in many great and violent struggles, that the sons of the Southern Cross were their most difficult and skilful adversaries. **1943** M. LAMB *Red glows Dawn* 36 Until

Darwin was bombed .. no hostile, warring shot had ever reverberated through the land of the Southern Cross.

southerner. Used, esp. by residents of Queensland and the Northern Territory, to designate one normally resident in a southern State.

1878 *Queenslander* (Brisbane) 15 June 332/4 If the freshness of these men's complexions had not pointed them out to me as Southerners, their black hats and extra heavy swags would most assuredly have done so. **1903** *Bulletin* (Sydney) 17 Sept. 35/1 The Southerner mentally associates Bananaland mainly with heat. **1911** E.J. BRADY *King's Caravan* 215 A Southerner told me that he had been living for two years in Brisbane. **1964** *N. Austral. Monthly* Sept. 7 Self-satisfied Southerners who sit back complaining of our 'backwardness' while enjoying all the comforts and pleasures of city life themselves. **1967** *Kings Cross Whisper* (Sydney) xli. 6/2 'Southerners', as Queenslanders quaintly call everybody else, are particularly attracted to Surfers. **1975** X. HERBERT *Poor Fellow my Country* 1012 They were all big fellows, Southerners by the conventional dress of black pants, striped shirts, black patent-leather shoes.

southern lights. [Also used elsewhere.] AURORA AUSTRALIS.

1775 *Philos. Trans. R. Soc. London* LXVIII. 409 Some Southern lights, very rare and motionless. **1870** *Age* (Melbourne) 7 Apr. 2/8 The Southern lights .. were visible all over the colonies. **1920** *Huon Times* (Franklin) 26 Mar. 2/5 The last couple of nights have witnessed very fine displays of the 'Southern Lights', the sky being illuminated with various coloured lights. **1971** G. WISEWOULD *Outpost* 154 On occasions during summer one sees the 'southern lights', long after sunset, gleaming pale on the horizon, sometimes green—sometimes green and gold.

South Land. Australia, esp. in the collocation **Great South Land.**

1671 J. OGILBY *America* 654 On the eighth of *Octob.* Tasman stood over to the *South-Land*, near which he was surpris'd by a violent Storm. **1813** J. BURNEY *Chron. Hist. Voyages* III. 181 Throughout the Instructions to Tasman for his second voyage, the *Terra Australis* is called the *Groote Zuid-land*, or *On-bekende Zuid-land*. i.e. The *Great* or the *Unknown South Land*. **1839** *S. Austral. Rev.* 13 'The Great South Land', as the island-continent was named by the early navigators. **1852** F. LANCELOTT *Aust. as it Is* I. 2 A century ago the mere coast line of this 'Great South Land' was an unsolved geographical problem. **1935** B.E. PHELPS *Austral. tells England* 18 On Captain Phillip's return to England he spoke in very definite terms of the golden prospects and splendid opportunities of the growing colony in the Great South Land. **1936** C.P. CONIGRAVE *N. Aust.* 14 The Dutch East India Company . . attempted to find out the truth about the South Land. **1957** F. CLUNE *Fortune Hunters* 138 A new deal for the Australian blacks is coming up fast, and the visit of Albert Namatjira to Sydney proved that public conscience is at last awake to our responsibilities to these ancestral folk of the Great South Land. **1976** K. CLIFT *Soldier who never grew Up* 30 Yes, we'll miss you native Southland the eucalypt, the wattle.

souvenir, *v.* [Used elsewhere but recorded earliest in Aust.: see OEDS *v.* 3.] *trans.* To appropriate; to steal; to take as a 'souvenir'. Also *absol.* and as *ppl. a.*

1918 C. GARSTIN *Mud Larks* 18 My batman tro. ..e underfoot at seven next morning. 'Goin' to be blinkin' murder done in this camp presently, Sir,' he announced cheerfully. 'Three officers went to sleep in bivvies larst night, but somebody's souvenired 'em since, an' they're all lyin' hout in the hopen now, Sir.' **1919** *Aussie: Austral. Soldiers' Mag.* Mar. 1/1 I'm just waiting for this photo bloke to get knocked. I want to souvenir his camera! **1926** *Bulletin* (Sydney) 27 May 22/2, I don't think 'Wang' need worry about the effect of war-souvenired cartridges dumped into municipal incinerators. **1932** J.J. HARDIE *Cattle Camp* (1944) 280 Ummm!—'Spose you souvenired it off one of your Fritz prisoners. **1935** J.P. MCKINNEY *Crucible* 150 The builders of it had started out very ambitiously with material evidently 'souvenired' from R.E. dumps, salvage-heaps and local barns. **1956** S. HOPE *Diggers' Paradise* 83 Early, too, numbers of youngsters show that tendency to 'souvenir' which is the euphonious term for pilfering. **1963** *Bulletin* (Sydney) 26 Jan. 3/2 Kelly's bones were souvenired as late as 1937. **1976** K. AMOS *New Guard Movt.* 72 Lady Game wrote to her mother that her son Bill had wanted to souvenir the petition to hang it in St. Paul's College. **1980** F. MOORHOUSE *Days of Wine & Rage* 134 The pubs around the Rocks ran out of glasses during the crawl because people either souvenired them or left them in the streets along the way.

Hence **souvenirer** *n.*

1918 *Aussie: Austral. Soldiers' Mag.* Sept. 3/2 When the recent stunt had passed along over the broken remains of murdered villages, my crowd, the Pioneers (better recognised by the unofficial monicker, 'the Souvenirers'), proceeded to make possies for themself among the jumble.

sowl, var. SOOL.

sowsops, var. SOURSOB.

S.P., *attrib.* and *n. Racing.* [f. the initials of *starting price* the final odds on a horse or greyhound at the time of starting.]

A. Used *attrib.* in Special Comb. **S.P. betting** *vbl. n.*, the placing of a bet at starting price; also *attrib.*; **book,** a ledger in which such bets are recorded; **bookie, bookmaker,** one who as a business accepts bets off the race-course, at starting price; so **bookmaking** *vbl. n.*; **job,** such a bet; **joint,** an establishment at which *S.P. betting* takes place; **man,** *S.P. bookmaker.*

1936 *Publicist* (Sydney) ii. 3/1 His song was unheeded by a crowd of whitefellows, who were congregated at that place for the purpose of engaging in **S.P.** illicit **betting**. **1941** *Bulletin* (Sydney) 26 Mar. 17/3 Bung had been cleaned up for s.p. betting, and in order to allay suspicion he'd removed the wireless from the bar. **1948** G. MEREDITH *Lawsons* 86 What do you want to know about S.P. betting for? The boss'll have plenty to say if he hears you've been havin' a few bob on. **1962** J.T. LANG *Great Bust* 335 They said we would ruin racing. That we would only drive people away from the courses and promote S.P. betting. **1972** *Bulletin* (Sydney) 13 May 13/1 Police difficulties in closing down SP betting shops on the NSW south coast recall the Chester Hill Fortress nonsense of 1968. **1948** G. MEREDITH *Lawsons* 86 What about racing? Maybe Foley is running an **S.P. book** or something, and Chris won it from him. **1962** J.T. LANG *Great Bust* 335 The war between the law and the **S.P. bookies** was unending. **1965** I. HAMILTON *Persecutor* 47 Although s.p. bookies are illegal the biggest of them get well known and by some triumphant miracle of the law they get away with it, though life is hotter for them now the legal betting shops are in action. **1965** *Coast to Coast 1963–64* 30 Business—of the S.P. bookmaking kind. **1979** B. DELANEY *Narc* 11 Why, to this day, do S.P. bookies openly take bets in the public bars in Sydney hotels? **1956** V. COURTNEY *All I may Tell* 165 Another said that he knew I was in the pay of the **S.P. bookmakers** because our paper had favoured the licensing of betting. **1978** WARD & SMITH *Vanishing Village* 95 Then we're responsible for what we call the licensing work, the S.P. bookmakers and the hotels—making sure they abide by the law. **1982** *Bulletin* (Sydney) 24 Aug. 41/1 SP bookmaking is still a multi-million dollar business, according to investigators, even though the TAB was set up in Victoria in 1961 to stamp out the then $324 million a year illegal turnover. **1984** *Canberra Times* 10 Nov. 1/1 Only a concerted national approach could beat the SP bookmakers. **1958** F. HARDY *Four-Legged Lottery* 175 An **SP job** (a horse backed away from the course); or a horse from a non-betting stable that drifts in the market because of pressure of money for other horses. **1965** —— *Yarns of Billy Borker* 107 'It's an SP job', I tells him, 'they'll back it off the course.' **1954** H.G. LAMOND *Manx Star* 107 I'll turn over a new leaf: there's good money to be made running a sly-grog shop or a **S.P. joint**. **1964** K. TENNANT *Summer's Tales* 22 You might want to get into an S.P. joint, buy a chicken farm, garage, something like that. **1969** W. MOXHAM *Apprentice* 24 He'd been main cockatoo—sentry to the ignorant—at the biggest SP joint in town . . a hellish good business till it was ruined by the government when it brought in the TAB. **1932** *Truth* (Sydney) 9 Oct. 1/4 The friend stated that he had had a successful bet with the bookmaker and that apparently the **S.P. man** had given him the marked notes with which he afterwards liquidated his debt to the constable.

B. *n.* Abbrev. of *S.P. betting, bookmaker, bookmaking*; also as quasi- *adv.* (see quot. 1949).

1941 *Action Front: Jrnl. 2/2 Field Regiment* Nov. 5 A bit of S.P. on the quiet. **1949** L. GLASSOP *Lucky Palmer* 4 Whenever he could 'wag' it from school on Thursdays he did the call for Ross Harrison, who bet S.P. on a house verandah overlooking the track. **1958** F. HARDY *Four-Legged Lottery* 76 Illegal betting has become a normal part of our society. SPs flourish even in the remotest places. **1964** A. STAPLES *Paddo* 79 Saturday afternoon Tony kept the shop open but didn't sell much; it was the front for the S.P. **1965** G.H. FEARNSIDE *Golden Ram* 184 We've had an open slather with S.P. here. **1969** G. JOHNSTON *Clean Straw for Nothing* (1971) 79 We could do more than just sit on our fat arses talking about beer and sport and racehorses and the S.P.

Hence **S.P.-ing** *vbl. n.*

1985 M. STEWART *Autobiogr. of my Mother* 172 Queenie had what she called 'SP-ing' at the back of the building. She ran an illegal betting establishment and had a room lined with telephones to take bets.

spag, *n.*[1] [Br. dial. *spag* the house-sparrow: see EDD *spag* and also *spadge, spadger, spadgick.*] A sparrow.

1951 *Bulletin* (Sydney) 17 Jan. 12/2 The spag makes no attempt to attack, but waltzes round in a shocked upright posture. . . Soon a regular chorus of chirrups is in full swing as the junior members of the speckled tribe add their bit of cheek, and the sparrows retire beaten. **1960** *Ibid.* 9 Sept. 19/1, I had found a spag's nest in the letterbox. **1971** D. IRELAND *Unknown Industr. Prisoner* 130 'Those little birds in the yard?' 'Spags. Little brown sparrows.'

spag, *n.*[2] [See quot. 1966.] An Italian immigrant.

[**1966** S.J. BAKER *Austral. Lang.* (ed. 2) 344 *Spaggie*, an Italian. (Ex spaghetti.)] **1967** V.G.C. NORWOOD *Long Haul* 38 A large party of 'Spags'—a slang Aussie term for spaghetti-eating Italian emigrants. **1974** *Bulletin* (Sydney) 1 June 40/1 'Why do you think Al Grassby has lost the election?' .. 'Oh .. brought in all those migrants.' But the migration level had fallen under Labor. 'No, y' know, those coons and spags.' **1983** *Nat. Times* (Sydney) 25 Mar. 25/2 The word spaghetti or 'Spag' is synonymous with Italian. Someone is either a 'Spag' or married to a 'Spag'.

spangled drongo. The bird *Dicrurus hottentottus* of n. and e. Aust. and elsewhere, having glossy black plumage with irridescent blue-green spangles or spots.

1845 J. GOULD *Birds of Aust.* (1848) II. Pl. 82, *Dicrurus bracteatus* . . Spangled Drongo. **1898** E.E. MORRIS *Austral Eng.* 126 The name [Drongo] is applied in Australia to *Chibia bracteata* .. which is called the Spangled Drongo. **1941** *Bulletin* (Sydney) 5 Nov. 14/4 A pair of spangled drongos—bushmen call them king crows or fishtails—have chosen this S.Q. mountain-edge as a hunting-ground for insects. **1962** MARSHALL & DRYSDALE *Journey among Men* 91 Another beautiful tropical bird that we now saw on the trip for the first time was the curiously cavorting spangled drongo. This species is a pioneer, the sole representative in Australia of a family that spreads right across from Africa to Japan. **1984** M. BLAKERS et al. *Atlas Austral. Birds* 613 The Spangled Drongo ranges from southern Asia to New Guinea and Australia.

Spaniard. *Obs. Spanish dollar*, see SPANISH *a.* 1.

1827 *Monitor* (Sydney) 30 Aug. 623/2 Knowing where I could borrow a few dollars, we sallied out on that pursuit, and very soon had the pleasure of pocketing some Spaniards.

Spanish, *a.* and *n. Hist.*

A. *adj.*

1. In the collocation **Spanish dollar,** the foreign coin most common in the early days of the Australian Colonies, circulating at a value of five shillings sterling.

1791 D. COLLINS *Acct. Eng. Colony N.S.W.* (1798) I. 180 The Spanish dollar was the current coin of the colony. **1825** *Howe's Weekly Commercial Express* (Sydney) 7 July 1 The Spanish Dollar will be received, as heretofore, at Five Shillings; the Colonial Dollar, at Three-fourths of the Spanish Dollar; and the Dump, at One-fourth. **1833** *Launceston Advertiser* 16 May 3 The Public should be on their guard when receiving Spanish Dollars, as there are now a great many counterfeits in circulation. **1838** *Sydney Herald* 5 Sept. 2/3 It appears that these [Mexican] dollars have been brought here by the New Union Bank, and issued at the rate of the Spanish dollar. **1874** C. DE BOOS *Congewoi Correspondence* 81, I happened to rekerlect about a heaper Spanish dollars, but I disremember how many.

2. [Also used elsewhere: see OEDS *a.* 8 a. (*c*).] Used of sheep, wool, etc., to designate the merino breed. Also **Spanish merino.**

1799 J. HUNTER Let. to Sir J. Banks 1 June 5, I send you three Specimens of Wool. 1 is that of a Spanish Ram. **1803** *Sydney Gaz.* 26 Mar., Fleece of a ewe imported from the Cape of Good Hope, said to be of the Spanish Breed. **1805** *Ibid.* 28 July, Have you any true bred Spanish Sheep in your flocks? **1809** *Ibid.* 18 Jan., At Mr M'Arthur's Farm, Parramatta, Several Flocks of choice Ewes and Weathers [*sic*] of the *Spanish* race. **1826** *Monitor* (Sydney) 1 Dec. 226/3 It is said that one thousand Spanish Sheep are on their way out from Lisbon, for the Van Dieman's Land Company. **1828** *Tasmanian* (Hobart) 26 Dec. 2 Our climate is precisely that in which the Electoral sheep best thrive... We have seen an animal only once improved from the *Saxon*, the fleece of which is not only superior to any of the *Spanish* merino best improved which we have met with, in respect to quality, but also in weight. **1853** S. SIDNEY *Three Colonies* (ed. 2) 65 M'Arthur . . was steadily pursuing his great idea of naturalising the 'noble race', or Spanish merino, on the plains of Australia.

B. *n.* A Spanish dollar, esp. in the phr. **to speak Spanish,** to be in possession of money.

1827 *Monitor* (Sydney) 26 July 539/2 Lupus Longpocket, the sub-Clerk, to whom is entrusted the care of forwarding the applications, has signified as the cause of their detention, the applicant's ignorance of the 'Spanish Language'. 'He must *speak Spanish* first'; are the words of Lupus... The poor fellow picked up *two words of Spanish* and delivered them, but whether from a want of grace, or, what is more probable, from a want of *fluency in the delivery*, it produced no effect upon the *stoney* heart of Long-pocket. **1832** *Hill's Life N.S.W.* (Sydney) 3 Aug. 2 Not being able to speak *Spanish*, the Bench, of course, sent him to the stocks. **1833** *Currency Lad* (Sydney) 27 Apr. 2 We shall do it as cheap as any of them. This is what is vulgarly called '*speaking Spanish*', but it is the best way to be *understood!* **1843** *Parramatta Chron.* 26 July 1/2 He jumped up, ran to his trousers, and found, to his 'inexpressible' horror, the contents of the watch pocket had been 'fobbed', and beheld the back of a man who was leaving the house. He immediately gave Edith into custody, and subsequently her husband was taken, but as there was no evidence to prove that either one or the other had been the purloiners of the 'Spanish' belonging to a 'Briton', they were discharged.

spare, *v.* In the phr. **spare me** (or **my**) **days,** an exclamation, esp. of exasperation.

1915 C.J. DENNIS *Songs of Sentimental Bloke* 16 The music of the sorft an' barmy breeze... Aw, spare me days! **1919** C. DREW *Doings of Dave* 15 Spare me days. **1926** 'DRYBLOWER' *Verses* 5, I ain't no scientific bloke, but spare me dinkum days. **1945** K.D. YOUNG *Born to Adventure* 42 'Spare me bloody days!' he said, 'I've got the whole blanky train full already.' **1955** STEWART & KEESING *Austral. Bush Ballads* 233 But come and hear 'em at it. Spare me days! oh strike me pink! Come and hear 'em at it while we have a quiet drink. **1959** M. RAYMOND *Smiley roams Road* 157 'Spare me days,' roared Mitchum, coming round to the end of the bar. 'You get out of the pub or I'll stoush you.' **1967** *Coast to Coast 1965–66* 134 Spare me days, you go and toil your guts out [etc.].

spare-chain, *v. trans.* To haul (a load) along by securing it with a chain: see quot. 1851.

1847 A. HARRIS *Settlers & Convicts* (1953) 109 The obstacles to be overcome in getting the plank dragged out of such a hole (which had to be done by sparechaining it along the ground, a plank at a time). **1849** S. & J. SIDNEY *Emigrant's Jrnl.* 162 Other settlers do not burn off at all, but saw the logs into pieces and spare chain them off the land, and then form what we call a rough bush fence, capable of keeping off all animals. **1851** J. HENDERSON *Excursions & Adventures N.S.W.* I. 129 He has only to send his team to the brush, and sparechain these slabs. [*Note*] This is the term applied to dragging anything with bullocks, by means of the extra chain belonging to the dray. **1879** 'AUSTRALIAN' *Adventures Qld.* 95 It has been shown that one way of getting out of a bog [with a bullock dray] is to work on the principle of the Scotchman who, while getting over his neighbour's wall was caught and asked where he was going to—'Bock agen', he replied; but at times it is impossible to go 'bock agen', then there is nothing for it but to 'spoke' it, spare-chain it, or unload. **1903** *Bulletin* (Sydney) 24 Dec. 36/3 The sleepers are 'sparechained' out of the bush from where they have been cut—*i.e.* a chain is passed round a number of them, and the bunch is hauled along the ground to where the waggon has been left. This is also called 'snigging-out'.

sparrowhawk. [Transf. use of *sparrow-hawk* the hawk *Accipiter nisus* of Britain and elsewhere.] **a.** COLLARED SPARROWHAWK. **b.** *Nankeen kestrel*, see NANKEEN.

1878 R.B. SMYTH *Aborigines of Vic.* II. 38 White crane . . *Tirtgerawan*. Sparrow hawk . . *Tootooth gwan*. **1912** *Emu* XII. 113, I saw it was a Sparrow-Hawk with a young Parrot in its talons. **1934** H.G. LAMOND *Aviary on Plains* 13 Three sparrow-hawks (Nankeen Kestrels) are there. **1956** A.C.C. LOCK *Tropical Tapestry* 125 A nankeen kestrel, commonly called sparrowhawk, rose from the grass near the road. **1962** B.W. LEAKE *Eastern Wheatbelt Wildlife* 83 The sparrow hawk, whose markings are very similar to the goshawk is the smallest and most determined of the hawks. It tries—and sometimes succeeds in—killing small birds in cages. **1965** *Austral. Encycl.* III. 322 The nankeen kestrel . . is often termed 'sparrow-hawk', but this name gives an erroneous idea of its habits. Its food consists almost entirely of mice, lizards, and large insects. **1981** M. SHARLAND *Tracks of Morning* 78 Tasmania has three kinds of goshawk—the white, the brown, and a smaller species known commonly as sparrow-hawk.

sparrow-starver. A street-cleaner: see quot. 1965.

1950 'B. JAMES' *Advancement Spencer Button* 49 Loutish youths, tough, vocal, conceited and pugnacious, known to the vulgar as 'sparrow-starvers', plied to and fro with yard-brooms and a kind of tray on wheels, collecting the manure and other refuse. **1965** G. MCINNES *Road to Gundagai* 113 His humble but essential job was to clean up the droppings from the big drays and waggons that rumbled to and from the docks. He and his kind were known, with apposite Australian wit, as 'sparrer starvers'.

spear, *n.*

1. a. An Aboriginal spear: see quots.

1787 *Descr. Botany Bay, on East Side New Holland* 7 Their weapons are spears or lances of different kinds. **1792** *Hist. Rec. N.S.W.* (1893) II. 797 Their spears are made of the stem of the grass tree. **1825** B. FIELD *Geogr. Mem. N.S.W.* 40 A number of natives . . collected on the shore . . and we could perceive with the glass that they had all spears. **1828** *Austral. Q. Jrnl. Theol., Lit. & Sci.* Jan. 29 The spears of the Natives of Hanover Bay were headed with stone, having both edges serrated, and were impelled, like those to the Southward by means of the *womerah*. **1846** *Moreton Bay Courier* 19 Sept. 4/1 The Alligator Rivers and Port Essington, where the throwing stick and the goose spears are means of obtaining game, and the common spear made of wood or strong reeds, and headed with sharp quartzose stone, form their means of offence and defence. **1865** J.M. STUART *Explorations in Aust.* 249 They had left one of their spears behind, a formidable weapon about ten feet long, with a flat round point, the other end being made for throwing with the womera. **1892** J. FRASER *Aborigines N.S.W.* 72 Their spears are either of reed or of wood, and the wood-spear may be plain in its whole length, or with jagged barbs worked in the natural wood at the point, or with stone jags fixed in the wood there, or with one, two, or three barbs or prongs cemented and lashed on; or it may be furnished with a sharp point and head of stone. **1910** J. MATHEW *Two Representative Tribes Qld.* 122 The spears, or *koni*, were from 7 to 10 ft. in length; made of iron-bark saplings and hardened at the point by the application of fire.

b. Special Comb. **spear thrower,** WOOMERA.

1896 B. SPENCER *Rep. Horn Sci. Exped. Central Aust.* IV. 89 *Spear-throwers*—'Amera', one type only is used in the regions visited, viz: a broad leaf-shaped instrument which is not only used for throwing the spear, but serves many useful purposes as a working tool. **1931** A.W. UPFIELD *Sands of Windee* 110 Mertee used a spear-thrower, a perfectly balanced piece of flat wood with a socket at its extremity to hold the butt of the spear. **1948** C.P. MOUNTFORD *Brown Men & Red Sand* 170 The spear thrower of the desert people has several uses... It is an extended arm by which the weapon can be thrown further; as a cutting tool, it serves a multitude of uses; as a dish, the hollow body is utilized to contain food; and for fire-making the thin edge of the spearthrower is rubbed across a split log until the heat from the friction lights the powdered wood-dust. **1963** D. ATTENBOROUGH *Quest under Capricorn* 73 He also owned a few spears and a wommera or spearthrower.

2. *fig.* Dismissal, esp. in the phr. **to get the spear,** to be dismissed; to be 'fired'.

1897 *Worker* (Sydney) 11 Sept. 1/1 Poor Billy Mayne has got 'the spear' and Dick his mate is 'shot'! **1898** *Bulletin* (Sydney) Dec. 15/1 *Discharge*, sack, shot, or spear. **1905** *Shearer* (Sydney) 20 May 8/1 Yez has a son chewing sailing-wax in the State treasury in Sydney town, so that if yez get the 'spear' (sack) it doesn't matter. **1906** *Bulletin* (Sydney) 25 Oct. 16/1 We don't want swagmen here! And before you get the billet you will find you've 'got the spear'. **1912** STEWART & KEESING *Old Bush Songs* (1957) 273 I've been many years a shearer and I fancied I could shear, I've shore for Rouse of Guntawung and always missed the spear. **1962** D. MCLEAN *World turned upside Down* 121 Danny got the spear from the job.

3. *transf.* A pipe sunk to tap a shallow aquifer: see quot. 1947. Also *attrib.*

1924 *Inlander* Sept. 49 There the farmer merely drives down 'spears' (hollow pipes, perforated freely for a short distance close to their strong pointed heads) and pumps away to his heart's content. **1947** H. DRAKE-BROCKMAN *On N.-W. Skyline* 21 From the main pipe-line 'spears' are thrust down into the riverbed, going to depths of twenty to forty feet, dependent on where the plantation is situated... The 'spears' are made of galvanised piping, flattened at the end, with an added side opening after the fashion of organ-pipes. **1964** R. CONNOLLY *John Drysdale & Burdekin* 76 Today, more than seventy years later, John Drysdale's multiple spears are still the method of pumping water from drifts of the Burdekin Delta. **1975** *Groundwater Resources Aust.* (Austral. Water Resources Council) 2 Connolly . . shows that towards the end of 1888 an irrigation system utilising a spear point assembly extracted water from unconsolidated sediments adjacent to Sheep Station Creek.

spear, *v.* [f. SPEAR *n.* 2.] *trans.* To dismiss (someone) from employment; to 'fire'. Freq. as past pple.

1911 'S. RUDD' *Dashwoods* 13 If I was the boss here I would. I'd spear him without warnin'. **1917** *Truth* (Sydney) 21 Jan. 11/7 I've shorn in every woolshed, from the Barwon to the Bree, I got speared at Goorianawa before I raddled three. ***c* 1927** J. BRADSHAW *Highway Robbery under Arms* (ed. 5) 42, I got speared . . for butchering a sheep in a most horrible manner. **1936** A.B. PATERSON *Shearer's Colt* 27 Didn't he spear (dismiss) you for cutting a plateful of meat off one of them stud rams? **1958** *Bulletin* (Sydney) 11 June 19/1 Consider the number of ways an Aussie can be dismissed from his job... He can be sacked, fired, hoisted, speared [etc.]

spear grass. Any of many grasses (fam. Poaceae), esp. of the genera *Stipa, Heteropogon* and *Aristida*, bearing a seed with a pointed husk and twisted awn(s), capable of working its way into soil, clothing, etc.: see quot 1844. See also WIRE-GRASS. Also *attrib.*

1840 *S. Austral. Rec.* (London) 28 Nov. 349 A little examination will point out the difference between kangaroo grass and spear grass. **1844** L. LEICHHARDT *Jrnl. Overland Exped. Aust.* 20 Nov. (1847) 45 Very disagreeable, however, was the abundance of Burr and of a spear-grass (Aristida), which attached themselves to our clothes and blankets, and entered (particularly the latter) into the very skin. **1863** W.J. WILLS *Successful Exploration Interior Aust.* 129 On the plains the spear grass up to our knees. **1881** *Proc. Linnean Soc. N.S.W.* VI. 744 The 'Spear-grass', *Heteropogon contortus*, is common on the downs, though not plentiful, and but for its destructive seeds is one of our best pasture grasses. **1887** J.H. WRIGHT *Our Victorian Coalfields* 22 Some 13,000 acres of poor land, consisting, for the most part, of spear-grass plains, with stunted gum-trees. **1889** J.H. MAIDEN *Useful Native Plants Aust.* 110 *Stipa* spp...

These grasses are excellent feeding before the appearance of the inflorescence; afterwards they are known as 'Spear Grasses'. **1935** C.H. SOUTER *Lonely Rose* 62 But the sweet scent of the speargrass takes me right back Home! **1948** G. FARWELL *Down Argent Street* 90 Within the first few months nine different species of grass appeared, principally spear grass (*Stipa scabra*). **1965** R.H. CONQUEST *Horses in Kitchen* 212 We'd skittled a big log, hidden in high spear-grass. **1979** D. LOCKWOOD *My Old Mates & I* 153 As we drove out of Pine Creek huge fires were consuming square miles of tall dry spear grass, as they do each year. **1982** J.B. HACKER et al. *More Beef Spear Grass Country* 1 Graziers soon found that sheep were not suited to the region because the barbed and hygroscopically awned seed of spear grass .. caused serious wounds.

spearo. [f. *spear(-fisherman* + -O.] A spear-fisherman.

1963 B. CROPP *Handbk. for Skindivers* 138 This day will see well over a dozen fast boats lined up on a Sydney beach and dozens of 'spearos' preparing for a keen four-hour contest, while the women and children picnic on the beach and prepare refreshments for their return. **1970** J.S. GUNN in W.S. Ramson *Eng. Transported* 55 Some are trite and could fade away, for example, *spearo*, 'fisherman' [etc.].

spearwood. [See SPEAR *n.* 1 a.] Any of several plants furnishing wood traditionally used for making spears, incl. YARRAN and the small tree *Eucalyptus doratoxylon* (fam. Myrtaceae) of s.w. W.A. Also *attrib.*

1837 G.F. MOORE *Evidences Inland Sea* 14 A hedge of spearwood and sedge marking the course of the winter stream. **1837** *Perth Gaz.* 12 Aug. 951 A Flat of about 70 Acres adjoining to a valuable Spear-wood Swamp. **1838** *Swan River Guardian* (Perth) 15 Feb. 4 The Perth Natives use [for the making of spears] a species of Melaleuca, which grows in salt marshes; the plant is known to the Settlers by the name of spear wood, and it is very useful for battens and making fences. **1875** J. FORREST *Explorations in Aust.* 66 Thence to Cooroo, over grassy country, with spearwood thickets intervening. **1896** *Proc. Linnean Soc. N.S.W.* XXI. 443 *A[cacia] doratoxylon* .. has only previously been recorded in this colony from the interior, as the 'Spearwood of certain tribes'. **1897** L. LINDLEY-COWEN *W. Austral. Settler's Guide* 215 Spear-wood (*E. doratoxylon*). **1936** J.E. HAMMOND *Western Pioneers* 126 Spear-wood .. was used by the natives for spears and other weapons and tools. **1981** G.M. CUNNINGHAM et al. *Plants Western N.S.W.* 602 The canes of this [*sc. Pandorea pandorana*] or closely related species were reported to have been used by aborigines for spear shafts (hence spearwood).

spec, var. SPECK *n.* and *v.*

special, *n. Hist.* GENTLEMAN CONVICT.

1832 J. HENDERSON *Observations Colonies N.S.W. & Van Diemen's Land* 9 The gentlemen convicts, who are denominated specials, were in the habit of being sent to a depôt at Wellington. **1835** 'IMPARTIAL OBSERVER' *Illustr. Present State N.S.W.* 64 Here seems to be the place to speak of that class of convicts, who are called gentlemen-convicts or specials. **1844** *Life J. Knatchbull* 15 He arrived here in the month of April, 1825, and was immediately sent as a special to Wellington Valley, then termed the 'swell settlement' being the place where the better class and more educated of the criminals were generally sent. **1851** J. HENDERSON *Excursions & Adventures N.S.W.* II. 1 One of the specials whom I had on loan from the convict barracks in Port Macquarie, was a Roman Catholic priest. **1873** 'LADY IN AUST.' *Memories Past* 16 Our farm servants were prisoners, but we had only two black sheep out of ten, and one of these was a 'special' or gentleman prisoner. **1900** 'WOOMERA' *Life & Experiences Ex-Convict* 13 In the road party it was a funny sight to see some of the flash 'specials' using a crosscut saw. **1952** J. TUCKER *Ralph Rashleigh* p. vi, Writing a novel takes time, so that I felt he must have been what was called a 'special', that is, an educated convict employed at a special task.

special, *a. Hist.* In special collocations: **special country lot** *Vic.*, a small tract of land suitable for cultivation as opposed to grazing (see quot. 1855); **survey,** a survey of land carried out under certain conditions which varied from Colony to Colony; the land so surveyed.

1842 *Act* (G.B.) 5 & 6 Vict. no. 36 Sect. 11, In respect of any Part not exceeding One Tenth of the whole of the Lands of the Third Class for the First Time offered for Sale .. it shall be lawful for any such Governor .. to name an upset Price higher than the lowest upset Price of Waste Lands in the Colony, and such excepted Lands of the Third Class shall be designated as '**Special Country Lots**'. **1843** *Portland Mercury* 4 Oct. 3/5 The surveyors should lay off a number of special country lots in different parts of the district as near Portland and Belfast as possible. **1848** *Portland Gaz.* 9 June 3/2 The great want of dairy and farm produce, which has been long felt, induced Mr Henty to draw the attention of Mr La Trobe, on his Honor's recent visit to Portland, to the necessity of having a number of suburban and special Country lots immediately surveyed and put up to auction. **1855** E.H. HARGRAVES *Aust. & Goldfields* 198 Grazing lands will be sold by auction in sections, never exceeding 140 acres, or one square mile and .. lands suited for cultivation, or likely to be purchased for small farms, and which will be designated as 'special country lots', will be sold in portions of from 20 to 320 acres. **1838** *S. Austral. Rec.* (London) 13 Jan. 31 He is trying to buy town sections, and has been talking to Mr Fisher about a **special survey.** **1840** *Ibid.* 15 Jan. 10 We came to .. a special survey, where we obtained some fried pork and damper. **1841** *Port Phillip Gaz.* 20 Mar. 5 A special survey can only be granted for purchases of above five thousand acres. **1843** *Melbourne Times* 4 Aug. 3/1, I live on the special survey called Alger's Survey. **1845** *Portland Gaz.* 9 Sept. 3/5 The Port Fairy Special Survey—Most of the tenants on Mr Atkinson's special survey, either have or are about to flit; it appears that the agreement between these 'Cockatoo settlers' and their landlord, was merely verbal, and as the speculation was not found to answer, of course some 'mistake' touching the terms of the said agreement occurred, which may end in the abandonment of the survey. **1855** W. HOWITT *Land, Labor & Gold* I. 324, I believe it had been part of a special survey, a system which at an earlier period of the colony had formed the capitalist and land-jobber, at the expense of the poor man. **1886** *N.T. Times Almanac* 58 Persons desiring to purchase by private contract lands not yet surveyed must apply to the Minister for a special survey thereof.

specimen. *Gold-mining.* See quot. 1869. Also *attrib.*

1869 R.B. SMYTH *Gold Fields & Mineral Districts* 622 *Specimen*, a piece of quartz containing gold which is visible to the naked eye. **1887** 'OLD GOLD DIGGER' *Gold Digger's Guide* 8 Often gold is attached to quartz and other stones, which are called 'specimens'. **1891** *Hist. Wedderburn Gold Fields* 14 Having several times 'shouted' for all the company, and swallowed several bottles of beer himself, he retired to his 'bunk' to dream of nuggets and specimens. **1931** W. BARAGWANATH et al. *Guide for Prospectors in Vic.* 31 The discovery of 'specimens' (gold attached to quartz) during the early 'seventies' attracted the attention of the miners and led them to follow certain belts of strata where such specimens were more abundant than elsewhere. **1932** I.L. IDRIESS *Prospecting for Gold* 16 If you are in reef or 'specimen' country, keep an eye on any iron or quartz stones you pick from the bottom of the wash. **1977** J. DOUGHTY *Gold in Blood* 76, I only saw one of the 'specimens'. It was as large as a dinner plate, and almost as round. .. It was composed mainly of quartz, but gold ran through it thickly in lace-like patterns.

speck, *n.* Also **spec.**

1. *Gold-mining.* A small fragment of gold; FLY-SPECK 2. Also **speck gold.**

1852 J. BONWICK *Notes of Gold Digger* 12 The head stuff is removed to make way for you to get under, to work at the latent treasure of specs, nuggets and washing stuff. **1852** *Wanderer* (Adelaide) (1853) July 74 'Nugget' .. is applied to any bit or piece of gold larger than dust and 'specks'. **1853** R.S. ANDERSON *Austral. Gold Fields* (1956) 21, 100 specs in a dish is a very fair 'prospect'. **1855** G.H. WATHEN *Golden Colony* 66 When the 'specks' at last begin to show, Out comes the ready knife, Sir. **1866** *Austral. Monthly Mag.* (Melbourne) III. 87 Bits of quartz, in which 'specks'—although nearly microscopic—were discernable if looked at closely. **1871** *Austral. Town & Country Jrnl.* (Sydney) 11 Mar. 304/2 About twelve specs to the dish have been obtained. **1881** G.C. EVANS *Stories* 91 'Here is a nice speck,' and I stooped to pick up what I thought was a quarter-ounce nugget. **1925** J.E. LIDDLE *Selected Poems* 86 Oft he 'naps' reefs with his pick, If they have 'specks' he may 'costeen'. **1930** H. REDCLIFFE *Yellow Cygnet* 208 It was 'speck' gold—an amateur could have told that. **1946** K.S. PRICHARD *Roaring Nineties* 40 The wind blew off the dust and left the heavy specks of gold in the dish. **1964** H.P. TRITTON *Time means Tucker* 58 In a week we mastered the jargon of the goldfields and spoke wisely of .. colours, specks, slugs *etc.*

2. The (comparatively small) island of Tasmania; FLY-SPECK 1.

1916 *Bulletin* (Sydney) 8 June 24/4 Over the Speck they seldom split really big trees for posts. **1918** *Huon Times* (Franklin) 1 Nov. 2/7 Mainland people were fond of referring to Tasmania somewhat contemptuously as 'the speck'. **1922** *Bulletin* (Sydney) 6 July 22/2 The Speck's early settlers learned from the blacks. **1931** *Ibid.* 4 Feb. 20/4 The button-grass plains of the sou'-west Speck carry a fairly large 'roo population. **1943** *Ibid.* 22 Dec. 13/3 The curious point in the list of similarities between s.-e. Australia and the Speck .. is that it emphasises the much greater differences which exist as between the flora of s.-w. W.A. and the regions mentioned. **1955** *Ibid.* 12 Jan. 12/3 On the north-west corner of the Speck .. the average rainfall is from 50 to 60 inches.

speck, *v. Mining.* Also **spec.**

1. *intr.* To search (for surface gold or opal).

1888 *Bulletin* (Sydney) 22 Dec. 18/1 He used to go 'a-speckin'' and 'fossickin'' amongst the old mullock heaps. **1901** *Truth* (Sydney) 16 June 5/8 Gins specking after a heavy rainfall .. were successful in getting several bits or pieces. **1903** A.G. CHARLETON *Gold Mining & Milling W.A.* 42 Hundreds of ounces have thus been picked up by the first-comers, 'specking' for gold, as it is called. **1906** *Bulletin* (Sydney) 26 Apr. 15/1 With red dust all a-smother we raked the riddling sieve, Or 'specked' round Maritana when luck was fugitive. **1911** A.L. HAYDON *Trooper Police Aust.* 331 'Specking for slugs', that is, looking for surface gold. **1947** F. CLUNE *Roaming around Aust.* 70 The kids of Coolgardie always go out 'specking' after a shower of rain. **1948** H. DRAKE-BROCKMAN *Sydney or Bush* 26 Time of Kimberley gold rush. I reckoned to spec a bit up the coast. **1958** F.B. VICKERS *Though Poppies Grow* 169 His retort to padre Postle's rhetoric was: bull-dust. What the hell was this way of life? Was it himself specking for gold out where the eagle flew—where a man could do a perish for want of a drink? **1969** E. WALLER *And there's Opal* 116 A couple of tourists specking for bits of potch and opal. **1977** J. DOUGHTY *Gold in Blood* 202 As the gully itself was only a few feet wide, with a pale green schisty bottom, it seemed a likely place to go specking.

2. a. *trans.* To search (the surface of the ground) for gold or opal.

1921 W.H. PHIPPS *Bush Yarns* 24 Set to work with his dishes, meanwhile urging the natives to 'speck' the ground for gold. **1932** I.L. IDRIESS *Prospecting for Gold* 185 You may get a 'line' of floaters leading right to the reef. You 'speck' those floaters. **1946** K.S. PRICHARD *Roaring Nineties* 37 He prospected twenty miles out, as far as Red Hill and specked alluvial. We fossicked along the ridge. **1951** I.L. IDRIESS *Across Nullarbor* 96 Within a week or so they were specking gold at the foot of Maritana Hill.

b. *trans.* To discover (surface particles of gold or opal).

1926 *Bulletin* (Sydney) 11 Feb. 22/3 A friendly nig, especially if occasionally given a trifle of tea or sugar or part of a tin of 'dog', would bring to the tent of the fossicker small pieces of gold specked by him. **1928** *Ibid.* 19 Sept. 25/3 A black stockman 'specked' a £400 specimen for his squatter boss. **1932** I.L. IDRIESS *Prospecting for Gold* 230 That is how White Cliffs was found, a field that supported three thousand people for many years. A kangaroo shooter there 'specked' potch. **1946** K.S. PRICHARD *Roaring Nineties* 54 The spot where he and German-George had specked a few bits of alluvial. **1977** J. DOUGHTY *Gold in Blood* 204 Almost at the top of the gully .. I specked a round, rough piece of gold which later turned the scale at five pennyweights.

Hence **specked** *ppl. a.*, found on the surface of the ground.

1980 S. THORNE *I've met some Bloody Wags* 73

Occasionally a specker is lucky, but a lot of stones sold as 'specked' opal are in reality 'ratted' opal.

specker, *n.*[1] *Mining.* One who looks for surface deposits of a mineral.

1897 *Bulletin* (Sydney) 10 July 9/3 The Girilambone copper-speckers overdid it last Tuesday. **1903** *Ibid.* 17 Jan. 26/1 I've not had average specker's luck—Or chucked it when I did. **1906** *Ibid.* 26 Apr. 15/1 And when the nights are darkest I hear the rifles ring For some too-ardent 'specker' belated, wandering. **1955** STEWART & KEESING *Austral. Bush Ballads* 135 They sought for the specker's paradise, where some wind-worn, broken strands Torn from the Cloth o' Gold might lie. **1980** S. THORNE *I've met some Bloody Wags* 73 After a shower or storm the opal fields are swarming with 'speckers'—hopefuls wandering about, heads down, bums in the air, looking for any gems on the ground.

specker, *n.*[2] Alteration of 'speculator'.

1919 *Smith's Weekly* (Sydney) 5 Apr. 9/3 Recent N.S.W. rains caught produce 'speckers' badly... Lucerne dropped from £13 10s. to £9 per ton. **1966** M. CANNON *Land Boomers* 77 As his profits grew, and with them his taste for gracious living, Larkin decided to imitate the Collins Street 'speckers' by building his own mansion.

specking, *vbl. n. Mining.* The action of searching for surface gold or opal. Also *attrib.*

1894 F. HART *Miner's Handbk.* 30 Here are situated the celebrated 'specking' grounds, over which hundreds of men walked day after day, turning over every stone with a forked stick to see if it might not be a specimen or cover a nugget. **1894** A.F. CALVERT *Coolgardie Goldfield* 65 Almost everyone in the camp went for an afternoon's specking (which means walking about with one's eyes fixed on the ground, looking for nuggets). **1898** D.W. CARNEGIE *Spinifex & Sand* 107 We were precluded from the alluring search for alluvial, 'specking', as it is termed. **1903** *Bulletin* (Sydney) 7 Feb. 15/3 At first, Lake Way was a great 'specking patch', and the gins . . were great speckers, and brought in a lot of slug gold. **1910** H. LAWSON *Skyline Riders* 122 The 'specking' in old diggers' heaps for 'colours' after rain. **1914** N.F. SPIELVOGEL *Gumsucker at Home* 94, I remember making many a shilling at the exciting pastime of 'specking'. **1930** H. REDCLIFFE *Yellow Cygnet* 198 Among the prospectors there was a custom known as 'Specking'... The prospector might venture into the unworked country and often meet with fair success... The risk, not a remote one, was that of becoming lost in a waterless belt. **1945** *Walkabout* (Melbourne) Mar. 14 Most of the residents of Lightning Ridge are experts at the art of specking. **1955** A.C.V. BLIGH *Golden Quest* 17 Kurnalpi was a specking field, for the gold was mostly picked up on the surface. **1965** B. JAMES *Collecting Austral. Gemstones* 51 Promising dumps for specking pointed out on the way.

spectacled, *a.* Used as a distinguishing epithet in the names of animals: **spectacled flycatcher** (or **monarch**), the predom. grey, orange, and white bird *Monarcha trivirgatus* of rainforest in e. mainland Aust., and elsewhere; **hare-wallaby,** the small wallaby *Lagorchestes conspicillatus* of n. Aust.

1898 E.E. MORRIS *Austral Eng.* 149 **Spectacled F[lycatcher]**—*P[iezorhynchus] nitidus.* **1929** A.H. CHISHOLM *Birds & Green Places* 36 You may frequently see the spectacled and black-faced flycatchers. **1945** C. BARRETT *Austral. Bird Life* 138 The spectacled flycatcher (*Monarcha trivirgata*) ranges from Cape York to north-eastern New South Wales; also occurring in New Guinea, Timor and the Moluccas. **1973** S. & K. BREEDEN *Wildlife Eastern Aust.* 71 A trilling 'pree-pree' and a Spectacled Flycatcher, skeleton leaf in his beak, flies to his partly completed nest. **1976** *Reader's Digest Compl. Bk. Austral. Birds* 383 (*caption*) Large black eye-patches earn the spectacled monarch its name. **1894** R. LYDEKKER *Hand-Bk. Marsupialia & Monotremata* 52 **Spectacled Hare-Wallaby.** *Lagorchestes conspicillatus...* General colour coarsely grizzled yellowish-grey; under-parts mingled white and slaty-grey; a well-defined chestnut band round the eye. **1928** G.H. WILKINS *Undiscovered Aust.* 82 One of the rare animals in the district was the curious-looking spectacled hare-wallaby. It is an animal slightly bigger than a rat-kangaroo and stands about eighteen inches high. **1975** *Ecos* v. 28/1 The spectacled hare-wallaby . . shelters during the daytime in squats made in long grass... These wallabies were once so common . . near Alice Springs that stockmen used to course them for fun with their dogs. **1981** *Ibid.* xxix. 21/2 Smaller macropods (members of the kangaroo family), such as the spectacled hare-wallaby . . fared less well, becoming scarce or extinct with the disappearance of the long grass in which they had sheltered.

speedball. [See quot. 1965.] A rissole.

1965 J.S. GUNN *Terminol. Shearing Industry* ii. 26 *Speed balls,* breakfast mincemeat rolls which are reputed (no doubt by the cook) to make shearers faster. The explanation may lie in the effect on the shearers' bowels. **1978** J. DINGWALL *Sunday too far Away* 40 'Bloody good cook.' . . 'Speed balls. That was his specialty.' . . 'Rissoles.'

speel, var. SPIEL.

speeler, var. SPIELER.

Speewah /'spiwa/. Also **Speewa.** [See quot. 1977.] **a.** An imaginary station or place used as a setting for tall stories of the outback. **b.** *transf.* Such a story. Also *attrib.*

1890 *Truth* (Sydney) 16 Nov. 1/4 Dear Mr *Truth*—I have just returned from 'the Spewah Country', where we have to crawl on our hands and knees to get under the clouds. **1911** *Bulletin* (Sydney) 17 Aug. 14/3 If any snagger boasted of having shorn 32 sheep in the breakfast 'run', there was always someone present to mention that 'Crooked Mick', at Speewah, had done 33 in the same time. **1944** A. MARSHALL *These are my People* 154, I had heard of Speewa, that mythical station used as a setting for all the lies put over on new-chums. **1951** E. HILL *Territory* 445 On the Speewaa: A legendary station of doughty deeds—'I bet that happened on the Speewaa.' The original Speewaa Station is near Swan Hill on the Murray River, home of great men and tall tales in the very earlies. **1956** A. MARSHALL *How's Andy Going?* 77 The heroes of American folk tales are sissies compared to the men of Australia's mythical station, the Speewah. **1970** B. EASTERBROOK *Tom the Urger* 10 His feats of strength filled Speewah Mick with spleen. **1977** L. BLAKE *Place Names Vic.* 242 Speewa: Locality by Murray River, N.W. of Swan Hill; in outback legends name of mythical sheep station, home of tall tales, where men, their locale, and achievements were all exceptionally big. **1979** *Courier-Mail* (Brisbane) 12 May 1/2 Each must tell a speerwah, or bush yarn, for more than four minutes.

speiler, speler, varr. SPIELER.

spell, *n.* [Br. dial.: see OEDS *sb.*[3] 3 b.] A period of rest from work; a holiday. Also *attrib.*

1831 *Sydney Herald* 12 Sept. 3/2 Taking a *spell* from the labours of the pestle and mortar. **1840** *Adelaide Chron.* 18 Feb. 3/5 The second day's stage from Lake Bonney brought us to a range of sand hills; and as there was plenty of good feed in their neighbourhood, we gave the horses and cattle a day's 'spell'. **1844** *Parramatta Chron.* 2 Nov. 2/3 On being requested by his overseer to continue his work, he threw down his tools and proclaimed his desire of having a *spell* in the watch house for a few days. **1853** A. MACKAY *Great Gold Field* 60, I fell in with a rough fellow at Mr Howard's, at the village of Peel, going into Bathurst to enjoy himself, or, as he termed it, to have a 'week's spell'. **1868** C.W. BROWNE *Overlanding in Aust.* 36 He takes, too, the chance of getting down to see a little of town life, which he will probably have an opportunity of doing when he takes his 'spell' (holiday) at the end of his trip, when he will consider himself entitled to a month's relaxation. **1880** J.B. STEVENSON *Seven Yrs. Austral. Bush* 33 After a day's spell, we set out, and my first real work in the bush began. **1901** *Brisbane Courier* 5 July 2/6 At 6 o'clock the men commenced to work cargo and continued with the usual 'spells' until 4 o'clock on Wednesday morning, when the steamer got away. **1911** *Emu* XI. 17 As very few birds were then breeding, I decided to give the collecting a spell. **1929** F. MANNING *Middle Parts of Fortune* I. 6 We should get a spell out of the line now. I don't believe there are more than a hundred of us left. **1943** *Bulletin* (Sydney) 6 Oct. 10/1 The candidate must drink two bottles of beer in three minutes, have a five minute spell, spin ten times and then drink a third bottle in five minutes. **1959** H. LAMOND *Sheep Station* 124 Some of the shearers, and an old rouseabout, got their horses in from the spell paddock. **1977** W.A. WINTER-IRVING *Bush Stories* 81 I'll drive, give you a spell. **1986** *Sunday Examiner* (Launceston) 30 Mar. 38/4 Hula Chief would run . . at Randwick next Saturday and then be sent for a spell.

spell, *v.* [f. prec.]

1. *intr.* To rest.

1841 S. STANGER in G. Mackaness *Fourteen Journeys Blue Mountains* (1950) iii. 67 As they formed altogether a jolly company, and had been a week coming from Sydney, they thought well to 'spell' (as they termed it) another day. **1844** *Standard* (Melbourne) (1845) 5 Feb. 4/1 Sunday October 6 . . this day we spelled. **1852** J. MACGILLIVRAY *Narr. Voyage H.M.S. Rattlesnake* II. 235, I went on next morning, and felt very bad, and I spelled for two days . . and sat down there, and I wanted to spell a little there, and go on. **1862** J. MCKINLAY *Jrnl. Exploration Interior* 22 Mar. 64 Bullocks did not come up last night, so have had to send back to-day, consequently spelled. **1880** *Blackwood's Mag.* (Edinburgh) Jan. 59/2 You can spell to-day and look about you . . and tomorrow Stone here . . will put you up to it. **1889** E.B. KENNEDY *Blacks & Bushrangers* 125 They determined to 'spell' there a few days and explore the neighbourhood. **1897** J.J. MURIF *From Ocean to Ocean* 61 The few white men I met . . did what they could . . inviting me to 'spell' with them if they were 'spelling'. **1911** ST. C. GRONDONA *Collar & Cuffs* 82 They have dinner and spell till 1 o'clock. **1918** *Kia Ora Coo-ee* May 8/2 We had fixed up that little affair at Gaza, and were now back again at Khan Yums, 'spelling'. **1925** *Bulletin* (Sydney) 1 Jan. 22/4 For the last week or so I've been spelling among the grasshoppers in the North (N.S.W.), and they are a terror. **1935** H.H. FINLAYSON *Red Centre* 103 When the flies and ants and heat and sand could be endured no longer, we left the skinning and spelled. **1951** E. HILL *Territory* 302 'I'm crook,' he said to the ringers. 'I'll spell for a bit.' **1963** J. DUFFY *Outsville Pub* 12 Young station hands in high-heeled boots, 'spelling' in satin, eyes shaded by broad brimmed hats. **1978** D. STUART *Wedgetail View* 50 Sitting on a slope above the camp, spelling while a gang with shovels cleared away the spoil from their work.

2. *trans.* To cause or allow (an animal, person, etc.) to rest in order to recuperate; to leave (land) unused for a period in order to improve its productivity.

1846 J.L. STOKES *Discoveries in Aust.* II. 42 In order . . to spell the oars, we landed at a point on the east side. **1849** *Argus* (Melbourne) 16 Mar. 4/5, I changed horses, and rode a black colt, to spell the other. **1851** *Bell's Life in Sydney* 1 Apr. 3/2 When at fault they could build a block house in one or two days where five whites and two blacks might remain in safety, spell the stock and gain the confidence of the blacks. **1864** H. JONES *New Valuations* 23 We have certainly sold sheep, as every other squatter does; we have bred and bought others. We deny that we are 'spelling' the country, and can only repeat our former assertion that the run will not carry more. **1879** 'AUSTRALIAN' *Adventures Qld.* 6 About noon they reached a fine creek... There were several bullock-drivers, with their teams, in camp there for their mid-day meal, and to spell and feed their bullocks for an hour or two. **1887** MRS D.D. DALY *Digging, Squatting, & Pioneering Life* 337 They 'spelled horses' for a time. **1902** R.C. PRAED *My Austral. Girlhood* 162 He would be asked to 'spell' his horse for a day, and, if he proved agreeable, be pressed to stay longer. **1918** C.J. DENNIS *Digger Smith* 29, I seen 'im strugglin' with a bag uv spuds. 'Look 'ere', I sez, 'you let me spell yeh, Dad. You 'umpin' loads like that's a bit too bad.' **1927** A. WRIGHT *Squatter's Secret* 114 Great place, down there, to spell a horse. **1944** J.H. PICK *Aust.'s Dying Heart* (rev. ed.) 85 These leases were completely spelled for over twenty years. Despite this prolonged rest the frontages which were eaten out in the first occupation made absolutely no progress in the way of regeneration. **1955** P. WHITE *Tree of Man* 205 It is best for you to spell the Creek paddock after summer. **1960** R.S. PORTEOUS *Cattleman* 233 We could do with a drop of rain, and even if we did get rain I'd like to see the bullock paddock spelled for a few months. **1986** *Sunday Examiner* (Launceston) 30 Mar. 37/1 Ritchie said Bonecrusher would be spelled and brought back with the Japan Cup next November as his main mission.

Hence **spelled** *ppl. a.*, **spelling** *ppl. a.*

1891 D. FERGUSON *Vicissitudes Bush Life* 47 When you are well **spelled** after your long tramp, I may get the Coni to give you a job at hut keeping. **1903** *Bulletin* (Sydney) 30 May 35/1 It was taken up . . partly for a **spelling** and fattening paddock for his bullocks and partly as a home for his wife. **1952** W. OGILVIE *Saddle for Throne* 75 As we drove one day through the lignum swamp Where the spelling horses ran, A loose horse broke from the noonday camp And trotted beside our van. **1980** *Sydney Morning Herald* 23 Oct. 30/5 The Metropolitan runner-up raced poorly to finish 11th, and the trainer Tom Hughes said he would almost certainly go to the spelling paddock.

spell-oh. Also **spello.** [f. SPELL *n.* + -O: see quot. 1862.] A call signalling the beginning of a break from work; the break itself.

1862 G.T. LLOYD *Thirty-Three Yrs. Tas. & Vic.* 125 Four or five times in one day .. was the ever-welcome command, 'Spell O, and sling kettles', responded to with marked satisfaction. **1872** *Illustr. Sydney News* 13 Apr. 55/1 Every two hours or so, the cry of 'spelloh' resounds in the woolshed; and then, one by one, the shearers knock off work to enjoy a smoke and a pannikin of tea. **1879** 'AUSTRALIAN' *Adventures Qld.* 19 When a batch of letters and papers arrived, unless the work at the time on hand rendered it impossible, it was 'Spell, ho!' with all hands, until the cream of the news was skimmed. **1888** J. POTTS *One Yr. Anti-Chinese Work Qld.* 10 Then the welcome cry of 'Spell-ho, spell-ho', and down goes the swag. **1889** *Bulletin* (Sydney) 5 Oct. 8/4 'Twas good, when 'spell-oh' had been said, To watch the white smoke curl and cling Against the gravel roof o'erhead. **1900** H. LAWSON *On Track* 97 Bill .. was having a spell-oh under the cask when the white rooster crowed. **1903** *Bulletin* (Sydney) 16 Sept. 16/3 The cocky's dog .. relentlessly chews invading 'townies' .. with occasional spell-ohs to cool off in an adjacent dam. **1965** L. HAYLEN *Big Red* 175 There oughter to be some easy-going sheilas in the town who'd like to sleep with Harry Dale the drover. I'm going to try it. We've got a 'spello' here. **1974** J. GABY *Restless Waterfront* 109 We knew also that the men did arrange their spell-ohs for a billy of tea whilst the work still went on.

Hence **spell-oh** *v. intr.*, to rest.

1898 E. DYSON *Below & on Top* 139 You can spell-oh till you pick up a bit, an' then you can get down to graft. **1900** *Bulletin* (Sydney) 6 Jan. 14/1 W'en the taste in Life turns sour, An' yer best girl goes to hell—Spell-oh!

spider.

1. a. A drink usually consisting of brandy mixed with lemonade (but see quots. 1861 and 1872).

1850 *Monthly Almanac* (Adelaide) 7 'Shouting' signifies paying for nine nobblers, four spiders, various glasses. **1853** F.J. COCKBURN *Lett.* (1856) 3, I ascertained afterwards that a 'nobbler' is the Colonial slang for half a glass of spirits; another piece of Colonial slang is calling a glass of brandy and lemonade 'a spider'. **1856** W.W. DOBIE *Recoll. Visit Port-Phillip* 43 One of them had become gradually overpowered by his frequent potations of 'spiders'. **1861** H. EARLE *Ups & Downs* 283 They are .. up to unlimited 'spiders', or lemonade and sherry. **1872** W.H. THOMES *Bushrangers* 333 We .. made him give us a 'spider', or some brandy and beer mixed. **1893** J.H. SIMMONDS *Some Odd Memories* 2 Then our old friend the Doctor would these others mock, And say *he* preferred to have spiders—and hock. **1918** *Bulletin* (Sydney) 1 Aug. (Red Page), 'A spider' was compounded of lemonade and brandy, while in a 'stone fence' ginger-beer mingled with the brandy. **1928** N.F. SPIELVOGEL *Affair at Eureka* 31 Men smoked their pipes and listened, while waiters in felt slippers moved along the aisles with trays of cocktails and 'spiders' and 'gin-slings' and 'gold-top'.

b. A soft drink to which a serving of ice-cream has been added.

1941 *Coast to Coast* 229 'You've had your drink, so now you've got to buy us all a spider at Smith's.' .. I didn't want to .. sit in Smith's and drink silly coloured muck with ice-cream floating in it. **1955** M. CORBEN *Not to mention Kangaroos* 115 It was *ginger* ale and ice cream. This mixture the Australians have mysteriously named a 'spider'. **1965** K. SMITH *OGF* 40 Bill Chaffey's secondhand furniture auction; the 'Miami' milkbar ('Give our Spiders a Fly, 1s. 3d.')—they're all part of a typical suburban street. **1979** E. SMITH *Saddle in Kitchen* 107 The treat of the day for us would be a 'spider' at one of the Greek cafes; a generous scoop of ice-cream that fizzed and bobbed when added to a tall, thick milkshake glass full of cool drink. **1981** J. SAXTON *Something will Come* 159 A spider was a parfait glass filled with soft drink and topped off with a scoop of rainbow ice-cream.

2. *Mining.* A candle-holder having a spike able to be thrust into clay, timber, etc.: see quot. 1982.

1912 *Mercury* (Hobart) 17 Oct. 5/1 The following is the text of a letter found pinned to the timber by a miner's 'Spider' close to the body of J. McCarthy at the 700 ft. level. **1913** A. PRATT *Golden Kangaroo* 10 The candle that guttered in a 'spider' spiked in a neighbouring beam. **1921** K.S. PRICHARD *Black Opal* 56 He had taken up his father's gouging pick and spider. **1932** I.L. IDRIESS *Prospecting for Gold* 234 The spider is the twisted piece of fencing-wire or the bought steel spike, which holds your candle. **1940** E. HILL *Great Austral. Loneliness* (ed. 2) 261, I watched the opal miners .. peering with keen eyes through a candle held on a piece of twisted iron called a 'spider'. **1948** K.S. PRICHARD *Golden Miles* 72 A man had to .. pick up his crib bag, 'spider' and candle. **1958** M.D. BERRINGTON *Stones of Fire* 33 A candle in a 'spider' that queer, spiked holder that is used below ground. **1976** F.R. ST. JOHN *Verse in Retirement* 14 No spider holds a candle light, No miners search below None now holds a 'miners right' Nor pans the creek for show. **1982** M. WALKER *Making Do* 98 They were working underground by candlelight, held on the wall by a spider; it's a piece of twisted iron. It had a candle in the middle of it, they would push that into one of the legs, as they call it, which is a timber prop that held up the stopings.

3. A gig used in a trotting race.

1934 T. WOOD *Cobbers* 18 Watching horses race by electric light is increased by the sight of them pulling gigs. These are called 'spiders'. **1945** S.J. BAKER *Austral. Lang.* 175 *Spider* or *jinker*, a trotting gig. **1955** A. ROSS *Aust. 55* 34 The drivers, dressed in silks like jockeys, sit behind their animals in tiny carriages known as spiders. **1969** *W. Austral.* (Perth) 5 July 32/5 Causing Pyraket to strike and badly buckle the inside wheel of Master Flame's spider.

spider flower. Any of several species of *Grevillea* (see GREVILLEA) having spidery flowers.

1913 F. SULMAN *Pop. Guide Wild Flowers N.S.W.* 10 The well-known Spider Flowers .. are .. marked by a more or less spider-like flower arrangement. **1938** K. HIGGINS *Betty in Bushland* 38 He found a pretty red Spider-flower. **1948** P.J. HURLEY *Red Cedar* 31 It was a wonderful spot for wildflowers... They grew along the ridges in great colonies of spider flowers, dog-roses, teatrees. **1981** G. CROSS *George & Widda-Woman* 9 We gathered small bunches of flowers for Mum .. spider flowers, waratahs.

spider orchid. Any of several terrestrial orchids of the chiefly Austral. genus *Caladenia* (fam. Orchidaceae) having long, narrowed sepals and petals. Also **spider,** and formerly **spider orchis.**

1867 *Lang. Native Flowers Tas.* 6 Spider Orchis .. danger near. **1889** J.H. MAIDEN *Useful Native Plants Aust.* 11 *Caladenia, spp.* .. 'Spider Orchids'. These and other orchids have edible tubers. **1898** E.E. MORRIS *Austral Eng.* 429 Spider-Orchis .. name given in Tasmania to the Orchid *Caladenia pulcherrima.* **1911** E. DYSON *Tommy Hawker* 33 Carrying a bunch of wild white violets and 'spiders'—as we always called the exquisite little bush orchids. **1928** M.E. FULLERTON *Austral. Bush* 38 The little spider orchid drew its thin life. **1948** J.K. EWERS *For Heroes to live In* 32 They .. put glass jars of everlastings and blood-red spider orchids on the long trestle-tables. **1965** *Austral. Encycl.* VII. 410 Spider orchid (*Caladenia* spp. of the section Calonema). **1978** L. WHITE *Memories of Childhood* 1 All the small orchids; spiders, donkeys, yellows, enamels. **1985** MARIS & BORG *Women of Sun* 64 Delicate spider orchids began to venture forth in spots untouched by grazing.

spiel /spil/, *v. Obs.* Also **speel.** [Var. of Br. dial. and slang *speel* to move fast, esp. to make off: see OEDS *speel, v.*[2]] *intr.* To gallop.

1892 *Truth* (Sydney) 27 Mar. 1/6, I heard the throaty Hebrew shriek as past the post they spieled... If you ask me in strict confidence, I think that sheeny's mad. **1895** A.B. PATERSON *Man from Snowy River* 14 If Pardon don't spiel like tarnation And win the next heat. **1895** B. MORANT *Poetry* (1980) 27 No grass this side the Border-fence! and all the mulga's dead! The horses for a day or two will have to spiel ahead. **1905** A.B. PATERSON *Old Bush Songs* 56 No more shall we muster the river for fats, Or spiel on the Fifteen-mile plain. **1918** J.A. PHILP *Jingles that Jangle* 51 It looked good for him, as in the lead he spieled along.

Hence **spieling** *ppl. a.*

1899 J. BRADSHAW *Quirindi Bank Robbery* 42 We reached Tamworth after walking at a speeling rate just in time for tea.

spieler /ˈspilə/. Also **speeler, speiler, speler.** [Orig. U.S. and now chiefly Austral.: see OED(S.] One who engages in sharp practice; a swindler, orig. a card sharper (see quot. 1886).

1879 *Truth* (Sydney) 23 Dec. 5/4 Formerly a café keeper .. now a professional 'spieler'. **1880** *Bulletin* (Sydney) 12 June 20/2 The gambling mania has reached Auckland. Michael Gallagher, who keeps a 'sporting' house in that town, has been fined in the Police Court for allowing professional 'speelers' to play in his house. **1886** *Adelaide Observer* 29 May 41/5 A speler is known as a man that can do without working, and who travels from meeting to meeting with a pack of cards or a dice-box in his hand. To offer him work would be to take a liberty quite unwarranted. They are independent men; they have no need to work; they live by their wits, and I dare say make a good living at their calling. **1896** N. GOULD *Town & Bush* 222 The 'speilers' cluster together when the favourite wins, and the first backer of the winner, when he asks for his money, is politely told to wait, as an objection is about to be lodged. **1901** *Truth* (Sydney) 21 Apr. 4/7 These flash bodegas are principally patronised by capable spielers, who fleece the 'highly respectable' old gentlemen who wander thither. **1907** *Ibid.* 7 Apr. 10/6 The white man who comes to the Territory .. usually belongs to the shifty class; not infrequently he is a spieler. **1916** R. MACKAY *Recoll. Early Gippsland Goldfields* 67 Have you ever watched a game of poker, where two out of the seven players were spielers. **1926** S.F. CASHMORE *N. Coast Verses* 63 First night a sheila picked me up, Next day a spieler took me down. **1944** K.S. PRICHARD *Potch & Colour* 23 One of these broken-down aristocrat spielers; but a witty devil. **1956** A.C.C. LOCK *Tropical Tapestry* 290 It was now a haven for spivs, spielers, black marketeers, dope pedlars, hotel racketeers and swindlers. **1973** H. LEWIS *Crow on Barbed Wire Fence* 131 If some sharp spieler tried to jump his train he'd chuck him off over a bridge. **1984** W.W. AMMON et al. *Working Lives* 57, I wouldn't even risk cashing her with you mob of spielers around.

spieling, *vbl. n. Obs.* [f. *spiel* to gamble: see OEDS *v.*] The activity of card-sharping; swindling. Also as *ppl. a.*

[N.Z. **1869** *Auckland Punch* 153, I twigged you on your speeling lay.] **1879** *Truth* (Sydney) 23 Dec. 5/4 A gambling den of the most dangerous character, because the 'spieling' is to a great extent a howling swindle and a pitfall for 'mugs'. **1887** *Boomerang* (Brisbane) 10 Dec. 10/4 The 'spieling' fraternity are in considerable force in Brisbane just now, doubtless anticipating a harvest at the coming race meeting. **1903** J. MARSHALL *Battling for Gold* 33, I could see that the 'speiling' or rough fraternity, which at that time was very strong on the goldfields, was largely represented in the crowd, and trouble was sure to ensue. **1911** *Truth* (Sydney) 26 Mar. 4/3 The spieling sharks of the betting shops .. unlawfully flourish. **1973** J. MURRAY *Larrikins* 115 'The Juvenile Spieler' the *Bird o' Freedom* called him... He mostly lives by small spieling, sneak thieving, or upon the earnings of some girl, most likely younger than himself.

spike-rush. [U.S. *spike rush* any sedge of the genus *Eleocharis* in which the flowers grow in dense spikes.] Any of the chiefly perennial sedges of the genus *Eleocharis* (fam. Cyperaceae) of all States and elsewhere.

1909 F.M. BAILEY *Comprehensive Catal. Qld. Plants* (ed. 2) 591 *Heleocharis* (Eleocharis) .. Spike Rush. **1930** A.J. EWART *Flora Vic.* 223 *H[eleocharis] acuta* .. Common Spike-rush. A rhizomic perennial, 6 to 18 inches high. **1976** *Reader's Digest Compl. Bk. Austral. Birds* 93 The geese feed on the bulbs of spike-rushes, which they dig up from the bare, sun-baked mud of the plains, with their strong, hooked bills. **1985** I. & T. DONALDSON *Seeing First Australs.* 192 The spike-rush, *Eleocharis dulcis* .. whose sweet nutty corms are one of the chief foods of the Anbarra people.

spikey. [See quot. 1951.] Any of several fish, incl. the *long-spined flathead* (see LONG 2).

1906 D.G. STEAD *Fishes of Aust.* 198 The fish is known to the fishermen of Coogee by the .. name of 'Spikey'. .. It is of a light sandy colour, spotted over with small, brilliant, red or vermilion spots. **1951** T.C. ROUGHLEY *Fish & Fisheries Aust.* 138 The long-spined flathead has received its name from the prominence of a preopercular spine on each side of the head; this is very sharp and has earned for the fish the name of 'spikey'. **1986** *Canberra Chron.* 29 Jan. 19/2 Close inshore, all the way down past the Murrah, there are millions of spikeys with just an odd good fish among them.

spill. *Politics.* The vacating of other offices in a cabinet, party, etc., after one important change of office.

1956 J.T. LANG *I Remember* 311 There had to be an annual election of leader. That made it inevitable that some members would intrigue against the leader hoping for a Cabinet spill. **1973** L. OAKES *Whitlam PM* 74 In the Caucus, Whitlam demonstrated his anti-Grouper credentials when, in April, he moved for a 'spill' of all party offices except those of the leader and Caucus secretary. **1975** *Austral.* (Sydney) 18 Mar. 1/3 It will be left to Mr Fraser's supporters to force the issue and move against Mr Snedden through either a spill of leadership positions or a motion of no confidence. **1982** *Canberra Times* 9 July 1/6 He would not say whether he would resign at the meeting and stand for re-election, or whether there would be a 'spill', a declaration that all 'shadow ministries' were vacant. **1985** *Austral. Financial Rev.* (Sydney) 26 July 2/2 So suspicious is each of the other and so intense is Mr Howard's desire for the top job that a 'spill' for the leadership initiated by either man is seen by senior Liberals as highly likely.

spin, *n.*[1]

1. *Two-up.* The act of tossing the coins in the air.

1919 C.H. THORP *Handful of Ausseys* 247 All set 'n away she goes—a fair spin an' a good 'un; an' it's—'eads. **1925** A. WRIGHT *Boy from Bullarah* 18 From all around the ring head backers rose to gather in their winnings, and stake again on the next spin. **1971** G. MORGAN *We are borne On* 87 There were thousands of troops scattered around and a big two-up school operated day and night, so I adjourned with my five pounds to the school to try my luck. In my first two spins I lost three pounds.

2. With qualifying word: a (good, bad, rough, etc.) run of luck.

1917 W.V. WRIGHT Diary 10 Jan., Out of the line at last, by jove she's been a crook spin this trip. **1919** W.H. DOWNING *Digger Dialects* 47 *Spin*, see *Trot* [an experience (e.g., 'a rough trot'; 'a bad time').]. **1924** A.W. BAZLEY et al. Gloss. Slang A.I.F. 27 (typescript) *Spin* (a rough), a bad time. From 'two up'... It is applicable to the general experience of life. **1927** *R. Comm. Moving Picture Industry* 989, I endeavoured to assist him, as I would any other man who had had a 'rough spin', and was a stranger in a strange land. **1935** K.L. SMITH *Sky Pilot Arnhem Land* 167 This is the end. But I've had a fair spin and nothing to complain of. **1939** I.L. IDRIESS *Cyaniding for Gold* 86 Jim Albury and his mate on the Bowman River near Gloucester were suffering a bad spin. **1949** P.A. JACOBS *Lawyer Tells* 114 They insisted on a fresh race, from which Adrienne was to be excluded. This time, .. Adrienne's mother, thinking that her daughter had not had a fair spin, joined in the race and .. won in a canter. **1950** K.S. PRICHARD *Winged Seeds* 368 She married the wrong man, she says, and has had a crook spin ever since. **1958** G. CASEY *Snowball* 246 I've given her a rough spin, since them days. Got too big fer me boots, I s'pose. **1966** A. HOPGOOD *Private Yuk Objects* Pref., I'm an Australian, mate. .. That means I can have three meals a day, watch the telly every night, go to the footy or the races .. and generally get a good spin out of life. **1974** D. O'GRADY *Deschooling Kevin Carew* 107 He knew Kevin had had a rough spin since the withdrawal of the Education Department scholarship.

spin, *n.*[2] Abbrev. of SPINNAKER. Also *attrib.*

1941 *Coast to Coast* 225 'How'd you go at the two-up?' I asked. 'Aw, I got a spin,' said Tom... 'I was holdin' a score but I dropped most of it.' **1944** *Troppo Tribune* (Mataranka) 29 May 1 Five pounds is a 'spin'. **1953** B. SUTTON *Snow & Me* (1966) 5 It would be easier to get out of Chief Little Wolf's Indian deathlock than to get a spin out of Snow. **1955** *Bulletin* (Sydney) 12 Oct. 13/2 He was a 'spin-a-day' man temporarily employed to cut wood for the station. **1963** J. DUFFY *Outsville Pub* 10 A quick check-up located two spins in his hip pocket, and close on a quid in change besides... He could eat, and smoke and get a long way on nearly eleven quid. **1970** N. KEESING *Transition* 202, I knew that a spin was a five-pound note, or ten dollars. **1975** M.B. ROBERTS *King of Con Men* 69 He would thump the bench .. and bark, 'Fined five pounds'... Throughout the length and breadth of Australia he was known as 'Spin McGee'—'spin' being the slang term for £5. **1977** P. MOTHERWELL *Mr Bastard* 40 The kid hands him the spin. 'Jesus Christ! Not another one—I've had nothing but spins and bricks all day.'

spin, *v. Two-up.*

1. *trans.* To toss (the coins) into the air so that they revolve. Also *absol.*, and with the result of the toss as obj.

1913 *Bulletin* (Sydney) 30 Jan. 16/1 Binghi is the boss person of a two-up ring... As an expert spinner .. few of the thousands of habitual 'swi-up' players I have seen can spin decently without violently swinging the arm. **1916** *Battery Herald: Jrnl. 14th Field Artillery* 9 Oct. 8 Spinning tails about six times in succession. **1941** E. BAUME *I lived These Yrs.* 122, I have often seen at the two-up schools in Sydney, in the old days, five and six hundred pounds 'spun' for on one turn of the coins. **1948** *Khaki Bush & Bigotry* (1968) 30 I'll spin 'em for a quid... Get set in the guts... Come on now.

2. *intr.* With **out**: to lose the right to continue as spinner.

1951 E. LAMBERT *Twenty Thousand Thieves* 234 'It's rainin' heads.' 'Well, what are we waiting for?' 'He'll spin out in a minute. He's done four straight.' **1971** G. MORGAN *We are borne On* 87 Before I left I had headed the pennies fifteen consecutive times and spun out for practically nothing, as I could not get set. **1972** J. O'GRADY *It's your Shout, Mate!* 25 After two more spinners had 'spun out', the keeper announced, 'We've got a guest spinner'.

spinach. [Transf. use of *spinach* the cultivated plant *Spinacia oleracea*.] *Wild spinach*, see WILD 1.

1770 J. BANKS *Endeavour Jrnl.* (1962) II. 114 Spinage (*Tetragonia cornuta*). **1788** D. COLLINS *Acct. Eng. Colony N.S.W.* (1798) I. 7 Every species of esculent plants that could be found in the country were procured... Wild celery, spinach, and parsley, fortunately grew in abundance about the settlement. **1849** C. STURT *Narr. Exped. Central Aust.* I. 118 Those next the stream had numerous herbs, as spinach, indigoferae clover etc. **1872** MRS E. MILLETT *Austral. Parsonage* 101 The finest kind of prickly-seeded spinach grew spontaneously as a weed in our glebe... The plant was spoken of with opprobrium as 'that horrid double gee'. **1923** J. ARMOUR *Spell of Inland* 10 We have different varieties of creepers, wild melons, bindaii, spinach, and other herbs that cattle eat.

spine-bash, *n.* [See next.] A rest; a sleep; an act of loafing. Formerly also as **spine drill, hour, job.**

1940 *First Post: Mag. 2/1st Battalion A.I.F.* Sept. 11 The science of *spine drill* has been mastered by four Section. **1945** *Atebrin Advocate: Mag. 2/4 Austral. Armoured Regiment* Jan. 3 You blokes can work if you want to... It's a spine job for me. **1949** *Gremlin Jottings* (Canberra) Nov. 1 An hour when respectable people are still getting some 'spine hours' up. **1968** S. GORE *Holy Smoke* 52 All except Jonah. And he's so crook in the guts that he's down at the blunt end o' the boat havin' a spine-bash. **1976** *Tracks we Travel* 17 Old Arty had struggled awake after his spine bash.

spine-bash, *v. intr.* To rest; to loaf. Freq. as *vbl. n.*

1941 *Argus* (Melbourne) 15 Nov. (Week-End Mag.) 1/4 *Spine-bashing*, having a rest; loafing. **1944** J.D. PORTER *Our Fertile North* 75 'Spine-bashing' had by now become an accepted item in the day's doings, and the few hours' rest after the mid-day meal proved most beneficial. **1947** *Bulletin* (Sydney) 17 Dec. 36/1 We were spinebashing in the tent one wet afternoon. **1958** R. ROBINSON *Black-Feller White-Feller* 9 They would rather have stayed in the camp to spine-bash or go down to the swy game. **1963** J. O'GRADY *Things they do to You* 32 He spent many hours—when other blokes were spine-bashing—teaching me. **1965** K. TENNANT *Summer's Tales* 58 We did some spine-bashing and after some steak-and-eggs the boys began to revive. **1973** R. ROBINSON *Drift of Things* 266 Don't give way to going 'Troppo', as most of the fellows do. In your spare time, instead of lying on your bed and just 'spine-bashing', go out for walks. **1977** S. LOCKE ELLIOTT *Water under Bridge* 232 So what you did to get back at them was to catch them having a 'smoko' on duty or spine bashing over at the canteen and put them on an emu parade. **1983** B. DAWE *Over here, Harv!* 133, I was doing a bit of spine-bashing on the morning of the twenty-fifth of April, thinking with gratitude of all those Diggers who gave their lives so I could go on bludging furiously every Anzac Day.

Hence **spine-basher** *n.*

1945 'MASTER-SARG' *Yank discovers Aust.* 75 'A spine basher'—lazy or heavy sleeper. **1972** A. CHIPPER *Aussie Swearers Guide* 40 *Layabout*, self-explanatory description of someone expert in work evasion. (A pithy alternative, less frequently used, is *spine basher*.) **1976** *Sydney Morning Herald* 20 Mar. 14 The elbow-benders, spine-bashers, eternal babblers keep one ear to the loud-speakers, an ear to the ground.

spinebill. [See quot. 1909.] Either of two small honeyeaters of the genus *Acanthorhynchus*, *A. tenuirostris* (see *eastern spinebill* EASTERN 2), and *A. superciliosus* of s.w. W.A.; COBBLER'S AWL. Also **spine-billed honeyeater,** and *attrib.*

1843 J. GOULD *Birds of Aust.* (1848) IV. Pl. 61, *Acanthorhynchus tenuirostris* .. Spine-bill, Colonists of New South Wales. **1887** *Illustr. Austral. News* (Melbourne) 21 Dec. 218/1 The honey-eaters seen were nearly all of Tasmanian origin... Only the New Holland and spine bill honey-eaters resemble the Victorian. **1902** *Emu* II. 14 The Spinebill (*Acanthorynchus tenuirostris*) loves to pry into the flowers of the ironbarks or mistletoe. **1903** *Ibid.* 164 Spine-billed Honey-eater... Not uncommon in the forest. **1909** G. SMITH *Naturalist in Tas.* 63 Another peculiar Honey-eater, characterized by its exceedingly long curved bill and its chocolate breast, is the Spine Bill. **1929** A.H. CHISHOLM *Birds & Green Places* 118 Once a spine-billed honeyeater came into the nesting-tree. **1939** J. GALBRAITH *Garden in Valley* (1985) 64 A quick and slender bird, rufous and black and white, with slate grey wings... A swift fluttering, and there were two birds among the blossoms... The spinebills had come to their kingdom. **1980** J. WOLFE *End of Pricklystick* 222, I can hear the long, piping call of the Spinebills in the Albizzia tree.

spine drill (hour, job): see SPINE-BASH *n.*

spine-tailed, *a.* Used as a distinguishing epithet in the names of birds: **spine-tailed log-runner,** see LOG-RUNNER 2; **swift,** the bird *Hirundapus caudacutus*, which breeds in Asia and migrates southward to e. Aust. in summer (see quot. 1986).

[**1842** J. GOULD *Birds of Aust.* (1848) II. Pl. 10, The Spine-tailed Swallow may frequently be seen, either singly or in pairs, sweeping up the gullies or flying with immense rapidity just above the tops of the trees.] **1856** H.B. STONEY *Vic.* 212 Of seven Australian swallows, one, the spine-tailed swift, the largest known member of the family is occasionally seen about Sydney. **1903** *Emu* II. 171 This is the first autumn in which the Spine-tailed Swifts (*Chaetura caudata*) have been so scarce. **1922** *Bulletin* (Sydney) 12 Jan. 20/1 It is difficult even to estimate the time taken by certain birds that breed in the Far North to reach Australia, which is their summer restaurant. The pilgrims include the .. spine-tailed swift, etc. **1965** *Austral. Encycl.* VIII. 381 The spine-tailed swift, about 8 inches in length, is greenish on the wings, brown on the back, and white on the throat. **1986** *Canberra Times* 22 Jan. 17/2 These are white-throated needletails (also known as spine-tailed swifts) slicing through the air at up to 130 km/h as they hunt for insects... The tiny, needle-like protrusions on the tail which give it its common name are barely visible except at very close range. They are really modified feathers and are thought to act as a prop when the bird clings to vertical surfaces.

spinifex. [The plant genus *Spinifex* was named by Swedish naturalist Carl von Linné (Linnaeus) (*Mantissa Plantarum* (1771) II. 163), f. mod. L. *spina* spine + *-fex* maker, f. *facere* to make.]

1. a. Any of many tussocky, often spiny, perennial grasses of the genera *Triodia* and *Plectrachne* (both fam. Poaceae), chiefly of arid and semi-arid Aust., as *Triodia basedowii, T. irritans*, and *T. pungens*; PORCUPINE GRASS 1. **b.** The similar *Zygochloa paradoxa* (fam. Poaceae; formerly *Spinifex paradoxus*) of arid and semi-arid Aust. **c.** (Occas.) a prostrate grass of the genus *Spinifex* (fam. Poaceae), occurring on coastal sand dunes in Aust., and elsewhere. **d.** With distinguishing epithet, as **buck, old man:** see under first element. **e.** *ellipt., spinifex country*. Also *attrib.*

1825 B. FIELD *Geogr. Mem. N.S.W.* 285 This part of the country is a universal mass of rocks, heaped one upon the other, and the interstices filled with spinifex, a prickly useless grass, of a powerfully aromatic smell. **1841** G. GREY *Jrnls. Two Exped. N.-W. & W.A.* I. 95 The soil beneath our feet was sandy, and thickly clothed with spinifex (a prickly grass). **1856** A.C. & F.T. GREGORY *Jrnls. Austral. Explorations* 20 Jan. (1884) 12 The country . . is poor and stony, producing little besides a sharp grass triodia—this is the spinifex of some Australian explorers. **1882** *Illustr. Austral. News* (Melbourne) 25 Jan. 10/3 To adequately describe spinifex is hard. Let the reader imagine a thousand knitting needles thrown into a confused kind of tangle, with all the points sticking outwards. **1916** *Emu* XV. 157 Some of the more rounded hills were covered in porcupine-bush (*Triodia*). This prickly plant is more often, and incorrectly, called 'spinifex'. **1927** M. DORNEY *Adventurous Honeymoon* 22 Spinifex is very hardy and nearly always green. It grows in distinctly separated clumps, the leaves (if one can call them such) being like long slender straws with a needle-like point at the end of each. **1935** I.L. IDRIESS *Man Tracks* 23 They returned . . with news from the spinifex natives of the tracks of a white man. **1958** F.B. VICKERS *Though Poppies Grow* 17 If we'd wanted to be on our own we'd have stayed out in the spinifex. **1966** M. BROWN *Jimberi Track* 87 Along comes a spinifex 'bloke' from Alice Springs. **1979** L.G. PLATT *Survival 3* 26 He busied himself collecting clumps of spinifex. . . This resin-filled scrub, he'd been told, was the natives' favourite smoke-signal material. **1981** D. LEVITT *Plants & People* 144 One man reported that he had recently treated sores on his daughter's body using Spinifex [*sc. Spinifex longifolius*]. **1983** *Weekend Austral.* (Sydney) 8 Oct. 9/1 The Outback—that festering scab of shimmering salt lakes, red sands freckled with wiry spinifex, and once-great mountain chains ground down by time into relic ridges.

2. Comb. (chiefly in sense 1 a.): **spinifex country, farm, grass, plain.**

1875 J. FORREST *Explorations in Aust.* 212 Most miserable **spinifex country** all day. **1892** *Bulletin* (Sydney) 23 Apr. 17/2 For a man to wander away from camp in the Never-Never spinifex country and remain away for hours, is a most uncanny thing. **1911** *Huon Times* (Franklin) 19 July 4/1 The lameness of the camels is . . due probably to their having to cross wide tracts of spinifex country. **1936** Austral. Archives CRS F1 36/577, I understand that the country . . is not pastoral country, and that much of it is of the type seen between Cockatoo Creek and the Granites, viz: 'Spinifex' country. **1962** *N. Austral. Monthly* Feb. 23 Have found good water supplies out in spinifex country, agreeing with the 'old hands' who say every cattle station should have some spinifex country. **1936** C.T. MADIGAN *Central Aust.* 248 There was nothing else of any value to be seen on the whole field; the leases were very aptly called '**spinifex farms**'. **1972** *Austral. Lapidary Mag.* Sept. 10/2 The result was excess publicity by the newspapers, and so the rush to peg miles of the area, locally called the 'Spinifex Farms'. **1863** J. DAVIS *Tracks of McKinlay* 41 The ever-recurring **spinifex grass** indicated its accompanying poor soil. **1895** *Trans. & Proc. R. Soc. S.A.* (1896) XVI. 256 They constantly burn large patches of the 'spinifex' grass, which is one of the most easily ignited substances, green or dry. **1896** B. SPENCER *Rep. Horn Sci. Exped. Central Aust.* I. 34 On the flats surrounding the rivers were low lying shrubs and clumps of Spinifex grass. [*Note*] That is the true Spinifex grass (*Spinifex paradoxus*) and not the Porcupine grass (*Triodia* sp.) which is often but erroneously, spoken of as Spinifex. **1908** W.A. Archives 2864A/5, At night . . having scooped a hole in the ground for your hip and filled it with spinifex grass or perhaps having made a whole bed of spinifex you sleep comfortably enough under the sky. **1934** C. SAYCE *Comboman* 32 A narrow slit all round admitted a certain amount of light under the heavy thatch of spinifex-grass. **1950** C.E. GOODE *Yarns of Yilgarn* 79 Boiling our billy on a tuft of resinous spinifex grass. **1891** W.H. TIETKENS *Jrnl. Central Austral. Exploring Exped.* 40 The country opened out into **spinifex plains** with an occasional sandhill. **1955** A. UPFIELD *Cake in Hat Box* 55 Crossed this spinifex plain to reach that rock. **1965** L. WALKER *Other Girl* 52 A couple of stranded girls on a dirt track a hundred miles out on a spinifex plain. **1978** D. STUART *Wedgetail View* 57 Spinifex plains, wind-grass plains, mulga country.

3. Special Comb.: **spinifex gum,** a resin obtained from spinifex (sense 1 a.), esp. *Triodia pungens*, traditionally used in hafting stone tools.

1898 D.W. CARNEGIE *Spinifex & Sand* 245 Two neat articles were fashioned by stringing together red beans set in spinifex gum. **1936** C. CHEWINGS *Back in Stone Age* 42 The so-called spinifex gum is a resin that exudes from the stems of a species of spinifex . . that grows on or around the base of rocky ranges.

4. In the names of animals occurring in spinifex country: **spinifex parrot,** either of two parrots, NIGHT PARROT and PRINCESS PARROT; **pigeon,** the predom. brown, crested pigeon *Petrophassa plumifera* of central, n., and n.w. Aust.; *plumed pigeon*, see PLUMED; **rat** (or **wallaby**), a hare-wallaby, esp. *Lagorchestes hirsutus*, formerly widespread in arid and semi-arid Aust.; **snake,** a snake or snake-like lizard occurring in spinifex country.

1917 *Bulletin* (Sydney) 6 Dec. 22/1 Most notable bird voices are those of . . myrlumbing (night or **spinifex parrot**) [etc.]. **1935** G. MCIVER *Drover's Odyssey* 175 This desolate tract of country was then the home of the beautiful spinifex parrot. . . The varied tints and brilliance of its plumage were wonderful. **1898** D.W. CARNEGIE *Spinifex & Sand* 303 The prettiest of all the birds is a little plump, quail-like rock- or **spinifex-pigeon**, a dear little shiny, brown fellow with a tuft on his head. **1947** W.E. HARNEY *Brimming Billabongs* p. xvi, Like a spinifex pigeon that rises quickly from its cover, he carried on with his story. **1966** *Meanjin* 35 The spinifex still showed a tinge of green and looked like millions of sleek pin-cushions neatly arranged by some over-industrious housewife. In and out of them strutted the perfectly camouflaged 'spinifex pigeons', as yet unaware of man as an enemy. **1977** W.A. WINTER-IRVING *Bush Stories* 6, I saw some little spinifex pigeons running like large brown mice, each one with a tiny crest of feathers on its head and chestnut brown feathers on its wings. **1982** H.J. FRITH *Pigeons & Doves Aust.* 263 The name 'Spinifex Pigeon' implies a close association with the spinifex grasses *Triodia* and *Plectrachne*. This is justified but the birds are not strictly confined to spinifex nor are they found in all places where those grasses grow. **1895** [**spinifex rat**] *Trans. & Proc. R. Soc. S.A.* (1896) XVI. 240 The Blyth Range, Barrow Range, and Victoria Desert tribes inhabit 'spinifex country' where subsistence is difficult to maintain, and but for the numerously-occurring *Largochestes hirsutus* commonly called 'Spinifex-Wallaby' . . it would probably be impossible for them to live in such desolate districts. **1898** D.W. CARNEGIE *Spinifex & Sand* 179 The desert silence unbroken by any animal life, excepting always the ubiquitous spinifex rat. A pretty little fellow this, as he hops along on his long hind legs, bounding over the prickly stools like an animated football with a tail. **1903** H. BASEDOW *Jrnl. Govt. N.-W. Exped.* 4 May (1914) 89 The sandy mulga flats are followed by a sandy loam bearing giant saltbush in which the spinifex wallaby or 'paddy melon' (*Largochestes hirsutus*) is plentiful. **1935** —— *Knights of Boomerang* 210 He has tricked us and has made us appear as miserable spinifex-wallabies fallen to his snare. **1937** M. TERRY *Sand & Sun* 95 Six bucks had made a fire to cook some spinifex rats. **1983** R. STRAHAN *Compl. Bk. Austral. Mammals* 199 The Rufous Hare-Wallaby was once common . . particularly in the spinifex hummock grasslands of the sand plain and sand dune deserts. Aborigines hunted it for food and early explorers commented on the large numbers of 'spinifex rats' flushed from cover. **1955** F.B. VICKERS *Mirage* (1958) 155 A **spinifex snake** slid away. **1984** W.W. AMMONR et al. *Working Lives* 180 There . . was a metre-long green spinifex snake. . . (Such snakes are deadly poisonous and the venom takes effect very quickly.).

spinnaker. [Fig. use of *spinnaker* a large sail.] A five-pound note; the sum of five pounds. See also SPIN *n.*[2]

1898 *Bulletin* (Sydney) 1 Oct. 14/3 A few more W.Q. slang words . . £5 is a ' spinnaker'. **1941** S.J. BAKER *Pop. Dict. Austral. Slang* 70 *Spinnaker*, £5. **1955** N. PULLIAM *I traveled Lonely Land* 152 I'll bet the first Aussie taker a couple of spinnakers the Snowy Mountains dream comes true.

spinner. *Two-up.*

a. The player who tosses the coins.

1911 L. STONE *Jonah* 215 The spinner handed his stake of five shillings to the boxer, who cried, 'Fair go!' **1918** *Aussie: Austral. Soldiers' Mag.* Dec. 3/1 They were playing the good old game and a big dope they called Snow was spinner. **1925** A. WRIGHT *Boy from Bullarah* 17 For a few moments the spinner stood waiting, while the players noisily made their wagers, and then again the voice of the ring-keeper rang out. 'Fair go! Set a quid.' **1943** J. BINNING *Target Area* 48 Granny is the best spinner I've ever seen. **1954** T. RONAN *Vision Splendid* 230 Before I bring the spinner in, have any of you head-backers got a bob or two to pay for my boot leather and Darcy's time and trouble? **1977** R. BEILBY *Gunner* 180 A two-up game proceeded intermittently, the ring-keeper's calls pealing faintly.

b. In the phr. **come in spinner,** the call which signals to the spinner that all bets have been placed and that it is time to toss the coins.

1943 *Troppo Tribune* (Mataranka) 12 Apr. 2 The old saying 'Come in spinner' is now amended. **1951** CUSACK & JAMES *Come in Spinner* 8 'A quid wanted,' he called. . . 'Right!' The voice rose jubilantly. 'Come in Spinner!' The rattle of coins sounded again. **1965** L. HAYLEN *Big Red* 101 Outside he could hear . . 'Come in Spinner.' The two-up game! **1977** R. BEILBY *Gunner* 182 Set inna centre, get set onna side! Come in, spinner!

spiny, *a.* Used as a distinguishing epithet in the names of flora and fauna: **spiny anteater,** ECHIDNA; **-cheeked honeyeater,** the predom. grey-brown honeyeater *Acanthagenys rufogularis* of mainland Aust., having spiny feathers from the bill to the cheek; **emex,** DOUBLE-GEE a.

1827 E. GRIFFITH tr. *Cuvier's Animal Kingdom* III. 263 The Echidnes . . otherwise **Spiny Ant-eaters.** **1861** 'OLD BUSHMAN' *Bush Wanderings* 54 We had a curious species of hedgehog, or ant-eater . . the *Echidna* or *Spiny Ant-eater* of naturalists. **1884** G. WIGHT *Qld.* 83 The ornithorhynchus or duck-billed platypus, and the echidna or so-called spiny anteater of the Australian region, although, like other mammals, they suckle their young, lay eggs like birds. **1900** *Bulletin* (Sydney) 20 Jan. 14/2 Next to the bandicoot and the belar-forest 'possum, as an Australian dainty, comes the spiny ant-eater. **1926** A.S. LE SOUEF et al. *Wild Animals Australasia* 370 The echidna, or, as it is very commonly called, the spiny ant-eater or 'porcupine', is widely spread over Tasmania, Australia, and New Guinea. **1955** N. PULLIAM *I traveled Lonely Land* 150 The sticky-tongued echidna, or spiny anteater—an interesting but not very attractive creature. **1984** E. ROLLS *Celebration of Senses* 141 A Spiny Anteater crossed the road, surprisingly tall and fast on the run. One usually sees them rolled into spiky, defensive balls. **1844** J. GOULD *Birds of Aust.* (1848) IV. Pl. 53, The **Spiny-cheeked Honey-eater** ranges very widely over the interior of Australia. **1896** B. SPENCER *Rep. Horn Sci. Exped. Central Aust.* II. 94 *Acanthogenys rufigularis* . . Spiny-cheeked Honey-eater[s] . . were scattered all through Central Australia, and unlike most Honey-eaters, were frequently found on the ground. **1929** A.H. CHISHOLM *Birds & Green Places* 47 The striped and spiny-cheeked honeyeaters, and the stately ground cuckoo-shrike. **1945** C. BARRETT *Austral. Bird Life* 161 Though its range is Australia-wide, the spiny-cheeked honeyeater . . cannot be regarded as a familiar bird. **1963** W.E. HARNEY *To Ayers Rock & Beyond* 79 The chanters sang about mythical trees, which were the ones the 'titjearra' (spiney-cheeked honey-eaters) rested on. **1970** D. STIVENS *Horse of Air* 137 Spiny-cheeked honeyeaters . . and singing honey-eaters . . were feeding among the isolated flowering bloodwoods. **1921** J. MATTHAMS *Rabbit Pest in Aust.* 255 **Spiny Emex,** three cornered jack, or Cat's Head, *Emex Australis*. **1930** A.J. EWART *Flora Vic.* 438 Spiny Emex. . . Widely spread in Victoria. . . The spiny fruits are said to be mechanically injurious to cattle, sheep, and fowls when swallowed. **1983** *Mercury* (Hobart) 2 June 12/5 Some Tasmanian sheep dogs could soon be wearing leather boots because of spiny emex, a noxious weed imported to Tasmania in seed wheat from New South Wales and South Australia.

spit, *n.* In the phr. **to go for the big spit:** see BIG 3 d.

spit, *v. trans.* In the phr. **to spit chips.**

a. To feel extreme thirst.

1901 *Bulletin Reciter* 108 While you're spitting chips like thunder .. And the streams of sweat near blind you. **1940** *Bulletin* (Sydney) 27 Mar. 17/1 But, though he's spittin' chips hisself, he nacherally shrank From anythin' to spoil that lovely thirst. **1946** A. MARSHALL *Tell us about Turkey, Jo* 142, I was spitting chips. God, I was dry!

b. To manifest extreme anger.

1947 J. MORRISON *Sailors belong Ships* 189 Old Mick Doyle's with them. He's spitting chips because they're not using sea water. **1954** P. GLADWIN *Long Beat Home* 17 It's enough to make you spit chips when you think of Sydney—movies and vaudeville comedies and a decent musician once in two years. **1968** S. GORE *Holy Smoke* 14 When he comes rushing up—spittin' chips, he's so mad—young Dave only lets fly with one shot outa his ging, and the big bloke's stonkered.

spitfire. The larva of a sawfly, esp. of the genus *Perga*, as *P. dorsalis*, a large dark larva which exudes a sticky greenish fluid when disturbed; SPITTER.

1920 M.N. & A.A. BREWSTER *Life Stories Austral. Insects* 110 Family Tenthredinidae (Sawflies)... The larvae of this group are better known than the adults... They may be seen in clusters on the leaves of *Eucalyptus*, and when disturbed, they turn up their tails and eject a greenish fluid, hence the children call them 'spitfires'. **1950** *Bulletin* (Sydney) 4 Oct. 12/4 At a very youthful age I learned the strengths and weaknesses in the armaments of the wogs in my life. Hornets were essentially 'in-fighters'; at long-range they were harmless. 'Spitfires', on the other hand, could get in their dirty work from a distance of anything up to 3 ft. **1984** *Canberra Times* 22 Sept. 11/1 The unpleasant habits of larvae of the steel-blue sawfly, or 'spitfires'... A sticky secretion from their mouths .. was high in eucalyptus oil and caused severe pain if it got into the eyes.

spitter. SPITFIRE.

1944 C. FENNER *Mostly Austral.* 153 They develop into very handsome sawflies... Schoolboys call them 'spitters', from their habit of waving their bodies when disturbed, and at the same time emitting a greenish, strong-smelling fluid from their mouths.

split, *v.*

1. *trans. Hist.* [Used elsewhere but of local significance.] To split (a log of wood) with an axe or similar tool, for use as rails, shingles, slabs, etc.; to split (rails, etc.) from a log. Also *absol.*

1793 D. COLLINS *Acct. Eng. Colony N.S.W.* (1798) I. 334 For splitting paling for fences, and bringing it in from the woods, they charged from one shilling and sixpence to two shillings and six-pence per hundred. **1805** *Sydney Gaz.* 22 Sept., An iron instrument used for shingle splitting. **1827** *Tasmanian* (Hobart) 21 June 2 We heard .. that two men had been speared by the natives... They were, I understand, either splitting timber, or sawing in the bush. **1833** *Launceston Advertiser* 18 Apr. 1 Any Person or Persons found trespassing on the Farm of the Undersigned .. by cutting or splitting timber or otherwise, will be prosecuted. **1845** *Portland Gaz.* 7 Oct. 4/1, I live at Portland, and am splitting wood for a settler: I have no license to split. **1864** J. ARMOUR *Diggings, Bush & Melbourne* 13 The hut was roomy; the walls were formed of hard-wood slabs, split like huge laths from logs. **1874** J.J. HALCOMBE *Emigrant & Heathen* 34 *Slab* huts are built on the same plan; only that slabs, split from the gum or iron-bark. ***c* 1886** *Few Lett. from Qld. Farmers* 5, I thought I could do better by .. splitting slabs, palings, shingles, and doing anything else that came my way. **1899** *Bulletin* (Sydney) 26 Aug. 16/1, I was splitting posts on the Darling and felled a belar. **1906** *Ibid.* 29 Mar. 14/3 A man cuts down a tree, and perhaps even splits it, and then finds .. that he can't get any 'squares' out of it. **1918** B. REYNOLDS *Dawn Asper* 114 'This is Crown land you're splitting on, isn't it?' remarked the new ranger. **1922** *Smith's Weekly* (Sydney) 25 Feb. 17/4 Splitting shingles on Brown Mountain .. I was chased along a ridge by a pack of dingoes. **1928** *Bulletin* (Sydney) 14 Mar. 23/1 While splitting in the bush I have several times come across a peculiar fungus.

2. *intr. Obs.* Of cattle: to separate from the main group. Freq. as *vbl. n.*

1848 H.W. HAYGARTH *Recoll. Bush Life* 63 The most frequent and troublesome habit is that of breaking off from the main body, or 'splitting'. **1859** W. BURROWS *Adventures Mounted Trooper* 136 Some cattle have a very bad habit of 'splitting'—that is scattering in different directions. **1888** W.T. PYKE *Bush Tales* 34 From original mismanagement they had become so wild, and had acquired so firm a habit of 'splitting', that to muster them was an impossibility.

split, *ppl. a. Hist.* [f. SPLIT *v.* 1.]

1. a. Of timber: that has undergone the process of splitting.

1797 D. COLLINS *Acct. Eng. Colony N.S.W.* (1802) II. 23 The miserable quarters which those gentlemen occupied were originally constructed only of split cabbage trees. **1827** P. CUNNINGHAM *Two Yrs. in N.S.W.* II. 170 Houses on the first establishment are either formed of wattle and plaster, or of split timber and plaster. **1836** J. BACKHOUSE *Extracts from Lett.* (1838) iii. 64 Living in a rough hut of split timber and bark. **1853** W. WESTGARTH *Vic.* 256 There were some stores or shops constructed of sawn boards .. and others of split slabs. **1856** S.C. BREES *How to farm & settle in Aust.* 58 Shafts are regularly 'slabbed' down the sides with small split boards of the stringy-bark tree. **1861** T. MCCOMBIE *Austral. Sketches* 123 The first object that attracts attention is the wool shed, a large building of slabs or rough split logs.

b. In the collocation **split stuff,** wood split as required for a particular purpose.

1836 *Cornwall Chron.* (Launceston) 1 Oct. 3 On the estate there are upwards of 70,000 bricks, and about 6,000 of split stuff for fencing. **1840** *S. Austral. Rec.* (London) 17 Oct. 251 A load of split stuff is required for the barn. **1847** A. HARRIS *Settlers & Convicts* (1953) 72, I came away, signed an agreement with him for a large quantity of split stuff; for as much indeed as, together with the setting it up as a fence, occupied me for twelve months. **1852** MRS C. MEREDITH *My Home in Tas.* I. 159 These consisted of what is here technically termed 'sawed stuff' and 'split stuff', by which is meant timber which is *sawn* into regular forms and thicknesses, as flooring boards, joists, battens, &c., and that which is *split* into 'posts and rails', slabs or palings. **1857** W. WESTGARTH *Vic. & Austral. Gold Mines* 35 From the stringy bark and other members of the forest is derived the 'split stuff', a large item of early colonial commerce. **1883** E.M. CURR *Recoll. Squatting Vic.* 96 A common bark building .. with a wool-press of split stuff outside, to match. **1978** M. WALKER *Pioneer Crafts Early Aust.* 34 The stringy-bark eucalypt was the major resource of 'split stuff', the contemporary term for the riven gum tree produce.

2. a. Made from wood that has undergone the process of splitting.

1828 *Tasmanian* (Hobart) 11 Apr. 2 Sawn timber of various sorts, and sizes, shingles, split posts [etc.]. **1859** *Bell's Life in Sydney* 18 June 1/1 Split posts of iron bark, blood tree, or other durable timber are substituted for saplings. **1897** L. LINDLEY-COWEN *W. Austral. Settler's Guide* 633, 150 split posts. **1900** *Bulletin* (Sydney) 21 July 15/1, I was .. putting up a line of split-fence on a N.S.W. station.

b. Esp. in the collocations **split paling, rail.**

1833 *Launceston Advertiser* 27 June 2, 1000 **split palings.** **1843** *Teetotal Advocate* (Launceston) 26 June 1/2 The usual supply of cedar, New Zealand pine, and deals, and a large quantity of split paling, shingles, and stringy bark sawn timber on hand. **1861** L.A. MEREDITH *Over Straits* 96 Some are roughly 'run up', of the split paling, whereof Tasmania has exported such immense quantities to Victoria. **1944** *Bulletin* (Sydney) 27 Sept. 13/3 Wending along a split-paling fence .. I heard a quick pattering of feet. **1838** *Southern Austral.* (Adelaide) 17 Nov. 4/2 Thirty Cottages or town lands, to be formed of **split rails** for uprights .. and for rafters, and for walls and roofs. **1852** *Four Colonies Aust.* 49 Fields are enclosed with split rails, morticed into upright posts. **1900** H. LAWSON *Over Sliprails* 95 There was .. a thin 'two-rail' (dignified with the adjective 'split-rail'—though rails and posts were mostly of saplings split in halves) running along the frontage. **1905** *Bulletin* (Sydney) 18 May 16/1 So he's planted neath the wattles .. And they fence his grave with split rails. **1932** *Ibid.* 3 Aug. 21/1 Some of the split-rail fences on station properties have stood so long that they have acquired an historic interest. **1951** G. FARWELL *Outside Track* 116 Lichen growing on split-rail fences gives them a curiously un-Australian air. **1975** J. DAVIS *Shortened Chair* 14 As a split-rail fence is weathered by sun, rain, frost.

splitter. *Hist.* [Spec. use of *splitter* one who or that which splits.]

1. One whose occupation is the splitting of rails, shingles, slabs, etc., from logs. Also with qualifying word, as **rail-splitter.**

1826 *Colonial Times* (Hobart) 24 June, To Fencers and Splitters. Wanted Four Men, who will Contract to Put up and complete One Thousand Rods of four-railed Fence, near Cape Portland. **1836** *Hobart Town Almanack* 73 The large and ugly gum trees .. had been left by the sawyers and splitters as not fit and proper materials. **1839** *Port Phillip Patriot* 5 Sept. 10/1 Sawyers and Splitters residing in the interior, have now an opportunity of consigning their labour for sale monthly or otherwise. **1847** G.F. ANGAS *Savage Life & Scenes* I. 44 The timber of the stringy bark is used for fencing, 'shingles' for roofing houses and other purposes. The men who prepare the wood are called 'splitters'. **1851** J.H. BURTON *Emigrant's Man.* ii. 82 Next the sawyers, are the 'splitters' .. important in a land where the limited household accommodation is dependent on very rough woodwork. **1869** J. MARTINEAU *Lett. from Aust.* 93 Splitters are at work felling .. and clearing away the underwood. **1888** W.T. PYKE *Bush Tales* 27 Many a splitter heedless when in search of monster trees has penetrated the forest's deep recesses and got 'bushed'. **1897** J.D. HENNESSY *New-Chum Farmer* 1 Hire yourself out to a dairyman, take a contract with a rail-splitter, sign articles with a cockatoo selector, but don't touch land without knowing something about it. **1912** *Bulletin* (Sydney) 4 Apr. 14/1 A splitter rarely gets more than one cut of rails out of a Monaro tree. **1917** *Ibid.* 11 Jan. 22/2 A rail-splitter killed a large diamond snake. **1928** R.H. CROLL *Open Road Vic.* 65 Way to get to the splitters' hut. **1928** M.E. FULLERTON *Austral. Bush* 36 When not a landowner himself, is a rail-splitter, a bark-stripper, a 'possum-trapper maybe. **1961** M. KIDDLE *Men of Yesterday* 67 Sawyers and splitters, or tiersman as they were often called, usually worked in pairs. They built themselves huts in the stringybark forests. **1978** M. WALKER *Pioneer Crafts Early Aust.* 37 The other major forest craftsmen, the splitters, worked as mates, in twos or threes, cleaving messmate, mountain ash or other suitable straight-grained trees. These men were known in England as 'rivers', in the early days of settlement as 'tiersmen' and then by the widely-used term 'splitters'.

2. A tree, the trunk of which will split cleanly.

1959 *Overland* xv. 25 All around were gaunt, bent and cross-grained old iron-barks... He said to me, 'Can you pick a splitter, lad?' **1960** *Bulletin* (Sydney) 16 Mar. 19/2 The paling-splitter worked and lived in noble solitude, and because only one stick in a hundred was a 'splitter' he ranged widely and vetted a lot of trees.

splitting, *ppl. a. Hist.* [f. SPLIT *v.* 1.]

1. Used in the process of splitting timber.

1838 *Austral. Mag.* (Sydney) 137, 2 Sets Splitting Wedges. **1839** *Tegg's Handbk. for Emigrants* 12 Grubbing tools. Splitting tools.

2. Of timber: able to be split.

1841 *Port Phillip Gaz.* 16 June 1 Valuable Sawing and Splitting Timber. **1851** J. HENDERSON *Excursions & Adventures N.S.W.* II. 43 It is expensive, and (where good splitting wood is not found) difficult, to construct fencing. **1879** 'AUSTRALIAN' *Adventures Qld.* 128 There was not much splitting timber on the east side of the site, within easy distance. **1907** *Bulletin* (Sydney) 10 Jan. 15/2 Given good-splitting ironbarks either of these men would cut 18 'eights' in a day.

spons. *Obs.* Abbrev. of 'spondulicks', money.

***c* 1879** *Ye Prodigal* (Sydney) 201 Those three happy men .. soon stood within the .. deserted house, mourning .. the departed 'spons' that they had lavished with such an utter contempt of riches upon those run-away husseys. **1884** *Austral. Tit-Bits* (Melbourne) 19 June 15/2 Edwards has at last got a match on in America, Frank H. Hart, the colored long distance walker, having put up the spons. **1892** 'P. WARUNG' *Tales Convict System* 29 Yer might hev giv'n him er knife, or spons. (money), or er smoke, don' yer see? **1916** *Truth* (Sydney) 21 May 12/7 Yes, Ethel she had shopping gone, And being minus spons, Nicked what her giglamps lit upon, A statuette of bronze.

spoof. [Of unknown origin.] Seminal fluid. Also as *v. intr.*, to ejaculate seminal fluid.

1916 *Runic Rhymes: Souvenir H.M.A.T. 'Runic'* July 3 Baa Baa Black hand Have you any oof? Yes sir, Yes sir All that we can spoof. **1981** P. RADLEY *Jack Rivers & Me* 61 The amount of spoof is more important to Eternity than the size of your cock.

Hence **spoofie** *n.*, a sexually attractive young woman.

1973 *Bulletin* (Sydney) 13 Jan. 27/1 'Spunk bubbles' or 'spoofies' the life savers call the nubile teenagers.

sport. [Chiefly Austral.: see OED(S *sb.*[1] 8 e.] A familiar form of address: cf. MATE 4.

1923 G.S. BEEBY *Concerning Ordinary People* 305 All right, sport. No offence meant. **1935** G. BLUNDEN *No More Reality* 344 'Take another jolt, sport,' said Clarrie with a grin. **1942** *Whizz* (Perth) Aug. 1 Pull your skull in, sport. **1944** *Aust. Week-End Bk.* 110 'Cheerio, Sport,' one of them shouted. **1956** *Overland* vii. 16 Sydney tram conductors have been ordered not to call passengers 'mate' or 'sport'. **1957** J. NAIRN *Out of Back Streets* 98 That's the first time I've heard one of the Chums calling anyone 'Sport'. You're getting more like a dinkum-di Australian every day. **1969** G. JOHNSTON *Clean Straw for Nothing* (1971) 135 Let's tackle the problem very seriously, sport. Let's you and me get properly pissed! **1977** S. LOCKE ELLIOTT *Water under Bridge* 196 She'll castrate you in the end, sport. **1982** H. KNORR *Private Viewing* 104 Don't get y' knickers in a knot, sport!

spot, *n.* [Spec. use of *spot* a small quantity; in Br. use usu. with *of*: see OED(S *sb.*[1] 7 d.]

1. A drink of alcoholic liquor, not necessarily small.

1922 H. LAWSON *Lett.* (1970) 235 There's no pub here. We can only gather .. and hope for demijohns from Narrandera (we call 'em 'jars' or 'spots'). **1924** *Bulletin* (Sydney) 22 May 24/3 There's a near-white youngster of 50-odd up in N. Queensland who almost keeps himself in 'spots' by winning bets from strangers over the strength of his teeth. **1927** A. WRIGHT *Squatter's Secret* 171 Have another spot, boss; you'll need it. **1932** H.V. HORDEN *Googlies* 44 There was a keg of beer as an incentive! This was duly consumed, and a few more 'spots' besides. **1934** 'E.N. SPEER' *Destiny* 236 There's that old cow Dan. Come here, Dan, and have a spot with an Old Contemptible! **1942** L. MANN *Go-Getter* 188 It's a time since I saw you, Chris. What about a spot? **1982** N. KEESING *Lily on Dustbin* 140 'A spot', meaning an alcoholic drink, seems by the 1980s to be a predominantly feminine usage... In the 1930s it was a vogue phrase used by both sexes and perhaps owing a good deal to P.G. Wodehouse.

2. The sum of one hundred pounds (or dollars).

1945 S.J. BAKER *Austral. Lang.* 109, £100—*spot.* **1950** *Austral. Police Jrnl.* Apr. 118 *Spot*, £100. **1967** *Kings Cross Whisper* (Sydney) xxxix. 4/5 *Spot*, one hundred dollars or pounds. **1976** S. WELLER *Bastards I have Met* 103 In gambling parlance, money-wise, 10's a 'brick', 100's a 'spot', 500's a 'monkey', etc. **1980** M. WILLIAMS *Dingo!* 83 'Let us go, and we'll give you a 'spot' each.' 'We couldn't do that,' he said. 'Anyway, what's a spot?' 'A hundred quid!' Dave told him. **1983** HIBBERD & HUTCHINSON *Barracker's Bible* 29 A 'spot' is $100.

spot, *v.* [Back-formation f. U.S. *spot-fire* a fire started by flying sparks at a distance from the main fire.] *intr.* Of a bushfire: to break out in patches ahead of the main fire (see quot. 1983). Also as *vbl. n.*

1978 LUKE & MCARTHUR *Bushfires in Aust.* 102 Spotting distances are abnormally high in some rough-barked eucalypts. **1981** *Bega District News* 27 Nov. 5/6 While Milliner was working at the top of the ridge the fire spotted across the gully and crossed the track. **1983** *Blue Mountains Gaz.* 3 Aug. 7/1 The program will also study the behaviour of bushfires, and the process of 'spotting' where firebrands are blown downwind to start new fires ahead of the main fire.

spotted, *ppl. a.* Used as a distinguishing epithet in the names of flora and fauna: **spotted bower-bird,** the spotted brown bird *Chlamydera maculata* of drier mainland Aust.; **ground-bird** (or **ground-thrush**), *spotted quail-thrush*; **gum,** any of several trees of the genus *Eucalyptus* (fam. Myrtaceae), esp. *E. maculata* of e. mainland Aust. and *E. henryi*, both having a colourful mottled trunk; the wood of the tree; **harrier,** the bird of prey *Circus assimilis*, widespread in mainland Aust. and occurring elsewhere, having blue-grey and chestnut plumage with white spots; **native cat,** *native cat* NATIVE *a.* 6 b.; **nightjar,** the nocturnal *Caprimulgus guttatus* of mainland Aust. (except the e. coastal region) and elsewhere, a mottled brown, grey and black bird with conspicuous white spots on the wing; **pardalote** (or **diamond bird**), the small bird *Pardalotus punctatus* of s.w. W.A. and e. Aust. incl. Tas.; see also *diamond sparrow* DIAMOND *n.*[1]; **quail-thrush,** the ground-dwelling thrush *Cinclosoma punctatum* of s.e Aust. incl. Tas., having quail-like plumage and shape; *spotted ground-bird*; **-sided finch,** *diamond firetail*, see DIAMOND *n.*[1]; **whiting,** the carnivorous marine fish *Sillaginodes punctatus* of s. Aust. incl. Tas., valued as food; KING GEORGE WHITING.

1841 J. GOULD *Birds of Aust.* (1848) IV. Pl. 8, *Chlamydera maculata.* **Spotted Bower-bird.** **1845** *Atlas* (Sydney) II. 318/3 The spotted bower-bird .. is .. exclusively an inhabitant of the interior of the country. **1901** K.L. PARKER in M. Muir *My Bush Bk.* (1982) 124 The spotted bower bird, whose voice anyone might well mistake for that of a cat. **1916** S.A. WHITE *In Far Northwest* 68 After a time a beautiful male spotted bower bird .. came. **1929** A.H. CHISHOLM *Birds & Green Places* 47 The talented spotted bower-bird. **1948** R. RAVEN-HART *Canoe in Aust.* 28 It was a bower-bird .. (the Spotted Bower-bird): 'They'll imitate anything.' **1962** MARSHALL & DRYSDALE *Journey among Men* 112 The spotted bower-bird .. gathers principally pale or reflecting objects—bleached bones and shells, and latterly, broken glass, bits of tin, thimbles, screws, spoons, forks, coins and the like. **1975** X. HERBERT *Poor Fellow my Country* 465 Red quandong cherries were the spotted bower birds' offering. **1840** [**spotted ground-bird**] J. GOULD *Birds of Aust.* (1848) IV. Pl. 4, The Spotted Ground-Thrush gives a decided preference to the summits of low stony hills and rocky gullies, particularly those covered with scrubs and grasses. **1899** *North-Western Advocate* (Devonport) 9 Aug. 2/3 A spotted ground thrush flew out. **1901** *Emu* I. 26 A nest containing eggs of the Spotted Ground Bird (*Cinclosoma punctatum*). **1945** C. BARRETT *Austral. Bird Life* 202 Quail-Thrushes or ground-birds (*Cinclosoma*) .. live 'close to the ground'... The spotted ground-bird (*C. punctatum*) inhabits southern Queensland, New South Wales, Victoria, South Australia, and Tasmania. **1824** *Austral.* (Sydney) 21 Oct. 2 He found a great deal of pine and iron bark; she oak, swamp oak, and a kind of **spotted gum.** **1826** J. ATKINSON *Acct. Agric. & Grazing N.S.W.* 15 *Spotted Gum.*—Found in abundance about Shoal Haven and Jervis's Bay. **1844** L. LEICHHARDT *Jrnl. Overland Exped. Aust.* 22 Oct. (1847) 20 Spotted-gum and Ironbark formed the forest. **1880** *Proc. Linnean Soc. N.S.W.* V. 452 *E. maculata* .. or 'The Spotted Gum', is a fine tree rising to 100 feet and upwards, and sometimes 80 or 90 feet without a branch. **1891** *Ibid.* VI. 408 *Eucalyptus goniocalyx* .. usually known as 'Spotted Gum' in Victoria, but not to be confused with the common N.S.W. 'Spotted Gum' (*E. maculata*). **1904** J.H. MAIDEN *Notes on Commercial Timbers N.S.W.* 13 Spotted gum .. is a smooth-barked tree, which has blotches of a whitish colour on the bark, owing to the outer layer of bark peeling off in patches. **1911** E.J. BRADY *King's Caravan* 230 He knew by long experience .. that cabbage gum makes good felloes and spotted gum good shafts. **1935** DAVISON & NICHOLLS *Blue Coast Caravan* 26 There were red flowering bottle-brushes .. with young spotted gums... Their trunks and limbs .. were dappled mauve and cream and green. **1955** N. PULLIAM *I traveled Lonely Land* 168 There are silver-leafed ironbarks .. and spotted gums .. which are prized for their resistance to the voracious ants. **1985** *Canberra Times* 23 Jan. 18/2 A mud-brick house among the spotted gums and ironbarks. **1898** E.E. MORRIS *Austral Eng.* 193 Harrier .. English bird-name .. assigned .. in Australia to *C[ircus] assimilis* .. called **Spotted Harrier.** **1902** *Emu* II. 10 The Spotted Harrier (*Circus jardinii*) .. preferring for its domain a patch of reed beds. **1945** C. BARRETT *Austral. Bird Life* 39 The spotted harrier .. frequents plains and open country generally. **1984** E. ROLLS *Celebration of Senses* 20 The big Spotted Harrier, a handsome blue-grey and chestnut, that flies slow, metre-high transects up and down our paddocks, causes little panic. **1933** C.W. PECK *Austral. Legends* (ed. 2) 225 The movement of .. the **spotted native cat** and the wallaroo. **1962** B.W. LEAKE *Eastern Wheatbelt Wildlife* 17 Australia itself is very free of carnivorous animals, and except for the dingo and spotted native cat, there are only odd very small mouse like creatures. **1980** G. ELLIS *Hey Doc, me Mate's Sick!* 82 Coen has an abundance of the spotted native cats (*Dasyurus*—not pussycats) and it was not uncommon for us to hear the lid of a trap shutting in the night and find a trapped native cat in the morning. **1896** B. SPENCER *Rep. Horn Sci. Exped. Central Aust.* II. 108 *Eurostopodus guttatus.* **Spotted Nightjar** .. I had hoped of securing .. but was disappointed. **1933** F.E. BAUME *Tragedy Track* 103 Rogers, who explored the district in 1911, gives the following list of native birds .. spotted night jar [etc.]. **1964** M. SHARLAND *Territory of Birds* 84 Spotted Nightjars were as thick as moths around a candle, their eyes gleaming like little pink lights as they squatted on the road. **1984** E. ROLLS *Celebration of Senses* 76 A Spotted Nightjar that did not catch enough insects at dusk is on the wing again, hawking. **1844** J. GOULD *Birds of Aust.* (1848) II. Pl. 35, *Pardalotus punctatus* .. **Spotted Pardalote** .. *Diamond Bird*, Colonists of New South Wales. **1896** F.G. AFLALO *Sketch Nat. Hist. Aust.* 137 The Spotted Diamond Bird (*Pardalotus punctatus*), known to aboriginals from its peculiar cry as the 'Weedupwee', burrows in the earth. **1917** *Bulletin* (Sydney) 19 July 24/1 The spotted diamond-bird (pardalote family) .. builds in a tunnel up to 5 ft. long and the entrance is just large enough to allow the occupier to enter. **1945** C. BARRETT *Austral. Bird Life* 181 The spotted pardalote .. is the best known species [of pardalote]. **1976** *Reader's Digest Compl. Bk. Austral. Birds* 517 Tiny white jewel-like spots adorn the forehead, wings and tail of the male spotted pardalote, and the wings and tail of the female. **1984** *Age* (Melbourne) 10 Apr. 28/7 Spotted Pardalotes are dumpy little birds which nest in holes in banks and sometimes in piles of builder's sand. **1965** *Austral. Encycl.* VII. 315 The only species of the group that are at all familiar, even to naturalists, are the **spotted quail-thrush** .. and the chestnut-backed quail-thrush. **1984** T.R. GARNETT *Stumbling on Melons* 120 One of the mystery birds of these ranges is the spotted quail-thrush, a greyish-brown bird with white tips to its tail. **1843** J. GOULD *Birds of Aust.* (1848) III. Pl. 86, *Amadina lathami.* **Spotted-sided Finch.** **1861** 'OLD BUSHMAN' *Bush Wanderings* 155 By far the most elegant, and in our district the rarest of all, was the *Spotted-sided Finch.* **1906** *Emu* VI. 31 Where is the sense in calling .. their Spotted-sided Finch (*Stagonopleura guttata*) the Diamond Sparrow? **1968** R. HILL *Bush Quest* 14 Various honeyeaters, wrens, red-browed and spotted-sided finches all came to drink while we watched. **1906** D.G. STEAD *Fishes of Aust.* 112 The **Spotted Whiting** .. may be at once distinguished .. by .. the presence of pretty Trout-like spots all over the upper half of the body. **1951** T.C. ROUGHLEY *Fish & Fisheries Aust.* 49 The spotted whiting .. as food .. is regarded by some as the finest of all Australian whitings. **1967** H. ANDERSON *Fish & Fisheries* 40 Spotted whiting is the largest of the whitings in Australia and the most important in the southern States.

spout, *n.*

1. *Shearing. Obs.* Used *attrib.* with reference to the practice of washing sheep under falling water: see quot. 1842. Esp. as **spout-washed** *ppl. a.*, **-washing** *vbl. n.*

1842 *Portland Mercury* 14 Sept. 4/4 Latterly a great improvement has been introduced, of washing them [*sc.* sheep] under spouts constructed where the river has a fall, by which the fleece is effectually cleansed with very little hand labour. As, however, nearly all Australian rivers cease flowing in severe droughts, the spout system cannot be put in practice then, nor in various extensive districts in the colony, where chains of ponds supply the place of running brooks. **1847** *Port Phillip Herald* 16 Nov. 3/5 It is a very superior run, and watered by the Lardarch and Werriby (both running streams), giving every facility for spout-washing. **1848** W. WESTGARTH *Aust. Felix* 252 The spout-washing process is usually very effectual. **1871** *Austral. Town & Country Jrnl.* (Sydney) 28 Jan. 103/2 The sheep gave an average of 3½ lb., spout-washed. **1927** A. CROMBIE *After Sixty Yrs.* 115, I can assure you, Crombie, Learmouth took seven shillings a head off all their spout washed sheep.

2. A hollow stump left on a tree (usu. a gum tree) where a branch has broken off.

1840 J. GOULD *Birds of Aust.* (1848) II. Pl. 2, During the day it [*sc.* the owlet nightjar] resorts to the hollow branches or spouts as they are called. **1902** *Emu* II. 36 The nesting place was in the spout of a gum-tree, about

30 feet from the ground. **1918** *Ibid.* XVII. 221 Nests seen in high gum-tree spouts in October to January.

spout, *v. Obs. Shearing. trans.* To wash (a sheep) under falling water. Also as *vbl. n.* and *ppl. a.*

1871 *Austral. Town & Country Jrnl.* (Sydney) 4 Feb. 138/3 Immediately spouted by the ordinary process, entirely dispensing with hot water, soap, or soda. *Ibid.*, I then found that the proportion of bright spouted sheep was small. **1873** A. TROLLOPE *Aust. & N.Z.* I. 122 There are various modes of washing—but on the stations which I saw on the Darling Downs the sheep were all 'spouted'... But before .. the spouting there is a preliminary washing... The sheep are passed on, one by one, into the hands of the men at the spouts. At one washpool I saw fourteen spouts at work, with two men at each spout... The sheep goes out of the spouter's hands, not into the water, but on to steep boards, arranged so as to give him every facility for travelling up to the pen which is to receive him.

Hence **spouter** *n.*

1873 [see SPOUT *v.*].

sprag, *v.* [Fig. use of *sprag* to stop (a wheel) by the use of a chock or bar which acts as a brake: see OED *v.* 2.]

1. *trans.* To obstruct (a plan, etc.); to thwart.

1911 *Bulletin* (Sydney) 2 Nov. 14/1 Some of these mean whites dummy leases for Chows... But the Commonwealth has got hold of things, and the oldest inhabitants who spragged the wheels of the Territory will have to alter... Nearly every mining lease in the Territory is being worked by Chows and dummies. **1965** U.R. ELLIS (*title*) Attempt to sprag New State Referendum. **1976** L. OAKES *Crash Through* 61 At the beginning of December, talking about the loan, Connor complained to his staff: 'Treasury's trying to sprag it. They're always trying to sprag things.' The word 'sprag' was one of his favourites, presumably picked up in Wollongong in the pre-Depression years.

2. To accost truculently; to pester.

1915 'LANCE-CORPORAL COBBER' *Anzac Pilgrim's Progress* (1918) 82 He's no bully, doesn't mag, Doesn't swank around an' sprag, You will never hear him brag Like a Hun. **1915** C.J. DENNIS *Songs of Sentimental Bloke* 130 *Sprag*, to accost truculently. **1935** L. LUARD *Conquering Seas* 41 'Twas only to save you from getting spragged. **1962** D. STUART *Yaralie* 127 He spragged me down on the jetty, asked me for a bit of bait, and hands over this money. **1973** *Kings Cross Whisper* (Sydney) cxlvii. 3/1 He gets a cab home and sprags them. **1979** D.R. STUART *Crank back on Roller* 95 This cove, Pommy, all mo. an' buck teeth, he sprags me an' Joey an' nothin'll do but he's gotta buy us grog.

spread. A distribution or scattering of stock over a wide area, esp. in the phr. **to have** (or **get**) **a spread on** and varr.

1903 *Bulletin* (Sydney) 17 Jan. 16/2 If there was a big spread on the sheep the men could not have sighted and 'cleared' every part of the paddock—the true definition of mustering—in time to count 80,000 sheep. **1904** *Emu* III. 174 They can be seen feeding sometimes as far as the eye can reach, in pairs or small mobs, like a flock of sheep 'on a good spread'. **1931** F.D. DAVISON *Man-Shy* (1962) 85 And don't let them get a spread on! **1936** I.L. IDRIESS *Cattle King* 60 The pikers among them would surely have a spread on by now.

spring, *v.* [Spec. use of *spring* to cause to appear.] *trans.* To discover or come upon (something or someone, usu. a concealed object or someone engaged in an illicit activity); esp. in the phr. **to spring the plant** (see PLANT *n.*[1] 1 b.).

1812, etc. [see PLANT *n.*[1] 1 a.]. **1842** *Geelong Advertiser* 18 Apr. 2/5 Having received certain information and a guide, Mr Le Seouff set out about eight days since to 'spring' an illicit still, which he had been told was in full play in the tea-tree scrub at Dandenong. **1845** *Cumberland Times* (Parramatta) 25 Oct. 2/4 The cordial comfort of a bottle of brandy was found concealed on his person, and on the Turnkey springing it, he begged him to 'ball it off' and say nothing. **1875** *Illustr. Adelaide News* ii. 11/3 It was Californian Jack, who, having unintentionally 'sprung' the lovers, was hastily 'backing out'. **1893** M. JEFFREY *Burglar's Life* (1968) 40 My brother Luke whispered to me, 'I've sprung a haul.' .. He had discovered money in the inside pocket of an overcoat. **1967** *Kings Cross Whisper* (Sydney) xxxix. 4/5 *Spring*, to be sprung, one is caught in the act of doing something highly irregular. **1968** L.H. EVERS *Fall among Thieves* 68 She springs right away that we've been lagged for sure. **1980** HEPWORTH & HINDLE *Boozing out in Melbourne Pubs* 42 A friend of ours, who spends part of his time as a married man, has used the Bayview as a discreet boozer to which he lures his female prey. He figured that nobody would ever spring him, but he figured wrong. **1981** B. DICKINS *Gift of Gab* 24 Our science teacher .. sprung me acting the goat and I was bumwallopped.

springboard. *Timber-getting.* [Orig. U.S.: see OED(S 3.] See quot. 1920. Also *attrib.*

1912 L. ESSON *Red Gums* 39 The mountain ashes Round the 'springboard' high. 'Cut the calf!' Splitters laugh At the reel and ruction. **1920** C.W. BRYDE *Chart House to Bush Hut* 103 Terry was great on springboard work. A springboard is a six-inch by one-inch board four feet long, with a horseshoe bolted on one end point up. You cut a notch two inches deep in a tree, insert the board, and stand on it to chop, the point of the shoe being driven by your weight into the upper edge of the notch and holding firm... I have heard it described as chopping with one foot in the grave and the other on a bit of orange peel. **1937** *Bulletin* (Sydney) 1 Sept. 20/4 Scrub-felling from spring-boards may be thrilling. **1959** *Overland* xv. 14 In no time I was climbing up onto the springboard up the trunk and putting in the belly cut while one of them put in the back cut. **1981** J.P. GABBEDY *Forgotten Pioneers* p. xi, Boards (often referred to as Springboards) are in sets of three—length 140 cm. (4 ft. 7 in.), width (at base) 19 cm. (7½ in.), at extremity 9 cm. (3½ in.); weight, approx. 9 lbs.; constructed from oregon.

springer.

1. *Obs.* An improvised fishing-rod; see quot. 1900.

1900 *Bulletin* (Sydney) 21 July 15/1 A springer is a tapering mallee rod, perhaps 10 feet long, pointed at the thick end. **1917** C. THACKERAY *Goliath Joe* 46, I was jest skinnin' a black maggy fer bait fer my 'and-line wen I seen my springer bend.

2. A spring-operated trap.

1909 *Emu* VIII. 220 As a boy I did a good deal of trapping .. and a favourite place to set a 'springer' was just where a wallaby would land after leaping over a gully. **1920** *Bulletin* (Sydney) 8 Apr. 22/1 Cut out poison, springers, dog-traps, fencing-wire nooses, 'figgers o' four', and such-like and sink pit-traps.

sprooker, var. SPRUIKER.

spruik /spruk/, *n.* [f. SPRUIK *v.*] A speech; a rant.

1911 *Truth* (Sydney) 3 Dec. 1/4 Why not call Sir Edward's spruik a great speech. **1916** *Ibid.* 23 July 1/5 Let Cann and Wade cross spruiks in petty strife While Willie views the beauties of Fiji. **1953** T.A.G. HUNGERFORD *Riverslake* 40, I usually go and have a bit of a spruik to him when I knock off.

spruik /spruk/, *v.* [Of unknown origin.] *intr.* To hold forth (in public); to deliver a harangue, esp. to advertise a show, etc.: see quot. 1912. Also *trans.*, to discourse on (a subject).

1902 *Truth* (Sydney) 14 Sept. 5/6 'Lockie the Spruiker' that 'spruiked' for years at the Gaiety door, Has gone out of the 'spruiking' business, and never will 'spruik' any more. **1907** *Ibid.* 26 May 1/3 Some of the women spruiking politics and posing as patriots are paid pimps of the Liberal League, and householders should shoo them off the premises. **1912** *Bulletin* (Sydney) 4 Apr. 14/4 *Spruik?* I just *could*! And wot was more, I used to *look* me part, A-standin' on them marble steps to give the show a start! And talkin' big, and talkin' fast, and poet-like, and free, About the noble fillums wot there was inside to see! **1918** N.P.H. NEAL *Back to Bush* 32 The parson bloke, after spruiking for a while, started waving his arms, and asked wildly, 'Is there anyone .. who isn't in love?' **1928** J. POLLARD *Bushland Vagabonds* 279 I'm no good at spruikin'. Take it on yourself. You've got the way, an' know all the youngsters. All you've got to do is to wish 'em a Merry Christmas an' 'and out the toys. **1954** N. BARTLETT *Pearl Seekers* 122 Spruiked for a circus in the U.S.A. **1969** W. MOXHAM *Apprentice* 31 He's always spruiking about this university degree he's supposed to have. **1982** *Bulletin* (Sydney) 26 Oct. 51/2 MacGregor .. didn't mention it (and the man himself has not been heard spruiking the fact).

Hence **spruiking** *vbl. n.* and *attrib.*

1925 *Bulletin* (Sydney) 16 July 47/2, I was lobbying the licensed victuallers' headquarters in the town for a spruiking job. **1955** E.O. SCHLUNKE *Man in Silo* 26 'Well, you'd do the spruiking all right,' Birnie admitted grudgingly. Henzel was a great reciter at parties and speaker at all public functions. **1980** M. WILLIAMS *Dingo!* 65 Algy followed the crowds with the hot dog can, and I did the spruiking. **1986** *Bulletin* (Sydney) 25 Mar. 97/2 Wakefield .. mounted the pulpit to harangue the audience... Such spruiking was interspersed with .. musical commentary.

spruiker /sprukə/. Also **sprooker.** A speaker employed to attract custom, esp. to a sideshow; a barker; an eloquent speaker.

1902 [see SPRUIK *v.*]. **1910** W.C. WALL *Sydney Stage Employee's Postal Ann.* 100 Mick was also a 'sprooker' for his own and other shows. **1916** *Truth* (Sydney) 25 June 9/5 In the courts he's a great spruiker, There he's pleading almost daily; His graceful arguments much weight they carry. **1924** *Smith's Weekly* (Sydney) 26 Apr. 25/4 The spruiker at the Melbourne Aquarium claims credit for bringing thousands of visitors to see the exhibit. **1933** J. MCCARTER *Love's Lunatic* 282 An' now y'll see how me little talks—like th' wireless spruikers say—have been goin'. **1944** *Aust. Week-End Bk.* 117 The greatest of all lion-tamers. The spruiker would blare out his name. **1956** A. MARSHALL *How's Andy Going?* 57 Outside I could hear the spruiker shouting, 'Shabaka, the great Egyptian Soothsayer. Tells your fortune for threepence.' **1965** K. SMITH *OGF* 207 Guy .. was .. a spruiker with a travelling sideshow in North Queensland, telling jokes outside the tent or posing as a hostile stranger in the crowd, yelling 'I'll have a go at 'im' when the boxers came out. **1977** C. MCCULLOUGH *Thorn Birds* 93 'Come on, chaps, who'll take a glove?' the spruiker was braying. **1983** *Canberra Times* 1 Oct. 23/6 A vacancy exists for a casual Spruiker to promote merchandise for all departments at our Belconnen store.

spud cocky. [f. *spud* potato + COCKY *n.*[2]] A potato farmer.

1950 *New Settler in W.A.* (Perth) Mar. 21 My next job was with a 'Spud Cocky' (potato farmer) digging taters for 10s. a week plus 1s. a bag bonus. **1985** P. CAREY *Illywhacker* 228 When some stirrers .. tried to organize a strike against the spud farmers .. I was called a scab... It was us scabs who brought in the spuds for those celebrated spud cockies.

spunk. A person sexually attractive to members of the opposite sex. Also *attrib.*

1978 J. ROWE *Warlords* 205, I mean I can always round up a boatload of horny looking young spunks, but there's no guarantees for old gits like us from the amateurs. **1979** CAREY & LETTE *Puberty Blues* 5 It was Darren Peters—the top surfing spunk of sixth form. **1981** *Age* (Melbourne) 21 Aug. 11/4 The show attracts a lot of 'spunk mail' from viewers (i.e. Dear John, you are a real spunk, please send me a photo). **1982** *Sydney Morning Herald* 18 Sept. 1/2 Teenagers still rage at weekends, check out spunks of both sexes and try to avoid hassles with the olds.

spunky, *n.* and *a.*

A. *n.* SPUNK.

1967 *Kings Cross Whisper* (Sydney) xxxix. 4/5 *Spunky*, young female. **1979** *Nat. Times* (Sydney) 17 Nov. 54/4 When we were surfie chicks they used to drive past yelling sexual insults to us. Now we drive past and yell 'Eh, spunky!'

B. *adj.* Sexually attractive.

1979 CAREY & LETTE *Puberty Blues* 5 Sue and I checked out the guys. They were spunkier at North Cronulla. *Ibid.* 9 Once you made it into the surfie gang, you were a top chick, with a spunky boyfriend. **1984** *Good Weekend* (Sydney) 6 Oct. 28/2 Gynaecologists in Sydney have been known to leave their wives for younger, spunkier patients.

spur-winged plover. [See quot. 1822.] The wading bird *Vanellus miles novaehollandiae*, chiefly of e. and s. Aust. incl. Tas., having predom. olive-brown and white plumage, yellow facial wattles, and a loud call; ALARM BIRD 1. Also **spur-wing plover.**

1822 B. FIELD *Geogr. Mem. N.S.W.* 11 Oct. (1825) 442 A bird is frequent here, called the spur-winged plover. It has a dull yellow lappet-like hood and is armed with a claw of the same colour, on the shoulder of each wing. It is a species of jacana. **1845** C. HODGKINSON *Aust., Port Macquarie to Moreton Bay* 207 In the more open inland parts of Australia, where other birds are somewhat scarce, the spur-winged plover is to be met with. **1861** 'OLD BUSHMAN' *Bush Wanderings* 111 The *Spur-wing Plover* . . is a fine bold-looking bird, considerably larger than the British lapwing. **1901** *Emu* I. 86 Spur-winged Plover . . though regarded as inhabiting the island [*sc.* Tasmania] many years ago . . was a rare bird until the 'eighties'. **1944** J. DEVANNY *By Tropic Sea & Jungle* 157 The spur-winged plover's cry is like a dingo's howl. **1975** X. HERBERT *Poor Fellow my Country* 428 A couple of spur-wing plovers swept up shrilly calling from the earthern tank behind a netting fence.

square, *n.* [From the shape of the bottle in which gin was customarily sold; used elsewhere but recorded earliest in Aust.] Gin. Also as **square cut, square face, square gin.**

1868 *Frank Gardiner, or Bushranging in 1863* 6 Let's have a taste of old square-cut, there, for the rain has almost drowned me. **1865** *Wallaroo Times* (Kadina) 18 Feb. 3/3, I do believe he's adulterated this water with 'square' or whisky. **1871** *Austral. Town & Country Jrnl.* (Sydney) 4 Mar. 266/2 On receipt of the reward, they immediately purchased 'square gin'. **1874** J.T. FALLON *Murray Valley Vineyard* 30 The laboring classes now prefer colonial wine, which can be obtained by them at colonial wine-shops in Melbourne, at the cheap rate of two-pence per glass, instead of bad brandy and worse 'square gin'. **1884** 'LOCAL LETTER CARRIER' *After Twenty Yrs.* 54 The pedestrian . . had the bottle of square carefully tucked under his arm. **1887** A. NICOLS *Wild Life & Adventure* 185 Send us a bottle of 'square' from the store. **1903** H. TAUNTON *Australind* 192 For days after, the changes would be rung on fried, boiled, roasted, poached, and scrambled eggs, not to mention the mighty number that would be eaten raw or beaten up in whisky, 'squareface' or 'shypoo', as the case might be. **1910** *Bulletin* (Sydney) 14 July 13/1 The old fellow barters the children with the heathens for tobacco, square gin or tucker. **1915** E.R. MASSON *Untamed Territory* 82 The main room has a table with sauces, bottles of 'square', and a tin or two upon it. **1940** E. HILL *Great Austral. Loneliness* (ed. 2) 83 Glass after glass of squareface was raised to the luck of the new beauty. **1942** F. CLUNE *Last of Austral. Explorers* 133 After . . a priming of 'Squareface' (gin) the tourists farewelled their navvy friends. **1965** L. HAYLEN *Big Red* 133 Red wondered: Wasn't it all plonk? Wasn't it all square face? He daren't show his ignorance again.

square, *a. Obs.* [Spec. use of *square* honourable, upright.] Of a female: respectable.

1892 *Bulletin* (Sydney) 5 Nov. 17/2 An tho', in her entirety, the Crimson Streak 'was there', I grieve to state the Crimson Streak was not a 'square affair'. **1916** *Truth* (Sydney) 29 Oct. 5/6 A prostitute is a prostitute and she seldom cares who knows it, but those 'half square' girls (as some of your correspondents call them) are the hussies that make the mischief. **1916** *Ibid.* 3 Sept. 10/2 Re 'love birds' and 'half-square' girls, they are more dangerous than any prostitutes. **1941** S.J. BAKER *Pop. Dict. Austral. Slang* 70 *Square Jane And No Nonsense*, a firm-minded girl of conservative instincts.

square, *v. intr.* With **off**: to set matters right; to settle a difference. Also *trans.*, to conciliate (a person).

1943 *Blitz & Pieces: Transport Weekly 2/101 Austral. Gen. Transport Co.* 8 Mar. 1 The officer . . was merely trying to 'square off', we've heard the story . . before. **1953** D. STIVENS *Gambling Ghost* 62 You'll have to square off with the boys. How much sugar have you got? **1968** S. GORE *Holy Smoke* 56 So what about givin' a man another go, now he's squared off with you? **1973** J. POWERS *Last of Knucklemen* (1974) 21 What I don't twig is how he'll square off with the brass? **1976** *Nature* (London) 19 Feb. 519/2 Squaring off the proprietors of the three national chains of newspapers, whose unquestioning support he [*sc.* Mr Fraser] enjoyed throughout the campaign. **1976** A. STRETTON *Furious Days* 203 Rex, tell him he has got the powers of the Australian Government—his orders can only be countermanded by Gough or myself. We will square off with other ministers later.

squarehead. A person with no criminal convictions.

1939 K. TENNANT *Foveaux* 312 'Never attack a squarehead' had always been Curly's motto. There was too much danger that a squarehead would top-off to the police in a jam. **1950** *Austral. Police Jrnl.* Apr. 119 *Squarehead*, one who has no convictions. **1967** *Kings Cross Whisper* (Sydney) xxxix. 4/5 *Square head*, a conformist. An unconvicted person. **1971** J. MCNEIL *Chocolate Frog* (1973) 41 Here we are, with the squareheads payin' fer our tucker, while we're trainin' ter get out and rob 'em again. **1984** *Bulletin* (Sydney) 20 Mar. 47/2 He was a one-off offender, a 'squarehead'.

square-tailed kite. The bird of prey *Lophoictinia isura* of mainland Aust.

1841 J. GOULD *Birds of Aust.* (1848) I. Pl. 22, *Milvus isurus* . . Square-tailed Kite. **1845** L. LEICHHARDT *Jrnl. Overland Exped. Aust.* 7 July (1847) 321 We cut up . . the emu . . but we had to guard it by turns, whip in hand, from a host of square-tailed kites. **1901** *Emu* I. 137 Square-tailed Kite . . —Shot at Killalpaninna. **1945** C. BARRETT *Austral. Bird Life* 40 The square-tailed kite . . met with in pairs as a rule, though widely spread on the mainland, is a scarce bird in southern parts of Australia. **1976** *Reader's Digest Compl. Bk. Austral. Birds* 119 Although the square-tailed kite might occur over any forested country, it is reasonably abundant only over sandplain country, particularly in Western Australia.

squarie. Also **squarey.** A young woman; a girlfriend. See SQUARE *a.*

1917 *Flotilla Echo: On Board H.M.A.S. No. 79* Dec. 8 Goes along to a stationer's shop. . . The 'squarie' behind the counter. **1945** *Buzz Rev.: H.M.A.S. 'Manoora'* 11 Mar. 4 A letter from his squarie. **1953** J.E. MACDONNELL *Wings off Sea* 73 The signalman was thinking the same thoughts about James's obvious lack of sex appeal. 'Poor coot. With that dial he couldn't raise a squarie even in Sydney.' **1959** J. WYNNUM *Down Hatch* 51 Who comes in but old Slops 'ere and within five minutes he's latched on to a squarie. He buys her a glass of suds. **1968** G. DUTTON *Andy* 203 His awe of his mate's squarey, this serious girl, overcame the slight delirium of the Do-What-You-Will atmosphere of Lydford's castle by the mountain. **1970** *R.A.N. News* (Sydney) 21 Aug. 12 You bloody beaut . . we'll be back outside with our squaries! **1984** V. DARROCH *On Coast* 33 *Squarie* (R.A.N.), girlfriend of sailor. Probable derivation from 'square rig', colloquial for R.N. blue-jacket uniform, to distinguish it from the rig of Petty Officers—called 'fore and aft' rig.

squat, *v. Hist.* [U.S. *squat* to settle on unoccupied land without legal title: see OED *v.* 9.]

1. *intr.* To occupy a tract of Crown land in order to graze livestock (a practice sanctioned in 1836 by the introduction of a licensing system). Occas. as **squat down.**

1827 P. CUNNINGHAM *Two Yrs. in N.S.W.* II. 162 They have therefore nothing to lose and much to gain by new settlers 'squatting' near their locations. **1835** *Sydney Herald* 27 Aug. 2/7 Nothing has been more common, for some years past, than to see an assigned convict stockman when free, either by ticket-of-leave or servitude, squat in some convenient place with an hundred or two, if not more, head of his own. **1836** *Colonist* (Sydney) 25 Feb. 57/1 Of all the verbs in Johnson's Dictionary, the one which is most frequently conjugated, in all its possible moods and tenses, in this colony is the verb *To squat*; which signifies to *sit down* with a number of sheep or cattle on Crown land in the interior, either within or beyond the boundary. **1839** W. MANN *Six Yrs.' Residence* 242 A family named Henty have squatted here, who have considerable numbers of cattle and sheep grazing on the waste lands of the colony. **1844** *Atlas* (Sydney) I. 52/3 He . . came to Colonize but has been obliged to Squat. **1847** J.D. LANG *Phillipsland* 113 On her arrival in the Colony, Miss Drysdale determined to 'squat', as it is styled in the phraseology of the country; that is, to settle on a tract of unoccupied Crown land, of sufficient extent for the pasturage of considerable flocks and herds, with their increase for several years—a tract, in all likelihood, from twenty to fifty square miles in extent. **1852** G.B. EARP *Gold Colonies Aust.* 98 The remaining mode of occupying land in New South Wales is to 'squat', i.e. to lease a large tract from the Government for purposes purely pastoral. **1857** 'RETURNED DIGGER' *Six Yrs. in Aust.* 24 Beyond the settled districts lies the bush, or wild uncultivated country, in which the sheep and cattle farmers are squatted on the soil or crown lands. **1864** *Bell's Life in Sydney* 2 Apr. 3/1 It was all very well for squatters to squat here for a very short time, and when they had squatted sufficiently, to go home and squat in their mansions and not think or care a hang for the country that set them on their legs. **1872** 'RESIDENT' *Glimpses Life Vic.* 31 The bright and fertile spot on which my friend and I had *squatted.* **1895** J.T. RYAN *Reminisc. Aust.* 128 They were the first to squat down on that lovely spot called Kelso. **1933** W.L. OWEN *Cossack Gold* 69 Two years later he 'squatted' with his brother Harding at Mallina. **1957** F. CLUNE *Fortune Hunters* 15 The vested interests of the absentee-owned pastoral companies . . squat on the river-frontages, where their forebears squatted a hundred years ago. **1972** ANDERSON & BLAKE *J.S. Neilson* 4 Here Cameron squatted to graze cattle and horses, and later, sheep. **1982** *Daily Mirror* (Sydney) 2 Nov. 21/3 So he squatted—that is he grazed his flocks and herds on Crown lands not yet officially recognised as being open to settlement.

2. *transf.*

1856 *Jrnl. Australasia* I. 247 They invariably seek to procure land adjoining unsold sections, that their own flocks and herds may 'squat' at will over an extended range.

squatocracy, var. SQUATTOCRACY.

squatocratic, var. SQUATTOCRATIC.

squattage.

1. *Hist.* Those leasing Crown land for grazing purposes, viewed collectively (see SQUATTER 2).

1845 *Standard* (Melbourne) 29 Jan. 3/3 Speaking of Mr Scott, the Parliamentary agent for the 'Squattage', he says that the opposition party in the Legislative Council 'will have now an agent in the House of Commons'. *Ibid.* 12 July 3/2 In the secession of Mr Walker, the 'Squattage' has lost a powerful advocate. **1847** *Atlas* (Sydney) III. 222/2 Aroused the ire of our correspondent and caused him to attack the 'squattage' upon the old principle of the 'fox and the grapes'.

2. *Hist.* The occupation of land in this fashion. Also *attrib.*

1847 *Port Phillip Herald* 8 Apr. (Suppl.), 'Settled districts' . . designates the region of lawful 'squattage'. **1847** *HRA* (1925) 1st Ser. XXVI. 122 Occupied under what may be termed Squattage tenure. **1972** W.K. HANCOCK *Discovering Monaro* 6 Let us look quickly at successive maps of Monaro, starting with the map of the Squattage District (called later the Pastoral District) as it was in 1840.

3. A tract of grazing land leased from the Crown; a substantial stock-raising establishment.

1846 *Portland Guardian* 25 Dec. 3/1 Then squattages were unequal to the demand; now the demand is unequal to the supply. **1849** A. HODGSON *Emigration Austral. Settlements* 19 The frequent changes in the Government Regulations respecting the Bush shook the settler's confidence in the tenure of his squattage. **1867** 'CLERGYMAN' *Aust. as it Is* 135 The squattages are let on fourteen years' leases, but are to be re-valued at that period. **1882** W.B. CHRISTIE *Our Land Laws* 7 The so-called 'squatting' districts of the colony are divided into 4329 runs or squattages. **1911** E.J. BRADY *River Rovers* 46 Next night found us at Boomanoomanah station, one of the finest squattages along the Murray on the New South Wales side. **1919** *Smith's Weekly* (Sydney) 1 Mar. 6/3 Gleeson . . took up a selection near Wollar in 1861. To this block, known as Coomealla homestead, he added from time to time, until he had acquired a small squattage. **1924** *Ibid.* 27 Dec. 23/5 Some farback Queensland squattages, though they are mostly cattle runs, can muster thousands of horses. **1942** H.H. PECK *Mem. of Stockman* 160 Instead of simply acquiring leaseholds of their squattages as was usual then, they bought the freeholds.

squatter. [U.S. *squatter* one settling on land with no legal title: see OED(S *sb.*[1] 1.]

1. *Obs.* One, esp. an ex-convict, who occupies Crown land without legal title.

1828 *Hobart Town Courier* 14 June 3 The measure gives great satisfaction to the settlers generally, with but few if any exceptions, among whom we may include those called squatters. **1832** *Colonist* (Hobart) 21 Dec. 3/1 The Police Magistrate of Campbell Town is directed to turn out the *squatter* as he is designated; although this *squatter* has an order for a second class allotment in Ross. **1835** J. Lhotsky *Journey from Sydney* 46 She and her husband were *Squatters*, the name given in the Colony to persons who cultivate unoccupied Ground, belonging therefore, as they say to Government. **1836** C. Darwin *Jrnl. Researches Geol. & Nat. Hist.* (1839) III. 527 A 'squatter' is a freed, or 'ticket of leave' man, who builds a hut with bark on unoccupied ground, buys or steals a few animals, sells spirits without a licence, receives stolen goods—and so at last becomes rich and turns farmer: he is the horror of all his honest neighbours. **1837** *Rep. Select Committee Transportation* 35 Are the squatters all from that class of individuals who were originally convicts, or from the class of emigrants? I think I have known a solitary instance of an emigrant being a squatter, but should say that it is very rare indeed. **1844** *Duncan's Weekly Register* (Sydney) 27 Apr. 552/1 'A *small* squatter' is necessarily either 'a sly grog seller, or a cattle stealer'. **1848** W. Westgarth *Aust. Felix* 246 A set of men who were to be found upon the borders of every large estate, and who were known by the name of *squatters*. These were ticket-of-leave holders or freed-men, who .. immediately became the nuisance of the district.

2. One who occupies a tract of Crown land in order to graze livestock, having title by either licence or lease.

1837 *S. Austral. Rec.* (London) 11 Apr. 53, I am now, therefore, what is termed here a 'squatter'—that is, to occupy, on a rental of £10 per annum, government land beyond the boundaries of land allotted for location. **1838** *Austral. Mag.* (Sydney) 137 You can .. form your head establishment on your own land, without any fear of being turned off by government at a short notice; and you can at the same time hold a squatter's license for unlocated crown lands. **1839** J.G. Johnston *Truth* 21 This is a recent settlement, which the Government has been forced to colonize in a regular manner, by numbers of squatters taking up their residence and pasturing their flocks and herds. **1844** *Colonial Times* (Hobart) 5 June, Squatting .. is .. favouring certain aristocratic parties, who being the licensed occupiers frequently of twenty miles square .. prevent the more humble squatter from seating himself in front of the located country. **1849** J.P. Townsend *Rambles & Observations N.S.W.* 18 Some are both farmers and squatters, having their farms within the boundaries, and their sheep and cattle stations beyond them; and, since wool and tallow are the exports of the colony, the settlers who produce these, and not the mere farmers, are the monied men. **1859** R.H. Horne *Austral. Facts & Prospects* 101 The method of reclaiming the lands must be without doing any gross injustice to the squatters. They were the pioneers and first settlers in the country. **1867** 'Clergyman' *Aust. as it Is* 104 The occupiers of the land—that class of the community called *squatters* or *Crown-tenants*—not being required to purchase the land of which they hold possession, they enjoy the full use and benefit of every farthing of their capital. **1874** *Illustr. Sydney News* 30 May 15/4 Squatters here are allowed to renew their leases, without any increase being made in their rent, on condition that the run is improved. **1886** W.J. Woods *Visit to Vic.* 25 My brother's place at Porcupine Ridge is a Selection, as distinguished from a Station, and he is a Selector as distinct from a Squatter. A Victorian squatter is a capitalist who leases large areas of pasture-land from the Government, and who must move on whenever it suits the authorities to sell his ground. **1903** E. Palmer *Early Days N. Qld.* 8 The name 'squatter' was given in the early days to the pastoral tenants of the Crown, who rented pasture lands in their natural state.

3. One who grazes livestock on a large scale (without reference to the title by which the land is held); such a person as being of an elevated socio-economic status. Also *attrib.*

1841 G. Arden *Recent Information Port Phillip* 27 Tobacco .. has been cultivated by squatters .. in quantities sufficient to supply their ordinary demands for *sheep dressing*. **1843** *Melbourne Times* 17 June 3/1 The extension of the franchise to gentlemen settlers, designated squatters. **1845** *Portland Gaz.* 15 Apr. 2/5 The whole history of the Squatters proves that they are the least avaricious—the most self denying, and, in every sense of the term, the most liberal class of men on the face of the earth. **1846** C.P. Hodgson *Reminisc. Aust.* 4 Squatters .. are generally allowed to be the aristocracy of the colony. **1854** W. Howitt *Boy's Adventures* 10 A squatter, that is a gentleman settler, often with fifty or a hundred thousand pounds, but still delighting in the name of squatter. **1861** L.A. Meredith *Over Straits* 119 The dashing tandem of the sporting squatter whirls past. **1867** 'Colonist' *Life's Work* 90 No men have made wealth faster in this colony than 'squatters'; that is, in plain English, sheep and cattle owners. **1872** A. McFarland *Illawarra & Manaro* 117 One firm of squatters had lately as many as 60,000 sheep. **1873** W. Thomson-Gregg *Desperate Character* II. 43 The squatters, for the occupants of the room belonged to that hyper-aristocratic section of colonial society, looked up. **1884** A.W. Stirling *Never Never Land* 19 'Is it a crime, Sir', began the hon. member, 'to be a squatter? Is it a sin, Sir, to be a grazier?' **1891** *Quiz* (Adelaide) 16 Jan. 7/1 There is a mean South Australian squatter who owns two or three runs. **1900** *Pastoral Times* (Deniliquin) 5 May 4/1 From the large station to the forty acre holding—in vulgar parlance from the 'squattah' to the 'cockie'. **1906** *Truth* (Sydney) 22 July 1/3 The devil sent the squatter, and the Lord sent the rabbits to oust him, and Bunny looks a winner. **1919** C.A. Bernays *Qld. Politics during Sixty Yrs.* 16 Bell was a squatter pure and simple, with all the high regard which a squatter of those times had for his own importance—living in a day when the squatter claimed the whole earth and the fullness thereof, and when the selector was regarded as being more or less of an impertinent interloper. **1926** A.A.B. Apsley *Amateur Settlers* 4 The word 'squatter' .. is now used in Australia only to denote a long-established and wealthy settler. **1942** H.H. Peck *Mem. of Stockman* 65 When in town was turned out to match the swellest squatter, with silk top-hat, and umbrella. **1944** J.H. Pick *Aust. Dying Heart* (rev. ed.) 44 City residents who have interests in the outback, 'suitcase squatters', who have neither the practical knowledge not the specialised interest. **1961** *Bulletin* (Sydney) 8 Feb. 15/3 King's School has one squatter scion, Geelong Grammar another who like being schoolmasters. **1976** L. Oakes *Crash Through* 35 The marriage united the Frasers with one of the wealthiest and most prominent squatter families of northern Victoria, the Sandford Beggs.

4. Abbrev. of *squatter pigeon*: see sense 5 below.

1872 C.H. Eden *My Wife & I in Qld.* 122 On the plains you find different kinds of pigeons, the squatters being most common .. crouching down to the ground quite motionless as you pass. **1887** S. Newland *Far North Country* 22 The beautiful topknotted pigeon, known in the old days on the Darling as 'the squatter', from its sitting so still when approached quite closely. **1912** J. Bowes *Comrades* 179 There's no need to go out that distance if its pigeons you're after. I saw quite a number of 'squatters' and 'bronze-wings', as I passed the two-mile water-hole yesterday. **1948** H.A. Lindsay *Bushman's Handbk.* 21 There is also the squatter, a big pigeon of the open plains, which makes a loud whistling with its wings as it flies. **1964** M. Sharland *Territory of Birds* 81, I saw another interesting pigeon, known widely in the North as the 'Squatter' from its habit of sitting quietly on the ground until danger is past. .. But this, of course, was not the true Squatter, although in some ways resembling it. It was the northern Partridge Pigeon, with handsome dark brown plumage, white face, slightly spangled breast, and large red eye-patch.

5. Special Comb. and collocations: **squatter chair, delight,** an outdoor, reclining chair consisting of a wooden frame from which a length of canvas is suspended and having a leg rest; also **squatter's chair, delight; king,** one who grazes livestock on a more than usually large scale; **pigeon,** any of several pigeons, esp. the ground-dwelling *Geophaps scripta* of Qld. and N.S.W.; see also Partridge pigeon.

1880 *Blackwood's Mag.* (Edinburgh) Jan. 59/1 John took possession of a **squatter's chair.** **1886** P. Fletcher 'Hints to Immigrants' in P. Fletcher *Qld.* 41 Then there is the squatter's or verandah chair, which is very comfortable to rest and smoke in, but which takes up too much room to be used indoors. **1902** E.B. Kennedy *Black Police Qld.* 218 Pushing them aside he sat down in one of the 'squatter' chairs and lit his pipe. **1926** M. Forrest *Hibiscus Heart* 25 Now, seated in his squatter chair, with his feet, sockless for coolness sake, thrust into an old pair of kangaroo-hide slippers. **1947** M. Raymond *Smiley gets Gun* 27 The sergeant .. got out of the squatter's chair and went muttering into his office. **1965** R.H. Conquest *Horses in Kitchen* 23 He'd sit on the veranda after dinner in one of the battered squatter's chairs. **1975** G.A.W. Smith *Once Green Jackaroo* 167 There was Jack dead drunk in the squatter chair. **1986** *Nat. Times* (Sydney) 21 Feb. 14/1 The old moneyed establishment .. clings to its gracious timber colonial mansions on stilts with wide verandas, squatter's chairs and ceiling fans. **1862** R. Henning *Lett.* (1952) 53 Mr Hedgeland has just been making for the veranda two of the easy-chairs called '**squatter's delights**'. They are made of two straight poles, which are leant against the wall of the house ladderwise. These are held together by two cross-bars, and to the bars is nailed a strip of strong canvas, such as we use for wool-bagging, and this forms the seat and back of the chair. The materials are simple enough, but I think it is the most comfortable kind of easy-chair I know. **1876** J.A. Edwards *Gilbert Gogger* 85 Would have pined to death had he not been able to sit in his squatter's delight under the kitchen verandah, and hold forth to his wondering auditors. **1879** 'Australian' *Adventures Qld.* 12 After tea, all but Mrs Brown adjourned to the verandah to recline in those rough but comfortable contrivances called 'squatter's delights', without which a bush verandah was incomplete. **1878** 'Ironbark' *Southerly Busters* 84 The **squatter kings** of New South Wales. **1886** 'Thirty-Five Yrs. Colonist' *Hard Times* 72 Shall squatter kings deny the land While hungering thousands idle stand? **1898** *Western Champion* (Barcaldine) 19 July 3/1 The squatter king, McCaughey, holds 100,000 acres. **1905** *Truth* (Sydney) 8 Jan. 1/7 The list of rents fixed by the Western Lands Board for pastoral leases is an interesting document. It shows that the great bulk of the land is held by banks and trading companies. The day of the squatter kings has passed. **1919** *Smith's Weekly* (Sydney) 1 Mar. 6/3 He thought he was a second Tyson, who was then the Squatter King. **1946** C. Fenner *Gathered Moss* 70 Melbourne had become the retiring place of squatter-kings and business men. **1860** 'Lady' *My Experiences in Aust.* 123 The **squatter pigeon** in particular is so little frightened at the approach of man that it seems almost cruel to betray its confidence. **1872** G.S. Baden-Powell *New Homes for Old Country* 353 Perhaps the best of the Australian birds for the table .. is the little 'squatter' pigeon. **1887** W.S.S. Tyrwhitt *New Chum in Qld. Bush* 159 The pretty little squatter pigeon .. will sit on her nest on the ground till your horse treads on her tail feathers. **1933** *Bulletin* (Sydney) 22 Mar. 21/3 A desirable little bird that is reported to have almost disappeared is the squatter pigeon (*Geophaps scripta*). **1956** A.C.C. Lock *Tropical Tapestry* 19 He flushed a squatter pigeon from almost under his feet. **1976** *Reader's Digest Compl. Bk. Austral. Birds* 243 Squatter pigeons feed on the ground and their diet is mainly seeds.

squatterdom. The squatters collectively (see Squatter 2 and 3); the practice of leasing Crown land for grazing purposes.

1855 W. Howitt *Land, Labor & Gold* II. 132 A perpetual squatterdom would be a perpetual disgrace to our science of colonization. **1859** W. Kelly *Life in Vic.* I. 143 The abolition of squatterdom and unlocking the lands was not regarded as cause and effect. **1875** 'Capricornus' *Squatting System Aust.* 11 Sydney .. was well irrigated by the golden shower that followed the rise of squatterdom. **1891** *Bulletin* (Sydney) 15 Aug. 18/1 Central Queensland squatterdom has made J.M. Niall its organiser. **1901** *Ibid.* 6 July 14/4 Squatterdom wears gloves because its hands are not clean. **1906** M. Cannon *That Damned Democrat* (1981) 88 *Plute against people.* Squatterdom scores. **1963** X. Herbert *Larger than Life* 94 There is now no 'done thing' in the doings of squatterdom half so classy as an 'eagle shoot'.

squatteress. A female squatter; a squatter's wife (see Squatter 3).

1878 G. Walch *Australasia* 18 Tom Talfourd .. had left her a wealthy squatteress, squattess, squattrix, or whatever the proper term may be. **1889** H. Egbert *Pretty Cockey* 114 Before the physician came, the squatteress was beyond his skill. **1909** E. Waltham *Life & Labour in Aust.* 30 On the occasion of our visit we were fortunate enough to witness the wedding of a young squatter and a more juvenile squattress. **1939** Franklin & Cusack *Pioneers on Parade* 11 It was a charming letter, though it contained no offer to pay the old squatteress's expenses. **1975** X. Herbert *Poor Fellow my Country* 681 Somewhat horse-faced young squatteress visiting from the South.

squatterie. *Hist.* Squattage 3.

1847 *Atlas* (Sydney) III. 62/2 Purchases a dray and

bullocks, loads with supplies, and off all start for new Providence squatterie. **1849** *Bell's Life in Sydney* 27 Jan. 3/4 Where'er we go, from North to South, In City, Town, or Squattery.

squatting, *vbl. n. Hist.* [f. SQUAT *v.*]

1. a. The action of occupying Crown land for grazing purposes; the system which allowed this. Also *attrib.*

1836 *Sydney Herald* 14 Apr. 3/4 An article, purporting to be a petition to the government to prevent improper squatting, has been drawn up. **1848** J.C. BYRNE *Twelve Yrs.' Wanderings* I. 186 *Squatting* in New South Wales, is the occupation without purchase of the Crown Lands, within the bounds of the colony, and of the vast extent of territory beyond the frontiers. **1857** W. HOWITT *Tallangetta* I. 158 How could such a thing as squatting exist when all the world was running at full speed? **1861** T. M'COMBIE *Austral. Sketches* 119 Not only squatting but even convictism . . have been of use in the early stages of colonisation. **1875** 'CAPRICORNUS' *Squatting System Aust.* 9 Squatting was hardening fast into an institution; grass claims were already spoken of as 'properties'. **1869** *Colonial Soc.* (Sydney) 18 Feb. 10 In the wild and squatting regions lived a youth, to fortune and to fame unknown. That is he lived up the country. **1890** W.F. BUCHANAN *Aust. to Rescue* 37 Squatting (pastoral occupation) is completely played out in New South Wales.

b. Special Comb. **squatting act,** any of several squatting acts introduced to restrain the unauthorized occupation of Crown land; **district,** an area available for squatting; **interest,** the squatters (see SQUATTER 2 and 3) collectively, esp. as a political force; **land,** *squatting district*; **lease,** an agreement under which Crown land is occupied for grazing purposes; the land so occupied; **licence,** a permit to occupy Crown land for grazing purposes; **question,** the subject of the squatting system as a matter of debate; **regulation,** a rule governing the practice of squatting; **run, station,** an area of Crown land occupied for grazing purposes (see also RUN 2 and STATION 2 a. and 3); **system,** the practice of occupying Crown land for grazing purposes; the allowing of this.

1840 *S. Austral. Rec.* (London) 29 Aug. 132 By the **Squatting Act** it is provided, that no sawyer shall cut in any district without a license. **1841** G. ARDEN *Recent Information Port Phillip* 114 There is a small assessment upon stock under the squatting act. **1846** *Moreton Bay Courier* 26 Dec. 2/3 *(heading)* The squatting act. **1857** *Illustr. Jrnl. Australasia* III. 124 Those who came after him were enabled to occupy large tracts at a nominal rent under the provisions of what is termed the Squatting Act. **1841** *Port Phillip Patriot* 16 Aug. 2/6 It was proposed to divide the country into **squatting districts.** **1845** *Atlas* (Sydney) I. 268/1 Had indeed the squatting districts occupied the whole territory of the British Crown in New South Wales, there might have been a shadow of an excuse. **1849** J.P. TOWNSEND *Rambles & Observations N.S.W.* 186 When railways shall be established, some squatting districts will doubtless become agricultural districts. **1859** W. FAIRFAX *Handbk. to Australasia* 187 Casino is in the squatting district of Clarence. **1869** *Bushmen, Publicans, & Politics* 18 Let us suppose a surveyed village situated in the centre of a squatting district ten miles all round it. **1882** W.B. CHRISTIE *Our Land Laws* 7 The so-called 'squatting' districts of the colony are divided into 4329 runs or squattages. **1842** *Colonial Observer* (Sydney) 24 Aug. 421/3 It was, in fact, an attempt to try the strength of the '**squatting interest**' against the strength of the government, in the administration of the government domain, and the protection of the aborigines. **1843** *Ibid.* 6 Sept. 1281/2 The Governor . . has repeatedly expressed himself unfavourably towards the squatting interest of the Colony. **1845** T. MCCOMBIE *Adventures of Colonist* 55 In New South Wales, the industry of the squatting (grazing) interest has forced the Colony to advance. **1847** *Port Phillip Herald* 2 Sept. (Suppl.), The public knew full well that the squatting interest was the true colonial interest. **1851** J.H. BURTON *Emigrant's Man.* i. 40 The 'great squatting interest', as it is termed, is now the leading aristocratic power in Australia. **1861** C. CAMPBELL *Squatting Question Considered* 5 Between 1840 and 1844, the squatting interest had become powerful. **1918** C.H. NORTHCOTT *Austral. Social Dev.* 65 Another phenomenon of great sociological significance, namely, the squatting interest. Squatters were the owners of large herds and flocks who moved them, without license or right of occupation, into the crown lands. **1846** *Moreton Bay Courier* 5 Sept. 2/4 The judicious and permanent regulation of the **squatting lands**—will be found in the Constitution. **1855** *Moreton Bay Free Press* 21 Aug. 3/2 Throughout the length and breadth of the squatting lands, large reserves for small farms have been laid out in all eligible situations, sufficient and more than sufficient to satisfy the requirements of small settlers for years to come. **1872** 'RESIDENT' *Glimpses Life Vic.* 12 A large proportion of the former squatting lands. **1859** W. FAIRFAX *Handbk. to Australasia* 195 At present much of it is shut up in the **squatting leases.** **1859** P. JUST *Aust.* 181 No squatting leases will be issued. **1877** 'CAPRICORNUS' *Land Law of Future* 12 The squatting lease was always and is still a valid transferable title. **1839** *Sydney Standard* 18 Mar. 4/3 Rents should be paid, as the fees for **Squatting Licenses** now are, to the Colonial Treasurer. **1840** A. RUSSELL *Tour through Austral. Colonies* 164 The original claimants to squat on such places, government protects on their paying the squatting licence. **1845** *Atlas* (Sydney) I. 555/1 The Squatting Licenses which profess upon the face of them to be licenses to use crown land for pasturage for one whole year on payment in advance of a con-si-der-a-tion of ten pounds sterling, have this year been materially altered. **1848** *Observer* (Melbourne) 19 Oct. 247/2 The landholders would be benefitted by prohibiting the holders of small Squatting Licenses from bringing any portion of their land into cultivation. **1852** G.B. EARP *Gold Colonies Aust.* 55 The number of squatting licenses issued is upwards of 1,500. **1884** 'R. BOLDREWOOD' *Old Melbourne Memories* 35, I had but to receive my squatting license, under the hand of the Governor of the Australias, for which I had paid ten pounds, and no white man could in any way disturb, harass, or dispossess me. **1846** *Moreton Bay Courier* 10 Oct. 2/3 The price of land has little to do with the **squatting question,** and any reduction in price could not affect the interests of graziers any more than it would those other classes of colonists. **1848** *HRA* (1925) 1st Ser. XXVI. 169 On the Squatting question, for instance, it considers that the system is too favourable for the large Graziers. **1856** *Jrnl. Australasia* I. 41 The great Squatting question . . may now be considered at rest. **1861** C. CAMPBELL *Squatting Question Considered* 3 The settlement of the squatting question is the natural supplement of legislation for the sale of Crown Lands. **1844** *Duncan's Weekly Register* 4 May 566/2 A meeting was held at Windsor, for the consideration of the new **squatting regulations.** **1845** *Portland Guardian* 27 Sept. 3/1 The squatters beyond the boundaries, it is probable, will be favored by the squatting regulations about to be promulgated. **1862** G.T. LLOYD *Thirty-Three Yrs. Tas. & Vic.* 381 There has ever been a strong feeling of opposition, on the part of the non-squatting community, to the holding of large tracts of country under the liberal squatting regulations. **1848** *Port Phillip Herald* 27 Apr. 2/4 The **Squatting runs** of the Port Phillip district are nearly equal to the surface of Scotland. **1849** *Belfast Gaz.* (Port Phillip) 20 Apr. 3/5 The Boards for examining Claims for Leases of Squatting Runs would probably be appointed on the return of the Governor to Head Quarters. **1851** *Empire* (Sydney) 24 Apr. 2/4 We may cite the sale by a city member of a squatting run for £1000. **1879** E. TRENERRY *Descr. Plan Austral. Trans-Continental Railway* 14 Even down to the year 1875 we find that the squatting runs were 865 in number, their average size being 26,552 acres. **1891** *Nineteenth Century* (London) Apr. 527 The drought of 1886 caused the abandonment of 5,000,000 acres of squatting runs in Queensland alone. **1841** *Port Phillip Patriot* 25 Feb. 4/4 Twenty of the principal **squatting stations** are already marked out for selection. **1843** J.F. BENNETT *Hist. & Descr. Acct. S.A.* 96 The only erections at a squatting station are a turf or slab hut, or probably a tent. **1848** *Information for Emigrants* ii. 22 Owing to the great extent of land occupied by each squatting station—on an average in some districts of from one hundred to a hundred and twenty square miles, and for the occupation of which, the sum of ten pounds is annually paid to Government—the country available for such pursuits is soon taken up. **1851** H. MELVILLE *Present State Aust.* 106 Locations that are 'beyond the boundaries' are what are called the squatting stations. **1853** MOSSMAN & BANISTER *Aust. Visited & Revisited* 67 A run or squatting station is composed of a number of these out-stations surrounding the home-stead at distances of four or five miles from each other. **1867** J. BONWICK *J. Batman* 35 He came here to prevent the country being a squatting station. **1878** R.B. SMYTH *Aborigines of Vic.* II. 275 *Wengal* obtained a good situation at a squatting station. **1837** *Colonist* (Sydney) 23 Mar. 95/2 The inroad upon his property is so great as to drive him to the **Squatting System**, actually abandoning all idea of improving the land he has purchased so dearly, and going off miles and miles into the interior beyond all social intercourse with his fellow creatures. **1845** C.J. BAKER *Sydney & Melbourne* 51 The squatting system is almost universally adopted throughout New South Wales by both graziers and sheep-farmers. **1849** *Sydney Guardian* 1 Jan. 125/3 The squatting system necessarily isolates and uncivilises those engaged in it. **1855** W. CAMPBELL *Crown Lands Aust.* 49 It is rather amusing to observe avowed opponents of the present squatting system . . unwittingly proposing a *second edition* of the present system. **1861** C. CAMPBELL *Squatting Question Considered* 4 By the end of 1839, the country was occupied as far as the dividing range, under a general squatting system, which authorised the occupation of any crown lands on payment of a license at the rate of £10 per annum.

2. a. Sheep or cattle raising by squatters (chiefly senses 2 and 3); stockholding. Also *attrib.*

1845 *Port Phillip Gaz.* 4 June 2 Squatting is, by far, the most gigantic interest in Australia. **1859** W. BURROWS *Adventures Mounted Trooper* p. xi, Twelve years ago, the chief employment of the Australian settler was sheep-rearing—or squatting. **1865** G.F. ANGAS *Aust.* 273 Grazing is called in Australia 'squatting', and the graziers are known by the singular appellation of 'squatters'. **1873** A. TROLLOPE *Aust. & N.Z.* I. 115 Unless rain came soon squatting affairs would begin to 'look blue'. **1876** J.B. STEPHENS *Hundred Pounds* 188 Some of those lazy intervals which all dwellers on cattle-stations are familiar with, when there is neither mustering, nor tailing, nor branding. . . One of those lulls from work during which 'squatting' approaches most nearly to a literal fact. **1884** G. WIGHT *Qld.* 67 Two of Queensland's greatest industries—Squatting and Agriculture. **1896** *Austral. Agriculturist* (rev. ed.) 157 Victoria and our own southern districts offer striking examples of successful change from the old style of squatting to a system of grazing-farming. **1900** T. MAJOR *Leaves from Squatter's Note Bk.* p. ix, Australian squatting is sick unto death. **1919** *Smith's Weekly* (Sydney) 1 Mar. 6/3 Squatting pays well these times; and it was worth while even in the old days when £3 was thought a good price on the hoof for store bullocks.

b. Comb. **squatting firm, industry, property.**

1879 S.W. SILVER *Austral. Grazier's Guide* 18 While the colonies are full of instances of prosperous **squatting firms,** the number of pastoral or agricultural companies which have survived their initiation may be counted upon one's finger. **1883** C. PROUD *Murray & Darling Trade* 17 In one instance twelve boxes were sent up by one of our largest squatting firms to the Upper Darling. **1897** T.W. BEILLEY *Australasia's Goldfields* 58 A well-to-do squatter, possessed of a magnificent fattening station, free of debt or liability . . agreed to the proposal of the managing partner of a squatting firm. **1886** J.F. CONIGRAVE *S.A.* 104 The progress of the **squatting industry** can be judged by the following returns of South Australian grown wools sold in the London auctions. **1921** L.G. JONES *Flockmaster's Companion* p. iv, He is a grandson of the late Mr Robert Jones, a pioneer of the squatting industry of that colony. **1927** A. CROMBIE *After Sixty Yrs.* 88 The leading representatives of the squatting industry. **1871** *Austral. Town & Country Jrnl.* (Sydney) 21 June 92/2 Money being again sufficiently plentiful to cause capitalists to look to **squatting properties** as a safe investment. **1879** *Hist. Berry Ministry* 20 It is reported that the Premier has invested in a large squatting property. **1881** J.C.F. JOHNSON *To Mount Browne & Back* 12 Carona . . is one of the most extensive squatting properties in the North-East. **1880** *S.-E. District S.A.* 22 Another squatting property which we passed to our right is Moyhall. **1889** *S.A. Parl. Papers* II. no. 77 48 About twenty years since I purchased a squatting property in Queensland.

squatting, *ppl. a.* [f. SQUAT *v.*] Of a person, etc.: that occupies land as a squatter (see SQUATTER 2 and 3); associated with such occupation.

1835 *True Colonist* (Hobart) 31 July 3/1 To scare away such squatting intruders as Mr Bateman, and his gigantic Company. **1845** C. GRIFFITH *Present State & Prospects Port Phillip* 19 Wheat will be raised on cheaper terms by persons who apply themselves wholly to this pursuit than it can be by the squatting stockholders of the present day. **1849** *Britannia* (Hobart) 3 May 3/5 Unprecedented dry weather is giving serious apprehension to our squatting community. **1856** J. BONWICK *W. Buckley* 75

The Moravian teachers near Lake Boga have been compelled to return home, chiefly through the opposition of some of their squatting neighbours. **1875** 'CAPRICORNUS' *Squatting System Aust.* 10 With the issue of the leases in 1846 the first squatting dynasty . . reached the height of its power. **1883** R.E.N. TWOPENY *Town Life Aust.* 244 The squatting class in Australia correspond to the landed gentry of England. **1898** D.W. CARNEGIE *Spinifex & Sand* 329 It is hardly fair to class the whole squatting population as savage ruffians. **1908** *Bulletin* (Sydney) 5 Mar. 14/2 Reasonable squatting men want to merely kill a freezing and export business. **1921** C.E.W. BEAN *Official Hist. Aust. 1914–18* I. 138 An officer of the citizen forces, an Australian pastoralist coming of an old 'squatting' family. **1953** C. WILLS *Austral. Passport* 63 This neighbour . . was a member of one of the big 'squatting' (landowning) families. **1961** *Bulletin* (Sydney) 8 Feb. 15/3 The squatting blood, in fact, has integrated itself into that of the national pool of ability very well.

squattocracy. Also **squatocracy.** The squatters as an interest group; the squatters as a socio-economic group (see SQUATTER 2 and 3).

1843 *Sydney Morning Herald* 6 July 2/7 The proceeds to be derived from the dairy, will set our squatocracy to rights before Christmas. **1844** *Bee of Aust.* (Sydney) 2 Nov. 4/1, I propose the grumbling squattocracy to tax, And to stick to the rich grazing community like wax. **1855** E.H. HARGRAVES *Aust. & Goldfields* 189 Owners of vast herds of cattle, droves of horses, and flocks of sheep . . have raised up a kind of estate . . or class . . known by the name of the 'Squatocracy'. **1862** C. ASPINALL *Three Yrs. Melbourne* 235 The Squattocracy are proverbially kind and open-hearted. **1878** *Squatters' Plum* 5 So long as the squattocracy are permitted to grasp the best acres in the country, who will be satisfied with the refuse? **1890** MRS R.D. DOUGLAS *Romance at Antipodes* 169 The 'squatocracy', which is really the aristocracy of Australia, is well represented here. **1906** *Gadfly* (Adelaide) 7 Mar. 5/1 The farmer . . wants land for his sons. . . To expect to get that from a party largely made up of the Squattocracy would be altogether too confiding on the part of the farmer. **1919** C.A. BERNAYS *Qld. Politics during Sixty Yrs.* 193 The first hint that in addition to a squattocracy there was a baby democracy claiming a share in the government of the country. **1930** 'BRENT OF BIN BIN' *Ten Creeks Run* (1952) 34 She was no rider, and had not been accepted by the squattocracy as she had hoped. **1950** G.S. CASEY *City of Men* 27 He was a perfect picture of that class of arrogant, big landholders to whom the Australians referred, with grudging respect and hearty hatred as 'the squatocracy'. **1967** A. SEYMOUR *One Day of Yr.* 105 All the best land had gone umpteen years ago, back in the 80s, the 70s, to the big boys, the squattocracy. **1983** *Canberra Times* 2 Oct. 8/4 The scrapbook of an artistically inclined daughter of the squattocracy.

Hence **squattocrat** *n.*, a member of the squattocracy.

1910 *Bulletin* (Sydney) 14 Apr. 14/1 The squattocrats never coined more cash in their lives than they have done during the past five years.

squattocratic, *a.* Also **squatocratic.** Of or pertaining to the squattocracy, or to one of its members. Also **squattocratical** *a.*

1843 *Maitland Mercury* 26 Apr. 2/5 The pernicious code was the offspring of *squattocratical* influence. **1846** *Bell's Life in Sydney* 27 June 2/3 After a rapid transit from the flat (not flats) of Campbellfield to the luxurious and fertile, though at this stage *raythe*r frigid, Plains of Bathurst, our Racing Reporter reached the squatocratical District of Wellington. **1854** *Melbourne Morning Herald* 18 Feb. 4/5 Squattocratic impudence. **1858** E.A. MARTIN *Life & Speeches D.H. Deniehy* (1884) 70 An attempt on the part of the Tory Squattocratic party to wrest the prize of responsible government for the purpose of perpetrating their own dominance. **1891** D. FERGUSON *Vicissitudes Bush Life* 2, I prepared to start for Australia to join a wealthy, 'squatocratic' relative. **1897** *Tocsin* (Melbourne) 16 Oct. 3/2 At last this constituency seems to have a chance of shaking off the squattocratic Staughton. **1963** X. HERBERT *Larger than Life* 94 It was inevitable that the aeroplane should replace the horse as the squatter's mount for hunting, for the squattocratic 'shoot'. **1975** —— *Poor Fellow my Country* 31 Not that Piggy would admit anything of the sort . . with his squattocratic wife and daughters.

squaw. *Obs.* [Transf. use of *squaw* a North American Indian woman or wife.]

1. An Aboriginal woman or wife. Also *attrib.*

1837 E. FRASER *Narr. of Capture* 7 About half an hour after the departure of the savages, I was visited by a very great number of their squaws, accompanied by their children. **1847** E.W. LANDOR *Bushman* 191 Why . . should he be violently dragged from the arms of his *wilgied* squaws, and his little pot-bellied piccaninnies. *c* **1856** F. GERSTAECKER *Life in Bush* 19 It was Cloko, his black squaw, whom he had been on the point of leaving. **1867** 'COLONIST' *Life's Work* 94 You give us tucker . . squaw very bad, tumble down sick; big lot pain, very ill want good tucker.

2. Special Comb. **squaw man,** a white man consorting with an Aboriginal woman.

1911 L.C.E. GEE *Gen. Rep. Tanami Goldfield* 20 The gin helper was not much in evidence. There were not many 'Komboes' or Squaw men. Still, I am sorry to say that it is a 'custom of the country' throughout the Territory.

squeaker.

1. Any of several birds to which a squeaking call is attributed, as the *noisy miner* (see NOISY), WHITEFACE, and (chiefly *W.A.*) *grey currawong* (see GREY *a.*).

1848 J. GOULD *Birds of Aust.* II. Pl. 45, *Strepera anaphonensis.* Grey Crow-Shrike. . . *Dje-läak*, Aborigines of Western Australia. *Squeaker*, of the Colonists. **1889** *Proc. Linnean Soc. N.S.W.* IV. 409 *Xerophila leucopsis* . . local name 'Squeaker'. **1905** *Emu* IV. 147 'Squeaker', which is a vernacular for the Leaden Crow-Shrike (Strepera) in Western Australia. **1927** J. POLLARD *Rose of Bushlands* 76 She heard a double high-pitched squeak come from the same direction and recognised the voice of a squeaker. Squeakers, the bell-magpies, were plentiful in the South. **1933** J.L. GLASCOCK *Jarrah Leaves* 81 The bush was alive with darting parrots and magpies and 'squeakers', with their incessant 'Squeak-squeak-squawk-squawk: It's gonna rain, it's gonna rain'. **1945** C. BARRETT *Austral. Bird Life* 189 The eastern whiteface (*A[phelocephala] leucopsis*) . . despite its cheerful song, is called 'squeaker'. **1965** *Austral. Encycl.* VIII. 258 Squeaker, a name commonly used in Western Australia for the grey currawong or crow-shrike (*Strepera versicolor*) because one of its notes has been likened to the mewing of a cat or the sound of a small tin trumpet.

2. Any of several small cicadas of the genera *Melampsalta* and *Pauropsalta*.

1907 W.W. FROGGATT *Austral. Insects* 353 Some species [of *Melampsalta*, cicada] are very numerous in early summer, and are known as 'Squeakers' on account of their musical notes. **1935** K.C. MCKEOWN *Insect Wonders Aust.* 195 The popular interest in cicadas . . is indicated by their common names . . the Squeaker and the Floury Miller—since popular names are bestowed only upon very familiar creatures. **1959** S.J. BAKER *Drum* 147 *Squeaker*, a type of cicada. **1965** *Austral. Encycl.* II. 380 Many small species [of cicada] are grouped together in the genera *Melampsalta* and *Pauropsalta* ('squeakers'), some species of which have been recorded as damaging fruit-trees while laying their eggs.

3. BETTONG.

1941 E. TROUGHTON *Furred Animals Aust.* 155 A variety of more or less local popular names have been applied to the animals [*sc.* Short-nosed Rat-Kangaroos], including Bettongs . . and Squeakers. **1954** C. BARRETT *Wild Life Aust. & New Guinea* 10 In South Australia brush-tailed Bettongs were used for coursing. Dealers sold them in hundreds at ninepence a-piece. 'Squeakers', as they were called . . have become rare. **1965** *Austral. Encycl.* V. 157 The short-nosed rat-kangaroos . . are grouped in the genus *Bettongia*. . . Once very plentiful, these attractive marsupials were known as 'squeakers' by the whites and 'tungoos' by the aborigines in South Australia.

squib, *n.* [Spec. use of *squib* 'a mean, insignificant or paltry fellow': see OED(S *sb.* 4.] A horse lacking stamina; hence, a spineless person, a coward.

1908 E.S. SORENSON *Squatter's Ward* 122 It's a monty the little squib would let out a yell jest as I was gettin' clear. **1915** DREW & EVANS *Grafter* 68 'The second horse don't count. . . He's a squib, and is liable to turn it up any minute. What did I tell you,' he cried, as the second horse fell back. **1918** A. WRIGHT *Breed holds Good* 15 'That squib won't see the mile out,' exclaimed Tom. **1933** *Bulletin* (Sydney) 15 Nov. 8/4 In the result stayers reproducing the old-time qualities of the Australian thoroughbred became rare; but speedy squibs abounded. **1945** 'MASTER-SARG' *Yank discovers Aust.* 46 Dingo is the slang word for coward. . . The dingo strikes by stealth and will avoid danger or a fight at any cost—thus the slang term for a 'squib'—another Australianism for coward, though not quite so strong. **1954** J. WATEN *Unbending* 143 A big mob came round last night and they made a lot of noise. But they were big squibs. **1965** F. HARDY *Yarns of Billy Borker* 19 Biggest squib that ever played, but keen. **1968** J. ALARD *He who shoots Last* 12 'I'm no squib,' he thought, 'I'll show them.' **1978** *Telegraph* (Brisbane) 8 Feb. 20/1 Don Ash is the sort of bloke who makes you feel a squib for crying off with some minor ache or pain from that daily canter around the block. **1984** *Sun-Herald* (Sydney) 26 Feb. 78/3 It has been said, among other things, that the Golden Slipper is a race for speedy squibs.

squib, *v.* [Prob. Br. dial. *squib* to run away: see EDD *v.*[2]]

1. *trans.* To evade (a difficulty or responsibility); to shirk through fear or cowardice (freq. with **it** as obj.). Also *intr.*

1918 G. DALE *Industr. Hist. Broken Hill* 170 All the employers had agreed to fight the Union, but had squibbed it at the last moment. **1919** *Aussie: Austral. Soldiers' Mag.* Jan. 11/1 A certain Rosella in the Aussie Army is . . always regarding a soldier proceeding in a direction other than towards the Front line as squibbing it. **1923** *Bailey, M.L.A. Exonerated* (Austral. Workers Union) 54 The words he used were, 'If you vote solid for the Executive and meet organisation with organisation, that's the only chance of beating it,' and I said I was not going to squib it. **1932** *Austral. Ring* II. xxv. 13 Phil Boulton, middleweight wrestler, wishes it to be known that he is not 'squibbing it' by not accepting Joe Keato's recent challenge for a match with a £20 side bet. **1943** *Southerly* i. 19 The mob roared in his ears. 'Go on! Hit him! Don't squib it! Dingo!' **1946** K. TENNANT *Lost Haven* 308 You'll probably squib out of it at the last moment. **1951** S. HICKEY *Travelled Roads* 41 W.M. Hughes has squibbed it at the outset by voting against the measure. **1965** R.H. CONQUEST *Horses in Kitchen* 59 A young fellow like you—a bloke who's never been hurt real bad, and who won't squib the challenge horses. **1978** K. GARVEY *Tales of my Uncle Henry* 22 Tiger's supporters couldn't believe that their champion had squibbed it, and Stevo come in for a good bit of chiackin' which didn't improve his temper much.

2. *intr.* To fail to act; to back down; to give in. Also with **on**: to betray or let down.

1934 *Red Star* (Perth) 9 Nov. 3/3 (*heading*) Lang candidate squibbing. **1945** *Coast to Coast 1944* 5 I'll let him through; it's better to squib than to wreck old Dutch and myself too. **1954** J. WATEN *Unbending* 87 'I won't squib on my mates over there,' he concluded pointing to the northern wall. **1956** B.J. RAYMENT *My Towri* 49, I agreed to catch one of the broken-in stallions if Bill would catch the other. I caught and removed mine but he squibbed. **1962** *Coast to Coast 1961–62* 83 He could finish on a good wicket in anything. And never squib on a bloke. **1984** *Sydney Morning Herald* 23 Feb. 9/6 The Treasury-types' eternal search for 'a politician with some guts' is futile. Mr Fraser looked tough enough at the time, but he squibbed.

squire. A young SNAPPER: see quot. 1969.

1874 *N.S.W. Rep. R. Comm. Fisheries* (1880) 10 The ordinary schnapper, or count fish, implies that all of a certain size are to count as twelve to the dozen, the shoal or school-fish, eighteen or twenty-four to the dozen; and the squire, thirty or thirty-six to the dozen. **1895** C. THACKERAY *Amateur Fisherman's Guide* 60 Splendid schnapper are caught, also sargent-baker, mowang, carp, squire. **1917** —— *Goliath Joe* 24 Bill copped a coupler groper, an' two squire. **1935** DAVISON & NICHOLLS *Blue Coast Caravan* 166 The squire—young schnapper we believe—were pink with silver underpants. . . The pink part of the body was spangled with kingfisher blue. **1969** J. POLLARD *Austral. & N.Z. Fishing* 712 At about a foot in length they are called squire, and having reached a legally and domestically acceptable size they are a welcome addition to the angler's catch.

squirrel.

1. A gliding possum (see *flying possum* FLYING); (chiefly *Qld.*) GREATER GLIDER. Also *attrib.*

1788 *HRA* (1914) 1st Ser. I. 31 Many trees were seen with holes that had been enlarged by the natives to get at the animal, either the squirrel [etc.]. **1794** G. SHAW *Zool. New Holland* 29 *Didelphis Sciurea.* The Squirrel Opossum . . has so much the appearance of a squirrel, that on a cursory view it might readily pass for such. A more exact inspection into its characters will however evince it to be a genuine Opossum. **1804** G. CALEY in A.E.J. Andrews *Devil's Wilderness* (1984) 95 In the night a Squirrel made a noise. **1820** C. JEFFREYS *Van Dieman's Land* 108 The wild animals consist of . . the opossum, the squirrel, the bandy-coat. **1842** R.G. JAMESON *N.Z., S.A., & N.S.W.* 116 This conformation [*sc.* marsupial] is common to all the quadrupeds of Australia, except the dingo. It comprehends the genera of . . *phalangista* or squirrel, *didelphys* or opossum. **1879** 'AUSTRALIAN' *Adventures Qld.* 15 Cutting out opossums, squirrels, or wild honey, from the hollow branches. **1910** J. MATHEW *Two Representative Tribes Qld.* 121 The women made dillie-bags of various patterns and sizes, the material being grass or string of squirrel fur. **1926** A.S. LE SOUEF et al. *Wild Animals Australasia* 256 As with most of the marsupials, the young 'squirrel' is born in June. **1956** K. TENNANT *Honey Flow* 189 We had convinced Bidgee that we must leave the squirrel possum in the grass where his mother could find him.

2. Special Comb. **squirrel glider,** the gliding possum *Petaurus norfolcensis* of e. mainland Aust., the soft fur of which is greyish above with a dark central stripe, and pale beneath; see also *sugar squirrel* SUGAR 3; formerly also **squirrel flying phalanger.**

c **1880** *Cassell's Nat. Hist.* III. 207 (OED) The Squirrel Flying Phalanger . . *Petaurus sciureus* . . has been called the Squirrel Flying Phalanger by mistake. **1894** R. LYDEKKER *Hand-Bk. Marsupialia & Monotremata* 104 Squirrel flying phalanger. *Petaurus sciureus* . . size medium; fur soft and silky, slightly woolly. General colour soft pale grey. **1943** C. BARRETT *Austral. Animal Bk.* 65 The squirrel flying phalanger or squirrel glider (*Petaurus norfolcensis*) . . has been known for more than a century and a half, having first been described as 'The Norfolk Island Flying Squirrel', in 1789. **1965** *Austral. Encycl.* VII. 235 The larger squirrel-glider (*Petaurus norfolcensis*) more nearly resembles the American grey squirrel, with its fluffier tail, which is about 9 inches long and has fur about 1½ inches long on the tail-base. **1970** W.D.L. RIDE *Guide Native Mammals Aust.* 79 Squirrel Gliders will readily take small birds, and mice, too. **1983** R. STRAHAN *Compl. Bk. Austral. Mammals* 140 Almost twice the size of the Sugar Glider, the Squirrel Glider is otherwise similar to it in appearance and gliding ability.

squirt, *n.*[1] A revolver.

1899 J. BRADSHAW *Quirindi Bank Robbery* 36 He covered me with his squirt, and sang out 'Bail up, or may Hall admire me if I don't blow the stuffing out of you in a slantingdicular direction.' **1912** —— *Highway Robbery under Arms* (ed. 3) 39 There they were, six of them, with guns, squirts, tomahawks. **1925** J.E. LIDDLE *Selected Poems* 82 Rifle and shot-gun, squirt and swag. **1941** *Salt* (Melbourne) 22 Dec. 34 *Squirt,* revolver.

squirt, *n.*[2] *Shearing. Obs.* Rhyming slang for EXPERT *n.* a.

1912 R.S. TAIT *Scotty Mac* 78 'Git the squirt'. . . 'Wanted, expert,' he yelled. **1915** *Bulletin* (Sydney) 28 Oct. 22/3 The expert who attends all machinery is invariably 'the squirt'.

squiz, *n.* Also **squizz.** [See next.] A look; an inspection.

1913 C.J. DENNIS *Backblock Ballads* 199 *Squiz,* a glance. **1915** —— *Songs of Sentimental Bloke* 15 Jist take a squiz at this, an' tell me can Some square an' honist tom take this to be 'Er own true man? **1947** F. CLUNE *Roaming around Aust.* 43 Or perhaps the Dutch Government might be persuaded to make a present of Dirck's original plate, to be preserved at Canberra, where historians could have a squiz at it. **1959** M. RAYMOND *Smiley roams Road* 33 'You can stay here if you like,' he told his mate. 'I'm going to have a squiz.' **1965** K. SMITH *OGF* 195 Hey, youse blokes! Come over here and take a squiz at *this!* **1973** J. POWERS *Last of Knucklemen* (1974) 38 Take a squizz out that window. Have a look at it. **1980** M. BAIL *Homesickness* 64 Have you been to the Imperial War Museum. I'd always wanted to have a squiz there.

squiz, *v.* [Br. dial.: see EDD.] *intr.* To look (at). Also *trans.*, to inspect.

1941 S.J. BAKER *Pop. Dict. Austral. Slang* 71 *Squiz,* to look at, inspect. **1949** C.B. MAXWELL *Surf* 4 He only wanted to squiz at the beach from the best vantage point of all, the balcony of the club. **1979** J. WILLIAMS *White River* 49 The mechanic refuelled and no doubt squizzed the plane's cargo.

stab, *n. Australian National Football.* [Spec. use of *stab* a vigorous thrust.] Used *attrib.* in Special Comb. **stab kick, (a)** a fast, low kick to a team-mate; **(b)** one skilled at so kicking; **pass,** *stab kick* (a); so **stab-passing** *vbl. n.*

1936 E.C.H. TAYLOR et al. *Our Austral. Game Football* 19 **Stab Kick**—This kick is most effective when short passing is necessary. **1963** *Footy Fan* (Melbourne) I. i. 21 Haydn Bunton was not a great stab-kick for those times but he would have passed in the present day speed game. **1964** J. POLLARD *High Mark* 23, I remember how I first gained a clue or two watching Bobby Rose, the neatest, most accurate stab-kick I have ever seen. **1973** P. MCKENNA *My World of Football* 76 (*caption*) The stab kick is a short distance, accuracy kick. **1982** *Bulletin* (Sydney) 28 Sept. 37/2 The increasing speed of the game stimulated the replacement of the two kicking styles which were once thought to represent the ultimate. . . The first to go was the stab kick, the grass-cutting drop kick pass which players . . could drill into a team-mate's chest at 40 paces. **1960** *N.T. News* (Darwin) 12 Jan. 8/3 Like lightning it was Tahs again for Vierk to take a **stab pass** and find the big timber. **1963** L. RICHARDS *Boots & All!* 47 Little Thorold was certainly spectacular and one of the best exponents of the stab-pass ever to play. **1969** A. HOPGOOD *And Big Men Fly* 36 A beautiful stabpass, right down the throat of team-mate Morris. **1972** J. HIBBERD *Stretch of Imagination* (1973) 47 Two minutes of silence for Mort, a man who was once the life of the party, who always did the right thing, a digger who has ceased to shovel, an Einstein of the stab pass and brindle chuck. **1973** J. DUNN *How to play Football* 35 Of course, the idea of the stab-pass is to find a team-mate's chest. **1982** *Bulletin* (Sydney) 28 Sept. 37/2 Many stab passes failed to reach their targets, and in any case stab passing was impossible on muddy grounds. The drop kick itself was subject to this limitation, and players of the late 1960s no longer had the time to steady before delivering it properly.

stab, *v. Australian National Football.* [f. prec.] *trans.* To execute (a stab pass).

1964 J. POLLARD *High Mark* 23 Once clear, he suddenly steadied a step, and stabbed the pass.

stack, *v. trans.* With **on**: to contrive; to produce. See also BLUE *n.*[2] 4 and TURN *n.* 2.

1965 J. WYNNUM *Jiggin' in Riggin'* 54 'I'm not stacking on any act, believe me,' moaned Stripey. **1979** B. HUMPHRIES *Bazza comes into his Own,* No worries, Ron, you'll stack on a beaut corroborree dance as soon as youse cop this Abbo style music.

stag. [Br. dial.: see OED *sb.*[1] 3.]

1. A beast castrated after reaching maturity; an inferior bullock.

1848 *Adelaide Miscellany* 2 Dec. 280 My bucolic knowledge . . left me in total ignorance of the nice distinction between yearlings, steers, heifers, stags [etc.]. **1876** J.A. EDWARDS *Gilbert Gogger* 120 Get that old stag that is in the paddock. **1880** J.B. STEVENSON *Seven Yrs. Austral. Bush* 39 A stag is a bullock which is coarse about the head and horns. **1915** G. SARGANT *Sweet Heart of Bush* 148 The cattle they were after were a mob made up of a bull, two stags, and a few stores and poddies. **1923** J. BOWES *Jackaroos* 84 Among the rejects was a roan stag, a coarse bullock of inferior quality. **1932** H. PRIEST *Call of Bush* 206 There were cattle to be mustered and 'stags' (bulls that have been emasculated when full grown, and that by their sheer savageness oust the effective males from the herd) to be 'cut out'. **1982** N. KEESING *Lily on Dustbin* 168 A calf is also known as a 'poddy', and if male and allowed to grow up so, it is called successively a 'bull calf', a 'bull' and, if castrated in adulthood, a 'stag'.

2. Shortening of *ram stag* (see RAM *n.* 1).

1919 *Bulletin* (Sydney) 11 Dec. 20/2 A Westralian shearer barbered 321 jumbucks in one day. True, he was paid for 321, but he took the overcoats off only 180. A large number of them were stags and rams, which were counted as 'doubles'.

staggering bob. [Br. dial.: see OED *staggering, ppl. a.* 1 d.] A newly-born calf; veal (see also quot. 1978).

1874 C. DE BOOS *Congewoi Correspondence* 157 Well, there wasn't nothing handy afore I'd cooled down, and so master Staggerin Bob got orf that time, and I was saved from makin a fooler myself. **1879** 'OLD HAND' *Journey Port Phillip to S.A.* 45 We were compelled to live upon what the men called 'staggering bob'—that is, newly born calves. **1900** 'WOOMERA' *Life & Experiences Ex-Convict* 15 He used to go about with two old caps tied up around his feet for shoes, and his 1 lb. of 'staggering bob', when cooked and eaten, was almost as nothing to him by way of checking hunger. **1901** *Bulletin* (Sydney) 7 Dec. 30/2 The very youngest calf, the merest staggering-Bob two days old, will lie as close as a snake in cover if left in hiding by his mother. **1903** E. PALMER *Early Days N. Qld.* 119 All their rations and ammunition were spoilt, and they had to live on young calf, 'staggering bob', as they called it. **1959** M. DURACK *Kings in Grass Castles* 230 They had been forced to dispose of no less than thirteen hundred new-born calves during the trip. It was a complete waste, for stockmen were oddly squeamish about eating veal or 'staggering Bob' as it was known in the cattle camps. **1978** F. HOWARD *Moleskin Gentry* 23 The serve of instant veal or calves offal, known on the Lachlan as 'staggering Bob' . . was cut from a fresh-killed beast and cooked over a camp fire.

stagger juice. [Used elsewhere but recorded earliest in Aust.: see OED(S *stagger, sb.*[1] 4.] Alcoholic liquor. Also *attrib.*

1896 *S.A. Parl. Debates* 14 July 141 The beautiful barmaids could only be regarded as the polished fangs of the stagger-juice rattlesnake. **1899** K. O'MALLEY *Second Message Sovereign Electors Encounter Bay* 9 When the city sharper is after the good young man from the country, does he invite him to a prayer meeting? No; but *to a drunkery,* and when he is full of stagger juice he empties his pockets and clears. **1907** A. MACDONALD *In Land of Pearl & Gold* 11, I sat on a barrel and lit a cigarette, knowing that a real 'stagger-juice' thirst would soon stop Bill's flow of eloquence. **1908** *Clipper* (Hobart) 18 Jan. 10/1 Recent investigations into the quality of the 'stagger-juice' retailed in these parts has produced a mild sort of scare. **1916** *Fort Critic* (Geelong) 17 June 1/2 Refrain from . . stagger juice and all other sorts of juices. **1938** W. DENNING *Capital City* 62 King O'Malley . . had a few violent prejudices. One of these was against high officials, whom he designated . . 'the gilt-spurred roosters'. . . Malted and spirituous liquors . . he designated as 'stagger-juice'. **1962** J. WYNNUM *Tar Dust* 82 'These two bowls of punch look exciting'. . . 'Well now, that one . . is our customary Stagger Juice.'

Hence **stagger juicerie** *n.*, a public house.

1899 K. O'MALLEY *Second Message to Sovereign Electors Encounter Bay* 32 They did not see that the Sunday-closing law was observed. The law was violated by stagger juiceries and booseries in an open way.

stagger-weed. The introduced European annual herb *Stachys arvensis* (fam. Lamiaceae), naturalized in temperate Aust.

1903 *Proc. Linnean Soc. N.S.W.* XXVIII. 766 *Stachys arvensis.* . . The common weed known as 'Stagger Weed' on the mainland. **1920** J.H. MAIDEN *Weeds N.S.W.* 5 *Stachys arvensis,* the so-called 'Stagger Weed', is . . widely distributed. **1926** *Bulletin* (Sydney) 11 Nov. 24/1 Another curse has come to blight the lives of N.S.W. sheep farmers. It is the 'stagger' or 'shiver' weed, technically *Stachys arvensis,* a native of Europe and Western Asia. The symptoms of poisoning are similar to those of the well-known sheep poisons 'marsh-mallow' and 'stagger-nettle', with the additional shivering. **1965** *Austral. Encycl.* IX. 227 Staggerweed (*Stachys*) is injurious to stock after prolonged feeding. **1981** G.M. CUNNINGHAM et al. *Plants Western N.S.W.* 577 In general, animals should not be grazed on pastures infested by stagger-weed.

staghorn. [See quot. 1852.] An epiphytic fern of the genus *Platycerium* (fam. Polypodiaceae), esp. the commonly cultivated *P. superbum* of Qld., n. N.S.W., and Malaysia. Also **staghorn fern, stag's horn (fern).**

1852 G.C. MUNDY *Our Antipodes* II. 27 On the forks of some of the older timber-trees grew, also, the stag-horn fern, as large as the biggest cabbage, the fronds exactly resembling the palmated antlers of the moose and reindeer. **1855** W. HOWITT *Land, Labor & Gold* II. 356 *Platycerium grande*, great staghorn fern, New South Wales. **1867** *Lang. Native Flowers Tas.* 7 Stag's Horn Fern . . I attach myself to you. **1882** *Austral. Handbk.* 392 Three fourths of Australian ferns belong to this colony. Amongst these are the 'Stag's horn' (*Platycerium grande* . .) [etc.]. **1887** H. GULLETT *Tropical N.S.W.* 9 Let us take a single tree—say, for instance this venerable teak. . . See the enormous bird's-nest ferns and immense staghorns growing in its forks. **1888** *Sydney Morning Herald* 24 Jan. (Centennial Suppl.) 1/6 The stag's horn ferns (*platycerium*), which are remarkable as being true epiphytes, attaching themselves to trees or rocks, also grow to an extraordinary size. **1899** R. SEMON *In Austral. Bush* 129 Amongst the branches . . mighty epiphytic ferns luxuriate, amongst others the 'crow-nest fern' (*Asplenium nidus*) and the 'stag-horn fern' (*Platycerium alcicorne*). **1903** *Emu* III. 81 'Staghorn' and other hardy ferns flourished luxuriantly. **1920** B. CRONIN *Timber Wolves* 44 Enough staghorn fern to bed a cow, and a morsel of prickly moses. **1948** P.J. HURLEY *Red Cedar* 143 Staghorns, Elkhorns, and Birds' Nest Ferns festooned the tree trunks. **1959** *Meanjin* 135 He raises his eyes to the staghorns that droop from the boles of the tall Burdekin plums or follows the flight of a black-and-orange regent-bird. **1984** K.A.W. WILLIAMS *Native Plants Qld.* I. 238 Staghorn. . . This species [*sc. Platycerium superbum*] forms a single plant. It becomes increasingly larger. . . Aged specimens . . may weigh upwards of 80 kg.

stain. *Obs.* The stigma of convict ancestry; TAINT. See also BIRTHSTAIN.

1872 'TASMANIAN LADY' *Treasures, Lost & Found* 134 It will be long, long years before the stain of our birthmark shall wear away; it will break out again and again; it will cling to us as Gehazi's leprosy clung to his accursed and suffering offspring. **1893** S. NEWLAND *Paving Way* 74 Love her! my God, I do love her! but if there is this convict stain, what am I to do?

stand, *n.* The position occupied by a shearer in a shearing shed; a shearing job; the shearer occupying a stand. Also *attrib.*, as (six, etc.)-**stand shed,** a shed having (a specified number of) stands.

1888 *Boomerang* (Brisbane) Mar. 3 His next 'stand', who was a good man with the clippers, challenged him to a brush for a score. **1895** *Worker* (Sydney) 5 Jan. 3/3 He changed his song before very long, For he learned that to obtain a stand He'd have to revoke, at a single stroke, His liberties at the squatter's command. **1904** *Shearer* (Sydney) 30 July 7/1 Members desirous of obtaining stands in any of the following sheds, in which there are vacancies, can obtain same by applying to Head Office. **1918** R.H. KNYVETT *Over there with Australs.* 30 They wanted to finish the shed so as to get a 'stand' at the commencement of shearing near by. **1913** J. TRURAN *Where Plain Begins* 148 Bradley's was only a 'six-stand' shed; that is, there were six machines, each with its pen for the shorn and unshorn sheep. **1946** F. CLUNE *Try Nothing Twice* 89 There were fifty stands in Kerabury shed, all driven by the traction engine. **1960** *Bulletin* (Sydney) 6 July 16/3 It was an old-time shed, holding a couple of thousand sheep or more, 50 stands (meaning 25 pens, races and other inconveniences), all of which had to be filled. **1973** R. ROBINSON *Drift of Things* 73 The first shed was a sixteen stand shed—eight shearers on either side of the board.

Also (ten, etc.)-**stander.**

1978 J. DINGWALL *Sunday too far Away* 17 'How many sheep at this shed of yours?' . . 'Forty thousand. Thereabouts.' . . 'What is it, a ten stander?' . . 'Eight.'

stand, *v. intr.* With **over**: to intimidate or threaten; to extort money from (someone).

1939 K. TENNANT *Foveaux* 173, I just had Thompson in here and he stood over me for three quid. **1950** *Austral. Police Jrnl.* Apr. 119 *Stand over*, to threaten, menace, or use duress on someone for the purpose of gain. **1958** F. HARDY *Four-Legged Lottery* 192 We'll have to stand over him to get our money. **1967** K. GILES *Death & Mr Prettyman* 58 'You couldn't, but you could stand over—pardon, persecute—me', said Baker, 'but believe me I'm clean. If I can help you get that bloody old bag count me in.'

standover.

a. An intimidatory tactic. Also as **standover tactic.**

1939 K. TENNANT *Foveaux* 180 'Struth, you earn your money on a stand over. **1954** L.H. EVERS *Pattern of Conquest* 198 Don't come the stand-over tactics you used with Charlie. **1957** J. WATEN *Shares in Murder* 63 He can't come this standover on me. He's got nothing on me and you know it.

b. Special Comb. **standover man, merchant,** one who engages in intimidatory tactics.

1939 K. TENNANT *Foveaux* 174 He didn't deserve to be a 'standover man' if he couldn't move quicker. **1951** CUSACK & JAMES *Come in Spinner* 355 It was Joe's bodyguard, Curly—stand-over man as well, they said. **1952** T.A.G. HUNGERFORD *Ridge & River* 209 Now they'll hate my guts for a while, and Wilder'll be the poor down-trodden guy that's being stood over—you know how they hate a stand-over merchant, don't you? **1957** J. WATEN *Shares in Murder* 79 He might end up as a common bully, a standover man. **1962** A. MARSHALL *This is Grass* 60, I guessed he was a stand-over merchant and that he had brought these two men with him like a hunter who goes out with his dogs. **1975** *Bulletin* (Sydney) 26 Apr. 44/3 The heavies (standover men) and the bludgers who neither worked nor stole but were simply professional parasites.

star grass. [Transf. use of *star-grass* any of several grass-like plants with stellate flowers or a stellate arrangement of leaves.] WINDMILL GRASS.

1844 L. LEICHHARDT *Jrnl. Overland Exped. Aust.* 16 Dec. (1847) 77 The chains of water-holes within the scrub are covered with stiff star-grass, having a great number of spikes rising from the top of the stem. **1880** J. BONWICK *Resources Qld.* 46 Star grasses are extending to the injury of better plants, since the sheep do not eat its flowers. **1901** K.L. PARKER in M. Muir *My Bush Bk.* (1982) 63 The grasses on the ridges were principally kangaroo grass and star grass. The latter looks like toy windmills, and whirls about in the wind like roly-polies, while building grass walls against the fences. **1907** F. TURNER *Anderson's Man. Vegetable Garden* 55 Star or windmill grass (*Chloris truncata*) is a perennial found over an immense area of country both east and west over the Dividing Range. **1917** *Bulletin* (Sydney) 9 Aug. 24/1 Young sheep get the wool on their foreheads matted with the seed of the star-grass. **1938** C.T. WHITE *Princ. Bot. Qld. Farmers* 203 Many other grasses go to make up the mixed native pasture . . Oat Grasses, Star Grasses, &c.

star lot. [Spec. use of *star lot* a starred item in a sale catalogue: see OED *sb.*[1] 20 and quot. 1928.] A small parcel of wool bales.

1899 G. JEFFREY *Princ. Australasian Woolclassing* 92 Lots of three bales or under are marked in the catalogue 'star lots', and are sold by themselves after the larger lots are disposed of. **1921** L.G. JONES *Flockmaster's Companion* 81 Any number of bales of five or under is called a star lot, and any number over five is called a bulk lot. **1928** C.E. COWLEY *Classing Clip* 165 The name *star lot* originated from the London method of wool-selling where both large and small parcels are shown, catalogued and sold together, but the small lots are indicated to the buyers by an asterisk being prefixed to the lot number. Thus in course of time, such lots became known as *star lots*. The term has become a generic one in the wool-trade. **1951** *Concerning Wool* (Austral. Wool Board) 103 *Star lots*, parcels or lots of wool containing less than the number of bales specified for sale in the main sale room.

Star of Bethlehem. Also **Stars of Bethlehem.** [Transf. use of *Star of Bethlehem* a plant of the genus *Ornithogalum*, esp. *O. umbellatum*, having white star-like flowers.] Any of several plants bearing a star-like flower, incl. the herb *Chamaescilla corymbosa* (fam. Liliaceae) of s. Aust. incl. Tas.; the flower of one of these plants.

1857 D. BUNCE *Australasiatic Reminisc.* 25 On the pasture lands were many of the pretty bulbous plants called Star of Bethlehem by the colonists, but by botanists known as *Anguillaria*, of which two species clothed the pasture. **1898** E.E. MORRIS *Austral Eng.* 435 Star of Bethlehem. . . The name is given in Australia to *Chamaescilla corymbosa*, and in Tasmania to *Burchardia umbellata* . . both of the *Liliaceae*. **1922** L. RODWAY *Some Wild Flowers Tas.* 104 Star of Bethlehem has white flowers in a loose terminal head. . . The fruit is a three-angled capsule. **1938** C.A. GARDNER *West Austral. Wildflowers* 8 Blue Tinsel Lily (*Calectasia cyanea*) . . known to some as the 'Star of Bethlehem', is restricted to sandy soils. **1939** M.B. ELDERSHAW *My Aust.* 219 Among the more modest are the white stars of the Wedding Bush and the blue Stars of Bethlehem. **1967** B.Y. MAIN *Between Wodjil & Tor* 97 Dark purplish-blue, yellow-centred 'stars of Bethlehem' studded the *Callithryx* shrubs fringing the pine grove.

starve, *v.* In the phr. **starve the rats** (or **roan bullock**): see CROW *n.*[1] 3 and LIZARD 2.

1908 *Bulletin* (Sydney) 9 Jan. 14/2 'Starve the rats' and 'snake's head' are two more poetical phrases that the Adelaide lad is godfather of. **1977** F.B. VICKERS *Stranger no Longer* 147, I was surprised to hear a publisher say: 'Starve the roan bullock! You're the first musterer's cook I've ever seen in a bloody hombburg.'

starver.

1. An animal which is starving because of a lack of pasture, esp. as caused by a drought.

1902 *Bulletin* (Sydney) 29 Nov. 15/1 'Starvers' are being travelled in thousands. **1904** M. WHITE *Shanty Entertainment* 8 Padding along behind or in front of his weak-kneed starvers. **1911** I.A. ROSENBLUM *Stella Sothern* 9 Your business was the sale of some Queenslanders—cattle, you know. They were regular starvers when I bought them at four pounds per head. **1922** 'J. NORTH' *Black Opal* 35 That's the place they sends orf ther starvers to in drought time. **1946** *Bulletin* (Sydney) 18 Dec. 28/2 Bought a big mob o' starvers at a bob a head an' kept 'em alive till the drought broke.

2. A saveloy.

1941 S.J. BAKER *Pop. Dict. Austral. Slang* 71 *Starver*, a saveloy. **1959** D. NILAND *Big Smoke* 211, I know what the things I eat cost me. Starvers, crumpets, stale cakes, specked fruit, pies. **1981** P. RADLEY *Jack Rivers & Me* 154 Indian dicks (thin sausages), thick-dick saveloys (called starvers in the Depression), and much grog.

starving, *ppl. a.* Of stock: suffering from a lack of pasture (see prec.).

1903 *Bulletin* (Sydney) 3 Jan. 17/1 The Victorian railway department allows a free pass for every truck in a starving-stock train, so when cockie has six trucks of 'starving stock' going practically free, he and five of his friends travel 'on the nod'. **1935** N. HUNT *House of David* 119 Rowel has a thousand 'store cattle'. . . He bought them as 'poor' and 'starving' for a pound. He'll sell them for ten or fifteen.

State.

1. Used *attrib.* in Special Comb. to designate financial support given by a government or a project so supported, as **State aid,** financial assistance, now esp. that given to private schools; **child (boy, kid, orphan,** etc.), a ward of the State; **school,** PUBLIC SCHOOL 1; also *attrib.*

1856 *Jrnl. Australasia* I. 246 He is the opponent of **State Aid** to Religion. **1859** P. JUST *Aust.* 292 A considerable portion of the public revenues have hitherto been set apart for the maintenance of religious worship, until the ability of the colonists to pay for its support by voluntary contributions has rendered it of less consequence to seek state aid. **1899** *North-Western Advocate* (Devonport) 8 Mar. 4/1 The need for state aid to enable them [*sc.* drought-stricken settlers] to remain on the soil. **1909** H.I. JENSEN *Rising Tide* 71 The Grammar Schools and High Schools, in receipt of State aid in some States. **1973** *Bulletin* (Sydney) 20 Jan. 40/2 Daniel Deniehy . . opposed State Aid, Chinese immigration and the squatters. **1978** G. HALL *River still Flows* 96 Possibly most people concealed the cogency of the Catholic argument, 'One brick in every four of your public schools is paid for by Catholics.' State Aid had come to stay. **1901** *Bulletin* (Sydney) 5 Oct. 36/1 How different are these bright-eyed youngsters from the usual **State-children** of school age! **1903** *Truth* (Sydney) 25 Oct. 1/8 Complaints are made in Bathurst that 'boarded out' State children cause great annoyance to residents by begging from door to door. **1905** *Bulletin* (Sydney) 6 July 36/2 Hard by was an undersized dairy farm run by a hungry couple and four hungrier State kids. **1913** *Truth* (Sydney) 6 Apr. 5/4 A young dairyman . . was . . charged with assaulting a State boy. *Ibid.*, People who took State children were allowed to chastise them. **1914** M. HALL *Woman in Antipodes* 149 The only other member of the household is a 'State boy', or what we should call a foundling. **1917** A.L. BREWER *'Gators' Euchre* 14 One State orphan was asked, long ago: he glanced fearfully in the direction of the farmer who kept him, shook his little head desperately in the negative, and . . ran behind a barn. **1934** J.C. LEE *Bosh-stralians* 18 The maid-of-all-work . . had been a member of the Maxwell family for the last ten years. 'State Child' covered her derivation. **1959** D. HEWETT *Bobbin Up* 104 You only took State kids when you were on the bones of your arse. Their miserable ten bob a week from the Government helped to feed your kids and kept *them* out of a Home. **1878** *Illustr. Austral. News* (Melbourne) 13 May 74/2 Our artist has depicted a few of the scholars who may be selected out of almost any **State school** in the colony, and has placed them graphically before us. **1892** H.C.J. LINGHAM *Juvenal in Melbourne* 26 Scarce in his teens, and from the State school freed, To earn his living see the lad proceed! **1927** J. LYNG *Non-Britishers in Aust.* 107 Children of Italian origin in all the State schools. **1936** E.C.H. TAYLOR et al. *Our Austral. Game Football* 77 The Public Schools of New South Wales and Queensland are devotees of the Rugby game, but rapid strides are being made towards establishing the Australian code in the State schools. **1954** J. WATEN *Unbending* 282 I'm really glad that you want to return to the State school and not to some other school. **1985** *Canberra Times* 1 Sept. 8/4 No wonder we 'Micks' used to have slanging matches . . with the State-school kids.

2. a. The designation which replaced 'colony' after Federation in the names of New South Wales, Queensland, South Australia, Tasmania, Victoria, and Western Australia. Freq. *attrib.*

1891 *Braidwood Dispatch* 1 Apr. 3/1 The Federation Bill was tabled this afternoon. . . Each colony shall hereafter be designated a state. **1900** *Advocate* (Burnie) 8 Dec. 1/8 When the Commonwealth comes into existence the federating colonies will drop the name of 'colonies' and be henceforth designated as 'States'. **1911** R.G.S. WILLIAMS *Austral. White Slaves* 78 There will be nothing left to the States that the Federal Government would take as a gift after April next. **1927** *R. Comm. on Wireless* 1885 The State Government had issued a booklet called 'Wireless and the Settler'. **1941** C. BARRETT *Aust.* 30 It's a State Forest . . and, Pan be praised, they've saved from the axe a stand of forest giants in a permanent reserve of one thousand acres. **1965** G. MCINNES *Road to Gundagai* 30 One day he opened an atlas of Australia and asked us to point out the six state capitals. **1973** *Bulletin* (Sydney) 27 Jan. 12/1 The state governments formally still have a colonial relationship to Britain. **1983** *Open Road* Apr. 2/1 N.S.W. is burdened with an inadequate road system, yet this financial year will receive back for roads only about 22 per cent of total State and Federal fuel tax revenue collected from N.S.W. motorists.

b. Special Comb. **State Governor,** the principal representative of the sovereign in one of the Australian States (see also GOVERNOR 1); **Premier,** see PREMIER 1; **rights,** the administrative and legislative responsibilities reserved to a State as distinct from the Federal government; also **State's right** and *attrib.*; **State righter,** one who supports the protection of a State's powers.

1900 *Advocate* (Burnie) 24 Aug. 2/4 The question of the status of **state Governors** is being largely discussed throughout the colonies. **1917** *Mercury* (Hobart) 24 Mar. 6/3 The functions and opportunities of a State Governor are circumscribed by the Constitution. **1936** H.V. EVATT *King & his Dominion Governors* 127 Mr Amery . . suggested that for the future, appointments to the position of State Governor should be made from Australian citizens. **1950** *Sydney Morning Herald* 16 Sept. 4/2 The State Governor, Sir John Northcott visited Junee today. **1973** *Bulletin* (Sydney) 27 Jan. 12/2 State governors formally have the power to 'reserve' legislation passed by the state governments. **1984** *Woman's Day* (Sydney) 29 Oct. 14/1 Sir Roden Cutler, Australia's longest-serving State Governor, believes the time is rapidly approaching when a woman will be appointed to the position. **1901** *Truth* (Sydney) 9 June 4/7 The highest interests and cherished **States Rights** of the Mother State. **1910** *Huon Times* (Franklin) 19 Feb. 2/2 Some producers argue that it would be another encroachment on State rights. **1931** *Century of Journalism* 386 As we have seen, practically all the problems that had worried the *Herald* in 1891 had been those represented by 'States' rights' and 'Senate representation'. **1944** G. COCKERILL *Scribblers & Statesmen* 105 Lyne was a thorough going Protectionist. . . Further, he was a 'State rights' man, whose support for the Federal movement was only nominal. **1981** *Canberra Times* 12 Nov. 2/6 It would be all too easy for objectors to mount a simplistic States' rights campaign. **1944** G. COCKERILL *Scribblers & Statesmen* 134 Former **'State-righters'** became earnest Federalists. **1955** G. HEALEY *A.L.P.* 195 Holman a State Righter, was, I believe, completely out of step with the party. **1956** V. COURTNEY *All I may Tell* 44 He was a bitter State Righter, and never seemed to realise that Australia had become a nation and we were part of it.

station. [Spec. use of *station* a place where soldiers are garrisoned, a military post: see OED(S *sb.* 11 (but see also *sb.* 13 a. and d.).]

1. a. *Hist.* An outpost of a colonial government, esp. as established for the employment of convict labour on public works; *convict station*, see CONVICT B. 3; *penal station*, see PENAL.

1816 *Hobart Town Gaz.* 28 Sept., His Excellency . . having been pleased to appoint Assistant Commissary General Broughton to take the Charge of the Commissariat Department at this Station . . he is directed to assume the Duties of his Office. **1820** *HRA* (1921) 3rd Ser. III. 129, I shall in the interim be enabled to communicate with you more particularly as to the days of Muster at the different Stations. **1822** J.T. BIGGE *Rep. State Colony N.S.W.* 26 The gangs vary from 30 to 60 each; and as their work proceeds, they remove their huts, which are always constructed of the branches and bark of the eucalypts, from one station to another. **1833** *N.S.W. Mag.* (Sydney) I. 62 Due notice will be given . . by the Principal Superintendent of Convicts, of the date when, and at what stockade, the prisoner can be obtained, in order that he may be applied for at that station. **1848** R. MARSH *Seven Yrs. of my Life* 71 At these different stations, are road parties, some fifty, one hundred, and two hundred men. **1854** H.B. STONEY *Yr. in Tas.* 37 But, alas! save at the stations, built alone for the punishment of crime, no human dwelling meets the eye. **1872** 'TASMANIAN LADY' *Treasures, Lost & Found* 127 The ruins of a wooden hut, with a tramroad running past it. . . ''Tis only an old station. Years ago the Government had a gang at work here.'

b. *transf.* A tract of land recognized as being occupied by Aborigines; a reserve for Aborigines, esp. as established by a religious mission (see also *mission station* MISSION 1) or government agency. Also *attrib.*

1825 B. FIELD *Geogr. Mem. N.S.W.* 57 The principal station of the tribe . . was about two miles higher up the Pumice-stone River. **1833** *Currency Lad* (Sydney) 26 Jan. 3 *The aboriginal mission.* We have been at some trouble to enquire into the proceedure [*sic*] of this undertaking lately commenced at the distant station of Wellington Valley. **1841** *Port Phillip Patriot* 16 Sept. 5/2 There is no station reserved for the tribe the prisoner belongs to. **1858** *V & P* (Vic. L.C.) (1858–59) no. D8 3 What do you mean by stations—do you mean small reserves of ground with provisions. **1886** *N.T. Times Almanac* 96 The Catholic Church Mission to the Aborigines has a station on a piece of land kept as an Aboriginal Reserve at Rapid Creek. **1889** *Illustr. Austral. News* (Melbourne) 1 Aug. 6/1 A suggestion has been made to utilise the Station for Aborigines at Coranderrk as a dairy farm school. **1950** V.E. TURNER *Ooldea* 8 The Aborigines' Board received the proposal to open the Station with sympathy, and eventually removed the ration depot from Tarcoola to Ooldea, Miss Lock becoming the rationing officer. **1963** 'E. LINDALL' *Springs of Violence* 39 These are tribal natives. They don't mix with the station crowd. **1974** J. HORNER *Vote Ferguson* 13 The staff positions on thirty Aboriginal stations were taken by Europeans. The manager of a 'station' and his wife as the matron, were chosen by the sub-committee of the Protection Board for their managerial experience. **1980** L.R. SMITH *Aboriginal Pop. Aust.* 109 Some people who were legally Aborigines resided on controlled stations managed by the Board for the Protection of Aborigines.

2. a. A tract of grazing land, usu. having a discernible centre of occupation: see quot. 1822. Also with distinguishing epithet, as **cattle, dairy, grazing, sheep, squatting, stock** (see under first element). See also RUN *n.*[2] 1 a.

1820 *HRA* (1921) 3rd Ser. II. 207 The Herds at each Station are to be Surveyed by a Committee. **1822** J.T. BIGGE *Rep. State Colony N.S.W.* 161 All persons who apply for the temporary occupation of a large tract of land, for the purpose of grazing . . shall employ an overseer, who shall be a free and unconvicted person, and require his constant residence at the principal station. **1824** *Austral.* (Sydney) 21 July 4 The applications of a growing farming community . . for further stations to sustain its rapidly increasing stock. **1826** J. ATKINSON *Acct. Agric. & Grazing N.S.W.* 5 The graziers who were forming new stations . . have hitherto created a temporary and local demand for wheat. **1835** J. BACKHOUSE *Extracts from Lett.* (1838) iii. 18 These stations, as they are called, usually belong to opulent settlers, living in town, or near, who derive a great part of their wealth from their large flocks of sheep and herds of cattle, which their servants (many of whom are prisoners) tend. **1845** W. WESTGARTH *Commercial, Statistical, & Gen. Rep. Port Phillip* 26 The custom of having a married couple, instead of two single men, for the duties of 'hutkeeping' and shepherding at the stations, is now more common. **1848** *Sidney's Austral. Hand-Bk.* 7, I lived in the far interior . . (the nearest of my stations being 300 miles, and the farthest more than 500 miles, from the settled districts). **1884** A.W. STIRLING *Never Never Land* 26 Mr M.C. Mason, of Headington Hill, general manager of all Mr C. Fisher's extensive stations on the Darling Downs. **1895** E.T.H. HUTTON *Narr. Tour of Inspection N.S.W.* 6 Barnato Station is an out-station of Nelyambo Station on the Darling, distant sixty miles. **1982** R. ELLIS *Bush Safari* 96 The ruins of Annandale Station, one of Sir Sidney Kidman's early runs, and the most remote station he ever owned.

b. *Hist.* In the phr. **right of station,** legal entitlement to the use of a tract of grazing land. See also RUN *n.*[2] 1 c.

1839 *Port Phillip Patriot* 24 Apr. 6/3 These cattle and the right of station Mr Bringle sold to Mr Ward Stephens. **1841** *Ibid.* 13 Sept. 4/6 The undersigned has for sale some herds of cattle, together with flocks of sheep, with right of stations. **1844** *Portland Mercury* 31 Jan. 2/1 *W.M. M'Dowell* Will sell . . *a mixed herd* of about 1000 head of superior cattle . . with right of station within five miles of Belfast. **1847** *Port Phillip Gaz.* 30 June 3, 8,392 Sheep, with right of Station given in, situate near the Murray River.

c. *Home station*, see HOME *attrib.*[2] b.

1840 T. SOUTHEY *Treatise on Sheep* 54 What in England is called a *homestead*, or, in Colonial idiom, a *station*, that is, the farm-yard and out-houses for sheep, cattle, etc. together with the other buildings requisite for the accommodation of the colonist's family. ***c* 1844** E. & F. ARTHUR *Jrnl. Events Melbourne to Mount Schank* (1975) 16 At the top of the hill, a mile on the road, we passed the Derwent Company's weather-boarded station. **1849** S. & J. SIDNEY *Emigrant's Jrnl.* 11 *Station* is the house, hut, and residence of the occupant, whether master or overseer. **1868** 'J.A.B.' *Meta of Gaindara* 37 We saw before our gladdened face, That welcome sight, a dwelling place, They here a 'station' call. **1873** A. TROLLOPE *Aust. & N.Z.* I. 119 It is a rule of life on a sheep-run that the station is never so full that another guest need be turned away. **1881** W. FEILDING *Austral. Trans-Continental Railway* 44 An hour's travelling over well-grassed plains . . brought us to a bark humpy which does duty for a station on Mr Sutherland's run of Elders Creek. **1886** P. CLARKE *'New Chum' in Aust.* 160 Near the homestead or station the paddocks are usually smaller, for the convenient working of the sheep to the 'yards', and the easy catching of the horses. **1914** 'B. CABLE' *By Blow & Kiss* 20 He's watchin' for some o' them bringin' down a few cattle. The station sent over yesterday for meat. **1934** 'S. RUDD' *Green Grey Homestead* 127 The old station was more like a rising township now than a squatter's headquarters. It had a row of shingle-roofed huts, spacious stables, a carpenter's shop, butcher's shop, store, and blacksmith's forge. **1963** V.B. CRANLEY *27,000 Miles through Aust.* 65 It was the usual Australian 'station'. Tin-roofed, slightly shabby, it surprisingly enough sported a lawn in front. **1979** *Quieter Moments* 28 Scores of men and women worked, to raise a station grand. A homestead and a shearing shed where twenty men could stand.

3. An extensive sheep or cattle raising establishment. See also RUN *n.*[2] 2 and under first element as for sense 2 a.

1843 R.D. MURRAY *Summer at Port Phillip* 151 Few in this country are aware of the vast tracts of land sometimes comprehended in the 'station' of a single individual. In one or two instances, they exhibit the dimensions of a small county. **1846** *Sydney Morning Herald* 11 Aug. 2/6 The word *station*, when applied to the small farms of Illawarra, may be likened to a man calling a *river* the *sea*. A station is generally understood to apply to a large tract of land. **1865** G.F. ANGAS *Aust.* 273 The large sheep and cattle farms, or 'stations' as they are termed in the colonies. **1876** 'RESIDENT' *Girl Life in Aust.* 137 Grandpapa had a station up bush, and the natives were just like flies—such a plague . . he got a lot of white stuff and mixed it with their flour—arsenic it was—and they died round the homestead. **1881** A.C. GRANT *Bush-Life Qld.* I. 42 Soon they passed a head-station, as the homestead and main buildings of a station are invariably called. **1882** *Bulletin* (Sydney) 23 Sept. 1/3 Our standard industry would be best conducted on a sheep-farm—larger than a selection, smaller than a station. **1890** *Sydney Morning Herald* 14 Oct. 3/6 The station is 40 per cent red soil, which holds tough leopardwood. **1893** 'TIMES SPECIAL CORRESPONDENT' *Lett. from Qld.* 73 The smallest station that I was on covered 200 square miles, and carried 66,000 sheep besides cattle and horses. **1912** L. ESSON *Time is not yet Ripe* 5 He has a big station in the Riverina, and goodness knows how many sheep. **1931** 'L. KAYE' *Tybal Men* 102 It makes me sick to hear it called a station. It's only a little poky farm. **1950** 'N. SHUTE' *Town like Alice* 81 'Wollara's two thousand seven hundred square miles'. . . 'But is that all one place—one farm, I mean?' 'It's one station,' he replied. 'One property.' **1965** L. WALKER *Other Girl* 81 The whole district wraps up for a week-end when a big station entertains. **1986** *Centralian Advocate* (Alice Springs) 15 Jan. 12/2 The stations he managed included Undoolya and later the Barron Creek Pastoral Company properties.

4. Comb. in sense 3: **station boss, cattle, cook, dog, hand, holder, homestead, horse, house, life, manager, overseer, owner, paddock, property, stock, work, yard.**

1936 *Bulletin* (Sydney) 1 Apr. 20/3 The **station boss** was liverish, so we were out of sight. But the new wood-and-water joey didn't know the signs. **1963** R.H. CONQUEST *Spurs are Rusty Now* 159 He was dressed in 'station boss' style—grey trousers, tan shoes, white shirt and blue tie. **1984** B. DIXON *Searching for Aboriginal Lang.* 122 Among those propping up the bar was a brawny female station boss mixing her beers—and her oaths—with those of the stockmen. **1902** *Bulletin* (Sydney) 7 June 16/3 In Queensland, the cattle-ticks and sequent redwater are obliterating **station cattle. 1909** *Ibid.* 14 Oct. 14/2 Station cattle . . have to be checked in the crush, or they will rush through too quickly. **1917** A.L. BREWER *'Gators' Euchre* 97 The station cattle are turned after a determined resistance. **1878** *Squatter's Plum* 42 Pity the shameless indifference to which men are reduced by continual begging from station-managers and hungry fawning on **station-cooks. 1888** *Illustr. Austral. News* (Melbourne) 22 Dec. (Suppl.) 2/1 The station cook is immeasurably his superior. **1893** 'OLD CHUM' *Chips* 43 At large stations the shearers often have a 'mess' of their own, and appoint their own cook but at our station they were fed by the station cook. **1903** *Bulletin* (Sydney) 9 July 16/2 The old station-cook thrust a greasy newspaper into the new book-keeper's hand. **1934** C. SAYCE *Comboman* 138 He engaged Mick as station cook. **1872** G.S. BADEN-POWELL *New Homes for Old Country* 337 Young kangaroo . . readily make friends with the **station-dogs. 1886** P. CLARKE *'New Chum' in Aust.* 192 They are always in trouble with the station-dogs. **1970** K. WILLEY *Naked Island* 141 Ranging about the cattle were half a dozen dingoes, most of them yellow or reddish, but a couple with darker coats revealing a cross with some station dog. **1872** 'RESIDENT' *Glimpses Life Vic.* 175 The kitchen, where the **station-hands** were assembled. **1885** MRS C. PRAED *Austral. Life* 63 The station hands had been getting in scrubbers, and the carcases of the wild bulls lay in the stockyard. **1905** *Bulletin* (Sydney) 3 Aug. 17/2 A station-hand is a 'pound-a-week' man, supposed to be generally useful. **1921** *Ibid.* 7 July 22/1, I . . know a general station-hand who travels by Ford. **1935** R.B. PLOWMAN *Boundary Rider* 27 Once a fortnight a station-hand brought out the rations. **1965** H. ATKINSON *Reckoning* 129 She quickly returned to her usual manner with the constable, which was not unlike that of a grazier's wife towards her husband's station hands. **1981** P.B. CRESWELL *Granite Peak* 3 A well had been sunk here by . . a Lake Violet stationhand, who had taken up a block of country. **1869** *Bushmen, Publicans, & Politics* 4 To demand that they shall be fed by such **station holders** as they may travel among until they get another 'job'. **1898** *Bulletin* (Sydney) 22 Oct. 14/2 A canny N.S.W. station-holder tells how he was getting a demi-john of brandy. **1916** T. WARLOW *By Mirage & Mulga* 2 The 'old bloke' . . was a friend of Alf.'s father; also a large stationholder, passing his time travelling from run to run. **1894** A.A. MACINNES *Straight as Line* 293 The carefully tended garden plots surrounding the comfortable, roomy **station homesteads. 1957** R.S. PORTEOUS *Brigalow* 21 It looked like a small village . . with its array of sheds, stockmen's quarters, and yards. Unlike so many barren station homesteads, this one was blessed with a fine collection of shade trees. **1965** L. WALKER *Other Girl* 129 The party was on a look-see of the outback and only stayed at the very best of station homesteads. **1900** R. BRUCE *Benbonuna* (1904) 261, I don't think you will find it all plain sailing, especially if any of the **station horses** have been running about there lately. **1934** 'S. RUDD' *Green Grey Homestead* 117 Those station horses . . stood there in the yard, flash and well-bred. **1965** R.H. CONQUEST *Horses in Kitchen* 148 Bushrangers . . specialized in the stealing of station horses. **1977** W.A. WINTER-IRVING *Bush Stories* 114 Their grey brumby mounts . . could tear through the scrub and contorted timber avoiding a collision with far more confidence than the station horses which were more comfortable to ride. **1840** *Sydney Herald* 31 Aug. 6/7 We have since heard that the sheep were not above a mile from the **station-house. 1859** W. BURROWS *Adventures Mounted Trooper* 122 This may possibly account for its superiority in comfort to the generality of station-houses. **1887** A. NICOLS *Wild Life & Adventure* 60 The long, low verandah which surrounded the station-house. **1895** K. MACKAY *Yellow Wave* 191 When the pioneers took possession of Afton Downs, they turned the old station-house into a species of club. **1934** T. WOOD *Cobbers* 13 The older station-houses—places where the guest, at dinner, must be as alert with the talk and the forks as he would have to be in a country house at home. **1937** J.M. HARCOURT *It never Fails* 179 Before the depression you could get a square meal and a handout at any farm or station-house on your way. **1972** M. CASSIDY *Dispossessed* 59 Back to the station-house. **1880** J. BONWICK *Resources Qld.* 31 One need but go to the Darling Downs . . to find **station life** associated with high civilization. **1886** R. HENTY *Australiana* 60, I got some idea of station life and management, as well as excellent sport, of which wild pig shooting formed a considerable part. **1910** *Huon Times* (Franklin) 30 Mar. 4/2 There are numerous arguments in favour of families growing up to the ways of station life. **1927** A. CROMBIE *After Sixty Yrs.* 144 He gave up station life long ago. **1937** G.H. SUNTER *Adventures Trepang Fisher* 107 My people in Adelaide wrote up and said they noticed that I had gone back to station life again for I was referred to as a 'well-known pastoralist'. **1969** L. HADOW *Full Cycle* 251 Twenty years of station life. **1878 station manager** [see *station cook*]. **1901** *Truth* (Sydney) 16 June 5/7 The Sultan of Turkey is not more jealous of his veiled mistresses than is a Westralian station manager of his stark naked lubras. **1915** *Bulletin* (Sydney) 26 Aug. 22/4 The station manager was riding round the run, when he was overtaken by a flash blackfellow. **1925** *Ibid.* 12 Feb. 22/2 A blue-tongue is a station manager, from the usual color of his remarks when addressing common lizards. **1925** *Ibid.* 9 Apr. 24/1 The station-manager is known as the 'trump'. **1947** E. HILL *Flying Doctor Calling* 14 A stockman's lot is a lonely one. Until he becomes a station-manager, somewhere about the age of forty-five, he has no shelter to offer a wife. **1965** L. HAYLEN *Big Red* 143 The station manager was a business man with a degree in Commerce. **1980** S. THORNE *I've met some Bloody Wags* 17 The hat, a flash pork-pie town job, belonged to a fairly plastered young station manager... How did I know he was a manager? Easy! He was wearing their uniform—flat-heeled elastic sides, cream trousers, plaited roohide belt, and a pale blue countryman shirt with a notebook and pen in one front pocket. **1897** *Tocsin* (Melbourne) 9 Dec. 10/2 The hero is a young **station overseer**, who marries the daughter of a shanty-keeper. **1965** R.H. CONQUEST *Horses in Kitchen* 80 Andy had but one ambition—he wanted to be a station overseer. **1873** A. TROLLOPE *Aust. & N.Z.* I. 96 The station passes . . into the hands probably of some huge **station owner**, who having commenced life as a shepherd or a drover, has now stations of his own. **1879** S.W. SILVER *Austral. Grazier's Guide* 1 The Australian stock-farmer, settler, squatter, station-owner, or run-holder, as he is indifferently termed. **1914** *Pastoral Rev.* 15 Jan. 61 Confidently recommended to . . Station Owners as an Absolutely Safe Wool Marking . . oil. **1932** R.W. THOMPSON *Down Under* 73 One would not realise the wealth of some of these way-back Queensland station owners, to look at them in their rough clothes with their gnarled hands. **1955** F. LANE *Patrol to Kimberleys* 145 Both station owners and their overseers are out mustering. **1965** L. WALKER *Other Girl* 62 Funny to be so near people who were kings of whole countries of land, as these station-owners were, and not feel anything very much. **1981** A.B. FACEY *Fortunate Life* 116 The station owners told Bill that I should go to Geraldton or Carnarvon. **1906** W.A. HORN *Notes by Nomad* 82 The traveller simply turns his horse into the **station paddock. 1910** *Huon Times* (Franklin) 12 Nov. 6/1 Mr John Huxley . . was severely injured by a bull in the station paddock on Monday last. **1923** *Bulletin* (Sydney) 29 Mar. 24/2 Are Australian-bred sheep changing their camping habits? Forty or fifty years ago a big leafy tree was selected for a camp and used year after year. The 'camping-tree' was a landmark in each station paddock. **1877** 'CAPRICORNUS' *Land Laws of Future* 6 The Land Board shall then procure . . a return specifying the sales of **station properties. 1890** W.F. BUCHANAN *Aust. to Rescue* p. xxii, We have great pleasure in submitting for your consideration a very fine station property. **1935** N. HUNT *House of David* 114 Buy 'Welloonga', the station property . . owned by this squatter. **1959** *Bulletin* (Sydney) 11 Nov. 16/3 Station-properties . . were forfeited by drought-hit owners. **1977** B. SCOTT *My Uncle Arch* 139 There had been that fellow from the station property, a grazier. **1880** *Austral. Town & Country Jrnl.* (Sydney) 14 Feb. 314/4 The **station stock** seldom feed near the road. **1903** *Bulletin* (Sydney) 17 Sept. 16/2 Your station stock are often on *my* country! **1981** A.B. FACEY *Fortunate Life* 167 We were crossing through cattle country so the Boss had put two extra men on the scouting team to help clear any station stock. **1879** *Kelly Gang* 15 The ostensible occupations of the two elder sons have been horse-breaking and farm and **station work. 1884** J.B. MARTIN *Reminisc.* 4 The stations were managed by superintendents, sometimes with the help of the 'young master' sent to learn station work. **1933** J. MCCARTER *Love's Lunatic* 43 Somehow, he had reckoned she was a new chum to station work from the jump-off. **1943** H.G. LAMOND *From Tariaro to Ross Roy* 27 Shearers then were bushmen, all round men, who did all classes of station work. **1950** G.M. FARWELL *Land of Mirage* 163 No black may now be engaged for station work in Queensland without a legal agreement, which must be signed by the manager and the local policeman, who represents the Queensland Protector. **1922** W.R. EASTON *Rep. N. Kimberley District W.A.* 1 We were able to make our starting depot at the Homestead, thus having the use of the **station yards** equipment. **1938** J.F.W. SCHULZ *Destined to Perish* 21 The only part of the gate visible, which was standing slightly ajar, was the sign itself, drift-sand having been piled fence-high all along the station-yard. **1963** M. BRITT *Pardon my Boots* 80 The tailing yard was a single large yard used when it was not necessary to take cattle all the way to the station yards.

5. Special Comb. **station Abo, black, (a)** an Aboriginal employed on a sheep or cattle station; **(b)** an Aboriginal residing at a reserve or mission station; **boy,** an Aboriginal male employed on a sheep or cattle station; **-bred** *a.*, (of an animal), bred on the property; also as quasi-*n.*; **camp,** a place on a station where stock are mustered for a particular purpose; the personnel, etc., so employed; **country,** land chiefly occupied as sheep or cattle stations; **gin,** an Aboriginal woman employed on a sheep or cattle station; **jack** *obs.*, see quot.; **keeper** *obs.*, HUT-KEEPER; **keeping** *vbl. n., obs., hut keeping*, see HUT-KEEP; **man,** one employed on, or one who owns, a sheep or cattle station; so **people; ration,** an allowance of provisions made to an employee on a sheep or cattle station (see RATION *n.* 1 a.); **rouse-about,** ROUSEABOUT a.; **run, (a)** an air service using the privately-owned landing fields on stations; **(b)** a stretch of grazing land on a station; **store,** the depot on a station from which supplies are dispensed or sold (see STORE 3); *pl.*, the supplies themselves; so **storekeeper.**

1938 *Bulletin* (Sydney) 1 June 21/1 The **station abo.** usually bears a white-fellow nickname. **1955** J. CLEARY *Justin Bayard* 292 He's only a bush myall. Not even a station abo. **1958** E. SALTER *Will to Survive* 214 It was odd, come to think of it, that a station abo should possess a boomerang. **1870** E.B. KENNEDY *Four Yrs. in Qld.* 67 Anyone who is really acquainted with the matter . . from having been not only amongst **station** and town

Blacks, but also for years in the same country with perfectly wild Blacks. **1896** W.H. Willshire *Land of Dawning* 11 When night comes on the station blacks have a wild and weird corroborree [*sic*] amongst themselves. **1911** *Bulletin* (Sydney) 7 Sept. 13/2 After a gorge of meat, the station blacks were suffering from internal cramps. **1922** 'J. Bushman' *In Musgrave Ranges* 82 These niggers are wild. . . They're different from the camp blacks who hang round stations. They'll likely be station blacks themselves some day, for the wild nigger's dying out. **1957** F. Clune *Fortune Hunters* 60 The 'station blacks' here were giving no trouble. **1961** *Bulletin* (Sydney) 14 Oct. 30/2 Down at the camp of the station blacks size didn't matter. **1890** A.J. Vogan *Black Police* 90 The hunted-thief look one nearly always sees on the face of the average '**station boy**' (squatter's aboriginal servant) is absent. **1895** *Bulletin* (Sydney) 9 Nov. 28/3 Topknot was a nigger with a bad reputation. He was a good enough station-boy when it so pleased him. **1882** Armstrong & Campbell *Austral. Sheep Husbandry* 242 Wild Horses . . when taken young . . are no more difficult to break in and handle than are ordinary **station-bred** horses. **1905** *Bulletin* (Sydney) 23 Feb. 16/3 He takes in at 9d. a head, a train-load of horses, mostly young station-breds. **1945** E. Mitchell *Speak to Earth* 114 The station-breds would be sold as fats next summer. **1977** H. Towson *Black & White* 69, I had to rely on the horse to take me home and luckily for me he was a station-bred horse. **1937** W. Hatfield *I find Aust.* 149, I looked for a job with a road mob and joined the **station camp** till they were ready to start. **1938** J.F.W. Schulz *Destined to Perish* 23 The station camp at the Big Bend is only periodically used by the stockmen. **1954** T. Ronan *Vision Splendid* 145 Next morning he started work bullock-tailing in the station camp. **1977** F.B. Vickers *Stranger no Longer* 99, I could see a windmill and tank, a horse yard and a corrugated iron hut of a station out-camp. **1884** J. Baker *Diary & Sketches Journey S.A.* 18 Oct. 15 Left farming district and started for **station country** thro pass in hills. **1915** A.J. Dawson *Rec. N. Freydon* 87 Up in the station country they never refuse a man rations, anyway; it's in the town the trouble is rations. **1950** C.E. Goode *Yarns of Yilgarn* 83 This was now station country and we passed a few sheep and opened an occasional fence that ran across the puzzle of worn-out tracks. **1962** Marshall & Drysdale *Journey among Men* 75 As we passed through the station country we asked men whether they had heard of the green-and-yellow night parrot. **1980** Ansell & Percy *To fight Wild* 7, I shouldn't have had my vehicle on station country without permission. **1895** L. Becke *Ebbing of Tide* 187 Chow Kum . . giving away so much rations to the **station gins**. **1913** *Bulletin* (Sydney) 6 Mar. 16/2 The boss decided to send her to the head station, where she would have the benefit of the station gins' attention. **1853** E. Mackenzie *Emigrant's Guide to Aust.* 112 Let the Sunday share be soaked on the Saturday, and beat it well with a rolling-pen, as this makes it more tender, take a seventh portion of the flour, and work it into a paste; then put the beef into it, boil it, and you will have a very nice pudding, known in the bush as '**station-jack**'. **1850** W. Gates *Recoll. Van Dieman's Land* (1961) II. 39 Each shepherd has in charge one thousand sheep. To each station are three shepherds, and at the hut—or station is another person, styled **station-keeper,** who remains there. *c* **1856** F. Gerstaecker *Life in Bush* 3 Among the guests was a station-keeper from Kangaroo Island. **1856** S.C. Brees *How to farm & settle in Aust.* 11 They can then decide between going into quartz-crushing, store-keeping, cultivating, or **station-keeping,** or breeding and fattening cattle. **1872** 'Resident' *Glimpses Life Vic.* 175 The **station-men** . . slunk away to their sleeping apartment. **1916** *Bulletin* (Sydney) 12 Oct. 24/1 Paddocks showed no sign of the station-man's stand-by—the Mitchell grass. **1927** A. Crombie *After Sixty Yrs.* 169 Station men (they are now termed graziers) had mustered. **1974** P. Hall *Sun & Grey Shadow* 5 The station man, Preston, was uneasy. He fumbled in his pockets, and took out a sweat-stained letter. **1948** P.J. Hurley *Red Cedar* 23 Terrigal, popular surf and seaside resort . . a summer residence for '**station people**' from the inland. **1965** L. Walker *Other Girl* 71 His own people were station people. **1976** K. Brown *Knock Ten* 239 Of course food was planned ahead, too. Some station people were already feeding batches of wild pigs that men caught along the river-banks. **1903** *Bulletin* (Sydney) 30 May 35/1 His wife . . objected to being carried up and down the road . . among **station-rations** and sundries. **1958** G. Casey *Snowball* 34 They reckon station rations are miles better for everybody, now. **1948** B. Cronin *How runs Road* 31 In Australia, very little more than half a century ago, bishops and **station rouseabouts** rubbed shoulders amicably in box-seat conversation. **1965** R.H. Conquest *Horses in Kitchen* 79 Probably few city people realize it, but there are subtle differences in Australia between cowboys, jackeroos and station rouseabouts. **1951** G. Farwell *Outside Track* 176 Normanton is much more in the swing of modern life. To start with, it enjoys two air services a week, in addition to an enterprising '**station run**' that follows the coastline as far north as Mitchell River. **1951** *Aircraft* Feb. 21 One of the oldest and most exemplary of the outback services in ANA's weekly 'Station Run', from Cairns via Croydon and Normanton to a chain of cattle stations running as far up the west coast of Cape York Peninsula as the Mitchell River Mission. **1972** M. Gilbert *Personalities & Stories Early Orbost* 21 The red cattle graze on the grass of the wide station run. **1980** W.H. O'Rourke *My Way* 207 To travel in an Avro Anson on the 'station run' was an education in itself. These trips certainly demonstrated the part that airways were playing in breaking down the isolation of these far-flung areas. **1872** 'Resident' *Glimpses Life Vic.* 169 Six drays accompanied us, loaded with **station stores.** **1889** H. Egbert *Pretty Cockey* 63 After shearing and wool-washing, Smith was summoned to the Station Store. This establishment was the office as well. **1890** 'R. Boldrewood' *Colonial Reformer* I. 187 What they drew from the station-store was accurately debited to them. **1976** B. Scott *Complete Bk. Austral. Folk Lore* 376 Rations were often of the cheapest and poorest quality. Another economy practised by station storekeepers was the supply of what the ration men called 'post and rail' tea, mainly consisting of the stalks and roughest leaves. **1979** D. Lockwood *My Old Mates & I* 171 Articles they had 'booked up' at the station store.

steady, *v. Droving.* [Spec. use of *steady* to cause to go at a more regular pace.] *trans.* To regulate the progress of (a travelling mob).

1884 'R. Boldrewood' *Old Melbourne Memories* 134 Was there another man 'steadying the lead' on the opposite side, right well mounted also. **1909** *Bulletin* (Sydney) 28 Oct. 13/3 It's not always easy to steady a big mob and make them feed again. . . Of course, they *can* be stopped. **1923** *Ibid.* 4 Jan. 22/2 In the case of a dusty camp, after you steady the mob and are ringing them up, the dust rises in clouds and half blinds them.

steaka-da-oyst, var. Steakdahoyst.

steak and kidney. Rhyming slang for 'Sydney'. (Quot. 1945 refers to an Australian cruiser of that name.)

1905 J. Meredith *Learn to talk Old Jack Lang* (1984) 12 No doubt you have wondered how your old *thief and robber* has been doing since you went back to the *steak and kidney*. **1945** *Dit* (Melbourne) Apr. 3 The old 'Steak and kidney' once fought a battle off Singapore. **1967** *Kings Cross Whisper* (Sydney) xxxix. 4/5 *Steak and kidney*, Sydney.

steakdahoyst. Also **steaka-da-oyst.** [Joc. representation of an Italian pronunc.] A café or restaurant specializing in steak and oyster dishes.

1916 *Truth* (Sydney) 2 July 6/8 This is nothing to the rough estimate of shells the collective oyster-openers at the numerous city steakdahoysts let fall on Saturday nights. **1928** *Bulletin* (Sydney) 4 Apr. 23/2, I earned £3 2s. over the open season whilst the local steaka-da-oysts had to draw their fish supplies from Melbourne.

steam, *n.*

1. *Hist.* Used *attrib.* with reference to the process of separating fat from an animal carcass by the application of steam.

1840 *Port Phillip Gaz.* 30 Nov. 3 Melbourne. *Melting Establishment, the first steam establishment formed in the colonies.* The Proprietors are purchasers of fat Stock or will melt down for the settlers upon Reduced terms. **1844** *Portland Mercury* 20 Mar. 2/5 We were gratified by an inspection of a complete and ingeniously fitted up steam-melting establishment. **1849** *Bell's Life in Sydney* 1 Dec. 4/4 The superiority of steam-rendered tallow.

2. In the phr. **like steam,** furiously; with gusto.

1905 H. Lawson *When I was King* 39 We was draftin' 'em out for the homeward track and sharin' 'em round like steam. **1944** L. Glassop *We were Rats* 129 Did those Eyeties have plenty of cognac? All the boys got blind. And we reefed watches and rings off 'em like steam. **1960** K. Smith *Word from Children* 156 They'd sell like steam. **1979** B. Hardy *World owes me Nothing* 102, I hammered at the door like steam and over he came and opened it.

3. Cheap wine; such wine strengthened with methylated spirits; methylated spirits.

1941 S.J. Baker *Pop. Dict. Austral. Slang* 71 *Steam*, cheap wine, esp. laced with methylated spirits. **1942** *Sun* (Sydney) 26 Aug. 4/8 Bombo has replaced plonk as a term for cheap wine, and less popular, but equally descriptive, is the use of 'steam' for wine. When a man 'flies for the bombo' or 'raises steam', he is on quite a bender. **1950** *Dark People in Melbourne* (Victorian Council Social Service) 27 'Steam' or wine mixed with methylated spirits may be purchased from 'sly grog' shops. **1953** T.A.G. Hungerford *Riverslake* 169 I've got a bottle of steam in my room—I think I'll have a snort and turn in. *Ibid.* 183 Look out for that bottle of steam. . . We've got to have something to drink the toasts with. **1960** D. Ireland *Image in Clay* (1964) 80 Only one thing in the world he likes better than a bottle of steam, and that's that gun. **1970** *Kings Cross Whisper* (Sydney) lxxxiv. 9/3 Those who curl up in the park with a bottle of steam will have to make their own arrangements. **1973** J. McNeil *Old Familiar Juice* 55 Rum, brandy, whisky, gin . . sting, steam, bombo . . *plonk*!

steam, *v. Hist. trans.* To separate fat from (an animal carcass) by the application of steam. Also with **down,** and as *vbl. n.*

1844 *Parramatta Chron.* 22 June 3/1 Mackellar and White's steaming establishment is going on swimmingly, having more than they can manage. Large quantities of tallow are being produced daily, which, with skin and hides, can find a ready market. . . Messrs. Benjamin and Moses have a large establishment in the course of erection, with steaming-house apparatus, and everything desirable to carry on the rendering system on a very large scale. **1844** *Sydney Morning Herald* 20 Aug. 2/6 We were invited to inspect the steaming down establishment belonging to Mr George Brown, at Dapto. **1849** *Bell's Life in Sydney* 1 Dec. 4/6 Steaming down 400 bullocks or 4000 sheep per week. . . The quantity obtained is greater than by the method of boiling down. **1851** H. Melville *Present State Aust.* 74 Last year, 120,690 sheep, and 5,545 head of cattle, were steamed, producing 27,725 cwt. of tallow.

steamer. *Obs. Kangaroo steamer*, see Kangaroo *n.* 6.

1820 C. Jeffreys *Van Dieman's Land* 70 Their meal consisted of the hind-quarters of a kangaroo cut into mince-meat, stewed in its own gravy, with a few rashers of salt pork, this dish is commonly called a steamer. **1829** H. Widowson *Present State Van Diemen's Land* 186 The flesh of the kangaroo . . may be dressed various ways, but the principal and best method is, by what is termed, a 'steamer'. **1839** W.H. Leigh *Reconnoitering Voyages* 83 Kangaroo would be a great acquisition to our English bill of fare. . . The colonists stew them; the dish is called a steamer. **1851** H. Melville *Present State Aust.* 311 The 'steamer' . . is made by mincing the flesh of the kangaroo, and with it some pieces of pork or bacon. **1862** G.T. Lloyd *Thirty-Three Yrs. Tas. & Vic.* 434 We saw delicious gravy 'steamers'. **1880** R. Rowe *Roughing It* 13 Tea, 'damper' and 'steamer' formed the evening meal at Broadoaks house that night. **1903** *Truth* (Sydney) 1 Oct. 17/1 The menu was curried rabbit and 'kangaroo steamer', and I was the only guest who didn't beam upon the 'steamer' with joy.

steel. Used *attrib.* in Special Comb. **steel band,** a hard thin layer of sandstone immediately above an opal-bearing stratum; **mill** *obs.*, a portable wheat-grinder.

1950 *Bull. no. 17* (Bureau Min. Resources, Geol. & Geophys.) 27 In many places the first or upper level is indicated by the presence of a very thin and hard band of siliceous sandstone known as the '**Steel Band**'. . . Both in the 'Steel Band' . . and in the Opal Dirt, opal may be found. **1960** D. McLean *Roaring Days* 62 When you strike what you call the 'steel band' of hard sandstone you know you're on the last layer before the opal dirt. A jeweller's shop might be under your feet. **1962** Whiting & Relph *Occurrence of Opal* 9 Precious opal occurs within the Finch Claystone, usually at or near its junction with the overlying Wallangulla Sandstone and underneath the 'steel-band' which is sometimes formed at this junction. This 'steel-band' is a thin (up to one foot) layer of hard siliceous sandstone. **1967** *Sunday Mail Mag.* (Brisbane) 8 Jan. 6/7 Then comes eight to twelve feet of quartzite . . and often after that, a layer of hard siliceous sandstone known as the 'steelband'. **1826** J. Atkinson *Acct. Agric. & Grazing N.S.W.* 30 Perhaps the Settler is sufficiently rich or has credit to procure a small **steel mill** and wire sieve for grinding and dressing his wheat into flour. **1839** D. MacKellar *Austral. Emigrant's Guide* 9 Steel mill, £4. **1870** M. Cash *Adventures* 12, I was obliged to apply myself diligently to an old rusty steel mill . . in order to grind a portion of my allowance of wheat. **1875** Campbell & Wilks *Early Settlement Qld.* 3, I had brought out wheat. . . Accordingly I set up a steel mill . . and set them to grind wheat. **1983** J. Birmingham et al. *Industr. Archaeol. Aust.* 28 The commonest one-man (or one-woman) grinder was made of iron. The so-called 'steel mill' was small enough to be portable and continued to be used in remote places until the late Victorian era or even later.

stepper. *Obs.* [Used elsewhere but recorded earliest in Aust.: see OED(S 2 a.] The treadmill.

1832 *Sydney Herald* 23 Jan. 2/4 Frank Howard, having moistened his clay the previous evening until he was unable to walk, was sentenced to try 'the stepper' for ten days. **1843** *Guardian* (Hobart) 26 Jan. 3/2 Out after hours; 2 months on the 'stepper'. **1845** *Melbourne Standard* 15 Mar. 2/6 Our justices, in sentencing delinquents to imprisonment and hard labour, seem to be ignorant of the fact that there is no hard labour to which the men can be placed since the 'stepper' is out of order.

Hence **stepping** *vbl. n.* and *attrib.*

1830 *Sydney Monitor* 14 Aug. 2/3 The sentences to the mill vary from seven to twenty-eight days. . . The stepping hours are in winter from six to twelve, and from one to six. **1832** *Sydney Herald* 27 Feb. 3/2 For which, seven days stepping was prescribed.

sterks, *pl.* Also **sturks.** [Perh. formed from *stercoraceous* pertaining to excrement.] A fit of exasperation or depression, in the phr. **to give** (one) **the sterks.**

1941 S.J. Baker *Pop. Dict. Austral. Slang* 71 *Sterks, give one the,* to infuriate, annoy, depress. **1959** 'D. Forrest' *Last Blue Sea* 24 He just gives me the sturks. **1968** S. Gore *Holy Smoke* 26 Gorblimey, you'd give a man the sterks, bludgin' there in bed as if it was the Palace Hotel or somethin'! **1972** N. Miles *Opal Fever* 98 'Wouldn't it give you the sturks?' complained Bill.

Hence **sterky** *a.*, frightened.

1944 J. Devanny *By Tropic Sea & Jungle* 162 The croc disappears, and there's Ernest, standing up to his waist in the water . . scared as hell, but too game to come out. . . So my dad goes in. He's a bit sterky too.

sterling. *Hist.*

1. British currency circulating in the Australian colonies. Also **sterling money** and *attrib.*

1806 *Sydney Gaz.* 2 Nov., All Checks and Promissory Notes issued shall by Public Proclamation be drawn payable in Sterling Money. **1811** *Ibid.* 8 June, Payment to be made in sterling money or colonial currency. **1828** *Tasmanian* (Hobart) 5 Sept. 2 When you go to the Merchant's Warehouse or Store to buy a bag of Sugar or a chest of Tea, you must pay *Sterling.* **1832** J. Busby *Authentic Information N.S.W. & N.Z.* 4 The shop-keepers and dealers in Sydney came to the resolution of abolishing the *currency prices,* and substituting sterling prices in their stead.

2. A non-convict, British-born resident of Australia. Freq. *attrib.*

1825 *Austral.* (Sydney) 1 Sept. 3 The idea originated in the best intentions . . to do honour to the strangers by bringing together all the Australian and Sterling Beauties of the Colony. **1827** P. Cunningham *Two Yrs. in N.S.W.* II. 53 Our colonial-born brethren are best known here by the name of *Currency,* in contradistinction to *Sterling,* or those born in the mother-country. **1829** E.G. Wakefield *Let. from Sydney* 129 That low-lived Englishman who, in the pride of his John Bull breed, and of his condition as paymaster to an exiled marching regiment, distinguishing the Emigrant and Native population of New South Wales, by nicknaming the one Sterling, and the other Currency, was no doubt, a man of taste. **1833** *Currency Lad* (Sydney) 12 Jan. 2 The names of Currency and sterling . . became at once badges of inferiority and superiority. **1844** Mrs C. Meredith *Notes & Sketches N.S.W.* 50 The natives (not the aborigines, but the 'currency', as they are termed, in distinction from the 'sterling', or British-born residents) are often very good-looking when young. **1854** W. Shaw *Land of Promise* 49 The terms 'currency' and 'sterling' which are class appellations, were formerly much in vogue, the former signifying those native born, the latter, emigrants. **1964** J.S. Manifold *Who wrote Ballads?* 24 The *sterling* classes—the non-convict English, whether administrators, settlers, or servicemen, who regarded the colony as a place of temporary exile.

Stewart's Ballarat seedling. A variety of apple: see quot. 1984. Also **Ballarat (seedling), Stewart's (seedling).**

1893 D.A. Crichton *Australasian Fruit Culturist* 183 *Stewarts Seedling.*—An excellent Victorian variety, raised in the Ballarat district . . a first-class dessert Apple; also suitable for export. **1917** *Jrnl. Dept. Agric. Vic.* XV. 543 That very fine quality, double purpose, and profitable apple the Stewart's, formerly known as Stewart's Seedling. The tree is a thrifty, good doer, whose rather large fruit ripens late and keeps well. **1984** *Age* (Melbourne) 19 June 27/2 It's a big round apple, green with a dull, pink blush on one side, and in its time it was also known as Ballarat Seedling, Ballarat, Stewart's, and Stewart's Ballarat Seedling. Its names suggest its history. It was first grown in Ballarat and exhibited there by a Mrs Stewart of Soldier's Hill. A nurseryman of Buninyong, Francis Moss, propagated the variety commercially and named it Stewart's Ballarat Seedling in the 1870s. It grew best in Victoria.

stick, *n.*

1. *pl. Australian National Football.* The goal-posts.

1876 T.P. Power *Footballer* 9 Let us suppose then the fray fairly begun by kicking off the ball toward the adversaries' sticks. **1890** *Bull-Ant* (Melbourne) 8 May 14/1 He reaches th' lether up outer th' ruck . . and lands th' blooming sfere round the Richmond sticks pretty quick. **1908** *Clipper* (Hobart) 19 Sept. 2/3 Simpson saved again between the sticks. **1928** G. Moriarty *Teaching Game of Football* v. 4 The *Full Forward* who should be in goals as a 'blind' in order to keep the opposing *Full Back* between the 'sticks' will dash out and mark the ball. **1944** *Fortress Chron.* (Torres Strait Islands) 25 May 1/1 Scored with a . . kick plumb between the sticks.

2. In the phr. **to have had the stick,** *to have had the dick,* see Dick.

1953 T.A.G. Hungerford *Riverslake* 49 When are you bunnies going to wake up that you've had the stick? **1973** D. Wolfe *Brass Kangaroo* 281 Look at this truck now. . . She's just about had the stick. Just about wore out.

3. Special Comb. **stick-picker,** see quot. 1959; so **-picking** *vbl. n.*

1959 H.P. Tritton *Time means Tucker* 58 Burning-off dead timber is a hot game. . . There were 40 men on the job, made up of six axe-men, 30 'stick-pickers' . . whose job was to pack the timber in heaps. **1964** *Ibid.* (rev. ed.) 87 We . . went to Wingadee to work for a contractor at burning off. This work is also known as 'stick-picking'. **1970** J.S. Gunn in W.S. Ramson *Eng. Transported* 56 The obsolete *stick-picker,* who gathers branches fallen from ringbarked trees. **1981** Ngabidj & Shaw *My Country of Pelican Dreaming* 25 The council also used its two vehicles for contract work . . and 'stick picking' on the Packsaddle Plain to clear future farmlands.

stick, *v.*

1. *trans.* With **up.**

a. *Obs.* To pierce (a piece of meat) with a spit and roast it before a fire: see Sticker-up 1. Also as *ppl. a.*

1837 S. Hack Lett. Nov., Cut from the hindquarters of a kangaroo and stuck up before the fire to roast, called in colonial phrase 'stick ups'. **1852** Mrs C. Meredith *My Home in Tas.* I. 55 'And gentlemen', as dear old Hardcastle would have said, if he had dined with us in the bush, 'to men that are hungry, stuck-up kangaroo and bacon are very good eating.' Kangaroo is, in fact, very like hare. **1854** *Courier* (Hobart) 3 Apr. 2 Christmas Day. . . This day we had a 'glorious feed' for dinner. Two black swans, one roasted (stuck-up), the other was made into sea-pie.

b. [Now also used elsewhere: see OED(S *v.*[1] 34 k.] *trans.* Of an (armed) bushranger: to stop by force and rob (a person or persons) on the road; to rob (a building, coach, etc., or the occupants thereof) under threat of violence. See Bail *v.* 2 a.

1843 F. Landon *Exile from Canada* (1960) 218 There are quite a number more bushrangers but they are not so daring, they do not stick folks up at the houses and rob so openly. **1848** *Maitland Mercury* 27 May 4/3 On Thursday week the bushrangers visited Mr Brock's farm, at the Black River, between Emu Bay and Circular Head, 'stuck up' several men, and supplied themselves with provisions, ammunition, &c. **1853** J. Rochfort *Adventures Surveyor* 46 'Stuck up' is a colonial expression for being robbed with a pistol at your head. **1864** *Bell's Life in Sydney* 23 Jan. 2/6 Mr Inspector Turnstern was 'stuck up' by two desperate old women in York-street and robbed of a large amount of self-esteem. **1865** J.F. Mortlock *Experiences of Convict* 114 To 'stick up' a person, house, or dray, means, in Australian 'flash' phraseology, to come suddenly with presented arms upon them, and threaten to kill any body who stirs, while the accomplice goes round and collects money, watches, jewellery, etc., and perhaps binds them. **1882** A.J. Boyd *Old Colonials* 4 I've had many a spear shied at me, and once a big mob stuck up my humpie. **1893** S. Newland *Paving Way* 288 He and his gang left us then, after sticking up the station. **1905** *Truth* (Sydney) 19 Nov. 1/4 Another coach stuck up during the week. **1911** *Huon Times* (Franklin) 25 Mar. 6/4 On Wednesday they stuck up a Chinese gardener on the Leichhardt River, tied him to a tree, took all his ammunition. **1928** M.E. Fullerton *Austral. Bush* 83 'Stuck up' by Power. The 'sticking up' was but a request for some matches. **1935** F. Clune *Rolling down Lachlan* 163 It seemed to be the height of their [*sc.* bushrangers'] ambition to 'stick-up' the troopers. **1950** G.M. Farwell *Land of Mirage* 171 Many a man who stuck up a gold escort or a Cobb & Co. coach had started out as a mere gully-raker, putting his brand on scrubbers.

c. *trans.* To frustrate the activity of (a person, etc.); to hamper.

[N.Z. **1863** S. Butler *First Yr. Canterbury Settlement* 68 At last we came to a waterfall. . . This 'stuck us up', as they say here concerning any difficulty.] **1879** *Kelly Gang* 135 We are stuck up; the Kellys are here, and the police are also stuck up. **1888** A.P. Martin *Oak-Bough & Wattle-Blossom* 132 We had been over six weeks stuck up by the floods. **1894** *Bulletin* (Sydney) 10 Mar. 7/4 Less water than ever at Coolgardie; teams stuck up, soakages dry. **1904** *Shearer* (Sydney) 6 Aug. 6/5 The union recently 'stuck up' without notice one of the company's colliers.

d. *trans.* To bring (an animal) to bay.

1884 'R. Boldrewood' *Old Melbourne Memories* 24 We knew then that she had 'stuck up' or brought to bay a large forester. **1891** 'Smiler' *Wanderings Simple Child* (ed. 3) 87 Let him get his dog to stick up an 'old man' [kangaroo] and then go quietly up, and gently raise the marsupial's off eyelid. **1910** *Huon Times* (Franklin) 24 Aug. 3/3 There were plenty of opossums. The dogs would stick them up in the day time.

e. *intr.* Of an animal: to stand at bay.

1893 E.D. Cleland *White Kangaroo* 55 He was certain the kangaroo would not go far before 'sticking up' and showing fight. This proved to be the case for very soon the 'old man' faced suddenly round, and sitting erect upon his hind legs he showed a bold front to his pursuers.

2. [Used elsewhere but recorded earliest in Aust.] In the phr. **to get stuck into,** to lay into, to make a physical assault on (someone); to attack (a project, meal, etc.) with gusto.

1941 S.J. Baker *Pop. Dict. Austral. Slang* 31 *Get stuck into,* to engage a person in a bout of fisticuffs. To tackle a job with a will. **1944** C. Wilmot *Tobruk* 40 When your mates've copped it, you want to get stuck into the bastards. **1953** T.A.G. Hungerford *Riverslake* 121 What was the trouble, Con? I saw you stuck into a Balt across the press as I come down. **1955** D. Niland *Shiralee* 30 'Never mind that,' he grunted. 'Get stuck into your tucker.' **1963** W.E. Harney *To Ayers Rock & Beyond* 66 With the coming of water Len got stuck into things with a will. **1966** *Mirage* Mar. 5 Noticed old J.D. was getting stuck into a feed in the Flight kitchen yesterday. **1971** *Kings Cross Whisper* (Sydney) cvii. 4/1 He said wine-drinkers would be well advised to run a geiger counter over their Hunter River '57, before getting stuck into it. **1977** A. Mackay *Life Pieces* I. 118 So we took some cans down to the beach and really got stuck into it. **1980** Holth & Barnaby *Cattlemen of High Country* 86 Once . . a cow wandered inside the lean-to and 'got stuck into' the feed. **1985** *Sunday Territorian* (Darwin) 24 Feb. 6/5 He got stuck into the Feds for providing 'little or nothing' for Northern Australian development.

sticker-up.

1. *Obs.* [See Stick *v.* 1 a.] A method of cooking meat out of doors (see quot. 1852); the meat so cooked. Also *attrib.*

1830 *Hobart Town Almanack* 112 Steaks . . which he cooked in the mode called in colonial phrase a sticker up. **1842** *S. Austral. Mag.* Oct. 21 The sticker-up, which, broiled before the flame, Did, with the ash-baked damper, well agree. **1852** Mrs C. Meredith *My Home in Tas.* I. 54 Here I was first initiated into the bush art of 'sticker-up' cookery. . . The orthodox material here is of course kangaroo, a piece of which is divided nicely into cutlets two or three inches broad and a third of an inch thick. The next requisite is a straight clean stick, about four feet long, sharpened at both ends. On the narrow part of this, for the space of a foot or more, the cutlets are spitted at intervals, and on the end is placed a piece of delicately rosy fat bacon. The strong end of the stick-pit is now stuck fast and erect in the ground, close by the fire, to leeward; care being taken that it does not burn. **1862** G.T. Lloyd *Thirty-Three Yrs. Tas. & Vic.* 103 Pounds of rosy steaks . . skilfully rigged after the usual approved fashion (termed in Bush phraseology a 'sticker up'), before the brilliant wood fire.

2. [f. Stick *v.* 1 b.] One who robs a person under threat of violence.

1855 W. Howitt *Land, Labor & Gold* II. 43 What are called Bendigo Faugh-a-ballahs, the same class of mortals as M'Ivor Stickers-up and Ballarat All-serenes—in plain English, thieves. **1866** *Illustr. Sydney News* 16 Nov. 3/1 Two 'stickers-up' at Adelaide have been captured. **1907** C. MacAlister *Old Pioneering Days* 232 Oh! don't you remember old Melbourne, Ben Bolt, When gold nuggets first were found out? When, mid five feet of mud on the wharves and the streets, And all night, 'stickers-up' roamed about.

sticking up, *vbl. n.* [f. Stick *v.* 1 b.] The action of robbing a person or persons under threat of violence. Also *attrib.*

1853 *Guardian* (Hobart) 10 Aug. 3/2 'Sticking up' still continues in Melbourne and on the roads to a fearful extent. **1862** *Bell's Life in Sydney* 21 June 2/1 A much more 'gentlemanly' affair than the vulgar 'sticking up' of the Escort. **1874** *Illustr. Sydney News* 39 Jan. 10/2 'Sticking up' was the colonial and genteel term applied to highway robbery. **1891** J. Singleton *Narr. Eventful Life Physician* 147 Their first adventure was the 'sticking up' of a tent, in which lived a schoolmaster and his family. **1900** C.H. Chomley *True Story Kelly Gang* 20 Power, a solitary rover . . had terrorised a large part of the colony by his 'sticking-up' exploits, though murder was a crime of which he was never guilty.

stick-nest rat. [See quot. 1941.] Either of the two rats of the genus *Leporillus, L. apicalis* (prob. extinct) and *L. conditor* (of Franklin Is., S.A.), both of which build a dwelling of sticks containing a soft nest or burrow. See also *rabbit rat* Rabbit A 1. Also **stick-nest building rat.**

[**1838** T.L. Mitchell *Three Exped. Eastern Aust.* I. 305 A species of rat was remarkable for the formidable fabric it raised to secure itself from the native dog, or birds of prey. This consisted of a rick or stack of small branches, commonly worked around and interlaced with some small bush.] **1923** *Rec. Austral. Museum* XIV. 23 While on a collecting expedition . . at various stations on the Trans-Australian Railway, I secured several specimens of a stick-nest building rat. **1941** E. Troughton *Furred Animals Aust.* 309 Stick-nest Rats. Genus *Leporillus*. . . The rats of this genus were originally known as the 'Native Rabbit' or 'Rabbit-Rat'. . . They are gregarious creatures, two species being communal house-builders, an unusual habit which provides the present popular name for the genus. **1984** *Age* (Melbourne) 10 Apr. 28/8 Native Stick-Nest rats have apparently become extinct on the mainland, although between 1500 and 2000 individuals live on Franklin Island in the Nuyts Archipelago in South Australia.

stick-up.

1. [Orig. Austral. but now chiefly U.S.: see OEDS *sb.* 2.] An instance of Sticking-up. Also *attrib.*

[**1887** W.H. Suttor *Austral. Stories Retold* 41 A body of men, mostly armed, met us. We at first thought it was a case of 'stick up'.] **1910** H. Lawson *Skyline Riders* 62 Scott that fired at Brummy Hughson, when the 'stick-ups' used to be. **1942** A.L. Haskell *Waltzing Matilda* 111 Brother Jim was prevented from joining through a ten-year sentence, result of his failure as a 'stick-up man' in New South Wales.

2. The place where an animal is held at bay. See Stick *v.* 1 d.

1978 A. Bentley *Introd. Deer Aust.* (ed. 2) 296 As Harry gets near the 'stick-up' he is cautious and only moves when the hounds are barking and stops when they stop.

sticky. Abbrev. of Stickybeak *n.* 1 and 2. Also as *adj.*

1941 S.J. Baker *Pop. Dict. Austral. Slang* 72 *Sticky* (adj.), curious, inquisitive. **1946** *Bulletin* (Sydney) 23 Jan. 12/3 Being a natural 'sticky' I climbed the ladder to see the cause of the man's interest. **1974** D. Ireland *Burn* 139 Have a gander. Perhaps your mates'd like a bit of a sticky too.

stickybeak, *n.*

1. An inquisitive person; one who 'sticks his (or her) nose into' the affairs of others. Also *attrib.*, and *transf.*

1920 B. Cronin *Timber Wolves* 159 I've told the girls to give out that we've gone fishing, if any sticky-beaks get to asking why we ain't visible no more. **1933** H.B. Raine *Lash End* 200 If that stickybeak pressman hadn't poked his nose into our business, none of this would have happened. **1943** *Bulletin* (Sydney) 29 Dec. 12/1 When two channels about six inches by a yard sprouted out of one side the stickybeak in me prevailed. 'What's this, a dam?' I asked. **1951** *Ibid.* 25 Apr. 12/2 Cows are natural sticky-beaks. **1965** K. Smith *OGF* 31 Other stickybeaks were pressing in around Miss Hairworth with more questions. **1972** J. Searle *Lucky Streak* 96 Flaming stickybeak. . . Poking, around putting her nose in everything. **1982** R. Hall *Just Relations* 231 Disguised as a mobile heap of blankets in case some stickybeak might be awake and prying.

2. An inquisitive look.

1971 *Bulletin* (Sydney) 21 Aug. 14/1 An old Digger type who was just having a bit of a stickybeak gets spun out of the crush.

stickybeak, *v.* [f. prec.] *intr.* To pry; to snoop.

1933 J. Truran *Where Plain Begins* 13 'So you're the bloke that's been robbin' me traps, are yer?' said the man. 'Serves yer right for stickybeakin' where you 'ad no business.' **1947** *Bulletin* (Sydney) 26 Mar. 45/1 Wait for sunset to stickybeak on platypuses. **1959** *Ibid.* 3 June 18/3 A chook, escapee from the fowlyard, paused to stickybeak at a fence-post, then bogged-in with great relish. **1960** *Khaki Bush & Bigotry* (1968) 260 You think of some old crone in a boarding-house, or something, stickybeakin' round. And that sort, too, she'd be sure to be in with the police. **1978** H. Haenke *Bottom of Birdcage* 47 Who wants sticky-beakin' down a sewer? Catch y' death.

Hence **stickybeaking** *vbl n.* and *ppl. a.*

1948 H. Drake-Brockman *Sydney or Bush* 230 Flat-chested old sticky-beaking romancer, that's what she is! **1965** R.H. Conquest *Horses in Kitchen* 103 'Are you satisfied now?' he said grimly to me. 'See what your sticky-beaking has done?' **1982** R. Hall *Just Relations* 357 'Bloody stickybeaking old bat,' growled George.

sticky wattle. The shrub *Acacia howittii* (fam. Mimosaceae) of e. Vic., cultivated as an ornamental. Also **sticky acacia.**

1930 A.J. Ewart *Flora Vic.* 600 *A[cacia] Howittii* . . Sticky Acacia. A viscid shrub. **1973** G.R. Cochrane et al. *Flowers & Plants Vic.* (rev. ed.) 197 The Sticky Wattle . . of South Gippsland hills . . is resinous with an aromatic scent, and has become a popular garden subject. **1985** *Canberra Times* 15 Aug. 11/2 The sticky wattle from Victoria makes a fine rapidly grown screening shrub.

stiff, *a.* [Prob. f. Br. slang *stiff* a penniless person: see OED(S *sb.* 4.]

1. Penniless. Hence, unlucky. Also as *n.*

1898 *Bulletin* (Sydney) 17 Dec. 15/2 Hard-uppishness a shearer confesses when he says he's *stiff.* **1899** *Ibid.* 19 Aug. 32/1 They weren't quite 'stiff', and scorned to eat Union tucker while they could buy—or steal—from the squatters. **1903** *Ibid.* 22 Oct. 35/4 He cannot . . travel 100 miles with a cheque in his pocket and keep it 'unbroken'. Once 'stiff', he can go from Sydney to the Gulf 'on his cheek'. **1909** A. Wright *Rogue's Luck* 197 'I'm stiff; ain't got er quid ter me name,' growled the man. **1918** *'Billjim' at Sea: Souvenir Voyage Modern Transport* 8, I reckon a man is stiff when he enlists and snuffs it before he gets a chance to fire a shot. **1922** C. Drew *Rogues & Ruses* 53 We're stiff enough to get cut up for broom handles. **1931** O. Walters *Shrapnel Green* 9 'Two flaming nicks,' he said, and flung the kip down in the mud. 'God spare me days, a man is stiff enough.' **1940** *Bulletin* (Sydney) 28 Feb. 16/4 The big fellow was stiff in a Victorian dairy town, so he took a job with a cow-cocky at 25s. a week and keep. **1943** S.W. Keough *Around Army* 59 Pick on someone else, can't y', an' give us a chance to get our Oscar back. *He* might get skittled an' then *we'll* be stiff!' **1960** R. Boyd *Austral. Ugliness* 61, I recall . . a waiter . . responding to my circumspect enquiry about the possibility of a glass of wine with the succinct phrase: 'I think you'll be stiff, mate.' **1972** J. de Hoog *Skid Row Dossier* 58 A favourite definition of the word stiff: 'a bloke who's got nothin' and never will have nothin'.'

2. Bad, hard, 'tough'; esp. in the collocation **stiff luck** and varr., 'hard lines'.

1900 *Bulletin* (Sydney) 28 Apr. 14/1 Recently read a stiff yarn about an orchid in Cuba which dropped its tendrils at night and drew up and strangled some Yankee sailors. **1919** *Remnants from Randwick* ii. 73 It 'ud be stiff luck to 'ear your cliner 'ad been pinched. **1922** F.C. Green *Fortieth* 15 Stiff luck! He was going on leave to-morrow. **1938** F. Clune *Free & Easy Land* 153 Compensation to the cow-cocky Gordons for their stiff luck. **1942** I.L. Idriess *Guerrilla Tactics* 50 It would be stiff luck to tackle a man who'd put in half his life at a wrestling-school. **1944** C. Wilmot *Tobruk* 17 If we take them by surprise, it'll be all right. If not, well—it may be a stiff go. **1968** S. Gore *Holy Smoke* 60 So he wouldn't have minded leasin' the joint to some blokes who'd been having a bit of a stiff trot, and was too skint to start up on their own d' y' see? **1972** *Bulletin* (Sydney) 15 July 15/1 Stiff luck there, we made a mistake. **1979** B. Humphries *Bazza comes into his Own*, If you're an English Aborigine wanting to migrate to Oz—it's stiff cheese! **1980** *Westerly* iv. 30 'People always think I am Aboriginal.' 'Stiff shit.'

3. In the phr. **stiff and swagless:** see *swagless* Swag *n.*

Hence **stiffness** *n.*, bad luck.

1918 *Aussie: Austral. Soldiers' Mag.* Dec. p. ii, Cripes! there's stiffness fer yer! We've just finished building this bonzer possie, stove and all, ready for the Winter, and now they go and make an Armistice!

stiffener. [Used elsewhere but recorded earliest in Aust.: see OEDS 3.] A fortifying or reviving alcoholic drink.

1864 J. Armour *Diggings, Bush & Melbourne* 14 They adjourned to the tap-room for 'a stiffener'. **1893** D. Healey *Cornstalk* 99 What with 'stiffeners' in him, his can under his arm, He was fortified inside and out with a charm. **1914** W. Collin *Life & Adventures* 147 Seeing the longing look in his face, I offered him what we then called a 'stiffener'. **1937** A.W. Upfield *Winds of Evil* 233 'Here, Barry! Have a stiffener,' Lee said kindly, proffering a tin pannikin. **1940** —— *Bushranger of Skies* 58 'I feel like a good stiffener.' 'So do I, though I seldom drink,' said Boney.

sting. [f. Br. slang *stingo* strong beer.]

1. Strong drink.

1927 K.S. Prichard *Brumby Innes* (1974) 68 Old Jack's been boozin' up a bit. Never touched a woman in all his born days, he says, but he ain't so teetotal about sting. **1929** —— *Coonardoo* (1961) 169 I'd stay and manage Nuniewarra for him until he pegs out—see he gets all the sting he wants. **1972** J. de Hoog *Skid Row Dossier* 4 You can share a bottle of sting (methylated spirits) down a lane. **1978** D. Stuart *Wedgetail View* 39 'Anyway, I'll set up a bit of a sting, eh?' The pair of them . . sat slowly drinking.

2. A drug, spec. one given illegally to a racehorse by injection.

1949 L. Glassop *Lucky Palmer* 36 They're going to

give it the sting. They'll hit it with enough dope to win a Melbourne Cup. **1950** *Austral. Police Jrnl.* Jan. 118 *Sting*, dope. **1958** F. HARDY *Four-Legged Lottery* 180 A man should only bet when he's got inside information—and if its information from a stable with a jigger or a good sting, all the better.

Hence as *v. trans.*, to administer an illegal drug to (a racehorse).

1978 H.C. BAKER *I was Listening* 109 This feller comes to me and wants me to 'sting' one of his horses. I told him, 'Look, there's nothing I can give you that'll make a horse do better than his best. If he's good enough he'll win; if he ain't, he'll lose.'

stingaree /'stɪŋəri, stɪŋə'ri/. Also **stingeree.** [Altered form of *stingray* a fish of the fam. Dasyatidae.] Any of several rays, esp. *Urolophus testaceus*, commonly found on muddy or sandy flats in shallow waters from Qld. southwards to S.A.

1830 R. DAWSON *Present State Aust.* 313 There is a common fish in the colony called a stingaree; its tail is pointed, and so sharp that the natives in bathing near a low shore are frequently wounded by it in the feet. **1841** *Geelong Advertiser* 27 Feb. 2/5 A seaman .. was wounded in the thigh by the fish called Fire Flare or Sting Ray (corrupted into Stingaree by the colonists). **1850** *Britannia* (Hobart) 17 Jan. 3/1 One of the largest Stingerees ever before seen, the monster being nearly eight feet long, and of nearly equal dimensions in breadth. **1872** C.H. EDEN *My Wife & I in Qld.* 250 They were the tails of 'stingarees', a large flat fish like a skate. **1918** *Truth* (Sydney) 28 July 9/4 Everybody remembers how stingarees were sold in the Government fish depots under the name of 'skate'. **1927** M. TERRY *Through Land of Promise* 302 Sharks, sword fish and stingerees—fish with stings in their tails. **1952** *Austral. Museum Mag.* June 310 Tailor and Stingaree are as much American as Australian. **1974** T.D. SCOTT et al. *Marine & Freshwater Fishes S.A.* 47 The name stingaree is often used synonymously with the name stingray, but should be restricted to those rays which possess both a barbed tail spine and a caudal fin. All species are included in a single genus, *Urolophus*.

stinger.

1. An exceptionally hot spell of weather.

1867 *S.A. Parl. Papers* no. 14 69 It would not find a purchaser at a much higher rate than you suggest?—I do not know; I think people have had such a stinger, there would be no buyers except just to put stock on in good seasons. **1899** 'S. RUDD' *On our Selection* 32 'My! it'll be a stinger to-night,' Dad remarked .. as he staggered inside with an immense log for the fire. **1942** E. LANGLEY *Pea Pickers* 220 The next day was a stinger; and we had to pick in Greenfeast's dry, starved bean crop.

2. Shortened form of STINGING TREE.

1941 H.D.A. JOSKE *Life to Live* 186 There are also several plants whose touch is extremely painful, the worst of them being the 'stinger'. **1976** E. WORRELL *Things that Sting* 47 A group of prickly-barked, pink-berried trees known as Stinging Trees or Stingers.

3. BOX JELLYFISH. Also *attrib.*

1981 *Ecos* xxviii. 21/1 This lake could prove particularly popular for recreation in summer, when marine 'stingers' (box jellyfish) are a hazard on the coast. **1984** *People Mag.* (Sydney) 7 May 10/3 Stingers will venture into ankle-deep water in search of their diet of small crustaceans and plankton... The canny stingers steer clear of coral, because their tendrils may become entangled. **1984** *N.T. News* (Darwin) 9 Nov. 32/4 Stinger suits, box jellyfish at Keith Kemps, Knuckey St sports store.

stingeree, var. STINGAREE.

stinging bush, stinging-nettle: see STINGING TREE.

stinging-ray. A stingray. Also *attrib.*

1804 *Sydney Gaz.* 30 Sept., A ludicrous contest some days since took place, the parties engaged in which were a seine attendant and a *stinging rae-fish*. **1862** G.T. LLOYD *Thirty-Three Yrs. Tas. & Vic.* 51 The ray is termed in the colonies the 'stinging-ray', from its possessing a barbed spear-bone. **1935** A. FRANCIS *Then & Now* 165 The sting-a-ree, or more properly, stinging-ray, is a flat, repulsive-looking fish, four or five feet across, which lies upon the bottom in shallow water. It has a long, whip-like tail, on the under surface of which is an ivory serrated spike six or more inches long, which is a dangerous weapon, as it produces a lacerated poisoned wound.

stinging tree. Any of several trees or shrubs of the genus *Dendrocnide* (fam. Urticaceae) of N.S.W., Qld., and elsewhere, characterized by stinging hairs, esp. on the leaves and small branches; NETTLE TREE. See also *giant stinging tree* GIANT, GYMPIE. Also **stinging bush, stinging-nettle tree.**

1836 J. BACKHOUSE *Narr. Visit Austral. Colonies* (1843) 431 We measured three Stinging-trees, *Urtica gigas*, eighteen, twenty, and twenty-one feet in circumference. **1851** J. HENDERSON *Excursions & Adventures N.S.W.* II. 231 The Nettle, or Stinging-tree .. attains a good size; its wood is white and soft; its blossom a beautiful scarlet, and its leaves are large, rough, and dark, inflicting a very poisonous sting. **1873** C.H. EDEN *Fortunes of Fletchers* 76 The stinging-nettle tree .. the intensity of whose poison is so violent that the man or horse unlucky enough to be brought into a prolonged contact with its branches is stricken with a numbness resembling paralysis. **1902** *Bulletin* (Sydney) 7 June 16/3 Clearing-work on the Mareeba-Atherton railway (N.Q.) has been suspended owing to the presence of some scrub abounding in 'stinging-tree'. **1918** G. WHITE *Thirty Yrs. Tropical Aust.* 19 The stinging tree *Urtica gigantica*, a giant nettle, twelve to eighteen feet in height, whose sting causes acute pain, which is renewed for some months after whenever the part stung is brought into contact with water. **1930** *Bulletin* (Sydney) 2 Apr. 23/3 Bordering the bush track through the Government reserve on the way to Minnamurra Falls (N.S.W.) there are some giant stinging-nettle trees. **1944** *Ibid.* 3 May 12/2 As one to whom the gates of Sheol have been opened by the stinging-tree of N.Q. I can't understand its absence from the reports of patrol activity in N.G. **1952** T.A.G. HUNGERFORD *Ridge & River* 145 'Bloody stinging-bush,' Wallace swore, sweeping the leaves from his shoulder. **1965** *Austral. Encycl.* IV. 406 In 1868 the name was altered to Gympie, an aboriginal term for the stinging trees found in the district. **1980** B. SCOTT *Darkness under Hills* 20 They dodged between the heart-shaped leaves of the stinging trees that grow thickly on the edge of the jungle.

stinkbird. Either of two birds of the genus *Sericornis, S. fuliginosus* of s.e. Aust. incl. Tas., and *S. campestris* of heathland and drier parts of s. mainland Aust.

1883 A.J. CAMPBELL *Nests & Eggs Austral. Birds* p. xxviii, The Striated Calamanthus .. is not without interest... The [Tasmanian] Islanders call it by the somewhat uneuphonious name of 'Stink-bird' or 'Stinker', because it emits a gamey scent, and dogs sometimes point at it. **1918** *Bulletin* (Sydney) 14 Feb. (Red Page), *White-browed Field-Wren* (Field Warbler, Stink-Bird). **1925** *Ibid.* 23 Apr. 23/2 The learned ornithologists have given us atrocities such as .. the olivaceous thick-head, and the stink-bird. **1954** C. BARRETT *Wild Life Aust. & New Guinea* 159 We have four field-wrens, the best known being the striated species, which sportsmen have given an ugly name—'stink-bird'; the little striped songster leaves a strong scent trail, which sporting dogs refuse to follow.

stinkfish. [See quot. 1906.] Any of several marine fish of the fam. Callionymidae, esp. those of the genus *Callionymus*, some of which are poisonous.

1900 *Proc. Linnean Soc. N.S.W.* XXV. 476 Mr D.G. Stead exhibited a specimen and described the effluvium-producing powers of the so-called 'Stink-Fish'. **1906** D.G. STEAD *Fishes of Aust.* 208 One species [of Dragonet] well-known in Port Jackson (because of the offensive smell exhaled from the gill-openings) is the Stink-Fish (*Callionymus curvicornis*). **1926** *Advertiser* (Adelaide) 18 Aug. 15/1 Some Italians caught and cooked a similar fish a few days ago. The fishermen 'only had a taste of it, and spat it out, owing to the bitter flavour; they were bad all day, feeling sick... ' Mr H.M. Hale .. reports that the fish responsible for the trouble is known as the stink fish (*Callionymus calauropomus*)... He said:- 'In certain fishes (for instance, in some of the toad fishes) poisonous alkaloids are present in the body, and are often most developed during the spawning season; such fishes cause serious trouble if used as food.' **1965** *Austral. Encycl.* III. 280 Dragonets are often called stinkfish, for they have a disagreeable odour rather like that of a cucumber. **1976** E. WORRELL *Things that Sting* 53 The flesh of poisonous *Stinkfish* tastes so bad that it is unlikely to be eaten by anyone.

stinking Roger. [Spec. use of *stinking Roger* any of several evil-smelling plants.] The strongly aromatic, tall, annual, American herb *Tagetes minuta* (fam. Asteraceae), naturalized in e. mainland Aust.

1871 *Austral. Town & Country Jrnl.* (Sydney) 426/2 'What is that tall bright-green feathery looking plant?' That is .. a Chinese medicinal plant, introduced here rashly at a venture, and dubbed by the euphonious epithet of 'Stinking Roger'. **1890** F.M. BAILEY *Catal. Indigenous & Naturalised Plants Qld.* (ed. 2) 103 Stinking Rodger—Tagetes glandulifera. **1898** *Bulletin* (Sydney) 8 Jan. 32/2 The grass along the headlands was almost as tall as the corn; the Bathurst-burr, the Scotch-thistles, and the 'stinking Roger', were taller. **1914** H.M. VAUGHAN *Australasian Wander-Yr.* 237 Along the banks of the creeks were flourishing a few coarse and strongly aromatic weeds, mostly owing [*sic*] such expressive names as 'Stinking Roger' and 'Cobbler's Pegs'. **1949** B. O'REILLY *Green Mountains* 142 Roger .. had been named because his natal bed had been a trampled mass of 'Stinking Roger'. **1979** E. SMITH *Saddle in Kitchen* 20 The creek ran out onto a flat, marshy patch that was overgrown with a tall, rank weed we called 'stinking Roger'.

stinkwood. [Spec. use of *stinkwood* a name for any of several plants the wood of which has an unpleasant smell.] Any of several trees or shrubs, esp. *Zieria arborescens* (fam. Rutaceae) of s.e. Aust., the leaves of which smell unpleasant when crushed, and *Jacksonia scoparia* (see DOGWOOD).

1827 *HRA* (1923) 3rd Ser. VI. 267 'Stink Wood' .. I believe has some what the appearance of Elder, with a very disagreeable smell. **1846** J. GOULD *Birds of Aust.* (1848) IV. Pl. 57, Called by the colonists of Swan River the stinkwood. **1847** D. BUNCE *Australasiatic Reminisc.* (1857) 129 The wood of the *Jacksonia* when burnt gives out a disagreeable, foetid smell, from whence it has derived the name of stink-wood. **1872** MRS E. MILLETT *Austral. Parsonage* 95 The burning of even a small bit of the tree commonly called 'stink-wood' will make the inmates of a room fly out of it, to avoid the terrible odour. **1897** L. LINDLEY-COWEN *W. Austral. Settler's Guide* 219 Stinkwood if cut down, dies out. **1927** T.S. GROSER *Lure of Golden West* 256 Stinkwood, banksia and the small blue-gum. **1981** G.M. CUNNINGHAM et al. *Plants Western N.S.W.* 399 The wood emits a most offensive odour when burning, hence two of its common names, stinkwood and dogwood.

stipe. [Transf. use of Br. slang *stipe* stipendiary (magistrate); chiefly Austral.] Abbrev. of 'stipendiary racing steward': see quot. 1983.

1902 *Sporting News* (Launceston) 6 Dec. 1/3 Where were the eyes of the stewards and 'stipe' in the first race? **1928** L.A. SIGSWORTH *Various Verse* 27, I am the man who owns the quadruped That sundry racing scribblers write about. It's me who takes the blame when he is 'dead'; When punters urge the stipes to 'rub him out'. **1956** S. HOPE *Diggers' Paradise* 141 According to the 'stipe', who evidently had failed to find a permanent job to his liking in Britain, Sir Gordon Richards was in the 'kindergarten class' so far as knowledge of racing was concerned. **1969** *Sporting Globe* (Melbourne) 2 July 5/7 Simpson told the stipes that Ridicule .. was slow to find his feet. **1979** S.W. DUTHIE *Fidlers Creek* 14 Of course the stipes ask some awkward questions but Carter shows he plonks a fair bit on his nag and he is more crook on it than all the flaming stewards put together. **1983** HIBBERD & HUTCHINSON *Barracker's Bible* 197 *Stipes*, the Stipendiary Stewards, who for their 'stipend' are charged with the enforcement of the Rules of Racing, and a fair crack of the whip for all concerned especially in matters vetinary [*sic*] and pharmacological.

stir, *v.* [Spec. use of *stir* to move to action: see *stir the possum* POSSUM *n.* 3. Used elsewhere but recorded earliest in Aust.]

a. *intr.* To cause trouble for its own sake.

1969 *Sunday Mail Mag.* (Brisbane) 22 June 11/4 'Groovy people', 'good clothes', anybody who can stir. **1972** J. DE HOOG *Skid Row Dossier* 110 Excitement was whipped up over the tiniest incident and when several youths went 'stirring' one day—riding up and down on the lifts of large office blocks—conversations dwelt on and enlarged every action. **1976** B. Bennett *New Country* 42 More interested in stirring than they are in abo poets. **1980** E.R. Hall *Can you hear Me?* 128 Throughout the years there were radio members who would 'stir' mainly in an effort to get the 'System' to work for the individual.

b. *trans.* To provoke (someone) into exhibiting exasperation, etc.

1972 L. Irish *Time of Dolphins* 33 'You know, Mrs Ro, you've got really nice legs.' 'Not all oldies have fat legs.' . . (You're a woman Ama Ro, oh yes, and she's damned well stirring you.) **1974** Buckley & Hamilton *Festival* 187 Stirring teachers was our favourite sport. **1977** D. Williamson *Club* (1978) 20 What role have you been taking in this, Laurie? Have you been stirring the lads? **1978** B. St. A. Smith *Spirit beyond Psyche* 180 She . . had often 'stirred' him about his pretty hair, but secretly she had been proud of him.

Also as *n.*

1981 Smolicz & Secombe *Austral. School through Children's Eyes* 82 We tend to speak the Polish language among ourselves 'for a stir'.

stirrer. [f. prec.; chiefly Austral.] An agitator; a trouble-maker.

1966 *R.A.N. News* (Sydney) 7 Jan. 8 Leg pulling . . is often used, discreetly, to test the quality of a man. The exponents of this art [are] usually called 'stirrers'. **1969** *Bulletin* (Sydney) 1 Mar. 18/3 Much more, and sooner, whatever the cost or trouble, is likely to be the 'stirrers'' slogan. **1971** *Ibid.* 10 July 22/1 Editorial writers have blustered that he isn't welcome as a 'stirrer' in this country. . . He led the Stop the Seventies Tour movement in Britain last year. **1973** D. Wolfe *Brass Kangaroo* 12 Big Mervyn complained of 'commos' and 'stirrers'. **1976** *Tracks we Travel* 162 Not that he was a stirrer wanting to stage a strike. **1982** *Bulletin* (Sydney) 6 July 25/2 The preselection contest could come down to a race between a younger activist—'a stirrer in the best traditions of the Senate' . . and a 61-year-old party man. **1983** *Ibid.* 1 Nov. 84/1 We were happy . . until stirrers like you came and started *their* stirrers demanding Award rates of pay and Land Rights and protection of Sacred Sites.

stirry, *a.* Of an animal: bad-tempered; restive.

1976 S. Weller *Bastards I have Met* 116 One big brahman bullock had bailed up. He was real stirry—would blow snot and throw dirt even if you looked his way. **1979** J. Lindeman *Red Rumps & White Faces* 29 The calves usually ran well; my worst worry was when a big 'stirry micky' attacked me from behind.

stobie pole. *S.A.* [f. the name of J.C. *Stobie* (1895–1953), engineer.] A pole of steel and concrete carrying electricity lines.

[**1953** *Advertiser* (Adelaide) 17 Aug. 2/7 Mr James Cyril Stobie designer of the concrete and steel posts . . died on Saturday night at his home in . . Malvern. In 1924 he designed the new-type electricity poles which were afterwards named after him.] **1970** *S. Austral. Electrical Contractor* Dec. 43 Stobie Poles. Much to do about them at present, their safety and their appearance. To me I cannot understand why wiring does not go underground. **1980** N. Jose *Possession of Amber* 83 Stobie poles and hamburger joints are as beautiful as everything else. **1983** *Advertiser* (Adelaide) 12 Dec. 3/3 A 27-year-old man died . . after the car he was driving . . hit a stobie pole. **1984** *Canberra Times* 7 Oct. 2/2 Clifton Pugh painted a naked Eve on a telegraph pole (or 'stobie pole' as the pie-floater-eating South Australians call them). **1985** *Advertiser* (Adelaide) 4 Jan. 1/6 That blight of the Australian landscape, the stobie pole, has angered S.A. motorists, town planners and conservationists for decades.

stock. [Spec. use of *stock* livestock: see OED(S *sb.*[1] 63 a. for numerous Comb. of local significance but well attested elsewhere.]

1. Used *attrib.* in Comb. **stock feed, feeding, owner, pen, train, work, yard.**

1890 A. Mackay *Austral. Agriculturist* (ed. 2) 67 When half a bushel of tares or vetches are sown with the rye, the mixture is excellent for **stock feed,** or making ensilage. **1930** A.E. Yarra *Vanishing Horsemen* 11 Charlie, the King of the Tamporinas, was chopping down young mulga trees for stock-feed. **1972** *Bulletin* (Sydney) 26 Feb. 57/3 The other way the sheep and wheat men have been saving themselves has been through a move to producing stockfeed. **1853** J.R. Godley *Extracts Jrnl. Visit N.S.W.* 9 The present governing, or rather legislating, class . . are, to a preponderable extent, men of considerable fortunes derived from **stock-feeding.** **1880** J. Bonwick *Resources Qld.* 61 The red [sweet potato], bearing wonderfully, is admirable for stock-feeding. **1804** *Sydney Gaz.* 18 Nov., I am . . anxious to propose, the establishment of a subscription fund, to be raised and supported by the **stock owners** in each particular district. **1817** *Hobart Town Gaz.* 31 May, It will be at the option of any Settler or Stock-owner to admit or refuse the Inspection of his Herds. **1827** *Hobart Town Courier* 1 Dec. 1 The country stock-owners count upon a strong muster of the Hobart-town butchers on this occasion. **1839** *Sydney Standard* 18 Mar. 4/3 Stock-owners and agriculturists . . cannot find men. **1858** *Illustr. Jrnl. Australasia* IV. 197 The stock-owners were the pioneers of civilization into the Australian wilderness. **1882** Armstrong & Campbell *Austral. Sheep Husbandry* 238 All stockowners have to pay an assessment *per capita*, for all sheep and cattle depastured on their runs. **1903** *Bulletin* (Sydney) 29 Oct. 17/1 As a mate for cocky, 'stocky' (small stock-owner) is new to me. **1924** *New Settlers' Handbk. Vic.* 67 The stockowners' guide. **1980** *Sydney Morning Herald* 22 Apr. 1/4 Mr Wallace is one of hundreds of stock owners driving herds on the roads in search of food throughout the State in the 1980 drought. **1808** *Sydney Gaz.* 2 Oct., The deceased went with others to rob the **stock pens** of Robert Ritchie. **1838** *Southern Austral.* (Adelaide) 3 Nov. 4/3 The dairy stock may be seen daily after the hour of four p.m., at the stock pens of J.W. Bull in Gilles-street. **1840** *S. Austral. Rec.* (London) 28 Nov. 348 The country gets somewhat enclosed, stock-pens are erected. **1903** *Bulletin* (Sydney) 20 Aug. 17/2 They meet the **stock-trains** Nor'ward And the trains from out the West. **1911** *Ibid.* 30 Nov. 14/1 What is the slowest journey on record? (Snails and congested stock trains barred.) **1923** A. Wright *Gambler's Gold* (ed. 2) 115 He'll get you a berth in a stock train, easy. **1943** H.G. Lamond *From Tariaro to Ross Roy* 23 The drudgery of **stock-work** . . galls so many white men. **1944** *Bulletin* (Sydney) 20 Dec. 13/3 In stock work a really good cutting-out horse is nothing else but a trick horse. **1954** T. Ronan *Vision Splendid* 306 Never done any stockwork. I don't like cattle. **1956** —— *Moleskin Midas* 114 The use of knives in this district is restricted to butchering and stockwork, and if you want to carve your name look for a carbean tree. **1960** R.S. Porteous *Cattleman* 209 Scrubber had finally decided that he was getting too old for stock-work, and the gardening job appealed to him. **1961** *Bulletin* (Sydney) 18 Nov. 31/1 In retirement he used to take on stockwork for 'grog money'. **1794** D. Collins *Acct. Eng. Colony N.S.W.* (1798) I. 336 All the people employed about the **stockyard.** **1805** *Sydney Gaz.* 17 Mar., Making for the Stock yard amused himself for some time at the expence of the poultry. **1820** C. Jeffreys *Van Dieman's Land* 59 The ground Mr Miller cultivated had been for some time before occupied as stock yards for cattle and sheep. **1832** *Hill's Life N.S.W.* (Sydney) 7 Sept. 2 The heifer was slaughtered in Mr Sparke's stock-yard, in the presence of all his government men. **1848** H.W. Haygarth *Recoll. Bush Life* 69 A stock-yard, or enclosure for cattle and horses, which no station in the interior of Australia is without, is usually erected on a flat, or gentle slope. . . The fence is five-barred, and of very strong construction. . . It is built entirely of wood, strong rails of which are firmly driven into mortised posts, sunk into the ground to the depth of three feet and upwards, and rammed down hard at the butt end. Nails are not used in any part of it. The size of an enclosure varies with the quantity of stock it is intended to contain. **1860** 'Lady' *My Experiences in Aust.* 168 Beyond the vineyard was the stockyard, used for containing the wild cattle and horses, when driven from different parts of the run, for the purpose of being branded, or at a general mustering time. **1884** 'R. Boldrewood' *Old Melbourne Memories* 30 The cattle were put into the stock-yard for the night. **1916** *Emu* XV. 155 Our host and I repaired to the well-built station stockyards. **1947** W.E. Harney *Brimming Billabongs* 151 We had paddocks between the rivers with a block of post and rails made at the narrowest part of the open end. Our stock yards were of the chock and log type—chocks between two posts, rails resting on chocks. **1983** M. Hayes *Prickle Farm* 115 The Department of Ag in Yass . . agreed to lend us some weld mesh to use as stockyards.

2. Special Comb. **stock agent,** one who deals in the buying and selling of stock; **boot** *obs.*, *stockman's boot*, see Stockman 2; **boy,** an Aboriginal male employed to look after stock; **country,** an area in which stock-raising is the principal industry; an area suitable for this; **driver** *obs.*, Drover 1; **-driving** *vbl. n.*, Droving 1; **establishment,** a sheep or cattle farm; **horse,** a horse trained to work with stock; **house** *obs.*, a building in which stock is accommodated; **hut** *obs.*, *stockman's hut*, see Stockman 2; **inspector,** an official employed to ensure that regulations concerning stock are complied with; **market** *obs.*, a place where sheep and cattle are sold; trade in sheep and cattle; **master, proprietor** *obs.*, Stockholder; **property** *obs.*, *stock establishment*; **reserve,** *travelling stock reserve*, see Travelling stock 2; **-rider,** Stockman 1; so **-ride** *v. intr.*; **-riding** *vbl. n.* and *attrib.*; **route,** *travelling stock route*, see Travelling stock 2; also *attrib.*; **run,** see Run *n.*[2] 2; **saddle,** a heavy saddle made for a stock horse; **station** *obs.*, see Station 2 a. and 3; **water,** water suitable for stock; **woman,** Stockholder; a woman employed to tend stock.

1819 *Sydney Gaz.* 20 Feb., An action for breach of agreement as **stock agent** for 3 years. **1839** *Southern Austral.* (Adelaide) 2 Oct. 3/1 A *fine young Entire cart horse* . . will stand at cover during the season . . at the stock yard of J.W. Bull, stock agent. **1888** 'R. Boldrewood' *Robbery under Arms* (1937) 95 You go to the stock agents, Runnimall and Co. **1942** H.H. Peck *Mem. of Stockman* 4 The earliest stock agent I can remember was Mr William Kissock. **1977** *Weekly Times* (Melbourne) 19 Jan. 11/3 Barney, the stock agent, was looking him straight in the eye when he said: 'If I were you, Clarence, I'd sell the lot and run some sheep.' **1981** *Austral. Country* May 70/3 Banks and stockagents need to be made aware of sharestocking. **1841** *Geelong Advertiser* 11 Oct. 1/4 Superior Wellington, Clarence, Blucher, and **Stock Boots.** **1845** *Port Phillip Gaz.* 23 July 3 Stock boots and slop clothing. **1850** *Perth Gaz.* 19 July 1 Strong Stock Boots 10s. and 9s. **1935** K.L. Smith *Sky Pilot Arnhem Land* 106 We cantered along the bush track, following the **stockboy,** who now had a fresh horse. **1938** X. Herbert *Capricornia* 83 Mark gave Jock one of his halfcaste piccaninnies for a stock-boy. **1955** F. Lane *Patrol to Kimberleys* 65 There'll be blacks with the cattle—stockboys and drovers. **1963** I.L. Idriess *Our Living Stone Age* p. xi, To this homestead, in many an area, clung the first blackboys to break away from the tribe as stockboys. **1847** A. Harris *Settlers & Convicts* (1953) 128 The country we passed through to-day was a very fine **stock-country,** beautiful flats of open meadow on river banks, and fine gentle grassy hills. **1898** D.W. Carnegie *Spinifex & Sand* 35 Given a good supply of water, it should prove valuable stock country. **1965** R.H. Conquest *Horses in Kitchen* 82 These days, licensing laws are strictly enforced in the stock country and the unlicensed revolver is now taboo. **1836** *Bent's News* (Hobart) 3 Sept. 3 You have among you so many good bush men, with **stock drivers** and pack bullocks at command. **1839** *Port Phillip Patriot* 13 Mar. 4 A celebrated stock-driver was showing off his dexterity, by cracking his cattle whip, which nearly severed (from his head) the *ear*, of a gent. who was passing by. **1846** *Cumberland Times* (Parramatta) 2 May 3/1 *A stock driver*, a man named Dwyer . . had taken 63 head of cattle from Mr Mayne, at Toongabee, to drive to Mudgee, and had procured an advance. **1849** A. Harris *Emigrant Family* (1967) 18 Kicking up the clouds of dust that furnishes the stock-driver with one of the principal parts of his professional avocations, that of chewing sand all day. *Ibid.* 20 Having now given the reader a sufficient sketch of the customs of **stock-driving.** **1857** J. D'Ewes *China, Aust. & Pacific Islands* 55, I had . . an opportunity of witnessing all the daring and hazardous exploits of stock-driving. **1891** D. Ferguson *Vicissitudes Bush Life* 113 Having such an inefficient mount for stock-driving, I had not provided myself with a stockwhip. **1831** *Sydney Herald* 23 May 3/4 Superintendent and Overseer. Wants a Situation, in an Agricultural or **Stock Establishment.** **1843** *Teetotal Advocate* (Launceston) 15 May 3/2 They robbed the stock establishment of Mr John Espie. **1838** D.L. Waugh *Three Yrs.' Practical Experience N.S.W.* 26 The **stock horses** know this as well as possible. **1839** *Sydney Standard* 11 Mar. 4/5 Stock horses should be included, otherwise breeding mares would be occasionally rode for the purpose of calling them stock horses, to avoid the tax. **1854** S. Sidney *Gallops & Gossips* 38 John was on a piebald stock-horse, an ugly brute, but perfect for mountain work. **1872** G.S. Baden-Powell *New Homes for Old Country* 201 The stock-horses are quite *sui generis* for the way in which they travel over rough country. **1888** *Centennial Mag.* 178 Quondong—the best hack and stock-horse in these parts. He can walk as fast as some horses can trot, cut out any beast that ever stood on a camp, and canter round a cheese plate. **1914** C.H.S. MATTHEWS *Bill* 99 One specially good man, who sleeps in his clothes, with an extra good stock-horse saddled ready. **1930** E.R. GRIBBLE *Forty Yrs. with Aborigines* 32 Found beside his stock-horse. **1935** R.B. PLOWMAN *Boundary Rider* 175 Hearing them coming the stock-horse only went faster. **1965** R.H. CONQUEST *Horses in Kitchen* 144 The Australian stock-horse of today, in my opinion, is the best of its type in the world. **1981** A. WILKINSON *Up Country* 23 He is a splendid stock horse, doing the 'cattle dog' thing of nipping a stubborn cow on the rump. **1801** *HRA* (1915) 1st Ser. III. 11 The want of **stock-houses** for Government cattle has been a great disadvantage to them, and the sheep in particular. **1808** *Sydney Gaz.* 29 May, 225 acres, with a good dwelling house, barn, stable, stock houses, and a capital stock yard. **1828** *Tasmanian* (Hobart) 9 May 3 *A farm* of 100 Acres, with a Stock House thereon, situate at the Black Brush. **1833** *Perth Gaz.* 16 Feb. 26 Many valuable and useful projects are either discontinued or abandoned for the want of a trifling sum, for which the parties could either in Stock Houses, Furniture or Land give ample security. **1826** *Colonial Times* (Hobart) 27 May, The same fate attends many other articles which we had prepared, viz . . on the means of preventing sheep stealing and runaways, particularly as connected with the evils attending the remote **stock huts.** **1831** *Ibid.* 24 Sept., An Aboriginal Tribe attacked the Stock Hut of Mr Stocker . . and speared a female child. **1839** *Tasmanian Weekly Dispatch* (Hobart) 11 Oct. 1/2 My Stock Hut at Prosser's Plains, in the absence of the stock-keeper, was robbed. **1847** *Britannia* (Hobart) 16 Sept. 3/1 The stock huts of a gentleman in the interior had been seven times robbed. **1890** W.F. BUCHANAN *Aust. to Rescue* 106 Hoping to see a cheering light ahead, from some solitary stock-hut. **1896** W.H. WILLSHIRE *Land of Dawning* 86 You shall be a **Stock Inspector** to investigate the red-water disease amongst cattle. **1912** *Bulletin* (Sydney) 15 Aug. 15/3 The stock-inspector in Western Queensland has to be a person of judicial mind. . . Hyphen . . and Asterisk, owner of the Y1T ranch, were pirating Mitchell grass on the mile-wide stock route. **1935** D.G. STEAD *Rabbit in Aust.* 12 This district has done more consistently good work, under its very efficient and able Stock Inspectors, in restricting the activities of the Rabbit pest. **1945** F. CORK *Tales from Cattle Country* 25 At the border the mob is met by the police and stock inspector who rides through the herd in search of 'lumpies'—cancery cattle —which are cut out and turned bush. **1960** *N.T. News* (Darwin) 5 Feb. 18/8 He challenged the big stock inspector to a duel with fists in the bush at Winnellie. **1834** *Perth Gaz.* 8 Nov. 387 These increased demands upon the **stock market** . . add to the advantage of the speculations which are afloat for the importation of a quantity of Sydney sheep. **1840** *S. Austral. Rec.* (London) 26 Dec. 410 It was ultimately fixed that the stock market should be held on Wednesdays. **1845** *Melbourne Standard* 11 Jan. 2/1 *Melbourne stock market.* Cattle have been in demand this week. **1890** 'R. BOLDREWOOD' *Colonial Reformer* II. 251 A favourable change would take place in the stock-market. **1839** *Port Phillip Gaz.* 27 Nov. 1 Mr Lewis Robertson . . announces to the Gentlemen and **Stockmasters** generally of Australia Felix, that he intends practising his profession as a *veterinary surgeon.* **1847** A. HARRIS *Settlers & Convicts* (1953) 112 Great numbers of men . . held cattle; many indeed became large stock-masters. **1854** W. SHAW *Land of Promise* 92 The interests of stock-masters were in much jeopardy. **1959** H. LAMOND *Sheep Station* 15 He . . had . . implicit faith in his judgement as a stock-master. **1829** *Tasmanian Almanack* 95 Fresh meat taken into the Commissariat Stores, for some years, at 6d. per lb. from **Stock-proprietors** only. **1839** *Port Phillip Gaz.* 13 Nov. 3 Several large stock proprietors are possessed of from twenty to thirty assigned servants. **1845** *Portland Guardian* 30 Aug. 4/2, I am a stock-proprietor, and . . lately came overland from Portland. **1853** A. KINLOCH *Murray River* 15 The land on the Murray to this point (the Darling) is all occupied, chiefly by large stock proprietors or squatters. **1828** *Tasmanian* (Hobart) 26 Sept. 3 Mr Bryant's valuable **stock property** fetched extremely satisfactory prices yesterday. **1839** *Port Phillip Gaz.* 21 Dec. 3 Any party requiring an Overseer or Manager on his Estate or large Stock Property. **1897** *Tocsin* (Melbourne) 16 Dec. 5/2 No attempt was made to let them [*sc.* sheep] encroach upon his well-grassed paddocks, which skirted the **stock reserve.** **1901** *Bulletin* (Sydney) 16 Nov. 14/4 At the dividing-fence between Mumbledool and the stock-reserve the rabbits play 'under and over' along the wire. **1949** *Coast to Coast 1948* 1 Old Ben had turned the mob of shorthorns through the gate into the stock reserve. **1844** N.L. KENTISH *Work in Bush Van Diemen's Land* (1846) 13 Messrs Field's cattle are driven occasionally to or from Middlesex Plains by their **stock-riders** in dry summer weather. **1859** W. KELLY *Life in Vic.* I. 78 Mad cattle fresh from the Bush, driven frantically backwards and forwards by yelling stockriders. **1869** J. MARTINEAU *Lett. from Aust.* 40 The toils and pleasures of stock-riding on cattle-stations . . are almost at an end in Victoria. **1870** J. BONWICK *Last Tasmanians* 110 A stock-rider found himself suddenly beset by a mob in the Abyssinian Marshes. **1885** MRS C. PRAED *Austral. Life* 126 My brother Jim, on a stock-riding beat, met one of these gentlemen. **1886** P. FLETCHER 'Hints to Immigrants' in P. Fletcher *Qld.* 4 Learn to milk, break in heifers . . stock-ride and slaughter. **1887** A. NICOLS *Wild Life & Adventure* 48 In Harold . . he saw a promising stock-rider and generally useful man on a station. **1898** *Western Champion* (Barcaldine) 18 Jan. 3/4, I have three sons in Queensland—first-class bushmen and stock riders. **1901** *Advocate* (Burnie) 8 June 4/2 The Duke expressed a desire to see a cattle draft, and in 'cutting out' certain animals and clearing them off, very fine stockriding was shown. **1903** E. PALMER *Early Days N. Qld.* 186 *The stockman, or stockrider* . . is a man of some importance in the daily life of a station. **1956** H. FRAUCA *In New Country* 24 My romanticised picture of the dinkum Aussie stock-rider. . . He wore a broad-brimmed hat, a red scarf tied round his neck, tight-fitting khaki slacks and huge spurs strapped onto his elastic-sided boots. **1973** *Parade* (Melbourne) Sept. 30/2 The authorities were able to choose exactly the sort of men they wanted from the hundreds of adventurers, prospectors, settlers and stock-riders who offered their services. **1884** W.J. O'DONNELL *Diary Exploring Exped.* 20 From the telegraph line (Northern Territory) we have proved that a good **stock route** can be made to the Ord River. **1898** D.W. CARNEGIE *Spinifex & Sand* 201 This small oasis . . is bound to play an important part in any scheme of a stock route from the cattle-stations of Central Australia to the Murchison or Coolgardie Goldfields. **1909** *Bulletin* (Sydney) 30 Sept. 14/1 The S.A. Government lately sent out a well-sinking party to open up a stock route. **1923** F.A.C. BISHOP *Rep. on Inspection Barkly Tableland* 5 The stock route comes out at this bore and continues on to the Crow's Nest bore, 16 miles on. **1934** 'E.N. SPEER' *Destiny* 242 He was overtaking a travelling mob of sheep, hoping he would reach them before they left the main road for the two-mile wide stock route. **1948** R. RAVEN-HART *Canoe in Aust.* 82 The main road there . . was a stock-route, very wide, with gates at intervals separating properties or paddocks. **1960** *N.T. News* (Darwin) 8 Jan. 4/3 The department has built dipping yards and inoculation depots at stock route junctions in the Territory. **1966** *Bulletin* (Sydney) 26 Mar. 22/3 After five months the stock routes were . . eaten out. **1983** C. BINGHAM *Beckoning Horizon* 5 The stock route was theoretically 660 feet wide on either side of the black-soil unsealed road that ran almost parallel to the Flinders, and along this narrow passage-way the drovers shepherded great mobs of sheep and cattle. **1822** *Hobart Town Gaz.* 9 Mar. (Suppl.), On or about the 22d of February last, Three Hundred and Sixty Sheep were stolen from my **Stock Run.** **1830** *Hobart Town Almanack* 81 On the right . . is the extensive grazing country called Abyssinia, principally occupied as stock runs. **1848** *Bell's Life in Sydney* 29 Jan. 2/2 Higson was charged with 'misconduct', in being absent from the stock-run. **1975** X. HERBERT *Poor Fellow my Country* 431 They left the ravaged country, to enter another shitty hoof-ripped tooth-torn stock-run, yellow earth and mean trees. **1887** A. NICOLS *Wild Life & Adventure* 211 Harold settled the **stock-saddle** on its back. **1932** J.J. HARDIE *Cattle Camp* (1944) 18 The girl swung stiffly into the big stock-saddle and settled herself behind the knee-pads. **1938** *Bulletin* (Sydney) 19 May 20/2 Just why stock-saddle makers can't take a leaf out of the military books has always been a puzzle to me in regard to swinging stirrup-irons. **1963** M. BRITT *Pardon my Boots* 98 The stock-saddles were so heavy and clumsy, with their deep seats, knee-pads and long flaps, that I always had difficulty in putting mine on Red. **1980** S. THORNE *I've met some Bloody Wags* 17 The hat, a flash pork-pie town job, belonged to a fairly plastered young station manager who was straddling one of the stock saddles on display in the window. **1824** *Sydney Gaz.* 26 Aug., Attacks on the **stock stations** there, putting some of the keepers to cruel deaths. **1828** *HRA* (1922) 1st Ser. XIV. 303 Conveying provisions and necessaries to their distant Stock Stations. **1834** H. CARMICHAEL *Hints relating to Emigrants* 17 A section of 640 acres . . will serve him as a stock-station; where he may erect . . a dairy-establishment. **1840** *S. Austral. Rec.* (London) 1 Jan. 3/3 The numerous farms and stock stations radiating in all directions from Adelaide. **1849** C. STURT *Narr. Exped. Central Aust.* I. 66 There can be no doubt but that in the course of a few years the stock stations from the respective colonies will meet. **1853** S. SIDNEY *Three Colonies* (ed. 2) 284 Recently a few stock stations have been taken up on the island, and about one hundred persons are resident there. **1882** ARMSTRONG & CAMPBELL *Austral. Sheep Husbandry* 223 Wells yielding . . a constant supply of good **stock water.** **1931** MRS E.P. HALFORD *Pioneers of Yesterday* 31 It is very good stock water. **1835** *Colonist* (Sydney) 10 Sept. 291/4 Any person can become a *stockholder* now, without the least ado, and without the least indelicacy, whether *stockman,* or **stockwoman.** **1902** R.C. PRAED *My Austral. Girlhood* 264 The stockwoman stayed away for a week. **1947** W.E. HARNEY *Brimming Billabongs* 124 The other stockwomen tended me as Nalyinda was born.

3. In the collocation **stock and station.**

a. Used *attrib.* to designate firms or their employees dealing in farm land, products, and supplies.

1872 *Causes Ruinous Condition Coal Trade N.S.W.* 15 He may . . invest one portion of his means in a coal-mine, another portion . . in a copper-mine, whilst these two may be supplemented by run-holding and stock and station agency. **1901** *Brisbane Courier* 2 July 3/3 The Company also undertake Stock and Station Business Generally, giving Special attention to Sales of Station Properties, Stores, and Fat Stock, &c. **1914** *Pastoral Rev.* 15 Jan. 62 The Company also undertakes all kinds of Stock and Station Business. **1943** A. DAWES *Soldier Superb* 81 A very gallant company commander . . was in the stock and station side of Dalgety's. **1955** J. CLEARY *Justin Bayard* 88 After that he went into a stock and station agency. **1965** G. MCINNES *Road to Gundagai* 113 Here were the big mortgage and stock-and-station houses where wool was finally baled and cleaned for export. **1960** R.S. PORTEOUS *Cattleman* 73 I've been thinking of branching out, expanding really, by starting a stock and station agency. **1981** *Austral. Women's Weekly* (Sydney) 11 Nov. 30/2 The stock and station fellows and the squattocracy were there after a cattle and pig sale.

b. Comb. **stock and station agent.**

1884 G. RANKEN *Dry Country* ii. 2 In my business of stock and station agent, I am . . behind the scenes. **1898** *Bulletin* (Sydney) 20 Aug. 14/1 In the cattle-duffing days a N.S.W. country stock-and-station-agent was offered 200 head of cattle at £2 per head. **1930** *Ibid.* 1 Jan. 19/4 A telegram from a firm of stock-and-station agents giving latest market prices for store sheep! **1950** *Coast to Coast 1949–50* 48 Her uncle . . had found this job with a stock-and-station agent in a country town. **1965** G.H. FEARNSIDE *Golden Ram* 154 A stock-and-station agent, Billy had campaigned on the grounds that he 'understood the problems of the man-on-the-land'. **1973** R.J. DOOLIN *Boy from Bush* 30, I took out an Auctioneers' Licence and started as a stock and station agent. **1985** *Bombala Times* 18 July 6/4 Concern was raised over the possibility of vandalism if a phone was installed . . and over whether or not the stock and station agents really wanted one.

stockade. *Hist.* [Transf. use of *stockade* a military fortification.] A structure in which convict gangs working in outlying districts were accommodated. Also **stockade station** and *attrib.*

1832 N.S.W. Mounted Police Troop Order Bk. 10 Dec. I. 49 The Trooper now stationed at the Fish River be removed from thence to the New Stockade on Cox's River where the Iron Gang is working. **1833** *N.S.W. Mag.* (Sydney) 61 Due notice will be given . . by the Principal Superintendent of Convicts, of the date when, and at what stockade, the prisoner can be obtained, in order that he may be applied for at that station. **1836** J. BACKHOUSE *Extracts from Lett.* (1839) iv. 9 Though this station is called a stockade, there is no defence around it; but no prisoner can wander off the premises, on account of the military guard. **1841** *Colonial Observer* (Sydney) 9 Dec. 78/1 Three prisoners of the Crown belonging to the stockade at Grose Farm effected their escape. **1843** *Sydney Morning Herald* 31 Oct. 2/7 David Ambrose, from Wollongong stockade, guilty of stealing and being a runaway. **1845** *Star* (Sydney) 11 Oct. 4/1

Fitzpatrick, the Stockade prisoner, found guilty . . of the murder of his fellow convict, is ordered for execution. **1850** C.A. KING *Life* 26, I was . . sentenced to fifty lashes, with orders to be sent to a Stockade station.

stockholder. A sheep or cattle farmer.

1804 *Sydney Gaz.* 14 Oct., The great increase of Male Stock . . requires the Price of Animal Food being reduced in proportion thereto; and any Combination or Monopoly, either on the part of the Stockholders or the Butchers, being counteracted. **1821** T. GODWIN *Descr. Acct. Van Diemen's Island* 7 Near this is Oreilton Park . . the property of E. Lord, Esq. the principal merchant, and largest stock-holder on the island. **1840** *S. Austral. Rec.* (London) 20 June 340 Several large stock-holders have chartered the *Cleveland*, to proceed with bullocks and sheep to King George's Sound. **1852** J. CAPPER *Philip's Emigrants' Guide* 42 Some of the South Australian stock-holders lead a very comfortable life, residing within or near the capital. **1890** 'R. BOLDREWOOD' *Squatter's Dream* 15 I'm bent on being a large stockholder, or none at all. **1930** BILLIS & KENYON *Pastures New* 21 The more lordly landowners, stock-holders and graziers usually lived in the town and kept superintendents to look after their stations.

So **stockholding** *vbl. n.*

1844 S. DAVENPORT *Let.* 29 Feb. in *S. Australiana* (1967) Sept. 74 Land may rise or fall as circumstances occur, but it has always value in conjunction with stock-holding, both as giving a run and being more or less improved by the stock. **1845** C. GRIFFITH *Present State & Prospects Port Phillip* 50 Stockholding squatters . . are completely at the mercy of the government. **1854** W. SHAW *Land of Promise* 243 Stock holding, which is a very important interest, ought to be next considered for a considerable portion of the wealth of the settlers consists in their flocks and herds.

stock-keep, *v. Obs.* [f. STOCK-KEEPER.] *intr.* To own stock; to tend the stock of another. Freq. as *vbl. n.*

1828 *Tasmanian* (Hobart) 24 Oct. 2 You have several branches of business here, that may be followed successfully; but pray how does stock-keeping get on? **1839** J. STEPHENS *Land of Promise* 170 The ordinary profits of stock-keeping in Australia are from 50 to 70 per cent. **1851** *Empire* (Sydney) 1 Apr. 3/3 For £25 to £27 per annum they stock-keep and fight the blacks. **1853** S. SIDNEY *Three Colonies* (ed. 2) 338 He said that he had stock-kept there for nearly twenty years. **1876** *Austral. Town & Country Jrnl.* (Sydney) 9 Sept. 422/1 'What can you do, young man?' 'Well, most things,' answered the Australian with quiet confidence—'Fence, split, milk, drive bullocks, stock-keep, ploughing.' **1880** J.B. STEVENSON *Seven Yrs. Austral. Bush* 36 The first duty I was called upon to perform in the stock-keeping line, was to assist in killing a beast. **1890** 'R. BOLDREWOOD' *Squatter's Dream* 72 If these here fences is to be run up all along the river, any Jackeroo can go stock-keeping! **1954** T. RONAN *Vision Splendid* 158 A man who has been a stockman from boyhood does not . . worry about provision for his old age. If he did he found some job less risky than stock-keeping. **1962** —— *Deep of Sky* 3 This job was relegated to Dad who, at the time, was looking after Sedan, the Welford bullock run. 'Riding the run', 'stockkeeping', these are now archaic expressions in the cattle industry, but in that age they signified the most important part of a cattleman's job.

stock-keeper. *Obs.*

1. STOCKMAN 1.

1795 S. MACARTHUR ONSLOW *Some Early Rec. Macarthurs* (1914) 49 Mr Macarthur has frequently in his employment 30 or 40 people. . . Eight are employed as stock-keepers, in the garden, stables and house. **1804** *Sydney Gaz.* 5 May, David Dyer . . had the charge of a Gentleman's Cattle as stock keeper. **1816** *Hobart Town Gaz.* 3 Aug., Considerable damage having been done through the neglect of Stock-keepers to my Farm . . all Stock found trespassing . . will be impounded. **1823** *Ibid.* 1 Mar. (Suppl.), The witness asked him, what would become of the poor stock-keeper (meaning the prosecutor's shepherd). **1843** J.F. BENNETT *Hist. & Descr. Acct. S.A.* 100 The persons who have charge of the herd . . are called stockmen, or stock keepers. **1848** J. BYRNE *Twelve Yrs.' Wanderings* I. 214 Stock-keepers have a more exciting life, which they spend entirely on horseback as it would be impossible to manage the wild cattle of Australia on foot. **1855** *Illustr. Sydney News* 7 Apr. 156/3 A wild bullock followed by a stock-keeper on horseback dashed through the toll-bar and into George-street. **1875** CAMPBELL & WILKS *Early Settlement Qld.* 26 Some of the larger stations were presided over by a 'super', but more generally by a stock-keeper and hut-keeper only. **1905** J. FURPHY *Rigby's Romance* (1946) p. xxi, The station stock-keeper had then been approached.

2. In special collocations: **stock-keeper's boot, hut,** *stockman's boot, stockman's hut*, see STOCKMAN 2.

1828 *Tasmanian Almanack* 45 It will . . be the duty of the master to furnish each servant with two suits of woollen slop clothing, three pair of **stock-keeper's boots**, four shirts, and one cap or hat, per annum. **1833** *Trumpeter* (Hobart) 10 Dec. 263 He has on hand a large stock of stock-keepers boots of the best quality, at . . low prices. **1847** *Guardian* (Hobart) 7 Aug. 1/1 A large quantity of Strong Stock-keeper's Boots from 5s. 5d. **1821** *Sydney Gaz.* 21 Apr., An information was exhibited against John Fewins, for the wilful murder of George Hancock, on the 9th of August, last, at a **stock-keepers'** [*sic*] **hut** on Jacob's Plains. **1840** *S. Austral. Miscellany* June 181 They attacked a stock-keeper's hut at the river Shannon. **1843** C. ROWCROFT *Tales of Colonies* (1858) 17 These mocassins I got at a stock-keeper's hut, who let me fit the sheep-skin warm to my feet.

stockman. Also **stocksman.** [Used elsewhere but recorded earliest in Aust.]

1. One employed to tend livestock, esp. cattle.

1803 Banks Papers VIII. 124 What was my nonsensical pursuit to the lives of the stockmen and stock. **1804** *Sydney Gaz.* 18 Nov., The stockman, whose immediate duty it is to provide by unweaned vigilance for the security of his inoffensive charge, would arouse from a state of blissful inactivity which he seems to have inherited from the first founders of his very ancient Order. **1817** *Hobart Town Gaz.* 22 Mar., For the same Farm, Two Stockmen are wanted, who has [*sic*] been accustomed to the Care, and understands the Management of Horned Cattle. **1828** *HRA* (1923) 3rd Ser. 799 Our Stockman goes some miles into the Woods daily with the Cattle. **1839** D. MACKELLAR *Austral. Emigrant's Guide* 6 The stockman is generally provided with a horse, and is in constant attendance upon the cattle. **1847** *Moreton Bay Courier* 3 July 4/2 During the day the cattle were 'tailed' by a stockman, and at night they were secured in a large paddock. **1853** H.B. JONES *Adventures in Aust.* 112 Bullock drivers and stocksmen, far from medical advice in the interior. **1867** G. WALCH *Fireflash* 44 Black Jem, the stockman, broke his neck a-trying of it after dark. **1884** 'R. BOLDREWOOD' *Old Melbourne Memories* 22 My stockman and I spent our days in 'going round' the cattle; shooting and kangaroo hunting in odd times. **1901** *Bulletin* (Sydney) 7 Dec. 30/2 A quiet milking-cow will 'plant' a young calf with such skill that 10 stockmen cannot find him in a one-mile paddock. **1922** *Ibid.* 4 May 22/4 Can any modern stockman or duffer beat Tom Hanson's record at spaying cows? **1945** A.W. UPFIELD *Death of Swagman* 152 Never did he leave a homestead without taking the mail for lonely stockmen stationed on the track ahead. **1965** R. OTTLEY *By Sandhills* 173 Many of the stockmen on the cattle-stations are aborigines, usually working happily alongside their white counterparts or under overseers. **1981** A. MARSHALL *Aust.* 27 Today . . our stockmen are often referred to as cowboys.

2. In special collocations: **stockman's boot** *obs.*, an (elastic-sided) riding boot; **stockman('s) cut,** a narrow-legged style (of trousers, etc.); also *attrib.*; **stockman's hat,** a broad-brimmed felt hat; **stockman's hut,** a dwelling provided for a stockman; **stockman's saddle** *obs., stock saddle*, see STOCK 2; **stockman's whip** *obs.*, STOCKWHIP 1.

1839 *Port Phillip Gaz.* 25 Dec. 3 **Stockmen's Boots,** and excellent Strong Shoes. **1845** *Portland Gaz.* 21 Oct. 3/5 A goodly assortment of every description of Boots and Shoes, from the stout stockman's boot to the lady's slipper. **1848** *Sydney Daily Advertiser* 12 Sept. 2/3 He . . requested Mr Olbrecht's shopman to furnish him with . . twelve pair [*sic*] of stockmen's boots. **1882** *Bulletin* (Sydney) 5 Aug. 6/3 The 'Plume' Brand Moleskin Trousers White And Printed, In **Stockman's** Or Ordinary **Cut.** **1953** *Ibid.* 16 Dec. 12/1 Before the war a Queensland firm with a big outback trade used to sell stockman's-cut pants made of a dark-blue material as thin as shirting. **1976** K. BROWN *Knock Ten* 66 The girl in her sweaty, greasy, slop-made man's stockman-cut dungarees, man's cotton shirt and old shapeless felt hat. **1950** G. FARWELL *Surf Music* 28 His weathered face under the tall crown of his **stockman's hat** was seamy and shrivelled as a claypan. **1965** G. MCINNES *Road to Gundagai* 248 With his portly paunch, his leathern gamecoat, florid face, and battered stockman's hat. **1806** *Sydney Gaz.* 30 Nov., Four muskets, taken from his **stockmen's huts** during the night time. **1842** *Sydney Morning Herald* 1 Aug. 1/6 On the Cattle station is a good substantial Stock-yard, with Milking-yards, Stockman's Hut, &c. **1855** W. HOWITT *Land, Labor & Gold* II. 389, I . . told my guide that we must return to the stockman's hut for the night. **1977** J. WALLACE *Memories Country Childhood* 11 The black dirt road that led to the woolshed and the stockmen's huts. **1837** *Colonist* (Sydney) 5 Jan. 3/4, 90 **Stockmans Saddles** at 25s. each. **1846** *Portland Guardian* 4 Sept. 2/2 Stockmen's saddles. **1864** W.H. THOMES *Gold Hunters' Adventures* 29 With many a sharp crack of the **stockman's whip**, we crossed the stream, and once more pursued our way towards Ballarat. **1891** 'SMILER' *Wanderings Simple Child* (ed. 3) p. iv, He has been with the pioneers, wielded the miner's pick, and the stockman's whip, swung the axe in the forest, and tramped many a league through the trackless back blocks of our southern wonderland.

stockwhip.

1. A whip used in the handling of cattle: see quot. 1845.

1839 J.C. CRAWFORD *Diary* 11 Mar. in *S. Australiana* (1964) Mar. 63 Mr Coutts and I rode at the leading party at full gallop with our stockwhips. **1845** D. MACKENZIE *Emigrant's Guide* 128 Each rider is armed with a stock-whip, the handle of which is only a little more than a foot in length, while the thong is twelve or fourteen feet long. **1852** *Four Colonies Aust.* 52, I have seen a pewter quart pot all but cut in two by one flourish of the stock-whip. **1868** *Mr Newcome in Search of Cattle Station* 17 On our getting up we cracked our stockwhips two or three times loudly as a signal for all hands to turn out. **1885** MRS C. PRAED *Austral. Life* 52 My father sat plaiting a thong for his stock-whip. **1900** R. BRUCE *Benbonuna* (1904) 24 I'll cut the liver out of you with a stock-whip if you do. **1907** *Truth* (Sydney) 7 Apr. 9/7 'But they use them on the stations?' 'Oh, yes, they use them, gins and bucks. Soon as they get tame enough, both squatters and missionaries run 'em in, and the one lot can use the stockwhip just as well as another.' **1915** V. PALMER *World of Men* (1962) 33 He was plaiting a stockwhip with that care and love men bestow on things they live by. **1926** A.A.B. APSLEY *Amateur Settlers* 90 The Australian stock-whip is made of plaited kangaroo hide. The expert is . . particular about its balance, finish, length of thong, silk 'flash' and raw-hide 'dropper'. **1955** F.B. VICKERS *Mirage* (1958) 154 Ted and Freddie uncoiled the stock whips from the pommels of their saddles. **1978** D. STUART *Wedgetail View* 3 He let each beast feel the sting of the stockwhip.

2. Special Comb. **stockwhip bird,** the bird *Psophodes olivaceus* (see WHIPBIRD).

1861 'OLD BUSHMAN' *Bush Wanderings* 151 The *Stock-Whip Bird* . . had rather the appearance of the pied wagtail at home . . a grating call-note, something similar to the springing of an old watchman's rattle, but of course not so loud, ending with a sharp smack. **1886** W.J. WOODS *Visit to Vic.* 24 The Coach-whip, and Stock-whip birds, whose call is like the spring of a watchman's rattle, ending with the crack of a whip. **1906** A. FRANCIS *Francis Family* 14 Laughing-Jackasses, Satin and Stockwhip-birds lived all around us. **1938** C.P. CONIGRAVE *Walk-About* 21 Hedges were alive with stock-whip birds.

stone, *n.*[1]

1. Used *attrib.* to designate an Aboriginal weapon or implement fashioned from stone.

1835 J. BATMAN *Settlement in Port Phillip* 7 June (1856) 22 The chiefs of the Port Phillip tribes made me a present of three stone tomahawks . . and other weapons of warfare. **1841** *Sydney Herald* 30 Apr. 2/2 Very often the camp is made the scene of strife and contention, which issues in blows with the waddies, and cuts with the stone knives. **1843** W. PRIDDEN *Aust.* 108 The dextrous savage then pulls out his hatchet, a rude *stone hatchet.* **1856** J. BONWICK *W. Buckley* 52 He would cut notches in the bark for his toes with a stone hatchet. **1874** J.J. HALCOMBE *Emigrant & Heathen* 109 The blows of the *stone tomahawk*, with which the natives had cut out for their food opossums or the tree grubs. **1892** J. FRASER *Aborigines N.S.W.* 76 Another implement that should be noticed is the stone hammer. It is a large stone, or, perhaps, two stones, one end being blunt for hammer work, and the other sharpened as an axe. **1896** B. SPENCER *Rep. Horn Sci. Exped. Central Aust.* IV. 98 *Stone Axe or Tomahawk—'Illipa'* . . is used in the Arunta tribe, and . . the material of the stone head is diorite. **1923** T. HALL *Short Hist. Downs Blacks* 17 *Muggin or stone tomahawk* . . was made from the blue metal or Whinstone to be found in our basalt country about the mountain precipices. . . There were two kinds of tomahawks, one for stripping bark, with a longer handle than the other, and much lighter. **1930** C.C. TOWLE *Certain Stone Implements* 10 The coastal tribes did not use any implement similar in any respect to the long flaked knife or the stone spear head.

2. Special Comb. **stone country,** *gibber country*, see GIBBER 2; **fence** *obs.* [U.S. in both senses], **(a)** a dry-stone wall; **(b)** an alcoholic drink (see quots. 1853 and 1918); **hut,** a dwelling made of blocks of stone.

1927 M.H. ELLIS *Long Lead* 138 In long grass, 'devil devil' and **stone country**. **1946** W.E. HARNEY *North of 23°* 168 Knowing that she belonged to what we called the 'stone' country and had never been in salt water. **1978** D. STUART *Wedgetail View* 1 It's stone country right through to the next pool, but there's good feed all the way. **(a) 1861** H. EARLE *Ups & Downs* 125 A small track of ground . . had been securely preserved from the intrusive and destructive tread of cattle by means of a '**stone fence**', formed of small pieces of burnt rock. **1904** *Publicist* (Sydney) 24 Nov. 18/2 He . . worked for five hours carrying rocks to a marked line where a stone fence was to be built. **(b) 1853** F.J. COCKBURN *Lett.* (1856) 3 A glass of sodawater and brandy is termed a '**stone fence**'. **1869** 'E. HOWE' *Boy in Bush* 84 There's a whole mob of fellows shouting for spiders and stone fences at the 'Macquarie Arms'. **1881** *Echoes from Bushland* 19 'Bring Mr MacLean a stone fence'; and the effervescing fluid gurgled pleasantly down Rory's parched gullet. **1918** *Bulletin* (Sydney) 1 Aug. (Red Page), In a 'stone fence' ginger-beer mingled with the brandy. **1845** *S. Austral. Odd Fellows' Mag.* Jan. 11 Some men are felling trees, some are building **stone huts.** **1868** J.K. TUCKER *Aborigines & Chinese Question* 6 Two stone huts . . had been erected. **1875** J. FORREST *Explorations in Aust.* 124 There was a substantial stone hut. **1950** A. GROOM *I saw Strange Land* 204 The iron-roofed, stone huts of Mount Quinn Station.

3. In the names of flora and fauna: **stone curlew,** CURLEW; **-fish,** [see quot. 1965, and also OED(S *sb.* 20 b.], any of several venomous fish of the fam. Synanceiidae of n. Aust. and elsewhere in the tropics, having dorsal spines capable of inflicting a painful, and potentially fatal, sting; **plover,** CURLEW.

1855 W. HOWITT *Land, Labor & Gold* II. 78 The **stone curlew.** These birds abound all along the creeks and water sides, and during the night make the loudest and most extraordinary cries. **1872** G.S. BADEN-POWELL *New Homes for Old Country* 349 The stone-curlew appears in most parts. **1917** *Bulletin* (Sydney) 5 July 22/2 The keenness of the aborigine's ear for bird notes is evidenced in the names resembling their call which he gave to familiar species. . . The stone curlew was called weelo, or weeloo. **1965** *Austral. Encycl.* III. 148 The stone-curlew (*Burhinus*), also called stone-plover and land-curlew . . is a sturdy, quietly-coloured bird of the forests. **1908** E.J. BANFIELD *Confessions of Beachcomber* 143 Beware of the **stone fish** (*Synanceia horrida*), the death adder of the sea, called also the sea-devil, because of its malice. **1935** F. BIRTLES *Battle Fronts Outback* 99 The dreaded stone-fish—a squat, ugly, drab fellow who lay in the sand with his poisonous barbs only too ready to be used on the offensive. **1948** W. HATFIELD *Barrier Reef Days* 29 '*Stone fish*' he said then with as much excitement as the children had ever heard in his voice. **1965** *Austral. Encycl.* VIII. 305 Stone-fishes, venomous fishes of the family Synancejidae. Their popular name is explained by their remarkable resemblance when in the water to blocks of eroded rock or weathered coral. **1971** *Bulletin* (Sydney) 23 Oct. 20/3 The poison barbs of the stone-fish will go through the thickest of sandshoes. **1984** B. DIXON *Searching for Aboriginal Lang.* 133 Most fishes are *bayi*, but the stone-fish and the toad-fish—which can inflict injury on a person—are specially marked by being *balan*. **1878** R.B. SMYTH *Aborigines of Vic.* II. 4 **Stone plover** . . *Wooloo-look*. **1901** *Emu* I. 131 The Stone Plover (*Burhinus grallarius*) also lives on the ground. **1928** C.G. LANE *Adventures in Big Bush* 235 The wailing of curlews (stone-plover). **1945** C. BARRETT *Austral. Bird Life* 109 These long-legged birds with swollen ankle-joints (hence 'thick-knees') more correctly are called stone-plovers though usually termed curlews. **1962** B.W. LEAKE *Eastern Wheatbelt Wildlife* 89 The curlew or stone plover . . will seek protection for hatching out and rearing its young much more so than the plover.

4. Intensively, in adj. relation to a noun, as **stone end** (or **finish**), the 'limit', the bitter end.

1946 K. TENNANT *Lost Haven* 22 She had kept her temper so far, she shouted, but this was the 'stone finish'. **1950** E.M. ENGLAND *Where Turtles Dance* 181, I can cure Dirk. To go back to Cooranga might be the stone end. We must have him at Wyuna. **1968** S. GORE *Holy Smoke* 36 Well, this is the stone end! If thouse weren't all so thick in the skull, thouse'd flamin' know the Lord's bound to give you an innings in the long run. **1973** C. EAGLE *Who could love Nightingale?* 237 It'll be the end of Edward! Absolutely the stone end of him. **1974** B. ROLAND *No Ordinary Man* 144 'Archie Bond won first prize in the lottery?' 'No! That'll be the stone end of Archie.' **1975** X. HERBERT *Poor Fellow my Country* 1151 If that was the game, arming the Bush Boongs, then for chrissake, that was the stone-end of everything!

stone, *n.*[2]

1. *Gold-mining.* Quartz.

***c* 1860** 'AURIFERA' *Victorian Miners' Man.* 104 *Stone*, vein-stone; quartz. **1966** *Prospectors' Guide* (Vic. Dept. Mines) 120 *Stone*, miner's name for quartz.

2. *Opal-mining.* Opal or opal-bearing material; an opal. In the phr. **to be on stone,** *to be on opal*, see OPAL 2.

1895 *Rep.* (N.S.W. Dept. Mines) 68 A patch of stone was taken about the end of the year which brought £1,200. **1921** K.S. PRICHARD *Black Opal* 33 You don't suppose Jun'd try to take the stones off of him, do you? **1924** T.C. WOLLASTON *Opal* 61 The men were not 'on stone' it seemed, but perhaps I could change the luck? **1932** I.L. IDRIESS *Prospecting for Gold* 236 These opals are called stones or nobbies, because they look such; little nobbies of opal camouflaged with opal dirt. Often they are the shape of a walnut. **1967** A. KALOKERINOS *In Search of Opal* 18 Stones that are worth $2,000 or more on the field are found at a rate that would not exceed one per week.

stonewall, *n. Obs.* [Fig. use of *stone-wall* barrier, prob. infl. by the nickname of Thomas Jonathan ('*Stonewall*') Jackson (1824–63), Confederate general during the American Civil War.] The obstruction of parliamentary business; a strategem used for this.

1875 *VPD* XXII. 1387/2 Wished to ask the honourable member for Geelong West whether the six members sitting beside him (Mr Berry) constituted the 'stone wall' that had been spoken of? Did they constitute the stone wall which was to oppose all progress—to prevent the finances being dealt with and the business of the country carried on? It was like bully Bottom's stone wall. It certainly could not be a very high wall nor a very long wall if it only consisted of six. **1904** *Advocate* (Burnie) 15 Nov. 4/3 The stonewall is a most legitimate weapon of party warfare. **1909** W.G. SPENCE *Aust.'s Awakening* 299 The Labor Party put up a stonewall in the Assembly against the proposals. **1919** [see *stonewalling, vbl. n.* STONEWALL *v.*].

stonewall, *v. Obs.* [f. prec.]

1. *trans.* To obstruct (a piece of parliamentary business).

1880 *Argus* (Melbourne) 16 Feb. 5/2 Advised the commission to comply with the demand, as otherwise the unsatisfied demanders might stonewall the bill. **1889** J.L. HUNT *Bk. of Bonanzas* 60 A sleep as sound as that of a Cabinet Minister when an Opposition member is 'stonewalling' a Government Bill at 4 o'clock in the morning. **1909** W.G. SPENCE *Aust.'s Awakening* 394 They deliberately stonewalled these measures for weeks.

2. *intr.* To engage in the obstruction of parliamentary business.

1880 *Argus* (Melbourne) 12 Feb. 9/5 The Opposition 'stonewalled' a whole night. September 3, sitting up until half-past 10 the following morning, in order to exact a pledge from the Government. **1892** *Truth* (Sydney) 15 May 2/7 Fur ye've just the schoolin' Bailes to be foolin' Wid a foony roolin', Shud he dar' stonewall.

Hence **stonewalling** *vbl. n.* and *attrib.*

1898 *Truth* (Sydney) 2 Oct. 1/5 The stonewalling tactics of the Opposition in N.Z. Parliament against the Old Age Pension Bill were a disgrace. **1913** J. ACKERMAN *Aust. from Woman's Point of View* 203 Stonewalling and gag methods were freely applied by members who were able to secure the floor for the greatest length of time. **1919** C.A. BERNAYS *Qld. Politics during Sixty Yrs.* 159 When his party banded together to resist some Government proposal, and set up a stonewall, Higg's stonewalling was inimitable.

stonewaller. *Obs.* One who obstructs parliamentary business.

1904 *Advocate* (Burnie) 15 Nov. 4/3 The artistic stonewaller tries to give some coherence and semblance of relevance to his remarks. **1905** *Shearer* (Sydney) 2 Dec. 4/1 He was journeying [to Melbourne] to help resist the pestiferous 'stonewallers', then active in the Federal Parliament. **1919** C.A. BERNAYS *Qld. Politics during Sixty Yrs.* 120 Tozer, that man of iron jaw . . established a reputation as a stonewaller. . . Tozer spoke for eight hours.

stonker, *v.* [Prob. f. *stonk* the stake in a game, esp. of marbles.] *trans.* To kill; to defeat; to outwit.

1918 *7th Field Artillery Brigade Yandoo* Jan. 95 How to stonker your cobber. **1920** W.H. DOWNING *To Last Ridge* 48 We just go into the line again and again until we get knocked. We'll never get out of this. Just in and out, in and out, and somebody stonkered every time. **1937** G.D. MITCHELL *Backs to Wall* 84 'If Fritzy stonkers Mitch in the next stunt', said Matthews, 'I'll go crook a treat.' **1946** *Bulletin* (Sydney) 28 Aug. 29/2 'Enery sez ter me: 'Watch me stonker the silly coot,' an' up 'e goes onter the stage. **1954** A. UPFIELD *Death of Lake* (1956) 141 What a ruddy mess! Stonker the crows! **1978** T. DAVIES *More Austral. Nicknames* 95 A teacher guaranteed to stonker any student with ideas above his ability.

stonkered, *ppl. a.* [f. prec.] Exhausted; 'finished'; (very) drunk.

1918 *Aussie: Austral. Soldiers' Mag.* Apr. 14/1 Make way for the wounded! Damn the war! . . It's this rotten pack. By Heaven, I'm feeling stonkered! **1924** *Truth* (Sydney) 27 Apr. 6/3 *Stonkered*, to be very drunk. **1937** G.D. MITCHELL *Backs to Wall* 197 We played poker on credit. I won all round, but never collected. The losers were all stonkered before they handled money again. **1946** *Southerly* ii. 75 'Tastes absolutely bonzer. . . ' 'I'm out to get stonkered good and proper.' **1956** *Bulletin* (Sydney) 15 Feb. 12/1 Our carriage was invaded by a couple of half-stonkered ringers from way back who had a good supply of bottled-stuff to help them onward. **1963** D.H. CRICK *Martin Place* 204 Gee, I'm stonkered, Danny. Been celebrating all afternoon. **1978** K. GARVEY *Tales of my Uncle Harry* 44 One Sunday night he produces a couple of bottles of rum, and we gets really stonkered. **1981** C. WALLACE-CRABBE *Splinters* 18 The stonkered pink cat growled straight round and came to a halt. **1985** P. CAREY *Illywhacker* 150 She ate heartily . . only announcing herself stonkered after scraping clean the large monogrammed plate of steamed pudding.

Also **stonkering** *vbl. n.*, drinking.

1950 N. LINDSAY *Dust or Polish* 103 'Can't you do your stonkering up here. . . ' 'Not me. I like a free leg when I'm out for a proper booze-up.'

stonkie. [f. *stonk* a coloured marble + -Y.] A coloured marble.

1915 N. LINDSAY *N. Lindsay's Bk. II.* 85 'How many marbles had you. . . ' 'Fifty-eight allies 'n two stonkies.' **1941** C. BARRETT *Aust.* 45 'Bluey likes anything purple or blue,' Harry told me. 'He collected some of our blue stonkies once.' 'Marbles,' the teacher explained. **1957** A. MARSHALL *Aust.* (1981) 74 Marble games seemed to vary in each State. Even the terms used were different. The names we gave to the cheapest marbles were 'shooks' and 'stonkies'.

stony, *a. Obs.* (except in place-names). In the collocation **stony rise:** see quot. 1846.

1846 W. WESTGARTH *Rep. Conditions Austral. Aborigines* 8 To the west and south west of Mount Rouse, there occur extensive tracts of those curious formations termed by the settlers 'stony rises', and consisting of innumerable heaps of fragments of rocks, forming hillocks or ranges, in general not exceeding 20 to 50 feet in height, distributed in endless variety, and traversing every possible direction. **1853** —— *Vic.* 42 Loose surface stones give quite a characteristic feature to many parts of Victoria, forming ridges and hillocks in endless diversity, and, under the local name of 'stony-rises', covering many square miles of surface. **1857** —— *Vic. & Austral. Gold Mines* 29 A feature usually accompanying these extinct volcanoes, is the 'Stony Rises'. **1861** 'OLD BUSHMAN' *Bush Wanderings* 112 The plover of the plains frequents the most desolate open stony rises.

stoom, *v.* [f. STUMER.] *trans.* To break (a person) financially. Chiefly in pass. Also *transf.*, to knock (someone) unconscious; to kill.

1898 *Bulletin* (Sydney) 17 Dec. 15/2 Hard-uppishness a shearer confesses when he says he's . . *stoomed.* **1908** E.S. SORENSON *Quinton's Rouseabout* 119 Garron . . 'as a kick-up with the ole gerl over something—God knows wot—an' she stooms him out—accidental, as yer might say. **1925** —— *Murty Brown* 68 'The scamps!' said Murty sympathetically. 'Might a 'urt yer!' "Urt me!' Charcoal snorted. 'Might a stoomed me out!'

stoomer, var. STUMER.

stop, *v. trans.* In the phr. **to stop one (a pint,** etc.), to have an alcoholic drink.

1924 LAWRENCE & SKINNER *Boy in Bush* 251 A man whom they knew from the north . . hailed them. 'Come an' stop one on me, maties.' **1926** M. FORREST *Hibiscus Heart* 92 Their owners were inside the bar 'stopping one'. **1942** L. MANN *Go-Getter* 8 But if he should recognise any one, he could scarcely avoid asking: 'Could you stop a pint?'

stoppers, *pl. Shearing. Obs.* See quot. 1965.

1895 *Worker* (Sydney) 28 Sept. 4/1 And set to work with my file—Levelled my knockers quickly, and then I rigged them up in style: Put on the stoppers, and shoved them away After the usual test. **1896** *Ibid.* 24 Oct. 3/3 Each man stepped up to his stand and drew off his stoppers . . with the set determination to do his level best to give satisfaction. **1956** R.G. EDWARDS *Overlander Songbk.* 91 So, lads, put on your stoppers, and let us to the hut, Where we'll gather round and have a friendly game. **1965** J.S. GUNN *Terminol. Shearing Industry* ii. 27 In the days of hand shears stoppers were pieces of material over the closed points of the blades to stop them springing open when not in use. It became a natural transition to say 'put on your stoppers' instead of stop work, stop taking, etc.

store.

1. *Hist.*

a. Abbrev. of *public store* (see PUBLIC *a.* 2).

1789 D. COLLINS *Acct. Eng. Colony N.S.W.* (1798) I. 88 There was a sort of sacredness about our store; and its preservation pure and undefiled was deemed as necessary as the chastity of Caesar's wife. **1790** *Copies & Extracts Lett. Governor Phillip* 17 June (1792) 110 Superintendants [*sic*] and storekeepers must be sent with convicts who are detached, and stores must be erected. **1791** *HRA* (1914) 1st Ser. I. 229 The Lieutenant-Governor's plan for rendering convicts independent of the store is enclosed. **1792** *Ibid.* 390, I think it highly probable that the store will be eased of two hundred people if the crops belonging to private persons turn out good. **1808** 'GENTLEMEN JUST RETURNED FROM SETTLEMENT' *Acct. Eng. Colony Botany Bay* 10 The first settler in this country who declared himself able to live on the produce of his farm, without any assistance from the stores, was James Ruse. **1819** W.C. WENTWORTH *Statistical, Hist., & Pol. Descr. N.S.W.* 26 The public buildings are a church . . a school house and stores for the reception and issue of provisions to such of the settlers in the adjacent districts as are victualled at the expense of the government. **1822** J.T. BIGGE *Rep. State Colony N.S.W.* 42 On Saturdays the convicts leave their work at ten in summer and eleven in winter, to enable them to attend at the store to draw their rations.

b. *spec.* In the phr. **off** (or **on**) **the store,** (not) in receipt of provisions, etc. from the public store.

1792 D. COLLINS *Acct. Eng. Colony N.S.W.* (1798) I. 208 Some had become settlers; some had left the country; others, to use their own expressions, had taken themselves **off the stores,** that is to say, had declined receiving any farther provisions from the public stores, or doing any public labour. **1802** *Gen. Orders issued by Governor King* 12 Jan. 75 Any person applying for prisoners off the Store, who does not employ them on their own grounds, suffers them to be on their own hands, or hires them out, will, on conviction before two Magistrates, forfeit £10 to the Orphan School, besides 2s. 6d. for every day such prisoner has been from Government Labour. **1805** *N.S.W. Gen. Orders* (1806) 14 July 168 Several of the Prisoners under Sentence of the Law who have been indulged with Permission to be off the Stores on Tickets of Leave, having neglected to attend the Public Muster yesterday, are ordered to Public Labour, and to be sent to some other Settlements. **1809** *N.S.W. Pocket Almanack* 7 Those taken off the stores to be employed on their masters' grounds only, and in no case be permitted on their own hands, or let to hire. **1813** *Ibid.* 61 *Convicts*—off the store on certificate not to be insolent to an officer, soldier, or constable. **1817** *HRA* (1917) 1st Ser. IX. 406 The Hardship they suffer by having their Families Struck off the Store. **1827** *Monitor* (Sydney) 23 Mar. 356/1 It is notorious the settlers will take off the stores, i.e. hire at their own cost, and employ free of all expense to the crown, more prisoners by half than the Governor has it in his power to assign to them. **1832** *HRA* 1st Ser. XVI. 805 He is first of all taken off the Stores, as it is technically called. **1801** *Gen. Orders issued by Governor King* 20 June (1802) 51 A General Muster of all the Male Prisoners, off and **on the Stores,** also Free Men of all descriptions . . on or off the Stores, will be taken at Hawkesbury, Parramatta and Sydney. **1803** *Sydney Gaz.* 17 Apr., The prisoner . . declared that he had been induced to commit the offence from a wish to be put on the Store: This was readily acquiesced in by the Magistrates, who ordered that he might labour for the Crown Two Years. **1813** *HRA* (1916) 1st Ser. VII. 726, I have however taken upon myself the Responsibility of putting himself and his Family on the Store for Eighteen Months. **1817** *Ibid.* (1917) 1st Ser. IX. 406 The Commissariat Officers were kept on the Stores. **1828** L.E. THRELKELD *Statement* 59 The Governor has kindly acceded to my request that four prisoners of the Crown shall be allowed me 'on the stores'.

c. Special Comb. **store receipt,** a receipt specifying the monetary value of produce accepted at a public store: see quot. 1810.

1810 E. BENT Let. 9 Mar. 130 When any persons deliver Beef, corn, flour . . into the Stores of the King, they receive for the Quantity delivered in, at a fixed price, which are signed by the Storekeeper, and are called Store Receipts. These are current for their amount, & are considered as good as Paynotes, because they also on every Quarter day are consolidated in like manner by Bills on the Treasury, on being presented to the Commissary. **1819** *HRA* (1917) 1st Ser. X. 110 Issuing Store-receipts . . is fraught with Evil. **1826** J. ATKINSON *Acct. Agric. & Grazing N.S.W.* 132 The drafts of the Commissariat Officers at the out-stations, termed store-receipts, upon the Commissary at Sydney, for supplies furnished at those stations, were negociable instruments, and were much used in making payments.

2. [Orig. U.S.] A shop stocking a wide range of necessary items, as clothing, hardware, provisions, etc., GENERAL store; a shop (usu. large and with a number of departments). Also *attrib.*

1825 *Austral.* (Sydney) 19 May 1 William Powditch having himself experienced the great want of a Store, or General Warehouse at Newcastle, for the supply of the Hunter's River Settlers, has determined upon opening a house of that nature immediately, upon his allotment at Newcastle, where he hopes the business will be conducted with such attention, liberality, and undeviating fairness, as to ensure the support of the numerous and respectable body of settlers in that fine district. **1827** P. CUNNINGHAM *Two Yrs. in N.S.W.* I. 51 Merchandise of every description can generally be bought at one and the self-same shop (or *store*, as we, like the Americans, call it). **1840** *S. Austral. Rec.* (London) 28 Mar. 148 Here you will find shops (or, as they are called, stores) of every description, where you may purchase the produce of the whole world. **1851** C. ROWCROFT *Emigrant in search of Colony* 405 He was a general dealer, and kept what is called 'a store' . . a place where every imagineable saleable thing is to be bought, from a lucifer match to a service of plate. **1860** 'LADY' *My Experiences in Aust.* 101 Contains many large stores—I was going to say 'notion shops'—from which the settler in the far interior gets his supplies of flour, tea, sugar, wearing apparel, and other necessaries of bush-life. **1872** MRS E. MILLETT *Austral. Parsonage* 16 The larger and more important shops, or rather 'stores', of the chief traders of the town. **1881** J.C.F. JOHNSON *To Mount Browne & Back* 4 There is the inevitable 'pub', store, and blacksmith's shop that go to make a township in Australia. **1895** *Western Champion* (Barcaldine) 30 July 1/1 As soon as the average Labor member puts on 'store clothes' he begins to despise the working man. **1919** *Wilson's Newcastle, Maitland & Cessnock Districts Street Directory* 24 (Advt.), Ophir tea is sold by all stores. **1938** *Australasian Grocer* June 147 If a department store closes on Saturdays, the small stores around it suffer. **1903** *Bulletin* (Sydney) 15 Oct. 35/1 A dashing young softgoodsman came from Sydney to take a billet in the leading store in Quantook. **1950** G.S. CASEY *City of Men* 243 When they have money they throw it away, and when they have not they retire to the bush and live on hope until they get enough colour to settle their store-bills. **1966** *Austral. Financial Rev.* (Sydney) 4 Mar. 2/3 Closing of stores at 12 noon every Saturday is a restriction of freedom. **1985** *Austral.* (Sydney) 18 Aug. 1/2 N.S.W. is the only state which allows general and department stores to open at weekends.

3. A depot on a rural property holding supplies for issue or sale to employees: see quot. 1833. Also *attrib.*

1833 J. KING *Information Van Diemen's Land* 15 Almost every person of property is a store-keeper for all kinds of goods; farmers keeping a store from which they supply all who work for them, and if they happen not to have any article that is wanted, they procure it, and charge the consumer a profit upon the colonial price. **1847** *Port Phillip Herald* 3 June 3/6 The improvements on the station consist of a good homestead, on which is erected a house, store, and kitchen, with two paddocks securely fenced in. There are also two out-stations, with every convenience. **1859** J.D. MEREWEATHER *Diary Working Clergyman* 95 The out-buildings consist of a store—where are kept the flour and other provisions of the establishment—a stable and a dray-shed. **1867** A.K. COLLINS *Waddy Mundoee* 9 A few yards away another hut is occupied by the overseer and the storekeeper; and hard by, is the store. **1872** MRS E. MILLETT *Austral. Parsonage* 245 The system, which universally prevailed in the colony, of paying wages by truck, every up-country settler keeping a shop or store for his labourers, and uniting in his own person the various callings of grocer, flour dealer, butcher, bootmaker. **1885** MRS C. PRAED *Austral. Life* 33 The drays were delayed by flooded creeks, and the store was empty of flour, tea, sugar, and all other groceries. **1900** *Tocsin* (Melbourne) 9 Aug. 6/1, I took a journey to a 'store'—that is to say, a selector's homestead where sufficient supplies were kept to lead to occasional visits from neighbours to make some emergency purchase. **1923** *Bulletin* (Sydney) 11 Oct. 24/4 As a rule native races possess good teeth. . . But put them on 'store' tucker *i.e.*, salmon, rice, sugar, etc., for any length of time, and almost always they develop dental trouble.

storekeep, *v. intr.* To keep a shop. Chiefly as *pres. pple.* and *vbl. n.*

1856 S.C. BREES *How to farm & settle in Aust.* 11 He can then decide between going into quartz-crushing, store-keeping . . or breeding and fattening cattle. **1872** MRS E. MILLETT *Austral. Parsonage* 62 The mysteries of stores and store-keeping in Western Australia were not to be fathomed in a single visit; they were such as could only be revealed by time accompanied with dear-bought experience. **1904** *Bulletin* (Sydney) 11 Feb. 16/2, I was storekeeping at Hoskins Town . . 30 years ago.

storekeeper.

1. *Hist.* A person employed to administer a public store: see STORE 1 a.

1793 J. HUNTER *Hist. Jrnl. Trans. Port Jackson* 308 Great care is to be taken of all the tools; each man taking his axe or hoe to his tent, or delivering them to the store-keeper. **1801** *HRA* (1915) 1st Ser. III. 251 Storekeepers at Parramatta have yesterday, through obstinacy and neglect, issued the full ration of meat. **1814** *N.S.W. Pocket Almanack* 112 No storekeeper or other person shall make any distinction between the higher and lower orders of persons in issuing provisions from the stores. **1829** R. DAWSON *Statement* 14 A large tent was pitched as an issuing store, under the management of a brick-layer (who was the *only* storekeeper provided by the committee for a period of *twenty two months*).

2. a. [Orig. U.S.] One who keeps a shop: see STORE 2.

1828 *Hobart Town Courier* 12 July 4 Mr John MacLeod of Elizabeth River, Storekeeper, has executed an Assignment of all his real and personal Estate and Effects. **1837** *S. Austral. Rec.* (London) 11 Nov. 14, I hourly regret I have no one here with whom I could enter into partnership in a general store. . . I think I may say that the storekeepers . . are getting 70 per cent clear. **1843** J.F. BENNETT *Hist. & Descr. Acct. S.A.* 128 There are merchants, shopkeepers (or storekeepers as is the Colonial phrase). **1853** J. SHERER *Gold Finder Aust.* 318 The gold-buyer's, at which we now arrived, was likewise a storekeeper. **1870** W.B. WITHERS *Hist. Ballarat* 216 Thou shalt not 'blatherskite' about 'new rushes' to thy neighbor that thou mayest benefit a storekeeper. **1887** W.S.S. TYRWHITT *New Chum in Qld. Bush* 89 The store-keeper generally ranks next to the police magistrate in Bush township society. **1910** *Huon Times* (Franklin) 16 Nov. 2/7 Just imagine storekeepers not stocking their staple products. **1928** B. CRONIN *Dragonfly* 74 There were those so hopelessly in debt to McMurtrie that they dare do no other than he told them. Not that the storekeeper made a showing of his authority. **1934** 'S. RUDD' *Green Grey Homestead* 96 'D'you know who's come home for Christmas?' you'll hear from the bustling storekeeper as you step on the verandah and reach the door. **1978** D. STUART *Wedgetail View* 13 Every poor bastard with a problem of rent or the money for the butcher or the storekeeper. **1985** *Harden-Murrumburrah Express* 30 Sept. 1/1 The publican was peeved because the wake would be not at his hotel but at the 'restaurant' run by storekeeper 'Windy' Regan.

b. In the special collocation **storekeeper's rush,** a gold rush occasioned by a false rumour (see quot. 1869); the rumour itself; also *fig.*

1869 'E. HOWE' *Boy in Bush* 213 We've heard of *storekeeper's rushes* before now, haven't we? . . Those fellows would make out that there was gold in the moon, if people could get there to buy their damaged goods. **1894** A.F. CALVERT *Coolgardie Goldfield* 20 There are new rushes breaking out at short intervals, but they are merely 'store keepers' rushes', as store keepers and teamsters can treat diggers how they like in this Colony, as they all work together for the one purpose. **1913** *Bulletin* (Sydney) 2 Jan. 15/1 Many "storekeepers" rushes on the goldfields have been put down to the big bird's fondness for picking up a bright article. In this way a small slug of gold of three or four dwt. has been unloaded in the bush, and that one piece has led to tons of earth being chucked about by eager hunters for more. **1920** A.G. HALES *McGlusky Gold-Seeker* 49 A storekeepers' rush, son, is a fake find got up by storekeepers. **1977** J. DOUGHTY *Gold in Blood* 74 It was contemptuously called a 'storekeeper's rush' designed to revive interest in Larkville and bring men to the town.

3. One employed to run a store on a rural property: see STORE 3.

1833 [see STORE 3]. **1843** *Sydney Morning Herald* 2 Oct. 3/1 Men Wanted—A man and his wife, the former as Storekeeper and the latter as Cook . . to proceed to New England. **1867** A.K. COLLINS *Waddy Mundoee* 9 A few yards away another hut, is occupied by the overseer and the storekeeper; and hard by, is the store. **1883** R.E.N. TWOPENY *Town Life Aust.* 244 The storekeeper is the lowest official on a station. **1891** *Truth* (Sydney) 15 Feb. 7/2 He makes his sons overseer, sheep overseer, storekeeper, bookkeeper. **1913** H. LAWSON *Triangles of Life* 166 Take some tucker along to the Mile Hut, and give it to the new shepherd you'll see there. Go to the storekeeper, and he'll give you a bag of ration. **1926** *Bulletin* (Sydney) 11 Nov. 22/2 The new Pommy knit his brows when the hatter included in his supply order: '2 tins of cocky's delight and a bottle of Mallee marmalade.' How was he to know that treacle and tomato sauce were indicated?

storm bird. [Transf. use of *storm-bird* a bird, the movements or cries of which are supposed to presage a storm.] Any of several birds, esp. the CHANNEL-BILLED CUCKOO.

1904 *Emu* IV. 46 Channelbill (*Scythrops novaehollandiae*), or 'Storm-Bird' as it is universally called out here, was first heard in 1902. **1921** S.A. WHITE *Bunya* 42 It was the harsh, loud cry of the channel-billed cuckoo or 'stormbird'. **1947** W.E. HARNEY *Brimming Billabongs* 34 The storm bird can tell when the shade leaves a person's body and he is about to die. **1949** B. O'REILLY *Green Mountains* 249 Cuckoos are our most renowned harbingers of rain, and any species of the large family may be known in some corner or other of Australia by the vernacular of 'rain bird' or 'storm bird'. **1981** A.B. FACEY *Fortunate Life* 90 The blue bird was about the size of the peewit too, but had a black head and a very light blue body. This bird was sometimes called a Storm bird on account of it appearing more frequently just before the weather turned stormy.

stoush /staʊʃ/, *n.* Also **stouch.** [Prob. f. Br. dial. *stashie, stushie* an uproar, disturbance, quarrel: see EDD.]

1. a. Fighting; violence; 'punishment'; a brawl or fight; a punch. Also *transf.* and *fig.*, and as **stoush up.**

1893 *Bulletin* (Sydney) 30 Dec. 4/4 The law of New South Wales . . has practically decided that Government by 'stoush' is an allowable process, so the practice of hiring bulky pugilists to attend political meetings and disfigure anybody who isn't in accord with Freetrade principles will doubtless grow and prosper. **1911** *Truth* (Sydney) 7 May 8/3 The charges . . were found proved, and the following stouch was ladled out to them:- Sebbens, for riotous behavior, £2, £1 1s. professional costs, and 8s. court costs. . . Boyd, fined £2, £1 1s. professional costs, and 6s. court costs. **1919** *Smith's Weekly* (Sydney) 19 Apr. 18/1 A certain Sydney artist received in an altercation with a brother-brush a hefty stouch on the eye. **1929** 'F. BLAIR' *Digger Sea-Mates* 73 One mob in the joint nearly 'ad a real stoush up over some slurs at a bloke with an outsize in appetites. **1936** *Publicist* (Sydney) i. 7/1, I look forward to the pleasure of handing out a considerable amount of stoush to some of these supra-cultured critics. **1945** *Bulletin* (Sydney) 14 Mar. 15/3 I've been attacked by total strangers thrice, and each time didn't learn what their grouch was until the stoush was over. **1958** *Coast to Coast 1956–57* 85 Ladies and gents, there's a question of a bit of stoush, and I'm here to see it's a fair dinkum bit of stoush. **1958** *Swag* (Sydney) ii. 20 How long since you last saw a full-scale all-in stoush? . . I'm talking about those magnificent dustups when 50 or 60 bruisers used to erupt in a seething mass of boots, knees, knuckles and chains. **1979** R. ENGLISH *Toxic Kisses* 162 So we've all been on that trip. Whether it was . . with an erudite ex-professor or with Len Evans at one of his stoushes, where the quality of the rain-affected early Shiraz was more important than how the condition of your liver was yellowing your eyes. **1986** *Bulletin* (Sydney) 28 Jan. 22/1 Hayden . . is prepared to take risks, even a stoush with the Left if necessary.

b. In the phr. **to deal out stoush:** see DEAL 2.

2. A war; military service. In the phr. **the Big Stoush,** the war of 1914–18.

1901 *Tocsin* (Melbourne) 29 Aug. 1/1 'In South Africa I'll get my rations and a chance to pick up some boodle by stoush.'—Explanation vouchsafed by one contingenter who is going back. **1919** O. HOGUE *Cameliers* 52 Quite a number of Light Horsemen, hearing 'the call of Stoush', and thinking that Sinai would not provide them with sufficient excitement, stowed away on the transports. **1920** *Aussie* (Sydney) Sept. 50/2 Returning from the fields of stoush last year, I came across a tough-looking Digger. **1941** *Cobbers* (Brisbane) 31 Jan. 14 It was a quiet moment in the last stoush. **1945** D. ROBINSON *Pop's Blonde* 79 Bill was an experienced housebreaker, having been 'inside' only three times since the finish of the 'Big Stoush'. **1952** A.W. UPFIELD *New Shoe* 124 Been cobbers since kids and wanted to keep together in the Great Stoush. **1960** *Bulletin* (Sydney) 22 June 16/3 Towards the end of Stoush II a party of us were stationed in the Admiralty Islands. **1963** A.E. FARRELL *Vengeance* 23 A broad leather belt . . bearing the inscription—*Gott Mit Uns*, Billy's souvenir of the 'Big Stoush' of 1914–18. **1969** *On Guard* (Broken Hill) Mar. 5 During the first 'stoush' he served overseas. **1978** M.J. BURTON *Bush Pub* 73 Archie was a returned soldier who had been wounded a few times. One of his souvenirs from the stoush was a metal plate in his skull.

3. Special Comb. **stoush-artist,** an accomplished and habitual fighter (see ARTIST).

1932 J. MCCARTER *Pan's Clan* 133 Stoush-artists from other places . . come the proverbial gutzers in Longreach. **1960** *Bulletin* (Sydney) 19 Oct. 16/1 The travelling bee-herds never back-chatted 'Hungry'; he had a good reputation as a stoush artist. **1966** D. NILAND *Pairs & Loners* 38 From Lurobodalla to Caddibarrawirracanna, he was a known stoush-artist and fearless roughrider.

stoush /staʊʃ/, *v.* Also **stouch.** [f. prec.]

a. *trans.* To punch, strike, or thrash (a person). Also *fig.*

1893 J.A. BARRY *Steve Brown's Bunyip* 66 I'll get stoushed over this job yet. Brombee's got it in for me. **1896** *Bulletin* (Sydney) 23 May 3/2 You remember the night when the traps got me for stoushing a bleeding Chow. **1904** *Truth* (Sydney) 15 May 7/2 'In the tenth year of the reign of Governor Macquarie', whom it was expected Bigge came out to 'stouch'. **1916** C.J. DENNIS *Moods Ginger Mick* 17 Mick never reely stoushed 'im, but 'e used 'im fer a mop. Then someone doused the bloomin' glim, an' Foo run fer a cop. **1925** *Bulletin* (Sydney) 26 Feb. 22/1 We stoushed a cop at Bredbo who'd surprised us after six. **1939** K. TENNANT *Foveaux* 142 It would just serve you right, if we let you loose, and you did stouch a copper and get pinched. **1952** C. MACINNES *June in her Spring* 88 You're a bit cheeky, aren't you? . . Of course, I don't want to stoush you in front of a girl. **1965** E. LAMBERT *Long White Night* 79 There was no mistaking that voice. 'Get out of that bloody car while I stoush yer!' **1979** S.W. DUTHIE *Fidlers Creek* 61 Instead of this geezer going up and stoushing this bum at the top end of the bar he picks on young Clem. **1982** R. HALL *Just Relations* 52 The two branches of Swans having a shot at one another, somebody forever getting stoushed.

b. *intr.* To fight; to struggle.

1909 *Truth* (Sydney) 16 May 12/4 Sisters stouch. Maria and Kate uncoil themselves in University Street. **1929** W.J. RESIDE *Golden Days* 375 When Fortune felt inclined to stoush I never missed a crack! **1954** J.E. MACDONNELL *Jim Brady* 45 He was in a position to stoush with the local larrikins. **1957** *Bulletin* (Sydney) 11 Dec. 36/1, I have often come upon a couple of big red old-man roos stoushing. **1965** R.H. CONQUEST *Horses in Kitchen* 47 The fellow who invented Rafferty's Rules was a dinkum innocent compared with some of the gents who stoushed in hobo camps.

Hence **stousher** *n.*, a fighter; **stoushie** *n.*, a soldier; **stoushing** *vbl. n.*, fighting; beating.

1909 *Truth* (Sydney) 28 Feb. 3/8 A **stousher** stoushed. For assaulting Harold Weekly . . a weed of a young fellow named Albert Margetts was fined £2. **1973** J. MURRAY *Larrikins* 99 The *Age's* fear was that the pushes and their larrikin members would turn into 'gaol-hardened brutes' because 'the larrikin will inevitably develop into the *stousher*'. **1941** *Action Front: Jrnl. 2/2 Field Regiment* Sept. 9 A real good bunch of **stoushies.** **1898** *Worker* (Sydney) 1 Jan. 7/1 The **stoushing** of the coppers by the push in particular. **1920** *Aussie* (Sydney) Apr. 31/2 We also have another record that will take some stoushing. **1927** F.C. BIGGERS *Bat-Eye* 14 Their nights fer bucks 'Oo bog in straight, an' try their 'and at stoushin's arts. **1963** J. WYNNUM *No Boats to Burn* 40 Pack it up you two! . . There's enough stouching going on in the world without you two mugs spoiling for a brawl.

stove, *v. trans.* To remove (a tree stump) by burning it in the ground: see quot. 1972. Also as *vbl. n.*

1897 L. LINDLEY-COWEN *W. Austral. Settler's Guide* 229 A plan . . has been adopted in South Gippsland, Victoria, for the last seven or eight years, of burning out or stoving trees or stumps, instead of grubbing. . . Other farmers about there told me it was only half the cost of grubbing to stove the stumps. **1972** K. SILLCOCK *Three Lifetimes* 33 'Stoving' . . was done by digging beside the stump and setting a roaring fire in the hole. . . When there was a good body of live coals the fire was covered over with sods of earth which allowed only a limited supply of air to enter. If this was tended every day or two . . the stump would smoulder for days as the fire followed and burned out all the main roots, finally consuming the aerial part of the stump or making it easy to remove to a heap.

straggler. [Spec. use of *straggler* an animal that strays from its habitat or companions.]

a. A stray or unbranded animal.

1846 S. DAVENPORT *Let.* 9 July in *S. Australiana* (1977) Sept. 157 The cattle had arrived in safety, a few stragglers only having escaped on the journey, which will work their way back to the Murray. **1848** H.W. HAYGARTH *Recoll. Bush Life* 56 Innumerable animals of every kind of brand, and others with no brand at all, and known as 'stragglers'. **1865** *Illustr. Sydney News* 16 Mar. 4/1 On stations not too heavily timbered or interspersed with thick scrub, mustering is easy enough, the stockmen marking their camping place for their cattle and have only to round up the stragglers. **1893** S. NEWLAND *Paving Way* 77 You had better collect all the stragglers, in any case, before I leave for the overland trip. **1914** R. KALESKI *Austral. Barkers & Biters* 39 A pup has got a fair idea of work (putting stragglers back into the mob). **1935** *Red Star* (Perth) 5 Apr. 3/1 At one part of the mustering when looking for the 'stragglers' the food was of the roughest, 'spuds' baked in the fire being a principal item. **1944** *Bulletin* (Sydney) 26 July 12/3 When, years ago, I was backtracking stragglers, night often found me *minus* nap and tucker.

b. *spec.* A sheep which is overlooked when the flock is rounded up for shearing. Also **straggler sheep.**

[N.Z. **1860** G. DUPPA in S.S. Crawford *Sheep & Sheepmen Canterbury* (1949) 46 Complete dipping flock .. deliver stragglers.] **1897** *Worker* (Sydney) 11 Sept. 1/2 The sheep are 'jumbucks', 'woollies' have the fleece still on their back, And 'stragglers' are the last to come along the woolshed track. **1905** *Shearer* (Sydney) 29 Apr. 4/4 The quality of the offerings was, with few exceptions, poor, and .. was comprised in the grease of the lamb's wool and clearing-up lots from stragglers, &c. **1913** H. LAWSON *Triangles of Life* 231 Jack Mitchell and I were 'carrying swags' west from the Darling in hopes of 'stragglers' to shear. **1972** *Bronze Swagman Bk. Bush Verse* (1973) 18 He must get those sheep... The stragglers all that missed the shear. **1977** F.B. VICKERS *Stranger no Longer* 111 At the finish of the main run of shearing I went back over my tracks with two shearers .. to comb the Murchison .. for any straggler sheep a squatter might want shearing... We all vowed never to go straggler shearing again.

c. Special Comb. **straggler shearing,** see quot. 1898; also **stragglers' shearing**.

1898 *Bulletin* (Sydney) 17 Dec. 15/2 *Stragglers* are the sheep missed in the general shearing. They are mustered afterwards, and shorn at the second or *straggler-shearing*. **1926** *Ibid.* 8 Apr. 22/2 Dawdling down the Diamantina, squandering days where the deep pools chain, Scorning a sheep-king's straggler-shearing, bulging the packbags once again! **1959** H. LAMOND *Sheep Station* 42 Later .. they had a stragglers' shearing of something over thirty-two thousand! **1977** [see sense b.].

straight, *a.* Used as an intensive in the collocation **straight goer,** an honest person. See also *straight dinkum* DINKUM C b. and c., *straight oil* OIL *n.* 2, and *straight wire* WIRE 1.

1899 *North-Western Advocate* (Devonport) 8 Feb. 2/6 Several years of experience in the produce trade, and is known as a 'straight goer'. **1901** *Truth* (Sydney) 7 Apr. 4/6 The present Council were elected on the cry of 'reform' and as 'straight goers'. **1909** *Ibid.* 2 May 9/1 Moncrieff has the reputation of being a straight-goer, and the men under him need not be scared about receiving a fair deal. **1925** A. WRIGHT *Boy from Bullarah* 142 You don't object to a straight-goer, I hope, Bill. **1948** M. UREN *Glint of Gold* 201 It was the sergeant, who was looked on as a very straight goer and one who rarely took a drink. **1953** 'CADDIE' *Caddie* 239 The Missus up at the pub told me about you... She recommended you to me; said you were a straight goer.

strain, *n.* The stretch of fencing wire between two strainers.

1930 D. COTTRELL *Earth Battle* 302 Many found the fence gaps and were through. Many more crashed in headlong flight against the uncut strains. **1937** A.W. UPFIELD *Mr Jelly's Business* 49 'E can put up a mile of fence whiles any ordinary man is putting up a cuppler strains. **1978** *Jrnl. Agric. W.A.* 71 For ease of working strains of about 2 km. seem best, although up to 7 km. strains are satisfactory using plain wire.

strain, *v.* In the phr. **to strain the potatoes** (or **spuds**): of a male, to urinate.

1965 *Times Lit. Suppl.* (London) 16 Sept. 812/2 Among his many idiosyncrasies a desire to pass water at the most inopportune moments has become increasingly manifest... McKenzie employs a number of colourful and expressive Australianisms to describe this prosaic function; straining the potatoes [etc.]. **1967** *Kings Cross Whisper* (Sydney) xl. 4/5 *Strain the spuds*, use the toilet. **1974** *Bulletin* (Sydney) 10 Aug. 41/3 Later McCarthy in Bazza style wishing to strain the potatoes is wandering around the hospital. **1982** P. BURGESS *Money to Burn* 114 Keep Ted's chair for him. He's only gone out to strain the spuds.

strainer. [Ellipt. form of *straining-post*: see OED *straining, vbl. n.* 6.] A strong post against which the wires of a fence are tightened; *fence strainer*, see FENCE *n.*[1] 1 a. Freq. as **strainer post.**

[N.Z. **1880** E.R. CHUDLEIGH *Diary* (1950) 289 Smith undertakes to cart my posts .. 5d. a post, strainers to count as three posts.] **1891** *Truth* (Sydney) 26 Apr. 7/3 Call that a fence! Look! Crooked as a ram's horn. Posts not rammed; strainers not big enough. **1914** *Fences & Fencing* (ed. 2) 31 *Strainer Posts* are the mainstay of a wire fence, and should be of the best timber procurable, with a diameter of not less than 12 inches. **1920** *Bulletin* (Sydney) 8 July 26/1 The fencer bent down and squinted through. 'That's all right', he said, 'it's only the strainer.' **1937** A.W. UPFIELD *Winds of Evil* 225 He sat with his back to a strainer-post which was a foot higher than the ordinary posts. **1940** I.L. IDRIESS *Lightning Ridge* 131 If the wires weren't slack I'd have to walk to the strainer post where the ends of the long wires are strained. With a key (wire straining key) I'd quickly untwist the two top wires and pull the ends through the post. **1949** *Bulletin* (Sydney) 13 July 10/4 Don and Joe were replacing a strainer-post of the roadside fence. **1953** *Meanjin* 6 His fences were straight and taut with huge strainer-posts. **1959** *Bulletin* (Sydney) 18 Nov. 19/3 Joe went to a land-owner and asked permission to cut a strainer from the timber in the creek-paddock. **1962** E. LANE *Mad as Rabbits* 165 Even the men, who'd been standing like strainer-posts until now, began to fidget and feel a bit silly. **1974** J. POLLARD *One for Road* 143 The fences consisted of widely spaced strainers, large and solid, and between them light stringers supporting the wires but only resting on the ground. **1981** *Practical Farm Fencing* 8 The strainer posts we found most effective were the single span using two 2.4 meter strainer posts and up to 3.0 meter stays.

'Stralia. Abbrev. of 'Australia'.

1955 F. LANE *Patrol to Kimberleys* 84 Course, there's only about nine million people in all of 'Stralia. **1973** H. LEWIS *Crow on Barbed Wire Fence* 5 'Like 'Stralia?' 'Very much,' I said and was glad I said it.

stranger.

1. An animal which has strayed from a neighbouring flock or herd. Also *attrib.*

1845 D. MACKENZIE *Emigrant's Guide* 132, I have never attended a muster .. without seeing several stray cattle (or *strangers*, as they are called) among every mob. **1885** *Illustr. Austral. News* (Melbourne) 30 Sept. 162/3 The duties of a boundary rider .. consist in riding round the fences .. blocking up any panels that may be broken, putting out strangers (that is stock that have strayed on to the run). **1888** 'R. BOLDREWOOD' *Robbery under Arms* (1937) 16 Jim and I knew the four calves were all strangers, but we didn't know the brands of the mothers. **1900** *Bulletin* (Sydney) 10 Mar. 31/2 I've seen many a one as would muster a cattle paddock, an draft out the strangers before puttin' 'em in the yard. **1945** F. CORK *Tales from Cattle Country* 23 When the muster falls due, the managers of neighbouring stations are notified and each sends a tender—sometimes two—who are responsible for their 'strangers' who have wandered out of bounds. **1955** J. CLEARY *Justin Bayard* 28 They had changed the brand on the stranger bullocks. **1965** J.S. GUNN *Terminol. Shearing Industry* ii. 28 *Stranger*, a strange sheep, probably from an adjoining property, which has joined the flock being shorn.

2. *Rock whiting*, see ROCK *n.* 2.

1873 F. DE CASTELNAU *Edible Fishes Vic.* 14 The *Stranger* (*Odax Richardsonii*) .. is very common in all seasons on the market. It is remarkable by its parrot-like beak and its colours, which are sometimes very beautiful. **1896** F.G. AFLALO *Sketch Nat. Hist. Aust.* 238 The little Rock Whitings, so-called (*Odax*) allied to the Melbourne 'Stranger' and the Kelp-fish of Hobart. **1906** D.G. STEAD *Fishes of Aust.* 146 In Victoria and Tasmania, this fish [*sc.* the Rock-Whiting] is known as 'Stranger'; this name even being occasionally used in the Sydney markets. **1933** D. MACDONALD *Brooks of Morning* 180 The 'tailer', well known in Sydney, is a 'stranger' in Melbourne, though the stranger is another fish altogether. **1969** J. POLLARD *Austral. & N.Z. Fishing* 749 Stranger[:] Fish of the family Neoodaciidae, also known as weedy whiting or rock whiting.

strapped, *a.* Of trousers: having a strip of material inserted down the back of the leg (see quot. 1899, 2).

1895 *Worker* (Sydney) 29 June 4/1 One of those slight, active, little fellows whom we used to see in cabbage-tree hats, Crimean shirts, 'strapped' trousers, and 'lastic sided boots. **1899** *Bulletin* (Sydney) 25 Feb. (Red Page), 'How did that cove Tom's horse do?' asked the man in strapped pants. **1899** H. LAWSON *Autobiogr. & Other Writings* (1972) 39 Stockmen wore strapped trousers... Rip the side and 'tween-leg seams of a pair of pants, take the back out altogether and put a new one in of a different colour .. for riding.

strata, *pl.* [Pl. of *stratum* a layer.] Used *attrib.* to designate a system of registering ownership of strata of air space in multi-storey buildings, esp. in the Comb. **strata title** (see quot. 1971).

1961 *Act* (N.S.W.) no. 17 Sect. 2, 'Strata plan' means a plan which .. shows the whole or any part of the land comprised therein as being divided into two or more strata. **1962** A.F. RATH et al. *Strata Titles* 11 The provisions .. have been criticised .. as casting on persons wishing to search a strata title the unnecessary burden of inspecting an additional document. **1971** CONRICK & THOMSON *Sale Real Property N.S.W.* 10 The Strata Titles Act enables land to be divided horizontally as well as by the traditional vertical division. It enables a party to hold ownership of a slice of airspace many feet above the ground, as distinct from ownership of the ground itself. **1982** *Advertiser* (Adelaide) 8 Aug. 33/5 Impressive single storey strata title home unit. **1986** *Austral. Financial Rev.* (Sydney) 4 Mar. 27/1 This elegant building has been completely renewed throughout to provide a total of 16 strata title office suites.

strawberry box. A cardboard container provided in aircraft, ships, etc., as a receptacle for vomit.

[N.Z. **1936** 'R. HYDE' *Passport to Hell* 93 The ship struck heavy weather... Up galley stairs and down corridors, life just one strawberry-box after another.] **1948** *Gremlin Jottings* (Canberra) May 4 Paper bags and cardboard 'strawberry boxes' are in frequent demand and use. **1965** G. MCINNES *Road to Gundagai* 35 All about us they were vomiting into 'strawberry boxes' while we raced up and down deck.

straw hat. A dandy. Also *attrib.* as **straw hat push,** the 'smart set', and **straw hatter.**

1902 *Truth* (Sydney) 30 Mar. 5/3 So-called 'respectably connected' persons of the class euphemistically known as 'the Straw Hat Push'. **1903** *Ibid.* 25 Jan. 1/5 'Cashier required for leading house, with knowledge of ladies' underclothing.' This looks like a good job for one of the lascivious straw hat push. **1917** *Ibid.* 15 Apr. 9/4 Aspiring flappers and would-be straw-hatters .. are a type I used to bump whilst in the police. **1930** H. REDCLIFFE *Yellow Cygnet* 20 'There ain't much of the 'straw 'at''—a slang phrase for dandy—'about that nipper.'

straw-necked ibis. [From the yellow straw-like neck plumage of the bird.] The predom. black and white wading bird *Threskiornis spinicollis*, chiefly of mainland Aust.

1841 *Port Phillip Patriot* 9 Aug. 4/3 Thousands of straw-necked Ibises (*Ibis spinicollis*), and of other species of the feathered race, were performing their allotted parts. **1845** L. LEICHHARDT *Jrnl. Overland Exped. Aust.* 19 July (1847) 334 Two straw-necked Ibises and seven ducks were shot. **1890** G.J. BROINOWSKI *Birds of Aust.* II. Pl. 26, The Straw-Necked Ibis has a most stately walk and dignified manner. **1912** *Emu* XII. 120 *Carphibis spinicollis.* Straw-necked Ibis .. very common. **1945** C. BARRETT *Austral. Bird Life* 54 The white ibis .. and the straw-necked ibis .. are widely spread and very abundant, the latter especially. **1962** B.W. LEAKE *Eastern Wheatbelt Wildlife* 78 Straw necked ibises were first seen (in large numbers) during the winter of 1892. **1979** D. LOCKWOOD *My Old Mates & I* 76 Straw-necked ibis and pied geese came in hundreds to the watered playing fields of Darwin where they might find worms and grubs.

streak. [Used elsewhere but recorded earliest in Aust.: see OEDS *sb.*[1] 4 b.] A tall, thin person.

[**1937** E. PARTRIDGE *Dict. Slang & Unconventional Eng.* 838 *Streak*, a very thin person: mostly Australian and N.Z.] **1941** S.J. BAKER *Pop. Dict. Austral. Slang* 73 *Streak*, a tall, lean person. **1946** J.J. FAHEY *Slim Sullivan hits Wallaby* 15 O.K., you long streak. You can try that again after the game. **1946** K. TENNANT *Lost Haven* 57 Thank goodness he hadn't told that long gabbling streak about Cherry. **1957** D. NILAND *Call me when Cross turns Over* 25 'Gorblimey, haven't they buddy well hanged you yet?'

greeted Fiddley Dick. 'Be quiet, you miserable streak,' said Resurrection Jim, grinning. **1967** *Kings Cross Whisper* (Sydney) xl. 4/5 *Streak of misery*, a tall thin person, not necessarily an unhappy one. **1972** W. WATKINS *Don't wait for Me* 3 Arsey Arkin .. was a goof. A long streak.

strength. [Spec. use of *strength* the demonstrative force of an argument; chiefly Austral. and N.Z.]

1. With **of**: the point or meaning of; the truth about; STRONG 1.

[N.Z. **1906** *N.Z. Truth* (Wellington) 26 Aug. 5 Wants a friend to get the strength of things.] **1908** H. FLETCHER *Dads & Dan* 112 'So yous thinks I'se wore out .. an' past patchin' an' mendin'?' 'That's about ther strength uv it.' **1926** K.S. PRICHARD *Working Bullocks* 136 'Now', she continued .. 'I'll just give you the strength of Red Burke.' **1939** K. TENNANT *Foveaux* 154, I see there's been some sort of a league or committee or something on the move... What's the strength of it? Any idea? **1950** F.J. HARDY *Power without Glory* 566, I told her she could have it. She said you had refused... What's the strength of it? **1963** A.E. FARRELL *Vengeance* 16 What's the strength of it all? Are you divorced or separated? **1977** B. SCOTT *My Uncle Arch* 119, I asked him what was the strength of him asking the Union meeting before he asked the blokes on the job. **1980** G. DUTTON *Wedge-Tailed Eagle* 93 What's the strength of this Nikolai? .. I mean, what sort of a bloke is he?

2. In the phr. **to get the strength of,** to comprehend; *to get the strong of*, see STRONG 2.

1904 H. FLETCHER *Dads Wayback* 34 About this forchin-tellin' game; it takes er bit o' knowin' ter get ther full strength of it. **1915** A. WRIGHT *Sport from Hollowlog Flat* 14 From Grif he got the 'strength' of the 'good thing'. It was Stars and Stripes, a pony. **1921** E.F. O'FERRALL *Bodger & the Boarders* 52, I see that Barnstorer bloke an' got the strength of the whole thing. **1947** V. PALMER *Hail Tomorrow* 20 You've about got the strength of it, Mick. **1969** *Advertiser* (Adelaide) 12 May 5/4 Get the strength of this: You talk about bankos and trunks.

stretcher. [Transf. use of *stretcher* camp-bed, spec. in a military or hospital context: see OED(S *sb.* 9.] A (folding) bed, made of canvas, hessian, etc., on a frame: see quot. 1857. Also **stretcher-bed.**

1834 N.S.W. Magistrates' Deposition Bk. 29 Oct., I found fault with the Prisoner for using a Stretcher which I kept for the use of my guests—without Leave and gave him Permission to sleep in the Dairy. **1840** A. RUSSELL *Tour through Austral. Colonies* 162 The beds used in the most of those stations I visited, were what are called *stretchers*, being similarly constructed to a camp stool, and about six feet in length. **1857** J. ASKEW *Voyage Aust. & N.Z.* 145 Here I first became acquainted with a 'stretcher', which is a very convenient kind of bed, made by nailing a piece of canvass to two pieces of wood, about six feet long and three inches square, these rest upon legs made in the form of the letter X, and are fastened at the crossings by an iron bolt, so as to allow them to separate as far as the canvass will permit. **1869** E.C. BOOTH *Another England* 21 He threw himself on his stretcher (for so the bedstead of the bush is called), and gave himself up to a few minutes' day-dreaming. **1888** J. FREEMAN *Lights & Shadows* 242 A stretcher, flock mattress, and two blankets comprised the bedding. **1916** T. WARLOW *By Mirage & Mulga* 72 McInverness .. lay on a stretcher-bed made up on the side verandah. **1934** 'E.N. SPEER' *Destiny* 245 An unused stretcher-bed was leaning against the wall of the verandah. **1961** *Bulletin* (Sydney) 14 Oct. 30/2 The camp is an open-air job with stretcher-beds, trucks and refrigerators standing about under the sparse trees. **1978** D. STUART *Wedgetail View* 120 He waited, sitting on Colin's stretcher while Martin washed the dishes.

striated pardalote. The small bird *Pardalotus striatus* of all States, having a black crown sometimes streaked with white.

1844 J. GOULD *Birds of Aust.* (1848) II. Pl. 38 *Pardalotus striatus* .. Striated Pardalote. **1896** B. SPENCER *Rep. Horn Sci. Exped. Central Aust.* II. 68 Striated Pardalote .. were shot in mallee scrub near Stevenson's Creek. **1945** C. BARRETT *Austral. Bird Life* 181 The striated pardalote (*P[ardalotus] striatus*) occurs in Tasmania as well as southern Victoria and South Australia. **1984** E. ROLLS *Celebration of Senses* 77 The little Striated Pardalote beats out its two notes astonishingly loudly.

strife. [Weakened use of *strife* contention, dispute.]

a. Trouble, disgrace, difficulty; conflict.

1931 'BRENT OF BIN BIN' *Back to Bool Bool* 320 Laleen does not want to come back here and make strife amongst her relatives. **1937** *Bulletin* (Sydney) 17 Mar. 20/2 If 'Dipso' waits until he is well and truly sprung and then swallows about a pint of ice-cream he can have a really enjoyable afternoon and then go home to face the strife without a wobble in his walk or speech. **1952** C. SIMPSON *Come away, Pearler* 223 You get a fair amount of strife in a place like this, but the pearlers aren't a bad bunch—three or four bad hats—you know. **1960** *N.T. News* (Darwin) 5 Feb. 3/2 Many outback roads were cut and some are still impassable, but the strife in the path of the rain was nothing when compared to the benefits. **1968** D. O'GRADY *Bottle of Sandwiches* 16 The bull-dust gave us some strife for a while. **1979** S.W. DUTHIE *Fidlers Creek* 45 Racing can .. cause of a bit of domestic strife. **1985** *Harden-Murrumburrah Express* 3 Oct. 15/4 First born child—I gave you life, Why do you cause me all this strife?

b. Esp. in the phr. **in(to) strife.**

1950 J. MORRISON *Port of Call* 174 It isn't good for a bloke to be on his own when he's in strife. **1959** D. HEWETT *Bobbin Up* 198 They'd really be in strife now, both out of a job and the venetians to pay off and owing all that on the house. **1963** J. O'GRADY *Things they do to You* 189 A fellow .. got into strife through eating crayfish. **1972** J. DE HOOG *Skid Row Dossier* 60, I met my wife at Newtown when I was 23 and I got her inta strife, so we got married. **1976** B. HOWARD-SMITH *Adult Gift Bk. Poetry* 20 Well I'd better be off if I value my life Can't cross the missus Or I'll be in strife. **1986** *Canberra Times* 13 Feb. 1/4, I suggested .. that they complain to people higher up but they believed they would get into strife if they did that.

strike, *v.* [Fanciful var. of *strike me blind, dumb, lucky*, etc.: see OED(S *strike, v.* 46 c.]

a. Used as a mild oath, esp. in the phr. **strike me blue (dead, fat, handsome, pink, roan).**

1916 'MEN OF ANZAC' *Anzac Bk.* 127 An' then—oh, **strike me blue** an' pink—Then don't the Turkies swear! **1954** A. UPFIELD *Death of Lake* (1956) 142 'Strike me flamin' blue!' exploded MacLennon. **1976** C.D. MILLS *Hobble Chains & Greenhide* 177 Wally said, 'Strike me blue, I've ridden the bloody thing a thousand times. *Its seventeen miles.*' **1977** B. SCOTT *My Uncle Arch* 71 'Strike me blue,' said Angus. **1932** J.J. HARDIE *Cattle Camp* (1944) 188 **Strike me** flamin' **dead**! I could write all he knows about cattle on a fly's eye with a lump of charcoal! **1955** D. NILAND *Shiralee* 152 Strike me dead, I curl up inside a wool-pack, overcoat on .. and yet duggar me if I can sleep. **1974** J. GABY *Restless Waterfront* 228 The surprised wharfie nearly fell off the seat. 'Well, strike me dead!' **1978** R.H. CONQUEST *Dusty Distances* 132 Strike me dead, it's young Ginger! [**1891** **strike me fat**: 'SMILER' *Wanderings Simple Child* (ed. 3) 19 'Sailor Bill' was accorded the privilege of acting as taster, to see how the cooking was going on... At length the mariner declared that he'd be 'struck fat' if the 'Kake' wasn't just about ripe.] **1895** *Bulletin* (Sydney) 15/4 Lord strike me fat! what yer givin' us? **1915** *Ibid.* 7 Jan. 13/1 Them New Year resoloooshins! Strike me fat, A man's a mug wot takes on makin' vows. **1945** *Ibid.* 2 May 12/4 I'm headin' west. Milk bar! Strike me fat! **1955** D. NILAND *Shiralee* 92 God strike me fat! Look who's here! **1980** BRENNAN & WHITE *Keep Billy Boiling* 49 I've struck some bogs, and some glue-pot clogs, And some porridge heaps I've seen But, strike me fat! there's none like that From Bourbah to Bullagreen. **1955** N. PULLIAM *I traveled Lonely Land* 390 **Strike me handsome** .. an exclamation like our 'Well, for goodness sake', 'You don't say', etc. **1959** R. MOORE *Smiley roams Road* 17 Spare me days and strike me handsome. **1968** S. GORE *Holy Smoke* 28 'Well, strike me handsome!' he says. 'Young Joe, eh?' **1892** *Truth* (Sydney) 15 May 1/5 **Strike me pink** if I tell a lie. **1901** *Ibid.* 9 June 5/8 My colonial, you were blank shikkered last night; strike me pink, you were, mister. **1916** 'MEN OF ANZAC' *Anzac Bk.* 47 'E says: 'Strike me pink! But where's them Turks.' **1940** *Digger Yarns: Cream of 'Aussiosities'*, 'Strike me pink!' burst out the Digger, 'be a bit more—careful—you.' **1955** D. NILAND *Shiralee* 120 Strike me pink, Mac, you're not leaving? **1969** B. GARLAND *Pitt Street Prospector* 82 Strike me pink! These blokes don't give a man a chance. Do they? **1976** C.D. MILLS *Hobble Chains & Greenhide* 177 'Strike me pink,' he moaned, 'I haven't got a thing cooked,' and almost went into a flat spin. **1917** *All abaht It* (London) Feb. (1919) 12 **Strike me rone** .. I had to laugh. **1955** D. STIVENS *Ironbark Bill* 47 Strike me roan if we are! **1976** B. NORMAN *Bush Pilot* 246 Strike me roan. Here I am trying to find Georgetown and he asks me for his stethoscope... 'Yes, doctor, here it is.' **1982** *Overlander* Sept. 27 Strike me roan! It's a heap faster than Sydney's transport.

b. In the phr. **strike a light**: see LIGHT *n.* 2.

c. As **strike (me)!** *ellipt.* of phr. in sense a. above.

1915 C.J. DENNIS *Songs of Sentimental Bloke* 57 O, strike! I could 'a' blubbed before 'em all! But I sat tight. **1918** *Huon Times* (Franklin) 2 Aug. 3/1 I'll bet you £800, strike me if I won't. **1921** F. GROSE *Rough Y.M. Bloke* 26 Strike me! Yer should er seen the feed they slapped up that night! **1935** K. TENNANT *Tiburon* 27 'There's me an' the missus an' the kid.' 'Strike! Don't stand there in the rain. Bring 'em in.' **1950** K.S. PRICHARD *Winged Seeds* 261 'Strike!' Bill laughed. **1954** *Coast to Coast 1953–54* 78 'Strike me', says Time-Table Tommy, 'things has changed all right and no mistake.' **1968** S. GORE *Holy Smoke* 110 *Strike!* Expression of astonishment, even awe.

strike camp. *Hist.* A camp formed by striking shearers; *union camp*, see UNION.

1891 *Great Qld. Strike* (United Pastoralists Assoc. Qld.) 14 During the present strike .. 'sundowners' are nowhere to be seen on the stations in Queensland... They are to be found in the strike camps, living on the strike funds. **1899** *Bulletin* (Sydney) 19 Aug. 32/1 They had avoided strike-camps as far as possible; they weren't quite 'stiff', and scorned to eat Union tucker while they could buy—or steal—from the squatters. **1901** *Illawarra Mercury* 5 Jan. 2/6 Pumpkins have been the mainstay of several shearers' strike-camps. **1908** *Bulletin* (Sydney) 23 Jan. 14/2 He fell into a strike camp, where he was tuckered for nearly six months. **1944** R. BEDFORD *Naught to Thirty-Three* 249 The strike-camps in the bush were models of discipline. **1963** D. WHITINGTON *Mile Pegs* 65 There were no shearers' cheques, because the regular men were living in strike camps or the cities .. and the scabs .. were being rushed away. **1982** L. MATHER *First Notes of Drum* 42 Trouble broke out on Meteor Downs... The bushmen struck and formed a strike camp down on the creek, away from the homestead, from whence they could sit the dispute out and picket the shearing shed at the same time.

Strine /straın/, *a.* and *n.* [Repr. an alleged Austral. pronunc. of *Australian*, coined by A.A. Morrison (b. 1911) in 1964.]

A. *adj.* Australian.

1964 *Sydney Morning Herald* 19 Dec. 13/6 (*heading*) New light on the Strine language, by Afferbeck Lauder, Professor of Strine Studies, University of Sinny. **1979** B. HUMPHRIES *Bazza comes into his Own*, This is your actual Strine wine bar mate. **1983** *Weekend Austral.* (Sydney) 8 Oct. 3/7 The flowers are 'strine', with arrangements of banksia and bush flora.

B. *n.*

a. An Australian.

1964 *Sydney Morning Herald* 19 Dec. 13/5 Selected translations of everyday words .. will be of interest .. also to overseas vistas and to the many New Strines in our mist. **1965** *Oz* (Sydney) 17 June 1 (*heading*) The Strines they are a-changing.

b. Australian English; a stylized representation of Australian speech characterized by excessive assimilation, elision, metanalysis, etc.

1965 *Sydney Morning Herald* 6 Jan. 1/10 The first advertisement in pure Strine reached our 'classified' department yesterday. It advertised a 'gloria soame' of 14 squares, with amenities. **1967** E. HUXLEY *Their Shining Eldorado* 30 There was a craze for Strine when I was in Sydney—or Sinny, as it is rendered in this ear-teasing tongue. **1972** R. BOYD *Great Austral. Dream* 30 Many will entertain you, as an Overseas Visitor, by adopting an especially exaggerated twist in vowel sounds in order to demonstrate what we jokingly call 'Strine', because every Australian, with characteristic modesty, believes that he himself does not possess an Australian Accent. **1974** ADAMSON & HANFORD *Zimmer's Essay* 20 Helm's strine shifted into a put-on pommie drawl. **1979** *Platypus* Nov. 17 Australia is a multi-racial society and newly-arrived settlers need some time before they have a substantial grasp of English or, as it is becoming known, Australian-English or 'strine'. **1983** M. FIELD *Oz Shrink Lit.* 76 Professor Afferbeck Lauder, That intrepid word-hoarder, With the guile of a dingo Shrink-litted our lingo, Made four syllables combine And christened it Strine.

Hence **strined** *ppl. a.*, Australianized.

1974 R. ROBINSON *Give it Bloody Go, Mate!* 74 'Can't you understand bloody English?' Well I thought I could, but when it was 'strined' like this it was a job.

string, *v.*[1] [Spec. use of *string* to move in a string.]

a. *intr.* Of a mob of sheep or cattle: to stretch out in a straggling line; to move as in a file. Also with **off** and **out,** and as *ppl. a.*

1876 J.A. EDWARDS *Gilbert Gogger* 144 A great number of the sheep had moved from off their camping ground, and were stringing away into the darkness of the bush. **1889** F. CRAWFORD *Native Companion Songster* 21 We are home at the yards, but the cattle may string. **1898** *Bulletin* (Sydney) 1 Jan. 3/2 You can see the front lot stringing, but the tail is out of sight. **1907** *Ibid.* 11 Apr. 15/3 Cattle stringing off here!! **1922** J. LEWIS *Fought & Won* 57 Although the cattle were lying down, we thought it well to be on the alert in case any of them should 'string off'. **1933** A.J. COTTON *With Big Herds in Aust.* 82 The two leading men take care not to close them in too much, otherwise they would walk too fast and, what is termed, 'string out'. **1938** BRIGGS & HARRIS *Joysticks & Fiddlesticks* 162 There is a circling mob of overlanding cattle, which . . break out into long, stringing flight. **1944** *Bulletin* (Sydney) 4 Oct. 15/2 He was tapping at a stone . . when the ballies strung past. **1954** H.G. LAMOND *Manx Star* 261 Stock 'string' when they walk in a long line.

b. *trans.* To cause (sheep or cattle) to move in a line. Also with **off** and **out.**

1920 J.N. MACINTYRE *White Aust.* 142 Two other members of the party . . were some distance away stringing the mob through the narrow gorge. **1923** *Bulletin* (Sydney) 4 Jan. 22/2 If you have a long dry stage to do, start early and let them get over the bad part as soon as possible. It may be advisable to string them. **1944** *Ibid.* 19 July 13/4 Charlie . . stringing the ballies for a count . . discovered two were missing. **1938** F. BLAKELEY *Hard Liberty* 169 At break of day they strung the cattle out towards the well. **1950** I. SHACKCLOTH *Call of Kimberleys* 51 Stringing out the sheep to the water-holes occupied long wearysome hours. **1960** R.S. PORTEOUS *Cattleman* 88 They were stringing the cattle off the dinner camp when the policeman rode up.

Hence **string** *n.*, a line of sheep or cattle.

1931 F.D. DAVISON *Man-Shy* (1961) 24 The cattle, in little strings and squads, were grazing their way in towards the waterholes. **1945** E. MITCHELL *Speak to Earth* 49 Slowly the strings and mobs of cattle collect. . . The 'fats' are chosen and carefully cut out of the mob.

string, *v.*[2] [Spec. use of orig. U.S. slang *string* to fool, deceive: see OED(S *v.* 15.] *trans.* With **on**: to deceive (someone), to 'string along'.

[N.Z. **1881** A. BATHGATE *Waitaruna* 142 A barmaid . . makes herself agreeable to those who frequent the house, and so she 'strings them on' and induces them to spend their money there.] **1888** 'R. BOLDREWOOD' *Robbery under Arms* III. 81 Mr Hamilton waited for about an hour so as to be sure they weren't stringing him on to go into the open to be potted at. ***c* 1907** W.C. CHANDLER *Darkest Adelaide* 1, *Don't worry!* On all Private Complaints, *male* and *female*, Consult *free* the Successful Practitioner, *Prof. A. Mills* who will Guarantee a cure in each case he undertakes. No stringing on, but a Speedy Cure always. **1970** J.S. GUNN in W.S. Ramson *Eng. Transported* 61 *String on*, deceive.

stringy.

1. Abbrev. of STRINGYBARK 1. Also *attrib.*

1901 *Bulletin* (Sydney) 7 Dec. 20/3 It was a small, two-roomed, stringy shanty, built near the foot-track. **1906** *Ibid.* 21 June 16/1 Snug in tent and stringy-shack the eight-hour sweaters snore. **1916** *Ibid.* 28 Sept. 24/4, I saw an old stringy bashed to pieces that yielded 2500 posts. **1945** *Coast to Coast 1944* 144 The low scrub and fringing bloodwoods and stringies melted into the night.

2. *Obs.* Used *attrib.* in the sense of STRINGYBARK 2.

1845 *Star* (Sydney) 25 Oct. 1/2 Then they shouted—'Braveo Billy! You're a right good, proper mark; There's no stringy stuff about you, You're the real iron-bark.'

3. *Obs.* Abbrev. of STRINGYBARK 3.

1871 *Austral. Town & Country Jrnl.* (Sydney) 1 Apr. 389/3 Its [*sic*] not everybody that does care about 'stringy', whether it be the real Tooth's, or Castlemine, or Parramatta, or even the renowned 'wallop' of the Western line. . . I well remember a governor of Victoria regaling his guests at the Queen's Birth-night ball, with 'Murphy's entire', the stringy of his colony. **1899** 'T. BLUEGUM' *Backblocks' Parson* 172 In the centre of the building was situated a public bar, furnished with strong liquors answering to the euphemisms, 'Stringy', 'Shandy', Tanglefoot', etc.

stringybark.

1. [See quot. 1904.] Any of many trees, chiefly of s.e. mainland Aust., of the genus *Eucalyptus* (fam. Myrtaceae) having a characteristically thick, rough, persistent, long-fibred bark; the bark or wood of the tree. Also with distinguishing epithet, as **red, swamp, white, yellow** (see under first element). Also *attrib.*, esp. as **stringybark tree.**

1799 D. COLLINS *Acct. Eng. Colony N.S.W.* (1802) II. 238 The remains of a canoe made of the stringy bark were lying upon the shore. **1801** *HRA* (1915) 1st Ser. III. 414 The finest stringy-bark and black-butted blue-gum trees I ever saw. **1809** *Sydney Gaz.* 28 May, Both the dead man's hands being to all appearance bound behind with a band of stringy bark. **1823** *Hobart Town Gaz.* 21 June, To be Sold about 1100 feet of seasoned 2 inch Stringy Bark Plants. **1827** P. CUNNINGHAM *Two Yrs. in N.S.W.* I. 202 If a red cedar drops upon a stringy-bark-boarded floor, it will smoulder away without bursting into flame. **1854** G.H. HAYDON *Austral. Emigrant* 99 The hut was roofed with broad sheets of stringey bark. **1873** J.C.F. JOHNSON *Christmas on Carringa* 13 The fire's a coming . . and'll be among the messmates and stringy-barks in less than half an hour. **1897** *Bulletin* (Sydney) 11 Dec. 7/2 Through stringy-bark and blue-gum, and box and pine we go; New camps are stretching 'cross the plains the routes of Cobb and Co. **1904** J.H. MAIDEN *Notes on Commercial Timbers N.S.W.* 10 The term 'Stringybark' is applied to trees having thick, fibrous bark—bark which is comparatively loose in texture, and which (for a Eucalyptus bark) possesses considerable tenacity. **1914** C.H.S. MATTHEWS *Bill* 54 He chooses a good, straight, likely looking 'box' or 'stringy-bark'—these are two well-known Australian eucalyptus trees. **1928** M.E. FULLERTON *Austral. Bush* 108 Stringy-bark (the outer covering of the stringybark-tree) was a great friend to the early-day settler. Of it he built his bush house, roof and walls. **1950** G. FARWELL *Surf Music* 45 The sappy eucalyptus smell of stringybark under his cross-cut saw. **1965** G. MCINNES *Road to Gundagai* 78 A coupler of clothesline with skinned stringy-bark props. **1972** ANDERSON & BLAKE *J.S. Neilson* 19 Margaret Neilson cooked over an open fire under the stringy-bark chimney. **1981** Q. WILD *Honey Wind* 32 The Stringybark was used when the wet season came. Then the bark could easily be stripped from the trees. **1986** *Weekend Austral. Mag.* (Sydney) 4 Oct. 16/5 Stringy-bark honey from the Tumut district of N.S.W., a strongish, medium amber honey, good for cooking, with a nice peppery finish in the throat.

2. Used allusively as an emblem of the unsophisticated, the remote, and the rustic. Freq. *attrib.*, passing into *adj.*

1833 *N.S.W. Mag.* (Sydney) I. 171 The workmanship of which I beg you will not scrutinize, as I am but, to use a colonial expression, '*a stringy-bark carpenter*'. **1836** J.F. O'CONNELL *Residence Eleven Yrs. New Holland* 49 Let us suppose the suitor an old 'stringy-bark', such being the soubriquet in which inland settlers rejoice. **1845** *Bell's Life in Sydney* 18 Jan. 2/1 The 'stringy bark' cove, sooner than not have a turn-up with this Liverpool 'Achilles', would fight him for 'love'. **1861** H. EARLE *Ups & Downs* 59 She would never have had the bad taste to prefer a stringy bark like me to such a fine-looking, first-class fellow as yourself. **1890** 'R. BOLDREWOOD' *Colonial Reformer* II. 249 I'd give a tenner out of my own pocket they was all out of that and back at Bowning or some other stringy-bark hole as is fit for 'em. **1892** H. NISBET *Bushranger's Sweetheart* 30 He was a larikin of the larikins, this tiny Stringy Bark, who haunted my thoughts. **1897** *Worker* (Sydney) 30 Oct. 3/4 The stringy-bark party will expire with this Parliament. **1914** E. DYSON *Spats' Fact'ry* 149 So obviously from the bush you might have combed the stringy-bark from his whiskers. **1966** *Southerly* ii. 110 Fish in the creek, rabbits, possums and roos to trap . . he was happy in his mindless, stringybark seclusion. **1978** SAW & MILLBANK *Back to Back Tango* 35 Six or seven generations earlier his parents . . had been among the first ticket-of-leavers to set up stringybark grog-shops in the bush between Sydney Town and Rose Hill.

3. Beer, esp. of poor quality.

1848 *Bell's Life in Sydney* 13 May 2/3 The Drunkards' Sheet at the Police-office on Monday numbered forty male and female sacrificants to hard stuff, stringy bark, and gin and bitterness. **1873** S.H. BANKS *Vice & Victims Sydney* 18 They are glad to spend, perhaps, their last threepence in a pint of 'stringy bark'. **1874** *Illustr. Sydney News* 22 Aug. 10/1 Tattoed dames . . hobbled unsteadily to Johnny Ward's for the inevitable pint of 'stringy-bark'. **1891** H. NISBET *Colonial Tramp* II. 30 Oceans of 'stringy-bark' and adulterated brandy. **1973** J. MURRAY *Larrikins* 43 Beer . . varied, from 'stringy-bark' to 'colonial', and was invariably blamed for much of the drunkenness in the cities.

4. Comb. **stringybark forest, range, slab.**

1837 H. WATSON *Lecture on S.A.* (1838) 19, I rode to the **stringy-bark forest.** **1851** *Illustr. Austral. Mag.* (Melbourne) Feb. 72, I found myself a considerable distance from home, in a dense stringy-bark forest; which from the effects of a recent bush-fire, presented a dark and dismal appearance. **1976** *Ecos* vii. 5 In . . the stringybark forests of south-eastern Australia . . fuel quantities may exceed 50 tonnes per hectare after only 15 fire-free years. **1841** *S. Austral. Mag.* July 9 Our **stringy bark ranges,** which are considered the most barren land we have, would answer excellently [*sc.* as land for vineyards] when cleared. **1861** 'OLD BUSHMAN' *Bush Wanderings* 46 It is principally found, I think, in the high Stringy-bark ranges. **1893** 'PIONEER' *Reminisc. Austral. Early Life* 35 Difficult to shepherd a flock of sheep to advantage in, being composed of stringybark and box ranges. **1838** T. WALKER *Month in Bush Aust.* 6 The offices are . . mostly built of stone or brick . . not made of the uncouth, rough **stringy-bark slabs,** of which such buildings are usually made in the colony. **1949** G. FARWELL *Traveller's Tracks* 27 This is not to suggest that there is some inherent virtue in stringybark slabs.

5. Special Comb. **stringybark beef,** tough beef; **cockatoo, settler,** a farmer of small means; **squatter,** see quot.

1848 *Bell's Life in Sydney* 19 Aug. 2/4 Beating up for recruits among the voters of those shady and sequestered regions so dear to the devotees of blady-grass, pork, and **stringy bark beef.** **1867** A.K. COLLINS *Waddy Mundoee* 16 Don't ye send more stringy bark beef to me than to anyone here? **1905** A.B. PATERSON *Old Bush Songs* 45 The old cocky, he grew jealous, and he thumped me black and blue, And he drove me off without a rap—the **stringy-bark cockatoo.** **1958** R. WARD *Austral. Legend* (1970) 5 Dad and Dave were not pastoral workers, bushmen proper, but poor selectors, 'stringybark cockatoos', who were sneered at. **1976** B. SCOTT *Complete Bk. Austral. Folk Lore* 19 These were the selectors, the stringybark cockatoos, the failed goldseekers turned settlers, battling it out on the thin edge of survival. **1836** 'W. R-s' *Fell Tyrant* 46 Poorest of all is the **stringybark settler.** **1845** J. TUCKER *Jemmy Green in Aust.* (1955) 52 He's got the regular cut of a stringy-bark settler now from top to toe. **1853** C.R. READ *What I heard, saw, & Did* 53 Imagining a 'stringy bark settler' to be some savage or other in the forest. **1864** *Illustr. Sydney News* 16 June 10/1 This hamlet . . consisted then, whatever it may be now, of about a dozen little huts or shanties inhabited by what are termed . . 'Stringybark settlers'. **1862** C. MUNRO *Fern Vale* I. 47 One or two settlers of minor importance, and dignified with the title of '**stringy bark**' or 'cockatoo **squatters**'.

striped honeyeater. The honeyeater *Plectorhyncha lanceolata* of inland e. mainland Aust.

1898 E.E. MORRIS *Austral Eng.* 199 Striped H[oney-eater]—*Plectorhyncha lanceolata.* **1909** *Emu* VIII. 242, I was also able to approximate some of the notes to those of the Striped Honey-eater. **1929** A.H. CHISHOLM *Birds & Green Places* 47 The striped and spiny-cheeked honey-eaters. **1945** C. BARRETT *Austral. Bird Life* 154 Greyish-brown, with blackish-brown stripes on the upper surface, the striped honeyeater . . may easily be recognized even though one is unfamiliar with its cheerful, whistling call. **1976** *Reader's Digest Compl. Bk. Austral.*

Birds 462 The striped honeyeater .. has a generally streaked appearance, with .. long and spiky feathers on the throat and upper breast.

stripey. Pl. **stripeys, stripies.** Any of several (usu. horizontally) striped marine fish, incl. *Latris lineata* (see TRUMPETER *n.*[1] 1), *Microcanthus strigatus* of s.w., n., and e. Aust. and the skipjack tuna, *Katsuwonus pelamis.*

1924 LORD & SCOTT *Synopsis Vertebrate Animals Tas.* 71 The Real or Tasmanian Trumpeter, .. is often referred to as the 'Stripey'. **1965** *Austral. Encycl.* IX. 52 It [*sc. Latris lineata*] is one of the choicest and commonest food-fish in the Tasmanian market, where it is often called 'stripey' on account of the longitudinal bars on the side of the body. **1978** N. COLEMAN *Austral. Fisherman's Fish Guide* 125 A common resident of tropical coral reefs, the 'stripey' is mostly encountered in schools. **1980** —— *Austral. Sea Fishes* 180 Stripeys swim in small, closely compacted schools... These fish are easy to keep in aquaria. **1986** *Canberra Chron.* 29 Jan. 19/2 The stripies are around but mostly staying well out, beyond the Four Mile.

stripper. [Spec. use of *stripper* a machine for stripping.]

1. A machine used to harvest grain: see quot. 1927.

1867 *Official Rec. Intercolonial Exhib. Australasia* 381 The Jurors award *medals* to the Wind Engine and Stripper, and *honourable mention* to Thresher and Smut Machines. **1875** *Illustr. Adelaide News* xiv. 7/1 In these illustrations the manner in which the wheat crop is harvested in South Australia is shown. The first engraving represents the strippers at work. These machines are adapted only for localities where extreme heat prevails during the harvest season. **1880** *Argus* (Melbourne) 13 Jan. 7/6 The Torrumbarry Plains are now quite bare, and the cattle and sheep are dropping for want of pasture. The wasteful policy of using only strippers is now plainly demonstrated, as there is not even straw to feed the cattle upon. **1894** J.K. ARTHUR *Kangaroo & Kauri* 40 The 'stripper' is employed, which plucks off the ears of corn, leaving the straw standing. **1922** J. LEWIS *Fought & Won* 6 The first strippers used in South Australia were drawn by bullocks, and had a long steering pole at the back of the machine. **1927** T.S. GROSER *Lure of Golden West* 144 The stripper is an enormous box-like machine, with spiked prongs or teeth projecting in front, which, drawn through the cornfield, pluck the ears from the stalks. **1946** A.J. HOLT *Wheat Farms Vic.* 1 Australia has made some notable contributions to the world pool of agricultural technology. These include the stripper. **1962** E. IRVIN *Early Inland Agric.* 66 McKay invented his harvester in 1883. It was a direct descendent of John Ridley's stripper, invented in South Australia some forty years earlier. **1981** A.B. FACEY *Fortunate Life* 66 The only method of harvesting was to strip the crop with a machine called a stripper. This had a comb arrangement that could be lowered or raised according to the height of the crop and it had to be kept just below the grain heads.

2. Special Comb. **stripper harvester,** a machine which harvests grain and frees it of chaff: see quot. 1979.

[**1885** *Vic. Govt. Gaz.* 12 June 1723 Patent for invention entitled 'Improvements in the raising and lowering of the front end of stripping and harvesting machines'.] **1891** *Australasian Ironmonger* Oct. 329 Stripper-harvester improvements... A revolving screen or separator arranged within the body or housing of a stripper-harvester or winnower, for separating the grain from chaff and unthreshed heads. **1906** *Cwlth. Parl. Papers* IV. 133 The stripper-harvester is described as a composite machine, made up of at least two distinct and pre-existing devices, viz., the stripper and the winnower. **1911** H.G. TURNER *First Decade Austral. Cwlth.* 125 Scheduling a scale of duties on stripper harvesters, Australian drills, and other agricultural machinery. **1978** A.E. COSH *Jumping Kangaroos* 20 The next invention was the complete stripper-harvester, which gathered and cleaned the grain while in motion. **1979** J. BIRMINGHAM et al. *Austral. Pioneer Technol.* 27 James Martin had already tried unsuccessfully to combine the stripper and winnower in one mobile machine. This was achieved by H.V. McKay in 1885, and in 1887 his new 'stripper-harvester' won a government prize for a reaping machine.

stroke. [Spec. use of *stroke* an amount of work: see OED *sb.*[1] 11.]

1. *Gold-mining.* In the phr. **to do a (good, great, fair) stroke,** to mine profitably.

1851 *Empire* (Sydney) 22 Oct. 282/6 The Wallaby is again getting into favour; and Pattison's Point, between the last named spot and the sheep station, has a few on it doing 'a great stroke'. **1852** *Ibid.* 23 Jan. 602/4 Washing tailings on the rich points is becoming very common, and many do a fair stroke at it. **1853** R.M. THOMAS *Present State Melbourne* 34 We hear occasionally of large nuggets being found, of men doing what is called *'the good stroke'*, or *'taking the trick'*—fortunes being made in a very short time. **1855** *Illustr. Sydney News* 28 Apr. 200/2 Waterford's party obtained fifteen ounces of gold during the week, and they expect to do a good stroke after they have finished their ground sluicing. **1856** *Moreton Bay Free Press* 18 Aug. 2/7 As regards my own party, we have been reported as doing a great stroke. Before last week we were clearing £6 per week; and last week we cleared seven ounces per man. **1859** *Colonial Mining Jrnl.* June 163/1 Yet many are quietly doing what is termed, in digging parlance, a very good 'stroke'. **1883** G.E. LOYAU *Personal Adventures* 16 Miners who had 'done a stroke', and whose claims were still being worked by their mates, came by.

2. In the collocation **government stroke**: see GOVERNMENT B. 4.

strong.

1. With **of**: STRENGTH 1.

1915 DREW & EVANS *Grafter* 54 'Hello, Grafter!' .. 'What's the strong of this? I thought you were fielding on the Outer?' **1919** A. WRIGHT *Game of Chance* 57, I knew the boy, and had the strong of him to a certain extent. **1922** C. DREW *Rogues & Ruses* 8 'Well, what's the strong of it all?' he questioned. **1938** X. HERBERT *Capricornia* 566 What's the strong of you? What's the questioning for? I've done nuthin. **1949** G. BERRIE *Morale* 27 On the outskirts of the crowd they stopped to draw breath, and the Bushman asked: 'What's the strong of all this?' **1968** S. GORE *Holy Smoke* 58 'That's about the strong of 'em,' he agreed. 'Pretty thick in the skull in the normal way, but cunnin' as sewer rats when they're trying to lumber someone under the Act.' **1976** D. IRELAND *Glass Canoe* 77 'Well, pants man,' the Great Lover said. 'What's the strong of you?' **1983** B. DAWE *Over Here, Harv!* 118 H-hey fellers... What's the strong of this—empty glasses? C'mon it's my shout. What're we having?

2. In the phr. **to get the strong of,** *to get the strength of,* see STRENGTH 2.

[N.Z. **1917** *Chrons. N.Z. Exped. Force* 19 Sept. 63 We sees a new stunt goin' on .. 'n we just halts for a second to get the strong of it.] **1923** C.E. SAYERS *Jumping Double* 50 Until you get the strong of the horse. **1950** G. FARWELL *Surf Music* 92 Maybe it was over before they got the strong of it. The long fissure opened black rock above their heads. **1970** R. BEILBY *No Medals for Aphrodite* 268 'Is that all you're worrying about?' Harry sounded incredulous. 'You know, I'll never get the strong of you.'

strong-billed honeyeater. The honeyeater *Melithreptus validirostris* of Tasmania and adjacent islands.

1845 J. GOULD *Birds of Aust.* (1848) IV. Pl. 70, *Melithreptus validirostris* .. Strong-billed Honey-eater. **1903** *Emu* II. 207 *Melithreptus validirostris* (Strong-billed Honey-eater)—This powerfully built bird is ever on the move. **1945** C. BARRETT *Austral. Bird Life* 153 The black-headed honeyeater .. and the strong-billed honeyeater .. are restricted to Tasmania and Bass Strait islands. **1976** *Reader's Digest Compl. Bk. Austral. Birds* 490 The strong-billed honeyeater finds larval and adult insects by prizing bark off trees with its stout bill.

strongfish. The greyish marine fish *Dactylophora nigricans* of s. Aust.; TILLYWURTI.

1924 LORD & SCOTT *Synopsis Vertebrate Animals Tas.* 70 Butter fish (of Tasmania) .. is known in New South Wales as the Dusky Morwong, and in South Australia as the Strong Fish or Tillywurti. **1963** B. CROPP *Handbk. for Skindivers* 116 Butterfish (*Dactylopagrus morwong*). This is the Victorian name for the dusky morwong, which inhabits Victoria, Western Australia, Tasmania and South Australia, the latter state giving it the name of strongfish. **1980** N. COLEMAN *Austral. Sea Fishes* 217 Dusky morwong, strongfish .. *Dactylophora nigricans.*

Stuart's bean tree. [f. the name of the explorer John McDouall *Stuart* (1815–1866) + BEAN TREE.] The deciduous tree *Erythrina vespertilio* (fam. Fabaceae) of n. Aust., having a corky bark and red pea-flowers. See also BEAN TREE.

1873 W.C. GOSSE *Rep. & Diary Central & Western Exped.* (1974) 3 Country still sandy, but not so thickly timbered. Noticed some fine specimens of Stuart's bean-tree. **1896** B. SPENCER *Rep. Horn Sci. Exped. Central Aust.* IV. 104 Occasionally, however, rather pretty necklaces are worn of the vermilion-red fresh, or yellow bleached, seeds of Stuart's Bean Tree (*Erythrina vespertilio*). **1903** H. BASEDOW *Jrnl. Govt. N.-W. Exped.* 12 Apr. (1914) 61 Mr McGuire, the overseer, has successfully grown two specimens of Stuart's Bean Tree (*Erythrina*) from seeds collected in the Northern Territory. **1936** C. CHEWINGS *Back in Stone Age* 6 The trays, troughs, and shields were mostly made from the light, soft wood of that beautiful drooping willow-like tree commonly known as Stuart's bean-tree. **1955** DEAN & CARELL *Dust for Dancers* 123 The natives call the bean tree Yinendi .. and it is sometimes known among Europeans as Stuart's Bean Tree. Its colourful red berries are not edible.

stubble quail. [See quot. 1846.] The bird *Coturnix pectoralis*, chiefly of s. Aust., having predom. grey-brown plumage with pale and dark streaks.

1846 J. GOULD *Birds of Aust.* (1848) V. Pl. 88, The chief food of this species is grain, seeds and insects, the grain as a matter of course being only procured in cultivated districts; and hence the name of Stubble Quail has been given to it by the colonists of Van Diemen's Land, from the great numbers that visit the fields after the harvest is over. **1861** 'OLD BUSHMAN' *Bush Wanderings* 106 We used to kill a large variety of the common quail, which we called the *Stubble Quail.* **1912** *Emu* XII. 118 Stubble Quail .. interesting birds in captivity. **1945** C. BARRETT *Austral. Bird Life* 67 The stubble quail (*Coturnix pectoralis*), chief victim of quail shooters, ranges widely over the mainland. **1980** *Ecos* xxvi. 29/2 There is a case for postponing the opening of the season for shooting stubble quail in Victoria and South Australia.

stubby.

1. a. A short, squat beer bottle, esp. one with a capacity of 375 ml.; the contents of such a bottle. See also *Darwin stubby* DARWIN. Also **stubby bottle.**

1966 J. IGGULDEN *Summer's Tales* 123 Drinking beer from small, cold stubbies. **1967** *Kings Cross Whisper* (Sydney) xli. 5/1 Darwin kids get a free stubby of either Vic. or Swan at lunch-time. **1970** *Bulletin* (Sydney) 16 May 22/1 The stubbie is one of the most malevolent inventions of the decade. **1975** *Ibid.* 3 May 42/1 The entrance to his establishment is a 20-foot high glass tower made entirely of stubbies... He has used only standard South Australian stubbies. **1978** C. RUHEN *Crocodile* 79 Catching Switch Gale's eye behind the bar, he grinned broadly, and winked. She smiled back at him, and snapped some more stubbies from the glass-fronted refrigator. **1984** *Canberra Times* 11 Apr. 14/9, I killed a gin at Mount Isa in September. I don't feel sorry for them. I carved her up about the neck with a stubby bottle.

b. Special Comb. **stubby cooler, holder,** a casing made of an insulating material, in which a stubby is held while the contents are being drunk.

1984 *Tourist: Ansett Airlines Mag.* Jan. 11 An Oz flag or that even more patriotic emblem, a folding **stubby cooler.** **1981** *Woman's Day* (Sydney) 9 Sept. 45/3 When we arrived to visit our son and daughter-in-law after a long trip, our son offered his father a stubby bottle of beer and his wife produced a **stubby holder**, saying, 'Here, Dad, put your beer in this.' And that is what he did—literally. Then he yelled, 'How silly can you get! This so-and-so thing has holes in it.' **1983** *Austral.* (Sydney) 14 Feb. 4/7 When campaigning on York Peninsula, Mr Thomson hands out stubby holders which proclaim: 'The North is Thomson Territory.'

2. *pl.* The proprietary name of a brand of shorts.

1973 *Austral. Official Jrnl. Patents* (Canberra) 3602, A263,605... Class 25. Goods: outer wear. *Stubbies.* **1977** *Austral.* (Sydney) 7 Apr. 3/4 Stubbies—the football shorts with pockets—have become an international fashion... Although the Stubby is a very Australian name—thought of in the context of short shorts to go with short bottles of beer—Mr Phillips is confident they will become as American as apple pie. **1980** B. HORNADGE *Austral. Slanguage* 230 The word *stubbie* can also be the cause of confusion in another direction, as it is the slang word used for football shorts with pockets. **1984** P. JARRATT *Aussie* 38 The flabby, white bellies of the ockers who wear Stubbies and terry-towelling hats and leer at topless girls. **1984** A. LANE *Barbie-up-Back* 59 He met all the folks and he laughed at their jokes and he wore his short Stubbies with pride. **1986** *Bulletin* (Sydney) 22 Apr. 30/1 Men in Stubbies and heavy boots fell about laughing at the notion that a scribe might actually get his soft, white hands dirty.

stub fence. See quot. 1901. Also **stub wall.**

1882 ARMSTRONG & CAMPBELL *Austral. Sheep Husbandry* 179 A stake fence (by some erroneously called stub) may be erected. **1901** W.G. ACOCKS *Settlers' Synopsis Land Laws N.S.W.* 116 *Schedule of classes of fencing usually prescribed by local land boards...* A 'drop' or 'stub' fence, not less than four feet in height, composed of saplings or split rails not more than ten feet in length.. held between two posts or uprights of split or barked round timber.. and tied firmly at the tops with wire of not less than No. 8 gauge. **1911** *Bulletin* (Sydney) 30 Mar. 44/2 Here and there stub walls have been built as partial protection. **1920** G. SARGANT *Winding Track* 135 You see this spud paddock is fenced with a stub fence—rough slabs standing on end. **1980** M. DUGAN *Early Dreaming* 6 A stub fence is posts in the ground close together and touching. They are different heights, so the top is gap-toothed.

stud.

1. An Aboriginal woman as the source of a white man's sexual gratification. Also **stud gin.**

1929 K.S. PRICHARD *Coonardoo* (1961) 46 'No stud gins for mine—no matter what happens,' he swore. **1934** *Red Star* (Perth) 23 Mar. 2/3 The squatters cynically referred to the aboriginal women who had been forced to become objects for the gratification of their sexual desires as 'stud gins'. **1956** T. RONAN *Moleskin Midas* 134 Don't like putting on other people's blacks, but this stud said she wouldn't stay with you if the police took her back on the chain. **1958** W.E. HARNEY *Content to Lie* 45 The 'Rib-binder' was a neat chap and a great one for the 'studs', his name for the 'girls'. **1963** *Sociol. Rev.* (Keele) Mar. 40 It has been a common practice for a 'small' cattleman.. to settle down with his 'stud' (aboriginal wife or mistress) with the express purpose of 'breeding his own stockmen', raising a family of half-caste boys who can help him with droving and station work. **1981** NGABIDJ & SHAW *My Country of Pelican Dreaming* 45 Billy Weaber helped another bloke put a station there... My sister came with me to be his stud.

2. Special Comb. **stud book** *N.T.*, a nickname for the register of wards of the State.

1960 *N.T. News* (Darwin) 15 Jan. 9/3 Lucky that Bobby Daly Waters' name is not in the Register of Wards—widely known in the Territory as 'The Stud Book'. **1975** K. WILLEY *Ghosts of Big Country* 134 At that time nearly all of the Territory's 17,000 Aborigines.. were entered in the Register of Wards, known.. to other Territorians as 'The Stud-Book'.

stud fence. [f. *stud* a wooden post of any kind.] See quot. 1928.

1918 *Bulletin* (Sydney) 21 Feb. 22/2 The alleged new fence.. is a 'stud fence' in the bush glossary. The studs of course are the rails. **1928** C.E. COWLEY *Classing Clip* 159 The most satisfactory yards are those built of posts and rails, or what is commonly known as a 'stud' fence; that is, made of saplings—one resting upon the end of the one in the previous panel, and so on.

stud gin: see STUD 1.

stumer /'stjumə, 'stumə/. *Obs.* Also **stoomer.** [Prob. transf. use of Br. slang *stumer* a forged or dishonoured cheque: see OED(S.)] One who is penniless. In the phr. **to come a stumer,** to lose one's money. See also STOOM.

1898 *Bulletin* (Sydney) 17 Dec. (Red Page), A *stoomer* or *stumer* is a man without money. **1910** O'BRIEN & STEPHENS Materials Dict. Austral. Slang, Come a *stoomer*, stake a bet and lose everything. **1941** S.J. BAKER *Pop. Dict. Austral. Slang* 73 *Stumer*, (in gambling or racing) a bankrupt, a defaulter... *Come a stumer*, to crash financially, esp. in a racing bet.

stump.

1. A pile supporting a dwelling; esp. in Qld. (see quot. 1959). Also *attrib.*

1910 *Huon Times* (Franklin) 13 July 4/3 Police found the traces of a man having stood on one of the stumps on which the building is built. **1951** P. MAYES *Austral. Architects Price Bk. & Guide* (ed. 11) 47 Add stump caps (24 Gauge Galv. Iron). **1959** E. DARK *Lantana Lane* 42 In these parts most houses stand up on stumps high enough to provide room beneath the floorboards for innumerable things, including, of course, the family's motor vehicle. **1983** *Weekend Austral. Mag.* (Sydney) 7 May 2/3 It finally dawned on me why the first Queenslanders built their homes on stilts, or 'stumps' as they call them up here. **1984** D. MALOUF *Harland's Half Acre* 144 The land sloped, so that the house.. sat on stumps that were five feet high at the front and eighteen at the back. **1986** *Nat. Times* (Sydney) 17 Jan. 22/2 It was a small place, few rooms and a veranda, set on capped stumps to keep the white ants out.

2. Used *attrib.* in Special Comb. **stump-grubbing** *vbl. n.*, the removal, by manual or mechanical means, of the stumps of felled trees; also *attrib.*; **hole,** the hole left when a stump has been removed, esp. by fire; **-jump** *a.*, used to designate a machine designed to operate on land from which the tree stumps have not been cleared, esp. as **stump-jump plough** (see quot. 1962); also *absol.* as *n.*, and **stump-jumping** *ppl. a.*; **-picking** *vbl. n., stump-grubbing*; also as *pr. pple.*

1896 *Bulletin* (Sydney) 4 Apr. 25/2, I would prefer a man that knows something about **stump-grubbing.** **1902** *Ibid.* 18 Oct. 15/1 Stump-grubbing is practically obsolete in Gippsland. **1908** *Ibid.* 15 Oct. 15/2 One of the largest stump-grubbing contests on record has just been completed in S. Aus. A new stock route.. has been cleared.. mostly through dense mallee scrub, for a distance of 150 miles. **1948** *Ibid.* 7 Apr. 23/2 Old Sam paused in his stump-grubbing as the car from the township pulled up. **1970** J.S. GUNN in W.S. Ramson *Eng. Transported* 61 Jobs like *sleeper cutting, stump grubbing* [etc.]. **1827** P. CUNNINGHAM *Two Yrs. in N.S.W.* II. 174 It is long before grasses grow upon the places out of which stumps have been burnt... But it is astonishing to observe what a height of richness wheat will attain on these spots, every **stump-hole** being easily reckoned in a field of wheat from this great luxuriance alone. **1845** *Bell's Life in Sydney* 20 Dec. 1/3 The late heavy fall of rain would render the stump-holes very dangerous. **1846** *Cumberland Times* (Parramatta) 28 Mar. 4/1 Andrew Liddell, surgeon, of West Maitland, saw a body in a stump hole. **1849** J.P. TOWNSEND *Rambles & Observations N.S.W.* 15 The ashes of the wood fires contribute much to the improvement of the soil; and a 'stump-hole' is always indicated by the superior luxuriance of the wheat immediately around it. **1852** G.C. MUNDY *Our Antipodes* I. 337 The hardness of the ground, the stump-holes, sun-cracks and deep fissures caused by water. **1882 [stump-jump]** *SAPD* 2nd Sess. 5 Sept. 565 Bonus to Mr R.B. Smith for his invention of the stump-jumping plough, £500. **1886** N. ROBINSON *Stagg of Tarcowie* 14 May (1977) 67, I was ploughing today with the stump-jump, or more properly it should be called a stone-jumper because it is very little better than any plough among roots, but a great deal better among stones. **1886** J.F. CONIGRAVE *S.A.* 75 It appears that the invention of the stump-jumping ploughs ranks next to Ridley's stripper. **1897** L. LINDLEY-COWEN *W. Austral. Settler's Guide* 112 Five years ago.. there was not a stump jump plough in the district. **1910** 'YARRAN' *Mallee* 5 A stump jump drill is being used with success. **1911** E.M. CLOWES *On Wallaby through Vic.* 297 Before the days of the axe and saw, the 'stump-jump', and the 'mallee roller'. **1916** 'T.O. LINGO' *Austral. Comic Dict.* 22 Stump Jumping Plough—the irresistible getting over the impregnable. **1927** T.S. GROSER *Lure of Golden West* 226 'Stump-jump' ploughs are employed... The construction of these implements.. enables the share or the disc, as the cases may be, to ride over any sunken roots, as they work on a pivot, and lift or 'jump' when striking an object. **1936** J.E. HAMMOND *Western Pioneers* 65 The old wooden ploughs were blunted.. by stones and roots... The modern stump-jump plough is not hampered. **1952** *New Settler in W.A.* (Perth) July 31 Cheap land, fairly easy clearing of the more or less useless native vegetation, stump-jump plough.. all assisted rapid extension especially in the 11 to 20 inch rainfall country of the wheat belt. **1960** *Bulletin* (Sydney) 8 June 18/2 The stump-jump harrow.. was another asset to mallee-country development. **1962** O. PRYOR *Aust.'s Little Cornwall* 180 Stump-jump ploughs had been invented by R.B. Smith, in 1876, and others, and had shares that were carried on hinged arms which would ride safely over the immovable stumps and then dig themselves into the ground again. **1986** *Search* Jan.–Feb. 17 The drawings of the stump-jump plough. **1926** *Bulletin* (Sydney) 25 Feb. 24/1 The dormouse opossum is not as rare as correspondents seem to believe. While in Parilla (S.A.) **stump-picking,** or 'emu-bobbing' as the old hands termed it, I came across several of the little chaps. **1932** J. TRURAN *Green Mallee* 120 Rafe Burtonwood finished his ploughing and stump-picking on Hoffmeyer's wilderness-block.

stump-jumper.

1. *Stump-jump plough*, see STUMP 2.

1882 R. SHAPLAND *Stump-Jumping Plough* 2 It cannot be disputed that the principle of the Stump-jumper was in use for many years before Mr Smith, Mr Shapland, or Mr Branson came before the public as inventors. **1885** N. ROBINSON *Stagg of Tarcowie* 17 Feb. (1977) 47 A Trial of stonejumpers came off in Hill's paddock, a large concourse of people was on the ground. Six, three furrow stumpjumpers competed. Mr Striker's of Caltowie gained the first prize, it hooked the stones out best. **1892** E.H. HALLACK *Our Townships, Farms, & Homesteads* 29 On the slope to the right land, which has been and is still being cleared of timber.. the stump-jumper is seen preparing it for cultivation. **1902** *Bulletin* (Sydney) 8 Feb. 3/2 Much of the mallee.. was originally cleared and grubbed before the 'stump-jumper' came into use. **1921** *Ibid.* 22 Sept. 20/1, I coax the old stump-jumper over snags an' river bars.

2. *transf.* and *fig.* See quot.

1985 *Sydney Morning Herald* 7 Dec. 47/3 He now hopes he has added a new definition, 'stump-jumper: a self-made, resilient Australian achiever of vision', to our national identity.

stump lizard. *Obs.* BOBTAIL.

1861 'OLD BUSHMAN' *Bush Wanderings* 136 If by chance a snake or stump-lizard shows a head, a congregation of miners will soon gather round it. **1896** F.G. AFLALO *Sketch Nat. Hist. Aust.* 178 The Stump Lizard (*Trachysaurus rugosus*) is.. hideous and inoffensive.

stumpy. Abbrev. of STUMPY TAIL.

1933 *Bulletin* (Sydney) 31 May 21/2 One fox would probably do more harm.. than a thousand 'stumpies'. **1956** A.C.C. LOCK *Tropical Tapestry* 107 Alan swerved to avoid running over a sleepy lizard... The stumpy, or bob-tail lizard of schoolboys, known to scientists as *Trachysaurus rugosus* is viviparous. **1967** R. HAWKER *Emu in Fowl Pen* 115 Out in the paddock there were stumpy-tailed lizards... The stumpies were the ones found run over on the main road, where they had not reckoned on passing traffic.

stumpy tail. BOBTAIL. Also **stump** (or **stumpy**)-**tailed lizard.**

1914 *Emu* XIV. 83 We witnessed a fight between two stump-tailed lizards (*Trachydosaurus rugosus*). **1925** *Bulletin* (Sydney) 18 June 24/1 The lizard is very much like the common stumpy-tail, but its scales are finer and the tail is more pointed. **1934** T. WOOD *Cobbers* 140 The stumpy-tailed lizard hid in shady patches of sand among the roots. **1967** U. TAYLOR *Bird of Wonder* 232 Nannies and English gardens were a far cry from hunting stumpy tails in the bush. **1972** ANDERSON & BLAKE *J.S. Neilson* 41 When the sand warmed in the spring sunshine, the stumpy tails and blue tongues.. and others of the lizard fraternity drowsed in comfort.

stung, *ppl. a.* [Prob. formed on STING *n.* 1.] Drunk. Also with **up.**

1913 *Bulletin* (Sydney) 25 Sept. 22/2 Me for 'Inebriated'... In the number, aptness and variety of its colloquial equivalents I consider it commandeers the pastry. For instance.. ripe, rolling, paralytic, stung [etc.]. **1920** W.H. DOWNING *To Last Ridge* 95, I was a bit doubtful and Nug was a bit stung. **1945** *Bulletin* (Sydney) 7 Feb. 13/4 In came another cane-knife buyer, half-stung, who butted in with maundering remarks. **1948** R. RAVEN-HART *Canoe in Aust.* 154 In Australian slang to be 'stung' is to be drunk. **1953** T.A.G. HUNGERFORD *Riverslake* 24 Jerry's nice and stung today—the third in a row. **1971** D. IRELAND *Unknown*

Industr. Prisoner 166 In order to have me my Dad and Mum got .. stung. **1981** A. WELLER *Day of Dog* 49 Pretty Boy, Doug and Micky drink three bottles of green ginger wine... Afterwards half stung up, they decide to catch a taxi.

sturks, var. STERKS.

Sturt. [f. the name of Charles *Sturt* (1795–1869), explorer.] In special collocations: **Sturt's desert pea,** the annual or perennial herb *Clianthus formosus* (fam. Fabaceae) of sandy soils in arid parts of all States except Vic. and Tas.; the pea-like flower of this plant, usu. bright red with a shiny black boss, the floral emblem of S.A.; *desert pea*, see DESERT; also **Sturt (desert) pea; Sturt's desert rose,** the shrub of arid central Aust. *Gossypium sturtianum* var. *sturtianum* (fam. Malvaceae); the large flower of this plant, usu. mauve and with a dark red basal spot, the floral emblem of the N.T.; *desert rose*, see DESERT; **Sturt's (terrible) rite** *obs.*, subincision (see WHISTLE-COCK a.).

1862 C. ASPINALL *Three Yrs. Melbourne* 165 The most beautiful flower which I saw in Australia was the Clianthus Dampiera, or Captain **Sturt's desert pea. 1898** *Bulletin* (Sydney) 26 Nov. 3/2 Oh, the new-made grave-mound, and the scarlet Sturt-pea wreath! **1914** T.C. WOLLASTON *Spirit of Child* 91 The soldier crabs too, those splendid fellows in black and red jackets like Sturt peas. **1935** G. MCIVER *Drover's Odyssey* 262 He took off his felt hat and there in the crown of it was a newly-plucked bloom of Sturt's desert pea. **1939** M.B. ELDERSHAW *My Aust.* 221 Sturt's Desert Pea, the long red flower with the black eye and the Red Runner, which has two valves and a tongue in hard red .. smack of a diagram of obscene organs in a medical text-book. **1948** E.H. COLLIS *Lost Yrs.* 101 Around the gold-fields and farther north is the vivid scarlet of Sturt's Desert Pea. **1958** F.B. VICKERS *Mirage* (ed. 2) 156 There were scarlet patches of Sturt Pea, long red tongues with black eyes and red pixie ears, smothering the vine they grew from. **1978** K. WILLEY *Joe Brown's Dog* 20 Sturt's desert pea spreads as a vine covering the red clay with green, then bursting into glorious crimson flowers. **1985** *Woman's Day* (Sydney) 1 July 20/2 Jack helped raise money by selling bunches of Sturt desert peas to transcontinental train passengers. **1904** *Proc. Linnean Soc. N.S.W.* XXIX. 137 *Gossypium sturtii* .. the 'native cotton' or, as it is sometimes called, '**Sturt's desert rose**'. **1928** M.E. FULLERTON *Austral. Bush* 101 Sturt's desert rose—a species of hibiscus. **1980** N. WATKINS *Kangaroo Connection* 92 He wore a Sturt Desert Rose, in the lapel of his white Saigon linen coat, and which he said he had discovered was the emblem of the Northern Territory. **1895** *Trans. & Proc. R. Soc. S.A.* (1896) 249 All the aborigines of the interior circumcise, and also slit the urethra. [*Note*] This mutilation is by different writers variously alluded to as the 'terrible rite', the 'mika operation' or '**Sturt's rite**'. **1901** *Brisbane Courier* 19 July 7/4 He speaks emphatically of the practice in vogue of performing what is known as 'Sturt's terrible rite' on the young of both sexes by the elders of the tribe. By this means the increase of the population is most seriously affected, and the prevalence of the practice he largely ascribes to the difficulty they experience in finding food. **1937** *Oceania* VIII. 197 This is another of the bewildering variety of names by which subincision is known, some others which have been commonly used are: division, *urethrotomia externa*, Sturt's rite, terrible or gruesome rite, artificial hypospadias, whistle, *mika, kulpi, arrilta, yerrupe*, etc.

stu-vac /ˈstju-væk/. [f. abbrev. of *stu(dent* + *vac(ation*.] In a university, college, etc.: the period between the end of classes and the beginning of examinations.

1970 E. & D. CAMPBELL *Demonstrator* 29 Did the university get sick of you or is this another of those long stu-vacs?

sub. [Abbrev. of *subterranean clover*.] In the phr. **sub and super,** applied to the sowing of subterranean clover with superphosphate as a means of establishing or improving pasture.

1977 *Ecos* xii. 6/2 Sowing 'sub and super' brought large areas of southern Australia into more-intensive use... Even the 'sub and super' formula didn't work on all land, especially on the more-sandy soils. **1986** *Austral. Garden Jrnl.* Aug. 230 The pastures were soon invaded by weeds, most of them from the Mediterranean and South Africa. Later, the now degraded pastures were made productive by the sub-and-super revolution, using introduced pasture grasses.

sub-artesian, *a.* [Used elsewhere but of local importance.]

1. Of a bore or water in an artesian basin: see quot. 1965.

1927 M. DORNEY *Adventurous Honeymoon* 31 There is much contention about the word 'sub-artesian'. Out in the back country all water that does not rise to the surface is referred to as sub-artesian although, I believe, that any water which, when it is tapped, rises above its original level, is really artesian. **1951** G. TAYLOR *Aust.* 261 The term *sub-artesian* is often used in Australia, rather loosely, for a series of deep wells apparently fed from a common basin, but in which the water does not rise to the surface. For instance, the wells on the Barkly Tableland, about 200 feet deep, are usually termed sub-artesian. Such wells obviously grade into the ordinary ground-water wells already discussed. The present writer thinks that the term 'sub-artesian' should be accurately defined where it is used in scientific writings. **1965** *Austral. Encycl.* I. 262 If the pressure is such that water is forced up above the ground surface the bore is said to be artesian; if the water rises, but to a point below the surface, it is said to be sub-artesian.

2. Comb. **sub-artesian bore, water.**

1926 A.A.B. APSLEY *Amateur Settlers* 132 Examine one of the **sub-artesian bores. 1954** H.G. LAMOND *Manx Star* 38 That was a sub-artesian bore, about 300 feet deep, equipped with an earth tank of a capacity of about 300,000 gallons, a line of troughs at which stock could water when water was pumped at the dry end of the year. **1965** A.W. UPFIELD *Lure of Bush* 111 The hut was old, but weather-proof, and was built but a few yards from the subartesian bore, at which a small petrol-engine lifted the water into three large receiving tanks. **1925** M. TERRY *Across Unknown Aust.* 135 The **sub-artesian water** .. was all right for drinking purposes. **1926** A.A.B. APSLEY *Amateur Settlers* 133 An endless stream of artesian water. If it does not quite rise to the top and has to be assisted by a wind pump, it is called 'sub-artesian water'. **1965** *Austral. Encycl.* I. 262 Artesian and sub-artesian water is known to exist in areas comprising about one-third of the Australian continent and is of considerable economic importance.

subbie, var. SUBBY.

sub-bore. Shortened form of *sub-artesian bore* (see SUB-ARTESIAN 2).

1956 B.J. RAYMENT *My Towri* 60 Although I had worked in many wells, I knew very little about sub-bores.

subby. Also **subbie.** [f. *sub(-contractor* + -Y.] A sub-contractor.

1978 *Sun-Herald* (Sydney) 4 June 21/1 Most owner-drivers or subcontractors, as they are known in the business have to overload if they want to make ends meet. For the independent 'subbie' a couple of extra tonnes over the legal limit is often the only thing separating a profitable run from a straight-out loss. **1981** *Truckin' Life* IV. xii. 37/1 By using subbies already partly loaded on the Sydney-Canberra-Adelaide run, one prime contractor is said to have slashed the rate by $12 a tonne. **1983** *Age* (Melbourne) 6 Oct. 5/5 Contractors .. withold 10 per cent of payments to sub-contractors unless the 'subbies' have exemption certificates or certificates stipulating a lower percentage. **1985** J. SCHULTZ *Steel City Blues* 108 I'm building a house... I've done it all myself—well, I've got in a few subbies.

subterranean orchid: see UNDERGROUND ORCHID.

suburban swagman: see SWAGMAN b.

suck, *n.*[1] [Prob. Br. dial. var. of SOAK.] SOAK.

1857 *Adelaide Times* 2 Nov., Two small land sucks. **1955** S. OSBORNE *Duck Shooting Aust.* 29 The fresh water sucks during the warmer months of the year do not show much water if any during the day time, but on the setting of the sun the evaporation of surface water becomes less and the sucks flow freely. **1974** J. BYRNE *Duck Hunting Aust. & N.Z.* 36 If the sun is hot, the presence of the seepage water, or 'sucks' as they are called, shows up only as a dampish spot on the sand in day-time.

suck, *n.*[2] In the phr. **fair suck of the sauce bottle**: see FAIR *a.*[1] 3 a.

sucker, *v.*: see SUCKER-BASH.

sucker, *n.* [Spec. use of *sucker* a shoot arising from the base of a plant, esp. from the underground root; a lateral shoot.] Esp. of eucalypts: see quot. 1903.

1903 *Proc. Linnean Soc. N.S.W.* XXVII. 566 The term 'sucker' is strictly confined in botany to young plants formed on underground rootstocks, while in Australia the same term is popularly applied to adventitious growths on various parts of the stem or branches caused chiefly by that particular part of the tree being either cut or bruised. **1942** T. KELAHER *Digger Hat* 49 Three-year-old gum suckers rustling in the breeze. **1973** C.E. GOODE *Stories Strange Places* 127 The Eastern-stater saw this chap in town one afternoon, and took him home to clear a field of mallee suckers.

sucker-bash, *v. intr.* To cut down suckers or new growth on newly-cleared land: see quots. 1945 and 1981. Freq. as *vbl. n.*, and *ellipt.* as **sucker** (see quot. 1942).

1942 *Bulletin* (Sydney) 1 July 12/4 Sucker bashing is a costly business, especially when the country has to be gone over a couple of times. Box and broad-leaf iron-bark are the worst timbers to sucker. **1945** J.A. ALLAN *Men & Manners* 89 The settlers had cut the scrub a foot above the ground, piled the refuse round the stumps, and fired it as the new shoots appeared. Even after that, 'sucker-bashing' .. had still been needed. **1973** R. ROBINSON *Drift of Things* 79 Tom would take on any job of bush work—fencing, clearing .. or 'sucker-bashing'. **1978** L. WHITE *Memories of Childhood* 25 He .. breaks the axe-handle when he's set down to sucker-bash. **1981** L. MCLEAN *Pumpkin Pie* 88 Dad said he might be able to get him a job 'sucker-bashing', a term used [*sic*] to knock new shoots off ring-barked trees.

Hence **sucker-basher** *n.*

1966 C. MCGREGOR *Profile Aust.* 297 They are the 'abos' most Australians know, living in tin humpies next to the town rubbish tip, scrounging drinks around the pub, working as pea-pickers, suckerbashers, ring-barkers and casual labourers. **1972** *Bulletin* (Sydney) 11 Nov. 61/2 One job that gave me great pride, if only from an etymological point of view, was that of ring-barker, sucker-basher.

suckhole. A sycophant. Also as *adj.*, sycophantic.

1943 D. FRIEND *Gunner's Diary* 37 Rank exhibitionism, of course (gipped up with the 'suckhole' motive). *Ibid.* 53 These sub-sections organise themselves to be bound by strong unwritten laws, and abide by them; thus in the troop, such-and-such a tent (*not* any of the six or eight inhabitants individually) is regarded as being good, bad, 'suckholes' or 'loafers', as the tribal dialect translates it. **1958** F.B. VICKERS *Mirage* (ed. 2) 110, I feeds the workers. Them's the ones I feed. Union man, me. I ain't one of the suck-hole cooks that stick to the boss. **1966** P. MATHERS *Trap* 12 Our progressive mayor .. and his pack of scabby suckhole mates.

Hence as *v. intr.*, to toady.

1969 F.B. VICKERS *No Man is Himself* 72, 'I know yous, yous bastard. You'll suckhole to him. Give it to him straight,' he shouted. *Ibid.* 112 I've had this suckholin' to get a job. Me an' Ted have tried hard. **1986** *Good Weekend* (Sydney) 3 May 12/2 Here I am on top of the entertainment world suckholing to a self-effacing reporter from a major metropolitan daily.

suffer, *v.* In the phr. **to suffer a recovery:** see RECOVERY.

sugar.

1. Used *attrib.* in Comb. which have a local significance but may not be excl. Austral., as **sugar district, experiment station, farm, farmer, -farming, field, land, -lander.**

1880 J. BONWICK *Resources Qld.* 73 The marvellous extent of sugar lands .. places Queensland at a great advantage. **1886** F.A. HAGENAUER *Rep. Aboriginal Mission Ramahyuck, Vic.* 36 The plantations or sugar fields are smaller or larger tracts of the richest land. **1902** *Bulletin* (Sydney) 11 Oct. 16/4 Protector Meston wants to collect the blacks to work on the sugar lands. **1903** *Truth* (Sydney) 6 Dec. 1/7 There is no possibility of plutocratic slave-owners in the sugar districts getting supplies of fresh niggers. **1905** *Bulletin* (Sydney) 12 Oct. 14/2 The number of drinking shops in the sugar districts of N.Q. might very well be reduced. **1911** *Ibid.* 8 June 14/2 Finding the climate of the Mallee, Victoria, uncongenial, a mate and I decided to migrate to the sugar fields of Queensland. **1930** V. PALMER *Passage* (1957) 64 Got a chance to buy into a sugar-farm with his brother. **1930** W.K. HANCOCK *Aust.* 81 Polynesians in their wild state never clamoured for admission to the Queensland sugar-fields. **1936** J. DEVANNY *Sugar Heaven* 9 The loose informal attitudes he had assumed since arriving in the sugar lands startled her. **1938** F. CLUNE *Free & Easy Land* 172 For years Sugarlanders have advocated the production of power alcohol from molasses. **1946** *Bulletin* (Sydney) 10 Apr. 15/2 We were loafing .. past the sugar-experiment station near Mackay (N.Q.). ***c* 1960** C. MACKNESS *Clump Point & District* 29 They also burned coral for lime which they transported by boat to South Johnstone, for sale to sugar-farmers. *Ibid.* 80 The Government had opened it up in 1924 as a sugar farming soldier settlement. **1962** *Daily Mercury Centenary Story* 15 In addition to raising .. seedlings, the Mackay sugar experiment station has tried the best overseas commercial canes.

2. Special Comb. **sugar beer,** a beer which is brewed using sugar instead of malt; also *attrib.*; **cocky,** *cane cocky*, see CANE 2; **doodle,** a tumble; a somersault; **mat,** SUGAR BAG 2 a.; **-squeezer,** one who is employed in the processing of sugar cane.

1831 *Sydney Monitor* 17 Sept. 2/2 The **sugar beer** sells as fast as it can be made, whereas the malt beer, *not being so sweet*, is not half so well relished, especially by the native-born. **1855** W. HOWITT *Land, Labor & Gold* II. 122 Beer they have little or none, except a species of hog-wash, honored with the name of sugar-beer. **1872** MRS E. MILLETT *Austral. Parsonage* 258 The native hop is a little ground-plant, named by botanists *Erythrea Australis*, with which, on account of its intensely bitter taste, sugar-beer used to be flavoured when English hops could not be procured. **1924** H.E. RIEMANN *Nor'-West o' West* 111 Billy Pollock was cook and sugar-beer brewer of Mollyanna sheep station. **1909** *Bulletin* (Sydney) 6 May 14/3 That **sugar-cocky**-fellow .. told me I would find a cane knife outside. **1915** *Ibid.* 25 Mar. 24/1 The Queensland sugar cocky has been working overtime. **1904** L.M.P. ARCHER *Bush Honeymoon* 9 'By George! he'll get a **sugar doodle** out of that van,' says Fred. **1919** C. DREW *Doings of Dave* 174 She'll do a sugar doodle. **1925** M. TERRY *Across Unknown Aust.* 123 'E did the finest sugar-doodle I've seen in all me born days. **1848** *Sydney Daily Advertiser* 1 Sept. 2/4 Obstructing the footway in the narrow part of King-street, by leaving a quantity of **sugar mats** upon it. **1888** J.C.F. JOHNSON *Austral Christmas* 78 Frequent domiciliary visits were paid to the composite tenement, constructed of kerosene cans, sugar-mats, and gunny bags. **1903** *Bulletin* (Sydney) 6 June 16/4 Charles Kingston's visit to this piebald land upset all calculations. The **sugar-squeezers** and the huge C.S.R. monopoly were aghast at his splendid reception. **1916** *Ibid.* 16 Mar. 22/3 For fair, honest, straight up and down drinking give me the sugar-squeezers, cane-choppers and all connected with the great treacle industry.

3. In the names of flora and fauna: **sugar ant,** any of several stingless ants of the genus *Camponotus*, as the common *C. nigriceps*, having an orange thorax and legs and black head; **glider,** the gliding possum *Petaurus breviceps* of n. and e. Aust. incl. Tas., and New Guinea; see also *sugar squirrel*; **grass,** the tufted perennial grass *Eulalia fulva* (fam. Poaceae), palatable to stock, of mainland Aust. and parts of s.e. Asia; **gum,** any of several trees of the fam. Myrtaceae, esp. *Eucalyptus cladocalyx* of s. S.A. incl. Kangaroo Island, widely planted as a windbreak (see quot. 1889); **squirrel,** (or **possum**), any of several arboreal marsupials, esp. the *sugar glider* and the similar, larger *squirrel glider* (see SQUIRREL 2).

1861 'OLD BUSHMAN' *Bush Wanderings* 208 Ants of every variety and size, from the little **sugar-ant** up to the great red soldier-ant. **1862** A. POLEHAMPTON *Kangaroo Land* 101 There is also the sugar-ant, so named from its particular weakness for sweets. **1891** M. ROBERTS *Land-Travel & Sea-Faring* 100 The ground, especially about our kitchen, was covered with countless swarms of ants, bull-dogs and sugar-ants [etc.]. **1916** S.A. WHITE *In Far Northwest* 120 These are formed by the natives when in search of sugar ants... These ants were described in 1880 by Sir John Lubbock as Camponotus inflatus. **1926** A.S. LE SOUEF et al. *Wild Animals Australasia* 371 It is specially fond of the large sugar-ant (*C. nigriceps*). **1967** B.Y. MAIN *Between Wodjil & Tor* 35 Golden-bodied, dark headed 'sugar ants' wandered over the ground .. solitarily. **1972** J. HIBBERD *Stretch of Imagination* (1973) 12 Sprinkle arsenicals on the sugar-ants and aphis and weevils as they struggle past in search of a bite to eat. **1941** E. TROUGHTON *Furred Animals Aust.* 95 '**Sugar Glider**' is now adopted as being brief and suitable for popular use, reflecting the captive's love of sugar derived from the blossom-eating habit, as well as the volplaning ability due to the presence of gliding membranes between the limbs. **1955** N. PULLIAM *I traveled Lonely Land* 150 The engaging sugar glider and the pygmy possum. **1975** *Ecos* vi. 7/2 The sugar glider probably occurs southwards from Cooktown. **1985** *Age* (Melbourne) 20 Sept. (Suppl.) 13/1 Something small moved on one of the felled branches... A bush rat perhaps, I thought. On closer inspection, it turned out to be two entwined tiny sugar glider possums. **1889** J.H. MAIDEN *Useful Native Plants Aust.* 106 *Pollinia fulva* .. the '**Sugar Grass**' of colonists, so called on account of its sweetness; it is highly productive, and praised by stockowners. **1897** L. LINDLEY-COWEN *W. Austral. Settler's Guide* 414 *Pollinia fulva* .. is a superior pasture grass, and is much praised by stockowners, who have given it the name of 'sugar grass', on account of the sweetness of its stems and foliage. **1930** D. COTTRELL *Earth Battle* 314 The fire had .. reached the five-foot sugar grass of a dried swamp. **1954** T. RONAN *Vision Splendid* 196 March, with the sugar grass, even in a light season, denser and taller than any planted crop. **1888** *Proc. Linnean Soc. N.S.W.* III. 509 *Eucalyptus gunnii.* .. In Tasmania this is known as 'Cider Gum', and in South-Eastern Australia occasionally as the '**Sugar Gum**'. **1889** J.H. MAIDEN *Useful Native Plants Aust.* 442 *Eucalyptus corynocalyx* .. (Syn., *E. cladocalyx*)... Sometimes called 'Sugar Gum', on account of its sweetish foliage, which attracts cattle and sheep. **1918** A.M. MOORE *Autumn Grey* 45 His hut of galvanised iron, shaded by a group of young bronze-tipped sugar-gums. **1948** J.K. EWERS *For Heroes to live In* 61 The trees had come while she was away—a hundred sugar gums and a mixed lot of ornamental trees for round the house. **1980** P. PEPPER *You are what you make Yourself* 56 We pulled the bark off the sugar gums and there's a little white speck in there and we'd stick our fingers on it and eat that. It's sweet and that's how it got the name of sugar-gum tree. **1846** *Portland Guardian* 22 Sept. 4/2 At Port Essington oppossums [*sic*] and **sugar squirrels** (*Petaurus sciures* [*sic*]) had been very numerous according to Captain Macarthur, but had now almost disappeared. **1851** J. HENDERSON *Excursions & Adventures N.S.W.* II. 173 There is a small kind [of flying squirrel], about the size of a mouse, which is called the sugar-squirrel, and is found about the huts occasionally. It has a strange tail, flat and resembling a feather. **1861** 'OLD BUSHMAN' *Bush Wanderings* 47 The *little Sugar Squirrel* is not at all uncommon among the honeysuckle and small gums in all the forests. **1919** *Bulletin* (Sydney) 31 July 20/2 South Coast (N.S.W.) sleeper-cutters come upon the big black, or 'magpie', squirrel occasionally in felling tall stringy-bark or box-trees... The fur is .. not nearly so fine as that of the little grey sugar-squirrel. **1921** *Ibid.* 13 Jan. 20/3 The sugar-possum, being no larger than a mouse, is hard to find. **1941** E. TROUGHTON *Furred Animals Aust.* 95 Because of the general appearance [of *Petaurus breviceps*], and readiness in taking honey, sugar and jam when captured, the bushmen's name of 'Sugar Squirrel' is easily understood. **1948** A. MARSHALL *Ourselves writ Strange* 314, I sat .. watching two phalangers—sugar squirrels—leap on to his shoulders and forage in his pockets. **1954** C. BARRETT *Wild Life Aust. & New Guinea* 21 The short-headed, or sugar-glider, popularly called 'sugar-squirrel', measures only fifteen inches in length.

sugar bag. Also **choogar bag** (only in sense 1). [Spec. use of *sugar bag* a bag for containing sugar.]

1. *Austral. pidgin.* **a.** The honey of the wild bee; its honeycomb or hive. **b.** *transf.* A bee of any kind; the honey of such a bee. See also quot. 1985. Also *attrib.*

1830 R. DAWSON *Present State Aust.* 136 The strange native pointed with his tomahawk to the tree and .. repeated the words, 'Choogar-bag, choogar-bag, choogar-bag!' (sugar-bag) their English expression for honey or anything sweet. **1846** T.H. BRAIM *Hist. N.S.W.* II. 247 Wild Honey, or, as the natives call it, Choogar Bag, is collected by a small stingless bee, not so large as the common fly. **1870** E.B. KENNEDY *Four Yrs. in Qld.* 78 The Aboriginals .. cut out 'possums from a tree or sugar bag (wild honey) by means of a tomahawk of green stone. **1881** A.C. GRANT *Bush-Life Qld.* I. 67 The regular sharp chop-chop of the tomahawks could be heard here and there, where some of them [*sc.* Aborigines] had discovered a sugar-bag .. on a tree. [*Note*] A nest of honey. **1892** J. FRASER *Aborigines N.S.W.* 54 After another Bora, he may eat the 'sugar-bag', that is, the honey of the bee; a step higher, and he may eat the male of the opossum, and so on until his initiation is complete, and then he may eat anything. **1902** E.B. KENNEDY *Black Police Qld.* 83 Ever and anon would he cast his eyes aloft and scan the spouts of the gumtrees within view looking for 'sugar bag'—wild bees' nests. **1922** *Bulletin* (Sydney) 31 Aug. 22/3 How's this for a record sugar-bag (English bees)? **1935** T. RAYMENT *Cluster of Bees* 513 With the advent of the white man, the more comprehensive term, 'Sugar-bag' was used by the blacks for all species of social bees. **1947** W.E. HARNEY *Brimming Billabongs* 136 They found a 'sugar bag' in one of the stunted gums that grew along the stony ridges of the pocket; and when it was cut out of the log, what a feast, as they sat down to scoop out the honey with their fingers. **1964** B. CRUMP *Gulf* 124 String that had been waterproofed with the black wax from the hives of the small stingless sugarbag-bees. **1979** D. LOCKWOOD *My Old Mates & I* 39 Sugarbag from the Swamplands. Natural wild honey, complete with honeycomb and a few wild black bees adhering. These are especially favoured by the North Australian tribesmen. Mr Y.B. Alderson reports: 'My son, Mick, is the sugarbag expert in the family. I've known him to get four gallons of wax-honey in an hour. When he sees bees flying around a hollow tree trunk he chops it down and we gorge ourselves on this delicacy.' **1985** B. ROSSER *Dreamtime Nightmares* 69 'She used to get sugarbags.' 'Sugarbags?' 'Honey ants.'

2. a. A bag of fine sacking made for containing sugar; such a bag as used subsequently for a variety of purposes. Also *attrib.*

1850 *Bell's Life in Sydney* 9 Nov. 1/2 Boots, scraps of paper, torn rags, old sugar-bags, and other useless refuse. **1872** MRS E. MILLETT *Austral. Parsonage* 105 The natives .. consider an empty sugar bag a great prize. **1895** P.W. MCNALLY *Irish Immigrant* 13 The youngsters on the sugar-bags ceased their play. **1915** G. SARGANT *Sweet Heart of Bush* 21 The customers, who generally called for their meat with a sugar bag rolled under their arm. **1938** D. BATES *Passing of Aborigines* 19 My feet immediately swelled with some swift poison, until I could fit them into nothing smaller than two sugar-bags. **1946** F. CLUNE *Try Nothing Twice* 82, I left Warby's with my sugar-bag swag and took the long, long trail a-winding. **1951** *Bulletin* (Sydney) 14 Mar. 12/1 He took small yellowtail and 'old wives' off the hook and flung them contemptuously into his sugar-bag. **1958** *Overland* 12/7 For a pillow, a sugar bag, stuffed with feathers. **1970** M. VODICKA *Track to Rum Jungle* 51 Walks for miles to do her shopping with a sugar bag. **1981** *Austral. Women's Weekly* (Sydney) 26 Aug. 20/3 Tess, who at times has had 12 men on her payroll, remembered when she first came to Triple Chance with her first husband and they slept under sugar bags. They built a sugar bag shanty and things were very tough for the two fossickers.

b. *transf.* See quot.

1978 H.C. BAKER *I was Listening* 70 A 'sugar bag carpenter' suggested a bush-carpenter or tommyhawk carpenter, which were the most disparaging appellations to be flung at a tradesman. An advertisement in the *Sydney Morning Herald* once read: Carpenters wanted. No sugar bag tradesmen need apply.

3. *fig.* One who accepts bribes or 'sweeteners'.

1877 *Vagabond Papers* 3rd Ser. 139 The warder who overlooks these little things, and who will make [*sic*] presents of tobacco, or traffic, is called a 'sugarbag'. I expect I was about the sweetest sugarbag they have had in Pentridge for a long time. **1924** *Aussie* (Sydney) Mar. 34/1 Th' game's right enough .. w'ere yer 'as the same camp an' 'as a sugar-bag of a ganger, an' can go slow a bit. **1950** F.J. HARDY *Power without Glory* 444 You are playing the public for suckers. And you get away with it, because you have made sugar-bags of the men who should expose you. **1968** L.H. EVERS *Fall among Thieves* 68 She knows that the copper who's number one is a sugar-bag so she talks to him half-cunning about a little something in his hand. **1972** BERMAN & CHILDS *Why* *isn't she Dead!* 66 If a policeman is called a 'sugarbag' by other police or the underworld he is on the take, the sugar merely sweetens or lightens any offence.

sugar-bagging, *vbl. n.*

1. The collecting of wild honey.

1906 *Bulletin* (Sydney) 10 May 40/1 There was the hunting and shooting and sugar-bagging.

2. *fig.* The practice of carrying provisions in a sugar bag: see SUGAR BAG 2 a. (*attrib.* in quot.).

1979 B. HARDY *World owes me Nothing* 138 There was plenty of scope for them in the 'sugar-bagging' system shearers had to put up with in these closely-settled areas. The men had to travel to work each day, taking their own tucker.

sugaropolis. A name applied to any of a number of towns in Queensland associated with the sugar industry.

1884 *Qld. Handbk. Information* (Burns, Philp & Co.) 31 Mackay is today the Sugaropolis of Queensland. **1899** *Progress* (Brisbane) 6 May 7/2 An old Laidley resident took a trip via the North Coast Line to Sugaropolis and—the home of black labour. **1915** *Bulletin* (Sydney) 16 Sept. 24/4 Races were to be held in Sugaropolis and the gang drew lots to decide who should stay at home as caretaker. **1926** *Smith's Weekly* (Sydney) 2 Oct. 19/2 In the sugaropolis of Bundaberg (Q.) .. the footballers wear hats. **1962** *Daily Mercury Centenary Story Mackay* 2 Mackay, the sugaropolis of Australia, and the 'Gateway to the Great Barrier Reef' looks forward to another one hundred years of progress.

sugary, *a. Mining.* [Br. dial.: see EDD *a.* 3.] Friable.

1846 F. DUTTON *S.A. & its Mines* 284 A kindly spar is intermingled with copper ore; 'sugary spar' is in considerable quantity. **1848** *S. Austral. Register* (Adelaide) 11 Oct. 2/4 At intervals, the ore is displaced by very sugary quartz. **1982** M. WATTONE *Winning Gold in W.A.* 70, I bent down and picked up a sugary quartz specimen which contained 2 oz. of gold.

sugee, var. SOOGEE.

suicide, *a. N.T.* Of the 'wet' or rainy season: unendurable.

1971 P. BODEKER *Sandgropers' Trail* 11 We close the dry winter season for our six months' fishing because summer up north is 'the wet', a contrasting period of searing heat and tropical floods, known in the Territory as the 'suicide months'. **1975** K. WILLEY *Ghosts of Big Country* 143 Those inhabitants who during the Wet—also known as the Suicide Season—would sometimes creep off into the cane-grass and there slit their throats. **1978** M. DOUGLAS *Follow Sun* 167 The locals call it 'suicide month'—November, that unendurable time of the year when the 'wet' begins in Australia's north.

sujee, var. SOOGEE.

sulky, *n.* [Transf. use of *sulky* a light two-wheeled carriage or chaise seated for one person.] A light horse-drawn vehicle used as a conveyance.

1902 *Bulletin* (Sydney) 31 May 14/1 The sulkies are always well-stocked with 'wobble Charlie' (rum), and the gins now spend their time on a steam merry-go-round in the township. **1912** T.E. SPENCER *Bindawalla* 36 Leslie and I drove in, in the sulky. **1927** T.S. GROSER *Lure of Golden West* 130 A drive with him through the Bush in his sulky. **1956** 'B. JAMES' *Bunyip of Barney's Elbow* 66 The sulky was an absurd arrangement with shafts, home-made of string-bark and nearly a mile long, with a fiery young colt towards the front end of them. **1964** A. STAPLES *Paddo* 21 We went seven miles to school in the sulky. **1981** *New Idea* (Melbourne) 3 Oct. 24/2 The sight of Leo and Lenny Bell trundling down the country roads near Ipswich, Q., high in the seat of their 1931 sulky, is one of peace and tranquility reminiscent of a time long past.

sulky, *a. Austral. pidgin.* Angry; unco-operative. In the phr. **to die sulky,** to die out of favour with one's community. Also **sulky fellow.**

1841 G. GREY *Jrnls. Two Exped. N.-W. & W.A.* I. 363 'Mr Grey sulky yu-a-da'; by which he intended to say '.. Mr Grey is not angry with you.' **1845** *Sentinel* (Sydney) 5 Feb. 3/3 Mount Macedon tribe .. all who die sulky left unburied. Goulburn, as Mount Macedon—All who die sulky left unburied. **1846** 'COLONIAL MAGISTRATE' *Remarks on Probable Origin* 25 Ceremonies are denied to those who die 'sulky'; that is in ill favour with their family or tribe. **1872** MRS E. MILLETT *Austral. Parsonage* 84 'Quiet fellow' and 'sulky fellow' have an almost equally wide range, the first signifying any conceivable degree of amiability, either in man or beast, and the latter ferocity to a like extent. **1879** 'AUSTRALIAN' *Adventures Qld.* 8 If black-boys were not satisfied—i.e., fed to repletion—they usually became sulky, and little good could be got out of them. **1910** *Emu* IX. 188 In the end I had to enact the 'sulky pfellow', and only exchange food for weapons. **1969** F.B. VICKERS *No Man is Himself* 8 Tallish and slim, and sulky-fella by the attitude of her, he thought.

sulphur-crested cockatoo. [See quot. 1849.] *White cockatoo* (a), see WHITE *a.*² 1 b.). Also **sulphur-crested white cockatoo.**

[**1787** J. LATHAM *Gen. Synopsis Birds* Suppl. I. 63 The Great Variety of the *Cockatoo* with a *yellow crest*, was seen in vast flocks in *New South Wales*, making an horrible noise. **1822** —— *Gen. Hist. Birds* II. 133 *Sulphur-headed parrot*... Head, and beneath, pale sulphur yellow; forehead crimson; cheeks blue... Inhabits New South Wales.] **1849** C. STURT *Narr. Exped. Central Aust.* II. 35 App. Cacatua Galerita—*Sulphur-crested Cockatoo.* This Cockatoo, the most common in Australia, is snow-white, with the exception of its crest, which is of a bright sulphur. **1865** *Illustr. Sydney News* 16 Nov. 12/1 A flock of sulphur-crested cockatoos twisted about the twigs. **1893** J. DEMARR *Adventures in Aust.* 93 Thousands of sulphur-crested white cockatoo had made these trees their roosting place. **1909** *Emu* VIII. 267 A very striking sight during the morning is a huge flock of Sulphur-crested Cockatoos. **1924** L. ST. C. GRONDONA *Kangaroo keeps on Talking* 128 The sulphur-crested cockatoo often finds his way to England... But the large black cockatoo .. will not adapt himself to captivity. **1945** C. BARRETT *Austral. Bird Life* 73 The sulphur-crested white cockatoo .. ranges over the continent generally, except in the west. **1956** A.C.C. LOCK *Tropical Tapestry* 256 They are homes of countless sulphur-crested cockatoos. **1981** *Bulletin* (Sydney) 30 June 13/2 Their wives and girlfriends .. were .. screeching like sulphur-crested cockatoos.

summer. Used *attrib.* in the names of flora and fauna: **summer bird,** any of several birds appearing in an area in summer, esp. the WOOD SWALLOW and the *black-faced cuckoo-shrike* (see BLACK *a.*² 1 b.); **grass,** any of several native or introduced grasses (fam. Poaceae) able to make rapid growth in summer, esp. the naturalized annual *Digitaria sanguinalis* and the similar *D. ciliaris.*

1861 'OLD BUSHMAN' *Bush Wanderings* 135 Another summer migrant to our district was the **Summer-bird,** about the size of the jay at home. **1895** *Argus* (Melbourne) 29 Nov. 6/7 The wood-swallows, known to us old colonists as summer birds, are migratory, making their appearance about September and disappearing about the end of January. **1900** A.J. CAMPBELL *Nests & Eggs Austral. Birds* 96 Under various trivial vernacular names, such as Blue Dove, Summer Bird, etc., the Black-faced Cuckoo Shrike is found through the length and breadth of Australia. **1931** M. TERRY *Hidden Wealth* 324 The birds included .. many small doves, summer birds, budgereegahs. **1979** *N.S.W. Parl. Papers* (1980–81) IV. 633 The old bird that used to come here every year, the summer bird, does not come any more to let us know that the summer is coming. **1846** *Sydney Morning Herald* 28 Feb. 2/6 The grass called joint grass, or water or **summer grass. 1889** J.H. MAIDEN *Useful Native Plants Aust.* 102 *Panicum sanguinale* .. 'Summer Grass'. A creeping, quick-growing grass; a great pest to farmers. **1923** E. BREAKWELL *Grass & Fodder Plants N.S.W.* 67 Summer Grass (*Panicum sanguinale*). This is well named Summer grass, as it is most conspicuous during the hottest days of summer. **1981** G.M. CUNNINGHAM et al. *Plants Western N.S.W.* 86 Summer grass *Digitaria ciliaris*... An annual grass which makes rapid growth during the summer months.

sun-bake, *v. intr.* To sun-bathe. Freq. as *vbl. n.* and *ppl. a.*

1910 *Truth* (Sydney) 9 Oct. 2/8 If those sun baking barrackers really desire to get sun baked in 'the altogether', why do they not repair to Tamarama Bay. **1918** *Bulletin* (Sydney) 10 Jan. 24/4 She was at Manly when she last wrote—sun-baking. **1927** 'S. RUDD' *Romance of Runnibede* 130 There was a lot of hard work and hard knocks, and sun-baking attached to it. **1934** E. STOREY *Eve's Affairs* 28 Outside was gorgeous .. the sort of day I guess nude sun-baking was invented. **1957** D. WHITINGTON *Treasure upon Earth* 62 Sun-baking later on the sand she told him a little of herself. **1965** *Kings Cross Whisper* (Sydney) Dec. 3/4 Found sun-baking in a small shed near Bandywhallop. **1977** W.G. HOWCROFT *Black with White Cockatoos* 84 A young country lass was sunbaking naked and face down on the roof of a motel in Surfers' Paradise. **1985** J. CLANCHY *Lie of Land* 106 Maureen and Sarah had got bored and were lying sunbaking.

Hence **sun-bake** *n.*, **sun-baker** *n.*

1940 *Digger Yarns: Cream of 'Aussiosities'*, We was in support, a nice cushy possie without much excitement. I'd been 'avin' a bit of a **sunbake** all the mornin'. **1967** D. HORNE *Educ. Young Donald* 10, I would walk there to have a swim and a sunbake. **1949** C.B. MAXWELL *Surf* 41 A **sunbaker** sat up and pushed forward a well-filled pot. 'Have a beer, sergeant!'.

sundown, *v.* [Back-formation f. SUNDOWNER.]

a. *intr.* To travel as a sundowner. Freq. as *vbl.n.*

1882 ARMSTRONG & CAMPBELL *Austral. Sheep Husbandry* 245 An undeserving scoundrel, who spends the greater part of his time 'lounging' or 'sundowning'—*i.e.*, spending his time under a shady currajong, or other sleep-inspiring tree. **1892** 'E. KINGLAKE' *Austral. at Home* 133 The effect .. was to make sundowning an intolerable nuisance. **1900** *Pastoral Times* (Deniliquin) 6 Jan. 2/5 We wakked [*sic*] the bottle between us, and then started to do a bit of sundownin'. **1909** E. WALTHAM *Life & Labour in Aust.* 22 Others again, having taken the tide at the ebb, have wandered on the track—sundowning—and on the 'wallaby'. **1925** J.E. LIDDLE *Selected Poems* 63 Yes, he had sundowned twenty years, Among the 'back-blocks'. **1946** F. CLUNE *Try Nothing Twice* 7 The place where Edward Hammond Hargraves sun-downed was the homestead. **1946** D. BARR *Warrigal Joe* 68 Sundowning had got into Joe's blood. Though not one of the cadging sort, he liked an easy life, and was as happy as Larry when on the wallaby.

b. *trans.* To importune (someone) for sustenance.

1924 H.E. RIEMANN *Nor'-West o' West* 58 'Hoped to pay me when he struck it rich.' .. 'That wouldn't be Palmer. A bloke with two thousand quid wouldn't sundown you for flour and sugar, that's certain.'

sundowner. An itinerant, ostensibly seeking work, who arrives at a place at the end of the day: see quots. 1886.

[**1846** C.P. HODGSON *Reminisc. Aust.* 303 This day's work is what is generally though not elegantly termed 'eye-balling', and its duration amounted in colonial phraseology, to a 'Sundowner', neither word is to be found I believe in an English dictionary, but both have very expressive meanings.] **1868** *Sydney Punch* 14 Nov. 198 (*heading*) The song of the sundowner. **1870** *Lictor* (Sydney) 5 May 1 If anyone should doubt the distressed state of our laboring population let him advertise for a servant of any kind, and mark the result; if still further proof be required let him go into the country districts and note the numbers of unemployed who are wandering up and down seeking work, and living on charity, after allowing a fair per centage for 'sundowners'. **1872** 'RESIDENT' *Glimpses Life Vic.* 222 An earlier arrival would be impolitic, as they would be exhorted to march onwards to the next station; of this the 'sun-downer' is fully aware. **1886** P. CLARKE *'New Chum' in Aust.*, I have spoken of 'sundowners' before now... The article is of the animal kingdom, genus *homo*, and generally tramps along during the day from station to station seeking work, timing his way so he may reach a station before 'sundown' in time for tea and bed. **1886** R. HENTY *Australiana* 178 These men were mere loafers or 'sundowners'—fellows who didn't want work, but who sponged upon the settler for a night's lodging and supper. **1891** H. NISBET *Colonial Tramp* 214 A sundowner is a gentleman who has all the instincts of a nobleman about him, but has been unfortunate in the choice of his parents. **1911** *Bulletin* (Sydney) 2 Nov. 14/3 The lady sundowner is an abundant feature of the Riverina river bends... They are popular visitors at the sheds and carry A.W.U. tickets to a girl. **1928** M. FORREST *Reaping Roses* 41 He wondered where these sundowners slept when they came to town. **1938** *Bulletin* (Sydney) 12 Jan. 21/1 Something new in the way of sundowners turned up at the homestead last week. Complete with swag, whiskers and bobbing hat corks, he added a novel touch by including a golf-club carried just abaft of the tucker-bag. **1959** *Ibid.* 7 Oct. 19/2 The sundowner .. would extort a drink from Bung by casually producing a matchbox, saying it contained his pet termites and drawing a graphic word-picture of the ravages they would make on a wooden pub if they were to escape. **1965** F. HARDY *Yarns of Billy Borker* 48 Did I ever tell you about the sundowner who paid his fare out of Wagga Wagga? **1980** J. WRIGHT *Big Hearts & Gold Dust* 220 You see I'm just a tramp, a sundowner.

sundries, *pl. Cricket.* [Chiefly Austral.: see OED(S.] The extras, or runs scored otherwise than off the bat.

1867 *Australasian* (Melbourne) 16 Mar. 332/1 With sundries forty-five, the innings closed for the very long score of 111. **1900** *Truth* (Sydney) 4 Mar. 2/5 Glass, not out: 0; Sundries: 20. **1912** *Australasian* (Melbourne) 2 Mar. 481/1, 12 sundries had been recorded in 24 runs. **1924** *Ibid.* 29 Nov. 1279/5 Osborne, b Hornibrook .. 1; Sundries .. 13; Total .. 111. **1947** *Sydney Morning Herald* 3 Jan. 7/8 T. Brookes, not out .. 8; Sundries .. 9; Total .. 379. **1968** J. POLLARD *Ampol Bk. Austral. Sporting Recs.* 105 *Most sundries allowed in a test:* 83 by England v. Australia, 1934. **1983** K. DUNSTAN *Cricket Dict.* 28 Extras. Or in politer circles, sundries.

sunnies, *pl.* [f. *sun(-glasses* + -Y.] A pair of sunglasses.

1981 *Sun-Herald* (Sydney) 11 Jan. 9/2 On his head was a top hat adorned with dark glasses ('sunnies'). **1984** *Sydney Morning Herald* 4 Feb. 35/2 A mob in mirrored sunnies (essential accessories at Narana along with the Molly Meldrum slouch hat and studded belt). **1984** P. JARRATT *Aussie* 60 Two .. items which have been pretty much standard for more than twenty years: tee shirt and sunnies... The sunglasses change shape with the seasons. **1985** *Health Standard* Nov. 5/1 *Sunnies* must now be labelled under a new safety standard which places them in three categories .. sunglasses suitable for everyday use [etc.].

sunset.

1. The western part of New South Wales and Queensland; the west. See also *back o' sunset* BACK D., *west of sunset* WEST. Also **sunset country** and *attrib.*

1908 *Bulletin* (Sydney) 7 May 15/2 During my divagations through the Sunset-country stations, I frequently found that the shearers and co. were decently housed, because of the S.A.A. **1910** *Ibid.* 2 June 15/1 I'll never forget .. one sunset track. I had trudged two tuckerless 16-mile stages... Then I struck my hospitable friend. **1916** *Ibid.* 28 Dec. 24/1 In my early days out in the Sunset .. wild cats had distributed themselves many hundreds of miles from any human habitation. **1919** R.J. CASSIDY *Gipsy Road* 88 Back to the Sunset Tracks. **1982** J.A. SHARWOOD *Vocab. Austral. Dried Vine Fruits Industry* 34 Severe dust storms .. roll in from the *sunset country* to the west of the Darling.

2. Special Comb. **sunset rum,** see quot. 1951.

1951 E. HILL *Territory* 124 When grog was short they made their own .. methylated spirit and kerosene mixed with Worcestershire Sauce and flavoured with ginger and sugar, known to the diggers as Sunset Rum. **1980** R. SHEARS *Gold* 30 Breweries sprang up selling dubious liquors ranging from amber-coloured water to 'sunset-rum'. This was brewed from methylated spirit, kerosene and Worcestershire sauce and flavoured with ginger and sugar.

Sunshine State. A name for Queensland.

1962 'C. ROHAN' *Delinquents* 128 'If you ask me, all Brisbane's full of coppers and all of them bastards,' she said, expressing in one concise sentence the full theory of central government of the sunshine state. **1965** R.H. CONQUEST *Horses in Kitchen* 128 My idea here is to try to explain Queensland .. to those who occasionally seek information about that part of Australia so often referred to as Bananaland, or the Sunshine State. **1980** S. THORNE *I've met some Bloody Wags* 15, I declined Hungry Proctor's offer of a further year's employment, and headed back to the Sunshine State. **1984** *Bulletin* (Sydney) 12 June 82/1 Small but insistent reminders of being in the Sunshine State. All those middle-aged men in safari suits, long socks and shorts.

super, *n.*[1] [Spec. use of *super*, abbrev. of *superintendent.*] The manager of a rural property (see also quot. 1967).

1849 *Stephen's Adelaide Miscellany* 8 Nov. 81 There are numberless other characters peculiar to the Bush, all of which are generally denoted very graphically by the technical terms that severally represent them, as—the 'flash gentleman' .. the 'super's man', 'the crawler' [etc.]. **1851** *Illustr. Austral. Mag.* (Melbourne) Apr. 224 Coming to Smith's station one night, where a whole lot of us supers and settlers had met for a christmas jollification. **1862** C. MUNRO *Fern Vale* I. 47 The party consisted of individuals called 'supers', or more properly speaking, the superintendents of stations, the owners of which were not resident on their properties. **1875** CAMPBELL & WILKS *Early Settlement Qld.* 26 Some of the larger stations were presided over by a 'super', but more generally by a stock-keeper and hut-keeper only. **1881** A.C. GRANT *Bush-Life Qld.* I. 62 The 'super' drives four-in-hand, wears kid gloves on the run, keeps racehorses, and leaves the work to a couple of overseers. **1898** C.G. DUFFY *My Life* 158 It is a .. common practice to squat in the Melbourne Club and leave the run to be managed by a 'super'. **1932** *Bulletin* (Sydney) 10 Feb. 21/2, I was struck by the reference to the man in charge of the station as 'the super', a title long ago superseded by 'manager'... The average out-backer accosted .. with the question, 'Where's the super?' would naturally associate it with phosphates. **1967** G. JENKIN *Two Yrs. Bardunyah Station* 66 But for the lowly rouseabout there is no battle—only work and a bit of skylarking when the boss-of-the-board (known usually as the 'Expert' or the 'Super') isn't looking.

super, *n.*[2]

1. Abbrev. of 'superphosphate'. Also *attrib.*

1925 *Bulletin* (Sydney) 20 Aug. 24/3 Has .. 'Jackeroo' noticed the inordinate desire stock .. show for feeding in paddocks which have been top-dressed with superphosphate? It's not the grass they seek, for the 'super' paddock is picked almost bare. **1943** *Ibid.* 6 Jan. 12/4 Heavy dressings of super .. promoted the growth of clover in my lawns. **1953** *Ibid.* 21 Jan. 12/2, I dug up six tons of super. Enough for two-hundred acres. **1965** G.H. FEARNSIDE *Golden Ram* 18 He said all his money was being continually poured back into the paddocks in the form of super and seed [etc.]. **1971** *Bulletin* (Sydney) 9 Jan. 54/2 The old recommendation for maintaining a good pasture—'a bag of super to the acre'. **1985** *Canberra Times* 21 Aug. 27/3 'We were really, genuinely, proud of this car, and very happy with it.' That in spite of critical comments from schoolmates who reckoned you had to put a bag of super in the back to make it handle properly.

2. In the phr. **sub and super:** see SUB.

super, *v.*

1. *trans.* Abbrev.of 'superannuate', to pension off.

1978 R.H. CONQUEST *Dusty Distances* 7, I ruined me back workin' as a ganger on the railways so they've super-ed me out on compo.

2. *intr.* To treat soil with superphosphate. (As *vbl. n.* in quot.)

1980 G. ROBINSON *Decades of Duntroon Bastard* 195 Profligate 'supering' with super-phosphate and drainage, had worked wonders.

superb, *a.* Used as a distinguishing epithet in the names of birds and animals: **superb blue** (or **fairy**) **wren,** the small bird *Malurus cyaneus* of s.e. Aust. incl. Tas., the breeding male having light and dark blue plumage; see also *blue wren* BLUE *a.*, *superb warbler*; **lyre-bird,** the bird *Menura novaehollandiae* (see LYRE-BIRD 1); BULLAN BULLAN; **parrot,** the bright green parrot *Polytelis swainsonii* of inland s.e. Aust.; also *ellipt.*; **snake,** COPPER-HEAD; **warbler,** *blue wren*, see BLUE *a.*

1945 C. BARRETT *Austral. Bird Life* 192 First of the fairy-wrens to be discovered was .. the **superb blue wren** or superb warbler. **1978** B.P. MOORE *Life on Forty Acres* 98 Among the really tiny birds that grace the property, the Superb Blue Wren (*Malurus cyaneus*) is undoubtedly the gem. **1984** E. ROLLS *Celebration of Senses* 78 As I sit writing, a male Superb Blue Wren makes a morning inspection of the gauze on the open window thirty centimetres from my shoulder. **1984** *A.N.U. Reporter* (Canberra) 26 Oct. 5 A female superb Fairy-Wren had just commenced constructing her dome-shaped nest... Her mate, in his contrasting blue and black colours, fed on insects amongst the ivy. [**1801 superb lyre-bird:** J. LATHAM *Gen. Synopsis Birds* Suppl. II. 271 Menura .. Superb M... This singular bird is about the size of a *Hen Pheasant*... The tail .. is of a singular construction.] **1929** A.H. CHISHOLM *Birds & Green Places* 89 In the richly vegetated areas of the east coast of Australia .. along the coast of New South Wales (the superb lyre-bird). **1945** C. BARRETT *Austral. Bird Life* 110 Convicts were members of the minor expedition which collected the first known specimen of *Menura novae-hollandiae*, the superb lyre-bird. **1984** SIMPSON & DAY *Birds of Aust.* 319 Male Superb Lyrebirds are polygamous and perform no parental duties. **1917** *Bulletin* (Sydney) 7 June 24/4 Another rare parrot is the green leek, or **superb parrot**... The common green, or swift parrot .. is very often styled 'green leek', though the real Simon Pure is a very different bird. **1945** C. BARRETT *Austral. Bird Life* 78 Long-tailed birds are .. the 'green leek' or superb parrot (*Polytelis swainsoni* [*sic*]) [etc.]. **1975** *Bulletin* (Sydney) 22 Feb. 20/2 The more exotic parrots, such as Golden Shoulders and Superbs fetch $10,000 a pair without difficulty. **1984** M. BLAKERS et al. *Atlas Austral. Birds* 262 The Superb Parrot .. inhabits woodland dominated by river red gum. **1902** *Encycl. Brit.* XXV. 795/1 The death adder, the brown, the black, the **superb** and the tiger **snakes** [of Australia]. **1906** *Bulletin* (Sydney) 12 July 16/1 The diamond snake .. is known as the copper-headed snake in Victoria, and is called the superb snake in N.S.W. Its scientific name is *Denisonia superba.* **1918** *Ibid.* 14 Nov. 22/4 There is one sure thing about the 'winders' of Tasmania. They are all of a kind and poisonous... Only three species occur: the tiger (*N. scutatus*), the copper-headed or superb (*D. superbus*) and the whip. **1953** K. GRAVES *Tasmanian Pastoral* 81 Even the Tasmanian copperhead or superb snake, a small snake but much the most aggressive of the tribe, is nearly two-and-a-half times more venomous than the cobra. **1783** J. LATHAM *Gen. Synopsis Birds* II. 502 **Superb W[arbler]** *Motacilla cyanea* .. inhabits *Van Diemen's Land*, the most southern part of *New Holland.* **1789** A. PHILLIP *Voyage to Botany Bay* 157 Superb Warbler. The length of this beautiful species is five inches and a half... The epithet of *superb* applies very ill to the female. **1808** J.W. LEWIN *Birds New Holland* 19 Superb Warbler .. inhabits woods, frequenting thick and low bushes, and creeping close to the ground in search of its food. **1827** P. CUNNINGHAM *Two Yrs. in N.S.W.* I. 231 We have the lively 'superb warbler', with his blue shining plumage and his long tapering tail, picking up the crumbs at our doors. **1841** J. GOULD *Birds of Aust.* (1848) III. Pl. 24, *Malurus lamberti* .. Lambert's Wren .. Superb Warbler. **1844** L. LEICHHARDT *Jrnl. Overland Exped. Aust.* 20 Dec. 80 We also observed the superb warbler, Malurus cyaneus of Sydney. **1861** 'OLD BUSHMAN' *Bush Wanderings* 148 The *Superb Warbler* is certainly rightly named, for I don't think there is a handsomer warbler in the world. **1887** *Illustr. Austral. News* (Melbourne) 21 Dec. 218/1 The superb warbler is much brighter than the Victorian, and has more color, especially the male bird. **1919** *Bulletin* (Sydney) 16 Jan. 24/4 We've hit it right sometimes with our bird *aliases* .. 'cocktail' (superb warbler). **1928** W. ROBERTSON *Coo-ee Talks* 42 Superb warblers, fantails .. and thornbills.

supplejack. [Spec. use of *supple-jack* any of several climbing or twining shrubs.]

1. Any of several plants having tough, flexible stems, esp. the climber *Flagellaria indica* (fam. Flagellariaceae) of n. Aust. and the vine or tree *Ventilago viminalis* (fam. Rhamnaceae). Also *attrib.*

1788 *HRA* (1914) 1st Ser. I. 21 The trees [on Norfolk Island] are so bound together by a kind of supple-jack that the penetrating into the interior parts of the island was very difficult. **1821** J. WALLIS *Hist. Acct. Colony N.S.W.* 8 When the first settlers landed, there was not a single acre clear of wood on the island; and the trees were so bound together by a creeping shrub called supple jack .. that it was very difficult to penetrate far among them. **1891** H. NISBET *Colonial Tramp* I. 263 Festooned with sassafras and supple-jacks. **1900** *Proc. Linnean Soc. N.S.W.* XXV. 593 *Ventilago viminalis* .. (Supple Jack). This vernacular name arose from the fact that the branches and stems of these trees often entwine, thereby presenting some similarity to the vines known as Supple Jack on the coast. **1912** *Emu* XII. 75 The cunnyanna tree (*Ventilago viminalis* ..) here is remarkable; when it grows up isolated from other trees &c., it develops into a tree growth, but if it happens to be near anything it can creep on it takes the form of a vine, and climbs all over the tree it touches; it is also known as supplejack. **1920** G. Sargant *Winding Track* 34 The boys peeped through the cracks in the slabs, while one of them very quietly and slowly riggled a snake-like supplejack stick through a hole in the fire place. **1938** C.T. White *Princ. Bot. Qld. Farmers* 31 *Flagellaria*, a 'Supple Jack' of the coastal 'brushes' or scrubs. **1951** J. Devanny *Travels N. Qld.* 140 The emu apple and supplejack were trees new to me. **1984** E. Rolls *Celebration of Senses* 37 Supplejack, a small twisted tree, acknowledges its need for company. Its young growth is too pliant to support it, so it writhes about on the ground till it finds something to climb up.

2. *Obs. fig.*

1843 *Colonial Observer* (Sydney) 1 Feb. 785/1 Such admirable *supple-jacks* .. as the would-be member for Illawarra. **1847** G.F. Angas *Savage Life & Scenes* I. 174 One of these fellows was a perfect supple-jack: he danced and capered about as though he was filled with quicksilver.

surf, *n.* [Spec. use of *surf.* Of local significance but not always excl. Austral.: see OED(S *sb.*]

1. The surf as a place of recreation. Also *attrib.*

1908 *Truth* (Sydney) 20 Dec. 5/5 The Manly maidens shoot the surf, or bake their bingies on the shingly shore. **1910** *Ibid.* 14 Aug. 5/3 Sun-baking, after a dip in the surf. **1916** *Ibid.* 26 Mar. 6/6 A *Manly Beach surf siren* suffered from sun-burn. **1925** A. Wright *Boy from Bullarah* 157 Again the call of the surf. Who could resist it. **1930** *Surf: All abaht It* 4 Perhaps you've looked at the surf-aces sometimes, as they've come tearing in to the beach on a foaming express-train, and wondered how they do it. **1931** *Century of Journalism* 516 The cult of the surf in Sydney dates back to less than 30 years ago. There are upwards of a dozen ocean beaches within easy distance of the city, and to-day surfing is the most popular of all summer pastimes. **1939** H.W. Dinning *Austral. Scene* 26 Three weeks of picnicking—of living half-nude between surf and table. **1963** *Bulletin* (Sydney) 23 Nov. 16/3 *Surf's up*, big surf. **1968** B. Humphries *Wonderful World Barry McKenzie*, I was sittin in the surf, When a mate of mine called Murf, Asks if he can crack a tube or two with me. **1979** T. Astley *Hunting Wild Pineapple* 148 A large and shambling young man who .. appeared to have no regular employment though his desperate search for work had taken him to every surf-spot on the eastern seaboard. **1986** *Bulletin* (Sydney) 14 Jan. 30/3 I'm getting blokes my own age all surf-stoked again.

2. A swim in the surf, esp. with the intention of riding waves; the riding of a wave.

1934 C. Mackness *Young Beachcombers* 46 Wish we had brought togs for a surf. **1967** *Surfabout* (Sydney) III. vii. 8 The other popular surf, the left beachbreak, works best at 3–4 feet on high tide. **1967** D. Horne *Educ. Young Donald* 11 Then go for another stroll down to the beach, and another surf. **1975** *Westerly* ii. 25 Two aboriginal children go off to Bondi for a surf.

3. Abbrev. of Surfer.

1975 *Nat. Times* (Sydney) 13 Jan. 40/1 If you are a 14-year-old schoolgirl and you have just discovered boys are not the same thing as your brothers, what really sends your heart into turmoil is the sight of a blond, long-haired, blue-eyed, sun-bronzed surf wearing board shorts and bare feet. **1979** *Westerly* ii. 10 We tried to stay clear of the surfs because they razzed us all the time.

4. In the collocation **surf and turf,** a dish in which lobster and beefsteak are served together.

1975 *New Press* (Perth) II. i. 29/3 Girl chose scallops en brochette and I had 'surf n turf' because I was curious to see what I could get for $1 extra. The answer was a lemon, or a quarter of one, sitting beside a shelled cray. It was accompanied by a minute fillet steak.

5. Special Comb. **surf beach,** a beach from which people surf; **board,** a board on which a surfer rides a wave; so **surf-boarding** *vbl. n.*; **carnival,** a competitive display of the skills of a *surf life-saver*; **club,** abbrev. of *surf life-saving club*; **life-saver,** a member of a *surf life-saving club*; also *attrib.*; **life-saving** *vbl. n.*, the action of saving a swimmer from drowning; the organized safe-guarding of swimmers in the surf; also *attrib.* in **surf life-saving club,** a voluntary organization formed to safe-guard lives in the surf; the premises of such an organization; **shooter,** Surfer; **ski,** a long, narrow board propelled with a paddle by the rider; so **-skiing** *vbl. n.*; **team,** a team of *surf life-savers*.

1929 *Bulletin* (Sydney) 13 Feb. 20/4 Off and on the Portugese man-o'-war or 'bluebottle' has been making itself a nuisance on Sydney **surf beaches** this summer. **1936** N. Caldwell *Fangs of Sea* 29 There are several fine surf beaches; tropical palms and coconut trees line the waterfront. **1941** C. Barrett *Aust.* 16 Dreams of surf-beaches in summertime. **1956** S. Hope *Diggers' Paradise* 246 The racecourses, cricket ovals and the surf-beaches symbolic of a carefree way of life. **1965** G. McInnes *Road to Gundagai* 68 Sydney's great surf beaches. **1930** V. Palmer *Passage* (1957) 127 Hughie would take his **surf-board** and make his way along the sands to Lavinia beach. **1934** T. Wood *Cobbers* 201 Over all this, riding it like a surf-board rides the waves, was a shouting. **1956** S. Hope *Diggers' Paradise* 167 It was a Hawaiian, the famous swimmer Duke Kahanamoku, who introduced the surfboard to Australia during his visit in 1914. **1959** R. Burns *Mr Brain knows Best* 12 I've got a bloody great bruise on my bottom where the surf-board hit me. **1964** *Sunday Mail Mag.* (Brisbane) 17 May 1/4 Surfboarding was virtually forgotten until the late 1930s. **1969** W. Moxham *Apprentice* 29 There was this surf board Rufe had been keen to buy. **1970** J.S. Gunn in W.S. Ramson *Eng. Transported* 60 The young Australians' sport of surfboarding has usually been content to adopt a great deal of established American terminology. **1914** R. Stock *Pyjama Man* 93 Manly was *en fête*. A **surf carnival** was in progress. **1956** S. Hope *Diggers' Paradise* 170 Splendid surf boats manned by stalwart young crews from the Life Saving Clubs, are usually out for practice when not racing at one or another of the Surf Carnivals held up and down the New South Wales coast during the summer season. **1963** J. Pollard *Austral. Surfrider* 132 The first Australian paddlers had their surf skis built for rescue work. Racing was introduced at surf carnivals to encourage them. **1913** *Newcastle Morning Herald* 31 Dec. 5/4 Such dangers as these have brought into existence the '**surf clubs**', which are life-saving clubs. **1930** V. Palmer *Passage* (1957) 72 There were .. two men with the badges of a well-known surf-club on their chests. **1957** *New Settler in W.A.* (Perth) May 5 Today, practically every popular beach in Australia has its lifesaving surf club. **1964** A. Staples *Paddo* 105 Every surf club will tell you the same as every sports club tells you, we may not be the premiers, but our members are the best, our beach has the best surf, our blokes stick together the most. **1968** M. Hilliard *Excuse me, Mr Sweetenham* 170 He said he was off to a dance at the Surf Club. **1963** V.B. Cranley *27,000 Miles through Aust.* 78 We had been invited out to attend the christening of a new lifeboat donated to the local **surf life-savers**. Their performance of swimming and rescue work was really outstanding. **1965** C. Johnson *Wild Cat Falling* 42 A brawny surf-lifesaver type passes along the sea front. **1942** M.L. Macpherson *I heard Anzacs Singing* 20 The **Surf Life-Saving** Association of Australia was founded in 1907 for the purpose of making the beaches safe for bathing. **1956** T.I. Thompson *Pop. Handbk. Swimming* 1 The glamour of surf life-saving. **1963** J. Pollard *Austral. Surfrider* 72 I'm not condemning the Surf Lifesaving movement. It has done a tremendous job over the years, saving thousands of lives and establishing a world-wide reputation. **1964** *Austral. Surf Life Saving Competition Handbk.* (Surf Life Saving Assoc. Aust.) 22 Signals are an essential part of surf life saving and any lack of knowledge, more particularly of those from the beltman or patient to the beach, may result in tragedy. **1972** *Bulletin* (Sydney) 8 Jan. 26/1 Surf life saving needs you. **1915** *Byron Bay Rec.* 2 Jan. 8 The members of the local **Surf** and **Life-Saving Club** were in evidence. **1956** S. Hope *Diggers' Paradise* 40 From the experience of that trek, I learned when to put special cream on my lips and nose, as do many of the members of the Surf Life-Saving Clubs. **1963** J. Pollard *Austral. Surfrider* 106 In the way they mould the careers of young men like myself, the Australian Surf Lifesaving Clubs have an important practical influence on the community. **1930** *Surf: All abaht It* 9 Getting on to a wave .. is one thing. Stopping on is another. It is at this stage, indeed, that the expert **surf-shooter** .. begins to leave the rough-and-ready novice far behind. **1949** C.B. Maxwell *Surf* 9 Old hands will still insist that time has not produced a surf-shooter to equal Freddie Williams. **1956** *Truth* (Sydney) 1 Jan. 44/4 Two surf boats and a small flotilla of **surf skis** and rubber floats were used to rescue screaming men and women and children struggling for life 200 yds. from the beach. **1956** S. Hope *Diggers' Paradise* 193 A number of young Sydneysiders have taken to a new thrill which combines surf-skiing and spear-fishing. **1963** B. Cropp *Handbk. for Skindivers* 31 Surf skis were first introduced to spearfishing over 10 years ago by divers operating at Byron Bay, New South Wales. In 1953, spearmen at Tweed Heads commenced to use skis extensively on offshore reefs. **1963** J. Pollard *Austral. Surfrider* 133 Surf skis are a purely Australian invention. When they were first built, they were made of cedar planking. .. These models have now been largely replaced by plywood models. **1964** *Austral. Surf Life Saving Competition Handbk.* (Surf Life Saving Assoc. Aust.) 14 In **surf teams** races, the team which first has all members of the team to finish shall decide placings in the event of a dead-heat. **1981** *Nat. Times* (Sydney) 20 Dec. 26/5 In 1965 Rodgers went to America with the Australian surf team, and he won the Iron Man contest there. .. Until 1969 he was Australia's Iron Man.

surf, *v.* [Used elsewhere but recorded earliest in Aust.: see OED(S *v.* 2.]

1. *intr.* Abbrev. of Surf-bathe and now the preferred term; now esp. to ride waves on a board. See also Body surf.

1913 [see *surfing, vbl. n.*]. **1914** *Truth* (Sydney) 13 Dec. 1/7 Most of our women .. have more clobber on them when in surfing than they do in the theatres and on the block. **1930** K.S. Prichard *Haxby's Circus* 313 The boys sprawled on the beaches, surfed and swam all day. **1946** 'A. Spence' *Mystery of Red Gum* 112 Mary, who had never surfed in her life, and was quite unaccustomed to large vicious breakers, lay for a moment breathless and a little stunned. **1959** E. Webb *Mark of Sun* 162 You came yesterday late, and surfed by yourself. **1964** *Surfabout* I. vi. 9 A hard place to surf as there is no beach, just rock. **1969** D. Cusack *Half-Burnt Tree* 196 Your Boss at the camp won't worry since you both go surfing together without any clothes on. **1981** *Nat. Times* (Sydney) 20 Dec. 27/4 I've been in the club since 1930 .. and I've surfed every day since, except for the war.

2. *trans.* To surf at (a specified place).

1964 *Surfabout* I. vi. 20 Those of you who have not surfed North Narrabeen, make it a must .. when it's a 'big day' and the ride will leave you really stoked. **1981** *Meanjin* 160 He .. had swum the rivers, surfed the whole coast, camped out in all the bush and hunted there.

Hence **surfing** *vbl. n.* and *ppl. a.*

1913 *Bulletin* (Sydney) 6 Mar. 16/2 The pest of 'bluebottles' (Portugese men-of-war), now infesting the N.S.W. surfing resorts. **1914** H.M. Vaughan *Australasian Wander-Yr.* 22 Of recent years 'surfing' has come into fashion on the ocean beaches, especially at Manly and Bondi. **1916** *Truth* (Sydney) 12 Mar. 1/6 Our surfing women's tight clobber (what there is of it) seems to go to waist, almost to surf-occasion. **1928** A. Wright *Good Recovery* 67 Betty went to her room, found and clothed her supple form in the costume of her surfing days. **1939** E.H. Lane *Dawn to Dusk* 43 On Sundays, bathing in the baths at Coogee .. was my greatest recreation, as surfing was then unthought of in Australia. **1948** J. Cleary *You can't see round Corners* 103 'Where d' you live?' .. 'Coogee.' 'Do much surfing?' **1956** S. Hope *Diggers' Paradise* 166 The most truly 'Australian' of all Australia's national pastimes is surfing, and the bounteous sea provides the best surf in the world. **1969** K. Leopold *My Brow is Wet* 30 Another weekend that would shatter the myth of the suitability of Queensland's southern coast for year-round surfing. **1978** L. O'Charley *Anatomy of Strike* 25 The spectre of surfing bums .. had faded from the scene.

surface, *n. Mining. Hist.* Used *attrib.* in Special Comb. **surface digging** *vbl. n.* [also U.S.], the mining of a deposit at or near the surface; (usu. *pl.*) the site of such a deposit; **stuff,** the material excavated in *surface digging*; **washing** *vbl. n.*, the washing of a surface deposit for gold, etc.; the deposit itself; **working** *vbl. n.*, the place at which a surface deposit is being mined.

1853 J. Sherer *Gold Finder Aust.* 56 In reference to the kinds of digging, they consist of two, technically denominated **surface-digging** and hole-digging. **1853** A. Mackay *Great Gold Field* 10 There have been some surface diggings on some of the slopes and low rises on the creek, which have turned out very well. **1855** W. Howitt *Land, Labor & Gold* I. 219 This is what may be called surface-digging, for the gold lies near the surface of the bottom of the creek. **1859** R.H. HORNE *Austral. Facts & Prospects* 31 They opened up new surface diggings, all of which were prolific. **1872** 'TASMANIAN LADY' *Treasure, Lost & Found* 148 These surface diggings are quickly worked out. **1855** W. HOWITT *Land, Labor & Gold* II. 239 Crowds began digging up **surface-stuff**, and carting it down to the gullies. **1872** 'QUIRIS' *Port Darwin* 11, I have traced it from the gully up on to the reef by washing the surface stuff. **1851** *Empire* (Sydney) 13 Dec. 464/5 As the surest plan I would recommend **surface washing** to all beginners, at which from one ounce to four ounces a-day can be obtained, according as they possess facilities for carting the stuff to the cradle. **1853** J. SHERER *Gold Finder Aust.* 176 There is some good surface-washing on the side of the hills, at times on the top of them and sometimes on the flats. **1856** S.C. BREES *How to farm & settle in Aust.* 57 This practice of superficial digging and surface washing has since been generally, although not wholly, given up. **1864** J. ARMOUR *Diggings, Bush & Melbourne* 8 We tried surface washing, but got only sore backs by it, and returned to the sinking. **1851** *Empire* (Sydney) 13 Sept. 152/1 It is rather thin, but firm in texture, and of a size something less than a threepenny piece; it was found in a **surface workings.** **1863** J.B. AUSTIN *Mines S.A.* 21 The surface workings present a very animated appearance. **1865** *Wallaroo Times* (Kadina) 5 July 3/3 My examination of the mine was confined to a portion of its surface workings.

surface, *v. Mining. Hist. intr.* To mine at or near the surface; to wash a surface deposit for a mineral, esp. gold.

1853 *Illustr. Sydney News* 12 Nov. 43/1 The sinking is from ten to fifteen feet but a great portion of the diggers are still surfacing, waiting for the drier weather.

Hence **surfacer** *n.*

1852 *Moreton Bay Free Press* 21 Dec. 4/3 A number of diggers here are only surfacers, that is, are only searching for gold about a foot or sometimes less from the surface. **1868** J. BAIRD *Emigrant's Guide Australasia* 171 The diggers were of diverse kinds—surfacers, shallow-sinkers, deep-sinkers, and quartz crushers—some being all these in turn.

surface tank: see TANK *n.*[1] 1.

surfacing, *vbl. n. Mining. Hist.*

1. The mining of a surface deposit; the washing of material from a surface deposit to extract a mineral, esp. gold.

1852 Tas. Non-State Rec. 56/1 15 June, Every gulley crossed more or less occupied. Some at surfacing, some digging. **1853** S. SIDNEY *Three Colonies* (ed. 2) 375 Surfacing is as uncertain as sinking. You may wash a whole day and get nothing, or you may happen upon some ounces in a square foot. **1857** W. WESTGARTH *Vic. & Austral. Gold Mines* 181 What is commonly called surfacing, or digging everywhere among the surface gravel and the upper layers of a light but variably coloured shale called the pipe-clay. **1868** J. BAIRD *Emigrant's Guide Australasia* 171 By shallow-sinking and surfacing whatever of the precious metal lay within easy reach was got at. **1885** N.W. SWAN *Couple of Cups Ago* 27 I've moved the pegs to the size of a prospecting claim, and it makes the spot where the horse-shoe was the heart of the ground where the surfacing will begin. **1896** B. SPENCER *Rep. Horn Sci. Exped. Central Aust.* III. 76 'Surfacing' has been attempted in a few places, notably on the western side of Kangaroo Creek, where the surface was removed to a depth of six to eight inches. **1931** C.B. SMITH *Austral. Gold Prospectors' Handbk.* 67 Where the prospector works among the surface deposits on the edges of rivers and creeks it is referred to as 'surfacing'.

2. Material taken from a surface deposit to be washed for gold, etc.

1852 A. ADAMSON *Lett.* 9 May (1901) 25 On Wednesday Joseph and I went out prospecting to Spring Gully; tried about a dozen pans of surfacing, but found nothing. **1852** J. BONWICK *Notes of Gold Digger* 18 The surfacing . . was . . immensely rich. **1859** *Colonial Mining Jrnl.* May 145/1 Following this course the diggings would lead to surfacing, which would, no doubt, with a good supply of water in the rainy season, pay very well. **1871** *Austral. Town & Country Jrnl.* (Sydney) 3 June 687/2 The whole of the surfacing and quartz . . seems to abound with gold. **1890** 'R. BOLDREWOOD' *Miner's Right* 153 It seems they have been mopping up some rich surfacing.

surf-bathe, *v. Obs.* [Also used elsewhere: see OED(S *sb.* 3.] *intr.* To swim in the sea, esp. to ride waves. Freq. as *vbl. n.*

1906 [see *surf-bather, n.*]. **1907** *Truth* (Sydney) 21 Apr. 1/6 The raising of false alarms on the surf-bathing beaches is nothing short of criminal. **1908** *Bulletin* (Sydney) 27 Feb. 14/3, I have been surf-bathing. **1912** *Truth* (Sydney) 18 Feb. 8/3, I think respectable people may go surf-bathing and, still remain respectable, but people who aren't moral and respectable do not become so by shooting the breakers and airing their figures on the beaches. **1912** *Ibid.* 10 Nov. 10/4 'Oh, Auntie', said the child, 'what's surf-bathing?' 'Something the savages do on boards,' replied the aunt vaguely. **1916** I.L. IDRIESS Diary 23 June iii. 90 We went out this afternoon, and above all things, went surf bathing! Glory of glories! Surf bathing. **1919** *Smith's Weekly* (Sydney) 1 Mar. 1/1 Surf-Bathing is dangerous for women. **1956** S. HOPE *Diggers' Paradise* 37, I had a natural appreciation for the beauty and charm of the Sydney girls, and sometimes lingered in mixed youthful society to surf-bathe.

Also **surf-bather** *n.*

1906 *Truth* (Sydney) 21 Jan. 1/6 Coogee Bay offers exceptional advantages to surf-bathers. **1913** *Bulletin* (Sydney) 6 Mar. 16/2 The Shocked . . watching the female surf-bather. **1915** N. LINDSAY *N. Lindsay's Bk. II* 28 Her body, of which nine-tenths is visible, is just tinted with the nice ruddy brown of the devoted surf-bather. **1932** R.W. THOMPSON *Down Under* 37 We met a few of our ship acquaintances on our prowls around, and took some of them with us on our drives in my friend's old Bentley to the beaches—Bondi, Coogee, Bronte—with their crowds of surf-bathers. **1963** J. POLLARD *Austral. Surfrider* 140 The Mayor of Waverley, pointing a finger of scorn at Bondi, declared: 'Some of these surfbathers are nothing but exhibitionists, putting on vee trunks and exposing themselves twisted into all shapes in the sand.'

surfer. [Used elsewhere but recorded earliest in Aust.: see OEDS.] One who swims in the surf, esp. one who does so to ride waves, either as a *body surfer* (see BODY SURF) or on a surfboard. Also *attrib.*

1913 W.K. HARRIS *Outback in Aust.* 93 Out of his hide they commenced to manufacture beautiful bags . . and, most novel of all, a 'surfer's companion', a dainty article intended to hold bathing suit and wet towel in a water-proof case. **1916** O. HOGUE *Trooper Bluegum at Dardanelles* 146 The Turks are not the surfers the Australians are. **1930** V. PALMER *Passage* (1957) 126 Never had Lavinia been more gay than that summer, with crowds of brown-limbed surfers sprawling on the white beaches. **1932** *Austral. Ring* II. xxv. 5 Surfing has now become his favorite pastime. He spends all his spare time down at Bondi learning to 'shoot' the breakers. Although he has only had a few lessons, he looks like becoming as efficient a surfer as he is a boxer. **1946** *Bulletin* (Sydney) 23 Jan. 12/2 Surfers on S.Q. beaches will have good reason to remember the first week of 1946. **1949** C.B. MAXWELL *Surf* 12 Residents petitioning councillors because these creatures without shame, these—these *surfers* occupied seas in the light of day, disrobing anywhere. **1963** B. JOHNSON *Surf Fever* 4 The Surfer, as he is commonly termed, is an everyday figure along the East Coast. **1966** *Surfabout* III. v. 33 A Surfer is a devoted and inconspicuous person in the sport. . . A Surfie is usually the exact opposite. He has a loud mouth and no respect for other people. **1984** P. JARRATT *Aussie* 50 Radio stations ran surfer stomps in surf clubs and on promenades and, for a while there, before the Beatles . . it seemed like the reckless hedonism of the surfing lifestyle was simply going to take over.

surfie. Also **surfy.** [f. SURF(ER + -Y.] A surfer, esp. one dedicated to surfboard-riding; one who frequents surfing beaches (see quots. 1964 and 1982). Also *attrib.*

1962 *Austral. Women's Weekly* (Sydney) 24 Oct. (Suppl.) 3/4 *Surfie*, a fond term for a good and keen surfer. **1963** *Bulletin* (Sydney) 30 Mar. 9/2 The catalyst which caused the interest in the board-riders, or Surfies, was their clash with the Rockers. **1964** M. HILLIARD *Running through Rain* 176 It was a gang of Surfies—bronzed youths who lived on the beaches in summer, lolling on the sand . . bleaching their hair. **1968** A. CLIFFORD *Send her down, Hughie* 130 There were surfers and surfies. Surfies bleached their hair, carried boards on their trucks, and lay on the beach—but did no actual surfing. **1970** P. SLATER *Eagle for Pidgin* 3 Twitty lot of ghastly giggling females and scurfy surfy males with fibreglass where their brains should be. **1975** *Bulletin* (Sydney) 18 Jan. 11/3 It's as worth while to pay surfies to surf as it is to pay poets to write poetry. Surfing is an art form. **1979** CAREY & LETTE *Puberty Blues* 1 Us little surfie chicks, chirping our way down on the train. **1982** *Bulletin* (Sydney) 19 Oct. 92/3 A 'monosyllabic cretin' . . who speaks two words of English—'Yeah' and 'Man'—streaks his hair with Clairol . . and, worst of all, drinks milk. In other words, a Bondi surfie.

Surfoplane. Also **surfoplane.** [Proprietary name.] An inflatable rubber mat used esp. for riding waves. Also *attrib.*

1934 *Sydney Morning Herald* 2 Apr. 13/8 Dee Why Surf Life-saving Club had the distinction of promoting the last carnival of the season. . . Results . . Surf-o-plane race—J. Watson (Bondi). **1955** *Gear & Equipment Handbk.* (Surf Life Saving Assoc. Aust.) 33 The rubber surf board or surfoplane is used extensively on surfing beaches. **1964** *Sunday Tel.* (Sydney) 23 Feb. 32/6 A three-year-old boy fell off his surf-o-plane into a hole that had developed on the northern end of the beach. **1972** K. WILLEY *Tales Big Country* 71 He would also pick up a few bob by working for the surf-o'-plane man on Dee Why beach. **1981** *Nat. Times* (Sydney) 20 Dec. 27/4 The prototype of the rubber surfoplane was a blown-up pillow case.

surfy, var. SURFIE.

surround, *v. Obs. trans.* To drink (alcoholic liquor).

1904 *Bulletin* (Sydney) 1 Dec. 40/1 He used to surround a good deal of liquor and then go down to the camp and 'deal it out' to the little woman for spite. **1907** *Ibid.* 28 Feb. 15/3 Seventeen beer-chewers went into a Winton (Q.) bar the other day, and came out an hour later, having . . surrounded 28 drinks each.

survey, *n.*[1] *Obs.* [Transf. use of *survey* the process of surveying a tract of ground.] A tract of land which has been surveyed.

1840 *S. Austral. Rec.* (London) 6 June 302 Newly arrived emigrants and the South Australian public generally, are invited to examine section 4208, part of Mr Dutton's splendid survey, at Mount Baker. **1844** *Portland Mercury* 10 Jan. 4/1 On the company's survey near the Albert, and adjoining the government township of Alberton, the embryo township of Victoria is situate. **1848** *Portland Gaz.* 7 July 3/1 The splendid surveys which that gentleman has purchased and, we know, *paid for.* **1861** 'OLD BUSHMAN' *Bush Wanderings* 95 A great country for pigeons is about the Survey, on the coast, forty miles from Melbourne.

survey, *n.*[2] *S.A. Hist.* [A term used by Cornish miners: see EDD.]

1. The letting of work in a mine.

1844 *S. Austral. Register* (Adelaide) 30 Mar. 2/2 A *survey* will be held at the Montacute Copper Mine, this day (Saturday), for letting the various works of the said Mine. Persons desirous of engaging on the said works are requested to be in attendance at from 12 to 1 o'clock. *Ibid.* 27 Sept. 1/3 Two of the Directors of the Belvedere Mining Company will attend at the mine for the purpose of holding a Survey. **1874** *Yorke's Peninsula Advertiser* (Moonta) 10 Feb. 2/4 'Big Survey' took place on Saturday when the number of men assembled in front of the office were computed at no fewer than twelve hundred. There are two kinds of surveys held on the mines, one denominated the little survey and the other the big survey, each taking place at intervals of nine weeks.

2. Special Comb. **survey-day,** the day appointed for the letting of work in a mine.

1848 *S. Austral. Register* (Adelaide) 12 Apr. 3/2 A new lode has been discovered since the last survey day. **1865** *Wallaroo Times* (Kadina) 22 Apr. 6/3 Saturday the 8th instant, was survey day at this mine. **1869** *Ibid.* 10 Feb. 2/4 'Survey day' . . i.e. the day upon which various operations to be carried on during the ensuing month are let by contract to the miners. **1962** O. PRYOR *Aust.'s Little Cornwall* 54 The old Cornish custom of Survey Day when men bargained publicly for work to be done underground lasted for about twenty years at Wallaroo and Moonta but was then superseded by private tenderings.

sus /sʌs/. *Hist.* Also **suss.** Abbrev. of SUSTENANCE. Also in the phr. **on (the) sus.**

1972 G.C. BOLTON *Fine Country to starve In* 99 Many regarded going 'on sus' as the last extremity. **1978** B. ST. A. SMITH *Spirit beyond Psyche* 132 His wife, a tiny wisp of a woman, looked after two sons in their twenties, both out of work and doing a bit of state relief work on the roads when compelled to, but mostly living on the 'Suss', the Sustenance allowance, on State Relief.

susso /'sʌsoʊ/. *Hist.* [f. SUS(TENANCE + -O.]

a. SUSTENANCE. Also in the phr. **on (the) susso.**

1941 S.J. BAKER *Pop. Dict. Austral. Slang* 51 *On the susso*, in receipt of unemployed sustenance. **1968** K. DENTON *Walk around my Cluttered Mind* 167 We've done a nice little ostrich trick about the queues for the Dole and the Susso and the sight of six thin men sharing one thin cigarette. **1971** G. WISEWOULD *Outpost* 16 Men on 'Susso'—the government allowance of six shillings a week to a man unable to obtain work. **1977** J. CARTER *All Things Wild* 7 A children's parody of the era reflected the shame many people felt if they had to accept government assistance: 'We're on the susso now; we can't afford a cow; we live in a tent, we pay no rent; we're on the susso now.' **1984** *N.T. News* (Darwin) 17 Sept. 7/2 During the great depression my father was forced to work for the Susso (sustenance payments or dole) for five days a week—no work—no money.

b. One who is in receipt of SUSTENANCE. Also *attrib.*

1947 V. PALMER *Cyclone* 8 He thinks it puts hair on his chest knocking around with the sussos. **1958** F. HARDY *Four-Legged Lottery* 44 Some of those who still had work looked down on the unemployed, the 'sussos' as they were contemptuously called. **1960** *Realist* (Sydney) iii. 22 The very thought . . of the contempt the respectable held for the sussos, changed his mood to defiance. **1964** K. TENNANT *Summer's Tales* 32 A beach strewn with susso Adonises already grilled walnut. **1969** P. ADAM SMITH *Folklore Austral. Railwaymen* 190 When war was declared all our big 'susso' camps folded up overnight. **1978** G. HALL *River still Flows* 57 Almost incredibly, instead of uniting the jobless workers in their misfortune, the 'Sussoes' themselves were often divided into factions. **1986** *Age* (Melbourne) 6 May 39/3 You can see the bluestone rim of the Boulevard built by 'susso' workers in the Depression.

sustenance. *Hist.* Any of several forms of unemployment relief provided, orig. by State governments, during the Depression.

1932 *Act* (Vic.) no. 4079 Sect. 3, 'Sustenance' includes shelter, clothing, and firewood, and references to receiving sustenance include references to obtaining sustenance. **1933** *Admin. Social Services* (Vic. Dept. Labour, Sustenance Branch) 11 Municipalities are entitled to demand work at Award Rates from any male person in receipt of sustenance, as head of a family unit, and from any single male person whether a traveller or resident. **1934** *International Labour Rev.* July 40 In Victoria alone has any concerted effort been made to require recipients of sustenance to give work in return. **1936** *Labour Rep.* (Cwlth. Bureau Census & Stat.) xxv. 113 *Western Australia*. . . From the 1st August, 1933, employment upon relief works has been on a rotary basis, which provides four weeks' full-time work followed by further full-time work equivalent in value to that of the periods of sustenance, set out in Column 'B' hereunder. *Ibid.* 114 When work for sustenance is performed payment is made in cash. When no work is performed sustenance orders on the various storekeepers are issued to the men. **1937** R.H. CROLL *Wide Horizons* 28 So many of the inhabitants are in receipt of aid from the Government in the form of 'sustenance' or the old-age pension. **1942** L. MANN *Go-Getter* 182 He would call at the Returned Soldiers' League and put himself on the list for sustenance there. **1956** V. COURTNEY *All I may Tell* 117 Many folk were short of the bare necessities of life and had to rely on dole tickets for their sustenance. A new term 'Sustenance Worker' came into the language, but the so-called sustenance was not really sufficient for children. **1958** F. HARDY *Four-Legged Lottery* 45 Before the end of 1930, Tom Roberts was forced to register for sustenance—at first a bag of groceries each week, later a small wage for which he had to work. **1963** 'C. ROHAN' *Down by Dockside* 21 Lila's baby was not at all well, and the social worker who went the rounds of the Port Melbourne sustenance houses advised her to take him to hospital. **1964** G. JOHNSTON *My Brother Jack* 162 They brought in the dole, and then the dole became 'the sustenance'. **1970** R. BEILBY *No Medals for Aphrodite* 86 The Depression had beaten him . . relegating him to that scrap-heap of the unemployed, the Sustenance Gang, one week's work in every three and that one spent 'pushing the banjo' with road-making gangs in the bush. **1977** J. CARTER *All Things Wild* 7 Men preferred to eke out an independent existence from the bush than accept what was to them the humiliation of the government dole or 'sustenance' work. **1978** B. ST. A. SMITH *Spirit beyond Psyche* 132 Two sons in their twenties, both out of work and doing a bit of state relief work on the roads when compelled to, but mostly living on the 'Suss', the Sustenance allowance.

swag, *n.* [Transf. use of *swag* a thief's plunder or booty: see OED *sb.* 9.]

1. The collection of possessions and daily necessaries carried by one travelling, usu. on foot, in the bush; esp. the blanket-wrapped roll carried, usu. on the back or across the shoulders, by an itinerant worker.

1841 *Sydney Herald* 10 Nov. 2/6 They gave me back my horse, and on him we fastened 'our swags' (for be it known, they scorned to take our dirty linen). **1849** J. PATTISON *N.S.W.* 115 It is advisable to take a pack-horse to carry that grand essential to bush-travelling called a 'swag'. **1853** C.R. READ *What I heard, saw, & Did* 6 His wife bringing up the rear, with a child on her back, who generally got a cheer from passers-by, or a question, as to how much she'd take for her '*swag*'. **1859** 'EYE WITNESS' *Voyage to Aust.* 18 The digger's mode of travelling is very distressing, as they generally carry with them all their utensils and tent covering; the weight of these things approaching near one hundred weight [*sic*]. The term or name given to this load is 'swag', which is made up in the following manner; his blankets are spread out, the shirts and small clothing are laid on them and rolled like a thick rope until it resembles a horse's neck-collar with both ends tied; this is thrown across the shoulders as a sportsman carries his shot-belt; to this is tied a pannikin, an axe to cut wood, a billy to carry and boil water in one hand, and a green bough in the other to ward off the flies from his eyes. **1870** C.H. ALLEN *Visit to Qld.* 248 Walking along one day with his 'swag' or knapsack on his shoulder, he met a man, driving a mob of sheep. **1879** 'AUSTRALIAN' *Adventures Qld.* 36 The blacks when caught had their heads pillowed on the spoils of the hut. They had taken the shepherds' rations, clothes, and blankets, making them up into convenient-sized 'swags' to travel with. **1890** *Bulletin* (Sydney) 30 Aug. 21/3 Did you ever take 'the wallaby' along some dreary track With that hideous malformation, called a swag, upon your back. **1905** *Ibid.* 15 Oct. 14/4 The hairy man with his brown paper swag and empty treacle tin. **1915** N. DUNCAN *Austral. Byways* 112 The bushmen travel amazingly light. A billy-can and a blanket—the 'swag' of the bush—are equipment enough for any frugal man in places within reach. **1929** W.J. RESIDE *Golden Days* 365 To-day he runs a motor-car, I sweat beneath a swag. **1941** K. TENNANT *Battlers* 39 Would you believe it, they'd soon got half the table talking about swags and showing how you rolled them with the serviettes. **1954** *Coast to Coast 1953–54* 20, I tell you both before youse throw the swags in it ain't any use you comin' out if you can't handle hay. **1962** V.C. HALL *Dreamtime Justice* 25 'Where are your teeth, Mr Morck?' There was a placatory note in the old mail-rider's voice as he told her his teeth were in his swag. **1981** A.B. FACEY *Fortunate Life* 78 She said, 'I didn't know you. Your swag is bigger than you are. Surely you never carried it all the way from Phillip's place.'

2. *spec.* A bed-roll.

1865 J.O. TUCKER *Golden Spring* 86 Disengaging myself of the cumbrous weight of blankets that comprised my 'swag'. **1924** J. HARPER *Splashes from Narran* 15 Shouldering his swag, one well-worn Government blanket, he lit out. **1947** E. HILL *Flying Doctor Calling* 14 He is a nomad for most of the year, tailing cattle and mustering, riding from waterhole to waterhole, sleeping in his swag on the ground for weeks . . and often with no comrades but the blacks. **1960** E. O'CONNER *Irish Man* 229 He lay in half-wakeful rapture, curled in his swag on the hard ground. **1975** X. HERBERT *Poor Fellow my Country* 152 'You didn't bring a swag.' 'Swag?' 'Bedding.' **1978** D. STUART *Wedgetail View* 40 He fumbled with the groundsheet and blankets and at last curled awkwardly into the swag. **1979** K. DUNSTAN *Ratbags* 10 She refused to get out of her swag. **1982** R. ELLIS *Bush Safari* 15 Another frugal meal of 'tinned dog', a couple of flats to mend, and straight into our swags.

3. *Obs.* Abbrev. of SWAGMAN a.

1910 'H.H. RICHARDSON' *Getting of Wisdom* 217 Her time was spent . . in taking long, solitary evening walks . . till Mother, haunted by a lively fear of encounters with 'swags' or Chinamen, put her foot down and forbade them.

4. In phr.: **to up swag,** to pack up one's possessions and set out on a journey; **swag up,** carrying a swag.

1873 *Australasian Sketcher* (Melbourne) 1 Nov. 133 (*caption*) **Up Swag.** **1877** *Free Trade Papers* xi. 4 Tell you what, mate, lets up swag and make to-night for the Reefs. **1902** R.C. PRAED *My Austral. Girlhood* 52 There was nothing for it but, as the old hands would have said, 'to up swag and shift further out'. **1919** A. WRIGHT *Game of Chance* 53 Up swag and ho for the Riverina. **1901** *Bulletin* (Sydney) 12 Oct. 16/1 Woman, with a **swag up,** recently passed through Walgett. **1938** F. BLAKELEY *Hard Liberty* 15 Since the first man was forced on the track with swag-up giving the evening hand-out has been part of the job of managing big runs. **1964** G. GELBIN *Australs. have Word for It* 144 Years ago I've seen this place lousy with men, all with the swag up, waiting for the sheds to start.

5. Special Comb. **swag carrier,** SWAGMAN a.; **swag-carrying** *vbl. n.* and *ppl. a.*; **cover,** a waterproof cover for a swag; **strap,** a strap with which a swag is held together and secured to the bearer.

1881 [**swag-carrier**] *Adventures of Strollers Otway Ranges* 7 Feeling just a trifle tired at the usual occupation of swag-carrying, we determined to 'make assurance double sure'. **1896** H. LAWSON *While Billy Boils* (1975) 21 A wretchedly forlorn specimen of the swag-carrying clan whom a boundary-rider had found wandering about the adjacent plain. **1898** *Bulletin* (Sydney) 26 Feb. 14/1 John Godkin, Tas. prospector, well-remembered in connection with the great Godkin mining case, 'lays over' all swag-carriers in the Land of Sleep-a-Lot. **1944** *Ibid.* 6 Dec. 13/3 Y'hear a lot about the mateship of swag-carriers. **1902** H. LAWSON *Children of Bush* 212 When the ground got a little drier we rigged a bit of shelter from the showers with some sticks and the oil-cloth **swag-covers.** **1934** *Bulletin* (Sydney) 26 Sept. 20/3 My best bed was of spinifex placed spiny side downwards. You need a good canvas swag-cover to spread over it. **1954** *Ibid.* 16 June 12/4 No self-respecting bushman would wrap a swag in a blanket—he uses a 'swag-cover'. This varies from the light duck of a 'boong's swag' to the heavier tarpaulin types. **1958** J.R. SPICER *Cry of Storm-Bird* 38 'What do you reckon we're goin' to sleep on?' 'Our swag-covers,' said Rob. **1979** R. EDWARDS *Skills Austral. Bushman* 17 The inland can be bitterly cold during the night despite the high temperatures of the day. There are often numbing winds or heavy, soaking dews and the swag cover is essential to protect both the sleeper and his bedding. **1981** G. MACKENZIE *Aurukun Diary* 50 A swag-cover thrown over a low branch of a tree made a blackboard, and school was in on the sandy bank. **1902** *Bulletin* (Sydney) 18 Oct. 15/1 When a **swag-strap** or anything else is lost a chest-inspection is commenced. **1915** *Ibid.* 11 Nov. 22/3 I'm game to bet my new swag-strap. **1965** R.H. CONQUEST *Horses in Kitchen* 42 The swagman . . rolled his belongings into a bag, which he tied to a swag-strap and dangled over his chest so as to balance the swag. **1980** ANSELL & PERCY *To fight Wild* 41 The swag of blankets and tarpaulin, with two swag straps, one in two sections connected by the swivel chain from a set of hobbles.

Hence **swagless** *a.*, without a swag, esp. in the phr. **stiff and swagless,** without money or possessions (see also STIFF 1); **swaglike** *a.* and *adv.*

[N.Z. **1885** A.H. BURTON *Maori at Home*, We horsemen found ourselves **swagless.**] **1906** *Bulletin* (Sydney) 12 July 17/1 When the nomad is utterly stiff and swagless, he obtains three or four discarded corn sacks and sews them together. **1920** *Smith's Weekly* (Sydney) 28 Aug. 9/4 That wanderer was not a waster. He was stiff and swagless, and no traveller likes to be on the road without a bluey of ordinary dimensions. **1928** *Bulletin* (Sydney) 29 Aug. 19/2 That wanderer happened to be stiff and swagless. **1890** *Argus* (Melbourne) 2 Aug. 4/2

He strapped the whole lot together **swag-like.** **1926** L.C.E. GEE *Bush Tracks & Gold Fields* 73 The swaglike object in the back part of the boat.

swag, *v.*

1. *intr.* To carry one's swag; to travel as a swagman. Also with **it.**

1859 'EYE WITNESS' *Voyage to Aust.* 21 All parties coming into the colony, with few exceptions, have to swag it for a time. **1861** T. M'COMBIE *Austral. Sketches* 5 This load is called 'the swag' and the mode of travelling, 'swagging it'. **1878** W. EVANS *Diary Welsh Swagman* (1975) 84, I prepare to swag again, but I fear I shall be unable to get work. **1889** *Bulletin* (Sydney) 15 June 13/4 If in luck, inclined to brag it, 'No up-country' *then* he votes, When he's down he'll gamely swag it, *Then* new chummy *minus* 'notes'. **1895** *Ibid.* 22 June 3/2 'Swagging' up the long divide that leads to Daybreak Range. **1908** E.G. MURPHY *Jarrahland Jingles* 16 It was on the old Kalgoorlie track we met him swagging in. **1918** *Huon Times* (Franklin) 20 Dec. 3/1 He took the train from York to Albany, and then swagged it on up to Coolgardie. **1934** 'E.N. SPEER' *Destiny* 243 Dave knew the ropes; how to fence, ride, cook, swag, how to be useful on a run. **1943** C.E. GOODE *Bridge Party at Boyanup* 15 They swagged it to Coolgardie in the good old 'roaring days'. **1956** *Bulletin* (Sydney) 1 Feb. 12/3 Swagging it in Queensland from Hughenden to Winton, I struck the pub on St. Patrick's Day in 1904.

2. a. *trans.* To travel through (the country) or along (a road) as a swagman.

1871 W. EVANS *Diary Welsh Swagman* (1975) 21 At Ballarat I visited Mr Roberts, the photographer, and asked him to take my portrait . . swagging the Bush with my billy-can. **1882** E.B. BAYLY *Alfreda Holme* 352 He might leave his luggage under Mr Hart's kind roof, and start with a bundle on his shoulders to 'swag' the country. **1903** *Bulletin* (Sydney) 21 Mar. 16/3 Among the large army of 'come-downers', swagging the bush, many have excellent references. **1960** 'A. CARSON' *Rose by any Other Name* 50, I was swagging my way up to the Northern Territory.

b. *fig.* To support (someone).

1896 *Bulletin* (Sydney) 23 May 3/2 Hold up, Billy; I'll stick to you; they've hit you under the belt; If we get the waddle I'll swag you through, if the blazing mountains melt.

Hence **(be-)swagged** *ppl. a.*, **swagging** *vbl. n.*

1881 *Adventures of Strollers Otway Ranges* 6 And what of W--? Robed and **swagged** like B--, coatless, with a slouching black billy-cock hat. **1906** *Bulletin* (Sydney) 24 May 14/1 Be-swagged, unsteadily he strode To pad it to his native land. **1898** *Ibid.* 20 Aug. (Red Page), It's a tedious job—like **swagging. 1911** E.J. BRADY *River Rovers* 45 The rheumatics had got into his right leg, and his swagging days were over. **1927** J. MATHIEU *Backblock Ballads* 1, I don't succumb to swagging, July fogs, or charcoal tarts. **1934** 'E.N. SPEER' *Destiny* 239 Neville had been initiated into 'swagging' and all its wrinkles. He had been shown how to roll 'fags', how to make damper, how to boil the billy, how to grill chops in the ashes. Finally, he was taught how to roll the fly and blankets into the swag.

swagger. [f. SWAG *n.* or *v.*] SWAGMAN a. Also *attrib.*

1855 *Argus* (Melbourne) 19 Jan. 6/1 We have observed a great influx of swaggers lately—all seemingly bound for Smith's Creek. **1882** E.B. BAYLY *Alfreda Holme* 135 They're a greater nuisance than swaggers at the hut. 'Swaggers', be it known, are men who roam the country, carrying all their worldly goods in a little 'swag' or bundle, on their shoulders, professedly in search of work, but in fact, living on the hospitality universal in the bush, where no man is refused a supper, night's lodging, and breakfast. **1888** G. ROCK *Colonists* 57 Now, mates, I'm only a poor swagger. **1894** *Bulletin* (Sydney) 13 Jan. 7/4 Close the swagger's port of departure—the lambing-down shanty. **1898** *Ibid.* 12 Feb. 14/3 A swagger struck Foxton . . and went round to the back-door of the local storekeeper and quietly asked for a bit of tucker. **1916** *Truth* (Sydney) 21 May 12/7 (*heading*) Australian swagman. Swagger work of art. **1976** B. SCOTT *Compl. Bk. Austral. Folk Lore* 374 Next morning an old swagger, passing by the dell, Saw the remains, stifled a sigh, and muttered another by hell.

swaggie. [f. SWAG *n.*[1] + -Y.]

a. A SWAGMAN or SWAGWOMAN. Also *attrib.*

1891 *Truth* (Sydney) 19 Apr. 7/3 Many a swaggy has to thank Charlie and the missus . . for a bit of tobacco and a feed. **1894** *Western Champion* (Barcaldine) 5 June 2/1, I had a good square (all round, too) look at the swaggie, and concluded some beer would set him up a bit if he had some dry clothes on. **1898** *Bulletin* (Sydney) 9 Apr. 14/1 Female 'swaggies' are becoming comparatively common in South Australia. **1911** *Ibid.* 10 Aug. 14/2 The bike seems to lend an air of business, which lifts a man right out of the swaggie class. **1918** A. WRIGHT *Over Odds* 85 At the Sundown camp . . a goodly number of swaggies had foregathered. **1935** F. CLUNE *Rolling down Lachlan* 47 Another swaggie . . had a wheelbarrow, and was lying on his back beside the fire, while the billy boiled. **1948** R.A. PEPPERALL *Emigrant to Aust.* 128 An enormous black jowl, which never appeared to have been adequately shaved, together with a disregard for his general appearance, often led him to be classed as a 'swaggie'. **1964** P. ADAM SMITH *Hear Train Blow* 119, I wished I could have worn a hat like this real swaggie. His felt hat had strings with corks on the ends hanging down all round the brim to keep the flies off his face. **1977** *Bronze Swagman Bk. Bush Verse* 30 And I've camped with the Swaggie, and drunk billy tea. **1981** A. MARSHALL *Aust.* 17 A swagman is generally patronised. . . The swaggie learns to encourage this attitude.

b. *fig.*

1943 'MRS E.F. BOSWORICK' *Amateur* 11 The wise old swaggy moon.

Hence **swaggying** *pres. pple.* and *vbl. n.*, leading the life of a 'swaggie'.

1905 *Bulletin* (Sydney) 2 Feb. 16/4 Swaggying is a varied and reasonably exciting profession in Westralia. **1923** *Smith's Weekly* (Sydney) 16 June 19/5 The next time I go swaggying I'll put an electric fan in my swag.

swagman. Formerly also **swagsman.**

a. One who carries a swag; an itinerant worker, esp. one in search of employment, who carries a swag; a tramp.

1869 W.M. HUGO *Hist. First Bushmen's Club* (1872) 30 Sir—A swagsman, and not ashamed to own it. I have done the 'wallaby' for years past in search of a billet. **1878** *Squatters' Plum* 42 A swagsman, who has travelled 200 or 300 miles in search of work without getting it, can tell a widely different tale. **1886** P. CLARKE *'New Chum' in Aust.* 122 Three miles farther on a couple of 'swagsmen'—workmen on the look-out for work, and carrying a swag, or bundle of their household goods—assured me that Bulli was then only five miles off. **1899** *Worker* (Sydney) 14 Jan. 5/2 A swagman named Walter Kirby has been found dead at Ursino, on the Paroo. . . A billy was found close by, on which was inscribed, 'Perished from want of water.' **1916** *Truth* (Sydney) 21 May 12/7 Charged . . with the theft of a bronze statuette of an Australian swagman, with a billy-can in his hand, and a dog beside him. **1926** G. BLACK *Hist. N.S.W. Political Labor Party* vi. 21 A swagman, minus an aeroplane, had voted in 26 electorates. **1934** T. WOOD *Cobbers* 200, I heard tales of drivers who had given swagmen a lift in return for gate-opening, and had then been confronted at the end of the day with a claim for wages, based on the standard rate as laid down by the Arbitration Courts of Queensland. **1956** A.C.C. LOCK *Tropical Tapestry* 107 Swagmen are a class of nomads who have disappeared from the Australian landscape. Some were sons of distinguished families. They had drifted with the current of social disfavour. **1963** 'E. LINDALL' *Springs of Violence* 37 'More likely a swagman's breakfast,' Walter grunted. 'What's that?' . . 'You don't know? . . It's a piss an' a look around.' **1971** *Bulletin* (Sydney) 4 Sept. 42/2 A nameless swagman who, about 80 years ago, jumped into Combo waterhole, sooner or later haunts all Australians. **1982** *Ibid.* 18 May 78/1 The boy's grandfather . . recognises as a swagman the scruffy man with the rolled blankets who had been propping himself up against the fence. . . He had told him to get moving but later feels guilty.

b. In the collocation **suburban swagman:** see quots.

1902 *Bulletin* (Sydney) 14 June 14/1 A curious institution is the Sydney suburban swagman. He 'works' his 'beat', or 'round', starting from Willoughby, where he lives in a tent or cave. Sometimes he travels what is known as the 'single triangle'—along Lane Cove-road to Hornsby, thence to Parramatta, and thence back, via Sydney, to his base of operations. He is generally in search of. . odd jobs. The 'double triangle' man usually 'works' from Parramatta to Penrith. Thence to Windsor, and back to the 'Bridge Hotel', Parramatta. **1905** W. MOORE *City Sketches* 46 The genteel cadger, known professionally as the suburban swagman, frequents other haunts than those of his Yarra-banking brother. **1911** *Bulletin* (Sydney) 6 Apr. 14/1 A long, attenuated, ungainly, awkward, suburban swagman was caught robbing the boss's best bulb beds.

swagwoman. A woman who carries a swag.

1894 *Bulletin* (Sydney) 7 Apr. 13/1 The swagwoman is becoming one of the sights of Maoriland. **1896** *Ibid.* 13 June 28/2 A swagwoman on the way to South Australia was arrested in Bendigo the other day as a vagrant. **1909** *Ibid.* 26 Aug. 14/4 A swagwoman is not a very common happening, but a few days ago an old travelling lady . . passed through Moree. **1980** BRENNAN & WHITE *Keep Billy Boiling* 86 Occasional swagwomen were to be found, usually characters of note such as 'Menindee Mary' and the 'Portia of Pooncarrie'.

swainsona /sweɪnˈsoʊnə/. Also **swainsonia.** [The plant genus *Swainsona* was named by R.A. Salisbury (*Parad. Lond.* (1806) Pl. 28) after English naturalist Isaac *Swainson* (1746–1812). The form *Swainsonia* has also been used as a name for the genus.] Any plant of the chiefly Austral. herbaceous genus *Swainsona* (fam. Fabaceae), perennials or annuals, esp. of drier Aust., having pinnate leaves and colourful pea-flowers. See also *Darling pea* DARLING.

1857 W. HOWITT *Tallangetta* I. 23 Interspersed amongst these were large purple vetches, or Swainsonias, of a most delicious vanilla scent. **1931** M. TERRY *Hidden Wealth* 324 On this station were noted two species of swainsona. **1946** C.T. MADIGAN *Crossing Dead Heart* 122 In the lower ground there were wide areas covered with the purple flowers of a creeping plant, a very attractive Swainsona. **1975** R.O. MOORE *Sunlit Plains Extended* 34 On the plains in good seasons both the dark and light lavender Swanisonia pea grew in abundance.

Swainson's phascogale. [First applied as the specific epithet *Swainsonii* by the English naturalist G.R. Waterhouse, after William Swainson (1789–1855), naturalist.] The small marsupial *Antechinus* (formerly *Phascogale*) *swainsonii* (fam. Dasyuridae) of Tas. and s.e. Aust., esp. in mountainous areas. Also **Swainson's pouched mouse.**

1894 R. LYDEKKER *Hand-Bk. Marsupialia & Monotremata* 171 Swainson's Pouched Mouse. *Phascologale swainsoni*. . . Fur very long, soft and thick. General colour deep rufous or umber-brown, under-parts dull brownish-grey . . length of head and body about 5 inches; tail of 4 inches. **1926** A.S. LE SOUEF et al. *Wild Animals Australasia* 334 Swainson's phascogale is a cold-country species, living in Tasmania and in the mountains of Victoria and Northern New South Wales. **1968** D. FLEAY *Nightwatchmen* 25 As I sat motionless a bright-eyed Swainson's phascogale (pouched mouse) emerged from a hollow log and ran perkily up and down my trouser leg.

swallow, *v. Obs. trans.* In the phr. **to swallow bobby,** to make a false statement.

1847 A. HARRIS *Settlers & Convicts* (1953) 51 Some of the first 'nobs' in the colony used to 'swallow bobby' (make false affidavits) to an enormous extent. **1970** J.S. GUNN in W.S. Ramson *Eng. Transported* 63 Other imminent or actual losses which seem regrettable to me are . . *square*, 'sober', *swallow bobby*, 'make a false statement to avoid customs duty'.

swallow-catch, *v. intr.* Of a horse: to run a race in fast time. (As *vbl. n.* in quot.)

1904 L.M.P. ARCHER *Bush Honeymoon* 70 'That's a good horse of yours, miss', he said coolly, 'bit of blood? They're doing some *swallow-catching* to-day; you ought to give him a cut—might win a quid or two.'

Hence **swallow-catcher** *n.*

1913 A. PRATT *Wolaroi* 128 Beehive, a noted swallow-catcher, was the first of all the horses to get moving.

swamp, *n.* Used *attrib.* in the names of flora and fauna having a swampy or periodically flooded habitat: **swamp box,** any of several trees, esp.

Lophostemon suaveolens (fam. Myrtaceae) of n. Aust., which is also known as *swamp mahogany*; **grass,** any of several native or introduced grasses (fam. Poaceae), incl. the American *Echinochloa crus-galli*, naturalized in all States; *water grass*, see WATER; **gum,** any of several trees of the genus *Eucalyptus* (fam. Myrtaceae), esp. *E. ovata* of s.e. Aust. incl. Tas., *E. microtheca* (see COOLIBAH), and (*Tas.*) *E. regnans* (see *mountain ash* MOUNTAIN); the wood of the tree; also *attrib.*; **harrier** (or **hawk**), **(a)** *obs.*, *spotted harrier* (see SPOTTED); **(b)** the bird of prey *Circus approximans*; **hen,** the bird *Porphyrio porphyrio* of Aust. and elsewhere, having blue and black plumage with a bright red bill and head shield; BALDCOOT; see also *red bill* RED *a.* 1 b.; **lily,** either of two perennial herbs, the tall, bulbous *Crinum pedunculatum* (fam. Liliaceae) of swampy land in coastal Qld. and N.S.W., bearing fragrant white flowers, and the aquatic *Ottelia ovalifolia* (fam. Hydrocharitaceae) of mainland Aust.; **mahogany,** any of several trees, esp. the rough-barked coastal species *Eucalyptus robusta* (fam. Myrtaceae) of e. Qld. and N.S.W., yielding a durable red timber, and *Lophostemon suaveolens* (see *swamp box*); the wood of the tree; **oak,** any of several trees or shrubs of the fam. Casuarinaceae, esp. *Allocasuarina paludosa* of s.e. Aust. incl. Tas., and *Casuarina glauca* of near-coastal s.e. N.S.W. to s.e. Qld.; the wood of the tree; also **she-oak; parrot** (or **parakeet**), the bird *Pezoporus wallicus* (see *ground parrot* GROUND *n.*[1]); **pheasant,** *pheasant coucal*, see PHEASANT 2; **quail,** *brown quail*, see BROWN *a.* 1; **rat,** a native rodent of the genus *Rattus*, esp. the grey or greyish brown *Rattus lutreolus* of e. Aust. incl. Tas.; **stringybark,** the small tree *Eucalyptus conglomerata* (fam. Myrtaceae) of s.e. Qld.; **tea-tree,** any of several shrubs or trees of the fam. Myrtaceae, as *Melaleuca ericifolia* of s.e. Aust. incl. Tas., and *Leptospermum myrtifolium* of e. mainland Aust.; **wallaby,** the dark-coloured wallaby *Wallabia bicolor* of areas of dense moist undergrowth in e. mainland Aust.

1878 R.B. SMYTH *Aborigines of Vic.* I. 220 The hunter, in places far removed from permanent water, has to draw his supply of that element from the roots of the **swamp-box** and the weir-mallee, which run a few inches below the surface of the earth. **1902** *Proc. Linnean Soc. N.S.W.* XXVII. 228 *Eucalyptus melanophloia* . . is regarded by bushmen as 'Swamp Box'. **1935** *Bulletin* (Sydney) 13 Mar. 20/2 The apple exudes a red gummy sap from the limbs. . . The swamp-box weeps only when rain is threatening. **1978** K. MCARTHUR *Pumicestone Passage* 43 Most of the canoe trees so far found from the Noosa River to the Passage shores have been swamp box (*Tristania suaveolens*). **1840** *S. Austral. Rec.* (London) 20 June 333 The cart was upset, nearly killing one of the men, whose life was only preserved by a bunch of **swamp-grass** and sedge, which prevented the load from crushing him to death. **1885** P.R. MEGGY *From Sydney to Silverton* 120 The fairy-like swamp grass, so-called because it flourishes in the track of swamps. **1927** *Bulletin* (Sydney) 1 Sept. 29/3 Swamp-grass, or water-grass, which forms broad patches and long, green points in swamps, and is often dense enough for water-fowl to walk on, grows to the surface from surprising depths. **1970** N.T. BURBIDGE *Austral. Grasses* III. 32 The name of Swamp Grass has been used for *E*[*chinochloa*] *walteri* and for related species, and it has, unfortunately, also been attached to other grasses. It is used here pending the discovery of a better name. **1832** *Colonist* (Hobart) 21 Sept. 1/5 For Sale . . a large quantity of excellent **swamp gum** shingles. **1854** W. HOWITT *Boy's Adventures* 209 The trees . . were of that gigantic species of red-gum, called swamp-gum, from its love of growing by water. **1872** 'TASMANIAN LADY' *Treasures, Lost & Found* 95 The graceful tree-fern, the sassafras, and that magnificent species of swamp-gum that fringes the banks of the Mingah. **1896** B. SPENCER *Rep. Horn Sci. Exped. Central Aust.* I. 13 The lines of the water-courses are marked by belts of gum trees and acacias . . *Eucalyptus microtheca*, the swamp gum [etc.]. **1926** A. EDEN *Places in Sun* 72 The ash or swamp-gum towers to 300 feet and more, a glorious, gracious tree. **1946** C.T. MADIGAN *Crossing Dead Heart* 43 This was a delightful spot, with gidgee again at the cliffs, and box and swamp gum. **1967** E. HUXLEY *Their Shining Eldorado* 172 The swamp gum or mountain ash—*Eucalyptus regnans*—survives here [*sc.* Florentine Valley, Tas.] probably in greater numbers than anywhere else on earth. **1985** *Trees & Natural Resources* Sept. 32 Students from Kyneton High School planting Swamp Gums to create a waterfowl sanctuary. **1843** [**swamp harrier**] J. GOULD *Birds of Aust.* (1848) I. Pl. 26, *Circus assimilis* . . Swamp Hawk, of the Colonists. **1861** 'OLD BUSHMAN' *Bush Wanderings* 123 One of the commonest of all the hawks with us was the large *Marsh Harrier*, or, as we used to call it, the *Swamp Hawk*. **1889** W.H. TIETKENS *Jrnl. Central Austral. Exploring Exped.* 27 Apr. (1891) 17 Noticed a few swamp hawks hovering over the camp. **1930** D. COTTRELL *Earth Battle* 61 The big brown swamp-hawks wheeled overhead and tilted up sideward a hundred feet. **1945** C. BARRETT *Austral. Bird Life* 39 Our two harriers are familiar birds, especially the swamp-hawk or Gould's harrier (*Circus gouldi*) usually seen flying, in a leisurely manner, over swampy places, crops and reedbeds. **1964** M. SHARLAND *Territory of Birds* 104 One immediately became the target for a Swamp Harrier which swung down towards it, struck and missed, and flew angrily round a point. **1986** *Parkwatch* (Vic. Nat. Parks Assoc.) Mar. 13 A swamp harrier soars over the lake-margins. **1833** *Perth Gaz.* 2 Mar. 35 Wild Birds, the . . **swamp hen** Pigeons, &c. &c., have been offered for sale more generally of late, than usual. **1841** J. GOULD *Birds of Aust.* (1848) VI. Pl. 70, *Porphyrio bellus* . . Swamp-Hen, Colonists of Western Australia. **1873** W.L. BULLER *Hist. Birds N.Z.* 186 The Swamp-hen is widely distributed over Tasmania, the greater part of the continent of Australia [etc.]. **1948** R. RAVEN-HART *Canoe in Aust.* 24 A pair of what Jack called 'waterfowl' (Eastern Swamp Hen), with bits of sealing-wax on their noses. **1955** *Bulletin* (Sydney) 2 Nov. 13/2 The blue bald coot—the swamp-hen of W.A.—walks through the tea-tree thicket with as much assurance as it roams around the edges of the swamp. **1968** R. HILL *Bush Quest* 11 From the opposite bank a swamp-hen came, flicking its black and white tail and bobbing its head as it fed amongst the trailing water weeds. **1982** R. ELLIS *Bush Safari* 124 Purple Swamphens strutted like large bantams along mud banks. **1867** *Lang. Native Flowers Tas.* 6 **Swamp Lily** . . Perishable beauty. **1909** *Bulletin* (Sydney) 16 Dec. 13/2 The many swamps and shaking-bogs wear a sheen of purple swamp-lilies. **1935** M. & E. DURACK *All-About* (1940) 63 From everywhere comes a scent of white swamp-lilies. **1970** BURBIDGE & GRAY *Flora A.C.T.* 16 Shallow pools in woodland habitats of lower elevations; widespread on Australian mainland; introduced in New Zealand. 'Swamp Lily' . . *O*[*ttelia*] *ovalifolia*. **1979** WRIGLEY & FAGG *Austral. Native Plants* 105 *C*[*rinum*] *pedunculatum* . . Swamp lily. Large plant with upright leaves 1 m. long. . . Bears open, white flowers on thick stem. . . Makes an excellent feature plant. **1817** A. CUNNINGHAM in I. Marriott *Early Explorers Aust.* (1925) 176 *Eucalyptus robusta* (white or **swamp mahogany**). **1836** J. BACKHOUSE *Narr. Visit Austral. Colonies* (1843) 422 Cedar, Sassafras, Swamp-mahogany . . form a striking contrast to the low forest. **1861** *Catal. Natural & Industr. Products N.S.W.* 28. Swamp Mahogany. . . A crooked growing tree, the timber much valued for knees and crooked timbers of coasting vessels. **1882** *Proc. Linnean Soc. N.S.W.* VII. 623 It was not . . until . . 1866 . . that *E*[*ucalyptus*] *robusta* was found to be the tree known to workmen as 'Swamp Mahogany', the original specimens of which were probably collected in low and swampy ground near Sydney. **1903** *Austral. Handbk.* 279 Large trees . . which furnish hard durable timber are . . 'Swamp Mahogany' (*Tristania suaveolens*), 'Brisbane Box' (*T. conferta*). **1909** R. KALESKI *Austral. Settler's Compl. Guide* 37 Swamp mahogany . . so called because its timber has a figure like Honduras mahogany. **1935** T. RAYMENT *Cluster of Bees* 463 A river-flat, which was not swampy, but covered with grass and a thick growth of 'swamp mahogany'—a *Eucalyptus*. **1974** N. CATO *Brown Sugar* 51 At first wool was exported . . then the valuable native timbers: red cedar, swamp mahogany. **1983** K.W. MANNING *In their Own Hands* 204 Messmate (swamp mahogany) could scarcely be coaxed to burn. Its pungent smoke would gum up flues and the wood generally was an invitation to domestic discord. **1801** *HRA* (1915) 1st Ser. III. 170 There are gum-trees, **swamp-oak,** the tea-tree. **1824** *Hobart Town Gaz.* 1 Oct., Colonial Timber may at any time be purchased of an inhabitant of this town . . Forest & Swamp Oak, for furniture, fuel, and boat timbers. **1832** *Sydney Herald* 7 May 3/1 A swamp oak tree at the lower end of George street . . has been lately cut down. . . This tree was considered sacred by Governor Macquarie, and the old hands of the Colony. **1851** J. HENDERSON *Excursions & Adventures N.S.W.* II. 215 The Swamp-Oak is not unlike that of the forest, but it grows by the sides of swamps, creeks, and rivers. **1880** R. ROSE *Austral. Guide: S.A.* 11 What may not be improperly designated the Australian fir tribe (*Casuarinas*), colonials have invested with very singular names. Thus, we find there . . the 'swamp-oak' (*C. paludosa*). **1901** *Proc. Linnean Soc. N.S.W.* XXVI. 687 *C*[*asuarina*] *Cunninghamiana* is, so far as I have been able to observe, purely a fresh water tree, and must not be confused with the Swamp Oak, *C. glauca*, often found near salt water along the coast. **1936** J.E. HAMMOND *Western Pioneers* 19 We could not make a fire and had to sit up all night getting . . shelter . . under a swamp oak tree. **1983** *Canberra Times* 24 Dec. 7/4 A Canberra firm has won a $617,000 contract to plant 500,000 swamp sheoaks at Brisbane's new airport. **1984** L. RICHARDSON *Bitter Yrs.* 2 The coastal frontage behind the swampy margins of Lake Illawarra were badly drained, the soil acidic and able to support only swamp oaks. **1833** [**swamp parrot**] *Trumpeter* (Hobart) 8 Nov. 227 *To Naturalists.* To be sold . . birds, in skins . . Swamp Parroquite. **1844** G.F. ANGAS *Savage Life & Scenes* 30 Apr. (1847) I. 152 Occasional swamp parrots fluttered up from the grass. **1845** J. GOULD *Birds of Aust.* (1848) V. Pl. 46, *Pezoporus formosus* . . Ground Parrot . . Swamp Parrakeet, Colonists of Van Diemen's Land. **1861** 'OLD BUSHMAN' *Bush Wanderings* 164 We had a curious ground parrot, common in the long grass in the plains, on the heather, and often in low tea-tree scrub . . called the *Swamp Parrot*. **1929** A.H. CHISHOLM *Birds & Green Places* 156 In the wallum country there is at least one bird, the swamp-parrot, unknown to any other island [than Fraser Island] (except Tasmania) and very rare on the mainland. **1962** MARSHALL & DRYSDALE *Journey among Men* 76 We carried with us the battered skin of a swamp parrot—a bird that looks not unlike the night bird we wanted to find. **1976** *Reader's Digest Compl. Bk. Austral. Birds* 272 There are only three ground-living parrots in the world: the swamp parrot, the night parrot and, in New Zealand, kakapo *Strigops habroptilus*. All three species are now extremely rare. **1825** B. FIELD *Geogr. Mem. N.S.W.* 46, I shot two **swamp pheasants** (a pretty black bird not unlike the English pheasants in shape). **1830** R. DAWSON *Present State Aust.* 14 It was known in the colony as the *swamp pheasant*, which inhabits the shores near the sea, and which is extremely rare, disappearing always when the country becomes settled. **1845** C. HODGKINSON *Aust., Port Macquarie to Moreton Bay* 209 The swamp-pheasant . . is a stupid inactive bird, generally found among swamp-oak thickets, bordering on marshes. **1872** C.H. EDEN *My Wife & I in Qld.* 121 The swamp pheasant (*Centropus Phasianus*) a pretty bird, but much smaller than its English relative. **1889** R.B. ANDERSON tr. Lumholtz's *Among Cannibals* 94 Although it really is a cuckoo, the colonists call it the 'swamp pheasant', because it has a tail like a pheasant. **1921** G.A. BELL *Under Brigalows* 133 The bubbling notes of the swamp pheasant. **1967** E. HUXLEY *Their Shining Eldorado* 331 The clumsy . . swamp pheasant . . runs swiftly on the ground but when it takes to the trees might almost be thought to have got at the grog. **1980** B. SCOTT *Darkness under Hills* 43 He built his fire . . and roasted a swamp-pheasant and some scrub turkey eggs. **1849** C. STURT *Narr. Exped. Central Aust.* II. 47 App. Synoïcus Australis—**Swamp Quail,** or Partridge . . is generally found in marshes, or marshy ground, and frequently in bevies. **1898** E.E. MORRIS *Austral Eng.* 374 Brown Q[uail]—*Synoicus australis* . . (Called also Swamp-Quail.) **1911** A. MACK *Bush Days* 56 A sudden 'whir-r-r' makes us jump back a pace as a swamp quail rises. **1933** F.E. BAUME *Tragedy Track* 103 The swamp quail is often to be seen. **1965** *Austral. Encycl.* VII. 316 The brown quail, or swamp quail, is found from the Moluccas through Australia to Tasmania. **1926** A.S. LE SOUEF et al. *Wild Animals Australasia* 118 The **swamp-rat** is found in swampy country all over South Australia. **1941** E. TROUGHTON *Furred Animals Aust.* 280 Swamp-Rats appear to be strictly vegetarian by nature. **1976** *Ecos* viii. 19 The swamp rat forages by day for grass, herbs, mushrooms, seeds, and insects. **1978** S. KELLY *Eucalypts* II. 44 **Swamp stringybark** has a very restricted natural distribution, on the flat land near the coast about 60–150 km. north of Brisbane. **1981** PRYOR & BRIGGS *Austral. Endangered Species* 50 Swamp stringybark grows on coastal flats or slight depressions in gently undulating areas which are wet and swampy during the wet season. **1832** J. BACKHOUSE *Narr. Visit Austral. Colonies* (1843) 58 They cross the mouth of the harbour on floats, in the form of a boat, made of bundles of the paper-bark of the **Swamp Tea-tree.** **1883** E. PALMER *Plants N. Qld.* 18 *Thryptomene oligandra* . . a small tree, called Swamp ti-tree, grows in sandy country near swamps. **1906** *Emu* VI. 54 A frail little nest of this species was found . . in a swamp tea-tree (*Melaleuca ericifolia*). **1935** D. THOMSON *In Arnhem Land* (1983) 67 We threaded our way among glades of swamp tea-tree, chiefly *Melaleuca leucadendra*. **1946** W.E. HARNEY *North of 23°* 30 That knadjebut, or swamp ti-tree, is good above ground. **1970** BURBIDGE & GRAY *Flora A.C.T.* 267 Shrub 1–2 metres high . . of forested gullies and high mountain valleys and ridges, commonly near seepage or swamps . . 'Swamp Tea-tree' . . *L[eptospermum] myrtifolium.* **1896** F.G. AFLALO *Sketch Nat. Hist. Aust.* II. 40 Into the specific descriptions of the rock, **swamp,** brush, scrub and other **wallabies** I shall not enter. **1904** *Shearer* (Sydney) 27 Aug. 7/2 *Marsupial-skins.*—Strong demand in force for swamp and rock wallaby and bear skins, prices showing an upward tendency. **1926** A.S. LE SOUEF et al. *Wild Animals Australasia* 189 *M. ualabatus,* known as the black and also as the swamp wallaby, inhabits scrubby damp gullies, through which it has well-marked paths or 'wallaby tracks'. **1946** K. TENNANT *Lost Haven* 233 Alec was amused by Dipper, a good bloke, but nervous as a swamp wallaby. **1965** *Austral. Encycl.* V. 160 The solidly-built and rather shaggy-haired swamp or black-tailed wallaby (*W[allabia] bicolor*), with a dark brown back and reddish-yellow belly. **1985** *New Idea* (Melbourne) 7 Dec. 25/1 Three young reds share the limelight with . . a swamp wallaby.

swamp, *v.*[1] *trans.* To drink, esp. in the phr. **to swamp one's cheque,** to spend one's entire earnings on alcoholic liquor.

1850 *Bell's Life in Sydney* 12 Jan. 2/7 Other members stayed away because they had taken their dinner before the hour of meeting and some, several of whom had been 'swamping it' at Botany on the previous day, had experienced that the water they then and there tested, disagreed with them. **1879** 'AUSTRALIAN' *Adventures Qld.* 2 They were . . denying themselves almost the necessaries of life, to save every farthing of their wages for months and months together; then to pay a flying visit to Old Rickets, and 'swamp their cheques like men'. **1894** *Bulletin* (Sydney) 3 Nov. 14/3 When riding homeward penniless, you light your pipe and think *This* somewhat like the time you 'swamped' your hard-earned cheque in drink. **1920** *Smith's Weekly* (Sydney) 28 Aug. 9/4 No traveller likes to be on the road without a bluey of ordinary dimensions. A man might 'swamp his cheque' . . but he won't part with his bundle.

swamp, *v.*[2] [Transf. use of U.S. *swamp* to clear a road: see OED(S *v.* 5.] *intr.* To travel as a SWAMPER (senses a. and b.); to work as an assistant to a bullock driver or other carrier (see quot. 1944); to work casually in this capacity (see quot. 1944). Also *trans.*, to obtain (a lift), and as *vbl. n.*

1897 *Bulletin* (Sydney) 6 Mar. 28/4 We were swamping back from Lake Darlot rush last winter with Billy Mills's camels. **1926** K.S. PRICHARD *Working Bullocks* 101 Billy Williams the bullocky, and Ern Collins who was swamping for him, turned their team into the yards on the following Monday. **1937** E. HILL *Great Austral. Loneliness* 96 In they come, across the jagged Leopolds, or up from the desert, 'swamping' with a bullocky, staggering behind a pack donkey, or on Shank's pony with a blackboy. **1941** D. O'CALLAGHAN *Long Life Reminisc.* 239 A few weeks after the sensational news . . people swamped from here and there. **1944** M.J. O'REILLY *Bowyangs & Boomerangs* 6 My duties were to help to load and unload, bring the horses in the morning, to harness up, help to corduroy bad patches on the track, draw water for the horses at the soaks and wells, hobble out the horses at night, put the bells on, etc. These duties were then known as 'Swamping', a very appropriate name, especially after heavy rains, when the waggons would sink to the axle. All this work for the privilege of having one's tucker, tools, and swag carried on the waggon. Fortunately the chap I 'swamped' for was an exceptionally good sort. **1954** T. RONAN *Vision Splendid* 92 This isn't my camp, I'm only swamping a ride. **1964** —— *Packhorse & Pearling Boat* 170 If I broke it for a tenner, I'd roll my swag and swamp my way back to Queensland. **1984** W.W. AMMON et al. *Working Lives* 156 He promised that if I gave him a hand to load the big wagon I could swamp up with him for as far as I wanted to go.

swamp cancer. [From the popular belief that the disease is associated with swampy land.] A skin disease of horses, in which a growth of granulation tissue occurs as the result of the presence of larvae of a thread-like parasitic worm of the genus *Habronema.*

1880 J.J. JONES *Openings for Emigrants* 21 Horses that suffer from swamp cancer are hurried off to the saltbush. **1898** D.W. CARNEGIE *Spinifex & Sand* 366 This habit of standing up to the girth in water has given rise to a horse-sickness known as 'swamp-cancer'. The skin under the belly becomes so soft that at last a raw place is formed, and this aggravated by the flies, spreads until it becomes a serious disease. **1911** *Cwlth. Parl. Papers* III. 5/9 There are three diseases, however, that seem to constitute drawbacks, to horse breeding in this part of the country. These are commonly known as (1) the 'Walk-about' disease, which is generally fatal; (2) the 'Puffs', and (3) the so-called 'Swamp-cancer'.

swamper. [See SWAMP *v.*[2]]

a. One who travels on foot but whose baggage is carried on a wagon.

1894 *Bulletin* (Sydney) 28 Apr. 9/3 Teamsters are now arriving with nothing but swags aboard, the 'swamper's' baggage being more remunerative than ordinary loading. **1896** *Ibid.* 18 Apr. 3/2 When you've anted five-and-sixpence for a bottle full of plums, You've to travel as a swamper, if you ain't a wealthy jay. **1897** A.F. CALVERT *My Fourth Tour W.A.* 58 A 'swamper', it appears, is a 'swagsman' without his 'swag', which is on one of the waggons. **1917** T.J. BRIGGS *Life & Experiences Successful W. Austral.* 126, I had with me two drivers and nine swampers. These latter were men who were making for the goldfields with their swags, and they paid me £4 each to carry their swags, and walked themselves. **1930** H. REDCLIFFE *Yellow Cygnet* 123 Swampers . . were those who, having no carriage but their legs, at a price arranged with the teamster, dumped their swags containing food and blankets on his dray, while they followed on foot throughout the journey. Probably the term of swamper was derived from the fact of the men with their water bags exhausting the small water holes. **1954** T. RONAN *Vision Splendid* 21 If Sidi picked up any swampers it was a safe bet that some of the luxury goods would be short on arrival. **1972** N. KING *Nickel Country* 48 Many men loaded on their swags and walked beside the wagons. They became known as 'swampers' and they soon learned to walk ahead of the wagons to avoid the choking dust. **1983** P. ADAM SMITH *When we rode Rails* 70 Some who walked while paying to send their swags ahead on a wagon were called 'swampers'.

b. One who obtains a lift.

1964 H.M. BARKER *Camels & Outback* 14 On this journey one of my three passengers (or 'swampers') would ride ahead on the horse to pick a camp. **1966** T. RONAN *Once there was Bagman* 15 My . . fellow swamper tossed his swag off [the mailman's truck] here; he was home.

swan. [Spec. use of *swan* a large swimming bird of the genus *Cygnus.*] *Black swan,* see BLACK *a.*[2] 1 b.

1801 M. FLINDERS *Observations Coasts Van Diemen's Land* 8 These swans are black, the wing feathers excepted. **1833** *Perth Gaz.* 7 Sept. 144/3 *Market prices* . . swan, 6 at 8s. **1852** J. MORGAN *Life & Adventures W. Buckley* 30, I could see an abundance of ducks, and geese, and swans. **1935** F. CLUNE *Rolling down Lachlan* 196 Here, ibis, ducks, and swans swam in the shade of box-trees mixed with belahs and yarran.

Swan River mahogany. [f. the name of the river in W.A., on which Perth stands.] JARRAH 1.

1847 E.W. LANDOR *Bushman* 396 We have just inspected about two tons of wood brought to this town (Leeds) under the name of Swan River Mahogany. **1924** A.B. PEIRCE *Knocking About* 171 A trip was made to Perth and Fremantle on the Swan River in Western Australia (a locality noted for a hard and soapy red gum called Swan River mahogany which is extensively used in the sheathing of vessels). **1974** *Bulletin* (Sydney) 18 May 24/2 The best bauxite tends to be found under the best jarrah—or Swan River mahogany as it was originally known.

swatser /'swɒtsə/. *Obs.* Also **swatzer.** [f. G. *schwarzer* a black (male) person.] An Aboriginal.

1896 *Truth* (Sydney) 7 June 5/5 They are supposed to repeat Her Majesty's monniker three times, and if the 'swatzer' doesn't halt, they can let go. **1898** *Bulletin* (Sydney) 1 Oct. 14/3 A few more W.Q. slang words . . a blackfellow is a 'swatser'. **1970** J.S. GUNN in W.S. Ramson *Eng. Transported* 134 Early migration from the German-speaking countries has enriched Australian English vocabulary with . . *swatser* (German *Schwarzer*), 'blackfellow, native'.

sweat, *v.* [Joc. use of *sweat* to give (a horse) a run for exercise.]

1. *trans.* To borrow (a horse) without the owner's permission. Also as *vbl. n.*

1869 *Bushmen, Publicans, & Politics* 6 The *sweating* of a horse is a good joke. **1904** L.M.P. ARCHER *Bush Honeymoon* 115 There were a lot of 'travellers' on the river, and if they struck her, they would probably *collar* the pack and *sweat* her for a week or two. **1922** *Bulletin* (Sydney) 23 Feb. 22/1 In the old days in N.S. Wales the law—in practice, if not by Act of Parliament—made a distinction between horse-stealing and horse-sweating. . . Borrowing a horse without the owner's knowledge or consent, and turning it adrift at the end of the ride, was called 'sweating'; and though it was punishable by law, the penalty was usually light. **1944** *Ibid.* 3 May 12/4 Our neighbor . . always declared that somebody 'sweated' one of his mokes every dance night.

2. To squander (one's own or someone else's earnings).

1882 *Bulletin* (Sydney) 21 Oct. 8/4 He had sweated his cheque at the hotel, and found himself a boosted-up community, with brain on fire, coppers hot, and a throat like the stove-pipe of Gehenna. **1956** R.G. EDWARDS *Overlander Songbk.* 77 We steer up to the girls, that ring themselves with grandeur, And while they sweat our cheques—they swear, they love the overlander.

sweating pen. A holding pen; orig. a covered lean-to shelter in which sheep, sweating from being mustered or driven, were confined while drying out before being moved to the holding pen in the shearing shed: see quot. 1980. See also *holding pen* HOLDING.

1882 ARMSTRONG & CAMPBELL *Austral. Sheep Husbandry* 175 A narrow race is made, which is filled from the sweating, or night pens. **1883** *Illustr. Austral. News* (Melbourne) 28 Nov. 194/3 Now the 'jumbucks' have all been penned up in the immense 'sweating pen' or covered in shed—fully 3000 or more. **1896** G. SUTHERLAND *Australasian Live Stock Man.* 208 In the case of a run employing about a dozen men at shearing time, this dry-shed or sweating-pen may be capable of holding fully 1000 sheep. **1928** C.E. COWLEY *Classing Clip* 147 The bulk of the sheep that will be kept under cover in the shed will be in what are commonly known as 'the sweating pens'. **1937** W.R. GLASSON *Musings in my Saddle* 76 He scrutinized the floor of the shed closely, the wool room, the shearing board and the sweating pens. **1965** J.S. GUNN *Terminol. Shearing Industry* ii. 29 *Sweating pen,* sometimes used in the same sense as 'holding pen', although there is no longer any suggestion of deliberately 'sweating' the sheep. **1979** HARMSWORTH & DAY *Wool & Mohair* 138 The pens in which the sheep are held before shearing are sweating pens and can be of any size, although very big pens are inconvenient to work . . it is customary to have the sweating pens of such a size that they will hold enough sheep for one day's shearing. **1980** P. FREEMAN *Woolshed* 18 The sheep enter the Kingsvale woolshed on slotted ramps and are directed by gates into 'sweating' pens. The term is an old one, for it recognises that shearers have always refused to shear 'wet' sheep, and that the sheep require time in these pens to cool down preparatory to shearing.

sweep. Pl. **sweep, sweeps.** [Of unknown origin, but see quot. 1857.] Any of several marine fish, usu. of the fam. Scorpidae, esp. those of the genus *Scorpis,* as *S. lineolatus* of s.e. Aust. incl. Tas.

1840 F.D. BENNETT *Narr. Whaling Voyage* I. 23 They were chiefly of the kinds known as . . 'sweeps', and 'rudder-fish', or scad. **1857** J. ASKEW *Voyage Aust. & N.Z.* 229 There is a curious little flat fish, called 'the sweep', of which many are caught. When first taken out of the water it is bright as silver, but in a few seconds it turns as black as a sweep, hence its name. **1880** *Proc. Linnean Soc. N.S.W.* V. 397 *Scorpis aequipinnis* . . '*The Sweep*' of the Sydney Fishermen. **1896** F.G. AFLALO *Sketch Nat. Hist. Aust.* 205 The little Sweep . . is the only edible member of the Coral Fishes (Chaetodontidae). ***c* 1905** *Tourists' Guide Geelong* 38 A fish but little known, and yet of great delicacy, is the sweep, which commands a price equal to soles or flounders, and weighs from 2½ to 5 lb. **1974** T.D. SCOTT et al. *Marine &*

Freshwater Fishes S.A. 249 Family Scorpidae. The fishes of this family are known generally as Sweeps. **1980** G. DUTTON *Wedge-Tailed Eagle* 36 We anchored off the rocks . . and caught sweep and parrot-coloured cod.

sweeper. *Shearing.* One who is employed to sweep pieces of wool which fall during shearing or the handling of the fleece from the floor of a shearing shed: see quot. 1918.

1910 C.E.W. BEAN *On Wool Track* 197 The locks are always being swept up by special boys—'sweepers'. **1918** R.H. KNYVETT *Over there with Australs.* 29 The 'sweeper' gathers into a basket the trimmings and odd pieces. **1980** P. FREEMAN *Woolshed* 20 There are three main types of shorn wool; the 'locks', from the sheep's legs, that are swept up and emptied into baskets by the 'sweepers'; the 'bellies' from the sheep's underside, which are carefully removed by sweepers and thrown into other baskets; and the 'fleece' itself.

sweepy. *Obs. Shearing.* [f. *sweeper* + -Y.] SWEEPER.

1898 *Bulletin* (Sydney) 20 Sept. 11/4 The 'sweepy', that swept the board.

sweet, *a.*[1] Used as a distinguishing epithet in the names of plants: **sweet bursaria,** see BURSARIA; **plum,** *Burdekin plum*, see BURDEKIN; **tea,** the wiry climbing plant *Smilax glycophylla* (fam. Smilacaceae) of e. N.S.W. and Qld. (see quot. 1790); SARSAPARILLA b.; see also *native sarsaparilla* NATIVE *a.* 6 a.; also **sweet tea plant.**

1874 LINDLEY & MOORE *Treasury of Bot.* (rev. ed.) 1324 *Owenia cerasifera* is called the **Sweet Plum.** **1888** *Proc. Linnean Soc. N.S.W.* III. 534 *Owenia cerasifera* . . 'Sweet plum' . . bears a fine juicy red fruit with a large stone. **1909** F.M. BAILEY *Comprehensive Catal. Qld. Plants* (ed. 2) 124 *Pleiogynium* . . *Solandri* . . Sweet Plum. . . The wood somewhat resembles American walnut; dark and heavy. **1965** *Austral. Encycl.* IV. 227 *Pleiogynium cerasiferum*, Burdekin plum or sweet plum (Anacardiaceae) . . the purplish stone fruits, 1–2 inches in diameter, have a very acidic taste, but if kept for several days they become palatable and refreshing. **1790** J. WHITE *Jrnl. Voyage N.S.W.* 155 That which we call the **sweet tea** is a creeping kind of vine, running to a great extent along the ground. . . Of this the convicts and soldiers make an infusion which is tolerably pleasant, and serves as no bad succedaneum for tea. **1835** J. BACKHOUSE *Narr. Visit Austral. Colonies* (1843) 292 The Sweet Tea, *Smilax glyciphylla*, abounds. It is a low, climbing plant, with narrow, heart-shaped leaves, having a taste something like Spanish Liquorice. **1860** G. BENNETT *Gatherings of Naturalist* 368 The Sarsaparilla, or Sweet Tea-plant of the colonists . . is very common in the vicinity of Sydney, climbing the trees, or trailing along the ground . . forming a mass of green foliage, diversified by the beautiful reddish tinge of the young leaves and clusters of black berries. **1888** *Proc. Linnean Soc. N.S.W.* III. 391 'Sweet Tea.' This plant has been recommended as an alterative, tonic, and antiscorbutic. **1929** *Aussie* (Sydney) 15 Oct. 42, I do my botanising in the Municipal Market, Sydney, and it was there that I learned about the 'sweet-tea' plant. It is the native sarsaparilla . . and it used to be extensively used for making tea. It is not to be confounded with tea-tree.

sweet, *a.*[2]

1. Good; all right; advantageously situated.

1898 *Bulletin* (Sydney) 17 Dec. (Red Page), *Krook* or *kronk* is bad; while *sweet, roujig,* and *not too stinkin'* are good. **1904** *Sporting News* (Launceston) 2 Jan. 3/1 A three year old colt by Pilgrim's Progress from Nellie, was thought to be a sweet thing, but he failed to find his feet. **1939** K. TENNANT *Foveaux* 312 'I brassed a mug yesterday', he told her, 'and everything's sweet again.' He flashed a roll of notes as big as his fist. **1951** E. HILL *Territory* 308 Gener'ly a big mob of myalls round there, but they're sweet for tabacca. **1964** *Sydney Morning Herald* 10 Aug. 2/5 The saying 'he's making his marble good' was one of the commonest of sayings in my school days. It meant what a schoolboy might say today: 'He's making himself sweet with teacher.' **1967** J. WYNNUM *I'm Jack, all Right* 21 We'd be sweet to pick up a couple of dolls. **1978** J. COLBERT *Ranch* 35 Well, all home to the ranch and see if we're sweet with the babbling brook. **1983** A.F. HOWELLS *Against Stream* 1 The job was a bit of a bore, but I'd had worse. And I was pretty sweet with the boss.

2. In phr.

a. she's sweet and varr., 'all is well'.

1942 *Khamseen Kronikle* 10 Sept. 1 Mick blushed pink and shuffled his feet, Twitched his moustache and murmured 'she's sweet'. **1961** *Realist* (Sydney) vii. 5 Whenever Harry had taxed Barney about taking a serious stand Barney had always repeated stubbornly, 'She's sweet for me'. **1964** K. TENNANT *Summer's Tales* 67 'Everything O.K.?' 'Yep,' said the scrawny man beneath us. 'She's sweet.' **1968** D. O'GRADY *Bottle of Sandwiches* 94 Righto, mate. She'll be sweet. Want a brew? **1979** *Bronze Swagman Bk. Bush Verse* 82 When yer board me ute, be careful where yer put yer plates-o'-meat—If yer'll just avoid me dog-traps, mate, I reckon she'll be sweet.

b. to cop it sweet, to accept a set-back with equanimity; to be fortunate.

1964 *Footy Fan* (Melbourne) II. ii. 13 The result was, down went Martyn, and credit to him, he 'copped it sweet' and for the rest of the day both boys played football. **1967** *Kings Cross Whisper* (Sydney) xxxiii. 40/4 *Cop it sweet*, never divulging information to the police. Take the blame rightly or wrongly. **1979** B. HUMPHRIES *Bazza comes into his Own*, Thanks to Alan Hopkinson, an old friend of the family, Barry has copped it sweet at Australia House with his own office in the migrant counselling dept. **1984** *Sun-Herald* (Sydney) 29 July 60/1 It was surprising that jockey Bruce Compton, rider of Missile runner-up Buena Gold, copped the flag start so sweet.

3. In the special collocation **sweet cop,** an easy task; an enviable situation.

1918 *Kia Ora Coo-ee* Oct. 9/3 Foraging was no sweet cop, let me tell you. **1951** *Tobruk to Borneo* (Perth) Mar. 5 We always did believe these pay sergeants had a sweet cop. **1968** D. O'GRADY *Bottle of Sandwiches* 6 'You're not right in the scone,' the boss said. 'Leavin' a sweet cop like you got here.' **1979** B. HUMPHRIES *Bazza comes into his Own*, 'I got no job and I'm down to me last razoo!' 'No problem, Barry me boy . . how's about I fix youse a nice sweet cop here at Oz House? I can swing you a beaut little lurk.'

sweetlip. Also **sweetlips.** [See quot. 1965.]

1. Any of many thick-lipped fish, esp. those of the fam. Haemulidae (Pomadasyidae) and some members of the fam. Lethrinidae (see EMPEROR), both predom. tropical families.

1928 S.E. NAPIER *On Barrier Reef* 81 'Sweet Lips', a perch-like fish. **1934** T. WOOD *Cobbers* 223 We could not haul up fast enough . . parrot fish . . sweet lip. **1965** *Austral. Encycl.* VIII. 381 Sweetlips, a name applied to several tropical fishes of the genus *Plectorhinchus*, remarkable for their greatly thickened lips. **1968** J. O'GRADY *Gone Troppo* 68 'What sort is it?' 'Wouldn't have a clue. On the guests' menu it's called Reef Fish. Could be anything. Probably Sweet lip'. **1974** J.M. THOMSON *Fish Ocean & Shore* 142 When most people talk about sweetlip they are referring to one or other of the emperors. **1980** T.A. ROY *Vengeance of Dolphin* 16 He was carrying by the gills a large sweetlip—a fine eating fish that abounds in the Great Barrier Reef waters.

2. Special Comb. **sweetlip emperor,** the fish *Lethrinus chrysostomus* of coral reefs in Qld.; any of several related fish. Also *ellipt.* as **sweetlip** (see sense 1).

1951 T.C. ROUGHLEY *Fish & Fisheries Aust.* 75 The sweet-lip emperor . . is one of the best eating fish of the Barrier Reef, its flesh being white,flaky, and of delicate flavour. **1969** J. POLLARD *Austral. & N.Z. Fishing* 194 Sweetlip emperors are olive green on top, silvery below, and their bodies are slashed with dark vertical bands. Their heads vary from salmon pink to vivid red. **1983** *Ecos* xxxv. 5/2 Three species of monocle bream and eight species of sweetlip emperor—all of them important fish in the market-place.

sweet-lips, *pl. Shearing. Obs.* A pair of hand shears.

1895 *Bulletin* (Sydney) 13 July 23/2 And there isn't any hurry, as it takes you all the day To get the 'sweet-lips' going. **1895** *Worker* (Sydney) 28 Sept. 4/1 In fact they were just what you might call grand, With their blades so straight and long—Regular 'sweet lips', just to my hand; Lively, but not too strong.

Sweet William. [Transf. use of *sweet-william* any of several small European sharks of the fam. Carcharhinidae.] The small shark *Mustelus antarcticus* (see GUMMY 2); the flesh of the shark.

1926 L.C.E. GEE *Bush Tracks & Gold Fields* 101 A couple of small ground sharks, commonly known as 'Sweet Williams'. **1937** *Bulletin* (Sydney) 25 Aug. 21/4 In the last 12 months the consumption of gummy shark has increased in Melbourne by over 200 p.c. . . Of course, you don't ask for gummy fillets. 'Sweet William' is the moniker. **1965** *Austral. Encycl.* IV. 401 Gummy (*Emissola antarctica*) . . has a curious odour and is therefore sometimes called 'Sweet William'. **1974** T.D. SCOTT et al. *Marine & Freshwater Fishes S.A.* 32 Gummy Shark; Sweet William. *Mustelus antarcticus* . . Marine.

swelling blight. BUNG EYE.

1859 W. BURROWS *Adventures Mounted Trooper* 149 The dust frequently causes them to be affected by what is called 'blight'. This disorder is attended with a peculiar redness of the eyelids, and an irritation causing the eyes to water considerably, accompanied with a smarting sensation. There are . . two kinds of this complaint, commonly known as 'sandy' and 'swelling' blight. **1872** C.H. EDEN *My Wife & I in Qld.* 150 Every two men you meet out of three have either the sandy or swelling blight—a species of ophthalmia. **1889** G.T. BLAKERS *Useless Young Man?* (1986) 120 There are two kinds of blight of the eyes in Australia: sandy blight and swelling blight. The latter . . is a more temporary, and quite painless swelling. . . Sometimes it lasts several days, sometimes only a few hours. **1901** K.L. PARKER in M. Muir *My Bush Bk.* (1982) 116 Sometimes they would only have swelling blight—'bungey eye' colloquially called—from a fly sting which the blacks used to cure by pressing on hot budtha twigs, and the whites with the blue-bag; but more often, the sandy blight—granulation of the eyelids.

swey, swi, varr. SWY.

swiftie. A piece of sharp practice; an act of deception; a trick; esp. in the phr. **to pull a swiftie.**

1945 S.J. BAKER *Austral. Lang.* 265 Swiftie . . will . . be heard in male conversation to describe a joke or trick that is either agreeable or disagreeable. **1946** *Austral. New Writing* 39 Hello—someone has worked a 'swifty'. **1962** *N.T. News* (Darwin) 13 Jan. 1/1 Not many opportunities for pulling a swifty you'd think. **1966** D. NILAND *Pairs & Loners* 177 He knew, of course, that vindictiveness was the reason Tiny was trying to pull a swifty. **1972** R. MAGOFFIN *Chops & Gravy* 21 A swiftie is something a bloke gets away with when he cons you, takes you down, takes you for a ride, puts one over you, or just plain *has* you. **1978** B. ST. A. SMITH *Spirit beyond Psyche* 209 Since the ole Jim's been out at the Farm an' they've let that stupid electrical contractor inter the factory on maintenance, me work as foreman 'as just about doubled. A man's gotta watch the cow all the way, otherwise he's liable t' pull a swifty, as y' might say.

swift parrot. [See quots. 1840 and 1976.] The predom. green parrot *Lathamus discolor* of e. Aust., which breeds in Tas.; *red-shouldered parakeet*, see RED *a.* 1 b. Also **swift(-flying) lorikeet,** and formerly **swift parakeet.**

1833 *Trumpeter* (Hobart) 8 Nov. 227 *To Naturalists.* To be sold . . birds, in skins . . Swamp Parroquite . . Swift ditto. **1840** J. GOULD *Birds of Aust.* (1848) V. Pl. 47, *Lathamus discolor.* Swift Lorikeet. . . Swift Parrakeet, Colonists of Van Diemen's Land. . . Small flocks of from four to twenty in number are also frequently to be seen passing over the town [of Hobart], chasing each other with the quickness of thought, and uttering at the same time a shrill screaming noise, like the Swift of Europe, whence in all probability has arisen its colonial name. **1909** G. SMITH *Naturalist in Tas.* 46 Another brilliantly coloured bird, with red and blue plumage . . is the small Swift Parakeet. **1945** C. BARRETT *Austral. Bird Life* 76 The swift-flying lorikeet or swift parrot (*Lathamus discolor*) . . is similar to the other small lorikeets in its habits. **1976** *Reader's Digest Compl. Bk. Austral. Birds* 274 Swift parrots live up to their name, for their flight is extremely swift and direct.

swill.

a. The rapid consumption of drinks in public houses at the end of the working day, as occasioned by the (former) six-o'-clock closing regulations. Also *attrib.*

1945 J. HOLMES *Is it Dinkum?* 6 And as its getting on for six, they are drinking now at will, And 'mobs' are flocking to the bars partaking of the 'swill'. **1952** *Newspaper News* (Sydney) 1 Apr. 10/4 Scotch is as hard to get as dry change in an hotel bar at swill time. **1956** E. LAMBERT *Watermen* 90 Inside Finnigan's the 'swill' was well under way. **1958** G. COTTERELL *Tea at Shadow Creek* 147 You ought to see the swill hour in New Zealand, five o'clock to six o'clock.

b. *spec.* In the collocation **six o'clock swill.**

1955 A. ROSS *Aust. 55* 81 This evening ritual, known amongst Australians as the 'six o'clock swill', is supported by two large and powerful groups: the brewers and the Methodists, 'wowsers' as they are called here. **1964** *Bulletin* (Sydney) 15 Feb. 22/2 He was puzzled by the term 'six o'clock swill'. He actually made a tour of hotel bars and he was surprised by the number of places in which the phenomenon did not occur. **1965** *Ibid.* 27 Mar. 18/2 The days of Victoria's 'six o'clock swill' are numbered and the Chief Secretary, Mr Rylah, may well usher in the spring by introducing legislation to extend drinking hours to 10 p.m. **1966** G. MCINNES *Humping my Bluey* 69 From the open doors of pubs came the deafening noise of the 'six o'clock swill'. **1978** G. HALL *River still Flows* 95 To show that we really were an enlightened people .. the Government decided to end that 'six-o'clock-swill' and give us more leisure in which to take our grog. **1984** S. DOWSE *Silver City* 73 It's a funny place... The men drink on their own, standing up, as fast as they can, before the pubs shut. The 'six o'clock swill', it's called.

Hence **swiller** *n.*

1964 *Bulletin* (Sydney) 15 Feb. 22/3 Mr Phillips was not a regular swiller for, according to the law, no drinks must be served after 6 p.m. **1966** G. MCINNES *Humping my Bluey* 148 'Good on ya mate!' roared the five o'clock swillers.

swimmers, *pl.* A swimming costume.

1967 *Sunday Truth* (Brisbane) 23 July 1/1 Bikini girls at Parliament House .. when a parade of new season's swimmers .. will be on show. **1975** S. FRENCH *Hey Phantom Singlet* 48 Mr Brown, now in his swimmers, swam across to the other side of the creek. **1978** *Courier-Mail* (Brisbane) 22 Feb. 1/9, I am not an exhibitionist and if I go swimming on the main beach, I would wear swimmers. **1986** *Sydney Morning Herald* 25 Jan. 1/5 So Darwin's citizens are being invited to bring their swimmers to the town pool for greasy pole games.

swimming togs: see TOGS.

swing, *v.* In phr.

a. to swing the gate, to be the fastest shearer in a shearing shed.

1898 *Bulletin* (Sydney) 1 Oct. 14/3 To 'ring' the shed or shear most sheep is to 'swing the gate'. **1915** *Ibid.* 18 Nov. 24/4 The fastest jumbuck-barber on a board .. is said to be 'ringing the shed', 'in the lead', 'out in front', 'swinging the gate' [etc.]. **1949** *Ibid.* 23 Feb. 14/4 Another common way to describe the ringer is to say that he 'swung the gate'. **1955** STEWART & KEESING *Austral. Bush Ballads* 234, I heard The Flyer ringing Orange Plains and Compadore; He 'swung the gate' at Netley in Eighteen eighty-four, In those days he was a goer, but the happy time has gone; He thought that Howe deserved the belt for his three-twenty-one. **1965** J.S. GUNN *Terminol. Shearing Industry* ii. 12 A ringer is .. said to 'swing the gate', presumably because he keeps the catching-pen gate swinging.

b. to swing Douglas, Kelly, the banjo: see DOUGLAS, KELLY *n.*[2], BANJO 2.

c. to swing the billy: see BILLY *n.*[1] 6.

d. to swing the bag, (of a bookmaker) to take bets at a race meeting.

1962 E. LANE *Mad as Rabbits* 192 Until that momentous decision he used to 'swing the bag' at every race meeting within a fifty-mile radius, and even after he had reformed he didn't dispose of his double-headed penny. **1982** P. ADAM SMITH *Shearers* 308 Jacky was swinging the bag and he didn't want either horse to win.

swing-gate. [Spec. use of *swing-gate* a gate constructed to swing to or shut of itself.] *Drafting gate*, see DRAFTING 2. Also **swinging gate.**

1865 *Argus* (Melbourne) 7 Feb. 6/6 Again, in 1847, I made another invention, known as the swing-gate. **1886** *Vic. Parl. Papers* I. D4 p. ii, Mr Lockhart Morton's 'Sheep Dip' and 'Swing-gate' have been, from the time of their invention, and still are, in general use in Victoria, and .. in the opinion of your Committee, they have been of immense practical benefit. **1890** 'R. BOLDREWOOD' *Squatter's Dream* 91 Mr Stangrove .. has no more idea of a swing-gate than a shearing machine. **1896** G. SUTHERLAND *Australasian Live Stock Man.* 487 The swing gate is so called because instead of being brought to a standstill when it comes into a line with the fence to which it belongs it may be swung further in either direction, thus facilitating the checking of the sheep as they move forward and admitting of counting and inspection, &c. **1897** R. NEWTON *Work & Wealth Qld.* 75 He stands all day working a swing gate in a race, till the two living streams have flowed into separate yards. **1921** *Bulletin* (Sydney) 8 Sept. 22/4, I have heard many an argument as to who invented the 'swinging-gate' in drafting yards. The consensus of opinion among the old hands awards the honour to Thos. Hungerford, of Walgett. **1965** J.S. GUNN *Terminol. Shearing Industry* i. 24 The 'swing gate' invented for drafting .. has proved of inestimable worth to the sheep industry.

swipe. Formerly **swipes.** [Spec. use of Br. slang *swipes* poor, weak beer: see OED.] A disparaging term for beer, esp. (formerly) that brewed in an Australian Colony; any beer. Also *attrib.*, and *transf.*

1843 *Satirist & Sporting Chron.* (Sydney) 1 Apr. 2/4 The waiter being called, each gent. ordered his ball or pot of swipes which ever suited his palate. **1851** *Empire* (Sydney) 23 Sept. 183/6 There was an extensive demand for ale and porter, and as you may suppose, these 'swipe' manufacturers vegetated wonderfully on the temperance cause. **1858** R. ROWE *Peter 'Possum's Portfolio* 94 The indignation of a colonial publican when I refuse to drink colonial ale (whatever Australians may think of themselves or their country, they certainly ought to think small beer of their 'swipes'). **1887** *Illustr. Austral. News* (Melbourne) 25 June (Suppl.) 4/2 The narrator, when he had told a 'good 'un', would be refreshed with a pint of devilish brew, called 'swipes', *i.e.*, a beverage in more polite parlance called colonial beer. **1916** *Truth* (Sydney) 18 June 1/8 Swipe-shops, gin-palace, and the gambling-den! **1929** W.J. RESIDE *Golden Days* 375, I only went to church one night—because a feed was on, And looked with scornful eye such swipe as lemonade upon. **1976** B. SCOTT *Complete Bk. Austral. Folk Lore* 320 Well, I'd had my bite o' tucker an' a glass or two o' beer An' was sittin' there a-fillin' of my pipe, When in comes Mad Macarthy an' Long Jim of Bundaleer, An' my word! but they was well upon the swipe.

swizzle-stick. [Transf. use of *swizzle-stick* a stick used for stirring a drink.] A twig from the shrub *Alyxia ruscifolia* (fam. Apocynaceae) of N.T., Qld., and N.S.W.; the shrub itself. Also *attrib.*

1886 H. FINCH-HATTON *Advance Aust.* (rev. ed.) 31 That's nothing short of a swizzle-stick and it grows on a tree that is peculiar to the Mackay district. **1890** F.M. BAILEY *Catal. Indigenous & Naturalised Plants Qld.* (ed. 2) 103 Swizzle-stick Shrub—Alyxia ruscifolia. *c* **1910** W.R. GUILFOYLE *Austral. Plants* 50 *Alyxia ruscifolia* .. 'Swizzle-stick Bush' (evergreen shrub, 8 to 10 ft.), f[lowers] white. **1949** D. WALKER *We went to Aust.* 48 This rum, and this rum alone, was 'the real Mackay'. And they found it was even better if stirred with a twig from the local bush; and the name of this twig was the 'swizzlestick'.

sword. *Obs.*

1. An Aboriginal weapon. In quots. 1796 and 1863 the weapon referred to is a boomerang.

1796 'SOCIETY OF GENTLEMEN' *New & Correct Hist. New Holland* 35 They have, besides, long wooden swords, shaped like a sabre, capable of inflicting a mortal wound, and clubs of an immense size. **1863** W.J. WILLS *Successful Exploration Interior Aust.* 330 He was killed by a stroke from what the natives call a sword (an instrument of semicircular form, five to eight feet long, and very formidable). **1870** E.B. KENNEDY *Four Yrs. in Qld.* 77 The coast Blacks carry a vast wooden sword. **1878** R.B. SMYTH *Aborigines of Vic.* I. p. xlv, The *Kul-luk* of the Gippsland natives, the *Bittergan* of the north-east coast, and the large sword made by the people of Rockingham Bay, were no doubt in their earlier forms like clubs, but they are to be classed rather with the *Lil-lil* and the *Quiriang-an-wun* than with the *Kud-jee-run*.

2. *fig.* A knife; esp. *attrib.* as **sword-swallower** (see quot. 1965); also **sword-swallowing** *vbl. n.*

1941 S.J. BAKER *Pop. Dict. Austral. Slang* 74 *Sword-swallowing*, the practice of eating with one's knife. **1965** J.S. GUNN *Terminol. Shearing Industry* ii. 30 *Sword swallower*, the fellow who uses his knife as a spoon and eats all his food off it. He is particularly resented by shearers, who are rather fastidious where food is concerned when he uses his knife in the butter. **1982** P. ADAM SMITH *Shearers* 278 'The babbler headed for the mulga saying he'd not cook for a sword swallower.' Translation: .. The cook left, saying he'd not cook for a man who ate off his knife.

sword-grass. [Transf. use of *sword-grass* any of several plants having sword-shaped leaves, applied more specifically in Aust. to such a plant when its leaves are capable of inflicting lacerations.] Any of several plants having long serrated leaves, esp. a sedge of the genus *Gahnia* (fam. Cyperaceae), as *G. sieberana* of e. mainland Aust. and elsewhere. See also CUTTING GRASS.

1879 *Kelly Gang* 38 The level space .. on the right hand side has a patch of very tall spear or sword-grass, which affords a jungle-like cover. **1887** J.H. WRIGHT *Our Victorian Coalfields* 40 He clutches at whatever is nearest to his hand. If this happen to be a bunch of sword-grass, he is safe to get his fingers cut to the bone. **1898** *Proc. Linnean Soc. N.S.W.* XXIII. 142 *Gahnia xanthocarpa* .. known as 'Sword Grass'. **1920** B. CRONIN *Timber Wolves* 91, I sits up in the middle of a clump of sword-grass and cusses. **1934** C. SAYCE *Comboman* 41 They had been rising over a hard stony plain with tufts of dry sword-grass here and there. **1979** K.A.W. WILLIAMS *Native Plants Qld.* I. 128 *Gahnia sieberana* .. Sword Grass... The long, narrow leaves have small serrations along the edges. This makes them very dangerous to handle... Even accidentally brushing against these 'blades' can cause quite deeply incised wounds.

swottie. Alteration of 'swaddy', soldier.

1944 *Action Front: Jrnl. 2/2 Field Regiment* May 7 A 'Swottie' team won the boat race to the consternation of the matelots. **1945** *Dit* (Melbourne) Aug. 82 Look at that swottie signalling the ship! **1952** *Bulletin* (Sydney) 12 Mar. 13/4 Cruiser Hobart had just hit port after pulling out the British swotties from Berbera. **1953** J.E. MACDONNELL *Gimme Boats* 73 One of them AWAS. Living among them swotties—I dunno. You know what they are with a bit of skirt!

swy. Also **swey, swi, zwei.** [a. G. *zwei* two.]

1. a. A two-shilling coin.

[**1898** *Bulletin* (Sydney) 1 Oct. 14/3 'Deuce of bobs' given in *Bulletin*, 27/8/'98, as Western slang term for florin. Western Queensland slang term is 'swideener'. **1924** *Truth* (Sydney) 27 Apr. 6/3 *Swy*, two.] **1941** S.J. BAKER *Pop. Dict. Austral. Slang* 75 *Swy*, the game of two-up. (2) A sentence of two years' gaol. (3) A florin. **1946** G. READING *Papuan Story* 12 When it came to pounds, shillings, and pence, with the infinite Australian variations such as trey, deenah, bob, zac, swy, caser, quid. **1963** J. DUFFY *Outsville Pub* 18 'Here's a swy,' he said, ringing it down on the table. 'Buy yourself one on me.' **1974** *Warrumbungle Bk. of Verse* (1978) 20 Another swy in the guts boys For two-up is the game Somebody kick the can boys Another two of the same. **1983** *Age* (Melbourne) 15 Dec. 13 (*caption*) Exhibition of used coin of the realm: bank notes, collector's items, swys, deaners, zacs, treys, brass razoos.

b. *transf.* A two-year prison sentence.

1975 *Bulletin* (Sydney) 26 Apr. 44/1 'So the low creeps got me a swy with a one.'.. He was sentenced to two years' imprisonment with a minimum of one year to be served, depending on how the parole board assessed his case at the end of that year.

2. TWO-UP *n.* Also as **swy-up** and *attrib.*

1913 *Bulletin* (Sydney) 30 Jan. 16/1 Few of the thousand of habitual 'swi-up' players I have seen can spin decently without violently swinging the arm. **1941** *Action Front: Jrnl. 2/2 Field Regiment* Aug. 5 His income from 'Swi' will be a thing of the past. **1944** *Aust. Week-End Bk.* 109 "Zwei?" What is 'zwei'?' asked the policeman... 'Two-up, an *illegal* Australian gambling game,' grinned one of the Aussie provosts. **1950** K.S. PRICH-

ARD *Winged Seeds* 63 What set the whole town agog . . was their attempt to visit the 'swy': the famous two-up ring on a sand hill near the old Rising Sun Inn. **1956** 'A.B.C.' *What is A?* 4 An Aussie is truth with a sunburned face, reassurance with a grin a mile wide and the hope of the future—heading for a game of Swy! **1960** *Centralian Advocate* (Alice Springs) 22 Jan. 3/3 The games of swy and in-and-outs, the feature of Tennant's night life, were also in smoke. **1967** F. HARDY *Billy Borker yarns Again* 2 Any experienced swy player can pick a butterflied penny from the genuine spinning article. **1977** R. BEILBY *Gunner* 8, I play two-up. You know—swy.

3. Special Comb. **swy game,** a game of two-up; **school,** a group of persons who have assembled to play two-up.

1946 *Bulletin* (Sydney) 24 July 29/3 The usual **'swi' game** was in progress. **1956** *Ibid.* 17 Oct. 12/2 That story . . took me back to '44 and the big swy-game behind the canteen at the 12-mile peg down the highway from Darwin. **1972** K. CLIFT *Saga of Sig* 21 He disclosed that he was quite well cashed up having been . . at the swy game. **1944** *Aust. Week-End Bk.* 107 The **'zwei' school** behind the canteen always claimed him. **1945** D. ROBINSON *Pop's Blonde* 20 He had spun six heads yesterday, at the 'swey' school in the camp and his pockets were full of piastres. **1953** *Bulletin* (Sydney) 21 Jan. 12/1 The swy-school is held each Sunday in a disused quarry just outside the town. **1960** S. WOODFIELD *A for Artemis* 156 The old bakery where he had his first swy school—gone.

Sydney. [The name of the capital city of New South Wales.]

1. Used *attrib.* in Special Comb. **Sydney duck** *hist.* [orig. U.S. (see Mathews)], a name given to an Australian immigrant to the Californian goldfields, esp. an ex-convict (see quots.); **-side,** New South Wales, as being on the other side of a natural barrier or border; see also SIDE *n.*[1] 1; the city of Sydney and its environs; also as *adj.*; **-sider,** a non-Aboriginal person native to or resident in **(a)** New South Wales, **(b)** Sydney, **(c)** Australia.

1889 T.W. KNOX *Boy Travellers in Australasia* 296 He then explained that **Sydney ducks** can hardly be said to exist at present, the term having been applied to runaway convicts, ticket-of-leave men, and other waifs and strays. **1889** J.H.L. ZILLMANN *Past & Present Austral. Life* 62 Botany Bay has still an unsavoury odour about it in England and the States; and to this day the name of 'Sydney ducks' is one of general opprobrium in California. **1927** *Aussie* (Sydney) Feb. 40/2 'Sydney ducks' . . were . . blamed for the terrible conflagrations that wiped San Francisco almost clean off the map. . . Those alleged Sydney ducks, who were convicts, who had stolen the vessels they arrived in, or had stowed away among the crowds of diggers who left these shores for the Eldorado . . and said that they had 'swum across, like the ducks'. . . They did dinkum Australians a lot of harm, even up to as recently as 25 years ago, when the epithet was still applied to visitors from Sydney. **1956** S. HOPE *Diggers' Paradise* 86 The mass of respectable Australians deplore manifestations that perpetuate the memory of the once-notorious convicts known as the Sydney Ducks. **1976** B. SCOTT *Complete Bk. Austral. Folk Lore* 15 The slang word mentioned above, 'kangaroo court', that is, a place where a man is judged by a self-constituted body, is still used in America to describe a trial with no legal standing. The phrase echoes the origin of the defaulters they were instituted to deal with, the 'Sydney Ducks'. **1846** S. DAVENPORT *Let.* 29 Apr. in *S. Australiana* (1977) Sept. 130 The discovery of a large grazing district to the north by Dr Leichhardt may likely lead to the investment of fresh capital on the **Sydney side** in its occupation with stock. **1853** W. WESTGARTH *Vic.* 89 On the Sydney side (to use the distinctive mode of speaking that was in use prior to the separation of Victoria), this system had commenced in rapine and disorder. **1859** W. KELLY *Life in Vic.* I. 179, I have never been on the Sydney side, and am therefore unable to speak . . of . . the Turon diggings. **1873** J.C.F. JOHNSON *Christmas on Carringa* 3 Mullockville, as probably most of you are aware, is a mining township on the Sydney side. **1888** 'R. BOLDREWOOD' *Robbery under Arms* (1937) 1 My name's Dick Marston, Sydney-side native. **1893** S. NEWLAND *Paving Way* 99 'Let me see him,' replied Roland. 'I've been looking for a Sydney-side crack ever since I came to the colony.' **1900** H. LAWSON *Verses Pop. & Humorous* 10 For in loneliness and hardship—and with just a touch of pride—Has my heart been taught to whisper, 'You belong to Sydney-Side'. **1914** *Bulletin* (Sydney) 22 Oct. 13/4 Shearing cut out at Glengarrie . . yesterday. A barber . . who comes from Sydneyside, I think, put up, on the last day, the respectable total of 304. **1918** W.M. MCDONALD *Soldier Songs Palestine* 32 He's from Sydney-side, and his virtues died. **1933** C. FENNER *Bunyips & Billabongs* 3 Early Sydneyside records of the marsh monster. **1954** N. BARTLETT *Pearl Seekers* 181 Used to say that divers had as many double-dealing tricks as Sydneyside confidence men. **1965** D. MARTIN *Hero of Too* 36 She came from Sydneyside. **1984** G. BLAINEY *Our Side of Country* 22 Close to the river, Joseph Hawdon and John Gardner, two of the first men to drive livestock overland from the Sydney-side, established their rural properties. **1865** *Macmillan's Mag.* (London) Jan. 163 The difference of intercolonial tariffs will make as handsome a cause for a very pretty squabble as the devil himself could desire. 'General Peter Lalor crossed the Murray yesterday, and attacked the enemy's earthworks at Three Mile Creek. He was forced to retire with a loss of 400 men. The **Sydney-siders'** loss is considered by him to have been far greater.' How pretty that will read! **1879** *Austral.* II. 681 You're from Melbourne, no doubt, ma'am. Saw it at once. Too much blow about these Sydney-siders. **1906** *Truth* (Sydney) 5 Aug. 1/5 The St. Kilda team of kickballers arrived in Sydney . . their mission being to popularise what is termed the Australian game of football. Sydneysiders have hitherto resented the purely Melbourne game being called 'the Australian game'. **1917** *Ibid.* 13 May 1/8 The Dominion soldiers look so much nicer than the Sydneysiders . . because they have their uniforms made to order. **1933** *Melbourne Univ. Mag.* Sept. 39 The Sydneysider is genuinely sorry for, but not contemptuous of the Melburnian. **1952** *Bulletin* (Sydney) 30 Apr. 16/1 Sydneysiders all talk as if their 'Arbor Bridge was a marvellous engineering feat, but, cripes, there was nothing to it! The water was there, stationary; it was just a matter of slinging the bridge across. **1965** G. MCINNES *Road to Gundagai* 71 'I spent a week in Melbourne.' 'When was that?' 'On a Sunday,' was the Sydneysider's counter jibe. **1986** *Nat. Times* (Sydney) 10 Jan. 12/2 My Sydney-born friends tell me that aliens can qualify to be called Sydney-siders after 20 years' continuous residence.

2. In the names of flora and fauna: **Sydney blue gum,** the tall, smooth-barked tree *Eucalyptus saligna* (fam. Myrtaceae) of e. N.S.W. and e. Qld.; the wood of the tree; **cedar** *obs.*, the tree *Toona australis* (see CEDAR 1); the wood of the tree; **funnel web (spider),** the spider *Atrax robustus* (see FUNNEL WEB); **rock (oyster),** the oyster *Saccostrea commercialis* (see *rock oyster* ROCK *n.* 2); *Moreton Bay oyster*, see MORETON BAY; also **Sydney oyster; silky (terrier),** *Australian terrier*, see AUSTRALIAN *a.* 4.

1904 J.H. MAIDEN *Notes on Commercial Timbers N.S.W.* 18 **Sydney blue gum** (*Eucalyptus saligna*) . . requires some distinctive designation to prevent its confusion with the pale-coloured blue gum (*Eucalyptus globulus*) of Tasmania and Victoria. **1915** *Forestry Question in N.S.W.* (Austral. Forest League) 4 The Sydney Blue Gum is comparatively easy to work, and, therefore, a favourite hardwood amongst shipwrights and carpenters. **1956** N.K. WALLIS *Austral. Timber Handbk.* 4 On the local market Sydney blue gum and rose gum are used for shipbuilding, flooring and general building and construction work. **1983** *Victorian Timber News* Apr. 8/2 Sydney Blue Gum . . has pink to red heartwood, paler sapwood, and gum veins. **1838** T.H. JAMES *Six Months S.A.* 29 **Sydney cedar** and laths and shingles from Van Diemen's Land in every direction. **1855** *Ovens & Murray Advertiser* (Beechworth) 20 Jan. (Suppl.) 1/4 Sydney cedar, from ½ in. to 3 in. **1875** R. & F. HILL *What we saw in Aust.* 61 The casements, wainscots, and doors, throughout the house of Sydney Cedar, might have passed for oak to the undiscriminating eye. **1965** *Austral. Encycl.* VIII. 234 As for the **Sydney funnel-web** spider, six human deaths have been recorded for this species since 1927, all in the neighbourhood of Sydney. **1980** R. MASCORD *Spiders of Aust.* 30 The range of *Atrax robustus* is known to extend from Newcastle, New South Wales, to Nowra, New South Wales, and westwards as far as Lithgow-Oberon, so the so-called Sydney Funnel-web does not belong to Sydney alone. **1985** *Blue Mountains Gaz.* (Springwood) 18 Dec. 3/1 The Blue Mountains funnel web (*Atrax versutus*) is the most common species on the Mountains, although the Sydney funnel web (*Atrax robustus*) is also met with on the Lower Blue Mountains. **1851** [**Sydney rock**] *Illustr. Austral. Mag.* (Melbourne) May 303 Bread and cheese, potatoes . . and Sydney oysters, raw and stewed . . gave us all a most agreeable repast. **1861** 'OLD BUSHMAN' *Bush Wanderings* 249 A very pretty little shell-fish, which they call the Sydney oyster. **1868** *Mope-Hawk* 53 Remember if you please that oysters are in season at present; 'Sydney rocks' are the best, I think, and besides they are the cheapest. **1917** F.J. MILLS *Dinkum Oil* 97 'Oysters' shouted Jensen . . and in a moment we were all sitting round picking the 'Sydney Rocks' from the cliff. **1933** S. GRIFFITHS *Rolling Stone on Turf* 30 Drop into Ned Bitton's oyster saloon . . and have a large plate of Sydney rocks. **1956** S. HOPE *Diggers' Paradise* 242 He had chewed 'ancient haddock' for long enough in Fleet Street, and was not averse to a dozen succulent Sydney rock oysters. **1977** *Commercial Fish Aust.* (Dept. Primary Industry) 94 Sydney rock oysters are found in southern Queensland, New South Wales and eastern Victoria particularly on rocky substrate in the intertidal zone of bays and estuaries. **1984** *Bulletin* (Sydney) 18 Dec. 43/3 There were always Sydney oysters—beaut, sweet, small and reasonably inexpensive. **1986** *Ibid.* 4 Feb. 25/2 The Sydney rock oyster (*Crassostrea commercialis*) has been commercially cultivated since 1870. **1915** *Ibid.* 25 Feb. 22/1 For the bark the gull had copied a lively little **'Sydney silky'** terrier kept in the same house. **1953** D. CUSACK *Southern Steel* 301 A small dog—perhaps a Sydney Silky. **1974** *Meanjin* 130 Miss Kerr had a Sydney silky. . . Once you took on the dog it was a responsibility. **1981** *Bulletin* (Sydney) 10 Mar. 46/1 My brother had two Sydney silkies, which slept *under* the bedclothes.

3. In the phr. **Sydney or the bush,** all or nothing (see quot. 1980); also used allusively with reference to the extremes of urban and rural life.

1915 DREW & EVANS *Grafter* 43 'Oh, well, Sydney or the bush', I said to myself, 'and I told him all about it.' **1930** E. SHANN *Econ. Hist. Aust.* 365 'Sydney or the bush!' cries the Australian when he gambles against odds. **1945** C. MANN *River* 45 But now he bet weakly, like a bank clerk. He bet on a Sydney or the Bush basis; and now, tomorrow, it was the Bush. **1947** F. CLUNE *Roaming around Aust.* 1 There's an old saying, 'Sydney or the Bush'. Well, I was going bush, leaving Sydney far behind. **1953** T.A.G. HUNGERFORD *Riverslake* 127 'Spin for five,' Murdoch suggested to Novikowsky. 'Sydney or the bush!' **1957** F. CLUNE *Fortune Hunters* 8 'Sydney or the Bush!' We threaded our way through the sprawl of the metropolis for fifteen miles to Parramatta, and then another nineteen miles to Penrith, on the Nepean River, through built-up areas practically all the way; but there Sydney finishes and the West begins, with the climb up and over the Blue Mountains. **1960** N. CATO *Green grows Vine* 128 These people are unhappy, they don't fit into either world, Sydney or the Bush. **1976** N.V. WALLACE *Bush Lawyer* 2 To the citizens of Adelaide, a village like Naracoorte was part of that huge area always referred to as 'the bush'. It is so in every State in Australia; 'Sydney or the bush' is one of our oldest phrases. **1977** F.B. VICKERS *Stranger no Longer* 28 Yes—It's going to be Sydney or the bush for me—and you're going to help me make it Sydney, Bert. **1980** B. HORNADGE *Austral. Slanguage* 110 The long-used expression *Sydney or the bush*, meaning 'all or nothing'. Originally it was used in the context of a man who gambled on making a fortune and living a life of ease in the city, with the penalty for failure being the need to seek a more difficult livelihood in the outback.

symph. [Abbrev. of *symphony*.] A symphony; a symphony orchestra.

1892 *Bulletin* (Sydney) 14 May 7/4 The missionary's daughter was About to play the symph. **1965** K. SMITH *OGF* 220 Limbering up for a session with the Sydney Symph.

T

tab, *n.*[1] *Obs.* [Abbrev. of *tabby* a young woman.] A (young) woman.

1918 *Aussie: Austral. Soldiers' Mag.* Dec. 5/1 Last night I struck a dinkum little tab and route-marched her to Hyde Park. **1919** *7th Field Artillery Brigade Yandoo* 20 Mar. 138 An excuse was found to run a Telephone Line across a window where . . Moroney had seen a couple of nice 'Tabs'. **1920** C.L. Hartt *More Diggerettes* 9 That's the worst of them French tabs. They look oright, but they're as ignorant as blanky bandycoots. **1932** H. Simpson *Boomerang* 276 We pay our tabs . . when we want 'em, and tell 'em to get to hell out of it when we don't.

TAB /ti eɪ 'bi, tæb/, *n.*[2] Also **T.A.B., tab.** [Acronym f. the initial letters of *Totalizator Agency Board*, the name of a government agency which controls off-course betting.] The Totalizator Agency Board; a branch or agency of this body; a bet placed with it.

[N.Z. **1953** *Evening Post* (Wellington) 16 Jan., There is ample evidence that the T.A.B. has captured the interest of our teen-agers.] **1961** *Herald* (Melbourne) 8 Mar. 34/1 There will be no radios at T.A.B. agencies. **1964** *Sydney Morning Herald* 20 May 10/2 The TAB has signed a contract to buy a building in Harris Street. **1965** *Ibid.* 15 Feb. 2/1 How long will it be before TAB does in fact take over and eliminate the vast illegal s.p. business which has been tolerated for years. **1968** F. Hardy *Unlucky Australs.* 7 TAB or not TAB? That is the question. . . Hope I don't lose today—I need the money. **1971** *Bulletin* (Sydney) 24 Apr. 61/3 It beats TAB cold. The bookies are a friendly looking mob of bandits. **1973** J. Powers *Last of Knucklemen* (1974) 51 On Saturdays I'll punt. Not big stuff like Pansy. But I got a system worked out that oughtta cover my tabs—for a while at least. **1981** K. Garvey *Rhymes of Ratbag* 42 Priests and parsons all inform us Gambling's bad, and we agree When we find our loss enormous On the hungry T.A.B. **1982** N. Keesing *Lily on Dustbin* 61 Both patronise the TAB (Totalizator Agency Board) often known as 'th' tab'.

table. *Shearing.* Abbrev. of *wool table* (see Wool 2). Also *attrib.* as **table hand, man,** one who trims and rolls a shorn fleece.

1905 *Shearer* (Sydney) 23 Dec. 7/5 They strut and skite round the woolroom and the galley-fire like 'first-battle' grenadiers to the great amusement of the . . two or three educated and travelled 'loppies' . . generally to be found amongst 'table-men'. **1908** W.H. Ogilvie *My Life in Open* 38 In front of the tables stand the 'wool-rollers', men whose business it is to 'skirt' the fleeces. **1928** C.E. Cowley *Classing Clip* 33 The table-hands know exactly where to find the skirtings, and can thoroughly trim the fleece in the quickest time. If the fleece is badly 'thrown out', that is, not well spread, or broken, or thrown across the table, the table-hands are compelled to devote time to getting the fleece into a more suitable position. **1965** L. Walker *Other Girl* 73 It was quite a scene that Friday afternoon in the shearing-sheds. . . Buck came down on to the table to clear the 'backs' to assist the table man.

table-drain. A very shallow surface drain.

1968 *Swag* (Sydney) i. 42 He was standing, mud-bespattered and forlorn, by the roadside, with his vehicle anchored in the table-drain below him. **1978** C. Green *Sun is Up* 25 It had been raining for three weeks. . . The thirsty paddocks drank deep, the table drains gurgled.

table-top. A vehicle for the carriage of goods, having a (large) flat tray.

1898 W. Ogilvie *Fair Girls* (1906) 113 There were side-rail tubs and table-tops, coaches and bullock-drays, Brown with the Barcoo Wonders, and Speed with the dapple greys Who pulled the front of his wagon out. **1936** I.L. Idriess *Cattle King* 75 His wagon . . was the old time table-top type, one with comparatively small front wheels but large rear ones. The flat top of the body came well out over the wheels, unlike the box wagon with the low wheels that came into fashion later. **1944** E.M. Anderson *Typist Tales* 106 He saw . . a table-top waggon loaded with fencing wire. **1974** W. Roediger *We Survived* 68 The waggons rolled into the wheat yards continuously. Some great table tops carrying big loads. **1980** M. Stringer *Austral. Horse Drawn Vehicles* 236 The class of waggon, known as the table-top . . is used in New South Wales and Queensland for the purpose of conveying wool and other produce to the railway. It has an immense carrying capacity, the extreme length over the back and front rails being within two inches of 20 ft., and the width outside the frame 7 ft. 1 in.

tacker. [Br. dial. *tacker* a small child, esp. a boy: see EDD *sb.*[2]] A small boy.

1942 P. Somerville *Not only in Stone* 101 Allen were only a little tacker at the time, an' 'e got lost an' went to sleep with daisies all about un. **1962** D. McLean *World turned upside Down* 109 When he was a little tacker, he used to wander. . . He was only a little nipper. **1980** M. Bail *Homesickness* (1981) 52 Ms Cathcart bent down before getting in, 'And what's this little tacker's name?' The boy pointed to himself.

TAFE /teɪf/. [Acronym f. the initial letters of *Technical and Further Education.*] A system of tertiary education offering courses mainly in technical and vocational subjects; an institution offering such courses. Also *attrib.*

[**1973** *Austral.* (Sydney) 27 Apr. 4/1 The Federal Minister for Education . . yesterday named a committee on technical and further education.] **1974** *TAFE in Aust.* (Austral. Committee Techn. & Further Educ.) 11 The systems of TAFE are not . . responsible for ensuring the structural mix or balance of the labour force. **1976** *Canberra Times* 27 Aug. 2/1 The setting-up of the Commission on Technical and Further Education (TAFE) has brought into national focus the deficiencies in our methods of recruiting and training skilled people. **1978** *Mercury* (Hobart) 25 Apr. 3/5 Mr Dean said that TAFE should receive its full funds so that technical education could play its part in getting the Australian economy back on its feet. **1979** *Herald* (Melbourne) 30 Oct. 6/2 TAFE was a fast-growing area of education providing part-time courses for people learning skills in industry, commerce, agriculture and public services. **1980** *Nat. Times* (Sydney) 10 Feb. 49/4 The barriers between TAFE and advanced education remain although there are hopeful signs that they may be removed. **1984** *Canberra Times* 28 Feb. 8/2 At least 60,000 people had been turned away from technical and further education colleges throughout Australia because resources provided to TAFES were inadequate. **1984** *Bulletin* (Sydney) 11 Dec. 34/2 The present TAFE system offering trade courses, and the theoretical side of apprenticeship training. **1985** *Canberra Times* 19 Sept. 3/4 He is now in the first year of a two-year licensed plumbing course at Canberra TAFE. **1985** *Blue Mountains Echo* (Katoomba) 23 Dec. 22/5 The nature of employment is changing . . with more and more young people turning to Technical Colleges because High Schools are not equipping them with the work skills they need. . . TAFE is preferred because of the contents of the courses, but also because it is less authoritarian.

tag-a-long. See quot. 1963. Also *attrib.* as **tag-a-long tart.**

1956 J.E. Webb *So much for Sydney* 64 Our Girls are most 'teenagers', and it doesn't matter whether they are socialites, shopgirls or 'tagalong tarts'. **1963** *Bulletin* (Sydney) 23 Nov. 16/3 *Tag-a-long*, a girlfriend (or boyfriend).

tail, *n.*[1]

1. [Transf. use of *tail* the rear end of a marching column: see OED(S *sb.*[1] 4 c.] The rear of a travelling mob of sheep, cattle, etc.

1849 A. Harris *Emigrant Family* (1967) 16 My cattle travel very wild; some of them are off down every gully they see:—you can . . stick to the tail of 'em. **1888** 'R. Boldrewood' *Robbery under Arms* (1937) 35 The dog stopped behind; he knew he'd have to mind the tail—that is the hindmost cattle. **1891** —— *Sydney-Side Saxon* (1925) 106 It took some time for the 'tail', with all the slower quiet cattle and calves to clear the forest. **1954** T. Ronan *Vision Splendid* 150 Then he noticed a milker's poddy bullock which had always been on the tail when he had been looking after the mob. **1980** Ansell & Percy *To fight Wild* 80 My father taught me to ride when I was about four or five, and my brothers and sisters. That was doing cattle work, pushing up the tail of the mob, that kind of thing, on quiet horses.

2. A fine strip of hide, etc., at the end of the thong of a whip: see quot. 1859.

1859 W. Burrows *Adventures Mounted Trooper* 133 Their 'stock-whips' . . are made of hide, plaited into a heavy thong, from nine to fifteen feet in length, the thickest part being about an inch in diameter, at the end of which is a 'tail' or point of green hide, crowned with a cracker of twisted raw silk. **1893** 'Old Chum' *Chips* 52 That merciless whip, with a short handle about a foot long, heavy and tapering to a point with a heavy whip some ten or twelve feet long, a long 'tail' and 'cracker' at the end of it. **1919** V. Marshall *World of Living Dead* 64 The flogger raised above his head the thick, short-handled 'cat' from which drooped down in murderous array its knotted 'tails' of hide.

3. A thread or train of particles of mineral, esp. alluvial gold: see quot. 1898.

[N.Z. **1898** 'H' *Grain of Gold* 12 By a peculiar motion of the wrist, Old Grit separated the lighter iron-sand from a smaller quantity of heavier copper pyrites, and draws the last into a long string into the bottom of the dish, called 'the tail'.] **1937** M. Terry *Sand & Sun* 75 Gold . . should show up in a bright yellow 'tail' behind the iron and such things. **1946** K.S. Prichard *Roaring Nineties* 40 Every dish Dinny panned off showed a fat tail of fine gold. **1959** D. Stuart *Yandy* 15 He knew the feel of a panning-off dish in his hands, and the dryness in mouth and throat when the tail of gold showed in the angle of the dish after he had washed a sample.

tail, *n.*[2] *Mining.*

1. Usu. in *pl.* as *n.*, in *sing.* when *attrib.* Abbrev. of 'tailings', mining refuse.

1855 *Illustr. Sydney News* 12 May 231/3 Puddling machines are daily getting more numerous on these diggings and form no very inconsiderable means of surfacing and tail-stuff washing; these machines use a great quantity of water in their washing operations and they are on such an account condemned by the diggers. **1859** W. Kelly *Life in Vic.* I. 203, I began by trying some dishes of tail-dirt. **1939** I.L. Idriess *Cyaniding for Gold* 163 Test your 'heads'—the slime as it goes into the mixer. Test for gold, acid, alkalinity, mineral combinations. Test your 'tails' (finished slime when discharged).

2. Special Comb. **tail race,** a channel through which the waste material from alluvial mining is carried away.

1856 G. Willmer *Draper in Aust.* 89 Another man was placed at the 'tail race' . . whose business was to throw up on either side of it the dirt and stones which would otherwise have choked up our stream. **1889** *Braidwood Dispatch* 25 Sept. 2/1 Mr Newman has commenced the construction of the tail race for the sluicing company. **1932** I.L. Idriess *Prospecting for Gold* 266 *Tail-race*, the channel in which tailings, suspended in water, are conducted away. **1980** J. WRIGHT *Big Hearts & Gold Dust* 146 There'd been a tail-race there many years ago.

tail, *n.*[3] *Two-up.*

1. *pl.* A fall of the coins in which the tails face upwards; a bet that the coins will fall this way.

1911 A. WRIGHT *Gamblers' Gold* (1923) 55 Throwing a coin on to the bag-covered floor, he called: 'Heads a shilling!' 'Tails one!' **1919** *Ross's Monthly* Dec. 4/2 Its tails you lose, and heads I win, The game is fair as day—I'll help you pray your soul from sin, And 'rook' you while we pray. **1919** A. WRIGHT *Game of Chance* 32 What about some dough? I'm pretty well emptied out. Been having a trot of tails.

2. Comb. **tail-backer, -bettor.**

1922 C. DREW *Rogues & Ruses* 138 'Has he got you going, too?' laughed a **tail backer.** **1925** A. WRIGHT *Boy from Bullarah* 18 Once again the coins went up, accompanied by the curses of the tail backers. **1954** T. RONAN *Vision Splendid* 231 Most of the tail backers were broke. **1959** *Never kill Dolphin* (Writer's Guild Qld.) 68 There was the old man on the mat with the tail-backers all round him and Shorty heading them again and again. **1946** *Austral. New Writing* 36 **Tail bettors** toss in their money and soon the pound is covered. Again the side bettors 'get set'. **1953** T.A.G. HUNGERFORD *Riverslake* 125 They stopped at the outer edge of the crowd . . to have a look at how the pennies were falling and to search for the tail-betters.

tail, *v.*[1] [See TAIL *n.*[1] 1.] *trans.* To follow, herd, and tend (livestock): see quot. 1905. Also with **out** and **up.**

1843 *Port Phillip Patriot* 11 May 3/2 The cattle . . were left in the yard all night, and tailed in the day. **1848** *Sidney's Austral. Handbk.* 57 When a herd has been purchased and brought upon a fresh run (or new pasture) they must be *tailed* for four or six months, that is to say, one or two horsemen must follow them from sunrise to sundown. At sundown they are driven into the stock-yard for the night. **1855** W. HOWITT *Land, Labor & Gold* I. 439 A boy was some time ago tailing out the horses, that is, watching them in the bush. **1860** *S. Austral. Advertiser* (Adelaide) 2 July 2/4 Boys to tail cattle, £10 to £13 per week, with the usual Rations. **1884** J.B. MARTIN *Reminisc.* 18 Some even 'tailed' herds, *i.e.* had them tended by men on foot as sheep were. **1895** G. RANKEN *Windabyne* 228 It ended in their engaging to herd, or 'tail' as it is called, the heifers now in their hands. **1905** L. BECKE *Tom Gerrard* 251 'I'll turn the rest over to you to tail.' 'Tail'—a drover or stockman who is set to keep a mob of cattle from straying 'tails' them—*i.e.*, follows at their tails. **1929** K.S. PRICHARD *Coonardoo* (1961) 14 Wanna or one of the younger boys tailed the night horses. **1936** C.P. CONIGRAVE *N. Aust.* 118 Many times their only companion being the native boy who tails up the police-horses. **1957** R.S. PORTEOUS *Brigalow* 127 Every day for a week we would drive them out and tail them on good feed. At sundown we would yard them . . run them through the drafting yards before breakfast and then tail them out again for the day. **1980** ANSELL & PERCY *To fight Wild* 102 There are places where they can use a plane or a helicopter to muster but still handle cattle in the traditional manner where each beast is important, where the weaners are tailed—held in a mob for a couple of days and educated by men on horseback, so that they get used to being handled—where the mickeys are cut and branded and put in a bullock paddock.

tail, *v.*[2] *Two-up.* [f. TAIL *n.*[3] 1.] In the phr. **to tail them** (or **'em**), to toss the coins so that they fall with the tail upwards.

1911 A. WRIGHT *Gamblers' Gold* (1923) 58 Tails some money. Any part of a quid tails. I'll lay odds he tails 'em. **1931** O. WALTERS *Shrapnel Green* 26, I was bettin' a dollar he'd tail them. . . Proved I was showin' good judgement when the ringkeeper said, 'Nicks are right!' **1953** T.A.G. HUNGERFORD *Riverslake* 126 'Ten bob he tails 'em!' he intoned. . . 'I got ten bob to say he tails 'em.' **1977** R.E. GREGORY *Orig. Austral. Inventions* 117 If they finish the same side up . . the players shout, 'He's headed them,' or 'He's tailed them.'

tail, *v.*[3] *intr.* With **out:** to work as a TAILER-OUT.

1919 C.J. DENNIS *Jim of Hills* 40 An' there he put me tailin' out.

tailer, var. TAILOR.

tailer, *n.*[1] [f. TAIL *v.*[1]]

a. An animal which is being herded; an animal at the 'tail' of a mob; a straying animal.

1890 MRS H.P. MARTIN *Under Gum Tree* 15 The two white stockmen being at an out station with a mob of 'tailers', or weaned heifers. **1900** *Western Champion* (Barcaldine) 10 July 18/1 For the 'tailers' begin to run cunning, And the mob is just going to split. **1914** C.H.S. MATTHEWS *Bill* 100 The man who was on watch rides behind and keeps the tailers up as far as possible. **1932** J. McCARTER *Pan's Clan* 184 He accidentally on purpose cut out about three hundred sheep from th' mob—off th' tailers. **1938** D. BATES *Passing of Aborigines* 57 About 400 tailers, cows and calves, were left to three of us to water. **1946** W.E. HARNEY *North of 23°* 11 Then herds go by, the drovers pass, The leaders feed along the route While cunning tailers nip the grass, Linger, then trot when whips are out. **1960** I.L. IDRIESS *Wild North* 194 The pack-team mooched contentedly along. . . Silent Jim and I brought up the 'tailers'.

b. One who herds livestock; one who rides at the 'tail' of a travelling mob; a horse used for this. Also *transf.* (see quot. 1930).

1895 K. MACKAY *Yellow Wave* 203 Taking out enough quiet horses to act as 'tailers', a dozen men . . made out early in the morning to where the horses 'ran'. Rounding up the 'tailers' in the bottom of one of the ravines . . the party, leaving half a dozen men in charge, rode off in threes. **1904** *Bulletin* (Sydney) 8 Dec. 36/4 There was a sufficient number of them to drive even such a mob as was on that plain. Flankers, leaders and tailers, plenty there. **1920** *Ibid.* 25 Mar. 22/2 The best horsetailer I ever knew was on a large Queensland cattle-run. . . He bet the cook a pound of tobacco that before leaving the camp he would tell him where every horse was running. . . We were all borrowing a pipeful of tobacco from the tailer. **1930** HIVES & LUMLEY *Jrnl. of Jackaroo* 21 On our way we collected the milking herd, consisting of ten quiet beasts, and drove them slowly in the direction the approaching cattle would have to go. These would act as 'tailers', and show the way to their wilder companions through the yard gates. **1934** M. GILMORE *Old Days* 168 You must not confuse the stockman with the 'tailer'. The tailer, and, for years the later rouseabout on the sheep-run, were no-account men. They were weaklings; they were menial; and could be asked to cut wood and would do it as a part of their lowly, wretched, and good-for-nothing lot. **1968** F. ROSE *Aust. Revisited* 269 *Tailer*, the man or more usually the youth responsible for the horses of a group of men working stock. The 'tailer' has the responsibility of hobbling the horses out at night and bringing them back in the early morning. **1976** C.D. MILLS *Hobble Chains & Greenhide* 4 With saddle hastily swapped, the rider races at a tangent, cuts the tracks and again picks up with the mob. The 'tailer' brings the used horses along at a steadier pace.

tailer, *n.*[2] TAILER-OUT.

1937 *N.S.W. Parl. Papers* (1938–40) 2nd Sess. VII. 667 The Aborigines Protection Board is running this sawmill. . . The tailer gets 22s. 6d. a week and the edging jerker £1 a week.

tailer-out. In a saw-mill: the employee responsible for guiding timber as it comes off the saw.

1895 *Bulletin* (Sydney) 3 Aug. 3/2 Few know the song—for the tailer-out, And the benchman swart, and his underlings, And the truckerman, and the trammer stout, Have their souls in the flitch and in wooden things. **1901** *Advocate* (Burnie) 2 Mar. 3/6 Wanted—sawmill hand, must be a thoroughly good tailer-out. **1916** *Bulletin* (Sydney) 18 May 24/3 All hands at Priest's sawmill . . were at a loss to account for a smell that . . nearly drove the sawyer, handle-man and tailer-out from their positions. **1929** C.H. WINTER *Story of 'Bidgee Queen* 30 He keeps the logmen busy and the tailer-out as well. **1959** M. RAYMOND *Smiley roams Road* 121 You're going to get a job this arvo straight after dinner. You're going to be tailer-out at the little bandsaw.

tailie. *Two-up.* [f. TAIL *n.*[3] 1 + -Y.] One who bets on the coins falling tails upwards; *tail-backer*, see TAIL *n.*[3] 2.

1919 W.H. DOWNING *Digger Dialects* 49 *Tailie*, a man who backs 'tails' in the game of two-up. **1944** *Observer: 2/6 Austral. Field Survey Battery R.A.A.* May 45 Want a taily; any more tailies. **1946** *Austral. New Writing* 36 Ten bob wanted to fill the gutz. We're right. Set 'em between yourselves. Get set on the side. Taily wanted for a dollar. **1949** L. GLASSOP *Lucky Palmer* 176 'Gents,' he cried, 'now isn't there a taillie in the school?' **1977** R. BEILBY *Gunner* 296 What about a bitta chop from you tailies? Come on, ya've hada good run. What about a sling?

tailing, *vbl. n.*

1. The herding and tending of livestock: see quot. 1848.

1848 H.W. HAYGARTH *Recoll. Bush Life* 56 When cattle are first brought to a new country they are subjected to a process called 'tailing', which consists in watching them with horsemen by day, and driving them into their enclosures every night: they grow very much out of condition under this treatment, but it must be continued as long as they show any inclination to ramble back to their old pastures, and usually lasts from three to five weeks, according to circumstances. **1876** J.B. STEPHENS *Hundred Pounds* 188 One of those lazy intervals which all dwellers on cattle-stations are familiar with, when there is neither mustering, nor tailing, nor branding, nor any other bucolic operation going on. **1936** W. HATFIELD *Aust. through Windscreen* 61 Tailing is a term used for checking the mob within reasonable limits instead of holding them tightly rounded up, which with fresh cattle demands riding at full gallop almost constantly till they settle down. **1938** D. BATES *Passing of Aborigines* 53 The long day's tailing made riding very wearisome.

2. The docking of an animal's tail.

[N.Z. **1864** E.R. CHUDLEIGH *Diary* (1950) 130, I tailed about 600 lambs.] **1916** *Bulletin* (Sydney) 6 July 22/3 Five catchers were allotted to each man, who had to do his own tailing and earmarking. **1955** J. MORRISON *Black Cargo* 57 He and Collins, the overseer, did all the knife-work—castrating, ear-marking, and tailing.

3. Special Comb. **tailing yard,** an enclosure into which cattle are herded temporarily: see quot. 1963.

1930 A. GROOM *Merry Christmas* 158 The cattle could be seen moving quietly to the tailing yards. **1954** T. RONAN *Vision Splendid* 145 He and the boys would take the bullocks out of the big wire tailing yard in the first light of morning. **1963** W.E. HARNEY *To Ayers Rock & Beyond* 45 The iron ring was cursed by the stockmen as something that gave lumpy-jaw to the cattle, but they did not alter the method until the drafting-yards was [*sic*] superseded by the 'tailing yard'. **1963** M. BRITT *Pardon my Boots* 80 This morning, the cattle, which had been mustered the day before and held in the 'tailing-yard' overnight, were to be drafted. The tailing yard was a single large yard used when it was not necessary to take cattle all the way to the station yards, or when they were to be held just for a night.

tailor. Also **tailer, taylor.** [Orig. U.S.: see OED *sb.* 2. See also quot. 1969.] The marine fish *Pomatomus saltator*, a voracious feeder occurring in coastal waters. See also CHOPPER 2. Also **tailorfish.**

1827 *Tasmanian Almanack* 142 Taylor . . 1s. 6d. each. **1847** E.W. LANDOR *Bushman* 393 There are immense quantities of fish upon this coast. The best kind are called tailors, and have a good deal of the mackerel flavour. **1857** J. ASKEW *Voyage Aust. & N.Z.* 228 The harbour abounds with fish, of which the schnapper, jewfish, tailerfish . . are used for food. **1895** C. THACKERAY *Amateur Fisherman's Guide* 3 The fisherman suffers much tribulation when a leatherjacket or tailer bites his line and clears off with his hook. **1909** *Bulletin* (Sydney) 22 Apr. 13/2 One of the most popular amusements along the Vic. coast is catching tailer or skipjack with a piece of white rag on a hook. **1932** R.W. THOMPSON *Down Under* 242 We caught forty Taylor and a good-sized Jew fish in the first hour. **1969** J. POLLARD *Austral. & N.Z. Fishing* 793 These [teeth] intermesh so closely when the fish bites that it is able to shear a garfish or a fine nylon line through with one chop. This shearing action of its teeth undoubtedly gave rise to the name of tailor. **1984** *Canberra Chron.* 16 May 23/1 Live bait, preferably small tailor or yellowtail.

tailor-bird. [Transf. use of *tailor-bird* any of several Asiatic birds stitching leaves to form their nests.] *Golden-headed fantail warbler*, see GOLDEN 3.

1854 W. HOWITT *Boy's Adventures* 43 We have never yet seen the nest of the bower bird . . though we have seen one of the tailor bird, suspended from the bough of a tree. **1861** J.D. LANG *Qld., Aust.* 152 On the extremity of these twigs, and generally within six or seven feet of the water, were numerous nests of the tailor bird. **1952** B. BEATTY *Unique to Aust.* 52 The Golden-headed Fantail Warbler, after building its coned nest, sews on leaves using cobwebs and gossamers for thread and its beak for a needle. Because of its deftness .. it is frequently referred to as Australia's tailor bird. **1964** M. SHARLAND *Territory of Birds* 32 (*caption*) The Tailor-bird gets its vernacular name from its habit of sewing leaves round its nest, using cobweb for thread.

tailorfish: see TAILOR.

taint. *Obs.* STAIN.

1841 *Port Phillip Patriot* 10 June 4/3 The progeny of the convict immigrants—persons who have always been free, but have a 'taint' in their blood.

Hence **tainted** *ppl. a.*, of convict descent.

1905 *Horlick's Mag.* (London) Feb. 175/1 The bulk of the population, excluding, of course, the tainted element from the penal colonies, was of the best men of the Old Country.

taipan /'taɪpæn/. [a. Wik Munkan *dhayban.*] The brownish snake *Oxyuranus scutellatus* of n. and n.e. Aust. and s. New Guinea, the longest Austral. venomous snake.

1933 *Proc. Zool. Soc. London* 858 The name 'taipan', by which *O[xyuranus] scutellatus* is known to the aborigines of Cape York Peninsular, is an excellent vernacular name for the species. The natives hold the taipan in great dread, and it appears to have been responsible for many deaths among them. **1958** E. WORRELL *Song of Snake* 110 Despite its shy nature the taipan is still without question the largest and deadliest of our venomous snakes. **1965** R.H. CONQUEST *Horses in Kitchen* 132 The deadly taipan, found mainly in the tropical north, is a coppery brown colour, usually about seven feet long, has a thin black neck and a long, oval-shaped head which expands when he attacks. **1976** S. WELLER *Bastards I have Met* 85 Our woodheap must have been alive with taipans. **1980** B. SCOTT *Darkness under Hills* 157 The fangs of the taipan—the huge, warlike brown snake of the scrubs.

take, *v.*

1. *trans.* [Used elsewhere, esp. in U.S., but of local significance: see OED *v.* 90 d. (b) and DAE *v.* 10 a.] With **up:** to acquire (land) from the Crown as owner or as tenant.

1831 J.G. POWELL *Narr. Voyage Swan River* 130 All the good land is already taken up on both sides of the Swan and Canning Rivers. **1840** A. RUSSELL *Tour through Austral. Colonies* 164 Land .. is more taken up for sheep runs than cattle walks. **1855** N.L. KENTISH *Question of Questions!* 40 They might locate on any 'country' they chose to 'take up', *i.e.*, to select to any extent. **1864** R. HENNING *Lett.* (1952) 72 You inquire about Biddulph's new 'purchase', but taking up country is not exactly a purchase... By the new Land Act, whoever just puts his stock on a new piece of country and then puts in his tenders for it to Government has the right of occupying that country as a sheep-run. **1879** E. TRENERRY *Descr. Plan Austral. Trans-Continental Railway* 14 Upwards of a thousand squatters .. had 'taken up', as the operation was called, vast principalities under Government regulations. **1890** W.F. BUCHANAN *Aust. to Rescue* 22 The pioneer squatter taking up country for stocking purposes, invariably drove the blacks still further back. **1910** *Huon Times* (Franklin) 17 Sept. 6/3 They had been assured in London that there was no need to go more than 20 miles from a railway to take up land. **1930** D. COTTRELL *Earth Battle* 82 Old H.B. rode back .. having made his two thousand pounds and ready to inspect and take up Tharlane. **1939** J.G. PATTISON *'Battler's' Tales Early Rockhampton* 9 At Rannes the Archers were joined by Mr Spencer. I rather think he was the same man who took up Mount Spencer, in the Nebo district. **1946** J.G. EASTWOOD *More about Cairns* 39 The land that I took up was 160 acres bordering on Janetta Creek, selected before survey. **1963** W.E. HARNEY *To Ayers Rock & Beyond* 35 Arthur was the son of a well-known pioneer settler called Billy Little who took up this country in 1927. **1976** B. SCOTT *Complete Bk. Austral. Folk Lore* 101 Oh Willy, dearest Willy, then stay at home with me. We'll take up a selection and a farmer's wife I'll be. **1981** A.B. FACEY *Fortunate Life* 49 A settler could take up land and settle on it without much or any money.

2. a. In the phr. **to take it out,** to undergo a punishment; esp. to serve a sentence of imprisonment instead of paying a fine.

1838 *Cornwall Chron.* 1 Sept. 3 James Smith was fined 5s. for being drunk, and not paying, he was ordered to take it out in wood [*sc.* to be put in the stocks]. **1888** *Bungendore Mirror* 27 June 2 At the Police Court on Saturday a woman was awarded a month's jail for obtaining goods under false pretences from P. McDonald, storekeeper. She goes to Goulburn to 'take it out'. **1901** *Advocate* (Burnie) 15 Feb. 2/4 Fined 5s., with the alternative of 48 hours, for having misconducted himself. Defendant elected to 'take it out'. **1904** *Ibid.* 11 June 3/2 Fined 40s., or three weeks' imprisonment. He 'took it out'. **1943** K. TENNANT *Ride on Stranger* 176 George Benson told her briefly he would see her husband had a lawyer. He would probably get a month at the most and he'd better 'take it out'.

b. *trans.* With **out:** to win (a prize, etc.).

1976 *Austral.* (Sydney) 15 July 2/2 Helen Morse .. takes out the Australian Film Institute's top actress award. **1979** *Advertiser* (Adelaide) 23 July 7/6 (*heading*) Flautist takes out title.

take-all.

1. [Used elsewhere but recorded earliest in Aust.: see OED(S *take-*.] A disease of wheat and other cereals caused by the fungus *Gaeumannomyces graminis*, producing root rot and causing the death of plants. Also *attrib.*

1866 *S. Austral. Register* (Adelaide) 11 May 2/7 The 'takeall', so called, is too well known in Tasmania... The farmers there find they can grow peas on land so infected .. and eventually return to wheat. **1882** *Three L's* 249 Mr Fox had begun farming in those good old days when red-rust and takeall were unknown. **1924** *Jrnl. Dept. Agric. Vic.* XXII. 605 Several other factors may result in the dying back of wheat plants, e.g., grubs may attack the roots of young wheat plants and cause decay and symptoms somewhat similar to takeall. But in such cases the whole of the crop is usually destroyed, and the disease does not occur in circular patches characteristic of takeall. **1949** *Coast to Coast 1948* 87 They had a good look at the crop, and after vain attempts to prove that it was 'frosted' and that it was suffering in part from 'foot-rot' and 'take-all' .. had to admit that it was an excellent crop. **1962** E. IRVIN *Early Inland Agric.* 51 The wheat yield throughout was estimated at 20 bushels to the acre, the oats being an unknown quantity due to take-all, strawing and other factors. **1984** *Advertiser* (Adelaide) 3 Jan. 15/2 Farmers and scientists are learning how to handle rhizoctonia and take-all diseases.

2. *transf.* A cutworm. Also *attrib.*

1899 *North-Western Advocate* (Devonport) 6 Jan. 2/1 The crops continue to look well, and the present rain will greatly benefit the potatoes and interfere with the peregrinations of the 'take all'. **1900** *Advocate* (Burnie) 14 Aug. 4/2 Mr Chapman moved that the subject be 'The life, history and habits of the underground grub, commonly known on the North-West Coast as 'take-all''. **1928** R.H. CROLL *Open Road Vic.* 102, I have seen these moths in millions on the summit of Mount Bogong itself... When one remembers that they are the 'cutworm' or 'take-all-grub' in its winged form. **1931** *Listening Post* (Perth) Sept. 30 Dairymen .. have suffered .. through the ravages of 'Take-all' or white grubs.

talent. The underworld; those who frequent it; an organized gang of these.

1879 D. MAYNE *Westerly Busters* 18 The 'talent', the 'fancy', the 'crushers', were there. **1882** *Sydney Slang Dict.* 8 The Talent—low gamblers, sharpers, larrikins and their girls, confirmed prostitutes, and 'the fancy' generally who frequent their resorts. **1893** D. HEALEY *Cornstalk* 66 The remaining larrikins are all members of organized gangs, called 'pushes' or 'talents'... As these .. gangs, the members of which range in age from 15 to 30 years, have feudal quarrels raging between them, a war of extermination is being continuously waged. **1899** *Truth* (Sydney) 15 Jan. 2/4 Three or four of a talent known as the Cow Lane Push. **1908** L. ESSON *Round Corner* 88 The talent pours in—thieves, pickpockets, vagrants, flash spielers, sailors who have gone down to the pub from ships, gaudily dressed women, Asiatics—they all add spice and colour to the narrow streets. **1917** A.B. PATERSON in C. Semmler *World of Banjo Paterson* (1967) 115 Now and then a van, laden with ten or eleven of 'the talent', and drawn by a horse that cost fifteen shillings at auction, rolled softly along in the same direction. Those were dog-fighters who had got 'the office', and knew exactly where the match was to take place. **1928** 'BRENT OF BIN BIN' *Up Country* 151 The elder won by telling his son he could use the Waterfall stallion as a saddle-horse in the off-season, and have him for his own in place of Black Belle, on condition that he left the talent of Eagle Hawk Gullies strictly alone. **1953** D. CUSACK *Southern Steel* 31 He'd learn responsibility quicker married than he would knocking about the ports with the rest of the talent. **1973** J. MURRAY *Larrikins* 185 The 'silver-tails' receive the one that is sharp; but the 'mugs' whom the 'talent' does not recognise suffer .. and they make suitable complaints as both hair and face are brought within the regulations.

talking stick. MESSAGE-STICK.

1913 *Bulletin* (Sydney) 31 July 15/2 'How do you know .. that this corroboree is going to take place?' 'Oh, news come roun',' he answered. My mind jumped to 'talking sticks', smoke signals and so on. **1928** R.M. MACDONALD *Opals & Gold* 200 He held aloft a small piece of pointed wood about four inches long; its surface was roughly tarred with shorthand-like marks and some symbols were also burned into the wood. 'It's a talking stick,' he continued.

tallegalane /tə'lɛgəleɪn/. Also **tallegallan, talleygallan.** [Prob. f. a N.S.W. Aboriginal language.] The fish *Myxus elongatus* (see *sand mullet* SAND).

1879 *Proc. Linnean Soc. N.S.W.* IV. 426 *Myxus elongatus* .. are known among the Sydney fishermen as the 'Sand Mullet' and 'Tallegallan'. **1896** F.G. AFLALO *Sketch Nat. Hist. Aust.* 232 The Sand Mullet or Talleygallan (*Myxus*) .. frequents the rivers, but goes down to the sea each winter. **1906** D.G. STEAD *Fishes of Aust.* 75 The Mullet which is also known as Tallegallane or Lano (*Myxus elongatus*). **1952** *Austral. Museum Mag.* June 310 The Australian aborigines had their names for fishes... I need only mention the following .. Morwong, Nannygai, Tallegalane, [etc.]. **1965** *Austral. Encycl.* VI. 195 The sand mullet or tallegalane .. of New South Wales is less valuable as a food fish, although it is at times plentiful in the markets.

tall oat grass. The tall, perennial grass *Themeda avenacea* (fam. Poaceae) of mainland Aust. See also OAT GRASS.

1895 F. TURNER *Austral. Grasses* I. 8 Between Nyngan and Bourke I once saw the 'tall oat grass' growing higher than the railway fences... The seeds are large, and in appearance somewhat resemble oats. **1903** G. SUTHERLAND *Australasian Live Stock Man.* (ed. 2) 389 *Anthistiria avenacea*, or 'Tall Oat Grass', is one of the grasses recommended for permanent pasture in the western districts of New South Wales. **1923** E. BREAKWELL *Grasses & Fodder Plants N.S.W.* 18 *Themeda avenacea* (Tall Oat or Wild Oat grass). Abundant on good plain soils throughout the interior. **1981** G.M. CUNNINGHAM et al. *Plants Western N.S.W.* 148 Tall oat-grass *Themeda avenacea* .. resembles kangaroo grass (*T. australis*) but is often taller (to 1.7 m. high).

tallow. *Obs.* Used allusively to designate a squatter (one who has grown 'fat' as a grazier).

1869 *Colonial Soc.* (Sydney) 18 Feb. 11 To tell you the truth, I should enjoy a peep at the tallow-ocracy of Australia. *Ibid.* 18 Mar. 6 I'm a swell! I'm a swell, of the Tallow-crat style, Who out of my sheepskins extracted a pile; I'm coarse and untutored, but feel it no shame—By right of my cash I am *crème de la crème*! **1892** *Truth* (Sydney) 24 Apr. 1/4 And the proper landed gent here is the hearty tallow fat, With his miles of water frontage with his miles away outback. **1902** M. CANNON *That Damned Democrat* (1981) 122 Balfour .. succeeded in getting his fellow Tallow Fats to amend the Education Act.

tallow-wood. [See quot. 1894.] The tall tree *Eucalyptus microcorys* (fam. Myrtaceae) of n.e. N.S.W. and s.e. Qld.; the greasy, strong, durable wood of the tree; (occas.) a similar eucalypt, or its wood. Also *attrib.*

1884 A. NILSON *Timber Trees N.S.W.* 67 *E[ucalyptus] microcorys.*—Tallowwood; Mahogany.—A tall tree, with a persistent furrowed fibrous bark. **1894** G. SCOTT *N.S.W. Hardwood Timber* 5 Tallow Wood .. is one of our most valuable timbers, and derives its local name from the fact of its being of an oily or rather greasy nature. **1900** *Proc. Linnean Soc. N.S.W.* XXV. 104 *Eucalyptus affinis*, sp. nov... A tree of moderate size, attaining a height of 80 feet... *Vernacular names.*—'Tallow Wood' at Murrumbidgerie, owing to the greasy nature of its wood. **1912** *Bulletin* (Sydney) 22 Feb. 13/1 The non-conductive properties of the tallow-wood yokes probably saved the life of every bullock. **1935** DAVISON & NICHOLLS *Blue Coast Caravan* 14 Ocean-going vessels came to the little port for cargoes of blackbutt, blue-gum, and tallow-wood logs. **1941** *Bulletin* (Sydney) 8 Jan. 17/2 The tallowwood bridge across Blicks River, on the Grafton-Armidale road was erected 60 years ago. **1979** J. BIRMINGHAM et al. *Austral. Pioneer Technol.* 33 Tallowood, though it resisted white-ant attack, was less liked on account of its poor splitting quality. **1982** R. HALL *Just Relations* 177 Billy levered up the tallow-wood threshold and used it to sledgehammer the lower part of the chimney. **1985** *Parks & Wildlife News* Summer 18 Tallowwoods, up to 70 m. in height and 8 m. in girth.

tally. [Spec. use of *tally* a count, a number, the record of this: see OED(S *sb.*[1] 2 e., and 5 a. and d.]

1. The number of sheep shorn by an individual shearer in a specified period; the record of this; a high number of sheep shorn (see quot. 1897); a call to mark a stage in the counting (see quot. 1886).

1870 *Austral. Town & Country Jrnl.* (Sydney) 29 Oct. 10/3 At five o'clock the bell rings; the day's labour is over; the men wait to see the sheep counted, and to hear their 'tallies'—the sums total of the day's shearing—read aloud. **1874** *Australasian Sketcher* (Melbourne) 31 Oct. 119/3 The men adjourn work for a smoke, and the 'tallies', representing the count of each man, are distributed to them in the evening. **1886** P. CLARKE *'New Chum' in Aust.* 175 As a 'hundred' is called, one of us calls out 'tally', and cuts one notch in a stick. **1887** *Bungendore Mirror* 12 Nov. 2 The highest tally we have heard of this season comes from the Narrowmine Shed. **1897** L. LINDLEY-COWEN *W. Austral. Settler's Guide* 635 Cuts in the skin are frequent with careless shearers, anxious only to make a tally. **1900** *Bulletin* (Sydney) 13 Jan. 32/3 The shearers are racing each other for tallies. **1909** E. WALTHAM *Life & Labour in Aust.* 174 As a rule the counter will station himself at one of the side posts, and will count in threes or fives. As soon as the hundred is reached, he calls out 'Tally' and a man standing near with a stick in his hand will notch it as the counter calls. **1917** T.J. BRIGGS *Life & Experiences Successful W. Austral.* 101 The tallies were not so high. However, I made a decent cheque as I put through about 100 jumbucks a day. **1930** *Bulletin* (Sydney) 8 Oct. 21/4 Not so long ago tomahawking was common among both good and bad shearers—the former when racing for a big tally. **1944** *Ibid.* 19 Apr. 12/1 Not a gun as far as pace was concerned—his tally .. was rarely more than 120 a day. **1946** *Ibid.* 11 Dec. 21/1 Those of us station-hands who could handle the bogai were set to barbering the woolled stragglers which had eluded the shearing-time musterings. 'You'll be on shed-hand rates,' said the overseer. 'So don't go for tallies; take your time and don't rough 'em.' **1955** E. BARNES *Easier Shearing* 15 As my tally was one hundred and fifteen, a few sheep above the average shorn by the seventy-five shearers, I was very pleased with myself. **1980** P. FREEMAN *Woolshed* 20 On completion of shearing, the sheep is dispatched unceremoniously down a sloped ramp into 'counting-out' pens, where the particular shearer's tally of shorn sheep is counted at the welcome 'smoko' and lunch breaks.

2. As **tally-hi.** [f. sense 1 + *hi(gh.*] See quot. 1964. Also *attrib.*

1964 *Sydney Morning Herald* 6 Apr. 2/6 The new 'tally-hi' shearing method .. cuts out some 15 blows (shearing strokes) a sheep and allows shearers to increase their tally by 20 or 30 sheep the first week they use it. This is not the only advantage of the tally-hi system. It is easier on the shearer because he does not have to lift the sheep or strain across it as much as he used to. It is easier on the sheep, reducing rough handling and the number of skin cuts. And it almost eliminates second cuts... 'The basis of the tally-hi system is that you shear down the sheep instead of across its body,' said Kevin Sarre. **1967** *Guide to 'Tally-Hi'* (Austral. Wool Board) 10 First introduced in mid-1963, the Tally-Hi shearing method was the result of a nation-wide survey to see what could be done to develop a standard method of shearing. **1979** HARMSWORTH & DAY *Wool & Mohair* 154 The feature of this *Tally Hi* method, as it is called, is the way that the strokes of the shearing handpiece progress in a rapid and smooth manner from one shearing position to the next.

tally-walka /'tæli-wɔkə/. Also **tally-walker.** [a. Bagandji *dali valga.*] See quot. 1947, and cf. ANABRANCH.

1900 *Pastoral Times* (Deniliquin) 10 Mar. 1/7 That proposal embodied water conservation by using the cowls, tally-walkas, billabongs, and branches of rivers. **1947** M. MACLEAN *Drummond of Far West* 92 Further along the road, we passed a 'tally-walker', which was a new one to us city folk. According to my informant, a billabong is a backwater of a river, or was so until the water receded and left the billabong isolated. He said a tally-walker is much the same thing, but it rejoins the river farther along again, when flowing sufficiently.

tamar, var. TAMMAR.

tamarind. [Transf. use of *tamarind* the tree *Tamarindus indica* and its fruit.] *Native tamarind*, see NATIVE *a.* 6 a.; the wood of a native tamarind.

1871 *Austral. Town & Country Jrnl.* (Sydney) 18 Mar. 330/4 A sample of the tamarind in this brush used in a bridge. **1902** *Bulletin* (Sydney) 6 Sept. 17/2 Near Hawkwood and Miles the wild lemon and tamarind trees, which have been regarded by bush naturalists as drought-proof, are dying.

tambaroora /tæmbə'rurə/. Also **tamberoora, tambooroora.** [The name of a goldfield north of Bathurst, N.S.W.]

a. A game in which each participant contributes an agreed sum to a pool which is then gambled for, the winner being required to buy drinks for the participants with (some of) the winnings: see quot. 1882.

1882 A.J. BOYD *Old Colonials* 63 It may be that the exciting game of Tambaroora is not familiar to all my readers... Each man of a party throws a shilling, or whatever sum may be mutually agreed upon, into a hat. Dice are then produced, and each man takes three throws. The Nut who throws highest keeps the whole of the subscribed capital, and out of it pays for the drinks of the rest. The advantage of the proceeding lies in this: Where drinks are charged at sixpence, the subscription is double that amount for each... Thus if ten Nuts go in for a Tambaroora, with nobblers at sixpence, the winner pockets five shillings by the transaction. **1895** *Bulletin* (Sydney) 26 Oct. 7/4 Service was being held on a Northern N.S.W. river, in a hall near the hotel. The landlord's little son .. seeing the priest, a great favourite of his, walked in and took a seat by his friend. The collection-box having been passed round, the child waited till the money was poured on the table in front of the clergyman, and then .. whispered—'Say, shall I run and tell dad you are going to have a tambooroora?' **1900** *Truth* (Sydney) 11 Feb. 7/3 A sort of tamberoora, each one paying a shilling to enter the ring and get all he could. **1916** A.I. MACLEOD *Hack's Brat* (1920) 11 Stingo Jamieson rose after a while to 'spout a spell', and MacLure began to edge his way towards the door. Most of the others had begun to play 'tamberoora' in spite of Stingo's ringing eloquence. **1923** J.A. PHILP *Songs Austral. Fascisti* 17 There were no Tambarooras at the old Dog and Duck.

b. Special Comb. **Tambaroora muster:** see MUSTER *n.* 5.

tame, *a. Obs.* [Transf. use of *tame*, as applied to an animal; rarely applied elsewhere to a person but cf. *tame Indian*, Mathews *tame, a.* 2.] Of an Aboriginal: not overtly hostile to the colonists. See also CIVILIZED.

1842 *Portland Mercury* 7 Sept. 3/5 Many of the blacks engaged in this outrage had been for a long time domiciled on the station of Messrs Winter Brothers; in fact, scarcely any attack on any station has been made by the natives save under the guidance of a 'tame black'. **1843** J. HOOD *Aust. & East* 190 Even the '*tame*' blacks, as they are called, are still a savage race. **1845** *Portland Guardian* 6 Sept. 3/2 They are divided into two parties; the wild natives forming one, the tame the other; the latter is said to number three hundred. **1857** J. BONWICK *Early Days Melbourne* 9 By the help of .. a few words understood by the tame blackfellows, Mr Batman told them what he wanted. **1870** —— *Last Tasmanians* 116 Some of them came across to the hut and said that all the party were tame Blacks .. meaning they were all peaceable. **1898** D.W. CARNEGIE *Spinifex & Sand* 154 It is marvellous how soon a tame boy comes to despise his own people, when he far outstrips any white man in his contemptuous manner of speaking about a '... black-fella'. **1907** *Truth* (Sydney) 7 Apr. 9/7 'But they use them on the stations?' 'Oh, yes, they use them, gins and bucks. Soon as they get tame enough, both squatters and missionaries run 'em in.' **1968** W. HILLIARD *People in Between* 67 Some 'boys' who were intelligent could be trained and 'tamed'. Carnegie's standard for 'tameness' is interesting. A 'tame' native was one who spoke English! No other requirements necessary!

tamma /'tæmə/. *W.A.* [Prob. f. a W.A. Aboriginal language.] A vegetation community consisting of low, thick, shrubby growth, the dominant plants incl. *Allocasuarina campestris* and *A. corniculata* (fam. Casuarinaceae) of W.A.; the plants themselves. Also *attrib.*

1905 *Rep. W.A. R. Comm. Immigration* 217, I have cultivated scrub plains—tamma scrub and blackboy country. **1926** J. POLLARD *Bushland Man.* 17 The sunlight .. showed up the darker patches where the taller scrubs and thickets of mallee and tamma and wodgil grew. **1971** B.Y. MAIN *Twice Trodden Ground* 33 The protection of tamma and acacia thickets was gone. **1973** R. ERICKSON et al. *Flowers & Plants W.A.* 190 Another vegetation type is tamma which is also a shrub formation but is less than 2 m. high and is dominated by *Casuarina campestris.*

tammar /'tæmə/. Also **tamar** and formerly **dama, damar, tamma.** [a. Gaurna *tarnma.*] The greyish-brown wallaby *Macropus eugenii* of s. S.A. and s.w. W.A. (incl. adjacent islands). Also *attrib.*, esp. as **tammar wallaby.**

1847 E.W. LANDOR *Bushman* 367 Our guides agreed .. to take us to a hill where a curious species of Kangaroo called 'Damar' by them, would be met with. **1891** P. O'FARRELL *Lett. from Irish Aust.* (1984) 86 We are going tamar hunting this evening. It is a small animal of the kangaroo species and very numerous. **1903** *Emu* III. 105 This scrub is the home of numerous tamma. **1926** A.S. LE SOUEF et al. *Wild Animals Australasia* 199 Dama wallaby. *Macropus eugenii*... South-western Australia and islands off coast. **1937** A.R. GRANT *Memories of Parliament* 3 The tamar, a most engaging little beast, provided sport and food. Indeed the tamar, whose hind quarters are baked in a camp oven, hath no fellow. **1943** E. TROUGHTON *Furred Animals Aust.* (rev. ed.) 194 The specific name *eugenii* is correctly used for all races of the Dama Pademelon. **1952** J.F. HADDLETON *Katanning Pioneer* 9 Jam stakes were put in side by side standing six feet above the ground .. to keep out the wild marsupials consisting of .. tamars and various other pests that would come at night to feed on the wheat. **1967** E. HUXLEY *Their Shining Eldorado* 217 The Tammar wallaby, now virtually extinct on the mainland but still to be found on the Abrolhos islands off the coast near Geraldton. **1978** *Ecos* xv. 27 A colony of tammar wallabies turned up in bush near Cleve on the Eyre Peninsula. **1985** *Austral.* (Sydney) 7 Nov. 8/1 Tamar wallaby joeys, ranging in age from 15 to 70 days, are decapitated, some are killed by night, some by day.

tangle. *Obs.* [Abbrev. of U.S. *tanglefoot* strong drink: see Mathews.] Alcoholic liquor.

1879 *Truth* (Sydney) 6 Nov. 8/1 A wicked female .. had imbibed more 'tangle' than she was able to accommodate without personal inconvenience. **1892** *Bulletin* (Sydney) 3 Sept. 22/1 And if he saw them coming, and rolled it out, perhaps He'd find his hard-earned tangle would be soaked up by the chaps. **1902** *Truth* (Sydney) 19 Oct. 8/1 Discussing club matters in the hotel bar over pints of tangle. **1907** *Ibid.* 17 Nov. 1/6 The curse of too much tangle. Saw a smart-looking chap, who formerly had a snug billet in the Civil Service, acting as a groom at a Nyngan hotel.

Hence **tangled** *ppl. a.*, drunk.

1899 J. BRADSHAW *Highway Robbery under Arms* (1912) 33 These two men were pannikin overseers, who had got a bit tangled with rum, and were trying the speed of their mokes. **1913** *Bulletin* (Sydney) 25 Sept. 22/2 Me for 'Inebriated' when we open the Multi-Synonymous

Word Competition. In the number, aptness and variety of its colloquial equivalents I consider it commandeers the pastry. For instance:- Loaded, primed .. tangled, outed [etc.].

tanglefoot. The deciduous shrub or small tree *Nothofagus gunnii* (fam. Fagaceae) having wiry, tangled branches, and occurring in the mountains of Tas.; *deciduous beech*, see BEECH; (occas.) any of several other plants of similar habit, as *Bauera rubioides* (fam. Saxifragaceae).

1891 W. TILLEY *Wild West of Tas.* 7 Bauera shrub, whose gnarled branches have earned for it the local and expressive name of 'tanglefoot' or 'leg ropes'. **1945** M. HODGES *Veil of Time* 89 Of the native trees all are evergreen, save one, a beech (Fagus Gunnii), called 'tanglefoot' by bushmen, which sheds its leaves yearly. **1969** HOLLIDAY & HILL *Field Guide Austral. Trees* 196 Tanglefoot .. is a truly deciduous species from alpine Tasmania. **1980** G.R. COCHRANE et al. *Flowers & Plants Vic. & Tas.* 115 The common name, Tanglefoot, serves to emphasise the density of the plant in exposed areas.

tank, *n.*[1] [Anglo-Indian *tank* artificial reservoir f. Gujarati *tankh* or Pg. *tanque* pond: see OED *sb.*[1]]

1. An artificial reservoir; DAM 1, esp. as excavated to provide water for livestock. Also **earth tank, surface tank.**

1791 D. COLLINS *Acct. Eng. Colony N.S.W.* (1798) I. 189 The governor had employed the stone-mason's gang to cut tanks out of the rock, which would be reservoirs for the water large enough to supply the settlement. **1833** *N.S.W. Mag.* (Sydney) 312 Sydney is supplied with water from tanks, that are filled by a small stream that runs through part of the town. **1851** H. MELVILLE *Present State Aust.* 32 The fresh water .. was .. formed into what were called the Tanks, reservoirs where the water was dammed up to prevent any waste. **1868** J. BAIRD *Emigrant's Guide Australasia* 17 What are called tanks up here [*sc.* the Warrego region] are more properly reservoirs, inasmuch as they are not lined with metal or timber... Tanks are usually made in swamps, which dry up in summer, for the sake of drainage. **1875** R.P. FALLA *Knocking About* (1976) 28 Those selectors who have sunk tanks or dams have sufficient water to last through the summer. **1889** E. GILES *Aust. twice Traversed* II. 15 Gibson dug a small tank, and the water soon cleared for itself a beautiful little crystal basin of the purest liquid. **1899** *Austral. Mag.* (Sydney) May 156 The crops have withered from the ground, The tank's clay bed is glarin'. **1909** *Bulletin* (Sydney) 10 June 13/2 Among the big cockies of Riverina at the present day is a desire to possess the largest surface-tank in the district. **1930** A.E. YARRA *Vanishing Horsemen* 75 They .. would otherwise have to drink the same water as the horses, from the slimey, clayey 'tanks' on the route. **1940** G. MORPHETT *Simple Story Rural Dev.* 2 My husband and I next started to excavate a tank .. 10 feet deep and 25 ft. in diameter, and gathered a heap of limestone which we burned .. to make mortar to build the tank floor and wall. **1960** *N.T. News* (Darwin) 4 Mar. 5/3 Tilmouth went to Inverway to build some earth tanks. **1982** G.B. EGGLETON *Last of Lantern Swingers* 59 Kangaroos and emus gathered at the tanks, bogging in the muddy edges, and, as tank after tank dried out, the wild creatures converged on the remaining water, compounding the situation.

2. Comb. **tank-keeper, -sinker, -sinking, town.**

1913 H. LAWSON *Triangles of Life* 234 Mitchell went, with the billy, into the little galvanized iron pumping-engine room, where the **tank-keeper** (an old sailor) was. **1946** K.S. PRICHARD *Roaring Nineties* 45 The tank-keeper refused to let him have water for his horses although he had a good supply. **1881** W.E. ABBOTT *Notes Journey on Darling* 60 The station-buildings are erected, stock bought, and fences and **tank-sinkers** set to work in all directions. **1886** P. CLARKE *'New Chum' in Aust.* 201 We pass the tank-sinkers' camp which we visited yesterday, and find that they have had to 'knock off' for the day, as the clay is as tenacious as glue. **1907** *Bulletin* (Sydney) 25 July 14/4 Across his chest lay a tank-sinker just as full. **1922** V. PALMER *Boss of Killara* 138 She was merely the daughter of Ned Langton, the tank-sinker. **1935** B.E. PHELPS *Austral. tells England* 198 A kindly tanksinker .. made an underground dairy for the selectors. **1946** *Coast to Coast 1945* 144 Of the three tank-sinkers he was a special cobber of mine. **1965** *N. Austral. Monthly* Oct. 15 It was too bulky to pack in a swag; it was used in a fixed camp only—a tank-sinker's plant or some kindred thing. **1890** E.T. TOWNER *Selectors' Guide Barcoo* 15 The other method of conserving water is by **tank sinking.** **1913** H. LAWSON *Triangles of Life* 180 Mrs Foster's husband and sons were away mostly, working with the drays—tank-sinking, dam-making, etc. **1952** F.W. GUNNING *Lure of North* 93 There was much tank-sinking going on at this time. John Cashan said that Johnny Musk was the first man to plough and scoop a tank on the Gascoyne for Gooch. **1968** LINKLATER & TAPP *Gather no Moss* 84 A group who had been tank-sinking on Brunette Downs started in with good cheques for a rest and a change of diet. **1979** B. HARDY *World owes me Nothing* 3 They were big men, and very fit from hard work on their father's tank-sinking plant. **1948** G. MEREDITH *Lawsons* 1 Wongalee is .. an impressive little one-horse town whose few hundred yards of bitumen, straggling at each end into dusty dirt roads, rouse no excess of enthusiasm. The visitor to all such country towns wonders why they don't plant a few trees... The answer is, of course, that they are mostly **tank towns** and trees are thirsty things.

tank, *n.*[2] [Spec. use of *tank* artificial receptacle.]

1. A safe. Also *attrib.*, esp. as **tank man,** a safe-breaker.

[N.Z. **1937** E. PARTRIDGE *Dict. Slang & Unconventional Eng.* 864 *Tank*, .. a safe: New Zealand c. (--1932).] **1950** *Austral. Police Jrnl.* Apr. 119 *Tank*, a safe. **1967** *Kings Cross Whisper* (Sydney) lxi. 4/2 *Tank*, a safe. People who specialise in robbing tanks are naturally known as tank men. **1974** C. PATON *I was Prison Parson* 40 As a 'tank' man (safe-blower) Harry had seen a lot of gaol. **1975** *Bulletin* (Sydney) 10 May 51/1 Safes were built which were almost impregnable and slowly the old lag 'tank man' went out of business. **1981** *Sydney Morning Herald* 2 Mar. 1/7 Dugan claimed that more than 30 years ago a friend had been arrested, convicted and sentenced for a Sydney 'tank' robbery—a safe cracking—which he had not done. Dugan said he knew this because he had done the job himself.

2. Special Comb. **tank-stand,** a structure which supports a tank in which water is stored.

1902 *Pastoralists' Rev.* Feb. 834 An earth tank stand for large stock tanks .. is constructed of earth bound together with logs scarfed into each other, to prevent the earth from spreading. **1914** C.E. MAYES *Austral. Builders & Contractors' Price Bk.* (ed. 8) 308 Angle steel tank stands. Complete with H.W. Decking. **1941** *Coast to Coast* 146 She crept off the veranda and went down under the tankstand. The soil under the tank was a rich chocolate brown, and there were drips of water coming from the tap. **1947** K. MCCONNEL *Planning Austral. Homestead* 89 The tank stand, which was 20 ft. high, was placed on the river bank between the river and the underground watertank. **1977** C. MCCULLOUGH *Thorn Birds* 116 A drover whose cross said only *Tankstand Charlie he was a good bloke.* **1983** B. CORBETT *Fistful of Buttercups* 45 My mother suggested that Tiger would be safer sleeping outside under the tank-stand.

Tanna. *Obs.* TOMMY TANNA.

1906 *Bulletin* (Sydney) 3 May 14/1 Why does the allegedly humane missionary insist on Tanna squeezing his expansive feet into a No. 8 shoe?

Tanner's curse. [See quot. 1897.] DOUBLE-GEE.

1897 L. LINDLEY-COWEN *W. Austral. Settler's Guide* 541 My [*sc.* Baron von Mueller's] informant is Mr D. Wansborough, who landed at Fremantle in 1831. He, with his wife, came from England under contract with Mr William Tanner. On their way out the ship put in at the Cape of Good Hope, where Mr Tanner obtained the seed. Eighteen months after arrival in Western Australia Mr Wansborough .. sowed a bed with the seed of this 'Cape spinach'... The seed was obtained from Mr Tanner... However, the plant did not prove a very palatable spinach, and soon became a troublesome weed, causing constant annoyance to the workmen, on account of its spinous seeds... It received the name of 'Tanner's curse' throughout the settlement. **1980** J. FITZPATRICK *Bicycle & Bush* 140 It has been called 'doublegee' .. 'Tanner's curse', [etc.].

Tantanoola tiger /tæntənulə 'taɪgə/. [f. the name of a town in s.e. S.A.] An animal reportedly seen at Tantanoola *c* 1889; a fabulous animal.

1893 *S. Austral. Advertiser* (Adelaide) 11 May 5/2 The Tantanoola 'tiger' is the 'lion' of the hour *writes the South-Eastern Star*). **1893** *Adelaide Observer* 13 May 25/1 Bunyips, sea serpents, and Tantanoola tigers are animals to be believed in when captured—but not before. .. The Tantanoola tiger, though not a probability, is always a possibility. *Ibid.* 30 Sept. 31/5 No sooner does any really reliable and startling information come to hand with reference to the famous Tantanoola 'tiger' than some one steps in with a cold matter-of-fact explanation. **1894** *Ibid.* 4 Aug. 31/5 Mounted-Constables Russell and Foote returned this evening from the search for the Tantanoola tiger in the Hundred of Kongorong. **1895** *Bulletin* (Sydney) 4 May 24/1 The famous 'Tantanoola tiger', which appears intermittently in S.A. and Victoria .. which fills the blank left by innumerable bunyips and the Dora-Dora blacks, is alleged to be identical with a cub which escaped from a travelling menagerie at Mt. Gambier (S.A.) thirteen years ago. **1903** *Truth* (Sydney) 27 Dec. 1/7 With the approach of the festive season, the Tantanoola tiger has again made its appearance at Snake Valley (Vic.). The inhabitants in that region appear to have made an early start on the 'moisture'. **1907** *Bulletin* (Sydney) 28 Mar. 14/3 A relative of the Tantanoola tiger .. has been causing a scare in South Gippsland (Vic.) .. so a terrified community .. takes its gun when it goes cow-hunting. **1909** *Truth* (Sydney) 11 Apr. 1/6 The Tantanoola tiger's brother has turned up in the vicinity of Kiama, where his long body, short legs, and big cat's head is fairly well known to one of the residents. **1911** *Bulletin* (Sydney) 5 Jan. 13/4 He will fight anything from a cockroach to a Tantanoola tiger. **1976** B. SCOTT *Complete Bk. Austral. Folk Lore* 11 Then tamed a Gippsland bunyip, and sooled him on to capture the Tantanoola Tiger and Fisher's Ghost.

taori, var. TOWRI.

tarantula. [Transf. use of *tarantula* a European spider of the fam. Lycosidae.] HUNTSMAN SPIDER.

1824 J. LYCETT *Views in Aust.* 4 Of poisonous reptiles, the centipede, tarantula, scorpion .. are the most hurtful. **1839** W.H. LEIGH *Reconnoitering Voyages* 131 An enormous tarantula marching majestically along. **1855** J. BONWICK *Geogr. Aust. & N.Z.* (ed. 3) 200 The Tarantula has poisonous saliva. **1870** E.B. KENNEDY *Four Yrs. in Qld.* 122 The 'Tarantula' is common, and sheds his skin like a snake. **1881** A.C. GRANT *Bush-Life Qld.* II. 18 The tarantula spiders—heavy, fat-bodied, horrid creatures, almost as large as small birds, with legs fully two inches long—spread their webs everywhere between the trees. **1900** *Bulletin* (Sydney) 27 Jan. 14/2 Last night my office companion, a huge tarantula, was mute and motionless on the wall as usual. **1934** C. MACKNESS *Young Beachcombers* 95, I have to fish the contrivances out and root out all the tarantulas that are nesting in them. **1946** *Victorian Naturalist* LXII. 228 In Australia the name 'Tarantula', as well as its corruption 'Triantelope', is applied to those large spiders belonging to the family *Eusparassidae*, the Crab or Huntsman Spiders. **1985** N. KEESING *Just look out Window* 36 The large brown hairy Huntsman spider, usually called 'tarantula' or 'triantelope', often enters houses.

tar-boy. *Shearing.* A hand employed chiefly to apply a disinfectant, orig. tar, to a wound accidentally inflicted on a sheep.

1871 *Austral. Town & Country Jrnl.* (Sydney) 21 Jan. 82/2 As a rule, the quickest men shear the best, and call less for the 'tar-boy'. **1888** *Boomerang* (Brisbane) 3 Mar. 13/3 The tar-boy was not called into requisition once during the day, and I felt elated. **1906** J. BARBOUR *Pencillings on Wallaby* 8 When the big guns open for a record score, And the tar-boys gather Round the ringer's door. **1922** 'J. NORTH' *Black Opal* 35 The bleating sheep, the cursing men, the yelling tar-boys and pickers-up. **1933** J. TRURAN *Where Plain Begins* 148 'Tar', cries the shearer; a dab or two with the brush where the cutter has drawn blood (but not too many dabs, for it goes against a man if he is always shouting for the tar-boy). **1942** *Bulletin* (Sydney) 4 Feb. 13/1 Soon as a ticky fleece hit the wool-table there was a cry of 'Salt!' and the tar-boys rushed up with a bucket of it and rubbed it well into the fleece. **1972** W. WATKINS *Suddenly of Age* 30 If he cut a sheep he'd yell, 'Tar! Christ, where's that bloody tar boy!' **1979** K. GARVEY *Absolutely Austral.* 19 The tar-boy by fly-strike kept running.

tarpaulin. Abbrev. of *tarpaulin muster* (see MUSTER *n.* 5).

1946 J.H. FAHEY *Slim Sullivan hits Wallaby* 11 'What

about a 'tarpaulin' for a new rifle for Slim?' 'Too right.. I'll sport a quid.'

tart. [Prob. abbrev. of *jam tart* (see quot. 1864), itself prob. rhyming slang for 'sweetheart'. Also used pejoratively, as elsewhere: see OED(S *sb.* 2.] A girl-friend or 'sweetheart'; applied generally to a girl or woman but usu. implying admiration.

[**1864** J.C. HOTTEN *Dict. Mod. Slang* (ed. 3) 254 *Tart*, a term of approval applied by the London lower orders to a young woman for whom some affection is felt. The expression is not generally employed by the young men, unless the female is in 'her best', with a coloured gown, red or blue shawl, and plenty of ribbons in her bonnet—in fact, made pretty all over, like the jam tarts in the swell bakers' shops.] **1892** *Truth* (Sydney) 1 May 2/7 They were very fond of music, were this baldy and his 'tart'. **1894** *Bulletin* (Sydney) 16 June 20/3 It may be merely the affectionate anxiety of a 'bloke' for his 'tart'. **1905** *Ibid.* 13 July 18/2 We 'ad a tart stayin' at our place once what 'ad the beautifulest 'ead uf 'air yer ever sighted. **1916** C.J. DENNIS *Moods Ginger Mick* 25 Mick listens, while I tells 'im 'ow they starts Be burnin' pore coves 'omes an' killin' kids, An' comin' it reel crook wiv decent tarts. **1924** F.J. MILLS *Happy Days* 118, I was on with a taxi-driver named Phyllis. Now, she was the neatest tart outside of a baker's shop... She 'ad the bonzerest ankles I ever seen. **1937** A.W. UPFIELD *Mr Jelly's Business* 28 I'm in love with a tart. Her name's Lucy Jelly. She is the loveliest girl within a thousand miles of Burracoppin. Twenty years old she is. Her father is a cocky four miles out. He doesn't seem to mind me courting his daughter, but he doesn't give me a chance to do any courting. **1965** G. MCINNES *Road to Gundagai* 28, I looked up to see the same Digger who had teased me earlier in the voyage about 'getting a tart'. **1972** D. SHEAHAN *Songs from Canefields* 132 If you fell in love and got on with a tart—'Twas happy she'd be to go out in a cart—And after the wedding she'd chatter for hours Of sight and scenes that she saw at the Towers. **1977** T. RONAN *Mighty Men on Horseback* 52 Hangin' around my tart?

tar tree. [See quot. 1948.] The tree *Semecarpus australiensis* (fam. Anacardiaceae) of n. Aust. and elsewhere.

1938 C.T. WHITE *Princ. Bot. Qld. Farmers* 176 Family Anacardiaceae.. represented in Queensland by seven native species. These include.. the Tar Tree (*Semecarpus australiensis*) [etc.]. **1948** H.A. LINDSAY *Bushman's Handbk.* 142 On the sea-coasts of Queensland, New Guinea and the Indies there grows a large tree with thick foliage... It can be recognized.. by the black, thick, tar-like sap which flows from any wound in the bark. This is the tar-tree whose sap causes bad ulcers. **1952** A.C.C. LOCK *Travels across Aust.* 78 Fastened to it is a notice: 'Beware. This is a tar-tree', and a further warning stated that the sap caused poisoning if it touched the flesh. **1978** R.J. BRITTEN *Around Cassowary Rock* 133 We got across the creek and tied the dinghy up to a tar tree. **1985** *Flora Aust.* XXV. 178 Tar Tree, Marking Nut.. occurs in north coastal N.T. and north-eastern Qld.; also extends to the Aru Is., New Guinea and New Britain.

tart shop. Used allusively of political office, esp. as able to be exploited by its occupants.

[**1904** A. DEAKIN in J.A. la Nauze *A. Deakin* (1965) 378, I do not propose to reply to him except by saying he presents to you as undignified a spectacle as does the ill-bred urchin whom one sees dragged from a tart-shop kicking and screaming as he goes.] **1908** *Truth* (Sydney) 13 Dec. 1/5 The Reid gang reckon they wouldn't occupy the tart shop if they had the chance, yet the envious hungry crowd are flattening their noses against the outside window like a lot of famished school kids. Could Rumpty's push scoff a tart in the shape of a Ministerial portfolio? **1908** *Ibid.* 27 Dec. 1/5 'Caryegraph', because its own pals are in the tart shop, says the development of the country warrants the present enormous loan expenditure. **1945** E.W. CAMPBELL *Hist. Austral. Labour Movt.* 151 It became clear to the job conscious politicians that Lang would never lead them back into 'the tart shop'. **1962** J.T. LANG *Great Bust* 72 It was about the same time that Menzies and the Young Liberals were waging war on the Country Party in Victoria, and Gullett was their spokesman in Canberra on behalf of the Outs. They wanted their share of the tart shop. **1982** *Sydney Morning Herald* 24 Dec. 12/5 Why should retired politicians, whose superannuation is already generously subsidised from the public purse, get free rides as well? The tart shop, it seems, is not just open to the railway unions.

tarwhine /'tawaɪn/. [a. Dharuk *darawayn* a fish.] The silvery marine fish *Rhabdosargus sarba* of Aust. and elsewhere.

c **1790** W. DAWES Grammatical Forms Lang. N.S.W., *Tar-ra-wine*, a fish. **1880** J. INGLIS *Our Austral. Cousins* 298 In the brackish waters near Lake Macquarie, are most plentiful supplies of black bream, tarwine.. and others. **1883** E.P. RAMSAY *Notes on Food Fishes N.S.W.* 12 The black bream (*Chrysophrys australis*) and the tarwhine (*Ch. hasta*) are both valuable food-fish... They attain a weight of 4 to 5 lbs. **1906** D.G. STEAD *Fishes of Aust.* 129 The Tarwhine (*Chrysophrys sarba*).. is more of a tropical species... Consequently it becomes more common on our coast as we proceed in a northerly direction. **1946** *Coast to Coast 1945* 11 He was a regular crank on fishing. Great red-shouldered jewfish that he could hardly lift.. bream and tarwhine. **1952** *Austral. Museum Mag.* June 310 The Australian aborigines had their names for fishes, of course, and still have in the more remote places, and some of these, even though tribes which invented them have become extinct or have 'lost their tongues', are currently used in everyday speech. I need only mention the following.. Tallegalane, Tarwhine, [etc.]. **1983** *Ecos* xxxv. 5/2 Closer investigation.. has now turned up evidence for sex inversion in yellowfin bream, tarwhine, snapper.. all of them important fish in the market-place.

Tasmaniac. A nickname for a non-Aboriginal person native to or resident in Tasmania.

1867 *Sydney Punch* 23 Feb. 101/1 'Fill we tankards to the brim', Thus Tasmaniacs used to cry. **1886** *Tasmanian* (Hobart) 20 Mar. 28, I'm full of information as regarding the Tasmaniacs. **1891** *Bohemia* (Melbourne) 25 June 7 Well, a second 'limb' representing Lord Ancrum duly arrived, and was also introduced to the tottering Tasmaniac. **1906** *Gadfly* (Adelaide) 7 Mar. 15/1 Hobart residents who join in the hue and cry against Tattersall's sweeps are popularly known as 'Tasmaniacs'. **1982** *Bulletin* (Sydney) 16 Nov. 42/2 In Sydney.. they are called Tasmaniacs.

Tasmanian, *a.* and *n.* [f. *Tasmania*, the name of an island lying south of s.e. Aust., and one of the federated States of Australia.]

A. *adj.*

1. Of or pertaining to the island of Tasmania or to its inhabitants.

1824 *Hobart Town Gaz.* 22 Oct., The *Tasmanian Fleece*, in our Gazette of the 9th of July last, we published some interesting Correspondence on the subject of wool exports from Van Diemen's Land. **1833** H.W. PARKER *Rise, Progress, & Present State Van Dieman's Land* 162 To impress upon the minds of the Australian and Tasmanian farmers. **1840** *S. Austral. Rec.* (London) 22 Feb. 58 It is on account of the name of the discoverer, that to the affairs and inhabitants of this country the epithet 'Tasmanian' is so frequently applied. **1860** *S. Austral. Advertiser* (Adelaide) 2 July 3/1 It was in July, the Tasmanian winter. **1889** J.H. WIGMORE *Austral. Ballot System* 82 The 'Tasmanian dodge' (which appeared in Australia once only, in 1868, where it was immediately detected..), consists in sending in a voter who manages to deposit a counterfeit ballot.. and to bring out his own genuine one; which is then marked in ink by the local manager without, and given to another henchman, who in turn brings out a fresh ballot, and the process is repeated. **1913** W.K. HARRIS *Outback in Aust.* 115 A family makes a meal off something which resembles a 'Tasmanian Mud' (a very sodden, badly-baked damper). **1928** A.W. LOONE *Tas.'s N.-E.* 29 Tasmanian working men are nearly all good workers. **1949** C. TURNBULL *Charm of Hobart* 22 Tasmanian history runs in a fairly level line. **1966** *Mercury* (Hobart) 13 July 3/6 A Tasmanian holiday sounds good—except for the food. **1986** *Nat. Times* (Sydney) 31 Jan. 4/1 'Having a good day?' asks Tasmanian Premier Robin Gray, pumping the sticky hand of an ice cream-eating voter.

2. In the names of flora and fauna: **Tasmanian barber** *obs.*, the marine fish *Caesioperca rasor* of Tas., Vic., S.A., and s. W.A.; **blackwood,** BLACKWOOD, esp. the wood of the tree; **blue gum,** the tree *Eucalyptus globulus* subsp. *globulus* (fam. Myrtaceae) of Tas. and s. Vic., the floral emblem of Tas.; the wood of the tree; **devil,** the carnivorous marsupial *Sarcophilus harrisii*, a black animal with white markings, mainly carrion-eating but of fierce appearance, now occurring only in Tas.; *bush devil*, see BUSH C. 3; DEVIL 1; *native devil, native hyena* (b), see NATIVE *a.* 6 b.; **lilac,** either of two shrubs or trees of s.e. Aust. of the genus *Prostanthera* (fam. Lamiaceae), *P. lasianthos* (see *Christmas bush* (a), CHRISTMAS) and *P. rotundifolia*, bearing white or lilac flowers; **myrtle,** MYRTLE 1; **native hen,** the plump, brown bird *Gallinula mortierii*, occurring in fields near water throughout Tas., excl. the south-west; see also *native hen* (a), NATIVE *a.* 6 b.; **oak,** the timber of the trees *Eucalyptus obliqua* (see MESSMATE), *E. regnans* (see *mountain ash* MOUNTAIN), and ALPINE ASH; (occas.) one of the trees themselves; **tiger,** the carnivorous marsupial *Thylacinus cynocephalus*, having sandy brown fur with dark brown stripes across the back and rump, now poss. extinct (see quots. 1885 and 1947); HYENA; *marsupial wolf*, see MARSUPIAL 1; *native hyena* (b), *native tiger*, see NATIVE *a.* 6 b.; *Tasmanian wolf*; THYLACINE; TIGER *n.* 1; see also WOLF a.; **trumpeter,** the fish *Latris lineata* (see TRUMPETER *n.*[1] 1); **waratah,** the shrub *Telopea truncata* (see WARATAH 1); **wolf,** *Tasmanian tiger*.

1842 *Tasmanian Jrnl. Nat. Sci.* I. 59 The *Serranus Rasor*, or **Tasmanian Barber,** is a beautiful fish. **1873** J. BONWICK *Tasmanian Lily* 27 The Tasmanian Barber is one of the Serrani... The colour is reddish brown. A bright blue stripe runs round the eye, and along the side. **1886** *T.H.A.J.* no. 69 6 **Tasmanian blackwood** .. will ever hold its own against all competitors as to quality, cost, and easy means of transit, whilst for furniture and all decorative purposes it is most valuable. **1903** *Proc. Linnean Soc. N.S.W.* XXVII. 575 *Acacia melanoxylon* is the same as the famous Tasmanian Blackwood, but in New South Wales it does not grow into such fine trees. **1918** *Huon Times* (Franklin) 23 July 3/3 The Warden then unveiled the board which was seen to be a handsomely polished memorial of Tasmanian blackwood. **1947** W.A.W. DE BEUZEVILLE *Austral. Trees* 122 Blackwood.. makes an excellent shade tree and is very hardy. Usually known as the Tasmanian Blackwood, the timber is ornamental and valuable. **1984** *Tasmanian Wood* July-Aug. 17, I have noted the great number of finely carved honour rolls, panelling and furniture throughout Tasmania, much in Tasmanian blackwood. **1880** C. PROUD *S.-E. District S.A.* 45 The longitudinal timbers are of jarrah, and the decking of **Tasmanian bluegum.** **1905** *Emu* V. 79 A fine clump of transplanted Tasmanian blue gums burst into early blossom. **1952** E. WALLING *Austral. Roadside* 58 These particular trees are the Victorian Blue Gums (*Eucalyptus bicostata*) as distinct from the Tasmanian Blue Gum (*Eucalyptus globulus*)... The seed vessels of the Tasmanian species are almost twice the size of those of *bicostata*. **1984** D.J. BOLAND et al. *Forest Trees Austral.* (rev. ed.) 458 Tasmanian blue gum occurs mainly along the east coast of Tasmania, mostly within 20 km. of the sea... It also occurs on Flinders and King Islands in Bass Strait, around Cape Otway, the Strzelecki Ranges and on Wilsons Promontory in southern, coastal Victoria. **1857** W. HOWITT *Tallangetta* I. 217 You have seen the **Tasmanian devil**—a furious beast that will devour its own species when wounded. **1867** *S. Austral. Register* (Adelaide) 30 Apr. 2/5 He also obtained five specimens, male and female, of the Tasmanian devil. **1885** *Illustr. Austral. News* (Melbourne) 19 Dec. 218/3 In the older geological time of the pleistocene period it seems to have existed on the mainland, like the so-called Tasmanian devil, now also confined to Tasmania, but very common in the fossil state in the pleistocene deposits about Melbourne. **1914** H.M. VAUGHAN *Australasian Wander-Yr.* 128 The Tasmanian Devil (*Sarcophilus ursinus*) is a powerful but sluggish creature. **1926** A. EDEN *Places in Sun* 77 The 'Tasmanian Devil' is well named. This animal also is only found in Tasmania. Black with a few small white patches, about the size of a badger, and with something of the appearance of a giant rat, it is the most bad-tempered of beasts imaginable. **1937** D. GLASS *Austral. Fantasy* 18 Tasmanian Devils exist in actual fact, jet-black sinners burrowing like badgers. **1964** B. WANNAN *Fair Go, Spinner* 70 He swam like an elephant, ate like a threshing machine and fought like a bagful of Tasmanian devils. **1985** *Mercury* (Hobart) 29 Oct. 30/1 Having recently graduated from the University of Tasmania, I read with concern the report of complaints made by animal liberationists about experiments performed upon Tasmanian Devils. **1892** M. NORTH *Recoll. Happy Life* II. 174 Shrubs of many kinds, that called the **Tas-**

manian lilac (*Prostanthera lasianthos*) being the most striking. **1914** H.M. VAUGHAN *Australasian Wander-Yr.* 119, I was delighted with the so-called Tasmanian Lilac. **1833** J. BACKHOUSE *Narr. Visit Austral. Colonies* (1843) 159 The **Tasmanian Myrtle,** *Fagus Cunninghamii*, here forms trees of moderate size. **1846** N.L. KENTISH *Work in Bush Van Diemen's Land* 21 *Tasmanian Myrtle* . . classes with the English Beech. **1931** *Bulletin* (Sydney) 25 Mar. 21/3 There is at least one Australian timber that is better appreciated abroad than at home—Tasmanian myrtle. **1943** *Pre-School Child* (Vic. Dept. Health) p. vi, In regard to timbers available for planks, etc. . . Tasmanian Myrtle . . should be good, as it is close grained and free from splinters. **1936** *Smith's Weekly* (Sydney) Apr. 20/4, I nominate the **Tasmanian native-hen** as the speediest of Australia's waterfowl. **1976** *Ecos* viii. 28 Studies . . on the Tasmanian native hen showed that any really intensive campaign to eradicate these flightless relatives of the mainland moorhens from agricultural areas would drive them to extinction. **1919** *Huon Times* (Franklin) 24 Oct. 5/1 Immediately opposite was a dining suite in **Tasmanian oak. 1943** *Bulletin* (Sydney) 4 Aug. 12/3 Many a piece of stringybark has been worked into cheap furniture as Tasmanian oak. **1956** N.K. WALLIS *Austral. Timber Handbk.* 8 The Tasmanian timber industry has always been an important contributor to Victorian and South Australian markets. The main timbers in plentiful supply are messmate, stringybark, alpine ash and mountain ash (collectively known as Tasmanian oak, and used for general building purposes including flooring, weatherboards and joinery, and for furniture and cooperage). **1967** E. HUXLEY *Their Shining Eldorado* 174 Stringybark (*E. delegatensis*) sometimes called Tasmanian oak and sometimes called Alpine ash. **1986** *Age* (Melbourne) 28 Oct. 30/3 Use treated pine or a durable hardwood such as jarrah for any outdoor project, and for Australian oak buy Tasmanian oak (if you're a free spender) or kiln-dried hardwood—usually mountain ash—(if you're not). **1833** J. BACKHOUSE *Narr. Visit Austral. Colonies* (1843) 30 Apr. 144 Great Swan Port. Upon one part of the beach . . and in several places, we saw the foot-prints of the **Tasmanian Tiger. 1855** J. BONWICK *Geogr. Aust. & N.Z.* (ed. 3) 200 The Dasyurus family is carnivorous. Of this, are the Thylacinus or Tasmanian Tiger, five feet long, with short legs and striped body. **1867** *S. Austral. Register* (Adelaide) 30 Apr. 2/5 The Doctor has also the promise of the Tasmanian tiger (*Thylacinus cynocephalus*). **1885** *Illustr. Austral. News* (Melbourne) 19 Dec. 218/3 The group of the marsupial wolf, or Tasmanian tiger . . is now entirely confined to Tasmania. . . In the older geological time of the pleistocene period it seems to have existed on the mainland. **1917** *Huon Times* (Franklin) 17 Aug. 2/5 The arms consist of two Tasmanian tigers guarding a shield with symbols representing the staple industries of the State. **1926** A.S. LE SOUEF et al. *Wild Animals Australasia* 330 He heard a rustle in the scrub, and on looking round saw what he describes as a beast 'larger and darker than the Tasmanian tiger'. **1947** MRS A.H. GARNSEY *Romance Huon River* 32 The Tasmanian Tiger . . is now protected, though thought to be extinct, as it was much hunted. **1963** V.B. CRANLEY *27,000 Miles through Aust.* 110 The *Thylacinus cynocephalus*. Back in 1808 the zoologist, G.P.R. Harris, Tasmania's first 'deputy surveyor' described him, and because of the tiger-like stripes covering his back, named him the Tasmanian Tiger. **1974** *Ecos* i. 26/2 The paintings of animals have produced surprises. One is said to undoubtedly represent the Tasmanian tiger, a species not known from live specimens or as fossils in northern Australia. **1981** *Bulletin* (Sydney) 3 Nov. 5/1, I . . agree . . that the Tasmanian Tiger . . still lives on. There are many sightings (mostly at night) for it is a nocturnal animal. **1906** D.G. STEAD *Fishes of Aust.* 118 The **Tasmanian Trumpeter** (*Latris hecateia*) . . has only been taken so far on the coasts of Tasmania, Victoria and South Australia. **1936** T.C. ROUGHLEY *Wonders Great Barrier Reef* 245 The Tasmanian trumpeter is a fish of extraordinarily fine flavour. **1984** *Canberra Chron.* 23 May 27/2 Some superb snapper and huge Tasmanian trumpeter. **1835** *Hobart Town Almanack* 110 *Telopea Tasmaniana.* **Tasmanian warratah. . .** The beautiful crimson flowering shrub, with dark green rhododendron like leaves, which grows in the upper region of Mount Wellington. It has not yet been successfully cultivated about Hobarttown. **1852** MRS C. MEREDITH *My Home in Tas.* I. 24 The Tasmanian Waratah is a shrub or bushy tree, with handsome dark-green foliage, and bright red flowers. **1942** C. BARRETT *Austral. Wild Flower Bk.* 24 The Tasmanian waratah usually is a shrub and, like its cousin of New South Wales, grows commonly on hillsides. **1980** G.R. COCHRANE et al. *Flowers & Plants Vic. & Tas.* (rev. ed.) 110 Tasmanian Waratah *Telopea truncata*. An erect, spreading, green-leafed shrub to small tree. **1855** W. HOWITT *Land, Labor & Gold* II. 392 The **Tasmanian wolf,** or hyena, as they call it here . . is a long, smooth-haired animal, of a grayish-brown, with black stripes across its back. **1914** H.M. VAUGHAN *Australasian Wander-Yr.* 128 The Tasmanian tiger, or wolf . . which is one of the most ancient animals left in the world, is a strange, ungainly creature. **1933** H.J. CARTER *Gulliver in Bush* 168, I had only this short view, but am convinced that the animal could only have been the Tasmanian wolf—rarely seen outside a zoo.

3. In the collocation **Tasmanian bluey,** a woollen outer garment (see BLUEY 3); the material of which such a garment is made.

1910 *Huon Times* (Franklin) 8 June 4/1 A bluish grey blanket overcoat, known as a Tasmanian bluey. **1934** T. WOOD *Cobbers* 86 A pair of them . . dressed in the manner of the craft—a slouch hat, trousers tucked into heavy boots, and a seamless coat of 'Tasmanian bluey', cut low round the neck and under the arms. **1962** E. LANE *Mad as Rabbits* 63 Mother used to buy Father's . . Tasmanian-bluey coats for winter that way. **1977** JOHNS & GREEN *Dog's Grave* 10 To protect the men from the intense cold of the mountain nights, drovers donned the famous Tasmanian Bluey made from pure wool and shower proof. **1982** *Canberra Times* 19 Nov. 3/3 The claim is for two pairs of overalls, a pair of safety boots and a coat known as a Tasmanian Bluey, to be worn for those doing outdoor work during inclement weather.

B. *n.*

1. A non-Aboriginal person native to or resident in Tasmania.

1833 W.H. BRETON *Excursions* 389 Tasmanians find great fault with those horses that are imported from Sydney. **1836** *Colonist* (Sydney) 22 Sept. 297/3 The existing race of Tasmanians . . first took up their abode at Port Phillip for the purpose of founding a British colony. **1841** *Colonial Mag.* (London) IV. 59 The blow under which Van Diemen's Land now staggers. This report struck with astonishment every absentee Tasmanian. **1851** H. MELVILLE *Present State Aust.* 62 The Tasmanians are therefore deeply interested in the success of their gigantic infant. **1852** J. WEST *Hist. of Tas.* I. 64 To both these tribunals the Tasmanians were amenable. **1860** *Bell's Life in Sydney* 26 May 3/2 My fellow passengers in the steamer, Tasmanians, South Australians, and Victorians. **1900** *Advocate* (Burnie) 8 Mar. 4/2 Taking up a safer position, the Australians covered the Tasmanians' retirement. **1920** *Huon Times* (Franklin) 21 July 2/5 The Tasmanian is not, as a rule, a demonstrative person. **1937** E.T. EMMETT *Short Hist. Tas.* 134 There were several battalions which were composed partly of Tasmanians. **1949** C. TURNBULL *Charm of Hobart* 21 He was a Tasmanian as a matter of course. **1969** *Mercury* (Hobart) 15 May 3/5 Mr Reece said he was making the attack because he was a Tasmanian 'and I fight for Tasmania'. **1985** *Ibid.* 16 May 9/3 For almost three years Mr Gray gave Tasmanians the brazen image the commentators dubbed 'the whispering bulldozer'.

2. A member of one of the Aboriginal peoples of Tasmania; a descendant thereof.

1844 C. LYON *Narr. & Recoll. Van Dieman's Land* 30 The ensanguined administration of Sir George Arthur, has destroyed a great part of the native foresters, and reduced the number from seventeen-hundred to about sixty, who are cooped up on a small island in Bass Straits, where they are continually dwindling away. . . The Tasmanians will rest amid the thousand wrecks of innocence, that England delights to crush when it is in her power. **1878** R.B. SMYTH *Aborigines of Vic.* I. p. lxxii, It is difficult to believe that the Tasmanians were scions of the continental tribes. **1944** C. FENNER *Mostly Austral.* 13 Did the Tasmanians use Australia as a stepping-stone to reach their island? **1968** R. TRAVERS *Tasmanians* 13 The Tasmanians were never very numerous. **1976** V.R. ELLIS *Trucanini* 1 The Tasmanians were a unique people whose origins have not yet been defined. **1981** *Canberra Times* 4 Nov. 13/1 The surviving Tasmanians struggle not only with the problems of all Aborigines in south-east Australia but, more, they have had to prove they existed at all.

tasmanite. A sulphur-rich hydrocarbon compound occurring in laminated shales in the Mersey River, n. Tas. Also *attrib.*

1864 A.H. CHURCH *Phil. Mag.* XXVIII. 465 (OED) Tasmanite, a new Mineral of Organic Origin. *Ibid.* 467 When Tasmanite is heated in the air, it burns readily with a very smoky flame and offensive odour. **1881** *T.H.A.J.* no. 55 7 Under application for lease for mining Tasmanite. **1900** *Proc. Linnean Soc. N.S.W.* XXV. 649 'Tasmanite' and Australian 'White Coal'. **1929** G. MEUDELL *Pleasant Career Spendthrift* 110 For years I have been intrigued by the rich possibilities of treating successfully the tasmanite or kerosene shale deposits of Northern Tasmania. **1965** *Austral. Encycl.* II. 83 Australia contains extensive deposits of oil-shale, which term is taken to include . . shales that contain free oil (for instance tasmanite-shale) . . in the Permian coal measures of Tasmania.

Tasmanoid, *a.* [f. TASMANIAN *n.* 2.]

1. Of, allied to, or resembling the ethnological type of the Aborigines of Tasmania. Cf. AUSTRALOID. Also as *n.*

1925 H. BASEDOW *Austral. Aboriginal* Pl. 3, Supraorbital, deep notch at root of nose, prognathism (Tasmanoid features), and female beard, Denial Bay tribeswoman. **1939** *Trans. R. Soc. S.A.* LXIII. 302 The prehistoric Australian race was not a pure one, but the result of the fusion of an Australoid with a Tasmanoid stock. **1952** R.M. & C.H. BERNDT *First Australs.* 25 Except for the Tasmanoids . . they represent some conformity of physical type, but much diversity in headshape and stature. **1969** A.A. ABBIE *Original Australs.* 13 There is also disagreement over whether . . they were the first inhabitants of Australia or dispossessed a yet earlier 'Tasmanoid' people.

2. *transf.* See quot.

1982 *Bulletin* (Sydney) 16 Nov. 42/1 Oh, but it's called Tasmanoia: it's an island state of mind. There are Tasmanoids everywhere. Even here in Melbourne the Tasmanians stick together.

Tassie , *n.* and *a.* Also **Tassey, Tassy, Tazzie.** [f. *Tas(mania* or TAS(MANIAN *n.* 1 and *a.* + -Y.]

A. *n.*

1. Tasmania.

1892 *Bulletin* (Sydney) 17 Dec. 19/1, I took a turn in New South, and tried Tassy and New Zealand. **1895** *Ibid.* 13 July 23/2 Men are there from cold Monaro, 'cockatoos' from further down, Men from Maoriland and Tassy, men from every smoky town. **1904** *Truth* (Sydney) 19 June 1/6 Tassy has decided to reduce the salary of its Governor. **1914** H.M. VAUGHAN *Australasian Wander-Yr.* 118 Fern Tree Bower . . is one of the Meccas of the Australian tourist in the island of 'Tassie', as it is sometimes familiarly called. **1923** M.B. PETERSEN *Jewelled Nights* 11 This is . . the 'ighest made road in 'Tassy'. **1942** *Welcome to Aust.* 7 *Tazzie*, Tasmania. **1953** L. & C. REES *Spinifex Walkabout* 15 Some of those cases will be sent as far as Melbourne and Tassie to cash in on the big money! **1955** N. PULLIAM *I traveled Lonely Land* 222 Every state has 'em, of course—except Tazzie, that is. **1967** *Kings Cross Whisper* (Sydney) xxxi. 3/4 Tassie aids Mainland. The Tasmanian Government has opened an appeal to relieve suffering in mainland cities. **1981** Q. WILD *Honey Wind* 73 Tassie's pretty, very English.

2. A non-Aboriginal person native to or resident in Tasmania.

1899 *North-Western Advocate* (Devonport) 27 Feb. 3/3 This time the Tassy happened not to win. **1905** A.B. PATERSON *Old Bush Songs* 51 Once more the Maorilander and the Tassey will be seen Cooking johnny cakes and jimmies on the plains of Riverine. **1918** *Aussie: Austral. Soldiers' Mag.* 18 Jan. 3/1 A Tassie indignantly urges us to deny the Furphy that Tasmania is seeking a separate peace. **1976** S. WELLER *Bastards I have Met* 54 You know I can always pick a Tassy. **1981** A.B. FACEY *Fortunate Life* 271 Our Engineers were sent to report on the ways and means of taking the ridge from the Turks. The Tassies had raided it earlier.

B. *adj.* Tasmanian.

1916 *Bulletin* (Sydney) 8 June 24/3 Tassy bushmen . . never spoke of 'carfing' a tree when they meant chopping or sawing it down. **1925** *Ibid.* 1 Jan. 22/3 This is the greatest number of whales ever washed up on the Tassie coast. **1940** E.A. MCCOMBE *Whales & Whalers* 30 We shall be referred to as Tassie boys, because the big majority had never been beyond the bush clad coast of the island of apples. **1956** *Bulletin* (Sydney) 26 Sept. 13/2 The Tassie devil has distant marsupial relatives; the Tassie tiger is unique. **1980** N. WATKINS *Kangaroo Connection* 21 Bet, Stinger Davis will wish he'd been up here, instead of hunting for those Tassy Devils down in Tasmania! **1984** *Bulletin* (Sydney) 25 Sept. 48/1 Tassie blueys—a heavy wool, fireproof, waterproof and bush-proof jacket with a leather collar.

Taswegian, *a.* and *n.* [f. TAS(MANIAN *n.* 1 and *a.* + -*wegian* as in *Glaswegian*, etc.]

A. *adj.* Tasmanian.

1961 *Bulletin* (Sydney) 24 May 8/1 The bracing Taswegian climate does not encourage Hobart citizenry to move far from their TV-sets. **1979** P. ADAMS *More Unspeakable Adams* 101 We do not propose to make the same mistake as our Taswegian forebears did with the Abos.

B. *n.* A non-Aboriginal person native to or resident in Tasmania.

1972 W. WATKINS *Don't wait for Me* 3 A dumb Tasmanian, called a Taswegian. **1973** H. LEWIS *Crow on Barbed Wire Fence* Pref., Regardless of whether you're . . a Taswegian or a Whatever-they-call-people-who-live-south-of-the-Murray, you're going to enjoy this book. **1981** A.J. BURKE *Pommies & Patriots* 56 The problem was never properly solved by the Victorian Yarra Yabbies, the New South Wales Corn Stalks, the West Australian Sand Gropers, the South Australian Crow Eaters, the Canberra ACTS, the Taswegians or the Queensland Cane cutters.

tats, *pl.* Also **tatts.** [Fig. use of *tats* dice; chiefly Austral.: see OED(S *tat, sb.*[1]] Teeth; usu. false teeth.

[N.Z. **1906** *N.Z. Truth* (Wellington) 28 July 1 When swift as a flash, she swished a stinging left hook on to his chin and—presto—his whole set of upper front 'tats' fell into his long beer!] **1919** W.H. DOWNING *Digger Dialects* 49 *Tats*, teeth. **1938** F. CLUNE *Free & Easy Land* 253 Took out his false 'tatts' and placed them alongside his bunk. **1939** *Bulletin* (Sydney) 26 Apr. 21/2 Where will you find a man willing to crawl up behind a horse and fasten his tats in its fetlock? **1943** S.W. KEOUGH *Around Army* 20 There is the classic case of the Western Front bab. who in 18 months had never boiled it once when making the tea. As he used to say to his offsider, 'Let the blankards strain the leaves through their tatts!' **1949** R. PARK *Poor Man's Orange* 254 He heard her calling after him, 'Hey, you forgot yer tats! Don't you want yer teeth?' **1970** R. BEILBY *No Medals for Aphrodite* 240 Snow's false teeth were the joke of the section. His 'tats', he called them. They were army issue and ill-fitting.

Tatts. Also **Tatt, tatt.** Abbrev. of 'Tattersall's Sweep', the name of a lottery established in 1881 by George Adams (1839–1904), licensee of Tattersall's Hotel, Sydney. Also **Tatt's sweep.**

1896 *Bulletin* (Sydney) 22 Feb. 27/2 Mr Murphy . . had drawn a minor prize in a Tatt. sweep, and he had been 'on a fair bend' for a week. **1897** *Tocsin* (Melbourne) 9 Dec. 9/2 The lucky drawers of starters in 'Tatt's' sweep were all so anxious to have a fair go with their 'neddies' that they laid the individuals named large sums to nothing in the event of a win. **1901** *Bulletin* (Sydney) 5 Oct. 16/4 Three black gins . . drew first prize in Tatt.'s special on Metrop. Stakes. **1916** O. HOGUE *Trooper Bluegum at Dardanelles* 252 When . . four soldiers crawled uninjured from the debris, their mates called out, 'Your luck's in. Get a ticket in Tatt.'s.' **1924** L. O'NEIL *Dinkum Aussie* 37, I worked an' belonged to me union, an' drew down a sizeable screw; Took tickets in Tatt's an' the Casket; was fairly contented with life. **1938** *Point* (Melbourne) I. ii. 24 He again attacked with the suggestion that I take so-and-so's place in the 'Try Again' syndicate in Tatts. **1955** N. PULLIAM *I traveled Lonely Land* 259 'Tatts' had always been in Tasmania and they could scarcely bear to let it go. **1965** *Coast to Coast 1963–64* 100 He gives her five bob each pay-day to buy a Tatts ticket in their joint names. **1979** H. POST *Maintain your Rage* 56 The man who has nothing and wins half a million in tatts may burst his best part through happiness.

taurai, tauri, varr. TOWRI.

tawarang /'tæwəræŋ/. *Hist.* Also **tourang, towerang.** [a. Dharuk *dawaraŋ*.] An Aboriginal shield: see quot. 1798.

1790 D. SOUTHWELL Corresp. & Papers, *D'tar-warra*, implement used to fend or ward off blows, a weapon of defence. **1798** D. COLLINS *Acct. Eng. Colony N.S.W.* I. 585 Ta-war-rang . . is about three feet long, is narrow, but has three sides, in one of which is the handle, hollowed by fire. The other sides are rudely carved with curved and waved lines, and it is made use of in dancing, being struck upon for this purpose with a club. **1847** G.F. ANGAS *Savage Life & Scenes* II. 248 They have also a species of triangular shield called a *tawarang*. **1851** J. HENDERSON *Excursions & Adventures N.S.W.* II. 150 The *tourang* is another sort of shield, used for causing missiles to glance aside. It is a solid piece of wood from two to three feet long, pointed at the ends, four-sided, with a hole cut through one edge, at the centre, to hold it by, while the opposite edge, or apex, is presented to the threatening spear. It is not used in those parts of the country where the *heelaman* is known. It is commonly carved all over. **1881** E. DAVIES *Story Earnest Life* 129 The savages were still yelling and beating on their towerangs with waddies. **1894** *Proc. Linnean Soc. N.S.W.* IX. 513 It is the *Tawarang* from high up the Murray River, and other parts of N.S. Wales. Dr Knight in his account of the savage weapons displayed at the Philadelphia Exhibition in 1876 called this shield *Towerang*.

tawny frogmouth. The frogmouth *Podargus strigoides* of all States, a mottled grey to brown nocturnal bird having a low, soft call; MOPOKE *n.* 1 b. See also PODARGUS. Formerly also **tawny-shouldered podargus.**

1840 J. GOULD *Birds of Aust.* (1848) II. Pl. 3, *Podargus humeralis* . . Tawny-shouldered Podargus. **1849** C. STURT *Narr. Exped. Central Aust.* II. 18 App. Tawny-shouldered Podargus. . . The appearance of this uncouth bird is very absurd, with his enormous mouth that literally reaches from ear to ear, and his eyes half shut. **1903** *Emu* III. 95 *Podargus strigoides* (?) (Tawny Frogmouth). . . It is strange that the natives here call the bird 'Morepork', which appears to be the general name all over Australia. **1923** *Bulletin* (Sydney) 2 Aug. 22/3 That useful and interesting night bird the tawny frogmouth . . depends altogether on his protective coloring in times of danger. **1968** D. FLEAY *Nightwatchmen* 143 The Tawny Frogmouth . . has a tremendously wide habitat and is quite numerous and well known over most parts of Australia and Tasmania. **1985** C. PALLIN *Bat came to Stay* 2 A pair of tawny frogmouths waited for someone to push food into their gaping beaks.

taylor, var. TAILOR.

tea.

1. [Spec. use of *tea* a meal at which tea is served: see OED(S *sb.* 4.] A substantial meal, usu. eaten in the early evening.

1863 *Jrnls. & Rep. Two Voyages Glenelg River* 24 July (1864) 21 For tea there was the usual dish of salt beef, and in addition a side dish of Fricassee à l'alligator, which under the name of stewed cobbler obtained but a qualified approval. **1871** *Emigrant's Wife* I. 118 They were astonished, as indeed most English people would be at the substantiality of an Australian tea. **1887** *Illustr. Austral. News* (Melbourne) 21 Dec. 218/1 On the way the hunter's dogs, which accompanied the party, killed several wallabies, so all had fresh meat for tea. **1924** H.E. RIEMANN *Nor'-West o' West* 113 That night after tea ('tea' is the designation of the evening meal among the shearers) he showed it to the camp. **1934** T. WOOD *Cobbers* 96 Tea . . one menu card could be used throughout the State. It would say soup, fried steak with two veg., corned beef or cold mutton, sweets. . . Speculation is a waste of time until the second course is cleared. Then you are free to wonder which of the two traditional sweets will appear . . port-wine jelly . . apple-pie. **1950** 'N. SHUTE' *Town like Alice* 177 Stupefied by the heavy meal of roast beef and plum pudding that the Queenslanders call 'tea' she sat in a deck-chair. **1965** K. MCKENNEY *Hide-Away Man* 27 'Put me tea in the oven, love,' he said. **1984** B. DIXON *Searching for Aboriginal Lang.* 69 In Australia 'tea' is the main meal of the day—a big slap-up feast with lots of meat, two or three vegetables, slices of bread and butter, and then a helping of pudding.

2. a. In the phr. **Tea and Sugar,** the name of a train conveying supplies to settlements along the Trans-Australian Railway. Also **Tea and Sugar train.**

1937 E. HILL *Great Austral. Loneliness* 225 The 'Trans' and its people are a little world sufficient for themselves, a remarkable colony of government servants. . . With . . week-end dances at Cook, and a weekly shopping orgy on the 'Tea and Sugar' train that brings their water and supplies. **1943** *Coast to Coast 1942* 188 Only staff men on duty bothered about the expresses, though there was always a bit of a stir when the Tea-and-Sugar groaned in, bringing supplies. **1956** B. BEATTY *Beyond Aust.'s Cities* 93 The coming of the 'Tea and Sugar' is regarded as the social event of the week. The little train is never in a hurry, and housewives can casually stroll over to make their purchases, collect parcels, or give their orders for next week's call. **1974** P. ADAM SMITH *Desert Railway* 84 The Tea and Sugar came along the line every week, stopping at every camp, no matter how small. **1977** B. FULLER *Nullarbor Lifelines* 39 It is the custom for the 'Tea and Sugar' to draw off onto a side line for the night, a procedure known as 'stabbing'.

b. In the collocation **tea and sugar burglar (bandit, bushranger),** a swagman; a petty thief. Also as **tea and sugar burgling.**

1900 H. LAWSON *On Track* 130 Could I explain that I 'jabbed trotters' and was a 'tea-and-sugar burglar' between sheds. They'd think I'd been a tramp and a beggar all the time. **1930** *Aussie* (Sydney) July 27/1 Other ways of referring to the pastime are 'humping your drum' . . and 'tea and sugar burgling'. **1945** T. RONAN *Strangers on Ophir* 52 Every tea-and-sugar bushranger who rats a boundary rider's hut thinks he's another Ned Kelly. **1967** *Kings Cross Whisper* (Sydney) xxxxi. 4/2 *Tea and sugar bandit*, a petty thief. Usually the type of person who is too lazy to work and too frightened to steal large quantities of other peoples' goods.

3. Special Comb. **tea billy,** a billy in which tea is brewed (see BILLY *n.*[1] 1); **bucket** *obs., tea billy*; **-dinner** *obs.*, TEA 1.

1889 E. GILES *Aust. twice Traversed* II. 67 While some were unyoking the horses, some were boiling the **tea-billies.** **1902** *Bulletin* (Sydney) 11 Jan. 32/1 Every traveller has . . one or two billies. Some have three—of varying sizes to fit one in the other. The tea-billy and meat-billy are the most common; the third is an auxiliary. **1931** *Ibid.* 16 Dec. 24/3 Hard up he was, with a fruit-tin for a tea-billy. **1965** A.W. UPFIELD *Lure of Bush* 112 He noted also the absence of the usual canvas water-bag, and the small tea-billy. **1903** *Bulletin* (Sydney) 23 May 17/1 O where's the old cooks smilin', the big **tea buckets** bilin'. **1926** K. DAHL *In Savage Aust.* 203 To hang the tea-bucket over the fire. **1855** W. HOWITT *Land, Labor & Gold* I. 126 Our **tea-dinner,** you will admit, is not to be sneezed at. **1867** G. WALCH *Fireflash* 27, I was warmly welcomed and enjoyed a substantial tea-dinner. **1871** 'IOTA' *Kooroona* 49 'I will order what is called here, a tea-dinner, immediately,' she continued.

tea bush. *Obs.* Any of several shrubs: see quot. 1900.

1839 W.H. LEIGH *Reconnoitering Voyages* 127 Wild indigo, or a solitary tea bush. **1886** N. ROBINSON *Stagg of Tarcowie* (1977) 30 June 73, I grubbed teabushes today, or what I call teabushes. They have a dark green leaf, very small, and white flowers in their season and plenty of prickles which any person who grubs them feels to his sorrow. **1900** *Proc. Linnean Soc. N.S.W.* XXV. 598 *Eremophila latifolia* . . (Tea Bush, because a beverage fit to drink is said to have been made from the leaves).

teak. [Tranf. use of *teak* the tree *Tectona grandis* of s.e. Asia, and its wood.] Any of several trees yielding a durable timber resembling teak, esp. CROW'S ASH.

1849 R.J. MANN *Emigrant's Guide Aust.* 75 Good teak and oak for repairing ships are found at the same place [*sc.* Port Essington]. **1866** LINDLEY & MOORE *Treasury of Bot.* 1128 *Teak, or Teakwood* . . *New South Wales*. Eudiandra [*sic*] glauca. **1887** H. GULLETT *Tropical N.S.W.* 9 Let us take a single tree—say, for instance this venerable teak. . . See the enormous bird's-nest ferns and immense staghorns growing in its forks. **1909** R. KALESKI *Austral. Settler's Compl. Guide* 30 The richness of the soil . . is shown by the forests, yielding valuable timbers, such as teak. **1926** *Qld. Agric. Jrnl.* XXV. 433 There is a Crow's Ash in Queensland which is called Teak in New South Wales, yet it is unlike Teak, whilst the wood that is of the Teak type in structure, uses and botanical order has been dubbed Beech after the European Beech, to which incidentally it bears no resemblance whatever. **1965** *Austral. Encycl.* VIII. 445 The Indian teak, *Tectona grandis* (family Verbenaceae), grows in a few gardens in North Queensland, but in Australia the name teak is applied to *Flindersia australis*.

tear. [Spec. use of U.S. *tear* a spree.] In the phr. **on the tear,** engaged in a drinking bout.

1898 *Bulletin* (Sydney) 23 Apr. 14/1 Our doctor and a huge bushman had been 'on the tear' for some days. **1908** *Truth* (Sydney) 26 Apr. 1/6 William Bates, who got on the tear (and the Ocean Beach, Manly) on Easter Monday, was fined 5s. **1920** 'J. NORTH' *Harry Dale's Grand National* 127 You look as if you'd been on the tear, young fellow, me lad. **1945** *Mud & Blood* 8 The soldier who went on the tear in Perth. **1955** R. LAWLER *Summer of Seventeenth Doll* (1965) 73 They wanted to know if we'd go out with 'em on the tear sometime. **1979** *Sporting Globe* (Melbourne) 19 Sept. 2 Chairman of selectors Wes Lofts was detailed to track down Young—but to no avail as the young Carlton player was dining with his parents, who were over from Tasmania. I think Wes thought Michael might have been out on the tear.

tea scrub. *Obs.* TEA TREE 1.

1842 *Geelong Advertiser* 28 Feb. 4/1 The country in the vicinity of the township is described as a useless barren track, covered with dense tea scrubs, intersected here and there with salt water marshes, and a few fresh swamps. **1855** W. HOWITT *Land, Labor & Gold* II. 387 We were neither come to the tea-scrub swamp nor the peppermint scrub. **1878** R.B. SMYTH *Aborigines of Vic.* II. 39 Tea scrub on hummocks.

tea-tree. Also **ti-tree.** [Transf. use of *tea-tree* the shrub yielding tea: see quot. 1843.]

1. Any of many often aromatic trees and shrubs of the fam. Myrtaceae, incl. those of the genus *Melaleuca* (see MELALEUCA) and esp. those of the chiefly Austral. genus *Leptospermum*; the wood of the tree; TEA SCRUB. Also *attrib.*

[**1773** J. COOK *Voyage towards South Pole* May (1777) 99 We at first made it of a decoction of the spruce leaves; but finding that this alone made the beer too astringent, we afterwards mixed with it an equal quantity of the tea plant (a name it obtained in my former voyage from our using it as tea then, as we also did now).] **1790** J. WHITE *Jrnl. Voyage N.S.W.* 229 Tea tree of New South Wales. Melaleuca? [*sic*] trinervia. This is a small shrub, very much branched. **1793** J. HUNTER *Hist. Jrnl. Trans. Port Jackson* 514 A little boy . . carried the fire, which was a piece of the bark of the tea-tree. **1805** J.H. TUCKEY *Acct. Voyage to establish Colony Port Phillip* 227 The tea-tree has its name from the leaf. . . It is small and very curly. **1833** *Perth Gaz.* 21 Sept. 151 At the conclusion of 15 miles we entered a dense forest of gum and tea-trees. **1843** J. BACKHOUSE *Narr. Visit Austral. Colonies* xxxiii, The genera *Leptospermum* and *Melaleuca* are, in the Island [*sc.* Tasmania], indiscriminately called 'Tea-tree', without reference to species. The leaves of some of them have been used as a substitute for tea; but the flavour is too highly aromatic to please the European taste. **1847** *Moreton Bay Courier* 23 Jan. 4/1 The tea-tree, or *Melaleuca*, is beginning to be much valued for boats. **1875** P.E. WARBURTON *Journey across Western Interior* 106 The banks of the stream itself overhung by the graceful foliage of the cajeput, or tea-tree (*Melaleuca leucodendron*). **1880** A. FORREST *N.-W. Exploration* 5 Followed a line of ti-trees which skirted a spinifex rise. **1888** *Proc. Linnean Soc. N.S.W.* III. 522 *Leptospermum scoparium* . . 'Tea tree'. It is said that this is the shrub the leaves of which were utilised by the crews of Captain Cook's ships for the purpose of making 'tea'. **1896** *Worker* (Sydney) 16 May 6/3 On the very spot where stood the old ti-tree humpy stands a neat brick cottage. **1898** *Bulletin* (Sydney) 8 Jan. 29/2 It is a stupid error to call the Australian tea-tree a 'ti-tree'. More than this it is a new-chumism, a relic of Gov. Phillip, a Botany Bayism. **1911** *Ibid.* 9 Mar. 15/1 The Melaleuca . . is the ti-tree, or, more properly, tie-tree. The strips of bark were used by the firsters at Ports Jackson, Phillip and Arthur. **1926** *Illustr. Tasmanian Mail* (Hobart) 31 Mar. 6/2 Remains of a forest, including the stumps of grass trees and the roots and leaves of tea-trees. **1938** C.T. WHITE *Princ. Bot. Qld. Farmers* 190 The name Tea-tree is due to the fact that Dr Anderson, who was the surgeon and naturalist on Cook's third voyage, mistook a species of *Leptospermum* for a North American plant which was then being used as a substitute for ordinary tea. **1950** *Bulletin* (Sydney) 2 Aug. 12/2 I've never encountered a piece of tea-tree so tough that nails cannot be driven into it. **1964** P. WHITE *Burnt Ones* 18 She was listening to the leaning tea-tree continue to saw at the gutter. **1979** DOUGLAS & HEATHCOTE *Far Cry* 112 The fence was made of tea-tree. **1984** *Southern Cross* (Melbourne) 5 Dec. 3/7 The Elwood foreshore area where work is under way on a ti tree area.

2. Comb. **tea-tree bark, brush, bush, creek, flat, scrub, swamp.**

1825 B. FIELD *Geogr. Mem. N.S.W.* 57 Their huts are built of long slender wattles . . and the whole is covered with **tea-tree** (melaleuca armilliaris) **bark,** in such a manner as to be quite impervious to the rain. **1842** *Colonial Observer* (Sydney) 27 July 355/1 The natives . . made a hut of tea-tree bark for us. **1844** J. TUCKER *Ralph Rashleigh* (1952) 80 Some got a few sheep skins, which . . they sewed . . rolling themselves up in them at night; while those who hadn't the luck . . had lately found out a way to prepare tea-tree bark for the same purpose. **1863** J. BONWICK *Wild White Man* 65 Teatree bark bandages were applied to the arm. **1870** E.B. KENNEDY *Four Yrs. in Qld.* 80 We . . found . . a novel carefully wrapped up in tea-tree bark. **1892** J. FRASER *Aborigines N.S.W.* 81 The bottom of the grave is then lined with 'ti'-tree bark, the body is laid thereon. **1810** *HRA* (1921) 3rd Ser. I. 774 The Island is . . covered with Thick **Tea Tree Brush.** **1829** *Hobart Town Almanack* 36 On the right is a branch road . . passing through the Tea tree brush. **1848** *Bell's Life in Sydney* 19 Aug. 2/4 An expedition of discovery among green wattle scrubs, tea-tree brushes . . and apple-tree flats. **1820** C. JEFFREYS *Van Dieman's Land* 133 For tea, they drink a decoction of the sassafras and other shrubs, particularly one which they call the **tea-tree bush.** **1831** *Acct. Colony Van Diemen's Land* 93 In crossing the little stream we chanced to strike against his large iron pot hid in a tea tree bush. **1859** W. BURROWS *Adventures Mounted Trooper* 69 Some quiet pool, overhung by tea-tree bushes. **1898** D.W. CARNEGIE *Spinifex & Sand* 261, I took the opportunity of writing . . under our solitary ti-tree bush. **1920** B. CRONIN *Timber Wolves* 50 She'd swept the floor with a tea-tree bush. **1952** A.W. UPFIELD *New Shoe* 5 Low clumps of tea-tree bush scattered upon the grassland to the verge of the cliffs. **1845** L. LEICHHARDT *Jrnl. Overland Exped. Aust.* 18 Sept. (1847) 408 Two **tea-tree creeks** . . contained fresh water in the upper part of their short courses. **1854** W. SHAW *Land of Promise* 149 The hounds . . were now careering the scent breast-high down to a tea-tree creek. **1889** W.H. TIETKENS *Jrnl. Central Austral. Exploring Exped.* 15 Mar. 3, I then struck a small ti-tree creek. **1845** C. HODGKINSON *Aust., Port Macquarie to Moreton Bay* 52 We started across a grassy **tea-tree flat.** **1880** J.B. STEVENSON *Seven Yrs. Austral. Bush* 96 Great numbers of wild bulls on the run . . were generally to be found in the tea-tree flats near the coast. **1889** 'SALTBUSH' *Sydney to Croyden* 31 Our route lies through miserable-looking country, the principle features consisting of level teatree flats, with patches of quinine and coolabah, all of stunted growth. **1835** *Jrnl. Australasia* (1856) I. 55 A dense **tea-tree scrub,** which we knew to be the surest indication of good water in its neighbourhood. **1846** G.H. HAYDON *Five Yrs. Experience Aust. Felix* 33 A great quantity of the tea tree (*leptospermum*) scrubs . . formerly lined both banks of the Yarra. **1861** 'OLD BUSHMAN' *Bush Wanderings* 32 A cone-shaped hut of tea-tree scrub, in which the hams should smoke for three or four days. **1872** 'RESIDENT' *Glimpses Life Vic.* 299 A small gum-forest, Ti-tree scrub. **1916** J.M. CREED *Recoll. Aust.* 19 Some small tree frogs . . sitting in a fork of ti-tree scrub. **1935** H. MCCRAE *My Father* 42 Gordon, practically destitute, went into the tea-tree scrub at Hampton, where he destroyed himself. **1956** E. MITCHELL *Black Cockatoos* 86 Along the banks the teatree scrub made dark tunnels for the water. **1827** *HRA* (1922) 3rd Ser. V. 853 Through low meadows with **Tea-tree swamps.** **1847** E.W. LANDOR *Bushman* 362 We reached Yeinart, a tea-tree swamp. **1861** J.D. LANG *Qld., Aust.* 122 Good agricultural country, intersected by patches of wallom flats and tea-tree swamps. **1895** W.H. WILLSHIRE *Thrilling Tale Real Life* 35 At noon we sighted the Lake, and got plenty of fresh water in little ti-tree swamps. **1934** WARBURTON & ROBERTSON *Buffaloes* 102 The truck . . led us . . through forest country with occasional tea-tree swamps. **1981** A. WILKINSON *Up Country* 129 The treacherous, bone-filled ti-tree swamp, where we, too, lost a cow.

3. Special Comb. **tea-tree oil,** a volatile essential oil distilled from species of the genus *Melaleuca* (fam. Myrtaceae), esp. from *M. alternifolia* of Qld. and N.S.W.; also *attrib.*

1933 *Bulletin* (Sydney) 12 July 19/2 The distillation of essential oil from *Melaleuca alternifolia* (tea-tree) has become an established N.S.W. industry. . . Some 40 tea-tree oil preparations are on the market. **1954** *Econ. Bot.* (N.Y.) VIII. 324/1 Tea-Tree Oil. . . Collection of leaf material differs from that in operation for eucalyptus leaves. **1965** *Austral. Encycl.* VIII. 445 The valuable tea-tree oils, much used as germicides and solvents and in perfumery, are distilled from arboreal *Melaleuca* species of the east coast of Australia, principally *M. alternifolia*, but also *M. linariifolia.* **1985** P. CAREY *Illywhacker* 222 We were on our way up to Darkville where one of Barret's clerks now had a still for making tea-tree oil.

technicolour, *a.* Also **technicolor.** In the collocation **technicolour yawn (chunder, laugh, yodel),** the act of vomiting.

1964 B. HUMPHRIES *Nice Night's Entertainment* 77 But when I'd swallowed the last prawn I had a Technicolor yawn And I chundered in the old Pacific sea. **1967** *Kings Cross Whisper* (Sydney) xxxii. 1/2 It will be available in the form of pills which will . . produce a technicolor chunder. **1967** F. HARDY *Billy Borker yarns Again* 63 Calling for Herb, see, that's one of the many euphemisms for vomit, others include . . throw, the whip o' will, the technicolour laugh and, in Queensland, the chuckle. *Ibid.* 66 Each one sang his own theme song between the technicolour yodels. **1972** *Bulletin* (Sydney) 14 Oct. 44/1 He made a quick dash across the acting area, made the head of the broad wooden staircase which leads up to the theatre and let fly with a series of resounding technicolor yawns. **1974** *Ibid.* 9 Mar. 10/1 The sick-making sequences will probably have less impact in this country because we've all been well initiated with Bazza McKenzie and his technicolor yawns.

teddy bear. Rhyming slang for LAIR *n.* a.

1953 S.J. BAKER *Aust. Speaks* 135 *Teddy bear*, a flashily dressed, exhibitionistic person; by rhyme on *lair*. **1965** W. GROUT *My Country's Keeper* 55 Umpire Col Edgar was so furious at this amateurish attempt at time wasting that he snapped to the Pakistani bowler: 'Get up you Teddy Bear' (an Australian expression not meant to be complimentary). **1974** STACKPOLE & TRENGOVE *Not just for Openers* 128 When Parfitt made the catch Greig jumped in the air, and, as he landed, thumped his fist into the pitch. . . I said to Greig as I walked past, 'You're nothing but a bloody Teddy Bear.' He returned the pleasantries.

telegram. *Obs.* BUSH TELEGRAPH *n.* 1.

1899 G.E. BOXALL *Story Austral. Bushrangers* 230 During the afternoon a number of other persons were brought into 'the camp'. All except one man were allowed to move about freely. This one man was tied, and was spoken to very roughly and uncivilly. The man was supposed to be 'a telegram', and this show of harshness 'a stall'. **1911** A.L. HAYDON *Trooper Police Aust.* 148 He was well served, also, by 'bush telegraphs'. . . There was reason to believe that the organisation of this service was so thorough that every township had its 'telegram'. Certain it is that throughout a wide extent of country the bushrangers were kept fully posted as to the movements of the police by their many friends.

telegraph, *n.*

1. Abbrev. of BUSH TELEGRAPH *n.* 1.

1864 *Goulburn Herald* 17 Aug. 2/3 These young scoundrels have got their 'telegraphs' in town, and there is not a stir the police can make but it is known. *Ibid.* 12 Oct. 4/5 It would make me look a gamer man to the police and other people as has got a down on me for being a telegraph to you chaps. **1888** 'R. BOLDREWOOD' *Robbery under Arms* (1937) 211 We sent Warrigal out to meet one of our telegraphs at a place about twenty miles off. **1902** J.S. HASSALL *In Old Aust.* 107 The network of 'telegraphs' . . in a great measure used to prevent their apprehension. **1907** C. MACALISTER *Old Pioneering Days* 290 This wood was brought by a man who was suspected as acting as 'telegraph' (or accessory) of Crookwell. **1948** F. CLUNE *Wild Colonial Boys* 329 The police were a quarter of a mile away, but they saw him and beckoned. Charters . . galloped away at full speed. . . 'A telegraph!' yelled Sanderson. 'Follow him, men!'

2. *Obs.* BUSH TELEGRAPH *n.* 2.

1856 *Tumut & Adelong Times* 1 Jan. 2/3 They approached to within one hundred yards of the camp unobserved, and then it was apparent that the 'telegraph' had done its work.

3. Abbrev. of BUSH TELEGRAPH *n.* 3.

1955 F. LANE *Patrol to Kimberleys* 23 News had a way of filtering in by smoke signal, message stick, or by native runner. This mysteriously accurate 'telegraph' spanned the vast and seemingly impenetrable stretches of the Australian outback.

4. *Obs.* A system of communication between prisoners: see quots. Also *attrib.*

1891 'OLD TIME' *Convict Hulk 'Success'* 20 The 'telegraph' was very extensively worked on board these hulks... The 'telegraph' was a system of speaking from one cell to another by means of tapping on the walls, a certain number of taps meaning a particular letter. **1903** *Bulletin* (Sydney) 10 Jan. 33/1 Gentleman Fred knocked . . so loud that 3rd Class Warder Downey . . caught the 'telegraph-operator' red-handed.

telegraph, *v. trans.* Abbrev. of BUSH TELEGRAPH *v.*

1937 M. TERRY *Sand & Sun* 80 We had been observed on the hilltop and the news was being telegraphed through the bush—a mulga wire.

telopea /tə'loʊpiə/. [The plant genus *Telopea* was named by British botanist R. Brown in 1809 (see quot. 1809), f. Gr. τηλο—comb. form of τῆλε afar + ὠπή sight, view, with reference to the conspicuous flower-head of the plant.] A shrub or tree of the genus *Telopea* (see WARATAH 1).

[**1809** *Trans. Linnean Soc. London* (1811) X. 197 *Telopea* . . Etym. τηλωπας qui e longinquo cernitur, quod de his fruticibus, floribus coccineis speciosis valet.] **1825** B. FIELD *Geogr. Mem. N.S.W.* 422 The shrubs and flowers are beautiful . . telopea the magnificent and thysanotus the lovely. **1832** J. BACKHOUSE *Narr. Visit Austral. Colonies* (1843) 114 The numerous brooks . . are margined with . . Blackwood and Telopea; the flowers of the last abound in honey. **1870** J. BONWICK *Last Tasmanians* 273 The Waratah, or Telopea, threw out its gorgeous crimson blossoms. **1929** *Aussie* (Sydney) Nov. 51/1 Ho, let me sing of the crimson telopea—Waratah, that is.

ten. In the phr. **ten, (ten,) two, and a quarter,** a week's ration of food as issued to a hand by an employer on a rural property: see quots. 1867 and 1957, and also EIGHT.

[**1867** 'CLERGYMAN' *Aust. as it Is* 179 The rations for one man are the well-known weekly allowance of 10 lbs. of flour, 10 lbs. of meat, 2 lbs. of sugar, and a quarter of a pound of tea.] **1903** J. FURPHY *Such is Life* 84 He has some hundreds of pounds lent out (without interest or security) though his pay is only fifteen shillings a week—with ten, ten, two, and a quarter. **1911** W.G. SPENCE *Hist. A.W.U.* 43 In many places the old ten, ten, two and a-quarter ration system was still in vogue. **1935** R.B. PLOWMAN *Boundary Rider* 186 *Ten, two, and a quarter.* Wherever there are sheep and boundary-riders these cryptic words have a world of meaning... On every sheep or cattle station where men are provided with rations, one man's needs are allotted on the basis of ten pounds of flour, two pounds of sugar, and a quarter of a pound of tea. **1957** J. HAWKE *Follow my Dust* 60 The food was reasonable, based on the old formula of Ten-Two-and-a-Quarter. Ten pounds of flour, two of sugar, a quarter of tea, with tomato sauce and unlimited mutton.

Tench. *Obs.* [Shortened form of *penitentiary* a prison.] A name for the convict barracks in Hobart: see quot. 1829. Also *attrib.*

1829 H. WIDOWSON *Present State Van Diemen's Land* 24 At the back . . is the prisoner's [*sic*] barracks, *alias* the Penitentiary, *alias* 'The Tench', by which latter name it is most frequently called by its inmates. **1841** B. WAIT *Lett. from Van Dieman's Land* (1843) 261 The prisoners were all landed *en masse*, and marched to the 'Tench' (prison barracks). **1848** R. MARSH *Seven Yrs. of my Life* 102 Myself and eight others were the last; we were escorted to Hobart town, and put in the prisoner's barracks, or tench. **1892** 'P. WARUNG' *Tales Convict System* 37 The sound of a bell came floating on the pellucid atmosphere to the ears of the dense, waiting crowd. 'That ain't the 'Tench clapper yet, surely?' exclaimed a bleary-eyed old ticket-of-leave man.

Hence **Tenchman** *n.*, an inmate, or former inmate, of the 'Tench'.

1869 *Colonial Soc.* (Sydney) 14 Jan. 6 The Model Country Loafer is usually an old lag. His experiences of Van Diemen's Land are large and instinctive in their nature. He tells some peculiar stories of adventures that happened to him when a 'Tenchman.

tender.

1. A representative of the owner of stray cattle sent to attend a *tender muster*.

1945 F. CORK *Tales from Cattle Country* 23 When the muster falls due, the managers of neighbouring stations are notified and each sends a tender—sometimes two—who are responsible for their 'strangers' who have wandered out of bounds. Visiting tenders are given complete charge of the cattle from the stations they represent.

2. Special Comb. **tender muster,** a round-up of all the cattle in a particular district at which owners lay claim to their strayed cattle.

1979 C. STONE *Running Brumbies* 35 For a tender muster, two or more cattle stations get all their men together on one of the stations to muster all the cattle in the area.

teno /'tɛnoʊ/. Abbrev. of 'tenosynovitis'. Freq. *attrib.*

1984 *Canberra Times* 19 Aug. 5/1 Teno has come in from the cold... The problems that repetition-strain injuries create are now being widely accepted by employers. *Ibid.* 7 Oct. 3/3 Some dodgy operators are jumping on the 'teno' bandwaggon. **1986** *Ibid.* 19 Feb. 14/5 (*heading*) $120,000 in 'teno' case.

tent. *Obs.* Used *attrib.* in Special Comb. **tent hut,** a temporary dwelling made of canvas, etc., stretched over a frame; **-keeper,** one who takes care of a tent, etc. (see HUT-KEEPER).

1804 *Sydney Gaz.* 26 Aug., He had created a **tent hut** with a chimney thereon. **1847** A. HARRIS *Settlers & Convicts* (1953) 99 When we went to bed in our little tent hut, we left the fire in front cheerfully blazing. **1849** —— *Guide Port Stephens* 34 Proceed next to put up your hut. You can have a tent hut at first, and a square hut afterwards, if you choose; but it will be better to put up a fair hut at once. **1845** C. HODGKINSON *Aust., Port Macquarie to Moreton Bay* 55, I can give credit to my **tent-keeper's** and bullock driver's account. **1852** D. MACKENZIE *Gold Digger* 52 All except the tent-keeper were out at their daily work. **1857** J. D'EWES *China, Aust. & Pacific Islands* 40 Superior officers individually, and others collectively, were allowed servants, or as they were termed, tent-keepers, with pay of 8s. per diem with tent and rations. **1859** P. JUST *Aust.* 50 We will give you a pound a-day and your grub to be our tent-keeper. **1888** G.O. PRESHAW *Banking under Difficulties* 21, I was to act as tent-keeper.

teraglin /tə'ræglən/. [Prob. f. a N.S.W. Aboriginal language.] The marine fish *Atractoscion aequidens* of N.S.W., s. Qld., and S. Africa; TRAG. Also **traglin.**

1880 *Proc. Linnean Soc. N.S.W.* V. 48 *Otolithus teraglin.* . . This fish is abundant on our coasts and attains a very considerable size—three or four feet in length. It is known to the fishermen as the 'Teraglin', and I have made that its specific name. **1896** F.G. AFLALO *Sketch Nat. Hist. Aust.* 205 The Pig-Fish, the Sergeant-Baker, Traglin. **1906** D.G. STEAD *Fishes of Aust.* 116 So far the Teraglin has only been obtained along the New South Wales coast, where at times it appears in very large numbers. **1945** J. DEVANNY *Bird of Paradise* 104 The traglin was dark green with gold around the gills. I have never tasted a more delicious fish than traglin and Byron Bay is the only place I have seen it. **1985** *Bulletin* (Sydney) 13 Aug. 56/3 When Doyle's opened, teraglin—known as 'trag'—was the staple fish served.

terrace. Abbrev. of 'terrace house'.

1894 *Bulletin* (Sydney) 3 Feb. 13/1 Formerly, the grasping 'trap', hurrying to get rich and own his little terrace, moved heaven and earth to get on to a 'Chow' beat. **1899** *Tocsin* (Melbourne) 30 Mar. 1/1 Madden has a terrace now at Flemington. The family is getting on. Its ambition is to own the whole earth. **1971** *Bulletin* (Sydney) 24 Apr. 83/1 One . . has sold many of the restored terraces in Sydney's Paddington-Woollahra area. **1972** *Southerly* vi. 281 The terrace he lived in was a ruin of decay and dilapidation and uncleanliness, his own room an oasis of elegant colours and culture, where music always played. **1981** B. OAKLEY *Marsupials & Politics* 39 If I find a guy who's stone deaf, partially sighted and without his sense of smell, I'll have a chance to sell your charming little weatherboard terrace.

terrible rite. *Obs.* The Aboriginal practice of subincision (see WHISTLECOCK a.).

1886 E.M. CURR *Austral. Race* I. 74, I refer to circumcision, which is performed with a jagged flint, and what I have already spoken of as the *terrible rite*. Of the latter, Eyre gives a sufficient description when he says *funditur usque ad uretheram à parte infera penis.* **1895** *Trans. & Proc. R. Soc. S.A.* (1896) XVI. 249 All the aborigines of the interior circumcise, and also slit the uretha. [*Note*] This mutilation is by different writers variously alluded to as the 'terrible rite', the 'mika operation' or 'Sturt's rite'. **1928** W. ROBERTSON *Coo-ee Talks* 59 The '*Mai-ing boomung* oath' was classed with the Terrible-Rites of initiation; it was used for the specific purpose of sealing the lips of the initiate, who had passed the three stages of the *Bora*.

Territorian. A non-Aboriginal person native to or resident in the Northern Territory.

1882 W. SOWDEN *N.T. as it Is* 41 The Territorians attempt races between the animated clothes-horses dubbed equines here. **1897** J.J. MURIF *From Ocean to Ocean* 183, I had heard that the Territorians were the essence of hospitality, and now I fully believe it. **1920** J.N. MACINTYRE *White Aust.* 131 Does anyone think that any Territorian who has fought the blacks in the early days, and drought and hardships and all the dangers and inconveniences of the empty North for years, deserved such legislators? **1930** J.S. LITCHFIELD *Far-North Memories* 57 A number of Territorians considered they had a right to take forcible possession of any lubra. **1950** *New Settler in W.A.* (Perth) Feb. 51 Somehow it never occurs to the Territorian that he might live somewhere else. **1960** *N.T. News* (Darwin) 5 Feb. 18/4 Former Territorian Bobby Liddle earned high praise . . at the Festival Hall in Melbourne last Friday. **1971** *Southerly* ii. 137 I'm a Territorian, Kenny Buckman's my name. **1985** *Bulletin* (Sydney) 28 May 39/3 The Territorians have their own flag and a quaint, old fashioned pride in their regional identity.

Territory.

1. Abbrev. of 'Northern Territory'. Also *attrib.*

1882 W. SOWDEN *N.T. as it Is* 150 The country on this run is some of the best in the Territory. **1886** *Adelaide Observer* 31 July 31 He leaves a comfortable home in Palmerston, which he has earned by many years of rough work in the Territory. **1898** A.B. PATERSON in C. Semmler *World of Banjo Paterson* (1967) 81 The man who once goes to the Territory always has a hankering to get back there. **1906** *Bulletin* (Sydney) 30 Aug. 16/4 Met a man back in the Territory who had 'done-in' a station. **1919** *Huon Times* (Franklin) 24 Jan. 4/4 The nearest doctor is 250 miles away, the only one in the Territory being resident in Darwin. **1944** A.S. SMITH *Boys write Home* 203, I even thought it was a bit of a thrill to be wheeling 1500 head of stampeding territory pikers on a black night down the Georgina. **1960** N. CATO *Green grows Vine* 33, I reckon this steak came from the Territory, Mrs Binks . . and I reckon it walked all the way. **1979** D. LOCKWOOD *My Old Mates & I* 95 The Territory was once a sanctuary for absconding husbands and other ne'er-do-wells. **1983** *Canberra Times* 26 Oct. 23/1 The Territory boasts the lowest unemployment rate in Australia though more than half the Aboriginal population is out of work.

2. Special Comb. **Territory rig,** *Darwin rig*, see DARWIN.

1964 A.H. AFFLECK *Wandering Yrs.* 39 It has taken a third of a century and a visit by a down-to-earth member of the Royal Family to make official in those parts the commonsense dress of slacks, shirt and tie known as 'Territory rig'. **1964** K. WILLEY *Eaters of Lotus* 12 Nott soothed rising tempers by defining a 'Territory rig' as 'white long-sleeved shirt, tie or bow tie, long trousers and dark shoes'. Socks, presumably, are optional. Territory rig has been in force ever since. **1984** (Invitation), *The Government of the Northern Territory* requests the pleasure of the company of Dr & Mrs I. Cook at the Official Opening of The Menzies School of Health Research by His Excellency the Governor-General of Australia... Dress: Territory Rig.

the, *dem. adj.* Used with the names of some towns (esp. in n. Aust.) freq. with ellipsis of a secondary element of the name, as **the Alice, Isa, Tennant** (for Alice Springs, Mount Isa, Tennant Creek): see quot. 1979.

1883 E.M. CURR *Recoll. Squatting Vic.* 165 (*note*) In Australia it is not unusual to prefix the definite article to the names of places; as *the* Moira, *the* Terricks, *the* Wee-waa, &c. **1900** *N.T. Times* (Darwin) 1 June 2/5 He . . will be bringing Stuart . . along in a few weeks. At present the latter is being quietly trained at the Katherine. **1922** J.J. Parker *N.T.* 7 The region between the Katherine and Darwin holds splendid possibilities for rice and cotton. **1938** F. Blakeley *Hard Liberty* 192 We had left the Marbles at half-past two . . a station boy told the telegraph master at the Tennant that three men and a dog were approaching from that place. **1950** A. Groom *I saw Strange Land* 75 It was good to see the Alice again. **1956** H. Hudson *Flynn's Flying Doctors* 220 We . . then saw beneath us the poppet-heads and iron roofs of Tennant Creek—a mining town, scattered among red rounded hills. 'The Tennant' is a gold field. **1965** K. McKenney *Hide-Away Man* 16 Reckon we could do with a trip to the Isa? **1972** W. Watkins *Wayward Gang* 42 She's stuck with him all the way; even when he went up to the Isa. . . He stiffened at the memory of Mount Isa. **1979** D. Lockwood *My Old Mates & I* 2 My friend said, 'At least you're not short of definite articles.' I knew what he meant. The Isa. The 'Loo. The Tennant. The Alice. The Elliott. The Kath-er-ine. The Daly. The 'Curry. Yet it's strange that I've never heard The Darwin or The Batchelor or The Renner or The Pine Creek. Some names just seem to fit naturally with an article, others are awkward.

thick-billed grass-wren. The small bird *Amytornis textilis* of w. and central Aust., having predom. brown plumage and a stout bill.

1913 *Emu* XII. Suppl. 79 *Amytornis modesta* . . thick-billed Grass-Wren. **1945** C. Barrett *Austral. Bird Life* 188 The thick-billed [grass-wren] . . inland districts of New South Wales, western Victoria, and South Australia. **1984** *Age* (Melbourne) 27 Mar. 24/8 Declining are the thick-billed grass-wren and . . the Plains Wanderer (of which the latest reports are that new populations have been discovered).

thickhead. [See quot. 1898.] Whistler 1.

1837 W. Swainson *On Nat. Hist. Birds* II. 250 Pachycephala . . Thickhead. **1890** *Act* (Vic.) 54 Vict. no. 1095 3rd Sched., Thick-heads. From the first day of August to the twentieth day of December next following in each year. **1898** E.E. Morris *Austral Eng.* 336 They . . are called *Thickheads*. . . The name is from Greek παχύς, thick, and κεφαλή, the head. **1911** A. Mack *Bush Days* 52 Thickheads burst into song as they flew into the white branches above. **1924** Lord & Scott *Synopsis Vertebrate Animals Tas.* 207 The Whistlers, or 'Thickheads' as they are often termed, constitute one of the delights of the Tasmanian bush. **1941** C. Barrett *Aust.* 15 Yellow robins build in silver wattles, and those songsters once called 'thickheads', with plumage as golden as their voices. **1984** Simpson & Day *Birds of Aust.* 322 Whistlers . . are robust birds with relatively large heads (hence the name 'thickheads').

thirds, *pl. Hist.* In the phr. **(up)on (the) thirds,** an agreement between an owner of livestock and a landholder, whereby the stock are pastured and tended by the landholder in return for one third of the profits: see esp. quot. 1834.

1823 *Hobart Town Gaz.* 29 Nov., Captain Welsh having made Enclosures on his Farm at the Coal River, for the purpose of protecting Cattle, will take Sheep or Cattle on the Thirds on the usual terms. **1829** *Launceston Advertiser* 4 May 1 *A gentleman* having an extensive Stock Run, is desirous of having a small flock of good woolled *sheep* on the thirds. **1834** T.P. Besnard *Voice from Bush* 11 Apr. (1839) 14 These sheep I have put out to graze, according to the custom of the country, on *thirds*—that is, the person who grazes and takes care of the flock is entitled to one-third of the produce of the wool, and one-third of the lambs that are dropped. **1847** A. Harris *Settlers & Convicts* (1953) 61 He knew of one settler, a magistrate, who had a fine run over the Hawkesbury River among the mountains, who had very few cattle on it, and was taking any he could get to graze on the thirds. **1874** *Illustr. Sydney News* 28 Feb. 15/3 He had a flock of sheep on 'the thirds', and kept two convicts as shepherds. **1898** G.J. de Winton *Soldiering Fifty Yrs. Ago* 49 'Theirs upon thirds' refers to the terms upon which sheep and cattle were grazed for other parties. **1946** A.J. Holt *Wheat Farms Vic.* 37 'Farming on thirds' . . is first recorded in Victoria in documents referring to Lascelles and his 'tenant' farmers of Lake Coorong.

thong. A flat-soled sandal held on the foot by a bifurcated thong passing between the first and second toes.

1960 *N.T. News* (Darwin) 8 Jan. 2/7 Just Arrived . . ! Thongs Scuffs Plastic Children's shoes. **1964** *Bulletin* (Sydney) 18 Jan. 12/2 It's not very easy for a man who has worn a suit every day of his life . . to learn to walk around in a beach shirt, shorts and thongs. **1969** *On Guard* (Broken Hill) Feb. 10 The wearing of . . shorts with thongs is not permitted. **1973** *Bulletin* (Sydney) 20 Jan. 10/1 Pat Troy of the Australian National University's urban research unit . . usually wears shorts and thongs to work at this time of year. **1986** *Ibid.* 28 Jan. 29/3 The dress regulations are 'Gold Coast casual—no thongs or uncovered swimwear'.

thornback. [Transf. use of *thornback* the British ray *Raja clavata*.] The marine fish *Raja lemprieri* of Tas., Vic., and S.A., having thorn-like spines on the dorsal surface. Also **thornback skate.**

1786 *Hist. Narr. Discovery New Holland & N.S.W.* 10 The sea-fish seen here were . . skates, thornbacks, and other fish. **1827** *Tasmanian Almanack* 142 Thornback [4s. to 6s. each]. **1875** *Melbourne Spectator* 28 Aug. 201/3 A thornback skate . . weighing 109 lbs., has been caught . . at North Arm, South Australia. **1881** *Proc. Linnean Soc. N.S.W.* VI. 375 *Raja lamprieri* [*sic*] . . '*Thorn Back*' of the Melbourne fishermen. **1974** T.D. Scott et al. *Marine & Freshwater Fishes S.A.* 57 Thornback skate. *Raja lemprieri* . . colour of disc greyish-black above, edges pinkish, white below.

thornbill. [Transf. use of *thornbill* an American humming-bird.]

1. Any of the small, plump birds of the genus *Acanthiza* of Aust. incl. Tas., and sub-alpine New Guinea. See also Tit, Tomtit.

1900 A.J. Campbell *Nests & Eggs Austral. Birds* 230 (*footnote*) Some recent authors use the term Thornbill a name already applied to a number of Humming Birds—as a vernacular name for the Acanthizas. **1905** *Emu* IV. 147 There is some objection to the term 'Thornbill' being applied to the Acanthizas. **1942** C. Barrett *From Bush Hut* 25 Scrub-wrens and thornbills lived among the tea-trees and silver wattles. **1973** V. Serventy *Desert Walkabout* 75 It was in this piratical way that the thornbill gained much of its food. **1985** Maris & Borg *Women of Sun* 68 A group of tiny thornbills with pale yellow breasts and green wings flitted about, calling to one another in their sweet, high-pitched voices.

2. With distinguishing epithet, as **brown, yellow-tailed:** see under first element.

thorny devil. [From the appearance of the lizard.] *Mountain devil* (a), see Mountain. Also *attrib.*

1904 *World's News* (Sydney) 9 Apr. 9 Seeing two illustrations of Moloch Horridus . . which were called 'Thorny Devils'. **1938** *Bulletin* (Sydney) 16 Mar. 21/3 'Thorny devil' (mountain devil we call it in W.A.). **1967** M. & M. Leyland *Where Dead Men Lie* 106 He was a Thorny Devil, a very repulsive looking, but none-theless harmless and gentle lizard . . nine inches long and a beautiful green and orange colour. **1985** *New Idea* (Melbourne) 2 Nov. 33 The thorny devil lizard (Moloch horridus) is extremely difficult to keep in captivity—it feeds only on small black ants, and can't live in a humid climate.

three-cornered jack. [f. *three-cornered*, prob. from the three spines of the fruit + *jack*, as used in the pop. names of various plants.] Double-gee. Also **three corner jack.**

1897 J.J. Murif *From Ocean to Ocean* 74 Three-cornered Jacks are another enemy to the cyclist. **1912** Spencer & Gillen *Across Aust.* 17 Its dry prickly seed cases . . popularly known as 'three-cornered Jack', are more than irritating when you have to come amongst them. **1936** C. Chewings *Back in Stone Age* 81 The elopers had taken a route that led over rough stony ground, infested with three-cornered jacks—a very bad prickle. **1944** *Bulletin* (Sydney) 23 Aug. 12/1 The pig, its hard little hooves impervious to the three-cornered Jacks which littered the plain, cantered away to safety. **1958** W.E. Harney *Content to Lie* 15 It is good to walk along the sand beaches free from stubbles of grass and three-cornered-Jacks that cover the earth in sandy patches. **1978** M.J. Burton *Bush Pub* 107 Swaller a certain amount of it [*sc.* curare] and you take orf like a goanna that's stood on a three-cornered jack. **1986** *Austral. Garden Jrnl.* Apr. 142 There is quite an infestation of rabbits and some weed problems, particularly box-thorn and three corner jack.

three-quarter caste, *a.* Of an Aboriginal: having one non-Aboriginal grandparent; (loosely) an Aboriginal of part-white descent. Also as quasi-*n.*

1900 *Advocate* (Burnie) 27 July 4/2 Joe Governor, a three-quarter caste. Another was . . a full-blood black-fellow. **1970** *Bulletin* (Sydney) 24 Oct. 30/3 Michael Anderson is 19, a three-quarter caste Aboriginal.

three-rail fence. A fence having three wooden rails as its horizontal members. Also **three-railed fence.**

1837 *Colonist* (Hobart) 11 May 152/2 The purchaser will have the option of renting from fifty to one hundred acres of land . . part of which is now enclosed with a three-railed fence. **1838** T.H. James *Six Months S.A.* 178 We presently came up to . . a three-rail fence. **1846** F. Dutton *S.A. & its Mines* 203 It takes about 4,500 pieces to inclose an eighty acre section with a three rail fence. **1859** H. Kingsley *Recoll. Geoffry Hamlyn* III. 125 The Sydney ghost actually did sit on a three-rail fence. **1882** A.J. Boyd *Old Colonials* 19 Things have come to a pretty pass, when a feller's only offered five bob a rod for a three-rail fence, slip panels included! **1914** *Bulletin* (Sydney) 19 Mar. 22/1, I have seen on the Dorrigo . . a three-railed fence of rosewood post and cedar rails.

three-up. *Obs.* A game in which three coins are tossed and bets laid on the fall, the toss being invalid unless the three display the same face on landing. See Two-up *n.* Also *attrib.*

1845 *Parramatta Chron.* 15 Mar. 2/1 The charged was . . descanting most learnedly on the evolution and revolutions of 'three up' . . with upturned eye and outstretched body intently watching the fall of some 'Browns'. **1849** A. Harris *Emigrant Family* (1967) 335 The evolutions of three penny pieces in the air; or, as he himself would have designated the game, 'three-up'. **1858** C.R. Thatcher *Colonial Songster* (rev. ed.) 16 The pleasures found in history, Some fools will prate about; 'Tis insignificant, compared With 'three up', or 'odd man out'. **1869** M. Clarke *Peripatetic Philosopher* 24 He would learn how to play 'props', and would not be entirely ignorant of the charming game of 'three-up'. **1888** J. Freeman *Lights & Shadows Melbourne Life* 216 A 'three-up' room . . is a room where gambling was carried on by tossing with three coppers. **1892** *Truth* (Sydney) 17 apr. 2/7 Hon. members can . . relieve the monotony of their duties by such innocent recreations as devil's pool, dominoes, draughts . . and 'Three-up'. **1907** C. MacAlister *Old Pioneering Days* 191 Some of them were, for instance, ardent followers of the 'three up school' and at such a game I discovered a man who had been recommended as a likely buyer.

throat. In the phr. **to have (got) the game** (or **it**) **by the throat,** to have control of a situation.

1947 J. Morrison *Sailors belong Ships* 15 We're sailors, see? Two sailors. We got the game by the throat. **1960** R. Tullipan *Follow Sun* 105 'Think we'll get it done today?' Brady asked. . . 'Can't miss. . . We have it by the throat now all right.' **1974** D. Ireland *Burn* 58 'I'm right. Gordon'll fix everything for me,' the boy's mother says. . . 'So you got the game by the throat, eh?'

throw, *n.* [Alteration of *froe*: see quot. 1916.] A tool for cleaving staves, etc., from a block of wood, having the handle at right angles to the blade.

1913 H. Lawson *For Aust.* 14 The crow-bar, pick-axe and the 'throw'—the axe that morticed well. **1916** *Bulletin* (Sydney) 4 May 22/3 'Coolibah' . . mentions the coastal bullocky's 'Flindozy' (for Flindersia), and writes of splitting timber with the paling 'throw'. Always in the bush I have heard it called throw, but lately in a hardware catalogue I saw the word printed 'froe'.

throw, *v.*

1. *trans.* To cast (an animal) to the ground, preparatory to branding, etc. Also *absol.*

1847 A. Harris *Settlers & Convicts* (1953) 28 In latter days it has been found that sometimes the beast has been thrown and the branded section of the hide actually flayed off. **1849** —— *Emigrant Family* (1967) 132 We can brand her without the catching rope... I'll catch her and throw her. **1902** *Bulletin* (Sydney) 13 Sept. 16/3 It is quite a usual thing, on cattle stations, to 'throw and tie' a wild beast. When let up, the animal will drive quietly enough with coachers—quiet cattle. **1912** *Ibid.* 11 July 14/2, I saw woman and girls toiling in the branding yard. They used to rope and help to throw a colt. **1916** *Ibid.* 22 June 24/4 Why do vets... persist in throwing colts for castration? .. The only man I know .. who emasculates without ropes is Harry Dempsey. **1942** *Ibid.* 1 July 12/3 Droving our scrubbers to the butcher, all previously thrown and tied, the first two nights were the worst. **1949** I.L. Idriess *One Wet Season* 240 Each difficult, swift action must necessarily be done in a split second. To throw a galloping beast thus necessitates a trained stock-horse, an expert rider, tenacious agility and nerve. **1960** R.S. Porteous *Cattleman* 170 I'm a bloody cattleman! The scrubber I couldn't throw and tie hasn't been born yet. **1980** Ansell & Percy *To fight Wild* 52 It's not as dangerous as throwing off a horse.

2. In the phr. **to throw off,** to engage in provocative banter; with **at,** to chaff or ridicule (someone); *chuck off,* see Chuck *v.* 1; *sling off,* see Sling *v.* 3. As *n.*, an instance of this.

1812 J.H. Vaux *Mem.* (1819) II. 218 *Throw off,* to talk in a sarcastical strain, so as to convey offensive allusions under the mask of pleasantry, or innocent freedom; but, perhaps, secretly venting that abuse which you would not dare to give in direct terms. **1911** E.S. Sorenson *Life in Austral. Backblocks* 247 Some hard case is bound to 'throw-off' at him at such times. **1917** C. Thackeray *Goliath Joe* 69 He had .. absorbed some of the local bucolic 'throws-off' at the men dressed in English knee-breeches. **1935** K. Tennant *Tiburon* 253 'You're not being funny, are you? Sort of throwing off?' He looked injured. **1962** D. Cusack *Picnic Races* 183 You're like all the townies. Throwing off at the people on the land.

throw-down. A type of small firework: see quot. 1922.

1890 *Truth* (Sydney) 16 Nov. 1/6 The remedy is to carry a supply of the 'throw downs' or detonators, which boys use on Queen's Birthday. **1896** E. Turner *Little Larrikin* 321 Lol was .. projecting jumping Jacks and throwdowns on the floor, and keeping the cook .. on the table. **1922** L.M. Pyke *Jack of St. Virgil's* 138 'Throw-downs?' .. 'You know, crackers that go off with a bang when you throw them down.' **1974** M. Paice *Dolan's Roost* 36 Ekka came away clutching a pocketful of throwdowns... Dobbo couldn't raise much of an interest in cracker night... Every year it had been great, saving up to buy fireworks.

throw-in. [f. *to throw in* to add to a bargain.] A stroke of unexpected good fortune.

1871 *Austral. Town & Country Jrnl.* (Sydney) 11 Feb. 186/1 The owner of Sunbeam took his grueling kindly, and I trust when next the two cracks meet he (Mr Henry) may have better luck. Mr Henry is every inch a sporting man, and deserves to have his throw in sometimes. *Ibid.* 25 Feb. 249/3 One of Mr Town's [horses] can hardly fail of winning the Grand Stand Stakes. Altogether the meeting promises a great 'throw in' for Mr Town's lot. **1884** *Austral. Tit-Bits* (Melbourne) 3 July 14/1 Leporello's win was a throw in for the books. **1900** J. Bradshaw *Highway Robbery under Arms* (*c* 1927) 110 This was a throw in for me. When Holt went to get his grog I placed or packed in at the bottom of his pint pannikin the crumb part of bread, and when Holt got his whack I would take the crumb part of bread out of Holt's pannikin, and squeeze it between my hands into my pannikin. **1976** C.D. Mills *Hobble Chains & Greenhide* 7 It was really quite a throw-in, for the plant, well yard-broken, raced down the wing and the dust obscured the rails.

throwing stick. a. Woomera (see quot. 1770). **b.** Boomerang *n.* 1. **c.** A straight stick of wood used as a missile.

1770 J. Cook *Jrnls.* 23 Aug. (1955) I. 396 They throw the Dart with only one hand, in the doing of which they make use of a peice [*sic*] of wood about 3 feet long made thin like the blade of a Cutlass, with a little hook at one end to take hold of the end of the Dart, and at the other end is fix'd a peice of bone about 3 or 4 inches long; the use of this is, I beleive, to keep the dart steady and to make it quit the hand in a proper direction; by the help of these throwing sticks, as we call them, they will hit a Mark at the distance of 40 or 50 Yards. **1790** R. Clark *Jrnl.* 16 Feb. 135 A Native on the Shore with two Spears and a throwing stick. ***c* 1795** G. Barrington *Voyage to Botany Bay* 58 The shell fixed on the throwing stick is intended for sharpening the point of their lance. **1820** C. Jeffreys *Van Dieman's Land* 126 They do not use the throwing-stick in the same manner as the natives of Port Jackson. **1833** *Perth Gaz.* 13 July 110, The natives then began to fix their spears in their throwing-sticks. **1846** *Moreton Bay Courier* 19 Sept. 4/1 At the Alligator Rivers and Port Essington .. the throwing stick and the goose spears are means of obtaining game. **1859** W. Burrows *Adventures Mounted Trooper* 97 Both kinds are thrown with a 'woomera' or throwing stick, which is a piece of wood about three feet in length, with a barb at the point that fits into a notch in the end of the spear; it is retained in the hand after the spear is thrown. **1883** F. Bonney *On Some Customs Aborigines* 6 A downward stroke with the pointed end of a throwing stick (*pirrah*), forces the tooth out. **1920** E. Wood *Under Southern Cross* 93 Found him with a leg buckled beneath his body, and a throwing stick, complete with spear, in his hand. **1943** *Bulletin* (Sydney) 29 Dec. 13/1 They were daring waders, often walking into swamps and lagoons chin-deep to retrieve wild duck brought down by kylie or throwing-stick. **1965** *N. Austral. Monthly* Dec. 10 Spears made of mulga each of which has a single point—sometimes a barb; heavy throwing sticks used to kill birds and small game. **1980** B. Scott *Darkness under Hills* 119 Bororen sang and tapped his throwing sticks together while Benarby danced the story about an elder.

throw-stick. *Obs.*

1. Boomerang *n.* 1.

1847 G.F. Angas *Savage Life & Scenes* II. 274 Who taught them the use of the *Boomerang,* which is depicted in the tombs of Egypt, and called by Wilkinson the *Throw-stick?*

2. Woomera.

1884 W.H.G. Kingston *Adventures in Aust.* 62 The throwing or throw-stick, is to serve the purpose of a sling for casting the spear. A heavy flat piece of wood, between two and three feet long, has at one end a slight hollow into which the end of the spear is fitted while at the other is a heavy weight, thus assisting the hunter in the art of throwing the spear. **1892** J. Fraser *Aborigines N.S.W.* 72 Another curiosity of Australian invention is the throw-stick, with which many of the war-spears are impelled from the hand of the owner. This is already known by the name of 'womara', and I think that the use of any other name for it causes confusion.

thrummer. *Obs.* [f. Br. slang *thrum(s*: see OEDS.] A threepenny piece; Scrum; Scrummy.

1898 *Tocsin* (Melbourne) 24 Nov. 5/3 This has been Charity and Show week with us in Ballarat, and we have been making our annual show of charity in the churches by putting a tanner in the plate instead of the usual thrummer. **1900** *Pastoral Times* (Deniliquin) 6 Jan. 2/5, I had accommodated a thrummer .. but Tom, Jack and 'Arry 'adn't a bean. **1907** *Truth* (Sydney) 30 June 9/5 Con can 'turn upon a thrummer' When he does a clever twist. **1911** A. Needham *Radicals* 31 Cadging, crawling for a 'thrummer', just to drive dull care away. **1944** *Bulletin* (Sydney) 1 Mar. 12/2 Mac stopped dead, the thrummer half out of his pocket.

thrush. [Transf. use of *thrush* the musical bird *Turdus philomelos,* and other birds of the fam. Turdidae or Muscicapidae. The word is used in Aust. for such birds, incl. the naturalized *T. philomelos.*] Any of several birds having a melodious song, esp. those of the genus *Colluricincla* (see *shrike-thrush* Shrike) and those known as *ground thrush* (see Ground *n.*[1]).

1794 G. Shaw *Zool. New Holland* 25 *Turdus Punctatus.* The Spotted-shouldered Thrush... Greyish-brown Thrush dashed with blackish. **1804** G. Caley in A.E.J. Andrews *Devil's Wilderness* (1984) 66 Saw 2 thrushes. **1818** J. Oxley *Jrnls. Two Exped. N.S.W.* 4 Aug. (1820) 256 There is a great diversity of birds, some of which have the most delightful notes, particularly the thrush. **1848** J. Gould *Birds of Aust.* II. Pl. 75, *Colluricincla rufiventris* .. Thrush, of the Colonists [of W.A.]. **1852** W. Hughes *Austral. Colonies* 83 The ordinary song-birds are almost entirely absent: there are, indeed, some among the native birds to which the names of thrush, lark, and other well-known warblers are given. **1909** G. Smith *Naturalist in Tas.* 66 One of the few mellow-voiced birds in Tasmania is the Thrush or Whistling Dick (*Colluricincla selbii*). **1935** F. Clune *Rolling down Lachlan* 12 The birds of the bush were befriended at the homestead .. soldier-birds and thrushes. **1965** *Austral. Encycl.* VIII. 494 Other Australian birds known as thrushes, but more correctly shrike-thrushes, are members of the genus *Colluricincla.*

thumb-piece. [Br. dial.: see OED b.] A piece of bread, with cheese or meat, held between the thumb and the finger.

1885 N.W. Swan *Couple of Cups Ago* 122 It [*sc.* the public] could eat its thumb-piece on a bit of bread, and go visiting in crimean shirts and lace-ups. **1951** E. Hill *Territory* 293 Breakfast is a thumb-piece and a quart of tea, standing up.

thunder-bird. [See quot. 1827.] Either of two birds of the genus *Pachycephala,* the *golden whistler* (see Golden 3), and the *rufous whistler* (see Rufous); Ring-coachman.

***a* 1827** *Trans. Linnean Soc. London* XV. 239 *Pachycephala .. Gutturalis...* 'This species', Mr Caley says, 'is called *Thunder-bird* by the colonists... The natives tell me, that, when it begins to thunder, this bird is very noisy.' **1848** J. Gould *Birds of Aust.* II. Pl. 64, *Pachycephala gutturalis* .. Thunder Bird, Colonists of New South Wales. **1891** G.J. Broinowski *Birds of Aust.* V. Pl. 43, One peculiarity about its note .. is that it is nearly always heard before a thunderstorm, a circumstance which has procured for it the name of 'Thunder Bird'. **1918** *Bulletin* (Sydney) 14 Feb. (Red Page), Yellow-breasted Whistler, Rufous-breasted Whistler (Mock Whip-birds, Thunder-birds). **1944** L. Welsh *Kookaburra* 10 One of the earliest of dawn-singers is the Rufous-breasted Whistler, alias the .. Thunder Bird. **1981** G. Cross *George & Widda-Woman* 88 The thunderbirds, the silver-eyes, the warblers and the whipbirds in the scrub beneath.

thunder egg. [U.S.: see OEDS *thunder, sb.* 6.] See quot. 1970.

1965 B. James *Collecting Austral. Gemstones* 21 Essentially it is a broken 'thunder-egg' with half the casing of rhyolite remaining. **1967** R.O. Chalmers *Austral. Rocks* 162 'Thunder eggs'. This rather meaningless term is being used rather loosely in Australia. The name is applied to material that occurs only in Oregon in the United States. **1970** J.A. Talent *Minerals, Rock & Gems* 261 *Thunder egg*—a hollow concretion consisting of layers of siliceous material (usually agate) with a lining of siliceous crystals. **1981** A. Wilkinson *Up Country* 16 We have found .. thunder eggs just lying on the track after a particularly heavy rain.

thylacine. /ˈθaɪləsin/. [The animal genus *Thylacine* was named by mammalogist C.J. Temminck (*Monogr. de Mammalogie* (1824) I. 23), f. Gr. *θύλακ-ος* pouch + L. suffix *-inus* of or pertaining to.] *Tasmanian tiger,* see Tasmanian *a.* 2.

1838 *Geol. Soc. London* III. 19 In the numbers of the grinders the Phascolothere resembles the Opossum and Thylacine. **1891** *Daily News* 5 May 5/5 (OED) The Zoological Society have just acquired a pair of thylacines—a somewhat rare, carnivorous marsupial, from Tasmania. **1911** C.E.W. Bean *'Dreadnought' of Darling* 119 The animal is differently known as the marsupial Wolf, or thylacine, or Tasmanian tiger. **1926** A.S. Le Souef et al. *Wild Animals Australasia* 318 The thylacine hunts singly or in pairs, feeding on wallabies, small rodents, and birds. **1975** *Ecos* v. 26/3 The thylacine .. was common in Tasmania during early settlement. This marsupial carnivore was almost certainly shot out because of its reputation as a sheep-killer. **1983** J. Hepworth *Birds & Beasties Aust.*, The Thylacine is now so rare It maybe isn't even there. And if it *is,* it well might think It safer to *pretend* extinct. **1984** *Age* (Melbourne) 18 Aug. 6/1 The Tasmanian tiger, or Thylacine, seems to have expired in 1934 when the last known animal passed away peacefully, behind bars, in the Hobart zoo.

tick.

1. Used *attrib.* and in Comb. with reference to the control or eradication of cattle-infesting ticks.

1898 *Bulletin* (Sydney) 23 July 15/2 T'other day a celestial cart was crossing the bridge that leads into the N.S.W. hamlet. Tick-inspector vociferates: 'Grease your horse, John!' **1911** E.J. Brady *King's Caravan* 209 After seeing the coach-horses from Nerang anointed with a smellful coat of tick-wash in the autumn morning . . we commenced. **1919** *Pastoral Rev.* 16 Jan. 42 Stress is laid on the good work done by Mr A.H. Cory, Chief Inspector, and Mr G.E. Bunnino, a member of the Tick Board, in their recent visit to the far north-west. **1956** *Bulletin* (Sydney) 4 July 13/2 A North Coast (N.S.W.) cocky, ordered by a tick-control inspector to dip a three-day-old calf . . threw *him* into the dip. **1956** T. RONAN *Moleskin Midas* 209 He was south of the Quarantine Line with tick-free cattle.

2. Special Comb. **tick fence,** a fence erected to prevent the movement of tick-infested cattle, etc., into a tick-free area; **gate,** an opening in such a fence at which travelling stock are subject to inspection; **line,** an imaginary line marking the boundary of a tick-infested area from which the movement of stock is prohibited.

1906 *Bulletin* (Sydney) 11 Oct. 17/1 A gatekeeper on the **tick fence** (Queensland border) is a State official. **1919** *Pastoral Rev.* 16 Jan. 42 At the mouth of the Tweed River the tick fence divides the two portions of the residential area, one portion being in Queensland and the other in New South Wales. **1933** H.J. CARTER *Gulliver in Bush* 80 One direction—the northern road—led us to the 'tick fence'. This was a strong double line of fencing separated by a wide swathe, guarded by a sort of blockhouse and its janitor, which the experts of the day vainly imagined would prevent the dreaded cattle-tick from crossing the border into New South Wales. **1927** *Bulletin* (Sydney) 15 Dec. 27/1 It wanders from the **tick-gate** where the main road's traffic spills. **1963** J. O'GRADY *Things they do to You* 119, I knew a bloke worked on a tick gate once. **1980** R.C. STIBBARD *Not Dream* 57 Coming home from the coast a few years ago, I was bringing a small bag of sand from the beach, and was told at the tick gates to throw it away, which I did. **1901** *Western Champion* (Barcaldine) 16 July 14/4 He proposed 'That this meeting strongly protests against the interference of traffic in and about Longreach caused by the **tick line** surrounding the town.' **1901** *Pastoralists' Rev.* Dec. 666 The new tick lines appear to be giving satisfaction, as they allow cattle west of a line joining Emerald and Bowen, and north of the former prohibited area, to travel South after dipping. **1943** H.G. LAMOND *From Tariaro to Ross Roy* 121 Though the country is clean, the cattle are tied up on account of a fanciful tick line drawn between that station and the markets. **1976** M. BROWN *Black Eureka* 4 Nearby was a roadblock, the so-called tick line which was not only used for disinfecting cattle on the move, but for blocking Aborigines from going north or south.

tick bush. (Chiefly *N.S.W.*) A shrub of the genus *Kunzea* (fam. Myrtaceae), esp. the white-flowering *K. ambigua* of N.S.W., Vic., and Tas.

1935 W.W. FROGGATT *Austral. Spiders* 77 *Ixodes holocyclus.* (The Dog or Bush Tick). . . The white flowering *Kunzia capitata* is popularly known about Port Jackson as 'Tick Bush', because it is one of the abundant bushes in the locality upon which these ticks abound. **1958** D.S. LESLIE *Green Singers* 202 Away to the east . . towards Megalong Valley, glowed . . wattle, amid . . tick-bushes and pin-leafed ti-trees. **1968** D. IRELAND *Chantic Bird* 24 A few hundred yards away from the house is the ti-tree bush, we called it tick-bush.

ticket, *n.*[1] *Hist.*

1. TICKET OF LEAVE 1. Also *attrib.*

1819 *HRA* (1921) 3rd Ser. II. 539 Specifying those whose Tickets are made for this Settlement. **1828** *Austral. Almanack* 87 Ticket of Leave Men, who habitually neglect to attend Divine Worship will be deprived of their Tickets. **1838** *HRA* (1923) 1st Ser. XIX. 604 Each punishment, which an assigned servant receives, puts him back a year in getting his Ticket. **1846** L.W. MILLER *Notes of Exile Van Dieman's Land* 350 On the 22nd February 1842, they received the promised *tickets* . . confining them to six districts in the interior. **1866** *Austral. Monthly Mag.* II. 179 When I gets to Hobart Town, what does I see? Lots of coves, well fed, well looked after; some in quod, some ticket coves. **1898** *Western Champion* (Barcaldine) 20 Dec. 1/3 What d'ye mean, Mr Goodyer, in asking Dr Thursby for a ticket for me? What business is it of yours whether I'm free or bond? **1900** W. DELAFORCE *Life & Experiences Ex-Convict Port Macquarie* 6 If he happened to prove himself a success at any particular vocation, he would never get his 'ticket', as the master for whom he was working would arrange with one of the other servants to quarrel with the handy man, and he would be sent to the lockup to be flogged, and get an addition to his sentence.

2. In the phr. **ticket of exemption (from Government Labour** or **Service),** a permit issued to a convict allowing residence with a spouse: see esp. quots. 1831, 1836, and 1837.

1830 *Sydney Monitor* 2 June 3/6 All holders of tickets-of-leave and tickets of exemption are to be mustered once a month by the Magistrates of the respective districts. **1831** *Austral. Almanack* 78 *A Ticket of Exemption from Government Labor* differs from a Ticket of Leave, in conferring no permission for the individual to employ himself for his own benefit or to acquire property, but simply the privilege of residing until the next 31st December, with the person therein named. **1836** J.F. O'CONNELL *Residence Eleven Yrs. New Holland* 47 Convicts are discharged from the factory by three methods—tickets of leave at the expiration of half their time of sentence, tickets of exemption upon the arrival of their husbands in the colony, and tickets of exemption upon the application of a suitor, who must marry, forthwith, the damsel whose liberty he seeks. **1837** *Rep. Select Committee Transportation* 11 Ticket of exemption . . has been discontinued for some years; but a ticket of exemption was given to men where they were assigned to their wives, or where they were allowed to live with their wives. **1849** A. HARRIS *Emigrant Family* (1967) 114 How easily you can get rid of your ticket of exemption from Government service.

3. Comb. in sense 1: **ticket holder, man, woman.**

1845 *Parramatta Chron.* 31 May 4/1 The man . . turned out to be a **ticket-holder** named Connell, lately . . liberated from custody, on a charge of murder, owing to the evidence against him being defective. **1852** J. WEST *Hist. of Tas.* I. 277 The formation of a new settlement was the grand expedient. Vessels bringing convicts to Van Diemen's Land were to convey ticket holders to North Australia. **1873** A. TROLLOPE *Aust. & N.Z.* II. 94 The rural labourers are ticket-holders—or expirees who were convicts. **1827** *Monitor* (Sydney) 23 Mar. 356 **Ticket men** up the country have a poor life of it under the present regulations. **1833** *Currency Lad* (Sydney) 2 Mar. 2 When he writes of ticket men, his remarks, if taken in earnest, are most unjust and cruel. **1861** M.A. BAIN *Ancient Landmarks* (1975) 265 It will not grievously affect religion as convicts, with few exceptions do not bother with it. The Ticket men scarcely visit a place of worship. **1897** *Bulletin* (Sydney) 24 July 11/1 How many Bulletin readers have ever seen a ticket-of-leave? Picked one up the other day, and for the first time understood why a ticket-man so rarely exhibits his 'certificate of freedom'. . . On the back of the ticket the description of the 'freed' prisoner is set forth under the following headings: Name, grade, native place, height without shoes, age, complexion, head, hair, whiskers, visage, forehead, eyes, nose, mouth, chin, remarks. **1847** *Britannia* (Hobart) 17 June 2/5 A **ticket woman**, flashily dressed.

Hence **ticketer** *n.*, one to whom a ticket of leave is granted. Also *transf.*

1844 *Colonial Times* (Hobart) 2 Nov., He was sent for two months on the roads, his Worship observing that there was rather too much of this sort of work now carrying on amongst the ticketers. **1865** 'SPECIAL CORRESPONDENT' *Transportation* 9 Every other man he sees is a 'ticketer'—as the criminal class, whether bond or free, are termed. **1872** *Punch Staff Papers* 63, I found everybody kind and friendly; and day after day passed in pleasant company (some of the most agreeable I must admit were 'ticketers'). **1924** LAWRENCE & SKINNER *Boy in Bush* 237 A lag is a ticketer: one who's out on lease.

ticket, *n.*[2]

1. A document certifying that the bearer is a member of a trade union.

1899 *Bulletin* (Sydney) 19 Aug. 32/1, I want to see his tickets. . . The 'Rep' opened the book and sorted out a bundle of grimy Union tickets. **1911** *Ibid.* 2 Nov. 14/3 The lady sundowner is an abundant feature of the Riverina river bends. . . They are popular visitors at the sheds and carry A.W.U. tickets to a girl. **1920** *Huon Times* (Franklin) 6 Jan. 3/4 A young woman was deprived of work because she had refused to take out a ticket. **1946** A.J. HOLT *Wheat Farms Vic.* 93 One interviewed said he had 'taken out a ticket' with the Australian Workers' Union. **1957** *Overland* ix. 10 'You've got a ticket, I suppose?' 'Ticket? . . What kind of ticket?' 'What kind of ticket—why, a Union ticket.' **1978** H.C. BAKER *I was Listening* 134 He had been in the building trade all his working life and held 'tickets' as a hoist driver, plant-operator, scaffolder, rigger and everything else covered by the Builders' Labourers' Union. **1981** *Bulletin* (Sydney) 9 June 28/2 Gallagher as much as said 'Go and get stuffed. There's no way you're going to get your tickets back.'

2. A piece of paper impregnated with lysergic acid diethylamide, the hallucinogenic drug LSD: see quot. 1969.

1969 *Pix* (Sydney) 19 Apr. 11 It [*sc.* LSD] is sold usually in absorbent paper in a portion of 120 micrograms known as a ticket. When you take a ticket you are on a trip.

3. In the phr. **to have tickets on** (a person or thing), to hold in high esteem; esp. **to have tickets on oneself,** to be conceited.

[N.Z. **1908** W.H. KOEBEL *Anchorage* 140, I don't know whether she's got any tickets on me.] **1918** B. REYNOLDS *Dawn Asper* 5 There is a current slang phrase . . 'She hasn't many tickets on herself!' Now, as far as Dawn Asper was concerned, this was perfectly true—she had *no* tickets on herself! **1948** K.S. PRICHARD *Golden Miles* 29, I had tickets on her once. But she never had an eye for any man but her husband. **1965** R. STOW *Merry-Go-Round* 132 'You've got tickets on yourself,' he finished, lamely. **1975** *Sun* (Sydney) 8 May 5/5 What I really had was tickets on myself, I suppose. **1981** P. BARTON *Bastards I have Known* 93 She dressed me up fit to kill. . . She'd done a good job and I must confess I had a few tickets on myself as I walked up the stairs.

ticket of leave. [Spec. use of *ticket of leave* a ticket or document giving leave or permission.]

1. A permit entitling a convict to live and work as a private individual within a stipulated area until the expiration or remission of sentence. Also *attrib.*, and *transf.*

1801 *HRA* (1915) 1st Ser. III. 48 All prisoners whose terms of transportation is [*sic*] not expired and are off the stores, or those with settlers, are to attend at the Secretary's office at Sydney . . to receive their tickets of leave. **1804** *Sydney Gaz.* 27 May, Under the indulgence of a Ticket of Leave, they obtained a very comfortable subsistence. **1813** *N.S.W. Pocket Almanack* 53 No application for Tickets of Leave will be attended to till the applicant has served Government, or those Settlers to whom assigned, for 3 years. **1824** E. CURR *Acct. Colony Van Diemen's Land* 39 A '*ticket of leave*' . . is a dispensation from Government labour granted . . for . . supposed meritorious conduct. **1832** *Colonial Times* (Hobart) 16 May, John Fletcher, Maria, is deprived of his Ticket of Leave, in consequence of improper conduct. **1843** *Sydney Morning Herald* 6 Oct. 3/1 He was travelling from Sydney to Goulburn, for which district he had a ticket-of-leave. **1850** *Illustr. Austral. Mag.* (Melbourne) Sept. 171 It is argued that Van Diemen's Land takes every opportunity, covert, or open, of shifting her convictism by means of tickets of leave, to the great Australian continent. **1859** W. FAIRFAX *Handbk. to Australasia* 61 By the regulations now in force . . prisoners . . receive tickets of leave if well conducted, when they have served half of their sentences; these tickets of leave enable them to reside and work for their own advantage in any district in the colony they may select; but places them under the surveillance of the police, to whom they are required to report their residences. **1874** *Illustr. Adelaide Post* 6 Aug. 19/1 Sulky Joe was an old hand and a bolter besides, that is, having obtained a ticket-of-leave from the Sydney authorities, he had taken French leave by crossing the Murray into Victoria, and was thereby liable to be arrested at any time. **1881** *Echoes from Bushland* 32 Moleskins of the 'ticket-of-leave' cut—that is, supernaturally tight at the knees and covering his toes. **1901** *Bulletin* (Sydney) 7 Sept. 14/2 In consideration of good conduct . . he is now on duty as black tracker under a sort of ticket-of-leave. **1921** J.T. SUTCLIFFE *Hist. Trade Unionism Aust.* 26 The English Government began to send out shiploads of ticket-of-leave men, who were still legally convicts and subject to police supervision. **1971** *Bulletin* (Sydney) 20 Feb. 17/2 Delamothe has also introduced a 'ticket-of-leave' system under which long-term prisoners nearing the end of their term are released each day to go to work.

2. One to whom a ticket of leave is granted.

1826 *Monitor* (Sydney) 1 Sept. 123/3 The other witness . . was reminded by the Magistrate, previous to his deposition, '*that he was a ticket-of-leave*'. **1838**

Cornwall Chron. (Launceston) 20 Jan. (Suppl.), Duncan Caton, ticket-of-leave, was fined 5s. for drunkenness. **1841** *Van Diemen's Land Papers Legis. Council* no. 26 62, I have 8 free men, 6 ticket-of-leave, and the rest assigned servants. **1847** *Port Phillip Herald* 15 Apr. 2/6, I did my best for the emancipists and tickets-of-leave.

3. Comb. **ticket of leave class, constable, convict, farmer, holder, lady, man, servant, woman.**

1851 H. MELVILLE *Present State Aust.* 139 The **ticket of leave class** possess about the same privileges in the colony, as the Jews now do in Great Britain. **1852** MRS C. MEREDITH *My Home in Tas.* I. 41 After remaining the allotted number of years in the ticket-of-leave class, the deserving convicts .. received a 'conditional pardon', which permitted them the range of the Australian colonies; and to some was granted a 'free pardon'. **1837** *Rep. Select Committee Transportation* 119 A **ticket-of-leave constable** was sent down to Sydney in charge of the prisoner. **1842** *Geelong Advertiser* 7 Mar. 2/3 A ticket-of-leave constable may, if he take the trouble, virtually become the *Acting* Police Magistrate. **1849** *Belfast Gaz.* (Port Phillip) 18 May 3/3 A man named M'Carrick, lately ticket-of-leave constable in Melbourne, drowned himself in the Barwon, at South Geelong. **1849** *Britannia* (Hobart) 24 May 2/6 From the bad characters we have had sent us under the denomination of exiles and **ticket-of-leave convicts.** **1857** J. ASKEW *Voyage Aust. & N.Z.* 251 There was a young man, a ticket-of-leave convict from Morton Bay [*sic*], who was in a dreadful state. **1862** G.T. LLOYD *Thirty-Three Yrs. Tas. & Vic.* 21 Numbers of **ticket of leave farmers** .. were arrested. **1880** R. ROWE *Roughing It* 8 The neighbouring ticket-of-leave farmers acted as 'fences', in more senses than one, for the thieves. **1835** *Colonist* (Sydney) 2 July 213/2 In the code of Regulations recently published, there is no requisition for the attendance of **ticket-of-leave holders** at public worship on Sabbath. **1842** *Colonial Observer* (Sydney) 19 Oct. 552/4 A number of ticket-of-leave holders, it appears, have got their names placed on the citizen list, much to the annoyance of all good citizens. **1846** *HRA* (1925) 1st Ser. XXV. 190 Free passages to be granted to the Wife and children of Bryan Veech, a Ticket of leave holder. **1848** J.C. BYRNE *Twelve Yrs.' Wanderings* II. 56 The ticket-of-leave-holder is left to shift for himself as he best can, being, however, under surveillance, that he may not leave the island. **1870** *Illustr. Sydney News* 6 Sept. 393 A ticket-of-leave holder .. was so severely injured that he died. **1891** J. FENTON *Bush Life Tas.* (1964) 45 Ticket-of-leave holders were convicts who had served a certain time in the colony, and from their good conduct were permitted to go at large within the boundaries of whatever police district they wished to reside in. **1902** *Bulletin* (Sydney) 15 Feb. 16/3 From Feb. 15 the new 'Regulations for Ticket of Leave Holders' came into force in W.A. **1840** *Tasmanian Weekly Dispatch* (Hobart) 6 Mar. 7/1 Ann Burton, a **ticket-of-leave-lady.** **1807** *Hist. Rec. N.S.W.* (1898) VI. 292 A considerable injury to the colony had crept in: that of **ticket-of-leave men**—men that were taken off the stores, and permitted to work for themselves. **1817** *HRA* (1917) 1st Ser. IX. 517 Ticket of Leave Men are to muster on the Right of the assigned Government Men. **1827** *Monitor* (Sydney) 24 Feb. 324/3 Ticket-of-leave-men, in Macquarie's time, were allowed to go where they liked. **1846** *Moreton Bay Courier* 19 Sept. 3/1 At the Police-office yesterday, Mrs Clarke, wife of a shoemaker in North Brisbane, was charged with having violently assaulted a ticket-of-leave man, named Zernan Herman, a Hottentot. **1854** *Illustr. Sydney News* 11 Feb. 148/1 It was very unbecoming of the defendant, simply a ticket-of-leave man, to wear a moustache and be decked out in the guise in which he was. **1873** A. TROLLOPE *Aust. & N.Z.* II. 129 The ticket-of-leave men are deterred from violence simply by fear. **1891** *Bohemia* (Melbourne) 29 Oct. 13 The U.K. had an unholy dread of the ticket-of-leave man. **1920** W. MCGUFFIN *Austral. Tales of Border* 9 'Ticket of leave men'—the 'Van Diemens' .. flocked over to Victoria when the gold diggings first broke out. **1965** G.H. FEARNSIDE *Golden Ram* 14 Old Matthew, who boasted of being able to trace back through his ancestors without finding a convict or ticket-of-leave man amongst them, was grateful for a direct rail-link with the capital. **1972** W.K. HANCOCK *Discovering Monaro* 43 Ticket-of-leave men .. sometimes received sheep and cattle in lieu of money wages. **1829** H. WIDOWSON *Present State Van Diemen's Land* 53 **Ticket-of-leave servants** .. will ask the same wages as the free man. **1839** *Sydney Standard* 11 Mar. 3/1 Ticket-of-leave servants may be, in many respects, better suited to colonial employers than servants of untainted character. **1820** *Sydney Gaz.* 19 Sept., On Wednesday the 27th Instant, for all the Free Women and Female Convicts, including **Tickets of Leave Women,** on or off the Stores. **1832** *Hill's Life N.S.W.* (Sydney) 30 Nov. 2 Her mistress was a ticket-of-leave woman, and not entitled by the Act to a female servant. **1837** *Cornwall Chron.* (Launceston) 2 Dec. 2 Catherine Gent, a ticket-of-leave woman, rather the worse for liquor. **1851** J. HENDERSON *Excursions & Adventures N.S.W.* 126 A lonely sawyer and his dirty and forbidding wife, or mistress, probably a ticket-of-leave woman or emancipist.

4. Special Comb. **ticket of leave muster,** a compulsory assembling of convicts holding tickets of leave: see MUSTER *n.* 1.

1837 *Cornwall Chron.* (Launceston) 2 Sept. 2 The Town has been *enlivened* this day with another of this [*sic*] disgraceful exhibitions, arising out of the Ticket-of-leave musters. **1845** *Port Phillip Gaz.* 31 Dec. 2 *Ticket of leave Muster*—The annual Muster of Ticket-of-leave holders will take place to-morrow morning, at the Melbourne police office. Ticket-of-leave holders by neglecting this muster will subject themselves to the loss of their indulgences. **1848** *Sydney Morning Herald* 14 Jan. 2/7 The annual ticket-of-leave muster has also taken place, but the gentry holding that indulgence are by no means punctual in reporting themselves to the magistrate. **1850** *Britannia* (Hobart) 12 Dec. 3/2 On a ticket-of-leave muster, ticket-of-leave constables only should attend.

Hence **ticket of leaver,** *ticket of leave holder.*

1852 G.C. MUNDY *Our Antipodes* I. 228 The overseer .. may be a hireling convict-emancipist, expiree, or ticket-of-leaver. **1853** S. SIDNEY *Three Colonies* (ed. 2) 176 Prisoners who had passed through a course of penal discipline in English gaols were landed and almost immediately set at liberty, either as exiles or 'ticket-of-leavers'. **1880** R. ROWE *Roughing It* 20 They came upon the rough homestead of one of the ticket-of-leavers. **1964** D. ROWBOTHAM *Man in Jungle* 98 Underdogs: former felons, ticket-of-leavers, and their women, all haunted by the Government arrow. **1978** SAW & MILLBANK *Back to Back Tango* 35 Six or seven generations earlier his parents had been transported in chains from County Mayo .. and had been among the first ticket-of-leavers to set up stringybark grog-shops in the bush between Sydney Town and Rose Hill.

ticket of occupation. *Hist.* A permit to pasture stock on a specified area of Crown land: see quot. 1826. See also LICENCE 1. Also **ticket of occupancy.**

1820 *HRA* (1921) 3rd Ser. III. 304 Do you consider that the Person, who has stock but has no Land, and only a Ticket of occupation, is as much entitled to supply meat as the person who has less stock but possesses Land? **1820** *AJCP* 110 C.O. 201/122 fo. 208, Is any & what fee paid on granting these tickets of occupancy? There is a fee of 7s. 6d. **1822** J.T. BIGGE *Rep. State Colony N.S.W.* 107 The boundaries of these tracts are described in the tickets of occupation by which they are held, and which are made renewable every year, on payment of a fee to the lieutenant-governor's clerk. **1826** J. ATKINSON *Acct. Agric. & Grazing N.S.W.* 65 This permission, or *ticket of occupation*, as it is termed .. conveys to the stock-owner a right to occupy a tract usually extending two miles in every direction from his stock-yard; always, however, holding himself in readiness to quit at six months notice from the Surveyor-General, should the land be wanted for the purpose of colonization; and also prohibited from cutting down or removing any timber, except what may be required for stock-yards or huts. **1836** *Bent's News* (Hobart) 9 July 2 Every Magistrate in the Island might possess a discretionary power to grant Tickets of Occupation to all industrious and deserving individuals of good character, to take possession of small portions of the whole of the unlocated Crown Lands throughout the Island. **1848** *Britannia* (Hobart) 2 Nov. 3/2 Mr Graves holds a ticket of occupation, in the name of his son, a minor, for the whole of Satellite Island. **1852** J. WEST *Hist. of Tas.* 69 The interior of the country being quiet, tickets of occupation were granted to settlers.

tickey. *Obs.* Also **ticky.** Alteration of TICKPENS.

c **1907** W.C. CHANDLER *Darkest Adelaide* 80 They wear an oily, unctuous expression calculated to deceive the most uncompromising cynic extant, they smoodge for 'tickeys', tea and cake, beer and wide, socks and slippers, and everything they can get for nothing. **1908** C.H.S. MATTHEWS *Parson in Austral. Bush* 272 Most of the boys were puttin' down a quid a time and losin' without a word, but there was one bloke only puttin' down a 'ticky' and losin' like the rest, and he was grousin' and grumblin'.

tickie. [f. *tick(inspector* + -Y.] An official responsible for the eradication of ticks.

1981 K. GARVEY *Rhymes of Ratbag* 51 With five hundred woody weaners We came droving from the east Where the pompous tick inspectors Think there's bugs on every beast. And beside a lonely border gate I saw a tickie sit. **1981** A. WILKINSON *Up Country* 86 Lawrie and 'the tickies' roared with laughter .. watching Hannibull .. try as he always does to jump the dip.

tick-jammer. *Shearing.* Also **tick-jamber.** One who operates a wool press.

1897 *Worker* (Sydney) 11 Sept. 1/1 'Tick-jammer' is the chap who puts the wool into the bales. **1898** *Bulletin* (Sydney) 1 Oct. 14/3 In a shearing shed: The boss is the 'finger' .. the wool-pressers 'tickjambers'. **1905** *Shearer* (Sydney) 4 Feb. 4/2 What do you know of .. 'tick-jammers', or of 'lizards' and 'wire inspectors'?

tickpens. *Austral. pidgin. Obs.* Also **tickpen.** [Alteration of 'sixpence'.] Money; SIXPENCE.

1838 J. BACKHOUSE *Narr. Visit Austral. Colonies* (1843) 539 They [*sc.* the Aborigines] quickly recognized us again and began to beg for 'tickpens', as they call sixpences to buy bread with. **1903** *Bulletin* (Sydney) 15 Oct. 17/1 The blackfellow had (sometimes in consideration of 'tickpen') .. shifted his quarters.

ticky, var. TICKEY.

tidal wave. *Obs.* See quot. 1895.

1878 'IRONBARK' *Southerly Busters* 203 Swore they should crush those sons of lush Who dealt in 'tidal-waves'. **1895** 'H. GOLDSMITH' *Euancondit* 178 The tidal wave .. turned out to be the largest glass of colonial beer that could be purchased for sixpence.

tier. Chiefly *Tas.* and *S.A.* [Spec. use of *tier* a row, rank.] A usu. forested range of hills or mountains, esp. one of a series; a mountain; in S.A. used with reference to the Mount Lofty Ranges and hence also to the forests located there (see esp. quots. 1849, 1882, and 1897). Freq. in *pl.*

1826 Tas. Colonial Secretary's Office Rec. 1/10 214, I was with my Sheep up in the Tier. **1833** J. BACKHOUSE *Extracts from Lett.* (1838) i. 76 Proceeded over 'tiers' of woody hills, which we passed without difficulty, by following the cattle-tracks. **1837** *Cornwall Chron.* (Launceston) 16 Dec. (Suppl.) 5 He had worked as a sawyer in the tiers. **1839** *Southern Austral.* (Adelaide) 17 July 1/5 Some impudent insinuations having been made respecting my having slaughtered a bullock at my house in the Tiers, I beg leave to inform the public, that I have done so. **1846** G.H. HAYDON *Five Yrs. Experience Aust. Felix* 48 The tier of mountains, the loftiest yet discovered in New Holland. **1849** G.B. WILKINSON *Working Man's Handbk. S.A.* 74 The large stringybark tiers or forests supply abundance of straight barrelled trees. **1854** F. TRELOAR Extracts from Diary 5 Mar. 17 My wife and Mr and Mrs Colliver started for Adelaide by mail cart. . . I catted [*sic*] 100 posts from the Teers to fence in a garden. **1861** L.A. MEREDITH *Over Straits* 6 Riding over the 'Tier' as our mountain-range is termed; and taking our departure by sea from Launceston. **1867** 'COLONIST' *Life's Work* 25 Towards the end of winter the *Tiers* (that is what in England would be called forests). **1868** J. BAIRD *Emigrant's Guide Australasia* 27 The Governor's country-house .. ought to have been built on the first tier of the Blue Mountain range. **1882** A. TOLMER *Reminisc.* II. 18 The country is nothing but a dense forest of stringy bark, similar to the 'tiers' near Adelaide. **1890** 'MRS A. MACLEOD' *Austral. Girl* (1894) 275 He was anxious about one of the patients he visited that day—a splitter living among the great tiers of peppermint eucalyptus that lay behind the Messmate Ranges. **1892** E.H. HALLACK *Our Townships, Farms, & Homesteads* 28 Approaching the headland of the Cape the tiers are met with, and there is a change of vegetation to yackas and bracken. **1897** H. HUSSEY *Colonial Life & Christian Experience* 64 There were several places where these marauders could carry on their nefarious practices, and there were suitable hiding-places for them—especially in the 'Tiers' in the Mount Lofty ranges. **1908** *Emu* VII. 143 The tract is bounded on all sides but the west by high tiers, rising abruptly from the upland, which has a general elevation of about 800 to 840 feet. **1924** B. Wannan *Treasury Austral. Frontier Tales* (1961) 35 Arctic storms that whitened the sheep-runs, and turned the jagged 'Tiers' to glittering icebergs. **1978** D. Vawr *Ratbag Mind* 96 Tasmania is probably the only place in the world where ranges are called 'tiers'. **1985** *Mercury* (Hobart) 15 Nov. 1/4 'We are on a crisis footing,' Dr Brown said... 'I think the people of Tasmania are not going to stand back and see bulldozers run to the top of the Western Tiers and chainsaws on the fringes of Federation Peak.'

tiersman. Chiefly *S.A.* One whose occupation is felling timber in the tiers.

1840 *S. Austral. Rec.* (London) 12 Sept. 167 Intemperance .. prevails chiefly among tiersman, splitters, and sawyers. **1846** F. Dutton *S.A. & its Mines* 203 The splitting of posts and rails gives occupation to a number of men, who are called 'tiersmen', from their avocations lying principally in the Bark Tiers or Ranges. **1852** F. Lancelott *Aust. as it Is* II. 115 Splitters, or as they are commonly called tiersmen, reside in the forests of stringy bark. **1891** Mrs J.I. Waterhouse *Bowled Out* 157 The clattering of horses' hoofs could .. be heard by those within, and the tiers-men appeared to think it would be prudent to retire. **1899** J.C. Hawker *Early Experiences S.A.* 67 A numerous party of the 'Tiersmen' were in Adelaide and an attempt would be made to rescue the prisoners. **1961** M. Kiddle *Men of Yesterday* 67 Sawyers and splitters, or tiersmen as they were often called, usually worked in pairs. They built themselves huts in the stringybark forests. **1978** M. Walker *Pioneer Crafts Early Aust.* 37 The other major forest craftsmen, the splitters .. were known in England as 'rivers', in the early days of settlement as 'tiersmen'.

tie-wire. A piece of wire used to fasten two objects, or two parts of an object, together.

1927 J. Pollard *Rose of Bushlands* 141 'Look for holes in the netting and broken tie-wires,' he told her. **1978** D. Stuart *Wedgetail View* 13 Their broken boots held together with cunningly contrived twitches of tie-wire.

tiger, *n.*

1. *Tasmanian tiger*, see Tasmanian *a.* 2 (see esp. quot. 1852). Also **tiger-wolf.**

1805 R. Knopwood *Diary* 18 June (1977) 85 They informed me that on the 2 of May when they were in the wood, they see a large tiger; that the dog they had with them went nearly up to it, and when the tiger see the men .. it went away. **1827** Tas. Colonial Secretary's Office Rec. 1/50 147, My son pack'd the [sheep] skins up one corner of the room with four Tigers skins over them. **1829** R. Mudie *Picture of Aust.* 174 They have vulgarly been called .. hyaenas, tigers, and even devils, according to the fancy of those by whom they have been seen. **1832** J. Henderson *Observations Colonies N.S.W. & Van Diemen's Land* 141 It is called by the settlers the Van Diemen's Land *Tiger*, and proves very destructive to sheep. **1841** *Morning Advertiser* (Hobart) 17 Sept. 2/4 Two pounds for the destruction of a native Dog or Tiger. **1852** J. West *Hist. of Tas.* I. 322 The Tiger or Hyaena of the colonists (*Thylacinus cynocephalus*) .. is of a tawny or brownish yellow color, with numerous black bands arranged transversely along the back, from the shoulders to the tail; hence the erroneous names tiger and hyaena, given to it by the early settlers. **1863** F. Algar *Handbk. to Colony Tas.* 9 Skins of the tiger and native cats are suitable for muffs. **1865** G.F. Angas *Aust.* 76 The *Thylacinus*, or 'tiger-wolf' and the *Sarcophilus*, or 'native devil', are the two largest and most ferocious of all the Australian carnivorous pouched animals. **1880** R. Rowe *Roughing It* 45 Presently he saw two golden-green eyes looking at him half fiercely, half fearfully between the leaves, and off scuttled a striped, stumpy-legged 'tiger'. **1886** M. Clarke *'New Chum' in Aust.* 320 The tiger-wolf and the 'native devil' are to be seen by penetrating still farther into the long mountainous ranges of the interior. **1900** *Advocate* (Burnie) 15 Dec. 2/6 Yesterday another tiger's head was presented at the Police Court for the usual reward... The animal was captured by Mr Thomas Allen, of Guilford. **1968** V. Serventy *Southern Walkabout* 51 Of course like every naturalist who visits Tasmania we kept our eyes open for the 'tiger'. **1978** *Ecos* xvii. 32/1 In 1966 an almost complete mummified carcass of a tiger was found in a cave near Eucla, W.A. Its age has been put at about 4600 years.

2. [Spec. use of *tiger* liveried servant, outdoor servant as a groom, etc.: see OED(S *sb.* 6.] One engaged in menial outdoor employment (see quots. 1853 and 1865); a shearer.

1853 H.B. Jones *Adventures in Aust.* 130 We left .. for the bush, respectively mounted on Admiral, Abelard, and Polka, with a young 'tiger' carrying our saddle bags and 'swag'. **1865** G.S. Lang *Aborigines of Aust.* 37 Nearly all the squatters, at some time or other adopt black boys, keeping them as 'tigers' or horse-breakers. **1897** *Bulletin* (Sydney) 20 Feb. 3/2 And tigers might have *heard* the Boss ere any harm was done—For when he passed it it was a sort of dot and carry one. **1899** *Ibid.* 19 Aug. 32/1 Even in Union sheds some of the shearers—'slow tigers' and Victorian cockies, mostly—objected to 'feedin' travellers'. **1956** F.B. Vickers *First Place to Stranger* 135 Those tigers (he meant the shearers) will make you dance. **1959** C.V. Lawlor *All This Humbug* 23 If you don't mind, Missus, I'd like to be sure I'm not drinking out of the same cup as the new 'Tiger'.

3. [Used elsewhere but recorded earliest in Aust.] One who has an insatiable appetite for work, etc. (see quots.).

1896 *Bulletin* (Sydney) 24 Oct. (Red Page), His father thought a lot of Henry; he used to call him a tiger for work. **1935** W. Hatfield *Black Waterlily* 20 'Tiger for work, aren't you?' he smiled. 'A good fault, of course, if you don't carry it to extremes.' **1953** D. Cusack *Southern Steel* 249 I'll hand it to you. You were always a tiger for work. **1959** D. Hewett *Bobbin Up* 79 'He's a real tiger for his tucker,' Linnie said, smiling wanly through her tears. **1965** J. Wynnum *Jiggin' in Riggin'* 28 'Some people never learn,' moaned Dinger. 'All I can say is you're a tiger for punishment, Stripey.' **1965** E. Lambert *Long White Night* 74, I patted her shoulder. 'Mum, you're a tiger for punishment!'

4. Alcoholic liquor; one who consumes this with enthusiasm.

1901 *Truth* (Sydney) 26 May 1/7 The people of New South Wales spent £4,744,000 on 'tiger' during the past year. **1929** H. Eyre *Hilarities* 8 They noticed that after the three cheers were given at the end Dame Nellie called for a 'Tiger'. Well she glanced at me when she said it. **1955** N. Pulliam *I traveled Lonely Land* 383 *On the tiger*, deliberately getting drunk. **1978** T. Davies *More Austral. Nicknames* 99 *Tiger.* He likes getting tanked.

5. Remote and inaccessible country. Chiefly as **tiger country.**

1945 E. George *Two at Daly Waters* 89 The territory a hundred and sixty miles west of Daly Waters and thence to the Western Australian coast is .. dreaded by aviators and generally called by them 'tiger country'. **1947** E. Hill *Flying Doctor Calling* 83 He was a story only when he crashed .. and he crashed three times in one year, in urgent night-flights in sudden blinding squalls, in jungle swamps, or 'out in the tiger' of unexplored range and unknown river. **1961** G. Farwell *Vanishing Australs.* 20 A Kimberley settler in the undeveloped 'tiger country', away on the wrong side of the rough-shod King Leopold Range. **1979** D. Lockwood *My Old Mates & I* 136 Between him and Arnhem Land proper there was no other white man and few who were black. Tiger country, jump-ups, escarpments, heavily timbered, unknown.

6. Special Comb. **tiger cat,** the large, carnivorous marsupial *Dasyurus maculatus* of e. Aust. incl. Tas., having brown fur with white spots on the body and tail; **flathead,** the marine fish *Platycephalus richardsoni*, predom. brown with darker bands or blotches, of s. N.S.W., e. Vic., and e. Tas., an important commercial species; **prawn,** a large prawn of the genus *Penaeus*, esp. *P. monodon* and *P. semisulcatus* of n. Aust. and elsewhere, and *P. esculentus* of n. Aust.; **snake,** either of the two snakes of the genus *Notechis*, both highly venomous, *N. scutatus* of s.e. mainland Aust. and *N. ater* of s.w. and s. Aust. incl. Tas.; also *attrib.*, and *ellipt.* as **tiger.**

1830 T. Betts *Acct. Colony Van Diemen's Land* 80 Kangaroo and other skins, such as those of the opossum, **tiger cat**, and plattypus .. are exported. **1851** H. Melville *Present State Aust.* 310 There is the tiger-cat; and a smaller species, called the native cat. **1887** *Illustr. Austral. News* (Melbourne) 21 Dec. 218/1 Tiger cats, larger than the Victorian ones, being plentiful, and requiring the inhabitants to shut up their poultry very closely, as one of these animals killed 25 fowls at Currie Harbor in a single evening. **1909** G. Smith *Naturalist in Tas.* 88 The two Tasmanian species known respectively as Native Cat (*Dasyurus viverrimus*) and Tiger Cat (*D. maculatus*) are distributed over the island and are quite commonly met with; they occur also on the Australian mainland. **1923** M. B. Petersen *Jewelled Nights* 40 The sharp penetrating cry of a tiger-cat was heard. **1949** B. O'Reilly *Green Mountains* 23 It was a spotted tiger cat, which had been eating a freshly-killed ring-tailed possum. **1981** J. Burt *Shutterbug in Bush* 213 The animal that interested me most .. was the tiger cat. This narrow-faced marsupial with white spots marking its brown coat and extending down its long waving tail stopped briefly in the beam of my torch before hurrying away. **1918** 'J. Scott' *How, when & where to catch Fish* 22 There is also the 'outside' flathead, which is rarely, if ever, caught inside, and it is generally known as the '**Tiger Flathead**'. **1962** 'N. Culotta' *Gone Fishin'* 87 Those are flathead. They call 'em tiger flathead. **1977** *Commercial Fish Aust.* (Dept. Primary Industry) 14 Tiger flathead occur along the coast of New South Wales, Victoria and Eastern Tasmania... They are a popular table fish. **1986** *Canberra Chron.* 29 Jan. 19/2 The tiger flathead have come in very close and in some instances have been taken only 1.5 km. off-shore. **1893** J.D. Ogilby *Edible Fishes & Crustaceans N.S.W.* 203 (OEDS) This [*sc. Penaeus monodon*] is the '**Tiger Prawn**' of the Sydney fishermen... This species is at times common in the Sydney market, but is irregular in its appearance. **1952** W.J. Dakin *Austral. Seashores* 176 The tiger-prawn is a large northern species that .. has dark vertical bands on its body. It is one of the commercial edible prawns of southern Queensland. **1976** *Ecos* ix. 24/3 The area also harbours large populations of greasyback and tiger prawns. **1986** *Bulletin* (Sydney) 1 Apr. 34/3 The Gulf fleet's capacity to capture what was almost 10,000 tonnes of tiger and banana prawns last season will not diminish. **1859** *Bell's Life in Sydney* 3 Dec. 3/2 Procured a black snake and a **tiger snake.** **1868** *Colonial Monthly* June 294 *The Tiger or Yellow Snake* of the colonies is, with the rest of its genus, peculiar to Australia. **1898** W. Redmond *Shooting Trip* 88 The tiger snake, so called from the yellow bands which mark it, is not so long as either the brown or the black. **1909** G. Smith *Naturalist in Tas.* 89 The two deadly kinds are firstly the Black, Tiger, or Carpet Snake (for it goes under all these names according to whether it is black, banded with yellow, or more irregularly blotched), *Hoplocephalus curtus* [etc.]. **1916** L. Ferris *John Heathlyn of Otway* 146 These fine September days invite the copper-heads and tigers out, as well as the black-fellows. **1936** J.C. Downie *Galloping Hoofs* 131, I could see by the firelight a pair of cruel eyes. It was a seven-foot tiger snake! **1971** *Bulletin* (Sydney) 23 Oct. 20/3 The venom of the tiger snake is stronger than that of the taipan, but the taipan has a more sophisticated biting mechanism. **1979** C. Thiele *River Murray Mary* 29 'What's the matter with him?' 'Snakebite... Probably over by the woodheap. This is the time for tigers.' **1986** *Mercury* (Hobart) 19 Feb. 16/5 Tiger snake antivenene was released in 1930, marking the beginning of a long CSL program which led to the development of antivenenes against all major Australian venomous snakes and spiders.

tiger, *v. intr.* To toil (see Tiger *n.* 2); to 'rough it'. Freq. as *vbl. n.*

1957 Stewart & Keesing *Old Bush Songs* 257 Your delicate constitution Is not equal unto mine, To stand the constant tigering On the banks of the Condamine. **1973** R. Robinson *Drift of Things* 385 He was a well-built young man, and a good worker as I was to find out; but then I had done my share of tigering and I reckoned I could hold my own.

tight little island. England; also *transf.*, Tasmania.

1868 *Sydney Punch* 25 Jan. 70/1 When you get back to the 'tight little island', otherwise known as England, I hope you'll be able to give a satisfactory account of the antipodes. **1880** *Bulletin* (Sydney) 10 July 13/4 He is convinced that the 'tight little island' is a treasure house. **1899** *Austral. Tit-Bits* (Sydney) 18 Feb. 24/2 It is said that the prettiest girls in Australia hail from 'the tight little Island', Tasmania. **1919** J.J. Kennedy *Whale Oil Guards* 31 Tasmania .. had declared war on the Commonwealth, that the Tight Little Island was now a republic.

tike, var. Tyke.

'Tilda. Also **'Tilder.** Shortened form of MATILDA 1.

1899 *Bulletin* (Sydney) 5 Aug. 35/1 I've dossed in such cabooses out-back that old 'Tilda has nearly crawled away from me. **1912** *Ibid.* 8 Aug. 15/1 We dumped our 'Tilders in the bar to take a little rest. **1920** *Ibid.* 30 Sept. 26/4 Whilst out for an airing with 'Tilda I dropped into the Wombat Inn. **1955** N. PULLIAM *I traveled Lonely Land* 379 Whether prospector, miner, shearer, stockman or what have you, the man on the move devised numerous names for the bluey and its contents: swag, knot, tilda [etc.].

tilly, *n.*[1] [f. MA)TIL(DA 1 + -Y.] MATILDA 1.

[N.Z. **1906** *N.Z. Truth* (Wellington) 24 Feb. 5 After 8 hours with Tilly up, our destination loomed up at last.] **1927** *Bulletin* (Sydney) 23 June 19 With my old soot-coated billy an' my leather-twisted Tilly I can laugh at every collared city swell.

tilly, *n.*[2] [f. U)TIL(ITY + -Y.] UTILITY.

1957 R.S. PORTEOUS *Brigalow* 26 They rarely showed fear of us, even when Carson careered round a mob in the rattling tilly. **1960** —— *Cattleman* 223 He's driving down in the tilly and he'll be here between eight and nine. **1977** V. PRIDDLE *Larry & Jack* 14 'What makes you walk out here in this heat, George? What's wrong with the old 'Tilly'?' 'I never drive the old bus when I know I'm going to have a few grogs.'

tillywurti /tɪli'wɜti/. Chiefly *S.A.* Also **tilliwurty.** [Prob. f. a S.A. Aboriginal language.] STRONGFISH.

1924 LORD & SCOTT *Synopsis Vertebrate Animals Tas.* 70 Butter fish (of Tasmania) . . is known . . in South Australia as the Strong Fish or Tillywurti. **1974** T.D. SCOTT et al. *Marine & Freshwater Fishes S.A.* 233 This species [*sc. Psilocranium nigricans*] which is also known as the 'Tillywurti' and 'Nuncla', is most abundant in shallow rocky areas off our coasts. **1980** G. DUTTON *Wedge-Tailed Eagle* 35 We went fish-spearing that night and I brought up a ten pound tilliwurty.

tilting the ring. A game played on horseback: see quot. 1980. Also **tilting in the ring.**

1901 *Advocate* (Burnie) 1 Feb. 2/4 An exhibition of tilting the ring was given when four out of six competitors managed to lift the ring once but could not repeat the performance. **1980** C. BARTLETT *Busy Life* 8 They used to play a game of 'tilting in the ring' on the horses. They had six poles round in a circle of about a hundred yards with short pieces of wire protruding from which was hung a wire ring about 2 inches across. They raced round trying to spear the rings with a long bamboo pole as they went by.

timber. Used *attrib.* in Special Comb. **timber getter,** one employed in felling trees for their wood; so **-getting** *vbl. n.* and *ppl. a.*; **jinker,** see JINKER *n.* 1; **licence,** a permit to fell timber on Crown land.

1849 A. HARRIS *Emigrant Family* (1967) 150 The saw and axe of the **timber-getters.** *Ibid.* 85 Many of them keep timber-getting establishments, and supply Sydney with building stuff. **1876** 'EIGHT YRS.' RESIDENT' *Queen of Colonies* 127 To keep these mills in raw material, principally pine, numerous parties of lumberers, or as they are more frequently called timber-getters, find remunerative occupation. **1896** *Bulletin* (Sydney) 18 Apr. 27/1 All these words were scattered by the pioneer timber-getters, settlers, or squatters, from Sydney to the Gulf of Carpentaria. **1909** H.I. JENSEN *Rising Tide* 97 The supervision of timber getters by Crown rangers has been so slack. **1917** *Bulletin* (Sydney) 4 Jan. 22/4 A few timber-getting families are . . the only dwellers. . . The piners formerly went nearly 100 miles up the Gordon, disregarding its rapids. **1928** A. WRIGHT *Good Recovery* 60, I live out here, a timber-getter, getting props for the mines, cutting sleepers, anything, and I make wages. **1958** H.D. WILLIAMSON *Sunlit Plain* 121 The timber-getter tugged at his shuddering gear lever. **1968** K. DENTON *Walk around my Cluttered Mind* 10 'What the hell's a timber-getter?' 'Fellow who chops down trees. Very hard work.' **1986** *Canberra Times* 3 Feb. 2/2 There are no Aussie 'lumber-jacks' . . they are timbergetters. **1916** J.B. COOPER *Coo-oo-ee!* 1 Heavy **timber-jinkers** groaned, on their way to the Ironbark Saw mill. **1840** *Port Phillip Gaz.* 24 Oct. 3 **Timber licenses** . . £64. **1848** *Britannia* (Hobart) 19 Oct. 2/6 The indiscriminate granting of Timber Licences for the Lands of the Crown. **1886** *N.T. Times Almanac* 75 A timber or bark licence will not authorise the holder to fell, cut, or remove timber, strip bark, on or from any lands surveyed, or under course of survey.

time. *Obs.* [Spec. use of *time* prescribed or allotted term: see OED(S *sb.* 7 d. Used elsewhere of a sentence of imprisonment but recorded earliest in Aust.] The duration of a sentence of penal servitude.

1790 *HRA* (1914) 1st Ser. I. 154 The answer you gave to the convict who came to tell you his time was expired—'Would to God my time was expired, too!'—was not calculated to make him satisfied with his situation. **1791** *Copies & Extracts Lett. Governor Phillip* 5 Nov. (1792) 126 The first settler was a convict, whose time being expired, a hut was built and one acre and an half of ground cleared for him at Parramatta. **1793** W. TENCH *Compl. Acct. Settlement* 147 Not out of his time; but allowed to work here at his leisure hours, as he has declared his intention of settling. **1796** *Instruct. for Constables Country Districts* 13 All those who shall offer themselves to hire without being possessed of Certificates signed by the Acting Commissary of their Time being expired. **1799** D. COLLINS *Acct. Eng. Colony N.S.W.* (1802) II. 142 A numerous body of the Irish convicts, many of whom had but lately arrived, insisted that 'their times were out'.

time-expired, *a. Hist.* [Spec. use of *time-expired* whose term of engagement has expired.]

1. Of an indentured labourer from the Pacific islands (see KANAKA *n.*): whose contracted term has been served.

1894 *Bulletin* (Sydney) 7 July 11/3 Gangs of time-expired N.Q. Kanakas are combining to cut cane by contract. **1897** *Ibid.* 26 June 16/4 A number of kanaka regulations were framed *compelling* time-expired boys to re-engage at the close of one month. **1903** *Ibid.* 3 Sept. 16/2 A time-expired Kanaka . . was sentenced to 14 days. **1970** K. WILLEY *Naked Island* 152 Captain Rogers landed eleven 'time-expired' natives at Wanderer Bay.

2. Of a convict: whose term of sentence has expired.

1929 'OLD STOCKMAN' *Sensational Cattle-Stealing Case* 77 The time-expired men have been let go, and the long-timers have been sent back to Bathurst. **1940** *Bulletin* (Sydney) 10 July 17/1 When I was a nipper many time-expired convicts from Tasmania were to be met with in Victoria.

time on. *Australian National Football.* Time added to the normal playing time at the direction of a field umpire to compensate for an interruption to the game.

1931 J.F. MCHALE et al. *Austral. Game of Football* 52 The field umpire shall instruct the time-keepers to add 'Time on'. **1936** E.C.H. TAYLOR et al. *Our Austral. Game Football* 45 The field umpire shall instruct the time-keepers to add 'Time on' by blowing his whistle and waving his arm to the timekeepers. **1973** B. HOGAN *Follow Game* (rev. ed.) 14 'Time on' or 'added time' is sometimes incorrectly referred to as 'time off'. 'Time on' is added to the time allocated for each quarter and is added during the quarter in which the 'time on' occurs.

time stick. *Obs.* CLAP STICK.

1856 J. BONWICK *W. Buckley* 59 We distinguish . . the tapping of time sticks. **1896** W.A. SQUIRE *Ritual, Myth, & Customs Austral. Aborigines* 14 Amid the sudden hideous uproar of beaten time-sticks, bullroars and maniacal shouts, supposed to prevent the women from noticing the departure.

Timor. [The name of an island off the n.w. coast of Aust., part of which was formerly a Portuguese colony.] Used *attrib.* esp. as **Timor pony,** to designate a small stocky horse of a breed imported from Timor; also *transf.* (see quot. 1916), and *ellipt.*

1828 *Tasmanian* (Hobart) 11 July 3 *Launceston, July 7.* The Timor Ponies were sold here on Saturday last. **1830** *Launceston Advertiser* 4 Jan. 4 We beg to deprecate the highly censurable conduct of persons, who owning those exotic nuisances called 'Timor Ponies', permit such as are entire, to run at large; by which means, several fine Yearling Fillies, depasturing in the suburbs, have become in foal. **1841** *Port Phillip Patriot* 1 July 1/5 A handsome pony gig suitable for a small timor. **1843** *Ibid.* 16 Jan. 3/4 *Found* straying in the neighbourhood of No Good Damper, a bay Timor mare pony. **1859** J.D. MEREWEATHER *Diary Working Clergyman* 65 Mounted on a Timor pony of astonishing strength and endurance. **1896** A. MACKAY *Austral. Agriculturist* (rev. ed.) 173 Whether we are interested in the midget Shetlanders or Timours, or the farm horse hackney or the blood horse, it is now felt that animals reared without the advantages of early handling . . require to be put through the process known as 'breaking'. **1916** J.M. CREED *Recoll. Aust.* 265 Ponies were also brought from the Malay Islands, being called 'Timor', though but a small number came from that island and those not the best. **1934** WARBURTON & ROBERTSON *Buffaloes* 240 Fifty Timor ponies, bright chestnuts and bays with flowing manes and tails, dashed off. **1947** W.E. HARNEY *Brimming Billabongs* (1963) 23 We lads would hunt in packs, for we were frightened of the dingoes and also of the 'jarungs', those little horses which you call Timor ponies. **1978** B. MULLINS *Horses & Ponies* 6 The little Timor pony . . though not a very handsome breed is sure-footed, even-tempered, eager and remarkably hardy.

timothy. [Of unknown origin.] A brothel.

1953 S.J. BAKER *Aust. Speaks* 124 *Timothy*, a brothel. **1967** *Kings Cross Whisper* (Sydney) lxi. 4/3 *Timothies*, houses in areas where if the rent is paid two weeks in a row the law calls round to see where the money came from. **1977** D. STUART *Drought Foal* 151 You've got to start thinking about a shielah [*sic*] in a timothy! **1978** —— *Wedgetail View* 49 I'm like the proverbial moll in the timothy. You've talked me into it. **1982** *N.T. News* (Darwin) 8 May 9/5 There were 17 men in the 'Timothy' when it 'went off'.

tin, *n.*[1]

1. Used *attrib.* in Comb. to designate an artefact made from tin-plate, as **tin billy, pot.**

1881 A.C. GRANT *Bush-Life Qld.* II. 231 Here a party of footmen tramped along with their swags rolled up on their backs, and the **tin-billies** in their hands. **1888** A.P. MARTIN *Oak-Bough & Wattle-Blossom* 128 A quart pot of tea within reach. A tin billy, containing a piece of salt beef, simmered on the fire. **1894** 'H. GOLDSMITH' *Our Alma* 39 In his left hand he carried a small tin billy. **1821** *Austral. Mag.* 91 The corpse having been let down into the grave, they proceeded, as is their custom, to place his spears, waddie, booncooring, net, **tin-pot,** and in short, all his worldly riches, by his side. **1834** G. BENNETT *Wanderings N.S.W.* I. 113 Tea, sugar, a tin-pot, and a blanket, are the requisites for a bush traveller. **1838** *S. Austral. Rec.* (London) 12 Dec, 138/2 Squatters . . galloping about the country with a 'short black pipe' in their mouths, and the 'tin pot of tea'. **1848** H.W. HAYGARTH *Recoll. Bush Life* 21 The tin quart pot, which has been dangling all day at the saddle-bow, boils at the crackling log fire. **1865** J.F. MORTLOCK *Experiences of Convict* 146, I often used to carry, for miles, some [water] in a convenient tin pot with lid and semi-circular wire handle.

2. Special Comb.

a. With reference to the mining of the metal: **tin-digger,** a tin-miner; **-diggings,** a place where tin is mined; **rush,** a sudden influx of miners to a site where deposits of tin have been found; the site itself; **-scratcher,** one who mines surface deposits of tin; any tin-miner; so **tin-scratching** *pres. pple.*; **show,** a tin deposit.

1899 R. SEMON *In Austral. Bush* 269 The **tin-diggers,** on leading their aqueduct from a source near the mountain-top to their camp, had cut a passage into the wood. **1899** *Western Champion* (Barcaldine) 7 Feb. 5/3 Late in the seventies two young men . . struck their camp on one of the Queensland **tin diggings. 1917** W. LEES *Coaching in Aust.* 47 Rough country to the Herberton tin diggings. **1893** *Braidwood Dispatch* 31 May 2/4 The numbers on the **tin rush** are increasing. **1899** *Western Champion* (Barcaldine) 7 Feb. 5/3 After passing through the bark township, now absolutely deserted from a tin rush some miles further down the creek, they made for Tenterfield. **1910** *Bulletin* (Sydney) 28 Apr. 14/1, I met the Baron on a tinfield. . . One night the **tin-scratchers** asked the Baron to sing. **1918** *Ibid.* 28 Feb. 24/1 You can tell a tin-scratcher wherever you meet him. . . He will be condemning the storekeeper for the high price of tucker . . and the low price of tin. **1928** B. CRONIN *Dragonfly* 28 There are about twenty inhabitants, mostly tin-scratchers and abos. **1937** WISBERG & WATERS *Bushman at Large* 98 Try tin-scratching for a while. . . Mount Garnett is a good place to try your luck. **1945** *Bulletin* (Sydney) 31 Jan. 14/3 Jim, the sole tin-scratcher on the creek, seemed pretty surly. **1954** T. Ronan *Vision Splendid* 113 Marty Boylan was tin-scratching at Hard Rock. **1963** I.L. Idriess *Our Living Stone Age* 156 The discovery and rich returns from the Empress, New Anniversary, and Gadfly made all men's mouths water, no matter whether we were gold-diggers, tin-scratchers, or silver-gougers. **1979** R. Edwards *Skills Austral. Bushman* 27 When the old-time north Queensland tin scratcher put down a shallow shaft he would sometimes construct what was known locally as a Jacob's ladder. **1920** B. Cronin *Timber Wolves* 28 A bunch of city mining men . . locate a **tin show.** **1952** C. Simpson *Come away, Pearler* 135 Billy's tin show must have duffered out by now.

b. tin lid, rhyming slang for 'kid', a child.

1905 J. Meredith *Learn to talk Old Jack Lang* (1984) 14 He introduced me to his *cheese and kisses* and four *tin lids*, two *mother's joys* and two *twist and twirls*. **1936** K.L. Smith *Sky Pilot's Last Flight* 29 Well . . 'trouble and strife' means a wife, and a 'tin lid', or 'God forbid' is a kid! **1968** S. Gore *Holy Smoke* 12 He's been a bash artist ever since he was a tin lid. **1981** B. Dickins *Gift of Gab* 2 What are the things of light that made me bawl as a tinlid?

3. *fig.* in the phr. **in the tin,** in a tight spot.

1940 P. Kerry *Cobbers A.I.F.* 13 Then young Johnny swam in slowly, an' 'is face wus one big grin, As he menshuned ter the breakers, 'Whacko, Serg.! Yer in the tin!' **1950** G. Farwell *Surf Music* 40 'Be two months before we're crushing. . . ' 'Plenty o' time.' . . 'All right for you. . . If I don't get some sugar soon, I'll be in the tin.'

tin, *n.*[2] [Fig. use of *tin* money, cash.]

1. Luck.

1918 [see Tinny *a.*]. **1945** *Atebrin Advocate: Mag. 2/4 Austral. Armoured Regiment* 24 Feb. 1 But ask Headquarters batsmen 'How is he for tin?'

2. Special Comb. **tin arse (back, bum),** an usually lucky person; also as **tin-arsed** *a.*

1898 *Bulletin* (Sydney) 4 June (Red Page), And a 'tin-back' is a party Who's remarkable for luck. **1941** S.J. Baker *Pop. Dict. Austral. Slang* 76 *Tin-ar--ed*, unusually lucky. **1955** D. Niland *Shiralee* 158, I come up with a stone worth five hundred quid. . . Tin-bum, they call me. **1959** —— *Gold in Streets* 164 Danno Costello met Chicker Foy: old tinarse, always holding well. **1965** K. McKenney *Hide-Away Man* 41 'You damned tin arse,' he said. 'You must have won a packet?' **1971** R.F. Brissenden *Winter Matins* 25 This tin-arsed character Hasn't been there six months before he starts To fidget, gets to grizzling in his beer About the wife and kids. **1975** L. Ryan *Shearers* 79 Good on yer, Joe. You always were a tin-arse.

tin-dish.

1. *Gold-mining.* A shallow vessel in which alluvial soil, gravel, etc., is washed to separate out gold. Also *attrib.* See Dish *n.* 1.

1851 *Empire* (Sydney) 6 Aug. 19/4 About twenty men at work at the diggings, all gathering a good harvest, though in sad want of utensils, there being only one cradle on the ground, all the operations being conducted with a tin dish. **1851** *Ibid.* 13 Sept. 151/7 The tents are struck—the tribes of cradlemen, and the tin dish helotry, have dispersed to the neighbouring tiers—bark huts look desolate and the gunyas are deserted. **1851** *Goldfield's Reminisc.* (1884) 3, I personally witnessed two men wash out one day before breakfast 10 pounds 4 ounces of pure gold from two tin dishes. **1853** Mossman & Banister *Aust. Visited & Revisited* 57 The residue is taken out and washed in a tin dish. **1859** F. Sinnett *Acct. 'Rush' Port Curtis* 77 The first tin dish I saw washed yielded about a penny-weight and a half. **1864** J. Armour *Diggings, Bush & Melbourne* 5 We have learnt how the diggers wash their bottom stuff, and hurry up for some of our tin dishes. **1911** *Bulletin* (Sydney) 19 Jan. 13/4 So far as I know the Westralian gold rushes of the early '90s never had a lynching; but two fellows at Kurnalpi, back of Hannan's, only missed it by a few minutes. . . At supper . . we heard a rattle of tin dishes, which meant a roll-up. **1943** A. Dawes *Soldier Superb* 59 There was . . more than one perspicacious prospecting Australian soldier, whose pack held a tin dish as well as the usual marshal's baton.

2. Special Comb. **tin-dish fossicking** *vbl. n.*, the process of washing for gold in a tin-dish; gold-mining in a small way (see Fossick *v.* 1); **washing** *vbl. n.*, see quot. 1853 (2).

1852 J. Bonwick *Notes of Gold Digger* 8 A good living may be got . . in a little **tin-dish fossicking** in deserted holes. **1853** Mrs C. Clacy *Lady's Visit to Gold Diggings* 85 A very fair amount of gold-dust may be obtained in either by the new-comer by tin-dish fossicking in deserted holes. *Ibid.* 64 **Tin-dish-washing** is generally done beside a stream. **1853** J. Sherer *Gold Finder Aust.* 281 The operation which procured . . three guineas' worth of gold is technically called tin-dish washing, and is very simply performed. The pan . . is generally about eighteen inches or more across the top, and three or four inches deep, with sloping sides. Into this vessel, the earth—which is technically called 'dirt'—is thrown . . and immersed in water several times.

Hence **tin-disher** *n.*

1882 W. Sowden *N.T. as it Is* 59 Mr Furner—no tin-disher, by the way—dug out a pie-tin full and washed a couple of pennyweights.

tin dog: see Dog *n.*[1] 2 c. and d.

Tingaringy gum /tɪŋgəˈrɪŋgi gʌm/. [f. the name of Mt. *Tingaringy*, n.e. Victoria, where the type specimen was collected in 1887.] The tree *Eucalyptus glaucescens* (fam. Myrtaceae) of scattered mountainous areas in e. Vic. and s.e. N.S.W.

1967 N.A. Wakefield *Naturalist's Diary* 26 There were thickets of the mallee-like Tingaringy Gum. **1981** L. Costermans *Native Trees & Shrubs S.-E. Aust.* 391 Tingaringi [*sic*] Gum (*E[ucalyptus] glaucescens*) was originally described as being a 'mallee' or small tree near the East Gippsland/N.S.W. border, but was later discovered as a tall tree near Mt Erica, almost 200 km. westward.

tin hare.

1. [Chiefly Austral.] An electric hare used in greyhound racing; also allusively, greyhound racing. Also *attrib.*

1927 *Sydney Morning Herald* 12 Sept. 6/3 Mr Beer's remarks re the Sports Ground for tin hare racing are quite illogical. **1932** *NSWPD* 2nd Ser. vol. 131 7906, I have been out to the 'tin hares' myself; it is a poor person's pastime and quite a lot of cash changes hands there. **1943** *Hindquarters Bull.: On Active Service* (New Guinea) 10 Mar. 2 It's not the RSPCA . . or a tin hare outfit. **1969** *N.T. News* (Darwin) 19 Apr. (Focus '69) 109/1 Many top notch tin hare chasers tried at open coursing are 'left for dead' by very ordinary live hare chasers. **1972** W.H. Bracht *Greyhounds* 123 In mechanical lure racing, often referred to as tin-hare racing, dogs chase an electrically or mechanically powered artificial lure on a circular or straight track.

2. *transf.* A nickname for a train, esp. a rail-motor. Also *attrib.* and as *v. intr.*

1938 F. Clune *Free & Easy Land* 190 We tin-hared sixty miles to Ayr on the Burdekin Delta. There is only one class on the tin-hare (rail motor). **1941** K. Tennant *Battlers* 159 The 'Tin Hare's' whistle was heard in the distance. **1965** M. & M. Leyland *Great Ugly River* 9 Now we rocked along in the two-carriage train known to the locals as the 'Tin Hare'. **1983** *Sydney Morning Herald* 8 Oct. 37/1 It is the last of the 'tin-hare' rail-motors.

tinned dog: see Dog *n.*[1] 2 c.

tinny, *n.* [f. *tin* + -Y.] Also **tinnie.**

1. A can of beer; the contents of such a can.

1964 B. Humphries *Nice Night's Entertainment* (1981) 79 So we all shacked up there with stacks of the old *glein*, a few crates of tinnies, a couple of little snow bunnies and no complications. **1976** M. Powell *Down Under* 48 The driver was . . complete with a crate of cold tinnies which we all swooped on as though it was manna from heaven. **1980** M. Grant *Barrier Reef* 194 Got a few tinnies and barbecued some fish and had a good sleep on the beach. **1981** Q. Wild *Honey Wind* 131 He likes to carry a 'cold tinnie' around on the job with him. **1982** *Canberra Chron.* 3 Mar. 5/2 Asked if they would prefer tea or coffee, one member said, 'Nothing, thanks, love. I'll have a tinny.' **1984** *N.T. News* (Darwin) 1 June 38/7 A mess which included literally hundreds of that notorious item which could one day join the Sturt's Desert Rose on the Territory flag—the empty tinnie. **1986** *Canberra Times* 15 Feb. 4/4 A tinnie or two may be good for you.

2. A boat with an aluminium hull.

1979 *Herald* (Melbourne) 7 June 35/1 The aluminium 'tinnie' has long been a major force in the Australian boat market for its low initial cost, durability and ease of use. **1982** *Sun-Herald* (Sydney) 5 Sept. 112/1 Tinnies offer value, fun. Dollar for dollar it's hard to go past the simple aluminium dinghy as a versatile fun boat. **1984** *N.T. News* (Darwin) 28 Sept. 37/8 Wanted, Tinny, 13 ft. 6 in.—15 ft. Prefer with trailer and no engine. Will pay up to $1500 for right boat.

tinny, *a.* [See Tin *n.*[2]] Lucky. Also as **tinny luck,** exceptional luck.

[N.Z. **1918** *Chrons. N.Z. Exped. Force* 7 June 205 Remarks are heard on the 'tinny' luck.] **1919** W.H. Downing *Digger Dialects* 50 *Tinny*, lucky. **1920** —— *To Last Ridge* 47 McAlister had tinny luck. Got a piece on the leg and went off in a stretcher as happy as Larry. **1938** *Kalgoorlie Digger* Oct. 5 Frank can hit the balls harder than any man . . and isn't he 'Tinny'. **1944** J.F. Dettman *Here was Glory* 25 P'raps yer'd like ter 'ear th' story uv 'is sudden reformation From a cheap 'Ack-Willie' artist an' a tinny 'Two-up' king. **1959** D. Niland *Gold in Streets* 165 And there was Chicker; lucky cow; collecting from Tommy and Tipslinger. Cleaning Tommy out. Talk about tinny. **1981** *Sun-Herald* (Sydney) 27 Sept. 9/3, I developed a technique and skills in gambling and I reckon I could still win a lot of money. As it is, I'm what you might call tinny. The only time I ever pulled the handle of a poker machine after I was converted, I won a jackpot.

tip, *n.*[1] *Obs.* [Deteriorated use of *tip* a gratuity.] A bribe; also, without article, bribery.

1812 J.H. Vaux *Mem.* (1819) II. 219 *Tip*, to give, pay, or bribe. To *take the tip*, is to receive a bribe in any shape; and they say of a person who is known to be corruptible, that he will *stand the tip*. *The tip* is a term frequently used to signify the money concerned in any dealings or contract existing between parties; synonymous with *the dues*. **1828** *Tasmanian* (Hobart) 25 Jan. 3 There is a long investigation going on concerning the *tip* (a bribe) said to have been received by some of the constables, at the late Sandy Bay races. *Ibid.* 29 Aug. 3 It came out, also, in evidence on these trials, that *tip* had been taken by certain parties, from several licensed victuallers. **1832** *Currency Lad* (Sydney) 6 Oct. 3 The whole fraternity of constables (save the mark!) as lovers of *tip*, purchaseable at any time for a pot of beer, or a king's picture. **1835** *True Colonist* (Hobart) 27 Mar. 3/3 The Police can have but little to live upon unless they take 'tip'. **1843** *Melbourne Times* 25 Mar. 4/4 He drew from his pocket a one pound note and flashing it in the eyes of constable Heffeman wished to know if he would take 'tip'. **1847** *Port Phillip Herald* 4 Feb. (Suppl.), *The Police Corps.* A complaint of taking what is commonly denominated 'tip', has been recently preferred against two members of this force. **1855** *Illustr. Sydney News* 20 Jan. 31/1 The Commissioners returned from Bendigo and resumed their inquiry into allegations of 'tip' and extortion against several officials of this district.

Tip, *n.*[2] *Obs.* Also **Tipp.** [Abbrev. of *Tipperary*, the name of a county in Eire.] An Irishman, esp. a gold-miner.

1862 C.R. Thatcher *Canterbury Songster* 19 To rescue him this rowdie Tip unto his mates he hollered. **1880** 'Erro' *Squattermania* 174 'I was all through the Tipperary rows.' 'What were they about?' asked Sutton. 'Why, the Tips, you see, got so fast and rowdy, that they took to mobbing claims and bullying the rightful owners clean out of their ground.' **1888** G.O. Preshaw *Banking under Difficulties* 59, I do not for one moment refer to those curses of a goldfield, the low Irish 'Tips'. **1892** 'R. Boldrewood' *Nevermore* III. 105, I paid you honest for Number One South, which I stand a good show of losin' if you don't come out and prove your pegs. The Tips are trying the bluff game, and if you don't stand by me I'll be regular jumped and run off the field.

tip, *v.*[1] *Obs.* [f. Tip *n.*[1]] *trans.* To bribe.

1845 S. Sidney *Three Colonies* (1853) 162 On his road, with his sheep, looking for a new station, he meets Timmins, an old 'lag', who, by 'tipping' the Clerks at the Crown Land Office, has had his run kept out of the government sales. **1847** A. Harris *Settlers & Convicts*

(1953) 49 All these except old Dennis were at this very time prisoners of the Crown, but got out of barracks by 'tipping' (bribing) the watchman and constables.

tip, *v.*[2] [Transf. use of *tip* to give a piece of information.] *trans.* To guess.

1955 R. LAWLER *Summer of Seventeenth Doll* (1965) 51 'Until last Saturday I didn't know you had any—de facto wives.' .. 'But I haven't! Ooh, what you mean is my kids? .. I tipped it'd be like that. Yes, kids I got all right. In three states.' **1977** R. BEILBY *Gunner* 301, I tipped who ya was.

tip-dray. A dray so constructed as to tilt in order to release its load: see DRAY 1.

1899 *North-Western Advocate* (Devonport) 30 June 2/4 We have been shown a very useful tip-dray... The wheels and undercarriage are of Victorian wood and the body of Tasmanian timber. **1901** H. LAWSON *Joe Wilson & his Mates* 79 I'd sold the two tip-drays that I used for tank-sinking and dam-making. **1961** *Meanjin* 357 The grey stallion carried Gourlay, on the floor of the tip-dray, uphill in the morning, curvetting with kittenish grace, as though the tip-dray were a chariot. **1962** E. LANE *Mad as Rabbits* 214 He had bought himself a horse and a tip-dray and settled down to work very soberly for several years for the Council, road-making.

Tipp, var. TIP *n.*[2]

tip-slinger. A racecourse tipster (see also quot. 1962).

1915 A. WRIGHT *Sport from Hollowlog Flat* 16 Tip-slinger Grif came and whispered, 'You're on a cert., she's the only trier.' **1919** V. MARSHALL *World of Living Dead* 69 The truly light-fingered gentry, the racecourse urger (tip slinger), the magsman [etc.] .. never hesitate to express their contempt for the more roughly inclined of the profession. **1934** *Bulletin* (Sydney) 15 Aug. 49/1 By their conversation most of them were tipslingers or urgers. **1944** *Full-Times Gaz.* (Rockhampton) 24 Feb. 1 Being the Official organ of the Tale tellers, tip slingers and time killers. **1962** J.T. LANG *Great Bust* 335 On the air the tip-slingers like Rufe Naylor sold their wares.

tissue. Chiefly *Tas.* A cigarette paper. Also **tisher.**

[N.Z. **1952** *Here & Now* Jan. 32/2 See if the parole-jumper in Number 8 has got any tissues left.] **1966** H. PORTER *Paper Chase* 202 In Hobart and Tasmania, the collecting of local idiosyncracies of vocabulary and custom .. suddenly seems the most trivial of things to do. I note that tissue is used for cigarette-paper. **1981** D. STUART *I think I'll Live* 122 Have you noticed that the Tasmanians to a man always refer to a cigarette paper as a 'tisher'?

tit. [Transf. use of *tit* a small bird of the fam. Paridae.] A small bird, esp. a THORNBILL or *scrub wren* (see SCRUB *n.* 5).

1901 *Emu* I. 60 The familiar Tits (*Acanthiza chrysorrhoa*) .. often build their bulky nests in conspicuous places. **1916** S.A. WHITE *In Far Northwest* 153, I was fortunate in discovering quite a new tit, which I have described as the Everard Range tit (*Acanthiza marianae*). **1948** P.J. HURLEY *Red Cedar* 33 Tits, pardalotes and other small fry often used these ironbarks as a hiding place.

ti-tree, var. TEA-TREE.

tizzy, *a.* [Prob. f. *tizzy* a state of excitement.] Gaudy; showy.

1953 S.J. BAKER *Aust. Speaks* 103 *Tizzy*, an adjective applied to ostentatious or 'flashy' dressing, or dressing with bad taste. **1969** G. JOHNSTON *Clean Straw for Nothing* (1971) 20, I was also going to say I send you lots of presents. Nice things, too. Nothing tizzy.

tizzy, *v.* [f. prec.] *trans.* To titivate (a person); also *transf.* (see quot. 1977). Usu. with **up** and freq. as *ppl. a.*

1960 K. SMITH *Word from Children* 72 According to children mothers get all 'tizzied up' before they go out. **1968** S. GORE *Holy Smoke* 28 While you're gettin' tizzied up I'll word yer Mum to slaughter a fatted calf. **1977** T.A.G. HUNGERFORD *Wong Chu* 86 A lot of places had been tizzied up. **1986** *Canberra Times* 3 Apr. 2/2 Basically, a mob of tizzied-up birds strutting round the place without contributing much to the common good isn't really what battling out a living from the Great Australian Loneliness is about, eh?

tjuringa, var. CHURINGA.

toa /ˈtoʊə/. [Prob. a. Diyari *tuwa.*] An Aboriginal direction-marker: see quot. 1981.

1927 *Bulletin* (Sydney) 27 Oct. 27/2 *Toas* or direction-finders are in use among the abos. in the Lake Eyre district, Centralia. **1977** P.J. UCKO *Form in Indigenous Art* 77 Toas are direction signs which signify particular localities and they were used by the Duri and neighbouring tribes of the Lake Eyre region of Central Australia. **1981** J. MULVANEY et al. *Aboriginal Aust.* 11 Very interesting examples of native constructions .. are the little-known Aboriginal directional markers from the Lake Eyre region known as 'toas'. Made of an amalgam of gypsum, wood and feathers, they were stuck in the ground on departure from a camp to communicate the destination of a departing group to anyone able to read them. **1986** *Bulletin* (Sydney) 25 Mar. 99/2 The toas are small Aboriginal sculptures made of wood, sometimes incorporating bits of gypsum, feathers, bones, human hair, woven fibres, grass, twigs, lizards' feet... They are thought to have acted as sign posts or message sticks around Lake Eyre and the Simpson Desert.

toad-fish. [Spec. use of *toad-fish* any of several fish of toad-like appearance.] Any of many self-inflating, usu. poisonous and spiny, marine and estuarine fish of the fam. Tetraodontidae.

1801 *HRA* (1915) 1st Ser. III. 171 One he said was killed by natives, the other eat [*sic*] a toad fish. **1825** *Australasian Pocket Almanack* 111 John Buff, a crown servant, poisoned by eating the toad-fish, dying in 20 minutes after he partook of the noxious animal, at Parramatta. **1836** BACKHOUSE & TYLOR *Life & Labours G.W. Walker* (1862) 12 Apr. 240 Several Toad-fish, a spotted flabby fish, short and thick in proportion to its length, which might be four to six inches. **1861** 'OLD BUSHMAN' *Bush Wanderings* 254 There are several nasty-looking fish in these bays—the poisonous toad-fish, the prickly porcupine-fish, and others. **1877** *Proc. Linnean Soc. N.S.W.* II. 248 *Tetrodon staigeri* .. comes from the Brisbane River, where Mr Staiger says it is called *Toad Fish.* **1909** H. BUTTON *Flotsam & Jetsam* 71 We caught a number of toadfish (*Apistes marmoratus*), a handsome spotted but poisonous fish. **1963** *N. Austral. Monthly* Nov. 26 The green toadfish is just about the greatest pest there is to line fishermen in saltwater creeks in the North in Winter. **1984** B. DIXON *Searching for Aboriginal Lang.* 133 Most fishes are *bayi*, but the stone-fish and the toad-fish—which can inflict injury on a person—are specially marked by being *balan.*

toadie, var. TOADY.

toado. [f. TOAD(-FISH + -O.] TOAD-FISH.

1906 D.G. STEAD *Fishes of Aust.* 225 The Toado (*Tetrodon hamiltoni*) .. is sometimes caught on the small-boy's line with a 'fly-hook'. **1911** A. MACK *Bush Days* 108 The toadfish, or 'toad-oes' of our childhood; quaint little chaps they are with their speckled brown and white skins, and stumpy tails. **1930** C.M. YONGE *Yr. on Great Barrier Reef* 88 The most remarkable is the 'toado' or balloon fish. **1965** *Austral. Encycl.* VIII. 512 In Australia more than 30 species of toadoes are found. Generally, they are less than 8 inches long and pear-shaped. **1976** E. WORRELL *Things that Sting* 52 Toadfish, often called Toadoes, are easily recognised. They have a thickset body without scales, a broad head with wide beak-like chopping teeth and a fan-tail.

toadskin. *Obs.* [Also U.S. for a green banknote.] FROGSKIN.

1924 A.B. PATERSON *Old Bush Songs* (ed 4) 65 With a toadskin in my pocket I borrowed from a friend, Oh, isn't it nice and cosy to be campin' in the bend.

toady. Also **toadie.** [f. TOAD(-FISH + -Y.] TOAD-FISH. Also **toady-fish.**

1935 DAVISON & NICHOLLS *Blue Coast Caravan* 281 A toady-fish .. who, on being approached, blew himself up into the semblance of a football covered with spines. **1939** *Bulletin* (Sydney) 31 May 21/4 Wouldn't doubt that a very small toadie (we call them blowfish in W.A.) will stiffen the poultry-yard. **1945** *Ibid.* 24 Jan. 13/4 These toadies, skinned, promised a fine feast, but two deaths resulted.

to and from. Rhyming slang for POM.

1946 R.D. RIVETT *Behind Bamboo* 399 *To-and-from*, a Pommy, i.e. Englishman. **1963** R. MCGREGOR-HASTIE *Compleat Migrant* 16 'You a to and from?' 'I'm English,' you say, guessing rightly that a to and from is Aussia [*sic*] rhyming slang for Pom. **1982** *Weekend Austral. Mag.* (Sydney) 6 Mar. 8/8 As a 'To-and-From', one of the things that baffled me in this Australian leisure lifestyle when I first arrived here many years ago was the esky routine.

toby. [Transf. use of *Toby*, familiar form of the name *Tobias.*]

1. *Shearing.* See quot. 1964.

1957 STEWART & KEESING *Old Bush Songs* 273 I've been shearing on the Goulburn side and down at Douglas Park, Where every day 'twas 'Wool away!' and Toby did his work. **1964** H.P. TRITTON *Time means Tucker* (rev. ed.) 41 Raddle was a stick of blue or yellow ochre, also called 'Toby' which was used to mark badly shorn sheep. **1965** J.S. GUNN *Terminol. Shearing Industry* ii. 33 *Toby*, another name for the raddle stick.

2. A 'willing horse'.

1941 S.J. BAKER *Pop. Dict. Austral. Slang* 77 *Toby*, a man silly of mind and clumsy of hand, but willing to do whatever asked. **1944** A. MARSHALL *These are my People* 155 I'm not much chop on pies, but I'm a toby on puddin's.

toe. Strength; speed.

1889 *Bulletin* (Sydney) 21 Dec. 15/3 But the goat made it clear each time he drew near That he had what the racing men call 'too much toe' for him. **1891** *Truth* (Sydney) 1 Feb. 6/2 Bushman hadn't the toe. **1900** *Bulletin* (Sydney) 8 Sept. 16/2 Johnnie was .. fired with the ambition to make his mark as a ped. He was convinced that he possessed more than ordinary 'toe'. **1922** C. DREW *Rogues & Ruses* 163 He has got two horses in the Handicap, and is bemoanin' his fate that both can't win. They're both got plenty of toe. **1958** *R.A.N. News* (Sydney) 5 Sept. 10 The bomb had plenty of toe. **1969** *Sun* (Melbourne) 12 July 58/1 The North half-forward line .. has a ton of toe and could give Richmond's novice half-back line a torrid afternoon. **1983** *Sun-Herald* (Sydney) 23 Oct. 73/4 In Lawson and Hogg we have two penetrating fast bowlers who have enough 'toe' to keep any batsman honest.

toe-rag. *Obs.* [Used elsewhere but recorded earliest in Aust.: see OEDS and EDD.]

1. A strip of cloth wrapped round the foot and worn inside a boot, in place of a sock; see also PRINCE ALBERTS. Also *attrib.* as an emblem of poverty or disreputableness.

1865 J.F. MORTLOCK *Experiences of Convict* 80 Stockings being unknown, some luxurious men wrapped round their feet a piece of old shirting, called, in language more expressive than elegant, a 'toe-rag'. **1888** *Centennial Mag.* (Sydney) 232 One of his feet had been bleeding, I could see from his 'toe-rag', which stuck out on one side. **1898** *Truth* (Sydney) 13 Feb. 3/5 In the early days of the colonies, squatters did not usually keep socks in their stores... Many wore boots only, and those who wished for other protection, tore off square pieces of old shirts and wrapped them round their feet. These were called 'toe-rags'... A common expression with the shearers is, 'Oh, you belong to the toe-rag mob', meaning .. too poor, or mean, to buy socks. **1901** *Ibid.* 18 Aug. 5/3 After a few years of 'battling' in the Chow's baneful brothel, they were cast adrift to swell the ranks of the toe-rag crowd. **1944** M.J. O'REILLY *Bowyangs & Boomerangs* 45 The sensible swaggie, if ever there were such an animal, did not bother about socks. 'Toe rags' .. were more suitable. **1966** S.J. BAKER *Austral. Lang.* (ed. 2) 105 *Toe-rags*, otherwise known as *Prince Alberts* or *Prince Alfreds*, were worn by tramps of low degree.

2. *transf.* A one-pound note.

1895 *Bulletin* (Sydney) 16 Feb. 21/2 'Toe-rag'—larrikinese for £1-note, from the odour thereof. **1945** S.J. BAKER *Austral. Lang.* 109 *£1* .. toe-rag.

toe-ragger. [f. TOE-RAG 1.]

1. A tramp; a 'down-and-out'.

1891 *Truth* (Sydney) 1 Feb. 6/4 They receive a consideration to ring in the name of every toe-ragger who may degrade the assembly when a boxing match is made. **1898** *Ibid.* 13 Feb. 3/5, I .. have never heard the word 'toe-ragger'. My son .. has heard it this last few years. . . A new word, and no doubt derived from toe-rag. **1941** S.J. BAKER *Pop. Dict. Austral. Slang* 77 *Toe-ragger*. . a person of no position, wealth or attainments. **1955** N. PULLIAM *I traveled Lonely Land* 47 A billabong where the swagman and the toe-ragger sat and boiled their billies. **1966** G.W. TURNER *Eng. Lang. Aust. & N.Z.* 144 The battler seems to have been the poorest itinerant. The toeragger was not much wealthier than the battler.

2. *transf.* One who is sentenced to a short term of imprisonment.

1918 J. MARSHALL *Jail from Within* 45 Christ Orlmighty, some o' you toeraggers (short-timers) take the cake. **1962** D. MCLEAN *World turned upside Down* 114 He's only a 'toe-ragger', that's what they call a short-term prisoner.

toey, *a.*

1. Restive, touchy; ill-at-ease.

1930 *Bulletin* (Sydney) 8 Oct. 35/2 Wise Force was 'toey' before the race, and behaved in alarming fashion on his way to and at the post. **1959** *Overland* xiv. 20 The other umpire a bit toey out there at square leg. **1967** J. WYNNUM *I'm Jack, all Right* 25 'How've you two been making out? All right?' 'Getting a bit toey,' Ginger told him. **1972** A. MACDONALD *Ukulele Player* 204 The lady was much set aback by this attitude. Turning very toey, she said, 'Very well, Mr Kreisler. But as this will be a purely commercial arrangement, I shall not expect you to meet or mingle with my guests. **1982** D. HARRIS *Drovers of Outback* 58, I had an old night horse which seemed to sense trouble and if the cattle were quiet he would get very 'toey'!

2. Fast.

1977 B. SCOTT *My Uncle Arch* 35 They had a getaway that Roger Bannister would have envied. Real toey, Arch reckoned.

togs, *pl.* A swimming costume. Also **bathing togs, swimming togs.**

1918 *Kia Ora Coo-ee* Apr. 7/1 Some of the Queenslanders are revelling in the opportunity of getting out in this hot weather in their bathing togs! **1930** V. PALMER *Passage* (1957) 72 'You nip in and get my togs.' He was more at ease in his bathing-trunks than in his double-breasted serge suit. **1944** *Aust.: Nat. Jrnl.* Apr. 65 She struts by swimming togs and towel across one arm. **1959** M. RAYMOND *Smiley roams Road* 48 'Come on boys, get your togs.' 'Now we'll see if we can shoot the breakers,' remarked Fred Stephens to Smiley and Joey. **1969** B. GARLAND *Pitt Street Prospector* 111 Get yer flamin' swimmin' togs on. **1978** G. LANGFORD *Death of James Dean* 21 Go back and get your togs. **1982** N. KEESING *Lily on Dustbin* 105 Once when Australians went to the beach for a 'dip' they carried . . togs.

Tojo. [The name of Hideki *Tojo* (1884–1948), Japanese army officer who became chief of staff and military dictator during the war of 1939–45.] A member of the Japanese armed forces; these forces collectively.

1943 J. BINNING *Target Area* 22 The monotone of the bombers is easing. Tojo is on his way out and now it is safe to get up. **1944** *Barging About: Organ 43 Austral. Landing Craft Co.* Nov. 1 You can call it idle boasting; But we'll have the Tojos toasting. **1985** N. MEDCALF *Rifleman* 113 You should have seen those Tojos run!

Hence **Tojo-land** *n.*, Japan; **Tojo-lander** *n.*, a Japanese person.

1943 *Camp Capers: Official Organ 157 Austral. Gen. Transport Co.* Aug. 12 If 'e ever gets to **Tojo-land** the Japs will die of fright. **1942** *Plane Speaking from R.A.A.F.* 8 We'd rather be in Tokio drinking Jappo beer, Throwing all the empties at some **Tojo-lander's** rear.

tom, *n.*[1] *Mining.*

1. [U.S.: see Mathews.] Abbrev. of LONG TOM 1.

1852 A. MACKAY *Great Gold Field* (1853) 5, I fell in with a mulatto . . who was working a small 'tom' by himself, with which he had cleared half an ounce up to twelve o'clock that morning. **1856** G. WILLMER *Draper in Aust.* 78 Without delay, I procured one of the long troughs known in digging parlance as a 'tom'. **1877** G. WALCH *Hash* 61 Two of my mates had gone off down the creek to fix the toms and the sluice boxes for the next washing up. **1890** 'R. BOLDREWOOD' *Miner's Right* 129 We separated it from the attendant clay and gravel by the old fashioned expedient of a 'tom'. **1900** *Bulletin* (Sydney) 9 June 31/2 The German . . was panning off the sand from his slides in the 'tom'. **1980** M. TEMPLE *Goers & Shicers*, It was put in a bucket and washed on a 'tom'—a sloping table about 2 feet wide with side and cross grooves to catch the gold.

2. [Also U.S.] A prop, as of timber: see quot. 1932.

1932 I.L. IDRIESS *Prospecting for Gold* 237 An odd 'tom' is occasionally put in underground when you strike an exceptionally large patch of opal and have to chamber out a huge space in the opal dirt. . . A tom is a prop, you jam one end under the roof with the other end resting on the floor. **1948** K.S. PRICHARD *Golden Miles* 93 Tom did not like the look of that greasy graphite on the west wall. He pointed it out to the shift boss. 'Christ, I'll get a couple of 'toms' for her, Ted,' Abel exclaimed affably. 'Now y're showin' values she's worth shorin' up.' **1977** J. DOUGHTY *Gold in Blood* 90, I wedged in the short 'toms' of timber to support the 'back' (roof) while I lay on my side, squeezed under the overhang.

tom, *n.*[2] Abbrev. of 'tom-tart' (see quot. 1882), a jocular formation on TART.

[**1882** *Sydney Slang Dict.* 8 *Tom-tart*, Sydney phrase for a girl or sweetheart. N.Z. **1906** *N.Z. Truth* (Wellington) 31 Mar. 6 For he tells you, not being prudy, That our love's a 'Tom' or 'tart', Or a 'clinah' or a 'Judy'.] **c 1907** W.C. CHANDLER *Darkest Adelaide* 9 If his 'tom' had even the inkling of an idea that he was not true to her in word and deed there would be merry L to pay. **1914** E. DYSON *Spats' Fact'ry* 115 Cake walkin' on the King's 'ighway with a flash tom on each fin. **1915** C.J. DENNIS *Songs of Sentimental Bloke* 15 Bli' me, look at me! Jist take a squiz at this, an' tell me can Some square an' honist tom take this to be 'Er own true man? **1933** N. LINDSAY *Saturdee* 181 Who's yer tom? She must be yer sweetheart. Why don't yer up an' kiss her? **1942** M.L. MACPHERSON *I heard Anzacs Singing* 33 In Australian . . a girl is a cliner or a tom. **1951** D. STIVENS *Jimmy Brocket* 102 'You did, Darling', one of the little social toms said. She was a nuggety little sheila.

tom, *v.*[1] *Obs.* [U.S.: see Mathews.] *trans.* To wash (auriferous material), using a long tom.

1855 W. HOWITT *Land, Labor & Gold* II. 261 When we went up this gully we found the whole of it most carefully dug out and tommed. **1862** J.A. PATTERSON *Gold Fields Vic.* 12 Wash-dirt had to be carted across the plain to the banks of the river, to be there 'cradled' or 'tommed'.

Hence **tommer** *n.*, one who washes auriferous material using a long tom.

1855 W. HOWITT *Land, Labor & Gold* II. 193 It will not pay the cradler or the tommer to put through much rough earth.

tom, *v.*[2] [Of unknown origin.] *trans.* To bounce: see quot. 1976. Also *intr.*

1947 *Coast to Coast 1946* 182 The tractor stormed ahead, filling the bush with its clamour. 'See how the log toms along,' said Blue watching it. **1976** C.D. MILLS *Hobble Chains & Greenhide* 29 They were yoked four abreast, and the outside string drew from the outside hub of the front wheel to enable them to swing, or 'tom' the front wheels away from an obstruction.

tom, *v.*[3] [f. TOM *n.*[1] 2.] *trans.* With **up:** to shore.

1979 J. WILLIAMS *White River* 57 We'd sailed together once on an Iron boat. . . Heavy weather in the Bight had set her rolling and locomotive wheels that hadn't been properly tommed up started chasing us around the hold.

tomahawk, *n.* Also **tommyhawk.** [Transf. use of *tomahawk* the axe of the North American Indian.] A hatchet; the stone hatchet of the Aborigines (see quots. 1840 and 1870).

1808 *Sydney Gaz.* 18 Sept., They never burden themselves with any other luggage than a spear or two, and a short club, unless they have been fortunate enough to get possession of a tomahawk. **1833** W.H. BRETON *Excursions* 239 The tomahawks . . that they use are very clumsy. **1840** A. RUSSELL *Tour through Austral. Colonies* 259 The principal tool used is the tomahawk, a piece of flint ground into a wedge shape, having a twig twisted or tied round the head, leaving a handle some inches long, according to the weight or size of the stone or flint required; the whole being much in shape to a hammer. **1845** *Sentinel* (Sydney) 5 Feb. 3/2 The grave is filled up by hands and tomahawk, not too hastily; they occasionally stop to trample it down. **1854** H.B. STONEY *Yr. in Tas.* 190 Obtained the necessary supplies of bacon and biscuit, tea and sugar, tomahawks, and other indispensables for a bush expedition. **1863** J. MORRILL *Sketch of Residence* 23 Their tomahawks (*bullgoo*) are made of stone, and latterly they have got a good deal of iron (*bingulburra*) among them. **1870** E.B. KENNEDY *Four Yrs. in Qld.* 78 The Aboriginals . . cut out 'possums from a tree or sugar bag (wild honey) by means of a tomahawk of green stone; the handle is formed of a vine, and fixed in its place with gum. **1890** *Braidwood Dispatch* 17 May 2/4 The mainland blacks made a murderous attack at Thursday Island on Wednesday night on Pitt's Beche-de-mere station. . . Pitt went aboard the lugger Annie, lying at anchor and found the cabin besmeared with blood, and tomahawk cuts on the hatch and scuttle. **1914** *Bulletin* (Sydney) 17 Sept. 22/2 With a tommy-hawk, or, rather, a half-handled 'Douglas', the gum is chipped off. **1928** R. ROSS *Reminisc.* 16 July in *S. Australiana* (1973) Sept. 49, I saw 1 blackfellow leave the camp with tommy hawk, spear and so forth. **1935** G. MCIVER *Drover's Odyssey* 50 These newcomers brought the boomerang, the ground tomahawk with a wooden handle. **1956** *Hardware Yr. Bk.* A56 The same dependable steel is also forged into Hytest three-quarter Axes and Tomahawks. **1966** *Hoofs & Horns* Feb. 34 They caught the horses with balls of mud, led them over to the store verandah, got out tomahawks and blocks of wood to chop the mud off, and, in effect to bang-tail them. **1986** *Canberra Times* 8 Apr. 1/3 The other man . . is to be extradited, on bail, to Queensland to face a charge of attempting to murder, by the use of a tomahawk, a 74-year-old man.

tomahawk, *v. Shearing.* Also **tommyhawk.** [f. prec.] *trans.* To shear (a sheep) roughly (see esp. quots. 1864 and 1895); to cut (a sheep) during shearing. Also *absol.*, and as *vbl. n.* and *ppl. a.*

1859 H. KINGSLEY *Recoll. Geoffry Hamlyn* II. 25 The poor sheep got fearfully 'tomahawked' by the new hands. **1864** J. ARMOUR *Diggings, Bush & Melbourne* 17 We had several who shore sixty, a few eighty, and one or two a hundred, but the latter were often brought to task for 'tomahawking', or leaving ridge-and-furrow shear-marks. **1879** 'AUSTRALIAN' *Adventures Qld.* 112 Most of them, though very good shearers if they liked, were in the habit of 'tomahawking'—hacking both wool and skin off the wretched animals in junks, and leaving as much wool on them in great ridges as would have paid for the shearing. **1890** *Bulletin* (Sydney) 20 Sept. 11/4 The 'ringer' that shore a hundred as they never were shorn before, And the novice, who toiling bravely, had 'tommy-hawked' half a score. **1895** J. KIRBY *Old Times in Bush* 147 The shearer did not care how much wool he left on the sheep, all his look out was, 'the count'. . . He would not scruple to leave half an inch long ridges of wool on the sheep, so long as he could get paid for the shearing. This kind of shearing was called 'Tom-a-hawking'. **1905** *Shearer* (Sydney) 23 Dec. 7/5, I once had the doubtful pleasure, many years ago, of working in a woolshed along with a 'tomahawking' . . shearer. **1912** J. BRADSHAW *Highway Robbery under Arms* (ed. 3) 7 But I'd rather tomahawk every day and shear a flock, For that's the only way I make some tin. **1930** *Bulletin* (Sydney) 8 Oct. 21/4 The jumbuck these days has to be 'pinked' without being butchered, but not so long ago tomahawking was common among both good and bad shearers—the former when racing for a big tally. **1982** P. ADAM SMITH *Shearers* 278 The Sweat Lover says he'll tell the Cocky if I tomahawk another.

tomahawker. Also **tommyhawker.** A shearer, esp. one who shears roughly.

1901 *Bulletin* (Sydney) 5 Oct. 16/3 Surely . . bush-workers are as worthy of consideration as the 'swaggers', 'tomahawkers', and 'loppies' of N.S.W. **1912** R.S. TAIT *Scotty Mac* 70 He even recognised the Tommyhawker shearing on the board. **1927** *Bulletin* (Sydney) 20 Jan. 24/2 At Wondong station, in seven and a half hours, 2472 jumbucks were undressed. . . The slowest tomahawker on the board accounted for a mere 176. **1960** D. MCLEAN *Roaring Days* 40, I pick up the fleece and take it to the classer. Without me they'd get nowhere. I'm the vital link between the tommyhawkers and the blokes who complain about them. **1964** H.P. TRITTON *Time means Tucker* (rev. ed.)

40 Tomahawkers were shearers whose sheep looked as though the wool had been chopped with an axe.

tomato sauce. Rhyming slang for 'horse'.

1905 J. MEREDITH *Learn to talk Old Jack Lang* (1984) 13 A *pot and pan* driving a nice high stepping *tomato sauce* in a flash *big an' bulky* pulled up. **1968** J. ALARD *He who shoots Last* 86 'Nice weak tomato sauce ta be puttin' money on,' said the Wrecker.

tommer: see TOM *v.*[1]

tommy-axe. [Shortened form of TOMAHAWK *n.* + *axe.*] A hatchet.

1898 E.E. MORRIS *Austral Eng.* 474 *Tommy-axe*, a popular corruption of the *Tomahawk*. **1938** X. HERBERT *Capricornia* 358 Cutting a strip of bark from the tree with the tommy-axe. **1965** G. MCINNES *Road to Gundagai* 145 He would chop its head off neatly with a tommy-axe.

tommyhawk, var. TOMAHAWK *n.* and *v.*

tommyhawker, var. TOMAHAWKER.

tommy rough. Also **tommy ruff.** [f. *Tommy* + transf. use of *ruff* a small fresh-water fish of the perch fam., having rough scales: see OED *sb.*[1] 2.] The marine fish *Arripis georgianus*, valued as food; HERRING 1 b.; *native herring*, see NATIVE *a.* 6 b.; ROUGHY a.

1886 J.F. CONIGRAVE *S.A.* 166 The popular opinion in favour of the 'snook' and 'tommy rough' is well grounded. **1903** W.J. SOWDEN *With Nor'-West Mail* 4 You fall into the hands of stewards, whose mania for tips is like a shark's appetite for tommyroughs. **1923** E.R. WAITE *Fishes S.A.* 9 Under the name *Arripis georgianus* it may be recognized . . by zoologists in London, Tokyo, Capetown, New York, Buenos Ayres, i.e., the world over, but by the name of 'Tommy Rough' it would be unknown outside Australia. **1970** L. WEDLICK *What Fish is That?* 37 Ruff *Arripis georgianus* . . called Tommy Rough in South Australia, Sea Herring in Western Australia, and Roughy in Victoria. **1984** E. ROLLS *Celebration of Senses* 56 South Australians fishing for the little, good-eating Tommy Ruffs.

Tommy Tanna /tɒmi 'tænə/. *Hist.* [f. *Tommy* a personal name + TANNA the name of an island of Vanuatu (formerly the New Hebrides).] A nickname for a Kanaka; usu. used generically.

1903 *Bulletin* (Sydney) 6 Dec. 1/7 It is only now, when there is no possibility of plutocratic slave-owners in the sugar districts getting supplies of fresh niggers to replace the 'returns', that the inhumanity of sending Tommy Tanna home has been discovered. **1905** *Ibid.* 12 Oct. 14/2 The number of drinking shops in the sugar districts of N.Q. might very well be reduced in the interests of white workers who are to take the place of disappearing Tommy Tanna. **1974** N. CATO *Brown Sugar* 28 'Tommy Tanna' was a nick-name for a Kanaka, just like 'John Chinaman' or 'Jacky' for an Abo.

Tom Thumb. [Used elsewhere but recorded earliest in Aust.] Rhyming slang for 'rum'.

1905 J. MEREDITH *Learn to talk Old Jack Lang* (1984) 14, I can go into the *rubbity dub* and have a lemonade, breasting the *near and far* with booze hounds drinking *Tom Thumb*. **1940** *Sixer* (Mornington) 22 May 9 *Tom Thumb*, rum. **1967** *Kings Cross Whisper* (Sydney) xli. 4/4 *Tom Thumb*, rum. Also rhyming slang for the drum, give the strong tip, drum a person up; give him the mail.

tomtit. [Transf. use of *tomtit* a bird of the genus *Parus*, and other small birds.] Any of several small birds, often a THORNBILL, and esp. the *yellow-tailed thornbill* (see YELLOW 1).

1883 A.J. CAMPBELL *Nests & Eggs Austral. Birds* p. iv, On the sunny side of prickly acacia hedges we found numerous nests of Tomtits or Yellow-tailed acanthizas. **1900** *Tocsin* (Melbourne) 2 Aug. 6/1 We had now subsisted four days on a yam, a tomtit, the snack of damper to which the old miner had invited us, and a taste of burnt sugar spoilt with wet flour. **1917** *Bulletin* (Sydney) 19 July 24/4, I plump for the little tit-warbler, or little tomtit (*Acanthiza nana*) and the barley-bird . . as the two smallest Australian birds. **1962** B.W. LEAKE *Eastern Wheatbelt Wildlife* 87 Yellow tailed thornbills or tom-tits have the cosiest nest made principally of grass and lined with feathers. **1981** A.B. FACEY *Fortunate Life* 89 And there was the little brown and grey tom tit.

tongs. *Shearing.* A pair of hand shears.

c **1895** CLARK & WHITELAW *Golden Summers* (1986) 133 When the Cove sez. Sez he, that shearing wont [*sic*] do my man. So I ship my b--y tongs across the dancing board, straddles my crock, & takes to the water like a b--y rat. **1897** *Worker* (Sydney) 11 Sept. 1/1 When by chance he gets a 'pen' he buys a pair of 'tongs'. **1906** *Bulletin* (Sydney) 30 Aug. 16/4 Once a pair of 'tongs', a strong wrist, and a stronger vocabulary were a shearer's outfit. **1912** J. BRADSHAW *Highway Robbery under Arms* (ed. 3) 23 We then picked our tongs, and started for the hut to prepare things for graft in the morning. **1929** *Aussie* (Sydney) Apr. 17/2 'Come, come, my man,' said the red light. 'This kind of shearing won't do me.' So I wrapped the turkey, closed the tongs, cuddled Matilda and here I am. **1951** G. PIKE *Campfire Tales* (1981) 104 Jacky Howe with the tongs (as shearers in those days referred to the blades).

tonic. [Joc. use of *tonic* a tonic medicine.] Alcoholic liquor.

1944 F. BERKERY *East goes West* 69 It also used to be the delightful practice of some of the 'dags' to journey on this train to Augusta to arrange for supplies of tonic, and to have a blow-out. . . No liquor was allowed on any of the trains . . but the harder they tried to enforce the rule, the more the grog came in.

tonicked, *ppl. a.* [Joc. use of *tonic, v.* to administer a tonic.] Drunk.

1911 *Bulletin* (Sydney) 12 Oct. 14/2 Who ever hears . . of a man being 'drunk'? . . The staid and dignified citizen will say he is 'intoxicated'. . . The average boy that he is 'shickered', 'blithered' or 'tonicked'. **1912** *Ibid.* 1 Feb. 13/1 When 'twas seen That his team was tonicked only to the verge of talking fight, Not a sober man would back him for a bean. **1961** F. LEECHMAN *Opal Bk.* 57 But the wicked old lout had been 'tonic'd' as they call it and had wandered about bushed for twenty-four hours.

tonk. [Of unknown origin.]

a. A male who in speech or manner appears to set himself above his fellows (see quot. 1965); a fool.

1941 S.J. BAKER *Pop. Dict. Austral. Slang* 77 *Tonk*, a simpleton or fool . . a dude or fop . . a general term of contempt. **1965** G. MCINNES *Road to Gundagai* 92 Just the same you couldn't help noticing that the Grammar boys came from the wealthiest homes, were C of E and Establishment and blessed by the Anglican Bishop and had ivy-covered walls and generally behaved as if they owned the place. They were known to us as *tonks*, which is an onomatopoetic [*sic*] description of what they were. **1970** *Coast to Coast 1967–68* 2 He had gone to agricultural college till he was eighteen, but like most farmers' sons had tended to disguise the fact in his speech. One taunting cry of 'Tonk!' and country boys felt they were ruined for life. **1970** R. BEILBY *No Medals for Aphrodite* 32 It was their lack of vocabulary that filled him with despair. . . 'You're a good bloke, Turk, but sometimes you talk like a tonk,' one of them had told him in a moment of bibulous candour. And so he took care not to talk like a tonk. **1983** *Weekend Austral.* (Sydney) 27 Aug. 20/8 Australian slanguage is well stocked with words and phrases to describe those who are a bit slow off the mental mark, who are—well, to put it bluntly, drongos . . tonks [etc.].

b. A male homosexual.

[N.Z. **1943** *Penguin New Writing* XVII. 83 The cook got my goat when he started trying to do the same thing. He was a tonk all right, just a real old auntie.] **1964** G. JOHNSTON *My Brother Jack* 115 He'll either pick up a dose, or he'll get her up the duff. . . Either that or he'll end up a tonk. **1965** H. PORTER *Stars Austral. Stage & Screen* 280 During the last ten years or more, there have been imported a coterie of *untalented* English homosexuals, English tonks unheard of outside their home country. **1970** *TV Times* (Sydney) 15 July 41/3 There was also a homosexual (who was referred to as a 'tonk'—thereby dating Mr Porter rather badly).

ton-work. *S.A. Mining. Obs.* [f. *ton* a measure of weight + *work*, by analogy with *tut-work*, designating a system of payment by measure of work done: see OED *tut, sb.*[2]] Piece-work.

1846 *S. Austral. Register* (Adelaide) 21 Oct. 3/4 At tut-work, tribute or ton-work the earnings of miners has been considerable. **1848** J. STEPHENS *Voice from Aust.* 16 There is no lack of employment, either at the mines, where 25s. per week can be reckoned upon, as permanent weekly wages, even by men who are not practical miners, but, in general, a great deal more has been earned by the 'job', or by what they call ton-work, tut-work, or tribute. **1850** *S. Austral. Register* (Adelaide) 18 Nov. 2/5 They are going through courses of ore which will be worked either on ton-work or tribute at a low rate. **1971** *AUMLA* xxxvi. 170 Work in the mines fell broadly into two categories, tutwork or ton-work, and work on tribute.

tooart, tooat, varr. TUART.

toodlembuck /'tudləmbʌk/. Also **toodle-em-buck.** [Prob. f. *tootle* to walk, wander + *th)em* + *buck* gambling marker.] A gambling game played by children: see quot. 1960.

1959 A.D. MICKLE *After Ball* 75 There was 'Toodle-em-buck'. That was purely a gambling game. **1960** K. SMITH *Word from Children* 155 Another gay, carefree kind of toy, designed to develop the gambling instinct in innocent children, was the Toodlembuck. It consisted of a disc of cardboard mounted on a cotton-reel and slipped over an old wooden meat-skewer. The top of the disc was divided into segments with a horse's name on each, such as 'Spearfelt', 'Carbine', or 'Heroic'. A pointer was fitted to the skewer and the disc was spun roulette-wise while the young bookie yelled, 'Who'll have a go on me old toodlembuck?'

toolache /tu'leɪtʃi/. Also **toolach,** and formerly **toolatchee, dulachie.** [a. Adnyamadhanha *tuligi.*] The large wallaby *Macropus greyi*, formerly of s.e. S.A. and adjacent Vic., now prob. extinct. Also *attrib.*

1879 'OLD HAND' *Journey Port Phillip to S.A.* 35 Kangaroos, Kangaroo rats, toolatchee and wallaby were abundant. **1885** *Eng. Illustr. Mag.* (London) X. 398 There were lots of dulachies, which are smaller than a brown kangaroo, and are grey-haired and red-headed. **1890** J.I. WATTS *Family Life S.A.* 182 There was a species [of kangaroo] that I had not seen on this side of the Murray, called by the blacks Toolaches. They are not so large as the common kangaroo, but are remarkably graceful animals. **1926** A.S. LE SOUEF et al. *Wild Animals Australasia* 189 Grey's wallaby, known as the 'toolach', is now very scarce. It is confined, as far as can be ascertained, to a small area of scrub-land inland from the mouth of the Murray River, South Australia. **1984** *Age* (Melbourne) 18 Aug. 6/1 Like many of its fellow victims, the toolache wallaby was too good-looking to live. . . Such a beautiful creature was doomed by exploitation for its fur.

too right: see RIGHT *a.* 3.

tooroo /'turu/, *int.* [Var. of *toodle-oo* 'goodbye' (see OEDS); the form *tooraloo* is used elsewhere but recorded earliest in Aust. (see OEDS).] 'Goodbye'. Also **tooraloo,** and as *n.*

1916 *Truth* (Sydney) 23 Jan. 10/5 Page said, 'Well, too-ra-loo; I'm getting off here.' 'Hoo-roo, Page,' he replied. **1927** *Bulletin* (Sydney) 14 Apr. 24/2 Does anybody know the derivation of 'tooroo', used out back in the same sense as 'so long' or 'good-bye'? It may be abo. **1927** *Ibid.* 12 May 27/3 A man from Windsor (N.S.W.) parting from me a few days ago, said, 'Well, tooroo—see you in Liverpool.' Thirty years ago, 'tooroo' or 'tooraloo' was commonly used about Sydney. The expression seems to have come from the chorus of a then popular song, commencing 'If I had the wings of a turtle-dove', the last line being 'I tooral looral I ay'. **1942** A.L. HASKELL *Waltzing Matilda* 38 'S'long Bill.' 'Too roo, Joe.' **1948** J.K. EWERS *For Heroes to live In* 3 'Oh, well! Too-roo!' He touched Darkie's flank with his heel, gave a wave to both girls and was soon out of sight. **1964** *N. Austral. Monthly* Dec. 8 We . . swapped any news, the petrol tanks were 'topped up' and with a cheery 'Too-roo' we were off again. **1970** R. BEILBY *No Medals for Aphrodite* 273 He had never been much of a one for good-byes. 'Tooroo, I'll be seeing you, be good,' had always seemed quite adequate. **1983** B. DAWE *Over here, Harv!* 122 The ambulance whanged by again, on its way to the morgue. . . And the ambulance bell kept yelling a last tooroo.

toot /tʊt/. [Prob. transf. use of Br. dial. *tut* a small seat or hassock: see OED *sb.*[1] 2.] A lavatory.

1965 J. O'GRADY *Aussie Eng.* 36 A toilet. Also known as a 'dunny', a 'shouse', a 'toot'. **1969** E.D. PRICHARD *Bachelor's Guide Sydney* 100 'Toot' or 'loo' is a toilet. **1974** *Westerly* i. 14 He'd been sleeping in Shelley Beach toot for a fortnight. **1978** J. ROWE *Warlords* 258 Waldon added over his shoulder, 'Gobind's in the toot. He'll be right out.'

tooth-billed cat bird. [f. *tooth-billed*, referring to the double notch at the tip of the bird's stout black bill + *cat bird* (see CAT A.).] The bird *Scenopoeetes dentirostris* of rainforest in n.e. Qld. Also **tooth-billed bower-bird.**

1904 *Emu* III. 188, I am sending you a photo. of the finest playground we found of the Tooth-billed Bower-Bird (*Scenopoeus dentirostris*). **1929** A.H. CHISHOLM *Birds & Green Places* 173 The tooth-billed cat-bird . . is confined to a jungle area in northern Queensland. **1945** C. BARRETT *Austral. Bird Life* 119 Departing from the age-old habit of bower-birds, the tooth-billed species . . instead of building a playhall, clears a space, roughly circular . . and decorates it chiefly with long leaves. **1976** *Reader's Digest Compl. Bk. Austral. Birds* 558 Mountain rainforests of north-east Queensland ring continuously with the loud song of male tooth-billed catbirds during the breeding season.

tooth man. A hearty eater.

1954 *Barbed Wire & Bamboo* (Sydney) Oct. 8 Rex, Trudy and Mrs Hearne admit to having seen some of the best in tooth men. **1967** *Kings Cross Whisper* (Sydney) xli. 4/4 *Tooth man*, a good eater.

top, *n.* Northern Australia, esp. in the phr. **up top.** See also TOP END 1.

[**1905** *Adelaide Observer* (Sydney) 26 Aug. 47/1 The train from Quorn to the 'top' north.] **1951** R. DORIEN *Venturing to Aust.* 181 The occupants liked living 'up top', would not live anywhere else. **1955** N. PULLIAM *I traveled Lonely Land* 221 He . . went on, 'He's good with stock . . and the cattlemen at The Top need him.' **1969** J. DINGWELL *One String* 100 First time in Australian history that Up Top has had these experiences. **1978** H.C. BAKER *I was Listening* 127 Months of enforced idleness in remote places. . . 'Up top' he had been a member of a gang.

Hence **up topper** *n.*, one native to or resident in northern Australia.

1969 J. DINGWELL *One String* 109 Up Toppers called the fresh-water Johnstone crocodile an alligator.

top, *v.* [Spec. use of *top* (usu. with *off* or *up*) to put the finishing touch to a process.]

1. *trans.* With **off** or **up:** to fatten (livestock) for market. Also *intr.*

1889 *Illustr. Austral. News* (Melbourne) 2 Sept. 18/1 Time passes on and he increases in size; but being brought in to be 'topped off' in the fattening paddock he shows a bit of the old leaven to the disgust of the sundowner, who spends the night in the sapling instead of in the men's hut. **1890** 'R. BOLDREWOOD' *Squatter's Dream* 50 The sheep were good sheep; they had well-grown fleeces, rather coarse; but that did not matter with fattening sheep; they were large and would make good wethers when topped up. **1901** *Advocate* (Burnie) 15 Feb. 3/4 For Sale—27 well-grown Store Pigs, fit for topping up. **1920** *Land of Lyre Bird* (S. Gippsland Pioneers' Assoc.) 125 About that time the scourge of caterpillars was very bad, recurring for several years, just at the season when the cattle should be topped off. **1923** J. BOWES *Jackaroos* 101 The cattle . . had 'topped up', and were on their way south to a distant market. ***c* 1960** C. MACKNESS *Clump Point & District* 61 Bringing cattle down from the Tableland in its dry season to be 'topped off' on his new pastures.

2. [Prob. joc. alteration of *tip off.*] *intr.* With **off:** to divulge information. Also *trans.*, to betray (someone).

1939 K. TENNANT *Foveaux* 312 There was too much danger that a squarehead would top-off to the police. **1941** S.J. BAKER *Pop. Dict. Austral. Slang* 77 *Top-off, to* . . to act as a police informer. **1959** D. NILAND *Gold in Streets* 94 I'll think up something and keep in her good books while I'm doing it, the slut, or she'll top me off.

top end.

1. Freq. with initial capitals. The northern part of the Northern Territory: see quot. 1963. Also *attrib.*

1933 F.E. BAUME *Tragedy Track* 158 No party ever given in Australia could reach the heights of that which farewelled a bushwoman of bushwomen when she passed through the Alice from the 'top end' on her way to Adelaide. **1936** C.T. MADIGAN *Central Aust.* 10 The Top End, the coastal region of the north is a different country altogether, with its rivers that always contain water, its alligators, its cattle-tick, its attempt at agriculture, its strikes and disorders. **1943** *Frontier News* Mar. 5/3 Having had it well impressed upon me from Broken Hill onwards that 'this is a man's country, and women are a nuisance', by one Roy—then driving the 'top-end' mail from Broken Hills [*sic*] to Cordillo Downs. **1954** T. RONAN *Vision Splendid* 224 Mr Toppingham hated the place; hated all towns; all people except a few Top End cattlemen and old Marty. **1960** *N.T. News* (Darwin) 5 Jan. 1/7 Meanwhile the 'top end's' vast buffalo herds, with the wet season on are starting to move south to watering places. **1963** F. FLYNN *Northern Gateway* 72 The Northern Territory may be divided into two parts—'The Centre' and the 'Top End'. The Centre has Alice Springs as its 'capital', or administrative base. In the Top End, Darwin is episcopal headquarters and the home of the Northern Territory's Administrator. **1972** *Bulletin* (Sydney) 22 Apr. 27/3, I am informed that the areas where wildlife, in particular birds, are most abundant, are in the Top End. **1980** N. WATKINS *Kangaroo Connection* 5 The Territory's 'dry' season lasts from April to October. The 'wet' commences in October and runs through to April, with rainfalls between fifty to sixty inches at Gregory's Creek Number Two, which was in the area known as the 'Top End'. **1986** *Centralian Advocate* (Alice Springs) 5 Feb. 37/2 The Alice Springs representative side fight against one of the Top End teams.

2. In local use: the Murray River upstream of its junction with the Darling River: see BOTTOM END, esp. quot. 1947. Also *attrib.*

1947 W. LAWSON *Paddle-Wheels Away* 102 A dozen river-men, swearing and shouting, erupted into the bar. 'Where are the 'top-end' crawlers? Come and fight, you dingoes.' **1956** [see BOTTOM END].

top-ender.

1. Freq. with initial capital. One native to or resident in the northern part of the Northern Territory.

1941 C. BARRETT *Coast of Adventure* 14 The old Top-ender drank beer, which, to the men up there, is more desirable than iced nectar is to gods. **1961** T. RONAN *Only Short Walk* 52 Any 'Top-Ender' who wanted an hotel booking, a tip for the races, or the loan of a fiver . . went to Billy. **1976** A. STRETTON *Furious Days* 204 Knowing the independent character and resourcefulness of the top-enders, I believed that if they were properly organized they could do the job quicker than the Armed Forces. **1984** *N.T. News* (Darwin) 21 Dec. 7/5 How many Top Enders must have marvellous memories.

2. A member of the crew of a Murray River boat.

1953 [see *bottom-ender* BOTTOM END]. **1976** DRAGE & PAGE *Riverboats & Rivermen* 212 Alec and David were 'top enders' who spent much of their lives in the Darling, Murrumbidgee, and Edwards rivers.

top feed. [f. *top* upper + FEED.] The foliage of bushes and trees, which provides pasture for livestock.

1931 M. TERRY *Hidden Wealth* 36 The top feed (edible bushes), associated with buck spinifex . . is raising some of the highest priced wool in Australia. **1946** W.E. HARNEY *North of 23°* 99 The cattle now look for the 'top feed', the edible bushes which keep them going till the wet returns. **1955** M. CORBEN *Not to mention Kangaroos* 31 Wandering cattle lived on 'top feed' from edible bushes and trees. **1962** *N.T. News* (Darwin) 13 Jan. 4/7 This will help freshen top feed and put more juice into it. And with so many stations left with only top feed for stock this will be some improvement. **1964** D. LOCKWOOD *Up Track* 48 In bad seasons I have seen fat cattle . . fattened on what is known as top-feed—the leaves of mulga and other edible trees and bushes. **1976** C.D. MILLS *Hobble Chains & Greenhide* 82 In common with all cameloid ruminants 'Humps' are mainly top-feeders and revel in such timbers as gidyea, mulga, blue-bush and cassia. . . A pet camel that has been 'poddy-reared' is a menace about a homestead. It will reach out and eat anything available.

topknot pigeon. A pigeon having a crest, esp. *Lopholaimus antarcticus* (see FLOCK PIGEON b.), and *Geophaps lophotes* (see *crested pigeon* (a), CRESTED). Also *ellipt.* as **topknot.**

1841 J. GOULD *Birds of Aust.* (1848) V. Pl. 61, *Lopholaimus antarcticus* . . Top-knot Pigeon of the Colonists of New South Wales. **1875** P.E. WARBURTON *Journey across Western Interior* 169 The Crested Dove, or Top-knot Pigeon of Warburton (*Ocyphaps Lophotes*) . . being exclusively an inhabitant of the plains of the interior . . can never become an object of general observation. **1890** G.J. BROINOWSKI *Birds of Aust.* III. Pl. 1, The Flock (*Carpophaga leucomela*) . . and the Top-knot (*Lopholaimus antarcticus*) Pigeons may be cited as typical [fruit eating pigeons]. **1901** F.J. GILLEN *Diary* 3 June (1968) 102 Number of beautiful topknot pigeons came in to water. **1916** *Bulletin* (Sydney) 23 Nov. 24/2 The 'Big Scrub', towards the Tweed (N.S.W.) and the jungles further north, once teemed with pigeons, among them the 'superb' . . and 'topknot'. **1923** J. BOWES *Jackaroos* 62 The crested pigeons, locally-known as 'top-knots'. **1932** H. PRIEST *Call of Bush* 116, I had hit a small crested pigeon, locally known as the Topknot, or Crested Bronzewing, which follows the traveller in the river country. **1956** A.C.C. LOCK *Tropical Tapestry* 109 Gidgee . . provided . . homes for hundreds of crested wood pigeons. This bird is also called the top-knot pigeon and crested bronzewing. It is, perhaps, the most common of native pigeons, but is none the less beautiful. **1976** *Reader's Digest Compl. Bk. Austral. Birds* 229 The nomadic topknot pigeon gets its name from its peculiar rust-red crest, which is unlike that of any of the other pigeons.

top-notcher. See quots.

1978 M. WALKER *Pioneer Crafts Early Aust.* 36 The top sawyer was the master craftsman, often termed a 'top notcher'. He was responsible for the sharpening and care of the tools and his partner was the general labourer, both around the site and in the pit. **1981** J.P. GABBEDY *Forgotten Pioneers* 16 'I was a top-notcher'. . . He . . went on to explain that he had been a pit-sawer for half of his life, and that the top-notcher was the man who stood on the top-side of the log and guided the cut along the chalked (or ash-marked) line.

top-off. [Prob. alteration of *tip-off.*] An informer. Also **top-off man,** etc.

1941 S.J. BAKER *Pop. Dict. Austral. Slang* 77 *Top-off*, a police informer. **1944** L. GLASSOP *We were Rats* 133, I haven't forgot . . how he pooled me with the Q.M. Just a top-off merchant, that's all he is. **1957** D. WHITINGTON *Treasure upon Earth* 93 'I don't want any insolence. Clear that road and then keep off our land, or you'll find yourself in gaol.' 'Just a bloody top-off.' **1964** K. TENNANT *Summer's Tales* 99 By all accounts he's been top-off man for the cattle thieves ever since he could walk. . . The sergeant told me he'd never catch any of those poddy dodgers out while the kid's in the district. **1968** *Kings Cross Whisper* (Sydney) lv. 11/2 (*heading*) Australia's most famous top-off galah, Andrew Dobber, M.P., has put his foot in it again. **1972** K. WILLEY *Tales Big Country* 24 'You'd better watch out for the police,' I said. 'That's against the law and there's a few top-offs around here.' **1978** H.C. BAKER *I was Listening* 16 'Don't have much to say to that bloke', he advised, 'he's a top-off.'

top-rail.

1. The upper horizontal member of a fence. Also *fig.* and *attrib.*

1898 G. DUNDERDALE *Bk. of Bush* 102, I . . saw the bandicoot sitting on a top-rail, watching me, and dangling her feet to and fro. She wore towzled red hair, a short print frock, and a look of defiance. . . You bandicooted my potatoes last night, and you've left the marks of your dirty feet on the ground. **1930** 'BRENT OF BIN BIN' *Ten Creeks Run* (1952) 1 Among the top-rail critics and advisers were neighbouring squatters and station-hands. **1958** F.B. VICKERS *Mirage* (ed. 2) 48 On the top rail of the yard sat the musterers.

2. See quot. 1921.

1915 V. PALMER *World of Men* (1962) 35 He always was a grip rider. . . No broncho-straps, or monkey-straps or top rails for him. He'd as soon ride without a saddle as not. **1921** G.A. BELL *Under Brigalows* 122 Some of them had rolled up a bundle of twigs in a bit of saddle cloth, and running straps through the 'dees' on the front of the saddle, strapped it across to give a firmer hold to their legs—top rails or kids they called these inventions.

Torrens. [Used elsewhere but recorded earliest in Aust.] The name of Robert *Torrens* (1814–84), first Premier of South Australia, used *attrib.* in Comb. with reference to a simplified method of land-title registration devised by him, and introduced into South Australia in 1858, as **Torrens system, title.**

1863 R.R. TORRENS *Transfer of Land by 'Registration of Title'* 1 Transfer of land by 'registration of title' as now in operation in Australia, under the 'Torrens System'. **1877** A. OLIVER *Collection of Acts relating to Land* p. ix, The attempt to substitute a system of transfers, accompanied by instruments declaring trusts .. may be the logical outcome of the Torrens system of registration. **1888** W. BADGER *'Land Transfer' Laws* p. vii, The 'Land Transfer', or 'Torrens' system of land alienation, takes its rise in South Australia. **1895** *Bulletin* (Sydney) 6 July 7/4 The simple and effective Torrens Title almost abolished the great conveyancing swindle in Australia. **1920** H.J. RUMSEY *Pommies* 154 As the property was under 'Torrens' title, it did not take long to arrange the transfer. **1938** W.M. ALEXANDER *Titles Office Practice* 3 A word of praise must be given to the originator of the Torrens Title, Mr., afterwards Sir Robert Richard Torrens. **1949** G.A. JESSUP *Course of Lectures Lands Titles* 21 The .. Torrens system .. establishes the title to all other alienated land per medium of the Certificate of Title. **1971** CONRICK & THOMSON *Sale Real Property N.S.W.* 55 The vendor's solicitor submits particulars of the title sufficient to enable the purchaser's solicitor to prepare the transfer. For Torrens Title if the contract was well drawn these will be the same as in the description of the property in the contract. **1981** G.F. BUGDEN *Unit & Group Titles Managem. Practice Qld.* 1 The principal system of title registration in Queensland is the 'Torrens System'.

Torres Strait pigeon. [f. the name of the strait between Cape York Peninsula and the s. coast of New Guinea.] The fruit-eating pigeon *Ducula bicolor* of n. Aust., s. New Guinea, and adjacent islands; *nutmeg pigeon*, see NUTMEG 2.

1843 J. GOULD *Birds of Aust.* (1848) V. Pl. 60, This bird [*sc. Carpophaga luctuosa*] is commonly known by the name of Torres Strait Pigeon, from its being so abundant there that few voyagers pass the straits during its breeding-season without seeing it. **1872** C.H. EDEN *My Wife & I in Qld.* 293 In the month of November, the annual migration of the Torres Strait pigeon commences. **1896** F.G. AFLALO *Sketch Nat. Hist. Aust.* 148 If there is a better eating than the Wonga, it is surely the Torres Strait, or White Nutmeg pigeon (*Myristicivora spilorrhoa*), the latter name being in allusion to its favourite food. **1936** C.P. CONIGRAVE *N. Aust.* 141 Torres Strait pigeon, snowy-white with the exception of the black points to its plumage. **1956** A.C.C. LOCK *Tropical Tapestry* 283 A pair of Torres Strait pigeons swept along speedily... These birds are protected; but that does not prevent bush people from shooting them when they feel like a change of diet. **1972** K. WILLEY *Tales Big Country* 174 Once he shot one of the Torres Strait pigeons. These glorious birds .. migrate down from the Pacific to nest in small islands of the Barrier Reef.

toss, *v.*

a. [Fig. use of *to toss* (etc.) *in the towel* to admit defeat: see OEDS *towel, sb.* 1 b.] In the phr. **to toss in the towel,** to die.

1937 V. PALMER *Legend for Sanderson* 32 Tossed in the towel. Seventy-four: he'd had a good spin.

b. In the phr. **to toss it in,** to finish; to give up. See also ALLEY 1.

[N.Z. **1952** THOMSON *Deer Shooter* 21 And though a few had stuck it out .. others had decided out of hand that deer-shooting was not for them and had tossed it in.] **1954** *Tobruk to Borneo* (Perth) Feb. 15 They got me Jack... You'd better toss it in. **1958** *Bulletin* (Sydney) 11 June 19/1 Consider the number of ways an Aussie can be dismissed from his job... He can be sacked, fired, hoisted [etc.]... Should he decide to beat the boss to the punch he may .. pull-out, toss it in [etc.].

tote. [Used elsewhere but recorded earliest in Aust.: see OED(S *sb.*[1] 2.]

1. a. Abbrev. of 'totalizator'. Also *attrib.*

1890 *Truth* (Sydney) 9 Nov. 1/5 He backed the horse on nearly every 'tote' in town, and drew altogether about £300. **1900** *Ibid.* 10 June 1/7 So sure as man gives lovely woman a vote, She'll prohibit the booze and shut down on the tote. **1912** L. ESSON *Time is not yet Ripe* 50 He alleges he is bursting to reform things—the tote, the tariff—bible readings in State Schools .. when the time is ripe... But it never is. **1918** *Truth* (Sydney) 13 Jan. 1/7 The tote is a failure as a revenue producer. **1926** A.A.B. APSLEY *Amateur Settlers* 214 The large rings of bookmakers, whose business seems in no way interfered with by the 'tote'. **1950** F.J. HARDY *Power without Glory* 24 'Tote' operators took a percentage of all takings. For them there were no losing races. **1970** K.E.C. GRAVES *Third Chance* 17 His fancy ran second—the tote pay-out was more than for the winning ticket. **1985** *Bulletin* (Sydney) 4 June 60/2 The local boys .. landed the contract for the new tote boards at Sha Tin, Hong Kong... Designed in Australia, they are years ahead of any other tote... Fitted with special patented glass which cuts out reflection; each tote has 950 computer outlets.

b. In the collocation **blind tote,** a totalizator which registers but does not indicate to a bettor the details of wagers laid.

1904 *Sporting News* (Launceston) 16 July 1/3 The committee of the Hobart Trotting Club has made an innovation... They have now instituted what is known as the 'blind tote' in order that owners who desire to back their horses without letting the public into the 'know' can do so. *Ibid.* 30 July 1/3 The blind tote was an innovation... So far as the owners were concerned, it was not a success, for the favorites rarely got home through the afternoon. **1933** S. GRIFFITHS *Rolling Stone on Turf* 35 A rough and ready 'blind tote' had also been installed... At this time the 'tote' was illegal in New South Wales; but the contraption was called a 'blind bookmaker', and the sporting police also were suddenly afflicted with defective vision.

2. Special Comb. **tote shop,** an illegal betting establishment.

1894 *Bulletin* (Sydney) 20 Jan. 6/4 If Parliament will pass an act decreeing that the landlord of every gambling den, 'tote'-shop, and house of ill-fame shall be imprisoned .. it will begin to look as if it was reasonably serious in the matter. **1897** *Tocsin* (Melbourne) 11 Nov. 9/1 Traps and D's .. must wipe out Tote-shops—dens of vilest sin. **1909** C. CROWE *Inquiry Agent* 47 After the passage of the Anti-Gambling measure, business was carried on at the 'Tote' shop, the betting club, and the hazard school. **1962** J.T. LANG *Great Bust* 313 W.E.V. Robson recalled when the tote shops flourished in King Street. When the workers had come out to their lunch they had flocked into the tote shops to back their fancies.

tother side.

1. OTHER SIDE 1.

1858 C.R. THATCHER *Colonial Songster* (rev. ed.) 77 He stuck up to a gal named Moggy, A big stout lass from t'other side. **1889** *Bulletin* (Sydney) 5 Oct. 8/2 In the rouse-abouts' hut .. they always spoke of the Cabbage Garden as 'Port Phillip', of the Holy Land as 'tother side.

2. OTHER SIDE 2 b.

1865 'SPECIAL CORRESPONDENT' *Transportation* 33, I found them all eager for information regarding the 'tother side', as they call the eastern colonies. **1963** X. HERBERT *Disturbing Element* 168 To scoot to T'otherside by way of the new Transcontinental Railway.

tothersider.

1. *W.A.* A person from an eastern State; OTHERSIDER. Also *attrib.*

***c* 1872** J.C.F. JOHNSON *Over Island* 1 (*note*) 'Over the Island.' The term used by old bushmen, more especially the 't'other siders', to imply all over the colonies. **1891** *Rec. Castlemaine Pioneers* 26 June (1972) 128 If a man was seen wearing a black beaver hat .. he was regarded with suspicion, and looked upon as a 'tothersider'. **1908** *Bulletin* (Sydney) 27 Feb. 15/3 Billy, like other old Gropers, resents the advent of the 'T'othersiders'. **1933** W.L. OWEN *Cossack Gold* 142 Western Australia is remarkable as a psychological and political paradox... The remaining inhabitants of the continent have always been 'T'othersiders', distrusted as a community and politically disliked. **1950** K.S. PRICHARD *Winged Seeds* 30 Unemployed from all over the country swarmin' here, t'other siders as well as W.A. blokes. **1963** X. HERBERT *Disturbing Element* 2 My parents .. were what were called T'othersiders, meaning people who had come to West Australia from the other side of the continent. It was a proud title, distinguishing those qualified to hold it from the local born, the Sand Gropers, and the New Chums from Britain. **1972** N. KING *Nickel Country* 63 These adventurers were mainly 'T'othersiders', men who came from the New South Wales and Victorian goldfields and the copper mines in South Australia. **1983** *Sydney Morning Herald* 7 Feb. 7/3 Kalgoorlie was a huge seat with a big population of radical T'Othersider miners. **1985** M. WALSH *May Gibbs* 29 The inhabitants of Perth felt isolated from the other Australian colonies .. and .. remained much closer to Mother England than did 'tothersiders'—those of the eastern cities.

2. In Tasmania, a person from the mainland; on the s.e. mainland, a person from Tasmania.

1899 *Mercury* (Hobart) 18 Mar. 3/7, I, a 'Tother-sider', have been a resident of Hobart for the past three years. **1899** G.E. BOXALL *Story Austral. Bushrangers* 139 It was popularly supposed that these bushrangers were all convicts from 'Van Diemen's Land' hence they were known as .. 'Tother siders'. **1940** *Bulletin* (Sydney) 10 July 17/1 When I was a nipper many time-expired convicts from Tasmania were to be met with in Victoria. These gentry were generally known as 'T'othersiders'.

tourang, var. TAWARANG.

touri, var. TOWRI.

tourist. [Ironic use of *tourist* a holidaymaker.] An Australian soldier posted to a European front during either of the world wars. Also *attrib.*

1916 *7th Field Artillery Brigade Yandoo* Aug. 19 *Who said* .. that stew does not agree with five-bob-a-day tourists. **1917** C.E.W. BEAN *Lett. from France* 224 The sort of Australian who used to talk about our 'tinpot navy' labelled the Australians who rushed at the chance of adventure the moment the recruiting lists were opened 'the six bob a day tourists'. Well—the 'Tourists' made a name for Australia such as no other Australians can ever have the privilege of making. **1919** A. WRIGHT *Game of Chance* 13 'And went away, but I became ill in Egypt and was sent back—'... "Tourists' they call them, do they not?' **1941** *Furphy Flyer: Official Organ 2/24 Austral. Infantry Battalion* 6 Oct. 1 They call us Tovell's tourists I'm damned if I know why. **1944** F. BRUNO *Sa-eeda Wog* 1 The first signs of the generation of returned 'blitzkrieg tourists'—swing through the crowd.

tournefortia /tʊən'fɔtiə/. [Transf. use of *Tournefortia* a plant genus named by Swedish botanist Carl von Linné (Linnaeus) (*Species Plantarum* (1753) 140), after French botanist J.P. de *Tournefort* (1656–1708).] The shrub or small spreading tree *Argusia* (formerly *Tournefortia*) *argentea* (fam. Boraginaceae) of seashores in n. Aust. and elsewhere.

1928 S.E. NAPIER *On Barrier Reef* 85 The tournefortia, a bushy shrub. **1936** T.C. ROUGHLEY *Wonders Great Barrier Reef* 17 An occasional Tournefortia-tree, much smaller and with silvery green lustrous foliage. **1965** *Austral. Encycl.* IV. 377 The pisonia tree .. is abundant on many of the islands, and so too is the tournefortia (*Messerschmidia argenta* [*sic*]). **1978** N. COLEMAN *Look at Wildlife Great Barrier Reef* 26 Tournefortias are moderately low, wide-spreading trees.

towel, *v.* [f. Br. slang *towel* to thrash: see OED(S *v.* 2.] *trans.* With **up:** to beat; to thrash. Also *fig.*, and as *vbl. n.*

1919 C. DREW *Doings of Dave* 170 Eileen will give her such a towelling up. **1927** A. WRIGHT *Squatter's Secret* 136 Dee will towel him up on that. **1951** CUSACK & JAMES *Come in Spinner* 372, I think you deserve the V.C. for the way you towelled old Mole up. **1955** R. LAWLER *Summer of Seventeenth Doll* (1965) 32 Instead of pointin' out that he had a bad back, he puts himself to work by this Dowd—gunna show him up, see. Well, that's just what he shouldna done, the kid towelled him up proper. **1969** A. BUZO *Rooted* (1973) 42 Gary got his big serve working, I chipped in at the end and we were laughing. Towelled them up in no time.

towerang, var. TAWARANG.

towie. [f. *tow(-truck* + -Y.] The driver of a tow-truck.

1975 *Bulletin* (Sydney) 6 Sept. 72/3 People in the tow-truck business say that the average time it takes the first 'towie' to get on the crash scene in a built-up area is between two and three minutes. **1979** *Truckin' Life* III. iv. 23 Paul, 28, is one of scores of 'towies' in Melbourne battling to earn a living as the State's traffic control system and breathalyser tests by police cut back the number of accidents. **1984** *Ibid.* VII. v. 16 Presently a towie for Top Transport, Michael has been on the road as an owner-driver for four years. **1984** R. CASWELL *Scales of Justice* 38 Any of you towies got your Authorities signed?

town.

1. [Br. dial. *town* a (small) group of dwellings, a village or hamlet with little or no local organization: see OED *sb.* 3.] A (small) cluster of dwellings and other buildings recognized as a distinct place: see quots.

1818 W. LAWRY in Methodist Missionary Soc. Rec. 9 Oct., My first place of preaching is Parramatta, a charming village (called a Town in New South Wales). **1824** E. CURR *Acct. Colony Van Diemen's Land* 50 Elizabeth's Town contains but one house; and in its suburbs, on Richmond Hill, is a cottage lately erected as a place of retirement for the lieutenant-governor. If this be a town, what is a desert? **1830** R. DAWSON *Present State Aust.* 370 The town of Bathurst consists of but few houses. **1839** W.H. LEIGH *Reconnoitering Voyages* 149 A kind of hovel called a store . . added to some half-dozen miserable and comfortless-looking sledge huts, is the 'town of Glenelg'. **1848** J. SYME *Nine Yrs. Van Diemen's Land* 156 In Van Diemen's Land . . the rank of a town is conferred upon places, not for what they are, but for what they may hereafter become. **1853** S. SIDNEY *Three Colonies* (ed. 2) 259 Within the Sydney district are the towns of Paramatta, Windsor, and Liverpool; but, in consequence of the dispersion incident to the pastoral pursuits which have hitherto formed the chief employment of Australia, there are really no towns in the European sense of the word. **1864** 'E.S.H.' *Narr. Trip Sydney to Peak Downs* 6 The town is composed of two public-houses and a few bark huts. **1878** E. BRADDON *Lett. to India from Tas.* (1980) 20 The Town of Hamilton (or Forth), called 'Town' out here . . would be styled a village anywhere in England. **1926** K. DAHL *In Savage Aust.* 220 A couple of gold batteries, a collection of low huts for the Chinese crew, and a couple of European houses constituted the 'town'. The name of 'town' is, however, in Australia employed with great generosity. 'A shop, a pub and a jail, that's a town', is an Australian saying, and in many cases it is literally true. **1977** W.A. WINTER-IRVING *Bush Stories* 17 Kalkadoon is just better than a hamlet, except that nobody living there would know the meaning of the word hamlet. So it's a town; small, remote, away out in the sticks as they say, far away from the railroad.

2. Used *attrib.* in Comb. designating a surveyed tract of land within a town, as **town acre, allotment, land, lot.**

1838 *S. Austral. Rec.* (London) 13 June 66 **Town acres** are in many situations not to be purchased at all. **1840** *S. Austral. Register* (Adelaide) 27 Feb. 9 The Town Surveyor is prepared to give over the boundaries of the following Town acres to the agents or proprietors of the same. **1849** G.B. WILKINSON *Working Man's Handbk. S.A.* 7 Town acres should be put up to public auction, at £2 10s. per acre. **1812** *HRA* (1916) 1st Ser. VII. 549 He also received a **Town Allotment** in Sydney, which he enclosed for the purpose of converting into a garden. **1817** *Hobart Town Gaz.* 4 Oct., All Persons, Free as well as Bond, who may be desirous of applying for Town Allotments of Ground to Build upon, are invariably to send in their applications to the Secretary's Office. **1832** *Hill's Life N.S.W.* (Sydney) 17 Aug. 1 *Two town-allotments* in the pleasant village of Liverpool, at the rear of the Church, and containing in all about two acres and a half; fenced in. **1842** *Colonial Observer* (Sydney) 5 Nov. 585/3 He got a large share of this valuable tract of land as his grant, together with the splendid *town allotment* of Elizabeth Bay. **1854** H.B. STONEY *Yr. in Tas.* 282 The town allotments of Birnie, till very lately, were to be sold at reasonable prices, as well as the suburban lots of fourteen to fifty acres. **1870** C.H. ALLEN *Visit to Qld.* 110 A newly formed Australian town is not a very beautiful object. Broad, straight streets, running in parallel lines, cut the square town into numerous smaller squares, which form what are called 'blocks'. Each block consists of about ten divisions, containing some two roods of land. These are put up and sold by the Government, and it is by buying such town-allotments, in the centres of rising places like Melbourne and Sydney, that enormous sums of money have been made. **1889** R.W. DALE *Impressions Aust.* 80 Town allotments of one quarter of an acre are sold at prices varying from £20 upwards, and villa or suburban allotments of two acres and a half at £100. **1899** *Progress* (Brisbane) 26 Aug. 9/3 One Town Allotment, Town of Yandina, having frontage to Scott-street. **1946** J.G. EASTWOOD *More about Cairns* 31 A week or two of spell in Brisbane was followed by getting work at Southport clearing scrub land ready to be cut up into Town allotments. **1837** *Colonist* (Sydney) 16 Mar. 88/1 The settlers . . were anxiously waiting the completion of the survey of the **town lands,** when they might commence building. **1839** R. COCK *S.A.*, The value of Town Lands in Adelaide . . is from £70 to £1600 per acre. **1852** D. MACKENZIE *Ten Yrs. Aust.* 4 The first Government Land Sale took place in June, 1837. A mania originating in the townland speculations of South Australia . . seized the colonists and the emigrating public. **1863** *Cassell's Emigrants' Handy Guide N.S.W.* 13 Crown lands are divided into four classes, viz: 'town lands' . . 'suburban lands' . . 'first-class settled districts' and 'second-class settled districts'. **1893** D.J. FROST *Crown Lands N.S.W.* 53 Town Lands cannot be sold in areas exceeding half an acre, or at a lower upset price than £8 per acre. **1835** R. TORRENS *Colonization of S.A.* 45 The proprietor of **town lots** could neither erect houses in the cheapest way, nor, when erected, dispose of them to advantage. **1839** *Dublin Rev.* VI. 456 The speculation in town lots has hitherto been almost the only occupation of the settlers. **1843** *Colonial Observer* (Sydney) 24 May 1045/1 The town lots are in Kiama, Narellan, Appin, Dungog, Scone. **1851** J.H. BURTON *Emigrant's Man.* ii. 7 Town lots—comprising all lands within the limits of any existing town specially named and described by the governor, or within any locality specified by the governor as the site of an intended town. **1897** L. LINDLEY-COWEN *W. Austral. Settler's Guide* 97 Three townsites are laid out along the line within the area—Woodanilling, Moojebing, and Pinwernying, and for the encouragement of village settlement, 304 town and suburban lots of from three-quarters of an acre to one-eighteen acres have been surveyed.

3. Special Comb. **town bike,** see BIKE 1; **black,** an Aboriginal who lives in a town (see quot. 1870, 1); see also TOWNY 3; **gang** *hist.*, a party of convicts assigned to hard labour on public works in a town; **reserve** *hist.*, land set aside as the site of a town (see quot. 1857).

1870 C.H. ALLEN *Visit to Qld.* 180 The **'town blacks'** are distinguished from those of the wild interior by the smattering of English they have picked up, and by their love of 'seexpences' and tobacco. **1870** E.B. KENNEDY *Four Yrs. in Qld.* 67 Not only amongst station and town Blacks, but also for years in the same country with perfectly wild Blacks. **1890** A.J. VOGAN *Black Police* 133 Frazer went about for years shooting all and every native he could see, 'station boys', warragals, or town blacks—he was not very particular. **1956** T. RONAN *Moleskin Midas* 152 The voices of town blacks and visiting blacks joined in greeting. **1796** D. COLLINS *Acct. Eng. Colony N.S.W.* (1798) I. 485 The **town gang** was employed delivering the storeships. **1804** *Sydney Gaz.* 2 Sept., The Inhabitants of Sydney are desired to send Assistance to the Superintendant who has the direction of the repairs wanting to the Public Roads leading towards Parramatta . . the Government Town Gangs being now at work thereon. **1810** *Ibid.* 10 Feb., The Town gangs are employed in clearing out the Tanks, which have long been filled with sand, washed in by heavy rains. **1825** *HRA* (1917) 1st Ser. XI. 728, I wished to get him out of the Town Gang at Windsor. **1839** *Port Phillip Patriot* 20 Mar. 4/3 W. Nichols absconding from the Town gang on Feby. the 11th, *fifty lashes* on the *naked* back. **1847** J. LACKLAND *Common Sense* 8 The town gang, at sixpence a-day, would cost £13 10s. **1858** N.L. KENTISH *Treatise Penal Discipline* 12 Such men as might happen to remain unassigned, would have to go out with all other men attached to, or temporarily placed in the barracks, to work upon the roads and streets in Sydney, as the 'Town Gang', under the supervision of overseers. **1873** J. BONWICK *M. Howe* 64 He was now thrown into the Town Gang. **1836** J. BACKHOUSE *Narr. Visit Austral. Colonies* (1843) 392 The **town reserve,** of Muscle Brook, is marked by a small, weatherboard inn. **1841** *Port Phillip Patriot* 31 May 3/1 The first special survey at Gipps' Land was taken by the Port Albert Company, on the express condition that . . they should be allowed to select the land immediately bordering upon the town reserve. **1857** W. WESTGARTH *Vic. & Austral. Gold Mines* 83 The map of the colony is plentifully studded with little shaded squares, some of which rejoice in a distinct name, while others are as yet under the generic designation of 'town reserves'.

townee, towney, townie, varr. TOWNY.

township.

1. *Hist.* A site reserved for and laid out as a town. Also **township reserve.**

1789 *HRA* (1914) 1st Ser. I. 127 You are . . to lay out townships of a convenient size and extent, in such places as You, in Your discretion, shall judge most proper. **1800** D. COLLINS *Acct. Eng. Colony N.S.W.* (1802) II. 312 A small township marked out. **1824** E. CURR *Acct. Colony Van Diemen's Land* 13 The road leads by the newly marked township of Brighton. . . The township is not distinguished by a building of any description. **1830** *Hobart Town Almanack* 29 The village of Oatlands . . was marked out as a township, together with Perth, Campbell town and Brighton by General Macquarie in May 1821. **1839** *S. Austral. Rec.* (London) 1 Nov. 261 *Township of Glenelg* ·The plan of this valuable township has, we understand, been laid before the Governor and Resident Commissioner, and finally approved of by his Excellency. **1841** *Sydney Herald* 6 Mar. 2/6 In this township there is no house of any description, neither is there any in its neighbourhood, except one public house, and a blacksmith's shop. **1855** G.H. WATHEN *Golden Colony* 30 Numerous inland *townships* are marked down on the government maps of the colony. These have sometimes no existence except on paper. **1861** L.A. MEREDITH *Over Straits* 40 It used to seem to me a strange colonial anomaly to call a very small village a 'township', and a much larger one a 'town'. But the former is the term applied to the lands reserved in various places for future towns. **1870** *Sydney Morning Herald* 2 July 5/5 Calling the at present unnamed township reserve, on which the works are situated, 'Gladstone'. **1886** *N.T. Times Almanac* 56 (*note*) A new township has recently been surveyed at a bend in the McKinley River, named Burrundie.

2. Such a site at an early stage of its occupation and development (see quots. 1830 and 1873); a small town (see quot. 1886). Also *attrib.*

1790 *HRA* (1914) 1st Ser. I. 196 The fixing the first settlers in townships will, I fear, prevent that increase of live stock which would be raised in farms at a distance from a great body of people. **1806** *Ibid.* (1915) 1st Ser. V. 750 In a situation calculated for that purpose in the Township of Sydney. **1819** *Sydney Gaz.* 23 Jan., Two or more Carts were Robbed on the Road leading to Liverpool within four miles of that Township. **1830** R. DAWSON *Present State Aust.* 377 Here is a small township, which as yet resembles a large village rather than a town. **1835** J. LHOTSKY *Journey from Sydney* 16 We arrived at Bong Bong, a Township of about twenty hearths. **1844** MRS C. MEREDITH *Notes & Sketches N.S.W.* 84 Bathurst, being the last township on the 'up-country road', is comparatively a place of some importance. **1860** 'LADY' *My Experiences in Aust.* 283 Tamworth . . is rather a nice little township, as colonial towns go. **1873** R.P. WHITWORTH *Lost & Found* 25 Jim and I went into the next township, if a congregation of tents and shanties might be called a township. Township now though, for it was embryonic Ararat. **1886** D.M. GANE *N.S.W. & Tas.* 151 To those unacquainted with Australian colloquialisms the word 'township' is misleading. One is reluctant to give to a little hamlet, containing barely a dozen houses, a title which would more properly apply to a town of moderate size. But, nevertheless, of that character are the majority of colonial townships. **1898** *Tocsin* (Melbourne) 1 Dec. 7/2 Dyson is equally at home on the selection as he is in the mining township. **1916** 'T.O. LINGO' *Austral. Comic Dict.* 16 Township—A store, an hotel, a post office, a blacksmith's shop, twenty-seven adults, seventy-five children, nineteen dogs, and Mrs O'Toole's pig. **1926** 'S. WESTLAW' *White Peril* 103 He looked at first sight quite the usual type of township lounger. **1948** R. RAVEN-HART *Canoe in Aust.* 56 It figured in the road-map as a township, Australian for village, 'pop. 37'. **1960** *N.T. News* (Darwin) 5 Jan. 2/1 He settled at Batchelor township, which now houses the Rum Jungle workers but was then a vacant block of bushland. **1980** F. MOORHOUSE *Days of Wine & Rage* 393 A township sprang up with a milkbar-general store and a petrol pump; and then a hall, then a camping ground, and then, by gradual 'improvements', a replica of a city suburb with mown lawns.

Townsville stylo. [f. the name of a coastal city of n.e. Qld. + *stylo*, abbrev. of *Stylosanthes*.] The annual or perennial herbaceous legume *Stylosanthes humilis* (fam. Fabaceae) of South America, used as a pasture plant in n. Aust. and elsewhere. Also **Townsville lucerne.**

1937 *Jrnl. Council Sci. & Industr. Research* 201 The so-called wild or Townsville lucerne . . was introduced accidentally into north Queensland. **1960** *N.T. News* (Darwin) 8 Jan. 1/3 Para grass has been sown. Buffel grass and Townsville lucerne will be planted later. **1971** *Bulletin* (Sydney) 3 Apr. 56/2 The principal crops at Willeroo will be grain sorghum and Townsville stylo (or lucerne)—a legume which makes excellent feed for cattle because it retains its protein content of nine or ten percent when bone dry. **1977** A.V. BOGDAN *Tropical Pasture & Fodder Plants* 402 (OEDS) *Stylosanthes humilis* was known as Townsville lucerne until about 1968–9 when the Queensland Herbage Plant Liaison Committee recommended that the name should be changed to Townsville stylo in order to avoid confusion with species of *Medicago*. **1985** *Nat. Farmer* (Windsor) 5 Sept. 47/2 Many of the species scientists first enthused over have dropped from the scene. Townsville stylo, once the leguminous coloniser of the north, has bitten the dust of disease.

towny. Also **townee, towney, townie.** [f. *town* + -Y. Used elsewhere but recorded earliest in Aust. (see OED(S *towny, sb.* 1 and also *townee, sb.*).]

1. A newly-arrived immigrant (*spec.* one from London).

1825 *Austral.* (Sydney) 29 Sept. 3 At peep of day, several persons . . assembled on a spot of ground suitable enough for witnessing a pulley hauley match between two ladies of the fancy; the one a towny, and the other of currency worth. **1847** A. HARRIS *Settlers & Convicts* (1953) 50 Was not I a Towny too?—'An emigrant: here about twelve months, and a Londoner.' **1898** *Bulletin* (Sydney) 26 Feb. 14/1 He once started from Waratah to the '13-Mile', the whole distance on 'cords', with a newchum. Godkin left with 75 lb., the towny with about 30 lb. **1956** A. UPFIELD *Battling Prophet* 19 Ben Wickham had been a newchum, a towny, an outsider lost in a rough man's country.

2. *transf.* A town-dweller, as distinguished from a country-dweller.

1827 P. CUNNINGHAM *Two Yrs. in N.S.W.* II. 245 The English convicts divide themselves into the two great classes of *townies* and *yokels*. **1837** *Cornwall Chron.* (Launceston) 21 Oct. (Suppl.) 6 This impoliticly exposed pigmy mimicry of thirty six, was made up of *Townies* and Country Residents. **1848** *Portland Gaz.* 13 Oct. 3/5 'Bushman' . . says that he entirely coincides with 'Towney'. **1873** 'LADY IN AUST.' *Memories of Past* 105 Our horses were undergoing an inspection from the 'townies', who considered us very courageous people to have trusted ourselves on such skeletons. **1893** G.E. LANGRIDGE *Side Lights of Labour* 16 A towney will find the hammering along the hard high road too much. **1915** E.M. WEETWOOD *Lure of Land* 88 Let the townies see what real Australia can do. **1928** *Bulletin* (Sydney) 30 May 25/2, I see that bushies are preferred to townies for the police force. **1946** *Ibid.* 18 Sept. 29/1 The cocky uses fencing-wire; the townie gets most things done with the yard of string and a good lick. **1963** R.H. CONQUEST *Spurs are Rusty Now* 203 My great-grandpa came from Sydney to Brisbane 'way back in 1870. We've always been 'townies', same as your people have always been 'bushies'. **1981** C. WALLACE-CRABBE *Splinters* 21 She looked forward to getting back into the city and enjoying its crowding sense of anonymity. . . She was, as always, a townie through and through.

3. *spec.* An urbanized Aboriginal. See also *town black* TOWN 3.

1959 D. LOCKWOOD *Crocodiles & Other People* 169 The sophisticated 'townies' who keep Darwin's army of civil service clerks in heavily starched white shirts and boiled trousers . . are fed during the week on steak stews and rice puddings. **1962** —— *I, Aboriginal* 94 Too many are becoming helpless townies, completely dependent on can-openers for their food, and bottle-openers for their drink. They would starve if forced to hunt. This is one of the tragic effects of our rapidly increasing assimilation into the white community. **1977** K. COOK *Man Underground* 29 Detribalized outcasts who hang around the mullock heaps picking up a few scraps of missed opal to trade for liquor. . . The favourite method of straightening out a townie.

towri /'taʊri/. Also **taori, taurai, tauri, touri, tyri.** [a. Kamilaroi *dauray*.]

1. COUNTRY 2: see quot. 1892.

1872 G.E. LOYAU *Colonial Lyrics* 23 The native tribes had made their 'towri' here. **1888** *Centennial Mag.* (Sydney) 224 They lived where God placed them; they hunted and fished from one side of their 'tauri' to the other. **1892** J. FRASER *Aborigines N.S.W.* 36 It is well-known here that each tribe had its own 'taurai'—territory or hunting-ground—usually determined by natural boundaries, such as mountain ridges and rivers. **1899** R.H. MATHEWS *Folklore Austral. Aborigines* 15 The chief of a Kamilaroi tribe whose *taori* comprised the district around Kunopia. ***c* 1900** R. PORTER *Eumalga* 2 His towri or kingdom extended to . . Dubbo. **1918** *Bulletin* (Sydney) 12 Dec. 24/1 A towri is the ground hunted and fished over by a tribe. **1921** G.A. BELL *Under Brigalows* 76 As a rule if blacks from another 'tyri' trespassed they were instantly killed. **1942** L. & K. HARRIS *Lost Hole Bingoola* 203 *Towris*, tribal hunting grounds of the Aboriginals. ***c* 1956** B.J. RAYMENT *My Towri* 96 In their wild state they had their schools and laws. The schools taught the geography of their towri and what part of their towri and when to obtain food, medicine, etc. **1964** J.S. RYAN *Land of Ulitarra* p. xi, The tribes were many more in number and their *touris* (or special territories) were much smaller than in other parts of the Continent. **1972** M. CASSIDY *Dispossessed* 7 All the white-fellas would honour Paddy-jack and he would return to their towri in the bush.

2. *transf.* A white person's 'stamping ground'.

1873 *Illustr. Sydney News* 5 July 11/1 The stock-keeper, as may be surmised, means one having the care of stock. He is usually found located at a cattle station far out on the Baloore or Barwon; though the 'towri', or portion of country he inhabits, is not restricted to these neighbourhoods. **1893** J.A. BARRY *Steve Brown's Bunyip* 79, I never was on this field before. Down about the Lachlan's my *towri*.

Tozer /'toʊzə/, *v.* and *n. Obs.* [f. the name of Horace *Tozer* (1844–1916), Queensland politician.]

A. *v. trans.* To remove (a person) from office in response to pressure exerted by another.

1896 *Truth* (Sydney) 7 June 1/6 Mr Reid has incurred the gratitude of all etymologists. . . Mr Reid has given us a new word, and in future, when one person is shunted by another in deference to the wishes of an influential third, he need not labour for a phrase to describe his case; he will say, 'I was tozered'. *Tozer*: verb active, to yank off; to slip, to politely shunt when politic. Queensland papers please copy.

B. *n.* A statement which is inaccurate or untrue. Also *attrib.* and as **Tozerism.**

1898 *Truth* (Sydney) 1 May 1/7 News that the heiress to the Figian [*sic*] throne is *en route* to England husband hunting. . . Now is not that a nice Tozer tale! **1909** W.G. SPENCE *Aust.'s Awakening* 165 Under a cross-examination of Labor members in the House, Tozer became so notorious for the unreliability of his statements that all over Queensland today, when you don't believe a statement, you say, 'That's a Tozer'. **1919** C.A. BERNAYS *Qld. Politics during Sixty Yrs.* 131 He was one of those comprehensive politicians who never allowed himself to be cornered through the absence of a plausible explanation, and just as in modern times in the House of Commons 'terminological inexactitude' was coined as a synonym for something which is supposed not to lead us to Heaven, so a 'Tozerism' was the invention of John Macrossan to distinguish something which might be true but probably was not.

trac. [Shortening of *intractable*.] A refractory prisoner. Also *attrib.*

1967 *Kings Cross Whisper* (Sydney) xli. 4/4 *Trac*, intractible prisoner. **1968** J. ALARD *He who shoots Last* Pref., These tough boys (the Tracs) are stripped, booted and bashed until their bowels work. **1980** SIMMONDS & GOLLAN *For Simmo* 138, I was three years in the 'trac' section at Grafton after attempting to escape from Goulburn in 1965. **1984** *Nat. Times* (Sydney) 1 June 15/4 They sent me to the tracs and the Blockhouse.

track, *n.*

1. WALLABY TRACK 2 a., esp. in the phr. **on the track.** See also *tucker track* TUCKER *n.*[1] 3.

1869 M. CLARKE *Peripatetic Philosopher* 41 The Wimmera district is noted for the hordes of vagabond 'loafers' that it supports, and has earned for itself the name of 'The Feeding Track'. I remember an old bush ditty, which I have heard sung when I was on the 'Wallaby': Hurrah! hurrah! for the feeding track, I've left the Avoca behind my back, Hurrah! hurrah! for the feeding track Hurrah! hurrah! for the Wimmera. **1873** J.C.F. JOHNSON *Christmas on Carringa* 19 'Tis Christmas Eve again today, And I am on 'the track'. **1894** *Bulletin* (Sydney) 14 Apr. 24/3 With an empty pocket and burdened back, He 'tackled the track' to the Thirsty Land. **1913** H. LAWSON *Triangles of Life* 247 Cooney, who had rolled his swag at daylight, took the track. **1938** *Bulletin* (Sydney) 5 Jan. 21/1 Putting rum in one's boots . . is by no means restricted to old battlers on the track. **1949** J. CLEARY *Long Shadow* 82 You met lots of blokes on the track and it was interesting to know their background. **1959** D. HEWETT *Bobbin Up* 124 In the years when men married and had families, he'd been 'on the track', one of an army of jobless men, strung out along the endless, dusty roads of New South Wales, harried from one dole centre to the other. **1965** F. HARDY *Yarns of Billy Borker* 50 'Struth,' Tommy says, 'things have changed on the track: sundowners paying for steak and grillers.' 'You been on the track?' the sundowner asks. 'Yeh, before the war.' **1977** F.B. VICKERS *Stranger no Longer* 101, I had learned on the track that the unemployed didn't enjoy the privileges of the 'swaggie' of better days who could always 'front up' to the cook and get a sit-down meal.

2. a. The route followed by a drover. See also *cattle track* CATTLE 2, *dry track* DRY *a.* 1, ROAD 2.

1880 'ERRO' *Squattermania* 128, I heard you had gone up the track with a mob of cattle. **1902** H. LAWSON *Children of Bush* 195 We went with Bob Baker, the drover, overland with a big mob of cattle, way up into Northern Queensland. We couldn't get a job on the home track. **1919** *Bulletin* (Sydney) 9 Jan. 22/3 Sheep are quiet things on the track; but they rush sometimes. **1932** W. HATFIELD *Ginger Murdoch* 162 You had to tell which way you came, what the track was like for grass and water, the stages you had made. **1942** H.H. PECK *Mem. of Stockman* 78 He was selling bullocks regularly in all four markets—Adelaide, Melbourne, Sydney and Brisbane—and had many thousands on the tracks. **1960** *N.T. News* (Darwin) 8 Jan. 3/3 The Jervois and Phillipson tracks are still the only ones carrying a reasonable amount of feed. **1978** D. STUART *Wedgetail View* 110 'You've been on the track with horses?' Colin asked. 'I was horsetailer with a mob of cattle from the Gulf down to the top end of New South Wales.'

b. *transf.* and *fig.*

1939 J.G. PATTISON *'Battler's' Tales Early Rockhampton* 7 On the track for the 'Morning Bulletin' for eight years.

3. That part of the Stuart Highway which runs between Darwin and Alice Springs.

1935 R.B. PLOWMAN *Boundary Rider* 207 Another turn-out had started just before him—a family wagonette from 'up the track'. **1942** *Sun* (Sydney) 26 Aug. 4/9 Darwin is said to be 'up in the blue', and to leave that happy spot is to 'go down the track' or 'go south'. **1944** J.D. PORTER *Our Fertile North* 12 Used by touring motorists as overnight stopping places on the long journey up 'the track' to Darwin. **1960** *N.T. News* (Darwin) 26 Feb. 6/3 The society plans to start work on their very big Fannie Bay block . . after two major Territory projects down the track are completed. **1963** *N. Austral. Monthly* Dec. 4/1 The never to be forgotten journey down the 'Track', as the nine hundred and fifty-four miles of the Stuart Highway linking Darwin with Alice Springs is locally known. **1965** *Ibid.* June 2 Sixteen miles 'down the Track' from Darwin is the turn-off to Howard Springs. . . Next spot is Berry Springs. **1977** K. COLE *Winds of Fury* 33 Some took to their battered cars, cleared a way through paths and streets, and roared and rattled off down the 'Track' (the Stuart Highway linking Darwin with Adelaide and Brisbane via the Barkly Highway). **1980** B. SANSOM *Camp at Wallaby Cross* 5 There is one main road out of Darwin. . . The road links the 'Top End' to 'The Centre' and the road itself features in local parlance as 'The Track'. **1984** *N.T. News* (Darwin) 10 Sept. 22/4 Now calling for expressions of interest from performers including those 'down the track'. 'We want to cover the whole of the NT.'

4. *fig.* The course or progress of an event, action, etc.

1945 L. JILLET *Moresby's Few* 13 The real war is much farther along the track now. **1984** *Canberra Times* 29 Apr. 1/4 An Australian Bill of Rights, was 'a long way down the track'.

5. Used *attrib.* in Comb. with reference to the practice during the Depression of the 1930s of issuing dole cards to unemployed itinerants but not allowing them to remain in any one place, as **track bloke, card, dolie, man, rations** *pl.*: see quots. 1941.

1934 *International Labour Rev.* July 37 (*note*) Travellers' or 'track' rations are an illustration of the change which has accompanied the systematisation of relief. Many who in pre-depression days only occasionally drew 'track' rations from the police now do it as a matter of course, since they have to be registered to be eligible for any relief at all. **1935** K. TENNANT *Tiburon* 167 The travelling unemployed . . occasionally settle in a town but are usually kept on the move in a wide area in search of work where there is no work. They live on track rations, charity or relief work, according to the type of town they find themselves in. **1941** —— *Battlers* 17 Thursday all over the West is dole day, when the track men come in to have their cards stamped at the police-station and get their rations to carry them to the next 'dole town'. *Ibid.* 24 The men with track-cards . . wander the country in search of work, getting their food-orders from declared 'dole stations' in towns fifty or sixty miles apart. **1944** *Bulletin* (Sydney) 27 Sept. 13/2 The police sergeant . . had a reputation for brusqueness to swagmen calling in for track rations. **1948** *Ibid.* 2 June 28/2 I've had enough o' you loafin' track blokes. **1962** J.T. LANG *Great Bust* 208 Provision was later made for track rations. **1966** E.J. WALLACE *Sydney & Bush* p. i, 'Track dolies'—swaggies or baggies, who had given up their homes to go on the road—were compelled to keep moving to collect their rations. **1978** W. LOWENSTEIN *Weevils in Flour* 1 A track man looks back with pity on the farmer: 'They had it worse . . lumbered with debt, and with a family. We could just pick up and go!'

6. Special Comb. **track mate**, a travelling companion.

1914 *Bulletin* (Sydney) 19 Mar. 24/1 The bloke who waltzes Matilda falls in with a varied assortment of track mates. **1917** *Ibid.* 16 Aug. 22/1 We were camp-mates on the rivers, We were track-mates on the plains. **1981** R. EDWARDS *Yarns & Ballads* 27 And it's told far and wide that stretched out by his side Was his track-mate—the old cockatoo.

track, *v.* [Fig. use of *track* to follow a path, to go, to travel: see OED(S *v.*[1] 3.] In phr.

a. to track with, to keep company with (a person of the opposite sex), to court: see TRAVEL 4.

1910 *Bulletin* (Sydney) 28 Apr. 13/2 He soon became the recognised bloke that Lizzie was 'tracking' with. **1915** C.J. DENNIS *Songs of Sentimental Bloke* 51, I swear I'll never track wiv 'er no more; I'll never look on 'er side o' the street. **1926** K.S. PRICHARD *Working Bullocks* 47 Combo's what they call a man tracks round with a gin in the nor'-west. **1948** *Bulletin* (Sydney) 8 Dec. 29/1 Cockie Rogers's daughter had been 'tracking' with Dan Matthews for some time, and the district predicted a match. **1954** T.A.G. HUNGERFORD *Sowers of Wind* 270, I bet it's that cross-eyed harlot he's been tracking with. **1978** D. STUART *Wedgetail View* 76 Maybe some married couple'll move in with a daughter for you to track with.

b. to track square (or **straight**) (with): see quot. 1919.

1919 W.H. DOWNING *Digger Dialects* 50 *Track square*, to pursue an amorous enterprise with honorable intentions. **1931** *Bulletin* (Sydney) 21 Jan. 20/1 'At last', said Dave, 'I think I've met me fate. I'm trackin' straight As fine a sheila as you'd wish to see.' **1940** *Sticking Plaster: Souvenir Issue 2/2 Field Ambulance* Feb. 10 The bloke what's trackin' square with my missus. **1949** A. MARSHALL *How Beautiful are thy Feet* 64 He wants me to track square with him. To look at him you'd never think he could talk seriously. He talked for a long while about tracking square. **1964** G. JOHNSTON *My Brother Jack* 161 He's been at me for years about how irresponsible I am, and the first time I come back with a girl I'm tracking square with, I get hoisted! **1980** E.R. HALL *Can you hear Me?* 61 He was not that type and in any case at the time he was tracking square with his future wife. **1982** LOWENSTEIN & HILLS *Under Hook* 121, I was a shearer and I was tracking square with my girl, so I decided to have a rest from shearing and go on the wharf.

tracker. [Spec. use of *tracker* one who tracks.] An Aboriginal employed by police to track down missing persons, esp. fugitives from the law; *black tracker*, see BLACK *a.*[1] 6; *native tracker*, see NATIVE *a.* 5; *police tracker*, see POLICE. Also *attrib.*

1826 *HRA* (1919) 1st Ser. XII. 534, I recommend that . . a party of the Black people on this side be taken out as trackers. **1839** *Sydney Standard* 18 Mar. 4/5 An Aboriginal native for each police station . . would serve as trackers. **1848** C. COZENS *Adventures of Guardsman* 152 He had been pursued . . by a party of four mounted police, and two aboriginal natives as *trackers*. **1862** *Bell's Life in Sydney* 21 June 2/5 Yesterday morning Sir F. Pottinger, with eleven troopers, twenty settlers, and two trackers, got on the track of the bushrangers. **1885** *S.A. Parl. Papers* III. no. 54 2 A fully equipped party to go in search. I offered on behalf of the Government the services of a couple of the native police as trackers. **1897** *Proc. R. Geogr. Soc. Australasia: S.A.* (1899) 119 The African 'spoor'-artist is good; the American 'trail-hunter' is better; but our own soft-tongued aborigine 'tracker' is a prince in comparison with them all. **1906** *Bulletin* (Sydney) 26 July 16/4 Victorian blacks have not been used as trackers for a number of years, the office being filled by importations from Queensland. **1926** *Ibid.* 8 July 22/2, I lost a valuable boy, a phenomenal tracker. I thought he'd simply 'gone bush'. **1938** X. HERBERT *Capricornia* 364 O'Crimnell took him over to the police-station and set his tracker-boy to work on him. **1955** F. LANE *Patrol to Kimberleys* 18 Glen learned that all the police stations in the outback employed trackers. **1979** C. JOHNSON *Long Live Sandawarra* 112 The six men do not cover their tracks well and the Queensland trackers can easily follow them towards the wild Wandjina gorge.

track-ride, *v. intr.* See quot. 1978 (here as *vbl. n.*). Also as **track rider** *n.*

1959 E. WEBB *Mark of Sun* 58, I made out that he had been a track rider on a station somewhere when he was younger, and that's where he'd picked up his bit of white-man's lingo. **1978** TEECE & PIKE *Voice of Wilderness* 21 It was necessary to do what was called 'track riding', looking for tracks of cattle that had strayed across the invisible boundary of the station.

traditional owner. An Aboriginal who is a member of a local descent group having certain rights in a tract of land, esp. as recognized under the *Aboriginal Land Rights (Northern Territory) Act 1976*: see quot. 1976. Also *attrib.*

[**1964** R.M. & C.H. BERNDT *World First Australs.* 344 Tribal or clan land itself is not transferable, but regarded as being held in trust by living men and women for past, present and future members of that unit. Their ownership, in this special sense of the term, is supernaturally sanctioned.] **1974** *Cwlth. Parl. Papers* I. no. 69 53, I have no doubt that the Larrakia people were the traditional owners of what is now the whole Darwin area. **1976** *Act* (Cwlth. of Aust.) no. 191 Sect. 3, 'Traditional Aboriginal owner', in relation to land means a local descent group of Aboriginals who—(a) have common spiritual affiliations to a site on the land, being affiliations that place the group under a primary spiritual responsibility for that site and for the land; and (b) are entitled by Aboriginal tradition to forage as of right over that land. **1978** *Nat. Times* (Sydney) 21 Oct. 22/3 One of the main concerns of the traditional owners is that mining pits be filled on completion of mining. **1981** *Cwlth. Parl. Papers* VI. no. 61 9, Questions may arise as to the identity of the traditional owners of the land which the seas adjoin but I suggest that . . some general evidence based on reputation within the community may be sufficient to establish and identify traditional owners. **1982** *Sydney Morning Herald* 17 July 1/3 Surrounding his house are the galvanised iron huts and tents of his brothers, sisters, uncles, aunts and cousins and their children—members of . . one of the two traditional owner clans of the region. **1984** *Bulletin* (Sydney) 6 Mar. 54/2 The claimants became reduced to one. Among his difficulties, he was unable to persuade the commissioner that he was a traditional owner. **1985** *Ibid.* 23 July 17/3 All this is brought about at the whim of a small group of traditional owners, trading on privileges that no other Australian has and financed to a large extent by our taxes. **1986** DAYLIGHT & JOHNSTONE *Women's Business* 63 Women from Numbulnar . . declared . . that this right is not being automatically accorded them as traditional owners.

trag. Pl. **trag, trags.** Shortened form of TERAGLIN.

1951 T.C. ROUGHLEY *Fish & Fisheries Aust.* 73 Teraglin (Trag, *Atractoscion atelodus*). **1973** *Kings Cross Whisper* (Sydney) xlv. 16/4 A nice haul of snapper, mowies and even a dozen or so trag. **1984** *Sunday Tel.* (Sydney) 5 Aug. 122/6 Tailor and teraglin could also put in an appearance, with the moon beginning to grow larger. One area which usually produces 'trags' is the Coogee ground.

traglin, var. TERAGLIN.

train, *n.* [Cf. *to pull a train* to copulate successively with more than one partner (see OEDS *pull, v.* 11 g.)] See quot. 1976.

1976 *Nat. Times* (Sydney) 29 Nov. 10/1 A National Times team has interviewed a number of people in a small cane-growing community in north Queensland, where a sexual practice called 'the train' occurs. . . A train might begin at the Saturday night cabaret, as a couple left together. Other men made a yanking motion in the air, like a conductor pulling the cord, and shouted, 'Too-hoot' All Aboard! And they would follow, and as many as 50 men would have sexual intercourse with the woman. **1980** B. HORNADGE *Austral. Slanguage* 191 A different kettle of fish entirely is the *train*, a subtle form of pack rape achieved by peer group pressures.

train, *v.* [f. prec.] *trans.* To subject (a female) to sexual intercourse with a succession of males.

1976 *Nat. Times* (Sydney) 29 Nov. 10/2 (*heading*) How women are trained. If it's not rape what is it? **1978** P.R. WILSON *Other Side of Rape* 115 A variety of derivations set the phrase in a more illuminating context—how women are trained, we want to train your women, and so on. **1983** G. LEWIS *Real Men like Violence* 81 The notorious gang rapes which occurred at Ingham, North Queensland, in 1977 were based on this kind of male bonding. Gang rape there was referred to as 'training' the local girls.

Hence **trainer** *n.*

1976 *Nat. Times* (Sydney) 29 Nov. 13/4 She knew the three men who raped her; they were leading 'trainers'.

tram. In the phr. **to be on the wrong tram,** to be pursuing an unproductive course.

1955 J. MORRISON *Black Cargo* 223 No, son, you're on the wrong tram with me. **1968** J. ALARD *He who shoots Last* 86 'Looks like we're on da wrong tram,' agreed the Wrecker. **1982** *Bulletin* (Sydney) 19 Jan. 27/3 What McMahon will be telling his former parliamentary colleagues is that the Fraser Government is, in his judgement, on the wrong tram economically.

trammie. [f. *tram* + -Y.] The driver or conductor of a tram.

[N.Z. **1912** *N.Z. Truth* (Wellington) 3 Feb. 5 Many there were who refused to believe the 'Trammies' would do such a thing, but . . the conductors and the motormen meant it, and the street cars were gradually deserted.] **1919** C. DREW *Doings of Dave* 160 'Say, trammie.' . . The tram-guard shook his head. **1934** *Red Star* (Perth) 23 Mar. 1/3 The trammies must be prepared to put up a fight against the action of the department. **1946** F. CLUNE *Try Nothing Twice* 13 An alliance was formed between the trammies and us newsies. They let us travel free, and we kept nit for them. **1959** R. BURNS *Mr Brain knows Best* 19 The seamen, the wharf labourers, the trammies, and the Bulk Handlers have all voted solidly for Marxist leadership. **1971** *Kings Cross Whisper* (Sydney) cxviii. 2/3 *Trammie tramped.* An all-night tramways bus driver was sentenced to three years gaol. **1983** D.J. BAILEY *Holes in Ground* 12 When 400 trammies marched on eight hour day 1911, Badger closed the company recreation room to them.

tramp, *v.* [Fig. use of *tramp* to stamp on: see OED *v.*[1] 2.] *trans.* To dismiss (a person) from employment.

1941 S.J. BAKER *Pop. Dict. Austral. Slang* 78 *Tramped*, dismissed from employment. **1948** *Bulletin* (Sydney)

16 June 23/4 During a recent shearing he sacked a man; but the wife, seeing the shearer walking to the office to get his cheque, stopped him. He told her that he'd been 'tramped'. **1953** T.A.G. HUNGERFORD *Riverslake* 213 It's like Con says, Carmichael tramps Hughie for a bit of a thing like that and if he gets away with it it'll be curtains for conditions in this place for a while. **1964** H.P. TRITTON *Time means Tucker* (rev. ed.) 11 'Less talk and more work, or I'll tramp you.' I tossed my shovel away. **1975** B. FOLEY *Shearers' Poems* 2 His dread of getting 'tramped' Because his eyes were on the blink Nearly drove him up the flamin' wall Then back down to demon drink. **1982** M. WATTONE *Winning Gold in W.A.* 66, I went to the surface and immediately was tramped (sacked).

tram troub. Also **tram trube.** TROUB.

1912 *Truth* (Sydney) 1 Dec. 3/3 (*heading*) Tricky tram troub's tart. **1914** *Ibid.* 19 July 1/3 The fairest of all fares? The tram troub's tart. **1915** L.C. REEVES *Australs. in Action New Guinea* 12 The uniform of the 'Tram Troub' was well displayed in the ranks and . . one heard such remarks as 'Fares Please', 'Hurry on Please'. **1916** *Truth* (Sydney) 5 Mar. 2/6 A tram troub named Austin Ritchie would appear to be anything but 'Fair please' at times. **1979** D. MCCARTHY *Fate of O'Loughlin* 144, I looked up and there's the conductor grinning at me . . a bloody tram trube.

Hence **tram troubing** *vbl. n.*

1914 *Truth* (Sydney) 18 Oct. 11/4 (*caption*) Blake makes a break. Takes to tram troubing.

transport, *n. Hist.* [Spec. use of *transport* one under sentence of transportation: see OED *sb.* 5.] One sentenced in the British Isles to a term of servitude in a penal colony in Australia.

1803 *Sydney Gaz.* 10 Apr., On Wednesday 10 prisoners who were capitally convicted at the last Criminal Court were respited by His Excellency, on condition of their becoming Transports for Life. **1808** *HRA* (1916) 1st Ser. VI. 515 Once a Seven Years Transport in this Colony. **1820** H.G. BENNET *Let. to Earl Bathurst* 44, I should recommend, for the future, that the transports for each colony, both of male and female, should be selected at home. **1830** *Monitor* (Sydney) 9 Oct. 2/4 Transports who have moved in good society at home; we mean convicted clergymen, officers in the army, navy. **1838** *Rep. Select Committee Transportation* 12 Apr. 130 The greater part are what are termed 'transports for life'. **1850** J. PLATT *Horrors of Transportation* 6, I was described as a run-away transport from my master. **1862** F.J. JOBSON *Aust.* 118 A few remain . . who are immediate descendants of 'transports'. **1893** J. DEMARR *Adventures in Aust.* 44 A man who was transported was said to have been 'lagged' and a transport was an old 'lag'.

transport, *v. Hist.* [Spec. use of *transport* to carry into banishment, as a criminal or slave: see OED *v.* 2 c.]

1. *trans.* To deport (a person sentenced in the British Isles) to a penal colony in Australia.

1788 *HRA* (1914) 1st Ser. I. 87 The knowing when the time expires for which the convicts have been transported is very necessary. **1801** G. BARRINGTON *Sequel to Voyage N.S.W.* 62 James Harris, James Ruffler, and Richard Partridge, who were all transported for life, received a pardon. **1815** *HRA* (1916) 1st Ser. VIII. 499 The necessity of allowing Persons, transported as Felons, to practise as Attornies. **1823** *Ibid.* (1917) 1st Ser. III. 80 Touching the behaviour of Female Convicts transported to this Colony. **1829** 'FORMER POLICE OFFICER' *Adventures I. Solomons* 19 About the year 1811, Isaac was tried at the Old Bailey, for picking the pocket of a gentleman, and sentenced to be transported for seven years. **1849** A. HARRIS *Emigrant Family* (1967) 84 'I never could think how she could come to be transported.' 'Was she, then, a convict originally.' **1860** 'LADY' *My Experiences in Aust.* 24 This worthy was transported in the early times of the colony, and from conducting himself properly while passing through the usual gradations of a convict's lot, he obtained in due time his ticket-of-leave, and set up as an auctioneer.

2. a. RETRANSPORT.

1811 *Sydney Gaz.* 16 Feb., *James Frazer* was found *Guilty* . . and sentenced to be transported to Newcastle, and kept to hard labour for the term of seven years. **1821** *HRA* (1921) 3rd Ser. IV. 13 Two Convicts . . runaways from Port Jackson under a former Sentence, and now transported for a new Crime. **1839** *Sydney Standard* 21 Jan. 3/2 *Patrick Lynch*, bond, house robbery, transported to a penal settlement for life. **1847** A. MARJORIBANKS *Travels N.S.W.* 105 Banishment from Australia, for the natives and free persons, is now to Norfolk Island, if for the first offence; but doubly convicted felons—that is, prisoners transported from this country convicted of new crimes there, are now all sent to Van Diemen's Land.

b. *transf.* Of an Aboriginal: to remove forcibly.

1835 H. MELVILLE *Hist. Van Diemen's Land* 25 He was transported from New Holland, and was employed in this Colony as a stock-keeper from which situation he was taken to assist in capturing the bushrangers. **1911** ST. C. GRONDONA *Collar & Cuffs* 60 The blacks have all been transported to Frazer, the dingoes are nearly all poisoned, and the fox has not penetrated so far north as this yet, consequently the turkey flourishes.

transportable, *a. Hist.* Attracting a sentence of transportation to a penal colony in Australia. Also *fig.*

1833 *HRA* (1923) 1st Ser. XVII. 306 Persons who had never been convicted of Felonry or any transportable Offence. **1846** *Ibid.* (1925) 1st. Ser. XXV. 57 If he commit transportable offence. **1849** *Bell's Life in Sydney* 10 Nov. 2/1 He also admits, 'that the report in the 'Sydney Morning Herald' would *seem* to imply that the second clause of the Bill referred only to persons convicted . . of any capital or transportable offence.' **1854** G.H. HAYDON *Austral. Emigrant* 91 You shall hear no more of this joke of yours (by the bye, it is a transportable one you know).

transportation. *Hist.* [Spec. use of *transportation* removal or banishment, as of a criminal to a penal settlement: see OED 2 c.]

1. The deportation to a penal colony in Australia of a person sentenced in the British Isles.

1789 W. TENCH *Narr. Exped. Botany Bay* 143 When the term of their transportation shall be expired. **1791** *Copies & Extracts Lett. Governor Phillip* 5 Nov. (1792) 125 Those convicts whose sentences of transportation expired, and have been permitted to become settlers at or near Parramatta, are to be supported and clothed from the public store for eighteen months. **1808** *Sydney Gaz.* 23 Oct., Charles Thorpe, a prisoner under sentence of transportation for 14 years. **1822** J.T. BIGGE *Rep. State Colony N.S.W.* 3 There are instances on record, in which convicts have expressed their desire that the sentence of transportation might be commuted, even for the utmost rigour of the law. **1827** G. HOLFORD *Let.* 7 The injustice of sending females, who were under sentence of transportation for seven years only, to New South Wales, without affording them some means of return . . was . . generally admitted. **1838** *Rep. Select Committee Transportation* p. iii, The punishment of Transportation is founded on that of exile, both of which are unknown to common law. **1839** *Sydney Herald* 9 Oct. 2/1 *Transportation has ceased.* This welcome fact was announced by the Governor yesterday. **1845** M. COLLISSON *S.A.* 28 In Van Diemen's Land, the proportion of bond to free is now as one to one; but the stream of transportation continues to flow in upon that devoted island. **1849** J.P. TOWNSEND *Rambles & Observations N.S.W.* 150 He appeared inclined to regret the cessation of transportation; and I doubt not that, in his heart, he was sometimes ready to exclaim with Sir John Falstaff, 'O for a fine thief of two-and-twenty or thereabouts! I am heinously unprovided.' **1865** *Glenorchy Murders* 7 He was sentenced to seven years' transportation. Under this sentence he arrived in Tasmania . . on the 31st July, 1852. . . Soon after his arrival he was assigned to Mr Turnley. . . While in his assigned service he frequently manifested habits of intemperance.

2. The committal to a penal settlement of a person sentenced in Australia.

1799 *HRA* (1914) 1st Ser. II. 306 Sentenced to fourteen years' transportation to Norfolk Island. **1808** *Ibid.* (1916) 1st Ser. VI. 395 Convicted of wilful and corrupt Perjury and sentenced to seven Years Transportation. **1818** *Hobart Town Gaz.* 3 Jan., His Excellency . . has been pleased to extend Clemency to 7 persons who were condemned to death at the late Criminal Sessions, commuting their sentence to transportation for life. **1820** C. JEFFREYS *Van Dieman's Land* 76 It is to be regretted, that, by the colonial orders, it is transportation to the coal-mines for any of the inhabitants to have wash, or wort, in their possession. **1833** *HRA* (1923) 1st Ser. XVII. 51, I would recommend that the Sentence of Mac Grath be commuted to Transportation for Life to Norfolk Island. **1836** J.F. O'CONNELL *Residence Eleven Yrs. New Holland* 66 The sale or gift of arms or ammunition to a bushranger is punishable by transportation to a penal settlement. **1844** *Sydney Morning Herald* 14 Oct. 2/6 A soldier of the 99th Regiment, was convicted of stealing in a dwelling-house, and in passing sentence of transportation for fifteen years upon the prisoner, the Chief Justice expressed his sorrow to find that there are so many bad characters among the military. **1850** *Irish Exile* (Hobart) 9 Mar. 6/4 The defendant arrived in this colony . . in 1840, under a sentence of seven years transportation; and . . at the Hobart Town Quarter Sessions held on the 25th of May, 1848, he received a sentence of imprisonment in H.M. gaol here, for the term of two years. He was now sentenced to seven years transportation. **1853** *Illustr. Sydney News* 12 Nov. 43/3 The four soldiers lately convicted at Launceston of an assault of William Henry Nash, have had their sentence of death commuted to transportation for ten years.

3. Comb. in sense 1: **transportation question, system.**

1847 *Britannia & Trades' Advocate* (Hobart) 15 Apr. 2/2 We solicit attention to that most important of all important matters connected with our colonial interests, namely, the **Transportation question.** **1848** *Moreton Bay Courier* 5 Feb. 4/2 The Transportation *Question* is, we understand, set at rest by the arrival of the ship, *Marion*, at Hobart town, with exiles for this colony and Port Phillip. **1851** *Empire* (Sydney) 1 Aug. 1/1 Upon the Transportation Question, I repeat my desire is never to see the system, again introduced to this colony. **1852** *Four Colonies Aust.* 16 On the transportation question, the Home Government was defeated, and suffered to retain only Van Diemen's Land as a settlement to which felons might be transported. **1853** W. WESTGARTH *Vic.* 167 The Transportation Question . . could scarcely now be discussed with temper. **1825** B. FIELD *Geogr. Mem. N.S.W.* 458 The evils and expense of the **transportation-system** would certainly be lessened, by placing the convicts more in the service of farming and grazing settlers, out of the reach of the temptations and evil communications of great towns. **1834** J.D. LANG *Hist. & Statistical Acct. N.S.W.* II. 219 The transportation-system . . constitutes the grand objection to New South Wales as a place to reside in. **1842** *Colonial Observer* (Sydney) 13 Aug. 393/2 The Home Government have partially but most absurdly retained the Transportation system at Norfolk Island. **1847** *Maitland Mercury* 18 Sept. 2/3 Those who had emigrated to New South Wales in former times, wrote then to their friends describing the horrors and contamination around them under the working of the transportation system. **1851** H. MELVILLE *Present State Aust.* 52 The transportation system cannot be otherwise than beneficial.

transportationist. *Hist.* One who favours the continuance of the convict system. Also **pro-transportationist.** See also ANTI-TRANSPORTATION.

1847 *Abolitionists & Transportationists* p. x, If he were a Transportationist, it would be cutting the throat of his own argument. **1850** *Sydney Morning Herald* 27 Sept. 2/2 The great, the only argument, of the transportationists is, that convicts make cheap servants. **1850** *Irish Exile* (Hobart) 21 Dec. 2/3 We can scarcely imagine it possible for a pro-transportationist to be returned for any one district in the island. **1852** J. WEST *Hist. of Tas.* I. 280 A few transportationists induced a respectable shopkeeper to propose thirty-nine reasons for the continuance of transportation. **1867** *Launceston Examiner* 19 May 316/4 We are told by the transportationists that they overflow with regard to the poor convict.

transported, *ppl. a. Hist.* [f. TRANSPORT *v.*]

1. Deported as a convict to a penal colony in Australia.

1822 J. DIXON *Narr. Voyage N.S.W. & Van Dieman's Land* 65 There is a . . factory of a very handsome appearance for such transported females as are not taken into the service of those settlers who require female servants. **1836** J.F. O'CONNELL *Residence Eleven Yrs. New Holland* 100 Beside the transported population, there are growing generations of Anglo-Australians. **1843** *Sydney Morning Herald* 23 May 2/8 Whence the cause of this rise in wages and loss to the graziers? I answer, the substitution of immigrant labour for transported labour was the cause. **1871** C.L. Money *Knocking about N.Z.* p. vii, The creature sustains life on 'forty pounds a-year and his tucker' at the remote station of a transported friend of the family.

2. In collocations: **transported convict, felon, offender.**

1824 *Australasian Pocket Almanack* 82 In the Grants is contained a proviso, that the grantee, his heirs and assigns, shall .. procure to be assigned to his or their service .. one **transported convict** for every 100 acres of the said land. **1847** J.B. Atkinson *Penal Settlements* 9 Until the year 1804, all our transported convicts were sent to New South Wales. **1853** W. Westgarth *Vic.* 167 In the Melbourne gaol, the more atrocious offenders were .. old transported convicts. **1863** C. Gibson *Life among Convicts* II. 216 The Act 5 Geo. IV.c.84, gave the governor of a penal colony a *property* in the services of a transported convict, and authorized him to assign the prisoner to any other person. **1840** *HRA* (1924) 1st Ser. XX. 527 Every **transported Felon** should, during the period of at least two years, receive no indulgence whatever. **1841** *Port Phillip Patriot* 1 Nov. 3/1 The Act of General Darling was passed at a period when the Colony of New South Wales was exclusively considered as the receptacle of transported felons. **1843** C. Rowcroft *Tales of Colonies* (1858) 245 The condition of the transported felon is much better than that of the honest labourer in England. **1829** *Colonial Times* (Hobart) 28 Nov., Occupiers of House etc., receiving therein any **transported offender** for the purpose of drinking or gambling, without the leave of such offender's employer, to be liable to penalties. **1835** *True Colonist* (Hobart) 21 Aug. 8/1 We have heard the opinion mooted .. that the *descendants* of 'transported offenders' ought not to be received into society until the third generation. **1840** *Tasmanian Weekly Dispatch* 21 Feb. 7/1 Indicted for being illegally at large, *being transported offenders.*

trap, *n.*[1] [Survival of Br. slang *trap* one whose business is to 'trap' offenders: see OED(S *sb.*[1] 6 and quot. 1859.] An officer of the law, esp. a police officer.

1812 J.H. Vaux *Mem.* (1819) 220 *Traps*, police officers, or runners, are properly so called; but it is common to include constables of any description under this title. **1817** *Hobart Town Gaz.* 26 July, They said 'they had suffered enough by the b--dy *traps* and would kill them all'. **1827** *Monitor* (Sydney) 8 Oct. 694 It is owing to such literal *traps* as Izzy, that the Police, the public Officers, and the Governor himself, are all brought into needless popularity. **1847** *Heads of People* (Sydney) 20 Nov. 44 Kemble .. appealed to his 'friend' the Chief Constable to preserve order, the chief trap finding his orders despised, made a touching appeal to the military. **1859** W. Kelly *Life in Vic.* I. 185 The police in the diggings went by the name of traps—an obsolete sobriquet at home. **1872** W.H. Thomes *Bushrangers* 30 The reward which the governor has offered .. has set all the *traps* of Melbourne on the alert. **1891** —— *Belle of Aust.* 45 You must marry the lady or die, for all the traps of Melbourne, with me at their head, could not preserve your life. **1907** *Truth* (Sydney) 14 July 9/4 From the spouts and ditches peeping, every 'trap' was bent on reaping The reward which zeal doth bringeth, both to 'ranker' and to 'sub'. **1921** G.A. Bell *Under Brigalows* 31 Yes, I durned well knew they two coves was traps, though they was mighty careful not to give theirselves away. **1948** F. Clune *Wild Colonial Boys* p. xix, 'Many a time my father sent me galloping through the bush with a message that the traps were coming.' 'Traps?' 'Mounted troopers.' **1965** D. Martin *Hero of Too* 248 The traps don't say pooh. They're ready to pay good money to find out who he is. **1978** K. Garvey *Tales of my Uncle Harry* 35 Muldoon heads for town and gets the traps.

trap, *n.*[2] [Spec. use of *trap* a snare in which animals are caught.] In the phr. **to go round the traps** and varr., to make a tour of inspection. Freq. *fig.*

1933 J. Truran *Where Plain Begins* 224 Reuben and his brother were 'going round the traps'. They carried no lantern; as the traps belonged to somebody else, that would have been an unwise procedure. **1965** J. Wynnum *Jiggin' in Riggin'* 124 So yesterday she made a trip around the traps, throwing out a few hints, is that it? **1965** W. Moxham *Follow That Horse* 105 Mrs Goldstone was .. the owner of a string of dress shops... Mrs Goldstone had been away in Queensland going around her traps.

trap-yard. An enclosure into which wild cattle, horses, etc., are driven and confined: see quots. 1880 and 1963. Also **trapping yard.**

1880 J.B. Stevenson *Seven Yrs. Austral. Bush* 93 Our first work was to construct a number of trap yards. These are small but high enclosures which we placed upon some of the most frequented tracks, generally concealed near a sudden turn, wings being run out on either side of the track for some distance. When we started a mob of horses we endeavoured to drive them along one of these tracks; and if we succeeded in this we generally managed to yard the greater part of the mob. **1898** C.L. Morgan *Rabbit Question in Qld.* 121 The most wholesale method of trapping [*sc.* rabbits] is by means of trap yards. **1913** *Bulletin* (Sydney) 24 Apr. 13/2, I came across some old trap-yards... The brumbies were yarded by stratagem and hard riding; the gate was then thrown open, and a half-cooked devil, armed with a shear-blade on a stick, stabbed them in the flank as they galloped out, and disembowelled them—this to avoid having a horse's corpse on the premises. **1926** J. Pollard *Bushland Man* 57 A trapping-yard had to be built at the pool in which to corral the horses, and the mob yarded when they came to drink. **1937** D. Gunn *Links with Past* 81 The stallion was running with wild horses .. so they erected a trap yard there and were fortunate enough to yard the mob. **1944** *Bulletin* (Sydney) 9 Aug. 13/1 The wild cattle seldom mixed with animals from the settled country; when they did, the combined herds were promptly run off to one of the many trap-yards built by scrubber-hunters. **1963** W.E. Harney *To Ayers Rock & Beyond* 48 The wide gate of the fenced-in enclosure was left open, but when the cattle of that part were to be mustered, the gate was shut and the only entry into the place was through a contraption called a 'bayonet' which was built with logs having sharpened ends in the same manner as a fish-trap. Once the cattle went inside the 'trap-yard' they could not get out.

travel, *v.*

1. *intr. Obs.* Of livestock: to be driven through the country, freq. in search of pasture.

1849 A. Harris *Emigrant Family* (1967) 16 My cattle travel very wild; some of them are off down every gully they see: you can .. stick to the tail of 'em. **1851** *Britannia* (Hobart) 21 Apr. 3/4 Through this line of country upwards of 80,000 sheep are 'travelling' in search of grass. **1870** *Sydney Morning Herald* 2 July 3/6 *For sale.* 800 mixed Cattle, near Dubbo, travelling southwards. **1887** W.S.S. Tyrwhitt *New Chum in Qld. Bush* 172 Drovers are wanted to take sheep and cattle to market when fat .. and in bad seasons to take them travelling for grass.

2. *trans.* To drive (sheep or cattle) through the country, freq. in search of pasture. Also *intr.*

1870 E.B. Kennedy *Four Yrs. in Qld.* 148 Travelling the sheep has to be resorted to when the country is short of water and grass. **1880** J. Bonwick *Resources Qld.* 35 Many are compelled to *travel* with stock when their own feed at home is destroyed by drought. **1890** 'R. Boldrewood' *Squatter's Dream* 182, I shall lose a lot of my lambs and calves, have to travel all the sheep. **1907** *Bulletin* (Sydney) 15 Aug. 14/2 The boss was to travel sheep—a week's journey—to the northern Mallee. **1916** T. Warlow *By Mirage & Mulga* 11, I had bought a mob of sheep from him, travelled them for sale, didn't sell them very well, and had altogether a bad time of it. **1930** 'Brent Of Bin Bin' *Ten Creeks Run* (1952) 2 In droughty summers he also travelled his sheep up. **1942** H.H. Peck *Mem. of Stockman* 61 Some of the leading drovers .. travelled the big mobs of bullocks from the pastures. **1960** R.S. Porteous *Cattleman* 86 'Got your waybill on you?' 'Yes. You didn't think I'd be mug enough to travel a mob without one, did you?'

3. *transf. intr.* To journey through the country, usu. on foot and freq. in search of work: see Traveller 1. Also *trans.*

1892 'J. Miller' *Workingman's Paradise* 105 Live on rations that the squatters serve out to keep men travelling the country so they can get them if they want them. **1903** W.L. Ogilvie *Hearts of Gold* 77 We were travelling down the Bogan where the scrubs are deep and dense. **1912** J. Bradshaw *Highway Robbery under Arms* (ed. 3) 27 Two men .. asked me to travel with them, and said that I would enjoy myself up to dick. **1960** *N.T. News* (Darwin) 22 Jan. 6/3 Bella was a first-class bush cook and very generous in her handouts to many a battler travelling this district in the depression days. **1965** R.H. Conquest *Horses in Kitchen* 9 In those days a swaggie coudn't draw rations in the same town two weeks running. He had to 'travel for rations'.

4. *intr.* To keep company (with a person of the opposite sex). Also *trans.*, to court. See Track *v.*

1892 *Bulletin* (Sydney) 5 Nov. 17/2 Tho' Bleeders deemed the square affair's white innocence a myth, She differed much from other girls that Bill had travelled with. **1901** *Truth* (Sydney) 21 Apr. 5/1 If the girl happened to have 'knocked about' or 'travelled' to any extent, she would not get employment. ***c* 1907** W.C. Chandler *Darkest Adelaide* 8 'E was in awful trouble over the female wot 'e was travellin'.

traveller.

1. One who journeys through the country (in search of work); Swagman a.

1845 *Bell's Life in Sydney* 22 Nov. 2/1 The publican can pretty well make the distinction between a 'traveller' and a 'pot-wolloper'. **1868** *Australasian* (Melbourne) 5 Sept. 305/3 'Travellers' would not unfrequently spend the afternoon at one of the three hotels .. and having 'liquored up' extensively, stagger up to the station, and insist upon lodging and food—which they got. **1872** 'Resident' *Glimpses Life Vic.* 221 Hordes of 'travellers' .. frequented the Bush. **1877** *Austral. Town & Country Jrnl.* (Sydney) 24 Feb. 303/1 A mounted tramp or 'traveller' looking for work, with no great hope of, or indeed concern about, finding it. **1893** *Southerly* (1964) iii. 204 Men tramping in search of a 'shed' are not called 'sundowners' or 'swaggies'; they are 'trav'lers'. **1896** *Bulletin* (Sydney) 1 Feb. 11/1 The writer knows a N.Q. run-manager whose custom is to talk to 'travellers' thus: 'Look here, men. If you're hungry to need's extent, kill a sheep, and I'll never say a word. But don't you set fire to my grass.' **1908** *Truth* (Sydney) 12 Apr. 11/4 Hardly a station will give a traveller a job. **1921** K.S. Prichard *Black Opal* 14 If a traveller—swagman—died on the road, it was Michael who saw he got a decent burial. **1933** J. Truran *Where Plain Begins* 140 The roads are as full o' travellers as a Chinaman's dog is o' fleas, an' some o' the poor coots seem t' have given up all 'opes o' workin' any more. **1941** K. Tennant *Battlers* 165 The travellers were just as much a separate race, distinct from the people who lived in towns, as the blacks were. **1959** *Bulletin* (Sydney) 7 Oct. 19/2 A match lighted and dropped when the grass was dry and long was a risk against which the old-time squatters insured by the system of handouts listed on the books as 'travellers' rations'. **1965** R.H. Conquest *Horses in Kitchen* 45 Queensland during the depression years attracted the maximum number of travellers during the winter months.

2. In special collocations: **travellers' flour,** flour of inferior quality (see quot. 1895); **hut,** a dwelling provided on a rural property for the accommodation of travellers (see quot. 1892); **sugar,** sugar of inferior quality.

1895 *Worker* (Sydney) 9 Feb. 4/2 One squatter on that creek charged me 5d. a lb. for flour of the most inferior quality, and alive with weevils. Storekeepers generally term it **'travellers' flour'**. **1898** *Ibid.* 1 Jan. 7/2 I've known storekeepers who kept special bins labelled 'travellers' flour', 'travellers' sugar' and so on. **1868** C.W. Browne *Overlanding in Aust.* 63 You go up to the **'travellers hut'**, to see if you can get any traveller going through to accompany you. **1887** A. Nicols *Wild Life & Adventure* 188 Men in twos and threes .. rode in .. and took up their quarters in the wool-shed and the travellers' hut. **1892** 'E. Kinglake' *Austral. at Home* 132 The number of 'sundowners', and the frequency of their visits, was the cause of the establishment of what is called the 'travellers' hut'. **1903** R.J. Clow *Pillar of Salt* 25 Leaving their swags in the travellers' hut they breasted up to the kitchen door. **1913** W.K. Harris *Outback in Aust.* 2 For three days he was laid up in the 'Traveller's Hut' (to be found on almost every sheep-station, for the use of 'swaggies'). **1898 travellers' sugar** [see *travellers' flour*].

traveller's joy. [Transf. use of *traveller's joy* the trailing plant *Clematis vitalba.*] *Old man's beard*, see Old man *n.* 3.

1881 *Proc. Linnean Soc. N.S.W.* VI. 741 *Clematis microphylla* or 'Traveller's Joy' which covered the bushes with its slender twining branches. **1985** *Canberra Times* 20 June (Suppl.) 1/5 *Clematis aristata* (traveller's joy or old man's beard) is a feature of the bushland in moist, sheltered gullies of Queensland, N.S.W., Victoria and Tasmania... It bears masses of creamy-white flowers in spring which are followed by fluffy, white seed heads.

travelling, *vbl. n.*

1. In the senses of TRAVEL. Also *attrib.*

1880 J.B. STEVENSON *Seven Yrs. Austral. Bush* 57 A mob, in travelling, generally takes the form of a wedge, the strongest and best travelling beasts going ahead. **1888** T.V. FOOTE *My Weird Wooing* 102 The monotony of sheep and cattle travelling. **1894** M. ROBERTS *Red Earth* 98 As the Australian system of travelling leads men to place after place looking for work, most station owners have the refusal day after day of many men. **1915** *Bulletin* (Sydney) 14 Oct. 24/4 Tell me a profession with more *aliases* than the swagmans? Here are a few: 'Waltzin' Matilda', 'paddin' the hoof', 'travellin'' [etc.]. **1974** D. STUART *Prince of my Country* 108 With the feeling of being hemmed in, caught, 'But I've got nothing, just a travelling swag.'

2. Special Comb. **travelling ration,** a ration of provisions, a dole (see TRACK *n.* 5); **statement,** a document in which the details of a travelling herd are recorded (see quot. 1920).

1959 *Overland* xv. 31 Scores of thousands of 'travellers'—who generally called themselves 'bagmen'—were scouring the roads and railway lines in search of **travelling rations.** **1977** J. DOUGHTY *Gold in Blood* 22 In the Queensland of those days, there was no need to work if you did not feel like working; you could enjoy the life of a gypsy. Nearly all police stations issued 'travelling rations'. **1977** L. FOX *Depression Down Under* 71 In those days you had to go to the police to get travelling rations—get the dole. **1878** *Act* (N.S.W.) 41 Vict. no. 19 Sect. 5, Every drover in charge of any travelling sheep and every drover in charge of travelling horses or cattle shall be provided at the time of his departure with a '**travelling statement**'. **1901** *Ibid.* no. 27 Sect. 69, All travelling stock shall be taken by the drover thereof by any direct road ordinarily used for the purpose of travelling stock to the place of destination mentioned in the permit or travelling statement. **1920** J.B. CRAMSIE *Managem. & Diseases Sheep* 36 He should produce, on demand, his permit and travelling statement, duly signed by a Stock Inspector, setting out full particulars of his sheep, brands, marks, owner, destination, etc., to any police officer, J.P., or Stock Inspector. **1932** J. MCCARTER *Pan's Clan* 155 I've th' travellin' statement in my pocket, with brands and ear marks shown, also the permit to travel.

travelling, *ppl. a.*[1] [f. TRAVEL *v.* 1 and 2.]

1. Of livestock: being driven through the country.

1872 G.S. BADEN-POWELL *New Homes for Old Country* 124 Station shepherds, who feed along the road, may be forewarned, and thus save their own flocks getting 'boxed' with the travelling 'lots'. **1880** G.A. BROWN *Sheep Breeding in Aust.* 331 They were of the flocks known as 'Stationary', as distinguished from the 'Travelling' flocks. **1904** *Bulletin* (Sydney) 10 Nov. 19/1, I believe *Bulletin* would allow a teamster, or a mob of travelling jumbucks to camp in its office before outback squattocracy would allow a swagman to look over the stock route or reserve fence. **1915** *Ibid.* 23 Sept. 22/4 A mob of travelling cows was put on camp. **1923** F.A.C. BISHOP *Rep. on Inspection Barkly Tableland* 4 On examination of the lung, I found it to be affected with pleuro-pneumonia, which clearly told me the travelling mobs ahead were affected. **1934** 'E.N. SPEER' *Destiny* 242 He was overtaking a travelling mob of sheep, hoping he would reach them before they left the main road for the two-mile wide stock route.

2. In collocations: **travelling sheep, shepherd, stockman.**

1864 H. JONES *New Valuations* 24 From 100,000 to 150,000 sheep leave the North annually for the other colonies... The feed, for a mile to a mile and a half in width, is either eaten or destroyed by these **travelling sheep.** **1880** P.R. GORDON *Drover's Guide* 9 Every drover in charge of travelling sheep in New South Wales must be provided with a 'travelling statement', signed by the owner. **1895** A.B. PATERSON *Man from Snowy River* 50 A man must cover with travelling sheep a six-mile stage a day. **1917** —— *Saltbush Bill* 3 We have sung the song of the droving days, Of the march of the travelling sheep. **1932** J. MCCARTER *Pan's Clan* 155 Every one of the jumbucks has a T branded on his rump, so we are O.K. with the travelling sheep laws. **1942** W. GLASSON *Our Shepherds* 9 Travelling sheep are often camped in a lane near this homestead. **1860** 'LADY' *My Experiences in Aust.* 126 A **travelling shepherd** or gold-digger would ask permission to boil his quart-pot at our fire. **1880** J.B. STEVENSON *Seven Yrs. Austral. Bush* 133 A stage manager and scene painter having been discovered in the person of a travelling shepherd, he was immediately engaged. **1835** J. LHOTSKY *Journey from Sydney* 9 Here the **travelling stockmen** remain with their herds for refreshment. **1939** J.W. COLLINGS *8000 Miles by Air* 7 A travelling stockman wires to another station, notifying them of his delay.

travelling, *ppl. a.*[2] [f. TRAVEL *v.* 3.] Engaged in journeying through the country (in search of work).

1909 *Bulletin* (Sydney) 26 Aug. 14/4 A swagwoman is not a very common happening, but a few days ago an old travelling lady .. passed through Moree. **1917** H. LAWSON *Lett.* (1970) 290 My old travelling mate and stationary friend. **1935** K. TENNANT *Tiburon* 167 The travelling unemployed .. occasionally settle in a town but are usually kept on the move in a wide area in search of work where there is no work.

travelling manager. On a rural property: a relieving manager (see quot. 1954).

1891 *Truth* (Sydney) 15 Feb. 7/2 There is (as in some woolclassing) a sort of archangel, called the 'superintendent' or 'travelling manager', but his face cannot be looked upon by the ordinary whaler who would live. **1954** T. RONAN *Vision Splendid* 100 'This Vincent who's travelling manager is a damned old fule and no cattleman'... Vincent.. was a hard man to place so, as there was nearly always some station manager away on holiday, Vincent acted as a sort of permanent relieving manager for the firm's northern properties. **1960** *N.T. News* (Darwin) 5 Jan. 5/4 Last I heard of him he was travelling manager for a well-known cattle company in the eastern states.

travelling stock.

1. Livestock being driven through the country. Also *attrib.*

1872 G.S. BADEN-POWELL *New Homes for Old Country* 122 One meets or passes 'travelling stock'—herds of more or less wild 'beasts' and flocks of sheep, each marked with a tar T, to show that they are 'travelling', *i.e.* moving from one place to another. **1890** *Braidwood Dispatch* 8 Jan. 2/2 This publication .. gives a return of the depth of water and condition of the pasture on the various routes for travelling stock throughout the colony, so that by referring to this a person in Braidwood with a mob of cattle or sheep en route from say Wagga or Albury knows exactly the state of the country in which are his stock. **1920** H.F. MOLLARD *Humour of Road* 41 A Government tank, for travelling stock, was passed on the left some miles further on, the long troughs being capable of watering hundreds of sheep at one time. **1932** J. MCCARTER *Pan's Clan* 155 When waterless stages precluded adherence to the travelling stock laws, the mileage was increased. **1935** K. TENNANT *Tiburon* 7 By Dwyer's farm, is the travellers' camp on a stretch of grazing-land rightly belonging to the Pastures Protection Board and reserved for hungry travelling stock. **1950** G.M. FARWELL *Land of Mirage* 42 An out-station hut built many years ago by Kidman, the Cattle King .. used to house a couple who looked after his travelling stock. **1956** T. RONAN *Moleskin Midas* 66 Harland .. had a fad for reading and expounding the laws and regulations concerning travelling stock.

2. Special Comb. **travelling stock reserve,** an area of Crown land set aside for the overnight accommodation of travelling stock (see quot. 1977); **route,** a strip of Crown land set aside as a right of way for travelling stock (see quots. 1881 and 1977); formerly also **travelling stock road.** See also T.S.R.

1930 A.E. YARRA *Vanishing Horsemen* 151 Charlie had located the probable site of the cattle camp in the daytime, on a **travelling stock reserve.** **1977** T.L. MCKNIGHT *Long Paddock* 25 Another variable in the spatial extent of TSRs involves areas set aside as overnight or holding paddocks. These paddocks, which are located on or adjacent to the stock routes, are normally identified as Travelling Stock Reserves, although in common parlance 'Routes' and 'Reserves' are often interchangeable. **1986** *Canberra Times* 12 Mar. 3/2 Camping in the Cooma Road travelling-stock reserve. **1881** [**travelling stock route**] A.C. CRUTTWELL *Sketches of Aust.* 42 A travelling stock-road is a straight strip of country, a mile broad, left by the Government for the purposes of large and small cattle travelling from one part of the country to another; they are wire fenced on both sides; but, except in this particular, are undistinguishable from the rest of the country they pass through. **1901** *Bulletin* (Sydney) 26 Oct. 16/3 Squatters .. lay phosphorised pollard on travelling-stock-routes and public roads. **1914** C.H.S. MATTHEWS *Bill* 97 He lived near one of the great Travelling Stock Routes. These T.S.R.s, as they are called, are simply tracks cut through the bush, running down from Queensland to New South Wales. **1935** D.G. STEAD *Rabbit in Aust.* 104 Many of the pastures protection authorities .. are carrying out eradicatory measures on Travelling Stock Routes. **1946** A.W. NOAKES *Life of Policeman* 60 The hotel was at the junction of several travelling stock routes. **1977** T.L. MCKNIGHT *Long Paddock* 1 Travelling Stock Routes are livestock driveways that are designed for the overlanding of stock, mainly cattle and sheep, from one area to another. The actual land occupied by the routes is government owned. The management and administration of the routeways is vested either in regional pastoral associations, in local governing bodies, or in the state department of agriculture. Normally any grazier may utilise the stock routes, providing he abides by the gazetted regulations and pays fees.

trawler. [Fig. use of *trawler* a fishing vessel.] A police vehicle.

1923 *Austral.* (Sydney) Apr. 56 The trorler is a 'nother name for th' p'leece patrol waggin, on account of it grabbin' up everything it comes across. **1933** H.B. RAINE *Lash End* 95 'Is the trawler here?' .. 'Coming round the corner now, sir'... He ran downstairs to tell the 'Black Maria' driver to open the door leading to the female half of the big vehicle. **1947** C.K. THOMPSON *Yes, your Honour!* p. xiv, The driver of the Black Maria, the 'trawler', or in polite language, the police patrol .. offered me a lift from the police-station to the court. **1977** D. FOSTER *Escape to Reality* 91 A trawler came cruising by.

tray. The flat, open part of a truck on which goods are carried.

1960 'N. SHUTE' *Trustee from Toolroom* 100 The semitrailer stood by the aircraft with the sausage-like component on the tray swathed in hessian. **1980** P. DAVIS *Australs. on Road* 125 Ford management conceived the idea of producing .. a passenger-type cab, married to an enclosed load tray; it was called the coupé utility.

tray, var. TREY.

tray-bit, var. TREY-BIT.

traymobile. A small table or stand on wheels or castors for use in carrying or serving food, drinks, etc.

1929 *Austral. Woman's Mirror* (Sydney) 26 Nov. 30/2 Many women fail to realise the labor-saving there is in the systematic use of the traymobile—dumb waiter is the old-fashioned name. Chiefly it is employed for carrying food and table furnishings from kitchen to dining-room, but there are several other ways in which it may be made to fulfil its duty of saving a woman's steps. **1941** *Countrywoman in N.S.W.* 1 Aug. 23 Other gifts were a traymobile from a 'Well wisher'. **1948** V. PALMER *Golconda* 169 Her attention was on the traymobile the girl had wheeled in beside her. She began to pour out the tea. **1958** M. WARREN *No Glamour in Gumboots* 143 'Have a drink', offered our hostess, wheeling forward a traymobile splendid with chrome. **1965** G. MCINNES *Road to Gundagai* 79 Against the vacant wall is the 'dumb waiter' or 'traymobile' on which food and crockery come in from the kitchen next door. **1977** *Meanjin* 176 The cleaner brought in the cakes and tea on a traymobile.

treacle-trousers, *pl.* A jibe levelled at a person wearing trousers which are too short. Also ellipt. as **treacle.**

1924 F.J. MILLS *Happy Days* 112 There was a space of three inches between the bottom of each leg and the top of each boot... Other boys 'barracked' him about it .. calling him 'treacle-trousers'. **1944** E.H. BURGMANN *Educ. Austral.* 23, I was growing fast, and as a gap between the top of my boots and the bottom of the legs of my trousers appeared slightly greater day by day I was greeted by the cry of 'treacle'.

tree. Used *attrib.* in the names of flora and fauna: **tree-bear** *obs.*, KOALA 1; **fern,** any of many ferns, esp. of the fam. Cyatheaceae, Dicksoniaceae, and Athyriaceae, having a tall woody trunk topped by large fronds; *fern tree*, see FERN 2; MAN FERN; **grub** (or **maggot**) *obs.*, WITCHETTY 2; **-kangaroo,** a tree-dwelling macropodid of the genus *Dendrolagus* of New Guinea and n.e. Qld., the two Austral. species being *D. bennettianus* and *D. lumholtzi* (see BOONGARRY); *climbing kangaroo*, see CLIMBING; also **tree-climbing kangaroo; lizard** *obs.*, GOANNA 1; **lucerne,** either of two introduced plants of the fam. Fabaceae, the s. European shrub *Medicago arborea*, and the shrub or small tree *Chamaecytisus prolifer* of the Canary Islands, an ornamental and fodder plant widely naturalized in s. Aust.; **martin,** the migratory bird *Cecropis nigricans* of Aust. incl. Tas., and nearby parts of the s.w. Pacific, usu. nesting in a hole in the trunk or bough of a tree; see also MARTIN; also **tree swallow; nettle** *obs.*, STINGING TREE.

1889 *Fortnightly Rev.* (London) Mar. 425 Kangaroos or little brown **tree-bears** or troops of parrots and cockatoos bring sound and movement into these vast solitudes. **1916** E. & M.S. GREW *Rambles in Aust.* 23 Unfortunately some of the most interesting cannot be kept in captivity. This applies, for instance .. to the koala, or little tree-bear. **1832** J. BACKHOUSE *Narr. Visit Austral. Colonies* (1843) 34 In damp places, by the side of the brook, a princely **tree-fern**, *Cybotium Billardieri*, emerged through the surrounding foliage. **1853** S. SIDNEY *Three Colonies* (ed. 2) 274 At Illawarra the palm and the tree-fern flourish. **1884** G. WIGHT *Qld.* 82 *Ferns* exist in great variety, from the splendid tree fern to the modest maiden-hair. **1908** E.J. BANFIELD *Confessions of Beachcomber* 252 The core of the tree fern ('kalo-joo') .. would stand as vegetables. **1926** M. FORREST *Hibiscus Heart* 118 All along the banks were piccabeen and full-skirted tree fern, while in the boughs overhead a bird's nest fern flourished. **1935** DAVISON & NICHOLLS *Blue Coast Caravan* 73 A company of tree-ferns growing not, as is usual, in a narrow gully, but in a wide one. **1949** E. NAPIER *Winter is in July* 188 Treeferns whose heads were like a whorl of green lace. **1967** V.G.C. NORWOOD *Long Haul* 73 The misty dark green and growths of soft tree-ferns with fronds sprouting from masses of reddish brown 'hair'. **1982** R. HALL *Just Relations* 36 A freak of light picking out one treefern with unnatural clarity. **1837** [**tree grub**] E. FRASER *Narr. of Capture* 14 To catch large tree-maggots. **1839** W.H. LEIGH *Reconnoitering Voyages* 163 Many they eat from pure choice, particularly the tree-maggot, which, when cooked, is said to be like Devonshire cream. I am sorry that my respect for the real Devon prevented me from indulging in this antipodean imitation. **1845** C. HODGKINSON *Aust., Port Macquarie to Moreton Bay* 224 The tree grub, which is very similar to the common nut maggot .. is also swallowed raw not only by the blacks, but by many of the whites. **1854** MRS C. CLACY *Lights & Shadows* I. 35 Tree-grubs, or maggots, and a few snakes, had been all on which he had subsisted for the last three days. **1874** J.J. HALCOMBE *Emigrant & Heathen* 109 The blows of the *stone tomahawk*, with which the natives had cut out for their food opossums or the tree grubs. **1886** R. HENTY *Australiana* 9 He was one of my instructors in the mysteries of .. finding the great white tree grub (an excellent morsel). **1866** *Illustr. Sydney News* 16 Aug. 19/3 There are more than fifty kinds of kangaroos in Australasia—the kangaroo proper .. and the **tree kangaroo** tribe, the last mentioned family being found in New Guinea only. **1889** R.B. ANDERSON tr. Lumholtz's *Among Cannibals* 102 It had a very long tail, and was as large as a medium-sized dog, climbed the trees in the same manner as the natives themselves, and was called *boongary*. I was sure that it could be none other than a tree-kangaroo (*Dendrolagus*)... None had yet been found on the Australian continent. **1899** R. SEMON *In Austral. Bush* 256 'Rock-wallaby' .. sometimes climb slanting trees, and are therefore confounded with the real tree-kangaroo, Dendrolagus, a very different animal. **1909** G. SMITH *Naturalist in Tas.* 132 [In] the damp tropical and sub-tropical region, including New Guinea and the North Queensland coast .. the curious Tree-climbing kangaroo (*Dendrolagus*) may be mentioned. **1913** *Bulletin* (Sydney) 5 June 15/4 The boongarry was long thought an aboriginal myth, like the bunyip; but it isn't, and the Melbourne Zoo has a couple to prove it... It is more of a tree wallaby than a kangaroo. A distinct species is Bennett's tree kangaroo. Both have a limited range on the Herbert and Bloomfield. **1918** G. WHITE *Thirty Yrs. Tropical Aust.* 20 The curious 'tree-climbing kangaroo' was first found within a few miles of Herberton. **1929** H. MACQUARRIE *We and Baby* 95 In a small enclosure lived a tree-kangaroo, presumably a species of large opossum. **1952** B. BEATTY *Unique to Aust.* 26 The Tree-Climbing Kangaroo is a strange type found only in North Queensland. When fully grown it is about two feet tall and has bluish-grey fur... The tree kangaroo possesses strong forearms with sharp claws. **1966** —— *Around Aust.* 302 Few Australians have seen a Tree Kangaroo in its wild state. **1983** R. STRAHAN *Compl. Bk. Austral. Mammals* 263 The forelegs are stouter and more muscular than those of typical kangaroos and the hindfoot, instead of being markedly elongate, is almost rectangular in shape, with a uniformly granular sole. Despite these adaptations, tree-kangaroos are ungainly in trees. **1984** B. DIXON *Searching for Aboriginal Lang.* 60 He's like a tree-climbing kangaroo sitting high in a tree eating malagan vines, that white man there. **1846** G.H. HAYDON *Five Yrs. Experience Aust. Felix* 75 The gigantic, or **tree lizard,** attains to the enormous length of two yards. **1855** W. HOWITT *Land, Labor & Gold* I. 118 Every now and then we came to a great iguana or tree-lizard. **1860** 'LADY' *My Experiences in Aust.* 145 Here, basking on the branch of a tall tree, I saw for the first time an Iguana, or tree lizard, a common enough reptile in the bush. **1880** R. ROWE *Roughing It* 79 In Australia there is a great tree-lizard, called the iguana, with a scaly skin of a greenish brown colour, which looks like dried up mud. **1910** *Advocate* (Burnie) 6 Jan. 2/7 The planting of sugar gums, currajungs, **tree lucerne.** **1925** T. RAYMENT *Profitable Honey Plants* 113 Tree Lucerne (*Medicago arborea*). Similar to the previous plant [*sc. Cytisus proliferus alba*] in many respects. The flowers, however, are yellow. **1935** F. CLUNE *Rolling down Lachlan* 107 In the foreground, a gum-tree .. also a small tree-lucerne. **1944** G.C. MORPHETT *Reminisc. Charles H. Field* 10 'True tree lucerne' .. is not the tree lucerne called 'tagasasti', but a different and much more valuable shrub, comparatively unknown in New South Wales. **1965** *Austral. Encycl.* V. 383 The white-flowered tagasaste of Teneriffe (*Cystisus proliferus*), which is a very large broom, is often known in Australia as tree lucerne, a name strictly applicable to the yellow-flowered bush *Medicago arborea.* **1986** *Western Farmer* (Perth) 15 May 15 Mention the name tree lucerne to researchers these days and you are likely to find yourself quickly corrected. The tree legume most farmers would know of as tree lucerne now is being promoted by its native Canary Island name of tagasaste. **1842** J. GOULD *Birds of Aust.* (1848) II. Pl. 14, *Collocalia arborea.* **Tree Martin.** **1883** A.J. CAMPBELL *Nests & Eggs Austral. Birds* p. i, One of us climbed a neighbouring tree, a large red-gum, and secured from its many holes and hollows a number of the eggs of the Tree Swallow. **1902** *Emu* II. 15 Colonies of the Tree Martin (*Petrochelidon nigricans*) share numerous dry trees on the river flats. **1945** C. BARRETT *Austral. Bird Life* 167 The tree martin .. nests in tree hollows and spouted branches, also deep crevices in cliffs. **1964** M. SHARLAND *Territory of Birds* 146 Another small decimator of flies, and always prominent because of its large flocks, is the Tree Martin, which is also called Tree Swallow. **1830** W.J. HOOKER *Bot. Miscellany* I. 254 Two *Eillmans*, or shields, of the wood of *Urtica Gigas*, or the **Tree Nettle,** as light as cork. **1855** *Illustr. Sydney News* 14 Apr. 172/3 The large leaves of the tree nettle spread conspicuously among the branches of the red cedar. **1882** A.J. BOYD *Old Colonials* 185 The stinging tree-nettle .. grows to an enormous size—I have seen them six feet in diameter, and sixty feet high—and the climate is most favourable to the development of its terrible stinging powers.

treecreeper. [Transf. use of *tree-creeper* any of several birds of the fam. Certhiidae.]

1. Any of the several small birds of the fam. Climacteridae, members of which hunt for insects on tree trunks and branches. See also WOODPECKER 1.

1855 W. HOWITT *Land, Labor & Gold* I. 63 There is a tree-creeper, which keeps up a perpetual pee! pee! pee!—never stopping for a moment, apparently, to take breath, as it runs up the loftiest tree from foot to summit, searching all the way for insects. **1871** C. DARWIN *Desc. Man.* II. 206 An Australian tree-creeper (*Climacteris erythrops*). **1919** *Bulletin* (Sydney) 16 Jan. 24/4 'Woodpecker' (tree-creeper) is only technically correct. We have no true woodpecker. **1944** P. PAXTON *Bush & Billabong* 54 The little Blue Tit was filled with pity... He thought of his cousin the Tree-Creeper, who was the best climber in the whole of the Australian Bush. **1956** E. MITCHELL *Black Cockatoos* 202 This was the one time of the year when all the whistlers were in the garden—thrushes, tree-creepers, rufous whistlers and eastern spinebills. **1965** *Austral. Encycl.* IX. 21 Treecreepers, small arboreal birds of the genus *Climacteris*, which is peculiar to the Australian region. **1976** *Reader's Digest Compl. Bk. Austral. Birds* 452 Treecreepers are small, brown birds with relatively short tails, fairly long bills and large, strong legs and feet.

2. With distinguishing epithet, as **brown, rufous, white-browed, white-throated:** see under first element.

trevally /trəˈvæli/. Also **trevalli,** etc. [Poss. an alteration of *cavally* horse-mackerel: see OED *sb.* 2.] Any of several marine fish of the fam. Carangidae (many of which are fished commercially), esp. of the genera *Caranx, Usacaranx*, and *Pseudocaranx.*

1871 *Industr. Progress N.S.W.* 791 Morwong, travally, salmon .. may be taken by the line in almost unlimited quantities. **1883** E.P. RAMSAY *Notes on Food Fishes N.S.W.* 20 The white trevally, *Caranx georgianus* .. on the New South Wales coast .. seldom .. weighing over 1½ to 2 lbs., is found on the shores of Queensland of a much greater size. **1897** 'OLD HOUSEKEEPER' *Austral. Plain Cookery* 46 *Trevalli and schnapper* .. must be cut across, in pieces about half an inch in thickness, or may be filleted. **1925** *Bulletin* (Sydney) 29 Oct. 24/3 The Australian term 'trevally', with its variations of 'trevalli' and 'trevalla', is a corruption of 'cavally' or 'cavalli', by which name the fish is known in Europe. **1939** *Ibid.* 1 Mar. 21/2 'Nor'-west' and I talk two different languages... I come from Queensland and know its northern coastal waters. With us a skipjack is a Long Tom, an alligator gar, and never trevally. **1946** *Ibid.* 14 Aug. 29/2 The W.A. skipjack is the eastern trevally. **1962** N. MONKMAN *Quest Curly-Tailed Horses* 210 Just beneath the sardines were big trevally—swift killers—streamlined like torpedoes, moving in an effortless patrol. **1984** *Canberra Chron.* 23 May 27/1 They .. took a few tiny trevally.

trewhella jack. Also **trawalla, trewhalla jack.** [Proprietary name.] *Wallaby jack*, see WALLABY 6.

1898 G.W. WALKER *Notes on Aborigines Tas.* 136 With axe, shovels, 'trewhalla' jacks, saws, horse and bullock teams, the settlers gradually cleared the grounds. [**1903** *Australasian Hardware* 13 *Timber jack* manufactured by *W. Trewhella* Trentham, Vic.] **1964** *Overland* xxx. 14 No bull-dozers! Axe, monkey-grubber, and trawalla-jack—and fire.

trey /treɪ/. *Hist.* Also **tray.** [Used elsewhere but recorded earliest in Aust.]

1. Abbrev. of TREY-BIT.

1896 *Bulletin* (Sydney) 15 Aug. 3/2 Then the jay what takes the plate around an' snipes the people's 'trays' 'Ud leave his prayers now an' then an' knock us gutter-ways. **1907** *Truth* (Sydney) 23 June 5/6 The receipts panned out *just twenty-one shillings*—not even a zac or a tray over. **1918** *Huon Times* (Franklin) 1 Nov. 3/1 When a conductor on a George-street tram asked whether he had tendered a 'trey' or a 'zack' for his fare, he was not at all sure as to how this was to be interpreted. **1925** *Aussie* (Sydney) Oct. 19/2 Refreshed and all content were they With purchase value of a 'tray'. Threepence held then by any man Received respect from publican. **1938** *Point* (Melbourne) I. ii. 23 That's why he didn't have many treys to give small boys in those days. **1948** R. RAVEN-HART *Canoe in Aust.* 186 Far too many threepenny bits ('trays'). **1968** J. BEGLEY *Block with One Holer* 4 Tom was saying, 'Bet you a trey'. **1980** C. JAMES *Unreliable Mem.* 15 My mother had naturally spiced the pudding with sixpences and threepenny bits, called zacs and trays respectively.

2. Special Comb. **tray-trapper,** one who takes up, or is the recipient of, a collection of money.

1905 *Truth* (Sydney) 12 Mar. 2/5 One of Booth's local tray trappers, a lovely Salvarmy lassie, has skipped by the light of the moon. **1959** D. NILAND *Gold in Streets* 106 'I'm surprised at the Father going him in public.' .. 'You know Liz it puts a new light on that tray-trapper for me.'

trey-bit /'treɪ-bɪt/. *Hist.* Also **tray-bit.** [Spec. use of *trey* the number three.] A threepenny piece.

1898 *Bulletin* (Sydney) 1 Oct. 14/3 A few more W.Q. slang words . . 3d. . . 'traybit' [etc.]. **1899** *Ibid.* 1 July 32/2 Den I socked me bit upon 'er—Ev'ry traybit I could bring. **1902** *Truth* (Sydney) 16 Mar. 4/4 The popular 'tray-bit', 'thrum', 'scrum', or 'boozer's life-saver'. **1916** *Ibid.* 5 Mar. 1/5 If, as some papers assert, most men follow the trade of their father, Sydney must have had at one time a goodly crowd of tray-bit sparrers. **1929** 'F. BLAIR' *Digger Sea-Mates* 131 There's the bloke coming to collect; a 'tray-bit' every time you sit down in these chairs. **1944** *Bulletin* (Sydney) 12 July 14/1 The New Year [plumduff], heavily charged with spice, fruit and trey-bits, was cooked and then hung in its rag to the rafters of the skillion at the back of our humpy. **1963** J. DUFFY *Outsville Pub* 56 If he had a trey bit in his pocket, it was because it had slipped his notice when he turned the lining inside out. **1973** H. LEWIS *Crow on Barbed Wire Fence* 18, I was pleased to have been 'requested' for a traybit. It made me feel part of the Australian scene.

triangle. *Hist.* [Spec. use of *triangle* a tripod, orig. formed of three halberds stuck in the ground and joined at the top, to which soldiers were formerly bound to be flogged. Used elsewhere but recorded earliest in Aust.: see OED 2 l.] A tripod to which a convict (later a prisoner) was bound before being flogged.

1829 *Cornwall Press* (Launceston) 24 Mar. 35/2 The compassion with which we listened to the shrieks of the beings in human shape suffering at the triangle, was only to be equalled by our disgust at their loud and abandoned laughter at being untied. **1838** A. MACONOCHIE *Thoughts on Convict Managem.* 2 Idleness and insolence of expression, or even looks, subjects them to the chain-gang or the triangle. **1841** B. WAIT *Lett. from Van Dieman's Land* (1843) 266 The *peacher* gets the triangle (place where a man is tied for a flogging), solitary, six months on the roads. **1850** C.A. KING *Life* 15 Four men (at all times), were kept at this place for the purpose of flogging, twenty-five lashes being given by a right handed man, and twenty-five by a left-handed. . . A bucket of water stood under the triangles, to revive the fainting spirits of the bleeding man or boy. **1883** *Bulletin* (Sydney) 30 June 6/2 Scarcely a week passes but some wretches are marched into a gloomy looking yard in the Melbourne gaol, stripped to the waist, bound to a triangle, and lashed. **1894** *Ibid.* 27 Jan. 13/1 Since Government *will* keep on flogging, why not, with a view to revenue, take the floggees' yells down in the phonograph, and then place the instrument in convenient spots, with a notice affixed something like this: 'Put a penny in the slot and hear Maguire at the triangles.' **1919** *Smith's Weekly* (Sydney) 1 Mar. 8/2 Flogging is a class punishment. . . Who ever saw a silk hat and a broad-cloth coat doffed at the triangles? **1929** 'OLD STOCKMAN' *Sensational Cattle-Stealing Case* 77 You should see the lock-up and triangles at Nanima. . . It is all done away with now.

triantelope /traɪ'æntəloʊp/. [Altered form of TARANTULA.] HUNTSMAN SPIDER.

1845 C. GRIFFITH *Present State & Prospects Port Phillip* 128 There is a great variety of spiders, the largest of which is called the tarantula, and by the old hands the *triantelope.* **1853** *Austral. Gold Digger's Monthly Mag.* iv. 123 *Triantelopes* . . had a liking for dry leaves. **1878** *Austral. Handbk.* 101 Spiders of all sizes, from the tarantula (or triantelope, as it is more vulgarly called) downwards, flourish in all parts. **1912** S. LOCKE *Dawsons' Uncle George* 120 A triantelope bit me. **1936** K.C. MCKEOWN *Spider Wonders Aust.* 79 The origin of the name 'Triantelope' is lost. **1941** *Bulletin* (Sydney) 26 Mar. 16/2 The big Mallee 'triantelopes' are three times the size of trapdoor spiders. **1976** E. WORRELL *Things that Sting* 33 The rock-dwelling Triantelope is reputed to give a painful bite.

tribal, *a.* Of or pertaining to a traditional Aboriginal community.

1882 W. SOWDEN *N.T. as it Is* 43 On one of those hills were curious stone erections, marking boundaries of natives' tribal territory. **1890** 'R. BOLDREWOOD' *Squatter's Dream* 266 The spot where the unlucky camp-fire had been lighted was within a short distance of the ancient and scarcely-observed tribal boundary. **1949** I.L. IDRIESS *One Wet Season* 102 The first to fall . . was an aboriginal shepherd boy who had been brought from the south by the whites. Poor Neah, speared to death far from his tribal country. **1959** L. ROSE *Country of Dead* 80 It was a symbol of Uncle Bertie's tribal totem, and on its surface was traced a ritual design of Lieri country. **1960** *N.T. News* (Darwin) 5 Jan. 1/1 The laws of the Northern Territory do not regard a tribal marriage of one of the parties as a bar to contracting a legal marriage with a third party. **1962** D. LOCKWOOD *I, Aboriginal* 31 We all belong to the Alawa tribe and the Roper River district, but every man among us owns a particular plot of tribal ground which he calls 'My Country'. **1977** H. TOWSON *Black & White* 15 The Aboriginals went to their tribal grounds during their walkabout.

tribe. A name applied, orig. by the colonists, to a traditional Aboriginal community, and also (see quot. 1845) to a company of Aborigines.

1790 D. COLLINS *Acct. Eng. Colony N.S.W.* (1798) I. 144 The different tribes (for we had thought fit to class them into tribes). **1805** *Sydney Gaz.* 31 Mar., The varying hand of nature had distinguished different *tribes* by a difference of feature and complexion. **1818** *Hobart Town Gaz.* 31 Jan., His Excellency the Governor held his usual annual Meeting of the Native Chiefs and their Tribes at Parramatta. **1833** *Launceston Advertiser* 31 Oct. 2 The Lieutenant Governor has much pleasure in announcing Mr Robinson's safe return from the coast, with an additional tribe of natives, whom he has after exceeding peril and much fatigue, induced to surrender. **1838** J. BACKHOUSE *Extracts from Lett.* (1839) v. 40 Several of these families residing in a district, form what the white people call a tribe, but these tribes are not subject to any recognized chief. **1845** *Port Phillip Gaz.* 13 Sept. 4 A small tribe of strange blacks . . consisting of four men and five lubras. **1854** E.S. PARKER *Aborigines of Aust.* 12 These petty nations have been erroneously designated '*tribes*', as 'the Port Phillip tribe' . . but the term tribe is more correctly applicable to an association of families and individuals . . owning some individual as their head or chief. And this distinction exists mostly clearly. . . Each of the nations or languages . . is divided into several tribes. **1868** J.K. TUCKER *Aborigines & Chinese Question* 10 Beside the shores of the Coorong, a few years ago, there were separate clans or tribes of the aborigines who were often engaged in war. **1878** R.B. SMYTH *Aborigines of Vic.* I. p. xxiv, A tribe is in fact but an enlargement of a family circle, and none within it can intermarry. **1889** J.H.L. ZILLMANN *Past & Present Austral. Life* 128 The black police are, as a rule, the pick of their tribe. **1910** J. MATHEW *Two Representative Tribes Qld.* 128 The term tribe as applied to the aborigines is somewhat vague. It has no reference to numbers, or extent of territory, or political unity. The bond of tribal affinity, that has generally been recognised, is community of language. **1925** *Smith's Weekly* (Sydney) 7 Feb. 17/7 In the aborigine towris of the lower Murray, the members of the tribes that were chosen as ambassadors . . were generally of lower mentality than the average. **1949** B. O'REILLY *Green Mountains* 141 The only proof a whitefellow can give a blackfellow that he is to be trusted is to become an integral part of the tribe.

Hence **tribesman,** an Aboriginal male; **tribespeople,** the members of an Aboriginal community.

1960 *N.T. News* (Darwin) 2 Feb. 1/5 Two of three Centralian aborigines who pulled a 'Houdini style' escape . . have been re-arrested. The natives were reported to be chained and handcuffed after police had seized arms in possession of a group of **tribesmen.** *Ibid.* 12 Feb. 3/6 She was taken back . . to her old life in a squalid humpy outside Hall's Creek. . . Her parents are trying to force her to marry the tribesman she was 'given' to at birth. *Ibid.* 23 Feb. 1/1 Look out Melbourne . . the high flying tribesmen of Maningrida settlement in Arnhem Land are after your blood . . on the Australian Rules field. **1980** ANSELL & PERCY *To fight Wild* 123 Soon after when the mission was started at Port Keats, the **tribespeople** moved over there.

trick. [Orig. U.S.: see OED(S *sb.* 6.] See quot. 1916.

1916 V.G. DWYER *Conquering Hal* 120 'Isn't she a trick?' . . 'A—I beg your pardon?' 'A trick, you know. No one's ever dull when Vi's about. She's real good fun—so full of life, you know, and something smart and funny to say about everybody.' **1934** 'E.N. SPEER' *Destiny* 238 You're a trick, Tinny, but, drunk or sober, you're as right as the bank. **1943** *Bulletin* (Sydney) 4 Aug. 12/1 He's a trick, isn't he? But young magpies are always mischievous. **1963** *Sunday Mail* (Brisbane) 10 Mar. 19/1 My wife was mystified when somebody in Brisbane described our daughter Sally, who is nearly five, as a 'trick'.

tricoloured chat. *Crimson chat*, see CRIMSON. Also **tricoloured bush chat** and formerly **epthianura.**

1842 J. GOULD *Birds of Aust.* (1848) III. Pl. 66, *Epthianura tricolor* . . Tri-coloured Epthianura. **1849** C. STURT *Narr. Exped. Central Aust.* II. 26 App. *Tricoloured Epthianura.* This beautiful little bird was procured, both on the summit of the Barrier Range, and on the plains to the westward of it, generally inhabiting open brush. **1901** *Emu* I. 127 Nests of the . . Tricoloured Chat . . with four eggs. **1904** *Ibid.* IV. 44 Tri-coloured Bush-Chat . . undoubtedly, I think, a migratory bird. **1916** S.A. WHITE *In Far Northwest* 70 The Tricoloured Chat . . flecked the landscape with jets of flame. **1945** C. BARRETT *Austral. Bird Life* 164 Both the tri-coloured or crimson chat . . and the orange-fronted species . . inhabit dry saltbush country.

trier. [Spec. use of *trier* one who tries to do something.] A racehorse which is being ridden to win.

1915 A. WRIGHT *Sport from Hollowlog Flat* 16 Tipslinger Grif came and whispered, 'You're on a cert., she's the only trier.' **1968** J. ALARD *He who shoots Last* 204 The contributing factor is that he does not ride many triers. **1977** W.A. WINTER-IRVING *Bush Stories* 129 At bush meetings, some horses are not exactly triers.

trifecta /traɪ'fɛktə/. [U.S. *trifecta*, f. *tri-* + *per)fecta* a method of betting in which the bettor must pick first and second: see OEDS *perfecta.*]

1. A method of betting in which the bettor must pick the first, second, and third finishers in a race in the correct order.

1968 *Sporting Globe* (Melbourne) 10 July 20/2 Trifecta: (per $1.00 unit): $21.80. **1977** *Courier-Mail* (Brisbane) 6 Apr. 1/3 To win the trifecta, he must pick the place-getters in finishing order. **1978** R.H. TUCKWELL *Aspects Gambling Market* 4 The turnover of bookmakers . . is several times that of the tote, possibly five or six times if the exotic-type of tote betting, such as quinellas and trifectas, is ignored. **1981** K. GARVEY *Rhymes of Ratbag* 25 'It's super' says the bloke who has a win on the trifecta.

2. *transf.* A run of three 'wins'.

1982 N. KEESING *Lily on Dustbin* 62 A Sydney woman said of a friend's daughter that she had won the daily double but missed out on the trifecta: the young woman in question was having her wedding at the fashionable St Marks, Darling Point, the reception at the Royal Sydney Yacht Squadron, but had missed out on the honeymoon in Fiji. **1983** *Sun-Herald* (Sydney) 6 Mar. 130/5 If they're super Sloanes they'll have the trifecta—a wedding at St Marks, the reception at *the* Golf Club and a honeymoon in Fiji. **1984** *Bulletin* (Sydney) 20 Mar. 54/1 The South-West of New South Wales struck the trifecta last week—the Riverina Merino Field Day, the opening of the duck season and a visit by Prime Minister Bob Hawke.

trigger plant. [See quot. 1984.] Any plant of the large, chiefly Austral. genus *Stylidium* (fam. Stylidiaceae); HAIR-TRIGGER. Also **trigger flower.**

1884 W.A. MILLER *Dict. Eng. Names of Plants*, Trigger-plant, *Stylidium graminifolium* and other species. **1901** M. VIVIENNE *Travels in W.A.* 61 The little trigger (candolea) [*sic*] plant, with its white flower suffused with shades of pink and yellow. **1926** J. POLLARD *Bushland Man* 207 They plucked . . rosy trigger-plants, pink boronia. **1939** M.B. ELDERSHAW *My Aust.* 221 The Trigger Plants are so called for their ingenious method of pollination. **1965** *Austral. Encycl.* IX. 36 Except for four species that extend to China, Ceylon and India, all of the 122 different trigger-flowers are exclusively Australian. **1984** E. WALLING *On Trail Austral. Wildflowers* 58 The base of the flower is sensitive to touch and when the pollen is ripe a little hammer springs down and dusts an insect . . with pollen. That is why it is called Trigger-plant.

trimmer. [*Transf.* use of *trimmer* 'one who trims or trounces': see OED(S 6.] A person (or thing) outstanding in some respect.

1878 'IRONBARK' *Southerly Busters* 11, I thought thee a regular 'trimmer', I thought thee a generous man.

1943 *Signals* (Melbourne) Christmas 14 You see, she lived with an aunt, and believe me, her aunt was a trimmer. **1953** D. STIVENS *Gambling Ghost* 100 You trimmer! Won by streets, didn't you? **1955** R. LAWLER *Summer of Seventeenth Doll* (1965) 22 You little trimmer, Emma, you little beauty. **1965** E. LAMBERT *Long White Night* 135 A schooner of beer would go down like a trimmer after driving twenty miles along dirt roads on a boiling hot day. **1976** C.D. MILLS *Hobble Chains & Greenhide* 94 'I'll take the cooking off your hands for a spell—if it suits you, of course.' 'You little trimmer. It'll suit me down to the ground,' George grinned.

triple antigen. [See *triple vaccine* (OEDS *triple, a.* 5).] A vaccine administered, usu. in infancy, as protection against diphtheria, whooping cough, and tetanus.

1953 *Med. Jrnl. Aust.* Nov. II. 742 Triple antigen contains 30 flocculation units of diphtheria toxoid, 10 flocculation units of tetanus toxoid and 20,000 million *H. pertussis* organisms per millilitre. **1967** *Cwlth. Serum Laboratories Comm. Ann. Rep.* 4 C.S.L.'s Triple Antigen vaccine, administered widely to generations of school children, has virtually rid Australia of the disease. **1986** *Age* (Melbourne) 2 Sept. 21/7 Her final triple antigen injection at the Infant Welfare Centre, for example, was faced with grace and courage .. by me.

triss. Also **trizz.** [Of unknown origin.] A male homosexual.

1953 K. TENNANT *Joyful Condemned* 165 Think I'm going round flapping my mouth to every silly triss that gets shoved in [the cell] with me? **1983** *Bulletin* (Sydney) 14 June 59/3 What on Earth's wrong with terms such as pouf, fag, fairy, dike, trizz, queer or pansy? Why 'gay'?

Hence **trissy** *a.*, homosexual.

1982 *Sydney Morning Herald* 4 Aug. 8/2 This is where Brideshead fails utterly; with the one exception of the scandalously trissy but minor character Anthony Blanche, they are all such dreary people.

trizzie. [Prob. alteration of TREY.] A threepenny piece.

1941 S.J. BAKER *Pop. Dict. Austral. Slang* 78 *Trizzie*, a 3d. piece. **1942** *Ack Ack News* (Melbourne) 1 Jan. 4 Speaking of Christmas pudding, a certain very high ranker left behind nine-pence in trizzies in the pud. **1953** 'CADDIE' *Caddie* 216 He was searching his pockets for the extra threepence he knew he didn't have. 'Blimey, I'm sure I 'ad another trizzy somewhere.' **1966** *Sunday Truth* (Brisbane) 23 Dec. 22/1 When you peppered the Christmas pud. with trey-bits this year we hope you remembered they will be scarcer next Yuletide and unless you hoard some there will be no trizzies at all for .. the 1968 plum-duff.

troll. Abbrev. of 'trollop'.

1963 J. CANTWELL *No Stranger to Flame* 75, I killed her because she was a troll. I'd been doing her for a year. I was ready to marry her. **1966** P. COWAN *Seed* 152 He had had her watched. Like one of his shady clients. Like some suburban troll. **1966** G. WYATT *Strip Jack Naked* 75 'You knocked the troll rotten?' Evan asked. 'No, I pinched the beer that was left'... 'That should teach her a lesson.'

trooper. *Hist.* [Transf. use of *trooper* a cavalry soldier.] A mounted police officer; *police trooper*, see POLICE.

[**1803** *HRA* (1915) 1st Ser. IV. 169 The horses pressed, the Government men decoyed To act as troopers, and to be employed About the person of our K--g and foe. **1830** *Ibid.* (1922) 1st Ser. XV. 770 The Mounted Police, which at present consists of about 68 Troopers.] **1840** *Sydney Herald* 11 Nov. 2/4 As a trooper of the border police was coming to Sydney to attend a trial .. he apprehended two men on suspicion of their being runaways. **1847** J.D. LANG *Phillipsland* 99 A few Scotch troopers of the Mounted Police, hastily assembled in the residence of the Crown Lands' Commissioner of the District. **1855** R. CARBONI *Eureka Stockade* 13 On crossing the holes, up to the knees in mullock, and loaded like a dromedary, 'Got your licence?' was again the cheer-up from a third trooper or trap. **1870** W.B. WITHERS *Hist. Ballarat* 198 The flag was hauled down by trooper, or policeman, John King. **1882** W. SOWDEN *N.T. as it Is* 47 A trooper combines police with postal duty. **1900** *Tocsin* (Melbourne) 9 Aug. 6/2 A trooper came up. He said he had noticed a smoke, and came to see what it meant. **1910** *Emu* X. 91 We .. met a trooper engaged in collecting census returns. **1936** W. HATFIELD *Aust. through Windscreen* 99 The trooper's cattle-dog bailed him up, and he stood glaring at us. **1944** *Bulletin* (Sydney) 2 Aug. 15/3 Our trooper, of the lean and lanky, sun-tanned outdoor type, grows ironical about the amount of desk work he gets these days. **1958** H.D. WILLIAMSON *Sunlit Plain* 179 The trooper had entered and was asking for information about a quarter-wool skin hanging over a wire. **1978** B. OAKLEY *Ship's Whistle* (1979) 31 Seventy thousand men out on the goldfields and five hundred troopers to watch 'em. I'm not raising the licence fee till I get more men, I don't care what Sydney says.

troppo /'trɒpoʊ/, *a.* [f. *trop(ic* + -O.]

a. Mentally disturbed, allegedly as a result of spending too much time (orig. on war service) in the tropics; mad, crazy. Also as *n.*

1941 *Army News* (Darwin) 14 Nov. 6/3 Some can still take life seriously despite the fact that the majority are slightly 'troppo'. **1943** *Troppo Tribune* (Mataranka) 6 Sept. 4 The paper is 'Troppo', the chaps are 'troppo', the times are 'troppo'; anybody who doesn't claim to be 'troppo' should go to see the M.O. **1944** *Fortress Chron.* (Torres Strait Islands) 4 Mar. 1/1 A typical, tropical 'troppo'. **1946** A. GREEN *We were (Riff) R.A.A.F.* 16 Men of the unit had a variety of hobbies, particularly the veterans or the 'troppos' as we called them. **1959** D. CUSACK *Say no to Death* 15 He'd seen a lot of homecomings where coves had been swept off, half-troppo, in a whirlwind of confetti and wedding breakfast and honeymoon, and only come up for air when it was too late. **1962** *N.T. News* (Darwin) 4 Jan. 15/2 It was a gay and hilarious party attended by the Western sheriff and his 'Troppo' wife and many other amusing .. characters. **1968** E.M. NOBLET *Winds that Blew* 162 'He must be troppo,' I said. Troppo, a much abused word, was a very real thing, an insidious thing, a thing that crept into a man and pulled invisible strings, cordoning him off from his fellows, caging him to be laughed at, sneered at, persecuted. **1970** M. VODICKA *Track to Rum Jungle* 60 Never mind that you are slightly blotto—Without a drink the climate would send you troppo. **1980** R. DAVIDSON *Tracks* 21 The range .. has .. a profound psychological effect on the puny folk below. It sends them troppo.

b. Esp. in the phr. **to go troppo,** to become so disturbed.

1943 *Troppo Topics* 11 Jan. 7 Nearly everyone has gone 'troppo'. **1945** G. POWELL *Two Steps to Tokyo* 149, I might have wondered at what stage I had reached in the process of going 'troppo'. It was a common saying with us that a man was beginning to go 'troppo' when he started talking to the lizards. **1955** J. CLEARY *Justin Bayard* 282 She was just unbalanced. I saw it happen in New Guinea during the war. We called it *going troppo* then. **1965** W. WATKINS *Wayward Gang* (1972) 148 God damn it, Rinso's gone troppo since that kid's death! **1979** B. HUMPHRIES *Bazza comes into his Own*, Am I going troppo? Mum's gettin' hitched again? **1985** *Good Weekend* (Sydney) 12 Oct. 7/2 It was just the culmination of the songs, the musicians and the director all of my choice and really for the first time having a great time and people going troppo for it.

trot.

1. *pl.* [Spec. use of the pl. of *trot* a trotting-race. Used elsewhere but recorded earliest in Aust.: see OEDS *sb.*[1] 2.] A race-meeting at which the programme consists of trotting and pacing races; orig. (see quot. 1890) a series of trotting races in a mixed meeting.

1890 *Australasian* (Melbourne) 22 Mar. 569/5 A goodly number of people assembled at Elsternwick-park on Saturday, and, excepting the trots, which were of a very uninteresting character, the sport was up to the average. **1899** *Bulletin* (Sydney) 21 Jan. 24/2 At the recent big M.L. trots horses well-known this side carried off their full share of prize-money. **1934** G. PORTER *Wanderings in Tas.* 279 Good-bye to your beauty-spots .. your 'trots' and your 'chops' and your tickets at Tatt's, the crayfish I could not eat and the trout I could not catch. **1945** *Bulletin* (Sydney) 1 Aug. 12/1 In 'the trots' at Hughenden (Q.) show a touchy chestnut colt with an abo. aboard lashed out at a sulky wheel. **1955** N. PULLIAM *I traveled Lonely Land* 297 Perth's big boasts, however, are her racecourse and the Friday night event held there under the bright lights, the Trots. **1963** R. MCGREGOR-HASTIE *Compleat Migrant* 13 The taxi-driver, who is telling her all about the Trotting Races (The Trots). **1973** J. ROMERIL *I don't know who to feel sorry For* 57 A few sheilas, the trots, some quiet music. **1979** J. WILLIAMS *White River* 4 Grandma said she was taking me to the Trots.

2. An uninterrupted sequence, esp. in a game of chance; a run of good or bad luck.

1911 L. STONE *Jonah* 216 A trot or succession of seven tails followed, and the kip changed hands rapidly. **1917** C. DREW *Reminisc. D. Gilbert* 73 There had been a big 'trot' of 'tails' just previous to this. **1922** —— *Rogues & Ruses* 102 You've stopped the trot at last. **1943** *War Drum* (Brisbane) Oct. 2 Our battalion .. was having a pretty bad trot. **1955** N. PULLIAM *I traveled Lonely Land* 76 When a player seems to be in a streak of winning luck, he's said to be 'having a good trot'. **1969** G. JOHNSTON *Clean Straw for Nothing* (1971) 217 Heard you were back in the Old Dart and having a bit of a tough trot. **1977** *Drag Show* 61 Oh, sometimes it might have been a broken love affair and sometimes it was simply a hard trot. **1985** N. MEDCALF *Rifleman* 160 Those poor buggers are having a tough trot back home.

troub /trub/. [Joc. use of *troubadour.*] A tram-conductor; TRAM TROUB. Also *transf.*, a bus conductor.

1910 *Truth* (Sydney) 13 Mar. 1/6 Troubs at times have a lot to put up with. On Thursday, on a Paddington tram, a fat duchess berated a conductor. **1912** *Ibid.* 24 Nov. 1/8 Now, I've frequently heard, and I've frequently read Of those 'terrible fellows the Troubs'. *Ibid.* 29 Dec. 5/6 Unlike our precious 'Pomegranates', the Melbourne troubs do not consider it a huge joke to toss an old gent off a car by starting too soon, or to leave an aged woman standing in the street. **1967** *Kings Cross Whisper* (Sydney) lxi. 4/4 *Troub*, a bus conductor, or conductress. From the two words tram and bus.

trouble. In the phr. **my troubles,** a dismissive exclamation: see quot. 1895.

1895 C. CROWE *Austral. Slang Dict.* 89 *My troubles*, what do I care. **1905** N.F. SPIELVOGEL *Gumsucker on Tramp* 90 Off again; round Leuwin Cape; rough seas; My troubles! I'm coming home. **1924** 'R. DALY' *Outpost* 84 Even the girls at school didn't like me, and weren't slow in showing it. My troubles, though! **1947** G. CASEY *Wits are Out* 44 'You better lay off Kitty while the old man's about, or there'll be one more out-of-work motor salesman kicking round the city,' Syd suggested. 'My troubles!' Jerry jeered. **1955** N. PULLIAM *I traveled Lonely Land* 382 *My troubles!*—exclamation like our 'I couldn't care less'.

trout. [Transf. use of *trout* a fresh-water fish of the fam. Salmonidae, esp. of the genus *Salmo*. The name is applied also to some naturalized fish of this fam.] Any of several native fish, esp. of the fam. Galaxiidae: see quot. 1965.

1833 J. BACKHOUSE *Narr. Visit Austral. Colonies* (1843) 179 Some of the pools near George Town produce a small speckled fish, which is named Trout, but is far inferior to the Trout of Europe. **1855** W. HOWITT *Land, Labor & Gold* I. 64 What they call black-fish and trout, to us quite a new fish. **1878** R.B. SMYTH *Aborigines of Vic.* I. 203 Amongst the fish commonly taken by the blacks are .. the gudgeon or trout of colonists (*Galaxias ocellatus* and *G. attenuatus*). **c 1905** *Tourist's Guide Geelong* 37 There [*sc.* at Barwon Heads or Ocean Grove] the fish that most delight the angler are to be found in large numbers and varieties, the chief perhaps being bream, silver bream, mullet, trout .. and black perch. **1965** *Austral. Encycl.* IX. 50 Some native fishes, such as the jollytails (*Galaxias*) and the Australian salmon or salmon trout (*Arripis*), are often regarded as trout, though they have little resemblance to and no affinities with the Salmonidae.

troy. [Of unknown origin.] A gambling game. Freq. *attrib.* as **troy school.**

1944 J. DEVANNY *By Tropic Sea & Jungle* 27 Tully was full of gambling joints, poker schools, troy schools. **1948** H.W. CRITTENDEN *Rogues' Paradise* 155 In Queensland the police protection given to gambling shops called 'troy schools' .. is notorious. **1961** *Bulletin* (Sydney) 22 Mar. 28/1 Ollie .. had been unsuccessfully trying to live on the game (troy) in Cairns since he'd had his clavicle broken.

trucker. *Mining.* [Spec. use of *trucker* a labourer who uses a truck or trolley.] One employed in a mine to shift ore in a skip or trolley: see quot. 1946.

1882 L.M. WILLIAMS *Diary of Disaster* (1982) 23 We were the only two working in that drive. We had no truckers, but trucked for ourselves. **1890** *Bulletin* (Sydney) 5 Apr. 5/4 Yes the truckers' toil is rather heavy grafting as a rule—Much heavier than the wages, well I know. **1895** *Ibid.* 5 Oct. 28/1 On going to the bottom level that night, and threading the course of the long, tortuous main drive, the trucker found the water below the incline higher than usual. **1913** A. PRATT *Golden Kangaroo* 5 A crowd of miners, mullockers and truckers. **1934** *Red Star* (Perth) 17 Aug. 4/1 Truckers are nearly suffocated with dust due to the dry nature of the dirt. **1946** W.E. HARNEY *North of 23°* 36, I became a trucker in the Duchess mine, my duties being to push a skip of ore to the flat so that the ore could go to the surface. **1948** K.S. PRICHARD *Golden Miles* 335 Tom blamed the contract system for a lot of the risks the men took. Most machine men worked by contract: truckers and shovellers were on wages. **1974** J. GABY *Restless Waterfront* 59 He was slow of movement, and if a foreman were placing him from a strange pick-up, he'd be most inclined to start him off as a trucker.

truckie. [f. *truck (driver* lorry driver + -Y.] A (long-distance) truck driver.

1958 *Coast to Coast 1957–58* 201 The truckie looked upwards. 'Whaddya want, mate?' **1961** *Realist* (Sydney) vi. 10/2 A truckie slews a moment with a bale And leaves his fingers on the leaning rail. **1972** *Bulletin* (Sydney) 29 July 41/3 For all his fond claims about being just a 'simple truckie' . . Thomas was never just an ordinary truck driver. **1976** *Truckin' Life* I. iv. 21 The average Aussie Truckie has a heart as big as his rig. **1979** D. LOCKWOOD *My Old Mates & I* 85 Down south they have Transport Regulation Boards and other fancy departments to make sure a truckie doesn't exceed his hours of work or the load he puts on the road. **1981** *Overland* lxxxv. 17 Stop for a feed at the truckie's cafe in Spencer Street.

trugo /'trugoʊ/. *Vic.* [f. *tru(e* + *go*: see quot. 1982.] A game in which a disc is struck towards a goal with a mallet: see quots.

1979 *Sunday Press* (Melbourne) 2 Dec. 44/2 Trugo has a following of more than 400 players. . . The disc (plastic these days) is placed between the feet, the back is turned to the opposite end of the rink and the disc is hit 28 metres—hopefully between the posts which are almost two metres apart. **1982** *Weekend Austral. Mag.* (Sydney) 2 Jan. 10/2 There's even a section on that unique Australian sport of trugo, invented at the Newport railway workshops in Melbourne. The game started in the 1920s when a group of workers with little or nothing to do at lunchtime started hitting a round rubber disc with a mallet towards two markers. One worker scored a goal and shouted to his mates: 'Hey that was a true go.' Hence, trugo. There are 12 clubs in Melbourne now, with more than 100 men and 60 women playing in regular competition. **1984** *Over Fifty Yrs. Trugo* (Victorian Trugo Assoc.) 10 The name of the game is Trugo and the chances are that most people have never heard of it, let alone played it. But that is hardly surprising because the game is played only in Melbourne and only by pensioners.

trump. [Fig. use of *trump* a card of a suit which ranks above the others.] A person in authority.

1925 *Bulletin* (Sydney) 9 Apr. 24/1 The station-manager is known as the 'trump'. **1942** *Sun* (Sydney) 26 Aug. 4/9 Officers are trumps, and reinforcements reos. **1956** *Bulletin* (Sydney) 5 Dec. 12/4 The young learner-shearer was having a rough time. . . A slip of the handpiece and there was one dead sheep. Sheepishly he asked the trump what he would do with the carcass. 'Oh, don't worry,' said the boss. **1975** R. MERRITT *Cake Man* (1978) 38 'You the trump around this rat's nest?' . . 'I beg your pardon?' . . 'Are you responsible, I mean, for keeping these black bastards on this reservation and away from decent people's property?' **1978** D. STUART *Wedgetail View* 74 From what I hear there'll be quite a show there in a few months' time, an' I think the trump might be just about ready to put on a few extra hands.

trumpeter, *n.*[1] [See quot. 1885.]

1. Any of several fish of the fam. Latridae, esp. *Latris lineata* of coastal waters of s.e. Aust., and New Zealand, and fish of the genus *Latridopsis*. See also HOBART TRUMPETER, STRIPEY, *Tasmanian trumpeter* TASMANIAN *a.* 2.

1827 *Tasmanian Almanack* 142 Trumpeter, very large, 2s. ditto. **1831** *Acct. Colony Van Diemen's Land* 127 The trumpeter . . is considered the most epicurean dish of the finny tribe of this island. **1851** *Guardian* (Hobart) 25 Oct. 3/2 It is the general practice of fishermen to work along Tasman's Peninsula, where large trumpeters are found in abundance. **1873** J. BONWICK *Tasmanian Lily* 2 The seamen amused themselves with fishing, and brought up that splendid fish the Trumpeter, a great luxury to those who have long feasted on salt junk. **1885** *Adelaide Observer* 18 Apr. 29 The fish known to Port Adelaide fishermen as the 'silver fish', and sometimes as the trumpeter (from the peculiar squeaking noise made by them when caught). **1944** J. DEVANNY *By Tropic Sea & Jungle* 81 The trumpeter is a tenor. . . He's usually about a pound and a half in weight, with a tough skin that gives him the name leather-jacket. **1978** N. COLEMAN *Austral. Fisherman's Fish Guide* 92 Jetties and wharves would never be the same without trumpeters and kids to haul them in, one after another, plopping them into the bait bucket or pail of water and listening with rapt fascination to the grunts, trumpets or croaks of this 'talking' fish. **1985** *Mercury* (Hobart) 27 Mar. 15/2 To a seafood gourmet a fresh trumpeter is more appealing than a frozen barracouta.

2. Special Comb. **trumpeter whiting,** any of several fish of the whiting fam., esp. *Sillago maculata* of n., e., and w. Aust.

1878 *Proc. Linnean Soc. N.S.W.* III. 380 *Sillago Bassensis.* . . Called at Sydney *Trumpeter Whiting*. . . Very common also at Brisbane, where it is the common whiting. **1906** D.G. STEAD *Fishes of Aust.* 111 The Trumpeter Whiting [*sc. Sillago maculata*] is principally an inhabitant of the waters of New South Wales and Queensland. **1918** J. SCOTT *How, when & where to catch Fish* 27 Whiting are undoubtedly the most highly prized as table fish. . . Trumpeter whiting are somewhat similar in appearance, being a darker brown, and slightly mottled along the back, and are not nearly as plentiful as sand whiting. **1965** *Austral. Encycl.* IX. 298 The trumpeter whiting (*S[illago] maculata*) is a northern fish ranging from the tropics southward to Port Jackson.

trumpeter, *n.*[2] *Hist.* A type of fetter: see quot. 1894.

1892 *Bulletin* (Sydney) 2 July 21/4 'I thought he was celled?' 'So he is, sir. No. 5!' 'And ironed?' 'Trumpeters—fifteen's [*sic*]—and wall-cuffs!' **1894** 'P. WARUNG' *Tales Early Days* 131 A brace of staples apiece driven in, and twenty-pound trumpeters, will hold 'em in, or else my name isn't Wright. [*Note*] Trumpeters, irons which connected the ordinary leg-chains with a bazil riveted around each leg immediately below the knees. **1937** W. & T.I. MOORE *Best Austral. One-Act Plays* 262 You can give me double darbies, solitary, wall cuffs, tube-gag, trumpeters . . I don't give a bugger.

try, *v. Mining.* [Spec. use of *try* to endeavour to ascertain by experiment.] *trans.* To test (soil, gravel, etc.) for the presence of a precious mineral.

1876 'EIGHT YRS.' RESIDENT' *Queen of Colonies* 134 With a pick, shovel, tin dish, and bag as tools, a blanket, billy, and quart-pot as equipment, they swarm over the country 'trying' it. Wherever they come across a 'likely-looking spot' they dig or 'bottom' a hole, take out a dishful of the 'wash-dirt', if any is found, and try it by washing at the nearest water-hole. **1888** G. ROCK *Colonists* 52 'Let's try a tubful o' stuff, anyhow.' They throw some dirt in the pudding tub, and are about to perform the operation of 'trying a prospect'. **1902** E.B. KENNEDY *Black Police Qld.* 66, I made up my mind to try a spec., so from Grafton I did wander, And bought a mob of nuggets there to begin as an overlander.

try diver. *Pearling.* An apprentice diver: see quot. 1956.

1913 *Cwlth. Parl. Papers* III. 691 Of the divers licensed, however, there are a number of learners—men known as 'try' divers. **1956** S. GORE *Overlanding with Annabel* 85 Pearl-divers are not born—they are made. A likely man serves one season as a 'try-diver', during which time he is head-crew of the boat, his assorted duties at sea leaving him only Saturday afternoons free to serve his apprenticeship in the diving dress, at all depths from seven to seventeen fathoms. **1964** T. RONAN *Packhorse & Pearling Boat* 166 They carried a crew of seven—one diver, one tender, and five deck hands, of whom one would be 'try' (that is, learner) diver.

try the acid: see ACID.

T.S.R. *Travelling stock route, reserve,* see TRAVELLING STOCK 2.

1897 *Bulletin* (Sydney) 11 Dec. 30/1 We were camped in ridgy country with a homestead fence aback And twenty chains of T.S.R. to shield us from the track. **1903** *Ibid.* 21 Mar. 16/2 Camping reserves for travelling stock, which are reserved from sale and lease, are placed at suitable distances along almost every T.S.R. for the convenience of drovers. **1913** W.K. HARRIS *Outback in Aust.* 149 Our course lay along a 'T.S.R.' (travelling stock route) for a few miles. **1942** L. & K. HARRIS *Lost Hole Bingoola* 203 *Travelling Stock Route*, or '*T.S.R.*', a right-of-way, half a mile wide, for drovers and their herds of cattle, with artesian bores or other water supplies available at frequent intervals. **1966** E.J. WALLACE *Sydney & Bush* 31 'Just remember—camp by a cemetery or a T.S.R.' 'T.S.R.?' Pete queried. 'What's that, Fred?' 'Travelling stock reserve. There's always water laid on there too.' **1977** T.L. MCKNIGHT *Long Paddock* 2 Now that road transport has become so widespread . . it may be that TSRs are more important as supplemental grazing areas than as accessways to market.

tuan /'tjuən/. [a. Wathawurung *duan*.] **a.** PHASCOGALE. **b.** *Flying possum*, see FLYING. Formerly also **tuan-tuan.**

1842 H. MCCRAE *Georgiana's Jrnl.* 16 Dec. (1934) 71 'Murray' brought us a live 'tuan-tuan'—a sort of flying squirrel, with extremely soft fur. **1845** MRS THOMSON *Life in Bush* 20 We sometimes got some skins of the . . flying-squirrel, or tuan, from the natives. **1859** H. KINGSLEY *Recoll. Geoffry Hamlyn* II. 280 The Touan, the little grey flying squirrel. **1886** R. HENTY *Australiana* 76 The Tuam is known commonly as the flying squirrel of Victoria. **1979** DOUGLAS & HEATHCOTE *Far Cry* 121 The Tuan, or brush-tailed phascogale (pencillata) [*sic*] is a Dasure, like the spotted native cat.

tuart /'tjuat/. Formerly also **tooat, tooart.** [a. Nyungar *tuwart*.] The medium to tall tree *Eucalyptus gomphocephala* (fam. Myrtaceae) of coastal s.w. W.A.; the strong, hard, yellowish wood of the tree. Also *attrib.*

1836 H.W. BUNBURY *Early Days W.A.* (1930) 71 We now came into a more open country with a good deal of grass growing on a light soil under very large White Gums, called by the natives 'Tooats'. **1842** 'J.K.C.' *Jrnl. of Voyage* 19 The different varieties of trees hereabouts are the red, white, and flooded gums . . and a few tuarts. **1847** *Britannia* (Hobart) 6 May 3/3 The wood of the *banksia* and the *tuart* are described as possessing qualities of great value for machinists and coach builders. **1850** *Ibid.* 12 Sept. 4/3 'The Tuart timber of the Deep River' is spoken of in the highest terms. **1869** F. ALGAR *Hand-Bk. Qld.* 13 Those [*sc.* trees] chiefly valuable for ship-building purposes are known by the native names of the Jarrah and Tooart. **1870** W.H. KNIGHT *W.A.* 23 The white-gum, or tuart, (*eucalyptus gomphochephala* [*sic*]). **1898** L. LINDLEY-COWEN *W. Austral. Settler's Guide* 662 On the limestone coast ranges east of the Darling ranges, the tooart. **1928** J. POLLARD *Bushland Vagabonds* 157 The railways use plenty of it. They replaced the steel under-carriages of the trucks with tuart. So it must be pretty strong. **1952** *New Settler in W.A.* (Perth) July 3 The flowers of the Tuart yield a profuse good quality nectar and Tuart honey is light in colour, of a pleasing flavour, and fine-grained when candied. **1967** U. TAYLOR *Bird of Wonder* 49 The trees—tuart gums had been decided on. **1985** *Austral. Garden Jrnl.* June 127 Tuart trees are indigenous to Western Australia, and have been planted widely throughout the drier rural areas along the southern coast.

tub. *Gold-mining. Obs. Puddling tub*, see PUDDLING 2.

1852 *Argus* (Melbourne) 8 Mar. 2/7 The 'rush' has left little elbow-room for those who are lucky enough in finding places for their tubs and cradles. **1857** 'ONE WHO KNOWS THEM' *Chinese Question Analyzed* 11 They are sufficiently in funds to purchase their own tubs and cradle. **1869** MRS W.M. HOWELL *Diggings & Bush* 48 They're getting half an ounce to the tub. **1871** J. BALLANTYNE *Homes & Homesteads* 40 With his 'cradle' he could wash his gravelly soil, or with his 'tub' he could puddle his clayey gatherings.

tube.

1. *Shearing. Obs.* A tubular casing containing the flexible shaft which drives the shears. Also *fig.*

1904 *Shearer* (Sydney) 29 Oct. 4/2 The tubes at Rhodesia are swinging with a will, and the tallies that will be cut at that shed will cause a panic in the opposition camp. **1905** *Ibid.* 19 Aug. 3/5 'My pets', as the 'Worker' terms them, have the tubes swinging at Coombe-Martin, and they will keep them swinging (D.V.) right on to the cut-out at that shed. **1963** *Sydney Morning Herald* 17 Aug. 11/7 I've shorn in hundreds of sheds with thousands of shearers. . . Get off the tube (out of the game) while you are young enough.

2. A can (or sometimes a bottle) of beer.

1964 B. HUMPHRIES *Nice Night's Entertainment* (1981) 77 We were on the beach or in the surf club cracking the tubes or demolishing a twelve. **1965** *Kings Cross Whisper* (Sydney) Oct. 2/4 All my life I have been a bottle man. These tin tubes are wrong. How can you have any fun when you're out on a tour by chucking tin tubes out of the car? **1971** F. HARDY *Outcasts of Foolgarah* 1 A lot of people drink canned beer these days; we're becoming a race of tube suckers. **1973** J. POWERS *Last of Knucklemen* (1979) 19 Moments like these are the glory of bein' old. You can just sit back an' suck on your tube an' watch. **1983** HIBBERD & HUTCHINSON *Barracker's Bible* 52 A tube is a tall can of beer in the Southern States, a bottle of beer in N.S.W.

tucker, *n.*[1] [f. Br. slang *tuck* to consume (food or drink): see OED *v.*[1] 10.]

1. a. *Obs.* A meal.

1833 *Launceston Advertiser* 24 Oct. 3 They then asked for a 'tucker' (the slang word for a meal), which was supplied. **1845** *Standard* (Melbourne) 8 Feb. 3/2 A tucker gratis. . . The Major . . called the Doctor's attention to the *Tucker* he had provided expressly for him, when the Doctor got into a *Scot*, but was finally appeased by finding that he was '*a day after the fair*'. He complained of the Major inviting him too late *to a Tucker*. **1846** L.W. MILLER *Notes of Exile Van Dieman's Land* 280 The wardsmen . . got all their hard labour performed by gorging the scoundrel with a '*good tucker*', as it was called.

b. Food. Also *attrib.*

1850 *Monthly Almanac* (Adelaide) 44 So hearing that 'plenty tucker' was their desire, I let them know by signs that I was not the sort of fellow to offer opposition to their very proper request. **1864** N. SHREEVE *Short Hist. S.A.* 25 The manner in which they make the agreement is, by giving them £1 each, and plenty of 'tucker' (a word for food). **1877** *Vagabond Ann.* 148, I got round into the Sydney-road, and stopped some draymen, asking them for some tucker. **1889** R.W. DALE *Impressions Aust.* 89 A young man . . on a station in South Australia . . was receiving 20s. a week and his 'tucker' as a boundary rider. **1895** *Worker* (Sydney) 5 Jan. 3/4, I was paid for all I shore; the tucker and cook would be deducted. **1905** *Truth* (Sydney) 6 Aug. 1/4, I didn't marry her to look at her. I married her to cook my tucker. **1916** 'MEN OF ANZAC' *Anzac Bk.* 44 What we frequently distrust in the way of tucker holds no terror for the Gallipoli flies. **1935** *Red Star* (Perth) 16 Aug. 3/2 The overseer claimed it would cost him £50 for shed hands' wages and tucker. **1948** M. UREN *Glint of Gold* 157 The tucker carried would be flour, sugar, tinned meat and fish, tea and coffee, dried vegetables, dried fruits, currants and raisins. **1965** F. HARDY *Yarns of Billy Borker* 25 'And what was the tucker like in Paris?' another fellow queried. **1977** S. LOCKE ELLIOTT *Water under Bridge* 226 We've all been off our tucker with the worry. **1981** D. STUART *I think I'll Live* 86 Yeah, she's a good tucker joint, this Java, be the look of it. Plenty o' fruit, bananas, all that stuff. **1986** *Bulletin* (Sydney) 7 Jan. 82/3 The fish is superbly fresh unless conditions are impossible, and that's when owner-fisherman George Mure becomes impossible: 'How can I serve decent bloody tucker when the seas have been as high as they have been?'

c. In the collocation **saddle-pouch tucker:** see quot. 1947.

1947 V.C. HALL *Bad Medicine* 14 Out on the run with the cattle he lives on 'saddle-pooch tucker' of damper and salt beef, and as one of them told me without a smile, 'a couple of tins of jam in case of sickness'. **1970** J.S. GUNN in W.S. Ramson *Eng. Transported* 63 Such food references as *saddle pouch tucker* . . are well left to history.

d. A supply of provisions.

1933 J.M. HARCOURT *Pearlers* 146 We've got to live till the boats come in again at the end of the first tucker.

2. Comb. **tucker bill, pack, time.**

1897 *Worker* (Sydney) 18 Sept. 3/4 The **tucker bill** at Mooloomon amounted to 21s. 2d. per man per week, the prices charged for rations being something dreadful, as the above figures go to show. **1912** R.S. TAIT *Scotty Mac* 77 Their share of the tucker bill would probably be about eighteen shillings. **1957** V. PALMER *Rainbow-Bird* 9 'I've had my full issue,' he told the men crowding round him. 'Seven years' battling in the spinifex, with that Indian storekeeper holding a tucker-bill two yards long against me whenever I made a strike.' **1962** *Meanjin* 50 'Hardly a day passes but you bring in fish to be cooked.' 'It helps out with tucker bills.' **1922** 'J. BUSHMAN' *In Musgrave Ranges* 237 His own **tucker-packs** had not been interfered with. **1949** I.L. IDRIESS *One Wet Season* 174 A fool black boy had mixed up the tucker-packs with the branding-irons and hobbles. **1954** T. RONAN *Vision Splendid* 37 Pulling things out of his tucker packs. **1976** C.D. MILLS *Hobble Chains & Greenhide* 174 Chuckera had brought a light tucker-pack, and had a fire going at the gates. **1912** *Bulletin* (Sydney) 1 Aug. 15/2 They're always ready for **tucker-time.** **1921** *Ibid.* 17 Nov. 20/2 At tucker-time we placed our guns . . on the ground and tackled the lunch in our bags. **1954** *Ibid.* 3 Mar. 12/2 Our chooks are swift off the mark at tucker-time.

3. Special Comb. **tucker bag,** a provision bag, esp. as carried by a swagman; **box,** a box for the storing or conveyance of provisions; **cart,** a vehicle for the conveyance of provisions; **shop,** a food shop; a restaurant; **track,** a route followed by itinerant rural workers and other travellers, judged according to the generosity with which provisions are supplied along the way (see WALLABY TRACK 2 a.).

1885 *Bulletin* (Sydney) 5 Sept. 5/3 Is your brain 'on the gutter'—a fanciful 'drunk'? Have your pannings today made the **tucker bag** right? **1893** *Ibid.* 16 Dec. 17/2, I suppose he's tramping somewhere where the bushmen carry swags, Cadging round the wretched stations with his empty tucker-bags. **1905** *Observer* (Adelaide) 2 Sept. 47/3 He produced from his tucker bag, and allowed us to sample, one of the choicest ox tongues ever seen inside or outside of a butcher's shop. **1923** J. MOSES *Beyond City Gates* 92 Never known to turn a man away with an empty tucker bag. **1938** *Bulletin* (Sydney) 12 Jan. 21/1 Complete with swag, whiskers and bobbing hat corks, he added a novel touch by including a golf-club carried just abaft of the tucker-bag. **1953** A.W. UPFIELD *Murder must Wait* 158 Do you happen to have an empty sugar sack I could use as a tucker bag? **1968** J. WOODBERRY *Come back Peter* (1974) 51 Paul had already tied his swag behind the leather, and he now fixed his tucker bag in front. **1980** ANSELL & PERCY *To fight Wild* 120 Then Luke said they didn't have much in the tucker-bags, just a bit of flour and sugar and so on. **1897** A.F. PATERSON *'Mid Saltbush & Mallee* 30 'Now, Miss Kerr . . will you . . help me to pack the **tucker box.**' 'Tucker box, what is that?' 'Well, perhaps I ought to say lunch box; for in the bush we do not boast of hamper baskets.' **1901** H. LAWSON *Joe Wilson & his Mates* 59, I . . got a gin case we used for a tucker-box, the frying pan and billy down. **1918** J.L. BURTON *Across Aust. in Seven Days* 4 We constructed a special tucker box, which we could lift out on to the ground, and this proved a jolly fine arrangement. **1923** J. MOSES *Beyond City Gates* 27 And the dog sits on the tucker box, Nine miles from Gundagai. **1932** J. TRURAN *Green Mallee* 107 He opened his tucker-box to look for something to eat. . . 'Well, ah'll be jiggered,' he said . . as he peered into the kerosene-case in which he was accustomed to store his eatables. **1955** F. LANE *Patrol to Kimberleys* 79 He filled the billy can with water from a canvas bag and, unlashing the tucker box, took out some bush bread and salt beef. **1965** A.W. UPFIELD *Lure of Bush* 151 She undid the strap securing the small 'tucker-box' to one of the running-boards, and produced tin pannikins, a bottle of milk, tea, sugar and sandwiches. **1978** D. STUART *Wedgetail View* 7 He put the plate and knife and fork back in the tuckerbox. **1905** *Bulletin* (Sydney) 20 Apr. 19/2 **Tucker cart** broke down. **1934** J.S. NEILSON *Autobiogr.* (1978) 90, I had a good job, I was driving the tucker cart & doing some grubbing. **1937** *Bulletin* (Sydney) 14 July 20/1 The thresher gang had put in the usual two hours work before breakfast when the tucker-cart hove in sight. **1957** J.M. HOSKING *Aust. first & Last* 30 With the cattle dog under the tucker cart and the flankers swinging wide, And my horse just wanting to gallop fast, I settle down for a ride. **1978** D. STUART *Wedgetail View* 12 Godjesus that had been a cold winter, but at least Reggie had kept a good tucker cart; plenty of everything, bread, milk, pickles. **1907** A. MACDONALD *In Land of Pearl & Gold* 110 You should make for Sydney too, Dave. . . There's some good **tucker-shops** there. **1984** W.W. AMMON et al. *Working Lives* 190 The hotel was a good tucker shop as Mrs Neville was a fine cook. **1896** H. LAWSON *While Billy Boils* (1975) 54 The men get a little more sociable . . and exchange hints as to good **tucker-tracks,** and discuss the strike, and curse the squatter. **1900** —— *Verses Pop. & Humorous* 58, I know the tucker tracks that feed—or leave one in the lurch—The 'Burgoo' (Presbyterian) track—the 'Murphy' (Roman Church). **1910** *Bulletin* (Sydney) 15 Sept. 13/3 A good tucker track pays the suppliers, and if a far-out track gets a bad name it is shunned until the scarcity of labor sends wages to balloon altitudes. **1930** E. ANTONY *Hungry Mile* 39 Go search along the highways, the hungry tucker tracks, In the huts of the cane-cutters, and the dirty cocky's [*sic*] shacks. **1982** R. HALL *Just Relations* 133 And then for any job of work I was prepared to try, But now I've found the tucker-track, I'll stop here till I die.

tucker, *n.*[2] and *attrib.* [Transf. use of TUCKER *n.*[1]]

A. *n.* The means of subsistence, esp. in the phr. **to make tucker.**

1858 *Colonial Mining Jrnl.* Oct. 23/2 They seemed to think that to work for any wages at all, over and above 'tucker' would be considerably to improve their fortunes. **1859** 'EYE WITNESS' *Voyage to Aust.* 18 The great hold the gold fields has of diggers and miners is simply this, things must work very bad with them if they cannot make their tucker out, this is the term given their food. **1864** *Port Denison Times* 10 Sept. 2/4 In their characteristic, but not very elegant language, they say they can make 'tucker'. **1870** C.H. ALLEN *Visit to Qld.* 249 There are few fields in which he may not find what is called 'tucker', that is to say, enough to provide the necessaries of life. **1878** *Illustr. Austral. News* (Melbourne) 10 June 107/1 Men have been known to work for years scarcely making what is colonially called 'tucker'. **1893** *Braidwood Dispatch* 29 July 2/4 We have . . in this district plenty of miners, who with a good deal of knowledge, find great difficulty in rubbing along—men who are well known for their indomitable pluck in sticking to a claim while it will pay 'tucker'. **1904** *Bulletin* (Sydney) 15 Sept. 40/3 When we . . look at the scrub in front of us, we know . . that we will have to go all the time to make more than tucker. **1915** 'ALPHA' *Reminisc. Goldfields* i. 47 Our average earnings during the whole time building the bridge and working the claim being only £6 per week. This we then considered as only a trifle over tucker. **1945** J. DEVANNY *Bird of Paradise* 24, I make out with about nine pounds a week. . . An inexperienced man wouldn't make his tucker. **1950** K.S. PRICHARD *Winged Seeds* 23 Some blokes were shovellin' dirt and not makin' tucker for months. **1973** C. AUSTIN *I left my Hat in Andamooka* 60 There are worse ways of living to a ripe old age, even if you only find enough opal to 'make tucker'.

B. *attrib.* Subsistence; yielding only the means of subsistence.

1882 A.J. BOYD *Old Colonials* 142, I spent a week prospecting about, and got good tucker gold. **1892** *Bulletin* (Sydney) 17 Dec. 19/1 Struck some tucker dirt at Armstrong's, and just lived at Pleasant Creek. **1900** *Worker* (Sydney) 15 Sept. 8/2 Windourin, New Wanganella, and Morago have cut out. The two latter were tucker sheds only. **1902** *Bulletin* (Sydney) 5 Apr. 15/1 They *do* peddle . . but at best it is only a tucker-business. **1905** *Ibid.* 14 Dec. 36/1 The gold-yield of the dirt he had tapped was far below tucker-standard. **1908** *Ibid.* 3 Dec. 14/1 We've worked it nigh a year, An' hardly took out tucker stuff—it hasn't run to beer. **1929** W.J. RESIDE *Golden Days* 340 Employed at a mere 'tucker' wage. **1964** D. LOCKWOOD *Lizard Eater* 126 Country around Kungarri rockhole which is claimed by the people to be better 'tucker country' than that further west.

2. In Comb. designating a mine or mining area, as **tucker claim, diggings, field, ground, show.**

1859 *Colonial Mining Jrnl.* Jan. 76/1 All are not,

however, lucky enough to strike even upon a **'tucker' claim,** and shicers are neither few nor far between. **1895** 'H. GOLDSMITH' *Euancondit* 174 Dick and his mate had only a 'Tucker claim': one that kept them in the bare means of subsistence. **1904** *Shearer* (Sydney) 10 Sept. 4/4 So the Woolgar, Mulgrave and Hodgkinson fields are duffers, or tucker-claims at best. Why not go round to Broome, W.A., and have a cut at the pearling? **1874** C. DE BOOS *Congewoi Correspondence* 115 There's no mistake about the Treasurer bein a fust-rate fossicker. My word! Why, if he was on a **tucker diggins** I believe he'd fossick good wages in the old drives. **1880** *Argus* (Melbourne) 17 Feb. 9/4 The miners' verdict used to be that it was a 'tucker' diggings. That would mean rather a profitable field elsewhere, for tucker in so remote and inaccessible a locality must mean a considerable weekly sum. **1933** W.L. OWEN *Cossack Gold* 92 When the richest plums had been picked it became a **'tucker-field'** to which the diggers returned to feed on the duff. **1980** N. KING *Colourful Tales* 96 While these men . . were successful in finding slugs of gold the area was not classed as being a 'tucker' or 'poor man's field'. **1869** R.B. SMYTH *Gold Fields & Mineral Districts* 624 **Tucker Ground,** ground which yields only sufficient gold to provide miners with *tucker.* **1884** *Austral. Tit-Bits* (Melbourne) 25 Dec. 18/2 A man don't care about killing himself working at tucker ground. **1895** J.W. ANDERSON *Prospector's Handbk.* (ed. 6) 167 *Tucker ground* (Australia), poor ground, just rich enough to allow a miner to buy food and the bare necessaries of life. **1906** E. DYSON *In Roaring Fifties* 99 He didn't believe he'd got a **tucker show,** and sadly advised Mike to shepherd a hole down to the left. **1909** H.I. JENSEN *Rising Tide* 44 If, after years of arduous toil in the back blocks, a fossicker is lucky enough to make a mineral discovery which promises to be become something better than a mere tucker show he must find capital. **1944** M.J. O'REILLY *Bowyangs & Boomerangs* 40, I worked mates with him for a time, but as it was only a 'tucker show' I moved on. **1977** J. DOUGHTY *Gold in Blood* 81 Though the claims stretched for nearly a mile, and some of them yielded 'wages', the majority were not even 'tucker shows'.

3. Special Comb. **tucker job,** a poorly paid job; **money,** a small sum of money; a pittance.

1905 *Bulletin* (Sydney) 13 Apr. 19/1 If a bootless man happens along, as is sometimes the case in Victoria, he is offered a **'tucker' job;** and a real good-natured cocky has been known to throw in a pair of his own cast-off 'crabs'. **1983** K.W. MANNING *In their Own Hands* 215 Late in 1914, in urging a prices conference with millers, Philip Kirwan declared that growing cane under present conditions was 'only a tucker job and not a very good one at that'. **1984** W.W. AMMON et al. *Working Lives* 42 With fencing you never had a dog's chance. It was seldom more than a tucker job, even to efficient men. **1892** 'MRS A. MACLEOD' *Silent Sea* I. 236 He had gone almost hungry, certainly very dirty, and in very broken boots, once when he was working in a poor patch of country, which did not yield **'tucker' money.** **1932** I.L. IDRIESS *Prospecting for Gold* 3 You of course have the chance of winning a little gold from the start, 'tucker money'. **1954** T. RONAN *Vision Splendid* 98 It's only tucker money, but Ettrick agreed to do the job for a tenner and situated as I am I could hardly ask for more.

tucker, *v.*[1] [f. TUCKER *n.*[1] and *n.*[2]]

1. a. *intr.* To eat food; to take a meal.

1870 G.P. DEANE Diary 10 Feb., They shifted us out of our Mess hut. Tuckering now in the stable shed. **1889** *Bulletin* (Sydney) 14 Sept. 22/1 She brought me eggs and cakes, for I was 'tuckering' in the hut. **1891** *Truth* (Sydney) 15 Mar. 7/3 But the most difficult step of all is from hut to barracks. I know some young and some old station hands who would lose ten years of their life to *tucker in the barracks.* **1896** *Worker* (Sydney) 26 Sept. 3/4 We are tuckering with the shearers. **1964** *N. Austral. Monthly* Nov. 19 We 'tuckered' wherever we happened to be except in some cases when we took dinner with us to save time. **1978** D. STUART *Wedgetail View* 61 A greasy chop an' a hunk o' bread . . an' y' reckoned you were tuckerin' like a lord. **1979** B. MARTYN *First Footers S. Gippsland* 109 She had Alec Ricketts 'tuckering' at her table and was relieved that Joe was able to have someone to help him.

b. *intr.* To subsist.

1925 E. MCDONNELL *My Homeland* 24 Loafed about the camp, tuckering mostly on damper and tea.

2. a. *trans.* To supply (a person) with food or provisions. Also *refl.* and *absol.*

1891 E.H. HALLACK *W.A. & Yilgarn Goldfields* 13 'What about tucker, have you any?' I was asked before starting. A reply in the negative caused the obliging Manager to arrange with the driver to take sufficient to 'tucker' me. **1901** *Bulletin* (Sydney) 15 June 14/3 Nine men are tuckered here (a Vic. station) for as nearly as possible 7s. 6d. each per week. **1911** *Truth* (Sydney) 10 Sept. 1/7 She loses sight of the fact that hubby has been tuckering, roosting, and clothing her for all these years. **1920** B. CRONIN *Timber Wolves* 40, I got a friend hereabouts that tuckers me when I'm along this way. **1943** *Bulletin* (Sydney) 27 Oct. 12/1 What I can't understand is how the devil he's goin' to keep her. Took him all his time to tucker himself. **1956** K. TENNANT *Honey Flow* 18 After tea—we tuckered the Muirdens that night because we had plenty of food and they had been 'doing a starve'. **1960** M. VIZZERS *She'll do Me!* 20 My best plan would be take a room in a cheap residential, do my own 'tuckering' and start looking for a job, any job. **1964** B. WANNAN *Fair Go, Spinner* 126 In those days, the shearers had to provide their own food supplies—'to tucker themselves', as they put it. **1973** J. MORRISON *Austral. by Choice* 45 They'd take us out and supply us with everything. Shovels and bars and post and wire. Tucker you, too. If you was far out from the homestead they'd send out once or twice a week, flour and meat and sugar and tea and take it off your cheque when you cut out.

b. *intr.* With **up:** to acquire a supply of food or provisions.

1915 E.R. MASSON *Untamed Territory* 53 The Japanese . . then return to Darwin, where they hand over their shell, and 'tucker up', as provisioning is called. **1940** F.D. DAVISON *Woman at Mill* 143 We were counting on it [*sc.* a money order] to tucker up with in Bairnsdale. **1948** H. DRAKE-BROCKMAN *Sydney or Bush* 115 Four, five weeks later, *Denny* comes in to tucker up. Citrine gets himself rowed ashore at once in the dinghy. **1969** J. DINGWELL *One String* 64 'I expect you've come to tucker up,' he asked the geologist presently.

tucker, *v.*[2] [U.S. *tucker* to tire: see Mathews.] *intr.* With **out** or **up:** to tire. Freq. as **tuckered out** (or **up**) *ppl. a.*, exhausted.

1911 A.L. HAYDON *Trooper Police Aust.* 390 He had been travelling round about a good part of the night and was fairly tuckered out. **1920** A.G. HALES *McGlusky Gold-Seeker* 54 That grey mare . . looks a bit tuckered up to *me.* **1969** A. HOPGOOD *And Big Men Fly* 46 I'm exhausted. I'm fair tuckered out. **1976** C.D. MILLS *Hobble Chains & Greenhide* 4 On the day of the 'run', fresh horses are tied up all over the area towards which the horses are expected to head, and as each ridden horse tuckers out a quick swing into the bush gives a fresh mount.

tuckerless, *a.* Without food or a means of subsistence.

1910 *Bulletin* (Sydney) 2 June 15/1 I'll never forget . . one sunset track. I had trudged two tuckerless 16-mile stages . . then I struck my hospitable friend, and inquired . . where the Government tank resided. **1926** *Ibid.* 28 Oct. 22/4 A tuckerless fortnight is more than enough for the average man. **1937** E. HILL *Great Austral. Loneliness* 82 The rind of the pods . . makes an acrid but nourishing food . . that tides over the tuckerless white man to the next out-camp.

tuckeroo /tʌkəˈru/. [Prob. f. a Qld. Aboriginal language.] The tree *Cupaniopsis anacardioides* (fam. Sapindaceae) of n. and e. Aust., cultivated as an ornamental.

1889 J.H. MAIDEN *Useful Native Plants Aust.* 410 *Cupania anacardioides* . . 'Brush Deal' and 'Tuckeroo' are Queensland colonial and aboriginal names respectively. **1909** F.M. BAILEY *Comprehensive Catal. Qld. Plants* (ed. 2) 113 *Cupania anacardioides* . . 'Tuckeroo' of Moreton Bay natives. **1965** *Austral. Encycl.* VIII. 4 C[*upaniopsis*] *anacardioides* ('tuckeroo') . . is a tree up to 40 feet high, ranging from Sydney around the coast to Arnhem Land and preferring brush forests in the neighbourhood of salt water. **1985** N. & H. NICHOLSON *Austral. Rainforest Plants* 23 Tuckeroo makes a handsome small to medium-sized shade tree for coastal areas.

tuck-out. *Obs.* [Transf. use of *tuck-out* a hearty meal, a 'blow-out': see OED *tuck, sb.*[1] 6.]

1. A beating; a fight.

1832 *Hill's Life N.S.W.* (Sydney) 31 Aug. 3 (Advt.), Bill Dargin was beaten by me; and I think never before or since received such a *tuck-out.* **1847** *Bell's Life in Sydney* 25 Dec. 2/2 A hostile meeting took place this morning . . on the Richmond Bottoms, for what is vulgarly termed a *tuck-out,* not of *bacon and eggs,* or roast beef and plum-pudding, but a reciprocal interchange . . between two very formidable farmers of the locality.

2. *Austral. pidgin.* Food.

1847 [see sense 1]. **1863** J. BONWICK *Wild White Man* 66 The aborigines were . . regaled with 'plenty tuck out'. **1890** J.I. WATTS *Family Life S.A.* 186 They were good-sized—about as long as a dessert plate—and I have no doubt very good eating. . . Some blacks came a week or two afterwards, and assured us they were very good 'tuck-out'. **1893** H.J. WHITE *Round Camp Fire* 56 Tho' promised they were a budgeree whack, Of tuckout and bacca. **1896** W.H. WILLSHIRE *Land of Dawning* 11 The lazy old men and women sit in the shade in the day, stroking poor lean dogs, and sending the youngsters out for 'tuckout'. **1915** J.R.B. LOVE *Aborigines* 18 The young men and women . . procure native food supplies ('bushy tuckout'). **1935** F. BIRTLES *Battle Fronts Outback* 80 The piccaninnies, too, had been earning their 'tuck-out', digging down into the soft soil at the foot of long creeping vines, for the yam roots.

Hence as *v. trans.*, to eat.

1981 NGABIDJ & SHAW *My Country of Pelican Dreaming* 66 We used also to tuck out goose—that was good food.

tug. [Of unknown origin.] A sharper (but see quots. 1896 and 1898). Also *attrib.*

1896 *Bulletin* (Sydney) 11 Apr. 17/4 Quite a number of bookies are migrating in view of the dull Australian winter tug-catching season. **1898** *Ibid.* 4 June (Red Page), And a sharper is a 'spieler' And a simpleton's a 'tug'. **1911** *Ibid.* 23 Nov. 13/4 Micko, from Collingwood, may be a 'tug' or a 'crook' or a 'rough-up' [etc.]. **1914** E. DYSON *Spats' Fact'ry* 124 You're the king tug, 'n' I'm just nothin'. **1927** J. MATHIEU *Backblock Ballads* 52 She had 'shouted' when 'Paroo' Showed the classic art of shearing on a pup . . And took lessons from a tug in picking up. **1933** A. REID *Those were Days* 55 So that chaps could know why a top-notch tug Can work 'his' ramps in a card-room snug.

tula /ˈtula/. Also **tuhla.** [Poss. a. Luritja dial. of Western Desert *tula.*] An Aboriginal tool used for wood-working: see quot. 1981.

1930 C.C. TOWLE *Certain Stone Implements* 10 The coastal tribes . . did not possess symmetrical types, of which the gouge (or adze, or tuhla) was the most widely distributed. **1975** T. MCCOURT *Aboriginal Artefacts* 119 The greatest range of scrapers is found wherever the tula and the unifaced point are found. However, scrapers of some sort or another have been used all over Australia. **1981** J. MULVANEY et al. *Aboriginal Aust.* 70 (*caption*) Tula adze, or woodworking chisel, from Barrow Creek, Northern Territory . . exhibits the characteristically curved and stout handle, with stone tip firmly fixed with *Triodia* cement.

tulip oak. [With reference to the grain of the timber which is reminiscent of that of the oak *Quercus* and SILKY OAK.] BOOYONG; the wood of this tree.

1938 C.T. WHITE *Princ. Bot. Qld. Farmers* 212 *Tarrietia* (Booyongs, Tulip Oaks or Stave Woods). **1956** A.C.C. LOCK *Tropical Tapestry* 45 Different species of fern leaves waved against the background of . . tulip oaks, sassafras and beeches. **1962** *Daily Mercury Centenary Story Mackay* 6 Apr. 43 The more popular scrub woods include satin oak, tulip oak. **1985** *Austral. Garden Jrnl.* Oct. 17 Do look down at the tulip oak flooring as you walk around the corner.

tulip tree. *Obs.* WARATAH 1. Also **tulip.**

1831 *Acct. Colony Van Diemen's Land* 66 The whole of this country is also interspersed with that magnificent shrub called Warrataw or tulip tree and its beautiful scarlet flowers. **1835** *Hobart Town Almanack* 110 *Telopea Tasmaniana.* . . The generic name is derived from *telopos* seen at a distance, its fine red blossoms being seen at a distance in the bush. It has been corrupted into tulip tree, to which it bears not the least resemblance. **1852** J. SHAW *Tramp to Diggings* 246, I met with a splendid shrub, called by the natives the Tulip-tree or shrub (*Telopea speciossima* [*sic*]). **1860** 'LADY' *My Experiences in Aust.* 310 Our green-house would be but ill stocked with Australian flowers; a few Warratahs (the tulip-tree of the colony), a Bigonia, and three or four specimens of the Norfolk Island pine. **1898** E.E. MORRIS *Austral Eng.* 498 The generic name *Telopea* .. has been corrupted into *Tulip.*

tulipwood. Any of several trees yielding an attractively streaked timber, esp. *Harpullia pendula* (fam. Sapindaceae) of rainforest in n.e. N.S.W. and e. Qld., which is cultivated as an ornamental; the wood of the tree. Also *ellipt.* as **tulip.**

1830 W.J. HOOKER *Bot. Miscellany* I. 239 Extensive brushwoods, the latter exhibiting a profusion of *Yellow Wood,* (*Oxleya xanthoxyla*) and *Tulip Wood.* **1845** J.O. BALFOUR *Sketch of N.S.W.* 39 The tulip wood, with its variegated flowers, and delightful perfume, grows in abundance. **1847** J.D. LANG *Cooksland* 138 Tulip-Wood—'This wood is suitable for fancy, cabinet and turning-work.' **1880** J. BONWICK *Resources Qld.* 82 The Tulip Wood, *Harpulla* [*sic*] *pendula,* is as beautiful for growth, as its wood is beautiful for cabinet work. **1915** *Forestry Question in N.S.W.* (Austral. Forest League) 5 Tulipwood is one of the handsomest of Australia timbers, and is only one example of the many native brush timbers whose commercial value has not yet been thoroughly appreciated. **1921** *Smith's Weekly* (Sydney) 1 Jan. 9/3 Saw a walking-stick the other day made from tulip. **1935** DAVISON & NICHOLLS *Blue Coast Caravan* 124 We learnt to know new trees .. tulipwood [etc.]. **1970** J.V. MARSHALL *Walk to Hills of Dreamtime* 157 *Tulipwood* Or *Cabinet-tree,* so called because of its hard close-grained wood. *Harpullia pendula*: a graceful eighty foot tree with yellow flowers, red-cum-yellow fruit and spectacular masses of berries. **1985** N. & H. NICHOLSON *Austral. Rainforest Plants* 37 Tulipwood has also been named Black Tulip for its beautiful timber, highly figured with contrasting dark and light bands.

tumble down, *v. Austral. pidgin. Obs.*

1. *intr.* To die; to fall down. Also *fig.*

1803 J.G. GRANT *Narr. Voyage N.S.W.* 113 Through Euranabie .. I found the bones were those of a white man that had come in a canoe from the southward, where the ship *tumble down,* the expression he made use of for being wrecked. **1827** P. CUNNINGHAM *Two Yrs. in N.S.W.* II. 22 Their common practice of fighting amongst themselves is still with the *waddie,* each alternatively stooping the head to receive the other's blows, until one tumbles down. **1848** *Atlas* (Sydney) IV. 359/2 Occasionally they tell of some one 'tumble down' from bite of myall snake. **1856** *Full & True Acct. Murder of P. Brown,* So now, my dear friends, we shall tumble down too, The white-fellows will hang us, and you will all view! We shall very soon die, but then, yes, oh then, We'll tumble down black, and jump up *white men.* **1867** 'COLONIST' *Life's Work* 94 You give us tucker... Squaw very bad, tumble down sick; big lot pain, very ill want good tucker. **1878** R.B. SMYTH *Aborigines of Vic.* I. 464 (*note*) At last he would 'tumble down'—the blacks' expression for 'die'. **1889** J.J. EAST *Aborigines S. & Central Aust.* 6 It is doubtless this custom of keeping the body so long until it cracks or begins to fall away that the native terms now generally used to signify death, viz., 'tumble down' and 'crack-a-back', originated. **1921** *Bulletin* (Sydney) 6 Jan. 20/3 An old mammie ran to our hut and called us—'Piccaninny tumble down,' she whispered. **1933** R.B. PLOWMAN *Man from Oodnadatta* 195, I have told the blacks that I am going to shoot the moon and that it is going to tumble down (die).

2. *trans.* To kill. (As *vbl. n.* in quot.).

1834 G. BENNETT *Wanderings N.S.W.* I. 131 Unceasingly complained of the 'tumbling down him brother'.

tumble down, *n. Austral. pidgin. Obs.* [f. prec.] Alcoholic liquor.

1827 P. CUNNINGHAM *Two Yrs. in N.S.W.* I. 236 A good jorum of *bull* (washings of a sugar bag) or *tumble down* (grog) at the conclusion of the harvest, sends them all merrily and gaily away. **1837** *Rep. Select Committee Transportation* (1838) 43 They would come to my farm and go into the huts, and if the men have any spirits (it is commonly called 'bull', but in addition they call it 'tumble down') they get it from them. **1843** W. PRIDDEN *Aust.* 143 Tobacco and spirits, which the poor natives call '*tumble-down*', are articles in constant request.

tumbling-tommy. [Alteration of *tumbling tom*: see OED *tumbling.*]

1. A horse-drawn scoop, having a tipping bucket and used esp. for earth-moving. Also *attrib.*

1934 *Bulletin* (Sydney) 9 May 20/2 Drawing .. water for stock from a well .. the bucket came off the 'tumbling-tommy' hook and sank to the bottom. **1943** H.G. LAMOND *From Tariaro to Ross Roy* 108 Steel wire took the place of the old soft iron wire... Tumbling Tommies and other automatic tin scoops took the place of the cumbersome slide. **1977** B. FULLER *Nullarbor Lifelines* 56 A 'tumbling tommy' was horse-drawn, the animal being controlled by means of long reins held by a driver who either walked well behind or else to one side. **1979** W.K. BECKINGHAM *Red Acres* 37 During the Depression I joined a Government dam-sinking team, and worked with a quarter-yard 'Tumbling Tommy' scoop with two horses, working in the corners where the tractors couldn't go. **1981** G. ELLIS *Hey Doc, let's go Fishing* 67 Early in this century a canal was cut from Basalt River to Lolworth to water some intervening country... In those days bulldozers and scrapers weren't known and it was a case of Tumbling Tommies, horse-drawn ploughs and wheelbarrows.

2. *transf.* See quot. 1977.

1977 B. FULLER *Nullarbor Lifelines* 56 Oddly enough, scoop men were known as 'tumbling tommies' after the small ground-clearing implements they drove.

tunnel. *Surfing.* The hollow curve of a breaking wave; a 'tube'.

1963 J. POLLARD *Austral. Surfrider* 104 There's a story about Mickey Munez, one of the great Hawaiian riders starting into a tube just after taking off on Rincon Point. He disappeared... They reckon he was inside that tunnel for 20 seconds. **1964** B. HUMPHRIES *Nice Night's Entertainment* (1981), When we weren't zipping, cutting and flicking the boards through tunnels and wipe-outs .. we were on the beach or in the surf club.

tupong /'tupɒŋ/. [a. Gangubanud *dubaŋ.*] The small, chiefly marine fish *Pseudaphritis urvilli* of s.e. Aust. incl. Tas.

1897 *Proc. Linnean Soc. N.S.W.* XXII. 557 Some months ago I received .. three fine specimens of a *Pseudaphritis* from the fresh waters of Victoria, where it is known to anglers as the 'Tupong'. **1952** *Austral. Museum Mag.* June 310 The Australian aborigines had their names for fishes, of course, and still have in the more remote places, and some of these, even though tribes which invented them have become extinct or have 'lost their tongues', are currently used in everyday speech. I need only mention the following .. Tupong, Turrum, [etc.]. **1974** L. WEDLICK *Sporting Fish* 17 The tupong is dark blue to purple on the back, and silver on the belly. *Ibid.,* All early articles referred to this fish as marble trout, freshwater flathead or congolli, the last name being the only by which the tupong is known in South Australia.

turkey, *n.*[1] [Transf. use of *turkey* a large gallinaceous bird.]

1. Either of two birds, the *wild turkey* (see WILD 1), and the *brush turkey* (see BRUSH *n.*[1] B. 2); *native turkey,* see NATIVE *a.* 6 b.

1827 *Monitor* (Sydney) 20 Aug. 599/1 Entered a thick shrub, at the foot of Mount Dumuresq [*sic*] .. found several turkies, and a remarkably large pigeon, upwards of three pounds weight. **1847** G.F. ANGAS *Savage Life & Scenes* I. 164 Mr Burr had shot a turkey, which was roasted on a stick. **1855** W. HOWITT *Land, Labor & Gold* I. 367 The so-called turkeys here are bustards. **1878** R.B. SMYTH *Aborigines of Vic.* II. 314 The patience shown by the blacks in snaring game is very great, and I have known a man spend hours in catching a turkey. **1883** W.J. O'DONNELL *Diary Exploring Exped.* 11 Aug. (1884) 16 Mr Linacre had shot a fine turkey, which was most acceptable to us in our reduced condition. The gizzard of this turkey when opened was found to contain a full-grown lark, which had been swallowed, feathers and all. **1911** ST. C. GRONDONA *Collar & Cuffs* 60 The fox has not penetrated so far north as this [*sc.* central Qld.] yet, consequently the turkey flourishes. **1926** A.A.B. APSLEY *Amateur Settlers* 96 We used to see .. the bustard known as 'turkey'. **1963** *N. Austral. Monthly* Dec. 33 Scrub turkeys—the brush turkey—were very plentiful then, but without a 'turkey dog' you could walk for hours, and perhaps days, without even hearing or seeing one. **1973** R. ROBINSON *Drift of Things* 418 The gang at the end of our section told us of the turkeys they shot. They were in mungerai (a succulent plant) country and we were in parakelia country.

2. With other distinguishing epithets, as **plain, scrub:** see under first element.

3. *transf.* SWAG *n.* 1; also a packhorse.

1905 *Shearer* (Sydney) 17 June 6/2 If you meet him on the track with your 'turkey coiled' (swag) no introduction is necessary. **1906** *Bulletin* (Sydney) 31 May 40/2 So you pack your bloomin' 'turkey', and you take the Northern train. **1911** *Ibid.* 27 July 13/4 'Turkey' is the term used for 'horse' by every shearer who disdains the common, garden names. **1912** 'IRONBARK' *Ironbark Splinters* 6 *Turkey,* bushman's slang for 'swag', a bundle of blankets and clothes. The term is sometimes also applied to a pack-horse.

4. In the phr. **head over turkey** and varr., 'head over heels'; also *fig.,* in disarray.

[**1906** E. DYSON *Fact'ry 'Ands* 234 One was dumped down two flights, 'ead over tuck, with a fat punch.] **1915** C.J. DENNIS *Songs of Sentimental Bloke* 43 'E swallers lysol, throws a fancy fit, 'Ead over turkey, an' 'is soul 'as flit. **1955** A. MARSHALL *I can jump Puddles* 46 Before I quieten her, I knock Sir Frederick Salisbury, or whatever his name is, head over turkey into a clump of peacocks. **1979** DUSTY & LAPSLEY *Walk Country Mile* 136 'Christ, there goes the bloody washing,' cursed Bridget. 'Look at it. Arse over turkey. I'll have to do the lot again.'

5. Special Comb. **turkey bush,** ELLANGOWAN POISON BUSH; *emu bush* (a), see EMU *n.*[1] 3; also *attrib.*; **nest dam** (or **tank**), a reservoir built in flat country where there is no natural run-off, having high earth walls and so resembling the mound of the brush turkey (see quot. 1974); also *ellipt.* as **turkey nest.**

1899 *Western Champion* (Barcaldine) 15 Aug. 5/1 All the wattle trees and bloodwoods have been killed for miles around... Wonder if it affected the **turkey bush.** **1927** *Bulletin* (Sydney) 14 Apr. 27/2 A large area of country south of the Escape River, Cape York Peninsula, is .. covered by the accursed 'turkey bush' scrub. **1936** F. CLUNE *Roaming round Darling* 163 Turkey-bush flower—white and small, having five petals to each bloom, like an English daisy. **1944** *Bulletin* (Sydney) 6 Dec. 12/2 A cane cocky out from Mackay (Q.) had a 20-acre block, mostly lantana and turkey-bush. **1957** R.S. PORTEOUS *Brigalow* 41 Once they hit the wilga and turkey bush they split up and vanished. **1963** M. BRITT *Pardon my Boots* 52 Thickly dotted with turkey-bush (a dry shrub). **1981** G.M. CUNNINGHAM et al. *Plants Western N.S.W.* 615 As with other species of the .. [Myoporaceae] family, the fruits of this plant are eaten by emus and plains turkeys, hence 'turkey-bush', one of the common names by which it is known. **1961** [**turkey nest dam**] J.W. JORDAN *Practical Sheep Farming* 66 The finished earth works and embankments form a nest-shaped storage, called a 'turkey-nest'. **1968** D. CAMPBELL *Drought* 104 The grazier on dead flat country .. may require bores or specially constructed 'ring' dams or 'turkey-nest' dams with a system of sprays for a limited crop area. **1974** F. STEVENS *Aborigines in N.T. Cattle Industry* 119 (*note*) A 'turkey-nest' tank is so described because of its appearance. Normally built in plains country, the earth walls of the dam usually rise 20 or 30 feet above the surrounding countryside, holding anywhere up to 20,000 gallons of water. **1978** M. NIXON *Rivers of Home* 7 These are commonly named 'turkey nest dams', in reference to the birds which build their nests on the ground in a similar manner with sticks and leaves. **1982** D. HARRIS *Drovers of Outback* 36 Next morning I went back to the turkey nest tank and climbed up the mill to have a look around.

Turkey, *n.*[2] Also **Turkie.** [The name of the country in s.e. Europe and s.w. Asia.]

1. In Services' speech: a Turkish soldier.

1916 'MEN OF ANZAC' *Anzac Bk.* 127 An' then—oh, strike me blue an' pink—Then don't the Turkies swear! **1916** O. HOGUE *Trooper Bluegum at Dardanelles* 191 But at other times he stalked back as if he had won the battle of Anzac 'on his own'. 'Killed three Turkeys,' he cried. And then he was as happy as Larry all day. **1974** D. STUART *Prince of my Country* 102 Knock the Turkey out, up through the Balkans an' in through the back door.

2. Special Comb. **turkey lolly,** a confection of spun sugar; *fairy floss*, see FAIRY *n.*[1] 2.

1971 J. HETHERINGTON *Morning was Shining* 45 In those days Turkey Lolly was sold on the Sandringham beach on hot summer afternoons by a tall copper-hued man who wore a turban. . . He would dip his dark hand into the tub and shovel the filmy confection into funnel-shaped home-made bags. **1978** L. WHITE *Memories of Childhood* 44 He had knowing blue eyes and curly fair hair like turkey-lolly. **1981** P. HAY *Meeting Sighs* 144 It may still be bought in some of our shops and stalls, masquerading under the name of 'Fairy Floss'. But what could equal genuine Turkey lolly: thin, brittle threads of coloured sweetness, manufactured by a real man of India, and exchanged for a copper coin or an empty beer bottle.

turn, *n.* [Transf. use of *turn* an item in a variety entertainment.]

1. A party.

1953 T.A.G. HUNGERFORD *Riverslake* 94 The Causeway's all right—a damned sight better than the turns up at the Albert Hall. Anyway, it's a football dance, not just one of those . . turns they slap on for the locals. **1965** K. TENNANT *Summer's Tales* 58 'Tell me, have you ever been to this Barmaids' Picnic before?' . . 'Never,' the thin man beside him answered. 'I hear it's quite a turn.' **1969** A. BUZO *Front Room Boys* (1970) 21 Went to a turn at Collaroy. Some bird's twenty-first. **1972** G. MORLEY *Jockey rides Honest Race* 127 The phone in the flat rang constantly with people ringing up inviting Kon to cocktail parties, art showings and fashion parties. Kon would only go to a few. He would send Phil or myself to the other turns. **1979** B. HUMPHRIES *Bazza comes into his Own*, Jeez, no bastard tipped me the wink this turn was fancy dress!

2. In the phr. **to stack on a turn,** to make a fuss.

1953 T.A.G. HUNGERFORD *Riverslake* 173 'When we got back—stone the crows, I thought she'd shed her blasted skin!' 'You might've told her before.' 'Like hell! She would've just stacked on a turn.' **1967** J. HIBBERD *White with Wire Wheels* (1970) 159 'How was she? Stacking on a turn?' . . 'Not Sue. She's as placid as they come.' **1973** J. POWERS *Last of Knucklemen* (1974) 23 I've done *thousands* on single bets, and I've never stacked on a turn like you do over a few lousy cans of beer! **1981** *Weekend Austral.* (Sydney) 21 Nov. 19/8 For reasons best known to himself, Mr Bjelke-Petersen stacked on a turn and the negotiations broke down.

turn, *v.*

1. *trans. Obs.* With **in:** to return (an assigned convict) to official custody. Also in the phr. **to turn** (a convict) **in to government.**

1830 R. DAWSON *Present State Aust.* 201, I asked him . . the reason of his having been 'turned in', as they call it, to government. **1831** *Sydney Herald* 1 Aug. 4/1 The Police Office is not so troubled as usual with servants who used to be turned in at the caprice of the master. **1835** *Cornwall Chron.* (Launceston) 18 Apr. 2 As a last resource, to prevent ourselves being further taxed with the support of a saucy servant, we '*turn him in*'. **1843** *Sydney Morning Herald* 26 Sept. 4/5, I went to Mr Sparke's place in search of him, and was told there that he had been turned into Government. **1900** C. WHITE *Hist. Austral. Bushranging* 113 The Bench ordered his ticket be taken away and him to be 'turned in to Government', i.e., returned to the Government gang of convicts to finish his original sentence.

2. *intr. Obs.* With **out:** to become a bushranger.

1862 *Western Post* (Mudgee) 24 Sept. 2/2 He was immediately told by the robber they ought to turn out. **1875** *Austral. Town & Country Jrnl.* (Sydney) 19 June 983/4 I'm not sure that you won't get off light. You have had the luck not to have killed anybody, that I know of, since you turned out. **1888** 'R. BOLDREWOOD' *Robbery under Arms* (1937) 3 How do you think a chap that's taken to the bush—regularly turned out, I mean, with a price on his head . . can stand his life if he don't drink? **1899** G.E. BOXALL *Story Austral. Bushrangers* 274 At this time the reward offered for the capture of Thomas Clarke was raised to £1000 while £500 was offered for his brother John, who had just 'turned out'. **1910** J. CAMERON *Spell of Bush* 131 [The bush] had been his home; for even before he had 'turned out', four walls had never held Michael Moran for long.

3. *trans.* Chiefly *N.T.* [Also U.S.] With **off:** to consign (livestock) to market.

1942 H.H. PECK *Mem. of Stockman* 103 Tatong always turned off many fat bullocks. **1960** *N.T. News* (Darwin) 26 Feb. 3/1 He predicted many stations would switch from breeding fat cattle up to four and five years old and turn off 18 months to two-year-old stores instead.

4. *trans.* With **on:** to provide (refreshments, esp. alcoholic liquor). Freq. in the phr. **to turn it on.**

1941 S.J. BAKER *Pop. Dict. Austral. Slang* 79 *Turn it on*, to provide liquor at a party . . to 'shout' drinks. **1944** P.C. NEASBEY *Blokes I Knew* 20 A crowd of admiring 'Diggers' proceeded to 'turn it on' to such effect that the guest of honor was soon hopelessly drunk. **1955** *Bulletin* (Sydney) 9 Feb. 12/3, I have seen beer turned-on at the cut-out in old-fashioned style by the owner, and left untouched by independent shearers. **1965** K. MCKENNEY *Hide-Away Man* 72 You wouldn't like to come down to James Sharkey's with me. He's turning it on this morning. I mean, cold beer and all that. **1977** B. SCOTT *My Uncle Arch* 109, I thought I'd die laughing at the big dinner the firm turned on. . . All the grog you could drink and baretop gogo dancers.

5. *trans.* To earn (a sum of money).

1960 R. PULLAN *Hardskins* 29 New Australians . . chase all over, looking for bargains, trying to beat you down, anything to turn a quid. **1968** A. LINKLETTER *Down Under* 20 The . . Aussies have since contracted with the Japanese to recover for scrap the metal of these ships which clog Darwin's harbor. 'They gave it to us,' a pub owner commented. 'Might as well turn a bob and sell it back to them.' **1976** F. MOORHOUSE *Conference-Ville* 106 Just been turning a quid.

turnipwood. Any of several trees the bark or wood of which has a turnip-like smell, as *Dysoxylum muelleri* (see *red bean* RED *a.* 1 a.), and esp. *Akania lucens* (fam. Akaniaceae) of n.e. N.S.W. and s.e. Qld.; the wood of the tree. Formerly also **turnip-tree.**

1871 *Austral. Town & Country Jrnl.* (Sydney) 18 Mar. 330/4 Another peculiar tree is detected by its smell to be the turnip-tree, from its aroma resembling the smell of Swede turnips. **1889** J.H. MAIDEN *Useful Native Plants Aust.* 420 *Dysoxylon Muelleri* . . 'Turnip-wood'. . . Timber of a rich red colour; used for cabinet-making and window work. When fresh cut the wood has much the smell of a Swedish turnip. **1898** E.E. MORRIS *Austral Eng.* 484 Turnip-wood. . . The timbers of the trees *Akania hillii* . . and *Dysoxylon Muelleri* . . from their white and red colours respectively. **1932** R.H. ANDERSON *Trees of N.S.W.* 169 Turnipwood . . is a handsome tree up to 40 feet in height, with large pinnate leaves. **1984** WRIGLEY & FAGG *Austral. Native Plants* (ed. 2) 431 Turnipwood. Small tree to 10 m. . . Has great potential for indoor plant work. Beautiful foliage.

turn-off. Chiefly *N.T.* [f. TURN *v.* 3; also U.S.] The quantity of marketable livestock produced by a rural property or district. Also *attrib.*

1960 *N.T. News* (Darwin) 11 Mar. 7/3 There is sufficient feed throughout the Alice Springs district at present to ensure a good turnoff by the middle of the year. **1962** *N. Austral. Monthly* Feb. 17 In 1961 the whole turn-off of several well-known cattle stations has been moved by road trains. **1966** J.H. KELLY *Struggle for North* 20 Within this classification I assessed regional cattle-carrying and turn-off capacities. [*Note*] The term 'turn-off' is of common usage in northern Australia. It is used to denote the number of cattle that are, or could be marketed annually, from individual cattle properties or from particular cattle regions. **1968** F. ROSE *Aust. Revisited* 269 *Turn-off cattle*, those cattle marketed from a property or station.

turpentine. [See quot. 1904.]

1. Any of several trees, usu. of the fam. Myrtaceae, esp. the tall *Syncarpia glomulifera* (syn. *S. laurifolia*) of e. N.S.W. and e. Qld., having a thick fibrous bark and yielding a reddish timber valued for its durability in sea water; the wood of the tree. Also *attrib.*, esp. as **turpentine-tree.**

1803 *Sydney Gaz.* 26 June, Timber in this colony includes Turpentine etc. **1805** J.H. TUCKEY *Acct. Voyage to establish Colony Port Phillip* 226 Turpentine is a small wood of no service but in flooring houses. **1818** J. OXLEY *Jrnls. Two Exped. N.S.W.* (1820) 331 The timber was chiefly black butted gum, stringy bark, turpentine tree and forest oak. **1870** *Sydney Morning Herald* 2 July 8/4 A sleeper of ironbark and one of turpentine . . have lately been taken up from our locomotive line. **1891** *Proc. Linnean Soc. N.S.W.* VI. 422 *Eucalyptus microcorys* . . called 'Turpentine' in Queensland, but not to be confused with the New South Wales Turpentine (*Syncarpia*). **1901** *Ibid.* XXVI. 209 Among the Mallee, about here there is often a spreading Pine, *Callitris verrucosa* . . which grows with a short stem and branches out almost from the ground. . . South of the Lachlan this tree is sometimes called Turpentine. **1904** J.H. MAIDEN *Forest Flora N.S.W.* I. 16 'Turpentine-tree.' It is so-called because of the resinous exudation which flows from between the bark and the wood when the timber is cut into. It is an unfortunate name, as it suggests inflammability, and turpentine is one of the most uninflammable of timbers. . . Turpentine timber has scarcely any odour. **1935** DAVISON & NICHOLLS *Blue Coast Caravan* 40 Valleys dotted with dark clumps of bush apple and turpentine. **1951** G. FARWELL *Outside Track* 27 His training had taught him to recognize the fibrous bark of the turpentine as the best material for roofing, since their gumminess preserved it against weather. **1969** W. MOXHAM *Apprentice* 10 His skin was like the bark of a turpentine tree, rough and grooved and hairy. **1981** G. CROSS *George & Widda-Woman* 88 Practically all the pylons for the wharves in Sydney Harbour were made from our turpentines. **1986** *Canberra Times* 1 Feb. 13/3 The boxes are made from 90-year-old turpentine-wood water pipes unearthed during the La Trobe Valley Water and Sewerage Board's pipeline upgrading program.

2. Special Comb. **turpentine bush,** any of several often resinous or aromatic shrubs, esp. some species of the genera *Beyeria* (fam. Euphorbiaceae) and *Eremophila* (fam. Myoporaceae) incl. *E. sturtii* of e. mainland Aust. Also *ellipt.* as **turpentine.**

1885 P.R. MEGGY *From Sydney to Silverton* 124 Another feature of the vegetation is the turpentine bush, remarkable for its irritating properties. **1910** *Emu* X. 17 Our road was now skirting the Barrier Range, through blue-and salt-bush country, with occasional turpentine-bushes. **1932** M.R. WHITE *No Roads go By* 53 They spread out, curling around the low scrubby mauve-flowering turpentine bushes. **1935** D. THOMSON *In Arnhem Land* (1983) 34 A splendid shrub known as the 'Turpentine bush' (*Calythrix microphylla*)—a blaze of rich purplish hue like heather; a really splendid thing. **1965** K. MCKENNEY *Hide-Away Man* 60 A clay road between grey gums and brown turpentine bush. **1977** *Ecos* xiii. 17/3 Unfortunately, the important weed, turpentine (*Eremophila sturtii*) escaped unscathed. **1985** *Austral. Financial Rev.* (Sydney) 18 Dec. 25 Noxious and inedible shrubs—like turpentine, punty and hopbush.

turps. [Transf. use of *turps* abbrev. of *turpentine.*] Alcoholic liquor. Esp. in the phr. **on the turps.**

1865 H. KINGSLEY *Hillyars & Burtons* 294 They tossed for a go of turps and a hayband—I ask your ladyship's pardon, that means a glass of gin and a cigar. **1944** *Newsreel* (Launceston) Dec. 16 What is the exact meaning of 'sucking the turps'? **1953** D. STIVENS *Gambling Ghost* 71 He went straight to the poison shop and proceeded to give the turps a John L. Sullivan of a bash. **1968** D. O'GRADY *Bottle of Sandwiches* 174 He's a bastard when he gets on the turps. **1980** S. THORNE *I've met some Bloody Wags* 36 Dan was a good bloke, but a terror on the turps. Once he started on rum—look out!

turquoise wren. The bird *Malurus splendens callainus* of arid central Aust.

1898 E.E. MORRIS *Austral Eng.* Turquoise W[ren]—*Malurus callainus.* **1916** S.A. WHITE *In Far Northwest* 25 One or two birds were met with and here for the first time, the turquoise wren . . which is a gem among birds. **1945** C. BARRETT *Austral. Bird Life* 193 The turquoise wren . . ranges from Spencer Gulf to Central Australia. **1976** *Reader's Digest Compl. Bk. Austral. Birds* 410 There are three subspecies of splendid wren, which were, until recently, regarded as separate species . . the turquoise wren [etc.].

turrum /'tʌrəm/. [Prob. f. a W.A. Aboriginal language.] Any of several large marine fish of n. Aust., of the fam. Carangidae, valued as game fish, incl. *Carangoides fulvoguttatus* and *Caranx ignobilis.*

1936 T.C. ROUGHLEY *Wonders Great Barrier Reef* 196 The most stubborn fighter of the reef is probably the turrum, a giant trevally which attains a weight of upwards of seventy pounds. **1952** *Austral. Museum Mag.* June 310 The Australian aborigines had their names for fishes, of course, and still have in the more remote places, and some of these, even though tribes which invented them have become extinct or have 'lost their tongues', are currently used in everyday speech. I need only mention the following . . Tupong, Turrum, [etc.]. **1981** G. ELLIS *Hey Doc, let's go Fishing!* 14 The turrum belongs to the trevally family, but it is a very deep chunky fish with shoulders (if such a description can be used of fish) like a working bullock.

tussock: see TUSSOCK GRASS b.

tussock, *v. Obs.* [f. *tussock*, abbrev. of TUSSOCK GRASS.] *intr.* To clear land of tussock grass. Chiefly as *vbl. n.*

[N.Z. **1866** J. MURRAY *Descr. of Southland* 28 [The intending farmer] will do well to 'tussac' a few acres;— that is chip off with an adze the flax and coarse grass growing on the land.] **1888** *Devon Herald* (La Trobe) 6 Mar. 2/2 We would remind persons interested that tenders invited by Mr G. Atkinson for tussocking on Pig Island, close tomorrow. **1904** *Bulletin* (Sydney) 7 Jan. 16/2 The swagman . . may obtain a little 'tussocking' at a contract price.

tussock grass. a. Any of several tussock-forming plants, usu. perennial grasses of the genus *Poa* (fam. Poaceae), esp. *P. labillardieri* of e. Aust. incl. Tas., and the related *P. sieberana*. **b.** (Freq. *ellipt.* as **tussock**) SERRATED TUSSOCK. Also *attrib.*

1870 J. BONWICK *Last Tasmanians* 243 The Bishop of Tasmania described it in 1854 as 'little more than a succession of sand heaps, covered here and there with tussock and stunted shrubs'. **1871** *Austral. Town & Country Jrnl.* (Sydney) 15 July 34/3 The tussac grass . . grows freely in most places in Australia where the soil is sufficiently rich. **1874** *Illustr. Sydney News* 19 Sept. 21/3 Dr Schomburk of Adelaide has succeeded in growing tussock grass there. It is regarded as a most nutritious food for sheep or cattle. **1896** A. MACKAY *Austral. Agriculturist* (rev. ed.) 335 Top-dressing with manure, and harrowing the dry soil, helps the grasses to get ahead of their weed enemies, amongst which 'tussock grass' is becoming very serious. **1909** E. WALTHAM *Life & Labour in Aust.* 109 Chinese clearing away the wire grass, tussocks and any useless débris. **1940** A.W. UPFIELD *Bushranger of Skies* 123 Country appearing to the uninitiated as semi-desert despite the growth of buckbush, cotton- and flannel-bush and the green sprouting tussock grass. **1968** J.N. WHITTET *Weeds* (rev. ed.) 364 Small areas of tussock can be removed by spraying with 8 lbs. of 2,2-DPA in 40 gallons of water and oversowing. **1968** N.T. BURBIDGE *Austral. Grasses* II. 36 Tussock Grass is a useful constituent of native pastures on the Tablelands, and the plants are grazed during the winter when little else is available. **1983** *Warwick Daily News* 14 June 3/1 Stands of apple box . . and tall tussock grassland. **1983** *Weekend Austral.* (Sydney) 30 July 4 Mrs Fisher informed the council of her intention to clear 16 ha. of tussock each year by mattocking and ploughing.

tussy-jumper. [f. TUSS(OCK GRASS + -Y + *jumper*.] One employed as a hand on a rural property.

1967 G. JENKIN *Two Yrs. Bardunyah Station* 6 All the tussy-jumpers there . . Give up a mournful moan. **1975** M. THORNTON *It's Jackaroo's Life* 64 So with tussie jumper Harry and the ute filled up with gas.

twang. [Prob. back-formation f. *Twankay* a variety of green tea.] Opium.

1898 *Bulletin* (Sydney) 1 Oct. 14/3 A few more W.Q. slang words . . opium 'twang', a Chinaman a 'canary' [etc.]. **1910** O'BRIEN & STEPHENS Materials Dict. Austral. Slang, *Twang*, opium. **1945** T. RONAN *Strangers on Ophir* 68 The honest Chinese limits himself to his one pipe of 'Twang' per night. **1961** I.L. IDRIESS *Tracks of Destiny* 94 This Chinaman was a 'runner', carrying smuggled 'twang' (opium) from Port Darwin to his compatriots inland at the Creek. **1966** S.J. BAKER *Austral. Lang.* (ed. 2) 157 Opium was once known as *twang* in bush slang.

tweed-capper. *Obs.* A British immigrant.

1912 *Truth* (Sydney) 31 Mar. 5/1 The jimmygrants . . tough tweed-cappers and verdant mugs. **1912** *Bulletin* (Sydney) 15 Aug. 15/2 A newly arrived 'Jimmy Grant' passed a paddock of dead, ring-barked timber. . . 'Crikey!' he howled, 'have all those trees been struck by lightning?' This part (Moombooldool) is thick with tweed-cappers, and the mistakes they invent keep the countryside from ever feeling dull.

tweeds, *pl.* Trousers. Also *transf.*

1954 T.A.G. HUNGERFORD *Sowers of Wind* 117 'I take my coat off every day, and it don't stop the flaming traffic!' 'Try taking your tweeds off, boof-head!' **1969** A. BUZO *Rooted* (1973) 85 Susan was a lovely girl. She never dropped her tweeds for anyone. **1980** M. BAIL *Homesickness* (1981) 161 'Should always lock the door, Shiel,' he said, giving his tweeds a hitch.

twelve apostles, *pl.* Freq. also as sing. See APOSTLE. Also **twelve apostle (bird).**

1889 *Proc. Linnean Soc. N.S.W.* IV. 412 *Struthidea cinerea*. . . About Cobbora [N.S.W.] they are known as 'Twelve Apostles', a title shared by *Pomatostomus*. **1901** *Emu* I. 113 Variously known as . . 'The Twelve Apostles' and 'Seven Sisters' . . my particular flock numbers twelve usually. **1911** ST. C. GRONDONA *Collar & Cuffs* 62 The twelve apostles, or family bird, as it is called locally, black and white jays and other members of that family are numerous. **1921** 'J. O'BRIEN' *Around Boree Log* 31 Happy Jacks (*alias* Gray-crowned Babblers) are brown with white markings; Twelve Apostles (*alias* Apostle Birds) are gray with brown wings. **1930** A. RUSSELL *Sunlit Trails* 53 The babblers are often erroneously called the 'jumpers', a name which should only be applied to the Apostle bird, the 'Twelve Apostle' . . of the bushman. **1934** H.G. LAMOND *Aviary on Plains* 189 There are exceptions, of course, as proved by the choughs—happy families, twelve apostles, quakers, or whatever might be the district name for that bird. **1963** O. RUHEN *Flockmaster* 93 On a bloodwood tree, a busy family of the Twelve Apostle birds, skipping from twig to twig as though they played some organised game. **1963** I.L. IDRIESS *Our Living Stone Age* 78 A mob of Twelve Apostles started a noisy brawl up above in the branches of the Leichhardt tree. **1972** J. JONES *Memories Golden Gate* (rev. ed.) 8 Other birds which were plentiful in the area were the . . Twelve Apostles.

twenty-eight. [See quot. 1843.] The parrot *Barnardius zonarius semitorquatus* of s.w. W.A., a predom. green bird with a black head, red bar on forehead, and yellow collar; (esp. *W.A.*) more generally, any subspecies of PORT LINCOLN PARROT. Also **twenty-eight parrot** and formerly **twenty-eight parakeet.**

1843 J. GOULD *Birds of Aust.* (1848) V. Pl. 19, While on the wing . . it often utters a note, which from its resemblance to those words has procured for it the appellation of 'twenty-eight' Parrakeet from the colonists; the last word or note being sometimes repeated five or six times in succession. **1847** *Atlas* (Sydney) III. 111/2 A new and beautiful variety of the parrot tribe is to be seen . . somewhat less in size than that commonly known as the 'twenty-eight'. **1872** MRS E. MILLETT *Austral. Parsonage* 217 As cage birds they are much valued, are soon tamed, and easily taught to whistle; I have heard a *Twenty-eight* that could even manage a few bars of the 'Prairie flower'. **1890** G.J. BROINOWSKI *Birds of Aust.* III. Pl. 31, Commonly known as the 'Twenty-eight' Parrakeet . . the *Platycercus semi-torquatus* is a bird of restricted habitat. **1941** D. O'CALLAGHAN *Long Life Reminisc.* 138, I came on a fine flock of Ring Necked Parrots, often called '28s'. **1957** J. NAIRN *Out of Back Streets* 172 They watched the green *twenty-eight* parrots, and the gaily coloured *galahs*. **1981** A.B. FACEY *Fortunate Life* 90 The 'twenty-eight' . . was most destructive on cereal crops and fruit.

twicer.

1. *Obs.* One who has been convicted of a criminal offence twice.

1856 *Moreton Bay Free Press* 28 Apr. 3/5 He was at once despatched on board a steamer for the Hunter, in company with a female who has by marriage, since, changed her name and by two 'twicers' from Norfolk Island, who were to put the man out of the way and pay themselves.

2. *transf.* [Used elsewhere but recorded earliest in Aust.: see OEDS 3.] One who engages in double-dealing.

1879 *Truth* (Sydney) 24 Oct. 4/4, I . . cannot fail to observe the evil intention lurking beneath that stamps the writer as the *twicer* he is. **1915** *Ibid.* 26 Sept. 3/1 Like all such 'trimmers' and 'twicers', however, he is beginning to get 'hot coffee' from both sides. **1951** S. HICKEY *Travelled Roads* 106 The Emperor expressed regrets for the necessity of the recent massacre which, he said, brought deserved retribution on the authors of the conspiracy. This Royal Aztec strongly conveys the conviction that when he was up against it he was a thorough 'twicer'. **1966** D. NILAND *Pairs & Loners* 68 She was no good, anyway; putting over her people like that, the twicer.

twining fringed lily: see FRINGED LILY.

twitch-stick. [f. Br. dial. *twitch* to draw tight: see OED *v.*[1] 6.] A forked stick used to tighten a securing rope: see quot. 1908.

1901 *Proc. Linnean Soc. N.S.W.* XXVI. 330 *E[ucalytus] viridis*. . . Over the Macquarie and Lachlan country it is the most eastern of all the Mallees, and in approaching its habitat its presence is often indicated by the fact that the straight tough stems of these little trees may be seen on the carrier's wagons, where they are used as 'twitch sticks' to tighten the ropes which fasten the loads. **1908** W.H. OGILVIE *My Life in Open* 50 Powerful ropes— as thick as a man's wrist—are used, and the system by which they are drawn tight is that of 'twitch sticks'. A rope is slung loosely round the second tier of bales and held in position from below by men holding the forked sticks. The teamster then inserts a short, strong twitch stick into the looped slack of the rope, and turning it over and over draws the rope tighter. . . Then he lays the stick level along the rope, and with strong twine binds stick and rope together. **1927** A. CROMBIE *After Sixty Yrs.* 76, I then with a twitch-stick took a reef in the line which bound his arms.

two-bob, *a.* and *n.*

A. *adj.*

1. Cheap; of little consequence.

1944 L. GLASSOP *We were Rats* 144 Bert was more the 'two-bob lair' type. **1949** G. FARWELL *Traveller's Tracks* 52 The 'two bob seats' round the fire are butter boxes. **1969** F.B. VICKERS *No Man is Himself* 105 Two-bob blackfellers—that's all me and Mavis are. **1973** J. POWERS *Last of Knucklemen* (1974) 30, I don't get hustled into punch-ups with two-bob lairs like that Hun. **1975** *R.A.N. News* (Sydney) 23 May 9 It was just a Boy Scout, two-bob compass anyway—the kind you buy in a supermarket. **1978** M.J. BURTON *Bush Pub* 30 Despite her new respectability she could not resist the lure of two-bob wine. **1984** *Nat. Times* (Sydney) 23 Mar. 31/1 Curtis used to be a two-bob revolutionary, wearing a North Vietnam badge on his school uniform and clutching Martin Sharp's Oz.

2. a. In the phr. **silly** (or **mad**) **as a two-bob watch,** unpredictable; very silly.

1954 P. GLADWIN *Long Beat Home* 72 There now, I clean forgot. I'm getting silly as a two-bob watch. **1965** F. HARDY *Yarns of Billy Borker* 140 He's there on his Pat Malone, see, talking to himself, silly as a two-bob watch. **1968** S. GORE *Holy Smoke* 47 '*Strike!*' says Nebuchadnezzer, feelin' as silly as a two-bob watch. **1973** J. POWERS *Last of Knucklemen* (1974) 56 You're as mad as a two-bob watch, Tassie. **1985** N. MEDCALF *Rifleman* 112 You're as mad as a two-bob watch!

b. In the phr. **to go off like a two-bob watch:** (of a woman) to be sexually very responsive.

1971 B. HUMPHRIES *Bazza pulls it Off*, I reckon she would have dropped her harolds and gone off like a two bob watch at the first Pom to have a Captain Cook at her bloody norks! **1976** J. JOHNSON *Low Breed* 231 Good fucks these educated birds, they went off like two bob watches!

B. *n.*

1. In the phr. **two-bob-in,** a collection to which subscriber donates two shillings (see BOB-IN).

1934 T. WOOD *Cobbers* 218 Experts who began the day with 'two-bob-in'. This means that everybody put a florin into a hat and the money went to him who caught the first fish: sharks barred. (A well-established custom. On the Day of Judgement all the Australians present will have two-bob-in for the first man who gets past Peter.) **1954** T. RONAN *Vision Splendid* 117 Bridge or poker at night with 'wet' two-bob-ins after every couple of hands.

2. In the phr. **to have two-bob each way,** to arrange one's affairs so that one cannot lose, to 'hedge one's bets'; also **two-bob each way** as *adj. phr.*, uncommitted.

1967 C.W. WILLIAMS *Yellow, Green & Red* 239 Some

of the Queensland Trade-Hallers in their 'wishy-washy' 2-bob each way, attitude. **1973** M. HARRIS *Angry Eye* 186, I suspect our elegant French trading friends are having two bob each-way in the Australian sex-aid market. **1984** *Age* (Melbourne) 16 July 12/7 Mr Hawke has gone down in my estimation also, he seems to want two bob each way on this one.

two kilometre law. *N.T.* A law prohibiting the consumption of alcoholic liquor out of doors within 2 km. of licensed premises: see quot. 1985.

1982 *Weekend Austral.* (Sydney) 28 Aug. 13/5 It is known throughout the Territory as the two kilometre law, and it is due to come into force at the end of the month. **1985** *Canberra Times* 17 Dec. 11/2 The Northern Territory Government's 'two-kilometre law', established several years ago prohibits Aborigines from drinking in public places, such as the Todd River bed, because it is within two kilometres of licenced liquor outlets. **1986** *Centralian Advocate* (Alice Springs) 5 Feb. 6/6 He said it appeared that the problem *was* the 'place alcohol is consumed at, rather than the consumption of it'. It had been worsened since the 'two kilometre law' and by visitors from out bush.

two ones: see ONES.

two pot screamer: see SCREAMER.

two-rail fence. A fence having two horizontal members. Also **two-railed fence,** and *ellipt.* as **two-rail.**

1840 *Port Phillip Gaz.* 5 Sept. 6 The whole of it is fenced in with a substantial two-rail fence. **1844** *Sydney Morning Herald* 8 Apr. 1/5 Fenced in with a two-railed fence. **1848** *Maitland Mercury* 19 Aug. 2/4 On Wednesday this waterhole, which looks like a stable yard, as expressively described by a witness at the inquest, was fenced in with a substantial two-rail fence. **1882** W. SOWDEN *N.T. as it Is* 35 There is a cemetery .. enclosed by a two-railed fence. **1891** G. DUNDERDALE *Prairie & Bush* 164 We came to St. Francis Church, at that time enclosed with an old two-rail fence. **1900** H. LAWSON *Over Sliprails* 95 There was .. a thin 'two-rail' (dignified with the adjective 'split-rail'—though rails and posts were mostly of saplings split in halves) running along the frontage. **1915** *Bulletin* (Sydney) 28 Jan. 22/3 A newchum in the Never Never is quickly introduced to a two-rail fence covered with sand past the top rail.

two-up, *n.* and *attrib.*

A. *n.* A gambling game in which two coins are tossed in the air and bets laid as to whether both will fall heads or tails uppermost; SWY 2. Also **two-up game.**

1884 *Adelaide Observer* 4 Oct. 30/4 Since his arrival the Sergeant has incarcerated one bibulous visitor for mulcting a publican .. and just lately gave another individual a 'Barcoo start' in consequence of an irrepressible predilection for the game known as 'two up'. **1893** *Western Champion* (Barcaldine) 27 June 1/5 The men were amusing themselves on the 'off-day' by playing cards, &c., one group playing 'two-up'. **1903** *Sporting News* (Launceston) 25 Apr. 4/6 The spectators, who had paid their 'bob-a-head', then indulged in a game of 'two up' on the course. **1914** C.H.S. MATTHEWS *Bill* 139 'Two-up' was going on in the back yards of all the pubs.—what you call 'pitch and toss' in England, I believe. **1933** F.E. BAUME *Tragedy Track* 166 It was too wet, even, for 'two up' outside the hotel. **1948** H.I. JENSEN *Dan Green* 16 He wanted .. to go down and play 'two up' with the workmen, about 100 of whom spent hours every night on this absorbing game, on a vacant allotment beside the hotel. **1954** J. CLEARY *Climate of Courage* 152 They're just starting a two-up game down at the back of the kitchens. **1971** *Bulletin* (Sydney) 27 Mar. 41/2 Commonwealth car-drivers playing two-up in a laughing circle. **1986** *Ibid.* 28 Jan. 29/1 It was almost impossible to get within cooee of the two-up game.

B. 1. *attrib.*

1886 *Austral. Town & Country Jrnl.* (Sydney) 3 July 23/2 The other class, as described by your contributor 'A. Sullivan', as 'two-up men', should be culled as soon as discovered. **1902** *Bulletin* (Sydney) 5 Apr. 15/1 There is an allied class known as buskers, jugglers, 'forties', two-up men, tramp-journalists, tinkers, raffle promoters, and other industrials not often heard of by the city dweller. They are all typical of this country and its people. **1905** *Shearer* (Sydney) 29 Apr. 5/2 The human dissections discovered in the .. watercourse are the remains of a 'two-up' speculator named Skinner. He was known to have a bit of stuff about him when last seen, having won considerable sums in the navvies' camp. **1916** *Truth* (Sydney) 25 June 11/6 This subscription-cadging practice is a standing inducement to every loafing parasite, two-up spieler, and shypoo joint-runner to bludge on the bona-fide toiler. **1918** N.P.H. NEAL *Back to Bush* 8 The Padre believed the 'Two-up' artist who told him they were only tossing to see who should have shore leave. **1929** W.J. RESIDE *Golden Days* 145 The 'two-up academy' was the favourite resort. **1945** *Bulletin* (Sydney) 4 Apr. 12/4 English pennies are in favor in Victorian two-up circles. **1960** S. WOODFIELD *A for Artemis* 34 Fondy, in the days of struggle had run an S.P. and two-up joint with Bill. She was his cockatoo. She would let out a screech when the cops turned into her street. **1980** M. WILLIAMS *Dingo!* 13, I got a job being the cockatoo for the two-up players, watching out for coppers.

2. Special Comb. **two-up king,** a successful promoter of two-up games; **kip,** KIP; **ring,** see RING *n.*[2] 1; **school,** a group of persons who have assembled to play two-up; the place where such an assemblage is regularly held (see also SCHOOL 3).

c **1930** 'N. GHURKA' *Graft* 12 Henry Stokes, Melbourne's erstwhile **two-up king,** originally rented the premises. **1948** G. FARWELL *Down Argent Street* 4 There are ambling miners .. tight-mouthed underground foremen, young fellows slewing after girls, the two-up king on nodding terms with half the town. **1981** F. HARDY *Who shot George Kirkland?* 8 Harry Stokes, the two-up and baccarat king. **1922** *Sydney Morning Herald* 1 July 17/6 Binghi is an expert with a **two-up kip.** He seems to 'swing' only with his wrist, instead of with his whole arm, and he is able to make the coins spin faster and cleaner than most white men. **1955** N. PULLIAM *I traveled Lonely Land* 380 *Two-up kip*, a narrow strip of wood about eight inches long and wide enough to hold two pennies. Used for tossing the coins in the game of two-up. **1897** *Worker* (Sydney) 18 Dec. 3/4 The town's **'two-up' school** met and duly opened 'biz' in the backyard of 'The Traveller's Rest Hotel'. **1911** *Huon Times* (Franklin) 3 June 6/5 She conducted services at Wooloomooloo, when members of 'two-up' schools were present. **1919** O. HOGUE *Cameliers* 212 It has been said that the first thing the Australians did in the Holy Land was to start a 'Two-up School'. **1937** E. HILL *Water into Gold* 113 Even the layreader ran a two-up school. **1948** C.B. MAXWELL *Cold Nose of Law* 60 The cemetery land where .. operates a big two-up school on railway pay days. **1962** J.T. LANG *Great Bust* 180, I reminded them of their old story that it was no use paying single men high wages because they would be frittering it away on the racecourse and in two-up schools. **1973** D. FOSTER *North South West* 22, I showed her where all the two-up schools and sly grog shops were. **1982** *Bushdriver* Oct. 10 Ford! F100 4WD diesel was about as popular as a policeman at a two-up school.

Hence **two-uppian** *a.*, of or pertaining to the game of two-up.

1916 *Truth* (Sydney) 19 Mar. 1/8 *The twouppian era.* I love to look on a scene like this Of wild and careless play.

two-upper. One who plays the game of two-up.

1905 *Truth* (Sydney) 11 June 1/3 The 'two-upper' spins and reaps, yet the Holy Joes don't consider him an ideal citizen. **1908** *Ibid.* 14 June 7/6 *Two-uppers.* Coin tossers caught at Camperdown. **1955** N. PULLIAM *I traveled Lonely Land* 76 The cockie okays or rejects the credentials of the players—the two-uppers—and you've got to be vouched for 'absolutely' before you can get in.

two ups, in: see UP *n.*

tyke. Also **tike.** [Prob. alteration of *Teague* a nickname for an Irishman, perh. infl. by Br. dial. *tike* churlish fellow (see EDD *sb.*[1] 2).] A Roman Catholic. Also *attrib.*

1902 *Truth* (Sydney) 27 Apr. 8/1 The 'Tike's concerts', was the usual manner among the Wesleyan class of referring to Amy Castles' season here. **1902** *Ibid.* 20 July 6/4 He's a tyke. He's a Mick. Chuck him out. **1941** S.J. BAKER *Pop. Dict. Austral. Slang* 76 *Tike, tyke*, a Roman Catholic. **1957** D. WHITINGTON *Treasure upon Earth* 57 Too many bloody tykes in the Labor Party. **1955** *Khaki Bush & Bigotry* (1968) 120 Why can't we get married? Why can't we? .. You know why you can't. .. It's just because he's a tyke. **1970** J. CLEARY *Helga's Web* 55, I thought you hinted this morning she wasn't good enough for me. Not being a Tyke or an Australian. **1977** R. MCKIE *Crushing* (1978) 135 She was taking her .. first communion at the R.C. church. She sicked up the wafer, the host, in a flower-bed outside. Old Tom—he's a tike—saw it happen. **1983** P. WHITE *Netherwood* 21 Don't want ter listen to any of yer tyke arguments.

Hence **tykery** *n.*, a Roman Catholic school.

1963 K. COOK *Stormalong* 84 'An old boy of St. Ignatius College, Boroen'. .. 'That's a tykery, isn't it?'

tyri, var. TOWRI.

Tyson. The name of James *Tyson* (1819–1898), rural land-holder, used allusively as the type of richness, parsimony, or enterprise.

1877 L.T. HERGENHAN *Colonial City* (1972) 387 When the stranger hears that the magnificent and park-like lands through which he drives are the property of 'Scabby Moffatt', 'Hungry-man Tyson', and 'Pig-pig Carter', he is apt to understand why a witty barrister called the squattocracy of the colonies the wealthy lower orders. **1890** *Bulletin* (Sydney) 4 Oct. 11/1 'Hungry Tyson' gave $2,000 to the Sydney Royal Naval Home. **1898** *Ibid.* 17 Dec. (Red Page) 'As mean as Hungry Tyson' (used by people who know nothing of Tyson). **1909** *Ibid.* 22 Apr. 13/4 Until you have manufactures, and more people in the towns, cockying here won't make any Jimmy Tysons. **1928** A. WRIGHT *Good Recovery* 8 Th'old bloke's as rich as Tyson. **1950** *Coast to Coast 1949–50* 190 No more bunging a job in at a minute's notice and walking off with a billycan and a roll of blankets, as independent as Tyson. **1962** T. RONAN *Deep of Sky* 30 He never subscribed to the 'hungry Jimmy Tyson' legend.

U

uey /'jui/. Also **uy, youee.** [f. *U(-turn* + -Y.] A U-turn. Also *fig.*, and *attrib.*

1973 F. MOORHOUSE *Austral. Stories* 58 Before they'd done the Uey, he'd brushed his hair back, lit a Rothman's and had the window down and his arm in place. **1973** R.D. JONES *Mad Vibe* 28 You describe the quiet sunday when you caught a bus home in sunlight warmth and almost rural day but actually is [*sic*] suspect you of chucking a Uy. **1976** *Bulletin* (Sydney) 28 Feb. 27/3 Ted Heath, like Fraser, began as a professed opponent of big government but was soon 'doing a youee' (U-turn) all over the place. **1983** *Truckin' Life* VI. xi. 70 The turning circle is 15.2 m. (49.8 ft.). Not natural U-ey material but adequate for a six tonner.

ugari /'jugəri/. *Qld.* Also **eugari, yugari.** [a. Jagara *yugari.*] PIPI. Also *attrib.*

1917 *Bulletin* (Sydney) 16 Aug. 22/4 The shell-fish *Donax deltoideus*, commonly called 'ugari' in Southern Queensland, seem gifted with intellect or reasoning powers. **1941** H.D.A. JOSKE *Life to Live* 29, I did learn the art of collecting pippies, which I found later were called in Queensland by their native name of eugaries. **1968** V. SERVENTY *Southern Walkabout* 21 Along the sandy beaches of Australia lives a small shellfish. The kind found along the east coast is known to the locals by its Aboriginal name of pipi, sometimes spelled pippie. South Australians know it as the Goolwa cockle while in Queensland it is called ugari. **1980** T.A. ROY *Vengeance of Dolphin* 144 There was the inner core ready to eat with the wallaby, the baked fish, big pearl shell oysters in their shells, and yugari shell-fish.

ugly Australian. [Prob. following *ugly American*: see OEDS *ugly, a.* 4 b.] OCKER *n.* 2. Also *attrib.*

1971 *Bulletin* (Sydney) 8 May 32/1 There was an 'Ugly Australian' parallel during the Cook Bi-Centennial celebrations last year, when attention was paid to Australia's responsibilities in the Pacific. **1975** D. WHITINGTON *Witless Men* 48 He fitted the Barry Humphries version of an Ugly Australian—noisy, extrovert, anti-intellectual, devoted principally to beer drinking, horse racing, football and any other of the pastimes regarded as typically Australian. **1980** *Southerly* ii. 146 Our Ugly Australian, our professional Ocker, had boasted he'd brought forty pounds of *proper* food from Hong Kong 'ter see me through'.

Ulysses butterfly. [See quot. 1911.] The large swallowtail butterfly *Papilio ulysses joesa* of n. Qld. and elsewhere, having brilliant metallic blue, black-bordered wings. Also *ellipt.* as **Ulysses.**

1911 E.J. BANFIELD *My Tropic Isle* 106 The great high-flying Ulysses, first observed in Australia on this very island over half a century ago. It was but a passing gleam, for the visiting scientist lamented that it flew so high over the tree-tops that he failed to obtain the specimen. True to name, the Ulysses still flies high and wide—a lustrous royal blue with black trimmings and dandified tails to his wings that answer the dual purpose of use and ornament. **1951** C. BARRETT *Butterflies Aust. & New Guinea* 17 The 'great high-flying Ulysses', first observed in Australia on Dunk Island more than sixty years ago. **1982** K. MCARTHUR *Bush in Bloom* 20 The Ulysses or Mountain Blue butterfly occurs naturally only as far south as Sarina, just south of Mackay, Queensland. **1985** *Melbourne Winners Weekly* 16 Dec. 4/1 A waterfall tumbles into a little terraced valley so that visitors look down from an aerial walk for a different view of the . . glorious turquois Ulysses butterflies. The Ulysses are being sponsored by Dunk Isle resort, of which they are the emblem.

umbrella. Used *attrib.* in the names of plants having some resemblance to an open umbrella: **umbrella fern,** any of several ferns of the fam. Gleicheniaceae, esp. *Sticherus flabellatus* of e. Aust. and elsewhere; **grass,** any of several grasses (fam. Poaceae), esp. perennials of the pantropical genus *Digitaria*, and *Panicum decompositum* (see *native millet* NATIVE *a.* 6 a.); **tree,** the tree *Schefflera actinophylla* (fam. Araliaceae) of Qld. and N.T., cultivated as an ornamental and an indoor plant; a similar plant (see quot. 1970).

1898 E.E. MORRIS *Austral Eng.* 143 **Umbrella F[ern],** Tasmanian name for Fan F[ern, *Gleichenia flabellata.*] **1941** C. BARRETT *Aust.* 22 Umbrella ferns cover a mound by the creek. **1956** T.Y. HARRIS *Naturecraft in Aust.* 115 Umbrella Fern and Coral Fern are . . hardy ferns growing in moist, rocky situations as a rule. The tough wiry fronds are repeatedly forked, giving an umbrella-like appearance. **1982** N.C.W. BEADLE et al. *Flora of Sydney Region* (ed. 3) 47 In moist gullies, in eucalypt forests on hillsides or along creeks at the edges of rainforests. New Caledonia, N.Z., Australia (Q., N.S.W., Vic.). Umbrella Fern. **1883** E. PALMER *Plants N. Qld.* 10 *Panicum decompositum*. . . The **'umbrella' grass;** grows on all western country with a fine branching seed-head and broad leaves. **1897** L. LINDLEY-COWEN *W. Austral. Settler's Guide* 628 Umbrella or spider grass (*Chloris acicularis*). Grows throughout the interior of the continent. A good pasture grass, growing on sandy or light loamy soils. It seeds freely, and stock like it. **1923** E. BREAKWELL *Grasses & Fodder Plants* 73 Owing to the shape of its flowering panicle the grass is often called Umbrella grass. **1936** F. CLUNE *Roaming round Darling* 57 We watched ants climb umbrella-grass. **1975** A.B. & J.W. CRIBB *Wild Food in Aust.* 102 *Panicum decompositum* . . Native Millet, Umbrella Grass. This common grass of the interior has a branching inflorescence which breaks off at maturity and is widely distributed by wind. **1870** E.B. KENNEDY *Four Yrs. in Qld.* 141 The **umbrella-tree,** with its large dark shiny leaves, of which there are usually five growing at the end of each stalk, and surmounted by its crimson flowers, forming brilliant stars, each red spray being fifteen inches long. **1898** E.E. MORRIS *Austral Eng.* 487 Umbrella-tree. . . Name given to *Brassaia actinophylla* . . from the large leaves being set, like umbrella-ribs, at the top of numerous stems. **1934** C. MACKNESS *Young Beachcombers* 123 Under a graceful umbrella-tree at the edge of the clearing, a young man sat on a low camp-stool. **1965** *Austral. Encycl.* IX. 72 Umbrella-tree . . is a handsome glabrous tree growing to about 40 feet in height and has dark, soft but close-grained wood. **1970** W.D. FRANCIS *Austral. Rain-Forest Trees* (ed. 3) 344 *Polyscias murrayi*. . . Sometimes called Umbrella tree. **1979** WRIGLEY & FAGG *Austral. Native Plants* 372 *Schefflera actinophylla* (Syn. *Brassaia actinophylla*) . . Umbrella Tree. . . Grown commonly as a tree in Brisbane, Adelaide and warmer northern areas. Very common as indoor or tub plant in most countries.

ump: see UMPY.

umpie, var. UMPY.

umpty-doo, *a.* Also **humpty-doo.** [Prob. joc. formation on *Humpty-Dumpty.*] **a.** Intoxicated. **b.** Topsy-turvy.

1911 *Bulletin* (Sydney) 12 Oct. 14/2 Who ever hears . . of a man being 'drunk'? . . The words supplied by individual fancy, such as 'skew-whiff', 'umpty-doo', etc., who would undertake to number them? **1913** *Ibid.* 25 Sept. 22/2 Me for 'Inebriated'. . . In the number, aptness and variety of its colloquial equivalents I consider it commandeers the pastry. For instance . . full, tiddley, umpty-doo. **1936** W. HATFIELD *Aust. through Windscreen* 143 Humptydoo (presumably from the nursery rhyme of Humpty-Dumpty) connotes in Australian slang a state of everything gone wrong. **1955** F. LANE *Patrol to Kimberleys* 105 Still, there are some queer animals in Australia. Take the platypus. That's the humptydoo cove what had all the professors scratchin' their heads when they first saw him.

umpy. Chiefly *Australian National Football.* Also **umpie.** [f. *ump(ire* + -Y.] An umpire. Also **ump.**

1963 *Footy Fan* (Melbourne) I. vii. 22 That case was summarily dismissed, much to the chagrin of the boundary 'ump' who vowed he would never again report a player. **1973** *Austral.* (Sydney) 4 Aug. 18/2 Then there's our recreations Like tossing cans at umpies Or molesting Abo sheilas And burning down their humpies. **1979** *Herald* (Melbourne) 2 June 32/5 Umpy kicked: boy is outed. A teenage footballer has been suspended until the 1981 season for kicking an umpire. **1981** *Sun-Herald* (Sydney) 18 Jan. 63/2 The ball was going so far down the leg side Howarth must have thought someone had moved the stumps when he saw the umpy's finger go up.

underground mutton: see MUTTON 2.

underground orchid. Either of two completely subterranean saprophytic orchids (fam. Orchidaceae), *Rhizanthella gardneri* of s.w. W.A. and *R. slateri* of e. Aust. Also **subterranean orchid.**

1968 C.A. GARDNER *Wildflowers W.A.* 16 The subterranean orchid . . has a lily-like inflorescence with crowded, dark coloured flowers in the base of its tube. **1973** R. ERICKSON et al. *Flowers & Plants W.A.* 190 The famous Underground Orchid, *Rhizanthella gardneri*, was first described from a plant collected near decayed stems of the Broom Honeymyrtle in 1928. The white stem was 30 cm. below ground level. **1985** *Canberra Times* 12 Nov. 1/3 Australia has the only two underground orchids in the world, and there is intense interest in their evolution and biology.

underscrub: see SCRUB *n.* 2 b.

undress, *v.* [Joc. use of *undress* to divest of clothes.] *trans.* To shear (a sheep).

1927 *Bulletin* (Sydney) 20 Jan. 24/2 At Wondong station, in seven and a half hours, 2472 jumbucks were undressed. **1930** D. COTTRELL *Earth Battle* 33, I undressed fifty-one full-wooled [*sic*] wethers at Sunda's Plain last month in a two-hour run! **1984** W.W. AMMON et al. *Working Lives* 155 In it were five shearers, all full of whisky. . . They had been knocking down several cheques . . and were heading up to Byro Station . . to 'undress the woollies'.

unfinancial, *a.* Insolvent. See also FINANCIAL.

1891 *Bulletin* (Sydney) 26 Dec. 14/1 The present 'unfinancial' condition of one or two titled Southern citizens is a miserable satire upon the 'handles' they wear. **1935** N. HUNT *House of David* 129 The continuance of the 'bad' year . . had from the first been compelling the 'weak'—unfinancial—men to send their stock regardless of condition or prices to the markets to 'lighten off'.

uni /'juni/. Abbrev. of 'university'. Also *attrib.*

1898 *Bulletin* (Sydney) 17 Dec. (Red Page), The only classical idioms I have found . . are *rotter, i.e.*, an adept in learning anything; and *panem agere*, Sydney Uni. slang for 'doing a loaf'. **1906** *Truth* (Sydney) 11 Feb. 3/3 Garrulous 'grads' from Sydney's unique 'Uni'. **1915** *Ibid.* 3 Oct. 1/2 Uni. undergrad takes umbrage. **1925** *Bulletin* (Sydney) 22 Oct. 24/3 According to Professor Barker, of Leeds Uni., it may soon be possible to get two or three shearings a year. **1940** *Ibid.* 15 May 16/1 Old Baldy wasn't too shook on the pair of Uni. undergraduates who pitched their natty tent close to his own humpy on the Murray. **1960** J.E. MACDONNELL *Subsmash!* 32 At the Uni. I'm doing medicine. Final year, in fact. **1971** *Bulletin* (Sydney) 24 Apr. 47/2 You've spent three years at the uni, where you've learnt some very bad habits like getting up late, wearing wild clothes, going to the beach in the afternoon. **1984** *Austral.* (Sydney) 29 Aug. 17/1 (*heading*) Unis look to industry for more funds.

union. *Hist.* [Shortened form of *trade union.*] Used *attrib.* in Special Comb. **union camp,** STRIKE CAMP; **cut,** a shearing job for which the rate of pay is in accord with union scales; **tucker,** food provided for the inhabitants of a strike camp.

1889 *Braidwood Dispatch* 28 Aug. 2/4 Although all approaches to the station are blocked by **union camps**, work is still proceeding under the shed rules. **1911** 'ROSE BOLDREWOOD' *Complications at Collaroi* 20 There's a big union camp near Rocky Point . . and . . Warnock and I were left with a board of *seven*! **1917** R.D. BARTON *Reminisc. Austral. Pioneer* 255 They won't get to the station, the union camp is on the road, and the road is blocked. **1899** *Bulletin* (Sydney) 19 Aug. 32/2 The mates again battled out across the whitening plains in search of a '**Union cut**'. **1951** S. HICKEY *Travelled Roads* 25 Many of the dyed-in-the-yarn (union shearers) rode and led packhorse a hundred miles out and home without getting a 'union cut'. **1896** *Worker* (Sydney) 5 Sept. 3/3 Buttabone camp has broken up, and a great number of the members of it, who ate good **Union tucker,** turned dog and went into the Buttabone shed at the reduced price. **1899** *Bulletin* (Sydney) 19 Aug. 32/1 They had avoided strike-camps as far as possible; they weren't quite 'stiff', and scorned to eat Union tucker while they could buy—or steal—from the squatters.

Union Jack. [Of unknown origin.] A cicada; formerly applied to the large black and orange *Macrotristria angularis* of e. Aust., and later to the *double drummer* (see DOUBLE *a.* 2).

1895 *Proc. Linnean Soc. N.S.W.* X. 529 *Macrouistria* [*sic*] *angularis* . . ('The Union Jack'). . . This Cicada does not appear about Sydney every year, but during this last season it was comparatively numerous. **1903** *Agric. Gaz. N.S.W.* XIV. 340 This cicada has several trivial names among the Sydney boys, and though the male is well known as the 'Double Drummer' on account of the large swollen covers over the drums, it is also known as the 'Union Jack'. **1965** *Austral. Encycl.* II. 380 The double drummer (*Thopa saccata*) is a large black and orange insect remarkable for its swollen tympana; it is sometimes known as the Union Jack.

unit. [Spec. use of *unit* accommodation unit in a larger building or group of buildings: see OEDS *sb.* 2 f.] Abbrev. of *home-unit* (see HOME *n.*[2] 2).

1949 *Sydney Morning Herald* 3 May 11/4 *Flatettes*, Paddington. 5 fullfurn. units in exc. condition. Beaut home and profits. **1961** *Bulletin* (Sydney) 8 July 27/3 Another class of home unit dweller is the country family. . . The country people often use their unit for only a couple of months of the year. **1969** A. BUZO *Rooted* (1973) 60 How can Simmo possibly move in here? This is my unit. That's my stereo set. You're my wife. **1974** *Meanjin* 130 She was only being sensible. But it meant a girl in a unit must be moderate. **1977** H. TOWSON *Black & White* 101 'Could you see me very plainly?' I asked, slowing the vehicle down to a stop in front of the girl's unit. **1980** *Westerly* iii. 31 After returning to her unit, she switched the electricity off, wrote a note to me and her past lover, walked into the middle of the busy street, and was mown down immediately by a milk truck. **1982** N. KEESING *Lily on Dustbin* 78 Nowadays 'units' are popular, home units being what the Americans call 'condominiums'.

unity ticket. In a (trade-union) election: an alliance of candidates, of differing political or ideological persuasion, united for electoral advantage (see esp. quot. 1980).

1961 *Bulletin* (Sydney) 15 Feb. 11/2 In these days of frequent unity-tickets between the Communist party and A.L.P. members it is unusual to discover that any State A.L.P. branch recognises the position. **1978** F. DALY *A to Z Politics* 110 *Unity tickets*, the name applied to groups of candidates of differing political or ideological points of view uniting to win office in trade unions. **1978** B. JONES *Cup Full River* 107 The Country Party won twenty seats in both 1969 and 1972. . . In the Senate it operates on a unity ticket with the Liberals which ensures it is over-represented there too. **1980** *Dict. Austral. Politics* 276 *Unity tickets*, how-to-vote cards issued for trade union elections on which the names of *Communist Party* candidates appeared jointly with those of ALP members.

unlocated, *ppl. a. Hist.*

1. Of land: not allocated to a settler. See LOCATED.

1821 *Sydney Gaz.* 20 Jan., At the back of the Land is an extensive range of hills unlocated, capable of maintaining a numerous herd of cattle, exclusive of the run on the Farm. **1823** *Hobart Town Gaz.* 7 June, To be Sold, or exchanged for unlocated Land, an old Freehold Grant of Land. **1828** *Hobart Town Courier* 19 Apr. 1 Lands, the property of the Crown and unlocated or adjoining remote and scattered Stock Huts, are not to be deemed settled Districts. **1831** *Van Diemen's Land Corresp. Military Operations* 23 Feb. 80 He does not think the Natives could now be induced to . . occupy the unlocated parts of the island. **1838** *Colonist* (Sydney) 20 Oct. 1/1 Extensive runs for Cattle on the unlocated Government Land with which the Estate is surrounded. **1846** *Portland Gaz.* 16 Oct. 3/3 The settlers pushing down the Macintyre have joined issue with those pushing up the Barwin, and there is now no unlocated country betwixt them.

2. In the collocation **unlocated grant** (or **order**), an entitlement to the choice of a specified area of unidentified land (see LOCATE *v.* 1).

1823 *Hobart Town Gaz.* 4 Oct., To be Exchanged for an Unlocated Grant, a Farm of 700 acres. **1832** *Colonial Times* (Hobart) 17 July, Wanted to Purchase, an Unlocated Grant, from 80 to 100 acres. **1833** *Trumpeter* (Hobart) 21 May 21 For Sale by Private Contract . . an unlocated maximum Grant. **1836** *Bent's News* (Hobart) 17 Sept. 1 *Location Order for Sale.* To be sold, an Unlocated Order for 2,000 Acres—and also two other Location Orders. **1838** R. GOUGER *S.A. in 1837* 7 Orders for land were frequently issued to favoured individuals . . who not intending to use that land, did not even trouble to select it. These 'unlocated orders', as they are called, are now often sold by auction. **1840** *Tasmanian Weekly Dispatch* (Hobart) 19 June 2/1 For Sale, an unlocated order for One Thousand and Seventy Acres of Land.

unlock, *v. Hist.* In the phr. **to unlock the land,** to release for occupation by small farmers Crown land already leased as grazing land; also in the imperative, as a political slogan. See also LOCK.

1855 *Ovens & Murray Advertiser* (Beechworth) 3 Mar. (Suppl.) 5/3 *Unlock the lands*—It is gratifying to find that the Government has at length seen the necessity for throwing open the lands in the vicinity of the gold fields for farming and agricultural purposes. . . The Government surveyor, is now employed in laying out farms in the neighbourhood of the Three-mile Creek, which . . will vary in extent from 10 to 50 acres. **1859** W. KELLY *Life in Vic.* I. 143 The abolition of squatterdom and unlocking the lands was not regarded as cause and effect. **1861** C. CAMPBELL *Squatting Question Considered* 11 The cry of unlock the lands was raised by the press to humour a restless people. **1886** 'THIRTY-FIVE YRS. COLONIST' *Hard Times* 5 For upwards of thirty years past, there has always been an outcry to unlock the land.

unmade, *ppl. a.* In the collocation **unmade road,** a vehicular way which has been cleared of vegetation but not formed. See MADE 1.

1857 W. WESTGARTH *Vic. & Austral. Gold Mines* 197 We had now the unmade or bush road to put up with. **1902** *Bulletin* (Sydney) 8 Nov. 36/1 The hedge of 'prickly-bush' . . sprawled half way across the unmade road. **1920** *Smith's Weekly* (Sydney) 13 Nov. 17/5, I lived for years on an unmade road, where bullockies passed each day.

unoccupied, *ppl. a.* Of land: not taken up by a settler or settlers.

1803 S. MACARTHUR ONSLOW *Some Early Rec. Macarthurs* (1914) 71 Permission to occupy a sufficient Track of unoccupied Lands to feed his flocks. **1862** C. MUNRO *Fern Vale* I. 4 You say the country is quite unoccupied: will not the natives be dreadfully wild. **1924** LAWRENCE & SKINNER *Boy in Bush* 366 Right away from Perth. Into the unoccupied country. Into the North-West.

unsettled, *ppl. a. Hist.*

a. Orig. used to designate Crown land which was inalienable; (loosely) unpopulated, or very sparsely populated, other than by Aborigines. See SETTLED 1.

1842 *Penny Mag.* (London) Jan. 2/1 Agricultural and pastoral pursuits are carried on in the 'bush', that is in the unsettled parts of the district. **1847** *HRA* (1925) 1st Ser. XXVI. 36 Relieving me from the invidious duty of defining Lands to be classified as 'unsettled'. **1853** S. SIDNEY *Three Colonies* (ed. 2) 188 The governor shall divide the lands of the colony into three districts, to be called the 'settled', 'intermediate', and 'unsettled'. . . In the unsettled lands, every holder of a licence is entitled to *demand* a lease for fourteen years. In the intermediate districts the lease is to be for eight years only, and the land is liable to be sold at the end of every year. **1859** W. FAIRFAX *Handbk. to Australasia* 115 About one-third of the island is little known, being designated 'Unsettled'. **1879** *Kelly Gang* 14 He chose this locality in preference to . . more unsettled parts . . because it supplied the necessity of propinquity to a public school. **1901** *Advocate* (Burnie) 4 Feb. 2/5 Extinguish any fires they may make to boil the 'billy' even in unsettled localities. **1961** M. KIDDLE *Men of Yesterday* 63 It was impossible to prevent scabbed sheep being moved through unsettled country.

b. *spec.* In collocations: **unsettled district, land.**

1844 *Colonial Times* (Hobart) 23 Jan., In the **unsettled districts,** free persons attached to the Convict Establishments . . are to be supplied by the Contractors with Rations. **1847** *Port Phillip Herald* 8 Apr. (Suppl.), The division of Crown lands into 'unsettled, intermediate, and settled districts', is not sufficiently defined. **1861** C. CAMPBELL *Squatting Question Considered* 8 The rush of population was chiefly to the unsettled district. **1869** *Bushmen, Publicans, & Politics* 3 The experience of many years in what, till lately, were the unsettled districts. **1880** J. BONWICK *Resources Qld.* 13 Queensland is divided into *Settled* and *Unsettled* Districts. **1891** J. FENTON *Bush Life Tas.* (1964) 18 No one dared venture out into the unsettled districts. **1845** *Atlas* (Sydney) I. 241/1 'All went merry as a marriage bell' whilst, in the natural order of things, convict labour was employed in preparing hitherto **unsettled lands** for settlement and sale. **1848** W. WESTGARTH *Aust. Felix* 233 *The division of all the crown lands into three classes*, namely, the settled, intermediate, and unsettled. The settled lands comprehend the nineteen old counties of the colony. . . The intermediate lands comprehend all the remainder of the counties not already included in the settled territory. . . The unsettled lands comprise the rest of the territory. **1851** J.H. BURTON *Emigrant's Man.* ii. 20 With regard to unsettled lands, the governor is empowered to grant leases of runs. **1909** H. BUTTON *Flotsam & Jetsam* 212 As my memory now serves me, this 'unsettled' land was open for sale.

unshingle, *v. Obs.* [f. *shingle* house-tile.] *trans.* To knock a hat from a person. Usu. as *ppl. a.* and *vbl. n.*

1827 *Hobart Town Courier* 10 Nov. 3/2 A man is said to be well shingled when he has a new English hat upon his head, worth 50s. and when the person that remarks it runs up behind him in the evening and carries off his hat, the bareheaded gentleman is said to be *unshingled.* **1836** *Hobart Town Almanack* 98 It was a very common practice to run up behind a well dressed person and whipping off his hat, to run away with it. This was called 'unshingling', or taking off a man's roof. **1857** D. BUNCE *Australasiatic Reminisc.* 58 The system of *unshingling*, or taking a hat from the traveller's head in the darkness of night, during his wanderings through the streets, did not fall to our lot to experience.

up, *n.* In the phr. **in two ups,** 'in two shakes', in a trice.

1934 T. WOOD *Cobbers* 25 He said we'd be there in two ups. **1941** S.J. BAKER *Pop. Dict. Austral. Slang* 79 *Two ups, in*, in a brief space of time. **1954** T. RONAN *Vision Splendid* 90 The trouble is . . that I'm only a swamper in the camp. Otherwise I'd have that son of a bitch off his horse in two ups. **1956** A. MARSHALL *How's Andy Going?* 159 This fire behind Barret's is only a scrub fire, but a north wind would whip it into a crown fire in two ups and where would we be then? **1968** S. GORE *Holy Smoke* 52 They go to the pack straight orf. And in about two ups they're all slingin' their stuff overboard and callin' on their gods 'n' that.

up, *adv.*

a. In the phr. **up the country,** away from a centre of population; into the interior of the country. Also as quasi-*n.*

1805 J. GRANT Let. 28 Apr., Capⁿ Bishop . . resided upon Prospect-Hill 20 miles up the Country. **1825** *London* Mag. May II. 52 It is seldom that any thieves is sent up the country, as most of the gentlemen resides in Sydney, and would sooner take for his servant a man that he knows has been a regular thief at home, than one of those barn dore gentlemen. **1832** *Sydney Herald* 6 Feb. 4/1 Mr Windeyer, the Assistant Police Magistrate, has proceeded up the country . . to recruit his health. **1841** G. GREY *Jrnls. Two Exped. N.-W. & W.A.* I. 159, I shouldn't think nothing at all of having shot that there black fellow; why, Sir, they're very thick and plentiful up the country. **1845** E.J. EYRE *Jrnls. Exped. Central Aust.* I. 17 The whole party (except the overseer who was at a station up the country) proceeded to Government House. **1855** W. CAMPBELL *Crown Lands Aust.* 58 It is better for the employer to give a higher rate to men upon the ground, than to be at the expense and risk of carrying new arrivals up the country. **1869** J. MARTINEAU *Lett. from Aust.* 37 It is a pleasant life to have a station up the country (but not too far up). **1880** J. BONWICK *Resources Qld.* 56 Abundance of good ground . . is known further up the country. **1896** H. LAWSON *In Days when World was Wide* 156 You'll admit that Up-the-Country, more especially in drought, Isn't quite the Eldorado that the poets rave about. **1919** T.G. RABBETS *Whimplin Whimsies* 43 The man from up the country has arrived in Brisbane town, To see his annual picture show and laugh at the circus clown. **1965** G.H. FEARNSIDE *Golden Ram* 172 So roll up your bundle and let us make a push, I'll take you up the country and show you the Bush. **1971** A. BUZO *Macquarie* (1973) 41, I hear Macquarie's up the country granting land to the Aborigines.

b. Also as **up (in, to) (the) bush** (or **mulga**).

1840 A. RUSSELL *Tour through Austral. Colonies* 86 When up in the bush, we met several females employed in chopping wood with axes. **1857** 'RETURNED DIGGER' *Six Yrs. in Aust.* 21 Even carters, up the bush, get £2 a week. **1862** A. POLEHAMPTON *Kangaroo Land* 213, I . . engaged myself as a sheep-washer up the Bush. **1867** 'CLERGYMAN' *Aust. as it Is* 272 The merchants of Sydney know well that bad goods, bad everything, are sent up to the bush. **1876** 'RESIDENT' *Girl Life in Aust.* 137 Grandpapa had a station up bush. **1957** J. NAIRN *Out of Back Streets* 188 Charlie was feeling as though he belonged to Australia after he had been 'up the bush' on three different occasions. **1968** S. GORE *Holy Smoke* 58 'Man ought to get his head seen to,' he said moodily. 'Stuck up here in the mulga, when he could be earning good money down in the city.'

c. Ellipt. for *up the country.*

1852 J. BONWICK *Notes of Gold Digger* 4 Tools are dearer up than in town. **1904** L. HOPKINS *On the Hop* p. xxii, *Old colonist* (to a new chum who is up for colonial experience). You see that shed yonder? Well, that's where we keep the rock-salt for the cattle to lick. **1965** G. MCINNES *Road to Gundagai* 248 Though he might speak *de haut en bas* to a young fellow 'up from town' or to one of his social equals whom he happened to dislike, he was on terms of free and easy yet dignified familiarity with the stockmen and the boundary riders and even with the itinerant shearers.

d. *transf.* With reference to specific locations.

1884 *Austral. Tit-Bits* (Melbourne) 26 June 13/3 Decency is at a discount with certain folks up Shields way. **1941** *Ack Ack: Jrnl. 2nd Anti Aircraft Regiment* 1 May 7 Thoughts going ever to those cobbers 'up the desert'. **1956** R. THROSSELL *Day before Tomorrow* (1969) 79 Will you come outside with me? Up the back. You know you said you would. **1962** E. LANE *Mad as Rabbits* 49 No longer, when sent up the paddock to cut shoots, did they cut just enough to build a mia-mia and then spend the rest of the day lying in its shade. **1971** D. WILLIAMSON *Don's Party* (1973) 27 She's got a job in Queensland. . . That Uni up Townsville. **1980** M. WILLIAMS *Dingo!* 45 Dad sat up the back yard talking to himself.

e. *spec.* In the phr. **up east,** along the coast of W.A., north and east of Broome.

1913 *Cwlth. Parl. Papers* III. 739 Yes, from Broome is . . 80 miles to the 90-mile beach. We used to go up east for eight or nine months at a time. **1933** J.M. HARCOURT *Pearlers* 38 Waller had come to Broome from Aru, bringing a fleet of nine ketches through the wild and treacherous waters of 'up East', as the badly charted coast from Derby to Wyndham was known to the pearlers of Broome. **1940** E. HILL *Great Austral. Loneliness* (ed. 2) 242 You hire an old lugger at Broome for £1 a month . . and set out for where you fancy 'up east'.

up-country, *a., adv.,* and *n.* [Used elsewhere (though rarely in Brit.) but of local significance: see OED(S.]

A. 1. *adj.* Situated in, belonging or relating to, etc., country which is inland and away from a major centre of population.

1816 [see *up-country settler*, sense 2 below]. **1826** *Austral.* (Sydney) 5 Jan. 2/4 Many Up-country people are in want of assigned servants. **1839** *Sydney Herald* 27 Sept. 2/1 It is the up-country landholders and stockholders who chiefly make up the revenue of the colony. **1851** *Empire* (Sydney) 9 July 4/1 We fancy that the up-country waters have not yet come down. **1862** H. BROWN *Vic. as I found It* 65 If Melbourne was not pleasant to me, up-country life would be worse. **1872** G.S. BADEN-POWELL *New Homes for Old Country* 120 Preconceived ideas of Australia are strangely upset by the numbers of people to be met with on the up-country roads. **1886** P. CLARKE *'New Chum' in Aust.* 235 The thin-blooded up-country man may wish that he could turn himself inside out to give his interior a chance of being equally cooked with his exterior. **1903** *Advocate* (Burnie) 1 Dec. 3/5 Wanted to sell. Roller Flour made from up-country wheat. **1916** E. & M.S. GREW *Rambles in Aust.* 31 Yet it is 'up-country' men that Australia wants, to clear, saw, and till her rich, fertile soil. **1930** K.S. PRICHARD *Haxby's Circus* 83 Lord Freddie . . was working as yard-man in an up-country hotel. **1955** STEWART & KEESING *Austral. Bush Ballads* 266 It was on a Sunday morning, the church was far away, They used to keep the Sabbath in their own up-country way. **1970** K.E.C. GRAVES *Third Chance* 7 There must be lorries operating to take the stock to the up-country sales. **1980** A.S. VEITCH *Run from Morning* 22 I'd hate to count the number of times I've had to sit behind an Austral Felix semi-trailer on an up country road!

2. In collocations: **up-country mail, settler, station, town, township.**

1855 *Bell's Life in Sydney* 12 May 3/2 The whole of the **up-country mails.** **1869** MRS W.M. HOWELL *Diggings & Bush* 252 We shall laugh heartily as we talk about the up-country Australian mail. **1876** *Willmett & Co.'s Cooktown Almanac* 26 The Bark Store, Upper Cape . . this being the receiving and dispatching office for all the up-country mails; and is the *rendezvous* for all up-country mailmen who meet there on mail days. **1816** *Hobart Town Gaz.* 7 Sept., The Black Natives of this Colony have for the last few weeks manifested a stronger Hostility towards the **Up-Country Settlers.** **1829** *Sydney Monitor* 3 Jan. 1450/1 Mr Richard Naylor begs to announce to his friends in Sydney, and the Up-country settlers, that he has opened the 'Bee Hive Inn'. **1842** *Sydney Morning Herald* 4 Aug. 1/3 It has been matter of regret amongst up-country settlers, that trusses could not hitherto be obtained for their establishments. **1872** MRS E. MILLETT *Austral. Parsonage* 245 The system . . universally prevailed in the colony, of paying wages by truck, every up-country settler keeping a shop or store for his labourers. **1845** C.J. BAKER *Sydney & Melbourne* 31 Change of air and scene may be obtained by visiting the **up-country station** of some friend. **1865** J.F. MORTLOCK *Experiences of Convict* 82 Mr Beaumont Smith . . had been promoted at an up-country station, from the scavengers' gang to be goat-minder. **1898** A.P. MARTIN *Beginnings Austral. Lit.* 20 As he had spent a couple of years on an 'up-country' station, he should write another novel dealing with what I have called the 'Pastoral Epoch'—the period of the pioneer squatters. **1902** *Sporting News* (Launceston) 13 Dec. 3/5 This horse, after doing stud duty on an up-country station. **1896** N. GOULD *Town & Bush* 224 The amateur bookmaker resides in the **up-country town** near which the picnic races take place. **1907** C. MACALISTER *Old Pioneering Days* 146 One morning, in an up-country town, I witnessed a fierce brawl between an aggressive bagman and a tipsy shearer. . . The 'drummer' got the worst of the fistic argument. **1871** *Austral. Town & Country Jrnl.* (Sydney) 1 Apr. 390/2 The various **up-country townships** in Victoria signalized the day fixed for the marriage of the Princess Louise . . by liberal displays of bunting. **1886** P. CLARKE *'New Chum' in Aust.* 156 A stranger in an up-country township soon exhausts the pleasures(!) of a place never intended for aught but the utilitarian purpose of money-making and spending.

B. *adv.* In or to country which is inland and away from a major centre of population.

1854 MRS C. CLACY *Lights & Shadows* I. 39 It was some one going up country and lost their track. **1861** 'OLD BUSHMAN' *Bush Wanderings* 36 Congregated over a dead carcass on the plains up country. **1871** *Austral. Town & Country Jrnl.* (Sydney) 25 Feb. 241/1 He left the swamp and again made his way up-country, and was at last arrested near Goulburn. **1882** J. SCHLEMAN *Life in Melbourne* 16 The cry for workmen up country was as earnest when I left as when I landed. **1897** E. SOLDENE *My Theatre & Mus. Recoll.* 210 It seemed terrible when people one knew said they had been 'up country' in the 'back blocks', in 'the bush' for six months at a time. **1914** C.H.S. MATTHEWS *Bill* 23 He was crossing the Blue Mountains, going up-country. **1926** A.A.B. APSLEY *Amateur Settlers* 38 You won't want to spend much money up-country. **1940** J.A. BROOK *Jim of Seven Seas* 67 The altitude at Canberra was the highest I had experienced. . . We had, as at all times when working up-country, to provide our bed and bedding. **1951** G. FARWELL *Outside Track* 23 After that encounter with . . the 'big smoke' . . he went back up country. **1971** G. WISEWOULD *Outpost* 163 There is fire somewhere and one looks to find its location, five miles, twenty miles or a hundred miles 'up country'. **1984** W.W. AMMON et al. *Working Lives* 155, I told him that I wanted to break up-country to try my luck on one of the sheep stations.

C. *n.* Country which is inland and away from a major centre of population.

1872 G.S. BADEN-POWELL *New Homes for Old Country* 374 The rivers of the up-country . . are mere long chains of water-holes. **1916** E. & M.S. GREW *Rambles in Aust.* 27 She came from up-country, and was able to tell us that two handsome large grey and black birds with a singularly limpid note were 'rain birds'. **1929** C.H. WINTER *Story of 'Bidgee Queen* 18 As the light of dawning breaks On the western plains and rivers, and the great 'up-country' smiles. **1934** T. WOOD *Cobbers* 90 Hereabouts a man can truthfully say that he is going down to the up country. In the South West 'up' is the commonest syllable on the map. . . The native word for a water-place. **1948** G. FARWELL *Down Argent Street* 3 Some . . have come straight from up-country, the names of pastoral companies lettered on doors. **1978** G. HALL *River still Flows* 16 We come from up country, we come from out back, The homestead, the hut and the wallaby-track, We come from the land where the riders are made, And we're all of us mates in the Bushman's Brigade.

uphill, *a.* [Transf. use of *uphill* presenting difficulties.] Hard-pressed.

1945 T. RONAN *Strangers on Ophir* 184 Peter'll be a bit uphill getting Luke out of the cooler, won't he? **1954** T.A.G. HUNGERFORD *Sowers of Wind* 141 He'll certainly be uphill now, trying to stack Lefevre for leave. **1978** *Sun-Herald* (Sydney) 15 Jan. 44/3 The Opposition . . will be uphill in persuading the voters to reject this opportunity to have the Council democratically elected.

up-jump. [f. *jumped-up* newly risen in status, arrogant.] An upstart; also as a general term of abuse. Also *attrib.*

1919 W.H. DOWNING *Digger Dialects* 51 *Upjump*, upstart; interloper. **1967** *Kings Cross Whisper* (Sydney) xliii. 11/2 *Upjump*, an upstart, a tear-away, general nuisance. **1968** D. O'GRADY *Bottle of Sandwiches* 89 Bloody rotten up-jump never-come-down . . rotten mongrel bloody stinkin' flamin' mongrel bloody bastard.

Hence **up-jumped** *a.*, upstart; disagreeable.

1938 X. HERBERT *Capricornia* (1939) 285 He told Frank that . . he was considered too superior to associate with an up-jumped yeller-feller. **1968** D. O'GRADY *Bottle of Sandwiches* 60 That damn up-jumped storm had followed the coast all the way down, and we were right behind it. *Ibid.* 89 'Bloody useless up-jumped offspring of a mongrel whore,' he said.

upter, *a.* Also **upta,** and formerly **up to.** [Abbrev. of *up to putty* (see PUTTY).] Bad; hopeless; no good.

1918 C.L. HARTT *Diggerettes* 19 With four hours to go and a booze-inflated headpiece, the outlook was 'up to'. **1919** W.H. DOWNING *Digger Dialects* 52 *Upter*, a corruption of 'Up to Putty'. **1919** C.H. THORP *Handful of Ausseys* 110 'How're things?' 'Up to—no blanky bon, diggers.' **1947** J. CLEARY *You can't see round Corners* 167 'How you going?' 'Upta. I've lost on every race so far.'

1952 E. LAMBERT *Twenty Thousand Thieves* (ed. 2) 130 Go Through slapped Happy's shoulder. 'How are yer, Hap, old feller?' 'Up ter,' replied Happy. **1953** 'CADDIE' *Caddie* 219 Dadda made some derogatory remark about the tucker. 'If it's upter why don't you 'ave a go?' **1970** R. BEILBY *No Medals for Aphrodite* 174 'How's the feet, Private Wilkinson?' 'Upta, sir. Can't get me boots on this mornin'.'

upya. Alteration of 'up you!', an exclamation of contemptuous rejection.

1941 S.J. BAKER *Pop. Dict. Austral. Slang* 79 *Upya!*, a contemptuous ejaculation. **1955** D. NILAND *Shiralee* 101 No, he said, I won't truckle to you. Upya for the rent.

urger.

1. One who gives (unsolicited) tips at a race meeting; a tipster: see quot. 1958.

1919 V. MARSHALL *World of Living Dead* 69 The truly light-fingered gentry, the racecourse urger (tipslinger), the magsman .. never hesitate to express their contempt for the more roughly inclined of the profession. **1932** C. HADE *Ebenezer* 8 There's Watto, an 'intellectual' in his day, A racecourse urger's part always prepared to play. **1946** R.D. RIVETT *Behind Bamboo* 164 Professional 'urgers' and hangers-on in the best traditions of the racetracks. **1958** F. HARDY *Four-Legged Lottery* 175 That's old 'Don't tell a soul', the urger. He gives you a tip and then persuades you to put a few quid on it for him. Gives a different horse to every victim. **1969** W. MOXHAM *Apprentice* 8 Scooter, who was a tipper—a word he like better than urger, tout, any of that lot—preferred Royal Randwick to the other city racetracks. **1981** *Sunday Mail* (Brisbane) 25 Oct. 11/7 Last week urgers were a problem at Eagle Farm.

2. *transf.* One who takes advantage of others; a petty racketeer.

1943 *Troppo Tribune* (Mataranka) 25 July 2 Who is the bloke from No. 1 earning the reputation of being an urger? **1953** T.A.G. HUNGERFORD *Riverslake* 3 Urgers, touts .. and straight-out crooks. You know. **1960** *Tobruk to Borneo* (Perth) Sept. 14 It was a haven for non-workers .. work-shy and urgers of all types. **1965** K. SMITH *OGF* 77 Two tough-looking urgers in silk shirts were moving among the crowd called the winning numbers in a raffle for a pair of dressed ducks. **1976** S. WELLER *Bastards I have Met* 76 One show time a bloke had a sort of 'Test your breath' turnout where, for a deener, you could blow and see what you could register on the dial. If you went past a certain number you won a box of chocolates. The bloke looking after it was a real good urger and he's got a wing of young blokes around him giving them the spiel. **1983** STURGESS & BIRNBAUER *Journalist who Laughed* 79 Clancy was a free enterprise man. He thought all unionists were urgers.

uro, var. EURO.

useful. A general factotum, esp. in a public house. Formerly also **general useful, generally useful.**

[**1866** R. HENNING *Let.* 16 May (1966) 218 There are three men employed about the place [*sc.* a logging business]. The bullock-driver, the punt-man and a 'generally useful' man.] **1891** *Bulletin* (Sydney) 4 Apr. 15/1 A 'billiard-marker and generally useful', engaged by a Macalister River .. hotel-keeper .. arose early on the morning after his arrival and proceeded to energetically scrub-brush the billiard-table with hot soap-and-water. **1907** W.R.O. HILL *Forty-Five Yrs. Experience N. Qld.* 30, I had a young fellow named Jack Hoare working for me as a 'general useful'. **1911** *Bulletin* (Sydney) 31 Aug. 13/1, I am the Rouseabout! The Generally Useful A mere social microbe. **1933** R.D. TATE *Doughman* 88 It was an old-fashioned building with one private and one public bar, together with a dubious room into which helpless patrons, both male and female were unceremoniously bundled, and their pockets scrupulously 'skinned' by a pockmarked 'useful'. **1940** *Sydney Morning Herald* 6 Jan. 28/8 *Situations wanted*... Gardener-useful, lawns, hedges, handy tools, repairs. **1953** *Sun* (Sydney) 27 July 1 At six o'clock the useful would take off his apron, jump the counter and go along closing and bolting the doors. **1960** J. WYNNUM *Sailor Blushed* (1962) 13 A 'useful' clattered round their stools with his broom, whilst a barmaid busily slapped a damp cloth around and under their glasses. **1972** *Kings Cross Whisper* (Sydney) cxxxviii. 2/3 Bertram Baits .. for some times was engaged as useful at the pub.

ute /jut/. Also **ut.** Abbrev. of UTILITY.

1943 *Troppo Tribune* (Mataranka) 8 Feb. 4 Drives round in his ute Now isn't that cute? **1944** S. KELLEN *Camp Happy* 11, I drove the 'ut' among narrow, dangerous curves. **1946** *Austral. New Writing* 37 The Lieutenant's Utility Truck or the 'Lute's Ute', as it is more often called. **1955** *Bulletin* (Sydney) 2 Feb. 13/1 Charley, caught well out in the blacksoil country in his utility .. glanced over his shoulder—the back of the ute was loaded with hailstones! **1964** P. WHITE *Burnt Ones* 289 The back of the ute was at least private, though it wasn't no Customline. **1976** *Bulletin* (Sydney) 3 July 58/2 In Canberra at least the traditional unit of volume is the 'ute load', since the utility, or a similarly sized trailer, is the main form of transport for firewood. My estimate is that at least the larger 'ute load' is a cubic yard, and, heaped right up so that some risks being lost on bumps in the road, it represents a good round metre measure, the cubic metre. **1985** *Overlander* Aug. 38 It's as much a part 20th century Australian rural history as tractors, headers and wire strainers... It's the ute.

utility. A small truck, having a cab and a tray used for carrying light loads: see quot. 1985. Also **utility truck,** and *attrib.*

1935 K.L. SMITH *Sky Pilot Arnhem Land* 96 In 1931 an old T-model Ford was converted into a utility truck and pressed into service. **1938** A. UPFIELD *Bone is Pointed* (1966) 259 Gordon hurried back to the now unloaded utility and, with the blacks beside him on the running-boards, he drove to the tall leafy tree. **1950** G.M. FARWELL *Land of Mirage* 107 They had a little green utility, and got within two miles of us. **1960** *N.T. News* (Darwin) 22 Jan. 3/4 Nancy tried to make passionate love to him in the police utility after he arrested her. **1972** *Southerly* i. 3 Trucks, Landrovers, utilities and new cars already scratched and dinted were drawn up beside the verandah. **1979** W.K. BECKINGHAM *Red Acres* 49 My first vehicle was a Cleveland utility. **1985** *Overlander* Aug. 38 Australia developed the ute. For lore has it that in 1933/34 it produced the world's first utility—a 'coupé utility'—in response to a farmer's wife bewailing the fact that no-one produced a vehicle suitable for work during the week that would double to go to church on Sunday.

uy, var. UEY.

V

vag, *n.* and *a.* [U.S., abbrev. of *vagrant* or *vagrancy*: see OEDS.]

A. *n.*

1. A vagrant.

1888 J. FREEMAN *Lights & Shadows Melbourne Life* 100 A few 'vags' of all ages and both sexes, who have just left the holes and corners where they have passed the night, prowl about the carts and stalls. **1905** W. MOORE *City Sketches* 48 The poor help the poor, and the vag. helps the vag. **1916** *Truth* (Sydney) 17 Dec. 1/6 A vag at the Scentral the other day claimed to be that weak that he couldn't lift his voice. **1942** *Bulletin* (Sydney) 1 July 13/4 It was near to closing time when the town's chief vag. entered my favourite pinky shop with a quart wine bottle that he had salvaged somewhere around the parks. **1979** M. RUTHERFORD *Departmental* 69 The vag waited but the policeman just walked past him to a car.

2. a. Vagrancy, esp. in the phr. **on** (or **under**) **the vag,** on a charge of vagrancy. Also *attrib.*

1877 *Vagabond Ann.* 58 Many young larrikins are brought up 'on the vag'. **1891** *Truth* (Sydney) 10 May 3/3 The young victim of a constable's malevolence was charged 'under the vag.', with having no visible lawful means of support. **1903** *Ibid.* 18 Jan. 1/7 For sitting on the street at Newtown on Sunday last, and telling a constable she had 'nowhere to go', an old woman was sent up for a month under the vag. **1919** V. MARSHALL *World of Living Dead* 12 Three charges agin' me—righteous, vag, an' resisting. **1937** WISBERG & WATERS *Bushman at Large* 87 You'll be up before the beak for an on-the-vag charge. **1951** CUSACK & JAMES *Come in Spinner* 261 She'd heard about lots of girls being picked up under the Vag., some of them the wrong girls too, like Monnie. **1965** *Coast to Coast 1963–64* 116 Harriet's doing six months on a vag rap. **1978** K. GILBERT *People are Legends* 21 Each other week I'm in 'pokey'—pigs charge me with drunk Or on vag. No place of abode I sleep by the road.

b. A charge of vagrancy; imprisonment as the result of such a charge.

1896 *Bulletin* (Sydney) 11 Apr. 17/4 A layer and a backer were run in at a Perth (W.A.) rural meeting, though everybody else was betting all day... Under W.A.'s precious law if they again offend they are liable to 12 months 'vag'. **1936** *Red Star* (Perth) 7 Feb. 1/1 Destitute men camping round Kalgoorlie are hunted away on threat of the 'vag'.

B. *adj.* Vagrant.

1963 *N.T. News* (Darwin) 3 Jan. 10/5 They asked me if I was working and I said no .. then the copper said 'you're vag' and they arrested me.

vag, *v.* [U.S.; f. prec.] *trans.* To arrest (a person) for vagrancy. Freq. in *pass.*

1903 *Truth* (Sydney) 22 Feb. 3/2 (*heading*) Two University Park sirens vagged, and sent to Bileola. **1913** J.B. CASTIEAU *Reminisc. Detective-Inspector Christie* 35 If you do not clear out of this at once I'll 'vag' you, as I know you are a magsman. **1922** D. COLLINS *Stolen or Strayed* 49 The offence alleged against Tim Hanson on the charge-sheet was that he had 'no visible means of support', otherwise he was 'vagged'. **1933** H.B. RAINE *Lash End* 50 The harlots who hang about with the Chinese always go back, for the Chinks pay their fines. The police vag. these girls sometimes, but what can they do? The Chinamen swear they are keeping them, the girls prove they have 'lawful' means of support, and are freed. **1950** K.S. PRICHARD *Winged Seeds* 221 The johns'll vag a single bloke and run him out of town if he's caught askin' for tucker. **1965** R.H. CONQUEST *Horses in Kitchen* 70 She never stayed anywhere long, and although she was vagged a few times, the authorities after cleaning her up a bit and sticking some proper tucker into her, always sent her on her way. **1984** P. READ *Down there with me on Cowra Mission* 57, I walked into town .. and I got vagged... Got ten days out of it.

values, *pl. Mining.* [Also U.S.] Payable quantities of a mineral. In the phr. **to make values,** to yield such quantities. See also MAKE *v.*[1] b.

1911 E.D. CLELAND *W. Austral. Mining Practice* 14 Occasionally values are found along the fault-lines .. but as a general rule, values are not found in appreciable quantity along the fault-lines. **1939** I.L. IDRIESS *Cyaniding for Gold* 184 You may locate such an outcrop. Sink on it, for gossan often 'makes' values at shallow depth. **1944** M.J. O'REILLY *Bowyangs & Boomerangs* 40 The method is to knap off part of the reef, powder it in a 'Dolly pot', and wash in a gold dish, where values, if any, will show up. **1948** K.S. PRICHARD *Golden Miles* 93 'I'll get a couple of 'toms' for her, Ted,' Abel exclaimed affably. 'Now y're showin' values she's worth shorin' up.' 'Get em, right away, or I'll be snatchin' me time,' Ted replied. 'Values, or no values, this place is a death trap without a bit of timberin'.'

Vandemonia. *Hist.* [f. *Van Diem(en's Land*, the name given to Tasmania by its discoverer Abel Tasman in 1642, in honour of Anthony *Van Diemen* (1593–1645), governor of the Dutch East Indies + *demon* + *-ia.*] A name for Tasmania, esp. as a penal colony.

1838 *Cornwall Chron.* (Launceston) 15 Sept. 1 Was Vandemonia formed but to propagate the convict's foul breath? **1892** *Bulletin* (Sydney) 2 Apr. 9/4 He was .. transported to Van Demonia for forgery. **1903** *Truth* (Sydney) 1 Mar. 1/6 One-sided summings up .. may please the social vampires and political pirates of Vandemonia. **1905** *Ibid.* 7 May 1/4 'Colonel' Davis, from Vandemonia .. has more intimate and precise notions about convictism than he has about Federalism.

Vandemonian, *n.* and *a. Hist.* Also **Vandiemenian, Vandiemonian.** [f. prec.]

A. *n.*

a. A non-Aboriginal person native to or resident in Tasmania. Formerly also **Vandiemener.**

1828 *Hobart Town Courier* 12 July 2 You have frequently expressed yourself interested much in us Van Diemeners. **1832** *Sydney Herald* 9 Apr. 2/3 We perceive that the Vandiemonians are not less in raptures than the Sydneyites. **1839** *Port Phillip Patriot* 24 Apr. 4 Would not a standing committee be useful in our rising Capital? Could we not meet in such a committee, not as Vandemonians, or Sydneyites, but as Australia Felixians? **1849** J.P. TOWNSEND *Rambles & Observations N.S.W.* 119 Of the natives of Tasmania few remain. All that the 'Van-Demonians' could catch were sent to Flinder's Island, in Bass' Straits. **1873** A. TROLLOPE *Aust. & N.Z.* II. 3 The Van Diemonians—as colonists from other colonies are wont to call them in jeering mirth—had a spirit of their own. **1889** *Bulletin* (Sydney) 21 Sept. 7/3 A vandalistic Vandemonian writes .. irreverently respecting tragedian Miln's recent boom in the Tight Little Island. **1910** *Huon Times* (Franklin) 12 Nov. 6/4 Some remarks unfavourable to the Vandemonians on the diggings, brought another old Tasmanian, a Mr Denny, to his feet. **1961** M. KIDDLE *Men of Yesterday* 45 For good and ill the Vandiemonians had founded the new colony. **1973** J. MURRAY *Larrikins* 56 In Melbourne, 'Vandemonians' seem to have found it a way to the heart of the mainland.

b. A convict who has served a sentence in Tasmania.

1847 *Port Phillip Herald* 12 Jan. 2/5 The Van Diemonians are, it appears, resolved to go to work at last, as no less than two gross robberies, accompanied by violence, were committed in the town of Melbourne on the night of Friday last. **1858** N.L. KENTISH *Treatise Penal Discipline* 44 All criminals are not Van Diemonians or Sydney convicts. **1865** 'SPECIAL CORRESPONDENT' *Transportation* 55 The free colonies plead that the Vandemonians by whom they have been outraged came, not as escaped convicts, but as men free in one form or another, by pardon or servitude. **1880** *Argus* (Melbourne) 27 Jan. 7/2, I deny calling his friends Vandemonians, or that I conducted myself in an unseemly manner. **1893** S. NEWLAND *Paving Way* 235 'An old lag', 'a Van Diemenian', he was a living reproach to the arbitrary, unjust, and iniquitous laws of his country. **1909** E. ASH *Austral. Oracle* 13 Among the old Vandemonians and ticket-of-leave men there was the scruff of the earth. **1940** *Bulletin* (Sydney) 10 July 17/1 When I was a nipper .. time-expired convicts from Tasmania .. were occasionally referred to as 'Vandemonians'. **1948** F. CLUNE *Wild Colonial Boys* 136 So we leave Darkie Christie languishing in the company of the Vandemonians at Pentridge. **1978** B. OAKLEY *Ship's Whistle* (1979) 25 A bit of a monster, Colonel .. like Old Craft here when he's crossed. He's an old Vandemonian—convict brotherhood.

B. *adj.*

a. Of, belonging to, or inhabiting Tasmania.

1832 *Currency Lad* (Sydney) 25 Aug. 2 The unlimited admission of Vandemonian wheat. **1840** *Port Phillip Gaz.* 21 Mar. 3 Several of the Vandemonian journals enjoy a considerable circulation in Melbourne. **1852** J. BONWICK *Notes of Gold Digger* 23 Ere's your Van Demonian Happles, and them as don't like the country needn't buy 'em. **1887** *Illustr. Austral. News* (Melbourne) 25 June (Suppl.) 10/3 We are under the necessity of trusting our first number (in print) to a Van Diemenean youth of 18. **1896** *Bulletin* (Sydney) 29 Feb. 25/2 Yes, Vandemonian trains are slow. **1903** *Truth* (Sydney) 1 Mar. 1/4 Vandemonian lawyers—with but two or three notable exceptions, squirm and whine, but never dare to kick—old convict customs, imported into the modern courts. **1976** B. SCOTT *Complete Bk. Austral. Folk Lore* 15 There were American sealers harvesting the islands in Bass Strait and to the south of New Zealand along with their Currency and Vandiemonian cousins.

b. *spec.* Of or pertaining to Tasmania as a penal colony or to one who has served a sentence of transportation there.

1847 L. FROST *No Place for Nervous Lady* (1984) 175 Nearly all the men about this part are old Vandemonian convicts and a notable set they are, but I trust their days of extortion and impudence are nearly over. **1852** *Murray's Guide to Gold Diggings* 48 The Van-Diemonian expirees are the most fortunate of the diggers. **1857** J. D'EWES *China, Aust. & Pacific Islands* 38 The diggers formed the carcase upon which the old convicts, or Vandemonian vultures gathered together. **1880** *Argus* (Melbourne) 27 Jan. 7/2, I deny that I insulted Mr Woods in any way unless he was insulted when I, in reply to an insulting remark from him, told him that he had better leave his Vandemonian proclivities behind him. **1961** M. KIDDLE *Men of Yesterday* 26 The corrupting processes of the British and Vandiemonian penal systems.

Van Diemen's Lander. *Obs.*

1. An Aboriginal native to Tasmania.

1825 B. FIELD *Geogr. Mem. N.S.W.* 207 The difference between the New Hollander and the Van Diemen's-lander is slight in the skull.

2. A non-Aboriginal person native to or resident in Tasmania.

1888 *Sydney Morning Herald* 24 Jan. (Centennial Suppl.) 2/3 Tasmania runs so smoothly in all its forms that if the people owning it have little interest in the discoverer from whom they received the name, they ought at least to be grateful for their escape from being Dutched 'Van Diemenslanders'.

Vandy, *n.* and *a. Obs.*

A. *n.* Abbrev. of VANDEMONIAN *n.* b.

1858 'A. PENDRAGON' *Queen of South* 80 Tacks, abashed at this attack, ventured, in a low tone, to mutter something about strangers, and 'sticking-up' and 'Vandies'. **1873** W. THOMSON-GREGG *Desperate Character* I. 181 Jones started when he heard the Irishman speak of 'Vandies' .. and .. perceived three rough-looking fellows.

B. *adj.* Abbrev. of VANDEMONIAN *adj.* a.

1896 *Bulletin* (Sydney) 29 Feb. 25/2 Vandy girls are quick!

varando, var. VERANDAH.

varied lorikeet. The lorikeet *Psitteuteles versicolor*, a red-capped bird with green, yellow, and pink plumage, occurring in woodlands and forests of n. Aust.

[**1822** J. LATHAM *Gen. Hist. Birds* II. 182 Varied Parrot. *Psittacus multicolor* .. bill black; plumage in general emerald green; on the forehead yellow; across the crown chestnut... Met with at Spencer's Gulf, on the south side of New-Holland.] **1842** J. GOULD *Birds of Aust.* (1848) V. Pl. 51, *Trichoglossus versicolor* .. Varied Lorikeet .. *Wĕ-ro-ole*, Aborigines of Port Essington. **1903** *Emu* II. 218 Varied Lorikeet (*Ptilosclera versicolor*)—I am forwarding the skin of a Lorikeet. **1964** M. SHARLAND *Territory of Birds* 37 The Varied Lorikeet, another bushland inhabitant, was in big flocks.

variegated wren. The small bird *Malurus lamberti lamberti* of the e. slopes of the central part of the Great Dividing Range; more generally, any bird of the widespread species *M. lamberti*; LAMBERT'S WREN. Also **variegated fairy wren,** and formerly **variegated warbler.**

1822 J.W. LEWIN *Nat. Hist. Birds N.S.W.* 15 (*caption*) Variegated Warbler .. inhabits thick brushy woods; frequents the low bushes, creeping close to the ground in search of its food. **1841** J. GOULD *Birds of Aust.* (1848) III. Pl. 24, *Malurus lamberti* .. Lambert's Wren .. Variegated Warbler. **1900** A.J. CAMPBELL *Nests & Eggs Austral. Birds* 176 The Variegated Wren is one of the few common birds of Australia of which Gould was unable to find the nest. **1945** C. BARRETT *Austral. Bird Life* 193 Of the red-winged forms, the variegated or Lambert's wren (*M[alurus] lamberti*) is typical. **1976** *Reader's Digest Compl. Bk. Austral. Birds* 413 (*caption*) Variegated wrens live on the eastern slopes of the Great Divide. **1984** M. BLAKERS et al. *Atlas Austral. Birds* 438 The Variegated Fairy-wren includes a high proportion of plant bugs and weevils in its diet.

vegetable John. *Hist.* A Chinese greengrocer.

1922 *Smith's Weekly* (Sydney) 15 July 17/4 My vegetable John told me that at one time he was a heavy opium smoker. **1982** N. KEESING *Lily on Dustbin* 118 The horse of the Chinese 'vegetable John' pulled a distinctive open cart covered by a brown awning.

velvet. Abbrev. of *black velvet* (see BLACK *a.*[1] 6).

1956 T. RONAN *Moleskin Midas* 106 This bitchin' country is going to the dogs. You got to pay so much for a bit of velvet that it'd be nearly as cheap to get married.

verandah, *n.* and *attrib.* Also **veranda** and formerly **varando, viranda.** [Used elsewhere of similar structures but important because of its frequency in Aust.: see OED(S.]

A. *n.*

1. a. An open-sided, roofed structure abutting on one or more faces of a domestic or commercial building, the main purpose of which is the provision of shelter: see quots. 1872 and 1886.

1805 *Sydney Gaz.* 17 Feb., A Varando in front, with a small room at each end. **1811** *Ibid.* 8 June, Government House was ornamented in a superior style of taste and elegance; the Viranda was arched with boughs fancifully dispersed between the colonades. **1835** *Cornwall Chron.* (Launceston) 21 Feb. 3 *To let* .. those Premises .. containing an excellent *shop*, with a verandah in front. **1844** *Sydney Morning Herald* 18 Oct. 2/7 It would be a great improvement if a light verandah were thrown over the entire footpath to the edge of the curb. **1857** J. ASKEW *Voyage Aust. & N.Z.* 62 The shops of the green grocers are .. protected from the sun's rays by verandahs, which cover the pathways. **1872** MRS E. MILLETT *Austral. Parsonage* 55 A verandah, formed by the continuation of the roof itself, until its eaves came to within seven feet of the grounds. **1886** D.M. GANE *N.S.W. & Vic.* 54 The chief peculiarity .. about Australian towns in general is the verandah. Few houses are without this necessary shelter. The shops, too, in the principal thoroughfares, by means of their broad porticoes, afford the pavements a cooling atmosphere. **1904** M. WHITE *Shanty Entertainment* 1 Congregated under the verandah of 'The Seventy Mile'. **1913** H. LAWSON *Triangles of Life* 109, I was already used to the absence of verandahs, and felt just as much at home as if I were walking down George St. from Redfern. **1926** A.A.B. APSLEY *Amateur Settlers* 88 The wide veranda above. **1943** *Coast to Coast 1942* 82 It had a wide veranda round three sides of it like a squatter's.

b. *spec.* Such a structure abutting a commercial building as a place where business is customarily transacted. Freq. in the phr. **under the verandah.**

1842 *Royal S. Austral. Almanack* p. xxi (Advt.), An extensive Verandah runs round the whole of the Market Place, under which the business can be conveniently transacted in all weathers. **1868** *Australasian* (Melbourne) 8 Feb. 178/2 The Victorian broker .. begins to be known, he is seen under the 'Verandah', and lunches at the Criterion. **1870** *Lectures delivered before Early Closing Assoc.* 8 So that these gambling frauds in the good old times were not confined to a few gentlemen who, it is said, may be seen 'Under the Verandah' (laughter). **1873** 'DEMONAX' *Mysteries & Miseries* 6, I always keep my eyes and ears open when on the Verandah. You want your eyes and ears there, I can tell you. **1880** *Argus News Summary* 5 Feb., In consequence of improvements in Collins-street west, and the enlargement of the Hall of Commerce into an exchange, the well-known 'Verandah' has been taken down. For many years past all brokers' business in stocks and shares has been conducted on the pavement under this verandah. **1898** E.E. MORRIS *Austral Eng.* 489 Verandahs .. are an architectural feature .. of most City shops, where they render the broad side-walks an almost continuous arcade. 'Under the Verandah' has acquired the meaning, 'where city men most do congregate'.

2. Such a structure which is either partially or fully enclosed to provide additional living space.

1839 W.H. LEIGH *Reconnoitering Voyages* 120 Thermometer in the evening stood at .. 130° in the verandah. **1849** A. HARRIS *Guide Port Stephens* 61 The verandah in Australia is indispensable. Washing is commonly done in the verandah. Ladies cannot walk about the bush for several hours a day... If there be a good verandah, they can sit or walk with a degree of pleasure. **1876** 'RESIDENT' *Girl Life in Aust.* 78 Round this central room spread a huge verandah, divided into bedrooms, windowless, and lighted and most sufficiently ventilated by about a foot from the roof being left exposed to the air. ***c* 1877** W. ARCHER in R. Stanley *Tourist to Antipodes* (1977) 31 No squatter's house in Queensland is without a verandah, long, deep and low. It is, if the expression may be allowed, the sitting-room, smoking-room, promenade and sometimes even the dining-room of the family, at least in the summer months. It is always provided with sofas, rocking-chairs and lounging chairs. **1892** MRS F. HUGHES *My Childhood in Aust.* 117 We often sat out in the verandah in the evening to listen to them. **1922** J.H. BIRDWOOD *Visit Aust. & N.Z.* 35 The girls all sleep in the verandah. **1981** A.B. FACEY *Fortunate Life* 53 They had only a two-roomed bag hut with a small lean-to verandah built on the north side. I was to sleep in the lean-to.

3. Such a structure which is floored and used as a place for relaxation.

1843 *Teetotal Advocate* (Launceston) 17 July 2/2 One of them kept sentry on the verandah. **1878** G. WALCH *Australasia* 19 The unconscious object of his threats was seated on the verandah of the bachelors' quarters. **1895** A.C. BICKNELL *Travel & Adventure Northern Qld.* 39 At night a drunken swagman, who had pitched his camp on the verandah outside our room, had a bad attack of delirium tremens. **1924** *Bulletin* (Sydney) 30 Oct. 24/4 The customer who has blewed his cheque .. is no ornament to a pub verandah, and various methods are employed by the out-back Bung to shift the shiftless ones. **1937** I.L. IDRIESS *Forty Fathoms Deep* 81 On shaded verandas of the pearlers' pretty bungalows easy chairs and hammocks were overworked. **1960** —— *Wild North* 156 Old Peter Sloane sat on his humpy veranda gazing wistfully at the huge bulk of Mount Finlayson. **1979** *Westerly* ii. 33 On the hospital verandah, he talked of the parrots.

4. With distinguishing epithet, as **back verandah, front verandah, side verandah.**

1849 A. HARRIS *Emigrant Family* (1967) 404 Mary stood a little way from the **back verandah. 1891** 'SMILER' *Wanderings Simple Child* (ed. 3) 14 I've seen a man in his shirt dancing up and down the back verandah for the last three-quarters of an hour. **1911** L. STONE *Jonah* 85 She had left Packard's without ceremony on her wedding-day, and was spending her honeymoon on the back veranda. Her tastes were very simple. Give her nothing to do, a novelette to read, and some lollies to suck, and she was satisfied. **1919** T.G. RABBETS *Whimplin Whimsies* 61 He closed the back veranda in, And there they all 'aboded'. **1937** A.W. UPFIELD *Winds of Evil* 155 The shower is on the back veranda. **1956** *Bulletin* (Sydney) 2 May 13/1, I sleep on a back-veranda and every night my rest is disturbed. **1981** Q. WILD *Honey Wind* 75 This cove has officially learned how to .. build a back verandah, raise six kids on the basic wage. **1849** A. HARRIS *Emigrant Family* (1967) 402 Mary and Margaret sat in the **front verandah. 1911** 'S. RUDD' *Bk. of Dan* 66 'Here he comes .. ' Duncan remarked, gazing off the end of his front verandah. **1934** C. MACKNESS *Young Beachcombers* 38 The front-veranda, which is the tropical equivalent to a sitting-room, was occupied by one forlorn little figure only. **1947** G. CASEY *Wits are Out* 163 On the front veranda old Kingston and his wife were just leaving. **1978** *Westerly* iii. 6 Louise, or Lois: up against the brick veneer of her front verandah. **1916** T. WARLOW *By Mirage & Mulga* 72 McInverness .. lay on a stretcher-bed made up on the **side verandah. 1938** X. HERBERT *Capricornia* 142 On a side veranda he stopped to look into a lounge-bar. **1967** M. HORNER *Austral. One-Act Plays: Bk. 3* 85 We were married after about a month .. on the side veranda. A minister came from the aboriginal mission.

B. *attrib.*

1. *Obs.* Of a building: having a verandah, as **verandah cottage, house, store.**

1819 *Hobart Town Gaz.* 16 Oct. (Suppl.), Mr W.A. Brodrebb .. has opened an Office at the Veranda House, Elizabeth Street. **1825** *Howe's Weekly Commercial Express* (Sydney) 26 Sept. 1 *To be let or sold*, a neat Verandah *cottage*. **1838** *Southern Austral.* (Adelaide) 30 June 2/4 *Verandah Store*, North Terrace, near the bank. *On sale*. **1861** R. HENNING *Lett.* (1952) 37 A pretty veranda house, with a grove of wattle-trees round it. **1870** *Sydney Morning Herald* 2 July 3/5 There is a pretty 4-room Verandah Cottage, with cellar. **1887** A. NICOLS *Wild Life & Adventure* 401 A half-finished verandah 'house' near by.

2. *fig.* Of a person: inclined to direct from afar and to take no active part, 'arm chair': see quot. 1973.

1929 K.S. PRICHARD *Coonardoo* (1961) 195 Yet Hugh Watt slogged on; no verandah manager about him. **1947** F. CLUNE *Roaming around Aust.* 158 Ted Norman wasn't a 'verandah pearler'. He went out with the luggers, like his Dad before him. **1951** W. HATFIELD *Wild Dog Frontier* 26 That dog's going to be sorry he didn't emigrate to New South to plague the verandah-riders down there. **1952** C. SIMPSON *Come away, Pearler* 51 Gympie Lewes can rub more sense out of the side of his snoot—about boats and shelling in general—than any bloody veranda pearler. **1973** H. HOLTHOUSE *S'pose I Die* 34 Paddy was what they called a 'veranda boss'—he did most of his supervising from the house. **1970** G. BAHNEMANN *Calling Reef* 88 The *Groper's* crew .. had never dared talk of the rich bed of gold-lip shell at Osprey Reef, for fear their masters—the 'Veranda Pearlers' who owned the luggers but did not themselves go to sea—might order them to go down. **1978** TEECE & PIKE *Voice of Wilderness* 199, I was no 'verandah manager'. I did not employ a head stockman; I filled both capacities and it meant I was away for six weeks at a time in the mustering camps.

3. Comb. **verandah post.**

1825 *Austral.* (Sydney) 21 July 2 These two rushed into the house, seized the overseer, tied his hands behind his back and then to one of the verandah posts .. and then plundered the house. **1882** W. SOWDEN *N.T. as it Is* 41 The verandah-posts clad with greenery, made the otherwise homely publichouse look almost romantic. **1916** C.L. HARTT *Humorosities* 9 'What do you think of London, mate?' 'There ain't a blessed verandah-post in it!' **1932** J. TRURAN *Green Mallee* 3 He pulled up again, and tethered the mare to Mr Gilson's veranda-post. **1948** *Coast to Coast 1947* 124 There was the usual crowd sitting on benches or leaning against veranda-posts outside the hotel.

4. Special Comb. **verandah bed,** a bed in a *verandah room*; **chair,** *squatter chair*, see Squatter 5; **room,** a room made out of part or the whole of an enclosed verandah (see *n.* 2).

1950 G.S. Casey *City of Men* 210 Just before lunchtime he rolled out of his **verandah bed** at his boarding-house. **1886** P. Fletcher 'Hints to Immigrants' in P. Fletcher *Qld.* 42 Then there is the squatter's or **verandah chair,** which is very comfortable to rest and smoke in, but which takes up too much room to be used indoors. **1896** A. Mackay *Austral. Agriculturist* (rev. ed.) 39 Verandah Chair—This is a really comfortable rest for a tired housewife, or the man after his day's work is done. **1848** *Maitland Mercury* 10 May 2/3 About eleven o'clock, he noticed a light in the **verandah room** of Mr Ballard's inn, the door of which room was open, although no-one was in it. **1902** A. Busby *Bathurst in Thirties* 2 The only shop in the whole district was carried on in a small end-verandah room of one of the public houses. **1933** J. McCarter *Love's Lunatic* 236, I run t' their verandah bedroom where th' missus was asleep in their canvas chair. **1960** C. Morse *Guest Yrs.* 15 Finally, I showed Thelma the bedrooms known as the 'veranda rooms'. Like the rest of the hotel, these rooms were on ground level.

Hence **verandahless** *a.*, lacking a veranda.

1910 *Bulletin* (Sydney) 7 July 44/1 One small, oblong, weather-board, bare, verandah-less 'cottage'. **1960** D. McLean *Roaring Days* 223 Mrs Withers was standing at the door of her verandah-less house as we drove up.

vermin, *collect.* [Spec. use of *vermin, collect.* animals of a noxious or objectionable kind.] Animals which prey upon crops, etc., esp. rabbits and dingoes. Used *attrib.* and in Comb., esp. as **vermin (proof) fence.**

1905 *Bulletin* (Sydney) 2 Nov. 14/2 Queensland keeps an expensive vermin fence going on the S.A. border. **1927** J. Pollard *Rose of Bushlands* 175 Joseph's idea . . is worth trying everywhere where there are rabbits. Many years will pass before all the Roads and Vermin Boards adopt the same plan. **1931** Mrs E.P. Halford *Pioneers of Yesterday* 5 You could drive . . over the top of the vermin-proof fence. **1957** J. Hawke *Follow my Dust* 73 He patrolled a section of some eighty miles of Momba's vermin fences. **1970** P. Slater *Eagle for Pidgin* 51 It looks as if wedgies could come off the vermin list sometime in the near future, anyway. **1972** Anderson & Blake *J.S. Neilson* 35 Concern with the increasing amount of rural depredation by the plague of rabbits caused the State Government on 2 March to declare that three vermin-proof fences would be erected in the north-west.

Victorian, *n.* and *a.* [f. the name of the State of *Victoria*, officially named in 1851 after Queen Victoria, reigned 1837–1901.]

A. *n.* A non-Aboriginal person native to or resident in Victoria.

1850 *Irish Exile* (Hobart) 28 Dec. 7/2 The Port Phillipians—we beg their pardon, the Victorians—have displayed their loyalty. **1858** *Bell's Life in Sydney* 23 Jan. 2/2 The Victorians were puzzled at the underhand bowling. **1869** *Notes of Excursion Blue Mountains & 'Zig-Zag Works'* 3 The excursionists were a party of Victorians then on a visit to the sister colony. **1884** *Austral. Tit-Bits* (Melbourne) 10 July 13/2 This seems to be about up to the standard of the Sydneyites, so Victorians can judge pretty well of the mental calibre of the audiences. **1898** H. Matthews *Chat about Aust.* 11 Victorians in general, and Melbournites in particular . . take the palm from all Australians for their partiality to holidays and sports of various kinds. . . Who . . has not heard of Cup Day? **1926** A. Eden *Places in Sun* 61 Victorians—we use the word in its geographical and not in its chronological sense. **1934** A. Pratt *Centenary Hist. Vic.* 214 In the field of Art, Victorians have won decided eminence. **1951** *Sydney Morning Herald* 23 Feb. 1/1 Six Victorians die from rare disease. **1973** *Age* (Melbourne) 9 Mar. 11/6 He said Labor spoke for more Victorians in Parliament than did the Government. **1986** *Canberra Times* 3 Mar. 1/1 (*heading*) Victorian to direct Office of Status of Women.

B. *adj.* Of or pertaining to the State of Victoria or to its inhabitants.

1855 W. Howitt *Land, Labor & Gold* II. 246 Reselling it at a truly Victorian profit. **1869** E.C. Booth *Another England* 1 These Victorian Britons have given to the rivers and the mountains of this other England they have founded in the south, the old-land names and titles. *c* **1883** C.F. Roberts *Iniquities of Lunacycraft* 43 Dr McCreery . . had *not the humanity* to offer me *any* help. Such was Victorian lunacycraft to me. **1899** H. Furniss *Austral. Sketches* 75 The science of the Victorian game of football may be too quick for a stranger to grasp at first sight. **1911** St. C. Grondona *Collar & Cuffs* 33 They are all bullicks here or milbries when they are yearlings; bullock is quite Victorian. **1934** A. Pratt *Centenary Hist. Vic.* 212 Many Victorian professors have achieved an international reputation in scholarship. **1954** *Victorian Hist. Mag.* June 115 He wrote to his Irish friends to tell them about the progressive measures being passed by the Victorian legislators. **1973** K. Dunstan *Sports* 223, 1908 was a big year. . . The Prime Minister, Mr Alfred Deakin, proposed the toast of Australian Rules Football . . and it was Victorian Rules no longer. **1984** G. Blainey *Our Side of Country* 46 The secret ballot was introduced for the first time in the world at the elections of 1856, and in the United States it became known as 'the Victorian ballot'.

Victoria rifle-bird. [f. *Victoria*, first applied as the specific name *Victoriae* by English zoologist J. Gould (see quot. 1849) + Rifle-bird.] The bird *Ptiloris victoriae* of tropical rainforest in n.e. Qld. See also Bird of Paradise 2. Also **Queen Victoria rifle-bird.**

[**1849** *Proc. Zool. Soc. London* 111 *Ptiloris Victoriae*. . . There are few [birds] from any part of the world that can vie with it in the richness of its colouring; and I cannot possibly have a better opportunity than now presents itself of paying a just tribute of respect to our most gracious Queen, by bestowing upon this lovely denizen of the Australian forests the specific appellation of *Victoriae*.] **1856** H.B. Stoney *Vic.* 215 The *Ptiloris paradisea*, or rifle bird, is well known to collectors. . . The smaller one . . has been deemed worthy to be associated with the name of our Queen, and is known as the Victoria rifle-bird. **1909** *Emu* VIII. 240 A splendid specimen of the Victoria Rifle-Bird . . was perched on an upright stick about 4 feet from the ground. **1945** C. Barrett *Austral. Bird Life* 128 The Victoria rifle-bird . . is restricted to North Queensland. **1980** M. Grant *Barrier Reef* 161 There were bowerbirds like . . the Prince Albert Rifle Bird and the Queen Victoria Rifle Bird.

vigoro /ˈvɪgərəʊ/. [Prob. formed on *vigour*.] A game played by women, combining elements of baseball and cricket. Also *attrib.*

c **1930** *Laws of Vigoro* 1 The Game 'Vigoro' (a combination of Cricket and Baseball) was invented to give the world a game—simple to interpret, interesting and exciting—which would enable all to became efficient players. **1931** *Sydney Morning Herald* 19 Mar. 13/4 *Vigoro.* New South Wales wins Dodge Cup. *Ibid.* 23 Mar. 13/7 The final of the first of the series of interstate vigoro matches to be held between New South Wales and Queensland was played at Randwick Racecourse on Saturday afternoon. **1951** *Ibid.* 4 Mar. (Sports Section) 14/2 N.S.W., 56 and 10–66, beat Queensland, 59 and 62, in the women's interstate vigoro carnival yesterday.

village. *Obs.*

1. A small (rural) settlement. See also Township 2.

1803 J. Grant *Narr. Voyage N.S.W.* 82 Paramatta . . is a very pretty village. **1820** C. Jeffreys *Van Dieman's Land* 55 New Town is a pleasant village about three miles N.W. of Hobart. **1830** *Hobart Town Almanack* 29 The village of Oatlands . . was marked out as a township, together with Perth, Campbell town and Brighton by General Macquarie in May 1821. **1845** *Star* (Parramatta) 11 Jan. 2/3 The village of Petersham (Sydney Road) was sold by auction last week at the rate of £400 per acre, for front, and £200 per acre for back allotments. **1853** Mossman & Banister *Aust. Visited & Revisited* 173 The township or village of Canbury, with its little church, sufficiently large to accommodate the scattered population hereabouts. **1863** T. Foster *Rev. Several Explorers Aust.* 3, I propose to follow the white man from his small village on Port Jackson to his rich settlement along the borders of the great Interior. **1882** *Bulletin* (Sydney) 3 June 10/1 The village of Queanbeyan has become a cock-pit. **1893** *Ibid.* 19 Aug. 20/4 There are no 'villages' in Australia—there are townships, and bush towns, and country towns, but the term 'villages' is merely an atavistic paroxysm. **1907** *Ibid.* 4 Apr. 15/3 Pine Creek (N.T.) . . is now a one-horse village. No one there but Government servants, a pub, saddler and storekeeper.

2. A cluster of Aboriginal dwellings.

1827 P. Cunningham *Two Yrs. in N.S.W.* I. 134 A stately healthy race, easy to be civilized. Their huts form villages of forty or fifty. **1835** J. Batman *Settlement Port Phillip* 29 May (1856) 11 We came upon, apparently quite fresh, tracks of the natives, leading to a village of huts or gunyahs. **1848** *Maitland Mercury* 5 July 3/1 Unlike most of the natives of Australia as yet discovered, they have fixed habitations, dwelling in little villages of six or seven huts in a cluster. **1862** Backhouse & Tylor *Life & Labours G.W. Walker* 243 The Aborigines had a little village of huts made of bark.

3. Special Comb. **village reserve,** a site reserved for a small rural settlement; **settlement, (a)** Village 1; **(b)** a government-sponsored co-operative farming community; **settler,** a member of a *village settlement* (b).

1837 *Tegg's N.S.W. Pocket Almanac* 67 On its banks are grants belonging to Messrs Percy Simpson, Tingecombe, and Campbell, also a **village reserve. 1842** *Melbourne Times* 22 Oct. 3/6 This valuable property is situated within a short distance of the Yarra Yarra, and abuts on the Heidelberg Village Reserve. **1851** J. Henderson *Excursions & Adventures N.S.W.* I. 93 Kyama is a village reserve, that is, a place set apart by the Government for a future village. **1840** *S. Austral. Rec.* (London) 7 Mar. 98 A community has been formed for the purpose of purchasing a special survey of 4,160 acres, 80 acres of which will be laid out in a central situation, as a **village settlement,** and divided into 320 allotments of a quarter of an acre each. **1891** 'Agricola' *New Earth* 1 Village Settlement is but another name for Co-operative Farming. **1892** *Bulletin* (Sydney) 14 May 11/2 The Victorian experiment of village-settlements as one narrow sluice valve of opportunity for surplus labour . . will be watched with interest. **1900** *Ibid.* 6 Jan. 5/1 The S.A. village settlements nowadays pin their faith chiefly to wheat-crops. The average settler doesn't think much of the communistic business, and wants a block of his own to work on. **1937** E. Hill *Water into Gold* 159 There was one Village Settlement in Victoria, one only—Nyah. **1976** Drage & Page *Riverboats & Riverman* 12 A scheme started by the South Australian Government to help the unemployed. Over a period of two or three years they sent families up the Murray to establish what they called 'village settlements' at Holder, New Era, Waikerie, Gillen East, Moorook, Kingston-on-Murray, Pyap, and Lyrup. **1894** *Bulletin* (Sydney) 3 Nov. 15/1 The child of a **village settler** at Kardella (Vic.), died of starvation, the other day. **1902** *Ibid.* 24 May 32/2 Johnson was a village settler, the generality of which class are the failures in every other walk of life, thrown by a fostering Government on to the primal resource—the land. **1937** E. Hill *Water into Gold* 156 The Village Settlers had contracted to grow . . wheat.

vine scrub. Formerly, any tropical or sub-tropical rainforest; now spec. a seasonally dry forest of this type. Formerly also **vine brush.**

1826 J. Atkinson *Acct. Agric. & Grazing N.S.W.* 3 Vine brushes are mostly found on the sides and summits of steep mountains near the sea. It is here we may see the vegetable kingdom in its most magnificent form, lofty cedar and turpentine trees of the grandest dimensions, with large vines or parasitical plants of various kinds, thick as a man's leg, twining up to their very tops, catching hold of other trees in all directions, until an immense net-work is formed, impervious to the sun's rays. **1827** P. Cunningham *Two Yrs. in N.S.W.* I. 151 You come to a thick vine brush of the richest soil. **1846** *Melbourne Argus* 16 June 2/2 A dense vine scrub, through which they had to cut their way. **1853** J. Sherer *Gold Finder Aust.* 98 (*note*) *Vine brush* is almost impenetrable forest, where vast numbers of parasitical plants, climbers, and underwood are all tangled together, usually upon a good soil. **1870** E.B. Kennedy *Four Yrs. in Qld.* 206 The Mary river . . banks were fringed by luxuriant 'vine'-scrubs. **1876** 'Capricornus' *Colonisation* 23 You had better take your women and children up the pine-covered mountains to the vine-brushes. **1889** R.B. Anderson tr. Lumholtz's *Among Cannibals* 25 Vitis in great abundance and of many varieties are found especially in the scrubs, hence the colonists call this sort of brush, *vine-scrub*. **1938** C.T. White *Princ. Bot. Qld. Farmers* 212 The vine scrubs or jungles (rain-forests) reach their greatest development in Australia in coastal Queensland. **1961** *Overland* xx. 21 The vine-scrub spurs and valleys where little creeks hid under the tangle of wait-a-while and massive trees. **1984** K.A.W. WILLIAMS *Native Plants Qld.* II. 224 Native Mulberry . . is a very common plant . . in the dry vine scrubs that grow on lava flows.

violet wood. *Obs.* The violet-scented wood of any of several trees; a tree having such wood.

1847 E.W. LANDOR *Bushman* 395 There is another highly-fragrant wood peculiar to this colony, called by the settlers 'raspberry jam', from its resembling that sweet meat in its scent. A small quantity sent to Tonbridge-Wells, was worked up into boxes, and highly approved of by the cabinet-makers, who gave it the name of 'violet wood'. **1861** F. ALGAR *Handbk. to Colony Qld.* 7 Violet Wood, Silk Oak, Tulip Wood, and Forest Oak . . are plentiful.

viranda, var. VERANDAH.

Vitamizer. Also **vitamizer.** [Proprietary name.] An appliance for blending cooking ingredients or for reducing raw fruit and vegetables to liquid form.

1951 *Austral. Official Jrnl. Patents* (Canberra) 3922 *Vitamizer* 102,530. 16th May, 1950. Food and drink mixing machines. Semak Electrics Pty. Limited. **1959** B. HUMPHRIES *Nice Night's Entertainment* (1981) 38 The wife's crying out for a vitamiser so I get her one. Must have used it once in six months. Fifteen quid for a glass of carrot juice. **1969** *Meanjin* 361 From a pocket he produces carrots in a plastic bag. His vitamiser whines. 'Carrot juice. I live on it.'

vulpine opossum. *Obs.* [See quot. 1848.] *Brush-tailed possum*, see BRUSH-TAILED.

1789 A. PHILLIP *Voyage to Botany Bay* 150 (*caption*) Vulpine Opossum. **1832** J. BACKHOUSE *Narr. Visit Austral. Colonies* (1843) 29 The Vulpine Opossum—the Common Opossum of this land—abounds. **1848** *Bell's Life in Sydney* 20 May 1/2 The opossum is something like a fox (and thence called the vulpine opossum) but inferior in size. **1865** G.F. ANGAS *Aust.* 74 Six species of opossum are inhabitants of Australia. The most abundant kind is the common or vulpine opossum.

W

wacker, var. WHACKER.

wacko, var. WHACKO.

waddy /ˈwɒdi/, *n.*[1] Also **waddi, waddie, wody, woodah.** [a. Dharuk *wadi* a tree, a stick of wood, a wooden weapon (see quots. 1790 in senses 1 a. and b.).]

1. a. An Aboriginal war-club; a piece of wood used as a club. In quot. 1798 the weapon referred to is apparently a boomerang.

1790 D. SOUTHWELL Corresp. & Papers, *Wad-di* or *wad-dy*, a stick or club. **1793** J. HUNTER *Hist. Jrnl. Trans. Port Jackson* 410 *Woo-da*, a club. **1798** M. FLINDERS *Voyage Terra Australis* (1814) I. p. cxxxix, He was of a middle age, unarmed, except with a *whaddie*, or wooden scimitar. **1803** J.G. GRANT *Narr. Voyage N.S.W.* 108 An elderly man made Euranbie a present of a *waddie*, or club. **1825** *Howe's Weekly Commercial Express* (Sydney) 2 May 3 Her enamoured swain . . sneaking softly behind her, with one blow of his *waddie* stretched her quivering at his feet. **1832** J. BACKHOUSE *Narr. Visit Austral. Colonies* (1843) 90 The chief instrument used in the chase by these people is a Waddy, a short stick about an inch in thickness, brought suddenly to a conical point at each end, and at one end a little roughed, to keep it from slipping out of the hand. **1841** *Geelong Advertiser* 27 Dec. 3/2 He was at a corrobory on Friday night, and had been knocked down with a waddy. **1850** *Monthly Almanac* (Adelaide) 44, I found myself in the middle of a party of natives. . . One of them played pretty with a waddy in the region of my bump of philoprogenitiveness. **1862** *Melbourne Punch's Almanack* 14 She was bent upon declining altogether to be struck on the head with the matrimonial waddy. **1880** 'OLD HAND' *Experiences of Colonist* (ed. 2) i. 37 They were also serviceable in occasionally providing food for the party, as they could with their waddies knock over a wallaby or a bandicoot, and thus ensure a good palatable meal. **1901** *Bulletin* (Sydney) 5 Oct. 17/1 You must see the native throwing . . to understand what woolanä-throwing is. Unlike the spear, the woolanä cannot be dodged, and escape depends on the manipulation of the shield or woodäh. **1935** H. BASEDOW *Knights of Boomerang* 63 The wounded bird could not travel fast. . . It was overtaken . . and struck on the head with a waddy. **1946** D. BARR *Warrigal Joe* 13 The boys were knocked over with waddies and finished off with spears. **1963** I.L. IDRIESS *Our Living Stone Age* 204 Gleefully they are hoping . . that there will be a fight and this old wretch will get his skull cracked by a waddy—an ironwood nullah, hard and heavy.

b. Chiefly *Austral. pidgin.* A tree; a piece of wood. Also *attrib.* and as *adj.* (see quot. 1856).

c **1790** W. DAWES Grammatical Forms Lang. N.S.W., *Wad-day*, wood (lignum). **1793** J. HUNTER *Hist. Jrnl. Trans. Port Jackson* 410 *Wad-dy*, a stick or tree. **1830** R. DAWSON *Present State Aust.* 78 Seeing some wood lying in my path, he gently took hold of my arm: 'Massa', said he, 'waddy (wood) you tee, (see).' **1846** MRS C. MEREDITH *Notes & Sketches N.S.W.* 106 The word 'waddie' though commonly applied to the weapons of the New South Wales aborigines, does not with them mean any particular implement, but is the term used to express wood of any kind, or trees. 'You maan waddie 'long of fire', means 'Go and fetch firewood.' **1856** W.W. DOBIE *Recoll. Visit Port-Phillip* 93 Borak you ever see black fellow with waddie (wooden) leg. **1859** W. BURROWS *Adventures Mounted Trooper* 102 The answer he got, in his own lingo, was, 'suppose you no cut waddy (wood) you bale get tucker'. **1870** C.H. ALLEN *Visit to Qld.* 181 In Queensland . . two or three tribes . . hang about the towns, and pick up a precarious living by begging or chopping 'waddy' or wood. **1884** A.W. HOWITT *On Some Austral. Ceremonies Initiation* 9 The Baiangal are . . correctly speaking, 'Tree-climbers' . . as distinguished from the Katungal, who live on fish . . and are therefore properly spoken of as 'Fishermen'. The whites know them by this name, but speak of the others as 'Waddy men', from the word *waddy*, colonially used for *tree.* **1956** B.J. RAYMENT *My Towri* 96, I can only recall odd words of their language and am not certain about some of them. Yowi, yes; bal, no . . wody, wood [etc.].

2. a. A club or cudgel as used by a person other than an Aboriginal; a piece of wood used as a weapon.

1809 *Sydney Gaz.* 14 May, Several depredations . . attributed to the offenders who have betaken themselves to the woods. . . A man, who resides at Hawkesbury was attacked and severely wounded in the head with a *waddy or club.* **1824** *Austral.* (Sydney) 30 Dec. 3, On Sunday night, a book-binder residing in Phillip-street, named Welsh, while in a state of intoxication, was attacked by three soldiers, who with waddies beat him in a most dreadful manner. **1841** *Geelong Advertiser* 27 Sept. 4/3 The prisoner . . returned to his hut about half an hour after sun-down . . and told his mate . . to provide himself with a waddy to protect himself. **1851** *Empire* (Sydney) 10 Nov. 346/7 A private watchman of Rogers's with a poised stick in hand, ordered him to stand 'or', said he, pushing the end of the waddy against his abdomen, 'I'll blow your brains out.' **1888** W.T. PYKE *Bush Tales* 36 A man is stationed, armed with a 'waddy', or green sapling, about as thick and four times as long, as an Irish shilelagh. **1891** *Truth* (Sydney) 22 Mar. 1/5 The latest tuberculosis cure is advertised by a picture of a man knocking the microbes out with a waddy. **1907** *Ibid.* 12 May 8/5 (*heading*) Woodford wields a waddy *and mangles Monoghan's melon.* **1930** K.S. PRICHARD *Haxby's Circus* 236 The men grabbed seats, started to smash them up, and use them as waddies. **1948** I.L. IDRIESS *Opium Smugglers* 188 Pick a good waddy . . a heavy one. . . If he's there then hit him a clout over the head. **1981** L. MCLEAN *Pumpkin Pie* 79 They could possibly have . . 'jumped the rattler' . . but knew that extra inspectors had been employed to hunt the free riders. . . Most of them carried a piece of wood, called a 'waddy', and would hit anyone unlucky enough to be caught on the train.

b. *fig.* In the phr. **to take up the waddy,** to engage in a vigorous defence (cf. 'to take up the cudgels').

1907 *Bulletin* (Sydney) 7 Feb. 15/1, I beg to take up the waddy of disputation on behalf of 'Crossnibs'.

waddy /ˈwɒdi/, *n.*[2] [a. Western Desert *wati.*] An Aboriginal male.

1935 H.H. FINLAYSON *Red Centre* 68 Over large portions of the interior the aborigine distinguishes himself from the white man by the term 'waddi' and this might perhaps serve as a name for the race. **1963** O. RUHEN *Flockmaster* 58 Some waddy's got himself lost—he's got a woman with him. They're out of tucker . . a bit lucky I came along.

waddy /ˈwɒdi/, *v.* [f. WADDY *n.*[1]]

a. *trans.* To strike, beat, or kill (an animal or person) with a waddy (see WADDY *n.*[1] a.). Also *intr.* and as *vbl. n.*

1833 *Launceston Advertiser* 31 Oct. 3 The spearing and waddying are yet of too recent occurrence to be remembered with indifference by our settlers. **1840** *Sydney Gaz.* 10 Sept., We learnt . . that three males and one female belonging to the brig *Maria*, had been waddied in the day time. **1847** *Moreton Bay Courier* 9 Oct. 4/3 Another woman of the same tribe, whom I had seen a short time before with a 'white child' upon being questioned what had become of it said, 'it plenty cry, we plenty waddy it'. **1857** J. BONWICK *Early Days Melbourne* 33 The women gathered roots, and picked out grubs, while the men waddied down birds, netted fish, speared kangaroos, and pulled opossums from their holes. **1863** —— *Wild White Man* 48 An unhappy girl . . had been waddied. **1888** H.S. RUSSELL *Genesis Qld.* 365 Calvert and Roper were severely wounded, and 'waddied'. **1903** *Bulletin* (Sydney) 22 Oct. 35/4 He *did* 'do it again', and returning from town with his mate—both 'tanked'—was waddied to death. **1914** T.C. WOLLASTON *Spirit of Child* 191 A good many people would succeed better in life if they were periodically *waddied.*

b. *fig.* To importune.

1880 H. KENDALL *Songs from Mountains* 201 Laura's lovers every day In sweet verse embody her. Katie's have a different way, Being frank, they 'waddy' her.

waddy wood. [See WADDY *n.*[1] a.] Any of several trees yielding a hard wood, esp. *Acacia peuce* (fam. Mimosaceae) of s.w. Qld. and N.T., and WHALEBONE TREE; the wood of the tree. Also **waddy tree,** and *attrib.*

1912 *Mod. Dict. Eng. Lang.* 803 *Wad'-dy-wood* . . a Tas. tree yielding a dense, hard, white wood which was used by aborigines for making waddies. **1929** W.D. FRANCIS *Austral. Rain-Forest Trees* 61 *Pseudomorus Brunoniana* . . Whalebone tree . . Waddy wood. . . The wood has been used for axe-handles and for the handles of other tools. **1940** *Bulletin* (Sydney) 4 Dec. 17/3 Its local name is 'waddy wood', botanical name *Acacia puece* [*sic*]. It grows about 12 miles north of Birdsville, in Western Queensland, near the S.A. border. **1946** C.T. MADIGAN *Crossing Dead Heart* 35 Near the bore there was a patch of 'waddy' trees, tall, straight trees some fifty feet high, with thin and drooping foliage and seeds in long pods. **1967** M. & M. LEYLAND *Where Dead Men Lie* 133 The moon shone through the chinks in the Waddy wood walls as I listened to the sounds of the others breathing. **1980** J. WOLFE *Crocodile Soup* 138 The professor was intrigued to inspect the strange 'Waddy' trees north of Birdsville. The trees are very beautiful, with long weeping foliage similar to a casuarina, and sigh in the ever-blowing wind from the surrounding desert.

wadgula /ˈwaɪdʒələ, ˈwɒdʒələ/. *Austral. pidgin.* Also **waigella, waijela.** [Alteration of WHITE FELLOW.] A white person.

1923 A.G. BOLAM *Trans-Austral. Wonderland* 76 'Waijela bool-ga munda?' (Whitefellow dig big earth?). **1938** D. BATES *Passing of Aborigines* 182 'Blak-fella king belong to this country!' shouted Nyimbana in English. 'We don't want waijela here! This *gabbi* our *gabbi*.' **1957** F. CLUNE *Fortune Hunters* 55 Then we put *poona* (sticks) all around hole *waipella* (whitefellow) fashion.' **1969** L. HADOW *Full Cycle* 157 'Hah, ha!' Jimmy Dabchick turned a cartwheel. 'Us all N-Yoongars. What she? Sister Merry Christmas only Waigella!' **1975** R. BEILBY *Brown Land Crying* 2 Pink as a white person's hands. Just like a wadjullah's. **1981** A. WELLER *Day of Dog* 7 We'll go and pick up a woman for ya, Dougo. Would ya like a big fat wadgula or a skinny little gin?

wadna /ˈwɒdnə/. *S.A. Obs.* [a. Gaurna *wadna.*] An Aboriginal hunting weapon: see quots.

1842 *S. Austral. News* (London) 46/2 The larger [skins] have their inner layers shaven off by the katta, kandappi, or wadna. **1845** E.J. EYRE *Jrnls. Exped. Central Aust.* II. 280 A strong sharp-pointed stick, flattened on one side near the point (called in the Adelaide dialect, 'Wadna', in that of Moorunde 'Ngakko'). **1846** C.W. SCHÜRMANN *Aboriginal Tribes Port Lincoln* 4 The wadna, is the boomarang of other Australian tribes, only that it is longer, thinner, and clumsier. **1847** G.F. ANGAS *Savage Life & Scenes* I. 111 Their weapons are the throwing-stick (*midlah*), which is made of the she-oak wood, larger and more clumsily shaped than that of the Adelaide tribes . . the *wadna*, for striking fish. **1860** *Trans. & Proc. R. Soc. Vic.* (1861) 170 The 'wadna' is a kind of weapon about three feet long, with a knee in the middle. It is never used as a weapon for fighting, but only for killing large fish.

wage. Usu. as **wages.**

1. Used *attrib.*, with reference to an amount paid periodically to an employee, in Special Comb. **wage plug,** *wages man*; **wages award,** AWARD *n.*; **board,** a body responsible for determining conditions of employment; also *attrib.*; **man,** one who works for a wage.

1918 G. DALE *Industr. Hist. Broken Hill* 206 The **wage-plug** on the surface is keeping in motion the machines of production. **1920** *Ross's Monthly* May 5/1 'E dances an' romances with the wage-plugs' daughters, too An' 'grashusly' selects a tart wot's pretty—wouldn't you? **1928** *Aussie* (Sydney) Oct. 6/1 Mum was an educated woman, and kept the farm books for Dad, who had started as a wage plug before he had reached his teens. **1931** 'BRENT OF BIN BIN' *Back to Bool Bool* 154 The Australian working-man is the richest wage-plug on God's earth, and the most leisured. **1954** A. UPFIELD *Death of Lake* (1956) 5 The great homestead .. comprised eight hundred thousand acres and was populated by sixty thousand sheep in the care of some twenty wage plugs. **1971** F. HARDY *Outcasts of Foolgarah* 22 Yes, a grand place to live is Foolgarah, even for wage-plugs. **1983** *Newcastle Herald* 19 Apr. 2/7 The value of this package of extras differs between Members, but it makes sure that the actual level of salary is less important to the MP than it is to the ordinary wage plug. **1933** R.D TATE *Doughman* 42 Three or four had been finishing very late—and that was dangerous, the **Wages Award** expressly stating that every carter must be off the premises on the stroke of six. **1945** *Bulletin* (Sydney) 26 Dec. 12/2 Murphy .. sidestepped wages awards by promising bonuses that never materialised. **1909** *Truth* (Sydney) 25 July 1/3 'Are you a married man?' was asked a witness at a **Wages Board.** **1915** M. ATKINSON *Trade Unionism in Aust.* 21 Undoubtedly the most important and significant activity of trade unionism has been in the sphere of the Wages Board system. **1918** C.H. NORTHCOTT *Austral. Social Dev.* 29 The Wages Board of Victoria were [*sic*] strongly opposed at their inauguration. **1922** C. DALEY *Early Squatting Days* 14 The minimum wage, the Wages Board, the Arbitration Court, even the eight hours system, were beyond the ken of worker and employer alike. **1871** *Austral. Town & Country Jrnl.* (Sydney) 21 Jan. 71/1 The cause is the old one of defective timbering, and it is somewhat queer that in both cases it is **wages men** that have been hurt. **1876** 'EIGHT YRS.' RESIDENT' *Queen of Colonies* 147 The last we heard of him, he was working as a 'wages-man' on a reef. **1891** *Truth* (Sydney) 26 Apr. 7/3 Fencing, ringbarking, dam-sinking and scrub-cutting are rarely done by wages men on a station. **1894** *Bulletin* (Sydney) 31 Mar. 9/4 The granting of 12 days' exemption at Coolgardie to enable leaseholders to get men would seem to indicate that wages-men were scarce. **1948** V. PALMER *Golconda* 132 Few of the gougers had families, and the wives of the wages-men whose tents and shanties she dropped into were wrapped up in their own concerns. **1957** —— *Seedtime* 165, I was one of the first wages-men on the field and I don't forget the way you worked to get us a little bit more than the current award. **1962** O. PRYOR *Aust.'s Little Cornwall* 52 A miner willing to take a chance preferred to work on tribute. They worked to the limit during the two-month time limit .. at the end of which time .. wages men might be given the potch to work.

2. Chiefly *Mining.* In *pl.*

a. *transf.* A sum sufficient to live on, esp. in the phr. **to make wages,** to earn an adequate living; **to pay wages,** (of a mine, a mineral deposit, etc.) to yield an adequate return.

1853 J.R. GODLEY *Extracts Jrnl. Visit N.S.W.* 19 'Making wages' .. in the mouths of diggers means earning 10s. a day, or £3 a week. **1855** *Ovens & Murray Advertiser* (Beechworth) 27 Jan. 4/2 It requires a great amount of patience and labour to work the claims, which in many instances barely pay wages to the parties working them. **1858** *Colonial Mining Jrnl.* Nov. 44/2 The companies that have bottomed and struck the gutter, are obtaining very fair wages. **1859** *Ibid.* July 189/2 A narrow gutter is said to have been struck, and to pay good wages. **1871** *Austral. Town & Country Jrnl.* (Sydney) 22 Apr. 495/1 The prospect is not rich but will yield good wages if steadily worked. **1928** A. WRIGHT *Good Recovery* 60, I live out here, a timber-getter, getting props for the mines, cutting sleepers, anything, and I make wages. **1944** M.J. O'REILLY *Bowyangs & Boomerangs* 60 We worked a few months there and just made wages.

b. *Attrib.* passing into *adj.* Modestly profitable.

1871 *Austral. Town & Country Jrnl.* (Sydney) 13 May 591/1 Nine claims are known to be on payable gold, while three or four more can obtain what is called a 'small wages prospect'. *Ibid.* 10 June 711/4 Even at this low return it is said the claim will pay; but if so, it will be merely a wages' claim, and the fortunes anticipated from it have vanished into thin air. *Ibid.* 15 July 79/3 In Rouse's paddock, the number of claims on gold is on the increase; the yield is nothing sensational, but is what is generally termed as 'good wages' ground. **1968** M.T. CLARKE *Spark of Opal* (1973) 54 The yield being enough to cover their overhead expenses—a 'wages' claim.

Wagga /ˈwɒgə/, *attrib.* and *n.* Also **Wogga, Wogger.** [Abbrev. of *Wagga Wagga* a town in s. N.S.W.: see B. quot. 1913.]

A. *attrib.* In Special Comb. **Wagga blanket, rug,** an improvised covering, usu. of sacking (see esp. quot. 1906); **pot (bell),** a cattle bell.

1933 J. TRURAN *Where Plain Begins* 143 He laid his blankets .. covering everything with what bushmen call a '**Wagga blanket**', that is, three or four wheat sacks sewn together, side by side. **1948** R. RAVEN-HART *Canoe in Aust.* 31 Though it was a blanket from Wagga, it was not a 'Wagga blanket' .. slang for an old corn-sack, used as a blanket for tramps. **1900** H. LAWSON *Over Sliprails* 62 The live cinders from the firebox .. fell in showers on deck. Every now and again a spark would burn through the '**Wagga rug**' of a sleeping shearer, and he'd wake suddenly and get up and curse. **1900** *Bulletin* (Sydney) 21 Apr. 32/2 A cast-off wool-bale is his eider-down, or, as he call [*sic*] it, his 'Wagga-rug'. **1906** *Ibid.* 9 Aug. 17/3 This is the only genuine 'Wagga rug'. Take three wheat or corn sacks and sew them together with a packing-needle and twine, side to side. Nothing more is needed. **1926** *Aussie* (Sydney) Aug. 50 The 'Wagga rug' .. was .. a split bag, but with an old woollen blanket, now too thin to keep out the cold, sewn on for lining. **1933** J. McCARTER *Love's Lunatic* 285 Back in their bedroom, Digger Whelan kicked off his elastic-side boots and sprawled on his Wagga rug. **1945** *Bulletin* (Sydney) 17 Jan. 15/4 The old chap snuggles under a pile of Wagga rugs and wallaby skins. **1960** *Ibid.* 10 Aug. 19/1 Best blanket I ever slept under was one that could be dignified as an improved Wagga-rug—two layers of corn-sacks, between which was stitched a layer of tea-tree bark. **1976** B. SCOTT *Complete Bk. Austral. Folk Lore* 380 A Wagga Rug is a sheet of paperbark between two opened out chaff bags. **1983** A.F. HOWELLS *Against Stream* 58 A bagman .. could usually find a place to doss .. unless he preferred to sleep beneath the stars under a Wagga Rug (corn sack). **1903** J. FURPHY *Such is Life* 19, I swapped her for a new thirty-by-twenty-four wool-rug, and a **Wagga pot,** good for eight or ten mile on a still night. **1946** *Hoofs & Horns* Mar. 28 The Wagga Pot .. was not quite as good as the Condamine. I believe it originated, and was made, at Wagga. It was just an oval cylinder with a flat top. **1981** A. MARSHALL *Aust.* 111 Mennicke of Wagga made a bell sometimes referred to as the 'Wagga Pot Bell'.

B. *n.* Short for *Wagga blanket, rug.*

1904 *Worker* (Sydney) 3/3 Oh the days along the river, Round the fires of bleak July, And the nights of cold and shiver In our Waggas 'neath the fly! **1913** *Bulletin* (Sydney) 27 Nov. 22/2 As for Wagga, it is written on the doors and walls of travellers' huts in three States that, in that town, age and dirt and many rents alone can save Matilda from the paws of the marauder. Hence 'Wagga' or 'tiger skin', meaning three or four frayed, disreputable bales sewn together and wrapped around a swag as an earnest of hopeless poverty. **1936** *Ibid.* 1 July 21/1 In bygone years at various times I tested All sorts of Waggas, and it's only fair To say the best 'neath which I ever rested Were wool packs which had seen a bit of wear. **1948** M. UREN *Glint of Gold* 161 The bunk consisted of oat bags sewn together and nailed on to a framework of poles. . . For winter warmth oat bags in two layers, called a 'wagga', were built. This was used as a quilt. **1957** *Overland* ix. 5 Some blankets and one of those bushman's quilts known as a 'wagga' were on the bunks. **1969** L. HADOW *Full Cycle* 248 'You must have a rug.' 'I'll be all right.' He knew they were short of coverings. She went to his camp bed. 'Take your wagga, then.' **1978** S. BALL *Mama's Boarding House* 24 As blankets became threadbare and unattractive they were converted into the ubiquitous wogger. This creation was achieved by machining two or three thin blankets together, then covering them in a flowered cretonne with a quilted stitch. The finished wogger made both a gay eiderdown and an incredibly warm covering. **1979** G. STEWART *Leveller* 20 A bagman was an unemployed person whose only possessions were bags: a water bag, a tucker bag, flour bags washed and sewn together called a Wogga; all carried in yet another bag. **1982** P. ADAM SMITH *Shearers* 207 A wagga can range from sacks sewn together and padded with 'spare' wool to the rather folksy waggas made by mothers from scraps of old warm material sewn together and padded with less respectable looking scraps of woollen odds and ends, like old socks.

waggy. [f. WAG(TAIL + -Y.] WILLY WAGTAIL.

1921 *Bulletin* (Sydney) 17 Nov. 20/3 Only three of our bush birds will attack man in defence of their nest. They are the willy-wagtail, the magpie and the butcher-bird. I think Waggy must be given the palm for downright pluck in view of his size. **1948** *Ibid.* 4 Feb. 29/3 There is a shed built from undressed bush timber where two waggies have nested for three seasons at least.

wagtail. [Transf. use of *wagtail* a small bird of the fam. Motacillidae, having a characteristic wagging tail.] Any of several small birds, usu. fantails of the fam. Muscicapidae, esp. WILLY WAGTAIL.

1831 G.F. MOORE *Diary Ten Yrs.* 4 Nov. (1884) 87 A young wagtail, which has as varied a style of singing as it has varied names, being called, besides the name just stated, razor-grinder, and superb-warbler. **1842** *S. Austral. Mag.* June 379 The liveliest of all our birds, the wagtail, with its snowy breast and deep black wings, attends our cattle as they crop the green herbage, to feast on the flies. **1889** *Proc. Linnean Soc. N.S.W.* IV. 407 *Sauloprocta motacilloides* .. known as 'Wagtail'. **1908** W.H. OGILVIE *My Life in Open* 5 The black wagtail, the 'shepherd's companion' of the Bush. **1948** P.J. HURLEY *Red Cedar* 33 Birds of all kinds found this sanctuary .. harsh-voiced friar-birds .. and cheeky wagtails. **1960** M. HENRY *Unlucky Dip* 15 The two children .. descending on the governess like a couple of wagtails harrying a peewee. **1974** BUCKLEY & HAMILTON *Festival* 71 His eyes darted like a wagtail in search of solidity.

wahbegong, var. WOBBEGONG.

waigella, waijela, varr. WADGULA.

wait-a-while. [Transf. use of *wait-a-bit* or *wait-a-while* any of several S. African thorny plants, incl. various species of *Mimosa.*] Any of several plants which may impede passage with their spiny leaves or prickles, esp. the tangled shrub *Acacia colletioides* (fam. Mimosaceae) of drier s. Aust., the similar *A. nyssophylla,* and LAWYER VINE. Also **wait-a-bit,** and *attrib.*, esp. as **wait-a-while bush.**

1889 J.H. MAIDEN *Useful Native Plants Aust.* 306 *Acacia colletioides* .. 'Wait-a-while' (a delicate allusion to the predicament of a traveller desirous of penetrating a belt of it). **1897** A.F. PATERSON *'Mid Saltbush & Mallee* 31 It is a wonder the trees ever come to maturity, but they sometimes grow in the wait-a-while bushes, then nothing can touch them. **1898** *Proc. Linnean Soc. N.S.W.* XXIII. 128 *Caesalpinia Bonducella*. . . This handsome, hooked trailer is called 'Wait-a-while' for obvious reasons. **1908** 'FIFTY-THREE YRS.' MINER' *So Long* 20 The gully was a 'rough shop', being full of 'lawyer' and 'wait-a-while' vines. **1911** ST. C. GRONDONA *Collar & Cuffs* 70 'Wait-a-bit', so-called from the difficulty experienced by a stockman in pulling a switch. **1935** E. COLEMAN *Come back in Wattle Time* 37 Spreading acacia (*A. diffusa*)—Rigid, green quadrangular phyllodes, with pungent points. Hence the bushman's name, 'Wait-a-while'. **1952** A.C.C. LOCK *Travels across Aust.* 68 Thorny ropes of 'wait-awhile' .. exercised strangle-holds. **1965** L. WALKER *Other Girl* 163 Always the men had their doze after lunch—propped against trees or under the scanty shade of a wait-a-bit bush. **1977** B. SCOTT *My Uncle Arch* 94 Little creeks hid under the tangles of wait-a-whiles and massive trees.

wait for a death, to: see DEATH.

Wakefield. *Hist.* [f. the name of Edward Gibbon *Wakefield* (1796–1862), author and colonist.] Used *attrib.* esp. in Comb. **Wakefield principle, system, theory,** to designate the application of Wakefield's doctrines of colonization to South Australia and, in a modified form, in other Australian Colonies (see quots.).

1842 *Geelong Advertiser* 9 May 4/1 Government . . is to borrow money on the '**Wakefield principle**', for colonization. **1848** J. STEPHENS *Voice from Aust.* 6 It is the first colony established on the Wakefield principle, according to which all the land was to be sold at a fixed price, and the money thus raised applied to emigration. **1852** J.D. LANG *Austral. Emigrant's Man.* 89 Land in New South Wales is sold at not less than a pound an acre, and the proceeds of such sales are expended in sending out suitable persons and families of the humbler and industrious classes, to supply the requisite amount of labour. This is what is called the 'Wakefield' principle. **1882** J. ALLEN *Hist. Aust.* 145 Its press joined with the press of the other colonies in denouncing what it called in derision the 'Wakefield', or self-supporting principle. **1839** *S. Austral. Rec.* (London) 9 Oct. 248 Comparing the operation of the **Wakefield system** in South Australia with that of the free-grant system in Canada. **1844** *Colonial Times* (Hobart) 2 June, That infamous imposture, 'the Wakefield system' . . has been productive, in a great measure, of the misery which exists in New South Wales. **1849** 'BUSHMAN' *Sidney's Austral. Handbk.* 17 The Wakefield system. The theory of this system consists in making the acquisition of land difficult, of reserving it for great capitalists, and of employing the proceeds of the land sales in importing labourers to be employed by those capitalists. **1863** F. ALGAR *Handbk. to Colony S.A.* 2 The principles of the Wakefield system were soon broken through. **1843** *N.S.W. Monthly Mag.* Oct. 619 'Sell the land to the capitalists', cried Wakefield, 'and with the proceeds export labourers to till the land thus sold.' In these few words is comprised the whole of what has somewhat ambitiously been called, 'The **Wakefield Theory** of Colonization'. **1849** *Perils, Pastimes, & Pleasures of Emigrant* 10 The 'Wakefield Theory' burst upon the world as a new discovery in economical science.

Hence **Wakefieldism** *n.*, this set of doctrines; **Wakefieldite** *n.*, WAKEFIELDIAN *n.* (*attrib.* in quot.).

1844 *Atlas* (Sydney) I. 25/2 Socialism, and **Wakefieldism,** and wild doctrines of a kindred nature run rampant. **1849** S. & J. SIDNEY *Emigrant's Jrnl.* 201 The exaggerated pictures of 'the felony of New South Wales', to use a **Wakefieldite** phrase.

Wakefieldian, *a.* and *n. Hist.* [f. WAKEFIELD.]

A. *adj.* Of or pertaining to the doctrines of Wakefield, esp. as these were implemented in South Australia.

1843 *Sydney Morning Herald* 19 Aug. 3/1 He must say from what has taken place in this colony since the introduction of the Wakefieldean system that the free grant system was the true system. **1844** *Atlas* (Sydney) I. 1/2 Some of us may think that the sudden cessation of transportation, or the application of the Wakefieldian theory to the sale of our lands . . are the sources of the mischief. **1855** W. HOWITT *Land, Labor & Gold* I. 147 The fatal Wakefieldian system of only selling colonial lands at a high price, and only where government pleases. **1858** *Illustr. Jrnl. Australasia* IV. 197 The adjoining colony of South Australia was settled on what is termed the Wakefieldian plan of colonization, the leading feature in which was 'a sufficient price'.

B. *n.* A supporter of the doctrine of Wakefield.

1847 *Heads of People* (Sydney) 18 Dec. 68/1 Arguments which have been sneered at, but never answered, by the Wakefieldians.

wake-up. Also **awake-up.**

1. An alert and resourceful person, esp. one who is alert to the possibilities of a situation.

1916 *Rising Sun: On Board 'Themistocles'* 26 Aug. (Suppl.), Now, boys, when you arrive at your destination, be the true Australian 'wake up'. **1934** W.S. HOWARD *You're telling Me!* 6 Well, I'm a wake-up; they don't get nothing out of *me*! **1944** *Austral. New Writing* 13 The average bloke in camp is very tolerant, and not a wake-up. But here is one bloke who is a wake-up! **1959** C. PEARL *So, you want to be Austral.* 24 Be warned—or as we Ordinary Australians say, be a wake-up. **1975** L.H. CLARK *Rouseabout Reflections* 100 The game was over, 'Right,' roared Snowie, 'I'm a wake-up now'; Ted pumped his hand, 'You've proved your mettle son.'

2. Passing into *adj.* In the phr. **to be** (or **take**) **a (full) wake-up** (to someone or something), to be (or become) (fully) alert to, or aware of, the intentions of a person or the possibilities of a situation.

1930 *Bulletin* (Sydney) 16 Apr. 58/2 'Cripes you're a full wake-up to that at last, are you?' Snow exclaimed. **1932** L. MANN *Flesh in Armour* 237 She would see, then, that he was no fool, and take a full wake-up to it. **1942** *Truth* (Sydney) 31 May 12/2 There is not the slightest doubt that customers are now a 'wake up' and have policed this health law themselves. **1945** D. CUSACK *Shoulder Sky* (1950) 114 No; Ginger wasn't like that. I'm awake-up to that kind. She was just nice and friendly. **1949** L. GLASSOP *Lucky Palmer* 185 Every time you make a bet kid it's four times as big as it really is. If you want a spin on say you want twenty quid on it. Spiro'll be a wake up it's for a fiver. **1957** D. WHITINGTON *Treasure upon Earth* 146, I should have been a wake up to you. I should have known you for the bastard you are. **1961** X. HERBERT *Soldiers' Women* 305 I'm a wake-up to you! I wish I'd been a wake-up from the start. **1968** W.N. SCOTT *Some People* 119 Now, this cocky was a shrewdie and he took a wake-up to Arch early on and sneaked round and watched what Arch was doing from behind the guava bushes near the dunny. **1979** S.W. DUTHIE *Fidlers Creek* 9 However the handicapper is now a wake-up to her and this day we are talking about down in the pub she gets done by half a length.

wal /wɒl/. Abbrev. of WALLOPER.

1944 *Quickmatch: Souvenir Mag. H.M.A.S. 'Quickmatch'* 42 By this time all dinner was eaten and the 'Wals' were asleep again. **1966** *Kings Cross Whisper* (Sydney) July 8/3 Rub shoulders with the socially prominent, the sportsman, the crims and maybe even a wal or two. **1968** J. ALARD *He who shoots Last* 19 Da Wals packed up young Kenny.

waler, var. WHALER *n.*[1]

waler. Also **whaler.** [f. shortened form of *New South) Wale(s + -er.*]

1. A horse bred in Australia, esp. in New South Wales, and imported into India; a light, Australian-bred horse.

1849 J. PATTISON *N.S.W.* 65 The colonial-bred horses, or Walers, as they are called in India. **1852** G.C. MUNDY *Our Antipodes* I. 265 Some of the 'Walers' have, I understand, greatly distinguished themselves in Indian racing. **1871** *Austral. Town & Country Jrnl.* (Sydney) 29 Apr. 525/3 Has finished by ruining the horse trade of the colony, and terribly damaging the character of the 'waler' in foreign markets. **1879** *Austral.: Monthly Mag.* (Sydney) II. 531 The blue flag shewed that Melbourne was leading, but the Walers were hanging in their skirts, and the two length's lead was going down. **1900** W.T. REAY *Australs. in War* 141 The second draft of horses for the Australian Regiment had arrived. . . There was a larger proportion of 'walers' in the first draft. **1919** E. DYSON *Hello, Soldier* 16 There was one pertickler whaler, known aboard ez Marshal Neigh, Whose monkey tricks with Privit Rowe was better than a play. **1930** *Bulletin* (Sydney) 2 Apr. 25/1 When old John Box drove the mail to Coonabarabran His reins were made of rawhide, his lash of kangaroo; He'd four grey Walers in his own brown shandrydan. **1956** T. RONAN *Moleskin Midas* 190 J.J. Harland, mounted on a big grey waler, trotted down to the post. **1972** *Ten Award Winning Stories* 11 For the walers and West Australian remounts who stood quietly in the sun the dry veldt was no novelty. **1981** D. STUART *I think I'll Live* 140 Australian horses. . . Couldn't find any brands I knew, but they're Walers right enough.

2. Abbrev. of NEW SOUTH WALER; also, loosely, an Australian. In quot. 1906 the reference is to the New South Wales Government.

1880 J. INGLIS *Our Austral. Cousins* 159 In the matter of awnings and verandahs the 'Walers' had a grand chance for a bright, cheerful . . display. **1891** *Truth* (Sydney) 26 Apr. 3/7 He'd better for to have plotted To rob the wealthiest bank owned by 'the Walers'. **1906** *Gadfly* (Adelaide) 11 Apr. 5/1 Item No. 7 on the agenda stands in the Wailers' name. **1943** S. BROGDEN *Sudan Contingent* 44 So the New South Welshmen lined up ashore . . trying not to grin as the Tommos found a nickname for them—'Walers'.

walk, *v. Austral. pidgin.*

a. *intr.* With **about:** to travel across country without restriction.

1828 *Sydney Gaz.* 2 Jan., When the executioner had adjusted the rope, and was about to pull the cap over his eyes . . he said, in a tone of deep feeling, which it was impossible to hear without strong emotion, 'Bail more walk about', meaning that his wanderings were all over. **1836** *Tegg's Monthly Mag.* I. 247 Black fellow make it constable good as white fellow, that look it out croppy, make it walk about. **1847** G.F. ANGAS *Savage Life & Scenes* II. 272 'Too much dibble-dibble walk about'; for they greatly fear meeting the 'dibble' or some evil spirit in their rambles. **1863** J. BONWICK *Wild White Man* 86 Ah! all gone now, all gone; only me left to walk about. **1894** *Bulletin* (Sydney) 5 May 9/3 The Bananaland free Kanaka waxes in years and in wisdom. If asked to take under 10s. a week . . he smiles and says, 'Me walk about one week.' **1916** S.A. WHITE *In Far Northwest* 21 It is a strange thing with camels, once they want (as the natives say) to 'walk about' there may be an abundance of their choicest food, yet they will ramble all night long. **1965** R. OTTLEY *By Sandhills* 38 'Me walk-about'. . . His voice hissed. . . 'Bye an' bye, maybe two, t'ree weeks, come back.'

b. *Obs.* Also **to walk all about.**

1847 J.D. LANG *Cooksland* 270 The very prohibition of the Aborigines to 'walk all about', as they express it themselves in their broken English. *Ibid.* 468 No doubt it is your own country, the place where you were born, and you have no place else to 'sit down and walk all about', to hunt and to gather *bangwall*. **1849** J.P. TOWNSEND *Rambles & Observations N.S.W.* 119 If Devil-Devil, when ' walking all about', should see the heads, and willed that it might be so, the defunct might jump-up again. **1851** H. MELVILLE *Present State Aust.* 114 Squatters take possession of the hunting grounds, the natives to whom they belong have no land to call their own—no country as they term it to 'walk all about'. **1861** J.D. LANG *Qld., Aust.* 392 You are not to 'sit down' or 'walk all about' over it, to hunt the kangaroo and opossum, or to gather *bangwall* any more.

walkabout. [f. WALK a.]

1. a. *Austral. pidgin.* One who travels on foot; a swagman or traveller. Also *attrib.*

1872 MRS J. FOOTT *Sketches Life in Bush* 28 We had visitors every day in the shape of travellers, or, as the blacks call them, 'walkabouts'. **1878** R.B. SMYTH *Aborigines of Vic.* II. 305 There are certain old men who were described to me as 'walk-about old men', who travelled among the neighbouring tribes carrying news, and were not meddled with. **1893** S. NEWLAND *Paving Way* 264 'That one stupid walk-about white fellow, bale black fellow', was their comment when spoken to on the subject. **1907** *Native Companion* Sept. 43 A motley variety of sundowners, swaggies, walkabouts, gypsies, and wanderers. **1980** L.G. FOGARTY *Kargun* 55 We must note in our minds that our people were sometimes walkabouts so our homes were everywhere.

b. *spec. Hist.* A Kanaka whose initial contract has expired and who remains in Australia: see quot. 1899. Also *attrib.* as **walkabout Kanaka.**

1895 *Bulletin* (Sydney) 21 Sept. 16/3 Again the walk-about Kanaka. It is now suggested that restrictive legislation be introduced. **1899** *Progress* (Brisbane) 13 May 1/2 The whites, even in the districts where kanaka labour is most employed, are beginning to find out that the 'walk about' is a nuisance. It appears from our exchanges that the kanaka who has put in one period of service is not compelled to enter into another engagement or go back to his island. He puts a price on his services and hangs about at Kanaka boarding-houses, until there is a scarcity of labour and he can secure full wages. **1900** *Bulletin* (Sydney) 28 Apr. 31/3 There is a numerous population of assorted niggers, the most ferocious of which is yclept the 'walk-about kanaka'. **1911** E.J. BRADY *King's Caravan* 242 He dreaded alligators and walk-about Kanakas.

2. COUNTRY 2.

1899 W.E. ROTH Rep. to Commissioner Police 3 Their walk-about extends on the one hand up the *Eastern* coast of the Peninsula as far as perhaps as the Stewart River. **1935** M. GILMORE *More Recoll.* 34 'The Dead Water' was a . . waterhole at which no black sat, because all the group in whose walk-about it had been were killed out.

3. a. A journey on foot, as undertaken by an Aboriginal in order to live in the traditional manner (esp. one undertaken as a temporary withdrawal from white society). See also PINK-EYE *n.*[2] Also *attrib.*

1910 *Bulletin* (Sydney) 22 Dec. 13/4 Shearing over,

black brother was sent off on his walk-about, the squatter supplying him with . . a few garments. **1911** E.S. SORENSON *Life in Austral. Backblocks* 43 She leaves the station with her followers pretty frequently for a 'walk-about', for the call of the wild comes irresistibly, no matter how long she has mixed with the whites. **1915** *Bulletin* (Sydney) 4 Nov. 26/1 A walkabout Binghi of the same colony of abos. told him he had been 'boned'. . . He took to his humpy, and in 10 days' time was dead meat. **1925** M. TERRY *Across Unknown Aust.* 101 Their explanation is that a 'corroboree' (native dance) must be attended, or a 'walk-about' taken for their health. **1926** L.C.E. GEE *Bush Tracks & Gold Fields* 12 The walk-about period generally synchronizes with the wet season. **1937** *Bulletin* (Sydney) 3 Mar. 20/2 Our abo. scrubfallers were on walkabout when a strange black-boy arrived. **1937** M. TERRY *Sand & Sun* 49 Mangey curs, from the camp of some walkabout blacks . . leapt up. **1938** D. BATES *Passing of Aborigines* 2 The blacks insisted on a 'pink-hi' or walkabout season—they could not live without it. **1947** W.E. HARNEY *Brimming Billabongs* (1963) 101 Walkabout time made the natives poor and eager to work when the stock season began. **1950** V.E. TURNER *Ooldea* 69 His father went off on the usual 'walkabout' after the funeral, caring nothing for the welfare of his two children. **1954** T. RONAN *Vision Splendid* 26 The timber was good walkabout country, which the open downs definitely were not. **1959** H. MYERS *Regions of Courage* 18 The regular boys and their giggling lubras were anxious to start on their walkabout, so were lined up at the store and issued dry rations—tea, flour, tobacco, sugar along with many small gifts. Their rations would be supplemented with bush tucker—wildfowl, lily roots, yams, grass-root nuts, snake and other foods. **1959** D. STUART *Yandy* 5 Others of the walkabout blackfellers might return to the evening fires empty handed, but not Warrie. **1962** D. LOCKWOOD *I, Aboriginal* 9 It was one walkabout time at Mount Saint Vidgeon in the Never-Never Land south of the Roper River that the Medicine Man, the Doctor Blackfellow, tried to kill me. **1965** A.W. UPFIELD *Lure of Bush* 74 Even the semi-civilized blacks must go on a walkabout when the call is heard; and it is the same call which urges a bushman suddenly to leave his job, break for the nearest hotel to spend his cheque, and then take his walkabout before settling again for a little while in a new job. **1969** H. HUTT *Ballad of Boot* 7 'What you're looking for', he decided, 'are 'walkabout' aborigines. That is, tribal aborigines who take an annual stroll through the bush living on snakes and roots and—er—wild biscuits and the like.' **1970** J.V. MARSHALL *Walk to Hills of Dreamtime* 19 It was the season of walkabout: the season-before-the-wet when, from all over the outback, tribes and individuals were making their way to the sites of the corroborees in the lands that had given them birth. **1979** D. LOCKWOOD *My Old Mates & I* 183 Soon he *was* an Aboriginal, able to undertake walkabouts of a hundred miles and live by his wits and hunting skill. **1979** *N.S.W. Parl. Papers* (1980–81) 3rd Sess. IV. 598 White people think walkabout is going for a walk into the bush and lying in the sun and doing a bit of fishing. Walkabout the Aboriginal way is where a man or a woman goes out to a sacred place. As you go to a cathedral the Aboriginal does this. **1984** B. DIXON *Searching for Aboriginal Lang.* 81 Rosie continued on the imaginary walkabout. Cutting out a palm-heart, and some lawyer cane, and boiling them up.

b. Quasi-*adv.* in phr. **to go** (or **send walkabout**). Also *transf.* and *fig.*

1927 R.S. BROWNE *Journalist's Memories* 291 Black brother and his spouse, or sister, or mother may 'go walk-about', and live on 'possum. **1934** *Red Star* (Perth) 6 Apr. 4/3 Also, the station manager used to hold mock courts to 'try' the blacks for offences against the management, and delivered sentences for going 'walk about' and such like. **1944** 'S. CAMPION' *Pommy Cow* 250 Oh, Mo, my mind's going walkabout. **1956** T. RONAN *Moleskin Midas* 192 Yates . . sent his blacks walkabout. **1964** *N. Austral. Monthly* Nov. 21 Even aborigines get homesick. . . About a dozen men and boys, who had been brought from Central Australia . . went walkabout, and were found about fourteen miles south of Darwin by the Welfare officers. **1973** M.T. CLARK *Spark of Opal* (rev. ed.) 212 They had to move from place to place—'go walkabout'—in search of food. **1974** *Bulletin* (Sydney) 25 May 23/1 He has noticed that maggots 'go walkabout', and after some research he learned that they look for sand or soil in which to develop to their pupae stage. **1977** T.A.G. HUNGERFORD *Wong Chu* 31 It's like the gins used to say up in the station when I'd tell them it was time they stopped going walkabout. No more, Missus.

4. a. *transf.* A period of rest; a holiday.

1908 MRS A. GUNN *We of Never-Never* 218 The day after that was filled in with preparations for a walkabout. **1912** *Bulletin* (Sydney) 10 Oct. 15/3 Mrs L. seized the biggest nulla in the camp, rushed at Sally, and laid her flat with one dreadful blow. . . The head quickly healed, but she had to take a 'walk-about' to let the storm of gossip blow over. **1934** WARBURTON & ROBERTSON *Buffaloes* 11 Blacks returning after a 'walk-about', which is their expressive term for a short holiday in Darwin, or elsewhere. **1942** J. & R. ACKLAND *Word from John* 11 May (1944) 173 Just returned from a four days' walk about, and we are not sure whether we feel the better or the worse for it as the trip included two nights in Tel Aviv. **1959** *Bulletin* (Sydney) 6 May 16/2 The latest for N.T. abos. is three weeks walkabout on full pay, as they are now holding their jobs long enough to get paid annual holidays at native resorts such as Snake Bay, Shoal Bay, and various islands. **1974** D. IRELAND *Burn* 15 You like Billy the best even though he's gone away on walkabout and Gordon's got brains and working in the city.

b. A straying; a journey; a 'look around'. Also *attrib.*

1926 A.A.B. APSLEY *Amateur Settlers* 114 The bulls go on what the blacks call a 'walk about'. **1928** R.H. CROLL *Open Road Vic.* 8 The corner of Spring and Flinders Streets . . might well serve as a starting place for a little 'walk-about', with an eye open for things of interest. **1937** *Bulletin* (Sydney) 1 Sept. 21/1 You wake up in the morning and find that your pack-prads have gone on a walkabout. **1940** *Sentry Go* (Keswick) Sept. 11/1 Our Band had a smart walk-about to Mitcham and back. **1961** *Bulletin* (Sydney) 1 Feb. 32/2 Bill Harney will come under critical scrutiny in the next few weeks as he sets out on his annual walkabout through the vast metropolitan hunting-grounds of the literary tribes. **1965** A.W. UPFIELD *Lure of Bush* 115 Whilst I take a walkabout around the place . . Mr Thorton . . would not mind making you a plan showing all the watering places. **1983** C. BINGHAM *Beckoning Horizon* 33 How far the goats roamed depended on grass and water. There was also a 'walkabout' time, which could lead to our scouring the country up to 10 miles from the township.

5. See WALKABOUT DISEASE.

walkabout disease.

a. A disease of horses, generally *Kimberley disease* (see KIMBERLEY). Also *ellipt.* as **walkabout.**

1911 *Cwlth. Parl. Papers* III. 519 There are three diseases, however, that seem to constitute drawbacks to horse breeding in this part of the country. These are commonly known as (1) the 'Walk-about' disease, which is generally fatal [etc.]. **1919** *Ibid.* (1917–19) VI. 1165 'Walk-about disease', the nature of which is yet undetermined, is responsible for an annual mortality of horses. . . The indications so far are that it is of plant poison origin, and associated with hepatic disturbance. **1932** W. HATFIELD *Ginger Murdoch* 20 Afraid to hang about that part 'cause the Birdsville weed's bad thereabouts, horses likely to get walk-about disease. **1953** J.K. EWERS *With Sun on my Back* 133 They would go foraging . . and . . find a clump of whitewood or one of the other noxious plants which, when eaten to excess caused the dread disease 'walkabout'. Year after year hundreds of horses die in the Kimberleys from this disease. **1976** C.D. MILLS *Hobble Chains & Greenhide* 1 'Walkabout' and Birdsville had taken heavy toll of our horses.

b. *transf.* and *fig.*

1951 E. HILL *Territory* 260 Wanderlust . . walkabout disease . . call it what you will. They called it 'ridin' around'.

walkabout Kanaka: see WALKABOUT 1 b.

walking man. *Obs.* SWAGMAN a.

1904 *Bulletin* (Sydney) 24 Nov. 18/2 'Any chance iv a job, mister?' said the swaggie. 'Dunno,' replied the man on the fence. 'If you like to tackle clearin' the rocks outer this yer paddock I'll gi' yer fi' bob a day. . . ' The walking man suggested 6s. **1910** *Ibid.* 7 July 13/2 The patience and long-suffering of the Australian walking-man had touching expression in rhyme.

walking-stick palm. [See quot. 1981.] The small palm *Linospadix monostachyus* (fam. Arecaceae) of s.e. Qld. and n.e. N.S.W.

1869 R.T.M. PESCOTT *W.R. Guilfoyle* (1974) 46 *Chamaedon* or walking stick palm is very plentiful. **1880** *Argus* (Melbourne) 5 Jan. 6/7 In the new conservatory the walkingstick palm of Queensland and New South Wales (Kentia monostylis). **1927** *Bulletin* (Sydney) 1 Sept. 26/4 The walking-stick palm . . is of the dwarf family, and grows abundantly on the gravelly banks of coastal ridge creeks in N.S. Wales. **1959** M. RAYMOND *Smiley roams Road* 196 Smiley plunged on . . through the walking-stick palms and tree ferns and bootlace trees. **1981** PUGH & RITCHIE *Guide to Rainforests N.S.W.* 4 Moving back into the forest you will find the smaller Walking Stick Palm, so named because its slender trunk with its knob on the end has been used for walking sticks.

walk-in, walk-out. Used to designate a method of selling a rural property, house, livestock, etc., by which the purchaser agrees to take possession unconditionally. Freq. *attrib.*

1930 *Bulletin* (Sydney) 4 June 20/1 Woolpacks acquired Whoopybilla Downs on walk-in walk-out terms. **1931** *Ibid.* 19 Aug. 21/4 If 'Bangtail' . . ever contemplates buying a cattle-run on a walk-in-walk-out basis, he would be well advised to insist on a bangtail muster. **1940** G. MORPHETT *Simple Story Rural Dev.* 4 In 1910 we sold the farm on a walk-in walk-out basis and retired to Adelaide. **1948** R.A. PEPPERALL *Emigrant to Aust.* 61 The practice common in Australia of 'Walk-in: walk-out', where it is rarely worth a settler's while to move his belongings when leaving a district owing to the high cost of transport. **1959** E. WEBB *Mark of Sun* 240 Nothing was altered in the cottage except that it was tidier than I had ever seen it before. Ana had intended to sell it, walk in, walk out. **1974** W. ROEDIGER *We Survived* 41 Dad finally sold them all to a butcher, walk-in walkout, for a trifling sum.

wallaby /ˈwɒləbi/, *n.* Formerly also with much variety, as **wallaba, wallabee, wallabi, wollaba, wollabi,** and with pl. **wallaby.** [a. Dharuk *walaba.*]

1. a. Any of many smaller marsupials of the fam. Macropodidae (see KANGAROO *n.* 1 a.), of several genera as *Macropus, Wallabia, Lagorchestes, Lagostrophus, Onychogalea, Petrogale, Thylogale,* and *Setonix.* Also *attrib.* **b.** With distinguishing epithet, as **agile, Bennett's, black-gloved, brush, hare, nail-tailed, parma, red-necked, rock, scrub, swamp, tammar, whiptail:** see under first element.

1798 D. COLLINS *Acct. Eng. Colony N.S.W.* I. 614 *Wal-li-bah,* black [kangaroo]. **1799** *Ibid.* (1802) II. 167 The grey kangooroo . . abounded in the open forest; the brushes were tenanted by the smaller black kind, or, as it is named by the natives of Port Jackson, the Wal-li-bah. **1802** Banks Papers 1 June VIII. 103 A Brush Kangoroo (Walaby) which is of a blackish colour. **1805** *Sydney Gaz.* 16 June, Then anxious, my eyes each direction pursue, Till the fleet-footed *wallaba* rises to view! **1824** *Sydney Herald* (1831) 4 July 3/1 Pheasants, and the black brush Kangaroo, called Wallaby, were plentiful. **1826** J. ATKINSON *Acct. Agric. & Grazing N.S.W.* 23 The kangaroos are of four kinds, viz. the buroo or forest kangaroo; the wallabee, or brush kangaroo [etc.]. **1827** *HRA* (1923) 3rd Ser. VI. 269 The only kind of much nutriment is a Grass in miniature on which the Wallabies feed. **1833** W.H. BRETON *Excursions* 251 Wallaba. Dark brown: it is found in brushes. **1835** T.B. WILSON *Narr. Voyage round World* 201 The dogs . . caught two *wallabi.* **1838** *Proc. Zool. Soc. London* VI. 23 Mr Ogilvy exhibited and characterized, under the name of *Macropus rufiventer,* a new species of Kangaroo which Mr Gould had received from Tasmania, where it is known by the name of Wallabee. **1839** *Southern Austral.* (Adelaide) 10 May 3/5 We have occupied their country—driven away their food—their kangaroos, their emu, their wallaby. **1844** *Dispatch* (Sydney) 27 Jan. 2/3 We trust a good collection of Kangaroos, Wild-dogs, Oppossums, Wollabi . . and wild Indians, will be got together to welcome the strangers, and we doubt not Zoological gardens on an extensive scale may soon be formed. **1845** E.J. EYRE *Jrnls. Exped. Central Aust.* I. 48 Several of a species of wallabie, very much resembling a hare in flavour, were shot. **1849** W. CARRON *Narr. Exped. Rockingham Bay & Cape York* 57 Wall shot a wallaby of a light grey colour, long soft fur, and rather bushy tail. **1852** *Austral. Gold Digger's Monthly Mag.* i. 21 The Wallaby of Tasmania is the Red-bellied Kangaroo, having a short black tail, brown back, and reddish-yellow belly. **1852** W. HUGHES *Austral. Colonies* 78 The wallabi is comparatively small in size; it makes an excellent soup. **1856** *Jrnl. Australasia* I. 112 A porcupine and a wollaba had been caught. **1874** *Austral. Handbk.* 71 The kangaroo takes precedence in size. . . Wallabys and paddy-melons are a smaller species. **1888** 'R. BOLDREWOOD' *Robbery under Arms* (1937) 25 Where's he to get a big mob there in that mountainous, beastly place, where the cattle all bolt like wallabies. **1902** R.C. PRAED *My Austral. Girlhood* 125 At four o'clock, the wallabis stir, and towards dusk, the curlews begin their melancholy wail. **1916** D.V. HACKETT *Austral. Household Guide* 574 *Wallaby, roasted.* Take 1 wallaby, some veal forcemeat, milk and butter. **1946** M. FRANKLIN *My Career goes Bung* 51 The skilled shearers had not yet returned to their little homes in the wallaby scrubs around us. **1952** B. BEATTY *Unique to Aust.* 26 The smaller Wallabies are a miniature species living in hill and scrub country. Apart from size there is little difference between kangaroos and wallabies. **1970** W.D.L. RIDE *Guide Native Mammals Aust.* 44 In some parts of Australia, and in particular where great kangaroos are rare, such as in Tasmania, or in the Kimberley, the local people may refer to large wallabies as kangaroos. **1984** B. DIXON *Searching for Aboriginal Lang.* 23 Among the rich jungle vegetation . . bustled wallabies.

2. a. WALLABY TRACK 2 a., esp. in the phr. **on the wallaby.**

1867 *Austral. Monthly Mag.* (Melbourne) IV. 41, I have just had a row with my people and am off anywhere, on the *wallabee*, to try my luck. **1871** *Illustr. Sydney News* 23 Dec. 210/1 Men 'on the wallaby' are those who continue to exist without a settled home and with little work or none at all. **1886** 'THIRTY-FIVE YRS. COLONIST' *Hard Times* 22 We find . . thousands on the 'wallaby' looking for work. **1893** J.A. BARRY *Steve Brown's Bunyip* 126 I'm on the wallaby, looking for shearing, and, worse luck, haven't got no gold. **1903** *Bulletin* (Sydney) 2 May 35/1 He began his training for the wallaby when he started going to school. **1915** A.J. DAWSON *Rec. N. Freyden* 86 It would be necessary for him . . to pack his swag and be off 'on the wallaby'; on the tramp, that is, putting in an occasional day's work, where this might offer, and sleeping in the bush. **1927** *Bulletin* (Sydney) 28 July 27/1 The man on the wallaby almost invariably makes his night-camp under a tree. **1946** D. BARR *Warrigal Joe* 8 I'm on the wallaby, but don't mind takin' a job; so long as you do all the work! **1962** J.T. LANG *Great Bust* 214 Question time had passed uneventfully on June 19, 1930. Speaker Norman Makin was in the chair. A Labor member wanted to know whether the unemployed on the wallaby could draw rations in Canberra. **1974** M. TERRY *War of Warramullas* 143 A station cook . . had taken to the wallaby and camped with me in western Queensland.

b. *transf.* and *fig.* The 'circuit'; **on the wallaby,** on the move.

1887 *Bulletin* (Sydney) 19 Nov. 5/1 An obviously inspired paragraph is going the journalistic wallaby—we have even seen it in the Argus and S.M.H. **1906** *Ibid.* 19 Apr. 14/3 In Central Australia the black . . is incessantly 'on the wallaby', so as to procure food. **1913** H. LAWSON *For Aust.* 50 But Freedom's on the Wallaby, She'll knock the tyrants silly. **1918** *7th Field Artillery Brigade Yandoo* June 105 Next morning, the Brigade was on the 'wallaby'. **1973** P. ADAM SMITH *Barcoo Salute* 2 Up to the age of seventy my mother was still 'on the wallaby' even with the frugal means at her disposal. However, to the surprise of everyone who knows her, she has now lived in the same house for four unbroken years, the longest residence in any one place in her life.

3. An itinerant rural worker; SWAGMAN a. Also *attrib.*

1869 M. CLARKE *Peripatetic Philosopher* 41 At the station where I worked for some time (as 'knock-about man') three cooks were kept during the 'wallaby' season—one for the house, one for the men, and one for the travellers. **1890** *Quiz* (Adelaide) 19 Dec. 17/2 One of the boys of the olden time had been working for this Croesus. . . When the employer had made up the accounts . . the wallaby took his cheque. **1898** *Bulletin* (Sydney) 8 Oct. 15/2 When I wore the Order of the Wallaby . . swag was fastened near the ends with the binders. **1918** *Ibid.* 19 Dec. 22/1 The queerest strike I ever bumped was in a wallaby camp on the Maranoa. **1927** W. BLACKET *May it please your Honour* 2 Clearly, if either of these events was to be described as a 'lynching' it could prove 'one of them wallabies' that the selector, following the precedent established by the late Mr Weller, suggested that his attorney should get in order to secure his acquittal at the Quarter Sessions holden at Woop Woop. **1956** H. FRAUCA *In New Country* 59 We didn't know his kind existed in Australia any longer, but there he was, a real swagman walking down the road. . . We waved at him but he didn't wave back at us. 'He's probably a 'wallaby',' said Wally. **1976** B. SCOTT *Complete Bk. Austral. Folk Lore* 207 And when our cheques are drained we will take the road again, Lime-burners in the Wallaby Brigade.

4. *pl.* The name of the Australian international Rugby Union team; in *sing.*, a member of such a team. Cf. KANGAROO *n.* 3 b. and SOCCEROO.

1908 *Referee* (Sydney) 4 Nov. 9/2 The discussion as to the name by which the team should be called was settled by the 'Daily Mail' wiring to the 'Wallabies', asking them to choose and nominate their sobriquet. They duly chose the name 'Wallabies' at a special meeting. 'Rabbits' has, therefore, been dropped by many papers. **1939** *Sydney Morning Herald* 26 Oct. 13/1 *Wallabies 'cruise' ends.* . . The New South Wales and Queensland members of the Australian Rugby Union team, the Wallabies, returned to Sydney yesterday morning. **1947** *Ibid.* 5 Aug. 10/6 The Wallabies sip afternoon tea ruefully watching other passengers demolish pastries. **1957** *Sun* (Sydney) 13 Apr. 5/1 If original plans stand the Australian Rugby Union selectors on August 25 will name 30 players to make what is regarded as the best sporting trip available to Australians. *Twenty three* days later they will set off—as the Wallabies—for the United Kingdom on a tour that will take in France, Italy and the USA. **1976** *Austral.* (Sydney) 22 Oct. 20/1 Driving rain, a wet ball and slippery conditions put the Wallabies on the way to the third defeat of their French Rugby Union tour yesterday.

5. Comb. **wallaby hunt, hunting, scalp, skin, stew, trap, trapping.**

1896 *Bulletin* (Sydney) 4 July 28/1 When it was not a bees-nest to chop out it was a **wallaby-hunt,** or an unbranded calf. **1885** D.E. MCCONNELL *Austral. Etiquette* 467 It is impossible to devote space to a full description of the exciting and pleasurable features of kangaroo-hunting, or of that other native sport, **wallaby-hunting,** which latter is pursued in a similar way to kangarooing, though the subject is a tempting one. **1885** *Bulletin* (Sydney) 5 Dec. 10/4 Kangaroo scalps are paid for at the rate of 9d. each. . . **Wallaby scalps** are only worth 4d. **1906** *Ibid.* 21 June 17/2 Two scalpers entered a liquor house in Springsure (C.Q.), ordered two pints, and passed a dingo scalp over the bar in payment. Mrs Public-house . . handed over as change three wallaby scalps. **1832** BACKHOUSE & TYLOR *Life & Labours G.W. Walker* 12 Oct. (1862) 104 The natives carried our bush apparatus, consisting of one of our water-proof covers, a **wallaby-skin** coverlet [etc.]. **1845** C. HODGKINSON *Aust., Port Macquarie to Moreton Bay* 213, I was riding in the forest . . attired in . . thin Wallabi-skin boots. **1877** H. TAYLOR *Emigration S.A.* 20 Tanning is a growing industry; the wallaby skin, tanned and dressed, is said to make the very finest and most durable leather, much superior to kid. **1891** J.J. ROCHE *Life J.B. O'Reilly* 648 You smoke? That's good for there's plenty of weed In that wallaby skin. **1930** 'BRENT OF BIN BIN' *Ten Creeks Run* (1952) 81 Aileen flung herself on the wallaby-skin beside her bed. **1938** D. BATES *Passing of Aborigines* 50 Three pairs of laced wallaby-skin shoes. **1895** *Devil in Sydney* 61, I consider a **wallaby stew** one of the greatest delicacies a person can sit down to. **1905** A.B. PATERSON *Old Bush Songs* 44 Quondong duff, paddy-melon pie, and wallaby Irish stew We used to eat while reaping for the stringy-bark cockatoo. **1974** *Austral. Folksongs* (Folk Lore Council Aust.) 102 Stir the wallaby stew, make soup of the kangaroo tail, I tell you things are pretty crook since Dad got put in gaol! **1930** 'BRENT OF BIN BIN' *Ten Creeks Run* (1952) 246 Abracadabra, a mountain-bred horse, had fallen into old Billy Heffernan's **wallaby-traps.** **1906** *Bulletin* (Sydney) 18 Oct. 44/1 Dave goes to look after his private enterprise of **wallaby trapping,** and Dad to the 'cultivation' he has already spent months clearing.

6. Special Comb. **wallaby drive,** an operation in which wallabies are herded, trapped and slaughtered, or otherwise hunted; **jack,** a heavy-duty, lever-action jack used for lifting logs, stumps, etc. (see also FOREST DEVIL, *kangaroo jack* KANGAROO *n.* 6); **net,** a net used by Aborigines to snare wallabies; **rug,** a rug made from wallaby skin; **tail,** the tail of a wallaby as an article of food, esp. *attrib.* as **wallaby-tail soup.**

1882 *Bulletin* (Sydney) 15 July 13/1 A **Wallaby drive** took place in the Bulli Mountains last week. **1897** *Western Champion* (Barcaldine) 31 Aug. 3/1 At a wallaby drive outside Gulgong recently 307 kangaroos and wallabys were killed. **1923** T. HALL *Short Hist. Downs Blacks* 20 No woman took part in the wallaby drive. **1949** B. O'REILLY *Green Mountains* 247 No manly old-world sport ever came so near to real warfare as did that true Australian sport, the Wallaby Drive, and it is easy to see the influence of its traditions in the Australian Light Horse. **1906** *Australasian* (Melbourne) 7 July 2/4 The **wallaby jack** is suitable for a great variety of purposes, besides the usual stump grubbing. **1909** *Anthony Hordern Catal.* 867 Trewhella's Wallaby Jack . . to lift 2½ tons . . Trewhella's Monkey Jack with Guide and 3 Spears. **1914** *Australasian* (Melbourne) 21 Mar. 642/3 'Monkey' winches 'monkey' and 'wallaby' jacks, that will save your time, increase your cultivation area, and, incidentally, your profits. **1920** *Hardware & Machinery* 30 June (Advt.) 58 'Wallaby jacks' are valuable assistants in any Lifting, Pulling Old Fences, Stump Grubbing, Log Rolling, &c. We make a large assortment of patented Stump and Tree Pullers. **1931** *Ibid.* 27 Apr. 17 'Wallaby jacks' are valuable assistants in any Lifting, Pulling Old Fences, Stump Grubbing, Log Rolling, etc. **1949** B. O'REILLY *Green Mountains* 107 The great pine trees were felled and 'barked'. . . Finally, with the aid of wallaby jacks they were set in motion and shot like meteors to the bottom of the gorge. **1883** E. PALMER *Plants N. Qld.* 18 A tall, shady tree, called Kurrijong. . . Inside bark worked up into strong cord for **wallaby nets** and bags. **1923** T. HALL *Short Hist. Downs Blacks* 11 It was the duty of the old women and widows to teach the girls to cook the food and train the children, also to make . . wallaby nets. **1832** BACKHOUSE & TYLOR *Life & Labours G.W. Walker* 12 Oct. (1862) 105 We composed ourselves to rest, making the best use we could of the **wallaby rug.** **1839** W.H. LEIGH *Reconnoitering Voyages* 141 We had no bed but a bundle of rags, in a frail rush hut, which admitted the rain most copiously. We had, however, a wallaba rug. **1892** 'R. BOLDREWOOD' *Nevermore* II. 159 Lance was invited to avail himself of a comfortable shake-down, where . . wallaby rugs protected him from the searching night air. **1839** W.H. LEIGH *Reconnoitering Voyages* 126 The **wallaba tails** again continually passing round our circle, to enable every one to suit himself. **1852** G.C. MUNDY *Our Antipodes* I. 43, I found myself sipping doubtfully . . a plate of wallabi-tail soup. **1930** HIVES & LUMLEY *Jrnl. of Jackaroo* 68 Drank the wallaby-tail soup. **1979** D. LOCKWOOD *My Old Mates & I* 69 And wallaby tail soup! She has a recipe she could sell for a thousand dollars if enough people were hungry castaways with money to spend.

7. In the names of flora and fauna: **wallaby grass,** any of many perennial grasses, usu. of the genus *Danthonia* (fam. Poaceae) of Aust. and elsewhere, typically fine-leaved tussocky plants valued as winter fodder; **rat** *Tas.*, the long-nosed potoroo *Potorous tridactylus apicalis.*

1889 J.H. MAIDEN *Useful Native Plants Aust.* 82 *Danthonia penicillata* . . '**Wallaby Grass**'. This perennial grass is useful for artificial mixed pasture. **1897** L. LINDLEY-COWEN *W. Austral. Settler's Guide* 409 *Danthonia semiannularis* . . 'Wallaby' grass. **1898** *Proc. Linnean Soc. N.S.W.* XXIII. 143 *Oplismenus compositus* . . var. *setarius.*—On the island [*sc.* Lord Howe Is.] they call it 'Wallaby Grass' and 'Dog's Medicine Grass'. The origin of the latter name is obvious; that of the former not so, as there are no wallabies on the island. **1923** E. BREAKWELL *Grasses & Fodder Plants N.S.W.* 229 *Danthonia* grasses . . often receive the names Silver-top, White-top or Fluffy-top. The old vernacular name, Wallaby grass, is not now nearly so common. **1935** C.W. WINDERS *Managem. Sown Pastures* 713 The native pasture, as such, is very valuable on the Downs, as it contains a large proportion of winter-growing species, such as wallaby grass. **1979** DOUGLAS & HEATHCOTE *Far Cry* 14 After the trees had fallen there was a thick growth of wallaby grass which choked out the wild-flowers, but was good fodder. **1909** G. SMITH *Naturalist in Tas.* 85 Besides the Wallabies, there are two similarly shaped animals known as Kangaroo and **Wallaby Rats** (*Bettongia cuniculus* and *tridactylus*), small black creatures about the size of a Hare. **1954** C. BARRETT *Wild Life Aust. & New Guinea* 11 The 'wallaby-rat' of Tasmania is one of the long-nosed, broad-faced rat-kangaroos, called *potoroos* by the natives who lived around Port Jackson.

wallaby /ˈwɒləbi/, *v. Obs.* [f. WALLABY *n.* 2.] *intr.* To journey through the country, to go 'on the wallaby track'.

1885 *Australasian Printers' Keepsake* 26 The white-folk wallaby, in numbers vast, Fill all the valleys where my fathers sprang when Jacky Jacky hurled his boomerang. **1906** *Bulletin* (Sydney) 31st May 40/2 So you wallaby and wander North and South, and East and West.

wallaby track.

1. The path worn by a wallaby.

1846 J.L. Stokes *Discoveries in Aust.* II. 390 In some parts of the tall scrub were wallaby tracks. **1926** A.S. Le Souef et al. *Wild Animals Australasia* 189 *M. ualabatus*, known as the black and also as the swamp wallaby, inhabits scrubby damp gullies, through which it has well-marked paths or 'wallaby tracks'.

2. a. *transf.* The route followed by one who journeys through the country in search of seasonal work (but see also quot. 1871); esp. in the phr. **on the wallaby track.**

1849 *Stephen's Adelaide Miscellany* 4 Oct. 42 The police themselves are usually well-treated in the bush . . they make a 'round' through the district, and get a meal at every hut, and one man from every said hut (besides those mobs on the 'wallaby track') stops for a night at the police-station in return. **1861** *Bell's Life in Sydney* 9 Nov. 4/2 And once more we were on the 'Wallaby Track' making our way from Cowra to 'the Flat'. **1871** *Illustr. Sydney News* 18 Mar. 154/1 'On the Wallaby track'. This expression designates a peculiar phase of Australian life. It is applied to a class of men who contrive to exist in the bush without a home, and, in a great measure, without work. **1887** 'Australian' *Our Homes* 8 With billy in hand and my swag at my back, I wander away on the Wallaby track. **1900** R. Bruce *Benbonuna* (1904) 70 The station hands, many of whom soon found themselves on what they called the 'wallaby track'—walking from station to station in search of employment, with their sole worldly effects rolled tightly as a 'swag' in a pair of red or blue blankets, and strapped to their shoulders. **1918** J.P. O'Donnell *Songs of Anzac* 15 Give me gums and the whiff of the wattle, The Wallaby track all the day. **1932** J. Truran *Green Mallee* 217 South Australia was still a long way off; too far for sore feet that were not used to the wallaby-track. **1974** *Austral. Folksongs* (Folk Lore Council Aust.) 59 The hills and the plains are well trodden By the men of the wallaby track. **1979** W.D. Joynt *Breaking Road for Rest* 21 We decided to put swags on our backs and go 'on the wallaby track'.

b. A tramp.

1865 *Sydney Punch* 23 Sept. 555/1 The principal animals in the district are wallaby tracks, and the principal birds, Cockatoo settlers.

Hence **wallaby tracker** *n.*

1888 E. Finn *Chron. Early Melbourne* I. 371 The 'wallaby trackers' would, on a certain evening, treat all the blacks that might cross the river. **1904** *Bulletin* (Sydney) 14 Apr. 15/2 Of all the wallaby-trackers' substitutes and make-shifts for tobacco I find honeysuckle . . the best-flavoured. **1905** *Ibid.* 12 Oct. 15/2, I have read . . about the mystic signs Hindu hawkers, wallaby trackers, etc. leave behind them to signify the dispositions of residents along the tracks of trade, truck and cadge.

wallaroo /wɒlə'ru/. [a. Dharuk *walaru.*] Any of several large, stocky kangaroos of rocky or hilly country, most commonly *Macropus robustus*, esp. the dark, shaggy-haired *M. robustus robustus* of N.S.W. and s. Qld.; Hill kangaroo. See also Euro, *rock kangaroo* Rock *n.* 2. Also *attrib.*

1826 J. Atkinson *Acct. Agric. & Grazing N.S.W.* 24 There is also found far in the interior another variety, called wallaroos. **1835** *Proc. Zool. Soc. London* II. 151 A specimen was exhibited of a *Kangaroo*, recently brought from New Holland, by Capt. Sir W. Edward Parry, R.N.. . . Mr Bennett . . stated it to be his intention to describe it in detail under the name of *Macropus Parryi*. . . The animal in question is known to the natives in the neighbourhood of Port Stephens (lat. 32° S.) by the name of *Wŏllăroo*. **1845** L. Leichhardt *Jrnl. Overland Exped. Aust.* (1847) 17 Nov. 481 Charley shot a Wallooroo just as it was leaping, frightened by our footsteps, out of its shady retreat to a pointed rock. **1891** *Bulletin* (Sydney) 19 Dec. 19/4, I bought a run a while ago, On country rough and ridgy, Where wallaroos and wombats grow—The Upper Murrumbidgee. **1899** R. Semon *In Austral. Bush* 256 The Australian colonists call all the larger kinds 'kangaroos', and only designate one big, heavy and nearly black species peculiar to mountainous districts (*Macropus robustus*) as 'Wallaroo'. **1924** *Bulletin* (Sydney) 27 Nov. 4/2 One of my tame grey wallaroos died, leaving a joey four months old in the pouch. **1943** S.W. Keough *Around Army* 57 What sort of gay-and-frisky do you call this, Arthur? I've tasted better stuff in a billabong full of dead wallaroos. **1974** *Southerly* ii. 147 I'd like a nice black wallaroo rug for my room. **1985** *New Idea* (Melbourne) 7 Dec. 25/1 Some of their more adventurous charges, such as a resident wallaroo, wander off into the bush.

wall-cuff. *Obs.* A manacle securing a prisoner's wrist to a wall-staple.

1892 *Bulletin* (Sydney) 2 July 21/4 'I thought he was celled?' 'So he is, sir. No. 5!' 'And ironed?' 'Trumpeters—fifteen's [*sic*]—and wall-cuffs!' **1937** W. & T.I. Moore *Best Austral. One-Act Plays* 262 You can gi'e me double darbies, solitary, wall cuffs, tube-gag, trumpeters . . . I don't give a bugger.

wallom, var. Wallum.

wallop. [Used elsewhere but recorded earliest in Aust.: see OEDS *sb.* 4 c.] Alcoholic liquor, esp. beer. Also *attrib.*

1871 *Austral. Town & Country Jrnl.* (Sydney) 1 Apr. 389/3 Not everybody . . does care about . . the real Tooth's, or Castlemine, or Parramatta, or even the renowned 'wallop' of the Western line. **1901** *Tocsin* (Melbourne) 22 Aug. 4/4 We was in the pub down near the river this morning, when the 'special' wot was supposed to be watching it came in for his drop of wallop. **1909** *Bulletin* (Sydney) 7 Jan. 39/2 Jigger . . made for Mander's wallop shop. **1933** *Ibid.* 15 Nov. 20/1 A skinful of wallop like this, by the Fates, Would leave us, I reckon, in perilous straits.

walloper. [f. *wallop, v.* to beat, belabour.] A policeman; also *transf.* (see quot. 1968).

1945 S.J. Baker *Austral. Lang.* 137 We also call a policeman a . . walloper. **1950** F.J. Hardy *Power without Glory* 33 Police! Everyone out! The bloody wallopers are on their way! **1963** J. O'Grady *Things they do to You* 141 Fifty or sixty knots in a thirty-mile zone, an' a motor-cycle walloper gets on his tail. **1968** F. Rose *Aust. Revisited* 78 'We're from the Attorney General's Department.' The Australian Security Intelligence Organisation was nominally under the control of the Attorney General's Department although answerable only to the Prime Minister. *So that's it: two Security wallopers.* **1974** N. Phillipson *As Other Man* 91 'Have you ever been in the hands of the police?' . . Even if the wallopers did believe his story, Mike would tear him limb from limb. **1983** A.F. Howells *Against Stream* 25 The two wallopers dragged him to his feet and tried to frog-march him off.

wallow. *Mining. S.A.* [Poss. f. *wallow* to abound (in wealth, etc.).] A rich deposit of ore.

1914 *Wallaroo & Moonta Mines* 20 These [deposits] formed a series of small 'bonanzas' ('wallows' in local phrase). **1962** O. Pryor *Aust.'s Little Cornwall* 52 A very rich pocket of ore was known as a 'wallow'. The largest wallow found at Moonta was struck in the Prince Alfred shaft in 1870.

wallum /'wɒləm/. Formerly also **wallom.** [a. Gabi *waalum.*] **a.** The shrub or tree *Banksia aemula* (fam. Proteaceae) of s.e. Qld. and e. N.S.W. **b.** The sandy coastal heathland in which the plant grows; more generally, an area of coastal heath (see quots. 1979 and 1980). Also *attrib.*, esp. as **wallum country.**

1861 J.D. Lang *Qld., Aust.* 122 Good agricultural country, intersected by patches of wallom flats and tea-tree swamps. **1869** *Wallaroo Times* (Kadina) 12 May 6/1 He must have passed over many miles of country thickly studded with 'wallum' or stemless grass-tree. **1876** 'Eight Yrs.' Resident' *Queen of Colonies* 104 Patches of most excellent land will be found here and there, usually on the banks of the streams, which will abruptly terminate in that worst of all coast-land 'wallum country', as it is called, from the native name of the shrub which principally grows on it. The soil in this wallum country is of the vilest description, producing scarcely any grass and only a few stunted honeysuckle and gum-trees, besides the never-ending wallum. **1879** 'Australian' *Adventures Qld.* 24 The country soon became rougher, and the grass trees and *wallum* so thick, as to render a slower pace absolutely necessary. **1929** A.H. Chisholm *Birds & Green Places* 156 In the wallum country there is at least one bird, the swamp-parrot, unknown to any other island (except Tasmania) and very rare on the mainland. **1938** C.T. White *Princ. Bot. Qld. Farmers* 209 The term 'Wallum' is applied in Queensland to barren country in the coastal belt covering large areas, particularly in the Moreton Bay, Wide Bay, and Harvey Bay districts. It consists largely of peat swamps, in some places very wet, alternating with sandy ridges covered with a fairly dense woodland consisting of low, stunted eucalypts, *Banksia aemula*, &c. This latter is the characteristic tree of much of the sandy tracts, and is itself known as 'Wallum'. **1967** E. Huxley *Their Shining Eldorado* 357 A Banksia shrub known as wallum (*Banksia aemula*), all gnarled and twisted branches and greeny-grey leaves, with a bottle brush flower. **1979** K.A.W. Williams *Native Plants Qld.* I. 70 In many parts of coastal Queensland south of the Tropic of Capricorn, there are areas of forest, woodland and heathland that have developed on acid, sandy soils of sandhills, sand dunes, and on flat or gently undulating sandy country with a high water table. Generally these areas are known as 'Wallum', a name derived from the Aboriginal word for *Banksia aemula*, a conspicuous tree of the habitat. **1980** E. McDonald *Wildflowers of Wallum* Dustjacket, Nowadays, by popular consent, the term 'Wallum' is not confined to the heathy country on which the Wallum tree grows, but is used to include all parts of the coastal lowlands having low natural fertility but which yet enjoys high rainfall. It embraces a wide variety of habitats. **1983** B. Corbett *Fistful of Buttercups* 163 The summer rains started in the wallum country, then moved westwards into the Dividing Range.

walnut. [Transf. use of *walnut* a tree of the genus *Juglans.*] Any of several trees, usu. of the fam. Lauraceae, having attractively figured wood supposed to resemble that of the Northern Hemisphere walnut; the wood of the tree. Also *attrib.*, and with distinguishing epithet, as *Queensland walnut* (see Queensland 2).

1926 *Qld. Agric. Jrnl.* XXV. 437 *Beilschmiedia elliptica* . . Walnut (Fraser Island). **1944** J. Devanny *By Tropic Sea & Jungle* 130 Some of our hardwoods compare with the soft woods for beauty. The heavy dark walnut for one. **1965** *Austral. Encycl.* IX. 150 Walnut. . . The name is . . given in the Australian timber trade to the woods of various trees of the laurel family. **1985** *Age* (Melbourne) 31 Oct. 11/3 There is no evidence that the animals which cannot survive in logged areas move to unlogged areas. People sitting at their blackbean and walnut tables don't think about that.

wambat, var. Wombat.

wambenger /'wɒmbɛŋgə/. [Poss. a. Nyungar *wambanoŋ.*] Phascogale 1 a.

1928 *Pop. Names for Marsupials* (Public Library, Museum, & Art Gallery W.A., Museum Leaflet no. 1), *Phascogale penicillata* . . Wambenger. **1955** *Bulletin* (Sydney) 28 Dec. 12/4 The brush-tailed phascogale (or wambenger), is disturbing poultry in the lower sou'-west. **1970** W.D.L. Ride *Guide Native Mammals Aust.* 112 The wambengers are arboreal and appear usually to make their nests in hollows.

wampoo pigeon, var. Wompoo pigeon.

wanderer. [See quot. 1926.] The migratory, predom. reddish-brown and black butterfly *Danaus plexippus* of Aust. and elsewhere.

1926 J. Pollard *Bushland Man* 227, I captured an interesting fellow . . one of the 'wanderers', a fine big fellow with golden-feathered wings, the veins forming a mazy black pattern. It had brushy feet and a downy body. . . He is well called a wanderer, for he is known in many countries. . . He has another name 'monarch'. **1948** R. Raven-Hart *Canoe in Aust.* 192 Butterflies came and sat on the rocks beside us as we sun-dried, fine big things with glowing red-brown wings that Robin called 'Wanderers'. **1986** *Age* (Melbourne) 6 May 36/3 You will see Common Browns floating through your garden and throughout the countryside. Do not confuse this butterfly with the Monarch or Wanderer, a butterfly that is also reasonably common in Victoria. This large and darker orange-brown butterfly has distinctive black wings, veins and margins to the wings. It is an American butterfly that spread to Australia and other parts of the world more than 100 years ago.

Wandjina /wɒn'dʒinə/. Also **Wondjina.** [a. Ngarinjin *warnjina* the quasi-ancestor, the one who lies across (mythological) time and law; f. *warn* across + *djina* this one.] A category of spirit people depicted in rock paintings of the Kimberley Ranges in Western Australia: see esp. quot. 1969.

1930 *Oceania* I. 259, I shall describe the paintings of this site... The most striking of these is a large man, about thirteen feet from the sole of his foot to the top of his hair, depicted horizontally along the rock-face. He has eyes and nose but no mouth. His face is partly surrounded by a horse-shoe shaped head-dress. [*Note*] Figures of this kind are called *wondjina* in the language. **1938** A.P. Elkin *Austral. Aborigines* 179 Each gallery includes at least one painting of a personal being known as Wondjina, associated with the sky, rain, rainbow, the rainbow-serpent, spirit-children and the increase of natural species. **1958** E.D. McCarthy *Austral. Aboriginal Rock Art* 53 Of all the pictographs in Australia none has caused so much interest nor produced a larger body of literature than the huge Wandjina .. paintings of the Kimberleys. **1969** Edwards & Guerin *Aboriginal Bark Paintings* 23 The Wandjinas of the Kimberleys are creative ancestral beings. When first discovered their white bodies and halo-like headdresses led to some fanciful theories linking them with Christian myths... To the Aborigines, the Wandjinas are not just paintings, but spirits.

wandoo /wɒn'du/. Formerly also **wando.** [a. Nyungar *wandu.*] The tree *Eucalyptus wandoo* (syn. *E. redunca* var. *elata*; fam. Myrtaceae) of s.w. W.A., usu. having a smooth mottled white or grey bark; the very hard, strong, durable wood of the tree. Also *attrib.*

1837 G.F. Moore *Evidences Inland Sea* 15 The trees are .. Wando (white gum with a rusty tinge). **1893** A.F. Calvert *W.A. & its Gold Fields* 16 *Eucalyptus redunca* (or Wandoo) the principal white gum-tree of Western Australia, derives its name from the hue of its bark, which on friction imparts a white colour. **1897** L. Lindley-Cowen *W. Austral. Settler's Guide* 108 The valley of the Marradong through to the Williams river is a comparatively narrow strip of good land, 40 miles long, timbered with wando, white gum, blue and red gums. **1908** J. Mann *Suitability Australasian Timber* 4 Timbers in which the grain is closely twisted and interwoven, are in general very hard, dense, and heavy... Such timbers as wandoo [etc.]. **1929** *Bulletin* (Sydney) 24 July 23/4 Westralian wandoo .. will show points to supplejack .. for toughness. **1948** H.A. Lindsay *Bushman's Handbk.* 13 Jarrah saplings are full of water and so are those of the karri and wandoo. **1956** N.K. Wallis *Austral. Timber Handbk.* 8 Wandoo (heavy constructional work, waggon building, sleepers and cross-arms) is in limited supply. **1966** *Realist* (Sydney) xxiv. 20 They rode out .. into the bush, picnicking by the dry creek-bed in the shade of the white wandoos. **1981** J.P. Gabbedy *Forgotten Pioneers* 72, I was one of a busy-bee group .. cutting wandoo poles for our tennis court fence.

wanga-wanga, var. Wonga-wonga.

wangi, var. Wongi *v.*

wangie, var. Wongi *n.*[1]

wanna /'wɒnə/. Also **wonna, wonnah.** [a. Nyungar (and other w. Austral. languages) *wana.*] An Aboriginal digging-stick. Also *attrib.*

1841 G. Grey *Jrnls. Two Exped. N.-W. & W.A.* II. 320 They came .. slowly forward with their *wan-nas* (a long stick they use for digging up roots) in their hands. **1878** R.B. Smyth *Aborigines of Vic.* II. 276 The old hag .. perfectly naked, but grasping a *wanna* in both hands, was running backwards and forwards before her hut. **1895** *Trans. & Proc. R. Soc. S.A.* (1896) XVI. 254 The 'wanna' and the 'wera' are the constantly accompanying implements of the blacks of the interior... The wanna is used for loosening the soil .. and with the wera the loosened stuff is scooped up. **1902** *Proc. R. Soc. Qld.* (1903) 69 The ordinary yam-stick (won-na) was a rounded piece of wood, not quite as thick as a broom-handle, about 6 feet long, scraped, and hardened with fire at one extremity. **1920** *Smith's Weekly* (Sydney) 25 Sept. 17/4 In the northern parts of West Australia the gins all carry a stick about five feet long and 1½ inches thick (the 'wonnah'), which they use when digging for grubs. **1950** V.E. Turner *Ooldea* 109 The women carried the babies on their backs and a 'weerah' full of water on their heads, leaving the hands free .. for the inevitable 'wonna', or digging stick. **1962** B.W. Leake *Eastern Wheatbelt Wildlife* 57 The women never failed to carry a Wanna stick. One of these would be about five feet long and one and a half inches in diameter, made out of a white gum or jamwood sapling.

wap, var. Wop.

waratah /'wɒrətə/. Formerly also **warata, warratah, warrataw, warrettah.** [a. Dharuk *warata.*]

1. Any shrub or small tree of the genus *Telopea* (fam. Proteaceae) of s.e. Aust., esp. *T. speciosissima* (the floral emblem of N.S.W.) and (*Tas.*) *T. truncata*; the striking, bright red flower-head of the plant, for which it is often cultivated; Tulip tree. See also *native tulip* Native *a.* 6 a., Telopea.

1788 J. Hunter Birds & Flowers N.S.W. Pl. 62, *Wara-ta.* **1791** J. Cobley *Sydney Cove* 3 Dec. (1965) 176, I send you a drawing of the War-ret-tah, several plants of which are in the tubs. **1793** J.E. Smith *Specimen Bot. New Holland* 19 The most magnificent plant which the prolific soil of New Holland affords is, by common consent both of Europeans and Natives, the Waratàh. **1797** *HRA* (1914) 1st Ser. II. 13 We can have no prospect of getting the warata plant home. **1805** Banks Papers 12 Jan. VIII. 172, I have not been able to send any seeds of the Warratah this time; by the natives having burned the woods. **1838** J. Martin *Austral. Sketch Bk.* 22 One of his pupils borne down by an immense bundle of *warrataws*, or colonial tulips. **1846** *Tasmanian Jrnl. Nat. Sci.* II. 134 That floral ornament the Warratah (*Telopea truncata*) grows on the summit of the range (near the brow), and for miles down the Liffy. **1852** G.C. Mundy *Our Antipodes* I. 183 In the bush we found the Waratah growing in great perfection. Its noble crimson core, shaped like a large artichoke, crowns a straight stem of hard wood, from five to ten feet high. **1873** J. Bonwick *Tasmanian Lily* 76 The wonder of all, the floral Queen of Tasmania, was the Waratah of the Natives, the Telopea of Whites. **1903** *Tasmanian Timbers* (Tas. Lands & Survey Dept.) 29 Waratah (*Telopea truncata*) .. may be got up to six inches in diameter. It is famed for its flowers. **1912** *Truth* (Sydney) 29 Dec. 3/6 Let Waratah, then, name the place Which we the capital have styl'd; The name has all that native grace, Which suits our nation'l new-born child. **1925** M. Gilmore *Tilted Cart* 67 But for us in the South, Where the Southern Cross shows, Like a kiss on the mouth The Waratah blows. **1948** E.H. Collis *Lost Yrs.* 101 In eastern Australia the gorgeous waratah has largely disappeared from the coastal districts. **1972** *Bulletin* (Sydney) 26 Aug. 6/1 If New South Wales has the waratah as its state emblem then surely the shark should be the emblem of Victoria. **1984** *Courier-Mail* (Brisbane) 8 Dec. 26/5 Dr Webb says we are only just beginning to throw off what he has called our botanical cringe. Judith Wright has written about this. We much prefer the gladioli to the waratah.

2. Abbrev. of *Waratah Festival*, a celebratory occasion (in quot. *transf.*).

1975 E. Goolagong et al. *Evonne* 189 When would they stop clapping? Not for five minutes, according to the journalists who timed it. It was a regular waratah (party) in the stadium.

3. Special Comb. **Waratah (Spring) Festival,** a carnival formerly held annually in Sydney, usu. in spring.

1956 *Sydney Morning Herald* 12 Sept. 4/4 The city will be dressed with flowers, flags and bunting for Sydney's first Waratah Spring Festival. **1967** *Ibid.* 20 Sept. 19/2 Mrs Sharry would like to see the Waratah Festival become bigger and bouncier than it is. **1974** *Ibid.* 2 Aug. 1/5 The Waratah Spring Festival will not be staged this year, the first time since it began in 1957. **1984** P. Jarratt *Aussie* 204 Sydney once had its Waratah Festival in which there was a parade and little else.

warb /wɔb/. Also **waub, worb.** [Prob. f. *warble* the maggot of a warble-fly: see OED *sb.*[2] 3.]

1. An idle, unkempt, or disreputable person: see quot. 1959.

[**1917** *Barrack: Official Organ Imperial Camel Corps* 1 July 6/2 The wowsers have another win; Two million beer warps die.] **1933** Murdoch & Drake-Brockman *Austral. Short Stories* (1951) 215 We were both of us what, in the back country, are called 'warbs', meaning confirmed and irredeemable loafers. **1956** Park & Niland *Drums go Bang* 126 Alongside this masterpiece he felt the warbiest of the warbs, the shabbiest of the shabs. **1959** S.J. Baker *Drum* II. 155 *Warb*, a low-paid manual worker... A dirty or untidy person... A simpleton or fool. **1967** K. Tennant *Tell Morning This* 201 But it's a no-hoper's jail—a lot of old warbs and kids mixed up with coves like Amos the Cannibal and chaps that razors bounce off. **1974** *Bulletin* (Sydney) 2 Nov. 57/2 In London a Jew is a fiveter—five-to-two. In Melbourne a Jew is a warb, which is short for warby, which rhymes with forby, which is short for four-by-two. **1979** Dusty & Lapsley *Walk Country Mile* 147 On one run I hired a warb called Bluey who thought he was something of a ladies' man. The trouble was the ladies didn't agree. **1981** P. Barton *Bastards I have Known* 53 Together with a couple of warbs (homeless alcoholics) and a few other social misfits. **1984** *Sydney Morning Herald* 4 Feb. 37/2 She picks up an intoxicated person (police call them waubs, slang passed down from they don't know where).

2. An unskilled circus hand.

1945 S.J. Baker *Austral. Lang.* 249 *Warb*, a circus labourer. **1956** Park & Niland *Drums go Bang* 174 I'm classed as a warb, but I do everything. I help pull down and put up the Big Top, play recorded music, bang the cymbals. **1967** J. Yeomans *Scarce Australs.* 30 There are four general hands (known in Australian circus slang as worbs).

warbler. [Transf. use of *warbler* any of many small birds of the fam. Sylviidae.]

1. Any of many small birds of several fam., usu. having a melodic call, esp. those of the genus *Gerygone* and other members of the fam. Acanthizidae, and of the fam. Maluridae and Ephthianuridae.

1790 J. White *Jrnl. Voyage N.S.W.* 257 *Motocilla*, or *Warbler.* Motacilla Pusilla... This little bird is about the same size with [*sic*] the Superb Warbler. **1836** *Sydney Herald* 21 Mar. 2/4 Among the birds we noticed .. an almost innumerable variety of finches, fly-catchers, warblers. **1849** *Tasmanian Jrnl. Nat. Sci.* III. 105 The fan-tailed fly-catcher and a warbler of the reeds cheered us with their pretty song by day. **1896** F.G. Aflalo *Sketch Nat. Hist. Aust.* 136 The Wrens and Warblers—chiefly *Maluri*, with the allied *Amytis* and *Stipiturus*—are purely Australian. **1945** C. Barrett *Austral. Bird Life* 183 We have about ninety species of warblers and they form the largest group of Australian birds. **1958** M.D. Berrington *Stones of Fire* 13 Friar birds are having a savage duel with countless warblers and fairy wrens. **1985** *Age* (Melbourne) 9 Sept. 15/5 The Australian wrens, warblers and robins are quite unrelated to their namesakes in the Northern Hemisphere.

2. With distinguishing epithet, as **brown, reed, rock, superb, white-throated:** see under first element.

warbling grass parakeet. Budgerigar. Also **warbling grass parrot.**

1840 J. Gould *Birds of Aust.* (1848) V. Pl. 44, *Melopsittacus undulatus* .. Warbling Grass-Parrakeet... Betcherrygah, Natives of Liverpool Plains. **1841** *Sydney Herald* 4 May 2/5 The Warbling Grass Parrakeet .. is remarkable for the 'inward warbling song' which is kept up during the day. **1865** G.F. Angas *Aust.* 94 The little 'warbling grass parrakeet' appears in vast flocks in South Australia during the Summer. **1901** *Emu* I. 138 Warbling Grass-Parrakeet .. Fairly abundant between Poonaranni and Oanna. **1916** S.A. White *In Far Northwest* 152 The warbling grass parrot (or more commonly known as the shell parrot) were met with, but not in numbers. **1934** H.G. Lamond *Aviary on Plains* 8 That's a mob of budgerigars (Warbling Grass-parrots).

warby, *a.* [See Warb.] Of clothes, etc.: shabby, decrepit. Also, unappealing.

1923 *Aussie* (Sydney) 15 Nov. 39 When your overcoat's warby, and turned to bottle-green, And the whole of your outfit's not fit to be seen. **1941** K. Tennant *Battlers* 207 'Of all the warby ideas', he said .. 'the warbiest is you going on your own.' **1947** *Bulletin* (Sydney) 19 Mar. 28/1 The rather warby-looking man with the sad expression and the faded blue eyes shuffled into Flanagan's shanty pub. **1959** D. Niland *Gold in Streets* 43 Danno and Johnny went to Mass in their neat but warby suits. **1965** E. LAMBERT *Long White Night* 135 That was one of the funniest sights the main street ever saw—my old man's warby old Model A towing Foran's dirty big gleaming new Packard! **1978** R.H. CONQUEST *Dusty Distances* 123 They're old police boots, a bit worn down in the heels and warby in the soles. **1981** C. WALLACE-CRABBE *Splinters* 37 It's hard to get rid of This warby smile.

warden. *Hist. Gold warden*, see GOLD 3.

1855 *Ovens & Murray Advertiser* (Beechworth) 7 Apr. 3/4 The present expensive staff of commissioners is to be entirely abolished; and the management of each district entrusted to one officer of high rank, and invested with grave authority, called a *warden*, who is to be directly responsible to the Government for his actions. **1861** L.A. MEREDITH *Over Straits* 141 The chief official in a digging settlement . . is entitled the Warden. **1890** A.J. VOGAN *Black Police* 34 The professional jumper of claims . . figures more often in the Warden's Court than the 'm drives' and 'cross cuts' of the field. **1898** R. RADCLYFFE *Wealth & Wild Cats* 34 The goldfields are ruled by Wardens, and each Warden has a district over which he is practically an absolute monarch. He marries, he tries all the varied assortment of drunks, he watches the 'spielers', sits upon the professional jumper, settles all mining disputes. **1938** C.P. CONIGRAVE *Walk-About* 12 Warden Finnerty . . had gone to inspect the new rush.

warragal, warragul, var. WARRIGAL.

warran /'wɒrən/. *Obs.* Also **warrein.** [a. Nyungar *warran.*] ADJIGO.

1840 *S. Austral. Rec.* (London) 21 Nov. 324 The warran, or native yam . . always grows in the most fertile tracts. **1863** *Jrnls. & Rep. Two Voyages Glenelg River* 1 Aug. (1864) 27 Edible roots, two species of which we recognised; they are identical with those of Champion Bay (warrein and ɔdjiko). **1878** R.B. SMYTH *Aborigines of Vic.* II. 245, I have . . seen both men and women sinking in loose sandy soil for an edible root called *warran*, one of the dioscoreae.

warratah, warrataw, var. WARATAH.

warra-warra /'wɒrə-wɒrə/. *Obs.* [a. Gaurna *warra warra.*] KORADJI.

1842 *S. Austral. News* (London) 15 Nov. 55/1 Their influence is counteracted by major evolutions, chiefly by the *yammai ama* or *warra-warra* (sorcerers). **1843** J.F. BENNETT *Hist. & Descr. Acct. S.A.* 67 There are among them professed sorcerers, called *warra-warra.* **1863** J. BONWICK *Wild White Man* 56 These Boylyas, Warrawarras, or doctors can . . carry themselves into the camp of an opposing tribe.

warregal, var. WARRIGAL.

warrein, var. WARRAN.

warrettah, var. WARATAH.

warrigal /'wɒrəgəl/, *n.* and *a.* Formerly also **warragal, warragul, warregal, warrigul, worrogal.** [a. Dharuk *warigal.*]

A. *n.*

1. DINGO *n.* 1.

c **1790** W. DAWES *Grammatical Forms Lang. N.S.W., Wor-re-gal*, a dog. **1793** J. HUNTER *Hist. Jrnl. Trans. Port Jackson* 411 *Waregal*, a large dog. **1798** D. COLLINS *Acct. Eng. Colony N.S.W.* I. 614 Tein-go, Din-go, Wor-re-gal, *Dog.* **1834** G. BENNETT *Wanderings N.S.W.* I. 125 Like a warragul, or native dog. **1851** *Illustr. Austral. Mag.* (Melbourne) Sept. 178 The 'worrogal' finds it is becoming serious . . then he tries to shake his pursuers off. **1867** A.K. COLLINS *Waddy Mundoee* 12 Them Warregals is most owdacious bad about us. They was howling and yelpin' around Crowther's Creek last night. **1874** C. DE BOOS *Congewoi Correspondence* 127 There was the dog, a reglar old man warrigal, with the ends of his red hair turnin' grey. **1892** HILL & THORNTON *Notes on Aborigines N.S.W.* 4 They are firm believers in the doctrine of Metempsychosis . . and have a firm conviction that a . . sly sneaking fellow will be a 'Warrigal', or native dog. **1911** E.J. BRADY *King's Caravan* 105 A warrigal yapped in the scrub. **1933** C. FENNER *Bunyips & Billabongs* 141 The dingo, or warrigal, the aboriginal's dog, is widespread throughout Australia, and has been throughout historic time; but it never got across Bass Strait. **1954** C. BARRETT *Wild Life Aust. & New Guinea* 46 The wild dog, called *warrigal* by blackfellows . . has been warred against with poison, trap and gun. **1970** K. WILLEY *Naked Island* 133 The dingo was cautious. . . He was a creamy fawn color, long and built comparatively close to the ground . . one of the last of the pure-bred warrigals whose ancestors had come to Australia with the Aborigines eons ago and run wild. **1980** C. ALLISON *Hunter's Man. Aust. & N.Z.* 17 The warrigal comes in a variety of sizes: small, medium, and large; long and lean, short and fat; without a true general form, although the great majority of wild dogs are not much larger than a mature kelpie at the shoulder and only slightly longer.

2. MYALL *n.*[1] 2.

1847 *Port Phillip Herald* 21 Jan. 2/6 On his way to the scrub, one of the Warrigals yabbered to him, which seemed to frighten him. **1863** J. BONWICK *Wild White Man* 80 The Warriguls, or wild blacks, of Gipps Land, dwelt in the rocky fastnesses of the Australian Alps. **1890** A.J. VOGAN *Black Police* 133 Frazer went about for years shooting all and every native he could see, 'station boys', warragals, or town blacks—he was not very particular. **1900** T. MAJOR *Leaves from Squatter's Note Bk.* 2 The tame blacks residing on the station termed these new arrivals 'Warragals' ('wild'). **1912** J. BOWES *Comrades* 235 The warrigal fell on his back, and lay clawing the air, beetle-like, with his hands and feet. **1920** *Smith's Weekly* (Sydney) 28 Aug. 9/4 Sub-inspector Kaye was killed by warrigals near Woolgar diggings 40 odd years ago. **1936** C. CHEWINGS *Back in Stone Age* 96 My boy's friend was a warrigal, that is, he could neither speak nor understand any English. **1977** LESLIE & COWIE *Wind still Blows* 39 The country of the dreaded Warrigals—that being the name given to the so-called wild natives of Gippsland.

3. The plant *Tetragonia tetragonoides* (fam. Aizoaceae), occurring in Aust. and elsewhere, having fleshy leaves used as a vegetable. In full **warrigal cabbage.**

1861 *Bell's Life in Sydney* 2 Feb. 2/6 The land's first rate, you all must know, It's 'bosh' to say that nought will grow Save cabbage known as 'Warrigal'. **1890** 'R. BOLDREWOOD' *Squatter's Dream* 67 Never seen a green thing except marshmallers and Warrigal Cabbage. **1904** *Proc. Linnean Soc. N.S.W.* XXIX. 135 Such annuals as . . *Tetragonia expansa* . . 'Warrigal Cabbage', are often the predominant plants. **1932** M.R. WHITE *No Roads go By* 45 In season, given the rain, wild spinach or warrigal cabbage and other types of luscious herbage flourished at the more-or-less sheltered base of the sandhills. **1981** J.A. BAINES *Austral. Plant Genera* 368 *T[etragonia] tetragonioides*, NZ Spinach, Warrigal Cabbage, all States and NZ. . . Early settlers actually cooked it like spinach.

4. A wild or untamed horse. Also *transf.*

1881 *Australasian* (Melbourne) 21 May 647/4 How we ran in 'The Black Warrigal'. **1891** 'SMILER' *Wanderings Simple Child* (ed. 3) p. iv, As good a horseman as ever straddled a warrigal. **1899** G.E. BOXALL *Story Austral. Bushrangers* 191 The story of warrigals, or wild horses, tempting working horses away was a common fiction. **1905** J. FURPHY *Rigby's Romance* (1946) p. xviii, These were warrigals, even as scrub-bred cattle. . . You know the class—long-bodied, clean-flanked, hard-muscled, ardent-eyed, and always in the same advanced-store condition. **1916** O. HOGUE *Trooper Bluegum at Dardanelles* 25 Wild warrigals of the West; bucking brumbies that beat the band; old outlaws off the grass that the station hands could never master. **1927** 'JULIET' *Devotion* 77 He broke her in himself—and a nice job he had of it, for the colt was a real warrigal. **1935** G. MCIVER *Drover's Odyssey* 204 When the white stockman could not . . ride a wild horse or 'warrigal' from fear of being thrown, the black would be ordered to mount him.

B. *adj.*

1. MYALL *n.*[1] B. 2 a.

1847 *Atlas* (Sydney) III. 21/3 They discovered two Warrigal natives who had been fishing for eels. **1853** J. SHERER *Gold Finder Aust.* 233 Warrigal (wild) black fellow work, work, work. **1888** W.H. WILLSHIRE *Aborigines of Central Aust.* 16 There was another warregal blackfellow higher up the bank, who looked on grinning. **1909** *Bulletin* (Sydney) 23 Sept. 15/1 An old warrigal nigger was passing close to the station homestead. **1920** C.H. SAYCE *Golden Buckles* 119 Tynan despatched a warragal nigger from the black's camp, to The Cliff telephone station.

2. Wild; untamed. Also *fig.*

1881 *Australasian* (Melbourne) 21 May 647/4 The 'Pet of the Devil' looked awfully grand, Spieling well out on the wing, With four mares without ever a brand, Loping in to the Warrigal spring. **1889** *Illustr. Austral. News* (Melbourne) 1 May 74/2 Should perchance one of the old warrigal bulls get cut off from the herd, he will not be satisfied until he has had his revenge on some of the musterers. **1893** *Bulletin* (Sydney) 18 Feb. 15/2 The word 'warrigal' was current aboriginee ere the British Lion deposited 'our forefathers' here. Since then, the word has been applied, both by blacks and whites, to anything wild, from the warrigal steer to the warrigal cabbage. . . But during the idyllic era of Australia—extending from the year 1 A.M. [*sic*] to 1788 A.D.—'warrigal' signified 'out-law'. **1904** *Truth* (Sydney) 31 July 9/5 The warrigal wowsers of Waine were conspicuous by their absence. These lewd, larrikin louts, who seek fatuously to foster the cause of pure, pious, parson-petted Jack Wayne. **1933** D. MACDONALD *Brooks of Morning* 49 The 'smokers' seem to be interested in the seed of warrigal melons, for one flushed them from every patch. **1946** K.S. PRICHARD *Roaring Nineties* 230 Con had a bad time with his warrigal camel. After a few good feeds, the brute started bucking, head down, and bolted. **1955** D. NILAND *Shiralee* 111 The warrigal wind shouldered the door in, swooped under the papers on the table, and upset the gin-bottle. **1978** D. STUART *Wedgetail View* 229 Half a dozen real warrigal knock-about men, proper bloody tearaway types.

war service home. A house purchased under a scheme providing for assistance to returned services personnel or their dependants: see quot. 1936.

1918 *Act* (Cwlth. of Aust.) no. 43 Sect. 1, This Act may be cited as the *War Service Homes Act* 1918. **1920** *Smith's Weekly* (Sydney) 9 Oct. 3/3 The Digger is given 37 years in which to pay for his War Service Home. **1922** *Daily Mail* (Sydney) 10 Jan. 7/3 The State Savings Bank Commissioners will take over the control of the building of war service homes in Victoria. **1933** *Whiz-Bang* (Brisbane) 1 May 5 No eviction of war service homes purchasers. **1936** E. SCOTT *Aust. during War* in *Official Hist. Aust. 1914–18* XI. 840 Under the War Service Homes Act the persons who were eligible to apply for assistance were returned soldiers or sailors who were married, or about to marry, or who had dependants for whom it was necessary to provide homes; or any soldier's widow, or the mother of a deceased soldier who had been dependant upon him before his enlistment, or who was a widow, or who, if she had a husband, was not supported by him owing to his incapacity. **1973** L. OAKES *Whitlam PM* 48 There was relief on all sides when the war service home the Whitlams were building in Wangi Ave., Cronulla was finally completed.

warty-faced honeyeater. *Regent honeyeater*, see REGENT 2.

[**1808** J.W. LEWIN *Birds New Holland* 7 Warty-Faced Honeysucker. . . Birds of this beautiful species were seen near Paramatta, in great numbers in the Spring of 1805.] **1843** J. GOULD *Birds of Aust.* (1848) IV. Pl. 48, *Zanthomyza phrygia* . . Warty-faced Honey-eater. **1849** C. STURT *Narr. Exped. Central Aust.* II. 28 App. *Warty-faced Honey-eater.* This Honey-eater, with alternate black and yellow plumage, frequented all the sand hills where *Banksias* grew. **1861** 'OLD BUSHMAN' *Bush Wanderings* 143 The *Warty-faced Honey-eater* is a very pretty bird . . of a deep black colour, spotted with bright yellow. **1902** *Emu* II. 14 The Warty-faced Honeyeater . . gives a decided touch of colour. **1976** *Reader's Digest Compl. Bk. Austral. Birds* 467 Regent honeyeater *Xanthomyza phrygia*. . . Other names . . warty-faced honeyeater.

waub, var. WARB.

Warwick Farm. [The name of a racecourse in Sydney.] Rhyming slang for 'arm'. Also *ellipt.* as **Warwick.**

1944 *Biscuit Bomber Weekly: Mag. 1st Austral. Air Maintenance Co.* 4 Nov. 2 So I put my Warwick-Farm around her bushel-and-peck and kissed her on the North-and-South. **1962** D. MCLEAN *World turned upside Down* 40, I don't want to get elephants. I just want a drop of dad 'n' mum to loosen up me warwicks. **1967** *Kings Cross Whisper* (Sydney) xliii. 11/2 *Warwick Farms*, arms.

wash, *n. Obs.* Abbrev. of WASH-POOL.

1886 R. HENTY *Australiana* 216 There were four of these paddocks between the 'wash' and the shed, and when the sheep arrived at the last paddock, near the shearing shed, it was put into the shed for the night and shorn the next day.

wash, *v.*[1] *Obs. intr.* (in quots.) SHEEP-WASH. Freq. as *vbl. n.*

1847 *Bell's Life in Sydney* 28 Aug. 3/5, I understand washing and shearing commence at Boyd and Co.'s next month. **1854** *Illustr. Sydney News* 18 Nov. 378/1 Lambing is now over or nearly so... Washing has commenced on many of the stations and shearing will soon be in full operation. **1874** R.P. FALLA *Knocking About* (1976) 21 Mr G. Rutherford is the only one on the Lower Avoca who will wash this shearing. **1880** *Blackwood's Mag.* (Edinburgh) Jan. 69/2 Men.. kept arriving, inquiring as to the terms of shearing and washing. The washers were, as a class, considerably below the shearers.

wash, *v.*[2] *Gold-mining. intr.* Usu. with **up.** To wash for gold in a sluice-box, etc., esp. after accumulating a quantity of wash-dirt; (of a claim, etc.) to yield gold through this process. Also *trans.*, with **off,** and freq. as **washing-up** *vbl. n.*

1859 *Colonial Mining Jrnl.* Apr. 123/3 The miners are not yet washing up. *Ibid.* May 145/2 Those machines, much as they facilitate the process of washing up, nevertheless are susceptible of great improvement. **1862** J.A. PATTERSON *Gold Fields Vic.* 128 The stuff is.. piled at the bottom till the supply of water permits 'washing-up' to take place. *Ibid.* 180 'Washing-off'.. takes place in the afternoon of every day. **1871** *Austral. Town & Country Jrnl.* (Sydney) 28 Jan. 113/1 The Enterprize Company had a splendid washing up last week; the yield was 70 oz. for about a fortnight's crushing. *Ibid.* 8 Apr. 431/2 Very few washings have taken place during the week, but the claims that did wash up yielded up to the average. **1872** 'DEMONAX' *Mysteries & Miseries* 17 They washed off the first lot, and the result was 12½ oz. of gold. This was left in the washing-off dish. **1884** *Goldfield's Reminisc.* 50 A well-known miner.. was on his usual spree after a good 'washing up'. **1889** *Braidwood Dispatch* 18 Sept. 2/1 Have run out the boxes, and intend washing up about the end of the week as it will be necessary to get new boxes. **1892** 'R. BOLDREWOOD' *Nevermore* I. 179 Why, they say he's worth forty or fifty thousand, if he's worth a penny, and the claim washing-up better and better every week? **1892** *Braidwood Dispatch* 21 Dec. 2/3 Money is not so scarce amongst the country folks as many persons would imagine. The diggers always manage to have a fair washing up at Christmas and the farmer has sources of raising a few pounds. **1896** J.W. ROBERTS *Mining Industry N.S.W.* 57 After these men had got out 'paddocks' of wash-dirt and were preparing for washing up, they were informed that their licenses did not include water rights. **1896** J. HOLT *Virgin Gold* (Advt.), Your machines were inspected by two experienced battery owners from Wyalong, who saw the machines at work, saw the result of half a day, and saw us wash up. They both pronounced them perfect gold savers. **1944** *Bulletin* (Sydney) 26 July 12/4 He took a sample, dollied it and washed up a few specks of color.

washaway. [Used elsewhere but chiefly Austral.: see OED.] The removal of earth by flood; the washing away of a portion of a railway line, road, etc., by flood; the hole or channel caused by this.

1893 *Westminster Gaz.* (London) 7 Mar. 8/3 The new railway also suffered severely, and traffic has been interfered with owing to several washaways. **1899** *Western Champion* (Barcaldine) 25 July 3/2 Up a grass slope, to a string-bark ridge. Through some broken washaways on the fall, and into spewy brigalow. **1910** *Huon Times* (Franklin) 6 Aug. 6/3 A washaway occurred on Millar's Karra and Jarrah Company's Karridale line last week, with the result that a timber train was derailed. **1927** K.S. PRICHARD *Brumby Innes* (1974) 71 *May*: .. Nyedee Hills, Unk, that range at the back of the run? *John*: (nodding) Steep as the back of your hand, all tussocky spinifex and wash-aways. **1938** F. RATCLIFFE *Flying Fox & Drifting Sand* 73 Driving a buggy over bush tracks—dashing off right or left into the forest wherever a wash-away.. makes a détour necessary—is a high art. **1951** *New Settler in W.A.* (Perth) Feb. 7 We came across a big Chrysler wedged hard in a three-foot deep washaway in the crumbling, red, clayey soil bank of a wide watercourse. **1962** J. HEDGE *Trout Fishing N.S.W.* 117 Opposite, on the left, are the shearing sheds. The old crossings to reach 'Koorabri' have now been discarded owing to the river having caused washaways. **1969** P. ADAM SMITH *Folklore Austral. Railwaymen* 16 One year between Oodnadatta and Finke there were washaways before and after us.

washer. A face-cloth.

1951 D. CUSACK *Say no to Death* 194 Doreen had given her a washer and a drop of warm water to wash the sleep out of her eyes. **1970** P. WHITE *Vivisector* 236 He was reminded of an old face-washer, often grubby, one of the maids had crocheted for him, in wide mesh. **1974** A. BUZO *Coralie Lansdowne says No* 71 I'll get you a cold washer.

washing, *vbl. n. Obs.*

1. Used *attrib.* with reference to the washing of sheep before shearing.

1847 *Bell's Life in Sydney* 24 July 3/1 Upon arriving at the banks of the Campaspie the river was 'up' and the opposite side presented a small pavement where sheep were driven down in the washing season. **1854** W. HOWITT *Boy's Adventures* 213 It was now the busy part of the squatter's year—washing and shearing time. **1891** H. NISBET *Colonial Tramp* I. 132 In the way of wool-sheds, sheep-pens, washing-ponds, &c.

2. Special Comb. **washing pen,** WASH-PEN; **washing-pool,** WASH-POOL.

1847 *Bell's Life in Sydney* 25 Sept. 3/3 In commencing operations for washing, there is frequently considerable difficulty to make the sheep enter the **washing pen.** **1841** *Port Phillip Gaz.* 7 Aug. 1 **Washing pools** of size to wash all sheep in the district. **1843** J. HOOD *Aust. & East* 151 Every morning Mr B-- starts for the washing pool.. and there overlooks the shearers. **1844** *Sydney Morning Herald* 8 Apr. 2/6 The labours of the field, the stockyard, the washing-pool, and the wool-shed, would also proceed far more quickly and pleasantly.

washing stuff. *Gold-mining. Obs.* Wash-dirt. Also **wash-stuff.**

1852 J. BONWICK *Notes of Gold Digger* 10 Most of that through which you are now digging may prove 'washing stuff'. **1853** J. SHERER *Gold Finder Aust.* 177 The gold.. lies upon a sort of pipe-clay, called by the diggers 'washing stuff'. **1854** *Illustr. Sydney News* 28 Feb. 163/3 A third party washed eighty pounds of gold from two tubs of washing stuff. **1855** G.H. WATHEN *Golden Colony* 55 Another gully has been deserted because the water-holes were dried up and the 'washing-stuff' wouldn't pay to cart to the nearest creek. **1858** *Illustr. Jrnl. Australasia* IV. 80 Into that vessel they put the 'washing stuff' (that is, the ferruginous quartz gravel and fine clay picked out of their stratum at the bottom of the hole). **1869** MRS W.M. HOWELL *Diggings & Bush* 48 They're getting half an ounce to the tub, all fine gold, in three or four feet of washing stuff. **1872** 'RESIDENT' *Glimpses Life Vic.* 274 The heaps of washstuff and clay thrown up by the miners. **1891** *Braidwood Dispatch* 15 Apr. 2/3 *Mining at Jembaicumbene*... The gold in Smith's being very fine and in the swamp very coarse, the washing stuff and stripping being also dissimilar. **1915** L. ROSS *From Rossiville to Victorian Goldfields* 56 On Bendigo Creek the miners were putting the wash stuff through the 'cradles' to get the gold it contained, and some others were 'panning it'.

wash-pen. *Obs.* [f. WASH *v.*[1]] An enclosure into which sheep are driven preparatory to being washed. Also *attrib.*

1847 *Maitland Mercury* 29 Sept. 2/5 This gate, during the time the sheep are being driven into the wash-pen, should be closed, that the water may not be seen. **1871** *Austral. Town & Country Jrnl.* (Sydney) 28 Jan. 103/2 The wool at Mr Sutton's had to be shorn in the grease, as both the river and creek were too high to put up a good wash-pen, but the staple is remarkably clean for greasy. **1879** S.W. SILVER *Austral. Grazier's Guide* 48 The wash-pen is so constructed as to overhang the water in a tolerably deep place, so that the sheep can be plunged in from the 'stage' or advanced platform of the wash-pen. **1890** 'R. BOLDREWOOD' *Squatter's Dream* 52 A black fellow or two would be handy at the wash-pen—the sheep having rather a long swim. **1942** W. GLASSON *Our Shepherds* 20 Washing sheep was strenuous work... At the end of the day a rum ration would be distributed among the wash pen workers.

wash-pool. *Obs.* [f. WASH *v.*[1] In Br. use but chiefly Austral.: see OED.] A pool, usu. in a natural watercourse, in which sheep are washed before shearing.

1830 R. DAWSON *Present State Aust.* 291 A large party of natives was taken up the country to assist in making a wash-pool at the river for sheep. **1843** *Colonial Observer* (Sydney) 12 July 1154/3 One of the Australian Agricultural Company's sheep watchmen was stopped on the road near the washpool by an armed bushranger. **1860** 'LADY' *My Experiences in Aust.* 176 The washpool is generally formed in a creek or river, where the natural body of water is increased by the construction of a rude dam... The sheep are flung out, one by one, into the pool. **1872** G.S. BADEN-POWELL *New Homes for Old Country* 176 In some handy creek the wash-pool is made. **1887** A. NICOLS *Wild Life & Adventure* 62 Down the creek was a 'wash pool', which might have been expressly designed by nature for cleansing the fleeces of the squatter's sheep preparatory to shearing them. **1928** M. FORREST *Reaping Roses* 146 Across the lagoon was the long galvanized iron-roofed wool-shed, and, some miles out, an up-to-date wash-pool for the scouring of the fleeces.

wash stuff: see WASHING STUFF.

wash-up. *Gold-mining. Washing-up,* see WASH *v.*[2]

1880 *Austral. Town & Country Jrnl.* (Sydney) 3 July 30/3 As soon as we had finished the next wash-up, I was to go back to Yatala. **1886** H.W.H. STEPHEN *Lily's Fortune* 74 He had bought into some really good claims, but there was no water and there had not been a wash-up for six weeks. **1897** T.W. BEILLEY *Australasia's Goldfields* 12 The alluvial gold obtained from its rocky bed near Anderson's Creek (shovelfuls, to author's knowledge, from occasional wash-ups of sluice boxes). **1913** H. LAWSON *Triangles of Life* 187 One morning in the New Year after the wash-up (and the claim panned out very well), the four of them went away.

waste, *a. Obs.* [Spec. use of *waste* uncultivated and uninhabited.] Of land: unalienated from, and unimproved by, the Crown; esp. in the collocation **waste land (of the Crown).**

1804 *HRA* (1921) 3rd Ser. I. 246 Two Acres for every Acre of Waste Land. **1826** *Ibid.* (1922) 3rd Ser. V. 322 The granting and settlement of the waste Lands of the Crown in New South Wales. **1835** *Colonist* (Sydney) 1/1 Discontinue the practice of granting waste land to free emigrants in the Australian colonies. **1840** *Port Phillip Gaz.* 25 Jan. 4 No sheepholder can be persuaded of his offence in grazing his flocks upon the waste pastures of the territory. *Ibid.* 25 Apr. 2 The banks, ever ready to 'make hay while the sun shines', hastened to meet with open coffers persons desirous of their assistance in the purchase of waste territories. **1843** *N.S.W. Monthly Mag.* Oct. 596 Is the £167,000 to be advanced on *Waste Land?* It will not be right to call it 'Pasture Land', for it is waste, or pasture, according to whether it has stock upon it or not. **1848** *HRA* (1925) 1st Ser. XXVI. 691 All the Waste Lands within the Settled Districts allotted to Commissioners of Crown Lands were already occupied. **1867** 'CLERGYMAN' *Aust. as it Is* 137 The 'Crown lands' are very frequently, in Government phrase, styled 'the waste lands of the Crown'. They cannot, however, with propriety be called waste lands, for they are applied to the only purpose, speaking of them in general, to which they can ever be applied—grazing. **1886** J.F. CONIGRAVE *S.A.* 62 A grant of land of five acres, on North-terrace, was made for the University buildings, together with a dedication of 50,000 acres of waste lands of the province for endowment purposes. **1890** 'R. BOLDREWOOD' *Squatter's Dream* 43 He once more sighted the unromantic but priceless waters of the Warroo, and beheld, with the eye of a proprietor, the 'waste lands of the Crown'—most literally deserving that appellation. **1934** 'S. RUDD' *Green Grey Homestead* 151 'The Mount' consisted of waste country reserved by a Government of squatters for 'closer settlement'.

watch-box. *Obs.* [Spec. use of *watch-box* a small structure providing shelter for a person on watch.] A movable sleeping compartment provided for the use of a watchman: see quot. 1848.

1826 J. ATKINSON *Acct. Agric. & Grazing N.S.W.* 74 The watchman is provided with a moveable watch-box, and usually two or three dogs, and generally keeps up fires all night. **1842** *Sketch of Shepherd's Duties N.S.W.* 49 The duty of a watchman is as easy as that of the shepherd; he sleeps by the fold, in a watch-box, trusting to his dogs to awaken him in case of the approach of a native dog. **1848** H.W. Haygarth *Recoll. Bush Life* 44 He resigns all charge of them to the watchman, who passes the night alongside the folds in a 'watch-box'. This is simply a sort of wooden frame, covered with hides, or the bark of trees, and standing about a foot from the ground, with an opening on one side large enough to admit a small mattress and blankets. **1873** 'Lady In Aust.' *Memories Past* 63 We found . . an old watch-box that some shepherd had used as a bedstead in days gone by. **1911** *Bulletin* (Sydney) 26 Oct. 14/2 The watch boxes, once used as portable sleeping apartments by sheep tenders, have long since been thrown into the rubbish tip. **1937** D. Gunn *Links with Past* 207 In the early days, when the hut-keeper watched the sheep, he used to sleep at the gate of the yard in what was called a watch-box. This was just a long box, on wooden wheels, in which the man could sleep if he wished. . . When the hurdle yard was moved, the watch-box was moved too. The shepherd's hut was a permanent residence.

watch-house. [Survival of *watch-house* a house used by municipal night-watchmen for the temporary custody of persons under arrest: see OED.]

1. A building, now usu. attached to a police station, in which suspected law-breakers are held under temporary arrest.

1810 *Sydney Gaz.* 29 Dec., The District Constable shall every Night place in the Watch-house, at Sun-set, a Constable to be called the *Constable of the Night*. **1824** *Australasian Pocket Almanack* 46 In each district there shall be built a watch-house, for the reception of such persons as shall be found in the streets after hours, *idle, disorderly*, or *suspicious*. **1842** *Hunter River Gaz.* 8 Jan. 3/4 Christmas has passed over without any rioting; not a single person having been sent to the watchhouse for drunkenness. **1863** J.H. Pope *Stumps & Rags* 7 Hence we have watch-houses for drunkards, lunatic asylums for madmen, government offices for ---, and jails for thieves. **1889** *Braidwood Dispatch* 9 Oct. 2/5 About half-past 8 this morning a man giving the name of Edward Woolf, 50 years of age, presented himself at the Russell-street watchhouse and made a statement. **1901** *Bulletin* (Sydney) 26 Oct. 16/3 The lockup-keeper of Fitzroy (Melb.) watch-house was absent on leave when a drunk was run-in. **1919** *Argus* (Melbourne) 1 Sept. 6/6 Detectives . . arrested George Ames Whitney . . and locked him up at the City Watchhouse. **1933** *Ibid.* 16 Dec. 23/4 Later, at the watchhouse, a painter, aged 34 years, and a woman, aged 24 years, were charged with house-breaking. **1955** *Sun* (Melbourne) 19 Nov. 2/5 He was later charged at the City Watchhouse with having stolen four cars. **1963** *Bulletin* (Sydney) 13 Apr. 10/2 One Brisbane police officer has said: 'I would hate to see any relative or friend of mine in the city watch-house.' **1978** R. Coleman *Pyjama Girl* 78 At 2 p.m. that day he was taken to the city watchhouse and charged with the murder of his wife.

2. Comb. **watch-house keeper.**

1835 *Colonist* (Sydney) 243/1 The police force at present consists of fifteen constables . . lock-up keeper, watch-house keeper, and scourger. **1847** *Melbourne Argus* 1 Oct. 2/3 Convicted upon his own confession of having escaped from the custody of a watchhouse keeper at the Broken River. **1855** G.H. Wathen *Golden Colony* 149 The clerk's room of the Swanston Street watchhouse . . within were several of the detective officers, and two watchhouse keepers at the books. **1888** G.O. Preshaw *Banking under Difficulties* 14 The watch-house-keeper said that I might deposit £5 as bail, and appear at ten o'clock. **1899** *Western Champion* (Barcaldine) 23 May 3/3 After sentence he was handed over to the lockup keeper, and in the evening he asked permission to go to the back part of the premises, and was allowed to do so, the watchhouse keeper accompanying him.

Hence **watch-house** *v. trans.*, to confine (someone) in a watch-house.

1829 *Sydney Monitor* 4 July, Had we not been considerate, the man would have been watch-housed.

watchman. *Obs.* [Spec. use of *watchman* a person employed to guard private property.] One who is employed to watch over sheep during the night: see quot. 1848.

1825 B. Field *Geogr. Mem. N.S.W.* 445 The settlers' convict-servants (stockmen and sheep watchmen) do little but drone about their filthy turf-huts. **1827** P. Cunningham *Two Yrs. in N.S.W.* I. 268 Three flocks are always penned together in contiguous hurdles under the charge of a watchman, who counts them regularly *in* at night, and the shepherds again count them *out* in the morning. . . The watchman has a small weather-proof watch-box to sleep in. **1840** *S. Austral. Rec.* (London) 30 May 284 The custom is that two shepherds, and another man called watchman, whose duty it is to be hut-keeper during the day, and watch the flocks whilst in their folds at night, occupy one hut or dwelling, and this is usually situated at a distance of a few miles from any other dwelling. **1848** H.W. Haygarth *Recoll. Bush Life* 44 For every flock two men are required, the shepherd, and another called the watchman, whose duty consists in taking care of the station, preparing the meals, watching the sheep at night, and shifting the folds every day. **1852** S. Mossman *Gold Regions* (ed. 2) 67 A watchman . . armed with a musket . . sleeps in a moveable watch-box, having spokes like a sedan-chair, and placed close by the sheep-yard.

water. Used *attrib.* in the names of flora and fauna: **water bush,** any of several plants, esp. *Myoporum acuminatum* (see *native myrtle* Native *a.* 6 a.), common along inland watercourses, *Adriana hookeri* (fam. Euphorbiaceae) of sandy soils in all mainland States, and (*W.A.*) shrubs of the Austral. genus *Bossiaea* (fam. Fabaceae) incl. *B. aquifolium*; **couch,** either of two perennial grasses (fam. Poaceae) of damp or wet places in Aust. and widespread elsewhere, *Paspalum distichum* of all mainland States and *P. paspalodes* of all States; **dragon** (formerly **iguana**), any of several lizards occurring near water, esp. those of the fam. Agamidae, as *Physignathus lesueurii* of e. mainland Aust; **goanna,** any of several species of goanna (see Goanna 1) occurring near water, usu. in n. Aust., esp. *Varanus mertensi*; **grass,** *swamp grass*, see Swamp *n.*; **gum,** any of several trees of the fam. Myrtaceae, esp. *Tristaniopsis laurina* (also called Kanooka) and the rainforest tree *Syzygium francisii* of n.e. N.S.W. and s.e. Qld.; (formerly) any of several trees of the genus *Eucalyptus* (fam. Myrtaceae) occurring along watercourses (see quots. 1826 and 1834); **-holding frog,** any of several burrowing frogs of drier inland Aust., esp. *Cyclorana platycephalus* of all mainland States exc. Vic.; **mallee,** any of several mallee eucalypts the roots of which are a source of water, as *Eucalyptus dumosa* and *E. oleosa* (fam. Myrtaceae); also *water tree*; **mole** *obs.*, Platypus 1; also *attrib.*; **rat,** the large aquatic rodent *Hydromys chrysogaster*, widespread near water in Aust. and occurring elsewhere, having dense soft fur and webbed hind feet; Beaver rat; **tree,** any of many trees yielding water from the roots, or from hollows in the trunk, esp. *water mallee*, some species of *Acacia* (fam. Mimosaceae), *Brachychiton* (fam. Sterculiaceae), and *Hakea* (fam. Proteaceae), as *H. leucoptera* (see Needlewood); **vine,** any of several climbing plants, esp. the woody *Cissus hypoglauca* (fam. Vitaceae) of e. Aust.; see also *wild grape* Wild 1.

1893 D. Lindsay *Jrnl. Elder Sci. Exploring Exped.* 6 The sandhills were covered with the green **water-bush** (*Pollechia Zeylanica*). **1898** C.L. Morgan *Rabbit Question in Qld.* 130 The rabbits are barking the edible bushes. . . These are generally emu bush, sandal-wood, water bush. **1935** H.H. Finlayson *Red Centre* 31 Water-bush, turpentine bush. **1946** C.T. Madigan *Crossing Dead Heart* 74 Water bush and many other herbs and grasses on the ridges. **1981** G.M. Cunningham et al. *Plants Western N.S.W.* 453 This species [*sc. Adriana hookeri*] is often called 'water bush' from the belief that it grows in places where water can be found at shallow depths. **1982** Elliott & Jones *Encycl. Austral. Plants* II. 355 *Bossiaea*. . . A common name in W.A. is water bush, derived from the fact that after rain, water is often retained between the leaves and stems. **1882** *Proc. Linnean Soc. N.S.W.* VII. 312 *Paspalum distichum* or the **Water-Couch** . . has established itself on the banks of our rivers. **1897** L. Lindley-Cowen *W. Austral. Settler's Guide* 402 There are also [among native Western Australian grasses] several species of the following genera . . *Paspalum* ('water couch') [etc.]. **1941** *Qld. Agric. Jrnl.* LV. 10 Water couch and salt water couch are closely allied grasses. **1968** N.T. Burbidge *Austral. Grasses* II. 152 Water Couch . . grows in shallow water or in lawns and, as its common name indicates, it has a spreading habit with a number of more or less horizontal stems rooting at the nodes. **1899** [**water dragon**] R. Semon *In Austral. Bush* 183 The water 'guanas (*Physignathus Lesueuri*) are expert swimmers. **1923** *Bulletin* (Sydney) 11 Jan. 24/3, I confess to having frequently mistaken the 'eastern water dragon' (*Physignathus lesueurii*) for the varanus. **1944** J. Devanny *By Tropic Sea & Jungle* 59 It was other-world . . to see a five-foot water-dragon slide from the rocks. **1978** B.P. Moore *Life on Forty Acres* 106 The semi-aquatic Water Dragon (*Physignathus lesueri*), occurs regularly along neighbouring creeks . . boldly barred with black on a brownish-red or greenish ground, and with a spiny crest on the head and much of the back. **1901** *Bulletin* (Sydney) 23 Mar. 14/4 **Water-'goannas'** are very common on Condamine river. **1915** *Ibid.* 7 Jan. 14/1 They cannot get the water gohanna to eat in captivity. **1935** D. Thomson *In Arnhem Land* (1983) 29 Someone would sight a water 'goanna' or monitor lizard (*Varanus*) sunning itself on a mangrove limb overhanging the water. **1977** H. Butler *In Wild* 17 Here's a Water Goanna, one of the Racehorse Goanna group. This one is totally adapted for water life: in fact most people who see them think they're crocodiles. **1829** *Sydney Monitor* 26 Jan. 1480/1 We were in the midst of bull-rushes and coarse **water-grass.** **1846** *Sydney Morning Herald* 28 Feb. 2/6 The grass called joint grass or water or summer grass. **1860** J.M. Stuart *Exploration of Interior* 3 A swampy flat on each side, in which are growing reeds, rushes and watergrass. **1874** *Illustr. Sydney News* 28 Mar. 19/2 Watergrass or Panicrum cras-galli [*sic*] is also sought after for the same purpose. Near Windsor the latter has been found growing several feet high, and assuming the appearance of millet. **1895** *Bulletin* (Sydney) 19 Jan. 24/2 Abe Saunders was down at what used to be the creek, trying to drag out his last milking cow from the place when [*sic*] she had bogged in a vain effort to find water-grass. **1927** *Ibid.* 1 Sept. 29/3 Swamp-grass, or water-grass, which forms broad patches and long, green points in swamps, and is often dense enough for water-fowl to walk on, grows to the surface from surprising depths. **1826** J. Atkinson *Acct. Agric. & Grazing N.S.W.* 14 *Flooded* or **Water Gum**—is found in low situations. **1834** G. Bennett *Wanderings N.S.W.* I. 187 A canoe . . had been scooped by Mr Manton's servants from the solid trunk of a 'water gum' tree, (*Eucalyptus sp.*). **1847** *Maitland Mercury* 13 Oct. 3/1 We came to a river from the northward, with high but irregular banks, lined with large water-gum. **1893** D.J. Frost *Crown Lands N.S.W.* 19 Mountain brush . . water gum . . have been . . proved suitable for engraving. **1911** E.J. Brady *King's Caravan* 230 He knew by long experience that water gum was best for hammer handles and mallets. **1921** *Aussie* (Sydney) Apr. 50/1 'My word! that's a lovely clump of Water-gums over there!' . . 'Cripes yes! I've got a dozen bosker axe-handles out of it already.' **1929** W.D. Francis *Austral. Rain-Forest Trees* 286 The name 'Water Gum' originated from the fact that quantities of a watery sap are sometimes contained in a central cavity or pipe of the stem, and it flows out when the trees [*sc. Eugenia francisii*] are being felled. *Ibid.* 305 *Tristania laurina*. . . This tree is called Water Gum probably because it often grows near streams. **1938** C.T. White *Princ. Bot. Qld. Farmers* 190 The name 'Water Gum' is one rather loosely used in Queensland for a number of Myrtaceous trees, being applied to species of *Tristania* and *Agonis*. **1948** P.J. Hurley *Red Cedar* 28 Tall Water Gums (*Tristania laurina*) reared their white arms loftily above lesser stringies. **1975** X. Herbert *Poor Fellow my Country* 12 Along the creek-bank, where water-gums . . and the like grew stoutly. **1896** B. Spencer *Rep. Horn Sci. Exped. Central Aust.* I. 21 The most interesting animal is the Burrowing or **Water-holding Frog** (*Chiroleptes platycephalus*). As the pool begins to dry up it fills itself out with water, which in some way passes through the walls of the alimentary canal filling up the body cavity and swelling the animal out until it looks like a small orange. **1935** H. Basedow *Knights of Boomerang* 87 Most of the Central Australian tribes . . are aware of the existence of water-holding frogs in the clays, loams and sands surrounding, or forming the bottom of, any dry waterholes and creek-beds. **1975** H.G. Cogger *Reptiles & Amphibians* 51 *Cyclorana platycephalus*. . . A burrowing frog which appears above ground only after rain. . . This is the best-known of Australia's 'water-holding' frogs; after rainy spells it burrows deep into the soil where it makes a 'cocoon'-like chamber . . which together with the frog's bladder is filled with water. **1855** J. Bonwick *Geogr. Aust. & N.Z.* (ed. 3) 202 The red or **water mallee,** from the cut rootlets of which water may be procured. **1899** *Bulletin* (Sydney) 18 Mar. 14/3 *Re* water-mallee as a thirst-quencher. **1901** *Proc. Linnean Soc. N.S.W.* XXVI. 199 The Red Mallee, *Eucalyptus oleosa*. In South Australia this tree is sometimes called Water Mallee because the roots yield a considerable quantity of water. **1935**

H. BASEDOW *Knights of Boomerang* 88 In the waterless tracts north of the Great Australian Bight . . the tribes could exist entirely on the fluid stored in the root-system of a species of eucalyptus popularly known as water-mallee. **1948** H.A. LINDSAY *Bushman's Handbk.* 8 The most famous of all our water-trees, the water mallee. **1975** A.B. & J.W. CRIBB *Wild Food in Aust.* 167 In dry country, the shallow roots of eucalypts have been the main suppliers of emergency water. . . Best known of these eucalypts are *E[ucalyptus] dumosa* (. . bull mallee, water mallee . .) and *E. oleosa.* **1800** Banks Papers 20 Sept. VII. 100, I send you . . *a cask in which is a* **Water Mole.** **1815** *HRA* (1916) 1st Ser. VIII. 573 In the reaches or pools of the Campbell River, the very curious animal called the Paradox, or Watermole is seen. **1837** *Lit. News* (Sydney) 21 Oct. 105 In the course of time, we might have become expert 'water-mole' hunters. **1860** G. BENNETT *Gatherings of Naturalist* 113 Very late in the evening we watched two Water-Moles paddling about in a small pond of the river. **1872** *Illustr. Sydney News* 28 Sept. 14/3 The watermole is a most extraordinary little animal. It is usually about a foot and half long, with the body stout, but somewhat depressed in form and tapering towards the extremities. The head is small, and is provided with five claws. The male having, in addition, a large spur similar to that of a game cock, upon each of the hinder feet. Its tail is short, broad and depressed. **1888** *Sydney Morning Herald* 24 Jan. (Centennial Suppl.) 1/5 The platypus, or water-mole, is remarkable in that, whilst it is a warm-blooded animal and lays eggs, it also afterwards suckles its young. **1902** G.F. TRAIN *My Life in Many States* 169 The most marvellous of all the queer things of Australia, to my mind, was the animal that laid eggs like a hen, suckled its young like a goat, and was web-footed like a duck. This was the duckbill, or water-mole, which the Australians call the Patybus [*sic*]. **1834** G. BENNETT *Wanderings N.S.W.* I. 306 An animal, called **'Water-rat'** by the colonists, and Biddunong by the aborigines, burrowed in the banks. **1841** *Sydney Herald* 20 May 2/3 The water rat is larger than the common rat, and burrows in the banks of rivers. **1876** W. HARCUS *S.A.* 282 The curious water-rats or beaver-rats must be mentioned as being purely Australian. **1913** C.G. LANE *Creature-Life* 59, I must not omit to mention the aquatic, rat-like rodents usually termed 'water-rats' in the bush, though known to naturalists as beaver-rats. **1941** E. TROUGHTON *Furred Animals Aust.* 264 According to a report in an oversea newspaper of June 1937, Australian dealers were turning to the native water-rat owing to a shortage of muskrat furs, and had been paying up to 4s. 6d. a single raw skin. **1977** H. BUTLER *In Wild* 84 One of the most beautiful animals . . it's the Water Rat or Beaver Rat. He's not a marsupial, he's a native rodent. See his big webbed back feet? The front feet are still rat-like for digging. **1895** *Proc. R. Geogr. Soc. Australasia: S.A.* (1899) 72 Several varieties of acacia are referred to by explorers and bushmen as **'water trees'**, the roots yielding a fair supply. **1903** *Proc. Linnean Soc. N.S.W.* XXVII. 577 *Eucalyptus maculata* (Spotted Gum) . . are known to residents and regular travellers as the 'Water Trees', owing to the fact that they have small hollows in the base of the trunks which hold water nearly all the year round. **1915** N. DUNCAN *Austral. Byways* 98 There may be no 'water trees'. **1928** *Bulletin* (Sydney) 12 Dec. 25/4 In the mulga country of Westralia there grows what is commonly known as the water-tree. In appearance it resembles a mulga, only the leaves are larger and greener. **1948** H.A. LINDSAY *Bushman's Handbk.* 3 On reaching the crest of the ridge you . . survey the scrub, looking for water-trees . . water mallees, a needlebush . . a banksia. *Ibid.* 7 There is only one real water-tree in the goldfields' area and it is known as *the* water-tree . . *Grevillea nematophylla*. . . It looks like a small she-oak. **1965** *Austral. Encycl.* IV. 411 *H[akea] leucoptera* has been called water-bush and water-tree because aborigines (and probably thirst-stricken explorers) have obtained water from the fleshy roots by digging them up, cutting them into pieces, and placing one end in a slow fire. **1908** *Emu* VII. 203, I saw a female Rifle Bird fly . . down upon a **water vine** (*Vitis hypoglauca*). **1914** *Bulletin* (Sydney) 5 Mar. 22/2 The Vitis, or water vine . . grows plentifully on our North Coast (N.S.W.) districts and in the Queensland coastal scrub. **1949** B. O'REILLY *Green Mountains* 100 The long, tough ropes of water-vine with which the whole jungle roof is interwoven, making a bridge from one tree to another. **1965** *Austral. Encycl.* IX. 209 Water-vine, a name given to several large vines in the rain-forests of eastern Australia. . . If a piece of the spongy stem . . is cut it drips a clear water which is drinkable. **1978** R.J. BRITTEN *Around Cassowary Rock* 101 Big heavy water-vines . . hang down out of trees like ship's hawsers.

water-bag. [Spec. use of *water-bag* a bag of skin or leather used for holding or carrying water.] A canvas bag used to carry water whilst travelling: see quot. 1914. See also quot. 1964.

1879 *Illustr. Austral. News* (Melbourne) 22 Jan. 7/3 We found at this camp two riding saddles, two pack saddles, six ten-gallon water-bags, three blankets, some tea and sugar. **1887** 'COMMERCIAL TRAVELLER' *Diary Three Months Trip Qld.* 29 Water bags (canvas) are much in vogue. **1896** D. STEWART *Thousand Miles & More* 2 On January 6th, 1896, I left Kanowna . . equipped with my water bag and tucker bag. **1914** C.H.S. MATTHEWS *Bill* 88 A water-bag . . i.e. a canvas bag in which water is carried for drinking purposes. The water percolates through the canvas and evaporates on the outside of the bag, absorbing heat as it does so, and so keeping the water inside the bag beautifully cool. **1934** T. WOOD *Cobbers* 194 A water-bag, the one cool thing on the train, dangling in the breeze at the end of the coach. **1939** J.G. PATTISON *'Battler's' Tales Early Rockhampton* 27 Ice and water bags were unknown, some few of the families had drip stones (imported), convict-made at Norfolk Island. **1950** 'N. SHUTE' *Town like Alice* 258 Suspended from the rafters was a large canvas water-bag cooling the draught. **1964** *N. Austral. Monthly* July 13 A common sight in most homes is a waterbag, suspended from a piece of wire in the shade. **1982** R. INGPEN *Austral. Inventions* 13 The famous canvas waterbag so often seen in the bush was invented by Thomas Livingstone Mitchell who observed that Aborigines carried their water in kangaroo skins.

water-burner: see WATER-SCORCHER.

water core. A disease of apples: see quot. 1891. Also as **water-cored** *ppl. a.*

1891 *Braidwood Dispatch* 22 Apr. 2/4 Water-core is easily known by the watery or waxy appearance it gives either the whole or part of an apple. **1915** DARNELL-SMITH & MACKINNON *Fungus & Other Diseases Apple & Pear* 39 Glassiness, or Water Core of the Apple. . . Externally the portion affected has frequently a waxy or glassy appearance. . . The cells composing glassy tissue are fully distended and turgid. The glassy portion . . when analysed . . is found to contain an excess of water. **1930** *Jrnl. Council Sci. & Industr. Research* 177 The fact that water-cored apples are subject to breakdown is well known. . . Water core is of two types. The first is developed in immature fruit and involves more or less of the core. . . The second type develops in maturing fruit and does not involve the tissues within the core line of vasculars. **1948** *Council Sci. & Industr. Research Bull.* no. 283 26 Watercore or Glassiness. This disorder is recognizable as a glassy translucent condition of the flesh of apples not necessarily in the core region as the name might imply. **1956** *Jrnl. Dept. Agric. S.A.* Dec. 214 Watercore is not a storage disorder but develops in fruit while it is still on the tree.

water frontage: see FRONTAGE 1.

waterhole. [Used elsewhere but of local significance: see OED.]

1. a. A depression in which water collects; a pond or pool, which may be of considerable extent.

1817 J. OXLEY *Jrnls. Two Exped. N.S.W.* (1820) 154 At the eighth mile we came upon a small water-hole, which our poor horses soon emptied. **1827** *Monitor* (Sydney) 30 Aug. 619/1 In the interior . . the supply of water depends on the creek and 'water holes'. **1839** S. BUTLER *Hand-Bk. Austral. Emigrants* 78 Many farms in the colony . . have no other water than what is . . collected from the surface during heavy rains in natural basins, or *water-holes*, as they are called by the colonists. **1847** *Atlas* (Sydney) III. 2/2 We crossed an extensive flat, at the end of which, and near the foot of some gentle and thinly wooded hills, was a long serpentine reedy water hole or lagoon. **1853** MOSSMAN & BANISTER *Aust. Visited & Revisited* 62 A glimpse of small sheets of water like the Serpentine, to which the colonists apply the homely term of 'water-hole'. **1874** R.P. FALLA *Knocking About* (1976) 5 The length of this magnificent water-hole cannot be less than two miles. **1880** 'ERRO' *Squattermania* 375 Coming to several long ponds or water-holes—as they are colonially termed—Dan jumped off his horse. **1898** D.W. CARNEGIE *Spinifex & Sand* 47 He presently took us to a small granite rock and pointed out a soak or rock-hole, we could not say which. . . We stooped to examine the water-hole. **1914** H.M. VAUGHAN *Australasian Wander-Yr.* 264 It was intersected by the broad Callide Creek, and was also supplied with a considerable number of pools or 'water-holes'. **1925** G. WIRTH *Round World with Circus* 6 Playing round a waterhole in our backyard in Dalby (Q.). **1950** G.M. FARWELL *Land of Mirage* 89 The waterhole was very picturesque, a large boomerang-shaped expanse, shallow, screened by coolabahs and wattle bush. **1975** G. BLAINEY *Triumph of Nomads* 178 For much of the year the aboriginals here came to rely on small waterholes in the great granite outcrops and soaks which yielded a little shallow water to those who scratched or dug at appropriate places in the sandy beds of creeks. Here and there a native well went down perhaps fifteen or twenty feet. **1986** *Sydney Morning Herald* 12 Apr. 1/4 Waterholes between Nyngan and Bourke are as exhausted as the farmers' bank balances.

b. An artificial reservoir for the collection or retention of water.

1827 P.P. KING *Narr. Survey Intertropical & Western Coasts* I. 13 Our water-holes . . dug at the edge of the sand, within thirty yards of the vessel. **1830** *Sydney Monitor* 7 Apr. 2/4 The water . . procured from a small lagoon which is daily drying up as the summer advances; indeed, so much so, that they are now compelled to sink . . water holes in the very centre of the lagoon! **1843** *Sydney Morning Herald* 24 May 3/6 A large waterhole or dam is now being constructed, which will insure a supply of water during the driest seasons. **1846** *Ibid.* 11 Aug. 2/7 The proprietors will not take the trouble to make water holes for the cattle, or even to clean out such as are already made and become useless for want of a little labour to deepen them, and make a hard bottom. **1859** 'EYE WITNESS' *Voyage to Aust.* 19 They endeavour to save the rain-water in large water-holes dug out for that purpose. **1895** R.J. CONINGSBY *Discovery Gold Aust.* 23 Now and again the downcast pilgrims would come to a tiny 'soak' or water hole which had been made by natives.

c. A cavity in the bed of a watercourse, esp. one that retains water when the main stream dries up: see quot. 1869.

1843 R.D. MURRAY *Summer at Port Phillip* 119 It is rare to find the channel of one of these streams without some portion of its contents remaining in those deep pools of water that occur at greater or less intervals in its course, and in colonial phrase are termed 'water-holes'. **1855** *Ovens & Murray Advertiser* (Beechworth) 27 Jan. 4/3 The water holes in the river have paid and are paying very handsomely; the dry season, otherwise so unfavourable to pastoral purposes has been a great benefit to the diggers, in aiding them in working their bed claims. **1869** E.C. BOOTH *Another England* 18 In seasons of extreme drought, the river would . . cease to run; but at frequent intervals, reaches of from a few hundred yards to five miles in length were met with and upon the banks, the flocks and herds could drink in the driest season. These reaches (water-holes is the homely colonial name for them) have, many of them, depths not yet fathomed. **1889** W.H. TIETKENS *Jrnl. Central Austral. Exploring Exped.* 31 Mar. (1891) 8 At 4.30 reached a clay-water channel with some very nice waterholes in it which were now quite full; around this spot mallee timber was observed. **1913** M.A. McMANUS *Reminisc. Maranoa District* 20 At night he put them in a large 'break', or half-yard on one side of which was a large waterhole in the Maranoa River. **1926** *Smith's Weekly* (Sydney) 22 May 19/5 The large waterholes in Koopa Creek (Q.) . . are known as cockatoo holes, the birds flocking there at sundown to drink, and camp in the trees near by. **1936** C. CHEWINGS *Back in Stone Age* p. xiv, The creek-bed, occupying nearly the full width of the pass, was filled with high reeds and deep waterholes. **1951** G. FARWELL *Outside Track* 93 The yarn flowed as sluggishly as his river, with many anabranches, and deep waterholes of reminiscences, and irrelevant snags and sandspits to check its course. **1960** R.S. PORTEOUS *Cattleman* 17 He knew every water-hole in every creek on the stock-routes of Queensland. **1977** W.A. WINTER-IRVING *Bush Stories* 17 Kalkadoon sits on a large waterhole that, unlike so many river waterholes, never quite dries up.

2. *transf.* A public house or bar, esp. one frequented by a coterie; a 'watering hole'.

1968 D. O'GRADY *Bottle of Sandwiches* 191 There was a water-hole on the corner, so we left old Nebby where she was and visited it. 'Hey, mate—no dogs in the bar.'

1976 D. IRELAND *Glass Canoe* 1 The Mead was our territory, the Southern Cross our waterhole. The next tribe drank at the Bull, and on the other side the nearest tribe holed up at the Exchange. While your tribe's waterhole flowed, you never went walkabout to another tribe's waterhole. **1983** *Truckin' Life* VII. ii. 25 Billo Mullane . . a few Saturdays back after a prolonged stop-over at the . . water hole on Friday night.

3. Special Comb. **waterhole squatter,** *claypan squatter*, see CLAYPAN 2.

1904 *S. Austral. Public Service Rev.* Dec. 27 We picked out the best way we could . . and in a few miles came to another watering place where another resident of the district, of the waterhole squatter variety, had his headquarters. **1905** [see *claypan squatter* CLAYPAN 2].

water-joey. One who is employed to carry water to supply the needs of a group. See WOOD-AND-WATER JOEY a.

1916 *Bulletin* (Sydney) 14 Dec. 24/4 A young half-caste aborigine . . for a screw of 12 bob a day, is water-joey to the gangs. **1936** C.P. CONIGRAVE *N. Aust.* 147 One of the party . . went off . . to get water. . . Suddenly the 'water joey' yelled out. **1981** D. STUART *I think I'll Live* 235 No water to be drunk except it's boiled first. No one to go to the river 'cept the water joeys.

water-scorcher. An inferior cook. Also **water-burner.**

1916 *All abaht It* (London) Nov. 27 Commotion caused after tea—stretcher seen with our poor water-scorcher aboard. **1964** K. TENNANT *Summer's Tales* 42 This payment included use of a communal kitchen. I was a water-scorcher. Cooks had for me, and still have, something of the witch-doctor quality of pianists. **1982** P. ADAM SMITH *Shearers* 264 They call him the water burner, cookoo, Silly Look, baitlayer, babbling brook.

watersider. WATERSIDE WORKER.

[N.Z. **1914** *Evening Post* (Wellington) 4 Feb. 10 Watersider (signature to letter).] **1937** L. ROSS *W. Lane & Austral. Labor Movt.* 124 The A.L.F. called on the watersiders. The watersiders responded. **1969** *N.T. News* (Darwin) 11 July 8/2 Darwin watersiders now officially have a guaranteed minimum wage of $200 a month, but will continue to press for permanent employment with a minimum weekly wage. **1971** *Bulletin* (Sydney) 30 Oct. 26/1 Burly ex-boxer and watersider Charlie Wells. **1974** J. GABY *Restless Waterfront* 10 Times without number the water-sider, or wharf-labourer as he was generally known in those early days, walked in through the gate at eight one morning and walked out again at seven o'clock the following morning, tired and dirty after the long twenty-three hour shift. **1978** *Cattleman* (Rockhampton) Sept. 1/1 (*caption*) Watersiders will load beef.

waterside worker. One who is employed to load and unload a ship's cargo; a wharf-labourer.

1903 *Waterside Workers' Gaz.* Sept. 5/3 Waterside workers have sometimes good grounds for complaining that they do not get their full pay. **1911** *Huon Times* (Franklin) 11 Oct. 2/3 The waterside workers would in all probability be persuaded to refuse to handle fruit picked or packed by what, in union parlance, is known as 'scab' labor. **1955** J. MORRISON *Black Cargo* 25 The Waterside Workers' Federation is the original and bona-fide trade union on the waterfront. **1973** D. WOLFE *Brass Kangaroo* 308 You heard of the Waterside Workers? The wharfies, they call 'em. **1982** LOWENSTEIN & HILLS *Under Hook* 20 Most waterside workers lived close to their jobs—the nature of the industry demanded it.

Watson. [See quot. 1966.] In the phr. **to bet like the Watsons,** to bet heavily.

1949 L. GLASSOP *Lucky Palmer* 163 Bet well? You bet like the Watsons. **1954** T. RONAN *Vision Splendid* 76 The survey-party is chequed up to the skies and while they've got it they'll bet like the Watsons. **1966** S.J. BAKER *Austral. Lang.* (ed. 2) 273 *Watson's, bet like the*, to wager heavily. There were apparently two Watson brothers, but legend disagrees when they operated—it varies from the 1880s to 'about 1910'. They are alleged to have been born at Bendigo, Victoria, and also to have been Sydney hotel-keepers and outback N.S.W. shearers. **1967** F. HARDY *Billy Borker yarns Again* 140 I'd bet like the Watsons meself if I had a million quid in the bank. **1972** *Bulletin* (Sydney) 12 Aug. 7/2 You never hear now of a punter betting like the Watsons.

wattle. [Transf. use of *wattle, pl.* and *collect. sing.* rods or stakes interlaced with branches in the construction of fences or wattle-and-daub buildings, from the use of the branches of wattles and similar plants for this purpose: see quots. 1790 and 1803.]

1. a. Any plant of the largest Austral. plant genus *Acacia* (fam. Mimosaceae), of which there are in Aust. nearly 800 described species, widespread elsewhere, esp. in the Southern Hemisphere; the wood of many of these species. The plants usu. have pale cream to orange-yellow, often fragrant flowers in spikes or globular heads, and vary in growth habit from prostrate shrubs to tall trees. Also *attrib.*

[**1790** W. TENCH *Compl. Acct. Settlement* (1793) 78, 32 houses . . built of wattles plastered with clay.] **1796** D. COLLINS *Acct. Eng. Colony N.S.W.* (1798) I. 556 The fizgig is made of the wattle. [**1803** *Sydney Gaz.* 20 Nov., A few pannels of houses built upon the principle of ancient colonial architecture were washed down. . . The crash of decayed posts and wattles was repeated but fortunately without injury to any of the tenants.] **1823** *Hobart Town Gaz.* 15 Feb. (Suppl.), A woman . . also swore to having seen a pot boiling there, with wattle-tan in it. **1826** *Monitor* (Sydney) 15 Dec. 247/2 Last Friday, I took an excursion to the North Shore, and in my peregrination met with Bungaree and his sable tribe, very contendedly seated beneath the shade of a wattle. **1829** R. MUDIE *Picture of Aust.* 138 Very many species of *acacia* are found in Australia. . . Locally, they are known by the name of wattles, from the slender twigs being used for that purpose. **1839** *Tasmanian* (Hobart) 8 Feb. 42/2 Happy to make arrangement with the Trade to supply them with Wattle faggots. **1843** *Teetotal Advocate* (Launceston) 22 May 4/2 The wattle is indigenous; that is, peculiar to the country. **1846** G.H. HAYDON *Five Yrs. Experience Aust. Felix* 38 The land . . is lightly timbered with blackwood, hickory and wattle (*acacia affinis*). **1855** J. BONWICK *Geogr. Aust. & N.Z.* (ed. 3) 202 There are 120 species of Acacia: as,—the Wattle, Mimosa, and Blackwood or Lightwood. **1857** J. ASKEW *Voyage Aust. & N.Z.* 259 A neat little bathing-house, with . . a space in front entirely surrounded with a sharkproof netting of wattles. **1870** J. BONWICK *Last Tasmanians* 119 A soldier . . was sitting amongst some young wattles, peeling the twigs for a bird cage. **1914** E.E. PESCOTT *Native Flowers Vic.* 40 The name Wattle is purely an Australian one, and has been adapted from the practice of 'wattling', or the weaving of the young pliable growths of these shrubs in the early days, to make fences and even houses—'wattle and daub', or 'wattle and dab', as the method was called. **1917** G.C. COOPER Diary 21 Nov., Proceeded back to Yebna and camped the night, passed through some beautiful country and lanes of a kind of wattle which had a beautiful scent. **1930** V. KENNEDY *By Range & River* 73 A full list of Atherton timbers would include such building timbers as . . wattle, spurwood, penda. **1934** W.A. OSBORNE *Visitor to Aust.* 63 Botanically known as acacias and resembling, though far eclipsing, the mimosas of Southern Europe, the wattle constitutes the largest genus in Australia. **1962** C. GYE *Cockney & Crocodile* 151 All around the soak grew wattles in flower and to our surprise a clump of 'blackboys'. **1971** A. BUZO *Macquarie* (1973) 54 He gave me a locket and a sprig of wattle which I still treasure to this very day. **1982** R. HALL *Just Relations* 453 The plants themselves tell their own saga, geraniums among grevillea, honeysuckle behind the wattle.

b. With distinguishing epithet, as **black, cedar, coast, Cootamundra, golden, green, pycnantha, sally, sandhill, scrub, silver, willow**: see under first element.

c. Rarely, and usu. with distinguishing epithet, a tree of another genus, as a species of *Albizia* (see ACACIA 2). See also *black wattle* (b), BLACK *a.*[2] 1 a.

1902 J.S. HASSALL *In Old Aust.* 145 The first building ever set up in Australia for the worship of God was erected by the Reverend Richard Johnson. . . It was built of wattle, not the tree we know by that name, but a sort of Christmas bush, *Callicoma serratifolia*. **1903** *Proc. Linnean Soc. N.S.W.* XXVIII. 747 *Albizzia lophanthus* . . a native of Western Australia and well acclimatised. Known as 'Wattle'. ***c* 1910** W.R. GUILFOYLE *Austral. Plants* 49 *Albizzia lophantha* . . 'Green Crested Wattle' . . (evergreen tree, 20 to 30 ft.) . . W. Aust.

2. The flower of the wattle; also *fig.*, and as the floral emblem of Australia (see also *golden wattle* GOLDEN 3).

1858 W.A. CAWTHORNE *Legend of Kupirri* 28 The cricket chirps beneath the grass, The wodlalla bends beneath the blast; The fragrant wattle scents the air, The yerké skips around his lair. **1878** *Illustr. Austral. News* (Melbourne) 2 Sept. 154/1 What the oak and the elm are to the Briton the gum and the wattle are to the Australian. **1889** F. CRAWFORD *Native Companion Songster* 21 Tread lightly, where wattles Their sweet perfume shed, And tall gum trees shadow The Stockman's last bed. **1891** *Worker* (Brisbane) 16 May 8 We'll make the tyrants feel the sting O' those that they would throttle; They needn't say the fault is ours, If blood should stain the wattle. **1911** *Huon Times* (Franklin) 10 June 5/1 Mr Chapman also suggested the use of the waratah instead of the wattle as the Australian National emblem. **1925** M. TERRY *Across Unknown Aust.* 171 A grove of wattle in full bloom, Australia's national flower. **1955** N. PULLIAM *I traveled Lonely Land* 214 The wattle, of the genus *Acacia*, is the national flower of Australia. Its dainty blossoms are reproduced on the Australian coat of arms, the perfect accompaniment to the figures of the kangaroo and the emu which support the shield. **1956** J.T. LANG *I Remember* 197 His own epitaph to fit the occasion would have been . . 'I held Australia first, I wrote for her, I fought for her And when at last I lie, Then who to wear the wattle has A better right than I?' **1981** G. CROSS *George & Widda-Woman* 9 We gathered small bunches of flowers for Mum . . native roses, wattle, bottle-brush. **1985** *Age* (Melbourne) 20 Sept. (Suppl.) 12/3 It was a beautiful Monday morning on the Number 85 inbound to the city. The smell of wattle thrummed through an open window. All the others were closed tight against the chance of a winter comeback.

3. In the phrase **up a wattle (tree),** *up a gum tree*, see GUM TREE 2.

1941 *Pow-Wow* (Shepparton) July 3 We think she was well kidded right up the wattle-tree. **1963** *Gumsuckers' Gaz.* (Melbourne) July 2 *Up a gum-tree*, in a quandary (a variant is *up a wattle*).

4. Comb. **a.** In sense 1: **wattle bush, scrub, tree.**

1837 Tas. Non-State Rec. 157/1 19 Nov., In this Colony [*sic*] . . though I Could not find a Furze Bush I Could find A **Wattle Bush.** **1852** J. WEST *Hist. of Tas.* II. 86 Excepting a small group of wattle bushes, at the distance of ten yards, the ground was free of all but the lofty trees. **1902** *V & P* (W.A.) III. no. 46 6 Passed 'Ghondamile Soak' (dry) at five miles, then came more mulga and exellent herbage, and at 11 miles good, red, sandy soil . . mulga, and wattle-bush (*acacia*). **1853** J. SHERER *Gold Finder Aust.* 227 The robbers . . ordered them to proceed with their cart into an adjacent **Wattle Scrub.** **1881** G. WALCH *Vic.* 52 The paddock was densely covered with gum-trees and wattle-scrub. **1900** T. MAJOR *Leaves from Squatter's Note Bk.* 54 An eagle hawk left his perch and alighted in a wattle scrub. **1927** M. TERRY *Through Land of Promise* 222 The wattle scrub and bushes growing therein. **1954** T. RONAN *Vision Splendid* 155 Spinifex ridges, wattle scrubs and long, sour-grassed flats succeeded each other with nerve-racking regularity. **1966** P. COWAN *Seed* 107 The lake was screened from the road by thick wattle scrub and paperbarks. . . She said: 'I'll change my shoes. I bought a pair of thongs for walking.' ***c* 1810** *Trans. Linnean Soc. London* (1827) XV. 239 This species . . is called *Thunder-bird* by the colonists. . . It frequents the *green* **wattle-trees** in Parramatta. **1829** *Launceston Advertiser.* 10 Aug. 2 Such is the forward state of the spring that the wattle trees in this county are generally almost in full bloom. **1859** H. KINGSLEY *Recoll. Geoffry Hamlyn* II. 16 Lay down on the long grass, under the flowering wattle-trees. **1880** J. BALLANTYNE *Our Colony* 92 The Acacias, of which upwards of one hundred varieties are known (one popularly called the wattle tree) . . yield a bark which is found useful for tanning purposes. **1902** *Emu* II. 102 To feed sheep on hay and chopped-up wattle tree. **1911** E.S. SORENSON *Life in Austral. Backblocks* 28 Mention of the log-and-pug recalls that it was from this kind of building that our wattle-trees got their name.

b. In sense 2: **wattle ball, bloom, blossom, gold.**

1963 R. STOW *Tourmaline* 24 The single soft **wattle-ball** of the evening star, which does not, alas, belong to me. **1884** D.B.W. SLADEN *Summer Christmas* 14 'Twas Christmas-eve, and they sat round Th' hearth filled with **wattlebloom** still found on stray trees. **1895** J.B.

O'HARA *Songs of South* 22 Yet the spring sheds blossoms around the ruin... The wattle bloom that the sun-god knows. **1857** J. BONWICK *Early Days Melbourne* 14 **Wattle blossoms** perfumed the country. **1878** *Illustr. Austral. News* (Melbourne) 2 Sept. 154/1 The milkwhite flower of the former [*sc.* the hazel] is not more cherished by English children than the wattle blossom by our own. **1894** A. ROBERTSON *Nuggets in Devil's Punch Bowl* 62 The honey was coming from the sack as clear as amber and smelling of wattle-blossom. **1916** 'T.O. LINGO' *Austral. Comic Dict.* 9 *Wattle blossom*, puffy nuggets; spring's currency circulating in the blood of every good Australian. The gold that perishes not. **1935** E. COLEMAN *Come back in Wattle Time* 9 During the Great War, thousands of Australian soldiers received a spray of wattle-blossom in their letters from home. **1954** J.E. MACDONNELL *Jim Brady* 7 Ridges golden with a froth of wattle-blossom. **1870** A.L. GORDON *Bush Ballads* 9 In the Spring, when the **wattle gold** trembles 'Twixt shadow and shine. **1883** 'KEIGHLEY' *Who are You* 54 My wealth has gone, like the wattle-gold You bound one day on my childish brow. **1916** J. FURPHY *Poems* Pref., While billies boil, and the wattle gold gets sicklied over with the anaemia of the drawing-room ballad-monger.

5. Special Comb. **wattle bark,** the bark of any of several species of wattle, some of which are cultivated commercially for the high tannin content of their bark; also *attrib.*; so **wattle-barker** (or **-stripper**), **wattle-barking** *vbl. n.*, **wattle bark stripping** *vbl. n.*; **extract** [used elsewhere but recorded earliest in Aust.], a concentrated tannin-rich substance produced from wattle bark; **gum,** a gum exuded from the trunk and branches of species of wattle.

1824 *Austral.* (Sydney) 16 Dec. 3 **Wattle-bark,** it is said, has been successfully tried in the sister colony for the purposes of tanning. **1836** *Cornwall Chron.* (Launceston) 27 Feb. 4 *Wanted to purchase, from* 50 to 100 tons good dry Wattle Bark, chopped or unchopped. **1845** *Portland Guardian* 30 Aug. 4/2 A bill, the object of which is to protect the growth of the native wattle for the sake of the gum, has passed the Council, and the exportation of the wattle bark from this colony, will be suspended for the next two years. **1878** R.B. SMYTH *Aborigines of Vic.* I. 264 The blacks treat boils and swellings thus: when hard, they lotion the part well with decoction of wattle bark; when obstinate, they boil wild marsh-mallow, and poultice. **1886** J.F. CONIGRAVE *S.A.* 125 Tanning and wattle bark-stripping, wine making, olive oil making, and fruit preserving are occupations particularly adapted to this climate and soil. **1891** J. FENTON *Bush Life Tas.* (1964) 20 Mr Charles Friend had a party of wattle strippers at Port Sorell. **1898** *Tocsin* (Melbourne) 6 Jan. 3/1 A grave slur has been cast on Australian leather, and more especially upon the wattle bark method of tanning by the late action of the War Office authorities. **1898** *Bulletin* (Sydney) 26 Feb. 14/2 Amongst the community of wattle-barkers in the vicinity of Warrayadin, the marriage ceremony is regarded .. as a wasteful and ridiculous business. **1905** *Ibid.* 26 Oct. (Red Page), The wattle barkers had been there years before. **1909** *Ibid.* 8 Apr. 14/1 Wattle-bark stripping is my own favourite job... The bark season is limited—from September to January in Victoria. **1920** *Ibid.* 6 May 20/2 About the toughest of all bushwork, not excepting wattle-barking or log-fencing, is burning. **1925** *Makeshifts & Other Home-Made Furniture* (New Settlers' League Aust.) 19 Sheepskins make good, warm mats. Soak the skins in a tub of wattle bark liquid for long enough to tan them. **1931** *Bulletin* (Sydney) 26 Aug. 21/4 'Wattle-barkers' were the pioneers of Australia's pioneers. **1938** C.T. WHITE *Princ. Bot. Qld. Farmers* 181 The story of the wattle-bark industry is a very sad one for Australia. About fifty years ago South Africa established wattle-bark plantations from seed collected in Australia. To-day 300,000 acres are under plantation in that colony. **1965** *Austral. Encycl.* IX. 219 The most satisfactory time to strip wattle bark is spring or early summer. **1981** A.B. & J.W. CRIBB *Useful Wild Plants Aust.* 51 Wattle bark is one of the most important tannin sources in the world and, particularly in earlier times, the local product was extensively used in Australian tanneries... At one time up to 20,000 tonnes of wattle bark were exported annually from Australia. However, since about 1905 there has been, in general, a decline in production here. [**1889 wattle extract:** J.H. MAIDEN *Useful Native Plants Aust.* 308 As far back as 1823 a fluid extract of Wattle Bark was shipped to London, fetching then the extraordinary price of £50 per ton, one ton of bark yielding 4 cwt. of extract of tar consistence.] **1927** *Council Sci. & Industr. Research Bull.* no. 32 13 Of more recent origin is the wattle extract industry of South Africa. **1969** T.C. THORSTENSEN *Practical Leather Technol.* 141 The main source of wattle extract is the *Acacia mollissima*, or Black Wattle. **1843** *Portland Mercury* 10 May 3/1 The Countess of Durham, the last wool ship of the season, had on board 581 bales of wool .. 2 casks of **wattle gum** [etc.]. **1892** MRS F. HUGHES *My Childhood in Aust.* 53, I remember that we very much enjoyed collecting and eating wattle-gum, a sticky secretion which comes on the wattle-trees. **1914** *School Paper* (Melbourne) 1 June 85 A sweetish, clear liquid to flow from cracks and holes in the wattles .. we call it wattlegum. **1953** *Bulletin* (Sydney) 4 Nov. 13/4 Along with wattle-gum as a free bush sweet went 'puddins'. **1965** H. ATKINSON *Reckoning* 76 He walked fast, chewing a wad of wattle gum, spitting the brown juice in jets between his teeth.

6. In the names of insects feeding on the wattle: **wattle goat moth,** any of several cossid moths of the genus *Xyleutes*, esp. the large *X. eucalypti* and *X. liturata*, the larvae of which are among the insects called witchetty grubs; **grub,** a grub, prob. a WITCHETTY 2; **pig,** the weevil *Leptopius duponti.*

1885 F. MCCOY *Prodromus Zool. Vic.* I. iii. 47 *Zeuzera (Eudoxyla) Eucalypti* .. the **Wattle Goat-Moth** .. common in the winged state about February, flying in the twilight, in all parts of the colony where Wattle trees abound. **1890** *Agric. Gaz. N.S.W.* (1903) XIII. 714 *The Wattle Goat-Moth...* This goat-moth caterpillar destroys an immense number of fine wattles. **1926** *Illustr. Tasmanian Mail* (Hobart) 5 May 57/3 The wattle goat moths have appeared in numbers all over the country. **1968** H. FRAUCA *Bk. of Insects* 52 Among the world's most spectacular moths are some native species in the family Cossidae .. one of which is the Wattle Goat Moth... The female of this species has a wingspan of about seven inches and her fur-covered body is larger than a mouse. **1854** W. HOWITT *Boy's Adventures* 301 The women .. hunt for the **wattle grub**, a great luxury of these people. **1892** C.C. JENKYNS *Hard Life in Colonies* 250 We avoided them, our tastes not having been educated up to wattle-grubs. **1898** *Bulletin* (Sydney) 3 Dec. 14/1 At Ross (Tas.) nearly every boy had his tomahawk and grub-tin, and, on holidays, used to go out after wattle-grubs. **1974** L. WEDLICK *Sporting Fish* 28 Wattle grubs are a good bait in the Gippsland streams. **1907** W.W. FROGGATT *Austral. Insects* 183 *L[eptops] tribulus*, often called by the Sydney boys the **'Wattle Pig'**, feeds on the foliage of the black wattle; it is .. about 1 inch in length. **1926** R.J. TILLYARD *Insects of Aust. & N.Z.* 242 *L[eptops] tribulus* .. is the common 'Wattle Pig Beetle', dark brown .. with short, blunt spines on elytra. **1968** V. SERVENTY *Southern Walkabout* 26 On a flowering wattle, at the edge of the lawn, Karen found a striking beetle, bright green in colour. Or so I thought at first, but a closer look showed it had a black undercoat with a metallic sprinkling of green scales... The local children call it the wattle pig. **1978** B.P. MOORE *Life on Forty Acres* 138 The well named 'wattle pigs' (*Leptopius duponti*), a dull black, warty weevil with a rather long snout.

wattle bird. a. Any of the several birds of the genus *Anthochaera* of s. Aust., large honeyeaters having loud harsh calls, two species of which have conspicuous facial wattles; GILL BIRD. **b.** With distinguishing epithet, as **brush, little, red, yellow:** see under first element.

1819 W.C. WENTWORTH *Statistical, Hist., & Pol. Descr. N.S.W.* 119 The wattle bird .. is about the size of a snipe, and considered a very great delicacy. **1831** *Acct. Colony Van Diemen's Land* 88 The wattle bird .. flew, uttering its singular note, with its long yellow pendants or ear-drops, from tree to tree. **1849** C. STURT *Narr. Exped. Central Aust.* II. 33 App. The *Anthochaera carunculata* is the largest of the wattle birds in South Australia. **1855** J. BONWICK *Geogr. Aust. & N.Z.* (ed. 3) 198 The Wattle bird, with its pendants, makes a noise like a person vomitting. **1855** W. HOWITT *Land, Labor & Gold* I. 111 There is a sort of large, dark-colored thrush called the wattle-bird, not because it haunts the wattle-trees, but because it has wattles like a domestic fowl. This bird frequents the Banksias, sucking the honey from their flowers, and has a crow and voice very like a pheasant. **1878** MRS MEREDITH *Grandmamma's Verse-Bk.* 23 '*Coruckity-cuck*! Coruckity-coo!' (Says the Wattle-bird up in the tree). **1886** *Mercury* (Hobart) 26 May 2/6 Wattle bird shooting commenced yesterday. **1892** E.H. HALLACK *Our Townships, Farms, & Homesteads* 20 He could always get employment of some kind, and if things came to the worst he could go gumming or shoot wattle birds to fill up time. **1920** J.J. GLADSTONE *Tragedy of Gallipoli* 38 Have you heard the wattle-bird rejoice When the glow of Spring is in the land? **1952** *Coast to Coast 1951–52* 107 In the garden behind the house the wattle birds called from the banksia-trees. **1984** SIMPSON & DAY *Birds of Aust.* 329 The large wattlebirds .. use the richest and most dense nectar sources (*Banksia, Eucalyptus*) and aggressively exclude smaller species from these.

Wattle Day. An annual celebration, the date of which varies locally, of the blossoming of the wattle.

1910 *Bulletin* (Sydney) 29 Dec. 14/3 The R.C. mission, near Geraldton (W.A.) .. instituted what are called 'gohanna days', which, in black brother's mind are equivalent to our Empire Day or Wattle Day. **1914** H.M. VAUGHAN *Australasian Wander-Yr.* 67 'Wattle Day', which has been fixed for 1st September, now being kept universally as a public holiday. **1924** *Sydney Morning Herald* 31 July 8/6 Wattle Day, which serves as propaganda in a picturesque form for the planting of wattles, and which aims at the cultivation of Australian national sentiment, by the distribution and wearing of the national flower, will be celebrated on Friday. **1935** E. COLEMAN *Come back in Wattle Time* 13 Wattle Day, now an Australian institution, has done much to popularise the wattles. **1974** *Southerly* i. 56 'Today is Wattle Day, an important anniversary for all Australians because the wattle is .. ?' 'Our national flower, and we should never forget it'... 'I hope you'll remember that the first of August is always celebrated as .. ?' 'Wattle Day,' the whole school replied. **1985** *Canberra Chron.* 21 Aug. 3/1 Today is Wattle Day in the ACT—the middle of the Week of the Wattle, which began on Sunday and will end on Saturday.

wattled bee-eater. *Obs.* WATTLE BIRD.

1788 J. WHITE *Jrnl. Voyage N.S.W.* (1790) 144 The Wattled Bee-eater .. fell in our way... Under the eye, on each side, is a kind of *wattle*, of an orange colour. **1801** J. LATHAM *Gen. Synopsis Birds* Suppl. II. 150 Wattled Bee-eater... Their chief food is insects, but they likewise are very fond of sucking the honey from the different kinds of *Banksia*. **1812** G. SHAW *Gen. Zool.* VIII. i. 173 *Wattled bee-eater.* Merops carunculatus... Beneath the eye on each side [of] the head, beyond the base of the lower mandible, is a lengthened pendent wattle of an orange-colour. **1847** J. GOULD *Birds of Aust.* (1848) IV. Pl. 55, *Anthochaera carunculata* .. Wattled Bee-eater .. Wattle Bird of the Colonists.

wax. Used *attrib.* in the names of plants having waxy or glossy fruits or flowers: **wax-cluster** *obs.*, the shrub *Gaultheria hispida* (fam. Ericaceae) of Tas.; **flower,** any of several plants having waxy flowers, esp. species of the genus *Eriostemon* (fam. Rutaceae) occurring in all States but not N.T., and cultivated as ornamentals; also *attrib.*; **-lip (orchid),** either of the two terrestrial orchids of the genus *Glossodia* (fam. Orchidaceae) of s.e. Aust. incl. Tas.

1834 *Hobart Town Almanack* 133 *Gaultheria hispida*—The **wax cluster,** abundant in the middle region of Mount Wellington. **1857** D. BUNCE *Australasiatic Reminisc.* 15 *Gaultheria hispida* (wax-cluster)—this plant was laden with beautiful clusters of pure white semi-transparent wax-like berries. **1888** *Proc. Linnean Soc. N.S.W.* III. 516 'Wax-cluster.' The fruit is eatable... The taste is something like that of young gooseberries. **1898** E.E. MORRIS *Austral Eng.* 505 Wax-cluster .. an Australian shrub... A congener of the English winter-green, or American checkerberry. ***c* 1910** W.R. GUILFOYLE *Austral. Plants* 182 *Gaultheria hispida* .. 'Wax-cluster', or 'White Cluster-berry' (evergreen shrub, 3 to 5 ft.) f[lowers] white. *Ibid.* 158 *Eriostemon obovalis* .. 'Fairy **Wax-flower**' (evergreen shrub, 2 to 3 feet). *Ibid.* 174 *Eupomatia Bennettii* .. 'Wax Flower Bush' .. f[lowers] yellow and dark red. **1914** E.E. PESCOTT *Native Flowers Vic.* 29 The wax flower of the Bendigo district must not be passed by. This is Eriostemon obovalis. **1934** W.A. OSBORNE *Visitor to Aust.* 154 No botanical knowledge will be necessary to appreciate .. Sturt's desert pea, wax flower, Swan River hibiscus. **1956** T.Y. HARRIS *Nature-craft in Aust.* 159 The Wax Flowers have five petals and ten stamens. **1986** *Your Garden* Jan. 61 The native Waxflowers are usually reproduced by cuttings although a high percentage 'take' is not always achieved. **1931** *Victorian Naturalist* XLVIII. 160 Of orchids, those found were mainly **Waxlips** (*Glossodia*).

These were growing in profusion. **1935** T. RAYMENT *Cluster of Bees* 146 Double-tails (*Diuris*) and wax-lips (*Glossodia*) are .. abundant. **1947** T.Y. HARRIS *Wild Flowers Aust.* (rev. ed.) 45 Wax-lip Orchid *Glossodia major.* The solitary purple or blue flowers, on their slender stems, are very lovely. **1985** *Age* (Melbourne) 20 Sept. (Suppl.) 7/1 Wax-lips, fringed hares and many varieties of greenhoods are like scattered, tiny gems in a sea of muted green.

waxie. [f. *wax* + -Y.] A wax match.

1928 *Bulletin* (Sydney) 29 Feb. 21/2 We were out of matches except for a chip from the head of a waxie found in my 'bumper' pocket. **1959** D. LOCKWOOD *Crocodiles & Other People* 70 'Throw a match into that grass,' Jack yelled. . . Before I could stop him he had struck a waxie and tossed it into the matted tangle beside the track.

wayback, *adv., a.,* and *n.* Also **away back.** [U.S. *wayback*: see OEDS.]

A. *adv.* OUTBACK *adv.*

1899 *Bulletin* (Sydney) 14 Jan. 14/1 Some years ago, when school-mastering way back, had occasion to call on Mrs Casey. **1903** *Advocate* (Burnie) 10 Feb. 3/4 One of the settlers away back. **1916** *Truth* (Sydney) 3 Sept. 9/3 To-day, I'm in the backblocks, way, way back, where the wool grows, and the station folk are bright and happy, for the squatter is experiencing very fortunate times. **1927** T.S. GROSER *Lure of Golden West* 173 Large tracts of country were being opened up 'wayback'. Every week saw large batches of settlers going further and further inland. **1936** E. HARRINGTON *Boundary Bend* 45 When you're way back again in the country.

B. *adj.* OUTBACK *a.*

1899 *Bulletin* (Sydney) 28 Jan. 14/3 On a N.S.W. wayback selection lives a family containing three male idiots. **1907** *Truth* (Sydney) 13 Jan. 1/5 'It is easier to get ten wives than one servant,' said a way-back farmer, bemoaning the dearth of domestics. **1926** *Smith's Weekly* (Sydney) 28 Aug. 18/3 Am betting the next new waggons on wayback roads will be called 'Miss Australia'. **1932** R.W. THOMPSON *Down Under* 73 One would not realise the wealth of some of these way-back Queensland station owners, to look at them in their rough clothes with their gnarled hands. **1967** *Southerly* iii. 205 This sun-baked, squalid .. wayback establishment.

C. *n.*

1. OUTBACK *n.*

1899 *North-Western Advocate* (Devonport) 21 Apr. 4/2 A man writes from way-back. **1900** *Bulletin* (Sydney) 14 July 15/1 There are worse moves than running a big herd of goats in the wayback. **1911** I.A. ROSENBLUM *Stella Sothern* 103 'How do the unskilled girls of Wayback make such delicacies .. ?' 'Australian bush girls can do anything.' **1929** W.J. RESIDE *Golden Days* 319 One camped in the way-back with an English chap. **1947** V.C. HALL *Bad Medicine* 261 He's an auld dingo-poisoner, Doctor. About 75. Come in from 'way back' with a load of scalps. **1956** *Bulletin* (Sydney) 15 Feb. 12/1 Our carriage was invaded by a couple of half-stonkered ringers from way back who had a good supply of bottled-stuff to help them onward.

2. OUTBACKER *n.*[1]

1903 *Bulletin* (Sydney) 11 Apr. 16/3 He had been a red-headed jackaroo but had evoluted to a perfect 'wayback' and attained management of a small station. **1915** A. WRIGHT *Sport from Hollowlog Flat* 21 At the table was an unmistakable 'wayback' .. down from Hollowlog Flat for a holiday. **1929** *Bulletin* (Sydney) 26 June 23/1 All the blokes an' janes up 'ere were waybacks wild an' green. **1937** *Australasian* (Melbourne) 38 A 'wayback' .. was searching in all his pockets and muttering: 'I ought to 'ave it; I 'ad it a minit ago.' **1956** T. RONAN *Moleskin Midas* 165 Of course, I'm only a wayback meself with no schoolin' so I wouldn't know.

waybacker. [f. prec.] OUTBACKER *n.*[1]

1899 *Bulletin* (Sydney) 5 Aug. 35/1 That's the Waybacker's ambition, to get 'paralytic drunk'. **1920** *Land of Lyre Bird* (S. Gippsland Pioneers' Assoc.) 383 Of medium height and wiry, and with a bushy black beard when I first knew him, he looked a typical 'waybacker'. **1927** T.S. GROSER *Lure of Golden West* 277 Lightening the lot of the 'way-backer'.

weaner.

1. [Used elsewhere but recorded earliest in Aust.] An animal, usu. a lamb or calf, weaned during the current year. Also *transf.* and *attrib.*

1865 R. HENNING *Lett.* 19 Aug. (1966) 208 He takes the heaviest flock of all, 2,200 weaners. **1872** C.H. EDEN *My Wife & I in Qld.* 67 You would never mix ewes and wethers or hoggets (two-year old sheep and weaners). **1888** 'R. BOLDREWOOD' *Robbery under Arms* (1937) 39 Our hungry weaners spread out and began to feed. **1895** G. RANKEN *Windabyne* 43 This was the cattle-run proper. Smaller paddocks were made lower down the river for weaners, heifers, and fattening stock. **1922** V. PALMER *Boss of Killara* 9 Most of the blackboys were herding weaners at another part of the run. **1932** W. HATFIELD *Ginger Murdoch* 203 We came across quite a few 'weaners' bawling through little mobs as though looking for their mothers. **1948** J.K. EWERS *For Heroes to live In* 2 He poured the peelings and scraps into the trough and the weaners buried their heads in the mush with squeals of delight. **1967** F.T. MACARTNEY *Proof against Failure* 49 The job was punching weaners, which means mustering ewes with lambs to separate the latter when weaned. **1980** ANSELL & PERCY *To fight Wild* 84 Came across a couple of weaner buffalo feeding right on the edge of the river. **1985** *Austral. Agric. Yr. Bk.* (Nat. Farmers' Federation) 219 Good lines of weaner and yearling heifers can be purchased without difficulty, and stud cattle of excellent quality are available.

2. *fig.* One who is young and inept; one who is new to a particular situation.

1892 *Truth* (Sydney) 22 May 1/5 Young Australia has too big a percentage of black sheep amongst its weaners. **1944** C. WILMOT *Tobruk* 43 We overtook a column of prisoners. . . An Australian sergeant hopped on the running-board and said, 'Would you drive us along a bit? I want to head these bloody weaners off down the road to Bardia.'

weaning paddock. An enclosure in which animals being weaned are confined.

1845 D. MACKENZIE *Emigrant's Guide* 120 Without a weaning or heifer paddock, you will be obliged to allow your calves to continue sucking their mothers for a whole year. **1847** *Atlas* (Sydney) III. 107/3 On the station are two cultivation paddocks, one horse paddock, and one large weaning paddock. **1945** E. MITCHELL *Speak to Earth* 149 A morning spent in the first weaning-paddock yard was quite exciting.

weatherboard, *a.* and *n.* [Transf. use of *weatherboard* a series of boards nailed horizontally, with overlapping edges, as an outside covering for walls.]

A. *adj.*

1. Of a building: having external walls covered with overlapping horizontal boards; weatherboarded.

1827 [see *weatherboard hut*]. **1847** *Moreton Bay Courier* 13 Nov. 3/1 We understand that a weatherboard building .. was blown down during the storm on Thursday evening. **1861** L.A. MEREDITH *Over Straits* 135 Substantial buildings are surrounded by the heterogeneous crowd of weather-board, slab, paling, and calico tenements always found in digging locations. **1871** *Austral. Town & Country Jrnl.* (Sydney) 15 Apr. 462/4 Most of the buildings are slab or bark, with weather-board fronts. **1900** H. LAWSON *Over Sliprails* 45, I had to pass the Bank on the way. It was the usual weatherboard box with a galvanised iron top. **1919** *Our Empire* (Melbourne) 18 Sept. 9 We have heard of a weatherboard hall being erected as a soldiers' memorial. **1926** 'S. WESTLAW' *Mystery of Lombardy Chambers* 128 The body had been removed in a spring cart to a room in the back of the weather-board Post Office. **1961** *Realist* (Sydney) vii. 13 Her eyes swept distastefully the ageing yellow weather-board portables, the rotting fence, the ancient shelter shed, the pot holed playground. **1972** ANDERSON & BLAKE *J.S. Neilson* 44 Down near the Well men had built a little weatherboard church.

2. In collocations: **weatherboard cottage, house, hut.**

1837 BACKHOUSE & TYLOR *Life & Labours G.W. Walker* (1862) 277 It already consists of nearly a hundred buildings, chiefly **weather-board cottages,** and a few rude, turf huts. **1848** H.W. HAYGARTH *Recoll. Bush Life* 6 As the royal Sydney mail subsides into a vehicle little better than a market-cart, so the stone or brick hotel gives place to the weatherboard cottage, and this in due time dwindles down to the slab hut beyond the boundaries of the colony. **1879** 'RECENT SETTLER' *Emigration to Tas.* 5 A weather-board cottage can be erected in a fortnight. **1897** R. NEWTON *Work & Wealth Qld.* 34 The modest weatherboard cottage, which has satisfied Mr Free's notions of comfort for many years, has not been replaced in his days of affluence by a more pretentious structure. **1910** *Bulletin* (Sydney) 7 July 44/1 One small, oblong, weather-board, bare, verandahless 'cottage'. **1956** A.C.C. LOCK *Tropical Tapestry* 246 We went along to a neat little weatherboard cottage. **1972** *Bulletin* (Sydney) 2 Dec. 51/1 (*caption*) Melbourne's first Post Office was a weatherboard cottage. **1984** P. CUFFLEY *Chandeliers & Billy Tea* 39 The simple weatherboard cottage became a universal symbol for the basic Australian home. **1847** *Moreton Bay Courier* 11 Sept. 3/2 In addition to these, several **weather-board houses** in various parts of the town are fast approaching towards completion. **1879** 'RECENT SETTLER' *Emigration to Tas.* 70 A fire is very acceptable after sunset, especially in a weatherboard house. **1886** P. CLARKE *'New Chum' in Aust.* 77 The coach stopped for dinner at an inn, or 'hotel' (as these unpretentious-looking weatherboard houses-of-call pretentiously style themselves). **1929** A. SMITH *Austral. Home Carpenter* 120 Front view of the weatherboard house into which an attic is to be built. **1951** D. COLLINS *Vic.'s my Home Ground* 24 In the early days, so Jim O'Brien told me, he and his five brothers and three sisters grew up happily in a slab-and-bark house, but in '92 an eight-roomed weatherboard house was built. **1965** G. MCINNES *Road to Gundagai* 36 The contrast between this dun-coloured weatherboard house with its tin roof and any other conceivable dwelling place was so enormous that to live in the house was an adventure in itself. **1827** P. CUNNINGHAM *Two Yrs. in N.S.W.* I. 163 From hence to the **Weather-board hut,** on King's Table Land, the distance is sixteen miles. **1851** C.P. FORD *Emigrant Family* 42 We removed to a nice weatherboard hut, with plenty of room in it, an underground dairy .. altogether a very respectable place. **1879** 'RECENT SETTLER' *Emigration to Tas.* 48, I saw .. two or three weather-board huts or cottages. **1986** *Age* (Melbourne) 13 Mar. (Green Guide) 8/1 We walked among the old green weatherboard huts of the repatriation centre at the Concorde Hospital in Sydney where the Diggers from both wars are looked after.

B. *n.* A weatherboarded building, usu. a dwelling. Also *attrib.*

1921 *Bulletin* (Sydney) 14 Apr. 56/3 When Joseph Appleby bought Mon Rèpos, Beach-road Carragool, he went straight to his friend Briggs to get it fully insured. . . 'Against fire, yes,' said Briggs. 'Though the premium is stiff for seaside weatherboards.' **1935** L. MANN *Human Drift* 238 Magnificently the two stories [*sic*] of Geelong weatherboards, new that year, overlooked on the ridge. **1956** E. LAMBERT *Watermen* 33 The fishing families lived mainly, as they had for generations, in the little weatherboards that lined the beach between the bridge and the pier. **1968** *Bulletin* (Sydney) 31 Aug. 42/3 Out in the older weatherboard suburbs, the three-yearly paint job is still the only defence against the subtropical seediness. **1986** *Ibid.* 29 Apr. 85/2 Dreyfus and his wife . . live in an unassuming weatherboard in a not very well cared for part of one of Melbourne's eastern suburbs.

weather shed. SHELTER-SHED; now usu. a structure in a school playground.

1889 *Braidwood Dispatch* 17 Aug. 3/5 Residence of 4 rooms with . . weather sheds. **1961** *Realist* (Sydney) xii. 14 Outside the weathershed he stopped. **1973** *Southerly* ii. 105, I called in at the school and found it was still one room and a verandah with hat pegs and a weather shed out the back that let the rain in every time. **1980** M. WILLIAMS *Dingo!* 25 After school most of the boys in Number Seven home hung around me in the weathershed.

wedding bush. [See quot. 1981.] Any of several white-flowered shrubs of the Austral. genus *Ricinocarpos* (fam. Euphorbiaceae).

1914 E.E. PESCOTT *Native Flowers Vic.* 100 The 'wedding bush' is a free-flowing heath-like bush, covered with masses of white starry flowers, . . botanically known as Ricinocarpus pinifolius. **1935** T. RAYMENT *Cluster of Bees* 46 During October .. the small tea-tree and the creamy wedding-bush cover the landscape. **1959** *Meanjin* 291 Tea-tree in full blossom, and wedding-bush even whiter. **1981** J.A. BAINES *Austral.*

n.

quot. 1900.] *Murray cod*, see MURRAY 2.

ee Whale *v.*] **1900** *Tocsin* (Melbourne) 6 Sept. d being a large fish, is by reason of his size termed a whale, and his captor a whaler. **1926** *Aussie* (Sydney) Aug. 50/1 The Mur- whalers were mostly old men, and their re Murray cod.

phr. **a whale in the bay,** a person with spend.

E. HARNEY *Grief, Gaiety & Aborigines* 20 I heard the term . . 'a whale in the bay' and se it meant someone was in town who had end. **1978** D. STUART *Wedgetail View* 30 of those hoons round the pubs, hangers- g for the old proverbial whale in the bay. MMON et al. *Working Lives* 22 Word had got here were a couple of whales in the bay, as already filling. **1984** *Austral.* (Sydney) r Read said he . . had told his staff the a poor horse could possibly win such a ring-in'. 'I knew there had to be some the bay for this kind of activity to go

. **to play the whale,** to vomit. PHRIES *Wonderful World Barry McKenzie,* elp me—you know . . *play the whale.* ulls it Off, I think I'm going to be sick. the whale. **1974** *Bulletin* (Sydney) 19 always getting full and playing the

uot. 1878.]

vel along (the banks of a river) as a g., and as *vbl. n.*

NSON *Christmas on Carringa* 16 Men through the Riverina country often e and a hook to catch cod or black- 'Murrumbidgee Whaling'. **1911** *ers* 45 He had 'whaled' the river for t the rheumatics had got into his wagging days were over. **1912** *Splinters* 45 The stations gives no ugar, beef, nor tea, An' Murrum- he game it used to be. **1924** E.J. 14 After leaving Newcastle, we ith the unrestraint of old bush- d' the rivers of prosperity in com- hoof across arid plains of life. a swagman along the banks of

) 2 July 6/1 There are thousands un-scorched grassless plains of and down the muddy streams by the politicians who ride in *sin* (Melbourne) 13 Sept. 6/1 In gga we had passed a proper rayed in garments of sacking fly from bark. **1907** *Bulletin* he Murrumbidgee whaler is only a very rare specimen **1918** D.H. MEIKLE *Humorous* park dosser Turnin' out to he Murrumbidgee Don't yer **6** R.G. EDWARDS *Overlander* utton . . just a bit cut off the jolly to be whaling in the

uot. 1965.] The rainforest (fam. Moraceae) of e. Guinea. See also WADDY

tive Plants Aust. 591 *Pseudo-* Whalebone Tree' in South- ood light brown, close- **29** W.D. FRANCIS *Austral.* *s Brunoniana* . . Whale- een used for axe-handles ols. **1965** *Austral. Encycl.* sented in Australia by *P.* which possesses a very branches, by virtue of whalebone-tree. **1984** *Qld.* II. 270 *Streblus pen-* is a small tree ± 5 m. the branches tending downwards.

whaler, var. WALER.

whaler, *n.*[1] Also **waler.** [See WHALE *n.*[1] and *v.*]

a. A swagman whose route follows the course of a river.

1878 'IRONBARK' *Southerly Busters* 177, I know the Murrumbidgee's bends, Though not a 'whaler' now, And many a score of sheep I've shore For good old Jacky Dow. **1889** *Bulletin* (Sydney) 5 Oct. 8/4 His constant care is to increase his slender store so that he may retire to some secluded bend where he can mend his diet with a few cod-fish (hence the name 'Whaler'). **1902** *Ibid.* 15 Nov. 31/2 'Swaggie comin',' said Bill. 'Whaler, too; I'll bet. I know by the swing of him.' **1913** W.K. HARRIS *Outback in Aust.* 144 On the Murrumbidgee we asked several questions of an old 'whaler' as to roads and grass and water ahead. **1925** M. GILMORE *Tilted Cart* 49, I toast my bit of bacon on A length of fencing wire—And it's so does every Waler! **1941** C. BARRETT *Aust.* 61 I've been a whaler . . since I was a nipper, mostly on the Murray. **1953** H.M. EASTMAN *Mem. of Sheepman* 70 'Walers' . . were a carefree lot. **1969** J. CARTER *Four-Wheel Drive Swagman* 71 (*caption*) In the old days, men like these who wandered the banks of the Murray were known as 'whalers'. **1983** A. CANNON *Bullocks, Bullockies & Other Blokes* 67 There were two types of whaler. One was rapt with the river. . . But the man before me was the other type—the scholar, the philosopher. . . He held deep views on politics.

b. *spec.*, as **Darling, Murray, Murrumbidgee whaler.**

1894 G. BOOTHBY *On Wallaby* 318 The '**Darling whalers**', as they are called: idle, loafing, thieving tramps, somewhat after the fashion of the 'Travellers' in North Queensland, who move up and down the river (up one bank and down the other), from year's end to year's end, doing no work and depending for their existence upon the charity of the unfortunate squatter. **1903** C. VON HAGEN *Plunder & Hunger* p. vii, The compulsory acceptance of the pannikin of flour, and the bit of tea and sugar, the impossibility of securing continuous work, the despair resulting from failure, the break that had taken place in all that tied him to relatives in the old country, the long, weary, heart-breaking tramp, tramp, tramp, from station to station, had, in a few short years converted a bright, intelligent young man full of hope and energy, into a confirmed 'Darling whaler' and vagrant. **1951** G. FARWELL *Outside Track* 19 There is no call for the writer to treat of the bush as though we were still living in Lawson's day. The lonely swagman and Darling whaler do not reflect the modern spirit. **1982** P. ADAM SMITH *Shearers* 224 'The Darling whalers' were known to the shearers for fifty years: swagmen in canoes, they bartered their catch of fish to the bladesmen waiting on the banks up and down the rivers. **1926** L.C.E. GEE *Bush Tracks & Gold Fields* 69 Those curious people, 'the **Murray whalers**'. **1936** *Bulletin* (Sydney) 13 May 20/1 Joe had been an old Murray whaler, and I asked him why he travelled alone. **1966** G.W. BROUGHTON *Men of Murray* 109 The people one met . . were 'Murray whalers', fishermen, engineers, or farmers. **1878** *Squatters' Plum* 15 At length he is advised to take to the bush and crawl from station to station looking for employment, and the adoption of this step gives him a new designation, that of Sun-downer, or **Murrumbidgee Whaler.** **1918** A. WRIGHT *Over Odds* 37 He was an ancient, properly-accoutred sundowner—the Murrumbidgee whaler that they'd heard about but had never seen in real life. **1953** A. RUSSELL *Murray Walkabout* 147 He was a 'Murrumbidgee whaler', the river prototype of the tramping sundowner. **1983** A.F. HOWELLS *Against Stream* 60 There were still a number of the old-time Murrumbidgee Whalers scattered along the river. These exswaggies had taken up permanent residence in huts and shacks of their own built on crown land. . . They received the pension and a few of them did a bit of fishing, trapping or tinkering.

c. In the collocation **whalers' delight:** see quots.

1901 *Bulletin* (Sydney) 14 Sept. 16/4 'Murrumbidgee jam' consists of brown sugar muddled up with cold tea. . . It is also called Whaler's Delight. **1920** *Ibid.* 24 June 22/3 'Murrumbidgee jam'—brown sugar made into a thick paste by mixing it with cold tea . . was also well known as Whalers' Delight.

whaler, *n.*[2] [See quot. 1969.] Any of several sharks of the fam. Carcharhinidae, esp. the large bronze whaler *Carcharhinus brachyurus* of s. Aust. and elsewhere in temperate seas. Also **whaler shark.**

1882 J.E. TENISON-WOODS *Fish & Fisheries N.S.W.* 92 It is very probable that the majority of our sharks have a very wide range. . . The following list includes all that are known to occur in our seas . . the Whaler, *Galeocerdo rayneri* [etc.]. **1887** *Proc. Linnean Soc. N.S.W.* II. 164 *Carcharias macrurus*, n.sp. . . This Shark is said to be not uncommon on the New South Wales Coast, where it is called the 'Whaler'. **1906** D.G. STEAD *Fishes of Aust.* 232 Amongst the Sharks may be mentioned . . the 'Whaler', sometimes known as 'River' Shark (*Carcharias brachyurus*). **1936** N. CALDWELL *Fangs of Sea* 9 The whaler shark, probably the most numerous of all Australian sharks, has a hide of medium thickness. **1951** T.C. ROUGHLEY *Fish & Fisheries Aust.* 249 There are several species of whaler sharks in Australian waters, including the black whaler (*Galeolamna macrurus*), the smaller bronze whaler (*G. ahena*), and the cocktail shark of South Australia (*G. greyi*), known in Western Australia as the Swan River whaler. **1969** J. POLLARD *Austral. & N.Z. Fishing* 686 The name whaler appears to go back to the days of the old whalers at Twofold Bay, on the New South Wales south coast, where they were among the most common species seen around the whales. **1974** J.M. THOMSON *Fish Ocean & Shore* 114 The whalers commonly move in packs and have been known to demolish a whale carcase in a few minutes. **1981** G. ELLIS *Hey Doc, let's go Fishing!* 50, I have often read of a shark's feeding frenzy, but I'd never seen anything quite as savage as this and decided that as I had no desire to share the boat with a maddened bronze whaler, it was time to call it a day.

whaling station. *Hist.* [Used elsewhere but recorded earliest in Aust.: see OEDS *whaling, vbl. sb.* 2.] A port serving as a base for whalers. See also *fishing station* FISHING.

1833 *Launceston Advertiser* 17 Oct. 3 The brig Socrates is entered at the Custom House for Portland Bay (whaling station). **1842** *Sydney Morning Herald* 6 Aug. 3/2 We believe that the whaling stations in Van Diemen's Land and Australia are all exempt from duty on spirits and tobacco. **1847** *Moreton Bay Courier* 3 July 4/1 A whaling station has been formed by the convict department at Fortescue Bay, Van Diemen's Land. **1878** R.B. SMYTH *Aborigines of Vic.* II. 244 Wherever whaling stations have been established, the natives have proved themselves to be very valuable assistants. . . They enter heartily into the sport, and make excellent 'pull-away hands' in the whale-boat. **1977** C. MCCULLOUGH *Thorn Birds* 20 The eleven men . . came out at the whaling station at Hobart.

whampoo pigeon, var. WOMPOO PIGEON.

wharfie. [f. WHARF(-LUMPER or *labourer* + -Y.] WATERSIDE WORKER.

1911 *Truth* (Sydney) 16 Apr. 5/8 *'Wharfies' take a hand.* . . The wharf laborers have good cause to thank 'Truth'. **1919** *Smith's Weekly* (Sydney) 8 Mar. 9/5 A pet method is to dump a case of whisky or wine on the wharf so darned hard that a few bottles break. What comes out of the box at the corners belongs to the wharfie, and is caught in a crib-tin. **1934** *Red Star* (Perth) 26 Oct. 4/1 Once again, safety first—for the cargo, the wharfie—doesn't matter. **1950** J. MORRISON *Port of Call* 15 'Not until the longshoremen begin coming back?' 'We call 'em wharfies here. You're off the Canadian?' **1958** C. KOCH *Boys in Island* 60 The men were waterfront workers, this was a wharfies' pub they had invaded. **1965** G. MCINNES *Road to Gundagai* 114 The docks themselves were a wonderful litter of bales and crates among which the 'wharfies' moved with lazy loose-limbed nonchalance like bronzed giants in the sun: blue dungarees, grey flannel singlets edged with navy cotton tops and big wideawake hats, bashed-in, stained and noble. **1976** *West of Peesey* (Warooka Hist. Committee) 20 There were days when the wheat and barley was shipped by ketches from the Point Turton jetty, and the fishermen became 'wharfies' and lumped the bags onto the boats. **1983** *Daily Tel.* (Sydney) 26 Feb. 1/2 His wife was the reason the former wharfie, brickie, bridge rigger, and battler got his start in television.

wharf-lumper. [f. *wharf* + *lumper* a labourer employed in loading or unloading cargo.] A wharf-labourer; WATERSIDE WORKER.

1899 *North-Western Advocate* (Devonport) 8 Mar. 2/8 Short strike amongst Hobart wharf lumpers. **1911** *Truth* (Sydney) 5 Feb. 1/7 It is an ironical fact that houses

Plant Genera 320 Wedding Bush . . a bushy shrub with white flowers like those traditionally used for weddings.

wedgebill. Either of two conspicuously-crested brown and grey birds of the genus *Psophodes, P. cristatus* of drier e. Aust. and *P. occidentalis* of drier w. Aust.

1841 J. GOULD *Birds of Aust.* (1848) III. Pl. 17, *Sphenostoma cristatum* . . Crested Wedge-bill. **1890** *Act* (Vic.) 54 Vict. no. 1095 3rd Sched., Wedge-bill. From the first day of August to the twentieth day of December next following in each year. **1896** B. SPENCER *Rep. Horn Sci. Exped. Central Aust.* II. 74 Crested Wedge-bill . . are also often heard singing at all hours of the night. **1916** S.A. WHITE *In Far Northwest* 8 The wedgebill, another bird which came under our notice, was smart-looking, with crest and long tail. **1945** C. BARRETT *Austral. Bird Life* 177 That fine songster and ventriloquist, the wedgebill . . inhabits dry inland areas. **1962** J. MARSHALL *Journey among Men* 46 Perhaps the wedgebill, even more than the bellbird, is the characteristic voice of the mulga. **1975** X. HERBERT *Poor Fellow my Country* 465 Crested wedgebills . . showed him pods opening to shed seeds that made good nutty munching.

wedge-tailed, *a.* Used as a distinguishing epithet in the names of birds: **wedge-tailed eagle,** the large eagle *Aquila audax*, widespread in Aust. incl. Tas., and occurring in s. New Guinea, having dark brown plumage and a wedge-shaped tail; *mountain eagle*, see MOUNTAIN; WEDGIE; see also EAGLE HAWK; also **wedge-tail, wedge-tail(ed) eagle(-hawk); shearwater** (formerly **petrel**), the dark brownish-black sea bird *Puffinis pacificus* of coastal e. and w. Aust., and elsewhere in the Indian and Pacific oceans.

1832 J. BACKHOUSE *Narr. Visit Austral. Colonies* 28 Dec. (1843) 118 Two **Wedge-tailed Eagles,** called in the colony Eagle Hawks, showed a disposition to carry off a small dog. **1865** G.F. ANGAS *Aust.* 87 Amongst the birds of prey inhabiting Australia the largest is the wedge-tailed eagle, a noble bird, about the size of the golden eagle of Europe. **1896** F.G. AFLALO *Sketch Nat. Hist. Aust.* 143 The Wedge-tailed Eagle (*Aquila audax*) . . is easily approached when gorged from a recent feed. **1912** SPENCER & GILLEN *Across Aust.* 67 However bad the season may be, you are certain to see great wedge-tailed eagle-hawks . . hovering about or perched on trees. **1935** T. RAYMENT *Cluster of Bees* 63 The majesty of the wedge-tail eagle cleaving the air to pick up deftly with its talons the timorous rabbit. **1942** C. BARRETT *From Bush Hut* 98 A pair of wedge-tails built a great stick nest in the big tree. **1978** D. STUART *Wedgetail View* 2 The wedgetails would plane in on wide wings to land awkwardly. **1984** M. BLAKERS et al. *Atlas Austral. Birds* 102 The Wedge-tailed Eagle is sometimes killed by poison at carcasses of animals. Though in most places the bird is protected, it is sometimes shot by farmers who regard it as a predator of sheep. **1848** [**wedge-tailed shearwater**] J. GOULD *Birds of Aust.* VII. Pl. 58, *Puffinus sphenurus* . . Wedge-tailed Petrel. **1902** *Emu* II. 36 The Wedge-tailed Petrel (*Puffinus chlororhynchus*) had prepared their burrows for laying in November. **1928** S.E. NAPIER *On Barrier Reef* 41 The mutton-bird—*alias* the Wedge-tailed Shearwater. **1955** V. SERVENTY *Aust.'s Great Barrier Reef* 57 The Wedge-tailed Shearwater . . is closely related to the common muttonbird of Bass Strait, and is a very similar bird in its habits. **1976** *Reader's Digest Compl. Bk. Austral. Birds* 57 Even when the wedge shape of its large tail is not clearly visible, the wedge-tailed shearwater can be distinguished at sea from other similar dark petrels.

wedgie. [f. WEDGE(-TAILED + -Y.] *Wedge-tailed eagle*, see WEDGE-TAILED.

1941 *Bulletin* (Sydney) 26 Mar. 17/2 On several occasions lately I have lost the services of my trapdog through the wedgies chasing him home. **1964** M. SHARLAND *Territory of Birds* 195 On the highway linking Darwin with Alice Springs . . 'Wedgies' are seen every few miles on the lookout for food. **1970** P. SLATER *Eagle for Pidgin* 50 In most countries people go for miles to see an eagle. . . Anyway scientific studies show only the odd wedgie will take a lamb.

weeai, weeay, varr. WEEI.

weebill. [See quot. 1984.] The smallest Austral. bird, *Smicrornis brevirostris*, an olive-brown to yellowish bird widespread in mainland Aust.

1931 J. DEVANEY *Earth Kindred* 14 The weebill, hid in his sapling top Whistled as tho' he would never stop. **1946** *Bulletin* (Sydney) 23 Jan. 12/2 A clump of tall sapling in a bend of the creek is the undisputed domain of a colony of Australia's tiniest birds, the weebills. **1964** M. SHARLAND *Territory of Birds* 140 The North is full of contrasts. . . The Weebill is yellow-tinted here, instead of brown as it is in the South. **1984** SIMPSON & DAY *Birds of Aust.* 326 The Weebill . . is thornbill-like but has a small, short bill.

weegie, var. WIDGIE.

weei /'wiaɪ/. Also **weeai, weeay, wei.** [a. Aranda *wiya.*] An Aboriginal boy.

1886 D. LINDSAY *Exped. across Aust.* (1889) 12 They also promised to bring in a *wei* (small boy) for me next day, in exchange for our dog 'Toby'. **1902** R. SCHLANK *Austral. Poems & Ballads* 9 When it's 'Wei! Catch the Boss, there!' [*Note*] Wei (boy), native word. **1931** M. TERRY *Hidden Wealth* 221 A mob of old blacks teaching several 'wee-ies' (young boys) how to spear cattle. **1933** R.B. PLOWMAN *Man from Oodnadatta* 46 The rest of the team consisted of one adult blackboy, two wee-ais (small blackboys) and a donkey. **1935** H.H. FINLAYSON *Red Centre* 63, I went on down with four camels, taking along three of the bucks and two 'weeis'; bright young boys of about fourteen. **1965** F.G.G. ROSE *Wind of Change* 169 Weeai is the local lingua franca word for young, uninitiated men or boys. In the same way Queeai is used for women and girls. These are not local words. **1973** *Bronze Swagman Bk. Bush Verse* (1974) 46 I'm a wee-i in my mia-mia on the Mulligan. **1974** N. PHILLIPSON *As Other Men* 121 A wife could find another buck and weeays could die; tribal groups could be dispossessed. **1976** C.D. MILLS *Hobble Chains & Greenhide* 72 The 'weeais' usually scored knives and mouth organs. A pocket knife was highly prized and carefully guarded. **1981** A. GRANT *Camel Train & Aeroplane* 104 All the riders taking up positions in the lead and only a small wei or gin keeping the stragglers up.

wee juggler /wi 'dʒʌglə/. Also **weejugla.** [a. Wiradhuri *wijugula.*] MAJOR MITCHELL COCKATOO.

1898 D.W. CARNEGIE *Spinifex & Sand* 274 Throughout the day, galahs, wee-jugglers . . and an occasional hawk or crow, came to the spring. **1904** *Bulletin* (Sydney) 4 Feb. 17/1 *Re* age of cockatoos. I know of a 'wee juggler' (pink with yellow crest) that was trapped . . on the Lachlan, in 1884. **1921** *Ibid.* 5 May 22/1 The wee-jugla, or pink cockatoo . . keeps religiously to itself. **1943** C. BARRETT *Austral. Animal Bk.* 183 'Wee juggler' is another popular name for this cockatoo, but nearly always it is called 'Major Mitchell'. **1976** N.K. WALLACE *Bush Lawyer* 129 The pretty white cockatoo with its pink front called the wee juggler or cockarina.

weekender. [Used elsewhere but recorded earliest in Aust.] A holiday house.

1921 *Bulletin* (Sydney) 14 Apr. 56/3 A man . . bought a week-ender which he confessedly didn't intend to inhabit for more than four months of the year. **1935** DAVISON & NICHOLLS *Blue Coast Caravan* 75 Holes had been hacked in the forest for room to plant untastefully designed, unpainted, tin-roofed 'week-enders'. **1944** L. GLASSOP *We were Rats* 266 It was just a 'week-ender', like any of the other thousands scattered sparsely around the edge of Lake Carraday. **1953** *Bulletin* (Sydney) 4 Nov. 12/2 At intervals of seven or eight weeks we visit our N.S.W. south-coast weekender. **1967** D. HORNE *Educ. Young Donald* 10 An inlet of Port Hacking . . where my grandfather had his 'weekender'. To get to the weekender, we would walk along a sandy bush track. **1971** *Bulletin* (Sydney) 9 Oct. 65/1 Once upon a time building a weekender for holidays—and eventual retirement—was an integral part of the Australian dream, like owning a Holden, a Victa lawnmower, and one's own home. **1981** B. OAKLEY *Marsupials & Politics* 52 Fifteen years ago we had a nice house in Melbourne, a weekender in the country, friends, parties, restaurants.

weelo /'wiloʊ/. Also **weeloo, weelow.** [a. Nhanta-anmaŋu (and other w. Austral. languages) *wilu.*] CURLEW.

1845 J. GOULD *Birds of Aust.* (1848) VI. Pl. 5, At night it [*sc.* the 'Large-billed Plover'] is said to utter a loud scream or cry, resembling the word *Weê-lo*, whence its Aboriginal name: it is somewhat singular that the same name is applied to the *Oedicnemus grallarius* by the natives of Western Australia . . the cry of the two birds being similar. **1904** *Emu* III. 174 *Burhinus grallarius* (Stone Plover, Wee-loo) . . pass the day sleeping on the stony ranges. *Ibid.* 175 *Orthorhamphus magnirostris* (Long-billed Stone-Plover)—The native name for this bird is 'wee-lo', same as for the preceding species, on account of the similarity of the cry. **1908** E.J. BANFIELD *Confessions of Beachcomber* 123 Many of the birds are distinguished and named in accordance with their notes. . . 'Wee-loo' the stone plover. **1917** *Bulletin* (Sydney) 5 July 22/2 The keenness of the aborigine's ear for bird notes is evidenced in the names resembling their call which he gave to familiar species. . . The stone curlew was called weelo, or weeloo. **1962** B.W. LEAKE *Eastern Wheatbelt Wildlife* 89 The curlew or stone plover . . called weelow by aborigines will seek protection for hatching out and rearing its young.

weeping, *ppl. a.* Used as a distinguishing epithet in the names of plants: **weeping fig,** the large, spreading tree *Ficus benjamina* (fam. Moraceae) of n. Qld. and elsewhere, cultivated as an ornamental; **gum,** any of several trees of the genus *Eucalyptus* (fam. Myrtaceae) esp. (*Tas.*) *E. pauciflora* (see *snow gum* SNOW 1); **myall,** the tree *Acacia pendula* (see MYALL *n.*[2]); **Polly grass,** a grass of the genus *Poa.*

1890 F.M. BAILEY *Catal. Indigenous & Naturalised Plants Qld.* (ed. 2) 103 **Weeping Fig**—*Ficus Benjaminea.* **1920** *Bulletin* (Sydney) 18 Mar. 24/2 Up in N.Q. Binghi makes music not only with a gum-leaf, but also with the leaf of the weeping-fig. **1935** DAVISON & NICHOLLS *Blue Coast Caravan* 107 The tree . . has drooping branches which form an invitingly dark enclosure with an outer lacing of golden-tipped leaves . . a weeping fig. **1965** *Austral. Encycl.* IV. 59 The weeping fig . . is exceedingly handsome, has been extensively planted, and is a feature of most coastal towns in Queensland. **1984** WRIGLEY & FAGG *Austral. Native Plants* (ed. 2) 438 *Ficus benjamina* Weeping fig. . . Used extensively as street tree in Brisbane and centres to the north. **1836** J. BACKHOUSE *Narr. Visit Austral. Colonies* (1843) 440 Goulburn Plain is an extensive down . . with thinly scattered trees, such as **Weeping Gum.** **1852** MRS C. MEREDITH *My Home in Tas.* I. 169 A kind of *Eucalyptus*, with long drooping leaves, called the 'Weeping Gum'. **1896** *Proc. Linnean Soc. N.S.W.* X. 599 *Eucalyptus coriacea* . . goes under the name of 'Weeping Gum' in Tasmania, owing to its scrambling habit; the name is also in use at Uralla, N.S.W. **1903** *Tasmanian Timbers* (Tas. Lands & Survey Dept.) 20 *Weeping gum* . . is a mountain species, and does not grow to a great size. **1981** M. SHARLAND *Tracks of Morning* 71 Specimens of the cabbage gum or weeping gum, always picturesque and lovers of high moist places. The specific botanical name of this attractive old tree is *pauciflora*, meaning poor blossom. **1848** *Maitland Mercury* 6 Dec. 4/3 The road is tolerably well defined, and passes through groves of **weeping myall** (acacia pendula). **1857** D. BUNCE *Australasiatic Reminisc.* 91 In places which were slightly elevated, many species of *Acacia* made their appearance, including the celebrated Weeping Myall (*A. pendula*). **1880** J. BONWICK *Resources Qld.* 82 The Weeping Myall, whose wood is turned into tobacco-pipes and sent far and wide. **1890** 'MRS A. MACLEOD' *Austral. Girl* (1894) 271 There was an artesian well ten miles off, on the plain of weeping myalls. **1903** G. SUTHERLAND *Australasian Live Stock Man.* (ed. 2) 385 Weeping Myall is another species of true acacia growing to a considerable height . . principally in the marshy tracts of land surrounding the lagoons and back waters of the creeks and rivers of Queensland and New South Wales. **1934** W.A. OSBORNE *Visitor to Aust.* 64 The wood of the Weeping Myall has a violet-like odour. **1880** J. BONWICK *Resources Qld.* 45 The *Poa brownii* is good in all seasons; the *P. cespitosa* [*sic*], or **Weeping Polly grass,** though tufty, is sweet and indicates good soil. **1889** J.H. MAIDEN *Useful Native Plants Aust.* 106 'Weeping Polly-Grass' . . is a rich and succulent grass, forming a fine fodder. **1981** E. ROLLS *Million Wild Acres* 28 The best grass, the tall sparse-seeded Oat Grass . . all but disappeared. So did *Poa caespitosa*, the Weeping Polly Grass of rich damp places.

weero /'wiroʊ/. [Prob. f. a W.A. Aboriginal language.] COCKATIEL.

1948 D.L. SERVENTY *Handbk. Birds W.A.* 3 Some aboriginal names . . have passed into use as vernacular names, either locally or generally. Such include . . 'Weero' for the Cockatoo Parrot. **1962** B.W. LEAKE *Eastern Wheatbelt Wildlife* 78 Budgerigars and cockatoo parrots or weeros appear in flocks when conditions are very dry further north. **1973** D. STUART *Morning Star, Evening Star* 59 Then after a while, the others, all round the dishes outside. Wagtails and finches . . and weeros once.

weet-weet /'wit-wit/. [a. Wuywurung *wij wij*.] An Aboriginal weapon and toy: see quot. 1967.

1878 R.B. SMYTH *Aborigines of Vic.* I. 353 Weet-Weet . . the plaything . . called by the natives of the Yarra *Witch-Wi-tch, We-a-witch, Weet-weet*, or *Wa-voit*, is one of the most extraordinary instruments used by savages. **1904** *Bulletin* (Sydney) 11 Feb. 16/3 The 'weet-weet' . . is still occasionally used by the blacks on the Coranderrk (Vic.) mission station. . . When well-thrown, this missile travels an astonishing distance. **1929** *Austral. Aborigines & South Sea Islanders Implements, Weapons & Curios, Tyrrell's Museum* 5 Weet Weet, Aboriginal toy or sporting implement, when thrown along the ground it describes a number of irregular gyratory movements or springs, much to the delight of the natives, who frequently throw small clubs, boomerangs, etc., at it for practice. . . The weight of the Weet Weet is usually a little more than 1 oz. Length varies from 12 in. to 24 in. 7s. 6d. and 12s. 6d. each. **1944** S.J. ENDACOTT *Austral. Aboriginal Native Words* 41 *Weetweet*, toy missile. **1967** D.J. MULVANEY *Cricket Walkabout* 65 Blood sports were exceptional, and throwing the 'kangaroo-rat' was no exception. The name is misleading. Normally termed a 'weet-weet', this weapon consisted of a solid wooden or bone knob on a flexible handle about two feet in length. It was normally used for bringing down birds or small animals. After it had been swung rapidly backwards and forwards to gather momentum and flex the weapon, it was skimmed low along the ground with an underarm jerky motion.

wei, var. WEEI.

weight. *Gold-mining.* Abbrev. of 'pennyweight', 20th part of 1 oz. Troy or 1.55 g.

1890 *Argus* (Melbourne) 9 Aug. 4/6 Tried a crushing and didn't get four weights to the ton. **1896** *Bulletin* (Sydney) 12 Dec. 26/4 Just a weight! And she bottomed at forty—A miner will know what it means. **1911** E.S. SORENSON *Life in Austral. Backblocks* 41 Her lot is a hard one, and yet she is happy in a way if there are a couple of 'weights' to clean out of the black sand by the slush lamp at night. **1923** M.B. PETERSEN *Jewelled Nights* 65 Sam and Dosey went down to see and they got a 'weight' in two 'dishes'! **1931** C.B. SMITH *Austral. Gold Prospectors' Handbk.* 30 Every day you add a few grains, a few 'weights' (pennyweights), or perhaps an ounce or two, to the precious yellow metal that gleams in your bottle. **1946** W.E. HARNEY *North of 23°* 13, I think of Ruby Ridge and our 'dryblowing' in search of the elusive weight. **1948** K.S. PRICHARD *Golden Miles* 27 The majority of workin' miners don't take the game seriously. If they get away with a few 'weights now and then, its only to show they've got the guts.

weir mallee /'wɪə mæli/. *Obs.* [a. Wergaia *wiar(gadjin* water tree + MALLEE 1 a.] The mallee or small tree *Eucalyptus dumosa* of drier s.e. mainland Aust.

1858 *Trans. Philos. Inst. Vic.* III. 32 The water-yielding Malleè, called the Weir Malleè, was known to the natives long before the arrival of the whites. **1878** R.B. SMYTH *Aborigines of Vic.* I. 220 Stanbridge says that the hunter, in places far removed from permanent water, has to draw his supply of that element from the roots of the swamp-box and the weir-mallee, which run a few inches below the surface of the earth. **1888** *Proc. Linnean Soc. N.S.W.* III. 509 *Eucalyptus dumosa* . . 'Weir-Mallee' of aboriginals.

welcome swallow. [See quot. 1945.] The swallow *Hirundo neoxena* of Aust. and, recently, New Zealand.

1842 J. GOULD *Birds of Aust.* (1848) II. Pl. 13, *Hirundo neoxena* . . Welcome Swallow. **1896** B. SPENCER *Rep. Horn Sci. Exped. Central Aust.* II. 68 At Henbury they were seen flying in company with the Welcome Swallow. **1903** *Emu* II. 210 Welcome Swallow . . are winter visitors to us. **1945** C. BARRETT *Austral. Bird Life* 166 The welcome swallow (*Hirundo neoxena*) is happily named, for no bird enjoys a larger share of public favour. Welcome wherever it appears, the common swallow nests above shop doorways and windows in suburbia, and beneath verandahs and the eaves of houses. **1962** B.W. LEAKE *Eastern Wheatbelt Wildlife* 89 The welcome, fairy and white headed swallows are all migratory, the first being very sociable. **1982** R. ELLIS *Bush Safari* 34 The Welcome Swallows nesting under the eaves of the wide verandah.

well-in, *a.* Affluent, well-to-do.

1845 T. MCCOMBIE *Adventures of Colonist* 241 They had a pretty little farm, and were well in. **1874** L.T. HERGENHAN *Colonial City* (1972) 331 When we wished to give a man the highest praise, we spoke of him as being 'well-in', or 'having made his pile'. **1891** 'R. BOLDREWOOD' *Sydney-Side Saxon* Introd., He's a well-in squatter, that took up runs or bought them cheap before free selection. **1899** 'S. RUDD' *On our Selection* 84 He was reputed to be well-in, though some said that if everybody had their own he wouldn't be worth much. **1922** A. WRIGHT *Colt from Country* 83 'Said to be well in, is he not?' queried Mrs Whinstun. **1927** K.S. PRICHARD *Brumby Innes* (1974) 96 He's rough as bags; but he'll treat Mrs Innes proper. He's well-in too. Can give her anything she wants if she only handles him right. **1936** H. DRAKE-BROCKMAN *Sheba Lane* 139 I've just told you we were pretty well in. Emily had all the things a girl likes. **1954** T.A.G. HUNGERFORD *Sowers of Wind* 35 He was an architect before the war, and pretty well in. **1976** D. IRELAND *Glass Canoe* 180 Someone saw her at the trots with some of the trotting men who were really well in, and she was regarded with awe ever after.

Welshie. [f. WELSH(MAN + -Y.] NEW SOUTH WELSHMAN.

1923 'J. NORTH' *Son of Bush* 115 Tommy ther drover! W'y, 'e wuz a Welshie, not er furriner!

Welshman. NEW SOUTH WELSHMAN.

1891 H. NISBET *Colonial Tramp* I. 171 On this side of the bridge which crosses the Murray the Echucans are rabid Victorians, on the other side they are rabid Welshmen. **1925** *Australasian* (Melbourne) 3 Jan. 27/1 Criticisms . . have been made regarding the preponderance of Welshmen over Victorians in the first Test.

welter. [Spec. use of Br. dial. *welter* something exceptionally big or heavy of its kind, a 'whopper': see OED *sb.*[3] 2.] In the phr. **to make** (something) **a welter, to make a welter of it,** to engage (in an activity) to excess.

1918 *Kia Ora Coo-ee* May 5/2 She was apparently English, and was making arm in arm with a Tommy. My oath! he was making a welter of it. **1918** A. WRIGHT *Breed holds Good* 10 Frank had gone into town, and . . made the pace a 'welter'. **1919** *Our Empire* (Melbourne) 18 Feb. 7 The lads cannot altogether be blamed for 'making it a welter'. **1932** M.R. WHITE *No Roads go By* 141 Cecil, intent on slapping together a good cheque, had lost sight of everything but the fact that the Boss was away, and now was his chance to make a welter of it. **1947** G. CASEY *Wits are Out* 55 'He goes the slops too heavy, though,' someone else stated. 'Old Ray'd go a long way, if he'd just lay off it a little bit. He's got the brains, but he makes a welter of it.' **1952** J. CLEARY *Sundowners* 227 'I don't want you to make a welter of it,' she said as she walked in behind the bar. . . 'Anyone who gets noisy drunk or tries to start a fight gets locked up until he sobers up.' **1978** D. STUART *Wedgetail View* 76 Martin rarely came back before midnight, and each morning Colin had to wake him. 'There's no doubt about it,' he said. . . 'You're making a welter of it, mate.' **1984** D. MARR *Ivanov Trail* 300 Barker was able to demonstrate that Hawke had no grounds on which to argue that Combe had or would make a welter of his party connections.

west, *adv.* Chiefly in N.S.W. and Qld.: west of closely settled districts; beyond the limits of settled, and by implication, civilized districts, esp. in the phr. **west of sunset.** See also SUNSET 1.

1905 *Truth* (Sydney) 19 Nov. 1/6 There is evidently a drought out west of West, even yet, for a Barringus correspondent writes that a wave of rabbits is on them from the West, evidently starved out. **1910** *Bulletin* (Sydney) 7 Apr. 14/1 In a West-o'-Sunset township two station hands argued all night. **1911** *Ibid.* 12 Oct. 13/2 During the past few years of my wanderings West-o'-Sunset and nearer-in I have seen only one of those elastic-sided guns, and the average youngster has grown to love the birds. **1916** *Ibid.* 17 Feb. 24/4 Barns was cursed from Holman's store to west of sunset. **1931** *Ibid.* 18 Nov. 21/1, I wish to God—I do indeed!—That I were West o' Sund'y. **1968** W. GILL *Petermann Journey* 127 Unfortunately life can become just as involved 'west of the black stump' as it can anywhere else.

western, *a.* Used as a distinguishing epithet in the names of animals: **western black cockatoo,** *red-tailed black cockatoo*, see RED *a.* 1 b.; **bristlebird,** the rare, ground-dwelling, brownish bird *Dasyornis longirostris* of s.w. W.A.; **brown snake,** the venomous snake *Pseudonaja nuchalis* (see *brown snake* BROWN *a.* 1); **grey kangaroo,** the kangaroo *Macropus fuliginosus* of s.w. and central s. Aust.; see also *grey kangaroo* GREY *a.*; also *ellipt.* as **western grey; rosella,** the predom. red, black, and green parrot *Platycercus icterotis* of s.w. W.A.; **whipbird,** the predom. olive-green bird *Psophodes nigrogularis* of coastal heaths and mallee scrubs in parts of s. Aust., lacking the distinctive cracking call of *P. olivaceus* (see WHIPBIRD).

1847 J. GOULD *Birds of Aust.* (1848) V. Pl. 9, *Calyptorhynchus naso* . . **Western Black Cockatoo** . . Red-Tailed Black Cockatoo of the Colonists. **1917** *Bulletin* (Sydney) 5 July 22/2 Karrak (the western black or redtailed cockatoo). **1896** B. SPENCER *Rep. Horn Sci. Exped. Central Aust.* I. 31 At the Goyder was secured the first specimen of the Western black cockatoo (*Calyptorhynchus stellulatus*), which does not appear to extend further south than this. [**1945 western bristlebird:** C. BARRETT *Austral. Bird Life* 191 The eastern bristlebird (*D[asyornis] brachyptera*) inhabits eastern New South Wales. . . The western form (*D. longirostris*) is confined to South-western Australia.] **1976** *Reader's Digest Compl. Bk. Austral. Birds* 422 The western bristlebird was formerly more abundant and had a greater range. . . The decline of the bird into a rare species is undoubtedly due to the large-scale clearing of its habitat for pastoral activities. **1983** *Western Farmer* (Perth) 10 Nov. 59/4 A search will start at Twertup on Saturday for the rare western bristle bird. **1967** H. COGGER *Austral. Reptiles* 98 The **Western Brown Snake** is similar in shape, size and habits to the Eastern Brown Snake, but is much more variable in colour. It varies from olive-grey to rich brown above. **1981** A. WILKINSON *Up Country* 168 At our feet . . was a 'chucked' beer can. Protruding from it . . was the body of a newly dead western brown snake. **1941** E. TROUGHTON *Furred Animals Aust.* 218 **Western** Forester or **Grey Kangaroo** . . *Macropus ocydromus*. . . This rather warmly coloured western member of the great-grey group is generally regarded as a geographical race of the eastern species, *M. major*. **1970** W.D.L. RIDE *Guide Native Mammals Aust.* 42 There are five species of Great Kangaroo: two of these, the Eastern and Western grey Kangaroos, are so alike that they were only separated with certainty as a result of studies on breeding biology and blood characteristics in 1966. **1983** *Mercury* (Hobart) 8 Sept. 16/2 There were about . . 1,800,000 western greys predominantly in South Australia. **1984** *Age* (Melbourne) 3 Sept. 12/1 The increase in one species, the western grey kangaroo, has endangered the ecological balance. **1945** C. BARRETT *Austral. Bird Life* 80 The **western rosella** . . (*P[latycercus] icterotis*) inhabits South-western Australia. **1962** B.W. LEAKE *Eastern Wheatbelt Wildlife* 85 The Western Rosella was quite numerous at the beginning of settlement. **1984** M. BLAKERS et al. *Atlas Austral. Birds* 277 The Western Rosella inhabits open and partly cleared eucalypt woodland and forest but not heath. **1945** C. BARRETT *Austral. Bird Life* 137 The **western whipbird** (*P[sophodes] nigrogularis*) had not been met with for many years in South-western Australia . . when it was re-discovered, in Mallee country near the South Australian-Victorian border. **1986** *West Austral.* 26 Mar. 30/3 Miss McNee recommended that a further survey be made of western whipbirds to see whether they used crown reserves in the wheatbelt.

western grey kangaroo: see KANGAROO *n.* 2.

westie, *n.* and *a.* [f. *west(ern suburb* + -Y.]

A. *n.* A resident of one of the western suburbs of Sydney.

1977 *Sea Notes* June-July 10/4 In Sydney, anyone who lives west of *you*, can be broadly dismissed as a 'Parra', or a 'Westie'. The first of these much loved expressions deriving from that satellite city of Sydney's, Parramatta. **1981** *Sydney Morning Herald* 20 Oct. 13/1 Bondi attracts all sorts. The eastern suburbs trendies, the 'westies' (anyone who lives west of the Harbour Bridge), the families, the migrants, the vagrants, the rich, the poor, the beautiful and the ugly. **1984** *Ibid.* 19 June 1/7 Westie-bashing is alive and well and living in State Parliament. After the Labor member for Blacktown, Mr John Aquilina, told the House he was proud to represent the people of Blacktown, the National Party member for Coffs Harbour, Mr Matt Singleton, replied: 'Yes, because you have 90 per cent of the drones, drongos and idiots in the community voting for you. The other 10 per cent don't even bother at all. There are plenty of these people out around Blacktown so easily 90 per cent of them would vote for you.' **1986** *Nat. Times* (Sydney) 10 Jan. 24/1, I met some young people we'd call 'westies' through a self-help organisation and I got on well . . but I would probably be embarrassed to bring them to a club or a party with my school friends.

B. *adj.* Of, pertaining to, or belonging to a resident of a western suburb of Sydney.

1982 *Austral. Women's Weekly* (Sydney) 10 Feb. 108/2 Incidentally, in the patois of the Bondi car park, panel vans are considered 'Westy'—a reference to Sydney's beachless western suburbs. **1986** *Nat. Times* (Sydney) 10 Jan. 24/4, I like wearing stylish, snobby clothes that are not 'westy'.

Westralia. Shortened form of 'Western Australia'.

1893 *Bulletin* (Sydney) 29 July 7/4 A Melb. timber-merchant formed a syndicate . . to prospect Westralia for gold. **1898** R. RADCLYFFE *Wealth & Wild Cats* 48 All Westralia was crying out for water. **1916** *Truth* (Sydney) 25 June 8/1 The Governor-General and Lady Helen left Melbourne on Friday, en route to Westralia. **1929** W.J. RESIDE *Golden Days* 49 Land of politicians silly, Land of dust and willy-willy, Land of blanket, tent and billy, Westralia? **1946** *Bulletin* (Sydney) 25 Sept. 28/1 In Westralia there is nothing better than redgum or kino for the tanning of fishing nets or lines. **1957** J.M. HOSKING *Aust. first & Last* 89 Westralia's own Swan Bitter too, Will make you hop like a kangaroo. **1969** L. HADOW *Full Cycle* 123 All well in Westralia stop.

Westralian, *n.* and *a.* [f. prec.]

A. *n.* A non-Aboriginal person native to or resident in Western Australia.

1891 E.H. HALLACK *W.A. & Yilgarn Goldfields* 34 Parting advice to Westralians is—try and inculcate the principles of self-help. **1894** *Bulletin* (Sydney) 7 July 23/4 Westralians are the dirtiest, laziest, and most disobliging white people he ever came across. *c* **1907** W.C. CHANDLER *Darkest Adelaide* 16 John Connolly . . is a Westralian. **1922** A. WRIGHT *Colt from Country* 14 He had become wise to Frank Helyer, the 'wealthy Westralian', as he was beginning to be called in Manly. **1942** *Bulletin* (Sydney) 7 Jan. 17/3 About this time of the year what the Westralians prosaically call 'red gums' are in vermilion flower, rivalling the Illawarra flame-tree in brilliance of hue. **1977** C.T. CASSIDY *Random Thoughts* 1 And gather here Westralians all, By birth, adoption, distant call, In confirmation of that day, When this State started on its way.

Hence **Westralienne** *n.*, a female Westralian.

1956 J.E. WEBB *So much for Sydney* 61 Westraliennes were equally loyal to Agnes Robertson.

B. *adj.* Of or pertaining to Western Australia.

1896 *Worker* (Sydney) 7 Mar. 1/3 What *can* you expect after a diet of 'tinned dog', the great Westralian standby, and when on your cuticle you've got a crust of real Westralian dirt—*not* 'wash' dirt? **1901** *Truth* (Sydney) 16 June 5/7 The Sultan of Turkey is not more jealous of his veiled mistresses than is a Westralian station manager of his stark naked lubras. **1912** *Bulletin* (Sydney) 10 Oct. 15/2 My Westralian township bears a name like a beer-logged person hooting huskily for Charon's ferry. **1929** W.J. RESIDE *Golden Days* 380 They travel, costlier freighted, Beneath Westralian suns. **1948** R.A. PEPPERALL *Emigrant to Aust.* 24 As we drew near the 'Westralian' coast they evinced signs of eagerness to get home. **1953** *New Settler in W.A.* (Perth) Mar. 39 All the main North-West centres are now served by one or other of the Westralian air services.

westringia /we'strɪndʒiə/. [The plant genus *Westringia* was named by English botanist J.E. Smith (*Vet. Akad. Handl. Stockh.* (1797) 171) after the Swedish physician J.P. Westring, a student of lichens.] Any plant of the genus of shrubs *Westringia* (fam. Lamiaceae) of temperate Aust., having white or bluish flowers and whorled leaves.

1814 R. BROWN *Gen. Remarks Bot. Terra Australis* 33 Westringia and Prostanthera, with the genera nearly related to each of these, are the most worthy of notice among Labiatae, all of them are limited to Terra Australis. **1827** A. CUNNINGHAM *Gen. Remarks Vegetation* 14 Upon Dirk Hartog's Island . . as also at Rottnest Island, Westringia was observed, of species . . common to the South Coast. *c* **1910** W.R. GUILFOYLE *Austral. Plants* 365 *Westringia rigida* . . 'Narrow-leaved Westringia' (evergreen shrub, 5 to 8 ft.). **1930** A.J. EWART *Flora Vic.* 981 *W[estringia] senifolia* . . Alpine Westringia. A shrub, 2 to 4 feet high. . . Confined to S. and N.E. Victoria. **1967** N.A. WAKEFIELD *Naturalist's Diary* 29 Westringia . . a remarkable shrub, forming clumps which apparently spring from the solid rock of sheer cliffs. **1984** E. WALLING *On Trail Austral. Wildflowers* 51 A Westringia with dainty white flowers spotted with purple and whorled leaves covered with white hairs on the under surface.

wet, *a.* and *n.*

A. *adj.*

1. In the collocation **wet season,** a period of substantial rainfall; a rainy season.

1842 *Austral. & N.Z. Monthly Mag.* 29 The wet season commences with slight showers in April. **1843** W. PRIDDEN *Aust.* 45 By *dry season*, or *wet season*, in Australia, we are . . to understand . . a series of *dry* or *wet years*. **1848** T.L. MITCHELL *Jrnl. Exped. Tropical Aust.* 76 In a wet season . . the country . . had been impassable. **1864** R. HENNING *Lett.* (1952) 69 This wet season has been very unhealthy, especially on the low-lying stations. **1882** A.J. BOYD *Old Colonials* 157 During the wet season the bush banker has a hard time of it. **1907** A. SEARCY *In Austral. Tropics* 2 The wet season begins about the end of October, and lasts approximately five months [in the Northern Territory]. **1922** J.N. MACINTYRE *High Explosive* 33 Our wet season was on, we had grass from two feet to six feet high. **1934** J.S. NEILSON *Autobiogr.* (1978) 68, 1905 opened up as a wet season. **1938** X. HERBERT *Capricornia* 374 Pommies and Dagoes and all, will get the Wet-Season feelin' and down tools. **1965** R.H. CONQUEST *Horses in Kitchen* 129 In north Queensland, during the wet season, even the frogs get rheumatism. **1984** B. DIXON *Searching for Aboriginal Lang.* 1 The first big storm of the wet season had just started.

2. Of sheep: having a fleece which is too damp to be shorn. Also as quasi-*adv.*

1894 *Bulletin* (Sydney) 20 Jan. 9/4, I can recall many instances of *some* shearers voting 'wet sheep' while at the hut. **1904** *Shearer* (Sydney) 3 Dec. 4/1 Owing to a couple of showers and a slight disagreement on that fruitful topic—wet sheep—shearing at Tara finished on November 14th. **1910** C.E.W. BEAN *On Wool Track* 181 A shearer half-way down the board stopped and hung up his machine. The slip of a boy shearing next to him looked up. 'Reckon they're wet?' he asked. The first shearer was putting on his coat. He nodded. 'I've been thinking so too, this half-hour,' said the youngster. It spread down the shed just like fire in stubble. **191**[illegible] *Bulletin* (Sydney) 2 Mar. 13/1 What sort of bloke is th[illegible] shed-boss? . . If he is a 'fair cow', and doesn't want 'wet' vote, the sheep will be wet . . for to suit t[illegible] 'rousies'' book the sheep should be wet pretty oft[illegible] **1926** *Ibid.* 11 Feb. 24/1 While the sheep stay 'wet', [illegible] the grub runs up, a mug Chow's 'broken the sch[illegible] **1918** R.H. KNYVETT *Over there with Australs.* 29 Whe[illegible] shearers want a spell I have known them declare majority vote that the sheep were 'wet', though had not been any rain for months! **1958** *Bulleti*[illegible] ney) 24 Sept. 18/2 Old Jacky Howe would be ro[illegible] he could see how the modern shearer fills in t[illegible] after he has 'voted 'em out' (wet). **19**[illegible] CHARLWOOD *Afternoon of Time* 55 The shearers . ewes and lambs, declared them 'wet' and kno[illegible] **1975** B. FOLEY *Shearers' Poem* 10 We'll shear 'e[illegible] do 'em clean, And remove the wet vote b[illegible] P. ADAM SMITH *Shearers* 228 Before the [illegible] founded, voting 'wet' was one of the few [illegible] against the squatter that the men had. . . Af[illegible] for retaliation was past, the use of a 'wet' [illegible] handy for the odd days off.

3. *fig.* Irritable; exasperated. Freq. i[illegible] **wet.**

1898 *Bulletin* (Sydney) 17 Dec. (Red [illegible] *narked* is to lose your temper; also expr[illegible] *dead wet*. **1915** C.J. DENNIS *Songs of Sent*[illegible]

Romeo gits wet as 'ell. **1941** [illegible] *tral. Slang* 81 *Wet, get*, to b[illegible] **1977** B. SCOTT *My Uncle Arch*[illegible] wet as hell. Pushing a pump[illegible] Friday night didn't make [illegible]

B. *n.* Chiefly *N.T.* Ab[illegible]

1908 *Truth* (Sydney) 2 [illegible] they are waiting for the [illegible] *turous Honeymoon* 85 The [illegible] comes down in torrent[illegible] *Land* 76 The 'wet' was d[illegible] five months. **1948** *Kh*[illegible] Wet's just about on us[illegible] yet? **1951** R. DORIEN [illegible] rential and erratic ra[illegible] the soil soggy as wet [illegible] talk about 'the wet'. [illegible] Huge holes appear [illegible] viously breaking u[illegible] *Verse* (1973) 44 We[illegible] come As the big [illegible] (Darwin) 15 Sept. [illegible] before the wet. [illegible]

whacker. Als[illegible] liar.] A fool; a[illegible] *adj.*

1966 D. N[illegible] out. 'You liste[illegible] the grouch a[illegible] you're going [illegible] again.' **196**[illegible] we'd proba[illegible] yuh anyw[illegible] bastards a[illegible] (1974) 21, [illegible] the worl[illegible] don't ha[illegible] *Sunday* [illegible] bation [illegible] name. [illegible] teen d[illegible] he str[illegible] witho[illegible] Boys [illegible] awa[illegible] hate[illegible]

wh[illegible]

-o. [illegible]

O[illegible]

built for wharf-lumpers and coalies should have a rent which only a middle-class semi-genteel city coin-counter . . could look at. **1933** A.J. COTTON *With Big Herds in Aust.* 52 There was a strike on among the wharf lumpers at the time we arrived. **1957** V. PALMER *Seedtime* 68 He had later carried his swag round the north, picking up jobs as cane-cutter, wharflumper, auctioneer's clerk. **1965** N. LINDSAY *Bohemians of Bulletin* 15 The old man's a wharflumper.

Also **wharf-lumping** *pres. pple.* and *vbl. n.*

1898 *Worker* (Sydney) 23 Apr. 5/2 If I were asked which was the best for a man to do—go gold-digging or stick to comping—I would say go 'wharf-lumping' or anything else. **1921** *Bulletin* (Sydney) 7 July 20/3 Here are the countries represented in a wharf-lumping gang that lately worked a steamer at Thursday Island: Britain, Russia, Germany, Denmark, Greece, Ceylon, Malay States, South Sea Islands. . . They all get award rates.

wheat. [Spec. use of *wheat* the cereal plant.] Used *attrib.* in Special Comb. **wheat cocky,** a wheat farmer; see COCKY *n.*[2]; also *attrib.*; so **wheat cockying** *vbl. n.*; **lumper,** one employed to load or unload sacks of wheat; so **wheat lumping** *pres. pple.* and *vbl. n.*; **paddock,** an enclosure in which wheat is grown; see PADDOCK *n.* 1 a.; also *attrib.*

1908 *Bulletin* (Sydney) 17 Dec. 15/1 The **wheat cockies** upon the Vic. northern plains are singing out that they cannot get enough men to do the harvesting. **1935** *Ibid.* 20 Feb. 20/3 A wheat cocky in a straw-decker . . would look . . incongruous. **1946** P.J. HURLEY *From Kosciusko to Sea* 97 Wheat 'cockies' mostly had a rough time. **1949** G. BERRIE *Morale* 218 What about you, Mac? Going back to wheat cockying? **1960** *Encounter* (London) May 26/2 The smaller brothers of the sheepman, the wheat-cocky and cow-cocky, have absorbed his style. **1971** W.G. HOWCROFT *This Side Rabbit Proof Fence* 68 A bachelor wheat-cocky neighbour arrived one evening in an ancient touring car. **1977** J. DOUGHTY *Gold in Blood* 15 The wheat cocky interested me because he had been a soldier, and because he had prospected in the Gippsland mountains for gold. **1911** *Bulletin* (Sydney) 16 Feb. 13/3 This man was filling-in time trying to beat out the fire, when a **wheat lumper** carrying a large billycan of beer transpired. **1925** *Ibid.* 16 Apr. 24/2 A fight started between two wheat-lumpers. **1933** J. MCCARTER *Love's Lunatic* 91 I'm like a wheat lumper when it comes t' handlin' th' ladies th' right way, aren't I? **1946** *Bulletin* (Sydney) 2 Jan. 13/2 I'm wheatlumpin' at Cowangie with four other blokes. **1952** A.W. UPFIELD *New Shoe* 65 A toughened wheat lumper could carry up a dead man, and arrive 'blown out'. A lesser man could not accomplish it. **1964** P. ADAM SMITH *Hear Train Blow* 185 'Gooda lucka,' called Chella Valenti, the wheat-lumper from southern Italy. **1975** R. BEILBY *Brown Land Crying* 179 Now they got this bulk-'andlin', tipped out from the 'arvesters inta a truck an' inta them bins at the railway. No wheat-lumpin' any more. **1981** A.B. FACEY *Fortunate Life* 220 Mr Adams gave me a job wheat-lumping at the Wickepin railway yard. **1981** D. STUART *I think I'll Live* 279 You mug, my old man was a wheat lumper in the Mallee country. **1846** *Moreton Bay Courier* 12 Dec. 2/4 A short time ago as Robert Tomlinson, a farm servant . . was reaping in the **wheat paddock,** a green snake bit him on the hand. **1879** *Native Tribes S.A.* 99 Jackson was working by himself at the wheat-paddock fence. **1916** F.S. ALFORD *Bulk Handling Wheat* 16 Sometimes the wheat paddock would be a mile away or more. **1964** P. ADAM SMITH *Hear Train Blow* 65 Curlews cried . . on the edges of the wheat paddocks.

wheat-eared Mitchell: see MITCHELL GRASS 2.

wheel, *n.*

1. [Chiefly Austral.: see OEDS *wheel, sb.* 7 b.] In the phr. **to be on** (someone's) **wheel,** to hound, or put pressure on (a person).

1922 C. DREW *Rogues & Ruses* 34 Me and Finger was on their wheels, but by the time we hit the ring Smiles' mount was three to one on. **1954** V. KELLY *Shadow* 89 Down there the cops'll give you a go. Here they're on your wheel all the time. **1959** A. UPFIELD *Bony & Mouse* 104 I'll be ready for it. I'm going to be right on Tony's wheel when it happens. **1969** O. WHITE *Under Iron Rainbow* 118 The inspector's been on my wheel to trace him.

2. In the phr. **silly as a wheel,** very silly.

1952 T.A.G. HUNGERFORD *Ridge & River* 57 Oscar was sound, but silly as a wheel. **1966** *Coast to Coast 1965–66* 157, I warned Rose. She was as silly as a wheel, too, but a man's got to do what he can to protect his daughters. **1985** J. CLANCHY *Lie of Land* 112 Father Tierney was mad. Cracked as an egg, some boys said, silly as a wheel, mad as a two-bob watch.

wheel, *v.* [Spec. use of *wheel* to turn (a person, animal, or thing) round or aside.]

1. *trans.* To cause (a stampeding mob of cattle, etc.) to turn back or to the side.

1872 G.S. BADEN-POWELL *New Homes for Old Country* 186 People will risk their necks merely to turn or 'wheel' a mob of cattle. **1891** 'R. BOLDREWOOD' *Sydney-Side Saxon* (1925) 104 It'll take some galloping to wheel that poley brindle's mob, and if they once break there's no headin' 'em! **1895** A.B. PATERSON *Man from Snowy River* 6 So Clancy rode to wheel them—he was racing on the wing Where the best and boldest riders take their place. **1915** V. PALMER *World of Men* (1962) 36 The obvious thing was for Denison to be smashed up in the timber that night when he rode to wheel the mob. **1939** J.G. PATTISON *'Battler's' Tales Early Rockhampton* 65 We generally worked in relays, the light weights on fast horses to take their place in the run, after the first burst was over, and wheel the lead in the desired direction. **1943** H.G. LAMOND *From Tariaro to Ross Roy* 38 He continued with his work, as stockmen will. After he had wheeled the fliers into the coachers he returned to the granite. **1957** R.S. PORTEOUS *Brigalow* 87 Though I told them that Carson had definitely refused to allow us to go after the scrubbers the boys were cheerfully optimistic. . . 'Give 'im another go tonight. . . You'll wheel 'im.' **1972** *Bronze Swagman Bk. Bush Verse* (1973) 9 'Twixt the river bank and the myall scrub Where Gold Star wheeled the lead.

2. *transf.* To discountenance (someone).

1912 *Bulletin* (Sydney) 28 Nov. 16/4 One of the fraternity confided to me on the board . . that he 'had peeled 88, and was dragging the chain behind Nugget Smith', but had bet him 'a bottle of sheep dip' that he'd 'wheel him next day'. This being translated means my friend had shorn 88 sheep, which was the lowest tally. The next most meagre barbering was that of the aforesaid Nugget, and my friend had wagered him a bottle of whisky he would disrobe more jumbucks than Nugget on the following day. **1915** *Anzac Rec. Gaz.* (Alexandria, Egypt) 12 Nov. 2/2 He had the good luck to miss being 'wheeled' many a time.

wheelbarrow. *Austral. pidgin. Obs.* A dray.

1848 C. COZENS *Adventures of Guardsman* 127 On perceiving what they termed the 'wheelbarrow' approaching, they set up a simultaneous shout, running to meet us . . readily lending their assistance in unloading the dray. **1848** H.W. HAYGARTH *Recoll. Bush Life* 108 In talking to a black, a dray, cart or vehicle of any sort, is expressed by a 'wheelbarrow'. ***c* 1879** A. MACPHERSON *Mount Abundance* 14 They knew the words 'white fellow' and 'wheelbarrow' (their corrupt word for *drays*)—words got from some semi-civilised tribes on the Lower Balonne.

wheeler. *Mining.* One employed underground to haul skips or trolleys of ore: see quot. 1962.

1901 *Illawarra Mercury* (Wollongong) 5 Jan. 2/3 The miners' wheelers held another meeting on Saturday last and decided that the wheelers do not return to work unless guaranteed the advance as agreed upon by the joint committee. **1904** *Worker* (Sydney) 17 Sept. 7/3 The pair of wheelers reached Balaklava by 4.30. **1950** H.C. WELLS *Earth cries Out* 3 Would a wheeler get enough for him and Beth to get married on? Anyway, he'd got a job at a pit. **1962** O. PRYOR *Aust.'s Little Cornwall* 35 The ore in the underground workings was hauled from chutes to the haulage shaft in wooden barrows, often through levels where the roof was so low that the wheelers had to walk with bent backs. **1983** D.J. BAILEY *Holes in Ground* 7 Interviewed in 1967 Harry William Lattimore, who started in the industry as a wheeler in the Rankin mine at 13 said: 'I was wheeling off my uncle and you had to be a good wheeler to earn 6s. a day. . . You worked from 8 o'clock until 5 o'clock. There was no air, and it was no wonder I got phthisis.'

wheel of fire tree: see FIRE-WHEEL TREE.

Whelan the Wrecker. The trading name of a demolition contractor, applied allusively to a demolitionist or vandal (see quot. 1929).

[**1929** *Melbourne Telephone Directory* May 390/2 Whelan the Wrecker—Sydney rd Cobg N13.] **1940** *Puckapunyal: Official Jrnl. 17th Austral. Infantry Brigade* Apr. 15 Did anyone see anything happen on the last train from Spencer Street . . Whelan the Wrecker was abroad apparently. **1980** *R.A.N. News* (Sydney) 13 June 5 Knocking it down? Send for Whelan the Wrecker.

wherang, var. WIRRANG.

whingeing pom. See quot. 1962. See also POM and POMMY. Also **whingeing pommy.**

1962 MARSHALL & DRYSDALE *Journey among Men* 189 The British national pastime of 'grousing' (to use an English phrase) has given rise in Australia to the derisive expression *wingeing pommy.* **1972** T. KENEALLY *Chant of Jimmie Blacksmith* 17 It'll pass a law to give every single wingein bloody Pommie his fare home to England. Back to the smoke and the sun shining ten days a year and shit in the streets. Yer can have it. **1974** W.F. MANDLE *Going it Alone* (1978) 45 Whingeing Poms make me ill. **1978** WARD & SMITH *Vanishing Village* 186 We do have some of the 'whingeing poms', although not many of them, but I've got one this year who is off back to England as fast as she can go. **1980** *Sydney Morning Herald* 1 Aug. 28/2 The Australian press chose to label Mike Brearley's Englishmen 'whingeing Poms'. **1982** *Austral.* (Sydney) 2 Nov. 2/5 'Whingeing Poms' are purely mythical, according to a survey by the Australia Britain Society and the N.S.W. Department of Immigration. It revealed that only 4 per cent of British migrants in the Sydney region were dissatisfied with their adopted lifestyle, compared with 58 per cent who claimed they were more than satisfied with their new home. **1984** *Sydney Morning Herald* 3 Feb. 8/7 What happened to the 'whingeing Pom' school of thought, and jokes like 'Grow your own dope—plant a Pom'?

whip, *n.*

1. *pl.* [Br. dial. *whips* 'lashings', an abundance: see OED(S *sb.* 3 c.] An abundance.

1890 *Quiz* (Adelaide) 5 Dec. 6/3 In what Literary Society are the terms, 'That's fair dinkum' and 'Oh, yes, whips' to be heard? **1898** *Critic* (Adelaide) 26 Feb. 5/3 A trifle o' tucker an' whips o' beer, Is all that I ask—meself. **1908** 'FIFTY-THREE YRS.' MINER' *So Long* 20 In the gully there was 'whips' of water, while wonga pigeons fluttered in the thick foliage. **1918** *Aussie: Austral. Soldiers' Mag.* Sept. 17/2 There's whips of Aussie tarts. **1934** 'S. RUDD' *Green Grey Homestead* 97 Tell him I've got whips of room for him. **1961** G. FARWELL *Vanishing Australs.* 182 Then you want capital—whips of it. **1972** R. EDWARDS *Austral. Folk Songs* 27 There's whips of tea in the billy, boy, And Johnny cakes and jam. **1978** D. STUART *Wedgetail View* 33 Soothes all the gut, good hot tea with whips o' sugar.

2. In the phr. **when the whips are cracking,** 'when the action starts'.

1906 A.B. PATERSON *Outback Marriage* 243 The boco's one eye's worth any horse's two. Me an' the boco will be near the lead when the whips are crackin'. **1955** H.G. LAMOND *Towser* 270 *Take tea with 'em,* be there at the finish of a long run. . . Whips are cracking. **1960** *Bulletin* (Sydney) 28 Sept. 16/3 In more-closely-settled areas the dogs don't understand the command, 'Go bogey', which used to send my outback hounds streaking half-a-mile to the nearest waterhole. But don't worry—they'll be there when the whips are cracking. **1977** R. BEILBY *Gunner* 116 I'll be there when the whips're crackin'! I'll keep up with you blokes if I hafta crawl!

3. In the phr. **fair crack of the whip:** see FAIR *a.*[1] 3 a. and b.

4. Special Comb. **whip mark,** used allusively of meat to indicate toughness.

1917 *'Brisbane' R.A.N.: On Board H.M.A.S. 'Brisbane'* I. 26 Look at the whip marks on the beef. **1941** *Men may Smoke* (Sydney) May 6 Pork . . its Buffalo! There's whip-marks on its hide.

whip, *v.* [Transf. use of Br. dial. and colloq. *to whip the cat,* used in various senses: see OED(S *v.* 16 a.] In the phr. **to whip the cat,** to suffer remorse; to complain; to 'cry over spilled milk'.

1847 A. HARRIS *Settlers & Convicts* 349 And now it was my turn to 'whip the cat'. **1876** J.A. EDWARDS *Gilbert*

Gogger 138 Whipping the Cat. [*Note*] Whipping: regretting past follies. **1896** H. LAWSON *While Billy Boils* (1975) 15 'Where's your mate?' 'Oh, he's round at the back. He'll be round directly; but he ain't drinking this morning.' Stiffner laughed that nasty empty laugh of his. He thought Bill was whipping the cat. **1905** *Truth* (Sydney) 30 Apr. 7/6 The prohibitionists of Campsie whipped the cat when they found they had to pay the fee of their own solicitor. **1908** 'FIFTY-THREE YRS.' MINER' *So Long* 68 But now you're down on your uppers, after trying your best, it's no use 'whipping the cat'. **1926** M. FORREST *Hibiscus Heart* 100 They are pretty disgusting . . but they never realize it when in liquor . . and whipping the cat afterwards doesn't seem to cure them. **1941** *Air Force News* (Melbourne) 3 May 3 He, the—sucker . . must stay and whip the cat. **1946** K.S. PRICHARD *Roaring Nineties* 136 We never seen colours on that trek, got wind of Paddy Hannan's reward on our way back, and Gord, did we whip the cat! **1968** S. GORE *Holy Smoke* 56 It's no good whipping the cat if a man's such a dill as to come the double on anyone . . and then gets the mockers put on him.

whipbird. [Shortened form of 'coach(man's) whip bird': see COACHMAN and COACH-WHIP.] Either of two predom. olive-green birds of the genus *Psophodes*, esp. the common *P. olivaceus* of e. mainland Aust., also known as COACHMAN, COACH-WHIP, *stockwhip bird* (see STOCKWHIP 2). See also *western whipbird* WESTERN.

1843 R.D. MURRAY *Summer at Port Phillip* 196 Terms such as the bell-bird and whip-bird denote two little birds that tinkle their bells and crack their whips with a surprising likeness to the original sounds. **1870** C.H. ALLEN *Visit to Qld.* 129 The 'Whip bird', also very frequent here. **1915** *Bulletin* (Sydney) 4 Mar. 14/4 There is also . . the sharp, bursting noise of the whip-bird. **1945** C. BARRETT *Austral. Bird Life* 136 The whip-bird or coachwhip bird (*Psophodes olivaceus*) ranges through Eastern Australia, from North Queensland to Victoria. **1955** V. PALMER *Let Birds Fly* 25 Whipbirds calling from one ferny hillside to another. **1976** *Bulletin* (Sydney) 11 Dec. 35/2 A whip-bird gave its wonderful, almost electronic call. **1980** J. WOLFE *End of Prickly-stick* 7 And one pair of whipbirds still. After the crack of the whip, listen closely and you will hear the female reply to her mate.

Hence **whip-birding** *pres. pple.*, imitating the sound made by a whipbird.

1909 *Bulletin* (Sydney) 26 Aug. 40/2 Some of the youngsters were shouting and whip-birding again, attracting everybody's attention.

whipping side. *Shearing.* [f. *whip, v.* to move (something) vigorously or quickly, with reference to the stroke of the shears.] The last side of the sheep to be shorn.

1899 J. BRADSHAW *Quirindi Bank Robbery* 3 Put me on a shearing floor and it's there I'm game to bet That I'd give to any ringer ten sheep start; When on the whipping side away from them I slide, Just like a bullet or a dart. **1906** J. BARBOUR *Pencillings on Wallaby* 10 While Mulga Joe, stripped to the waist, Speeds down the whipping side. **1911** 'S. RUDD' *Bk. of Dan* 132 Dan . . flew down the 'whipping side', set the sheep on its legs and booted it into the pen before his opponent was a quarter way through. **1929** *Aussie* (Sydney) Apr. 17/1 'I went from the sneezer to the breezer in three chops up the nick and down the whipping side in a couple more'. . . That is to say, he did one side of a sheep in three blows of the shears, then shore the neck and the last side in a couple more. **1955** E. BARNES *Easier Shearing* 41 And now we come to the 'whipping' or last side. . . While shearing the whipping side, the left hand has not been idle. **1964** H.P. TRITTON *Time means Tucker* (rev. ed.) 40 Bill would shear a sheep to the 'whipping side', then pass it to me, and as it was straight going, seven or eight blows would complete the job. **1979** 'BLUE SHEARER' *First Clip* 21 Alongside all the shearing 'giants', I suppose she wasn't much, But I loved to watch her whipping side, And I loved to see her crutch. **1982** *Sydney Morning Herald* 23 Oct. 29/3, I grabbed my boggi and ran her down the whipping side.

whippy. [Of unknown origin.]

1. The base in a kind of hide-and-seek game.

1964 *Bulletin* (Sydney) 22 Aug. 31/3 The Tree was the whippy for hidings, the base for releasings. **1980** C. JAMES *Unreliable Mem.* 34, I noticed a girl using the fence as a whippy. She was leaning against it with her face buried in her folded arms while other girls hid. If some other girl got to the whippy while she was away searching, there would be a cry of 'all in, the whippy's taken'.

2. *transf.* A place in which money is kept; the money in such a place.

1973 *Kings Cross Whisper* (Sydney) cliv. 16/2 I've never yet met a Kiwi who didn't cry poor mouth while he snipped you bone dry and all the time had a secret whippy tucked away somewhere you didn't know about. **1980** *Sun-Herald* (Sydney) 27 Jan. 66/4 Fair dinkum, if a man had enough in the willy, I mean whippy, I'd get myself a charlie . . and shout her seven or so ounces of sheer joy.

whip snake. [See quot. 1893.] Any of several slender, whip-like snakes, esp. of the genus *Demansia* of mainland Aust. and New Guinea, esp. the widespread, venomous *D. psammophis*.

1844 *Duncan's Weekly Register* (Sydney) 16 Nov. 246/1 All the whip snakes are proverbially dangerous and the poison most active and fatal. **1847** *Moreton Bay Courier* 29 May 4/2 The Whip Snake is usually of a light grey colour. . . They frequent the banks of rivers, creeks and nestle in the earth or in hollows of trees. **1863** J. MORRILL *Sketch of Residence* 24, I was also bit by a whip snake, which made me swell up for two days. **1893** J. DEMARR *Adventures in Aust.* 206 A whip-snake is so called, owing to its resemblance in length and thickness to the thong of a whip. **1909** G. SMITH *Naturalist in Tas.* 90 The little whip snake (*Denisonia coronoides*) . . is generally found in dry localities away from water. **1928** E. FOREMAN *Hist. & Adventures Qld. Pioneer* 105 Thrilling adventure . . with a whip snake. **1965** *Austral. Encycl.* VIII. 167 Most other small species, mainly of the inland areas, are referred to in general terms as whip-snakes or saltbush snakes. **1983** H.G. COGGER *Reptiles & Amphibians* (rev. ed.) 430 Black Whip Snake *Demansia atra*. . . Body slender; tail thin and whip-like. 1 metre (total length).

whipstick. [Transf. use of *whip-stick* a pliant stick used as a whip.]

1. a. A form of growth (usu. of mallee eucalypts) characterized by a number of erect, slender stems; a tree of this habit. **b.** An area of vegetation dominated by such trees. Also *attrib.*

1855 *Illustr. Sydney News* 9 June 296/1 A considerable number of diggers have located themselves at the 'whip-sticks', with the view of giving the celebrated Scrub . . a thorough prospecting this winter. **1857** W. HOWITT *Tallangetta* I. 268 Why, it's not very pleasant, In the dark whipstick bush, To be shot down like a pheasant, Or pulled up like a rush. **1862** J.A. PATTERSON *Gold Fields Vic.* 11 Some of the men . . found themselves in the vicinity of a few white tents, half hidden in the whipstick. **1907** *Jrnl. Dept. Agric. Vic.* V. 433 It is more than probable that an acre of 150 [black wattle] trees will produce more bark . . than an acre of 500 whipsticks that can only produce thin, inferior bark. **1928** B. CRONIN *Dragonfly* 51 A natural windbreak of tumbled hill . . was crowned with whip-stick, like the hairs on the back of a caterpillar. **1931** F.D. DAVISON *Man-Shy* (1961) 78 Thin whip-sticks, growing close together, and as high as a man's head, covered large areas of ground. **1981** L. COSTERMANS *Native Trees & Shrubs S.-E. Aust.* 374 If the aerial parts of the plant are burnt or broken off, new shoots will sprout from the lignotuberous root-stock, usually producing the 'whip-stick' type of growth. **1983** M. HAYES *Prickle Farm* 44 We'd even braved the elements to collect a van load of wood from out in the whipstick somewhere.

2. Comb. **whipstick mallee, scrub.**

1900 *Proc. Linnean Soc. N.S.W.* XXV. 602 *E*[*ucalyptus*] *viridis* . . is known as **Whipstick Mallee** from its erect slender stems. **1944** *Bulletin* (Sydney) 12 July 14/3 Next time I'm bushed well out in the whipstick mallee I'll . . drum on a dead tree with the back of my axe in order to call attention. The only difficulty will be to find a dead tree thicker than my wrist in that country. **1962** H.J. FRITH *Mallee-Fowl* 54 On very sandy soils or where limestone is close to the surface the eucalypts have many thin stems, only about an inch in diameter. These types are known as whipstick mallee. **1983** *Bogong* IV. v. 4 Mallee may be from two to eight metres tall, with stems 3–20 cms. in diameter, the smaller stemmed mallee being called 'whipstick', the large mallees being 'bull mallee'. Variation in mallee growth is determined by soil type—whipstick mallee grows on sandy dunes while bull mallee occupies troughs of heavier soils. **1853** C.R. READ *What I heard, saw, & Did* 53 *Find* a track through the **whip stick scrub.** **1855** W. HOWITT *Land, Labor & Gold* II. 96 The valleys are covered with what they call the whipstick scrub; a scrub of dwarf gum-trees, which run about twelve feet high or so, growing densely, side by side. **1905** J. FURPHY *Rigby's Romance* (1946) 63 I'll be waiting for you that evening at sunset, in the whipstick scrub. **1936** *Bulletin* (Sydney) 4 Mar. 21/1 What about the 'brushers', long, oarlike blades of wood we used to brush aside the whipstick scrub when mustering cattle out from the Wakool? **1949** G. FARWELL *Traveller's Tracks* 38 Only a few weed-grown mullock piles among whipstick scrub. **1978** W. LOWENSTEIN *Weevils in Flour* 47 You'd cut the whip-stick scrub, get paid for how much oil came out of it. **1984** E. WALLING *On Trail Austral. Wildflowers* 45 The Whipstick scrub lies to the west of Bendigo Valley, and it's called Whipstick from early digging days when branches of the Green Mallee tree were used for whips.

whiptail wallaby. [See quot. 1941.] The wallaby *Macropus parryi* of e. Qld. and e. N.S.W., light to brownish-grey in colour, having a long, slender, dark-tipped tail; PARRY'S WALLABY; PRETTY FACE. Also **whiptail, whip-tailed wallaby.**

1900 *Bulletin* (Sydney) 7 July 15/1 The white-bellied wallaby, known in Q. as the 'whiptail', is even a better jumper than the 'roo. **1924** *Ibid.* 3 Jan. 22/2 A whip-tail wallaby and a rock wallaby in captivity. **1941** E. TROUGHTON *Furred Animals Aust.* 200 *Wallabia elegans*. . . This is . . generally known as the Whip-tail owing to the great length of the slender tail, which equals that of the combined head and body. **1949** B. O'REILLY *Green Mountains* 95 Time for winter walkabout came and the whiptail wallabies went far back into the ranges. **1986** *Sydney Morning Herald* 15 Jan. 5/2 High killing quotas, illegal interstate trade in skins and constant pressure from the shooting industry have put the future of red kangaroos and the whip-tailed wallaby in jeopardy in Queensland.

whirley, whirlie, varr. WURLEY.

whirly. Also **wurley.** [f. *whirl(wind* + -Y.] WILLY WILLY 1. Also **whirly-wind, wind-whirly.**

1894 H. NISBET *Bush Girl's Romance* 9 Only the Wurley caused any discomfort, or an occasional bush-fire made them apprehensive. **1925** *Bulletin* (Sydney) 12 Feb. 24/1 He watched the whirlies lift The sand off the grassless plain. **1931** J.R. FIDDIAN *R. Mitchell of Inland* 98 The 'whirlies', in which, in a narrow compass, the wind whirled round and round and up into a towering pillar which swept imposingly across the landscape. **1942** *Aust. Week-End Bk.* 174 Bursts of Wurlies. These dust storms are so bad that lights have to be turned on in the main street at 3 o'clock in the afternoon. **1954** A. UPFIELD *Death of Lake* (1956) 11 The 'whirlies' had danced all day. **1964** *Mount Isa Mail* 10 Mar. 3/6 A large section of a roof was ripped off a building by a 'whirly' in Camooweal Street this afternoon. . . The whirly passed through town at about 1.30 p.m. **1974** *Bronze Swagman Bk. Bush Verse* 62 Over went the locust tree, The chooks blew away. Blimey, what a whirly-wind We had that day. **1980** J. WRIGHT *Big Hearts & Gold Dust* 9 Wind whirlies, like mischievous boys, plucked the flower petals from pear and apple trees.

whirly-whirly. Also **wurly-wurly.** [Reduplication of WHIRLY, by analogy with WILLY WILLY.] WILLY WILLY 1.

1926 *Bulletin* (Sydney) 25 Feb. 1/1 The 'wurly-wurly' of the native has become the 'willy-willy' of the white. **1969** R. OTTLEY *Brumbie Dust* 21 Where the mirages dance on the horizon and the dust whirls and capers into fantastic whirlie-whirlies. **1972** *Southerly* i. 4 A small whirly-whirly swept down the verandah, lifting dust and lolly papers in a mini-spiral. **1976** F.R. ST. JOHN *Verse in Retirement* 42 And those ozonic vapours as change of wind cuts capers Along the sands the whirly-whirleys grow.

whirly-wind: see WHIRLY.

whisperer. A racecourse tipster.

1914 M. CANNON *That Damned Democrat* (1981) 97 His non-productiveness surpasses that of the bookmaker . . and the professional 'whisperer' on racecourses all rolled into one. **1918** *Euripidean: Troopship Souvenir* 6 Well, wot didn't they call me . . speiler, rook, whisperer and the like. **1920** 'J. North' *Harry Dale's Grand National* 101 He got a tidy income as a 'whisperer', one of that small army of turf hangers-on who impart information. **1936** A.B. Paterson *Shearer's Colt* 37 'Did you ever hear of a whisperer?' 'I have', said Fitzroy, 'plenty of 'em. They're fellows who come to you on the race-course and whisper to you what'll win.'

whistle, *v.* [See Whistlecock a.] *trans.* To perform subincision upon (an Aboriginal male). The examples are *vbl. n.*

1897 W.E. Roth *Ethnol. Studies* 177 Introcision, otherwise known as 'Sturt's terrible rite', 'whistling', artificial hypospadias, &c., is met with throughout the Boulia, Leichhardt-Selwyn, and Upper Georgina Districts. **1974** *Forum* vii. 37 Some scientists say whistling was a form of population control.

whistlecock. a. In an Aboriginal initiation ritual: the slitting of the underside of the penis in order to make a permanent opening into the urethra; subincision. **b.** An Aboriginal male on whom this operation has been performed. Also **whistle-prick,** and as *v. trans.* See also *Sturt's rite* Sturt, Terrible rite.

1969 A.A. Abbie *Original Australs.* 147 One Australian name for subincision is *mika* while Curr calls it the 'terrible rite'. Outback whites familiar with Aborigines refer to the condition as 'whistle-cock'. **1970** N.A. Beagley *Up & Down Under* 52 The virile youths were operated on with a piece of sharp stone and made 'whistle cocks'... I asked were they married. 'Oh yes.' 'Any children?' 'No, me whistle cock.' **1972** N. Miles *Opal Fever* 151 'So he won't pass on his faults to the next generation, they make him a whistle-cock.' 'Whistle-cock. What's that?' 'It's a simple operation. They make a small hole in the base of his cock, so that none of his semen will enter the woman.' **1973** D. Wolfe *Brass Kangaroo* 88 He raised his penis with one hand and I saw the small incision, at the base, underneath. 'That's true whistlecock, Sam.' **1974** *Forum* vii. 37 That whistle-prick no good. Just wettem libral's arse. **1985** B. Rosser *Dreamtime Nightmare* 75 'How do they whistle-cock them?' 'They put a kangaroo bone down the hole [of the penis] then they rip them up with a sharp stone.'

whistler.

1. Any of the small, insectivorous birds of the chiefly Austral. genus *Pachycephala*, typically having a rich, whistled song; Thickhead.

1924 Lord & Scott *Synopsis Vertebrate Animals Tas.* 207 The whistlers, or 'thickheads', as they are often termed, constitute one of the joys of the Tasmanian bush. **1929** A.H. Chisholm *Birds & Green Places* 13 No mistaking the voice of any one of Australia's several species of birds indefinitely known as 'whistlers'. **1945** C. Barrett *Austral. Bird Life* 177 The ten species of whistlers (*Pachycephala*), formerly called 'thickheads', are placed in the family of song-shrikes, Pachycephalidae. **1965** *Austral. Encycl.* IX. 292 All whistlers build cup-shaped nests of either bark or twigs. **1984** Simpson & Day *Birds of Aust.* 322 Whistlers .. are robust birds with .. distinctive voices—some are among Australia's most beautiful songsters, with variable repertoires of rich, melodic phrases.

2. With distinguishing epithet, as **golden, rufous:** see under first element.

3. See *whistling duck* (b), Whistling.

whistling, *ppl. a.* Used as a distinguishing element in the names of fauna: **whistling dick** (esp. *Tas.*), *grey thrush*, see Grey *a.*; **duck, (a)** either of two ducks of the genus *Dendrocygna* of n. and e. Aust., *D. eytoni* (see *plumed tree duck* Plumed) and *D. arcuata* of Aust. and elsewhere in the Indo-Pacific region; also **whistling tree duck; (b)** *pink-eared duck*, see Pink *a.*; also **whistle-duck, whistler; eagle** (or **kite**), the dark and light brown bird of prey *Haliastur sphenurus* of Aust. and elsewhere, having a loud whistling call; formerly also **whistling hawk; tree frog,** the frog *Litoria verreauxi* of s.e. mainland Aust.

1848 J. Gould *Birds of Aust.* II. Pl. 77, *Colluricincla Selbii* .. **Whistling Dick,** of the Colonists of Van Diemen's Land. **1903** *Emu* III. 23 Whistling Shrike-Thrush (*Collyriocincla rectirostris*)—This bird is known to most Tasmanians as the 'Whistling Dick', on account of its noisiness and general cheerfulness... It always makes its presence known long before it can be seen with its loud and melodious whistling notes. **1918** *Huon Times* (Franklin) 15 Oct. 3/2 It would be a fine thing if the shooting of the 'whistling dick' could be stopped. There is no doubt he is a splendid little bird for the orchardist. **1924** C.E. Lord *Synopsis Vertebrate Animals Tas.* 208 The 'Whistling Dick', as the species is called by bushmen. **1952** J.R. Skemp *Memories Myrtle Bank* 248 One or two blue wrens and whistling dicks (grey thrushes) would take the food from my hand. **1770** J. Banks *Jrnl.* 8 July (1896) 286 On our passage down we met several flocks of **whistling ducks,** of which we shot some. **1849** C. Sturt *Narr. Exped. Central Aust.* II. 56 App. Malacorhyncus Membranaceus .. is very common on most of the Australian creeks and streams, and is called the Whistling Duck. **1857** H. Turnbull *Leichhardt's Second Journey* (1983) 46 The whistling duck, a very pretty bird peculiar to the north-west coast of New Holland. They go in large flocks and make a strange whistling noise. They roost on the trees and are delicious eating. **1872** A. McFarland *Illawarra & Manaro* 143 The 'whistling duck' is .. found in some parts of Manaro. **1896** F.G. Aflalo *Sketch Nat. Hist. Aust.* 100 The Whistling Tree Duck (*Dendrocygna*), so-called from the peculiar whistling note it utters on the wing, has an allied species, which also whistles, on the north-west coast. **1901** G. White *Across Aust.* 13 Frew's Ironstone Lagoon, a beautiful waterhole... Four whistling ducks were disporting themselves on its bosom. **1926** K. Dahl *In Savage Aust.* 167 Another species of whistler (*Dendrocygna Eytoni*). **1934** H.G. Lamond *Aviary on Plains* 64 There's a big mob of whistlers (Whistling Ducks) in this country. **1945** C. Barrett *Austral. Bird Life* 48 The whistling tree-duck .. at times appears in southern Australia. **1955** S. Osborne *Duck Shooting Aust.* 11 *Pink-eared duck*... Also known as Whistling or Zebra Duck and Widgeon. **1964** M. Sharland *Territory of Birds* 105 Here also was a pair of unusual perching ducks, the handsome *Dendrocygna*, commonly called 'Whistler', and in ornithological vernacular 'Plumed Tree Duck'. *Ibid.* 105 A second species, the Whistling Tree Duck, much like it in general appearance, but without the plume-like flank feathers, is more commonly dispersed and occurs on lagoons close to Darwin. **1974** J. Byrne *Duck Hunting Aust. & N.Z.* 191 The long legs and neck of the Whistle-ducks are quite distinctive on land, and in flight, the legs trail behind the tail and the neck is bent downwards in a characteristic attitude. **1827** [**whistling eagle**] *Trans. Linnean Soc. London* XV. 187 It is called the Whistling Hawk by the settlers. **1843** J. Gould *Birds of Aust.* (1848) I. Pl. 5, Its flight, when high in the air, is buoyant and easy, and it frequently soars to a great altitude, uttering at the same time a shrill whistling cry, from which circumstance it has obtained from the colonists the name of the Whistling Hawk, and by which it is at once distinguished from all the other members of the family inhabiting Australia. *Ibid.*, I may mention that, having winged a very rare Tern on the surface of a lagoon, a Whistling Eagle immediately descended and carried it off. **1849** C. Sturt *Narr. Exped. Central Aust.* II. 13 App. *The Whistling Eagle* .. is a dull and stupid bird, and is easily approached. **1860** G. Bennett *Gatherings of Naturalist* 176 The Whistling Hawk of the colonists, (*Haliaëtus canorus*). **1896** B. Spencer *Rep. Horn Sci. Exped. Central Aust.* II. 106 Whistling Eagle .. appear to feed on any dead animal. **1935** Davison & Nicholls *Blue Coast Caravan* 18 Whistling eagle, little lorikeet, crimson parrot. **1956** A.C.C. Lock *Tropical Tapestry* 278 In the horizontal branch of a tall poplar gum a whistling eagle (*Haliastur sphenurus*) flew from its nest, a big flat pile of sticks and twigs. **1968** R. Hill *Bush Quest* 135 The next and last hawks of the day were four whistling kites... Their sandy and vandyke-brown plumage looked very handsome against the deep blue sky. **1982** R. Hall *Just Relations* 87 It was his grandfather who pointed out the whistling eagle's nest in August and the death adder's nest in May. **1984** M. Blakers et al. *Atlas Austral. Birds* 96 As with other carrion eaters, the Whistling Kite has probably benefited greatly from agriculture, farming providing carcasses and clearing making them visible. **1969** D. Clyne *Austral. Frogs* 77 *Hyla verreauxi*, **Whistling Tree Frog...** The call is .. long and shrill, rather like a series of whistled notes... Queensland and N.S.W. **1978** B.P. Moore *Life on Forty Acres* 115 The Whistling Tree Frog (*Litoria verreauxi*) is another species that keeps mostly away from permanent water and its pleasant and extended musical trill can be heard almost anywhere and at any season, after rain.

white, *n.*[1], *a.*[1] (and *attrib.*), and *adv.* [Spec. use of *white* a person of a race distinguished by a light complexion.]

A. *n.* White man 1.

1818 *Hobart Town Gaz.* 26 Dec., The blows and cries of the Blacks, excited to uproar and outrage by the Whites, who take pleasure in the sufferings of their fellow men. **1827** P. Cunningham *Two Yrs. in N.S.W.* II. 34 If a *white* injures them, they generally satisfy their rage upon the first of that colour they can conveniently meet with. **1839** *Sydney Standard* 11 Mar. 4/2 A police force .. keeping order amongst the lower classes of Whites. **1852** J. Morgan *Life & Adventures W. Buckley* 122 The gentlemen .. on coming up to where we were—whites and blacks—appeared to be very much astonished. **1865** G.S. Lang *Aborigines of Aust.* 29 The native spectators groaned whenever a blackfellow fell, but cheered lustily when a white bit the dust. **1884** A.W. Howitt *On Some Austral. Ceremonies Initiation* 2 The accounts .. have been at second-hand, derived from the statements of blackboys living with the whites. **1897** J.J. Murif *From Ocean to Ocean* 62 From Hergott to Alice Springs the population is grouped under three generic headings—'Whites', 'Afghans', and 'Blackfellows'. **1922** 'J. Bushman' *In Musgrave Ranges* 63 The three whites were sitting near an open pack-bag, eating damper and salt meat, and drinking tea from the drover's quart-pot. **1941** *Bulletin* (Sydney) 23 Apr. 16/2 No whites within 35 miles. **1965** *N. Austral. Monthly* Jan. 24 Bill is ever remembered up here by whites and blacks alike. **1983** *Truth* (Sydney) 14 Feb. 7/8 The racial antagonisms are not confined to the whites. **1986** *Centralian Advocate* 15 Jan. 5/2 There are numerous bush foods all over Australia which have been discarded by whites in their attempts to cart England around with them.

B. *adj.* (and *attrib.*)

1. Of British or European descent; of or pertaining to a person of such descent, or to such people collectively.

1835 J. Bonwick *W. Buckley* (1856) 20 The commission of any outrages upon the White Immigrants. **1848** T.L. Mitchell *Jrnl. Exped. Tropical Aust.* 388 The first white female he could ever have seen. **1856** J. Bonwick *W. Buckley* 90 They were acquitted for want of white evidence. **1863** —— *Wild White Man* 76 The overlanders with stock were more than once waylaid .. and white blood shed in the struggle. **1885** *Rec. Castlemaine Pioneers* 28 June (1972) 139 At the Maloga Station .. blacks with a suspicion .. of a white taint can be taught to pray and sing and marry. **1895** *Worker* (Sydney) 26 Jan. 3/2 He was speculator, storekeeper, and gambler, and made no more flies about robbing his own countryman than he did the 'White Devils'. **1920** *Smith's Weekly* (Sydney) 11 Sept. 17/6 About 'white trackers'. When it's a life-and-death matter, Binghi's the man for the job every time. **1945** E. George *Two at Daly Waters* 39 Very proud of being allowed to tend the white piccaninny, Maggie carefully gave her the bottle. **1955** D. Niland *Shiralee* 135 He hated the ignominy of capitulating to a harlot, and a black one at that. Macauley, the gin-jockey, they could say. The black velvet for Macauley; he can't get the white satin, poor sod. **1986** *Canberra Times* 15 Mar. 2/4 White settlement, white cattle and sheep have destroyed many of the traditional food sources.

2. [Used elsewhere but recorded earliest in Aust.: see Mathews *a.* 1.] Of exemplary character. See also White man 2.

1856 J. Bonwick *Bushrangers* 94 According to the testimony of his overseer, Connell, he was 'the whitest man on the farm'. **1883** *Sydney Mail* 5 May 823/4 He was always the same. The whitest man I ever knew, or ever shall—that I say and stick to. **1891** *Truth* (Sydney) 19 Apr. 3/3 A whiter fellow than him, I know, Don't stand to-day on the earth below. **1904** *Shearer* (Sydney) 17 Sept. 4/4 The boss is a good sort and has always been reckoned one of the 'whitest' men in the West. **1925** M. Terry *Across Unknown Aust.* 252 Dick proved himself to be 'white' right through, by insisting on carrying the load. **1934** J.S. Neilson *Autobiogr.* (1978) 96 My boss was as white a man as ever I worked for and he was very anxious that I should keep on. **1948** K.S. Prichard *Golden Miles* 374 Tom Gough's one of the finest, whitest men ever drew breath. There's not two like him born in a century. **1965** D. Martin *Hero of Too* 248 He's the whitest yellow man of them all. Where would our boy be without Lammy, and him doing all the dirty work? **1980** Holth & Barnaby *Cattlemen of High Country* 63 In deference to his experience, bushcraft and reputation as a 'white bloke', Wally Ryder has been tacitly acknowledged as Ben's successor as the boss at the big muster. In cattlemen's terms, to be called a 'white bloke' is the greatest praise.

3. Exclusive of non-whites.

1901 *Bulletin* (Sydney) 11 May 14/1 M'Parritch was very strong against the admission of aboriginal children to 'white' schools. *Ibid.* 19 Oct. 14/2 Roebourne . . consists of two towns; the brown, yellow and black conglomeration on one side of a creek, and on the other the so-called 'white' town. **1911** *Ibid.* 10 Aug. 14/2 Menzies (W.A.) . . confessed shamefacedly to two Jap laundries and numerous 'Ghan camel-drivers. But the local miners' union got busy, and established a 'white' laundry. **1936** C.P. CONIGRAVE *N. Aust.* 250 Who can say . . Australia may not be called upon to defend her persistence in putting a white fence around her continent.

4. In Comb. and collocations in sense 1 (*n.* and *a.*): **white labour, person, population.**

1899 *Progress* (Brisbane) 29 Apr. 9/1 The return of a **white labour** candidate for such a multi-coloured district as Cairns, is one more indication that the revolt against the rule of the black-labour party will come from the white men who have the misfortune to live in those parts of the colony where the Curse most abounds. **1905** *Tocsin* (Melbourne) 16 Nov. 7/2 The extra cost of raising shell by white, as compared with coloured, labour ranged from £45 to £83 per ton. **1909** A. FISHER *Policy for Aust.* 21 We have made a success of the white-labour policy. Nearly all our sugar now is produced by white labour. **1941** J.W. DAFOE *Under Southern Skies* 26 The white Australia policy implies that all the work of Australia, household, menial, routine and heavy, shall be done by white labour. **1808** *Sydney Gaz.* 19 June, A boat was upset off Bradley's Head, in which there were three **white persons** and two natives. **1838** BACKHOUSE & TYLOR *Life & Labours G.W. Walker* 29 Jan. (1862) 285 They . . have cut off a number of white persons. **1843** *Port Phillip Mag.* Feb. 88 As to medicine they never knew that such a powerful means of relief existed until the arrival of the **white population.** **1858** T. MCCOMBIE *Hist. Colony Vic.* 90 From Gipps Land, and all the outlying districts, news was arriving of aboriginal aggressions, and the white population, not very numerous at this period, began to dread a general attack. **1898** D.W. CARNEGIE *Spinifex & Sand* 327 The white population numbers so few.

5. In Special Comb. and collocations: **white brother,** used ironically to designate a non-Aboriginal Australian male; cf. *black brother* BLACK *a.*[1] 5; **gin, lubra** *Austral. pidgin*, a white woman; see GIN 1, LUBRA 1; **Mary,** see MARY c.; **native,** NATIVE *n.* 2; **settlement,** SETTLEMENT 1 b.; **settler,** SETTLER 1.

1913 *Bulletin* (Sydney) 30 Jan. 16/1 Binghi . . runs risks which would end in serious disablement for **White Brother.** **1925** *Smith's Weekly* (Sydney) 21 Feb. 20/5 The Australian abo. is seldom credited with the capacity for using his brains to make money. But one dusky dogger showed his white brother points. **1843** *Sydney Morning Herald* 19 Sept. 2/7 He rushed past me towards the women, saying—white fellow have black gins, now black fellow have **white gins.** **1849** S. & J. SIDNEY *Emigrant's Jrnl.* 123 There was a white gin (woman), the stockman's wife, both cockneys. **1888** W.T. PYKE *Bush Tales* 11 The bushrangers demanded why the blacks had dared to threaten a white gin. **1912** J. BRADSHAW *Highway Robbery under Arms* (ed. 3) 21 All the same white gin, too many whitefellow no good. **1843** *Portland Mercury* 20 Dec. 3/2 She stated she had been sent by the owner of the house (**white loubra**). **1845** MRS THOMSON *Life in Bush* 21 The sight of a 'white leubra', as she called her, seemed for a time to take away her speech. **1856** W.W. DOBIE *Recoll. Visit Port-Phillip* 77, I sometimes found myself addressing her in the jargon in use with the black fellows, with whom I could converse much more fluently than with this white lubra. **1900** R. BRUCE *Benbonuna* (1904) 23 White lubra say him big one poorly. **1949** I.L. IDRIESS *One Wet Season* 119 She could find the haunts of birds and animals, reptiles and fish. This was a real white lubra who actually could live on the bush. **1830** T.J. MASLEN *Friend of Aust.* 132 There are now . . many **white natives** in Australia. **1852** W. HUGHES *Austral. Colonies* 112 The colonial-born portion of the Australian population—that is, the white natives of the different colonies—are distinguished by the same general spareness of form, and pallidness of complexion, which characterises the people of the United States. **1865** J.F. MORTLOCK *Experiences of Convict* 92 The white natives of Van Diemen's Land are generally tall, muscular, and good looking. **1886** R. HENTY *Australiana* 36, I, son of Stephen Henty, am the first white native of this first settlement. **1909** *Bulletin* (Sydney) 21 Oct. (Red Page), It has been urged locally that the adjective 'Australian' should be reserved for that literature in English which has been produced by the white natives of Australia. **1849** A. HARRIS *Guide Port Stephens* 71 Those who remain wandering about in the **white settlements** half-civilized. **1864** J. MORRILL *Sketch of Residence* 215 Hoping . . we should be able to reach some white settlement. **1898** D.W. CARNEGIE *Spinifex & Sand* 253, I . . had no longer any purpose than that of traversing the region that lay between us and 'white settlements'. **1840** *S. Austral. Register* (Adelaide) 23 July 8 Surveys carried on by modern **white settlers.** **1865** G.S. LANG *Aborigines of Aust.* 38 They have been deprived of their hunting grounds without any provision being made for them, the country having been occupied by the white settlers. **1879** *Native Tribes S.A.* p. xi, All who have written upon the subject of the Australian native tribes acknowledge that they vanish before the white settler. **1973** *Bulletin* (Sydney) 27 Jan. 40/2 The early attempts of white settlers to comprehend and use their new continent.

C. *adv.*

1. Honourably; in the manner of a WHITE MAN 2.

1897 *Worker* (Sydney) 11 Sept. 1/1 A pound a hundred, 'in or out', with rules and tucker fair, He designates as 'working white' and shearing 'on the square'.

2. In the phr. **to live white,** (of an Aboriginal) to live in the manner of white people.

1940 E. HILL *Great Austral. Loneliness* (ed. 2) 273 Since he died, the policeman at Beltana and the Chief Protector of Aborigines in Adelaide have written to me, asking if I would leave the camp and live white again. **1951** —— *Territory* 217 The harbour swarmed with crocodiles, for the blacks, 'living white' for a generation, had given up hunting their eggs.

white, *a.*[2] and *n.*[2] [Spec. use of *white* the colour.]

A. *adj.*

1. a. Used as a distinguishing epithet in the names of plants: **white apple,** any of several trees, esp. the tall *Syzygium cormiflorum* (fam. Myrtaceae) of n. Qld., having round white edible fruits, and the similar *S. forte*; **ash,** any of several trees, usu. of the genus *Eucalyptus* (fam. Myrtaceae), esp. *E. fraxinoides* of easternmost Vic. and s.e. N.S.W., having a white smooth upper trunk and strong whitish timber, and *E. oreades* of e. N.S.W. and s.e. Qld.; the wood of the tree; also **white mountain ash; beech,** see BEECH; **box,** any of several trees, usu. of the fam. Myrtaceae, esp. *Eucalyptus albens* of s.e. mainland Aust., yielding a pale, strong timber; the wood of the tree; **cedar,** the deciduous tree *Melia azedarach* var. *australasica* (fam. Meliaceae) of Qld., N.S.W., and New Guinea, widely cultivated, esp. as a street tree, having a furrowed bark and strongly scented, lilac-coloured flowers; the attractively figured wood of the tree; LILAC; also *attrib.*; **cypress pine,** see *white pine*; **gum,** any of many trees of the genus *Eucalyptus* (fam. Myrtaceae) having a smooth, whitish bark; the wood of the tree; also *attrib.*; **honeysuckle,** the tree or shrub of coastal e. Aust. *Banksia integrifolia* (fam. Proteaceae), having leaves which are white underneath; the wood of the tree; **ironbark,** any of several trees of the genus *Eucalyptus* (fam. Myrtaceae), incl. *E. leucoxylon* (see YELLOW GUM 2); **lily** *obs.*, a plant of the genus *Crinum* (fam. Liliaceae), perh. *Darling lily* (see DARLING); **mahogany,** any of several trees of the genus *Eucalyptus* (fam. Myrtaceae), esp. *E. acmenioides* of n.e. N.S.W. and e. Qld., yielding a hard, durable, brown timber; the wood of the tree; **mangrove,** the tree or shrub *Avicennia marina* var. *resinifera* (fam. Verbenaceae), widespread in coastal mainland Aust., having leaves glossy above and whitish below; *grey mangrove*, see GREY *a.*; **mountain ash,** see *white ash*; **oak,** any of several trees yielding a whitish wood, esp. *Lagunaria patersonia* (fam. Malvaceae) of e. Qld., Norfolk Is., and Lord Howe Is.; **pine,** the straight-trunked tree *Callitris glaucophylla* (fam. Cupressaceae) of s. mainland Aust., having aromatic green to grey-green foliage; the close-grained, termite-resistant, fragrant wood of the tree; see also *Murray pine* MURRAY 2, *Murrumbidgee pine* MURRUMBIDGEE A.; also **white cypress (pine); punk,** the white, spongy fruiting body of the bracket fungus *Piptoporus portentosus*; see also PUNK; **sally,** any of several trees, esp. *E. pauciflora* (see *snow gum* SNOW 1); **stringybark,** any of several rough-barked trees of the genus *Eucalyptus* (fam. Myrtaceae) yielding a pale timber, esp. *E. eugenioides* and *E. globoidea* of s.e. mainland Aust.; **waratah,** the shrub or small tree *Agastachys odorata* (fam. Proteaceae) of Tas., bearing spikes of fragrant white flowers.

1852 J. MACGILLIVRAY *Narr. Voyage H.M.S. Rattlesnake* II. 152 Sixty feet high, the straight trunks rising twenty or thirty feet from the ground to the branches. . . We called it the **white apple.** It is a species of *Eugenia.* **1890** F.M. BAILEY *Catal. Plants Qld.* 103 White Apple—Eugenia grandis. **1909** —— *Comprehensive Catal. Qld. Plants* 208 *Eugenia cormiflora* . . a White Apple. 'Mooroolʼ of Barron River natives. **1932** R.H. ANDERSON *Trees of N.S.W.* 129 *Endiandra virens*, sometimes known as White Apple, is . . a small to medium sized tree, with rather sparse, light green foliage and large yellowish fruits which form in great profusion. **1935** *Bulletin* (Sydney) 13 Mar. 20/2 'Quareef's' flowering gums . . have a peculiarity in common with the white-apple and swamp-box trees in southern Queensland. The apple exudes a red gummy sap from the limbs. . . The swamp-box weeps only when rain is threatening. **1985** N. & H. NICHOLSON *Austral. Rainforest Plants* 60 Like all the Lilly-pillies, White Apple makes a handsome tub plant when young. **1898** *Proc. Linnean Soc. N.S.W.* XXIII. 412 *Eucalyptus fraxinoides*, sp. n. . . Because of its resemblance to American Ash it goes under the name of **White Ash;** it also goes under the name of Mountain Ash, a name which, however, should be reserved for *E. Sieberiana.* **1900** *Ibid.* XXV. 109 *Eucalyptus stricta*. . . We have received this species from Mr R.H. Cambage from the top of Pigeon-house Mountain . . near Milton. It is known locally as 'White Ash'. **1926** *Qld. Agric. Jrnl.* XXV. 435 *Flindersia Bourjotiana* . . White Ash. **1947** W.A.W. DE BEUZEVILLE *Austral. Trees* 166 White Mountain Ash . . is very similar to the Blue Mountain Ash. . . The timber is . . sought after for construction of propellor blades for aircraft, car body building, etc. **1963** C. BURGESS *Blue Mountain Gums* 41 *'Blue mountain ash'*, *'white ash'* or *'smooth-barked mountain ash'* was described by R.T. Baker in 1899 and named *Eucalyptus oreades*. . . The bark is smooth, white and deciduous in ribbons. **1985** P. CAREY *Illywhacker* 117 We would want mountain ash or white ash for spars. **1867** A.K. COLLINS *Waddy Mudoee* 7 On the Condamine . . where the myall flourishes, and the **white box,** and sandal-wood, and pine, spring into glorious life. **1887** *Proc. Linnean Soc. N.S.W.* II. 278 *Eucalyptus . . hemiphloia*. . . Two distinct trees in this district are known as white-box. **1902** *Ibid.* XXVI. 557 *E[ucalyptus] Stuartiana* . . is the 'Apple-tree Gum' of Mr De Coque. . . In New England I have often heard it called 'White Box' to this day. **1919** R.T. BAKER *Hardwoods of Aust.* 174 The timber is pale-coloured, very durable, and much resembles 'White Box'. **1936** F. CLUNE *Roaming round Darling* 161 White box is a good burning wood, sheds a brown bark in springtime, then it has a white surface. **1965** *Austral. Encycl.* III. 406 The common names are often derived from the colours of bark, timber or foliage . . white box (*E[ucalyptus] albens*, having pallid glaucescent foliage). **1808** J.W. LEWIN *Birds New Holland* 9 These birds . . are fond of the berry of the **white cedar** of the colony. **1825** B. FIELD *Geogr. Mem. N.S.W.* 320 The white cedar (melia azedarach) is a very tough and straight-grained wood. **1865** G.F. ANGAS *Aust.* 122 The white cedar-tree, or Australian lilac, emits from its pendulous clusters of lilac blossoms a delightful fragrance. **1902** *Emu* II. 101 The Bower-Birds appear to be living almost solely on white cedar berries. **1935** F. BIRTLES *Battle Fronts Outback* 93 A big white cedar . . was to be our future craft—a dugout canoe. **1984** E. ROLLS *Celebration of Senses* 39 Old planted White Cedars, one of the few seasonally deciduous trees in Australia, mass themselves in lilac each spring before they break into leaf. **1793** J. HUNTER *Hist. Jrnl. Trans. Port Jackson* 525 The face of the country . . was a poor soil, but finely formed, and covered with the stately **white gum**-tree. **1798** D. COLLINS *Acct. Eng. Colony N.S.W.* I. 550 We passed a tree (of the kind named by us the white gum, the bark of which is soft) that we judged to be about one hundred and thirty feet in height. **1814** *HRA* (1916) 1st. Ser. VIII. 221 The White Gum Bark as near the last as possible in every respect. **1828** *Hobart Town Courier* 5 July 3 The brig Tranmere . . sailed for London on Sunday, with . . considerable shipments of the different sorts of timber indigenous in the island, as .. stringy bark and white gum. **1832** G.F. MOORE *Diary Ten Yrs. W.A.* 14 Sept. (1884) 135 The white or blue gums (there seems to be a confusion about the names), have a bark not unlike that of beach [*sic*], of a light slate-colour, and smooth. **1852** G.C. MUNDY *Our Antipodes* I. 156 There is the White Gum, with its smooth, polished, round and naked boughs, looking so like human limbs as to be almost indecent in their nudity. **1871** *Illustr. Austral. News* (Melbourne) 2 Jan. 22/2 The toorat wood is the most valuable. It is a variety of white gum, close grained, not to be split, very hard, and capable of enduring a great amount of heat without rending. **1890** J.I. WATTS *Family Life S.A.* 97 It is a thousand pities that the really magnificent white gum trees, which flourished on the banks of the Torrens .. were allowed to be cut down. **1922** E. MERYON *At Holland's Tank* 27 The hut was built of white gum slabs. **1941** C. BARRETT *Aust.* 27 At the base of a very old white gum nodding greenhoods abound. **1965** G. MCINNES *Road to Gundagai* 74 A strip of buffalo grass with a single twisted white gum, separates the pavement from the street. **1977** *Ecos* xiv. 21/3 *Eucalyptus alba*, the white gum of northern Australia, Papua New Guinea, and Timor. **1801** *HRA* (1915) 1st Ser. III. 175 The hills are covered with excellent verdure without trees, except in the valleys, and they are chiefly Banksia new, or what is commonly called the **white honeysuckle.** **1904** J.H. MAIDEN *Notes on Commercial Timbers N.S.W.* 26 White honeysuckle (*Banksia integrifolia* ..) is a pinkish timber showing a neat grain. **1938** W.A. GOODACRE *Honey & Pollen Flora N.S.W.* 70 White Honeysuckle (*Banksia integrifolia*) varies in size from a shrub to a medium-sized tree. .. It .. is characterized by having untoothed leaves which are whitish underneath with a close felt of hairs. **1843** *Sydney Morning Herald* 6 May 1/7 Building and sawn timber, cut from **white iron bark.** **1880** *Proc. Linnean Soc. N.S.W.* V. 503 *E[ucalyptus] paniculata*, varies in the colour of the wood from white to red, and, therefore, is sometimes called 'White', and sometimes 'Red Ironbark'. **1909** R. KALESKI *Austral. Settler's Compl. Guide* 32 In the *coastal district* we find .. white and red ironbark. **1857** D. BUNCE *Australasiatic Reminisc.* 91 In the richest soil .. large groups of the *Crinum*, **white lily.** *Ibid.* 95 The white lily grew here in patches, on the red puffy soil, producing a large coated bulb like the onion; its seeds are spongy and resemble the human testes, and from this circumstance the natives call it Byarrong, their name for that part of the body. **1870** E.B. KENNEDY *Four Yrs. in Qld.* 141 Wild jessamine, and large white lilies, with bulbous roots, grow in the lowest parts of the scrubs. **1880** *Proc. Linnean Soc. N.S.W.* V. 455 The **White Mahogany** (*E[ucalyptus] acmenoides*) was regarded by Mr Bentham as a variety of *E. pilularis*, but this cannot be the case. **1904** J.H. MAIDEN *Notes on Commercial Timbers N.S.W.* 12 *White mahogany* .. is a pale-coloured timber, which bears no resemblance either to the mahogany of commerce or to the red or forest mahogany of New South Wales. **1909** R. KALESKI *Austral. Settler's Compl. Guide* 37 There is a whitish timber called white mahogany, but really not a mahogany at all; this is equal to mahogany for all purposes. **1926** *Qld. Agric. Jrnl.* XXV. 433 There is another tree resembling Red Mahogany in bark and habit, which, as a corollary, has been called White Mahogany because the wood is white. **1962** *Daily Mercury Centenary Story Mackay* 43 The best known forest hardwoods are .. red and white mahogany. **1979** J. BIRMINGHAM et al. *Austral. Pioneer Technol.* 182 The sleepers were cut by broadaxe and adze. Eucalypt hardwoods were invariably used, usually from the lower slope forest areas (ironbark .. tallowood, white mahogany). **1888** *Proc. R. Soc. Qld.* (1889) V. 11 *Avicennia officinalis*. .. Many cattle that would, doubtless, have perished during the recent protracted drought from failure of other fodder, were sustained by browsing on the foliage of the **white mangrove.** **1908** E.J. BANFIELD *Confessions of Beachcomber* 252 The broad beans of the white mangrove ('kum-moo-roo') would stand as vegetables. **1936** T.C. ROUGHLEY *Wonders Great Barrier Reef* 175 The timber of the white mangrove is peculiar in the arrangement of the annual rings; the fibres .. forming a sort of plywood which adds greatly to its strength. **1983** *Austral. Fisheries* Aug. 16/1 'Dieback disease' was held responsible for deaths of the grey mangrove, *Avicennia marina* var. *australasica* (also known as the white mangrove). **1835** J. BACKHOUSE *Narr. Visit Austral. Colonies* (1843) 258 Scattered on the grassy hills, is *Hibiscus* or *Lagunea* Patersonii, which forms a spreading tree of forty feet in height; it is called here **White Oak.** **1855** J. BONWICK *Geogr. Aust. & N.Z.* (ed. 3) 203 The Bread-fruit of Norfolk Island runs 20 feet and the White Oak 80 feet. **1898** *Proc. Linnean Soc. N.S.W.* XXIII. 124 *Lagunaria patersoni* .. known as 'Sally' on Lord Howe Island, but 'White Oak' in Norfolk Island. The wood is put to no purpose except to yield grubs for fishing. **1926** *Qld. Agric. Jrnl.* XXV. 436 *Stenocarpus sinuatus* .. White Oak. **1965** *Austral. Encycl.* VI. 350 Today the island [*sc.* Norfolk Island] has a well-wooded appearance. .. White oak (*Lagunaria patersonii*) mingles here and there with the pines. **1896** *Proc. Linnean Soc. N.S.W.* XXI. 464 *C[allitris] columellaris* .. '**White Pine**'. **1901** *Bulletin* (Sydney) 4 May 14/2 The barrackers for new railways always end up by stating that 'the proposed line will tap large forests of white pine'. **1918** C.E. BOSWORTH *Shoe & Leather Trade* 38 A recent development in the domestic supply of tanbarks is the discovery of valuable tannin in the .. 'white pine' (*Callitris glauca*). **1938** C.T. WHITE *Princ. Bot. Qld. Farmers* 66 Plants which are found growing thickly together, forming at times almost pure stands, are said to be gregarious. Examples in Queensland are .. White Cypress (*Callitris glauca*) [etc.]. **1956** T.Y. HARRIS *Naturecraft in Aust.* 120 White Cypress Pine extends over much of inland Australia, sometimes confined to the ridges. **1976** *Ecos* viii. 10/2 A large region of woodland—dominated mainly by bimble box (a eucalypt), mulga, and white pine. **1984** E. ROLLS *Celebration of Senses* 28 A bigger farm on sandy loam scattered with Kurrajongs and White Cypress Pines. **1941** J.H. WILLIS *Victorian Fungi* 62 The name '**White Punk**' has been applied to *Polyporus eucalyptorum*—a large, spongy bracket .. appearing at a considerable height on the boles of eucalypts throughout the State. **1968** V. SERVENTY *Southern Walkabout* 132 One large white bracket in our garden was called by the early settlers, the 'white punk' because it could be used for tinder. **1896** *Proc. Linnean Soc. N.S.W.* X. 599 *Eucalyptus coriacea* .. '**White Sally**' is a name in use at Queanbeyan. **1934** E. COLEMAN *Come back in Wattle Time* 38 White Sally (*A[cacia] floribunda*)—A graceful shrub, with narrow, ribbon-like phyllodes, much thinner than those of the Sallow Acacia. **1942** E. ANDERSON *Squatter's Luck* 21 Tailed orchids, white and blue, Wattle, white-sally. **1963** C. BURGESS *Blue Mountain Gums* 47 '*Snow gum*' or '*white sally*' was named *Eucalyptus pauciflora* by Sieber and the description published in 1827. **1880** *Proc. Linnean Soc. N.S.W.* V. (1881) 491 *E[ucalyptus] piperita* .. is sometimes called, especially to the Southward, '**White Stringy Bark**'. *Ibid.* 492 Mr Bentham considered *E[ucalyptus] eugenioides*, or the White Stringy Bark to be a variety of *E. piperita*. **1904** J.H. MAIDEN *Notes on Commercial Timbers N.S.W.* 10 White Stringybark is usually so called in this State from the circumstance of its colour being paler than that of the other stringybarks. **1932** R.H. ANDERSON *Trees of N.S.W.* 110 *Eucalyptus globoidea*, a species closely related to the white stringybark [*E. eugenioides*] occurs as a small to medium-sized tree. .. The pale, almost white, timber is generally useful. **1981** A.B. & J.W. CRIBB *Useful Wild Plants Aust.* 193 The bark of the white stringybark, *E[ucalyptus] globoidea* .. and of the blue-leaved stringybark .. have been .. found to yield a fibre suitable as a substitute for the imported sisal and coconut fibre. **1903** L. RODWAY *Tasmanian Flora* 307 **Waratah, white:** *Agastachys odorata*. **1933** C.W. PECK *Austral. Legends* (ed. 2) 70 There is really a white waratah. **1983** *Ecos* xxxvii. 6/1 Some shrubs, in particular white waratah (*Agastachys odorata*), can be used to determine a site's fire history.

b. In the names of animals: **white-backed magpie** (formerly **crow-shrike**), a magpie having a white back, as *Gymnorhina tibicen hypoleuca* of Vic., S.A., and Tas., and *G. tibicen dorsalis* of w. Aust.; **-backed swallow,** the black and white bird *Cheramoeca leucosternum* of drier mainland Aust.; *black and white swallow*, see BLACK *a.*[2] 1 b.; **-bearded honeyeater,** *New Holland honeyeater*, see NEW HOLLAND 2; **-bellied** (or **-breasted**) **sea eagle,** the large, grey and white bird of prey *Haliaeetus leucogaster* of Aust. and elsewhere; **-breasted cormorant,** the black and white bird *Leucocarbo fuscescens* of rocky coasts of s. Aust. incl. Tas.; **-breasted robin,** the small, grey bird *Eopsaltria georgiana* of s.w. W.A., having a whitish breast; formerly also **white-bellied robin, white-breasted flycatcher; -breasted wood swallow,** the dark grey and white bird *Artamus leucorhynchus* of Aust. and the s.w. Pacific; also **white-rumped wood swallow; -browed babbler,** the greyish-brown and white bird *Pomatostomus superciliosus* of s. mainland (exc. easternmost) Aust., having a long white eyebrow; see also HAPPY JACK; **-browed scrub wren,** the small bird *Sericornis frontalis* of e. and s. Aust., having brownish upper parts and a white eyebrow; **-browed treecreeper,** the predom. brown bird *Climacteris affinis* of inland s. Aust., having a white streak above the eye; **-browed wood swallow,** the predom. slaty-grey and chestnut bird *Artamus superciliosus*, having a white stripe above the eye; also **white-eyebrowed wood swallow; -capped noddy,** the sooty black bird *Anous minutus* of n.e. Aust. and elsewhere in the tropics, having a white crown and forehead; **-cheeked honeyeater,** the bird *Phylidonyris nigra* of e. and s.w. Aust.; **cockatoo, (a)** the cockatoo *Cacatua galerita* of n., e., and s.e. Aust. incl. Tas., New Guinea, and New Britain, a predom. white bird with a curving yellow crest and raucous call, popular as a pet; *lemon-crested cockatoo*, see LEMON 1; SULPHUR-CRESTED COCKATOO; *yellow-crested cockatoo*, see YELLOW 1; **(b)** any of several other, predom. white, cockatoos, esp. the *long-billed corella* (see LONG 2); **crane** (or **egret**), the white, long-necked wading bird *Egretta alba*, widespread in Aust. and elsewhere; **cray** *W.A.*, the crustacean *Panulirus cygnus* (see *rock lobster* ROCK *n.* 2), having a pale colour after ecdysis; WHITE *n.*[2] 2; also **white crayfish; death,** *white pointer*; **eagle** *obs.*, *white goshawk*; **-eared honeyeater,** the predom. olive-grey honeyeater *Lichenostomus leucotis* of s. and e. mainland Aust., having a black face and white ear-patch; **-eye,** *silver-eye*, see SILVER 1; **-eyebrowed wood swallow,** see *white-browed wood swallow*; **-eyed crow,** either of two large black birds of the genus *Corvus*, *C. coronoides* (see RAVEN) and *C. orru* of Aust. and New Guinea; **-eyed duck,** the duck *Aythya australis* of all States, the mature male having predom. brown plumage and a white eye; PUNKARI; **-faced** (or **-fronted**) **heron,** the predom. grey, white-faced wading bird *Ardea novaehollandiae*, widespread and common in Aust. and occurring elsewhere; *blue crane*, see BLUE *a.*; **-faced storm-petrel,** the migratory *Pelagodroma marina*, a greyish and white sea-bird, breeding on islands of s. Aust. and elsewhere; **-faced xerophila** *obs.*, WHITEFACE; **-fronted chat,** the white, black, and grey bird *Epthianura albifrons* of s. Aust. incl. Tas.; NUN; also **white-fronted bush chat; -fronted falcon** *obs.*, *little falcon*, see LITTLE 2; **-fronted honeyeater,** the honeyeater *Phylidonyris albifrons* of drier mainland Aust.; **-gaped honeyeater,** the greyish honeyeater *Lichenostomus unicolor* of n. Aust.; **goshawk** (or **hawk**), the bird of prey *Accipiter novaehollandiae*, of n. and e. Aust. incl. Tas. and elsewhere, in its white-plumed phase; *white eagle*; **-headed fishing-** (or **fish-**) **eagle,** either of two white-headed birds of prey, the *white-bellied sea eagle* and the *red-backed sea eagle* (see RED-BACKED); **-headed pigeon,** the pigeon *Columba leucomela* of e. Qld. and e. N.S.W., the mature male having a dark body and white head; **-headed sea eagle,** *red-backed sea eagle*, see RED-BACKED; **-headed stilt,** the long-legged, black and white wading bird *Himantopus leucocephalus* of Aust. and elsewhere; **ibis,** the black and white wading bird *Threskiornis molucca* of Aust. and elsewhere; **kangaroo,** an albino kangaroo; **-naped honeyeater,** the olive and white honeyeater *Melithreptus lunatus* of forests in e., s.e., and s.w. mainland Aust., having a black head with a white nape; see also *black cap* BLACK *a.*[2] 1 b.; **-necked (Pacific) heron,** *Pacific heron*, see PACIFIC; **-plumed honeyeater,** the honeyeater *Lichenostomus penicillatus* of mainland Aust. exc. the n., n.e., and s.w., a predom. olive, yellow, and grey-brown bird with a white tuft behind the ear; **pointer** (or **shark**), the large shark *Carcharodon carcharias* of s. Aust. incl. Tas., and worldwide in temperate and tropical seas; *white death*; **-quilled pygmy goose,** the waterbird *Nettapus coromandelianus* (see *pygmy goose* PYGMY); also **white-quilled goose; -quilled rock pigeon,** the predom. brown pigeon *Petrophassa albipennis* of N.T. and n. W.A.; see also *rock pigeon* ROCK *n.* 2; **-rumped wood swallow,** see *white-breasted wood swallow*; **-shafted fantail,** CRANKY FAN; **-shouldered caterpillar-eater,** *white-winged triller*; **-tailed black cockatoo,** either of two black cockatoos of s.w. W.A. having a broad white band on the tail, *Calyptorhynchus latirostris* and the long-billed black cockatoo, *C. baudinii*; also **white-tailed cockatoo; -tailed kingfisher,** the migratory kingfisher *Tanysiptera sylvia* of rainforest in n. Qld., and New Guinea; **-throated grass-wren,** the bird *Amytornis woodwardi* of Arnhem Land, N.T., having black, brown, and white plumage with a white throat and breast; **-throated honeyeater,** either of two white-throated honeyeaters of n. Aust. and elsewhere, *Conopophila albogularis* and (more often) the black, olive-yellow, and white *Melithreptus albogularis*; **-throated nightjar,** the nocturnal bird *Caprimulgus mystacalis*, having mottled black, grey, and brown plumage with white throat markings, and occurring in e. mainland Aust. and nearer Melanesia; **-throated thickhead,** *golden whistler*, see GOLDEN 3; **-throated treecreeper,** the bird *Cormobates leucophaea* of e. Aust., having dark olive-brown upper parts and a white throat; (occas.) a similar treecreeper; **-throated warbler** (or **flyeater**), the woodland bird *Gerygone olivacea* of n. and e. Aust., having a grey back, white throat, and yellow breast; *bush canary*, see BUSH C. 3; see also *native canary* NATIVE *a.* 6 b.; **-winged chough,** see CHOUGH; **-winged triller,** the migratory bird *Lalage tricolor*, widespread in mainland Aust., the breeding male having a loud chattering song; *white-shouldered caterpillar-eater*; **-winged wren,** the small bird *Malurus leucopterus* of drier mainland Aust., the breeding male having bright blue plumage with white wings.

1844 [**white-backed magpie**] J. GOULD *Birds of Aust.* (1848) II. Pl. 47, *Gymnorhina leuconata* . . White-backed Crow-Shrike. **1849** C. STURT *Narr. Exped. Central Aust.* II. 21 App. *The White-backed Crow Shrike* . . is somewhat larger than, and very much resembles a magpie, but the proportion of white is greater and there is no metallic or varied tint on the black feathers as on the European bird. **1896** B. SPENCER *Rep. Horn Sci. Exped. Central Aust.* II. 70 It is possible that these specimens are hybrids between the White-backed and the Black-backed Crow-Shrike. **1911** A. MACK *Bush Days* 36 The white-backed magpies of the south. **1933** H.J. CARTER *Gulliver in Bush* 168 The white-backed magpie was . . as musical as his cousins in New South Wales. **1945** C. BARRETT *Austral. Bird Life* 219 The term 'piping crow-shrike' rarely is used now. There are only three species; the white-backed magpie (*Gymnorhina hypoleuca*) [etc.]. **1986** *Canberra Times* 19 Feb. 21/6 In the wake of last week's column about white-backed and black-backed magpies two people have reported sightings of grey magpies. **1945** C. BARRETT *Austral. Bird Life* 167 Ranging widely over the continent, the **white-backed** or white-breasted **swallow** (*Cheramoeca leucosterna*) is an inland species in the eastern states, but in South and Western Australia also frequents coastal districts. **1953** A. RUSSELL *Murray Walkabout* 115 At Cooltong Reach . . I saw the most striking picture of the social habits of the white-backed swallows that has come my way. . . I struck the face of the cliff. . . Forty-three 'white-backs' issued from that tunnel-mouth. **1984** M. BLAKERS et al. *Atlas Austral. Birds* 344 The White-backed Swallow nests either singly or colonially in sandy banks and was found in the early days of European settlement in the South-West in burrows of bandicoots and rat-kangaroos. **1902** *Emu* II. 24 Late in January last a nest of the **White-bearded Honey-eater** (*Meliornis novaehollandiae*) was taken in a briar bush close to a public road, a few miles from Hobart. **1918** *Bulletin* (Sydney) 14 Feb. (Red Page), *Honey-Birds* generally, specially the . . *White-bearded Honey-eater* (yellow-wings). **1945** C. BARRETT *Austral. Bird Life* 159 Banksia groves and coastal heathlands best suit the handsome, noisy New Holland or white-bearded honeyeater. **1841** J. GOULD *Birds of Aust.* (1848) I. Pl. 3, *Ichthyiaëtus leucogaster*. **White-bellied Sea-eagle.** *Ibid.* Pl. 4, The White-breasted Sea Eagle is very common on the northern and eastern portions of Australia. **1855** J. BONWICK *Geogr. Aust. & N.Z.* (ed. 3) 197 There are large Wedge-tailed and white-bellied Sea Eagles. **1903** *Emu* II. 140 *Haliaëtus leucogaster* (White-bellied Sea-Eagle). . . The stick nest of this bird was found. **1926** K. DAHL *In Savage Aust.* 165 We saw the large white-bellied sea-eagle. **1945** C. BARRETT *Austral. Bird Life* 32 All around Australia's coastline of 12,000 miles the white-breasted sea-eagle occurs at intervals. **1968** R. HILL *Bush Quest* 19 In one ancient towering eucalypt I found the nest of a white-breasted sea eagle. **1986** *Canberra Times* 2 Apr. 23/1 An ornithologist tells me that formal studies of hit-miss ratios have shown that even the white-bellied sea eagle, which looks like a splendidly efficient machine, often has to try lots of times before it gets a fistful of something. **1843** J. GOULD *Birds of Aust.* (1848) VII. Pl. 69, *Phalacrocorax leucogaster* . . **White-breasted Cormorant.** **1903** *Emu* II. 167 White-breasted Cormorant (*Phalacrocorax gouldi*) . . on the plains . . also in Corio Bay. **1974** C. THIELE *Albatross Two* 110 'Look at that white-breasted cormorant.' . . 'That's a shag.' **1846** [**white-breasted robin**] J. GOULD *Birds of Aust.* (1848) III. Pl. 13, The White-bellied Robin is a native of Western Australia, but only to be met with in the hilly portions of the country. **1880** 'OLD HAND' *Experiences of Colonist* (ed. 2) ii. 50 The white-breasted flycatcher would hover around, warbling lowly its sweet liquid notes. **1945** C. BARRETT *Austral. Bird Life* 176 The white-breasted robin (*Quoyornis georgianus*) occurs only in South-western Australia. **1966** SLATER & LINDGREN *Wildlife W.A.* 21 The White-breasted Robin is confiding by nature and can be called up to within three feet of the diligent observer. **1984** M. BLAKERS et al. *Atlas Austral. Birds* 372 The White-breasted Robin feeds on insects collected in sallies from a bare twig or other vantage point. **1842** [**white-breasted wood swallow**] J. GOULD *Birds of Aust.* (1848) II. Pl. 33, *Artamus leucopygialis* . . White-rumped Wood Swallow. **1903** *Emu* II. 148 *Artamus leucogaster* (White-rumped Wood-Swallow). . . Only one nest of this bird was found. **1934** *Bulletin* (Sydney) 16 May 34/4 The white-rumped wood-swallow . . is found through eastern and northern Australia and in Malaysia. [**1945** C. BARRETT *Austral. Bird Life* 201 All but three of the seventeen members of the wood-swallow family are confined to the Australian region. . . The white-breasted species (*Artamus leucorhynchus*) is distributed over Australia generally.] **1964** M. SHARLAND *Territory of Birds* 92 After I arrived at the Darwin cottage in March, the White-breasted Wood-swallow population on the wires reached seventy-eight. **1982** *Reader's Digest Compl. Bk. Austral. Birds* (rev. ed.) 570 The white-breasted wood swallow is seldom found far from fresh or brackish water and is mainly a bird of the tropics. **1898** E.E. MORRIS *Austral Eng.* 13 **White-browed B[abbler]**—*P[omatostomus] superciliosus*. **1900** A.J. CAMPBELL *Nests & Eggs Austral. Birds* 272 *White-browed babbler* . . Mr James G. McDougall informs me he has taken the eggs of this species in South Australia . . early in July. **1931** M. TERRY *Hidden Wealth* 326 Birds observed included . . white-browed babblers. **1962** B.W. LEAKE *Eastern Wheatbelt Wildlife* 87 White-browed babblers or apostle birds travel around in groups from seven to twelve. They are noisy birds, and often sound as if they are scolding one another. **1984** M. BLAKERS et al. *Atlas Austral. Birds* 424 Groups of 3–15 White-browed Babblers live together and breed communally. **1898** E.E. MORRIS *Austral Eng.* 408 **White-browed S[crub]-W[ren].**—*S[ericornis] frontalis*. **1903** *Emu* II. 163 White-browed Scrub-Wren . . very abundant in the salt-bush scrub. **1929** A.H. CHISHOLM *Birds & Green Places* 136 Mockery is authenticated in the cases of . . the white-browed scrub-wren, one or two thornbills. **1945** C. BARRETT *Austral. Bird Life* 185 The white-browed scrub-wren . . is at home among coastal tea-tree. **1977** *Ecos* xi. 21/2 One particular white-browed scrub wren was first banded on a forestry access road 14 years ago. In the intervening years it has been caught in a mist net no less than 18 times. **1984** *A.N.U. Reporter* (Canberra) 26 Oct. 5/2 Near Forestry, a pair of White-browed Scrubwrens were carrying food to nestlings housed in a well-camouflaged nest, close to the ground and amongst thick bushy growth. **1913** *Emu* XII. Suppl. 84 *Climacteris superciliosa* . . **White-browed Tree-creeper**. . . Range: S. Queensland, New South Wales, Victoria, S., Central, and W. Australia. **1945** C. BARRETT *Austral. Bird Life* 170 The white-browed tree-creeper (*C[limacteris] affinis*) enjoys a wide range. **1976** *Reader's Digest Compl. Bk. Austral. Birds* 454 The unobtrusive, little-known white-browed treecreeper is the member of its family best adapted to life in the desert. **1983** *Age* (Melbourne) 31 Aug. 12 Is the rare white-browed tree-creeper of no concern to the Fund for Animals? **1842** [**white-browed wood swallow**] J. GOULD *Birds of Aust.* (1848) II. Pl. 32, *Artamus superciliosus* . . White Eye-browed Wood Swallow. **1849** C. STURT *Narr. Exped. Central Aust.* II. 20 App. *Artamus Superciliosus* . . White eye-browed wood Swallow. A white line over the eye is the distinguishing mark of this bird. **1898** E.E. MORRIS *Austral Eng.* 449 White-browed Wood S[wallow]—*A[rtamus] superciliosus*. **1902** *Emu* II. 59 White-browed Wood-Swallow. *Artamus superciliosus*. . . They are now feeding upon the honey-laden flowers, and this perhaps accounts for their brush tongues. **1919** *Bulletin* (Sydney) 9 Jan. 24/4 The white-eyebrowed wood-swallow has just arrived in this (the Bega, N.S.W.) district. **1934** *Ibid.* 16 May 34/4 The white-browed wood-swallow . . often called the summer martin—the most handsome member of the family, slaty-grey above, chestnut below, with a white patch above the eye. **1945** C. BARRETT *Austral. Bird Life* 201 Some of our species are migratory, notably the handsome white-browed wood-swallow . . and the masked wood-swallow. **1984** M. BLAKERS et al. *Atlas Austral. Birds* 632 The White-browed Woodswallow inhabits woodlands. It is usually in large flocks, often in company with the Masked Woodswallow. **1898** E.E. MORRIS *Austral Eng.* 322 **White-capped N[oddy]**—*A[nous] leucocapillus*. **1928** S.E. NAPIER *On Barrier Reef* 51 Lady Musgrave Island and N.W. Islet are the special reserves of . . the white-capped noddies. **1955** V. SERVENTY *Aust.'s Great Barrier Reef* 51 The White-capped Noddy is a more ambitious nest builder. **1982** *Reader's Digest Compl. Bk. Austral. Birds* (rev. ed.) 223 The food of the white-capped noddy is mainly fish. **1843** J. GOULD *Birds of Aust.* (1848) IV. Pl. 25, The **White-cheeked Honey-eater** is an inhabitant of New South Wales, and certainly proceeds as far to the eastward as Moreton Bay. **1898** E.E. MORRIS *Austral Eng.* 199 White-cheeked H[oneyeater]—*Meliornis sericea*. **1945** C. BARRETT *Austral. Bird Life* 159 The white-cheeked honeyeater . . inhabits heath country and open timbered areas. **1965** *Austral. Encycl.* IV. 528 The genus *Meliornis* contains two species . . marked with black and white on the head and breast, and with a good deal of yellow in the wings. The most plentiful is the New Holland . . honeyeater; the white-cheeked honeyeater is very similar, but has more white on the head and is not so common. **1984** M. BLAKERS et al. *Atlas Austral. Birds* 553 The White-cheeked Honeyeater nests colonially. Many gather on flowering shrubs such as banksias and dryandras. [**1770** **white cockatoo:** J. COOK *Jrnls.* 4 Aug. (1955) I. 367 The Land fowls we met with here . . were . . Cockadores of two sorts the one white and the other brown.] **1788** J. WHITE *Jrnl. Voyage N.S.W.* 22 Apr. (1790) 148 We made a kettle of excellent soup out of a white cockatoo and two crows. **1834** G. BENNETT *Wanderings N.S.W.* I. 243 The field of wheat at this station being just ripe, a man was obliged to be almost constantly on the watch, to prevent the 'white cockatoos' from attacking and destroying it. **1848** H.W. HAYGARTH *Recoll. Bush Life* 138 A large white cockatoo . . is perhaps the best talking bird yet discovered. **1852** G.C. MUNDY *Our Antipodes* I. 286 The fields were covered, as by a snow-drift with flights of the large white cockatoo. **1872** MRS E. MILLETT *Austral. Parsonage* 221 The white cockatoo lives chiefly upon roots, which Nature has enabled the bird to dig for in the driest weather, by furnishing him with a large bill shaped exactly like a pick-axe. **1893** F.W.L. ADAMS *Australs.* 95 Flights of white cockatoos stream out, shrieking like evil souls. **1911** O. LEWIS *Collection of Verses* 29 Come wagtail and plover, bell bird and curlew, 'Australia for ever' screech white cockatoo. **1934** W.A. OSBORNE *Visitor to Aust.* 79 White cockatoos go in flocks like European rooks, and have a call not dissimilar. **1963** X. HERBERT *Disturbing Element* 40 White cockatoos having a last row in some distant tree over who was going to sleep with whom. **1970** P. SLATER *Eagle for Pidgin* 45 A flock of white cockatoos—corellas I thought . . their pale wings flushed pink as the sun lit them. **1980** M. GRANT *Barrier Reef* 59 The common old white cockatoo sells for $1000 in America and is a prestige pet on the West Coast. **1814** M. FLINDERS *Voyage Terra Australis* II. 226 The aquatic birds were blue and **white cranes,** sea-pies, and sand-larks. **1836** *Sydney Herald* 21 Mar. 2/4 Among the aquatic birds we recognised the . . white crane, and Ibis. **1846** J. GOULD *Birds of Aust.* (1848) VI. Pl. 58, *Herodias imaculata* . . White Crane of the Colonists. **1904** *Emu* III. 235 A White Crane's or Egret's nest (*Mesophoyx plumifera*) with two large young ones was seen. **1932** H. PRIEST *Call of Bush* 125, I saw the rare White Ibis . . and the rarer still White Egret (*Herodias timoriensis*). **1935** DAVISON & NICHOLLS *Blue Coast Caravan* 16 White cranes roosting on snags in a marsh at the back of the mill. **1945** C. BARRETT *Austral. Bird Life* 54 Of egrets we have three species: the white egret (*Egretta alba*), the plumed egret . . and the little egret. **1977** *Ecos* xi. 21/2 Bird experts were surprised to find that the white ibis, little egret, and white egret all move between southern Australia and New Guinea. **1958** [**white cray**] *Austral. Jrnl. Marine & Freshwater Research* 538 Towards the end of the period in which whites are caught the colour of the white crayfish tends to deepen and these crayfish are often referred to as 'pinks'. **1985** *West Austral.* (Perth) 21 Nov. 41/1 The 1985 season opened slowly on Friday with the start of the white cray run. White crays are young adults four or five years old. **1948** R.S. CLOSE *Morn of Youth* 62 Our twenty-foot shark . . was still far short of the record **White Death** (. . *Carchardon Albimors*), caught . . off Port Fairy, Victoria. **1951** T.C. ROUGHLEY *Fish & Fisheries Aust.* 246 The largest dangerous shark is the white shark (*Carcharodon carcharias*) or 'great white death', as Zane Grey called it, which is common round the Australian coast but has not been recorded from Tasmania. **1980** H. LUNN *Behind Banana Curtin* 32 In Queensland these sharks are also called the 'White Death' because they are proven man-eaters. **1840** T.J. BUCKTON *W.A.* 77 The most singular among the rapacious birds is a **White Eagle.** **1863** F. ALGAR *Handbk. to Colony S.A.* 6 The birds are equally singular with the beasts, there being white eagles and black swans. **1822** J. LATHAM *Gen. Hist. Birds* IV. 186 **White-eared Honey-eater** .. common about Port Jackson, Sydney, and Parametta [*sic*], in thick woods, at all seasons. **1846** J. GOULD *Birds of Aust.* (1848) IV. Pl. 36, The White-eared Honey-eater enjoys a very wide range of habitat. **1903** *Emu* II. 164 White-eared Honey-eater (*Ptilotis leucotis*).—Not uncommon in the forest. **1952** B. BEATTY *Unique to Aust.* 52 The white-eared Honey-eaters .. are called Hairdressers by bushmen. These odd birds generally use animal hair for lining their nests but much prefer human hair if available. **1978** B.P. MOORE *Life on Forty Acres* 96 This spring (1975) I detected a pair of handsome green and yellow White-eared Honeyeater (*Meliphage leucotis*) visiting my grevilleas. **1986** *Your Garden* Jan. 35 (*caption*) A White-eared Honeyeater makes use of this handy perch over the water surface. **1843** J. GOULD *Birds of Aust.* (1848) IV. Pl. 81, *Zosterops dorsalis* .. **White-eye,** Colonists of New South Wales. **1906** *Emu* VI. 53 *Zosterops caerulescens* .. 'White-eye', the appellation usually in vogue .. arisen from the fact that a ring of very short white feathers surrounds each orb. **1933** D. MACDONALD *Brooks of Morning* 24 The White-eye, and it may be other birds as well, like their apples neither too acid nor too sappy. **1984** SIMPSON & DAY *Birds of Aust.* 333 White-eyes. Family Zosteropidae. These .. olive-green and yellow birds, usually with white eye-rings, are found in the Old World and in Australia. **1845** J. GOULD *Birds of Aust.* (1848) IV. Pl. 18, *Corvus coronoïdes* .. **White-eyed Crow.** **1849** C. STURT *Narr. Exped. Central Aust.* II. 32 App. *White-eyed Crow.* This bird approaches somewhat to the raven. **1931** *Bulletin* (Sydney) 1 Apr. 21/4 A sagacious scamp is the Australian raven, known in the bush as the white-eyed crow. **1847** J. GOULD *Birds of Aust.* (1848) VII. Pl. 16 *Nyroca australis* .. **White-eyed Duck.** **1896** B. SPENCER *Rep. Horn Sci. Exped. Central Aust.* II. 110 White-eyed Duck .. were shot at Owen Springs. **1945** C. BARRETT *Austral. Bird Life* 50 The white-eyed duck .. commonly known as 'hardhead' and 'bar-wing', actually has white eyes. **1976** *Reader's Digest Compl. Bk. Austral. Birds* 108 Only the male white-eyed duck has a white-eye; the female is brown-eyed. **1789** [**white-faced heron**] A. PHILLIP *Voyage to Botany Bay* 163 White-Fronted Heron... This bird was sent from Port Jackson in New Holland, and as it has not been noticed by any author, we consider it as a new species. **1801** J. LATHAM *Gen Synopsis Birds* Suppl. II. 304 White-fronted H[eron] .. twenty-eight inches in length... Inhabits New Holland. **1847** J. GOULD *Birds of Aust.* (1848) VI. Pl. 53, *Ardea novae-hollandiae* .. White-fronted Heron. **1896** B. SPENCER *Rep. Horn Sci. Exped. Central Aust.* II. 105 White-fronted Heron .. proved to be rather wary. **1916** S.A. WHITE *In Far Northwest* 189 A white-fronted heron, commonly called the blue crane, sat upon an old tree stump. **1926** A.S. LE SOUEF et al. *Wild Animals Australasia* 322 A tiger-cat carefully stalking a white-fronted heron which was feeding on a mud-flat. **1944** J. DEVANNY *By Tropic Sea & Jungle* 74 The blue crane, now—some people call it the white-faced heron—he roars if you like. **1965** *Austral. Encycl.* III. 362 The commonest member of the group [of egrets and herons] as a whole throughout Australia and Tasmania is the white-fronted heron. **1968** R. HILL *Bush Quest* 21 The brolga or native companion is one of Australia's largest birds and our only crane—despite the popular use of the name 'blue crane' for the white-faced heron. **1984** *A.N.U. Reporter* (Canberra) 26 Oct. 5 (*caption*) A White-faced Heron skims over the placid waters of Sullivans Creek. **1845** J. GOULD *Birds of Aust.* (1848) VII. Pl. 61, *Thalassidroma marina* .. **White-faced Storm-Petrel.** **1913** *Emu* XII. Suppl. 28 *Pelagadroma marina* .. White-faced Storm-Petrel... Range: Seas of S. Queensland, New South Wales, Victoria, S. and W. Australia, Tasmania. [**1945** C. BARRETT *Austral. Bird Life* 89 Only one of the five storm-petrels .. on the Australian list has become well-known to our bird-lovers: the dainty white-faced species.] **1977** *Ecos* xi. 19/1 In Australia, bands were first used in 1912, when members of the Melbourne Bird Observers' Club .. placed them on Tasmanian mutton-birds .. and on white-faced storm petrels. **1985** *Age* (Melbourne) 19 Mar. 12/1 South Channel Island supports one of only three Victorian breeding colonies of an attractive seabird, the white-faced storm petrel. **1844** J. GOULD *Birds of Aust.* (1848) III. Pl. 67 *Xerophila leucopsis* .. **White-faced Xerophila.** **1896** B. SPENCER *Rep. Horn Sci. Exped. Central Aust.* II. 82 White-faced Xerophila .. were met with in nearly every place where mulga scrub exists. [**1842 white-fronted chat:** J. GOULD *Birds of Aust.* (1848) III. Pl. 64, *Epthianura albifrons.* White-fronted Epthianura.] **1903** *Emu* II. 163 White-fronted Chat... Plentiful all over the plains. **1918** *Bulletin* (Sydney) 14 Feb. (Red Page), *White-fronted Bush-Chat* (Tang, Nun, Tintac) and other members of the genus *Epthianura.* **1962** B.W. LEAKE *Eastern Wheatbelt Wildlife* 88 Groundlarks as their name implies are ground birds, and like the banded plover, and white-fronted chat are very useful insectivorous birds. **1984** M. BLAKERS et al. *Atlas Austral. Birds* 572 The White-fronted Chat feeds mainly on ground-dwelling insects. **1841** J. GOULD *Birds of Aust.* (1848) I. Pl. 10, *Falco frontatus* .. **White-fronted Falcon** .. Little Falcon, Colonists of Western Australia. **1849** C. STURT *Narr. Exped. Central Aust.* II. 14 App. *The White-fronted Falcon* .. was generally hid in the trees, and would descend like an arrow .. frequently carrying off two of the little *Amadina castanotis.* **1896** B. SPENCER *Rep. Horn Sci. Exped. Central Aust.* II. 55 White-fronted Falcon .. is generally found near the rocky ranges. **1822** J. LATHAM *Gen. Hist. Birds* IV. 173 **White-fronted Honey-eater** .. inhabits New South Wales; said to be fond of honey, but will also feed on flies. **1843** J. GOULD *Birds of Aust.* (1848) IV. Pl. 29, *Glyciphila albifrons* .. White-fronted Honey-eater. **1896** B. SPENCER *Rep. Horn Sci. Exped. Central Aust.* II. 92 White-fronted Honey-eater .. was shot as it was feeding on a cluster of Loranthus. **1916** S.A. WHITE *In Far Northwest* 50 Among the blossoms .. was a small party of white-fronted honey-eaters. **1945** C. BARRETT *Austral. Bird Life* 155 The white-fronted honeyeater .. frequents dry scrubs and its range includes Central Australia. **1976** *Reader's Digest Compl. Bk. Austral. Birds* 499 The white-fronted honeyeater is a cautious bird, in appearance slender and sinuous, with a conspicuous white forehead and face. **1898** E.E. MORRIS *Austral Eng.* 199 **White-gaped H[oney-eater]**—*Stomiopora unicolor.* **1901** *Emu* I. 100 White-gaped Honey-eater .. is very quiet, so much so that I have never heard its note. **1964** M. SHARLAND *Territory of Birds* 70 The rollicking calls of White-gaped Honeyeaters are particularly musical. **1976** *Reader's Digest Compl. Bk. Austral. Birds* 481 (*caption*) The white-gaped honeyeater is a noisy bird which can easily be recognised as it has no adornment except its white gape. **1790** [**white goshawk**] J. WHITE *Jrnl. Voyage N.S.W.* 250 The White Hawk. *Falco albus...* With black beak, cere and legs yellow. **1831** *Hobart-Town Almanack* 260 White hawk. Astur Novae Hollandiae. **1843** J. GOULD *Birds of Aust.* (1848) I. Pl. 14, *Astur novae-hollandiae* .. Albino. White Goshawk... White Hawk, of the Colonists. **1857** *Illustr. Jrnl. Australasia* III. 168, I brought a splendid pair of white hawks, taken near Hobart Town. **1861** 'OLD BUSHMAN' *Bush Wanderings* 122 The *White Goshawk* is by far the chastest in appearance of all the Australian hawks. **1903** *Emu* II. 161 White Goshawk .. fairly common in the forest. **1931** J. DEVANEY *Earth Kindred* 16 The white hawk hovered harpy-like. **1981** M. SHARLAND *Tracks of Morning* 78 The white goshawk is a beautiful forest-loving species. **1856** H.B. STONEY *Vic.* 212 The large **white-headed fishing-eagle** of Australia may daily be seen about the harbour. **1926** K. DAHL *In Savage Aust.* 301 Small white-headed fish-eagle (*Haliastur girrenera*). **1928** C.G. LANE *Adventures in Big Bush* 207 He was a magnificent specimen of the eagle family; a full-grown, white-headed Fishing-eagle, of powerful build, majestic mien, and dauntless courage. **1898** E.E. MORRIS *Austral Eng.* 156 **White-headed** F[ruit]-**P[igeon]**—*Columba leucomela.* **1916** *Bulletin* (Sydney) 23 Nov. 24/2 The 'Big Scrub', towards the Tweed (N.S.W.) and the jungles further north, once teemed with pigeons, among them the .. 'white-headed' and 'topknot'. **1945** C. BARRETT *Austral. Bird Life* 62 'Baldy' is the white-headed pigeon's nickname. **1984** M. BLAKERS et al. *Atlas Austral. Birds* 220 Last century the White-headed Pigeon was commonly seen by settlers clearing the rainforest. It became rare but has recently begun to increase again. **1852** J. MACGILLIVRAY *Narr. Voyage H.M.S. Rattlesnake* I. 105 A pair of **white-headed sea-eagles** had established their aërie in a tree. **1903** *Emu* II. 140 *Haliastur indus*, sub-species *Girrenera* (white-headed Sea-Eagle)... Eight nests with fresh eggs in were found. **1841** J. GOULD *Birds of Aust.* (1848) VI. Pl. 24, *Himantopus leucancephalus* .. **White-headed Stilt.** **1855** *Illustr. Sydney News* 24 Feb. 82/1 The White Headed Stilt .. is a native of Australia known to the colonists as the Stilt Bird... Its easy and graceful bearing render it an ornament to the secluded spots it inhabits. **1912** *Emu* XII. 119 White-headed Stilt... Their cry resembles a puppy's bark. **1945** C. BARRETT *Austral. Bird Life* 104 We have three long-legged members of the great Plover family: the white-headed stilt [etc.]. **1965** *Austral. Encycl.* VIII. 295 The white-headed stilt .. is largely white with darker plumage on the hind-neck, back and wings. **1973** V. SERVENTY *Desert Walkabout* 61 Hundreds of pelicans .. white-headed stilts and various species of ducks were feeding in the shallows. **1842** J. GOULD *Birds of Aust.* (1848) VI. Pl. 49, Straw-necked and **White Ibises** (*Ibis spinicollis* and *Ibis strictipennis*). **1847** G.F. ANGAS *Savage Life & Scenes* I. 57 A few scattered gum-trees grow along the water's edge; and these are the resort of multitudes of black shags, or the less numerous white ibis, which roost on their decayed branches. **1901** *Emu* I. 138 White Ibis (*Ibis molucca*).—The only bird of this species was seen near Kalamurina. **1932** H. PRIEST *Call of Bush* 125, I saw the rare White Ibis .. and the rarer still White Egret. **1968** R. HILL *Bush Quest* 16 Straw-necked and white ibis fed in scattered flocks through the reeds and on the banks. **1974** *Ecos* ii. 26/3 We do know that the white ibis, straw-necked ibis, and the Murray cod—a native fish— .. breed only after flooding. **1878** R.B. SMYTH *Aborigines of Vic.* I. 250 The **white** and red **kangaroo**, sleeping very fast, have their own way to guard themselves against being surprised. **1902** *Sporting News* (Launceston) 22 Nov. 3/5 An experienced bushman, who can prove that white kangaroos are by no means rare in this State. **1919** C.A. BERNAYS *Qld. Politics during Sixty Yrs.* 72 Passed in 1901 the Act which gave significance to the white kangaroo which subsequently appeared upon our postage stamps. **1822** J. LATHAM *Gen. Hist. Birds* IV. 168 **White-naped Honey-eater...** One, supposed to differ in sex, had the band across the nape pale blue, instead of white. **1903** *Emu* II. 165 White-naped Honey-eater (*Melithreptus lunulatus*).—Have not seen this bird on the plain. **1945** C. BARRETT *Austral. Bird Life* 153 'Black-cap', the white-naped honey-eater .. is a very common bird of the mainland, being found in all the states, though absent from Northern Australia. **1984** *A.N.U. Reporter* (Canberra) 26 Oct. 5/2 The honeyeaters were feeding in a variety of ways. The White-naped hung from the very ends of twigs, gleaning insects from the leaves. **1847** J. GOULD *Birds of Aust.* (1848) VI. Pl. 52 *Ardea pacifica* .. Pacific Heron .. **White-necked Heron** of the Colonists. **1901** *Emu* I. 138 White-necked Heron (*Notophoyx pacifica*)... One or two others were noted. **1945** C. BARRETT *Austral. Bird Life* 55 The white-necked Pacific heron (*N[otophoyx] pacifica*) is a larger bird than the 'blue crane', and comparatively rare. **1984** B.A. LANE et al. *Birds Port Phillip Bay* 28 The White-necked Heron is present in smaller numbers with up to 10 being seen on each of the Bay's major wetlands. **1845** J. GOULD *Birds of Aust.* (1848) IV. Pl. 43, *Ptilotis penicillatus* .. **White-plumed Honey-eater.** **1902** *Emu* II. 14 The White-plumed Honeyeater .. is not seen at all here. **1948** R. RAVEN-HART *Canoe in Aust.* 86 Mildura has good streets .. noisy with 'linnets' (White-plumed Honey-eaters). **1984** *A.N.U. Reporter* (Canberra) 26 Oct. 15/2 White-plumed Honeyeaters were feeding their fledglings, lumbering inexpertly about the branches and squawking with characteristic calls of young birds. **1881** *Proc. Linnean Soc. N.S.W.* VI. 358 *Carcharodon rondeletii* .. 'The **White Pointer**' of Sydney Fishermen. **1898** E.E. MORRIS *Austral Eng.* 412 White S[hark]—*Carcharodon rondeletii* .. called also the White-Pointer. **1937** G.H. SUNTER *Adventures Trepang Fisher* 30 Sharks are very numerous... The 'white pointer' .. grows up to forty feet. **1956** S. HOPE *Diggers' Paradise* 183 A white pointer looks an ugly monster slung by the tail at a weighing station ashore. **1965** *Austral. Encycl.* IX. 297 White shark (*Carcharodon albimors*), one of the most ferocious of marine animals .. being provided with many rows of large triangular teeth, well adapted for tearing flesh. **1974** J.M. THOMSON *Fish Ocean & Shore* 112 Of all sharks, perhaps, the name white death, otherwise the white pointer (*Carcharodon carcharias*), strikes the greatest terror in human hearts... Despite its name only the belly of this shark is white; the general coloration is a dark grey or black. [**1898 white-quilled pygmy goose:** E.E. MORRIS *Austral Eng.* 165 Goose-teal... The English name for a very small goose of the genus *Nettapus.* The Australian species are—Green, *Nettapus pulchellus* .. White-quilled, *N. albipennis.*] **1913** *Emu* XII. Suppl. 41 *Nettapus albipennis* .. White-quilled Pigmy-Goose... *Range*: Queensland, New South Wales. **1945** C. BARRETT *Austral. Bird Life* 47 The green species (*Nettapus pulchellus*) perhaps is more attractive than its ally, the white-quilled pygmy goose (*N. coromandelianus*). **1964** M. SHARLAND *Territory of Birds* 105 There is a second species of *Nettapus*, the White-quilled Pigmy Goose. **1980** C. ALLISON *Hunter's Man. Aust. & N.Z.* 122 The White pygmy or White-quilled goose and the Cape Barren goose. **1913** *Emu* XII. Suppl. 25 *Petrophassa albipennis* .. **White-quilled Rock-Pigeon...** *Range*: N.W. Australia. **1943** C. BAR-

RETT *Austral. Animal Bk.* 160 The white-quilled rock pigeon (*Petrophassa albipennis*) . . is nowhere plentiful. **1964** M. SHARLAND *Territory of Birds* 172 There is only one other kind [of Rock Pigeon], also restricted in its range, which is the White-quilled Rock Pigeon. **1984** M. BLAKERS et al. *Atlas Austral. Birds* 235 The White-quilled Rock-Pigeon . . is confined to sandstone gorges with permanent water. **1840** J. GOULD *Birds of Aust.* (1848) II. Pl. 83, *Rhidipura albiscarpa* . . **White-shafted Fantail.** **1902** *Emu* II. 12 The White-shafted Fantail . . are, as usual, among the commoner birds. **1918** *Bulletin* (Sydney) 31 Jan. 24/3 A pair of white-shafted fantails ('cranky fan') plastered their ethereal wineglass-shaped nest this season on the low twig of a laurel bush. **1942** C. BARRETT *From Bush Hut* 78, I found nests of the white-shafted fantail. . . 'Cranky Fan'—a nickname for this little grey bird with white-striped tail feathers—builds a dainty nest. **1981** M. SHARLAND *Tracks of Morning* 80 For producing the prettiest nest of any bird, I give full honours to the white-shafted fantail—the 'cranky fan', as it's commonly known. **1901** *Emu* I. 127 The following day, nests of the **White-shouldered Caterpillar-eater** (*Lalage tricolor*), with young. **1916** S.A. WHITE *In Far Northwest* 123 The white-shouldered caterpillar-eater . . were met with. **1945** C. BARRETT *Austral. Bird Life* 198 The white-shouldered caterpillar-eater or white-winged triller . . ranks high as a songster, with its trilling canary-like strain. Both sexes sing, though the female triller is less gifted than her mate. **1846** J. GOULD *Birds of Aust.* (1848) V. Pl. 13, *Calyptorhynchus baudinii* . . **White-tailed Black Cockatoo** of the Colonists. **1903** *Emu* III. 12 We also secured the eggs of the White-tailed Cockatoo. **1945** C. BARRETT *Austral. Bird Life* 72 The white-tailed black cockatoo (*C[alyptorhyncus] baudini*) . . differs from all the other species of its genus in having brownish-black and white plumage. **1985** *West Austral.* (Perth) 3 July 60/2 Swarms of feral bees are known to drive white-tailed black cockatoos out of their nesting holes in the South-West. **1896** F.G. AFLALO *Sketch Nat. Hist. Aust.* 117 The **White-tailed Kingfisher** (*Tanysiptera sylvia*) is found only in the Cape York Peninsula. **1923** *Bulletin* (Sydney) 11 Oct. 24/2 The rare white-tailed kingfisher of the Far North and the beautiful parrakeet of coastal Bananaland break into the ground mounds of white-ants. **1945** C. BARRETT *Austral. Bird Life* 139 The white-tailed kingfisher . . is a strikingly handsome bird. **1965** *N. Austral. Monthly* Dec. 17 The White-tailed Kingfisher, a migrant from New Guinea . . frequents the rain forests of the coastal districts of North Queensland, thus differing in habitat from the other kingfishers. Deep blue above, chestnut below with scarlet bill and feet, it has very long white tail plumes—a truly handsome bird. **1982** *Reader's Digest Compl. Bk. Austral. Birds* (rev. ed.) 326 White-tailed kingfishers eat insects, frogs and lizards. **1926** *Official Checklist Birds Aust.* (R. Australasian Ornith. Union) p. v, A few long names such as **White-throated Grass-Wren** . . have so far defied efforts for improvement. **1964** M. SHARLAND *Territory of Birds* 180 It was elusive, as was the uncommon White-throated Grass-wren. **1984** M. BLAKERS et al. *Atlas Austral. Birds* 446 The endemic White-throated Grasswren is confined to the sandstone country of the Arnhem Land escarpment. **1843** J. GOULD *Birds of Aust.* (1848) IV. Pl. 51, *Entomophila albogularis* . . **White-throated Honey-eater.** **1848** *Ibid.* Pl. 74, *Melithreptus albogularis* . . White-throated Honey-eater. **1913** *Emu* XII. Suppl. 86 White-throated Honey-eater. . . Range: N.W. Australia, Northern Territory, Queensland, New South Wales (New Guinea). [**1945** C. BARRETT *Austral. Bird Life* 154 The golden-backed honeyeater . . is found in . . mid-western . . Australia . . while the white-throated species . . ranges from New Guinea to Northern Australia.] **1968** R. HILL *Bush Quest* 51 A single white-throated honey-eater followed me for a while, scolding from the cover of the dusty gum leaves. **1976** *Reader's Digest Compl. Bk. Austral. Birds* 491 White-throated honeyeaters keep mostly to the upper foliage of trees, where their white throats, black heads and extensive white crescents on the back of their heads contrast conspicuously with the green leaves. **1865** J. GOULD *Handbk. Birds Aust.* I. 96 *Eurostopodus albogularis.* **White-throated nightjar.** . . In the daytime it sleeps on the ground on some dry knoll or open part of the forest, and as twilight approaches sallies forth . . in search of insects. **1900** A.J. CAMPBELL *Nests & Eggs Austral. Birds* 536 The first egg of the White-throated Nightjar that came into my possession was a fine specimen taken in the scrubby country adjacent to Lake King, Victoria. **1929** A.H. CHISHOLM *Birds & Green Places* 157 A 'laughing owl', the white-throated nightjar of ornithology. **1968** D. FLEAY *Nightwatchmen* 153 The White-throated Nightjar and its allies represent the ultimate in clever camouflage or 'invisibility'. **1984** M. BLAKERS et al. *Atlas Austral. Birds* 317 The White-throated Nightjar takes many large nocturnal insects, disturbing them from the treetops. **1902** *Emu* II. 14 Just in this country, too, the **White-throated Thick-head** (*Pachycephala gutturalis*) is found. **1917** *Bulletin* (Sydney) 16 Aug. 22/3 Golden-breasted whistler (also called white-throated thick-head). **1841** J. GOULD *Birds of Aust.* (1848) IV. Pl. 95, From the manner of its [*sc.* the Red-eyebrowed Tree-Creeper's] ascending the trees and keeping almost entirely to the small upright stems of the *Casuarina*, I believed it to be the **White-throated Tree-Creeper** (*Climacteris picumnus*). **1903** *Emu* II. 165 White-throated Tree-Creeper (*Climacteris leucophaea*). . . Plentiful in the Otways. **1945** C. BARRETT *Austral. Bird Life* 170 The white-throated tree-creeper . . ranges from southern Queensland to Victoria, and South Australia. **1965** *Austral. Encycl.* IX. 21 Nine species occur in Australia, perhaps the best-known ones being the brown, white-throated and red-browed treecreepers. **1984** SIMPSON & DAY *Birds of Aust.* 327 (*caption*) The pale wing bars of the White-throated Treecreeper are exposed in flight. [**1847 white-throated warbler:** J. GOULD *Birds of Aust.* (1848) II. Pl. 97, *Gerygone albogularis* . . White-throated Gerygone.] **1900** A.J. CAMPBELL *Nests & Eggs Austral. Birds* 155 *Gerygone albigularis* . . white-throated fly eater. . . From its song . . and partly on account of its yellow breast, it has gained the local name of 'Native Canary'. **1929** A.H. CHISHOLM *Birds & Green Places* 109 It may be that the white-throated warbler will tell you a story. **1948** J. FAIRFAX *Run o' Waters* 112 The swift rising scale of that lovely little flautist, the white-throated fly eater. **1956** A.C.C. LOCK *Tropical Tapestry* 245 The air was again sweet with the perfume of frangipane, among which the yellow wee-bill and white-throated warbler searched for insects and nectar. **1976** *Reader's Digest Compl. Bk. Austral. Birds* 448 Each spring the familiar liquid song of the white-throated warbler heralds the bird's arrival in the southern parts of its range. **1926** *Official Checklist Birds* (R. Australasian Ornith. Union) p. v, Some long formal names such as . . White-shouldered Caterpillar-eater, and Rose-breasted Cockatoo, have been replaced by . . **White-winged Triller,** and Galah respectively. **1948** J. FAIRFAX *Run o' Waters* 110 We camped that night on a tiny island . . the home of the white-winged trillers, which gladdened us with their song. **1984** E. ROLLS *Celebration of Senses* 77 The White-winged Triller makes long rolls of two notes. **1841** J. GOULD *Birds of Aust.* (1848) III. Pl. 25, *Malurus leucopterus* . . **White-winged wren.** **1903** *Emu* III. 36 *Malurus leucopterus* (White-winged Wren) . . was nowhere abundant except after the hurricane of 1898. **1964** M. SHARLAND *Territory of Birds* 139 The White-winged Wren . . prefers the cover of low bushes and grass around lagoons and on treeless flats. **1976** *Reader's Digest Compl. Bk. Austral. Birds* 415 There is a black-and-white form of the white-winged wren.

2. In special collocations: **white choker** [used elsewhere but recorded earliest in Aust.], a clergyman; also *attrib.*; so **white chokerism** *n.*; **house,** aperient salts; **lady,** a drink, one ingredient of which is methylated spirits; also *attrib.*; **leghorn,** a female player of lawn bowls; also *attrib.*; **money** *Austral. pidgin, obs.*, a silver coin; **wing(er),** one who refuses to join a trade union (see also quot. 1982, 1); also **white wings** and *attrib.*

1851 *Bell's Life in Sydney* 19 Apr. 1/4 Despite the croaking anathemas of pseudo-saints and whinings of **white-chokers.** **1867** *Sydney Punch* 29 June 45/2 The utter extermination of chicanery, charlatanism, white-chokerism, and cant. **1894** A.B. BELL *Oscar* 64 When she told me as how it wouldn't be proper for our parson to marry hisself, I took care to bring another white choker along. ***c* 1907** W.C. CHANDLER *Darkest Adelaide* 58 'But surely', I said . . 'a child like you should be home instead of accosting men old enough to be your father in the streets.' 'Garn', she said, 'I suppose you are one of those white-choker blokes who mother told me to dodge.' **1943** S.W. KEOUGH *Around Army* 25 There is still something that the M.O. can try on him—**white-house;** the only reason he hasn't ordered it so far is that it doesn't go with Number Nines and oil. **1947** M. MACLEAN *Drummond of Far West* 96 One medicine he sometimes ordered for them was the kind of salts known as 'whitehouse'. **1935** K. TENNANT *Tiburon* 24 The exceptions were two old men in the corner lying stupified over a mixture of **'white lady'**—boiled methylated spirit with a dash of boot-polish and iodine, which they had spent the afternoon concocting. **1940** *Sentry Go* (Keswick) Aug. 29 A White Lady case. Methylated spirit drinker. **1960** *N.T. News* (Darwin) 26 Jan. 5/3 He had been drinking 'white lady'—a potent mixture of methylated spirits and powdered milk. **1969** P. ADAM SMITH *Folklore Austral. Railwaymen* 13 At the construction works at Kyogle [N.S.W.] the navvies drank 'Lantana Rum'—a mixture of methylated spirits ('White Lady'), flyspray and Kiwi boot polish. One man went mad on it, many more were silly for weeks at a time. **1972** L.A. MURRAY *Poems against Economics* 16 But see You can't trust even half a whitefeller. You died of White Lady through me. **1978** K. GILBERT *People are Legends* 22 Gimme the price of some plonk Brother 'White Lady' white metho despair. **1983** *Overlander* Jan. 70 A White Lady is equal parts of meths and ammonia. **1975** L. RYAN *Shearers* 155 **White leghorn:** Breed of fowl. Colloquial term for a woman bowler. **1982** N. KEESING *Lily on Dustbin* 59 Since bowling clubs, and some golf clubs, segregate the sexes, Ladies' Day at the bowling club is 'White Leghorn Day'. **1983** HIBBERD & HUTCHINSON *Barracker's Bible* 230 *White leghorn day*, . . ladies' Lawn Bowls afternoon. **1984** *Bulletin* (Sydney) 3 Apr. 50/3, I wrote recently about lawn bowlers, known affectionately as the 'White Leghorns'. Gwen Dunn, of Blakehurst, N.S.W., writes to tell me they are now wearing 'mini-beige' instead of white. **1839** W. MANN *Six Yrs.' Residence* 153 After receiving a few shillings, which they call **white money,** they retired. **1845** *Melbourne Standard* 1 Mar. 2/6, I think he can be made to understand the difference between right and wrong, as he knows the difference between black and white money, and also the comparative value of a bob and a tanner. **1848** *Adelaide Miscellany* 16 Sept. 106/2, I had been importuned by almost every man, woman, and child for black money, white money, and 'baccar'. **1853** E. SAUNDERS *Our Austral. Colonies* 4 As many as 50 natives . . display considerable ingenuity and importunity in getting 'white money' (as they call silver) from visitors. **1864** *Illustr. Sydney News* 15 Oct. 13/3 The aborigines . . persistently dogged . . one of them for 'white money, massa'. **1896** M. HORNSBY *Old Time Echoes Tas.* 24 Sidling up to 'The Vet.' they began to clamour for 'bacca, white money, and so on. **1898** *Worker* (Sydney) 30 July 3/3 Men are still scarce in these parts, but those who are here are of a superior class to what we have had during the few seasons since '94, the **'White Wings'** gentry must have received their just deserts—the dirty kick-out. **1911** *Huon Times* (Franklin) 30 Sept. 6/2 He was followed by an assistant from No. 1 establishement, who explained that he was 'a white wing'. **1982** LOWENSTEIN & HILLS *Under Hook* 63 There was some Union members took out a licence before the Union said, 'Okay, we'll go back as a body and take out licences'. These fellers, even though they're not scabs, they're classed as 'white wingers'. Not really accepted. **1982** P. ADAM SMITH *Shearers* 127 Whitely King, secretary of the Pastoralists' Union, unwittingly lent his name to a whole army of men when the 'free' labourers became known as 'White Wings'.

B. *n.*

1. *Australian National Football.* In the phr. **the man in white,** a referee or umpire.

1968 EAGLESON & MCKIE *Terminol. Austral. Nat. Football* ii. 22 *Man in white* . . (a) field umpire . . (b) referee, (c) umpire. **1971** A. BUZO *Roy Murphy Show* (1973) 107 It's all very well to knock the men in white, Mike, but you must bear in mind that referees have many difficulties confronting them and they do have a most insidious task to perform. **1973** *Sun-Herald* (Sydney) 16 Sept. 63/6 Refereeing continued to be a pain in the neck, with the public asking only one thing from the men in white—consistency. **1982** *N.T. News* (Darwin) 31 Dec. 13/4, 12 women umpires have been sharing the solitary shower at Gardens Oval, with the men in white (not all at the same time) while waiting for extra showers to be installed. **1984** *Sun* (Melbourne) 16 July 68/5 An earlier incident involving Footscray skipper Jim Edmond and Swans defender David Ackerley went unseen by the men in white.

2. *W.A. White cray*, see WHITE *a.*^{2} 1 b. Also *attrib.*

1958 *Austral. Jrnl. Marine & Freshwater Research* 542 It . . seems . . that whites are not a species distinct from the reds, but are, in fact, animals in one of the many moult phases in the life history of the crayfish *Panulirus longipes*. . . Some crayfish marked in the white phase have been recaptured as reds, while penned whites have deepened in colour to red after 2 months. **1973** *W. Coast Fisherman* Sept. 3 It is during November and December—the 'white' season—that most fishermen expect to earn enough to tide them over the less productive summer months. They could not survive without the 'whites'. **1982** *West Austral.* (Perth) 16 Dec.

7/1 'The whites are on the run.' This is when the young crayfish—usually about four years old—begin to move from shallow coastal waters into the deep. They are called whites because of their new pale-coloured shells. **1983** *Ibid.* 28 Dec. 57/2 The crayfish season began on November 15. . . 'The whites have not started to really run yet.'

white, *v.* In the phr. **to white it out,** to serve a gaol sentence.

1885 *Australasian Printers' Keepsake* 25 He caught a month, and had to 'white it out' At diamond-cracking in Castieau's Hotel. **1955** N. PULLIAM *I traveled Lonely Land* 393 *White it out,* serve a jail sentence.

white ant, *n.* [Fig. use of *white ant* termite.]

1. Used of a person's failing sanity or intelligence, as if white ants were the agents of its attrition. Esp. in the phr. **to have white ants,** to be eccentric or 'dotty'.

1908 *Austral. Mag.* (Sydney) Nov. 1250/1 If you show signs of mental weakness you are either balmy, dotty, ratty, or cracked, or you may even have white ants in your attic. **1926** L.C.E. GEE *Bush Tracks & Gold Fields* 65 In the unsteady glance of his honest, old eyes and his disconnected speech, I read the mark of the Australian solitudes—'white ants' they call it up north. **1937** I.L. IDRIESS *Forty Fathoms Deep* 87 A hardened old nor'-wester can develop a few 'white ants', as well as the veriest new-chum. **1948** V. PALMER *Golconda* 49 They had a definite respect for Christy. He might have a few kinks . . but there was something dinkum about him, and if there were white ants behind his forehead they had a lot of work ahead of them. **1983** *Weekend Austral. Mag.* (Sydney) 27 Aug. 20/8 Australian slanguage is well stocked with words and phrases to describe those who are a bit slow off the mental mark. . . Suffering from white ants upstairs, to put it succinctly.

2. A saboteur; one who undermines (a political party, policy, etc.).

1969 J. O'GRADY *O'Grady Sez* 54 'Wine . . is the oldest drink known to man.' A white ant from the temperance society said, 'What about water?' **1972** A. CHIPPER *Aussie Swearers Guide* 70 *White ant,* someone who betrays his fellow workers.

white-ant, *v.* [Used elsewhere but recorded earliest in Aust.: see OEDS *v.*] *trans.* **a.** To destroy (a wooden structure) in the manner of white ants. **b.** *fig.* To undermine or sabotage (an enterprise, organization, etc.).

1922 *Daily Mail* (Sydney) 9 Jan. 4/3 Any man who attempts by insidious means to white-ant our White Australian policy should be firmly handled. **1923** J.A. PHILP *Songs Austral. Fascisti* 10 The Caucus platform's rotting . . White-anted by the Bolshies. **1944** *Action Front: Jrnl. 2/2 Field Regiment* May 4 Let us build our house upon a rock for it will not then be white-anted. **1948** V. PALMER *Golconda* 251 'Have to hunt jobs like most other poor coots in this country, so got to be at home wherever we dump our swags.' 'Or wherever you see a chance of white-anting the union, eh?' **1965** R. STOW *Merry-Go-Round* 172 '*Maplestead & Mackay*—hairy socks for phoney Englishmen.' 'He's off again', Rick said, 'white-anting the Empire.' **1978** SAW & MILBANK *Back to Back Tango* 75 She refused to discuss anything at all with me. She white-anted all the orders I gave to the Staff. **1982** *Bulletin* (Sydney) 16 Mar. 17/3 The Australian Federal Police were created in 1979. They have attempted to become a real police force by 'white-anting' State and Territory police forces, duplicating their investigations and on occasions obstructing them.

Hence **white-anted** *ppl. a.*, **white-anter** *n.*, **white-anting** *vbl. n.* and *attrib.*

1936 F. CLUNE *Roaming round Darling* 205 The piece of the boat is five feet long and is made of soft wood, badly **white-anted. 1940** E. HILL *Great Austral. Loneliness* (ed. 2) 332 Murramurie will cheerfully rig herself out in a white-anted flour-bag if necessary. **1951** —— *Territory* 238 He was out with a gang of black wharfies to the white-anted landing in the mud. **1955** N. PULLIAM *I traveled Lonely Land* 393 *White-ant,* to sabotage a labor movement. **White-anter,** one who does so. **1980** H. LUNN *Behind Banana Curtain* 155 Anyone who has been seeing your girlfriend or wife on the side in Queensland is condemned not as a cad or a bounder, but as a 'whiteanter'. **1930** H. REDCLIFFE *Yellow Cygnet* 46 He was in no error in regard to the upright character of the young man, and that it would require much '**white-anting**' and the use of insidious and convincing argument to undermine his integrity. **1936** E. SCOTT *Aust. during War* in *Official Hist. Aust. 1914–18* XI. 695 The leaders of unionism were under no delusions . . as to the destruction of unionism itself by the process which, a little later, came to be known as 'white-anting'. **1968** G. SINGER et al. *On how to keep your Gown Clean* 22 This account of the dangers inherent in a naïve approach to the student problem by the unwary academic would not be complete without mentioning the white-anting, or fifth column, tactics adopted by the graduate student. **1976** K. AMOS *New Guard Movt.* 38 Signs of dissension . . Campbell put down to 'white-anting' tactics on the part of the Old Guard and the 'Establishment'. **1985** *Bulletin* (Sydney) 11 June 34/3 Hawke and his staff, on an overseas trip . . formed the suspicion that Hayden was doing a white-anting job back in Australia.

white Australia.

1. a. Used *attrib.* and *absol.* to designate a *white Australia policy* (see sense 2).

1898 *Tocsin* (Melbourne) 3 Feb. 7/1 'A white Australia is the most sacred article in the creed of every Australian.'—Premier Reid. **1904** *Shearer* (Sydney) 10 Sept. 3/3 The Federal Labour Party secured the passage into law of a measure restricting alien races coming into the Commonwealth. Indeed a 'White Australia' has been and still is one of the chief planks of the party. **1911** R.G.S. WILLIAMS *Austral. White Slaves* 131 The future leaders while shrieking 'White Australia' are doing their best to ensure that the country must eventually come under the rule of foreigners. **1929** P.R. STEPHENSEN *Bushwhackers* 43 White Australia began in a drinking-song bellowed in pubs on the gold-fields and in townships: Rule Britannia, Britannia rule the Waves! No more Chinamen allowed In New South Wales. **1946** R.D. RIVETT *Behind Bamboo* 117 This last serves to stir up great controversy over such questions as immigration, abolition of State Parliaments, continuance of White Australia. **1955** G. HEALEY *A.L.P.* 31 There is, of course, no reference to the term 'White Australia' anywhere in our legislation; but the exclusion of any person thought undesirable for any reason is effected by an education test. **1963** *Bulletin* (Sydney) 6 July 35/1 It is surely a trifle premature to brand White Australia as a lost cause. **1977** R. MACKLIN *Paper Castle* 182 We've got enough on our hands without White Australia rearing its ugly head again, especially now.

b. Australia as a society into which immigration of non-whites is restricted.

1901 PARSONS & HOLTZE *N.T. of S.A.* 8 This is not high class humanitarianism, but it is probably necessary for race preservation, and it will maintain a 'White Australia' in the only sense compatible with the development of its agricultural resources. **1903** *Truth* (Sydney) 4 Jan. 7/3 Station managers give the preference of work to the heathen Chinee at the lucrative consideration of 25s. per week, while some of the station (general) hands—white men—only receive £1 per week. How is this for a white Australia, eh? . . The lynx-eyed 'Johns' are engaged . . while 'yours truly' and his fellows are 'padding the hoof'. **1905** *Ibid.* 5 Mar. 1/7 It is bad enough that White Australia should be over-run with dirty pagan Hindoos . . but when some horrible Hindoo scoundrel gets hold of one of our young girls and handles her in a revolting manner it is enough to make a white man's blood boil. **1909** H.I. JENSEN *Rising Tide* 120 We must maintain a White Australia, and we may have to fight for it. **1910** *Huon Times* (Franklin) 12 Nov. 6/6 But if our girls do not marry, what of a White Australia? **1916** *Truth* (Sydney) 22 Oct. 7/8 We want a white Australia, No other shall she be.

c. A white person, considered as representing white Australia (see sense 1 b.).

1913 *Bulletin* (Sydney) 10 Apr. 14/3 White Australia and Black Australia were engaged taking out the bottom wire of the station boundary fence.

2. Special Comb. **white Australia policy,** a policy of restricting immigration into Australia to white people.

1901 *Truth* (Sydney) 10 Mar. 1/4 Barton's white Australia policy will yet secure for him Reid's soubriquet of Yes-No. **1905** *National Rev.* (London) 544 There is consequently no party, and no leader in the Commonwealth, in 1905, not pledged to the 'White Australia' policy. **1918** N.P.H. NEAL *Back to Bush* 15 First debate held on fore deck. Subject: 'That in the opinion of this House the White Australia Policy is fully justifiable.' **1934** *Red Star* (Perth) 23 Mar. 4/2 Comrade Mountjoy said that the Party would concentrate on the exposure of the White Australia policy which intensified racial hatred. **1952** J.R. TYRRELL *Old Bks.* 4 He was on the Lambing Flat diggings . . notorious for the fierce rioting of the diggers, resenting an Asiatic invasion of swarms of Chinese. This was one of the incidents building towards the later political catch-cry and eventual national article of faith, the White Australia Policy. **1963** D. ROBERT *Look at me Now* 113 In no other country in the world do white men cut cane. In Queensland they have done so since the 'White Australia policy' took away the coloured labour imported for the purpose. **1973** *Bulletin* (Sydney) 17 Feb. 52 *(caption)* Bloody nerve! Copying our White Australia policy and then using it to keep out white Aussies! **1982** *Ibid.* 6 Apr. 29/2 Just as many Asians suspect, the Department of Immigration and Ethnic Affairs does operate a White Australia policy of a sort.

white Australian.

1. AUSTRALIAN *n.* 2. Also as *adj.*

1847 A. HARRIS *Settlers & Convicts* (1953) 205, I should suppose there are few races, if indeed there is any race of men, in the habitual enjoyment of such sound health as the white Australians. Most of the young men are of very good stature; a great number extraordinarily so. The most obvious characteristic of the Australian white women is peculiar and striking womanliness; a strongly feminine aspect and a tone of voice; and I think I may add that the same quality runs no less distinctly into their style of thought and general mental character. **1910** *Bulletin* (Sydney) 29 Jan. 15/1, I was witness to a brawl in a pub yard . . between five inked-up Hindus and two half-inked white Australians. **1937** *Publicist* (Sydney) xvii. 5/2 Fair treatment of Aborigines puts White Australian decency to the test! **1942** T. KELAHER *Digger Hat* 55 We go to spoil another Axis feast—To guard our own good white Australian land. **1944** E.M. ANDERSON *Typist Tales* 115 Real good blokes those Czechos. . . Charge 'em same ruddy price as anybody else—same as white Australians. **1967** D. HORNE *Educ. Young Donald* 12 The mahogany stain that marked the true White Australian. **1986** *Canberra Times* 15 Feb. B4/1 White Australians, it would seem, have lived for the past 100 years on this continent in a virtual state of paranoia.

2. A supporter of a *white Australia policy* (see WHITE AUSTRALIA 2).

1901 *Truth* (Sydney) 1 Sept. 5/7 Being . . a white Australian 'to the backbone and spinal marrow'. **1906** *Bulletin* (Sydney) 26 July 16/1 The sturdy 'White Australians' are disloyalists and cranks. **1924** H.E. RIEMANN *Nor'-West o' West* 103 'Welly fine day, Mister Hullicane Joe,' he said in feeble tones. Joe was a keen White Australian. 'That's all right,' he said stiffly.

whitebait. [Transf. use of *whitebait* a small fish used as food.] Any of several fish caught small and eaten whole, as *Lovettia sealii* and the young of the JOLLYTAIL.

1861 E.P. RAMSAY-LAYE *Social Life & Manners* 99 We had caught a famous basketful of a little fish called *whitebait*, from its resemblance to the old country fish of that name. **1873** F. DE CASTELNAU *Edible Fishes Vic.* 16 *Engraulis Antarcticus*, or the *whitebait*, is very common in the fish market. **1882** *T.H.A.J.* no. 92 p. lv, The Jollytails, Sand-smelts, and Smelts are frequently termed 'Whitebait', and are esteemed a great delicacy for the table. **1951** T.C. ROUGHLEY *Fish & Fisheries Aust.* 157 The Tasmanian whitebait consists of adult fish that are making their way into the rivers to spawn. **1974** *Ecos* i. 6/3 At the University of Tasmania Mr M. Cassidy . . has shown that a local fish, *Galaxias* (often known as whitebait or native trout), cannot detect low concentrations of cadmium in streams.

White Elephant. [Spec. use of *white elephant* a burdensome possession.] A name applied metaphorically to the Northern Territory. Also **White Elephant of South Australia.**

1887 MRS D.D. DALY *Digging, Squatting, & Pioneering Life* 209 The Northern Territory . . the 'White Elephant of South Australia'—to use a term very freely used for the Territory in the colonies. **1891** *Quiz* (Adelaide) 9 Jan. 15/3 If a man were to sit down to write a sober history of the Northern Territory in its social aspect he would probably run the risk of having his name bracketed with that of Ananias. . . The following little story . . will illustrate the peculiar condition of things in the land of the White Elephant. **1936** C.T. MADIGAN *Central Aust.* 10 The Northern Territory . . has often been called Australia's 'White Elephant'.

whiteface. Any of the three species of the genus *Aphelocephala* of s. and central mainland Aust., small brownish birds, the most common and widespread being *A. leucopsis*; (formerly) *white-faced xerophila*, see WHITE *a.*[2] 1 b. See also SQUEAKER 1.

1903 *Emu* III. 72 Near Jan Juc, close to the edge of the coastal ranges, the Whiteface (*Xerophila leucopsis*), an inland species, was seen breeding. **1945** C. BARRETT *Austral. Bird Life* 189 Those quaint little birds, the white-faces (*Aphelocephala*) . . frequent open forest country and open scrublands. **1981** M. SHARLAND *Tracks of Morning* 110 Tapping a post may bring from an old knot hole a small, modest looking bird called the whiteface.

white fellow, *n.* and *a. Austral. pidgin.* Also **white fella, white feller.**

A. *n.* A non-Aboriginal person.

1826 R. DAWSON *Private & Confidential* 5 This was not the first time they had seen White 'Fellows' as they call us. **1836** J.F. O'CONNELL *Residence Eleven Yrs. New Holland* 87 They appear to have recognised their title 'black fellows', and in return dub the English 'white fellows', seemingly perfectly content with the distinction, and considering white the worse hue, decidedly. **1847** *Atlas* (Sydney) III. 8/2 It was the first white-fellow's [*sc.* a woman] blood he had ever shed. **1859** W. BURROWS *Adventures Mounted Trooper* 100 White fellow big fellow fool work like it bullock, what for not make it's lubra work, like it black fellow? **1871** *Austral. Town & Country Jrnl.* (Sydney) 17 June 748/1 They are generous to the very last morsel, and are otherwise willing to assist, as they say, 'white fellow'. **1898** D.W. CARNEGIE *Spinifex & Sand* 284 He knew the words 'white-fella' and 'womany', and had certainly heard of a rifle. **1911** A.L. HAYDON *Trooper Police Aust.* 268 As a precaution against any meddling on the part of the natives the telegraph men gave many of them electric shocks from the wires. . . The 'white fellow's devil' was held in such awe far and wide that no-one dared touch the wires. **1936** *Publicist* (Sydney) ii. 3/1 His song was unheeded by a crowd of whitefellows, who were congregated at that place for the purpose of engaging in S.P. illicit betting, and not for the purpose of hearing Jacky sing. **1967** M. BARRETT *Gold of Lubra Rock* 26 The white-fellers wanted it. **1980** ANSELL & PERCY *To fight Wild* 119 And there was this bloke, riding a mule. A whitefellow, dressed in black.

B. *adj.* Non-Aboriginal; alien (to the Aborigines).

1834 G. BENNETT *Wanderings N.S.W.* I. 210, I was accosted by a native black, who asked, whether 'I white feller parson, for me want shilling'; but not being of the clerical profession, I did not consider myself liable to be placed under contribution. **1861** *Burke & Wills Exploring Exped.* 12 The flour, 50 lb. of which I gave them, they at once called 'white-fellow nardoo'. **1951** E. HILL *Territory* 20 No need to promise 'white-fella tucker' when lily-time is here. **1962** V.C. HALL *Dreamtime Justice* 32 Commonwealth Police Tracker Jarat, whose white-fellow name was Big Pat, looked at his subordinates on the opposite side of the camp-fire. **1962** D. LOCKWOOD *I, Aboriginal* 206, I had put all my tribal ways behind me and attempted to live and behave in the whitefeller way. **1967** M. SELLARS *Carramar* 44 Their staple diet, bully beef, damper, and tea ('white-feller tucker'). **1977** X. HERBERT *Dream Road* 16 Anybody talk white-feller way here get sick. **1980** ANSELL & PERCY *To fight Wild* 133 The ranges on the boundary they called High Lonesome. These are all whitefellow names, but they have blackfellow or old-time names for the same places.

whiteheads, *pl.* [See quot. 1956.] Of wheat: diseased or dead plants, affected by root rot such as TAKE-ALL 1.

1833 *Sydney Monitor* 20 Apr. 3/3 The machine will . . clean 100 bushels of wheat a day, dividing the white-heads and chaff, and leaving the grain free from dirt. **1885** N. ROBINSON *Stagg of Tarcowie* 27 Jan. (1977) 19 Cleaning the screenings and white heads. From the white we got 3 bags clean wheat, out of the screenings 9 bags fit for crushing for the horses. **1905** *Shearer* (Sydney) 7 Jan. 4/1 Whiteheads and smut are plentiful and will reduce the yields. **1924** *Jrnl. Dept. Agric. Vic.* XXII. 605 Takeall and Whiteheads are two phases of the one disease. With Takeall the whole plant dies and fails to produce an ear. Whiteheads, however, occur when the fungus has not been able to progress sufficiently to completely destroy the plant. **1956** CALLAGHAN & MILLINGTON *Wheat Industry Aust.* 296 The plants may be killed [by root rot] at a comparatively early stage of growth or they may be killed after heading but before the formation of grain in the ear. These are termed, from their bleached appearance, 'whiteheads' and they constitute a major loss of yield in affected crops.

Whiteley King. [f. the name of John *Whitely King* (1857–1905), president of the Pastoralists' Union of N.S.W., 1890–1902: see quots.] Used *attrib.* and *absol.* to designate an improvised billy-can.

1902 *Bulletin* (Sydney) 1 Feb. 16/2 A billy fashioned from a fruit tin is universally known as a 'Whiteley King', from the secretary of the Pastoralists' Union, who, during the shearing troubles, sent out bands of non-unionists furnished with these impromptu utensils. **1904** *Shearer* (Sydney) 24 Dec. 3/3 The number of hopeless, penniless, and soapless boys of tender years carrying old coal sacks, hessian or 'shook' shop-window-blinds for swags, and burnt-out lead tins, syrup tins, or half kerosene tins for billies—real Whiteley King outfits! **1911** *Bulletin* (Sydney) 24 Aug. 14/2 'Ah' . . asks why any old tin used instead of the orthodox billy is called a 'Whiteley King'? During the shearers' strike the 'free' laborers, sent by Whitely and Co., to take the place of the shearers on strike, almost invariably sported an old treacle pot, or some similar makeshift thing, presumably from motives of economy. **1919** *Port Hacking Cough* (Sydney) 11 Jan. 65 Three small puppies played around a time-worn 'Whiteley King' billy-can.

white man. [Spec. use of *white man* a man belonging to a race having naturally light-coloured skin or complexion.]

1. A non-Aboriginal inhabitant of Australia, usu. of British or European descent. Also as adj. (in *Austral. pidgin.*).

1833 *Perth Gaz.* 7 Sept. 143 A wish, that 'white man' would go into the bush with them, and 'boo' (shoot) black man. **1838** *Southern Austral.* (Adelaide) 22 Dec. 4/3 On the part of the blacks the foundation of their wrongs has been simply yet strikingly expressed by their proverb of 'whiteman come, kangaroo go'. **1848** T.L. MITCHELL *Jrnl. Exped. Tropical Aust.* 12 Under this unfavourable aspect the white man first comes before the aboriginal native; were the intruders accompanied by women and children, they could not be half so unwelcome. One of the most striking differences between squatting and settling in Australia consists of this. **1859** J.D. MEREWEATHER *Diary Working Clergyman* 180 These stupid blacks mistook this poor American black for one of themselves. . . A black expressed to me to-day great indignation at their stupidity, saying, that they ought to have known the difference between 'black fellow' and 'white man's black fellow'. **1872** 'CAPRICORNUS' *Bush Essays* 42 Many of the Bush population, the naturalised immigrants . . would scorn, in their dirty pride as 'white men', to learn a lesson in industry and respectability from the Asiatics. **1897** J.J. MURIF *From Ocean to Ocean* 118, I had been three days and two nights without eating 'white man's tucker'. **1918** G. WHITE *Thirty Yrs. Tropical Aust.* 63 Many politicians of to-day advocate a white-worked shelling industry, and a few declare it should be made white man's industry solely. Shellers contend this cannot be done. **1954** T. RONAN *Vision Splendid* 120 The north, in the wet season, was certainly not a white man's country. **1977** X. HERBERT *Dream Road* 78 First the whiteman's greeting, the handshake. **1981** NGABIDJ & SHAW *My Country of Pelican Dreaming* 9, I had to distinguish between the 'white man way' whereby relationships are described in terms of actual 'blood' ties, and 'blackfeller Law' by which persons become classificatory kin (sometimes referred to as the 'skinning Law').

2. [U.S.: see Mathews 2.] A person of impeccable character. See also WHITE *a.*[1] 2.

[N.Z. **1888** P.W. BARLOW *Kaipara* 192 A 'white man' as a good fellow is called out here.] **1891** *Truth* (Sydney) 19 Apr. 1/5 Queensland shearers regard Sir Charles Lilley as a white man from his boots to his bell-topper. **1895** *Worker* (Sydney) 27 Apr. 3/2 Donnelly . . is a close personal friend of mine, and a real *white man*, as straight as they make 'em. **1908** C.H.S. MATTHEWS *Parson in Austral. Bush* 85 The miners are, most of them, full of energy and grit, ready to do anything for the parson, if once they believe him to be, in their own phrase, 'all right' or 'a white man'. **1914** —— *Bill* 130 It's a funny thing, but it's true, that the law always punishes you worse for anything done to a 'scab', though that sort of scum deserves all it gets, than it would if you had done the same thing to a Union man—or, as we say in Australia, 'a white man'. **1929** W.J. RESIDE *Golden Days* 197 'A white man', was how he was described. **1972** J. JONES *Memories Golden Gate* (rev. ed.) 10 Generally speaking they were fine people there in those days—hard working, independent, happy and friendly with high standards of what was the right thing to do. To use an expression common in those days, they were 'white men'. **1978** S. BALL *Muma's Boarding House* 129, I don't like Paddies much but I've seen a lot of Arthur up at the hospital and I can see he's a real white man.

whitewash, *v. Shearing. trans.* To shear (a sheep, esp. a lamb) lightly. Also as *ppl. a.*

1905 *Shearer* (Sydney) 23 Dec. 7/5, I once had the doubtful pleasure, many years ago, of working in a woolshed along with a 'tomahawking' and 'whitewashing' shearer who rejoiced in or groaned under the suggestive 'monniker' of 'More Tar'. **1925** *Bulletin* (Sydney) 21 May 22/2 If a lamb is 'whitewashed' (that is, merely 'topped') at, say, five months old, the fleece 12 months later will be even in length. **1982** P. ADAM SMITH *Shearers* 406 *Whitewashing*, shearing very young lambs.

whitewash gum. [See quot. 1928.] Any of several trees of the genus *Eucalyptus* (fam. Myrtaceae) having a smooth, whitish bark, incl. GHOST GUM.

1926 A.A.B. APSLEY *Amateur Settlers* 131 Tall white-wash gums. **1928** B. SPENCER *Wanderings in Wild Aust.* 366 Now and again there were a few beautiful white-stemmed, or white-wash, gum-trees. This special kind (*Eucalyptus terminalis*) is especially abundant in this part of the Centre. . . The bush men call them white-wash gums for the simple reason that their trunks and boughs are coated with a fine pure white powder that rubs off. **1936** C.T. MADIGAN *Central Aust.* 85 The watercourses . . are thickly lined with splendid eucalypts, mainly a white gum, *Eucalyptus papuana*, locally called whitewash gum, as the limbs are smooth and white, as if they had been whitewashed. **1965** *Austral. Encycl.* III. 406 White-bark or 'whitewash gum' (*E[ucalyptus] apodophylla*) of Arnhem Land has perfectly smooth trunks covered with a white mealy 'bloom' that rubs off when touched.

whitewood. [Transf. use of *whitewood* a tree with light-coloured wood.] Any of many plants yielding a pale wood, esp. the small tree or tall shrub *Atalaya hemiglauca* (fam. Sapindaceae) of drier inland Aust., having waxy grey-green leaves and generally valued as fodder (although the fruits can be poisonous to horses). Also **whitewood tree.**

1826 J. ATKINSON *Acct. Agric. & Grazing N.S.W.* 3 Here are found . . the whitewood or boula tree, with its dark green foliage and smooth bark, resembling the beech of Europe. **1843** *Portland Mercury* 5 Apr. 3/2 These samples consist of extracts from the bark of the mimosa, honeysuckle, and whitewood. **1862** W. LANDSBOROUGH *Jrnl. Exped. from Carpentaria* 71 The soil was rich . . and slightly wooded with whitewood. The whitewood I take to be the tree Mr Gregory calls the erythuna [*sic*]. **1884** E. PALMER *Notes Austral. Tribes* 15 They sometimes use the winged seed of *Atalaya hemiglauca* (the whitewood), the gyrations of which cause them amusement. **1911** ST. C. GRONDONA *Collar & Cuffs* 70 Whitewood is a stunted tree, the light-grey leaves of which horses are especially fond. **1935** H.H. FINLAYSON *Red Centre* 109 The woody, bright orange fruit of the white wood, *Atalaya* sp., which is intolerably bitter but which the camels will seek out. **1953** H.G. LAMOND *Big Red* 133, I saw ninety-three bodies of dead 'roos under a clump of whitewood trees. **1978** D. STUART *Wedgetail View* 58 Straggling lines of whitewood on the floodflats.

whiting. [Transf. use of *whiting* a European gadoid fish, *Merlangius merlangus*, valued as food.]

1. Any of several marine fish of several fam., esp. of the Indo-Pacific fam. Sillaginidae, valued as food.

1792 *Hist. Rec. N.S.W.* (1893) II. 794 The best fish that are caught are . . flatheads, salmon, whitings. **1803**

J.G. GRANT *Narr. Voyage N.S.W.* 109, I . . caught more whitings and small snappers. **1821** T. GODWIN *Descr. Acct. Van Diemen's Island* 9 Fish are caught in abundance. . . Those most known are . . sole, mackerel, whiting. **1851** H. MELVILLE *Present State Aust.* 44 The whole coast of New South Wales abounds with fish . . among which the epicures select the whiting and mullet. **1878** *Proc. Linnean Soc. N.S.W.* III. 380 *Sillago maculata* . . very common in the Sydney market, and known as the *Whiting.* **1895** C. THACKERAY *Amateur Fisherman's Guide* 70 Whiting, sand flathead and jewfish are the best fish caught off the beaches. **1918** 'J. SCOTT' *How, when & where to catch Fish* 27 Of the large number of different kind of fishes to be caught in New South Wales waters, whiting are undoubtedly the most highly prized as table fish. **1948** F.D. MARSHALL *Let's go Fishing* 80 Of all sea fish the whiting ranks among the very best table fish. **1974** T.D. SCOTT et al. *Marine & Freshwater Fishes S.A.* 208 Family Sillaginidae. The fishes of this family are known popularly as Whiting. However, they should not be confused with European Whiting, which are members of the family Gadidae. . . Members of the Sillaginidae are restricted to the western Pacific region.

2. With distinguishing epithet, as **King George, rock, sand, spotted, trumpeter**: see under first element.

whombat, whombatt, varr. WOMBAT.

wicked willainy. *Obs.* [Repr. non-standard pronunc. of *wicked villainy.*] The illicit distillation of spirits; such spirits. Also *attrib.*

1844 *Bee of Aust.* (Sydney) 26 Oct. 2/5 It . . will, doubtless, cause the eyes of the honest good man 'wot despises wicked willainy' to be suffused with tears at finding what extensive *plants* there were to *cooper* his fair trade. **1845** *Parramatta Chron.* 8 Mar. 2/2 *Joseph Fubbs,* appeared on summons to account for the proprietorship of two vessels of 'wicked willainy' seized on the 21st ultimo, by the Chief Constable, at a waterhole at the head of Saltpan Creek. *Ibid.* 19 Apr. 1/3 Wicked Willainy seems *running* its illicit course in this district; a large double still, capable of containing 100 gallons, having been found in a scrubby creek in the bush, near the premises of Mr Rourke, a short distance from Newcastle. **1845** *Star* (Sydney) 15 Nov. 2/3 In fine, although there has been no wicked willainy discovered, there has been a vast quantity of *still* life. **1846** *Cumberland Times* (Parramatta) 3 Jan. 2/2 *Wicked willainy case.*—On Monday Mr Patrick Hayes, out on bail, appeared to answer the charge of working an illicit still upon his premises at the Emu Brewery.

wicket. [Fig. use of *wicket* a cricket pitch. Used elsewhere but recorded earliest in Aust.: see OEDS 3 d.] In the phrase **to be on a good wicket,** to be in an advantageous or comfortable position.

1910 L. ESSON *Woman Tamer* (1976) 70 We were on a good wicket when Pete says to his bit o' fluff: 'Would you like to see a real solid bracelet, duckie?' **1913** W.K. HARRIS *Outback in Aust.* 10 It is no uncommon sight for half a dozen 'swaggies' to arrive at the house at the same time, and, to use a slang expression, they are always on a 'good wicket'. **1957** V. PALMER *Rainbow-Bird* 94 They're on a good wicket now because for the first time in their lives the jobs are chasing them. **1965** H. ATKINSON *Reckoning* 30 It's better than that bloody humpy yer bin livin' in. Yer on a good wicket. **1966** D. NILAND *Pairs & Loners* 46 I'm on a good wicket, making a packet. Everything's fine.

wide, *a.* In the phr. **the wide brown land,** Australia.

1908 *Call* (Sydney) Nov. 7 Her beauty and her terror—The wide brown land for me. **1934** J. & G. MACKANESS *(title)* The wide brown land. **1966** J. SMITH *Ornament of Grace* 33 A nice myth to be dusted off every Anzac Day, about bronzed heroes of the wide brown land. **1970** *Sunday Tel.* (Sydney) 9 Aug. 16/1 *(heading)* The wide brown land is up for sale (cheap). **1973** *Austral.* (Sydney) 4 May 11/4 Migrants are staying away in droves from the widest and brownest part of this wide, brown land.

wideawake. A wallaby, perh. a HARE-WALLABY.

1863 J.B. AUSTIN *Mines S.A.* 30 During the journey we saw innumerable Kangaroo rats, 'wideawakes' (a variety of the wallaby) a few Kangaroo and some five turkeys. **1902** R. BRUCE *Reminisc. Old Squatter* 152 The dark fur and long ears of a wideawake (wallaby). **1909** LINDSAY & HOLTZE *Territoria* 24 Kangaroo rats, wideawakes, and mountain devils.

wide comb: see COMB 2.

wide working, *vbl. n.* Of a sheep-dog: the controlling of the movement of sheep while remaining at some distance from them. See WORK 2.

1902 *N.S.W. Sheepbreeders Yr. Bk.* 41 The awards shall be by points. The following are the maximum number of points—Under command 30, activity 15, wide working 15, steadiness 15, putting through hurdles, poles and yarding 25, total 100. **1914** R. KALESKI *Austral. Barkers & Biters* 55 When the trials started a few years ago, lots of the dogs were 'sneakers'. That is, they crept about close to the sheep, and dodged them through. Owing to 35 points being given for activity and wide working, this style has about died out. **1923** *Austral.* (Sydney) June 11 The dog is racing them again. He keeps well out from the woollies. Wide-working is a test of his worth.

Hence **wide worker** *n.*

1977 *Working Dog* (Vic. Dept. Agric., N.E. Region) 12 Some dogs are bred to be wide workers and it can be very difficult, at times impossible, to make these dogs work in close. **1983** P. VIDLER *Border Collie in Australasia* 20 She 'was the widest worker I have seen; setting off at a jog behind me, she almost disappeared in the distance before she would turn and put on any pace'.

widgeon. [Spec. use of *widgeon* a wild duck.] Any of several ducks, esp. *pink-eared duck* (see PINK *a.*).

1840 *Corresp. on Secondary Punishment* (Great Brit. Parl.) 27 Feb. (1841) 32 Called by one of the men who had been at Macquarie Island, where they are in great abundance, a widgeon . . a very pretty bird, delicate eating. **1898** E.E. MORRIS *Austral Eng.* 511 Widgeon. . . In Australia, it is used as another name for the *Pink-eyed* (or *Pink-eared*) *Duck.* It is also used, as in England, by sportsmen as a loose term for many species of Wild-Duck generally. **1924** LORD & SCOTT *Synopsis Vertebrate Animals Tas.* 177 The Pink-eared Duck is not a common species in Tasmania. . . On the mainland this bird is sometimes referred to as the 'Widgeon' by shooters. **1954** *Coast to Coast 1953–54* 15 He saw the wide shovel-bills, the heavy heads, the set-back wings of the widgeon as they banked and turned for the open swamp. **1980** C. ALLISON *Hunter's Man. Aust. & N.Z.* 115 The beautiful Pink-ear is known in some places as the Zebra or Widgeon.

widgery, var. WITCHETTY.

widgie. Also **weegie.** [Of unknown origin.] The female counterpart of a BODGIE *n.*[1] Also *attrib.*

1950 *Sun* (Sydney) 5 July 19/3 There'll be prizes . . for the most colorfully dressed 'bodgy' and 'weegie'. **1951** *Argus* (Melbourne) 11 Dec. 5/3 He had become a member of the 'bodgie-widgie cult', and they had got the idea to go with other 'bodgies' and 'widgies' to Sydney. **1955** *Sydney Morning Herald* 11 Feb. 4/9 Constable Waldon said: 'A widgie, as she is known to me, is generally dressed in a very tight blouse, mostly without sleeves, and generally with a deep, plunging front. The blouse closely conforms to the lines of the body. In addition, she usually has a form-fitting skirt, which is very tight, especially around the knees. The skirt flares out a little below the knees and generally has a split either at the side or at the rear to enable her to walk. A widgie wears a short-cropped haircut.' Judge Curlewis said the detective's description of a widgie was the best he had heard in a Court. **1957** J.M. HOSKING *Aust. first & Last* 93 New South Wales girls are like honey, But they cost you lots of money. . . There are widgies there and the bodgies, But you won't find many 'stodgies'. **1963** R. MCGREGOR-HASTIE *Compleat Migrant* 53 There's none of this class distinction in Australia. Anybody can be a bodgie (male) or a widgie (female). **1967** G. JENKIN *Two Yrs. Bardunyah Station* 6 Where the nags are wild as widgies on the old Tarcoola side. **1971** *Bulletin* (Sydney) 17 Apr. 43 *(caption)* Shirley . . recollects her teenage life with her family, her experiences as a bike-gang widgie. **1980** S. ORR *Roll On* 67 The shifty-eyed inheritors of the long-gone bodgie and widgie set, slide on. **1983** *Age* (Melbourne) 12 Aug. 2/7 The word 'widgies' came from the . . black market rag trade. Mr Hewett says it is derived from the Australian term 'ridgee-didge'. 'It meant that something was good, and when somebody bought some good quality American cloth it was called 'ridgee-didge'. Later the bodgies' girlfriends got called widgies,' he says.

wife-starver. A husband who defaults on the payment of maintenance to a wife or ex-wife.

1966 S.J. BAKER *Austral. Lang.* (ed. 2) 155 *Wifestarver,* a prisoner confined under the provisions of the Deserted Wives and Childrens Act, 1901–6. **1976** D. HEWETT *Golden Oldies* (1981) 47 He's left her, alright, run off to Darwin where all the wife-starvers go. **1982** P. ADAM SMITH *Shearers* 201 Contractors are used to bodgy names—there are always some who don't travel with their own names: they had their own reasons. You met plenty of 'wife starvers' out west, cleared out to get out of paying maintenance for wife and kids.

wig, *n. Shearing.* The wool which grows above and around the eyes of a sheep.

1964 R. WARD *Penguin Bk. Austral. Ballads* 228 Two blows to chip away the wig. **1972** G.W. TURNER *Good Austral. Eng.* 61 One thing I did notice about shearing was . . two terms for the one idea . . for example . . topknot/wig.

wig, *v. Shearing. trans.* To clip wool from about the eyes of (a sheep). Freq. as *vbl. n.*

1913 W.K. HARRIS *Outback in Aust.* 151 'Wigging' . . consists of shearing the wool away between the eyes . . to prevent the sheep being blinded by the seeds. **1914** *Pastoral Rev.* 16 Mar. 242 Treatment of wool-blind sheep (wigging) is also very desirable. **1930** D. COTTRELL *Earth Battle* 123 Fifty rams and wethers . . had been flyblown, and needed shearing round the belly and horns—'wigging and bellying' as it was called. **1967** F.T. MACARTNEY *Proof against Failure* 46, I learnt all about . . wigging (removing wool over-growing the eyes, from which at the same time grass seeds had often to be removed as capable of causing blindness). **1975** L.A. POCKLEY *Handbk. for Jackeroos* 88 When sheep are shorn around the faces . . they are said to be 'wigged'.

So **wiggings** *pl.,* the pieces of wool so removed.

1958 H.D. WILLIAMSON *Sunlit Plain* 204 Regan bent down to look behind a bale of wiggings. He pulled a skin out by the tail. **1975** L.A. POCKLEY *Handbk. for Jackeroos* 88 Sheep are shorn around the faces. . . This wool is sold separately as 'Wiggings'.

wigwam. *Obs.* [Transf. use of *wigwam* the dwelling of the North American Indian.]

1. A name applied by the colonists to an Aboriginal's dwelling (see GUNYAH 1); also *transf.,* a roughly-constructed dwelling occupied by a white person.

1792 W. BLIGH *Voyage to South Sea* 214 The wigwam and turtle shell, were proofs that the natives at times visited this place. **1828** H. DANGAR *Index & Directory River Hunter* 113 It is a custom amongst these aboriginals . . to make the women perform every drudgery. . . The men seldom do more than hunt and build their wigwams. **1837** E. FRASER *Narr. of Capture* 1 Mrs Fraser . . after having been compelled to take up her abode in a wigwam and to become the adopted wife of one of the Chiefs . . was providentially rescued from her perilous situation. **1843** MACARTHUR & THERRY *Election County of Camden* 37, I asked him in what consisted his qualification, and find it to consist of a lease-hold in land on which a few gunyas or wig-wams were erected, and no house worth £200 a-year, I told him—and I think satisfied him—that he was not qualified to be an elector. **1853** W. WESTGARTH *Vic.* 253 The punch of an iron tree waddy upon the skull of an aboriginal lubra, whose noisy jealousy amongst her several rivals had disquieted the family wigwam.

2. *fig.* In the phr. **a wigwam for a goose's bridle,** used as a reply to an unwanted question: see quot. 1982.

1960 K. SMITH *Word from Children* 155 In more colourful times, thirty years ago, a stickybeak would be told 'It's a wigwam for a goose's bridle' or, 'The first prize in a mind-your-own-business contest'. **1965** G. MCINNES *Road to Gundagai* 24 When we pressed Thirk more closely all he would say was 'What they need is a wigwam for a goose's bridle' which was his way of shutting us up. **1982** N. KEESING *Lily on Dustbin* 68 'A wigwam for a goose's bridle' . . is one of the most used and widespread of all snubs and put-downs to children in Australia.

Wilcannia shower /wɪlkænjə ˈʃaʊə/. [f. the name of a town in w. N.S.W.] A dust storm.

1903 J. FURPHY *Such is Life* 290 Here was the true key to the Wilcannia shower. **1961** G. FARWELL *Vanishing Australs.* 174 There was the day the *Florence Annie* was bushed in a Darling dust storm—a 'Wilcannia shower', as they used to be called.

wild, *a.*

1. Used as a distinguishing epithet in the names of flora and fauna: **wild banana,** *native banana,* see NATIVE *a.* 6 a.; **carrot,** *native carrot,* see NATIVE *a.* 6 a.; **celery** *obs.*, a herbaceous plant of the genus *Apium* (fam. Apiaceae), esp. *native parsley* (see NATIVE *a.* 6 a.); **cherry,** CHERRY 1; **clematis,** any of several vigorous climbing plants of the genus *Clematis* (fam. Ranunculaceae), incl. *C. microphylla, C. pubescens, C. glycinoides,* and *C. aristata* (see *old man's beard* OLD MAN *n.* 3); **cucumber,** any of several plants bearing a melon-like fruit, esp. naturalized species of the genus *Cucumis* (fam. Cucurbitaceae); **currant,** *native currant,* see NATIVE *a.* 6 a.; **dog,** DINGO *n.* 1; **fig,** any of several plants of the genus *Ficus* (fam. Moraceae); the fruit of the plant; **geranium,** any of several introduced or native plants of the fam. Geraniaceae, esp. the perennial *Pelargonium australe* of all States; **ginger,** any of several plants of the fam. Zingiberaceae, esp. of the genus *Alpinia* of n. Aust. and elsewhere; **goose** *obs.*, **(a)** *Cape Barren goose,* see CAPE BARREN; **(b)** *magpie goose,* see MAGPIE *n.* 2; **grape,** any of several plants bearing a grape-like fruit, incl. the climber *Legnephora moorei* (fam. Menispermaceae) of Qld. and N.S.W., and species of *Cissus* (see *water vine* WATER); the fruit of the plant; **hop** (usu. in *pl.*), *native hop,* see NATIVE *a.* 6 a.; also *attrib.*; **indigo** *obs.*, INDIGO a.; also *attrib.*; **lemon,** any of several trees or shrubs supposed to resemble the lemon, esp. *Canthium oleifolium* (fam. Rubiaceae) of inland Qld. and N.S.W., bearing fragrant white flowers; also *attrib.*; **lime,** *native cumquat,* see NATIVE *a.* 6 a.; **melon,** any of several plants bearing a melon-like fruit, esp. the naturalized perennial *Citrullus colocynthis* (fam. Cucurbitaceae), the fruit of which has a bitter flesh, and *C. lanatus* (see PIE-MELON); the fruit of the plant; **nutmeg,** NUTMEG 1; also *attrib.*; **onion,** *onion weed* (c), see ONION 1; **orange,** any of several often spiny, small trees or shrubs of the genus *Capparis* (fam. Capparaceae) of mainland Aust., esp. the inland *C. mitchellii,* bearing an edible, rounded fruit with numerous seeds; the fruit of the plant; BUMBLE TREE; *native pomegranate* (a), see NATIVE *a.* 6 a.; see also *native orange* NATIVE *a.* 6 a.; also *attrib.*; **parsley,** the shrub *Lomatia silaifolia* (fam. Proteaceae) of e. N.S.W. and e. Qld.; **parsnip,** any of several herbs of the genus *Trachymene* (fam. Apiaceae) having a pale, fleshy root, esp. *T. anisocarpa* of s. Aust. incl. Tas.; the root of the plant; **passionfruit,** any of several plants, esp. native or introduced tendril-bearing climbers of the genus *Passiflora* (fam. Passifloraceae); **peach,** any of several plants incl. the tree *Terminalia carpentariae* (fam. Combretaceae) of n. Aust.; the wood or fruit of the plant; **pineapple,** any of several species of MACROZAMIA; **plum,** *native plum,* see NATIVE *a.* 6 a.; also *attrib.*; **raspberry,** *native raspberry,* see NATIVE *a.* 6 a.; **rhubarb,** any of several plants incl. the naturalized succulent annual *Rumex vesicarius* (fam. Polygonaceae) of mainland Aust.; **sorghum,** any of several grasses (fam. Poaceae) incl. *Sorghum leiocladum* of e. mainland Aust.; **spinach,** any of several plants used as a green vegetable incl. WARRIGAL *n.* 3 and some plants of the fam. Chenopodiaceae; SPINACH; **tobacco,** any of several plants incl. the naturalized shrub or small tree *Solanum mauritianum* (fam. Solanaceae) of disturbed land in parts of e. Aust., and species of *Nicotiana,* esp. the S. American *N. glauca,* naturalized in mainland Aust. and elsewhere; see also *native tobacco* NATIVE *a.* 6 a.; also *attrib.*; **turkey,** the large, nomadic, often solitary game bird *Ardeotis kori,* of mainland Aust. and New Guinea; *plain turkey* (a), see PLAIN 2; see also TURKEY *n.*[1] 1; **turnip,** any of several plants, usu. naturalized herbs of the fam. Brassicaceae, and esp. the annual *Brassica tournefortii* naturalized in mainland Aust.; **violet,** any of several plants bearing bluish-violet or white flowers, usu. of the genus *Viola* (fam. Violaceae), esp. the perennial herb *V. hederacea* of e. and s.e. Aust.; **yam,** YAM.

1864 J. MORRILL *Sketch of Residence* 228 A **wild banana,** full of black seed, and very little flesh. **1960** I.L. IDRIESS *Wild North* 213 Should he jump now he would alight on the fronds of . . wild banana and cable vine and creeper. **1844** *Swan River News* June 47/2 The **wild carrot** is . . an excellent vegetable, and from its root rich wine has been extracted. **1848** T.L. MITCHELL *Jrnl. Exped. Tropical Aust.* 352 The wild carrot, *Daucus brachiatus,* with an annual wiry root, was also seen in the rich ground near the river. **1880** J. BONWICK *Resources Qld.* 44 The best . . grasses . . of Darling Downs, the kangaroo, blue, and wild-carrot. **1931** F.D. DAVISON *Man-Shy* (1962) 7 They knew where the crowfoot and wild carrot would be springing fetlock deep. **1961** A.M. DUNCAN-KEMP *Our Channel Country* 10 Herbage of many varieties forms a vast carpet inches thick and feet high. Verbine . . wild carrot, balsam grass. **1788** *HRA* (1914) 1st Ser. I. 23 The heaths that are free from timber are covered with a variety of the most beautiful flowering shrubs, **wild celery** [etc.]. **1833** *Jrnls. Several Exped. W.A.* 197 Wild celery grew very abundant [*sic*] on the side of the estuary. **1898** *Proc. Linnean Soc. N.S.W.* XXIII. 129 *Apium prostratum* . . known locally as 'Wild Celery'. King informed me that this plant has been cultivated on the island [*sc.* Lord Howe Is.], and an inferior celery produced. **1871** 'IOTA' *Kooroona* 60 The beautiful tree to which English settlers have given the name of the **wild cherry. 1928** M.E. FULLERTON *Austral. Bush* 130 Most tangy and unfruitlike of berries is the fruit of the wild cherry-tree. **1972** ANDERSON & BLAKE *J.S. Neilson* 17 Protesting flocks of white cockatoos and galahs arose from the wild cherry trees. **1984** K.A.W. WILLIAMS *Native Plants Qld.* II. 136 *Exocarpos cupressiformis* . . Cherry Ballart . . Wild Cherry. . . As the fruit matures the stem swells and when this fleshy portion is deep red in colour and soft it is sweetly palatable. Otherwise it is very astringent and is like biting a green persimmon. **1845** *Sydney Morning Herald* 14 Jan. 4/4 Here the scene changes to a brush of cedar . . over which the **wild clematis,** and fifty other specimens of woodland creeper, either hang in festoons . . or playfully arch themselves over the brook in beautiful luxuriance. **1878** R.B. SMYTH *Aborigines of Vic.* I. 276 The band tied round the head [as worn by the aborigines of the Lower Murray] . . is made of the fibrous root of the wild clematis. **1933** C.W. PECK *Austral. Legends* (ed. 2) 25 Wild clematis and Wonga wonga vine climbed from shrub to shrub. **1866** *Australasian* (Melbourne) 25 Aug. 665/2 There are a variety of herbs on which stock are found to thrive exceedingly; amongst which may be enumerated . . **'wild cucumber'** and 'carrots'. **1871** *Austral. Town & Country Jrnl.* (Sydney) 6 May 557/4 The ill effects of the colycynth or wild cucumber growing so profusely. **1916** *Bulletin* (Sydney) 6 July 24/3, I have . . tried to swallow a mouthful of the deceitful wild orange. . . The wild cucumber found in the north-east parts of South Aus. is more satisfying. **1948** H.A. LINDSAY *Bushman's Handbk.* 58 Wild cucumbers are fairly common; they are too like the domestic variety to need any description, but one species is so bitter that it is quite inedible. **1965** P. JONES *Johnny Lost* 52 Weeds grew overnight in the vegetable patch—stickfast and wild cucumber and cobbler's peg. **1803** *Sydney Gaz.* 26 June, After they had eaten their provisions they found nothing to subsist on but **wild-currants** and sweet-tea leaves. **1846** G.H. HAYDON *Five Yrs. Experience Aust. Felix* 18 The wild currant (*leucopogon Richei*), a small bushy shrub, with fruit about the size of the English description, but of a more acid flavour. **1859** J.M. STUART *Explorations in Aust.* 24 Nov. (1865) 103 The wild currant, or rather grape, grew in great abundance. . . There were two kinds; one grew upon a dark-green bush, and had a tart and saltish taste, the other grew upon a bush of a much lighter colour. **1947** W.E. HARNEY *Brimming Billabongs* 163 During the good seasons . . we found the 'munagidje' or wild currant. **1949** B. O'REILLY *Green Mountains* 89 Wild currants, red and black . . grew thickly over the rocky ridges. **1955** M. BUNDEY *My Land* 18 They used to have their lessons out under a large wild currant tree. **1793** W. TENCH *Compl. Acct. Settlement* 172 The Indians sometimes kill the kanguroo, but their greatest destroyer is the **wild dog,** who feeds on them. **1827** *Monitor* (Sydney) 30 Mar. 363 A small paddock is enclosed adjoining the garden for a menagerie, and we have in it, the Kangaroo, Opossum, Emu, black Swan, spotted wild Cat, wild Dog, and the Bear found in the mountains. **1841** *Port Phillip Patriot* 15 Mar. 4/1, 5s. for every wild dog we kill. **1865** G.F. ANGAS *Aust.* 80 The 'Dingo' or wild dog . . is found all over the Australian continent (though it does not occur in Tasmania). **1884** E. PALMER *Notes Austral. Tribes* 6 They can feign death as well as their companion the wild dog. **1911** *Huon Times* (Franklin) 24 June 5/3 People living in settled districts in Australia in these days have little conception of the extent to which the Australian wild dog has still to be reckoned with. **1932** C.M. GRAY *Western Vic. in Forties* 8 The wild dogs, which were then very numerous, kept up a howl during the whole night round my cart. **1948** P.J. HURLEY *Red Cedar* 78 The sheep were broken up in small flocks. . . Adjustable yards and a watchman kept the 'wild dogs' (dingoes) off by night. **1788** *HRA* (1914) 1st Ser. I. 23 The heaths that are free from timber are covered with a variety of the most beautiful flowering shrubs, wild celery, spinages, samphose, a small **wild fig. 1841** J. GOULD *Birds of Aust.* (1848) V. Pl. 61, Among other substances found in the stomachs of those specimens . . I dissected were the wild-fig and the large round berries of the cabbage palm. **1865** G.F. ANGAS *Aust.* 123 Amongst the few barely edible fruits indigenous to Australia may be mentioned the wild fig. **1883** W.J. O'DONNELL *Diary Exploring Exped.* 16 Apr. (1884) 3 The Victoria River . . is a noble river, and is heavily timbered with such trees as . . wild fig, curryjohn, melaleuca, and numerous others. **1925** *Smith's Weekly* (Sydney) 18 July 15/5 In the Bega (N.S.W.) district are hundreds of large bushy trees, known locally as wild figs. **1952** N. GOREY *Alice* 22 Wild figs are small brown fruits of a tree which has a leaf quite unlike a fig. **1978** D. STUART *Wedgetail View* 58 Deep gorges where the wild fig clung to precipitous slopes above tangled masses of spindly creek wattles. **1839** *S. Austral. Rec.* (London) (1840) 18 July 45 Thousands and tens of thousands of acres of land, fit for the plough and level as a bowling-green, covered with thousands of **wild geraniums** and other flowers. **1853** *Illustr. Sydney News* 15 Oct. 10/3 We see in the meadows the wild geranium, pink and blue. **1912** SPENCER & GILLEN *Across Aust.* 17 Then again, there was the wild geranium. **1947** T.Y. HARRIS *Wild Flowers Aust.* (rev. ed.) 54 Wild Geranium or Austral Storksbill *Pelargonium australe.* Like most of its kind, this *Pelargonium* is a lover of sandy soils, and is found in the poor coastal country of all the eastern States and Tasmania. **1870** E.B. KENNEDY *Four Yrs. in Qld.* 142 **Wild ginger** of an excellent quality is found everywhere. **1893** 'TIMES SPECIAL CORRESPONDENT' *Lett. from Qld.* 7 They merely escape from the undergrowth of wild ginger and tree-fern and stinging bush which fringes the scrub. **1935** DAVISON & NICHOLLS *Blue Coast Caravan* 124 The china-blue berries of the wild ginger. **1981** J.A. BAINES *Austral. Plant Genera* 26 *A[lpinia] arundelliana,* Wild Ginger, in E. Aust. **1770** J. COOK *Jrnls.* 4 Aug. (1955) I. 367 Some of our gentlemen . . in the Country heard and saw **wild Geese** in the night. **1844** *Port Phillip Gaz.* 6 July 3 The Cape Barren or wild goose, is about the same in size as the tame bird, but when dressed is of a far superior flavour. **1845** L. LEICHHARDT *Jrnl. Overland Exped. Aust.* 3 Sept. (1847) 386 We encamped . . in a fifth creek, which lower down contained . . reaches of brackish water covered with wild geese (Anseranas melanoleuca). **1882** W. SOWDEN *N.T. as it Is* 36 The croaking of frogs. . . Plaintively mingle with it the cackling of wild geese. **1852** J. MORGAN *Life & Adventures W. Buckley* 101 We made a lengthy halt at Mangowak where we lived on . . a sort of **wild grape** which grows in great abundance thereabouts. **1859** J.M. STUART *Explorations in Aust.* 28 Nov. (1865) 105 There are large quantities of the wild grape growing here, both red and white. They are very good indeed, and, if cultivated, would, I think, become a very nice fruit. **1870** E.B. KENNEDY *Four Yrs. in Qld.* 138 There are wild grapes, and many other kinds of fruit. **1916** *Bulletin* (Sydney) 13 Apr. 24/3 Kosciusko and the Kiandra country, in midspring and early summer . . become matted with the variegated red, pink and yellow hop-scrub, wild-pea, purple wild-grape and starry prickly bush [etc.]. **1947** T.Y. HARRIS *Wild Flowers Aust.* (rev. ed.) 35 Wild grape *Cissus Baudinianus* syn. *Vitis Baudiniana.* In the richer jungle country of the coast of New South Wales this climbing plant is common. . . The berries are round and black. **1979** K.A.W. WILLIAMS *Native Plants Qld.* I. 170 *Legnephora moorei* Menispermaceae. Wild Grape: A strong, twining climber. . . The common name could be misleading with regard to the edible qualities of the attractive fruit. It is suspected of being toxic and therefore should be avoided. **1854** W. HOWITT *Boy's Adventures* 5 He . . browses on the acacia trees and the bitter **wild hop** shrub. **1885** P.R. MEGGY *From Sydney to Silverton* 54 Wild hops, prickly acacia, and box flats. **1902** *Proc.*

Linnean Soc. N.S.W. XXVII. 588 In going southerly for 18 miles from Oberon towards Swatchfield .. other trees are .. *Goodenia ovata* .. a shrub locally known as Wild Hops [etc.]. **1948** G. Farwell *Down Argent Street* 87 Wild hops whose red leaves glow amid the brilliant hues of Salvation Jane. **1979** B. Martyn *First Footers S. Gippsland* 14 Pungent smelling wild hops. **1804** *HRA* (1915) 1st Ser. IV. 602, I send some samples of the produce extracted from the **Wild Indigo** Plant of this Country. **1839** W.H. Leigh *Reconnoitering Voyages* 127 A majestic forest of brobdignag looking gum-trees, all clear under their towering heads save the beautiful plants of the wild indigo. **1848** T.L. Mitchell *Jrnl. Exped. Tropical Aust.* 278 Covered with luxuriant anthistiria and wild indigo. **1880** J. Bonwick *Resources Qld.* 47 Among poison plants are .. the wild Indigo. **1861** *Sydney Mail* 6 July 3/3 *P[ittosporum] revolutum* .. is locally designated the '**Wild Lemon**' from the colour of its fruit. **1892** *Proc. Linnean Soc. N.S.W.* VII. 41 Mr Maiden exhibited a series of specimens of *Capparis nobilis*, the 'Wild Lemon' of the Richmond River. **1900** *Ibid.* XXV. 598 *Canthium oleifolium* .. (Wild Lemon, from the colour of the leaves, and general appearance of the tree, but the fruits are quite small and in clusters). **1926** *Qld. Agric. Jrnl.* XXV. 440 Citrus australis .. Wild Lemon. **1966** A. Morris *Plantlife W. Darling* 79 *Canthium latifolium* .. 'Wild lemon'. Small tree growing on the granite of Tibooburra, and sandstone at Mootwingee. Rare. **1981** G.M. Cunningham et al. *Plants Western N.S.W.* 623 Wild lemon suckers freely from the roots and this no doubt accounts for the characteristic thickets in which it usually occurs. **1901** K.L. Parker in M. Muir *My Bush Bk.* (1982) 103 Gaengaen, the olive-foliaged **wild limes,** whose miniature lemon-like fruit is a boon in a thirsty climate, ripening as it does in summer. **1944** *Bulletin* (Sydney) 29 Nov. 13/3 What has come over the Queensland wild lime? This tree was once found only in widely separated clumps, generally on broken-plain country. .. But now the little tree has gone mad, overrunning forests and open-scrub country. **1849** J.P. Townsend *Rambles & Observations N.S.W.* 181 On some stations in the district it [*sc.* the feed] is composed of barley grass, wild carrots, and **wild melons.** Of the long runners of the last the cattle are very fond. **1881** J.C.F. Johnson *To Mount Browne & Back* 11 The little bitter wild melon, common near Adelaide. **1885** P.R. Meggy *From Sydney to Silverton* 121 The ground was covered with wild melons of enormous size, from which the best jam is said to be made. **1911** C.E.W. Bean *'Dreadnought' of Darling* 135 Out there they have a theory that the blindness is due to eating a small green herb with a fruit like a gooseberry, which they call 'wild melon'. **1923** J. Armour *Spell of Inland* 10 We have different varieties of creepers, wild melons, bindaii, spinach, and other herbs that cattle eat. **1973** W.T. Parsons *Noxious Weeds Vic.* 139 There can be some confusion between colocynth and wild melon (*Citrullus lanatus*). Wild melon differs in being an annual with a much less robust taproot. **1829** R. Mudie *Picture of Aust.* 152 On the tropical shores, a species of **wild nutmeg** (*myristica insipida*) is not uncommon, but it is perfectly useless. **1841** G. Grey *Jrnls. Two Exped. N.-W. & W.A.* I. 85 The space between these trees and the cliffs was filled by a dense forest, principally composed of the Pandanus and wild nutmeg trees. **1870** E.B. Kennedy *Four Yrs. in Qld.* 142 The wild nutmeg grows .. in good sized bushes, both male and female. **1880** *Austral. Handbk.* 359 The rivers are on each side clothed with .. wild nutmegs. **1984** B. Dixon *Searching for Aboriginal Lang.* 23 Trees with edible fruit like the black pine, the finger cherry and the wild nutmeg. **1864** 'E.S.H.' *Narr. Trip Sydney to Peak Downs* 11 Crinum Creek .. is so named from the lilies, which travellers call **wild onions.** **1901** J.H. Maiden *Plants reputed to be Poisonous* 30 *Bulbine bulbosa* .. 'Native or Wild Onion' .. has several times been sent to me as a poisonous weed. **1979** W. Hartley *Checklist Economic Plants Aust.* 69 *Nothoscordum inodorum* .. Wild Onion. **1885** P.R. Meggy *From Sydney to Silverton* 124 **Wild oranges** as bitter as gall .. may be occasionally seen on the plains. **1900** *Proc. Linnean Soc. N.S.W.* XXV. 593 *Capparis Mitchelli* .. (Wild Orange, as it bears a fruit somewhat similar to an orange in shape and size, and moreover the trees are thorny). **1901** K.L. Parker in M. Muir *My Bush Bk.* (1982) 101 The fruit, known as the wild orange, is more like a pomegranate in structure, when ripe, dark green outside and yellow within. This fruit has a perfectly delicious aromatic scent. **1912** B. Spencer *Wanderings in Wild Aust.* 12 Nov. (1928) 902, I watched one woman making little dampers .. out of a big lot of wild orange (Capparis) seed that she pounded up on stone. **1952** B. Beatty *Unique to Aust.* 66 Caper butterflies .. feed upon the Wild Orange or Caper bush of the interior. **1986** *Age* (Melbourne) 6 May 36/5 The Caper White larvae feed on plants of the genus *Capparis*. The wild orange, *C. mitchellii* is the best known. **1947** T.Y. Harris *Wild Flowers Aust.* (rev. ed.) 68 **Wild Parsley** *Lomatia silaifolia* .. is a small shrub with deeply-toothed, divided leaves and long, loose spikes of cream flowers. **1965** *Austral. Encycl.* VII. 29 Wild Parsley .. is also applied to the proteaceous shrub *Lomatia silaifolia* in eastern sandstone areas of New South Wales. **1805** *Acct. Voyage to establish Colony Port Phillip* 162 Of potable vegetables, wild celery, **wild parsnip,** scurvy-grass .. were found in great abundance. **1835** F.C. Irwin *State & Position W.A.* 23 The principal root they use is the eringo, or wild parsnip. **1889** J.H. Maiden *Useful Native Plants Aust.* 142 Recently (December 1887) the sudden death of numbers of cattle in the vicinity of Dandenong, Victoria, was attributed to their having eaten a plant known as the wild parsnip. **1917** R.D. Barton *Reminisc. Austral. Pioneer* 119 Some people call it the 'wild parsnip', but the right name is the berang (the blacks' name). **1965** *Austral. Encycl.* VIII. 546 *T[rachymene] anisocarpa* (syn *Didiscus pilosus*) is the so-called wild parsnip of sandy coastal country all around southern Australia. .. *T. glaucifolia*, the wild parsnip of inland plains. **1975** A.B. & J.W. Cribb *Wild Food in Aust.* 154 Wild parsnip is a pretty little wildflower of coastal districts. .. There is a thickened taproot like a small parsnip. This is parsnip-like in flavour as well, and can be eaten with pleasure either raw or cooked. **1984** K.A.W. Williams *Native Plants Qld.* II. 286 *Trachymene ochracea* .. Wild Parsnip .. has a swollen underground stem which is much like a white carrot and tends to grow fairly deep into the soil. **1870** E.B. Kennedy *Four Yrs. in Qld.* 142 **Wild passion-fruit,** bearing red flowers, handsomer than the cultivated ones, creeps in and out of the bushes. **1911** St. C. Grondona *Collar & Cuffs* 69 The wild passion fruit, or 'split jack', as it is locally called, is a very common creeper, with a fruit which .. splits when ripe. **1923** *Bulletin* (Sydney) 27 Dec. 23/4 To .. blue couch .. I can add another common bush plant with generally unsuspected poisonous properties. This is the wild passion-fruit. **1948** H.A. Lindsay *Bushman's Handbk.* 58 The wild passionfruit, which is similar to the domestic variety, but much smaller, and the fruit, yellow when ripe, is carried inside a hairy network. **1980** E. McDonald *Wildflowers of Wallum* 38 Wild Passion-fruit. *Passiflora alba*. .. The dainty white blossoms .. flower alongside the pale green globules of fruit, which look tempting to eat. **1985** *Austral. Plants* June 131 Wild Passionfruit [*sc. Capparis spinosa* var. *nummularia*] grows as a low shrub up to 4 metres high. .. The edible part is the flesh between the seeds. **1853** A. Kinloch *Murray River* 16 The only fruit .. in use amongst the whites is that called the 'quondong'—a species of **wild peach,** which is largely used as a preserve. **1928** E.H.F. Swain *Timbers & Forest Products Qld.* 467 Wild Peach *Trema aspera*. **1948** *Austral. Bushcraft* (Austral. Army Educ. Service) 9 For the firestick you should select .. a slab of 'snap and rattle' mallee wood, or wild peach. **1981** D. Levitt *Plants & People* 36 Wild Peach, Red Cement Tree (*Terminalia carpentariae*). .. The fruit, which resembles a small green peach about 1.5 to 2.5 cm. in size, was eaten raw, including the skin. **1901** J.H. Maiden *Plants reputed to be Poisonous* 31 *Macrozamia* spp.—'Zamia palm', 'Burrawang', '**Wild pine-apple**' .. are gregarious plants. **1938** C.T. White *Princ. Bot. Qld. Farmers* 134 Burrawang or Wild Pineapple is a name frequently given to species of Macrozamia, particularly to *M. spiralis*. All the Australian members have a bad reputation as plants poisonous to stock. **1984** K.A.W. Williams *Native Plants Qld.* 186 Once again attention is drawn to an unsuitable and misleading common name. 'Wild Pineapple' may indicate edibility. The fruit is poisonous and although eaten by the aboriginal people, they were treated beforehand. **1849** J.P. Townsend *Rambles & Observations N.S.W.* 131 Amongst the trees .. in this district is the gigantic fig-tree. It is produced by a seed deposited by birds, in an undigested state, in the cleft of a gum or of a **wild plum**-tree. **1872** C.H. Eden *My Wife & I in Qld.* 208 We used to find a great variety of wild plums (*Achras Australis, Owenia venosa*). **1926** K. Dahl *In Savage Aust.* 199 Having found and eaten a kind of wild plum (a species of *Terminalia*). **1949** G. Farwell *Traveller's Tracks* 87 There was a 'forest' of wild plum, at least six inches high, with more exposed roots than branches. **1977** W.A. Winter-Irving *Bush Stories* 141 On Rocklands Station at Camooweal the rare wild plum trees grow in a creek bed. The leaves of these heavily foliaged trees are a deep reddish-purple. **1845** R. Howitt *Impressions Aust. Felix* 75 The bramble, too, with a red berry instead of a black, called here the **wild raspberry,** yet the fruit neither tasting like the one nor the other. **1859** R.H. Horne *Austral. Facts & Prospects* 170 The wild raspberry hooks off his clothes, and tears his flesh. **1897** Mrs L. Rawson *Austral. Cook & Laundry Bk.* 80 Wild Raspberry .. make a very nice preserve, insipid as they are in a raw state. **1905** *Emu* V. 3 Groped our way in the dark through thick tangles of wild raspberry and other prickly bushes. **1935** T. Rayment *Cluster of Bees* 256 The cat-head ferns trembled in amongst the long hooked vines of the wild-raspberry. **1949** B. O'Reilly *Green Mountains* 149 There were three kinds of wild raspberries. **1878** R.B. Smyth *Aborigines of Vic.* II. 173 **Wild rhubarb** .. Lanangárangal. **1903** *Proc. Linnean Soc. N.S.W.* XXVIII. 541 *Emex australis*. .. This maritime plant has been found at New Angledool .. in the northern interior where it is locally known as 'Wild Rhubarb'. **1948** G. Farwell *Down Argent Street* 92 Red dock (Rumex vesicarium), otherwise known as wild rhubarb. **1895** F. Turner *Austral. Grasses* 49 In the New England district the '**wild sorghum**', when in flower, is quite a feature in the pastures, and is described as a valuable grass. **1903** G. Sutherland *Australasian Live Stock Man.* (ed. 2) 390 *Andropogon Australis* is sometimes called 'wild sorghum', and is fairly palatable to sheep in the cooler parts of Australia. **1907** *Emu* VI. 107 Seeds of what is locally called wild sorghum (*Chionachne barbata*). **1961** A.M. Duncan-Kemp *Our Channel Country* 10 Parakeelya, wild sorghum, rice-grass and barley grasses thrive there. **1793** J. Hunter *Hist. Jrnl. Trans. Port Jackson* 63 A convalescent [from scurvy] who had been sent from the hospital to gather **wild spinach** or other greens, was murdered by the natives. **1829** R. Mudie *Picture of Aust.* 149 Culinary vegetables there are none, with the exception of a species of wild spinach, which is found on the sandy shores, and which, though eagerly sought for there, would not be much esteemed in any other country. **1863** W.J. Wills *Successful Exploration Interior Aust.* 156 The banks are well lined with .. wild spinach. **1912** *Emu* XII. 84 A weed plentiful on the sand-ridges .. is known as wild spinach (*Tetragonia expansia*). **1918** C. Fetherstonhaugh *After Many Days* 238, I had a fine piece of spiced beef, also potatoes and some 'fat hen' (wild spinach). **1932** M.R. White *No Roads go By* 45 In season, given the rain, wild spinach or warrigal cabbage and other types of luscious herbage flourished at the more-or-less sheltered base of the sandhills. **1979** B. Hardy *World owes me Nothing* 25 Beside garden fruit and vegetables there were wild ones collected in the bush .. pigweed, wild spinach, and milk thistle. **1827** *HRA* (1923) 3rd Ser. VI. 267 An unpleasant smelling viscous plant, called by the Sealers '**Wild Tobacco**'. **1834** J.D. Lang *Hist. & Statistical Acct. N.S.W.* I. 371 My father .. pointed out to me several plants of wild or indigenous tobacco, which he had observed growing in the .. dry bed of a lagoon. **1887** *Illustr. Austral. News* (Melbourne) 21 Dec. 218/2 On the way many miles had to be forced through a species of wild tobacco plant common in Tasmania. **1903** *Proc. Linnean Soc. N.S.W.* XXVIII. 745 The Jew's Ear fungus .. is a regular article of export. .. It is chiefly collected on Wild Tobacco (*Solanum auriculatum*). **1921** K.S. Prichard *Black Opal* 79 A sulphur-coloured butterfly fluttered .. over a wild tobacco plant. **1973** R. Erickson et al. *Flowers & Plants W.A.* 198 In sheltered spots such as breakaways, delicate herbs are found, e.g. wild tobacco, *Nicotiana* species. **1986** *Your Garden* Jan. 23 *Solanum mauritianum* wild tobacco tree (NSW). **1825** *Howe's Weekly Commercial Express* (Sydney) 1 Aug. 3 Our **wild turkeys** are a species of bustard. **1839** J. Stephens *Land of Promise* 59 The finest bird of the game kind is the bustard or wild turkey. .. It is nearly as large as an English goose, and is delicious, but generally manages to keep out of the reach of a gun. **1850** *Australasian Sporting Mag.* 104 The .. Wild Turkey is a capital fellow, and an excellent dish. **1861** 'Old Bushman' *Bush Wanderings* 62 The *Wild Turkey* .. is a species of bustard, smaller, however, than the European bustard. **1881** *Illustr. Austral. News* (Melbourne) 7 Sept. 170/4 The Australian Bustard (choriotis Australis), or wild turkey, is to be found in many parts of Victoria. **1935** F. Birtles *Battle Fronts Outback* 53 The wild turkey .. is a grey bird standing about three feet high and weighing up to twenty pounds. **1970** K. Willey *Naked Island* 136 At dusk he killed a wild turkey, the big, slow bustard of the plain. **1899** *North-Western Advocate* (Devonport) 5 May 3/5 The land .. was literally covered with **wild turnip** of abnormal growth. **1966** A. Morris *Plantlife W. Darling* 64 *Sisymbrium orientale* .. very common. Introduced. Weed. Throughout the district. **1986** *Trees & Natural Resources* Mar. 2 The annual, Wild Turnip (*Brassica tournefortii*) and Poached Eggs Daisy .. became the dominant plants in the dune grasslands. **1916** *Bulletin*

(Sydney) 13 Apr. 24/3 Kosciusko and the Kiandra country, in midspring and early summer . . become matted with . . swamp lilies, the feathery **wild violets,** butter-cups, yams and thousands of unnamed plants. **1926** J. POLLARD *Bushland Man* 127 'This', he said, separating one, 'is the wild violet.' **1984** E. WALLING *On Trail Austral. Wildflowers* 5 Wild Violets, with their fan-like leaves of fresh rich green which carpet the ground . . and with their white and purple throated flowers. **1770** J. COOK *Jrnls.* 29 June (1955) I. 353 We found some **wild Yamms** or Coccos growing in the swampy grounds. **1820** C. JEFFREYS *Van Dieman's Land* 133 They are subject to numerous privations, particularly in the articles of tea, sugar, tobacco and bread; for this latter article, however, they substitute the wild yam. **1901** G. WHITE *Across Aust.* 5 The blacks gather the wild yams when in season. **1963** O. RUHEN *Flockmaster* 62 Having noticed . . the foliage of wild yams growing in a bushy glade, she took the knife and went to dig them. At least they would give body to the soup.

2. Of an Aboriginal or group of Aborigines, in the collocations **wild Aboriginal, black, blackfellow, fellow** (also *attrib.*), **man, native, nigger, tribe:** used **(a)** by whites, to designate an Aboriginal who is hostile to white society or who lives in a traditional manner and is independent of it; **(b)** by Aborigines, to designate an Aboriginal from another group or tribe.

1848 *Bell's Life in Sydney* 5 Feb. 1/2 The **wild aboriginal** stood on the banks of the brawling current. **1858** T. MCCOMBIE *Hist. Colony Vic.* 86 The semi-civilized tribes are far more deserving of pity than the wild free aborigines of the interior. **1896** W.H. WILLSHIRE *Land of Dawning* 72 The *Sydney Bulletin* holds the proud sway over all Australian print productions. It not only reaches the combos and stockmen of Central Australia, but . . wild aboriginals have used its red cover as the salient point of their costume. **1912** *Bull. N.T.* i. 48 Amongst the 'wild' aborigines no fever was present. **1959** A. UPFIELD *Bony & Mouse* 64 The wild aborigines have given examples of extraordinary proficiency, and for them foot-tracking is, indeed, an exact science. **1838** *S. Austral. Rec.* (London) (1839) 13 Mar. 159 We have no **wild blacks** nor wild beasts here. **1845** J. DREDGE *Brief Notices* 8 Europeans . . have found it impossible to avail themselves of the assistance of the native to any extent beyond their own country, unless they could well satisfy them of protection against the 'wild blacks'. **1855** G.H. WATHEN *Golden Colony* 74 They are regarded by the genuine diggers very much as 'native dogs' and wild blacks are by the squatters—a public pest, to be hunted down and exterminated. **1878** R.B. SMYTH *Aborigines of Vic.* I. 359 The natives of Gippsland were always regarded by their neighbours as 'wild blacks'. **1890** R.S. BROWNE *Romances Gold Field & Bush* 33 The wild blacks get away as quickly as possible after a raid. **1926** A.A.B. APSLEY *Amateur Settlers* 76 (*note*) 'Wild blacks' are those who have not come in contact with white men. **1981** A.B. FACEY *Fortunate Life* 29 He had been brought up in the bush with the wild blacks. **1842** *Portland Mercury* 7 Sept. 2/5 The aboriginal Roger . . still denies that he committed the murder, and says that it was done by other **wild black fellows.** **1846** *Portland Gaz.* 15 Sept. 4/5 Each tribe denominates as 'wild blackfellows' all others who are beyond the limits of its acquaintance. **1861** *Burke & Wills Exploring Exped.* 11 Our black boys are continually in dread lest the 'wild black fellows' should poison them by some means. **1906** *Bulletin* (Sydney) 22 Mar. 15/2 The 'smell' of a wild blackfellow is bad at any time; but, after a couple of feasts of goose-eggs—phew! **1916** S.A. WHITE *In Far Northwest* 36 During the afternoon the boys became very excited, and, pointing to footprints in soft sand, repeated 'Wild Blackfeller' several times. **1961** *Polynesian Soc. Jrnl.* (Wellington, N.Z.) June 203 Several older Adelaide women have said they would not visit the west coast . . for fear of unwittingly offending the 'wild blackfellers' who will always have their revenge. **1927** M. DORNEY *Adventurous Honeymoon* 34 Consider themselves a peg or two above the '**wild-feller** myall' who roams the bush and is not employed by the whites. **1935** H. BASEDOW *Knights of Boomerang* 20 Between themselves they had the closest ties of kinship. . . All outside the clique were 'wild-fellows'. **1867** J. BONWICK *J. Batman* 18 Now comes the interesting entry about the **wild man.** **1881** A.C. GRANT *Bush-Life Qld.* II. 189 They had come in sight of the wild men's camp. **1827** P. CUNNINGHAM *Two Yrs. in N.S.W.* II. 40 You must never strike one of the **wild natives,** unfamiliarized to Europeans, even if you detect them in theft—or they will revenge themselves by taking your life some time or other. **1845** *Portland Guardian* 6 Sept. 3/2 The aborigines in the district have been, we hear, mustering in large numbers near the big swamp, for the purpose of displaying their courage and dexterity in war. They are divided into two parties; the wild natives forming one, the tame the other, the latter is said to number three hundred. **1847** *Port Phillip Patriot* 23 Feb. 3/2 There is not now any European woman among the wild natives in Gipps Land. **1896** W.H. WILLSHIRE *Land of Dawning* 5 We all pretty well know why we carry revolvers on our belts—not only for **wild niggers.** **1893** *Bulletin* (Sydney) 9 Sept. 7/2 A Boulia (W.Q.) storekeeper has billed a certain quarrelsome wild-nigger partnership with the cost of 'nine paddlocks and two pairs of chains'. **1896** W.H. WILLSHIRE *Land of Dawning* 65 Neither the wild nigger up the tree nor my blackboys understood one word of that eloquent address. **1907** A. SEARCY *In Austral. Tropics* p. viii, A party of whites were on the island, and a mainland black boy they had with them was speared by the wild niggers. **1846** *Portland Guardian* 8 Dec. 3/3 It is hard to surmise what has been their fate, for it is evident that they were with the **wild tribes,** as the remains of their mia mias and capups are still in existence. **1878** R.B. SMYTH *Aborigines of Vic.* I. 367 This is one of the best native tomahawks I have seen. It was obtained from a wild tribe quite unacquainted with the acts of Europeans. **1886** F.A. HAGENAUER *Rep. Aboriginal Mission Ramahyuck, Vic.* 4, I have successfully completed the long desired missionary journey to the wild tribes of Aborigines in North Queensland.

3. Of a tract of land, in the collocations **wild bush, country, ground, land, pasture, territory:** unalienated; unimproved. See also WASTE.

1832 *Sydney Monitor* 11 Aug. 2/1 We are Colonists old enough to remember, when Liverpool was the **wild bush,** with a few acres of the trees felled, but not burnt off. **1852** *Austral. Gold Digger's Monthly Mag.* iii. 82 There was so much romance in the thing; being in the wild bush with kangaroos. **1877** *Illustr. Austral. News* (Melbourne) 14 May 74/4 The former 'wild bush' has been turned into grazing paddocks and orchard land. **1905** *Truth* (Sydney) 12 Mar. 3/2, I let a contract to have the land cleared and fenced in, as it is only wild bush. **1949** I.L. IDRIESS *One Wet Season* 95 A sixty mile ride was ahead, a rough sixty miles with no track, only wild bush. **1942** C. BARRETT *From Bush Hut* 7, I 'killed' and scattered my last camp-fire, coming down from **wild country,** the old way of living seemed to go. **1957** F. CLUNE *Fortune Hunters* 57 He made several long-distance patrols into 'wild' country. **1849** S. & J. SIDNEY *Emigrant's Jrnl.* 162, I will begin by describing the operations on taking a bush farm, that is, **wild** government **ground** covered with trees and grass never used before, except for feeding black fellows, kangaroos, cattle, horses and sheep. **1856** W.H.G. KINGSTON *Emigrant's Home* 10 They would buy two or three hundred acres of wild ground. **1839** *Sydney Standard* 1 Apr. 3/3 An appropriation of the *nett* proceeds of **wild lands,** has been very earnestly recommended. **1840** *Port Phillip Patriot* 23 July 2 The nett proceeds of the sales of wild lands . . should be applied to the purposes of immigration. **1841** *Launceston Courier* 15 Mar. 2/2 In Van Diemen's Land . . 12,090,476 acres of wild land remain ungranted. **1849** 'BUSHMAN' *Sidney's Austral. Handbk.* 61 In wild land, away from stations, as when on an overland journey to Port Philip and South Australia. **1839** *S. Austral. Rec.* (London) 10 Apr. 171 It may be expedient to reduce the rent of the **wild pastures.** **1840** *Sydney Herald* 19 June (Suppl.) 1/3 The Land Fund, arising from the sale of the **wild territory** of the Colony is to be reserved for immigration.

4. Of a domesticated animal: used to designate one which has strayed and established itself in the wild, and the progeny of such animals, esp. in the collocations **wild buffalo, cattle, herd, horse, mob, pig.**

1841 *Geelong Advertiser* 20 Sept. 4/2 It was in these luxuriant tracts that we started up large numbers of **wild buffaloes** and ponies, all as fat as our cattle at home when driven to market at Christmas time. **1910** *Huon Times* (Franklin) 2 Apr. 3/2 In the rich pastoral country along the Daly and Adelaide rivers in the north of Western Australia there are estimated to be . . 60,000 head of wild buffaloes. **1801** *HRA* (1915) 1st Ser. III. 11 Of the **wild cattle,** no other calculation can be made of them than that they are alive and increase fast in numbers. **1807** *Ibid.* (1916) 1st Ser. VI. 154 By the Wild Cattle is to be understood Animals which no barrier practicable to be made by us at present can confine. **1829** *Cornwall Press* (Launceston) 24 Mar. 36/2 Large numbers of wild cattle without any brand, were met with by the party lately in quest of the natives, among the fine marshes near St. Patrick's Head. **1846** *Cumberland Times* (Parramatta) 7 Feb. 4/2 Intelligence has been received that Captain Sturt was on his return from Adelaide. In the course of the expedition numberless herds of wild cattle were fallen in with, which were supposed to be composed of cattle that have strayed from the farthermost stations on this side of the continent, and those who have broken away from the overlanders, and their consequent (and in this colony rapid) increase. **1868** *Illustr. Sydney News* 7 Aug. 19/3 The increase of wild cattle in the thinly settled districts of Australia has long been a source of annoyance to the squatters. **1888** W.T. PYKE *Bush Tales* 34 Half-wild cattle have a constant tendency to acquire bad habits. **1920** *Smith's Weekly* (Sydney) 16 Oct. 17/4 As a wild-cattle persuader I haven't seen the equal of Albert Widders. . . He would, within an hour, without bail or leg-rope, milk a cow that was never before yarded. **1934** C. MACKNESS *Young Beachcombers* 162 When he wanted to pay his rates or invest in a chest of tea, he sold off some of his wild cattle, knowing that they would escape into the jungle and return to him when their unlucky purchaser took delivery. **1944** *Bulletin* (Sydney) 9 Aug. 13/1 The wild cattle seldom mixed with animals from the settled country. **1806** *HRA* (1915) 1st Ser. V. 675 The **Wild Herds** . . are now the exclusive property of the Crown. **1817** *Ibid.* (1917) 1st Ser. IX. 348, I do not believe there is above one fourth now remaining of the Wild Herds I saw myself. **1849** A. HARRIS *Emigrant Family* (1967) 64 Very wild herds . . require great height and strength of fence. **1881** A.C. GRANT *Bush-Life Qld.* I. 206 Numbers of ill-shaped, badly-bred bulls wander among the quiet cattle, and the presence of the wild herd induces the desertion to the scrubs of many of its members. **1854** S. SIDNEY *Gallops & Gossips* 40 It was at a spring in this flat that Long Peter, while cutting out some wild honey with a black, had caught sight of the **wild horses.** **1880** J.B. STEVENSON *Seven Yrs. Austral. Bush* 92 Thick vine-scrubs cover the sides and tops of the ranges, and through these the wild horses had cut numerous paths. **1896** N. GOULD *Town & Bush* 213 Occasional wild-horses, may be found in this mountainous district. **1881** A.C. GRANT *Bush-Life Qld.* I. 200 He is a large roan bullock . . that has been missing from the run for the last year or two, and has been seen to-day for the first time in that period. Most probably he has been away in the scrub with a **wild mob.** **1895** *Bulletin* (Sydney) 21 Dec. 27/4 To strongholds where the wild mobs hide The gully-rakers go. **1934** 'S. RUDD' *Green Grey Homestead* 61 How they knew the lay of the country, those two fellows, and every move of the wild mobs! **1854** F. ELDERSHAW *Aust. as it really Is* 122 Some of the Coast Scrubs are infested with large numbers of **Wild Pigs.** **1886** P. CLARKE *'New Chum' in Aust.* 214 The squatter has another enemy in the shape of wild pigs, the progeny of those long ago introduced by the early settlers. **1916** *Bulletin* (Sydney) 10 Feb. 24/3 Wild pig hunting is a profitable week-end spree. **1942** I.L. IDRIESS *Guerrilla Tactics* 7 Many a time I've gone wild-pig hunting with the northern abos into the jungle. **1980** *Sydney Morning Herald* 13 Oct. 3/4 The grass vanished, and paddocks became nothing but dirt, and wild pigs wore a clearly defined track to the station food bins.

5. In the collocation **wild colonial boy,** a bushranger (see quot. 1905); a larrikin (see LARRIKIN 2 a.).

c **1881** R.G. EDWARDS *Index Austral. Folk Songs* (1971) (song title), The wild colonial boy. **1905** A.B. PATERSON *Old Bush Songs* 33 'Tis of a wild Colonial boy, Jack Doolan was his name, Of poor but honest parents he was born in Castlemaine. **1948** F. CLUNE *Wild Colonial Boys* 27 A few bushrangers lived in caves and other hiding places . . harried by police and occasionally making raids. . . These were the original 'Wild Colonial Boys'. **1964** B. BEAVER *Hot Men* 77 Bert had chimed in with his sourly affectionate Cockney tones, 'Hark at that, Len, the original wild colonial boy'. **1967** R. STOW *Midnite* 127 Talked about the old days when Midnite was a wild Colonial boy. **1984** R.F. BRISSENDEN *Gough & Johnny were Lovers* 21 Oh, so loverly when professors never make a noise; Universities don't like the wild colonial boys.

6. In the adj. phr. **wild and woolly,** 'rough and ready'.

1936 I.L. IDRIESS *Cattle King* 85 Where shall we go now. . . Well then, say Queensland and the wild and woolly Paroo? **1941** *Somers Sun* 24 July 2 You have a wild and woolly time. **1965** R.H. CONQUEST *Horses in Kitchen* 194 The time the first mass-medium entertainment, radio, reached the wild-and-woolly parts. **1981** Q. WILD *Honey Wind* 77 Everyone pretends Australia is a wild and woolly country... 'But we've gone the way of the bush... Got too many shire engineers and council inspectors.'

wild cat, *n.*[1] *Native cat*, see NATIVE *a.* 6 b.

1831 *Acct. Colony Van Diemen's Land* 227 The skins of the opossum, of the wild and tiger cat . . and of several other animals, also fetch a tolerable price in England. **1845** J.O. BALFOUR *Sketch of N.S.W.* 26 The wild cat is the size of a rabbit, and is covered with a beautiful and speckled fur. **1859** W. KELLY *Life in Vic.* I. 240, I was promised some genuine . . wild-cat worrying. **1869** MRS W.M. HOWELL *Diggings & Bush* 16 'What is a wild cat like, papa?' 'It is a cat, my dear, with a small head and a spotted skin, which is very handsome.' **1884** *Austral. Tit-Bits* (Melbourne) 25 Dec. 14/2 My only companion being the native bear, opossum and wild cat, and even these seemed to make fun of me. **1962** B.W. LEAKE *Eastern Wheatbelt Wildlife* 51 This Wild cat (Dasyurus geoffroyi fortis) was more slender than the domestic cat, but very strong for its size.

wild cat, *n.*[2] [U.S. *wild cat* 'a mine of doubtful value or one serving as the basis of fraudulent transactions': see Mathews *n.* 2 b.] An unproductive mine; one falsely represented as productive. Also **wild-cat mine.**

1892 'A.M.' *From Aust. & Japan* 10 His prospects . . struck me about being on a par with those of a Queensland wild-cat mine after the directors and promoter-shareholders have succeeded in unloading every share of their scrip on a gullible London public. **1898** G.T. BELL *Coolgardie* 51 They get fat fees for their reports, but oft times they get rats, When the ten-ounce reef a duffer proves and the mines are called 'wild cats'. **1922** J. LEWIS *Fought & Won* 170 After some discussion M'Culloch told me that he would drive me around to see the other 'wild-cats' I was looking at. **1930** H. REDCLIFFE *Yellow Cygnet* 127 While they sat at their meal they spoke of gold; of the fields that were prospering; of those that were only 'wild cats'. **1936** J. KIRWAN *My Life's Adventure* 59 After these mines were pegged out there were many who condemned them as 'wild cats'. It was said that it was a shame to attempt to foist them on the public as worth working. **1947** F. CLUNE *Roaming around Aust.* 76 As a result, Pearce and Brookman kept on pegging—and they pegged out 'the Golden Square Mile'. Everybody said it was a 'Wild Cat'. **1962** O. PRYOR *Aust.'s Little Cornwall* 92 Not all the mining shows outside the original Wallaroo and Moonta leases of the type known in business circles as 'wild cats'.

wilga, var. WILGIE.

wilga /'wɪlgə/. [a. Wiradhuri *wilgar*.] A shrub or small tree of the genus *Geijera* (fam. Rutaceae), esp. *G. parviflora* of inland e. Aust., having a spreading crown and pendulous foliage; SHEEP BUSH. Also *attrib.*

1887 W.H. SUTTOR *Austral. Stories Retold* 127 Near the hut is a large wilgar tree, the most shapely and beautiful of all trees in that region. **1889** J.H. MAIDEN *Useful Native Plants Aust.* 130 *Geijera parviflora* . . 'Wilga'... Sheep only are particularly fond of this bush, and it seems quite unaffected by droughts. **1891** 'R. BOLDREWOOD' *Sydney-Side Saxon* (1925) 182 She'd always said she'd like to be buried there, down by the creek, and under a spreading wilga tree. **1903** F. TURNER *Bot. Darling, N.S.W.* 410 The 'wilga' (*Geijera parviflora*) . . is often, and I think rightly, described as the most graceful tree of the interior. **1915** E.M. WEETWOOD *Lure of Land* 43 A small clump of beehive-shaped wilgas grew inside the enclosure. **1936** F. CLUNE *Roaming round Darling* 120 The wilga is specially suited for sheep, who . . squat on their haunches and nibble the leaves overhead. **1957** —— *Fortune Hunters* 13 Level sheep country, sparsely treed with wilga, mulga, saltbush and bastard box. **1978** K. GARVEY *Tales of my Uncle Harry* 28 He staggers up to a wilga and collapses in the shade. **1986** *Sun-Herald* (Sydney) 26 Jan. 7/1 Property owners had begun noticing kurrajongs and wilgas losing their leaves.

wilgie /'wɪlgi/. Chiefly *W.A.* Also **wilga, wilghi, wilgi, wilgy.** [a. Nyungar *wilgi*.] A red ochre used by Aborigines to paint the body on ceremonial occasions.

1836 H.W. BUNBURY *Early Days W.A.* (1930) 83 The Wilghi, which is a preparation of red earth and grease, constitute their favourite ornament and covering. **1840** T.J. BUCKTON *W.A.* 96 Both smear themselves with a pigment they call wilga, which is red, and mixed with grease. **1857** W.S. BRADSHAW *Voyages* 101 The natives are a very dirty race, they take a delight in smearing themselves with grease and wilgie. **1902** *Proc. R. Soc. Qld.* (1903) XVII. 58 A sort of red ochre, wil-gi . . was used with fat for smearing over the body. **1929** W.J. RESIDE *Golden Days* 162 Native ochre, or what the natives call 'wilgi', is the material used for the painting of their bodies. **1962** B.W. LEAKE *Eastern Wheatbelt Wildlife* 58 Among granite hills in the Eastern Wheatbelt caves are often located, under the inside roofs of which an aborigine has at some time held one hand firmly with the fingers spread out and sprinkled wilgie (the natives reddish powdered paint) between the fingers and around the hand. **1970** J. DAVIS *First-Born* 23 He squats on a narrow ledge in the summer shade; A spear and an axe of stone lay at his side: The wilgy, gently moulded, mixed with care and pride. **1985** M. WALSH *May Gibbs* 31 The Gibbs . . were involved in the establishment in 1890 of a society to encourage the development of young artists' work called the Wilgie Club—'wilgie' being a native name for coloured clay.

wilgied, *a.* [f. prec.] Painted with WILGIE.

1840 A. HASLUCK *Portrait with Background* (1955) 192 They dislike Flowers, and will not suffer any one to be placed on their heads... I never knew any but one . . who permitted me at Augusta to place a large piece of the crimson Antirrhinum in his Wilgied Locks. **1847** E.W. LANDOR *Bushman* 191 Why . . should he be violently dragged from the arms of his *wilgied* squaws, and his little pot-bellied piccaninnies. **1863** *Jrnls. & Rep. Two Voyages Glenelg River* 30 July (1864) 24 There is a red ochreous stain upon them [*sc.* Aborigines' canoes] here and there to be detected, but we account for these as having been communicated from the wilgied persons, or they possibly have been designedly covered with wilgi (red ochre).

wilgy, var. WILGIE.

wilja, var. WILTJA.

will, *v.* In the interrogative phr. **wouldn't it?,** see WOULD.

William.

1. Joc. substitution for BILLY *n.*[1] 1.

1902 *Bulletin* (Sydney) 26 Apr. 3/2 The William-cans are loaded at the hostel 'cross the road. **1908** *Ibid.* 2 Jan. 15/1 None but a flaming jackass would credit two light twigs with power to restrain a william-full of water. **1920** *Land of Lyre Bird* (S. Gippsland Pioneers' Assoc.) 73 It is astonishing how unshapely the William can be without interfering with its capacity for producing the bushman's elixir of life, billy tea. **1925** *Bulletin* (Sydney) 19 Mar. 24/2, I left my william-can at home one day.

2. In the phr. **William the Third,** rhyming slang for 'turd'.

1968 *Swag* (Sydney) iv. 26 What a nasty-minded, thoroughly suspicious little William the Third he is. **1972** *Bulletin* (Sydney) 19 Aug. 6/3, I understand from producer Phillip Adams, they needed a special truck filled with rubbish to give Earls Court the ideal English atmosphere. They even had to gather dog 'William the Thirds' to put on the pavement. **1979** B. HUMPHRIES *Bazza comes into his Own*, Them robbers always leave a helluva lot of William the Thirds on the carpet when they've done some poor bastard's nice home.

willie wagtail, var. WILLY WAGTAIL.

willing, *a.* [Spec. use of *willing* without reluctance.] Vigorous; aggressive. Freq. in the collocation **willing go,** a vigorous contest.

1899 *Bulletin* (Sydney) 12 Aug. 14/2 Came across two wallabies having such a 'willing go' that they let me come within a dozen yards. **1907** *Truth* (Sydney) 28 July 5/8 The battle for the Lachlan promises to be 'a willing go' between little Jimmy Caroll . . and Anti-pothat 'Andy' Kelly, the present Labor member. **1921** C.E.W. BEAN *Official Hist. Aust. 1914–18* IV. 339 The fighting (says Sergeant Downes, who was present) was 'very willing', the Germans coming at the bombing parties several times. **1975** *Bulletin* (Sydney) 26 Apr. 45/3 He was willing (courageous and daring) and would jeopardise his own safety . . so that the bagman (the take man carrying a bag) could get out of the store with the booty.

willow. [Transf. use of *willow* a plant of the genus *Salix*, having long, narrow, pendulous leaves and occurring along watercourses.]

1. Any of several trees or shrubs resembling the willow, incl. species of *Acacia* (fam. Mimosaceae), and *willow myrtle*. Also *attrib.*

1826 J. ATKINSON *Acct. Agric. & Grazing N.S.W.* 4 In willow brushes the ground is more or less covered with the white or woolly gum trees, and underneath thickly covered with what is termed in the Colony willow brush, growing to the height of 2 or 3 feet. **1831** W. BLAND *Journey of Discovery Port Phillip* 58 Mr Hume recognized . . the willow of the colony . . which is common in Van Diemen's Land . . and is there called the black wood. **1846** C.W. SCHÜRMANN *Aboriginal Tribes Port Lincoln* 6 The willow, and another shrub named purrenye, exude . . some gum of the colour and transparency of sugar-candy. **1889** J.H. MAIDEN *Useful Native Plants Aust.* 306 *Acacia calamifolia* . . 'Willow', or 'Broom Wattle'. 'Wallowa' of the aboriginals at Lake Hindmarsh Station (Victoria). **1902** *Emu* II. 71 Some 'willow' undergrowth in a karri forest. **1915** *Bull. N.T.* xiv. 10 In Coomera Valley (metamorphic) we find . . a fodder acacia (known as willow) . . and various other trees. **1928** J. POLLARD *Bushland Vagabonds* 212 The forest floor was clean by comparison with the karri-clad slope, where . . bottlebrush, willow, and others climbed with and closely hugged the grand white trees. **1934** W.A. OSBORNE *Visitor to Aust.* 62 The visitor, therefore, when he hears such terms as . . willow (the indigenous and not the imported), box, hickory, and others must not expect striking resemblances to the originals.

2. Special Comb. **willow myrtle,** the tree or shrub *Agonis flexuosa* (see PEPPERMINT 2); **wattle,** any of several trees or shrubs of the genus *Acacia* (fam. Mimosaceae), usu. having pendulous foliage and occurring along watercourses, esp. *A. salicina* (see COOBA); formerly also **willow-leaved acacia.**

1898 E.E. MORRIS *Austral Eng.* 513 **Willow Myrtle** . . a tree, *Agonis flexuosa* . . native of West Australia, and cultivated for ornament as a greenhouse shrub. **1965** *Austral. Encycl.* VI. 237 The willow myrtle . . is much planted in the eastern States for shade and ornament; it has pendulous branches and drooping willow-like foliage. **1986** *Age* (Melbourne) 28 Oct. 32/2 *Agonis flexuosa*, also called the willow myrtle (in both green and variegated forms) and a number of callistemon . . are other native trees which would have pride of place. **1835** [**willow wattle**] *Hobart Town Almanack* 62 *Acacia saligna?* Willow leaved Acacia. A fragrant flowering species, forming a large shrub. **1860** *Sydney Mail* 27 Oct. 3/3 Our botanist may find . . some of the willow-leaved acacias, &c., here. **1914** E.E. PESCOTT *Native Flowers Vic.* *Acacia salicina*, the 'willow wattle', so called from the similarity of its foliage to that of the willow, is a very decorative species. **1921** A.J. CAMPBELL *Golden Wattle* 50 The Willow Wattle . . of Riverina also sometimes flowers during 'Fiery February'. **1965** *Austral. Encycl.* III. 38 Cooba, the aboriginal name and still the vernacular for the pendulous and mainly riparian inland tree *Acacia salicina*, for which 'willow wattle' has now been standardized in the timber trade. **1981** L. COSTERMANS *Native Trees & Shrubs S.-E. Aust.* 107 Small tree; green leaves thinnish, willowy . . Willow Wattle.

willy, *n.*[1] Abbrev. of WILLY WILLY 1.

1906 *Bulletin* (Sydney) 23 Aug. 16/3 A recent 'willy' unroofed a house on the outskirts of the township. **1929** W.J. RESIDE *Golden Days* 341 Soon gathered to witness the 'willy'. **1935** H.H. PARRY *Girl of West* 13 In the land where the 'willies' blow. **1950** A.W. UPFIELD *Widows of Broome* 10 Every house is protected with storm shutters, some even wire-cabled to the ground, for when the summer willies blow they are apt to lift more than dust. **1977** B. FULLER *Nullarbor Lifelines* 40 There is nothing to break the force of the winds, and they blow very fiercely at times... The 'willies' are the terror of all, especially of the boarding house people.

willy, *n.*[2] [Unexplained use of a form of the name

William.] The amount of money at one's disposal, esp. for betting; money; a wallet.

1949 L. GLASSOP *Lucky Palmer* 36 Two quid? Break it down. That's me willie. That's all I got. **1967** *Kings Cross Whisper* (Sydney) xliii. 11/3 *Willy*, a wallet. **1975** *Bulletin* (Sydney) 26 Apr. 45/3 'So we send in Limp to tug the tart minding the willy.' . . It was this woman who was guarding the willy (money). **1977** J. RAMSAY *Cop it Sweet* 96 *Willy*: Supply of betting money; wallet.

willy nilly. [f. *willy-nilly, adv.* whether one likes it or not.] Fanciful alteration of WILLY WILLY 1.

1920 *N.T. Times* (Darwin) 10 Jan. 5/2 The men were Japanese and had been fishing and had secured a good haul when a willy nilly came along and upset the boat. **1946** K.S. PRICHARD *Roaring Nineties* 245 Sometimes a willy-nilly would whirl along, deluging dinner and diners with red dust. **1955** J. CLEARY *Justin Bayard* 185 A willy-nilly of dust rose up and spun away over the trees.

willy-wag.

1. Abbrev. of WILLY WAGTAIL.

1938 F. BLAKELEY *Hard Liberty* 178 It is almost impossible to hunt if a couple of willy-wags decide to accompany the hunter. **1958** *Bulletin* (Sydney) 24 Sept. 18/3 A jacky-winter . . is on equal terms with the willy-wag and not over-awed even by a maggie.

2. Rhyming slang for 'swag'.

1905 J. MEREDITH *Learn to talk Old Jack Lang* (1984) 12, I . . finished up in the dead house, broke to the wide. But they left me my *Willy Wag* and gave me a bit of tucker. **1964** D. LOCKWOOD *Up Track* 100 'Well, mate,' George said, 'I'm going to roll out the willy-wag. I'm on watch at three-thirty for two and a half hours.'

willy wagtail. Also **willie wagtail.** [Transf. use of *willy-wagtail* the water wagtail *Motacilla lugubris*.] The black and white bird *Rhipidura leucophrys*, widespread in Aust. and occurring elsewhere, sometimes confused with the RESTLESS FLYCATCHER; *black and white fantail*, see BLACK *a.*[2] 1 b.; SHEPHERD'S COMPANION; WAGGY. See also WAGTAIL.

1885 MRS C. PRAED *Head Station* II. 151 A brisk little willy-wagtail hopping about on the gravel. **1896** A.J. NORTH *List Insectivorous Birds N.S.W.* i. 13 'Black and White Fantail'. . . From this bird's habit of constantly swaying its lengthened tail feathers from side to side it is locally known in many districts as the 'Willy Wagtail'. **1905** *Steele Rudd's Mag.* (Brisbane) Oct. 833 She's got setch a haughty walk with her, swingin' her hind skirts about east and west like a Willie-Wagtail. **1917** *Bulletin* (Sydney) 17 May 22/2 The vocabulary of willy wagtail, or black and white fantail (jirri jirri and pulcherry of the blacks) is about the best known of any bird in the bush. **1933** N. LINDSAY *Saturdee* (1936) 46, I been missin' eggs for a long time. . . Lost two willie-wagtails and a bonzer white spadger's. **1953** D. CUSACK *Southern Steel* 138 The beer's on the nose and the plonk'd make a willy-wagtail fight an emu. **1973** *Meanjin* 254 The chirpings of birds woke him at daylight. He lay still, trying to identify them. One he was sure was a willi-wag-tail. **1984** SIMPSON & DAY *Birds of Aust.* 323 The familiar, misnamed Willie Wagtail is a fantail, not a wagtail (Motacillidae); it occurs throughout Australia (except Tasmania).

willy willy /'wɪli wɪli/. Chiefly *n.w. Aust.* [a. Yinjibarndi *wili wili*.]

1. A whirlwind: see quot. 1898.

1894 *Age* (Melbourne) 20 Jan. 13/4 The Willy Willy is the name given to these periodical storms by the natives in the north west. **1898** R. RADCLYFFE *Wealth & Wild Cats* 70 'Willie-willies' . . are water-spouts made of sand instead of water. . . They usually begin upon a very small scale . . a dancing column of dust, dung, dead flies, and old paper. Give them time and they will show sport. But the 'willie-willie' has no perseverance; he lacks continued effort, and the slightest opposition in the shape of a tin hut or a telegraph pole so destroys his symmetry that he dies of disgust in a small heap of refuse. But with plenty of room he becomes rampant. When he gets over fifty feet high his power is vast. **1909** *Bulletin* (Sydney) 4 Feb. 13/1 And paint the town till, dazed and dilly, With drinking, girling, The world seems one vast willy-willy, About us whirling. **1918** *Truth* (Sydney) 3 Feb. 1/6 Westralia has its Willy-Willys. On this side we have Willie and Billee. All stormy subjects. **1933** J.M. HARCOURT *Pearlers* 18 The pearling crews feared them only less than the 'willy-willies', the cyclones of the Nor'-west coast. **1944** 'S. CAMPION' *Pommy Cow* 268 Several hundred little inch-high willy-willies, bred by the parent storm, continuing their spinning dance along the desert. **1961** *N. Austral. Monthly* Dec. 44 Willy-willies sent reddish spirals upwards as they advanced across the drought-stricken plains. **1975** X. HERBERT *Poor Fellow my Country* 421 They saw a pillar of the dust rising like a willy-willy. **1981** Q. WILD *Honey Wind* 11 He came in over the long expanse of hot bitumen and saw the willy-willies churning the dust beside him.

2. *transf.* and *fig.* Also *attrib.*

1928 J. POLLARD *Bushland Vagabonds* 8 The little black pony Johnny was riding shied nervously as the dust rose about her feet in a tiny willy-willy. **1939** K. TENNANT *Foveaux* 254 A willy-willy of words sprang up, a blown dust-spout in the path of an oncoming storm. **1950** G. FARWELL *Surf Music* 133 Now, a man, caught up in these willywillies of his passion, doesn't stop to analyse things. **1972** *Bulletin* (Sydney) 29 July 44/1 Woodsreef Mines Ltd. has . . overcome what must be something of a record willy-willy of directors, to put together and get working Australia's largest asbestos operation to date. **1974** C. THIELE *Albatross Two* 135 Andy ran hands through his willy-willy hair. 'Aren't we poetic this morning?'

3. Comb. **willy-willy season.**

1914 *Pastoral Rev.* 16 Feb. 110 The summer rains already received . . will be followed up during the Willy Willy season in March. **1937** I.L. IDRIESS *Forty Fathoms Deep* 161 March is a dangerous month in the willy-willy season. **1947** H. DRAKE-BROCKMAN *On N.-W. Skyline* 34 It was the Lay-up—the willy-willy season when all the fleet was in. **1954** N. BARTLETT *Pearl Seekers* 122 They spent most of this money in the pubs at Cossack and Roebourne during the enforced lay-up, from November to March, the dreaded willy-willy season.

wiltja /'wɪltjə/. Also **wilja.** [a. Western Desert language *wilja*.] An Aboriginal shelter. See also GUNYAH.

1950 V.E. TURNER *Ooldea* 136 There are three kinds of native homes—houses (karrpa), shelter (wilja) and breakwinds (yaw). **1974** *Rep. Desert Housing Task Force* (R. Austral. Inst. Architects) 3 As an alternative cover for steel or water pipe framed wiltjas, the Task Force recommends . . glass reinforced plastic with an aluminium coating. **1979** M. HEPPELL *Black Reality* 143 Transition to European-style houses is one of these. It must be recognised by those in authority that transition from *wiltja* to house does not involve only a modification to customs. **1983** N. GREEN *Desert School* 4 Soon the mission grew quiet as Aborigines and Wyalpula withdrew into the shade of wiltjas and houses to escape the hellish sun. **1986** *Good Weekend* (Sydney) 26 Apr. 62/3 The local community is building a traditional wiltja (hut).

Wimmera /'wɪmərə/. [The name of a region of w. Victoria.] Used *attrib.* in the name of **Wimmera rye-grass,** the Mediterranean annual grass *Lolium rigidum* (fam. Poaceae), widely sown as a pasture grass, and also naturalized and sometimes regarded as a weed. Also **Wimmera rye.**

1920 *Proc. R. Soc. Vic.* XXXII. 199 'Wimmera Rye Grass'. . . This is a new record as a naturalised alien in Victoria. **1923** E. BREAKWELL *Grasses & Fodder Plants N.S.W.* 175 *Lolium subulatum* (Wimmera Rye grass) . . is really a form of *Lolium rigidum* and has gained some reputation as an annual winter grass in the Wimmera districts of Victoria. **1928** R.G. STAPLEDON *Tour in Aust. & N.Z.* 74 A grass which has come into great prominence in recent years is the so-called Wimmera rye-grass (*Lolium subulatum*). It would seem as if this grass first appeared in Victoria, presumably as a stowaway, about thirty years ago. **1966** N.T. BURBIDGE *Austral. Grasses* I. 118 Wimmera Rye . . is one of the most important annual grasses in improved pastures, especially when used in rotation with cereals.

wind-grass. The grass *Aristida contorta* (see *mulga grass* MULGA B. 3).

1845 L. LEICHHARDT *Jrnl. Overland Exped. Aust.* 21 July (1847) 339 This was not covered with the stiff grass, nor the dry wind-grass of the plains north of the Staaten. **1863** G.W. EARL *Handbk. for Colonists Tropical Aust.* 45 The scrubby country had a good supply of tufty wind-grass. **1929** K.S. PRICHARD *Coonardoo* (1961) 69 He saw wind-grass growing among the rocks, tufts as fine and yellow as mulga blossom. **1978** D. STUART *Wedge-tail View* 57 Spinifex plains, wind-grass plains, mulga country.

Windies, *pl.* [Contraction of *West Indies*. Used elsewhere but recorded earliest in Aust.] A nickname for the West Indian cricket team. Also in *sing.*, a member of this team.

1964 K. MACKAY *Slasher opens Up* 89 This impulsive batting is crowd-pleasing stuff, but should never be recommended. But the 'Windies'—and more power to them—are not meant to be shackled by convention. **1975** *Herald* (Melbourne) 11 Oct. 27/1 Whirlwinds from the Windies. . . It won't be another Bodyline series, but the Tests between Australia and the West Indies this summer will be a blood and guts battle of brute speed. **1978** *Sporting Globe* (Melbourne) 1 Apr. 3/2 Stormy blast hits Windies. **1984** P. JARRATT *Aussie* 109 It doesn't matter whether he's a Pommie, Windie or Kiwi, if he hits our Lillee or Lawson over the fence. **1985** *Sun* (Melbourne) 7 Jan. 31/2 Banners tacked to the fence forecast the Windies ugly fate.

windmill grass. [See quot. 1983.] Any of several grasses (fam. Poaceae), usu. bearing a digitate flower-head; often of the genus *Chloris*, esp. the widespread *C. truncata* of all mainland States; STAR GRASS.

1889 J.H. MAIDEN *Useful Native Plants Aust.* 80 *Chloris truncata* . . 'Windmill Grass' . . is perennial and showy, an excellent summer and autumn grass, of ready growth, and relished by stock. **1905** *Proc. Linnean Soc. N.S.W.* XXX. 48 The 'windmill grasses' (*Chloris* spp.) and species of *Eragrostis* are also prominent amongst the pasture herbage. **1923** E. BREAKWELL *Grasses & Fodder Plants N.S.W.* 182 Star or Windmill grass comes very quickly on land that has been cultivated. **1968** N.T. BURBIDGE *Austral. Grasses* II. 144 Windmill Grass is a widespread summer-growing native species which may behave as an annual under dry conditions. **1983** G.G. ROBINSON *Native Grasses Northern Tablelands* 11 Windmill grass is easily recognised by its windmill like flower. It forms a dense turf of pale green folded leaves. On the tablelands it is not a highly productive species and its hard leaves are not relished by sheep.

windmill magistrate. *Obs.* See quot. 1869.

1869 J. MARTINEAU *Lett. from Aust.* 134 Lest the term *Windmill Magistrate* should be unintelligible to those who are not fully initiated into the mysteries of colonial democracy, perhaps I should explain that there have been persons aspiring . . to the honour of being magistrates whose early education was not very comprehensive, and who, not being able to sign their names, were in the habit of affixing their mark X instead. The supposed resemblance of this mark to the sails of a windmill suggested the term. **1918** *Bulletin* (Sydney) 1 Aug. (Red Page), During one of the Ministries of Henry Parkes in the 'seventies, that consummate old general smoothed out a somewhat ruffled political situation by a judicious and generous creation of Jay Pees. So generous . . that a number . . could not read or write and signed their names with an X. The resemblance of this monogram to the sails of a windmill suggested the happy appellation of 'windmill magistrates'.

wind-whirly: see WHIRLY.

wine. Used *attrib.* in Special Comb. **wine cask,** see CASK; **dot** [pun on *Wyandotte* a breed of fowl], an habitual drinker of cheap wine; **saloon,** an establishment licensed to sell wine only; **shanty,** SHANTY *n.*[1] a.

1940 *Sentry Go* (Keswick) Dec. 24/2 In an hotel near Adelaide . . a chap, apparently a '**wine-dot**'. **1953** T.A.G. HUNGERFORD *Riverslake* 35 'Is he a wine-dot?' 'Is he hell! . . He's never off it.' **1968** J. ALARD *He who shoots Last* 229 Obviously an old wine dot whose reeking body . . bore grim evidence of the downward path the poor unfortunate had trodden. **1980** HEPWORTH & HINDLE *Boozing out in Melbourne Pubs* 15 Those who followed the Bacchic way were variously known as plonk fiends or artists, plonkos, winos, bombo bashers, winedots and wyandottes. **1933** H.B. RAINE *Lash End* 88 She strutted away to the nearest **wine saloon.** **1963** X. HERBERT *Disturbing Element* 164 Of course the wine saloon has been an all-Australian institution; but I don't think the attitude to wine drinking was ever in the other States what it was in W.A. **1878** *Squatter's Plum* 16 As a rule, he [*sc.* the station hand with cheque] has not far to go in search of friendly voices. The sly grog-shop or the **wine-shanty** stands on the road-side ready to receive him with open door... At length, partially drugged with the insidious liquor, he consents to trust his cheque in the publican's possession, and 'shouts' at random for all comers. **1972** ANDERSON & BLAKE *J.S. Neilson* 18 Abe Crabtree conducted the mail depot and a wine shanty. **1975** *Bulletin* (Sydney) 12 July 5/2 This precludes the setting up of any so-labelled 'wine shanties': it requires considerable capital investment, plus stringent council requirements and regulations, to set up a cider tavern with all the facilities that must be included. **1978** W. HOWCROFT *Dungarees & Dust* 41 Two itinerant workers in a bush wine shanty began quarrelling violently.

wing, *n.*[1]

a. A fence, usu. one of a pair, built out from a stock yard and serving to guide or channel stock towards its entrance: see quot. 1888 (2). Also **wing fence.**

1887 K. MACKAY *Stirrup Jingles* 16 Gone is the rush and rattle Of pikers on the rails, When wings were full of cattle, And thongs came down like flails. **1888** 'R. BOLDREWOOD' *Robbery under Arms* (1937) 14 There was a 'wing' ran a good way out through the scrub—there's no better guide to a yard like that. **1888** W.T. PYKE *Bush Tales* 37 Two side fences, called 'wings', are carried out in front of the enclosures, extending to a distance of 10 or 12 roods. These are sufficiently wide at the outer extremities to admit at once the whole herd. **1891** D. FERGUSON *Vicissitudes Bush Life* 7 See how long he's been putting up the stockyards and wing fences to run her into. **1892** B. MORANT *Poetry* (1980) 5 Our stockwhips in the stilly night like rifle-shots would ring When we beat them on the Bilbee Flat and slewed 'em to the wing; And when we had 'em yarded [etc.]. *c* **1899** 'SANDALWOOD NUTT' *Tarragal* 24 We have had two good yards erected, with long wings, so that with a fair run of luck, we should make a good haul out of the Warrigals. **1962** *N.T. News* (Darwin) 4 Jan. 11/4 Council had inspected the existing set-up which has a gap between two wing fences at the Northern end.

b. Special Comb. **wing yard,** a stock yard of this sort; also **winged yard.**

1916 *Bulletin* (Sydney) 13 July 24/1 The whole district turned out to round up kangaroos and yard them. We camped out overnight and started the 'drive' at daybreak into a wing-yard. **1945** F. CORK *Tales from Cattle Country* 34 Well-trained 'coachers' lure the brumbies into a winged yard. The 'coachers' are broken station horses which have been at the game for years.

2. a. The flank of a travelling mob of sheep, cattle, etc. Also *attrib.*

1895 A.B. PATERSON *Man from Snowy River* 6 So Clancy rode to wheel them—he was racing on the wing Where the best and boldest riders take their place. **1913** W.H. OGILVIE *Overlander* 66 The sheep are running a mile a-head, And there, whenever the leaders string, Laggards loiter, or wing-sheep spread, Every kelpie's a king. **1917** A.L. BREWER *'Gators' Euchre* 96 The lead drover digs his spurs into his horse's sides; the animal plunges forward towards the right wing; and he canters round and shouts a few words to one of the wing drovers. **1919** *Bulletin* (Sydney) 17 July 22/3 'Steve Hart' asked.. whether a dog 'on the wing', or ringing a mob of sheep, should turn out or in when coming back. **1920** L. ESSON *Dead Timber* 40 That baldy-faced piker gets slewing out on the left wing. **1931** F.D. DAVISON *Man-Shy* (1962) 85 'Barney,' he added, 'you and Splinter had better take one wing.' **1954** T. RONAN *Vision Splendid* 156 Mr Toppingham, being on the wing or the tail, had no chance to see they had left the stock pads.

b. *transf.* A number of livestock detached from the main body, esp. illicitly.

1943 H.G. LAMOND *From Tariaro to Ross Roy* 33 The sheep were shepherded and enclosed in brush yards at night. If a wing of a flock was lost.. that lost flock would be torn by dingoes. **1947** W.E. HARNEY *Brimming Billabongs* 153 So we would go over the hills to the big cattle runs and there would take over a 'wing'—a certain number of mixed cattle—and these we would drive home, to hold them in the pockets of the salt-water arms until the calves were big enough to be weaned from their mothers and branded with Bob's station brand. **1966** T. RONAN *Strangers on Ophir* (rev. ed.) 52 Some of those blokes from the Georgina could slip and lift a wing of good butchers' cattle before you knew anything about it.

c. A team or group.

1976 S. WELLER *Bastards I have Met* 76 The bloke looking after it was a real good urger and he's got a wing of young blokes around him giving them the spiel.

wing, *n.*[2] *Obs.* [Of unknown origin.] A penny.

c **1907** W.C. CHANDLER *Darkest Adelaide* 58 What, 'arfa caser, and I have to sling a bob for the room out of it. Only eighteen wing for myself? Can't do it. **1936** W. HATFIELD *Aust. through Windscreen* 2 'I've only one-and-six.'.. 'Tell you what... Gimme the eighteen wing and we'll go inside and shout the house.'

winger. [f. WING *n.*[1] 2 a.] A stockman controlling the flank of a travelling mob.

1951 E. HILL *Territory* 293 A ringer riding ahead, wingers on the flank, and the boss drover behind, they string out and move off.

wingman. *Australian National Football.* A player in the wing position.

1931 J.F. MCHALE et al. *Austral. Game of Football* 60 The half-backs on the flanks and the wing men should in most cases play out towards the fence, unless the centre and the half-forward centre are absolutely unguarded, when an easy pass is possible. **1963** L. RICHARDS *Boots & All!* 133 Dixon must be rated as one of the best wingmen Melbourne has ever had. **1973** J. DUNN *How to play Football* 62 It is obvious.. that pace is tremendously important for the wingman, and it is more than just an Australian Rules tradition. Let's face it, the wingman has to send his team into attack and must always be alert for breakaways that can slice open even the tightest defences.

winking owl. [See quots. 1905 and 1968.] *Barking owl*, see BARKING.

1844 J. GOULD *Birds of Aust.* (1848) I. Pl. 34, *Athene connivens.* Winking Owl. **1905** *Emu* IV. 128 Winking Owl (*Ninox connivens*)... The.. eyes.. constantly 'winking' (conniving), hence the specific name. **1916** *Bulletin* (Sydney) 20 Jan. 24/4 Along the creek the gooragang (winking owl) and the boobook shout greetings all night. **1968** D. FLEAY *Nightwatchmen* 71 Known as the Winking Owl in the official checklist and in various bird books, this strong, golden-eyed bird actually does not blink or wink any more than do other Australian owls.

wipe, *v. trans.* To dismiss, discard, disown (esp. a person).

1941 K. TENNANT *Battlers* 196 Giving her money.. in the casual manner that wiped her from all consideration as a human being. **1946** *Coast to Coast 1945* 123 Listen pal—your girl wiped you, didn't she? **1954** T.A.G. HUNGERFORD *Sowers of Wind* 162 She dumped me, wiped me like a dirty nose. **1965** E. LAMBERT *Long White Night* 64 'We'll have a drink,' I told them. 'Then I'm wiping you two like a dirty floor. I've got a message from Australia to deliver to one of the local citizens. I'll see you tonight.' **1975** R. BEILBY *Brown Land Crying* 295 You can wipe that idea, if that's what you're thinking. **1983** P. WHITE *Netherwood* 36 Suspended once—but they didn't wipe me.

wipe-off.

1. A total loss, a 'write-off'.

1945 *Victory Roll* 59 One slip in this work and pilot and aircraft were a 'wipe-off'. **1945** L. JILLETT *Moresby's Few* 96 The Kittyhawk.. was a 'wipe-off'.

2. A 'sure thing'.

1946 *They wrote it Themselves* (W.A.A.A.F.) 18 *It's a wipe-off*, or I *thought I could swing it* both mean *it's in the bag.*

wira, var. WIRRA *n.*[1]

wire.

1. In the phr. **straight wire.**

a. The complete truth; an honest account.

1892 'J. MILLER' *Workingman's Paradise* 104 If I was pretty flush.. I'd waltz right up to him.. to ask the time, and if he came any of his law-de-dah squatter funny business on me I'd give him the straight wire, I promise you. **1920** A.G. HALES *McGlusky Gold-Seeker* 205 Is that a straight wire or a leg pull? **1955** N. PULLIAM *I traveled Lonely Land* 237 Why I'd even make it for the Olympics.. and that's the straight wire.

b. As adj. phr., honest.

1908 'FIFTY-THREE YRS.' MINER' *So Long* 20 Is it another 'fairy' or a 'straight-wire' yarn?

c. As adv. phr., truly; honestly.

1917 P. AUSTEN *Bill-Jim* 27 These 'ighfaluten tikes gives me th' 'ump—Straite wire, I'd like ter douse em in th' pump. **1949** C. BENHAM *Diver's Luck* 108 Well, Jim, I'm telling you, straight-wire, that I won't get drinking.

2. Special Comb. **wire door,** *fly door*, see FLY *n.*[1] 1; **fake,** *v. intr.*, to make wire clothes pegs, toasting forks, etc.; freq. as *vbl. n.*; so **faker; inspector,** *boundary rider*, see BOUNDARY B. 2; **strainer,** an implement used to tighten the horizontal wires of a fence.

1935 F. CLUNE *Rolling down Lachlan* 129 The kitchen **wire-door** slapped and re-clapped. **1957** R. BEYNON *Shifting Heart* (1960) 7 The porch or back verandah—is in full view, with a wire door centre back. **1973** F. MOORHOUSE *Stories* 32 The wire door squeaks open and bangs. **1978** C. RUHEN *Crocodile* 126 The wire door at the back of the house slammed, and she heard Wes stamping into the kitchen. **1935** K. TENNANT *Tiburon* 29 'What's 'e doing?' '**Wire-fakin'**.' 'He would be... Man's a genius. Make any mortal thing out of wire—clothes-pegs, bottle-cleaners, anything.' **1970** J.S. GUNN in W.S. Ramson *Eng. Transported* 63 No one wants a revival of the need for.. *wire faking* or other terms of depression years. **1977** L. FOX *Depression Down Under* 99 Men would go 'wire-faking'. Out of wire they would create toasting forks with long handles, meat holders for open fire grilling, even a strong wire clothes peg. *Ibid.*, The wire-fakers raised a few shillings from their craft. **1905** *Shearer* (Sydney) 4 Feb. 4/2 What do you know of.. 'tick-jammers', or of 'lizards' and '**wire inspectors**'? **1906** *Bulletin* (Sydney) 19 Apr. 15/1 Lately, one of two 'wire-inspectors', camped at an out-station in C.Q., killed and brought home to show his mate, a beautifully-marked whip-snake. **1911** ST. C. GRONDONA *Collar & Cuffs* 57 The emu.. is only of use.. to give the boundary riders and wire inspectors something to do. **1936** *Bulletin* (Sydney) 29 Jan. 20/4, I have heard boundary-riders referred to by many names. Blue-tongues, lizards, hatters, boundary-jerkers, wire-inspectors [etc.]. **1882** ARMSTRONG & CAMPBELL *Austral. Sheep Husbandry* 204 Novel **Wire Strainer**... This instrument.. should be made of light iron... Three short spikes, or legs, should be fixed behind, so as to give the instrument a grip of the post as soon as the wire is tightened. **1931** 'L. KAYE' *Tybal Men* 79 Vivian slung a rifle and wire-strainer at his saddle. **1936** F. CLUNE *Roaming round Darling* 169 A wire-strainer is a peculiar little dibdab with three contraptions which are supposed to grip the wire while you twiddle the handle. **1959** A. UPFIELD *Bony & Black Virgin* 209 'What kind of wire-strainer does Nuggety Jack use?' 'Forked stick he can get out of the scrub,' replied Pointer. 'Doesn't do too good a job, though.' 'Our man used a patent chain wire-strainer he bought at a store.'

wiree /'waıri/. [See quot. 1965.] *Rufous whistler*, see RUFOUS.

1921 'J. O'BRIEN' *Around Boree Log* 15 Did you wonder why the wiree comes to sing his sweetest song? [*Note*] Also known as the Chocolate Wiree (pronounced 'wiry'): a very fine songster, called by ornithologists 'Rufous-breasted Whistler'. **1965** *Austral. Encycl.* IX. 292 The rufous whistler.. proclaims its presence with a song that is remarkably melodious and sprightly... Other names based on the bird's calls are 'ee-chong' and 'wiree'.

wire-grass. Any of many perennial grasses, usu. of the genus *Aristida* (fam. Poaceae), having a tufted or tussocky habit and stiff, wiry stems.

1817 J. OXLEY *Jrnls. Two Exped. N.S.W.* 1 June (1820) 52, I wish the grass had proved equally good, but there is nothing for them but dead wire-grass (*ira*). **1834** G. BENNETT *Wanderings N.S.W.* I. 138 The 'wire-grass' is said to indicate good soil, being found growing in alluvial soil, in clumps. **1887** J.H. WRIGHT *Our Victorian Coalfields* 39 The worst obstacle to progress is the wire-grass, so named from its resemblance to stout wire. **1920** J.N. MACINTYRE *White Aust.* 77 The country is poorly grassed with spinifex, wire-grass, and turpentine-grass. **1933** J.L. GLASCOCK *Jarrah Leaves* 12 He gazed rapturously in front of him at the clumps of wire grass on the plain. **1945** A.W. UPFIELD *Death of Swagman* 72 It was useless to attempt to track across that dense growth of wire grass growing to a height of eighteen inches. **1972** M. CASSIDY *Dispossessed* 103 He could dodge you for hours among this wire grass. **1982** *Ecos* xxxiii. 17/1 It is all very well to read in an old diary that 'the country was a sea of wire-grass', but how much was 'a sea'? And which species of 'wire-grass' did the writer have in mind? **1985** J. GALBRAITH *Garden in Valley* 9 Dense shrubs and tangles of wiregrass grew on the sheltered slopes.

wireweed. Any of several plants having wiry stems, usu. herbs of the genus *Polygonum* (fam. Polygonaceae), esp. *P. aviculare* of all States, and allied species.

1875 *Papers & Proc. R. Soc. Tas.* (1876) 96 Underneath there is generally a tall and tangled growth of wireweed (*Bauera*) . . with horizontal scrub (*Anodopetalum*). **1919** *Agric. Gaz. N.S.W.* XXX. 814 A Muswellbrook correspondent . . had discovered wire weed . . to be making serious inroads on his stand of young lucerne. **1966** A. MORRIS *Plantlife W. Darling* 53 *Polygonum Aviculare*. . . 'Wire-weed'. Cultivated ground. Introduced weed. July 1920. **1985** *Weekly Times* (Melbourne) 7 Aug. 6/4 Brome grass and wireweed were perennial problems on his land. Spraying the year before on ground that was going to be cropped helped to control them.

wirilda /wəˈrɪldə/. [a. Yaralde *wurrulde*.] The shrub or small tree *Acacia retinodes* (fam. Mimosaceae) of S.A., Vic., and Tas., cultivated as an ornamental. Also **wirilda wattle.**

1930 A.J. EWART *Flora Vic.* 596 *A[cacia] rhetinodes* [*sic*] . . Wirilda. Glabrous shrub or small tree. **1935** E. COLEMAN *Come back in Wattle Time* 40 *Wirilda wattle* . . flowers practically all the year round—with restraint during the winter. **1939** J. GALBRAITH *Garden in Valley* (1985) 107 The Wirilda . . is shining through the rain, a lovely tree with blue-green leaves and primrose flowers. **1981** L. COSTERMANS *Native Trees & Shrubs S.-E. Aust.* 319 Wirilda . . flowers (mostly spr-sum): Pale-yellow . . rarely profuse.

wirra, var. WIRRI.

wirra /ˈwɪrə/, *n.*[1] Also **wira, wirree, worra.** [Prob. f. a N.S.W. Aboriginal language.] A shallow wooden scoop used by Aborigines as a container and as a digging implement.

1897 K.L. PARKER *Austral. Legendary Tales* (ed. 2) 16 Ye have filled your goolays and comebees with fruits, and your wirrees with honey. **1935** H.H. FINLAYSON *Red Centre* 79 The *wirra* is a shallow wooden dish which functions as a sand scoop. **1936** J.E. HAMMOND *Western Pioneers* 216 Worra, for digging up roots for food and digging graves etc. **1940** L.E. SHEARD *Austral. Youth among Desert Aborigines* (1964) 77 The men then scraped the earth with a 'wira' completely covering the grave. **1969** A.A. ABBIE *Original Australs.* 78 If water supplies are scanty and undependable, the women collect what water they can in their wooden vessels (*wirras, pitchis, coolamons*) and carry these carefully on their heads throughout the day's march. **1973** V. SERVENTY *Desert Walkabout* 26 The wooden bowls were called wirras by these people.

wirra /ˈwɪrə/, *n.*[2] [a. Diyari *wirra*.] The plant *Acacia salicina* (see COOBA).

1906 J.H. MAIDEN *Wattles & Wattle-Barks* (ed. 3) 90 *A[cacia] salicina*. . . Following are some additional aboriginal names . . 'Wirrha', Cooper's Creek, near Lake Eyre. **1941** I.L. IDRIESS *Great Boomerang* 102 Burned leaves of the wirra (a species of acacia, the leaves of which when burned yield a powder of potash).

Wirra /ˈwɪrə/, *n.*[3] Abbrev. of 'Wirraway', the name of an Australian modification of the North American NA/6 military aircraft.

1941 *Air Force News* (Melbourne) 15 Nov. 5 All eyes go up as the 'Wirras' dive. **1968** G. DUTTON *Andy* 47 Do you think I enjoy pushing a bloody great Wirra into a hangar?

wirrah /ˈwɪrə/. [Prob. f. a N.S.W. Aboriginal language.] Either of two marine fish of rocky reefs of the genus *Acanthistius, A. ocellatus* of s.e. Aust. and *A. serratus* of s.w. Aust.

1880 *Proc. Linnean Soc. N.S.W.* V. 324 *Plectropoma ocellatum*. . . This is the 'Wirrah' of the aborigines, a common fish, but valueless for food. **1895** C. THACKERAY *Amateur Fisherman's Guide* 78 *Rose Bay*, is a favourite ground. . . Wirrah and ling, are constantly caught. **1906** D.G. STEAD *Fishes of Aust.* 103 The name of Wirrah is of native origin. I have heard also the names of 'Pepper Cod' and 'Peppermint Rock-Cod' applied to this fish. **1949** *Bulletin* (Sydney) 28 Sept. 10/4 The 'wirrah', also known among rockhoppers as 'old boots' . . is tough. . . I dropped a four pounder into the basket. **1978** N. COLEMAN *Austral. Fisherman's Fish Guide* 16 Most commonly found in shallow water around rocky reefs, the wirrah is often termed as a 'boot'. This is due to the fishes' poor eating qualities which in no uncertain terms resemble a 'boot', both in texture and lack of flavour. **1985** *Canberra Chron.* 13 Nov. 19/2 The best catch of fish I saw was a load of wirrahs, catties, eels and ling. Not exactly the most exciting fishing in the world.

wirrang /ˈwɪræŋ/. Also **wherang, wirring, woorang, worrung.** [a. Wiradhuri *weerung*.] *Rock wallaby*, see ROCK *n.* 2.

1833 W.H. BRETON *Excursions* 251 Wirrang.—Bittang. Rock kangaroos. **1850** *Australasian Sporting Mag.* 92 The Woorang or Wirring, as it is there called, is the Rock Wallaby. They average about twenty five pounds weight, and would bother a chamois with their pace over a country all but impracticable to human beings. **1855** R. AUSTIN *Jrnl. Interior W.A.* 14 Several worrungs, a small and very beautiful species of kangaroo, about the size of a rabbit, were shot today. **1900** *Bulletin* (Sydney) 21 July 15/1 'Coolawine' and 'wherang' (orthography not guaranteed) for bear and rock-wallaby, are commonly used on some of the coastal rivers.

wirree, var. WIRRA *n.*[1]

wirri /ˈwɪri/. *Obs.* Also **wirra.** [a. Gaurna *wirri*.] An Aboriginal weapon, used as a club or missile: see quot. 1860.

1841 C.G. TEICHELMANN *Aborigines S.A.* 10 His coming they prevent by striking with their *wirri*, the air around the hut in different directions. **1842** *S. Austral. News* (London) 15 Oct. 46/1 Smaller animals, as birds, &c., are thrown at and killed by the wirri. **1843** J.F. BENNETT *Hist. & Descr. Acct. S.A.* 62 The *wirri*—generally called by the Settlers *waddie*—is a kind of club about two feet long, having a knob at one end, and the other cut in a rude manner, something in the form of a screw, to ensure a firm hold in the hand. **1847** G.F. ANGAS *Savage Life & Scenes* I. 58 A tall, muscular native, perfectly naked, armed with a wirri and a spear. **1858** W.A. CAWTHORNE *Legend of Kupirri* 18 They lift no spear, they lift no *wirri*, Powerless before Kupirri. **1860** *Trans. & Proc. R. Soc. Vic.* (1861) 170 Another weapon, called 'wirra', is made of the stem of young trees, about one and a-half feet long, and barely an inch thick. The thin end, which serves for the handle, is generally notched, while towards the thicker end it is a little bent, somewhat in the shape of a sword. . . This weapon the natives use for killing kangaroo rats and other small animals. **1862** C. WILHELMI *Manners & Customs Austral. Natives* 14 Smaller animals . . they kill by throwing at them (when started) clubs called 'wirra'. **1868** *Illustr. Sydney News* 28 Dec. 108/1 The ease, the grace, and the sure aim with which a native throws his wirri, or waddy . . are matters of surprize to the civilized white men. **1879** *Native Tribes S.A.* 214 Wirris, by the whites incorrectly called waddies, are also made of gum saplings.

wirring, var. WIRRANG.

wise man. *Obs.* KORADJI.

1805 J. TURNBULL *Voyage round World* I. 85 This operation is performed very simply by their curradiges or wise-men. **1841** G. GREY *Jrnls. Two Exped. N.-W. & W.A.* I. 215 The cave was frequented by some wise man or native doctor, who was resorted to by the inhabitants in cases of disease or witchcraft. **1847** G.F. ANGAS *Savage Life & Scenes* I. 86 The sick are either entrusted to the care of sorcerers, or 'wise-men'. **1857** J. BONWICK *Early Days Melbourne* 38 The doctors, or wise men, are dreaded by the others.

witarna /wɪˈtanə/. [a. Baŋgala *witarna*.] An Aboriginal ceremonial object: see quot. 1846 and BULL-ROARER.

1846 C.W. SCHURMANN *Aboriginal Tribes Port Lincoln* 5 The witarna, an oval chip of wood, say eighteen inches long and three or four broad, smooth on both sides and not above half an inch thick. By a long string which passes through a hole at one end, the native swings it round his head through the air, when it gradually, as the string becomes twisted, produces a deep unearthly sound. **1860** *Proc. R. Soc. Vic.* (1861) 172, I have to mention another instrument, quite different from any of those above, viz.: the 'witarna', a piece of wood 18 inches long, 4 inches broad, 1/4 inch thick, which, tied to a long string, they swing above their heads, and thus produce a low rumbling sound. **1878** R.B. SMYTH *Aborigines of Vic.* I. p. xxiii, In Africa . . the fetich-man blows a kind of whistle made of hollowed mangrove wood, and the sound is probably a signal to those not privileged to keep away; just as the *Witarna* is used for this purpose in Australia.

witchetty /ˈwɪtʃəti/. Also with much variety, as **widgery, witchety, witjuti.** [a. Adnyamadhanha *wityu* hooked stick used to extract grubs + *varti* grub.]

1. *Obs.* A hooked stick for obtaining witchetty grubs. Also *attrib.*

1862 W.R.H. JESSOP *Travels & Adventures* II. 214 Besides the yam-stick, which is made of the hardest wood, there is the grub stick, called witchertie, a small hooked twig, which the women carry in the nose, and the men in a fillet round the head: this last is used for extracting the grub from crevices and holes. **1925** H. BASEDOW *Austral. Aboriginal* 125 This implement is from four to six inches long and is usually cut from a small pronged twig. . . The stick is inserted into the hole occupied by the witchedy grub, hook foremost, and pushed in until the grub is penetrated. . . The witchedy-hook is known throughout central and southern Australia.

2. *transf.* The large, edible, wood-eating larva or pupa of any of several moths, esp. cossids of the genus *Xyleutes*, and beetles of the fam. Cerambycidae; GRUB; MARGOO; *tree grub*, see TREE; *wood grub*, see WOOD *n.*[1] 3 b. See also BARDIE. Also **witchetty grub** (sometimes *attrib.*).

1891 *Trans. R. Soc. S.A.* XIV. 158 They did, however, eat one 'witchety', the native name of large white grubs, much relished by the blacks as an article of food, which are the larval forms of certain Longicorn beetles and Lepidoptera. **1894** R. LYDEKKER *Hand-Bk. Marsupialia & Monotremata* 191 The Marsupial Mole . . 'was fed on the 'witchetty' (a kind of grub)'. **1897** J.J. MURIF *From Ocean to Ocean* 176 The best bait one can use is a section of widgery (or 'witchery', a grub three or four inches in length, found at the roots of gum trees, and tasting, when slightly roasted, not unlike a hen's egg). **1900** A.A. DAVIDSON *Jrnl. of Explorations Central Aust.* 3 June (1905) 25 Traces of natives were found about the water. They have been cutting out witchities. **1901** F.J. GILLEN *Diary* 3 May (1968) 63 My old friend Unchalka head of the Udnirringita or Witchetty grub totem to which I have the honour to belong. **1925** H. BASEDOW *Austral. Aboriginal* 124 The witchedy grub is extracted from its hiding place by means of a light hooked stick. **1927** M.H. ELLIS *Long Lead* 48 The witchedee grub which every true black Australian relishes. **1936** C.T. MADIGAN *Central Aust.* 198 There, set out before the fire . . a row of beautifully browned 'widgettie' grubs, all ready to be devoured. **1938** D. BATES *Passing of Aborigines* 209 The mawgu, or witchetty, a delicate white grub found in the roots and bark of mallee and mulga and other trees. **1948** H.A. LINDSAY *Bushman's Handbk.* 36 Three main types of witchetty grub. The smallest . . is the larva of the longicorn beetle, and seldom exceeds two inches. . . The second . . attains a length of three inches . . with a circumference about that of a man's finger; it is the larva of the wood moth. The third is the larva of the ghost moth, which attains a length of five or six inches and a circumference of three. **1949** H.C. JAMES *Gold is where you find It* 139 A patch of small umbrella-like acacia bushes, half dead. He uprooted them one by one, and from each root he levered out a big, curled-up, white widgee grub. The niggers ate them. **1953** *Trans. R. Soc. S.A.* LXXVI. 59 Aborigines with access to *witjuti* grubs usually are healthy and properly nourished. **1959** E. WEBB *Mark of Sun* 75 When the witchetties were cooked, she rolled them on a piece of thin bark. **1962** D. LOCKWOOD *I, Aboriginal* 91 They are horrified that we eat witchetty grubs and yet they regard snails and frogs as delicacies. **1970** *Insects of Aust.* (CSIRO) 798 The larva of the small *X[yleutes] leucomochla* . . which . . feeds externally on the roots of *Acacia ligulata* in inland South Australia, is the true witchetty grub of the Aborigines. **1982** HADLINGTON & JOHNSTON *Introd. Austral. Insects* 61 The witjuti . . a South Australian species, lives in the soil. **1986** *Bulletin*

(Sydney) 25 Mar. 90/3 Chefs . . were asked to work with . . witchetty grubs. . . At $3 each, plus air delivery they were still expensive.

3. Special Comb. **witchetty bush,** any of several plants of the genus *Acacia* of drier Aust., esp. the shrub or tree *A. kempeana* of all mainland States exc. Vic.

1935 H.H. Finlayson *Red Centre* 30 The broad-leafed mulga or witchetty bush, the roots of which harbour a grub beloved by the blacks. **1940** L.E. Sheard *Austral. Youth among Desert Aborigines* (1964) 108 We travelled on gradually getting into the wide arms of the Musgraves, where the mulga became thicker and there were some places with thick witchety bush scrub. **1950** A. Groom *I saw Strange Land* 191 Njunowa knocked low *Acacia Kempeana* (witchetty) bushes over, and pulled from the fractured roots white grubs. **1980** R. Davidson *Tracks* 90 There was nothing but the still, olive-green witchetty bushes, and miles of broken red rock and dust. **1982** Elliot & Jones *Encycl. Austral. Plants* II. 70 *Acacia kempeana* . . Witchetty Bush. . . The common name arises because the trunk and branches are often infested with witchetty grubs.

wizard. *Obs.* Koradji. Also *attrib.*

1884 A.W. Howitt *On Some Austral. Ceremonies Initiation* 4 The doctors and wizards of some distant tribes . . might . . become acquainted with the leading Wolgal men. **1886** E.M. Curr *Austral. Race* I. 45 It is an universal belief of the Blacks that a conjuror, wizard, or doctor . . can charm. **1888** *Proc. Linnean Soc. N.S.W.* III. 422 Mr Froggatt exhibited a fine collection of native weapons and implements. . . It comprises spears . . coolamons . . wizard-stick used for bewitching enemies.

wobbegong /ˈwɒbigɒŋ/. Also **wahbegong, wobbygong, wobegong.** [Prob. f. a N.S.W. Aboriginal language.] Any of several slow-moving, bottom-dwelling sharks of the fam. Orectolobidae, esp. of the genus *Orectolobus*, commonly found among seaweed-encrusted rocks; *carpet shark*, see Carpet.

1852 G.C. Mundy *Our Antipodes* I. 392 The most hideous to behold of the shark tribe is the wobegong, or woe-begone, as the fishermen call it. **1874** *N.S.W. Rep. R. Comm. Fisheries* (1880) 19 The wahbegong, of which there are several varieties on this coast, is chiefly nocturnal. **1896** F.G. Aflalo *Sketch Nat. Hist. Aust.* 221 A Tiger Shark (*Galeocerdo*) . . lay alongside our steamer off Cairns. . . The variegated pattern on its back was not unlike that of the Wobbegong or Carpet-Shark of Sydney. **1921** *Bulletin* (Sydney) 14 July 26/2 The wobbegong, or carpet shark, first turned up in Sydney Cove. One was caught by Lieut. Watts . . in 1788. **1930** C.M. Yonge *Yr. on Great Barrier Reef* 93 The wobbegong or carpet shark (*Orectolobus devisi*) is a somewhat rarer but more handsome beast, coloured grey with a variegated pattern, and equally harmless. **1975** A. O'Grady *Sugar-Coated Comfortable* 33 'I don't eat wobbegong, but maybe you boongs do.' He ducked a blow from Katherine, who was part aboriginal. She said, 'The damn thing wouldn't mind eating you, it's a shark, isn't it?' **1981** *Bulletin* (Sydney) 9 June 56/2 Wobbygongs have teeth similar in size and shape to those of the grey nurse. Althought much more docile in appearance, wobbygongs or carpet sharks have an aggressive nature. They will bite a diver and frequently take speared fish.

wobbles, *pl.* [See quot. 1897.] An affliction of stock, usu. of cattle, attributed to consumption of the leaves of plants of the fam. Zamiaceae, and characterized by loss of control, and gradual loss of use, of the hindquarters.

1894 *Jrnl. Bureau Agric. W.A.* I. xviii. 225 The disease 'wobbles' is essentially peculiar to zamia districts. **1897** L. Lindley-Cowen *W. Austral. Settler's Guide* 587 The macrozamia . . has long been known to possess deleterious properties, due partly to indigestibility, but more from the poisonous constituents that bring on in the animals feeding on them a series of symptoms ending in partial paralysis of their hind quarters. The disease is known by the names 'rickets' and 'wobbles', from the 'wobbling' character of the gait of the animal affected by it. **1956** Gardner & Bennetts *Toxic Plants W.A.* 6 'Rickets' or 'wobbles' in cattle due to poisoning with *M[acrozamia] Reidlei* was a widely recognized condition of common occurrence in the southern parts of Western Australia from the earliest days of settlement until more recent times when the extension of pasture development has greatly reduced access to the plant by stock. **1974** S.L. Everist *Poisonous Plants Aust.* 167 The commonest condition brought about by consumption of leaves is inco-ordination in the hind limbs known as 'rickets', 'Zamia staggers' or 'wobbles'. . . Leaves of several species in at least three Australian genera (*Cycas, Macrozamia* and *Bowenia*) can produce a characteristic disturbance of gait (ataxia). . . The condition is irreversible. **1980** O. Ruhen *Bullock Teams* 187 Eating burrawongs, or indeed any of the cycads in the *Macrozamia* family can also cause the 'staggers' or 'wobbles' as they were alternatively called. The bullocks seemed to lose control over the hips and back.

wobbygong, wobegong, var. Wobbegong.

wodgil /ˈwɒdʒəl/. *W.A.* Also **wodjil.** [Prob. f. a W.A. Aboriginal language.] A vegetation community of tall shrubby growth dominated by plants of the genus *Acacia*, esp. *A. neurophylla*; the wood of the plants. Freq. *attrib.*, esp. as **wodgil scrub.**

1948 J.K. Ewers *For Heroes to live In* 5 The wodgil and wattle scrub had been cleared in the early days to make a horse yard. **1950** *Bulletin* (Sydney) 3 May 12/2 In the Westralian wheatbelt . . the cockies reckon jamwood-posts will outlast practically any other timber except wodgil. **1962** B.W. Leake *Eastern Wheatbelt Wildlife* 103 The mountain devil likes gravelly scrub and wodgil country, but will wander far from this. *c* **1968** J.S. Beard *Wildflowers Northwest* 18 The wodjil is basically a thicket of dense shrubs of 'broombrush' habit, that is they bear very numerous erect branches arising from the base and forming a domed crown. **1973** R. Erickson et al. *Flowers & Plants W.A.* 190 On poor sandy clays there is frequently a tall thicket formation known as wodjil. **1973** C.E. Goode *Stories Strange Places* 11 About half a mile away, in a dense patch of wodgil scrub ending in a line of breakaways, was suitable stone.

wog, *n.* [Of unknown origin.]

1. A name applied to various insects and grubs, esp. those regarded as predatory or otherwise disagreeable.

[**1909** F.E. Birtles *Lonely Lands* 111 The little water that remained was filled with a kind of water beetle, locally known as 'wee woggies'.] **1938** *Bulletin* (Sydney) 7 Sept. 20/2 As the water moves slowly down the bays countless root-eating 'wogs' break for cover and an irregular line of starlings perform efficient mopping-up. **1940** *Ibid.* 4 Dec. 16/2 Of all the miscellaneous assortment of wogs that bountiful Nature inflicts on her sons, the 'itchy grub' is the most insidious. A harmless-looking hairy caterpillar, about two inches long, it leaves an invisible irritant behind that lingers long after it has gone. **1943** J. Devine *Rats of Tobruk* 39 She had lovely hair, and we did not discover for a long while that it was full of wogs. **1950** *Bulletin* (Sydney) 4 Oct. 12/4 At a very youthful age I learned the strengths and weaknesses in the armaments of the wogs in my life. Hornets were essentially 'in-fighters'; at long-range they were harmless. 'Spitfires', on the other hand, could get in their dirty work from a distance of anything up to 3 ft. . . The 'itchy grub' (processional caterpillar) left behind a powerful irritant where'er he walked. **1956** D. Rowbotham *Town & City* 76 It's a menace, a breeding place for mosquitoes and God knows what variety of wogs. **1960** *N.T. News* (Darwin) 19 Jan. 7/2 Mr Wilson of the City Council was present also and answered questions on treatment of grubs and 'wogs' on foliage. **1976** B. Scott *Complete Bk. Austral. Folk Lore* 379 Re 'stinking, stinking wogs' mentioned in the poem; these are undoubtedly the little beetles known in Innisfail as the 'lavender' bug, or 'stink' bug. When distressed these squirt out a corrosive fluid or gas which stings severely, especially if it gets you in the eye. **1982** J.A. Sharwood *Vocab. Austral. Dried Vine Fruits Industry* 32 A grower . . who is *chasing the wogs* is examining his vines closely for signs of insect damage.

2. A microbe or germ, a 'bug'; an illness. Also *attrib.*

1941 S.J. Baker *Pop. Dict. Austral. Slang* 82 Wog, a germ or parasite. *c* **1946** J.E. Purtill *Farewell 'Robbie'* 25 The Padre looked along the line—boys with the 'flu and 'wog', Then went off with his cobber to eat the poor girl's dog. **1948** *Bulletin* (Sydney) 11 Feb. 23/3 Alf . . watched them pack and head for the falls on Crow Bend, where, after testing the wog-content, the scientific bloke voted it safe to drink. **1951** D. Cusack *Say no to Death* (1959) 97 'Hasn't your boy-friend ever heard about infection?' . . 'Probably he doesn't know what the wog means.' **1956** J.F. Macdonnell *Commander Brady* 224 'What actually was wrong with him?' Number One looked at him steadily. 'Like I said. A wog.' 'Yes, I heard that. What sort of wog?' . . 'Malaria,' he said briefly. **1963** J. O'Grady *Things they do to You* 14 Medical science . . discovered a multitude of wogs. **1973** *Bulletin* (Sydney) 17 Feb. 43/2 The great decimator that has plagued man for centuries . . since he became so mobile and began moving the wog around the globe may come under control. **1978** C. Green *Sun is Up* 26 A ''flu wog' struck, and several families of children were absent with, as their neighbours put it, 'terrible hackin' coffs'. **1983** *Nichigo Press* July 14/4 Have you been in bed with a wog? Oh no, I'm married!

wog, *v.* [f. *wog*, a colloq. name for a foreigner.] *trans.* In Services' speech: to buy (goods) from or sell to the local inhabitants.

1940 *Action Front: Jrnl. 2/2 Field Regiment* Oct. 5 Whilst short of cash, he wogged his fountain pen. **1941** *Vic Eddy: Signals 7th Austral. Division*, We have 'wogged' the office boy's . . suit, and with the lucre obtained from that transaction [etc.]. **1981** D. Stuart *I think I'll Live* 103 Some of my blokes have been seeing a few of the locals at night, at a corner of the back fence, an' wogging a bit of gear.

Wogga, Wogger, var. Wagga.

wogoit /ˈwoʊgɔɪt/. [Prob. f. a N.T. Aboriginal language.] *Rock ringtail*, see Rock *n.* 2. Also *attrib.*

1926 K. Dahl *In Savage Aust.* 203 Upon my questions as to the nature of the 'wogoit', he informed me that the wogoit was a large kind of opossum which spent the days in hollows and crevasses among the rocks, feeding in the trees at night. **1942** C. Barrett *From Bush Hut* 37 *Wogoit* (that's a blackfellow name for the rock-possum). **1946** D. Barr *Warrigal Joe* 20 Poor country; but worse lay ahead of them—'wogoit' land. It was walk-march for the horses, from the time the outfit left camp.

woilie, var. Woylie.

wolf. [Transf. use of *wolf* the large canine *Canis lupus.*] **a.** Any of several carnivorous native quadrupeds, esp. *Thylacinus cyanocephalus* (see *Tasmanian tiger, wolf* Tasmanian *a.* 2). **b.** Dingo *n.* 1. Also **wolf-dog.**

1770 J. Cook *Jrnls.* 4 Aug. (1955) I. 367 Here are wolves. **1805** J.H. Tuckey *Acct. Voyage to establish Colony Port Philip* 201 Four large wolves were seen at Western Port. **1829** R. Mudie *Picture of Aust.* 174 The Australian animals that may strictly speaking be considered as wild beasts, that is, as subsisting on animal food, form a genus which is peculiar to Australia, and to which, in consequence of their rough appearance, the name of *dasyuris* has been given. They have vulgarly been called bears, wolves, hyaenas, tigers, and even devils, according to the fancy of those by whom they have been seen. **1837** E. Fraser *Narr. of Capture* 8 The kangaroos and wolf-dog are the chief quadrupeds. **1845** *S. Austral. Odd Fellows' Mag.* Aug. 107 At that time the district was approached with great difficulty, the roads over hill and dale being infested with wild dogs (*wolves*). **1898** E.E. Morris *Austral Eng.* 514 It [*sc. Thylacinus*] is the largest carnivorous marsupial extant, and is so much like a wolf in appearance that it well deserves its vernacular name of Wolf, though now-a-days it is generally called Tiger.

wollaba, wollabi, var. Wallaby.

wollamai /ˈwɒləmaɪ/. [a. Dharuk *walamay.*] The marine fish *Chrysophrys auratus*, a Snapper.

1790 D. Southwell Corresp. & Papers, *Woa-la-mi*, snapper. **1906** D.G. Stead *Fishes of Aust.* 127 'Wollomai' is a name given by some New South Wales blacks to these old examples of the Snapper. **1952** *Austral. Museum Mag.* June 310 The Australian aborigines had their names for fishes, of course, and still have in the more remote places, and some of these, even though tribes which invented them have become extinct or have 'lost their tongues', are currently used in everyday speech. I need only mention the following . . Turrum . . Wobbegong, and Wollomai.

Wolseley. *Obs.* [Proprietary name, f. the name of F.Y. *Wolseley* (1837–1899), inventor.] A Wolseley shearing-machine. Freq. *pl.* for *sing.*

[**1889** H. Egbert *Pretty Cockey* 5 A public trial of Mr

F.Y. Wolseley's patent sheep-shearing machine was made yesterday at the wool stores of Messrs R. Goldsborough & Co.] **1897** *Bulletin* (Sydney) 20 Feb. 3/2 And Bogan laid his 'Wols'ley' down and knocked that rouser out. **1899** *Western Champion* (Barcaldine) 1 Aug. 11/1 The announcement of 30,000 sheep to be shorn was received with very mixed feelings by the forty good men and true who, for the past eleven weeks, had been wielding the Wolseleys with such unremitting vigor upon the Wellshot jumbucks. **1905** A.B. PATERSON *Old Bush Songs* 26 I've pinked 'em with the Wolseleys and I've rushed with B-bows. **1905** J. MEREDITH *Learn to talk Old Jack Lang* (1984) 13, I can blind Tom Power with wool with the Wolseleys and give Jacky Howe a fifty start. **1906** *Pastoralists' Rev.* 15 Feb. 24 (Advt.), The Wolseley. The only *reliable* sheep shearing machine. **1923** *Austral. Official Jrnl. Patents* (Canberra) 194 Wolseley. 34,205. . . Sheep-Shearing Machines, Cream Separators, Milk Cleansers and Milking Machines.

woma, var. WOMMA *n.*[2]

wombat /'wɒmbæt/, *n.* and *attrib.* Formerly also with much variety, as **wambat, whombat, whombatt, womat, wombach, womback.** [a. Dharuk *wambaty*.]

A. *n.*

1. Any of the several thickset, burrowing, herbivorous marsupials of the fam. Vombatidae of s. and e. Aust. incl. Tas., the commonest and most widespread of which is *Vombatus ursinus*. See also BADGER. Also *attrib.*, and with distinguishing epithet, as **hairy-nosed** (see under first element).

1798 *Hist. Rec. N.S.W.* (1895) III. 821 Different animals, one of which Wilson called a whom-batt, which is an animal about 20 inches high, with short legs and a thick Body forwards, with a large head, round ears, and very small eyes; is very fat. **1798** Banks Papers 5 Aug. XIX. 48 A new animal discovered on an island on the coast of New South Wales . . the Mountain Natives call it Wombach. . . One is female and has the false belly for the security of its young. **1798** D. COLLINS *Acct. Eng. Colony N.S.W.* (1802) II. 99 The mountain natives named this new animal Wom-bat, and said it was good eating; but it was wholly unknown to those who were admitted into the settlement. **1799** *Ibid.* 153 The *Wom-bat* (or, as it is called by the natives of Port Jackson, the *Womback*). **1801** M. FLINDERS *Observations Coasts Van Diemen's Land* 26 The new animal called, Womat, by the natives at the back of Port Jackson, is found in no inconsiderable numbers upon Cape-Barren Island. **1806** *Hist. Rec. N.S.W.* (1898) VI. 66 The native told me that the porcupine ant-eater and the whombat must be common by his frequent seeing their tracks, and our dog catching one of both. **1814** M. FLINDERS *Voyage Terra Australis* I. p. cxxxv, Clarke's Island afforded the first specimen of the new animal, called *womat*. . . This little bear-like quadruped is known in New South Wales, and called by the natives *womat, wombat*, or *womback*, according to the different dialects, or perhaps to the different rendering of the wood rangers who brought the information. **1829** R. MUDIE *Picture of Aust.* 170 The *Wombat* (*phascolomys*) has considerable resemblance to the koala, only instead of climbing trees like that animal, it burrows in the earth. **1834** C.O. BOOTH *Jrnl.* 8 Mar. (1981) 172 Massacred a brace of Kangaroo and pair of very fine Badgers (very improperly so named) called Wambats by the Natives. **1841** *S. Austral. Mag.* Dec. 211 Genus *Phascolomys*.—Phas. ursinus—the wombat . . common. **1846** *Tasmanian Jrnl. Nat. Sci.* II. 117 A young wombat, stuffed and roasted whole in the same manner as a sucking pig, makes a most delicious dish. **1865** G.F. ANGAS *Aust.* 76 The wombat is a curious creature, of which four distinct species have been met with in the southern portion of Australia. **1884** 'R. BOLDREWOOD' *Old Melbourne Memories* 157 Where the wombats dug their treacherous shafts and galleries, how many a good steed and horseman have I seen overthrown. **1896** E. DYSON *Rhymes from Mines* 124 Time was when Death sat by me, and he stalked me through the trees. . . I was sullen as a wombat on such still, wan days as these. **1930** 'BRENT OF BIN BIN' *Ten Creeks Run* (1952) 6 Anyone with as much gumption as a wall-eyed wombat can see some things for himself. **1938** D. BATES *Passing of Aborigines* 135 That wombat was four hours in the hot ashes before it became edible—tender and tasty as roast pork. **1962** J. HEDGE *Trout Fishing N.S.W.* 20 A wombat is rather short-sighted. It is rarely seen in the daytime, and on such a meeting with the children was probably more scared than they, and wished only to run home to its den. **1971** D. WILLIAMSON *Don's Party* (1973) 89 You've got about as much sensitivity as a geriatric wombat. **1982** P. GOLDSWORTHY *Archipelagoes* 43 The old wombat joke—it eats roots and leaves. **1986** *Canberra Times* 2 Apr. 23/4 A wombat, not at all amused by the fact that the porch of its home beside the Goodradigbee River near Wee Jasper had been used as a dump for some campers' beer bottles, beer cans, empty Cheezel packets and other debris . . flung them all out again.

2. a. A slow or stupid person. Also *attrib.*

1905 *Bulletin* (Sydney) 3 Aug. 16/2 Murphy was a member of Jackson's road gang, in the wombat country, near where Bill Lyne gets his votes. **1964** *Southerly* ii. 108 And wombat novelists rise, as erst they rose, To praise their country in illiterate prose. **1979** T. SCHURMANN *Showie* 43 Tommo called out, 'Why don't you put the policeman off the ground, you great half-witted wombat!' **1984** *Bulletin* (Sydney) 20 Nov. 33/1 Those who follow Sinclair on his mostly rural election train are known as wombats. They wear ties with yellow wombats on them. They read Phantom comics.

b. Appled *fig.* in allusion to the wombat's ability to burrow.

1917 *Byron Bay Rec.* 7 July 4 In addition to the important work of tunnelling, units under the supervision of officers and n.c.o.'s, thousands of infantrymen, the greater majority of whom were entirely ignorant of underground work, have been transformed into excellent wombats. **1984** *Bulletin* (Sydney) 13 Nov. 32/3 Men known colloquially as 'wombats', says Costigan, illegally transmit prices to an operator outside racetracks by talking into radio devices in their pockets.

B. *attrib.*

1. Of a tract of land: inhabited by wombats.

1824 W. BLAND *Journey of Discovery Port Phillip* 7 Oct. (1831) 2 In the evening pass through Wombat brush. [*Note*] This brush, like most other parts of the country frequented by the animal from which it takes its name, is an excellent light soil. **1845** C.J. BAKER *Sydney & Melbourne* 68 Wombat ground is not uncommon in Australia, though some districts are entirely free from it. **1880** R. ROWE *Roughing It* 75 Tom Todd took him to a regular wombat warren. **1913** W.M. ANDERSON *Rhymes of Rouseabout* 6 With the wombat range before us and another league of plain.

2. Of a hole: made by a wombat. Also *fig.*

1845 E.J. EYRE *Jrnls. Exped. Central Aust.* I. 190 There were in places a great many wombat holes. **1847** *Britannia* (Hobart) 26 Aug. 4/3 Some pushed into wombat burrows. **1849** C. STURT *Narr. Exped. Central Aust.* I. 197 The dogs took shelter in wambut holes. **1854** W. HOWITT *Boy's Adventures* 47 Today Alfred found an American digger going down into a wombat-hole. It was circular and perpendicular, and there he was with his tin dish. **1882** A. TOLMER *Reminisc.* I. 191 Near the wombat hole . . we found two broken muskets. **1908** *Bulletin* (Sydney) 2 July 15/3 Many other creepy crawly things do inhabit wombat holes. **1930** 'BRENT OF BIN BIN' *Ten Creeks Run* (1952) 92, I suppose your father thinks anything big above a spring-cart and those wombat holes about Little River. **1945** J. DEVANNY *Bird of Paradise* 134 The first thing should be to cut out all these here State Governments. They're jest wombat holes for grafters to crawl into. **1948** R. RAVEN-HART *Canoe in Aust.* 165 Did you see the wombat-wells? They dig holes in the sand, maybe six feet or so from the lake, and the water comes up in them fresh.

3. Special Comb. **wombat berry,** the climbing plant *Eustrephus latifolius* (fam. Liliaceae) of e. mainland Aust. and elsewhere, bearing a globular orange berry and cultivated as an ornamental.

1880 *Argus* (Melbourne) 12 Jan. 6/7 In the borders many interesting plants are in flower, notably . . the wombat berry (Eustrephus) [etc.]. **1914** E.E. PESCOTT *Native Flowers Vic.* 91 Eustrephus Brownii, the 'wombat berry', is a climbing liliaceous plant, with small pink flowers. In the autumn it is covered with abundant clusters of bright orange berries. **1930** A.J. EWART *Flora Vic.* 285 *Eustrephus* . . only a single species, confined to Australia. *E. latifolius* . . Wombat Berry. . . The small Tubers are sweet and edible. **1967** N.A. WAKEFIELD *Naturalist's Diary* 7 Along these creeks there are huge gnarled kanooka trees, lilly-pillies and blackwoods. These are festooned with jungle lianas such as Wombat Berry (*Eustrephus latifolius*). **1979** K.A.W. WILLIAMS *Native Plants Qld.* I. 122 Wombat Berry . . cannot tolerate wet or boggy conditions.

Hence **wombat** *v.*, to dig or tunnel, like a wombat; also as *vbl. n.*, **wombatty** *a.*, heavily populated by wombats (see quots.).

1852 J. BONWICK *Notes of Gold Digger* 12 The constraint of body in work, the damp, the closeness of the atmosphere, the gloom, the fear of impending rocks, with occasional raps of knuckles and skull against the sides and roof, altogether make this **wombatting** not the most amusing operation in life. **1973** D. WOLFE *Brass Kangaroo* 143 Above the road a bent figure scratched around in the last remnants of the morning mist. 'And that there's old Clarrie trying to wombat the spuds out.' **1908** *Bulletin* (Sydney) 2 July 15/3 It is my ill-fortune to live in what is the **wombattiest** region on earth.

womera, var. WOOMERA.

womera /'wɒmərə/. Also **womerang, woomera,** and with much variety. [a. Dharuk *wumeraŋ* a club, the form prob. infl. by WOOMERA.] An Aboriginal club; an Aboriginal weapon (in quots. 1821, 1832 (1), and 1843, a boomerang). Also **womera-spear.**

1798 D. COLLINS *Acct. Eng. Colony N.S.W.* I. 613 *Wo-mur-rǎng* [in a list of the names of clubs]. **1821** S. LEIGHT in Methodist Missionary Soc. Rec. 18 Nov., The Wamareen. This Instrument or Weapon is made of heavy wood and is intended to disperse a Crowd, the skill which they have acquired in throwing it is highly wonderful. **1827** *Monitor* (Sydney) 8 Nov. 752/1 One of our people had his arm broken by a wooden womara, which the Natives threw in great numbers. **1832** J. HENDERSON *Observations Colonies N.S.W. & Van Diemen's Land* 151 A womroo . . resembles the blade of a sabre, imitated in wood, and deprived of the handle; both ends are however similarly pointed, and the general curve possesses a considerable convexity. It is thrown, with the concave side towards the object, and is made to revolve horizontally. **1832** *Hill's Life N.S.W.* (Sydney) 21 Sept. 4 Unerring his aim when his barbed spear flew, Nor less so, when wamrah, or bomring, he threw To lay the wing'd game at his feet. **1843** C. ROWCROFT *Tales of Colonies* II. 34 Almost before I could take aim at the native, the womera, skimming through the air, returned to the spot from which the native had cast it. **1847** *Bell's Life in Sydney* 20 Nov. 4/1 Aye Zytta, bid the *wommera* kill! Since Noona cannot fill thy heart. [*Note*] Wommera, a stem of the grass tree 5 or 6 feet long, the point hardened by fire. **1864** J. ROGERS *New Rush* 46 Next—high in air the womerang-spear he flings. **1871** *Austral. Town & Country Jrnl.* (Sydney) 13 May 598/3 Sumpy first struck him with the tomahawk, and the other two finished him with their womeras. **1910** *Huon Times* (Franklin) 19 Mar. 5/2 Their opponents had only the ordinary bush waddies and woomeras. **1928** W. ROBERTSON *Coo-ee Talks* 66 The performers looked terrible as they rushed upon each other with woomera-spears. **1930** J.S. LITCHFIELD *Far-North Memories* 38 Dick made a vicious swipe at it with a wommera. **1931** *N.T. Times* 9 Jan. 3/1 A number of the married men wanted to buy the woomeras that the bucks used for beating their wives. **1935** M. GILMORE *More Recoll.* 266 He was scarcely right on his feet till a wammerah whizzed at his head.

womma /'wɒmə/, *n.*[1] [a. Yankundjara dial. of Western Desert *woma*.] *Honey ant*, see HONEY.

1916 S.A. WHITE *In Far Northwest* 120 These are formed by the natives when in search of sugar ants, which they call 'womma'. These ants were described in 1880 by Sir John Lubbock as Camponotus inflatus. **1932** *Bulletin* (Sydney) 13 Jan. 21/2 The sugar-ant provides a choice dainty. Binghi digs down into the nests, being very careful not to damage the 'womma' he is after.

womma /'wɒmə/, *n.*[2] Also **woma.** [a. Diyari *wama*.] The python *Aspidites ramsayi* of arid Aust.

1935 H. BASEDOW *Knights of Boomerang* 75 Rock-pythons attain a length of from fifteen to seventeen feet. In Central Australia the recognised delicacy . . is a large brown variety of the carpet-snake. . . By nature it is sluggish and voracious, and therefore usually well-nourished and fat. . . It is known as 'womma', which means 'fat'. **1950** G.M. FARWELL *Land of Mirage* 96 The snake was a *womma*, a harmless sandhill variety, like a carpet snake. **1967** H. COGGER *Austral. Reptiles* 80 The Woma inhabits the arid centre of Australia, extending outwards into the dry inland of all mainland States except Victoria. **1973** A. BURNETT *Wilful Murder in Outback* 51 There is a snake peculiar to the area called the womma, a green reptile which is not venomous and grows to twelve feet long. The aborigines regard it as a delicacy and I have eaten it on several occasions.

wommara, wommera, var. WOOMERA.

wompoo pigeon /ˈwɒmpu ˈpɪdʒən/. Also **wampoo, whampoo pigeon.** [Imitative: see quot. 1976.] The fruit-pigeon *Ptilinopus magnificus* of near-coastal rainforest in n.e. Aust., also occurring in New Guinea; *king pigeon*, see KING *n.*[1] 2; *magnificent fruit pigeon*, see MAGNIFICENT; *painted pigeon*, see PAINTED.

1870 E.B. KENNEDY *Four Yrs. in Qld.* 111 One may find a large one with green back and purple and yellow breast, called the Whompoa, or painted pigeon. **1901** *Truth* (Sydney) 10 Mar. 5/5 Whampoo pigeons, green and rich gold, crowd the showers of ruddy-berries to the ground. **1910** *Emu* X. 207 A pair of the Purple-breasted Fruit Pigeons (*Megaloprepia magnifica*) commonly known as the 'Whampoo', on account of their deep note. **1931** *Bulletin* (Sydney) 29 July 20/3 The wompoo pigeon sends a man off with 'Good luck to you!' **1944** J. DEVANNY *By Tropic Sea & Jungle* 157 The wampoo pigeon's a good beefy bloke, and fine eating too. **1976** *Reader's Digest Compl. Bk. Austral. Birds* 227 (*caption*) The wompoo pigeon—named for its booming, far-carrying call. **1978** *Ecos* xv. 32/1 The wompoo pigeon . . is a large green bird with grey head, purple breast, and yellow abdomen, and its loud bubbling call is a familiar sound in tropical rainforest during the dry season. **1985** *Parks & Wildlife News* Summer 19 Four endangered bird species have their home in this park—the . . Wompoo Pigeon [etc.].

wompy, *a.* [Of unknown origin.] Ill. Also as *n.*, something liable to make one ill.

1920 *Bulletin* (Sydney) 24 June 20/2, I have seen seasoned breakers and horsemen . . get very 'wompy' inside after riding two or three willing three-year-olds in quick succession. **1982** P. RADLEY *My Blue-Checker Corker* 47 A guy called Nickie Johnson went on the piss . . with half a gallon of wompy, a toothbrush and a small tin of red paint.

womra, var. WOOMERA.

Wondjina, var. WANDJINA.

wonga, var. WONGI *v.*

wonga: see WONGA-WONGA 1.

wonga /ˈwɒŋgə/, *n.*[1] [a. Wergaia dial. of Wemba *waŋgal* reed-bed, bulrush.] BULRUSH.

1865 *Trans. Philos. Soc. N.S.W.* 361 In this part of the county where extensive reed beds are of common occurrence, the natives live for several months during the year on 'Typha roots', or Wongal (*Typha Shuttleworthii*). **1888** *Proc. Linnean Soc. N.S.W.* III. 550 *Typha angustifolia* . . is the 'Wonga' of the Lower Murray aboriginals. The young shoots are edible, and resemble asparagus. **1965** *Austral. Encycl.* IX. 347 'Wonga' is a Lower Murray aboriginal word conveying the idea of 'quivering motion' or 'suddenly springing up' and was originally applied to *Typha angustifolia*, the reed mace.

wonga /ˈwɒŋgə/, *n.*[2] [Prob. f. a W.A. Aboriginal language.] CORROBOREE *n.* 1. Also *attrib.*

1946 W.E. HARNEY *North of 23°* 220 The aboriginals are singing and stamping their feet down in the camp, for they are dancing a wonga, the trade dance of these people. **1955** F. LANE *Patrol to Kimberleys* 8 'The others are in Derby for the big fella wonga—that's the corroboree.' 'Corroboree?' 'That's a native shindig they put on when they get together.' *Ibid.* 133 Later many of Tiger's 'plays' had been pirated by less talented wonga makers.

wongai /ˈwɒŋgaɪ/. [Prob. f. a Qld. Aboriginal language.] A tree occurring on the islands of n.e. Aust., bearing an edible fruit, as *Zizyphus jujuba* (fam. Rhamnaceae) and a species of *Terminalia* (fam. Combretaceae); the fruit of these trees. Also *attrib.*, esp. as **wongai tree.**

1904 *Emu* III. 183 The date-like fruit of the terminalia (native 'wongai'). **1947** I.L. IDRIESS *Isles of Despair* 146 All the yams and berries and wongais will soon ripen. **1952** C. SIMPSON *Come away, Pearler* 14 Her mouth had the fullness and colour of the ripe red-purple plums of the wongai-tree. **1968** *Courier-Mail* (Brisbane) 10 July 2/8 Thursday Island . . has an informal charm and friendliness which easily tempts one to bite into the sticky fruit of the wongai tree. If you eat this fruit, legend says, you are bound to return.

wonga-wonga /ˈwɒŋgə-wɒŋgə/. Also **wanga-wanga.** [a. Dharuk *waŋa waŋa.*]

1. The ground-feeding, grey and white pigeon *Leucosarcia melanoleuca* of e. mainland Aust. Also *attrib.*, esp. as **wonga-wonga pigeon,** and freq. abbrev. as **wonga (pigeon).**

1821 L. MACQUARIE *Jrnls. of Tours* 20 Nov. (1956) 223 Major Morisett has most kindly sent his young friend Lachlan the following very handsome present of pets; vizt. four black swans . . and one wanga-wanga pigeon. **1827** P. CUNNINGHAM *Two Yrs. in N.S.W.* I. 321 We have a large pigeon named the *wanga-wanga*, of the size and appearance of the ringdove. **1833** W.H. BRETON *Excursions* 270 The most common is the bronze-winged about the size of a tame pigeon; but although a handsome bird, it is very far inferior to the won-ga won-ga. **1843** J. GOULD *Birds of Aust.* (1848) V. Pl. 63, While traversing these arborean solitudes, one is frequently startled by the sudden rising of the Wonga-wonga, the noise of whose wings is quite equal to, and not very different from, that made by a Pheasant. **1860** G. BENNETT *Gatherings of Naturalist* 4 The Wonga-Wonga among the Pigeon tribe is not less esteemed, its flesh being white, delicate, and of surpassing flavour. **1868** J. BAIRD *Emigrant's Guide Australasia* 39 The wonga wonga pigeons, each weighing about a pound, were delicious. **1872** G.S. BADEN-POWELL *New Homes for Old Country* 353 The beautiful light-grey wonga-wonga is found chiefly in scrubs. **1890** G.J. BROINOWSKI *Birds of Aust.* III. Pl. 11, In the Burragorang Valley . . the Wonga is found in great numbers, attracted by the Black Wattle. **1896** *Bulletin* (Sydney) 18 Apr. 27/1 From Botany came the words wombat, wommera, yarraman, wonga-wonga. **1899** *Austral. Mag.* (Sydney) 29 Apr. 104, I saw a pair of beautiful round-breasted wonga pigeons, parading on a log. **1904** *Emu* III. 236, I have at last seen a Wonga's (*Leucosarcia picata*) nest. **1917** *Bulletin* (Sydney) 9 Aug. 24/4 'E.S.S.' . . says the wonga is the pick of the bush pigeons. Guess he hasn't tasted the green-pigeon, which . . excels the wonga as the latter excels the brown-pigeon. **1922** R.L. JACK *Northmost Aust.* I. 314 Scrub turkeys, wonga wongas and Torres Strait pigeons were seen. **1935** F. CLUNE *Rolling down Lachlan* 45 They . . caught a wonga pigeon for breakfast. **1965** *Austral. Encycl.* VII. 112 The largest member of the family is the wonga pigeon, an inhabitant of the heavy forests of eastern Australia from Cape York to Victoria; it gets the name 'wonga' from its curious, oft-repeated call. **1984** M. BLAKERS et al. *Atlas Austral. Birds* 238 The Wonga is a ground-feeding pigeon that lives mainly in rainforest and eucalypt forest.

2. Special Comb. **wonga-wonga vine,** the climbing plant *Pandorea pandorana* (fam. Bignoniaceae) of e. Aust. incl. Tas., bearing clusters of showy pale-coloured flowers and cultivated as an ornamental. Also **wonga vine.**

1895 J.H. MAIDEN *Flowering Plants & Ferns N.S.W.* 33 The Wonga Wonga Vine. *Tecoma australis* . . a tall, woody, glabrous climber, with more or less twining branches. **1901** 'A. FERRES' *Free Selector* 114 In the happy days of long ago, Beneath the wonga vine. **1914** H.M. VAUGHAN *Australasian Wander-Yr.* 279 The elegant white-blossomed 'Wonga-wonga vine', or wild tecoma of Australia. **1936** F. CLUNE *Roaming round Darling* 162 Another shrub was the wonga-wonga vine. It has white flowers, and the blacks used to hollow the stems and make whistles from them. **1945** *Queanbeyan Age* 30 Oct. 3/1 Bignonia Australis is better known as the Wonga Wonga vine, and with its bell-shaped blooms of purple-spotted petals, is a showy representative of its race. **1985** *Canberra Times* 20 June (Suppl.) 4/2 *Pandorea pandorana* (wonga vine) is . . an extremely floriferous, strong-growing climber with a twining habit. . . The creamy or pale-brown flowers are borne in loose clusters. The throat of the floral tube may be dotted or wholly suffused with colours varying from red to purple or maroon.

wongi /ˈwɒŋgi/, *n.*[1] *Austral. pidgin.* Also **wangie, wongie, wongy.** [f. WONGI *v.*] A conversation; a chat; also the local idiom (see quot. 1931). Also *attrib.*

[**1895** *Port Augusta Dispatch* 27 Sept., We camped together that evening and had a good *wang* (talk). Then we parted again next morning.] **1903** *Folklore* (London) XIV. iv. 342 Jack went to have a *wangie* (talk) with the native who gave it. **1929** K.S. PRICHARD *Coonardoo* 243 He . . had seen smoke . . and come in for a bit of sugar and a wongie. **1930** *Listening Post* (Perth) Aug. 19 Barney dearly loves a wongi. **1931** O. WALTERS *Shrapnel Green* 33 The wongi was 'ard to get on to. . . A shanty was sometimes a caffey. **1945** *Frontier News* June 6/2 Those of us . . who used to pull up, whenever we did meet someone on the track, to boil the billy and have a 'wongy'. **1950** K.S. PRICHARD *Winged Seeds* 315 Occasionally Bill mentioned having met some goldfields boys and foregathered with them for a 'wongie' about home. **1962** *Texas Q.* 29 If a bloke comes in in the middle of the afternoon when there's only you and the blowfly on the window in the bar and if he asks you to have one, well, he's out for a wongi. **1968** W. GILL *Petermann Journey* 6 As we parted, I was invited to his camp for a 'wongi'. **1984** *Sunday Independent* (Perth) 28 Oct. 8/4 Senator Withers plays down his role and dislikes the term 'Peacock's right-hand man'. 'Call me his 'wongi man'—I'm just someone he can have a chat with at the end of the day,' he said with a smile.

wongi /ˈwɒŋgi/, *n.*[2] [Prob. f. a W.A. Aboriginal language.] An Aboriginal from the vicinity of Kalgoorlie, W.A. See also quot. 1981.

1950 K.S. PRICHARD *Winged Seeds* 161 'Bob Brown'd never forgive us if he heard we'd been calling on the wongi and hadn't paid him and his missus a visit,' Dinny chuckled. **1981** A. WELLER *Day of Dog* 61 Charley's woman, a shy dark wongi from Kalgoorlie, comes out and takes the baby. . . [*Note*] Really the people from Kalgoorlie way, but any full-blood Aboriginal. **1986** —— *Going Home* 68 He is a Wongi from out near Laverton, and he can hardly speak English. When he first came to Perth many years ago, he huddled in the back of the police Land Rover and moaned in terror.

wongi /ˈwɒŋgi/, *v. Austral. pidgin.* Also **wangi, wonga.** [a. *waŋka* to talk, common to most w. Austral. languages.] *intr.* To talk; also *trans.*, to tell.

[**1835** G.F. MOORE *Diary Ten Yrs. W.A.* (1884) 5 July 271 Weeip . . asked me to 'paper wonga' the Governor about it. **1842** —— *Descr. Vocab. Aborigines W.A.* 100 *Wan-gow, verb*—Pres. part., Wangowin; past tense, Wangyaga. To speak; to talk.] **1872** MRS E. MILLETT *Austral. Parsonage* 79 'Womany drunk', he said with an air of careless dignity; 'I tell him let her *wonga*' (*i.e.* talk)—'morning all right.' **1927** K.S. PRICHARD *Brumby Innes* (1974) 60 You wongie them not to be damn fools, Polly. **1938** A. UPFIELD *Bone is Pointed* (1966) 231 'Do you know anything about the boning of the detective?' . . 'Yes, John . . I wongied with Nero and Wandin, and they agreed to get the bone.' **1955** F.B. VICKERS *Mirage* (1958) 26 'White fella all time wangi,' Bungil said. **1976** C.D. MILLS *Hobble Chains & Greenhide* 35 We used to 'wongi' in the dialect, and I owe most of my knowledge of it to his teaching. *Ibid.* 103 This was the first chance I had to get close to the camp, and we 'wongied' with our toes in the ashes until late that night.

wonguim /ˈwɒŋgwəm/. [a. Wathawurung and Wuywurung *waŋim.*] A boomerang which can be made to return to the thrower.

1878 R.B. SMYTH *Aborigines of Vic.* I. 317 The *Wonguim*, the weapon that has a return flight. **1886** F. COWAN *Aust.* 24 His Won-guim: Boomerang of play: an Eucalyptus-leaf-like toy of wood. **1965** A.W. UPFIELD *Lure of Bush* 69 'There are three kinds of boomerang,' he went on. 'The Wonguim, which returns in its flight to the thrower; the Kirras, which does not return; and the very heavy Murrawirrie.'

wongy, var. WONGI *n.*[1]

wonk. [Prob. f. *wonky* unstable, faulty.]

1. A white person; also *transf.* as a generalized term of abuse.

1938 X. HERBERT *Capricornia* 252 He went to the Dagoes and Roughs of second-class and won their friendship by . . telling them how he had been cast out by the Wonks of the saloon. **1951** *Bulletin* (Sydney) 6 June 15/4 'What's a soda?' repeated the big bloke. 'Why a soda's a woolly, o' course. I mean, it's—Well he's a wonk.' The bloke looked more confused than before. 'What, don't you know what a wonk is either?' Hec scowled at him. 'Well, look here, it's a . . a dill, see?' **1959** S.J. BAKER *Drum* 157 *Wonk*, a white man or white woman. Aborigines (esp. half-castes) use this pejorative much as whites use the word *boong* to denote an Aboriginal. **1959** E. WEBB *Mark of Sun* 20 Sometimes whites would get out of cars along the road and walk over to the Camp and peer inside the humpies, or rough bough shelters, curious to see how the abos lived. . . One of the boys nailed a board up on a tree near the road with '*wonks*—keep out!' on it. **1967** R. DONALDSON et al. *Cane!* 235 'Good on y', y' fat-gutted wonk.' 'An you, Elephant-belly.'

2. An effeminate or homosexual male.

1945 S.J. BAKER *Austral. Lang.* 123 An effeminate male is a . . gussie, spurge and wonk. **1970** P. WHITE *Vivisector* 213 I'd have to have a chauffeur to drive me about—with a good body—just for show, though. I wouldn't mind if the chauffeur was a wonk.

wonky, *a.* [Spec. use of *wonky*: see prec.] Mad. Also **wonkyite** *n.*, a mad person.

1959 A. UPFIELD *Bony & Mouse* 76 Plenty of wonkyites down at Dryblowers, but not that bad. Take a ride over that way and look-see for yourself. Characters, all of 'em. No, this feller muderin' people isn't that sort of lunatic. **1973** J. GREENWAY *Down among Wild Men* 102 One could let one's tongue slip easily into 'wonky'—bush yabber for 'crazy'.

wonna, var. WANNA.

wood, *n.*[1]

1. *Obs.* Applied to a tract of naturally treed land, and now superseded by BUSH *n.* 1.

1770 J. BANKS *Endeavour Jrnl.* (1962) II. 56 Dr Solander and myself went a little way into the woods and found many plants, but saw nothing like people. **1788** *HRA* (1914) 1st Ser. I. 21 Lieut. King describes this island [*sc.* Norfolk] as one intire wood. **1804** S. MACARTHUR ONSLOW *Some Early Rec. Macarthurs* (1914) 85 The Universal mode of feeding Sheep in that Country has been by driving them into the Woods, on the Natural Pasturage. **1821** J. WALLIS *Hist. Acct. Colony N.S.W.* 8 When the first settlers landed, there was not a single acre clear of wood on the island; and the trees were so bound together by a creeping shrub called supple jack . . that it was very difficult to penetrate far among them. **1828** *HRA* (1923) 3rd Ser. VI. 799 Our Stockman goes some miles into the Woods daily with the Cattle. **1844** J.S. PROUT *Jrnl. Voyage Plymouth to Sydney* 21 Except those parts surrounding the settlers' houses, the face of the country appears covered with bush or wood. **1853** J. GODLEY *Extracts Jrnl. Visit N.S.W.* 4 The Australian woods, composed chiefly of different species of eucalyptus, or gum-tree, are sparse, scanty, and altogether destitute of shrubs and parasites. **1872** 'RESIDENT' *Glimpses Life Vic.* 5 Life in the woods. **1892** 'MRS A. MACLEOD' *Silent Sea* III. 171 The wide shadowy woods and softly swelling rises that succeeded the boundless horizons and arid monotony of that region exhilarated the spirits like an escape from captivity.

2. *Obs.* In phr. with various verbs of motion, esp. **to take to the woods,** (of a convict) *to take to the bush*, see BUSH *n.* 4 a.

1788 *HRA* (1914) 1st Ser. I. 57 A convict who fled to the woods after committing a robbery, returned after being absent eighteen days. **1790** D. COLLINS *Acct. Eng. Colony N.S.W.* (1798) I. 139 They took to the woods, having more than once or twice robbed their companions. **1801** G. BARRINGTON *Sequel to Voyage N.S.W.* 21 The Irish Convicts, who had taken to the woods were soon apprehended. **1809** *Sydney Gaz.* 14 May, We should fairly wish to persuade others from so stupid a conduct as that of taking to the woods, under a notion of *bettering* their condition. **1818** T.E. WELLS *M. Howe* (1945) 17 He eloped into the Woods and joined twenty-eight felons at that time at large committing depredations. **1827** P. CUNNINGHAM *Two Yrs. in N.S.W.* II. 194 Some . . will occasionally take to the woods, and subsist by plundering the settlers around. . . This method of robbery is denominated 'bush-ranging'.

3. Special Comb. **a.** In sense 1. (*Obs.*): **wood man, native,** an Aboriginal living in the bush; **ranger,** one who travels through the bush (cf. BUSHRANGER 2).

1798 D. COLLINS *Acct. Eng. Colony N.S.W.* I. 555 The hut of the **woodman** is made of the bark of a single tree. **1800** *Ibid.* (1802) II. 300 With the **wood natives** he had sufficient influence to persuade them that he had once been a black man. **1811** G. PATERSON *Hist. N.S.W.* 106 These wood natives make a paste formed of the fern-root and the ant bruised together. **1804** *Sydney Gaz.* 30 Sept., *To Stock-keepers, and* **Wood Rangers,** lost, a Brindled Cow. **1807** *HRA* (1921) 3rd Ser. I. 668 In consequence Labour stood still, and the Inhabitants became a set of Wood-Rangers; and I much fear it will be some time before they are brought to . . industrious habits. **1814** M. FLINDERS *Voyage Terra Australis* I. p. cxxxv, This little bear-like quadruped is known in New South Wales, and called by the natives *womat, wombat* or *womback*, according to the different dialects, or perhaps to the different rendering of the wood rangers who brought the information.

b. Used to designate the habitat of animals: **wood adder,** any of several small, harmless lizards of the fam. Gekkonidae, esp. *Diplodactylus vittatus* of s. mainland Aust; **duck,** the perching duck *Chenonetta jubata*, occurring in lightly-wooded country near water in Aust. incl. Tas; MANED GOOSE; **grub,** WITCHETTY 2.

1903 *Bulletin* (Sydney) 9 July 17/1 The **'wood-adder'** of western N.S.W., a lizard about 3½ in. long, dark brown with blue-black markings is reputed to be venomous. **1935** *Ibid.* 13 Feb. 21/4 We went through that lot—frill lizard, carney, jew, blue-tongue, wood-adder, and at that we groped for another mental inspiration. **1965** *Austral. Encycl.* V. 346 Because of the rather grotesque appearance of some geckos, they are frequently referred to as 'wood adders' or 'rock adders' and regarded as poisonous. Actually they are absolutely harmless and inoffensive. **1825** B. FIELD *Geogr. Mem. N.S.W.* 440 Shot a **wood-duck** for breakfast. **1849** C. STURT *Narr. Exped. Central Aust.* II. 54 App., In the colony they are called the wood duck, as they rest on logs and branches of trees, and are often in the depth of the forest. **1861** 'OLD BUSHMAN' *Bush Wanderings* 81 The Wood Duck, take it altogether is, I think, the handsomest little duck in the colony. **1892** 'R. BOLDREWOOD' *Nevermore* 172 They stepped lightly out, bearing with them a goodly assortment of wild-fowl—noble black duck, delicate teal, and that lovely minute goose, the *Anas boscha*, commonly known as the 'wood duck'. **1933** W.L. OWEN *Cossack Gold* 130 The most graceful of the floating birds, and very good to eat, were the 'wood-ducks'. **1953** E. MITCHELL *Flow River, blow Wind* 91 Wood-duck, grey and white, flew up in golden spray. **1973** V. SERVENTY *Desert Walkabout* 59 Next morning I went bird-watching at the billabong and met a large party of wood ducks. **1986** *Sydney Morning Herald* 13 Feb. 3/2 The other problem is the shooting of protected ducks, such as the freckled duck, and other water birds . . which live among the game species . . chestnut teal, wood duck [etc.]. **1827** P. CUNNINGHAM *Two Yrs. in N.S.W.* I. 345 Our **wood-grub** is a long soft thick worm, much relished by the natives, who have a wonderful tact in knowing what part of the tree to dig into for it. **1851** H. MELVILLE *Present State Aust.* 346 The wood grub was, to them, a great delicacy. **1902** *Bulletin* (Sydney) 8 Nov. 3/2 And if occasion'ly he cooks Some wood-grubs in a pan, Or carnies roasts in lonely nooks, 'They fill,' says Bogan Dan.

c. Used to designate the material: **wood-chop,** CHOP *n.*[2]; also as **wood-chop contest;** and *attrib.*; **joey,** one who is responsible for maintaining a supply of firewood; **line,** a railway constructed for the transport of timber; also *attrib.*; **splitter,** SPLITTER 1; also **splitting** *pres. pple.*

1918 *Bulletin* (Sydney) 16 May 48/2 Bill Lucas will chop against a local champion. . . After the **wood-chop** five rounds between. **1929** 'A. RUSSELL' *Bungoona* 134 There were little groups . . discussing the chances of the various candidates in the competitions listed for the afternoon. 'Red Jerry for the wood-chop!' a man was shouting. **1948** *Bulletin* (Sydney) 17 Mar. 23/2 The woodchop at the up-country show brought a good entry. **1952** *Ibid.* 23 Apr. 16/3 Most of that day he spent watching the woodchops. **1977** *Nat. Capital Agric. Soc., Canberra Nat. Show* 105 The National Capital Agricultural Society *presents* the 1977 '1,000' national woodchop . . *sponsored by* Tooheys Limited. **1981** J.P. GABBEDY *Forgotten Pioneers* p. xi, All logs for woodchop contests shall be classified by diameter and not by girth or circumference. **1986** *Sunday Examiner* (Launceston) 30 Mar. 33/1 George and David Foster cruised to victory in the Royal Easter Show's woodchop arena. **1963** X. HERBERT *Disturbing Element* 74 That firewood business made Mother angry, when she saw the way Phil and I leapt into it. She yelled at Dad: 'Making **wood-joeys** of my sons!' **1929** W.J. RESIDE *Golden Days* 24 Our return journey on the **wood-line** train. **1944** M.J. O'REILLY *Bowyangs & Boomerangs* 42 The Kurrawang woodline near Kalgoorlie, where a gentleman named Hedges had the contract of supplying firewood to the Kalgoorlie and Boulder mines. **1950** *Coast to Coast 1949–50* 149 Toni had come to Western Australia to work on the wood-line up on the goldfields. **1972** B. FULLER *West of Bight* 66 So railways were built. These became known as 'woodlines'. The Gwalia woodline tapped the mulga forest around Leonora and was perhaps the best known. **1979** J. WILLIAMS *White River* 81 The old woodline, where my grandfather Seagrim had gone in the early 1900's and worked felling wood to keep the boilers hissing steam for the gold mine. **1855** G.H. WATHEN *Golden Colony* 91 We had with us as guide through the forest a **wood-splitter.** **1861** 'OLD BUSHMAN' *Bush Wanderings* 216 On their own resources, living by wood-splitting, shooting, etc. **1865** J.J. WESTWOOD *Jrnl.* 391 The woodsplitter tore his blanket in half to keep me warm. **1899** *Austral. Tit-Bits* (Sydney) 25 Mar. 111/2 A wood-splitter was at work, getting posts and rails, and he was engaged on a big log. **1903** *Bulletin* (Sydney) 16 July 16/4 Astonishing the carelessness with which some stumpers and wood-splitters deal with dynamite.

wood, *n.*[2] [Prob. in fig. allusion to WOODEN or WOODENER.] In the phr. **to have the wood on** (someone), to have an advantage over (someone).

[N.Z. *c* **1926** 'MIXER' *Transport Workers' Songbk.* 7, I hold the 'wood' on those who work.] **1949** L. GLASSOP *Lucky Palmer* 156 She's got you taped, too, kid. She's got the wood on all of us. **1954** T.A.G. HUNGERFORD *Sowers of Wind* 264 That's the trouble with you puffed-up bastards—you never know when to call it a day with your big ideas about yourselves. Can't you realize I've got the wood on you? You've got two minutes. **1965** J. O'GRADY *Aussie Eng.* 88 'He's got the wood on me'—he has some kind of advantage over me, which forces me to do whatever he wants me to do. **1971** D. IRELAND *Unknown Industr. Prisoner* 53 You know what the secret is to beat this company? How we always have the wood on them? It's the fantastic unity amongst the men, that has this company on its knees! **1974** D. STUART *Prince of my Country* 66 It looks as if Father has the wood on this sour old man right from the start. **1977** N. MANNING *Us or Them* (1984) 46 We've got the wood on Wilkie and McKenzie. . . I caught them smoking pot in the out-of-bounds area.

woodah, var. WADDY *n.*

wood-and-water joey. [f. *wood-and-water*, in allusion to 'hewers of wood and drawers of water' (*Josh.* ix. 21) + JOEY *n.*[2] 2.]

a. An unskilled labourer who performs the menial tasks of an establishment; USEFUL.

1882 *Sydney Mail* 1 Nov. 783/4 Bobby, he don't know a p'leeceman from a wood-an'-water joey. **1891** *Truth* (Sydney) 3 May 7/4 The wood-and-water Joey scrubbed the pots, pans and floors, and washed up. **1902** E.B. KENNEDY *Black Police Qld.* 74 It appeared that he was known in the town, having been wood and water 'Joey' at one of the stores some months previously. **1915** 'ALPHA' *Reminisc. Goldfields* i. 58 She was the only single girl on the creek—sweet 17 at that—for whom I sometimes acted as wood and water 'joey'. **1930** V. PALMER *Passage* (1957) 31, I wanted you to be something different from a wood-and-water joey, earning a few pounds here and there from men like Kunkel. **1941** *Bulletin* (Sydney) 8 Oct. 15/3 The wood-and-water joey was told to split up the last big log on the woodheap. **1955** G. HEALEY *A.L.P.* 226 As an active member of a branch of the party, I have kept close contact with the real life blood of this great Movement—those unselfish, devoted little people who, in the political movements, as in all phases of human activity, provide the workers, the shock troops, the cannon fodder, the 'wood and water joeys', and finally the inspiration for all things worth while. **1965** R. OTTLEY *By Sandhills* 174 At the lower end of the scale is a boy, called a 'wood-and-water-joey'. His job is to cut wood for the kitchen-stove, clean watering troughs, and do many other odd jobs, such as helping with the killing of animals. **1978** D. STUART *Wedgetail View* 46 You might consider taking a job here with me, wood-and-water joey, general rouseabout.

b. *fig.* A servile employee or hanger-on, a 'bum boy'.

1898 *Truth* (Sydney) 14 Aug. 4/2 You acted as Parkesian wood-and-water joey. **1901** *Ibid.* 13 Jan. 5/1 This fashionable young man, the *fidus Achates*, or social wood and water joey of local squatterdom. **1916** *Ibid.* 26 Mar. 6/6 He may serve yet a while as a wood-and-water Joey for the Tories. **1919** *Bulletin* (Sydney) 8 Mar. 6/3 Australians . . had been told so often, by immigrants mostly, that they were poor things fit only to produce wool and other raw material, and to be wood-and-water Joeys for the Old World. **1949** I.L. IDRIESS *One Wet Season* 230 The old fool thinks I'm going to take it lying down. . . And he thinks I'm going to be a wood-and-water joey for him and his flash young girl. **1963** R.H. CONQUEST *Spurs are Rusty Now* 144 'Can't he get his own beer?' I asked. 'How long have you been that old sinner's wood-and-water Joey?'

Hence **wood-and-water joeying** *vbl. n.*

1917 A.B. PATERSON in C. Semmler *World of Banjo Paterson* (1967) 254 He was to do a year in the shops, and pick up all the wrinkles, and get a car for the old man. Bit better than wood and water joeying wasn't it? **1943** *Bulletin* (Sydney) 4 Aug. 13/1 The boss . . said he could do a bit of wood-and-water joeying.

Woodbine. [Transf. use of *Woodbine* the proprietary name of an English cigarette.] An English person, esp. a soldier. Also *attrib.*

1919 W.H. DOWNING *Digger Dialects* 54 *Woodbine*, an English soldier, so called from the name of a cheap brand of cigarette favored by Englishmen. **1923** *Bulletin* (Sydney) 18 Jan. 24/3, I . . know a Pitt street Digger who . . wanted to see his best girl in a neighbouring village so badly that he lifted a prad from the nearby Woodbine lines for the purpose. All went well till the ardent one bumped an astonished Tommy officer. **1934** V. PALMER *Sea & Spinifex* 154 It's too late to try and crayfish now. You were eating steak and chips down the street to-night with that bunch of woodbines. **1937** E. HILL *Water into Gold* 192 Bagtown became 'Woodbine Ave' . . so-called for the number of English settlers in residence. [**1977** R. BEILBY *Gunner* 43 'Inglesi,' he grinned. 'Pommies. Chooms. 'Bines. That's what we call them.']

wooden, *v.* [Formed after *stiffen* to make a corpse of, but cf. WADDY *v.* a.] *trans.* To strike; to knock down; also *fig.*, to stun. Also with **out.**

[N.Z. **1904** 'G.B. LANCASTER' *Sons o' Men* 252 He'll wooden more of you out if you scare him.] **1905** *Truth* (Sydney) 9 July 1/7 A Perth (W.A.) paper says that 'the proportion of Dagos to the British population is nothing less than alarming and that a secret society exists among the savage scum for woodening-out the white'. **1911** 'S. RUDD' *Dashwoods* 25, I never saw him any more till I see you going to wooden him with the furniture. **1929** C.H. WINTER *Story of 'Bidgee Queen* 65 It flattened Mrs Doolan out, and 'woodened' Johnson's mare. **1936** J. DEVANNY *Sugar Heaven* 255 That woodened the organisers properly. They couldn't reply. **1938** W. HATFIELD *Buffalo Jim* 84 Finding it a bit different to 'woodening' a drunk at the back of the pub in the dark, aren't you? **1957** J. HAWKE *Follow my Dust* 174 He'll be having the ding-bats in no time. Best thing is to wooden him with a shovel. **1959** A. UPFIELD *Bony & Mouse* 59 Got woodened with something wot wasn't a bike chain. **1968** S. GORE *Holy Smoke* 88 Steer clear of all these bludgers that's goin' around town only lookin' for an excuse to wooden some poor coot on the noggin with a bottle. **1981** A.B. FACEY *Fortunate Life* 70 He had picked up a stick about four feet long and one and a half inches thick, and intended to wooden me out.

woodener. [See prec.] A staggering blow; a knock-out punch. Also *fig.*

1899 *Bulletin* (Sydney) 2 Sept. 14/3, I gave him a regular woodener on the jaw and stretched him. **1900** *N.T. Times* (Darwin) 19 Jan. 2/7 She . . poured 'a real woodener' of raw three-star brandy into her. **1901** *Bulletin* (Sydney) 5 Jan. 14/1, I gave the bloke that rushed me a fair woodener! *He'll* be more careful who he tackles when he gets out of hospital again—if ever he does get out. **1903** 'BOONDI' *Boondi's Bk.* 49 Caught him what 'Little Geordie' called 'a woodener' fair on the nose. *c* **1907** W.C. CHANDLER *Darkest Adelaide* 56 When he had recovered from the woodener he had received he made for the exit door with the agility of a rabbit running from a dog. **1922** 'J. NORTH' *Black Opal* 54 A woodener on the jaw . . sent him down for the count.

wooden pear. [See quot. 1865.] Any of the several shrubs or small trees of the Austral. genus *Xylomelum* (fam. Proteaceae), of Qld., N.S.W., and s.w. W.A. See also *native pear* NATIVE *a.* 6 a., PEAR 1. Also **woody pear,** and *attrib.*

1835 J. BACKHOUSE *Narr. Visit Austral. Colonies* (1843) 292 He told us, that the leaves of the Wooden-pear, *Xylomelum pyriforme*, dye wool yellow. **1865** G.F. ANGAS *Aust.* 121 Amongst the anomalies of the Australian vegetable world are the 'wooden pear tree' and the native cherry: the former, which grows near Sydney, has a seed vessel in size and aspect like an ordinary pear, but which consists entirely of hard wood, enclosing a few flat seeds in the centre. **1929** *Bulletin* (Sydney) 27 Nov. 25/4 Growing in the 'wallum' lands of coastal southern Queensland is a tree known as wooden pear. **1965** *Austral. Encycl.* IX. 521 *X*[*ylomelum*] *pyriforme* (native or wooden pear) . . occurs frequently on Hawkesbury sandstone formations. **1967** B.Y. MAIN *Between Wodjil & Tor* 10 Clumps of woody pear trees (*Xylomelum angustifolium*) grew on the sandy slope on the other side of the ridge. **1985** *Blue Mountains Gaz.* (Springwood) 18 Dec. 35/1 Botanical highlights of the walk include the largest stand of woody pears in the Upper Mountains.

woodheap, *n.* A pile or stack of wood, esp. firewood.

1918 *23rd: Voice of Battalion* 15 Oct. 15 Papa Dear—I hope you're well. . . How's the wood heap. **1941** *Coast to Coast* 3 There was a dogleg fence around it and a pepper-tree drooping over the wood-heap. **1962** 'D. FORREST' *Hollow Woodheap* Dustjacket, The Bank, paternal, sanctimonious, an edifice of assumption based on a grain of truth, is a hollow woodheap. **1966** H. GYE *Father clears Out* 77 Father was out at the woodheap chopping Mother's wood for her. **1979** *N.S.W. Parl. Papers* (1980–81) 3rd Sess. IV. 701, I had to work on the wood heap and carry my swag.

woodheap, *v. trans.* [f. prec.] **a.** To ostracize (a fellow worker). **b.** To require (an itinerant worker, swagman, etc.) to cut firewood in exchange for a meal.

1932 *Bulletin* (Sydney) 9 Nov. 21/2 A shearer up Armidale way had been 'woodheaped' for refusing to take out his A.W.U. ticket. 'Woodheaping' is about as old as shearing in Australia. In pre-union days it was applied to the man who made himself a general nuisance. . . It consists in expelling the offender from the shearers' mess, with the result that he has to have his meals in solitude, sitting on the woodheap, which lies behind every shed cookhouse. **1957** D. WHITINGTON *Treasure upon Earth* 90 Mick inquired about the attitude of station owners on the roads leading south. 'No handouts. . . They'll woodheap you on Yarranook and Wineba, but the rest'll turn the dogs on you.' **1977** —— *Strive to be Fair* 114 'He'd woodheap yer' . . refers to a station boss too lousy to give you a feed for nothing. He puts you on the woodheap first.

woodpecker.

1. [See quot. 1965.] TREECREEPER 1; SITTELLA.

1833 *Trumpeter* (Hobart) 8 Nov. 227 *To Naturalists.* To be sold . . birds, in skins . . Woodpecker, Green Linnet, Goldfinch. **1922** L.G. CHANDLER *Bush Charms* 107 We have no true Woodpeckers in Australia. The Brown, White-browed, and White-throated Tree-Creepers of the open timber, and the Red-browed Tree-Creeper of the ranges are, in Victoria, the Woodpeckers of country-dwellers. **1956** A.C.C. LOCK *Tropical Tapestry* 125 Tree climbers, dainty in their rich shades of brown, were plentiful. School children call them woodpeckers. **1965** *Austral. Encycl.* IX. 21 Their [*sc.* treecreepers'] habit of pecking at the bark has given them in Australia the name of woodpeckers; but they are not related to the true woodpeckers, which are unaccountably absent from Australia. **1981** A.B. FACEY *Fortunate Life* 89 The woodpecker was bigger than the wagtail and would run up any tree by digging its sharp claws into the wood.

2. [U.S.: see OEDS 3.] A machine-gun.

1943 A. DAWES *Soldier Superb* 59 The throb of enemy aircraft engines and the cough of enemy 'woodpeckers' always menacing in your ears. **1944** *Barging About: Organ 43 Austral. Landing Craft Co.* Oct. 10 Up on Shaggy Ridge things were pretty stinking what with Nips up trees, mortars and woodpeckers. **1946** A.J. MARSHALL *Nulli Secundus Log* 90 We struck Jap bunkers for the first time. He had dug in on the high ground and each 'woodpecker' was protected by light machine-guns and riflemen. **1985** N. MEDCALF *Rifleman* 197 Find that bloody woodpecker. You will not . . attack it! I don't want nine . . men arguing with a heavy machinegun.

woodser. Abbrev. of JIMMY WOODSERR

1942 *Bulletin* (Sydney) 23 Sept. 12/2 He was too well known to risk going to the bar for a 'woodser'. **1976** S. WELLER *Bastards I have Met* 21 Of course we enjoy our beer too. But this is only secondary. If it wasn't you'd see a lot more blokes drinking 'woodsers'.

wood swallow. A bird of the genus *Artamus*, chiefly of mainland Aust. See also *blue martin* (b), BLUE *a.*, *summer bird* SUMMER. Also with distinguishing epithet, as **black-faced, little, masked, white-breasted, white-browed** (see under first element).

1827 *Trans. Linnean Soc. London* XV. 211 Artamus . . Albovittatus . . called *Wood Swallow*, as we find in Mr Caley's notes. **1842** J. GOULD *Birds of Aust.* (1848) II. Pl. 27, *Artamus sordidus* . . Wood Swallow of the colonists. **1861** 'OLD BUSHMAN' *Bush Wanderings* 141 The wood swallow is nearly as large as the British starling. **1895** *Argus* (Melbourne) 29 Nov. 6/7 The wood swallows are somewhat sluggish and slow in their flight, and thus fall an easy prey to either the gun or the murderous and detestable 'shanghai'. **1901** *Emu* I. 72 That favourite little bird, known here as the Summer Martin or Wood Swallow, arrived today. **1929** A.H. CHISHOLM *Birds & Green Places* 62 These wood-swallows are among the few Australian birds which eat bees. **1955** F. LANE *Patrol to Kimberleys* 121 Disturbed from the grass, wood-swallows and bush-larks rose in clouds which momentarily obscured the sun. **1984** SIMPSON & DAY *Birds of Aust.* 340 Woodswallows' movements are in response to the availability of their main food item, namely, flying insects.

woody pear: see WOODEN PEAR.

wool.

1. In the imperative phr. **wool away!** the call of a shearer to a picker-up, requesting the clearing away of the fleece just shorn.

1879 S.W. SILVER *Austral. Grazier's Guide* 55 The fleece is thrown upon the shed-floor, the words 'Wool away!' are shouted, and another sheep caught. **1895** *Bulletin* (Sydney) 13 July 23/2 But the next day things have altered, and the short, hoarse, 'Wool away!' Replaces reminiscent jokes and latest 'leary' lay. **1908** K. MACKAY *Songs Sunlit Land* 12 From where boards are white with fleeces, And the cry is 'Wool away'. **1917** *Truth* (Sydney) 21 Jan. 11/7 I've been shearing on the Goulburn side, I've shorn at Douglas Park—Where all the day 'twas 'Wool away!' and Toby did his work. **1943** C. SHAW *Outback Occupations* 29 'Wool away', you roar happily as you throw the ewe between your legs into the branding pen. **1965** R.H. CONQUEST *Horses in Kitchen* 193 No bleating sheep . . no bellowed 'wool away'. **1982** *Sydney Morning Herald* 23 Oct. 29/4 There are cries of . . Wool Away! when the fleece piles up around the shearers' feet and the picker-up is busy elsewhere.

2. Special Comb. **wool barber,** a shearer; **bin,** any of several boxes or compartments into which a wool classer directs graded fleeces; **blind** *a.*, (of a sheep) having wool growing over the eyes; also as *n.*; hence **blindness** *n.*; **book,** see quot. 1979; **cheque,** the amount received from the sale of a season's wool by a sheep-farmer or by the sheep-farmers of a district, etc., collectively; **-classer,** one who grades fleeces; **classing** *vbl. n.*, the grading of fleeces; also as *pres. pple.*; **clip,** the annual wool production of a sheep-farmer, or of sheep-farmers of a district, etc., collectively; **dray** *obs.*, a wagon in which wool is carried; see DRAY 1; **hawk,** a shearer; **hook,** a hook used to manoeuvre a bale of wool; **house** *obs.*, a building for the storage or processing of wool, esp. when shearing is done out of doors; **king,** a large-scale sheep-farmer; **man,** a sheep-farmer; **press,** a machine which compresses bales of wool; **presser,** one who operates a *wool press*; **pressing** *vbl. n.*, the compressing of wool bales in a *wool press*; **roller,** see quot. 1979; so **rolling** *vbl. n.* and *attrib.*; **room,** that part of a wool shed in which the shorn fleeces are processed and packed; **scour,** a shed where wool is washed; **screw** *obs., wool press*; **season,** the period during which sheep are shorn and the wool marketed; **shed,** *shearing shed*, see SHEARING B. 3; also *attrib.* as **wool shed dance,** a dance held in a wool shed, esp. an annual dance held to celebrate the end of shearing; **sorter** *obs., wool-classer*; **store,** a warehouse in which wool is stored; **table,** the table on which a shorn fleece is processed; **team,** a team of draught animals used to pull a vehicle carrying wool; **track,** the route by which consignments of wool are conveyed to a port; **wash,** *wool scour*.

1962 T. RONAN *Deep of Sky* 58 They're short of shearers. . . Old Beadsman has picked up enough to beat anything that those **wool-barbers** will own. **1984** W.W. AMMON et al. *Working Lives* 191 During the shearing season the passing teams of 'wool barbers' helped a lot as they earned good money and were big spenders. **1879** S.W. SILVER *Austral. Grazier's Guide* 54 The fleece is spread out by the wool-roller, preparatory to being folded up and tossed into a **wool-bin.** **1953** A.W. UPFIELD *Venom House* 116 The presses were in the same shut-off part of the shearing shed as were your wool tables and bins? **1985** J. HARRISON *Bit of Dag* 23 Why not shove it under one of the wool bins until after smoko when you can figure out what to do with it? **1914** *Pastoral Rev.* 16 Mar. 242 Treatment of **wool-blind** sheep (wigging) is also very desirable. **1932** R.W. THOMPSON *Down Under* 60 Many of the sheep were now becoming wool blind. . . We therefore decided to tackle the job ourselves, only calling in one old shearer. **1935** R.B. PLOWMAN *Boundary Rider* 158 The sheep had been run in so that they could be gone over for wool blindness, and for blowfly damage. **1952** *Bulletin* (Sydney) 6 Aug. 16/2 The last half-dozen sheep, wool-blind wethers, balked. **1982** J. MORRISON *North Wind* 197 In addition the sheep were wet from the showers during the day. With a fading light it was going to be about ten times worse than pushing a mob of wool-blinds up the ramp of a shearing shed. **1961** *Bulletin* (Sydney) 15 Mar. 40/3 The admirable first type says: 'I'll leave the preparation of the clip to you.' . . You show him the lines, and except for an occasional look in the **wool-book** . . you scarcely see him. **1979** HARMSWORTH & DAY *Wool & Mohair* 177 The wool book is the official record of all bales pressed in the wool shed and in it are recorded the full details concerning the contents of the bales, their weight and number. **1930** A.E. YARRA *Vanishing Horsemen* 20 There isn't enough left from the **wool cheque** to pay the income tax people. **1937** *Publicist* (Sydney) viii. 12/1 A few millions annually is to be lopped off our wool cheque. **1951** G. FARWELL *Outside Track* 14 Our wool cheque for 1950–51 was over £600,000,000. **1974** J. HORNER *Vote Ferguson* 161 The station-owner joyfully showed Ferguson his last wool-cheque worth thousands of pounds. **1879** S.W. SILVER *Austral. Grazier's Guide* 78 The process of culling is generally performed by the aid of an experienced '**wool-classer**'. **1899** G. JEFFREY *Princ. Australasian Woolclassing* 38 If the sheep are properly drafted, that is, the different sexes, ages, and culls, etc. kept by themselves for the purpose of being shorn separately, the work of the Wool Classer is very much simplified, because he will be able to class each lot on its own merits. **1908** C.H.S. MATTHEWS *Parson in Austral. Bush* 138 The wool-classers at their tables test the fineness and strength of the wool. **1955** H.G. LAMOND *Towser* 193 One morning, due to an order by the wool-classer which the men resented, the rouse-abouts called a strike. **1982** *Weekend Austral. Mag.* 13 Nov. 16/2 He has encouraged his four sons. One is a shearer, another a wool classer. **1847** *Port Phillip Gaz.* 8 Nov. 3 He has commenced the business of **Wool** Sorting, **Classing,** Packing, and Purchasing and selling Wool on Commission. **1899** G. JEFFREY *Princ. Australasian Woolclassing* 41 In Australia the term 'Woolclassing' is applied to the work carried on at the station at shearing time, when the wool is being prepared for market. **1937** E. HILL *Great Austral. Loneliness* 266 Mrs Giles was wool-classing. . . She has a little flock that she 'puts through' herself for pin money. **1977** F.B. VICKERS *Stranger no Longer* 72, I was in a job, paying the basic wage, that permitted me to enrol for a course in wool-classing at the Perth Technical School. **1844** Macarthur Papers LXII. 215 It now becomes my duty to inform you that the whole of my private Property in New South Wales, with the exception of the **Wool Clip** of the approaching season, has been sold. **1884** A.W. STIRLING *Never Never Land* 53 The wool clip varies considerably, not only with the quality of the sheep, but with the season. **1937** *Publicist* (Sydney) vii. 10/2 Yorkshire's mills consume less than a quarter of the Australian wool clip. **1973** *Bulletin* (Sydney) 13 Jan. 17/2 Dry conditions, bordering on drought in much of south-east Australia have cut the wool clip. **1835** *Cornwall Chron.* (Launceston) 21 Feb. 3 *Tarpaulings* [*sic*] for covering of **wool drays.** **1843** *Sydney Rec.* 2 Dec. 68/3 It is wished that persons sending wool-drays to Sydney will have the goodness to allow the use of them on their return, for the conveyance of families into the several districts. **1853** J.R. GODLEY *Extracts Jrnl. Visit N.S.W.* 13 Wool drays, two-wheeled vehicles, drawn by from four to ten horses or bullocks, generally the latter, and carrying from one to two tons of wool in bales. **1892** *Truth* (Sydney) 1 May 1/7 A wool-dray is never unloaded, bar accidents, from start to finish of a journey. **1916** *Bulletin* (Sydney) 20 July 26/2 Among western **wool-hawks** the 'bindie-eye' ranks first of things that are forever accursed. It is a spidery vegetable that spreads over the sheepfolds and sheds innumerable spiny burrs into the jumbuck's overcoat. **1921** R.N. GUNN *Poems Pioneering Days* 32, I am a wool-hawk from the West; Can tear the wool off with the best. **1934** *Austral. Ring* IX. cvii. 4 Wool-hawks commended the clean-cutting 'tongs' Manufactured by 'Burgon and Ball'. **1955** STEWART & KEESING *Austral. Bush Ballads* 234 I'm king of all the wool-hawks—boss wherever shearers work. **1908** W.H. OGILVIE *My Life in Open* 45 All handling of wool bales is done with **wool hooks.** **1947** W.M. HUGHES *Crusts & Crusades* 39 The dining room was crowded with a mob of hungry men, most of them with wool-hooks in their belts. **1827** P. CUNNINGHAM *Two Yrs. in N.S.W.* I. 273 The fleeces are rolled and carried to the **wool-house**, being sorted according to their qualities into different binns, and weights being placed above them to press them down. **1843** *Sydney Morning Herald* 26 Dec. 2/3 There is also a wool house abutting on the Yarra, where the skins after being deprived of their wool, which is carefully washed and sorted, are cured and ready to be placed in the hands of the tanner. **1857** Tas. Non-State Rec. 103/4 9 Nov., I have got all the offices . . repaired and wool-house built, but I do not like the situation there for shearing being so very sandy. **1839** *Port Phillip Patriot* 3 Apr. 3 The actual murderers [of aborigines] appear to have been set on and supported by some of the **Wool Kings** of New South Wales. **1875** G. WALCH *On Cards* 3 The Director of the theatre, rigidly excludes colonial aristocracy, shoddy princes, wool-kings and all. **1905** *Shearer* (Sydney) 17 June 6/3 He clears out in high dudgeon, telling the trees . . that the wool king is a cow and a deep-dyed ruffian! **1936** E. SCOTT *Aust. during War* in *Official Hist. Aust. 1914–18* XI. 850 Sir Samuel M'Caughey was one of the best known and most successful graziers in Australia, one of those 'wool kings' of the great flock, founded by John Macarthur, who clipped fortune from the backs of their millions of sheep. **1950** *Bulletin* (Sydney) 8 Mar. 13/3 Two sons of local wool-kings leaned on . . two English sports-cars. **1850** *Irish Exile* (Hobart) 17 Aug. 4/3 *Bankers!* merchants, lawyers, **woolmen**—all of them. **1929** A.H. CHISHOLM *Birds & Green Places* 57 Among the wool-men of central Queensland! **1973** *Bulletin* (Sydney) 13 Jan. 18/1 With their average debt estimated at about $45,000 (for woolmen) graziers were more often than not locked in. **1829** *Hobart Town Almanack* 141 **Wool presses** on the different farms of the interior are also becoming more common every day. **1845** *Sydney Morning Herald* 8 Aug. 4/3 Containing a most splendid wool press, the original cost of which was £150. **1887** A. NICOLS *Wild Life & Adventure* 191 Sorting the fleeces according to quality, forming them into bales in the wool-press and marking them. **1912** J. BRADSHAW *Highway Robbery under Arms* (ed. 3) 38, I followed him and butted him into the wool press, and would have dumped him up with a bail of dags only for the other shearers pleading him off. **1934** T. WOOD *Cobbers* 191 To talk about shearing, and wool-presses, and cuts of lucerne. **1980** P. FREEMAN *Woolshed* 20 There are now various collections of wool bins and baskets which are fed separately into the 'wool press'. The wool is pressed into bales which are sewn up and stencilled. **1846** C.P. HODGSON *Reminisc. Aust.* 107 A man being on the alert to pick up the fleeces as soon as they are clipt, conveys them to the wool-sorter, who arranges them according to their quality; after that they are handed over to the **woolpresser** and by him to the bale. **1879** S.W. SILVER *Austral. Grazier's Guide* 55 The wool-pressers . . begin to think about making up a bale. **1889** H. EGBERT *Pretty Cockey* 45 There were generally about six wool-pressers. Some of them slept in the Wool Shed, some in the Men's Hut, and others in their own tents. **1933** C.H. HOLMES *We find Aust.* 156 The 'boss' of the board is in command of the shearers, wool classers, wool pressers, and rouse-abouts. **1965** R.H. CONQUEST *Horses in Kitchen* 188 There's the wool-presser, in greasy shorts and Jacky Howe singlet. **1984** *People Mag.* (Sydney) 7 May 40/2 My father was a woolpresser. **1848** S. & J. SIDNEY *Emigrant's Jrnl.* 66 **Wool-pressing** is done by the bale. **1879** 'AUSTRALIAN' *Adventures Qld.* 1 The pioneer squatters had to work and rough it with the meanest of their men. There was no kind of toil in which they did not take an active part—bullock-driving, splitting, building, fencing, shepherding, shearing, wool-pressing [etc.]. **1946** J.G. EASTWOOD *More about Cairns* 30, I . . got three weeks wool-pressing at Maxwelton woolshed. **1953** A.W. UPFIELD *Venom House* 78 'How many shearers?' 'Two. There was a picker-up. And Robin Foster's brother done the wool pressing.' **1879** S.W. SILVER *Austral. Grazier's Guide* 54 The fleece is spread out by the **wool-roller,** preparatory to being folded up and tossed into a wool-bin. **1882** ARMSTRONG & CAMPBELL *Austral. Sheep Husbandry* 174 The T shed . . is built as though it were two buildings—the one forming the cross of the T being used as a shearing board, sheep and sweating pens. This part of the building, and as much of the other as may be required for wool-classing, wool-rolling, etc., is built upon blocks. **1913** W.K. HARRIS *Outback in Aust.* 155 The wool-rollers then skirt and roll up each fleece. **1928** C.E. COWLEY *Classing Clip* 32 It can be 'thrown out' on the wool-rolling table. **1961** *Bulletin* (Sydney) 3 Feb. 44/2 The woolrollers rolled a million fleeces a day. **1979** HARMSWORTH & DAY *Wool & Mohair* 159 The men employed as wool rollers remove all faulty portions and roll the fleece into a compact bundle so that the bulk quality of the fleece is exposed to the classer's view. **1836** J. BACKHOUSE *Narr. Visit Austral. Colonies* (1843) 441 We . . returned to Goulburn, after having a meeting with about forty persons, in the **wool-room,** at Rossiville. **1845** *Sydney Morning Herald* 8 Aug. 4/3 Large and really substantial Wool Shed, with covered-in sheep-pen attached, besides a wool room. **1908** W.H. OGILVIE *My Life in Open* 38 At the end of the shed and under the same roof is a large wool-room. Here are placed the wool-tables and the bins in which the different sorts of wool are stacked. **1936** *Bulletin* (Sydney) 15 Apr. 21/1 It was Sunday morning, and all was still and quiet in the woolroom. **1980** P. FREEMAN *Woolshed* 161 The wool room accommodated 11 tables. **1896** T. HENEY *Girl at Birrell's* 68 Then there were the people wanting work in the **wool-scour,** the shearing-sheds, mustering-yard, shearers' hut and kitchen. **1911** C.E.W. BEAN *'Dreadnought' of Darling* 101 The wool . . goes on to be washed by machine in a second big shed, the wool-scour, so as to get the grease and dirt out of it. **1944** *Bulletin* (Sydney) 8 Nov. 13/2 We'd just finished tea at the woolscour on a Bogan (N.S.W.) station when a swaggie drew up. **1951** G. FARWELL *Outside Track* 138 Down by the waterhole are the crumbling walls of a wool scour, where some £100,000 worth of machinery lies rusting in the sun. **1827** P. CUNNINGHAM *Two Yrs. in N.S.W.* (ed. 2) II. 82 Wooden **wool-screw** (warranted) £15. **1844** *S. Austral. Register* (Adelaide) 21 Aug. 2/1 John Bentham Neales will sell on Saturday, a prime lot of cattle, after which a very powerful wool-screw. **1841** *Geelong Advertiser* 8 May 2/5 Ere the return of another **wool season** our bay will be crowded with a fleet of merchantmen. **1881** G. WALCH *Vic.* 123 In the 'wool season', as it is termed, Echuca presents a scene of great activity. **1908** C.H.S. MATTHEWS *Parson in Austral. Bush* 203 As the wool season was coming on, he had taken to the track again, hoping to be taken on in some of the sheds as a 'picker-up'. **1835** J. BACKHOUSE *Narr. Visit Austral. Colonies* (1843) 318 At Myami, a Sydney merchant, has erected some good, wooden buildings . . prisoners' huts, a large **wool-shed,** etc. Most of them are weatherboard, of the Pine of this neighbourhood. **1845** *Sydney Morning Herald* 8 Aug. 4/3 Large and really substantial Wool Shed, with covered-in sheep-pen attached, besides a wool room. **1865** G.F. ANGAS *Aust.* 276 The largest building on the whole establishment is the wool-shed, where the sheep are shorn, and the wool stowed. **1872** *Illustr. Sydney News* 13 Apr. 55/1 A woolshed on a large station, at shearing time, is a sight worth seeing. Twenty, thirty, mayhap forty men, all clipping the wool for dear life. **1884** A.W. STIRLING *Never Never Land* 152 On any large and well-managed there is a substantially built wool shed, the most approved pattern for which is T-shaped. **1913** W.K. HARRIS *Outback in Aust.* 154 In the wool-shed the heavy thrum of the machines driving the shears goes on from daylight to dark, with short intervals for dinner and 'smoke-oh!' **1935** R.B. PLOWMAN *Boundary Rider* 41 A large woolshed with its attendant yards, men's huts, a cottage . . and buggy sheds . . covered an area of several acres. **1965** L. WALKER *Other Girl* 51 A woolshed makes a first-class dance floor. **1985** *Austral. Agric. Yr. Bk.* (Nat. Farmers' Federation) 121 A typical viable sheep enterprise in the southern zone, with a market value of $500,000, has a homestead; accommodation complex comprising overseer's cottage, workmen's quarters, garage and store; shearers' quarters; woolshed [etc.]. **1965** L. WALKER *Other Girl* 190 The annual **woolshed dance** is always pandemonium. **1977** C. MCCULLOUGH *Thorn Birds* 227 Everyone came to a woolshed dance, from squatters' sons and daughters to stockmen and their wives if any, maidservants, governesses. **1805** S. MACARTHUR ONSLOW *Some Early Rec. Macarthurs* (1914) 113 A person who came with Mr McArthur said to be a professed **Wool-sorter.** **1834** J.D. LANG *Hist. & Statistical Acct. N.S.W.* I. 350 It [*sc.* the wool] . . is either bought or received for consignment by merchants in Sydney some of whom employ wool-sorters of their own to assort and repack it for the London market. **1872** G.S. BADEN-POWELL *New Homes for Old Country* 176 The wool-sorter, and his helps, tie up . . fleeces, and put them in their proper bins. **1890** 'R. BOLDREWOOD' *Colonial Reformer* II. 95 Grahame was obviously devoted to sheep. . . It would have been wrong to have withdrawn so promising a woolsorter from the establishment. **1840** *Port Phillip Gaz.* 13 June 1 Extensive **Wool Stores** at Williams Town are now completed, and ready for the reception of Wool. **1889** H. EGBERT *Pretty Cockey* 5 A public trial of Mr F.Y. Wolseley's patent sheep-shearing machine was made yesterday at the wool stores of Messrs R. Goldsborough & Co. **1901** H. LAWSON *Joe Wilson & his Mates* 88, I had had an idea of getting a billet in one of the big wool-stores—I was a fair wool expert. **1986** *Good Weekend* (Sydney) 1 Mar. 9/1 In the early 1980s, Myer bought a whole block of woolstores along the Geelong waterfront. [N.Z. **1865** M.A. BARKER *Let.* 1 Dec. in *Station Life N.Z.* (1870) 32 We next inspected the **wool tables,** to which two boys were incessantly bringing armfuls of rolled-up fleeces.] **1879** S.W. SILVER *Austral. Grazier's Guide* 40 Hogget fleeces . . make a very respectable show on the wool-table. **1904** *Bulletin* (Sydney) 1 Sept. 16/4 The picker-up running up and down the shearing board carrying fleeces to the wool tables. **1942** *Ibid.* 4 Feb. 13/1 Soon as a ticky fleece hit the wool-table there was a cry of 'Salt!' and the tar-boys rushed up with a bucket of it and rubbed it well into the fleece. **1981** A.B. FACEY *Fortunate Life* 186 Mr Kent showed me how to class wool and throw it so it would fall spread out over a special wool-table. **1836** *Cornwall Chron.* (Launceston) 31 Dec. 2 A great number of **wool teams** are on the road to Sydney. **1848** *Maitland Mercury* 18 Mar. 2/3 Between Merton and Singleton a great number of wool teams remain delayed, many of them so bogged that they cannot move till the roads have dried up somewhat. **1875** 'CAPRICORNUS' *Squatting System Aust.* 11 Citizens rubbed their hands with glee when they saw the wool-teams streaming into the town. **1909** W.G. SPENCE *Aust.'s Awakening* 140 The procession of wool teams paraded the streets, escorted by specials and foot and mounted police. . . The specials, being in plain clothes, and marching next the teams and between uniformed constables. **1934** T. WOOD *Cobbers* 208 Droves of cattle passed. . . Wool-teams passed us, wheels creaking. **1959** H.P. TRITTON *Time means Tucker* 41 Yarragrin . . was also famous as a camp for the wool-teams, coming in from the north-west. **1903** J. FURPHY *Such is Life* 248 These **wool-tracks,** that knew him so well, will know him no more again for ever. **1959** J. WRIGHT *Generations of Men* (1960) 217 They followed a line through the trees that led southward across the road, once an important wool-track to the coastal ports. **1900** H. LAWSON *On Track* 131 The engine drivers at the shed or **wool-wash.** **1908** *Truth* (Sydney) 2 Aug. 7/7 John . . worked at Hughes's woolwash at a wage of 42s. per week. **1955** *Bulletin* (Sydney) 16 Jan. 13/2 The chap was on his way home from work at a woolwash.

Woolloomooloo /wʊləmə'lu/, *attrib.* and *n.* [Transf. use of the name of a wharf-side suburb in Sydney.]

A. *attrib.*

1. Rough, uncultivated; thug-like.

1891 *Truth* (Sydney) 3 May 4/5 One prisoner is confined in No. 3 yard—a 'Queen's pleasure man'—and who is now perfectly sane, could tell you how he was pummelled by two Woolloomooloo bummers placed in charge of him. **1942** E. LANGLEY *Pea Pickers* 73 ''Ave er drink. . . 'Ave er drink,' he said, passing around his flask. 'No-one? All right, 'ere's the Woolloomooloo spit.' He spat and drank. **1965** A.W. UPFIELD *Lure of Bush* 154 'You—you blank Wooloomooloo rat!' Rainbow snarled. **1967** *Kings Cross Whisper* (Sydney) xliii. 11/3 *Woolloomooloo upper-cut*, a strategic boot in the groin.

2. Applied to one who affects the manner of the type specified: see quots. 1900 and 1984.

1900 *Truth* (Sydney) 28 Jan. 5/5 Other men . . could not tell a brigalow scrub from a dog-leg fence . . and . . ride a horse like a tailor, 'Woolloomooloo bushmen' in short. **1944** *Barging About: Organ 43 Austral. Landing Craft Co.* Nov., These Woolloomooloo tars are flouting us to our faces. **1984** V. DARROCH *On Coast* 42 *Woolloomooloo Yank*, a name applied to any seaman (or shore worker) of Australian origin who adopted an American accent—usually after his first short visit to the U.S.A.

B. *n.* A fight.

1981 P. RADLEY *Jack Rivers & Me* 95 Tony roared. . . 'Oh, my aching heart, what a name,' Connie said and then she roared like Tony. Nance put a stop to their private woolloomooloo.

woolly, *n.* and *a.*

A. *n.*

1. [Used elsewhere but recorded earliest in Aust.] A sheep, esp. one which is ready for shearing. Also *attrib.*

1897 *Worker* (Sydney) 11 Sept. 1/2 The sheep are 'jumbucks', 'woollies' have the fleece still on their back. **1909** *Bulletin* (Sydney) 28 Oct. 13/3 Only newchums and woolly-stockmen (i.e., sheep-men) use the whip as a plaything. **1943** *Ibid.* 6 Oct. 12/3 The number of freak woollies I've been mixed up with during the last quarter of a century is phenomenal. **1956** K. TENNANT *Honey Flow* 89 He couldn't be bothered, he said, waiting on a lot of woollies, crutching, shearing, ducking them and drenching them.

2. *transf.* A sheep-farmer.

1961 *Bulletin* (Sydney) 15 Mar. 40/1 There are many types of guessers. The ideal is the big-bull boy covered in competence, confidence, doctor's white coat and cook's white trousers. Many cockies are quite unimpressed with such sartorial ostentation; but one woollie maintains: 'You can get more out of the rousies if you lair up.'

B. *adj.*

1. In the collocation **woolly back** (or **coat**), a sheep.

1915 *Bulletin* (Sydney) 2 Sept. 26/4 A vegetable much abused in parts of Westralia is commonly known as 'blind grass'. . . The woolly-coats, as a rule, won't tackle it. **1926** *Ibid.* 22 July 22/1 Many thousand woolly-backs have invaded parts of the Gulf country once regarded as solely cattle land. **1977** F.B. VICKERS *Stranger no Longer* 107 We shore 42,000 sheep at Bindimia in that year—2,000 more woolly backs than in the previous year.

2. Oriented towards sheep-farming.

1942 *Bulletin* (Sydney) 23 Sept. 13/2 A hundred years ago Australia was more woolly than it has ever been since. In N.S.W. the whole country was arranged for the convenience of the woolgrower.

woolly bull. A one-piece garment worn under a flying suit. Also *attrib.*

1949 A. SCHOLES *Fourteen Men* 10 Tons of equipment, from 'woolly-bull' zipper flying suits to pre-fab huts . . had been accumulating at the Tottenham Air Force Depôt in Melbourne's western suburbs. **1969** J. PEARCE *Look Mum I'm Flying* 12 The next day we were issued with flying clothing. The inner suit called a Woolly Bull.

woolly bush. Any of several plants of the genus *Adenanthos* (fam. Proteaceae) having silky hairs on the leaves, esp. the shrubs *A. sericeus* and *A. cygnorum* of s.w. W.A.

1897 L. LINDLEY-COWEN *W. Austral. Settler's Guide* 182 The wooly bush has a characteristic which is worthy of note; it carries a fibre which would make a good rope. **1936** J.E. HAMMOND *Western Pioneers* 163 In the old days the side of the hill . . was one dense thicket of what was called 'woolly bush', in which the mosquitoes bred prolifically. **1958** F.B. VICKERS *Though Poppies Grow* 133 The scrub was looking rather tired and dusted, but all the little silver-eyes that nested in the thickets of woolly-bushes were having a last minute play-about. **1973** R. ERICKSON et al. *Flowers & Plants W.A.* 15 A shrubby member of the *Banksia* family, *Proteaceae*, is the Common Woollybush, *Adenanthos cygnorum*. . . This is a grey-green bush covered with soft, hairy leaves.

woollybutt. [See quot. 1965.] Any of several trees of the genus *Eucalyptus* (fam. Myrtaceae) having a rough bark on part or all of the trunk, esp. *E. longifolia* of e. N.S.W. and *E. miniata* of n. Aust.; the wood of these trees; WOOLLY GUM. Also *attrib.*, and formerly **woolly-butted gum.**

1836 J. BACKHOUSE *Narr. Visit Austral. Colonies* (1843) 445 One called here, the Woolly-butted Gum, seems identical with the Black-butted Gum of Tasmania. **1853** MOSSMAN & BANISTER *Aust. Visited & Revisited* 185 The trees about Major's Creek are the white-gum and woolly-butt. **1867** *Illustr. Sydney News* 16 Mar. 138/3 There, at the foot of a gigantic woolly-butt, lay the remains of what had once been a man. **1894** *Melbourne Museum Catal.—Economic Woods* 28 (Morris) The Woolly-butt grown at Illawarra is in very high repute for wheelwright's work. **1902** *Proc. Linnean Soc. N.S.W.* XXVII. 581 *Eucalyptus aggregata* follows alluvial flats or damp places on the tablelands. . . At Hobby's Yards . . the tree is known as Woolly-butt. . . Still it is very distinct from the various Woolly-butts . . of the coast districts. **1912** *Huon Times* (Franklin) 3 Jan. 2/4 Fine Victorian hardwoods, such as mountain ash, woolly butt, and spotted gum. **1927** M. TERRY *Through Land of Promise* 61 Common trees were woolibutt, bloodwood, coolibah and mimosa. **1936** J.C. DOWNIE *Galloping Hoofs* 54 Out of a wollybutt and boxwood clump, leaped half a dozen big grey kangaroos. **1949** I.L. IDRIESS *One Wet Season* 265 Soon the messmates and woollybutt . . would add yet more prettiness to the open bush above the lovely vistas of silky oaks. **1958** *Bulletin* (Sydney) 26 Nov. 19/2, I noticed two strange-looking bits of woollybutt-wood. **1965** *Austral. Encycl.* IX. 369 Woollybutt, the standardized name in the timber trade for *Eucalyptus longifolia*. . . The name refers to the thick fibrous bark, present only on the lower part of the trunk. Three other eucalypts . . are also known by this name. **1982** R. HALL *Just Relations* 164 He walked ahead into the bush . . for a moment blotted up by the shadow of a giant woollybutt.

woolly gum. *Obs.* WOOLLYBUTT.

1826 J. ATKINSON *Acct. Agric. & Grazing N.S.W.* 4 In willow brushes the ground is more or less covered with the white or woolly gum trees. **1827** P. CUNNINGHAM *Two Yrs. in N.S.W.* I. 200 Black-butted, and woolly, gums are so nominated from the corresponding appearance of their respective barks. **1839** T.L. MITCHELL *Three Exped. Eastern Aust.* (rev. ed.) II. 163 The woolly gum also grew there, a tree much resembling the box in the bark on its trunk. **1902** *Proc. Linnean Soc. N.S.W.* XXVI. 556 *E[ucalyptus] Stuartiana* . . is perhaps the 'Woolly Gum' of Berrima.

woolly kangaroo. *Obs.* A sheep. See also quot. 1829.

1829 R. MUDIE *Picture of Aust.* 168 In the interior a kangaroo has been met with, with fur so long and soft, as to get the name of the woolly kangaroo. **1856** J. BONWICK *W. Buckley* 90 They had a right to a few of the white man's woolly kangaroo. **1863** —— *Wild White Man* 13 If a native took a wooly kangaroo feeding upon his pastures, the owner of that sheep would soon retaliate. **1903** *Truth* (Sydney) 4 Jan. 8/1 The white man quarrelled with the black-fellows about their gins, and the latter naturally retaliated by stealing the 'woolly kangaroos'.

woomera, var. WOMERA.

woomera /'wʊmərə/. Also **womera, wommara, wommera, womra,** etc. [a. Dharuk *wumara.*] An Aboriginal implement used to propel a spear (see quot. 1963); *spear-thrower*, see SPEAR *n.* 1 b.; THROWING STICK a.

1793 J. HUNTER *Hist. Jrnl. Trans. Port Jackson* 410 *Womar*, a throwing-stick. **1798** D. COLLINS *Acct. Eng. Colony N.S.W.* I. 584 The wo-mer-ra, or throwing-stick, is . . about three feet long, with a hook at one end (and a shell at the other, secured by gum), to receive which there is a small hole at the head of the spear. **1803** J.G. GRANT *Narr. Voyage N.S.W.* 114 With the *womara*, or instrument they throw the spear with . . they make an incision from the throat down the breast to the lower part of the belly. **1814** M. FLINDERS *Voyage Terra Australis* II. 11 Our native did not understand a word of their language, nor did they seem to know the use of his *womerah* or throwing stick. **1819** W.C. WENTWORTH *Statistical, Hist., & Pol. Descr. N.S.W.* 116 The womera, or throwing stick, which enables the natives of Port Jackson to cast their spears with such amazing force and precision, is not used by them [*sc.* Tasmanian Aborigines]. **1835** J. BATMAN *Settlement Port Phillip* 6 June 19 After travelling about eight miles we were surprised to hear a number of voices calling after us, and on looking round encountered six men, armed with spears fixed in their wommeras. **1846** C.W. SCHÜRMANN *Aboriginal Tribes Port Lincoln* 3 The catch of the wommara is hooked, in throwing the spear. **1853** I. CHAMBERLAYNE *Austral. Captive* 145 All the editor knows of the *womra* is, that it is normally employed in launching the spear at a distant object. **1878** R.B. SMYTH *Aborigines of Vic.* I. 319 By means of the *Wammerah*, or throwing-stick, the spear is thrown with much greater momentum, and of course increased velocity. **1888** W.H. WILLSHIRE *Aborigines of Central Aust.* 28 The 'effective' range of a native spear, when thrown with the woomera, is about 50 yards. **1915** *Jrnl. R. Soc. W.A.* (1916) I. 57 The spears are thrown by the hand without the use of the 'womera' or 'yangal'. **1940** J. POLLARD *Out of West* 95 At once Moonda slipped his spear into his womera and threw it. **1952** I.L. IDRIESS *Outlaws of Leopolds* 26 We jumped up and fitted spears to wommeras and leaped out to meet them. **1963** D. ATTENBOROUGH *Quest under Capricorn* 73 He also owned a few spears and a wommera or spear-thrower, a long slat of wood shaped into a handle at one end and fitted with a spike at the other. **1974** D. IRELAND *Burn* 47 They had the grooved stick, the woomera thing to throw the spear. **1976** C.D. MILLS *Hobble Chains & Greenhide* 97 If the butt is towards you, he only has to swing it straight round to ship it in the woomera, then wallop-o, you cop it. **1978** 'B. WONGAR' *Track to Bralgu* 78 The *balanda* mob should have sensed, when they found my spear and wommera left lying on the ground, that I would have no further need to fight or even to hunt. **1984** B. DIXON *Searching for Aboriginal Lang.* 79 A party of hunters crept stealthily up, spears at the ready in their woomeras, to let loose an attack once they were close enough.

Woop Woop /'wʊp wʊp/. [Jocular formation, prob. infl. by the use of reduplication in Aboriginal languages to indicate plurality or intensity; but see also WOP-WOP.]

1. (The type of) a remote and supposedly backward rural town or district. Also (with **the** and without initial capitals) **woop-woops,** remote country. See also BULLAMAKANKA, OODNAGALAHBI.

1918 N.P.H. NEAL *Back to Bush* 32, I once went to church in Woop-woop. **1921** *Smith's Weekly* (Sydney) 17 Sept. 17/6 Dad from Woop Woop was keenly curious about jazz. **1932** *Whiz-Bang* (Brisbane) 1 Dec. 17, I wood not miss it fer anything even if I 'ad to walk from Woop Woop to attend. **1940** *Rip* (Port Phillip) 29 Oct. 1 If I go to the dance on Thursday, I'll have to walk from Woop-Woop. **1950** J. MORRISON *Port of Call* 241 'He's got to go to Mordialloc first to get spruced up. He ain't in the race.' 'That's what comes of living out in the woop-woops.' **1960** *N.T. News* (Darwin) 2 Feb. 1/2 The Fokker's list of calls reads like the report of a cross-country race in the 'Woop-Woop Gazette'. **1972** *Bulletin* (Sydney) 5 Feb. 29/3 A London taxi ground up to the front door and a sun-tanned, behatted head emerged from its window. 'That airport must have been in bloody Woop-Woop,' it said in unmistakeably Australian cadences. **1986** *Sydney Morning Herald* 1 May 13/1 It was like council night in Woop Woop—Federal Parliament on Tuesday, that is.

2. An inhabitant of such a place. Also **woop.**

1936 M. FRANKLIN *All that Swagger* 472 Adrienne was no blob or woop-woop. **1939** FRANKLIN & CUSACK *Pioneers on Parade* 73 'The Mitchell, what's that?' asked Willie. 'Don't be such a woop,' said Prim. 'It's a library.' **1950** *Coast to Coast 1949–50* 201 That'll be a job for you, Mum—feeding the chooks. I'll make a fair dinkum woop-woop out of you in no time.

woorang, var. WIRRANG.

wop. *Obs.* Also **wap.** [A coinage of popular journalism and unrelated to *wop* a southern European.] A 'whore'; used as a term of generalized abuse. Also **wopster.**

1899 *Truth* (Sydney) 5 Feb. 14/3 The peculiar notions of Mrs Grundy [*sc. The Sydney Morning Herald*], who, since her settlement in New South Wales, has gone from bad to worse until she has at last come to be derided and despised as the degraded, despicable sort of social 'wop' of the worst kind that she really is. **1902** *Ibid.* 20 July 4/4 By way of variety this wayward 'wop' became an inmate of one of the Salvation Army Female Refuges in London under the name of Margaret Herbert. **1904** *Ibid.* 18 Dec. 5/4 She got into gaol; and then she was known As a drunkard, a harlot, a wop. **1909** *Ibid.* 20 June 5/2 As a newspaper proprietor, he could confidently claim to have done more for the material and moral welfare of the People than all *the wowsers of Wellington* and their wopsters put together. **1910** *Ibid.* 4 Dec. 7/1 Without the wanging and whangdoodling of waps and Wowsers, or the discordant ding-dong din of cracked church and chapel bullock bells.

wop-wop. *Obs.* [Perh. f. Br. dial. *wap* (or *wop*) to wrap, to make a careless bundle of anything: see EDD *v.*[1] 1.] ROUSEABOUT *n.* a.

1900 *Bulletin* (Sydney) 18 Aug. 14/3 The shearer terms the rouseabout variously a 'loppy' . . 'wop-wop' [etc.]. **1904** *Ibid.* 1 Sept. 16/4 A new name now given to the rouseabout or loppy is 'wop-wop'. The term is said to have originated in the peculiar sound ('wop-wop, wop-wop') caused by the picker-up running up and down the shearing board carrying fleeces to the wool tables during shearing time. **1915** *Ibid.* 28 Oct. 22/3 A shed-hand is a 'rousie' . . or 'wop-wop'.

worb, var. WARB.

word, *n.* [Ellipt. form of *upon my word* assuredly, certainly: see OED(S *word, sb.* 15. In Br. use *my word* is an ejaculation of surprise.] In the phr. **my word,** an expression of emphatic agreement or endorsement; 'indeed'; 'my oath' (see OATH).

1857 *Illustr. Jrnl. Australasia* II. 179 'Surely the report of a pistol would bring some of you to my assistance.' 'My word!' cried the stockman, 'you may safely say it would bring me.' **1891** *Quiz* (Adelaide) 9 Oct. 7/1 'You been Christian along a mission station?' 'My word, yes, along a mission station—my word.' **1909** C. SHELDON *Chewin' Rag* 33 My word! Sandy's as sharp as a 'nife, but he's as streit as a di, you can bet on that. My-my-blest if I can get a word good enuf, 'colonial' isn't in it, Sandy's so streit. My word! **1948** R. RAVEN-HART *Canoe in Aust.* 29 'My word!' he said, that strongest of Australian affirmatives. **1952** 'N. SHUTE' *Far Country* 144 It was a heeler because it went for the heels of the cattle. . . 'Do you use them for sheep. . . ?' 'My word,' he said. **1967** G. JENKIN *Two Yrs. Bardunyah Station* 4 'Would you care for a cuppa tea mate?' I said, 'My word I would!'

word, *v. trans.* To speak to or tell; to accost. Also to rebuke.

1905 *Bulletin* (Sydney) 19 Nov. 5/1 A woman standing at the door 'worded' them, and asked them if they were not going to 'set 'em up'. **1910** L. ESSON *Woman Tamer* (1976) 70 We . . started wording the tarts. **1916** C.J. DENNIS *Moods Ginger Mick* 19 To fight an' forage. . . Spare me days! It's been man's leadin' soot Since 'e learned to word a tart an' make a date. **1919** V. MARSHALL *World of Living Dead* 22 There is the chance to 'word' a mate whom maybe one never sees elsewhere. **1944** K.S. PRICHARD *Potch & Colour* 106 There was a kid at the Three Mile could play dark horse, win like a streak of greased lightning, they said, and promised to word him. **1950** —— *Winged Seeds* 25 Paddy and Bill Matheson worded the blokes who were rushin' the lease. **1968** S. GORE *Holy Smoke* 28 Y' look as if you'd been dragged though a barb-wire fence backwards! Come on, and while you're gettin' tizzed up I'll word yer Mum to slaughter a fatted calf. **1973** J. MURRAY *Larrikins* 117 The 'donahs' would grimace and giggle, and the boys would 'word 'em'.

work, *v.*

1. *Hist.* In the phr. **to work in chains** (or **irons**).

a. Of a convict: to wear fetters while engaged in hard labour.

1790 D. COLLINS *Acct. Eng. Colony N.S.W.* (1798) I. 111 These were the people who were ordered by the justices to work in irons. **1816** *Hobart Town Gaz.* 14 Dec., Sentenced each of them to receive 200 lashes and to work in irons in the gaol gang for 12 calendar months. **1829** *Sydney Monitor* 19 Jan. 1467/3 His Excellency changed the punishment . . from assignment . . to *working in chains* on the roads, the said chains being superadded by an iron-collar with spikes, which besides its extra weight, pinched and scorched the men's necks. **1843** C. ROWCROFT *Tales of Colonies* (1858) 219 You must know that the different gangs that work in chains are watched by overseers, who have their eyes constantly on them. **1849** A. HARRIS *Emigrant Family* (1967) 189 The gangs working in or out of irons on the roads. **1865** 'SPECIAL CORRESPONDENT' *Transportation* 32 The re-convicted men remain there in the chain-gang and work in irons at a bridge which is being constructed over the Swan.

b. To cause (a convict) to labour in fetters. Chiefly in *pass.*

1807 W. PATERSON Let. to Sir J. Banks 13 Nov. 4 The most worthless characters might be worked in Irons as a punishment. **1827** P. CUNNINGHAM *Two Yrs. in N.S.W.* (ed. 2) II. 194 Decided receivers ought indeed to be worked in irons during the whole of their sentence, without a prospect of mitigation. **1837** W.B. ULLATHORNE *Catholic Mission Australasia* 20 The man is sent to an iron-gang, to be worked in chains for three months. **1844** *Sydney Morning Herald* 3 Feb. 2/5 A man of the name of Miers, a prisoner of the crown, residing with his wife has been sentenced to be worked in irons for twelve months for purchasing stolen goods.

2. *trans.* To herd (sheep, cattle, etc.). Also *transf.*, to accommodate (stock) and as *vbl. n.* See also WIDE WORKING.

1880 J.B. STEVENSON *Seven Yrs. Austral. Bush* 115 A cattle yard capable of working a moderate herd of cattle usually covers about two acres, and is constructed of posts and rails. **1890** 'R. BOLDREWOOD' *Squatter's Dream* 140 The collie 'Help', then, as he grew up, showed great hereditary aptitude for every kind of knowledge connected with the 'working' of sheep. **1897** L. LINDLEY-COWEN *W. Austral. Settler's Guide* 632, I have owned a good-sized flock, which was generally worked without a dog. **1901** *Bulletin* (Sydney) 7 Dec. 30/4 A collie puppy will amuse himself by yarding fowls into a stable, 'working' them with a knowledge which was instilled into his mother. **1924** *Ibid.* 24 July 24/4 A neighbour of mine while working cattle had worn the horsehair cracker on his whip back to the knot. **1936** W. HATFIELD *Aust. through Windscreen* 85 Not that an Englishman couldn't work stock in the Northern Territory. **1942** *Bulletin* (Sydney) 22 July 13/2 Long Paddy . . had worked a calf to the outskirts of the mob. **1956** B.J. RAYMENT *My Towri* 18 Harry Rayment worked cattle for about a year on Swanvale Station. **1960** E. O'CONNER *Irish Man* 210 He and Paula and Dalgliesh mustered near the homestead, and worked cattle in the yards close to the house. **1975** R. MACKLIN *Queenslander* 108 We've been working cattle all week and I've been so buggered.

3. In the phr. **to work back,** to work overtime.

1926 'S. WESTLAW' *Mystery of Lombardy Chambers* 10 Ralph Harding was 'working back'. Business at present was pretty brisk; and besides, he was keen to get on. **1939** K. TENNANT *Foveaux* 363 'I want to get off at seven,' Linda said obstinately. 'I'll work back any other night, George.' **1946** *They wrote it Themselves* (W.A.A.F.) 22 Nights of 'working back', doing rush repair jobs in the unaccustomed glare of the electric light. **1960** R. PULLAN *Burning of Albie* 144 Towards Summer, Netta worked back a lot at the office, sometimes until eight. **1970** D. WILLIAMSON *Coming of Stork* (1974) 60 In about five years, Clyde will start stuffing his secretaries and telling Anna he's working back late. **1977** *Southerly* i. 64 Look, I'll be working back tonight at the college and I'll be going straight on to the wedding from there. **1986** *Poets' Lunch* (A.N.U. Staff Centre) 10 You mean you haven't met Cherisse? She's working back tonight.

worker. [Survival of Br. *worker* draught animal: see OED 2 d.] A draught bullock or horse.

1847 *Bell's Life in Sydney* 20 Mar. 3/1 Seed any workers this morning? I'se a missed two . . both on 'em was hobbled. **1873** J.C.F. JOHNSON *Christmas on Carringa* 13 Bullocky Bill . . was driving in his 'workers'. Tommy Banks, his bull-puncher, was over last night for to borrer some silk crackers off of me. **1888** 'R. BOLDREWOOD' *Robbery under Arms* (1937) 7 This was where our cattle ran, for, of course, we had a team of workers and a few milkers when we came. **1893** R. BRUCE *Echoes from Coondambo* 157 Now cunning old worker, crabbed and strong. **1936** *Bulletin* (Sydney) 27 May 21/3 My neighbor has a good pair of plough-horses, but, with a paspalum patch to break up for farming, *his* neighbor is on the job with two of his 'workers' behind the plough.

1959 H. LAMOND *Sheep Station* 74 Those sheep were let go in the horse-paddock—an area large enough to necessitate workers being hobbled and belled at night so they could be easily got next morning.

workers' compensation. a. Used *attrib.* to designate legislation which provides for the compensation of an employee who sustains an injury in the course of employment (see quot. 1906). **b.** A payment or series of payments made under this legislation (also *attrib.*).

1902 *Act* (W.A.) 1 & 2 Edw. no. 5 Sect. 1 (1), The short title of this Act is the Workers' Compensation Act, 1902. **1906** J.W. BLAIR et al. *Workers' Compensation Act* p. xxxi, By 'The Workers' Compensation Act of 1905' an entirely new principle was introduced. By this Act the worker is given a right to compensation from his employer for accidental injuries sustained in the course of the employment. **1927** TREATT & RAINBOW *Law relating to Compensation* p. iii, The *Act* of 1926 not only introduced an entirely new system of administration in matters of workers' compensation but has also introduced a number of radical changes. **1946** F. CLUNE *Try Nothing Twice* 49 In those days there was no worker's compensation or mollycoddling of workers. **1961** *Sydney Morning Herald* 4 Aug. 7/1 A male nurse who was injured while playing with the Callan Park Staff Soccer Club when off duty was entitled to workers' compensation. **1985** *West Austral.* (Perth) 12 June 10/4 Men in the WA workforce make four times as many workers' compensation claims each year as women, according to the TLC.

working, *ppl. a.* In special collocations: **working bee,** a gathering of volunteers to perform a (communal) task; **bullock, (a)** WORKER; **(b)** a hard-working person; a 'willing horse'; **gang** *hist.*, GANG; **mate,** see MATE 1 a.; **overseer** *obs.*, a person employed on a rural property both to work and to supervise the work of others.

1908 *Bulletin* (Sydney) 12 Mar. 15/1 The **Working Bee** of alleged farmers . . made a goodly stretch of the Prospect Road. **1914** *Truth* (Sydney) 15 Feb. 2/6 The Society's now notorious 'working' bee is 'alleged' to have lined a pavilion. . . This 'bee', which is mainly made up of large-bingied swells had been doing for nixie work on the show ground. **1944** A.J. & J.J. MCINTYRE *Country Towns Vic.* 118 The actual work necessary for, say, gardens, is sometimes carried out by the men of the town and district, in a 'working bee' led by the Progress Association. **1982** *Austral. Women's Weekly* (Sydney) 10 Feb. 22/2 On his NSW western highlands property east of Inverell, Jim Morse joined his fellow farmers and graziers in December in a working bee, and planted a woodlot of some 260 trees. **(a) 1805** *Sydney Gaz.* 24 Feb., The Stock consists of 2 **Working Bullocks.** **1824** E. CURR *Acct. Colony Van Diemen's Land* 27 The principal uses of this herd of cattle have been to supply working bullocks for the public service. **1845** G. FLAXMAN tr. Kavel's *S.A. as it Is* 309 Even the working bullocks look as fat, and indeed are so, as the fattened cattle in many parts of Germany. **1857** W. WESTGARTH *Vic. & Austral. Gold Mines* 122 Three, four, and even seven pairs of oxen, or working bullocks as they are colonially distinguished. **1887** 'COMMERCIAL TRAVELLER' *Diary Three Months Trip Qld.* 12 The occasional clang of the working bullock's bells, all of which sounded to me as if they were cracked. ***c* 1906** L. BECKE *Settlers Karossa Creek* 16 He . . had been looking for a couple of working bullocks, which had strayed. **1930** V. PALMER *Passage* (1957) 162 Hughie's career was a novelty and adventure in which she shared, while his own had been a mere plodding along the beaten track like a working-bullock. **(b) 1874** C. DE BOOS *Congewoi Correspondence* 168 It's because they're such reglar stickers that they say a feller's a reglar workin bullock when he does all he knows for his master or anybody else. **1891** *Truth* (Sydney) 29 Mar. 7/4 He must either be someone who can help him bodily and mentally, or simply a working bullock, generally an *idiot or 'looney'*. **1905** *Ibid.* 15 Jan. 1/1 The Assistant Clerk . . is the 'working bullock' of the House. **1790** D. COLLINS *Acct. Eng. Colony N.S.W.* (1798) I. 101 The **working gangs** being now so much reduced by the late embarkation, the hoy was employed in bringing the timber. **1810** *Sydney Gaz.* 21 Jan., In Consequence of His Excellency the *Governor* having been enabled to augment the Ration, the Hours of Labour for Working Gangs in the Employ of Government will be as follows. **1820** *Ibid.* 1 Apr., The several Working Gangs in the immediate Employment of Government, at Sydney and Elsewhere, do commence their daily work at Seven each Morning. **1835** J. BACKHOUSE *Narr. Visit Austral. Colonies* (1843) 275 We went about two miles into the bush, to visit some working gangs. **1848** J. SYME *Nine Yrs. Van Diemen's Land* 221 The records of marks . . were made up from the reports of . . the 'prison overseers', in charge of working gangs. **1833** *Launceston Advertiser* 4 July 2 *Wanted*, on a small Farm near Town, a **Working Overseer.** **1841** *Launceston Courier* 22 Feb. 3/4 *Wanted* a Working Overseer possessing a thorough knowledge of Agriculture, and competent to undertake the entire management of an Agricultural Farm. **1849** A. HARRIS *Guide Port Stephens* 54 You will do best, therefore, to get 1st What is called a 'Working Overseer'; that is to say, a trust-worthy and judicious man of the labouring order; he will give you information, look after the hands, and work himself. **1879** S.W. SILVER *Austral. Grazier's Guide* 34 With the assistance of his working overseer, he will 'put his sheep through the yards' . . separating all sheep of differing ages from flocks into which they may have strayed. **1891** 'R. BOLDREWOOD' *Sydney-Side Saxon* (1925) 183 If I couldn't go there myself, I was to get a good stockman and put him on as working-overseer.

working man's block. *Obs.* See quots. 1891 and 1901. Also *attrib.*, and as **working man's homestead block.**

1886 N. ROBINSON *Stagg of Tarcowie* 16 Apr. (1977) 65 He has one of the working man's blocks up the creek towards O'Grady's. **1890** *Quiz* (Adelaide) 4 July 2/1 Mr Cotton stuck to the working men's blocks system until it became an accomplished fact. **1891** J. HUGHES *Aust. Revisited* 129 Working men's homestead blocks, not exceeding twenty acres . . may be leased by auction at an upset price of sixpence per acre. **1901** *Austral. Handbk.* 95 Every person who does not own land within the Colony . . who is the head of a family, or a male who has attained the age of 18 years, shall be entitled to obtain a lease of lands *set apart for Working Men's Blocks.*

worra, var. WIRRA *n.*[1]

worrogal, var. WARRIGAL.

worrung, var. WIRRANG.

worry. In phr.

a. no worries: see NO *a.* 2.

b. my worries, *my troubles,* see TROUBLE.

1949 A. MARSHALL *How Beautiful are thy Feet* 50 'My worries,' said Correll, contemptuously gesturing, 'She's got nothing on me.' **1953** T.A.G. HUNGERFORD *Riverslake* 174 'And you're on the outer for sticking up for him?' 'My worries.' **1963** A. UPFIELD *Madman's Bend* 96 'It's going to be another fine day, isn't it?' 'My worries if it's fine or wet.'

would. [Ellipt. for *wouldn't it* (*make you sick*, etc.).]

a. In the interrogative phr. **wouldn't it,** an exclamation of dismay, exasperation, or disgust.

1940 *Wouldn't It: Souvenir Mag. H.M.T. 'Orcades'* 7 Feb., In this brief foreward to *'Wouldn't It'* . . one is tempted first to speculate on the origin of the name. A catch phrase . . obviously expressive of disgust. More often than not . . at the actions or orders of higher authority. Be that as it may *'Wouldn't It'* in common with so many equally succinct expressions coined by the old A.I.F. has apparently come to stay. **1941** *Argus Weekend Mag.* (Melbourne) 15 Nov. 1/3 Another universal favourite is still the famous 'Wouldn't it --!' Never given the final words (the completed sentence has several variations on 'Wouldn't it rock you!', or 'Wouldn't it rip you!'), the exclamation depends upon inflexion as to whether it conveys disgust, amazement, or pleasure. **1942** *Plane Speaking from R.A.A.F. Amberley* 1 Oct. 4 He was tired out. Because why? Because he went for a stroll around the park with his wife on Sunday afternoon and he carried the baby! Wouldn't it? It would! **1948** R. RAVEN-HART *Canoe in Aust.* 78 Jack's comment was a perfect example of the Australian economy of words: he looked at the muck and said, 'Wouldn't it!' **1957** 'N. CULOTTA' *They're Weird Mob* 66 He said, 'That's the number of yer cubicle. Leave yer clothes there. Lock 'em up, an' pin the key ter yer trunks. Got ut?' I said, 'Yes, I have it in my hand.' He said to his friend, 'Wouldn' ut?' His friend said, 'Yeah.' **1961** *Bulletin* (Sydney) 1 Mar. 32/3 The shearing-contractor's wife arrived with the bread in a newish Jag. My missus is driving a five-year-old Morris Minor. Wouldn't it? **1965** *Meanjin* 95 'And she got the ticket I'd have got. Ten thousand quid. I got the next one, one off the winner. Wouldn't it?' 'Wouldn't it.' **1972** J. O'GRADY *It's your Shout, Mate!* 14 The barmaid's sigh was greatly exaggerated. She said to the audience, 'Wouldn't it? It's just not my day.'

b. Similarly in the phr. **wouldn't it rip (root, rotate) you.**

1941 *Somers Sun* 24 July 1 Wouldn't it rip yer? **1945** S.J. BAKER *Austral. Lang.* 152 (*note*) The authentic digger form is *Wouldn't it root you!* A regimental paper 'Wiry' (1941) took its name from the first letters of the words in this phrase. **1961** L. GLASSOP *We were Rats* (ed. 3) 117 Well woulden it rotate ya? **1967** R. DONALDSON et al. *Cane!* 92 'Wouldn't it root you?' said Frank. **1982** *Bulletin* (Sydney) 25 May 50/3 Something really awful can cause you to cry aloud: *'Wouldn't it rip yer!'*

wowse /waʊz/, *v.* [Back-formation f. WOWSER *n.* 2.] *intr.* To preach; to behave puritanically. Also as *vbl. n.*

1906 *Truth* (Sydney) 24 June 1/7 Now then, ye wowsers—rise up and wowse violently. **1909** *Ibid.* 19 Sept. 1/8 On tea the crowd carouses, and the whiskered wowser wowses. **1913** *Bulletin* (Sydney) 3 Apr. 15/1 Spread the new gospel where the Wowsers wowse, And shed for lonely Bung a bitter tear. **1919** PIKE & COOPER *Austral. Film* (1980) 118, I, Egbert McWowse, hereby declare . . I shall no longer wowse, but will Jazz my way to destruction if I want to. And I don't give a dash what the congregation says. **1922** *Aussie* (Sydney) Oct. 10/3 Ut's no good. Ther parsons wowsing 'bout their evils uv divorce. **1968** *Bulletin* (Sydney) 9 Nov. 37/2 But, to be precise about wowsers, and wowsing (it declines beautifully), a wowser was not necessarily a teetotaller, it was not meant to describe the man who led a good and pure life, but the kill-joy, the professional moaner about everything that made life pleasant. **1983** *Nat. Times* (Sydney) 8 July 20/4 You bunch of wowsing do-gooders, I suggest you ring Keith Van der Linden, who is the company secretary, to register your complaint.

wowser /ˈwaʊzə/, *n.* and *a.* [Prob. f. Br. dial. *wow* to howl or bark as a dog; to whine, grumble, make complaint (see EDD *v.*[1]); claimed by John Norton (*c* 1858–1916), editor of the Sydney *Truth* (1891–1916), as his coinage: see quot. 1910 (2) at sense 2 of the *n.*, but also quots. 1879 and 1910 (3) at senses 1 a. and 2 respectively.]

A. *n.*

1. *Obs.*

a. A person who is obnoxious or annoying to the community or who is in some way disruptive. Also *transf.* [The final word of quot. 1879 is unlikely to be 'whores', which is used freely elsewhere in the text.]

[**1879** *Truth* (Sydney) 20 Nov. 5/1 Now she may be seen on Sydney streets—varying between a state of idiotic drunk and beastly drunk—generally in company with a very seedy and disreputable looking being of the masculine order. . . Who shall say our editor (who is so heavy on the Prostitution question) is wrong when he states that some women are born w--s?] **1899** *Ibid.* 8 Oct. 5/6 The Parraween push. A partisan protest. Willoughby 'wowsers' worried. The 'talent' get a 'turn'. **1900** *Ibid.* 21 Jan. 4/5 Seneschal was another 'wowser' that you and all the world wot of. He ran many races . . without being placed. **1901** *Ibid.* 28 July 1/3 For a short period, then, the whilom Wind Club wowsers were exceedingly quiet, but unfortunately this desirable state of affairs was not destined to continue, as the noxious men and women have again banded together for the purpose of carrying on their rascally, unmoral capers. **1902** *Ibid.* 23 Nov. 1/2 Another of his whims or freaks was to promise a number of wowsers of the 'wild woman' type (to use a term coined by Mrs Lynn Linton) that he would supplant men in the Public Service with women. **1904** *Ibid.* 31 July 9/4 Warn several hungry-looking Waine wowsers against the probable consequences of their conduct if they should dare to throw any of the *bags of flour* they had come armed with. A hint to his supporters to keep a sharp watch on these blackguards political meeting. *Ibid.* 9/5 The warrigal wowsers of Waine were conspicuous by their absence.

These lewd, larrikin louts, who seek fatuously to foster the cause of pure, pious, parson-petted Jack Wayne.

b. As a generalized term of abuse.

1899 *Truth* (Sydney) 26 Nov. 6/3 O is the ordeal of facing a mauser, P is the Paddington Popinjay wowser. Q are the qualms which made some heroes queer, R and the reasons (?) they'd not volunteer. **1900** *Ibid.* 11 Feb. 8/2 The officers are a sorry lot of *weird and worried wowsers* who can be safely trusted to get their men into serious trouble the first time an occasion presents itself. *Ibid.* 18 Feb. 5/5 Wollongong's magistrate. A weird old wowser. **1902** *Ibid.* 12 Jan. 4/8 To the bucolic mind any wowser who wears a black coat and a plug hat, and hooks himself on to the tail of a prominent politician, no matter how discredited and perjured, is a person to be cultivated. *Ibid.* 7 Sept. 5/2 Weary Wesleyan wowsers. **1915** B. Gammage *Broken Yrs.* (1974) 87 The *right* type of Australian is a real firm fellow and can't be beaten *anywhere*, that *does not* include the street corner wowsers of the towns but chiefly the country lads.

2. One who is publically censorious of others and the pleasures they seek; one whose own behaviour is puritanical or prudish. (Now the general use.)

1900 *Truth* (Sydney) 8 Apr. 7/1 That old Y.M.C.A. wowser, whose journalistic virtue is of such transparent purity that it could not be suffered to endure more wear and tear without a knighthood. **1903** *Ibid.* 2 Aug. 2/7 He ridicules the mournful croakings of *the wasted wowsers* who denounce every earthly pleasure as sinful. **1904** *Ibid.* 18 Sept. 1/7 The watery wowsers who wouldn't be seen sipping a nobbler in a public house, but who swig good stiff inches from the big black bottle on the bedroom shelf. **1906** *Ibid.* 25 Mar. 8/3 A wowser cannot walk through the Art Gallery without being shocked by seeing the picture of some well-proportioned goddess. *Ibid.* 5 Aug. 4/7 Those pious, Puritanical, pragmatical, pulpit-pounding self-pursuers whom we call wowsers. *Ibid.* 23 Sept. 11/3 Blow the trumpets, bang the drums! Hark!—the Holy Wowser comes! **1910** *Ibid.* 13 Feb. 1/8 Whose hand is cold, and limp, and dank, And breath most strange, and weird, and rank, A sort of human septic tank? The Wowser. *Ibid.* 8 May 1/5 Therefore, 'Palmam qui meruit ferat'—the motto of Lord Nelson. Let it be the motto of John Norton in the circumstances of this case, and for the purposes of establishing his claim to immortal glory as the inventor of the word Wowser. *Ibid.* 15 May 5/6 In the ordinary parlance of the proletariat, it [*sc.* wowser] signifies a 'bald-headed, bad-breathed, bible-banging bummer, who ought to be banged with a bowser, which is a wig for a wire-whiskered wowser'... There is no doubt you have enlarged the scope of, and popularised, the expression; but you have not in the least detracted from its original meaning... Of course, a false sense of public decency forbids the publication of the derivation and true meaning... From 'Subscriber and Constant Reader of 'Truth' who actually pays for the paper, and never forgets to 'rouse on' the agent when it is not delivered.' **1911** *Ibid.* 7 May 4/5 Moliere's Tartuffe was a Roman Catholic French Wowser. **1912** *Ibid.* 22 Dec. 11/7 Wowsers' physogs all remind us, It is bad to live on tea; And each time we gaze upon them, We go out upon the spree. **1915** *Ibid.* 30 May 1/4 The wowsers enjoy the whine of life. **1919** *Smith's Weekly* (Sydney) 1 Mar. 5/3 There are about as many unofficial booze factories as in that other wowser's paradise—the near-dry U.S.A. **1922** *Aussie* (Sydney) Feb. 17/1 Wowsers and gloom-merchants are always saying that we spend too much of our time in sport. **1930** *Surf: All about It* 18 Yet even today, the act of jumping into the Pacific with as little as possible on the body is regarded with gloomy suspicion by the *wowsers.* **1944** 'S. Campion' *Pommy Cow* 281 It was the local wowsers, mainly female, who worried about the plethora of hotels. **1957** 'N. Culotta' *They're Weird Mob* 50 'What are wowsers?' 'Blokes that don' drink.' **1975** *Bulletin* (Sydney) 18 Jan. 6/1 But members of this odd body of wowsers want the right to *force* their opinions on to others. **1986** *Ibid.* 4 Mar. 45/1 Victoria's publicans seem utterly to have lost their marbles. They have made common cause with the wowsers.

B. *adj.* (and *attrib.*) Of or pertaining to a wowser (see sense 2 above); (repressively) puritanical.

1913 *Bulletin* (Sydney) 11 Dec. 3/2 The primitive, pre-Wowser days, when Life, with hard knocks and rubs Was gradually and silently shaping in her fecund processes. **1916** *Truth* (Sydney) 4 June 6/6 Unless people get their backs up and fight this religious monster.. this will be the most wowser-ridden land on this old planet of ours. **1927** F.C. Biggers *Bat-Eye* 15 Although I own I thought th' worst Uv wowser blokes 'oo wears their collars back end first. **1934** *Bulletin* (Sydney) 12 Sept. 11/4 That morbid sex curiosity which is the curse of wowser-ridden communities. **1942** L. Mann *Go-Getter* 201 A few years ago the age was seventeen, but some old women got a wowser government to increase the age. **1957** F. Clune *Fortune Hunters* 28 Instead of buying a drink at the side-door of the closed bar, we raided our own emergency desert-crossing supplies, and drank damnation to Tom Playford's wowser laws. **1962** Marshall & Drysdale *Journey among Men* 195 Now we were at the gateway of the wowser belt. A wowser is a gentleman who uses a contraceptive as a book-mark for his Bible. Adelaide, and its larger south-eastern neighbour Melbourne, are traditionally the wowser cities... Adelaide and Melbourne both have a reputation for the repression of any books that may, from time to time, excite the disapproval of the small, but vociferous wowser groups that flourish there. **1972** *Bulletin* (Sydney) 10 June 16/3 The DLP is frank about seeking what it describes as the 'wowser vote'. **1982** R. Hall *Just Relations* 116 Annie.. leaves town to nurse in some ratbag Churchill war, reconciled with her wowser brother to make matters worse.

Hence **wowseress, wowserette, wowserine** *n.*, a female wowser.

1910 *Bulletin* (Sydney) 22 Dec. 13/4 The female is rather dingy-looking and might be a **Wowseress.** **1911** *Truth* (Sydney) 29 Jan. 1/6 The **wowserette**.. kept quiet on the subject of mixed bathing. **1917** *Bulletin* (Sydney) 22 Nov. 3/2 And now My Little **Wowserine** is tenant of my heart. (Excuse me while I make attempt a ruling right to get: Should she be 'Little Wowserine' or 'Little Wowserette'?).

wowserdom. Wowsers collectively: see Wowser *n.* 2.

1906 *Truth* (Sydney) 28 Oct. 5/5 Never before had Wowserdom received such a shock in its respectability weskit. **1907** *Ibid.* 20 Oct. 3/6 We merely pick up our pen in hand to jot down a few points in favor of the new rules and regulations of wowserdom. **1912** *Ibid.* 11 Aug. 3/6 And finally chuck in his marble in the odor of white-whiskered wowserdom. **1916** *Ibid.* 21 May 1/4 Wowserdom objects to the tights of a ballet girl. **1984** *Bulletin* (Sydney) 17 Apr. 47/1 As a veteran student of wowserdom, I will watch his progress with devoted interest.

wowserish, *a.* Puritanical or prudish.

1906 *Truth* (Sydney) 20 May 5/8 As long as they are not Wesleyan wowserish, pragmatically Puritanical, and noxiously Nonconformist-Conscience-like. **1914** *Bulletin* (Sydney) 27 Aug. 24/1 Gentlemen of a wowserish cast of whiskers are repudiating football's claim to be considered a desirable sport. **1933** F. Clune *Try Anything Once* 122 They looked much the same although it seemed to me they had lost their dash and grown wowserish. **1945** A.W. Upfield *Death of Swagman* 157 'I never read any novels.' 'Oh, come now! You mustn't be so wowserish, Padre!' **1968** *Swag* (Sydney) ii. 38/1 Don't have anything to do with the flat if the frig is one of those puny waist-high models, seemingly designed by members of the Temperence Union. I once had one of those. It accommodated only half a dozen bottles, and each time I opened the door, one would fall and smash on the floor. And I'm sure I heard the frig cackle with wowserish glee. **1983** *Age* (Melbourne) 3 Dec. 11/2 Coming hard on the heels of the casino inquiry, which also recommended in the negative, the Government's decision on poker machines may give it a puritanical or wowserish image.

wowserism.

a. An act or utterance characteristic of a wowser: see Wowser *n.* 2.

1904 *Truth* (Sydney) 3 Jan. 5 (*heading*) Wonders and 'wowserisms' of the week. **1975** *Bulletin* (Sydney) 19 Apr. 21/1 Not all the Rev Saunders' arguments against the club licence are wowserisms. He draws attention to the part booze plays in the road toll.

b. The behaviour or beliefs of such a person; puritanism.

1906 *Truth* (Sydney) 28 Oct. 10/4 An anti-Puritan league fights wowserism. **1912** *Ibid.* 18 Aug. 1/1 That spirit of meddlesomeness and prying prudery that Australians call Wowserism. **1921** *Ross's Monthly* (Melbourne) 25/2, I am coming back to Australia by hook or by crook—simply cannot stand this infernal Imperialist Hell-hole of wowserism and hypocrisy, worse than Adelaide at its worst. **1933** *Melbourne Univ. Mag.* 39 We have acquired a reputation for stolidness, wowserism and caution. **1947** N. Lindsay *Halfway to Anywhere* 191 Bill and Waldo had got the words and melody of 'The Giant' from Pointer Brindle... Oral tradition is still probably immortalizing it, such is the spiritual need to make some ribald retort to wowserism's restrictions. **1956** A. Upfield *Battling Prophet* 113 The excuse was Knocker's ulcers, which forbade him to join in the riot, when actually it was just plain wowserism. **1970** *Bulletin* (Sydney) 30 May 21/3 You have wowserism; we have Toronto. **1984** *Canberra Times* 11 July 5/4 The liquor poll is a curious survivor from the turn-of-the-century days when the country was in the grip of wowserism.

wowseristic, *a.* Puritanical; prudish: see Wowser *n.* 2.

1907 *Truth* (Sydney) 17 Mar. 6/6 Chain prayers. The latest production. A lamentable wowseristic exhibition. **1910** *Ibid.* 2 Jan. 4/7 As the result of the enforcement of numerous Wowseristic Acts of Parliament, gaiety is fleeing from this country. **1918** N.P.H. Neal *Back to Bush* 5 If the wowseristic minds of a few people are so distorted as to be shocked by the tone of some of our articles, we are sorry. **1951** D. Stivens *Jimmy Brockett* 207, I kept thinking of the beaut times I used to have with Jack Harper when we were good cobbers—that was before he went all respectable and wowseristic on me.

wowserly, *adv.* In the manner of a wowser: see Wowser *n.* 2.

1907 *Truth* (Sydney) 20 Jan. 1/4 Mem. for 'wowserly' females—'A woman can be serious without being sour.' **1963** X. Herbert *Disturbing Element* 164 Even we, reared in the wowserly tradition of Phil the Fluter, always had a flagon or two.

wowsery, *a.* Characteristic of a wowser: see Wowser *n.* 2.

1912 *Truth* (Sydney) 11 Aug. 8/5 Three petitions.. all of which were slightly wowsery in their tone. **1916** *Ibid.* 4 June 6/6 Some of those who at the present time advocate shorter hours for hotels are honest enough; but a big majority of the wowsery crowd have an eye open for their own special benefit. **1925** *Bulletin* (Sydney) 16 July 48/1 A more wowsery-looking person I never saw. **1926** 'S. Westlaw' *White Peril* 172 Melbourne.. has the reputation of being one of the most 'wowsery' cities in the Commonwealth, and the gloom of its sabbaths is proverbial. No trams or trains (except church trains) run in the suburbs on Sunday mornings, and in the evenings these conveyances retire from use at the godly hour of 10.15 or so. **1960** *Westerly* ii. 31 Probably some woman flying off the handle, about her near-inebriate spouse to a wowsery neighbour.

wowsey, *a. Obs.* [f. Wowse + -y.]

a. Sanctimonious.

1909 *Truth* (Sydney) 17 Oct. 1/6 Has it ever struck you lately Mister Norton, to be shure, That a smock-faced wowsey sperrit Hangs around about each dore?

b. Disorderly; disruptive.

1911 *Bulletin* (Sydney) 7 May 8/2 William Whitfield wollops the wowsey wasters... William James Whitfield summoned Hugh Sebbens for riotous behavior and assault on the 9th April last, the last named retaliating with a 'poultice' for assault.

woylie /'wɔɪli/. *W.A.* Also **woilie.** [Prob. f. a W.A. Aboriginal language.] The small marsupial *Bettongia penicillata* (see Bettong).

1928 *Pop. Names for Marsupials* (Public Library, Museum, & Art Gallery W.A., Museum Leaflet no. 1), *Bettongia penicillata* .. Woilie. **1941** E. Troughton *Furred Animals Aust.* 156 This animal (sometimes known .. by the aboriginal name 'Woilie' or 'Woyre' in the south-west) .. makes its grass nest in a hollow. **1962** B.W. Leake *Eastern Wheatbelt Wildlife* 45 The woilie (*Bettongia pencillata*) made a neat covered nest of rushes on the edges of sandplains. **1976** *Ecos* vii. 10/3 One scrub-inhabiting mammal, the woylie, seems to do best in areas of fairly frequent burning in the wetter southern forest. **1985** *West Austral.* (Perth) 6 Nov. 54/2 The long-term health of some W.A. woodlands could depend on a small fungus-loving marsupial, the rare and en-

X

xanthorrhoea /zænθəˈriə/. [The plant genus *Xanthorrhoea* was named by English botanist J.E. Smith (*Trans. Linn. Soc. London* (1798) IV. 219), f. Gr. ξανθός yellow + ῥοία flowing, referring to the yellow resin exuded by the type species, *X. resinosa*.] Any plant of the genus *Xanthorrhoea* (fam. Xanthorrhoeaceae) of all States, varying in form from herb-like plants to small trees, many species bearing a tall flowering spike rising from the crown of grass-like leaves. See also GRASS-TREE 1. Also *attrib.*, esp. as **xanthorrhoea resin.**

[**1798** *Trans. Linnean Soc. London* IV. 219 *Xanthorrhoea hexandria Monogynia*... Char. essent. *Corolla* infera [etc.].] **1814** R. BROWN *Gen. Remarks Bot. Terra Australis* 44 Xanthorrhoea .. is in habit one of the most remarkable genera of Terra Australis. **1822** B. FIELD in G. Mackaness *Fourteen Journeys Blue Mountains* 7 Oct. (1950) ii. 32 Xanthorrhoea, the sceptre of Flora... New South Wales is a perpetual flower garden. **1847** E.W. LANDOR *Bushman* 40 There is the xanthorea, or grass-tree, a plant which cannot be intelligibly described to those who have never seen it. **1855** J. BONWICK *Geogr. Aust. & N.Z.* (ed. 3) 202 The Xanthorrhea [*sic*] or Grass-tree throws up a spike of flowers, 5 to 8 feet high; the resin is a balsam. **1868** H. WATTS *Dict. Chem.* V. 1054 (OED) Xanthorrhoea resin. **1944** *Bull. Imperial Inst.* Jan.-Mar. 77 There are no recent figures for the availability of Xanthorrhoea resin. **1955** *Austral. Jrnl. Chem.* 263 The complex mixture of aromatic compounds found in Xanthorrhoea resins. **1974** *Ibid.* 331 Reported occurrences of compounds in all *Xanthorrhoea* resins are summarized.

X-ray. Used *attrib.* to designate a style of Aboriginal painting which originated in Western Arnhem Land and which is characterized by the depiction of internal as well as external organs of the subject: see quot. 1978.

1943 *Primitive Art Exhib. Catal.* (Nat. Gallery & Nat. Museum Vic.) 2 Some of them .. are likely to appeal more strongly to the European than the 'X-ray' paintings from the Northern Territory of Australia, with their representations of the spine, ribs and inner organs. **1958** F.D. MCCARTHY *Austral. Aboriginal Rock Art* 50 The Mangaridji or Ginbalanya tribe was chiefly responsible for the Oenpelli district paintings, but the Gunwinggu now living there also paint X-ray style. **1965** K. KUPKA *Dawn of Art* 73 The painters of the Stone Country produce a sort of anatomical painting which has acquired a certain fame as 'X-ray painting'. **1978** R. EDWARDS *Aboriginal Art in Aust.* 42 The famous X-ray paintings have their home in the west. In them, the artist portrays not only the external features of the animal, human or spirit being he is painting, but also the spinal column, heart, lungs and other internal organs. It is a conventional way of showing that there is more to a living thing than external appearances. **1981** *Aboriginal Aust.* (Austral. Gallery Directors Council) 186 The kangaroo is in 'X-ray' style, showing some of the internal organs and backbone. **1984** J. ISAACS *Arts of Dreaming* 174 The more recent polychrome figures and animals that show internal anatomical features have been called X-ray art.

dangered woylie. Sometimes called the bettong or the rat kangaroo, it is thought to be the main agent in spreading underground fungi that speed up plant regeneration after fires.

wrap *n.* and *v.*, var. RAP *n.* and *v.*

wrapped, *ppl. a.* [Blend of *wrapped* 'deeply interested, centred or absorbed, *in* a person or thing' (see OED 4) and *rapt* entranced, enraptured (see OED 1).] Overjoyed; with **in**, engrossed in; infatuated by. Also **rapt.**

1963 'C. ROHAN' *Down by Dockside* 212 She gave me a quid now and then. I never stood over her for it. She's wrapped in me, see. **1971** D. WILLIAMSON *Don's Party* (1973) 53 *Don*: How did she take it? *Susan*: I don't think she was wrapped. **1974** STACKPOLE & TRENGOVE *Not just for Openers* 114 Poor O'Keefe wasn't so rapt; he took none for 121. **1979** CAREY & LETTE *Puberty Blues* 49 'Look Debbie—Kim told me that Bruce's wrapped in ya,' it said. **1981** P. BARTON *Bastards I have Known* 152 The famous little Ferguson tractor . . helped to save the town of Wentworth during the big Murray River floods in the early 1950s. The people of the town were so rapt in the tractor that they erected a memorial to it. **1983** F. WILLMOTT *Breaking Up* 19 This girl . . reckons she's been rapt in me since the beginning of the year. **1984** *N.T. News* (Darwin) 2 Nov. 2/1 It goes without saying the whole family is absolutely thrilled by the result. 'I was wrapped!' **1986** *Mercury* (Hobart) 27 Mar. 40/1 Hoyer . . said he'd be 'rapt to be invited to train with them'. **1986** *Centralian Advocate* (Alice Springs) 2 May 1/1 The newly-chosen minister has declared he was 'rapt' with his new portfolio.

wren. [Transf. use of *wren* the small passerine bird *Troglodytes troglodytes* of Europe, and other related birds.] Any of many small, ground-frequenting, insectivorous birds, usu. having an upright tail, esp. those of the genus *Malurus* (see *fairy wren* FAIRY *n.*[1] 1) and others of the fam. Maluridae. Also with other distinguishing epithets, as **black-backed, blue, emu, Lambert's, purple-backed, purple-crowned, red-winged, scrub, superb blue, turquoise, variegated, white-winged:** see under first element.

1833 *Trumpeter* (Hobart) 8 Nov. 227 *To Naturalists.* To be sold . . birds, in skins . . House Robin . . Wren. **1847** J. GOULD *Birds of Aust.* (1848) III. Pl. 57, *Acanthiza apicalis* . . Wren, Colonists of Swan River. **1887** *Illustr. Austral. News* (Melbourne) 20 Aug. 147/1 A border of floral and ornithological emblems, of subjects peculiar to the colony. These include parrakeets . . wrens and other birds. **1932** A.H. CHISHOLM *Nature Fantasy in Aust.* 130 Rather more than forty varied species are airily associated under the name of *wren*. . . All are terrestrial, insectivorous birds. . . But the distinctive feature of the clan as a whole (with the exception of the scrub-wrens and fern-wren) is the long, quaintly erect tail. **1965** *Austral. Encycl.* IX. 511 Mainly . . the term 'wren' is applied to the tiny, long-tailed, brisk-voiced birds of the genus *Malurus*. . . These fairy wrens . . occur in various parts of Australia. **1985** *Age* (Melbourne) 9 Sept. 15/5 The Australian wrens, warblers and robins are quite unrelated to their namesakes in the Northern Hemisphere.

wriggle. In the phr. **to get a wriggle on,** to move with expedition; to 'get a move on'.

1911 ST. C. GRONDONA *Collar & Cuffs* 11 After the fire on 'Macara' station the sheep had to get a 'wriggle on' pretty quickly, as nearly the whole reserved paddocks suffered from the fire. **1912** M.C. DONALD *Real Austral.* 15 When he fights, the other fellow has to 'get a wriggle on', to use one of his many slang expressions. **1916** 'MEN OF ANZAC' *Anzac Bk.* 36 You'd better get a wriggle on. There's a short cut that way. **1918** *Fair Dinkum: On Board 'Nestor'* Mar. 4 Everybody must 'get a wriggle on' as all contests must be concluded. **1921** *Aussie* (Sydney) Apr. 28/3 There's a 13th back there says he's found the tunics if you get a wriggle on! **1962** MARSHALL & DRYSDALE *Journey among Men* 70 Ray . . clung like a possum to the rigging. . . The kid in the rigging exhorted the gunman not to waste time, to get a wriggle on, to wake up.

wriggler. A snake.

1927 *Bulletin* (Sydney) 3 Nov. 24/2 A handsome little wriggler is the red-naped or scarlet-spotted snake (*Pseudelaps diadema*). **1949** I.L. IDRIESS *One Wet Season* 60 Bert was whistling cheerily as they loaded up the car—until he thought of snakes. His wife was an experienced bushwoman, but if there was one thing she detested it was wrigglers. **1972** W. WATKINS *Wayward Gang* 144 'Let's go in here and get the wriggler.' 'The men will be home soon.' 'Bugger the men. . . The snake will have gone by then.'

wrought, var. RORT *n.*

wroughter, var. RORTER.

wurley, var. WHIRLY.

wurley /ˈwɜli/. Pl. **wurlies.** Also **whirley, whirlie, wurlie,** and formerly with much variety. [a. Gaurna (and related languages) *wa(d)li.*]

1. The temporary shelter of an Aboriginal; an Aboriginal dwelling (see quots. 1854, 1871, and 1975). See also GUNYAH 1.

1839 *Port Phillip Patriot* 10 June 6/1 The Governor has made good wurleys for them [*sc.* Aborigines] to sleep in when the nights are cold. **1843** *Adelaide Observer* 12 Aug. 6/2 They remained the whole day fetching wood and water, in return for a little sugar or biscuit, and left a little before sunset to go to their whurlies. **1854** W. SHAW *Land of Promise* 209 They live in what are termed 'whirleys', which are fragile erections made of rushes or bark, disposed in a conical shape, and about the size of an oven. **1860** J.M. STUART *Explorations in Aust.* 17 July (1865) 228 A little fellow . . was cleaning some grass seeds in a worley. **1863** J. DAVIS *Tracks of McKinlay* 231 A 'whirlie', or temporary shelter of the wandering natives. **1871** 'IOTA' *Kooroona* 188 When they arrive at a spot where they choose to 'sit down', for that is the literal meaning of the expression they use in place of the English word, 'camp', they break down a few small trees, lay them on the ground in a circle, a foot or at most two feet high, leaving a wide opening on one side, and there they sit, doing nothing, when tired of walking about. These small enclosures of boughs they call wurleys. **1898** D.W. CARNEGIE *Spinifex & Sand* 295 A dozen little 'wurlies' or branch-shelters were dotted about the foot of a sandhill. **1912** SPENCER & GILLEN *Across Aust.* 125 We found ourselves close to a number of wild, sand-hill natives who had here built their little 'wurleys' or lean-to shelters. **1939** T.E. JONES *These Twenty Yrs.* 52 The earth floor of a filthy 'wurly' is no place to bring children into the world. **1950** V.E. TURNER *Ooldea* 7 The natives picked up the sheets of twisted galvanized iron to build new wurlies. **1960** *N.T. News* (Darwin) 8 Jan. 6/8 He denied having shot a dog while it was lying on a blanket in a wurlie. **1975** *Bulletin* (Sydney) 16 Aug. 22/2 Also in sight are the wurlies made of corrugated iron, canvas sacks and rugs. These are occupied by the Aborigines and cost nothing. **1981** *Austral. Women's Weekly* (Sydney) 15 Apr. 62/1 Near Milparinka, in north-west NSW, the frames of a group of wurlies known to have been there for 100 years can still be seen. When in use they were covered in bushes. In Arnhem Land similar ones were covered in paper bark.

2. *transf.* Any temporary shelter.

1840 *S. Austral. Rec.* (London) 28 Mar. 143 What would you think in England of leaving a good bed and warm fireside, and going into the forest by some water hole, and making a break wind (or werlie) formed of boughs, to protect you from the wind and wet. [*Note* House or shelter in the native language.] **1847** G.F. ANGAS *Savage Life & Scenes* I. 162 We encamped at sunset in a green and fern-clad valley, where we each built ourselves small huts, or *wirleys*, of boughs. **1869** H. KENDALL *Leaves from Austral. Forests* 132 He took His axe, and shaped with boughs and wattle-forks A wurley, fashioned like a bushman's roof: The door brought out athwart the strenuous frame: The back thatched in against a rising wind. **1888** W.H. WILLSHIRE *Aborigines of Central Aust.* 5 Up to the present time it has been a 'camp' merely, my quarters consisting of wurlies constructed of boughs. **1931** J.R. FIDDIAN *R. Mitchell of Inland* 93, I made a sort of wurlie for protection against the wind. **1932** C.M. GRAY *Western Vic. in Forties* 14 We made our 'wirley' (breakwind of boughs), had supper and a pipe, spread our rugs on the ground, and lay down. **1957** F. CLUNE *Fortune Hunters* 95 He had no tent, but sheltered his party in a quickly-made 'wurley' of laced boughs. **1959** D. LOCKWOOD *Crocodiles & Other People* 71 'See that wurlie there?' Jack said, pointing to the skeleton of what had once been a rough bush shelter. **1980** M. DUGAN *Early Dreaming* 25 You stood one sheaf up like a tentpole, held it there, and laid other sheaves against it until you had a wurlie or wigwam of hay.

wurly-wurly, var. WHIRLY-WHIRLY.

wurrung /ˈwʊrʊŋ/. [a. Nyungar *wuruŋ*.] The nail-tailed wallaby *Onychogalea lunata* having a crescentic white shoulder marking, now presumed extinct; *crescent nail-tailed wallaby*, see NAIL-TAILED WALLABY.

1875 J. FORREST *Explorations in Aust.* 225 Shot a wurrung on our way. **1928** *Pop. Names for Marsupials* (Public Library, Museum, & Art Gallery W.A., Museum Leaflet no. 1), *Onychogale lunata* . . Wurrung. **1952** J.F. HADDLETON *Katanning Pioneer* 97 The wurrung . . is a little smaller than the tommer. . . You would mostly find him living in she-oak or stinkwood country. It lives on grass, has its young the same as the 'roo but when it was chased by a dog would run into a log. . . It has totally disappeared from this district. **1962** B.W. LEAKE *Eastern Wheatbelt Wildlife* 46 To procure Wurrungs for food, the aborigines used to light a fire and smoke them out.

Y

-y, *suffix.* Also **-ey, -ie.** [Orig. used to form pet names and familiar diminutives and now widespread as elsewhere in informal English, esp. as a mark of familiarity.] Added as a final syllable to: **(a)** discrete, usu. monosyllabic, forms (but see e.g. BULLOCKY *n.* 2 and 3), as BLOCKIE, BLUEY, BROOMIE, BROWNIE *n.*[1] and *n.*[2], BUSHY *n.*, CHALKIE, CREAMY, DOLEY, GREENIE, GUMMY, HEADY, JACKY *n.*[1] and *n.*[4], KIPPY, LITTLEY, MATEY, RINGIE, ROANY, ROUGHIE, SCALIE, SCHOOLIE *n.*[2], SCRUMMY, SHARPIE, SHORNIE, SHREWDIE, STONKIE, SWAGGIE, TAILIE, TINNY *n.*, TRAMMIE, TOWNY, UEY, WAXIE, YOUNGIE, ETC.; **(b)** shortened forms of words or collocations, as AUSSIE *n.*, BARBIE, BIKIE, BLOWEY *n.*[1] and *n.*[2], BODGIE *n.*[1], BOMMIE, BOSIE, BRICKIE, BRUMMY *n.*, BUDGIE, BULLY, BUNDY *n.*[3], CARBY, CHEWY, CHRISSY, COCKY *n.*[1] and *n.*[2], COLDIE, CONNIE, COSSIE, DECKIE, FOOTY, FOXIE, FRESHY, GROUPIE, GUVVIE, HALFIE, HIDEY, HODDIE, HOSTIE, HOTTIE, JEWIE, JUMMY, KINDY, KINGIE, KOOKY, LIMEY, LIPPY, LOBBY, LOWIE, MOSSIE, MOWIE, MUDDIE, NEWIE, NOGGY, OCKY, OSSIE, POKIE, POMMY, POSSIE, PREZZIE, ROUGHY, ROUSIE, SALTIE, SCHOOLIE *n.*[1], SICKIE, SLUSHY *n.*[2], SMOOY, SUBBY, SUNNIES, SURFIE, SWEEPY, TASSIE *n.*, TICKIE, TILLY *n.*[1] and *n.*[2], TOADY, TOWIE, TRUCKIE, UMPY, WAGGY, WEDGIE, WELSHIE, WESTIE *n.*, WHARFIE, WHIRLY, YACHTIE, etc. For forms previously used elsewhere, see BLACKIE, COVIE, MAGGIE, POLLY, SLUSHY *n.*[1], etc.

yaahoo, var. YAHOO *n.*[1]

yabber /'jæbə/, *n.* Also **yabba.** [f. YABBER *v.*]

1. Talk; conversation; discussion; language. See also *paper yabber* PAPER. ALSO **yabber yabber.**

1855 R. CARBONI *Eureka Stockade* 5 There was .. a great waste of yabber-yabber about the diggers not being represented in the Legislative Council. **1863** *Adelaide Observer* 18 Apr. 147/4 The natives of the North were described as a finer race of men than those of the South, very shrewd and intelligent, and in many cases possessing sufficient knowledge of the 'White man's yabber' to make themselves understood. **1876** J.A. EDWARDS *Gilbert Gogger* 187, I could learn the yabber of any tribe in a couple of months. **1888** 'R. BOLDREWOOD' *Robbery under Arms* (1937) 65 'What's all that lingo, Mr McIntyre!' called out Jim... 'Is it French or Queensland blacks' yabber?' **1900** W. DELAFORCE *Life & Experiences Ex-Convict Port Macquarie* 11 The aborigines came around us with their 'yabber', and it was but a short time before they were off to the police and informed them of our whereabouts. **1912** *Truth* (Sydney) 6 Oct. 7/8 There shouldn't be any trouble hitting on the most appropriate name for the new capital. What about a contraction of Yass-Canberra? We consider Yaberra would be sweetly pretty, and, as it will be the place where the Federal yabber-yabber will be held, the appropriateness of the name is unquestionable. By all means, let us have it—Yaberra. **1928** H.C. PERRY *Son of Aust.* 281 But by reason of their light-hearted nature they will with much greater relish join in a friendly 'yabba', hunt, or corroboree. **1938** F. CLUNE *Free & Easy Land* 186 There was excited yabber in the tribal parliament. **1949** C. BENHAM *Diver's Luck* 155 Get some more beer in an' we'll come along an' have another yabba-yabba some time. **1966** D. NILAND *Pairs & Loners* 80 After a couple of hours yabber and taking it easy we were good cobbers. **1984** B. DIXON *Searching for Aboriginal Lang.* 49 'Do any of the old blackfellows around here talk lingo still?' 'Oh yes .. you get the old yabber-yabber around town when they come in for rations.'

2. Special Comb. **yabber stick,** MESSAGE-STICK.

1893 *Trans. & Proc. R. Soc. S.A.* 243, I have, in travelling over the district, often carried 'Yabber-sticks' for the natives. **1942** L. & K. HARRIS *Lost Hole Bingoola* 16 The notched stick, the yabber stick, was a letter and would give more news than the smoke signal he had wondered about. **1958** *Coast to Coast 1957–58* 34 He had come to where, according to smoke signal, yabba-stick, and word of mouth, white men were making powerful magic. **1963** J.F. HARLEY *Mantle of Safety* 38 Or an aboriginal message was sent with a simple yabba stick—a piece of paper stuck into a cleft stick.

yabber /'jæbə/, *v.* Orig. *Austral. pidgin.* Also **yabba.** [Prob. a. Wuywurung *yaba.*]

1. *intr.* To talk; to converse. Also **yabber yabber.**

1841 *Port Phillip Patriot* 7 Jan. 2/3 A black named Winberry said he commanded the party. They pointed their guns at them. Deighton at last got out, and called upon Winberry to protect them. Winberry said he was no good, 'he' (meaning Deighton), 'too much yabber to master'. **1857** K. CORNWALLIS *Yarra Yarra* 5 Oh! I rejoice to think on Quilla Quah, The fairest virgin that o'er Mookerwaa Danced to the war-song of a naked throng, Or yabba yabbaad o'er old Burrendong. **1878** R.B. SMYTH *Aborigines of Vic.* II. 289 The fact of my being able to converse with them in their own tongue, gave me considerable influence. They used to say—'No stupid, Mr Locke; always yabba the same as black-fellow.' **1890** *Truth* (Sydney) 10 Aug. 3/3 He .. explained that when he stood opposite the man who had taken the axe it would 'yabber' and tell him the guilty person. **1905** J. FURPHY *Rigby's Romance* (1946) 27 Wonder why .. they never learn to yabber grammatical? **1922** 'J. BUSHMAN' *In Musgrave Ranges* 231 They collected in a bunch and yabbered excitedly. **1938** F. CLUNE *Free & Easy Land* 217 Jemmy Morrill was worth his weight in gold, as he yabbered with the aborigines. **1946** D. BARR *Warrigal Joe* 14 He dragged me up to the chief who yabbered away. **1969** *Kings Cross Whisper* (Sydney) lxix. 1/2 Few Australians can speak English. Most have learnt from disc jockeys and yabber in an odd language called Strine.

2. *trans.* To say; to ask.

1847 *Port Phillip Herald* 25 Feb. (Suppl.), Bobby cried out to Mr Beveridge, 'what for you yabber me cram jumbuck?' *anglice*, 'why did you charge me with stealing your sheep?' **1859** W. BURROWS *Adventures Mounted Trooper* 83 The missionaries yabber plenty daily bread and trippenny pieces. **1873** C.H. EDEN *Fortunes of Fletchers* 168 'That fellow yabber plenty questions?' asked George.

yabbering, *vbl. n.* [f. YABBER *v.*] Talking; conversing. Also as *ppl. a.*

1847 *Maitland Mercury* 16 Oct. 2/5 When .. within a few rods' distance of Five Dock, such a piercing cry of misery was raised, that Captain Morris at once stopped the steamer; and no sooner was this done than there was a tremendous 'yabbering' heard, the only distinguishable sounds amongst which however were 'Missa Boyd'. **1864** *Port Denison Times* 20 Aug. 2/3 After much 'yabbering', the mover rises to propose the motion. **1879** 'AUSTRALIAN' *Adventures Qld.* 38, I say Bony, what did you do down in the scrub? I heard a good deal of yabbering. **1900** T. MAJOR *Leaves from Squatter's Note Bk.* 51 We distinctly heard the yabbering of many blacks. **1911** A. SEARCY *By Flood & Field* 265, I heard the loud yabbering and laughing of blacks. **1960** J. WYNNUM *Pinch of Salt* (1963) 24 That seemed to do the trick—the yabbering ceased. **1968** D. O'GRADY *Bottle of Sandwiches* 211 Eventually we ignored the yabbering, jabbering and pointing people.

yabby /'jæbi/, *n.* Also **yabbie.** [a. Wemba *yabij.*]

1. Any of several fresh-water crayfish (usu. of the genus *Cherax*) valued as food, esp. the common *C. destructor*, native to s.e. Aust.; LOBBY. Also *attrib.*

[**1884** D.B.W. SLADEN *Summer Christmas* 87 A picnic they'd determinèd Into the forest, some to seek A dish of yabbers from the creek. [*Note*] Yabbers are small fresh water cray fish rather larger than prawns.] **1894** *Argus* (Melbourne) 6 Oct. 11/2 In the case of the small crayfish, called 'Yabbies' by the blacks in New South Wales, these may be found all over Australia, I think, both in large and small lagoons. **1910** *Bulletin* (Sydney) 11 Aug. 43/2 Each man has his own yabby-tin in these parts. **1921** *Austral. Museum Mag.* Dec. 88 The 'Yabbie' (*Parachaerops bicarinatus*), a freshwater crayfish well known for its depredations in artificially constructed dams in Western N.S. Wales .. riddles the banks with its burrows, causing them to collapse. **1923** H.C.A. HARRISON *Story of Athlete* 38 'Yabbies' .. are a kind of small crayfish, of a brownish colour, with long feelers, and, like the latter, turn red on being cooked. **1935** J.K. EWERS *Fire on Wind* 62, I keep a good table here... Parrot pie, braised wallaby, yabbi mayonaise. **1952** C. MACINNES *June in her Spring* 85 This bloody dam is full of yabbies. The bastards have been nipping me. **1962** J. HEDGE *Trout Fishing N.S.W.* 97 The Little Pied Cormorant is highly beneficial because of its intensive feeding on the destructive Yabby. **1977** P. ADAMS *Unspeakable Adams* 71 My epic is called *Claws* and it stars that most awesome of Antipodean creatures. the *Cherax*, otherwise known as the yabbie. **1981** C. WALLACE-CRABBE *Splinters* 16 Yabbies went scuttling from dam to dam in quest of fresh homes in the mud.

2. Chiefly *Qld.* NIPPER *n.*[1]

1952 W.J. DAKIN *Austral. Seashores* 199 This [*sc. Callianassa .. australiensis*] is the species that is popularly known in northern New South Wales and Queensland as the yabby. **1968** W.N. SCOTT *Some People* 132 The point is, as any Queensland fisherman can tell you, that a yabby is a sort of saltwater crayfish with claws, that looks as though someone has stepped on it.

3. *transf.* A wicket-keeper.

1983 HIBBERD & HUTCHINSON *Barracker's Bible* 235 *Yabbie* .. wicket keeper: from the curious stance and gauntlets of the pudgy breed.

yabby /'jæbi/, *v.* [f. prec.] *intr.* To fish for yabbies. Chiefly as *pres. pple.* and *vbl. n.*

1934 *Bulletin* (Sydney) 24 Oct. 21/2 Here's a sport for those who .. forget their bait when yabbying. **1941** K. TENNANT *Battlers* 53 They've gone yabbying. But they'll be in to lunch. **1962** E. LANE *Mad as Rabbits* 161 The glorious summer-time sport of yabbying. **1977** R. MCKIE *Crushing* (1978) 117 The dancing class was at first more absorbing than .. going yabbying. **1980** *Westerly* iii. 29 Gardener's Creek yabbying and tadpole hunting at weekends.

yacca, var. YAKKA, YAKKER.

yacca /'jækə/. Chiefly *S.A.* Also **yacka.** [a. Jagara *dakka.*]

1. GRASS-TREE 1 a. Also *attrib.*

1890 *Oldest Coursing Club in Aust., being Hist. Narracoorte Club* 16 The soil excellent and dotted over in places somewhat thickly with clumps of yacca grass. **1906** *Emu* V. 132 The 'yacca', as the grass-tree is often called, exudes from the lower portion of its trunk a rust-coloured resinous gum. **1917** F.J. MILLS *Dinkum Oil* 8 Men who'd got ashore was bein' bowled over like yaccas in a storm. **1925** *Smith's Weekly* (Sydney) 24 Jan. 23/7 Yacka .. is largely used as a substitute for firewood in the Hill River district of S.A., where there is little or no local timber. **1938** *Bulletin* (Sydney) 3 Aug. 20/4 In my S.A. district tenders were called for grubbing some yaccas. **1970** J.V. MARSHALL *Walk to Hills of Dreamtime* 64 They .. sat at their ease in the sun making yacca-wood spears. **1979** DOUGLAS & HEATHCOTE *Far Cry* 4 There was no green pasture .. or even English weeds among the yackas and stunted gumtrees.

2. Special Comb. **yacca gum,** *grass-tree gum*, see GRASS-TREE 1 c.

1908 M. VIVIENNE *Sunny S.A.* 405 A large trade is

being done with Germany in valuable 'yacca gum'. **1914** *Bulletin* (Sydney) 17 Sept. 22/2 There is one industry in Australia that's going to benefit by the war—and that's the 'jigging' of yacka gum in Kangaroo Island (S.A.).

yachtie. [f. *yacht(sman* + -Y.] A yachting enthusiast.

[N.Z. **1943** *Amer. Speech* XVIII. 88 Yachty.] **1951** L. D'ALPUGET *Let's go Sailing* 39 Any 'yachtie' who has crewed in a trans-Tasman can command a place in just about whatever boating company he chooses. **1965** G. MCINNES *Road to Gundagai* 184 One should never leave them [*sc.* bottles] bobbing about the bay the way the careless 'yachties' did. **1978** N. EVERS *Tas. Paradise & Beyond* 42 The young 'yachties' will tell you that he is a priceless source of guidance and practical help. **1984** *Weekend Austral. Mag.* (Sydney) 21 Apr. 20/1 Club members still faced levies to pay for the privilege of defending the Cup . . despite rumblings from some disaffected yachties.

yacka, var. YACCA, YAKKA.

yackai /'jækaɪ/, *n.* and *int.* Also with much variety (see quots.) [a. Wiradhuri (and many other languages) *yagay*.] A call used by an Aboriginal to command attention or express emotion. Cf. COOEE *n.* and *v.*

1887 W.H. SUTTOR *Austral. Stories Retold* 84 With much shouting of 'Yuccai!' ('Oh dear!'). **1903** H. BASEDOW *Jrnl. Govt. N.-W. Exped.* 16 May (1914) 104 We had not proceeded far when we heard the 'yackai' or 'coo-ee' of the tribe. **1951** E. HILL *Territory* 5 Plenty of fresh water for the ship and the Larrakia, who drank two quarts each with yacki of amazement and delight. **1964** *N. Austral. Monthly* Oct. 22 At the creek at Weipa we yelled a loud 'yakai' and lots of natives came down from the mission. **1967** R. DONALDSON et al. *Cane!* 34 A hundred *yack-ies* and *cooees* rang out over the corn. **1977** V. PRIDDLE *Larry & Jack* 70 In no time his brother Jack and three other searchers appeared and gave a 'Yakki' of delight when they saw Larry had the little girl.

Hence **yackai** *v. intr.*, to utter such a call; also as *vbl. n.*

1903 H. BASEDOW *Jrnl. Govt. N.-W. Exped.* 20 May (1914) 109 We can hear voices and the 'yackaiing' of the dusky folk in the neighbouring hills to-night. **1925** M. TERRY *Across Unknown Aust.* 126 In the North one hears them yackai-ing, laughing. **1958** F.B. VICKERS *Mirage* (ed. 2) 7 It's about time those devils had a spell from yackkying, he thought. And the natives themselves listened to that silence.

yacker, var. YAKKA, YAKKER.

yacker. Also **yakker.** [Var. of *yatter* idle talk, incessant chatter: see OEDS.] Talk; chatter.

1882 *Sydney Slang Dict.* 9 *Yacker*, talk. **1941** S.J. BAKER *Pop. Dict. Austral. Slang* 83 *Yacker*, talk. **1973** P. WHITE *Eye of Storm* 306 She wished it had been a hospital, when she could have produced a chart, handed over . . and swept off without further yakker. *Ibid.* 441 Couldn't get on with me work—not with all the yakker that was goin' on in 'ere.

yacker, var. YAKKA, YAKKER.

yahoo /ja'hu/, *n.*[1] *Obs.* Also **yaahoo, yahor.** [Prob. a. N.S.W. Aboriginal (poss. Dharuk) *yahoo* catbird, owl. See also quot. 1844.] **a.** A name given by Aborigines to an evil spirit (cf. BUGEEN). **b.** *transf.* A monster or 'hairy man' (see quots. 1847 and 1937).

1835 J. HOLMAN *Travels* IV. 480 The natives are greatly terrified by the sight of a person in a mask calling him 'devil' or *Yah-hoo*, which signifies evil spirit. **1843** *Sydney Morning Herald* 12 July 2/8 Several parties have been unexpectedly alarmed by the sudden appearance of a monster, which they designate a Yaa-hoo! **1844** MRS C. MEREDITH *Notes & Sketches N.S.W.* 94 The name Devil-devil is of course borrowed from our vocabulary. . . That of Yahoo, being used to express a bad spirit or 'Bugaboo', was common also with the aborigines of Van Diemen's Land, and is as likely to be a coincidence with, as a loan from, Dean Swift. **1847** *Moreton Bay Courier* 6 Feb. 4/3 In this locality it is called *Yaa-hoo*, and is described as having much resemblance in form to the human figure, but with frightful features. **1856** G. WILLMER *Draper in Aust.* 227 The evil spirit they term 'Yahor', (devil, devil) of whom they live in great terror. **1876** *Austral. Town & Country Jrnl.* (Sydney) 4 Nov. 729/2 For many years past it had been believed by the settlers of that wild part of the country, that the Walla Walla scrub was inhabited by a monster commonly called 'the hairy man of the wood', or what all the blacks stand so much in dread of—the Yahoo. **1893** J.A. BARRY *Steve Brown's Bunyip* 68 Tom won't try no more gammonin' to be a yahoo. He's full's a tick ov sich sport, he is. **1937** *Mankind* June 91 In the Mudgee district . . a scrubby place was reputed to be the abode of a 'Yahu', and a resident in the Maitland district told me a 'Yahu' was reputed to live in a thick scrub there. Each said he was a big hairy man.

yahoo /ja'hu/, *n.*[2] [Imitative (see quot. 1931): but see also prec.] *Grey-crowned babbler*, see GREY *a.*

1928 R.H. CROLL *Open Road Vic.* 49 Forceful note of the 'yah-hoo' or catbird. **1931** N.W. CAYLEY *What Bird is That?* 124 Grey-crowned Babbler *Pomatostomus temporalis* . . also called . . Yahoo [etc.]. . . Many of its calls are difficult to describe, but the loud 'Ya-hoo, Ya-hoo' is a very familiar call. **1948** R. RAVEN-HART *Canoe in Aust.* 99 A more official name is Grey-crowned Babbler but another popular name fits them even better, 'Yahoo', both imitating their call and suggesting their behaviour. **1977** G.C. JOYNER *Hairy Man S. Eastern Aust.* 12 The yahoo of the aboriginals is a large bird of the mopepoke or cuckoo species.

yahor, var. YAHOO *n.*[1]

yakka /'jækə/. Also **yacca, yacka, yacker, yakker.** [f. YAKKER.] Work; strenuous labour; esp. in the phr. **hard yakka.**

1888 *Boomerang* (Brisbane) 14 Jan. 13 The Brisbane wharf labourers are so accustomed to hard yacker that they can't be happy for a single day without it. **1894** *Western Champion* (Barcaldine) 5 June 2/1 Been hurrying to get here to do a bit of yacker for your grub, eh? **1905** *Shearer* (Sydney) 19 Aug. 8/3 If for 'yakker' you're a demon You can do *their* share as well! **1908** E.G. MURPHY *Jarraland Jingles* 39 Yacker allus 'as me beat. **1916** L. FERRIS *John Heathlyn of Otway* 68 Does a couple of weeks' hard yakker, then a few days' liquid refreshment. **1917** C.H. SOUTER *To Many Ladies* 32 'No kid-glove yacker!' says Sergeant Bill, As he charges with his men. **1930** J.S. LITCHFIELD *Far-North Memories* 16 'Them fellers is doing all the yakker, but it is Billy will get the splosh'; said the doleful miner. **1942** *Khamseen Kronikle* 27 Aug. 2 We didn't like the . . beer, the yacka or the oranges. **1942** L. MANN *Go-Getter* 12 Relief was, in a way, like work in the army. You did the job and had nothing much to think about. Even on this hot day Chris would rather have been doing such yacca than delivering bills. **1949** G. FARWELL *Traveller's Tracks* 25 A coal town like Cessnock is . . a base for the hard yacker of industry. **1959** *Bulletin* (Sydney) 14 Jan. 18/3 Old Harry . . reckons he got through a lifetime's hard yakka in his goldmining days. **1968** S. GORE *Holy Smoke* 18 'Ard yakka for God, that one. He's mak' im outa dirt. **1975** L.H. CLARK *Rouseabout Reflections* 131 It all begun [*sic*] the day that Thomson put two black boys on To do all heavy yakka round the joint. **1986** *Nat. Times* (Sydney) 21 Feb. 16/3 Child care remains women's responsibility. . . There's no evidence that men are taking part in the hard yakka.

yakker, var. YACKER.

yakker /'jækə/, *v.* Also **yacca, yacker.** [a. Jagara *yaga*.] *intr.* To work; to labour.

1847 J.D. LANG *Cooksland* 123 'What for Commandant yacca paper?' What is the gentleman working at the paper for? [*Ibid.* 447 The word *yacca* in the Moreton Bay dialect of the Aboriginal language, is one of those unfortunate words that has more than double duty to perform. It signifies everything in the shape of service or performance from the first incipient attempts at motion, to the most violent exertion, and it usually takes its signification from the noun to which it is appended, as in the instance I have given above, *mooyoom yacca*, to read, to write, or to cast accounts.] **1876** 'EIGHT YRS.' RESIDENT' *Queen of Colonies* 337 Whitefellow yacker (work), bullock yacker, yarraman (horse) yacker, baal gentleman. **1892** *Bulletin* (Sydney) 19 Nov. 19/1 The stevedore must yacker for the bit he gets to eat. **1899** *Truth* (Sydney) 15 Jan. 2/4 That class of sturdy young loafers . . won't attempt to 'yakker' while the 'old woman' can keep her wash-tub out of pawn. **1914** *Bulletin* (Sydney) 3 Dec. 13/2 When the bushman goes off to yakker in the big timber he does not, as a usual thing, carry a medical outfit. **1918** L.J. VILLIERS *Changing Yr.* 8 'Ow'd he fancy it fer yakkerin on a thresher?' ' 'Twould be beaut ter 'ave the cow w'ere he mus' foller suit.' **1926** *Bulletin* (Sydney) 24 June 22/2, I was yakkering on Brooklyn station, Windellama Creek (N.S.W.). **1934** *Ibid.* 10 Jan. 20/1 'Do we have to yacker this afternoon?' asked one of the hands.

yalka, var. YELKA.

yam. [Transf. use of *yam* the starchy, tuberous root of *Dioscorea* species.] Any of several plants having an edible tuberous root, incl. MURNONG, and species of the genus *Dioscorea* (fam. Dioscoreaceae) and of other families; the tuber of these plants; *native yam*, see NATIVE *a.* 6 a.; *wild yam*, see WILD 1. Also *attrib.*

1770 J. BANKS *Endeavour Jrnl.* (1962) II. 127 The only vegetables we saw them use were Yams of 2 sorts, the one long and like a finger the other round and coverd with stringy roots, both sorts very small but sweet. **1805** *Sydney Gaz.* 13 Jan., A very fine species of yam has been found at Port Dalrymple; the discovery of which was owing to the hogs sent there. **1845** L. LEICHHARDT *Jrnl. Overland Exped. Aust.* 9 May (1847) 249 They threw some yam-roots over to us, the plant of which we were not able to ascertain. **1879** 'OLD HAND' *Experience of Colonist* 31 Some tubercules of a plant called by the natives murnong and by the colonists yam. **1892** MRS F. HUGHES *My Childhood in Aust.* 51 There was a juicy plant we called yam, about three inches long, which we also ate by forties and fifties. **1926** A.S. LE SOUEF et al. *Wild Animals Australasia* 304 Occasionally bandicoots will take yams. **1947** W.E. HARNEY *Brimming Billabongs* (1963) 50 That yellow flower tells us we must be ready to dig this little yam. **1978** K. MCARTHUR *Pumicestone Passage* 45 Another delicacy was the root of the little ground orchid commonly called ladies tresses (*Spiranthes australis*) which an Aboriginal friend of the author called 'yams'.

yammagi /'jæmədʒi/. *W.A.* Also **yamagee, yamagi, yamidgee, yammagee, yammogee.** [a. Watjari *yamaji*.] A generic term for an Aboriginal; an Aboriginal male.

1925 J.E. LIDDLE *Selected Poems* 89 They talked of 'Yammogees' and 'Jinns'. **1926** *Bulletin* (Sydney) 14 Oct. 24/2 A pot-bellied old yammagi came along to the outcamp one evening, accompanied by several gins. **1937** E. MORROW *Law Provides* 145 You know 'em yamagi called Spider? **1963** R. MILLINGTON *Nation of Trees* 87 Some yamagies on their way through to town tell Sam and the others that there is a gathering of the clans. **1965** R. STOW *Merry-Go-Round* 186 'What's yamidgees?' said the boy. 'Boongs. Noogs. Coloured folk.' **1976** B. BENNETT *New Country* 42 That's her, over there. Holding court with the local yammagees. **1983** G.E.P. WELLARD *Bushlore* 55, I was standing outside the humpy discussing the days work with three of the Yamagee musterers. I use the word 'Yamagee' because that is the name they call themselves in that district. They never say 'Blackman' or 'Aborigine', it is always 'Yamagee'.

yam-stick. DIGGING STICK.

1846 F. DUTTON *S.A. & its Mines* 330 His 'gin' will ply the 'yamstick', and dig from the soil the same miserable subsistence as heretofore. **1859** W. BURROWS *Adventures Mounted Trooper* 99 The 'lubras', or 'gins', as they call their women, are generally to be seen carrying . . their yam-sticks; these are small sticks with a point at each end, and about three feet in length, used . . for the purpose of digging yams, which are small bulbs growing at the roots of tufts of grass, and tasting very like nuts. **1878** R.B. SMYTH *Aborigines of Vic.* I. 115 A blackfellow with a yam-stick can dig out a wombat, and two or three or four would quickly dig a grave four or five feet in depth. **1894** G.H. GIBSON *Ironbark Chips* 17 And he used to bang his lubra with a 'yam-stick' on the head. **1919** *Huon Times* (Franklin) 14 Mar. 3/7, I have often come upon gins on their knees in scrubs, digging great trenches with yamsticks, in quest of those delicious tubers (wild potatoes), or disembowelling the huge mounds in which the brush turkeys bury their eggs. **1929** *Bulletin* (Sydney) 6 Feb. 23/3 The inseparable companion of Miss Binghi is the yam-stick. **1947** W.E. HARNEY *Brimming Billabongs* (1963) 60 These yam sticks were fighting weapons too. **1969** A.A. ABBIE *Original Australs.* 75 Women are the main collectors of vegetable food. They always carry a fairly long 'digging-stick'. . . In the north where yams are the chief objective the stick is usually called a 'yam stick'.

yan /jæn/, *v. Austral. pidgin. Obs.* [a. Aboriginal *yan-* (common to most languages).] *intr.* To go; to move.

1839 T.L. MITCHELL *Three Exped. Eastern Aust.* (rev. ed.) II. 71 And then he yan (i.e goes) away! **1848** H.W. HAYGARTH *Recoll. Bush Life* 108 The phrase used by our tribe to signify a handsaw was taken from its motion when in action; they never could be persuaded to call it anything but a 'yan' (go) 'and come back again'. **1849** A. HARRIS *Emigrant Family* (1967) 222 You yan along a yerriman (shall go off on your horse). **1870** C.H. ALLEN *Visit to Qld.* 183 Native terms that are used by the whites also as a kind of colonial slang, such as . . 'yan', to go; 'cabon', much; and so on. **1882** A.J. BOYD *Old Colonials* 16 He shouted to them to 'yan' (clear out).

yanaman, var. YARRAMAN.

yandy /'jændi/, *n.* Also **yandi, yandie.** [a. Yinjibarndi *yanti.*] A shallow (wooden) dish used to separate seeds, etc., from refuse or particles of a mineral from alluvial material: see quot. 1914. Also **yandy-dish.**

1903 *Folklore* (London) XIV. iv. 349 The only other acquisition we have made is a 'Yandie', the native cradle or basket made out of a piece of bark. **1914** *Register* (Adelaide) 30 July 8/7 Moolyella has been a very rich tinfield. . . There are a number of aborigines in the locality, and the whites employ the gins to 'yandie' their tin—i.e., to clean it—which is done on a piece of wood hollowed out after the fashion of a butcher's tray, and described by natives as a 'yandie'. . . This contrivance is jugged [*sic*] by a peculiar motion of the wrist that impels the dirt in one direction while the tin goes the other. Only the gins do it. **1919** *Bulletin* (Sydney) 22 May 22/4 The yandy . . is a short piece of troughing, or curved bark, but the niggers get wonderful results from the deft way they have of shuffling dirt in it. **1943** *Ibid.* 7 July 12/1 The coolamon—it was known elsewhere as the pitchi or yandi—was the abo.'s one universal utensil. **1952** B. BEATTY *Unique to Aust.* 10 Simply a piece of upturned bark, the yandi is rocked in a curious way, one end held in each hand, the secret lying in a certain jerk of the wrist while the yandi is rocking. Its purpose is to separate one thing from another. **1956** *Bulletin* (Sydney) 13 June 12/3 After the natives had gathered what pods they could off the trees they got to work on the fallen seeds with yandi-dishes. **1962** *Texas Q.* 45 The women used a long, shallow, oval wooden dish called a yandy to separate grain from husks.

yandy /'jændi/, *v.* [f. prec.] *trans.* To separate (seeds, etc., or a mineral) from the surrounding refuse by shaking the raw material in a yandy: see esp. quots. 1914, 1933, and 1956. Also *absol.* and as *vbl. n.*

1914 [see YANDY *n.*]. **1919** *Bulletin* (Sydney) 22 May 22/4 At Moolyella, in the nor'-west of West, yandying lead is the chief industry of the tribes, who make a good thing out of it. **1933** C. FENNER *Bunyips & Billabongs* 158 When a gin has collected a coolamon (shallow wooden vessel) full of seed she has also a good deal of sand, dust, grass and leaves. But by shaking and twisting the coolamon in a particularly skilful way an almost perfect separation is made. This art of separation is called 'yandying'. **1944** M.J. O'REILLY *Bowyangs & Boomerangs* 48 Those who did not have dryblowers employed lubras to extract the fine dust and light debris from the tin after it went through a shaker. This process was called 'Yandying' by the natives. Yandying, in blackfellow language, means shake-about. It is the natives' method of separating the grass seeds from the husk. **1956** *Bulletin* (Sydney) 13 June 12/3 A gin who's a good hand at yandi-ing can separate white-ant eggs from dirt. **1962** *Texas Q.* 45 This unusual skill has now been successfully extended (generally with a similar dish made of sheet iron) to separate mineral from mullock in the small native mining shows. Now known as 'yandying' this skill was originally exclusively feminine. **1977** D. STUART *Drought Foal* 178 Comin' in with alluvial gold they'd yandied from the old alluvial patches. **1984** W.W. AMMON et al. *Working Lives* 63 Duster pulled in on his way back to his tin show at Nullagine where he had these young gins yandying for him.

Hence **yandier** *n.*, one who yandies.

1954 I.L. IDRIESS *Nor'-Westers* 165 A noted yandier, Mary Ann, had . . yandied a whole bag of stream tin.

yang yang, *n.* [Of unknown origin.] A cicada.

1926 L.C.E. GEE *Bush Tracks & Gold Fields* 93 And then, out of the branches of this tree, the yang yangs sing—I don't know what their proper name is (Cicada, I think).

yang-yang, *a.* [Of unknown origin.] Of a horse: spirited.

1976 C.D. MILLS *Hobble Chains & Greenhide* 149 If any of the storybook Romeos had tried any of those tricks on some of the 'yang-yang-yowadas' we had, they'd have been in strife. **1977** T. RONAN *Mighty Men on Horseback* 13 He's got a mob of yang-yang horses. **1982** P. ADAM SMITH *Shearers* 366 Those 'yang-yang' horses which were always left in the camp for some new chum stockman to ride do not exist.

Yankee. Used *attrib.* in Special Comb. **Yankee grab,** a game of chance played with dice, resembling craps; **grubbing** *vbl. n.*, see quot. 1914; also **grubbed** *ppl. a.*; **shout,** an occasion the expenses of which are shared by the participants.

1879 'NEW CHUM' *Ramble in Launceston* 53 The golden youth from the shops are here playing **'Yankee grab'** for shillings' [*sic*] till daylight dawns. **1888** J. FREEMAN *Lights & Shadows Melbourne Life* 47 The publican proposes a 'shake' for drinks, which means a game called 'Yankee grab', played with dice. **1892** *Western Champion* (Barcaldine) 21 June 13/1 The bar-room was full of squatters and drovers, bullock-drivers, stockmen, and jackeroos, all drinking whisky 'straight', and mostly playing 'Yankee Grab' at a pound a 'pop'. **1908** 'FIFTY-THREE YRS.' MINER' *So Long* 77 The everyday customers then had a 'Yankee grab' amongst themselves, and one of them 'shouted' for all hands. **1929** W.J. RESIDE *Golden Days* 375 And as for Yankee-Grab again—I'd never come at that. **1982** P. ADAM SMITH *Shearers* 280 These men remember the big tin shed on the banks of the Thompson River where they broke down their cut-out cheque playing local variants of Crap called Yankee Grab, Murrumbidgee and Sevens. **1914** *Pastoral Rev.* 15 Apr. 335 **Yankee grubbing** means the preparation of timbered land for cropping by grubbing all the small timber and cutting the large trees down just under the surface of the soil, so that stump-jump machinery can be used. **1930** O. RUHEN *Bullock Teams* 230, I always disliked having an onlooker when I was tree-pulling. We would often snag a 'Yankee-grubbed' stump—that is, a sapling cut just above the ground. **1945** S.J. BAKER *Austral. Lang.* 171 We have many versions of the shout, such as the *American shout*, **Yankee shout** (we also call it a *Yank* or *Yankee*), *Scotch shout*, etc. **1955** N. PULLIAM *I traveled Lonely Land* 387 *Yankee shout*—go Dutch, each pay for his own. **1964** *Bulletin* (Sydney) 30 May 37/2 We were agog to know who paid for the feast. It was a little disappointing to discover later that it was what we used to call a 'Yankee shout': everybody dubbed in.

Yank-happy, *a.* Of an Australian woman: favouring the company of an American serviceman.

1943 *Full-Times Gaz.* (Rockhampton) 13 Jan. 3 Most of our girls have gone Yank happy. **1944** *Wog Jrnl.: Mag. Headquarters 3rd Austral. Infantry Brigade* 16 Feb. 1 By the way you aren't Yank happy are you Cpl.? **1950** K.S. PRICHARD *Winged Seeds* 288 Pat had become 'Yank happy' like so many other girls who were fluttering gaily with American soldiers. **1968** G. DUTTON *Andy* 110 The Americans, with their retinue of Yank-happy sheilas and Australian racketeers.

Yan Yean /jæn 'jin/. [The name of a reservoir supplying water to Melbourne.] Tap-water. Also as quasi-*adj.*, 'as water is to wine'.

1868 *Australasian* (Melbourne) 25 Jan. 113/3 It might be thought that an occasional sprinkling of Yan Yean scattered upon him by a careless or lively city Aquarius would not cause him much chagrin. **1871** J. BALLANTYNE *Homes & Homesteads* 143 There is also on this floor a hydraulic lift, worked by means of the Yan Yean, which has been laid on by the proprietors all over the premises, in order, as much as anything, to ensure cleanliness. **1880** *Argus* (Melbourne) 6 Feb. 7/7 The gardens were in a very clean condition, and the ornamental portions were fresh and blooming, notwithstanding the extreme heat of the month—a proof of the efficacy of the Yan Yean supply. **1889** *Chron. Melbourne Beefsteak Club* I. 267 We have this year eaten ten dinners; we have consumed 122 plates of beefsteak; the liquids I approximate roughly at 50 gallons—beer, wine, coffee, lemon-squash, and 'Yan Yean', with, say, 500 cigars. **1923** *Woman's World* 1 Aug. 455/1 Mrs Brown puts some plums into a saucepan and adds as much Yan Yean as it will hold. **1972** J. HIBBERD *Stretch of Imagination* (1973) 18 Must have an 1876 Château Carbonnieux with the basted salamander, anything else would be unspeakably yan yean, eh Jeremy?

Hence **Yan Yean** *v. trans.*, to douse with water, to quench (in quot. *fig.*).

1885 *Austral. Tit-Bits* (Melbourne) 26 Feb. 11/1 One day they have had to fan the patriotic flame, and the next to Yan Yean it.

yapunyah /jə'pʌnjə/. [a. Gunya *yapan*ʸ.] Either of two trees of the genus *Eucalyptus* (fam. Myrtaceae), *E. ochrophloia* occurring along watercourses and seasonally inundated land in s.w. Qld. and n.w. N.S.W., and *E. thozetiana* of Qld. and N.T.; the wood of these trees; LAPUNYAH b; NAPUNYAH. Also **yapunyah-tree.**

1878 'IRONBARK' *Southerly Busters* 144 The tall yapunyah's shadow Rests upon the stockman's grave. [*Note*] A species of Eucalyptus which flourishes on the Paroo and in the west of Queensland. **1898** C.L. MORGAN *Rabbit Question in Qld.* 98 Posts to be of . . bendee or yapunyah. **1906** *Proc. Linnean Soc. N.S.W.* XXXI. 308 *E*[*ucalyptus*] *Thozetiana* . . is called 'Yappunyah', a name applied also to *E. ochrophloia* . . a far western species. **1942** F. CLUNE *Last of Austral. Explorers* 99 They reached the Paroo River, a chain of waterholes, fringed by yapunyah-trees. **1976** N.V. WALLACE *Bush Lawyer* 129 The most beautiful of all was the tan-barked yapunyah.

yard, *n.*

1. [Spec. use of *yard* an enclosure for poultry or cattle adjacent to a farm building: see OED *sb.*[1] 2.] An enclosure, sometimes makeshift and (formerly) movable, in which sheep, cattle, etc., are confined for a particular purpose. Also *attrib.*

1810 *Sydney Gaz.* 8 Dec., Grazing Farm—on which there is . . Dairy &c and good Yards well adapted for Horned Cattle or Sheep. **1824** E. CURR *Acct. Colony Van Diemen's Land* 70 The sheep fold is made of rough logs or of brushwood, and both the huts and the yard may be constructed in the course of two days. **1844** *Sydney Morning Herald* 17 Dec. 4/5 There is, I am aware, an objection with some graziers to the use of 'yards'. . . I am quite convinced that clean, dry, hard boarded yards are better in every respect for the sheep's health, and for the colour and condition of the wool, than hurdles. **1851** H. MELVILLE *Present State Aust.* 109 Yards are commenced; if for sheep, brush fence serves very well for a time—but for cattle more substantial work, such as log fencing, is required. **1868** *Mr Newcome in Search of Cattle Station* 10 It was not etiquette in New South Wales to go near the yard while slaughtering was going on. **1879** S.W. SILVER *Austral. Grazier's Guide* 34 With the assistance of his working overseer, he will 'put his sheep through the yards' . . separating all sheep of differing ages from flocks into which they may have strayed. **1893** 'PIONEER' *Reminisc. Austral. Early Life* 35, I was to keep the hut, shift the yards, cook, and do odd jobs about the hut. **1909** *Emu* VIII. 235 Secure our horses in a temporary but strong yard of saplings. **1921** G.A. BELL *Under Brigalows* 58 The yards for sheep are generally made of hurdles . . on account of the ease with which they can be shifted. **1928** B. SPENCER *Wanderings in Wild Aust.* 308 Small mobs of horses . . were under the charge of black boys who were employed to 'shepherd' them, that is, to look after them in the bush, and have them 'yarded', which means brought into a small space, roughly enclosed with bushes and dignified with the name of 'yard'. **1932** J. TRURAN *Green Mallee* 52 Six horses were feeding from boxes in a 'yard' made by running a strand of barbed wire around a number of bushes. **1944** E.M. ANDERSON *Typist Tales* 73 I'll have to put up some sort of a make-shift yard. **1955** *Bulletin* (Sydney) 18 May 13/1 The camp shifted into gidgee country for a yard-building job. **1978** D. STUART *Wedgetail View* 47 Bloody cattle drovin' or chasin' sheep in the yards at shearing time.

2. [Also Br. dial. and U.S.: see OED(S *sb.*[1] 3.] The

enclosed area surrounding a house; a domestic garden. See also BACK YARD 1.

1843 *Teetotal Advocate* (Launceston) 31 July 3/5 A four-roomed Cottage, with Garden or Yard behind. **1907** *Truth* (Sydney) 20 Jan. 9/8 You could not get your yard mowed or your housework done. **1935** K. TENNANT *Tiburon* 216 They did as best they could by tearing leaves off the lily plants Mrs Moore had planted round the yard. **1956** 'A.B.C.' *What is A?* 30 When the lawns are neat and smooth, Hubby can bring his cronies home to admire *his* well-kept yard. **1965** P. TODHUNTER *Aust. under Scalpel* 79 In Australian cities .. gardens are called yards. **1969** K. LEOPOLD *My Brow is Wet* 148, I was sittin' out in our yard gettin' a bit of fresh air. **1978** *Mud over Blood Chron.: 2/7 Austral. Infantry Batallion Assoc. Newsletter* Dec. 4 Besides, says Bernie, a house and a yard makes for much more pleasant living. **1982** N. KEESING *Lily on Dustbin* 77 The traditional Australian dream is to own a home with a garden which is called a 'yard'.

yard, *v.* [Also U.S.: see OED *v.*[1] 1.]

1. *trans.* To confine (livestock) in an enclosure, either overnight or for a particular purpose. Also *absol.* and as *ppl. a.*

1821 *Regulations respecting Assigned Convict Servants* 30 June 15 It is not deemed eligible in this island to yard the flocks at night. **1845** D. MACKENZIE *Emigrant's Guide* 114 You must build .. a stock-yard sufficient to contain your herd, as they must for the first few months be .. *yarded* or confined in the stockyard by night. **1856** W.W. DOBIE *Recoll. Visit Port-Phillip* 102 All hands are employed .. in yarding, throwing in, catching, and ducking the stupid animals, whose wool is for our use, and not their own. **1868** C.W. BROWNE *Overlanding in Aust.* 60 The system of yarding sheep and sending them out in charge of a shepherd, is adopted in Queensland. **1880** J.B. STEVENSON *Seven Yrs. Austral. Bush* 93 The men who took a mob in hand first could go a 'buster', making the pace as warm as possible .. till the mob was finally yarded. **1888** T.V. FOOTE *My Weird Wooing* 152 Shoot the scouring parties of police like yarded bullocks. **1898** *Bulletin* (Sydney) 12 Nov. 32/2 Then its feed the squealing 'dinnis', and its yard the milkers up. **1908** *Ibid.* 21 May 39/1 Selectors here and there shepherd a flock, but the work is done by the children .. who follow the woollies all day and yard them at night. **1920** *Ibid.* 2 Sept. 24/3 The station's beef rations had been yarded, and my father was preparing to finish the business with a .44 Winchester. **1932** J. MCCARTER *Pan's Clan* 155 Joe .. was to take complete charge of the steeds, and to erect the rope-break in ample time to yard the sheep on the night's camp. **1949** H.G. LAMOND *White Ears* 134 Stud sheep, and those upon which their owners placed a high value, were brought in to the head station and yarded during the night with watch-dogs chained about their enclosures. **1960** *Centralian Advocate* (Alice Springs) 15 Jan. 4/4 If two butchers yard on the same day they have to box the cattle to water them, because the receiving yard is the only yard serviced with water. **1978** D. STUART *Wedgetail View* 8 How strange it was that the same bullocks, yarded, or in any manner crowded together, should feel the urge to mount their fellow castrates and ape the bull.

2. *trans.* To round up and confine (wild cattle, pigs, etc.). Also with **up.**

1867 'COLONIST' *Life's Work* 47 They're a mob of the wildest cattle we ever yarded. **1872** A. MCFARLAND *Illawarra & Manaro* 116 Two of our graziers .. have taken in hand the destruction of such animals as roam at will upon their runs; having disposed of all they can yard to a 'Down the Mountain' buyer. **1891** T. BATEMAN *Valley Council* p. iii, We .. yarded-up brumbies or scrubbers from the back districts. **1915** *Bulletin* (Sydney) 26 Aug. 22/2 The scrub wildings wheeled from the clash and clatter coming in on their flank and were yarded. **1934** 'S. RUDD' *Green Grey Homestead* 113 'I never did any yarding of wild pigs,' young McCleverty will stutter... 'A cove would want to be on a pretty good horse .. to yard 'em in that sort of country.' **1944** J.J. HARDIE *Cattle Camp* (ed. 3) 16 He had ramped about the team as if he were yarding a mob of scrubbers.

3. a. *trans.* To secure (kangaroos, rabbits, etc.), preparatory to their slaughter.

1886 R. HENTY *Australiana* 224 Mr Moffat set out at once to round up the kangaroos, it being arranged that when sufficient had been yarded a signal would be given. **1900** *Bulletin* (Sydney) 1 Sept. 14/2 Recently saw a 'drive' in which 932 wallabies were yarded and killed with sticks. **1916** *Ibid.* 13 July 24/1 The whole district turned out to round up kangaroos and yard them. We camped out overnight and started the 'drive' at daybreak into a wing-yard. **1926** *Smith's Weekly* (Sydney) 22 May 19/7 The largest number of rabbits caught in one drive was 14,700 yarded years ago at Coonamble (N.S.W.) by an assorted crowd of bushmen and townspeople. **1943** H.G. LAMOND *From Tariaro to Ross Roy* 40 Each muster of 'roos was killed as soon as they were yarded.

b. *transf.* Also with **up.**

1930 V. PALMER *Passage* (1957) 184 The killers .. would yard a whale up like dingoes would a stray sheep. **1951** J. DEVANNY *Travels N. Qld.* 45 Only once did I see sharks engaged in what fishermen call 'yarding' their prey.

4. *transf.* and *fig.*

1892 *Bulletin* (Sydney) 31 Dec. 9/2 Yard-up, in one enclosed space, all the present Australian members of Parliament. **1899** *Ibid.* 11 Mar. 31/2 They had been .. yarding the rubbish. **1910** *Ibid.* 31 Mar. 14/2 We wasn't engaged, but it was a pretty well understood thing. Next time I yarded her was at a hop at Wattle Flat. **1915** *Ibid.* 23 Dec. 26/4 Some of these smart kelpies that can yard chickens back into their egg-shells ought to come to town and face city conditions. **1928** *Ibid.* 7 Mar. 23/1 The table manners of the abo... were perfect until the juggling of the hard-boiled peas tricked him... Calling for a glass he scooped the peas into it, and swallowed them, remarking as an after-thought: 'That's the best way to yard 'em.' **1941** *Ibid.* 5 Nov. 14/2 Mat was dead leary of women, going in mortal fear that one day one of them would yard and brand him in the good old church way. **1956** T. RONAN *Moleskin Midas* 111 Where's these bloody traps? Who said I tickled Mulvaney's Peter? I'm out here to be yarded. Come out, you khaki-clad bastards and yard me! **1963** M. BRITT *Pardon my Boots* 52 Jack had only brought him out of retirement for me to ride. 'You could yard a fly in a bottle on him,' he said, lovingly adjusting the bridle.

yarder.

1. One responsible for the yarding of animals, esp. of sheep prior to shearing. Also **yarder-up.**

1883 *Illustr. Austral. News* (Melbourne) 28 Nov. 194/3 Suddenly we come upon three individuals, whistling, shouting and yelling their level best—or their level worst. These are the 'yarders' who keep the shearers supplied from sunrise to sunset with a continual and incessant stream of living animals. **1893** S. NEWLAND *Paving Way* 340 He required a man to act as 'yarder up' and to drive sheep to and fro between the paddocks and the shearing-shed. **1894** *Western Champion* (Barcaldine) 16 Jan. 12/1 Now then, yarder, watch my pen. When my mate has caught the 'cobbler', for the ringer's racing then. **1899** *Bulletin* (Sydney) 1 Apr. 14/2 The real 'cobbler' was kept in the pen, perhaps all day, as the yarder-up used him as a decoy-sheep. **1923** *Ibid.* 1 Nov. 24/3 The 'yarder-up' .. often has a well-trained decoy to pilot the stubborn mobs into their pens.

2. *transf.* A horse used in yarding stock.

1927 K.S. PRICHARD *Bid me to Love* (1974) 6 My yarder's got out of the paddock. You might keep an eye out for him over your way.

yarding, *vbl. n.* [f. YARD *v.* 1.] The confining of animals in an enclosure; the animals so confined. Also with **up.**

1889 *Illustr. Austral. News* (Melbourne) 1 May 74/2 Then comes the excitement of yarding, the cracking of the stockwhips, and the shouting of the men, and finally, the most important of all, the drafting of the herd for both fats and stores. **1890** 'R. BOLDREWOOD' *Colonial Reformer* II. 108 But with this class of 'shorthorn' yarding is a much more rapid affair. **1931** 'L. KAYE' *Tybal Men* 16 There was a good yarding of stock as they passed through the pens toward the group surrounding that where the auctioneer was selling. **1936** *Bulletin* (Sydney) 8 July 2/2 Two brumby stallions .. picked up the trail of the station stock horses, and consequently found themselves trapped in the receiving yards. They were caught, a fortnight elapsing, between the two yardings. **1957** R.S. PORTEOUS *Brigalow* 38 And yarding-up on Yakaparni *was* a job. Nine times out of ten the leaders baulked at the wide-open gateways. **1963** M. BRITT *Pardon my Boots* 70 Jack rode over and told me that they were going to start yarding up, and that I had better ride away a bit to be out of the rumpus. **1985** *Austral. Town & Country Jrnl.* (Sydney) 15 July 16/3 A yarding of 650 cattle at Wednesday's cattle sale, including 240 stores.

yarn, *n.* [See YARN *v.*] A chat, a discussion.

1852 F.R. GODFREY *Extracts Old Jrnls.* 11 Aug. (1926) 137, I had a long 'yarn' with Pearson and Augusta about my affairs. **1859** 'EYE WITNESS' *Voyage to Aust.* 22 You are questioned all about home, what brought you out, and all such questions, until what is termed in the colony a good yarn is over, you may then be asked to have a nobler [*sic*]. **1870** J. BONWICK *Last Tasmanians* 116 They asked the Buxtons to come over to their camp, and have 'a yarn'. **1913** M.A. MCMANUS *Reminisc. Maranoa District* 39 He used to delight in going to travellers' camps to have a 'yarn' with them. **1929** 'OLD STOCKMAN' *Sensational Cattle-Stealing Case* 17, I got into a yarn with the Boss, and asked him if could [*sic*] find us a job. **1944** A.S. SMITH *Boys write Home* 58 There they all stood and had a bit of a yarn before they came home. **1952** J. CLEARY *Sundowners* 260 He'd have to have a yarn with Ida about getting so matey with the boss and his missus. **1969** A. BUZO *Front Room Boys* (1970) 23 Some of me old mates from the bush turned up for a beer and a yarn. **1986** *Sydney Morning Herald* 12 Apr. 1/2 He says he doesn't really want to do any sort of interview, but it doesn't take long to see that deep down, the man likes a good yarn.

yarn, *v.* [Transf. use of *yarn* to tell a tale. Used elsewhere but recorded earliest in Aust.: see OED(S *v.* 1.] *intr.* To talk; to chat. Also as *vbl. n.*

1847 A. HARRIS *Settlers & Convicts* (1953) 90 As R-- and his acquaintance 'yarned', I took up one of the books. **1868** 'S.S. JUNR.' *Travels & Adventures W.A.* 2, I thought it glorious fun, smoking our cigars and yarning until overcome by our long drive, we both fell asleep. **1884** A.W. STIRLING *Never Never Land* 39 The manager received me with open arms, and we 'yarned' far into the night over the old country. **1896** M. CLARKE *Austral. Tales* 7 By 'yarning', dear reader, I don't mean mere trivial conversation, but hard, solid talk. **1913** M.A. MCMANUS *Reminisc. Maranoa District* 39 In the course of their 'yarning' they informed him they were bound for Chinchilla. **1932** K.S. PRICHARD *Kiss on Lips* 179 B.Y. yarned with us awhile, asked after Jeff and Dick Morrison. **1948** V. PALMER *Golconda* 24 A few loungers stood yarning at McClintock's hessian store, where the trade was mostly in tobacco and tickets for the Casket. **1962** J. MARSHALL *Journey among Men* 131 It's hard work sinking bores, and after a few months on your own, with no one but a coupla abos to yarn to, you've gotta get stinkin' once in a while. **1976** C.D. MILLS *Hobble Chains & Greenhide* 25 A few of us had our 'toes in the ashes', and were smoking and yarning.

yarra /'jærə/, *n. Obs.* [Prob. a. Wiradhuri *yara.*] A name given to any of several trees occurring near watercourses, perh. chiefly *Eucalyptus camaldulensis* (see RED GUM 1): see quot. 1889. Also *attrib.*

1834 G. BENNETT *Wanderings N.S.W.* I. 251 Magnificent water gum-trees, (Dad'ha and Yarra of the aborigines). **1839** 'FRIEND TO TRUTH' *True Picture Aust.* 23 This reedy swamp was nearly a mile broad, and beyond it we found firm, open, and good ground; some very large trees of the 'yarra' species of *eucalptus* growing between it and the edge of the reeds. **1847** *Port Phillip Gaz.* 24 Mar. 4 The Yarra .. is a wildly beautiful stream, fringed with the Yarra and mimosa trees. **1861** J.D. LANG *Qld., Aust.* 106 No longer a chain of dry ponds in brigalow scrub, but a channel shaded by lofty yarra trees. **1887** *Proc. Linnean Soc. N.S.W.* II. 279 *Eucalyptus .. rostrata* .. 'River Gum', 'Yarrah'; grows only on river flats. **1889** J.H. MAIDEN *Useful Native Plants Aust.* 511 'Yarrah', according to Dr Woolls, is a name applied by the aboriginals to almost any tree. **1893** D. LINDSAY *Jrnl. Elder Sci. Exploring Exped.* 163 There are several beefwood or 'yarra' trees growing around the well.

yarra /'jærə/, *a.* [f. the name of a psychiatric hospital at *Yarra* Bend, Victoria.] Insane; stupid. Also as *n.*

[**1880** *Argus* (Melbourne) 24 Jan. 6/5 The demeanour of Government supporters, such as Mr *Tucker* and Mr *Andrew*, suggested to one member on the Ministerial side who did keep his temper, the idea that they would both have to be removed to the Yarra Bend.] **1943** S.J. BAKER *Pop. Dict. Austral. Slang* (ed. 3) 89 *Yarra* .. stupid, crazy. **1967** *Kings Cross Whisper* (Sydney) xliii. 11/3 *Yarra*, a stupid person. **1968** J. ALARD *He who shoots Last* 126 Da foist week I wuz here, I cracked it fer a load of da

Sandy McNabs; dey nearly drove me yarra. **1971** J. McNEIL *Chocolate Frog* (1973) 50 What'ser matter? You gone yarra, or somethin'? **1980** *Sydney Morning Herald* 20 Oct. 26/7 Kingston Town is a good horse . . but in my opinion he would not have lived with Phar Lap. I know a lot of people will say I'm 'Yarra'; but that's my belief.

Yarra-banker /jærə-'bæŋkə/. [f. the name of the *Yarra* River, upon which Melbourne stands.] **a.** *Obs.* A vagrant (see quot. 1895). **b.** A soap-box orator. See also DOMAIN. Also *attrib.*

1895 C. CROWE *Austral. Slang Dict.* 98 *Yarra bankers*, vagrants living on the banks of the Yarra. **1897** *Bulletin* (Sydney) 18 Sept. 20/2 Yarrabanker Fleming indulged in some pretty plain speaking. **1901** *Tocsin* (Melbourne) 3 Oct. 8/2 Mr Edgar complains that the 'Yarra Bankers' (as he contemptuously terms them) attack those placed in 'high places', such as the Government and members of Parliament. **1912** L. ESSON *Time is not yet Ripe* 32 The man's an agitator, a red-flagger, a Yarra-banker. **1916** 'T.O. LINGO' *Austral. Comic Dict.* 6 *Yarra Banker*, usually a man who stands on a soap box telling the great unwashed how 'dirty' the rich man is. **1962** J.T. LANG *Great Bust* 157 Curtin was suspect at that time as a militant. He had been a leader of the Victorian anti-Conscription fight, and had been a Melbourne Yarra-banker.

Hence **Yarra-banking** *ppl. a.*, 'tub-thumping'.

1905 W. MOORE *City Sketches* 46 The genteel cadger, known professionally as the suburban swagman, frequents other haunts than those of his Yarra-banking brother.

yarraman /'jærəmən/. Chiefly *Austral. pidgin.* Pl. **yarraman(s), yarramen.** Also **yanaman.** [Prob. a. Aboriginal *yiraman*, f. *yira-* teeth: see quot. 1984.] A horse.

1842 *Legends of Aust.* Mar. 49 'Got it coat, yarraman, and musket, just like it soger.' (Meaning that they were equipped with horses, fire-arms, &c., and drest like the mounted police.) **1848** T.L. MITCHELL *Jrnl. Exped. Tropical Aust.* 270 They exclaimed 'Yarra-man', the colonial natives' name for a horse. **1856** W.W. DOBIE *Recoll. Visit Port-Phillip* 61 In stalks a black-fellow, like an emissary of Satan, who . . tells him how that 'two big-fellow bushrangers pull away along o' creek, and look out yarramen (horses) belonging to station, and no gammon'. **1863** J. DAVIS *Tracks of McKinlay* 144 Natives . . using the word 'Yanaman' for horse, as in Sydney. **1876** F. NAPIER *Notes Voyage N.S.W. to N. Coast* 40 They told us that they had seen the captain on a 'yanaman' (horse). **1882** A.J. BOYD *Old Colonials* 69 Well, then there's seventeen yarramen—call 'em thirty pounds a head. **1892** *Western Champion* (Barcaldine) 9 Feb. 12/2 The astonished 'yarraman' gave one look round at old 'Polly' . . and started off across the plain like a toboggan slide on a down grade. **1916** *Bulletin* (Sydney) 12 Oct. 47/1 Sometimes, her yarraman lightly pacing, she came to their camp. **1923** J. BOWES *Jackaroos* 67 'Lot of pfellers go longa here.' 'How many yarramans?' **1931** *Listening Post* (Perth) Sept. 17 So you're leavin' me, old yarraman. **1946** A. THURIAN *Bush Tea & Overlanders* 23 The yarraman stood in a mob. **1976** C.D. MILLS *Hobble Chains & Greenhide* 13 'Properly good yarraman this one,' seemed to be the undeniable verdict. **1984** B. DIXON *Searching for Aboriginal Lang.* 72 In fact, *yarraman* 'horse' comes originally from a language just south of Sydney where it may have meant 'long teeth'. It was adopted into the peculiar pidgin that early settlers used in communicating with Aborigines. When the first white men came into Queensland, they used the word *yarraman* 'horse', thinking that they were speaking '*the* Aboriginal language'. The Aborigines imagined they were being taught an English word.

yarran /'jærən/. Also **yarren.** [a. Kamilaroi (and related languages) *yarran.*] The small to medium tree *Acacia omalophylla* (*A. homalophylla*) (fam. Mimosaceae) of inland N.S.W., Qld., and n. Vic., having a rough bark and smooth foliage; the dark brown, durable wood of the tree. Also *attrib.*

1882 ARMSTRONG & CAMPBELL *Austral. Sheep Husbandry* 196 Dry yarren makes the best fence. **1884** G. RANKEN *Dry Country* i. 6 Shrubs . . are in great variety, and are known by local names such as . . Yarran, Belah, and numerous others. **1887** W.H. SUTTOR *Austral. Stories Retold* 117 The yarran, an acacia, like the myall having violet-scented wood, is widely dispersed, and frequently fringes the myall patches with its olive-green foliage. **1903** J. FURPHY *Such is Life* 55 He had never concerned himself to know the difference between yarran and mallee. **1915** E.M. WEETWOOD *Lure of Land* 29 Allowed her to walk through the first belt of yarran from the tank. **1927** J. MATHIEU *Backblock Ballads* 55 But he crashes all unheeding, At the timber-tangled wall, Looking dense enough to stop a yarran spear. **1959** C.V. LAWLOR *All This Humbug* 14 They sat round a fire of dead yarran wood.

yartz /jatz/. [Coinage of Barry Humphries (b. 1934), entertainer and writer: see quot. 1978.] Fanciful alteration of 'the arts'.

1978 B. HUMPHRIES *Nice Night's Entertainment* (1981) 183 This pome is dedicated to something Australians hold very precious beginning with Y—'the Yartz'. **1983** *Sydney Morning Herald* 2 Mar. 24/4 Only a cultural philistine would disapprove of such generosity to the yartz. **1984** *Age* (Melbourne) 5 May 3/4 (*heading*) Horne looks forward to the end of the yartz. **1985** *Bulletin* (Sydney) 17 Dec. 74/1 The journalist had referred to Cohen as 'our Pattersonesque Minister for the Arts'. That's as in Les Patterson, Barry Humphries' salivating, lecherous and truly foul Minister for the Yartz.

yate /jeɪt/. Formerly **yeit.** [Prob. f. a W.A. Aboriginal language.] Any of several trees of the genus *Eucalyptus* (fam. Myrtaceae) of s. W.A., esp. the rough-barked *E. cornuta*, yielding a remarkably hard, strong timber; the wood of the tree. Also **yate tree,** and *attrib.*

1833 *Jrnls. Several Exped. W.A.* 142 A plain of sandy soil, and white gum and yeit trees. **1849** J.S. ROE *Rep. Exped. S.-Eastward Perth* 16 Famished animals were revelling in a beautiful patch of . . grass growing amongst yeit-trees. **1880** F. VON MUELLER *Select Extra-Tropical Plants* 110 Eucalyptus cornuta . . the Yate Tree of South-West Australia. A large tree of rapid growth, preferring a somewhat humid soil. **1907** *Westminster Gaz.* (London) 20 Nov. 12/1 The extraordinary properties of yate, believed to be the strongest of all known woods. **1912** 'IRONBARK' *Ironbark Splinters* 13 Where the breezes fan The 'jarrah' and 'yate'. **1938** *Bulletin* (Sydney) 6 July 21/3 The comparatively small yate tree, which occurs in forests in W.A.'s extreme sou'-west, produces one of the world's strongest timbers. **1965** A.R. BARRETT *Hist. War Service Land Settlement Scheme W.A.* 23 The Jerramungup Station Area was practically all Yate (*Euc. occidentalis*) country, a large proportion of which had been ringbarked. **1983** *Newsletter* (Soc. for Growing Austral. Plants, Canberra Region) June 20 The first eucalypt to be collected in Western Australia, the Yate.

yaw, var. YU.

yeelaman, yelaman, varr. HIELEMAN.

yelka /'jɛlkə/. Also **yalka, yulka.** [a. Aranda *yalke.*] Any of several sedges of the genus *Cyperus* (fam. Cyperaceae) yielding an edible tuber; the tuber itself. Also *attrib.*

1896 B. SPENCER *Rep. Horn Sci. Exped. Central Aust.* IV. 60 *Cyperus rotundus.* In almost every camp we saw large quantities of the tunicated tubers of this plant, which are generally called 'Erriákura' or 'Irriakura' by the Arunta natives. In some parts however the term 'Yelka', 'Yelki' or 'Yilka' is used, and this is the name by which it is generally known amongst the whites. **1933** W. HATFIELD *Desert Saga* 129 Grass-seed was a forgotten luxury, as were yams and yelkas and the roots of the nut-grass. **1936** C. CHEWINGS *Back in Stone Age* 2 If seeds require roasting . . or yelka-bulbs peeling, they are placed in this tray. **1947** W.E. HARNEY *Brimming Billabongs* 8 A group of women . . were hunting for 'yalka', a small grass nut that grows abundantly in the swamps. **1957** M. GARTRELL *Dear Primitive* 10 Along the creek-bank collected a few handfuls of yelka (a bulb-like grass-root that looks like an onion but tastes like a potato). **1969** A.A. ABBIE *Original Australs.* 74 In central Australia an important article of diet . . is a tuber—the 'yelka' of Aborigines—which can be eaten either raw or cooked and is highly nutritious. **1980** R. DAVIDSON *Tracks* 137 For me there were yalka (like tiny onions) to be dug up and roasted in the coals. **1981** G.M. CUNNINGHAM et al. *Plants Western N.S.W.* 164 Tubers formed at the base of yelka plants were eaten by aborigines in Central Australia. **1985** *Austral. Plants* June 127 *Cyperus bulbosus.* . . Widely known as 'Yulka' in central Australia, this sedge grows up to 40 cm. high. . . The edible part is the small tuber. It can be eaten raw or lightly roasted.

yellow, *a.* Also **yeller** (only sense 4).

1. Used as a distinguishing epithet in the names of flora and fauna: **yellow-bellied glider,** the gliding possum *Petaurus australis* of e. mainland Aust., having a greyish-brown back and yellow to white belly; formerly also **yellow-bellied flying phalanger;** also *attrib.*; **-bellied** (or **-breasted**) **shrike-tit,** *shrike-tit*, see SHRIKE; **-billed kingfisher,** the kingfisher *Syma torotoro* of Cape York Peninsula (n. Qld.) and New Guinea; **-billed** (or **-legged**) **spoonbill,** the spoonbill *Platalea flavipes* of all States, having white plumage and a yellow bill; **bloodwood,** any of several trees of e. Qld. and e. N.S.W. of the genus *Eucalyptus* (fam. Myrtaceae) having rough, tesselated, sometimes yellow bark, as *E. eximia* of N.S.W.; **bob,** *yellow robin*; **box,** any of several trees of the genus *Eucalyptus* (fam. Myrtaceae), esp. *E. melliodora* of s.e. mainland Aust.; the wood of the tree; also *attrib.*; **-crested (white) cockatoo,** the cockatoo *Cacatua galerita* (see *white cockatoo* WHITE *a.*[2] 1 b.); **-eye mullet,** the marine and estuarine fish *Aldrichetta forsteri* of s. Aust. and New Zealand, having a slender body and yellow eye; also *ellipt.* as **yellow-eye; -faced honeyeater,** the predom. grey-brown honeyeater *Lichenostomus chrysops* of e. Aust., having a broad yellow stripe, bordered by black, through the eye; **-footed rock wallaby,** the rock wallaby *Petrogale xanthopus* of S.A., w. N.S.W., and s.w. Qld.; **hammer,** *yellow robin*; **honeyeater,** the greenish-yellow honeyeater *Lichenostomus flavus* of n. Qld.; **jacket** (or **jack**), any of several trees, usu. of the genus *Eucalyptus* (fam. Myrtaceae) having at times a yellowish trunk or bark, incl. *E. similis* and *E. peltata* subsp. *peltata* of Qld., and *E. lirata* of the n. Kimberley region, W.A.; **monday** (also **munday, mundy**), the cicada *Cyclochila australasiae* of s.e. Aust., when yellow; see also GREENGROCER; **oriole,** the yellowish-green bird *Oriolus flavocinctus* of n. Aust. and elsewhere, having a loud, melodious call; **parrot,** see *yellow rosella*; **-plumed honeyeater,** the predom. olive-brown and grey honeyeater *Lichenostomus ornatus* of s. mainland Aust., having a yellow neck plume; **robin,** either of two small, predom. greyish birds of mainland Aust. having a partly or wholly yellow underside, **(a)** the eastern *Eopsaltria australis* (also **yellow-breasted robin**), **(b)** the western *E. griseogularis*; *yellow bob, hammer*; **rosella,** the parrot *Platycercus elegans flaveolus* of the Murray-Murrumbidgee Rivers region of inland s.e. Aust.; *Murray smoker*, see MURRAY 2; also **yellow parrot; -spotted honeyeater,** the dark olive-green honeyeater *Meliphaga notata* of rainforest in n.e. Qld., having a rounded yellow ear patch; **stringybark,** any of several rough-barked trees of the genus *Eucalyptus* (fam. Myrtaceae), esp. *E. muellerana* of e. Vic. and s.e. N.S.W.; the wood of the tree; **-tailed black cockatoo,** the black cockatoo *Calyptorhynchus funereus* of s.e. Aust. incl. Tas., having a broad yellow band on the tail; also **yellow-tailed cockatoo; -tailed** (or **-rumped**) **thornbill,** the small, predom. olive-grey and buff bird *Acanthiza chrysorrhoa* of all States; see also TOMTIT; also **yellow-rumped tit; -throat,** see *yellow-throated scrub wren*; **-throated miner,** the predom. grey-brown bird *Manorina flavigula* of mainland Aust., having yellow and black markings on the head and throat; **-throated scrub wren,** the small bird *Sericornis citreogularis* of forested parts of e. mainland Aust., having brown, black, and yellow plumage with a bright yellow throat; also **yellow-throat; -tufted honeyeater,** the predom. dark olive to olive-yellow honeyeater *Lichenostomus melanops* of s.e. mainland Aust.; **walnut,** the tall rainforest tree *Beilschmiedia bancroftii* (fam. Lauraceae) of n.e. Qld.; the wood or fruit of the tree; **wattle bird,** the brown and white streaked bird *Anthochaera paradoxa* of Tas., the largest Austral. honeyeater, having long orange-yellow facial wattles; **weebill,** the yellowish northern form, *Smicrornis brevirostris flavescens*, of the WEEBILL; **-wing,** *New Holland honeyeater*, see NEW HOLLAND 2; also **yellow-wings.**

1860 [**yellow-bellied glider**] G. BENNETT *Gatherings of Naturalist* 150 The Long-Tailed Flying Opossum, or

Flying Squirrel of the colonists (*Belideus flaviventris*) is widely distributed... It is also known as the Yellow-bellied Flying Phalanger. **1926** A.S. Le Souef et al. *Wild Animals Australasia* 256 The yellow-bellied flying phalanger is found in open timbered country. **1941** E. Troughton *Furred Animals Aust.* 98 Yellow-bellied Glider .. *Petaurus australis*... This largest member of the genus *Petaurus* inhabits the coastal forests of eastern Australia, from southern Victoria to southern Queensland. **1973** S. & K. Breeden *Wildlife Eastern Aust.* 123 The Yellow-bellied Glider's progress through the forests can be followed by sound—nearly every glide is accompanied by his wild call. **1986** *Sydney Morning Herald* 22 Feb. 11/1 Populations of yellow-bellied glider possums, one of Australia's most spectacular, colorful, and vocal, tree-dwelling marsupials. **1918** *Bulletin* (Sydney) 14 Feb. (Red Page), **Yellow-bellied Shrike-Tit** (Yellow-Hammer, Crested Tit). *Ibid.* 19 Sept. 24/2 For the most elegant nest of all Australian birds I plump for that of the yellow-breasted shrike-tit, or 'falcon shrike'. **1929** A.H. Chisholm *Birds & Green Places* 132 The yellow-breasted shrike-tit has been heard, in New South Wales, to utter 'one curious note, something between the miewing and spitting of a cat'. **1985** *Melbourne Winners Weekly* 9 Sept. 23/1, I feel in a mischevious [*sic*] mood. I saw a yellow bellied shrike-tit! **1898** E.E. Morris *Austral Eng.* 248 **Yellow-billed K[ingfisher]**—*Syma flavirostris*. **1945** C. Barrett *Austral. Bird Life* 144 There are several other northern species: the mangrove kingfisher .. the forest kingfisher .. and the yellow-billed kingfisher. **1965** *N. Austral. Monthly* Dec. 17 Australia has ten species of kingfishers, and North Queensland has them all, though one, the Yellow-billed Kingfisher, occurs only at Cape York, being mainly a New Guinea species. **1985** *R. Australasian Ornithologists Union Newsletter* Sept. 9, I found the Yellow-billed Kingfisher to be unafraid but difficult to see, because of its habit of perching motionless on low branches. However, after many days of searching, a patch of yellow caught my eye against the dark forest, and came into focus as this stunning, small bird, with its vivid, orange-yellow head and breast, satiny sea-green wings, and massive bill. **1842 [yellow-billed spoonbill]** J. Gould *Birds of Aust.* (1848) VI. Pl. 49, *Platalea flavipes* .. Yellow-legged Spoonbill. **1898** E.E. Morris *Austral Eng.* 430 Yellow-billed S[poonbill]—*P[latalea] flavipes*. **1901** *Emu* I. 138 Yellow-legged Spoonbill... Two or three flocks were seen at Kalamurina. **1968** R. Hill *Bush Quest* 3 A solitary yellow-billed spoonbill stood guard at the edge of the marshy ground. **1984** M. Blakers et al. *Atlas Austral. Birds* 67 The Yellow-billed Spoonbill is typically an inland bird. **1880** *Proc. Linnean Soc. N.S.W.* V. 467 *E[ucalyptus] eximia* .. the 'Smooth-barked', '**Yellow**', or 'Mountain **Bloodwood**'. **1926** *Qld. Agric. Jrnl.* XXV. 439 Eucalyptus trachyphloia, White, Yellow or .. Bastard Bloodwood. **1963** C. Burgess *Blue Mountain Gums* 19 'Yellow Bloodwood' .. *Eucalyptus eximia* .. is an attractive medium-sized tree of the poor sandstone foothills. **1984** D.J. Boland et al. *Forest Trees Aust.* (rev. ed.) 226 The outer layers are brown to yellowish-brown but the more recently formed bark is distinctly yellow. This bark is typical of the yellow bloodwoods. **1909** A.E. Mack *Bush Calendar* 68 Then a **yellow-bob** came to visit us. **1923** *Austral.* (Sydney) May 45 For serene unruffled beauty and unfailing trustfulness I know no equal of 'Yellow Bob'. **1944** L. Welsh *Kookaburra* 11 *The yellow robin.* One of the first birds in the bush to awaken and one of the last to go to rest... Popularly called 'Yellow Bob' .. it also has the pleasing title of the Dawn Singer. **1981** P. Hay *Meeting of Sighs* 143 In the scrubland Yellow Bob is singing in the light. **1877** F. von Mueller *Introd. Bot. Teachings* 15 The Honey-Eucalypt (*Eucalyptus melliodora*) .. passes by the very unapt vernacular name **Yellow Box**-tree, though no portion of it is yellow, not even its wood, and though the latter resembles the real boxwood in no way whatever. **1878** R.B. Smyth *Aborigines of Vic.* II. 160 Yellow-box—Tarrk. **1880** J. Bonwick *Resources Qld.* 79 *Yellow Box*, a Eucalypt, is hard, tough, and durable. **1901** *Proc. Linnean Soc. N.S.W.* XXVI. 211 In the Camp-belltown and Illawarra districts *E[ucalyptus] Bosistoana* .. is sometimes called Yellow Box, the local assumption in some cases being that it is a coast form of *E. melliodora*. **1919** R.T. Baker *Hardwoods of Aust.* 174 *Eucalyptus melliodora* .. 'Yellow Box'... The common name is not given to the tint of the timber, but from the yellow colour of the inside of the bark, by which character the bushmen distinguish the species. **1944** *Southerly* i. 14 Yellow box gives the best honey. They knew it all through the west. Yellow box honey. **1952** E. Walling *Austral. Roadside* 21 The prevalence of the Yellow Box .. is a sign of good sheep country. **1973** D. Wolfe *Brass Kangaroo* 194 A group of big, old yellow-box trees on the bank of the Latrobe River showed long scars where the aborigines had removed sheets of bark for their canoes. **1986** *Age* (Melbourne) 7 Feb. 2/4 The river red gums, black box and yellow box trees had all failed to flower, leaving many professional apiarists scraping the bottom of the jar. **1852** W. Hughes *Austral. Colonies* 82 The **yellow-crested** white **cockatoo** is very numerous, and is a great pest to the farmer. **1876** *Illustr. Austral. News* (Melbourne) 27 Dec. 202/1 The fussy and imperial yellow-crested cockatoo, whose monotonous screech, and grotesque and discordant egotism, always arrests attention. **1909** G. Smith *Naturalist in Tas.* 46 On the rather remote sheep-runs flocks of the large yellow-crested white cockatoo may be seen. **1928** G.H. Wilkins *Undiscovered Aust.* 143 Yellow-crested cockatoos were seldom seen. **1948** A.J. McLachlan *McLachlan* 12 The screech of the yellow-crested cockatoo was a familiar sound. **1984** B. Dixon *Searching for Aboriginal Lang.* 122, I sat and had lunch on the sandy river shore, to the annoyance of a yellow-crested cockatoo who insistently proclaimed from the top branch of a tea-tree that this was *his* territory. **1906** D.G. Stead *Fishes of Aust.* 79 The **Yellow-eye Mullet** .. is distributed right round the southern half of Australia. **1951** T.C. Roughley *Fish & Fisheries Aust.* 36 The yellow-eye mullet .. is a small but important species, and is the principal mullet marketed in South Australia. **1974** J.M. Thomson *Fish Ocean & Shore* 107 Except near Ceduna the yellow-eye mullet is more common than the sea mullet in Tasmania, Victoria and South Australia. **1983** *Canberra Chron.* 28 Sept. 19/1 He also took some good mullet to about 900 gm., which I presume were big yelloweye. **1846** J. Gould *Birds of Aust.* (1848) IV. Pl. 45, *Ptilotis chrysops*. **Yellow-faced Honey-eater.** **1883** A.J. Campbell *Nest & Eggs Austral. Birds* p. iii, We flushed a Yellow-faced Honey-eater from its neatly-made nest of moss and hair. **1932** A.H. Chisholm *Nature Fantasy in Aust.* 185 Walking recently in a patch of casuarinas I saw a pair of brown-headed honeyeaters and a pair of yellow-faced honeyeaters. **1986** *Canberra Times* 16 Apr. 19/2 Fleeing the impending gloom of a Canberra winter, the yellow-faced honeyeaters are on the move again. **1894** R. Lydekker *Hand-Bk. Marsupialia & Monotremata* 47 **Yellow-footed Rock-wallaby.** *Petrogale xanthopus*... Fur long, soft, and silky. General colour grey, white beneath... Tail ringed above and on the sides with dark brown and pale yellow. **1910** *Emu* X. 30 It seems a pity that the dainty little yellow-footed rock wallaby is not protected. **1926** A.S. Le Souef et al. *Wild Animals Australasia* 202 Yellow-footed rock-wallaby .. is one of the handsomest of the marsupials. **1941** E. Troughton *Furred Animals Aust.* 182 This handsome species is usually called the Yellow-footed Rock Wallaby in natural history books, in reference to the bright coloration of the feet .. but both the ear and tail coloration appear to present more striking individual features. **1984** *Courier-Mail* (Brisbane) 30 June 26 He had missed the chance to film one of the most sought after animals in Queensland—the yellow-footed rock wallaby. **1876** *Observer Miscellany* (Adelaide) 8 Apr. 257/2 **Yellow-hammers** are everywhere, and very tame. **1903** *Bulletin* (Sydney) 31 Jan. 36/1 We had no knowledge of scientific terms. To us they were .. yellow-hammers. **1944** L. Welsh *Kookaburra* 11 *The yellow robin.* One of the first birds in the bush to awaken and one of the last to go to rest... Popularly called .. 'Yellow Hammer'. **1845** J. Gould *Birds of Aust.* (1848) IV. Pl. 42, *Ptilotis flava* .. **Yellow Honey-eater.** **1898** E.E. Morris *Austral Eng.* 199 Yellow H[oney-eater]—*Ptilotis flavescens*. **1956** T.Y. Harris *Naturecraft in Aust.* 63 The Honeyeaters comprise about one-tenth of our bird species... Some, like the Yellow Honeyeater .. are confined to the tropical north. **1976** *Reader's Digest Compl. Bk. Austral. Birds* 481 The presence of yellow honeyeaters is heralded by their loud cheery calls and their scolding chatter. **1984** Simpson & Day *Birds of Aust.* 232 Yellow Honeyeater... *Habitat* coastal and riverine forests, mangroves, gardens. **1882** Armstrong & Campbell *Austral. Sheep Husbandry* 231 The trees found to die most quickly after being operated upon are box, peppermint, and '**yellow-jacket**'. **1899** *Proc. Linnean Soc. N.S.W.* XXIV. 462 There are several so-called 'Yellow Gums' in New South Wales, but they must not be confused with the 'Yellow Box' or 'Yellow Jacket' (*E[ucalyptus] melliodora*). **1919** *Bulletin* (Sydney) 30 Oct. 24/4 We 'drove' an enormous yellow-jacket gum into the ironwood, and that did the trick. **1934** 'E.N. Speer' *Destiny* 242 He moved to the side of the road and stopped under the shade of two yellow-jacket trees. **1943** *Coast to Coast 1942* 14, I tied the horse to a yellow jack and crept towards the river. **1952** R. Morgan *Reminisc. Aboriginal Station* 10 There is the black and grey box, the yellow jack, Murray pine and, along the river flats, the old red gums. **1984** D.J. Boland et al. *Forest Trees Aust.* (rev. ed.) 239 Two species, viz. the yellow jackets (*E[ucalyptus] lirata* and *E. similis*), have a yellow fibrous bark somewhat like yellow bloodwoods. **1895** *Proc. Linnean Soc. N.S.W.* X. 529 *Cyclochila Australasiae* .. ('The Green Monday')... This is our commonest Sydney Cicada... There is a yellow variety of this species, which is popularly called the '**Yellow Monday**'. **1905** *Bulletin* (Sydney) 16 Feb. 16/2 Where the locusts .. ? The trees in the parks are unscaled by eager imps, seeking on the brittle bough the 'floury baker' and the 'yellow munday'. **1922** *Austral. Museum Mag.* Dec. 204 The Yellow Monday has .. been the plaything of the boys of Sydney, probably since the earliest days of the colony. **1951** Cusack & James *Come in Spinner* 163 She uncurled her fingers and showed the jewelled head of a cicada. 'He's a Yellow Mundy.' **1965** *Austral. Encycl.* II. 379 *Cyclochila australasiae*, a common insect in the Sydney district, has three forms: a green, known as the green monday; a yellow, the yellow monday; and a black and green, the black prince. (Yellowmundee was the name of an aboriginal met by Watkin Tench near Parramatta in 1791, and it was later applied—as Yellow Monday—to a creek in the area.) **1982** N. Keesing *Lily on Dustbin* 95 His tally for today (which he keeps in a shoe box ..) has been two 'greengrocers', a 'black prince' and one 'yellow Monday'... It is a bumper year for cicadas. **1945** C. Barrett *Austral. Bird Life* 137 The **yellow oriole** (*Oriolus flavocinctus*) frequents palm scrubs and the mangroves. **1964** M. Sharland *Territory of Birds* 70 The Yellow Oriole was the leading performer, with mimicry that would have earned it an ornithological 'Oscar'. **1984** Simpson & Day *Birds of Aust.* 336 The Yellow Oriole's nest is often placed over a stream or pond. **1898** E.E. Morris *Austral Eng.* 199 **Yellow-plumed H[oney-eater]**—*P[tilotis] ornata*. **1903** *Emu* III. 11 The Yellow-plumed Honey-eater .. sought the 'white gums'. **1945** C. Barrett *Austral. Bird Life* 159 The yellow-plumed honeyeater .. inhabits Mallee and other dry scrubs and ranges from Victoria to South-western Australia. **1962** B.W. Leake *Eastern Wheatbelt Wildlife* 76 Practically gone are .. the large numbers of yellow plumed honeyeaters that used to feed on the nectar of the gimlet, salmon, white and York gums. **1984** M. Blakers et al. *Atlas Austral. Birds* 536 The Yellow-plumed Honeyeater lives in eucalypt woodland, mallee and acacia scrub. **1827** *Trans. Linnean Soc. London* XV. 242 [Pachycephala] .. Australis... 'This bird', Mr Caley says, 'is called **yellow Robin** by the colonists. It is an inhabitant of brushes.' **1843** J. Gould *Birds of Aust.* (1848) III. Pl. 11, *Eöpsaltria australis*. Yellow-breasted Robin... Yellow Robin, Colonists of New South Wales. **1902** *Emu* II. 14 The Yellow-breasted Robin .. one would hardly expect to find in this class of country. **1945** C. Barrett *Austral. Bird Life* 174 The friendly southern yellow robin .. lives in fern gullies, dense scrub along the banks of streams, and moist, thickly timbered country. **1951** A. Marshall *Aust.* (1981) 78 A yellow-breasted robin alighted on a small branch. **1981** G. Cross *George & Widda-Woman* 88 He taught her how to spot at a distance the yellow robins. **1849 [yellow rosella]** *Adelaide Miscellany* 20 Sept. 25 The bright yellow parrot of the Murray was flitting from tree to tree. **1921** *Bulletin* (Sydney) 29 Sept. 20/2 For the .. most beautiful of Australian parrots I plump for .. the yellow parrot or 'Murray smoker'. **1932** H. Priest *Call of Bush* 162 The yellow Rosella (*Platycercus flaveolus*)—a most beautiful bird, a living kaleidoscope of bright colours—green and yellow, jewelled with blue and red. **1948** R. Raven-Hart *Canoe in Aust.* 106 A lovely little blue-and-yellow parrot with a curious blue 'moustache', Yellow Rosella, alias Murray Smoker or Swamp Lory. **1969** J.M. Forshaw *Austral. Parrots* 185 The yellow rosella .. a riparian species closely associated with the Murray, Murrumbidgee and Lachlan Rivers. **1869** J. Gould *Birds of Aust.* Suppl. Pl. 41, *Ptilotis notata* .. **Yellow-spotted Honey-eater**... This species of Ptilotis is a native of the Cape-York peninsula, where appears to be tolerably common. **1903** *Emu* II. 147 *Ptilotis notata* (Yellow-spotted Honey-eater)... This lively bird generally prefers the thick scrub. **1929** A.H. Chisholm *Birds & Green Places* 79 The shrilling of 'Jacky', the yellow-spotted honey-eater. **1975** *Ecos* vi. 7/1 The yellow-spotted honeyeater is known to live both here [*sc.* between Cairns and Ingham, Qld.] and at the tip of Cape York. **1904** J.H. Maiden *Notes on Commercial Timbers N.S.W.* 12 *Blackbutt* (*Eucalyptus pilularis*) .. is a strong, durable, thoroughly safe and well-tried timber... There is a variety of it (var. *Muelleriana* ..), which sometimes goes under the name of '**yellow stringy-**

bark'. **1932** R.H. ANDERSON *Trees of N.S.W.* 110 Yellow Stringybark (*Eucalyptus Muelleriana*)... The vernacular name is derived from the yellowness of the inner bark... The timber is also yellowish in colour. **1965** *Austral. Encycl.* VIII. 507 Yellow Stringybark .. piles, poles, fence-posts, sleepers [etc.]. **1978** *Ecos* xv. 11/1 The main timber species affected [by dieback] are Silvertop ash .. and yellow stringybark (*E. muellerana*) in South Gippsland. **1837** J. BACKHOUSE *Narr. Visit Austral. Colonies* (1843) 505 There are also **Yellow-tailed** and Red-tailed **Black Cockatoos.** **1900** A.J. CAMPBELL *Nests & Eggs Austral. Birds* 603 The yellow-tailed Black Cockatoo, a bush barometer for storms up country in the old times, used to trace the creeks after wattle grubs. **1931** N.W. CAYLEY *What Bird is That?* 141 Yellow-tailed Black Cockatoo... Also called Funereal Black Cockatoo and Black Cockatoo. Usually in pairs or small flocks, frequenting heavily timbered mountain ranges and adjacent open forest lands. [**1945** C. BARRETT *Austral. Bird Life* 70 There are four species [of black cockatoo], three of them being distinguished by variously coloured tail-bands. The yellow-tailed or funereal species .. perhaps is the best known of all the black cockatoos.] **1980** L. FULLER *Wollongong's Native Trees* 48 Yellow-tailed black cockatoos (*Calyptorhynchus funereus*) are particularly fond of the wood-boring larvae of longicorn beetles. **1985** P. CAREY *Illywhacker* 493 The day he brought the yellow-tailed cockatoo down from the tree at Bendigo School. **1898** [**yellow-tailed thornbill**] E.E. MORRIS *Austral Eng.* 470 Yellow-rumped T[it]—*Geobasileus chrysorrhoea.* **1903** *Emu* III. 138 What difference can it make if I speak of .. the Tomtit instead of the Yellow-rumped Tit? **1933** *Bulletin* (Sydney) 5 Apr. 27/1 The yellow-tailed thornbill constructs a double nest, the lower cavity being lined with feathers and containing the eggs. **1948** R. RAVEN-HART *Canoe in Aust.* 194 A tom-tit (Yellow-tailed Thornbill), wearing a speckledy school-cap with a white piping and with a bright yellow patch in the seat of its trousers. **1976** *Reader's Digest Compl. Bk. Austral. Birds* 440 A bright yellow rump distinguishes the yellow-rumped thornbill from all other thornbills. **1978** B.P. MOORE *Life on Forty Acres* 98 Yellow-tailed Thornbills (*Acanthiza chrysorrhoa*), with their zip-zip call. **1984** M. BLAKERS et al. *Atlas Austral. Birds* 488 The Yellow-rumped Thornbill inhabits country ranging from eucalypt forest to eucalypt woodland with a grassy understorey. **1848** J. GOULD *Birds of Aust.* VI. Pl. 79, *Myzantha flavigula* .. **Yellow-throated Miner.** **1890** G.J. BROINOWSKI *Birds of Aust.* IV. Pl. 14, The Yellow-throated Miner .. is to be found in the belts of timber bordering the rivers of the interior, particularly the Namoi. **1945** C. BARRETT *Austral. Bird Life* 161 The yellow-throated miner (*M[yzantha] flavigula*) is found in the interior of the continent. **1973** V. SERVENTY *Desert Walkabout* 52 The yellow-throated miner is a bird of the west and inland. It is grey headed compared to the black head of the noisy miner. It also has a much whiter rump than the noisy species. **1984** M. BLAKERS et al. *Atlas Austral. Birds* 515 The Yellow-throated Miner feeds on nectar and seeks insects in crevices and under litter and cow-pats. **1898** E.E. MORRIS *Austral Eng.* 408 **Yellow-throated S[crub]-W[ren]**—*S[ericornis] citreogularis.* **1901** *Emu* I. 73 The small Brown Tit .. relines deserted domiciles of the Yellow-throated Scrub Wren. **1918** *Bulletin* (Sydney) 31 Jan. 24/4 The yellow-throated scrub-wren ('devil-bird') hangs its enormous nest from the twigs of sassafras. **1929** A.H. CHISHOLM *Birds & Green Places* 25 To see a little yellow-throated scrub-wren dance attendance upon the scratcher. The yellow-throat is also a ground-feeding bird. **1945** C. BARRETT *Austral. Bird Life* 185 The yellow-throated scrub-wren .. builds a large, elongated dome-like nest. **1965** *Austral. Encycl.* VIII. 48 The yellow-throat is further distinguished by the possession of a most spirited and melodious song, which frequently extends into admirable mimicry of the notes of other birds. **1976** *Reader's Digest Compl. Bk. Austral. Birds* 427 Of all the scrub wrens, the yellow-throated scrub wren is the brightest in colouring, though its colours camouflage it against the rainforest floor, where it lives. **1844** J. GOULD *Birds of Aust.* (1848) IV. Pl. 37, The **Yellow-tufted Honey-eater** is abundant in New South Wales, inhabiting at one season or other every portion of the country. **1902** *Emu* II. 14 Among the smaller saplings the Yellow-tufted Honey-eater (*Ptilotis auricomis*) lives contentedly. **1945** C. BARRETT *Austral. Bird Life* 158 'Yellow whiskers' seems an absurd name for such a beautiful bird as the yellow-tufted honeyeater .. but the tuft of golden-yellow feathers behind the ear suggested it to schoolboys of long ago. **1981** *Canberra Times* 16 Apr. 19/3 Many white-naped honeyeaters join the migration, and occasional eastern spinebills .. as well as the rare yellow-tufted honeyeater may be swept along with the excitement. **1926** *Qld. Agric. Jrnl.* XXV. 435 Cryptocarya Bancroftii **Yellow Walnut** (Atherton), Canary Ash. **1951** W.D. FRANCIS *Austral. Rain-Forest Trees* (rev. ed.) 403 *Beilschmiedia bancroftii* .. Yellow Walnut .. wood yellow, often with darker streaks. **1965** *Austral. Encycl.* I. 483 *B[eilschmiedia] bancroftii* (the canary ash or yellow walnut) is a large tree common on the Atherton Tableland, North Queensland. **1983** R. STRAHAN *Compl. Bk. Austral. Mammals* 133 The flowers of Brown Bollywood and the fleshy outer covering of the Yellow Walnut are also eaten [by the Lemuroid Ringtail Possum]. **1903** *Emu* II. 208 *Acanthochaera* [*sic*] *inauris* (**Yellow Wattle-bird**)—one pair noted feeding on a flowering blue gum tree. **1926** *Official Checklist Birds Aust.* (R. Australasian Ornith. Union) p. v, Mr Matthews considered it was fixed by Lesson in 1830 as the Yellow Wattle-bird. **1945** C. BARRETT *Austral. Bird Life* 162 Tasmania possesses the largest of the three species, the yellow wattle-bird. **1984** M. BLAKERS et al. *Atlas Austral. Birds* 503 The Yellow Wattlebird is considered to be a game bird. Though on the partly-protected list, an open season may be declared, the most recent of which took place in 1972. **1945** C. BARRETT *Austral. Bird Life* 187 The **yellow weebill** (*S[micrornis] flavescens*) is found in Central and North-western Australia, the Northern Territory and North Queensland. **1956** A.C.C. LOCK *Tropical Tapestry* 245 The air was again sweet with the perfume of frangipane among which the yellow weebill and white-throated warbler searched for insects and nectar. **1965** *Austral. Encycl.* IX. 224 The yellow weebill inhabits the far north of the continent. **1908** *Emu* VIII. 41 The white-bearded Honey-eater (*Meliornis novaehollandiae*), often called the '**Yellow-wing**' is to be seen flitting in the thick bushes. **1918** *Bulletin* (Sydney) 14 Feb. (Red Page), *Honey-Birds* generally, especially the .. *White-bearded Honey-eater* (Yellow-wings).

2. *Obs.*

a. Used of convicts (see also CANARY 1 a.) with reference to the colour of their clothing: see quot. 1826. Esp. in the collocation **yellow jacket.**

[**1826** Tas. Colonial Secretary's Office Rec. 1/34 133, I should recommend Yellow Jackets and Trowsers as being the most conspicuous... For the Goals [*sic*] I recommend a Party dress of Jackets and Trowsers, one half of which should be yellow—and the other half Black.] **1837** P. ADAM SMITH *When we rode Rails* (1983) 13 She was carried along the track on a kind of sedan chair, made of kangaroo skins spread over boards attached to two poles. These, she said, were 'strapped to two yellow men' (the convicts who wore sulphur coloured uniforms marked with the broad arrow). **1843** C. ROWCROFT *Tales of Colonies* (1858) 386 It was a road-gang of yellow-jackets going to work. **1846** —— *Bushranger Van Diemen's Land* I. 13 'I wish we had some grub,' said one of the yellow jackets. **1851** H. MELVILLE *Present State Aust.* 169 The jury .. are to try their '*peer*' the yellow-jacket. **1853** *Guardian* (Hobart) 12 Jan. 3/2 Josiah Hand you are a yellow bird, and glory in your irons.

b. In the collocation **yellow frigate,** a hulk used for the accommodation of convicts: see quot. 1859.

1859 W. BURROWS *Adventures Mounted Trooper* 171 After he had been for some time in fine, airy lodgings in the 'yellow frigates', as the hulks are called from their being painted yellow, he fancied he should like to get out. **1891** 'OLD TIME' *Convict Hulk 'Success'* 20 The convicts on board the 'yellow frigates' had a dull time of it.

3. [Used elsewhere but of local significance.] Having a yellowish complexion or skin, esp. in the collocations **yellow agony,** the Chinese in Australia; a member of this community; also *attrib.*; **peril,** immigration from Asian countries to Australia; the Asiatic peoples collectively; an Asiatic person.

1879 *Illustr. Austral. News* (Melbourne) 22 Jan. 18/2 Although a satisfactory settlement has been arrived at between the Sydney seamen and their employers as to the introduction of Chinese sailors, the agitation relative to the '**yellow agony**' question has by no means subsided. **1898** E. DYSON *Below & on Top* 105 He felt himself called upon, as a husband and father, to rise and enter a protest, which he did, pointing out to the Yellow Agony, in graphic and forcible language, the gross wickedness of robbing a struggling man. **1904** *Shearer* (Sydney) 3 Dec. 8/4 What with the clergy battling for the yellow agony and the support given to Chinese by members of the Legislative Council. **1908** *Bulletin* (Sydney) 10 July 14/3 The honor of introducing the yellow agony into Queensland rests with Arthur Hodgson of Eden Vale. A batch of Chinkies was landed at the station to do the shepherding. **1905** *Nat. Rev.* (London) 542 It was while he was a resident in South Australia and Victoria, and a Minister of the Crown in the latter State, that Professor C.H. Pearson .. wrote his book containing the earliest sufficient prophecy of the '**Yellow Peril**'. **1913** *Bulletin* (Sydney) 25 Dec. 22/1 The Darwin Chow .. informed 'J.C.C.' that his stock-in-trade consisted of gohannas' gall-bags... Almost any old gall is marketable with the yellow peril. **1920** H.F. MOLLARD *Humour of Road* 92 'Talking of Chinamen .. reminds me of --.' There was a movement at the door. The travellers off the Canowindra train were coming in, and those who had finished rose to make room for them. 'Saved from the Yellow Peril,' said Jim Turner. **1929** P.R. STEPHENSEN *Bushwhackers* 44 As Willy Ah Foo was the only Yellow Peril left in our district, pressure was put upon him to clear out. **1963** X. HERBERT *Disturbing Element* 34 A generation later, the annihilation of the Australian Nation by the Yellow Peril looked like becoming a frightful reality. **1971** *Bulletin* (Sydney) 18 Sept. 47/2 Australians did not invent the 'yellow peril'. The seeds had blown in from Europe, having been released around the world to serve the purposes of imperialism. **1980** C. JAMES *Unreliable Mem.* 141 National Service was designed to turn boys into men and make the Yellow Peril think twice about moving south.

4. Usu. **yeller.** Of mixed Aboriginal and white parentage, esp. in the collocation **yellow fellow.** Also *fig.* (see quot. 1965).

1913 W.K. HARRIS *Outback in Aust.* 115 We asked how they got on before the advent of the white man. The reply was not quite unexpected: 'Plenty tucker, no yeller-fellers' (half-castes). **1930** A.E. YARRA *Vanishing Horsemen* 126 Why that feller shook more cattle an' got more yeller piccaninny than you can shake a stick at. **1935** K.L. SMITH *Sky Pilot Arnhem Land* 269 The half-caste was the centre of an excited group of blacks and coloured folk. Poor girl! For one brief hour the 'outcast' was an envied heroine, and the once despised 'yellow fellow' reaped in the darkies' eyes a glory eclipsing that of a film star. **1938** X. HERBERT *Capricornia* 37 A half-caste—a yeller-feller! .. He had been trying to beget yeller-fellers for years. **1951** J. DEVANNY *Travels N. Qld.* 190 'My best stockman is a yellow-feller' (half-caste). **1958** O. RUHEN *Naked under Capricorn* 95 The blacks will stay on their tribal country; the yeller-fellers got no laws, they got no decency. **1964** *Meanjin* 57 Yeller boys can be difficult sometimes. **1965** M. PATCHETT *Last Warrior* 253 They are in towns now learning the white men's ways, becoming 'yellow boys'. **1975** X. HERBERT *Poor Fellow my Country* 52 Now, I'm using the term Black Velvet not simply to apply to fullblood women, but any of obvious Aboriginal strain, 'yeller girls', or 'creamy pieces', as they're called, half and quarter. **1976** K. BROWN *Knock Ten* 66 'How long has your baby been ill .. ?' 'It's not mine. It belongs to a yellow piece works on our place.' **1978** R.A.F. WEBB *Brothers in Sun* 126 The part-Aboriginal result of a drunken coupling in the dry bed of the River Todd or of the half-ashamed satisfaction of an urgent lust in the paddock behind a homestead, was unacceptable to both black and white society... Contemptuously referred to as 'yeller-fellers', those who survived existed precariously in a no-man's land between the communities.

yellowbelly. [f. the pale, sometimes yellow, underside of the fish.] *Golden perch*, see GOLDEN 3.

1880 *Proc. Linnean Soc. N.S.W.* (1881) 354 *Ctenolates ambiguus* .. the '*Golden Perch*' and '*Yellow belly*' of the Colonists. **1906** D.G. STEAD *Fishes of Aust.* 97 The Golden Perch or 'Yellow-belly' .. is abundant in all the western rivers of New South Wales. **1932** W. HATFIELD *Ginger Murdoch* 65 He grilled a yellow-belly on the coals—just as it was caught, fins, scales and all. **1950** G.M. FARWELL *Land of Mirage* 67 They would .. fish for bream and yellow-bellies in the placid centre of the lake. **1974** L. WEDLICK *Sporting Fish* 11 Once known as 'yellowbelly' this perch was officially called 'callop' but this name too was ousted and today the fish is both officially and colloquially known as a golden perch or yellowbelly. **1977** V. PRIDDLE *Larry & Jack* 15, I like to camp for the night on the bank of a big waterhole and do some fishing. Nothing nicer than a slab of yellow belly for breakfast. **1985** *Trees & Natural Resources* Dec.

29 They landed a Yellowbelly that fed five adults for breakfast.

yellow fever. *Obs. Gold fever*, see GOLD 3.

1849 *Argus* (Melbourne) 3 Aug. 4/2 The 'yellow' fever is very prevalent, many persons sacrificing their little all to hasten to the 'diggings'. **1852** D. MACKENZIE *Gold Digger* 29 The yellow fever seized on all classes of society. **1861** T. M'COMBIE *Austral. Sketches* 47, I began to experience evident symptoms of the return of the 'yellow' fever, and a journey to the new gold-fields seemed to be the only cure. **1878** P. FOX *Unsuccessful Colonist* 138 The large yields of gold for the first few years of the 'yellow fever', had settled down into one of mere supply. **1891** *Braidwood Dispatch* 4 July 2/4 *Nelligen mining.*—The 'yellow fever', and reefing mania is still influenziastically raging here. **1897** A.F. CALVERT *My Fourth Tour W.A.* 15 The air in Perth is full of the yellow fever. Its germs, in the shape of talk of reefs, leases, claims, yields, trial crushings, camels, syndicates, stocks, and company flotations, are as thick as a London fog.

yellow gum.

1. *Obs.* [See quot. 1834.] **a.** The yellow resin exuded by *Xanthorrhoea resinosa* (fam. Xanthorrhoeaceae), and allied species, used in medicines and as an adhesive. See also *grass-tree gum* GRASS-TREE 1 c. **b.** Any of these plants, occurring in e. Aust. Also *attrib.*, esp. as **yellow gum tree.**

1770 J. BANKS *Jrnl.* 23 May (1896) 271 The plant yielding the yellow gum, of which, though we saw vast numbers, we did not see any that showed signs of gum. **1789** A. PHILLIP *Voyage to Botany Bay* 60 (*caption*) Yellow gum plant. **1790** J. WHITE *Jrnl. Voyage N.S.W.* 151 Their spears are made of a kind of cane which grows out of the tree that produces the yellow gum. **1793** W. TENCH *Compl. Acct. Settlement* 190 The fish-gigs and spears are commonly (but not universally) made of the long spiral shoot which arises from the top of the yellow gum-tree. **1798** D. COLLINS *Acct. Eng. Colony N.S.W.* I. 551 To their hair, by means of the yellow gum, they fasten the front teeth of the kangooroo. **1829** R. MUDIE *Picture of Aust.* 136 *Xantorrhoea*, called the yellow gum, or yellow resin tree, and also the grass tree, is another of the singular vegetables of Australia. **1834** G. BENNETT *Wanderings N.S.W.* I. 62 It is named '*grass tree*' by the colonists for its long pendent grassy foliage, and '*yellow gum tree*' from secreting a quantity of yellowish gum. **1844** C. LYON *Narr. & Recoll. Van Dieman's Land* 38 The most remarkable is the yellow gum tree, which attains the height of our tallest beeches, growing straight for about fifteen or twenty feet, after which it branches out into long spiral leaves, which hang down on all sides, and resemble those of the largest kind of grass. **1886** F. COWAN *Aust.* 16 The grass-tree .. Yellow-gum: a monstrous aborescent [*sic*] Rush .. of divers uses .. from dyeing silk to making an illuminating gas.

2. [From the colour of the bark or wood.] Any of several trees of the genus *Eucalyptus* (fam. Myrtaceae) esp. *E. leucoxylon* of s.e. mainland Aust., having a mottled, sometimes yellow, smooth bark. See also *white ironbark* WHITE *a.*[2] 1 a.

1848 T.L. MITCHELL *Jrnl. Exped. Tropical Aust.* 107 We this day passed a small group of trees of the yellow gum, a species of eucalyptus growing only on the poor sandy soil near Botany Bay. **1901** *Proc. Linnean Soc. N.S.W.* XXVI. 135 The 'Yellow Gum' of St Vincent's Gulf, South Australia, we believe to be a form of *E. Gunnii.* **1942** R.T. PATTON *Know your Own Trees* 41 Botanically, Yellow Gum is a true Ironbark. It is the only one of that group without a black persistent bark. **1952** E. WALLING *Austral. Roadside* 109 The so-called Yellow Gum .. has smooth, yellow, deciduous bark. **1981** A.B. & J.W. CRIBB *Useful Wild Plants Aust.* 28 The yellow gum, *E[ucalyptus] leucoxylon*, of western Victoria and southern ranges of South Australia.

yellowtail. [Spec. use of *yellowtail* a name for various fish.] Any of several fish having a yellow caudal fin, esp. *Trachurus novaezelandiae* of estuaries and coastal waters, which is commonly used as bait, and *Seriola lalandi* (see KINGFISH).

1839 *Tasmanian* (Hobart) 26 Apr. 133/3 The fish was of the description called yellow tail or trumpeter. **1844** *Colonial Lit. Jrnl.* (Sydney) 21 Nov. 350/1 At last a greedy yellowtail Was caught. **1880** *Proc. Linnean Soc. N.S.W.* V. 540 *Seriola grandis* .. '*Yellow Tail*' of the Melbourne Fishermen. **1898** *Bulletin* (Sydney) 29 Jan. 31/1, I hated the term 'bung' because it meant yellowtail, and yellowtail were the only fish that I could catch. **1906** D.G. STEAD *Fishes of Aust.* 149 The Yellowtail (*Trachurus declivis*) .. is an almost cosmopolitan fish. **1933** D. MACDONALD *Brooks of Morning* 180 Sydney has a kingfish .. which we Victorians flippantly call a yellowtail. **1951** *Bulletin* (Sydney) 14 Mar. 12/1 He took small yellowtail and 'old wives' off the hook and flung them contemptuously into his sugarbag.

yellow-wood.

1. Any of several trees, esp. some species of the genus *Flindersia* (fam. Rutaceae), *Ristantia pachysperma* (fam. Myrtaceae) of lowland rainforest in n. Qld., and *Acronychia oblongifolia* (fam. Rutaceae) of e. Vic., N.S.W., and Qld.; the yellowish wood. Also *attrib.*

1791 P.G. KING in *Extracts Lett. Arthur Phillip* 10 Jan. 17 The live oak, yellow wood, black wood, and beech, are all of a close grain, and are a durable wood. **1814** *HRA* (1916) 1st Ser. VIII. 222 With the Yellow Wood also sent these Barks produce Olives of all Shades. **1836** J. BACKHOUSE *Narr. Visit Austral. Colonies* (1843) 365 *Oxleya zanthoxyla*, is the yellow wood, of Moreton Bay. **1848** *Portland Gaz.* 8 Apr. 4/4 The yellow-wood tree is the same as the fustic of South America—the low price of £4 per ton in the London market precludes the prospect of its ever being exported. **1882** *Austral. Handbk.* 391 Several species of *Flindersia* supply the timber known by the name of 'Yellow-wood'. **1920** B. CRONIN *Timber Wolves* 234 The smell of the burning yellow wood was jess great. **1984** *Townsville Bull.* 15 Sept. 11/7 Yellow wood contained a toxic substance called tannin which poisoned cattle through liver and kidney failure.

2. With distinguishing epithet: **deep** (or **dark**) **yellow-wood,** the rainforest tree *Rhodosphaera rhodanthema* (fam. Anacardiaceae) of Qld. and n.e. N.S.W., having a very scaly bark; the wood of the tree; **light yellow-wood,** any of several species of yellow-wood yielding a pale, yellowish timber; the wood itself.

1880 J. BONWICK *Resources Qld.* 82 **Dark Yellow Wood,** a *Rhus*, with a scaly bark and red flower, is eagerly sought after by sawyers for furniture use. **1885** F.M. BAILEY *Catal. Plants Two Metropolitan Gardens* 23 *Rhus rhodanthema* .. Deep Yellow-wood. **1903** *Proc. Linnean Soc. N.S.W.* XXVIII. 699 *Acronychia Endlicheri*... Called 'Big or Dark Yellow Wood'. **1926** *Qld. Agric. Jrnl.* XXV. 438 Rhodosphaera rhodanthema .. Deep Yellowwood. **1965** *Austral. Encycl.* IX. 527 The name deep yellow-wood is often applied to the tulip satinwood, *Rhodosphaera rhodanthema.* **1880** J. BONWICK *Resources Qld.* 81 The **Light-yellow Wood** is *Flindersia*, as useful as cedar, with excellent dyeing properties, and capable of good polish. **1888** *Proc. Linnean Soc. N.S.W.* III. 367 *Daphnandra micrantha* .. 'Light Yellow-wood'. **1928** E. FOREMAN *Hist. & Adventures Qld. Pioneer* 43 Light yellow-wood, tulip wood, iron wood.

yeo, var. YOE.

yike. [Of unknown origin.] A quarrel; a fight. Also as *v. intr.*

1940 *Mod. Standard Eng. Dict.* (Odhams Press, rev. ed.) *Yike, v.*, to fight. **1941** S.J. BAKER *Pop. Dict. Austral. Slang* 84 *Yike*, a row or argument. (2) A fight. **1945** 'R. RENE' *Mo's Mem.* 186 There's that tram connie having a yike with a drunk. **1952** T.A.G. HUNGERFORD *Ridge & River* 213 Don't let's yike about it. **1957** D. WHITINGTON *Treasure upon Earth* 25 'Seems like you got a yike on your hands, Loch,' Tom said. 'He's too small for me.' Lochie eyed his opponent doubtfully... 'I'm not really keen on fighting,' he said weakly. **1958** *Coast to Coast 1957–58* 196 'Bit of a yike on earlier, eh?' 'That Greek! .. Just says anything that comes into his head.' **1963** D. WHITINGTON *Mile Pegs* 210 This was no bar-room yike, Clancy was no shambling shearer or heavy-shouldered timber-worker. **1976** *Sunday Sun* (Brisbane) 11 Apr. 6/2 ALP circles have scoffed at suggestions of a political 'yike' between State Opposition Leader Tom Burns and TLC chief Egerton. **1984** *Business Rev. Weekly* (Sydney) 7 Jan. 18/1 We have had a couple of small yikes, mainly on things like contract prices.

yodel, *v. intr.* To vomit.

1965 J. WYNNUM *Jiggin' in Riggin'* 45 'Can you yodel?' grinned Cal. 'I understand that's a definite aid to sales.' 'Only in a bucket,' chortled Stripey. 'Six meals Muldoon the troops call him. Three down and three up. The most seasick sailor in the service.' **1971** B. HUMPHRIES *Bazza pulls it Off*, What bastard yodelled all over the Migrant Information Desk? **1979**—*Bazza comes into his Own*, The Robert Menzies Memorial Reading Room's over there, mate, but keep youse eyes peeled. Some dirty bastard from the Trade Commissioner's Department just yodelled on the wall-to-wall, and youse might slip and break youse neck!

yoe /jəʊ/. Also **yeo, yow, yowe,** and diminutive **yowie.** [Br. dial. form of *ewe*: see OED *yeo* and *yowie*, OED(S *yow(e)*.] A ewe.

1900 H. LAWSON *Verses Pop. & Humorous* 171 He thought that he'd be fined all right—he couldn't turn the 'yoe'. **1903** J. FURPHY *Such is Life* 233 Ole hon t'we gits a holt of 'em fellers' mongreals!—bin leavin' three o' hour gates hopen; an' the yowes an' weaners is boxed. **1904** J. FARRELL *My Sundowner* 73 I've been a sinner and I've stown the young of Your yowies. **1915** G. SARGANT *Sweet Heart of Bush* 131 You have only just started on the yoes (ewes). **1919** 'AIMSFELD' *Howls of Dingo* 31 The bleat of many thousand sheep, of wethers, lambs, and yeos. **1948** J. FURPHY *Buln-Buln & Brolga* 51, I was sent to Wagga with twelve hundred yowes. **1965** L. HAYLEN *Big Red* 100 The sweat of agony on their brows at 'spells', the deep gash in the bare-bellied 'yeo', the strident call for 'Tar!' **1973** R. EDWARDS *Austral. Folk Songs* 41, I struck a blow at a poor old yoe. **1974** *Austral. Folksongs* (Folk Lore Council Aust.) 53 The ringer looks around and is beaten by a blow And curses the old snagger with the bare-bellied yeo.

yohi /ˈjoʊwaɪ/, *adv. Austral. pidgin.* Also **ooah, oowa, yoi, youai, yowhi, yowi.** [a. Jagara (and many other languages) *yu, yuway.*] An affirmative reply, 'yes'.

1859 H. KINGSLEY *Recoll. Geoffry Hamlyn* II. 215 'Yowi; but mine want it big one flying doe.' [*Note*] Yowi means eys .. more of a Moreton Bay word. **1879** 'AUSTRALIAN' *Adventures Qld.* 65 'Did you see anything else, Tommy?' '*Yowi*—mine see him big bone belonging to *yarraman*, I believe.' **1881** A.C. GRANT *Bush-Life Qld.* I. 236 'You patter (eat) potchum?' 'Yohi' (yes) said John, rather doubtfully, for he is not sure how his stomach will agree with the strange meat. **1889** *Centennial Mag.* (Sydney) 775 'Youai,' said Pompey, pleased at this proof of the truthfulness of his tale. **1894** G.H. GIBSON *Ironbark Chips* 22 Then Billy murmured 'budgeree', and 'Yohi', meaning 'yes'. **1926** M. FORREST *Hibiscus Heart* 188 'You after honey, Tim?' .. 'Yowhi,' Tim grinned. **1927** W.M. FLEMING *Hunted Piccaninnies* 150 'You think it that always?' asked Joe. 'Yowi,' answered Coolamon readily. **1936** A. RUSSELL *Gone Nomad* 34 The big chief smiled, politely inscrutable. 'Oo-ah' (yes) he said. **1949** C. FENTON *Flying Doctor* 32 Yo-I boss, him Florina all right. **1965** F.G.G. ROSE *Wind of Change* 157, I asked him .. to which he answered with a smile '*Ooowa!*' (Yes!). **1978** J. & P. READ View of Past 197 (typescript) Throw away all that bush stuff? Youai.

yoke, *v.* [Elsewhere constr. without *up.*] *trans.* With **up:** to put a yoke on (draught animals).

1848 T.L. MITCHELL *Jrnl. Exped. Tropical Aust.* 107 The cattle were yoked up early and we travelled on over fine grassy plains. **1891** J. FENTON *Bush Life Tas.* (1964) 14 The drivers yoked up their bullocks, and started for Northdown. **1900** L. HENSLOWE *Ann.* 70 The horses not put to, or 'yoked up' as a colonial would express it.

yonnie /ˈjɒni/. Also **yonny.** [Poss. f. a Vic. Aboriginal language.] A small stone; a pebble.

1941 S.J. BAKER *Pop. Dict. Austral. Slang* 84 *Yonnie*, a small stone; a pebble. **1965** K. SMITH *OGF* 123 Fred Gadley called me an urger and threw a yonnie on the roof. **1977** W. MOORE *Just to Myself* 60, I slam the receiver on the hook and chuck a yonnie at the rooster because it's rooting a chook. **1979** *Age* (Melbourne) 2 July 9/8 You should have included 'brinny' and 'yonny' as synonyms for 'stone'. **1985** *Ibid.* 16 Aug. 19/2 Have you ever .. tried to skim flat yonnies across the ocean?

yoolahng /ˈjulæŋ/. Also **yoolang.** [a. Dharuk *yulaŋ.*] An Aboriginal ceremony during which a youth is initiated into manhood; the place where such ceremonies take place.

[**1796** D. COLLINS *Acct. Eng. Colony N.S.W.* (1798) I. 583 In alluding to this ceremony [*sc.* extraction of a front tooth] .. the words Yoo-lahng erah-ba-diahng were always used.] **1829** R. MUDIE *Picture of Aust.* 260 The first part of the ceremony consists in preparing the proper arena for the future operations, which is an oval of about twenty-seven feet by eighteen, cleared from grass and roots, and called the yoolahng. **1847** G.F. ANGAS *Savage Life & Scenes* II. 217 An open space, called Yoolang, had been cleared for the purpose. **1892** HILL & THORNTON *Notes on Aborigines N.S.W.* 8 A ceremony which is common among all tribes is that of conferring on youths the title of manhood, and this is called at any rate in the Sydney district 'yoolangh'. **1896** W.A. SQUIRE *Ritual, Myth, & Customs Austral. Aborigines* 7 The Bora, Kabbara, Yoolangh, or Kipperah, which is of a religious and civil character, is the great educational ceremony of the Murri or Australian race.

York gum. [f. the name of a town e. of Perth in W.A.: see quot. 1889.] The tree *Eucalyptus loxophleba* (fam. Myrtaceae) of s.w. W.A., varying in form from a rough-barked tree to a smooth-barked mallee; the wood of the tree. Also *attrib.* Quot. 1837 may refer to a different tree, the TUART.

1837 G.F. MOORE *Evidences Inland Sea* 15 The trees are .. Toart (the York gum). **1844** *Swan River News* June 48/1 The natives .. collect a description of manna from the leaves of the York gum, which yields a considerable quantity of saccharine matter. **1855** R. AUSTIN *Jrnl. Interior W.A.* 6 The jam and York gum forests growing on brown gravelly loam around the outcrop of the granite. **1872** MRS E. MILLETT *Austral. Parsonage* 93 Logs, especially those from the tree known as the York gum, will be found alight on the under side hours after the fire is supposed to have been extinguished. **1889** J.H. MAIDEN *Useful Native Plants Aust.* 448 *E[ucalyptus] loxophleba* is known by the aboriginal name of 'Yandee', but usually to the colonists of Western Australia as 'York Gum', as it is very abundant near the town of York. **1896** *Austral. Handbk.* 385 The indigenous trees comprise .. tuart, or tooart, (*Eucalyptus gomphocephala*) .. York gum (*Eucalyptus loxophleba*). **1908** J. MANN *Suitability Australasian Timber* 4 Timbers in which the grain is closely twisted and interwoven, are in general very hard, dense, and heavy. .. Such timbers as Wandoo, Tuart, and York Gum. **1936** J.E. HAMMOND *Western Pioneers* 92 All timber .. had to be shipped from Fremantle, except the jam-wood .. and York gum for cart and wagon building. **1952** A.C.C. LOCK *Travels across Aust.* 235 York gum is a hard, dense, heavy wood, with interlocked grain. **1973** W.G. WALKER *Gloss. Terms* 9 The next time, york gum and jam trees were planted to provide shade.

York road poison. [See quot. 1926.] The shrub *Gastrolobium calycinum* (fam. Fabaceae) of s.w. W.A., which is poisonous to stock. Also *ellipt.* as **York road,** and *attrib.*

1865 'SPECIAL CORRESPONDENT' *Transportation* 14 The York-road plant, a low bushy scrub, with narrow fresh green leaves, and a light-coloured stem. After a bush fire this is the first plant to spring up. **1897** L. LINDLEY-COWEN *W. Austral. Settler's Guide* 578 The well-known 'York road' occurs as a small shrub. **1926** *Poison Plants W.A.* (W.A. Dept. Agric.) 32 The name York Road Poison was given to it because of the heavy losses of stock from eating it along the York Road between Guildford and York [*sc.* W.A.] from 1854 onwards. **1981** A.B. FACEY *Fortunate Life* 96 There was a poison bush called York Road Poison .. and two or three mouthfuls would be sufficient to kill a cow.

youai, var. YOHI.

youee, var. UEY.

young, *a.* In special collocations: **young Australia,** the youth of Australia collectively; recently colonized Australia; **country,** applied to Australia as having only a short history since European settlement.

1848 *Sydney Morning Herald* 29 Jan. 3/1 We have Young France and Young England in Europe, and it is very obvious that we shall soon have **Young Australia.** **1884** *Austral. Tit-Bits* (Melbourne) 26 June 13/1 Young Australia cannot do better than go and see this fine old English comedy. **1897** *Bulletin* (Sydney) 11 Dec. 16/1 She objects to young Australia ungroomed and perfumed with colonial beer. **1927** A. CROMBIE *After Sixty Yrs.* 36 Upon failing to obtain water he thought he had about reached what young Australia now terms 'the limit'. **1929** P.R. STEPHENSEN *Bushwhackers* 42 The *Bulletin* and the *Worker* used to come out in those days with front-page cartoons indicating the Yellow Peril peering over the Great Wall at Young Australia, with horrible, sly grimaces. **1964** G. PETERS *Claw of Cat* 24 Shaking her head .. at the Americanisms Young Australia affected these days. **1971** *Bulletin* (Sydney) 27 Nov. 48/3 Telling of another part of contemporary 'Young Australia'. **1876** G.H. REID *Essay on N.S.W.* 81 It would be absurd to expect manufacturers in a **young country** under a policy of free trade, to appear .. imposing. **1882** W.B. CHRISTIE *Our Land Laws* 25 The lands of a young country like ours, are its best national securities. **1886** 'THIRTY-FIVE YRS. COLONIST' *Hard Times* 10 A young country like Australia. **1891** A. WEATHERHEAD *Leaves from my Life* 3 In a young country like this .. progress becomes every day more apparent. **1953** T.G. TUCKER *Aust. as Home* 5 Australia, like other portions of the world, colonized from Great Britain, is sometimes spoken of as a 'new' country, sometimes as a 'young' country.

youngie. [f. *young* + -Y.] A young woman; a young person. Also *attrib.*

1965 *Oz* (Sydney) xxiii. 8 So I figured that we'd have 250 fiddlies left for turps and a bit of youngie jumping. **1969** W. MOXHAM *Apprentice* 94 A lot of oldies didn't like youngies was the strength of it. **1971** *Bulletin* (Sydney) 17 Apr. 19/2 *Kids, just,* first launched as 'youngies', Youth Power has now become a conventional wisdom.

youngon, youngun, var. YUNGAN.

youse, *pers. pron.* and *possessive pron.* Also **yous.** [Prob. orig. in Irish English: see EDD (which cites Irish, U.S., and Austral. examples), OED *yez* and OEDS *yous.* In predom. sub-standard use in Aust.]

A. *pers. pron.*

1. Used when addressing more than one person; you (*pl.*).

1902 *Bulletin* (Sydney) May 642/2 The men persuaded us to try our luck with them, at least for a time. 'Yous can leave us when you like, if it doesn't pay.' **1920** *Aussie* (Sydney) Dec. 78/3 Larry is goin' ter tell youse blokes wot 'e thinks of Billy 'Ughes. **1937** C.E.W. BEAN *Official Hist. Aust. 1914–18* V. 586 'Never mind, kid', he said, 'the boys will hunt Fritz without yous kids.' **1944** P.C. NEASBEY *Blokes I Knew* 152 The first decent-looking sheila I see since leaving Aussie and I have to have a lot of mugs like youse with me. **1957** V. PALMER *Rainbow-Bird* 34 But I said that youse blokes were waiting for your tobacco, an' that nothing would stop me. **1974** *Bulletin* (Sydney) 19 Jan. 12/2 If youse want to know what bloke in Canberra I reckon really is a snappy dresser it's Senator Doug McClelland, no risk. **1984** P. READ *Down there with me on Cowra Mission* 23 Dad said we gotta keep away from youse.

2. Used when addressing one person; you (*sing.*).

1885 E. NEVILL *Gleanings with Meanings* 3 As he staggered along the footpath, he met a gentleman, whom he thus accosted, 'Plaise, sor, can yiz be afther tellin me which is the other soide ave the sthreet?' **1960** K. SMITH *Word from Children* 97, I 'ope youse are doin' good in your English and I 'ope youse got a good mark in spellin'. **1971** B. HUMPHRIES *Bazza pulls it Off,* See youse Blue—just shooting through to the Gents to shake hands with the unemployed. **1976** HURST & CAMERON *In Collaboration* 39 Listen Harry, if youse were an out of work streaker no one'd lend you a pair of strides.

B. *possessive pron.* Your.

1979 B. HUMPHRIES *Bazza comes into his Own,* Keep youse eyes peeled. **1983** E. JOLLEY *Mr Scobie's Riddle* 122 'Aw come on. Get all of youse things off,' she said.

yow, var. YOE.

yow. [Of unknown origin.] In the phr. **to keep yow,** *to keep nit,* see NIT 2.

1942 E. LANGLEY *Pea Pickers* 283 You keep yow .. and whistle .. if anyone comes along. **1965** G. MCINNES *Road to Gundagai* 206 Molly kept a look out ('kept yow', as we used to say). **1966** S.J. BAKER *Austral. Lang.* (ed. 2) 344 *Keep yow,* to maintain guard while some illegal activity is afoot.

Yowah nut /'jaʊə nʌt/. [f. the name of an opal field w. of Cunnamulla in s. Qld.] An ironstone nodule (see quot. 1972), occas. having a core of precious opal.

1932 I.L. IDRIESS *Prospecting for Gold* 249 Inside an occasional boulder is a 'kernel' of opal, hence 'kernel opal'. The 'Yowah nuts', in the Eulo district, are famous. These 'nuts' are ironstone packed like pebbles and the kernels have produced gems fit for a queen's purse. **1962** D. MCLEAN *World turned upside Down* 144 That piece that Narrow gave us will be the first profits in the partnership. It'll probably bring fifty quid an ounce and I estimate there's six ounces in it. It's what's known as boulder opal or a Yowah nut. **1972** S.N. BAWDEN *Austral. Gemstones* 68 Yowah Nut is the name given to almond-shaped nodules of ironstone on the opal fields at Yowah in south-western Queensland.

yowe, yowie, var. YOE.

yowhi, yowi, var. YOHI.

yowie /'jaʊi/. [a. Yuwaalaraay *yuwi* dream spirit.] An ape-like monster supposed to inhabit parts of eastern Australia: see quot. 1980 (1). Also *attrib.* and *transf.*

1975 *Bulletin* (Sydney) 17 May 20/1 The monster—the 'Yowie'—currently causing trouble in the central-west of N.S.W. **1977** K. GILBERT *Living Black* 241 We had the legendary bunyip, the giant water snake, the little people and the hairy youree—the huge shaggy man-like creature that the whites call 'yowie'. **1980** M. MCADOO *If only I'd Listened* ('George Nott'), 'E'd be about six foot easy tall, broad, an' a sort of brownish fur lookin' stuff all over 'im, an' standing up like a man. .. We didn't know what the name of it was then, but .. a lot of people've been seein' them around the eastern parts, an' they're known as the 'Yowie'. **1980** *Austral. Infantry* Dec. 10 Current equipment includes .. Denison smock or 'Yowie Suit'. **1982** ROBSON & BARNES *Dare to be Different* 31 The city fathers met and agreed to build a yowie. You know .. a yeti .. an abominable snowman. **1986** *Star Weekly* (Canberra) 10 Apr. 10/2 Last week I recounted my meeting with the yowie on the banks of the Murrumbidgee.

yu /ju/. Also **yaw.** [a. Western Desert language *yuu.*] An Aboriginal shelter, *spec.* BREAKWIND 1.

1950 V.E. TURNER *Ooldea* 136 There are three kinds of native homes—houses (karrpa), shelter (wilja) and breakwinds (yaw). **1979** M. HEPPELL *Black Reality* 144 The two traditional shelters of an Aboriginal camp are the *yu* (windbreak) and the *wiltja* (literally, shade). As their names imply, one is protection from the wind, the other is protection from the best of the sun.

yugari, var. UGARI.

yulka, var. YELKA.

yungan /'jʌŋən/. *Obs.* Also **youngon, youngun, yungun.** [a. Jagara (and neighbouring languages) *yaŋan.*] A dugong. See also MANATEE.

1836 J. BACKHOUSE *Narr. Visit Austral. Colonies* (1843) 368 The Blacks .. value the flesh of another cetaceous animal, called here Youngon, the Dugong of India, *Halicore Dugong.* **1841** *Sydney Herald* 5 May 2/5 Should any of the tribes on the sea coast have been so fortunate as to catch a sea-hog—called *youngun*—which sometimes is the size of a young bullock, intelligence of the event is immediately sent along the coast. **1847** J.D. LANG *Cooksland* 97 But the fish, or rather sea-monster, peculiar to Moreton Bay, and the East coast to the northward, is a species of sea-cow or manatee, called by the black natives *yungan.* **1852** J. MACGILLIVRAY *Narr. Voyage H.M.S. Rattlesnake* I. 48 The Australian dugong (*Halicore Australis*) which is the object of a regular fishery .. on account of its valuable oil .. and is harpooned by the natives, who know it under the name of *Yung-un.* **1861** J.D. LANG *Qld., Aust.* 339 Fish of all kinds, including the .. yungan and various kinds of shellfish .. contribute to .. their multifarious bill of fare.

yura, var. EURO.

Z

zac. Also **sac, zack.** [Prob. f. Scot. dial. *saxpence.*]

1. A sixpence. Also *transf.*, a trifling sum of money.

1898 *Bulletin* (Sydney) 1 Oct. 14/3, 6d. a 'zack'. **1908** *Truth* (Sydney) 8 Nov. 1/7 'Wanted, respectable person, all duties, wages 2s. 6d. per week!' Ye gods! respectability at two and a sac per week. **1919** C.H. THORP *Handful of Ausseys* 163 Muttering blasphemies against all '--s who are spongin' on their Governmints an drawin' ten an' a zack a day while they dodge a trip to the firin' line, the cold-footed --s'. **1929** F. BLAIR *Digger Sea-Mates* 148 'I've just spent me last brown, too. Frank's still holding.' 'His hat,' said I. 'I'm down to a zac.' **1945** *Aust. Week-End Bk.* 164 The only one who'd backed it had been his wife who'd had a zac each way. **1953** A.W. UPFIELD *Venom House* 101 It was the first time I got the notion I was worth a zac to anyone. **1965** K. SMITH *OGF* 120 The only State finances I see are the zacs and deeners people give me on the bus. **1986** *Nat. Times* (Sydney) 10 Jan. 42/4 No wonder Paul Keating has angrily refused to give the ABC another zac.

2. A prison sentence of six years or six months.

1919 V. MARSHALL *World of Living Dead* 84 Done the zac I got fer cattle duffin' up Gilgandra way, A zac's hard labour—wot I had ter do. **1971** J. MCNEIL *Chocolate Frog* (1973) 20 *Tosser*: How long are yer doin'? *Kevin*: Six months .. down at the Petty Sessions... *Shirker*: .. Why'd yer *get* the zac?

Zambuk /'zæmbʌk/. Also **Zambuck.** [The proprietary name of an antiseptic ointment.] A member of the St John's Ambulance Brigade, esp. such a person in attendance at a sporting event.

[**1902** *Truth* (Sydney) 21 Dec. 7/4 *Zam-buk.* Name carries no meaning. The ointment carries a blessing. **1918** N.Z. *Chrons. N.Z.E.F.* 21 June 221 The tenderfoot and Zambuk, Working madly in the trenches.] **1941** S.J. BAKER *Pop. Dict. Austral. Slang* 91 *Zambuck*, a first-aid man in attendance at a sporting contest. **1945** *Bandi Banner* (Bandiana) 21 Apr. 7 The R.A.P. staff could be 'Zambucks' at football matches. **1948** R. RAVEN-HART *Canoe in Aust.* 145 Play struck me as very clean, but accidents are frequent, and ambulance men, 'Zambuks' in Australian slang, are often busy. **1964** *Referee* (Sydney) 17 Apr. 3/3 Take it easy. The Zambuck is coming and it's a woman. **1976** *Sun-Herald* (Sydney) 5 Sept. 70/6 If you asked the kids of today what a zambuck was, they would probably tell you that he was some type of South African antelope. **1984** *Bulletin* (Sydney) 6 Mar. 43/1 If you don't know what a Zambuck is, it's someone in the black and white uniform of the St. John Ambulance Brigade doing honorary duty at a sports arena, ready to dash on the field with everything from linament to stretcher.

zamia /'zeɪmiə/. [Transf. use of the plant genus name *Zamia*, under which Austral. species of *Macrozamia* were formerly classified.] A cycad, esp. of the genus *Macrozamia* (see MACROZAMIA). Also *attrib.*, esp. as **zamia palm.**

[**1825** B. FIELD *Geogr. Mem. N.S.W.* 244 Generally the soil is rather barren, and is covered with low ferns, prickly shrubs, and a kind of dwarf palm, called *burrawang* by the natives (zamia spiralis).] **1838** J. BACKHOUSE *Narr. Visit Austral. Colonies* (1843) 541 In some places between Perth and Guildford the Zamias are very fine their trunks, which are always blackened by fire, being six or eight feet in circumference, and as much in height, and surmounted by fine crests, of stiff pinnate palm-like leaves four feet long or more... In this part the natives bury or macerate the nuts, till the rinds become half decomposed, in which state they eat the rind, ejecting the kernel; in N.S. Wales, they pound and macerate the kernels and then roast and eat, the rough paste. **1841** G. GREY *Jrnls. Two Exped. N.-W. & W.A.* II. 61 The native had at this time gone away to look for Zamia nuts. **1844** L. LEICHHARDT *Jrnl. Overland Exped. Aust.* 1 Dec. (1847) 60 The most remarkable feature in the vegetation, however, was an arborescent Zamia, with a stem from seven to eight or ten feet high, and about nine inches in diameter, and with elongated cones, not yet ripe. **1855** W. HOWITT *Land, Labor & Gold* II. 359 There the Zamia, like a young date palm, spreads out its rigid bushes. **1872** MRS E. MILLETT *Austral. Parsonage* 48 The waving bracts of the zamias, or palms as they are popularly called in the colony, imparted somewhat of a semi-tropical character to the foreground. **1897** L. LINDLEY-COWEN *W. Austral. Settler's Guide* 42 The zamia palm .. is commonly regarded as the cause of 'wobbles' in cattle and sheep. **1914** H.M. VAUGHAN *Australasian Wander-Yr.* 279 Some rocky ridges overgrown with zamia palms. **1925** H. BASEDOW *Austral. Aboriginal* 77 A kind of hand-ball is practised on Bathurst Island. The seeds of the zamia (cycas media) take the place of a small ball. **1935** DAVISON & NICHOLLS *Blue Coast Caravan* 165 They ate also the green heart of the piccabeen palm and the nuts of the zamia palm. **1938** C.T. WHITE *Princ. Bot. Qld. Farmers* 134 Zamia, Zamia Palm, or Zamia Fern are various popular names given in Queensland to different species of Cycads. **1964** R.M. & C.H. BERNDT *World First Australs.* 99 Grey .. also refers to natives of Western Australia as storing zamia nuts by burying them in the ground. **1977** V. PRIDDLE *Larry & Jack* 40 You'd be much better off cleaning up more Zamia country and improving the property instead of trying to pinch cleanskins. **1984** *Austral. Plants* Dec. 15 *Macrozamia riedlei* is commonly called the 'Zamia palm' by West Australians.

zebra. Used *attrib.* in the names of animals: **zebra duck,** *pink-eared duck*, see PINK *a.*; also *ellipt.* as **zebra; finch,** the small bird *Taeniopygia guttata* widespread in much of mainland Aust., having black and white tail bars, the mature male having a chestnut ear patch; *chestnut-eared finch*, see CHESTNUT *a.*; **fish,** any of several marine fish, usu. of s. Aust., esp. *Melambaphes zebra* and *Enoplosus armatus* (see OLD WIFE); **parrot** *obs.*, BUDGERIGAR; also **zebra parakeet.**

1955 S. OSBORNE *Duck Shooting Aust.* 11 They have most peculiar brown and white striped markings on their breast, and an inconspicuous pink marking near the ear; hence the name **Zebra** or pink-eared **duck.** **1966** P. COWAN *Seed* 141 Grey teal, Zebras, Black duck. Get some really good sport here. **1980** C. ALLISON *Hunter's Man. Aust. & N.Z.* 115 The beautiful Pink-ear is known in some places as the Zebra or Widgeon or even Pink-eye. **1936** C.T. MADIGAN *Central Aust.* 103 Flocks of the most typical bird of Central Australia, the pretty little **zebra finch,** with its husky chirp. **1940** *Bulletin* (Sydney) 20 Nov. 16/1 Watched a mob of waxbills (zebra finches) migrating from one bit of water to another across the Queensland downs country. **1952** A.M. DUNCAN-KEMP *Where Strange Paths go Down* 110 Suddenly the branches became animated with strange vitality, and myriads of zebra finches settled on the twigs, clustering on the dead wood like a fresh growth of leaves. **1964** M. SHARLAND *Territory of Birds* 137 Neither was the Zebra Finch ever seen far from water—house-tanks and cattle-troughs. **1984** M. BLAKERS et al. *Atlas Austral. Birds* 595 The Zebra Finch .. usually breeds in colonies of 40–100 birds. **1771** *Philos. Trans. R. Soc. London* LXI. 247 It is called by the Commodore the **Zebra fish.** **1896** F.G. AFLALO *Sketch Nat. Hist. Aust.* 225 The 'Old Wife' of Port Jackson and elsewhere is a remarkable little member of the perch family. The names by which it is known in the Melbourne Market, 'Zebra-fish' or 'Bastard Dory', are considerably more appropriate. **1956** B. BEATTY *Beyond Aust.'s Cities* 158 To the accompaniment of screams from the hundreds of terns circling your launch you land fish after fish after fish. Kingfish .. zebra-fish, and maybe a shark or two. **1974** T.D. SCOTT et al. *Marine & Freshwater Fishes S.A.* 227 The Zebra Fish is very common in shallow waters off our coasts... The flesh of fresh specimens is quite tasty. **1983** HUTCHINS & THOMPSON *Marine & Estuarine Fishes S.-W. Aust.* 42 Zebra Fish .. easily recognized by the light and dark cross-bars on body. **1860** G. BENNETT *Gatherings of Naturalist* 228 A very delicate and beautiful little Parrot .. is the Canary or **Zebra Parrot.** **1896** F.G. AFLALO *Sketch Nat. Hist. Aust.* 125 Grass Parrakeets .. feed .. mostly on the ground .. and almost the only one in evidence at the stores of London dealers is the favourite little warbling Bujerigar (*Melopsittacus undulatus*), or, as it is variously called, the 'Zebra Parrakeet' .. 'Shell Parrot', etc.

ziff. [Of unknown origin.] A beard; also *transf.*, an old man, a 'grey-beard'.

1917 *Stretcher* (Melbourne) Mar. 9 Z is for 'Ziff' which appears on the lip To call it a 'mo' would give one the pip. **1918** *Fair Dinkum: On Board 'Nestor'* Apr. 4 If on you a ziff does grow. **1922** *Bulletin* (Sydney) 19 Oct. 22/3 The miner's ziff was beaten by that of a man who used to knock about Sydney... His beard .. reached his feet and trailed 18 inches along the ground. **1924** *Aussie* (Sydney) Oct. 30/1 'Grey old ziffs,' youth lightly classes Hero-hearts of yesteryears. **1938** *Listening Post* (Perth) Nov. 21 It was found that the ziff.. was a serious impediment to the accurate fitting of the gas mask. **1948** *Bulletin* (Sydney) 21 Jan. 28/1 Grandpa Cresswell had returned from a city visit .. *minus* his luxurious ziff and been bailed up by the dogs. **1961** C. MCKAY *This is Life* 141 This brought the 'ziffs' into the picture—ancient white-bearded directors who should make way for young men. **1971** J. BARLOW *In All Good Faith* 16 'What's the ziff for?'... 'I'm an art student. Y'want to make something of it?' **1981** G. KELLY *Always Afternoon* 211 'Better get rid of that ziff,' she said pointing to his embryonic beard.

Hence **(be-)ziffed** *a.*, bearded.

1973 *Southerly* i. 7 Other foreigners in Ellie's court are from a nearby cell of the B.B.C., multi-lingual translators from the Foreign News Service, all with crystalline English accents .. and be-ziffed as wisdom-saturated Mamelukes. **1978** R.J. BRITTEN *Around Cassowary Rock* 53 The adventures of Long John Silver, Blackbeard, Bully Hayes and Mutiny on the Bounty all rolled up and thrown together in one big black-ziffed personage by the name of Glub.

zigzag.

1. *Hist.* A type of railway line designed for very steep gradients, having the track laid in the form of one or more Zs with reversing points where the line doubles back to enable a train to reverse its direction.

1871 *Austral. Town & Country Jrnl.* (Sydney) 13 May 590/3 The difficulties are comparatively removed now that railways and zig-zags carry us in comfort over what was at one time the worst parts of the road. **1880** *Bulletin* (Sydney) 13 Mar. 4/1 If you drive on the Blue Mountain zigzag in a railway car and have a smash you lose your life and go to glory. **1883** *Ibid.* 26 May 18/3 The coupling-chain on a Blue Mountain goods-train snapped, near the zig-zag. **1931** LAWSON & BRERETON *H. Lawson* 22 A party of us, 'The Mountain Push', as Henry called us, would take packhorses and ride down the steep Zig-Zag on Mount Victoria into the Kanimbla Valley. **1935** A. RAYMENT *Romance of Railway* 27 Mr Whitton's great engineering feat of the two Zig Zags;

the lesser, known as the Lapstone Zig Zag on the eastern approach and the Great Zig Zag near Lithgow.

2. Special Comb. **zigzag fence,** see quot. 1890. Also *ellipt.*, as **zigzag.**

1882 ARMSTRONG & CAMPBELL *Austral. Sheep Husbandry* 194 Zig-Zag Fence. This fence resembles the chock and log in its formation, but differs from it in having no chocks. **1890** A. MACKAY *Austral. Agriculturist* (ed. 2) 32 Zigzag Fence . . is made by embedding the butt end of one tree in a notch cut for the purpose in the top end of another, laying them along the ground in a zigzag form, so that each log intersects the entire line at an angle of forty-five degrees. When the logs have been piled up to the desired height, cross-logs and a heavy top-rail are then put up . . so as to bind the whole. **1897** L. LINDLEY-COWEN *W. Austral. Settler's Guide* 236 Zig-zag, and other purely timber fences, used to be common in the colony in the old days, prior to the introduction of wire netting. **1911** E.S. SORENSON *Life in Austral. Backblocks* 30 The fences near the homestead show some variety of style. There is the dog-leg . . the chock-and-log, the log-and-stub, the brush, cockatoo, sapling-rail, and the zig-zag. **1978** M. WALKER *Pioneer Crafts Early Aust.* 28 In the Wimmera about 1863–4, another type was termed 'zig-zag', being made up from five pine or buloke logs nine feet (2.7 m.) long each with a V-shaped indentation, top and bottom, allowing the logs to be seated securely one to the other.

zwei, var. SWY.

zygomaturus /zaɪgoʊmə'tjurəs/. [The animal genus *Zygomaturus* was named by W.S. Macleay (1792–1865), Trustee of the Australian Museum: see quot. 1857.] A large extinct marsupial of the Austral. genus *Zygomaturus.*

1857 *Sydney Morning Herald* 9 Sept. 2/6 Another characteristic of this new quadruped, which may be called Zygomaturus, is the great distance of the zygomaturic arch from the temporal bone. **1903** E. PALMER *Early Days N. Qld.* 243 The utter extinction of these gigantic species, comprising diprotodon, nototherium, and zygomaturus, and other species . . can only be accounted for by a great change of climate. **1986** *Sydney Morning Herald* 15 Jan. 24/4 The Victoria Cave was first explored in 1969. 'So far we have discovered 78 different species from frogs to the Zygomaturus, which is a very large quadruped marsupial, about as large as a bull.

SELECT BIBLIOGRAPHY
INTRODUCTION

This is a list of works quoted frequently in the dictionary and of those which it might be difficult to find from the short reference given in citations.

Pseudonymous works have usually been entered under the pseudonym, with the author's actual name added within brackets. Cross references have been included if warranted. Definite and indefinite articles preceding titles of journals and newspapers have been omitted.

Annual volumes of legislation, sessional publications of parliaments, and government gazettes have not been listed in the *Bibliography*. Where parliamentary publications are used as the source of citations, they have been referred to by abbreviations, the key to which will be found in the *List of Abbreviations* (p. XIV). Where legislation is the source of citations, references have been made in the following style:

(Year of enactment) Acts (state or country) (Regnal year, where applicable) (Number) (Section)

For example:

1896 *Acts* (N.S.W.) 59 Vic. no. 26 section 15.

Page numbers for such references have not been included.

Works held by the Australian War Memorial Library (many of which are ephemera and unlikely to be found elsewhere) are marked with an asterisk.

Pauline Fanning

SELECT BIBLIOGRAPHY

A.I.M. frontier news Sydney 1930–34 (continued by *Frontier news*)

'A.J.O.' (A.J. Ogilvy) *Sullivan and co.* Hobart 1905

'A.L.F.' (S. Terry) *The history of Samuel Terry in Botany Bay* London 1838

'A.M.' (J. Murdoch) *From Australia and Japan* London 1892

A.N.F.C. review, 1953 Melbourne 1954

ABBIE, A.A. *The original Australians* Wellington, N.Z. 1969

ABBOTT, J.H.M. *Tommy Cornstalk* London 1902

Dogsnose Sydney 1928

The King's School and other tales for old boys Sydney 1931

The abolitionists and transportationists: a satirical poem Hobart 1847

Aboriginal claims discussed, in a letter to a colonist in Western Australia London 1838

Aboriginal Australia see Mulvaney, D.J. et. al.

Aboriginal history Canberra 1977–84

Aboriginal news Canberra 1973–80

Aborigines of Australia: extract from a letter dated Perth, Swan River, Western Australia, July 17, 1836 London 1836

Aborigines protector: official organ of the Association for the Protection of Native Races Sydney 1935–41, 1946–48

ABSALOM, J. & R. *Outback cooking in the camp oven* Canterbury, Vic. 1982

An account of the colony of Van Diemen's Land in 1830, with a descriptive itinerary of the country London 1831

**Ack ack: journal of the 2nd Anti Aircraft Regiment A.I.F.* Puckapunyal, Vic. and Palestine 1940–41

Ack ack news: the monthly magazine of the Anti-Aircraft Units (R.A.A. and R.A.E.) in Victoria Melbourne 1941–43

ACKLAND, J. & R. eds. *Word from John* Sydney 1944

ACOCKS, W.G. *The settlers' synopsis of the land laws of New South Wales* Sydney 1901

Across country: Australia's national country music magazine Melbourne 1978–82

**'Action': magazine of the 6th Australian Advanced Workshops* Toowoomba, Qld. 1944–45

**Action front: journal of the 2/2 Field Regiment* Melbourne and In the field 1940–45

ADAMS, F. *The Australians: a social sketch* London 1893

ADAMS, P. *The unspeakable Adams* West Melbourne 1977

More unspeakable Adams West Melbourne 1979

*ADAMS, R.H. Diary. 1916

ADAM-SMITH, P. *Hear the train blow: an Australian childhood* Sydney 1964

Tiger country Adelaide 1968

The rails go westward South Melbourne 1969

The Barcoo salute Adelaide 1973

The desert railway Adelaide 1974

The Anzacs West Melbourne 1978

The shearers Melbourne 1982

When we rode the rails Sydney 1983

Australian women at war Melbourne 1984

ed. *Folklore of the Australian railwaymen* South Melbourne 1969

ADAMSON, A. *Letters: ed. by his daughters* Melbourne 1901

ADAMSON, R. & HANFORD, B. *Zimmer's essay* Sydney 1974

ADDISON, G.C. *The miners' manual* Sydney 1895

Adelaide chronicle and South Australian advertiser Adelaide 1839–40

Adelaide miscellany of useful and entertaining knowledge Adelaide 1848–49 (continued by *Stephen's Adelaide miscellany*)

Adelaide observer Adelaide 1843–1904 (continued by *The observer*)

Adelaide *punch* Adelaide 1868–84

Advertiser Darwin 1980–

Advocate Burnie, Tas. 1919– (continues *North western advocate)*

AFFLECK, A.H. *The wandering years* Croydon, Vic. 1964

AFLALO, F.G. *A sketch of the natural history of Australia* London 1896

'AGRICOLA' *The new earth* Brisbane 1891

Age Melbourne 1854–

**Air action No.1: stories of adventure in the sky* Melbourne [1963]

**Air Force news* Melbourne 1941

AKHURST, W.M. *Tom Tom, the piper's son* Melbourne 1867

The house that Jack built Melbourne 1869

ALARD, J. *He who shoots last* Sydney 1968

ALDRIDGE, J. *My brother Tom* London 1966

The untouchable Juli Boston 1975

ALEXANDER, A.J. *Alexander's colonial guide; or the emigrant's hand-book to the best colony* Melbourne 1862

ALFORD, F.S. *Bulk handling of wheat* Adelaide 1916

ALGAR, F. *A handbook to the colony of Queensland, Australia* London 1861

A handbook to the colony of New South Wales London 1863

A handbook to thc colony of South Australia London 1863

A handbook to the colony of Tasmania London 1863

A handbook to the colony of Victoria (Australia) London 1863

A handbook to Queensland London 1869

**All abaht it: journal of the 10th Field Ambulance* London 1916–19

ALLAN, J.A. *Men and manners in Australia* Melbourne 1945

ALLEN, C.H. *A visit to Queensland and her goldfields* London 1870

ALLEN, J. *South Australia as it is and how to get to it* London 1847

ALLEN, J. *Journal of an experimental trip by the 'Lady Augusta', on the River Murray* Adelaide 1853

ALLEN, J. *History of Australia from 1787 to 1882* Melbourne 1882

ALLEN, Mrs J.S.O. *Memories of my life from my early days in Scotland till the present day in Adelaide* Adelaide 1906

ALLEN, W. *Immigration and co-operative settlement on the waste lands of the colony along our railway lines* Brisbane 1881

ALLISON, C. *The hunter's manual of Australia and New Zealand* Sydney 1980

'ALPHA' *Reminiscences of the goldfields in the fifties and sixties: Victoria, New Zealand, New South Wales* Melbourne 1915

AMALGAMATED SHEARERS' UNION OF AUSTRALASIA *General rules of the Amalgamated Shearers' Union of Australasia adopted June, 1886 (revised January 1887)* Ballarat, Vic. 1887

AMMON, W.W. et al. *Working lives* Fremantle, W.A. 1984

AMOS, K. *The New Guard movement* Melbourne 1976

AMOS, P. *The silver kings* London 1970

ANDERSON, E. *Squatter's luck and other poems* Melbourne 1942

ANDERSON, E.M. *Typist tales and tales* Sydney 1944

ANDERSON, G. *Fixation of wages in Australia* Melbourne 1929

ANDERSON, H. *Colonial ballads* Ferntree Gully, Vic. 1955

Farewell to old England Adelaide 1964

Fish and fisheries Melbourne 1967

Larrikin crook: the rise and fall of Squizzy Taylor Milton, Qld. 1971

ANDERSON, H. & BLAKE, L.J. *John Shaw Neilson* Adelaide 1972

ANDERSON, J. *Tirra lirra by the river* South Melbourne 1978

The impersonators Melbourne 1980

ANDERSON, J.W. *The prospector's handbook* London 1886, 6th ed. 1895

ANDERSON, R. *On the sheep's back* Melbourne 1966

ANDERSON, R.B. see Lumholtz, C.

ANDERSON, R.S. *Australian gold fields: their discovery, progress and prospects* Sydney 1956 (first publ. Glasgow 1853)
ANDERSON, W.M. *Rhymes of a rouseabout* London 1913
ANDREW, B. *Australian football handbook* Adelaide 1971
ANDREWS, A. ed. *A sketch of the colony of Western Australia* London 1849
ANGAS, G.F. *Savage life and scenes in Australia and New Zealand: being an artist's impressions of countries and people at the Antipodes* 2 vols. London 1847
Description of the Barossa Range and its neighbourhood in South Australia, by 'Agricola' London 1849
Australia: a popular account of its physical features, inhabitants, natural history and productions, with the history of its colonization London [1865]
'AN ANGLO-INDIAN' *A visit to Tasmania* Murree, Pakistan 1877
ANSELL, R. & PERCY, R. *To fight the wild* Fremantle, W.A. 1980
ANTILL, H.C. *Early history of New South Wales: two old journals being the diaries of Major H.C. Antill on the voyage to New South Wales in 1809, and on a trip across the Blue Mountains in 1815* Sydney 1914
Antipodean: an illustrated annual Melbourne 1893–97
ANTONY, E. *The hungry mile* Sydney 1930
**Any complaints: official newspaper of the troops in camp at Rutherford* Newcastle, N.S.W. 1940
The Anzac book see *The men of Anzac*
'ANZAC-FRANCO-AUSSIE' see O'Donnell, J.P.
**Anzac records gazette* Alexandria, Egypt 1915–16
APSLEY, A.A.B. *Why and how I went to Australia as a settler* London 1926
The amateur settlers London 1926
Arbitrations between the proprietors Lambton Colliery and their miners and the Newcastle Coal Mining Co. and their miners Newcastle, N.S.W. 1886
ARCHER, L.M.P. *A bush honeymoon and other stories* London 1904
ARCHER, T. *The history, resources, and future prospects of Queensland* London 1881
Some remarks on the proposed Queensland trans-continental railway n.p. 1881
Alleged slavery in Queensland n.p. 1883
ARDEN, G. *Recent information respecting Port Phillip and the promising province of Australia Felix* London 1841
Arden's Sydney magazine Sydney 1843
ARGLES, T.E. see *Pilgrim*
Argus Melbourne 1848–1957 (continues *The Melbourne Argus*)
ARMOUR, James *The diggings, the bush and Melbourne* Glasgow 1864
ARMOUR, John *The spell of the inland: a romance of Central Australia* Melbourne 1923
ARMSTRONG, A.S. & CAMPBELL, G.O. *Australian sheep husbandry* Melbourne 1882
ARMSTRONG, H.J. *A handy-book on the management of mining companies in Victoria* Melbourne 1888
Army news Darwin 1941–46
ARTHUR, E. & F. *A journal of events: from Melbourne, Port Phillip to Mount Schank, in the district of Adelaide* Hobart 1975 (first publ. Sheerness, England 1844)
ARTHUR, J.K. *Kangaroo and kauri* London 1894
ASH, E. *The Australian oracle* Melbourne 1909
ASKEW, J. *A voyage to Australia & New Zealand* London 1857
**The asp; ammunition supply – petrol: unofficial official rag of 22 Coy. A.A.S.C.* [W.A.] 1942
ASPINALL, C. *Three years in Melbourne* London 1862
ASTLEY, T. *Hunting the wild pineapple* West Melbourne 1979
ASTLEY, W. see 'Warung, P.'
ASTON, T. *Memoirs of Tilly Aston* Melbourne 1946
**Astra: the official publication of the Third Divisional Train* [Melbourne] and Salisbury Plains [*sic*], England 1916
**Atebrin advocate: magazine of Headquarters, 2/4 Australian Armoured Regiment* In the field 1944–45
ATKINS, R. Journal. 1792–1810 NLA MS 4039
ATKINS, T. *Reminiscences of twelve years' residence in Tasmania and New South Wales, Norfolk Island and Moreton Bay* Malvern, England 1869
ATKINSON, G. *Everything you've ever wanted to know about Australian Rules football but couldn't be bothered asking* Canterbury, Vic. 1982
The book of Australian Rules finals Canterbury, Vic. 1983
ATKINSON, H. *The reckoning* London 1965
ATKINSON, J. *An account of the state of agriculture & grazing in New South Wales* London 1826
On the expediency and necessity of encouraging distilling and brewing from grain in New South Wales Sydney 1829
ATKINSON, J.B. *Penal settlements and their evils* London 1847
ATKINSON, L. *A voice from the country* Canberra 1978
Excursions from Berrima and a trip to Manaro and Molonglo in the 1870's Canberra 1980
ATKINSON, M. *Trade unionism in Australia: report of a conference held in June, 1915* Sydney 1915
ed. *Australia: economic and political studies* Melbourne 1920
Atlas: Sydney weekly journal of politics, commerce, and literature Sydney 1844–48
ATTENBOROUGH, D. *Quest under Capricorn* London 1963
ATTIWILL, K. *Cut-lunch commandos* Melbourne 1944
AUDAS, J.W. *Native trees of Australia* Melbourne [1934]
'AURIFERA' *The Victorian miners' manual* Melbourne [c.1860]
Aussie: the Australian soldiers' magazine In the field 1918–19
Aussie: the cheerful monthly Sydney 1920–32
AUSTAL, F. *City and country life* Sydney 1937
AUSTEN, P. *Bill-Jim* Sydney 1917
AUSTIN, C. *I left my hat in Andamooka* Melbourne 1973
AUSTIN, J.B. *The mines of South Australia* Adelaide 1863
AUSTIN, R. *Journal of Assistant-Surveyor R. Austin, commanding an expedition sent by the government to explore the interior of Western Australia* Perth 1855
Austral observer Melbourne 1882
Australasian Melbourne 1864–1946 (continued by *Australasian post)*
Australasian: a quarterly reprint of articles selected from the periodicals of the United Kingdom; with original contributions, chiefly on subjects of colonial interest Melbourne 1850–51
Australasian almanack Sydney 1827 (continued by *Australian almanack)*
Australasian farmer Melbourne 1885
Australasian pastoralists' review Melbourne 1891–1901 (continued by *Pastoralists' review)*
Australasian pocket almanack Sydney 1822–26 (continued by *Australasian almanack)*
Australasian printers' keepsake Melbourne 1885
Australasian sketcher with pen and pencil Melbourne 1873–89
Australasian sporting magazine Sydney 1850–51
Australia Sydney 1923–25 (continues *Australian)*
Australia directory London 1853–1907
Australia Felix monthly magazine Geelong and Melbourne 1849
Australia: or, which is the best colony for the emigrant? Dublin 1840
Australia, Van Dieman's Land, and New Zealand: their history and present state London 1840, rev. ed. 1849
Australia week-end book Sydney 1942–46
Australia: who should go; – how to go; – what to do when there Liverpool [c. 1854]
'AUSTRALIAN' *Adventures in Queensland* Hobart 1879
'AN AUSTRALIAN' *Our homes: and how to make them happy* Sydney 1887
Australian Sydney 1824–48
Australian Sydney 1923 (continued by *Australia)*
Australian Sydney 1964–
Australian: a monthly magazine Sydney 1878–81
Australian almanack Sydney 1828–35 (continues *Australasian almanack)*
Australian and New Zealand monthly magazine London 1842
Australian boys and girls: an illustrated annual Sydney 1895
Australian bushcraft issued by the Australian Army Education Service Melbourne 1948
Australian churchman Sydney 1867–86
'AN AUSTRALIAN COLONIST' *The resources of Australia* London 1841
A description of the settlement of King George's Sound in Western Australia London 1846
The Australian comic dictionary see 'T.O. Lingo'

Australian farm and station handyman Adelaide 1937–39
Australian farming Melbourne 1921–26
Australian financial review Sydney 1951–
Australian folksongs of the land and its people: compiled by the Folklore Council of Australia Kilmore, Vic. 1974
Australian forestry journal Sydney 1918–31
Australian gem and minerals fossicker Kenmore, Qld. 1974–75
Australian geographic: Dick Smith's journal of discovery and adventure Terrey Hills, N.S.W. 1986–
Australian gold digger's monthly magazine and colonial family visitor Melbourne 1852–53
Australian handbook London 1870–1906
Australian home beautiful Melbourne 1925– (continues *Australian home builder*)
Australian home builder Melbourne 1922–25 (continued by *Australian home beautiful*)
Australian law reports Sydney 1973–
Australian letters Adelaide 1957–68
Australian magazine; or, compendium of religious, literary, and miscellaneous intelligence Sydney 1821–22
Australian magazine Sydney 1838
Australian magazine Sydney 1899
Australian mammalogy: journal of the Australian Mammal Society Sydney 1972–
Australian medical journal Sydney 1856–June 1914 (title varies, continued by *Medical journal of Australia*)
Australian monthly magazine Melbourne 1865–67 (continued by *The colonial monthly*)
Australian museum magazine Sydney 1923–61 (continued by *Australian natural history*)
Australian musician Bondi, N.S.W. 1977–80
Australian national game of football: hints for umpires issued by the Australian National Football Council Richmond, Vic. 1950
Australian natural history Sydney 1962– (continues *Australian museum magazine*)
Australian new writing Sydney 1943–46
Australian official journal of patents, trade marks and designs Canberra 1931–
Australian one-act plays book 3, ed. by M. Horner Adelaide 1967
Australian plants: Commonwealth journal of the Society for Growing Australian Plants Sydney 1959–
Australian police journal Sydney 1946–
Australian quarterly journal of theology, literature and science Sydney 1828
Australian 'ring' Sydney 1932–34
The Australian settler, and the Australian shepherd London [1854]
Australian settlers guide or monthly journal Sydney 1835
Australian short stories Carlton, Vic. 1982–
Australian sportsman Sydney 1848–49
Australian surf life saving competition handbook 4th ed. Sydney 1964
Australian tit-bits Melbourne 1884–86
Australian tit-bits Sydney 1899–1900
Australian town & country journal Sydney 1871–1919
Australian trans-continental railway see Feilding, W.
Australian woman's mirror Sydney 1924–61
Australian women's weekly Sydney 1933–
Australian worker Sydney 1913– (continues *The worker*)
Australian writers' annual Sydney 1936
Australiana: a weekly paper Adelaide 1845
Awful execution of 17 convicts who were executed at Sydney, New South Wales, on May 22nd, 1852 for the horrid massacre of a tribe of natives Manchester [1852]
Axeman's journal and sporting news v.p. 1901–2 Jan. 1904 (continued by *Sporting news and axeman's journal*)

BAALMAN, J. *The Torrens system in New South Wales* Sydney 1951
BACKHOUSE, J. *Extracts from the letters* parts 1–5 London 1838–39
A narrative of a visit to the Australian colonies London 1843
BACKHOUSE, J. & TYLOR, C. *The life and labours of George Washington Walker of Hobart Town, Tasmania* London 1862
Back to the bush! 1914 1918 see Neal, N.P.H.
BADEN-POWELL, G.S. *New homes for the old country* London 1872
BAGLIN, D. & MULLINS, B. *Aborigines of Australia* North Sydney 1969
BAGLIN, D. & AUSTIN, Y. *Galvo country* Sydney 1979
BAHNEMANN, G. *The calling reef* Sydney 1970
BAIL, M. *Homesickness* Melbourne 1980, Ringwood, Vic. 1981
BAILEY, D.J. *Holes in the ground: Queensland coalminers in struggle, 1840–1980* Brisbane 1983
BAILEY, F.M. *A synopsis of the Queensland flora: containing both the phaenogamous and cryptogamous plants* Brisbane 1883
Catalogue of the indigenous and naturalised plants of Queensland Brisbane 1890
Comprehensive catalogue of Queensland plants 2nd ed. Brisbane, 1909.
The Queensland flora Brisbane 1899–1902
BAILEY, J. *The wire classroom* Sydney 1972
BAIN, E. *The ways of life* Perth 1976
BAIN, M.A. *Full fathom five* Perth 1982
BAINES, J.A. *Australian plant genera* Sydney 1981
BAIRD, D. *The incredible gulf* Adelaide 1970
BAIRD, J. *The emigrant's guide to Australasia. Australia: New South Wales, Western Australia, South Australia, Victoria, and Queensland* London 1868 new ed. [1871]
BAKER, A.M. see 'Hill, M.'
BAKER, C.J. *Sydney and Melbourne: with remarks on the present state and future prospects of New South Wales* London 1845
BAKER, G. *Montgomery and I* Melbourne 1968
BAKER, H.C. *I was listening: true Australian yarns about colourful men and women* Adelaide 1978
BAKER, J. Diary and watercolour sketches of a journey through the upper north and far north interior of South Australia. 1884–85 Mortlock Library D5863(L)
BAKER, L.A. *Lucy Marline; or, the bushrangers: a tale of New South Wales* Boston 1848
BAKER, R.T. *The hardwoods of Australia and their economics* Sydney 1919
BAKER, R.T. & SMITH, H.G. *A research on the pines of Australia* Sydney 1910
A research on the eucalypts especially in regard to their essential oils 2nd ed. Sydney 1920
BAKER, S.J. *A popular dictionary of Australian slang* Melbourne 1941
3rd ed. 1943
The Australian language Sydney 1945
2nd ed. 1966
Australia speaks: a supplement to 'The Australian language' Sydney 1953
The drum: Australian character and slang Sydney 1959
BALFOUR, J.O. *A sketch of New South Wales* London 1845
BALL, D. *The great Australian snake exchange* Richmond, Vic. 1978
BALL, S. *Muma's boarding house* Adelaide 1978
BALLANTYNE, J. *Homes and homesteads in the land of plenty* Melbourne 1871
Our colony in 1880 Melbourne 1880
BALLOU, M.M. *Under the Southern Cross* Boston 1888
**Bandi banner: unofficial organ of the 1st Australian Base Ordnance Depot* Bandiana, N.S.W. 1944–45
**Bandicog: magazine of 2/4 Australian Base Workshops A.E.M.E.* Bandiana, N.S.W. 1944
BANDMANN, D.E. *An actor's tour or seventy thousand miles with Shakespeare* 3rd ed. New York 1886
BANDSMA, A.T. & BRANDT, R.T. *Insects in Australia* Christchurch, N.Z. 1966
BANFIELD, E.J. *The confessions of a beachcomber* London 1908
BANKS, E.A. *Sunshine and shadow* Melbourne 1874
BANKS, J. Papers. ML MS
The Endeavour journal of Joseph Banks, 1768–1771 ed. by J.C. Beaglehole 2 vols. Sydney 1962
Journal of the Right Hon. Sir Joseph Banks during Captain Cook's first voyage in H.M.S. Endeavour in 1768–71 ed. by J.D. Hooker London 1896

BANKS, M.M. *Memories of pioneer days in Queensland* London 1931
BANKS, S.H. *Vice and its victims in Sydney: the cause and cure* Sydney 1873
BANNISTER, T. *A letter on colonial labour, and on the sale of lands in Austral-Asia* Hobart 1833
BANNOW, W. *The emigrant's hand-book to the British colonies* London 1887
The colony of Victoria socially and materially Melbourne 1896
BARBOUR, J. *Pencillings on the wallaby* Ballarat, Vic. 1906
BARCLAY, A. *Life of Captain Andrew Barclay of Cambock, near Launceston, V.D.L. Written from his own dictation at Cambock, February 19, 1836* Edinburgh, 1854
BARCS, E. *Backyard of Mars: memoirs of the 'reffo' period in Australia* Sydney 1980
**Barging about: the organ of 43 Australian Landing Craft Company* New Guinea 1944
BARKER, E.H. ed. *Geographical, commercial, and political, essays; including statistical details of various countries* (anon.) London 1812
BARKER, H.M. *Camels and the outback* Melbourne 1964
BARKER, J. *The two worlds of Jimmie Barker* Canberra 1977
BARKER, J. & GRIGG, G. *A field guide to Australian frogs* Adelaide 1977
BARKER, M.A. *Letters to Guy* London 1885
BARKER, W.H. *The gold fields of Western Australia* London 1894
BARKER, W.R. & GREENSLADE, P.J.M. eds. *Evolution of the flora and fauna of arid Australia* Frewville, S. Aust. 1982
BARLEE, C.H. *Humorous tales and sketches of colonial life* Sydney 1893
BARLOW, J. *In all good faith* London 1971
BARNARD, R. *Death of an old goat* London 1974
BARNES, L.C. & TOWNSEND, I.J. *Opal: South Australia's gemstone* Adelaide 1982
BARR, D. *Warrigal Joe: a tale of the never never* Melbourne 1946
**Barrage: magazine of Headquarters, R.A.A., 7th Australian Division* New Guinea 1943
**Barrack: the official organ of the Imperial Camel Corps* Cairo 1916–17
BARRETT, A.R. *History of the War Service Land Settlement Scheme, Western Australia* Perth 1965
BARRETT, C. *Koonwarra: a naturalist's adventures in Australia* London 1939
Australia: my country Melbourne 1941
Coast of adventure: untamed north Australia Melbourne 1941
From a bush hut Melbourne 1942
On the wallaby Melbourne 1942
An Australian wild flower book Melbourne 1942
An Australian animal book Melbourne 1943
Australian nature wonders Melbourne 1944
The platypus Melbourne 1944
Australian bird life Melbourne 1945
Parrots of Australasia Melbourne 1949
Wild life of Australia and New Guinea Melbourne 1954
BARRETT, J. *Falling in: Australians and 'boy conscription' 1911–1915* Sydney 1979
BARRETT, M. *Traitor at twenty fathoms* London 1963
The gold of Lubra Rock London 1967
The Barrier silver and tin fields in 1888 Adelaide 1888
BARRINGTON, G. *A voyage to Botany Bay with a description of the country, manners, customs, religion, &c. of the natives by the celebrated George Barrington. To which is added his life and trial* London [c.1795]
A sequel to Barrington's voyage to New South Wales London 1801
The history of New South Wales including Botany Bay London 1802
BARRY, G. *Bed and bored* Melbourne 1966
BARRY, J.A. *Steve Brown's bunyip and other stories* Sydney 1893
The luck of the native-born Sydney 1908
BARRY, W.J. *Up and down; or, fifty years' colonial experiences* London 1879
BARTLETT, N. *The pearl seekers* London 1954
Island victory Sydney 1955
BARTLEY, N. *Opals and agates* Brisbane 1892
BARTON, P. *Bastards I have known* Adelaide 1981
BARTON, R.D. *Reminiscences of an Australian pioneer* Sydney 1917
BASEDOW, H. *Journal of the government north-west expedition (March 30th–November 5th, 1903)* Adelaide 1914
The Australian aboriginal Adelaide 1925
Knights of the boomerang Sydney 1935
BASTARD, T. *The autobiography of 'Cockney Tom'* Adelaide 1881
BATEMAN, T. *The Valley Council; or leaves from the journal of Thomas Bateman of Canbelego Station, N.S.W.* ed. by P. Clarke London 1891
BATES, D. *The passing of the Aborigines* London 1938
BATMAN, J. *The settlement of John Batman in Port Phillip* Melbourne 1856
**Battery herald: journal of the 14th Field Artillery Brigade* In the field 1916
BAUME, F.E. *Tragedy track: the story of the Granites* Sydney 1933
BAXTER, P. *Growing fruit in Australia* Melbourne 1981
BAYER, L. *Muutchaka* Melbourne 1888
BAYLIS, H. *A reminiscence of the bush-ranging days in New South Wales* Sydney [c.1870]
BAYLY, E.B. *Alfreda Holme: a story of social life in Australia* London [1882]
*BAZLEY, A.W. et al. Glossary of slang & peculiar terms in use in the A.I.F. 1924
BEADELL, L. *Still in the bush* Adelaide 1975
Beating about the bush Adelaide 1976
BEADLE, N.C.W. et al. *Flora of the Sydney region* 3rd ed. French's Forest, N.S.W. 1982
BEAGLEY, N.A. *Up and down under* London 1970
BEAN, C.E.W. *On the wool track* London 1910
The 'Dreadnought' of the Darling London 1911
*Diary. 1915–16
Letters from France London 1917
The official history of Australia in the war of 1914–18 vols. I–VI. Sydney 1921–42
Here, my son: an account of the independent and other corporate boys' schools of Australia Sydney 1950
BEAR, J. *Impressions of a Victorian abroad; also confessions of a naughty boy of the fifties: being sketches of early Melbourne* Melbourne [c. 1896]
BEARD, W. ed. *Old Ironbark: some unpublished correspondence (1817–24) from and to William Lawson explorer and pioneer of Veteran Hall, N.S.W.* Sydney 1967
BEATTY, B. *Unique to Australia* Sydney 1952
Beyond Australia's cities Melbourne 1956
The awakening giant Sydney 1961
With shame remembered: early Australia Melbourne 1962
Around Australia Melbourne 1966
BEAUVOIR, L. de *A voyage round the world* vol. I. London 1870
BEAVER, B. *The hot summer* Sydney 1963
The hot men London 1964
You can't come back Adelaide 1966
BECKE, L. *Old convict days* London 1899
Breachley: black sheep London 1902
Tom Gerrard London 1905
The settlers of Karossa Creek London [1906]
BECKETT, J. A study of a mixed blood Aboriginal minority in the pastoral west of New South Wales. M.A. thesis. University of Sydney 1958
BECKETT, J. *A new-chum looks at Queensland* Ilfracombe, England [1965]
BECKETT, R. *Axemen stand by your logs!* Sydney 1983
BECKINGHAM, W.K. *Red acres* Perth 1979
BEDFORD, R. *Naught to thirty-three* Sydney [1944]
Bee of Australia Sydney 1844
BEESTON, J.L. *Five months at Anzac: personal experiences of the officer commanding the 4th Field Ambulance Australian Imperial Force* Sydney [1916]
Bega district news Bega, N.S.W. 1923–
BEGLEY, J. *The block with the one holer* Adelaide 1968
BEILBY, P. ed. *Australian TV: the first 25 years* Melbourne 1981

BEILBY, R. *No medals for Aphrodite* Sydney 1970
The brown land crying Sydney 1975
Gunner: a novel of the retreat from Crete London 1977
BEILLEY, T.W. *Australasia's goldfields' place in 'latter-day' world history* Melbourne 1897
Belfast gazette and Portland and Warrnambool advertiser Belfast, Vic. 1849–90 (continued by *The Port Fairy Gazette*)
BELL, A.B. *Australian camp fire tales* Brisbane 1894
Oscar: a romance of Australia & New Caledonia Brisbane 1894
BELL, G.A. *Under the brigalows* Melbourne [1921]
BELL, G.T. *Coolgardie ten years hence* Fremantle, W.A. [1898]
*BELLAMY, E. Diary. 1915–17
Bell's life in Sydney Sydney 1845–72
BELSCHNER, H.G. *Sheep management and diseases* Sydney 1950
Cattle diseases Sydney 1967
BENHAM, C. *Diver's luck: a story of pearling days* Sydney 1949
BENNET, H.G. *A letter to Earl Bathurst, Secretary of State for the Colonial Department, on the condition of the colonies in New South Wales and Vandieman's Land, as set forth in the evidence taken before the Prison Committee in 1819* London 1820
BENNETT, G. *Wanderings in New South Wales .. during 1832, 1833, and 1834* London 1834
Gatherings of a naturalist in Australia London 1860
BENNETT, J.F. *The South Australian almanack and general directory* Adelaide 1841, 1842
Historical and descriptive account of South Australia London 1843
BENNETT, S. *The history of Australian discovery and colonisation* Sydney 1865
BENT, E. Letterbook, 1809–11. NLA MS 195
BENTLEY, A. *An introduction to the deer of Australia with special reference to Victoria* 2nd ed. Melbourne 1978
Bent's news and Tasmanian three-penny register Hobart 1836–39
BERKERY, F. *East goes west* Melbourne 1944
BERN, J. Blackfella business: whitefella law. Ph.D. thesis. Macquarie University 1974
BERNDT, R.M. *Djanggawul: an Aboriginal religious cult of north-eastern Arnhem Land* Melbourne 1952
BERNDT, R.M. & C.H. *Sexual behaviour in western Arnhem Land* New York 1951
The first Australians Sydney 1952
Man, land and myth in north Australia Sydney 1970
Pioneers & settlers: the Aboriginal Australians Carlton, Vic. 1978
The Aboriginal Australians: the first pioneers Carlton, Vic. 1983
BERNDT, R.M. et al. *Aboriginal Australian art* Sydney 1982
BEROS, H.E. *The fuzzy wuzzy angels* Sydney [1943]
BERRIE, G. *Morale: a story of Australian light horsemen* Sydney 1949
BERRINGTON, M.D. *Stones of fire: a woman's experiences in search of opal* Melbourne 1958
BERRY, A. *Reminiscences* Sydney 1912
*BERRY, G.M. *Report to G.O.C. Light Horse Brigade* In the field 1916
BESNARD, T.P. *A voice from the bush in Australia* Dublin 1839
BEST, A.D.W. see Taylor, N.M. ed.
BETTS, T. *An account of the colony of Van Diemen's Land* Calcutta 1830
BEUKERS, J. *The humour and pathos of the Australian desert* London 1913
BEYNON, R. *The shifting heart* Sydney 1960
BICKFORD, J. *Christian work in Australasia* London 1878
BICKNELL, A.C. *Travel and adventure in northern Queensland* London 1895
BIGGE, J.T. *Report of the Commissioner of Inquiry into the state of the colony of New South Wales* London 1822
BIGGERS, F.C. *Bat-eye: a tale of the northern coalfields* Sydney 1927
BILLIS, R.V. & KENYON, A.S. *Pastures new: an account of the pastoral occupation of Port Phillip* Melbourne 1930
**'Billjim' at sea: souvenir of the voyage of a modern transport* London 1918
BINGHAM, C. *The beckoning horizon* Ringwood, Vic. 1983
BIRDWOOD, J.H. *A visit to Australia and New Zealand* London 1922
BIRMINGHAM, J. et al. *Australian pioneer technology: sites and relics .. towards an industrial archaeology of Australia* Melbourne 1979
BIRTLES, F.E. *Lonely lands: through the heart of Australia* Sydney 1909
Battle fronts of outback Sydney 1935
BISCHOFF, J. *Sketch of the history of Van Diemen's Land* London 1832
**Biscuit bomber weekly* Qld. and In the field 1944–45
BISHOP, F.A.C. *Report on an inspection of the pastoral holdings, stock routes, bores and dips on the Barkly Tableland* Melbourne 1923
BISKUP, P. *Not slaves not citizens* St. Lucia, Qld. 1973
'BLACK, D.' (J.L. Gray) *Red dust: an Australian trooper in Palestine* London 1931
BLACK, G. *A history of the N.S.W. Political Labor Party* Sydney 1926–29
BLACK, J.M. *Naturalised flora of South Australia* Adelaide 1909
Flora of South Australia Adelaide 1922–29
BLACKBURN, A.G. ed. *The management of booms and busts* Geelong, Vic. 1977
Blackwood's (Edinburgh) magazine Edinburgh and London 1817–
BLAINEY, G. *Triumph of the nomads* Melbourne 1975
All for Australia Sydney 1984
Our side of the country: the story of Victoria North Ryde, N.S.W. 1984
'BLAIR, F.' (S. Buckby) *Digger sea-mates* Sydney 1929
BLAIR, R. *President Wilson in Paris* Sydney 1974
BLAKE, B.J. *Australian Aboriginal languages* Sydney 1981
BLAKELEY, F. *Hard liberty* London 1938
Dream millions: new light on Lasseter's lost reef Sydney 1972
BLAKERS, G.T. *A useless young man? An autobiography of life in Australia, 1849–64* Ringwood, Vic. 1986
BLAKERS, M. et al. *The atlas of Australian birds* Melbourne 1984
BLAND, W. ed. *Journey of discovery to Port Phillip, New South Wales, by Messrs. W.H. Hovell, and Hamilton Hume in 1824 and 1825* Sydney 1831
New South Wales: examination of Mr James Macarthur's work, 'New South Wales, its present state and future prospects' Sydney 1838
New South Wales: review of the examination of Mr James Macarthur's work Sydney 1839
BLAXLAND, G. *A journal of a tour of discovery across the Blue Mountains in New South Wales* London 1823
BLAZEY, P. & CAMPBELL, A. *The political dice men* Fitzroy, Vic. 1974
BLEAKLEY, J.W. *The Aboriginals and half-castes of Central Australia and north Australia* Melbourne 1929
BLIGH, A.C.V. *The golden quest* Sydney 1955
BLIGH, W. *A voyage to the South Sea* London 1792
**Blitz and pieces: transport weekly of the 2/101 Australian General Transport Coy.* In the field 1943–44
The blossom Sydney 1828
BLOXSOME, C. *How Wonder won the cup* Glen Innes, N.S.W. 1924
'BLUEGUM, T.' *The backblocks' parson: a story of Australian life* London 1899
'BLUE THE SHEARER' *The first clip* Dubbo, N.S.W. 1979
BODEKER, P. *The sandgropers' trail* Sydney 1971
Bogong: journal of the Canberra and South-East Region Environment Centre Canberra 1980
Bohemia Melbourne 1890–92
BOLAM, A.G. *The trans-Australian wonderland* Melbourne 1923, 3rd ed. 1924, 4th ed. 1925
BOLAND, D.J. et al. *Forest trees of Australia* 4th ed. Melbourne 1984
'BOLDREWOOD, R.' (T.A. Browne) *Old Melbourne memories* Melbourne 1884
Robbery under arms London 1888
A colonial reformer 3 vols. London 1890
The miner's right London 1890
The squatter's dream: a story of Australian life London 1890
A Sydney-side Saxon London 1891, Sydney 1925
Nevermore London 1892
A romance of Canvas Town and other stories London 1898
In bad company and other stories London 1901

'BOLDREWOOD, Rose' (R. Browne) *The complications at Collaroi* London 1911

BOLTON, G.C. *A fine country to starve in* Perth 1972

'BONANZA' (S.W. Jonnes) *Goldfield's reminiscences* Melbourne 1884

BOND, C. *Goldfields and chrysanthemums* London 1898

BOND, G. *A brief account of the colony of Port-Jackson in New South Wales* Southampton 1803

BONNEY, F. *On some customs of the Aborigines of the River Darling, New South Wales* London 1883

BONWICK, J. *Notes of a gold digger* Melbourne 1852

Geography of Australia and New Zealand 3rd ed. Melbourne 1855

The bushrangers: illustrating the early days of Van Diemen's Land Melbourne 1856

William Buckley, the wild white man, and his Port Phillip black friends Melbourne 1856

Early days of Melbourne Melbourne 1857

The wild white man and the blacks of Victoria Melbourne 1863

John Batman, the founder of Victoria Melbourne 1867

Curious facts of old colonial days London 1870

The last of the Tasmanians; or, the black war of Van Diemen's Land London 1870

Mike Howe, the bushranger of Van Diemen's Land London 1873

The Tasmanian lily London 1873

The resources of Queensland London 1880

BONYTHON, K. *Ladies' legs & lemonade* Adelaide 1979

**Book of the Ballarat: left Australia 19 February, torpedoed Anzac Day 25 April 1917* London 1917

The boomerang Brisbane 1887–92

BOOMSMA, C.D. *Native trees of South Australia* Adelaide 1972 (S.A. Woods and Forests Dept. Bulletin no. 19)

2nd ed. 1981

'BOONDI' (J.I. Hunt) *Boondi's book* Sydney 1903

BOOTH, C.O. *Journal* Hobart 1981

BOOTH, E.C. *Another England: life, living, homes, and homemakers in Victoria* London 1869

BOOTH, J. *Only the tracks remain* Sydney 1972

BOOTHBY, G. *On the wallaby; or through the East and across Australia* London 1894

BORLASE, J.S. *The night fossickers and other Australian tales of peril and adventure* London 1867

**Bostall boshter: the Abbey Wood convalescent depot* Bostall Heath, England 1916

BOSWELL, A.A. *Recollections of some Australian blacks* n.p. 1890

BOSWORTH, C.E. *Shoe and leather trade in Australia* Washington 1918

BOURKE, J.P. *Off the bluebush* Sydney 1915

BOURNE, G. *Bourne's journal of Landsborough's expedition from Carpentaria in search of Burke and Wills* Melbourne 1862

BOWES, J. *The new-chums* London 1915

The jackaroos London 1923

BOXALL, G.E. *The story of the Australian bushrangers* London 1899

BOYCE, F.B. *Our church on the River Darling: a reminiscence* Sydney 1910

BOYD, A.J. *Old colonials* London 1882

BOYD, R. *Australia's home* Melbourne 1952

The Australian ugliness Melbourne 1960 rev. ed. Ringwood, Vic. 1968

The great Australian dream Sydney 1972

'BOYS IN UNIFORM' *Time off* Brisbane [1944]

BRACKEN, T. *Dear old Bendigo: (a sketch of the early digging days), and Rogers of Eaglehawk* Bendigo [1892]

BRADDON, E. *A home in the colonies: letters to India from north-west Tasmania, 1878* ed. by S. Bennett Hobart 1980

BRADDON, R. *Naked island* London 1961

BRADEN, L. *Bullockies* Adelaide 1968

BRADSHAW, W.S. *Voyages to India, China, and America, with an account of the Swan River settlement* London 1857

BRADY, E.J. *Bells and hobbles* Melbourne 1911

The King's caravan: across Australia in a wagon London 1911

The land of the sun London 1924

BRADY, J. *A descriptive vocabulary of the native language of W. Australia* Rome 1845

BRAHAM, N. ed. *The dwarf: selections from the McGregor literary competitions 1978–79* Toowoomba, Qld. 1979

Braidwood dispatch Braidwood, N.S.W. 1859–1970

BRAIM, T.H. *A history of New South Wales, from its settlement to the close of the year 1844* London 1846

**Bran mash: the Fourth Light Horse* Anzac Cove, Gallipoli 1915

BRASSEY, A. *The last voyage to India and Australia in the 'Sunbeam'* London 1889

BRAY, C. *Blossom like a rose* London 1969

Breakers of men: or torturing the twelve: published by the Industrial Workers of the World Prisoners Release Committee Melbourne [c. 1920]

BREAKWELL, E. *The grasses and fodder plants of New South Wales* Sydney 1923

BREEDEN, S. & K. *Wildlife of eastern Australia* Sydney 1973

BREES, S.C. *How to farm and settle in Australia* London 1856

BRENNAN, R.M. & WHITE, G. *Keep the billy boiling* Warren, N.S.W. 1980

BRENTNALL, T. *My memories* Melbourne 1938

'BRENT OF BIN BIN' (M. Franklin) *Up the country* Edinburgh 1928

Ten Creeks Run Edinburgh 1930, Sydney 1952

Back to Bool Bool Edinburgh 1931

BRETON, W.H. *Excursions in New South Wales, Western Australia, and Van Dieman's Land, during the years 1830, 1831, 1832, and 1833* London 1833

BREWER, A.L. *'Gators' euchre and other stories* Melbourne 1917

BREWER, G.F. *On the breadline: oral records of poverty* Melbourne 1980

BREYDOR, B. *Flying is for the birds* Sydney 1967

Thank God there's an Army London 1967

You oughta seen us! Sydney 1969

BRICE, J. *South Australia as it is: how to get to it, and what to do when there* Bristol 1848

BRIDE, T.F. ed. *Letters from Victorian pioneers* Melbourne 1898

BRIGGS, F.S. & HARRIS, S.H. *Joysticks and fiddlesticks* London [1938]

BRIGGS, T.J. *Life and experiences of a successful West Australian* Perth 1917

BRINSMEAD, H.F. *Under the silkwood* North Melbourne 1976

**'Brisbane' R.A.N.: being paper published on board H.M.A.S. 'Brisbane'* Malta 1917

Brisbane courier Brisbane 1864–1933 (continues *The courier*, continued by *The courier-mail*)

BRISSENDEN R.F. *Gough and Johnny were lovers* Ringwood, Vic. 1984

Britannia and trades' advocate Hobart 1846–53

British migrants' case for repatriation Adelaide 1932

BRITT, M. *Pardon my boots* Melbourne 1963

BRITTEN, R.J. *Around the Cassowary Rock* Adelaide 1978

BROCK, D.G. *Recollections of D.G.B. 1843* Adelaide 1981

Journal written during Sturt's northern expedition. Mortlock Library D4745(L) (publ. Adelaide 1975 under title *To the desert with Sturt 1844–46)*

BROCKMAN, F.S. *Report on exploration of north-west Kimberley, 1901* Perth 1902

BROGDEN, S. *Sudan contingent* Melbourne 1943

Sky diggers Melbourne [1944]

BROINOWSKI, G.J. *The birds of Australia* 6 vols. Melbourne 1890–91

BROMBY, R. *Rails to the Top End: the Adelaide-Darwin transcontinental railway* Sydney 1982

Bronze swagman book of bush verse Winton, Qld. 1973–79

The bronze trumpet: a satirical poem Sydney 1866

BROOK, J.A. *Jim of the seven seas* London 1940

BROOKS, A.E. *Australian native plants for home gardens* Melbourne 1959

BROOKS, J.M. *The opal witch* London 1967

BROPHO, R. *Fringedweller* Sydney 1980

BROUGHTON, G.W. *Men of the Murray: a surveyor's story* Adelaide 1966

BROUGHTON, W.G. *A journal of visitation by the Lord Bishop of Australia in 1845* London 1846

BROWN, F.H. *Songs of the plains* Sydney [1934]
BROWN, G. *My descent from soapbox to Senate* Brisbane 1953
BROWN, G.A. *Sheep breeding in Australia* Melbourne 1880
BROWN, H. *Victoria, as I found it, during five years of adventure* London 1862
BROWN, J. *Just for the record* Sydney 1984
BROWN, K. *Knock ten: a novel of mining life* Sydney 1976
BROWN, M. *The Jimberi track* Sydney 1966
The black Eureka Sydney 1976
BROWN, P.L. *Coast of coral and pearl* London 1972
BROWN, R. *Prodromus florae Novae Hollandiae et insulae Van-Diemen* London 1810
General remarks, geographical and systematical, on the botany of Terra Australis London 1814
BROWN, W.B. *Narrative of a voyage from London to South Australia* London 1850
BROWNE, C.W. *Overlanding in Australia* Melbourne 1868
BROWNE, F.C. *They called him Billy* Sydney 1946
The public be damned! Sydney 1947
BROWNE, R. *Aboriginal family* London 1983
BROWNE, R.S. *Romances of gold field and bush* Sydney 1890
A journalist's memories Brisbane 1927
BROWNE, T.A. see 'Boldrewood, R.'
BROWNE, T.F. de C. *The miners' handy book* Sydney [1882]
BROWNRIGG, M.B. *The cruise of the 'Freak'* Hobart [1872]
BRUCE, K. *Digger tourists* Melbourne [1940]
BRUCE, R. *The dingoes and other tales* Adelaide 1875
Echoes from Coondambo Adelaide 1893
Reminiscences of an old squatter Adelaide 1902
Benbonuna: a tale of the 'fifties' Adelaide 1900, London 1904
BRUNO, F. *'Sa-eeda wog'* Sydney [1944]
BRYDE, C.W. *From chart house to bush hut* Melbourne [1920]
BUCHANAN, A. *The real Australia* London 1907
BUCHANAN, C. *We have bugger all!: the Kulaluk story* Carlton, Vic. 1974
BUCHANAN, M.S. *Prospecting for opal in Australia* Campsie, N.S.W. [1931]
BUCHANAN, W.F. *Australia to the rescue: a hundred years' progress in New South Wales* London 1890
BUCKLEY, B. & HAMILTON, J. eds. *Festival and other stories* Melbourne 1974
BUCKTON, T.J. *Western Australia, comprising a description of the vicinity of Australind and Port Leschenault* London 1840
BUDDIVENT, P.L. *The 'Centennial'* Sydney 1888
BUFTON, J. *Tasmanians in the Transvaal war* Hobart 1905
BUGGY, H. *Let's look at football* Melbourne [1953]
BULEY, E.C. *Australian life in town & country* London 1905
Bull-ant Melbourne 1890–92
BULLEN, F.T. *Advance Australasia: a day-to-day record of a recent visit to Australasia* London 1907
Bulletin Sydney 1880–
Bulletin of the Northern Territory Melbourne 1912–36
**Bully tin: incorporating the Baronta bully tin, the voice of No. 7 Adv. Amn. Depot* Baronta, Qld. 1943–44
BUNBURY, H.W. *Early days in Western Australia* London 1930
BUNBURY, T. *Reminiscences of a veteran* 3 vols. London 1861
BUNCE, D. *Australasiatic reminiscences of twenty-three years' wanderings in Tasmania and the Australias* Melbourne 1857
BUNDEY, W.H. *A winter cruise on Australia's great waterway and what I saw at Mildura* Adelaide 1890
Bungendore mirror and Lake George advertiser Bungendore, N.S.W. 1887–88
BUNSTER, G. & THATCHER, R. *It runs in the blood* Bathurst, N.S.W. 1872
BURBIDGE, N.T. *Australian grasses* 3 vols. Sydney 1966–70
BURBIDGE, N.T. & GRAY, M. *Flora of the Australian Capital Territory* Canberra 1970
BURFORD, R. *Description of a view of the town of Sydney, New South Wales* London 1829
BURGESS, C. *Blue Mountain gums* Sydney 1963
BURGESS, P. *Money to burn* Ringwood, Vic. 1982
BURGMANN, E.H. *The education of an Australian* Sydney 1944
BURKE, A.J. *Bite the pineapple* Brisbane 1979
Pommies and patriots Brisbane 1981
The Burke and Wills exploring expedition: an account of the crossing the continent of Australia, from Cooper's Creek to Carpentaria: reprinted from 'The Argus' Melbourne 1861
BURKE, D. *Darknight* Sydney 1979
BURKE, K. *With horse and Morse in Mesopotamia: the story of Anzacs in Asia* Sydney 1927
BURN, D. *Vindication of Van Diemen's Land* London 1840
Narrative of the overland journey of Sir John and Lady Franklin and party from Hobart Town to Macquarie Harbour, 1842 Sydney 1955
An excursion to Port Arthur in 1842 Hobart 1892
BURNETT, A. *Wilful murder in the outback* Adelaide 1973
BURNS, R. *Mr Brain knows best* Sydney 1959
BURNS, T.E. & SKEMP, J.R. eds. *Van Diemen's Land correspondents* Launceston, Tas. 1961
BURROWS, W. *Adventures of a mounted trooper in the Australian constabulary* London 1859
BURT, J. *Shutterbug in the bush* Adelaide 1981
BURTON, B.K. *Teach them no more* Sydney 1967
BURTON, J.H. *The emigrant's manual: Australia, New Zealand, America, and South Africa* 2 parts. Edinburgh 1851
BURTON, J.L. *Across Australia in seven days* Sydney [1918]
BUSBY, A. *Bathurst in the thirties: some memories of the early days* Bathurst, N.S.W. 1902
BUSBY, J. *Authentic information relative to New South Wales, and New Zealand* London 1832
Bushdriver Sydney 1977–
BUSHELL, A. ed. *Yesterday's daughters: stories of our past by women over 70* Melbourne 1986
'A BUSHMAN' SEE *Sidney's Australian handbook*
'BUSHMAN, J.' (C.H. Sayce) *In the Musgrave Ranges* London [1922]
Bushmen, publicans and politics Deniliquin, N.S.W. 1869
BUSTARD, R. *Australian lizards* Sydney 1970
BUTCHER, A.D. *The freshwater fish of Victoria and their food* Melbourne 1946
BUTLER, A.G. *The digger: a study in democracy* Sydney 1945
BUTLER, H. *In the wild with Harry Butler* Sydney 1977
In the wild with Harry Butler Part two. Sydney 1979
BUTLER, S. *The hand-book for Australian emigrants* Glasgow 1839
BUTTON, H. *Flotsam and jetsam: floating fragments of life in England and Tasmania* Launceston 1909
BUZO, A. *Norm and Ahmed* 1968 see *Three plays*
The front room boys 1969 in *Plays* Melbourne 1970
Rooted 1969 see *Three plays*
Macquarie Sydney 1971
The Roy Murphy show 1971 see *Three plays*
Three plays Sydney 1971
Coralie Lansdowne says no Sydney 1974
Tom Sydney 1975
Martello Towers Sydney 1976
**Buzz review: weekly publication of the H.M.A.S. Manoora armed merchant cruiser* At sea 1945
BYERLEY, F.J. ed. *Narrative of the overland expedition of the Messrs. Jardine, from Rockhampton to Cape York, northern Queensland* Brisbane 1867
BYRNE, J. *Duck hunting in Australia and New Zealand* Sydney 1974
BYRNE, J. *Horse riding the Australian way* Melbourne 1972
BYRNE, J.C. *Emigrant's guide to New South Wales proper, Australia Felix, and South Australia* 4th ed. London 1848
Twelve years' wanderings in the British colonies, from 1835 to 1847 2 vols. London 1848
Byron Bay record Byron Bay, N.S.W. 1902–?1924

'CABLE, B.' (E.A. Ewart) *By blow and kiss* 2nd ed. London 1914
**Cacolet: journal of the Australian Camel Field Ambulance* Cairo 1917–18
Caddie: a Sydney barmaid London 1953
CALDWELL, N. *Fangs of the sea* Sydney 1936

CALDWELL, R. *The gold era of Victoria: being the present and future of the colony in its commercial, statistical, and social aspects* London 1855

In our great north-west Adelaide 1894

CALTHORPE, M. *The dyehouse* Sydney 1961

The defectors Sydney 1969

CALVERT, A.F. *Narrative of an expedition into the interior of north-west Australia* London 1892

Western Australia and its gold fields London 1893

The Aborigines of Western Australia London 1894

The Coolgardie goldfield: Western Australia London 1894

My fourth tour in Western Australia London 1897

CALWELL, A.A. *How many Australians tomorrow?* Melbourne 1945

Immigration: policy and progress Melbourne 1949

Be just and fear not Hawthorn, Vic. 1972

CAMERON, A. *Australia Felix, or Sir Valiant Love* Sydney 1892

CAMERON, D. *The mysteries and miseries of Scripopolis: an account of a week in Sandhurst. By 'Demonax'* Melbourne [1872]

CAMERON, J. *The fire stick: incidents in the shearers' strike. A tale of Australian bush life by Wulla Merii* n.p. [c. 1892.]

**Camp capers* [In the field] 1943

CAMPBELL, A.J. *Nests and eggs of Australian birds* 2 parts. Sheffield, England 1900

Renaming Australian birds: is it necessary? Melbourne 1918

Golden wattle: our national floral emblem Melbourne 1921

CAMPBELL, C. *The squatting question considered with a view to its settlement* Melbourne 1861

CAMPBELL, D. *Drought: causes effects solutions* Melbourne 1968

CAMPBELL, E.W. *History of the Australian Labor movement* Sydney 1945

CAMPBELL, J. *Nests and eggs of Australian birds* Melbourne 1883

CAMPBELL, Jean. *The babe is wise* London [1939]

CAMPBELL, John. *The early settlement of Queensland .. with which is also printed 'The raid of the Aborigines' by .. William Wilks* Ipswich, Qld. 1875

CAMPBELL, Joseph. *Norfolk Island and its inhabitants* Sydney 1879

CAMPBELL, N. *The dinky-di soldier* Sydney 1918

CAMPBELL, W. *The crown lands of Australia* Glasgow 1855

The discovery of gold in Victoria Edinburgh 1856

'CAMPION, S.' (M.R. Coulton) *Bonanza* London 1942

The pommy cow London 1944

Canberra times Canberra 1926–

CANNEY, E.H. *The land of the dawning* London 1894

CANNON, A. *Bullocks, bullockies and other blokes* Melbourne 1983

CANNON, M. *That damned democrat: John Norton, an Australian populist, 1858–1916* Melbourne 1981

CANNON, R. *Savage scenes from Australia* Valparaiso 1885

CANTWELL, J. *No stranger to the flame* London 1963

CAPLE, S.C. *The Ashes at stake: memories of Anglo-Australian cricket* Worcester, England 1961

CAPPER, H. *South Australia: extracts from the official dispatches of Colonel Light* London 1837

The Australian colonies: where they are, and how to get to them London 1855

CAPPER, J. *Philips' emigrants' guide to Australia* Liverpool 1852

2nd ed. 1853

3rd ed. London 1856

facs. ed. by D.J. Golding, Melbourne 1973

Australia: as a field for capital, skill, and labour London 1854

'CAPRICORNUS' (G. Ranken) *Bush essays* Edinburgh 1872

The squatting system of Australia Edinburgh 1875

Colonisation in 1876 Sydney 1876

The land law of the future Sydney 1877

CARBONI, R. *The Eureka stockade* Melbourne 1855

CARELL, V. *Naked we are born* Sydney 1960

CAREY, G. & LETTE, K. *Puberty blues* Melbourne 1979

CAREY, P. *Illywhacker* St. Lucia, Qld. 1985

CARNEGIE, D.W. *Spinifex and sand* London 1898

CARR, D.J. & S.G.M. eds. *Plants and man in Australia* Sydney 1981

People and plants in Australia Sydney 1981

CARR, R. *Surfie* Sydney 1966

CARRON, W. *Narrative of an expedition, undertaken under the direction of the late Mr Assistant Surveyor E.B. Kennedy, for the exploration of the country lying between Rockingham Bay and Cape York* Sydney 1849

CARSTAIRS, C. *The zero heroes* Sydney 1969

CARTER, B.A. *Lookin' for higher places* Albert Park, Vic. 1978

CARTER, H.J. *Gulliver in the bush: wanderings of an Australian entomologist* Sydney 1933

CARTER, J. *People of the inland* Adelaide 1966

Stout hearts and leathery hands London 1968

Four-wheel drive swagman Adelaide 1969

Wild country Adelaide 1971

All things wild Adelaide 1977

CASEY, G. *It's harder for girls and other stories* Sydney 1942, 1944

Birds of a feather Perth [1943]

Downhill is easier Sydney 1945

The wits are out Sydney 1947

City of men London 1950

Snowball Sydney 1958

Amid the plenty Sydney 1962

CASEY, G. & MAYMAN, T. *The mile that Midas touched* Adelaide 1964

CASH, M. *The adventures of Martin Cash* ed. by J.L. Burke Hobart 1870

CASH, S.J. *Prospecting for gold by the loaming system* Perth 1934

'CAS-HAMBA' *Sketchy characters of gold fields life* Sydney 1900

Cassell's emigrants' handy guide to New South Wales London [1863]

Cassell's emigrants' handy guide to Queensland London [1863]

Cassell's emigrants' handy guide to Tasmania London [1863]

Cassell's emigrants' handy guide to Victoria London [1864]

CASSIDY, C.T. *Random thoughts at Wyndham* n.p. [1977]

CASSIDY, M. *The dispossessed* London 1972

CASSIDY, R.J. *The land of the starry cross* Melbourne 1911

The gipsy road Sydney 1919

CASTIEAU, J.B. *The reminiscences of Detective-Inspector Christie* Melbourne [1913]

CASWALL, A. *Hints from the journal of an Australian squatter* London 1843

CATO, N. *Green grows the vine* London 1960

But still the stream London 1962

Brown sugar London 1974

Mister Maloga: Daniel Matthews and his mission, Murray River, 1864–1902 St. Lucia, Qld. 1976

The causes of the ruinous condition of the coal trade, in the northern district of New South Wales Newcastle, N.S.W. 1872

CAWTHORNE, W.A. *The legend of Kupirri; or the red kangaroo* Adelaide 1858

Census of the plants of Victoria with their regional distribution and the vernacular names as adopted by the Plant Names Committee of the Field Naturalists' Club of Victoria Melbourne 1923

Centennial magazine Melbourne and Sydney 1888–90

Central Australian land rights news Alice Springs, N.T. 1976–82 (continued by *Land rights news*)

Centralian advocate Alice Springs, N.T. 1947–

**Certo insana: unofficial organ of the 5th Australian Division Signals* [1939–45]

CHALMERS, O. *The observer's book of rocks and minerals of Australia* Sydney 1979

CHAMBERLAYNE, I. *The Australian captive; or, an authentic narrative of fifteen years in the life of William Jackman* Auburn, U.S.A. 1853

CHAMBERS, C.H. *Thumb-nail sketches of Australian life* New York 1891

CHANCY, W.S. see 'Rusticus'

CHANDLER, C.W. *Darkest Adelaide and sidelights of city life* Adelaide [c.1907]

CHAPMAN, H.S. *The new settlement of Australind* London 1841

Character glimpses: Australians on the Somme compiled by A.H. Cooper Sydney [1920]

CHARLESWORTH, J. *A visit to the diggings; or sketches of Australian life* Chatham, England 1855

CHARLETON, A.G. *Gold mining and milling in Western Australia* London 1903

CHARLWOOD, D.E. *An afternoon of time* Sydney 1966

CHAUNCY, W.S. *A guide to South Australia* London 1849
CHAUVEL, C. & E. *Walkabout* London 1959
**Cheeriodical: R.A.A.F. station, Rathmines, N.S.W.* [Rathmines], N.S.W. 1942
CHEWINGS, C. *Back in the stone age: the natives of Central Australia* Sydney 1936
CHILD, J. *Australian insects* Lane Cove, N.S.W. 1960, rev. ed. 1968
The children in the scrub see Tandy, S.
CHINNER, G.F. *Spray from the war wave* Sydney 1900
CHIPPENDALE, G.M. *Eucalypts of the Western Australian goldfields (and the adjacent wheatbelt)* Canberra 1973
CHIPPER, A. *The Aussie swearer's guide* Melbourne 1972
CHISHOLM, A.H. *Mateship with birds* Melbourne 1922
Birds & green places: a book of Australian nature gossip London 1929
Nature fantasy in Australia London 1932
Bird wonders of Australia Sydney 1934
The making of a sentimental bloke Melbourne 1946
ed. *Land of wonder: the best Australian nature writing* Sydney 1964
CHISHOLM, A.R. *The familiar presence* Melbourne 1966
CHISHOLM, C. *Emigration and transportation relatively considered* London 1847
CHISHOLM, J.K. *Speeches and reminiscences* Sydney 1907
CHOMLEY, C.H. *The true story of the Kelly gang of bushrangers* Melbourne 1900
CHUBB, C.F. *Fugitive pieces* Brisbane 1881
Citizen Sydney 1846–47
**Citizen soldier of Australia* Sydney 1937–38
CLACY, Mrs C. *A lady's visit to the gold diggings of Australia, in 1852–53* London 1853
Lights and shadows of Australian life 2 vols. London 1854
CLANCHY, J. *Lie of the land* Carlton, Vic. 1985
CLANCY, L. *The wife specialist* Melbourne 1979
Perfect love Melbourne 1983
CLARK, A. *Australian adventure: letters from an ambassador's wife* South Melbourne 1969
CLARK, D. *Boomer: the life of a kangaroo* New York 1955
CLARK, J. & WHITELAW, B. *Golden summers: Heidelberg and beyond* rev. ed. Melbourne 1986
CLARK, L.H. *Rouseabout reflections* Melbourne 1975
The secret springs Melbourne 1980
CLARK, R. Journal, 1787–92. ML MS Safe 1/27
CLARKE, A.E. *The man nobody understood* [Melbourne] 1941
CLARKE, M. *The peripatetic philosopher* Melbourne 1869
Old tales of a young country Melbourne 1871
Holiday peak and other tales Melbourne 1873
Australian tales Melbourne 1896
Stories of Australia in the early days London 1897
CLARKE, P. *The 'new chum' in Australia* London 1886
ed. *The Valley Council; or leaves from the journal of Thomas Bateman of Canbelego Station, N.S.W.* London 1891
CLARKE, W.B. *Researches in the southern gold fields of New South Wales* Sydney 1860
CLEARY, J. *You can't see around corners* New York 1947, Sydney 1948
The long shadow London 1949
Just let me be London 1950
The sundowners London 1952
The climate of courage London 1954
Justin Bayard London 1955
Back of sunset London 1959
Helga's web New York 1970
CLEARY, P.S. *The one big union: will it emancipate the worker?* Sydney 1919
CLELAND, E.D. *West Australian mining practice: a description of the mining methods followed by the principal gold mines of Western Australia* Kalgoorlie, W.A. 1911
CLELAND, J.B. *Some diseases peculiar to, or of interest in Australia* Sydney 1912
'CLERGYMAN' (J. Morison) *Australia as it is* London 1867
CLERK, A.T. *The prickly pear problem in Queensland* Brisbane 1913
CLIFFORD, A. *Send her down, Hughie!* Adelaide 1968
CLIFT, C. *Walk to the Paradise Gardens* London 1960
CLIFT, K. *The saga of a sig.: the wartime memories of six years service in the Second A.I.F.* Randwick, N.S.W. 1972
The soldier who never grew up Sydney 1976
Clipper Hobart 1893–1909
CLOSE, R.S. *Love me sailor* Melbourne 1945
Morn of youth Melbourne 1948
With hooves of brass Adelaide 1961
Of salt and earth: an autobiography Melbourne 1977
CLOW, R.J. *The pillar of salt: a story of station life* Balaklava, S. Aust. 1903
CLOWES, E.M. *On the wallaby through Victoria* London 1911
CLUNE, F. *Try anything once: the autobiography of a wanderer* Sydney 1933
Rolling down the Lachlan Sydney 1935
Roaming round the Darling Sydney 1936
Dig Sydney 1937
Free and easy land Sydney 1938
Last of the Australian explorers London 1942
The red heart: saga of Centralia Melbourne 1944
Try nothing twice Sydney 1946
Roaming around Australia Melbourne 1947
Wild colonial boys Sydney 1948
Overland Telegraph Sydney 1955
The fortune hunters: an atomic odyssey in Australia's wild west, and things seen and heard by the way of a jeep jaunt Sydney 1957
CLUTTERBUCK, J.B. *Port Phillip in 1849* London 1850
CLYNE, D. *Australian frogs* Melbourne 1969
A guide to Australian spiders Melbourne 1969
Coalition between the squatters and free selectors Sydney [1868]
Coast to coast: Australian short stories Sydney 1941–73
COBBER, Lance-Corporal see Lance-Corporal Cobber
**Cobbers: official organ of the A.I.F. Grovely camp* [Brisbane] 1940–41
COBBOLD, R. *The history of Margaret Catchpole, a Suffolk girl* 3 vols. London 1845
COCHRANE, A. *Granite rocks and ozone or two weeks' leave on full pay* Adelaide 1902
COCHRANE, G.R. et al. *Flowers and plants of Victoria* Sydney 1968 rev. ed. [1973]
Flowers and plants of Victoria and Tasmania Sydney 1980
COCK, P. *Alternative Australia: communities of the future?* Melbourne 1979
COCK, R. *South Australia* Adelaide 1839
COCKBURN, F.J. *Letters from the southern hemisphere* Calcutta 1856
COCKERELL, J.T. *Scenes behind the curtain; or, the acts and deeds of the convict detectives of New South Wales* Brisbane 1861
COCKERILL, G. *Scribblers and statesmen* Melbourne 1944
COE, J.J. ed. *Desperate praise: the Australians in Vietnam* Perth 1982
COGGER, H.C. *Australian reptiles in colour* Sydney 1967
Reptiles and amphibians of Australia Sydney 1975, rev. ed. 1983
COLBERT, J. *The ranch* Melbourne [1978]
COLE, K. *Winds of fury* Adelaide 1977
COLEMAN, E. *Come back in wattle time* Melbourne 1935
COLEMAN, N. *What shell is that?* Sydney 1975
A field guide to Australian marine life Adelaide 1977
A look at wildlife of the Great Barrier Reef Sydney 1978
Australian fisherman's fish guide Sydney 1978
Australian sea fishes south of 30° S Sydney 1980, rev. ed. 1983
Australian sea fishes north of 30° S Sydney 1981, rev. ed. 1986
COLEMAN, R. *The pyjama girl* Melbourne 1978
The colonial intelligencer; or, Aborigines' friend London 1847–58
COLLINGS, J.W. *8000 miles by air around Australia visiting Flying Doctor bases* Malvern, Vic. 1939
COLLINS, A.K. *Waddy Mundoee, or, the life and adventures of a pioneer squatter* Sydney 1867
COLLINS, B. *The second step* Sydney 1972
COLLINS, Dale *Victoria's my home ground* Melbourne 1951

COLLINS, David *An account of the English colony in New South Wales* 2 vols. London 1798–1802
COLLINS, S.H. *A geographical description of Australasia* (anon.) Hull, England 1830
'COLLINS, T.' see Furphy, J.
COLLINSON, J.W. *Early days of Cairns* Brisbane 1939
ed. *More about Cairns: 3. Recollections of a varied life* see Eastwood, J.G.
COLLISSON, M. *South Australia in 1844–45* Adelaide 1845
COLLUM, J.A. *New settlers' handbook for Queensland* Brisbane 1925
The colonial cook book London 1970 (first publ. Sydney 1864)
Colonial literary journal Sydney 1844–45
Colonial magazine and commercial-maritime journal London 1840–42
'A COLONIAL MAGISTRATE' (W. Hull) *Remarks on the probable origin and antiquity of the Aboriginal natives of New South Wales* Melbourne 1846
Colonial mining journal of Victoria, Australia, & adjacent colonies Melbourne 1858–?1861
Colonial monthly: an Australian magazine Melbourne 1867–70 (continues *The Australian monthly magazine*)
Colonial observer Sydney 1841–44
Colonial society Sydney 1868–69
Colonial times and Tasmanian advertiser Hobart 1825–57 (continues *The Hobart Town gazette*)
Colonist and Van Diemen's Land commercial and agricultural advertiser Hobart 1832–34 (continued by *True colonist and Van Diemen's Land political despatch* etc.)
Colonist: a weekly journal of politics, commerce, agriculture, literature, science, and religion, for the colony of New South Wales Sydney 1835–40
'A COLONIST' *Life's work as it is; or, the emigrant's home in Australia* London 1867
'A COLONIST OF TWENTY YEARS' STANDING' (C.R. Carter) *Victoria, the British 'El Dorado'; or Melbourne in 1869* London 1870
The Colony of Queensland as a field for emigration n.p. [1866]
Commercial journal and advertiser Sydney 1836–41 (continued by *Free press and commercial journal*)
'A COMMERCIAL TRAVELLER' *Diary of a three months' trip to the outlying districts of the north and north-west of Queensland, during the period of the late disastrous floods* Brisbane 1887
A concise history of the English colony in New South Wales, from the landing of Governor Phillip in January 1788, to May 1803 London [1804]
Conference between the Amalgamated Shearers' Union of Australasia, and the Pastoralists' Federal Council of Australia Newport, Vic. 1891
CONIGRAVE, C.P. *North Australia* London 1936
Walk-about London 1938
CONIGRAVE, J.F. *South Australia: a sketch of its history & resources* London 1886
CONIGRAVE, S. *Reminiscences of the early days* Perth 1916
CONINGSBY, R.J. *The discovery of gold in Australia* London 1895
CONNOLLY, E. *How Eric Connolly bets and wins* Sydney 1926
CONNOLLY, R. *John Drysdale and the Burdekin* Sydney 1964
CONQUEST, R.H. *The spurs are rusty now* Sydney 1963
Horses in the kitchen: true tales of outback Australia Sydney 1965
Dusty distances: yesterday's Australia Adelaide 1978
CONROY, J.M. *False, and other tales* Melbourne 1872
**Contact: journal of the Air Force Association Victoria division* Melbourne 1945–52
COOK, J. *The journals of Captain James Cook on his voyages of discovery: I. The voyage of the 'Endeavour', 1768–1771* ed. by J.C. Beaglehole London 1955
A voyage towards the South Pole and round the world performed in His Majesty's Ships the 'Resolution' and 'Adventure', in the years 1772, 1773, 1774, and 1775 2 vols. London 1777
COOK, K. *The man underground* Melbourne 1977
COOK, T. *The exile's lamentations* North Sydney 1978
COOMBE, F. *School days in Norfolk Island* London 1909
COOMBS, H.C. *Kulinma: listening to Aboriginal Australians* Canberra 1978
COOPER, E. *Forest culture and eucalyptus trees* San Francisco 1876
COOPER, F. de B. *Wild adventures in Australia and New South Wales, beyond the boundaries, with sketches of life at the mining districts* London 1857
*COOPER, G.C. Diary. 1916–18
COOPER, J.B. *Coo-oo-ee!: a tale of bushmen from Australia to Anzac* London 1916
COOPER, W. *Colonial experience* Sydney 1979
COOTE, W. *History of the colony of Queensland from 1770 to the close of the year 1881* Brisbane 1882
CORBEN, M. *Not to mention the kangaroos* New York 1955
CORBIN, H.H. et al. *Federal Capital Territory: reports relating to afforestation* Melbourne 1918
CORFIELD, W.H. *Reminiscences of Queensland, 1862–1899* Brisbane 1921
CORK, F. *Tales from the cattle country* Adelaide [1945]
*CORNEY, F.R. Letter 31 Oct. 1916
Cornhill magazine London 1871
'CORNSTALK, S.' (F.S. Walker) *Land of Australia* Sydney 1913
Cornwall chronicle Launceston, Tas. 1835–80 (incorporated in *The examiner*)
CORNWALLIS, K. *Yarra Yarra; or the wandering Aborigine* London 1858
Cornwall press and commercial advertiser Launceston, Tas. 1829
CORRIS, P. *White meat* Sydney 1981
The winning side Sydney 1984
COSH, A.E. *Jumping kangaroos: the life of an Australian pioneer settler's son* Armidale, N.S.W. 1978
COSTELLO, M.M.J. *Life of John Costello: being the adventures of a pioneer, pastoralist and explorer in Queensland and the Northern Territory* Sydney 1930
COSTERMANS, L. *Native trees and shrubs of south-eastern Australia* Adelaide, 1981
COSTIN, A.B. et al. *Kosciusko alpine flora* Melbourne 1979
COTTERELL, G. *Tea at Shadow Creek* London 1958
COTTON, A.J. *With the big herds in Australia* Brisbane 1933
COTTRELL, D. *Earth battle* London [1930]
Counsel for emigrants 3rd ed. Aberdeen, Scotland 1838
Countrywoman in New South Wales: official journal of the Countrywomen's Association of New South Wales Sydney 1937– (from 1957 has title *The country woman*)
COUPER, J.M. *The thundering good today* London 1970
Courier Brisbane 1861–64 (continues *The Moreton Bay courier*, continued by *The Brisbane courier*)
Courier Hobart 1840–59 (continues *The Hobart Town courier*)
Courier-mail Brisbane 1933– (continues *The Brisbane courier*)
COURTIER, S.H. *No obelisk for Emily* London 1970
Dead if I remember London 1972
COURTNEY, V. *All I may tell: a journalist's story* Sydney 1956
COWAN, F. *Australia: a charcoal-sketch* Greensburg, U.S.A. 1886
COWAN, P. *The unploughed land* Sydney 1958
Seed Sydney 1966
COWL, Mrs T. *Some of my experiences during a voyage to the Gulf of Carpentaria and three years' residence at Normanton in the early seventies* Brisbane [c.1907]
COWLEY, C.E. *Classing the clip: a handbook on wool-classing* Sydney 1928
COX, E.W. *The evolution of the Australian merino* Sydney 1936
COX, W. *A narrative of proceedings of William Cox, esq. . . in constructing a road . . over the Blue Mountains . . in the years 1814 & 1815* Sydney 1888
COX, W.G. *Irrigation with surface and subterranean waters and land drainage* Sydney 1906
COZENS, C. *Adventures of a Guardsman* London 1848
CRAIG, W. *My adventures on the Australian goldfields* London 1903
CRAMSIE, J.B. ed. *Management and diseases of sheep in Australia* Sydney 1920
CRANLEY, V.B. *27,000 miles through Australia* London 1963
CRAWFORD, F. *The native companion songster* Brisbane 1889
CRAWFORD, R. *Echoes from bushland* Sydney 1881
CREED, J.M. *My recollections of Australia and elsewhere 1842–1914* London 1916

CRESWELL, P.B. *Granite Peak 1929–1979* n.p. [1981]

CRIBB, A.B. & J.W. *Wild food in Australia* Sydney 1975
Useful wild plants in Australia Sydney 1981
Wild medicine in Australia Sydney 1981

CRICK, D.H. *Martin Place* Sydney 1963

CRISP, L.F. *The parliamentary government of the Commonwealth of Australia* Melbourne 1949

CRITCH, M. ed. *Our kind of war: the history of the VAD/AAMWS* [Perth] 1981

Critic Adelaide and Melbourne 1897–1924

CRITTENDEN, H.W. *Rogues' paradise: a critical survey of the Australian scene* Sydney [1948]

CRITTENDEN, V. *The front garden: the story of the cottage garden in Australia* Canberra 1979
An autumn visit: historic gardens in Sydney and the Blue Mountains Canberra 1982

CROCKER, A. *Australia hops in* Sydney 1941 (first publ. 1935)

CROLL, R.H. *The open road in Victoria: being the ways of many walkers* Melbourne 1928
Wide horizons: wanderings in Central Australia Sydney 1937
ed. *Smike to Bulldog: letters from Sir Arthur Stretton to Tom Roberts* Sydney 1946

CROMBIE, A. *After sixty years or recollections of an Australian bushman* Brisbane 1927

CROMPTON, W. *Convict Jim* Maryborough, Qld. 1894

CRONIN, B. *The coastlanders* London [1918]
Timber wolves London [1920]
Red Dawson London [1927]
Dragonfly London [1928]
Bracken London [1931]
How runs the road Melbourne 1948

CROOKSTON, R.M. The unseen tragedy of the Aborigines. Lutheran Church archives, Adelaide. c. 1934

CROSS, G. *George and the widda-woman* Adelaide 1981

CROWE, C. *The Australian slang dictionary* Melbourne 1895
The inquiry agent: a drama of real life played on the stage of the world Melbourne 1909
One big crime: startling stories of Australian crimes and corruption Melbourne 1920
Policemen and politicians Melbourne 1921

CRUMP, B. *Gulf* Wellington, N.Z. 1964

CRUTTWELL, A.C. *Sketches of Australia* London [1881]

'Cry havoc': H.M.S. Kanimbla [At sea] 1941–42

CULL, W.A. *At all costs* Melbourne [1919]

'CULOTTA, N.' (J.P. O'Grady) *They're a weird mob* Sydney 1957
Cop this lot Sydney 1960
Gone fishin' Sydney 1962
Gone gougin' Sydney 1975

Cumberland times Parramatta, N.S.W. 1845–1911 (title varies as *Cumberland times and Western advertiser, Parramatta chronicle and Cumberland general advertiser*, and others)

CUNNINGHAM, A. Comparative table of the different languages spoken by the Aborigines of the continent of Terra Australis at different parts of its coasts. 1817–22 ML MS A1752
A few general remarks on the vegetation of certain coasts of Terra Australis, and more especially of its north-western shores London 1827

CUNNINGHAM, G.M. et al. *Plants of western New South Wales* [Sydney] 1981

CUNNINGHAM, P. *Two years in New South Wales; a series of letters* 2 vols. London 1827, 2nd ed. 1827

CURR, E. *An account of the colony of Van Diemen's Land, principally designed for the use of emigrants* London 1824

CURR, E.M. *Recollections of squatting in Victoria then called the Port Phillip district (from 1841 to 1851)* Melbourne 1883
The Australian race 4 vols. Melbourne 1886–87

CURRAN, J. *Murder on the bore-drain* Quirindi, N.S.W. 1978

Currency lad Sydney 1832–33

CURRIE, G.A. *A report on a survey of weed problems in Australia* Melbourne 1936

CURTIS, L.S. ed. *The history of Broken Hill* Adelaide 1908

CURTIS, W.M. *The student's flora of Tasmania* part I. Hobart 1956
The student's flora of Tasmania part II. Hobart 1963

CURTIS, W.M. & MORRIS, D.I. *The student's flora of Tasmania* part I. 2nd ed. Hobart 1975

CUSACK, D. *Morning sacrifice* 1942 see *Three Australian three-act plays* Sydney 1950
Comets soon pass 1943 see *Three Australian three-act plays*
Shoulder the sky 1945 see *Three Australian three-act plays*
Three Australian three-act plays Sydney 1950
Say no to death London 1951, Berlin 1959
Southern steel London 1953
Picnic races London 1962
The half-burnt tree London 1969

CUSACK, D. & JAMES, F. *Come in spinner* Melbourne 1951

CUSACK, J.J. *The Cusack plan* Cooma, N.S.W. [1943]

DAFOE, J.W. *Under southern skies* Winnipeg [1941]

DAHL, K. *In savage Australia: an account of a hunting and collecting expedition to Arnhem Land and Dampier Land* London 1926

DAKIN, W.J. *Whalemen adventurers* Sydney 1934
Great Barrier Reef Melbourne 1950
Australian seashores: a guide for the beach-lover, the naturalist, the shore fisherman, and the student Sydney 1952 rev. ed. 1980

DALE, R.W. *Impressions of Australia* London 1889

DALEY, C. *Early squatting days: from the papers of the late A.F. Mollison* Melbourne 1922 (In *Victorian Historical Magazine* vol. 9 July 1922 pp. 1–25)

DALGLEISH, H.D. *Tie my swag to a rainbow* Perth 1968
No wonder the kookaburras laugh! Perth 1968 (vol. 2 of *Tie my swag to a rainbow*)

DALY, Mrs D.D. *Digging, squatting, and pioneering life in the Northern Territory of South Australia* London 1887

DALY, F. *From Curtin to Kerr* Melbourne 1977
A to Z of politics Melbourne 1978

DAMPIER, W. *A new voyage round the world* 3 vols.
vols. 1–2 3rd ed. London 1698–99, vol. 3 under title *A voyage to New Holland &c. in the year 1699* London 1703

DANGAR, H. *Index and directory to map of the country bordering upon the River Hunter* London 1828
Dark people in Melbourne: a study . . conducted . . for the Victorian Council of Social Service Melbourne 1950

DARNELL-SMITH, G.P. & MACKINNON, E. *Fungus and other diseases of the apple and pear* Sydney 1915

DARRELL, G. *The sunny south* Sydney 1975

Darwin: a way of life: issued by the Northern Territory Administration Darwin 1967

DARWIN, C. *Journal of researches into the geology and natural history of the various countries visited by H.M.S. Beagle, under the command of Captain Fitzroy, R.N. from 1832 to 1836* London 1839
Geological observations on the volcanic islands, visited during the voyage of H.M.S. Beagle . . 1832–1836 London 1844

DAVIDSON, A.A. *Journal of explorations in Central Australia . . 1898 to 1900* Adelaide 1905

DAVIDSON, G.F. *Trade and travel in the Far East* London 1846

DAVIDSON, R. *Tracks* London 1980

DAVIES, D.J. *A review of coal question: preceding and during the lock-out on northern coalfields 1929* [Sydney 1929]

DAVIES, E. *The story of an earnest life: a woman's adventures in Australia* Cincinnati 1881

DAVIES, J. *A souvenir of Kangaroo Island* Adelaide 1979

DAVIES, L. *Past master and other stories* [Perth] 1980

DAVIS, A.H. see 'Rudd, S.'

DAVIS, H.W. *Bachelors in the bush* Toowoomba, Qld. 1984

DAVIS, J. *Tracks of McKinlay and party across Australia* London 1863

DAVIS, J. *The first-born and other poems* Sydney 1970

DAVISON, F.D. *'Man-shy'* Sydney 1962 (first publ. 1931)
Dusty: the story of a sheep dog Sydney 1946
The road to yesterday Sydney 1964

DAVISON, F.D. & NICHOLLS, B. *Blue coast caravan* Sydney 1935
DAVITT, M. *Life and progress in Australasia* London 1898
DAWE, B. *Just a dugong at twilight* Melbourne 1975
Sometimes gladness: collected poems, 1954–1978 Melbourne 1978
Over here, Harv! Ringwood, Vic. 1983
DAWES, A. *'Soldier superb'* Sydney 1943
DAWES, E.N. *Australian proprietary and private companies: law and management* Sydney 1955
DAWES, W. Grammatical forms of the languages of N.S. Wales, in the neighbourhood of Sydney, in the year 1790. AJCP M686
Dawn: a magazine for the Aboriginal people of NSW Sydney 1952–54
DAWSON, A.J. see *The record of Nicholas Freydon*
DAWSON, R. *Private & confidential:* [*reproductions of a letter addressed to John Smith, M.P., dated Sydney, February 4, 1826, and extract of a letter to Mrs Dawson, dated Port Stephens, May 7, 1826*] London 1826
Statement of the services of Mr Dawson, as chief agent of the Australian Agricultural Company London 1829
The present state of Australia London 1830
DAY, A.S. *The democrat* Melbourne 1890
DEAN, B. & CARELL, V. *Dust for the dancers* Sydney 1955
DEAN, W. *Home and camp* Marrickville, N.S.W. [1906]
DEAN, W.B. *Notorious bushrangers of Tasmania by 'Cabby'* Launceston, Tas. 1891
DEBENHAM, A.E. *All manner of people* Sydney 1967
DE BOOS, C. ed. *The Congewoi correspondence* Sydney 1874
DE CASTELNAU, F. *Notes of the edible fishes of Victoria* Melbourne 1873
DE HOOG, J. *Skid row dossier* Melbourne 1972
DELAFORCE, W. *The life and experiences of an ex-convict in Port Macquarie, by 'Woomera'* Port Macquarie, N.S.W. [1900]
DELANEY, B. *Narc! inside the Australian Bureau of Narcotics* Sydney 1979
'DELANEY, D.' (J. Sandes) *The captain of the gang* Sydney 1913
The white champion Sydney 1917
DELBRIDGE, A. *Aussie talk* Sydney 1984
DEMARR, J. *Adventures in Australia fifty years ago* London 1893
'DEMONAX' see Cameron, D.
DENIEHY, D.H. *The life and speeches* see Martin, E.A.
'DENISON, C.' (E. Partridge) *Glimpses* London 1928
DENISON, W.T. *Varieties of vice-regal life* 2 vols. London 1870
DENNIS, C.J. *Backblock ballads* Melbourne [1913]
The songs of a sentimental bloke Sydney 1915
The moods of Ginger Mick Sydney 1916
Doreen Sydney 1917
Backblock ballads and later verses Sydney 1918 (first publ. 1913)
Digger Smith Sydney 1918
Rose of Spadgers: a sequel to 'Ginger Mick' Sydney 1924
Random verse Melbourne 1952
DENNY, W.J. *The diggers* London [1919]
A digger at home and abroad Melbourne 1941
DENTON, K. *A walk around my cluttered mind* Melbourne 1968
The breaker Sydney 1973
The thinkable man Sydney 1976
Derwent star and Van Diemen's Land intelligencer Hobart 1810–12
A description of Botany Bay, on the east side of New Holland, in the Indian Seas Lancaster [1787]
DESMOND, V. *The awful Australian* Sydney 1911
DETTMAN, J.F. *Here was glory* Sydney 1944
DEVANEY, J. *The vanished tribes* Sydney 1929
DEVANNY, J. *Out of such fires* New York 1934
Sugar heaven Sydney 1936
The killing of Jacqueline Love Sydney 1942
By tropic sea and jungle Sydney 1944
Bird of paradise Sydney 1945
Travels in North Queensland London 1951
Devil in Sydney; or, barmaids, baldheads, mashers, etc. Sydney 1895
DEVINE, J. *The rats of Tobruk* Sydney 1943
D'EWES, J. *China, Australia and the Pacific Islands, in the years 1855–56* London 1857
DE WINTON, G.J. *Soldiering fifty years ago* London 1898
The diary of an officer of the 16th (Queen's) Lancers. June 16, 1822, to June 16, 1840 Calcutta 1894
DICK, W. *A bunch of ratbags* London 1965
DICKINS, B. *The banana bender* [&] *The death of Minnie* Sydney 1981
The gift of the gab Melbourne 1981
The Crookes of Epping Carlton, Vic. 1984
Digger yarns: the cream of the 'Aussiosities' Sydney 1940
'DINGO, D.' *Australian rhymes and jingles* Fitzroy, Vic. 1871
DINGWALL, J. *Sunday too far away!* Richmond, Vic. 1978
DINGWELL, J. *One string for Nurse Bow* London 1969
The cattleman London 1974
Cane music London 1975
DINNING, H.W. *By-ways on service: notes from an Australian journal* London 1918
Australian scene Sydney 1939
**Dit: the R.A.N. bulletin prepared by the Naval Information Section* Melbourne 1944–45
DIXON, B. *Searching for Aboriginal languages: memoirs of a field worker* St Lucia, Qld. 1984
DIXON, James *Narrative of a voyage to New South Wales, and Van Dieman's Land in the ship Skelton, during the year 1820* Edinburgh 1822
DIXON, John *The condition and capabilities of Van Diemen's Land, as a place of emigration* London 1839
DIXON, R. *The story of J.T. Lang* [Sydney 1943]
DOBIE, W.W. *Recollections of a visit to Port-Phillip, Australia, in 1852–55* Glasgow 1856
DOBSON, R. *Over the frontier* Sydney 1978
DOLLMAN, W. *Bush fancies and campfire yarns* Adelaide 1898
**D.O.M.F. weekly lyre* Alice Springs, N.T. 1941
DONALDSON, R. et al. *Cane!* London 1967
'DOONE, J.' (V. Marshall) *Timely tips for new Australians* London [1926]
DORIEN, R. *Venturing to Australia* London 1951
DORNEY, M. *An adventurous honeymoon: the first motor honeymoon around Australia* Brisbane [1927]
**Double gee (Garners guerrillas): official organ of the A.W.L. League and G.U. depot* Kalgoorlie, W.A. 1943
DOUGHTY, J. *Gold in the blood* Adelaide 1977
DOUGLAS, M. *Follow the sun and other journeys* Adelaide 1978
DOUGLAS, M. & OLDMEADOW, D. *Across the top and other places* Adelaide 1972
DOUGLAS, N. *A far cry: Neil Douglas spinning yarns with Abbie Heathcote* Kangaroo Ground, Vic. 1979
DOUGLASS, Mrs R.D. *A romance at the Antipodes* New York 1890
DOW, J.L. see 'The Special Reporter of "The Leader"'
DOWNING, W.H. *Digger dialects* Melbourne 1919
To the last ridge Melbourne [1920]
DOYLE, M. ed. *Extracts from the letters and journals of George Fletcher Moore, Esq.* London 1834
DRAGE, W. & PAGE, M. *Riverboats and rivermen* Adelaide 1976
DRAKE-BROCKMAN, H. *Sheba Lane* Sydney 1936
On the north-west skyline Perth 1947
The fatal days Sydney 1947
Sydney or the bush Sydney 1948
Men without wives Sydney 1955
ed. *West Coast stories* Sydney 1959
DREW, C. *Reminiscences of Dick Gilbert* Sydney 1917
The doings of Dave Sydney 1919
Rogues & ruses Sydney 1922
DREW, C. & EVANS, I.B. *The grafter* Sydney 1915
'DRYBLOWER' (E.G. Murphy) *Jarrahland jingles* Perth 1908
Dryblower's verses 1894–1926 Perth [1926]
DRYSDALE, I. & DURACK, M. *The end of dreaming* Adelaide 1974
DUBOIS, B. ed. *The high light* Adelaide 1910
DUCKWORTH, A. see *The timber and forests of New South Wales*
DUFFIELD, R. *Rogue bull: the story of Lang Hancock: king of the Pilbara* Sydney 1979
DUFFY, C.G. *My life in two hemispheres* 2 vols. London 1898
DUFFY, J. *The Outsville pub* Sydney 1963

DUGAN, C.C. *An old Tasmanian road* Hobart 1920
DUGAN, M. ed. *The early dreaming: Australian children's authors on childhood* Milton, Qld. 1980
DUGUID, C. *From the Suez Canal to Gaza with the Australian Light Horse* Adelaide [c.1919]
DUNCAN, N. *Australian byways: the narrative of a sentimental traveller* New York 1915
DUNCAN, S.T. *Journal of a voyage to Australia* Edinburgh 1869
DUNCAN-KEMP, A.M. *Our sandhill country* Sydney 1933
Where strange paths go down Brisbane 1952
Our channel country Sydney 1961
Where strange gods call Brisbane 1968
Duncan's weekly register, of politics, facts, and general literature Sydney 1843–44
DUNDERDALE, G. *Prairie and bush* London 1891
The book of the bush London 1898
DUNN, J. *How to play football Australian style* Kent Town, S. Aust. 1973
DUNSTAN, K. *Knockers* North Melbourne 1972
Sports Melbourne 1973
Ratbags Sydney 1979
Footy: an Aussie Rules dictionary South Melbourne 1983
DURACK, M. *Keep him my country* London 1955, Sydney 1966
Kings in grass castles London 1959
Sons in the saddle London 1983
DURACK, M. & E. *All-about: the story of a black community on Argyle Station, Kimberley* Sydney 1935, Perth 1940
Dusts of time (gold dust, red dust and bull dust): Lake Cargelligo and district 1873–1973 [Lake Cargelligo, N.S.W.] 1973
DUSTY, S. & LAPSLEY, J. *Walk a country mile* Adelaide 1979
DUTHIE, G. *I had 50,000 bosses: memoirs of a Labor backbencher 1946–1975* Sydney 1984
DUTHIE, S.W. *Fidlers Creek* Adelaide 1979
Duties of a shepherd in New South Wales [London 1842]
DUTTON, F. *South Australia and its mines* London 1846
DUTTON, G. *Andy* London 1968
The wedge-tailed eagle South Melbourne 1980
DWYER, J.F. *Leg-irons on wings* Melbourne 1949
DWYER, V.G. *Conquering Hal* London 1916
DYER, J. *'Captain Blood'* London 1965
DYSON, E. *Rhymes from the mines* Sydney 1896
Below and on top Melbourne 1898
Fact'ry 'ands Sydney 1906
In the roaring fifties London 1906
The missing link Sydney 1908
Tommy the hawker and Snifter his boy Sydney 1911
Benno and some of the push Sydney 1911
The loves of Lancelot Sydney 1914
Spats' fact'ry Sydney 1914
'Hello, soldier!': Khaki verse Melbourne 1919

'E.H.' (E. Hulme) *Advance Australia: a settler's 35 years' experience in Victoria, Australia, and how £6 8s. became £8,000* Melbourne 1891
'E.S.H.' *Narrative of a trip from Sydney to Peak Downs, Queensland, and back* London 1864
EAGAR, E. *Letters to the Rt. Hon. Robert Peel .. on the advantages of New South Wales and Van Diemen's Land as penal settlements* London 1824
EAGLE, C. *Hail and farewell* Melbourne 1971
Who could love the nightingale? Melbourne 1973
Four faces, wobbly mirror South Melbourne 1976
EAGLESON, R.D. & MCKIE, I. *The terminology of Australian national football* 3 parts. Sydney 1968–69
EARDLY-WILMOT, C. *Six letters on subjects of colonial interest* Hobart 1855
EARL, G.W. *Enterprise, discoveries, and adventures in Australia* London [c. 1846]
A handbook for colonists in tropical Australia Penang 1863
EARLE, H. *Ups and downs; or incidents of Australian life* London 1861
Early days see *Western Australian Historical Society journal*
EARP, G.B. *The gold colonies of Australia* London 1852, rev. ed. 1853
ed. *What we did in Australia* London 1853
EAST, J.J. *The Aborigines of South and Central Australia* [Adelaide 1889]
EASTMAN, H.M. *Memoirs of a sheepman* Deniliquin, N.S.W. 1953
EASTMAN W.R. & HUNT, A.C. *The parrots of Australia* Sydney 1966
EASTON, W.R. *Report on the north Kimberley district of Western Australia* Perth 1922
EASTWOOD, J.G. *More about Cairns: 3. Recollections of a varied life* Brisbane 1946
Echoes from the bushland Sydney 1881
Eclectic: journal of the North Adelaide Young Men's Society Adelaide 1871–72
Ecos Canberra 1974–
EDEN, A. *Places in the sun* London 1926
EDEN, C.H. *My wife and I in Queensland* London 1872
The fortunes of the Fletchers London 1873
Australia's heroes 3rd ed. London [1875]
EDEN, G.E.M. *Bush ballads* London [1907]
EDMONDS, C. *Dangerous marine animals of the Indo-Pacific region* Newport, Vic. 1975
EDWARDS, J.A. *Gilbert Gogger; or, Australasia veritas* Mackay, Qld. 1876
EDWARDS, Reginald G. *The Australian garden book* Sydney 1950
EDWARDS, Robert *Australian Aboriginal art* Canberra 1979
ed. *Aboriginal art in Australia* Sydney 1978
EDWARDS, Robert & GUERIN, B. *Aboriginal bark paintings* Adelaide 1969
Arnhem Land in colour Adelaide 1970
EDWARDS, Ron *Australian folk songs* Holloway Beach, Qld. 1972
Australian bawdy ballads Holloway Beach, Qld. 1973
Australian traditional bush crafts Melbourne 1975
The Australian yarn Adelaide 1977
Skills of the Australian bushman Adelaide 1979
Yarns & ballads of the Australian bush Adelaide 1981
EDWARDS, S.H. *Shooting and shooting bushcraft* Sydney 1951
EGBERT, H. *Pretty cockey! or, the life & death of a terrible flirt* Newcastle, N.S.W. 1889
EGGLETON, G.B. *Last of the lantern swingers* Mildura, Vic. 1982
Eight hours' history Launceston, Tas. [1870] (reprinted from the *Australian journal*)
'EIGHT YEARS RESIDENT' (E. Thorne) *The queen of colonies; or, Queensland as I knew it* London 1876
Elders weekly Perth 1922– (1 Jan. 1963–14 Nov. 1974 as *Elders GM weekly*)
ELDERSHAW, F. *Australia as it really is* London 1854
ELDERSHAW, M.B. *My Australia* London 1939
ELDRIDGE, M *Walking the dog and other stories* St Lucia, Qld. 1984
ELIJAH, J.W. *The rural school: its problems and functions* Melbourne 1926
ELKIN, A.P. *The Australian Aborigines* Sydney 1938.
3rd ed. 1954, 4th ed. 1964
Aboriginal men of high degree Sydney 1946
ELLINGHAUS, R.M. *Coping with a bust* Prahran, Vic. 1979
ELLIOTT, B. ed. *The Jindyworobaks* St. Lucia, Qld. 1979
ELLIOTT, S. *Fifty years of colonial life* Melbourne [1887]
ELLIOTT, S.L. *Water under the bridge* South Melbourne 1977
ELLIS, D. *A screw loose* Sydney 1965
ELLIS, G. *Hey doc, me mate's sick!* Adelaide 1980
Hey doc, let's go fishing! Adelaide 1981
ELLIS, M.H. *The long lead: across Australia by motor-car* London 1927
The red road: the story of the capture of the Lang party by Communists, instructed from Moscow Sydney [1932]
ELLIS, R. *Bush safari* Adelaide 1982
ELLIS, V.R. *Trucanini* Hobart 1976
Elliston's Hobart Town almanack and (Ross's) Van Diemen's Land annual, for 1837 Hobart 1837
ELSUM, W.H. *Australia and other poems* Melbourne [1911]
EMERSON, E.S. *A shanty entertainment* Melbourne 1910 (first publ. 1904)
See also 'White, M.'
The emigrant's friend; or authentic guide to South Australia London 1848

The emigrant's guide to New South Wales, Van Diemen's Land, Lower Canada, Upper Canada, and New Brunswick London 1832
The emigrant's guide to Port Curtis and the Canoona gold regions . . by Leonard Pearson Melbourne 1858
Emigrants' letters . . published for the Committee of the Emigrants' School Fund London 1850
Emigrant's wife; or, one in ten thousand 3 vols. London 1871
EMMETT, E.T. *A short history of Tasmania* Sydney 1937
Empire Sydney 1850–75
Emu Melbourne 1901–
Emu Bay times see *North-western advocate*
'ENDEAVOUR', H.M. Bark. Log 1768, 69, 70 & 71. NLA MS 3
ENGEL, F.G. *The land rights of Australian Aborigines* [Sydney] 1965
England and her colonies considered in relation to the Aborigines London 1841
ENGLAND, E.M. *Where the turtles dance* Sydney 1950
Enobesra: cadets handbook Canberra 1972
ERICKSEN, R. *West of centre* London 1972
ERICKSON, R. *Orchids of the west* Perth 1951
Triggerplants Perth 1958
ERICKSON, R. et al. *Flowers and plants of Western Australia* Sydney 1973
Ern Malley's journal Melbourne 1952–55
'ERRO' *Squattermania; or, phases of Antipodean life* London 1880
ERSKINE, J.E. *A short account of the late discoveries of gold in Australia with notes of a visit to the gold districts* London 1852
An essay on politics in verse Ballarat, Vic. 1867
ESSON, L. *The woman tamer* Sydney 1976 (first publ. Melbourne 1911)
Three short plays Melbourne [1911]
Red gums and other verses Melbourne 1912
The time is not yet ripe Sydney 1973 (first publ. Melbourne 1912)
Dead timber London 1920 (first publ. Melbourne 1911)
The Southern Cross and other plays Melbourne 1946
ETHERIDGE, R. et al. *Lord Howe Island: its zoology, geology, and physical characteristics* Sydney 1889 (Australian Museum memoirs 2)
Eureka! selected poems and stories Canberra 1963
**Euripidean: the lighter moments of those who anticipate doing serious work* England 1916–18
**Euripides ensign: [journal published on board 'Euripides']* At sea May–June 1915
EVANS, G.C. *Stories told around the camp fire* Sandhurst, Vic. 1881
EVANS, G.W. *A geographical, historical, and topographical description of Van Diemen's Land, with important hints to emigrants* London 1822
EVANS, W. ed. *Diary of a Welsh swagman 1869–1894* South Melbourne 1975
EVANS, W.J. *Rhymes without reason* Adelaide 1898
EVATT, H.V. *The king and his dominion governors* London 1936
EVERETT, T.H. *Living trees of the world* London 1969
EVERIST, S.L. *Poisonous plants of Australia* Sydney 1974
EVERS, L.H. *Pattern of conquest* Sydney 1954
EVERS, N. & INGPEN, R. *Tasmania: paradise and beyond* Adelaide 1978
EWART, A.J. & DAVIES, O.B. *The flora of the Northern Territory* Melbourne 1917
EWERS, J.K. *Fire on the wind* London 1935
The story of the pipe-line: being an account of the construction of the Coolgardie water scheme Perth [1935]
Tales from the dead heart Sydney [1944]
For heroes to live in Melbourne 1948
With the sun on my back Sydney 1953
Long enough for a joke: an autobiography Fremantle, W.A. 1983
Examiner Launceston, Tas. 1901– (continues *Launceston examiner*)
**Exhaust manifold: safety valve of the 162 Australian General Transport Company* New Guinea 1943–44
**Expeditionary: official chronicle of the 6th and 7th Infantry Battalions A.I.F. voyage 'Hororata' A.20 194* At sea 1914
Express Sydney 1880–86 (continued by *Illustrated express*)
Extract of a despatch from Lieutenant-Governor Stirling to the Right Honourable Sir George Murray, dated Perth, Western Australia, 20th January 1830; containing information relative to the progress of the settlement at Swan River London 1830 (G.B.P.P. H.C. 675)
Extracts of letters from Arthur Phillip, Esq., Governor of New South Wales, to Lord Sydney; to which is annexed a description of Norfolk Island, by Philip Gidley King, Esq. London 1791
Extracts of letters &c. [from Swan River] series 1–3 London 1830
Extracts from the papers and proceedings of the Aborigines Protection Society London 1839
Extracts from Australian and Van Diemen's Land journals, referring to the constitutions proposed in 1849 for the different Australian colonies [London 1850]
Extracts from the Hobart Town gazette Hobart 1848–49
'EYE WITNESS' *A voyage to Australia and back, a visit to the gold diggings, and general information for emigrants* London 1859
EYRE, E.J. *Journals of expeditions of discovery into Central Australia and overland from Adelaide to King George's Sound in the years 1840–1* 2 vols. London 1845
EYRE, H. *Hilarities* Sydney 1929

FACEY, A.B. *A fortunate life* Fremantle, W.A. 1981
FADDEN, A. *They called me Artie: the memoirs of Sir Arthur Fadden* Milton, Qld. 1969
*FADDEN, R.M. Daily diary: Australian Land Clearing Team. 2 Mar.–28 Aug. 1968
FADEN, W. *A chart of the Indian Ocean* London 4 June 1803
FAHEY, J.J. *Slim Sullivan hits the wallaby* London [1946]
FAIR, R. *A treasury of Anzac humour* Brisbane 1965
FAIRBRIDGE, R. *Pinjarra: the building of a farm school* London 1937
**'Fair dinkum': journal published on board 'Nestor'* At sea 1918
FAIRFAX, J. *The colonies of Australia* London [1852]
FAIRFAX, J.F. *Run o' waters* Sydney [1948]
FAIRFAX, W. ed. *Handbook to Australasia* Melbourne 1859
FALK, D.G. *Rick: or, the récidiviste* London 1891
FALLA, R.P. *Knocking about* Donald, Vic. 1976
FALLON, J.T. *The 'Murray Valley vineyard' Albury, New South Wales, and 'Australian vines and wines'* Melbourne 1874
FARJEON, B.L. *In Australian wilds* London 1870
FARQUHAR, R.N. *Agricultural education in Australia* Hawthorn, Vic. 1966
Farrago Melbourne 1925–
FARRELL, A.E. *The vengeance* London 1963
FARRELL, J. *How he died and other poems* Sydney 1897
My sundowner and other verses Sydney 1904
FARWELL, G. *Down Argent Street: the story of Broken Hill* Sydney 1948
Traveller's tracks Melbourne 1949
Land of mirage Melbourne 1950
Surf music and other stories Sydney 1950
The outside track Melbourne 1951
Vanishing Australians Adelaide 1961
Cape York to the Kimberleys Adelaide 1962
FAULK, L.E & O.B. *The Australian alternative* New York 1975
FAVENC, E. *Reports on country in the Northern Territory* Adelaide 1883
The last of six: tales of the Austral tropics Sydney 1893
FAWCETT, J.W. *A narrative of the terrible cyclone and flood in Townsville, North Queensland, January 25th, 26th, 27th and 28th, 1896* Townsville, Qld. 1896
FEARNSIDE, G.H. *Sojourn in Tobruk* Sydney 1944
The golden ram Sydney 1965
Half to remember: the reminiscences of an Australian infantry soldier in World War II Sydney 1975
ed. *Bayonets abroad: a history of the 2/13th Battalion A.I.F. in the Second World War* Sydney 1953
FEARN-WANNAN, W. *Australian folklore: a dictionary of lore, legends and popular illusions* Melbourne 1970
See also Wannan, B.
FEILDING, W. *Australian trans-continental railway: diary of journey of the trans-continental railway survey expedition from Mitchell to Point Parker, Queensland* London [1881]
FELDT, E.A. *The Coast Watchers* Melbourne 1946

Fences and fencing 2nd ed. Sydney 1914 (N.S.W. Dept. of Agriculture. Farmers' bulletin no. 74)
FENNER, C. *Bunyips and billabongs: an Australian out of doors* Sydney 1933
Mostly Australian Melbourne 1944
Gathered moss Melbourne 1946
FENTON, C. *Flying doctor* Melbourne 1947
FENTON, F.W. *This side up* Melbourne [1878]
FENTON, J. *A history of Tasmania: its discovery in 1642 to the present time* London 1884
Bush life in Tasmania fifty years ago Devonport, Tas. 1974 (first publ. London 1891)
FERGUSON, C.D. *The experiences of a Forty-niner during thirty-four years' residence in California and Australia* Cleveland, U.S.A. 1888
FERGUSON, D. *Vicissitudes of bush life in Australia and New Zealand* London 1891
FERGUSON, J. *White Australia* Sydney [1914]
'FERRES, A.' (J.W. Kevin) *The free selector and other verses* Sydney 1901
FERRIS, L. *John Heathlyn of the Otway* London [1916]
A few letters from Queensland farmers and others London [c. 1886]
FIDDIAN, J.R. *Robert Mitchell of the Inland* Melbourne 1931
FIDLER, J.C. et al. *The biology of apple and pear storage* Canberra 1973
FIELD, B. *First fruits of Australian poetry* Sydney 1819
2nd ed. 1823
ed. *Geographical memoirs on New South Wales by various hands* London 1825
FIELD, C.F. *Reminiscences* see Morphett, G.C. ed.
FIELD, M. *Oz shrink lit.: Australian classic literature cut down to size* Ringwood, Vic. 1983
FIELD, R. *All over down under* London 1965
'FIFTY-THREE YEARS' MINER' *So long* Sydney 1908
Film weekly Sydney 1926–73
FINCH-HATTON, H. *Advance Australia!* 2nd ed. London 1886
FINGLETON, J. *Fingleton on cricket* London 1972
FINLAYSON, H.H. *The red centre* Sydney 1935
FINN, E. *The chronicles of early Melbourne 1835 to 1852 . . by 'Garryowen'* 2 vols. Melbourne 1888
**First aid post: official organ of 2nd Field Ambulance* Anzac 1915
**First post: magazine of the 2/1st Btn. A.I.F.* Palestine 1940–44
**First post: official camp newspaper of the 4th Infantry Brigade* Melbourne 1939
Fish & fisheries Sydney 1980
FISHER, A. *A policy for Australia: speech by A. Fisher at Gympie, 30th March 1909* Gympie, Qld. 1909
FISHER, E. *The kiss of Dolly Day* Melbourne 1912
Fishing information & services handbook Sydney 1983
FITZGERALD, J.F.V. *Australia* London 1881
FITZGERALD, R.T. *The secondary school at sixes and sevens* Hawthorn, Vic. 1970
FITZPATRICK, B. *Australian Natives' Association 1871–1961* Melbourne 1961
FITZPATRICK, J. *The bicycle and the bush* Melbourne 1980
FITZPATRICK, J.C.L. *'The good old days'* Sydney 1900
When we were boys together: reminiscences of the Hawkesbury district Windsor, N.S.W. 1909
The good old days of Molong Parramatta, N.S.W. 1913
Those were the days: being a record of the doings of the men and women of the Hawkesbury 50 years ago and more Sydney 1923
Five plays for stage, radio and television St Lucia, Qld. 1977
FLANAGAN, R.J. *The Aborigines of Australia* Sydney 1888
FLAXMAN, G. tr. *South Australia as it is: by the Rev. Augustus Kavel* Adelaide 1845
FLEAY, D. *Nightwatchmen of bush and plain* Brisbane 1968
FLEMING, W.M. *The hunted piccaninnies* London 1927
FLETCHER, C.B. *The Murray Valley: a three thousand mile run* Sydney 1926
FLETCHER, H. *The Waybacks in town and at home* Sydney 1902
Dads Wayback: his work Sydney 1904
FLETCHER, H.B. *Boundary riders of Egypt* Melbourne [1919]
FLETCHER, J.P. & HILLS, J.F. *Conscription under camouflage* [Adelaide 1919]
FLETCHER, L. ed. *Pioneers of education in Western Australia* Nedlands, W.A. 1982
FLETCHER, P. ed. *Queensland: its resources and institutions* Brisbane 1886
FLINDERS, M. *Observations on the coasts of Van Diemen's Land, on Bass's Strait and its islands, and on part of the coasts of New South Wales* London 1801
A voyage to Terra Australis; undertaken for the purpose of completing the discovery of that vast country, and prosecuted in the years 1801, 1802, and 1803, in His Majesty's Ship the Investigator 2 vols. London 1814
FLOOD, James *New Norcia: the remarkable Aborigines institution of the Australian Commonwealth* London 1908
FLOOD, Josephine *Archaeology of the dreamtime* Sydney 1983
**Flotilla echo* At sea and Malta 1917–18
FLYNN, E. *Beam ends* London 1937
My wicked, wicked ways London 1959
FLYNN, F. *Northern gateway* Sydney 1963
Northern frontiers Sydney 1968
FLYNN, J. *The bushman's companion: a handful of hints for outbackers* Melbourne 1910
FOGARTY, L.G. *Kargun* North Brisbane 1980
FOLEY, B. *Shearers' poems* Alfred Cove, W.A. 1975
FOLJAMBE, C.G.S. *Three years on the Australian station* London 1868
Football record Melbourne 1912–
FOOTE, T.V. *My weird wooing* Melbourne [1888]
FOOTT, Mrs J. *Sketches of life in the bush* Sydney 1872
Footy – and the clubs that make it Melbourne [1954]
Footy fan Melbourne 1963–64
FORD, C.P. *The emigrant family* London 1851
Ford news Sydney ?1937–58 (title varies as *Hastings Deerings news*)
FORDE, J.M. see 'Old Chum'
**Fore & aft: 42 Aust. Landing Craft Coy. A.I.F.* New Guinea 1945
FOREMAN, E. *The history and adventures of a Queensland pioneer* Brisbane 1928
The forestry question in New South Wales with special reference to the present and future timber supply: issued by the New South Wales branch of the Australian Forest League Sydney 1915
'A FORMER POLICE OFFICER' (I. Solomons) *Adventures, memoirs, former trial, transportation & escapes, of that notorious fence and receiver of stolen goods, Isaac Solomons* London 1829
FORREST, A. *North-west exploration: journal of expedition from De Grey to Port Darwin* Perth 1880
'FORREST, D.' (D. Denholm) *The last blue sea* London 1959
The hollow woodheap Brisbane 1962
FORREST, J. *Explorations in Australia* London 1875
FORREST, M. *Hibiscus heart* London 1926
Reaping roses London [1928]
FORSYTH, C. *The Governor-General* Camberwell, Vic. 1976
FORSYTH, W.D. *The myth of the open spaces* Melbourne 1942
**Fortress chronicle: weekly paper of the HQ Australian AA & Frt Coy RAE Torres Strait forces* In the field 1944
FOSTER, D. *North south west* South Melbourne 1973
Plumbum Ringwood, Vic. 1983
Dog rock Ringwood, Vic. 1985
FOSTER, J.F.L. *The new colony of Victoria, formerly Port Phillip* London 1851
FOSTER, T. *Review of the labours of several explorers of Australia* Melbourne 1863
Four colonies of Australia London 1852
FOWLER, F. *Southern lights and shadows* London 1859
FOX, F. *From the old dog* Melbourne 1908
FOX, L. *The strange story of the Eureka flag* Sydney 1963
ed. *Depression down under* Sydney 1977
FOX, M. *Possum magic* Adelaide 1983
FOX, P. *The unsuccessful colonist; his fortunes, misfortunes, observations, and opinions* Adelaide 1878

FRANCIS, Alexander *Then and now: the story of a Queenslander* London 1935
FRANCIS, Angela [*The Francis family: pioneer life in Queensland*] East Grinstead, England 1906
FRANCIS, W.D. *Australian rain-forest trees* Brisbane 1929
rev. ed. 1951
3rd ed. 1970
Frank Gardiner, or bushranging in 1863 Sydney 1863
FRANKLIN, Jane Diary of a visit to South Australia in December 1840 to January, 1841. NLA MS 114/7
FRANKLIN, John *Narrative of some passages in the history of Van Diemen's Land* n.p. [1845]
FRANKLIN, M. *My brilliant career* Edinburgh 1901
Some everyday folk and Dawn Edinburgh 1909
All that swagger Sydney 1936, 1980
My career goes bung Melbourne 1946
See also 'Brent of Bin Bin'
FRANKLIN, M. & CUSACK, D. *Pioneers on parade* Sydney 1939
FRASER, E. *Narrative of the capture, sufferings, and miraculous escape* New York 1837
FRASER, J. *The Aborigines of Australia: stories about the Kamilaroi tribe* Maitland, N.S.W. 1882
The Aborigines of Australia: their ethnic position and relations London [1888]
The Aborigines of New South Wales Sydney 1892
FRAUCA, H. *In a new country* Perth [1956]
Harry Frauca's book of insects Brisbane 1968
FREAME, W. *Old memories of the Hawkesbury, Nepean and Hunter River districts* Parramatta, N.S.W. 1918
FREEMAN, J. *Lights and shadows of Melbourne life* London 1888
FREEMAN, P. *The woolshed: a Riverina anthology* Melbourne 1980
FREEMAN, W.G. & CHANDLER, S.E. *The world's commercial products* London 1908
Freeman's journal Sydney 1850–1932 (continued by *Catholic freeman's journal*)
FRENCH, S. *Hey phantom singlet* Sydney 1975
Fresh evidence from early goldmining publications, 1851–1860 Sydney 1966 (University of Sydney Australian Language Research Centre. Occasional paper no. 9)
'FREYDON, N.' (A.J. Dawson) see *The record of Nicholas Freydon*
FRIEND, D. *Gunner's diary* Sydney 1943
'A FRIEND TO TRUTH' *A true picture of Australia, its merits and demerits* Glasgow 1839
FRITH, H.J. *The mallee-fowl* Sydney 1962
Waterfowl in Australia Sydney 1967
Pigeons and doves of Australia Adelaide 1982
FROGGATT, W.W. *Australian insects* Sydney [1907]
Australian spiders and their allies Sydney 1935
The insect book London 1948
Frontier news Sydney 1934– (continues *A.I.M. frontier news*)
FROST, D.J. *Crown lands of New South Wales: how and where to get them* Sydney [1893]
FROST, J. *The horrors of convict life* London 1856
FROST, L. *No place for a nervous lady* Ringwood, Vic. 1984
FROUDE, J.A. *Oceana: or England and her colonies* Hobart 1973 (first publ. London 1886)
FRY, H.P. *A letter to the householders of Hobarton, on the effects of transportation, upon the morals and moral condition of the colony* Hobart 1847
A full and true account of the murder of Peter Brown a shepherd who was killed at Franklin Harbour by four Aboriginal natives of Port Lincoln n.p. [1856]
FULLBROOK, G. *A house called Kangaroo* London 1968
FULLER, B. *The Nullarbor story* Adelaide 1970
West of the Bight Adelaide 1972
The Ghan: the story of the Alice Springs railway Adelaide 1975
Nullarbor lifelines Adelaide 1977
FULLER, L. *Wollongong's native trees* Wollongong, N.S.W. 1980
FULLERTON, M.E. *Bark house days* Melbourne 1921
The Australian bush London 1928
**Full-times gazette: magazine of the 13 Bn V.D.C.* Rockhampton, Qld. 1943–44
FURNISS, H. *Australian sketches made on tour* London [1899]
FURPHY, J. *Such is life: being certain extracts from the diary of Tom Collins* Sydney 1903
Poems Melbourne 1916
Rigby's romance Sydney 1946
The buln-buln and the brolga Sydney 1948
**Furphy flyer: official organ of the 2/24 Australian Infantry Battalion* Tobruk 1941–42

GABBEDY, J.P. *The forgotten pioneers: axemen – their work, times and sport* Fremantle, W.A. 1981
**Gabber: Queensland lines of communication Army Trade Training Depot* Queensland 1942–45
GABY, J. *The restless waterfront* Sydney 1974
Gadfly Adelaide 1906–09
GAFFNEY, J.H. *Populate or perish* [Perth, 1943]
GALBRAITH, J. *Wildflowers of Victoria* Melbourne [1950]
A field guide to the wild flowers of south-east Australia Sydney 1977
Garden in a valley Hawthorn, Vic. 1985 (first publ. 1939)
GALE, F. ed. *We are bosses ourselves* Canberra 1983
GALL, I. *Fishing for the fun of it* Milton, Qld. 1970
GALLOP, R.G. In the 'never never' land: essay describing life on Lanark Downs cattle station, Clermont, Queensland 11 Dec. 1886–19 Jan. 1887. ML MS 488
GAMMAGE, B. *The broken years* Canberra 1974
GANE, D.M. *New South Wales and Victoria in 1885* London 1886
GARDINER, J. *Twenty-five years on the stage* Adelaide [c.1891]
GARDINER, J.S. *Coral reefs and atolls* London 1931
GARDNER, A.F. *Flooding of the mine* Fitzroy, Vic. [c.1880]
GARDNER, C.A. *West Australian wildflowers* Perth 1938
Wildflowers of Western Australian 3rd ed. by H.F. Parkinson Perth, 1968
GARDNER, C.A. & BENNETTS, H.W. *The toxic plants of Western Australia* Perth 1956
GARE, N. *The fringe dwellers* London 1961
GARLAND, B. *The Pitt Street prospector* Barraba, N.S.W. 1969
GARNER, H. *Monkey grip* Melbourne 1977
Honour and other people's children Melbourne 1980
Postcards from Surfers Ringwood, Vic. 1985
GARNET, G. *A Barrier bride* Melbourne 1898
GARNETT, T.R. *Stumbling on melons* Melbourne 1984
GARNSEY, Mrs A.H. *The romance of the Huon River* Melbourne 1947
'GARRYOWEN' see Finn, E.
GARSTIN, C. *The mud larks* Sydney 1918
GARTRELL, M. *Dear primitive: a nurse among the Aborigines* Sydney 1957
GARVEY, K. *Tales of my Uncle Harry* Sydney 1978
Absolutely Australian Sydney 1979
Rhymes of a ratbag Richmond, Vic. 1981
GASK, A. *The secret of the garden* London 1924
GASTON, A. *Coolgardie gold* London [1939]
GATES, W. *Recollections of life in Van Dieman's Land* Lockport, U.S.A. 1850, Sydney 1961
GAUNT, M. *Dave's sweetheart* Melbourne 1894
Gayzette Sydney 1974
GEDNEY, C.W. *Foreign cage birds* 2 vols. London [1877–79]
GEE, L.C.E. *Bush tracks and gold fields* Adelaide 1926
Geelong advertiser Geelong, Vic. 1840–
GELBIN, G. ed. *Australians have a word for it* Berlin 1964
GENDERS, R. *Scented flora of the world* London 1977
General orders see *New South Wales general . . orders*
'A GENTLEMAN JUST RETURNED FROM THE SETTLEMENT' *An account of the English colony at Botany Bay, and other settlements in New South Wales, from their first establishment to the present time* London 1808
GEOGHEGAN, E. *The currency lass* Sydney 1976
GEORGE, E. *Two at Daly Waters* Melbourne 1945
January and August Melbourne 1947

re and the Aborigine in Australia 1770–1975 Brisbane

far from home London 1936
r cry: Neil Douglas spinning yarns with Abbie Heathcote
d, Vic. 1979
ng in New South Wales Sydney 1962
963
g: a season on Monaro Sydney 1968
to swim correctly Sydney 1930
827. University of Tasmania Archives R.12
vations on the colonies of New South Wales and Van
utta 1832
nd adventures in New South Wales 2 vols. London

Fanny: women's letters to and from New South Wales,
tters Bay, N.S.W. 1985
Birrell's London 1896
new-chum farmer Sydney 1897
s of Rachel Henning Sydney 1952, 1966
rrl': the first surveyor and other Aboriginal legends

nates ed. by B.L. Lawson & J. Le Gay Brereton

ney 1900–04
or my early life London 1886
ck reality: Aboriginal camps and housing in remote
979
Sydney 1978
an library 4 vols. Richmond, Vic. 1983
e, J. Boozing out in Melbourne pubs Sydney 1980
art 1845–46 (continues Hobart Town herald, con-
n herald or Tasmanian southern reporter)
Sydney 1938
n Sydney 1961
e Sydney 1963
nent Melbourne 1963
country Sydney 1975
dney 1977
ubble Sydney 1936
et Melbourne 1913
ization and depommification of an artful English
53
ustralian soldier Sydney [1944]
s shining London 1971
elbourne 1959
nes rolling home Sydney 1976
ses for Dolly [&] The Tatty Hollow story Sydney

ning [&] The golden oldies Woollahra, N.S.W.

warden, The Netherlands 1977
n tour at the Antipodes in 1861–1862 London

e wheels 1967 in Plays Melbourne 1970
ays Melbourne 1970
agination Sydney 1973
rne 1974
, G. The barracker's bible Melbourne 1983
' London 1925
ngwood, Vic. 1985
elbourne 1980
loneliness London 1937
ne 1940
elbourne 1937
g Sydney 1947
ney 1951
d nearest the stars: a journey by taxi across Aus-

ne 1968

Hill, R. & F. *What we saw in Australia* London 1875
Hill, R. & Thornton, G. *Notes on the Aborigines of New South Wales* Sydney 1892
Hill, W.R.O. *Forty-five years experience in North Queensland* Brisbane 1907
Hilliard, M. *Running through the rain* London 1964
Excuse me, Mr Sweetenham London 1968
Hilliard, W. *The people in between: the Pitjantjatjara people of Ernabella* London 1968
Hill's life in New South Wales Sydney 1832–33 (final issue has title *The weekly observer*)
Hindmarsh, M. *Letters 1821–1843* Sydney 1945
**Hindquarters bulletin* New Guinea 1943
Hinkins, J.T. *Life amongst the native race* Melbourne 1884
Hints on emigration to the new settlement on the Swan and Canning Rivers London 1829
An historical narrative of the discovery of New Holland and New South Wales London [1786]
History of Botany Bay, in New Holland Bristol [1787]
The history of New South Wales (by James O'Hara) London 1817
History of the Berry Ministry (issued by *The argus*) Melbourne 1879
Hives, F. & Lumley, G. *The journal of a jackaroo* London 1930
Hobart Town almanack Hobart 1829–38 (title varies as *Ross's Hobart Town almanack and Van Diemen's Land annual* (1835–36) and *Elliston's Hobart Town almanack, and Ross's Van Diemen's Land annual* (1837)
Hobart Town courier Hobart 1827–40 (continued by *The courier*)
Hobart Town gazette Hobart 1816–27 (20 Aug.–31 Dec. 1825 has title *Colonial times*)
Hobart Town herald Hobart 1845–47 (subtitle varies, July 1845–Mar. 1846 has title *Herald of Tasmania*)
Hobart Town magazine Hobart 1833–34
Hobarton guardian Hobart 1847–54 (continues *The guardian*, incorporated in *The Hobarton mercury*)
Hobarton mercury Hobart 1854–June 1860 (title varies, continued by *The mercury*)
Hodge, H. *Death in the morning* Sydney 1938
Hodges, M. *Veil of time* Melbourne 1945
Hodgkinson, C. *Australia, from Port Macquarie to Moreton Bay, with descriptions of the natives* London 1845
Hodgson, A. *Emigration to the Australian settlements* London 1849
Hodgson, C.P. *Reminiscences of Australia* London 1846
Hogan, B. *Follow the game* Melbourne 1968, 3rd ed. Adelaide 1973
6th ed. 1983
Hogan, T.M. & Gye, H. *The tight little island: a trip through Tasmania* Hobart 1914
'Hogbotel & Ffuckes' *Snatches & lays* Melbourne 1973
Hogue, O. *Trooper Bluegum at the Dardanelles* London [1916]
The cameliers London 1919
Holdsworth, P.J. *Station hunting on the Warrego: Australia: at the valley of the Popran: and other poems* Sydney 1885
Holford, G. *Letter to the Rt. Hon. the Secretary of State for the Home Department* London 1827
Holman, James *A voyage round the world, including travels in . . Australasia* vol. IV. London 1835
Holman, Joseph *'The Aussies' – they're a weird lot!* Edgecliff, N.S.W. 1980
Holmes, C.H. *We find Australia* London 1933
Holmes, E.L. *The pioneer motor car trip of Australia* Melbourne 1900
Holmes, J. *The punter* Adelaide 1944
Is it dinkum? Adelaide 1945
Holmes, O.W. *Poems of Oliver Wendell Holmes* rev. ed. Boston 1878
Holt, A.J. *Wheat farms of Victoria* Melbourne 1946
Holt, J. *Memoirs of Joseph Holt* ed. by T. Crofton Croker 2 vols. London 1838
Holt, W.E. *Your friend Ben* Adelaide 1945
Holth, T. & Barnaby, J. *Cattlemen of the high country* Adelaide 1980
Holthouse, H. *S'pose I die: the story of Evelyn Maunsell* Sydney 1973
Home beautiful see *Australian home beautiful*

George, R. *Sandy Lee live at Nui Dat* Sydney 1983
**Georges gazette: special number on WAAF AWAS MSL WRANS AAMWS AWLA etc.* Melbourne 1943
Gerald, F. *A millionaire in memories* London 1936
Gerstaecker, F. *Narrative of a journey round the world* London 1853
Life in the bush n.p. [c. 1856]
The two convicts London 1857
'Ghurka, N.' *Graft: startling disclosures of corruption in the Victorian police force* Melbourne [c.1930]
Gibbs, J. *A bitch called Tracy* Sydney 1975
Gibbs, M. *Gumnut babies* Sydney 1916
Snugglepot and Cuddlepie Sydney 1918
Gibson, C. *Life among convicts* 2 vols. London 1863
Gibson, G.H. see 'Ironbark'
Gilbert, K. *End of dreamtime* Sydney 1971
Because a white man'll never do it Sydney 1973
Living black Melbourne 1977
People are legends St Lucia, Qld. 1978
Gilbert, M. ed. *Personalities and stories of the early Orbost district* Orbost, Vic. 1972
Giles, E. *Giles's explorations, 1875* Adelaide, 1877 (S.A.P.P. 1876 vol. III. no. 22)
Australia twice traversed 2 vols. London 1889
Giles, J.M. *Migrant Australia* London 1960
Giles, K. *Death and Mr Prettyman* London 1967
Gilks, E. see Y.O.-B.A.
Gill, W. *Petermann journey* Adelaide 1968
Gillen, F.J. *Diary* Adelaide 1968
Gillespie, M. ed. *'Into the hollow mountains'* North Fitzroy, Vic. 1974
Gilmore, M. *Hound of the road* Sydney 1922
The tilted cart Sydney 1925
Old days: old ways, a book of recollections Sydney 1934
More recollections Sydney 1935
Giovanni in botany: or the libertine transported London 1822
Gladstone, J.J. *The tragedy of Gallipoli* Melbourne [1920]
Gladwin, P. *The desert in the heart* London 1952
The long beat home London 1954
Glass, D. *Australian fantasy* London 1937
Glasson, W.R. *Musings in my saddle* London 1937
Our shepherds Sydney [1942]
Glassop, L. *We were the rats* Sydney 1944 rev. ed. 1961, 1965
Lucky Palmer Sydney 1949
The rats in New Guinea Sydney 1963
Gleaner Sydney 1847–48 (continued by *Christian standard*)
Gleeson, T.P. *Essays on the Australian way of life* Melbourne [1950]
Glenfield, E. *On strike; or where do the girls come in?* Sydney 1890
Glennon, J. *The heart in the centre* Adelaide 1960
The Glenorchy murders: a full account of the capture, trial and execution of William Griffiths [Hobart] 1865
Godfrey, F.R. *Extracts from old journals written by Frederic Race Godfrey . . of Boort Station, Loddon district, Victoria 1846–1853* Melbourne 1926
'Godfrey, W.' *Malleson at Melbourne* London 1956
Godley, J.R. *Extracts from the journal of a visit to New South Wales in 1853* n.p. 1853
Godwin, T. *A descriptive account of Van Diemen's Island, being part of the British colony of New South Wales* London 1821
Goldsmith, A.J. *Reminiscences of an old engineer* Brisbane 1926
'Goldsmith, H.' (H.J.G. Armstrong) *Our Alma* London 1894
Goldsworthy, P. *Archipelagoes* Sydney 1982
Zooing North Ryde, N.S.W. 1986
Gomm, L.J. *Blazing the western trails: the story of the life and work of William Kennedy, pathfinder, preacher and pioneer* Sydney 1935
Goode, A.R. see 'Russell, A.'
Goode, C.E. *The grower of golden grain* Melbourne 1932
The bridge party at Boyanup Melbourne 1943
Yarns of the Yilgarn Melbourne 1950
Stories of strange places Melbourne 1973
Goode, J. *Guide to Australian insects* North Melbourne 1971
Goodge, W.T. *Hits! skits! and jingles* Sydney 1899

Goodhart, D. *We of the turning tide* Adelaide 1947
Good weekend Sydney 1985–
Gordon, A.L. *Bush ballads and galloping rhymes* Melbourne 1870
Gordon, A.S. *Mordecai MacCobber: the story of a Scotch Jew in Australia* 2nd ed. St Kilda, Vic. 1918 4th ed. 1929
Gordon, K.M. *Youth centres* Canberra 1944
Gordon, P.R. *Drover's guide* Brisbane 1880
Gore, S. *Overlanding with Annabel* Sydney 1956
Down the golden mile London 1962
Holy smoke: from the scriptures according to Saltbush Bill Sydney 1968
Gorey, N. ed. *The Alice . . compiled by the Alice Springs Branch of the Country Women's Association* Adelaide 1952
Gorman, C. *A night in the arms of Raeleen* [&] *The Harding women* Sydney 1983
Gosse, W.C. *Report and diary of Mr W.C. Gosse's central and western exploring expedition, 1873* Alice Springs, N.T. [1976]
Gouger, R. *South Australia in 1837* London 1838
Gould, J. *Monograph of the macropodidae, or family of kangaroos* 2 parts. London 1841–42
The birds of Australia 7 vols. London 1848
The mammals of Australia 3 vols. London 1863
Handbook to the birds of Australia 2 vols. London 1865
The birds of Australia. Supplement London 1869
Gould, N. *On and off the turf in Australia* London 1895
Town and bush London 1896
Gould, R.A. *Yiwara: foragers of the Australian desert* London 1969
Gouldstone, S. *Australia and New Zealand: guide to food bearing plants* Sydney 1978
Graham, J.R. *A treatise on the Australian merino* Melbourne 1870
'Grahame, S.' see Williams, G.
Grant, A. *Camel train & aeroplane: the story of Skipper Partridge* Adelaide 1981
Grant, A.C. *Bush-life in Queensland or John West's colonial experiences* 2 vols. Edinburgh 1881
Grant, A.R. *Memories of Parliament* Perth 1937
Grant, D. *Through six gaols* Sydney 1921
Grant, F. *Death on my wing* Sydney 1963
Grant, J. *The narrative of a voyage of discovery, performed in His Majesty's vessel the Lady Nelson . . to New South Wales* London 1803
Grant, J. Correspondence and journal 1805–10. NLA MS 737
Grant, M. *Barrier Reef* London 1980
Inherit the sun London 1981
Grasby, W.C. *Principles of Australian agriculture* London 1912
Grattan, C.H. *Introducing Australia* New York 1942
Graves, H.E. *Who rides?: events in the life of a West Australian police officer* London 1937
Graves, K.E.C. *Tasmanian pastoral* Melbourne 1953
The third chance Adelaide 1970
Gray, C.M. *Western Victoria in the forties* Hamilton, Vic. 1932
Gray, G.R. *The entomology of Australia in a series of monographs* London 1833
Gray, O. *Drive a hard bargain* Hobart 1958
Gray, R. *Reminiscences of India and North Queensland 1857–1912* London 1913
Gray, W. *Days and nights in the bush* Sydney 1935
Green, A. *We were the (riff) R.A.A.F.* Perth 1946
Green, B. *Small town rising* South Melbourne 1981
Green, C. *The sun is up* Richmond, Vic. 1978
Burn the butterflies Sydney 1979
Green, E. *Journeys with Gelignite Jack* Adelaide 1966
Green, F.C. *The Fortieth: a record of the 40th Battalion, A.I.F.* Hobart 1922
Green, J. *The story of the Australian Bushmen* Sydney 1903
Green, M. *After the Boolucburrers* n.p. [1966]
Greene, W.T. *Parrots in captivity* 3 vols. London 1884
Greenway, J. *Down among the wild men: the narrative journal of fifteen years pursuing the old stone age Aborigines of Australia's western desert* London 1973

GREER, G. *The female eunuch* London 1970
GREGOR, J. *The church in Australia. part II: two journals of missionary tours . . Moreton Bay* London 1845
GREGORY, A.C. & F.T. *Journals of Australian explorations* Brisbane 1884
GREGORY, J.W. *Dead heart of Australia: a journey around Lake Eyre in the summer of 1901–1902* London 1906
GREGORY, R.E. *Originally Australian inventions and ideas* Sydney 1977
Gregory's fishing guide 8th ed. Sydney 1973
Gregory's Sydney pocket guide Sydney [1978]
**Gremlin jottings* Canberra 1947–50
GREW, E. & M.S. *Rambles in Australia* London 1916
GREY, G. *Journals of two expeditions of discovery in north-west and Western Australia, during the years 1837, 38, and 39* 2 vols. London 1841
GRIBBLE, E.R.B. *Forty years with the Aborigines* Sydney 1930
The problem of the Australian Aboriginal Sydney 1932
GRIBBLE, J.B. *Black but comely* [London 1884]
GRIERSON, L. *Down by the riverside* London 1974
GRIFFITH, A. *The Griffith-Moroney debate* Sydney 1909
GRIFFITH, C. *The present state and prospects of the Port Phillip district of New South Wales* Dublin 1845
GRIFFITHS, O. *Darwin drama* Sydney 1947
GRIFFITHS, S. *Turf and heath: Australian racing reminiscences* Melbourne 1906
A rolling stone on the turf Sydney 1933
GRIMMETT, C.V. *Getting wickets* London 1930
GRONDONA, St.C. *Collar and cuffs: the adventures of a jackeroo* Melbourne [1911]
The kangaroo keeps on talking London 1924
GROOM, A. *I saw a strange land* Sydney 1950
Wealth in the wilderness Sydney 1955
GROSE, F. *1811 dictionary of the vulgar tongue* ed. by R. Cromie Chicago 1971
GROSE, F. *A rough Y.M. bloke* Melbourne 1921
GROSER, T.S. *The lure of the golden west: experiences and adventures in a Bush Brotherhood of Western Australia* London 1927
GROSVENOR, G.A. *A long way from 'Tipperary': 58 years of South Australian journalism* Hawthorndene, S. Aust. 1983
GROUT, W. *My country's keeper* London 1965
GROVER, M. *Minus quantity and other short plays* Sydney 1914
Guardian Sydney 1844
Guardian Hobart 1847 (continued by *The Hobarton guardian*)
GUBBIN, S.C. *A journey from Wilgera and Tancoola to the Everard Ranges . . in 1882* Adelaide 1902
Guide book for the use of prospectors in New South Wales 2nd ed. Sydney 1919
GUILFOYLE, W.R. *Australian botany* Melbourne 1878
Australian plants suitable for gardens, parks, timber reserves, etc. Melbourne [c. 1910]
*Guinea gold. In the field 1942–45
GULLET, H. *Tropical New South Wales* Sydney 1887
GULLETT, H.S. *The Australian Imperial Force in Sinai and Palestine* (Official history of Australia in the war of 1914–1918 vol. VII) Sydney 1923
Gumsuckers' gazette Melbourne 1960–63 (continued by *Australian tradition*)
GUNN, Mrs A. *The little black princess* London 1905
We of the never-never London 1908
GUNN, D. *Links with the past* Brisbane 1937
GUNN, J.S. *The terminology of the shearing industry* 2 parts. Sydney 1965
Research and Australian English Wagga Wagga, N.S.W. 1970
An opal terminology Sydney 1971
Distribution of shearing terms in New South Wales Sydney 1971
GUNN, R.N. *Poems of the pioneering days* Stanthorpe, Qld. 1921
GUNNING, F.W. *Lure of the north: seventy years' memoirs of George Joseph Gooch and his pioneer friends of Western Australia* Perth 1952
GUNTHER, A.C.L.G. *An introduction to the study of fishes* Edinburgh 1880
GUNTHER, J. Letters and journals of J. Gunther, missionary at Wellington Valley, New Holland, from Aug. 8th 1837–Dec. 31st 1840. Church Missionary Society. Records. AJCP M224 CN/047

GURNER, J.A. *Life's panorama* Melbourne 1930
GUTHRIE, J.F. *A world history of sheep and wool* Melbourne 1957
GYE, C. *The cockney and the crocodile* London 1962
GYE, H. *Father clears out: by 'James Hackston'* Sydney 1966

'H.J.L.' (H.J. Laplastrier) *The travels and adventures of Mr Newchamp* Melbourne 1854
**H.M.A.S. Westralia magazine* At sea 1944
HACK, S. Letters written from Sydney and Adelaide. 1837–39 NLA MS 140
HACKER, J.B. et al. *More beef from spear grass country: pasture research at Rodd's Bay, Central Queensland, 1945–1977* Brisbane [1982]
HACKETT, D.V. *The Australian household guide* Perth 1916
'HACKSTON, J.' see Gye, H.
HADDLETON, J.F. *Katanning pioneer* Perth 1952
HADE, C. *Ebenezer* [Sydney] 1932
HADOW, L. *Full cycle and other stories* London 1969
HAENKE, H. *The bottom of a birdcage* Brisbane 1978
HAGENAUER, F.A. *Report of the Aboriginal mission at Ramahyuck, Victoria, for the year 1885, and notes of a missionary journey to north Queensland* Sale, Vic. [1886]
HALCOMBE, J.J. *The emigrant and the heathen; or, sketches of missionary life* London [1874]
HALE, H.M. *The crustaceans of South Australia* 2 parts. Adelaide 1927–29
HALE, M.B. *The transportation question; or why Western Australia should be made a reformatory colony instead of a penal settlement* Cambridge 1857
HALES, A.G. *McGlusky the gold-seeker* London [1920]
HALFORD, Mrs E.P. *Pioneers of yesterday: the overland trip from South Australia to Western Australia, accomplished by the Halford family* Perth [1931]
HALL, E.R. *Can you hear me?* Box Hill North, Vic. 1980
HALL, G. ed. *Rhymes from the rivers* Lismore, N.S.W. 1976
The river still flows Lismore, N.S.W. 1978
HALL, H.L. *Victoria's part in the Australian federation movement 1849–1900* London 1931
HALL, M. *A woman in the Antipodes and in the Far East* London 1914
HALL, N. et al. *Forest trees of Australia* 3rd ed. Canberra 1970
The use of trees and shrubs in the dry country of Australia Canberra 1972
HALL, P. *Sun and grey shadow* London 1974
HALL, Robert *The useful birds of southern Australia* Melbourne 1907
HALL, Rodney *A place among people* St Lucia, Qld. 1975
Just relations Ringwood, Vic. 1982
ed. *Poems from prison* St Lucia, Qld. 1973
HALL, T. *A short history of the Downs blacks known as 'the Blucher tribe'* Warwick, Qld. [1923]
HALL, V.C. *Bad medicine* Melbourne 1947
Dreamtime justice Adelaide 1962
HALL, W.H. *Practical experience at the diggings of the gold fields of Victoria* 2nd ed. London 1852
HALLACK, E.H. *Western Australia and the Yilgarn goldfields* Adelaide 1891
Our townships, farms, and homesteads: southern district of South Australia Adelaide 1892
HALLAM, J. *The untold story* North Sydney 1983
'HAMER' (H.S. Mercer) *The search for the bonzer tart* Sydney [c. 1920]
HAMILTON, G. *Summer glare* Sydney 1959
HAMILTON, I. *The persecutor* New York 1965
HAMILTON, J. *Nights ashore* Sydney 1933
Sailor town shanties and troopship memories Sydney 1936
HAMILTON, J.C. *Pioneering days in western Victoria: a narrative of early station life* Melbourne [1913]
HAMILTON-WILKES, M. *Kelpie and cattle dog* Sydney 1967
HAMMOND, J.E. *Winjan's people: the story of the south-west Australian Aborigines* Perth [1933]
Western pioneers: the battle well fought Perth [1936]
HANCOCK, W.K. *Discovering Monaro* Cambridge 1972
HANDSLEY, G.W. *Two-and-a-half years a prisoner of war in Turkey* Brisbane [1919]

HANIGAN, P. & LINDSAY, R. *No tracks on the river* Wilcannia, N.S.W. 1978
HANMAN, E.F. *Twelve months with the 'Anzacs'* Brisbane 1916
HANNAH, H. *Together in this jungle scrub* Elands, N.S.W. 1981
HANRAHAN, B. ed. *Motor racing the Australian way* Melbourne 1972
HANSELL, H. *The everlastin' ballads* Melbourne [1920]
HANSON, J. *(Letter written) on board the Lord Lyndork to Captain Butterworth. At sea, January 9, 1832* Madras 1832
HARCOURT, J.M. *The pearlers* London [1933]
Upsurge London [1934]
It never fails London [1937]
HARCUS, W. ed. *South Australia: its history, resources, and productions* London 1876
HARDIE, J.J. *Cattle camp* Sydney 1932, 1944
HARDING, E. ed. *Alan Marshall talking* Melbourne 1978
HARDING, W.G. *An American looks at Australia* Washington 1943
HARDMAN, D.J. *The major tuna industries of the world* (issued by the) Fisheries Division, Department of Primary Industry Canberra 1962
HARDY, B. *The world owes me nothing* Adelaide 1979
HARDY, F. *Power without glory* Melbourne 1950
The four-legged lottery London 1958
The hard way London 1961
Legends from Benson's Valley London 1963
The yarns of Billy Borker Sydney 1965
Billy Borker yarns again Sydney 1967
The unlucky Australians Melbourne 1968
The outcasts of Foolgarah Melbourne 1971
Who shot George Kirkland? Port Melbourne 1981
'HARDY, P.' (V.H.P. Purnell) *The torch of remembrance* Brisbane 1941
HARDY, W. *The saltwater angler* Sydney 1966
HARE, F.A. *The last of the bushrangers* London 1892
HARGRAVES, E.H. *Australia and its goldfields* London 1855
HARNEY, W.E. *North of 23°* Sydney [1946]
Brimming billabongs Sydney 1947, 2nd ed. London 1963
Life among the Aborigines London 1957
Content to lie in the sun London 1958
Tales from the Aborigines London 1959
Grief, gaiety and Aborigines London 1961
To Ayers Rock and beyond London 1963
HARNEY, W.E. & LOCKWOOD, D. *The shady tree* Adelaide 1963
HARPER, E.L. *The king of ballyhoo* Hidden Valley, Qld. 1978
HARPER, J. *Splashes from the Narran* Sydney 1924
HARPUR, C. Kangaroo hunt. 1863 ML MS C377
HARRINGTON, E. *Boundary bend and other ballads* Melbourne [1936]
My old black billy and other songs of the Australian outback Melbourne 1940
The Kerrigan boys and other Australian verses Melbourne 1944
HARRIS, A. *Settlers and convicts* London 1847, Melbourne 1953
A guide to Port Stephens, in New South Wales London 1849
The emigrant family; or, the story of an Australian settler Canberra 1967 (first publ. London 1849)
HARRIS, D. *Drovers of the outback* Fitzroy, Vic. 1982
HARRIS, H.W. *Shearers or shorn* Brisbane 1891
HARRIS, L. & K. *The lost hole of Bingoola* Indianapolis, U.S.A. 1942
HARRIS, T.Y. *Wild flowers of Australia* rev. ed. Sydney 1947
Australian plants for the garden Sydney 1953
Naturecraft in Australia Sydney 1956
HARRIS, W.K. *Outback in Australia or three Australian overlanders* Letchworth, England 1913
HARRISON, H.C.A. *The story of an athlete* Melbourne 1923
HARRISON, J. *A bit of a dag: tales of a shearing gang* Buderim, Qld. 1985
**Harry Peck's post: official organ of the 2/5 Field Regiment Association* Sydney 1948–60
HART, F. *Western Australia in 1891* Perth 1892
The miner's handbook and investor's guide to Western Australia Melbourne 1894
Picturesque Western Australia London [c. 1897]
HARTIGAN, P.J. see 'O'Brien, J.'

HARTLEY, F.J. *Sanananda*
HARTLEY, W. *A checklist of*
HARTT, C.L. *Humorosities*
Diggerettes (digg
More diggerettes
HASKELL, A. *Waltzing Ma*
HASLUCK, A. *Portrait with* 1955
ed. *Audrey Te*
Audrey Lady
HASLUCK, N. *The hat o* 1978
The blue guita
HASLUCK, P. *An open g*
HASSALL, J.S. *In old A* bane 1902
HATFIELD, W. *Sheepm*
11th ed. 19
Ginger Mur
Desert saga
River crossi
Black wate
Australia t
Big timber
I find Aust
Buffalo Jin
Into the (g
Barrier R
Wild dog
**'Havildar' havaloo*
HAWDON, J. *Journa in 1838* Melbo
HAWKE, J. *Follow*
HAWKER, G.C. D Library D261
HAWKER, J.C. Di
Early e
HAWKER, R. *An*
HAWKES, J.G. e 1979
HAWKESWORTH 1930
HAWKESWORTH *present Majes* London 177
HAY, Mrs A. 1899
HAY, P. ed. Warrnamb
HAYDON, A.I
HAYDON, G.I
Th
HAYDON, T.
HAYES, M.
HAYGARTH,
HAYLEN, L.
T
e
HAYLES, K.
HAYNES, R
HAYTER, F
HAYTER, J
HAYWARD
HEAD, H.

Heads of
HEALY,

HEALY, J.J. *Literatu* 1978
HEALY, T.E.A. *And*
HEATHCOTE, A. *A f* Kangaroo Grou
HEDGE, J. *Trout fish*
rev. ed. 1
Trout fishi
HELLMRICH, D. *Hou*
HELLYER, H. Diary
HENDERSON, J. *Obse Diemen's Land* Ca
Excursions 1851
HENEY, H. ed. *Dear 1788–1857* Rushc
HENEY, T. *The girl at*
HENNESSEY, J.D. *The*
HENNING, R. *The lette*
HENRY, G.J. *'Girro g* Brisbane 1967
Henry Lawson, by his Sydney 1931
Henslowe's annual Syd
HENTY, R. *Australiana*
HEPPELL, M. ed. *A bl Australia* Canberra
HEPWORTH, J. *His book*
Little Austral
HEPWORTH, J. & HINDL
Herald of Tasmania Hob tinued by *Hobart To*
HERBERT, X. *Capricorni*
Soldiers' wom
Larger than li
Disturbing ele
Poor fellow my
Dream road Sy
HERRON, M. *Seed and st*
HERVEY, G. *Australians*
HESLING, B. *The dinkum immigrant* Sydney 19
HETHERINGTON, J. *The A*
The morning w
HEWETT, D. *Bobbin up* M
This old man co
Bon-bons and r 1976
Susannah's dre 1981
HEWISON, R. *Slocum* Leeu
HEYWOOD, B.A. *A vacatio* 1863
HIBBERD, J. *White with wi*
Who? 1968 in *P*
A stretch of the in
Dimboola Melbo
HIBBERD, J. & HUTCHINSON
HICKS, S. *'Hullo Australian*
HILL, A. *The Bunburyists* R
HILL, B. *Near the refinery* M
HILL, E. *The great Australia*
2nd ed. Melbou
Water into gold M
Flying doctor calli
The Territory Syd
'HILL, M.' (A.M. Baker) *Lar tralia* London 1955
HILL, R. *Bush quest* Melbou

Home building in the inland issued by the Flying Doctor Service of Australia Brisbane [c. 1947]
Home cookery for Australia 2nd ed. Melbourne 1906
**Home trail: souvenir issue of voyage of H.M.T. 'A.30'* At sea 1918
'Honk!' the voice of the benzine lancers and organ of the gear-box musicians France 1915
HOOD, J. *Australia and the East* London 1843
The land of the fern Melbourne 1885
Hoofs & horns Prospect, S. Aust. 1944–
HOOKER, W.J. *Botanical miscellany* 3 vols. London 1830–33
HOOKEY, M. ed. *Bobby Knopwood and his times* Hobart 1929
HOPE, J.L.A. *In quest of coolies* London 1872
HOPE, S. *Diggers' paradise* London 1956
HOPGOOD, A. *Private Yuk objects* Melbourne [1966]
And the big men fly South Yarra, Vic. 1969
And here comes Bucknuckle Richmond, Vic. 1980
HOPKINS, D.J. *Hop of the 'Bulletin'* Sydney 1929
HORDEN, H.V. *Googlies: coals from a test-cricketer's fireplace* Sydney 1932
Horlick's magazine and home journal for Australia, India and the colonies London 1904–05
HORN, W.A. *Notes by a nomad: an olla-podrida* London 1906
Horn boy Hobart 22 Aug. 1834–13 Dec. 1834
HORNADGE, B. *The Australian slanguage* North Ryde, N.S.W. 1980
HORNE, D. *The permit* Melbourne 1965
Southern exposure Sydney 1967
The education of young Donald Sydney 1967
HORNE, G. *Aboriginal stone implements of south-eastern Victoria* Melbourne 1921
HORNE, G. & AISTON, G. *Savage life in Central Australia* London 1924
HORNE, R.H. *Australian facts and prospects: to which is prefixed the author's Australian autobiography* London 1859
HORNSBY, M. *Old time echoes of Tasmania by 'the vet'* [Hobart 1896]
HORSPHOL, L. *Turn down an empty glass* Sydney 1978
HOSE, T. *The Australian magpie and the British Commonwealth of Nations* Melbourne 1936
HOSKING, J.M. *Australia first and last* Sydney 1957
HOTTEN, J.C. *A dictionary of modern slang, cant, and vulgar words* London 1859
2nd ed. 1860
3rd ed. 1864
rev. eds. 1865, 1870
HOUGHTON, N. *Beech Forest* Beech Forest, Vic. 1984
HOULDING, J.R. *Australian capers; or Christopher Cockle's colonial experience by Old Boomerang* London 1867
Australian tales and sketches from real life by Old Boomerang London 1868
HOVELL, W.H. *Reply to 'A brief statement of facts, in connection with an overland expedition from Lake George to Port Phillip, in 1824', published in May last, by 'Hamilton Hume'* Sydney 1855
HOWARD, F. *The moleskin gentry* Melbourne 1978
HOWARD, S. *Forty-six* Sydney 1934
HOWARD, W.S. *You're telling me!* Sydney 1934
HOWCHIN, W. *The geography of South Australia* Melbourne 1909
The geology of South Australia Adelaide 1918
HOWCROFT, W.G. *This side of the rabbit proof fence* Melbourne 1971
The farm that blew away Melbourne 1973
Sand in the stew Melbourne 1974
The old working hat Melbourne 1975
Dungarees and dust Melbourne 1978
The bushman who laughed Richmond, Vic. 1982
'HOWE, E.' (R. Rowe) *The boy in the bush* London 1869
HOWE, E.W. *Travel letters from New Zealand, Australia and Africa* Topeka, U.S.A. 1913
HOWELL, W.M. *Reminiscences of Australia: the diggings and the bush* London 1869
HOWELLS, A.F. *Against the stream: the memoirs of a philosophical anarchist, 1927–1939* South Yarra, Vic. 1983
Howe's weekly commercial express Sydney 1825
HOWITT, A.W. *On some Australian beliefs* London 1883
On some Australian ceremonies of initiation London 1884
Australian group relations Washington 1885
The Jeraeil or initiation ceremonies of the Kurnai tribe London 1885
On Australian medicine men London 1886
Notes on songs and song makers of some Australian tribes London 1887
The native tribes of south-east Australia London 1904
HOWITT, R. *Impressions of Australia Felix* London 1845
HOWITT, W. *A boy's adventures in the wilds of Australia* London 1854
Land, labor and gold: or two years in Victoria with visits to Sydney and Van Diemen's Land 2 vols. Boston 1855
Tallangetta, the squatter's home 2 vols. London 1857
HUDSON, H. *Flynn's flying doctors: an artist's journey through the outback and the story of the Flying Doctor Service in Australia* London 1956
HUELIN, F. *'Keep moving'* Sydney 1973
HUGHES, A.M. *Idylls of the bush* Melbourne 1886
HUGHES, C.A. *The government of Queensland* St Lucia, Qld. 1980
HUGHES, Mrs F. *My childhood in Australia* London [1892]
HUGHES, J. *Australia revisited in 1890* London 1891
HUGHES, R.D. *Living insects* Sydney 1975
HUGHES, W. *The Australian colonies* London 1852
HUGHES, W.M. *The case for Labor* Sydney 1910
Crusts and crusades Sydney 1947
Policies and potentates Sydney 1950
HUGO, W.M. *History of the first Bushmen's Club in the Australian colonies, established at Adelaide, South Australia* Adelaide 1872
HULL, H.M. *The experience of forty years in Tasmania* London 1859
HULME, E. see 'E.H.'
'HUMANITY' *Sketches of Chinese character, illustrative of their moral and physical effect on the rising generation of Victoria* Castlemaine, Vic. 1878
HUME, G. *River Murray fishing & boating guide* North Adelaide [1967]
HUME, F. *Madame Midas* London 1888
Hummer Wagga, N.S.W. 1891–Sept. 1892 (continued by *The worker*)
HUMPHRIES, B. *The wonderful world of Barry McKenzie* London 1968
Bazza pulls it off Melbourne 1971
Dame Edna's coffee table book Sydney 1976
Bazza comes into his own Melbourne 1979
A nice night's entertainment Sydney 1981
HUNGERFORD, R. ed. *The complete book of Australian fishing* 3rd ed. Cheltenham, Vic. 1982
HUNGERFORD, T.A.G. *The ridge and the river* London 1952
Riverslake Sydney 1953
Sowers of the wind Sydney 1954
Shake the golden bough Sydney 1963
Wong Chu and the queen's letterbox Fremantle, W.A. 1977
Stories from suburban road: an autobiographical collection 1920–1939 Fremantle, W.A. 1983
HUNGERFORD, T.G. *Diseases of livestock* 3rd ed. Sydney 1953, 6th ed. 1967, 8th ed. 1975
HUNT, H.A. et al. *The climate and weather of Australia* Melbourne 1913
HUNT, J.L. *Hunt's book of bonanzas* Sydney 1889
HUNT, N. *The house of David* Sydney 1935
HUNTER, J. Sketchbook: 100 original watercolours, birds, fishes, flowers, natives, New South Wales, 1788–1790. NLA NK 2039
An historical journal of the transactions at Port Jackson and Norfolk Island London 1793
Letter to Sir Joseph Banks 1 June 1799. NLA MS 9/87
HUNTER, L.R.M. *Woodline: five years with the woodcutters of the Western Australian goldfields* Forrestfield, W.A. 1976
Huon times Franklin, Tas. 1910–42 (from Dec. 1933 has title *Huon and Derwent times*)
HURLEY, P.J. *Red cedar: the story of the north coast* Sydney 1948
From Kosciusko to the sea Sydney 1946
HUSSEY, H. *More than half a century of colonial life and Christian experience; with notes of travel, lectures, publications, etc.* Adelaide 1897
HUTCHINS, B. *A guide to the marine fishes of Rottnest Island* Perth 1979
HUTCHINS, B. & THOMPSON, M. *The marine and estuarine fishes of south-western Australia* Perth 1983

HUTCHINSON, G. ed. *The great Australian book of football stories* South Yarra, Vic. 1983
HUTCHINSON, J.N. *North west Australian wildflowers* vol. I. Sydney 1971
HUTLEY, D.B. *Clement: a suburban romance* Sydney 1976
The swan Sydney 1978
HUTT, H. *The ballad of the boot* London 1969
HUTTON, E.T.H. *A narrative of the tour of inspection through the Western Division of New South Wales* Sydney 1895
HUXLEY, E. *Their shining Eldorado: a journey through Australia* London 1967
HYETT, J. *A bushman's harvest* Melbourne 1961

IDRIESS, I.L. *Diary 1915–18. AWM written records 1 DRL 373
Flynn of the inland Sydney 1932, 1975
Lasseter's last ride: an epic of Central Australian gold discovery Sydney 1931, 1932
Prospecting for gold Sydney 1932
The desert column: leaves from the diary of an Australian trooper in Gallipoli, Sinai, and Palestine Sydney 1932
Man tracks: with the Mounted Police in Australian wilds Sydney 1935
The cattle king Sydney 1936
Forty fathoms deep Sydney 1937
Cyaniding for gold Sydney 1939
Lightning Ridge Sydney 1940
Guerrilla tactics Sydney 1942
Horrie the wog-dog Sydney 1945
In crocodile land Sydney 1946
The opium smugglers Sydney 1948
One wet season Sydney 1949
Across the Nullarbor Sydney 1951
Outlaws of the Leopolds Sydney 1952
The Nor'-westers Sydney 1954
The silver city Sydney 1956
The wild north Sydney 1960
Tracks of destiny Sydney 1961
Our living stone age Sydney 1963
Opals and sapphires: how to work, mine, class, cut, polish, and sell them Sydney 1967
IGGULDEN, J. *The storms of summer* London 1960
The clouded sky New York 1964
Dark stranger London 1965
ed. *Summer's tales* Melbourne 1966
Illawarra mercury Wollongong, N.S.W. 1855– (from 1 Jan. 1950–12 Nov. 1955 has title *Illawarra daily mercury*)
Illustrated Adelaide news Adelaide 1875–80 (continued by *Pictorial Australian*)
Illustrated Adelaide post Adelaide 1867–?1874
Illustrated Australian magazine Melbourne 1850–52
Illustrated Australian news Melbourne 1862–?1896
Illustrated journal of Australasia Melbourne 1857–58 (continues *Journal of Australasia*)
Illustrated Melbourne post Melbourne 1862–68 (incorporated in *Illustrated Australian news*)
Illustrated Sydney news Sydney 1853–94
Illustrated Tasmanian mail Hobart 1921–35 (continues *The Tasmanian mail*, incorporated in *The mercury*)
'AN IMPARTIAL OBSERVER' (J. Lhotsky) *Illustrations of the present state and future prospects of the colony of New South Wales* Sydney 1835
Independent Launceston 1831–35
Industrial information bulletin Melbourne 1946–75
Industrial news Sydney 1921–22
Information for emigrants: in three parts. I. North America. II. New South Wales, Port Phillip, Cooksland, South Australia and New Zealand. III. The Cape of Good Hope, Algoa Bay, and Port Natal London 1848
INGAMELLS. R. *Conditional culture* Adelaide 1938
Sun-freedom Adelaide 1938
Australian Aboriginal words Melbourne 1955
INGLETON, G.C. *True patriots all: or news from early Australia – as told in a collection of broadsides* Sydney 1952
INGLIS, J. *Our Australian cousins* London 1880
INGPEN, R. *Australian inventions and innovations* Adelaide 1982
Inlander Sydney 1913–29, 1963
Inquirer: a Western Australian journal of politics and literature Perth 1840–55 (continued by *The inquirer and commercial news*)
Inquirer and commercial news Perth 1855–1901 (continues *The inquirer*, continued by *Morning herald*)
Intercolonial Exhibition of Australasia, 1866–67 see *Official record of the Intercolonial Exhibition*
Intercolonial quarterly journal of medicine and surgery Melbourne 1894–96
'IOTA' *Kooroona: a tale of South Australia* London 1871
IRBY, E. *Memoirs of Edward and Leonard Irby* Sydney 1908
IREDALE, F. *33 years of cricket* Sydney 1920
IRELAND, D. *Image in the clay* St. Lucia, Qld. 1964
The chantic bird New York 1968
The unknown industrial prisoner Sydney 1971
The flesheaters Sydney 1972
Burn Sydney 1974
The glass canoe Melbourne 1976
Irish exile and freedom's advocate Hobart 1850–51
IRISH, L. *Time of the dolphins* Sydney 1972
Iron Ned Kelly and his gang Sydney [c. 1900]
'IRONBARK' (G.H. Gibson) *Southerly busters* Sydney 1878
Ironbark chips and stockwhip cracks Melbourne 1894
Ironbark splinters from the Australian bush London 1912
IRVIN, E. *Early inland agriculture* Wagga, N.S.W. 1962
IRVING, D. *The destruction of Dresden* London 1963
IRWIN, F.C. *The state and position of Western Australia* London 1835
ISAACS, J. *Arts of the dreaming: Australia's living heritage* Sydney 1984
Island authors: an anthology of short stories, articles and poems by Tasmanian authors Hobart 1971

'J.A.B.' *Meta of Gaindara: an Australian poetical romance* Melbourne 1868
'J.W.T.' *The land question in Queensland* Brisbane 1866
JACK, R.L. *Northmost Australia: three centuries of exploration, discovery, and adventure in and around the Cape York Peninsula, Queensland* 2 vols. Melbourne 1922
'A JACKAROO' *The immigration question* Sydney 1870
**Jackass: First Australian General Hospital monthly* [In the field] 1918
JACKSON, A. *Robert O'Hara Burke and the Australian exploring expedition of 1860* London 1862
JACKSON, H. *Broken fleece* Sydney 1910
JACKSON, J.A. *National emigration considered chiefly with reference to the Australian colonies* London 1848
JACKSON, S.W. Field trip notebook. 1908 NLA MS 466/126
JACOBS, P.A. *A lawyer tells* Melbourne 1949
JAENSCH, D. *The government of South Australia* St Lucia, Qld. 1977
'JAMES, B.' (J. Tierney) *Cookabundy Bridge and other stories* Sydney 1946
The advancement of Spencer Button Sydney 1950
The bunyip of Barney's Elbow Sydney 1956
JAMES, B.S. *The Westralian goldfields* London 1896
JAMES, C. *Unreliable memoirs* London 1980
Charles Charming's challenges on the pathway to the throne London 1981
JAMES, G.L. *Shall I try Australia?: or health business and pleasure in New South Wales* Liverpool 1892
JAMES, G.P.R. *The convict: a tale* London 1851
JAMES, H.C. *Gold is where you find it* London 1949
JAMES, M.W. *The 'coo-ee' call* Adelaide [1917]
JAMES, P. *Stories of central Queensland* Spring Hill, Qld. 1982
JAMES, T.H. *Six months in South Australia* London 1838
JAMES, W. *Barrel and book: a winemaker's diary* Melbourne 1949
Janie stagestruck Sydney 1972
JARRATT, P. *Aussie: Australians at play* McMahons Point, N.S.W. 1984
'JASON' *The blowfly pest: experiences of Australian sheepowners with Cooper's powder dip* Sydney [1919]
JEFFERIS, B. *Half angel* New York 1959
One black summer New York 1967

JEFFREY, G. *The principles and practice of Australasian woolclassing* Adelaide 1899
JEFFREY, M. *A burglar's life; or the stirring adventures of the great English burglar* Launceston, Tas. 1893
JEFFREYS, C. *Van Dieman's Land: geographical and descriptive delineations of the island of Van Dieman's Land* London 1820
JENKIN, G. *Two years on Bardunyah Station* Adelaide 1967
JENKINS, J. *Diary of a Welsh swagman* see Evans, W. ed.
JENKYNS, C.C. *Hard life in the colonies, and other experiences by sea and land* London 1892
JENNER, D.G. *Darlings, I've had a ball* Sydney 1975
JENSEN, H.I. *The rising tide: an exposition of Australian socialism* Sydney 1909
Dan Green, mystery man Brisbane 1948
JERSEY, M.E. *Fifty-one years of Victorian life* London 1922
JESSOP, J. ed. *Flora of Central Australia* Sydney 1981
JESSOP, W.R.H. *Flindersland and Sturtland; or, the inside and outside of Australia* 2 vols. London 1862
Travels and adventures in Australia 2 vols. London 1862
JESSUP, G.A. *A course of lectures on land titles in South Australia* Adelaide 1949
Jest: a digestion of good humor Sydney [1943]
JEWSON, B. *Stir* East Melbourne 1980
JILLET, L. *Moresby's few* Narrabri, N.S.W. 1945
JOBSON, F.J. *Australia* London 1862
JOHNS, G. *Poems* [Canberra] 1971
JOHNSON, A.T.M. *Australian life or high jinks in the sunny south* London [1915]
JOHNSON, B. *Surf fever* Brisbane 1963
JOHNSON, C. *Wild cat falling* Sydney 1965
JOHNSON, F. *Frank Johnson's laugh special* Sydney 1944
JOHNSON, J. *A low breed* Adelaide 1976
JOHNSON, J.C.F. *Christmas on Carringa* Adelaide 1873
Over the island Adelaide [1873]
To Mount Browne and back Adelaide 1881
An Austral Christmas Melbourne 1888
JOHNSON, J.P. *Plain truths, told by a traveller regarding our various settlements in Australia and New Zealand* London 1840
JOHNSON, R. *An address to the inhabitants of the colonies, established in New South Wales and Norfolk Island* London 1792
Some letters of Rev. Richard Johnson, B.A., first chaplain of New South Wales ed. by G. Mackaness Sydney 1954
JOHNSTON, C.W. *The out-back homestead* Bathurst, N.S.W. 1904
JOHNSTON, G.H. *New Guinea diary* Sydney 1943
My brother Jack London 1964
Clean straw for nothing London 1969, 1971
A cartload of clay Sydney 1971
JONES, B. *Cup full of river* Brisbane 1978
JONES, D. *Palms in Australia* Sydney 1984
JONES, E. *Barlow down under* London 1977
JONES, F.W. *The mammals of South Australia* Adelaide 1923–25
JONES, H. *The new valuations; or, the case of the South Australian squatter fairly stated* Melbourne 1864
JONES, Mrs H. *Broad outlines of long years in Australia* London 1878
JONES, H.B. *Adventures in Australia* London 1853
JONES, J. *Memories of Golden Gate, North Queensland* 2nd ed. Seven Hills, Qld. 1972
JONES, J.J. *Condamine bells: songs and stories of the Australian outback* Perth 1961
JONES, L.G. *The flockmaster's companion* Brisbane 1921
JONES, P. *Johnny lost* London 1965
JONES, R.D. *The mad vibe* Cammeray, N.S.W. 1973
Walking the line Sydney 1979
JONES, R.W. *With the 'roos* [Ballarat, Vic. 1917]
JONES, T.E. *'These twenty years'* Sydney 1939
JORDAN, J.C. *The management of sheep and stations* Melbourne 1867
JOSE, N. *The possession of amber* St Lucia, Qld. 1980
Rowena's field Adelaide 1984
JOSKE, H.D.A. *A life to live* South Melbourne [1941]
JOST, J. *This is Harry Flynn* London 1974
Kangaroo court London 1979
JOUBERT, J. *Shavings & scrapes from many parts* Dunedin 1890
Journal and proceedings of the Royal Society of New South Wales Sydney 1867– (to 1875 has title *Transactions*)
Journal of agriculture, Western Australia Perth 1899–
Journal of agriculture and industry of South Australia Adelaide 1897–1904 (continued by *Journal of the Department of Agriculture* of South Australia)
Journal of Australasia Melbourne 1856 (continued by *Illustrated journal of Australasia*)
Journal of the Department of Agriculture of South Australia Adelaide 1904–76 (continues *Journal of agriculture and industry*, from Nov. 1963 *Journal of agriculture, South Australia*)
Journal of the Department of Agriculture, Victoria Melbourne 1902– (from 1957 *Journal of agriculture, Victoria*)
Journal of the Pioneers and Old Residents Association Castlemaine, Vic. 1889–1900
Journal of the Royal Australian Historical Society Sydney 1901– (title varies, to 1918 has title *Journal and proceedings of the Australian Historical Society*)
Journal of the Royal Historical Society of Queensland Brisbane 1914–
Journal of the Royal Society of Western Australia Perth 1914– (to 1924 has title *Journal and proceedings*)
Journals and reports of two voyages to the Glenelg River, and the north-west coast of Australia 1863–4 Perth 1864
Journals of several expeditions made in Western Australia, during the years 1829, 1830, 1831 and 1832 London 1833
JOYCE, A. *A homestead history: being the reminiscences and letters of Alfred Joyce* Melbourne 1942
JOYNER, G.C. *The hairy man of south eastern Australia* Canberra 1977
JOYNT, W.D. *Breaking the road for the rest* South Yarra, Vic. 1979
JUKES, J.B. et al. *Lectures on gold for the instruction of emigrants about to proceed to Australia* London 1852
'JULIET' (J.E. Levy) *Devotion* Melbourne [1927]
JUPP, J. *Ethnic politics in Australia* Sydney 1984
JURGENSEN, M. *Signs and voices* St Lucia, Qld. 1973
JUST, P. *Australia; or notes taken during a residence in the colonies from the gold discovery in 1851 till 1857* Dundee 1859
JUTE, A. *Festival* Melbourne 1982

KAHN, E.J. *G.I. jungle* New York 1943
KALESKI, R. *The Australian settler's complete guide, scientific and practical* Sydney 1909, 2nd ed. 1910
Australian barkers and biters Sydney 1914
**Kangaroosilite: [published on board 'Wandilla']* At sea Jan. 1916
**Kan-karroo kronikle: magazine of the voyage of the H.M.T.S. 'Karroo'* At sea 1914
KAVAL, A.L.C. see Flaxman, G. (tr.)
'KAYE, L.' (N.W. Norman) *Tybal men* London [1931]
Desert herbage London [1932]
Black wilderness London [1936]
KEESING, N. *Lily on the dustbin: slang of Australian women and families* Ringwood, Vic. 1982
Just look out the window: superstitions, odd beliefs and possibly the truth about the weather and your fortune Ringwood, Vic. 1985
ed. *Transition* Sydney 1970
'KEIGHLEY' (K. Goodchild) *Who are you?: A volume of verse* Echuca, Vic. 1883
KELAHER, T. *The digger hat and other verses* Sydney 1942
KELEN, C. *Punks travels* Sydney 1980
KELLEN, S. *Camp happy* Sydney 1944
KELLEY, R.B. *Animal breeding* London 1942
Sheep dogs 4th ed. Sydney 1970
The Kelly gang: or the outlaws of the Wombat Ranges Melbourne 1879
KELLY, J.H. *Struggle for the north* Sydney 1966
KELLY, M. *Spinifex* London 1970
KELLY, P. *The unmaking of Gough* Sydney 1976

KELLY, S. *Forty Australian eucalypts in colour* Sydney 1949
Eucalypts Melbourne 1969
vol. 2 1978
KELLY, V. *The shadow: the amazing exploits of Frank Fahy* Sydney 1954
The bogeyman: the exploits of Sergeant C.J. Chuck, Australia's most unpopular cop Sydney 1956
The greedy ones Sydney 1958
The shark arm case rev. ed. Sydney 1975
KELLY, W. *Life in Victoria or Victoria in 1853, and Victoria in 1858* 2 vols. London 1859
KELSEY, D.E. *The shackle: a story of the far north Australian bush* Blackwood, S. Aust. 1975
KEMP, E. *A voice from Tasmania* Hobart 1846
KENDALL, H. *Poems and songs* Sydney 1862
Leaves from Australian forests Melbourne 1869
Songs from the mountains Sydney 1880
KENEALLY, T. *The place at Whitton* London 1964
The cut-rate kingdom Sydney 1980
KENNA, P. *The slaughter of St Teresa's day* Sydney 1972
KENNEALLY, J.J. *The complete inner history of the Kelly gang and their pursuers* Melbourne 1929
KENNEALLY, K. ed. *The natural history of the Wongan Hills* Perth 1977
KENNEDY, B. *Silver, sin, and sixpenny ale: a social history of Broken Hill 1883–1921* Melbourne 1978
KENNEDY, Edward B. *Four years in Queensland* London 1870
Blacks and bushrangers: adventures in Queensland London 1889
Out of the groove: a romance of Australian life London 1892
The black police of Queensland London 1902
KENNEDY, Edmund B.C. *Extracts from the journal of an exploring expedition into Central Australia, to determine the course of the River Barcoo* [London] 1847
KENNEDY, J.J. *The whale oil guards* Dublin 1919
KENNEDY, M. *Born a half-caste* Canberra 1985
KENNEDY, V. *By range and river: in the Queensland tropics* Cairns, Qld. 1930
KENT, T. *A letter to Barron Field, esq.* London 1825
KENTISH, N.L. *The political economy of New South Wales* Sydney 1838
Work in the bush . . thoughts in the bush, and life in the bush . . of Van Diemen's Land Hobart 1846
Proposals for establishing in Melbourne . . the Victoria Sheep and Cattle Assurance Company Melbourne 1849
The question of questions! Melbourne 1855
Treatise on penal discipline Melbourne 1858
Valedictory ('P.P.C.') letter Melbourne 1858
KEOUGH, S.W. *Around the Army* Sydney 1943
KERR, B. *The silliad, a metrical travesty* Carlton, Vic. 1900
Kerr's Melbourne almanac and Port Phillip directory Melbourne 1841–42
KERRY, P. *Cobbers of the A.I.F.* Sydney 1940
KERSHAW, M. *Colonial facts and fictions* London 1886
KETTLE, E. *Gone bush* Sydney 1967
Khaki bush and bigotry: three Australian plays St Lucia, Qld. 1968
**Khamseen kronikle* [Egypt] 1942
Kia-ora coo-ee: the official magazine of the Australian and New Zealand forces Cairo 1918
KIDDLE, M. *Men of yesterday: a social history of the Western District of Victoria 1834–1890* Melbourne 1961
KIDMAN, B. *On the wallaby* Sydney 1974
KING, A. & C. *Australian holiday* Melbourne 1945
KING, A.R. *The efficiency of rural firefighters* Melbourne 1962 (CSIRO Chemical Research Laboratories technical paper no. 4)
KING, H.J. & BURNS, T.E. *Wildflowers of Tasmania* Milton, Qld. 1969
KING, J. *Information from Van Diemen's Land* London 1833
KING, N. *Colourful tales of the Western Australian goldfields* Adelaide 1980
KING, P.G. Journal of the Lieutenant-Governor of Norfolk Island 1791–96. NLA MS 70
KING, P.P. *Narrative of a survey of the intertropical and western coasts of Australia performed between the years 1818 and 1822* 2 vols. London 1827
KING, S. *Molly's year in camp: the actual diary – letters of an Australian girl, the names only being fictitious* London 1934
KINGHORN, J.R. *Snakes of Australia* Sydney 1929
'KINGLAKE, E.' (E. Garnsey) *The Australian at home* London [1892]
KINGSLEY, H. *The recollections of Geoffry Hamlyn* 3 vols. Cambridge 1859
KINGSMILL, J. *Advice to prisoners sentenced to transportation* London 1849
KINGSTON, W.H.G. *The emigrant's home; or how to settle* London 1856
Adventures in Australia London 1884
KINLOCH, A. *The Murray River* Adelaide 1853
Letters from South Australia (1853 to Feb. 1860) 2nd ed. London 1861
Kings Cross whisper Sydney 1965–
KIRBY, J. *Old times in the bush of Australia* Ballarat, Vic. 1895
KIRBY, W. *On the power wisdom and goodness of God as manifested in the creation of animals and in their history habits and instincts* 2 vols. London 1835
KIRWAN, J. *An empty hand: pioneers and pioneering in Australia* London 1934
My life's adventure London 1936
KITTLE, S. *A concise history of the colony and natives of New South Wales* Edinburgh [1814]
KITTO, R.L.M. *The goldfields of Victoria* London 1867
KLEIN, C. *The pomegranate tree* Newport, N.S.W. 1977
Women of a certain age Newport, N.S.W. 1979
KLEINSCHMIDT, H.E. & JOHNSON, R.W. *Weeds of Queensland* Brisbane 1977
KNIGHT, J.G. *A few particulars relative to the colony of Victoria (Australia)* London 1863
KNIGHT, J.J. *Brisbane: a historical sketch of the capital of Queensland* Brisbane 1897
In the early days: history and incident of pioneer Queensland 2nd ed. Brisbane 1898
KNIGHT, W.H. *Western Australia* Perth 1870
KNOWLES, F. *With the Dinkums: no. 1* Sydney 1918
KNOWLES, J.W. *Lonely rails in the Gulf country: the story of the Normanton–Croydon railway, Queensland* Brisbane 1983
KNOWLES, M.M. *Meg of Minadong* Melbourne 1926
KNOX, D.J. et al. *What is 'the red book'?* Melbourne [1946]
KNOX, T.W. *The boy travellers in Australasia* New York 1889
KNUDSEN, P.A. *The bloodwood tree* London 1962
KNYVETT, R.H. *'Over there' with the Australians* New York 1918
KOCAN, P. *The treatment* Sydney 1980
KOCH, C.J. *The boys in the island* London 1958
Across the sea wall London 1965
The year of living dangerously West Melbourne 1978
KUNRATHY, C. *Impudent foreigner* Sydney 1964
KUPKA, K. *Dawn of art: painting and sculpture of Australian Aborigines* Sydney 1965

Labor call Melbourne Nov. 1906–24 Sept. 1953 (continues *Tocsin*, continued by *Labor* to Sept. 1961)
LACKLAND, J. *Common sense: an enquiry into the influence of transportation on the colony of Van Diemen's Land* Launceston, Tas. 1847
LADDS, D.D. *We have our dreams* Brisbane 1957
'A LADY' (Mrs A. Macpherson) *My experiences in Australia: being recollections of a visit to the Australian colonies in 1856–7* London 1860
'A LADY IN AUSTRALIA' (A.M. Dawbin) *Memories of the past* Melbourne 1873
'A LADY LONG RESIDENT IN NEW SOUTH WALES' (C. Barton) *A mother's offering to her children* Sydney 1841
LAFFER, H.E. *The wine industry of Australia* Adelaide 1949
Lake Eyre, South Australia: the great flooding of 1949–50: the report of the Lake Eyre Committee Royal Geographical Society of Australasia, South Australian branch Adelaide 1955
LAMB, M. *'Red glows the dawn'* [Hartwell, Vic. 1943]
LAMBERT, E. *The twenty thousand thieves* Melbourne 1951, 1952
Glory thrown in London 1959
The long white night London 1965
LAMOND, H.G. *An aviary on the plains* Sydney 1934

From Tariaro to Ross Roy: Wm. Ross Munro Brisbane 1943
White Ears the outlaw Sydney 1949
Big Red London 1953
The manx star London 1954
Towser the sheep dog London 1955
Sheep station London 1959

'LANCE-CORPORAL COBBER' *The Anzac pilgrim's progress* London [1918]

LANCELOTT, F. *Australia as it is: its settlements, farms, and goldfields* 2 vols. London 1852

**Land Army gazette: magazine of the Queensland division Australian Women's Land Army* Brisbane 1943–44

The land of promise see Stephens, J.

Land of the lyre bird: a story of early settlement in the great forest of South Gippsland Published for the South Gippsland Pioneers' Association Melbourne 1920

Land rights news Alice Springs, N.T. 1983– (continues *Central Australian land rights news*)

LANDOR, E.W. *The bushman; or, life in a new country* London 1847

LANDSBOROUGH, W. *Journal of Landsborough's expedition from Carpentaria, in search of Burke & Wills* Melbourne 1862

LANE, A. *The barbie-up-the-back* Surry Hills, N.S.W. 1984

LANE, B.A. et al. *Birds of Port Phillip Bay* Melbourne 1984

LANE, C.G. *Creature-life in Australian wilds* London 1913
Adventures in the big bush: in the haunts of the Aboriginal London 1928

LANE, E. *Mad as rabbits* Adelaide 1962
Our Uncle Charlie Adelaide 1964

LANE, E.H. *Dawn to dusk* Brisbane 1939

LANE, F. *Patrol to the Kimberleys* New York 1955

LANE, R.D. *The romance of old Coolgardie* Perth 1929

LANE, W. see 'Miller, J.'

LANG, A. *Custom and myth* Oxford 1884

LANG, G.S. *Land and labour in Australia* Melbourne 1845
The Aborigines of Australia Melbourne 1865

LANG, J. *Botany Bay; or, true tales of early Australia* Melbourne 1885 (first publ. London 1859)

LANG, J.D. *Narrative of the settlement of the Scots Church, Sydney* Sydney 1828
An historical and statistical account of New South Wales 2 vols. London 1834
Cooksland in north-eastern Australia London 1847
Phillipsland; or the country hitherto designated Port Phillip Edinburgh 1847
The Australian emigrant's manual; or, a guide to the gold colonies of New South Wales and Port Phillip London 1852
Freedom and independence for the golden lands of Australia Sydney 1857
Queensland, Australia London 1861

LANG, J.T. *I remember* Sydney 1956
The great bust: the depression of the thirties Sydney 1962
The turbulent years Sydney 1970

LANGFORD, G. *The death of James Dean and other stories* Beecroft, N.S.W. 1978

LANGLEY, E. *The pea pickers* Sydney 1942

LANGRIDGE, A.K. *The Queensland Kanaka labour traffic since 1885* London [1892]

LANGRIDGE, G.E. *Side lights of labour* Hobart 1893

Language of the native flowers of Tasmania Launceston, Tas. 1867

Lantern [Adelaide] 1874–90 (continued by *Quiz and The lantern*)

LAPLASTRIER, H.J. see 'H.J.L.'

LAPTHORNE, A.M. *Mildura calling* Melbourne 1946

LARCOMBE, F.A. *The advancement of local government in New South Wales, 1906 to the present* Sydney 1978

LARWOOD, H. & PERKINS, K. *The Larwood story* London 1965

LASERON, C.F. *Laseron's direction finding by the sun and stars* Sydney 1942

LATCH, B. & HITCHINGS, B. *Mr X: police informer* Melbourne 1975

LATHAM, J. *A general synopsis of birds* 3 vols. London 1781–85
Supplement. 2 vols. London 1787–1801
A general history of birds 10 vols. Winchester 1821–24

Launceston advertiser Launceston 1829–47

Launceston courier Launceston 1840–43

Launceston examiner Launceston 1842–1900 (continued by *The examiner*)

'LAURIER, D.' (L. Sizer) *The two men from northern rivers* Adelaide [1935]

LAVERS, D. & ZWAR, D. *Vet in the clouds* London 1978

LAWLER, R. *Summer of the seventeenth doll* London 1965 (first publ. Sydney 1957)
The Piccadilly bushman London 1961

LAWLESS, W. *The Darcy story* Sydney [c.1919]

LAWLOR, C.V. *All this humbug* Sydney 1959

LAWRENCE, D.H. & SKINNER, M.L. *The boy in the bush* London 1924

LAWRY, W. Letters, 1818. (Methodist Missionary Society. Records AJCP M124)

Laws of the Australasian game of football as adopted by the Australasian Football Council Adelaide 1925

LAWSON, H. *Short stories in prose and verse* Sydney 1894
In the days when the world was wide and other verses Sydney 1896
While the billy boils Sydney 1896
On the track Sydney 1900
Over the sliprails Sydney 1900
Verses popular and humorous Sydney 1900
Joe Wilson and his mates Edinburgh 1901
Children of the bush London 1902
The elder son Sydney 1905
When I was king and other verses Sydney 1905
The rising of the court Sydney 1910
The skyline riders Sydney 1910
For Australia and other poems Melbourne 1913
Triangles of life and other stories Melbourne 1913
Letters 1890–1922: ed. by C. Roderick Sydney 1970

LAWSON, L. *'The lonely crossing'* and other poems Sydney [1904]

LAWSON, W. *Paddle-wheels away* Sydney 1947
Blue gum clippers and whale ships of Tasmania Melbourne 1949

LAZARIDES, M. *The grasses of Central Australia* Canberra 1970

LEACH, J.A. *An Australian bird book* Melbourne 1911
Australian nature studies Melbourne 1922

LEACH, W.E. *The zoological miscellany; being descriptions of new, or interesting animals* 3 vols. London 1814–17

LEAF, H. *Under the Southern Cross: a record of a pilgrimage* London 1923

LEAKE, B.W. *Eastern wheatbelt wildlife* Perth 1962

Leaves from the diary of a lunatic Melbourne 1937

LEE, C. *Bush week* Sydney 1980

LEE, J.C. *Boshstralians* London 1934

LEE, Mrs R. *Adventures in Australia* London 1851

LEECHMAN, F. *The opal book* Sydney 1961

LEEPER, G.W. *Introduction to soil science* Melbourne 1948
3rd ed. 1957

LEES, W. *The Aboriginal problem in Queensland* Brisbane 1902
Coaching in Australia: a history of the coaching firm of Cobb and Co. Brisbane 1917

Legends of Australia Sydney 1842

LEICHHARDT, L. *Journal of an overland expedition in Australia, from Moreton Bay to Port Essington . . during the years 1844–1845* London 1847

LEIGH, W.H. *Reconnoitering voyages and travels, with adventures in the new colonies of South Australia* London 1839
The emigrant: a tale of Australia London 1847

LEIGHTON, S. Australian journal and notes. 4 vols. 1868 NLA MS 360

LE LIEVRE, C. *Memories of an old police officer* Adelaide 1925

LENTZNER, K. *Dictionary of the slang-English of Australia* Halle-Leipzig 1892

LESLIE, D.S. *The green singers* London 1958

LE SOUEF, W.H.D. *Wild life in Australia* Melbourne [1907]

LE SOUEF, W.H.D. et al. *The wild animals of Australasia* London 1926

LESTER, B. *Verses of this and that* Ouyen, Vic. 1971

LETTE, K. *Hit and ms* Ringwood, Vic. 1984

Letters from South Australia Thrapston, England [1847]

Letters from a young Queenslander 2nd ed. Brisbane 1916

LEVITT, D. *Plants and people: Aboriginal uses of plants on Groote Eylandt* Canberra 1981

LEVY, J.E. see 'Juliet'

LEWIN, J.W. *Birds of New Holland with their natural history* vol. I. London 1808

Birds of New South Wales, with their natural history Sydney 1813

A natural history of the birds of New South Wales London 1822

LEWIS, B. *Sunday at Kooyong Road* Richmond, Vic. 1977

LEWIS, G. *Real men like violence* Kenthurst, N.S.W. 1983

LEWIS, H. *Crow on a barbed wire fence* Sydney 1973

LEWIS, J. *Fought and won* Adelaide 1922

LEWIS, J.H. *Stuart's journey into the interior of Australia* Adelaide 1860

LEWIS, O. *Collection of verses* Adelaide 1911

LEWIS, W.J. *The language of cricket* London 1934

LEYLAND, M. & M. *Great ugly river* Melbourne 1965

Where dead men lie Melbourne 1967

Untamed coast Melbourne 1969

L'HOTELLIER, A. *The green fields of Paraguay* [Melbourne 1920]

LHOTSKY, J. *A journey from Sydney to the Australian Alps, undertaken in the months of January, February, and March, 1834* Sydney 1835

see also 'An impartial observer'

Liberator Melbourne 1884–1904

Lictor Sydney 1869–70

LIDDLE, J.E. *Selected poems* Mullewa, W.A. [1925]

LILLEY, G.W. *Lengthening shadows: memoirs of a Queensland bushman and Queensland historical essays* Brisbane 1977

LILLEY, W.O. *Reminiscences of life in Brisbane, and reflections and sayings* Brisbane 1913

**The limbless soldier: magazine of the Limbless Soldiers Association of Victoria* Melbourne 1923–35

'LINDALL, E.' (E.E. Smith) *Springs of violence* London 1963

A kind of justice New York 1964

Northward the coast London 1966

A gathering of eagles London 1970

Search for tomorrow London 1974

A day for angels London 1975

Season of discovery Melbourne 1978

LINDEMAN, J. *Red rumps and white faces* n.p. [1979]

LINDLEY, J. & MOORE, T. eds. *The treasury of botany: a popular dictionary of the vegetable kingdom* 2 parts. London 1866, rev. ed. 1874

LINDLEY-COWEN, L. *The West Australian settler's guide and farmer's handbook* 6 parts. Perth 1897–98

LINDSAY, D. *An expedition across Australia from south to north, between the telegraph line and the Queensland boundary, in 1885–6* London 1889

Journal of the Elder Scientific Exploring Expedition, 1891–2 Adelaide 1893

LINDSAY, D. & HOLTZE, A.L. *'Territoria' 'land of the dawning'* Adelaide 1909

LINDSAY, H.A. *The bushman's handbook* Sydney 1948

LINDSAY, J. *Life rarely tells* London 1958

LINDSAY, N. *Norman Lindsay's book: no. II* Sydney 1915

'Saturdee' Sydney 1933, London 1936

Halfway to anywhere Sydney 1947

Dust or polish Sydney 1950

Bohemians of the Bulletin Sydney 1965

LINDSAY, R. *A letter from Sydney* Melbourne 1983

LINGHAM, H.C.J. *Juvenal in Melbourne* Melbourne 1892

'LINGO, T.O.' see 'T.O. Lingo'

**Link: Toc H journal of Australia* Melbourne 1926–

LINKLATER, W. & TAPP, L. *Gather no moss* South Melbourne 1968

LINKLETTER, A. *Linkletter down under* North Sydney 1968

**Listening post: official organ of the R.S.L. W.A. branch* Perth 1929–57

LITCHFIELD, J.S. *Far-north memories: being the account of ten years spent on the diamond-drills, and of things that happened in those days* Sydney 1930

Literary news: a review and magazine of fact and fiction Sydney 1837–38

'LITTLE JACOB' *Colonial pen-scratching; or sketches of South Australian life* Mount Barker, S. Aust. 1860

LITTLER, F.M. *A handbook of the birds of Tasmania* Launceston, Tas. 1910

LLOYD, E. see 'A squatter'

LLOYD, G.T. *Thirty-three years in Tasmania and Victoria* London 1862

LLOYD, K. *Black opal* London 1967

LLOYD, S. *The Lightning Ridge book* Mumbil, N.S.W. 1967

LLOYD, V.H. *The hidden enemy* Sydney 1957

'A LOCAL LETTER CARRIER' *After twenty years* Ballarat, Vic. 1884

LOCK, A.C.C. *Travels across Australia* Melbourne 1952

Tropical tapestry: from Capricorn to Cape York Melbourne 1956

LOCKE, E. *From shore to shore* Brisbane 1944

LOCKE, S. *Mum Dawson, 'boss'* Sydney 1911

The Dawsons' Uncle George Sydney 1912

LOCKWOOD, D. *Crocodiles and other people* Adelaide 1959

Fair dinkum London 1960

I, the Aboriginal Adelaide 1962

We, the Aborigines Melbourne 1963

The lizard eaters Melbourne 1964

Up the track Adelaide 1964

LONGMORE, C. *'Eggs-a-cook!': the story of the Forty-Fourth: war – as the digger saw it* Perth 1921

LOONE, A.W. *Tasmania's north-east* Launceston, Tas. 1928

LORD, C.E. & SCOTT, H.H. *A synopsis of the vertebrate animals of Tasmania* Hobart 1924

LORD, E.E. *Shrubs and trees for Australian gardens* Melbourne 1948

3rd ed. 1956

'LORENSKI, A. DE.' (M.J. Wade) *Australian and other poems* Maryborough, Qld. 1891

LORIMER, P.D. *Songs and verses* London 1901

LOVE, J.R.B. *The Aborigines: their present condition* Melbourne 1915

LOVEJOY, G.W. *'In journeyings often'* Dubbo, N.S.W. 1940

LOVELESS, G. *The victims of whiggery* London 1837

LOWENSTEIN, W. *Weevils in the flour: an oral record of the 1930s depression in Australia* Melbourne 1978

LOWENSTEIN, W. & LOH, M. *The immigrants* Melbourne 1977

LOWENSTEIN, W. & HILLS, T. *Under the hook: Melbourne waterside workers remember working lives and class war: 1900–1980* Melbourne 1982

LOWER, L.W. *Here's luck* Sydney 1930, new ed. 1955

LOYAU, G.E. *Colonial lyrics* Sydney [1872]

The personal adventures of George E. Loyau, written by himself Adelaide 1883

LUBBOCK, A. *Australian roundabout* London 1963

LUCAS, A.H.S. & LE SOUEF, W.H.D. *The animals of Australia* Melbourne 1909

The birds of Australia Melbourne 1911

LUMHOLTZ, C. *Among cannibals* tr. by R.B. Anderson New York 1889

LUNN, H. *Joh: the life and political adventures of Johannes Bjelke-Petersen* St Lucia, Qld. 1978

Behind the banana curtain St Lucia, Qld. 1980

Queenslanders St. Lucia, Qld. 1984

LYDEKKER, R. *A hand-book to the marsupialia and monotremata* London 1894

2nd ed. 1896

LYNG, J. *Non-Britishers in Australia: influence on population and progress* Melbourne 1927

LYNN-GUIST, A. see *Pilgrim*

LYON, C. *Narrative and recollections of Van Dieman's Land* New York 1844

'LYTH' *The golden south: memories of Australian home life from 1843 to 1888* London 1890

MABBUTT, J.A. *Desert landforms* Sydney 1977 (*An introduction to systematic geomorphology vol. II.*)

MACADAM, J.F. *Some poisonous plants in the north-west* Sydney 1966 (N.S.W. Dept. of Agriculture. Division of Plant Industry. Bulletin P331)

MCADOO, M. *'If only I'd listened to grandpa': recollections of the old days in the Australian bush* Sydney 1980

MacAlister, C. *Old pioneering days in the sunny south* Goulburn, N.S.W. 1907

McArdle, A.A. *Poultry management and production* Sydney 1961

Macarthur, J. *New South Wales: its present state and future prospects* (anon.) London 1837

Macarthur, J. & Therry, R. *Election for the county of Camden: the speeches of James Macarthur and Roger Therry, esquires* Sydney 1843

Macarthur, Mrs J. Extracts from letters of Mrs John Macarthur, 1789–1840. ML MS A2908

McArthur, K. *Bread and dripping days* Caloundra, Qld. 1977
rev. ed. 1981
Pumicestone Passage: a living waterway Caloundra, Qld. 1978

Macartney, F.T. *Proof against failure* Sydney 1967

McBryde, I. *Aboriginal prehistory in New England* Sydney 1974

McCarter, J. *Pan's clan* Sydney 1932
Love's lunatic Sydney 1933

McCarthy, D. *South-west Pacific area – first year* Canberra 1959
The fate of O'Loughlin Sydney 1979

McCarthy, F.D. *New South Wales Aboriginal place names* Sydney 1952
Australian Aboriginal rock art Sydney 1958

McCleary, G.F. *Cricket with the kangaroo* London 1950

McCombe, E.A. *Whales and whalers* Sydney 1940

M'Combie, T. *Adventures of a colonist; or Godfrey Arabin the settler* London 1845, 1850
Australian sketches Melbourne 1847
2nd series Melbourne 1861
The history of the colony of Victoria from its settlement to the death of Sir Charles Hotham Melbourne 1858

McConnel, K. *Planning the Australian homestead* Sydney 1947

McConnel, M. *Memories of days long gone by, by the wife of an Australian pioneer* [Brisbane 1909]

McConnell, D.E. *Australian etiquette; or the rules and usages of the best society in the Australasian colonies* Melbourne 1885

McCourt, T. *Aboriginal artefacts* Adelaide 1975

McCoy, F. *Prodromus of the zoology of Victoria* 2 vols. Melbourne 1885–90

McCrae, G.G. *Mamba* Melbourne 1867

McCrae, H. *My father and my father's friends* Sydney 1935
ed. *Georgiana's journal: Melbourne a hundred years ago* Sydney 1934

McCullough, C. *The thorn birds* New York 1977

Macdonald, A. *The ukulele player under the red lamp* Sydney 1972

Macdonald, D.A. *The bush boy's book* Melbourne 1911

McDonald, E. *Wildflowers of the Wallum* Ascot, Qld. 1980

Macdonald, J. *Thunderbolt: an Australian story* London 1894

Macdonald, J.G. *Journal . . on an expedition from Port Denison to the Gulf of Carpentaria and back* Brisbane 1865

Macdonald, R.M. *Opals & gold: wanderings & work on the mining & gem fields* London 1928

McDonald, W.M. *Soldier songs from Palestine* Melbourne [1918]

McDonnell, E. *My homeland* Wollongong, N.S.W. [1925]
The land of the budgeriga Newcastle, N.S.W. 1936

Macdonnell, J.E. *Wings off the sea* Sydney 1959 (first publ. London 1953)
Jim Brady, leading seaman London 1954
Commander Brady London 1956
Subsmash! London 1960

McDowall, R.M. ed. *Freshwater fishes of south-eastern Australia* Sydney 1980

McEvey, A. *John Cotton's birds of the Port Phillip district of New South Wales 1843–1849* Sydney 1974

McEwin, H. *The fruitgrower's handbook* 2nd ed. Melbourne 1913

McFarland, A. *Illawarra and Manaro: districts of New South Wales* Sydney 1872

M'Farland, J. *A digest of the law of mining in Victoria* Melbourne 1873

Macgill, P. *The diggers: the Australians in France* London 1919

Macgillivray, J. *Narrative of the voyage of H.M.S. Rattlesnake* 2 vols. London 1852

McGregor, C. *Profile of Australia* London 1966
Don't talk to me about love Sydney 1971
The see-through revolver St Lucia, Qld. 1977

McGregor-Hastie, R. *The compleat migrant* London 1963

McGuffin, W. *Australian tales of the border* Melbourne 1920

McGuire, P. *Australian journey* London 1939

McHale, J.F. et al. *The Australian game of football* Melbourne 1931

MacInnes, A.A. *Straight as a line: an Australian sporting story* London 1894

MacInnes, C. *June in her spring* London 1952

McInnes, G. *The road to Gundagai* London 1965
Humping my bluey London 1966

McIntyre, A.J. *Putting over a burst* Brisbane 1942

McIntyre, A.J. & J.J. *Country towns of Victoria* Melbourne 1944

MacIntyre, J.N. *White Australia: the empty north* Sydney 1920
A high explosive from the empty north Burketown, Qld. [1922]

Macintyre, S. *Militant: the life and times of Paddy Troy* Sydney 1984

McIver, G. *A drover's odyssey* Sydney 1935
The bunyip and other verses Sydney 1943

McJannett, R. *Saltbush Jim, V.C.: and other verses* Newtown, N.S.W. [c.1918]

Mack, A. *Bush days* Sydney 1911

Mackaness, G. ed. *Fourteen journeys over the Blue Mountains of New South Wales 1813–41* 3 parts. Sydney 1950–51

Mackay, A. *The great gold field: a pedestrian tour through the first discovered gold district of New South Wales, in the months of October and November, 1852* Sydney 1853
The Australian agriculturist and colonists' guide 2nd ed. Sydney 1890
The Australian agriculturist and guide for land occupation 3rd ed. Sydney 1896

McKay, C. *This is the life* Sydney 1961

Mackay, J. *Discovery of the Pioneer River, Q.* Singleton, N.S.W. 1892

Mackay, K. *Stirrup jingles* Sydney 1887
Out back London 1893
The yellow wave London 1895

Mackay, M. *Natives' Institution, King George's Sound, Western Australia* Sydney [1859]

Mackellar, D. *The Australian emigrant's guide* Edinburgh 1839

McKellar, J. *Sheep without a shepherd* Melbourne 1937

McKenna, P. *My world of football* North Sydney 1973

McKenney, K. *The hide-away man* London 1965

Mackenzie, D. *The emigrant's guide; or ten years' practical experience in Australia* London 1845
Ten years in Australia: being the results of his experience as a settler during that period 3rd ed. London 1852
The gold digger: a visit to the gold fields of Australia London [1852]

Mackenzie, J. *Australian paradox* London 1962 (first publ. 1961)

'Mackenzie, S.' (K.I. Mackenzie) *Dead men rising* London 1951

McKenzie-Hatton, E. *Moluscut: stories of work amongst the sugar doodles of Queensland* Sydney [c.1926]

McKeown, K.C. *Insect wonders of Australia* Sydney 1935
Spider wonders of Australia Sydney 1936
Australian insects Sydney 1942

Mackie, E. *Oh to be an Aussie!* Sydney 1977

McKie, R. *The mango tree* Sydney 1974
The crushing Sydney 1978
Bitter bread Sydney 1978

McKinlay, J. *McKinlay's journal of exploration in the interior of Australia* Melbourne [1862]

McKinney, J.P. *Crucible* Sydney 1935

Macklin, R. *The Queenslander* Sydney 1975
The paper castle Sydney 1977
Newsfront Melbourne 1978
The journalist Melbourne 1979

Mackness, C. *Gem of the Flat* Sydney [1914]
The young beachcombers London 1934
Clump Point and district: an historical record Clump Point, Qld. [c. 1960]

Macknight, C.C. *The voyage to Marege': Macassan trepangers in northern Australia* Melbourne 1976

McKnight, T.L. *The camel in Australia* Melbourne 1969

The long paddock: Australia's travelling stock routes Armidale, N.S.W. 1977
McLaren, J. *My crowded solitude* London 1926
New love for old London 1950
McLean, A. *Harry Bloomfield: or the adventures of an early Australian squatter* Melbourne 1888
McLean, D. *The roaring days* London 1960
The world turned upside down London 1962
McLean, L. *Pumpkin pie and faded sandshoes* Sydney 1981
Maclean, M. *Drummond of the far west* Manly, N.S.W. 1947
Maclehose, J. *The picture of Sydney: and strangers' guide in New South Wales, for 1838* Sydney 1838
McLelland, R. *Outback touring* Cammeray, N.S.W. 1978
McLennan, L. *The spirit of the west* Sydney 1943
Macleod, Mrs A. (C.E.M. Martin) *The silent sea* 3 vols. London 1892
An Australian girl London 1894 (first publ. 1890)
Macleod, A.I. *Hack's brat* Sydney 1920 (first publ. 1916)
McMahon, J.T. *The bushies' scheme at work in Western Australia* Perth [1939]
Macmahon, P. *The merchantable timbers of Queensland* Brisbane 1905
McManus, F. *The tumult & the shouting* Adelaide 1977
McManus, M.A. *Reminiscences of the early settlement of the Maranoa district* Brisbane 1913
McMichael, D.F. ed. *A treasury of Australian wildlife* Sydney 1967
MacMillan, W. *Australian gossip and story* Brisbane 1895
M'Nally, P.W. *The life and adventures of the wild Scotchman* Brisbane [1899]
McNally, W. *Man from zero* Melbourne 1973
McNeil, J. *The chocolate frog* [&] *The old familiar juice* Sydney 1973
How does your garden grow Sydney 1974
Maconochie, A. *Thoughts on convict management* Hobart 1838
General views regarding the social system of convict management Hobart 1839
On the management of transported criminals London 1845
On the management of prisoners in the Australian colonies London [c. 1845]
McPhee, D.R. *The observer's book of snakes and lizards of Australia* Sydney 1979
Macpherson, A. *Mount Abundance: or, the experiences of a pioneer squatter in Australia thirty years ago* London [c. 1879]
Macpherson, M.L. *I heard the Anzacs singing* New York 1942
The Macquarie dictionary St Leonards, N.S.W. 1981
Macquarie, L. *A letter to the Right Honourable Viscount Sidmouth* London 1821
Journals of his tours in New South Wales and Van Diemen's Land 1810–1822 Sydney 1956
MacQuarrie, H. *We and the baby* Sydney 1929
Macqueen, T.P. *Thoughts and suggestions on the present condition of the country* London 1830
Australia as she is and as she may be London 1840
McRoach, J.J. *A dozen dopey yarns* Fitzroy, Vic. 1979
McTavish, S. *Rafferty king of Australia* Melbourne 1931
Madigan, C.T. *Central Australia* London 1936
Crossing the dead heart Melbourne 1946
Magoffin, R.D. *We bushies* Ilfracombe, England 1968
Chops and gravy Charters Towers, Qld. 1972
Maiden, J.H. *The flowering plants and ferns of New South Wales* 7 parts. Sydney 1895–98
Plants reputed to be poisonous to stock in Australia Sydney 1901
Notes on the commercial timbers of New South Wales 2nd ed. Sydney 1904
The forest flora of New South Wales 8 vols. Sydney 1904–25
Wattles and wattle-barks 3rd ed. Sydney 1906
The weeds of New South Wales Sydney 1920
Main, B.Y. *Between Wodjil and Tor* Brisbane 1967
Twice trodden ground Milton, Qld. 1971
Spiders Sydney 1976
Main, W. *Bush solitudes and other verses* Melbourne 1896
Maitland mercury and Hunter River general advertiser Maitland, N.S.W. 1843–93 (continued by *The Maitland daily mercury*)
Major, T. *Leaves from a squatter's note book* London 1900
Makeshifts and other home-made furniture and utensils Melbourne 1925 (New Settlers League of Australia. Rural development booklets 2)
Malone, R.E. *Three years' cruise in the Australasian colonies* London 1854
Malouf, D. *Johnno* St Lucia, Qld. 1975
Harland's half acre New York 1984
Mander, A.E. *Our sham democracy* Sydney 1943
Mandle, W.F. *Going it alone* London 1978
Manifesto of the Federal Labor Executive on the unity negotiations of 1934 Brisbane [1934]
Mankind Sydney 1931–
Mann, A. *The goldfields of Australia* London 1852
Mann, D.D. *The present picture of New South Wales* London 1811
Mann, J.F. *Eight months with Dr Leichhardt, in the years 1846–47* Sydney 1888
Mann, L. *Flesh in armour* Melbourne 1932
Human drift Sydney 1935
A murder in Sydney London 1937
Mountain flat London 1939
The go-getter Sydney 1942
Mann, R.J. *Mann's emigrant's guide to Australia; including the colonies of New South Wales, Port Philip, South Australia, Western Australia, and Moreton Bay* London 1849
Mann, W. *Six years' residence in the Australian provinces, ending in 1839* London 1839
Manning, A.E. *The bodgie* Sydney 1958
Manning, F. *The middle parts of fortune* 2 vols. London 1929
Manning, K.W. *In their own hands: a North Queensland sugar story* Farleigh, Qld. 1983
Manning, N. *Us or them* Sydney 1984
Mant, G. *You'll be sorry* Sydney 1944
Maris, H. & Borg, S. *Women of the sun* Ringwood, Vic. 1985
Marjoribanks, A. *Travels in New South Wales* London 1847
Marriott, J.A.R. *Empire settlement* London 1927
Marsden, J.B. ed. *Memoirs of the life and labors of the Rev. Samuel Marsden* New York [1858]
Marsden, S. *Some private correspondence of the Rev. Samuel Marsden and family 1794–1824* Sydney 1942
Marsh, R. *Seven years of my life; or narrative of a patriot exile* Buffalo, U.S.A. 1848
Marshall, A. *Sunny Australia* London [1911]
Marshall, Alan *These are my people* Melbourne 1944
Tell us about the turkey, Jo Sydney 1946
Ourselves writ strange Melbourne 1948
How beautiful are thy feet Melbourne 1949
Bumping into friends Melbourne 1950
How's Andy going? Melbourne 1956
This is the grass Melbourne 1962
These were my tribesmen Melbourne 1965
Hammers over the anvil West Melbourne 1975
Alan Marshall's Australia South Yarra, Vic. 1981
Marshall, Alan John & Drysdale, R. *Journey among men* London 1962
Marshall, Alan John ed. *Nulli secundus log* Sydney 1946
Marshall, F.D. *Let's go fishing* Sydney 1948
Marshall, T.S. *Memoir of the Victorian Country Fire Service and other reminiscences* Melbourne 1930
Marshall, V. *Jail from within* Sydney 1918
The world of the living dead Sydney 1919
Martin, A.P. *The beginnings of an Australian literature* London 1898
ed. *An Easter omelette* Melbourne 1879
ed. *Oak-bough and wattle-blossom* London 1888
Martin, A.W. ed. *Essays in Australian federation* Melbourne 1969
Martin, C.E.M. see Macleod, Mrs A.
Martin, D. *The hero of Too* Melbourne 1965
Hughie Melbourne 1971

Frank & Francesca Melbourne 1972
MARTIN, E.A. *The life and speeches of Daniel Henry Deniehy* Sydney 1884
MARTIN, H.A. ed. *'Under the gum tree'* London 1890
Coo-ee: tales of Australian life London [c. 1891]
MARTIN, J. *The Australian sketch book* Sydney 1838
MARTIN, J.B. *Reminiscences by J.B.M.* Camden, N.S.W. 1884
MARTINEAU, H. *Homes abroad* London 1832
MARTINEAU, J. *Letters from Australia* London 1869
MARTYN, B. *First footers in South Gippsland* Dumbalk, Vic. 1979
MASCORD, R. *Spiders of Australia: a field guide* Sydney 1980
MASLEN, T.J. *The friend of Australia; or a plan for exploring the interior* London 1830
MASS, N. *Australian wild-flower fairies* Sydney 1937
MASS, O. *Dangerous waters* Adelaide 1975
MASSON, E.R. *An untamed territory* London 1915
'MASTER-SARG' *A Yank discovers Australia* Sydney [1945]
MASTERS, O. *Loving daughters* St Lucia, Qld. 1984
MATHERS, P. *Trap* Melbourne 1966
The Wort papers North Melbourne 1972
MATHESON, J. *Day dreams* Brisbane [1936]
MATHEW, J. *Eaglehawk and crow* London 1899
Australian echoes London 1902
Two representative tribes of Queensland London 1910
Ballads of bush life Melbourne 1914
MATHEWS, G.M. *A list of the birds of Australia* London 1913
MATHEWS, R.H. *Folklore of the Australian Aborigines* Sydney 1899
MATHIEU, J. *Backblock ballads and lignum lyrics* Brisbane [1927]
Matilda: a whole swagful of local verse compiled by the Winton Tourist Promotion Assoc. Winton, Qld. 1970
MATTHAMS, J. *The rabbit pest in Australia* Melbourne 1921
MATTHEWS, C.H.S. *A parson in the Australian bush* London 1908
Bill: a bushman London 1914
MATTHEWS, Harley *Saints and soldiers* Sydney 1918
ed. *Pillar to post* Sydney 1944
MATTHEWS, Herbert *Chat about Australia* Bournemouth 1898
MATTINGLEY, C. *The great Ballagundi damper bake* Sydney 1975
MAXWELL, C.B. *The cold nose of the law* Sydney 1948
Surf: Australians against the sea Sydney 1949
MAXWELL, J. *Hell's bells and mademoiselles* Sydney 1932
MAYES, C.E. *The Australian builders & contractors' price book* 8th ed. Sydney 1914
MAYES, P. *The Australian architects, builders and contractors price book and guide* Glebe, N.S.W. 1951
MAYNE, D. *Westerly busters* Bathurst, N.S.W. 1879
MAYNE, R.W. *The two visions* Sydney 1874
MAYNE, W. *Salt River times* West Melbourne 1980
Meanjin Brisbane 1940– (from 1945 publ. in Melbourne; title varies, from 1961 *Meanjin quarterly*)
MEDDING, P.Y. ed. *Jews in Australian society* Melbourne 1973
Medical journal of Australia Sydney July 1914– (continues *Australian medical journal*)
MEEHAN, B. *Shell bed to shell midden* Canberra 1982
MEGGY, P.R. *From Sydney to Silverton* Sydney 1885
MEIKLE, D.H. *Humorous and other verses* [Sydney 1918]
Melbourne argus Melbourne 1846–48 (continued by *The argus*)
Melbourne Christmas annual Melbourne [1880]
Melbourne monthly magazine Melbourne 1855
Melbourne punch Melbourne 1856–1900
Melbourne punch's almanack Melbourne 1862
Melbourne times Melbourne 1842–43
Melbourne university magazine Melbourne 1907–
Melbourne weekly courier Melbourne 1844–46
MELVILLE, H. *Two letters written in Van Diemen's Land* Hobart 1834
The history of the island of Van Diemen's Land, from the year 1824 to 1835 inclusive London 1835
Australasia and prison discipline London 1851
The present state of Australia London 1851
**Men may smoke: official journal of the 2/18th BN 8th Div A.I.F.* Sydney & Malaya 1940–41
'THE MEN OF ANZAC' *The Anzac book* London 1916
MENDELSOHN, O. *The earnest drinker's digest* Sydney 1946
A waltz with Matilda Melbourne 1966
MERCER, G. *Copy letter .. to the Principal Secretary of State for the Colonies* Edinburgh 1836
Mercury Hobart July 1860– (continues *The Hobarton mercury*)
Mercury and South Australian sporting chronicle Adelaide 1849–?1851
MEREDITH, G. *The Lawsons* Sydney 1948
MEREDITH, J. *Learn to talk old Jack Lang: a handbook of Australian rhyming slang* Kenthurst, N.S.W. 1984
MEREDITH, L.A. (Mrs C.) *Notes and sketches of New South Wales, during a residence in that colony from 1839 to 1844* London 1844
My home in Tasmania 2 vols. London 1852
Over the Straits: a visit to Victoria London 1861
Tasmanian friends and foes: feathered, furred, and finned Hobart 1880
MEREWEATHER, J.D. *Diary of a working clergyman in Australia and Tasmania, kept during the years 1850–1853* London 1859
MERRITT, R.J. *The cake man* Sydney 1978
MERYON, E. *At Holland's tank* Sydney 1922
METCALFE, E. *Garden party* [Perth] 1980
METHODIST MISSIONARY SOCIETY Records, 1812–26 AJCP M124
MEUDELL, G. *The pleasant career of a spendthrift* London 1929
MEYER, H.E.A. *Manners and customs of the Aborigines of the Encounter Bay tribe, South Australia* Adelaide 1846
MEYRICK, F.J. *Life in the bush, 1840–1847* London 1939
MICKLE, A.D. *The wee dog and other essays* Melbourne 1922
After the ball Melbourne 1959
MIKES, G. *Boomerang* London 1968
MILES, B. *The stars my blanket* London 1954
MILES, N. *Opal fever* London 1972
MILFORD, R.H. *Australia's backyards* Sydney 1934
MILL, G. *Nobody dies but me* North Sydney 1968
MILLER, H.M. *My story* South Melbourne 1983
MILLER, J. *Koori: a will to win* Sydney 1985
'MILLER, J.' (W. Lane) *The workingman's paradise* London 1892
MILLER, L.W. *Notes of an exile to Van Dieman's Land* New York 1846
MILLER, R. *Sugarbird lady* Adelaide 1979
MILLETT, Mrs E. *An Australian parsonage; or, the settler and the savage in Western Australia* London 1872
MILLIGAN, H. *A sprig of light* vol. 2 West Geelong, Vic. 1981
MILLINGTON, R. *A nation of trees: Australian rites* London 1963
MILLS, C.D. *The stockwhip and the spur* Sydney 1956
Hobble chains and green hide Mudgee, N.S.W. 1976
MILLS, F.J. *Dinkum oil* Adelaide 1917
Cheer up: 'a story of war work' Adelaide 1920
Happy days Adelaide 1924
MILLS, H.C. *No regrets* Belmont, Vic. 1981
MILNE, W. Notes of a journey to the south eastern district. January 1863 S. Aust. Archives D5139(L)
Miner and general advertiser Lambing Flat, N.S.W. 1861–62
Mining chronicle Melbourne 1882–83
**Mirage: RAAF Williamtown monthly* (title varies) Williamtown, N.S.W. 1967–69
MIRRITJI, J. *My people's life* Milingimbi, N.T. 1978
MITCHEL, J. *Jail journal* Dublin 1913 (first publ. New York 1854)
MITCHELL, Edmund *The labour question in Australia* Melbourne 1892
MITCHELL, Elyne *Speak to the earth* Sydney 1945
Flow river, blow wind Sydney 1953
Black cockatoos mean snow London 1956
MITCHELL, G. *The bush horseman: the horsemanship of the Australian outback* Sydney 1981
MITCHELL, G.D. *Backs to the wall* Sydney 1937
MITCHELL, T.L. *Three expeditions into the interior of eastern Australia* 2 vols. London 1838
2nd ed. 1839
Journal of an expedition into the interior of tropical Australia London 1848
MOBERLY, G.F. *Experiences of a 'dinki di' R.R.C. nurse* Sydney 1933

A modern dictionary of the English language with Australasian supplement London [1912]
MOFFITT, I. *The U-Jack society: an experience of being Australian* Dee Why, N.S.W. 1972
MOLESWORTH, W. *Report from the Select Committee of the House of Commons on transportation .. and notes by Sir William Molesworth, Bart., chairman of the Committee* London 1838
MOLLARD, H.F. *Humour of the road* Melbourne [1920]
MOLONEY, B. *Memoirs of an abominable showman* Adelaide 1968
MONEY, C.L. *Knocking about in N.Z.* Melbourne 1871
MONEY, L. *The footy fan's handbook* Melbourne 1981
Monitor Sydney 19 May 1826–11 Aug. 1828 (continued by *The Sydney monitor*)
MONKMAN, N. *Quest of the curly-tailed horses* Sydney 1962
Monthly almanac and illustrated commentator nos. 1–6 Adelaide 1850
MOODIE, P.M. *Aboriginal health* Canberra 1973
MOODY, C.P. *Australian cricket and cricketers 1856—1893–94* Melbourne 1894
MOORE, A.M. *Autumn grey* Melbourne [1918]
MOORE, B.P. *Life on forty acres: some experiences of a naturalist living in the Australian bush* Faringdon, England 1978
MOORE, G.F. *Extracts from the letters and journals 1834* see Doyle, M. ed.
Evidences of an inland sea, collected from the natives of the Swan River settlement Dublin 1837
A descriptive vocabulary of the language in common use amongst the Aborigines of Western Australia London 1842
Diary of ten years eventful life of an early settler in Western Australia: and also a descriptive vocabulary of the language of the Aborigines London 1884
MOORE, J.L. *The canine king: the working sheep dog* Cheltenham, Vic. 1929
MOORE, R.O. *Sunlit plains extended: the making of a bushman* Albury, N.S.W. 1975
MOORE, T.I. *Emu parade* Sydney 1941
MOORE, W. *Just to myself, but ..* Adelaide 1977
MOORE-BENTLEY, M. *Sketched from life* Sydney 1903
MOORE-ROBINSON, J. *A record of Tasmanian nomenclature with dates and origins* Hobart 1911
MOOREHEAD, A. *Rum Jungle* London 1953
Cooper's Creek London 1963
MOORHOUSE, F. *Futility and other animals: a discontinuous narrative* Sydney 1969
The electrical experience Sydney 1974
Conference-ville Sydney 1976
Days of wine and rage Melbourne 1980
The everlasting secret family and other secrets Sydney 1980
'MOOSAFIR' *The north-west coast of Tasmania* Melbourne 1889
MORAN, S. *Reminiscences of a rebel* Chippendale, N.S.W. 1979
MORANT, B. *The poetry of 'Breaker' Morant from the Bulletin 1891–1903* Gladesville, N.S.W. 1980
Moreton Bay courier Brisbane 1846–61 (continued by *The courier*)
Moreton Bay free press Brisbane 1850–59 (continued by *Queensland free press*)
MORGAN, J. *The life and adventures of William Buckley* Hobart 1852
MORGAN, R. *Reminiscences of the Aboriginal station at Cummeragunga and its Aboriginal people* Melbourne 1952
MORIARTY, G. *Teaching the game of football by post* Melbourne 1928
MORLEY, B.D. & TOELKEN, H.R. eds. *Flowering plants in Australia* Adelaide 1983
MORLEY, G. *Jockey rides honest race* Sydney 1972
MORLEY, R. *Cool change moving north* London 1966
Morning advertiser and colonial maritime journal Hobart 1841
Morpeth review Morpeth, N.S.W. 1927–34
MORPHETT, G.C. ed. *The life and letters of Sir John Morphett* Adelaide 1936
Reminiscences of Charles H. Field [Adelaide] 1944
MORPHETT, J. *South Australia: latest information .. in a letter .. dated Nov. 25th, 1836* London [1836]
Letter .. to his brother, received by the brig 'Rapid', Nov. 7th 1837 London 1837
MORRIS, A. *Rich river* Echuca, N.S.W. [1953]
MORRIS, E.E. ed. *Cassell's picturesque Australasia* 4 vols. London 1887–89
Austral English: a dictionary of Australasian words phrases and usages London 1898
MORRIS, G.S. *Convicts and colonies* London 1853
MORRIS, M. *Dark tumult* London 1939
The township Sydney 1947
MORRISON, J. *Sailors belong ships* Melbourne 1947
The creeping city Sydney 1949
Port of call Melbourne 1950
Black cargo Melbourne 1955
Twenty-three Sydney 1962
Australian by choice Adelaide 1973
North wind Ringwood, Vic. 1982
MORRISON, S. *Who's taking you to the dance?* Prahran, Vic. 1979
MORSE, C. *The guest years of my life* Sydney 1960
MORTLOCK, J.F. *Experiences of a convict* London 1865
MORTON, W.L. *Notes of a recent personal visit to the unoccupied portions of northern Queensland* [Melbourne 1860]
MOSES, J. *Beyond the city gates* Sydney 1923
Nine miles from Gundagai Sydney 1938, 1944
MOSSMAN, S. *A voice from Australia* London 1852
The gold regions of Australia: a descriptive account of New South Wales, Victoria, and South Australia, with particulars of the recent gold discovery 2nd ed. London [1852]
MOSSMAN, S. & BANISTER, T. *Australia visited and revisited* London 1853
MOTHERWELL, P. *Mr Bastard* Collingwood, Vic. 1977
Mount Isa mail Mount Isa, Qld. 1953–66
MOUNTFORD, C.P. *Brown men and red sand: wanderings in wild Australia* Melbourne 1948
Aboriginal paintings from Australia Milan 1964
Records of the American-Australian scientific expedition to Arnhem Land 4 vols. Melbourne 1956–64
MOWLE, M.B. Diaries 1850–55. ML MS 68
MOXHAM, W. *The longshot* Sydney 1964
Follow that horse Sydney 1965
The apprentice Adelaide 1969
MOYES, A.G. *Australian batsmen: from Charles Bannerman to Neil Harvey* Sydney 1954
MOYES, J.F. *Scrap-iron flotilla* Sydney 1943
MOYNIHAN, C. *The feast of the Bunya* Brisbane 1901
Mud and blood Melbourne 1945
MUDIE, J. *The felonry of New South Wales* London 1837
MUDIE, R. *The picture of Australia* London 1829
**Mud over blood chronicle: 2/7th Australian Infantry Battalion Association newsletter* Melbourne 1976–82
MUELLER, F. von. *Introduction to botanic teachings at the schools of Victoria* Melbourne 1877
Select extra-tropical plants Calcutta 1880
2nd ed. Sydney 1881 (first Australian ed. publ. Melbourne 1876, with title *Select plants readily eligible for industrial culture*)
MUGGRIDGE, W. *How to train a racehorse: Australian horse talk for horse men* Sydney 1920
MUIR, M. *My bush book: K. Langloh Parker's 1890s story of outback station life with background and biography* Adelaide 1982
MULLALLY, J. & SEXTON, I.P. *Stir the possum* [Albany, W.A.] 1976
Libra and the leprechaun Victoria Park, W.A. 1978
MULLEN, C.C. *History of Australian rules football 1858 to 1958* Carlton, Vic. 1959
MULLINS, B. & J. *Horses and ponies in Australia* Sydney 1978
MULVANEY, D.J. *Cricket walkabout: the Australian Aboriginal cricketers on tour 1867–8* Melbourne 1967
The prehistory of Australia London 1969
MULVANEY, J. et al. *Aboriginal Australia* Sydney 1981
MUNDY, G.C. *Our Antipodes: or, residence and rambles in the Australasian colonies with a glimpse of the gold fields* 3 vols. London 1852
MUNRO, C. *Fern vale or the Queensland squatter* 3 vols. London 1862

MURDOCH, J. see 'A.M.'
MURIF, J.J. *From ocean to ocean: across a continent on a bicycle* Melbourne 1897
MURNANE, G. *Tamarisk row* Melbourne 1974
A lifetime on clouds Melbourne 1976
MURPHY, E.G. see 'Dryblower'
MURPHY, H.M. *Strictly for soldiers* Sydney 1943
MURPHY, R.D. *Speak to strangers* Sydney [1960]
MURPHY, W.E. *History of the eight hours' movement* Melbourne 1896
MURRAY, J. *Larrikins: 19th century outrage* Melbourne 1973
MURRAY, L.A. *Poems against economics* Sydney 1972
MURRAY, P.J. *Not so bad as they seem: the transportation, ticket of leave, and penal servitude questions* London 1857
MURRAY, R.D. *A summer at Port Phillip* Edinburgh 1843
Murray's Austral-Asiatic review Hobart 1828 (continued by *The Tasmanian and Austra-Asiatic review)*
Murray's guide to the gold diggings: the Australian gold diggings: where they are and how to get at them Sydney 1956 (first publ. London 1852)
Muse: arts and entertainment in Canberra Canberra 1980–Jan. 1984 (continued by *Muse communique)*
Muse communique: muse – arts and entertainment in Canberra including communique, a 2XX subscriber's magazine Canberra Mar. 1984– (continues *Muse)*
MYATT, B. ed. *Australian and New Zealand gemstones* Dee Why West, N.S.W. 1972
Dictionary of Australian gemstones Dee Why West, N.S.W. 1974
MYERS, J. *The life voyage and travels of Capt. John Myers* London 1817

NAGLE, W. *The odd angry shot* Sydney 1975
NAISH, J. *The cruel field* London 1962
That men should fear London 1963
NANSON, E.J. *The real value of a vote and how to get it at the coming federal elections* Melbourne 1900
NAPIER, E. *Winter is in July* London 1949
NAPIER, F. *Notes of a voyage from New South Wales to the north coast of Australia* [Glasgow 1876]
NAPIER, S.E. *On the Barrier Reef: notes from a no-ologist's pocket-book* Sydney 1928
NATHAN, P. & JAPANANGKA, D.L. *Settle down country* Malmsbury, Vic. 1983
Nation Sydney 1958–July 1972 (merged with *The review* to form *Nation review)*
Nation review Melbourne 1972–79
National times Sydney 1971– (from 10 Aug. 1986–1988 had title *National times on Sunday)*
Native companion Melbourne 1907
Native tribes of South Australia : introd. by J.D. Woods Adelaide 1879
NEAL, N.P.H. ed. *Back to the bush! 1914 1918* Sydney 1918
NEASBEY, P.C. *Blokes I knew* Sydney 1944
NEEDHAM, A. *The radicals and other verse* Hobart 1911
NEEDHAM, H.M. *The morepork* Sydney 1929
NEILSON, J.S. *The autobiography of John Shaw Neilson:* introduced by N. Keesing Canberra 1978
NELSON, T. *Towards socialism in Australia: a worker draws conclusions from Labor history* Sydney [1940]
NESFIELD, H.W. *A chequered career* (anon.) London 1881
NEVILL, E. *Gleanings with meanings* Melbourne 1885
NEVILLE, M. *Murder and poor Jenny* London 1954
'NEW CHUM' *A ramble in Launceston* Launceston, Tas. 1879
New country: a selection of Western Australian short stories Fremantle, W.A. 1976
New idea Melbourne 1902–
New settler in Western Australia Perth 1950–60
New settlers' handbook to Victoria Melbourne 1924
New South Wales general .. orders 16 Feb. 1791–1815 (title varies) Sydney 1800–19
NEW SOUTH WALES. Governor. *Instructions for the constables of country districts .. Nov. 16 1796* Sydney 1796
Instructions to the watchmen of the town divisions .. Nov. 18 1796 Sydney 1796
New South Wales magazine Sydney 1833–34
New South Wales. Magistrates' deposition book. 1834–35 NLA MS 67
New South Wales monthly magazine Sydney 1843
New South Wales. Mounted Police. Troop order books 1832–41. 2 vols. NLA MS 3221
New South Wales pocket almanack Sydney 1806–21 (continued by *Australasian pocket almanack)*
NEW SOUTH WALES. Royal Commission .. to inquire into and report upon the actual state and prospect of the fisheries of this colony. *Report .. and appendix* Sydney 1880
New South Wales sheepbreeders year book Sydney 1898–1908
New South Wales sporting magazine Sydney 1848–49
Newcastle morning herald and miners' advocate Newcastle, N.S.W. 1861–
NEWLAND, S. *The far north country* Adelaide 1887
Paving the way London 1893
Land-grant railway across Central Australia Adelaide 1902
A band of pioneers: old-time memories Adelaide 1919
NEWMAN, G.M. *The Northern Territory and its gold-fields* Adelaide 1875
NEWMAN, H.W. ed. *Extracts & reports on the Lucknow, or Wentworth gold-field* Orange, N.S.W. 1888
NEWTON, R. *The work and wealth of Queensland* Brisbane 1897
NGABIDJ, G. *My country of the pelican dreaming* Canberra 1981
NIALL, B. *Seven little billabongs: the world of Ethel Turner and Mary Grant Bruce* Melbourne 1979
Nichigo press Sydney 1980–
NICHOLSON, J.H. *The opal fever* Brisbane 1878
NICHOLSON, N. & H. *Australian rainforest plants* Lismore, N.S.W. 1985
NICOLL, G.R. *Fifty years' travels in Australia, China, Japan, America, etc., 1848–1898* London 1899
NICOLS, A. *Wild life and adventure in the Australian bush: four years' personal experience* London 1887
NILAND, D. *The shiralee* New York 1955
Call me when the Cross turns over Sydney 1957
Gold in the streets London 1959
The big smoke London 1959
Dadda jumped over two elephants London 1963
Pairs and loners London 1966
Dead men running Sydney 1969
NISBET, H. *A colonial tramp: travels and adventures in Australia and New Guinea* 2 vols. London 1891
A bush girl's romance London 1894
NISBET, J. *Scraps* Bathurst, N.S.W. 1924
NIXON, M. *The rivers of home* Perth 1978
NOAKES, A.W. *The life of a policeman* Brisbane [1946]
Water for the inland Brisbane [1947]
NOBLET, E.M. *The winds that blew at Cossack* Sydney 1968
NOLAN, C. *A bride for St Thomas* London 1970
NOONAN, W. *The surprising battalion* Sydney 1945
NORMAN, B. *Bush pilot* Cairns, Qld. 1976
NORTH, A.J. *Descriptive catalogue of the nests & eggs of birds found breeding in Australia and Tasmania* Sydney 1889
A list of the insectivorous birds of New South Wales 6 parts. Sydney 1896–1905 (reprinted from *The agricultural gazette of New South Wales)*
NORTH, E. *Nobody stops me* New York 1960
'NORTH, J.' (P. Reay) *Harry Dale's Grand National* Sydney 1920
The black opal Sydney 1922
A son of the bush Sydney 1923
NORTH, M. *Recollections of a happy life* 2 vols. London 1892
North Australian monthly Darwin 1954–65
North Queensland guardian Townsville, Qld. May 1937–Nov. 1943 (continued by *Queensland guardian*, Brisbane)
North-western advocate West Devonport, Tas. Jan.–13 Nov. 1899 (incorporated in *North western advocate and Emu Bay times* , Burnie, Tas. and from 1919 continued by *The advocate)*
NORTHCOTT, C.H. *Australian social development* New York 1918

Northern herald: free every Thursday with the Sydney morning herald Sydney 1984–
Northern Territory news Darwin 1952–
Northern Territory times Darwin 1873–1932
NORTON, J. *Australian essays on subjects political, moral and religious* London 1857
The condition of the colony of New South Wales Sydney 1860
NORWOOD, V.G.C. *The long haul* London 1967
Notes of an excursion to the Blue Mountains and the 'zig-zag works' Melbourne 1869
NUGENT, J.F. *Lorblimey and other pious pieces* Melbourne [1916]
Number one Adelaide 1861
Nungalinya occasional bulletin Casuarina, N.T. 1976–

**O P: a literary chronicle of the 10th Battery A.F.A. at the front* London 1917
**O-pip: 'P' Battery, Australian Field Artillery* Melbourne 1943
OAKES, L. *Whitlam PM: a biography* Sydney 1973
Crash through or crash Richmond, Vic. 1976
OAKLEY, B. *A wild ass of a man* Melbourne 1967
A salute to the great McCarthy Melbourne 1970
Let's hear it for Prendergast Melbourne 1970
The ship's whistle Melbourne 1979
The great god Mogadon St Lucia, Qld. 1980
OAKMAN, H. *Garden & landscape trees in Australia* Adelaide 1979
OATES, A. & SEEMAN, A. *Victorian Aborigines: plant foods* Melbourne 1979
'O'BRIEN, J.' (P.J. Hartigan) *Around the boree log* Sydney 1921
O'BRIEN, S.E. & STEPHENS, A.G. *Materials for a dictionary of Australian slang* Sydney 1900–10
Materials for an Austrazealand slang dictionary Sydney [c. 1910]
Observer Adelaide 1905–31 (continues *The Adelaide observer*)
Observer Hobart 1845–46
Observer Melbourne 1848–49
Observer Sydney 1958–61
**Observer: 2/6 Australian Field Survey Battery, R.A.A.* Brisbane 1942–44
Observer miscellany Adelaide 1875–79
O'CALLAGHAN, D. *Long life reminiscences & adventures throughout the world* Sydney 1941
Oceania Melbourne (from vol. 3 publ. in Sydney) 1930–
O'CONNELL, J.F. *A residence of eleven years in New Holland and the Caroline Islands* Boston 1836
'O'CONNER, E.' (B. McNamara) *Steak for breakfast* Sydney 1958
The Irishman Sydney 1960
A second helping Sydney 1969
O'CONNOR, D.B. *Black velvet* Townsville, Qld. 1931
The belle of Barrine Brisbane [1932]
ODELL, C. *Working dogs* Sydney 1966
O'DONNELL, J.P. *Songs of an Anzac by an Anzac-Franco-Aussie* Dublin 1918
O'DONNELL, W.J. *Diary of the exploring expedition . . from Port Darwin to Cambridge Gulf* Melbourne 1884
O'DOWD, B. *The bush* Melbourne 1912
Beaufort: an ode Beaufort, Vic. 1927
O'FERRALL, E.F. *Bodger and the boarders* Sydney 1921
'AN OFFICER' *An authentic and interesting narrative of the late expedition to Botany Bay, as performed by Commodore Phillips, and the fleet of seven transport ships under his command* London 1789
'AN OFFICER OF THE LINE' *The military-sketch book: reminiscences of seventeen years in the service abroad and at home* 2 vols. London 1827
Official record of the Intercolonial Exhibition of Australasia Melbourne 1866–67
OGILVIE, W.H. *Fair girls and gray horses with other verses* Sydney 1898
Hearts of gold and other verses Sydney 1903
My life in the open London 1908
The overlander and other verses Glasgow 1913
OGILVY, A.J. see 'A.J.O.'
O'GRADY, A. *The sugar-coated comfortable* Sydney 1975
O'GRADY, D. *A bottle of sandwiches* Sydney 1968
O'GRADY, J.P. *The things they do to you* Sydney 1963
Aussie English Sydney 1965
Gone troppo Sydney 1968
O'Grady sez Sydney 1969
Aussie etiket Sydney 1971
It's your shout, mate! Sydney 1972
Survival in the doghouse Sydney 1973
There was a kid Sydney 1977
see also 'Culotta, N.'
O'HALLORAN, M. *Western Australian police manual: a catechism of the duties of police constables* Perth 1914
O'HARA, J. *The history of New South Wales* (anon.) London 1817
O'HARA, J.B. *Songs of the south* London 1895
'OLD BOOMERANG' see Houlding, J.R.
'AN OLD BUSHMAN' (H.W. Wheelwright) *Bush wanderings of a naturalist* London 1861
'OLD CHUM' (J.M. Forde) *Chips: or, Australia in the fifties* London [1893]
Some fragments of old Sydney Sydney 1898
'AN OLD COLONIST' *How constitutional government was won for Australasia* Rockhampton, Qld. 1898
**Old faithful: journal of the 3rd Battalion the Royal Australian Regiment* Korea 1953
'AN OLD GOLD DIGGER' *The gold digger's guide* Kadina, S. Aust. 1887
'AN OLD HAND' (G. Hamilton) *Experiences of a colonist forty years ago and a journey from Port Phillip to South Australia in 1839* Adelaide 1879
2nd ed. 1880
'AN OLD HOUSEKEEPER' *The Australian housewives' manual: a book for beginners and people with small incomes* Melbourne 1885 (first publ. 1883)
Australian plain cookery Melbourne [1897]
'OLD STOCKMAN' (A.H. Sutton) *Sensational cattle-stealing case* Dubbo, N.S.W. 1929
'OLD TIME' *The convict hulk 'Success'* Melbourne 1891
'AN OLD YET YOUNG COLONIST' *One mode of passing away a spare day* Adelaide 1857
The oldest coursing club in Australia, being a history of the Narracoorte Club from 1867 to 1889 Narracoorte, S. Aust. 1890
OLIVER, A. *A collection of Acts relating to the transfer of, or dealing with, land* Sydney 1877
O'MALLEY, K. *Second message to the sovereign electors of Encounter Bay* Adelaide 1899
'OMEGA' *Gold in Australia* [London 1851]
The sheep, long-woolled as well as short-woolled, for Victoria, Tasmania, & New Zealand Melbourne 1865
Omnibus and Sydney spectator Sydney 1841–43
**On guard: official organ of the Broken Hill sub-branch of the Returned Services League* Broken Hill, N.S.W. 1969–73
'ONE WHO HAS HANDLED THE SPADE' *Bounty immigration: a letter to the members of the Legislative Council* Melbourne 1855
'ONE WHO IS GOING' see Stephens, J.
'ONE WHO KNOWS THEM' *The Chinese question analyzed with a full statement of facts* Melbourne 1857
'ONE WHO WAS THERE' *Prison sketches* Hobart 1883
Once a month: an illustrated Australian magazine Melbourne 1884–86
O'NEIL, L.M.D. *Dinkum Aussie* Brisbane 1924
O'NEILL, C.T. *Soldiers' poems* Melbourne [1917]
ONSLOW, S.M. ed. *Some early records of the Macarthurs of Camden* Sydney 1914
Open road Sydney 1922–
OPITZ, J. *Cooinda in Kakadu: the personal story behind it* Darwin 1984
OPPEN, E.A. *A description of the Northern Territory of South Australia* Hertford, England 1864
O'REILLY, B. *Green mountains and Cullenbenbong* Brisbane 1949
O'REILLY, J.B. *Songs from the southern seas* Boston 1873
O'REILLY, M.J. *The pinnacle road* Hobart 1936
Bowyangs and boomerangs: reminiscences of 40 years' prospecting in Australia and Tasmania Hobart 1944
ORR, S. *Roll on brave new bloody world* Sydney 1980

OSBORNE, A. *Notes on the present state and prospects of society in New South Wales* London 1833
OSBORNE, J.P. *Nine crowded years* Sydney 1921
OSBORNE, O. *The golden jubilee* Melbourne [1901]
OSBORNE, S. *Duck shooting in Australia* Sydney 1955
OSBORNE, W.A. *The visitor to Australia* Melbourne 1934
O'TOOLE, A. *The coach from the city: a story about Australian rules football* Adelaide 1967
The racing game Adelaide 1969
OTTLEY, R. *By the sandhills of Yamboorah* London 1965
Brumbie dust New York 1969
The Bates family New York 1969
**Our empire: the official organ of the Sailors & Soldiers Fathers Association* Melbourne 1918–21
Ourselves and our land see 'R.T.H.'
OUTHWAITE, R.L. & CHOMLEY, C.H. *The wisdom of Esau* Melbourne [1941]
Ovens and Murray advertiser Beechworth, Vic. 1855–
Overland Mount Eliza, Vic. 1954–
Overlander Sydney 1976–
'OVERLANDER' *Australian sketches* London 1887
OWEN, W.L. *Cossack gold: the chronicles of an early goldfields warden* Sydney 1933
OXLEY, J. *Journals of two expeditions into the interior of New South Wales, undertaken . . in the years 1817–18* London 1820
Oz Sydney 1963–70
Ozbike Spit Junction, N.S.W. 1978– (from 1982 publ. Rydalmere, N.S.W.)

PACKER, J. *Leopard in the fold* London 1969
PAGE, G. *Smalltown memorials* St Lucia, Qld. 1975
PAGE, J.J. *Ross Island 'MUD-pickers': a history of Ross Island South Townsville state school* South Townsville, Qld. 1984
PAGE, M. & INGPEN, R. *Aussie battlers* Adelaide 1982
PAGRAM, E. *Never had it so good* Melbourne 1968
PAICE, M. *Valley in the north* Sydney 1957
Run to the mountains Sydney 1972
Dolan's roost Sydney 1974
Shadow of wings Sydney 1978
PALLIN, C. *A bat came to stay* Sydney 1985
PALMER, E. *On plants used by the natives of North Queensland, Flinders and Mitchell Rivers, for food and medicine* Sydney 1884
Concerning some superstitions of North Queensland Aborigines Brisbane 1886
Early days in North Queensland Sydney 1903
PALMER, G. *Kidnapping in the south seas* Edinburgh 1871
PALMER, K. & MCKENNA, C. *Somewhere between black and white: the story of an Aboriginal Australian* South Melbourne 1978
PALMER, N. *Talking it over* Sydney 1932
PALMER, V. *The world of men* Melbourne 1962 (first publ. 1915)
The prisoner 1919 see *The black horse*
The boss of Killara Sydney 1922
Telling Mrs Baker 1922 see *The black horse*
Travellers 1923 see *The black horse*
The black horse and other plays (The prisoner, Travellers, Telling Mrs Baker) Melbourne 1924
The passage London 1930, 1957
Separate lives London 1931
The Swayne family Sydney 1934
Legend for Sanderson Sydney 1937
Cyclone Sydney 1947
Hail tomorrow London 1947
Golconda Sydney 1948
Let the birds fly Sydney 1955
The rainbow-bird and other stories Sydney 1957
Seedtime Sydney 1957
The big fellow Sydney 1959
PALMER-ARCHER, L.M. see Archer, L.M.P.

Pan-Pacific worker: official organ of the Pan-Pacific Trade Union Secretariat Sydney 1928–32
Papers and proceedings of the Royal Society of Tasmania Hobart 1851–
PARANJPYE, S. *Three years in Australia* Poona 1951
PARER, J.J. *The Northern Territory* Melbourne 1922
PARK, R. *Harp in the south* Boston 1948
Poor man's orange Sydney 1949
A power of roses Sydney 1953
The companion guide to Sydney Sydney 1973
PARK, R. & NILAND, D. *The drums go bang!* Sydney 1956
PARKER, E.S. *The Aborigines of Australia: a lecture* Melbourne 1854
PARKER, H.W. *The rise, progress, and present state of Van Dieman's land* London 1833
PARKER, K.L. *Australian legendary tales* 2nd ed. London 1897 (first publ. 1896)
More Australian legendary tales London 1898
The Euahlayi tribe: a study of Aboriginal life in Australia London 1905
The walkabouts of Wur-Run-Nah Adelaide 1918
'PARKER, L.' (A.M. Thirkell) *Trooper to the Southern Cross* London 1934
PARKER, N. *Mystery aboard the Murrabit* Melbourne 1964
PARKER, R. *Fiddlers' place* London 1961
Boy on a chain London 1964
PARKES, H. *Stolen moments* Sydney 1842
Speeches on various occasions . . 1848–1874 Melbourne 1876
PARKINSON, S. *A journal of a voyage to the south seas, in His Majesty's Ship, the Endeavour* London 1773
Parks & wildlife news [Sydney], 1980–
Parkwatch: official journal of the Victorian National Parks Association Melbourne 1978– (continues *The VNPA journal*)
PARNELL, D. & ANDREW, B. *Australian football: hints and advice* Melbourne 1959
Parramatta chronicle and Cumberland general advertiser Parramatta, N.S.W. 1843–45
PARRY, H.H. *Girl of the west* Sydney 1935
PARSONS, F. *A man called Mo* Melbourne 1973
PARSONS, J. *Thirty-six years amongst criminals* St Kilda, Vic. 1906
PARSONS, W.T. *Noxious weeds of Victoria* Melbourne 1973
PARTINGTON, J.E. *Random rot* Altrincham, England 1883
PARTRIDGE, E. *A dictionary of slang and unconventional English* London 1937
2nd ed. 1938
5th ed. 1961
8th ed. ed. by P. Beale 1984
see also 'Denison, C.'
Pasquin: the pastoral, mineral, and agricultural advocate London 1882 (reprint of journal issued 1867–69)
**Passed by censor: souvenir of Australian Naval & Military Expeditionary Force, very late German New Guinea* In the field 1918
Pastoral review Melbourne 1913–Sept. 1935 (continued by *Pastoral review & graziers' record*)
Pastoral review & graziers' record Melbourne 1935–
Pastoralists' review Melbourne Mar. 1901–12 (continues *Australasian pastoralists' review* continued by *Pastoral review*)
PATCHETT, M. *The last warrior* London 1965
PATERSON, A.B. *The man from Snowy River and other verses* Sydney 1895
. . . the popular song Waltzing Matilda: words by A.B. Paterson . . music arranged by Marie Cowan Sydney [1903]
Rio Grande's last race London 1904
The old bush songs Sydney 1905
An outback marriage Sydney 1906
Saltbush Bill, J.P., and other verses Sydney 1917
Three elephant power and other stories Sydney 1917
The shearer's colt Sydney 1936
Singer of the bush: complete works 1885–1900 Sydney 1983
Song of the pen: complete works 1901–1941 Sydney 1983
PATERSON, A.F. *'Mid saltbush and mallee* Adelaide 1897
PATERSON, G. *The history of New South Wales from its first discovery to the present time* Newcastle upon Tyne 1811

PATERSON, W. Letter to Sir Joseph Banks 13 Nov. 1807 NLA MS 9/123
PATON, C. *I was a prison parson* Dee Why West, N.S.W. 1974
'PATRIUS' (G. Smith) *Hoisting our flag* Newcastle, N.S.W. 1917
PATTERSON, J.A. *The gold fields of Victoria in 1862* (anon.) Melbourne 1862
PATTISON, J. *New South Wales: its past, present, and future condition by a resident of twelve years' experience* London 1849
PATTISON, J.G. *'Battler's' tales of early Rockhampton* Melbourne 1939
PATTON, R.T. *Know your own trees: a short introduction to the study of our common eucalypts* Melbourne 1942
PAVY, P. *Bush surgeon* Adelaide 1979
PAYNE, G.A. *Original Australian verses* Adelaide 1912
PEARL, C. *So, you want to be an Australian* Sydney 1959
Morrison of Peking Sydney 1967
Beer, glorious beer Melbourne 1969
The pearling industry of Western Australia Perth 1979
PEARSE, A.W. *A windjammer 'prentice* Sydney 1927
PEARSON, L. see *The emigrant's guide to Port Curtis*
PEASE, Z.W. *The Catalpa expedition* New Bedford, Mass. 1897
PECK, C.W. *Australian legends: tales handed down from the remotest times by the autochthonous inhabitants of our land* 2nd ed. Melbourne 1933 (first publ. 1925)
PECK, H.H. *Memoirs of a stockman* Melbourne 1942
'PEGASUS' *So the drover said* Albury, N.S.W. [1917]
PEIRCE, A.B. *Knocking about* New Haven, U.S.A. 1924
PELLOE, E.H. *West Australian orchids* Perth 1930
'PENDRAGON, A.' (G. Isaacs) *The queen of the south* Gawler, S. Aust. 1858
PENTON, B. *Landtakers* Sydney 1934
Think – or be damned Sydney 1941
People Sydney 1950– (merged June 1972 with *Pix* , title varies)
People's horn boy Hobart 1834
PEPPER, P. *You are what you make yourself to be: the story of a Victorian Aboriginal family 1842–1980* Melbourne 1980
PEPPERALL, R.A. *Emigrant to Australia* London 1948
**Pepper box: printed on board the Malwa Dec. 1915* Colombo 1915
'PERAMBULATOR VON VELOCIPEDESTRIAN' *Anecdotes of Victoria* Melbourne 1869
PERCY, H. *Here's Hal Percy* Sydney 1941
Perils, pastimes, and pleasures of an emigrant in Australia, Vancouver's Island and California (by J. Ward) London 1849
PERKINS, C. *A bastard like me* Sydney 1975
PERKINS, R. *The 'drag queen' scene: transsexuals in Kings Cross* Sydney 1983
PERRY, N. & R. *Gemstones in Australia* Sydney 1979
Perth gazette and Western Australian journal (continued by *Perth gazette and independent journal of politics and news*) Perth 1833–47
PESCOTT, E.E. *The native flowers of Victoria* Melbourne [1914]
PETERS, G. *The claw of a cat* London 1964
PETERSEN, M.B. *Jewelled nights* London [1923]
Monsoon music London [1930]
PETHERAM, R.J. & KOK, B. *Plants of the Kimberley region of Western Australia* Nedlands, W.A. 1983
PETRIE, T. see *Tom Petrie's reminiscences of early Queensland*
PHELPS, B.E. *An Australian tells England* Sydney [1935]
PHILIP, G.B. *Sixty years recollections of swimming and surfing in the eastern suburbs* Sydney 1940
PHILLIP, A. *The voyage of Governor Phillip to Botany Bay* London 1789
Copies and extracts of letters London 1792
Philips' emigrants' guide to Australia see Capper, J.
PHILLIPS, N. & R. *Rogaining: cross-country navigation* Melbourne 1982
PHILLIPSON, N. *As other men* Melbourne 1974
PHILP, J.A. *Jingles that jangle* Brisbane 1918
PHIPPS, W.H. *Bush yarns and town sketches* Melbourne [1921]
PICK, J.H. *Australia's dying heart* 2nd ed. Melbourne 1944
PIDDINGTON, A.B. *Popular government and federation* Sydney 1898
PIKE, A. & COOPER, R. *Australian film 1900–1977* Melbourne 1980
PIKE, G. ed. *Campfire tales: an anthology of true stories of the pioneering days from 'Around the campfire' feature in the 'North Queensland register'* Mareeba, Qld. 1981
Pilgrim: a sensational weekly pamphlet by A. Lynn-Guist (T.E. Argles) Sydney 1878
PINNEY, P. *Road in the wilderness* Melbourne 1952
Restless men Sydney 1966
'A PIONEER' *Reminiscences of Australian early life* London 1893
PIRANI, L. *The old man river of Australia* Sydney 1946
PITTMAN, E.F. *The mineral resources of New South Wales* Sydney 1901
Plane speaking from R.A.A.F. at Amberley Amberley, Qld. 1942
PLATT, L.G. *Survival 3* Brisbane 1979
Platypus: Australian Federal Police official journal Canberra 1979–81
Plays Melbourne 1970
Plea for separation or the freedom and independence of Australia Melbourne 1888
PLOWMAN, R.B. *Camel pads* Sydney 1933
The man from Oodnadatta Sydney 1933
The boundary rider Sydney 1935
POCKLEY, L.A. *A handbook for jackeroos* Sydney 1975
Poems written by Australian soldiers at the Front [Adelaide 1918]
Point Melbourne 1938
Poison plants of Western Australia rev. ed. Perth 1926
POLEHAMPTON, A. *Kangaroo land* London 1862
'POLICEMAN' *Headlong rhymes* London 1843
POLLARD, Jack ed. *The Australian surfrider* Sydney 1963
High mark: the complete book on Australian football Sydney 1964
One for the road Sydney 1966, 1974
Australian and New Zealand fishing London 1969
POLLARD, James *The bushland man* London 1926
Rose of the bushlands London [1927]
Bushland vagabonds London 1928
ed. *Out of the west* Perth [1940]
POLLARD, R. *The cream machine* Sydney 1972
POLLOCK, W. *So this is Australia* London 1937
POPE, J.H. *Stumps and rags, and oedematology* Ballarat, Vic. 1863
POPESCU, P. *The last wave* Sydney 1977
Port Denison times Bowen, Qld. 1864–1910
**Port Hacking cough: a record of the returning home of the 1914–1919 on board H.M.A.T. D'34' S S Port Hacking* Sydney 1918–19
Port Lincoln herald Port Lincoln, S. Aust. 1839–40
Port Phillip gazette (title varies) Melbourne 1838–51
Port Phillip herald Melbourne 1840–48 (continued by *The Melbourne morning herald*)
Port Phillip magazine Melbourne 1843
Port Phillip patriot Melbourne, 1839–48
PORTEOUS, R.S. *Brigalow* Sydney 1957
Cattleman Sydney 1960
PORTER, G. *Wanderings in Tasmania* London 1934
PORTER, H. *A bachelor's children* Sydney 1962
The watcher on the cast-iron balcony: an Australian autobiography London 1963
Stars of Australian stage and screen Adelaide 1965
The cats of Venice Sydney 1965
The paper chase Sydney 1966
The extra Melbourne 1975
PORTER, R. *An historical story: Eumalga or the white chief* Orange, N.S.W. [c. 1900]
Portland gazette and Belfast advertiser Portland, Vic. 1844–49
Portland guardian Portland, Vic. 1842–1964
Portland mercury Portland, Vic. 1842–July 1844 (continued by *Portland gazette*)
POST, H. *Maintain your rage* Dandenong, Vic. [1979]
POSTLETHWAITE, D.G. *Home to the hill* Ilfracombe, England 1979
POTTS, J. *One year of anti-Chinese work in Queensland, with incidents of travel* Brisbane 1888
POWELL, G. *Two steps to Tokyo* Melbourne 1945
POWELL, M. *Margaret Powell down under* London 1976
POWER, F.R. *Stranger at the door* Melbourne 1967

My fight for 'crash' justice Victoria 1972
POWER, T.P. ed. *The footballer* Melbourne 1876
POWERS, J. *The last of the knucklemen* Melbourne 1974
The coach: a season with Ron Barassi Melbourne 1978
Pow-wow: 17th Garrison Battalion magazine Shepparton, Vic. 1941–42
PRAED, Mrs C. *Policy and passion: a novel of Australian life* 3 vols. London 1881
Australian life black and white London 1885
The head station 3 vols. London 1885
Miss Jacobsen's chance 2 vols. London 1886
The romance of a station: an Australian story London 1889
My Australian girlhood: sketches and impressions of bush life London 1902
PRATT, A. *The golden kangaroo* Sydney 1913
Wolaroi's cup Sydney 1913
PRESHAW, G.O. *Banking under difficulties: or life on the goldfields of Victoria, New South Wales & New Zealand: by a bank official* Melbourne 1888
PRESTIDGE, R. *Cataclysm* Norwood, S. Aust. 1976
PRICE, C.A. *German settlers in South Australia* Melbourne 1945
PRICE, J.M. *The land of gold* London 1896
PRICHARD, E.D. *A bachelor's guide to Sydney* Sydney 1969
PRICHARD, K.S. *The pioneers* London [1915]
The black opal London 1921
Working bullocks London 1926
Coonardoo Sydney 1929, 1961
Haxby's circus London 1930
Kiss on the lips and other stories London 1932
Intimate strangers London 1937
Moon of desire London 1941
Potch and colour Sydney 1944
The roaring nineties London 1946
Golden miles Sydney 1948
Winged seeds London 1950
N'goola Melbourne 1959
Subtle flame Sydney 1967
Brumby Innes, and Bid me to love : ed. by K. Brisbane Sydney 1974
PRIDDEN, W. *Australia, its history and present condition* London 1843
PRIDDLE, V. *Larry and Jack* Brisbane 1977
PRIEST, H. *The call of the bush: wanderings of a nature man on the Murray River* London 1932
PRIEST, J. *Virtue in flying: a biography of pioneer aviator Keith Virtue* Sydney 1975
'A PRISON CHAPLAIN' (C. Gibson) *The story of the life of Thomas Jones, an escaped Norfolk Island convict* London [c. 1860]
Proceedings of a general court-martial held at Chelsea hospital .. for the trial of Lieut.-Col. Geo. Johnston London 1811
Proceedings of the Linnean Society of New South Wales, 1875– Sydney 1877–
Proceedings of the Prehistoric Society Cambridge 1935–
Proceedings of the Royal Society of Queensland, 1884– Brisbane 1885–
Proceedings of the Royal Society of Victoria, 1888– Melbourne 1889– (continues *Transactions and proceedings*)
Proceedings of the Zoological Society of London London 1830–1965 (continued by *Journal of zoology*)
Ye prodigal: a weekly social and moral pamphlet Sydney [c. 1879]
Progress Brisbane 1899–1900
PROUD, C. *The south-eastern district of South Australia in 1880* Adelaide 1881
The Murray and Darling trade in 1883 Adelaide 1883
PRYOR, L.D. *Trees in Canberra* Canberra 1962
PRYOR, O. *Cousin Jack cartoons* Sydney 1945
Australia's little Cornwall Adelaide 1962
Publicist Sydney 1936–41
Puckapunyal: official journal of the 17th Australian Infantry Brigade Melbourne and Palestine 1940
PUGH, D. & RITCHIE, R. *A guide to rainforests of far north east New South Wales* n.p. 1981
PULLAN, R. *The burning of Albie* Sydney 1960
The hardskins Sydney 1960
PULLEY, K. *Marine fishes of Australian waters* Melbourne 1974
PULLIAM, N. *I traveled a lonely land: this is Australia and these are the Australians – as I saw them* Indianapolis 1955
Punch Melbourne 1900–25
Punch staff papers Sydney 1872
Punchialities from Punch Melbourne [c. 1884]
PURTILL, J.E. *Farewell 'Robbie': and other poems* n.p. [c. 1946]
PURVIS, A.V. Heroes unsung. Alice Springs Public Library MS
PURVIS, H. & PRIEST, J. *Outback airman* Adelaide 1979
PYKE, L.M. *Jack of St Virgil's* London [1922]
PYKE, W.T. ed. *Bush tales* Melbourne 1888
The coo-ee reciter Melbourne 1904
PYNE, A. *Reminiscences of colonial life* London 1875

Queensland agricultural journal Brisbane 1897–
Queensland government mining journal Brisbane 1900–
Queensland guardian Brisbane Dec. 1943–66 (continues *North Queensland guardian)*
Queensland: letters from emigrants with most recent intelligence London 1863
Queenslander Brisbane 1866–1939
Quickmatch: souvenir magazine of HMAS Quickmatch Bombay 1944
Quieter moments [Kent Town, S. Aust.] 1979
QUILTY, T. *The drover's cook* Sydney 1958
'QUIRIS' *Port Darwin: its soil, climate, and resources, and prospects as a goldfield* Melbourne 1872
Quiz Adelaide 1890 (continued by *Quiz and The lantern*)
Quiz and The lantern Adelaide 1890–93

'R.R.' ed. *Australia, Van Dieman's Land, and New Zealand* London 1840
'R.T.H.' *Ourselves and our land; some reflections on the present state of Australia* Melbourne [1911]
RAAF saga Sydney 1944
RAF RAAF: souvenir of a memorable voyage, Crenferry cruise no. 3 At sea 1944
Rabaul record (previously Namanula times): newspaper of the colony of German New Guinea, occupied by Australian Military Forces Rabaul 1916–18
RABBETS, T.G. *Whimplin whimsies and other selections* Brisbane 1919
RADCLIFFE, W. *The Port Arthur guide .. from original records at the Old Curiosity Shop, Port Arthur* Hobart 1932
RADCLYFFE, R. *Wealth and wild cats* London 1898
RADLEY, P. *Jack Rivers and me* North Sydney 1981
My blue-checker corker and me North Sydney 1982
RAE, J. *Gleanings from my scrapbook* Sydney 1874
Thirty-five years on the New South Wales railways Sydney 1898
RAESIDE, J. see Reside, W.J.
Rag: HMAS 'Orara', R.A.N. minesweeper At sea 1942–43
RAILTON, S.D. *Southern Cross* Sydney [1945]
RAINE, H.B. *The lash end* Sydney 1933
The whip-hand Sydney 1933
RAINS, F.L. *By land and ocean* London 1878
Rambles at the Antipodes (by E. Wilson) London 1859
RAMSAY, J. *Cop it sweet: a dictionary of Australian slang and common usage* Sydney 1977
RAMSAY-LAYE, E.P. *Social life and manners in Australia* London 1861
RAMSON, W.S. ed. *English transported* Canberra 1970
RANDALL, L. *Australian family plays* Macgregor, Qld. 1978
RANKEN, G. *The dry country .. also letters addressed to Mr Brodribb by gentlemen in the western districts of the colony* 2 parts. Sydney [1884]
ed. *Windabyne: a record of by-gone times in Australia* London 1895
see also 'Capricornus'
Rataplan: the magazine of the arts St Kilda, Vic. 1968
RATCLIFFE, F. *Flying fox and drifting sand* New York 1938
RATH, A.F. et al. *Strata titles* Sydney 1962
RAVEN-HART, R. *Canoe in Australia* Melbourne 1948
RAWSON, D.W. *Australia votes* Melbourne 1961

RAWSON, Mrs L. *Australian cook and laundry book* Melbourne 1897
RAYMENT, A. *The romance of the railway with reminiscences of a railway staff officer* Sydney 1935
RAYMENT, B.J. *My towri: to my sons and a few old cobbers* Brisbane 1956
RAYMENT, T. *A cluster of bees* Sydney 1935
RAYMOND, M. *Smiley gets a gun* London 1947
Smiley roams the road London 1959
READ, C.R. *What I heard, saw, and did at the Australian gold fields* London 1853
READ, J. & P. eds. A view of the past: Aboriginal accounts of Northern Territory history. 1978
READ, P. *Down there with me on the Cowra mission* Sydney 1984
Reader's digest complete book of Australian birds Sydney 1976
Realist writer (from Mar. 1960 issued as *Realist*) Sydney 1958–67
REAY, M. ed. *Aborigines now* Sydney 1964
REAY, P. see 'North, J.'
REAY, W.T. *Australians in war: with the Australian regiment from Melbourne to Bloemfontein* Melbourne 1900
A white Australia; the Kanaka labour question; sugar growing in Queensland; the part played by the black man Melbourne 1901
'A RECENT SETTLER' *Emigration to Tasmania* London 1879
The record of Nicholas Freydon: an autobiography (by A.J. Dawson) London 1915
Records of the Australian Museum Sydney 1890–
Records of the South Australian Museum Adelaide 1918–
Records of the Western Australian Museum Perth 1910–39
Red star Perth 1934–36
REDCLIFFE, H. *The yellow cygnet* London 1930
REDMOND, W. *A shooting trip in the Australian bush* Dublin 1898
REED, A.W. *Aboriginal words of Australia* Sydney 1965
Aboriginal place names and their meanings Sydney 1967
REED, B. *Mr Siggie Morrison with his comb and paper* South Yarra, Vic. 1972
Cass butcher bunting Port Melbourne 1977
Crooks Melbourne 1984
REEDER, F.A. *The diary of a rat* Canberra 1977
REES, L. ed. *Australian radio plays* Sydney 1946
REES, L. & C. *Spinifex walkabout: hitch-hiking in remote north Australia* London 1953
Coasts of Cape York Sydney 1960
REEVES, L.C. *Australians in action in New Guinea* Sydney 1915
Referee Sydney 1886–1939
Register Adelaide 1901–29 (continues *South Australian register* continued by *Register-News pictorial*)
Register of flashmen. 1841 N.S.W. State Archives, Benches of Magistrates, *etc.* 2/673
Regulations respecting assigned male and female convict servants, as set forth in proclamations and general orders Hobart 1821
REID, Alan *The Gorton experiment* Sydney 1971
The Whitlam venture Melbourne 1976
REID, Arthur *Those were the days* Perth 1933
REID, F. *The fighting cameliers* Sydney 1934
REID, G.H. *An essay on New South Wales, the mother colony of the Australias* Sydney 1876
REID, J. *The adventures of an Australian traveler* [Buffalo, U.S.A. 1864]
REID, J. Arbuckle *The Australian reader* Melbourne 1882
REID, James A. *A pioneer grazier in Australia* Geelong, Vic. 1924
REID, M. *The Australian businessman's digest* Melbourne 1978
REID, R.L. *Healthy eating in Australia* Melbourne 1984
REID, T. *Two voyages to New South Wales and Van Diemen's Land* London 1822
REIDY, D. *It's this way* London 1964
REILLY, J.T. *Reminiscences of fifty years residence in Western Australia* Perth 1903
**Remnants from Randwick written and illustrated by patients at No. 4 A.G.H. Randwick* Sydney 1918–19
RENAR, F. *Bushman and buccaneer: Henry Morant and his ventures and verses* Sydney 1902
'RENE, R.' (H.V. Sluice) *Mo's memoirs* Melbourne 1945
Representative: a daily journal of the election Sydney 1850
Report from the Select Committee on Transportation London 1837 (G.B.P.P. H.C. 518)
Ibid. 1838. (G.B.P.P. H.C. 374)
RESIDE, W.J. *Golden days being memoirs and reminiscences of the goldfields of Western Australia* Perth 1929
'A RESIDENT' *Social life and manners in Australia* see Ramsay-Laye, E.P.
'A RESIDENT' (J.H. Kerr) *Glimpses of life in Victoria* Edinburgh 1872
'A RESIDENT' *Girl life in Australia: a description of colonial life* Liverpool 1876
'A RESIDENT OF TWELVE YEARS' EXPERIENCE' see Pattison, J.
Retail merchandiser Melbourne 1953–67
'A RETURNED DIGGER' *Six years in Australia: its present condition and future* Manchester 1857
'A RETURNED SOLDIER' *Anzac memoirs: humorous sketches* Petersham, N.S.W. [1920]
Returns relative to the settlement on the Swan River London 1831 (G.B.P.P. H.C. 41)
'REV. F.T.P.' *Thirty-shilling horse; or Parson P's mission to the Wimmera District, Victoria . . Jy, 1874* Melbourne 1899
Review Melbourne 1970–72 (merged with *Nation* to form *Nation review*)
REYNOLDS, B. *Dawn asper* Sydney 1918
RHYS, L. *My ship is so small* Melbourne 1946
RICE-CHAPMAN, P. *Food at the top end* Darwin 1981
RICHARDS, L. *Boots and all!* London 1963
RICHARDS, M. *North coast run* Killara, N.S.W. 1977
RICHARDSON, A.J. *Private journal of the surveyor attached to Messrs. Frank and Alexander Jardine's overland expedition to Cape York* Brisbane [1867]
RICHARDSON, A.R. *Early memories of the great nor-west and a chapter in history of W.A.* Perth 1909
new ed. 1914
'RICHARDSON, H.H.' (E.F.L. Robertson) *The getting of wisdom* London 1910, 1960
RICHARDSON, L. *The bitter years!: Wollongong during the great depression* Marrickville, N.S.W. 1984
RIDE, W.D.L. *A guide to the native mammals of Australia* Melbourne 1970
RIDLEY, W. *Report laid before the Moreton Bay Aborigines Friends' Society, of a journey along the Condamine, Barwon, and Namoi Rivers* Sydney 1855
RIDPATH, P. *Possum moods* Sydney 1967
RIEMANN, H.E. *Nor'-west o' west* Sydney 1924
RILEY, E. *All that false instruction* London 1975
**Ringo: Second Battalion Royal Australian Regiment* Nui Dat, Vietnam 1971
**Rip: unofficial organ of the Port Phillip fortress* Port Phillip, Vic. 1940
**Rising sun: the chronicle of the 37th Battalion* Melbourne 1929–30
**Rising sun: journal published on board 'Themistocles'* At sea 1916
**Rising sun: paper published on board 'Kyarra' A.55* At sea 1916
RITCHIE, J.D. *Australia as once we were* Melbourne 1975
RITCHIE, J.E. *An Australian ramble or a summer in Australia* London 1890
RITCHIE, P.H. *North of the never never* London 1935
RITZ, H.B. *Speech of the Tasmanian Aborigines* Hobart 1909
RIVETT, R.D. *Behind bamboo* Sydney 1946
ROBB, E.M. *Lyrics* Prahran, Vic. [1928]
ROBERT, D. *'Look at me now': a sailor in the South Pacific* London 1963
Bellbird eleven London 1965
ROBERTON, H.S. *Now blame the farmer* Sydney 1945
ROBERTS, B. *The phantom boy* Burnie, Tas. 1976
Stones in the Cephissus Cook, A.C.T. 1979
The penalty of Adam Belmont, Vic. 1980
ROBERTS, C.F. *Iniquities of lunacycraft and hocus-pocus of three learned judges in the first law case of the kind on this side of the world* Melbourne 1882–83
ROBERTS, J. *Two years at sea: being the narrative of a voyage to the Swan River and Van Dieman's Land, during the years, 1829, 30, 31* London 1834

ROBERTS, J.P. *Massacres to mining* Melbourne 1981
ed. *The Mapoon story by the Mapoon people* Melbourne 1975
ROBERTS, J.W. *The mining industry of New South Wales* Sydney [1896]
ROBERTS, M. *Land-travel and sea-faring* London 1891
Red earth London 1894
ROBERTS, M.B. *A king of con men* Auckland 1975
ROBERTS, R. *The life and opinions of R. Roberts, a wandering scholar, as told by himself* ed. J.H. Davies Cardiff 1923
ROBERTS, S.H. *History of Australian land settlement* Melbourne 1924
ROBERTS, T. *Lindsay's boy* (in *Five plays*) St Lucia, Qld. 1977
ROBERTSON, A. *Nuggets in the devil's punch bowl and other Australian tales* London 1894
ROBERTSON, W. *Sunshine and shadow: sketches of a western parish* Sydney 1918
Coo-ee talks: a collection of lecturettes upon early experiences among the Aborigines of Australia delivered from a wireless broadcasting station Sydney 1928
ROBINSON, D. *Pop's blonde* Sydney 1945
ROBINSON, G. *The decades of a Duntroon bastard* Belmont, Vic. 1980
ROBINSON, G.A. *Friendly mission: the Tasmanian journals and papers .. 1829–34* ed. by J.A. Plomley Hobart 1966
ROBINSON, G.G. *The native grasses of the northern tablelands* Sydney 1983
ROBINSON, N. ed. *Stagg of Tarcowie: the diaries of a colonial teenager (1885–87)* Adelaide 1977
ROBINSON, Robbie *Give it a bloody go, mate!* Adelaide 1974
ROBINSON, Roland *Legend and dreaming: legends of the dream-time of the Australian Aborigines* Sydney 1952
Black-feller white-feller Sydney 1958
Altjeringa Sydney 1970
The drift of things South Melbourne 1973
The shift of sands Melbourne 1976
ROBISON, R. *The case of Captain Robison* London 1831
ROBSON, F. & BARNES, M. *Dare to be different* Milton, Qld. 1982
ROBSON, L.L. *The convict settlers of Australia* London 1965
ROCHE, J.J. *Life of John Boyle O'Reilly* New York 1891
ROCHFORT, J. *The adventures of a surveyor in New Zealand and the Australian gold diggings* London 1853
RODWAY, L. *The Tasmanian flora* Hobart 1903
Some wild flowers of Tasmania Hobart 1910
2nd ed. 1922
ROE, J.S. *Report of an expedition under the Surveyor-General, Mr J.S. Roe, to the south-eastward of Perth, in Western Australia, between the months of September, 1848, and February, 1849, to the Hon. the Colonial Secretary* London 1849
ROE, R. & SHAW, N.H. *Mint weed, salvia reflexa Hornem.: present distribution and status in Australia* Melbourne 1947 (C.S.I.R.O. bulletin no. 231)
ROEDIGER, W. *We survived* Tumby Bay, S. Aust. 1974
ROGERS, J. *The new rush* Melbourne 1864
ROGERS, R.S. *An introduction to the study of South Australian orchids* 2nd ed. Adelaide 1911
ROGERS, T. *Correspondence relating to the dismissal of the Rev. T. Rogers, from his chaplaincy at Norfolk Island* Launceston, Tas. [1849]
'ROHAN, C.' (D. Olsen) *The delinquents* London 1962
Down by the dockside London 1963
ROLAND, B. *No ordinary man* London 1974
ROLLS, E.C. *They all ran wild* Sydney 1969
A million wild acres: 200 years of man and an Australian forest Melbourne 1981
Celebration of the senses Melbourne 1984
Romantic career of George Adams (Tattersall) Launceston, Tas. [1939]
rev. ed. 1947
ROMERIL, J. *Chicago, Chicago* Melbourne 1974
I don't know who to feel sorry for Sydney 1973
The floating world Sydney 1975
RONAN, T. *Strangers on the Ophir* Sydney 1945
rev. ed. 1960
Vision splendid London 1954
Moleskin Midas London 1956
The pearling master London 1958
Only a short walk London 1961
Deep of the sky London 1962
Packhorse and pearling boat Melbourne 1964
Once there was a bagman Melbourne 1966
The mighty men on horseback Adelaide 1977
ROSE, F.G.G. *The wind of change in Central Australia* Berlin 1965
Australia revisited Berlin 1968
ROSE, L. *Country of the dead* Sydney 1959
ROSE, R. *The Australian guide* London 1880
The Victoria guide London 1880
ROSENBLUM, I.A. *Stella Sothern: a story of bohemia and the bush* Sydney 1911
ROSS, A. *Australia 55: a journal of the M.C.C. tour* London 1955
ROSS, C. *Observations and cultural notes on grapes* 3rd ed. Brisbane 1916
ROSS, L. *William Lane and the Australian Labor movement* Sydney [1937]
ROSS, M.I. *The Dawn Hill brand* Boston 1939
ROSSER, B. *This is Palm Island* Canberra 1978
Dreamtime nightmares: biographies of Aborigines under the Queensland Aborigines Act Canberra 1985
Ross's magazine of protest Melbourne Dec. 1915-May 1916 (continued by *Ross's monthly of protest*)
Ross's monthly of protest Melbourne June 1916-Nov. 1923
ROTH, H.L. *Sketches and reminiscences from Queensland, Russia and elsewhere* [Halifax, Canada 1916]
ROTH, W.E. *Ethnological studies among the north-west-central Queensland Aborigines* Brisbane 1897
Games, sports and amusements of the north Queensland Aboriginals Brisbane 1902
ROTHERHAM, E.R. et al. *Flowers and plants of New South Wales and southern Queensland* Sydney 1975
2nd ed. 1982
ROUGHLEY, T.C. *Fishes of Australia and their technology* Sydney 1916
Wonders of the Great Barrier Reef Sydney 1936
Fish and fisheries of Australia Sydney 1951, 1953, 1971
ROUGHSEY, D. *Moon and rainbow* Sydney 1971
'ROUSEABOUT' *The jackeroo: or, changes and chances in the life of a free selector* Corowa, N.S.W. 1891
ROWBOTHAM, D. *Town and city* Sydney 1956
The man in the jungle Sydney 1964
ROWCROFT, C. *Tales of the colonies* 3 vols. London 1843
new ed. 1858
The bushranger of Van Diemen's Land 3 vols. London 1846
An emigrant in search of a colony London 1851
ROWE, J. *McCabe P.M.* London 1972
The chocolate crucifix Melbourne 1972
The warlords Sydney 1978
ROWE, R. *Peter Possum's portfolio* Sydney 1858
Roughing it in Van Diemen's Land London [1880]
see also 'Howe, E.'
ROWLANDS, L. *A bird in the hand* Sydney 1965
ROY, T.A. *The vengeance of the dolphin* London 1980
Royal Australian Navy news Sydney 1958–82
Royal South Australian almanack and general directory Adelaide 1839–55 (from 1841–44 issued as *South Australian almanack*)
ROYDHOUSE, T.R. & TAPERELL, H.J. *The Labour Party in New South Wales* Sydney 1892
'RUDD, Steele' (A.H. Davis) *On our selection!* Sydney 1899
The book of Dan Sydney 1911
'Me an' th' son' Sydney 1924
The romance of Runnibede Sydney 1927
Green grey homestead Sydney 1934
RUDD, Stuart *Auburn by night: the life and experiences of Stuart Rudd* Parramatta, N.S.W. 1949
Far and near Silverwater, N.S.W. [1955]
RUHEN, C. *Wild beat* Sydney 1967
Crocodile Hong Kong 1978
RUHEN, O. *Naked under Capricorn* London 1958

The flockmaster London 1963
Bullock teams: the building of a nation North Ryde, N.S.W. 1980
RULE, E.J. *Jacka's mob* Sydney 1933
Rules & regulations for the management of the Aborigines or Black Native Institution of New South Wales; established at Parramatta on the 18th of January, 1815 Sydney 1819
RUMSEY, H.J. *The pommies or new chums in Australia* Dundas, N.S.W. 1920
Australian nuts and nut growing in Australia Dundas, N.S.W. 1927
**Runic rhymes: souvenir of H.M.A.T. 'Runic'* At sea 1916
RUSSELL, A. *A tour through the Australian colonies in 1839* Glasgow 1840
RUSSELL, Archer *Sunlit trails* Sydney 1930
A tramp-royal in wild Australia: 1928–1929 London 1934
Gone nomad Sydney 1936
Bush ways Sydney [1945]
Murray walkabout Melbourne 1953
'RUSSELL, A.' (A.R. Goode) *Bungoona* London [1929]
RUSSELL, H.R. *A short description of the Australian colonies* Sydney 1851
RUSSELL, H.S. *The genesis of Queensland* Sydney 1888
'RUSTICUS' (W.S. Chauncy) *How to settle in Victoria; or instructions on the purchase and occupation of the land, with observations on gardening and farming* Melbourne 1855
RUSTON, G. *The clock of time or from venturesome pom to dinkum Aussie* Perth 1983
RUTH, T.E. *Mannixisms* Melbourne 1917
RUTHERFORD, M. *Departmental* Woollahra, N.S.W. 1979
**Rutherford rumblings: journal of the 33rd Battalion New England Regiment* Tamworth, N.S.W. 1940
RUTTER, J.J. *Ulladulla to New England and back* Armidale, N.S.W. 1887
RUTTER, S. *Hints to gold hunters* Sydney 1851
RYAN, J.S. *'Splinters on the wall'* Sydney 1909
RYAN, J.T. *Reminiscences of Australia* Sydney [1895]
RYAN, L.D. *Sheep-shearing experting* Sydney 1957
Australian wool clip preparation Sydney 1968
The shearers Guildford, N.S.W. 1975

'S.S. JUNR' *The travels and adventures of two commercial travellers through the eastern districts of Western Australia* Fremantle, W.A. 1868
SABEY, I. *Noel nocturne* Adelaide 1944
Sabretache: journal of the Military Collectors Society of Australia (title varies) Melbourne 1958–
SADLER, J. *Lyrics and rhymes* Adelaide 1890
SADLIER, J. *Recollections of a Victorian police officer* Melbourne 1913
ST JOHN, F.R. *Verse in retirement (II)* [Point Lonsdale, Vic.] 1976
**St Kilda by the sea annual* Melbourne 1914–17
SAINT-THOMAS, H. *Night of the long shadows* London 1967
SALISBURY, R.A.T.G.C. *Lord Robert Cecil's gold fields diary: introd. and notes by E. Scott* 2nd ed. Melbourne 1945
SALISBURY, S. et al. *Fishermen's views: transcripts of interviews with senior members of the lower Clarence River fishing fleet* Canberra 1980
Salt: authorised education journal of Australian Army and Air Force (title varies) Melbourne 1941–46
'SALTBUSH' *Sydney to Croydon* Sydney 1889
SALTER, E. *Will to survive* London 1958
SAMPSON, R.S. *Through Central Australia* Perth 1933
SAMPSON, W.G. *Tuna fishing in Australia* Wellington, N.Z. 1962
'SANDALWOOD NUTT' *Tarragal: an Australian tale* Perth [c. 1899]
SANDERCOCK, L. & TURNER, I. *Up where, Cazaly?* London 1981
'SANDERS, D.L.' (L. Walker) *Ribbons in her hair* London 1957
SANSOM, B. *The camp at Wallaby Cross: Aboriginal fringe dwellers in Darwin* Canberra 1980
SANTAMARIA, B.A. *Against the tide* Melbourne 1981
SARGANT, G. *The sweet heart of the bush* Melbourne 1915
The winding track Melbourne 1920
SARGENT, G.E. *Frank Layton: an Australian story* London 1865
Satirist and sporting chronicle Sydney 1843
SAUNDERS, E. *Our Australian colonies: notes of . . a visit to Australia, Van Dieman's Land, and New Zealand, in the years 1852–3* Bath 1853
SAUNDERS, P. *Two years in Victoria from 1853 to 1855* Calcutta 1863
SAVERY, H. *The hermit in Van Diemen's Land* Hobart 1829
Quintus Servinton 3 vols. Hobart 1830–31
SAVILLE-KENT, W. *The Great Barrier Reef of Australia; its products and potentialities* London 1893
The naturalist in Australia London 1897
SAW, R. & MILBANK, I. *The back to back tango* Adelaide 1978
SAWER, G. *Australian government today* Melbourne 1948
Australian federal politics and law Melbourne 1956
SAXTON, J. *Something will come to me* Ilfracombe, England 1981
SAYCE, C.H. *Golden buckles* Melbourne 1920
Comboman London [1934]
SAYERS, C.E. *The jumping double* Sydney 1923
'SC-TT, I.' *How I stole over 10,000 sheep in Australia and New Zealand* London [c. 1894]
SCHLEMAN, J. *Life in Melbourne, Australia* London 1882
SCHLUNKE, E.O. *The man in the silo* Sydney 1955
The village Hampden Sydney 1958
Stories of the Riverina Sydney 1965
SCHMIDT, P.J. & YEATES, N.T.M. *Beef cattle production* 2nd ed. Sydney 1985
SCHULTZ, J. *Steel city blues* Ringwood, Vic. 1985
SCHULZ, J.F.W. *Destined to perish -!?* Tanunda, S. Aust. 1938
SCHURMANN, C.W. *The Aboriginal tribes of Port Lincoln, in South Australia* Adelaide 1846
SCHURMANN, T. *Shop!* Adelaide 1975
The showie Adelaide 1979
SCHWAB, L. *The Socceroos and their opponents* Melbourne 1979
Science of man Sydney 1898–1912
SCOTT, A. *A manual of Australian football* Melbourne 1965
SCOTT, B. see Scott, W.N.
SCOTT, E. *Australia during the war* Sydney 1936 (The official history of Australia in the war of 1914–1918 vol. XI.)
'SCOTT, J.' (D.W. Rudd) *How, when and where to catch fish* Sydney [1918]
SCOTT, N. *Wherever we step the land is mined* London 1980
SCOTT, T.D. *The marine and freshwater fishes of South Australia* 2nd ed. Adelaide 1974
SCOTT, W.N. *Some people* Milton, Qld. 1968
Complete book of Australian folk lore Sydney 1976
My Uncle Arch and other people Adelaide 1977
Tough in the old days Adelaide 1979
Darkness under the hills Melbourne 1980
'SCOTTY'S BROTHER' (C. Duguid) *The desert trail: with the Light Horse through Sinai to Palestine* Adelaide [1919]
SCOULER, I.A. *Dowerin story in pioneering days* Perth 1929
SEAGER, J. *Kangaroo Island doctor* Adelaide 1980
SEARCY, A. *In northern seas: being Mr Alfred Searcy's experiences on the north coast of Australia* Adelaide 1905
By flood and field: adventures ashore and afloat in north Australia London 1911
SEARLE, J. *The lucky streak* Sydney 1972
SEATON, R.C. *Six letters from the colonies* Hull 1886
SEKULESS, P. *Fred: an Australian hero* St Lucia, Qld. 1981
SELLARS, M. *Carramar* Brisbane 1967
SELLECK, R.J.W. *Frank Tate: a biography* Melbourne 1982
SEMMLER, C. *The Banjo of the bush* Melbourne 1966
ed. *The world of 'Banjo' Paterson* Sydney 1967
SEMON, R. *In the Australian bush and on the coast of the Coral Sea* London 1899
**'Sentry go': Fourth Garrison Battalion* Adelaide 1940
SERVENTY, D.L. & WHITTELL, H.M. *A handbook of the birds of Western Australia* 2nd ed. Perth 1951
SERVENTY, V. *Australia's Great Barrier Reef* Melbourne 1955
Nature walkabout Sydney 1967
Southern walkabout Sydney 1968
Wildlife of Australia Melbourne 1968

Around the bush Sydney 1970
Dryandra: the story of an Australian forest Sydney 1970
The singing land Sydney 1972
Desert walkabout Sydney 1973
**Serviceman: official magazine of the Woden Valley sub-branch R.S.L.* Canberra 1972–84
Settlers' handy pamphlet containing general information useful to new and old settlers [Perth] 1911
The 7th Field Artillery Brigade yandoo see Yandoo
SEYMOUR, A. *The one day of the year* London 1962
The one day of the year: a novel London 1967
SHACKCLOTH, I. *The call of the Kimberleys* Melbourne 1950
SHACKLETON, B. *'Karagi'* Wyong, N.S.W. 1980
SHANN, E.O.G. *Cattle chosen: the story of the first group settlement in Western Australia 1829 to 1941* London 1926
SHAPCOTT, T. *Stump & grape & bopple-nut* Toowong, Qld. 1981
SHAPLAND, R. *Stump-jumping plough* Adelaide 1882
SHARLAND, M. *Tasmanian birds: how to identify them* Hobart 1945
A territory of birds Adelaide 1964
Tracks of the morning Hobart 1981
SHARLAND, W.S. *The Sporting Globe football book* Melbourne 1930
SHARP, I.G. & TATZ, C.M. *Aborigines in the economy* Melbourne 1966
SHARP, M.E.P. et al. *Early days at St Peter's College, Adelaide 1854–1878* Adelaide 1936
SHARWOOD, J.A. *Vocabulary of the Australian dried vine fruits industry* Sydney 1982 (Sydney University Australian Language Research Centre. Occasional paper no. 20)
SHAW, A.G.L. *The story of Australia* London 1955
rev ed. 1969
SHAW, B. *Old Arthur Rae's amazing record* Sydney [1928]
SHAW, C. *Outback occupations* Sydney 1943
The Warrumbungle mare Sydney 1943
A sheaf of shorts Sydney 1944
SHAW, G. *Zoology of New Holland* London 1794
The naturalist's miscellany vol. X. London 1798–99
General zoology 14 vols. London 1800–26
SHAW, J. *A tramp to the diggings* London 1852
SHAW, W. *The land of promise; or, my impressions of Australia* London 1854
SHEARD, L.E. *An Australian youth among desert Aborigines* Adelaide 1964
Shearer Sydney 1904–06
SHEARS, R. *Gold!: where to go & how to find it* Sydney 1980
SHEARSTON, T. *Something in the blood* St Lucia, Qld. 1979
SHEEHAN, B. & WORLAND, D. *Glossary of industrial relations terms* Bundoora, Vic. 1979
2nd ed. 1981
SHELDON, C. *Chewin' the rag* Brisbane 1909
SHEPHERD, A.N. *Irrigation farming in New South Wales* Sydney 1925 (N.S.W. Dept. of Agriculture. Farmers' bulletin no. 148)
SHEPPARD, T. *Children of blindness* Sydney 1976
SHERER, J. ed. *The gold finder of Australia* London 1853
SHILLINGLAW, J.J. ed. *Historical records of Port Phillip* Melbourne 1879
Shire & municipal record Sydney 1908–
'The shock brigader' see Tramway workers
SHOLL, M. ed. *A handy book to Tasmanian mining and general investment, 1882–1883* Tasmania 1882
SHOLL, R.J. *Journal of an expedition from the government camp, Camden Harbour, to the southward of the Glenelg River in north-western Australia* (in *Journal of the Royal Geographical Society* London 1866 vol. 36)
SHORLEY, E.T. *Poetic reflections in rhyme and reason* Rockhampton, Qld. [1924]
SHORTT, K. *Echoes of the Clarence* Stanthorpe, Qld. 1980
SHREEVE, N. *A short history of South Australia* London 1864
SHUMACK, S. *An autobiography: or tales and legends of Canberra pioneers* Canberra 1967
'SHUTE, N.' (N.S. Norway) *A town like Alice* London 1950
The far country London 1952
Beyond the black stump London 1956
SIDNEY, J. *A voice from the far interior of Australia* London 1847
SIDNEY, N. *Beyond the bay* Melbourne 1966
The return Melbourne 1976
SIDNEY, S. *Female emigration* London 1850
The three colonies of Australia; .. London 1852
2nd ed. 1853
Gallops and gossips in the bush of Australia . . . London 1854
Sidney's Australian hand-book: how to settle and succeed in Australia: comprising every information for intending emigrants London 1848
9th ed. 1849
Sidney's emigrant's journal London 1849
**Signals: a journal compiled by the Signalwomen of the Australian Corps of Signals-L.H.Q.* Melbourne 1943
SIGSWORTH, L.A. *Various verse* Rockhampton, Qld. [1928]
Verse Rockhampton, Qld. [1933]
SILLCOCK, K. *Three lifetimes of dairying in Victoria* Melbourne 1972
SILVER, S.W. *Handbook for Australia & New Zealand* London 1874
3rd ed. 1880
SIMCOX, H. *Rustic rambles, in rhyme* Ballarat, Vic. 1866
SIMMONDS, J. & GOLLAN, A. *For Simmo* North Ryde, N.S.W. 1980
SIMMONDS, J.H. *Some odd memories of the Field Naturalist's Club* Brisbane 1893
SIMON, E. *Through my eyes* Adelaide 1978
SIMONS, K. *Not with a kiss* Sydney 1962
SIMPSON, C. *Adam in ochre* Sydney 1951
Come away, pearler Sydney 1952
The new Australia Sydney 1971
SIMPSON, H. *Boomerang* London 1932
SIMPSON, K. & DAY, N. *The birds of Australia* South Yarra, Vic. 1984
SIMPSON, W. *One of our pilots is safe* London 1942
SINCLAIR, A. *A clip of wool from shearing shed to ship* Sydney 1899
SINCLAIR, C. *Tall bronzed and handsome* Sydney 1968
Singabout: the magazine of the Bush Music Club Wooloomooloo, N.S.W. 1956–67
SINGER, G. et al. *On how to keep your gown clean* Melbourne [1968]
SINGLETON, C.C. & BURKE, D. *Railways of Australia* Sydney 1963
SINGLETON, J. *A narrative of incidents in the eventful life of a physician* Melbourne 1891
SINGLETON, J. *True confessions* Stanmore, N.S.W. 1979
SINGLETON, R. *The march past* Sydney 1957
SINNETT, F. *An account of the 'rush' to Port Curtis* Geelong, Vic. 1859
An account of the colony of South Australia London 1862
**Sixer: official organ of the Sixth Infantry Brigade and attached units* Mornington, Vic. 1940
SKEMP, J.R. *Memories of Myrtle Bank* Melbourne 1952
Sketch of a shepherd's duties in New South Wales see *Duties of a shepherd in New South Wales*
A sketch of Western Australia and of the Western Australian Company's settlement of Australind London 1843
SKEYHILL, T. *Soldier songs from Anzac* Melbourne 1915
SKINNER, M.L. *WX – Corporal Smith* Perth 1941
The fifth sparrow Sydney 1972
SKY, F.M. *Our most important problem: it is immigration: Australia's duty* Sydney 1926
SLADEN, D.B.W. *A summer Christmas and a sonnet upon the S.S. 'Ballaarat'* London 1884
Australian ballads and rhymes: poems inspired by life and scenery in Australia and New Zealand London 1888
SLATER, P. *A field guide to Australian birds* Adelaide 1970
SLATER, R. *Rod and line in Tasmania* Launceston, Tas. 1904
SLEEMAN, J.H.C. *Queer Queensland: the breeding ground of the Bolshevik* Brisbane [1918]
**Slipstream: No. 81 (Fighter) Wing Bofu, Japan* In the field 1946
SLOAN, E. *A kangaroo in the kitchen: and other adventures of an American family down under* New York 1978
'SMILER' (A.A.G. Hales) *The wanderings of a simple child* 3rd ed. Sydney 1891
SMITH, Alexander *The Australian home carpenter* Melbourne 1929
SMITH, Ann *A sad but true story concerning the death of John James Emanuel Smith* Hobart 1885

SMITH, A.S. ed. *The boys write home* Sydney 1944
SMITH, B.St.A. *The spirit beyond the psyche* Melbourne 1978
SMITH, C.B. *Australian gold prospectors' handbook* Sydney 1931
SMITH, C.H. *How y' going mate?* Mt Gambier, S. Aust. 1963
SMITH, E. *Saddle in the kitchen* East Perth 1979
SMITH, G. *A naturalist in Tasmania* Oxford 1909
SMITH, G.A.W. *Once a green jackaroo* London 1975
Riding high Adelaide 1977
SMITH, G.M. *The days of Cobb & Co.* Parramatta, N.S.W. 1906
SMITH, H.B. *The sheep and wool industry of Australasia* London [1914]
2nd ed. 1916
3rd ed. 1929
SMITH, Jan *An ornament of grace* Melbourne 1966
SMITH, John *The Congewoi correspondence* see De Boos, C.
SMITH, J.E. *A specimen of the botany of New Holland* London 1793
Tracts relating to natural history London 1798
SMITH, K. *A word from children* Adelaide 1960
OGF: being the private papers of George Cockburn, bus conductor, a resident of Hurstfield, a suburb of Sydney, Australia Sydney 1965
SMITH, K.L. *Sky pilot in Arnhem Land* Sydney 1935
Sky pilot's last flight Sydney 1936
SMITH, L.H. *The lyrebirds of Sherbrooke* Melbourne 1951
The lyrebird Melbourne 1968
SMITH, L.R. *Memories of Hall* Canberra 1975
The Aboriginal population of Australia Canberra 1980
SMITH, S. *Whether to go and whither?* London 1852
SMITH, S.C. *Original ideas and criticisms* Brisbane 1929
SMITH, W.R. *In southern seas: wanderings of a naturalist* London 1924
Smith's weekly Sydney, 1919–50, May–June 1968
Smoke signal: news-sheet of Palm Island Palm Island, Qld. 1974
Smoke signals Melbourne 1960–72
SMOLICZ, J.J. *Culture and education in a plural society* Canberra 1979
SMOLICZ, J.J. & SECOMBE, M.J. *The Australian school through children's eyes: a Polish-Australian view* Melbourne 1981
SMYTH, R.B. *The gold fields and mineral districts of Victoria* Melbourne 1869
The Aborigines of Victoria: with notes relating to the habits of the natives of other parts of Australia and Tasmania Melbourne 1878
SNODGRASS, J. *New South Wales, as it is* Dublin 1864
SNOW, E.C. *Leather, hides, skins & tanning materials* London 1924
Social horizons Sydney 1943–45
Socialist Melbourne 1906–23
'A SOCIETY OF GENTLEMEN' *A new and correct history of New Holland; with a description of that part of it called Botany Bay, and particularly Port Jackson* Glasgow 1796
**Soldier: journal of R.S.S.A.I.L.A. and V.D.C.* Julia Creek, Qld. 1944
Some account of the Mount Morgan gold mine see 'W.G.C.'
**Somers sun* Somers, Vic. 1941
SOMERVILLE, P. *Not only in stone* Sydney 1942
SOMMERLAD, E.C. *The land of 'the beardies': being the history of the Glen Innes district* Glen Innes, N.S.W. 1922
SORENSEN, J. *The lost shanty* Perth [1939]
Collected poems Perth 1950
SORENSON, E.S. *Quinton's rouseabout and other stories* Melbourne 1908
Life in the Australian backblocks London 1911
Chips and splinters Sydney 1919
SOUTER, C.H. *To many ladies* Adelaide 1917
The lonely rose Adelaide 1935
South Australian advertiser Adelaide 1858–99 (continued by *Advertiser and register*)
South Australian almanack see *Royal South Australian almanack*
South Australian gazette Adelaide 1836–39 (first issue 18 June 1836, publ. in London, continued by *South Australian register*)
South Australian magazine Adelaide 1841–43
South Australian miscellany, and New Zealand review Adelaide 1839–40
South Australian news London 1841–52
South Australian odd fellows' magazine Adelaide 1843–46
South Australian record London 1837–41
South Australian register Adelaide 1839–1900 (continues *South Australian gazette* continued by *The register*)
South Australian review for March, 1839 London 1839
South Australiana Adelaide 1962–
South Briton: or, Tasmanian literary journal Hobart 1843
SOUTHALL, I. *Woomera* Sydney 1962
Southerly Sydney 1939–
Southern Australian Adelaide 1838–51
Southern Cross Sydney 1859–60
Southern Cross and Antarctic gazette (publ. on board SS 'Croesus') 1854 (no. 1 has subtitle *South Atlantic gazette*)
**Southern Cross gazette: journal of H.M.A.T. 'Themistocles'* At sea 1917
Southern queen: a newspaper for the city and the bush, and the chronicle of the national church Sydney 1845
SOUTHEY, T. *A treatise on sheep, addressed to the flock-masters of Australia, Tasmania, and Southern Africa* London 1840
SOUTHWELL, D. Correspondence and papers, 1788–90. BL Add. MS 16383; AJCP M1538
SOWDEN, W.J. *The Northern Territory as it is* Adelaide 1882
With the nor'-west mail: a cruise on summer seas: notes on Western Australia .. pearl fishing Adelaide 1903
SPAWN, A.F. *New homes in the irrigation and fruit-growing colonies of Victoria, Australia* London [1891]
SPEARS, S.J. *Early works* Collingwood, Vic. 1978
'THE SPECIAL CORRESPONDENT OF THE "MELBOURNE ARGUS" ' *Transportation: the British convict in Western Australia* London 1865
'THE SPECIAL REPORTER OF "THE LEADER" ' (J.L. Dow) *Agriculture in South Australia* Adelaide [1874]
Spectator and Methodist chronicle Melbourne 1875–79
'SPEER, E.' (E.N. Hobson) *Destiny* Sydney 1934
'SPENCE, A.' (I.M. Murphy) *The mystery of red gum* Perth 1946
SPENCE, C.H. *Clara Morison: a tale of South Australia during the gold fever* 2 vols. London 1854
An autobiography Adelaide 1910
SPENCE, E. *The green laurel* London 1963
The nothing-place London 1972
SPENCE, W.G. *Australia's awakening: thirty years in the life of an Australian agitator* Sydney 1909
History of the A.W.U. Sydney 1911
SPENCER, B. *Report on the work of the Horn scientific expedition to Central Australia* 4 vols. Melbourne 1896
Native tribes of the Northern Territory of Australia London 1914
Wanderings in wild Australia 2 vols. London 1928
SPENCER, B. & GILLEN, F.J. *The native tribes of Central Australia* London 1899
The northern tribes of Central Australia London 1904
Across Australia 2 vols. London 1912
The Arunta: a study of a stone age people 2 vols. London 1927
SPENCER, J. *Cross section* Sydney 1966
SPENCER, T.E. *How M'Dougall topped the score and other verses* Sydney 1906
Budgeree ballads Sydney 1908
Bindawalla: an Australian story Sydney 1912
SPICER, J.R. *Cry of the storm-bird* London 1958
SPICER, W.W. *A handbook of the plants of Tasmania* Hobart 1878
SPIELVOGEL, N.F. *A gumsucker on the tramp* Ballarat, Vic. [1905]
The cocky farmer Melbourne [1907]
The gumsucker at home Melbourne [1914]
The affair at Eureka: the story of '54 Ballarat, Vic. 1928
Old Eko's note-book Sydney 1930
Sporting life Sydney 1954–57
Sporting news and axeman's journal Launceston, Tas. 1904
SPRY, C. *Real estate without headaches* Canberra 1979
SPURR, F.C. *Five years under the Southern Cross* London 1915
'A SQUATTER' (E. Lloyd) *A visit to the Antipodes: with some reminiscences of a sojourn in Australia* London 1846
'A SQUATTER' *A letter addressed to the squatters of New South Wales on the transportation & labour questions* Sydney 1851

The squatters' plum, or, immigration exposed Sydney 1878
SQUIRE, W.A. *Ritual, myth, and customs of the Australian Aborigines* Maitland, N.S.W. [1896]
SQUIRES, V. *Livestock management in the arid zone* Melbourne 1981
STAAL, P. *A foreigner looks at Australia* London 1936
STACKPOLE, K. & TRENGOVE, A. *Not just for openers* Abbotsford, Vic. 1974
STAMER, W. *Recollections of a life of adventure* 2 vols. London 1866
Standard and Port Phillip gazetteer Melbourne 1844–45
STANGER, Mrs J.C. *A journey from Sydney, over the Blue Mountains, to Bathurst, forty years ago* (anon.) Bathurst, N.S.W. 1882
STANLEY, R. ed. *Tourist to the Antipodes: William Archer's 'Australian journey, 1876–77'* St Lucia, Qld. 1977
STANLEY, T.D. & ROSS, E.M. *Flora of south-eastern Queensland* vol. I. Brisbane 1983
STANNAGE, C.T. ed. *A new history of Western Australia* Nedlands, W.A. 1981
STAPLEDON, R.G. *A tour in Australia and New Zealand: grass land and other studies* London 1928
STAPLES, A. *Paddo* Sydney 1964
Star, and working man's guardian Parramatta, N.S.W. 1844–46 (from 4 Oct. 1845 has title *The Star*)
STEAD. C. *Seven poor men of Sydney* London 1934, Sydney 1971
STEAD, D.G. *Crustaceans: ancient, modern and mythical* Sydney 1905
Fishes of Australia: a popular and systematic guide to the study of the wealth within our waters Sydney 1906
The rabbit in Australia Sydney 1935
Sharks and rays of Australian seas Sydney 1963
STEEL, M. *Red Rover* Adelaide 1973
Steele Rudd's magazine Brisbane 1905–07
STEPHEN, A.C. *An Australian in the R.F.A.: being letters and diary* Sydney 1918
STEPHEN, H.W.H. *Lily's fortune* Sydney 1886
STEPHENS, A.G. *The pearl and the octopus* Melbourne [1911]
STEPHENS, A.G. & O'BRIEN, S.J. see O'Brien, S.E. & Stephens, A.G.
STEPHENS, J. *South Australia an exposure* London 1839
The land of promise London 1839
A voice from Australia! London 1848
STEPHENS, J.B. *The black gin* Melbourne 1873
A hundred pounds Melbourne 1876
Miscellaneous poems Brisbane 1880
Fayette; or, bush revels Brisbane 1892
Stephens's Adelaide miscellany Adelaide 1849 (continues *The Adelaide miscellany*
STEPHENSEN, P.R. *The bushwhackers* London [1929]
STEPHENSON, H. *Cattlemen & huts of the high plains* Armadale, Vic. 1980
STEVENS, F. *Aborigines in the Northern Territory cattle industry* Canberra 1974
STEVENSON, J.B. *Seven years in the Australian bush* Liverpool 1880
STEWART, A. *Let's get cracking* Sydney 1943
STEWART, D. *A thousand miles and more: a tramp through the Coolgardie goldfields* Melbourne 1896
STEWART, D.A. *Sun orchids* Sydney 1952
STEWART, D.A. & KEESING, N. eds. *Australian bush ballads* Sydney 1955
Old bush songs Sydney 1957
STEWART, G. *The leveller* Perth 1979
STEWART, M. *Autobiography of my mother* Ringwood, Vic. 1985
STEWART, P. *Australian tales and verses* Melbourne 1908
**Sticking plaster: souvenir issue 2/2 Field Ambulance* Melbourne 1940
STIRLING, A.W. *The never never land: a ride in North Queensland* London 1884
STIRLING, E. & RICHARDSON, N.H. *Memories of Aberfeldy and memories of the Jordan in the depression* n.p. 1977
STIVENS, D. *The courtship of Uncle Henry* Melbourne 1946
Jimmy Brockett London 1951
The gambling ghost and other tales Sydney 1953
Ironbark Bill Sydney 1955
A horse of air Sydney 1970
The demon bowler and other cricket stories Collingwood, Vic. 1979
STOCK, R. *The pyjama man* Sydney [1914]
The stockowner's guide Sydney 1912
STOKES, J.L. *Discoveries in Australia* 2 vols. London 1846
STONE, C. *Running the brumbies* Adelaide 1979
STONE, D.M. *Gold prospecting* Lilydale, Vic. 1977
STONE, D.M. et al. *Metal detecting for gold and relics in Australia* Lilydale, Vic. 1980
STONE, L. *Jonah* London [1911]
Betty Wayside London [1915]
STONEY, H.B. *A year in Tasmania: including some months' residence in the capital; with a descriptive tour through the island* Hobart 1854
Victoria: with a description of its principal cities, Melbourne and Geelong: and remarks on the present state of the colony London 1856
STOW, R. *A haunted land* London 1956
The bystander London 1957
Tourmaline London 1963
The merry-go-round in the sea London 1965
Midnite: the story of a wild colonial boy Melbourne 1967
**Stretcher: journal of the Camel Brigade Field Ambulance* Melbourne 1917
STRETTON, A. *The furious days: the relief of Darwin* Sydney 1976
STRETTON, C. *Memoirs of a chequered life* 3 vols. London 1862
STRICKLAND, E. *The Australian pastor: a record of the remarkable changes in mind and outward estate of Henry Elliott* London 1862
Strictly personal: stories of re-establishment from the personal angle (issued by the Ministry of Post-War Reconstruction et al.) Melbourne [1946]
Stringybark & greenhide: folk magazine of Australia Newcastle, N.S.W. 1979–83
STRUTT, F.L. *The song of an outback bloke* Rockhampton, Qld. [1933]
STRUTT, W. *The Australian journal of William Strutt, A.R.A. 1850–1862* ed. by G. Mackaness Sydney 1958
STRZELECKI, P.E. de. *Physical description of New South Wales and Van Diemen's Land* London 1845
STUART, D.R. *Yandy* Melbourne 1959
The driven Melbourne 1961
Yaralie Melbourne 1962
Morning star, evening star Melbourne 1973
Prince of my country Melbourne 1974
Walk, trot, canter and die Melbourne 1975
Drought foal Melbourne 1977
Wedgetail view Melbourne 1978
Crank back on roller Melbourne 1979
I think I'll live Melbourne 1981
STUART, H.A. ed. *Bards of Burwood* Burwood, N.S.W. [1901]
STUART, J.M. *Exploration of the interior: diary . . from March 2 to September 3, 1860* Adelaide 1860
Explorations in Australia: the journals of John McDouall Stuart during the years 1858, 1859, 1860, 1861, & 1862 2nd ed. London 1865
STUART, R.P. & NAYLOR, T.B. *Norfolk Island 1846* Adelaide 1979
STURGESS, G. & BIRNBAUER, B. *The journalist who laughed* Richmond, Vic. 1983
STURT, C. *Two expeditions into the interior of southern Australia, during the years 1828, 1829, 1830, and 1831* 2 vols. London 1833
Narrative of an expedition into Central Australia, performed under the authority of Her Majesty's government, during the years 1844, 45, and 46; together with a notice of the province of South Australia in 1847 2 vols. London 1849
Style manual for authors, editors and printers of Australian government publications 3rd ed. Canberra 1978
SULMAN, F. *A popular guide to the wild flowers of New South Wales* 2 vols. Sydney 1913–14
SUMMONS, J. *Lamb of God* Sydney [1980]
Sun Sydney 1910–
Sun and New South Wales independent press Sydney 1843
Sun-herald Sydney 1952–
Sunday independent Perth, 1970– (continues *The independent*)

Sunday sun Brisbane Sept. 1971– (continues *Sunday truth*)
Sunday telegraph Sydney 1939–
Sunday truth Brisbane Oct. 1960–29 Aug. 1971 (continues *Truth*, continued by *Sunday sun*)
SUNTER, G.H. *Adventures of a trepang fisher* London 1937
Surf: all about it Sydney 1930
Surfabout Sydney 1963–68
**Survey sentinel: 2/1 Australian Army Topographical Survey Company* [In the field] 1941–43
SUTCLIFFE, J.T. *A history of trade unionism in Australia* Melbourne 1921
SUTHERLAND, G. *Tales of the goldfields* Melbourne 1880
The Australasian live stock manual and breeder's record Melbourne 1896
2nd ed. 1903
SUTTON, B. *Snow and me* Brisbane [1966]
Comrade George Fortitude Valley, Qld. 1976
SUTTOR, W.H. *Australian stories retold and sketches of country life* Bathurst, N.S.W. 1887
Swag Sydney 1968
SWAIN, E.H.F. *The timbers and forest products of Queensland* Brisbane 1928
SWAN, N.W. *A couple of cups ago, and other stories* Melbourne 1885
Swan River guardian Perth 1836–38
Swan River news and Western Australian chronicle London 1844–49 (continued by *The Western Australian*)
SWANTON, E.W. ed. *The world of cricket* London 1966
'SWEENEY, EX-CROOK' *I confess! (an expose of the Sydney underworld, compiled to assist in the prevention of crime)* Sydney [c. 1936]
SWEENEY, M. *Melbourne's armageddon* Melbourne [1912]
SWEET, R. *Flora Australasica* London 1827–28
Sydney daily advertiser Sydney 1848
Sydney gazette and New South Wales advertiser Sydney 1803–42
Sydney guardian Sydney 1848–50
Sydney herald Sydney 1831–42 (continued by *The Sydney morning herald*)
Sydney mail Sydney 1860–1938
Sydney monitor Sydney 1828–41 (continues *The monitor*)
Sydney morning herald Sydney 1842– (continues *The Sydney herald*)
Sydney punch Sydney 1864–88
Sydney record Sydney 1843–44
Sydney sentinel Sydney 1845–48
The Sydney slang dictionary Sydney [c. 1882]
Sydney standard and colonial advocate Sydney 1839
Sydney times Sydney 1834–38
SYME, J. *Nine years in Van Diemen's Land* Dundee 1848
SYMON, J.H. *The Australian Commonwealth Bill* Adelaide 1900

'T.O. LINGO' *The Australian comic dictionary* Melbourne [1916]
TV times Sydney 1959– (to Oct. 1959 has title *TV news-times*)
TV week Melbourne 1957–
TAFT, R. *From stranger to citizen* Nedlands, W.A. 1965
TAIT, R.S. *Scotty Mac – shearer* Sydney 1912
TALENT, J.A. *Minerals, rocks and gems* Milton, Qld. 1970
Talking football with the stars Melbourne 1954
TANDY, S. *The children in the scrub: a story of Tasmania* London [1878]
TAPLIN, G. ed. *The folklore, manners, customs, and languages of the South Australian Aborigines* Adelaide 1879
Tasmania. Colonial Secretary's Office. Records, 1824–55 Tasmania. State Archives. Record group CSO 1–83
Tasmanian non-state records. Tasmania. State Archives.
Tasmanian Hobart 1827–31 (continues *The Tasmanian and Port Dalrymple advertiser* continued by *The Tasmanian and southern literary and political journal*)
Tasmanian Launceston 1881–95 (continues *Weekly examiner*)
Tasmanian almanack Hobart 1825–30
Tasmanian journal of natural science, agriculture, statistics, &c. London 1842–49 (continued by *Papers and proceedings of the Royal Society of Tasmania*)
'A TASMANIAN LADY' *Treasures, lost and found: a story of life in Tasmania* London 1872
Tasmanian mail Hobart 1877–1921 (continued by *The illustrated Tasmanian mail*)
Tasmanian weekly dispatch Hobart 1839–41 (continues *The Tasmanian*)
TATE, R.D. *The doughman* Sydney 1933
TAUNTON, H. *Australind: wanderings in Western Australia and the Malay east* London 1903
TAYLOR, A.G. *The marble man* Sydney 1889
TAYLOR, E.C.H. ed. *Our Australian game of football* Melbourne 1936
TAYLOR, G.A. *Those were the days* Sydney 1918
TAYLOR, H. *Emigration to South Australia* London 1877
TAYLOR, H.S. *Pioneer irrigationists' manuals* Renmark, S. Aust. 1920
TAYLOR, K.G. *Pick and the duffers* Sydney 1930
TAYLOR, N.M. ed. *Journal of Ensign Best 1837–1843* Wellington, N.Z. 1966
TAYLOR, P. *An end to silence* Sydney 1980
TAYLOR, P.A. *The colony of Queensland and the alleged slave trade in the South Seas* London 1869
TAYLOR, T.E. *Peregrinations of an Australian prisoner of war* Melbourne 1920
TAYLOR, W.C. *Jottings on Australia: with remarks on the California route to New York and Liverpool* London 1872
'TE WHARE' *A bush cinema made in Australia* Sydney 1922
TEECE, C.W. & PIKE, G. *Voice of the wilderness* Rockhampton, Qld. 1978
Teetotal advocate Launceston, Tas. 1843
Teetotaller, and general newspaper Sydney 1842–43
Tegg's handbook for emigrants London 1839
Tegg's monthly magazine Sydney 1836
Tegg's New South Wales pocket almanac and remembrancer Sydney 1836–44
TEICHELMANN, C.G. *Aborigines of South Australia* Adelaide 1841
Telegraph Brisbane 1872– (from 1948–28 May 1955 has title *Brisbane telegraph*)
'TEMPE' see Willis, J.
Ten award winning stories by north-west Tasmanian writers [Burnie, Tas.] 1972
TENCH, W. *A complete account of the settlement at Port Jackson* London 1793
A narrative of the expedition to Botany Bay London 1789
TENISON-WOODS, J.E. *Fish and fisheries of New South Wales* Sydney 1883
TENNANT, K. *Foveaux* London 1939
The battlers London 1941
Ride on stranger London 1943
Lost haven New York 1946
The joyful condemned New York 1953
The honey flow London 1956
Tell morning this Sydney 1967
ed. *Summer's tales 1* Melbourne 1964
Ibid. 2 Melbourne 1965
TENNISON, P. ed. *Heyday or doomsday? Australia 2000* Melbourne 1977
TERRY, M. *Across unknown Australia* London 1925
Through a land of promise: with gun, car and camera in the heart of northern Australia London 1927
Hidden wealth and hiding people London 1931
'Out back' Sydney [1932]
Untold miles: three gold-hunting expeditions amongst the picturesque borderland ranges of Central Australia London 1933
Sand and sun London 1937
War of the Warramullas Adelaide 1974
TERRY, S. see 'A.L.F.'
TESHER, H.O. *The eleven days* Melbourne 1977
THACKERAY, C. *The amateur fisherman's guide* Sydney 1895
Goliath Joe, fisherman Sydney [1917]
THATCHER, C.R. *Thatcher's colonial songster* Melbourne 1858
The Victoria songster part 5. 2nd ed. Melbourne 1860
Thatcher's Invercargill minstrel Invercargill, N.Z. [1864]
THATCHER, R. *A travelled actor* Sydney 1881
ed. *Something to his advantage* Sydney 1875
Theatre magazine (title varies) Sydney 1904–26

THEODORE, E.G. *Some industrial problems and their solution* London 1920
THERRY, R. *Reminiscences of thirty years' residence in New South Wales and Victoria* London 1863
They wrote it themselves: a book of the W.A.A.A.F. Melbourne 1946
THIELE, C. *The sun on the stubble* Adelaide 1961
Albatross two Adelaide 1974
Chadwick's chimney Sydney 1979
River Murray Mary Adelaide 1979
THIELE, R. *Ketch hand* Epping, N.S.W. 1976
Things I hear .. a privately circulated digest for busy people Sydney 1946–81
'A THIRTY-FIVE YEARS' COLONIST' *Hard times and how to mend them, or the only real land reform* Brunswick, Vic. 1886
Thirty shilling horse see 'Rev. F.T.P.'
THOMAS, Amby *Moments of leisure* Brisbane 1919
THOMAS, Athol *Bulls and boabs* Adelaide 1980 (first publ. 1977)
THOMAS, M. *The diary and letters .. 1836–1866 being a record of the early days of South Australia:* ed. by E.K. Thomas Adelaide 1915
THOMAS, P. *Taming the concrete jungle: the builders laborers' story* Sydney 1973
THOMAS, R.M. *The present state of Melbourne and the gold fields of Victoria* London 1853
THOMAS, W.R. *In the early days* Broken Hill, N.S.W. 1889
THOMES, W.H. *A gold hunter's adventures; or, life in Australia* Boston 1864
The belle of Australia; or who am I? Chicago [1891]
Life at the gold mines of Ballarat London [1891]
THOMPSON, G. *Slavery and famine, punishments for sedition; or, an account of the miseries and starvation at Botany Bay* London 1794
THOMPSON, H. *Ballads about business and back-block life* Dunedin, N.Z. 1909
THOMPSON, R.W. *Down under: an Australian odyssey* London 1932
THOMSON, D.F. *Bindibu country* Melbourne 1975
Donald Thomson in Arnhem Land South Yarra, Vic. 1983
THOMSON, J.M. *Fish of the ocean & shore* Sydney 1974
A field guide to the common sea & estuary fishes of non-tropical Australia Sydney 1977
THOMSON-GREGG, W. *A desperate character* 3 vols. London 1873
THONEMANN, H.E. *Tell the white man: the life story of an Aboriginal lubra* Sydney 1949
THORNE, S. *I've met some bloody wags!* Adelaide 1980
THORP, C.H. *A handful of Ausseys* London 1919
THREADGILL, B. *South Australian land exploration: 1856 to 1880* 2 vols. Adelaide 1922
THRELKELD, L.E. *Aboriginal mission, New South Wales* Sydney 1825
A statement chiefly relating to the formation and abandonment of a mission to the Aborigines of New South Wales Sydney 1828
An Australian grammar Sydney 1834
The annual report of the mission to the Aborigines, Lake Macquarie, for MDCCCXXXVIII Sydney 1838
Specimens of the language of the Aborigines of New South Wales to the northward of Sydney *a.* 1859. ML MS A382
Australian reminiscences & papers: ed. by N. Gunson 2 vols. Canberra 1974
THROSSELL, R. *The day before tomorrow* Sydney 1969
Wild weeds and wind flowers: the life and letters of Katharine Susannah Prichard Sydney 1975
**Through: the official journal of Signals 8th Australian Division* Singapore 1941
THURIAN, A. *Bedouries and Queeop* Townsville, Qld. 1945
Bidgeroo and jumbucks Townsville, Qld. 1945
Bunyips and bushland Townsville, Qld. 1945
Bush tea and overlanders Townsville, Qld. [1946]
THWAITES, F.J. *Sky full of thunder* London 1968
THYER, R. & P. *Streetlight* Montmorency, Vic. 1984
Tibbs' popular song book Sydney 1887
TIETKENS, W.H. *Journal of the Central Australian Exploring Expedition, 1889* Adelaide 1891
TILLEY, W. *The wild west of Tasmania* Zeehan, Tas. 1891
TILLYARD, R.J. *The insects of Australia and New Zealand* Sydney 1926
The timber industry and forests of New South Wales (by A. Duckworth) Sydney 1902
TINDALE, N.B. *Aboriginal tribes of Australia: their terrain, environmental controls, distribution, limits, and proper names* Canberra 1974
**Tobruk to Borneo: quarterly journal of the 2/28 Battalion and 24th A/Tank Coy Association* Perth 1951–69
Tocsin Melbourne 1897–11 Oct. 1906 (continued by *Labor call*)
TODHUNTER, P. *Australia under the scalpel* London 1965
TOLMER, A. *Reminiscences of an adventurous and chequered career at home and at the Antipodes* 2 vols. London 1882
Tom Petrie's reminiscences of early Queensland (dating from 1837) recorded by his daughter Brisbane 1904
2nd ed. 1932
TOMLIN, J.W.S. *Australia's greatest need* Westminster 1914
The story of the Bush Brotherhoods London 1949
TOMPSON, C. *Wild notes from the lyre of a native minstrel* Sydney 1826
TORLESSE, C.O. *The Canterbury settlement topographically described in a report to J.R. Godley, Esq.* [London] 1851
TORRENS, Robert *Colonization of South Australia* London 1835
Emigration from Ireland to South Australia Dublin 1839
TORRENS, Robert Richard *Transfer of land by 'registration of title', as now in operation in Australia under the 'Torrens system'* Dublin 1863
Tourists' guide to Tasmania (issued by the) Union Line of Steamers Hobart 1898
TOURNAY-HINDE, E.E. *Minds unmoored* Burwood, N.S.W. [1936]
TOWLE, C.C. *Certain stone implements of the scraper family found along the coast of New South Wales* Sydney 1930
TOWNER, E.T. *The selector's guide to the Barcoo* Brisbane 1890
TOWNSEND, J.P. *Rambles and observations in New South Wales* London 1849
TOWNSHEND, D.J. *Gland time* London 1975
TOWSON, H. *The black and the white* Ilfracombe, England 1977
TRAMWAY WORKERS *'The shock brigader' 1933: containing essays, stories, verse, etc.:* by Tramway workers Melbourne 1933
Transactions and proceedings and report of the Philosophical Society of Adelaide, 1877/78–1878/79 Adelaide 1878–79 (continued by *Transactions and proceedings of the Royal Society of South Australia*)
Transactions and proceedings .. of the Royal Society of South Australia, 1879/80 (title varies) Adelaide 1880–
Transactions of the Linnean Society of London London 1791
Transactions of the Philosophical Institute of Victoria, 1855/56–1859 Melbourne 1857–60 (continued by *Transactions of the Royal Society of Victoria*)
Transactions of the Philosophical Society of New South Wales, 1862–1865 Sydney 1866
Transactions of the Royal Society of Victoria, 1860–1887 Melbourne 1860–88 (from 1865 *Transactions and proceedings*, continued by *Proceedings of the Royal Society of Victoria*)
Transactions of the Zoological Society of London London 1833/35–1984
Transportation news magazine Sydney 1935–Feb. 1940 (continued by *Truck & bus transportation*)
The transportation question considered Hobart 1847
TRAUTMAN, E. & J. *Jinkers and jarrah jerkers* Geraldton, W.A. 1980
TRAVERS, J.H. *Bull dust on the Brigalow* Toowoomba, Qld. 1976
TRAVERS, R. *The Tasmanians* Melbourne 1968
TREATT, V. & RAINBOW, A.E. *The law relating to compensation for injuries to workers* Sydney 1927
Tree lover: journal of the Australian Forest League Sydney 1933–41
Trees and natural resources Springvale South, Vic. 1985– (continues *Trees and Victoria's resources*)
Trees and Victoria's resources Springvale South, Vic. 1981–84 (continues *Victoria's resources*, continued by *Trees and natural resources*)
TREGASKIS, E.F. *Santa Claus' message: a Christmas story* Blackburn, Vic. 1921
TRELOAR, F. Extracts from the diary. 1823–79 Mortlock Library MS D4800(L)

TRENERRY, E. *Descriptive plan for a proposed great central Australian transcontinental railway* London 1879
TREVOR, P. *With the M.C.C. in Australia (1907–1908)* London 1908
Trifler and literary gleaner Launceston, Tas. 1842–43
TRIST, M. *In the sun* Sydney 1943
Now that we're laughing Sydney 1945
What else is there? Sydney 1946
Daddy Sydney 1947
TRITTON, H.P. *Time means tucker* Sydney 1959
rev. ed. 1964
TRITTON, N. *Poems* [Brisbane 1921]
TROLLOPE, A. *Australia and New Zealand* 2 vols. London 1873
Harry Heathcote of Gangoil London 1874
**Troop ship news* At sea 1941
**Tropic spread* New Britain 1945
**Troppo topics: official organ of 1 Lost Fd Coy R.A.E.* n.p. 1942–43
**Troppo tribune: news mouthpiece of 8 A.A.O.D. 14 a L. of C. sub area, Australia* Mataranka, N.T. 1942–44
TROST, G.F. *Call me a cabbie* Sydney 1966
TROTTER, F.E. *Tales of Billzac: being extracts from a digger's diary* Brisbane 1923
TROUGHTON, E. *Furred animals of Australia* Sydney 1941
Truck & bus transportation Sydney Mar. 1940– (continues *Transportation news magazine*)
Truckies: voice of the road transport industry Sydney 1978–81
Truckin' life Clayfield, Qld. 1976–
True colonist and Van Diemen's Land political despatch, and agricultural and commercial advertiser Hobart July 1834–Dec. 1844 (continues *The colonist and Van Diemen's Land commercial and agricultural advertiser*)
True sun, and New South Wales independent press Sydney 1844
Trumpeter Hobart 1833–?1849
Trumpeter general Hobart 1833–34
TRURAN, J. *Green mallee* Sydney 1932
Where the plain begins Sydney 1933
Truth Brisbane 1900–16 Oct. 1960 (continued by *Sunday truth*)
Truth Sydney 1879–80
Truth Sydney 1890–5 Oct. 1958 (continued by *Sunday mirror*)
TUCK, G. *A field guide to the seabirds of Australia and the world* London 1980
TUCKER, H.F. *The new Arcadia: an Australian story* London 1894
TUCKER, H.J. *The weather prophet and other verses* Adelaide 1929
TUCKER, J. *Ralph Rashleigh or the life of an exile:* ed. by C. Roderick Sydney 1952
TUCKER, J.K. *The Aborigines and the Chinese in Australia* Sydney 1868
TUCKER, J.O. *The golden spring and other poems* Melbourne 1865
The mute, and other poems Melbourne 1870
TUCKER, M. *If everyone cared* Sydney 1977
TUCKEY, J.H. *An account of a voyage to establish a colony at Port Philip in Bass's Strait, on the south coast of New South Wales, in His Majesty's Ship Calcutta, in the years 1802–3–4* London 1805
TULLIPAN, R. *Follow the sun* Sydney 1960
March into morning Sydney 1962
TURNBULL, C. ed. *Ned Kelly: being his own story of his life and crimes* Melbourne 1942
The charm of Hobart Sydney 1949
TURNBULL, H. *Leichhardt's second journey: a first hand account* Sydney 1983
TURNBULL, J. *A voyage round the world in the years 1800, 1801, 1802, 1803, and 1804* 3 vols. London 1805
TURNER, A. *Royal mail and other plays* Perth [1944]
TURNER, E. *Seven little Australians* London 1912 (first publ. 1894)
TURNER, F. *Australian grasses* vol. 1. Sydney 1895
Botany of the Darling, New South Wales Sydney 1903
Anderson's manual of the farm Sydney [1907]
TURNER, G. *The lame dog man* Melbourne 1967
TURNER, G.W. *The English language in Australia and New Zealand* London 1966
rev. ed. 1972
TURNER, H.G. *The first decade of the Australian Commonwealth: a chronicle of contemporary politics, 1901–1910* Melbourne 1911
TURNER, V.E. *'Ooldea'* Melbourne 1950
Twentieth century impressions of Western Australia Perth 1901
**21st on the 25th: 21st Australian Infantry Brigade* Palestine 1940
**Twenty-second's echo* In the field 1918–19
**The 23rd: the voice of the Battalion* In the field 1917–19
**Two bar four three bulletin* North Borneo 1945
**Two blues formerly the Bait: magazine of the 13th Battalion* France 1918
TWOPENY, R.E.N. *Town life in Australia* London 1883
TYERMAN, D. & BENNET, G. *Journal of voyages and travels* 2 vols. London 1831
TYLER, M.J. *Frogs* Sydney 1976
There's a frog in my stomach Sydney 1984
ed. *The gastric brooding frog* London 1983
TYRRELL, J.R. *Australian Aboriginal place-names and their meanings* Sydney 1933
Old books, old friends, old Sydney Sydney 1952
TYRWHITT, W.S.S. *The new chum in the Queensland bush* London [1887]

ULLATHORNE, W.B. *The Catholic mission in Australasia* Liverpool 1837
'ULOOLA' (G.D. Humphrey) *A fable: with other verses* Parramatta, N.S.W. 1900
UNION LINE OF STEAMERS see *Tourists' guide to Tasmania*
UPFIELD, A.W. *The sands of Windee* London [1931]
Wings above the Diamantina Sydney 1936
Mr Jelly's business Sydney 1937
Winds of evil Sydney 1937
The bone is pointed Sydney 1938, 1966
The mystery of Swordfish Reef Sydney 1939
No footprints in the bush New York 1944
Death of a swagman New York 1945
The bachelors of Broken Hill New York 1950
The widows of Broome New York 1950
The new shoe London 1952
Murder must wait New York 1953
Venom house Melbourne 1953
Death of a lake London 1954, 1956
Cake in the hat box Melbourne 1955
The battling prophet London 1956
Bony and the black virgin London 1959
Bony and the mouse London 1959
Madman's bend London 1963
The lure of the bush New York 1965
UREN, M. *Glint of gold: a story of the gold fields of Western Australia and the men who found them, especially the prospectors and one prospector known to his mates as Diorite* Melbourne 1948

The vagabond annual, Christmas 1877 Melbourne 1877
The vagabond papers: sketches of Melbourne life, in light and shade (by J.S. James) Melbourne 1876–77
The vagabonds or the bonded vags Sydney 1894
VANDERKISTE, R.W. *Lost – but not for ever* London 1863
VAN DIEMEN'S LAND. Lieutenant-Governor. *Government and general orders .. from February, 1813, to February, 1814* Hobart 1814
Van Diemen's Land almanack Hobart 1831–33 (continued by *The Van Diemen's Land annual*)
Van Diemen's Land chronicle Hobart 1841
Van Diemen's Land .. correspondence .. on the subject of the military operations .. against the Aboriginal inhabitants London 1831 (G.B.P.P. H.C. 259)
Van Diemen's Land gazette and general advertiser Hobart 1814
Van Diemen's Land monthly magazine Hobart 1835
Van Diemen's Land pocket almanack, for the year .. 1824 Hobart 1824
VAUDE, C. *Tivoli up-to-date: joke, parody & monologue* Melbourne 1916
VAUGHAN, H.M. *An Australasian wander-year* London 1914
VAUGHAN, M.K. *Wombat stew* Sydney 1984
VAUX, J.H. *Memoirs of James Hardy Vaux* 2 vols. London 1819

VAWR, D. *The ratbag mind of Dinas Vawr* Adelaide 1978
VEITCH, A.S. *Run from the morning* Sydney 1980
Roses and boronia: a mid-Victorian romance Sydney 1981
VEITCH, R. & SIMMONDS, J.H. *Pests and diseases of Queensland fruits and vegetables* Brisbane 1929
VERNON, B. *A big day at Bellbird* Sydney 1971
VESEY-FITZGERALD, B. & LAMONTE, F. *Game fish of the world* London 1949
'THE VET' see Hornsby, M.
'VIATOR' (J.A. Robinson) *From up along down under: with the Empire Parliamentary Delegation to Australia* Newfoundland 1927
VICARS, J. *The tariff, immigration, and the labour question* Sydney 1877
**Vic Eddy: produced by Signals 7th Australian Division for Christmas 1941* [Palestine] 1941
VICKERS, F.B. *The mirage* Melbourne 1955, Berlin 1958
First place to the stranger London 1956
Though poppies grow Melbourne 1958
No man is himself Sydney 1969
A stranger no longer Sydney 1977
Victorian agricultural & horticultural gazette Geelong, Vic. 1857–61
Victorian historical magazine Melbourne 1911– (from 1975 has title *Victorian historical journal*)
Victorian naturalist: the journal & magazine of the Field Naturalists' Club of Victoria Melbourne 1884–1953
Victorian poultry journal Melbourne 1919–56
Victorian review Melbourne 1879–86
Victorian timber news (title varies) Blackburn, Vic. 1981–
Victoria's resources Springvale, Vic. 1959–80 (continued by *Trees and Victoria's resources*)
VIDAL, M.T. *Tales for the bush* Sydney [1845]
VIDLER, E.A. *Our own birds of Australia* Melbourne 1931
VILLIERS, L.J. *The changing year* Adelaide 1918
VIRGO, C.J. *Australasian building knowledge* 4 vols. Brisbane 1947–52
VIVIENNE, M. *Travels in Western Australia* London 1901
Sunny South Australia .. 4,000 miles of travel, 1837–1908 Adelaide 1908
VODICKA, M. *Track to Rum Jungle* Ilfracombe, England 1970
VOGAN, A.J. *The black police* London 1890
The voice of the Battalion see *The 23rd*

'W.G.C.' *Some account of the Mount Morgan gold mine* Rockhampton, Qld. 1885
'W.R.L.' (W.R. Lawson) *Our wool staple: or a history of squatting in South Australia* Adelaide 1865
'W.R.-s.' *The fell tyrant: or the suffering convict* London 1836
'W.T.G.' *Quite colonial: or the mighty nugget of Slaty Creek* [Creswick, Vic. c. 1948] (first publ. 1862 in *Family herald*)
WACKETT, L.J. *Studies of an angler* Melbourne 1950
WADE, A. *Vagabond verse* Melbourne 1917
WADHAM, S.M. & WOOD, G.L. *Land utilization in Australia* Melbourne 1939
**'Wagflagger' Sig 6 Aust Div abroad* [Palestine] 1941
WAIT, B. *Letters from Van Dieman's Land, written during four years imprisonment for political offences committed in Upper Canada* Buffalo 1843
WAITE, E.R. *A popular account of Australian snakes* Sydney 1898
The fishes of South Australia Adelaide 1923
The reptiles and amphibians of South Australia Adelaide 1929
**Waiting times* [Belgium] 1919
WAKEFIELD, E.G. *A letter from Sydney, the principal town of Australasia:* ed. by R. Gouger London 1829
The new British province of South Australia London 1834
WAKEFIELD, N.A. *Ferns of Victoria and Tasmania* Melbourne 1955
Naturalist's diary Croydon, Vic. 1967
WAKEFIELD, S. *Poems* Murray Bridge, S. Aust. 1980
WALCH, G. *The 'fireflash'* Sydney 1867
True-blue beard Melbourne 1872
Australia Felix Melbourne 1873
On the cards; or, a motley pack Melbourne 1875
A little tin plate Melbourne [1881]
Victoria in 1880 Melbourne 1881
ed. *'Hash': a mixed dish for Christmas* Melbourne 1877
ed. *Australasia: an intercolonial Christmas annual* Melbourne 1878
ed. *The Victorian jubilee book* 1887
Walch's Tasmanian almanac Hobart 1863–1980
Walkabout: Australian geographical magazine Melbourne 1934–74
WALKER, D. *We went to Australia* London 1949
WALKER, G.W. *Friendly counsel addressed to the working classes, more especially to newly arrived emigrants* [Hobart] 1854
Notes on the Aborigines of Tasmania, extracted from the manuscript journals of George Washington Walker Hobart 1898
WALKER, J. *No sunlight singing* London 1960
WALKER, K. *The dawn is at hand* Brisbane 1966
WALKER, L. *The other girl* London 1965
The runaway girl London 1975
see also 'Sanders, D.L.'
WALKER, M. *Pioneer crafts of early Australia* South Melbourne 1978
Making do Ringwood, Vic. 1982
WALKER, T. *A month in the bush of Australia* London 1838
WALKER, W. *An account of the great flood on the Hawkesbury of June, 1864, and the lesser flood, of July following* Parramatta, N.S.W. 1864
'WALKER, W.H.' (G. Ranken) *The invasion* Sydney 1877
WALL, A.G.N. *Letters of an airman* Melbourne [1918]
WALLACE, E.J. *Sydney and the bush* Sydney 1966
WALLACE, J. *Memories of a country childhood* St Lucia, Qld. 1977
WALLACE, N.V. *Bush lawyer* Adelaide 1976
WALLACE, R. *The rural economy and agriculture of Australia and New Zealand* London 1891
WALLACE-CRABBE, C. *The emotions are not skilled workers* Sydney 1980
Splinters Adelaide 1981
WALLACE-CRABBE, R. *Feral palit* Prahran, Vic. 1978
The Wallaroo and Moonta mines Adelaide 1914
WALLER, E. *And there's gold out there!* Melbourne 1966
And there's opal out there Melbourne 1969
WALLING, E. *The Australian roadside* Melbourne 1952
On the trail of Australian wildflowers Canberra 1984
WALLIS, J. *An historical account of the colony of New South Wales and its dependent settlements* London 1821
WALSH, J.M. *The man behind the curtain* Sydney 1927
WALSH, M. *May Gibbs: mother of the gumnuts, her life and work* North Ryde, N.S.W. 1985
WALTERS, O. *Shrapnel green and other verses* 2nd ed. Perth 1931
WALTHAM, E. *Life and labour in Australia: being personal observations* London [1909]
Wanderer Adelaide 1853
'WANDERER' *'Down on their luck': a true narrative of Queensland* Brisbane 1887
WANNAN, B. *Chronicles of Boobyalla* Adelaide 1979
ed. *A treasury of Australian humour* Melbourne 1960
ed. *A treasury of Australian frontier tales* Melbourne 1961
ed. *Fair go, spinner* Melbourne 1964
ed. *Classics of Australian humour* Melbourne 1982
see also Fearn-Wannan, W.
**War drum: magazine of Q'land L. of C. area B.I.P.O.D.* Brisbane 1943–44
WARBURTON, C. *White poppies* Sydney 1937
WARBURTON, C. & ROBERTSON, W.K. *Buffaloes: adventure and discovery in Arnhem Land* Sydney 1934
WARBURTON, P.E. *Journey across the western interior of Australia* London 1875
WARD, E. *The vineyards and orchards of South Australia* Adelaide 1862
WARD, H. Diary containing the account of his voyage from England to South Australia, commencing 18th July 1838 and concluding upon arrival at Holdfast Bay December 1st 1838. Mortlock Library MS D6357
WARD, H.E. *Down under without blunder* Melbourne 1967
WARD, James see *Perils, pastimes and pleasures*
WARD, Jim & SMITH, G. *The vanishing village: a small Australian town in transition* Melbourne 1978

WARD, John Diary of a convict on Norfolk Island. 1841–42 NLA MS 3275
WARD, R. *The Australian legend* Melbourne 1970 (first publ. 1958)
WARDEN, I. *The worst of Warden* Canberra [1980]
WARDLEY, E. *The confessions of Wavering Worthy* Sydney 1864
WARLOW, T. *By mirage and mulga: the soldiers' cheer-up book* Adelaide 1916
WARNER, P.F. *England v. Australia: the record of a memorable tour* London 1912
Cricket reminiscences: with some review of the 1919 season London 1920
WARNER, W.L. *A black civilization* rev. ed. New York 1958
WARREN, J. *Australian football fundamentals* French's Forest, N.S.W. 1982
WARREN, L.A. *Speaking silence* Melbourne [c. 1923]
WARREN, M. *No glamour in gumboots* Sydney 1958
WARREN, W.H. *The strength and elasticity of New South Wales timbers of commercial value* Sydney 1887
Australian timbers Sydney 1892
The Warrumbungle book of verse Coonabarabran, N.S.W. 1978
'WARUNG, P.' (W. Astley) *Tales of the convict system* Sydney 1892
Tales of the early days London 1894
WATEN, J. *The unbending* Melbourne 1954
Shares in murder Melbourne 1957
Season of youth Melbourne 1966
WATERHOUSE, G.R. *The natural history of marsupialia or pouched animals* Edinburgh 1841 (The naturalist's library. Mammalia vol. XI.)
WATERHOUSE, Mrs J.I. *Bowled out: a story of bushranging in South Australia* Adelaide 1891
Waterside workers' gazette Melbourne 1903–14
WATHEN, G.H. *The golden colony: or Victoria in 1854* London 1855
WATKINS, N. *The kangaroo connection* Rabaul, P.N.G. 1980
WATKINS, W. *The wayward gang* Adelaide 1965
The perilous hours London 1966
Andamooka London 1967
Shadow of the whip London 1967
Don't wait for me I'm already gone Melbourne 1972
Suddenly of age Melbourne 1972
WATLING, T. *Letters from an exile at Botany-Bay* Penrith, England 1794
WATMOUGH, W. *The cult of the budgerigar* London 1935
WATSON, E.L.G. *But to what purpose* London 1946
Journey under the southern stars London 1968
WATSON, H. *A lecture on South Australia .. delivered .. Nov. 27, 1837* London 1838
WATSON, W.C. *The memoirs of a ship's fireman* Melbourne 1916
WATT, A. *The evolution of Australian foreign policy* Cambridge 1967
WATTONE, M. *Winning the gold in Western Australia* Scarborough, W.A. 1982
WATTS, C.H.S. & ASLIN, H.J. *The rodents of Australia* Sydney 1981
WATTS, C.S. *Selected verse* Sydney 1944
WATTS, J.I. *Memories of early days in South Australia* Adelaide 1882
Family life in South Australia fifty-three years ago Adelaide 1890
WAUGH, D. *Master White Grass* Melbourne 1974
WAUGH, D.L. *Three years' practical experience of a settler in New South Wales* Edinburgh 1838
We 5: a book for the season Melbourne [1879]
**'We of the A.I.F.': souvenir* (of the film) Melbourne 1939
WEATHERHEAD, A. *Leaves from my life* Bega, N.S.W. 1891
WEATHERLY, K. *The roo shooter* London 1968
WEBB, E. *The mark of the sun* New York 1959
WEBB, J.E. *So much for Sydney* Sydney 1956
WEBB, R.A.F. *Brothers in the sun: a history of the Bush Brotherhood Movement in the outback of Australia* Adelaide 1978
WEDGE, J.H. *The diaries of John Helder Wedge 1824–1835* Hobart 1962
WEDLICK, L. *Fishing in Australia* Sydney 1962
What fish is that? [Newport, Vic.] 1970
rev ed. 1980
Sporting fish of inland lakes and streams [Newport, Vic.] 1974
**Weekend magazine: 15 Aust Inf Bde* [Solomon Is.] 1945
Weekly observer Sydney 1833 (continues *Hill's life in New South Wales*)
WEETWOOD, E.M. *The lure of the land* Melbourne 1915
WELCH, D.M. *Aboriginal rock art of Kakadu National Park* Darwin 1982
WELCH, R.P. *Observations on convict and free labour for New South Wales* London 1847
Welcome to Australia (compiled by the Australian-American Cooperation Movement) Melbourne 1942
WELLARD, G.E.P. *Bushlore* Perth 1983
WELLER, A. *The day of the dog* North Sydney 1981
Going home North Sydney 1986
WELLER, H. ed. *Lip service* East Perth 1979
WELLER, S. *Bastards I have met* Charters Towers, Qld. 1976
Old bastards I have met Charters Towers, Qld. 1979
Wellington times and mining and industrial gazette see *North-western advocate*
WELLS, A.E. *Milingimbi* Sydney 1963
Forests are their temples Hobart 1979
WELLS, E. *Fragments from France and Gallipoli* Perth 1921
WELLS, H.C. *The earth cries out* Sydney 1950
WELLS, T.E. *Michael Howe: the last and worst of the bushrangers of Van Diemen's Land* : with introd. by G. Mackaness Sydney 1945 (first publ. Hobart 1818)
WELSBY, T. *Schnappering and fishing in the Brisbane River and Moreton Bay waters* Brisbane 1905
WELSH, L. *The kookaburra* [Ballarat, Vic.] 1944
WENHOLZ, H. *The improvement of Australian wheat* Sydney 1937
WENTWORTH, W.C. Miscellanea. 1816–45 ML MS A758
A statistical, historical, and political description of the colony of New South Wales and its dependent settlements in Van Diemen's Land London 1819
Australasia London 1823
WEST, J. *The history of Tasmania* 2 vols. Launceston, Tas. 1852
WEST, K. *Power in the Liberal Party* Melbourne 1965
West Australian Perth 1833–
West Australian selector's guide Perth 1907
West of the Peesey (compiled by the Warooka Historical Committee) Warooka, S. Aust. 1976
Westerly Perth 1956–
Western Australian Fremantle, W.A. 1831–32 (continued by *Western Australian colonial news*)
Western Australian colonial news Perth 1832–33 (continues *The Western Australian*)
Western Australian Historical Society journal and proceedings (title varies) Perth 1927– (from July 1963 has title *Royal Western Australian Historical Society etc.)*
Western champion Barcaldine, Qld. 1879–1937
**Westernlander .. and Ack ack* On board .. H.M.T. 'Westernland' 1941
WESTGARTH, W. *A commercial,statistical, and general report on the district of Port Phillip, New South Wales, for the half year ended 31st July, 1845* Melbourne [1845]
A commercial, statistical, and general report .. of Port Phillip, New South Wales, for the half year ended 31st of January, 1846 Melbourne [1846]
A report on the condition, capabilities, and prospects of the Australian Aborigines Melbourne 1846
Australia Felix; or, a historical and descriptive account of the settlement of Port Phillip, New South Wales Edinburgh 1848
Victoria; late Australia Felix, or Port Phillip district of New South Wales; being an historical and descriptive account of the colony and its gold mines Edinburgh 1853
Victoria and the Australian gold mines in 1857; with notes on the overland route from Australia, via Suez London 1857
Australia: its rise, progress, and present condition Edinburgh 1861
'WESTLAW, S.' (J. Pike) *The white peril* London [1926]
The mystery of Lombardy Chambers London [1926]
WESTWOOD, J.J. *The journal of J.J. Westwood* Melbourne 1865

'WHAKS LI KELL' (D. Healey) *The Cornstalk: his habits and habitat* Sydney 1893
What migrants need to know about Western Australia Perth 1968–72
WHEELHOUSE, F. *Digging stick to rotary hoe* Melbourne 1966
Wheels Sydney 1953–
WHEELWRIGHT, W.H. see 'Old Bushman'
WHITE, A. *A popular history of mammalia* London 1850
WHITE, C. *History of Australian bushranging* 2 vols. Sydney 1900
WHITE, C.T. *Principles of botany for Queensland farmers* Brisbane 1938
WHITE, D. *Packaging at its apostrophe best* Newtown, N.S.W. 1978
WHITE, G. *Across Australia: being the diary of a journey from Port Darwin to Adelaide during June, July, August, 1901* Melbourne [1901]
Thirty years in tropical Australia London 1918
WHITE, H.A. *Crime and criminals; or, reminiscences of the Penal Department in Victoria* Ballarat, Vic. 1890
WHITE, H.J. *Round the camp fire* Port Augusta, S. Aust. 1893
WHITE, J. *Journal of a voyage to New South Wales* London 1790
WHITE, J.C. *Queensland the progressive!* London 1870
WHITE, John C. & HALLIWELL, W.K. *Dole bludger's handbook* Melbourne 1983
WHITE, L. ed. *Memories of childhood* Fremantle, W.A. 1978
'WHITE, M.' (E.S. Emerson) *A shanty entertainment* Melbourne 1904
WHITE, M.R. *No roads go by* Sydney 1932
From that day to this Adelaide 1961
WHITE, O. *Under the iron rainbow: northwest Australia today* Melbourne 1969
Silent reach London 1978
WHITE, P. *The aunt's story* New York 1948
The ham funeral 1947 see *Four plays*
The tree of man New York 1955
Riders in the chariot London 1961
The season at Sarsaparilla 1961 see *Four plays*
A cheery soul 1962 see *Four plays*
Night on Bald Mountain 1962 see *Four plays*
The burnt ones London 1964
Four plays (The ham funeral, The season at Sarsaparilla, A cheery soul, Night on Bald Mountain) London 1965
The vivisector New York 1970, London 1970
The eye of the storm London 1973
Flaws in the glass London 1981
WHITE, S.A. *Into the dead heart: an ornithological trip through Central Australia* Adelaide 1914
In the far north-west: an expedition to the Musgrave and Everard Ranges Adelaide 1916
Bunya, or mystery mountains Adelaide [1921]
WHITECROSS, R.H. *Slaves of the son of heaven* Sydney 1951
WHITING, J.W. & RELPH, R.E. *The occurrence of opal at Lightning Ridge and Grawin, with geological notes on County Finch* Sydney 1962
WHITINGTON, D. *Treasure upon the earth* Melbourne 1957
Mile pegs Sydney 1963
In search of an Australian Melbourne 1967
'The witless men' Melbourne 1975
Strive to be fair: an unfinished autobiography Canberra 1977
WHITLAM, E.G. *Labor Party policy speech* Sydney 1972
WHITLEY, G.P. *Native freshwater fishes of Australia* Brisbane 1961
Marine fishes of Australia 2 vols. Brisbane 1962
More early history of Australian zoology Sydney 1975
Handbook of Australian fishes : ed. by J. Pollard North Sydney 1980
WHITTAKER, E.C. *Apple growing* 4th ed. Sydney 1966
WHITTELL, H.M. *The literature of Australian birds* Perth 1954
WHITTET, J.N. *Weeds* Sydney 1958, 2nd ed. 1968
WHITWORTH, R.P. *Lost and found: a romance of the desolate region* Melbourne 1873
Velvet and rags Melbourne [1886]
WHITWORTH, R.P. & WINDAS, W.A. *Shimmer of silk: a volume of Melbourne Cup stories* Melbourne 1893
**Whiz-bang* South Brisbane 1929–
**Whizz: a Fourteenth Battalion production* [Perth] 1942
WHYTE, W.F. *William Morris Hughes: his life and times* Sydney 1957
WIDOWSON, H. *Present state of Van Diemen's Land* London 1829
WILD, Q. *The honey wind* Bunyip, Vic. 1981
WILHELMI, C. *Manners and customs of the Australian natives* Melbourne 1862
WILKES, C. *Narrative of the United States Exploring Expedition* 5 vols. Philadephia 1844
WILKES, G.A. *A dictionary of Australian colloquialisms* London 1978, rev. ed. 1985
WILKINS, G.H. *Undiscovered Australia, being an account of an expedition to tropical Australia* London 1928
WILKINSON, F. *Australia at the Front: a colonial view of the Boer War* London 1901
WILKINSON, G.B. *The working man's handbook to South Australia* London 1849
WILLEY, K. *Eaters of the lotus* Brisbane 1964
Naked island and other South Sea tales Sydney 1970
Boss drover Adelaide 1971
Tales of the big country Adelaide 1972
Ghosts of the big country Adelaide 1975
Joe Brown's dog, Bluey Adelaide 1978
WILLIAMS, C. *Open cut: the working class in an Australian mining town* Sydney 1981
WILLIAMS, C.P. *Southern sunbeams* Melbourne 1879
WILLIAMS, C.W. *Yellow, green and red* Brisbane 1967
WILLIAMS, G. *New Australia: where socialism has failed:* .. by 'Stewart Grahame' London 1912
WILLIAMS, H. *My love had a black speed stripe* South Melbourne 1973
WILLIAMS, H.R. *Comrades of the great adventure* Sydney 1935
WILLIAMS, J. *Tom Collins and his house* Perth 1973
White River and other stories Fremantle, W.A. 1979
WILLIAMS, K.A.W. *Native plants of Queensland* 2 vols. North Ipswich, Qld. 1979–84
WILLIAMS, Max *Dingo! My life on the run* Melbourne 1980
WILLIAMS, Michael *The making of the South Australian landscape* London 1974
WILLIAMS, R.G.S. *Australian white slaves* Sydney 1911
WILLIAMS, V. *The years of big Jim* Victoria Park, W.A. 1975
WILLIAMS, W. *A vocabulary of the language of the Aborigines of the Adelaide district* Adelaide 1839
WILLIAMS, W.H. *Williams's illustrated Australian annual, 1869–70 – 1870–71* Melbourne 1870–71
WILLIAMSON, D. *The removalists* Sydney 1972
Jugglers three 1972 see *The coming of Stork*
Don's party Sydney 1973
What if you died tomorrow 1973 see *The coming of Stork*
The coming of Stork, Jugglers three, What if you died tomorrow Sydney 1974
The club Sydney 1978
WILLIAMSON, H.D. *The sunlit plain* Sydney 1958
WILLIS, J. *A summer holiday in Victoria and New Zealand; or leaves from a tourist's note book* : by 'Tempe' Singleton, N.S.W. 1883
WILLIS, J.H. *Victorian fungi* Melbourne 1941
WILLMER, G. *The draper in Australia: being a narrative of three years' adventures and experience at the gold-fields, in the bush, and in the chief cities of Victoria and New South Wales* London 1856
Willmett & Co's Cooktown almanac, North Queensland directory, and miners' and settlers' companion for 1876 Cooktown, Qld 1876
WILLS, C. *Australian passport* London 1953
WILLS, W.J. *A successful exploration through the interior of Australia* London 1863
WILLSHIRE, W.H. *The Aborigines of Central Australia* Port Augusta, S. Aust. 1888
A thrilling tale of real life in the wilds of Australia Adelaide 1895
The land of the dawning: being facts gleaned from cannibals in the Australian stone age Adelaide 1896
WILMOT, C. *Tobruk 1941* Sydney 1944
WILSON, A. *Lays and tales of the mines* Melbourne 1916

WILSON, B. ed. *Pasture improvement in Australia* Sydney 1968
WILSON, E. see *Rambles at the Antipodes*
WILSON, F.H. Overland expedition no. 2. 1855 DL MS 18
WILSON, F.S. *Australian songs and poems* Sydney 1870
WILSON, H. *The log of H.M.S. 'Encounter'* London [1913]
WILSON, H.H. *The golden age* Sydney 1959
Where the wind's feet shine Sydney 1960
WILSON, J. *Australian surfing and surf life saving* Adelaide 1979
WILSON, P.R. *The other side of rape* St Lucia, Qld. 1978
WILSON, T. *The luck of the draw* South Yarra, Vic. 1980
WILSON, T.B. *Narrative of a voyage round the world* London 1835
WINTER, C.H. *The story of 'Bidgee Queen* Sydney 1929
WINTER, T. *Mountain verse: a collection of Snowy Mountains poems* Canberra 1982
WINTER-IRVING, W.A. *Beyond the bitumen* Adelaide 1971
Bush stories Adelaide 1977
WINTON, T. *An open swimmer* Sydney 1982
Scission Fitzroy, Vic. 1985
WIRTH, G. *Round the world with a circus: memories of trials, triumphs and tribulations* Melbourne 1925
WIRTH, P. *The life of Philip Wirth: a lifetime with an Australian circus* Melbourne 1934
**Wiry: 6th Field Regiment* Ingleburn, N.S.W. [and] Overseas 1940–41
WISBERG, A. & WATERS, H. *Bushman at large* New York 1937
WISEWOULD, G. *Outpost: a doctor on the Divide* Kilmore, Vic. 1971
**With compliments: a souvenir written by Sgt. 'X' . . of the 4th Australian Garrison Battalion* [Adelaide 1942]
WITHERS, W.B. *The history of Ballarat* Ballarat, Vic. 1870
WITTON, G.R. *Scapegoats of the Empire: the story of the Bushveldt Carbineers* Melbourne 1907
**Wog journal: HQ 3rd Aust Inf Bde* n.p. 1942–44
WOLFE, D. *The brass kangaroo* Melbourne 1973
WOLFE, J. *The end of the pricklystick* Eden, N.S.W. 1980
Crocodile soup Eden, N.S.W. 1980
WOLLASTON, T.C. *The spirit of the child* Melbourne 1914
Woman's day Sydney 1948–
'WONGAR, B.' (S. Bozic) *The track to Bralgu* London 1978
WOOD, E. *Under the Southern Cross* London [c. 1920]
WOOD, G.A. *The Wood electoral system: electoral reform* Melbourne 1902
WOOD, J. *'Neath southern skies* Castle-Douglas, Scotland 1882
WOOD, J.G. *The natural history of man* 2 vols. London 1868–70
WOOD, O'H. *Cup week* Melbourne 1912
WOOD, T. *Cobbers: a personal record of a journey from Essex, in England, to Australia* London 1934
Cobbers campaigning Sydney 1940
WOODBERRY, J. *Floodtide for Rafferty* London 1960
Come back Peter Adelaide 1968
A garland of gannets Melbourne 1969
WOODFIELD, S. *A for Artemis* Sydney 1960
WOODHOUSE, A. *The man with the apples* Melbourne 1890
WOODS, J.D. *The province of South Australia* Adelaide 1894
WOODS, W.J. *A visit to Victoria* London 1886
WOOLCOCK, D.T. & C.E. *Australian terrestrial orchids* Melbourne 1984
WOOLLEY, P. *The art of living together* Camberwell, Vic. 1978
WOOLLEY, T. *Reminiscences of the life of a bushman* London 1850
'WOOMERA' see Delaforce, W.
WOORE, T. *Diary of Thomas Woore R.N. [1843–1935]* [Goulburn, N.S.W. 1935]
Worker Brisbane 1890–1974
Worker Sydney Oct. 1892–6 Nov. 1913 (continues *The Hummer*, continued by *Australian worker*)
The working dog (issued by the) Victorian Department of Agriculture Dookie, Vic. 1977
WORRELL, E. *Things that sting* Sydney 1976
WORSNOP, T. *The prehistoric arts, manufactures, works, weapons, etc., of the Aborigines of Australia* Adelaide 1897
**'The wouldn't it'* [At sea] 1940
The wrens & warblers of Australia Sydney 1982
WRIGHT, A. *A rogue's luck* Sydney 1909
Gamblers' gold Sydney 1923 (first publ. 1911)
In the last stride Sydney 1914
A sport from Hollowlog Flat Sydney 1915
Over the odds Sydney 1918
The breed holds good Sydney 1918
A game of chance Sydney 1919
Rung in Sydney 1921
A colt from the country Sydney 1922
The boss o' Yedden Sydney 1922
The boy from Bullarah Sydney 1925
The squatter's secret Sydney 1927
A good recovery Sydney 1928
WRIGHT, C. *Historic Melbourne* 1901–05 NLA News cuttings 994.51 WRI
WRIGHT, J. *The generations of men* Melbourne 1959
WRIGHT, J.H. *Our Victorian coalfields* Mirboo North, Vic. 1887
WRIGHT, W.V. Diaries 27 Oct. 1915–23 Mar. 1917 ML MS 1012
WRIGHTSON, P. *The ice is coming* Richmond South, Vic. 1977
WRIGLEY, J.W. & FAGG, M. *Australian native plants* Sydney 1979
2nd ed. 1984
WYATT, G. *Strip Jack naked* North Sydney 1966
A bit of a canter Sydney 1967
In Falconer's wake: an action-packed absorbing drama of the sea Sydney 1967
WYATT, R.T. *The digger on the 'Durham'* Sydney 1919
WYE, W.J. *Souvenirs of the sunny south* Melbourne 1915
WYNER, I. *With banner unfurled: the early years of the Ship Painters and Dockers Union* Sydney 1983
WYNNUM, J. *Down the hatch* London 1959
A pinch of salt Sydney 1963 (first publ. 1960)
The sailor blushed Sydney 1962 (first publ. 1960)
Storm in a port Sydney 1962
Tar dust Sydney 1962
No boats to burn Sydney 1963
Jiggin' in the riggin' Sydney 1965
I'm a Jack, all right London 1967

'Y.O.-B.A., Barrister-At-Law' (E. Gilks) *Proclamation!: a paper for everyone: the storm in a tea-cup; or, the end of the crisis in Victoria, 1878* Melbourne 1878
**Yandoo: the 7th Field Artillery Brigade* v.p. 1916–19
YARRA, A.E. *The vanishing horsemen* London 1930
'YARRAN' *The Mallee: Victoria's great wheat province* Melbourne 1910
YOFFA, A. *The real thing: adventures in the Australian bush* New York 1929
YONGE, C.M. *A year on the Great Barrier Reef: the story of corals & of the greatest of their creations* London 1930
Yorke's Peninsula advertiser Moonta, S. Aust. 1872–1922
YOUNG, G.C. *Rhymes from the front* [Warminster, England c. 1919]
YOUNG, K.D. *Born to adventure* London [1945]
YOUNGER, C. *Less than angel* London 1960
Yulngu: a magazine for Aborigines and their friends in the Katherine region Katherine, N.T. 1982–83

ZILLMANN, J.H.L. *Past and present Australian life* London 1889
Career of a Cornstalk including fifty years of Australian history with sketches of leading statesmen Sydney 1914
Zoological journal London 1824–1835